CONTEMPORARY
ARCHITECTS

CONTEMPORARY ARTS SERIES

CONTEMPORARY ARCHITECTS

SECOND EDITION

Editors:
Ann Lee Morgan and Colin Naylor

Advisers:
Thomas Hall Beeby, Jorge Czajkowski
Vittorio Gregotti, Anthony Jackson
William H. Jordy, Udo Kultermann
David Mackay, Esther McCoy
Wolfgang Pehnt, Mildred F. Schmertz
Harry Seidler, Arieh Sharon
Pierre Vago, Hiroshi Watanabe
Arnold Whittick

St J

ST. JAMES PRESS
CHICAGO AND LONDON

Front cover: John Burgee Architects with Philip Johnson—Republic Bank Center, Houston, Texas, 1981

© by St. James Press, 1987

ST. JAMES PRESS
425 North Michigan Avenue
Chicago 60611, U.S.A.
or
3 Percy Street
London W1P 9FA, England

First published in the U.S.A. and U.K. in 1987

British Library Cataloguing in Publication Data
Contemporary architects.——2nd ed.——
   (Contemporary arts series).
   1. Architects——Biography
   I. Morgan, Ann Lee   II. Naylor, Colin
   III. Series
   720′.92′2   NA40

   ISBN 0–912289–26–0

Filmsetting by Vantage Photosetting Co. Ltd,
Eastleigh and London
Printed in Great Britain at The Bath Press, Avon

CONTENTS

EDITORS' NOTE

In this first revision of *Contemporary Architects*, originally published seven years ago, every entry has been updated to reflect current bibliography as well as, for the living entrants, works produced since 1980 and biographical events, including awards and exhibitions. Many entries are illustrated with new photographs.

To strengthen the contemporary focus of this volume, we have added about forty architects and have deleted some whose activity ceased before World War II. In making these decisions, we have been assisted by an Advisory Board, listed on page ix. As in the first volume, we have continued to define the word "architect" very broadly, so as to include planners, theorists, structural engineers, and landscape architects whose work seems to be central to the enterprise of creating habitable spaces in our day.

We are grateful not only to our advisers but to the many contributors who revised their original essays or wrote new ones and, in many instances, offered useful advice. To the libraries that aided our research – especially that of the Royal Institute of British Architects – we owe a fundamental debt of gratitude. Most of all, for their generous cooperation, we thank the living architects, nearly all of whom provided information about themselves and their work, as did firms or families of many deceased ones.

ADVISERS/CONTRIBUTORS

Advisers

Thomas Hall Beeby, Jorge Czajkowski, Vittorio Gregotti, Anthony Jackson
William H. Jordy, Udo Kultermann, David Mackay, Esther McCoy
Wolfgang Pehnt, Mildred F. Schmertz, Harry Seidler, Arieh Sharon
Pierre Vago, Hiroshi Watanabe, Arnold Whittick

Contributors

Stanley Abercrombie, Friedrich Achleitner, Kurt Ackermann, Gerald Adler
W. H. Alington, Bob Allies, Anthony C. Antoniades, Katsuyoshi Arai
Christopher Arnold

Edmund N. Bacon, George Baird, Alan Balfour, Jonathan Barnett
T. Q. Battle, Stephen Bayley, Konstantin Bazarov, B. E. Biermann
Peter Blundell Jones, Oriol Bohigas, Harold Booton, Christian Borngräber
Michael Brawne, H. A. N. Brockman, H. Allen Brooks

Georges Candilis, Anton Capitel, Max Cetto, D. D. C. Chambers
Bernard Champigneulle, Ching-Yu Chang, Giuliano Chelazzi, Alson Clark
Ursula Cliff, Peggy Cochrane, James Codrington Forsyth, Carolyn Cole
Peter Collins, Peter Collymore, Brenda Colvin, Jeffrey Cook
Henry Cowan, Logan Cravens, S. Fiske Crowell, Jr., James Stevens Curl
William J. R. Curtis, Jorge Czajkowski, Teresa Czaplinska-Archer

Justus Dahinden, Eric de Maré, Mary Elizabeth Devine
Renée Diamant-Berger, John D. Dickson, Philip Drew, Martina Düttmann

Garrett Eckbo, Rita Eder, Julian Elliott, Muriel Emanuel
Richard England

Tobias Faber, Geoffrey Lee Farnsworth, Dimitris A. Fatouros, Chris Fawcett
Volker Fischer, John Furse

Darius Gilmont, Romaldo Giurgola, Jorge Glusberg, Gontran Goulden
James Gowan, Urs Graf, Cedric Green, Daniel Gregory, Anthony Gregson
Doreen Greig

Hans Hallen, Stephen P. Hamilton, Clinton Harrop-Allin, Lucinda Hawkins
Mary Hayes, Raija-Liisa Heinonen, Tom Heneghan, Gilbert Herbert
Paul Heyer, Don J. Hibbard, Donald Hoffmann, William Dudley Hunt, Jr.
Kent Hurley

Anthony Jackson, Geoffrey Jellicoe, Jürgen Joedicke, Joseph B. Juhasz

Diane Kell, Jonathan Kingdon, Robert E. Koehler, Otto Koenigsberger
Udo Kultermann, Bruce Kuwabara

Michael Laurie, Richard Lavenstein, Linda Legner, Ronald Lewcock
Michael Lloyd, Arnulf Lüchinger, K. C. Lye

David Mackay, Randell L. Makinson, Antero Markelin, Linda Martin
Lara-Vinca Masini, Robert Maxwell, Esther McCoy, J. M. McKean
Michael McMordie, Nory Miller, Edward D. Mills, Luciana Miotto-Muret
Flavio Motta, Elizabeth Murphy

Janet Nairn, Zdravko Natchev, Colin Naylor, Robert B. Nevel

Roger Osbaldeston, Timothy Ostler

Gordon Patterson, Roger Pegrum, Wolfgang Pehnt, Richard C. Peters
Julius Posener

Malcolm Quantrill

Andrew Rabeneck, Larry Richards, Ida Rodriguez, Abraham Rogatnick
Eugene Rosenberg, Michael Franklin Ross, Mitchell B. Rouda
Diana Rowntree, Paul Ryan, Joseph Rykwert

Manfred Sack, B. S. Saini, Asko Salokorpi, Mildred F. Schmertz
Norbert Schoenauer, Franz Schulze, Robert Segrest, Harry Seidler
Eduard F. Sekler, E. J. Seow, Dennis Sharp, Adrian Sheppard
Richard Sheppard, Nathan Silver, C. Ray Smith, Kevin Spencer
Paul Spreiregen, Ulrike Jehle-Schulte Strathaus, Pekka Suhonen

Howard Tanner, Jennifer Taylor

Günther Uhlig

Pierre Vago

Russell Walden, Hiroshi Watanabe, David Watson, Frank Werner
Arnold Whittick, Sheldon Williams, Stephanie Williams, Peter Willis
John Winter, Robert Winter

CONTEMPORARY
ARCHITECTS

Alvar Aalto
Raimund Abraham
Max Abramovitz
Kurt Ackermann
Ray Affleck
Steffen Ahrends
Ahrends Burton and Koralek
Takefumi Aida
Gregory Ain
Edouard Albert
Franco Albini
Christopher Alexander
Robert E. Alexander
W. H. Alington
Osvald Almqvist
Mario Roberto Alvarez
Sydney Ancher
Tadao Ando
John Andrews
Dimitris Antonakakis
Suzana Antonakakis
Antonini Schon Zemborain and Associates
Architects Co-Partnership Inc.
Nader Ardalan
Ove Arup
Yoshinobu Ashihara
Charles Herbert Aslin
Gunnar Asplund
Atelier 5
Ian Athfield
Gae Aulenti
Carlo Aymonino
Takamitsu Azuma

Sven Backström
Edmund N. Bacon
Daniel Badani
George Baird
Jacob Bakema
Gianluigi Banfi
Edward Larrabee Barnes
Jonathan Barnett
Luis Barragán
Otto Bartning
Baudizzone-Diaz-Erbin-Lestard-Varas
Paul Baumgarten
BBPR Architectural Studio
Eugène Beaudouin
Welton Becket
Thomas Hall Beeby
Günter Behnisch
Peter Behrens
Lodovico Belgiojoso
Pietro Belluschi
Sergio Bernardes
Max Bill
Gunnar Birkerts
Peter Blake
Charles Blessing
Holger Blom
Piet Blom
Aulis Blomstedt
Jørgen Bo
Vladimir Bodiansky
Ricardo Bofill
Helge Bofinger
Oriol Bohigas
Dominikus Böhm
Gottfried Böhm
Paul Bonatz
Pep Bonet
Mario Botta
Victor Bourgeois
Robin Boyd
Michael Brawne

Marcel Breuer
Johannes Brinkman
Samuel Brody
Charles William Brubaker
Erik Bryggman
Gordon Bunshaft
John Burgee
Roberto Burle Marx
Buszko and Franta

Charles Warren Callister
Cambridge Seven Associates
Felix Candela
Georges Candilis
Guido Canella
Douglas Cardinal
Hugh Casson
Casson Conder Partnership
Eduardo Catalano
William W. Caudill
Max Cetto
Rifat Chadirji
Chamberlin Powell and Bon
Pierre Chareau
Melvin Charney
Serge Chermayeff
Thomas D. Church
Mario J. Ciampi
Cristian Cirici
Lluis Clotet
Wells Coates
José A. Coderch
Colquhoun and Miller
Brenda Colvin
Amyas Connell
Peter Cook
Charles M. Correa
Peter Corrigan
Lúcio Costa
Keith E. Cottier
Philip Cox
Warren J. Cox
David A. Crane
Theo Crosby
Sylvia Crowe
James Cubitt
Edward Cullinan

Justus Dahinden
John Dalton
Trevor Dannatt
Gustavo da Roza
J. R. Davidson
Lewis Davis
Giancarlo De Carlo
Harald Deilmann
Alejandro De La Sota
Bernard de la Tour d'Auvergne
Enrique del Moral
Vernon DeMars
A. J. Diamond
Kamran Diba
Eladio Dieste
John Dinkeloo
Richard Döcker
B. V. Doshi
Alden B. Dow
Barry Downs
Philip Dowson
Constantinos Doxiades
Jane B. Drew
Macy DuBois
Willem Dudok
Werner Düttmann

Charles Eames
Norman Eaton
Garrett Eckbo
Michel Ecochard
Ezra Ehrenkrantz
Egon Eiermann
Peter D. Eisenman
Julian Elliott
Craig Ellwood
Richard England
Arthur Erickson
Ralph Erskine
Aarne Ervi
Joseph Esherick

Hassan Fathy
Hermann Fehling
Sverre Fehn
Bernard Feilden
Luigi Figini
João Filguéiras
József Finta
Kay Fisker
O'Neil Ford
Norman Foster
Revel Fox
Ulrich Franzen
Eugène Freyssinet
M. Paul Friedberg
Yona Friedman
E. Maxwell Fry
Bohuslav Fuchs
Hiromi Fujii
Buckminster Fuller
Don Hendry Fulton

Ignazio Gardella
Robert Geddes
Frank O. Gehry
Frederick Gibberd
Robin Gibson
Jean Ginsberg
Ernst Gisel
Romaldo Giurgola
Mathias Goeritz
Bruce Goff
Daniel Gogel
Bertrand Goldberg
Ernö Goldfinger
Myron Goldsmith
Gollins, Melvin, Ward
Teodoro González de León
Joan Goody
James Gowan
Bruce J. Graham
Giorgio Grassi
Michael Graves
Eileen Gray
Allan Greenberg
Charles Sumner Greene
Henry Mather Greene
Herb Greene
Vittorio Gregotti
Walter Gropius
Irving Grossman
Victor Gruen
Barnett Gruzen
Amancio Guedes
Joaquim Guedes
Rolf Gutbrod
Charles Gwathmey
Patrick Gwynne

N. John Habraken
Hans Hallen

Lawrence Halprin
Oskar Hansen
Norman Hanson
Hiroshi Hara
Hugh Hardy
Hugo Häring
Harwell Hamilton Harris
Wallace K. Harrison
George E. Hartman
Josef Havlíček
Zvi Hecker
John Hejduk
George F. Hellmuth
Hellmuth, Obata and Kassabaum
Helmut Hentrich
Ron Herron
Herman Hertzberger
Ludwig K. Hilberseimer
Tao Ho
Josef Hoffmann
Charles Holden
William Graham Holford
Hans Hollein
Wilhelm Holzbauer
Clemens Holzmeister
Sutemi Horiguchi
George Howe
Howell, Killick, Partridge and Amis
Richard Hughes

Kazuhiro Ishii
Arata Isozaki

Daryl Jackson
David Jackson
Arne Jacobsen
Hugh Newell Jacobsen
Helmut Jahn
Uttam C. Jain
Pierre Jeanneret
Geoffrey Jellicoe
John M. Johansen
Philip Johnson
R. N. Johnson
A. Quincy Jones
Alexis Josic
Josep María Jujol
Sumet Jumsai

Ely Jacques Kahn
Louis I. Kahn
Gerhard M. Kallmann
Dov Karmi
Ram Karmi
George Kassabaum
Tasso Katselas
George Fred Keck
György Kévés
Fazlur Khan
Frederick Kiesler
Kiyonori Kikutake
Dan Kiley
Edward A. Killingsworth
Ron Kirby
Josef Paul Kleihues
Edward F. Knowles
Knut Knutsen
Carl Koch
Pierre Koenig
Aris Konstantinidis
Rem Koolhaas
Arthur Korn
Arne Korsmo
Friedrich Wilhelm Kraemer
Ferdinand Kramer

Leon Krier
Rob Krier
Lucien Kroll
Ernest J. Kump
Kisho Kurokawa

Bohdan Lachert
Morris Lapidus
Albert Laprade
Denys Lasdun
John Lautner
Le Corbusier
Ricardo Legorreta
Ludwig Leo
Fritz Leonhardt
Richard Le Plastrier
William Lescaze
Rino Levi
Sigurd Lewerentz
David Lewis
William S. W. Lim
Datuk Lim Chong Keat
Horst Linde
Richard Llewelyn-Davies
Leandro V. Locsin
Marcel Lods
Berthold Lubetkin
Colin Lucas
Hans Luckhardt
Wassili Luckhardt
Anthony Lumsden
Kjell Lund
Victor A. Lundy
André Lurcat
Hans Luz
Donlyn Lyndon
Eric Lyons
Lyons, Israel, Ellis and Gray

David Mackay
Col Madigan
Robert Maillart
Fumihiko Maki
Imre Makovecz
Angelo Mangiarotti
Al Mansfeld
Manteola, Sánchez Gómez, Santos, Solsona,
  Architects
C. S. Mardall
Sven Markelius
Jerome Markson
Leslie Martin
Josep Martorell
Tomoya Masuda
Ernst May
Bernard Maybeck
Kunio Mayekawa
Gerald McCue
Raymond McGrath
Ian McHarg
Peter McIntyre
Noel Michael McKinnell
Richard Meier
Eric Mendelsohn
Paulo Mendes da Rocha
John Merrill
Hannes Meyer
Wilhelm O. Meyer
Giovanni Michelucci
Ludwig Mies van der Rohe
Henrique Mindlin
Ehrman B. Mitchell
José Rafael Moneo
Arthur Cotton Moore
Charles W. Moore

Riccardo Morandi
Jorge Machado Moreira
Luigi Moretti
William Morgan
Raymond Moriyama
Peter Moro
Bryce Mortlock
Werner M. Moser
Hidalgo Moya
Monta Mozuna
William C. Muchow
Peter Muller
Tohgo Murano
Glenn Murcutt
Stuart Murray
Barton Myers

Wallace Neff
George Nelson
Paul Nelson
Pier Luigi Nervi
Walter A. Netsch
Richard J. Neutra
Oscar Niemeyer
Matthew Nowicki
Eliot Noyes

Gyo Obata
Dieter Oesterlen
Juan O'Gorman
Shin'ichi Okada
Masato Otaka
Sachio Otani
Frei Otto
J. J. P. Oud
Nathaniel Owings

Mario Pani
John B. Parkin
John C. Parkin
Giovanni Pasanella
Mario Payssé-Reyes
I. M. Pei
Gustav Peichl
Cesar Pelli
Luis Peña
Fabio Penteado
Timo Penttilä
William L. Pereira
Enrico Peressutti
Lawrence B. Perkins
Auguste Perret
Charlotte Perriand
Marcello Piacentini
Renzo Piano
Reima Pietilä
Dimitris A. Pikionis
Gino Pollini
James Stewart Polshek
Gio Ponti
John Portman
Paolo Portoghesi
Philip Powell
James Pratt
Cedric Price
Jean Prouvé
Victor Prus

Ludovico Quaroni

Roland Rainer
Pedro Ramirez Vazquez
Ralph Rapson
John Rauch
Antonin Raymond

Yacov Rechter
Affonso Eduardo Reidy
Leif Reinius
Andrew Renton
Viljo Revell
Leonardo Ricci
Bruce Rickard
Mario Ridolfi
Gerrit Rietveld
Roberto Architects
Howard Robertson
Jaquelin Robertson
Kevin Roche
Archibald C. Rogers
Ernesto Nathan Rogers
Richard Rogers
Peter Rose
Eugene Rosenberg
Aldo Rossi
Alfred Roth
Pierre Roux-Dorlut
Michel Rouz-Spitz
Paul Rudolph
Aarno Ruusuvuori

Eero Saarinen
Eliel Saarinen
Francisco Saénz de Oiza
Moshe Safdie
Junzo Sakakura
Rogelio Salmona
Giuseppe Samonà
Brian Sandrock
Alberto Sartoris
Hideo Sasaki
Louis Sauer
Leonardo Savioli
Carlo Scarpa
Hans Scharoun
Rudolph Schindler
Frank Schlesinger
Dolf Schnebli
Rudolf Schwarz
Paul Schweikher
Michael Scott
Denise Scott Brown
Der Scutt
Walter Segal
Harry Seidler
Ivan Seifert
Robin Seifert
Werner Seligmann
Josep Lluis Sert
Arieh Sharon
Eldar Sharon
Sheppard, Robson and Partners

Kazuo Shinohara
Seiichi Shirai
John Ormsbee Simonds
Heikki Siren
Kaija Siren
Alvaro Siza
Louis Skidmore
Skidmore, Owings and Merrill
Nils Slaatto
Ivor Smith
Whitney R. Smith
Alison Smithson
Peter Smithson
Paolo Soleri
Raphael Soriano
Josep Maria Sostres
Ettore Sottsass, Jr.
Basil Spence
Mart Stam
Otto Steidle
Douglas Stephen
Robert A. M. Stern
Stillman and Eastwick-Field
James Stirling
Edward Durell Stone
Oscar Stonorov
Hugh A. Stubbins, Jr.
Helena Syrkus
Szymon Syrkus

Roger Taillibert
Minoru Takeyama
Kenzo Tange
Yoshiro Taniguchi
Bruno Taut
Max Taut
Team Zoo
Ivar Tengbom
Giuseppe Terragni
Heinrich Tessenow
Clorindo Testa
The Architects Collaborative
Paul Thiry
Ron Thom
Benjamin Thompson
Stanley Tigerman
Alexandros N. Tombazis
Eduardo Torroja y Miret
R. H. B. Toy
William Turnbull, Jr.
Oscar Tusquets

O. M. Ungers
Shizutaro Urabe
Jørn Utzon
Roelof S. Uytenbogaardt

György Vadász
Pierre Vago
Gino Valle
J. H. van den Brock
Cornelis van Eesteren
Aldo van Eyck
Jan van Wijk
Eva Vecsei
Robert Venturi
José Villagrán García
Carlos Raúl Villanueva
Alexander von Branca
Meinhard von Gerkan

Konrad Wachsmann
Derek Walker
David A. Wallace
Gregori Warchavchik
John Carl Warnecke
Miles Warren
Youji Watanabe
Clifford Wearden
John Weeks
Harry Weese
Richard S. Weinstein
Hanna Wejchert
Kazimierz Wejchert
Clifford Wiens
Philip Will, Jr.
Jean Willerval
Amancio Williams
Owen Williams
Clough Williams-Ellis
Colin St. John Wilson
Leslie Hugh Wilson
James Wines
Peter Womersley
Jackson C. S. Wong
Shadrach Woods
Ken Woolley
Frank Lloyd Wright
Lloyd Wright
William Wilson Wurster

Minoru Yamasaki
F. R. S. Yorke
Isoya Yoshida
Takamasa Yosizaka

Wojciech Zablocki
Abraham Zabludovsky
Marco Zanuso
Bernard Zehrfuss
Eberhard Zeidler

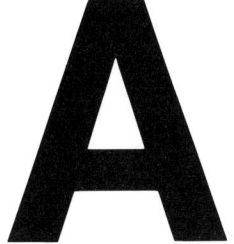

A

AALTO, Alvar.

Finnish. Born Hugo Alvar Henrik Aalto in Kuortane, near Jyväskylä, 3 February 1898. Educated at the Jyväskylä Lyseo, 1908-16; studied architecture, under Armas Lindgren, Technical University of Helsinki, 1916-21, Dip. Arch. 1921. Served in the Finnish Army in 1939. Married the architect Aino Marsio in 1924 (died, 1949); children: Johanna and Hamilkar; married the architect Elissa Mäkiniemi in 1952. Worked as an exhibition designer in Göteborg, Sweden, Tampere, Finland, and Turku, Finland, 1921-22; in private architectural practice, in Jyväskylä, Finland, 1923-27, Turku, Finland, 1927-33, and Helsinki, 1933 until his death in 1976: in partnership with Aino Aalto, 1924-49, and with Elissa Aalto, 1952-76. Established experimental plywood furniture workshop with Otto Korhonen, Turku, Finland, 1929, and ARTEK furniture design company, with Aino Aalto and Mairea Gullichsøn, Helsinki, 1935. Professor of Architecture, Massachusetts Institute of Technology, Cambridge, 1946-48. President of the Academy of Finland, 1963-68. Exhibitions: *Triennale,* Milan, 1933; *Alvar Aalto: Architecture and Furniture,* Museum of Modern Art, New York, 1938; *Alvar und Aino Aalto,* Kunstgewerbemuseum, Zürich, 1948; Ecole des Beaux Arts, Paris, 1950; *Möbel aus Holz und Stahl: Alvar Aalto—Mies van der Rohe,* Gewerbemuseum, Basel, 1957; Keski-Suomen Museum, Jyväskylä, Finland, 1962; Akademie der Künste, Berlin, 1963; Kunsthaus, Zürich, 1964; *Contemporary Finnish Architecture,* Smithsonian Institution, Washington, D.C., 1965; *L'Opera di Alvar Aalto,* Palazzo Strozzi, Florence, 1965; Ateneum, Helsinki, 1967;, Modern Museet, Stockholm, 1969; *Alvar Aalto 1898-1976,* Finlandia Hall, Helsinki, and Royal Academy, London, 1978 (travelled to Edinburgh and New York, 1978-79); *Alvar Aalto: das architektonische Werk,* Museum Folkwang, Essen, West Germany, 1979; *Alvar Aalto: Furniture and Glass,* Museum of Modern Art, New York, 1984 (toured the United States, Canada, and Europe, 1985-86). Recipient: First Prize in the competitions for Jyväskylä Workers' Club, 1923, Paimio Tuberculosis Sanatorium, 1927, Viipuri Municipal Library, 1927, Aitta Summer Houses, 1928, Finnish Pavilion for the Paris World's Fair, 1936, Finnish Pavilion for the New York World's Fair, 1938, Forum Redivium, Helsinki, 1948, Lahti Church, 1950, Säynätsalo Town Hall, 1950, Malm Funeral Chapel, 1950, Jyväskylä Teachers' University, 1950, Kuopio Regional Theatre, 1951, Rautatalo Office Building, Helsinki, 1951, Seinäjoki Church, 1952, Sports and Congress Hall, Vienna, 1953, Göteborg, Sweden Town Hall, 1955, Kiruna, Sweden Town Hall, 1958, Aalborg, Denmark Art Museum, 1958, Essen, West Germany Opera House, 1958, Seinäjoki Town Hall, 1959, and the Protestant Parish Centre, Zürich, 1967; other prizes include—Royal Gold Medal for Architecture, Royal Institute of British Architects, 1957; Sonningpriset, Denmark, 1962; Gold Medal, American Institute of Architects, 1963; Gold Cube, Svenska Arkitekters Riksforbund, Sweden, 1963; Cordon del Calli de Oro, Sociedad de Arquitetos, Mexico, 1963; Bronzeplakette, Freie Akademie der Künste, Hamburg, West Germany, 1965; Medaglia d'Oro, City of Florence, 1965; Diplome des Palmes d'Or du Mérite de l'Europe, 1966; Helsingin Yliopiston Ylioppilaskunnan Puheenjohtajiston merkki purppuranauhassa, Finland, 1966; Thomas Jefferson Medal, University of Virginia, Charlottesville, 1967; Alvar Aalto Medal, Finland, 1967; Litteris et Artibus Medal, Sweden, 1969; Médaille d'Or, Académie d'Architecture, Paris, 1972; Tapiola Medal, 1975; Outstanding Architect Award, National Arts Foundation, Liechtenstein, 1975. Honorary doctorates: Princeton University, New Jersey, 1947; Technical University of Helsinki, 1949; Norges Tekniske Højskole, Trondheim, Norway, 1960; Eidgenössische Technische Hochschule, Zürich, 1963; Columbia University, New York, 1964; Politecnico, Milan, 1964; Technische Hochschule, Vienna, 1965; University of Jyväskylä, 1969. Honorary Royal Designer for Industry, Royal Society of Arts, London; Senior Fellow, Royal College of Arts, London, 1950; Honorary Fellow, American Institute of Architects, 1958; Fellow, World Academy of Arts and Sciences, Israel, 1963. Honorary Member: Royal Institute of British Architects, 1937; Södra Sveriges Byggnadsteniska Samfund, Sweden, 1957; American Academy of Arts and Sciences, 1957; Accademia di Belle Arti, Venice, 1958; Association of Finnish Architects, 1958; Norske Arkitekterns Landsforbund, Norway, 1959; Västmanlands-Dala Nation, Uppsala, Sweden, 1965; Colegio de Arquitetos, Peru, 1965; Engineering Society of Finland, 1966; Bund Deutscher Architekten, Germany, 1966; American Academy of Arts and Letters, 1968; National Institute of Arts and Letters, U.S.A., 1968; Akademie der Bildenden Künste, Vienna, 1975; Royal Scottish Academy, 1975. Chevalier of the Légion d'Honneur, France, 1939; Kømmendors Korset av Dannebrogen, Denmark, 1957; Grand Cross of the Lion of Finland, 1965; Grande Ufficiale al Merito, Republic of Italy, 1966; Grand Croix de l'Ordre du Faucon, Iceland, 1972. *Died* (in Helsinki) *11 May 1976.*

Works:

1918 Aalto Family House remodelling, Alajärvi, Finland
     Belfry, Kauhajärvi, Finland
1921/
  22 Association of Patriots Building, Seinäjoki, Finland
1922 *Industrial Exhibition,* Tampere, Finland
1922/
  23 Two-family house, Jyväskylä, Finland
1923/
  24 Apartment building, Jyväskylä, Finland
1923/
  25 Workers' Club, Jyväskylä, Finland
1924 Church restoration, Äänekoski, Finland
     Church restoration, Anttola, Finland
1925 Church, Jämsä, Finland (competition project)
     Church remodelling, Viitasaari, Finland

1926/
  29 Church, Muurame, Finland
1927 Toolo Church, Helsinki (competition project)
     Church, Viinikka, Finland (competition project)
     Belfry restoration, Pylkönmäki Church, Finland
1927/
  28 Farmers' Cooperative Building and Finnish Theatre, Turku, Finland
     Apartment building, Turku, Finland
1927/
  29 Association of Patriots Building, Jyväskylä, Finland
     Turun Sanomat Newspaper Offices, Turku, Finland
1928 Summer houses, Aitta, Finland (competition project)
     Church restoration, Korpilahti, Finland
1929 Columbus Memorial Lighthouse, Dominican Republic (competition project)
     Church restoration, Kemijärvi, Finland
     7th Centenary Exhibition, Turku, Finland
1929/
  33 Tuberculosis Sanatorium, Paimio, Finland
1930 Institute for Physical Education, Vierumäkı, Finland (competition project)
     Michele Agricola Church, Helsinki (competition project)
     Stadium and Sports Centre, Helsinki (competition project)
     University Hospital, Zagreb, Yugoslavia (competition project)
1930/
  31 Cellulose factory, Toppila, Oulu, Finland
1930/
  35 Municipal Library, Viipuri, Finland (destroyed, 1943)
1932 Helsinki Stadium (competition project)
     Prefabricated one-family house (competition project)
     Enso-Gutzeit Weekend Cabin (competition project)
1932/
  33 Villa Tammekan, Tarto, Estonia
1933 Housing for the employees and doctors of the Tuberculosis Sanatorium, Paimio, Finland
     Redevelopment plan for Normalm, Stockholm (competition project)
1934 Railway station, Tampere, Finland (competition project)
     Stenius Housing Development, Munkkiniemi, Helsinki
     Exhibition Hall, Helsinki (competition project)
1934/
  36 Aalto House, Munkkiniemi, Finland
1936 Art Museum, Tallinn, Estonia (competition project)
1937 Finnish Pavilion, World's Fair, Paris
1936/
  39 Cellulose factory, Sunila, Finland (first stage of construction)
1937 Savoy Restaurant, Helsinki
     Nordic United Bank, Karhula, Finland

1937/
38 Director's house, Sunila, Finland
Two-storey housing, Sunila, Finland
Two-storey terrace housing, first and second groups, Sunila, Finland
1938 Forestry Pavilion, *Agricultural Exhibition*, Lapua, Finland
Blomberg Film Studio, Westend, Helsinki
University of Helsinki Library extension (competition project)
Anjala Paper Factory, Inkeroinen, Finland
1938/
39 Three-storey terrace housing, first and second groups, Sunila, Finland
Finnish Pavilion, World's Fair, New York
Elementary school, Inkeroinen, Finland
Anjala Apartments Buildings, first group, Inkeroinen, Finland
Anjala Terrace House, second group, Inkeroinen, Finland
Anjala Housing for Engineers, Inkeroinen, Finland
Villa Mäirea, Noormarkku, Finland
1938/
40 Terrace housing, Kauttua, Finland
1939/
45 Ahlströ Apartment Buildings, Karhula, Finland
1940 Haka Housing Development, Helsinki (competition project)
Traffic plan and design of Erottaja Square, Helsinki (competition project)
1941 Plan for an experimental town
1941/
42 Regional plan for the Kokemaki Valley, Finland
1942/
43 Women's dormitory, Kauttua, Finland
1942/
46 Urban design project for Säynätsalo, Finland
1943 Town Centre, Oulu, Finland (competition project)
Merikoski Power Station, Oulu, Finland (competition project)
1944 Town Centre, Avesta, Sweden (competition project)
Stromberg Housing Development, Vaasa, Finland
Extension to factory, Kauttua, Finland
1944/
45 Urban design for Rovaniemi, Finland (project)
Ahlström Mechanical Workshop, Karhula, Finland
1944/
47 Strömberg Meter Factory, Vaasa, Finland
Strömberg Terrace Housing, Vaasa, Finland
1945 Engineer's house, Kauttua, Finland
Sauna, Kauttua, Finland
ARTEK Exhibition Pavilion, Hedemora, Sweden
1945/
46 Sawmill extension, Varkaus, Finland
One-family housing development, Varkaus, Finland
1946 Heimdal Housing Development, Nynäshamn, Sweden (competition project)
Master plan for Nynäshamn, Sweden (competition project)
One-family house, Pihlava, Finland
1947 Strömberg Sauna and Laundry, Vaasa, Finland
Johnson Research Institute, Avesta, Sweden
1947/
48 Baker House Dormitory, Massachusetts Institute of Technology, Cambridge
1947/
53 Regional plan for Imatra, Finland
1948 Forum Redivivum: Cultural and Administrative Centre, Helsinki (competition project)
1949 Ahlstrom Factory Warehouse, Karhula, Finland
General plan for the Institute of Technology,

Otaniemi, Finland (competition project)
Woodberry Poetry Room, Lamont Library, Harvard University, Cambridge, Massachusetts
1949/
50 Tampella Housing, Tampere, Finland
1949/
54 Sports Hall, Otaniemi, Finland
1950 Church, Lahti, Finland (competition project)
Funeral chapel, Malm, Finland (competition project)
Kivelä Hospital, Helsinki (competition project)
1950/
52 Town Hall, Säynätsalo, Finland
1950/
55 Regional plan for Lappland
1951 Erottaja Pavilion, Helsinki
Regional Theatre, Kuopio, Finland (competition project)
Enso-Gutzeit Paper Factory, Kotka, Finland
One-family house, Oulu, Finland
Workers' housing, Inkeroinen, Finland
1951/
52 Typpi Oy Nitrogen Factory and housing for Typpi Oy employees, Oulu, Finland
1951/
53 Enso-Gutzeit Paper Mill, Summa, Finland
1951/
54 Paper mill, Chandraghona, Pakistan
Cellulose factory, Sunila, Finland (second stage of construction)
Three-storey apartment house, third group, Sunila, Finland
1952 Cemetery and funeral chapel, Kongens Lyngby, Copenhagen (competition project)
Association of Finnish Engineers Building, Helsinki
Enso-Gutzeit Country Club, Kallvik, Finland
1952/
54 Housing for the personnel of the Public Pensions Institute, Munkkiniemi, Finland
1952/
56 Public Pensions Institute, Helsinki
1952/
57 Pedagogical University, Jyväskylä, Finland
1953 Sports and Congress Hall, Vogelweidplatz, Vienna (competition project)
Imatra Centre Design Project
Aalto Summer House, Muuratsalo, Finland
1953/
55 Ruatatalo Office Building, Helsinki
1954 Studio R.S., Como, Italy
Housing Aero, Helsinki
1955 Urban design project for Summa, Finland
Bank building, Baghdad, Iraq (competition project)
Aalto Studio, Munkkiniemi, Finland
Theatre and concert hall, Oulu, Finland (project)
1955/
57 Apartment building, Hansaviertel, Berlin
Town Hall, Göteborg, Sweden (competition project)
1955/
58 House of Culture, Helsinki
1956 Main Railway Station: Drottningtorget, Göteborg, Sweden (competition project)
Director's house, Typpi Oy, Oulu, Finland
Master plan for the University of Oulu, Finland
Finnish Pavilion, *Biennale*, Venice
1956/
58 Operating Room, Tuberculosis Sanatorium, Paimio, Finland
Church, Vuoksenniska, Imatra, Finland
Villa Louis Carré, Bazoches, France
1957 Kampementsbacken Housing Development, Stockholm (competition project)
Town Hall, Marl, West Germany (competition project)
1957/
61 Korkalovaara Housing Development,

Rovaniemi, Finland
Sundh Centre, Avesta, Sweden
1958 Town Hall, Kiruna, Sweden (competition project)
Art Museum, Baghdad, Iraq
Post Office Administration Building, Baghdad, Iraq
Opera House, Essen, West Germany (competition project)
1958/
60 Church, Seinäjoki, Finland
1958/
62 Neue Vahr High-Rise Apartments, Bremen, West Germany
1959 Bjornholm Housing Development, Helsinki
Finnish War Memorial, Suomussalmi, Finland
1959/
62 Central Finnish Museum, Jyväskylä, Finland
Enso-Gutzeit Headquarters, Helsinki
Parish Centre, Wolfsburg, West Germany
1959/
64 New Centre, Helsinki
1960/
61 Shopping centre, Otaniemi, Finland
Lieksankoski Power Station, Lieksa, Finland
1960/
63 Cultural Centre, Wolfsburg, West Germany
Thermotechnical Laboratory, Institute of Technology, Otaniemi, Finland
1960/
64 Main Building, Institute of Technology, Otaniemi, Finland
1961/
62 Housing for nurses, Tuberculosis Sanatorium, Paimio, Finland
Office and apartment block, Rovaniemi, Finland
1961/
63 Town Hall, Seinäjoki, Finland
1961/
64 Opera House, Essen, West Germany (competition project)
1962 Apartment blocks, Tapiola, Finland
Enskilda Bank Building, Stockholm (competition project)
Cultural Centre, Leverkusen, West Germany (competition project)
Terrace housing, Jakobstad, Finland
Stockmann Department Store expansion, Helsinki (project)
1962/
63 Heating Plant, Institute of Technology, Otaniemi, Finalnd
Housing development, Rovaniemi, Finland
1962/
64 Scandinavia Bank Administration Building, Helsinki
1962/
66 Student hostel, Otaniemi, Finland
1963 Urban Centre, Rovaniemi, Finland
Swimming Hall extension, Jyväskylä, Finland
Student Union Building, Jyväskylä, Finland
Town plan for Otaniemi, Finland
1963/
65 Kaufmann Conference Suite, Institute of International Education, New York
Library, Seinäjoki, Finland
Student Association House, Västmanland-Dala, Uppsala, Sweden
Heilig-Geist-Gemeinde Kindergarten, Wolfsburg, West Germany
1963/
66 Parish Centre, Seinäjoki, Finland
1964 BP Administration Building, Hamburg, West Germany (competition project)
Wood Technology Laboratories, Institute of Technology, Otaniemi, Finland
Tuberculosis Sanatorium extension, Paimio, Finland
1964/
65 One-family house, Rovaniemi, Finland

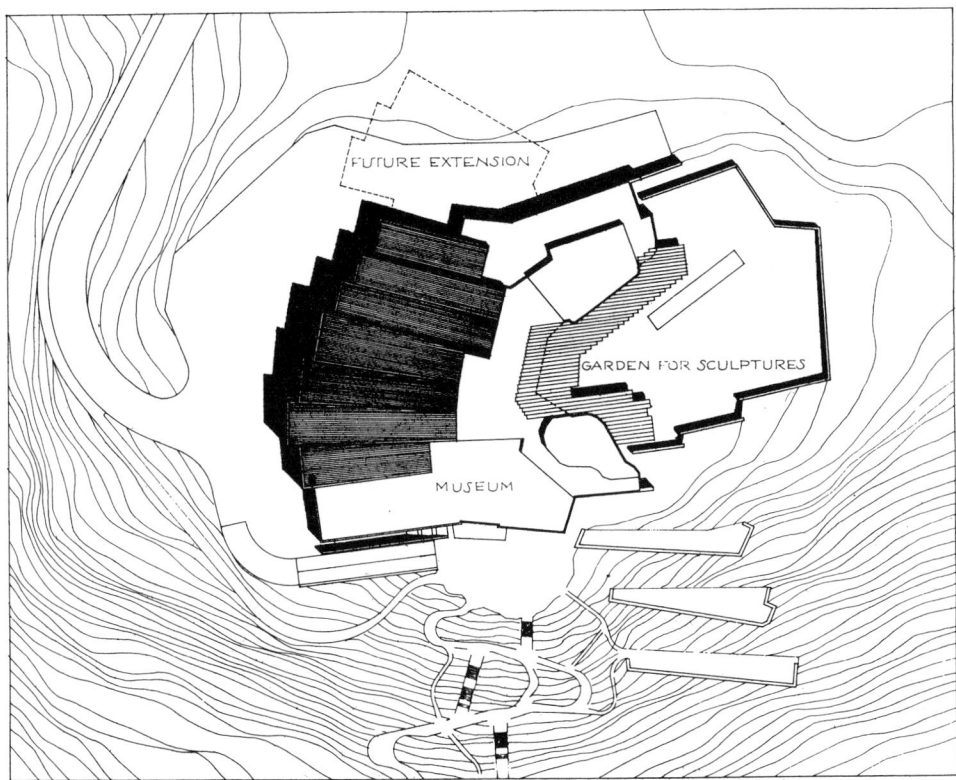

FUTURE EXTENSION

GARDEN FOR SCULPTURES

MUSEUM

Alvar Aalto: Project for the Shiraz Art Museum, Iran, 1970.

1964/
66 Urban design project for Stensvik, Finland
1964/
67 Ekenäs Savings Bank, Tammisaari, Finland
1965 Castrop-Rauxel Urban Centre, West Germany (competition project)
1965/
68 Scandinavian House, Reykjavik, Iceland
Library, Rovaniemi, Finland
Parish Centre, Detmerode, Wolfsburg, West Germany
Schönbühl High-Rise Apartments, Lucerne, Switzerland
1965/
69 Library, Institute of Technology, Otaniemi, Finland
1965/
70 Library, Mount Angel Benedictine College, Mount Angel, Oregon
1965/
72 Administration and Cultural Centre, Jyväskylä, Finland
1966 Experimental town, Gammelbacka, Porvoo, Finland (project)
Housing complex, Pavia, Italy (project)
Cultural Centre, Siena, Italy (project)
Theatre, Wolfsburg, West Germany (competition project)
Prototype for the administration building and warehouse of the Società Ferrero, Turin (project)
1966/
69 Academic Bookshop, Helsinki
Town Hall, Alajärvi, Finland
1966/
76 Riola Parish Centre, Bologna Italy
1967 Protestant Parish Centre, Zürich-Altstetten, Switzerland (competition project)
1967/
69 State Office Building, Seinäjoki, Finland
Kokkonen House, Järvenpää, Finland
1967/
71 Finlandia Hall, Helsinki
Institute of Physical Education, Jyväskylä University, Finland
1967/
73 City Electric Company Administration Building, Helsinki

1968/
69 Theatre, Seinäjoki, Finland (project)
1968/
71 Water Tower, Institute of Technology, Otaniemi, Finland
1969/
70 Villa Schildt, Tammisaari, Finland
Parish Centre, Alajärvi, Finland
1969/
75 Main Building extension, Institute of Technology, Otaniemi, Finland
1970 Church, Lahti, Finland
Art Museum, Shiraz, Iran
Police Headquarters, Jyväskylä, Finland
1970/
75 Theatre, first and second stages, Rovaniemi, Finland
1971 Alvar Aalto Museum, Jyväskylä, Finland
1972 Helsinki Central Plan, second stage
Art Museum, Aalborg, Denmark (with J.J. Baruel)
1973/
75 Finlandia Congress Hall, Helsinki
Swimming Hall, Jyväskylä, Finland
1974 Midwest Institute of Scandinavian Culture, Wisconsin (project)
1975 Town Hall, Jyväskylä, Finland
1975/
76 Master plan of the university area, Reykjavik, Iceland

Publications:

By AALTO: books—*An Experimental Town*, Cambridge, Massachusetts 1940; *Post-War Reconstruction*, New York 1941; *Alvar Aalto: Synopsis*, edited by Bernard Hoesli, Basel and Stuttgart 1970; *Alvar Aalto: Sketches*, edited by Göran Schildt, Helsinki 1972, Cambridge, Massachusetts and London 1978; articles—"Menneitten aikojen motivit" in *Arkkitehti* (Helsinki), no. 2, 1922; "André Lurcat" and "Abo stads 700-ars jubileum" in *Arkkitehti* (Helsinki), no. 6 1929; "Bostadsbebyggelse pagammal stadsplan" in *Byggmastaren* (Stockholm), 1930; "Rationalismen och Manniskan" in *FORM* (Stockholm), no. 7, 1935, reprinted in *Architectural Forum* (New York), September 1935; "Utställningar" in *Byggmastaren*

(Stockholm), no. 32, 1937; "Rakenteitten ja aineitten vaikutus nykaikaiseen rakennustaiteeseen" in *Arkkitehti* (Helsinki), no. 9, 1938; "The Humanizing of Architecture" in *Technology Review* (Cambridge, Massachusetts), November 1940, reprinted in *Architectural Forum* (New York), December 1940; "E. G. Asplund: In Memoriam" in *Arkkitehti* (Helsinki), nos. 11/12, 1940; "Euroopan jälleenrakentaminen tuo pinnalle aikamme rakennustaiteen keskeisimmän probleemin" in *Arkkitehti* (Helsinki), no. 5, 1941; "Bostadsutställningen en ateruppbyggnadsutställning" in *Arkkitehti* (Helsinki), nos. 9/10, 1941; "Finlands Arkitektförbunds standardiseringsarbete" in *Arkkitehti* (Helsinki), nos. 5/6, 1943; "Finsk Byggstandardisering" in *Byggmastaren* (Stockholm), no. 1, 1943; "D. Dahlberg: in Memoriam" in *Arkkitehti* (Helsinki), no. 1, 1944; "Rovaniemirediviva" in *Arkkitehti* (Helsinki), nos. 11/12, 1945; "Vad skall man göra med gardeskasernen?" in *Arkkitehti* (Helsinki), nos. 1/2, 1946; "Fin de la machine à habiter" in *Metron* (Rome), no. 7, 1946; "Un Sanatorium pour touberculeux en Finlande" in *Architecture française* (Paris), no. 62, 1946; "Architettura e arte concreta" in *Domus* (Milan), nos. 223/225, 1947; "Kulttuuri ja tekniikka" in *USA: Suomi-Finland* (Helsinki), no. 4, 1947; "The Decadence of Public Buildings" in *Arkkitehti* (Helsinki), nos. 9/10, 1953; "Rakennushallituksen Pää johtajan Virka" in *Arkkitehti* (Helsinki), no. 2, 1953; "Akademisk Arkitektförening 75 ar" in *Arkitekten* (Copenhagen), 1954; "Suomen Rakennustaiteen Museo" in *Arkkitehti* (Helsinki), no. 2, 1954; "Zwischen Humanismus und Materialismus" in *Der Bau* (Vienna), nos. 7/8, 1955, reprinted in *Baukunst und Werkform* (Darmstadt, West Germany), no. 6, 1956; "Problemi di architettura" in *Quaderni* (Turin), November 1956; "Annual Discourse" in *RIBA Journal* (London), May 1957; "Henry van de Velde: in Memoriam" in *Arkkitehti* (Helsinki), nos. 11/12, 1957; "Der Stadtplan von Imatra, Finnland" in *Werk* (Zürich), no. 11, 1959; "Il nuovo centro di Helsinki" in *Casabella* (Milan), August 1961; "Le Corbusier: In Memoriam" in *Progressive Architecture* (New York), October 1965; "Kaupunkisuunnittelu ja julkiset rakennukset" in *Arkkitehti* (Helsinki), nos. 3/4, 1967.

On AALTO: books—*Alvar Aalto: Architecture and furniture*, exhibition catalogue, New York 1938; *Space, Time and Architecture* by Siegfried Giedion, 2nd edition, Cambridge, Massachusetts and London 1949, and later editions; *Alvar Aalto* by Georgio Labò, Milan 1948; *Alvar Aalto and Finnish Architecture* by E. and C. Neuenschwander, London and New York 1954; *Scandinavian Architecture* by Thomas Paulsson, London 1959; *Alvar Aalto* by Frederick Gutheim, New York and London 1960, Milan 1963; *Alvar Aalto* by Göran Schildt and Leonardo Mosso, Jyväskylä, Finland 1962; *Alvar Aalto 1922-62*, edited by Karl Fleig, Zürich, London and New York 1963; *L'Opera di Alvar Aalto*, exhibition catalogue by Leonardo Mosso, Florence 1965; *Complexity and Contradiction in Architecture* by Robert Venturi, New York 1966; *Alvar Aalto* by Yukio Futagawa and others, Tokyo 1968, revised English edition as *Alvar Aalto* by George Baird and Yukio Futagawa, London 1970; *Alvar Aalto, vol. II: 1963-70*, edited by Karl Fleig, London 1971; *Alvar Aalto*, edited by Karl Fleig (adaptation of his previous books), London 1975, Zurich 1979; *Alvar Aalto* by Carlo Cresti, Florence 1975; *Architecture by Alvar Aalto*, Helsinki, no. 1-, from 1976; *Alvar Aalto and the International Style* by P. D. Pearson, New York and London 1978; *Alvar Aalto, Architectural Monographs 4* by Steven Groak, Liisa Heihonen and Demetri Porphyrios, London 1978; *Alvar Aalto, 1898-1976*, exhibition catalogue, by Aarno Ruusuvuori, Helsinki 1978; *Alvar Aalto*, edited by Göran Schildt, London and Cambridge, Massachusetts 1978; *Alvar Aalto—The Inner Process*, lecture paper by Malcolm Quantrill, London 1978; *Alvar Aalto*, edited by David Dunster, New York 1979; *Alvar*

Aalto: das architektonische Werk, exhibition catalogue, edited by Zdenek Felix, Essen, West Germany 1979; *Aino and Alvar Aalto: tutto il design* by Luciano Rubino, Rome 1980; *Alvar Aalto versus the Modern Movement*, edited by Kirmo Mikkola, Helsinki 1981; *Alvar Aalto als Designer*, by Werner Blaser, Stuttgart 1982; *Sources of Modern Eclecticism: studies on Alvar Aalto* by Demetri Porphyrios, London 1982; *Det vita bordet: Alvar Aaltos ungdom och grundlaggande konstnarlis ideer* by Göran Schildt, Stockholm 1982; *Alvar Aalto: A Critical Study* by Malcolm Quantrill, London 1983; *Alvar Aalto: The Early Years* by Göran Schildt, New York 1984; *Contemporary Designers*, edited by Ann Lee Morgan, New York and London 1984; articles— "The Work of Alvar Aalto" by P. M. Shand in *Architectural Review* (London) September 1931; "Alvar Aalto: Finland's Modern Master" in *Architectural Forum* (New York), April 1938; "Due ville di Alvar Aalto" by G. Pagano in *Casabella* (Milan), no. 145, 1940; "Trends in Factory-Made Furniture" by E. Race in *Architectural Review* (London), no. 617, 1948; "Alvar Aalto" by Siegfried Giedion in *Architectural Review* (London), February 1950; "Il lungo cammino di Alvar Aalto" by Carlo Santini in *Domus* (Milan), January 1951; "The One and the Few" by Reyner Banham in *Architectural Review* (London), April 1957; "Aalto and His Influence" by Dennis Sharp in *Architecture and Building* (London), December 1957; "Alvar Aalto from Sunila to Imatra: Ideas, Projects and Buildings" by Carlo Santini and Göran Schildt in *Zodiac 3* (Milan), 1958; special issue of *Arkkitehti* (Helsinki), January-February 1958; "Finland and Architect Aalto" by John Burchard in *Architectural Record* (New York), January 1959; "Alvar Aalto baut in Deutschland" by G. Kuhne in *Bauwelt* (Berlin), no. 41, 1962; "L'Opera di Alvar Aalto" by Alessandro Mendini in *Casabella* (Milan), November 1965; "Aalto Revisited" in *Architectural Forum* (New York), April 1966; "Alvar Aalto and the Ethos of the Second Generation" by Peter Smithson in *Arkkitehti* (Helsinki), nos. 7/8, 1967; "Aalto Ego" by Jane Holtz Kay in *Building Design* (London), August 1973; special number of *Arkkitehti* (Helsinki), no. 6, 1974; four articles by Louis Hellman in *Building Design* (London), February and March 1975; "Alvar Aalto: The Man and His Work," special issue of *Arkkitehti* (Helsinki), nos. 7/8, 1976; "Alvar Aalto: Architecture Was His Medium" by Karl Fleig in *Werk* (Zürich), October 1976; "Alvar Aalto," special issue of *Space Design* (Tokyo), January/February 1977; "On Aalto," special issue of *Progressive Architecture* (New York), April 1977; "Reflections on the Influence of Alvar Aalto" by George Baird in *Canadian Architect* (Toronto), May 1977; "Alvar Aalto: His Life, Work and Philosophy," special issue of *L'Architecture d'aujourd'hui* (Paris), June 1977; "An Architect of True Genius" by Malcolm Quantrill in *The Sunday Times* (London), 3 September 1978; "Alvar Aalto," special issue of *Architectural Association Quarterly* (London), no. 3, 1978; "Aalto Literature: Architecture in Buildings and Ideas" by Pekka Suhonen in *Arkkitehti* (Helsinki), no. 2, 1980; "Aalto and After" by Charles Knevitt in *Building Design* (London), 16 May 1980; "Hugo Alvar Henryk Aalto: A Bibliography" by Omri Eytan in *Affiche* (Greenbelt, Maryland), June/July 1980; "Alvar Aalto in Barcelona again" by Fernando Perez Oyarzum in *Arquitecturas bis* (Barcelona), April-June 1981; "Alvar Aalto in Context" by Robert M. Kliment in *Architectural Record* (New York), September 1981; "Currents and Undercurrents in Finnish Architecture" by Asko Salokorpi in *Apollo* (London), May 1982; "Aalto's Architecture Redefined?" by Bob Allies in *Architects' Journal* (London), 23 February 1983.

Bibliography: *Alvar Aalto: A Bibliography* by William C. Miller, Monticello, Illinois 1976, as *Alvar Aalto: An Annotated Bibliography*, 1984; *Alvar Aalto: Designer and Architect*, Monticello, Illinois 1980.

"Alvar Aalto's work has meant the most to me," Robert Venturi has written, "of all the work of the Modern masters," and there are many admiring references to Aalto in Venturi's *Complexity and Contradiction in Architecture*. Visually unrelated as Aalto's and Venturi's work may seem, this acknowledged link points to the adept manipulation of "complexity and contradiction" by the Finnish master, and even to the seeds of postmodernism in some of modernism's earliest monuments.

Aalto's architecture varied from International Style dogma in a number of ways: it was often rough in texture, natural in color, and lyrical rather than strictly ordered in its floor plans and even in its distribution of structural elements. In a time, now past, when the shared traits of the modern masters were being emphasized at the expense of their individuality, these variations were glossed over as the idiosyncrasies expected of an artist from such a remote land.

There is much, indeed, in Aalto's work that is perfectly fitting for the limited economic and natural resources (including limited sunlight) of Finland, and his earliest works—the Muurame Parish Church, for example, and the Farmers' Cooperative in Turku—were designed in the context of a new nation's natural self-consciousness. (Finland became an independent country only in 1917, when Aalto was 19.)

But from the completion of the Paimio sanatorium in 1933 and the Viipuri library in 1935, it was clear that Aalto was an architect of international stature. His Finnish pavilions for the Paris World's Fair of 1937 and the New York World's Fair of 1939 and the exhibition organized by John McAndrew at New York's Museum of Modern Art in 1938 established his reputation throughout the west. In the same decade, Aalto, his wife Aino, and Mairea Gullichsøn formed the Artek Company for the manufacture and distribution of the beginning of a series of modest but brilliant furniture designs, the most popular of these being Aalto's three-legged stacking stool, designed in 1938 and now ubiquitous.

Aalto's first permanent American design (there were to be only three major American works, including the handsome Kaufmann Conference Suite at the Institute of International Education in New York) was the 1948 Baker House dormitory at the Massachusetts Institute of Technology. Of rough brick, with two main elevations quite different in character, and sinuously curving in plan (to give rooms views up and down, not just *at* the adjacent river), Baker House was a clear break with modern purity, unity, and planarity. (Aalto's work on Baker house was interrupted by Aino's illness and death; it is important to note that both Aino and Aalto's second wife, Elissa, were collaborating partners in his work.)

Other major buildings of Aalto's maturity include the Gullichsøn house, Villa Mairea, of 1939, the modest but moving Säynätsalo Town Hall of 1952, the Public Pensions Institute, Helsinki, of 1956, the Helsinki House of Culture of 1958, the Vuoksenniska church of the same year, the Wolfsburg (Germany) Cultural Center, finished in 1963, and a number of buildings at the Institute of Technology, Otaniemi.

Throughout the whole scope of this work—from stools, vases, and lighting fixtures to the planning of entire urban areas—it is possible to see not only those personal inclinations and poetic "complexities" that separate Aalto from the mainstream of the modern movement, but also those touches of thoughtfulness and grace that raise his work above the mainstream of the architecture of any period. For Aalto was more than a master of artistic form and of intelligent planning; he was the master as well of the details that relate a building successfully to its users. He cared for the proper shape of a handrail, for the convenience of storage elements, for the texture of a wall, for the delights of natural light. He once advised the architecture students at M.I.T. to design their windows as if the girls they loved were sitting in them.

In Aalto's work, we find assuring precedents for some current trends, we find an honorable and simple humanism amongst modernism's pretensions, and we find the permanent pleasures of architecture at its highest level.

—Stanley Abercrombie

ABRAHAM, Raimund Johann.

Austrian. Born in Lienz, Tyrol, 23 July 1933; emigrated to the United States, 1965. Educated at the Realgymnasium, Lienz, 1944-52; studied architecture, Technische Universität, Graz, 1953-58, Dip.Ing. 1958. Married Henny Petri in 1964; children: Una and Wassily. In private practice as architect and industrial designer, Vienna, 1960-64; worked with the architect Frederick Kiesler, *q.v.*, New York, 1964; in private practice, Providence, Rhode Island, 1964-71; founder, with S. Thomasson, Studio of Environmental Technology, Providence, Rhode Island, 1968. Since 1971, in private practice, New York. Instructor in Architecture, Rhode Island School of Design, Providence, 1964-71; Professor of Architecture, Cooper Union, New York, and Adjunct Professor of Architecture, Pratt Institute, Brooklyn, New York, since 1971; Visiting Professor, Architectural Association School, London, 1972-73, University of Houston, Texas, 1981 and 1983, and the University of Strasbourg, France, 1985; Davenport Professor of Architecture, Yale University, New Haven, Connecticut, 1985. Exhibitions: *Work in Progress*, Rhode Island School of Design, Providence, 1964; *Aktion Architektur*, Graz, Austria, 1965; *L'Architettura Sperimentale*, National Institute of Architects, Rome, 1967; *Architectural Fantasies* (with Hans Hollein and Walter Pichler), Museum of Modern Art, New York, 1967; *Changing Form in Architecture*, at the *Triennale*, Milan, and the Institute for Advanced Studies, London, 1968; *Hyperspaces*, Architectural League, New York, 1969; *Zero-Zones*, Moderna Museet, Stockholm, 1969; *Architecture* (with A. Natalini, F. St. Florian, and M. Webb), Brown University, Providence, Rhode Island, 1972; *Works 1960-1973*, Galerie Grunangergasse, Vienna, 1973; *The House: Universe of Man*, Galeria Universitaria, Mexico City, 1975; *America-Europa*, at the *Biennale*, Venice, 1976; *Model as Idea*, Institute for Architecture and Urban Studies, New York, 1976; *Alternative Architecture*, Louisiana Museum, Humlebaek, Denmark, 1977; *Abraham/Eisenman/Hejduk/Rossi*, Cooper Union, New York, 1977; *Architecture I*, Leo Castelli Gallery, New York, 1977; *Seven Architects*, Institute of Contemporary Art, Philadelphia, 1978; *Fantastic Architecture*, Drawing Center, New York, 1979; *10 Immagini per Venezia*, Museo Correr, Venice, 1980; *City Segments*, Walker Art Center, Minneapolis, 1980; *Collisions*, Yale University, New Haven, Connecticut, 1981; *Urban Fragments*, Architectural Association, London, 1981; *Trends in Contemporary Architecture*, National Gallery, Athens, 1982; *Raimund Abraham: The Berlin Projects*, Aedes Gallery, West Berlin, 1983; *Follies*, Leo Castelli Gallery, New York, 1983 (travelled to Los Angeles, and Madrid, Spain); *Arte Austriacca*, Museum of Modern Art, Bologna, Italy, 1984; *Visionary Architecture*, Kunsthalle, Hamburg, and Akademie der bildenden Künste, Munich, 1984; *Abenteuer der Ideen*, Nationalgalerie, West Berlin, and at the *Triennale*, Milan, 1984; *Revision der Moderne*, Deutsches Architekturmuseum, Frankfurt, and Centre Georges Pompidou, Paris, 1984; *Terza Mostra d'Architettura*, at the *Biennale*, Venice, 1985. Recipient: Clawson Mills Fellowship, Architectural League, New York, 1968; First Prize, The City as Significant Environment Competition, Milan, 1972; First Prize, Rainbow Plaza Competition, Niagara Falls, New York, 1972; Graham Foundation Fellowship, Chicago, 1974; National Endowment for the Arts Grant, Washington, D.C., 1976; DAAD Fellowship, West Berlin, 1981; First Prize, IBA Competition, West Berlin, 1981; First Prize, Times Square Tower Competition, New York, 1984; Stone Lion Award, Third Architecture Biennale, Venice, 1985. Address: 44 Bond Street, New York, New York 10012, U.S.A.

Works:

1958 Pan-Arabian University City, Riyadh, Saudi Arabia (project; with F. Gartler and J. Lundberg)
1959 Cultural Centre, Leopoldville, Congo (project; with F. Gartler)
1959/
61 J. Dapra House, Salzburg, Austria (with F. Gartler)
1960 Vocational School, Vienna (project; with F. Gartler and W. Benedikt)
1960/
64 Pless House, Vienna (with F. Gartler and F. Max)
1961 Three Churches, Copenhagen (projects)
1962 Ideal Church (projects)
Compact Cities (theoretical project)
1963 House for Two Friends, Oggau, Austria (project; with Walter Pichler)
1963/
64 Linear City (theoretical project)
Metropolitan Core (theoretical project)
1963/
67 Dellacher House, Oberwarth, Austria
1964 Fountain, Benjamin Franklin Parkway, Philadelphia (project; with A. W. Galler)
1965 Mega Bridges (theoretical project)
Tegel Air Terminal, West Berlin (project; with F. St. Florian)
1966 Air Ocean City (theoretical project)
Universal City (theoretical project)
Experimental House, Connecticut (partially built)
1967 Transplantation I (theoretical project)
Radar Cities (theoretical project)
Urban Interchange (theoretical project)
Continuous Building (theoretical project)
Moon Crater City (theoretical project)
1968 Cultural Center, Binghamton, New York (project; with A. W. Geller)
1968/
69 Universal House (project)
Low-income Housing, Providence, Rhode Island (project; with F. St. Florian and S. Thomasson)
1968/
70 Prefabricated Houses, Providence, Rhode Island (with S. Thomasson)
1969/
70 M.A.Z.E. – Experimental Kindergarten (with S. Thomasson)
1970 Erde Wolken Haus – Earth Cloud House (theoretical project)
1971 House with Curtains (theoretical project)
Centre Georges Pompidou, Paris (competition project; with F. St. Florian)
1972 House with Two Halves (theoretical project)
House with Nine Rooms (theoretical project)
House with Permanent Shadow (theoretical project)
House with Three Rooms (theoretical project)
House with Path (theoretical project)
House with Three Walls (theoretical project)
1973 House with Two Horizons (theoretical project)
House with Flower Walls (theoretical project)
1974/
75 House without Rooms (theoretical project)
1976 Seven Gates to Eden: Penetration, Collision, Separation, Illumination, Projection, Isolation, Fragmentation (theoretical projects)

1977 House with Projected Landscapes (theoretical project)
1979 House for the Sun (project)
1979/
80 City of Twofold Vision, Venice (project)
1980 Wall of Lost Journeys, Venice (project)
Hospital of Canareggio, Venice (project)
Tower of Wisdom, Venice (project)
Monument to Aviation, Melbourne, Australia (project)
Anthology Film Archives, New York (project)
Congress Hall redevelopment, West Berlin (project)
Friedrichstrasse City Block development, West Berlin (project)
Les Halles redevelopment, Paris (project)
1981 Monument for the Absence of the Painting *Guernica*, Guernica, Spain (project)
1982 Church on the Berlin Wall (project)
Monument for the Berlin Wall (project)
Peak Development, Hong Kong (project)
1983 House for Euclid, Greece (project)
Opera de la Bastille development, Paris (project)
Prinz Albrecht Palais development, West Berlin (project)
1984 P. Vellat House, Colorado (project)
Times Square Tower, New York (project)
H-aus (theoretical project)
1985 New Accademia Bridge, Venice (project)
Palazzo Ca' Venier/Peggy Guggenheim Museum extension, Venice (project)
Rainbow Plaza, Niagara Falls, New York (with G. Fiorenzoli and A. W. Geller)
Residential and Office Building, Friedrichstrasse, West Berlin
Anthology Film Archives, New York

Publications:

By ABRAHAM: books—*Elementare Architektur*, with photographs by Josef Dapra, Salzburg 1963; *L'Architettura Sperimentale*, with Friedrich St. Florian, Rome 1967; *Modular Housing*, with Friedrich St. Florian and S. Thomasson, Providence, Rhode Island 1968; *Maze*, with S. Thomasson, Providence, Rhode Island 1969; *Works 1960-1973*, exhibition catalogue, Vienna 1973; *The House: Universe of Man*, exhibition catalogue, Mexico City 1975; *Urban Fragments*, exhibition catalogue, London 1981; *Raimund Abraham: Berlin Projects*, exhibition catalogue, West Berlin 1983; article—"Negation and Reconciliation" in *Perspecta* (New Haven, Connecticut), no. 19, 1982.

On ABRAHAM: books—*Architektur in Wien* by Ottokur Uhl, Vienna 1965; *Architectural Fantasies*, exhibition catalogue by Arthur Drexler, New York 1967; *Experimental Architecture* by Peter Cook, London 1970; *L'Architettura Radicale* by P. Navone and B. Orlandoni, Milan 1974; *Architecture I*, exhibition catalogue by Pierre Apraxine, New York 1977; *Europa-America*, edited by Franco Raggi, Venice 1978; *Fenster: Raimund Abraham*, Innsbruck, Austria 1979; *Architektur aus Osterreich seit 1960* by Peter M. Bode and Gustav Peichl, Salzburg and Vienna 1980; *Raimund Abraham: Obras y Proyectos 1960-83* by Alberto Campo Baeza, Kenneth Frampton and others, Madrid 1983; *Follies: Architecture for the Late-Twentieth-Century Landscapes* by B. J. Archer and A. Vidler, New York 1983; *Moderne und Postmoderne: Architektur der Gegenwart 1960-1980* by Heinrich Klotz, Braunschweig and Wiesbaden, West Germany 1984; *La Terza Biennale d'Architettura*, exhibition catalogue by Aldo Rossi, Venice 1985; articles—"L'Architettura Sperimentale" by A. Mendini in *Casabella* (Milan), no. 314, 1967; "The Mechanistic Image" by Peter Cook in *Architectural Design* (London), June 1967; "Hyperspaces" in *Architectural Design* (London), July 1969; "Due Austriacci a una Scuola

Americana: Imaginary Architecture" in *Domus* (Milan), October 1970; "Dreamhouses di Raimund Abraham" by A. Natalini in *Domus* (Milan), June 1971; "Winners in the Shinkenchiku Residential Design Competition" in *Japan Architect* (Tokyo), December 1976; "Formalism and Realism in Architecture" in *L'Architecture d'Aujourd'hui* (Paris), no. 190, 1977; "Imaginary Architecture I: Raimund Abraham" by Arata Isozaki in *Space Design* (Tokyo), March 1977; "City Segments", special issue of *Design Quarterly* (Minneapolis), no. 113/114, 1980; "Ten Architects in Venice" by F. Dal Co in *Architecture + Urbanism* (Tokyo), October 1980; "Modern Greek Dramas" in *Building Design* (London), 28 January 1983; "Architecture Is More Than Pretty Words" by A. Campo Baeza in *Q* (Barcelona), May 1983.

*   *   *

Collision as a metaphor plays a salient role in my work as a physical or syntactic manifestation. I believe that the dialectical principle of "collision" is the ontological basis of all architecture. Above all it addresses itself to the archetypical site of the horizon where the earth meets the sky. Any architectural endeavor is an interference with this site. One either builds up into the sky or down into the earth. This interference is the quintessence of the architectural act; one which is totally antithetical to any form of aesthetic or historical speculation. The process of design is only a secondary and subsequent act whose purpose is to reconcile and harmonize the consequences of the initial collision. I think it is possible to develop a taxonomy of collisions in architecture: the collision of the "object with time"—an intersection one might say with a "frame of time" as in the split axis of my chair project which implies the temporal intervention of the body; the collision of the "body with architecture" as in the *House Without Rooms*; the collision of an "object with architecture" as in my *Monument to Aviation*; the collision of the "site or the architecture with light" as in the *House with Permanent Shadow* or in the Guernica project; the collision of "architecture and landscape" as in the *House With Projected Landscapes* in which the surrounding topography literally inscribes itself on the section of the house—the converse is a situation in which the architecture inscribes the topography as in *House With Path*: the collision of "architecture with architecture" as in the *Seven Gates of Eden*.

The phenomena of collision leads rather directly to the complex process of decomposition, as an agent by which to pursue the act of making a *critique*. Modern art in general is the first art epoch in history to predicate itself not only on the criticism of all cultural antecedents but also on the criticism of art *in se*. In architectural terms, decomposition can be seen as the negation of the architectural entity, of a whole, which, in the last analysis, can only be understood through the truth of its elements. The physical relations between architectural components can also be interpreted as a series of collisions, as a set of interpenetrations, if you like, in which the "horizon" always establishes the grammatical clarity of the elemental relationships.

In metaphysical terms, architecture has always been a monument to the eternal, commemorating both the absence and presence of man. For all its paradoxical nature, the eternal has endured as the mainspring of architecture. Today, however, the time-honored reciprocity between the eternal and the apocalypse has been fundamentally transformed. Where formerly the apocalypse had only a metaphysical status, today it has become only too realizable in terms of our own capacity for physical destruction.

More specifically, architecture can only be understood as a polarity between geometric and physiological space or as collision between the ideal and matter, and while the ideal represents the notion of infinity or, let us say, the eternal, matter can be regarded as the symbolic representation of the body—its presence and its absence. To put it in

other words, while man's conceptual powers aspire to the infinite, his body is essentially fragile, temporal, a corpus which will be laid waste, like material itself, by the unremitting action of time. If there remains any hope for recreating the iconic in the modern world, then surely this will only come from a reinterpretation of the archetypal existence of man; that is to say, new icons cannot possibly be established on the basis of motifs drawn or transposed from lost historical epochs. New icons will either come from a recognition of our intrinsic ontological limits or they will not arise at all.
—Raimund Abraham

Architectural drawing occupies as central a position in the work of Raimund Abraham as the actual realization of his projects. His first houses were built between 1960 and 1964, in part collaboration with Walter Pichler. In New York in 1964 Abraham worked alongside Frederick Kiesler. A participant in the Viennese architectural scene of the early sixties, influenced by Pichler and Hollein, St. Florian and Peichl—and undertaking collaborative projects with most of these architects—Abraham developed the architectural drawing as a medium of architectonic expression in its own right, defending its importance thus: "Drawing is for me an equivalent to building. I only ever start to draw once I have fully formulated an architectonic idea, that is, the abstract concept. Then I begin to build, as I draw. (. . .) There are a number of different languages which can be used to put an architectural idea into practice. One possibility is drawing. And I don't mean that an architectural drawing is an intermediate product: the result of frustration when building projects are lacking. It's a great mistake to think that drawing can be classified as an intermediate product."

Between 1962 and 1967 Abraham produced series of drawings of imaginary cities—for example, Compact Cities (1962), Mega Bridges (1965), Air Ocean City (1966), Universal City (1966), Radar Cities (1967) and Moon Crater City (1967)—which featured high-tech and utopian megastructures like the works of the English group Archigram and Adolfo Natalini's Italian team. But unlike these works with their astronautic optimism deriving from pop art, Abraham's drawings convey in their almost neurotic linemasses the metaphysical fear that such hyperstructures of town planning inspire in him. Abraham imagines not only the technically realizable but also its psychological effect on the users and inhabitants. The cylinders, discs, concrete blocks and pipelines take on an almost organic quality which is more important than the functional, sociological or ergonomic source of the architectural forms.

In such projects a specifically Viennese mentality is apparent, the same mentality that defines the ephemeral (though aimed at actual realization) architectonic works of Coop-Himmelblau and Haus-Rucker-Co. Such an architectonic mentality, dialectically linking technics with psychology, rationalism with poetry, and reality with fiction, enabled Abraham too, in 1970, to free himself from his technological utopias. His megastructures already contained an inherent critique. In the space of five years Abraham now produced ten "poetic" house designs, whose subjective-mythical quality brings them closer to architectural poems or paraphrases than realizable buildings. At the same time Abraham worked nine of these houses into a huge, coloured triptych. The designs were intended to reflect an inner psychological reality, a world of fantasy, of intuition and dream, as the titles themselves indicate: "House with permanent shadow", "House with two horizons", or "House with flowery walls". The "Nine Houses" describe or construct archetypes and metaphors for houses. The open, isometric perspectives form a contrast with the misty fragments of landscape, street and countryside, within which the houses are arranged side by side. Abraham's triptych summarizes his architec-

tural conception of the seventies. Alongside such draughtsmen as Massimo Scolari, Leon Krier, Hans Dieter Schäal and John Hejduk, all of whom have been strongly influenced by him and with whom he has been teaching at the Cooper Union School in New York since 1971, Abraham is the most important and till now most influential representative of a conception of architecture which sees the drawing as its self-justifying end product. With the "built drawing", architecture as a category of art not only recapitulates an essential part of its own history (from Piranesi to Boullée), but also approaches current art forms like individual mythologies, Concept Art and Environmental Art.

Those imaginary architectural forms have often evolved to meet the concrete needs of town planning, especially in the course of competitions. Despite the fact that he has won several first prizes, the number of actual buildings realized from Abraham's designs is small: about ten in 25 years. Like SITE or Peter Eisenman, Abraham has a concise architectonic theory, to which both his drawings and his buildings submit. The central notion is one of "collision": understood as dialectical principle and ontological basis of all aritecture. Every type of building is either built upwards towards the sky or sunk downwards into the earth; at the same time man-built areas not only define the relationship that exists between inside and outside with regard to man and his environment, but they are also operations which alter the horizon in the widest sense of the word: in spatial, spiritual and psychological terms, and also in terms of history and the history of development. The design is as a result only a secondary act, having the objectives of harmonizing that "collision" and transforming it into spatial experience. The design principle is de-composition, understood as the negation of existing architectonic entities, which are put together in new ways. The redefinition of existing factors takes place, according to Abraham, in the polarity between geometric and physiological space, and only from this standpoint can he imagine a development for the present of a new iconography, a new representationalism in architecture. The objective of a present-conscious architectonic thinking cannot be the rediscovery of historical forms: it must be the progressive recognition of the ontological limits inherent in human existence.

Thanks to this conception, and its formulation in design terms that are not only theoretically but also aesthetically brilliant, Abraham has become in recent years one of today's most influential teachers in the study of architectonics. His defiant, poetic, at times surreal alternative to the usual oppressive utilitarianism of our built environment strikes a clear chord in our modern world.
—Volker Fischer

ABRAMOVITZ, Max.
American. Born in Chicago, Illinois, 23 May 1908. Educated at the University of Illinois, Urbana-Champaign, 1925-29, B.S. 1929; Columbia University, New York, 1929-31, M.S. 1931; did postgraduate work at the Ecole des Beaux-Arts, Paris, 1932-34. Served as a Lieutenant-Colonel in the United States Army, in America and in the China theatre, 1942-45; Legion of Merit Award; served as a Colonel in the United States Air Force, serving at the Pentagon, Washington, D.C., 1950-52; Special Assistant to the Assistant Secretary of the United States Air Force, 1952. Married Anne Marie Causey in 1937 (divorced, 1964); children: Michael and Katherine; married Anita Zeltner Brooks in 1964. Associate Professor, School of Fine Arts, Yale University, New Haven, Connecticut, 1939-42; Partner, with Wallace

K. Harrison, q.v., Harrison and Arbramovitz, New York, 1945-76; Deputy Director of Planning, United Nations Headquarters, New York, 1947-52. Since 1976, Partner, Abramovitz-Harris-Kingsland, New York. Governor, New York Building Congress, 1957-64; Chairman of the Board, American Society of Civil Engineers, 1966-68. Director, New York Regional Plan Association; Trustee, Mt. Sinai Hospital, and Mt. Sinai Medical Center, New York. Exhibitions: University of Illinois, Urbana-Champaign campus and Chicago Circle campus, 1963; University of Michigan, Ann Arbor, 1964; Virginia Polytechnic Institute, Blacksburg, 1964; Parsons College, Fairfield, Iowa, 1964. Archive Collection: Syracuse University, Syracuse, New York, and University of Wyoming, Laramie. Recipient: President's Award, Columbia University, 1960; Achievement Award, University of Illinois Alumni Association, 1963. D.F.A.: University of Pittsburgh, Pennsylvania, 1961; University of Illinois, Urbana-Champaign, 1970; Fellow, Brandeis University, Waltham, Massachusetts, 1963. Fellow, American Institute of Architects, 1952. Address (office): 630 Fifth Avenue, New York, New York 10020, U.S.A.

Works:

1947/
53   United Nations Headquarters, First Avenue, New York (as Deputy Director of Planning; Wallace K. Harrison, Chairman of the Board of Design and Director of Planning; with advisory team of Architects, including Le Corbusier, Oscar Niemeyer, and Sven Markelius)
1951   Corning Glass Center, Corning, New York
1952   United States Embassy, Havana
         United States Embassy, Rio de Janeiro
1955   Inter-Faith Chapels, Brandeis University, Waltham, Massachusetts
1957   Commercial Investment Trust Building, New York
1958   Corning Glass Building, New York
         Loeb Student Center, New York University, New York
1960   Gateway 4 Building, Equitable Life Assurance Society, Pittsburgh, Pennsylvania
1961   Central Intelligence Agency Building, Langley, Virginia
1962   Philharmonic Hall (now Avery Fisher Hall), Lincoln Center, New York (interior rebuilt, 1976)
         Columbia University Law School and Plaza, New York
1963   Assembly Hall, University of Illinois, Urbana-Champaign
1964   Phoenix Mutual Life Insurance Building, Hartford, Connecticut
         Bell Telephone Building, World's Fair, New York
         Institute of International Education, 809 United Nations Plaza, New York (with Wallace K. Harrison and Michael M. Harris)
1965   Erieview Plaza, Cleveland, Ohio
1966   860 United Nations Plaza Building, New York
         Hilles Library, Radcliffe College, Cambridge, Massachusetts
1967   Union Bank Square, Los Angeles
         Temple Beth Zion, Buffalo, New York
1969   Erie County Bank and Office Building, Buffalo, New York
         Cincinnati Center, Ohio
         Fiberglas Tower, Toledo, Ohio
         Krannert Center for the Performing Arts, University of Illinois, Urbana-Champaign
1970   Westinghouse Building, Pittsburgh, Pennsylvania
         Banque Rothschild Building, Paris
         Brandeis University Master Plan and Academic Buildings, Waltham, Massachusetts

Currier Houses, Radcliffe College, Cambridge, Massachusets

School of International Affairs, Columbia University, New York

Fine Arts Center, University of Iowa, Iowa City

1971 United States Steel Building, Pittsburgh, Pennsylvania

1972 First National Bank Building, Louisville, Kentucky

Music School, University of Iowa, Iowa City

Hancher Auditorium, University of Iowa, Iowa City

1976 GAN (Groupe des Assurances Nationales) Tower, La Défense, Paris

1977 GAN Building, Bordeaux, France

Nationwide Insurance Company Plaza, Columbus, Ohio

Mead Tower, Dayton, Ohio

Dayton Power and Light Building, Ohio

1979 Hebrew Union College-Jewish Institute of Religion, New York

1982 Owens-Illinois World Headquarters, Toledo, Ohio

1984 Jewish Chapel, United States Military Academy, West Point, New York

Publications:

By ABRAMOVITZ: books—*Architecture and the University*, Princeton 1954; *The Architcture of Max Abramovitz*, Champaign-Urbana, Illinois 1963; tapes—*Oral Memoir of Max Abramovitz*, New York 1976; articles—"An Architect's Message" in *Opera News* (New York), 29 September 1962; "The City of Tomorrow" in *Pitt* (Pittsburgh, Pennsylvania), October 1963; "Programming and the Client-User" in *Progressive Architecture* (New York), October 1965; "Designing for the Performing Arts" in *Journal of Aesthetic Education* (Urbana, Illinois), January 1969; "The Susan Morse and Frederick Wiley Hilles Library at Radcliffe College" in *Harvard University Library Bulletin* (Cambridge, Massachusetts), October 1969.

On ABRAMOVITZ: book—*The Story and Facts about the Krannert Center for the Performing Arts*, Urbana, Illinois 1969; articles—"Student Religious Center based on Synagogue" in *Architectural Record* (New York), June 1948; "Embassy Office Building" in *Progressive Architecture* (New York), October 1951; "Three Chapels" in *Architectural Record* (New York), September 1954; "New York's Biggest Building in 25 Years" in *Architectural Forum* (New York), January 1955; "An Unusual Design for Collegiate Religion" in *Architectural Record* (New York), January 1956; "A Squat Headquarters for CIT" in *Architectural Forum* (New York), January 1958; "The Big Mirror" in *Architectural Forum* (New York), May 1959; "Student Center for Big City University" in *Architectural Record* (New York), May 1960; "Lincoln Center, New York: Philharmonic Hall" in *Architectural Record* (New York), September 1962; "Panther Hollow Redevelopment, Pittsburgh, Pennsylvania" in *Progressive Architecture* (New York), July 1963; "Temple Beth Zion" in *Architectural Record* (New York), March 1968; "Architecture for the Arts of Music, Dance and Drama" in *Architectural Record* (New York), November 1969; "U.S. Steel Headquarters Building" in *Civil Engineering* (New York), April 1970; "Recu Chez Rothschild—La Banque Rothschild" in *Connaissance des arts* (Paris), May 1970; "Big Steel Spike: The U.S. Steel Building" in *Architectural Forum* (New York), December 1971; "Bank in Paris—Rothschild Bank" in *Réalités* (New York), October 1972.

Bibliography: *Max Abramovitz and University Architecture: An Introductory Bibliography*, Monticello, Illinois 1983.

*

I am trying to find in architecture a rightness that transcends the fashionable, an architecture which contains a planned order, a rhythm, with an interrelationship of spaces that is vital—wherein there is nothing that can be taken away from the building without feeling a loss and where everything contributes to the desired expression.

A building or a space should make one feel that a thought is within it, that it is more than a shelter, as a good book is more than words put together, as music is more than an arrangement of notes.

I will use the full vocabulary available to me of structure, materials, technical devices, and, when and where necessary, develop new uses for materials and structure, but always within the framework of the search for the proper design concept. I have no desire to warp the individual to technology.

Architecture can tell us more about people and the man than the other arts because it has less opportunity to be irrelevant and trivial than the other arts. Since it is in and among our buildings that we live and move, it is in our buildings that our lives are revealed.

—Max Abramovitz

*

Max Abramovitz is best known, perhaps, as the "other half" of the partnership of Harrison and Abramovitz. This "second billing" is understandable enough; from Rockefeller Center to the United Nations to the New York State Capital, Wallace K. Harrison has been team leader of some of the most famous architecural works of the twentieth century. Yet, any examination of Abramovitz's works (the former partners freely credit each other's work) reveals that Abamovitz emerges from the thirty year partnership as very much an architect in his own right.

During the great building sprees of the 1900s in the large cities of the United States, there was a great deal of experimentation with new materials, and, like many others in that decade, Abramovitz was a great user of glass. The Corning Glass building, with the first full glass skyscraper wall, contains more glass than any building built to that time. Yet, as always with Abramovitz, there is more of interest than simply statistics; the Corning Glass Building and the earlier Glass Center interestingly present the material, and the buildings exude spaciousness, airiness, light, even levity.

Abramovitz is happy when he is working with large and lofty interiors, with bare areas. And, a notable aspect of his work, he is as interested in the spaces between his buildings and their settings as he is in the structures themselves.

The Inter-Faith Chapels at Brandeis University, consisting of three buildings for the Protestant, Catholic, and Jewish faiths, surround a pool; each has its own outside altar, so that joint services can take place. There is no outside "identification," but, though each building is of the same height and size and constructed of the same materials, each one has its own particular shape, the common theme appearing in the truncation of a geometric form. Glass, again, is an important feature: glass panels occupy the full height of the "cut-off" ends facing the pool. Much thought was given to detail, and advice was taken from the three religious authorities; inside each building, Abramovitz's attempt to convey the relevant spiritual mood has been entirely successful.

The Philharmonic Hall at Lincoln Center received a great deal of publicity, but more interesting is the Krannert Center for the Performing Arts at the University of Illinois, in which the truncated forms again appear. The Great Hall, seating 2100, is a complete rectangle; the Festival Theatre, seating 985, is an oval, cut across at both ends; and the playhouse, with 678 seats, is a similar basic shape, cut off at one end only; in addition, the Center includes an outdoor amphitheatre for 560 spectators and a Studio Theatre, almost square, for experimental drama, with seating for 150. Again, too, the spacing is interesting; the composition is reminiscent of a Roman Forum, a response to the obvious need for communicaion among the various theatres—a constant journeying from one to the other was obviously foreseen as part of the life of the Center.

Throughout his career, and throughout America, Abramovitz has built a number of important buildings. All of these works have something in common. Abramovitz believes that you cannot end up with a good result unless you start off with a good idea; from the beginning the plan and program must be based on what is wanted, not what the architect would like to impose. Ideas that are not there at the beginning will grow from discussions with the client, who must be advised about what is and what is not possible. In this way the architect involves his client in the process of design—not gratuitously, but to ensure that the building will "work" for its users, that it will be "appropriate." The fact that Abramovitz continues to be commissioned for auditoriums of all kinds, for places of worship, educational complexes, and office buildings, and by a variety of clients, suggests that more often than not he achieves his goal.

—Muriel Emanuel

ACKERMANN, Kurt.

German. Born in Insingen, Rothenburg ob der Tauber, 2 March 1928. Educated at the Oskar von Miller-Polytechnikum and the Technische Hochschule, Munich, 1949-54. Married Eleanore Höfter in 1958; children: Katrin, Peter, and Christoph. Since 1953, in private practice, Munich; Principal, Professor Kurt Ackermann und Partner, Munich, since 1969 (partners: Jürgen Feit, Peter Jaeger, and Richard Martin). Guest Lecturer at the Technical University, Vienna, 1971, and at the Technische Hochschule, Darmstadt, West Germany 1974. Since 1974, Professor of Design and Construction, University of Stuttgart; Guest Professor of Planning, Technical University, Vienna, 1979-80; Professor of Planning, University of Dortmund, West Germany, 1981. Member of the Executive Board, Bund Deutscher Architekten, in Bavaria, 1965-67; Member of the Governing Board, national Bund Deutscher Architekten, 1972-75; Member of the Editorial Committee, *Der Architekt*, Bonn, 1972-77. Member, Board of Patrons, *Bauen und Wohnen*, Zürich, since 1970; Member, Munich City Planning Commission, since 1973; Consultant to the Architectural Branch, German Research Organization, since 1975; Member of the Governing Council, Baden-Württemberg Building and Housing Research Society, since 1977. Exhibitions: *Zeit im Aufriss*, Munich 1983; Industriebau 1984, toured Germany, 1984. Recipient: Munich Culture Prize, for architecture, 1967; Bund Deutscher Architekten of Bavaria Prize, 1967, 1971 (twice), 1975, and 1983; German Brick Industry Prize, 1971; Munich Honor Prize, for housing construction, 1971; Munich Region Prize for City Design, 1979; Deutscher Architekturpreis, 1983; Mies van der Rohe Prize, 1984. Address: Professor Kurt Ackermann und Partner, Malsenstrasse 57, 8000 Munich 19, Germany.

Works:

1956 Gartner House, Gundelfingen, West Germany

1957 Holzbauer House, Gauting, West Germany

Primary school, Insingen, near Rothenburg, West Germany

1958 Dr. Peters House, Berg, West Germany

Hops warehouse, Mainburg, West Germany

Kurt Ackermann: Ice Skating Rink, Munich, 1983.

OSLW: Air Force Officers' School, Fürstenfeldbruck, West Germany

Heating Plant Building, Fürstenfeldbruck, West Germany

Esso Petrol Service Station, Munich (competition project)

1979 Administration Building, Munich

1981 Nationalgalerie extension, West Berlin (competition project)

1983 Post Office Savings Bank, Munich (competition project)

Märker Limestone Works, Harburg, West Germany

Skating Rink, Munich

1983/
85 Housing Development, Gottfried-Böhm-Weg, Munich

Winterling Housing Development, Munich

1983/
86 Footbridge, Kelheim, West Germany

1984 Bavarian Buildings Corporation Office, Munich

Post Office Headquarters, Regensburg, West Germany (competition project)

1984/
85 Housing on the Kulturforum, West Berlin

Langenscheidt Publishing Offices, Munich

1984/
86 Drainage Buildings and shoreline landscaping, Kelheim, West Germany

Student Housing Block, Freimann, Munich

Publications

By ACKERMANN: books—*Manifest für Architektur*, with the Architektenteam, Munich 1973; *Werkbericht Büro Prof. Kurt Ackermann + Partner*, Stuttgart 1978; *Grundlagen für das Entwerfen und Konstruieren*, Stuttgart 1983; *Industriebau*, Stuttgart 1984; articles—"Neuzeitliche Hopfenaufbereitungsanlagen" in *Hopfenrundschau* (Wolznach, West Germany), February 1959; "Der Architekt und das landwirtschaftliche Bauen" in *Baumeister* (Munich), January 1962; "Möbel kaufen in München" in *Bauwelt* (Berlin), no. 40, 1965; "Hardt-Schule in Weilheim" in *Baumeister* (Munich), February 1973; "Honorarreform ein Trauerspiel mit Ignoranz und Unvermögen" in *Architekt* (Stuttgart), September 1973; "Dieses Heft sieht anders aus" in *Architekt* (Stuttgart), January 1974; "Zum Entwerfen von Banken" in *Architekturwettbewerbe* (Stuggart), no. 77, 1974; "Der Architekt mit einem abermals anderen Gesicht" in *Architekt* (Stuttgart), January 1975; "Nachruf Karl Schwanzer" in *Architekt* (Stuttgart), October 1975; "Nostalgie—Laune oder Herausforderung" in *Bauen und Wohnen* (Zürich), December 1975; "Stellungnahme zur Gesamthochschulentwicklung" in *Architekt* (Stuttgart), December 1975; "Das Institut für Grundlagen des Entwerfens und Konstruierens" in *Baumeister* (Munich), April 1976; "Offene Umgänge an Verwaltungsbauten" in *Architekt* (Stuttgart), June 1976; "Planungs-und Bauablauf eines staatlichen Bauvorhabens" in *Architekt* (Stuttgart), February 1977; "Vorläufig nichts Neues unter der Sonne," with Paulhans Peters, in *Architekturwettbewerbe* (Stuttgart), no. 90, 1977; "Architekt and Bauingenieur" in *Glasforum* (Schorndorf, West Germany), March 1979; "Architekt und Ingenieur" in *Deutsche Bauzeitung* (Stuttgart), March 1981; "Das neue Bauen—Impulse der Olympischen Bauten" in *Sport und Design*, Baden-Baden, West Germany 1981; "Sportbauten—Synthese von Nutzung, Konstruktion und Form" in *Architekturwettbewerbe* (Stuttgart) no. 110, 1981; "Bauen mit Stahl" in *Deutsche Bauzeitung* (Stuttgart), January 1983.

On ACKERMANN: books—*Industriebau* by Walter Henn, Munich 1961, London 1965; *Stahlkonstruktionen im Hochbau* by Konrad Gatz and Franz Hart, Munich 1966; *Industriebau* by S. Nagel and S. Linke, Gütersloh, West Germany 1972; *Deutsche Kunst seit 1960, vol 4: Architecture* by Paolo Nestler and Peter M. Bode, Munich 1976; *Kurt Ackemann + Partner: Bauten, Projekte*, Stuttgart 1978; articles—in *Deutsche Bauzeitschrift* (Gütersloh, West Germany), July 1974 and September 1974; in *Bauen und Wohnen* (Zürich), April 1975; "Das dritte Dach" by Manfred Sack in *Die Zeit* (Hamburg, West Germany), 7 October 1983; "Schonheit des Technischen" by Christoph Hackelsberger in *Suddeutscher Zeitung* (Munich) 1983; "German Architecture Revitalized" by Manfred Sack in *Lufthansa Germany* (Frankfurt), June 1983.

If we look more closely at "anti-technical criticism," there emerges the almost schizophrenic contradiction of our age, which has the highest hopes in the perfection and automation of science, industry, housing, and leisure, and at the same time indulges in unrealistic daydreams of social utopias. Most publications on modern architecture deal more with ugliness than with beauty. Negative examples are legion, and no architect will deny his share of the responsibility. On the other hand, good work too is not spared. Outstanding buildings are denigrated as "solitaire" architecture, monuments to the architect, and they are often rated bad because they are new or large.

There is a distinct danger that violent rejection of aesthetic purism may issue in the opposite extreme, a revival of popular mannerism attended by arbitrary historicizing formalism. One thing, however, the negative publicity has done: it has sharpened our eye for the problems of historic monument preservation and has initiated a revision of our ideas of industrial architecture.

Nostaligia is a kind of longing. It leads to an attitude in which we merely look back; it leads to the obfuscation of problems and destroys the freedom of designer and builder. This lack of freedom can be overcome by group work on nostalgia-free social and environmental problems, by consistent and objective approaches to assignments, by the creation of alternatives as well as the technically adequate employment of materials.

The necessity of preserving historic buildings and the continuation of traditions must be taken for granted. Full of fascinated satisfaction, we have observed the rediscovery of the great values of old industrial buildings and industrially produced constructions of the last century. These products, on a high architectural level, and often designed by engineers, were scarcely noticed by their own age and their significance was not recognized.

It is not merely the historical interest in these astonishing buildings that strikes me as important in this change of outlook. They can also support us in our work, if we carefully study and analyze these buildings, not only with regard to the influence of engineering design on architecture, but also to clarify our own standpoint and to develop our own ideas of a more imaginative technology. Many people may notice only the decorations on these old buildings. We should not, however, be so superficial, but should derive from them a feeling for proportion, for naturalness and timelessness. Timelessness, too, is a notable feature of quality. Logical construction principles and the materials of steel and glass have not only led to bold forms but also to a new architecture. What is decisive about these buildings is their logic, precision, purity, elegance, and beauty.

Transparency articulates and lightens these buildings, which were not merely prestige structures but realized correctly understood basic functional principles. Both the aesthetic and the technical standpoints determined their expressive design.

I should now like to raise this question: What chance has such an architecture in our contemporary society? I think if clients attach the same importance to design as to function, we shall again have buildings that impose form on our environment, owing to their polyvalence, logical construction, and technical perfection. This means that we want more experimentation and research, more imagination, more technology, and more architecture.

* * * *

This article was written ten years ago. In principle, little has changed. The lustre of post modernism, after many realized projects, has faded severely. In some countries, the euphoric push for this architectural concept has obviously slowed down, although historical "quotations" are still in fashion.

In America, which I have just visited, an architecture of monumental and gigantic packaging is dominant. However, there is really little that is new. In England, on the other hand, there are excellent impulses in thought and form in the section of industrial buildings. Minted by technology, these examples emanate a new "technical esthetic" and show that the nostalgia wave really is the challenge of our time.

—Kurt Ackermann

Kurt Ackermann was one of the young German architects who began their professional careers after World War II and who based their work on that of those first and second-generation Modernists then still at the height of their creative powers. For Ackermann, the influence was, above all, Mies van der Rohe, whose buildings in Chicago were having great influence in Germany at that time. But this turning towards Mies was due not so much to any formal reason as to a certain way of looking at architecture, a way to which Ackermann had been dedicated from the start— the development of form from the created detail and the significance of construction itself as a medium of architecture.

Ackermann was also influenced, one might say, by the simple lines of those houses with clearly defined outlines; of brick, with gable roofs; concisely proportioned; their detail moulded with infinite care that Egon Eiermann, for example, built in the 1930s. There were similar buildings in Bavaria at the time— for instance, tha main Post Office—that must also have played their part in influencing him.

It is from these foundations, then, that Ackermann's work has developed in the last decade. His style is characterized by the clear arrangement of the architectural totality, the attempt to make the building readable, as it were, from its external appearance, to bring construction and form into a harmonious whole. In this way Gartner House in Gundelfingen (1970) uses the existing conditions in a layout which radiates outwards and in the centre of which lies the circular dining room.

Quite different in expression is the Air Force Officer's School in Fürstenfeldbuck, completed in 1977. Here it is not so much the steel and glass architecture that is characteristic as it is, rather, the placement of the buildings around garden squares. It is the spatial concept, rather than the technical detail, that decisively and fittingly expresses the character of the site.

Instead of employing the usual street edge construction, the Moll Housing Development in Munich (1970) was built in a horseshoe shape around a central inner courtyard. The individual homes are in blocks that are vertically staggered and horizontally displaced; it makes for a most unusual example of town building in Germany.

At a time when there is much questioning of values, Ackermann, in his work, shows how it is possible to base one's style upon traditional methods and yet progress further and simultaneously to remain aware that design must always be a combination of both construction and creation. What emerges is not a speculative architecture but one that uses the means of our time in order to give to the people of our time a fitting environment in which to live.

—Jürgen Joedicke

AFFLECK, Raymond Tait.

Canadian. Born in Penticton, British Columbia, 20 November 1922. Educated at West Hill High School, Montreal, 1935-39; McGill University, Montreal, 1941-47 (Hugh McLennan Travelling Scholarship; Royal Architectural Institute of Canada Medal; Louis Robertson Prize in Design; Lieutenant-Governor's Silver Medal), B.Arch. 1947; Eidgenossische Technische Hochschule, Zürich, 1948. Married Betty Ann Henley in 1950; children: Graham, Neil, Jane, Gavin, and Ewan. Architectural Assistant, McDougall Smith and Fleming, Montreal, 1948-50, and Vincent Rother, Montreal, 1950-51; Principal, R. T. Affleck, Montreal, 1952-55, and Affleck Desbarats Dimakopoulos Lebensold Sise, Montreal, 1955-69. Since 1969, Principal, Arcop Associates, Montreal (other principals: Fred Lebensold, Art Nichol, W. Paul Hughes, and Ramesh Khosla; associates: Imre Reichmann, Allan Thomas, Bruce Allan, Brian Hall, and Alan Woolham). Visiting Professor, McGill University, Montreal, since 1965. Exhibitions: *Architectural Work of Affleck Desbarats Dimakopoulos Lebensold Sise,* Montreal Museum of Fine Arts, 1965; *National Gallery of Canada Competition Exhibition,* National Gallery, Ottawa, 1978. Recipient: Massey Medal, 1961, 1964, 1967, and 1970; Canadian Centennial Medal, 1967. Honorary doctorates: University of Calgary, Alberta, 1972; Nova Scotia Technical College, Halifax, 1976; McGill University, Montreal, 1984. Fellow, Royal Architectural Institute of Canada, 1965; Academician, Royal Canadian Academy of Arts, 1967. Address: Arcop Associates, Post Office Box 900, Station H, 1440 St. Catherine Street West, Montreal, Quebec H3G 2L6, Canada.

Works:

1953   Klassen House, Montée des Trentes, St. Hilaire, Quebec
1954   Talbot Johnson House, Senneville Road, Senneville, Quebec
      Town of Mount Royal Post Office, Graham Boulevard, Quebec (with Jean Michaud)
1955   Queen Elizabeth Theatre, Vancouver, British Columbia
1956/
  65   Place Ville Marie, Montreal (with I. M. Pei)
1962   Summerlea Golf and Country Club, Pointeaux-Cascades, Quebec
1964   Robert Tilden House, Lac Tremblant, Quebec
1964/
  68   Place Bonaventure, Montreal
1965   Harry Hoy House, Lac Tremblant, Quebec
      Stephen Leacock Building, McGill University, Montreal
1966   Old Arts Building renovation, Montreal
1967   Arts and Culture Centre, St. John's, Newfoundland (with Cummings and Campbell)
1969   Life Sciences Centre, Dalhousie University, Halifax, Nova Scotia (with J. Davison)
1970   John Sparling House, Georgeville, Quebec
      Concourse, World Trade Center, New York (with Minoru Yamasaki)
1972/
  73   Long range plan for the Toronto Harbourfront
1974/
  79   Redevelopment plan for the Halifax-Dartmouth Waterfront, Halifax, Nova Scotia
      Market Square, Saint John, New Brunswick
1977   Les Terrasses de la Chaudiere, Hull, Quebec
1978/
  79   Core Action Program, Moncton, New Brunswick
1983   Alcan Company Headquarters, Montreal
      Place Air Canada, Montreal

Publications:

By AFFLECK: reports—*Recent Canadian Experience in Wall Design,* for the International Council for Building Research, Oslo 1967; *Exhibitions and International Fairs as a Means of Mass Communication,* for Unesco, Paris 1968; *Implications of the Changing Society on the College of the Future,* for the Ontario Department of Education, Toronto 1968; articles—"Place Bonaventure: The Architect's View" in *Architecture Canada* (Toronto), July 1967; "The City as Process" (RIBA Discourse) in *RIBA Journal* (London), June 1968; "Urban Renewal" in the *Montreal Star,* August 1968; "Place Bonaventure: Celebration of the Mixmaster" in *Modulus 5* (Charlottesville, Virginia), 1968; "An Approach to Architectural Education at the University of Toronto" in *Canadian Architect* (Toronto), 1969; "Architecture and Planning in the Post-Modern World" in *Contact* (Waterloo, Ontario) January 1982; "Three Decades of Modern Architecture in Quebec" in *Modern Architecture in Canada,* edited by Leon Whiteson, Toronto 1983; "Maison Alcan" in *The Montreal Gazette,* 24 October 1983; "The Changing Face of Architecture in Montreal" in *The Montreal Gazette,* 17 December 1983.

On AFFLECK: book— *Building with Words: Canadian Architects on Architecture ,* with introduction by W. Bernstein and R. Cawker, Toronto 1981; articles— "Stephen Leacock Building" in *Canadian Architect* (Toronto), May 1964; "Stephen Leacock Building" in *Architectural Record* (New York), February 1966; "R. T. Affleck: A Need for More Hands" in *Canadian Architect* (Toronto), September 1966; "Arts and Culture Centre, St. John's" in *Architecture Canada* (Toronto), January 1967; "Place Bonaventure, Montreal" in *Architectural Record* (New York), December 1967; "Place Bonaventure, Montreal" in *Architectural Design* (London), January 1968; "Place Bonaventure, Montreal" in *Progressive Architecture* (New York), July 1968; "The Unlikely Conversion of Ray Affleck" in *Saturday Night* (Toronto), May 1970; "National Arts Centre, Ottawa" in *Architecture d'aujourd'hui* (Paris), September/October 1973; "Place Bonaventure, Montreal" in *Landscape Design* (London), February 1977; "Planting with Evergreens" in *Concrete Quarterly* (London), April/June 1977; "Hotel Mughal, Agra, Headquarters" in *Architecture Concept* (Montreal), January/February 1981; "Hotel Mughal, Agra, India" in *Domus* (Milan), December 1980; "New Project for the Alcan Headquarters" in *Architecture Concept* (Montreal), January/February 1981; "From Mies to Metaphors" in *Canadian Architect* (Toronto), May 1983; "Maison Alcan" in *Arq* (Quebec), December 1983; "Market Square, Saint John, New Brunswick" in *Progressive Architecture* (New York), March 1984; "Maison Alcan, Montreal" in *Canadian Architect* (Toronto), April 1984; "Maison Alcan" in *Canadian Heritage* (Toronto), May/June 1984; "Market Square, Saint John, New Brunswick" in *Arq* (Quebec), August 1984.

A perennial concern in my work has been the individual's experience as he moves through a succession of spaces, an experience that is not primarily visual but involves a relationship of all the sense, especially the tactile. I have also been particularly interested in the social aspects of architecture, which, in my opinion, revolve around the sharing of space between a variety of people who are, in effect, in touch with each other through sharing the same space.

This preoccupation has been particularly significant in the design of complex mixed-use projects, such as Place Bonaveture, Montreal, or Market Square, Saint John, New Brunswick, as well as in urban design in general. This mode of perceiving architecture applies to interior space as well as exterior space and their interfaces. It applies equally well to the scale of a building or the scale of a city. Although one cannot see space, light, natural or artificial, helps to articulate space and plays a crucial role in perception and hence in the design process.

Generally speaking, I structure the design process by imagining the spaces that people will move through— not the objects they will look at. The imaging of experience is much more complex than the imaging of objects—but it is of the greatest importance to my work as an architect.

—Ray Affleck

Although in the largest city in Canada, and one that has included building spectaculars such as *Expo '67* and the 1976 Olympic Games, Montreal's architecture has had more notoriety abroad than influence at home. Similarly, its English-speaking school of architecture at McGill University has been an important source of ideas and people who have made their mark elsewhere and yet itself has failed to create a dynamic centre of its own. The exception is Ray Affleck whose profession stance and design approach have been widely influential.

Evolving out of a climate of unpleasant extremes and a city of grey stone buildings, Affleck's architecture is distinguished by its exterior heaviness and cavernous interior streets. Extending through not only his own designs but also those of adjacent buildings, this underground alternate environment concept has now spread to other urban centres. The phenomenon is an inversion of the vertical separation of vehicular and pedestrian traffic: automobiles exude their pollution into the open air while people inhabit an artificially controlled climate below the city surface. Comfortable at least for transients, if potentially as benumbing as Musak, this internal street system has other architectural advantages. Where the traditional street grid or its building equivalent, the corridor, is the pedestrian route, contemporary architects have felt impelled to get their effects by manipulating the building form, thereby producing arbitrary relationships with the urban facade, or by unnecessarily twisting the shape of rooms. By treating circulation as the experiential medium, the architect can leave the rooms functionally intact, while their juxtaposition creates the architectural space. The flowing space of early modern architecture, which necessarily opened by rooms into one another, is here confined to the link between them, producing another type of experience most nearly related to mediaeval squares or village high streets. The method has been to leave the planning elements—classrooms, stores—as standard units and to develop a multilevel, irregular spatial connection to them. While theoretically sound, the result is reminiscent of an experimental maze, especially when poorly lit and unrelated to outside reference points. Similarly the use of exposed concrete has been rationalized as an expression of its inherent integrity and as providing a neutral background for the imprint of its users' personalities, while in fact being depressingly grey and resisting any adornment.

The discrepancy between the informal, warm character of Affleck himself and that of his buildings also shows in the type of work for which he has been responsible, including the massive Place Bonaventure, which sits forebodingly in the centre of Montreal, a prototypical commercialized megastructure with its associated distortion of social values. Known for his support of such values, Affleck has nevertheless also evolved a technically sophisticated service to developers since his association with I.M. Pei and Webb and Knapp on Place Ville Marie established his initial partnership in the 1950s.

Recently, however, the impact of the conservation movement has encouraged a more sensitive approach to the redevelopment of cities. For the Alcan headquarters in Montreal, the historic Atholstan mansion was restored, the buildings along Sherbrooke Street retained, and an unpretentious, although elegant, office block inserted behind and connected to them by a skylighted atrium. Marking some thirty years of practice, it is fitting that the quality of this design reaffirms Affleck's position among the most respected architects in Canada.

—Anthony Jackson

AHRENDS, Steffen.

South African. Born in Berlin, Germany, 16 August 1907; emigrated to South Africa, 1936: naturalized, 1946. Educated at Landheim Schondorf, Bavaria, matriculated 1924; University of Berlin-Charlottenburg, 1924-25; Bauhochschule, Weimar, under Otto Bartning, *q.v.* and Ernst Neufert, 1925-29; sat special examination, University of the Witwatersrand, Johannesburg, 1937, Dip. Arch. 1938. Married Visino in 1930 (divorced, 1944); Ruth Napier in 1946 (divorced, 1963); Jackie Popper in 1964; children: Peter, Benjamin, Sebastian, and Katrina. Worked in his father's architectural studio, Berlin, 1930-31; joined Ernst May Group, Moscow, 1931-32; returned to his father's studio, Berlin, 1932-36. In private practice, Johannesburg, from 1938: in partnership with Robin Walker, 1948-53, Michael Sutton, 1952-64, and with Trevor Wellbeloved, 1965-78, and Adrian van Dongen 1969-78. Worked in Spain on cluster-group housing, 1972-75. Address: Casa Uno, Bahia de Casares, Estepona, Malaga, Spain.

Works:

1938/
78 500 houses in the Transvaal, Cape Province, Natal Province, and the Orange Free State of South Africa and in Rhodesia
1950 Club House, Bryanston Country Club, Sandton, Transvaal (destroyed by fire, 1953)

Huntingdon Shops and Flats, Sandown, Transvaal
1951 Matus Shops and Offices, Roodepoort, Transvaal
Revolf Shops and Flats, Greenside, Johannesburg
1952 Gold and Diamond Pavilions, Van Riebeck Festival, Cape Town
1952/
60 Suzmann Showroom, Warehouse, and Offices in Welkom, Orange Free State and Pretoria, Ermel, and Bethal, Transvaal
1953 Transvaal Chamber of Mines Pavilion, Rand Show, Johannesburg
Club House reconstruction, Bryanston Country Club, Sandton, Transvaal
1954 Engelhard Court House, Hurlingham, Transvaal
Bedelia Hotel, Welkom, Orange Free State
Daagbreek Hotel, Welkom, Orange Free State
Transvaal Chamber of Mines Pavilion, Bloemfontein, Orange Free State and Bulawayo, Rhodesia
B.S.A. Pavilion, Bulawayo, Rhodesia
1955 Harmony Hotel, Virginia, Orange Free State
30 housing units, Benoni, Transvaal
1958 Engelhard Guest House, Sabie River Bungalow, Transvaal
Anglo-American Corporation Guest House, Welkom, Orange Free State
Fibro Service Station, Bedfordview, Transvaal
Balalaika Hotel, Sandown, Johannesburg
1959 Total Oil Service Station, Fairview, Johannesburg
Callinicos Shops and Flats, Kensington, Johannesburg
1960 Barlows (Caterpillar) B.T. & M. Factory, Isando, Transvaal
1961 Total Oil Service Station, Illovo, Johannesburg
Bayers Agrochem. Factory, Isando, Transvaal
1962 Barclays Bank, Louis Trichard, Transvaal
Sanipass Hotel, Drakensberg, Natal

1962/
72 T and C Head Office and Warehouse, Isando, Transvaal
1962/
78 Grandstand and Club House, Johannesburg Turf Club
1963 Drum Rock Hotel, White River, Transvaal
Commissioner-General's Residential Units, Mafeking, Cape Province
Social Science and Speech Clinic, University of the Witwatersrand, Johannesburg
Transvaal Provincial Administration hostels and schools in Witbank, Sanieshof, Klersdorf, Koster, and Coligny, Transvaal
1963/
69 CPL (Agfa) Factory, Isando, Transvaal
1964 Barclays Bank Pavilion, *Rand Show,* Johannesburg
Sturrock and Robson Guest House, Dullstrom, Transvaal
Sabie Country Club House, Sabie, Transvaal
Barlows (Caterpillar) B. T. & M. Factory, Belleville, Cape Province
1965 Barlows (Hyster) Factory, Isando, Transvaal
Barlows Federated Timber Factory, Benoni, Transvaal
Gallo Pavilion, *Rand Show,* Johannesburg
1966 Mbula Guest House, Sabie, Transvaal
1967 River Club House, Sandton, Transvaal
Barlows Federated Timber Factory, Springs, Transvaal
1968 T and C Offices and Warehouse, Paarl, Cape Province
1970 SAFI Offices, Sabie, Transvaal
1971 T and C Offices and Warehouse, Milnerton, Cape Province
CPL (Agfa) Factory, Milnerton, Cape Province
3 houses at Sotogrande, Costa del Sol, Spain
1972/
75 Bahia de Casares (cluster housing), Estepona, Costa del Sol, Spain (with Aubrey David)
1974 Guest house, Piggs Peak, Swaziland

Steffen Ahrends: **Bahia de Casares cluster-housing, Estepona, Spain, 1972-75.**

Publications:

On AHRENDS: articles— "Gold Pavilion, Van Riebeck Festival, Cape Town" and "Diamond Pavilion, Van Riebeck Festival" in *Architect and Builder* (Johannesburg), May 1952; "Ranch House 'V' in Hurlingham" in *Architect and Builder* (Johannesburg), June 1952; "Chamber of Mines Pavilion, Rand Easter Show" in *Architect and Builder* (Johannesburg), June 1953; "New Bloemfontein Chamber of Mines Pavilion" in *Architect and Builder* (Johannesburg), June 1959; "Guesthouse Engelhard, Eastern Transvaal" in *Architect and Builder* (Johannesburg), March 1960: "Illovo Total Oil Service Station" in *South African Architectural Record* (Johannesburg), September 1961; "New Social Science and Speech Clinic, Witwatersrand University" in *South African Architectural Record* (Johannesburg), August 1967; "House Vladykin, Umhlanga Rocks, Natal" in *Artlook* (Johannesburg), February 1971; "House Skeen, Umhlanga Rocks, Natal" in *Architect and Builder* (Johannesburg), September 1971; "House Gevisser, Hyde Park" in *Habitat* (Johannesburg), 1974.

It may be that my particular interest in houses was awakened during my last three years in Germany, 1933-36. The modern house we believed in was soon taboo, even when treated in a moderate or disguised way. The progressive and cultured people who would have built modern houses were either emigrating or did not dare to express their innermost thoughts.

I probably realized at that time that the modern house (particularly the house of the 1930s belongs to the "International Style") requires a type of person who, although aware of the heritage of cultured tradition, is prepared consciously to break those ties in order to live in a *contemporary* way with a vision towards the future. It also came to me that a house is to a certain extent merely the shell that personifies the atmosphere of the particular mental world a person lives in. An architect may guide up to a certain point, but to transplant a person into a world he has neither the inclination nor the capacity to understand will finally create a dissonance (so often perceptible) in the relationship between the house and its owner, his furniture and paintings, and even his garden.

—Steffen Ahrends

Steffen Ahrends was one of the many talented people who came to South Africa as intellectual refugees from Nazi Germany in the 1930s. Of those who were architects, he made the greatest impact, and his works may be found from the Cape to Rhodesia. The large practice he achieved was the result of his training and outstanding talent combined with unfailing enthusiasm, a compelling personality, and, without being doctrinaire, an ability to influence conservative clients and builders to accept and appreciate new ideas about architecture. One of his tasks, particularly in regard to domestic work, was to overcome the always present need in the minds of white South Africans for the reassurance of the familiar symbols of stability and security which they identify with the past.

A varied practice gave Ahrends the chance to explore the two different but sometimes complementary architectural impulses of his mind—the rational and the romantic. The former directed his large, complicated but disciplined buildings commissioned for collective usage—a logical consequence of his architectural education at Weimar and Moscow under some of the advanced thinkers who contributed to the development of the international style and to modern urban planning in the 1920s and 1930s. His informed approach and creative handling of space, light, and form, an insistence on high standards of industrial technology, and a command of rationalized building processes make the larger buildings not only workable but also interesting.

The romantic impulse had been nurtured by his youthful response to the possibilities of the traditional materials used by craftsmen in the Gothic, The Baroque, and the vernacular domestic architecture he had studied in south Germany. The quality of his domestic work, which made him the most influential architect in that field in Johannesburg for more than thirty years, is generally considered to fall into this category.

Once he had taken the measure of South African social and geographical conditions, his designs for houses, large and small, country hotels, and clubs evolved as being eminently suitable for the climate and the way of life of his clients: they were planned with free-flowing spaces, conscious orientation, and protection from extremes of weather for outdoor life. He employed natural finishes for floors—flagstones, quarry tiles, brick—and rustic brick for walls, sometimes exposed, roughly plastered and colourwashed, internally and externally. He also experimented with local timbers and exposed the construction of the roofs, sometimes ceiling them with bound canes in the Old Cape Dutch fashion.

The importance that Ahrends gave to these roofs underlined his romanticism. The functions of the spaces they covered produced new angles, and by following the natural changes of site levels, he produced a variety of related forms which, with the textures and colours of their coverings of thatch, shingles, or differently shaped and coloured Mediterranean-like tiles, gave each house its own individuality. His houses are never boring. Moreover, whether the site was a flat one or on the side of a mountain, whether it was complemented with the kind of local planting he recommended or surrounded by semi-tropical growth or man-made forests, these beautiful buildings rest in complete harmony with their settings.

—Doreen Greig

AHRENDS BURTON AND KORALEK.
Partnership; established, London, 1961. Partners: Peter Ahrends, Richard Burton, Paul Koralek, Paul Drake, Patrick Stubbings, and John Hermsen. Exhibitions: *Ahrends Burton and Koralek: drawings and models*, RIBA Heinz Gallery, London, 1980 (travelled to Ireland, Germany and Finland, 1981-83); *Model Futures*, Institute for Architecture and Urban Studies, New York, 1983. Recipient: First Prize, Trinity College Library Competition, Dublin, 1960; EAHY Award, London, 1976; Structural Steel and *Financial Times* Award, London, 1976; Department of the Environment Design Awards(2), London, 1977; Southern Region Award, Royal Institute of British Architects, 1978; Structural Steel Design Award, London, 1980; Carpenters Award, London, 1981; Gold Medal, *Architectural Design*, London, 1982. Address: Unit 1, 7 Chalcot Road, London NW1 8LH, England.

Works:

1963 Kasmin Gallery, Bond Street, London
     Henry Moore and Ben Johnson exhibitions, New London-Marlborough Gallery, London
1964 St. Anne's Church, Soho, London (project)
     Bryan-Brown House, Thurleston, Devon
     New Inn Hall Street Development Plan, Oxford (project)
     Office building, London Road, Cheam, Surrey
1965 Chichester Theological College, Sussex
     Tate Gallery exhibition, London
1967 Library, Trinity College, Dublin
1968 Bell Tower, Canberra, Australia (competition project)
     Eastfield County Primary School, Thurmaston, Leicestershire
     South-West Area Development Plan, Basildon, Essex
     Graduate Centre Housing, Basildon, Essex (project)
1969 Centre for Management Studies, phase I, Kennington, Oxford
     Houses, Dunstan Road, Old Headington, Oxford
1971 Redcar Library, Yorkshire
1972 Maidenhead Library, Berkshire
     Roman Catholic Chaplaincy, Oxford
     St. Andrew's College, Booterstown, Dublin
     New Building, phase I, Keble College, Oxford
     Nebenzahl House, Jerusalem
1973 Ravelin House Development Plan, Portsmouth Polytechnic, Hampshire
     St. Martin's Youth Centre, Adelaide Street, London
     Plan Guinet, Valescure, Var, France (project)
     Kimbell Construction workshop, Brixworth, Northamptonshire
     Chahar Bagh Development Study, Isfahan, Iran (project)
1974 Centre for Management Studies, phase II, Kennington, Oxford
     Habitat Warehouse and Showroom, Wallingford, Berkshire
1975 Chalvedon Housing, area I, Basildon New Town, Essex
     Whitmore Way Housing, Basildon New Town, Essex
     Post Office Headquarters Redevelopment, St. Martins-Le-Grand, London (project)
1975/
  80 Felmore Housing, Basildon, Essex
1975/
  83 Cummins Engines Factory, Shotts, Lanarkshire, Scotland
1976 New Building, phase II, Keble College, Oxford
     Chalvedon Housing, area II, Basildon New Town, Essex
1977 Chalvedon Housing, area II, Basildon New Town, Essex
     Library, Portsmouth Polytechnic, Hampshire
     Headquarters, British Airports Authority, Gatwick Airport, Surrey (project)
1978 Northlands Housing, area I, Basildon New Town, Essex
     Arts Faculty Building, Trinity College, Dublin
     Johnson and Johnson Head Office, Slough, Berkshire (project)
1979 Collen House, County Wicklow, Eire
     Town Hall, Oldenburg, Germany (project)
1979/
  80 Bancroft 9 Housing, Milton Keynes, Buckinghamshire (project)
     Callands Action Area Plan, Warrington, Lancashire (as consultants)
1979 John Lewis Department Store, Kingston, Surrey (project)
1980 Mary Rose Ship Museum, Portsmouth, Hampshire (project)
1981 Merck Sharpe & Dohme chemical laboratories, Harlow, Essex (competition project)
     Sam Smith Brewery Building, Tadcaster, Yorkshire (project)
1981/
  82 Low Energy Hospital Study
1982/
  84 J. Sainsbury Supermarket, Canterbury, Kent
     W. H. Smith Offices, Greenbridge, Swindon, Wiltshire
1982 St. Mary's low-energy hospital nucleus and residences, Newport, Isle of Wight
     National Gallery extension, London (competition project)
     Shopping Complex, Sheffield, Yorkshire (project)

Ahrends, Burton and Koralek: J. Sainsbury Supermarket, Canterbury, Kent, 1982-84.

1983 Housing and Commercial Development, Kingston Power Station Site, Surrey (project)
      British Telecom Headquarters, Milton Keynes, Buckinghamshire (competition project)
1983 School for Woodland Industries, Hooke Park, Dorset (project)
1984 Royal Opera House Development, Covent Garden, London (project)

Publications:

On AHRENDS BURTON AND KORALEK: books—*Late-Modern Architecture* by Charles Jencks, London 1980; *Ahrends Burton & Koralek: architectural drawings and models*, exhibition catalogue, London 1980; *Model Futures*, exhibition catalogue by Bob Allies, New York 1983; articles—"Architects and Their Offices" by Mary Haddock in *Building* (London), November 1966; "Trinity College Library, Dublin" by Patrick Delaney in Architectural Design (London), October 1967; "Retreat for Executives" in *Architectural Forum* (New York), May 1970; "Easy Reading in Redcar" by David Roessler in *Architectural Forum* (New York), November 1971; "Easy Riders" by Tim Rock in *L'Architecture d'aujourd'hui* (Paris), December 1971/January 1972; "Profile of a Practice: Ahrends Burton and Koralek" in *The Architect* (London), December 1973; "Extrovert Library" by Lance Wright in *Architectural Review* (London), May 1974; "Five Works by Ahrends Burton and Koralek" in *L'Architecture d'Aujourd'hui* (Paris), September/October 1974; "ABK" by John Donat in *Architecture Plus* (New York), October 1974; "The Works of Ahrends Burton and Koralek" in *Architecture + Urbanism* (Tokyo), December 1974; "Designed for Flexibility" by Neil Steedman in *Building Design* (London), April 1975; "Art Object for the

Post Office" by Lance Wright in *Architectural Review* (London), July 1975; "House in Jerusalem" by Ulrik Plesner in *Architectural Review* (London), August 1975; "ABK Booterstown" by Lance Wright in *Architectural Review* (London), June 1976; "Quality Through Caring: The Practice of Ahrends Burton and Koralek" by Charles Knevitt in *Building Design* (London), November 1976; "As Easy as ABK" by Stephanie Williams in *Building Design* (London), June 1977; "Basildon Blend" in *Building* (London), June 1977; "ABK Housing in Basildon" by Peter Ellis and Richard MacCormac in *The Architects' Journal* (London), September 1977; "Unbuilt England" by Peter Cook in special issue of *Architecture + Urbanism* (Tokyo), October 1977; "Oxford: New Buildings at Keble and St. John's" by John Huniadis in *Architectural Review* (London), December 1977; "Bungalows Are Back" by Stephanie Williams in *Building Design* (London), February 1978; "Social Science, User Research and the Design Process" by Peter Ellis in *The Architects' Journal* (London), February 1978; "Reading Between the Lines" in *The Architects' Journal* (London), 26 July 1978; "A Precious Testimony of persistence: The Work of ABK" by Moriyuki Agawa in *SD: Space Design* (Tokyo), August 1978; "Recent Work of ABK" by Stevan Brown in *RIBA Journal* (London), January 1979; "Maidenhead Public Library" in *Industria delle Costruzioni* (Rome), July/August 1979; "Portsmouth Polytechnic Library" in *Architecture + Urbanism* (Tokyo), October 1979; "ABK on show" by Colin Davies in *Building* (London), 24 October 1980; "ABK gets hung" by Lynda Relph-Knight in *Building Design* (London), 24 October 1980; "Rose from the dead" in *Building* (London), 5 December 1980; "Richard Burton – a partner in Ahrends Burton and Koralek" in *New Zealand Architect* (Auckland), no. 2, 1981; "ABK Shotts" by Peter Buchanan in *Architectural Review* (London), February 1982; "Cummins Engine Company, Lanarkshire" in *Architecture + Urbanism*

(Tokyo), July 1982; "ABK criticise National Gallery Competition" in *The Architects' Journal* (London), 2 March 1983; "National Gallery Progress Report" by Peter Buchanan in *Architectural Review* (London), February 1984; "Mast Appeal" by John Winter in *The Architects' Journal* (London), 5 December 1984.

Implicit in our work is a search for quality which concerns the character and atmosphere of spaces. This has to be achieved amidst the constraints of a realistic and practical world. There are inevitable tensions between what is desirable and what is possible; between Utopian planning and society as it is; between the potential of technology and the realities of the building industry; between what one would like to spend and what one can afford. The process of design is an effort to close those gaps using such constraints as a springboard for ideas.

Each building is a response to a new and different situation, a personal interpretation and evaluation that grows out of attitudes and standards that are the cumulative product of experience and collaboration. It is a produce of shared thought and feeling and of the conviction that the quality of our surroundings cannot be dissociated from the quality of life.

—Ahrends Burton and Koralek

In the early 1950s, when Peter Ahrends, Richard Burton and Paul Koralek first began working together while students at the Architectural Association in London, the atmosphere around them was one of confidence, energy and enthusiasm. The agonies of the past decade had now been overcome while the potential of the new decade had been optimistically predicted by the *Festival of Britain*. Spontaneity overcame reflection; exploration superseded academicism; imagination overpowered theory.

This atmosphere engendered in Ahrends, Burton and Koralek an approach towards design that has stayed with them throughout their practice together. To each project they seek to bring certain analytical and organisational skills but no preconceived architectural theories or forms. The first stage of their work is one of enquiry, examining and, always, questioning the brief, seeking and exploring each possible direction. The second stage is one of discovery: the design emerges, or the design is found. The design proclaims itself. For Ahrends, Burton and Koralek believe that inherent within each brief and the social circumstances in which it arises, is the form of its architectural expression. And, conversely, the finished building should become the physical symbol of the activities and the aspirations on which the design was founded. An understanding of this attitude helps to explain the apparent diversity of their work. The series of buildings that they have completed show considerable development in technique and sophistication, but, more powerfully, each one stands independently of each other as a unique solution to its initial programme.

While it is true that Ahrends, Burton and Koralek have neither embraced any specific architectural theories nor used them polemically to influence others, two particular influences of their student days should be noted. The first was Frank Lloyd Wright, in particular his concept of an organic architecture, as well as his fluid, and fluent, planning of space; interestingly, their admiration for Wright went against the conventional wisdom at the Architectural Association at that time, which favoured Le Corbusier and Mies van der Rohe. The second major shared influences was a visit to Turkey and Iran in 1956, which opened up to the three students a new architectural vocabulary of decoration and natural light.

The majority of Ahrends, Burton and Koralek's commissions have involved the design of new buildings in the context of an historical city. The have shown great respect for the traditional, well-made buildings that have constituted their neighbours, and have responded to the particular qualities of these places with considerable sympathy. But they have not forgotten, or disregarded, the time, the age in which they are building, and have consistently made use of any new technologies, new materials, new components that are available. The resulting dialogue in their buildings between the old and the new, the traditional and the modern, the hand-crafted and the machine-finished, the soft irregularity of concrete and brick and the precision of steel and glass, has almost become a hallmark of their work as well as perhaps its most influential characteristic. If this dialogue is particularly articulate, it is because of the inventiveness and the care with which their buildings are put together, each detail referring back to, and thereby reinforcing, the primary characteristics of the design. If the dialogue is particularly compelling, it is because it is one of such significance today.

—Bob Allies

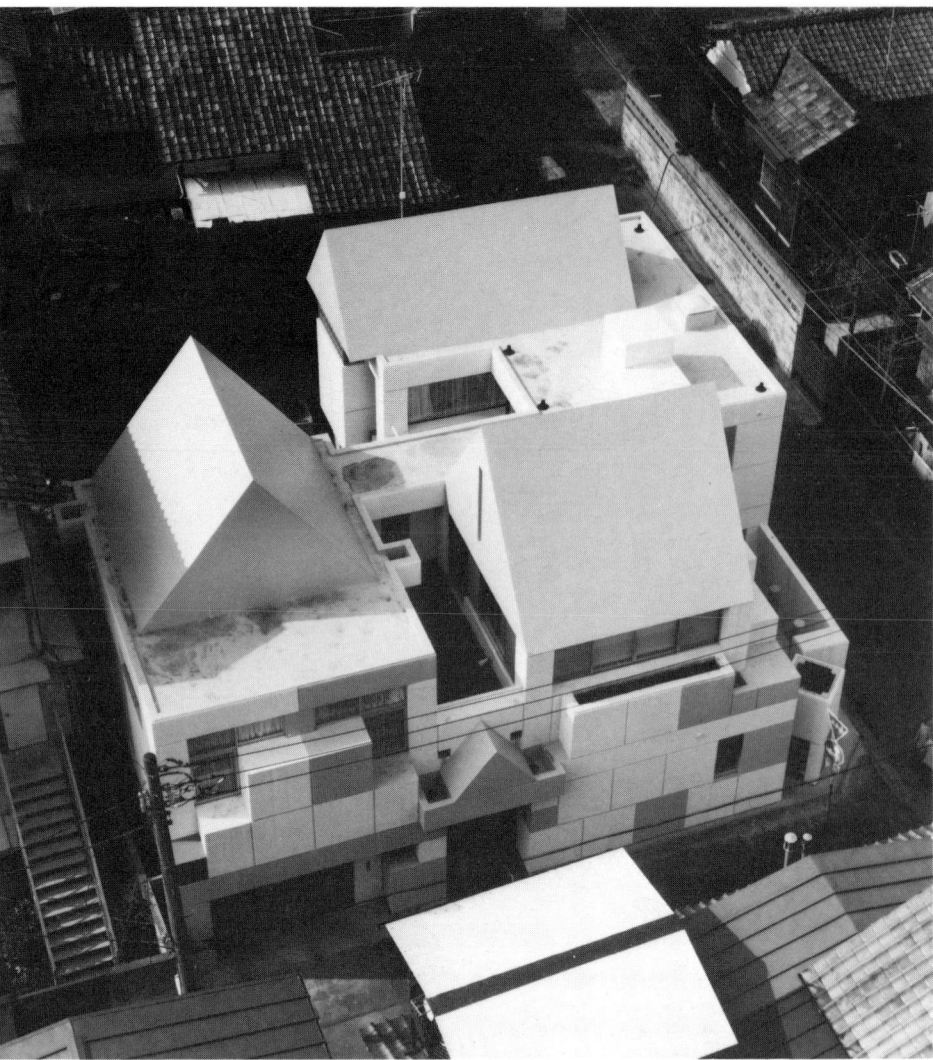

Takefumi Aida: Toy Block House III, Tokyo, 1981.

AIDA, Takefumi
Japanese. Born in Tokyo, 5 June 1937. Educated at Waseda University School of Architecture, Tokyo, B.Arch. 1960, M.Arch. 1966, D.Eng. 1971. Married Kazuko Hama in 1966; children: Aya and Akira. Since 1970, Principal, Takefumi Aida Architect and Associates, Tokyo. Lecturer, College of Technology, Waseda University, 1972-76; Assistant Professor, Shibaura Institute of Technology, Tokyo, 1973-76. Lecturer, Iwate University, since 1972, and Nagoya Institute of Technology, since 1976; Professor, Shibaura Institute of Technology, Tokyo, since 1977. Councillor, Kanto Area, Architectural Institute of Japan, 1976-78; Juror, American Institute of Architects, Seattle Chapter, 1978. Councillor, Architectural Institute of Japan, Tokyo, since 1978.

Member, ArchiteXt, with Takamitsu Azuma, *q.v.*, Mayumi Miyawaki, Makoto Suzuki, and Minoru Takeyama, *q.v.*, since 1971. Exhibitions: *Triennale*, Milan, 1973; *The Works of Takefumi Aida*, Tokyo, 1977; *New Wave in Japanese Architecture*, toured the United States, 1978; *Today: An Exhibition of Houses*, Tokyo, 1978; *Seven Architects*, Kobe, Japan, 1982; *Drawings of Japanese Architects*, Space Art Gallery, Seoul, Korea, 1983; *Architects' Drawings*, Sagacho Exhibit Space, Tokyo, 1984. Recipient: Merit Prize, Farmers' Housing Competition, Architectural Institute of Japan, 1967; Annual Newcomers Prize, Japan Architect Association 1982. Address: Takefumi Aida Architect and Associates, 3-2 Okubo 1-chome, Shinjuku-ku, Tokyo 160, Japan.

Works

1968   An Artist's House, Kunitachi, Tokyo
1971   Anti-Avant-Garde House, Fujisawa, Kanagawa, Japan
1972   Nirvana House, Fujisawa, Kanagawa, Japan
       Annihilation House, Mutsuura, Kanagawa, Japan
       Shike Showroom, Hodogaya, Kanagawa, Japan
1974   PL Institute Kindergarten, Osaka
       House Like a Die, Izu, Shizuoka, Japan
       Persona House, Suginami, Tokyo
1976   Stepped-Platform House, Kawasaki, Kanagawa, Japan
1977   Tamatsukuri Hot Springs Monument, Tamatsukuri, Shimane, Japan
       Pension-style Hotel at Shiobara, Tochigi, Japan

1979   Toy Block House I, Hofu, Yamaguchi, Japan
       Toy Block House II, Kawasaki, Kanagawa, Japan
1980   House Based on a Mondrian Pattern, Kodaira, Tokyo
1981   Toy Block House III, Nakano, Tokyo
1982   Toy Block House IV, Suginami, Tokyo
1983   Toy Block House VII, Meguro, Tokyo
       Toy Block House IX (Doll's House)
       Memorial on Brimstone, Io-to, Tokyo
1984   Toy Block House X, Shibuya, Tokyo

Publications:

By AIDA: books— translation of *Architecture: Action and Plan* by Peter Cook, Tokyo 1971; *Theory of Architectural Forms*, Tokyo 1975; translation of *Rivers in the Cities* by Roy Mann, Tokyo 1975; *Shin-Kenchikugaku-Taikei/Towards the Horizon of Architectural Forms*, co-author, Tokyo 1982; translation of *Architectural Drawing: The Art and the Process* by Gerald Allen and Richard Oliver, Tokyo 1983; *Toy Block House: Works of Takefumi Aida*, Tokyo 1984; articles— "Approach to the Urban Residence, Symbol of the Urban Residence" in *Shinkenchiku* (Tokyo), January 1967; "Urban Design Note: City and Factory" in *Shinkenchiku* (Tokyo), October 1967; "Wall House: The Concept of Encampment" in *Toshijutaku* (Tokyo), November 1968; "Can the House Serve as a Point of Origin" in *Toshijutaku* (Tokyo), September 1969; "Image of the House" in *Kindaikenchiku* (Tokyo), September 1969; "Architecture as Rearguard" in *Kenchikubunka* (Tokyo), February 1971; "Revitalized Architecture" in *Japan Architect* (Tokyo), July 1971; "Movement Toward the Primary" and "Plan for a Box House" in special edition of *Toshijutaku* (Tokyo), September 1971; "Robert Venturi from Our Viewpoint" in *Architecture + Urbanism* (Tokyo), October 1971; "Lightless Intellectuality" in *Shinkenchiku* (Tokyo), August 1972; "Speculation in the Dark" in *Japan Architect* (Tokyo), November 1972; "Twelve Memoranda on the House Like a Die" and "When Architecture Disappears" in *Japan Architect* (Tokyo), July 1974; "Scenery— Even at That, Can Architecture Continue Relating Something?" in *Space Design* (Tokyo), November 1974; "Function of Individual Housing: An Architect's View" in *Kenchikuzassi* (Tokyo), December 1974; "From the Awe-Inspiring to the World of Sensuality" in *Japan Architect* (Tokyo), February 1975; "Eliminating as a Method for Architectural Forms" in *Shotenkenchiku* (Tokyo), October 1975; "Forest Lawn Memorial Park and Mortuaries" in *Architecture + Urbanism* (Tokyo), November 1975; "Forms, Spaces of Silence, and Calm" in *Architecture + Urbanism* (Tokyo), December 1975; "About Silence" in *Shinkenchiku* (Tokyo), February 1976; "From Silence" in *Architecture + Urbanism* (Tokyo), May 1976; "My Esquisse" in *Kenchikuchishiki* (Tokyo), November 1977; "Silence: In the Culture of Sympathy" in *Architecture + Urbanism* (Tokyo), March 1978; "A New Wave of Japanese Architecture— Waving Back to the U.S.A." in *Architecture + Urbanism* (Tokyo), March 1979; "A Die Named Architecture," with Kazuhiro Ishii, in *Kenchiku Bunka* (Tokyo), July 1981; "On Playfulness" in *Shinkenchiku* (Tokyo), August 1981; "From the Lecture of Kenneth Frampton" in *Kenchiku Bunka* (Tokyo), September 1981; "Toy Blocks— The Concept of Coexistence of Construction and Destruction" in *Architecture + Urbanism* (Tokyo), February 1982.

On AIDA: books— *Architettura razionale* by Aldo Rossi, Milan 1973; *Japanese Contemporary Architecture 24*, Tokyo 1973; *Modern Movements in Architecture* by Charles Jencks, London 1973, Tokyo 1976; *A New Wave of Japanese Architecture*, with introduction by Kenneth Frampton, New York 1978; *Transformations in Modern Architecture* by Arthur Drexler, New York 1979; *Late-Modern Architecture* by Charles Jencks, London 1980; articles— "Nirvana House" in *Japan Architect* (Tokyo), August 1972, *Domus* (Milan), January 1974, and *Casabella* (Milan), January 1974; "PL Institute Kindergarten" by Takashi Hasegawa in *Shinkenchiku* (Tokyo), January 1974; "Stepped-Platform House" by Kazuyuki Honda in *Shinkenchiku* (Tokyo), June 1976; "The ArchiteXt Group," special edition of *Japan Architect* (Tokyo), June 1976; "Post Metabolism," special edition of *Japan Architect* (Tokyo), October/November 1977; "Ontology of House" by Chris Fawcett in *GA Houses 4*, Tokyo 1978; "AD Profile 28: Post-Modern Classicism" by Charles Jencks in *Architectural Design* (London), no. 5/6, 1980; "Apptel pension near Shiobara" in *Architecture Interieure Créé* (Paris), November/December 1980; "Mondrian Pattern: Sensed/Unsensed" by Kenshiro Takami in *Shinkenchiku* (Tokyo), August 1981; "Thirty Controversial Houses," special issue of *l'Architecture d'aujourd'hui* (Paris), April 1983; "Residential Architecture," special issue of *GA Houses* (Tokyo), July 1983.

Pleasure is the goal of play. The search for it is an important and integral part of human nature. Architecture is not just the concrete expression of function but is the expression of an architect's intentions as well. It is here that the issue of playfulness enters the picture.

Architecture is the product of a heightened sensibility. The extent to which a building can be the manifestation of an architect's sensibility determines the importance of architecture in a given culture

One enjoys a game because of developments that occur unexpectedly despite one's finest calculations.

A game is very similar to the process of architectural design in which the architect overcomes restrictions imposed by reality. The creative activity of an architect vis-a-vis society is a type of intellectual game.

Playing with toy blocks is a sophisticated game. It offers the challenge to create forms given the imposed conditions. It is a question of combining a limited number of pieces in order to create forms analogous to other forms. It is thus closely related to the creative activity of architects.

Architecture is produced within the framework of restrictions and conditions characteristic of an era, just as toy blocks are played within the framework of certain given conditions. We gain pleasure from toy blocks not only in piling them up, but also in seeing them collapse. There is pleasure in both their construction and destruction.

The most vital stage of the game is when one chooses pieces or combinations of pieces through trial and error. This corresponds to the *esquisse* in architecture design and is the stage of the intensive creative activity. Playfulness is a universal issue. Any ideas of playfulness can in a sense contribute to this search for what we all have in common.

—Takefumi Aida

"It is a lot easier and more natural to put a puzzle ring back together than to take it apart" (Kobo Abe).

Takefumi Aida's Artist's House, Kunitachi, Tokyo (1967) features an atelier as a bit of "displaced space" perched perilously on the roof of the house proper, like a bird uncertain of its roost. The three sections of the house— the residence, the staircase, and the atelier— are separated and handled as independent entities the arrangement of which on the site (we seem to see) can only be provisional; this architecture-by-parts, as if it were being rationed, is presented face on, in a literal and wry graph of house-in-the-city. It isn't comfortably honed down to a "controlling centre" with "assistant elements"; each part is shown to be something in itself. It is akin to Monta Mozuna's Anti-Dwelling in Hokkaido in its box form— but there the comparison ends; Monta moves from the arbitrary to the geometrical, but what Aida has done is to remove the boxes from the natural relationship to one another and then assign them quite arbitrary relations. As Onobayashi says of Artist's House, "The densest and most dramatic spatial sequence in the house is that leading from entrance to corridor and staircase." This is the main theme, and the other activity spaces are tucked away like closets in a sorcerer's castle. This approach reflects what Van Eyck calls "the clarity of the labyrinth."

In the Nirvana House, Annihilation House, House Like a Die, and the PL Institute Kindergarten, Aida has developed a "space of encounters"— "the very space I have been seeking is one born of a meeting between varying threads, one that produces an exalted tension as a result of that meeting." The "encounter" itself is formed by the conscious extraction and combination of straight and curved lines of hard and soft elements and by the fusion and revulsion among functional units. The "encounter" turns out to be a meeting between "consciousness and sporadic consciousness."

Aida's "speculation in the dark" concentrates on the "Ah-ness" of things *(Mono-no-aware);* his designs are token hints of the "eternal in the here and now" penultimate expression of what will never fully be said. In this sense, his work can't be properly called architecture but rather formulae for an architectural experience that sees all things as they are happening "by themselves" in miraculous spontaneity. *Yugen,* too, is alluded to, with all its haunting strangeness of Buddhist intimations and poetic shock. Annihilation House might well be summed up by Zeami's description of *Yugen:*

Over foam-flecked waves in the falling night,
The Wild Ducks' cries are dying, dim and white.

—Chris Fawcett

AIN, Gregory.

American. Born in Pittsburgh, Pennsylvania, 28 March 1908. Studied mathematics at the University of California at Los Angeles, 1924-26, and architecture at the University of Southern California, Los Angeles, 1927-28. Married Agnes Budin in 1929; married Ruth March in 1938; children: Emily and Christopher. Worked with R. M. Schindler, *q.v.*, Los Angeles, 1932, and Richard J. Neutra, *q.v.*, Los Angeles, 1932-35. In private practice, Los Angeles, from 1935. Visiting Professor of Design, University of Southern California, 1947-63; Professor, and Head of the School of Architecture, Pennsylvania State University, University Park, 1963-67. Exhibitions: *Built in USA: 1932-1944*, Museum of Modern Art, New York, 1944; Museum of Modern Art, New York, 1950 (individual show); *Sixteen Southern California Architects*, Scripps College, Claremont, California, 1950. Recipient: *House Beautiful* Award, 1937, 1938, 1940; Pittsburgh Glass Award, 1938; Guggenheim Fellowship, 1940. Fellow, American Institute of Architects. Address: 2830 Francis Avenue, Los Angeles, California 90005, U.S.A.

Works:

1936 Edwards House, 5642 Hollyoak Drive, Los Angeles
1937 Ernst House, 5670 Hollyoak Drive, Los Angeles
      Dunsmuir Flats, 1281 South Dunsmuir Avenue, Los Angeles
      Byler House, 914 Avenue 37, Mt. Washington, Los Angeles
1938 Brownfield Medical Building, Los Angeles
      Beckman House, 357 North Citrus Avenue, Los Angeles
      Kun House, 7947 Fareholm, West Hollywood, Los Angeles
1939 Daniel House, 1856 Micheltorena Street, Silver Lake, Los Angeles
      Hay House, 3132 Oakcrest Drive, Studio City, Los Angeles
      Tierman House, 2323 Micheltorena Street, Silver Lake, Los Angeles
      Vorkapich Garden House (pre-fabricated plywood house), 2100 Benedict Canyon Road, Beverly Hills, California
1941 Ain House, 7964 Willowglen Road, West Hollywood, Los Angeles
      Orans House, 2404 Micheltorena Street, Silver Lake, Los Angeles
1948 Mar Vista Housing Development (100 houses), Mar Vista, Los Angeles
      Avenel Housing Group, 2839-45 Avenel Street, Silver Lake, Los Angeles
      Hollywood Guilds and Unions Office Building, Cahuenga Boulevard, Los Angeles
      Miller House, 1634 Gilcrest, Beverly Hills, California
1949 Schairer House, 11750 Chenault Street, Los Angeles
      Wilfong House, Altadena, California
1950 House, 1350 Linda Ridge Road, Pasadena, California
      Beckman House, 15622 Meadowgate Road, Sherman Oaks, California
      Hurschler House, 1200 Hillcrest Avenue, Pasadena, California
      Museum of Modern Art House, New York
      Kun House, 7947 Fareholm, West Hollywood, Los Angeles
1951 Margolis House, 5786 Valley Oak Drive, Los Angeles
      Mesner House, 13957 Valley Vista Boulevard, Los Angeles
1952 Mesner House, 14571 Valley Vista Boulevard, Los Angeles
1954 Feldman House, 1181 Angelo Drive, Los Angeles

1955 Matthews House, San Rafael Avenue, Los Angeles
1957 153rd Street School, 1605 West 153rd Street, Los Angeles
     Asher House, 263 Loring Avenue, Los Angeles
1960 Gallas House, 5326 Sherbourne Drive, Los Angeles
1961 Elterman House, 15301 Kingswood Lane, Sherman Oaks, California
1962 Berg House, Malibu, California
1963 Lewin House, 15310 Jessen, La Canada, California

Publications:

By AIN: articles— "Small Scale Prefabrication" in *Arts and Architecture* (Los Angeles), March 1941; "In Search of Theory" in *Arts and Architecture* (Los Angeles), January 1966.

On AIN: books—*Built in USA: 1932-1944,* exhibition catalogue, New York 1944; *The Second Generation* by Esther McCoy, Salt Lake City, Utah 1984; articles— "Dunsmuir Flats" in *Architectural Record* (New York), February 1940; "Guest House" in *Architectural Record* (New York), April 1940; "Houses in Los Angeles" in *Architectural Forum* (New York), April 1940; "Los Angeles House for A. A. Ernst" in *Architectural Record* (New York), October 1940; "Tierman House" in *Arts and Architecture* (Los Angeles), April 1941; "Orans House" in *Arts and Architecture* (Los Angeles), April 1942; "Ain House" in *Arts and Architecture* (Los Angeles), May 1942; "Park Planned Homes" in *Progressive Architecture* (New York), July 1947; "100 Houses for Advance Development Company" in *Arts and Architecture* (Los Angeles), May 1948; "Basic Design for a 100-Unit Subdivision" in *Architectural Forum* (New York), April 1949; "Museum of Modern Art Exhibition House" in *Architectural Record* (New York), July 1950; "Avenel Housing Associates Project" in *Progressive Architecture* (New York), February 1951; "Two View House" in *Interiors* (New York), August 1951; "Retrospect: Gregory Ain's Social Housing" by Esther McCoy in *Arts and Architecture* (Los Angeles), Winter 1981.

Bibliography: *The Search for Low-Cost Housing in the Architectural Work of Gregory Ain: A Selected Bibliography* by Robert B. Harmon, Monticello, Illinois 1981.

I have always felt that the architect must not regard his work as an opportunity to demonstrate his virtuosity! Instead, his work is a step to enhance the quality of living, and it can be most effective when it is produced in collaboration with many other experts as well as other colleagues in his profession.

Most contemporary work is done in a fever of ruthless money-making— that attitude must be replaced by an entirely different set of values. The architectural profession can be truly effective only if it can join hands with all the other social scientists and work with them, and the public at large, to defeat ruthless piracy.

—Gregory Ain

Gregory Ain's impulse to study architecture came from an acquaintance as a youth with R.M. Schindler's Kings Road house, and his dissatisfaction with his Beaux Arts training determined him to work in the office of Richard Neutra. Combined in all his early work, which is his finest, are Neutra's repetitive windows and monoplanar surfaces and Schindler's broken planes and accommodation of shell to plan. In the 1939 Tierman house, the modular

fenestration is countered by a roof rising to a square skylight in the center of the plan and a dramatic brick chimney, the two-story height of which is exposed in the open stair-well to the lower level. In his Hay house of 1939, he breaks up the volumes by treating the recessed front door and patio door as dark panels which extend to the second story eaves.

Ain's interest in group housing for middle- and low-income families began in his 1937 Dunsmuir Flats, his most frequently published work. The best-known view is of four staggered, two-story, white blocks, the ceiling levels defined by continuous ribbon windows; not seen are the private porches and patios. The panel-post construction was an early effort to reduce cost, followed in 1939 by prefabricated plywood walls for a model house.

Ain received a Guggenheim Fellowship in 1940 to continue his researches in low-cost housing, and throughout the 1940s, he designed, with the participation of clients, a number of projects for attached and detached housing that were notable for site planning and innovative floor plans. Few were built because lending agencies opposed multiple ownership. One of the several schemes to be built was the 1948 Avenel housing for a musicians' union whose members worked in films. The twenty attached units were broken into two blocks for a hillside site, and private patios off the living rooms faced the view.

The 100-house Mar Vista development, begun the same year, used a staggered plan for the siting to insure greater separation; there were variations of the basic design, but the two-bedroom and sleeping alcove plan was common to all. The living room, kitchen, dining room, and bedroom alcove were essentially one space, which was opened by a glass wall to a patio.

For his more elaborate houses, he borrowed freely from the flexible plan of his low-cost housing, and in most cases, the alcove sleeping room became a library or guest room. Ain also adapted many contractors' practices for large or small houses to save construction time and reduce cost. Aside from Irving Gill, Ain was the first architect in California to refine and dignify low-cost housing.

—Esther McCoy

ALBERT, Edouard.

French. Born in Paris, 10 July 1910. Educated at the Lycée Voltaire, Paris, 1916-19; Collège Stanislas, Paris, 1920-28; Ecole Nationale Supérieure des Beaux-Arts, Paris, 1932-37, Dip.Arch. 1937. Served in the French Army Engineering Corps, 1931. Married Hélène Borel in 1942; children: Philippe, Anne, and Eve. Worked as an industrial designer, Paris, 1928-30; in private practice, Paris, 1938 until his death in 1968. Researcher, Alexis Carrel Foundation, Paris, 1941-44; Architect, Ministry for Prisoners and Deportees, Lorraine, 1945-46, and the Air Ministry, Paris, 1946-51; Chief Architect, Ministry of Education, Paris, 1963-68. Professor and Head of the Architecture Department, Ecole National Supérieure des Beaux-Arts, Paris, 1958-68. Member of the Jury, Grand Prix de Rome, Paris, 1960-68; member, Editorial Board, *L'Architecture d'aujourd'hui* Paris, 1960-68. Exhibitions: Gallery René Drouin, Paris, 1942; *Exposition des Arts Ménagers,* Paris, 1952; Musée des Arts Décoratifs, Paris, 1959, and Moscow, 1960; Musée Océanographique, Monaco, 1967; Musée des Arts Décoratifs, Paris, 1968; Mobilier Nal, Paris, 1969; Osaka, Tokyo, and Kyoto, Japan, 1969 (retrospective). Recipient: First Prize, Town Planning Competition, Vanault-les-Dames, Marne, 1941; Grand Prix d'Architecture, Centre d'Etudes Architecturales, Paris, 1957. *Died* (in Paris) *18 January 1968.*

Works:

1939 Metallurgical factory, Dreux, France
     Workmen's houses, Dreux, France
1941/
42 Town plans, Marne et Ardennes, France
1944/
45 7 hospital centers, Moselle and Lorraine, France
1946 Forge Factory, Dreux, France
1946/
52 Reconstruction of Lisieux, Calvados, France
1947/
48 "Philhome" Prefabricated Houses, for Dufay Chromex Ltd., England
1948 House, Oyonnax, Jura, France
1949/
52 Town plans for Ajaccio, Calvi, and Corte, Corsica
1950 Long Distance Emission Center, for the Air Ministry, Etampes, France
1952 House, Champagnolles, Jura, France
     Town Hall and School, Vanault-les-Dames, Marne, France
1953 Air France and Staff Restaurant, Orly Airport, France
1955 Office building (steel tubular structure), 85 Rue Jouffroy, Paris
1958 Air France Hotel interiors, Orly Airport, Paris
     Skyscraper (first in Paris), Rue Croulebarbe, Paris
1959 Air France Administration Building, Orly Airport, Paris
1960 3 churches in Vietnam
     Théâtre Populaire, Rond Point, La Défense, Paris (project; with Jean Vilar)
1961 Montconseil Chapel, Corbeil-Essones, France
1962 Vallourec Research Center, Aulnoye, Pas de Calais, France (with Champetier de Ribes)
1962/
68 Faculty of Literature and Human Sciences, University of Tours (project)
1963 Hotel Complex (arborescent structure), Place de la Résistance, Paris (project)
1963/
66 Housing, Maisons-Laffitte and Melun, France
1964 Faculty of Sciences, University of Paris
1965 Circular Tower, Place d'Italie, Paris (project)
1966 Artificial Island, Monaco (project; with Commander Cousteau)
1966/
67 Library, University of Nanterre, France (with Maroti)

Publications:

By ALBERT: book—*ABC of an Architect,* Algiers 1978; monographs—*Towards an Architecture in Space,* Dreux, France 1959; *Metallic Structures in Architecture,* Brussels 1960; *General Principles of a Contemporary Theatrical Architecture,* Paris 1963; *Arborèscent Structures,* Paris 1964; *A Contemporary Process of Thinking,* Beirut 1966.

On ALBERT: books—*New French Architecture* by Maurice Besset, London and Stuttgart 1967; *Guide: Architecture en France 1945-1983* by Marc Emery and Patrice Goulet, Paris 1983; articles—"Les Compagnons d'Oeuvre" by Jean Giraudoux in *Le Figaro* (Paris), 7 July 1942; "85 Rue Jouffroy, Paris" by J. de Bary in *L'Oeil* (Lausanne), April 1958; "Théâtre Populaire" in *L'Architecture d'aujourd'hui* (Paris), February/March 1964; "Un siècle d'architecte" in *L'Architecture d'aujourd'hui* (Paris), April/May 1964; "Artificial Island" in *L'Architecture d'aujourd'hui* (Paris), April/May 1967; "School Buildings" in *Acier/Stahl/Steel* (Brussels), May 1967; "School Buildings" in *Technique et architecture* (Paris), no.3, 1968; article in *Architectural Review* (London), April 1968; "Un grand vision-

naire, Albert" by Michel Ragon in *Planète* (Paris), no. 39, 1968; article by Pierre Joly in *L'Oeil* (Lausanne), February 1970; article by I. Schein in *Paris-Construit.* Paris 1970; "Faculté des Sciences" by Bernard Marrey in *Revue de l'art* (Paris), 1975.

Edouard Albert was an architect in tune with his times. He had a sharp appreciation of its specific needs and of the possibilities it offered. But he thought that, in comparison with other scientific and artistic disciplines, architecture remained inactive. "And yet," he wrote, "if the constructed environment is not in complete harmony with its age, it will soon be largely responsible for a mounting discontent among the coming generations and for the inevitable social reactions that will follow." A highly cultured man, profoundly human in the sense that nothing which touched sensibility and the arts remained foreign to him, poet and visionary, creative artist, professor of architecture, and moving spirit behind a Centre for Research into Structures, Albert was an architect convinced of the need to find new technical solutions that, together with new materials, would beget new forms.

Albert's professional life illustrated his beliefs. It is marked by works that reveal inventiveness and originality.

From 1945 he studied pre-fabrication, using lightweight materials (Dufaylite), for economical housing that could be dismantled, transformed, and transported and could be produced in aeronautical, naval or railway workshops. In 1950 he began to use hollow profiles; he initiated the use of the tubular steel framework in an office building in the rue Jouffroy in Paris in 1955, a building that can truly be called "revolutionary:

I thought that we had finally arrived at an age of permanent inventiveness and that we could no longer settle for methods that were cumbersome, slow, subject to the vagaries of climate and demanding highly-skilled manpower. It was probable that metal in tubular form would play an important role, because columns (which tubes resemble), like welded joints or connections, are aesthetically acceptable and because the concrete infill lowers the transmission of sound and heat to the point where the Fire Services accept it for very large buildings without also requiring an exterior steel protection.
Five other qualities had determined the choice of the tube: economy of weight (13T instead of 39 in classic IPN); economy in the use of ground space; compared to that of a concrete or coated steel framework; area gain; improved long-term conservation, because the cylinder has no return angle or edge; and the usefulness of tubes for conveying certain supplies and evacuations (electricity cables, rainwater conduits, etc.)

Albert continued his research in this direction in his building in the rue Croulebarbe, Paris, a skyscraper that is the same height as the towers of Notre Dame. Posts of considerable diametral dimensions and thickness carry up to 385T, with inter-axes of 1·50m. and tubular wind braces in the form of the cross of St. Andrew. The same principle was applied to the Air France Administration Building at Orly Airport and the Vallourec Research Center in Aulnoye, where square hollow tubes were adopted for the framework.

At the same time, Albert studied three-dimensional structures, convinced that this kind of tubular system would eventually predominate. He used very small-diameter tubes for the Montconseil Chapel at Corbeil-Essones. Then he moved on to larger projects—a Théâtre Populaire, which should have been built with Jean Vilar at La Défense, Paris, where the roofing structure and envelope is entirely three-dimensional, with post-stressed tubes on a network of tetrahedrons and octahedrons, and an

Edouard Albert: Hotel Complex, Place de la Resistance, Paris, 1963 (project).

artificial island off Monaco, which should have been built in collaboration with Commander Cousteau. The island forms a kind of atoll of 220m. diameter, with an inscribed diameter of 115m. The immersed section descends for 25m., the superstructures rise to 25m., and the spiral tower, topped with a beacon, reaches 100m. The arrangement of the floatation is made up of a 6m. diameter tube connected vertically by 5 tubes of the same dimension to the crown of dodecahedrons forming the enclosure. The wind braces are secured by a series of tetrahedrons of 3·50m. diameter tubes.

In 1963 Albert was commissioned to design a hotel complex in the Place de la Résistance in Paris opposite the Pont de l'Alma. The "given" of the architectural sector was the meeting on this site of the multiple paths along the Seine with the avenues that lead to it: the complex aimed to extend this greenery on a monumental scale by the erection of a lofty transparent structure bearing a series of suspended hotels, themselves covered in greenery. Albert's enormous "plant" emphasizes the curve of the river at the site. It is an arborescent structure containing two hotels on two levels, distributed in space at a height of 120m., allowing light and air to circulate among them.

When we are able, by means of studies, to master the relationships and to solve the equation of the smallest common divisor or module of the secondary structure at the same time as that of the largest common multiple or general rhythm of the primary structure, we shall be sure of the work's unity and of its scale in relationship to man and the site. By such a procedure, one gains in strength and economy, because the easy hyperstatic relations established in the three-dimensional provide that nothing useless is preserved and that the aspect is simplified. This alleviation allows a coherent liaison of architecture with space—like the trunk and branches of a tree—and also secures the disposal of dead weight. Gothic Art was already going in this direction, and its reference to the plant world was not without deep significance. As soon as there is a breach of the compact solid, it is normal to take an option on space, which alone contains everything.

Albert created a Studio of Scientific Research into treelike structures, believing that at a time when the range of possibilities offered by science made possible the realization of everything imaginable, art should refine techniques to ensure that they were not perverted by inconsiderate usage.

Professor at the Ecole des Beaux-Arts from 1959 until his death in 1968, Albert based his teaching on a removal of barriers between the arts; he tried to initiate his pupils into a broad general culture by means of conversations with the masters of different disciplines—engineers, mathematicians, composers, painters, sculptors, men of the theatre, etc. This open-mindedness led him to create in 1960 a student architect exchange scheme between Kyoto and Paris; it continued until his death. In the end, perhaps the best way to convey Albert's spirit is with his own words:

The "wonderful" is beginning to disappear from our planet by our constant stripping down of the magical content of things. How can we translate our eternal hope into a style that will define us in relation to our epoch? If we want to be skilled enough to build as the spirit commands, we must not allow ourselves to be overwhelmed by sterile positivism or intellectual scepticism—for the poet is always right: the spirit of inventiveness cannot be duped by sham separations between the real and the unreal, between the concrete and the abstract.

We have entered a new age. Its character is kinetic and universal. In the space age we should probably have a corresponding spatial architecture. Spatial architecture—like atonal music or nonrepresentional painting—are not only expressions invented to shock man out of his conventional thinking; they also, in themselves, possess harmonious lines of strength.

—Renée Diamant-Berger

ALBINI, Franco.

Italian. Born in Robbiate, Como, 17 October 1905. Educated at Polytechnic, Milan, Dip.Arch. 1929. Married; son: Marco. In private practice, Milan, from 1930; subsequently joined by the firm's current partners, Franca Helg, 1952, Antonia Piva, 1962, and Marco Albini, 1965. Lecturer, American-Italian Commission of Cultural Exchanges, Rome, 1954-63; Professor of Architectural Composition, Polytechnic, Milan, 1963-77. Member, Unesco Commission for the Renewal of the Museums of the United Arab Republic, 1968-9. Member of CIAM (Congrès Internationaux d'Architecture Moderne). Exhibitions: *Italian Contemporary Art, Decorative Art and Modern Architecture*, Stockholm and Helsinki, 1953; *Ten Italian Architects*, Los Angeles, 1967; *28/78 Architettura*, Palazzo delle Stelline, Milan, 1979; *Design & design*, Palazzo delle Stelline, Milan, and Palazzo Grassi, Venice, 1979; *Franco Albini: Architettura per un museo*, Galleria Nazionale d'Arte Moderna, Rome, 1980. Recipient: First Prize, Main Hall Competition, *Triennale*, Milan, 1954; La Rinascente Compasso d'Oro, Milan, 1955 1958, 1964; Bronze Medal, Parsons School of Design, New York, 1956; Olivetti National Medal for Architecture, Italy, 1957; IN-ARCH Award, Italy, 1963, 1965; Biscione d'Oro Award, *Ente Manifestazione Provinciale per il Turismo*, Milan, 1971; First Prize, Municipal Theatre Competition, Vicenza, Italy, 1971. Member, Italian Institute of Town Planning and of the Scientific Institute of the C.N.R. (National Research Centre of Museography). Member, Academy of San Luca. Honorary Royal Designer for Industry, Royal Society of Arts, London; Honorary Fellow, American Institute of Architects. *Died* (in Milan) *1 November 1977*.

Works:

1936   Design of the Dwelling Exhibition, *Triennale*, Milan (with R. Camus, P. Clausetti, I. Gardella, G. Mazzoleni, G. Minoletti, G. Mucchi, G. Palanti and G. Romano)
Design of the Antique Jewellery Exhibition, *Triennale*, Milan (with G. Romano)
Design of Room for a Man, *Triennale*, Milan
Fabio Filzi Workers' Housing Estate, Viale Argonne, Milan (with R. Camus and G.C. Palanti)
1938   Villa Levi alterations, Broglio, Varese, Italy
Villa Pestarini, Piazza Tripoli, Milan
Gabriele d'Annunzio Workers' Housing Estate, Milan (project; with R. Camus and G.C. Palanti)
Ettore Ponti Workers' Housing Estate, Milan (project)
Villa Toniolo, Piani d'Invrea, Riviera di Ponente, Italy
Villa Monzino alterations, Moltrasio, Italy
1940   "Criteria for the Modern Home," *Triennale*, Milan
Villa Neuffer alterations, Ispra, Lake Maggiore, Italy
1941   *Scipione Exhibition*, Galleria Brera, Milan
1944   Ceccon Garden, Erba, Italy
Furniture store, Via Verri, Milan (with BBPR, Ignazio Gardella, and G. Mucchi)
1945   Villa Picolli, Torno, Lake Como, Italy (project)
Master plan for the City of Milan (project; with others)
1946   *Home Furnishings Exhibition*, Palazzo dell Arte al Parco, Milan
Master plan for the centre of the City of Milan (with BBPR, Piero Bottoni, Luigi Figini, Gino Pollini, and others)
1947   Villa Levi Swimming Pool and Garden, Broglio, Varese, Italy (project)
1947/
48   Development plan for Reggio Emilia, Italy (with Giancarlo De Carlo)

1948/
49   Venetian Gallery reconstruction, Galleria Brera, Milan (with L. Castiglioni)
1949/
50   Pirovano Hotel/Mountain Refuge, Cervinia, Italy
1950   Istituto Nazionale Assicurazioni Office Building, Parma Italy
Istituto Nazionale Assicurazioni Workers' Housing Estate, Crescenzago, Milan (with F. Marescotti)
Mangiagalli Workers' Housing Estate, Via Jacopino da Tradate, Vialba, Milan (with Ignazio Gardella)
Office and residential building, Piazza Repubblica, Milan (project)
1950/
51   Instituto Nazionale Assicurazioni Workers' Housing Estate, Cesate, Milan (with others)
1950/
61   Palazzo Bianco conversion to a museum, Genoa
1952   Museo del Tesoro di San Lorenzo, Genoa
Salons, *Exhibition of Arts and Customs*, Palazzo Grassi, Venice
1952/
61   Palazzo Rosso conversion to a museum, Genoa
1952/
62   Municipal Offices, Genoa
1953   *Italian Contemporary Art, Decorative Art and Modern Architecture* exhibition, Stockholm and Helsinki
Villa alterations, Diano Marina, Italy
1954   Design of the Montecatini and Rhodatoce exhibitions, Trade Fair, Milan
Main Hall, *Triennale*, Milan
Arts Schools Section, *Triennale*, Milan
Salons, *Exhibition of Arts and Customs*, Palazzo Grassi, Venice
Design of the Italian State Exhibition, *Bienal*, São Paulo, Brazil
Società Gres Employees Residential Buildings, Colognola, Bergamo, Italy
1955   Istituto Nazionale Assicurazioni Housing Estate Creche-Kindergarten, Cesate, Milan (with G. Rigoli)
Valleta Cambiaso Public Gardens and Sports Grounds, Genoa
1955/
56   Villa Minorini, Parco del Tigullio, Italy
Villa Olivetti, Ivrea, Italy
1956   Palazzo dell'Arte Exhibition Galleries, Genoa (competition project; with M. Labo, Daneri, Grossi Bianchi and Zappa)
Delacroix exhibition, *Biennale*, Venice
Premio La Rinascente—Compasso d'Oro Exhibition, World's Fair, New York
Office and residential building, Turin (project)
Villa Zambelli, Forli, Italy
1957   Istituto Nazionale Assicurazioni Housing Estate, Scandino, Reggio Emilia, Italy
1957/
61   Istituto Nazionale Assicurazioni Office and Residential Buildings, Genoa-Piccapietra
La Rinascente Department Store, Piazza Fiume, Rome
1958   Farm building conversion, Gallarate, Varese, Italy
1959   Villa, Pearso, Italy (project)
Villa Strangalini, Pieve Ligure, Italy
1960   *International Glass and Steel Exhibition, Triennale*, Milan
History of Petroleum Exhibition, Automobile Museum, Turin (with C. Levi)
History of the Tyre Exhibition, Automobile Museum, Turin
1960/
72   5 residential buildings, Via Argelati, Milan
1961   Organization, Productivity, Market Pavilion, *International Work Exhibition*, Turin
Scientific Research Pavilion, *International Work Exhibition*, Turin

House, Punta Ala, Italy
1962 House, Galliate Lombardo, Italy
1962/
  63 New Egyptian Museum, Cairo, Egypt (project)
     Apartment building, Castellaro, Zoagli, Italy
     Building conversion, via San Maurilio, Milan
     Villa Osti, Bogliasco, Italy
1962/
  65 Villa alterations, via XX Settembre, Milan
1962/
  69 Stations for the first line of the underground
     (Subway), Milan
1963/
  67 Building, Via Moise Loria, Milan
1963/
  75 Sant'Agostino Museum, Genoa
1964 Italian industrial exhibition, World's Fair,
     New York
     Modissa Building, Bahnhofstrasse, Zürich
     (competition project)
     Forti District Landscaping Study, Genoa
1964/
  67 Building, via Fulvio Testi, Milan
     Hotel, Santa Cesarea Terme, Calabria, Italy
1965 *Guardi Exhibition,* Palazzo Grassi, Venice
     Villa, Cremella, Como, Italy
     Villa Contarini conversion, Valnogaredo,
     Padua

1965/
  67 Villa, Quinto, Genoa
1965/
  70 Apartment building, Courmayeur, Aosta,
     Italy
1965/
  72 Graeco-Roman Museum, Alexandria, Egypt
1966 Italsider Steel Pavilion, Trade Fair, Milan
     (with E. Gentili Tedeschi)
1966/
  70 Residential and office building, Piazza Arcole,
     Milan
1967 Italsider "Yesterday, Today, Tomorrow"
     Pavilion, Trade Fair, Milan (with E. Gentili
     Tedeschi)
     Thermal Bath Building, Salsomaggiore
     Terme, Italy
1967/
  69 Villa, Ponte dell'Olio, Piacenza, Italy
1967/
  70 Villa, Parma, Italy
1968 Italsider "Why Steel" Pavilion, Trade Fair,
     Milan (with E. Gentili Tedeschi)
     Alfa Romeo Technical Office Building, Arese,
     Italy (competition project)
     Breuil Centre, Cervinia, Italy
1968/
  69 Master plan for the Egyptian Museum and

Egyptian Museum Cultural Center, Cairo
     Villa, Cremella, Como, Italy
     SNAM G.N.L. Terminal landscaping, Lanig-
     aglia, La Spezia, Italy (consultancy project)
1968/
  70 Brionvega Storage, Display and Office Build-
     ings, Arzano, Padua and Florence
1968/
  71 Apartment and office building, Parma, Italy
1969 Villa, Padenghe, Lake Garda, Italy
1969/
  70 Medieval Tower conversion, Montecatini Val
     Cecina, Italy
1969/
  71 Villa, Rocca San Casciano, Forli, Italy
1969/
  73 Secondary school, Giussano, Milan
     SNAM Office Building III, San Donato
     Milanese, Milan
1969/
  74 Office and residential building, Madre di Dio,
     Genoa
     Civic Museum conversion, Eremitani Cloist-
     er, Padua
     Cassa di Risparmio conversion, Palazzo Pisa-
     roni, Piacenza, Italy
1971 Municipal Theatre, Vicenza, Italy (compe-
     tition project)

Franco Albini: Thermal Bath Building, Salsomaggiore Terme, Italy, 1967.

1971/
  72 Palladio Exhibition Plan, Basilica, Vicenza, Italy
1971/
  73 Villa, Daverio, Italy
1972 *Achievements of the Pahlavi Era* exhibition, Marble Palace, Tehran
      Domus Comestabilis Offices conversion, Vicenza, Italy
      Office and picture gallery conversion, Sforza Castle Milan
      Villa, Daverio, Italy
1972/
  75 Old town center building code study, Brescia, Italy
1973 *The School of Leonardo* exhibition, Palazzo Reale, Milan
      Houses, Gavirate, Italy (project)
      Villa, Daverio, Italy
1973/
  74 Civic Center and Canteen, Sassuolo, Modena, Italy (project)
1974 *The School of Leonardo* exhibition, Tokyo
      50 Years of Italian Painting in the Boschi-Di Stefano Collection exhibition, Palazzo Reale, Milan
      Kindergarten, Sassuolo, Modena, Italy (with A. Pastorini)
      Houses, Montichiari, Italy
      Country Club, Croara, Italy (project)
1974/
  75 Corso Garibaldi study, Milan
      Palazzo del Monte restoration, Piacenza, Italy
1975 Masmak restoration, Riyadh, Saudi Arabia (project)
      Public Gardens and Parks Study, Saudi Arabia (with A. Porcinai)

Also numerous furniture designs.

Publications:

On ALBINI: books—*Forme nuove in Italia* by Agnoldomenico Pica, Milan and Rome 1957; *Architettura italiana ultima/Recent Italian Architecture* by Agnoldomenico Pica, Milan 1959; *Storia dell'architettura moderna* by Leonardo Benevolo, 2 vols., Bari, Italy 1960; *The New Architecture of Europe* by G. E. Kidder Smith, New York and London 1961; *Franco Albini* by Giulio Carlo Argan, Milan 1962; *Dizionario enciclopedico di architettura e urbanistica,* edited by Paolo Portoghesi, Rome 1969; *Orientamenti nuovi nell' architettura italiana* by Vittorio Gregotti, Milan 1970; *Dizionario degli architetti,* edited by B. Oudin, Milan 1971; *Design in Italia 1945-1972* by Paolo Fossati, Milan 1972; *Franco Albini 1930-1970* by Franca Helg, Cesare De Seta and Marcello Fagiolo, Florence 1979, 1981, London, 1981; *28/78 Architettura,* exhibition catalogue, edited by Maria Grazia Mazzocchi Bonadonna, Milan 1979; *Franco Albini (1905-1977): Architettura per un museo,* exhibition catalogue, Rome 1980; articles—"Franco Albini and Architectural Culture in Italy" by Giuseppe Samona in *Zodiac* (Milan), no. 3, 1957; "Contemporary Italian Architects" in *Notiziario culturale italiano* (Paris), May 1963; "Recent Works by Albini-Helg" by F. Tentori in *Zodiac* (Milan), no. 14, 1965; "Realismo e architettura povera" by E. D'Alfonso in *Casabella* (Milan), no. 352, 1970; "The Work of Franco Albini," special issue of *Architettura* (Rome), October 1979; "The Rationalist Franco Albini" by Alberto Sartoris in *Domus* (Milan), February 1980; "Bourgeois, Architect, Reserved and a Poet—The Work of Franco Albini" by Alberto Ferrari in *Modo* (Milan), April 1980.

Although Franco Albini's work covered a wide range from furniture design to town planning projects, he became best known as an outstanding exhibition and display architect whose world stature led him to be entrusted with the project for the great new museums of Egyptians art in Cairo. His influence can be seen in museums throughout the world, though it was his work in Genoa that first made him famous. There, he remodelled the interiors of two Renaissance palace museums with rich art collections—the Palazzo Bianco, or White Palace, and the Palazzo Rosso, or Red Palace—displaying their art with abstract rigour yet sensitivity, so that it could be seen clearly and effectively to best advantage.

Also in Genoa he built a new museum to house the Treasury of the Cathedral of San Lorenzo, which possesses such fabulous objects as the Sacro Catino, a cup brought back from the Middle East by the Crusaders. Supposed to have been given to Solomon by the Queen of Sheba, it is the vessel from which Christ is claimed to have drunk at the Last Supper. Albini's new Museo del Tesoro di San Lorenzo is in the undercroft of the cathedral and is laid out geometrically as a series of circular rooms of various sizes with the objects dramatically lit.

Italian designers have been best known for such things as cars or Olivetti typewriters, but Albini made a major contribution to experiments in Italian furniture design, from compact dining room furniture in graded units which pack away into a small area to a variety of very comfortable, circular arm chairs, such as the elegant malacca and bamboo-cane Margherita, designed with his partner Franca Helg in 1950.

From his first villa in Milan in 1938, he was responsible for a great variety of works, including a number of stations for the Milan underground system. The most controversial of his buildings has been the large department store La Rinascente in Rome, the most interesting version of which was the original model, deeply influenced by the metal structures of the nineteenth century. As actually built, it is a savagely brutal structure with an exposed steel frame of almost windowless concrete walls built of pleated units.

Like Ignazio Gardella, with whom he worked on the development of the new Cesate district of Milan, he was one of the longest survivors of the first generation of Italian modernism or rationalism, with an exceptionally versatile career that made him a major influence in many fields of design.
—Konstantin Bazarov

ALEXANDER, Christopher.

British. Born in Vienna, Austria, of British parents, 4 October 1936. Educated at Oundle School, Northamptonshire; Cambridge University, 1956-59, B.A. in architecture, M.A. in mathematics; Harvard University, Cambridge, Massachusetts, 1960-63, Ph.D. in architecture 1963. Married; has two children. Worked for the Village Development Planning Department of the Government of Gujarat, India, 1962; Consultant in Urban Housing, Arthur D. Little Company, San Francisco, 1963; Consultant Architect, Bay Area Rapid Transit System, San Francisco, 1963-64; Consultant on User Needs, Ministry of Public Buildings and Works, London, 1965-66. Since 1967, Director, Center for Environmental Structure, Berkeley, California. Consultant Architect to the Ministry of Information and Tourism, Spain, 1975, and Ministry of Environment, Papua New Guinea, 1976; Architect and Planner, Jewish Agency and Ministry of Housing, Israel, 1978; Consultant Architect, Infonavit, Mexico, 1978. Assistant Professor, 1963, Professor in the Humanities, 1965-66, Associate Professor of Architecture, 1966-70, and since 1970, Professor of Architecture, University of California, Berkeley. Visiting Lecturer, Royal Institute of Technology, Stockholm, 1973, and University of Mexico, Mexicali, 1975-76. Recipient: International Design Award, Kaufmann Foundation, 1965; Research Medal, American Institute of Architects, 1972; Japanese Institute of Architects Prize, 1985. Member, Swedish Royal Academy, 1985. Address: Center for Environmental Structure, 2701 Shasta Road, Berkeley, California 94708, U.S.A.

Works:

1962 Master plan for the village of Bavra, Gujarat, India
      Bavra Village School, Gujarat, India (project; with Janet Johnson)
1963 Urban housing program, San Francisco
1963/
  64 Courtyard House, New Haven, Connecticut (project; with Serge Chermayeff)
1964 Rapid transit stations for the Bay Area Rapid Transit System, San Francisco (schematic design; with Van King and Sara Ishikawa)
1968 Multi-Service Center, Hunts Point, Bronx, New York (project; with Sara Ishikawa and Murray Silverstein)
1969 Community village of 1,500 houses, Lima, Peru (competition project; with Sanford Hirshen, Sara Ishikawa, Christie Coffin, and Shlomo Angel)
1970 "A Human City" Pavilion, World's Fair, Osaka, Japan (with Ronald Walkey and others)
      Berkeley City Hall Complex, California (project; with Ronald Walkey and Barbara Schreiner)
1970/
  73 Master plan for the University of Oregon, Eugene (with others)
1970/
  78 Experimental furniture designs
1971 Fourteen prototype houses, Lima, Peru
1971/
  74 Community Mental Health Center, Modesto, California (with Murray Silverstein and Nacht and Lewis)
      Master plan for the town of Marsta, Sweden (project; with Max Jacobson and Ingrid King)
1972 Mill Valley Housing Cooperative, California (project; with Sara Ishikawa)
1974 User-designed apartment building, St. Quentin-en-Yvelines, near Versailles (project; with Ingrid King and Walter Wendler)
      Master plan for a tourist resort, Fuerteventura, Canary Islands (with Ingrid King, Halim Abdelhalim, and Lisa Heschong)
      Tourist development, Malaga, Spain (project; with Halim Abdelhalim, Walter Wendler, Ingrid King, Donald Corner, and Howard Davis)
      Two-story building of featherweight concrete (project; with Walter Wendler, Donald Corner, and others)
      Master plan for the town square of Walnut Creek, Arizona (with Ingrid King)
1975 Rockbridge Plaza (shops and apartments), Oakland, California
1975/
  76 Experimental block production factory, Mexicali, Mexico
1975/
  78 Multi-colored experimental tiles and paintings
1976 Eight experimental houses, (with community facilities, Mexicali, Mexico
1977 Migrant worker's house (project: for the California Department of Migrant Services)
1977/
  78 Experimental designs in sprayed concrete
1978/
  79 Master plan for Moshav Sof Ma'arav, Galilee, Israel
      Experimental sprayed concrete house, Martinez, California

Christopher Alexander: User-designed apartment building, St. Quentin-en-Yvelines, France, 1974 (project).

1980 Tarrytown Conference Center extension, New York (project)
Restaurant and entertainment complex, Hudson River, New York (project)
Linz Cafe Building, Linz, Austria
1981 North Omaha Community Master Plan, Nebraska
Guasare New Town Master Plan, Maracaibo, Venezuela
Mr. and Mrs. Stuart Card House, Portola Valley, California (project)
1982 John and Mara Lighty terraced house, Lake Berryessa, California
Twenty Houses, Moshav Shorashim, Galilee, Israel (project; with Artemis Anninou)
Ten-storey Apartment Building, Sapporo, Japan (with Ingrid King)
Mr. and Mrs. Kinsey Anderson House, Bodega Bay, California (project)
1982/
83 Crawford Estate Mansion, Stinson Beach, California (project)
1982/
85 New Eishin School, Tokyo (project)
1983 Thirty houses, workshops and commercial complex, Moshav Shorashim, Galilee, Israel
Mr. and Mrs. Andre Sala House, Albany, California (with Gary Black)
Fresno Farmers Market, California (with Carl Lindberg and Jonathan Fefferman)

1984 John and Terry Naylor House, Orinda, California (project)
1984/
85 Low-cost housing development, Sao Carlos, Brazil (project)
1985 Outdoor Pavilion for the Omega Institute, New York (project)
Al and Katherine Haimson House, Woodside, California (project)
Anne Medlock/John Graham House, Whidbey Island, Seattle, Washington (project)
George Sarlo House extension and swimming pools, Sonoma, California
Office furniture for Haworth Furniture (with Artemis Anninou and Gary Black)
New Eishin University, Iruma shi, Tokyo (with Hajo Neis, Gary Black, Ingrid King and others)
Office furniture for Sweet Potatoes Factory, Berkeley, California
Carpentry Workshop, Martinez, California (with Gary Black)

Publications:

By ALEXANDER: books—*Community and Privacy: Towards a New Architecture of Humanism,* with Serge Chermayeff, New York 1963, Tokyo and London 1966, Buenos Aires 1967, Paris and Stuttgart 1972; *Notes on the Synthesis of Form,*

Cambridge, Massachusetts 1964, Milan 1967, Paris 1970; *Systems Generating Systems* (booklet), Chicago 1967; *A Pattern Language Which Generates Multi-Service Centers,* with Sara Ishikawa and Murray Silverstein, Berkeley, California 1968; *Houses Generated by Patterns,* with Sanford Hirshen, Sara Ishikawa, Christie Coffin, and Shlomo Angel, Berkeley, California 1969; *Tres aspectos de matematica y desegnò,* Barcelona 1969; *Mosaic of Subcultures,* Berkeley, California 1969; *A Human City,* Tokyo 1970; *La estructura del medio ambiente,* Barcelona 1971; *The Grass Roots Housing Process,* with Halim Abdelhalim and others, Berkeley, California 1975; *The New Apartment Building,* with Ingrid King and Walter Wendler, Berkeley, California 1975; *People Rebuilding Berkeley: The Self-Creating Life of Neighborhoods,* with Howard Davis and Halim Abdelhalim, Berkeley, California 1975; *The Oregon Experiment,* London 1975; *A Pattern Language,* London 1977; *The Timeless Way of Building,* London 1979; *The Linz Cafe/Das Linz Cafe,* New York and Vienna 1981; *Rebirth of the Inner City: The North Omaha Plan,* with Howard Davis, Nebraska 1981; *The Production of Houses,* with Howard Davis and others, New York 1985; *Battle: The Story of a Historic Clash Between World System A and World System B,* with Hajo Neis and others, New York 1985; *Sketches of a New Architecture,* New York 1985; *The Nature of Order,* New York 1985; *A New Theory of Urban Design,* with Hajo Neis and others, New York 1986; articles— "Perception and Modular Coordination" in *RIBA Journal* (London), October 1959; "The Revolution Finished Twenty Years Ago" in *Architects Yearbook*, London 1960; "A Result in Visual Aesthetics" in *British Journal of Psychology* (London), October 1960; "The Origin of Creative Power in Children" in *British Journal of Aesthetics* (London), July 1962; "Main Structure Concept," with B. V. Doshi, in *Landscape* (Berkeley, California), Winter 1963-64; "On Changing the Way People See," with A. W. F. Huggins, in *Perceptual and Motor Skills* (Missoula, Montana), July 1964; "The Theory and Invention of Form" in *Architectural Record* (New York), April 1965; "A City Is Not a Tree" in *Architectural Forum* (New York), April May 1965, reprinted in *Architecture, mouvement, continuité* (Paris), November 1967; "The Question of Computers in Design" in *Landscape* (Berkeley, California), Spring 1965; "Relational Complexes in Architecture," with Van Maren King and others, in *Architectural Record* (New York), September 1966; "From a Set of Forces to a Form" in *The Man-Made Object*, edited by Gyorgy Kepes, New York 1966; "The Pattern of Streets" in *Architectural Design* (London), November 1967; "Design Innovation," with others, in *Progressive Architecture* (New York), November 1967; "Subsymmetries," with Susan Carey, in *Perception and Psychophysics* (Austin, Texas), February 1968; "The Bead Game Conjecture" in *Lotus* (Venice), no. 5, 1968; "Thick Walls" in *Architectural Design* (London), July 1968; "Major Changes in Environmental Form Required by Social and Psychological Demands" in *Architectural Design* (London), March 1970; "The Environment" in *Japan Architect* (Tokyo), no. 165, 1970; "Interview with Maria José Rague Arias" in *California Trip*, Barcelona 1971; "Houses Generated by Patterns: Summary" in *The Growth of Cities* by David Lewis, London 1971; "The Atoms of Environmental Structure," with Barry Poyner, in *Emerging Methods of Design*, Cambridge, Massachusetts 1971; "A Refutation of Design Methodology," interview with Max Jacobson, in *Architectural Design* (London), December 1971; "An Attempt to Derive the Nature of a Human Building System from First Principles" and "The Invention of a Human and Organic Building System" in *Shirtsleeve Session on Responsive Housebuilding Technologies* by Edward Allen, Cambridge, Massachusetts 1972; "The Andalusian Project," with Halim Abdelhalim, Walter Wendler, and others, in *Architectural Design* (London), January 1975; "The Architect Builder" in *AIA Journal* (Washington, D.C.), September 1977; "Value: A Reply to Protzen" in *Concrete* (Slough, Buckinghamshire), no. 8, 1977; "Value in Design," with Jean-Pierre Protzen, in *Design Studies* (Guildford, Surrey), July 1980.

On ALEXANDER: book—*Christopher Alexander: The Search for a New Paradigm in Architecture* by Stephen Grabow, London 1983; articles— "The Death of the Beaux-Arts: The Cal-Oregon Experiment in Design Education" by M. A. Milne and C. W. Rusch in *AIA Journal* (Washington, D.C.), March 1968; "Pattern Language: The Contribution of Christopher Alexander's Center for Environmental Structure to the Science of Design" by Roger Montgomery in *Architectural Forum* (New York), January February 1970; "Design Method or Beaux-Arts? Four Notes on Design Method" by Juan Pablo Bonta in *Architectural Association Quarterly* (London), Autumn 1970; "Christopher Alexander ou le mythe de la création scientifique" by J. Dreyfus in *La Vie urbaine* (Paris), no. 2, 1971; "Dossier: Recherche Habitat" in *Architecture d'aujourd'hui* (Paris), July August 1974; "Christopher Alexander's Timeless Way of Building" by Kanna Hirata in *Architecture + Urbanism* (Tokyo), no. 3, 1975; "La Régression californienne ou la réificacion du mythe Christopher Alexander" in *Architecture, mouvement, continuité* (Paris), March 1976; "The Oregon Experiment" in *Building Design* (London), 10 February 1978;

"Alexander's Pattern Language", in *Architectural Association Quarterly* (London), no. 4, 1979; "Critical Analysis of 'A Pattern Language'" by M. Dominguez in *Arquitecturas bis* (Barcelona), September/December 1979; "Christopher Alexander and the Pattern Language" in *Architecture + Urbanism* (Tokyo), December 1979; "Patterns and Regeneration" in *Architectural Review* (London), December 1981; "The Linz Cafe" in *Baumeister* (Munich), April 1982; "Notes on the synthesis of Christopher Alexander" in *Fifth Column* (Montreal), Autumn 1982; "Towards an Architecture: Christopher Alexander and Pattern Language" in *Architects' Journal* (London), 5 January 1983; "Linz Cafe: The Architect's Evaluation" and "Contrasting Concepts of Harmony in Architecture" in *Lotus International* (New York), no. 40, 1983.

Christopher Alexander is a major voice among those trying to evolve a sound theoretical basis for architecture. His influence has been through his writing and teaching rather than through completed buildings. In recent years, however, he and his collaborators have produced a number of projects that have lent visual evidence to his theoretical position.

Educated both as an architect and as a mathematician at Cambridge, Alexander later obtained his Ph.D. in architecture from Harvard University. His doctoral work in 1962 and 1963 centered on the development of computer programs for the Hierarchical Decomposition of Sets or Systems having associated graphs (the programs were known as HI-DECS). The basic aim of this work was to develop techniques for the analysis of successful environments and for the creation of new environments. In particular, explicit analysis, it was hoped, would enable designers to capture the elusive qualities of traditional unselfconscious designs for buildings and settlements in a way that escapes the crude rationalism of conventional architectural design.

Alexander's criticism of existing design methods, implicit in the aims of his mathematical work, found expression in two books. *Community and Privacy: Towards a New Architecture of Humanism*, written with the modernist pioneer Serge Chermayeff, explored in particular notions of privacy within the home and between home and community. Many examples were given of courtyard houses and other house forms satisfying the complex criteria of sociability and privacy in the home. *Notes on the Synthesis of Form* was one of the most important books of the decade. It presented a coherent theoretical explanation of the shortcomings of crude rationalist design, the basis for the success of many unselfconscious designs, and the necessary methods for creating better designs in the future. The impact of the book was tremendous. Architects were quite unused to serious theoretical texts outside the traditions of art history. Alexander wanted to know what made places work, not what made them look as if they worked. The theory was based on the concept of "fit" between human needs/demands and possible forms, a central theme in Alexander's thought.

Following a brief spell in an experimental group at the British Ministry of Public Buildings and Works, Alexander took up a post in 1966 at the University of California, Berkeley, where he still teaches. At Berkeley he developed the theory of "fit" in terms of what he called "patterns"— the successful resolution of a specific problem within a specific context. Patterns can be seen as "correct" solutions to subproblems in design and can be combined into a "pattern language" accessible to all who wish to build, not merely to professional architects. The evolution of a pattern language by Alexander and his colleagues at his design and research organization, the Center for Environmental Structure, led to a diminished confidence in mathematical methods as a basis for better design, to be replaced by empirical research to support the hypotheses of patterns.

In 1971, in an interview, Alexander shocked the

large fraternity of design methodologists by condemning design methods as offering nothing useful on how to design buildings and as being obsessed with techniques leading nowhere. Since then, the work of CES has focussed on design projects. But more important for most architects has been the publication of three books: *The Timeless Way of Building*, which sets out the philosophical basis of the Pattern Language as a medium for articulating needs and for creating buildings and environments in an adaptive rather than a wholesale manner; *A Pattern Language*, which is a compendium of 253 patterns researched at CES and ranging in scale from demographic considerations to detailed questions of ornament; and *The Oregon Experiment*, which describes a specific cooperative planning experiment for the evolution of the 15,000-student Eugene campus of the University of Oregon.

Alexander has secured an important place in the history of twentieth-century architecture. His critics now accuse him of a progressive slackening of rigour and the glorification of self-building, manual work and crafts at the expense of confrontation with modern technology and social institutions. But he has great resilience and originality of thought. There is much of real value in the Pattern Language concept, and it promises much for the future of the built environment in a time of increasing disillusionment with more conventional approaches.

—Andrew Rabeneck

ALEXANDER, Robert Evans.

American. Born in Bayonne, New Jersey, 23 November 1907. Educated at Cornell University, Ithaca, New York, 1925-30, B.Arch. 1930. Married Eugenie Vigneron in 1931 (died, 1952); children: Lynne and Timothy; married Mary Starbuck in 1953 (divorced, 1982); son: Robert Jr.; married Nancy Jaicks in 1984. Partner, Wilson, Merrill and Alexander, Los Angeles, 1935-41; worked at Lockheed Aircraft, Burbank, California, 1942-45; in private practice, Los Angeles, 1946-49; in partnership with Richard J. Neutra, *q.v.*, Los Angeles, 1949-58. From 1958, Principal, Robert E. Alexander and Associates, Los Angeles. Member, 1945-51, and President, 1948-50, City of Los Angeles Planning Commission. Formerly, consultant to the Government of India, for the United Nations: Territory of Guam; University of California at San Diego; California Institute of Technology, Pasadena; Claremont Colleges, California; Public Housing Administration, Washington, D.C.; Federal Housing Administration, Washington, D.C.; United States Navy; General Services Administration, Washington, D.C.; and Office of Civil Defense Mobilization, Washington, D.C. President, Southern California Chapter, American Institute of Architects, 1970. Recipient: about thirty design awards, 1946-70, Honor Award, 1946, 1951, and 1954, and Twenty-Five Year Award, 1972, American Institute of Architects. Fellow, American Institute of Architects, 1956. Address: 2909 Regent Street, Apt. 3, Berkeley, California 94705, U.S.A.

Works:

1935/
42 Baldwin Hills Village, Los Angeles (with Wilson, Merrill, and Reginald D. Johnson; Clarence Stein, consultant)
1939 Estrada Courts, Los Angeles
1942 Lakewood City, Los Angeles
1946 Community Church, Baldwin Hills, Los Angeles
1946/
50 Shops, Baldwin Hills, Los Angeles

Robert Alexander: Baldwin Hills Village, Los Angeles, 1935-42.

1947/
49 Elementary School, Baldwin Hills, Los Angeles
1948 Pearce House, Los Angeles
Demonstration Elementary School, University of California at Los Angeles
1948/
55 Orange Coast College, Costa Mesa, California
1950 Urban redevelopment plan for Sacramento, California (project; with Richard Neutra)
1950/
53 Redevelopment plan for Elysian Heights, Los Angeles (project; with Richard Neutra)
1952/
54 Territorial plan, Governor's Residence, and three schools, Guam (with Richard Neutra)
1953 Community Hotel, San Pedro, California (with Richard Neutra)
1954 Child guidance clinic, Los Angeles (with Richard Neutra)
Business Education Building, Orange Coast College, Costa Mesa, California (with Richard Neutra)
Family housing, Mountain Home, Idaho (with Richard Neutra)
1955 Mellon Science Building and Francis Scott Key Auditorium, St. John's College, Annapolis, Maryland (with Richard Neutra)
1656 National Charity League Headquarters, Los Angeles (with Richard Neutra)
1957 Science Building, Arts and Music Auditorium, and Sports Facilities, Orange Coast College, Costa Mesa, California (with Richard Neutra)
Miramar Chapel, La Jolla, California (with Richard Neutra)
Ferro Chemical Company Office Building, Cleveland (with Richard Neutra)
Alamitos Intermediate School, Garden Grove, California (with Richard Neutra)
1958 Riviera Methodist Church, Redondo Beach, California (with Richard Neutra)
Fine Arts Building, University of Nevada, Reno (with Richard Neutra)
Palos Verdes High School, California (with Richard Neutra)

Fine Arts Center, California State University, San Fernando (with Richard Neutra)
Elementary Training School, University of California at Los Angeles (with Richard Neutra)
Visitors' Center, Gettysburg, Pennsylvania (with Richard Neutra)
Visitors' Center, Petrified Forest, Arizona (with Richard Neutra)
Police Facilities Building, Santa Ana, California (with Romberg and Lowry)
Family housing, Lemoore, California (with Richard Neutra)
1959 Museum of Natural History and Planetarium, Dayton, Ohio (with Richard Neutra)
Library, University of Nevada, Reno
1960 Megastructure, Caracas, Venezuela (project; with Richard Neutra)
Married student housing, University of Southern California, Los Angeles
1961 Great Western Savings and Loan Building, Los Angeles (with Skidmore, Owings and Merrill)
Catskill Elementary School, Los Angeles
International Student Center, University of California at Los Angeles
1962 Dining Facility, University of California at San Diego
1963 Swirlbul Library, Adelphi University, Garden City, Long Island, New York (with Richard Neutra)
United States Embassy, Karachi, Pakistan (with Richard Neutra)
Lincoln Memorial Museum, Gettysburg, Pennsylvania (with Richard Neutra)
1964 Hall of Records, Los Angeles (with Richard Neutra)
Richard J. Neutra Elementary School, Lemoore, California (with Richard Neutra)
1964/
71 School of Medicine, University of California at San Diego
1966 Residence Halls, Revelle College, University of California at San Diego
1968 Baxter Hall of Humanities and Social Sciences, and Ramo Lecture Hall, California Institute of Technology, Pasadena

1968 Bunker Hill Towers, Figueroa and 1st Streets, Los Angeles
1970 Los Angeles Central Library addition (project)
1972 Beckman Behavioral Biology Laboratories, California Institute of Technology, Pasadena
1976 Ridgecrest Mental Health Center, California
1979 Two schools in Japan (as consultant)
1983 Two schools in Okinawa (as consultant)

City plans for El Paso, Texas-Juarez, Mexico; Tulsa, Oklahoma; Anchorage, Alaska; and Sacramento, San Fernando, Vista, Norwalk, Escondido, and South San Diego, California

Publications:

By ALEXANDER: books—*Rebuilding the City: A Study of Redevelopment Problems in Los Angeles,* with Drayton S. Bryant, Los Angeles 1951; *The Rural City* (United Nations publication), New York 1952; *Environmental Quality and Amenity in California,* with Okimoto, Sacramento, California, 1966; articles— "Preview of a New Way of Life" in *Revere Magazine* (New York), no. 14, 1943; "The Suburban Campus" in *Urban Land* (Washington, D.C.), December 1966; "Southern California Transit: Too Little, Too Late, Too Bad" in *Cry California* (San Francisco), Spring 1968.

On ALEXANDER: articles— "Demonstration School" in *Architectural Forum* (New York), November 1951; "College Buildings: Space Analysis" in *Progressive Architecture* (New York), February 1952; "Planning Guam" in *Progressive Architecture* (New York), January 1953; "Guam: A Problem in Progress" in *Arts and Architecture* (Los Angeles), May 1953; "A Community Hotel" in *Arts and Architecture* (Los Angeles), September 1953; "Sacramento: A Model for Small City Redevelopment" in *Architectural Forum* (New York), June 1954; "Orange Coast College, Costa Mesa, California" in *Progressive Architecture* (New York), July 1955; "Second Group of American Embassy Buildings" in *Architectural Record* (New York), June 1956; "Genetrix: Personal Contributions to American Architecture" in *Architectural Review* (London), May 1957; "Office Building and Auditorium" in *Arts and Architecture* (Los Angeles), July 1957; "The Campus Library and the Architect" in *Architectural Record* (New York), August 1957; "An Airman's Chapel: Miramar Chapel" in *Arts and Architecture* (Los Angeles), April 1958; "Libraries: Gables and Garden for Nevada Campus" in *Architectural Forum* (New York), February 1963; "Campus Planning: Building Types Study 339" in *Architectural Record* (New York), November 1964; "College Dormitories: Building Types Study No. 349" in *Architectural Record* (New York), August 1965; "Library Buildings Award Program" in *AIA Journal* (Washington, D.C.), August 1966.

My work as an architect has been soul-satisfying. It has been important to the users and has satisfied their activities and feelings. The importance of the work as object is insignificant compared to the "glory of the action" of my involvement.

I have consciously managed a diverse practice in such a way that I have been personally involved in developing the concept design of almost everything with which my name is identified. Starting from a "left brain" saturation, I have tried to apply the "right brain" after the purposes of the program have been satisfied. Extensive work in "city planning" has been incorporated as a natural part of architecture, and my involvement in community and social issues as well as professional concerns has been constant.

—Robert E. Alexander

As a partner in a large firm, Robert Alexander made important contributions to the planning of Lakewood Village and the well-known Baldwin Hills Village in Los Angeles. Before starting his own practice he wrote, "The form of the house is absolutely unimportant. In the field of form the community plan is the only important thing. It must have a head, a heart, a soul and a purpose.... Tomorrow's client is the people and it is not a beast. We must take architecture to the people." This philosophy has been evident in all of his work.

Two of his first commissions contributed to the enrichment of the area surrounding Baldwin Hills Village. A nearby shopping center established a close relationship to the circulation patterns of the Village. A community church project is notable for its free form and the close integration of architecture and landscape architecture. The landscape architect had been brought in at the very beginning of the job.

A demonstration school built on the campus of the University of California at Los Angeles was freely disposed so that the stream running through the site was left in its natural state and became a "learning experience" for the children. In planning the individual classrooms, the architect brought "the people," in this case the faculty, into the planning process to an unprecedented degree. About Alexander's technology building at Orange Coast College, the editors of *Progressive Architecture* wrote, "one can hardly discuss the technology building's structure or acoustics individually; they are so interrelated that an analysis of one becomes a compendium of the other." For this job, Alexander hired a well-known artist as color consultant. The consultant conferred with teaching personnel before submitting swatch-abstracts for their approval. This was typical of the way the whole job proceeded. Once again, architecture was brought to the people.

Before all the buildings on the Orange Coast campus were completed, Alexander joined Richard Neutra in a partnership which lasted for a decade. Neutra's interest in form was greater than Alexander's so that the form of the later Orange Coast buildings and the other buildings executed by the partners bears the Neutra stamp. A project for a megastructure at the intersection of two highways in Caracas was probably an Alexander concept, as after the partnership was dissolved he became interested in planning a transit system for Los Angeles, with megastructures proposed for the principal intersections in the system.

As planner in charge of the new campus for the University of California at San Diego and as architect for a group of dormitories there, Alexander succeeded in humanizing the scheme. A group of interestingly spaced, lowrise dormitories was erected in place of the few highrise buildings that had originally been proposed.

As a concerned citizen of Los Angeles, Alexander became interested in saving the downtown urban core. He prepared a plan to save Bertram Goodhue's historic Los Angeles central library. His major commission downtown is the Bunker Hill Towers, a large apartment complex. It is one of the few recent developments in the area that respects the scale of the old city. The softened corners recall the Victorian buildings that once stood on Bunker Hill. Unfortunately its example has not been followed, and Bunker Hill Towers is overshadowed by fashionable monuments which lack the sense of appropriateness to site that Alexander has sought to achieve in all his commissions.

—Alson Clark

ALINGTON, William Hildebrand.
New Zealander. Born in Lower Hutt, 18 November 1929. Educated at the University of Auckland School of Architecture, 1951-55 (Senior Scholar, 1954), B.Arch, 1956: influenced by the government architect F. G. Wilson and by Professor R. H. Toy; University of Illinois, Urbana, 1957-59 (Fulbright Scholar), M.Arch. 1959: influenced by Professor A. R. Williams. Married Margaret Hilda Broadhead in 1955; children: Elisabeth, Giles, and Catherine. Draughting Cadet, 1950-55, and Architect, 1956-65, Ministry of Works, Wellington; Architect, Robert Matthew and Johnson-Marshall, London, 1956-57; Tutor, University of Illinois, 1958; Partner, with A. L. Gabites, J. A. Beard and D. J. Edmondson, Gabites and Beard, Wellington, 1965-71, with Gabites, Beard, Edmondson, D. J. Wilson, S. W. Toomath, D. G. Irvine and G. Anderson, Gabites, Toomath, Beard, Wilson and Partners, Wellington, 1971-72, and with Gabites and Edmondson, Gabites, Alington and Edmonson, Wellington, 1972-84 (office established in Christchurch, 1975); Director of Alington Group Architects, Wellington, since 1984. Assistant Editor, *New Zealand Institute of Architects Journal*, Wellington, 1964-69; Councillor and Vice-Chairman, New Zealand Institute of Architects, 1964-78; President, Architectural Centre Inc., 1970-72; Honorary Member of the Faculty of Architecture, 1975-78, Honorary Lecturer in Architecture, 1978-85, Victoria University of Wellington; Vice-Chairman, 1978, Chairman, 1979, 1980, Wellington Branch of the New Zealand Institute of Architects. Recipient: Bronze Medal, 1971, 1974, Silver Medal, 1972, Branch Awards, 1973, 1975, 1976, and National Award, 1977, New Zealand Institute of Architects. Associate, 1955, and Fellow, 1972, New Zealand Institute of Architects. Associate of the Royal Institute of British Architects, 1960. Address: Alington Group Architects, 126 The Terrace, Post Office Box 10403, Wellington, New Zealand.

Works:

1956 Standard Water Tower, Palmerston North, New Zealand
1962 Gisborne Courthouse, New Zealand
     Alington House, Wellington
1965 Meteorological Office, Wellington
1966 Civic Administration Building, Upper Hutt, New Zealand
1968 Civic Hall, Upper Hutt, New Zealand
1970 Halls of Residence, Massey University, Palmerston North, New Zealand
1972 Pedestrian precinct, Upper Hutt, New Zealand
     Helen Lowry Hall of Residence, Wellington
     Wesley Haven Geriatric Hospital, Lower Hutt, New Zealand
1974 New Zealand Chancery, New Delhi, India (project)
1976 Waipa County Council Office, Te Awamutu, New Zealand
     Waikanae Fire Station, New Zealand
     Horowhenua County Office, Levin, New Zealand
     Alington (Snr.) House, Wellington
1977 Waipa Lookout, Te Awamutu, New Zealand
     Public Library, Waikanae, New Zealand
     Karori Scout Hall, Wellington
1978 Public Library, Upper Hutt, New Zealand
     Wellington High School, Stage 1
     Wellington Planetarium
     Johnsonville Union Church, Wellington
     Anglican Chinese Mission Church, Wellington
1979 Wellington High School, Stage 2
1982 Morrison House, Levin, New Zealand
1984 School of Music, Wellington
     New Zealand Chancery, New Delhi, India

Publications:

By ALINGTON: books—drawings and appendix in *Frederick Thatcher and St. Paul's* by M. H. Alington, Wellington 1965; *Old St. Paul's, Wellington: A Pictorial Record,* with M. H. Alington, Wellington 1968; articles—"The Church and Architecture" in *Student* (Wellington), June 1955; "Mies van der Rohe" in *New Zealand Institute of Architects Journal* (Wellington), August 1963; "Francis Gordon Wilson," entry in the *Encyclopaedia of New Zealand,* vol. 3, Wellington 1966; "A Critique of Victoria University of Wellington Arts and Library Building" in *New Zealand Institute of Architects Newsletter* (Auckland), July 1967; "Some Comments on the Christchurch Town Hall" in *Landfall* (Christchurch), September 1972; "Christchurch Town Hall", with R. Muston and A. H. Marshall, in *Home and Building* (Auckland), 1 May 1973; "Comment" in *New Zealand Institute of Architects Journal* (Wellington), September 1974; "Architecture" in *Thirteen Facets,* edited by I. M. Wards, Wellington 1978.

On ALINGTON: articles—"Helen Lowry Hall of Residence" in *Home and Building* (Auckland), 1 October 1973; "Gabites, Alington, Edmondson" by Marjorie Lekner in *NZIA Journal* (Wellington) February 1974.

*

In our work we have aimed at achieving quality buildings that occupy an unobtrusive place in the community. The range of materials used is deliberately limited, and the occupants' requirements are not tightly accommodated within the buildings.

The planning is usually clear and uncomplicated, and the volumes and forms carefully proportioned to provide calm, stable spaces within buildings that take sympathetic cognizance of their surroundings.

In the design method followed, techniques and spatial relationships evolve from one project to the next. This form of development allows for careful analysis of previous projects and the production of work that has an immediate place in existing communities.

In most commissions the service to the clients includes the preparation of a brief of requirements and the design of the furnishings and gardens. Clients are constantly involved in the design process, as are all architectural partners, and all design policy is carefully analysed, documented, and presented to the clients for discussions and decisions.

Because of the very limited financial resources and the spasmodic nature of their availability in this country, we have found that a fragmentation of the building form is necessary if the project is to proceed as the finances become available. This results in the construction of smaller-scaled buildings which are appropriate for the size of the communities they serve. The construction period of the work is fully monitored, and the methods of contracting allow the architect to fully coordinate the work on the site and to maintain strict financial control of all phases. Advanced computer control of the contracting and construction periods are employed.

The methods and techniques used ensure that the design intentions are realized. The resulting efficiencies have allowed more and more time to be spent in canvassing many aspects of the clients' requirements and in developing the designs.

—W. H. Alington

*

W. H. Alington deserved the title of Architect. His work, set within the New Zealand landscape, possesses virtues of consistency, restraint, reason, order and sensitivity. Alington's concern as an architect, within the everyday realities and contingencies of professional life, is the pursuit of quality—quality of service and product. He views the role of the architect as that of a "master builder of things." This statement of belief is not simply the pragmatic position of *l'homme engagé;* for Alington, architecture has strong intangible characteristics.

W. H. Alington: Civic Administration Building, Upper Hutt, New Zealand, 1966.

His philosophy is built up from the idea that architecture is part of a much wider context. This realization helps him to strive for a sense of timelessness in his work. He avoids styling his buildings in a day-to-day sense. He believes in the classic need for a created order in which architecture finds a meaningful place. Yet, at the same time, he wants his work to be comprehensive enough to embrace a sense of warmth, comfort and well-being.

Intellectually Alington is a dualist. In his work one feels the desire for harmony and at the same time one senses his longing to capture a feeling of naturalness. This is clearly visible in the way he sets his buildings in the New Zealand landscape. (He is perhaps more a rural "spirit" than an urban dweller—a New Zealand characteristic.) As far as architectural space is concerned, Alington views it as a product of all objective faculties and subjective senses. Alington concurs with Kant in believing that the aesthetic experience is the process of all the faculties of concept, meshing together before the imaginative leap is taken.

Viewed as a logical sequence of events, Alington's architecture, from the Gisborne Courthouse, to the Meteorological Office placed high above Wellington's dramatic harbour, to the Civic Centre set within the valley of the Upper Hutt region, is a built vindication of his design philosophy and of his approach to architecture. It is a dualist synthesis of geometric resolution and his desire to embrace the natural. On visiting one of his buildings years after its completion, one still has the feeling of being in the company of a man who cares for this kind of synthesis in modern architecture.

—Russell Walden

ALMQVIST, Osvald.

Swedish. Born in Trankil, near Karlstad, Värmland, 2 October 1884. Educated at Karlstad School, 1900-09; Royal Institute of Technology, Stockholm, under L. I. Wahlman and Erik Lallerstedt, 1904-08; Royal Academy of Arts, Stockholm, 1909-10; with six fellow students, left the Academy and founded the independent Klara School of Architecture, Stockholm, with Carl Westman, Ragnar Östberg, Ivar Tengbom, q.v., and Carl Bergsten as teachers, 1910-11. Worked in the office of the architect Bodson, Brussels, 1908-09, in Dortmund, Germany, 1909, and in the office of Ivar Tengbom, Stockholm, 1910-11; in partnership with Gustaf Linden, Stockholm, 1911-13; in private practice, Stockholm, 1913-16; Architect and Engineer, Stora Kopparbergs Bergslag Company Domnarvet Ironworks, Dalecarlia, Sweden, 1916-20; returned to private practice, Stockholm, 1920. Member, Committee on Workers' Housing, Stockholm, 1920-21; Head of the Committee on Standardization of Kitchen Equipment, Stockholm, 1922-34; Acting Head of the Parks Department, Stockholm, 1936-38; Town Planner Adviser to Södertälje, Sweden, 1940-48. Recipient: First Prize, Sundsvall Elementary School Competition, Sweden, 1924; First Prize, with Sigurd Lewerentz, Jönköping Redevelopment Competition, Sweden, 1928. *Died (in Stockholm) 6 April 1950.*

Works:

1910/
11 National Monument, Stockholm (project)
1911/
13 Apartment building, Stockholm (with Gustaf Linden)
    Hotel, Nyköping, Sweden (with Gustaf Linden)
1914 Woodland Cemetery, Stockholm (Stockholm South Cemetery) (competition project)
1916/
20 Bergslagsbyn (model village for workers), at the Domnarvet Ironworks, Dalecarlia, Sweden
    Ironworks Manager's House, Domnarvet, Dalecarlia, Sweden
1917/
21 Forshuvudforsen Hydro-Electric Power Station, Sweden (with Vattenbyggnadsbyran)
1924 Elementary school, Sundsvall, Sweden (competition project)
1925/
28 Hammarforsen Hydro-Electric Power Station, northern Sweden (with Vattenbyggnadsbyran)
    Krangforsen Hydro-Electric Power Station, northern Sweden (with Vattenbyggnadsbyran)
1928 Plan for the redevelopment of 3 blocks in Jönköping, Sweden (4 competition projects; with Sigurd Lewerentz)
    Katarina Secondary School, Stockholm (competition project; with Sigurd Lewerentz)
1929 Chenderoh Hydro-Electric Power Station, Malaya (with Vattenbyggnadsbyran and Rendel, Palmer and Tritton)
1930 Terraced houses, furniture, industrial products in concrete (including conical flower pot later used by Stockholm Park Department), and prefabricated cast-iron staircase, *Stockholm Exhibition*
1931 Town plan for Stockholm (with Sigurd Lewerentz)
1931/
32 Workshop training school, Domnarvet, Dalecarlia, Sweden
1932 Museum, Malmö, Sweden (competition project; with Sigurd Lewerentz)
1933/
36 Vocational school, Lulea, Sweden

1939/
40 Development plan for the Årsta district of Stockholm (with Albert Lilienthal)

Publications:

By ALMQVIST: books— *Byggnadsplaner för Bostadsomraden, nagra Allmanna Synpunkter*, Stockholm 1921; *Köket och Ekonomiavdelningen*, Stockholm 1934; articles—"Forshuvudforsens Kraftverk" in *Byggmastaren* (Stockholm), no. 81, 1922; "Internationella Stadsbyggnadsutställningen ISBU" in *Byggmastaren* (Stockholm), no. 213, 1923; "Stadsplanefragor och Bostadsomradens Planläggning" in *Byggmastaren* (Stockholm), nos. 247, 259, and 275, 1923; "Gatubelysningsarmatur: Nagra Reflexioner i Anledning av Lyktstolpstävlingen" in *Byggmastaren* (Stockholm), no. 52, 1924; "Omputsning" in *Byggmastaren* (Stockholm), no. 361, 1924; "Sjätte Vaningen" in *Byggmastaren* (Stockholm), no. 48, 1925; "Kökets Standardisering: Nagra Synpunkter vid Pagaende Utredningsarbete" in *Byggmastaren* (Stockholm), no. 105, 1927; "Nyara Kraftverksanläggningar: Synpunkter pa deras Arkitektoniska Utformning" in *Byggmastaren* (Stockholm), no. 73, 1929; "Den Statsunderstödda Egnahemsverksamheten m.m." in *Byggmastaren* (Stockholm), no. 2, 1934.

On ALMQVIST: book— *Osvald Almqvist: En Arkitekt och Hans Arbete* by Björn Linn, Stockholm 1967.

As a student, Osvald Almqvist had travelled in Belgium and in Germany, but he was generally disappointed with modern architecture of the years before 1914. He seems to have derived much pleasure from what he saw of mediaeval towns, and in this respect he is similar to Camillo Sitte. In 1910, he left the Academy in Stockholm with other students to study at a private school with Östberg, Tengbom, Westman, and Bergsten as teachers. Two of his contemporary students were Gunnar Asplund and Sigurd Lewerentz, and with them, Almqvist developed an architecture of national realism that was very different from the neoclassicism taught at the Academy. From the summer of 1910, Almqvist studied the timber-framed buildings of Sweden and became steeped in the language of traditional structures and details. His early work at Nyköping with Gustaf Linden owes much to mediaeval apartment blocks and to traditional vernacular buildings.

Almqvist entered an unfinished scheme for the Stockholm Woodland Cemetery competition in 1914; it was won by Asplund and Lewerentz, but Almqvist's design clearly influenced the later realization of the project. The fact that the design was submitted in a sketchy state was an early indication of a distressing lack of decision and of slowness in Almqvist that was to become more acute as the years passed. His partnership with Linden was dissolved, and he became architect to Domnarvet Ironworks for which he created Bergslagsbyn, a model village for workers that incorporated some of the lessons of Swedish vernacular housing and those of European townscapes. His Forshuvudforsen Hydro-Electric Power Station of 1917-21 is regarded as one of the most important of early Swedish industrial buildings in an idiom that owed nothing to period precedent. From this time, he was to evolve his theory of sanitary aesthetics that would avoid inessentials and would express function honestly. In the years following 1922, he designed standard kitchen elements, and his ideas were consolidated in the publication of the Swedish kitchen standards in 1934 that have been the prototypes for much that is now taken for granted in domestic utilities. His most celebrated functional building is the power station at Chenderoh on the Berak River in Malaya, which he

designed in collaboration with Rendel, Palmer and Tritton of London. Its success made him an international authority on the design of power stations. He prepared several designs for the Stockholm Exhibition of 1930, including a house, some furniture, and a cast-iron staircase that became a classic.

In later years, Almqvist ran a small practice and became head of the Stockholm Parks Department in 1936, a post he relinquished two years later when it became clear that his administrative ability was unsuited to the job. His last works were in the planning of Årsta in Stockholm under Albert Lilienthal and as adviser on planning to the town of Södertälje. In 1950, he succumbed to the lung disease that had plagued him since 1921, surrounded by drawings of small projects that reflected his lifelong interest in Swedish vernacular housing.

—James Stevens Curl

ALVAREZ, Mario Roberto.

Argentinian. Born in Buenos Aires, 14 November 1913. Educated at the Colegio Nacional, Buenos Aires, 1926-32 (Gold Medal, 1932); University of Buenos Aires, Faculty of Architecture, 1932-37; (Gold Medal, and Annual Decorative Composition Prize, 1935; Gold Medal, 1937), Dip.Arch. 1937. Married Jorgelina Ortiz de Rosas in 1953; children: Juana and Mario Roberto, Jr. Since 1937, in private practice, Buenos Aires: as Mario Roberto Alvarez and Associates, since 1947. Architect, Ministry of Public Works, Buenos Aires, 1937-42; Municipal Architect, Avellaneda, Argentina, 1942-47; Adviser, Secretariat of Public Works of the City of Buenos Aires, 1958-62; Secretary to the World Football Cup Stadium Commission, Buenos Aires, 1972-78. Vice-President, Central Society of Archiects, Buenos Aires, 1953-55; Head of the Argentine Delegation, International Union of Architects Congress, London, 1961; Vice-President and Founding Associate, Faculty of Architecture and Town Planning, University of Buenos Aires, 1979; Commission Member for the Conservation of Artistic Sites and Buildings, Buenos Aires, 1979; Architectural Commission Member to the Secretary of Culture, Buenos Aires, 1980. Exhibitions: *Bienal*, Sao Paulo, 1957; Argentine Architects, Buenos Aires, 1958 (toured South America, the United States, and Europe); *10th Exhibition of School Architecture*, Building Center, Buenos Aires, 1967; *Architects of Buenos Aires*, Centro de Arte y Comunicacion, Buenos Aires, 1977. Recipient: First Prize, Town Hall Competition, San Luis, Argentina, 1937; Ader Fellowship, Buenos Aires, 1937; First Prize, San Martin Sanatorium Competition, Buenos Aires, 1939; Gold Medal, *Fourth National Salon of Architecture*, Buenos Aires, 1942; First Prize, Club Pelota Competition, Tres Arroyos, Argentina, 1942; First Prize, Pergamino Sanatorium Competition, Buenos Aires, 1943; First Prize, Sanatorium Competition, Avellaneda, Argentina, 1948; First Prize, Orthopaedic Sanatorium Competition, Buenos Aires, 1955; First Prize, Bank of Avellaneda, Argentina Competition, 1958; First Prize, Banco Italiano Competition, Buenos Aires, 1959; First Prize, Banco Popular Competiton, Buenos Aires, 1962; First Prize, Jockey Club Competition, Buenos Aires, 1963; First Prize, Somisa Headquarters Competition, Buenos Aires, 1966; First Prize, Meat and Animal Virus Technology Laboratories Competiton, Buenos Aires, 1967; First Prize, Faculty of Engineering Competition, University of La Plata, Argentina, 1967; First Prize, San Martin Railway Viaduct Competition, Buenos Aires, 1967; First Prize, Banco Industrial Competition, Bahia Blanca, Argentina, 1968; First Prize, Club Aleman Competition, Buenos Aires,

1968; First Prize, International University City Competition, Belgrano, Buenos Aires, 1970; First Prize, National Technical University Competition, Buenos Aires, 1971; First Prize, Argentina/Uruguay Hydro-electric Scheme Competition, 1973; Grand National Arts Prize, Ministry of Culture, 1976. Honorary Diploma, Peruvian Institute of Urbanism and Planning, and the Centro de Arte y Comunicacion, Buenos Aires, 1979; D.Arch.: Universidad Catolica de La Plata, Argentina, 1982. Honorary Fellow, American Insitute of Architects, 1976; Academician, Academia Nacional de Buenos Aires, 1983. Address: Mario Roberto Alvarez y Asociados, Solis 370, Buenos Aires, Argentina.

Works:

1937   San Martin Sanatorium, General San Martin, Buenos Aires
       Roncatti Restaurant, Julio A. Roca 537, Pergamino, Buenos Aires
1939   L.R.M. Radio Aconcagua Building, Avenida Emilio Civit, Mendoza, Argentina
1941   Portland Cement Housing, Buenos Aires (competition projects; with M. O. Ruiz)
1944   Emergency and Urological Block, Fiorito Hospital, Avellaneda, Buenos Aires
1945   Home for the Aged, Avellaneda, Buenos Aires
1947   Seven-storey apartment building, Avenida Mitry Lavalle, Avellaneda, Buenos Aires
1948   Health Center, Salta, Buenos Aires
       Health Center, Santiago del Estero, Buenos Aires
       Health Center, Corrientes, Buenos Aires
       Health Center, Catamarca, Buenos Aires
       Health Center, Tucuman, Buenos Aires
       Health Center, Jujuy, Buenos Aires
       M.A.D.A Sanatorium, Avellaneda, Buenos Aires (with M. O. Ruiz)
       Fourteen-storey apartment building, San Jose 1121-35, Buenos Aires (with M. O. Ruiz)
1949   Apartment building, Alsina 3263, Buenos Aires
1951   Six-storey apartment building, Pozos 825, Buenos Aires
       Three-storey apartment buildings, Humberto 1645, Buenos Aires
1953   Ten-storey apartment building, Parera 65-69, Buenos Aires (with M. O. Ruiz)
       Municipal Tennis Club, Olleros y. V. Alsina, Buenos Aires
       Municipal Theatre, General San Martin, Buenos Aires (with M. O. Ruiz)
1953/
64   Buenos Aires City Cultural Center
1954   Puentes House, Pirovano 1149, Martinez, Buenos Aires (with M. O. Ruiz)
       Podesta House, Pedro Goyena and L. Martinez, Martinez, Buenos Aires
1956   Dalbrollo House, Pergamino, Buenos Aires
1957   Thirteen-storey apartment building, Posadas 1695, Buenos Aires (with M. O. Ruiz)
1958   Mergherian House, La Lucila, Buenos Aires
       Banco Popular Main Office, Florida and Cangalla, Buenos Aires
       Banco Popular Branch Office, Pergamino, Buenos Aires
1959   Banco del Interior Building, Cordoba, Buenos Aires
       Nuevo Banco Italiano Building, San Justo, Buenos Aires
1960   City Grain Exchange Building, Avenida Corientes y Bouchard, Buenos Aires
       Association of Banks Monument, Avenida del Libertador, Buenos Aires
       Banco de Avellaneda Building, Quilmes, Buenos Aires
1961   Coca Cola Works, Luis Vale, Buenos Aires

Mario Alvarez: IBM Headquarters, Buenos Aires, 1978-84.

1961/
69 Cervantes National Theatre rebuilding and additions, Avenida Cordoba, Buenos Aires
1962 Argentine National Library, Buenos Aires (competition project)
1963 Jockey Club Headquarters, Florida 559, Buenos Aires (competition project; with J. M. Borthagaray)
Cup Hipico Argentino (stadium), Avenida Figueroa Alcorta 7285, Buenos Aires
Panedile Argentina (25-storey apartment building), Avenida Libertador 3754, Buenos Aires (with Aslan and Ezcurra, and Joselevich and Ricur)
1964 San Luis Clinic, San Martin de Tours 2980, Buenos Aires
Begrano Day School, Buenos Aires
Eighteen-story apartment building, Virrey Loreto y Arribenos, Buenos Aires
Sixteen-storey apartment building, Paraguay y Talcahuano, Buenos Aires
1965 Pruss House, 11 de Septiembre 1382, Buenos Aires
Bank of America Headquarters, Cangallo and San Martin, Buenos Aires (with Aslan and Ezcurra)
Office building, Carlos Pellegrini 313, Buenos Aires
Ministry of Defense Laboratories, Avenida General Paz y Zufriategui, Buenos Aires (with A. Dodds and M. Cattaneo)
Santa Fe-Parana River Tunnel, Entre Rios Province, Argentina
1966 Inge Argentina Shopping Center, with office and apartments, Acevedo 57, Buenos Aires
New Legislature Building, Buenos Aires (competition project)
Somisa Headquarters Building, Avenidas Belgrano y General Roca, Buenos Aires
Finanfor Building, Viamonte and Esmeralda, Buenos Aires
1966/
69 Covida Tower twenty-one-storey apartment building, Villaneuva y Teodoro Garcia, Buenos Aires
1967 Railway overpass, Avenidas Juan B. Justo y Cordoba, Buenos Aires
Faculty of Engineering Building, National University, La Plata, Argentina (competition project)
1968 Colon Theatre alterations and extensions, Buenos Aires
INTA Animal Virus Laboratories, Castelar, Buenos Aires (with Ralph M. Parsons Company)
1969 Centro Corrientes (office building), Corrientes 753-63, Buenos Aires
Banco Federal Building, Buenos Aires
Ken Brown Electronics Building, Lope de Vega y Margarinos Cervantes, Buenos Aires
Three-storey apartment building, Virrey Pino y Conde, Buenos Aires
El Continente (nineteen-storey apartment building), Avenida del Libertador y Basavilbaso, Buenos Aires (with L. Guidice)
Libertador Plaza Tower (twenty-storey apartment building), Avenida del Libertador 2140, Buenos Aires (with O. Zlotolow)
Playa Club Building, Miramar, Buenos Aires
Fifteen-storey apartment building, Avenida Presidente Figueroa Alcorta 3010, Buenos Aires
Hilton Hotel, Arenales y Esmeralda, Buenos Aires
1970 Office building, Rivadavia 540, Buenos Aires
Twelve-storey apartment building, Viamonte Libertad, Buenos Aires
Club Aleman, Corrientes 319-43, Buenos Aires (with B. Davinovic and G. Iturralde)
Guemes Sanatorium, stage I, Francisco Acuna de Figueroa y Cordoba, Buenos

Aires
Master plan for University City, Belgrano, Buenos Aires (competition project)
1971 Technology Buildings Complex, National Technical University, Buenos Aires (competition project; with M. Revol Luque, E. Diaz Garcia, and H. Hobbs)
Galeria Jardin Shopping Center, with offices and apartments, Florida 559, Buenos Aires
New Stock Exchange, Avenida Leandro Alem 344-66, Buenos Aires
1972 Master plan for the River Plate Athletic Club Complex, for the World Cup, Buenos Aires
Housing development, Avenida Colonel Roca, Buenos Aires (competition project)
Estadio Unico Stadium, La Plata, Argentina (competition project)
Office building, Avenida Leandro Alem 538, Buenos Aires
INTA Experimental Station Laboratories Building System (competition project)
1973 Office building, Avenida Corrientes y Reconquista, Buenos Aires (project)
Salto Grande Hydroelectric Dam, Argentine-East Uruguay Highway, Argentina (project; with Technical Commission Architects and Charles T. Main Company)
Housing development, Florencio Varela, Buenos Aires (competition project)
House for the Army Commander-in-Chief, Ruta Panamericana, Buenos Aires
Nujmovich House, La Pamba 3780, Buenos Aires
Diarben Company House, San Isidro Boating Club, Buenos Aires
1976 Office building, Sarmiento 1138, Buenos Aires
Banco Continental Building, Buenos Aires
Banco Credito Rural Argentino rebuilding, Buenos Aires
1977 Office building, Cangallo 715, Buenos Aires
Barreal Housing Development, Pampa del Indio, San Juan Province, Argentina
Pachon-Erizos Housing Development, San Juan Province, Argentina
1978/
80 Guemes Sanatorium, stage II, Francisco Acuna de Figueroa y Cordoba, Buenos Aires
Bianco Rio de la Plata Headquarters, Buenos Aires
Office building, Tucuman 744, Buenos Aires
Banco Financiero Argentino, Buenos Aires
Banco Mercantil, Buenos Aires
Office building, Avenida Leandro Alem and Paraguay, Buenos Aires
Office building, Avenida Leandro Alem 456-74, Buenos Aires
Office building, Chacabuco 271, Buenos Aires
Banco Rio de la Plata, Caballito, Buenos Aires
Chacofi Office Tower, Avenida Leandro Alem 538, Buenos Aires
Master plan for the Newman Country Club, Buenos Aires
Martens Office Building, Corrientes 355, Buenos Aires
1978/
84 Alto Palermo Community, Residential and Commercial Development, Buenos Aires
High rise Housing Block, Alvear y Parera, Buenos Aires
Sefaradi Educational Congregation Compex, Buenos Aires (project)
High rise Housing Block, Florida y Tucuman, Buenos Aires
Banco Feigin Headquarters alterations, Corrientes 341, Buenos Aires
Banco Provincia Branch Offices, Ricardo Rojas y Reconquista, Buenos Aires (project)
Stock Exchange Building, Rosario, Santa Fe Province, Argentina
Banco Nacion Building, Rosario, Santa Fe Province, Argentina

Office Building, Coronel Diaz y French, Buenos Aires
High rise Housing Block, Coronel Diaz y French, Buenos Aires
Higher Education Complex, University of Belgrano, Buenos Aires
Higher Education Complex, University of Technology, Buenos Aires
Majdalani Cooperative Housing, Virrey del Pino 3474, Buenos Aires
Melhem Family House, Punta del Este, Uruguay
Karagozlou Family House, La Lucila, Buenos Aires Province
Guemes Sanatorium, stage III, Francisco Acuna de Figueroa y Cordoba, Buenos Aires
Cooperative Housing, Gascon y Rivadavia, Buenos Aires
Cooperative Housing, Juncal 1897, Buenos Aires
Cooperative Housing, Las Heras y Billingshurst, Buenos Aires
Cooperative Housing, Las Heras y Rodriguez Pena, Buenos Aires
Cooperative Housing, Talcahuano 1279, Buenos Aires
Cooperative Housing, Avenida Libertador y Buschiazzo, Buenos Aires
Cooperative Housing, San Martin de Tours y Avenida Libertador San Martin, Buenos Aires
Cooperative Housing, Avenida Libertador, Buenos Aires
IBM Office Building, Catalinas Norte, Buenos Aires
Campomar Foundation Laboratory, Parque Centenario, Buenos Aires
Biochemical Research Institute of La Plata, Buenos Aires Province
Tiburon I High rise Housing Block, Punta Del Este, Uruguay
Tiburon II High rise Housing Block, Punta del Este, Uruguay
Pez Espada High rise Housing Block, Punta del Este, Uruguay
Delfin High rise Housing Block, Punta del Este, Uruguay
High rise Housing Block, San Martin de Tours II y Libertador, Buenos Aires
Teatro Argentina de La Plata Building, Buenos Aires Province (competition project)
Charity Lotteries and Casino Buildings, Buenos Aires (competition project)
Banco Provincia Misiones, Misiones Province, Argentina (competition project)
Renault Argentina Headquarters Building, Buenos Aires (competition project)
Central City Area Redevelopment, Buenos Aires (with others)

Publications:

By ALVAREZ: book— *Teatro Municipal General San Martin,* with M. Oscar Ruiz, Buenos Aires 1959; articles— "Buenos Aires y su arquitectura" in *El mundo* (Buenos Aires), 1960; "Buenos Aires 1990" in *Vision* (Buenos Aires), 1970; "Ciudad de Buenos Aires, su transformacion" in *Primera plana* (Buenos Aires), 1971.

On ALVAREZ: book— *Mario Roberto Alvarez* by Marcelo A. Trabuco, Buenos Aires 1965; articles— "Building for the Club Aleman" in *Neustra Arquitectura* (Buenos Aires), no. 486, 1973; special issue of *Summa* (Buenos Aires), September 1974; "Pruss Residence in Buenos Aires" in *Informes de la construccion* (Madrid), December 1974; "Somisa Building in Buenos Aires" and "Remodelling of the

Theatre Colon" in *Neustra arquitectura* (Buenos Aires), no. 492, 1975; "Single-family House at the Boating Club of San Isidro" in *Neustra Arquitectura* (Buenos Aires), no. 500, 1977; "Three Recent Works by Mario Roberto Alvarez Asociados" in *Summa* (Buenos Aires), June 1979; "The CHACOFI Tower Block, Buenos Aires" in *Summa* (Buenos Aires), September 1980; "Banco Rio, Caballito Branch, Buenos Aires" in *Summa* (Buenos Aires), November 1980; "IBM Argentina Building" in *Summa* (Buenos Aires), April 1981.

My aims and intentions over the past forty two years could be summarized as follows: I am not committed to one particular typology. It is more a question of making the complicated simple; achieving good, efficient workmanship (I am not interested in exciting attention or in being a fashionable architect); building durably; organizing space to allow for unknown activities in the future; integrating the plastic arts to architecture; keeping an eye on the quality of space, form, proportion, and detail; anticipating growth, flexibility, change, and the integration of new technology to the processes of construction; using good, honest materials and working hard, in order to make as few mistakes as possible.

—Mario Roberto Alvarez

Mario Roberto Alvarez has carried out so great a volume of work that he ranks as the most prolific architect in Argentina and perhaps in all of Latin America—yet, in more than forty years, there has never been any diminution in the virtues that were internationally recognized in his earliest constructions.

In his attitude towards architecture and in his work methods, Alvarez is a rationalist. But it is not a rationalism that involves a freezing of typologies invariably in time. His work is characterized by an adapting of form to function (therein lies the difference from Mies) and by a simplification and gemoetric definition of elements. Alvarez believes that permanent and universal values can be expressed through architecture. His perspective is classical, and his works contribute elements of order and clarity to the urban environment.

Alvarez's manifest intention is to "create good and enduring buildings in every aspect," an objective that he achieves both in his designs and in the choice of materials that prevent his building from showing the passage of years. Although the initial investment for the client may be somewhat high, because of the cost of high-quality materials and execution, the ease in upkeep more than compensates for that apparent disadvantage, and Alvarez himself contributes to keeping other costs down in his rational methods of design and his organization of the processes of construction.

Alvarez's output can be characterized as giving simple answers to complex requirements: there is always a concern with the quality of space and form, with proportion and control of details, with centering attention on a few elements for the purpose of achieving a stylistic synthesis. At the same time, Alvarez believes that an architecture of shape-for-shape's-sake is no longer valid, that objective reality makes it imperative that qualitative and quantitative changes that take place in time, which are useful to the community, should be allowed for in the design. His projects aspire to four conditions—growth, flexibility, change, and the integration of new technology—as the only way of allowing for the unknown activities of the future.

To achieve these various goals, Alvarez and his team involve themselves in every job from the drawing stage up to final and full operation of the building, along the way controlling and directing construction, rigorously analyzing all the details of the building and its mechanical equipment. The attention given to the "technical infrastructure" is

revealing of Alvarez's vision of "total building". Clarity and ease of maintenance is the basis of the correct operation of the building organism. Whether or not the architectural or mechanical elements are visible is irrelevant; they must be designed meticulously, as much for efficiency as for "formal appearance."

And it is also consistent with Alvarez's goals that he should be involved in projects not customarily part of the repertoire of architectural teams—a vehicular bridge, an underwater tunnel, a hydro-electric dam, and so forth. He points out that "the architect must furnish the engineer with images." Engineering works profit from the intervention of specialists in the planning of the physical environment, and they should participate in the project both in the formulation and the setting up of access elements and in the design of the structure itself so that it is formally integrated with the landscape and with other constructed elements. Including the architect in interdisciplinary teams contributes to the creation of a harmonious whole, one that is integrated into the surrounding space, within a common language, so that the structure does not stand out as foreign and unexpected but as natural and consequential within the treated and modelled space.

Alvarez is concerned with technological problems. An example is his proposal for prefabricated elements for a simple, functional, and economical construction system made up of materials produced by domestic industry, in which the number of components is reduced to a minimum and the total system can be easily disassembled and reconstructed. Another example of this interest is his Somisa Headquarters Building, the first building in Argentina to be built wholly of steel (concrete is the usual structural material) and the first in the world to be completely welded. Another of his characteristics—the exhaustive examination of factors not explicitly assigned to the architect by the client but which may be important for the appropriate resolution of the project—is perhaps best exemplified in his suggestion (which was finally put into practice) of incorporating a corner plot into the plan for the Municipal Theatre of Buenos Aires, thus allowing for the creation of an open plaza with offices giving onto it.

The meanings that can be read into Alvarez's works are those of contemporary rationalism, in which architecture seeks no references beyond architecture itself, rejecting mannerism or decoration which, as Alvarez maintains, are simply means of evasion from objective reality. These values are obviously appealng to non-professionals—to his clients—who hold him in high regard. When, in 1976, the American Institute of Architects made Alvarez an Honorary Fellow, it recognized the importance of a career that has enhanced and enriched architecture in Argentina.

—Jorge Glusberg

ANCHER, Sydney Edward Cambrian.

Australian. Born in Sydney, New South Wales, 25 February 1904. Educated at Sydney Technical High School, 1917-19; articled to the architect E. W. S. Wakeley, Sydney, 1924-26; studied at Sydney Technical College, 1925-29, Dip.Arch. 1929; worked in the offices of Wunderlich Ltd., Prevost Synnot and Ruwald, and Ross and Rowe, Sydney, 1926-30; awarded New South Wales Board of Architects Australian Medallion and Travelling Scholarship, 1930; travelled in England and on the Continent, 1930-36; Served in the Royal Australian Engineers, in the Middle East, 1940-41, and at Army Headquarters, Melbourne, 1942-45: Major. Married Leatha Hasemer in 1936 (died, 1970); sons: John and Paul.

Worked in London in the offices of Verity and Beverley, Joseph Emberton, Textaphote, and Thompson and Watford, 1930-36; returned to Australia and worked in the office of Emil Sodersten, Sydney, 1936; Partner, with Reginald Prevost, Prevost and Ancher, Sydney, 1936-39; worked in the Bank Section of the Commonwealth Department of Works, and in the office of John D. Moore, Sydney, 1939-40; Technical Officer, Commonwealth Experimental Building Station, Sydney, 1945-46; Principal, Sydney Ancher and Partners, Sydney, 1946-53; Partner, with Bryce Mortlock, *q.v.*, and Stuart Murray, *q.v.*, Ancher, Mortlock and Murray, Sydney, 1953-64, and, with Mortlock, Murray, and Ken Woolley, *q.v.*, Ancher, Mortlock, Murray, and Woolley, Sydney, 1964 until he retired in 1966. Design Teacher, Sydney Technical College, 1948-49, and Newcastle Technical College, Newcastle, New South Wales, 1949-50. Exhibitions: Contemporary Art Society, Sydney, 1948-52; Royal Australian Institute of Architects, Sydney, 1948-52; *Ancher, Mortlock, Murray and Woolley, Sydney Architects, 1946-74,* Art Gallery of New South Wales, Sydney, 1976, toured Australian galleries 1977. Recipient: Sulman Award, Royal Australian Institute of Architects, New South Wales Chapter, 1945; Gold Medal, Royal Australian Institute of Architects, 1976. Fellow, Royal Australian Institute of Architects; Associate, Royal Institute of British Architects. *Died, 8 December 1979.*

Works:

1946 Ancher House, 1 Maytone Avenue, Killara, Sydney
1948 Hamill House, 4 Maytone Avenue, Killara, Sydney
Ancher House II, 2 Maytone Avenue, Killara, Sydney
Farley House, North Curl Curl, Sydney
1949 English House, Killeaton Street, St. Ives, Sydney
1950 Riley House, Merrivale Road, Pymble, Sydney
1956 Ancher House III, 15 Bogota Avenue, Neutral Bay, Sydney
1956/
66 Shopping Centre, West Pymble, Sydney
Shopping Centre, East Lindfield, Sydney
Council Chambers rebuilding, Gordon, Sydney
Public library, Gordon, Sydney
Baby health centre, Lindfield, Sydney
Public golf club house, Gordon, Sydney
Three-level parking station, Gordon, Sydney
1960 Murphy House, 7 Ginahgulla Road, Bellevue Hill, Sydney
1963 Redman House, 24 Ross Street, Newport, Sydney
Stewart House, Richmond Avenue, St. Ives, Sydney
Housing, Northbourne Avenue, Canberra (with Stuart Murray)
1965 Students Union Building, Australian National University, Canberra

Publications:

By ANCHER: articles—"Travelling Scholar Returns" in *Architecture* (Sydney), March 1936; "Whither Architecture?" in *Architecture* (Sydney), June 1936; "Educating the Architect of Tomorrow" in *Architecture* (Sydney), May 1938; "The Evolution of Modern Architecture" in *Architecture* (Sydney), December 1939; "The Architect's Dilemma" in *RAIA News Bulletin* (Sydney), May 1976.

On ANCHER: books— *Australia's Home* by Robin Boyd, Melbourne 1952; *The Australian Ugliness* by Robin Boyd, Melbourne 1960; *Ancher, Mortlock,*

Murray and Woolley, Sydney Architects, 1946-76, exhibition catalogue, by David Saunders and Catherine Bourke, Sydney 1976; articles— "Sydney Ancher (1904-1979)" by Stuart Murray in *Architecture Australia* (Melbourne), March 1980; "Modern Australian Architecture," special issue of *Process: Architecture* (Tokyo), March 1981.

In the years immediately following World War II, I was able, for the first time, to shake off the tendency to think automatically of architecture along traditional lines.

A new resolve enabled me to design simple and straight-forward buildings, free from pre-conceived ideas on proportion and style. I came to believe that all work should possess a timeless quality. And I felt that if all buildings were designed in this way, they would contribute to the kind of unified character you find in the grouped buildings on a Greek island.

I was also early taken with the idea of developing an Australian style. Many things favoured such an approach, including the actual character of the typical Australian, which for good or bad is certainly quite distinctive. I later realized that, as there is no positively recognizable style of any other Western country, it seemed unlikely that an Australian style would emerge.

As an aid to maintaining the desired character in all designs, I have found it essential to constantly evaluate trends. These generally are merely fashion changes— in clothes, cars, and many other things which often affect our way of living. They are mostly quite transitory and, as such, are undesirable influences in the shaping of permanent things such as buildings. Some trends do result in changes for the good, but mostly their influence is not lasting.

Altogether, I find it satisfying to have evolved some direction for my work. I believe in a set line of development with leanings to simple, straightforward, perhaps even classic designs.

—Sydney Ancher (1979)

The unassuming architect Sydney Ancher was one of the most respected architects to have practised in Sydney this century. It is remarkable that Ancher, who designed relatively few buildings, mostly houses, and certainly nothing that would be considered a "major work," was such a pivotal figure for the local development of modern architecture. While Ancher was one of the first to introduce the International Style to Australia, he was a regional architect in every respect. Much of this country's better architecture has come from people who were influenced by Ancher. Of these, several worked with Ancher, worked for Ancher, or worked for someone who worked for Ancher—he was responsible for quite an extensive architectural family tree!

Australia is a conservative country and Ancher was among the few prewar "modern" architects. Between 1931 and 1936, he worked and travelled in Europe, and he returned there again in 1939. During these visits, he saw much of contemporary architecture, and was particularly impressed by the pure geometry and open planning of the work of Mies van der Rohe. After four years in the Army during the War, Ancher established his own practice. His most important works are the houses of the 1946-58 period. In Australia, postwar shortages of materials and skilled labour were acute, and the quality of new housing was low indeed. The average house was a stripped-down version of the typical bungalow: a box under a pitched roof, with punched holes for windows and compartmented interiors. These were visually depressing and climatically unsound. In his own quiet way, Ancher contributed to a domestic design revolution that established the basic Australian dwelling concepts, which persist today, despite differing expressions. Fundamental was his adaption of prewar European examples to the Australian climate, materials, building techniques, and way of life.

With the simplicity of their crisp, white forms, his early houses were considered by local councils to be an affront to decency! The order of their form and the solidarity and blankness of their colour contrast with, yet compliment, the rough Australian bush sites on which (even in suburbia) they often were built. Even so, native trees, rock outcrops, and variances in terrain were always respected and integrated with the strictly man-made structures. The Australian sun casts strong shadows of posts and planting on their white exteriors.

The houses are not large, often no larger than the average postwar dwelling, but with their flat roofs, which freed interior space, and the opening up of walls with glass, they appear generous and spacious. His plans, with central, "to-be-lived-in" living rooms and minimal, yet open, secondary spaces, reflect his "hatred of secrecy and holes in the corner." With generous outlooks and the extension of the houses by patios and verandahs, the outside was closely related to the interior. The use of the continuous flat slab made for easy movement between these areas. Increased air circulation and the protecting shade afforded by deep overhangs, pergolas, and wide, covered verandahs, kept them cool in summer. On occasion, the extensive, covered, outdoor spaces rivalled the interiors in area.

The houses received considerable publicity, and their relevance was soon widely recognised by the architectural profession. Ancher's planning and structural concepts were taken up and developed by others, but soon the prismatic white finishes gave way to the more rugged expression of materials "as found."

Although Ancher took no part in the designing of project housing, his firm's involvement helped introduce these buildings to the general market, and this has had a widespread effect on house design throughout the country. The further impact of this work is now evident in commercial, institutional, and retail buildings as well. The result has been an architecture more compatible with its context than the majority of prior solutions.

Ancher retired from active practice in 1965, and in 1976 the Royal Australian Institute of Architects

Sydney Ancher: H. S. English House, Saint Ives, Sydney, 1949.

Tadao Ando: Rokko Housing, Kobe, Japan, 1983.

acknowledged his contribution with the award of its Gold Medal. The importance of his work for Australian architecture cannot be overstressed. From the time of his initial, modest buildings, he was one of the few leaders towards major changes in Australian design. Ancher was alone in denying the significance of his efforts.

—Jennifer Taylor

ANDO, Tadao.

Japanese. Born in Osaka, 13 September 1941. Self-taught in architecture, 1962-69. Married Yumiko Kato in 1970; son: No. Travelled in America, Europe and Africa, 1962-70. Since 1969, Founder-Director, Tadao Ando Architect and Associates, Osaka (Associates: Takao Shima, Masataka Yano, Ko Nakakita, Fumihiko Iwama, Junya Toda, Kiyono Hane, Migiwa Hosoda, Nobuaki Ishimaru, Kazuya Okano, Takashi Yamaguchi, Hiroshi Nakanishi, Takaaki Mizutani and Yumiko Kato). Exhibitions: *A New Wave of Japanese Architecture*, Institute for Architecture and Urban Studies, New York, 1978 (toured the United States); *Tadao Ando: Architecture*, Union of Hungarian Architects, Budapest, 1979; *La Obra de Tadao Ando*, Colegio Oficial de Arquitectos, Madrid, 1982; *Tadao Ando: Minimalisme*, Institut Français d'Architecture, Paris, 1982; *Tadao Ando: Architecture*, Thermen

Museum, Heerlen, Netherlands, and Architectuur-museum, Amsterdam, 1982; *La Modernité—un projet inachévé*, at the Festival d' Automne, Paris, 1982; *Tadao Ando Architecture*, Lausanne, Switzerland, 1983; *Tadao Ando's Architecture*, Helsinki and Jyvaskyla, Finland, 1983; *Tadao Ando* (retrospective), toured Japan, 1983; *Tadao Ando: Architecture*, Vienna and Innsbruck, Austria, 1985; *Tadao Ando: Architecture*, Sofia, Bulgaria, 1985. Recipient: Annual Prize, Architectural Institute of Japan, 1979; Japan Cultural Design Prize, 1983; Alvar Aalto Medal, 1985. Address: Tadao Ando Architect and Associates, 5-23 Toyosaki, 2-chome, Oyodo-ku, Osaka 531, Japan.

Works:

1973 Tomishima House, Oyodo Ward, Osaka, Japan

1974 Uno House, Ukyo Ward, Kyoto, Japan
Tatsumi House, Taisho Ward, Osaka, Japan
Hiraoka House, Takarazuka, Hyogo Prefecture, Japan
Shibata House, Ashiya, Hyogo Prefecture, Japan

1975 Soseikan (Yamaguchi/Twin House), Takarazuka, Hyogo Prefecture, Japan

1976 Azuma House (Row-House Sumiyoshi), Sumiyoshi Ward, Osaka, Japan
Hirabayashi House, Suita, Osaka, Japan
Bansho House, Nishi-Kamo, Aichi Prefecture, Japan
Tezukayama Tower Plaza (commercial and residential complex), Sumiyoshi Ward, Osaka, Japan
Okamoto Housing, Higashi-nada Ward, Kobe, Japan (project)

1976/
77 Art Gallery Complex (project)

1977 Rose Garden Commercial Complex, Chuo Ward, Kobe, Japan
Manabe Residence (Tezukayama House), Abeno Ward, Osaka, Japan
Matsumoto House (House with Territory-Delineating Walls), Ashiya, Hyogo Prefecture, Japan
Kitano Alley Commercial Complex, Chuo Ward, Kobe, Japan

1978 Ishihara House (Glass-Block House), Ikuno Ward, Osaka, Japan
Koto Alley Commercial Complex, Nishinomiya, Hyogo Prefecture, Japan
Okusu House, Setagaya Ward, Tokyo
Sunny Garden Commercial Complex, Nishinomiya, Hyogo Prefecture, Japan

1979 Horiuchi House (Glass-Block Wall), Sumiyoshi Ward, Osaka, Japan
Matsutani House, Fushimi Ward, Kyoto, Japan
Ohnishi House, Sumiyoshi Ward, Osaka, Japan
Ueda House, Soja, Okayama Prefecture, Japan

1980 Steps (commercial complex), Takamatsu, Kagawa Prefecture, Japan
Matsumoto House, Wakayama, Wakayama Prefecture, Japan

Kitano Ivy Court (commercial and residential complex), Chuo Ward, Kobe, Japan

Fuku House, Wakayama, Wakayama Prefecture, Japan

Katayama House, Nihinomiya, Hyogo Prefecture, Japan

1981 Rin's Gallery (commercial complex), Chuo Ward, Kobe, Japan

Koshino House, Ashiya, Hyogo Prefecture, Japan

Portpia '81 Fashion Live Theater exhibition pavilion, Port Island, Kobe, Japan

Kojima House, Kurashiki, Okayama Prefecture, Japan

Tomishima House extensions, Oyodo Ward, Osaka, Japan

Bansho House extensions, Nishi-Kamo, Aichi Prefecture, Japan

1982 Sun Place (bank and commercial complex), Takamatsu, Kagawa Prefecture, Japan

Tadao Ando and Associates Studio, Oyodo Ward, Osaka, Japan

Izutsu (town-house in Kujo), Nishi Ward, Osaka, Japan

Ishii House, Hamamatsu, Shizuoka Prefecture, Japan

Bigi Atelier Building, Shibuya Ward, Tokyo

Soseikan Tea-House, Takarazuka, Hyogo Prefecture, Japan

Akabane House, Setagaya Ward, Tokyo

1983 Umemiya House, Tarumi Ward, Kobe, Japan

Rokko Housing, Nada Ward, Kobe, Japan

Ryukotsushin Building, Shinjuku Ward, Tokyo

Kaneko House, Shibuya Ward, Tokyo

1984 Motegi House, Nagata Ward, Kobe, Japan

Uejo House, Suita, Osaka, Japan

Koshino House extension, Ashiya, Hyogo Prefecture, Japan

Iwasa House, Ashiya, Hyogo Prefecture, Japan

Koreyasu House, Toyonaka, Osaka, Japan

Ota House, Takahashi, Okayama Prefecture, Japan

Minamibayashi House, Ikoma, Nara Prefecture, Japan

Festival Building, Naha, Okinawa Prefecture, Japan

Time's Building, Nakagyo Ward, Kyoto, Japan

Hata House, Nishinomiya, Hyogo Prefecture, Japan

Sinsaibashi To Building, Minami Ward, Osaka, Japan

Melrose Building, Meguro Ward, Tokyo

1985 Bigi Aobadai Building, Meguro Ward, Tokyo

Aoyama To Building, Minato Ward, Tokyo

Bigi Atelier House, Shibuya Ward, Tokyo

Nakayama House, Nara, Nara Prefecture, Japan

Bal Mon-Petit-Chou Building, Sakyo Ward, Kyoto, Japan

Publications:

By ANDO: books—*Tadao Ando*, Tokyo 1981, Barcelona 1985; *Tadao Ando: Monographies*, Paris 1982, Milan 1985; *Tadao Ando: Buildings, Projects, Writings*, New York 1984; articles—"A Wedge in Circumstances" in *The Japan Architect* (Tokyo), June 1977; "Conforming to the Environment" in *The Japan Architect* (Tokyo), August 1977; "New Relations Between Space and the Person" in *The Japan Architect* (Tokyo), October/November 1977; "Blank Space on the Site" in *The Japan Architect* (Tokyo), May 1978; "The Wall as Territorial Delineation" in *The Japan Architect* (Tokyo), June 1978; "The Emotionally Made Architectural Spaces of Tadao Ando" in *The Japan Architect* (Tokyo), April 1980; "Steps Upward Through Light" in *The Japan Architect* (Tokyo), July 1980; "Ryoheki House" in *Parametro* (Bologna, Italy), August/September 1981; "From Self-Enclosed Modern Architecture

Toward Universality" in *The Japan Architect* (Tokyo), May 1982; "Sun Place" in *The Japan Architect* (Tokyo), September 1982; "Interview with Tadao Ando" in *Techniques et Architecture* (Paris), December 1982/January 1983; "The Simple Relationship Between Human Beings and Space", Interview, in *Architectes* (Paris), March 1983; "Space Determined by Concrete Blocks" in *The Japan Architect* (Tokyo), October 1983; "Town House at Kujo" in *The Japan Architect* (Tokyo), November/December 1983; "Twin Wall" in *The Japan Architect* (Tokyo), August 1984.

On ANDO: books—*A New Wave of Japanese Architecture*, with introduction by Kenneth Frampton, New York 1978; *The New Japanese House* by Chris Fawcett, London 1980; *La Modernite—Un Projet Inacheve*, exhibition catalogue by J. P. Chimot, K. Frampton, B. Lubetkin and others, Paris 1982; *Tadao Ando—Minimalisme* by Francois Chaslin, Arata Isozaki, Vittorio Gregotti and others, Paris 1982; articles—"Up To Now" by Mayumi Miyawaki in *The Japan Architect* (Tokyo), June 1978; "The Post Metabolists" by A. MacNair in *Arquitectura* (Madrid), January/February 1979; "Nine Neo Wrinkles on the Water" by Hiroshi Watanabe in *AIA Journal* (Washington, D.C.), November 1979; "Japanese Minimalism" by David Morton in *Progressive Architecture* (New York), May 1980; "Tadao Ando: A Redefinition of Space, Time and Existence" by B. Bognar in *Architectural Design* (London), May 1981; "Japan Through the Looking Glass", special issue of *Domus* (Milan), June 1981; "Tadao Ando", special issue of *Space Design* (Tokyo), June 1981; "Tadao Ando—A Japanese Architect of the New Wave" by D. Peters in *Baumeister* (Munich), January 1982; "From Utopia to the Corner Drugstore" by Hiroshi Watanabe in *Art News* (New York), February 1982; "Tadao Ando", special issue of *The Japan Architect* (Tokyo), May 1982; "Tadao Ando—The Beauty of Simplicity" by F. Lamarre in *Architecture* (Paris), September 1982; "Tadao Ando Exhibition—The Destruction of Simplicity" in *De Architect* (The Hague), October 1982; "Rokko Housing" by Vittorio Gregotti in *Casabella* (Milan), October 1982; "Latest Work of Tadao Ando" by B. Bognar in *Architectural Review* (London), November 1982; "Solo Artist" by P. Popham in *Building Design* (London), 23 September 1983; "Architects and Builders: The Work of Fumihiko Maki and Tadao Ando" by Koji Taki in *The Japan Architect* (Tokyo), November/December 1983; "Tadao Ando: Heir to a Tradition" by Kiyoshi Takeyama in *Perspecta* (New Haven, Connecticut), no. 20, 1983; "Tadao Ando's Architectuur van Contradicties" by W. Arets in *De Architect* (The Hague), March 1984.

Modern Japanese architecture evolved in a very different way from modern European architecture, which developed out of centuries of history and endeavor. In late 19th and early 20th centuries, Japan blindly worshipped the West, and to attempt to modernize quickly, it introduced superficial aspects of Western culture and eliminated what was Japanese. Twenty years after World War II, as Japan entered a period of intensive economic growth, skyscrapers, all very much alike, began to be built, and national history, culture, aesthetics, and racial character—the factors that ought to provide a basis for architecture—were disregarded; economic principles came to rule architecture. Everything from materials and forms down to dimensional details such as ceiling heights came to be determined from a functional and economic standpoint. Even today, much of contemporary Japanese architecture represents half-digested modernism. In the past, the Japanese created a distinctive culture that was closely tied to climate. If one looks at the traditional style of life, one can see that the people of the past attempted to bring nature into the dwelling, even as they developed various domains to separate the dwelling from the surroun-

ding natural environment. Since Japan has distinctive seasons and a relatively mild climate, the Japanese looked on nature not as something to confront and overcome but as a thing to cherish and love. This viewpoint resulted in an architectural approach that sought to extend architecture through incremental additions into the natural environment, as in *sukiya* style architecture, the representative example of which is the Katsura Detached Palace. The goal was to always maintain absolute locational relationships and to create an aggregate of fragmentary views. Behind this was the Japanese belief that spirits dwell in every detail.

However, today as urbanization advances and we are flooded with information, a view of architecture as a totality, a view that assures the maintenance of architectural identity, is needed. I am interested both in Japanese aesthetics which places importance on parts and the application of reason which gives order to the whole. To give a stable order to the building as a whole, I use geometry. However, my concern is not geometric forms in themselves but the spaces to which they give birth. When natural light is introduced into the building and makes apparent the space that is there, geometric order recedes into the background. Patterns of shadow are thrown against the evenly finished concrete surface which softly envelop the space. I am always conscious of the nature of these times and of the needs of human beings, and my wish is to interpret in new ways and using contemporary materials and methods Japanese aesthetics which is being forgotten. Modern architecture was an "open" architecture; in "closing" it and endowing it with the regional character of Japan, I intend nevertheless to endow it with a universality and a creativity that transcends borders.

—Tadao Ando

Tadao Ando's rise within the last decade to his prominant place in the Japanese architectural firmament is commonly if not very imaginatively described as meteoric, but that astronomical metaphor with its suggestion of incandescence is the only thing even remotely flashy about the career of this Osaka designer. He eschews frivolity (and expressions of humor in any guise), and he does not discard an idea until he has explored all its possibilities in an entire series of buildings, unlike some of his more fickle Tokyo confreres who seem to develop a new style, accompanied by a completely revamped set of theoretical rationalizations, each week.

It is revealing that despite many, and often larger, subsequent commissions, the first work of his to gain public attention, the Azuma House of 1976, is still widely considered his representative building. The house presents to the street a sheer, unadorned wall of exposed concrete and makes no effort to ingratiate itself with its neighbors. The visitor ventures to enter the front door of this severe structure with some trepidation. Inside as well as outside, the texture of the concrete is the only surface decoration that the architect permits himself. As with practically all of Ando's houses, the building is divided into two parts. To get from the living room in the front section of the house to the dining room in the back, one must traverse an open courtyard, so that it is in the lap of the gods whether one walks under stars or storm clouds to reach one's supper. Ando's avowed purpose in providing such courtyards is to offer therapeutic exposure to nature to dwellers in arid urban environments. However, the nature that Ando will allow into his house is rendered highly abstract: a stone-paved courtyard or at the most a closely cropped lawn, unornamented by trees or bushes and given additional visual interest only by the vagaries of the weather.

Ando thus equates nature with purity—what could be more pure than an empty courtyard washed by sunlight or rain?—and his ultimate objective is to create an enclave within the contemporary city, whose consumer values he deplores, an enclave within which the simplest and most basic human activities are made resonant. One recalls that in early Zen monasteries, every human act, from eating and bathing to excretion of bodily wastes, was considered a part of the religious training of acolytes. In a world that puts a premium on creature comforts and convenience, one can too easily lose sight of one's existential condition, and it is to restore a sense of one's place in the universe that Ando creates his ascetic environents. If the task he has set for himself sometimes appears hopeless given the distractions of modern Japanese society, there is no denying the strength of his convictions and the expressive power of his work, and the fact that he has many admirers, particularly among younger Japanese architects, suggests that his quest may not be entirely quixotic.

—Hiroshi Watanabe

ANDREWS, John

Australian. Born in Sydney, New South Wales, 29 October 1933. Educated at North Sydney Boys High School; University of Sydney (Ormonoid Prize for Design, 1956), B.Arch. 1956; Harvard University, Cambridge, Massachusetts, under Josep Lluis Sert, *q.v.*, M.Arch. 1958. Married Rosemary Randall in 1958; children: John, Lee, Craig, and James. Worked for Edwards Madigan Torzillo, Sydney, 1957, and John B. Parkin, Don Mills, Toronto, 1958-62. Principal, John Andrews Architects, Toronto, since 1962, and John Andrews International Pty. Ltd., Sydney, since 1972. Member of Staff, 1962-69, and Chairman of the School of Architecture, 1967-69, University of Toronto. Exhibitions: *National Institute of Arts and Letters Exhibition,* New York, 1971; *Transformations in Modern Architecture,* Museum of Modern Art, New York, 1979. Recipient: Centennial Medal, Canada, 1967; Massey Medal, Canada, 1967; Arnold Brunner Award, National Institute of Arts and Letters, U.S.A., 1971; Honor Award, 1973, and Bartlett Award, 1973, American Institute of Architects; Design in Steel Citation, American Iron and Steel Institute, 1973; Award, Pre-stressed Concrete Institute, U.S.A., 1976; Bronze Medal, Queensland Institute of Architects, 1976; Award of Excellence, Concrete Institute of Australia, 1977(twice); First Prize, Intelsat Headquarters Competition, Washington, D.C., 1980; Gold Medal, 1980, Merit Award, 1982(twice), and Sulman Medal, 1983, Royal Australian Institute of Architects; Advance Australia Award, 1982. Associate, Royal Institute of British Architects; Fellow, Royal Architectural Institute of Canada; Life Fellow, Royal Australian Institute of Architects. Address: John Andrews International Pty. Ltd., 1017 Barrenjoey Road, Palm Beach, New South Wales 2108, Australia.

Works:

1962 Master plan for Scarborough College (University of Toronto), Scarborough, Ontario
1963 Scarborough College (University of Toronto), phase I, Military Road, Scarborough, Ontario
1964 Master plan for Erindale College (University of Toronto), Erindale, Ontario
1965 Bellmere Public School, Scarborough, Ontario
Student Housing Complex B, University of Guelph, Ontario
Apartment Tower, for the Stelco Steel Company (project)
1966 Master Plan of the St. George Campus of the University of Toronto

1967 Lecture Theatre, Boiler Plant, and alterations to the existing building, Prince of Wales College, Charlottetown, Prince Edward Island
African Place, *Expo '67,* Montreal
Activity Area F, *Expo '67,* Montreal
Commonwealth Place, *Expo '67,* Montreal (project)
Weldon Library, University of Western Ontario, London
Plan for the Metro Centre, Toronto
Student Centre, University of Toronto (project)
Seaport Passenger Terminal, Port of Miami, Florida
Redevelopment plan for the Civic Square, Hamilton, Ontario (competition project)
Plan for the Yorkdale Shopping Centre, Toronto
Student Residence, Brock University, St. Catherines, Ontario
Library/Instructional Center, Sarah Lawrence College, Bronxville, New York (project)
1968 Gund Hall: Graduate School of Design, Harvard University, Cambridge, Massachusetts
Art Complex, Smith College, Northampton, Massachusetts
1969 David Mirvish Gallery, Toronto
Scarborough College (University of Toronto), stage II, Scarborough, Ontario
1970 School of Art, Kent State University, Ohio
Feasibility study for the expansion of the Behavioral Science Department, Tufts University, Medford, Massachusetts
Student Residence, Australian National University, Canberra
1972 Pintannie Commercial Redevelopment (multi-storey office complex), Roma Street, Brisbane (project)
Plan for the Belconnen Town Centre Retail Mall, Canberra
1973 Woden East Government Offices, Canberra (project)
Student Residence, Canberra College of Advanced Education
Chemical Engineering Building, University of Queensland, Brisbane
Design guidelines for the retention of the Great Hall of Union Station in the Metro Centre development, Toronto
Master plan for Kelvin Grove College of Advanced Education, Brisbane
1974 Development plan I for Darling Downs Institute of Advanced Education, Toowoomba, Queensland
Development plan for Ithaca Technical College, Brisbane
Regional Shopping Centre, Sydney (project)
Design study of the retail centre of Belconnen, Canberra
Study of transportation interchange and commercial/sporting development, Canberra
1975 School of Australian Environmental Studies, Griffith University, Brisbane
Low Bay Low-Income Housing Complex, Sydney
Environmental guidelines study of Palm Beach, Sydney
Urban design study of the town centre of Monarto, South Australia
Master plan for Ipswich College of Technical and Further Education, Queensland
1976 Cameron Offices, Belconnen, Canberra
King George Tower, King and George Streets, Sydney
Andrews House (2), Palm Beach, Sydney (project)
Educational Resource Centre, Kelvin Grove College of Advanced Education, Brisbane, Queensland

Development plan II for Darling Downs Institute of Advanced Education, Toowoomba, Queensland
Belconnen Bus Terminal, Canberra
1977 Canadian National Tower, Metro Centre, Toronto
Library/Union, stage I, Royal Melbourne Institute of Technology (project)
Site location study of the Museum of Australia, Canberra
Development study of Sydney Central Station
Woden College of Technical and Further Education, stage I, Canberra
Lecture Theatre and Staff Office Buildings, Darling Downs Institute of Advanced Education, Toowoomba, Queensland (project)
Mandurah High School, Western Australia (project)
1978 Resource Material Centre, Ipswich College of Technical and Further Education, Queensland
Housing Village, Griffith University, Brisbane, Queensland (project)
Andrews Farmhouse, Eugowra, New South Wales
Bateman Catholic Centre, Perth, Western Australia (project)
Union Building, Royal Melbourne Institute of Technology, Melbourne
1979 Glebe Cluster Housing, Sydney (project)
1980 Intelsat Headquarters Building, Washington, D.C.
Garden Island Parking Structure, Woolloomooloo Bay, Sydney
1981 Merlin Hotel site development, Perth, Western Australia
1982 Physics, Chemistry, and Common Teaching Buildings, Australian Defence Forces Academy, Canberra
Railway Stations Area Redevelopment, Adelaide, South Australia (project)
1984 State Convention Centre, Melbourne
McNamara Group Office Building, Smith and Macquarie Streets, Parramatta, Sydney
1985 Standard Telephones and Cables High-Tech Centre Study (project)
National Sports Centre Field House Feasibility Study, Bruce, Canberra (project)

Publications:

By ANDREWS: book—*Architecture: A Performing Art* with Jennifer Taylor, Sydney 1980, Guildford, Surrey 1982; articles—"Conversations with John Andrews Architects," interview, in *Progressive Architecture* (New York), February 1972; "A. A. Interview" by John Witzig in *Architecture in Australia* (Sydney), June 1975; "Notes from Down Under," interview, in *Canadian Architect* (Toronto), June 1976.

On ANDREWS: books—*World Architecture 3,* edited by John Donat, London 1966; *Canadian Architecture 1960-70* by Carol Moore Ede, Toronto 1971; *Third Generation: The Changing Meaning of Architecture* by Philip Drew, London 1972; *Architecture in the Seventies* by Udo Kultermann, London 1980; *The Australian People* by Craig McGregor, Sydney 1980; *Megastructure* by Reyner Banham, London 1980; *Old Continent—New Building,* edited by Leon Paroissien and Michael Griggs, Darlinghurst, New South Wales 1983; articles—"The New Campus" by Oscar Newman in *Architectural Forum* (New York), May 1966; "Beyond the Individual Building" in *Architectural Record* (New York), September 1966; "Scarborough College" by Kenneth Frampton in *Architectural Design* (London), April 1967; "Dorm City" by Kenneth B. Smith in *Architectural Forum* (New York), December 1968; "City Within a City" in *The Architect and Building News* (London), 5 June 1969; "Some Comments on

the Building" by Peter Pragnell in *Architectural Forum* (New York), December 1969; "Design and Process: Four Projects by the John Andrews Office" in *Architectural Record* (New York), February 1970; "Passenger Terminal, Port of Miami" in *Canadian Architect* (Toronto), April 1970; "Conversations with the John Andrews Architects" in *Progressive Architecture* (New York), February 1972; "Gund Hall: Harvard's Graduate School of Design under One Roof" in *Architectural Record* (New York), November 1972; "D. B. Weldon Library, University of Western Ontario, London" in *Canadian Architect* (Toronto), November 1972; "Harvard's New Hall" by William Marlin in *Architectural Forum* (New York), December 1972; "Good Architecture—Bad Vibes" by Ada Louise Huxtable in *Canadian Architect* (Toronto), January 1973; special issue of *Architecture + Urbanism* (Tokyo), May 1974; "Five Projects by John Andrews International" in *Canadian Architect* (Toronto), July 1976; "King George Tower" in *New South Wales Builder* (Sydney), February 1977; "Civil Service City" by Jennifer Taylor in *Architectural Review* (London), March 1978; "Australia's John Andrews Wins $30 Million Competition" in *Architectural Record* (New York), June 1980; "Architecture as Urban Precinct: An Office Block by John Andrews" by J. T. Robertson in *Architectural Record* (New York), October 1980; "John Andrews, RAIA Gold Medallist, 1981" in *Architecture Australia* (Melbourne), May 1981; "Andrews House, Eugowra, NSW" in *Process: Architecture* (Tokyo), no. 22, 1981; "A High Down Under" in *Progressive Architecture* (New York), June 1982; "Merlin Hotel Centre" in *Constructional Review* (Sydney), November 1984; film—*Architecture: A Performing Art*, directed by Michael Robertson, 1979.

1962—Scarborough College, Toronto, Ontario Canada: "The students would spend five or six months, almost the full academic year, stumbling through wind, rain, sleet, and snow, from building to building, fumbling with coats and galoshes, getting wet, cold, and ill. It seemed much more sensible to connect all the buildings. Our approach was to provide a ground-level interior pedestrian circulation route with high use destinations plugged into it and secondary routes above and below it."

1979—Library and Union Facilities, Royal Melbourne Institute of Technology, Melbourne, Victoria, Australia: "It is fairly evident that at the moment there is no organization, no system of movement through the campus. This was an obvious opportunity to pull the whole thing together. It puts the library at the heart of the campus, it puts the major student facilities at the heart of the campus, and it pulls all of the ground level pedestrian circulation together into the one system, maximizing the opportunity for convenience and contact. That is an old story for me, regardless of whether it is in Melbourne or Toronto. It is still the major genesis of any building."

—John Andrews

John Andrews's architectural intentions in Scarborough College, Ontario—the work that established him as an architect of international importance—have tended to be ignored because its "form" coincided with the avant-garde architectural language of the 1960s. Although Andrews is a fluent stylist, he is less concerned with form and style than he is with finding the right approach for each problem. His best architecture demonstrates a

quality of geographical and existential appropriateness—which is "Australian" to the extent that Australia as a country is dominated by its geography. But "geography," with Andrews, refers to much more than the factors of climate and landscape; it implies the total physical environment of the building. Earl Berger has observed that Andrews's buildings "say something simply and easily understood about where you are and what you're doing there." Andrews's concern is with the rational and commonsensical solving of problems. He agrees with the anti-aesthetic sentiments expressed by Mies van der Rohe in 1923: "We reject: all aesthetic speculation, all doctrine, and all formalism."

The Rationalism of Andrews's architecture is expressed in the clear articulation of circulation and the emphasis on movement as a source of contact and interaction. The functional identity of the architectural elements is stressed rather than suppressed.

Though schizoid in its elevations, Scarborough College contains many of the innovations associated with Andrews, so it must be considered as a key work. His response to the harsh Canadian winter and the Scarborough site now seems both practical and beautiful. He intergrated all the college functions in phase I, within a single building complex that is linked by a monumental internal street. The building forms a wall that follows the escarpment edge of a deep ravine and is breached near its centre adjacent to the meeting place. There is an important difference between Scarborough College and later Andrews buildings: he usually tries to define spaces by walls and, where practicable, to avoid the use of internal columns—that is, he avoids placing columns inside his buildings and tends to externalize his supporting elements. The influence of Mies's "thinking" on Andrews reveals itself in his concern for the relationship of walls and columns—when they occur.

The Student Housing Complex at the University of Guelph has a strong, diagonally-aligned geometry based on Louis Kahn's dormitories at Bryn Mawr. The Housing Complex uses two distinct structural systems—loadbearing masonry walls in the courts for the small-span living quarters and long-span concrete structures for the streets, bridges, and dining halls, with no attempt to establish a coherent relationship. The importance of circulation and structure of the Miami Seaport Passenger Terminal has resulted in a powerful sculptural form that is much more unified than the Guelph Student Housing.

The Cameron Offices at Belconnen, in Canberra, is structurally perverse, even Mannerist. The complex consists of seven parallel office wings linked, at their ends, by a shaded walkway system. Whereas Mies exposed roof-beams above the roof in Crown Hall at Illinois Institute of Technology, Andrews has gone one step further and located his supporting structure in the courts adjacent to the office blocks. The staggered office floors are suspended on one edge, and supported at the other, from free-standing gallows supporting structures.

The King George Tower, on the corner of King and George Streets, Sydney, explores a fresh approach to sun control: it employs a common space frame on all three facades to support glass screens in a variety of configurations. The tower is splayed on the corner to open up the street intersection and to provide a sunken plaza.

Andrews intended that the open, staggered studio terraces of the Harvard Graduate School of Design would encourage a greater degree of interaction between students. The roof over the studios is supported by exposed steel trusses and stepped to admit daylight. He conceived the GSD as a nonspecific building in which learning would occur in an informal setting.

In the early 1970s, Andrews had a significant influence on Australian architects whose rustic romanticism was in marked contrast to his own vigorous rationalism.

—Philip Drew

ANTONAKAKIS, Dimitris.

Greek. Born in Chania, Crete, 22 December 1933. Educated at the Experimental School, University of Athens, 1939-51; National Technical University, School of Architecture, Athens, under Michelis, Dimitris Pikionis, *q.v.*, Liapis, Marthas, Speyer, and Fatouros, 1953-58, Dip.Arch. 1958. Served as a Reserve Officer in the Hellenic Air Force, 1958-61. Married the architect Suzana Kolokytha (*q.v.*: Suzana Antonakakis) in 1961; children: Aristides and Aekaterini. Since 1959, in partnership with Suzana Antonakakis, Athens: Founder-Principal, with Suzana Antonakakis, Atelier 66, architects, Athens, since 1965 (Associates: Gabriel Aidaonopoulos, Eleni Goussi-Dessylas, Dionissis Potiris, Efi Tsarmakli-Vrondissi, Costis Hadjimichalis, George Antonakakis, Aleca Monemvassitou-Antonakakis, Bouki Babalou-Noukakis, Antonis Noukakis, Irana Morettis, Alecos Polychroniadis, Dina Vaiou-Hadjimichalis, Dimitris Rizos, Theano Fotiou, and Costis Daskalakis). Assistant Instructor of Architecture, 1959-64, Instructor of Architecture, 1964-78, and since 1978, Lecturer in Architecture, National Technical University, Athens. Special Consulting Architect, Archaeological Service, Athens, 1961-62; Architect Consultant, Hellenic Committee for Nuclear Energy, 1962-63; Administrative Committee Member and Treasurer, 1962-63, and Member of the Special Committee for Information, 1971-74, Greek Architects Association; President, Association of Assistants and Instructors at the National Technical University, 1975-77; Vice-President, Central Administrative Committee, Association of Assistants and Instructors of Greek Universities, 1976-77. Exhibitions: *Modern Greek Architecture*, Patrai, Greece, 1967, 1978, and 1984; *Modern Greek Architecture*, Athens, 1971 and 1978; *Greek Furniture*, Athens, 1981; *Het werk van Dimitris en Suzanne Antonakakis*, Technische Hogeschool, Delft, Netherlands, 1981; *Traces of an itinerary: Suzana and Dimitris Antonakakis*, Architectural Association, London, 1982; *Urban buildings in Athens*, Athens, 1982; *L'Habitat urbain en Grèce 1900-1982*, Ghent and Liège, Belgium, and Athens, 1982-84; *Interarch '83*, Sofia, Bulgaria, 1983; *Prizes of Greek Architecture 1973-83*, Athens, 1984. Recipient: First Prize, 14th and 15th Public Schools Competition, Thessaloniki, Greece, 1961; First Prize, Archaeological Museum Competition, Chios, Greece, 1965; First Prize, Engineers and Contractors Association Summer Homes Competition, Spetsae, Greece, 1966; First Prize, Tourist Development Competition, Paleokastritsa, Corfu, Greece, 1966; First Prize, Old Castle Development Competition, Corfu, Greece, 1967; First Prize, Children's Summer Holiday Camp Competition, St. Andreas, Athens, 1972; Honour Award, Technical Chamber of Greece Competition, Athens, 1979; First Prize, Urban Park Competition, Trikala, Greece, 1980; First Prize, University of Crete Competition, Rethymnon, 1982; First Prize, Technical University of Chania, Crete, 1983. Address: Atelier 66, 118 Emmanuel Benaki Street, Athens 114 73, Greece.

Works (with Suzana Antonakakis):

1961 14th and 15th Public Schools, Thessaloniki, Greece (competition project)

1961/
62 Apartment building, Argolidos, Athens

1962/
63 Apartment building, Archelaou/Ellanikou, Athens
   Apartment interiors conversion, Acchelaon, Athens
   School for Handicapped Children interiors, Ag. Anarghyra, Athens

1962/
65 Private house, Phivis 15, Glyfada, Athens

1964 Reception Hall, International Fair, Thessaloniki, Greece (project)

Dimitris Antonakakis: Hotel at Chania, Crete, 1980-83.

1965 Private house, Chania, Kastelli, Greece
  (project)
  School complex, Thessaloniki, Greece
  (project)
  Hotel Chios, Greece
1965/
  66 Archaeological Museum, Chios, Greece
1965/
  67 Apartment interior conversion, Alfiou 9,
    Athens
1965/
  68 Private house additions, Hydra, Greece
    Hotel, Plepi, Greece
1965/
  69 Restaurant, Chania, Crete
1966 Tourist development in Paleokastritsa, Corfu,
    Greece (competition project)
    Tourist development at Aghi Apostoli Beach,
    Chania, Crete (project)
    Summer houses settlement, Spetsae, Greece
    Museum, Komotini, Greece (project)
    Old Castle Development, Corfu, Greece (com-
    petition project)
    Municipal Shopping Centre, Corfu, Greece
    (project)
    Tourist Pavilion, Amalias, Greece
1966/
  67 Private consulting room, Athens
1967 Private house, N. Kifissia, Athens
    Museum, Kastoria, Greece (project)
    Hotel and Restaurant, Paleokastritsa, Corfu,
    Greece (project)
    Consulting room and office furniture, Athens
1967/
  68 Holiday house, Portocheli, Greece
    House additions, Phaliro, Athens
1968 Tourist development at Phani Bay, Chios,
    Greece (project)
    House additions, Kifissia, Athens
    Park landscaping, Athens (project)

Hotel, Naxos, Greece (project)
Municipal Theatre, Athens (project)
1968/
  69 Tourist company offices, Asklipiou 3, Athens
    House extensions, Kallithea, Athens
1968/
  76 Hotel, Chania, Crete
1968/
  78 Tourist Complex, Plepi, Greece
1969 Mineworkers and Administrators Settlement,
    Distomo, Greece
    Private house, Chania, Crete
    Holiday house, Villia, Greece
    Olive mill/lecture hall conversion, Hydra,
    Greece
    Office building, Patission 12, Athens (project)
    Storehouse/cafe conversion, Chania, Crete
    Hotel furniture, Athens
1969/
  70 Apartment building, Ghizi 12, Psychiko,
    Greece
    Apartment building, Proklou 29, Athens
    Holiday house, Rea, Greece
    House additions, N. Psychiko, Athens
1969/
  71 Hotel, Chios, Greece
    Recreation development at Alcronafplia, Naf-
    plion, Greece
1970 City Centre, Karlsruhe, West Germany
    (project)
    House, Vrilissia, Athens
    Holiday house, Chania, Crete
    Foreign Languages Institute, Kallithea,
    Athens
    Wine Factory, Anthoussa, Greece (project)
    Akronafplia Night Club, Nafplion, Greece
    (project)
1970/
  71 House additions, Loutraki, Greece
    Hotel, Porto Ghermeno, Greece

Notary's office, Philonos 35, Piraeus, Greece
1970/
  72 House additions, Kallithea, Athens
1971 House additions, Chania, Crete
    Military hospital, Bengazi, Libya (project)
1971/
  72 House additions, Phaliro, Athens
    Hotel, Portocheli, Greece
1971/
  75 House, Chania, Crete
1972 House, Politia, Athens
    House, Ekali, Athens
    House, Mykonos, Greece (project)
    House, Hydra, Greece
    Town Hall, Tavros, Athens (project)
    Conservatory, Chania, Crete (project)
    Loukopoulos Sculpture Exhibition layouts,
    Greek Hellenic Union, Athens
    M. Kostakou Painting Exhibition layouts,
    Astor Gallery, Athens
1972/
  73 Apartment building, Phaliro, Athens
    House, Politia, Athens
    House, P. Penteli, Athens
    Apartment interior conversion, N. Kifissia,
    Athens
1972/
  74 House, Chania, Crete
    House, P. Penteli, Athens
1972/
  76 Hydra Beach Village, Plepi, Greece
1973 Environmental Protection Study, Cyclades,
    Greece
    Children's summer holiday camp, St.
    Andreas, Athens
1973/
  74 Apartment building, Emmanuel Benaki 118,
    Athens
    Pierrakos house, Oxylithos, Euboea, Greece
    Paint factory, Koropi, Greece

1973/
75 Hydra Beach Village New Town, Plepi,
Greece
1974/
75 Apartment building, Philothei, Athens
Holiday house, Alikianos, Chania, Crete
Holiday house, Spata, Greece
Apartment interior conversion, Ag. Para-
skevi, Athens
1974/
77 Hotel, Heraklion, Crete
1975 Holiday house, Kouvaras, Greece (project)
House, Politia, Athens
Holiday house, Chania, Crete
House, Hydra, Greece
Shopping Centre, Athens (project)
1975/
76 Bookstore, Athens
1975/
77 House, Ano Voula, Athens
1976 House, Kifissia, Athens
House, Vrilissia, Athens
Hotel, Vouliagmeni, Athens
Kanaghini Painting Exhibition layouts, Zo-
umboulaki Gallery, Athens
Voghiazoglou Ceramics Exhibition layouts,
French Institute, Thessaloniki, Greece
Kostakou Painting Exhibition layouts, Ora
Cultural Centre, Athens
1976/
77 Apartment building, Yakinthou 18, Athens
House, Saronis, Athens
1977 Apartment building, Helioupolis, Athens
Apartment building, Ano Voula, Athens
Painting and Sculpture Exhibition layouts,
Municipal Cultural Centre, Athens
1977/
78 House, Aegina, Greece
House, Oxylithos, Euboea, Greece
Office building, Navarinou, Athens
Apartments conversion, Denokratous 9,
Athens
Apartment Building, Sina, Athens
House at N. Pendeli, Athens
1977/
80 House at Glyfada, Athens
1977/
81 House at Kantza, Athens
1978/
80 House at Hydra II, Greece
House at Tragana, Greece
1978/
81 House near the Acropolis, Athens
House at Melissia, Greece
House at Ag. Paraskevi, Athens
1978/
82 House at Ano Voula II, Athens
Apartment Building, Lycabetus Hill, Athens
1978/
84 House at Monte Vardia II, Crete
1979/
83 House at P. Psychico, Athens (with Atelier 66
members)
1980/
82 House remodelling, Piraeus, Greece
House renovation, Atsipopoulo, Greece
1980/
84 Boarding house, Langadia, Greece (with
Atelier 66 members)
1980 House at Chania, Crete
Urban Park (recycling of a mill), Trikala,
Greece (with Atelier 66 members)
Central Office of the Technical Chamber of
Greece, Athens (with Atelier 66 members)
University of Industrial Studies, Athens (with
Atelier 66 members)
1981/
85 House at Perdika, Aegina, Greece
1981/
- Housing Development, Komotini, Greece
(with Atelier 66 members)
1982/
84 House at Ag. Paraskevi, Athens

1982/
- Public Hospital, Sitya, Crete (with Atelier 66
members)
House at Vamvakopoulo, Greece
1983/
85 Apartment Building, Ano Voula, Athens
1983 Technical University of Chania, Crete (with
Atelier 66 members)
House at Sifnos I, Greece
House at Sifnos II, Greece
1984 Office Building interiors, Holargos, Athens
(with Atelier 66 members)
House at Mitilyni, Greece

Publications:

By ANTONAKAKIS: book—*Cyclades: Identification and Recording of Important Settlements or Parts
of Them,* with Suzana Antonakakis and others, 6
volumes, Athens 1974; articles—translations of Le
Corbusier's "Argument," "Une Petite Maison" and
"Lettre al Martienssen" in *Subjects of Modern
Architecture,* Thessaloniki, Greece 1962; "Problems
of Tourist Development; or, How to Avoid Destruction of Form and Equilibrium in Entire Areas: An
Approach" in *Iconomikos Tachydromos* (Athens),
25 November 1971; "Notes on the Contact Limit of
Public and Private Space" in *Chroniko 1973,* Athens
1973: "Open Letter to a Friend, Now That Some-
thing can Possibly Change" in *Chroniko 1974,*
Athens 1974; "Unforeseen Changes in the Dwelling
Space," with Suzana Antonakakis and C. Hadjimi-
chalis, in *Design in Greece* (Athens), no. 6 1975;
"Three Apartment Buildings," with Suzana Anton-
akakis, in *Design in Greece* (Athens), no. 8, 1977;
"Apartment Houses in Athens: The Architects
Role," with Suzana Antonakakis, in *Architecture in
Greece* (Athens), no. 12, 1978; "Vacation Houses in
Attica," with Suzana Antonakakis, in *Design in
Greece* (Athens), no. 10, 1979; "Multi-Storey Town
House in Athens," with Suzana Antonakakis, in
Design in Greece (Athens), no.13, 1982; "Trikala's
Public Park Design," with others, in *Architecture in
Greece* (Athens), no. 16, 1982.

On D. and S. ANTONAKAKIS: books—*Architec-
tes de la Grèce contemporaine* by F. Loyer, Paris
1966; *Die Architektur der Moderne* by Kenneth
Frampton, Stuttgart 1983; *Post-War Architecture in
Greece, 1945–1983,* edited by O. B. Doumanis,
Athens 1984; *Regionalism and Greek Architecture:
The Architecture of Dimitris and Suzana Antonak-
akis,* thesis by V. Metallinou, Massachusetts Ins-
titute of Technology, Cambridge 1984: articles—
"Greek Art and Architecture 1945–1967" by
Dimitris Fatouros in *Balkan Studies,* Thessaloniki,
Greece 1967; "Schulmöbel für Geistigzurück-
gebliebene Kinder" by Aris Konstantinidis in *Möbel
Interior Design* (Stuttgart), no. 6 1967; "L'Architec-
ture en Grèce" by F. Loyer in *Architecture,
mouvement, continuité* (Paris), no. 167, 1968; "A
Critique of Modern Greek Architecture" by F.
Loyer in *Architecture in Greece* (Athens), no. 2,
1968; "Akronafplia: The Crown of Nafplion" by D.
Philippidis in *Architecture in Greece* (Athens), no. 9,
1975; "The Grid and the Pathway" by A. Tzonis
and L. Le Faivre in *Architecture in Greece* (Athens),
no. 15, 1981; "New Greek Architecture," special
issue of *Wonen-TA/BK* (Heerlen, Netherlands),
October 1981; "Traces of an Itinerary" in *Architectural Association Events List* (London), February
1982; "Architecture contemporaine et expression
régionale" by A. Tzonis and L. Le Faivre in *Le
Carré Bleu* (Paris), no. 2, 1982; "A Flavour of
Modernity in Greek Architecture" by G.
Simeoforidis in *International Architect* (London),
no. 8, 1982; "Prospects of a Critical Regionalism"
by K. Frampton in *Perspecta* (New Haven, Connecticut), no. 20, 1983.

Since the early years of our studies and professional
activity, we have worked under two main influences.

The first was defined by information about international modern art and architecture as it was
expressed in the School of Architecture of the
National Technical University of Athens through
the teachings of Michelis, Ghika, and the decisive
presence of J. Speyer, Professor at Illinois Institute
of Technology, Chicago, a Visiting Professor at the
N.T.U. from 1957 to 1961. Speyer's original, personal manner introduced us to the methods of
working and the teaching of Mies van der Rohe as
well as to the international debate of that time on
architecture and art.

The second influence found its origins in a more
general attitude that prevailed at the time in Greece,
an attitude that searched the essence of the Greek
cultural heritage, rejecting superficial imitation of
tradition forms. The deeper meaning of the work
and teaching of Pikionis, as well as the clarity of the
work of Aris Konstantinidis, exercised an important
influence in this direction.

In our travels through Greece since our school
days, we have searched to identify relationships
between open and closed, public and private space,
as they could be found in built environments as
expressions of socio-economic and human relations.
Our major goal was to express these relationships in
our own projects. We realized that the quality of
built environment is directly influenced by their
treatment.

We analyzed the characteristics of closed and
open space and became conscious of the value of
their complexity in traditional architecture. We
worked on the problem of correlating private and
public space as well as the problem of transition
from one to the other—establishing successive degrees of higher and lesser privacy in moving from
one space to the next. We try to realize in our
practical work and in a comprehensive way principles that are theoretically clear to us. This effort is
made not only in large-scale synthesis but also in
small-scale houses and apartment buildings, where
cost and construction limitations are great and of
crucial significance.

In the course of our work, we came to realize that
teamwork enriches each team member's experience
and pushes collective effort forward. Thus we
organized in 1964 an architect's atelier, later named
Atelier 66.
—Dimitris and Suzana Antonakakis.

The work of Dimitris and Suzana Antonakakis is not
only outstanding as architecture; it also offers a
creative way of thinking about the organization of
space that is valuable for Greek as well as international contemporary architecture. In their work,
the elements of space, materials, cost, geometry, and
social criticism are combined in a multi-variant and
consistent logical structure.

I believe that it is possible to distinguish four basic
organizing principles in their work:

1) The materials and methods of construction
correspond to the needs and possibilities of the
Greek environment without diminishing the technological level of the construction. As physical
elements, the constructions belong to the natural
and man-made native environment without being
"folksy."

2) Spatial organization is based on a downward
gradient transition from one category of space to
another, with different degrees of complexity.

3) The space produced is usually polyvalent. This
is true both in the so-called main or complex spaces,
such as a living room or an exhibition room, as well
as in the simple or secondary spaces, such as a
channel of communication. This is why, in the
Antonakakises' architecture, a corridor is not a
corridor: they create anti-institutional space.

4) Use or function in their work is always
determined by, or refers to, two basic socio-spatial
dimensions: the "closed-open" and the "private-
public." They coordinate the functions between
them. Their architectural work is usually organized

around some kind of open space, and the relation of building to street becomes of great importance and is treated with special care.

As a result of the consistent use of these organizing principles, the architecture of the Antonakakises presents these characteristics: each work has consistency and is coherent; their different works are coherent with each other (though this does not mean that they resemble one another); and their architecture is economical both in conception and realization.

No doubt these four organizing principles are not always clearly defined and clarified from the start, nor are they always apparent in every one of the Antonakakises' works. But the Antonakakises do make a continuous effort to define and clarify the ways in which their architectural work is composed; they are scrupulous and persistent in elaborating the problems of socio-spatial organization. (This is true of any creative/intellectual work: the gradual clarification of organizing principles also characterizes the evolution of the work of creative architects.)

I would cite three examples from their work in which the four principles have been successfully integrated:

The apartment building in Benaki Street, Athens: The spatial organization—with an elaborated system of different levels within the block and within each flat, and the relating of indoor with outdoor spaces (street and back yard)—results in a consistent and cohesive system. This work is, typically, of average cost. It proves how small-scale elements can play a constructive role in the man-environment relationship and how it is possible to transform and use in a positive way the restrictions of the conventional financial and building regulations of a typical urban milieu.

The Pierrakos House at Oxylithos: This country house involves a variation of the spatial system used in the Benaki Apartments. Here, the system is developed freely in space without well-defined limits, whereas in Benaki it is "enclosed" in a restricting "trunk."

The mineworkers housing at Distomo: This is a project of urban scale, organized according to the same spatial concepts as Benaki or Pierrakos but within a complex of many buildings differing in size and function. The complex is well integrated into the natural landscape, with a thoughtful interplay of open and covered streets, open and closed spaces, a response to the socio-cultural activities, and as a result of the physical organization, of the whole.

The Antonakakises' spatial thinking has proved successful not only in detached small and medium-scale buildings but also in larger urban complexes. Two large-scale projects, the school of Philosophy at Rethymno and the Technical University at Chania, Crete, create more complicated space systems than the earlier work. Both, with a clear urban character and a complexity, often in a state that might be called excitement, present a consistent evolution of their architecture.

A spatial network of activities and iconographic references is coordinated by a main piazza, one or two piazzettas, and a dominant main street. A setting tries to create a symbolic image without copying stylistic fragments to meet a difficult symbolic function.

—Dimitris A. Fatouros

ANTONAKAKIS, Suzana Maria.

Greek. Born Suzana-Maria Kolokytha in Athens, 25 June 1935. Educated at primary and secondary schools in Athens, 1942-53, including the French Institute, 1948-51; National Technical University, School of Architecture, Athens, under Michelis,

Dimitris Pikionis, q.v., Fatouros, Marthas, and Speyer, 1954-59. Married the architect Dimitris Antonakakis, q.v., in 1961; children: Aristides and Aekaterini. Since 1959, in partnership with Dimitris Antonakakis, Athens: Founder-Principal, with Dimitris Antonakakis, Atelier 66, since 1965. Architect/Consultant, Archaeological and Restoration Service, Athens, 1961-63; Administrative Committee Member, Greek Architects Association, 1971-72. Exhibitions: Poster Exhibition, International Fair, Thessaloniki, Greece 1964; Modern Greek Architecture, Patrai, Greece, 1967, 1978, 1984; Modern Greek Architecture, Athens, 1971 and 1978; Greek Furniture, Athens, 1981; Het werk van Dimitris en Suzanne Antonakakis, Technische Hogeschool, Delft, Netherlands, 1981; Traces of an Itinerary: Suzana and Dimitris Antonakakis, Architectural Association, London, 1982; Urban Buildings in Athens, Athens 1982; L'habitat Urbain en Grèce 1900-1982, Ghent and Liège, Belgium, and Athens, 1982-84; Interarch '83, Sofia, Bulgaria, 1983; Prizes of Greek Architecture 1973-1983, Athens, 1984. Recipient: First Prize, 14th and 15th Public Schools Competition, Thessaloniki, Greece, 1961; First Prize, Archaeological Museum Competition, Chios, Greece, 1965; First Prize, Engineers and Contractors Association Summer Homes Competition, Spetsae, Greece, 1966; First Prize, Tourist Development Competition, Paleokastritsa, Corfu, Greece, 1966; First Prize, Old Castle Development Competition, Corfu, Greece, 1967; First Prize, Children's Summer Holiday Camp Competition, St. Andreas, Athens, 1972; Honour Award, Technical Chamber of Greece Competition, Athens, 1979; First Prize, Urban Park Competition, Trikala, Greece, 1980; First Prize, University of Crete Competition, Rethymnon, 1982; First Prize, Technical University of Chania Competition, Crete, 1983. Address: Atelier 66, 118 Emmanuel Benaki Street, Athens 114 73, Greece.

Publications:

By ANTONAKAKIS: books—translation of Entretien by Le Corbusier, Athens 1971; Cyclades: Identification and Recording of Important Settlements or Parts of Them, with Dimitris Antonakakis and others, 6 volumes, Athens 1974; articles—"Unforeseen Changes in the Dwelling Space," with Dimitris Antonakakis and C. Hadjimichalis, in Design in Greece (Athens), no. 6, 1975; "Three Apartment Buildings," with Dimitris Antonakakis, in Design in Greece (Athens), no. 8, 1977; "Apartment Houses in Athens: The Architect's Role," with Dimitris Antonakakis, in Architecture in Greece (Athens), no. 12, 1978; "New Premises of the Technical Chamber of Greece" in Architecture in Greece (Athens), no. 15, 1981.

See ANTONAKAKIS, Dimitris

ANTONINI SCHON ZEMBORAIN.

Partnership; established, Buenos Aires, 1961, by graduates of the Universidad Nacional de Buenos Aires, Antonio Sergio Mauro Antonini (born 1936), Gerardo Saul Federico Schon (born 1936), and Eduardo Alejandro Zemborain (born 1936). Associates: Miguel Eduardo Hall (born 1943), since 1971; Juan Carlos Fervenza (born 1942), since 1973. Recipient: numerous first prizes in private and public architectural competitions in Argentina, including Ayacucho City Hall Competition, 1965; Omnibus Station Competition, Tandil, 1966; Tandil Cultural and Sports Center Competition, 1968; Chaco Provincial Bank Corporation, 1970; Government Administration Center Competition, La Plata, 1971; Civic Center Competition, San Juan, 1971; La Plata World Cup Football Stadium Competition, 1972;

Flores Housing and Urban Planning Competition, Rosario, 1974; University City Competition, San Luis, 1977; National Lottery Building Competition, Buenos Aires, 1981; Rio Cuarto Bus Station Competition, 1982. Address: Avenida Quintana 585, Buenos Aires 1129, Argentina.

Works:

1962/
63 Sol Petrol Refineries, Francisco Solano, Buenos Aires (as consultants)
1964 Argentine Tourism Pavilion, Fifth Cotal Congress, Rio de Janeiro
National Tourist Board Pavilion, Semana de Cordoba exhibition, Cordoba, Argentina
1964/
65 Office building, Chacabuco, Avellaneda, Buenos Aires
1964/
66 Apartment building, Repetto 473, Martinez, Buenos Aires
1965 Ayacucho Town Hall, Buenos Aires
1965/
66 Cine Majestic Building conversion, Villa Ballester, Buenos Aires
Cine Gran Liniers Building conversion, Liniers, Buenos Aires
1965/
67 Guillon Parish Church, Buenos Aires
1966 Exhibition stands, Effica 66, Buenos Aires
1966/
67 Camara Economica Mercedinia Headquarters, Mercedes, Buenos Aires (with Amaya, Devoto, Martin, Pieres and Lanusse)
1966/
69 Exhibition stands, Exposicion del Confort Humano, Buenos Aires
1967 Municipal building, 3 de Febrero, Buenos Aires (project)
1967/
70 Omnibus Terminal, Tandil, Buenos Aires
Apartment building, Gutierrez 2673, Buenos Aires (as consultant architects)
1968 Lakeside Hotel, Laguna de Monte, Buenos Aires
1968/
69 America Office Building (with cinema and car park), Avenida Callao 1057, Buenos Aires
1968/
70 Road/Rail Underpass, Avenida del Libertador, Buenos Aires (with Fernandez Long and Reggini)
Banco del Norte y Delta Argentino Computer Center, Avenida Figueroa Alcorta 7640, Buenos Aires (with Fernandez Long and Reggini)
Apartment building, Avenida del Libertador General San Martin 1080/84, Buenos Aires
1968/
71 El Chocon Housing and Community Development, Chocon Hydroelectric Works, Neuquen, Argentina (supervising architects; with Alexander Gibb and Partners and Llauro and Urgell)
1969/
70 Tandil Cultural and Sports Center Complex, Buenos Aires
Cine Ambassador Building conversion, Lavalle 777, Buenos Aires
Belgrano Athletic Club alterations and extensions, Buenos Aires (project)
Apartment building, Calle French 2377, Buenos Aires (as consultant architects)
Civic Center, La Rioja, Argentina (project)
Teatro Argentino/Channel Nine TV Studios conversion, Buenos Aires (as consultant architects)

Antonini, Schon, Zemborain and Associates: Project for the Retiro area of Buenos Aires, 1980.

1970 Soana Car-Wash Service Stations, Buenos Aires (project)
Plan for the Perito Moreno Highway, Buenos Aires (competition project; with Latinoconsult)
Development plan for the Ullum Tourist Resort, San Juan, Argentina (with Harz of Argentina and Edison Consult)

1970/
72 Apartment building, Blanco Encalada 5317, Buenos Aires
Campo del Pinazo Sports Fields, stages I and II, Belgrano Athletic Club, Buenos Aires

1971/
72 Naval Air Station, Ushuaia, Tierra del Fuego, Argentina (project)

1971/
73 Apartment building, Calle French and Calle Austria, Buenos Aires

1971/
74 Celulosa Argentina Building conversion, Avenida Paseo Colon y Mejico, Buenos Aires

1971/
75 El Embrujo Neighborhood Housing Development, El Talar, Tigre, Buenos Aires

1971/
79 Government Administration Center, La Plata, Buenos Aires (with Llauro and Urgell)
Chaco Provincial Bank Headquarters, Resistencia, Chaco, Argentina
Civic Center, Stage I, San Juan, Argentina

1972/
73 Alcopa Complex Temporary Planning Center, Rio Limay Hydroelectric Development, Alicura, Neuquen, Argentina (project)

1972/
75 Ingenio Providencia Administration Building, Rio Seco, Tucuman, Argentina

1973/
74 Dining Hall, Futaleufu Aluminum Plant, Puerto Madryn, Argentina (project)
Cerro Chapelco Tourist Complex, Neuquen, Argentina (project; with Latinoconsult)
Plan for the Grand Aqueducts System, Argentina (competition project)
Housing development, Rio Grande, Tierra del Fuego, Argentina

1974 Housing development, Finca Lules, Tucuman, Argentina
Housing development, San Pablo, Tucuman, Argentina

1974/
75 Single-family housing, Rio Seco, Tucuman, Argentina
El Embrujo Neighborhood Housing Development extension, El Talar, Tigre, Buenos Aires
Greater Buenos Aires Electrical Services Building (project)

1974/
76 Town development plan for Minera de Tio Turbio, Santa Cruz, Argentina (with STAFF architects)
Pre-fabricated housing development, Santa Cruz, Argentina (project; with STAFF architects)
Housing and community services buildings, Minera de Rio Turbio, Santa Cruz, Argentina (with STAFF architects)
Yacimiento Carbonifero Building, Rio Turbio, Santa Cruz, Argentina (with STAFF architects)
Barrio de Flores Neighborhood Housing Development, Rosario, Santa Fe, Argentina (with STAFF architects)

1975/
76 Hotel, Angostura, Neuquen, Argentina (project)
Civic Center, Angostura, Neuquen, Argentina (project)
Town development plan for Pocitos, San Miguel de Tucuman, Argentina

1975/
78 Mar del Plata World Cup Football Stadium and Sports Complex, Buenos Aires

1976 Plan for the center of Rosario, Santa Fe, Argentina

1976/
78 Civilian/Military Housing Development, Naval Air Station, Punta Indio, Veronica, Buenos Aires

1977 New School 4, Autopista 25 de Mayo, Buenos Aires (project; with ATEC)
Industrial plant, Comodoro Rivadavia, Chubut, Argentina (project)

1978 Urbanization Plan for the South Bank of the River Plate, Argentina
Rosario II Housing Complex, Rosario, Santa Fe, Argentina (with STAFF architects)
Hydroelectric Scheme Permanent Village, Argentine side of Yacyreta Island
Hydroelectric Scheme Permanent Village, Paraguayan side of Yacyreta Island
Avenida 9 de Julio Redevelopment, Buenos Aires
Lago Club Tourist Complex, Buenos Aires
DUT Club Hotel, Bariloche, Rio Negro, Argentina
Waterproof Cloth Plant, Comodoro Rivadavia, Chubut, Argentina
Municipal Garbage Transfer Plants, Buenos Aires

1979 Yacyreta Hydroelectric Scheme Relocation Plan, Posadas, Misiones, Argentina
Villa Lanus Housing Relocation Complexes, Posadas, Misiones, Argentina
Lomas Inn Residential Development, San Isidro, Buenos Aires Province
Colon and Guemes Apartments, Mar del Plata, Buenos Aires Province
Apartment Building, Cervino 3670, Buenos Aires
Costanera Norte Recreation and Sports Complex, Buenos Aires
Covered Stadium, Mar del Plata, Buenos Aires Province
Covered Ice Rink, Mar del Plata, Buenos Aires Province
Two sports centres, Buenos Aires (with SEPRA, Kocourek, Rana Veloso, Alvarez, and Forster)
School for Rosario Residential Complex, Santa Fe, Argentina (with STAFF architects)
Primary School, Villa Lanus, Posadas, Misiones, Argentina
Esso Foundation Engineering School, Campana, Buenos Aires Province (with SEPRA)
Sixty primary schools, Buenos Aires (with SEPRA, Kocourek, Rana Veloso, Alvarez, and Forster)
Espiritu Santo Parish Church, San Isidro, Buenos Aires Province
Health Assistance Centres, Posadas, Misiones, Argentina
Petrona Cordero General Hospital, San Fernando, Buenos Aires Province
Juan A. Fernandez General Hospital, Buenos Aires (with SEPRA and others)
Cosme Argerich General Hospital, Buenos Aires (with SEPRA and others)
Bridge over the Ana-Cua River, Misiones, Argentina

1980 North Riverside Urban Plan, Buenos Aires
Piedra del Aguila Hydroelectric Scheme Temporary Village, Neuquen, Argentina
Cielo Abierto Condominium, Punta del Este, Uruguay
A4 Relocation Housing, Posadas, Misiones, Argentina
25 de Mayo Elevated Turnpike Offices, Buenos Aires
Disco Supermarket, Emilio Mitre, Buenos Aires
Chacabuco Park Cultural and Sports Centre, Buenos Aires
Yacyreta Club, Ituzaingo, Corrientes, Argentina
Golf Driving-Range, Buenos Aires
Church in Villa Lanus, Misiones, Argentina
Chapel in Posadas, Misiones, Argentina
Ramon Sarda Maternity Hospital, Buenos Aires (with SEPRA and others)
Jose Maria Ramos Mejia General Hospital, Buenos Aires (with SEPRA and others)
Ignacio Pirovano General Hospital, Buenos Aires (with SEPRA and others)
Esso Refinery Master Plan, Campana, Buenos Aires Province
25 de Mayo Elevated Turnpike Air Terminal and Parking Garage, Buenos Aires
Retiro Urban and Traffic Development, Buenos Aires
Northern Area Urban and Traffic Development, Buenos Aires
Subway System extension and renovations, Buenos Aires

1981 9 de Julio Elevated Turnpike Service Buildings, Buenos Aires
9 de Julio Turnpike Northern and Southern Toll Areas, Buenos Aires
Esso Refinery Administration Building, Campana, Buenos Aires Province
National Lottery and Casinos Headquarters, Buenos Aires
Disco Supermarket, Avenida La Plata, Buenos Aires
Disco Supermarket, Martin Fierro, Buenos Aires
Disco Supermarket, Avenida Quintana, Buenos Aires
School for Mentally Handicapped Children, Mercedes, Buenos Aires Province
Piedra del Aguila Hydroelectric Scheme School and Hospital, Neuquen, Argentina

1982 Rio Cuarto Bus Station, Cordoba, Argentina
Disco Supermarket, Virrey del Pino, Buenos Aires
Palermo Shopping Mall, Buenos Aires
European Bank of Latin America (BEAL) Headquarters, Buenos Aires
European Bank of Latin America (BEAL) Liniers Branch, Buenos Aires
Automobile Mall, Buenos Aires
Disco Supermarket, Salguero, Buenos Aires
Sewage Treatment Plant, Munro, Buenos Aires
Disco Supermarket, Guido Spano, Buenos Aires

Publications:

On ANTONINI/SCHON/ZEMBORAIN: articles—"Workers' Housing for La Providencia Sugar Refinery in Tucuman Province" in *Nuestra arquitectura* (Buenos Aires), no. 500, 1977; "Zemborain, Schon and Antonini houses, San Isidro, Buenos Aires" in *Summa* (Buenos Aires), June 1979; "Administrative Offices of Ingenio La Providencia, Rio Seco, Tucuman Province" in *Summa* (Buenos Aires), August 1979; "Antonini Schon Zemborain and Associates—Projects of the Last Five Years," special issue of *Summa* (Buenos Aires), August/September 1981; "A Long Journey to the Supermarket," special issue of *Summa* (Buenos Aires), August 1982; "Antonini Schon Zemborain and Associates, 1981-1982," special issue of *Summa* (Buenos Aires), March 1983.

Collaborators since student days, the team of Antonini Schon Zemborain have worked together professionally for twenty-five years, yet they are still only fifty years of age. Throughout this period, they have developed the most varied of themes—from one-family and collective dwellings to civic and administrative centers, multi-functional complexes, housing developments, terminals, highways, and so forth, to the Mar del Plata Stadium, one of the sites of the 1978 World Soccer Championship. There is a certain stylistic evolution in their work, but basically it maintains a continuity of adherence to certain principles.

Their first notable work was the Ayacucho Town Hall in 1965. As one of the team puts it, the building "created a following," and they subsequently received commissions for other similar works. At that time the team considered themselves to be influenced by the new British architecture; in particular, they valued the durability rather than the formal language of buildings. They also believed in an architecture that is not too aggressive but is adequate to its use and appropriate to its environment, and it is this attitude that continues to inform their work. And, through a continuing self-criticism, and because they search out and respond to new tendencies in the architectural world, they keep their minds open to new solutions, an attitude that sets them apart from practitioners of spectacular but ephemeral fashions based on an a priori formalism.

But this is not to suggest that one work differs radically from another in either design or method. Each work is achieved by a very rigorous response to the program and by their as rigorously ensuring that everything—from the plan, as it were, to the carpentry—is controlled by a spatial module that acts not as a point of departure but as the coordinator of all architectural elements.

During the entire creative process, there is a set of design obligations that must be respected. These obligations are not imposed as a result of the team's adherence to some particular theory of form but as a result of their having determined the objective of each particular work, by testing alternatives against the program. When the design objective is established, they attempt synthesis with the spatial module—the method is highly analytical and highly controlled.

The adoption of a coordinating module does have several consequences. It allows for a simple building process. It creates a method of linkage of the various elements. The module is not necessarily a cube, but it *is* three-dimensional, and it can be clearly "read" in the building. It also allows for flexibility. In large-scale enterprises—The Civic Center at San Juan or the Government Administration Center at La Plata—the team has had to accept that parts of the complex may be used in ways different from their conception, that future growth must be allowed for, and that, as is frequently the case, the final purpose of the work may not be the same as the one that was initially envisaged by the program. Rigorous design criteria and a coordinating spatial module create not only the means but also the pattern for future change.

For the Government Administration Center at La Plata, Antonini Schon Zemborain created two towers facing a public square and flanking the City Hall. They chose a simple volumetric solution and avoided any need to "compete" with the environment. Set in two plots that are symmetrical in relation to the old building that they frame, the towers are both higher than the surrounding buildings and aligned to, and reflective of, each other, in their relation to the axis coordinating the whole. The City Hall rises above the axis. Because of the solution adopted, the City Hall stands out in the totality of the space, the different characters of the towers contributing to this effect. The towers were conceived by the team as an articulated set between which, as there was a correspondence in function, there would be a correspondence in form, in coordinating module.

The center is recognizable as the work of Antonini Schon Zemborain. So is the Civic Center of San Juan—though here different conditions were involved. Because earth tremors are common in the area, the structures had to be strong and earthquake-resistant. More important, in this work the team tried to create a "community space" within the downtown area, a space that the city's inhabitants would identify as their own, one that would become a distinctive element in the urban fabric. Defined by the team as a work "that has a strong existence achieved by means of simple elements," the Civic Center has achieved its goals.

Antonini Schon Zemborain finds it difficult to point to any one work as "characteristic." They prefer to talk about a spectrum of work. Yet the Mar del Plata Stadium does very well reveal the consistent patterns in their architecture. There is the subtle yet readable presence of the coordinating module, which generates more complex forms (the horizontally extended building, the curves) appropriate to function; the attention to environment and the relation of structure to surroundings (the treatment of park areas; the fluid conditions of access and circulation); simplicity of execution, the rigorous application of predetermines construction principles; and a flexibility achieved by clarity in design, so that the different parts of the complex can later be adapted to other uses. Moreover, a balanced image is maintained—despite a roofcovering that is a real structural accomplishment, it is not allowed to become the center of attention.

If, as they wish, one looks at their work as a whole—and if one looks at it not as a manifestation of a theory but as a series of works performing certain functions, making no reference to anything besides itself—then the best and nost obvious description of the buildings of Antonini Schon Zemborain is that they are classical—not classical in some stylistic or formal sense but in the manifest clarity and simplicity of their solutions.

—Jorge Glusberg

ARCHITECTS' CO-PARTNERSHIP

Company; established as Architects' Co-Operative Partnership, by eleven ex-students of the Architectural Association School of Architecture, London, 1939; reformed after the war, 1945, by eight of the original partners—Kenneth Capon, born 1915; Peter Cocke, born 1917; Michael Cooke-Yarborough, born 1915; Anthony Cox, born 1915; Michael Grice, born 1917; Michael Powers, born 1915; Greville Rhodes, born 1916, left the partnership 1947; and Leo de Syllas, born 1917, died 1964; subsequent partners: Philip Groves, born 1928, educated at Regent Street Polytechnic School of Architecture, London—joined, 1955, Partner, 1965, Director 1971; Hugh Durrant-Whyte, born 1931, educated at the University of the Witwatersrand, South Africa—joined, 1956, Director, 1971-80; John Jordan, born 1933, educated at the Birmingham School of Architecture—joined, 1959, Director, 1971-81; Roy Smith, born 1931, educated at North London Polytechnic School of Architecture—joined, 1958, Director, 1973; Kenneth Dalley, born 1942, educated at the Birmingham School of Architecture—joined, 1973, Director, 1977; Peter Nixon, born 1929, educated at North London Polytechnic School of Architecture—joined, 1950, Director, 1973; Sydney Peachment, born 1929, educated at North London Polytechnic School of Architecture—joined, 1951, Director, 1973; Terence Snow, born 1931, educated at North London Polytechnic School of Architecture—joined, 1960, Director, 1973. Name changed to Architects' Co-Partnership, 1953; office opened in Lagos, Nigeria, 1954; partnership changed to unlimited company, 1971; main office moved from central London to Hertfordshire, 1971. Recipient: Northern Region Award, 1967, London Region Award, 1968, and South East Region Award, 1971, of the Royal Institute of British Architects; Civic Trust Award, 1960, 1961, 1965, 1967, 1968, 1972; Housing Design Award, 1968; Queen's Award for Export Achievement, London, 1983. Address: Architects' Co-Partnership Inc., Northaw House, Potters Bar, Hertfordshire EN6 4PS, England.

Works:

1951 Various structures for the *Festival of Britain* exhibition, South Bank, London
1952 Rubber factory and offices, Brynmawr, South Wales
1953 Richard Lee Primary School, Coventry
1954 Science laboratories, Bryanston School, Blandford, Dorset
Housing, Pitstone, Buckinghamshire
1955 Margaret Wix Primary School, St. Albans, Hertfordshire
Bedwell East Primary School, Stevenage, Hertfordshire
Roundwood Park Primary School, Harpenden, Hertfordshire
Secondary modern school, Chaddesden, Derbyshire
Secondary modern school, Hurlfield, Sheffield
1956 Shepherd's Lane Primary School, Rickmansworth, Hertfordshire
Park Lane Primary School, Waltham Cross, Hertfordshire
Infant school, Alderman's Green, Coventry
1957 Batford Infant School, Harpenden, Hertfordshire
Secondary modern school, Bingham, Nottinghamshire
1958 Secondary modern school, Thornbridge, Derbyshire
Secondary modern school, Long Sutton, Lincolnshire
Secondary modern school, Tile Cross, Warwickshire
Science laboratories, Sherborne Girls' School, Dorset
Chemical factory, Berkhamsted, Hertfordshire
President's Lodge, Corpus Christi College, Oxford
1959 Thrift Farm Secondary School, Borehamwood, Hertfordshire
Secondary modern school, Newbold, Warwickshire
1960 Risinghill Comprehensive School, Finsbury, London
Secondary modern school, Waltheof, Sheffield
Chemistry laboratories, University of Leicester
Secondary modern school, St. Austell, Cornwall
Study bedrooms, St. John's College, Oxford
1961 Secondary modern school, Wilnecote, Warwickshire
Research laboratories, Liphook, Surrey
15 primary and secondary schools, Nigeria
Bristol Hotel, Lagos, Nigeria
1962 Tye Green area housing, Harlow New Town, Hertfordshire
Radiobiological laboratories, Wantage, Berkshire
Tutors' houses, St. John's College, Oxford
1963 Harris Technical College, Preston, Lancashire (with the Department of Education and Science)
Study bedrooms, King's College, Cambridge
School for spastics, Tonbridge, Kent
1964 Physics Laboratories, University of Hull
Beaufoy Comprehensive School, Lambeth, London
Community Centre, Bethlem Hospital, Beckenham, Kent
1965 Teachers' Training College, Trinity College, Carmarthen, Wales
Biochemistry Laboratories, Imperial College, South Kensington, London

Spastics training school, Meldreth, Cambridgeshire

Spastics hostel, Broadstones, Birmingham

1967   Ophthalmic Unit, Royal Berkshire Hospital, Reading

Spastics workshops Broadstones, Birmingham

Junior Health Training Centre, Greenwich, London

Dunelm House Student Community Building, University of Durham

Science and Mathematics Laboratories, University of Hull

Laboratories, University of Keele, Staffordshire

St. Paul's Cathedral Choir School, London

Housing, Kingsley Place, Highgate, London

Music School, Lancing College, Sussex

Physics Laboratories, University of Essex, Colchester

1968   Library, University of Essex, Colchester

1969   Chemistry Laboratories, University of Essex, Colchester

Chemistry Laboratories, University College, London

Study bedrooms, Goldney House, University of Bristol

1970   Staff Hostel and Nurses' School, Maudsley Hospital, Camberwell, London

Alexander Barracks, Pirbright, Surrey

Chemistry Laboratories, Imperial College, South Kensington, London

Computer Building, University of Essex, Colchester

1971   Study bedrooms, University of Essex, Colchester

1972   Royal School of Signals, Blandford, Dorset

3 boarding schools, Tunis, Sfax, and Le Kef, Tunisia

Wolfson Building (study bedrooms), Trinity College, Cambridge

1973   22 schools, Trinidad and Tobago, West Indies

1974   School of Environmental Studies, University College, London

Housing, Ethelred Street area, Lambeth, London

1975   Study bedrooms and theatre, Guy's Hospital, Southwark, London

1976   Arts Faculty Building, University of Durham

1977   Factory, offices and research laboratories, Swindon, Wiltshire

1978   Laboratories, Hatfield Polytechnic, Hertfordshire

Pavilions for the International Fair, Khartoum, Sudan

4 schools, Mutrah, Ruwi, Sohar, and Nizwa, Oman

Study bedrooms, Sinclair House, University of Bristol

Staff Training College, Central Electricity Generating Board, Hertfordshire

Teaching Hospital, Baghdad, Iraq

Five Hospitals, Saudi Arabia (as supervisors)

1979   University of Lagos Master Plan, Nigeria

General Hospital, Jordan

Hostel, Lambeth, London

1981   International Fair, Amman, Jordan

Research and Administration Facility, Swindon, Wiltshire

1982   Victoria Barracks, Windsor, Berkshire

Housing Development, Lambeth, London

Category "C" Prison, Bovingdon, Hertfordshire

1983   Housing renovation, Calne, Wiltshire

Department of Geography, University of Bristol, Avon

Category "C" Prison, Gaynes Hall, Cambridgeshire

Private Clinic, Oxford Street, London

1984   Computer Science Facility, Hatfield Polytechnic, Hertfordshire

District General Hospital, Plymouth, Devon

Department of Biotechnology, Imperial College of Science and Technology, London

Study bedrooms, seminar rooms, and shops, Trinity College, Cambridge, England

Computer Operations Facility, Innsworth, Gloucester, England

Prison extensions, Bedford, England

Publications:

By ACP: books—*Planning Buildings and Facilities for Higher Education*, London 1975; *Design for Health Care* by Anthony Cox and Philip Groves, London 1981; articles—"Building in the Tropics" in *The Architects Journal* (London), 16 May 1957; "Architect's Approach to Architecture" in *RIBA Journal* (London), June 1967; "Building for the Health Care Programme, Saudi Arabia" in *RIBA*

Architects Co-Partnership: Khartoum International Fair, Sudan, 1978.

Journal (London), June 1976; "Khartoum International Fair" in *RIBA Journal* (London), April 1978.

On ACP: articles—"Brynmawr" by R. Furneaux Jordan in *Architectural Review* (London), March 1952; "The Team in the Office" in *Architecture and Building* (London), April 1956; "Dunelm House, Durham" by John Donat in *Architectural Review* (London), June 1966; "Schools in Trinidad" in *Building* (London), 16 November 1973; "Frontline Design" by Gontran Goulden in *Building* (London), 21 March 1980; "Exporting the Best of British Architecture" by Charles McKean in *The Times* (London), 19 June 1980.

The original partners of ACP were nursed in the Modern Movement in architecture in the years immediately preceding the Second World War, when the work of the architectural Establishment seemed to them bankrupt and irrelevant. They began to practise in the post-war welfare state when local authority and government architects' departments were small, compared with what they have since become, and when there was an acute shortage of labour and materials, severe economic stringency, and great demands for new buildings for the community.

ACP was not so much concerned with creating architectural monuments as with the provision of humane and efficient shelter for social activities and by accident rather than by design found itself building for education, following the post-war bulge in the birth rate, through primary to secondary schools, generally using pre-fabricated systems of construction. With the subsequent expansion of the universities, its work extended into a wider field, where its largest single commitment was the master plan and most of the buildings for the new University of Essex, and also into buildings for health, medical research, and housing. Thus, the majority of its commissions have been in the public sector.

ACP has also always been concerned with the problems of design in the developing world and has worked in West Africa, the West Indies, and the Middle East, designing and building educational programmes for the World Bank, hospitals, low-cost housing, and a large exhibition centre in Khartoum.

—Architects' Co-Partnership

The fact that Architects' Co-Partnership was founded early in 1939 by eleven young architects from the Architectural Association School of Architecture as Architects Co-Operative Partnership explains much of the character and consistency of the architecture they produce. The group were brought up in the early days of modern architecture in Britain, and like many of their contemporaries, regarded the new approach to architecture proclaimed particularly by Le Corbusier as a crusade to which they could devote their energies and talents. Architecture through technology could be a powerful agent of the new good life in a just society.

The first major building designed by ACP in 1946 and built in 1948-52 was the new rubber factory at Brynmawr in South Wales. The site was difficult and bleak, but the architects produced a building that had a permanent effect on industrial building in Britain. By carefully analysing the factory process and interpreting this in a building of shell concrete domes and barrel vaults, approached by a communal pedestrian ramp and overlooking a man-made lake, they established an architectural standard for industry that has seldom been equalled. This building helped to make factory-building an acceptable subject for architectural study and development, and it will always be regarded as one of the 'classic' industrial buildings of the twentieth Century.

The postwar schools programme helped to establish ACP in the field of educational buildings. They were involved in school and college design, starting with the Hertfordshire "light and dry"

systems, and gradually evolved their own special architectural character. As the education programme developed, so ACP's work moved into the more complex university and polytechnic buildings and later into facility planning, medical building, and urban houising both in UK and overseas.

ACP were among the first UK firms to work overseas, mainly in education and health, and their buildings show that they have not lost their ability to adapt to changing social circumstances and climatic conditions; these works underline their continued faith in the essential social value of architecture, a 1930's belief that is equally valid in the present day.

Buildings designed by ACP, on their own admission, are not intended to be architectural monuments; they are meant to fill a social need economically and practically and give aesthetic satisfaction to their users. It is not surprising that ACP prefer to remain an anonymous architectural team and have reinforced their skills by setting up their own environmental engineering group known as Northaw Engineering Consultants (NECI).

Six of the founders are still active architects and, together with a new generation of partners, ACP has been able to demonstrate that the philosophy and attitudes that brought the original eleven together are still socially and architecturally relevant after forty years practice.

—Edward D. Mills

ARDALAN, Nader.

Iranian. Born in Tehran, 9 March 1939. Educated at the Carnegie Institute of Technology, Pittsburgh, Pennsylvania, 1956-61 (American Institute of Architects Scholarship), B.Arch. 1961; Harvard Graduate School of Design, Cambridge, Massachusetts, M.Arch. 1962. Married Laleh Bakhtiar (divorced, 1976); married Shahla Ganji in 1977; children: Mani, Iran, Karim, and Alireza. Designer, Skidmore, Owings and Merrill, *q.v.*, San Francisco, 1962-64; Head, Architecture and Engineering Section, National Iranian Oil Company, Masjid-i-Sulaiman, Iran, 1964-66; Design Partner, Abdolaziz Farmanfarmaian and Associates, Tehran, 1966-72; Managing Director, Mandala Collaborative, Tehran, 1972-79; President, Mandala International, Boston, since 1977; Principal, Nader Ardalan and Associates, Boston, since 1979; Senior Vice-President, Jung/Brannen International Ltd., Boston, since 1983. Visiting Critic in Architecture, Tehran University, 1969-73; Yale University, New Haven, Connecticut, 1977, Graduate School of Design, Harvard University, Cambridge, Massachusetts, 1977-78, and Massachusetts Institute of Technology, Cambridge, 1979-80; Visiting Critic in Urban Design, Harvard Graduate School of Design, 1977-78 and 1981-52; Member of the Designing for Islamic Cultures Workshop, Harvard University/Massachusetts Institute of Technology, 1980. Member, Steering Committee, Aga Khan Award for Architecture, 1970-80. Recipient: First Prize, Iran-America Society Culture Center Design Competition, 1975; Planning Award, *Progressive Architecture*, 1979. Address: Jung/Brannen International Ltd., 177 Milk Street, Boston, Massachusetts 02109, U.S.A.

Works

1962/
64   Engineering Sciences Building, University of California, Berkeley (with Skidmore, Owings and Merrill)
1964/
66   Housing and Community Facilities, National Iranian Oil Company, Kharg Island, Aghajari, Masjid-i-Sulaiman, Iran
1965 Dr. Ali Saidi House, Tehran

1966 Dr. A.G. Ardalan House, Caspian Sea, Iran
1968 Saman Apartments, Tehran (with Abdolaziz Farmanfarmaian and Associates)
1968/
72   Asian Games Sports Center, Tehran (with Abdolaziz Farmanfarmaian and Associates)
1970/
72   Mehrabad Airport expansion, Tehran (with Abdolaziz Farmanfarmaian and Associates)
      Malek House, Tehran
1971/
73   Iran Center for Management Studies, Tehran (with Abdolaziz Farmanfarmaian and Associates)
1971/
74   Behshahr Home Offices, Tehran (with Abdolaziz Farmanfarmaian and Associates)
1974 Arya Mehr University (master plan, university mosque, library, student union, and gateway), Tehran
      Jondi Shahpour New Town, Ahwaz, Iran (with Skidmore, Owings and Merrill)
1974/
76   Creative Arts Center, Tehran
      Pardisan Enviromental Park, Tehran
      Bandar Shahpour New Town, Persian Gulf, Iran (with Skidmore, Owings and Merrill)
1975 Urban design studies for the Abbassabad Development, Tehran (with Kenzo Tange and Louis Kahn)
      Master Plan for the Tappeh Eram New Community, Shiraz, Iran
      Master plan for Bu Ali Sina University, Hamadan, Iran (with Georges Candilis)
      Design of the *Sacred Space* exhibition, National Museum of Design, Smithsonian Institution, Washington, D.C. (with Karl Schlamminger)
1976/
77   Academic Buildings, Dormitories, and Administration Housing, Bu Ali Sina University, Hamadan, Iran (with Georges Candilis)
1977 Garden Apartment and Community Center, Monte Carlo Mosque, Tehran
1977/
78   Industrial Development Bank of Iran Headquarters Building, Tehran
1978 Mercantile Bank of Iran and Holland Headquarters Building, Tehran
      Tehran Center for the Celebration of Music
      Development plan, and first phase housing, Nuran Satellite Town, Isfahan, Iran
1979 University Mosque, Bu Ali Sina University, Hamadan, Iran
1981 Serena Hotels Master Plan and Design, Faisalabad, Pakistan
1982 Universal All-Religions Centre, Suresnes, France
1984 "Jerusalem Consciousness" Old-City Preservation Plan, Jerusalem, Israel
      International Hotel, Mersin, Turkey
1985 Ankara Sheraton Hotel Centre, Turkey

Publications:

By ARDALAN: books—*The Sense of Unity: The Sufi Tradition in Persian Architecture,* with Laleh Bakhtiar, Chicago 1973; *Habitat Bill of Rights,* with Josep Lluis Sert, Moshe Safdie, Balkrishna Doshi, and Georges Candilis, Tehran 1976; *Al-Masjid al-Haram: The History and Construction of the Holy Ka'ba,* Mecca 1976; *Blessed Jerusalem,* Cambridge, Massachusetts 1983; articles—"Model Islamic Neighborhood" in *The Arab City,* Riyadh, Saudi Arabia 1982; text, in *Awakening Through Architecture,* symposium report, Cambridge, Massachusetts 1983; "On Mosque Architecture" in *Architecture and Community: Building in the Islamic World Today,* edited by Renata Holod and Darl Rastorfer, Millerton, New York 1983.

On ARDALAN: book—*Iran: Elements of Destiny* by Roloff Beny, Toronto 1978; *Islamic Architecture*, exhibition catalogue, Venice 1983; articles— "Contemporary Iranian Architects" by M. Eshraq in *Art and Architecture* (Tehran), June/November 1973; "Iran Today" in *Newsweek* (New York), November 1974; "Architectures iraniennes" by Yvette Pontoizeau in *Architecture d'aujourd'hui* (Paris), February 1978; "Jondi Shahpour New Community: 1979 Award for Planning" in *Progressive Architecture* (New York), February 1979.

I believe that good architecture should reflect a holistic appreciation of reality. Reality, it is held, has a hierarchy of awareness levels within which there exists both outer and inner dimensions. The outer (ecological) dimension relates to a finite world of limited energy-income from the sun, of fixed energy reserves. The inner (cultural) dimension relates to human kind, who have an infinite, hidden reserve of energy—the spirit—that can often transcend the limited context of this phenomenal world. The creative imagination that has extended the art and architecture of humanity has primarily grown from this inner dimension.

It has, therefore, been my intention to develop a firm working understanding of how, traditionally, the proper and balanced relationship of both inner and outer energies has been achieved throughout history. The comparative study of outstanding traditional societies has always been undertaken with a view to discerning the underlying universal values and attitudes that are common to man. while appreciating the particular, adaptive strategies of each. The study of traditions in architecture or the normative ways of societies provide me with a sense of relaxed anticipation of the future that complements contemporary knowledge and technology.

This complementary view of existence and creativity has been applied systematically in my teaching, research, and work. At present the focus of my work centers on the re-creation of a minimum energy waste design, while my research is concerned with the aesthetics of energy in architecture.

—Nader Ardalan

Born in Iran, Nader Ardalan is now the principal of Mandala International, a group of architects and planners operating in Boston in association with the Mandala Collaborative of Tehran. Together, they have designed several buildings and planning schemes for Iran.

Ardalan's chief concern is with what he calls the "cultural dimension" of architecture. He is very disturbed that though its architectural theories have had a broad worldwide impact, a sense of culture hardly exists in the United States. Especially in developing countries struggling to maintain identity as they rapidly adopt modern technology, the importance of the "cultural dimension" cannot be overlooked.

"We are at the threshold of the development of new architectural theories, set against the background of the ashes of the International Style," Ardalan feels. "The means lie in the domain of universal concerns that range from spiritual considerations to biosphere ecology and renewable resource usage. Most design attitudes today are parochial and resource-unconsious, and ninety percent of the world cannot afford to emulate them."

Ardalan's architecture shows that he has learned a great deal from many Third World cultures. He has absorbed lessons not only from their ancient history but also from their recent historical struggles (successes and failures) with the industrialized world. His Tehran Center for the Celebration of Music is a case in point. Through a system of pedestrian walkways, the center is linked with several other cultural facilities in the immediate area, thus creating

Nadar Ardalan: Nuran Satellite Town, Isfahan, Iran, 1978 (model).

a cultural quarter that never existed before. The concept of walls, courtyards, outer and inner gardens, and a general progression of internalized spaces draws much from traditional Iranian design. The use of water and light (particularly dramatic is the light from the oculus above the theatre. Its shimmering opalescent surfaces add to the sense of depthless space created within the cone) make the building vibrant and inspiring.

Mandala's plan for Nuran, the City of Illumination, a new town to be built near Isfahan, is even more exciting. Within the context of plannned city, Ardalan has developed a strong sense of place, in striking contrast to so many of the new towns developed by other contemporary architects. The plan is structured with geometry, but two commercial paths designed for non-vehicular traffic meander through the town in amorphous routes. The primary axis of the town is aligned with two holy places, one to the east and one to the west, adding a spiritual justification to the plan. Parts of the plan are

symbolic; the west side of the town is the imaginative or spiritual head, while the east side is the thinking or material head of Nuran. The axial spine of Nuran is a traditional "paradise garden," which enforce the spiritual axis between the two shrines, creates a cool space that is easily accessible from all points, and further connects Nuran to regional cultural traditions.

Ardalan is a person dedicated to the search for origins, and it is because of that dedication that he has focussed so much attention on pure numbers, geometry, and his Islamic heritage. His designs are often highly geometrical, but his sense of geometry is finely tuned, developed from his study of Sufi traditions in ancient Persian architecture. His work should be a beacon not only for other architects practicing within the context of the developing world, but for architects in the west as well, who too often forget that without cultural connections, architecture is incapable of answering human needs.

—Mitchell B. Rouda

ARUP, Ove Nyquist.
British. Born in Newcastle upon Tyne, 16 April 1895. Educated at preparatory, primary and high schools in Germany and Denmark; studied philosophy and mathematics at the University of Copenhagen, B.A. 1916, and civil engineering at the Royal Technical College, Copenhagen, 1916-22, B.Sc. 1922. Married Ruth Sorensen in 1925; children: Anya, Jens, and Karin. Worked as a designer for Christiani and Nielson, Hamburg, Germany, 1922-23, then as Designer, 1923-25, and Chief Designer, 1925-34, for Christiani and Nielsen Ltd., London; Director and Chief Designer, J. L. Kier and Company Ltd., London, 1934-38; Director, Arup Designers Ltd. and (with his cousin) Arup and Arup Ltd., London, 1938-46; in private practice as an engineering consultant, London, 1946-49. Senior Partner, Ove Arup and Partners, London, since 1949, and Arup Associates, London, since 1963. Consultant Engineer to the Air Ministry, London, 1938-45. Visiting Lecturer, Harvard University, Cambridge, Massachusetts, 1955; Alfred Bossom Lecturer, Royal Society of Arts, London, 1970. Chairman, Society of Danish Civil Engineers in Great Britain and Ireland. 1955-59. Founder-Member, Modern Architecture Research Group (MARS), London, 1933; collaborated with the Tecton Group, London, 1933. Exhibition: Institute of Civil Engineers, London, 1981. Recipient: Design Award, 1954, 1956, 1958, 1960, 1961, 1962, 1964, 1966, 1967(3), 1968(2), 1970(2), 1971, 1972(3), 1973, 1974(2), 1975(2), 1976, 1977(5), 1978(2), 1979(2), 1980(2), 1982(2), 1983(3), and Gold Medal, 1966, Royal Institute of British Architects; Civic Trust Award, 1961(3), 1965, 1967(4), 1968(3), 1969(8), 1970, 1971, 1972(6), 1975, 1978, 1979(3), 1981, 1982, 1983, 1984(2); Massey Medal, Royal Architectural Institute of Canada, 1964; Structural Steel Design Award, 1969, 1970, 1971(2), 1974, 1976(2), 1984; Queen's Award to Industry, 1969, 1984; Department of the Environment Housing Award, 1970, 1979(2), 1980; A.C.E.A. Award of Excellence, 1972; Special Award, Institute of Structural Engineers, 1973, 1977; Business and Industry Environment Award, 1975, 1977, 1978; *Financial Times* Industrial Architecture Award, 1975, 1982, 1984; Concrete Society Award, 1976, 1979, 1980, 1983(2); European Steel Structure Award, 1977; *Progressive Architecture* Award, 1978; Brick Development Award, 1979; Aga Khan Architecture Award, 1980; British Steel Corporation Award, 1981; Natural Stone Design Award, 1981(2); Carpenters Award, 1981, 1983; French Steelwork Award, 1982. D.Sc.: University of Durham, 1967; University of East Anglia, Norwich, 1968; Tekniske Hojskole, Lyngby, Denmark, 1974; Heriot-Watt University, Edinburgh, 1976. Fellow, Institution of Structural Engineers, 1940, and Institute of Civil Engineers, 1951. Fellow, American Concrete Institute, 1975. C.B.E. (Commander, Order of the British Empire), 1953; Knight Bachelor, 1971. Chevalier, 1965, and Commander, 1975, Order of the Dannebrog, Denmark. Address: Ove Arup and Partners, 13 Fitzroy Street, London W1P 6BQ, England.

Works (as structural engineer):

1933 Cafe and shelter, Canvey Island, London
 Highpoint I (apartment building), Highgate, London
1939 Penguin Pool, London Zoo, Regent's Park, London
 Air-raid shelters for the Finsbury Borough Council, London

With Ove Arup and Partners:

1946/
 50 Brynmawr Rubber Company Factory, Gwent, Wales
1946/
 52 Bus Station, Dublin
1947/
 48 Mfantsipim School, Accra, Ghana
1947/
 52 Flats, Busaco Street, Finsbury, London
1948/
 51 CIBA (Aero Research Ltd.) Factory, Duxford, Cambridgeshire
1948/
 63 Ibadan University, Nigeria
1949/
 51 Various structures for the *Festival of Britain*, South Bank, London
1949/
 53 Gestetner Ltd. Offices, Tottenham, London
1950/
 54 Hunstanton Secondary Modern School, Nofolk
1950/
 56 Trades Union Congress Building, Great Russell Street, London
1951/
 54 Kidbrooke Comprehensive School, London
1951/
 62 Cathedral of St. Michael, Coventry, Warwickshire
1952/
 53 Mayfield School, Putney, London
1952/
 59 Flats, Sydenham Hill, London
1953/
 60 Housing, Golden Lane, City of London
1954/
 63 Civic Centre, Plymouth, Devon
1954/
 64 National Sports Centre, Cyrstal Palace, London
1955/
 60 Princess Margaret's Hospital, Swindon, Wiltshire
1956/
 61 Flats, St. James Place, London
1957/
 61 Bank of England Printing Works, Debden, Essex
1957/
 68 South Bank Development (Queen Elizabeth Hall), London
1957/
 73 Sydney Opera House, New South Wales
1958/
 62 Addenbrooke's Hospital, Cambridge, England
1958/
 64 Civic Centre, Hampstead, London
1959/
 72 Sussex University, Falmer, Sussex
1960/
 66 Massey-Ferguson Ltd. Factory, Coventry, Warwickshire
1960/
 67 British Petroleum Headquarters, Moorfields Project, Moorgate, London
1961/
 63 Kingsgate Footbridge, Dunelm House, University of Durham, England
1961/
 65 St. Katherine's Dock House, London
1961/
 66 Abbotsinch Airport, Glasgow, Scotland
1962/
 71 Stock Exchange Building, London
1963/
 66 Jebba Paper Mills, Nigeria
1963/
 67 Corporation Street Development, Birmingham, Warwickshire
1963/
 74 General Hospital, Kuala Lumpur, Malaysia
1964/
 66 University of East Anglia, Wivenhoe, Essex
1964/
 77 Royal Free Hospital, London
1965/
 71 Airdrie District General Hospital, Lanarkshire, Scotland
1966/
 74 Conference Centre and Hotel, Riyadh, Saudi Arabia
1967/
 74 Mosque, Conference Centre and Hotel, Mecca, Saudi Arabia
1969/
 71 Gateshead Bypass, Tyne and Wear
1969/
 72 Television Tower, Emley Moor, Yorkshire
1970/
 80 Wood Green Shopping City, London
1971/
 77 Centre Georges Pompidou, Place Beaubourg, Paris
1972/
 75 Berry Lane Viaduct, Chorley Wood, Hertfordshire
1972/
 78 Brighton Marina, Brighton, Sussex
1972/
 National Exhibition Centre, Birmingham, Warwickshire
1973/
 81 Byker Viaduct and Metro, Tyne and Wear
1974/
 80 Hoover Factory, Merthyr Tydfil, Wales
1975/
 University of Doha, Qatar
 British Library, Euston Road, London
1976/
 79 Trade Centre, Abu Dhabi, United Arab Emirates
 Sports Complex, Abdul Aziz University, Jeddah, Saudi Arabia
1977/
 79 Carlsberg Brewery, Northampton, England
1977/
 81 Sara Roads, Saudi Arabia
1977/
 82 National Concert Hall, Cardiff, Wales
1978/
 82 Kessock Bridge, Inverness, Scotland
1978/
 83 Foyle Bridge, Londonderry, Northern Ireland
1978/
 84 Art Gallery, Stuttgart
 Kylesku Bridge, Sutherland, Scotland
1978/
 85 Lloyds Headquarters, London
1979/
 85 Bank Misr, Cairo
1980/
 84 Renault Warehouse, Swindon, Wiltshire
1980/
 85 Hong Kong and Shanghai Bank Headquarters, Hong Kong
 Haifa Street Development, Baghdad, Iraq
1981/
 83 Saddam's Qadissiya Martyr's Monument, Baghdad, Iraq
 Central Bank Printing and Minting Works, Baghdad, Iraq
1982/
 84 British Oxygen Headquarters, Windlesham Surrey
1982/
 - Royal Holloway and Bedford Colleges, London
1983/
 - Royal Docks Development, London
 Schlumberger (Lightweight Structures) Factory, Cambridge, England
1984/
 - Clovis Community Hospital, California
 National Garden Festival Exhibition Hall, Stoke-on-Trent, Staffordshire

Publications

By ARUP: books—*Design, Cost, Construction and Relative Safety of Trench, Surface, Bombproof and Other Air Raid Shelters*, London 1939; *London's Shelter Problem*, London 1940; *Safe Housing in Wartime*, London 1941; articles "Subsidence under the Tidal Pressures" in *The Structual Engineer* (London), no. 12, 1929; "Planning in Reinforced Concrete," in 2 parts, in *Architectural Design*, (London), nos. 9 and 10, 1935; "Reinforced Concrete" in *The Architects Yearbook*, London 1945; "Shell Construction" in *Architectural Design* (London), no. 11, 1947; "Modern Architecture: The Structural Fallacy" in *The Listener* (London), no. 1375, 1955; "Design and Construction of the Printing Works at Debden," with Sir Howard Robertson and others, in *The Structural Engineer* (London), no. 4, 1956; "A Discussion about Future Developments in Building Techniques" in *Architectural Design* (London), no. 11, 1957; "The Architect and the Engineer," with E.D.J. Matthews, in *Journal of the Institution of Civil Engineers* (London), August 1959; "Reinforced Concrete Design" in *The Financial Times* (London), 13 November 1961; "Foreword" to *Candela, The Shell Builder* by Colin Faber, New York 1963; "Discussion of Form and Structure in Engineering" in *Journal of the Institution of Civil Engineers* (London), October 1964; "Problems and Progress in the Construction of the Sydney Opera House" in *Civil Engineering and Public Works Review* (London), no. 703, 1965; "Ove Arup Talks to Peter Rawstone" in *RIBA Journal* (London), no. 4, 1965; "Art and Architecture: The Architect-Engineer Relationship" in *RIBA Journal* (London), August 1966; "The Evolution and Design of the Concourse at the Sydney Opera House" in *Journal of the Institution of Civil Engineers* (London), no. 4, 1968; "From Gorillas at the Zoo to Aussies at the Opera," interview with Martin Pawley, in *Building Design* (London), May 1970; "I Am Not a Prophet" in *Contract Journal* (London), no. 4761, 1970; "The Potential of Prestressed Concrete" in *Concrete* (Slough, Buckinghamshire), no. 6, 1970; "Sydney Opera House," with G.Z. Zunz, in *Civil Engineering* (New York), no. 12, 1971; "Built Environment Professions: What's in a Name?" in *Built Environment* (London), March 1975; "I Only Used Ordinary, Plain Common Sense" in *New Civil Engineer* (London), April 1975; "Sir Ove Arup," interview in *Building* (London), October 1977; "FIP 8th Congress" in *Concrete* (Slough, Buckinghamshire), May 1978; "Development of English Architecture" in *Erhvervs Bladet* (Copenhagen), June 1979; "Arup Associations" in *Architectural Review* (London), January 1980; "Future Life Styles" in *RSA Journal* (London), July 1980; "My Architectural Theory" in *RIBA Journal* (London), November 1980; "Arup on Arup Associates" in *Architects' Journal* (London), 17 June 1981; and numerous articles and reports in the *Arup Journal* (London).

On ARUP: books—*University Planning and Design* by Michael Brawne, London 1967; *Cambridge New Architecture* by Nicholas Taylor and Philip Booth, London 1970; *Building, the New Universities* by T. Birks, Newton Abbot, Devon 1972; *Third Generation: The Changing Meaning of Architecture* by Philip Drew, London 1972; *Ove Arup and his collaboration with Berthold Lubetkin*, thesis by J. Sherrat, St. Andrews University, Fife, Scotland, 1982: articles—"Arup's First Ten Years" in *Architecture Plus* (New York), November/December 1974; "Piece Work" by Graham Hancock in *Building Design* (London), 5 September 1975; "The Award Winners: A Profile of Arup Associates" in *Building Design* (London), 11 June 1976; "Grand Master: The Career of Sir Ove Arup and His Influence on Post–1930 Architecture" in *Building* (London), 7 October 1976; "Arup Associates" in *Architecture + Urbanism* (Tokyo), December 1977; "Task Force from the Past" by Martin Pawley in *Building Design* (London), 25 June 1982.

Structure exists for a purpose and as part of an entity that also has its purpose; the efficiency of a structure can only be judged in the light of these various purposes great and small. We need to integrate the work of the various disciplines in the

Ove Arup: Footbridge, Dunelm House, University of Durham, 1967.

building industry, in order to achieve greater efficiency and greater artistic control. The plain facts are that architecture will die if it is not efficient and that we need an environment where we can feel at home—which is what architecture stands for. Such facts are no less true now that we are undertaking tasks of ever-increasing size and complexity, with ever more complex technical resources at our command. And when I say that design should aim at a practical fulfilment of purpose, this is the purpose I have in mind. But it is not the purpose that is forced upon us.

Totally integrated, comprehensive architecture will result in efficiency of execution, but will also require much effort and dedicated involvement on the part of the directing team. And the onslaught of mechanization and standardization, the compulsion to minimize human effort, to reduce cost at whatever cost, all this may spell—I am afraid—the end of design as an art. Of course, many people realise now that our economic thinking is faulty, that the cost in human happiness is too high, that we are frantically busy building on sinking foundations. We can afford, if need be, a lowering of material standards. What we can't afford is to lose our humanity.

—Ove Arup

Ove Arup is not an architect, yet one of the best architectural practices in Britain bears his name. This is as it should be. Few people understand architecture so well, possibly because few have the driving curiosity about the universe that led this tall, vague-seeming man to take a degree in philosophy before embarking upon structural engineering. In 1966 he told *The Architects' Journal*:

Architecture has been defined as "building plus delight".... We know roughly what a building is. A building has to do a job and... has to cost as little as is compatible with doing its job well. Only in a very few cases is cost of no importance. Delight, on the other hand, has nothing to do with cost. It is not safeguarded by spending a lot of money—it may even be had for nothing, or next to nothing. It is produced somehow by the creation of spaces, sculptural relationships, light and shade, colours and textures, and by the clarity or ingenuity with which its functional and structural problems are solved; but exactly *how* we do not know.... This is unfortunate because "delight" is what every architect wants to produce... So naturally he spends his energies on the pursuit of delight. And perhaps neglects the building. This is unfortunate because it endangers his whole quest for delight.

I do not suppose he had it quite so clearly worked out in the 1930's when he met Berthold Lubetkin, Max Fry, Ernö Goldfinger, Wells Coates, and other members of the MARS Group, but he already understood "the purpose of the whole exercise, which is not first of all to produce good plumbing, or good structure, but good architecture, total architecture, and with it delight." Ove enjoyed the enthusiasm of these pioneers, their belief in what they were doing. The social importance of architecture, he says, was rightly stressed. He shared their lively interest in the new material reinforced concrete and understood its limitations better than these architects for whom it was a symbol as well as a building material.

In order to work with Lubetkin on the design of Highpoint I, Arup joined J.L. Kier and Company, the structural contractors. The box structure they evolved together was elegant to inhabit, as well as mathematically elegant, having no clumsy framing to complicate the interior. The same period was enlivened by the spiral ramps of the Penguin Pool and overshadowed by a bitter fight with Finsbury Borough Council over air raid shelters.

From the increasingly restrictive field of contracting, Arup moved into consultancy and in 1949 set up Ove Arup and Partners, Consulting Engineers. Originally forty in London, plus five in Dublin to build Michael Scott's bus station, the firm now has nearly 2,000 in ten offices in the U.K. and 1,000 more in forty offices around the world.

Largeness is integral to the man—faintly Neanderthal in outline—his thinking, and activities, as it is to Philip Dowson of Arup Associates. Yet Arup well knows that architectural quality bears no relation to size, that the design process is essentially the same for a chess set as for an opera house. The Barbican project, the firm's largest, is a sizeable slice of the City of London; Sydney Opera House, their greatest challenge. Yet Arup has chosen to represent himself with the little footbridge over the Wear between Durham Cathedral and Dunelm House, a late building for The Architects Co-Partnership, one of his earliest clients. He was actively involved in the design of the footbridge, whereas his involvement in another felicitous work, the Maltings at Snape, was indirect. But nonetheless real. Its designers, Arup Associates—structural, electrical, and mechanical engineers, quantity surveyors, and architects—are the embodiment of Arup's belief that "when engineers and quantity surveyors discuss aesthetics and engineers study what cranes can do, we are on the right road."

Arup Associates, Architects and Engineers emerged as a separate entity from the consulting engineers in 1963. Arup's original partners in it were architect Philip Dowson and engineers Ron Hobbs and Derek Sugden, who led the Maltings team. Now there are six architect partners, three surveyors, and five engineers. They have made a telling contribution to university residences—at Somerville, Corpus Leckhampton, Trinity Hall, and St. John's, Oxford—using the structural frame to articulate the stack of small rooms. Loughborough was a new concept in university planning. The CEGB headquarters is an outstanding demonstration of how to articulate the living cells of a mammoth organization. The Festival Building at Liverpool merits its acclaim. Yet, I still think it is the firm's characteristic factory design, with the office block discretely slung within the industrial envelope, that best demonstrates the aesthetic gains that accrue from the full integration of the building professions.

—Diana Rowntree

ASHIHARA, Yoshinobu.

Japanese. Born in Tokyo, 7 July 1918. Educated at the University of Tokyo, 1940-42, B.Arch. 1942; Graduate School of Design, Harvard University, Cambridge, Massachusetts, 1952-53, M.Arch. 1953; doctorate conferred by the University of Tokyo, 1962. Served in the Japanese Army, 1942-45. Married Hatsuko Takahashi in 1944; children: Yukiko and Taro. Draftsman, Junzo Sakakura Architect and Associates, Tokyo, 1946-47, and Marcel Breuer Architect and Associates, New York, 1953-54. Since 1955, principal, Yoshinobu Ashihara Architect and Associates, Tokyo. Professor, Hosei University, Tokyo, 1959-64; Professor and Chairman, Musashino Fine Arts University, Tokyo, 1964-70; Professor, University of Tokyo, 1970-79. Director, 1959-61, and President, 1980-82, Japan Architects Association; Director, 1960-62, and Vice-President, 1976-78, Architectural Institute of Japan. Recipient: Award, 1960, and Special Award, 1965, Architectural Institute of Japan; Minister of Education Award, 1968; NSID Golden Triangle Award, U.S.A., 1970; Japan National Art Academy Award, 1984. Order of Commendatore, Italy, 1970; Honorary Fellow, American Institute of Architects, 1979. Address: Yoshinobu Ashihara Architect and Associates, Sumitomo Seimei Building, 31-15 Sakuragaoka-cho, Shibuya-ku, Tokyo 150, Japan.

Works:

1956 Chuo Koron Building, Tokyo
1959 Hotel Nikko, for Japan Air Lines, Tokyo
Nikko Youth Hostel, Nikko, Japan
1960 Yokohama Municipal Hospital
1962 Takamatsu Red Cross Hospital, Takamatsu, Japan
Ofuna Botanical Garden, Kanagawa, Japan
Okayama Prefectural Children's Hall, Okayama, Japan
1963 Kagawa Prefectural Library, Takamatsu, Japan
Master plan for the International Conference Hall, Kyoto
1964 Komazawa Olympic Gymnasium and Control Tower, Tokyo
Kawasaki Nikko, for Japan Air Lines, Kawasaki, Japan
Musashino Fine Arts University, Tokyo
1966 Ibaragi Prefectural Cultural Centre, Mito, Japan
Sony Building, Tokyo
1967 Japanese Pavilion, *Expo '67,* Montreal
Kiyose Housing Community Center, Tokyo
Suginami Ward Welfare Hall, Tokyo
1969 Fuji Film Building, Tokyo
Institute for International Studies and Training, Shizuoka, Japan
Australian Pavilion, *Expo '70,* Osaka
New Zealand Pavilion, *Expo '70,* Osaka
Italian Pavilion, *Expo '70,* Osaka
1970 Iwanami Publishers' Building, Tokyo
Sekai Boeki Kaikan (restaurant), Tokyo
1971 Ibaragi Prefectural Welfare Hall, Mito, Japan
1972 Health Department Hospital, Ryukyu University, Okinawa
Shiseido Building, Tokyo
1973 Mobil Sekiyu Head Office, Tokyo
1974 KPI Town, Chiba, Japan
IBM Building, Osaka
1975 Australian Pavilion, *Ocean Expo '75,* Okinawa
Mobi Sekiyu Pegasus House, Shizuoka, Japan
1980 Dai-ichi Kangyo Bank Head Office, Tokyo
National Museum of Japanese History, Chiba, Japan
1981 First Church of Christ Scientist, Tokyo
Vice-President's Official Residence, The House of Representatives, Tokyo
Civic Hall, Kanazawa, Japan

Publications:

By ASHIHARA: books— translation of *Sun and Shadow* by Marcel Breuer, Tokyo 1957; *Exterior Space in Architecture: From the Building to the City,* Tokyo 1962; *Exterior Design in Architecture,* New York 1970; *Gaibu Kukan no Sekkei,* Tokyo 1975; *Aesthetics in Townscape (Machinamino Bigaku),* Tokyo 1979; articles— "An amoeba-like city without a center" in *The Japan Architect* (Tokyo), June 1983; "Shinkenchiku Residential Design Competition 1983" in *The Japan Architect* (Tokyo), February 1984.

On ASHIHARA: books— *New Japanese Architecture* by Udo Kultermann, London 1960; *New Directions in Japanese Architecture* by Robin Boyd, London and New York 1968; *Nuova architettura giapponese* by Egon Tempel, Milan 1969; *Contemporary Japanese Architecture,* edited by Paolo Riani, Florence 1969; articles— "Suginami Public Hall" in *Kenchiku Bunka* (Tokyo), January 1968; "Head office of the Fuji Photo Film Company" in *The Japan Architect* (Tokyo), November 1969; "Institute for International Studies and Training" in *The Japan Architect* (Tokyo), April 1970; "New Developments in Japanese Architecture" in *Architectural Record* (New York), September 1970; "Institut fur internationale Studies, Fujinomiya" in

Baumeister (Munich), February 1971; "Head office of the Shiseido and Hirano Building" in *The Japan Architect* (Tokyo), October 1972; "Osaka IBM Building" in *The Japan Architect* (Tokyo), January 1973; "Japanese wedding hall in the Suginami district of Tokyo" in *Art et Architecture* (Paris), January/March 1974; "IBM Japan, Osaka offices" in *The Japan Architect* (Tokyo), August 1975; "Pegasus House" in *The Japan Architect* (Tokyo), October 1976; "House with three courts in Yokohama" in *Baumeister* (Munich), July 1977; "Head office of the Dai'ichi Kangyo Bank" in *The Japan Architect* (Tokyo), June 1981; "What future for architecture?", special issue of *Casabella* (Milan), November/December 1981.

Bibliography: *Yoshinobu Ashihara: Japanese Architect* by James P. Noffsinger, Monticello, Illinois 1981.

My efforts have been directed to the creation of architectural space, human and functional. In earlier works, I concentrated on the creation of interior space but soon I became equally interested in exterior space. In working on buildings of larger scale in recent years, I have tried to solve the problem of how to integrate interior and exterior space to make an organic unity.

In order to make space with human quality, we must try to organically combine spaces of varied sizes in a building, instead of merely filling stories of equal height with necessary functions. The use of floors of split levels is one of the answers to the problem. I have adopted this method in the Chuo Koron Building (1956) as well as in the Hotel Nikko (1958), a private house in Tokyo, clubhouse, library, and the Musashino Fine Arts University (1964).

The idea of using split levels was further extended in the Sony Building in the Ginza (1966): I made the entire interior space continuous by placing 27 floors on successive different levels. In the design of the Japanese Pavilion for the 1967 World Exhibition in Montreal, I produced continuous space by employing the same concept.

With the increase in size and number of buildings in one architectural complex, I have come to be interested in the problem of how to treat space between buildings. It is natural for an architect to study the space occupied by a building he is designing, but he should also give a meaning to the negative space not occupied by the building. My study on "exterior space in architecture" has been put to practical use in the design of the Olympic Gymnasium and the Control Tower in Komazawa Park (1964) as well as in the design of the Musashino Fine Arts University.

Architecture is the art of creating a space. We must make efforts to create space of better quality with full utilization of modern technology. My future endeavors will continue to be directed to the organic unity of interior and exterior space.

—Yoshinobu Ashihara

Yoshinobu Ashihara's most successful early work was the Sony Building in Tokyo. A cubic spiral of skip floors, it develops a space continuity that works its way throughout the built fabric, eating up the normally static and intractable elements, generating a fabulous appetite for all things spatial by the time it reaches roof level. This helter-skelter of internal connections still has time to present itself succinctly to the street—"the twenty-seven floors on successive, different levels, form a three-dimensional promenade.

From early on in his career Ashihara has pursued solutions to the questons of continuity and flow between interior and exterior spaces, but until his work on the Komazawa Gymnasium for the 1964 Tokyo Olympics he had concentrated primarily on interior spatial composition. For Komazawa, as well as for the Musashino Fine Arts University in Tokyo

and the Ibaragi Prefectural Cultural Center, he was able to evolve a distinct hierarchy at face value and apply it literally: he still possessed the wit to invest his external plazas with a certain quality of enclosure, while his interiors, fed by the quasi-external corridors, had a touch of the exterior about them.

This architecture-of-betweens, composed of discreet volumes set in "proud loneliness" and interconnected by a series of corridor-like life lines, is of course typical of Japanese retrospective space. The principle of space order involved is *Fu-seki* (placement due to circumstance), and the method of spatial composing synthesis is a cluster system *(Chidoregake)*, alterating turns (*Ore-magari*), deflected lines (*Tawani*), and recessed niches (*Kubomi*). The marrying system whereby these elements are brought together and rendered feasible for sustaining the idiosyncratic patterns of everyday social life owes much to Kurokawa's "Media-Space" or " *En*-Space." This architecture-of-the-street—or pilgrimage-space—is necessary for the activation of the scattered entities and can be known by any of these names: free space, play-space, equilibrium-zone, grey-zone, feeling of common possession, expanse for shadows, or in-between-condition.

What we have in Ashihara's work is a programme for an architecture of threshold theatre.

—Chris Fawcett

ASLIN, Charles Herbert.

British. Born in Sheffield, Yorkshire, 15 December 1893. Educated at Sheffield Central School, and the University of Sheffield. Served in the Royal Artillery, on the Western Front, 1916-19. Married Ethel Fawcett Armitage in 1920; had one daughter. Worked in the City Architect's Office, Sheffield, 1919-22; Architect, Borough Engineer's Office, Rotherham, Yorkshire, 1922-26; Deputy County Architect, Hampshire, 1926-29; Borough Architect, Derby, 1929-45; County Architect, Hertfordshire, 1945 until his retirement, 1958. President, Nottinghamshire, Derby and Lincoln Society of Architects, 1941-43; President, Royal Institute of British Architects, 1954-56. Recipient: Bronze Medal, Royal Institute of British Architects, 1957. Fellow, Royal Institute of British Architects; Associate, Institute of Civil Engineers, and Institute of Structural Engineers. Honorary Fellow, American Institute of Architects. *Died* (in Hertford) *18 April 1959.*

Works

1929/
45 New Exeter Bridge, Police Headquarters, Bus Station, Open Market, River Gardens, Exeter House, Central Improvement Scheme, Schools, Hospitals, etc.—all Derby
1946 Cheshunt Primary School, Cheshunt, Hertfordshire
1947 Junior Mixed School, Essendon, Hertfordshire
Wilbury Junior Mixed School, Letchworth, Hertfordshire
Strathmore Avenue Infants School, Hitchin, Hertfordshire
Belswains Junior Mixed School, Hemel Hempstead, Hertfordshire
Little Green Lanes Junior School, Croxley Green, Hertfordshire
Malvern Way Infants School, Croxley Green, Hertfordshire
Warren Dell Infants School, Watford, Hertfordshire
Highwood Junior Mixed School, Bushey, Hertfordshire

1948/
49 Spencer Junior School, St. Albans, Hertfordshire
Morgan's Walk Junior Mixed School, Hertfordshire
Monkfrith Infants School, East Barnet, Hertfordshire
Cowley Hill Junior School, Borehamwood, Hertfordshire
Leavesden Green Junior School, Watford, Hertfordshire
St. Mary's Infants School, Ware, Hertfordshire
Templewood Junior Mixed School, Welwyn Garden City, Hertfordshire
Highover Junior Mixed School, Hitchin, Hertfordshire
Batford Junior Mixed School, Harpenden, Hertfordshire
Gascoyne Cecil Junior Mixed School, Hatfield, Hertfordshire
Aboyne Lodge Infants School, St. Albans, Hertfordshire
Oxhey Wood Junior School, Oxhey, Watford, Hertfordshire
Casslobury Junior Mixed School, Watford, Hertfordshire
Maylands Junior School, Hemel Hempstead, Hertfordshire
Maylands Infants School, Hemel Hempstead, Hertfordshire
Whitings Hill Junior Mixed School, Barnet, Hertfordshire
South Hill Junior Mixed School, Hemel Hempstead, Hertfordshire
Mandeville Junior School, St. Albans, Hertfordshire
Fairlands Junior Mixed School, Stevenage, Hertfordshire
St. Meryl Junior Mixed School, Watford, Hertfordshire
1950 Oaklands Infants School, East Barnet, Hertfordshire
St. Mary's Infants School, Baldock, Hertfordshire
Blackthorn Junior School, Welwyn Garden City, Hertfordshire
Grange Junior Mixed School, Letchworth, Hertfordshire
Brookmans Park Junior Mixed School, Hatfield, Hertfordshire
Hazelwood Infants School, Abbots Langley, Hertfordshire
Little Furze Junior School, Oxhey, Watford, Hertfordshire
Little Furze Infants School, Oxhey, Watford, Hertfordshire
Bowmans Green Junior Mixed School, London Colney, Hertfordshire
Mill End Junior School, Rickmansworth, Hertfordshire
Stanstead Road Secondary Modern School, Hoddesdon, Hertfordshire
St. Julians Secondary Modern School, St. Albans, Hertfordshire
Adeyfield Secondary Modern School, Hemel Hempstead, Hertfordshire
Sandridgebury Lane Grammar School, St. Albans, Hertfordshire
Howard Secondary Modern School, Welwyn Garden City, Hertfordshire
1951 Greenfields Junior Mixed School, Oxhey, Watford, Hertfordshire
Kenilworth Drive Junior Mixed School, Borehamwood, Hertfordshire
Broom Barns Infants School, Stevenage, Hertfordshire
Cranborne Infants School, Hatfield, Hertfordshire
Brookfield Junior School, Borehamwood, Hertfordshire
Merydene Infants School, Borehamwood, Hertfordshire

Scots Hill Grammar School, Rickmansworth, Hertfordshire

1952 Lea Farm Junior School, Garston, Watford, Hertfordshire

Park Lane Junior Mixed School, Waltham Cross, Hertfordshire

Icknield Infants School, Letchworth, Hertfordshire

Havers Lane Junior Mixed School, Bishops Stortford, Hertfordshire

Livingstone Junior Mixed School, East Barnet, Hertfordshire

Hobbs Hill Junior School, Hemel Hempstead, Hertfordshire

Hobbs Hill Infants School, Hemel Hempstead, Hertfordshire

Saffron Green Junior Mixed School, Borehamwood, Hertfordshire

Site 7 Junior School, Oxhey, Watford, Hertfordshire

Barnet Lane Secondary Modern School, Barnet, Hertfordshire

Old Hale Way Secondary Modern School, Hitchin, Hertfordshire

1953/
58 Site 7 Infants School, Oxhey, Watford, Hertfordshire

New Green Farm Junior Mixed School, St. Albans, Hertfordshire

Bennetts End Junior Mixed School, Hemel Hempstead, Hertfordshire

Chaulden Junior School, Hemel Hempstead, Hertfordshire

Chaulden Infants School, Hemel Hempstead, Hertfordshire

Hillside Junior School, Abbots Langley, Hertfordshire

Bedwell East Junior School, Stevenage, Hertfordshire

Bedwell East Infants School, Stevenage, Hertfordshire

Broom Barns Junior School, Stevenage, Hertfordshire

Cowley Hill Infants School, Borehamwood, Hertfordshire

Blackthorn Infants School, Welwyn Garden City, Hertfordshire

West Shephall Secondary Modern School, Stevenage, Hertfordshire

Bennetts End Secondary Modern School, Hemel Hempstead, Hertfordshire

Bennetts End Grammar School, Hemel Hempstead, Hertfordshire

Leggatts Farm Secondary Modern School, Borehamwood, Hertfordshire

Potters Lane Grammar School, Borehamwood, Hertfordshire

Publications

By ASLIN: article—"Specialized Developments in School Construction" in *RIBA Journal* (London), no. 1. 1950.

On ASLIN: articles—"Charles Herbert Aslin" in *RIBA Journal* (London), May 1952; "Hertfordshire School Development" by K. C. Twist, J. T. Redpath and K. C. Evans, in *The Architects' Journal* (London), 12 May 1955, 26 May 1955, 11 August 1955, 19 April 1956, 2 August 1956; "Obituary: Mr. C. H. Aslin – prefabricated building" in *The Times* (London), 20 April 1959; "Obituary: Charles Herbert Aslin" in *RIBA Journal* (London), June 1959.

Charles Herbert Aslin is best known for his Hertfordshire School programme for building 175 schools in 15 years, which has become a well-known case study in the history of prefabrication. After previously working in various local government offices such as Derby, where he had been since 1929,

Aslin became County Architect for Hertfordshire in 1945. This was a crucial moment, because of the destruction caused by bombing in London and the Greater London Plan's overspill policy for the creation of four new towns: the Hertfordshire architect was faced with the challenge of providing enough school places for a deluge-rate of growth. Not only was there an acute shortage of school places, but this was also unfortunately accompanied by an acute shortage of manpower, particularly craftsmen in the building industry. Since there was also a shortage of traditional building materials such as timber and bricks, there was clearly a need for some "non-traditional" system of building. Aslin faced the challenge by using prefabrication—specifically by developing a component method for prefabrication (as distinct from the alternative total unit prefabrication method) of standardized factory-made units capable of simple erection on the site by a small number of semi-skilled men. The idea that the building should mainly consist of factory-made units simply erected was the basis of the whole development, and it took advantage of the production potential of light industry that had built up during the war.

Most of the schools were built in the constructional system that became known as the "Eight-foot three System"—a light frame with precast concrete walling and roofing units on an 8 foot 3 inch grid—of which the prototype was the Cheshunt Primary School, built in 1946. In the following years the annual plans demanded the building of an increasing number of schools. The great advantage of standardizing the component parts, rather than standardizing bay units as most manufacturers of the time had been doing, was that the component method gives much greater flexibility. As Aslin himself wrote, "If you design a whole room, all you can do with it is to stick a series on one end or the other and get something like a train; it only works on the flat. If, however you go in for small components, you have enormous flexibility, both horizontally and vertically, and can do anything you like." At Cheshunt the 8ft 3 inch grid was used with the concrete slabs horizontal externally, but after a short time the slabs were used vertically instead, since with 8 foot 3 inch slabs horizontally the only possible aperture in a bay was one of 8 foot 3 inch width, whereas with vertical slabs the opening could be any multiple of the width of the slabs. The 8 foot 3 inch grid was successfully applied to multi-storey buildings, and later other grid modules were also used. The flexibility was such that, with the subsequent improvement in the supply of building materials, such materials as timber could also be incorporated in the development.

The development work was of course not confined to the structure itself, but also covered the services, fittings and equipment of the schools, and Aslin also extended his ideas about prefabrication to such elements as heating and lighting. He also pioneered the use of bold, clear colours in schools.

—Konstantin Bazarov

ASPLUND, (Erik) Gunnar.

Swedish. Born in Stockholm, 22 September 1885. Educated at the Royal Institute of Technology, Stockholm, 1905-09; awarded Royal Institute of Technology Travel Scholarship, 1910: travelled in Germany; studied at the independent Klara School of Architecture, Stockholm, with Bergsten, Tengbom, Westman and Östberg, 1910-11. Married Gerda Sellman in 1918 (separated, 1934); Ingrid Katarina Kling in 1934. In private practice, Stockholm, 1911 until his death in 1940. Assistant Lecturer, 1912-13, Special Instructor in Ornamental Art, 1917-18, and Professor of Architecture, 1931-40, Royal Institute of Technology, Stockholm.

Editor, *Arkitektur,* Stockholm, 1917-20. Exhibitions: *The Architecture of Gunnar Asplund,* Museum of Modern Art, New York, 1978; drawings, Max Protetch Gallery, New York, 1984. Recipient: First Prize, Karlshamn (Sweden) Secondary School Competition, 1912; First Prize, Göteborg (Sweden) Law Courts Competition, 1913; First Prize, with Sigurd Lewerentz, Stockholm South Cemetery Competition, 1914; First Prize, Gustaf Adolf Square Competition, Göteborg, Sweden, 1918; First Prize, Kviberg Cemetery Competition, Göteborg, Sweden, 1926; First Prize, Kviberg Crematorium Competition, Göteborg, Sweden, 1936; First Prize, Stockholm Social Welfare Office Competition, 1938; First Prize, Stockholm City Archives Competition, 1939. *Died* (in Stockholm) *20 October 1940.*

Works:

1909 Elementary school, Hälsingborg, Sweden (competition project)
Swedish Church, Paris (competition project)

1912 Elementary school, Kalmar, Sweden (competition project)
Rosenberg Villa, Karlshamn, Sweden (project)
Timmermansorden (Order of Carpenters) Building, Stockholm (competition project; with Berven)

1912/
18 Secondary school, Karlshamn, Sweden

1913 Law Courts rebuilding and extension, Göteborg, Sweden (competition project)
Mixed school, Hedemora, Sweden (Competition project)
Selander Villa, Örnsköldsvik, Sweden
Sturegarden, Nyköping, Sweden

1914 Dr. Ruth's Villa, Kuusankoski, Finland
Stockholm South Cemetery (competition project; with Sigurd Lewerentz)

1915 Entrance buildings, Hammarby Sports Ground, Stockholm

1915/
24 Carl Johan Elementary School, Göteborg, Sweden

1916 Steel Rope Factory Housing, Ekaterinoslav, Russia
Law Courts rebuilding and extension, Göteborg, Sweden (2nd project)

1917 Workers' housing, Stockholm
Götatsplatsen Square, Göteborg, Sweden (competition project)
Interiors, *Home Exhibition of the Swedish Society of Arts and Crafts,* Stockholm

1917/
18 Snellman Villa, Djursholm, near Stockholm
Tisenhult Manor restoration, near Katrineholm, Sweden

1917/
21 Lister County Court, Sölvesborg, Sweden
Workers' housing, Tidaholms bruk, Sweden
Brokind Manor extension and restoration, Ostergotland, Sweden (project)
Gustaf Adolf Square redevelopment, Göteborg, Sweden (competition project)
Cemetery, Vasterås, Sweden (project)

1918/
20 Woodland Chapel, Stockholm South Cemetery

1919 St. Eriksplan Railway Goods Station, Stockholm (project; with Ture Tideblad)

1919/
20 Law Courts and Stock Exchange reconstruction, Gustaf Adolf Square, Göteborg, Sweden (project)

1920 Interiors, *Workshops Society Exhibition,* Stockholm

1920/
28 City Library, Stockholm

1921 Cemetery extension, Almunge, Sweden
Helgeandsholmen, Stockholm (competition project)

Prince Oscar Bernadotte's Family Vault, North Cemetery, Stockholm

1922 Bridge and road approaches, Klevaliden, Sweden

Royal Chancellery Buildings, Stockholm (competition project; with Ture Ryberg)

1922/
23 Skandia Cinema, Stockholm

1922/
24 Offices, South Cemetery, Stockholm

Pavilion, *Paris Exposition* of 1925 (competition project)

1924/
25 Admiral Sten Ankarcrona's Family Vault, North Cemetery, Stockholm

Assembly Hall interiors, Restaurant Gillet, Stockholm

1924/
29 Cemetery, Oxelösund, Sweden

1925 Law Courts reconstruction and extension, Göteborg, Sweden (3rd project)

Sculpture, City Library Park, Stockholm (competition project; with Ivar Johnsson)

Kviberg Cemetery, Göteborg, Sweden (competition project)

Odenhallen Market Hall, Stockholm (project)

1926/
28 Rettig Family Vault, North Cemetery, Stockholm

1927/
35 Park development plan for the City Library, Stockholm

1928 Arvfursten Palace reconstruction and extension, Stockholm (project)

1928/
30 *Stockholm Exhibition*

1929/
36 Secondary school extension, Karlshamn, Sweden

1931 Swedish Society of Arts and Crafts Building renovation, Nybrogatan 7, Stockholm

1932 Stockholm Breweries Apartment Building, Norr Mälarstrand, Stockholm (competition project)

Kviberg Cemetery Chapel, Göteborg, Sweden (competition project)

Malmö Museum, Sweden (competition project)

1933 Gustaf Carlström Houseboat (project)

National Museum interiors, Stockholm (project)

1933/
35 Bredenberg Department Store, Stockholm

1933/
37 State Laboratory for Biological Research, Stockholm

1934 Bromma Airport, Stockholm (project)

B. Beckstrom summer residence, Stavsnas, Sweden

1934/
37 Law Courts reconstruction and extension, Göteborg, Sweden

1935 Stockholm Tower, Skansen, Stockholm (project)

1935/
37 Chapel, Oxelösund, Sweden

1935/
40 Woodland Crematorium, South Cemetery, Stockholm

1936 Students Corps Building, Uppsala (project)

1936/
40 Kviberg Cemetery Crematorium, Göteborg, Sweden

Stennäs House (Asplund House), Sorunda Parish, Stockholm

Stockholm Tower and Square, Maritime Museum, Stockholm (project)

1937/
40 Skövde Crematorium, Sweden (not completed)

State Veterinary Bacteriological Laboratory, Stockholm (not completed)

1938/
39 Social Welfare Offices, Stockholm (competition project)

1939 Apartment block, Malmskillnadsgatan, Stockholm (project)

1939/
40 City Archives, Stockholm (not completed)

Publications:

By ASPLUND: articles—writings in *Arkitektur* (Stockholm), 1917-20, and *Byggmästaren* (Stockholm), 1920-40; "The City of Gothenburg" in *Byggmästaren* (Stockholm), no. 10, 1939; "The Cemetery of Stockholm" in *Byggmästaren* (Stockholm), no. 19, 1940.

On ASPLUND: books—*Swedish Architecture of the Twentieth Century* by Hakon Ahlberg, London 1925; *Verso un'architettura organica* by Bruno Zevi, Milan 1945; *E. Gunnar Asplund* by Bruno Zevi, Milan 1948; *Gunnar Asplund, Architect, 1885-1940*, edited by

Gunnar Asplund: Woodland Crematorium, Stockholm, 1940.

Gustav Holmdahl, Sven Ivar Lind and Kjell Odeen, Stockholm 1950; *Gunnar Asplund: A Great Modern Architect* by Eric de Maré, London 1955; *Gunnar Asplund*, dissertation by D. M. Spark, University of Newcastle 1959; *The Architecture of Erik Gunnar Asplund* by Stuart Wrede, London and Cambridge, Massachusetts 1980; *GA 62: Woodland Crematorium, Stockholm, 1935-40, Woodland Chapel, 1918-20, Stockholm Public Library, 1920-28*, edited by Yukio Futagawa, Tokyo 1982; articles—"Sweden's First Functionalist" by Bruno Zevi in *Architectural Record* (New York), April 1938; "The Crematorium in Stockholm" by Hakon Ahlberg in *Byggmästaren* (Stockholm), no. 19, 1940; "E. Gunnar Asplund: A Tribute" by P. Morton Shand in *Architectural Review* (London), May 1941; "L'Ultima opera di Asplund" by Attilio Podesta in *Casabella* (Milan), September 1941; "The Work of E. G. Asplund" by Francesco Fariello in *L'Architettura* (Rome), October 1942; "Asplund: Form and Metaphor" by Stuart Wrede in *Progressive Architecture* (New York), February 1980; "Stuart Wrede, Hakon Ahlberg and the Architecture of Gunnar Asplund" by Simo Paavilainen in *Arkkitehti* (Helsinki), no. 5, 1981; "The First Discovery of Asplund" by Francisco Mitjans Miro and Miguel Fisac in *Quaderns* (Barcelona), October 1981; "The Dwelling of Man beneath the Stars" by Luis Bravo in *2C Construccion de la Ciudad* (Barcelona), November 1981; "Erik Gunnar Asplund, September 22, 1885—October 20, 1940,"special issue of *Space Design* (Tokyo), October 1982.

Bibliography—*Erik Gunnar Asplund and the Development of Swedish Architecture* by Robert B. Harmon, Monticello, Illinois 1980.

Gunnar Asplund was Sweden's most important architect between the wars. He was not a great innovator, as were Le Corbusier, Gropius and Wright, but he was a great artist, and though by nature no doctrinaire teacher, he was a leading light in a generation of pre-war Swedish designers including Östberg, Tengbom, Eriksson, Hedqvist, Ahren, and Markelius, whose work brought worldwide respect. He is recalled by those who knew him as a man of great kindliness, warmth, and, in spite of his fame, surprising modesty. His early work belongs to that brilliant period of neo-classical romance called Swedish Grace—a term the functional puritans were to dub Pseudish Grace. Later, he was converted to the Modern Movement of the 1930s.

Born and bred in Stockholm, he was trained at the city's Technical High School and Academy of Art. After graduating in 1909, he entered a number of competitions, particularly for schools, in which he won two first prizes. His first major design was the extension to the Göteborg Law Courts, for which he gained first prize in a 1913 competition. This started a controversy that lasted twenty years, and his final design, a complete departure from the original, was not executed until 1937.

At the close of 1913, Asplund set off, with funds he had earned, on a Grand Tour of Europe. On his return the following year, he won, in partnership with his friend Sigurd Lewerentz, an important international competition for the layout of Stockholm South Cemetery with a design that sensitively exploited the Scandinavian pinewoods of the site. It was here that Asplund's greatest work, the Woodland Crematorium, was to be completed in 1940.

A number of commissions for other cemeteries, for private houses, and for small, provincial jobs followed. He also edited *Arkitektur* for a while. During the First World War, he won second prize for Göteborg's Carl Johan School, which was later commissioned, and he designed dwellings for the Russian Steel Rope Factory at Ekaterinoslav, some workers' emergency dwellings in Stockholm, and the charming, if stylized, Snellman Villa at Djursholm, near Stockholm. After the war, he won another first

in a competition for the layout of Gustaf Adolf Square in Göteborg, and at this time his enchanting little Woodland Chapel in the South Cemetery was built with its high-pitched roof and internal dome supported by Doric columns. A work of 1923 was the romantic and colourful fantasy of the Skandia Cinema in Stockholm, the overtones here being Pompeian pastiche. He then conceived his famous Stockholm City Library with a great central cylinder—a symmetrical, transitional design of geometrical modernity with eclectic detailing, in curious contrast with Östberg's City Hall, at last finished, after fourteen years' effort, the previous year, the swan song of Europe's Arts and Crafts Movement.

While the Library was nearing competition, the *Stockholm Exhibition* was being planned. In 1930 it burst upon an astonished public, trumpeting the new age of *Funkis*—of machine aesthetic and social realism. Le Corbusier had not shouted his staccato aphorisms in vain. Here, Asplund boldly but gracefully embraced the new creed. Though it had but a may-fly life, the exhibition was the herald of a revolution in Scandinavian architecture. It was not large, and it concentrated on housing and domestic artifacts, its first aim being to improve public taste in the design of everyday things made in factories.

Asplund's style had undergone a radical change, but he was too great a creative individualist to become firmly bound by the joyless rigidity of the new movement. His first important job after the exhibition was Stockholm's Bredenberg Department Store, which is uncompromisingly "modern" in its glass walls and engineered framework, though the detailing is as meticulous and elegant as ever. This was followed between 1935 and 1937 by the austere State Laboratory for Bacteriological Research in Stockholm and the Kviberg Cemetery Crematorium in Göteborg. A year later, he built for himself and his family a small and endearing summer residence in the Stockholm archipelago; it reveals his usual concern with marrying a building to its site. He then won two more competitions, but he did not live to see them accomplished: the Stockholm Welfare Offices and the Stockholm City Archives building.

Asplund's final work is an architectural landmark of our century. It has absorbed the crude but cleansing puritanism of Functionalism but goes beyond it to prove that simplicity need not be boring; monumentality, be pompous; refinement, be weak; nor romance, be sentimental. "Biblical" is the word the architect himself found to describe it. This is his masterly, timeless Woodland Crematorium where buildings and landscape form a single, moving entity. It was completed the year he died in 1940. *Si monumentum requiris. . . .*

—Eric de Maré

ATELIER 5.
Partnership; established, Bern, Switzerland, 1955. Partners: Jacques Blumer, born 1937; Anatole du Fresne, born 1939; Ralph Gentner, born 1929; Christiane Heimgartner, born 1936; Rolf Hesterberg, born 1927; Hans Hostettler, born 1925; Pierluigi Lanini, born 1938; Alfredo Pini, born 1932; Denis Roy, born 1935; Bernard Stebler, born 1935; Fritz Thormann, born 1930; administration—Christian Flückiger, born 1929. Recipient: First Prize, Lima, Peru International Housing Development Competition, United Nations, 1969; Housing Design Award, Department of the Environment, London, 1971; First Prize, Swiss National Bank Competition, Bern, 1974; Paul Bonatz Prize, Stuttgart, 1975; First Prize, Kunstmuseum Competition, Bern, 1976; Design Award, 1977, and Hugo Häring Award, 1978, Bund Deutscher Architekten;

First Prize, School Competition, Bösingen, Switzerland, 1977; First Prize, Teachers' College Competition, Thun, Switzerland, 1977; First Prize, Aarematte Plan Competition, Kirchlindach, Switzerland, 1981; First Prize, Schwarzenburg Hospital Competition, Switzerland, 1981; First Prize, Wittigkofen Nursing Home Competition, Bern, 1983; First Prize, Brugg Old People's Home Competition, Switzerland, 1984. Address: Atelier 5, Architekten und Planer, Sandrainstrasse 3, 3007 Bern, Switzerland.

Works:

1957 Flamatt I Rowhouses, Flamatt, Switzerland
1958 House, Rothrist, Switzerland (additions in 1964)
1959 House, Motier, Switzerland (additions in 1968)
    Apartment house, Seftigenstrasse, Bern
    Muller Factory, Thun, Switzerland
1960 Flamatt II Rowhouses, Flamatt, Switzerland
    Weekend house, Zofingen, Switzerland
    Apartment house, Weissenbuhlweg, Bern
1961 Taillepied Neighborhood Development Plan, Lutry, Switzerland (project)
    Halen Housing Estate, near Bern
    Two-family house, Bolligen, Switzerland
    Gfeller Company Factory, Flamatt, Switzerland
1962 House, Villars-sur-Glane, Switzerland
    Werkhof Burren Storage Building, Flamatt, Switzerland
1962/
76 Keller House alterations, Montet, Switzerland
1963 Apartment house, Biel, Switzerland
    Apartment house, Flamatt, Switzerland
    Radio Monitoring Station, Bern
    Belmont Museum, Lausanne, Switzerland (project)
    Migros Shopping Center, Roggwil, Switzerland
1964 Local plan for Bösingen, Switzerland
    Miroir New Town, Lutry, Switzerland (project)
    La Combe Neighborhood Development Plan, Lutry, Switzerland
    House, Carona, Switzerland
    Engineering School, Biberach, West Germany (competition project)
1965 Urban design for the Ruhwald District of Berlin (competition project)
    Rowhouses, Park Hill Village, Croydon, Surrey
    House, Gerlafingen, Switzerland
    Apartment house, Rodtmattstrasse, Bern
    Apartment house, Urtenen, Switzerland
1966 Town expansion plan for Karlstadt, West Germany (competition project)
    Town expansion plan, stage I, Steinhagen, West Germany
    District plan, stage I, for Werther, West Germany
    Neighborhood development plan for Bad Godesberg, Bonn (project)
    Two-family house with veterinary office, Kerzers, Switzerland
    Apartment building, Morillonstrasse, Bern
    Open space study for a cemetery at Lutry, Switzerland
1968 Local plan for Lutry, Switzerland
    Local plan for Zollikofen, Bern (competition project)
    Weekend house, Sardinia, Italy
    House, Boll-Sinneringen, Switzerland
    Apartment building, Lyss, Switzerland
1969 Local plans for Aarberg and Tafers, Switzerland
    Previ-Lima Housing Estate, Peru (competition project)
    Expansion plan for Solingen, West Germany (project)

National Building Code Study, Zürich
House with graphic arts studio, Oberhöchstadt, Frankfurt (additions in 1973)
1970 Regional plan for Burgdorf, Switzerland
Local plans for Bellmund, Bödeli, Interlaken and Neuenegg, Switzerland
Local plan for regional center, Lyss, Switzerland
Park Hill Village Neighborhood Development Plan, stage I, Croydon, Surrey
Brunnadern Apartments, Bern
Rainpark Rowhouses and Apartments, Brugg, Switzerland
Apartment building, Burgdorf, Switzerland
Highway retaining wall improvement, Flamatt, Switzerland
1971 Local plans for Flamatt, Frutigen, Ipsach, Plasselb, Port, and Reichenbach, Switzerland
School Design Competition Plan, Neuenegg, Switzerland
1972 Local plan for Sutz-Lattrigen, Switzerland
City center redevelopment, Solingen, Ohligs, West Germany (competition project)
Student housing, University of Stuttgart
Rowhouses, Regerstrasse, Solingen, West Germany
House, Bumpliz, West Germany
Meeting house, Charmey, Switzerland
Catholic church, Flamatt, Switzerland
Colora Printing Dyes Factory, Flamatt, Switzerland
1973 Economic development plan for Oberes Emmental, Switzerland (with the University of Bern Economic Study Group)
Local plans for Bühl, Kleinbösingen, Nidau, and Tauffelen, Switzerland
Neighborhood development plans for Radevormwald Dahlerau, West Germany, and Burgerbeunden Nidau and Risgrund Flamatt, Switzerland
Environmental study, Biel-Löhre, Switzerland
Buhnenberg Housing Estate, Oftringen, Switzerland (project)
Schroderweg Housing Estate, Dahlerau, West Germany (project)
Apartment building, Adelboden, Switzerland
Planning study, Bözingefeld, Switzerland
Local plan review, Ried Köniz, Bern
1974 Local plans for Albligen, Interlaken, Matten, Unterseen, and Sonceboz, Switzerland
Village center plans for Flamatt, Oftringen, and Thörishaus, Switzerland
Neighborhood development plan for Gwanne Reichenbach, Switzerland
Thalmatt Housing Estate, Bern
Galerie Bischofberger, Zürich
Gewerbehaus Thalmatt Office Building, Thalmatt, Switzerland (project)
1974/
75 Flückiger House annex, Zollikofen, Switzerland
1975 Economic development plan for Kandertal, Switzerland
Local plans for Alterswil, Barbereche, and Hochstetten, Switzerland
Village master plan for Lyss, Switzerland
Harbor neighborhood development plan, Seebucht Spiez, Switzerland
Building code regulations, State of Freiburg, Switzerland (as associates)
Fontana House, Bruzzella, Switzerland (project)
Railroad Workers' Housing extensions, Erstfeld, Switzerland (project)
Apartment building, Sandrainstrasse, Bern
1976 Economic development plan for Trachselwald, Switzerland
Local plan for Tramelan, Switzerland (project)
Village center master plan for Bösingen, Switzerland

Community development plan for Bernfeld Aarberg, Switzerland
Design for the Bern Festival
Lorraine Housing Estate, Burgdorf, Switzerland
Orangery Stadtgärtnerei Building alterations and restoration, Bern
Student Center and Dining Hall, University of Stuttgart
1976/
83 Art Museum reconstruction and additions, Bern
1977 Economic development plan for Center-Jura, Switzerland (with the Neuchâtel University Economic Studies Group)
Neighborhood development master plan for Scheuerfeld Tauffelen, Switzerland
Plan for a vacation community, Udrischa Ettenberg, Switzerland (project)
Staatsbank Headquarters Building, State of Freiburg, Switzerland (competition project)
School, Bösingen, Switzerland (competition project)
Meyer House, Lausanne, Switzerland (project)
Thormann House alterations, Halen, Switzerland
1977/
78 Gfeller-Corthésy House alterations, Mühlethurnen, Switzerland
Halter House alterations, Reistel, Switzerland
1977/
79 Frey and Barandun Houses, Bremgarten, Switzerland
1977/
85 Teachers' College extensions, Bern
1978 Commercial School alterations and renovation, Bern
Hohscheiderhof Urban Plan, Solingen, West Germany (project)
Piotr Kowalski schulture realisation, Winterthur, Switzerland (project)
1978/
79 Centennial Exhibition Designs, Art Museum, Bern
1978/
80 Milliet House alterations, Biel, Switzerland
State Teachers' College extensions, Thun, Switzerland
1978/
81 Swiss National Bank Building, Offices and Shopping Centre (conversion of the Kaiser Complex), Bern
Amthaus Building alterations and additions, Bern
Savings and Loan Bank alterations, Bern
1979 Aarbergergasse/Neuengasse Urban Design Studies, Bern
Environmental Plan, Kandertal Region, Switzerland
1979/
80 Environmental Plan, Oberes Emmental, Switzerland
Tourist Development Plan, Oberes Emmental, Switzerland
1979/
81 Solar Cell Development for Baude et Cie, Geneva
Daylight Deflecting Systems, Munich and Innsbruck, Germany (with Christian Bartenbach)
1979/
82 Brönnimann House, Mühlethurnen, Switzerland
1980 Atelier Hofkunst, Missy, Switzerland (project)
Mediaeval Town Centre Plan, Nidau, Switzerland
1980/
83 Vaucher House, Shop and Offices, Niederwangen, Switzerland
1981 Aarematte Neighborhood Plan, Kirchlin-

dach, Switzerland (competition project)
Henke House alterations, Fraubrunnen, Switzerland
Lorraine District Trade Schools Master Plan, Bern (project)
University Institutes Master Plan, Neubrückstrasse, Bern (project)
1981/
82 Freeway Sound Absorbing System, Freiburg, Switzerland (project)
1981/
85 Housing Pattern Research Programme for the Alpine Tourist Regions, Switzerland
Housing, Community and Commercial Buildings, Thalmatt Estate II, Herrenschwanden, Switzerland
1981/
86 Schurlirain Neighborhood Plan, Ipsach, Switzerland
1981/
87 Hospital, Schwarzenburg, Switzerland
1982/
83 Pia House alterations, Bern
1982/
86 PTT Bollwerk Telecommunications Centre renovations and additions, Bern
1983 Meret Oppenheim Fountain, Bern (with Meret Oppenheim)
Gallery Lighting Design for Baron Thyssen-Bornemisza, Villa Favorita, Castagnola, Switzerland
Uhlmann Offices, Bern
Aquatics Centre, Biel, Switzerland (project)
1983/
84 Burgunder Restaurant, Bern
River Aare and Thunersee Lakeshore Plan, Unterseen, Switzerland (project)
1983/
86 Gumme Neighborhood Plan, Port, Switzerland
Kapellacker Neighborhood Plan, Ueberstorf, Switzerland
Mont-Soleil Neighborhood Plan, St. Imier, Switzerland
Ried Housing Development, Niederwangen, Switzerland
1983/
88 Apprentices' Training Workshops, Bern
1983/
89 Psychiatric Clinic and Market-Garden Complex, Münsingen, Switzerland
1983/
90 Wittigkofen Nursing Home, Bern
1984 Blumer House alterations, Thalmatt Estate I, Switzerland
Von Muhlenen House alterations, Thalmatt Estate I, Switzerland
New Housing and Community Development, Kölliken, Switzerland (project)
1984/
85 Main Street Area Design, Beatenberg, Switzerland (project)
Christen House alterations, Habstetten, Switzerland
1984/
86 Old People's Home, Brugg, Switzerland
Thirteen terrace houses, Flamatt 3 Development, Switzerland
Ten houses, Langern, Oftringen, Switzerland
Town Centre Plan, La Neuveville, Switzerland
Stauble House alterations, Thalmatt Estate I, Switzerland
Talman House alterations, Ueberstorf, Switzerland

Publications:

By ATELIER 5: books—*Architektur und Tageslicht*, Zürich 1984; *Siedlungen* by Anatole du Fresne, Zürich 1984.

Atelier 5: Vaucher multi-purpose building, Niederwangen, Berne, 1980-83.

On ATELIER 5: books—*The New Architecture in Europe* by G. Kidder Smith, London and New York 1961; *Industrial Buildings: an International Survey* by W. Henn, Munich 1962; *New Swiss Architecture* by A. Altherr, Lausanne, Switzerland 1964; *The New Brutalism* by Reyner Banham, Stuttgart, London and New York 1966; *New Directions in Swiss Architecture* by Jul Bachmann and Stanislaus von Moos, New York 1969; *Entwurf und Planung Studentenheime* by Hans Schmalscheidt, Munich 1973; *Differentiated Housing Estates* by G. Schwab, Stuttgart 1974; *Architektur in Deutschland* by H. and M. Bofinger, J. Paul and H. Klotz, Stuttgart 1979; *Architecture in the Seventies* by Udo Kultermann, London 1980; *Architecture 70/80 in Switzerland* by Werner Blaser, Basel 1982; *Für das Kunstwerk* by Rémy Zaugg, Zürich 1983; articles—in *Werk* (Zürich), November 1958, May 1962, January 1963, March 1972, and March 1975; *Architectural Design* (London), November 1959, September 1962, February 1963, April 1965, and April 1970; *Casabella* (Milan), no. 258, 1961; *L'Architecture d'aujourd'hui* (Paris), no. 103, 1962, no. 131, 1965, February/March 1968, and November/December 1973; *Deutsche Bauzeitung* (Stuttgart), January 1966; *Baumeister* (Munich), September 1966, February 1970, March 1972, April 1972, December 1972, December 1973, May 1976, and March 1978; *Architecture + Urbanism* (Tokyo), December 1971, October 1975, December 1977, and March 1978; *Global Architecture* (Tokyo), no. 23, 1973; "Atelier 5" by Marcin Przytubski in *Arkitektura* (Warsaw), March/April 1979; "Atelier 5" by Bernhard Hoesli and others in *Bauen und Wohnen* (Zürich), July/August 1980; "Lorraine Housing Complex in Burgdorf", in *Deutsche Bauzeitschrift* (Gütersloh, West Germany), September 1981; "Two renovations in Berne" in *Baumeister* (Munich), December 1981; "Rehabilitation and Extensions to the 'Amthaus' in Berne" in *Werk, Bauen und Wohnen* (Zürich), June 1982; "Amthaus and Siedlung Thalmatt I" in *Abitare* (Milan), August 1982; "Savings and Loan Bank in Berne" in *Deutsche Bauzeitschrift* (Gütersloh, West Germany), September 1982; "Kunstmuseum Bern" in *Baumeister* (Munich), March 1984.

In our office an architectural design is never made by one single person, not even in the very first stage. From the beginning, there are always at least two persons working together. In general, the architects in charge discuss the different aspects of the problem before they begin to make the first drafts for its solution. Of course, we make sketches to arrive at a mutual understanding (but these sketches are not really drafts); in doing so, we discuss various ways of tackling the problem. We look for the essential crux of the problem, the way to give the most extensive but also the most typical expression to the problem.

For example, the design of the Student Center for the University of Stuttgart took shape when we decided to tackle the problem of relating each single place or table to its surroundings. The narrow column-grid originated from this, and when we carried through this fundamental idea, the building took its shape. The fundamental principle for the building therefore originated from an extreme simplification of the whole problem and from concentrating on a central idea which a simple sketch could illustrate. This principle was the starting point for the consequent execution of a very complex building.

As we often have long discussions before making an actual design, we almost never have to devise alternatives; they are discussed as possibilities in advance. We elaborate real alternatives only in cases where the original conditions are changed by the actual work or where the problem or program must be determined by the work. This process is valuable in planning and town-planning, when the program becomes part of the design.

In the beginning of Atelier 5, the search for form had a greater importance than it does now; that is, our designs were more the result of formal considerations. Today, form grows as we interpret a basic idea. The design of the Student Center would probably not have been possible fifteen years ago because the problem of the unitary form of the building would have been too important to us. In those days, we would have used more "traditional" methods to try to realize the program with harmonic cubical forms. Today, the form occurs when we elaborate the fundamental idea. We rarely proceed from formal conceptions because our designs are always the result of teamwork and because the same people do not always work together. Goals of essential content can be discussed, but formal conceptions are very difficult to discuss.

We see ourselves as both theorists and practitioners. Our plans always originate from theories that arise from a large number of influences from different fields—but they are not treated in a scientific manner. We work, according to our talents and experience, on a very wide basis. We always try to realize any commission by considering all the problems from as many aspects as possible, but we don't attempt to follow, or create, some theoretical treatise. All the same, we appreciate the work of the theorist who perhaps extends the profession of the architect to the point where he cannot himself build any longer because his theories can only find their realization in Utopia; the theorist can create attitudes that are important in the actual design process. The practitioner can as well be justified in developing theories about building and planning that will become a basis for carrying out actual building. In this sense, it is, for us, not a solution to unify completely the profession of architect because in that way the activity that can be influenced by the architect is narrowed.

Nor do we believe that the profession of the architect should be organized like an industrial concern, that there should be a division of labor, for example between design and executive work. Our way of working attempts a continuity from planning up to supervision of the building site—not only continuity of thought but also continuity of persons. We think that the "idea" of a building cannot be preserved when it passes through different departments if it is not accompanied by the same one or two persons from the beginning to the end. The profession of the architect should not be limited; it should be organized on a very wide basis.

—Atelier 5

Atelier 5 says, "In the beginning of Atelier 5, the search for form had a greater importance than it does now; that is, our designs were more the result of formal considerations. Today, form grows as we interpret a basic idea." This statement is particularly informative, for it calls attention to an essential aspect of the change in the ideas of the architectural avant-garde during the last twenty years. Until then, "the new"—in accordance with the pioneer ideologies of the first two decades of this century—had, to a large extent, appeared as a visible interpretation of a "Manifesto for Modern Construction." In contrast, since the beginning of the 1970s, a more complete relationship with the environment has begun to prevail, and greater importance is now placed on problems of historic continuity and formal integration. I don't refer to a renaissance of the ideas of the 1940s about a "native style" (though a trend in this direction, with modern trimmings, is distinctly apparent in one of the newest Swiss housing estates); I mean, rather, that contemporary avant-garde architects, and an ever-increasing circle of progressive thinkers concerned with architecture, recognize and accept as pertinent problems, in new building, the maintenance of existing constructions and a more meaningful use of human living space as a means of an improvement in the quality of life. There has been such a development in Atelier 5's conception of building, a development that is clear if one compares an early work, the Halen Housing Estate of 1961, with the Bern Kaiser development of twenty years later.

Halen is one of the best-known, and, among experts, the most popular, of the new housing estates in Switzerland. There was hardly an architectural student in the 1960s who didn't attempt a "Halen Project." Similarly, there were architects who constantly produced "Halen Variations." Even now, the influence of Halen in Swiss architecture remains strong. Yet Halen can in no way be taken as a model for a contemporary housing estate. It was exceptional in practically every respect—from the point of view of the planning concept ("collective estates for individualists"); in relation to the uniform class of the inhabitants (almost without exception, independent professional intellectuals); and, with regard to the particularly favorable topographical situation of the building site (a clearing surrounded on all sides by dense forest, an ideal prerequisite for an unique, architectonically planned, collective total concept).

The most characteristic feature of the total concept of Halen is the estate plan itself, which is based on the traditional grid plan of the Old Town of Bern, thereby creating an extremely interesting historical building dialogue. Yet, in spite of this remarkable integration of a planning principle rooted in local tradition in a housing estate conceived for contemporary needs, Halen dominates as a deliberate manifesto for "the new architecture," the form language of Le Corbusier, the architect that Atelier 5 regarded as its true mentor.

Typically, the initial planning and erection of Halen did not allow for any subsequent extensions or additions. But it remains unique; the designers have succeeded in an outstanding way in building an estate that, with one exception, the restaurant/community area, is a perfectly functioning realization of the goal of "more collectivity in planning on behalf of the greater individual freedom of all."

The original Kaiser complex was built in 1903 in a central position in the Old Town of Bern. In 1974 an architectural competition was organized for the erection of the Swiss National Bank on the same site, without modification of the existing facades, and Atelier 5 won the competition.

A direct comparison of Atelier 5's Kaiser design with that of the Halen Estate makes little sense. Much more interesting are the principles which lie behind these two projects. Twenty-five years ago, Atelier 5, with the building of Halen, brilliantly achieved the realization of a manifesto; Le Corbusier's language of form was central to their design. But Halen stood partially "on the green meadow," and did not need to take into consideration neighboring buildings. Kaiser, however, is an old building; it has been integrated for many years with the buildings of the Old Town of Bern; it is to be developed as a combined business, shopping, and office centre—and such a project involves essentially different demands from those of Halen.

On the basis of the competition program, Atelier 5 came to the conclusion that "the client, presented with the program for the future use of space, did not believe that it could be achieved by renovation of the old building." It says much for Atelier 5 that, in spite of this attitude, they recommended renovation and substantiated their recommendation with skilful argument, with the result that they were awarded execution of the project. Only coming years will show whether it will one day stand as a recommendation for the meaningful preservation of existing buildings and have as lasting an influence on the future

architectural scene as Halen has had on the architecture of the modern estate.

—Urs Graf

ATHFIELD, Ian Charles.

New Zealander. Born in Christchurch, 15 July 1940. Educated at Christchurch Boys High School, 1954-58; Auckland University School of Architecture, under R. H. Toy, 1961-63, Dip.Arch. 1963. Married Nancy Clare Cookson in 1962; children: Jesse and Zachary. Architect, Stephenson and Turner, Auckland, 1963; Architect, 1963-65, and Partner, 1965-68, Structon Group Architects, Wellington. Since 1968, Principal, with Ian Dickson and Graeme J. Boucher, Athfield Architects, Wellington. Exhibitions: *5 New Zealand Architects,* Wellington, 1974; *International Union of Architects Exhibition,* Vancouver Art Gallery, 1976. Recipient: Design Award, Auckland Architectural Association, 1968, 1972, 1978, 1982; Silver Medal, 1972, Bronze Medal, 1975, Gold Medal, 1982, and Design Awards, 1982, 1984, New Zealand Institute of Architects; New Zealand Tourist and Publicity Design Award, 1975; First Prize, International Housing Design Competition, Manila, Philippines, 1976; Joint First Prize, Low Cost Housing Competition, Fiji, 1978; Environmental Award, New Zealand Chamber of Commerce, 1979; AAA Monier Design Award, 1983. Address: Athfield Architects, P. O. Box 3364, 105 Amritsar Street, Wellington 4, New Zealand.

Works:

1968 Imrie House, Whangarei, New Zealand
       Multi-unit housing, Majoribanks Street, Wellington
       Athfield House, Wellington
       Jones House, Christchurch
       Hall, Waikoiwaiti, Otago, New Zealand
1969 McIntyre House, Wellington
       Slim House, Wellington
       Porteous House, Wellington
       Jackson House, Wellington
       Plimmers Emporium Shopping Centre renovations, Wellington
1970 Nathan House, Wellington
       Manson House, Wellington
       Buck House, Wellington
       James House, Wellington
       Johnson House, Wellington
       Sampsan House, Wellington
       Church Hall, Dannevirke, New Zealand
1971 Elder House, Wellington
       Merwood House, Wellington
       Sindall House, Wellington
       Coca-Cola bottlers' plant and offices, Upper Hutt, New Zealand
1972 Davis Mission House, Coromandel, New Zealand
       Wakatipu Trading Post Shopping Mall, Queenstown, New Zealand
       Motel Units, Queenstown, New Zealand
       House restoration, 12 Boulcott Street, Wellington
       St. Columban's Mission House and Offices, Lower Hutt, New Zealand
       Recreational Centre, Victoria University, Wellington
1973 Monopoli House, Nelson, New Zealand
       Grand Hotel restoration, Palmerston North, New Zealand
       Cole House, Auckland
       Bailey House, Wellington
1974 Carruthers House, Wellington
       Logan House, Wellington
       Cates House, Auckland

McKenzie House, Wellington
       Sparkes House, Wellington
       King House, Wellington
       Zander House, Wellington
       Jamieson House, Wellington
       Army Workshops, Waiouru, New Zealand
       Arlington Apartments, Wellington
1974/
   79 City Council Housing Project, Lower Hutt, New Zealand
1975 Cox House, Wellington
       Kenerdine House, Havelock North, New Zealand
1976 24-unit Village, Hastings, New Zealand
1977 Hogg House, Wellington
       Marlborough Club, Blenheim, New Zealand
       Eureka House shopping centre, Queenstown, New Zealand
       Chief Post Office, Nelson, New Zealand (project drawings only)
1977/
   79 Marsden Village shopping centre, Karori, Wellington
1978 National Publicity Studios renovations, Wellington
       Taita R.S.A. Building, Hutt Valley, New Zealand
1979 Porirua R.S.A. Building extensions, New Zealand
       G.E.C. Factory extensions, Porirua, New Zealand
       George and Sons shopping complex, Wellington
       Crown Fletcher House office building, 158 The Terrace, Wellington
       Cable Car Terminals, Wellington
       Hall and Community Centre, Maungaraki, New Zealand
       Felvin Hardware Building, Kaiwharawhara, Wellington
1980 Greta Point Tavern renovations, Wellington
       Bank of New Zealand Building, Lilbirnie, Wellington
       A.M.P. Society office building, Bloomfield Terrace, Lower Hutt, New Zealand
       Agriculture House, Wellington
       Buck House, Havelock North, New Zealand
1981 Shamrock Hotel restoration and relocation, Wellington
       A.M.P. Society office building, 138 The Terrace, Wellington
       Master Builders Association office building, Willis Street, Wellington
       Radfield Hospital, Blenheim, New Zealand
       Wrightson N.M.A. Building, Tapanui, New Zealand
       Wrightson N.M.A. Building, Napier, New Zealand
       Wrightson N.M.A. Building, Timaru, New Zealand
       Wrightson N.M.A. Building, Kaiwharawhara, New Zealand
       B.P. Petrol Service Station, Mana, New Zealand
       Custance House, Havelock North, New Zealand
1982 Western Park Tavern renovations, Wellington
       Wrightson N.M.A. wool store offices, Invercargill, New Zealand
       Motor Hotel, Lower Hutt, New Zealand
       Central Church of Christ additions and alterations, Wellington
       First Church of Christ Scientist new building, Wellington
       De Bretts Hotel, Wellington
1983 Law Offices alterations, Blenheim, New Zealand
       Cricket Centre, Wellington
       Cotton Precinct Buildings, Victoria University, Wellington
       Moore Wilson Warehouse, Wellington
1983/
   85 Baycourt Shopping Complex, Wellington

Ian Athfield: Buck House, Havelock North, New Zealand, 1980.

Energy Board office building, Hutt Valley, New Zealand

Hewlett Packard Headquarters Offices, Wellington

Erskine College Redevelopment, Wellington

Skyline Restaurant, Wellington

1984 Rankine Brown Courtyard, Victoria University, Wellington

Visitor's Centre, Hauraki Gulf Maritime Park, North Head, New Zealand

1984/
85 Odlins Building alterations, Queen Elizabeth II Art Council, Wellington

Office and Showroom conversion, Thorndon Quay, Wellington

Administrative Staff College, Waikanae, New Zealand

Town Square Development, Queenstown, New Zealand

Restaurant and Art Gallery, Petone, New Zealand

Publications:

On ATHFIELD: books—*Architecture an Involvement*, Wellington 1963; *The Architecture of Self-Help Communities* by Michael Seelig, New York 1978; *Joyful Architecture – The Genius of New Zealand's Ian Athfield* by Gerald Melling, Dunedin 1980; articles—"Houses for People or People for Houses" in *New Zealand Listener* (Wellington), August 1971;

"Bird of Paradise" in *Designscape* (Wellington), October 1972; "Winds of Change" in *New Zealand Home Journal* (Auckland), December 1972; "A House You Can't Ignore" in *Thursday* (Auckland), September 1973; "Kiwi Concrete" in *Design* (London), December 1974; "Lots of Ups and Downs" by Nanette Cameron in *Thursday* (Auckland), December 1974; "Medieval Disney" in *Australian Post* (Sydney), February 1975; "Intuitions by Athfield" in *New Zealand Listener* (Wellington), April 1976; "Human Settlements" in *Architectural Record* (New York), May 1976; "New Zealand Architect Flouts the Rules" by Paul Goldberger in the *New York Times*, June 1976; "Prelude au Congrès de Vancouver" in *L'Architecture d'Aujourd'hui* (Paris), July 1976; "Athfield under Attack" by Boyce Richardson in *New Zealander Listener* (Wellington), July 1976; "Habitat" by Ian Hagan in *RIBA Journal* (London), August 1976; three articles in the *Christian Science Monitor* (Boston), 6, 13 and 23 August 1976; "Habitat—Self-Help Housing" in *Designscape* (Wellington), October 1976; "Urban Revival" in *New Zealand Listener* (Wellington), July 1977; "The Perfect Family Home" in *Australian Women's Day* (Sydney), August 1977; "Squatter Space" in *New Zealand Listener* (Wellington), October 1977; "The Shamrock Hotel" in *New Zealand Architect* (Auckland), no. 1, 1980; "The contemporary architectural debate of the eighties" by Russell Walden in *New Zealand Architect* (Auckland), no. 2, 1980; "The Wellington Cable Car" in *Home and Building* (Auckland), no. 6, 1980; "The rise of the personal in

New Zealand Architecture" by Russell Walden in *New Zealand Architect* (Auckland), no. 4, 1981; "National Award 1982: the Greta Point Tavern" in *New Zealand Architect* (Auckland), no. 3, 1982; "New Zealand Rebel" by Russell Walden in *Architectural Review* (London), May 1982; film—*Architect Athfield*, New Zealand National Film Unit, Wellington, 1977; *Wellington Architecture*, TV New Zealand, 1981.

*

Athfield Architects is a co-operative, design-based practice of five people. The practice, which I started in 1968, has a strong influence on the current New Zealand architectural scene, albeit mainly through small-scale domestic buildings. International recognition was gained by the office in 1976 by winning the International Competition for the Urban Environment of Development Countries, Manila, Philippines. Current interests are in community-involved building projects and knocking the bastions of architectural professionalism, the sanctity of design and town planning.

—Ian Athfield

*

Ian Athfield's work as an architect, brief as it has been to date, has called into question many of the assumptions of the Modern Movement and is contributing to the reappraisal of architecture in New Zealand. Athfield's buildings, among the steep hills of Wellington, have from their inception commanded attention and consideration. Their apparent strident, arbitrary and flamboyant forms belie the strong sense of order and integrity in the use of materials and also the intense radical concern for society that informs Athfield's thinking.

Athfield spent his early years in Christchurch, where he was fortunate to experience a wave of enthusiasm, care and concern for buildings that was characteristic of that city in the early 1960's. Later, as a student, Athfield moved to the Auckland University School of Architecture and the tutelage of Professor R. H. Toy and Lecturer Peter Middleton. It was here in the 1960's—during the usual iconoclastic activities of students and the plethora of visual opportunities—that Athfield became attracted to the authentic use of materials in the work of Antonio Gaudi and Mies van der Rohe. He was conscious of the relationship of their work to its setting and aware of the necessity of communities to have a building heritage. He quickly set about obtaining a thorough understanding of materials and basic building techniques.

The dichotomy of allowing for complete and freeranging change and the desire for permanence and stability of strucutre have produced in Athfield the flowering of a Renaissance. A fundamental part of his quest has been the need to produce a philosophical framework capable of absorbing the variety of architectural forms, while at the same time maintaining some reality in a radically changing society.

Athfield's strong social concern and his attempts to understand and design within communities have led him into some exciting and frustrating programmes both overseas and in New Zealand. Reactions to his work have been equivocal, and the conflict he has had with planning bureaucracies has caused him to fear that we could very easily destroy ourselves in the quest for learning to cope with our society and environment. In spite of many setbacks, he has remained firm in his convictions as to the value of good building to a community's life and health.

Ian Athfield's contribution to the health of architecture in New Zealand has been quite profound, and his work to date in the midst of the New Zealand landscape promises well for a significant radical architectural stake in the future.

—W. H. Alington

AULENTI, Gae(tana).
Italian. Born in Palazzolo dello Stella (Udine), 4 December 1927. Educated at the Milan Polytechnic School of Architecture, Dip.Arch. 1954. In private architectural practice, Milan, since 1954; also exhibition and industrial designer, since 1960: collaborated with Olivetti company from 1966, and with Fiat car firm from 1968; stage designer, in collaboration with Luca Ronconi, Laboratorio di Progettazione Teatrale, Prato, 1976-78. Assistant Professor of Architectural Composition, Faculty of Architecture, University of Venice, 1960-62; Adjunct Assistant Professor of the Elements of Architectural Composition, Faculty or Architecture, Milan Polytechnic, 1964. Visiting Lecturer, College of Architecture, Barcelona, and the Cultural Center, Stockholm, 1969-75. Member, Editorial Staff, *Casabella,* Milan, 1954-63. Member, Board of Directors, *Lotus,* Venice, since 1974. Member, Studies for Architecture Movement, Milan, 1955-61. Member, Association for Industrial Design, Milan, since 1960 (Vice-President, 1966); Joint Executive Member, *Triennale* exhibitions, Milan, since 1977. Exhibitions: Triennale, Milan, 1960, 1963; *Aspects of Contemporary Art,* Aquila, Italy, 1963; *Gae Aulenti,* Gimbels, New York, 1967; *Italian Design,* Hallmark Gallery, New York, 1968; *Italy: The New Domestic Landscape,* Museum of Modern Art, New York, 1972; *Knoll au Musée,* Musée des Arts Décoratifs, Paris, 1972; *28/78 Architettura,* Palazzo delle Stelline, Milan, 1979; *Gae Aulenti,* Padiglione d'Arte Contemporanea, Milan, 1979; *The European Iceberg,* Art Gallery of Ontario, Toronto, 1985. Recipient: Grand International Prize, *Triennale,* Milan, 1960-64; First Prize, with V. Magistretti, Meda Elementary School Competition, 1967; First Prize, Directional Center Competition, Perugia, 1971. Honorary Member, Italian National Society of Interior Designers, 1967, and American Society of Interior Designers, 1976. Address (office): 4 Piazza S. Marco, 20121 Milan, Italy.

Works:

1956   House and Stable, San Siro, Milan
1959   Single Family House, Brianza, Italy
1960   *New Design for Italian Furniture* exhibition layouts, Milan
        Casa exhibit at the *XII Triennale,* Milan
1962   Elementary School, Monza, Italy (competition project)
1963   Holiday House, Tonale Pass, Italy
        Historical City Centre Plan, Milan (project)
        Villa in the Woods (project)
        Tempo delle Vacanze Pavilion, *Triennale,* Milan
1965   Max Mara Offices, Milan
1966   Garden, *Triennale,* Milan
        Olivetti Shop, Paris
1967   Elementary School, Meda, Italy (competition project; with Vico Magistretti)
1968   Fiat exhibit, *Salone dell'Automobile,* Turin and Geneva
1968/
69   Apartment interiors, Milan
1969   Fiat exhibit, *Salone dell'Automobile,* Turin and Geneva
1969/
70   Fiat Showroom, Zurich
1970   *Olivetti: Concept and Form* exhibition layouts, Paris, Barcelona, Madrid, London, Edinburgh and Tokyo
        Fiat Showroom, Brussels
        Fiat Showroom, Turin
        Garden, Granaiolo, Florence
        Boutique Cadette, Milan
        Fiat exhibit, *Salone dell'Automobile,* Turin and Geneva
1970/
71   Rodin Pavilion, Lugano, Switzerland (project)
1970/
75   Hotel alterations and renovations, Trieste, Italy (partly completed)
1971   Villa, Capalbio, Italy (project)
        Knoll Showroom, Boston, Massachusetts
        Directional Centre, Perugia, Italy (competition project)
1972   Apartment interiors, Rome
        Chateau de la Croe renovations (project)
1973   Fiat Showroom II, Turin
        Christo exhibition layouts, Rotonda della Besana, Milan
        Housing Development, Cinisello Balsamo, near Milan (project)
        Housing Development, Rome (project)
        Single-Family House, Pisa, Italy
        Villa, Parma, Italy
1974   Villa, San Michele, Italy
        Villa, Formentor, Mallorca, Spain
1975   *Barber of Seville* stage designs, Theatre de l'Odeon, Paris
        Basilicia Gardens, Galliano, Italy (project)
        Old House conversion, Portofino, Italy
        Weekend House, Emilian Plain, Italy
1976   Fiat exhibit, *Salone dell'Automobile,* Turin
1977   *The Wild Duck* stage designs, Teatro di Genova, Genoa
        Wozzeck stage designs, Teatro alla Scala, Milan
1978   Fiat exhibit, *Salone dell'Automobile,* Turin

1980/
81   *Donnerstag aus Licht* stage designs, Teatro alla Scala, Milan
1982   Gare d'Orsay Station/Museum conversion, Paris

Publications:

By AULENTI: books—*Un Nuova Scuola di Base,* with others, Milan 1973; *Il Laboratorio di Prato,* with Franco Quadri and Luca Ronconi, Milan 1981; articles—"Soviet Architecture" in *Casabella* (Milan), April 1962; "Marin County" in *Casabella* (Milan), April 1964.

On AULENTI: books—*Design Italia '70* by Davide Mosconi, Milan 1970; *Progetto e Utopia* by Manfredo Tafuri, Bari 1970; *Design Process Olivetti 1908-1978* by Nathan H. Shapira, Los Angeles 1979; *Gae Aulenti,* exhibition catalogue by Vittorio Gregotti, Emilio Battisti and Franco Quadri, Milan 1979; *Interior Views* by Erica Brown, London 1980; *The European Iceberg,* exhibition catalogue edited by Germano Celant, Milan 1985; articles—"Olivetti à Paris" in *L'Oeil* (Lausanne), May 1967; "Un Ambiente di Apparenza Magica" in *Domus* (Milan), July 1967; "Per la Moda" in *Domus* (Milan), August 1968; "Dottore Architetto Gae Aulenti" by Federico Correa in *Cuadernos de Arquitectura* (Barcelona) no. 74, 1969; "Il Luogo di una Collezione" in *Domus* (Milan), January 1970; "Gae Aulenti: New Force in Italian Design" in *Vogue* (New York), July 1970; "Knoll, New York" in *Architectural Forum* (New York), July/August 1970; "Medium Cool Message" by Alastair Best in *Design* (London), October 1970; "Une Architecture Intérieure pour mettre en Valeur de Précieuses Collections" in *Maison Francaise* (Paris), November 1970; "Knoll International à Boston" in *L'Oeil* (Paris), September/October 1971; "Private House, Milan" in *Japan Interior Design* (Tokyo), July 1972; "Italy: The New Domestic Landscape" in *Architectural Design* (London), August 1972; "Eine Wohnung in Mailand" in *Architektur und Wohnen* (Hamburg), February 1973; "Analisi di un Ambiente" in *Casa Vogue* (Milan), March 1973; "Vue Imprenable sur Rome" in *Connaissance des Arts* (Paris), November 1973; "Hall d'Exposition Fiat à Bruxelles" and "Hall d'Exposition Fiat à Zurich" in *L'Architecture d'aujourd'hui* (Paris), September 1975; "A Weekend Retreat on the Emilian Plain" in *Architectural Digest* (Los Angeles), November/December 1975; "The Design of Gae Aulenti" by Gabriella Drudi in *Craft Horizons* (New York) February 1976; "Living Around the World: Cave of Enchantment in Italy" in *Ideal Home* (London), August 1976; "Gae Aulenti – architecture, scene and design" by Pier Carlo Santini in *Ottagono* (Milan) December 1977; "The conversion of the Gare d'Orsay" in *Architecture Interieure Crée* (Paris) July/August 1982.

Nothing is built on stone; all is built on sand, but we must build as if the sand were stone (Jorge Luis Borges).

This quote headed Gae Aulenti's text in the catalogue of the *New Domestic Landscape* exhibition held at the Museum of Modern Art, New York, in 1972, and it is as relevant to her work now—such as the Turin Showroom, Turin, 1973, and the Theatrical Space Project of 1975—as it was to the work presented at that exhibition—a "House Environment" comprising differently articulated pyramids set up at the four corners of a square plinth: this design is made up of elements so composed as always to make their original purpose evident, while at the same time remaining open to a determination of their future purposes.

Gae Aulenti views the condition of architecture as being beyond the strife of governments, war, and hunger. It is concrete space, a positive thing that has as its substance the city, in which the private and collective "join to transform nature through the exercise of reason and memory." None of man's objects, whether monument or den, can escape their relationship to the city, "the place where the human condition is manifested." The existence of an object is defined by the actual circumstance of its own relationship to the city: an object is allowed to come into being and discover its own relationship to other objects by a process not announced by its own independent voice but with that of the city too. The objects with which we deal are very numerous, ranging from the unstable and changeable to the archetype, from the precious relic to the casualty of history.

If these generalizations are true, then "the process of design can only find its proper relationship in a field of which it does not constitute the centre." Aulenti maintains that a domestic environment should not be designed in its general form, for its positive qualities can reside only in the sum of the conditions in accordance with which its spatial elements and attribution of meanings approach a synthesis, "which is possible only by using and testing all the criteria applied to designing a city." Her concern, then, is to make things appear in all their complexity and density, even if the result can represent only a limited part of the whole field.

At present, our choice is restricted to recovering the positive significance of man, who finds fulfilment through creating for himself an aesthetic atmosphere with an aesthetic intention. This choice, which looks forward hopefully to a more authentic existence for man, the rediscovery of his stable and permanent values, has been a poetic one—an arbitrary selection; is has, therefore, an emblematic value, alluding to the exorcism of a new society.

—Chris Fawcett

AYMONINO, Carlo.
Italian. Born in Rome, 18 July 1926. Educated at the University of Rome School of Architecture, Dip.Arch. 1950. Married three times; children: Aldo, Livia, Silvia, and Adriano. Since 1951, in private practice, Rome; Founder/Director, with Maurizio Aymonino, Baldo de Rossi, and Alessandro de Rossi, Studio AYDE, Rome, since 1960. Assistant Lecturer, 1951-63, and Professor, since 1981, University of Rome School of Architecture; Lecturer, 1963-67, Professor, 1968-73, and Dean of the Graduate School of Architecture, 1973-79, University of Venice. Co-Editor, 1959-64, Editorial Board Member, 1977-79, and "Opinion" column editor, since 1982, *Casabella* magazine, Milan. Exhibitions: *Triennale*, Milan, 1969 and 1981; *Carlo Aymonino*, Galleria AAM, Rome, 1977; *Plans and Work*, Max Protetch Gallery, New York, 1980; *Architettura Berlino '84*, Florence, 1982; *Drawings*, Rizzoli Gallery, New York, 1983; *Colosso a Roma*, Fondazione Agnelli, Turin, 1983. Recipient: First Prize, San Giovanni a Teduccio Competition, Naples, 1953; First Prize, Pescara Covered Market Competition, Italy, 1954; First Prize, Chamber of Commerce Competition, Massa and Carrara, Italy, 1956; IN-ARCH Prize, Rome, 1964; Architecture Prize, Accademia di San Luca, Rome, 1976; First Prize, Largo Firenze Competition, Ravenna, Italy, 1982. Address: Vicolo di Santa Agata 19, 00153 Rome, Italy.

Works:

1950 INA-Casa Housing Development, Tiburtino, Rome (with Ludovico Quaroni, M. Ridolfi, and others)
1951 La Tartaruga, house, Via Innocenzo X, Rome

(with Ludovico Quaroni)
1953 San Giovanni a Teduccio Development, Naples (with Chiarini, Girelli, Lenci, Melograni, and Vandone)
1954 Covered market, Pescara, Italy (competition project; with others)
Spine Bianche housing development, Matera, Italy (with others)
1956/
60 Chamber of Commerce Building, Massa and Carrara, Italy
Cassa di Risparmio, Rovigo, Italy (competition project; with others)
1957/
59 "Trattturo dei Preti" (INA-Casa Housing Development), Foggia, Italy (with others)
Apartment building, Via Citerni, Rome (with others)
House, Lungotevere degli Inventori, Rome (with others)
National Library, Rome (competition project; with others)
House, via Tommaso Salvini, Rome (with others)
INA-Casa Housing Development, viale Ofanto, Foggia, Italy (with others)
"Commenda Ouest" (INA-Casa Housing Development), Brindisi, Italy (with others)
Cooperative residential developments, Lecce, Italy (with others)
Piazza Guerra redevelopment, Empoli, Italy (competition project)
Law Courts, Brindisi, Italy (with others)
Cooperative residential developments, Brindisi, Italy (with others)
1960 Condominium, Via Arbia, Rome (with others)
F. Vandone Polio Center, Ospedale Spallanzani, via Portuense, Rome (with others)
Institute of Technology, Brindisi, Italy (with others)
Villa di Giulio, Brindisi, Italy
1961 Law Courts, Lecce, Italy (competition project; with others)
Institute of Technology, Lecce, Italy (with others)
1962 Plan for the city center of Turin (competition project)
Manifatture Tabacchi planning study, Bologna, Italy (with Giordano)
Plan for the center of Breuil, Italy (competition project; with others)
Plan for the city center of Bologna, Italy (with others)
Condominium, Via Anagni, Rome (with others)
Apartment and office building, Savona, Italy (with others)
1963 Tor Carbone cooperative residential development, Rome (with others)
1964 Paganini Theatre reconstruction, Parma, Italy (competition project)
Tor de' Cenci housing development, Rome (with others)
1966 Chamber of Deputies Building, Rome (competition project)
1967 Psychiatric Hospital, Mirano, Italy (competition project; with Constantino Dardi)
Monte Amiata Housing Development, Gallaratese, Milan (with Aldo Rossi and others)
1968 Bank of Italy Headquarters, Grosseto, Italy
1970 Centre Beaubourg, Paris (competition project)
G. Marconi School of Science, Pesaro, Italy
High school campus, Pesaro, Italy
1971/
73 Plan for the old city center of Pesaro, Italy (with others)
Plan for the city center of Reggio Emilia, Italy (competition project; with Constantino Dardi)
Plan for the city center of Perugia, Italy (with Constantino Dardi)

Master plan for the University of Florence (competition project; with others)
Elementary school, Abbiategrasso, Italy
New University of Cagliari, Italy (competition project; with others)
New University of Calabria, Italy (competition project; with others)
Piazza XX Settembre redevelopment, Fano, Italy
Cassa di Risparmio, Fano, Italy
"Roma-Est" (housing development), Rome (project; with Constantino Dardi and R. Panella)
1976 National Academy of San Luca, Rome (competition project)
1977 Prager Platz redevelopment, Berlin (competition project)
Law Courts, Ferrara, Italy (with others)
1978 Plan for the city center of Florence (competition project; with Aldo Rossi and others)
1979 Civic Center, Pesaro, Italy
Semirurali housing development, Bolzano, Italy (with others)
1980 Public Housing Block, West Berlin (project; with A. Aymonino)
1981 Benelli Headquarters, stage 1, Pesaro, Italy (with F. Battimelli)
Mestre-Terraglio Hospital, Mestre, near Venice (project; with C. Mar, L. Calcagni, and G. Tamaro)
1982 Regional Government Headquarters, Umbria, Italy (competition project; with S. Giani)
Palazzo Scatolari renovations and alterations, Pesaro, Italy (project; with M. L. Tugnoli)
Largo Firenze area renovation plan, Ravenna, Italy (competition project; with A. Aymonino, B. Savoia, P. Zambelli, G. Barbini, A. Morelli, and V. Scardovi)
La Villette Development, Paris (competition project; with A. Zattera, G. Giacomo D'Ardia, V. Fraticelli, R. Nicolini, and G. C. Mainini)
Colossus Plan, Rome (project; with A. Aymonino, S. Giulianelli, and M. L. Tugnoli)
City Centre Plan, Abano Terme, Italy (project; with R. Panella, S. Rocchetto, and Scaeso)
Pomposa Abbey Plan, Pomposa, Italy (project; with G. Barnini, P. Zambelli, and A. Torti)
Ex IMA area redevelopment plan, Ferrara, Italy (project; with A. Veronese)
1983 Urban Plan and Building Development in Agrarian Syndicate area, Rovigo, Italy (project; with F. Bendazzoli and L. Semerani)
Edilgori prefabricated shop and office building, Orte, Italy (project; with S. Giani and M. L. Tugnoli)
San Cristoforo district urban plan, Udine, Italy (competition project; with G. Barnini)
Gymnasium and Swimming Pool, Atessa, Italy (project; with A. Aymonino, C. Baldisseri, and L. Sarti)

Publications:

By AYMONINO: books—*La città territorio*, editor, Bari, Italy 1964; *La formazione del concetto di tipologia edilizia*, Venice 1965; *L'Utopia della realtà*, editor, Bari, Italy, 1965; *Gli alloggi della municipalità di Vienna 1922-32*, Rome 1965; *Origine e sviluppo della città moderna*, Padua, Italy 1965; *I centri direzionali*, with Pierluigi Giordani, Bari, Italy 1967; *La città di Padova*, editor, Rome 1970; *Il significato delle città*, Bari, Italy 1975; *Giuseppe Samonà, 1923-1975: cinquant'anni di architettura*, exhibition catalogue, with others, Rome 1975; *Le capitali del XIX Secolo: I Parigi e Vienna*, with others, Rome 1975; *I catasti storici di Padova*, editor, Rome 1976; *Lo studio dei fenomeni urbani*, Rome 1977; *1977: Un*

Carlo Aymonino: Palace of Justice, Ferrara, Italy, 1977.

ation," with Thomas Maldonado and Pierluigi Cervellanti, in *Casabella* (Milan), September 1977; "Design at Different Scales of Reference" in *Architecture + Urbanism* (Tokyo), February 1978; "Roma—una città a parte," with Raffaele Panella, in *Casabella* (Milan), no. 487/8, 1983; "Il concorso ferroviario di Bologna" in *Casabella* (Milan), no. 497, 1983.

On AYMONINO: books—*Il concorso per i nuovi uffici della Camera dei Deputati* by Manfredo Tafuri, Rome 1968; *L'architettura di Roma capitale 1870-1970*, Florence 1971; *Il dibattito architettonico in Italia 1945-1975*, Rome 1977; *Global Architecture 45: Housing Complex at the Gallaretese Quarter, Milan* by Yukio Futagawa and Pierluigi Nicolin, Tokyo 1977; *Guida di Roma moderna* by I. de Guttry, Rome 1978; *Campus scolastico a Pesaro—collana cultura e territorio*, Rome 1980; *Carlo Aymonino: l'architettura non e un mito* by Claudia Conforti, Rome 1980; articles—"Architetture di Giovani" by Giuseppe Samonà in *Casabella* (Milan), no. 205, 1955; "Camera di Commercio, Industria e Agricoltura di Massa e Carrara" by Giuseppe Samonà in *L'Architettura* (Rome), no. 74, 1961; "Recente attivita dello Studio Architetti e Ingegneri" by Manfredo Tafuri in *'L'Architettura* (Rome), no. 93, 1963; "Montecitorio valle di lacrime" by G.K. Koenig in *Casabella* (Milan), no. 321, 1967; "Le Centre de direction de Bologna" by Marco de Michelis and Marco Venturi in *Espace et Sociétés* (Paris), March 1971; "Un contributo per la fondazione di una nuova scienza urbana" by M. Scolari in *Controspazio* (Bari, Italy), no. 78, 1971; "Roofless Homes" in *Casabella* (Milan), July 1974; "La Génération de l'incertitude" by F. Dal Co and M. Manieri-Elia in *L'Architecture d'aujourd'hui* (Paris), no. 181, 1974; "Carlo Aymonino" in *Architecture + Urbanism* (Tokyo), February 1978; "Il Palazzo di Giustizia di Ferrara" in *Casabella* (Milan), no. 479, 1982; "La casa parcheggio a Pesaro" in *Domus* (Milan), no. 637, 1983; "Centro direzionale Benelli a Pesaro" in *Casabella* (Milan), no. 497, 1983; "Bolzano, il quartiere delle semirurali" in *Baumeister* (Munich), no. 12, 1983; "Il palazzo di giustizia di Ferrara" by Paolo Portoghesi in *Epoca* (Milan), 1984.

Architectural and urban design require different scales of reference and, therefore, different techniques of representation. It is true, moreover, that these are not necessarily independent and unrelated, nor is the only possible relationship between them the strictly hierarchical one suggested by different methods of drawing and layout. Indeed, the more complete any proposed architectural solution, the greater the likelihood that it will also help to determine features at the various scales of reference involved in the project.

—Carlo Aymonino

progetto per Firenze, with others, Rome 1978; *Roma: continuità dell'antico*, Rome 1981; *Un progetto per il centro storico*, with Raffaele Panella, Rome 1983; *Architettura del presente e città del passato*, edited by Umberto Siola, Rome 1984; articles—"Un dibattito sulla tradizione in architettura" in *Casabella* (Milan), no. 206, 1955; "Cronaca e storia del quartiere Tiburtino" in *Casabella* (Milan), no. 215, 1957; "Inchiesta edilizia sulle città italiane: Brindisi" in *Casabella* (Milan), no. 222, 1958; "Matera: mito e realtà " in *Casabella* (Milan), no. 231, 1959; "Copenhagen" in *Urbanistica* (Turin), March 1960; "15 Anni di architettura italiana" in *Casabella* (Milan), no. 251, 1961; "Roma: il sistema dei centri direzionali" in *Casabella* (Milan), no. 264, 1962; "La condizione edilizia di Roma" in *Casabella* (Milan), September 1963; "Facolta di tendenza?" in *Casabella* (Milan), no. 287, 1964; "Berlino: una città aperta" in *Casabella* (Milan), no. 288, 1964; "Dibattito sulle tendenze attuali dell'architettura nel fasciolo dedicato a progetti di architetti italiani," with others, in *Casabella* (Milan), July 1964; "Ospedale psichiatrico di Mirano," with Constantino Dardi, and "Il P.R.G. di Bari" in *Lotus* (Venice), no. 6, 1969; "Progetto architettonico e formazione della città " in *Lotus* (Venice), no. 7, 1970; "Due insediamenti turistici nel mezzogiorno" in *L'Architettura* (Rome), May 1970; "Progetti dello Studio Semerani-Tamaro 1965-1971" in *Controspazio* (Bari, Italy), July/August 1971; "Roma-Est: proposta architettonica," with Constantino Dardi and R. Panella, in *Controspazio* (Bari, Italy), December 1973; "The Contribution of Oswald Mathias Ungers to Architecture," with Vanna Fraticelli, in *Controspazio* (Bari, Italy), November 1975; "Architecture of Aldo Rossi" in *Architecture + Urbanism* (Tokyo), no. 67, 1976; "Materia e materiali" in *Lotus* (Venice), June 1977; "Urban Centres: Conservation and Innov-

Carlo Aymonino has been involved in the architectural/cultural debate in Italy since 1950, when he collaborated with Ludovico Quaroni on the neo-realist experiment of the Tiburtino Quarter in Rome. Aymonino has arrived at his current theoretical position through a profound critical reappraisal of his own past experiments and from an analysis of the problems of contemporary life.

Aymonino's studies of "directional centres," which he interprets as associate organisms, polyfunctional "containers" (for a variety of purposes and functions) that will yet allow for continuity in the general form of a structural complex, are based on his conception of the "physiological process of present-day society" and on the essential needs of today's cities.

The directional centre forms a link between the city centre and its surroundings, a link created by Aymonino's revival of the historic concept of typology. There is, for example, the typology of the city itself, "a place created by history." There is the typology of the individual urban component—for example, the university, "a place that produces problems." Within the urban morphology, there is also an "ideological representative" component that is fundamental to society and to democracy. It is this concept of individual types within a whole, a whole given form by a directional centre, that Aymonino tries to implement in his work as a town planner.

He speaks of needing a "rule" rather than a "regulation." He follows a process of "fundamental architectural rebuilding" that takes into account various considerations from the ideological and sociological to the technical/scientific and formal/historical.

His best known work—it might be called the Aymonino paradigm—is the Monte Amiata Housing Development in the Gallaratese district of Milan. It impresses as a complex formal fantasy that makes use of expressionist ideas and multiple quotations, which Aymonino seeks to unify in a highly-defined polysemantic design in which the memory of the past combines with a projection of the future. Tafuri speaks of the Gallaratese complex as being autobiographical, like Fellini's film *8½*. And, indeed, the complex is full of expressiveness and emotion, emphasized by its proximity to Aldo Rossi's apartment complex, which is clinically and programmatically "abstract" in accordance with Rossi's views on the importance of the rational in Italian architectural culture.

—Lara-Vinca Masini

AZUMA, Takamitsu.

Japanese. Born in Osaka, 20 September 1933. Educated at the Osaka University School of Architecture, 1952-57, B.Arch. 1957. Married Setsuko Nakaoka in 1957; daughter: Rie. Designer, Ministry of Postal Services Architecture Department, Tokyo and Osaka, 1957-60; Chief Designer, Junzo Sakakura, Architect, and Associates, Osaka, 1960-63, and Tokyo, 1963-67. Since 1967, Principal, Takamitsu Azuma Architect and Associates, Tokyo. Lecturer in Architecture, Tokyo University of Art and Design, 1976-78; Tokyo Denki University, 1979-81; School of Architecture, Tokyo University, 1983-85; School of Architecture, Osaka University, since 1984. Lecturer in Environmental Engineering, Osaka University, since 1980. Member, ArchiteXt, with Takefumi Aida, *q.v.,* Mayumi Miyawaki, Makoto Suzuki and Minoru Takeyama, *q.v.,* since 1971. Exhibitions: *Today: An Exhibition of Houses,* Design Gallery, Tokyo, part I and II, 1978. Recipient: First Prize, Kinki Branch of the Japan Institute of Architects Competition, 1957; First Prize, Student Hall of the School of Engineering of Osaka University Competition, 1958. Address: Takamitsu Azuma Architect and Associates, 3-6-1 Minami-Aoyama, Minato-ku, Tokyo, Japan.

Works:

1966 Tower House, Jingumae, Shibuya-ku, Tokyo
1967 Akatsuka Lodge, Nojiriko-Daigaku-mura, Shinanomachi, Nagano, Japan
1968 Kawamoto House, Aoyama-dai, Suita, Osaka
Satoya House, Higashi-Toyomanka, Osaka
Yano House, Matsubara, Setagaya-ku, Tokyo
Taiyo-do Building, Nagaoka, Kyoto
Diamond Building, Higashiyodogawa-ku, Osaka
Nakahara House, Midori-dai, Kawanishi, Hyogo, Japan

1969 Inoue House, Kanagawa-ku, Yokohama
Nakamura Clinic Building, Minami-ku, Osaka
Fukunaga-Miyata House, Honmachi, Toyonaka, Osaka
Satsuki Nursery School, stage I, Ikeda, Osaka
Akatsuka Tower House, Kusaka-cho, Higashi-Osaka, Osaka
1970 Kawabe House, Ebina, Kouza-fun, Kanagawa, Japan
Komoro Drivers School, Komoro, Nagano, Japan
Oyama House, Kami-Shibutani, Ikeda, Osaka
Kano House, Shiromae, Gifu, Japan
Haijima Seaside Lodge, Iwafune, Ohara, Chiba, Japan
Mitsui Group Pavilion, *Expo '70,* Osaka (with others)
1971 Awatsuji House, Matsubara, Setagaya-ku, Tokyo
Hakusenken (Buddhist Temple), Arakawaku, Tokyo
Umezawa Clinic Building, Taito-ku, Tokyo
Takahashi House, Nada-ku, Kobe, Japan
Machida Lodge, Daigaku-mura, Agatsumagun, Gunma, Japan
Ito House, Kintei, Kawasaki, Kanagawa, Japan
1972 Machida House, Ichigaya, Shinjuku-ku, Tokyo
Airship Bowling Center, Takaishi, Osaka
Takaishi Drivers School, Takaishi, Osaka
1973 Nishimura House, Shichirigahama, Kamakura, Kanagawa, Japan
Chin House, Komaba, Shinjuku-ku, Tokyo
Ogita House, Hisagi, Zushi, Kanagawa, Japan
Komiya House, Sakurayama, Zushi, Kanagawa, Japan
Sumino House, Kurakuen, Nishinomiya, Hyogo, Japan
Satsuki Nursery School, stage II, Ikeda, Osaka
Seibu-Yatsugatake Lodge, Uminokuchi, Minami-Saku-gun, Nagano, Japan
Yamamichi Mountain Lodge, Karuizawa, Nagano, Japan
Araki House, Musashino, Tokyo
Yasumaru House, Hanayashiki, Takarazuka, Hyogo, Japan
1974 Miyota Civic Welfare Center, Kita-Saku-gun, Nagano, Japan
Itaya House, Kichijyoji, Musashino, Tokyo
Ohsawa House, Narita-Higashi, Suginami-ku, Tokyo
Taira House, Yohkoh-dai, Kohnan-ku, Yokohama
Matsumoto House, Minato-ku, Yokohama
Ohto Clinic Building, Iruma, Saitama, Japan
Mizuno House, Koyodai, Kawanishi, Hyogo, Japan
Seijin Nursery School, Jyojo, Kyoto
Yamazaki House, Tomizuka-cho, Hamamatsu, Shizuoka, Japan
Miyota Nursery School, Kita-Saku-gun, Nagano, Japan
1975 Yoshida House, Higashi-cho, Iwatsuki, Saitama, Japan
Shyomoto House, Hagoromo, Takaishi, Osaka
Fuji-kyuko Office and Dormitory Complex, Minato-ku, Tokyo
Green Camping Ground Center House, Fujiyoshida, Shizuoka, Japan
1976 Takahashi House, Tama-ku, Kawasaki, Kanagawa, Japan
Matsuda House, Motoazabu, Minato-ku, Tokyo
Yamamichi House, Kugenuma, Fujisawa, Kanagawa, Japan
Dantsuka Clinic and Hospital, Iruma, Saitama, Japan

Egawa House, Kohtohen, Nishinomiya, Hyogo, Japan
1977 Boh House, Nishi-Ochiai, Shinjuku-ku, Tokyo
Morita House, Sasuke, Kamakura, Kanagawa, Japan
Yamagami House, Midori-ku, Yokohama
Yonezawa Building, Nakagyo-ku, Kyoto
Wat House Complex, Yatsusaka, Iwaki, Fukushima, Japan
1978 Watanabe House, Yokohama
Kijima House, Moriyama, Komoro, Nagano, Japan
Ujiie House, Niiza, Saitama, Japan
1979 Fukuchi House, Iwaki, Fukushima, Japan
Low-rise housing, Minami-Momoyama, Kyoto
1980 Ozawa House, Ohno-mura, Ibaragi, Japan
Itoh House, Niigata, Japan
Seishin Nursery School, Jyojo, Kyoto
Haijima House, Ohara, Chiba, Japan
1981 Takahashi House, Kobe, Japan
House on Tama Hill, Tokyo
Yamaki House, Mekami-yama, Hyogo, Japan
House on Kobinata Hill, Bunkyo-ku, Tokyo
Katsumi House, Ohmiya, Saitama, Japan
Okahata House, Sakai, Osaka
Japan Baptist Center, Nerima-ku, Tokyo
Kijima House, Komoro, Nagano, Japan
House at Uenohara, Yamahashi, Japan
1982 House at Hanegi, Setagaya-ku, Tokyo
Ishikawa House, Kamakura, Kanagawa, Japan
1983 Biblical Church, Takada, Toshima-ku, Tokyo
Yoshikane House, Kohriyama, Nara, Japan
Matsuda House, Minato-ku, Tokyo
Azuma Architects Office, Minato-ku, Tokyo
Obata House, Shiga-cho, Shiga, Japan
Hirasawa House, Shinagawa-ku, Tokyo
1984 Hashimoto Baptist Church, Hashimoto, Wakayama, Japan

Publications:

By AZUMA: books—*Re-evaluation of the Residence,* Tokyo 1971; *Global Interiors 4: Southern Europe,* Tokyo 1972; *Planning Methodology for the Contemporary House,* Tokyo 1975; *The Philosophy of Japanese Traditional Architecture,* Tokyo 1981; *The Living Room in a House/The Park in the City,* Tokyo 1983; articles—"Discovery of Underground Spaces" in *Kenchiku* (Tokyo), March 1967; "Tower-like Residence: An Abstract Analysis" in *Kenchiku* (Tokyo), June 1967; "An Architect Must Have His Own Project" in *Japan Architect* (Tokyo), June 1967; "Terminal Zones as Urban Facilities: About Their Compounding and Ecology" in *Kenchikuzasshi* (Tokyo), October 1967; "Takamitsu Azuma's Activities and Works: A Seven Day Ulysses" in *Toshijutaku* (Tokyo), July 1968; "Theory of Open Space from the Design Standpoint" in *Toshijutaku* (Tokyo), March 1969; "A Hypothesis" in *Japan Architect* (Tokyo), November 1970; "Conception of a Creative Team System" in *Shotenkenchiku* (Tokyo), June 1971; "Living Space in the City" in *Japan Architect* (Tokyo), July 1971; "What Urban Space Is to Me" in *Toshijutaku* (Tokyo), September 1971; "Design Memo for the Awatsuji Residence" in *Japan Architect* (Tokyo), June 1972; "Proposal for an Image of Public Residential Spaces" in *Japan Interior Design* (Tokyo), July 1974; "What Can We Do for the Townscape" in *Shotenkenchiku* (Tokyo), June 1975; "Cognizance and Method" in *Japan Architect* (Tokyo), June 1976; "From the Individual to the Assembled Group" in *Japan Architect* (Tokyo), August 1978; "Slit—Heterogeneous Forms, Spaces and Actions" in *Japan Architect* (Tokyo), June 1981; "Polyphony in Architecture" in *Japan Architect* (Tokyo), February 1983; "Transformations of the Tatami-mind" in *Japan Architect* (Tokyo), May 1984.

Takamitsu Azuma: Biblical Church at Takada-no-Baba, Tokyo, 1983.

On AZUMA: articles—"ArchiteXt and the Problem of Symbolism" by Charles Jencks in *Japan Architect* (Tokyo), June 1976; "Post-Metabolism: The New Wave in Japanese Architecture" by K. Ishii and H. Suzuki in *Japan Architect* (Tokyo), October/ November 1977; "Wat House" in *Japan Architect* (Tokyo), August 1978; "Simplicity or Elegance" in *Japan Architect* (Tokyo), September 1980; "Three Houses by Takamitsu Azuma" in *Japan Architect* (Tokyo), October 1981; "Seishin Nursery School" in *Japan Architect* (Tokyo), September 1982; "Coincidentia Opposititorum: About the Works and Philosophy of Takamitsu Azuma" by Udo Kultermann in *Japan Architect* (Tokyo), February 1983; "SD Review 1983," special issue of *Space Design* (Tokyo) December 1983.

My cognition of the way architecture ought to be and the method I developed from it both depend entirely on a series of oppositional propositions: individuality and collectivity, enclosure and openness, continuity and separation, mixture and simplification, and so on. Each work includes many of these propositions, but the list given here by no means exhausts them. I often make deliberate differences between plan and section in order to generate a feeling of tension. I bring inside building elements that belong outside (urbanization of architecture) and sometimes I design the space around the building to the maximum by means of unifying it with the building (architecturalization of the city). These are the parts of many oppositional propositions that I have not explained. Many of the individual themes I employ are shared in the methods of other architects. But each architect wants to integrate his knowledge or his method and to express the resulting unity in an individualized way. Perhaps it is inconvenient to attempt to do this by organizing and preserving knowledge in the form of a series of oppositions.

Nevertheless, I want to preserve a strong feeling of tension by leaving the oppositions unresolved.

Furthermore, I wish to fuse these oppositions in the work of architecture. In other words, I want my architecture to be someting like a soup in which some of the vegetables remain undissolved and float about. Japanese cuisine emphasizes ways of combining the natural flavors of foods to best advantage. But one is always conscious of the tastes of the individual ingredients as one chews. I may be striving to achieve something similar in architecture. I believe that this is the only method that can result in a creative correspondence between the space created by an architect and the person who uses it. I feel that this element has been left behind in the methods of other architects. When all of the vegetables in a soup have dissolved, the only thing that remains is the blended flavor that the cook had in mind. In an architecture in which the oppositions remain unresolved, the user can select and combine the oppositions that suit his own needs and wishes at each time. Under such an arrangement, the architect prepares, and the user accepts and takes part in the creative act. The "polyphonic way of architecture", which supports my recent works, is developed from these cognitions and concepts.

—Takamitsu Azuma

Takamitsu Azuma is one of those sensitive, careful, dextrous architects whose work is a pleasure to experience, but he has never been quite innovative enough to attract an international following. After graduation from Osaka University in 1957, Azuma spent three years in relative obscurity working for the Ministry of Postal Services before he joined the offices of Junzo Sakakura. As chief designer with Sakakura from 1960 to 1967, Azuma developed his subtle, austere architectural style. After establishing his own office in 1967, Azuma, given a free hand, designed the Tower House for himself and his family. On a very narrow sliver of land in dense downtown Tokyo, Azuma developed an ingenious vertical sequence of spaces that expresses his individuality in a neighborhood of typical Japanese tile-roofed dwellings. The smooth, taut surfaces are punctured with pure openings, while the mass of the tower protrudes in bold diagonal cantilevers that extend the constricted space outward.

In 1971 Azuma helped form ArchiteXt, a group of five young, radical Japanese architects, who some thought would become the next Metabolist Group. ArchiteXt was composed of Azuma and Takefumi Aida, Mayumi Miyawaki, Makoto Suzuki, and Minoru Takeyama, and one of the purposes of the group was to attract attention to their unconventional wit and parody of modern architecture. Azuma was probably the least outrageous of the five, and yet in many ways his buildings seem some of the most lasting in their interest. The Seijin Nursery School, for example, presents a generally lean and blank facade to the street, but the uncommon cut-out entry indicates that something special lies within. Azuma has dextrously created a central space that serves as a private piazza for the children, with glimpses through geometric cut-outs into the building and out toward the street.

On yet another tight urban lot (are there any other kind in Japan?) Azuma has fashioned four superb apartments (called the Wat House) where two would have been tough. Employing the same simple, white, concrete surfaces of the Tower House and at the Seijin Nursery School, Azuma again carved out a private realm off the busy street. While the Wat House is part of its neighborhood, it is also a semi-private cluster of urban dwelling units—an opposition that interests Azuma, "the relation between individuality and collectivity." The resolution of these opposing forces in architecture is what Azuma describes as "Oppositional Harmony."

In his work, Azuma seeks to find a duality in which individual expression and contextualism can co-exist and in which the subjugation of the environment can occur without losing the respect for nature traditional to Japanese architecture. Thus far, he has achieved his goal on a limited scale. We must look toward his future projects for a further refinement of this most intriguing concept.

—Michael Franklin Ross

B

BACKSTRÖM, Sven Mauritz.

Swedish. Born in Havdhem, Gotland, 20 January 1903. Educated at the Högre Allmänna Läroverket, Visby, Sweden, graduated 1923; Royal Technical University, Stockholm, 1923-29, Dip.Arch. 1929; student/assistant, under Dag Ribbing and Eskil Sundahl, Kooperativa Förbundets Arkitektenkontor, Stockholm, 1929-32; in the studio of Le Corbusier, Paris, 1932-33; studied in England and Italy, 1934-36. Married Gunvor Holmgren in 1937; children: Adam, Marie, Mårten, and Pontus. In partnership with Leif Reinius, *q.v.*, Stockholm, since 1936. Architect for the Strömsholm Royal Palace, 1951-78. Recipient: Kasper Salin Award, Svenska Arkitekters Riksförbund, 1967; Prince Eugen Medal, 1970; Olle Engkvist Medal, 1973; Honorary Award, Stockholm Building Association, 1981. Member, Royal Academy for Free Arts, 1962. Knight Commander, Royal Order of Vasa, 1973. Address: Backström and Reinius, Storgatan 11, 114 44 Stockholm, Sweden.

Works:

1938 Unmarried women's living quarters, Stockholm
1939/
40 Community house and living quarters for old people, Alvik, Sweden
1943/
45 Point houses, Danviksklippan, Stockholm
Star Units Housing Development, Gröndal, Sweden
1946 Crematorium, Lund, Sweden
1946/
48 Nedre Norrland Law Courts, Sundsvall, Sweden
1946/
51 Terraced houses, Gröndal, Stockholm
Nockebyhov Housing and Family Hotel, Nockeby, Stockholm
1948/
51 Björnbo Service Flats for Old People, Lidingö, Sweden
1948/
52 Rosta Housing Development, with schools, Örebro, Sweden
1948/
65 Ekliden High School, Nacka, Sweden.
1953/
55 Vällingby Shopping Center, Sweden
1955/
62 Office Block 5, Sergels Torg, Stockholm
1956 Staff Quarters, Swedish Embassy, Neuilly, Paris
1956/
60 Farsta Shopping Center, Sweden
1957/
60 Crematorium additions, Lund, Sweden
1962/
64 Ahléns Department Store, Stockholm
1963 Staff Quarters, Joseph Rowntree Corporation, York, England
1964 Swedish Pavilion, World's Fair, New York

1964/
67 Police Headquarters, Göteborg, Sweden
1966/
69 PUNKT Department Store and Parking Garage, Västerås, Sweden
1968/
74 PK Bank Headquarters, with shops, Stockholm
1970/
73 Shops and Offices, Östra Nordstaden, Göteborg, Sweden
1972/
79 AMS Education Building (offices, industrial premises, workshops, and school), Stockholm
1973/
75 Housing complex, with school, Upplands Väsby, Sweden
1974/
76 Pauves Honteux Society Old People's Home, Nockeby, Stockholm
1974/
78 Office and Shop Complex, Stockholm
1975/
79 Sveriges Arbetsgivareförening Building, Stockholm

Publications:

By BACKSTRÖM: book—*Swedish Housing of the 'Forties*, Stockholm 1950; article—"Bank in Kungstandgarden, Stockholm", with Leif Reinius, in *Arkitektur* (Stockholm), February 1975.

On BACKSTRÖM and REINIUS: articles—"Vallingby City Centre" in *Jano Arquitectura* (Barcelona), February 1975; "Collaboration in Design ..." by Stig Alund in *Byggmastaren* (Copenhagen), June 1979; "Backström and Reinius—A Catalogue of Their Work over the Last Fifty Years", special issue of *Arkitektur* (Stockholm), August 1982; "Itineraire scandinave", in *Le Carré Bleu* (Paris), no. 1, 1984.

Swedish architecture divides neatly into ten-year periods. The 1930s were the years of functionalism—of internationalism, the legacy of the Bauhaus, flat roofs, and buildings that looked as if they were built of concrete using modern industrial techniques. The 1940s, by contrast, were for Sweden years of isolation due to the war in which the country was neutral, years

Sven Backström and Leif Reinius: PK Bank Headquarters, Stockholm, 1968-74.

in which the parallel of development of international architecture in Europe was brutally cut off at the root. Building in Sweden was thus affected by a dearth of foreign influences and at the same time by a dearth of certain materials. The result was the rise of an introspective, national style still (just) within the bounds of modern architecture. This was one of the high periods of Swedish architecture, and it made the country a Mecca for architects from abroad after the war. Sven Backström and Leif Reinius, more than any architects at the time, epitomize this era.

Their work was characterized by the use of natural materials such as brick in conjunction with plenty of timber, traditional roof-forms, and an elegant, refined detailing, which in the hands of their imitators was apt to become effeminate. Their buildings of the period had a very human scale, with liberal use of breaks and bay windows to reduce the visual impact of large buildings; they had a thoroughly non-industrial look, relying on a level of craftsmanship that at the time was probably unexcelled anywhere. One of the great inventions of the partnership was the "star" housing block, a three-storey, low-pitched-roofed, Y-shaped block with the three arms at an angle of 120° to each other and the staircase at the apex. These could be joined in almost unlimited numbers to form what were virtually hexagonal courts with two of the sides missing, giving pleasant proportions, human scale, and economical solutions. Perhaps the most notable scheme of this kind was Gröndal in Stockholm, a scheme that also included some very early stepped housing, where each flat had a large garden terrace, and a point block where the special characteristics of various floors were lovingly exploited.

By the 1950s, the pendulum was swinging back to the International Style, but Backström and Reinius kept to the course that they had set themselves and continued to produce humane and highly individual buildings. Now that the pendulum has again swung back to humanism and away from repetitiveness, it is remarkable to note how many ideas popular today were pioneered by Backström and Reinius thirty or forty years ago. The small scale, the feeling of individuality, and the hand-built look so typical of many recent schemes were typical of Backström and Reinius in the 1940s. Oddly enough, this has not caused Backström and Reinius—still going strong at around eighty—to emulate the new vernacular. Their later work, perhaps because it happens to cover the more prestigious end of the market, has harder and more elegant materials than before and perhaps pays less attention to the tiny detail and the human scale. As architects, they seem intent on pursuing a logical line of development to the end, rather than doing opportunist throw-backs to what undoubtedly was a High Period.

—James Codrington Forsyth

BACON, Edmund Norwood.
American. Born in Philadelphia, Pennsylvania, 2 May 1910. Educated at Cornell University, Ithaca, New York, 1927-32, B.Arch. 1932; Cranbrook Academy, Bloomfield Hills, Michigan, under Eliel Saarinen, *q.v.*, 1936 (graduate fellowship in city planning). Served as a Quartermaster 2nd Class in the United States Navy, 1943-45. Married Ruth Holmes in 1938; children: Karin, Elinor, Hilda, Michael, Kira, and Kevin. Architectural Designer, office of Henry Killam Murphy, Shanghai, China, 1934; worked for W. Pope Barney, Philadelphia, 1935; Supervisor of City Planning, Flint Institute of Research and Planning, Michigan, 1937-39; Managing Director, Philadelphia Housing Association, 1940-43; Co-Designer, *Better Philadelphia Exhibition,* and Senior Land Planner, Philadelphia City Planning Commission, 1946-49; Executive Director, Philadelphia City Planning Commission, 1949-70 (Development Coordinator, 1968-70). Since 1970, in private practice, Philadelphia; Vice-President, Mondev International Ltd., Montreal, since 1971. Adjunct Professor, University of Pennsylvania, Philadelphia, since 1950. Member, Task Force on the Potomac River Basin Plan, to the United States Secretary of the Interior, 1965-68; Member, Citizens' Advisory Committee on Recreation and Natural Beauty, to President Johnson, 1966-69, and on Environmental Quality, to President Nixon, 1969-70; Member, Urban Transportation Advisory Council, to the United States Secretary of Transportation, 1969-71. Member of the Board, Franklin Institute, Philadelphia, 1969-78. Recipient: Travel/Study Grant, Ford Foundation, 1959; Medal of Achievement, Philadelphia Art Alliance, 1961; Man of the Year Award, City Business Club, Philadelphia, 1962; Brown Medal, Franklin Institute, Philadelphia, 1962; Rockefeller Foundation grant, 1963; Distinguished Service Award, American Institute of Planners, 1971; Gold Medal, Royal Institution of Chartered Surveyors, London, 1974; Honor Award, Fairmount Park Art Association, Philadelphia, 1976; Medal, American Institute of Architects, 1976; R. S. Reynolds Memorial Award for Community Architecture, 1976; Philadelphia Award, 1983; Penn Club Award, 1984. Address (home/office): 2117 Locust Street, Philadelphia, Pennsylvania 19103, U.S.A.

Works:

1934   Residences, Shanghai, China (with Henry Killam Murphy)
1937   Traffic survey of Flint, Michigan
1941   Phillips House, Torresdale, Pennsylvania (with Oscar Stonorov)
1947   Design of the *Better Philadelphia Exhibition* (with Oscar Stonorov)
1952   Penn Center, Philadelphia (original concept; with Vincent Kling)
1957   Plan for Market East, Philadelphia (with W. von Moltke and Romaldo Giurgola)
1958   Plan for Society Hill, Philadelphia (with I. M. Pei)
1960   Comprehensive plan for Philadelphia (with Arthur T. Row)
1963   The Plan for Center City, Philadelphia
1966   Plan for Market East, Philadelphia (with Skidmore, Owings and Merrill)
1972   Plan for downtown Salem, Massachusetts (with Nelson W. Aldrich and John F. Collins)
1975   Plan for Westlake Mall, Seattle, Washington (with Romaldo Giurgola)
1978   Plan for Lafayette Plaza, Boston (with Romaldo Giurgola)

Publications:

By BACON: book—*Design of Cities,* New York 1967, revised edition 1974, London 1976; chapters—in *Man and the Modern City,* Pittsburgh, Pennsylvania 1963; *The Conscience of the City,* edited by Martin Meyerson, New York 1970; *American Civilization,* edited by Daniel Boorstin, London 1972; *Energy Use Management,* volumes III and IV, edited by Rocco Fazzolare and George B. Smith, New York 1978; articles—"A Case Study in Urban Design" in *Journal of the American Institute of Planners* (Washington, D.C.), August 1960; "Downtown Philadelphia: A Lesson in Design for Urban Growth" in *Architectural Record* (New York), May 1961; "Architecture and Planning" in *AIA Journal* (Washington, D.C.), June 1961; "American Homes and Neighborhoods, City and Country" in *Annals of the American Academy of Political and Social Science* (Philadelphia), July 1968; "Time, Turf, Architects and Planners" in *Architectural Record* (New York), March 1976; "The Design of Rome" in *Urban Design International* (Purchase, New York), January/February 1980; films—project director, *Understanding Cities,* series of five films.

On BACON: books—*The Art of Government* by James Reichley, New York 1959; *Cities in a Race with Time* by Jeanne R. Lowe, New York 1967; *The Last Landscape* by William H. Whyte, New York 1968; *The Future of the City* by Peter Wolf, New York 1974; *Downtown USA* by Kenneth Halpern, New York 1978; articles—"Philadelphia Does It: The Battle for Penn Center" by James Reichley in *Harpers'* (New York), February 1957; cover story in *Time* (New York), 6 November 1964; "A City's Future Takes Shape" in *Life* (New York), December 1965; "Recent Works of Edmund B. Bacon" in *Kenchiku Bunka* (Tokyo), February 1972; "Post-Renaissance Philadelphia" in *AIA Journal* (Washington, D.C.), March 1976; "Philadelphia Story" in *Progressive Architecture* (New York), April 1976; "Five Noted Thinkers Explore the Future" in *National Geographic* (Washington, D.C.), July 1976; "Philadelphia: A Lesson in Urban Design" by C. Curtis in *Planning and Building Developments* (Braamfontein, South Africa), July/August 1978; "Cities in the 1980s: A Dialogue" in *Historic Preservation* (Washington, D.C.), May/June 1981.

The building of cities is one of man's greatest achievements. The form of his city always has been and always will be a pitiless indicator of the state of his civilization. This form is determined by the multiplicity of decisions made by the people who live in it. In certain circumstances, these decisions have interacted to produce a force of such clarity and form that a noble city has been born. A deeper understanding of the interactions of these decisions can give us the insight necessary to create noble cities in our own day.

I should like to dispel the idea, so widely and uncritically held, that cities are a kind of grand accident, beyond the control of the human will, and that they respond only to some immutable law. I contend that human will can be exercised effectively on our cities now, so that the form that they take will be a true expression of the highest aspirations of our civilization.

With the enormous improvement in the techniques of mathematical manipulations of electronic computers applied to the problem of projecting past trends, we are in danger of surrendering to a mathematically extrapolated future which at best can be nothing more than an extension of what existed before. Thus, we are in danger of losing one of the most important concepts of mankind, that the future is what we make it.

Recent events in Philadelphia have proved incontrovertibly that, given a clear vision of a "design idea," the multiplicity of wills that constitute our contemporary democratic process can coalesce into positive, unified action on a scale large enough to change substantially the character of a city. It is my belief that a new awareness and understanding of "design idea" will enable the architectural profession over the years immediately ahead to become more relevant and effective in the building of our cities.

—Edmund N. Bacon

Edmund N. Bacon was with the Philadelphia City Planning Commission for 24 years—first as Senior Land Planner, then, from 1949 to 1970, as Executive Director. Few city planners or urban designers ever stay put that long. A typical planner may work for several years with a commercial development company that has hired him for his grasp of federal and local renewal policies and his ability to make imaginative use of local zoning law as well as federal, state, and local funding sources in the developer's behalf. For the next few years, he may be on the other side of the desk, this time in a public planning agency, devising ways to attract yet control development so that it will ultimately improve the life of the city or region. At some point in the planner's career he will probably be off to Third World countries to consult with rulers who wish to rebuild their cities in the image of the West. Is it possible to be a successful and effective planner and yet stay in one job for more than a quarter of a century? It may be the only way, if Bacon's achievement is to set the standard.

A city changes slowly, conforming to patterns imprinted by transportation systems, parks, plazas, footpaths, and other networks of open space, as well as landmark buildings that combine beauty with historic significance. The catalyst for change is economic; the physical form of change is shaped by zoning law. The nature of the growth of Philadelphia during Bacon's long term as Executive Director was to a significant degree established in advance by Bacon himself. What distinguishes him from almost all the planners of his own and succeeding generations is the fact that he elected to pay continuous attention to a single city over a long span of time. A street of shops reviving, a neighborhood of landmarks preserved, a subway line extended, a slum eradicated and the dwellers rehoused—all are catalysts for further change. Bacon's twenty-four years with the planning commission consisted of initiating such transforming ideas, getting them accepted by the public, and seeing them accomplished over decades.

Philadelphia's first planner was William Penn, who laid out the city in the eighteenth century. The City Hall was placed at the center of two perpendicular axes. A major rectangular park marks each of the four quadrants formed by these cross axes. As the city expanded through the nineteenth and early twentieth centuries, its urban core remained intact. In Bacon's vision, Philadelphia must continue to grow organically from this nucleus. He believes that the patterns of civic space, recreation, and transportation established during the city's beginnings and extended by succeeding generations of builders and planners must be understood, fostered, and continued—if the city is to prosper and grow in beauty.

In 1970, Bacon left the Philadelphia City Planning Commission to become Vice-President of Mondev International Ltd., based in Montreal. Today, the development he set in motion as Philadelphia's chief planner continues to be carried out within the framework and public consensus he established. That consensus did not always exist and, like all things political, is fragile.

Philadelphia was one of the first cities to begin to build again after the hiatus of World War II. It became a testing ground for the federal urban renewal and housing programs of the 1950s and 1960s. Because Bacon was eager to take advantage of these programs, he tried out most of them, finding out what worked and what didn't. Inevitably, the programs favored one social class over another, and Bacon became the target of the political left, who had begun to call the nation's urban renewal projects "negro removal." The epithet "gentrification" had yet to be invented, but Bacon was criticized for his efforts to bring the middle classes back from the suburbs to the city and accused of fostering the outward dislocation of the poor. His urban design ideas were characterized as mere efforts to hide the city's ill-housed and poor behind an "antiquated City Beautiful" facade.

Although these criticisms were valid in part, they have been muted in recent years as leftist polemic found new targets. Today, Philadelphia is visited regularly by busloads of planners, architects, historians, community leaders, teachers, and students. They all go to learn—how to preserve landmarks, to revive neighborhoods, to build playgrounds, to renew parks, to separate pedestrian and vehicular traffic, and to house the poor and elderly. The attention paid to Philadelphia today is a tribute to Bacon, the outstanding planner of his generation.

—Mildred F. Schmertz

Edmund Bacon: Plan for Center City, Philadelphia, 1963.

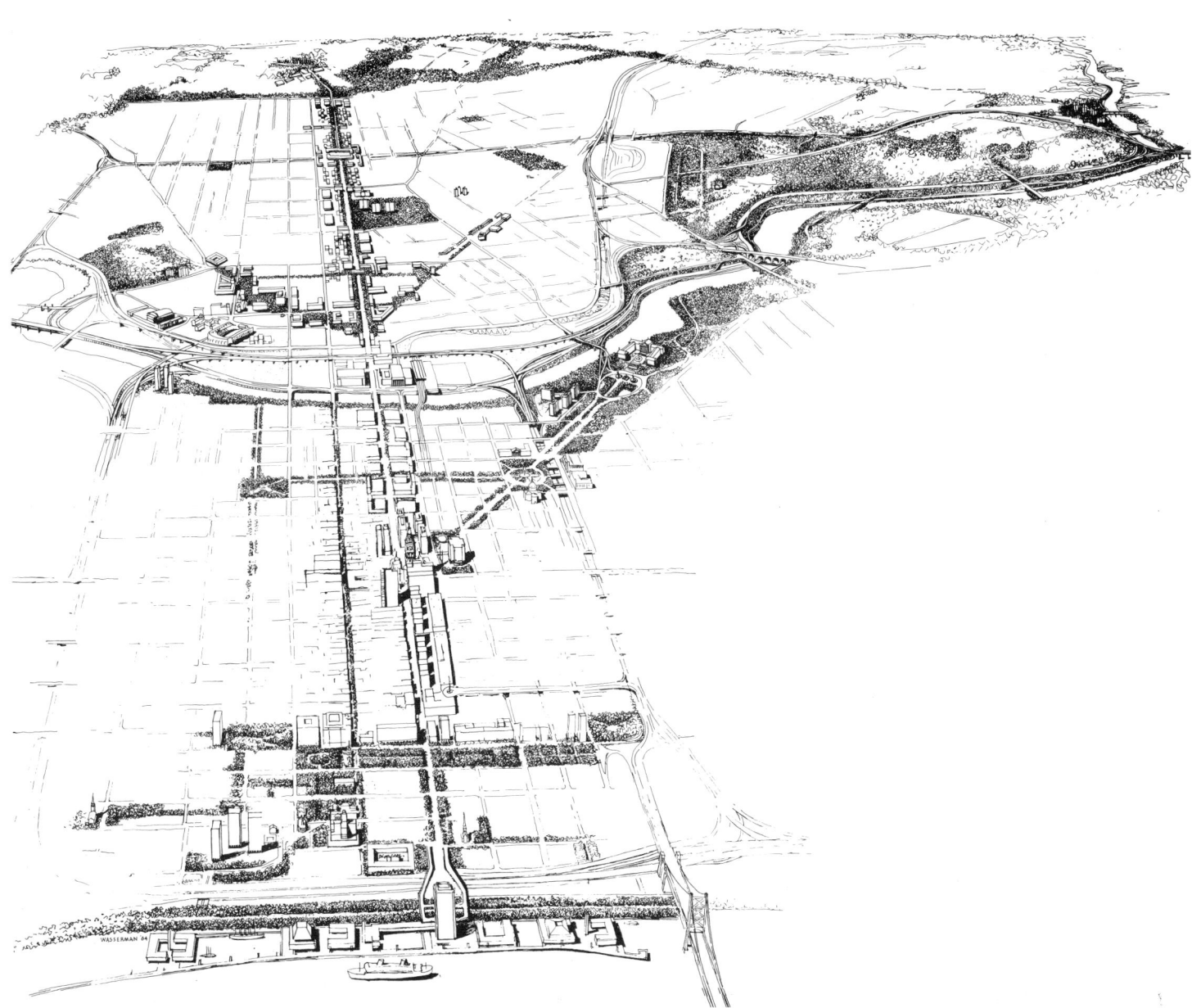

Daniel Badani: St. Louis Hospital, Paris, 1984 (model).

BADANI, Daniel Emile.

French. Born in Vincennes, 19 June 1914. Educated at the Lycée du Puy, Haute Loire; Ecole Nationale Supérieure des Beaux-Arts, Paris. Served in the Engineers, 12th Division of the French Army, 1939-40: Lieutenant. Married Jacqueline Chaleye in 1944; daughter: Laetitia. Since 1946, in private practice, with Pierre Roux-Dorlut, *q.v.*, Paris, Abidjan, Ivory Coast, and Bône, Algeria. Inspector-General of Urban Planning, Paris, 1944-50; Consultant Architect to the Ministry of Reconstruction and Development for the Languedoc-Roussillon region of France, 1950-60, and to the Development Bureau for the La Défense complex, Paris, 1969-72. Currently, Architect-in-Chief of Civic Buildings and National Monuments; Member of the General Council of Building for France; Consultant Architect to the Ministry of Reconstruction and Development for Paris; Consultant Architect to the Ministry of Equipment for Paris; Member of the Regional Commission on Architecture for the Paris region; Consultant on Urbanism and Architecture to the Mayor of Paris; and Member of the Editorial Board, *Architecture francaise,* Paris. Professor at the Ecole Nationale Supérieure des Beaux-Arts, Paris, 1946-55. President, Committee on Architects in Charge of Public Buildings and National Monuments, 1968-70, Syndicate of Parisian Architects, 1968-70, and National Union of French Architects, 1969-70. Exhibitions: Syndicate of Architects, Paris, 1960; Congress of Architects, London, 1960, Moscow, 1961; *Exposition internationale des formes industrielles,* Paris, 1963; International Exposition, Stockholm, 1963; *Architecture francaise de recherches,* Paris 1965; *Exposition nationale des beaux-arts,* Paris, 1977; *Salon d'automne,* Paris, 1977; *Decade d'architecture,* Bâtimat, Paris, 1983. Recipient: Silver Medal, Académie d'Architecture, Paris, 1968; Gold Medal, Société d'Encouragement à l'Art et à l'Industrie, Paris, 1972; Silver Medal, City of Paris, 1977. Member, l'Académie d'Architecture. Officer and Chevalier of the Légion d'Honneur; Chevalier des Arts et Lettres, France; Chevalier, l'Ordre de l'Etoile Noire du Benin. Address (office): 46 Avenue d'Iena, 75116 Paris, France.

Works:

1946 Seafront reconstruction at Sète, France
1947 Urban plan for Abidjan, Ivory Coast

Urban plan for Sassandra, Ivory Coast
Urban plan for Bouake, Ivory Coast
1950/
53 Four courtrooms, Palace of Justice, Abidjan, Ivory Coast
1950/
57 Central Posts and Telecommunications Building, Place Lapalud, Abidjan, Ivory Coast
Control Building and Hangar, Abidjan Airport, Ivory Coast
1952 Quai de la Consigne reconstruction, Sète, France
1952/
57 Cocody Mixed School, Abidjan, Ivory Coast
1953 Station, Bouake, Ivory Coast
1953/
54 Ministry of Public Works Offices, Abidjan, Ivory Coast
1953/
55 Abeille Company Offices and Commercial Buildings, Abidjan, Ivory Coast
Hôtel des Relais Aériens, Niamey, Nigeria
Bank of West Africa Building, Sassandra, Ivory Coast
1954 Urban plan for Toulouse, France
1954/
56 Palais du Grand Conseil (Palace of the National Assembly), Dakar, Senegal
1954/
57 Centre for Nuclear Studies, Marcoule, Gard, France
1955 School complexes, Herault, Vaucluse, and Var, France
1955/
57 Pont Lagunaire Rail Route, Abidjan, Ivory Coast
1956/
65 Housing, Saint Maurice-Vallon des Fleurs, Nice, France
1957 Fédération Nationale du Bâtiment Headquarters, Rue Laperouse, Paris
Canteen, Nuclear Centre, Le Bouchet, France
1957/
64 Villiers-le-Bel District Redevelopment, Paris
1958 Housing, administrative, community, and commercial development, Quarter Succi, Abidjan, Ivory Coast
Housing, Quartier N'Singa, Abidjan, Ivory Coast
Mixed Classical and Modern College, Bagnols-sur-Ceze, France
Master Plan for housing, Corneilles en Parisis, France
General hospital, Bouake, Ivory Coast

Palais de France Pavilion, World's Fair, Brussels
1959 Centre for Building Research and Development, Saint Remy les Chevreuses, France
1960 School complex, Villiers-le-Bel, Paris
Hippone-la-Royal Satellite City, Bône, Algeria (unfinished)
1960/
63 Centre for Nuclear Studies, Cadarache, Bouces du Rhone, France
Vincennes Stadium, France (competition project)
1962 Housing and commercial development, Quartier de la Grangette, Beziers, France
Cité Scolaire de la Dullague School and College Buildings, Beziers, France
1962/
67 Primary school, Adjame, Abidjan, Ivory Coast
1963 University, Constantine, Algeria (unfinished)
Anna Jacquin House, Boulogne, Paris
1964 Housing Quartier de l'Iranget, Beziers, France
Seafront development, phase I, Saint Raphael, France
1965 Urban plan for Champigny-Chennevieres, Val de Marne, France
Urban renewal plan for Avignon, France
Regional urban plans for Nice, Beziers, Saint Raphael, and Antibes-Vallauris, France
1966 Institut Francais de l'Afrique Noire Building, Abidjan, Ivory Coast
1966/
70 Housing, Quartier de las Planas, Nice, France
1967/
70 Secondary school, Mainvilliers, Paris
Secondary school, Gif sur Yvette, Paris
Secondary school, Saint-Denis, Paris
Secondary school, Vaux-le-Penil, Paris
Secondary school, Limours, Paris
1967/
74 Petit Defend Holiday Village, Saint Raphael, France
1968 Food warehouse, Chenneviers-sur-Marne, France
1968/
72 Tourist Centre, Maure-Viel Alpes Maritimes, France
La Rague Pleasure Port, Maure-Viel, Alpes Maritimes, France
1969 Apartment buildings and Quartier de la Balance renovations, Avignon, France
1969/
73 Agricultural administration Offices redevelopment, Montpellier, France

1969/
74 Single people's housing, Champigny sur Marne, France

1970 Residential and community development, Valenton, Paris

University Institute of Technology, Avenue de Versailles, Paris

University Institute of Technology, Amiens, France

University Institute of Technology, Clermont, near Paris

University Institute of Technology, Lyon-la-Doua, near Paris

1971/
73 New Prefecture Building, Créteil, Val de Marne, France

Housing and commercial development, Brunoy (Essone), Paris

1971/
74 Science Faculty Buildings, University of Clermont-Ferrand, France

1972 Seafront development, phase II, Saint Raphael, France

1972/
75 Housing, Quartier de Saint Augustin, Nice, France

1973 Housing development, Champigny sur Marne, Paris

Housing, Carros, Alpes Maritimes, France

1974 Hall of Archives, Créteil, Val de Marne, France

1975 Ministry of Defence Building renovations, Ilot St. Germain, Paris

Residential tower block, Courbevoie-La Défense, Paris

1976 Housing, Créteil (Orme St. Simeon), Paris

Parc St. Cloud Tunnel for the West Motorway, Paris

1976/
77 Courts of Justice, Créteil, Val de Marne, France

Alentours-Pont de Sèvres Road Traffic and Environmental Development, Boulogne, France

1977 Saint Bernard Gardens Development, Paris

1978 RNUR Road Station Complex, Boulogne, France

1979 Commercial Centre, Housing and Community Study, Zac Saint-Blaise, France

Postal and Telecommunications Centre, Boulogne, Paris

Eure-et-Loire Prefecture annexe, Chartres, France

Apartments (80), rue Lourmel, Paris

Housing (100 units), rue Nansouty, Paris

Housing (500 units), Chenneviers-sur-Marne, Paris

1981 New Prefecture Building for Var, Toulon, France

Palace of Justice, Toulon, France

Housing (625 units), Paris

Collective Housing, Villas and PAP Apartments, St. Laurent du Var, France

1982 Credit Mutuel Agricole du Midi branch offices, Lattes, near Montpellier, France

Prets Central Library, Nice, France

International Bank of West Africa Headquarters, Douala, Cameroons

Arnodet Housing Quarter renovations, Meudon, France

1984 Croce Spinelli Commercial and residential Building, Paris

Professional School of Commerce, Six Fours, Var, France

Institut Nationale Polytechnique de Lorraine, Nancy, France

Saint-Louis University Hospital Centre, Paris

Housing (83 units), Quai de Jemmapes, Paris

Publications:

On BADANI book—*Guide d'architecture contemporaine en France* by D. Amouroux, M. Crettol and J.P. Monnet, Paris 1974; articles—"Credit Agricole Mutuel du Midi" and "Créteil Law Courts" in *Mur vivant* (Paris), no 47, 1978; "Créteil: A More Accessible Justice" in *Crée* (Paris), February/March 1978; "Operation Pont-de-Sèvres" in *Mur vivant* (Paris), no. 49, 1978; "Tunnel for the West Motorway" in *Construction moderne* (Paris), Winter 1978; "Block of Flats in Nice" in *Construction moderne* (Paris), Spring, 1980; "A Prefecture Shaped Like a Fortress" in *Construction moderne* (Paris), March 1982; "Prefecture for Eure-et-Loire at Chartres" in *Recherche et architecture* (Paris), no. 49, 1982; "Prefecture Eure-et-Loire" in *Mur vivant* (Paris), no. 69, 1983.

*

Daniel Badani and Pierre Roux-Dorlut met in 1940 in Marseilles where Eugène Beaudouin had brought together various Parisian architects whose practices had been disrupted by the war. In 1946 Badani and Roux-Dorlut formed a partnership to study the rebuilding of the Languedoc, and today that partnership, based on a common architectural training and reinforced by a common regional background, is cemented by more than thirty years of work, struggle and friendship.

A "partnership" suggests reciprocal influence, complementary enrichment, a dialogue in which the naturel inclination of each partner is tempered by that of the other. However, for those who know Badani and Roux-Dorlut well, it is possible to discern the impact of the individual personality on their joint achievements. They carry out their professional programs together, but the final embodiment in form often reveals the dominant influence of one or the other.

Daniel Badani shows a certain classicism, even a taste for the baroque, tendencies curbed by Roux-Dorlut who, five years younger and of an austere and determined character, tends to simplify by finding everywhere a contemporary expression in architecture.

Their first achievements were in Africa, notably in Abidjan where they built, among other works, the courtrooms for the Palace of Justice, the Central Posts and Telecommunications Building, and various residential districts; in Dakar, where they built the Palais du Grand Conseil, which became the National Assembly of Senegal; and in Bouake, where they built the general hospital. In France they produced the principal plans and numerous buildings for the Centre for Nuclear Studies at Marcoule and at Cadarache, competition projects like the Vincennes Stadium, residential complexes both in the South and in the Paris area, and educational, industrial, public, and administrative buildings throughout the country.

Badani's influence shows most clearly in such works as the renovation of the Quartier de la Balance in Avignon, on the historic site of the Papal Palace, and in a special study commissioned by André Malraux as Minister of Culture, the development of a protected sector in the heart of Paris. Badani proposed that the importance of the Tuileries Gardens be emphasized by extending them to the arcades along the rue de Rivoli, freeing the area from traffic by the creation of underground streets and parking areas. The plan is bold, intelligent, and logical.

It was also with deference to an on-site-element—a large area of water—that Badani conceived the New Prefecture Building for the Val de Marne in Créteil. The most appropriate simile for the building is that it is like a ship. And Badani carefully studied the approaches, remodelled the ground, created gardens and pathways that not only provide entry but also invite one to regard the building from various aspects.

Roux-Dorlut's personal intervention is clearly evident in larger projects such as the University of Constantine, Algeria; the Hippone-la-Royal satellite city; the university of Clermont Ferrand; the new town of Bône; the building complex and urban development of the bridge quarter of Sèvres, Boulogne-sur-Seine; and in the recent University of Nancy. In all these projects, Roux-Dorlut expresses a preference for very careful organization of volumes, spaces, and open green areas in relation to their surroundings.

One of their most recent projects is St Louis Hospital, where he introduced new forms and volumes around a seventeenth-century historical monument with great sensitivity and respect. In the University of Nancy, the same care for compostition within an urban setting, the extremely well considered relationship between different buildings, and the choice of materials, show a remarkable sensitivity and elegance, as well as his tendency to research new forms for each project.

—Renée Diamant-Berger

BAIRD, George.

Canadian. Born in Toronto, Ontario, 25 August 1939. Studied at the University of Toronto, 1958-62, B. Arch. (Honours) 1962; post-graduate research studies, University College, London, 1964-67. Married Elizabeth Carol Davis in 1964. In private practice as George Baird Architect, Toronto, 1968-82. Since 1982, Partner, with Barry Sampson, Baird/Sampson Associates, Architects, Toronto. Visiting Lecturer, Royal College of Art, London, 1965-67; Tutor, Architectural Association School, London, 1968-72; Associate Professor of Architecture, 1972-82, Professor of Architecture since 1982, and Chairman of the Department of Architecture, 1983-85, University of Toronto; Visiting Professor of Architecture, Princeton University, New Jersey, 1983. Member of the Registration Board, Ontario Association of Architects, 1976-78; Editor, *Trace* magazine, Toronto, 1980-82. Exhibitions: *Prospectus '74*, David Mirvish Gallery, Toronto, 1974; *Documents of 35 Britain Street*, University of Toronto, 1976; *Architectural Drawings*, A.C.T. Gallery, Toronto, 1978; *Five Works from the Office of George Baird, Architect*, Princeton University, New Jersey, 1977; *City Segments*, Walker Art Center, Minneapolis, 1980; *Baird Sampson Associates*, Ballenford Books, Toronto, 1982 (travelled to the Nova Gallery, Vancouver, British Columbia, and the Technical University of Nova Scotia, Halifax); *Recent Works of Baird/Sampson Associates*, Clare Hall, Cambridge, England, 1985. Recipient: Ontario Renews Award, 1981; *Canadian Architect* Award of Excellence, 1985. Fellow, Royal Architectural Institute of Canada, 1985. Address: Baird/Sampson Associates, Architects, 35 Britain Street, Toronto, Ontario M5A 1R7, Canada.

Works:

1972 Ontario Housing prototypes (competition project)

1973 Archibald/Murray House additions and renovations, Victoria Park Avenue, Scarborough, Ontario

1974 Dunbarton-Fairport United Church reconstruction, Pickering, Ontario

Onbuildingdowntown: Core Area Design Guidelines, Toronto

1975 Inner Core Area Land-Use Study, Toronto

1976 Haig House additions and renovations, Farnham Avenue, Toronto

Regina Traces: Urban Development Plan, Regina, Saskatchewan (competition project)

1977 Small Town Arena System, Ontario

1978 Dufferin/St. Clair Library additions and renovations, Dufferin Avenue, Toronto

Three Ontario Towns: Historical Case Study

1979 Historic Shopping Area Study, Bowmanville, Ontario

1980 Ontario Trucking Association Headquarters, Rexdale, Ontario
St. Clair Silverthorn Library additions and renovations, St. Clair Avenue, Toronto
Spadina Quay Public Space Design, Harbourfront, Toronto
Spadina Quay Street Design, Harbourfront, Toronto
With Baird/Sampson Associates:
1982 Bathurst Quay Site Plan, Harbourfront, Toronto
Greening Downtown: Georgia-Robson Corridor Design Guidelines, Vancouver, British Columbia
City Hall, Edmonton Alberta (competition project)
Iler/Campbell Law Offices, Simcoe Street, Toronto
McGrath House addition and renovation, Unsworth Avenue, Toronto
1983 Church of the Epiphany and St. Mark additions and renovations, Cowan Avenue, Toronto
Regina Rail relocation, Regina, Saskatchewan
Trinity Square and Park, Toronto (competition project)
1984 Elliot Lake Auditorium for the Arts, Elliot Lake, Ontario (project)
National Capital Symbols Analysis Study, Ottawa, Ontario
Queen's Quay Streetscape, Harbourfront, Toronto
1985 Spadina Park, Harbourfront, Toronto
Old St. John's Church restoration, Stamford, Ontario

Publications:

By BAIRD: books—*New Towns for Old?*, editor, Stratford, Ontario 1969; *Meaning in Architecture*, editor, with Charles Jencks, London 1969, New York 1972; *Alvar Aalto*, with photographs by Yukio Futagawa, London 1970; *Artwork on Toronto*, Toronto 1984; articles—"Expression: An Argument" in *Architectural Review* (London), November 1965; "Paradox in Regent's Park" in *Arena* (London), April 1966; "La Dimension Amoureuse in Architecture" in *Arena* (London), June 1967; "Ask The People Who Live There . . .", with James Lorimer, in *Architecture Canada* (Toronto), May 1968; "A New Literacy" in *Architectural Design* (London), March 1969; "The Dining Position" in *Forum* (Hilversum, Netherlands), October 1976; "999 Queen Street: A Collective Failure of Imagination" in *City Magazine* (Toronto), Summer 1976; "Vacant Lottery" in *Design Quarterly* (Minneapolis), no. 108, 1978; "Main Street: Can It Survive the Shopping Centre?", with Barry Sampson, in *After the Developers*, Toronto 1981; "Northern Polarities", with George Kapelos, in *O Kanada*, exhibition catalogue, West Berlin 1982; "Think: Engage: Cross Disciplines: Persevere: Build" in *C Magazine* (Toronto), Summer 1985.

On BAIRD: book—*Building with Words: Canadian Architects on Architecture*, with introduction by W. Bernstein and R. Cawker, Toronto 1981; articles—"Seven Essays in Ontario Vernacular", in *Process: Architecture* (Tokyo), no. 5, 1978; "Regina Traces, Saskatchewan, 1975" in *Design Quarterly* (Minneapolis), no. 113/114, 1980; "Wraith Exquis" by

Nory Miller in *Progressive Architecture* (New York), February 1981; "The Edmonton City Hall Competition" by Larry Richards and Ina Wakefield in *Trace* (Toronto), July/September 1981; "Fiendishly Clever Renovation Is Eminently Sensible As Well" by Adele Freedman in *Globe and Mail* (Toronto), 5 November 1981; "Recycled Shell" in *Canadian Architect* (Toronto), June/July 1983; "Interview with Baird and Sampson Associates, Toronto" by Leo De Sorcy in *Fifth Column* (Montreal), Summer 1983; "Ontario Trucking Association Headquarters" in *Section A* (Montreal), August/September 1983; "Trinity Square Park Competition" in *Section A* (Montreal), December 1983/January 1984; "Greening Vancouver?" by Andrew Gruft in *Section A* (Montreal), February/March 1984; "At The Crossroads" by Susan Doubilet in *Progressive Architecture* (New York), August 1984; "Award of Excellence" in *Canadian Architect* (Toronto), December 1984.

We believe that modernism in architecture, as Jurgen Habermas has argued, is an "uncompleted project". We are well aware of the critiques which have been made of mainstream modernism, in the past decade or so. Nevertheless, we see in many anti-modern polemics a whole series of false dichotomies.

We refuse to accept, for example, the conventional current view that modern architecture cannot contribute to a rich tradition of urbanity. We are well aware that a quarter century of simplistic, second-generation modernism *was* anti-urban, and we deplore the work of this sad period after the second world war. But we insist that this simple-

George Baird: Edmonton City Hall, Alberta, 1982 (model).

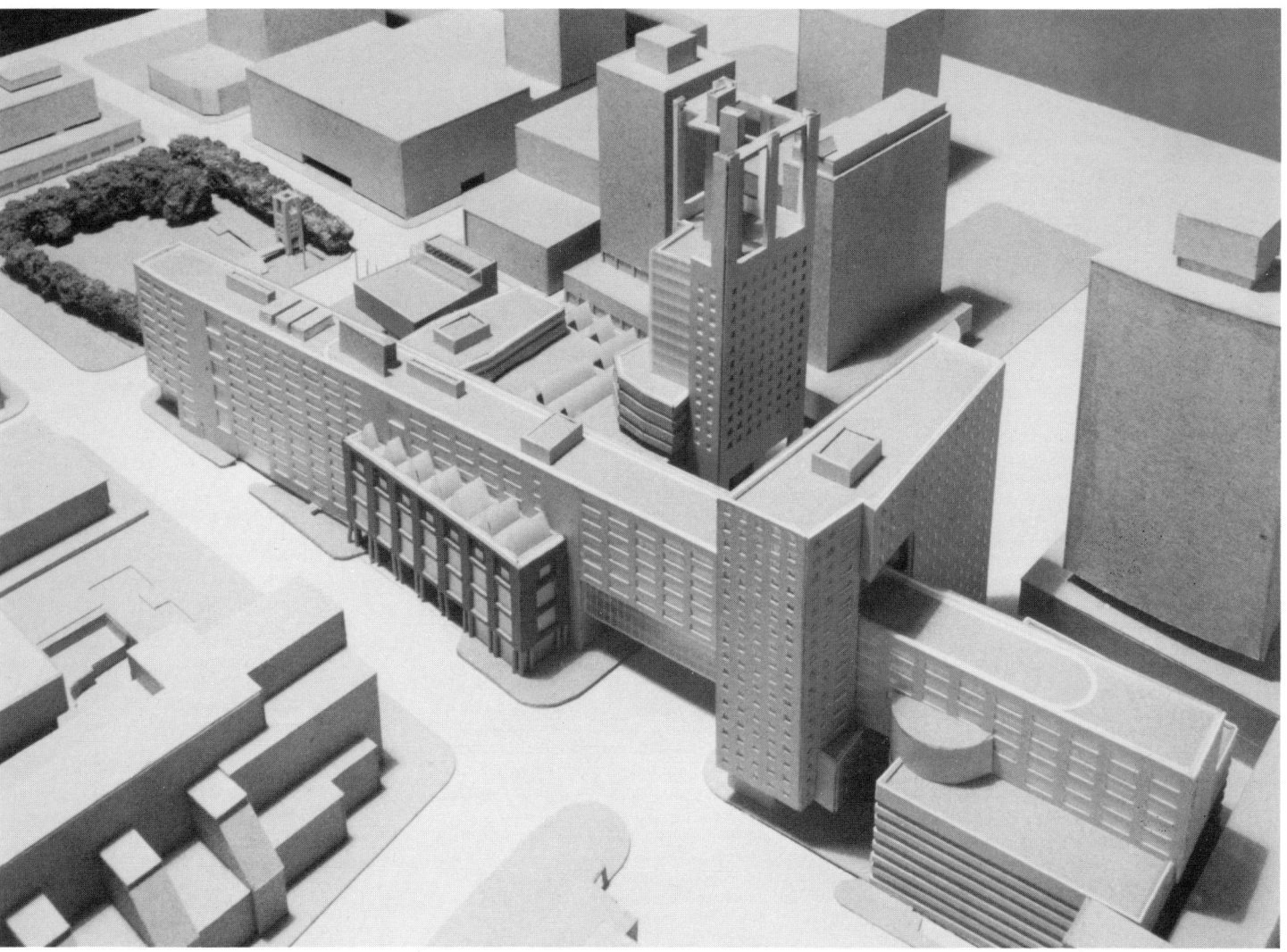

mindedness is not in any way inherent in modernism itself. We strive, in our own urban projects, simultaneously, to achieve the important qualities of modernity and of urbanity.

We refuse also to accept the common current view that architecture and social programs have nothing to do with one another. Indeed, we have noted with some irony how certain leftist and conservative critics of mainstream modernism have come to agree with one another in this regard. The leftists in question see formal values in architecture *sui generis* as elitist, and have convinced themselves that any interest in architectural form per se, is socially irresponsible. Their conservative allies on the other hand, hold that architecture must hold itself above social concerns altogether, being capable of being compromised by any concern for social issues. We deny both of these sad extremisms, believing instead that the evolution of social forms, remains, as, in our view, it always has been one of the most important generators of new formal possibilities in architecture.

We interest ourselves in the formal exploration of such possibilities. At the same time we recognize the necessity of architecture to go beyond the mere *expression* of social life, to yet more transcendent ends. We reject too, the supposition that socially responsible praxis precludes the possibility of symbolism, as well as the converse supposition that architectural modernism cannot be symbolic. We see it as the task of our generation to use social forms and contemporary building methods to generate new architectural symbols.

As a result of these convictions we hold for our own architecture two kinds of "both-and" objectives. We practise in a specific setting in the northern half of North America in the last quarter of the twentieth century, and we seek to give expression to an architectural discourse which addresses the large international issues in architecture in our time, *at the same time* that it openly acknowledges the local particularities of our own society. Similarly, we seek to contribute to the completion of the project of modernity in architecture in our time *at the same time* that we comment upon, enrich and elaborate the contextual traditions of architecture and urbanism in Canada.

Finally, seeing modernism as a socio-cultural phenomenon *not* of the past half century, but rather of the past *two* centuries or so, we see the continuation of this "uncompleted project" as encompassing proposals which link technological development to symbolic expression in a fashion which will long outlast ourselves and our practising contemporaries.

—George Baird and Barry Sampson

Educator, lecturer, author, editor, designer, consultant, Baird is unique in Canada. No other architect in the country has demonstrated that range and combination of talents which elsewhere in the world has characterized the membership of the avant-garde and made it such a potent force. Yet unlike his international counterparts, Baird has had little impact on the architectural scene, either in general, across Canada, or even in Toronto.

One of the reasons for this failure to influence his contemporaries probably lies in the quality and content of his work. A persistent concern among Canadian intellectuals has been the fear of provincialism. Baird himself has adressed this issue, arguing that architecture must be measured by international standards. The topic seems to be particularly troublesome in Toronto which, at least in the minds of its inhabitants, represents the best in Canada, yet still seems to place well behind New York and other important centres.

In his own work, Baird has shown intelligence, sensitivity and descrimination judged by the "progressive" architectural norms of the day. Perhaps this is where the paradox lies. Applying international models of theory and practice to the Canadian situation almost guarantees mediocrity.

Architecture is not just a fine art but also a social art; it owes much to its historic and geographic context. Transplanting solutions from one country to another usually reduces their value. Additionally, the derivative is seldom as interesting as the original, and Baird's work is no exception. It tends to follow foreign precedents rather than to advance them or question their validity.

Meanwhile, no new solutions are proposed for this country. Here is where leadership might emerge and worldwide attention be attracted. By adopting the position that the quality of architecture should be measured by the standards of its own avant-garde instead of by the success of its response to local conditions, beliefs and aspirations, Baird seems to have been diverted from viewing Canadian problems in a different and rewarding manner. This is to be regretted as no one else in his generation has shown the same potential to fulfill this role.

—Anthony Jackson

BAKEMA, Jacob Berend.

Dutch. Born in Groningen, 8 March 1914. Educated at the Technical High School, Groningen, 1932-37; Academy of Architecture, Amsterdam, 1937-41, Dip.Arch. (cum laude) 1941; Technical University, Delft, Netherlands, 1939-40. During World War II, prisoner of war in France, 1941; escaped and joined the underground movement in Groningen, 1942. Married Silina Th. van Borssum Waalkes in 1939; children: Brita, Erik, and Nils. Worked in the office of Cor van Eesteren, *q.v.*, Amsterdam, 1937-41, van Tijen and Maaskant, 1941, and in the Rotterdam Municipal Housing Department, 1945. Principal, with J. H. van den Broek, *q.v.*, (died 1978), Architectengemeenschap van den Broek en Bakema, Rotterdam (associates: J. Boot; J. M. A. de Groot; J. E. Rijnsdorp; J. M. Stokla), 1948 until his death in 1981. Extraordinary Professor of Architecture, Technical University, Delft, Netherlands, 1963-80; Professor in Urban Design, Staatliche Hochschule für Bildende Künste, Hamburg, West Germany, 1965-80. Visiting Professor, International Summer Academy, Salzburg, Austria, 1965-69, 1973-75, Columbia University, New York, 1970-71, and Cornell University, Ithaca, New York, 1972. Co-Editor, *Forum,* Hilversum, Netherlands, 1959-64; Member of the Board, *Architectura et Amicitia,* Amsterdam, 1965-67. Member of CIAM (Congrès Internationaux d'Architecture Moderne), 1947-81 (Member of the Board, 1953-59), and of Team 10, 1963-81. Exhibitions: *Bouwen voor een open samenleving,* Boymans Museum, Rotterdam, 1963, toured the Netherlands, Germany, Austria and Italy; *Pampus,* Stedelijk Museum, Amsterdam, 1965, toured the Netherlands, Austria and the United States; *Samen Bouwen,* Town Hall, Schoonhoven, Netherlands, 1972, toured Austria and Germany; *Progettie Opere,* Castello Nuovo, Naples, 1974, toured Italy. Recipient: Dutch Critics Prize, International Association of Art Critics, 1972; Camillo Sitteprize, Austria, 1977; Honorary Cross, Salzburg, Austria, 1978. Member, Akademie der Künste, Berlin 1971-81; Honorary Member, American Institute of Architects, Zentral Vereinigung Architekten Österreichs (Austria), Bund Deutscher Architekten (Germany), Association of Scottish Architects, and Suomen Arkkitehtiliitto (Finland). Officer, Orange-Nassau Order, Netherlands, 1958; Knight, Order of Nederlandse Neeuw, 1971. Member, Order of La Couronne, Belgium, 1958. *Died* (in Rotterdam) *20 February 1981.*

Works:

1947/
48 Social Centre, Rotterdam (demolished)

1947/
53 Cinema 't Venster, Rotterdam

1948/
50 Two semi-detached houses, Hornlaan, Beverwijk, Netherlands
Nederlandse Kroonkurk Mij. N.V. Factory and Office Building, Sluisjesdijk, Rotterdam

1948/
51 Termeulen-Wassen-van Vorst Shopping Bazaar, Binnenweg, Rotterdam

1948/
53 City Transport and Motor Services Building, Schiekanaal, Rotterdam

1949 Pendrecht Housing Estate, Rotterdam (project)
Artists Centre (project)

1949/
50 Layout and buildings for the *Rotterdam Ahoy* exhibition, Stadspark, Rotterdam
Zuid Shipping Union Medical Services Building, St. Jobsweg, Rotterdam

1949/
51 Van Houten and Zn. Metalworks Shop and Office Building, Bierstraat, Rotterdam
Mill and bakery extensions, Binnenhaven, Wageningen, Netherlands
Anthony Veder N.V. Shipping Bureau extensions, Westplein 11, Rotterdam

1949/
52 Van der Meer House remodelling, Prins Bernhardkade, Rotterdam

1949/
53 Lijnbaan Shopping Centre, Lijnbaan, Rotterdam
Ypenhof (van den Broek House), Kralingseweg 179, Rotterdam
Secondary school with gymnasium, Coppelstockstraat, Brielle, Netherlands

1950 Cinema, Hengelo, Netherlands (project)
Public housing, Drente, Netherlands (project)
van den Broek/Bakema Office extensions, Westerkade, Rotterdam
Van Leer Company Administration Building, Stadionplein, Amsterdam (competition project)
Auction Building, Marconistraat, Rotterdam (project)
Bataafse Petroleum Company Administration Building, The Hague (competition project)
Uttman House, Bennekom, Netherlands (project)

1950/
51 Aircraft hangar, Ypenburg, Netherlands
Terrace housing, Heeswijkstraat, Voorburg, The Hague

1950/
53 Holland-America Lines Works Building, Wilhelminakade, Rotterdam

1951 Hoving House, Drachten, Netherlands (project)
Pendrecht Housing Estate, Rotterdam (project; with Opbouw Group)
Sanders House, Vught, Netherlands (project)

1951/
52 Hispano Suiza N.V. Factory, Terheydenseweg, Breda, Netherlands
Esso Service Station, Ungerplein, Rotterdam

1951/
53 Zuid Shipping Union Station, Bananenstraat, Rotterdam
Veder N.V. Warehouse and Office Building, Ijsselhaven, Rotterdam
Public housing, Blankenburgersingel, Overschie, Rotterdam

1951/
54 Terrace shops and houses, Lange Nieuwstraat, Velsen, Netherlands

1951/
61 Metallurgy Laboratory, Technical University, Delft, Netherlands

1952 Veder House, Kralingseweg, Rotterdam (project)

Jacob Bakema: Town Hall, Terneuzen, Netherlands, 1961.

1952/
53 Niehuis-van den Bergh Works Building, with Housing, Havenstraat, Rotterdam

1952/
54 de Klerk Furniture Shop, Nieuwe Binnenweg, Rotterdam
   Public housing, Molenleystraat, Breda, Netherlands
   Huf Shoe Store, Hoogstraat, Rotterdam
   Horticultural School, Burgmeester H. van Sleenstraat, Brielle, Netherlands
   Public housing, with shops, Burgmeester Baumannlaan, Rotterdim
   Ten Cate and Company Administration Building, Spoorstraat, Almelo, Netherlands

1952/
55 Public housing, with shops and restaurant, Pleinweg, Zuidplein, Rotterdam
   Boilerhouse and Laboratory of Heating Techniques, Technical University, Delft, Netherlands

1952/
56 Terraced and public housing, Maarten Harpertszoon Trompstraat, Brielle, Netherlands

1953 Alexanderpolder Housing Estate, Rotterdam (project; with Opbouw Group)
   Van Giessen and Zn. Wharf, Office and 53 Shops enlargement, Krimpen an der Ijssel, Netherlands
   Veder N.V. Office remodelling, Westerkade, Rotterdam (project)
   Hotel, Rotterdam (project)

Van Ommeren N.V. Office Building, Westerlaan, Rotterdam (project)

1953/
54 Housing, Breedveldsingel, Rotterdam
   Layout and buildings for the E 55 exhibition, Rotterdam

1953/
55 Nurses' Home, Westersingel, Rotterdam
   Housing development, Geuzenveld, Amsterdam
   Navy Sports Centre, Schulpweg, Rotterdam

1953/
56 Rotterdamsche Kolen Centrale Office and Warehouse Building, Waalhaven, Rotterdam

1954 Sonneveld House Redevelopment, Schiedamsevest, Rotterdam

1954/
56 Public housing, with shops, Mariniersweg, Rotterdam

1954/
57 Galeries Modernes Department Store, Hoogstraat, Rotterdam
   Town Hall remodelling, Marktplein, Brielle, Netherlands (with Philippus Bolt and C. Baert de la Faille)

1954/
58 Reformed Church, Burgemeester Honnerlage Gretelaan, Schiedam, Netherlands
   T.N.O. Metallurgy Laboratories, Rotterdamseweg, Delft, Netherlands

1955 Civic Center, St. Louis, Missouri (project)
   Visser House, Papendrecht, Netherlands (project)

Zwolsman N.V. Head Office, Utrecht, Netherlands (project)
Sanders House, Juliaanlaan, Rotterdam
Sports Park, Madestein, The Hague (project)
Congress Hall, The Hague (project)

1955/
57 Shopping Centre, Zuiderwinkels, Nagele, Netherlands
   School for the Retarded, Burgmeester H. van Sleenstraat, Brielle, Netherlands
   Prefabricated public housing, Rijswijk, Netherlands

1955/
59 Terraced and public housing, Vrederust Oost, The Hague

1955/
60 Montessori School, Schimmelpenninckstraat 20, Rotterdam

1956 Hotel, Zeestraat-Javastraat, The Hague (project)
   Alexanderpolder Housing Estate, Rotterdam (project; with Opbouw Group)
   Single-family housing, Karpendonk, Eindhoven, Netherlands (project)
   Diepen House, Wassenaar, Netheulands (project)
   Youth Hostel, Oostvoorne, Netherlands (project)
   Theatre, Zwartenweg, The Hague (project)
   Nievelt-Goudriaan and Company Office Building, Veerkade, Rotterdam (project)
   Frik House extensions, Heerenveen, Netherlands (project)

Centre Building, Emmen, Netherlands (project)

1956/
57 Public housing, Hengelolaan, The Hague
Van Giessen and Zn. Offices remodelling, Krimpen an der Ijssel, Netherlands
Wieringa House, Hobbemastraat 2, Middelharnis, Netherlands

1956/
58 Klein Driene Development, Hengelo, Netherlands
Ierland-van Zanten Shop, Lijnbaan, Rotterdam

1956/
61 World Broadcasting Building, Witte Kruislaan 55, Hilversum, Netherlands

1957 Viewing Tower, Stadtpark, Rotterdam (project)
Shopping Centre, Vlaardingen, Netherlands (project)
Maritime Centre, Scheveningen, The Hague (project)

1957/
58 't Heechterp District Development, Leeuwarden Oost, Netherlands

1957/
59 Nord-Kennermerland Regional Plan, North Holland

1957/
60 Apartment tower block, Hansaviertel, Berlin
Diaconessenhuis Clinic extensions, Westersingel, Rotterdam
Medical Centre, de Cordesstraat, Hook of Holland

1957/
62 Aero- and Hydrodynamics Laboratories, Technical University, Delft, Netherlands
Het Parool Newspaper Building, Amsterdam

1958 Netherlands Pavilion, Worlds Fair, Brussels (with Gerrit Rietveld and Joost Willem Cornelis Boks)
Lummus Nedland N.V. Office Building, Plaspoelpolder, Rijswijk, Netherlands (project)
Landbouwhuis (Agricultural Centre), Paternosterstraat, Alkmaar, Netherlands (project)
Capital Centre, Berlin (competition project)
Ter Meulen House, Oude Zeeweg, Noordwijk, Netherlands (project)
Vlaardingen Nord Building, Vlaardingen, Netherlands (project)
Margarine AG/Unilever Office Building, Valentinskamp, Hamburg, West Germany (competition project)
Shopping Centre, Culemborg, Netherlands (project)

1958/
59 Van Welzenes N.V. Factory, Spijkenisse, Netherlands

1958/
60 Floriade horticultural exhibition layouts, Stadspark, Rotterdam
Reformed Church, Ring, Nagele, Netherlands
van Roosbroeck House, Barendrechtseweg, Barendrecht, Netherlands (demolished)

1958/
61 Dura N.V. Office Building, Raadhuisplein, Rotterdam
Analytical Chemistry Laboratories, Technical University, Delft, Netherlands

1958/
62 Town Hall, Marl, West Germany

1958/
63 Central Post Office Building, Prinses Beatrixlaan, The Hague

1959 De Nederlanden 1845 Insurance Building, Adelheidstraat, The Hague (competition project)
Shopping Centre, Laan van Meerdervoort, The Hague (project)

1959/
61 Meerwaldt House, Baarsweg, Hoogvliet, Netherlands
Lamers and Indemans N.V. Factory extensions, Parallelweg, 's Hertogenbosch, Netherlands
Shopping Centre, with maisonettes, Bergen, Netherlands
Terraced houses with shops, Prins Hendrikstraat, Hook of Holland

1959/
62 Grain Testing Laboratories, Technical University, Delft, Netherlands
Leeuwarden Noord Housing Estate, Leeuwarden, Netherlands
Shopping Centre, with houses, Binnenhof, Amstelveen, Netherlands

1959/
63 Road Construction Laboratories, Technical University, Delft, Netherlands

1959/
64 School of Engineering Lecture Building, Technical University, Delft, Netherlands
School of Architecture Lecture Building, Technical University, Delft, Netherlands

1960 World Health Organization Building, Geneva (competition project)
Radio and television station, Kuwait (project)
Cultural Centre, Leverkusen, West Germany (competition project)

1960/
61 Van Buchem House, Offenbachlaan 5, Hillegersberg, Rotterdam
Van Wijk House, Distelstraat 4, Hook of Holland
De Klerk House, Tsjaikofskilaan 7, Hillegersberg, Rotterdam

1960/
62 Post Office, Binnenhof 64, Amstelveen, Netherlands
Junior School and Kindergarten, Smeetslandsedijk, Rotterdam
Raiffeisenbank Building, Prins Hendrikstraat, Hook of Holland
Van Giessen and Zn. Canteen and Drawing Office, Krimpen an der Ijssel, Netherlands
Office building with shops, Tuftmarkt-Kalvermarkt, The Hague

1960/
63 High-rise apartment block, Mariahoeve, The Hague (project)
Office building, Oostingstraat, Emmen, Netherlands
Elementary School, Emmercompascum, Emmen, Netherlands

1960/
68 Town Hall, Terneuzen, Netherlands

1961 Elementary School, Erica, Emmen, Netherlands (project)
Fortgens House, Straatweg, Rotterdam (project)
Timp House extensions, Grindbank, Laren, Netherlands (project)
Steilshoop Housing Estate, Hamburg, West Germany (competition project)
Frik House, Heerenveen, Netherlands (project)
Shopping Centre, Heemskerk, Netherlands (project)
High School for the Social Sciences, Linz, Austria (competition project)
Plan for Wulfen New Town, Westphalia, Germany (competition project)
Shopping Centre, Jagershoef, Eindhoven, Netherlands (project)
High-rise apartment block, Rozenburg, Netherlands (project)

1961/
62 Auditorium, Technical University, Delft, Netherlands
Central Post Office, Velperweg, Arnhem, Netherlands
Wierda House, Burgemeester Falkenlaan, Heerenveen, Netherlands

1961/
63 Philips N.V. Works Housing, Strijpsestraat, Eindhoven, Netherlands
Van Wilgen House, Mahlersingel, Rotterdam

1962 Development plan for the Woensel District, Eindhoven, Netherlands
Town Hall, Offenbach am Main, West Germany (competition project)
Nordweststadt Centre, Frankfurt (competition project)
Centre Building, Spoorstraat, Nimwegen, Netherlands (project)
Van der Sande Wijbrand House, Straatweg, Rotterdam (project)
Lijnbaan Shopping Centre extension, Lijnbaan, Rotterdam
University of the Ruhr, Bochum, West Germany (competition project)
Philips N.V. Works Housing, Geldrop, Netherlands

1962/
63 Expansion plans for Hengelo North, Netherlands

1964 Protestant Student Community Centre, Mainz, West Germany (competition project)
Town Hall, Jerusalem (competition project)
Town plan for Skopje, Yugoslavia (competition project)
Sociedad Immobiliaria y del Gran Kursaal Maritimo S.A., San Sebastian, Spain (competition project)

1964/
68 Drachten Elementary School, Netherlands

1964/
69 Hermes Student Club, Rotterdam

1965 Zwijndrecht Secondary School, Netherlands
Leo van Ireland House, Rotterdam
Mobile Theatre, for the Dutch Opera Foundation (project; with Frei Otto)

1965/
70 M.B.O. Covered Shopping Centre, Leeuwarden, Netherlands

1965/
71 Drachten Elementary School for Handicapped Children, Netherlands

1965/
76 Town Hall, Ede, Netherlands

1966/
68 Corpac Office Building, Tilburg, Netherlands

1966/
69 Apartment building, Tilburg, Netherlands

1966/
73 Nurses' Dormitory, Leidschendam, Netherlands

1966/
74 I.C.Z. Hospital, Apeldoorn, Netherlands

1967 Sanders House reconstruction, Schiedam, Netherlands

1968 Medical School, Accra, Ghana
Urban district development plan for Diemen, Netherlands
Exotarium (tropical garden), The Hague
Town Hall, Amsterdam (competition project)

1968/
73 Cultural and Community Centre, Winschoten, Netherlands

1968/
76 D.S.H.B. Old People's Housing, Delft, Netherlands

1969 Shell Company Administration Building, Hamburg (competition project)
Lommerrijk Sports Centre Residential Buildings, Rotterdam
Town Hall and Apartments, Weert, Netherlands
University of Brussels (competition project)
Student Dormitories, Delft, Netherlands

1969/
77 Mummelmannsberg Comprehensive School, Hamburg, West Germany (with others)

1970 Netherlands Pavilion, World's Fair, Osaka, Japan (with Carel Weeber)

1971 University Economics Faculty Building extension, Rotterdam (project)

1971/
73 de Grave Home for the Retarded, Gorinchem, Netherlands

1971/
76 Erasmus College Secondary School, Zoetermeer, Netherlands
1973 Zeckendorf House, Bahamas
Sunter Town Plan, Djakarta, Indonesia
(project)
Kurhaus District redevelopment, Scheveningen, Netherlands (as supervising architects)
Barre Molen Windmill restoration, Zo-
eterwoude, Netherlands
1974 City Centre plan for Eindhoven (project; with
Herman Hertzberger)
World Trade Centre, Rotterdam (competition
project)
Traffic plan for Kloekamp and Main Railway
Station, The Hague
Kaatstraat renovation, Utrecht, Netherlands
1975 Renovation of the Weerdjes District, including apartment buildings, Arnhem,
Netherlands

Publications:

By BAKEMA: books—*Towards an Architecture for Society*, Delft, Netherlands 1963; *From Doorstep to Town*, Zeist, Netherlands, 1964; *Stadtebauliche Architektur*, Salzburg 1965; *L. C. van der Vlugt*, Amsterdam 1968; *Team 10 Primer*, with others, edited by Alison Smithson, London 1968; *Thoughts about architecture*, edited by Marianne Gray, London 1981; *Architektur der Zukunft, Zukunft der Architektur*, with Jürgen Joedicke, Egon Schirmbeck and others, Stuttgart 1982. articles—"Open Brief aan J.J.P. Oud," with J. H. van den Broek, in *De Groene Amsterdammer* (Amsterdam), 6 December 1952; "Building with Weathering Steel" in *Polytechnische Tijdschrift* (The Hague), December 1973; "BFU: Nine Evaluations," with others, in *Architecture Plus* (New York), January/February 1974; "Trees First, Then Houses" in *Bouw* (Rotterdam), May 1974; "Some Conditions Governing the Current Development of Architecture" in *Bauen und Wohnen* (Zürich), December 1975; "Bureaucracy Puts Architecture into Cold Storage" in *RIBA Journal* (London), October 1976; "Building in Urban Holland" in *Parametro* (Bologna), April 1979; "Once Again: Two Libraries and Architecture" in *Wonen-TA/BK* (Heerlen, Netherlands), June 1979.

On BAKEMA: books—*CIAM 1959 in Otterlo*, Stuttgart 1959; *Architektur und Stadtebau: Das Werk van den Broek und Bakema*, edited by Jürgen Joedicke, Stuttgart 1963; *Bouwen voor een open Samenleving*, exhibition catalogue, Rotterdam 1963; *van den Broek/Bakema*, edited by Camillo Gubitosi and Alberto Izzo, Rome 1976; *Architecture-Urbanism: Architecten-gemeenschap van der Broek en Bakema*, edited by Jürgen Joedicke, Stuttgart 1976; articles—"Het Bureau van den Broek en Bakema" by Willem van Tijen in *Forum* (Amsterdam), June 1957; "Costruzioni degli Architetti Jacob Bakema e Johannes van den Broek" by G. Perugini in *L'Architettura* (Rome), September 1959; "van den Broek und Bakema," special issue of *Bauen und Wohnen* (Zürich), October 1959; "Brinkman, Brinkman, van der Vlugt, van den Broek, Bakema" by B. Housden, special issue of *Architectural Association Journal* (London), December 1960; "Computer Centre of the Amro Bank, Amstelveen" in *Bauen und Wohnen* (Zürich) September 1973; "Comprehensive School in Mummelmannsberg, Hamburg" in *Baumeister* (Munich), February 1974; "New Education Centre in Mummelmannsberg" in *Polytechnisch Tijdschrift* (The Hague), March 1977; "Exhibition of Rotterdam Library Project" by Francis Strauven in *Wonen-TA/BK* (Heerlen, Netherlands), February 1979; "Obituary: Jacob Bakema" *Architects' Journal* (London), 4 March 1981; "Jacob B. Bakema: His Destiny and His Enduring Significance" by Wiek Roling in *Bouw* (Rotterdam), 21 March 1981; "Jacob Bakema, 1914-1981" in *Architecture d'aujourd'hui* (Paris), April 1981; "Bakema Speaks Again" in *De Architect* (The Hague), April 1981; "J. B. Bakema 1914-1981" in *Deutsche Bauzeitung* (Stuttgart), April 1981; "Jacob B. Bakema, 1914-1981" by Donald Grinberg in *Progressive Architecture* (New York), July 1981; "Jaap Bakema 1914-1981" by Aldo Van Eyck and others in *Forum* (Hilversum, Netherlands), July 1981; "Jacob B. Bakema 1914-1981" by Jetteke Bolten in *Dutch Art + Architecture Today* (Amsterdam), December 1981.

Urbanistic architecture can be more than functionalism of use; it can also involve functionalism of expression. Architecture without urban dimension in our days cannot give enough information. Man is living in a field of tension between his locality—town—region, and earth-moon universe. A living town-village can no longer be limited. Nowhere in the world has this proved to be possible. This is the time of total urbanization. But the process can be structured by architecture. Rhythmized and accentuated.

Perhaps, for the first time in history, art will be a condition of existence, and urbanization must find the right proportions between use and care. Architecture always was a process of proportioning. Interior is concentrated intensified exterior.

Knowing that property, power and defence can no more be continuous reasons for architecturban forms stimulates research into more universal motivation. Somehow the understanding that our existence-energy-being is a kind of network-like structure make us try even harder for solutions for clustering, knots and transitional elements with which the built environment can be shaped.

There are knots of connection: to research what elements can be connected or knotted without losing identity—wall-like buildings, towers, transitional elements, energy lines, clustering.

Sant' Elia, Terragni, Golosov, Rietveld and Duiker (during 1925-35) contributed to our architecturbanistic vocabulary. They expressed a new kind of simultaneity; the abandoning of hierarchy. But they could not know the problems of total urbanization of our days. The world must now deal with the worldwide administration of production and distribution.

The architectonic vocabularly has to be prepared for the expression of total urbanization. Town planning is also society planning. Clustering, wall-like buildings, transitional elements, rhythmizing and accentuation are events which can be experienced visually. They can refer to human relations and interests. Conceptions such as court, square and street are signs of relationship and contrast. Urbanistic structures and forms can influence human meeting and separation. To find out what sorts of clusters are appropriate is also a question about the relationships of social forms.

The building program is named: office, house, shop, church, post office, auditorium, hospital. Every name stands for a growing idea and in every building program there is that hidden relation with all other programs and their expression by space-form conception. Every building program is part of the total built environment. The participation of every building program in the total urban structure and the expression of both participation and independence is the proper exercise of architecturbanism: it gives social, economical and political consequence.

There can grow an urban image in which both parts and the whole can be expressed. Every building program can thus be activated to develop its relationship with all others. Transitional elements are important means of expression of these events: the telephone box, a flower stand, a canopy, offices over shops can be stepping stones. At a distance I see something high, and at the foot of it I discover the small elements. At the speed of cars, I can experience the high elements at a distance; at the speed of pedestrians, I become familiar with small elements. To be information and sign is the extension of use-functionalism.

This is extended to expressive functionalism. Visual clustering, grouping, and the structure of society are reciprocally defined concepts.

The space-plastic urban form is a problem of the relationship of volumes in space. The administrative urban form is, anyway, also a social political problem. It could be simpler for every user if urban forms and their areas of influence could be simultaneously an expression of the common interests of the user. As in history the town hall and church were meaningful, so our new form, should be the expression of the new distribution of power. (If we consider what forms, until now, have *not* been used to shape the built environment, we can better understand the expressionlessness of much modern architecture.)

There are many kinds of building programs that can stimulate and express an imaginative reality. Can we mobilize form to serve the coming total urbanization? Does our time have potential enough for such a task? Much will depend on the simultaneous employment of a lust-for-use and a lust-for-care. How does one find the architectonic expression of total urbanization?

—Jacob Bakema (1980)

Jacob Bakema was versed in technology and was tutored in hydraulic engineering as well as in architecture. He studied part-time in Amsterdam, where his final-year tutor was Mart Stam. As a native of Groningen, he was perhaps unsympathetic to the theories of the Delft School, where he attended selected courses in town planning as a part-time student, for the predominantly Roman Catholic ideals of Granpré Molière found more congenial ground in which to flourish in the southern provinces of Brabant and Limburg. The craft traditions that had been a feature of Dutch architecture since Berlage purified design of excessively applied ornament had flourished during the inter-war years. Functionalist ideas, as propounded by the followers of De Stijl, were seen to be radically to the left, and a more continuous traditional manner of design was thus in favour during times of international stress. Bakema remained convinced by modernist ideas and rejected the conservative-craft-oriented beliefs of the Delft School.

His experience from 1937 until 1941 in the office of Cor van Eesteren in Amsterdam and later contact with van Tijen, in whose office he worked from 1941 until 1943, brought him to know the partnership of Brinkman and van der Vlugt. He thus had a long connection with the firm that was later to consist of Brinkman and van den Broek. The partnership's buildings—such as the van Nelle factory and the Bergpolder block in Rotterdam—remained true to functionalism at a time where there was a reaction back to traditional architecture. Bakema joined van den Broek as a partner in 1948, and the older man was appointed professor at Delft, so the two partners were in a position to attack the conservative theories of the Delft School. In their attacks, they were supported by the survivors of the De Stijl movement.

Bakema was solely concerned with the designs for the 't Venster Centre in Rotterdam and for the civic centre plans for St. Louis; however, it is with the office of van den Broek that his most famous buildings were erected. The Lijnbaan Centre in Rotterdam in 1953 was an early version of the pedestrian shopping street. The partnership also produced a number of civic centres, that at Marl (the centre at Terneuzen is more satisfactory) being representative of a type that has become depressingly familiar all over western Europe and America. Four tower blocks linked by lower slabs, with a courtyard, the whole ensemble planned to get as far away as possible from any hint of formality, geometry, or classical memory, will be familiar to all those who have seen what has occurred in towns during the 1950s and 1960s.

Among other works by Bakema in partnership with van den Broek are schools at Brielle and for the Montessori Lyceum at Rotterdam; the Netherlands

Pavilion at the World's Fair in Brussels; the Rotterdam stores, Wassen van Vorst and Galeries Modernes; buildings for the Technical University at Delft; the Osaka Expo Pavilion; and severe modern churches at Schiedam and Nagele.

Bakema and van den Broek have been prolific and have had a great influence on developments in Britain and in Germany. The elegance of earlier works by the Brinkmann and van der Vlugt partnership is missing, however, and a certain brashness perhaps prevails. The assertion by Bakema that architecture is the three-dimensional expression of human behaviour savours of a certain cliché-ridden mentality that has bedevilled architectural thinking for so long. One suspects that any slick phrase can gain credence in a profession that has lost its values and is confused in its direction.

Bakema and van den Broek also established themselves in the field of town planning, and their proposals for the Kennermerland area of Holland set fashions in regional planning concepts during the 1950s and early 1960s (This scheme was presented by Bakema at the final meeting of C.I.A.M., a body with which he was closely involved during the postwar period). Indeed, the *opera* of Bakema and van den Broek are representative of trends in the architectural profession in the first two decades following World War II, exemplifying how traditional values were deliberately jettisoned. Little regard was paid to existing fabric (although Bakema appears in his writings to suggest the opposite), and the language of architecture, be it classical or vernacular, was ignored for an abstraction. The result of this revolution are visible in towns and cities all over Europe, especially in Britain. The insistence on brash concrete, large areas of glass, unrelated forms, crude junctions, and unrefined detail has been a familiar feature of architecture since the 1950s. Bakema's most famous work is the Lijnbaan in Rotterdam; a dispassionate examination of this large development will show that it has not worn well and that its modernity is neither elegant nor even remotely admirable.

—James Stevens Curl

BANFI, Gianluigi
Italian. Born in Milan, 2 April 1910. Educated at the Liceo Parini, Milan, 1921-27; Milan Polytechnic School of Architecture, 1927-32, Dip.Arch. 1932. Served in the Italian Army, 1932-34, and 1943 until the armistice, then with the Resistance: arrested by the Germans in 1944: deported to the concentration camp at Mauthausen where he died, 1945. Married Julia Bertolotti in 1939; son: Giuliano. Founder Partner, with Lodovico Belgiojoso, *q.v.* Enrico Peressutti, *q.v.* and Ernesto Nathan Rogers, *q.v.* BBPR Architectural Studio, *q.v.,* Milan, 1932 until his death. Member of CIAM (Congrès Internationaux d'Architecture Moderne), from 1935; Member, Commissione per Le Manifestazione d'Arte Moderne dell' Associazione trai i Cultori d'Architettura, 1935. *Died* (in Mauthausen) *10 April 1945.*

Publications:

By BANFI: articles— "Urbanistica Anno XII," with Lodovico Belgiojoso, in *Quadrante* (Milan), May 1934; "Urbanistica Corporativa," with Lodovico Belgiojoso, in *Quadrante* (Milan), August/ September 1934; "La Casa Contemporanea al Regime Corporativo" in *Domus* (Milan), November 1934; "Una Casa a Milano" in *Quadrante* (Milan), January 1935; "Abitare" in *Domus* (Milan), June 1938; "La Casa e la Finestra" in *Rassegna di Architettura* (Milan), September 1939; "Citta" in *Domus* (Milan), July 1941; "La Casa Ideale" in *Domus* (Milan), August 1942.

See **BBPR ARCHITECTURAL STUDIO**

BARNES, Edward Larrabee.
American. Born in Chicago, Illinois, 15 April 1915. Educated at Harvard University, Cambridge, Massachusetts, under Marcel Breuer, *q.v.,* B.S. (cum laude) 1938, M.Arch. 1942; awarded Sheldon Travelling Fellowship, 1941-42. Served as a Lieutenant in the United States Naval Reserve, 1942-47. Married Mary Elizabeth Coss in 1944; son: John. Since 1949, in private practice, New York. Architectural Design Critic and Lecturer, Pratt Institute, Brooklyn, New York, 1954-59, and Yale University, New Haven, Connecticut, 1957-64; Member of the Visiting Committee, Massachusetts Institute of Technology, Cambridge, 1965-68, and Graduate School of Design, Harvard University, Cambridge, Massachusetts, since 1978; Thomas Jefferson Professor of Architecture, University of Virginia, Charlottesville, 1980. Director, Municipal Art Society of New York, since 1960 (Treasurer, 1961); Trustee, American Academy in Rome, 1963-78 (First Vice-President, 1973; First Vice-Chairman, 1975); Member, Urban Design Council of New York, 1972-76; Trustee, Museum of Modern Art, New York, since 1975; Westchester Planning Board, New York, since 1976. Exhibitions: *Architecture for the Arts*, Museum of Modern Art, New York, 1971; *Edward Larrabee Barnes*, Scaife Gallery, Carnegie Institute, Pittsburgh, Pennsylvania, 1974; *Transformations in Modern Architecture*, Museum of Modern Art, New York, 1979; *New American Art Museums*, Whitney Museum, New York, 1982. Recipient: A. W. Brunner Prize, National Institute of Arts and Letters, 1959; Distinction in the Arts, Yale University, 1959; Design Awards, 1959 and 1963, and Honor Citation, 1974, *Progressive Architecture*, New York; Silver Medal, 1960, and Citation in Landscape Architecture, 1965, Architectural League of New York; First Honor Award, Federal Housing Administration, 1963; New York Chapter Medal of Honor, 1971, Collaborative Achievement Award, 1972, Honor Awards, 1972 and 1977, and Firm Award, 1980, American Institute of Architects; Harleston Parker Medal, Boston Society of Architects, 1972; Merit Awards, American Society of Landscape Architects, 1972 and 1978; Bard Award, City Club of New York, 1978; Louis Sullivan Award, 1979; Honor Award, Connecticut Society of Architects, 1980; Thomas Jefferson Medal, University of Virginia, 1981; Honor Award, Mayor of the City of New York, 1982; Honor Award, New Mexico Society of Architects, 1983. D.F.A.: Rhode Island School of Design, Providence, 1983; D.H.L.: Amherst College, Massachusetts, 1984. Fellow, American Institute of Architects, 1966. Associate, 1969, and Academician, 1974, National Academy of Design; Fellow, American Academy of Arts and Sciences, 1978. Address (office): 410 East 62nd Street, New York, New York 10021, U.S.A.

Works:

1955 Camp Bliss, Fishkill, New York
1958/
  65 Capitol Tower Apartments, 1500 Seventh Street, Sacramento, California (with Wurster, Bernardi and Emmons, and DeMars and Reay)
1959 Woodland House, Chappaqua, New York
1962 Haystack Mountain School of Arts and Crafts, Deer Isle, Maine
1963 El Monte Apartments, Hato Rey, Puerto Rico
  Henry House, Blue Mountain Lake, New York
  Pan American World Airways Ticket Office, Vanderbilt Avenue and East 45th Street, New York (with Charles Forberg)
  Neiman-Marcus Shopping Center, Fort Worth, Texas

1965 Helen Newberry Joy Residence for Women, Wayne State University, Detroit
1965/
  74 Master plan and major buildings for the State University of New York at Potsdam
1966 W. D. Richard Elementary School, Columbus, Indiana
1968 Wye Institute Camp, Cheston-on-Wye, Maryland
  Rochester Institute of Technology campus, Rochester, New York
1968/
  78 Master plan and major building for the State University of New York at Purchase
1969 Christian Theological Seminary, Indianapolis
  Residence Halls, Bennington College, Vermont
  Snell Music Center, William Moore Dietel Library, and Clementine Mille Tangeman Apartments, Emma Willard School, Troy, New York
  Dormitories, St Paul's School, Concord, New Hampshire
1971 New England Merchants National Bank Building, Boston
1973 Theatre and Outdoor Forum, Monterey Peninsula College, Monterey, California
  Crown Center (office building complex, retail complex, and parking), Kansas City, Missouri
  Rockefeller Hall, Harvard Divinity School, Cambridge, Massachusetts
1973/
  74 South Street Seaport Development Plan, New York (with Jonathan Barnett and James Ulmer)
1974 Walker Art Center, Minneapolis
  American Savings Bank, 31-02 Steinway Street, Queens, New York
  Cochrane-Woods Art Center, University of Chicago
1975 Sarah M. Scaife Gallery, Carnegie Institute, Pittsburgh, Pennsylvania
1976 House on the Maine coast, at Mount Desert
  Law School, Drake University, Des Moines, Iowa
1976 Indiana University/Purdue University Master Plan and Main Buildings, Indianapolis
1977 Farnum, Vanderbilt, and Durfee Halls renovation, Yale University, New Haven, Connecticut
  Chicago Botanical Garden, Glencoe, Illinois
  IBM World Trade/Americas Far East Corporation Headquarters, Mount Pleasant, New York
1978 Visual Arts Center, Bowdoin College, Brunswick, Maine
  Cathedral of the Immaculate Conception, Burlington, Vermont
1979 Main Gate and Conservatory restoration, New York Botanical Garden, Bronx, New York
1981 Asia Society Gallery and Office Building, New York
1982 Office Building, 535 Madison Avenue, New York
1983 Museum of New Mexico addition, Santa Fe
  IBM Offices, 590 Madison Avenue, New York
  Dallas Museum of Art, Texas
  Fuqua School of Business, Duke University, Durham, North Carolina
1984 Private House, Dallas, Texas
  Dormitory Building, University of Virginia, Charlottesville
  Mathematics and Computer Center, Amherst College, Massachusetts

Publications:

By BARNES: articles— "Defence Housing" in *Task* (New York), no. 2, 1941; "The Design Process" in *Perspecta* (New Haven, Connecticut), no 5, 1959;

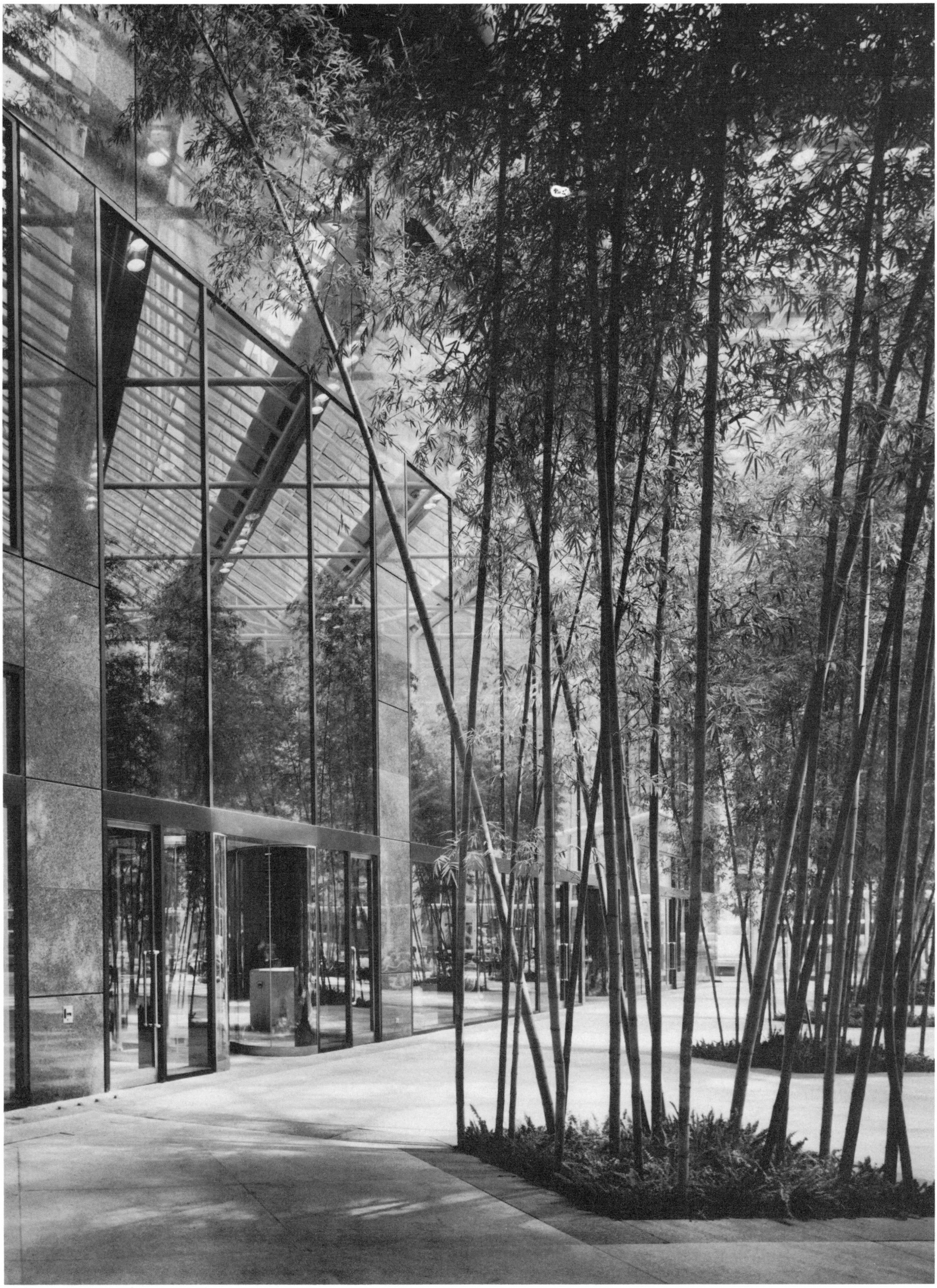

"Control of Graphics Essential to Good Shopping Center Design" in *Architectural Record* (New York), June 1962; "Remarks on Continuity and Change" in *Perspecta* (New Haven, Connecticut), no. 9/10, 1965.

On BARNES: books—*The Ideal Theatre: Eight Concepts*, New York 1962; *Architects on Architecture* by Paul Heyer, New York 1962; *American Architecture Now*, edited by Barbaralee Diamonstein, New York 1979; *Inside New York's Art World* by Barbaralee Diamonstein, New York 1979; *New American Art Museums*, exhibition catalogue, by Helen Searing, New York and Los Angeles 1982; articles—"Genetrix: Personal Contributions to American Architecture" in *Architectural Review* (London), May 1957; "Architecture of Ideas" in *House and Home* (New York), March 1962; "Architect Ed Barnes: Toward Simpler Details, Simpler Forms and Greater Unity" in *Architectural Forum* (New York), August 1963; "A Return to Absolute Simplicity" in *House and Garden* (New York), April 1965; "Lines and Volume: Two Recent Projects from the Boards of Edward Larrabee Barnes" in *Progressive Architecture* (New York), April 1969; "In Praise of the Unexciting Old Concepts Which Inspired the Work of Edward Larrabee Barnes for the College of Potsdam" in *Architectural Record* (New York), August 1972; "Crown Center: Urban Renewal for a Kansas City Grey Area" in *Architectural Record* (New York), October 1973; "Barnes Gratia Artis" in *Progressive Architecture* (New York), March 1975; "What Should a Museum Building Be?" by Paul Goldberger in *Art News* (New York), October 1975; "An Art Center by Edward Larrabee Barnes" by Mildred F. Schmertz in *Architectural Record* (New York), March 1978; "A Neo-Richardson Romanesque Cathedral by Edward Larrabee Barnes" in *Architectural Record* (New York), January 1979; "Visual Arts Centre, Bowdoin College, Brunswick, Maine" in *Baumeister* (Munich), March 1979; "IBM World Trade, America's Far East Headquarters" in *Architecture + Urbanism* (Tokyo), August 1979; "Profile of the Winner of the 1980 Firm Award" by Cervin Robinson in *AIA Journal* (Washington, D.C.), April 1980; "Restoring a Victorian Botanical Conservatory" in *Architectural Record* (New York), October 1980; "More on IBM's Blockbuster . . . " in *Interiors* (New York), November 1980; "A Master Mason Architect Carries Off the Louis Sullivan Trophy" in *Architecture Concept* (Montreal), January/February 1981; "Master of Sleek Restraint" by Douglas Davis in *Newsweek* (New York), 18 May 1981; "Edward L. Barnes' Design for the Performing Arts at Purchase" in *Architectural Record* (New York), August 1981; "Architecture's Master of the Middle Way" by Carter Wiseman in *Saturday Review* (New York), November 1981; "Dallas Museum of Fine Arts" in *Arts and Architecture* (Los Angeles) no. 1, 1983; "Skyscrapers in New York" in *Bouw* (Rotterdam), 28 May 1983; "Dallas Christens Its Exemplary Home-Grown Museum" by John Russell in the *New York Times*, 29 January 1984; "Nine Lively Acres Downtown" by Wolf Von Eckardt in *Time* (New York), 13 February 1984; "Art Oasis", in *Progressive Architecture* (New York), April 1984; "Art and Architecture in Dallas" in *Architecture* (Washington, D.C.), April 1984; "A Skyscraper in Context" by Mildred Schmertz in *Architectural Record* (New York), May 1984; "The IBM Garden Plaza" by Paula Deitz in *Architectural Record* (New York), May 1984; "In Deference: Museum of Fine Arts/Museum of New Mexico, Santa Fe, New Mexico" in *Architectural Record* (New York), May 1985.

Bibliographies: *The Architecture of Restraint in the Works of Edward L. Barnes: A Selected Bibliography* by Robert B. Harmon, Monticello, Illinois 1981; *Edward Larrabee Barnes* by Lamia Doumato, Monticello, Illinois 1982.

Edward Larrabee Barnes: IBM Building Garden Plaza, Madison Avenue, New York, 1983.

In a great variety of civic, educational and ecclesiastic buildings, and several urban and campus plans, Edward Larrabee Barnes has proven himself to be a serious, adept designer with a true finesse in using geometry to order without inhibiting space. His buildings are exacting; they are detailed meticulously and arranged precisely. Still, there is never a sense of the contrived; his buildings are clean and rational without being imposing. He is, amidst gestures that tend towards the monumental, acutely concerned with context, and his buildings rarely appear cold or out of place.

After working with both Gropius and Breuer, it is not surprising that Barnes displays such a love for the value of pure form. Complex programs are simplified by the employment of dominant shapes, and the final buildings are easily readable and abstract. Barnes's materials are generally homogeneous and stretch across large expanses of the external skin. This method eliminates multiple readings and aids in the clarification of the massing that characterizes his structures. In fact, very large glass walls and windows, topped by oversized spandrels, have become a trademark. His campus at Rochester Institute of Technology, the Christian Theological Seminary in Indianapolis, and the Sarah Scaife Gallery at the Carnegie Institute in Pittsburgh all contain this highlight.

In composing plans, Barnes often uses modules. Sometimes they occur in unusual forms or in repetition; at the Plants and Man Building of the New York Botanical Garden, for example, hexagonal glass volumes are repeated. Often, though, his modules are merely organizational devices that are barely visible when the building is complete. Precast concrete panels and large cut stone are common materials in Barnes's architecture, and both further impose modular dimension restrictions.

Some of Barnes's recent work exhibits a lighter approach to materials, but there is still a clear reference to geometry, formal order in the plan, and careful, precise detailing. They still incorporate abstract simplifications of massing and detail, and the results are not merely rational but also evocative, without seeming forced.

—Ching-Yu Chang

BARNETT, Jonathan.

American. Born in Boston, Massachusetts, 6 January 1937. Educated at the Noble and Greenough School, Dedham, Massachusetts, 1948-54; Yale University, New Haven, Connecticut, 1954-58, B.A. 1958; Cambridge University (Mellon Fellow), under Leslie Martin, *q.v.*, and Colin Rowe, 1958-60, B.A. 1960, M.A. 1967; Yale University, under Paul Rudolph, *q.v.*, 1960-63, M.Arch. 1963. Designer in the office of Haines, Lundberg and Waehler, New York, 1963-64; Associate Editor, *Architectural Record*, New York, 1964-67 (Editorial Consultant, since 1968); Principal Urban Designer, 1967-69, and Director of the Urban Design Group, 1969-71, New York City Planning Department. Since 1971, in private pracice, as consultant and urban designer, New York. Professor of Architecture, and Director of the Graduate Program in Urban Design, City College of New York, since 1971. Member of the Board, Municipal Art Society, 1970-78. Vice-President, 1968-70, and President, Architectural League of New York, 1977-81; Member of the Board, New York Landmarks Conservancy, since 1973; Member of the Executive Committee, New York Chapter, American Institute of Architects, 1977-79. Program Director, First National Conference on Urban Design, New York, 1978; President of the Architecture and Planning Section, Jubilee Congress of the Australian and New Zealand Association for the Advancement of Science, 1980. Exhibitions: *The New City: Architecture and Urban Renewal*, Museum of Modern Art, New York, 1966; *Urban Design in New York*, Architectural League of New York, 1969 (organized exhibition). Recipient: Jesse Neal Award, 1966; *Urban Design* Award, 1978. Address (office): 330 West 42nd Street, New York, New York 10036, U.S.A.

Works:

1966/
67 Twin Parks Urban Renewal Plan, Bronx, New York (with Giovanni Pasanella, J. T. Robertson, Richard Weinstein, and M. Weintraub)

1968 Standards for Planned Unit Development, New York (with Urban Design Group)
Special Theatre Zoning District, New York (with Urban Design Group)

1969 Downtown Brooklyn Development Plan, New York (with Urban Design Group and Vincent Ponte)
Negril Development Plan, Jamaica, West Indies (with Adelates Technical Services, Giovanni Pasanella, J.T. Robertson, and Richard Weinstein)
Comprehensive Plan for New York City

1970/
71 Rapid Transit Corridors Plan, for the New York City boroughs of Brooklyn, Queens, Bronx, and Manhattan (with Urban Design Group)

1973/
74 South Street Seaport Development Plan, New York (with James Ulmer and Company and Edward Larrabee Barnes)

1975 Various projects for Arlen Realty, in Dallas and Houston, Texas, Alexandria, Virginia, and New York (with Arlen Planning and Design Group and J. T. Robertson)

1976/
78 Development and management plans for the Gateway National Recreation Area, New York (with the National Park Service)

1977 Louisville Alley Study, Louisville, Kentucky (with the Community Design Center and Grady Clay)
Alaska State Capital Competition Plan, Willow, Alaska (with M. Paul Friedberg and Benjamin Thompson)

1977 Downtown development strategy for Pittsburgh, Pennysylvania

1978 Sha Tin and Tuen Mun town Centre Plans, New Territories, Hong Kong (as adviser to Yunken Freeman)
Crawford-Roberts Neighborhood Plan, Pittsburgh, Pennsylvania

1979 Manhattan Community Planning Board Studies no. 7, New York

1979 Downtown Urban Design Coordination, Pittsburgh, Pennsylvania

1980 New York City Convention and Exhibition Center Urban Design Study, New York
Downtown Design and Development Studies, Salt Lake City, Utah (with Philip G. Hammer)

1981 Downtown Urban Design Studies, Cleveland, Ohio
H. E. B. Grocery Company Landscape Designs (with Geiger-Berger engineers)

1982 Downtown Urban Analysis, Bridgeport, Connecticut (with Regional Plan Association and Design Development Resources)

1983 Downtown Design and Development Studies, Boise, Idaho
City Centre Development Controls, Yanbu, Saudi Arabia (with John Carl Warnecke and Associates, Archiplan, Madin, and URS International)

1983- ARCORP Project Urban Design, Weehawken and West New York, New Jersey (phase 1 with Cesar Pelli and Associates, Hillier Group, and Fisher-Friedman Associates)

1984 Downtown Urban Design and Action Plan, Bridgeport, Connecticut (with Halcyon Ltd., and Wilbur Smith and Associates)
Downtown Urban Design Coordination, Kansas City, Missouri
Downtown Urban Design Coordination, Charleston, South Carolina

Publications:

By BARNETT: books—*Urban Design as Public Policy*, New York 1974, Tokyo 1978; *The Architect as Developer*, with John Portman, New York 1976; *Introduction to Urban Design*, New York 1982; *The Elusive City*, New York 1985; articles—"A New Meaning for Modern Architecture" in *Architectural Record* (New York), July 1966; "Helping Downtown Compete with the Suburbs" in *Architectural Record* (New York), January 1974; "Future of the Office Building" in *Architectural Record* (New York), April 1974; "Wanted: Not-for-Profit Entrepreneur" in *Architectural Record* (New York), December 1974; "What To Do for an Encore..." in *Architectural Record* (New York), June 1976; "What's New in Downtown Planning?" in *Urban Design* (Purchase, New York), Spring 1977; "Enterprise Zone" in *Urban Design International* (Purchase, New York), May/June 1981; "Designing Downtown Pittsburgh" in *Architectural Record* (New York), January 1982.

On BARNETT: books—*American Architecture Now*, edited by Barbaralee Diamonstein, New York 1980; *Collaboration: Artists and Architects*, edited by Barbaralee Diamonstein, New York 1981.

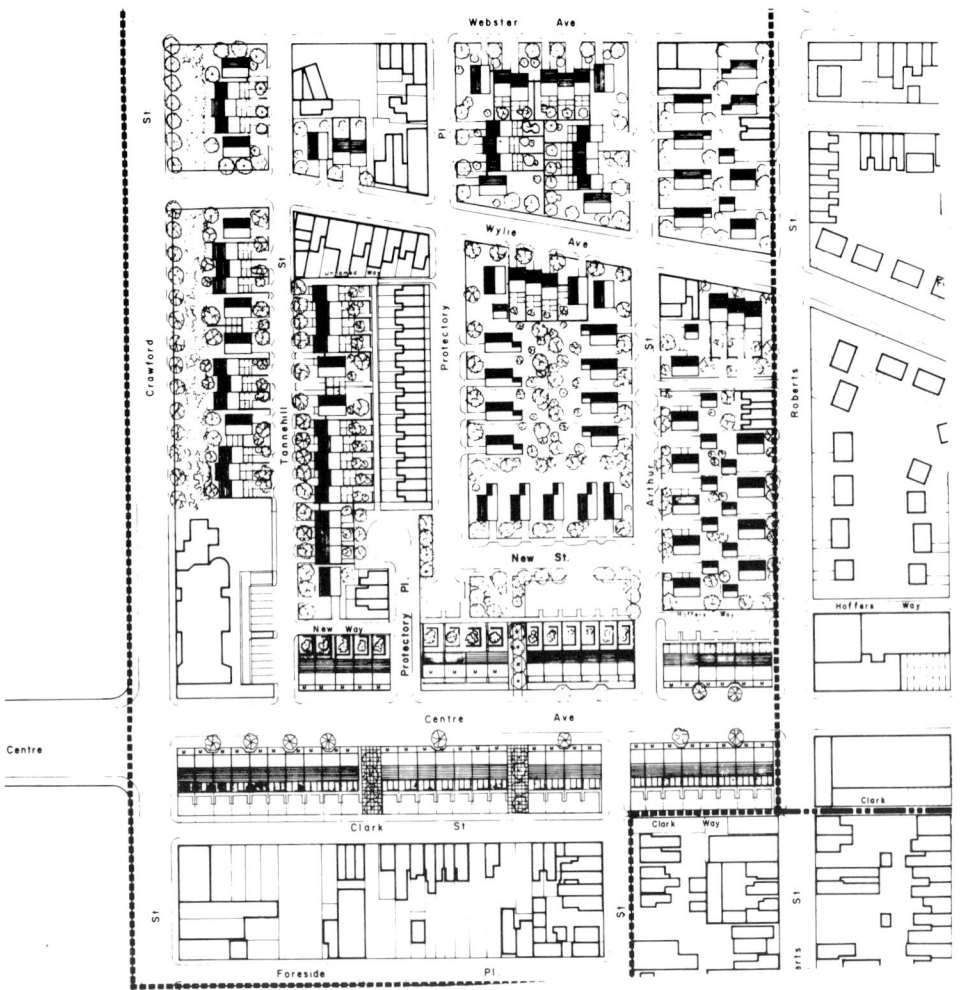

Jonathan Barnett: Crawford-Roberts Neighbourhood Plan, Pittsburgh, 1978.

Huge amounts of money are spent on cities, much of the time to do things badly. My work, whether teaching, writing, or consulting, is involved in redirecting the resources that are being expended in any case: on private development, government buildings, parks, highways, and the other major changes we make in our environment, to achieve both better design and long-range public interests. My practice is devoted to working with cities, federal agencies, community groups, private developers, or architects to develop, design, and effectuate large-scale new development or the conservation of existing neighborhoods and historic districts.

I direct a graduate program in urban design that accepts students who already have professional degress in architecture or landscape architecture and extends that education with the skills and insights that will enable them to use their talents at an urban scale. The program provides substantial course work in law and real estate, so that studenst will be equipped with the tools to negotiate effectively as either government officials or designers; intense case-study studio problems in consultation with the practitioners involved; part time apprenticeship in New York offices working on urban design commissions; and an intellectually rigorous instruction in the history and structure of contemporary cities and the pertinent social, economic, and planning issues of the foreseeable future.

My latest book, *The Elusive City*, is a history of the struggle in western civilization between attempts to design cities and relatively intractable social and economic forces. The book, in discussing not only the designs but the political and personal circumstances in which they were developed—and the often far-from-expected results—seeks to illuminate the pitfalls and possibilities for design on this scale. I have also written a textbook *Introduction to Urban Design*, for the beginning student, for whom no such text had been available.

—Jonathan Barnett

Jonathan Barnett began his career as an architect and an architectural writer, but his primary professional effort has been in the field of urban design. In many ways, Barnett is the father of this discipline.

In the mid-1960s, Barnett and a group of associates (who later were to become the Urban Design Group of New York City's Planning Department, with Barnett as director) rejected the existing model of unresolvable conflict between policitians, economists, and developers with little sensitivity to the potential of fine design on the one hand, and architects and urban planners, who saw little relevance in the realities of politics and economics, on the other.

Barnett and his group proposed careful environmental planning, taking full advantage of architectural design possibilities, composed with strict and genuine economic sensibility. Moreover, he stressed the importance of schemes that solved problems in totality, and he placed little faith in the ability of individual architectural solutions to solve complex urban dilemmas. When John V. Lindsay created the Urban Design Group in 1967, Barnett was given the opportunity to become a truly generative force, and he explored and implemented many of his most innovative ideas in this capacity. The work that he and his group performed experimentally has become a guide for all urban design work performed since then.

Their success was attributable to several key factors in Barnett's method of approach and philosophy of execution. Besides attempting to solve problems broadly, rather than imposing only one or two changes in the hope of aggregate growth, Barnett stressed close interaction with community forces. By working with local groups and individuals, he made sure that his designs were appropriate and met with general public receptiveness. With regard to implementation, Barnett realized that no plan could be

successful without great political struggle, and he often directly challenged those institutions that barred urban change. Finally, by enforcing urban design decision through modification of the existing network of zoning laws, Barnett was able to regulate neighborhoods and actively change existing patterns without violent renewal or conflict.

His many projects for New York include revamping of the Times Square area, the development of the Lincoln Center project, and urban renewal projects throughout the five boroughs. By implementing valid urban design via public policy, he has effectively transformed much of New York City.

Since his retirement from the Urban Design Group in 1971, Barnett has worked independently, both as a designer and an urban planning consultant. He has worked on the South Street Seaport Development, a nine-block historic district in lower Manhattan, in association with Edward Larrabee Barnes. He has developed the general management plan and environmental impact statement for the Gateway National Recreation Area, the first urban national park, located in New York City. He has also developed a series of prototype neighborhood plans with the Louisville Community Design Center, acted as consultant to the primary planners for two new town centers in Hong Kong, and produced studies for the new Alaska state capital.

Recently, Barnett has been a consultant to the Urban Redevelopment Authority of Pittsburgh on two projects. One is a development strategy for the downtown Golden Triangle area, which includes plans for the coordination of bus and rail rapid transit, public open space, new parking facilities, downtown housing, a retail shopping strategy, and revised zoning controls. The second is a project for low-income housing to be made up entirely of single-family row and detached houses.

—Ching-Yu Chang

BARRAGÁN, Luis.

Mexican. Born in Guadalajara, Jalisco, in 1902. Trained as an engineer, Dip.Ing. 1925; self-taught as an architect. Travelled in Spain and France, 1924-26; practised in Guadalajara, 1927-36; lived in Paris, attending Le Corbusier's lectures, 1931-32; has worked in or near Mexico City since 1936: concentrated on planning studies and real estate, 1940-45; Founder-Director, with Jose Alberto Bustamante, Jardines del Pedregal de San Angel, S.A., Mexico City, 1945-52; Co-founder, Las Arboledas Residential Zone Foundation, Mexico City, 1957, and La Hacienda Golf Club, Mexico City, 1958. Since 1976, Partner, with Raul Ferrera, Luis Barragan y Raul Ferrera Arquitectos, Mexico City. Exhibition: *The Architecture of Luis Barragán,* Museum of Modern Art, New York, 1976. Recipient: Pritzker Prize, 1980. Fellow of the American Institute of Architects; Honorary Member, American Academy and Institute of Arts and Letters, 1984. Address: Luis Barragan y Raul Ferrera Arquitectos, Calle General Francisco Ramirez 12, 11830 Mexico, D.F., Mexico.

Works:

1927 Robles Leon House restoration, Guadalajara
1928 Robles Leon Rental Houses, Guadalajara
Mrs. Harper de Garibi House, Guadalajara
E. Gonzalez Luna House, Guadalajara
Enrique Aguilar House, Guadalajara
1929 G. Cristo House, Guadalajara
Children's Playground, Parque de la Revolucion, Guadalajara
E. Gonzalez Luna Rental Houses, Guadalajara
1931 Barragán Family House restoration, Chapala, Jalisco, Mexico
1932 House restoration, Guadalajara (with engineer Juan Palomar)
1936 House for two families, Avenida Parque Mexico, Mexico City
Two rental houses, Avenida Mazatlan, Mexico City
1937 I. Pizarro Suarez House, Las Lomas de Capultepec, Mexico City
1940 Apartment building, Calles Lerma y Guadiana, Mexico City
Rental house, Calle Guadiana, Mexico City
Apartment building, Avenida Mississippi, Mexico City
Apartment building, Plaza Melchor Ocampo, Mexico City (with José Creixell)
Apartment building with adjoining single house, Avenida,Mississippi, Mexico City
Painters' studios building, Plaza Melchor Ocampo, Mexico City
Three low-cost apartment buildings, Calle de Elba, Mexico City
Eduardo Villasenor House, San Angel, Mexico City
1945 Four private gardens, Avenida Constituyentes y Calle General Francisco Ramirez, Mexico City
Three private gardens, Avenida San Jeronimo, San Angel, Mexico City
1945/
50 El Pedregal, formerly known as Parque Residencial Jardines del Pedregal de San Angel, Mexico City: master plan, three demonstration gardens, and entrances, including the Plaza de las Fuentes
1947 Luis Barragán House, Tacubaya, Mexico City
1948 Two houses, 10 and 12 Avenida de las Fuentes, El Pedregal, Mexico City (with Max Cetto)
1950 Eduardo Prieto Lopez House, El Pedregal, Mexico City
1953 La Plaza del Zocalo Fountain and Mall, Mexico City (project)
1955 Capuchinas Sacramentarias del Purismo Corazon de Maria Chapel, Tlalpan, Mexico City

Hotel Pierre Marquez gardens, Acapulco
Antonio Galvez House, Calle Pimentel 10, San Angel, Mexico City
Jardines del Bosque master plan, Guadalajara (project)
Capillo del Calvario Chapel, Jardines del Bosque, Guadalajara (project)
1957 Satellite City Towers, Queretaro Highway, Mexico City (with Mathias Goeritz)
1958 Las Arboledas master plan and building code, Mexico City
El Muro Rojo, Las Arboledas, Mexico City
1959 Plaza del Campanario, Las Arboledas, Mexico City
Plaza y Fuente del Bebedero, Las Arboledas, Mexico City
1964 Los Clubes master plan, public landscaping, and building code, Mexico City
Fuente de Los Clubes (Fuente de Los Amantes), Mexico City
1967 Lomas Verdes master plan and building code, Mexico City (project; with Juan Sordo Madaleno)
Open chapel for Lomas Verdes, Mexico City (project)
1968 San Cristobal stable, pools, and house for Mr. and Mrs. Folke Egerstrom, Los Clubes, Mexico City (with Andres Casillas)
1969 Service entrance gate, Los Clubes, Mexico City (with Raul Ferrera)
Cano master plan, near Tepotzotlan, Mexico

1971 Guadalajara Club and Race Track (project)
1972 Monumental fountain for Lomas Verdes, Mexico City (project; with Ricardo Legorreta)
1973 Pigeon Tower, El Palomar, Guadalajara (project; with Raul Ferrera)
1976 Gilardi House, Tacubaya, Mexico City (with Raul Ferrera and Alberto Chauvet)
Harris Bank of Chicago Offices, Mexico City (project; with Raul Ferrera)
1978 Jose Luis Carrete Penthouse interiors, Mexico City (with Raul Ferrera)
1979 Monumental projects, Monterrey, Mexico (with Raul Ferrera)
Silver Sculpture for Tane Orfebres (project; with Raul Ferrera)
Vitro Company Sports Club, Mexico City (project; with Raul Ferrera)
1980 Wind-music Tower, Mexico City (project; with Raul Ferrera)
Remanso Monument and Fountain, Mexico City (project; with Raul Ferrera)
Casolar Company House, Manzanillo, Colima, Mexico (project; with Raul Ferrera)
1980/
81 Visa Corporation Complex, Monterrey, Mexico (project; with Raul Ferrera)
1981 Golf Clubhouse and Grounds, Manzanillo, Colima, Mexico (project; with Raul Ferrera)

Luis Barragán: Plaza de las Fuentes, El Pedregal, Mexico City, 1950.

Red Plaque-Lighthouse of Commerce high-rise building, Monterrey, Mexico (project; with Raul Ferrera)

1982 Valdes House, Monterrey, Mexico
Benjamin Baldwin House, Sarasota, Florida (project; with Raul Ferrera)
Calvin Klein shops (prototypes for fifty-five shops; with Raul Ferrera)
Francis Ford Coppola Housing Development (Point of View), movie studios, and winery, California (project; with Raul Ferrera)

1983 Caballero House, Gomez Palacio, Durango, Mexico (with Raul Ferrera)

1984 Sumner Peck Land Development, Fresno, California (four projects; with Raul Ferrera)
Morrissey Beach House Development, Long Island, New York (project; with Raul Ferrera)

Publications:

By BARRAGÁN: articles—"Gardens for Environment—Jardines del Pedregal" in *Journal of the American Institute of Architects* (Washington, D.C.), April 1952; "The Construction and Enjoyment of a Garden Accustoms People to Beauty, to Its Instinctive Use, Even to Its Accomplishment" in *Via 1: Ecology in Design* (Philadelphia), 1968; "Luis Barragán y El Regreso a Las Fuentes," interview, with Damian Bayon in *Plural 48* (Mexico City), September 1975; "Luis Barragan," interview, with Jorge Salvat in *Archetype* (San Francisco), Autumn 1980.

On BARRAGÁN: books— *The New Architecture in Mexico* by Esther Born, New York 1937; *18 Residencias de arquitectos mexicanos* by Enrique Yanez, Mexico City 1951; *Mexico's Modern Architecture* by I. E. Myers, New York 1952; *Latin American Architecture since 1945* by Henry-Russell Hitchcock, New York 1955; *Mexican Journal: The Conquerors Conquered* by Selden Rodman, New York 1958; *Moderne Architektur in Mexiko* by Max Cetto, Teufen, Switzerland 1961; *Modern Gardens and the Landscape* by Elizabeth B. Kassler, New York 1964; *Mexican Homes of Today* by Warren and Verna Cook Shipway, New York, 1964; *Builders in the Sun: Five Mexican Architects* by Clive Bamford Smith, New York 1967; *Analisis critico de la arquitectura moderna in Mexico* by Hernandez Laos, Guadalajara 1968; *Art in Architecture* by Louis G. Redstone, New York 1968; *Mexican Landscape Architecture—From the Street and from Within* by Rosina Greene Kirby, Tucson, Arizona 1972; *The Architecture of Luis Barragán*, exhibition catalogue, by Emilio Ambasz, New York 1976; *GA 48: House and Atelier for Luis Barragan*, edited by Yukio Futagawa, Tokyo 1979; articles— "Mexican Villas: Luis Barragán, Architect" in *Architectural Record* (New York), September 1931; "Modernist Houses in Mexico Designed by Luis Barragán" in *House and Garden* (New York), October 1931; "Recent Work of a Mexican Architect—Luis Barragán" in Architectural Record (New York), January 1935; "The Gardens of Pedregal" by Mary Saint Albans in *Modern Mexico* (New York), April 1946; "Jardines del Pedregal, Mexico City" and "House by Luis Barragán, Architect" in *Arts and Architecture* (Los Angeles), August 1951; "Barragán's House" by Esther McCoy in *Los Angeles Times Home Magazine,* 19 October 1952; "Il Pedregal di Città del Messico" by Gio Ponti in *Domus* (Milan), March 1953; "Arbeiten von Luis Barragán, Mexico" by Horst Dohnert in *Baukunst und Werkform (* Darmstadt, West Germany), November 1954; "Master Designer, Luis Barragán" in *Interiors* (New York), December 1963; "The Private World of Luis Barragán" in *Vogue* (London), April 1966; "The House of Luis Barragán" in *Harper's Bazaar* (New York), July 1968; "Dans l'actualité le style mexicain, chez un architecte de Mexico" in *Elle* (Paris),

October 1968; "I muri di Luis Barragán" in *Domus* (Milan), November 1968; "El Palomar et son colombier géant" in *Vogue* (Paris), October 1974; "Luis Barragan" in *Arquitectura Mexico* (Mexico City), January/February 1977; "Luis Barragan and His Works" by M. Schjetnan Garduno in *Arquitectura Mexico* (Mexico City), September/October 1978; "Luis Barragan—Alchemist of Architecture" in *Arkkitehti* (Helsinki), no. 4, 1980; "The Haunting Art of Luis Barragan" in *AIA Journal* (Washington, D.C.), June 1980; "Pritzker Prize Awarded to Luis Barragan" in *Progressive Architecture* (New York), June 1980; "The Works and Background of Luis Barragan" in *Architecture + Urbanism* (Tokyo), August 1980; "The Influential Lyricist of Mexican Culture" in *Landscape Architecture* (Louisville, Kentucky), January 1982; "Modern Mexican Architecture," special issue of *Process: Architecture* (Tokyo), July 1983; "The Shaping of Space with Simple Means" in *Deutsche Bauzeitung* (Stuttgart), November 1983.

Bibliographies: *Architectural Splendor in the Sun— Mexico's Luis Barragan: A Selected Bibliography* by Robert B. Harmon, Monticello, Illinois 1980; *Luis Barragan, The Architect and His Work* by Florita Z. Louie de Irizarry, Monticello, Illinois 1983.

My house is my refuge, an emotional piece of architecture, not a cold piece of convenience. I believe in an "emotional architecture." It is very important for humankind that architecture should move by its beauty; if there are many equally valid technical solutions to a problem, the one which offers the user a message of beauty and emotion, that one is architecture.

Any work of architecture which does not express serenity is a mistake. That is why it has been an error to replace the protection of walls with today's intemperate use of enormous glass windows.

The construction and enjoyment of a garden accustoms people to beauty, to its instinctive use, even to its pursuit. I believe that architects should design gardens to be used, as much as the houses they build, to develop a sense of beauty and the taste and inclination toward the fine arts and other spiritual values.

—Luis Barragán

Luis Barragán is among the most perfectionist, poetic, and sublime of all contemporary architects. He is the spiritual leader of three generations of Mexican Minimalists and has become one of the revered mystics of architecture for an increasing number of designers, especially in the United States.

Working in an idiom that is at once spare and ascetic, abstract and monastic, Barragán evokes the tradition of anonymous building. He has long been interested in North African, Mediterranean, and Mexican village architecture, which he calls "architecture for the poor." Yet, in the same work he can ring the overtones of the rich, almost epic tradition of all architecture. He does it by a minimalist statement that echoes, like an epitome, the continuity of uninterrupted tradition.

His work is minimal, yet sumptuous in color and texture, in visual drama and stunning juxtapositions. It is composed with the purest of planes—either wall or water—with intersecting walls of strong and stark proportions, and, above all, with a clear sense of the interaction and the union between building components and nature—between stucco and timber and sky, trees, and water. Much of Barragán's work, in fact, has been in urban planning and in landscape architecture—at the edges of actual shelter, where buildings merge with the landscape. His most revered projects conjure up images of a roofless Barcelona pavilion, as if Mies had worked in adobe.

His early work of the 1920s consists of a number of residences in the early International Style, not unlike Le Corbusier's work at the same time. Since 1950,

color has played a significant role in his work, especially in the Satellite Towers of 1957, as it had with Le Corbusier at Ronchamps (1950-53) and La Tourette (1957-60). Barragán's vibrant colors on the exteriors of his works—pink, lemon, magenta, and coral—are quintessentially Mexican. His element is the climate of Mexico—somewhat like the Mediterranean—its light, air, and open simplicity.

A confirmed religious man, Barragán designs architecture that is almost mystical, as is visible in his serene chapel for the Capuchinas Sacramentarias in Tlalpan and in his seemingly ineffable gardens for meditation. A horseman by bearing and interest, Barragán achieves abstract yet mythical dimensions when he designs water troughs and fountains for horses within warm-up rings and resting places. Most celebrated of these are his projects at Las Arboledas, a residential subdivision in the suburbs of Mexico City, and the San Cristobal stable, horse pool, swimming pool and house (with Andres Casillas) for Mr. and Mrs. Folke Egerstrom in Los Clubes. There, the use of falling splashing water from overhead troughs recalls for him the aqueducts of his own childhood village Mazamitla.

In his own house in Mexico City, a view from the library toward the garden, over a series of interior partitions of varying heights, is like a Josef Albers painting in three dimensions—a live-in homage to the square. And the cruciform division of the window glazing is inescapable. A small, white-walled patio off his architecture workshop has a rectangular black pool fed by a trickle of water coming through an old timber that projects from the wall. It is a miniature aqueduct. Sunk in the pool is an ancient terracotta amphora; a cluster of other amphoras stands alongside the pool. In this exterior room—all white and black with the terracotta of the amphoras as accent and with the blue Mexican sky for its ceiling— a rustic door to the adjacent garden is painted shocking pink—softened only by the weathering of rains and the bleaching of the inevitable Mexican sun. There is no furniture. It is an abstract composition, made kinetic and full of life by its falling water, by the changing sky, and by its colorful surprise. It is a synthesis of life and the elements, of meditation and the permanence of change.

It is in a series of poetic extracts such as these—of schematic details standing as apparent symbols— that the totality of Barragán's work is known, primarily through the abstracted photographs of the architect's personally selected photographer Armando Salas Portugal. Through these images, most people have come to project the apparently infinite poetic genius—the epic unreality—of Barragán. And therein lies his influence, not as planner or provider of functional shelter, but as poet, as epitomizer.

Barragán has not been concerned with the larger demands of urban architecture or with the requirements of the poor for shelter—despite his admiration of anonymous building as a source of inspiration. He has remained aloof from this reality. He has built only what he himself has found interesting, primarily aesthetic problems of a romantic nature—towers, fountains, and pools. His disciples have questioned his courage and his refined goal of purity. For he has built comparatively little—less and less, it seems, as time has gone on—despite the growing reputation, respect, and demand.

Louis Kahn consulted him on the plaza design for the Salk Laboratories, but Barragán said there was no need for him because Kahn already knew the right thing to do—plant nothing, just reveal the view of the ocean. Later, Kahn flew Barragán to La Jolla to see the plaza when it was finished. Barragán approved. Unlike Kahn, who undid the day's work with new ideas each night, like Penelope taking out each day's weaving of the tapestry, Barragán simply did not get involved in numerous commissions offered to him. His disciple Ricardo Legorreta convinced him for a while to be a partner, yet after countless revisions, Barragán would say to a client that he did not like what they had finally decided to submit—and thereby undermine and undo it all. He has been invited to design a new stable in Oklahoma, and Americans hoped to have one of his projects nearby to see, but it looks, several years later, as if the stable will not come to pass.

Still, Barragán has been a deep influence on three generations of Mexican architects, including his own generation and architects in their forties, such as Legorreta, as well as a younger generation around thirty. Yet, he is determinedly modest, always emphasizing the continuity and continuum of Mexican architecture. He explains that he himself was influenced by an older generation—the sculptor and painter Jesus "Chucho" Reyes—and that his work has been influenced by his longtime colleague, the sculptor Mathias Goeritz, who collaborated on the Satellite Towers and who has been a seminal influence. He also maintains that he has been influenced by younger Minimalists. "We are all friends and discuss many of these things back and forth," he has pointedly stated.

What Barragán aims for is simplicity and refinement without denying the color or tradition of architecture. Although the extracted images of his architecture convey to us a kind of sculptural myth based in the realm of architecture, Barragán calls himself a landscape architect, intimating his deeper commitment to the cosmic realm of nature in its widest sense.

—C. Ray Smith

BARTNING, Otto.

German. Born in Karlsruhe, 12 April 1883. Educated at the Technische Hochschule, Charlottenburg, Berlin; Technische Hochschule, Karlsruhe; and Berlin University. In private practice, Berlin, from 1905. Director, Staatlichen Bau- hochschule, Weimar, 1926-30. Chairman, Deutsche Werkbund, 1946; President, Bund Deutscher Archiekten, 1950-59. Honorary Doctor of Theology, Albertus University, Königsberg, Germany, 1924. *Died* (in Darmstadt, West Germany), *20 February 1959*.

Works:

1906 Evangelical Church with Vicarage and Parish Centre, Peggau, Steiermark, Austria
1907/
08 Evangelical Church, Cogealac, Black Sea, Rumania
1908 Evangelical Parish Centre, Selzthal, Steiermark, Austria
Liebscher House, Peggau, Steiermark, Austria
1909 Evangelical Chapel, Schenkenham, Böhm. Isergebirge, Germany
1909/
10 High Lutheran Church with Vicarage, Essen, Germany
Pommer Country House, Mondsee, Pichl, Austria
Evangelical Parish Centre, Rottenmann, Steiermark, Austria
1910 Evangelical Parish Centre, Morchenstern, Böhmen, Germany
1910/
11 Woehler House, Hamburg
Westendorp House, Düsseldorf
Benfey House, Düsseldorf
Evangelical Church with Vicarage, Leibnitz, Steiermark, Austria
1911/
12 E. von Simson Country House, Dahlem, Berlin
Evangelical Church with Vicarage and Parish

Centre, Neustadt, Böhmen, Germany
Evangelical Church with Vicarage, Graslitz, Böhmen, Germany
Evangelical Parish Centre, Dzieditz, Schlesien, Germany
Hartmeyer House, Vienna
Evangelical Parish Centre, Mahrenberg, Steiermark, Austria
1912 Schwerdtfeger Mansions, Nieder-Sieggersdorf, Schlesien, Germany
Evangelical Parish Centre, Oberschreiberhau, Riesengebirge, Germany
1912/
13 Robert Friedlaender Country House, Dahlem, Berlin
Evangelical Church with Vicarage and Parish Centre, Krems, Donau, Austria
Hessel Country House, Grunewald, Berlin
1912/
14 Evangelical Church, Nassengrub, Böhmen, Germany
1913 A. Von Simson House, Charlottenburg, Berlin
1913/
14 Von Waetjen House, Düsseldorf
G. von Simson House, Caputh, Potsdam, Germany
1914 Office Building, Viktoriastrasse 25, Berlin
1914/
15 R. von Simson Country House, Dahlem, Berlin
1916 Friedlander-Fuld Office additions and alterations, Unter den Linden 9, Berlin
1918/
19 Von Bodenhausen House additions, Bendlerstrasse 6, Berlin
1919 Bendix Offices, Friedland, Germany
1919/
20 Cassirer House additions, Berlin
Krupp Company Offices, Berlin
1920 Shop building, Unter den Linden, Berlin
1921 Castle renovations, for Count Kalckreuth, Siegersdorf, Germany
1921/
22 Götz House, Sudpark, Cologne
1921/
23 Trabrennbahn Buildings, Mariendorf, Berlin
1921/
24 House, Wylerberg bei Cleve, Germany
1922 Danish Church, Berlin
Coal Works Water Tower, Zeipau, Germany
Sternkirche (Star Church) Model
1923/
24 Aschaffenburg Clothing Factory, Monchen Gladbach, Germany
Dr. Theo Meyer House, Zeipau, Germany
1924 Ceramics factory, Tempelhof, Berlin
Lieck und Heider Shop, Berlin
1924/
25 Workers' Housing, Zeipau, Schlesien, Germany
1924/
26 Merkelsdorf Warehouse, Böhmen, Germany
1925 German Red Cross Offices, Berlin
Metzger House, Potsdam, Berlin (project)
Gustav-Adolf Church, Charlottenburg, Berlin
1925/
26 Children's Home, Ruppin, Germany
German State Pavilion, Trade Fair, Milan
1926/
28 Housing development (48,000 units), Berlin
1927 Baptist Chapel, *Free Art Exhibition*, Berlin
1927/
28 Children's Hospital, Lichterfelde, Berlin
Elektro-Thermit Offices, Tempelhof, Berlin
1928 Geographical Foundation Headquarters renovations, Wilhelmstrasse 29, Berlin
Pressa Steel Church, Cologne
Evangelical Church, Wilhemshof an der Havel, Austria
1928/
29 State Music School, Frankfurt an der Oder, Germany
Theo Meyer Country House, Westend, Berlin

1929/
30 Jungfernheide Housing Development Berlin
Rundkirche (Round Church), Essen, Germany
1930/
31 Health Farm, Wilmersdorf, Berlin
Stahlkirche reconstruction, Essen, Germany
Evangelical Church, Dornbirn bei Bregenz, Austria
1931/
32 Bartning Wharf Building System
1931/
33 Gustav-Adolf Evangelical Church with Parish Buildings, Siemenstadt, Berlin
1932/
33 Haselhorst District Housing Development, Berlin
1933/
34 German Community Evangelical Church with Vicarage, Lisbon
1934 Evangelical Church, Heerlen, Netherlands
1934/
35 Astoria Hotel alterations, Berlin
St. Mark's Evangelical Church, Baden, Karlsruhe, Germany
1935/
36 Evangelical Church of the Holy Cross, Chemnitz, (now Karl-Marx-Stadt), Germany
1936 Evangelical Church, St. Blasien, Germany
1936/
37 Kippenberg Collection, Goethe Archives, Leipzig, Germany
Christian Science Building and Church, Wilmersdorf, Berlin
1937 Bartning House, Westend, Berlin
German Medical Insurance Office Building, Zehlendorf, Berlin
1937/
38 Evangelical Church with Vicarage, Stetten am Heuberg, Baden, Germany
Burkhardt House, Bodensee, Switzerland
Evangelical Church, Gorlitz-Rauschwalde, Germany
Tanello House, Lugano, Switzerland
Apartment house, Schoneberg, Berlin
1938 Wichernbundes Old People's Home, Baden, Karlsruhe, Germany
1938/
39 Mayrisch House, Cannes, France
Evangelical Church, Beirut, Lebanon
1939 Alb District Evangelical Church, Baden, Karlsruhe, Germany
1939/
40 Evangelical Church renovations, Bregenz, Austria
1940/
42 Evangelical Church with Vicarage and Parish Centre, Belgrade, Yugoslavia
1941/
42 German Protestant Church renovations, Paris
Evangelical Church with Vicarage, Barcelona
1943/
44 German Protestant Church renovations, Brussels
1946 Experimental Clay Building Development, Neckarsteinach, West Germany
Emergency pre-fabricated churches in timber, for the German Evangelical Relief Organization (prototypes)
1950/
51 Church of the Holy Trinity reconstruction, Worms, West Germany
Women's Clinic reconstruction, Darmstadt, West Germany
1953 Church of Christ, Bad Godesberg, West Germany (with O. Dörzbach)
1956/
57 Funeral Chapel, Bremen-Walle, West Germany (with O. Dörzbach)

Publications:

By BARTNING: books—*Vom neun Kirchbau,*

Berlin 1919; *Was ist Bauen?*, Stuttgart 1952; *Otto Bartning in kürzen Wörten*, Hamburg 1954; *Erde Geliebte*, Hamburg 1955; *Kirchen: Handbuch für den Kirchenbau*, with W. Weyres, Munich 1959.

On BARTNING: books—*Der Baumeister Otto Bartning und die Wiederentdeckung des Raumes* by Hans Meyer, Heidelberg, West Germany, 1951; *Bauten in Deutschland seit 1948*, edited by Erwin Gottschalk, Darmstadt, West Germany, 1959; articles—"The Work of Otto Bartning" by Jurgen Bredow and Helmut Lerch in *Der Architekt* (Stuttgart), January 1983; "On the Work of Otto Bartning, 1883-1959" by Jurgen Bredow and Helmut Lerch in *Archithese* (Zurich), March/April 1983; "Otto Bartning, 1883-1959" in *Bauwelt* (Berlin), 15 April 1983.

In addition to being an architect; Otto Bartning was a doctor of theology and deeply interested in the development of the Lutheran liturgy. He was primarily a designer of churches, which in his early days were strongly gothic in feeling, although they were stripped of all ornament and mouldings. Later, he experimented with many types of auditorium plan using modern construction techniques to create large, clear spans and wall panels mainly of glass.

His Sternkirche of 1922 was one of these designs, with a central altar, radiating aisles, and tiered seating. Daylighting was provided from curved dormer windows carried on the vaulting ribs. The steel-framed Rundkirche in Essen was a circular pepperpot in three stages with a belfry carried on the third stage. Inside, the steel was concrete-cased. It had a gallery. The congregation sat in a semi-circle in the main body of the church, and the general effect was hard and severe.

The Pressa Church in Cologne, also known as the Stahlkirche, is his best known work, with a steel frame and steel and glass walls. The steel-clad walls are in the shape of a hyperbola on plan and rise from within a low, square, flat-roofed base. The church is lit through stained glass in tall narrow windows and is totally without ornament.

The fan-shaped Gustav Adolf church in Berlin Siemensdadt has a concrete-framed tower at its apex. The wall opposite the tower is of brick, almost covered by the formally arranged organ. The side walls are of glass framed in concrete.

After World War II Bartning built almost fifty low-cost churches using bomb rubble for their concrete walls and factory-made timber trusses for their roofs.

In his early days he designed a number of large, rather strange, frankly expressionist country houses with polygonal rooms which produced elevations with irregular eaves levels and facetted walls.

Bartning's design for a ceramics factory at Berlin-Tempelhof in 1924 is sharp and clean in outline very much in the style of Arne Jacobsen whose work it antedates by thirty years.

—Gontran Goulden

BAUDIZZONE-ERBIN-LESTARD-VARAS.
Partnership; established as Baudizzone-Diaz-Erbin-Lestard-Varas, in Buenos Aires, 1966, by Miguel Andres Patricio Baudizzone, Antonio Diaz, Jorge Rufino Erbin, Jorge Horacio Lestard, and Alberto Jaime Varas; firm changed title to Baudizzone-Erbin-Lestard-Varas in 1979. Exhibitions: *Arquitectos de Buenos Aires*, Centro de Arte y Comunicacion, Buenos Aires, 1976; *Architecten van Buenos Aires*, International Cultureel Centrum, Antwerp, 1979. Recipient: First Prize, Cultural Center Competition, Mendoza, Argentina, 1971; First Prize, City Auditorium Competition, Buenos Aires, 1972. Address: 25 de Mayo 516, 11, Buenos Aires 1002, Argentina.

Works:

1965 Wilson Display Stand, *Argentine Rural Society Exhibition*, Buenos Aires
      Apartment building, Guido 1624, Buenos Aires
1966 Engineering Building, National Technological University, Avellaneda Campus, Buenos Aires
1967 Apartment building, Laprida 2044, Buenos Aires
1968 Gonzalez Porto Publishing Company Building, Avenida de Mayo 952, Buenos Aires
      Vincente Lopez Paper Factory, M. Moreno 4674, Buenos Aires
      Municipal Theatre of Balcarce City, Argentina
      Housing complex, Los Alamos Country Club, Pilar, Argentina
      Science Research Institute and Sciences Building, National University of La Plata, Argentina
1969 Travel Commission Exhibition Building, La Boca Sports City, Buenos Aires
1970 Tower apartment block, Zapiola 2191, Buenos Aires
      Apartment building, Coronel Diaz 2521, Buenos Aires
      Garay Sanatorium, Santa Fé, Argentina
1971 Bariloche Foundation Research Center, Bariloche, Rio Negro, Argentina (competition project)
      Brandsen Municipal Hospital, Buenos Aires
      Cultural Center, Mendoza, Argentina (competition project)
1972 Apartment building, Calle French 3680, Buenos Aires
      Housing development, San Clemente del Tuyu, Argentina
      Hidronor Administrative Headquarters, Neuquen, Argentina (project)
      City Auditorium, Buenos Aires (competition project)
1973 Housing development, Quilmes, Argentina (project)
      Community Medical Center, San Juan, Argentina
      Apartment building, Beruti 3180, Buenos Aires
      Prefabricated housing development, San Isidro, Buenos Aires (project)
1974 National Unversity of Rio Cuarto, Argentina (as construction advisers and planners)
      Lande House, Calle Saenz Valiente 1194, Buenos Aires
      Lopez Isnardi House, Pinamar, Province of Buenos Aires
      Bernardi House, General Pacheco, Buenos Aires
      Housing development, La Verde, Chaco, Argentina
      Office building, Calle Libertad, Buenos Aires
      Sports Complex, Corrientes, Argentina (competition project)
1975 Apartment building, Calle Aguero 2008, Buenos Aires
      Apartment building, Pueyrredon 1779, Buenos Aires
      Office building, Calle Reconquista and L. N. Alem, Buenos Aires
      Apartment building, Calle Juncal 3152, Buenos Aires
      Apartment building, Calle Maipu 1230, Buenos Aires
1976 Office building, Calle Marcelo T de Alvear and L. N. Alem, Buenos Aires
      Office building, Calle Viamonte and L. N. Alem, Buenos Aires
      Tower apartment building, Calle Salguero and Cabello, Buenos Aires
      Office building, Calle Reconquista 478, Buenos Aires
      Office building, Calle Tucuman 1400, Buenos Aires (project)

1977 Celorrio House, Punta del Este, Uruguay
      Office building, Calle Suipacha 68, Buenos Aires
      Office building, 25 de Mayo and Lavalle, Buenos Aires
      Banco Hispano Building, Esmeraldo 56, Buenos Aires
      Hotel San Martin de Los Andes, Neuquén, Argentina
      Bus Terminal, Buenos Aires (project)
1978 Municipal Bank of Rosario Headquarters, Buenos Aires (project)
      Two houses, Ingeniero Maschwitz, Province of Buenos Aires
1978/
79 Housing development, Santa Fé, Argentina
      Housing Development, Catamarca, Argentina
      Housing Development, Neuquén, Argentina
      Kraves House, Pilar, Buenos Aires Province
      CIMP Medical Psychoanalytical Institute, Buenos Aires
      Tornu Hospital renovations, Buenos Aires
      Hospital for Burns, Buenos Aires
      Hospital for Tumors, Buenos Aires
1980 Housing Development, Punta del Este, Uruguay
1981 Housing Development with Communal Services, Nazca Avenue, Buenos Aires
      San Miguel House, Buenos Aires Province
      Fideicom Banking Headquarters, Buenos Aires
      Kogan House, Bariloche, Argentina
      Tedim House, Bariloche, Argentina
1982 Hospital in Ushuaia, Tierra del Fuego, Argentina
      Miraflores Club Sports Centre, Buenos Aires
      Langer House Country Club, Escobar, Argentina
      Grain Exchange Market, Bahia Blanca, Buenos Aires Province
      Troncoso House in La Martona Country Club, Buenos Aires
      Nano House, Colon, Entre Rios, Argentina
      Housing Development (112 units), Perito Moreno, Santa Cruz, Argentina
      Housing Development (80 units), Puerto Deseado, Santa Cruz, Argentina
1983 Opera House, Paris (competition project)
      Penthouse renovations and alterations, Buenos Aires
      Ski Resort Housing and Facilities, Bariloche, Argentina
      Rio Grande Hospital, Tierra de Fuego, Argentina
1984 Lifshitz House, Miraflores, Argentina
      Housing Development (400 units), Rio Negro, Argentina
      Housing Development (76 units), Bahia Blanca, Buenos Aires Province
      Housing Development (476 units), Trelew, Rio Negro, Argentina
      Housing Development (250 units), Rosario, Santa Fé, Argentina

Publications:

On BELV: books—*New Directions in Latin American Architecture* by Francisco Bullrich, New York 1969; *Architecture of Baudizzone, Erbin, Lestard, Varas*, Miami, Florida 1980; articles—in *Summa* (Buenos Aires), October 1969, November 1971, and January 1975; *Hogar y arquitectura* (Barcelona), no. 103, 1973; *Architectural Review* (London), June 1973 and September 1975; *L'Architecture d'aujourd'hui* (Paris), July 1973; *Domus* (Milan), no. 525, 1973, and no. 545, 1975; *Academia Nacional de Bellas Artes: Anuario no. 4*, Buenos Aires 1976; "Torre del Rio Office Tower Block" in *Nuestra arquitectura* (Buenos Aires), no. 500, 1977; "Houses in Maschwitz, Buenos Aires Province" in *Summa* (Buenos Aires), July 1979; "Estuario Reconquista 1104 Office

Building" in *Summa* (Buenos Aires), December 1979; "Finvercon Office Building in Buenos Aires" in *Summa* (Buenos Aires), July 1980; "Tower Blocks at Maipu 1230, Buenos Aires" in *Summa* (Buenos Aires), November 1980; "Architecture under the Rules of Urban Construction" in *Summa* (Buenos Aires), May 1982; "Opinion de Alberto Varas" in *Dos puntos* (Buenos Aires), February 1983; "The Barrio Centenario in Santa Fe" in *Summa* (Buenos Aires), April 1983.

Despite their tacit support for systemization in what is obviously systematic in their own work, Baudizzone-Erbin-Lestard-Varas do not wish to be classified as "systems architects." There was a time however, when the studio regarded itself as a "laboratory" of systematic architecture. After re-examining its past activity, it began to value an analytical vision of architecture—architecture as a search for architectural elements; architecture as the exploitation of the expressivenes of those elements. The systematic conception of architecture is that "architecture is a set of related parts." The team carried out work as from this perspective, with the elements defined as "special typologies" to be related in networks and series of networks.

Perhaps their resistance to the "systems archi-tects" label derives from the fact that it is, as a definition, too encompassing; it might be said that all

architecture, and particularly contemporary archi-tecture, is systems-based. BELV has used elements from diverse sources in its buildings and used them according to their own criteria, adapting them in each case to the type of building with which they were dealing. Their dominant theory during the period 1966-75 was that there was no such thing as a single volume in which everything is situated, a conception that contradicts the ingenuous guidelines of sponta-neous or naive architecture, the tradition that a building is a box that contains internal components.

The City Auditorium of 1972 is the last of their buildings to be conceived totally in a systematic way. Their reaction against systematic conception is—according to some of the partners—a reaction against the work of the Japanese architect Isozaki, specifically Isozaki's rhetoric about architecture as a manifestation of architectural language falling back on itself, "producing a metaphor on the expressed language." In other words, architecture is meta-linguistic; it talks about itself in a kind of permanent reflection, a kind of vicious circle that does not take into consideration any elements of extra-architectural reality. For example, one can imagine constructing everything on the basis of a self-repeating modular structure, like a cube reproduced an infinite number of times.

After 1972 the team very clearly moved away from these kinds of ideas by incorporating into their works and projects non-architectural factors, that is, by

taking into account elements that lie beyond a particular work in itself. They make explicit their distance from modernism and the theories of Le Corbusier. Their concern has become architectural language but in the sense that the typological constitutes an important and abiding concern in the conception and design of their buildings. To a certain extent, they have returned to architectural classicism in an attempt to find a way of creating architecture that is based on their own knowledge of the laws of construction; they are concerned with the elements of architecture and their relative value.

The criticism of Le Corbusier is not directed against the man himself; it is the theoretical posture of Corb and his disciples that seems wrong. As far as BELV are now concerned, the modern movement left aside such concerns as symmetry, composition, and geometry—and it is these concerns that they now try to rescue and include in their work. Up to a certain point, this interest was merely notional; now it is obvious in their work, obvious and explicit. Their attitude with regard to architectural functionalism is now decidely hostile; its principles are rejected as chimerical and its forms as abnormal, repressing cultural values.

It is worth pointing out that in their current efforts, they are interested in the "ideology of the box." Their purpose is not to cover up the inside with the external skin but to allow the facade to be an exhibition of the building's structural elements, so that entrails are

Baudizzone-Erbin-Lestard-Varas: Nazca Housing Development, Buenos Aires, 1982 (model).

outside and the skin inside. Rather than being conceived as a product of analysis between its parts, the building is an investigation in architectural language: there is full consciousness of working with an architectural rhetoric, with a discourse in which buildings "speak" and allude to other things, behave, in short, as "signifying" elements that express languages that are technical, aesthetic, and so forth.

As well, there is in their work a typological discrimination, an historical reconnaissance of architecture, an accumulation of past and present references and experiences. The team believes that there is an historical continuity in the development (and elaboration) of construction, a natural evolution of the architectural, a continuum that modernism interrupted. Today, in their effort to overcome what they see as the dead end of modernism, the team has reverted to what is, in their view, the invaluable typological and historical dialogue of architecture.

—Jorge Glusberg

BAUMGARTEN, Paul.

German. Born in Tilsit, East Prusia, 9 May 1900. Educated at the Gymnasium, Inowrazlaw, 1907-17; Gymnasium, Nordhausen, 1919; Technische Hochschule, Danzig (now Gdansk, Poland), 1920-21; Technische Hochschule, Berlin, 1922-25, Dip. Eng. 1925. Served in the German Army, 1917-18. Married Margot Huebner in 1934. Worked as an Assistant, then Associate Architect in the office of Mebes and Emmerich, Berlin, 1925-34; manager of a private company building department, Berlin, 1934-35; Manager of the City of Berlin Building Department, 1936; Manager of the Building Derpartments of Ph. Holzmann Company, Frankfurt and Berlin, 1936-46; in private architectural practice, Berlin, from 1947. Professor of Architecture, Hochschule für Bildende Künste, Berlin, 1952-68. Exhibition: *German Architecture Today*, Royal Institute of British Architects, London, 1955. Recipient: Critics' Prize, Berlin, 1954; Berlin Art Prize, 1960; University of Tübingen Medal, 1968. Member, Akademie der Künste, Berlin, 1957. *Died* (in Berlin) *8 October 1984*.

Works:

1929/
   23 Housing estates, Berlin
1933 Water Sports Building, Berlin suburbs
1934 Berlin Refuse Disposal Department Office
      Building renovations

1935 Berlin Refuse Disposal Department loading site
1950 Rot-Weiss Club and Grounds, Berlin
1951 Hotel am Zoo reconstruction, Berlin
1953 Music Academy Concert Hall, Berlin
1955 Eternit Company Guest House, Berlin
1957 Eternit Company Industrial Buildings, Berlin
     Interbau House 25, Berlin
     Hotel am Zoo additions, Berlin
1958 Rot-Weiss Club House Buildings, Berlin
     Boris Blacher House, Berlin
     Ruhr Coal Company Office Building, Berlin
     Eternit Company Canteen Building, Berlin
1959 Church, Am Lietzensee, Charlottenburg, Berlin
1960 Old People's Day Centre, Wolfsburg, West Germany
     Volkswagen Company residential buildings, Wolfsburg, West Germany
1961 Shopping Centre, Wolfsburg, West Germany
1966 Dining Halls and related buildings, University of Tübingen, West Germany
1967 High rise building, Wolfsburg, West Germany
     BEWAG Company Building extensions, Berlin
1969 Federal Courts Building, Karlsruhe, West Germany
1970 Reichstag reconstruction, Berlin
1975 Music Academy Theatre, Berlin

Publications:

On BAUMGARTEN: books—*German Architecture Today*, exhibition catalogue, with foreword by C. H. Aslin and introduction by Otto Bartning, London 1955; *Neue deutsche Architektur* by Hubert Hoffmann and others, Stuttgart, Teufen and London 1956; *Planen und Bauen in neuen Deutschland*, edited by the Bund Deutscher Architekten, Cologne and Opladen, West Germany 1960; *Die Wiedergeburt der deutschen Städte* by Wilhelm Westecker, Düsseldorf and Vienna 1962; *Modern Architecture in Germany*, with introduction by Ulrich Conrads, London and Stuttgart 1962; *Architecture in Germany* by Alfred Simon, Essen, West Germany 1969; *German Architecture 1960-1970* by Wolfgang Pehnt, London and Stuttgart 1970; *Federal Republic of Germany: Planning and Building* by Alfred Simon, Bonn 1973; articles—"Reichstag Resurrection" by David Booth in *Architectural Review* (London), March 1975; "New Theatres in Arts Schools in Berlin, Hanover and Cologne" by Horst Birr in *Bühnentechnische Rundschau* (Velber, West Germany) December 1975; "Studio stage of the Hochschule der Künste in Berlin" in *Bauwelt* (Berlin), 6 May 1977; "Paul Baumgarten on his 80th Birthday" in *Bauwelt* (Berlin), 9 May 1980; "Lecture halls for the University of Tübingen" in *Deutsche Bauzeitsch-*

rift (Gütersloh, West Germany) May 1982; "Paul Baumgarten 1900-1984" by Günther Kühne in *Bauwelt* (Berlin), no. 41, 1984.

Some German industrial buildings of the middle 1930s after the Nazi seizure of power, stand comparison with the best of Italian rationalist architecture. Paul Baumgarten directed the building of the Berlin Refuse Disposal Department and, avoiding any kind of monumentality, fulfilled in the best sense the demands of New Building in relation to suitability of and respect for materials. His buildings of the period are not different in form from buildings of the 1920s: they have flat roofs, continuous window cramp irons with tubular steel profile, unclad steel supports.

Suitability for their purpose and unobtrusive elegance are also the characteristic features of Baumgarten's postwar buildings. He frequently uses glass walls to establish a connection between the interior and the outside world—whether in a concert hall, a factory, or a church. Experience of surrounding nature becomes part of the building's purpose. For example, the individual structures of the Federal Courts open onto the Botanical Garden in Karlsruhe (the initial plan was to build the Baden State Theatre there). And Baumgarten considered as his best his unexecuted design of five circular elements permeated by nature.

In the 1960s, the political differences between the two German states turned Baumgarten's reconstruction of the Reichstag in Berlin into a most exhausting task. But the result has been successful. The modern interior is in exciting contrast to the historical architecture of the building's original construction.

In the extension of the BEWAG Company Building, Baumgarten was able to alter the basic concept of his employers. They wanted to build directly onto the existing Shell-Haus. Baumgarten moved his multi-storey building away from Emil Fahrenkamp's famous building and therby emphasized the neighbouring building, preserving it as a monument, as an independent, historically valuable structure. Baumgarten's attitude involved a restraint rarely practiced by architects in the 1960s.

—Christian Borngräber

BBPR ARCHITECTURAL STUDIO.

Partnership; established, Milan, 1932, by Gianluigi Banfi, *q.v.* (died, 1945), Lodovico Belgiojoso, *q.v.*, Enrico Peressutti, *q.v.* (died, 1975), and Ernesto

Paul Baumgarten: Federal Courts Building, Karlsruhe, West Germany, 1969.

Nathan Rogers, *q.v.* (died, 1969). Exhibitions: *Ten Italian Architects,* Los Angeles County Museum of Art, 1967; *Utopia e crisi dell'antinatura,* at the *Biennale,* Venice, 1978; *Architetture italiane degli Anni '70,* Galleria Nazionale d'Arte Moderna, Rome, 1981; *BBPR a Milano,* Padiglione d'Arte Contemporanea, Milan, 1982. Recipient: First Prize, Warehouse Competition, Ente Nazionale Risi di Lombardia e Piedmonte, 1937. Address: via dei Chiostri 2, 20121 Milan, Italy.

Works:

1932   Hotel Quisiana and Church of Sant'Angelo, Rome (Banfi diploma project)
       Casa del Fascio Tipo per la Città (Banfi and Belgiojoso project)
1933   City plan for Pavia, Italy (project)
       Casa del Sabato per gli Sposi, *Triennale,* Milan (exhibition project; with Portaluppi, Fontana and Chiesa)
       Gairinge House interiors, Trieste
       Marietti House interiors, Palazzo Resta Pallavicini, Via Conservatorio, Milan
1934   Palazzo del Littorio, *Mostra della rivoluzione fascista,* Rome (competition project; with Luigi Figini, Gino Pollini, and Luigi Danusso)
       Ferrario House additions, Via Crocifisso, Milan (destroyed during World War II)
       Casa Qualunque, Via Vallazze, Milan (project)
       Exhibition Hall, *Mostra dell'Aeronautica,* Palazzo dell'Arte, Milan
       Samengo House interiors, Genoa
1935   Villa Morpurgo, Opcina, Trieste
       Home for Red Cross Nurses, Via Caradosso, Milan
       Tessiture Agosti Buildings, Legnano, Milan (project)
       Exhibition Halls, *Mostra dello sport,* Palazzo dell'Arte, Milan (with R. Guttuso and F. Melotti)
       Pavilion, *International Exposition,* Brussels
       Exhibition Halls, *Mostra del mare,* Trieste
       Cassa Malattie Office interiors, Trieste
       Enrico House interiors, Genoa
       Feltrinelli Studio interiors, Via Caserotti, Milan (with A. Belgiojoso)
       Feltrinelli Office/Apartment Building, Via Manin, Milan (with A. Belgiojoso)
1936   Villa Venosta conversion, Gornate Olona, Varese, Italy
       Hotel and restaurant, Opcina, Trieste (project)
       Bozzi and Crippa Society Pavilion, Fiera Campionaria, Milan
       Pavilion, *Triennale,* Milan (with G. Melotti and C. Cagli)
       Premoli House interiors, Corso Monforte, Milan
       Design for the "La Voce del Padrone" Radio (competition project)
1936/
37   Master plan for the Aosta Valley, Italy (with others)
1937   Palazzo della Civiltà Italiana, *International Exposition,* Rome (two projects)
       Warehouses, Ente Nazionale Risi di Lombardia e Piedmonte (competition project)
       Victory Monument, Piazza Fiume, Milan (competition project)
       Community shopping and nursery development, Vercelli, Italy (competition project; with E. Radice Fossati)
       Italian Shipping Companies' Floating Pavilion, World's Fair, Paris (with P. Zappa, M. Russo, and L. Fontana)
       Exhibition Halls, *Leonardo da Vinci Exhibition,* Milan
       Cinema Scenography Pavilion, *Mostra del teatro italiano,* Villa Olmo, Como, Italy

BBPR Architectural Studio: Chase Manhattan Bank Building, Milan, 1969.

       Banfi House interiors, Via Gustavo Modena, Milan
       Monselise House interiors, Via M. Fanti, Milan (with P. Filippini)
1938   Master plan for the Pavilions, Fiera Campionaria, Milan (project; with E. Radice Fossati)
       Heliotherapy Clinic, Legnano, Milan (demolished, 1956)
       School, Robbio Lomellina, Pavia, Italy (project)
       Romanin House interiors, Milan
1939   Tourist development plan for the Island of Elba (project)
       Salsomaggiore Town Centre Plan, near Parma, Italy (competition project)
       Le Grazie Workers' Housing, for the Cantoni Cotton Factory, Legnano, Milan
       Cucirini Milanesi Building interiors, Milan
       Cozzi House interiors, Treviglio, Bergamo, Italy
       Crippa Shop interiors, Montecatini Terme, Italy
       Rooms for the Luini and for the Leonardo schools, *Mostra Leonardesca,* Palazzo dell'Arte, Milan
       Children's Holiday and Health Centre, Legnano, Milan
       Villa G., Scorcola, Trieste (project)
       Gennarini-Gras House interiors, Milan
       Terni Pavilion, Fiera Campionaria, Milan
       Stipel Telephone Building interiors, Galleria Vittorio Emanuele, Milan
       Crippa House interiors, Caravaggio, near Bergamo, Italy
       Banfi House interiors, Via Moscova, Milan
1940   Urban plan for the Belsana Paper Industry (factory/office/housing development), Valle del Lerone, Lera, Genoa (project)
       Central Post Office Building, EUR Quarter, Rome

       San Simpliciano Cloisters restoration (including BBPR Studio), Milan (with E. Radice Fossati)
       Villa Gersony, Desenzano, near Verona, Italy (not completed)
       Forme nel Parco Pavilion, *Triennale,* Milan
       La Lampada Bookshop, Corso Vittorio Emanuele, Milan
       Belgiojoso House interiors, Via Perugia, Milan
       Spiga and Corrente Galleries interiors, Via Spiga, Milan
1941   Rural Casa del Fascio (competition project)
       Studio Formiggini interiors, Milan
1942   Ideal Homes for *Domus* magazine, Milan (projects)
       Furniture store, Via Verri, Milan (with Franco Albini, Ignazio Gardella, and G. Mucchi)
1943   Centre for Facial Injuries, Milan Policlinic, Via Lamarmora, Milan (project)
       Wooden House (project)
       Cabrini House interiors, Milan
1944   Belsana Building, Corso Matteotti, Milan
1945   Master plan for the City of Milan (project; with others)
       Residential development, Via Alcuino, Milan (with F. Ordanini Studio)
       Villa Salmoiraghi, Lanzo d'Intelvi, Como, Italy (not completed)
1946   Master plan for the centre of the City of Milan (with Franco Albini, Piero Bottoni, Luigi Figini, Gino Pollini, and others)
       Monument to the Victims of German Concentration Camps, Monumental Cemetery, Milan
       Banfi Gandini Tomb, Monumental Cemetery, Milan
1947   Villa Merlo, Via Duse, Vigevano, Italy
       Bertoletti Alpine Resthouse, Bormio, Sondrio, Italy
       Villa, Bormio, near Sondrio, Italy (project)

Exhibition Halls, *Mostra della resistenza italiana,* Palais de Trocadero, Paris (with G. Mucchi and M. de Micheli)

Villa Riva, Saronno, Italy

Flora Bar interiors, Via Manzoni, Milan

Ravelli Apartment interiors, Milan

Oggioni House interiors, Milan

Objects and Furnishing Units Pavilion, Triennale, Milan

1948 Apartment/Office Building, Piazza San Erasmo, Milan (with C. Monti)

Marzoli House interiors, Milan

Melzi d'Eril House interiors, Milan

1949 Oxilia House interiors, Milan

Cinema Rosa, Via Canonica, Milan

1950 Union of Manufacturers Textile Factory, Nerviano, Italy (with A. Radaelli Studio)

Palazzo Ponti restoration, Via Bigli, Milan (with C. Monti)

Pavilion and Riva Park, Saronno, Italy (with P. Porcinai and F. Ordanini Studio)

Stock Exchange and Chamber of Commerce Headquarters conversion, Via Meravigli, Milan (competition project)

Cultural Centre, Via Amedei, Milan (project)

Rollier House interiors, Via Poerio, Milan

1951 INA urban plan for Cesate, near Milan (project; with Franco Albini, G. Albricci, and Ignazio Gardella)

United States Pavilion (for the Museum of Modern Art, New York), *Triennale,* Milan

"Architecture, Measure of Man" Room, *Triennale,* Milan (Rogers only; with Vittorio Gregotti and G. Stoppino)

"Forme dell'utile" Room, *Triennale,* Milan (Belgiojoso and Peressutti only; with F. B. Ceriani and M. Huber)

First Class Lounge on the *Neptunia* cruise ship

Grandini House interiors, Milan

Longoni House interiors, Milan

Palazzo Venier dei Leoni restoration/ conversion, for the Peggy Guggenheim Museum, Grand Canal, Venice (project)

1952 Tower Apartment Buildings, Campi Elisi, Trieste (project)

Piccolo Teatro della Città di Milano conversion, Via Rovello, Milan (Rogers only; with M. Zanuso)

Camillo Olivetti Monument, Ivrea, Italy (project; with L. Fontana)

Matarazzo House, São Paulo, Brazil (project)

1953 INA housing developments at Albizzate, Varese, Baggio, Casorate-Sempione, Varese, Gambolo, Gazzada Schianno, Pinerolo Po, Pavia, and Sedriana, Italy

Aquila Service Station, Grumola, Port of Trieste

Ravelli Family Vault and Chapel, Bollote Cemetery, Milan

Cotonficio Valle Susa Depot and Offices, Turin

Grand Show Pavilion, *International Textile Exhibition,* Turin (with G. Lanzani Studio)

Design of the *Thonet Exhibition,* Museum of Modern Art, New York (Peressutti only)

Electric Advertisement Clock, for Soleri, Udine

1954 INA Housing Development, Bellinzago Lombardo, Italy

CUS Factory extension, Collegno, Italy

CUS Factory extension, Rivarolo, Italy

Villa Brusadelli, Capri (project)

"Labyrinth of the Children" Pavilion, *Triennale,* Milan (with S. Steinberg and A. Calder)

Italian Pavilion, *Bienal,* São Paulo (competition project)

Olivetti Showrooms, Fifth Avenue, New York

Recchia House interiors, Milan

1955 Borgo San Sergio Housing and Community Development Plan, Trieste (Rogers only; with W. A. Badalotti)

Palazzina Riva, Via Borgonuovo, Milan (not completed; with W. F. Masi and P. Portaluppi)

Apartment building conversion, Porta Vercellina, Milan (project)

Peressutti House interiors, Corso Magenta, Milan

1956 Sforza Castle conversion to a museum, stage I, Milan (with C. Baroni, R. Chiavelli, and G. Lanzani)

AGIP Office interiors, Milan

Rogers Apartment interiors, Via Bigli, Milan

Hotel, near Beirut, Lebanon (project)

1957 Rural plan for Trieste (Rogers only; with W. P. Cosulich and L. Semerani)

Sesto San Giovanni CECA Workers' Housing Development, Milan

La Loggetta CECA Workers' Housing Development, Naples

Villa Jucker, Zoagli, Genoa

Scotellaro Tomb, Tricarico Cemetery, Matera, Italy (with Carlo Levi)

ENI-AGIP Pavilion, Fiera Campionaria, Milan

Library interiors, *Biennale,* Venice (project)

Moriggia Housing Development, Gallarate, Italy

Civic Centre, Borgo San Sergio, Italy (with S. Bassani, S. Tintori, and L. Paiosa)

1958 Revised master plan for the centre of the City of Milan (Belgiojoso only; with L. Caccia Dominioni and P. Gazzola)

Valesca Tower Building, Milan (with A. Danusso, U. Rivolta, and F. Ordanini)

Aquila Building, Muggia, near Trieste (with S. Tintori and L. Paiosa)

Olivetti Technical and Mechanical Institute, Ivrea, Italy (project; with S. Tintori)

Italian Pavilion, World's Fair, Brussels (with Giancarlo de Carlo, Ignazio Gardella, G. Perugini, and Lodovico Quaroni)

Canadian Pavilion, *Biennale,* Venice (with G. Bay)

Primary school, Cesate, near Milan

Conference Hall, Unesco, Paris

Ravelli Apartment interiors, Via Borgogna, Milan

Designs for Arflex Furniture, Milan

1959 Moriggia Social Centre, Varese, Italy (project)

Società Reale Mutua di Assicurazione Building, Piazza Statuto, Turin (with others)

Casa Lurani Cernuschi restoration, Via Cappuccio, Milan

Plan for the La Rinascente Shop, Via Corso, Rome (competition project)

Housing development, Via San Vittore, Milan (project)

Velarca boat summer house conversion, Lake Como, Italy

1960 Tourist development plan for Punta Stella, Island of Elba (with P. Porcinai)

Development plan for Chiesa Rossa, Milan (competition project)

Santa Margherita Ligure Housing Development, Genoa (project; with Tekne and Bassani)

Primary school, Bellinzago Lombardo, Italy

Municipal Hall, Bellinzago Lombardo, Italy (project)

Mayer Building, Via Masolino da Panicale, Milan

Palazzina Mayer restoration, Via Bigli, Milan (with S. Steinberg and G. Lanzani)

Apartment building conversion, Tellaro, La Spezia, Italy

Randazzo Optical Shop interiors, Palermo, Sicily (with B. Munari, R. Chiavelli, and G. Lanzani)

Spazio and Arco metal furniture, for Olivetti, Milan

1961 Palace of Culture, Milan (Rogers only; project; with M. Zanuso)

Town Hall, Aver El Qasar, Khartoum, Sudan (competition project)

Villa Bartolini, Castiglione della Pescaia, Italy

Patrizi Family Vault, Monumental Cemetery, Milan

Martinoli House interiors, Piazza San Erasmo, Milan

Design of lamps Aglia, Enterprise, Polinnia, Ro, and Talia, for the Artemide Company, Milan

1962 Villa Stabilini, Daverio, near Varese, Italy

Italsider Kindergarten, Genoa (project)

Rafaello ship interiors (competition project)

Tourist development plan for Versilia, near Viareggio, Italy

1963 Sforza Castle Museum restoration, stage II, Milan (with C. Baroni, R. Chiavelli, and G. Lanzani)

Hotel Alfio, Punta Stella, Island of Elba

Tourist/residential development plan for Vecchiano, Pisa, Italy (project)

Apartment building, Via Vigna, Milan

Villa Zanetta, Lake Maggiore, Solcio di Lesa, Novara, Italy

Castello Bruni restoration, Jerago, near Varese, Italy

Orfonatrofio Femminile "Stellin" restoration, Corso Magenta, Milan (project; with J. Battistoni)

Memorial Museum to the Victims of Nazi Concentration Camps, Castello de Pio, Carpi, Italy (with R. Guttuso, M. Chiavelli, and G. Lanzani)

Shell Company Entrance Hall and Exhibition Rooms, London

Einaudi Books/Galleria interiors, Via Manzoni, Milan

1964 Villa, Punta Stella, Island of Elba (not completed)

Gratosoglio Housing and Community Development, stage I, Milan (with others)

Electric Sub-station and Warehouse, for the Milan Underground (Subway), Sesto San Giovanni, Milan (with S. Zorzi, F. Bertolini, P. Maffioletti, and L. Paiosa)

Villa Jucker, Roncano di Bavero, Novara, Italy (with P.Porcinai and A. Radaelli)

Esso Motel, Autostrada dei Laghi, Milan (competition project)

1965 Secondigliano Housing Development, Naples (competition project)

Hispano-Olivetti Building, Ronda de la Universidad, Barcelona (with J. S. Mauri, R. Casals, and L. Paiosa)

Albertini Apartment Building, Via Zezio, Como, Italy

Belgiojoso Building, Via Maddalena, Milan

Building restoration, Via San Andrea, Milan

Church restoration, Longarone, near Belluno, Italy (competition project)

Cicogna Family Vault and Chapel, Bisuschio, near Milan

1966 Master plan for the Town of Biella, Italy (project; with A. Belgiojoso)

Moriggia Nursery and Kindergarten, Italy

Tourist/residential development plan for Lake Garda, Lazise, near Verona (project; with A. Belgiojoso and A. Radaelli)

Banca Commerciale Italiana Building, Via Ruggero Settimo, Palermo, Sicily (with R. Guttuso, S. Bassani, R. Chiavelli, and G. Lanzani)

Banca Privata Finanziaria Building restoration and additions, Via Verdi, Milan

Jacini House restoration, Via dei Bossi, Milan

1967 Housing development, Via Beato Angelico, Milan

Andreatta Apartment Building, Pinzolo, Trento, Italy

Apartment/office building, Via Stampa, Milan

Villa Grandini, Luvinate, Varese, Italy

"Man in the Community" Pavilion, *Expo '67,* Montreal (Peressutti only; with F. Melotti and P. I. Tall)

Gratosoglio Housing and Community Development, stage II, Milan (with others)

IRFIS Headquarters interiors, Palermo, Sicily

Revised master plan for the Town of Biella, Italy (project; with others)

Memorial, Gusen, Mauthausen, Austria

1968 Apartment/office building, Via Toino, Milan

Convent of St. Francis restoration, Rimini, Italy (project)

Hispano-Olivetti Showrooms, Piazza de Espana, Madrid (with R. Casals and A. Rodriguez)

1969 Giornale di Sicilia Building, Via Lincoln, Palermo, Sicily

Apartment buildings, Via Pontaccio, Milan

Regional plan for the Metropolitana Veneta, Venice (as project consultants)

Reconstruction plan for the Old City of Kuwait (project; with A. Belgiojoso, G. Albertazzi, M. G. Sandri, and F. Ordanini)

Chase Manhattan Bank Building, Piazza Meda, Milan

Romagnoli House restoration, Via Annunciata, Milan

1969/
82 Lecco-to-Colico Motorway, Italy

1970 Gabriele d'Annunzio University, Chieti, Italy (with F. Ordanini and W. Passarella)

Motorways, throughout Italy (as consultants)

Tourist development plan for St. Vincent, Italy

Mazzocchi Tourist/Residential Development, Gabicce, near Ancona, Italy

Apartment/office buildings, Piazza Vittorio Veneto, Biella, Italy (project)

Inverigo Housing and Community Development, Como, Italy (project)

New India Assurance Building, Cooperage Road, Bombay (with National Design Institute of Bombay and Shri J. G. Bodhe)

Mediolanum Building, Corso Vittorio Emanuele, Milan (with Ligresti and Cattozzo, R. Coluccini, and L. Paiosa)

Migliorisi Building, Corso Buenos Aires, Milan (with F. Ordanini)

Apartment/office building, Via Solferino, Milan

Tourist development plan for Ascia, Naples

Urban development plan for Canzo, Italy (project)

Hotel, Capoliveri, Island of Elba

Romagnoli Apartment interiors, Milan

1971 Apartment/office building, Via Perugia, Milan

Apartment building, Corso Lodi, Milan

Holiday houses, Gabicce, near Ancona, Italy

San Simpliciano Cloisters restoration, for the Faculty of Theology, Milan

Exhibition Halls, Trade Fair, Dakar, Senegal (competition project)

Kindergarten, Concorezzo, Italy

1972 Central Square, Bellagio, Lake Como, Italy (project)

Ternate Quarries landscaping, Varese, Italy

Development plan for the Legnano Castle and Park, Milan

Apartment building, Viale Majno, Milan

Apartment/office building, Via Madonnina, Milan

B House, Maccagno, Italy

High school, Giussano, Italy

University of Calabria, Arcavacata, Cosenza, Italy (project)

Municipal Offices conversion, Concorezzo, Italy

St. Vincent Hotel, Sports and Cultural Centre, Aosta Valley, Italy

Circolo Hospital additions, Varese, Italy

Building conversions, Corso di Porta Nuova, Milan

1973 Plan for the Monti Berici Region of Italy (with (Technital)

Prefabricated elements, for Fintech Italcamus

M House, Milan

University of Messina, Sicily

Retirement home, Vanzago, Milan

Industrial development, near Choggia, Italy

(with Lodovico Quaroni)

1974 Development plan for the communities of Lake Garda, Italy

Development plan for Dubai (competition project)

Landscape development plan for Bellagio, Lake Como, Italy (project)

M House, Bonassola, Italy

V House, Jeddah, Saudi Arabia

Schools development, Cornaredo, Milan

Technical school, Catanzaro, Italy

Technical school, Modena, Italy

Spaltenna Castle conversion, Gaiole in Chianti, Italy

1975 Memorial to the Victims of Nazi Concentration Camps, Auschwitz, Poland

Tourist development plan for Milazzo, Italy (competition project)

1976 Development plan for the central area of San Pietro all'Olmo, Milan

National Housing Authority Residential Development, Kuwait

Residential development, Masate, near Milan

Residential development, Paullo, Italy

Housing developments at Riyadh, Qatif, Jeddah, and Khobar, Saudi Arabia (competition project)

High school, Concorezzo, Italy

Borgo S. Sergio Parish Church, Trieste

Apartment building conversion, Via Correnti, Milan

Building conversion, Corso S. Marta, Milan

Palazzo Bagatti-Valsecchi conversion, Via S. Spirito, Milan

Development plan for the Port of Venice (as consultants; with Technital)

Road plans for Lecco, Italy (competition project)

Housing development, Nigeria

1977 Stock Exchange Building conversion, Milan

Palazzo Reale alterations and renovations, Milan (project)

1978 Via Pontaccio and Via Garibaldi Development, Milan (project)

1980 Management Centre, Milan (competition project)

Publications:

By BBPR: books—*Stile*, Milan 1936; *Il piano regolatore della Valle d'Aosta*, with others, Ivrea, Italy 1943; articles—"Un programma di architetture," with others, in *Quadrante* (Milan), May 1933; "Relazione al progetto del Palazzo del Littorio," with Luigi Figini, Gino Pollini, and Luigi Danusso, in *Quadrante* (Milan), August/September 1934; "Il fatto esposizione" in *Quadrante* (Milan), June 1935; "Urbanistica corporativa" in *Quadrante* (Milan), September 1935; "L'Annata architettonica" in *Almanacco letterario Bompiani*, Milan 1936; "Il volto delle epoche" in *Enciclopedia pratica Bompiani*, Milan 1936; "Riorganizzazione dell'edilizia rurale," with E. Radice Fossati, in *Congresso Nazionale di Urbanistica* (proceedings), Rome 1937; "L'Architettura" in *Almanacco letterario Bompiani*, Milan 1942; "La città in cura" in *Tempo* (Rome), 1942; "Il piano A-R: la descrizione del piano," with others, in *Costruzioni-Casabella* (Milan), September 1946; "Stile del museo" in *Città di Milano*, Milan 1956.

On BBPR: books—*La cultura architettonica in Italia tra le due guerre* by Cesare De Seta, Rome 1972, 1983; *Città, museo e architettura: Il gruppo BBPR nella cultura architettonica italiana 1932-1970* by Ezio Bonfanti and Marco Porta, Florence 1973 (includes bibliography); *Immaginazione megastrutturale dal futurismo a oggi*, edited by Enrico Crispolti, Venice 1979; *Architetture italiane degli anni '70*, exhibition catalogue, edited by Giovanna De Feo and Enrico Valeriani, Rome 1981; *BBPR a Milano*, exhibition catalogue, edited by Antonio Piva, Milan 1982; articles—"Gli architetti BBPR" by L. Sinisgalli in *Comunità* (Milan), May/June 1950; "Continuità e coeranza dei BBPR" by E. Paci in *Zodiac* (Milan), April 1959; "Meda Offices: Architects BBPR" in *Architectural Review* (London), January 1974; "Castle into War Memorial, Capri, Italy" in *Architecture Plus* (New York), March/April 1974; "Project Barrier: Office Buildings, Piazza Meda, Milan" by Aileen Graham in *Architects' Journal* (London), June 1974; "In the Barracks of the Geometry of Death" by Renato Pedio in *Architettura* (Rome), November 1980; "The Architecture of Continuity" by Giuseppe Samonà in *Casabella* (Milan), December 1982.

*

BBPR Architectural Studio was founded in 1932, only five years after the setting up of an Italian CIAM group, an event that could be said to mark the arrival of Modern architecture in Italy. Despite the excitement created earlier outside Italy by Sant'Elia and the Futurists, modernist ideas had to overcome a fierce chauvinism within Italy. Italy is more accustomed to setting examples of style than to receiving them, particularly examples from the North. Gianluigi Banfi, Lodovico Belgiojoso, Enrico Peressutti, and Ernesto Rogers nonetheless produced resolutely modernist thesis projects in their final year at Milan Polytechnic.

Early projects included competitions, a plan for Pavia, and a witty, spectacular weekend house for the fifth *Triennale* in Milan. Following this early burst of activity, the BBPR Studio, along with many other Italian modernists, fell under the spell of Fascist patronage. Having encountered resistance to modernism among the establishment, they hoped that Fascism would favour progressive architecture. Their eagerness to build, and their relative youth, numbed them to the true implications of Mussolini's ambitions. True, in the late 1930s, BBPR did some remarkably sensitive and intelligent work, notably the Heliotherapy Clinic at Legnano of 1938. The restoration of the cloisters of San Simpliciano of 1940, which housed the firm's own offices, was a triumph of intelligent sympathy for the past, a quality to be seen again later in the magnificent conversion of the Sforza Castle to a museum (1954-56).

When Italy joined the German Axis, the progressive potential of Fascism vanished, just as Hitler had forced out German modernists as "radical" and "bolshevik." BBPR's Post Office complex of 1940 within Rome's EUR Quarter is the only building there to sustain the modernist spirit, while lesser architects "succumbed to the flattery of M. Piacentini, swallowing up and regurgitating arches, columns, pilasters, symmetrical plans, static volumes, pointless scenographic perspective," as Bruno Zevi has put it. The episode of EUR, the advent of war, and their own awareness of the failure of Fascism forced BBPR underground, Rogers to Lausanne, Banfi to die tragically at Mauthausen.

The war over, a renascence of Italian architecture began. Young architects who had been stifled by Fascism, able only to talk and reflect, burst on the scene and became part of the Italy the world turned to for inspiration in industrial design, naval architecture, sculpture, and fashion. Italy, as always, could provide elegance and style, both in great demand after wartime austerity. The architecture of BBPR, the more eclectic Gio Ponti, and many others, was very much part of this development.

The usual materials of modern architecture—glass, steel, and concrete—were now rationed, and BBPR sought new forms based on indigenous masonry, smaller windows, and careful planning. They and their colleagues such as Samonà, Quaroni, Gardella, and Albini, were well equipped for such discoveries. Their knowledge of architectural history was deep, and their love of Italy enriched by her recent horrible experiences. They began to produce a new type of modern architecture, one that did not turn its back on the past, was not frightened to copy what is good, and one that displayed great good humour—three attributes eschewed in the Anglo-Saxon interpretation of modernism, which is obsessed with originality, purity of form, and functional expressionism. The romanticism of the Italian movement, the concern for the symbolic rather than the expressive, was too much for the powerful British and American critics who, not seeing the wood for the trees, accused the Italians of gross eclecticism, whimsy, moral irresponsibility, and worse. So vituperative was this attack that even now, when the north is discovering what it calls postmodernism, the true genesis of that idea in the Italy of the 1950s remains unacknowledged. BBPR are among the masters of what is being learned today.

In particular, the Velasca Tower Building of 1955-58 is a seminal building. Although attacked in England for its allusive qualities (compared with mediaeval buildings) and berated for its lucid, organic structure, the building is a masterful synthesis of its complex functional requirements, Milanese traditions, structural possibilities, and great art. It is art that often seems to be lacking in northern architecture, and one can only hope that the scorn heaped on the great Italian postwar architects, especially BBPR, is inspired by envy.

It is worth remembering that Belgiojoso, Peressutti, and Rogers, along with other Italians whose best work was done in the postwar years, were people mature in the 1950s and 1960s who had seen great hopes frustrated; many of them had been fooled by Fascism; they saw their country ravaged by war; and they loved and understood their cultural heritage. The wisdom born of those experiences is felt in the maturity and great sophistication of their work. One day, the rest of the world is bound to acknowledge their contribution.

—Andrew Rabeneck

BEAUDOUIN, Eugène Elie.

French. Born in Paris, 20 July 1898. Educated at the Collège Lavoisier, Paris; Ecole Nationale Supérieure des Beaux-Arts, Paris; French Academy, Rome, 1929-32. Married the artist Josephine Cals in 1928; children: François, Sylvie, and Thierry. In partnership with Marcel Lods, *q.v.*, Paris, 1925-40. In private practice, Paris, since 1944. Chief Architect of Public Buildings and National Palaces, France, since 1933; Member, National Council of Architecture and Town Planning, since 1950. Director of Architectural Studies, University of Geneva, 1940-68. Professor of Architecture, Ecole Nationale Supérieure des Beaux-Arts, Paris, since 1946. President, International Union of Architects, 1960-64. Honorary President, French Town Planning Society, since 1965, Association of Architects' Councils of the Ministry of Equipment, since 1966, and of the Association of Chief Architects of Public Buildings and National Palaces, since 1969. Exhibition: *Het Nieuwe Bouwen Internationaal: CIAM*, Rijksmuseum Kröller-Müller, Otterlo (toured Netherlands), 1983. Recipient: First Prize, with Marcel Lods, World's Fair Competition, Paris, 1937. Officer of the Grimaldi Order, Monaco, 1958; Chevalier, Order of Merit, 1960; Officer of the French Academy, 1962; Member, Fine Arts Academy, Institut de France, 1963; Commander of the Légion d'Honneur, 1971; Commander of the Order of Arts and Letters, 1972. Honorary Fellow, Royal Institute of British Architects, American Institute of Architects, and Sociedad Central de los Arquitectos Argentinos. Address (office): 38 rue de l'Yvette, Paris 16, France.

Works:

1928 Town Plan for La Havane, France (with J.C.N. Forestier)

1930/
36   Plan for the Paris region (with Henri Prost)
1932 Cité des Oiseux (housing development), Bagneux, France
1933 Palais des Expositions, Paris (project; with Marcel Lods and Vladimir Bodiansky)
1934 Cité de la Muette (housing development), Drancy, France (with Marcel Lods and Vladimir Bodiansky)
1935 Open-Air School, Suresnes, France (with Marcel Lods)
1937 Aero-Club, Buc, France (with Marcel Lods and Jean Prouvé; demolished by the Germans during the Occupation, 1940-44)
Design of the World's Fair, Paris (with Marcel Lods)
French Embassy, Ottawa, Canada
1938 Dismantable Week-end House, *Exposition Habitation*, Paris (with Marcel Lods)
1939 Maison du Peuple, Clichy, Paris (with Marcel Lods, Vladimir Bodiansky, and Jean Prouvé)
1940 Town Plan for Cape Town (first project)
1941/
61   Plan for Monaco
1942/
43   Town Plan for Marseille
1948 Town Plan for Saigon
Town Plans for Montpellier and Toulon, France
French Embassy, Accra, Ghana
1949 Industrial complex, Sarre, France
1950 Industrial centers and residential complexes in Gabon and Cameroun
1951 Cité Rotterdam (housing development), Strasbourg
Joffre School, Montpellier, France
1954 Les Bas-Coudrais (housing development), Sceaux, France

Eugène Beaudouin: Cité de la Muette, Drancy, France, 1934.

Housing development, including Young Workers Dormitory, Cachan, France

University Residence Hall, Antony, France

1958 Decoration of Paris for the visit of H.M. Queen Elizabeth II

French Embassy, Pretoria, South Africa

1958/
74 Renovation of the Gare Montparnasse/Avenue du Maine District of Paris (with U. Cassan, L. de Marien, J. Warnery, J. Saubot, and R. Lopez)

1959 Ministries of Agriculture and Industry Building, rue Barbet de Jouy, Paris

Residence Hall, University of Clermont-Ferrand, France

1960 Mixed School, Antony, France

Town plan for Cape Town (2nd project)

1961 National School of Taxation, Clermont-Ferrand, France

1962 Faculty of Law, University of Clermont-Ferrand, France

Housing development, Eaubonne, France

1962/
74 Venissieux-les-Minguettes (satellite town), Lyons

1964 Town plan for Cape Town (3rd project)

Plan for the reconstruction of Suresnes, France

Housing development, Vernaison, Lyon

1964/
69 Z.U.P. Housing Development, Venissieux-les-Minguettes, Lyon

Z.U.P. Housing Development, La Foux, Saint Tropez, France

Tourist housing, Saint-Cyprien, Languedoc, France

1964/
76 Administrative Center, Eaubonne, France

1965 La Croix-Laval University Complex, Lyon

1966 Housing development, Angers, France

1966/
68 International Labor Organization Building, Geneva (with others; as Chief Architect)

1967 Post Office, Eaubonne, France

1967/
68 Mixed School, Meudon, France

1967/
73 Palais des Nations extension and remodelling, and new Conference Hall, United Nations, Geneva (with Pier Luigi Nervi and Alberto Camenzind)

1968 Plan for the Isfahan region of Iran

1968/
77 National Veterinary School, Lyon

1972 Housing development, Saint-Laurent du Var, France

1973/
74 Venissy Commercial Center, Venissieux-les-Minguettes, Lyon

1974 Montparnasse S.N.C.F. Railway Station Complex (station; housing; conference center; shops; hotels; cinemas; restaurants; and general services), Paris

1977 Apartment building, rue des Prairies, Paris

1978 Auteuil-Muette Tax Center, for the Finance Ministry, rue George Sand, Paris

Publications:

By BEAUDOUIN: articles—"L'Enseignement de l'architecture" in *Werk* (Zürich), June 1943; "L'Urbanisme et l'architecture au Cap" in *La Construction moderne* (Paris), April 1953; "De la Composition des plans-masse des groupes d'habitations" in *Forum* (Amsterdam), May 1953.

On BEAUDOUIN: books—*Guide de l'art dans la rue au XXe Siècle—Paris et sa banlieue* by Bernard Marrey, Paris 1974; *L'Architecture de la Réconstruction en France, 1945-1953* by Anatole Kopp, Frédéri-que Boucher and Danièle Pauly, Paris 1982; *Het Nieuwe Bouwen Internationaal: CIAM—Housing, Town Planning*, exhibition catalogue by R. D. Oxenaar and A. van der Woud, Delft, Netherlands 1983; articles—"Architects of Europe Today: Eugène Beaudouin" by George Nelson in *Pencil Points* (New York), February 1936; "Edificio de la Legación de Francia en Ottawa" in *Arquitectura* (Mexico City), January 1940; "Cité Rotterdam" in *Werk* (Zürich), September 1953; "Reconstruction and Housing in France," special issue of *Techniques et architecture* (Paris), November/December 1953; "Architecture sociale et hospitalière" in *L'Architecture française* (Paris), June 1960; "Maine/Montparnasse" in *Architecture française* (Paris), July/August 1973; "Maine/Montparnasse" in *Moderner Markt* (Frankfurt), January 1974.

In the practice of architecture and urbanism, I have tried to make it my object in all my work to provide "a service" to the client, to allow him a measure of control, and in this way to achieve a final result that is a collective effort.

My attitude, in all circumstances, is to work conscientiously and with complete sincerity.

—Eugène Beaudouin

Eugène Beaudouin followed in the great tradition of French architects by studying at the French Academy in Rome. However, the classical education that had had such immense international repercussions for students of the late eighteenth century was not to provide Beaudouin with his inspiration. Like so many others of his generation, he became concerned with the provision of low-cost housing for the poorer members of society. He worked for the public housing office of the Department of the Seine and, later, for the Société des Logements Économiques pour Familles Nombreuses. He realized that structural experiment was needed to provide low-cost housing and that it was essential to mix such experiment with modern distributive ideas.

His Cité de la Muette at Drancy, with Marcel Lods, was a mixed development of low- and high-rise buildings in which modern prefabricated concrete components were used. There were several four-storey blocks and five sixteen-storey towers built on a steel skeleton. Roofs and non-loadbearing walls were of precast concrete, as were the outer coverings, the stairs, and the balconies, so a rigorous quality control was possible in factory conditions when the units were manufactured. The circular staircases to the towers at Drancy were expressed in vertical fins of precast concrete, and each tower was constructed with panel effects, all in concrete. These system-built towers were early prototypes of high-rise housing blocks that became usual during the 1950s and 1960s and have since attracted universal anathema. Beaudouin's system of precast concrete was also used in his school at Suresnes of 1935.

Beaudouin prepared designs for the Unesco Building in Paris after World War II, but by then his aggressive dogmatism and the ferociously puritan effects of his housing designs had alienated many people. His designs were not felt to be what was required by the several distinguished architects who advised on the design of the headquarters.

Other schemes by Beaudouin include the Maison du Peuple at Clichy of 1939, the Cité Rotterdam housing estate at Strasbourg, and many other developments for public buildings and housing. He is also known in the field of town and regional planning, where his peculiar blend of French logic and a ruthless devotion to systems for building have tended to produce hard and uncompromising environments, with no redeeming feature to humanise and soften their impacts.

—James Stevens Curl

BECKET, Welton David.

American. Born in Seattle, Washington, 8 August 1902. Educated at the University of Washington, Seattle, 1923-27, B.Arch. 1927; Ecole des Beaux Arts, Fontainebleau, France, 1928. Married; sons; Bruce and Welton, Jr. Worked as a designer-draftsman for a small architectural office in Los Angeles, 1929; in private practice, Seattle, 1929-33; Partner, with Walter Wurdeman and Charles Plummer, Becket, Wurdeman and Plummer, Los Angeles, 1933 until Plummer's death in 1939, then as Becket and Wurdeman, 1939 until Wurdeman's death in 1949; Becket continued the firm as Welton Becket and Associates, serving as President, 1949-68, and Chairman of the Board, 1968 until his death in 1969 (firm now continues under the direction of Welton Becket, Jr.); offices established in San Francisco, 1949, New York, 1950, and Houston, 1960. Master Planner and Supervising Architect, University of California at Los Angeles, 1949-69. Recipient: First Place, Pan Pacific Auditorium Competition, Los Angeles, 1934; Honor Award, American Institute of Architects, 1936; Award, Pan American Congress of Architects, 1950. Fellow, American Institute of Architects, 1952. *Died* (in Los Angeles) *17 January 1969.*

Works:

1934 Pan Pacific Auditorium, Los Angeles (with Walter Wurdeman)

1940 Jai Alai Auditorium, Manila (with Walter Wurdeman)

1946 House of tomorrow, Los Angeles (with Walter Wurdeman)

1947 Bullocks's Department Store, Pasadena, California (with Walter Wurdeman)

1948 Prudential Square, Los Angeles (with Walter Wurdeman)

1949 General Petroleum Building, Los Angeles (with Walter Wurdeman)

1950 Bullock's Department Store, Westwood, California

1951 Stonestown Shopping Center, San Francisco, California

1955 Beverly Hilton Hotel, Beverly Hills, California

1956 Ford Motor Company General Office Building, Dearborn, Michigan

1957 Canyon Village, Yellowstone National Park, Wyoming

Hawaiian Village, Honolulu (with Edwin L. Bauer)

1958 Beach facilities, Santa Monica, California

Master plan for Century City, Los Angeles

1959 California Teachers Association Headquarters, Burlingame, California

Nile Hilton hotel, Cairo

Southland Center, Dallas (with Mark Lemmon)

Design of the *United States Exhibition*, Moscow

Los Angeles Memorial Sports Arena

1960 Kaiser Center, Oakland, California

Welton Becket and Associates Building, 10000 Santa Monica Boulevard, Los Angeles

1961 Neuropsychiatric and Brain Research Institute, University of California at Los Angeles

Veterans Administration Hospital, Palo Alto, California

1962 500 Jefferson Building, Houston, Texas

Gateway Building West, Century City, Los Angeles

Los Angeles International Airport (with Pereira and Luckman)

Marion Davies Children's Clinic, University of California at Los Angeles

1963 Cullen Center, Houston, Texas

Bullock's Department Store, Sherman Oaks, California

Hotel Sonesta, Houston, Texas

Welton Becket: Xerox Square, Rochester, New York, 1968.

Humble Oil Building, Houston, Texas (with Goleman and Rolfe, and Pierce and Pierce)
Civic Center, Orange, California
Security Pacific Bank Building, Tishman Airport Center, Los Angeles
U. S. Borax Building, Los Angeles
United States Embassy, Warsaw
1964 Ford Motor Company Pavilion, World's Fair, New York
General Electric Exhibit, World's Fair, New York
Gateway Building East, Century City, Los Angeles
The Meadows (apartments), San Rafael, California
Dorothy Chandler Pavilion, Los Angeles Music Center
Phillips Petroleum Building, Bartlesville, Oklahoma
1965 Beverly Hills/Westwood Office of the Automobile Club of Southern California, Century City, Los Angeles
Bullock's Department Store, Lakewood, California
North Carolina Mutual Life Building, Durham, North Carolina (with Marion A. Ham)

Pauley Pavilion, University of California at Los Angeles
Public Library, Pomona, California (with Everett and Tozier)
Institute for Chronic Disease, University of California at Los Angeles
Wells Fargo Bank, San Rafael, California
1966 Jules Stein Eye Institute, University of California at Los Angeles
Northgate Shopping Center, San Rafael, California
Center Plaza, Boston
Federal Office Building, Los Angeles (with Albert C. Martin and Associates, and Paul R. Williams)
First State Bank, Clear Lake City, Texas
1967 Fashion Island, Newport Beach, Calfornia
Gulf Life Tower, Jacksonville, Florida (with Kemp, Bunche and Jackson)
Hartford National Bank Building, Hartford, Connecticut (with Jeter and Cook)
Ahmanson Theatre, Los Angeles Music Center
Park Lane Apartments, Monterey, California
1968 Manila Hilton hotel (with C. D. Arguelles)
City Hall, Pomona, California (with B. H. Anderson)

Academic Building, United States Naval Postgraduate School, Monterey, California
School of Public Health, University of California at Los Angeles
Xerox Square, Rochester, New York
1969 Aetna Life and Casualty Building, San Francisco
Almaden Fashion Plaza, San Jose, California
Bullock's Department Store, La Habra, California
Canada College, Redwood City, California (with Chan Rader Associates)
Equitable Life Building, Los Angeles
Hoffman Medical Research Center, University of Southern California, Los Angeles
Mutual Benefit Life Building, San Francisco

Publications:

On BECKET: book— *Total Design: The Architecture of Welton Becket and Associates* by William Dudley Hunt, Jr., New York 1972; articles— "Recent Works of Welton Becket and Associates" in *Michigan Society of Architects Bulletin* (Detroit), June 1958; "Welton Becket and Associates" in *Interiors* (New York), September 1959; "Portrait of the Artist as a Businessman" by Robert Sheehan in *Fortune* (New York), March 1967; "Obituaries: Architect Welton Becket" in *Architectural Record* (New York), March 1969; "Obituary: Welton Becket" in *Progressive Architecture* (New York), April 1969.

Discussions between architects about the influence of architects on architecture are almost always concerned, sometimes exclusively, with the subject of design. And architectural design is often taken to mean, narrowly, the form of esthetics of buildings.

Welton Becket influenced the esthetic design of buildings, but much more important was his deep influence on the complete design of buildings, including not only their forms but also their plans, functions, interiors, systems, structures, and other aspects. Equally as important was Becket's contribution to the revolutionary changes that have taken place in architectural practice.

In the early 1930s Becket was one of the first architects to recognize that much of the architecture of the future world would consist of large, complex buildings and groups of buildings. He also foresaw that such buildings, more often than not, would be designed and constructed for corporations and other organizations of great size. The owners of such buildings, the clients of architects, would be, not individuals, but groups of people, mostly businessmen, the officers and boards of directors of the organizations.

In order to serve the needs of such corporate owners, Becket set out to build an architectural practice of sufficient size and capabilities to handle properly such large and complex work. Since it would be dealing with businessmen, Becket organized the firm in a businesslike manner, along the lines of the organizations for which it would perform architectural services. In order to serve all of the needs of the clients, the firm would offer not only the usual architectural services but also what Becket came to call total design, including master planning, site planning, engineering, interior design, landscape architecture, graphic design, and other services. Thus, the firm would be able to analyze problems, perform studies and research, solve problems through design, and transform the solutions into completed buildings and groups of buildings that were complete to the last detail.

Becket established his practice of architecture in 1933 and practiced continuously for thirty six years, devoting himself to all aspects of architecture in the broadest sense, but avoiding involvement in related but non-architectural activities, such as construction, real estate, or the financing of buildings. Unlike many of his contemporaries who often spent much of their time in non-practice pursuits, such as teaching or making speeches, Becket devoted himself entirely to the practice of architecture.

By the time he died, in 1969, Becket had developed one of the largest and most successful firms in the world. It was one of the first truly national, and later international, American architectural firms, with offices in a number of cities. Although he was proud of the awards his buildings earned at various times, Becket was most proud of the list of clients he developed and of the fact that many of them automatically came back to his firm, some on numerous occasions, when they had additional building projects in mind.

The firm established by Becket has continued to prosper, maintaining the same business principles and devotion to total design envisioned by its founder. Other large, multifaceted national and international firms are in practice today, but Becket pioneered the way for them.

—William Dudley Hunt, Jr.

BEEBY, Thomas Hall.

American. Born in Oak Park, Illinois, 12 October 1941. Educated at Lower Merion High School, Ardmore, Pennsylvania, 1955-58; Gresham School, Holt, Norfolk, England, 1958-59; Cornell University, Ithaca, New York, under Colin Rowe and John Hejduk, *q.v.* 1959-64, B.Arch. 1964; Yale University, New Haven, Connecticut, under Paul Rudolph, *q.v.* Vincent Scully, and Serge Chermeyeff, *q.v.* 1964-65, M.Arch. 1965. Married Marcia Dale Greenlease in 1960 (divorced, 1973); children: Donald and Mary Anne; Married Kirsten Peltzer in 1975; sons: Markus and Johannes. Associate, C.F.Murphy Associates, Chicago, 1965-71; Partner, with James Hammond, Hammond Beeby and Associates, Chicago, 1971-76. Since 1976, Partner, with Hammond (retired, 1983) and Bernard F. Babka, Hammond Beeby and Babka, Chicago. Associate Professor, Department of Architecture, Illinois Institute of Technology, Chicago 1973-80; Director, School of Architecture, University of Illinois at Chicago, 1980-85; Dean, School of Architecture, Yale University, New Haven, Connecticut, since 1985. Exhibitions; *100 Years of Architecture in Chicago,* Neue Sammlung, Munich, and Museum of Contemporary Art, Chicago, 1976; *Chicago Architects,* Co- oper Union, New York, and Time-Life Building, Chicago, 1976; *7 Chicago Architects,* Richard Gray Gallery, Chicago, 1976; *The Exquisite Corpse,* Walter Kelly Gallery, Chicago, 1977; *Designs for Urban Living,* Walker Art Center, Minneapolis, and Graham Foundation, Chicago, 1978; *Wishful Thinking,* Cooper Hewitt Museum, New York, 1979; *Bridging Chicago,* Graham Foundation, Chicago, 1979; *American Architectural Alternatives,* toured Europe, 1979-80; *Biennale,* Venice, 1980; *Late Entries to the Tribune Tower Competition,* Museum of Contemporary Art, Chicago, 1980; *Speaking a New Classicism,* Smith College of Art, Northampton, Massachusetts, 1981; *Chicago Architectural Club Exhibit,* Art Institute of Chicago, 1981, 1982, 1983, and 1984; *Chicago Art Fair,* Frumkin-Struve Gallery, Chicago, 1981; *Rooms* (with Irene Siegel), Young Hoffman Gallery, Chicago, 1981; *Room, Window, Furniture,* Cooper Union, New York, 1982; *Architecture de Chicago,* Paris Art Centre, Paris, 1983; *World's Fair Charrettes,* University of Illinois at Chicago, 1983; Recipient: Distinguished Building Award, American Institute of Architects, Chicago Chapter, 1976 (twice), 1977, 1978, 1979, 1980 (twice), 1983, and 1984, Illinois Chapter, 1981, and National Design Award, 1984. Address: Hammond Beeby and Babka, 1126 North State Street, Chicago, Illinois 60610, U.S.A.

Works:

1971 Malcolm X College, Chicago (with C. F. Murphy and Associates)
1975 One Woodfield place (office building), Schaumberg, Illinois
1976 Beider Conference Center, Chicago
First National Bank of Ripon, Wisconsin
1977 Champaign Public Library, Illinois
1978 Beasly House, Monroe, Wisconsin
Bank of the North Shore, Northbrook, Illinois
Doane Observatory, Alder Planetarium, Chicago
Hewitt Associates Office Building, Lincoln-shire, Illinois
Highland Lakes Office Building, Lombard, Illinois
Sanders House, Barrington, Illinois
1979 Dearborn Park townhouses, Chicago
Faltz House, Chesterton, Indiana
Tri-State Office Center, Northbrook, Illinois
North Shore Congregation Israel addition Glencoe, Illinois
Bush House, Harbour Island, Bahamas
Hild Library, Chicago
1980 Beasly House, Monroe, Wisconsin
Colorado Plaza, Denver
Illinois Hospital Association, Naperville, Illinois
1981 Art Institute of Chicago additions, Chicago
Building Rehabilitation, 11 South LaSalle Street, Chicago
Krehbiel House addition, Hinsdale, Illinois
1982 American Academy of Pediatrics, Arlington Heights, Illinois
Bannockburn Green Shopping Center, Bannockburn, Illinois
Shutack House, Oakbrook, Illinois
1984 Formica Showroom, Chicago
Hyde Park housing, Chicago
World's Fair Plan, Chicago

Publications:

By BEEBY: articles—"The Grammar of Ornament, Ornament as Grammar" in *VIA III* (Graduate School of Fine Arts, University of Pennsylvania, Philadelphia), 1977; "Vitruvius Americanus: Mies Ornament" in *Inland Architect* (Chicago), May 1977; "Flowering Grid" in *Architectural Review* (London), October 1977; "Of Manifest Destiny and the Death of Prophets" in *AIA journal* (Washington, D.C.), October 1978; "The Cultural Implications of Urban Form" in *Design Quarterly* (Minneapolis), 1978; "What's next?" in *AIA journal* (Washington, D.C.) May 1980; "The Song of Taliesin" in *Modulus* (Charlottesville, Virginia), Spring 1981; "Drygoods Box School" in *GA Houses* (Tokyo), May 1981, "Transatlantic Fantasies" in *Architectural Review* (London), May 1984; "Epilogue in *Visual notes,* edited by Norman Crowe and Paul Laseau, Princeton, New Jersey 1984.

On BEEBY: books—*100 Years of Architecture in Chicago,* exhibition catalogue, by Grube, Pran and Schultz, Chicago 1976; *Chicago Architects* by Stuart Cohen, Chicago 1976; *Ornamentalism* by Robert Jensen and Patricia Conway, New York 1981: *Postmodern* by Paolo Portoghesi, New York 1983; articles—"40 under 40" by Robert Stern in *Architecture + Urbanism* (Tokyo), January 1977; "Chicago 7" in *Architecture + Urbanism* (Tokyo), May 1977; special issue on Chicago of *Architectural Review* (London), October 1977; "The Diversity of Design in Chicago" by Peter Pran in *Architettura* (Milan), December 1977; "Ripon Pavilion" by David Morton in *Progressive Architecture* (New York), July 1978; "Chicago on the Drawing Board" by Nory Miller in *Horizons* (New York), September 1978; "Prime Square Footages" by John Dixon in *Progressive Architecture* (New York), October 1978; "Color in Architecture" by Nory Miller in *AIA Journal* (Washington, D.C.), October 1978; "Designs for Living" by Douglas Davis in *Newsweek* (New York), 6 November 1978; "The Exquistite Corpse" in *Architecture + Urbanism* (Tokyo), July 1978; "La Herencia Arquitectonica de Chicago: una imagen clasico-romantico" by Stanley Tigerman in *Arquitectura* (Madrid) March/April 1979; "Kaleido-scope" by Nory Miller in *AIA journal* (Washington, D.C.), May 1979; "Modernism and the Canonical Chicago Architectural condition" by Stanley Tigerman in *Harvard Architectural Review* (Cambridge, Massachusetts), Spring 1980; "Replicas" in *AIA Journal* (Washington, D.C.), May 1980; "The Chicago Seven" by Lance Knobel in *Architectural Review* (London), June 1980; "Hammond Beeby and Babka" by Suzanne Stephens in *Progressive Architecture* (New York), June 1980; "Chicago Story, Upon Story, Upon Story, Upon Story ..." by M. W. Newman in *Horizon* (New York) July 1980; "The Burham Library and Architecture Gallery" in *Inland Architect* (Chicago), July/August 1980; "The Presence of the Past" in *Domus* (Milan), October 1980; "Post Modern Classicism" by Charles Jencks in *Architectural Design* (London), November 1980; "Talk on Mies van der Rohe, Myron Goldsmith, Thomas Beeby and Masami Takayama" in *Architecture + Urbanism* (Tokyo), January 1981; "Chicago Slab" in *Architecture Review* (London), February 1981; "American Architecture after Modernism" in *Architecture + Urbanism* (Tokyo), March 1981; "An Experiment in Color" in *House Beautiful* (New York) May 1981; "Radiating Serenity" in *Interiors* (New York), May 1981; "Thomas H. Beeby—1981 projects" in *Controspazio* (Bari, Italy), April/June 1981; "Thonet Takes Five" in *Progressive Architecture* (New York), August 1981; "Beeby Branch Library" in *Architecture Review* (London), August 1981; "New Waves in American Architecture" in *GA Houses* (Tokyo), Fall 1981; "Traditional rekindled" in *Architectural Record* (New York), June 1983; "Historic Addition to a 60s Temple" by Nora Richater Green in *AIA Journal* (Washington, D.C.), May 1984; "A Villa in a Park: Offices for the American Academy of Pediatrics, Elk Grove Village, Illinois" in *Architectural Record* (New York), May 1985.

Bibliography: *The Chicago Seven* by Lamia Doumato, Monticello, Illinois 1982.

Our approach has been to utlize the lucid systematic qualities of construction long associated with the architecture of Chicago. We employ frame construction as a pragmatic necessity and an organizing aesthetic device. prefabricated systems and modular coordination play a major in the visual character of our buildings. We are also interested in as free an arrangement as possible. The Fluid spatial quality of early modern architecture has strongly influenced our work. We are concerned with expressive display of functional elements through arrangements of construction. This would equate with the volumetric and fenestration effects found in the nineteenth century balloon-framed houses prevalent in Chicago. Our interests also encompass the question of meaning of forms and their derivation form the ideas of the past.

These methods and ideas constitute neither a revolutionary nor a radical approach; however, the full implication of these combine concepts has never been fully explored. The great break in continuity of architectural development in Chicago occured during World War II when virtually all building stopped. At this time a schism developed which has increased with time. The choice has been between classicism pursuing pure construction and its conscious antithesis of picturesque romanticism. To explore synthesis has difficult and challenging aspects. The shift in our practice from primarily dealing with commercial buildings to the design of public and institutional structures has had a major effect on the iconography of the work, now that it is no longer based on generalized programs.

Thomas Hall Beeby: Hewitt Associates Office Building, Lincolnshire, Illinois, 1978.

Our work between 1979 and 1984 focused on the meaning of form with the increased integration of historical precedent as a design method. The constructional methodology, including structure and detailing, has maintained modern techniques, but the imagery has shifted toward more easily understood models. There has been a decrease in the level of abstraction with the notion of an increased comprehensibility.

—Thomas Hall Beeby

Thomas Hall Beeby is one of the leading younger figures of the post-Miesian generation in Chicago. Typical of the designers who matured in the city during the late 1960s and 1970s, Beeby has moved from an early, rather close fidelity to the principles of Miesian structural geometry to a gradually more personal idiom marked at times by a strikingly original quality of lyric fantasy.

Beeby spent his boyhood in the suburbs of Chicago and Philadelphia, and in Norfolk, England. His professional training led to a Bachelor of Science

in Architecture degree in 1964 from Cornell University, where he studied with John Hejduk and Colin Rowe, and a Master of Architecture in 1965 from Yale University, where he worked with Paul Rudolph. He accepted his first professional position with the firm of C. F. Murphy Associates, at that time one of the leading exponents of Miesian design in Chicago. Beeby quickly came under the influence of the two most talented architects on the Murphy staff, Gene Summers and Jacques Brownson. The lessons learned from that encounter are evident in the work Beeby did in the design of the Malcolm X College in Chicago.

In 1971 he joined James Hammond to form Hammond, Beeby and Associates, later (in 1977) Hammond Beeby and Babka. Two of the more important early works which Beeby executed for the partnership are Woodfield Place (eleven-story office building) in Schaumburg, Illinois, a clear expression of the Chicago frame, and the First National Bank of Ripon, Wisconsin. Thereafter, however, a tendency away from local formula toward more experimental forms became apparent; in his library for Cham-

paign, Illinois, the design is marked by curved walls and corrugated metal siding, as well as a free plan reminiscent of the earlier European work of Mies and Le Corbusier.

By 1979 Beeby had utilized curvilinear form to highly inventive advantage in the cylindrical volumes of the Doane Observatory in Chicago, as well as in the gleaming, round, white-brick box which houses the Bank of the North Shore in Northbrook, Illinois. For a 1978 exhibition of the Chicago Seven (a group of young local designers seeking alternatives to the traditional Chicago structuralist viewpoint), he submitted a series of drawings for a project, The House of Vergil, which suggested he had moved, at least at the level of imagination, into a realm of luxurious visionary form altogether removed from the sternness of his early manner. Still, among his completed works, such as the Hewitt Associates Office Building in Lincolnshire, Illinois, he has maintained a balance between what he himself has called "pure construction" and "picturesque romanticism."

—Franz Schulze

BEHNISCH, Günter.

German. Born in Lockwitz bei Dresden, 12 June 1922. Studied engineering at the Technische Hochschule, Stuttgart, 1947-51, Diplom-Ingenieur 1951. Oberleutnant, German Navy, 1939-45; prisoner-of-war in England, 1945-47. Married Johanna Fink in 1952; children: Sabine, Charlotte, and Stefan. Practised with Bruno Lambart, Stuttgart, 1952-56; practised on his own, Stuttgart, 1956-66; formed company, Behnisch & Partner, Stuttgart, 1966 (partners: Fritz Auer, Winfried Büxel, Manfred Sabatke, Erhard Tränkner, and Karlheinz Weber). Regional Director, Bund Deutscher Architekten, Baden-Württemberg, 1965-68. Professor, Technische Hochschule, Darmstadt, since 1975. Exhibition: *Zeit im Aufriss*, Herkulessaal der Residenz, Munich, 1983. Recipient: Paul Bonatz Prize, City of Stuttgart, 1963; Grand Architecture Prize, Bund Deutscher Architekten, 1972; Hugo Häring Prize, Bund Deutscher Architekten, Baden-Württemberg, 1972, 1974, 1977; Germany Architecture Prize, Bundesarchitektenkammer, 1977. Address: Behnisch & Partner, Mendelssohnstrasse 22, 7000 Stuttgart-Sillenbuch, Germany.

Works:

1957   District Council Office, Schwäbisch-Gmünd, Germany (with Bruno Lambart)
1959   Hohenstaufen Grammar School, Göppingen, Germany (with Bruno Lambart)
      Vogelsan School, Stuttgart (with Bruno Lambart)
1960   Technical School, Radolfzell, Germany
1961   Town Hall, Mannheim (project)
1963   State Technical College, Ulm
1965   Otto Hahn Grammar School, Furtwangen, Germany
      Grammar School, Deutenberg, Schwenningen, Germany
      Town redevelopment, Waiblingen, Germany (project)
1966   Droste-Hulshoff Grammar School, Freiburg
      Friedrich von Keller School, Neckarweihingen, Germany
1967   Design for a University, Bremen (project)
      District Hospital, Göppingen, Germany (project)

      Holiday House, Schlechtbach, Germany
      Sports Centre, Sindelfingen, Germany
1968   State Technical College, Aalen, Germany
      Salier Grammar School, Waiblingen, Germany
      Sports Hall, Schwenningen, Germany
1968/
  72   School, Radolfzell, Germany
1969   Pavilion, *Garden Exhibiton,* Dortmund
      Administration Building, Kronprinzenstrasse, Stuttgart
      In den Berglen School, Oppelsbohm, Germany
      Oskar-von-Miller School, Rothenburg, Germany
1970   Leisure Centre Park, Pfullingen, Germany (project)
      Friedrich-Schiller Grammar School, Marbach, Germany
      Sports Hall, Rothenburg, Germany
      Purchasing Centre, Waiblingen, Germany (project)
      Purchasing Centre, Ludwigsburg, Germany (project)
      Korber Hohe Physical Training Hall, Waiblingen, Germany
      Hymnus Choirboys Home, Stuttgart
1971   University Sports Centre, Bremen (project)
      European Patent Office, Munich (project)
      Nursing Home, Dahn, Germany (project)
1972   Bofingen Shopping Centre, Ulm
      Rechts d. Rems School Centre, Waiblingen, Germany
      Olympiapark, Munich (with Günter Grzimek)
1972/
  73   Auf dem Schafersfeld Grammar School stage I, Lorch, Germany
1972/
  76   Fritz Erler Technical School Centre, Pforzheim, Germany
      Bei der Bleiche School and Sports Centre, Rothenburg, Germany
1973   Geriatric and Nursing Home, Reutlingen, Germany
      Hospital, Waldkraiburg, Germany (project)
1973/
  77   Schlossvorhof Courtyard Development, Stuttgart

1973/
  80   Konigstrasse Pedestrian Zone, Stuttgart
1974   Josef Effner Grammar School, Dachau, Germany
      Thermal Baths, Baden-Baden, Germany (project)
      Olympiapark Company Administration Building, Munich
      Sports Hall, Lorch, Germany
1974/
  78   Schloss Platz Underground (Subway) Station, Stuttgart
1974/
  80   Assembly Hall and Parliament Buildings, Bonn
1974/
  82   Study Centre, Bruchsal, Germany
1976   Hospital, Pfaffenhofen, Germany
1976/
  78   Friedrich-Schiller Grammar School extensions, Marbach, Germany
1976/
  82   Health Resort Centre, Bad Salzuflen, Germany
1977   Neugereut Nursery School, Stuttgart
1977/
  79   Elementary and Grammar School, Alfdorf, Germany
1978/
  80   Parliament Buildings Development Plan, Bonn
1978/
  81   Kleine Schlossplatz redevelopment, Stuttgart
1978/
  82   August Kayser Foundation Geriatric and Nursing Home, Pforzheim, Germany
1979   New Town Hall, Reutlingen, Germany (project)
1979/
  82   Auf dem Schafersfeld Grammar School, stage II, Lorch, Germany
1980/
  81   Diakonische Werk Headquarters, Stuttgart (project)
      Catholic University Library, Eichstatt, Germany (project)
1980/
  82   Professional School, Herrenberg, Germany

Günter Behnisch: Olympia park, Munich, 1968-72.

Publications:

By BEHNISCH: books—*Buildings of 19th Century Paris,* Darmstadt 1974; *Buildings of 19th Century England,* Darmstadt 1976; *Backsteinbauten,* Darmstadt 1977; articles—"Looking for, and setting the place", interview with Wolfgang Pehnt, in *Bauwelt* (Berlin), 22 May 1981.

On BEHNISCH: books—*Behnisch & Partner: Buildings and Projects,* Stuttgart 1975; *Architecture in the Federal Republic* by Heinrich Klotz, Frankfurt, Berlin, and Vienna, 1977; *Architektur in Deutschland* by H. and M. Bofinger, J. Paul and H. Klotz, Stuttgart 1979; *Bauten des Bundes 1965-1980* by Wolfgang Leuschner, Karlsruhe 1980; *Zeit im Aufriss: Architektur in Bayern nach 1945,* exhibition catalogue by Christoph Hackelsberger, Munich 1983; *Architektur in Deutschland '83,* edited by Jurgen Joedicke, Stuttgart 1984; articles— "Flashback to Munich's Olympic Park" in *Bauen-Wohnen* (Munich), April 1978; "Vocational School in Pforzheim" in *Architektur und Wohnwelt* (Stuttgart), June 1978; "Gunter Behnisch—for a free and open architecture" in *Der Architekt* (Stuttgart), January 1979; "Lutheran Study Centre, Stuttgart" in *Baumeister* (Munich), November 1980; "Three works by Behnisch and Partner" by Renato Pedio in *Architettura* (Rome), May 1981; "Freedom and plurality in architecture—Behnisch and Partner", special issue of *Deutsche Bauzeitung* (Stuttgart), March 1982.

*

I am a university teacher and a "free-lance architect" in the partnership Behnisch & Partner: a free-lance architect has the opportunity and the responsibility to exercise a free and independent attitude to problems.

One consequence has been that, while we have not and would not reject such work in principle, we have not, as yet, worked for banks, combines, etc.; we have been much more involved with schools, old people's homes, kindergartens and other public-sector installations.

Practically all our commissions result from architectural competitions. In almost every case we have ourselves carried out all the architectural requirements up to the handing over of the complete project.

Our largest and most spectacular commission to date was for the Olympic Games site in Munich. The tent roof achieved notoriety because of technical, financial and labour problems, but the real achievement was in the successful integration into the structure of Munich of a site covering 3 × 1·5 kilometres. The park, with its sporting installations, sports grounds and recreational areas, met all the functional, technical, spatial, architectonic, organizational and financial requirements. The popular reaction is that surely it must always have been there. The Olympia Park is now the favourite recreational area in Munich, a town richly endowed in this respect.

The scale of a project is, however, not most important.

In 1977 we completed, in Stuttgart-Neugereut, a small kindergarten which, for us, is equally of great importance. It stands airy, distinctive, and carried out with affection in a new, much too densely built part of town, where the chief concern has been with the "return" on buildings. In our opinion it is an oasis, a world for children, and well worth working for.

Our next large-scale project is the Parliament Buildings in Bonn: the Upper and Lower Houses of the German Parliament together with related streets, squares and parks. An important undertaking for our company and one of interest for us. We will try to avoid representation as such, monumentality and the pursuit of the art object. We will endeavour rather to give architectonic expression to that which should distinguish a free society and which is commonly, too frequently suppressed.

—Günter Behnisch

*

I've asked Günter Behnisch what importance, for people, he would claim for archictecture. His answer involved the demands that are made on architecture, demands that can no longer, as in former times, be considered as separate from the building itself—such as the square metre, climate, construction techniques, light, building elements, gravity, geometry, and form, as well as financing and, finally, the symbolic nature of architecture. The manner in which the architect arranges and presents his priorities determines the value that attaches to these demands. For this very reason, architecture has, of necessity, been perceived and appreciated differently by different people in different ages and in different situations.

But the value of architecture for people today also depends on how far the natural world, creation, is burdened by our constructions and how far they do or do not satisfy aesthetic needs. In any aesthetic standard Behnisch wishes to be able to perceive a concern for people, their internal natures and their external surroundings— whether the architect takes the trouble to help people or whether he hands them over to the "powerful" of our age. Behnisch does not want to create forms that are empty of content in order to generate an aesthetic goal; he wants his forms to be the consequence of a comprehensive argument with reality. Behnisch conceives of reality as power, that force in society that wants to shape people, things and nature to its own end.

His attitude begs a few questions. Who wields this power? How does this power happen? Does it have any right at all to be reflected in our architecture? And, yet, the questions are beside the point. The history of architecture demonstrates that the architect's dialogue with temporal and spiritual powers and the conversion of their demands into forms have led to the most valuable and beautiful buildings. Power is not in itself negative, only its misuse. Architecture commissioned by the powerful is in no way, by definition, inhuman; the only question is whether artistry shines through.

Behnisch also precludes "closed formal principles" from his works. As far as he is concerned there is no autonomy of form, nor are human needs established and ordained in some psychological, philosophical or religious sphere. To some extent he also denies the influence of archetypes and any inevitable continuity of tradition. For Behnisch the most important buildings are those that reveal a changing vision of the world rather than a changing set of specifications. The known and lively project that fits eloquently into the present unique situation need not immediately reveal the signature of its creator but should bear witness that, in this particular case, the "right thing" has been done. For Behnisch this "right thing," in our increasingly crowded and highly organized world, is the creation of oases, free space for the perplexed.

Behnisch is not, however, optimistic about the future development of architecture. He sees too many architects as being in one of two categories— those who simply confirm reality and thereby increase its restraints and those who avoid reality by taking refuge in Art, in the commanding heights. Behnisch feels that such architects betray their brothers and surrender them to the powerful forces of our time, in that they aesthetize architecture, and place it on a pedestal; that is, they remove it from everyday life and render it incomprehensible.

Behnisch tries to be another sort of architect, and in that attempt he deserves our highest praise. He tries to achieve, and in his projects has achieved, an architecture totally related to people.

—Justus Dahinden

BEHRENS, Peter.

German. Born in Hamburg, 14 April 1868. Studied painting at the Künstschule, Karlsruhe, and in various painters' studios, Düsseldorf, 1886-89; travelled in the Netherlands: influenced by the work of the "luminist" painters, 1890. Married Lilli Kramer in 1889 (died, 1957). Moved to Munich, 1890; Co-Founder, Munich Secession group of painters, 1893; first woodcuts, 1896; Co-Founder, Union of Arts and Crafts Workshops, Munich, 1896; collaborated on the magazine *Pan,* Munich, 1898; first industrial designs for glass factory, Munich, 1898; joined the artists' group Die Sieben (The Seven), including architects J. M. Olbricht and P. Huber, painters H. Christiansen and P. Burck, and sculptors L. Habich and R. Bosselt, in Darmstadt, Germany 1899, and began architectural work, Darmstadt, 1900; Director, Nuremberg Master Course, 1902; Director, Kunstgewerbeschule, Düsseldorf, 1903-07; in private practice, Berlin, from 1907 (pupil/assistants included Le Corbusier, *q.v.,* Walter Gropius, *q.v.,* and Mies van der Rohe, *q.v.*); Director, Academy of Art, Düsseldorf, 1921-22; Professor, Academy of Fine Arts, Vienna, 1922-27; Head of the Department of Architecture, Prussian Academy of Arts, Berlin, 1936-40. Exhibitions: *Secession Exhibition,* Berlin and Vienna, 1893, Zürich, 1897, and Darmstadt, Germany, 1899; *Exposition of Decorative Arts,* Turin, 1902; World's Fair, St. Louis, Missouri, 1904; World's Fair, Ghent, Belgium 1913; *Gewerbeschau,* Munich, 1922; *Exposition des arts dé coratifs,* Paris, 1925; *Die Wohnung,* Stuttgart, 1927; *Peter Behrens 1868-1940,* Kaiserslautern, West Germany, 1966 (toured Hagen, West Germany; Berlin; Darmstadt, West Germany); *Peter Behrens und die AEG,* Internationale Design Zentrum, Berlin, 1978. *Died* (in Berlin) *27 February 1940.*

Works:

1900 Theatre (project)
1901 Behrens House, Künstler-Kolonie, Darmstadt, Germany
1902 Exhibition Stand, *Exposition of Decorative Arts,* Turin
1904 Restaurant, *Building Exhibition,* Düsseldorf
       Reading Room, City Library, Düsseldorf
1905 Showrooms and Garden, *Nordwestdeutsche Art Exhibition,* Oldenburg, Germany
1905/
06 Obenauer House, Saarbrucken, Germany
1906 Delmenhorster Linoleum Pavilion, German Arts Trade Fair, Dresden, Germany
1907 Crematorium, Delstern, near Hagen, Germany (with the painter E. R. Weiss)
       Warehouse (project)
1908/
10 Catholic Fellowship House, Neuss, Germany
1909 Schroeder House, Eppenhausen, near Hagen, Germany
1909/
10 AEG (German General Electric Company) Turbine Factory, Huttenstrasse, Berlin
1910 AEG (German General Electric Company) High Tension Plant, Berlin
1910/
11 AEG (German General Electric Company) Motor Factory, Berlin
       AEG (German General Electric Company) Workers' Apartment Buildings, Henningsdorf, near Berlin
       Cuno House, Eppenhausen, near Hagen, Germany
1911/
12 Frankfurter Gasgesellschaft Buildings, Oshafen, Germany
       German Embassy, Isaak-Platz, St. Petersburg (now Leningrad)
       Goedecke House, Eppenhausen, near Hagen, Germany
       Wiegand House, Peter-Lenne-Strasse, Dahlem, Berlin (now the German Archaeological Institute)

Continental Rubber Company, Hannover, Germany

1912/
23 Mannesmann Tube Co. Office Building, Düsseldorf

1915/
16 National Automobile Company Offices, Obserschoneweide, Berlin

1916 House of Friendship, Constantinople, now Istanbul

1917 Exhibition Building, *Deutsche Werkbund Exhibition*, Bern, Switzerland

1919 Garden Suburb, Neusaburg, near Berlin

1920 Garden Suburb, Nowawes, near Potsdam, Germany

Housing Estate, Altona, near Hamburg, Germany

1920/
24 Höchst Chemical Factory and Dyeworks, Frankfurt

1921/
25 Steelworks, Oberhausen, Germany

1922 Stumm Administration Building, Düsseldorf (project)

1924/
25 Monastery of St. Peter, Salzburg, Austria

1925 People's Building, Vienna

Tomb of Reichspresident Friedrich Ebert, Heidelberg Forest Cemetery, Germany

1926 Fashion House, Frankfurt

"New Ways" (house), Northampton, England

1926/
27 Terrace housing, Weissenhof Estate, Stuttgart

1928 Thyssen Company Administration Building, Düsseldorf (project)

1929/
31 Berolina Building Complex, Alexanderplatz, Berlin

1931 Clara Ganz Villa, Cronberg, Taunus, Germany

1931/
34 New Buildings for the State Tobacco Factory, Linz, Austria (with Alexander Popp)

Publications:

By BEHRENS: books—*Feste des Lebens und der Kunst*, Jena, Germany 1900; *Behrens Schrift*, Offenbach am Main, Germany 1902; *Beziehungen der künstlerischen und technischen Probleme*, Berlin 1917; *Vom sparsamen Bauen*, with H. de Fries, Berlin 1918; *Das Ethos und die Unlagerung der künstlerische Probleme*, Darmstadt, Germany 1920; *Terrassen am Hause*, Stuttgart 1927; articles—"Die Lebensmesse von Richard Dehmel" in *Die Rheinlande* (Mainz, Germany), April 1901; "Mein Sondergarten" in *Offizielle Ausstellungszeitung der internationalen Kunst- und Gartenbauausstleung Mannheim* (Mannheim, Germany), 1 May 1907; "Die Gartenstadt-bewegung" in *Berliner Tageblatt* (Berlin), 5 March 1908; "Die Zukunft unserer Kultur" in *Frankfurter Zeitung* (Frankfurt), 14 April 1909; "Uber Aesthetik in der Industrie" in *AEG-Zeitung* (Berlin), June 1909; "Kunst und Technik" in *Innendekoration* (Darmstadt, Germany), July 1911; "Peter Behrens aussert sich auf eine Rundfrage über die bauliche Entwicklung der Berliner City" in *Berliner Morgenpost* (Berlin), 27 November 1912; "Zur Erziehung des baukünstlerischen Nachwuchses" in *Peter Behrens und seine Weiner akademische Meisterschule*, edited by K. M. Grimme, Vienna 1930; "Die Baukunst und das Leben" in *Baugilde* (Berlin), no. 16, 1932.

On BEHRENS: books—*Entwicklungsgeschichte der modernen Kunst* by Julius Meier-Graefe, Stuttgart 1904; *Das Einzelwohnhaus der Neuzeit* by Erich Haenle and Heinrich Tscharmann, Leipzig, Germany 1906; *Moderne Baukunst* by Karl Scheffler, Berlin 1907; *Das neue Kunstgewerbe in Deutschland* by Joseph August Lux, Leipzig, Germany 1908; *Die*

Kunst Peter Behrens by Friedrich Hoeper, Berlin 1909; *Etude sur le mouvement d'art décoratif en Allemagne* by Le Corbusier, La Chaux-de-Fonds, Switzerland 1912; *Peter Behrens* by Fritz Hoeber, Munich 1913; *Peter Behrens: sein Werke von 1909 bis zur Gegenwart* by Paul Joseph Cremers, Essen, Germany 1928; *Peter Behrens und seine Wiener akademischen Meisterschule*, edited by K. M. Grimme, Vienna 1930; *Das Gesellenhaus und eine stadtebauliche Studie von Peter Behrens in Neuss* by E. Seipe, Neuss, Germany 1961; *Bauen in Berlin 1900-1964*, Berlin 1964; *Peter Behrens* by Lida Branchesi, Rome 1965; *Peter Behrens 1868-1940*, exhibition catalogue, by Wilhelm Weber, Herta Hesse-Frielinghaus, Stanislaus von Moos and others, Kaiserslautern, West Germany 1966; *Peter Behrens* by H. J. Kadataz, Leipzig, East Germany 1977; *Industriekultur: Peter Behrens und die AEG 1907-1914* by Tilmann Buddensieg and Henning Rogge, Milan and Berlin 1978; *Nicht gebaute Architektur: Peter Behrens und Fritz Schumacher als Kirchenplaner in Hagen* by W. Hoepfner and F. Neumeyer, Mainz, West Germany 1979; *Casa Behrens, Darmstadt* by C. Norberg-Schulz, Rome 1980; *Il Primo Behrens: origini del moderno in architettura* by Guglielmo Bilancioni, Florence 1981; *Peter Behrens, Architect and Designer* by Alan Windsor, London and New York 1981; articles—"L'Oeuvre de Peter Behrens" by Julius Posener in *L'Architecture d'aujourd'hui* (Paris), March 1934; "Peter Behrens" by P. Morton Shand in *Architectural Review* (London), September 1934; special number of *Casabella* (Milan), no. 240, 1960; "Peter Behrens" by L. Miotto Muret in *Architecture* (Paris), April 1976; "Peter Behrens and the AEG Architecture" in *Lotus* (Venice), September 1976; "Peter Behrens and the AEG" in *Bauwelt* (Berlin), 16 March 1979; "Peter Behrens: Haus Behrens 1901" in *Architectural Design* (London), no. 1/2, 1980; "Industriearchitektur—Exhibition on Peter Behrens and the AEG" in *L'Architecture d'aujourd'hui* (Paris), April 1980; "Peter Behrens and the Rathenaus AEG" in *Casabella* (Milan), April 1981.

Bibliography—*Peter Behrens* by Lamia Doumato, Monticello, Illinois 1983.

Peter Behrens's work covers a wide range. In the early part of his career, he worked mainly as a painter and engraver and as a designer of domestic and industrial equipment. In designing a wide variety of objects, he interpreted function in the simplest and most direct manner but with an eye to effective form. The designing of the good prototype for industrial production foreshadowed the methods of the Bauhaus. It also influenced Behrens's early work as an architect at the beginning of the century. He took advantage of new methods made possible by developments in the constructional application of concrete, glass, steel, and other synthetic materials and was among the first to use these with good effect. He can thus be regarded as one of the important pioneers of modern functionalism and the new architecture. At the same time, beginning as an architect in an age of eclecticism, he responded to various influences both traditional and contemporary, and was himself to some extent an eclectic—but a discriminating one. His work as an industrial architect is of a somewhat different character from his domestic work, although they are both aesthetically determined by classical feeling. The difference emerges to some extent from the type of building. Where the type has a long history, such as a house or the Monastery of St. Peter, Salzburg, then traditional influences are strong, but if the particular type has few precedents, as in much modern industrial building, then functionalism is correspondingly prominent.

Perhaps Behrens's best known building, and one of the most impressive of industrial buildings in Europe erected in the early years of the century, is the immense AEG Turbine Factory in the Huttenstrasse, Berlin. It is designed to admit the

maximum of light, and the large interior space is enclosed by extensive areas of glass between tapering steel uprights, canted forward a little so that a wide cornice is formed, indicating the demarcation of the glass roof. The building has a massive grandeur resulting not only from the simple, large-scale expression of function but also from the heavy masonry treatment of the corners and the cornice effect, neither of which is demanded by practical purpose; they are obviously the result of Behrens's liking for classical monumentality. In the AEG High Tension Plant, also in Berlin, motifs such as classical porticos with columns and pediments are introduced in a simplified form.

A good example of Behrens's functional determinism is the office building for the Mannesmann Tube Company at Düsseldorf. Here, the internal divisions are determined by the space required for the efficient operation of clerks, which in turn control the size of the standardized units in the construction of the building. The design of this building demonstrated the greater freedom of planning made possible by standardized, interchangeable parts of steel, concrete, and glass.

Although the planning of later industrial and office buildings was controlled by his logical interpretation of purpose, Behrens did introduce decorative motifs of a romantic or classical character. In the Hoag Steelworks at Oberhausen, the whole massing gives the building a monumental character—but with the introduction of contemporary horizontal motifs in the long canopies. In the Höchst Chemical Factory and Dye Works, Behrens gives a romantic character to the large entrance hall by the flute-like treatment of brickwork in various colours and a disposition of forms so as to introduce dramatic effects of light and shadow.

Response to contemporary trends is clearly apparent in the tobacco factory at Linz, which he designed in 1931 in collaboration with Alexander Popp. In this factory, the steel-frame construction is set back a little from the long, slightly convex facade; this allows for uninterrupted glass bands alternating with bands of rendered brickwork for the whole length of the building, a dramatic horizontal emphasis accentuated by wide, projecting caves. Only Mendelsohn's Schocken store at Chemnitz (now Karl-Marx-Stadt) has a comparable dramatic character. But even in this modern factory at Linz, classical motifs are introduced: the glass tower at the entrance with a band of symbolic sculpture is reminiscent in treatment of a Greek frieze.

Behrens's domestic buildings, which he began designing a little earlier than his industrial works, are the work of an eclectic. The influence of English domestic architecture is apparent in his own house at Darmstadt and in the Obenauer House at Saarbrucken, among others, in the garden suburbs he planned and built near Berlin, and in the Altona estate near Hamburg, which he built just after World War I. These houses are traditional in character with steeply pitched roofs. Among the best is the Obenauer House; with its large, plain, white walls and well-disposed windows, it clearly shows Voysey's influence.

A house by Behrens that attracted much attention in architectural circles when it was built was "New Ways" in Northampton, for it was regarded, in its simplicity, orientation, large windows, and flat concrete roof, as the first really modern house in England. Yet, it is also eclectic in design, planned with classical symmetry and with mediaeval decorative embellishments. This characteristic blending of tradition and progressive developments occurs again in the large Ganz Villa in the Taunus Mountains, which, although modern in appearance with flat roof, plain walls, and horizontal emphasis, is yet structurally traditional, with the room division of the upper floor dependent on the ground floor structure (unlike, say, Le Corbusier's houses of pole and slab construction, which make possible an independent and flexible planning of each floor). Because of its structure, the house retains a somewhat massive, traditional character, and like most of Behrens's work, it owes much to the classic tradition.

Behrens was an architect who combined modern functional design and the use of modern materials and methods with a degree of eclecticism, but always with an underlying classical and monumental determinism.

—Arnold Whittick

.

BELGIOJOSO, Lodovico Barbiano di.

Italian. Born in Milan, 1 December 1909. Educated at the Liceo Parini, Milan, 1921-27; Milan Polytechnic School Architecture, 1927-32, Dip.Arch. 1932. Served in the Italian Army, 1932-34, 1940; political prisoner in Germany, 1944-45. Married Carolina Cicogna Mozzoni in 1934; children: Margherita, Maria Luisa, Alberico, and Giovanni. Founder Partner, with Gianluigi Banfi, *q.v.,* Enrico Peressutti, *q.v.,* and Ernesto Nathan Rogers, *q.v.,* BBPR Architectural Studio, *q.v.,* Milan, since 1932. Member, Milan Building Commission, 1937-39; Member, Municipal Committee for the Master Plan for the City of Milan, 1946-47, and the revision, 1957-60; Member, Committee for the Lombardy Regional Plan, 1952-55; Consultant, Municipal Planning Department, Milan 1961-65. Administrative Director, INU (Istituto Nazionale di Urbanistica), since 1948 (President, Lombardy Section, 1951-52, 1953-54); Director, Technical Committee, PIM(Inter-Municipality Project), since 1962; Administrator, Research and Study Commission, Metropolitana Veneta, Venice, since 1967. Professor of Design, Architectural Institute, Venice, 1955-63.Since 1963, Professor of Design, Milan Polytechnic School of Architecture. Member of CIAM (Congrès Internationaux d'Architecture Moderne), from 1935; Member, Commissione per le Manifestazione d'Arte Moderna dell'Associazione tra i Cultori d'Architettura, 1935; Member 1945, and President, 1947, MSA (Movimento di Studi per l'Architettura); Member, Maison des Artistes, Lausanne, 1949; Founder Member, Société Européenne de Culture, 1950; Member, Institut d'Esthetique Industrielle, Paris, 1951; President Lombardy Regional College of Architects, 1959-60. Recipient: Cervo d'Oro, Italy, 1970. Member, Academy of Fine Arts, Genoa, 1949, and Venice, 1958; Member, National Academy of San Luca, Rome, 1960. Honorary Member, Royal Society of Arts, London, 1958. Address: Studio Architetti BBPR, via dei Chiostri 2, 20121 Milan Italy.

Publications:

By BELGIOJOSO: book— *Intervista sul mestiere di architetto,* edited by Cesare De Seta, Rome 1979; articles— "Urbanistica Anno XII," with Gianluigi Banfi, in *Quadrante* (Milan), May 1934; "Urbanistica Corporativa," with Gianluigi Banfi, in *Quadrante* (Milan), August/September 1934 "La Casa per la Famiglia" in *Domus* (Milan), August 1942; "Per Scegliere La Casa" in *Vie d'Italia* (Rome), November 1949; "L'Evoluzione del Metodo Espositivo nelle Passate Triennali" in *Casabella* (Milan), November/December 1954; "La Ricostruzione dei Musei del Castello Sforzesco" in *Aspetti, Problemi e Realizzazioni di Milano,* Milan 1957; "Processo Estetico alle Autostrade: La Parola all'Accusa" in *Quattroruote* (Milan), October 1962; "Lettera al Direttore" in *Quattroruote* (Milan), November 1962; "Il Lavoro della Giuria: Il Concorso per il Centro Direzionale di Torino" in *Casabella* (Milan), August 1963; "Commenti alle Nuove Autostrade" in *Quattroruote* (Milan), July/August 1967; "Problemi attuali nelle Realizzazioni dell'Edilizia Souvenzionata" in *Edilizia Popolare* (Rome), July/August 1967; "Si Progetta il Traforo dello Stelvio" in *Quattroruote* (Milan) January 1968; "Adaption of Housing to the Site" in *Revue de L'Union Internat-*

ionale des Architectes (Paris), July 1968; "Commenti alle Nuove Autostrade" in *Quattroruote* (Milan), July 1968; "Considerazioni di Ordine Urbanistico e Architettonico" in *Edilizia Popolare* (Rome), November/December 1968; "Il Salone di Torino visto da un Architetto" and "Un Buon Esempio" in *Quattroruote* (Milan), January 1969; "Commenti alle Autostrade: Quattro Recenti Construzzioni" in *Quattroruote* (Milan), January 1970; "Le Stazioni di Servizio nel Paesaggio" in *Quattroruote* (Milan), December 1970; "Un Nuovo Guasto Straddale in Toscana" in *Quattrorouote* (Milan), November 1971; "The residential quarter in Italy" in *Città e Società* (Milan), April/May 1982.

BELLUSCHI, Pietro.

American. Born in Ancona, Italy, 18 August 1899; emigrated to the United States, 1923; naturalized, 1929. Educated at the University of Rome, 1919-22, D.Eng. 1922; Cornell University, Ithaca, New York, 1924. Married Helen Hemmila in 1934 (died, 1962); children: Peter and Anthony; married Majorie Bruckner in 1965. Worked as a housing inspector in Rome, 1923; Electrical Helper, Bunker Hill and Sullivan Mining Company, Kellogg, Idaho, 1924-25; Draftsman, 1925-27, Chief Designer, 1924-42, and Associate, 1932-42, A. E. Doyle and Associates, Portland, Oregon; in private practice, Portland, 1943-50 (firm acquired by Skidmore, Owings and Merrill, *q.v.*); Dean of the School of Architecture and Planning, Massachusetts Institute of Technology, Cambridge, 1951-65. Since 1965, in private practice, Boston and Portland, Oregon. Consulting Professor of Architecture, University of Oregon, Eugene, 1965; Thomas Jefferson Professor of Architecture, University of Virginia, Charlottesville, 1966. President, Oregon Chapter, American Institute of Architects, 1943-44; Member, National Fine Arts Commission, 1950-55; Trustee, American Federation of Arts, 1954; Trustee, Boston Museum of Fine Arts, 1958-65; Trustee, Lahey Clinic, Boston, 1960-65. Trustee, Portland Art Museum, since 1932 (President, 1947-48). Recipient: Committee on Education Award, 1940, First Award, 1954 and 1956, Centennial Medal, 1957 Award of Merit, 1960, First Honor Award, 1963, and Gold Medal, 1972, American Institute of Architects; Design Award, *Progressive Architecture,* 1948, 1954, 1959, and 1964; National Council of Churches of Christ Award, 1956; Gold Medal, Memphis Chapter, American Institute of Architects, 1957; Award of Merit, Baltimore Chamber of Commerce, 1959; Distinguished Service Award, University of Oregon, 1959; Certificate of Merit, New York State Association of Architects, 1960; Citation of Excellence, Philadelphia Chapter, American Institute of Architects, 1960; First Honor Award, AIA/American Library Association, 1963; "People's Architect" Award, Rice University, Houston, 1963; Gold Medal, Italian Charitable Society, 1963; Honor Award, Portland Chapter, American Institute of Architects, 1965 and 1971; Office of the Year Award, *Administrative Management,* 1966; Wood Structure Design Award, National Forest Products Association, 1967; Medal of Excellence, Rhode Island Chapter, American Institute of Architects, 1967; PLAN Award, Junior League, Columbus, Ohio, 1969; Design Excellence Award, Oklahoma City Arts Council, 1970; Bard Award, City of New York, 1970; Architectural Award of Excellence, American Institute of Steel Construction, 1970 (three times); Design in Steel Award, American Iron and Steel Institute, 1971; Gold Medal, Dante Society of Massachusetts, 1971; Award of Excellence, American Concrete Institute, Oklahoma Chapter, 1974; Award of Excellence, Oklahoma Chapter, American Institute of Architects, 1974; Award, New England Regional Chapter, American Institute of Architects, 1974; Special Commendation, Western Massachusetts Chapter,

American Institute of Architects, 1974; Special Citation, American Association of School Administrators, 1974; Honor Award, Bay Area Chapter, American Institute of Architects, 1974; Gold Medal, University of Naples, 1974. LL.D.: Reed College, Portland, Oregon, 1950; Sc.D.: Christian Brothers College, Memphis, Tennessee, 1957; D.F.A.: Univeristy of Rhode Island, Kingston, 1963; University of Massachusetts, Amherst, 1967; University of Portland, Oregon, 1977; Pacific Northwest College of Art, Portland, Oregon, 1982; D.Arch.: University of Michigan, Ann Arbor, 1967; L.H.D.: University of Oklahoma City, 1968. Fellow, American Institute of Architects, 1948. Fellow, American Academy of Arts and Sciences, 1952; Academician, National Academy of Design, 1953; Member, National Institute of Arts and Letters, 1955; Member, Tau Beta Phi, 1961. Fellow, Royal Academy of Fine Arts, Copenhagen, 1954; Member, Instituto Marchigiano-Accademia Scienze, Lettere e Arti, Italy, 1975. Knight Commander (Commendatore), Republic of Italy, 1965. Address: Pietro Belluschi Inc., 700 Northwest Rapidan Terrace, Portland, Oregon 97210, U.S.A.

Works:

1932/
38 New wings for the Portland Art Museum, Oregon
1936 Belluschi House, Portland, Oregon
1937 Finley and Son Mortuary, Portland, Oregon
1938 Sutor House, Portland, Oregon
1941 Platt House, Portland, Oregon
 Myers House, Seattle
 Peter Kerr Beach House, Geahart, Oregon
 St. Thomas More Chapel, Portland, Oregon
 Ladd and Bush Bank Building additions, Salem, Oregon
 Wherrie Tailoring Shop Front, Portland, Oregon
1942 Boilermakers Union Building, Portland, Oregon
 McLoughlin Heights Shopping Center, Vancouver, Washington
 Bagley and Downs Shopping Center, Vancouver, Washington
1944 Belluschi Farmhouse, Aloha, Oregon
1945 Northwest Airlines Offices, Portland, Oregon
 Waddles Drive-In Restaurant, Portland, Oregon
1946 First National Bank, Salem, Oregon
 Electrical Distributing Company Building, Portland, Oregon
1947 Belluschi Office, Portland, Oregon
 Edris Morrison Photographic Studio, Portland, Oregon
1948 Oregon State Hospital, Salem
 Oregonian Newspaper Building, Portland, Oregon
 Equitable Building, Portland, Oregon
 Menefee House, Yamhill, Oregon
1949 Moore House, Portland, Oregon
1950 Zion Lutheran Church, Portland, Oregon
1951 Central Lutheran Church, Portland, Oregon
 First Presbyterian Church, Cottage Grove, Oregon
1952 Y.W.C.A. Building, Salem, Oregon
1954 Back Bay Center, Boston (project)
 Marion County Courthouse, Salem, Oregon
1955 Louis B. Skidmore House, Winter Haven, Florida
 Lutheran Church, Walnut Creek, California (with Skidmore, Owings and Merrill)
 Central Lutheran Church, Eugene, Oregon (with Skidmore, Owings and Merrill)
1956 Temple Israel, Swampscott, Massachusetts (with Carl Koch and Associates)
1957 First Lutheran Church, Boston
1958 Library, Bennington College, Vermont (with Carl Koch and Associates)
 Life Magazine House, Palo Alto, California

1959 Church of the Redeemer, Baltimore, Maryland (with Rogers and Taliaferro)

Dining Hall and Dormitory, Rhode Island School of Design, Providence (as consultant)

Temple Adath Israel, Philadelphia (with C. Frederick Wise)

Portsmouth Abbey Church and Monastery, Rhode Island (with Anderson, Beckwith and Haible)

1961 Park Avenue Congregational Church, Arlington, Massachusetts (with Carl Koch and Associates)

1962 Temple B'rith Kodesh, Rochester, New York (with Waasdorp, Northrup and Kaelber)

Pan American Building, New York (as consultant; with Walter Gropius, and Emery Roth and Sons)

1963 Goucher College Center, Towson, Maryland (with Rogers, Taliaferro and Lamb)

1964 Housing Complex, University of Rhode Island, Kingston (with Sasaki, Dawson, DeMay and Associates, and Kent, Cruise and Associates)

Engineering Complex, University of Colorado, Boulder (as consultant; with Sasaki, Walker and Associates, and Architectural Associates)

Trinity Church, Concord, Massachusetts (with Anderson, Beckwith and Haible)

Northern States Power Company Building, Minneapolis, Minnesota (as consultant to Ellerbe and Company)

1965 Rohm and Haas Office Building, Philadelphia (as consultant; with George M. Ewing and Company)

May Memorial Unitarian Church, Syracuse, New York (with Pederson, Hueber and Hares)

Public Library, Akron, Ohio (as consultant to Tuchman-Canute)

1966 Performing Arts Center, Ethel Walker Girls School, Simsbury, Connecticut (with Robert Brannen)

Equitable Center Office Building, Portland, Oregon (with Wolff, Zimmer, Gunsul, Frasca)

Science and Multipurpose Buildings, Portsmouth Abbey Boys School, Rhode Island (with Robinson, Green and Beretta)

First Methodist Church, Duluth, Minnesota (with Melander and Fugelso)

Sunset Mountain Park, California (as consultant; with Daniel, Mann, Johnson and Mendenhall)

1967 Unitarian Church of the Christian Union, Rockford, Illinois (with C. Edward Ware)

St. Margaret of Cortona Church, Columbus, Ohio (with Brubaker and Brandt)

Magsaysay Office Building, Manila, Philippines (as consultant to A. J. Luz Associates)

1968 Temple B'nai Jeshurun, Short Hills, New Jersey (with Gruzen and Partners)

Bishop W. Angie Smith Chapel, Oklahoma City University

St. Joseph's Church, Roseburg, Oregon (as consultant; with Wolff, Zimmer, Gunsul, Frasca)

1969 One Financial Center, Cambridge, Massachusetts (with Jung/Brannen Associates)

Library Building, School of Architecture, University of Virginia, Charlottesville (with Sasaki, Dawson DeMay and Associates, and Rawlings and Wilson)

Faculty Club Dining Room, Princeton University, New Jersey (with W. C. Harrison Hill)

Motion Picture Association of America Headquarters, Washington, D. C. (as consultant to Vlastimil Koubek)

1970 Bank of America World Headquarters, San Francisco (as consultant; with Wurster, Bernardi and Emmons, and Skidmore, Owings and Merrill)

Boston Company Building, Boston (with Emery Roth and Sons)

Undergraduate Dormitory, Massachusetts Institute of Technology, Cambridge (with The Architects Collaborative)

First National Bank, Seattle (as consultant; with Naramore, Bain, Brady, Joganson)

Juilliard School of Music and Alice Tully Hall, Lincoln Center, New York (with Eduardo Catalano and Helge Westmann and Associated Architects)

Wellesley Office Park no. 4, Massachusetts (with Jung/Brannen Associates)

Hawaiian Electric Company Building, Honolulu (as consultant to Au Cutting Smith and Associates)

Master Plan for the Boston Campus of the University of Massachusetts (with Sasaki, Dawson, DeMay Associates)

1971 St. Mary's Catholic Cathedral, San Francisco (as consultant; with Pierluigi Nervi, and McSweeney, Ryan and Lee)

University Lutheran Church, Philadelphia (with A. Ewing and Associates)

Portland Museum Art School addition and Sculpture Court, Oregon (with Wolff, Zimmer, Gunsul, Frasca and Ritter)

Courthouse complex for Baltimore County, Maryland (as consultant to the Office of Gadreau)

Covenant Presbyterian Church, Albany, Georgia (with Robert Brannan)

1972 Kah-Nee-Ta Lodge Hotel, Warm Spring Indian Reservation, Oregon (with Wolff, Zimmer, Gunsul, Frasca and Ritter)

Keystone Office Building, Boston (with Emery Roth and Sons)

Bystate West Urban Complex, Springfield, Massachusetts (with Eduardo Catalano)

Pacific Gas and Electric Company Building, San Francisco (as consultant to Hertzka and Knowles)

Fort Myer Post Chapel, Norfolk, Virginia (as consultant to Johnson and Johnson)

1973 Kerr-McGee Center, Oklahoma City

IBM Center, Baltimore (with Emery Roth and Sons)

1974 Community Center, Sacramento, California (as consultant; with Sacramento Architects Collaborative)

Sterling and Francine Clark Art Institute, Williamstown, Massachusetts (with The Architects Collaborative)

Tobin Elementary School, Cambridge, Massachusetts (with Sasaki, Dawson, DeMay Associates)

Wellesley Office Park no. 5, Massachusetts (with Jung/Brannen Associates)

One Main Savings Bank, Portland (with Jung/Brannen Associates)

1979 Pentagon City Office Building, Washington, D.C. (with Jung/Brannen Associates)

1980 San Francisco Symphony Hall, (with Skidmore, Owings and Merrill)

1981 Campbell House, on the MacKenzie River, Oregon

George Fox College Physical Education Center, Newburgh, Oregon (with DMJM)

Agronomy Building, Ohio State University, Columbus (with Brubaker and Brandt)

Lutheran Church, Silverton, Oregon.

Auditorium for Lingnan College, Hong Kong (as consultant to Arthur Kwok)

Concert Hall for Douglass College, Brunswick, New Jersey (with Jung/Brannen Associates)

1982 Christ the King Catholic Church, Milwaukie, Oregon (with Yost Grube Hall)

Baltimore Symphony Hall, Maryland (with Jung/Brannen Associates)

Papworth House, Portland, Oregon

No. 1 Post Office Square Tower, Boston (as consultant to Jung/Brannen Associates)

Meridien Hotel, Boston (as consultant to

Jung/Brannen Associates)

Classroom Building for Portsmouth Abbey, Rhode Island (with Jung/Brannen Associates)

1983 Ed Ball Office Tower, Miami, Florida (with Vlastimil Koubek)

Pavillon Hotel, Miami, Florida (with Vlastimil Koubek)

California State Office Building, Van Nuys (as consultant to Western Pacific Collaborative)

United States National Bank of Oregon Tower, Portland (as consultant)

1984 One Financial Center Tower, Boston (with Jung/Brannen Associates)

St. Matthews Lutheran Church, Beaverton, Oregon (with Yost Grube Hall)

Washington State Convention and Trade Center (project), Seattle (as consultant to TRA)

Stimpson Office Tower (project), Seattle, Washington (as consultant to John Graham Associates)

Publications:

By BELLUSCHI: articles— "Shopping Centers" in *Forms and Functions of Twentieth Century Architecture*, edited by Talbot Hamlin, New York 1952; "The Spirit of the New Architecture" in *Architectural Record* (New York), October 1953; "The Meaning of Regionalism in Architecture" in *Architectural Record* (New York), December 1955; "Architectural Milestones" in *AIA Journal* (Washington, D.C.), May 1973.

On BELLUSCHI: books—*The Modern House in America* by James Ford and Katherine Morrow Ford, New York 1940; *The Northwest Architecture of Pietro Belluschi*, edited by Jo Stubblebine, New York 1953; *Pietro Belluschi: Buildings and Plans*, edited by Camillo Gubitosi and Alberto Izzo, Rome 1974; *Frozen Music: A History of Portland Architecture* by Bosker and Lencek, Portland, Oregon 1985; articles—"An Eastern Critic Looks at Western Architecture" in *Arts and Architecture* (Los Angeles), December 1940; "Readiness for Better Architecture" in *Sunset* (Menlo Park, California), April 1943; "An Architect's Challenge" in *Architectural Forum* (New York), December 1949; "Belluschi Appraises the Gropius Challenge" in *Architectural Forum* (New York), May 1952; "Pietro Belluschi: The 1972 Gold Medallist" by Elisabeth K. Thompson in *Architectural Record* (New York), April 1972; "Lincoln Centre for the Performing Arts, New York" in *Architecture + Urbanism* (Tokyo), August 1973; "Growth of a University" by Ellen Perry Berkeley in *Architecture Plus* (New York), March April 1974; "The Gold Medallists" in *AIA Journal* (Washington, D.C.), June 1979; "Charleston" in *Urban Design International* (Purchase, New York), May/June 1980; "Cultural Colossi" in *AIA Journal* (Washington, D.C.), August 1981; "Belluschi's Equitable Building in Portland wins 25-Year Honor" in *AIA Journal* (Washington, D.C.), April 1982; "The Anatomy of Transition— Cathedral Building and Social Justice in San Francisco 1962-71" by James Gaffey in *Catholic Historical Review*, January 1984.

Bibliography: *Pietro Belluschi* by Lamia Doumato, Monticello, Illinois 1980.

In my long professional practice, tested in the winds of change, I have held to the belief that there are certain principles of honesty, integrity, and clarity that, applied in their own time and place, give meaning and permanence to architecture as a social art.

There are also trends towards the superficial and the ephemeral, perhaps as a protest against our old puritan culture. These trends now more than ever appear to be espoused by articulate, self-congratulating taste-makers engaged in the game of form-giving for its own sake.

These fickle arbiters demand new fashions every other day, soon to be bored by them, eagerly discarding them, further blurring the distinction between reality and make-believe. I don't consider these trends to constitute a "watershed," as they claim, but I am not so naive as to think that, given the subjective nature of the art, it is possible or even desirable to eliminate all attempts to escape reality.

—Pietro Belluschi

Pietro Belluschi, who has been described by the *New York Times* as "one of America's most respected modern architects," has maintained his belief in orthodox modernism throughout a long carreer ranging from modest, single-family houses in the Northwest to major private and public buildings on both coasts. In his early regional work, Belluschi stressed the need to "derive designs from functional demand," and as the keynote speaker at the American Institute of Architects 1979 convention, he reiterated this solution, attacking "today's architecture of appearances" based on "pre-conceived aesthetic theories" or cynical pandering to "mobile, rootless persons who want to be indulged with as many pleasurable sensations as possible."

Belluschi first came to national prominence in 1932 with his design for a new wing for the Portland Art Museum in a simple style, harmonious with the original building. This was followed by a second wing which added a dramatic skylit sculpture court and typically innovative monitor lighting in the new galleries. His continued work on the museum's development plan for forty years culminated in a new Museum Art School with three floors of studios, a gallery, auditorium, and offices adjacent to a new pedestrian mall.

In the Portland area, Belluschi designed a series of houses and churches in an elegantly simplified regional style that often suggested a distinct Japanese influence. The St. Thomas More Chapel, with its peaked roof and steeple, is reminiscent of New England churches in its simple exterior. The interior is "decorated" only by the crossed roof beams, but Belluschi reversed the traditional position of the steeple over the entrance, placing it instead over the altar, where its pleasant clerestory effect creates a subtle focal point for worship.

In another local church, the Zion Lutheran, the spire is retained for its symbolic value, with the roofline continuing over a deep, sheltering porch, contributing to the sense of safety and welcome. Here, the interior is marked by a rich use of contrasting textures—wood, brick, glass, copper—and the roof is supported not by crossbeams but by graceful, free standing, laminated wood arches.

Central Lutheran is a more complex design, using a solid, round, brick apse combined with an open-work wood nave and bell tower. Once again, the roof is supported by laminated wood arches but with a more horizontal emphasis. The building is sensitively sited both for privacy and views and in relation to the existing trees.

The simplicity and clarity of Belluschi's early small-scale buildings are evident in his larger works as well. The 1948 Equitable Building, made of reinforced concrete clad in aluminium, is an early example of curtain wall. The starkness of its flush exterior walls boldly reflects Belluschi's admonition "to eliminate, refine, and integrate." For the 1970 Boston Company Building, he worked closely with engineers on an ingenious structural system of corner columns round a central core, to give that city its first column-free interior space.

Perhaps the greatest challenge of Belluschi's career was the design for the new Juilliard School of Music and Alice Tully Hall, at Lincoln Center. The monolithic travertine facade of this building masks a teaching and performing complex of great intricacy, built four storeys below street level and six above on a tight, irregular site with severe height limitations. Three theatres, a library, recording and ballet studios, teaching rooms, and offices all had to be insulated from each other and from the nearby subway. It was designed and built over twelve years with inflation necessitating a continual paring down of details. The resulting simplicity, particularly the exposed-concrete and wood-paneled interior, is a welcome change from the unconvincing glitter of other Lincoln Centre buildings and a testament to Belluschi's adherence to his own dicta.

—Lucinda Hawkins

BERNARDES, Sergio Vladimir.

Brazilian. Born in Rio de Janeiro, 9 April 1919. Educated at the University of Brazil, Rio de Janeiro, Dip.Arch. 1948. Married Clarice Hermos Leal in 1941; children: Christina, Sergio, and Claudio; married Maria Clara Joppert; married Christian Guarana; daughter: Bernarda; married Miriam Guanas in 1976. Since 1948, in private practice, Rio de Janeiro. Professor of Architecture, University of Brazil, since 1958. Member of the Council, Brazilian Institute of Architects, 1948; Adviser to the Government of Guanabara State, Brazil, 1960-65. Exhibitions: *Bienal*, São Paulo, 1953 and 1967. Recipient: First Prize, Housing Competition, *Bienal*, São Paulo, 1951; First Prize, Industrial Architecture Competition, Venice, 1955; First Prize, Brasilia Airport Competition, 1960; First Prize, Sports Center Competition, Sao Bernardo do Campo, São Paulo, 1967. Member, Order of the Rio Branco, Brazil, and Order of Merit Tamandre, Brazil. Address: Sergio Bernardes Associados, Avenida Niemeyer 179, Rio de Janeiro, Brazil.

Works:

1945/
48   Model shop, Rio de Janeiro
    Eduardo Baouth House, Rio de Janeiro (project)
    Aviation City, Galeao Airport, Rio de Janeiro (project)
1951   Jadir de Souza House, Rio de Janeiro
1952   Guilherme Brandi House, Petrópolis, Brazil
    St. Dominic Church, São Paulo (competition project)
1953   Companhia Siderurgica Nacional Exhibition Pavilion, São Paulo
    M. C. Macedo Soares House, Rio de Janeiro
    Paulo Sampaio House, Rio de Janeiro
1954   Ivo Pitanguy House, Rio de Janeiro
1957   Brazilian Pavilion, *Bienal*, São Paulo
1958   Brazilian Pavilion, World's Fair, Brussels
1959   House, Waterloo, Belgium
    Costa Brava Building, Rio de Janeiro
1960   Ortemblad House, Rio de Janeiro
    Caldas Filho House, Bahia, Brazil
    Marinho Office Building, Brasilia
    Monumental axis extension, Supersonic Airport, Brasilia (project)
    Gentil House, Ceará, Brazil
    IAPB Building, Goias, Brazil
    Hotel/Commercial Center, Minas Gerais, Brazil (project)
    Lunardeli House, Minas Gerais, Brazil
    Ensch House, Minas Gerais, Brazil
    de Freitas House, Piaui, Brazil
    Railway and Highway City-to-Port Link, Rio de Janeiro (project)
    Sao Luiz Home for the Aged, Rio de Janeiro
    Correio da Manha Newspaper Agency, Rio de Janeiro
    Credito Real de Minas Gerais Bank, Rio de Janeiro

    Ducal Stores Chain, Rio de Janeiro
    Coca-Cola Factory, Rio de Janeiro
    Borges Bank Building, Rio de Janeiro
    Sao Cristovao Exhibition Pavilion, Rio de Janeiro
    Araruama Club, Rio de Janeiro
    Samambaia Residential Complex, Petrópolis, Brazil (project)
    Engineering Development Company Building, Rio de Janeiro
    Alves House, Rio de Janeiro
    Figueira House, Rio de Janeiro
    Guimaraes House, Rio de Janeiro
    Cabral House, Rio de Janeiro
    Adolfo Gentil House, Rio de Janeiro
    Sergio Bernardes House, Rio de Janeiro
    Caio Furtado de Mendonca House, Rio de Janeiro
    Luiz Carlos Peixoto House, Rio de Janeiro
    Carlos Lacerda House, Rio de Janeiro
    Newton Kubrusly House, Rio de Janeiro
    Carlos Albuquerque House, Rio de Janeiro
    Joaquim Bento A. de Lima House, São Paulo
    Joao Souza Dantas House, São Paulo
    Ludovico Gavazi House, São Paulo
    Niomar Muniz Sodre House, Rio de Janeiro
1961   City plan for Salvador, Brazil (project; with others)
    Hospital Network, Brasilia (project)
    Lake Hotel, Brasilia (project)
    Cota 1000 Club, Brasilia
    Sergio Correa Costa House, Brasilia
    Coacy Oliveira House, Brasilia
    Government Palace and Secretariats, Ceará, Brazil
    Marshall Humberto Castelo Branco Mausoleum, Ceará, Brazil
    Ouro Preto University, Minas Gerais, Brazil
    Varzea de Palma Irrigation Plant and Agrarian Development, Minas Gerais, Brazil (project)
    Cassio Lanari House, Minas Gerais, Brazil
    Marcelo Moreira de Andrade House, Minas Gerais, Brazil
    Guanabara State Plan, Brazil (project)
    Dix Building, Rio de Janeiro
    Bandeirantes Beach Club, Rio de Janeiro
    Flower Market, Rio de Janeiro
    Castelo Country Club, Rio de Janeiro
    Jose Olimpio Bookshop, Rio de Janeiro (project)
    Jose Luiz de Magalhaes Lins House, Rio de Janeiro
    Roberto Schwab House, Rio de Janeiro
    Ilha Porchat Building, São Paulo
    Commercial Center, Boqueirao, São Paulo
    Fernao Dias Inn, Rio de Janeiro
    Minas Gerais Bank Headquarters, Minas Gerais, Brazil
1962   City of Salvador Integration Plan, Brazil (project)
    Reconcavo Expressway Plan, Bahia, Brazil (project)
    Central Food Warehouse, Bahia, Brazil
    Salvador-Itaparica Linking Bridge, Brazil
    Jao Regatta Club, Goias, Brazil
    Rio Palace Hotel, Rio de Janeiro (project)
    Tres Solares Building, Rio de Janeiro
    Jose Colagrossi House, Rio de Janeiro (project)
    Francisco de Assis Figueiredo House, Rio de Janeiro
    Tito Zarvos Garage, São Paulo
    Sebastiao Almeida Ribeiro House, São Paulo
    Tower Building, São Paulo (project)
    Mendel Aronis House, São Paulo
1963   Floating University, Kuwait (project)
    Virgilio Tavora House, Ceará, Brazil
    Plan for Vidigal Beach, Rio de Janeiro
    John Kennedy Building, Rio de Janeiro
    Galeao International Hotel, Rio de Janeiro (project)
    Roberto Lanari House, Rio de Janeiro

Sergio Bernardes: Naval Ministry Compound, Brasilia, 1972 (project).

1964 Cocoa Bean Research Center (CEPEC), Bahia, Brazil
Copacabana-Niterói Tourist Bridge, Rio de Janeiro (project)
Enaldo Mendonca House, Rio de Janeiro
Plan for the city of Rio de Janeiro
Free Port, Rio de Janeiro (project)
Army Geographical Service Headquarters, Rio de Janeiro
Baronesa de Pocone Building, Rio de Janeiro
Beco Theatre, Rio de Janeiro
Rachel Demarchi House, Rio de Janeiro
Campinas University, São Paulo (project)
Orla Club, São Paulo
1965 President Strossner Port City, Paraguay (project)
Urban and Suburban Highway System, Rio de Janeiro (project)
Play Ball Bowling Alley, Rio de Janeiro
Sidney Latini House, Rio de Janeiro
Getulio Neves House, Rio Grande do Sul, Brazil
Thomaz Albomos House, Rio Grande do Sul, Brazil
Convergence Center, São Paulo (project)
Francisco Matarazzo House, São Paulo
Waler Building, Rio de Janeiro
1966 Francisco Souza Dantas House, São Paulo
Rialto Hotels, Italy (project)
Tourist development, Dubrovnik, Yugoslavia (project)
Ghana Embassy and Ambassador's Residence, Brasilia
Tambaú Hotel, Paraiba, Brazil
Highway/Railroad/Telecommunications System, Parana, Brazil (project)
Cargo Terminal, Rodotrem, Parana, Brazil
Favela Plan, Rio de Janeiro (project)
Cata-Vista Residential Complex, São Paulo
Jayme de Souza Dantas House, São Paulo
Pedro Leardi House, São Paulo
Joao Pessoa City Plan, Paraiba, Brazil (project)
Commercial Center, Parana, Brazil (project)
1967 Salvador Port, Brazil (project)
Flavio Guttierrez House, Minas Gerais, Brazil
Petite Art Gallery, Rio de Janeiro
G-4 Art Gallery, Rio de Janeiro
Ponta da Gavea Residential Complex, Rio de Janeiro (project)
Orcal Commercial and Residential Complex, Rio de Janeiro

Espacial Hotel, Rio de Janeiro (project)
Gerson de Freitas House, Rio de Janeiro
Sao Bernardo do Campo Satellite Town, São Paulo (project)
1968 Workers' Housing Development, Aratu, Brazil (project)
Tropical Hotel, Manaus, Brazil (project)
Industrial Center, Aratu, Bahia, Brazil
Study of the Alagados Poverty Areas, Bahia, Brazil
Victor Gradim House, Bahia, Brazil
Sao Luiz City Plan, Maranhao, Brazil (project)
Belem Telephone Company Building, Para, Brazil
Tropical Hotel, Recife, Pernambuco, Brazil (project)
Casa Alta Building, Rio de Janeiro
Tucuns Residential Complex, Cabo Frio, Rio de Janeiro (project)
Alvaro Salles House, Rio de Janeiro
Covered Stadium, Corinthians Club, São Paulo (project)
Araouara Club, São Paulo
Tourist plan for Campos do Jorao, São Paulo
1969 Jose Holanda House, Bahia, Brazil
Buriticupu and Pindare Basin Study, Maranhao, Brazil
Integrated Highway and Waterway Plan, Maranhao, Brazil
Forestry and Agrarian Development, Maranhao, Brazil (project)
Mangabeiras Farm Urban Development, Minas Gerais, Brazil
Boa Viagem Beach Club, Pernambuco, Brazil
Rio Tropical Hotel, Rio de Janeiro (project)
Swimming Pool, Yacht Club, Rio de Janeiro
Bonino Art Gallery, Rio de Janeiro
Petrobrás Research Center, Rio de Janeiro
Guanabara Pavilion, Providence Charity Fair, Rio de Janeiro
1971 Milhem Simao Racy Jr. House, São Paulo
Tourist development, Algarve, Portugal (project)
Brazilian Coffee Institute Headquarters, Brasilia (project)
Monument to the National Flag, Brasilia
Military Academy, Brasilia (project)
Cecilia do Rego Almeida House, Parana, Brazil
Sergio Alberto M. Carvalho House, Rio de Janeiro (project)

Roberto Boavista House, Rio de Janeiro
City Sector Plan, Albufeira, Portugal (project)
1972 Casa Forte Building, Bahia, Brazil
Super Block, Brasilia
COTELB Telephone Company Southern Peninsula Station, Brasilia
Navy Officers' Club, Brasilia (project)
Transbrasil Aircraft Hangars, Workshops and Administration Buildings, Brasilia
Naval Ministry Compound, Brasilia (project)
Human Resources Center, Brasilia (project)
Morada do Frade Hotel, Espirito Santo, Brazil
Dorio Cardoso House, Brasilia
Schering Chemical and Pharmaceutical Industry Factory, Rio de Janeiro
1972/
80 Convention Center Complex, Brasilia
1974 Free Point, Rio de Janeiro
Helio Prates da Silverra House, Rio Grande do Sul, Brazil
1975 Paco de Pedra Residential Development, Rio de Janeiro (project)
Alfio Russo House, Minas Gerais, Brazil
Brazilian Computers and Systems Factory, Rio de Janeiro
Hellan Siqueira House, Rio de Janeiro
Moacyr del Tedesco House, Rio de Janeiro
Jose Leme Lopes Filho House, Rio de Janeiro
Bicudo de Castro House, Rio de Janeiro
Rio Parque Sports Center, Rio de Janeiro (project)
1976 Caracarai Civic Center, Roraima, Brazil (project)
Caracarai Public Market, Roraima, Brazil (project)
Caracarai Town Hall, Roraima, Brazil (project)
Caracarai Bus Terminus, Roraima, Brazil (project)
Boa Vista Town Hall, Roraima, Brazil (project)
Boa Vista Municipal Chamber House, Roraima, Brazil (project)
Boa Vista Civic Square, Roraima, Brazil (project)
Sea Rescue Station and Service Facilities, Rio de Janeiro
Paqueta Tourist Hotel, Rio de Janeiro (project)
1977 Sernambetiba Residential Complex, Rio de Janeiro

Dulce Coelho House, Rio de Janeiro
Henrique Melman House, Rio de Janeiro
Jose Safra House, São Paulo
Sao Goncalo Urban Development, Taubate,
São Paulo (project)
Heavy Cargo Terminal, Rio de Janeiro
(project)
Play Center, Rio de Janeiro (project)
Master plan for Taubate, São Paulo
Municipal Technical Registry, Taubate, São
Paulo (project)
1979 Sergio Bernardes House alterations, Rio de
Janeiro

Publications:

By BERNARDES: book—*City: The Survival of
Power*, Rio de Janeiro 1975.

On BERNARDES: book—*Modern Architecture in
Brazil* by Henrique Mindlin, Rio de Janeiro 1956;
articles—"Habitations individuelles au Brésil" in
Architecture d'aujourd'hui (Paris), July 1948; "Twen-
tieth Century Domestic Architecture: Brazil" in
Architecture d'aujourd'hui (Paris), October 1953;
"Three Houses by Sergio Bernardes" in *Archi-
tectural Review* (London), March 1954; "Interconti-
nental Airport, Brasilia" in *Modulo* (Rio de Janeiro),
August 1960; "Brésil—Amazonie: Hotel 'Tropical' à
Manaos" in *Techniques et architecture* (Paris),
September 1969; "Flying Down to Rio" by James De
Long in *House Beautiful* (New York), June 1970;
"Rio—Zoo Project" by Celina Luz in *Modulo* (Rio
de Janeiro), April/May 1978.

My aim, both in theory and in practice, is to play a
part in the planning of man's environment, an
environment resulting from the different ways in
which man organizes himself and his space for work,
living and movement.

Two concerns predominate. The first is professional and involves my contribution to the
solution of specific problems, such as those of private
houses, flats, clubs, estates, commercial buildings,
and so forth—the whole range of specific projects the
design of which is determined by existing circumstances, without taking the overall view into
consideration.

We live in an age in which rapid communications
have changed our entire lifestyle. Our situation must
be completely reappraised if we are to consider the
advance that science and technology have made on
outdated notions. Nowadays, we think more in
square centimetres than in square metres; and a piece
of furniture that was made with the square metre in
mind will have to be reconsidered both in terms of its
size and its function. Transport, whether public or
private, will have to be restructured. A distinction
will have to be made between the right to own and the
right to build, so that we can create towns that can be
run economically, towns whose designers will aim at
a compact and harmonious fusion of work, circulation, and living areas. Indeed, there must be a total
reappraisal, from ideologies to religious views.

Spatial architecture is the art of concentration;
urbanism is the art of dispersion. The two must be
synchronized, yet their application is inevitably
expedient, catering to popular needs and determined
by the immediately prevailing circumstances.

The architect who created religious architecture,
rural and civil architecture, the architecture of ports
and armies, must now create an architecture of
politics, of law, of administration, of economics and
finance, in which the combined knowledge of these
sciences produces a new spatial architecture.

My second concern is also professional. It involves
my contribution to the solutions of problems of a
more general nature. For these wider problems, I
have been involved in the creation of L.I.C.—
Laboratório de Investigações Conceptuais (Laboratory of Conceptual Research)—which is, above all, a
political organization. We are a macrovision lobby.

By "lobby" I mean the "explicit and legitimate
articulation of the interests of any group, consisting
of clear, systematic, direct pressure applied to the
authorities with the aim of influencing decisions."
And "macrovision" implies a global consideration
of problems and a desire to solve them in the long
term. It has nothing to do with award-hunting or
academic results, nor does it succumb to the instant
solution of problems effected within the extremely
short terms of political and administrative office.

Non-conformism prevents us from accepting that,
by definition, certain tasks are the exclusive preserve
of universities or governments, especially when both
are handicapped by outdated notions; universities
create formal skills, and governments apply them. As
soon as materials, machinery, techniques, and
formulas are shown to be inefficient, ill-conceived,
costly, or counterproductive, there arises an opportunity for innovation and change. It is the responsibility of *all* of us to make the most of this
opportunity; it must not be left to institutions,
dubious consortia, or academics.

At the same time, it is not the intention of L.I.C.
simply to challenge the establishment for the sake of
challenge or to add fuel to the "modernist" fire. No
one should be excluded; on the contrary, I think the
channels of contribution should be broadened. We
must try to re-establish the practice of working
together—politicians working with technicians, professionals with academics, state institutions with
private institutions. There is no reason to perpetuate
a wasteful confrontation. The right way is in
understanding and cooperation, cooperation based
on a dialogue between equals. Healthy interaction is
not based on prejudice, and, as members of a team,
our prejudices must be forgotten. This interaction
will demand the best from each contributor, and the
interaction itself will be the test. It must be strong
enough to relinquish preconceived notions. The
languages of traditional education, of race, and of
class must no longer be used; they must give way to a
new language, more dangerous perhaps but a
language that will be free to redefine, free enough to
cater to the needs of people.

In the L.I.C., it is difficult to produce formal plans.
L.I.C. formulas and proposals often outstretch the
apparent dimensions of the problem. A laboratory is
a "place destined for the experimental study of any
type of science or for the practical application of
scientific knowledge" and conceptual research ought
to be concerned with questioning those views and
basic ideas that are supposed to be furthering the
technological advance but that are ultimately no
more than its straitjacket.

—Sergio Bernardes

The work of Sergio Bernardes is an elaboration of
three distinct, and sucessive, architectural visions. At
the beginning of his career in the late 1940s,
Bernardes's architectural aims—revealed chiefly in
the plans for private houses on which his reputation
is based—tended towards a plasticity, which, though
characteristic of Brazilian architecture of the period,
is peculiar to Bernades in its constant avoidance of
gratuitious formalism. The elegant detail, the simple
yet sophisticated plans, the fluid spaces, and the
pleasing shapes add up to works of great precision
and aesthetic appeal.

M.C. Macedo Soares House of 1953 was the start
of Bernardes's concern with the expression of the
construction materials themselves, this concern
became increasingly important in the years that
followed. This exceptional house links the rustic—
stone masonry, hand-made bricks—with the
industrial—large panes of glass and the light metal
trellis that holds up the roof of undulating aluminum
tiles. The house is a perfect metaphor, not only of the
contradictory nature of the Brazilian scene but
also—with its broad spacing—of the country's
continental vastness.

The increasing use of bare materials is notable in
several buildings that could be called transitional,
such as the Ivo Pitanguy House of 1954. This interest

led to a coherent rationalization of building
methods, which in turn initiated the second phase of
Bernardes's work: experimentation with brutalism.

A change in construction techniques is but one
aspect of a transformation that affected his whole
system of formulating space. The structural module
became the skeleton around which works were built;
it exerted a classicizing and compartmentalizing
influence both on internal space and also—by its
"legibility"—on external form. In the architect's
own house (1960), a work that symbolized the times
(it was altered in 1979), this characteristic is not so
evident, but in other works—the J.L.M.Lins House
of 1961, the Dantas House of 1966, and the Ceará
State Government Palace in 1961—the reference,
whether intentional or not, to traditional Brazilian
architecture is considerable.

The plastic unity that until then had predominated
was now broken down into component parts. The
architectural elements were no longer applied with
the same dynamism, and the spatial fluidity occurred
principally in the areas that link the interior with the
exterior, resulting in some notable verandas and
terraces. In the larger, non-residential buildings, the
module imposed a standardization particularly
suited to industry. This phase was also extremely
important in that it offered an alternative—both
logical and versatile—in an age in which the
exceptional and personal nature of Oscar Niemyer's
projects for Basilia offered no possiblity of imitation
or adaption in conventional architecture. The
Bernardes alternative, with its accent on construction technique, developed from Rio de Janeiro, and
influenced such younger architects as Arthur Licio
Pontual, Marcos Vasconsellos, and Marcello
Fragelli.

In 1964 Bernardes put forward a utopian plan for
the city of Rio de Janeiro. To an extent, this plan has
to do with Bernardes's activities in the field of design
and with the two exhibition pavilions he had
previously built—one in Sao Paulo for the Companhia Siderurgica Nacional in 1953, and the Brazilian
Pavilion at the 1958 Brussels World's Fair. Both were
notable for their daring suspended roofs. The first
formed a bridge spanning a stream in Ibirapuera
Park. It attracted attention for its lightness and for its
almost *chinoiserie* profile, defined by two inverted
parabolas and inclined lateral pillars. The Brazilian
Pavilion in Brussels was built around a central
"impluvium" covered by an enormous floating gas
balloon.

Meanwhile, Bernardes perfected and patented the
most various of industrial design projects: portable
roofs made of wood, steel or fibre-cement; several
construction materials; fittings and furniture; lighting and even motor-launches, a bicycle, a flexible car,
and the fuselage and nose of a small supersonic
aircraft.

It is between these two concerns—on the one hand,
a certain technological visionary approach the aims
of which transcend the brutalist phase; on the other
hand, a concern with design, with attention to
detail—that the genesis for the plan for Rio de
Janeiro occurrs. The plan is perhaps the only one of
its kind by a Brazilian architect in an era that was
noted, throughout the world, for the relative
abundance of this sort of work.

Among the proposals of the plan were the creation
of centers for capturing solar energy, processing
plants for converting sea water into drinking water,
and 500-metre telecommunication towers. The residential areas were concentrated in helical skyscrapers with staggered floors allowing an open
terrace for each apartment. A link between Rio and
Niterói, the town on the other side of Guanabara
Bay, was made by two bridges. The first, at the mouth
of the bay was a tourist bridge, supported by eight
hotels in the shape of inverted pyramids. The second,
the port of the bridge, consisted of hexagonal
"Islands," each side a dock 200 metres in length;
inside, there were four floors of warehouses, with
parking on the roof. The islands linked with the
industrial zones of both cities,

The technical/scientific theses of this project, and

the mental attitudes necessary to its conception, are reflected in all Bernardes's subsequent work. To provide for interdisciplinary research into his new concerns, Bernardes created the Laboratório de Investigações Conceptuais, L.I.C. The laboratory operates in conjunction with his office and aims "to reconsider the concepts that are at the base of all moral, ethical, political, judicial, administrative thought." The basic premises of the research are outlined in his book, *City: The Survival of Power*. In this third phase, prospective planning and theoretical considerations are the most important aspect of Bernardes's work.

Bernardes's tendency towards technology corresponds to the strengthening of a technocratic ideology in Brazilian national politics. It is significant that from the end of the 1960s Bernardes was not only invited to create various projects of a civil/official nature but also became architectural consultant to the governments of several states. In his architecture, the new phase is marked by a certain reworking of space—a tendency towards "astronautical," anti-organic shapes, often concentric, closed squares and circles as in the Tanbaú Hotel of 1966, the Petrobrás Research Center of 1969, and the projects for the Military Academy and the Human Resources Center in Brasilia in 1971-72. The "nomination" of materials is no longer the principal aspect of the architecture; rather, it is characterized by the plasticity favored during the first phase but now based on other premises.

Form remains important, but it is now related to the expression of the method of construction. It is synthetic when based on the structural technology of the more daring projects, and analytical when it is a reflection of the components of buildings erected with more conventional construction techniques. The form is a marriage—within a single architectural vision—of technology and design.

The buildings that look the simplest often have complex functions and house the most sophisticated equipment. In this group could be included the most pragmatic projects such as the Tambaú Hotel, the Casa Alta Building, and the factory for the Schering Chemical and Pharmaceutical Industry. These buildings set new architectural standards—yet, paradoxically, the most audacious, even visionary projects, such as the Tropical hotels in Manaus and Recife, and the Brazilian Coffee Institute and the Naval Ministry Compound in Brasilia, generally have functions that do not justify the singular quality of designs conceived out of a desire for technological experimentation.

Indeed, in this phase of the architect's work, concept and form are not always related. Perhaps this is why Bernardes's recent work has had so little influence on current Brazilian architectural thought. Yet Bernardes's theories are so stimulating and provocative that he is constantly being invited to give lectures and talks, more often than not to a non-architectural audience. He has become one of the main spokesmen of a wider architectural vision in Brazil.

—Jorge Czajkowski

BILL, Max.

Swiss. Born in Winterthur, 22 December 1908. Educated at the Kunstgewerbeschule, Zürich, 1924-27; Bauhaus School, Dessau, Germany, 1927-29. Served in the Swiss Army, 1939-45. Married Binia Spoerri in 1931; son: Johann. Has worked in Zürich as an architect, painter, sculptor, and graphic artist, since 1929, and as an industrial designer, since 1944. Lecturer on the Theory of Form, Kunstgewerbeschule, Zürich, 1944-45; Co-Founder and Rector, Hochschule für Gestaltung, Ulm, West Germany, 1951-56; Professor of Environmental Design, State Institute of Fine Arts, Hamburg, West Germany

1967-74. Member of the Communal Council, City of Zürich, 1961; National Councillor, Swiss Parliament, 1967-74. Member of the Central Board, Schweizerische Werkbund, 1952-62; Member, Swiss Federal Art Commission, 1961-69; Member of the Board, Geschwisten-Scholl Foundation, Ulm, West Germany, 1964; Member of the Superior Council (Creátion Esthetique Industrielle), French Ministry of Industrial and Scientific Development, 1971-73. Member: Abstraction-Création group, Paris, 1932-36; Allianz, Zürich, 1937; CIAM (Congrès Internationaux d'Architecture Moderne), 1938; UAM (Union des Artistes Modernes), Paris, 1949; Deutscher Werkbund, 1956. Exhibitions (paintings, sculpture, architecture, graphics): individual—Bauhaus, Dessau, 1928; Atelier des Künstlers, Zürich, 1929; Kunstmuseum, Basel, 1939; Galerie des Eaux-Vives, Zürich, 1946; Galerie d'Art Moderne, Basel, 1949; Museu de Arte Moderna, São Paulo, 1950; Ulm Museum, West Germany, 1956 (toured Germany); Helmhaus, Zürich, 1957; Städtisches Museum, Leverkusen, West Germany, 1959; Staatsgalerie, Stuttgart, 1960; Kunstmuseum, Winterthur, Switzerland, 1960; Staempfli Gallery, New York, 1963; Galleria Cadario, Milan, 1964; Kunsthalle, Bern, 1968; Kestner Gesellschaft, Hannover, West Germany, 1968; Kunstverein für die Rheinland und Westfalen, Düsseldorf, 1968; Gemeentemuseum, The Hague, 1968; Arts Club of Chicago, 1969; Centre National d'Art Contemporain, Paris, 1969; Musée de Peinture et de Sculpture, Grenoble, France, 1969; San Francisco Museum of Art, 1970; Musée Rath, Geneva, 1972; Marlborough-Godard Galerie, Toronto and Montreal, 1972; Marlborough Fine Art Gallery, London, 1974; Albright-Knox Art Gallery, Buffalo, New York, 1974 (toured the United States); Kunsthalle, Hamburg, West Germany, 1976 (toured Germany); Kunstmuseum, Düsseldorf, 1977; University of Parma, Italy, 1977; Moderne Galerie, Bottrop, West Germany, 1978; Museo de Bellas Artes, Caracas, 1979; Museo Español de Arte Contemporaneo, Madrid, 1980; Fundacion Miro, Barcelona, 1980; Villa Malpensata, Lugano, Switzerland, 1980; Honor Hall, Sculpture Biennale, Padua, Italy, 1981; Museum für Moderne Kunst, Goslar, West Germany, 1982; group—*Abstraction-Création*, Paris, 1933; *Konkrete Kunst*, Kunsthalle, Basel, 1944; *Pevsner/Vantongerloo/Bill*, Kunsthaus, Zürich, 1949; *Bienal*, São Paulo, 1951; *Monument to the Unknown Political Prisoner*, Institute of Contemporary Arts, London, 1952; *Biennale*, Venice, 1958; *Konkrete Kunst: 50 Jahre Entwicklung*, Kunsthaus, Zürich, 1960; *Max Bill/Le Corbusier*, Galerie Aurora, Geneva, 1968. Recipient: Grand Prize, *Triennale*, Milan, 1936, Kandinsky Prize, Paris, 1949; First Prize for Sculpture, *Bienal*, São Paulo, 1951; Grand Prize, Triennale, Milan, 1954; Gold Medal, Verucchio, Italy, 1966; City of Zürich Art Prize, 1968; Misha Black Award, Society of Industrial Artists and Designers, London, 1982; Kaiserring, City of Goslar, West Germany, 1982. Honorary Fellow, American Institute of Architects, 1964. Extraordinary Member, Akademie der Künste, Berlin, 1972; Honorary Member, Royal Flemish Academy of Sciences, Literature and Arts, 1973. Address: Albulastrasse 39 III, 8048 Zürich, Switzerland.

Works:

1928 Children's Garden and Shelter, Zürich (project; with Hans Fischli)
1932/
33 Max Bill House and Studio, Höngg, Zürich
1936 Swiss Pavilion, *Triennale*, Milan
1937 Waid Country Restaurant, Zürich
1938 Swiss Pavilion, World's Fair, New York
1939 City Building and National Planning Display, Swiss National Exhibition, Zürich (with Hans Schmidt)
1942 Villiger House, Bremgarten, Aargau, Switzerland

1949 Apartment Building, Zürich (project)
Seebach School Pavilion, Zürich (competition project)
Die Gute Form Pavilion, Swiss Industries Fair, Basel
1951 Swiss Pavilion, *Triennale*, Milan
1952 Swiss Pavilion, *Biennale*, Venice
Monument to the Unknown Political Prisoner, London (competition project)
1953/
54 Freudenberg Cantonal School, Zürich (competition project)
1953/
55 Hochschule für Gestaltung, Ulm, West Germany
1955 Ulm City Pavilion, *Baden-Württemberg Exhibition*, Stuttgart
1956 Georg Buchner Monument, Darmstadt, West Germany (project)
1957 Swiss National Monument (project)
Master plan for the Olma Agricultural Fair, St. Gallen, Switzerland (competition project)
Design of *The Unknown Present* exhibition, Globus Department Store, Basel, St. Gallen, Chur, and Aarau, Switzerland
1957/
58 Cinevox Cinema and Apartment Building, Neuhausen am Rhinfall, Switzerland (with Olivio Ferrari)
1959 Design of the *Swiss Design* exhibition, London
1960 Design of the *Konkrete Kunst: 50 Jahre Entwicklung* exhibition, Kunsthaus, Zürich
Design of the *Dokumentation über Marcel Duchamp* exhibition, Kunstgewerbemuseum, Zürich
Design Institute, Zürich (project)
1960/
61 Imbau Administration Building, Leverkusen, West Germany (with Olivio Ferrari and Rudolf Welter)
Lichtdruck Printing Works, Dielsdorf, near Zürich (with Peter Hofmann)
Fleckhaus (single-family house), Odenthall-Erberich, near Cologne (with Olivio Ferrari and Oswald Ungers)
1961 Fountain Courtyard, *International Hydraulic Engineering Exhibition*, Berlin
1962 Alcan Aluminium Museum, Montreal (project)
1963 Scenery for the play *Oedipus*, Municipal Theatre, Ulm, West Germany
1964 "Bilden und Gestalten" Section, *Swiss National Exhibition*, Lausanne
1964/
74 Radio Station Building (and studios), School of Applied Arts, Zürich (with Willy Roost)
1966/
67 Lavina-Tobel Bridge, near Tamins, Switzerland (with Aschwanden and Speck)
1967 Wind Column, *Expo '67*, Montreal (now in the Musée d'Art Contemporain, Montreal)
1967/
68 Max Bill House and Studio, Zumikon, Zürich
1968/
70 Design of the *Zürcher Künstler* annual exhibitions, Zürich
1971 Denis René/Hans Mayer Art Gallery, Düsseldorf
1976 Yaacov Agam Studio, Esbly, France

Publications:

By BILL: books—*Le Corbusier: Oeuvre Complet*, volume 3, editor, Zürich 1939, London 1964; *Quinze Variations sur un même thème*, Paris 1938; *5 Construktionen + 5 Compositionen*, Zürich 1941; *10 Original Lithos*, Zürich 1942; *X × X*, Zürich 1942; *Leo Leuppi: 10 Compositionen*, Zürich 1943; *Konkrete Kunst*, exhibition catalogue, with others, Basel 1944; *Hans Arp: 11 Configurations*, with others, Zürich 1945; *Wiederaufbau*, Zürich 1945; *Wassily*

Max Bill: Swiss National Exhibition, Lausanne, 1964.

Kandinsky: 10 farbige Reproduktionen, Basel 1949; *Robert Maillart: Brücken und Konstruktionen,* Zürich 1949; *Moderne schweizer Architektur 1925-45,* Basel 1950; *Wassily Kandinsky,* editor, Paris 1951; *Form: A Balance Sheet of Mid-Twentieth Century Trends in Design,* Basel 1952; *Über das Geistige in der Kunst,* editor, Bern 1952; *Mies van der Rohe,* Milan 1955; *Essays über Kunst und Künstler,* editor, Stuttgart 1955, Bern 1963; *Die Gute Form,* Winterthur, Switzerland 1957; *Punkt und Linie zu Flache,* editor, Bern 1959; *Enzo Mari,* with Bruno Munari, Milan 1959; *Konkrete Kunst: 50 Jahre Entwicklung,* exhibition catalogue, with René Wehrli and Margit Staber, Zürich 1960; *7 Scarions,* Genoa, Italy 1967; *Zürcher Künstler,* exhibition catalogues, Zürich, 1968, 1969; *11 × 4,* Zürich 1970; *Jahresgabe 1972,* Bern 1972; *System mit fünf vierfarbigen Zentren,* St. Gallen, Switzerland 1972; *8 = (2 × 4/4) = 8,* Neuchâtel, Switzerland 1974; *16 Constellations,* Paris 1974; *7 Twins,* Neuchâtel, Switzerland 1977; articles—"The Beginning of a New Epoch in Architecture" in *Architectural Design* (London), no. 11, 1955; "Le Corbusier" in *Neue zürcher Zeitung* (Zürich), no. 3867, 1965; "Das Individuelle und das Allgemeine in der Architektur" in *Diskussionsforum schöner Wohnen,* Stuttgart 1966; "Mes Rapports avec l'architecture grecque" in *Monde Grec,*

Fribourg, Switzerland 1966; "Responsibility in Design and Information" in *American Scholar* (Washington, D.C.), Spring 1966; "La Formation de l'architecte" in *Revue de l'Union Internationale des Architectes* (Paris), no. 44, 1967; "Walter Gropius" in *Universitas* (Stuttgart), no. 11, 1969; "Ludwig Mies van der Rohe 1886-1969" in *Neue zürcher Zeitung* (Zürich), August 1969; and numerous contributions to art journals and art exhibition catalogues throughout the world.

On BILL: books—*Max Bill,* Buenos Aires 1955; *Max Bill* by Eugene Gomringer, Max Bense and others, Teufen, Switzerland 1958; *Max Bill* by Margit Staber, London 1964, St. Gallen, Switzerland 1971; *Max Bill: The Graphic Work,* Nuremberg 1968; *Max Bill* by Eduard Huttinger, Zürich 1977; *Max Bill; ou la recherche d'un art logique* by Valentina Anker, Lausanne, Switzerland 1979; *Max Bill: Rassegna Internazionale delle arti e della cultura,* Lugano, Switzerland 1980; *Contemporary Designers,* edited by Ann Lee Morgan, New York and London, 1984; articles—"Variations on a Single Theme in the Fine Arts" by George Schmidt in *XX Siècle* (Paris), no. 4, 1938; "Complessità di Max Bill" by Vittorio Gregotti in *Casabella* (Milan), no. 228, 1959; "Max Bill 1963" by Max Bense in *Art International*

(Lugano, Switzerland), no. 3, 1963; "Max Bill" by Margit Staber in *Art International* (Lugano, Switzerland), no. 5, 1966; "Max Bill" by Shutaro Mukai in *The Essence of Present Design Theories,* Tokyo 1966; "Max Bill's Aesthetische Zustande" by Max Bense in *Artistik und Engagement,* Cologne 1970; special issue of *Nueva forma* (Madrid), September 1973; "Sculptor, Painter, Mathematician—Switzerland's Max Bill" by Nancy Tobin Willing in the *Courier Express Magazine* (Buffalo, New York), September 1974; "Superb Puritan" by Robert Hughes in *Time* (New York), November 1974; "Max Bill" by Pierre Joly in *L'Oeil* (Paris), September 1976; "Economy, Ecology and Ethic: Max Bill" by Jasia Reichardt in *Building Design* (London), 15 October 1982.

Max Bill the Builder. Of our few and talented contemporaries who can claim the soubriquet "Renaissance Man," Bill is redolent with qualifications.

Apart from being a busy writer (his writing generally concerns himself, his exploits, and his "confirmed" theories about colour, shape, content and mathematical dicta), he is also an acclaimed painter, strictly non-figurative with a Bauhaus-trained determination to delve deep into the logistics of form and colour. In addition, he is a sculptor able to translate mind into matter with a devastating precision that brooks no accidents, however happy. He is an ideas-man who, in the creation of stadiums, layouts of large and important national and private exhibitions, and big displays, is a sure-fire success (by his own standards and those of many others), even if the demands he makes on co-workers tend to be excessive. But perhaps—is "perhaps" the right word?—above all, he is a master builder, an architect who, even though many of his projects have never been realized, has left enough of his personalized edifices around the world, along with a deep pile of blueprints, sketches, designs, and plans, to ensure himself a nomination to the Empyrean where Wren rubs shoulders with Corb.

Yet a question nags: what is the true significance in world terms of Bill as an architect? Bill is a loner who has stepped outside so many magic circles that he has the doubtful distinction of being even more remote—in whichever artistic role he happens to be playing—from the *Geist unserer zeitgenossische Epoche* than Frank Lloyd Wright or Tatlin. The influence of this mighty theoretician upon other contemporary architects is limited to so narrow a circle that one is prompted to wonder if it contains anyone other than Bill himself. The question can be put another way: would it have made any difference to the development of twentieth-century construction if Bill the architect had never existed?

Whatever the answer to that question, one has to admit that there is a wealth of personal achievement, that for fifty years Bill has been an outstanding artist/creator. Of some forty-odd projects, he has seen—often in cooperation with other architects—at least three-quarters of them brought to completion; and this list includes a wide variety of works from houses to exhibition layouts, from theatre-decor to the joint undertaking, with Aschwanden and Speck, of the Lavinia-Tobel Bridge near Tamins, Switzerland.

The Lavinia-Tobel Bridge proved to be one of Bill's happiest commissions. (He would probably welcome other similar commissions.) His interest in bridge construction comes from his study of the Swiss bridge-designer Maillart about whom he wrote an informed monograph after the war, and it was through encountering the son of Ros (one of Maillart's strong adherents) that Bill came into contact with Aschwanden and Speck.

The very real success with the bridge came a few years after work on the Hochschule für Gestaltung in Ulm, started in 1953, which dragged on for two years and which Bill rated as a failure (he resigned his rectorship in 1957). Most of the buildings were allowed to fall into disuse, but the main structure won a conservation order and was converted by Ulm University into its Psychology Department; attempts have also been made to transform what remains of the accommodation area into living quarters for the university's professors and students.

Between Ulm and the Lavinia-Tobel Bridge came the "Bilden und Gestalten" Section of the *Swiss National Exhibition* at Lausanne; little of it remains today in its original Bill-conceived state except the theatre—a great and practical design in constant use.

From this brief summary, it will be obvious that Bill the architect is extremely difficult to "place." He certainly preserves the *art concret* purism of early Le Corbusier, but he is not beyond making it the formal basis from which outcrops, often aggressive outcrops, can occur. This rogue impulse—not really "rogue" or "impulse" at all because it is based on extremely sophisticated, no-nonsense mathematical formulae—is early in evidence in his work, in the original version of his own home-cum-atelier in Höngg in Zürich, which was completed as long ago as 1933.

Another distinguished factor about Bill the architect is that he is supremely practical, especially in the drawing up of attractively low tenders for any contract that comes his way. Individuality, cost, work-duration, and scientific investigation of acce-

ptable if heretical raw materials for building purposes all tend to answer the requirements of the most cash-conscious clients. The 1942 Villiger House in Bremgarten—prefabricated but also with wood-timbered character—was completed in five months!

As an architect, Max Bill has had his interesting successes; he has had just as many interesting failures. It is perhaps best to allow posterity the last word.

—Sheldon Williams

BIRKERTS, Gunnar.

American. Born in Riga, Lativia, 17 January 1925; emigrated to the United States, 1949: naturalized, 1954. Educated at the English School, Riga, 1939-44; Technische Hochschule, Stuttgart, 1945-49, Dip.Arch.Eng. 1949. Married Sylvia Zvirbulis in 1950: children: Sven, Andra, and Erik. Worked as a designer in the office of Perkins, *q.v.:* Lawrence B. Perkins, and Will, *q.v.:* Philip Will, Jr., Chicago, 1950-51, and in the office of Eero Saarinen, *q.v.,* and Associates, Bloomfield Hills, Michigan, 1951-54; Chief Designer, Minoru Yamasaki, *q.v.,* and Associates, Birmingham, Michigan, 1955-59; Principal, Birkerts and Straub, Birmingham, Michigan, 1959-62. Since 1962, President, Gunnar Birkets and Associates, Birmingham, Michigan. Assistant Professor, 1961, Associate Professor, 1963-69, and since 1969 Professor of Architecture, University of Michigan, Ann Arbor; Lawrence J. Plym Professor of Architecture, University of Illinois, Urbana-Champaign, 1982; T.S. Monaghan Professor, University of Michigan, Ann Arbor, 1984. Exhibitions: *Furniture Design Competition,* Cantu, Italy, 1954, Akron Art Institute, Ohio, 1954; *Bienal,* São Paulo, 1962; *40 under 40,* Architectural League of New York, 1965; Katonah Museum of Art, New York, 1970; Museum of Modern Art, New York, 1971; Notre Dame University, Indiana, 1973; *Design in Michigan,* Cranbrook Academy, Bloomfield Hills, Michigan, 1977; Museum of Modern Art, New York, 1979; Neuberger Museum, Purchase, New York, 1981; American Academy and Institute of Arts and Letters, New York, 1981; University of Illinois, Urbana-Champaign, 1983; Kingswood, Cranbrook Educational Community, Bloomfield Hills, Michigan, 1983; Ballenford Architectural Books, Toronto, 1983; Detroit Artists Market, 1984. Recipient: Young Designer of the Year Award, Akron Institute of Art, Ohio, 1954; First Prize, International Furniture Competition, Cantu, Italy, 1955; *Progressive Architecture* Award, New York, 1961; Award of Excellence, *Architectural Record,* New York 1961, 1968; First Honor Award, American Institute of Architects, 1962; Award of Merit, American Institute of Architects, Detroit Chapter, 1963 and 1967; Honor Award, Church Architecture Guild of America, 1964; Award of Merit, Michigan Society of Architects, 1967; Honor Award, American Insitute of Architects, 1970 and 1973; Bartlett Award, 1970; National Gold Medal in Architecture, Tau Sigma Delta, 1971; American Iron and Steel Institute Awards, 1973 and 1975; Honor Award, Consulting Engineers Council of the United States, 1973; Award of Honor, Michigan Society of Architects, 1974, 1977, 1979, 1980, 1981, and 1984; Award of Excellence, American Institute of Steel Construction, 1974 and 1979; Honor Award, and Gold Metal, American Institute of Architects, Detroit Chapter, 1975; Energy Conservation Award, Owens-Corning Fiberglas Corporation, 1977; Honor Award, American Institute of Architects, Detroit Chapter, 1978; Gold Medal, Michigan Society of Architects, 1980; Arnold W. Brunner Prize, American Academy and Institute of Arts and Letters, 1981; Silver Castle Award, United States Army Corps of Engineers, 1984. Fellow, American Institute of Architects, Latvian Architects Associ-

ation, and the Graham Foundation. Address: Gunnar Birkets and Associates, 292 Harmon Street, Birmingham, Michigan 48009, U.S.A.

Works:

1960 Schwartz Summer House, Northville, Michigan
Haley Funeral Home, Southfield, Michigan
1961 1300 Lafayette East Apartments, Detroit
1962 Peoples Federal Savings and Loan, Royal Oak, Michigan
Lillibridge Elementary School additions, Detroit
Marathon Oil Company Office Building, Detroit
1963 University Reformed Church, Ann Arbor, Michigan
1964 Lincoln Elementary School, Columbus, Indiana
1965 Public Library, Livonia, Michigan
Tougaloo College Library, Mississippi
Church of St. Bede, Southfield, Michigan
Glen Oaks Community College, Centreville, Michigan
1967 Ford Motor Company Pavilion, *Hemisfair 1968,* San Antonio, Texas
Federal Reserve Bank, Minneapolis
1968 Public Library, Duluth, Minnesota
1969 IBM Corporate Computer Center, Sterling Forest, New York
Contemporary Arts Museum, Houston
1970 Dance Instructional Facility, State University of New York, Purchase
1973 Municipal Fire Station, Corning, New York
1974 Calvary Baptist Church, Detroit
IBM Office Building, Southfield, Michigan
Law School additions, University of Michigan, Ann Arbor
1975 United States Embassy Office Building, Helsinki
1976 Museum of Glass, Corning Glass Works, Corning, New York
1979 College of Law Building, University of Iowa, Iowa City
1980 Private House, Kalamazoo, Michigan
Baldwin Public Library addition, Birmingham, Michigan
1981 District Office Building, Green Bay, Wisconsin
Uris Library addition, Cornell University, ithaca, New York
Chapel and Educational Facility, Camp Wildflecken, West Germany
1982 Woodbranch Energy Plaza, Houston, Texas
1984 St. Peter's Lutheran Church, Columbus, Indiana
Domino World Headquarters, Ann Arbor, Michigan

Publications:

By BIRKERTS: book—*Subterranean Urban Systems,* Ann Arbor, Michigan 1974; articles—"On Alvar Aalto" in *Progressive Architecture* (New York), April 1977; "A Steady Influence on a City of Turmoil," interview in *Dichotomy* (Detroit), Fall 1980; "Aalto's Design Methodology" in *Architecture + Urbanism* (Tokyo), May 1983; "Gunnar Birkets interviewed by G.B." in *Reflections* (Urbana, Illinois), Fall 1983.

On BIRKERTS: book—*Architecture and the College,* Urbana, Illinois 1968; *Architecture in a Revolutionary Era* by Julian Eugene Kulski, Nashville, Tennessee and London 1971; *The Visual Dialogue* by Nathan Knobler, New York 1972; *Arts of the Environment,* edited by Gyorgy Kepes, New York and London 1972; *Architecture in the United States* by Ralph W. Hammett, New York and London 1976; *Architecture in America* by G. Kidder Smith, fluence of program, money, and available technology and materials. He often speaks of his powers of synthesis and intuition but almost never of self-expression. "To synthesize," he has written, "is to consciously search for and analyze the intrinsic structure of any design problem, while intuition is the ability to subconsciously sense the intrinsic structure of the problem. One approach deals more or less with external factors, the other with internal feelings, but both are part of the struggle to respond to human needs as they appear out of the nature of the problem. I avoid overall theories about form and try to give each building its own theoretical base."

Birkets has always been interested in light as the means of bringing the sense of the outside to an interior space and increasing its apparent size. He borrows light from one space and transmits it to another either directly or by reflection. A second concern of his has been the simplification of form, details, and construction problems. To this end, he believes that he subordinates structure, never letting it become the principal element of architectural expression. Actually he does no such thing. Structure fascinates him. The Federal Reserve Bank of Minneapolis and the Tougaloo College Library in Mississippi are triumphs of structural expression.

Overriding each building's theoretical base, and the set of architectural rules that he lays down for himself, and what he take to be the operations of this conscious and unconscious in synthesis, is a powerful talent. His work remains remarkably creative and self-expressive, bursting out of its theoretical constrains. Like Saarinen, Birkets produces strong, unforgettable images that exist in an esthetic world that transcends their rationale.

—Mildred F. Schmertz

Gunnar Birkerts: Federal Reserve Bank, Minneapolis, 1967.

New York 1976; *New Architecture in the World* by Udo Kultermann, revised edition, London 1976; *Architects on Architecture*, edited by Paul Heyer, New York and London 1978; *Architecture and You* by William W. Caudill, Paul Kennon and William M. Pena, New York 1978; *GA 2: Gunnar Birkerts and Associates*, edited by Yukio Futagawa, Tokyo 1982; articles—"A Search for Architectural Principles— Some Thoughts and Works of Gunnar Birkerts" in *Progressive Architecture* (New York), September, 1964; "Newest projects of Gunnar Birkerts" in *Architectural Record* (New York), August 1966; "Three Colleges by Gunnar Birkerts" in *Architectural Record* (New York), October 1968; "Gunnar Birkerts—Architect" in *Architecture and Planning* (Taiwan), November 1969; "Gunnar Birkerts" in *Kenchiku Bunka* (Tokyo), March 1970; "Eine 'Bruecke' für die Federal Reserve Bank in Minneapolis" in *Werk* (Zürich), no. 4, 1970; "Bucher-Bruecke" in *Baumeister* (Munich), December 1970; "Opere e progetti di Gunnar Birkerts e Associati" in *Architettura* (Rome), May 1971; "Bridge for a Bank" in *Architectural Forum* (New York), June 1971; "To Amerikanske Biblioteksprosekter" in *Arkitekten* (Copenhagen), no. 9, 1971; "New Directions for Gunnar Birkerts" in *Architectural Record* (New York), October 1971; "Gunnar Birkerts," special issue of *Architecture + Urbanism* (Tokyo), July 1972; "This Building Is a Bridge" in *Popular Science* (New York), August 1972; "Liberating Lane" in *Progessive Architecture* (New York), March 1973; "Gunnar Birkerts" in *Kentiku* (Tokyo), December 1973; "A Minneapolis La Banca" in *Domus* (Milan), January 1975; "Aktualitat, Federal Reserve Bank of

Minneapolis" in *Bauen and Wohnen* (Zürich), April 1975; "Leading Architects of the World: Gunnar Birkerts" in *Nikkei Architecture* (Tokyo), 4 October 1976; "Architecture Who Puts Poetry into His Buildings" in *Saudi Gazette* (Saudi Arabia), 2 March 1978; "The Philosophy and Methodology of Gunnar Birkerts" in *Dichotomy* (Detroit), April 1979; "A New Glass House to House the Best of Beautiful Glass" in *Smithsonian* (Washington, D.C.), May 1980; "A New Museum for an Ancient Art" in *Time* (New York), 30 June 1980; "Birkerts' Library for Duluth" in *Architectural Record* (New York), November 1980; "The Long Baltic current" in *Inland Architect* (Chicago), November 1980; "Three Recent Works of Gunnar Birkerts" in *Space Design* (Tokyo), April 1981; "Underground Books" in *Architects' Journal* (London), 28 July 1982; "Splendor Beneath the Grass in Michigan" in *AIA Journal* (Washington, D.C.), January 1983; "Explorations: Four Projects of Gunnar Birkerts" in *Architectural Record* (New York), March 1983; "Fácoltà di Legge dell'Università del Michigan" in *Industria delle costruzioni* (Rome), May 1983; "Villa Ginny: The Next Architecture" in *Domus* (Milan), July/August 1984.

Gunnar Birkerts has been producing significant, controversial buildings for almost twenty-five years. Strongly influenced by Eero Saarinen, for whom he worked as a young apprentice, having newly arrived in the United States from Latvia, his work has been shaped, as he admits, more by the times we live in than by any current ideological position. Like all contemporary architects, he acknowledges the in-

BLAKE, Peter.

American. Born in Berlin, Germany, 20 September 1920; emigrated to the United States, 1940: naturalized, 1944. Educated at the Bootham School, York, England, 1935-38; University of London, 1938; Regent Street Polytechnic School of Architecture, London, 1939; University of Pennsylvania School of Architecture, Philadelphia, 1940-41; Pratt Institute School of Architecture, New York, 1947-49, B.Arch. (honors) 1949. Served as an Intelligence Officer, United States 5th Armored Division, 1944-45, and as a Staff Intelligence Officer, Headquarters, United States Forces in Europe, 1945-47. Apprentice to Serge Chermayeff, *q.v.*, London, 1938-39, and to George Howe, *q.v.*, Oscar Stonoroy *q.v.*, and Louis I. Kahn, *q.v.*, Philadelphia, 1940-42; Curator, Department of Architecture and Industrial Design, Museum of Modern Art, New York, 1948-50; Associate Editor, 1950-61, Managing Editor, 1961-64, and Editor-in-Chief, 1964-72, *Architectural Forum*, New York; Partner, Peter Blake and Julian Neski, Achitects, New York, 1956-60, and James Baker and Peter Blake, Architects, New York, 1964-71; Contributing Editor, *New York Magazine* 1968-76; Editor-in-Chief, *Architecture Plus*, New York, 1972-75; Chairman of the School of Architecture, Boston Architectural Center 1975-79. Since 1979, Chairman, Department of Architecture and Planning, Catholic Univesity, Washington, D.C. Chairman, 1962, and Member of the Board of Directors, 1965-73, International Design Conference in Aspen, Colorado; Chairman, Advisory Panel to the Shah of Iran on Housing, Urban Development and New Town Planning, 1976. Member, Board of Directors, City Walls, New York, since 1968; Member, Public Arts Council of the Municipal Arts Society, New York, since 1970. Recipient: Ford Foundation grant, 1960; Howard Myers Award for Architectural Journalism, 1960; Graham Foundation Fellowship, 1962; Architecture Critic's Medal, American Institute of Architects, 1975; Distinguished Designer

Fellowship, National Endowment for the Arts, 1984.
Fellow, American Institute of Architects, 1970.
Address: Department of Architecture and Planning
Catholic University, Washington, D.C. 20064,
U.S.A.

Works:

1955/
65   Numerous houses in the New York City area
1957 Design of the *America Builds* exhibition, West
     Berlin
1959 Design of the *U.S. Architecture* exhibition,
     Moscow
1960 Hollis Unitarian Church, Queens, New York
     Allen-Stevens Offices and Warehouse,
     Queens, New York
1961 Temple Emanu-El, Livingston, New Jersey
1963 Ideal Theatre, for the Ford Foundation
     (project)
1964 Library, Darrow School, New Lebanon, New
     York
     Plan for Tegel Airport, Berlin (competition
     project)
1965 Town plan for Manjstee, Michigan
     Institute buildings and housing, Max Planck
     Institute, Berlin (competition project)
1970 Mental Hygiene Center, Binghamton State
     Hospital, New York
1974 Roundabout Theatre Stage One, New York
1975 Neely Experimental Theatre, Vanderbilt Uni-
     versity Drama School, Nashville, Tennesee
1978 Puerto Rican Travelling Theatre, New York
1982 Vietnam Veterans Memorial, Washington,
     D.C. (competition project)

Publications:

By BLAKE: books—*Marcel Breuer: Architect and
Designer,* New York 1949; *An American Synagogue
for Today and Tomorrow,* New York 1954; *Sun and
Shadow,* London 1956; *The Master Builders: Le
Corbusier, Mies van der Rohe, Frank Lloyd Wright,*
New York and London 1960, revised edition New
York 1976; *The New Forces,* Melbourne 1971;
*Architecture for the New World: The Work of Harry
Seidler,* Sydney 1973; *God's Own Junkyard: The
Planned Deterioriation of America's Landscape,* New
York 1964; *Form Follows Fiasco: Why Modern
Architecture Hasn't Worked,* Boston 1977; *Subways,*
exhibition catalogue, New York 1977; *Australian
Embassy, Paris,* Sydney 1979; numerous articles in
architectural journals throughout the world.

On BLAKE: articles—"Bard College Student Hous-
ing, Annandale-on-Hudson" in *Architecture +
Urbanism* (Tokyo), June 1973; "Student Housing,
Bard College" in *Baumeister* (Munich), March 1974;
"A Teaching Theatre : An Ideal Theatre" by Stanley
Abercrombie in *Contract Interiors* (New York),
September 1978; "Towering over His Toy Town" by
Jasia Reichardt in *Building Design* (London), 18
March 1983; "Modernism: Is It Still Alive?" in *Inland
Architect* (Chicago), May/June 1984.

Like most young architects starting out in the United
States and in Europe in the 1950s, I was tremendous-
ly influenced by the clear logic and pure beauty of
Mies van der Rohe's work. I knew Mies quite well
and found his theories and his performance
enormously persuasive—especially since he was not
only a superb artist but also a man of enormous
charm and, believe it or not, of enormous humanity.
Not until after he died did I really begin to question
some of the hard-edged diagrams that he had built.

Since then I have been attracted increasingly to the
work of certain humanists—especially Alvar
Aalto—whom we used to consider rather too
sentimental for a rational age. I was asked recently to
identify the one building, in the Greater Boston area,

Peter Blake: Rehabilitation Center, Binghamton State Hospital, New York, 1970.

built since World War II, that had really stood the
test of time. Aalto's Baker House at M.I.T.,
completed in the late 1940s, was the obvious answer.

Today, I design and build—or try to design and
build—as simply as I can, as neatly as I can, as
modestly as I can, and as well as I can. And as
inexpensively as I can; I am very pleased that the
Rehabilitation Center in Binghamton, New York,
was constructed for about six per cent below the
allocated budget. That produced not merely a
building that I like very much indeed—but also a
building that returned some money to the people
who agreed to pay for such a generous gesture—in
this case, the taxpayers of Binghamton. I consider
myself some sort of populist, in that regard; and I
don't think I would know how to design a
monument—in the unlikely event that someone
asked me to design and build one.

I have an uneasy feeling that the modern
movement, in its preachings, has been extraordinarily arrogant—telling people what was supposedly good for them, instead of *listening* to their
needs and aspirations. It seems to me that the modern
movement has not, until quite recently, come to
terms with the idea of an egalitarian democracy—a
human condition which, for better or for worse, is
not compatible with super-planning à la Haussmann, Le Corbusier, Hilberseimer, or, for that
matter, Frank Lloyd Wright. If the choice is between
egalitarian democracy and modern architecture, I (a
modern architect) today prefer the former.

—Peter Blake

Peter Blake began his architectural career through a
somewhat conventional sequence of development.
He went to architectural school when the Modern
Movement was supplanting the Beaux Arts tradition
as the dominant theory expounded in architectural
academia in the United States. He studied the great
modern masters and professed his reverence for
Wright, Le Corbusier, and Mies van der Rohe in his
book *The Master Builders,* which he wrote in 1960.
His earlier buildings, while not numerous, exhibit a
strong influence of the masters. However, more

recently, as if not completely convinced of those
sacred cows of modernism, "form follows function,"
"less is more," and so forth, he has become a
successful critic of modern architecture, challenging
these time-honored beliefs in his publishing and in his
designs.

As a teacher and the editor of two successive yet
discontinued magazines, *Architectural Forum* and
Architecture Plus, he was constantly criticizing the
built examples of current trends and their creators'
adherence to or deviation from the precepts of the
accepted philosophy. In practice, increasing labor
expenses, energy conciousness, and governmental
regulation in a world where time is money and money
builds architecture, the phrases "shortened version,"
"instant house," "no frills," seem to have replaced
the sacred cows. In many respects, the Modern
Movement has failed to provide for us today. Well-
planned ideal cities, fashioned in bricks and mortar
from the concepts introduced by the architects of the
International Style, have developed into sterile
wastelands, irresponsible to the well being of the
individual.

The culmination of Blake's criticism of modern
doctrine is expressed in his 1977 book, *Form Follows
Fiasco: Why Modern Architecture Hasn't Worked.*
Here, he admits that the Modern Movement which
he so endearingly promoted has failed. His appreciation for his mentors has not been abandoned, but
their precepts cannot alone direct present day
building.

As a critic, Blake has the intelligence, knowledge,
wit, and honesty to be listened to and respected.
Though his essays and books speak more for his
reactionary attitude toward the direction of modern
architecture, his works have switched from pure
adherence to the dogma of the masters to an
architecture more responsive to contemporary constraints. The cost of his conventionally built Mental
Hygiene Center in New York State (1970), for
example, came in under budget because he cut out the
special details, expensive materials, even prefabricated components, and fit the building construction
method and its materials to those readily and
inexpensively available.

—Stephen P. Hamilton

BLESSING, Charles Alexander.

American. Born in Montrose, Colorado, 23 May 1912. Educated at the University of Colorado, Boulder, B.S.Arch. Eng. 1934; Massachusetts Institute of Technology, Cambridge, B.Arch. 1937, M.City Planning 1939. Served in the United States Army Engineers Office, 1943; Director of Urban Research, United States Navy Military Government Program, Princeton, New Jersey, 1944-45, and Monterey, California, 1945; City Planning Officer, SCAP Headquarters, Tokyo, 1945-46; Lieutenant. Married Elizabeth C. Long in 1940; children: Bayard and Curtis. Planning Engineer, New Hampshire Planning and Development Commission, 1940-41; City Planner, Chicago Plan Commission, 1942; Regional Planning Engineer, Greater Boston Development Committee, 1946-48; Director of Planning, Chicago Planning Commission, 1948-53; Director of City Planning, Detroit City Planning Commission, 1953-74. Since 1974, Director of Planning, Detroit Department of Community and Economic Development. Adjunct Associate Professor of City Planning, Wayne State University, Detroit, 1954-59. Currently, Professor of Architecture, Urban Design Studio, University of Detroit. Member, National Industrial Zoning Committee, 1949-53 and 1971-73; Vice-Chairman, Detroit Commission on Neighborhood Conservation and Improved Housing, 1955-60; President, American Institute of Planners, 1958-60; Member, Michigan Cultural Commission, 1961-62; Chairman, Urban Design Committee, American Institute of Architects, 1962-63; Member, National Planning Advisory Committee, Highway Research Board, 1964-67; Member, National Advisory Council, Urban America, 1966-67; Member of the Board of Registration, 1968-75, and Chairman of the Board, 1968-75, Professional Community Planners of Michigan. Recipient: Biennial Award for Design Excellence, United States Department of Housing and Urban Development, 1970; Urban Design Award, *Progressive Architecture*, New York, 1971; Gold Medal, American Institute of Architects, Detroit Chapter, 1972; Distinguished Engineering Alumnus Award, University of Colorado, 1972; American Institute of Architects Award, 1976. Fellow, American Institute of Architects. Address (office): 350 East Congress Street, Detroit, Michigan 48226, U.S.A.

Works:

1948/
53 Plans and planning proposals for the City of Chicago
1953/
74 Plans planning proposals for the City of Detroit

Publications

By BLESSING: book—*The Form of Cities in Perspective; The Graeco-Roman World 500 B.C.to A.D 200* exhibition catalogue, Ann Arbor, Michigan 1973; article—"Seeing the City Whole" in *AIA Journal* (Washington D.C.), September 1974, January 1975 and April 1976.

On BLESSING: articles—"Detroit and the Vision of Charles Blessing" by James Bailey in *Architectural Forum* (New York), June 1965; "The Other Architect" in *Architectural and Engineering News* (Philadelphia), February 1967.

Charles Blessing is an architect, yes, but he prefers to be called an urban planner. What he has done over the last quarter of a century is to combine the skills of both kinds of professional in a pioneering effort as director of city planning for Detroit.

Today, while he has retired from the position he held since 1953, he is just as busy as ever, having switched his visionary talents to a more specific place, the University of Detroit where he is a professor in the Urban Design Studio of the School of Architecture. Thus, in a sense, he has came full circle.

Meanwhile, he can look back with pride to that portion of his career spent serving a metropolis of more than one million people, which, surprisingly enough to some, was earning its share of recognition even though cities like Philadelphia seemed to be getting all the acclaim. Detroit, under Blessing's leadership was the first American city to become involved in social and community organizational work, and in the 1960s was honored by the American Institute of Planners and the American Institute of Architects for its contribution to urban design. What really has mattered the most over the years, however, was that Blessing is one of the most humane persons dealing with cities in our society.

In 1976 he was cited by the American Institute of Architects with a medal for his "unique and artistic documentation of many of the world's great cities." Said the jury in making the presentation: "During the course of his life as an architect and city planner, Blessing has documented the cities and places of his world as has no other person before him. His drawings . . .have become a more meaningful way of expressing and recording the drama, form and grain of the man-made environment."

Blessing understands—and visually interprets—cities in the large context of geography as well as in the intimate context of people as expressed through neighborhoods. he is broad and he is deep, going back to the ancient cities of Greece for his basic text and for a beginning to his own documentation.

When the *AIA Journal*, for its Bicentennial issue, queried professionals for a list of buildings that they felt had had the greatest influence in America, Blessing replied: "The design of the city represents the greatest challenge of the architect; the present confusion and disarray of the urban development is the real enemy of great architecture. This is not to say that no single building can qualify as an architectural masterpiece even if it lacks harmony with its surroundings, but rather to emphasize that urban visual chaos and ugliness can only be overcome by a level of thought and activity beyond the scale of a single building."

It is very likely beyond the scope of any one profession to manipulate the total form of the city, but perserverance in a search for the answers that satisfy the spirit is a must. Blessing is one of those professionals who is truly dedicated to continuing in that search, not only in Detroit but also everywhere he goes about the world in an attempt to foster a better understanding of the urban design process.

—Robert E. Koehler

BLOM, Holger.

Swedish. Born in Stockholm, 2 August 1906. Studied at the Royal Institute of Technology School of Architecture, Stockholm, 1924-28; Department of Art History, University of Stockholm, 1928-29; Royal Academy of Arts School of Architecture, Stockholm, 1930-32: Chancellor's Medal, 1932. Married Alla Feodorvna Doljencova in 1934; sons: Igor, Tarras, and Peter. Worked with Lars Israel Wahlman, Stockholm, 1928-29; studied and travelled in Europe, working in Paris and Amsterdam, 1929-31, and in the United States, Asia, and South America, 1965-75. In private practice, Stockholm, since 1931. Worked in the Stockholm City Planning Office, 1932, and in the Street Office, 1933-38, and served as City Garden Director (Chief of the Stockholm Parks Department), 1938-71. Working Member of the Stockholm Committee for the Embellishment of Public Places, 1962-83; Executive Secretary, Advisory Committee for the Preservation of the Beauty of Stockholm, 1972-83. Secretary, 1944-47, Chairman, 1948-50 and 1960-65, and Honorary Director, 1978, of the Society of Swedish Artists; President, Stockholm Rotary Club, 1973-74; Honorary Director, Association of Swedish Landscape Architects 1978; Founder-Member, International Federation of Landscape Architects. Exhibition: *Plock i parken,* Collector Gallery, Stockholm, 1971. Recipient: Gold Medal, Patriotic Society of Sweden; Medal of St. Erik, Stockholm; King Christian X Medal of Liberty, Copenhagen. Honorary Member: Swedish Society of Landscape Architects; Swedish Artists Club; British Society of Landscape Architects; Society of Venezuelan Landscape Architects. Knight Commander of the Royal Order of the North Star, Sweden; Knight of the Royal Vasa Order, Sweden; Knight Commander of the Order of Pope Gregory, Vatican; Officer of the Order of Oranje-Nassau, Netherlands. Address: Odengatan 15, 114 24 Stockholm, Sweden.

Works:

1932 Design for modern motor-hearse, Stockholm
Design of City Garbage Disposal Vehicles, Stockholm
1932/
35 Underground tramway stations, Stockholm
Slussen traffic cloverleaf, Stockholm (with Tage William-Olsson)
1932/
84 Numerous apartment buildings, terraced houses, villas and weekend cottages, with Jan I. Wahlman, including Villa Branner (1937) and the parks and landscaping projects, Tullgarden (1955), Trygg-Hansa Felminggaten (1979), and Galärvarvsparken (1981)
1933- Numerous street architecture projects, bus terminals and shelters, pedestrian subways, shopping centres, and open-air restaurants in Stockholm, including Norra Bantorget bus terminal (1936), Stureplan mushroom bus shelter (1938), and the Strömparterren park buildings (1968)
1934/
36 City Sanitary Department garages and employees' buildings, Stockholm
1936 Lövsata Refuse Destruction Building, Stockholm
1937/
72 Numerous city plans and systems for Stockholm parks, open spaces, festivals, sculptures, and monuments, including Björns trädgard park (1937), Berzeliipark (1940), Norr Mälarstrand seashore (1941-45), Fafängan park (1942), Tegnerlunden park (1942), Mosebacketorg park (1943), Kungsträdgarden park (1945-72), and the integrated suburban parks system (1940-72)

Publications:

By BLOM: numerous writings on landscape architecture and town-planning for the Royal Academy School of Stockholm, Technical University of Stockholm, and Swedish radio and television, including *Parks,* booklet, Stockholm 1952; *Se pa Slussen: fran Soderbo till Karusellen,* with Hans Eklund and others, Stockholm 1981.

On BLOM: books—*Trettiotalets Byggnadskonst i Sverige,* edited by Hans Brunnberg, Hans-Fedrik Neumüller and Ingra Mari Lönnroth, Stockholm 1943; *Sweden Builds* by G. E. Kidder Smith, New York and Stockholm 1950, London 1957; *Building Modern Sweden* by Bertil Hultén, : 'armondsworth, Middlesex 1951; *Modern Garden.* by Peter Shepheard, London 1953; *Playgrounds and Recreation Spaces* by Alfred Ledermann and Alfred Trachsel, Stuttgart and London 1959; *The Park and the Town* by George F. Chadwick, London 1966; *Planning for*

Holger Blom: Norr Malarstrand Seashore Park, Stockholm, 1941-45.

Play by Lady Allen of Hurtwood, London 1968; *Landscape of Man* by Geoffrey and Susan Jellicoe, London 1975.

The art of building parks is part of architecture. The materials are different, certainly, but the problems are similar. Solution in plan, the forming of space, the detail. With the ground and the plants, compositions in space and colour are produced that range from the most practical to the most solemn. And with these living materials, all human emotions and rational requirements can be expressed.

—Holger Blom

While World War II was devastating most of Europe, the Swedes were exploring new concepts of landscape, especially in cities. After the war, landscape architects and laymen in the war-torn countries were astonished by the originality and inventiveness with which Holger Blom, the director of parks in Stockholm, brought landscape into the busiest centres of the city. The Swedish summer is short but fairly predictable; the air has never been polluted by intensive industrialization, and public vandalism is minimal. Stockholm was the first major city to prepare and execute a comprehensive landscape plan, its general shape dictated by the powerful terrain of water and rock. From the surrounding country, green fingers of landscape penetrate right to the city centre where they seem to explode into flower at Blom's magic touch.

The most popular of all of Blom's inventions (soon to be copied throughout Europe and become hackneyed) were the portable containers on the pavements. These attractively-shaped, mass-produced concrete bowls were filled with plants in flower at a central depot, then placed wherever they could enrich an urban setting. Another of his

innovations was to plant the banks of the Malärstrand, the city's principal water scenery, not as a sophisticated park but as a reflection of the city's outer landscape, with wild plants and seats set among flowers. Blom also introduced children's climbing play sculpture; he designed small areas for unusual types of play activity, such as open air stages on which children could act. His structures were all in natural materials.

It can be said the the impetus given to simplicity and grace in civic landscape by Holger Blom inspired nearly every civilized society struggling to recuperate after the war. He lifted urban park design from the traditional borough surveyor's conception of art into one that is art itself.

—Geoffrey Jellicoe

BLOM, Piet.

Dutch. Born in Amsterdam, 8 February 1934. Educated at the Architecture Academy, Amsterdam, under Aldo van Eyck, 1956-62, Dip.Arch. 1962; awarded Prix de Rome, 1962. Married Elisabeth Margaretta Maria Abels in 1958; children: Hannah, Abel, and Betje. In private practice, Monickendam, Netherlands, since 1967. Exhibition: Gallery on the Spaanse kade bridge, Rotterdam, 1977. Recipient: Architectural Prize, West Berlin, 1976. Knight of the Order of the Oranje Nassau, The Hague. Address (office): School-straat 2, Monickendam, Netherlands.

Works:

1963 Boerderij Students Building (conversion of farm building), Twente Technical University, Enschede, Netherlands
1967/
   69 Bastille Students Building/Community Centre, Twente Technical University, Enschede, Netherlands
1972/
   73 Kasbah Housing Development, Hengelo, Netherlands
1975 Subterranean Development under the Rozengracht, Amsterdam (project)
   Jordaan District Redevelopment Plan, Amsterdam (project)
1975/
   78 Speelhuis Leisure Centre, with theatre, small halls, and housing, Helmond, Netherlands
1977 Apartment buildings, with shops and bridge, Spaanse kade, Rotterdam
   Housing, Spaanse kade, Rotterdam
   Minerva Academie, Groningen, Netherlands
1978/
   79 Apartment buildings (2), Rotterdam (project)

Publications:

By BLOM: article—"The Singular Opinions of Piet Blom" in *Bauwelt* (Berlin), 7 October 1974.

On BLOM: Books—*World Architecture 3*, London 1966; *Architectuur en Planning: Nederland, 1940-1980*, edited by S. Umberto Barbieri, Rotterdam and Amsterdam 1983; articles—"Kasbah Experimental Housing in Hengelo" in *Detail* (Munich), January/February 1974; "Trial for Helmond's 'Forest of Houses'" by Ruud Brouwers in *Wonen-TA/BK* (Heerlen, Netherlands), May 1974; "Team 10 + 20: Introduction and Conclusion," special issue of *L'Architecture d'aujourd'hui* (Paris), January/February 1975; "The Kasbah, Hengelo—A Real Experiment" by W. J. van Heuvel in *Polytechnische Tijdschrift* (The Hague), 25 June 1975; "Housing and Community Centre in Helmond" in *Bauen und Wohnen* (Zürich), January 1976; "The Dwelling Tree" by Pierluigi Nicolin in *Lotus* (Venice), no. 11, 1976; "Experimental Housing: Nine Years of Passive Conduct" by Aad Wassenaar in *Wonen-TA/BK* (Heerlen, Netherlands), March 1977; "Speelhuis Cultural Centre in Helmond" in *Polytechnische Tijdschrift* (The Hague), December 1977; "188 Homes in Helmond" in *L'Architecture d'aujourd'hui* (Paris), April 1978; "Boxing Clever" in *The Architects' Journal* (London), 10 May 1978; "Think of a Square and Cube It" in *Interior Design* (London), July 1978; "Het Speelhuis in Helmond" by Nathalie van den Eerenbeemt in *Bauwelt* (Berlin), 4 August 1978; "Art and Community Centre in Helmond" by Jurgen Joedicke in *Bauen und Wohnen* (Zürich), December 1980; "Structuralism as Planning Network and Double Land Use" by Wim J. van Hauvel in *Polytechnisch Tijdschrift* (The Hague), April 1981; "Piet Blom: The Homo Ludens of Dutch Architecture" by Jord den Hollander in *Dutch Art + Architecture Today* (The Hague), May 1981.

Piet Blom received his architectural education at the Architecture Academy in Amsterdam. One of his teachers was Aldo van Eyck, and van Eyck's progressive concepts exerted a decisive influence on Blom, as they did also on such architects as Herman Hertzberger and Jan Verhoeven. These architects are today described as adherents of Structuralism; as a reaction against decades of domination by Functionalism, it demands a humanization of architecture. The principles of Structuralism, all assimilated in Blom's work, are these: 1) Town planning should strive for a multiform urban landscape, the *casbah organisée*, instead of the garden city. 2) Town planning should be based on a "sense of place" concept, rather than on the "space-time" concept of the verdant functional town. 3) There should be a deliberate creation of a "realm of the intermediate," areas where the individual and community can meet—for instance, squares, streets, and apartment building galleries that are not only functional but also life-enhancing. 4) The shape, form, and identity of the town must come about according to the methods of architecture, not the scientific/analytic method of Functionalism. 5) There must be structural development, as opposed to arbitrary town growth. 6) Building mass must be articulated—as an alternative to amorphous town planning and mammoth building blocks. 7) Growth should be coherent to insure an atmosphere of order and repose. 8) The architect should prepare for future change by creating polyvalent forms and by allowing for individual interpretations, so that change is possible, so that the user may express his identity (the analogy is to the language model of linguistic Structuralism; the enemy is uniformity). 9) Time must be rendered transparent: the architect must study early and other cultures, he must offer new interpretations of these experiences for our time and place; the architect must create from the fund of knowledge in his "imaginary museum." 10) Before everything else, the architect must consider the archetypal behavior of man in a community; in his concern, he is similar to Structuralist anthropoligists such as Lévi-Strauss. All of Blom's works are attempts to realize his Structural ideals.

Boerderij, his first Students Building at the Twente Technical University: although Blom converted an existing farm building and continued to work with gable roofs, he was able to demonstrate his own formal language. The way he has handled the interior space with its empty areas and sloping views under the roof, as well as his skillful use of brick, roof tiling, and timber for the exterior, is remarkable. The individually set, gabled windows provide a particular emphasis. The building is architectonically very fine.

Bastille, the second Students Building at Twente: the basic plan is an extendable web of regularly ordered construction elements within which space and an organized structure are arbitrarily articulated.

Spielhuis Leisure Center, with theatre, small halls, and dwellings, in Helmond: it consists of cubes that stand on their corners. Because of the "utopian" nature of the project, the client asked for three trial prototypes. They were successful, and Blom used the shapes for the theatre in the centre of the town. Here, he proved that the slanting walls and window areas were no formal joke but a way to promote spatial

contact. The hall, painted like a circus tent, is also worthy of mention; so are the foyer, partly roofed in glass, the colorful interior decoration, and the clear structural organization. The dwellings are single cubes arranged around the theatre. Blom achieved a very successful work—with a delighted and critically engaged client.

Within the framework of a national experimental program, Blom tried to realize van Eyck's vision of the *casbah organisée* in his Kasbah Housing Development in Hengelo; it is perhaps his most vigorous attempt to realize the ideals of Structuralism. But, because the project was not built as originally planned, and because there is no polyvalent communication structure for the collective areas under the houses, it remains architectonically interesting, but its success with regard to municipal diversity is impossible to judge.

What can be said is that Blom is an original artist/architect who achieves his best work when his client is able to follow and, if necessary, influence his imaginative ideas. He has a predilection for sloping roofed buildings and natural materials and colors, and he has command over the proportions of his individual architectonic forms.

—Arnulf Lüchinger

BLOMSTEDT, Aulis.

Finnish. Born in Jyväskylä, 28 July 1906. Educated at the Institute of Technology, Helsinki, under Armas Lindgren and Lisko Nyström, 1924-30, Dip. Arch. 1930. Served in the Finnish Army in Helsinki, 1931-32, Vatnuori, 1939-40, and Vuosalmi, 1941-44: Lieutenant; awarded Cross of Liberty 4th Class. Married Heidi Sibelius in 1932; children: Juhana, Petri, Anssi and Severi. In private practice, Finland, 1945 until his death in 1979. Professor of Architecture (Public Buildings), Institute of Technology, Helsinki, 1958-66. Exhibitions (individual): Museum of Finnish Architecture, Helsinki, 1962; *Aulis Blomstedt: Serigraphies,* Artek Gallery, Helsinki, 1973; *Aulis Blomstedt, architecte: pensée et forme,* Fondation Le Corbusier, Paris, 1977; *Aulis Blomstedt,* Museum of Finnish Architecture, Helsinki, 1980. Recipient: State Award in Architecture, Finland, 1977. Honorary Member of SAFA (Finnish Architects Association), and of ORNAMO (Finnish

Designers Association). *Died* (in Espoo, Finland) *21 December 1979*.

Works:

1930/
32 Tehtaanpuisto Church, Helsinki (competition project)
1939 Apartment building, Pihlajatie 52, Helsinki
1946 University Library, Turku, Finland (competition project)
  Sauna Rysä Kallio, Kirkkonummi, Finland
1947 Walhalla Fort Restaurant, Suomenlinna, Helsinki
1948 Villa Salonen, Espoo, Finland
  "Kenno" Industrial Housing System (project)
  Imperial Palace, Addis Ababa, Ethiopia (competition project)
1950 Saimaanhovi Club Building, Imatra, Finland
  Pedagogical Institute, Jyväskylä, Finland (competition project)
1951 Apartment building, Asesepänkatu, Turku, Finland
  Villa Therman, Tolkkinen, Finland
1954 "Ketju" Terrace Houses, Tapiola, Espoo, Finland
  Apartment building, Kolmirinne, Tapiola, Espoo, Finland
1955 Artists' Terrace Houses, Tapiola, Espoo, Finland
1956/
57 Apartment building, Nallenpolku, Tapiola, Espoo, Finland
1958 Aulis Blomstedt Studio, Tapiola, Espoo, Finland
  Concert Hall, Oslo, Norway (competition project)
1959 Workers Institute Annex, Helsinki
1960 Villa Pettersson, Helsinki
  Finnish Architecture exhibition, Stockholm and Warsaw
1961 Apartment building, Riistapolku, Tapiola, Espoo, Finland
1962 Terrace houses, Nelikko, Tapiola, Espoo, Finland
1963 Citadelle Experimental House, Norrköping, Sweden (project)
1964 Terrace houses, Leppäkertuntie, Tapiola, Espoo, Finland
  Suvikumpu Housing Area, Tapiola, Espoo Finland (competition project)
1965 Apartment buildings, Kaskenpaja ja Allakka, Tapiola, Espoo, Finland

Aulis Blomstedt: Storage and industrial building for a bank, Konala, Helsinki, 1976.

1967 Congregational Hall, Kulosaari, Helsinki (competiton project)
1968 Villa Stig Weckström, Espoo, Finland
      Villa Bjorn Weckström, Espoo, Finland
      Parish Center, Maaselkä, Finland
1969 *Finland in Louisiana* exhibition, Louisiana Museum, Humlebaek, Denmark
      Cubic Exhibition Unit System
      Boarding School for Handicapped Children, Kuutinharju, Finland
1970 *Finnish Architecture* exhibition, Minsk, U.S.S.R.
1971 Beaubourg Centre, Paris (competition project)
      Villa Auramo, Bromarv, Finland
      Church Reconstruction, Kulosaari, Finland
1972 Pollution-Free House (project)
1973 Small House Unit Study (project)
      Cafeteria and Custodian's Apartment, Ainola, Järvenpää, Finland
1974 Puntarpää Apartment Building, Soukka, Espoo, Finland
      25th Anniversary Exhibition, Museum of Finnish Architecture, Helsinki
1976 Storage and industrial building for a bank, Konala, Helsinki
      Church Parish House Annex, Kulosaari, Finland
1978 Reconstruction plan for Walhalla Fort Restaurant, Suomenlinna, Helsinki

Publications:

By BLOMSTEDT: articles, all in *Arkkitehti* (Helsinki)—"Eliel Saarinen," no. 11/12, 1943; "Paul Nelson: The Suspended House," no. 9/10, 1945; "The Post-War Reconstruction of the World and the Architects," no. 6, 1955; "The Architect's Place Today in the Community," no. 9, 1956; "The General Foundations of House Planning," no. 3, 1957; "Public Buildings and Tradition," no. 5, 1958; "The Problem of Form in Architecture," no. 12, 1958; "Measure and Proportion," no. 9, 1962; "Urbanization and the Landscape," no. 4, 1963; "The Fourth Dimension of Architecture," no. 12, 1964; "Architectural Research," no. 6, 1967; "Man—The Measure of Architecture," no. 2, 1971; "Architect Training—From School into Life," no. 1, 1972; "Autonomy of Achitecture," no. 5, 1974; "The ABC of Architecture," no. 3, 1978; also "Prospects in Architecture," with commentary by Asko Salokorpi, in *Abacus* no. 3, 1982.

On BLOMSTEDT: book—*Aulis Blomstedt, architecte: pensée et forme,* exhibition catalogue, edited by Juhani Pallasmaa, Helsinki 1977; articles—"Aulis Blomstedt, 28.7.1906-21.12.1979" by Juhani Pallasmaa in *Arkkitehti* (Helsinki), no. 8, 1979; "Aulis Blomstedt, 1905-1979" by Juhani Pallasmaa in *Carré Bleu* (Paris), no. 1, 1980; "Aulis Blomstedt (1906-1979)" in *Building* (London), 7 March 1980; "Aulis Blomstedt 1900-1979" in *Projekt* (Bratislava), March 1981.

My architecture aims at simplicity and clarity. I mean that in arranging forms, I resort to as few basic geometric units as possible.

My plans for private family housing always take account of the residents' wishes.

Over a period of ten years, I have developed a modular system (canon, 60). It was first published in the magazine *Le Carré Bleu* in 1961. We use it, my assistant and I, in all projects. I always try to look for the largest square possible in the system for use as the basic module of the plan. The plan for a bank's central storage facilities (1976) consists of four squares of 48 metres each side. I pay particular attention to aesthetic proportions.

—Aulis Blomstedt (1979)

Aulis Blomstedt was one of Finland's most devoted students of the fundamental concepts of architecture and of shape and harmony. He created a theoretical basis for discussion of the aesthetic foundations and social applications of module systems. In the reconstruction period of the 1940s, he devised an industrially-produced cell construction system. From the 1950s, he concentrated mainly on a system of measurements based on the dimensions of the human body and on musical harmony.

Blomstedt's aim was primarily to discover the fundamental laws of architecture, the laws that govern the dimensions of a building. His (often aphoristic) comments stressed the importance of man, nature, and individual perception, but the ultimate object of his theoretical deliberations was the building itself, its plan and its model. His scale of materials was ascetic but often warm.

Whereas Blomstedt's work in the 1940s featured "romantic" applications of wood and stone, his work in the 1950s—for example, the row and apartment houses in Tapiola and the Workers Institute Annex in Helsinki—shows a dominant tendency towards clear and simple space and a perception of shape that follows from a predetermined dimensional harmony. This trend continues in Blomstedt's later work. There are sometimes bold, rhythmic patterns—yet they are always subject to an overall harmony. Blomstedt emphasized the importance of graphic composition in architecture. A graphic artist himself, he also designed jewellery in silver and gold and produced various works of graphic art.

—Pekka Suhonen

BO, Jørgen.

Danish. Born in Copenhagen, 8 April 1919. Educated at the Royal Danish Academy of Fine Arts School of Architecture, Copenhagen, 1936-41, Dip. Arch. 1941. Married Gerda Bennike in 1941 (divorced, 1966); children: Malene, Morten, Mikkel, and Marie. In private practice, Copenhagen, since 1943. Technical Consultant, Conservation Society, Denmark, 1946-52; Member, Conservation Board, Denmark, 1952-61. Teacher, 1946-59, Assistant Professor, 1959-60, and since 1960, Professor of Building Design, Royal Danish Academy School of Architecture. Member, Censorship Committee, Charlottenborg, Denmark, 1958-71; Member of the Committee, Slotsholmen, Copenhagen, 1961-63; Member, Management Committee, San Cataldo, Italy, 1966; Member, Governing Board, Danish Institute in Rome, 1968-70. Member of the Council, Royal Danish Academy, since 1959. Exhibition: Charlottenborg Exhibition Building, Denmark, 1983 (retrospective). Recipient: Lyngy-Taarbaek Municipality Award, 1948; Gladsaxe Municipality Award, 1955, 1956; The Wood Prize, Information Council of the Timber Trade, 1958; Eckersberg Medal, 1959, and C.F. Hansen Medal, 1983, Royal Danish Academy of Arts; Horsholm Municipality Award, 1962; Copenhagen Municipality Award, 1965; Award from the Committee for the Embellishment of the Capital, Copenhagen, 1965. Knight, 1966, Knight First Grade, 1977, Order of the Dannebrog. Address (office): Hovedvagtsgade 2, 1103 Copenhagen K, Denmark.

Works:

1945/
58   Terrace housing developments (Stengårdsparken, Skoleparken, Hyrdeparken, and City of Pre-fabricated Houses), near Copenhagen (with Knud Halberg)
1958 The Louisiana Museum, Humlebaek, Denmark (with Vilhelm Wohlert)

Westminster Department Store, Copenhagen
1959 Design of the *House and Garden* Exhibition, Copenhagen (with Vilhelm Wohlert)
      "Elm House," Elmvej 11, Vedbaek, Denmark (with Vilhelm Wohlert)
      Jensen House, Jacosmindevej 25, Humlebaek, Denmark
      Design of the *Danish Design* Exhibition, Stockholm
      Vime Supermarket, Århus, Denmark
1961 Blaagaard Teachers College and Enghavegaard Elementary School, Sborg, Denmark (with Karen and Ebbe Clemmensen)
      Malmmose House, Ishj, Denmark (with Vilhelm Wohlert)
1962 Andersen House, Rungsted, Denmark (with Vilhlem Wohlert)
      Design of the *Egyptian Art* Exhibition, Louisiana Museum, Humlebaek, Denmark (with Vilhelm Wohlert)
      Piniehj Terrace Houses, Rungsted, Denmark (with Vilhelm Wohlert)
1963 Overgård House, Vedbaek, Denmark (with Vilhelm Wohlert)
      Gyldendal Publishing Company Office/Dispatch Hall, Copenhagen (with Vilhelm Wohlert)
1964 Kirstineparken Terrace Houses, Hørsholm, Denmark
      "Parade of Northern Houses," Norköping, Sweden (with Vilhelm Wohlert)
      Lindevangsgården interiors, Birkerd, Denmark
1965 The Museum of Music History conversion, Copenhagen (with Vilhelm Wohlert)
1965/
67   Works for the Birkerd Municipality, Denmark
1967 Barfred House, Viborg, Denmark
1968 Louisiana Museum extension I, Humlebaek, Denmark (with Vilhelm Wohlert)
      Schitz House, Tibirke, Denmark
1968/
73   Danish Embassy, Brasilia (with Vilhelm Wohlert)
      I.B.M. Headquarters, Lundtofte, Denmark
1969/
75   Arthur K. Watson International Education Centre, for IBM, La Hulpe, Belgium
1973/
76   Carlsberg Foundation and Royal Danish Academy of Science and Letters restoration and interiors, Copenhagen
1971/
78   Ny Carlsberg Glyptotek, Copenhagen (as supervising architect)
1966- Thorvaldsens Museum restoration, Copenhagen (as supervising architect)
1970- Danish Institute in Rome (as supervising architect)
1970/
79   Ancient Barrows of Jelling Landscaping, Denmark
1972- Museum of the Castle of Snderborg interiors, Denmark
1975/
79   Ministry of Cultural Affairs restoration, Åbenrå 26-30, Copenhagen
1976/
79   I.B.M. Office/School Building, Lundtofte, Denmark
1976/
82   National Museum interiors, Copenhagen
1978/
82   Louisiana Museum extensions II, Humlebaek, Denmark (with Vilhelm Wohlert)
1978/
83   City Museum, Bochum, West Germany (with Vilhelm Wohlert)
1981- Office and apartment buildings, Khulafa Street, Baghdad, Iraq
1983 Culture/History Museum, Hamm, West Germany (with Vilhelm Wohlert)

A.K. Watson International Education Centre extensions, IBM company, La Hulpe, Belgium

1984- Danish National Museum mediaeval and antique gallery interiors, Copenhagen

Publications:

On BO: book—*Dansk Arkitektur* by Tobias Faber, Copenhagen 1963, 1976; articles—"The Louisiana Museum" in *Arkitektur* (Copenhagen), 3 and 4, 1959; "Various works by Jørgen Bo" in *Arkitekur* (Copenhagen), no. 5, 1963; "The Museum of Music History" in *Arkitektur* (Copenhagen), no. 1, 1968; "Blaagaard Teachers College and Enghavegaard Elementary School" in *Arkitektur* (Copenhagen), no. 2, 1969; "Extension to the Louisiana Museum" in *Arkitektur* (Copenhagen), no. 6, 1973; "Watson Education Centre, IBM Headquarters-Denmark, and The Danish Embassy in Brasilia" in *Arkitektur* (Copenhagen), no. 3, 1976; "The National Museum," "Castle of Snderborg," and "Thorvaldsens Museum" in *Arkitekten* (Copenhagen), no. 6, 1981; "IBM Office Building, Denmark" in *Arkitekten* (Copenhagen), no. 4, 1982; "Louisiana—extensions, 1971-82" in *Arkitekten* (Copenhagen), no. 7, 1982; "Museum Bochum" in *Arkitekten* (Copenhagen), no. 3, 1984.

To a great extent is has been my fate to deal with buildings placed in surroundings of scenic beauty. Adjusting the buildings to nature has consequently been a general theme in all my works. This applies not only to the choice of materials and their mutual connection with the locality but also to the way the shape of the building is adapted to local climatic conditions and to the proportions, rhythmics, and lines of the landscape. As a result my working method has often been, before the actual projecting has begun, to mark out the buildings on the site in such a way that it is possible to form an estimate of the connection between the interiors and the landscapes immediately outside of them, as well as of the lines of the building in relation to the ground. This thesis is best reflected in the Louisiana Museum which is, in principle, a covered walk through a varied garden where the plan of the building expresses the rise and fall of the ground and where large windows deliberately frame picturesque landscape topics, resulting in an unbroken dialogue between nature and art. However, in the more industrialized buildings, e.g. the buildings for IBM, the correlation with the surrounding landscape has also been of great importance to the projects.

The Danish Embassy in Brasilia has been built on ground falling steeply down towards an artificial sea, and the fall of the ground is the main motive in the general composition. The buildings have been placed on terraces, emphasizing the fall of the ground, and they have been given their special form—the relatively narrow depth of the houses and the very large projecting roofs—from the wish to produce a building milieu pleasant to live in, in this very warm area where rainfall is infrequent but heavy. It is the main principle of the buildings that all rooms should be naturally ventilated and completely protected against the sun. This means that sunblinds, Venetian blinds, and tinted glass can be avoided and that the sliding doors can be open practically twenty-four hours a day, covered only by mosquito curtains. This form of building has proved to be desirable in Brasilia, a city which is otherwise characterized by

completely sealed up and artificially ventilated buildings where the change between the internal and external climate is violent and inconvenient.

An essential part of my production concerns museum buildings or museum arrangements. In this connection, the correlation between the works of art, the building units, and the light plays an important role. The daylight lighting of museums is critical for the experience of the art. It is a very complicated study in which, in my opinion, the point is to find the most natural ways of lighting. These may vary a great deal, depending on the type of work in question: different forms of light-intake will result in different architectural expressions. The buildings are thus characterized either by large sidelights, by lantern constructions, or, as in the museum at Bochum, Germany, by tent-shaped skylight constructions through which an optimum lighting of the rooms is obtained without letting in any actual sunlight.

—Jørgen Bo

As a young architect, Jørgen Bo made himself known through architectural competitions, and early in his career he collaborated with the architect Knud Halberg on the design of a number of residential developments, chiefly one- and two-storey row-houses situated in green spaces, with fine relations between dwellings and communal areas: even today these houses hold their own among the best and most advanced residential developments of the time.

Bo soon manifested his great interest in and sensitivity to Danish scenery and the relationship of house/housing development and town/surrounding area, whether he was dealing with open landscape or existing buildings. This interest found its finest expression in the Louisiana Museum, which he designed with Vilhelm Wohlert. Here, a number of low-rise museum wings are integrated in undulating park grounds, with solitary large trees on a bankside sloping down to the Sound. In the Louisiana Museum, modern open-space architecture, carried out with traditional attention to detail and fine workmanship, is combined with the simplified, textural effect of whitewashed walls around large glazed areas and accentuated roof-bearing timber girders.

Alone or in collaboration with Wohlert, Bo has been in charge of the restoration and conversion of older buildings of high architectural quality: he has created delightful modern settings for new activities, yet always with a deep understanding of the distinctive character of the old buildings. Special mention should be made of the conversion of a former vicarage in central Copenhagen into the Museum of Music History and of the new exhibition rooms in Gottlieb Bindesbll's Thorvaldsen Museum of the 1880's, one of the major works of Danish architecture.

Bo has also designed a series of attractive one-family houses of distinction, and in recent years he has been awarded major commissions outside Denmark—the Danish Embassy in Brasilia, the IBM Education Centre in Brussels, and the art museum in Bochum in collaboration with Vilhelm Wohlert. These are buildings expressive of the very finest qualitites of Bo's talent: a simplified and well-defined functional arrangement within an architectural framework designed in harmony with the characteristics of the site and its environment, further enriched through the choice of materials and their textural treatment.

At an early stage of his career, Bo became a member of the teaching staff of Professor Palle Suenson's department of the School of Architecture of the Royal Danish Academy of Art. In 1960 he was made Professor of Buildings Design. Since then, by virtue of his forceful artistic personality and his profound engagement in the creative side of the architect's work, he has attracted many students and has become an inspiring teacher to future architects.

—Tobias Faber

Jørgen Bo: City Museum, Bochum, West Germany, 1978-83.

BODIANSKY, Vladimir.

French. Born in Kharkov, Russia, 25 March 1894; emigrated to France, 1917: naturalized, 1929. Educated at the Institute of Bridges and Causeways, Moscow, 1911-14, Dip. Ing. 1914; Ecole Nationale Supérieure de l'Aéronautique, Paris, 1919-20, Dip. Ing. 1920. Served as a Cavalry Officer, then as a Pilot-Aviator, Tsarist Army, Russia, 1915-17; Officer, French Foreign Legion, 1918-20. Married Xenia Loukomsky in 1928; children: Vladimir and Michel-Noel. Worked as an engineer for the Highways Department, Moscow, and on the Bokhara-Kabul Railway, Afghanistan, 1914-15; Chief Section Engineer, Great Lakes Railway, and Master-Planner, Town of Albertville, Lake Tanganyika, Congo, 1921-23; Engineer/Designer, Renault Car Company Research Center, Paris, 1923-24, and Caudron Aeroplane Company, Paris, 1924-25; Managing Director, Francois Villiers Aeroplanes, Paris, 1925-30; Director, Bodiansky Aeroplane Company, Paris, 1930-31; in private architectural-engineering practice, collaborating with Eugène Beaudouin and Marcel Lods, Paris, 1931-39; Managing Director, Mopin and Company, Paris, and Leeds, Yorkshire, England, 1933-39; Director, Department of Special Studies, Messier Technical Center, Pau, France, 1940-44; Member, French Town Planning and Housing Mission to the United States, 1945-46; Founder Member, 1946-49, and Director, 1949-66, ATBAT (Atelier des Bâtisseurs), Marseilles. Professor and Studio Master (Atelier Camelot-Bodiansky), Ecole Nationale Supérieure des Beaux-Arts, Paris, 1965-66. Adviser, Monnet Plan, Paris, 1946-47; Technical Consultant, United Nations Building Committee, New York, 1947; Technical Consultant to the town of Sabende, French Guinea, 1959-61; Technical Adviser, French Polar Stations at Adelaide Island, Antarctica and Arctic Greenland, and to High Altitude Stations in the Andes, 1954-59; Technical Adviser, United Nations Missions to Cambodia, 1961-63; Co-Rapporteur, United Nations Urban Development and City Planning Committee, Geneva, 1961-66. European Vice-President, Permanent Commission on Industrialization, CIAM (Congrès Internationaux d'Architecture Moderne), 1949-66; Vice-President, Cercle d'Etudes Architecturales, Paris, 1953-55; President, Interconsult (consulting engineers group), The Hague, 1956-57; Member of the General Council, ICRPD (International Center for the Development of Overseas Territories), Paris, 1962-66. Recipient: Gold medal, Society for the Encouragement of Arts and Industry, France, 1959. Chevalier, Légion d'Honneur. *Died* (in Paris) *10 December 1966.*

Works:

1914/
15 Bokhara-Kabul Railway constructions, Afghanistan

1920/
23 Great Lakes Railway constructions, Congo
Plan for Albertville, Lake Tanganyika, Congo
Furnaces, coal-mines, brickworks, plan for a river highway, etc., Congo

1924 "C.99" Reconnaissance Airplane, for the Caudron Company, Paris

1925/
30 Sea-Plane Prototypes, for the Francois Villiers Company, Paris
Bodiansky Prototype Airplane, Paris

1933 Palais des Expositions, Paris (project; with Eugéne Beaudouin and Marcel Lods)

1934 Cité de la Muette (housing development), Drancy, France (with Eugène Beaudouin and Marcel Lods)

1936 Circular Aircraft Hangar (project; with Marcel Lods)

1937 Quarry Hill Housing Estate, Leeds, Yorkshire, England (with R. A. H. Livett)

1937/
38 Suspended Highways (projects; with Azivessy and Nitzshke)

1939 Maison du Peuple, Clichy, Paris (with Eugène Beaudouin, Marcel Lods and Jean Prouvé)
1941/
42 Schmidt Telescope, and Equatorial Telescope, Pic-du-Midi Observatory, Bagneres, France
1946/
49 Unité d'Habitation (Cité Radieuse), Marseilles (with Le Corbusier)
1947/
49 France-U.S.A. Memorial Hospital, Saint-Lô, France (as technical consultant to Paul Nelson)
1951/
55 Musulman Collective Housing Development, Casablanca (with Georges Candilis and Shadrach Woods)
1952/
54 Master plan for Casablanca (with Georges Candilis and Shadrach Woods)
1954/
59 Plans for polar stations at Adelaide Island, Antarctica, and Greenland
    Igloo building for Paul-Emil Victor Polar Expedition
    High Altitude Observatory Station for Andes Expeditions (project)
1956/
61 Housing development, Bagnols-sur-Cèze, France (with Georges Candilis and Alexis Josic)
1959 Town development plan for Annassers, Algeria (with André Gomis)
1959/
61 Town plan for Sabende, French Guinea (as technical consultant)
    Urban development plans and buildings, French Guinea
    Redevelopment plan for the Dame-Blanche, Paris (with J. de Chalender)
1961/
63 South-Asia Olympic Stadium Complex, Phnom-Penh, Cambodia (with Van Moly Van, Um Samouth, Duchemin, Morin and Kandaouroff)
    Plans for various cities in Cambodia

Publications:

By BODIANSKY: book—*Chart de l'Habitat du Cercle d'Etudes Architecturales*, Paris 1957.

On BODIANSKY: books—*New French Architecture* by Maurice Besset, London and Stuttgart 1967; *Dizionario Enciclopedico di Architettura e di Urbanistica,* edited by Paolo Portoghesi, Rome 1968; *Architecture de la Reconstruction en France 1945-53* by Anatole Kopp, Frédérique Boucher and Danièle Pauly, Paris 1982; article—"The Work of Vladimir Bodiansky" by Marion Tournon Brahly, in *Architectural Design* (London), January 1965.

Vladimir Bodiansky was one of the most interesting, complex, exciting and extraordinary personalities among architects and builders in France from the 1930's to the 1960's. He took part in and influenced, directly or indirectly, a very large number of the most important achievements of this period.

Bodiansky was born in Kharkov in 1894; he received a higher technical education until it was interrupted by the War. As a young officer in the Tsarist Army he was forced to emigrate during the October Revolution. After an eventful journey across Siberia and China he returned to Europe and, like thousands of other white Russians, finally settled in Paris. During the 1920's he entered the Ecole National Supérieure de l'Aéronautique in Paris and became an aircraft builder. Young and enthusiastic, he wanted to revolutionize everything. His aircraft were distinctive in their originality; they announced a new wave before its time. After many difficulties, he abandoned everything and went off to the Belgian Congo to work on the construction of the railway. When he returned to France he worked again in aeronautics, then in the 1930's he turned to building construction as Chief Engineer for "Mopin" pre-fabrication processes. He directed the construction of the very important Quarry Hill Housing Estate in Leeds, England. Meanwhile, he had become acquainted with architecture and architects, in particular the team of Beaudouin and Lods. He had finally found his true vocation.

Bodiansky collaborated, as engineer, with the team of Beaudouin/Lods on several studies and completed works, among which were the project for the Palais des Exposition (Paris) in glass and steel; a project for a circular aircraft hanger; and in 1934, the Cité de la Muette in Drancy, an entirely pre-fabricated housing development—an event of some importance at that time.

During the Second World War Bodiansky met Le Corbusier, and together they assembled a team of architects and engineers, so that they might respond effectively to the problems of post-war reconstruction. Bodiansky was now convinced that the enormous demands of our time needed new skills and a new structuring of the profession of architect. He sought to combine the talents of architects, engineers and builders. This goal led to the birth of the Atelier des Bâtisseurs—ATBAT—which he founded with Le Corbusier, Wogensky, Lefèvre and the entrepreneur Py—builders like the German master builders of the Middle Ages.

As soon as the was was over Bodiansky took part in a study mission to the United States and recognized the enormous technical progress that the war had brought about in that country. Returning to France in 1946, he joined Le Corbusier to devote himself entirely to the first important achievement of ATBAT, the Cité Radieuse in Marseilles. For three years without a break the very happy collaboration continued: if it was Le Corbusier who spiritually conceived the Cité Radieuse, it was Bodiansky who was entirely responsible for its technical realization—a striking example of co-operation between architect and engineer. During this same period he accompanied Le Corbusier to New York to plan the United Nations Building: Bodiansky's participation in the team and his influence were most crucial. But at the end of the 1940's Le Corbusier withdrew from ATBAT. The collaboration of these two strong and extremely different personalities had led to an inevitable conflict.

Bodiansky continued to direct ATBAT's activities, which became more and more varied and important; it went on to produce polar habitat for Paul-Emil Victor; the France-U.S.A. Memorial Hospital at Saint-Lô, with the architect Paul Nelson; Musulman Collective Housing Development in Morocco, with the writer and Shadrach Woods; and many other noteworthy works. Among Bodiansky's personal achievements the Olympic Stadium in Pnom Penh is particularly outstanding.

Bodiansky also took part in all the activities and international conferences in the field of architecture and urbanism. In 1953 at the CIAM Congress in Aix-en-Provence he proposed a Habitat Charter that included ideas and suggestions that are still topical and valid today.

Towards the end of his life he devoted himself mainly to teaching: as Professor at the Ecole Nationale Supérieure des Beaux-Arts, he created the Bodiansky Atelier where he tried to define the necessary qualifications and skills of an architect for our time, a new kind of man who, like himself, combined the spiritual with the material, sensitivity with technical knowledge, the dream with the reality—in short, the synthesis of architect and engineer.

—Georges Candilis

BOFILL Levi, Ricardo.

Spanish. Born in Barcelona, 5 December 1939. Educated at the French Institute of Barcelona, until 1955; Escuela Tecnica Superior de Arquitectura, Barcelona, 1955-56; Architecture University of Geneva, 1957-60. Founded Taller de Arquitectura, Barcelona, 1960 (current staff: Peter Hodgkinson, J. Pierre Carniaux, Patrick Genard, Rogelio Gimenez, Fernando Trueba, José María Rocias, Paul Elliott, Rosaria Iacovino, Xavier Grau and Omar Migliore), and in Paris, 1971 (current staff: Ramón Collado, Thierry Recevski, Patrick Dillon, Hilario Pareja, Eric Ryser and Martín Andujar). Exhibitions: *Biennale*, Venice, 1976, 1980; Centre Georges Pompidou, Paris, 1978; *Setmanes Catalanes a Berlin*, Berlin, 1978; Museum of Modern Art, New York, 1979; Architectural Association, London, 1981; *Projects Francais - La Cité*, École Nationale Supérieure des Beaux-Arts, Paris, 1981; *Presence de l'Histoire*, Chapelle de la Salle Pêtrière, Paris, 1981; *The Presence of the Past*, Fort Mason Center, San Francisco, 1982; *El Jardi del Turia*, Palau de la Lonja, Valencia, 1982; *El Jardi del Turia - Metamorfosi della Citta*, Palazzo Braschi, Rome 1983; *The Folly*, Leo Castelli Gallery, New York, and James Corcoran Gallery, Los Angeles, 1983-84; *Architecture et Industrie*, Centre Georges Pompidou, Paris 1983; *Places d'Europe*, Centre Georges Pompidou, Paris, 1984; *L'Art Espanol*, Galerie Nouvelles Images, The Hague, 1984. Recipient: ADI – FAD Prize, Barcelona, 1964; Fritz Schumacher Prize, University of Hamburg, 1968; International Design Award, American Society of Interior Designers, 1978; First Prize, Balcon sur la ville housing competition, Dreux, France, 1981. Address: Taller de Arquitectura, Avenida de la Industria, 14, Sant Just D'Esvern, Barcelona, Spain; Taller de Arquitectura, 18 rue de l'Université, 75007 Paris, France.

Works:

1960 La Elviria Urban Development, Malaga (project)
1960/
62 Rubiol Apartment Building, Calle J. S. Bach 28, Barcelona
1961 Autorremolques Industrial Building, Tarragona, Spain
1962/
63 Bargallo Apartment Building, Calle Urgel, Barcelona
    Sargazo Holiday Apartments, Castelldefels, Spain
1962/
64 Ventura Apartment Building, Calle Viladomat, Barcelona
    Andreu Apartment Building, Calle Maestro P. Cabrero, Barcelona
1963 La Manzanera Resort Complex Master Plan, Calpe, Spain (project)
1963/
65 Schenkel Apartment Building, Calle Nicaragua 99, Spain
1964/
65 Apartment house, Calle J. S. Bach 4, Barcelona
1964/
72 Barrioa Gaudi Residential Complex, Reus, Spain
1965/
66 La Manzanera Apartment Building, Calpe, Spain
1965/
68 El Castell Apartment Building, Vallpineda, Sitges, Spain
1966 Riomar Hotel, Delta del Ebro, Spain (project)
1966/
67 Chemical factory, Granollers, Spain
    Mas-Pey Swimming Club, San Feliu de Guixols, Spain
    La Manzanera (Xanadu) Apartment House, Calpe, Spain

Ricardo Bofill: Le Viaduc Housing, St. Quentin-en-Yvelines, France, 1974.

1967/
68 La Manzanera Housing, Calpe, Spain
1968/
69 CEEX-1 City in Space, Madrid (project)
1968/
71 La Manzanera Housing II, Calpe, Spain
1968/
73 La Muralla Roja Holiday Apartments, Calpe, Spain
1969 El Caballo de Monte Carlo Multi-Sports Facility, Montecarlo, Concurso, Spain (project)
1969/
71 Urban, rural and residential proposal, Chile (project)
1970/
75 Walden 7 Residential Complex, Sant Just Desvern, Barcelona
1971/
72 Civic Centre, Evry, France (competition project)
1971/
73 La Petite Cathedral Residential Complex, Cergy-Pontoise, France (project)
1972 CEEX-1 City in Space reorganization, Madrid (project)
1972/
73 La Citadelle renovations, Fort St. Cyr, Trappes, St. Quentin en Yvelines, France (project)
1972/
76 Country house, Montras, Calella, Spain
1973 La Maison d'Abraxas Residential Complex, St. Quentin en Yvelines, France (project)
Assis Home for the Aged, Sabadell, Spain (project)
Champs Elysées/La Defénse Urban Study, Paris (project)
Forum Blanch Civic Centre, Paris (project)
1973/
74 Hotel, St. Quentin en Yvelines, France (project)
1973/
76 La Fabrica Cement Factory remodelling (Taller de Arquitectura offices), Sant Just Desvern, Barcelona

1973/
78 Meritxell Religious Centre, Andorra, Spain
1974 La Maison Verte, Abidjan, Ivory Coast, Africa (Project)
1974/
75 Point "M" Civic Centre, Paris (project)
Urban master plan for Carros, Spain (project)
Urban master plan for Cala Ratjada, Palma, Majorca, Spain (project)
1974/
76 Le Parc de la Marca Hispanica Monument, Le-Boulou-Le Perthus, France
1975 Cemetery at Montcada, Spain (competition project)
1975/
76 Le Lac Residential Complex, Trappes, St. Quentin en Yvelines, France
Le Couloubrier Residential Complex, St. Maxime, France (project)
Central Plaza, St. Maxime, France (project)
Harbour at St. Maxime, France (project)
1976 La Petite Cathedrale Residential and Commercial Complex, Meaux, France (project)
Les Illetes Luxury Tourist Complex, Palma, Majorca, Spain (project)
Prefabricated apartments, Guatemala (project)
Concurso Master Plan, Vitoria, Spain (project)
Castro-Urdiales Master Plan, Bilbao, Spain (project)
1977 Residential Complex with park and institutional buildings, Bilbao, Spain (project)
San Juan Despi District Plan, Barcelona (project)
Santa Maria de Gallecs New Town, Barcèlona (project)
1978/
80 Houari Boumedienne agricultural village, Abadla, Algeria
Village F linear city, Abadla, Algeria (project)
City extension, Bechar, Algeria (project)
Housing developments in Mosstagahnem, Oued Rhio, and Reliesam, Algeria (projects)
Housing development, Ain-Nadja, Algeria

(project)
Hall of Residence, Rouiba, Algeria
Administrative Town of Sibi Bel Abbes, Algeria (project)
1978/
83 Le Palais d'Abraxas housing development, Marne la Vallee, near Paris
1979 Ministry of Foreign Affairs building, Riyadh, Saudi Arabia (competition project)
1979/
83 Les Echelles du Baroque housing development, 14th arrondissement, Paris
Le Theatre-L'Arc housing development, Marne la Vallee, near Paris
Antigona Urban Plan and housing development, Montpellier, France
1980 Apartment building complex, Rotterdam (project)
Condominium complex, Houston, Texas (project)
1980/
83 El Anfiteatro housing complex, Calpe, Alicante, Spain
1981 Les Temples du Lac housing development, St. Quentin en Yvelines, France (project)
Le Balcon sur la Ville housing and municipal development, Dreux, France (competition project)
The Green Crescent housing and municipal development, Cergy Pontoise, near Paris (project)
Los Jardines Clasicos del Ensanche urban park, Barcelona (competition project)
Los Jardines de Catalunya parks plan, Barcelona (project)
Los Jardines del Turia parks plan, Valencia (project)
Terrace Housing, France (project)
Les Maisons Temple prefabricated housing, France (project)
1981/
83 Les Rives du Lez riverbank landscaping, Montpellier, France
1982 Bab El Sheikh Zone 6 housing and commercial complex, Baghdad, Iraq (project)
Parc de la Villette, Paris (competition project)

Publications:

By BOFILL: books—*Hacia una formalizacion de la
Ciudad en el Espacio*, Barcelona 1968; *CEEX 1, City
in Space Experience*, Barcelona 1970; *L'Architecture
d'un Homme*, Paris 1978; *El Taller y la Critica*,
Barcelona 1981; *Los Espacios de Abraxas - El Palacio
- El Teatro - El Arco*, Paris 1981; *Projets Francais
1978-81: La Cite - histoire et technologie*, exhibition
catalogue, Paris 1981; *Los Jardines del Turia*,
catalogue, Valencia 1982; *Taller de Arquitectura: city
design, industry and classicism*, Barcelona 1984;
articles—"Panorama historico de la arquitectura
moderna espanola", and "Ante proyecto de ordenacion de un barrio en Reus" in *Zodiac* (Milan) no.
15, 1965; "Xanadu, residence d'Alicante, laboratoire
Granollers" in *L'Architecture d'Aujourd'hui* (Paris),
no. 139, 1968; "La cimenterie" in *L'Architecture
d'Aujourd'hui* (Paris), no. 213, 1981; "Taller de
Arquitectura" in *GA Document* (Tokyo), Winter
1981.

On BOFILL: books—*Architecture 2000* by Charles
Jencks, London 1971; *Taller de Arquitectura* by Jose
Agustin Goytisolo, Barcelona 1977; *Structuralism in
Architecture and Urban Planning* by Arnulf Luchin-
ger, Stuttgart 1980; *GA 19: Taller de Arquitectura*,
edited by Yukio Futagawa, Tokyo 1980; *Late
Modern Architecture and other essays* by Charles
Jencks, London 1980; articles—in *Forum* (Hilver-
sum, Netherlands), June 1968, July/August 1969,
November 1969, May 1971; *Baumeister* (Munich),
June 1968, October 1969; *Nouvel Observateur*
(Paris), October 1974, June/August 1975; *Archi-
tectural Design* (London), July 1968, March 1970,
August 1971; *Bauen und Wohnen* (Zurich), June
1971; *Architektur und Wohnform* (Stuttgart), November 1971; *Architectural Review* (London), Nov-
ember 1973; "Esquisses pour Les Halles" in *L'Oeil*
(Lausanne), March 1975; *Progressive Architecture*
(New York), September 1975; *Technique et Architec-
ture* (Paris), October 1975; "Versailles pour le
peuple" in *Architecture d'Aujourd'hui* (Paris),
November/December 1975, October 1976; *Architecture + Urbanism* (Tokyo), December 1976; "Taller
de Arquitectura" by Anna Bofill in *Wonen - TA/BK*
(Heerlen, Netherlands), April 1979; "Architecture's
new ism" by Charles Jencks in *Sunday Times
Magazine* (London) 10 January 1982; "Ricardo
Bofill - Palace of Abraxas, Theatre and Arch, Marne
la Vallee" by Charles Jencks in *Architectural Design*
(London), February 1982; "Ricardo Bofill, ein Star
der Postmoderne" by Rudolf Schilling in *Tages
Anzeiger Magazin* (Berlin), 24 April 1982; films—
Barrio Gaudi by Hans Magnus Enzesberger, 1971;
Urbanisme et Desarroi by J. Darribehande and J. P.
About, 1971; *Taller de Arquitectura* by Robert
Cordier, 1976.

*

The Taller de Arquitectura is a multi-disciplinary
group involved in proposals and solutions for
physical design problems within a broad spectrum of
environmental issues. The atelier, which I founded in
1962, rapidly developed to include people from
architectural, artistic, literary, musical, philosophical and mathematical fields. These varied backgrounds and experiences provide the diversity of
viewpoints which is essential to the philosophy and
work of the Taller. However, the perception and
meaning of physical form as a container of life lie at
the center of the firm's approach.

Physical form is viewed by the Taller also within its
wider political-cultural context. The failure of the
"modern movement" to evoke or include this wider
context is evident. The continued degradation of the
landscape under the principles of the "modern
movement" demonstrates that "functionalism" is a
necessary but insufficient response to the problem.
Man requires a context for social activities which
cannot be defined solely in terms of use. As Adolf
Loos wrote, "Architecture provokes spiritual reactions in man . . . the mission of architects is to make
these explicit." The use of "zoning" as a method for
analyzing social structures and built form is another
example of this failure to include the political-
cultural context of the physical world. The results are
shallow environments, devoid of the rich fabric of
social interaction and meaning. It leads to an
unnatural division of human activities because of its
concentration on the functional relationship between a few aspects of life. These factors, plus the lack
of personal involvement in decisions concerning
one's surroundings, lead to the well-documented loss
of aesthetic dimension and the lack of interaction
with one's physical world.

The Taller, through its research of these immediate
problems, has developed various alternative solutions aimed at regaining the now-ignored quality
and value of life. A relationship between social reality
and urban and architectural forms has always
existed. Thus the Taller's solutions have been created
intentionally both within the existing milieu and with
the assumption of a change in present conditions.
The Taller has so defined a new position for itself in
its efforts to perceive and bring to reality new
possibilities of physical form. Obviously, creativity,
imagination and logical reasoning are the bases for
the transformation of the environment. However,
the physical designer needs new methods of synthesis
to control the contradictions inherent in the work
and to reach for new forms. The designer also has the
responsibility to provide the mediating framework to
coordinate specialists working towards the improvement of the landscape. Through the achievement of
this synthesis and through the research of the Taller,
several basic concepts, or tenets, have been explored.
These have then been further defined, and given
physical form in the projects themselves.

The first of these is the generation, through a
logical, abstract and recursive process, of a fabric
internal to a building or complex. This is derived
from the organization of space in a traditional
settlement of the Mediterranean. Dwelling units of
varying sizes are arranged in a three-dimensional
grid to form the complementary open spaces at all
levels including streets, squares, promenades, and
forums. This process is exemplified in Barrio Gaudi
in Reus or La Muralla Roja at Calpa, and especially
in City in Space, a generic study for a Mediterranean
town, and in Walden 7 in the suburbs of Barcelona,
which offers clear implications for the fabric in
surrounding areas, which is as yet unstructured.

The Taller also has been involved in research on
architectural objects as signs and symbols. The
church, the castle, and the monument have functioned historically to give orientation and identity to
an urban place. This led the Taller to a re-
examination of these forms in terms of more
contemporary activities. La Petite Cathedrale in
Cergy-Pontoise is an explicit example of this. The
forms and elements of the gothic cathedral provided
the inspiration for a linear development of residential, commercial and other uses intermingled along a
covered street. Another example is La Citadelle and
Abraxas in St. Quentin en Yvelines. In this a military
fortress was re-used by converting it into an
assemblage of dwellings and hotel-complex. It
formed a symbolic linear fabric and created an
imposing environmental feature.

A concern of the firm has always been the
common, public space. Thus the study of the
generation of architectural volumes, which can only
form ultimately enclosed space, naturally led to the
investigation of the negative space created by the
volumes. The goal has been the development of a new
typology of urban tissue based on the ambience of the
Medieval, Renaissance, and Baroque examples of
street, square and open space. This aspect began with
the project for the structuring of the center of the new
Nanterre. The Taller also has been able to take
advantage of exceptional situations to produce
examples such as Vitoria, Castro Nova, and Echevarria, Bilbao, all in the north of Spain. This interest in
shaping open space has also led to projects in
completely rural settings. The concern in these cases
has been the shaping of the environment on a
monumental scale to give significance to place. "El
Pont de Meritxell" is a cultural, religious, and
recreational center in Andorra, which forms a linear
structure linking two sides of the major valley. It is
part path, part bridge and part viaduct to mark the
location of the patron saint of the principality. "Le
Parc de la Marca Hispanica" is a symbolic pyramid
on the French-Spanish border in homage to
Cataluna.

Finally, the Taller has been involved in the
preservation and regeneration of existing urban
fabrics, and improvements to the city center. The
proposal for Les Halles in Paris is basically the return
to an ambience that could have existed originally
when the neighborhood, Le Marais, was built.
Unfortunately, the task was begun after the old
pavilions were already demolished.

The offices for the firm, which were renovated
from an old cement factory, are the most recent
example of this line of work.

—Ricardo Bofill

*

The key to Ricardo Bofill's work is imagination. The
strong, clear image of a central architectural idea
permeates the whole design process. This process is,
in itself, of almost child-like simplicity, based on the
possible permutations of aggregating modular
spaces that together give a built form to the image of
the initial idea. Other conditioning factors—
structural and constructive problems, building regulations, costs—are "subtracted" from the primary
image, so that the form is eroded by these conditions
rather than occurring as a result of them. Imagination and vision are given primacy of place, reviving
the cultural role of architecture in society. That this
revival takes physical rather than literary form
makes Bofill's ideas interesting. He has managed to
get his ideas built, first through family backing, then
later through agile and persuasive political
maneuvering, disarming the opposition through
personal charm, artistic conviction and hard
teamwork.

Bofill is not an academic; he failed to complete his
professional training at both the Barcelona School of
Architecture and at Geneva, and this probably
explains his fresh amateur approach to architecture
and his surprising nonchalance about details and
finishes, sadly reflected in the rather fragile durability and weathering of his buildings—like his low-
cost housing, Barrio Gaudi in Reus, or his apartments in Sitges. As a result of designing from mainly
models and large perspective drawings, the joints of
his buildings and the joining of different materials
are often crude and primitive—like the sanctuary of
Meritxell in Andorra. This indifference to detail
sometimes makes his buildings seem like full-size
models, with abundant redundancies, cardboard
images, as in the red-coloured apartments La
Muralla Roja in Calpe.

Bofill's own explanations of his work should be
treated with care as they are generally tactical and
meant for the gallery. His work has a far more serious

content: the role of architecture as a generator of urban spaces. In this role architecture must be clear and easily understood by the public, and there is no doubt that Bofill's proposals for Les Halles redevelopment in Paris contained all the elements for easy assimilation, with a formal, almost "beaux arts," layout and repetitive facades and galleries with their historical connotations.

These historical connotations are seldom absent in his work and are somewhat disconcerting. The modern movement in architecture has not, up to now, accommodated an eclectic decoration whimsically, albeit intelligently applied, in order to obtain certain theatrical effects upon the urban stage. Bofill's vocabulary is, in this respect, extraordinarily wide, dipping into both history and geography for inspiration—Egypt for Walden 7 and neo-Gothic for his renovation of the cement factory next door. This re-use of historical languages may be part of the modern movement's maturity, or part of "postmodern" architecture, but in Bofill's non-academic hands it appears as a provocatively polemical element.

Bofill's early buildings in the mid-1960's—the apartment houses in Barcelona, a number of private houses, a chemical factory near Granollers—fall clearly into the so-called "School of Barcelona" (neo-realist, brutalist, with strong inspiration in constructive detailing from the Modernisme architects in Barcelona at the turn of the century). The housing at Reus and the apartments at Sitges show the result of his model-making approach to design. Both projects pay for innovations by some very awkward spaces and places but these flaws are easily compensated for by the innate feeling of identity and ingenious play between public and private open areas. Walden 7, his utopian village in the sky, is an impressive tour-de-force, and makes a valid claim that architecture may yet be able to solve the problems of multi-storey dwellings.

His recent work in France in and around Paris, and more recently in Montpellier, shows him to be relying more and more on classical models treated with a monumental mannerism with rather dead-pan sexless detailing. His naif theory of the relationship between the discipline of technology and classicism, obviously meant for the gallery, has – as a side effect – dulled his own imagination. However, his innate knack of clear architectural concepts in the basic organization of his compositions indicates that he is still capable of producing architecture.

—David Mackay

BOFINGER, Helge.

German. Born in Stettin, Pommern (now Szczecin, Poland), 30 March 1940. Educated at the Volksschule and Ratsgymnasium, Goslar, 1947-59; studied architecture, Technische Universitat, Braunschweig, 1960-68, Dip.Ing.Arch. 1968. Married Margret Schreib in 1965. Student-assistant in several architectural studios, Braunschweig, 1962-68; since 1969, founder-partner, with Margret Bofinger, Bofinger und Partner, in Braunschweig (1969-81), Berlin and Wiesbaden. Technical Assistant to Zdenko Strizic, Technische Universitat, Braunschweig, 1968-69; Adjunct Professor, 1979-81, and Professor from 1985, University of Dortmund; Visiting Professor, Istituto Universitario di Architettura, Venice, 1984; Visiting Critic, University of Buenos Aires, 1985; also guest lecturer at the universities in Stuttgart, Hannover and Darmstadt, 1984. Director of Architecture and Monuments, 1972, Principal Member of the Braunschweig Section, 1973, and Federal Chairman from 1975, Bund Deutscher Architekten; Board Member, Society of the Friends of the German Architecture Museum, Frankfurt, 1985. Exhibitions: *Architekturzeichnungen 1479-1979*, Staatliche Museen Preussischer Kulturbesitz, Berlin, 1979, and Cologne, 1980; *Internationale Bauausstellung*, Berlin, 1984; *Bauen für Frankfurt*, Frankfurt, 1984; *Klassizismen und Klassiker*, Karlsruhe, 1985; *Bauen Heute*, German Architecture Museum, Frankfurt, 1985; *New Building in a Historic Context*, toured the United States, Canada, Italy and Israel, 1985-87. Recipient: Deubau Prize, Germany, 1979; First Prize, Wilhelmstrasse International Competition, Berlin, 1981; German Architecture Prize Special Appreciation, 1983. Honorary Professor, University of Buenos Aires, 1985. Addresses: Biebricher Allee 49, 6200 Wiesbaden, West Germany; Knesebeckstrasse 75, 1000 (West) Berlin, Germany.

Works:

1968 University, Bielefeld, Germany (competition project)
    School Centre, Bückeburg, Germany (competition project)
    County Administration Building, Minden, Germany (competition project)
    Shop within a shop, Commercial Centre, Berlin (project)
1969 University Hall, Dusseldorf (competition project)
    Commercial Centre with Parking Garage, Braunschweig, Germany (project)
    Town Hall, Göttingen, Germany (competition project)
    Town Hall, Bonn (competition project)
    Church Centre, Darmstadt-Kranichstein, Germany (competition project)
1969/
  70 New Ostsee Spa Development, Weissenhäuser Strand, Germany
1970 Dörfle Redevelopment Plan, Karlsruhe, Germany (competition project)
    Private Swimming Hall, Goslar, Germany
    School Centre, Cloppenburg, Germany (competition project)
    Vacation Centre with Hotels and Housing, Tettenborn, Harz, Germany (project)
    Office and Bank Building, Hannover (competition project)
    Cultural Centre, Herne, Germany (competition project)
    House in Göttingen, Germany
    School Centre, Unterweissach, Germany (competition project)
    Bank, Heiligenhaus, Germany (competition project)
    Housing (50 units), Braunschweig, Germany (project)
    School Centre, Volkmarode-Braunschweig, Germany (competition project)
    School Centre, Wattenscheid, Germany (competition project)
    Urban Development Plan, Göttingen, Germany (project)
1971 Urban Row-House, Braunschweig, Germany (project)
    School Centre, Schmallenberg, Germany (competition project)
    Urban Development Plan, Waltrop, Germany (project)
    Playground, Essen, Germany (competition project)
    Cemetery, Wiesbaden, Germany (competition project)
    Secondary School, Königslutter, Germany (competition project)
1971/
  74 Housing Development with underground garage, Göttingen, Germany
1972 Hotel and Convention Centre, Goslar, Germany (project)
    Housing Development (200 units), Braunschweig, Germany (project)
    Single-family House, Homburg, Saar, Germany (project)
    Single-family House, Braunschweig, Germany (project)
    Fairground layout, Munich (competition project)
    High-rise Housing Block, Salzgitter, Germany (project)
    Hotel and Housing Development, Goslar, Germany (project)
1972/
  74 Department Store, Braunschweig, Germany
    Underground Parking Garage, Braunschweig, Germany
    Public Tunnel Passage, Braunschweig, Germany
1973 Cafe Kröpke, Hannover (competition project)
    School Centre, Hankensbüttel, Germany (competition project)
    School Centre, Bad Zwischenahn, Germany (competition project)
    School Centre, Vecta, Germany (competition project)
    School Centre, Peine, Germany (competition project)
1973/
  74 Castle Park and Reading Pavilion, Braunschweig, Germany
1974 Office Building, Braunschweig, Germany (project)
    Parliament Building, Dusseldorf (competition project)
    Hospital, Reinickendorf, Berlin (competition project)
1975 Parking Garage, Braunschweig, Germany (project)
    Museum of Modern Art, Dusseldorf (competition project)
    School Centre, Berlin (competition project)
    School Centre, Bovenden, Germany (competition project)
    Commercial Centre and Urban Development, Braunschweig, Germany (competition project)
1976 Airport Administration Building, Munich (competition project)
    Office Building, Berlin (competition project)
    Department Store and Urban Development, Lübeck, Germany (competition project)
    County Administration Building, Osnabrück, Germany (project)
    Storage Building, Essen, Germany (project)
    Mechanised Warehouse, Essen, Germany (project)
1976/
  77 Ledenhof Piazza, over an underground garage, Osnabrück, Germany
1977 Domshof Piazza, Bremen, Germany (competition project)
    Housing and Commercial Development, Berlin (competition project)
    Spandau Market Place, Berlin (competition project)
1978 Housing and Commercial Development, Braunschweig, Germany (project)
    Hotel and Piazza, Berlin (competition project)
    Church Centre, Göttingen, Germany (competition project)
    Housing and Commercial Centre, Göttingen, Germany (project)
1978/
  79 Secondary School, Friedland, Germany
1979/
  82 Villa S., Kronberg, Germany
1979/
  84 German Cinema Museum, Frankfurt-am-Main
1980 Market Place, Ippenbüren, Germany (project)
    Colonia Insurance Company Headquarters, Cologne (competition project)
1981 Wilhelmstrasse Development, Berlin (IBA competition project)
1982 Postal Museum, Frankfurt-am-Main (competition project)

Helge Bofinger: House S., Kronberg, West Germany, 1979-82.

Vocational Training College, Kriftel, Germany (competition project)
1983 Music High School, Frankfurt-am-Main (competition project)
Federal Reserve Bank, Darmstadt, Germany (competition project)
Museum of Modern Art, Frankfurt-am-Main (competition project)
House H., Munich
Industrial Refuse System, Frankfurt-am-Main (competition project)
1984 Market Place, Osnabrück, Germany (competition project)
Dr. K. House, Zweibrücken, Germany
High-rise Tower with Fair Halls, Frankfurt-am-Main (competition project)
1985 Museum of Modern Art, Bonn (competition project)
School extensions, Frankfurt-am-Main
Block 19 Housing and Commercial Development (IBA), Berlin

Publications:

By BOFINGER: books—*Architektur in Deutschland*, with Margret Bofinger, Heinrich Klotz and Jurgen Paul, Stuttgart and Berlin 1979; *Junge Architekten in Europa*, with Margret Bofinger, Stuttgart and Berlin 1983; articles—"Architektur: Zwischen Tradition und Lebensangst", in *Das Kunstwerk* (Baden-Baden, Germany) no. 3/4, 1983; "Prefabricated Classicism", with others, in *Baumeister* (Munich) November 1983; "Joven arquitectura en Alemania, Analisi Teorico", in *On* (Barcelona) no. 5, 1984; "Die Kunst der Symmetrie", in *Daidalos* (Berlin) March 1985; "Helge Bofinger: European Aspects", in *Architecture + Urbanism* (Tokyo) no. 4, 1985.

On BOFINGER: books—*Deutsche Kunst seit 1960: Architektur* by Paolo Nestler and Peter M. Bode, Munich 1976; *Architektenzeichnungen 1479-1979*, Berlin 1979; *Die vergeudete Moderne* by Frank Werner, Stuttgart 1981; *Jahrbuch für Architektur 1983*, Braunschweig 1983; *E + P: Entwurfe und Planung* by Hermann Wachberger, Munich 1983; *Jahrbuch für Architektur 1984*, Braunschweig 1984; *Facades des Maisons Individuelles, 1945-1985*, compiled by Jean Pierre Dumont, Lausanne 1984; articles—"Projekte: Bofinger und Partner", in *Baumeister* (Munich) January 1971; "Three examples of housing", in *Bauwelt* (Berlin) 4 April 1975; "The Schlosspark and its pavilion in Braunschweig", in *Bauwelt* (Berlin) 16 July 1976; "From the geometry of the environs: Ledenhof in Osnabruck", in *Bauwelt* (Berlin) 15 December 1978; "Industrializzazzione dell'Edilizia e Prefabbricazione", in *Industria Italiana del Cemento* (Rome) no. 7/8, 1979; "Il Padiglione di Lettura nel Parco del Castello di Braunschweig", in *Industria Italiana del Cemento* (Rome) no. 10, 1979; "An urban space designed for a variety of uses", in *Domus* (Milan) October 1979; "Was ist, wohin geht's Architektur in Deutschland" by Manfred Sack in *Die Zeit* (Hamburg) no. 22/25, 1979; "Extension to a secondary school near Gottingen", in *Baumeister* (Munich) January 1980; "Haus S., Kronberg", in *Architektur und Wohnen* (Hamburg) no. 3, 1982; "IBA—Wettbewerb Wilhelmstrasse", in *Bauwelt* (Berlin) no. 3, 1982; "Berlin renewal", in *Domus* (Milan) April 1982; "Houses with a square plan", in *Bauwelt* (Berlin) 11 February 1983; "A new House of Glass", in *Domus* (Milan) no. 643, 1983; "A Residential Complex in Gottingen", in *Industria Italiana del Cemento* (Rome) no. 5, 1983; "Man sollte sich daran freuen durfen", in *Deutsche Bauzeitung* (Stuttgart) no. 7, 1983; "Architecture in Progress: IBA", in *Architectural Design* (London) no. 1/2, 1983; "Museums-Konzeptionen, Deutsches Filmmuseum", in *Werk, Bauen und Wohnen* (Zurich) no. 12, 1984; "Francoforte, La Riva dei Musei", in *Abitare* (Milan) nos. 6 and 8, 1984; "Helge Bofinger: Works", in *Architecture + Urbanism* (Tokyo) no. 7, 1984; "Maison entre pleins et déliés", in *Techniques et Architecture* (Paris) June/July 1984; "Musees dans la Ville: Musee Allemand du Cinema, Frankfurt", in *Techniques et Architecture* (Paris) no. 359, 1985; "German Cinema Museum", in *Architecture + Urbanism* (Tokyo) no. 2, 1985.

Following the experience of modernity with the dissolving of classical architectonic space (Mies and Le Corbusier) it has become impossible to build a symmetrically defined space without simultaneously canceling it again. Its irritation is almost a fundamental condition of the contemporary experience of space and the application of architectural order, because the relativity of time and space and the presence and availability of all history and all cultures is rooted so firmly in our consciousness that we find ourselves unable to tolerate architectural order other than in modified form.

The enlightening effect of this modified sense of space makes its impossible to recreate classical spatial order. It is the simultaneous overlapping of different architectural orders and spatial principles which constitutes the difference between the continuing modern movement and historical architecture that has recently become so popular once again.

It is the integration into another, abstract space enclosing the factual realm of architectural order—along with the light that defines it and the prospects that open up—which not only expands the dimensions of infinite space but also transforms it into an architectural volume as part of an enveloping space. Spatial penetrations have always been signs of a higher order. Whereas the baroque dome had to rely on the art of painting for creating the illusion of opening up into infinity, our modern technology of large glazed roofs enables us to introduce the reality of this celestial dome to our architectural space and to obliterate the boundary between inside and outside. We can use glass and mirrors to completely dissolve space into light and to disrupt the reality of its perspectively visible delimitations.

The irritation of our experience of space cancels out the so clearly defined classical principles of order, the symmetrical plan, and restores the freedom of appropriating space, the chance to imbue architecture with imagination and feeling—as the precondition for an open use of space.

The poetry of space derives from the suspension of its boundaries and of the defined architectural order, which is still and simultaneously the only way in which we can perceive it.

It is the feeling which is generated in the intermediate realm of these mutually exclusive principles in the human imagination, the ability to integrate such divergencies in our own complexity, that constitutes freedom. And that is what architectural order is supposed to ensure.

Yet it is more than a question of open doors and transparent façades. It is, in fact, a question of our imagination's choice of alternatives, for our thoughts are collages of memories.

—Helge Bofinger

With the energy crisis and the consequent deceleration in building, a generation of architects began to grow which, unpressured by the mechanistic vortex of postwar reconstruction needs, is discovering a taste for theoretical speculation, and allowing itself time and space for its "verification."

The term "designer architecture" serves to characterize a certain type of production which is basically more contemplative than practical. It is a preliminary attempt to repossess architecture as a global gestural act. The second step is the rediscovery of an enormous range of construction materials, from elegant metals such as bronze and stainless steel to the beauty of delicately coloured marbles. The most advanced construction techniques are wedded to traditional craft methods. Utopian projects of a better world are developed—utopias which Helge Bofinger opposes to dreams of an old and lost world.

It is a mode of thought riddled with ambiguity inasmuch as, in the context of the new culture, a concern for models of the past certainly exists while the capacity to assimilate them is overvalued. Less evident is the time factor; the cultural stance of modern man is so distant from that of preindustrial society that abstraction becomes inevitable. As Heinrich Klotz has warned: "Although the young generation of architects appears to be particularly rich in ideas, there is nevertheless the threat that a new unitarian style is being instituted that could begin to dominate and to impede inventive momentum, even before the new gestalt exists."

Bofinger certainly belongs to that generation of young architects sensitive to the new changes. His graphic research is careful, and already indicates a choice of materials in which can be seen a predilection for marble, the play of light filtering through generous fenestration into the depths of buildings, the extolling of each successive floor and for the brilliance of the materials. From the classical world comes the clarity and organization of his design. The plan of the villa at Kronberg, perfectly square, is divided into two equal but distinct sections linked together by the "public" space of the central fenestrated corridor. Every innovation has an air of the classical, as in the entrance hall, and the search for formal symmetry. The tempietto, conceived in the manner of Schinkel, is related to the morphology of the new generation of Rationalists from Botta to Isozaki, who prefer to display clearly the configuration of geometric proportions in which they use highly controlled openings to convey light to the interior. The Secondary School at Friedland offers another example. The didactic model of the Basarstrasse or Lernstrasse, followed in the 1970s as the standard vehicle of an acquisitive social/liberal conscience, is here abandoned. The whole plan converges radially upon a forum in the shape of a sloping amphitheatre with podia for spectators, while the entire corridor, with classrooms along the circle's outer face opening onto it, becomes the gallery of the theatre. The light flooding in from the large skylight accentuates the building's "public" forum-like character.

It is true that in Germany theoretical speculation in architecture has encountered resistance, perhaps because right here the momentum of the architectural avantgarde was violently broken by the advent of Nazism, and was thus left with a traumatic mark which has not yet been assimilated. Attentive to the inheritance of Miesian teaching and to archetypes from the fertile ground of the Bauhaus, German culture has refined construction techniques to cope with the immense effort of reconstruction.

The triumph of Richard Meier in the Frankfurt Craft Museum competition signalled a turning point. Some exhibitors, from Kleihues to Ungers, have quickly shown their openness to this compelling new language. Although most young architects still lack an objective international experience, the Europe of Natalini, Krier and Botta, Portzampar, and Bofinger is evolving rapidly. After an apprenticeship amidst utopian projections and the maturing of graphic means, it is now ready to translate speculation into concrete testimony.

—Giuliano Chelazzi

BOHIGAS Guardiola, Oriol.

Spanish. Born in Barcelona, 20 December 1925. Éducated at the Escuela Tecnica Superior de Arquitectura, Barcelona, 1943-51, Dip. Arch. 1951, Dr. Arch. 1963; studied town planning at the Instituto de Estudios de la Administracion Local, Barcelona, 1961. Served in the Spanish Army, Campamento de la Granja, Segovia, 1946-47. Married Isabel Arnau in 1957; children: Gloria, Maria, Eulalia, Pere, and Josep. In partnership with Josep Martorell, q.v., Barcelona, since 1951, and with Martorell and David Mackay, q.v., Barcelona, since 1962. Director, Spanish Technical Office of Jespersen Prefabricated Systems, Barcelona, since 1972; Director of Planning, City Council, Barcelona, 1980-84; Advisor on Urban Affairs, Barcelona, 1984. Senior Lecturer, 1964-66, Professor of Architectural Composition, 1971-80, and Director, 1977-80, Escuela Tecnica Superior de Arquitectura, Barcelona. Visiting Professor, Universidad Autonoma, Mexico City, and the College of Architecture, La Plata, Cordoba, and Rosario, Mexico, 1974, Ball State University, Muncie, Indiana, 1976, and Universidad de los Andes, Bogota, Colombia, 1982. Head of the Historical Archive, Colegio de Arquitectos de Cataluña, Barcelona, 1969; Member of the Editorial Board, Arquitecturas Bis, Barcelona, 1974; Editor, Lotus, Milan, 1975. Founder-Member, Grupo R, Barcelona, 1951. Associate Director, International Committee of Architectural Critics, 1977; President, Fundacio Miro, Barcelona, 1980. Recipient: Biennial Prize, 1968, and Puig i Cadafalch Prize, 1970, Colegio de Arquitectos de Cataluña, Barcelona. Corresponding Member, Colegio de Arquitectos de Venezuela, 1976; Member, Accademia Nazionale di San Luca, Rome, 1981. Address: Martorell-Bohigas-Mackay, Camp 61, Barcelona 6, Spain.

Publications:

By BOHIGAS: books—Un Segle de Vida Catalana, with others, Barcelona 1960; Tres Ensayos Polemicos sobre la Pintura de Todo, with others, edited by Joaquín Horta, Barcelona 1961; Llibre de l'Any 1962, with others, Barcelona 1962; Tres Ensays sobre de A. Cardona Torrandell, with others, Barcelona 1963; Barcelona entre el Pla Cerda y el Barraquisme, Barcelona 1963; Llibre de l'Any 1963, with others, Barcelona 1964; Plan Especial de Ordenacion de la Zona Sudoeste de Montjuich, with others, Barcelona 1967; Architectura Modernista, Barcelona 1968, Turin 1969; Les Escoles Tecniques Superiors y la Estructura Profesional, Barcelona 1968; Contra una Arquitectura Adjetivada, Barcelona 1969; La Arquitectura Española de la Segunda Republica, Barcelona 1970; Polemica d'Arquitectura Catalana, Barcelona 1970; Proceso y Erotica del Diseño, Barcelona 1972; Reseña y Catalogo de la Arquitectura Modernista, Barcelona 1972; The Anti-Rationalists, with others, edited by Nikolaus Pevsner and J.M. Richards, London 1973; Once Arquitectos, Barcelona 1976; Cataluñya: Arquitectura y Urbanisme durant la Republica, Barcelona and Bari, Italy 1978; Reconstruccio de Barcelona, Barcelona 1984.

See MARTORELL, BOHIGAS, MACKAY

BÖHM, Dominikus.

German. Born in Jettingen, 23 October 1880. Educated at the Technische Hochschule, Stuttgart, under Theodor Fischer. Served in the German Army, 1918. Married Maria Schreiber; children: Anton, Paul, and the architect Gottfried Böhm, q.v. In private practice, Cologne, 1903-52; in partnership with his son Gottfried, in Cologne, 1952 until his death in 1955. Professor, Kunstgewerbeschule, Offenbach, Germany, 1914-26, and Kölner Werkschule, Cologne, 1926-35 and 1945-50. Recipient: First Prize, International Cathedral Competition, San Salvador, 1953. Commander, Order of St. Sylvester, Vatican, 1953. Died (in Cologne) 3 August 1955.

Works:

1903 Kindergarten, Jettingen, Germany
　　　Herzog Guest House, Jettingen, Germany
1904 Garden Building for Karl Böhm House, Maximilianstraase, Bad Reichenhall, Germany
1908 Design of the Deutscher Künstlerbund Exhibition, Darmstadt
1909 Catholic church, Ürdingen, near Krefeld, Germany (project)
　　　Catholic church, Memmingen, Germany (project)
1910 Gymnasium, Wettenhausen, Germany
1911 House, Kurfürstenstrasse, Bingen am Rhein, Germany
　　　Church, Wriezen, Brandenburg, Germany (project)
1912 Walter Villa, Offingen, Germany
1913 Zimmer House, Blumenstrasse, Offenbach am Main, Germany
　　　Mayer House, Taunusring, Offenbach am Main, Germany
　　　Tomb for Clemens Böhm, Jettingen Cemetery, Germany
1914 St. Magdalena Catholic Parish Church, Nymphenburg, Munich (2 projects)
　　　St. Josef's Catholic Church, Offenbach, Germany (project)
　　　Seashore Hospital for the South Seas (project)
　　　Government Building, Cameroons (project)
　　　House, German South-East Africa (project)
　　　Catholic Church of the Heavenly Glory (project)
1915 Catholic church renovation, Offenbach am Main, Germany (project)

House renovation and Chapel, for Baroness Gumppenberg, Bad Reichenhall, Germany
1918 Catholic Garrison and Sister-Church, Parish of St. John the Baptist, Neu-Ulm, Germany (project)

St. Elisabeth's Catholic Parish Church, Donau, Ulm, Germany (project)

War Memorial, Pfauen Island, Lake Havelsee, Germany (project)

Hotel, Luisenbad, Bad Reichenhall, Germany
1919 Harbour-Site Monastery and Church (project)

St. Josef's Catholic Church, Offenbach am Main, Germany (project)
1920 Temporary Church of St. Josef, Offenbach am Main, Germany (demolished, 1947)

Catholic Chapel alterations, Heisterbacher-rott, Germany
1922 Catholic Church, Rhineland (project)

Tomb for Leonhard Thoma, Jettingen, Germany

Hotel rebuilding, Maria Laach, Germany
1923 Church of the Light of Christ (2 projects)

War Memorial Church, Göttingen, Germany (project)
1924 Munsterplatz Development, Ulm, Germany (project)

St. Josef's Catholic Church, Offenbach am Main, Germany (2nd project)
1925 Church with the Parabolic Vault (2 projects)

Monastery by the Sea (project)

St. Boniface Catholic Church, Frankfurt-Sachsenhausen am Main, Germany (project)

St. Josef's Catholic Church, Offenbach am Main, Germany (3rd project)
1926 Catholic Church of Christ the King, Bischofsheim, Mainz, Germany

St. Petrus Canisius Catholic Church, Offenbach am Main, Germany (project)

St. Martin's Catholic Church, Nuremberg, Germany (project)
1927 St. John the Baptist Catholic Parish Church and War Memorial, Neu-Ulm, Germany

Church enlargement, Grosswelzheim am Main, Germany

Catholic Church, Wiesdorf, near Leverkusen, Germany (project)

Church of the Three Kings, Bickendorf, Cologne (competition project)
1928 Catholic village church, Frielingsdorf, Germany

Catholic Church of Christ the King, Kuppersteg, Leverkusen, Germany

Mumbauer House, Bad Kreuznach, Germany

Catholic Chapel of the Immaculate Conception, *Presse Exhibition*, Cologne
1929 Catholic village church rebuilding, Freihalden, Germany

Hospital extension, Lindlar, Germany

St. Kamillusplatz Development, Hindenburg in Oberschlesien, Germany (2 projects)

Technical School, Hindenburg in Oberschlesien, Germany

Workers' Welfare Centre and Church and Monastery of St. Kamillus, Hindenburg in Oberschlesien, Germany

Kamillianer College, Berlin (project)

Cenotaph, Annaberg, in Oberschlesien, Germany (project)

Catholic village church, near Pfaffenhofen, Germany (project)
1930 Kolping Works General Secretariat, Kolpingplatz, Cologne

Catholic Church, Gleiwitz in Oberschlesien, Germany (project)

Catholic village church extensions, Birken bei Wissen/Sieg, Germany

St. Elisabeth's Church Facade and Porchway, Hagen, Germany
1931 St. Kamillus Monastery, Church and Asthma Clinic, Monchen-Gladbach, Germany

Seminary, Limburg an der Lahn, Germany

St. Josef's Catholic Church, Hindenburg in Oberschlesien, Germany

Zanders Paper Factory, Bergisch-Gladbach, Germany

Catholic Church, Norderney, Germany

St. Wolfgang Catholic Parish Church, Kumpfmuhl, Regensburg, Germany (project)

Catholic Church, Geilenkirchen, Germany
1932 Caritas Institute Hospital Church of St. Elisabeth, Hohenlinde, Cologne

St. Engelbert Catholic Parish Church, Riehl, Cologne

Church, Marienberg im Westerwald, Germany

Dominikus Böhm House, Marienburg, Cologne
1933 Catholic Parish Church of the Holy Cross, Osnabruck-Schinkel, Germany

Art Gallery, Old Botanical Gardens, Munich (3 projects)

St. Francis Catholic Parish Church, Rheydt-Geneicken, Germany
1934 Country Youth House, Voiswinkel, near Bergisch-Gladbach, Germany

Spahn Building, Kaiser-Wilhelm-Ring, Cologne (project)

Savings Bank, Meppen an der Ems, Germany (project)

Dr. Scheiber Memorial, Vocklamarkt, Germany

Franciscan Church and Monastery, Garnstock, near Eupen, Belgium

Village church, Lohne in Niedersachsen, Germany (project)

Catholic village church, Hallgarten in der Rheinpfalz, Germany (project)
1935 City Hall, Augsburg, Germany (project)

Central Garage, Cologne (project)

Catholic Church, Marienburg, Cologne (2 projects)

St. Marien Catholic Church, Nordhorn-Frenswegen, Germany
1936 St. Engelbert Catholic Parish Church, Essen, Germany

Catholic Parish Church of the Heart of Jesus, Neustadt, Germany

Village church, Ringenberg, near Wesel, Germany

St. Wolfgang's Catholic Parish Church, Regensburg-Kumpfmuhl, Germany (project)

Elementary school, Borger, near Meppen, Germany

Catholic Church, Duisburg, Germany (project)
1937 St. Josef's Catholic Parish Church, Lingen-Laxten, Germany

Catholic Church of the Holy Cross, Bocholt, Westphalia, Germany

Baptismal Chapel for the Catholic Church of St. Marien, Mulheim/Ruhr, Germany

Temporary church, Marl, near Recklinghausen, Germany (project)

Catholic Church, Werne an der Lippe, Germany (project)

Catholic Church, Velbert, Rheinland, Germany (project)

Heimat Church, Timbu, Brazil (project)

Catholic Church, Neustadt, Dresden (project)
1938 Hospital Chapel, Haselunne, Westphalia, Germany

Dr. Schilgen House, Münster, Germany

New church facade for St. Josef's Benedictine Abbey, Gerleve, Westphalia, Germany

Catholic Church, Gelsenkirchen-Buer, Germany (project)

Elementary school, Stadtchen an der Ems, Germany (project)

Elementary school, Papenburg an der Ems, Germany (project)

Catholic Church, Haltern, Westphalia, Germany (project)

Hugo Schmolz Tomb, Cologne

Catholic Church, Neuss-Reuschenberg, Germany (project)

1939 Catholic Church of the Holy Cross, Dulmen, Westphalia, Germany

Chapel extensions, Kunstrop, Westphalia, Germany (project)

Catholic Church, Hamborn, Westphalia, Germany (project)

Student House, Cologne (project)
1940 St. Wolfgang's Catholic Parish Church, Kumpfmuhl, Regensburg, Germany

Dominikus Böhm House, Jettingen in Schwaben, Germany
1941 Cinema, Weiden in der Oberpfalz, Germany (project)

Sawmill, Ottmarshausen, near Augsburg, Germany
1942 Temporary Church of the Heart of Jesus, Deuten, Germany

Community Centre and School, Jettingen in Schwaben, Germany (project)

St. Agritius Catholic Church, Trier, Germany (project)
1943 Roadside Chapel, Birken, near Wissen/Seig. Germany (project)
1944 Catholic Church, Neuburg an de Kammel, Germany (project)
1945 New buildings for the Church of the Holy Cross, Trier, Germany (project)
1946 St. Albert's Catholic Church, Saarbrucken, West Germany

St. Peter's Provost Church rebuilding, Recklinghausen, West Germany (project)

St. George's Catholic Parish Church reconstruction, Vreden, Westphalia, West Germany (project)

Asbach-Uralt Management Building, Rudesheim/Rhein, West Germany (project)
1947 Mortuary Chapel, Burtenbach, near Jettingen, West Germany (project)

Catholic Parish Church, Linz am Rhein, West Germany (project)
1949 Laurenz Brothers Textile Mills extensions, Ochtrup, Westphalia, West Germany

Sacristy, arcades, memorial and funeral chapels, Church at Kemnat in Schwaben, West Germany

St. Karl Borromaus Catholic Church, Münster, West Germany (project)

St. Matthias Catholic Church reconstruction, Bayenthal, Cologne
1950 St. Josef's Catholic Parish Church reconstuction, Duisburg, West Germany

St. Wendelin Catholic Parish Church, Dirmingen an der Saar, West Germany

Mortuary Chapel, Oberwaldbach in Schwaben, West Germany
1951 St. Moritz Catholic Parish Church reconstruction, Augsburg, West Germany

St. Martin's Catholic Parish Church extensions and new Parish House, Cochem an der Mosel, West Germany.

Catholic Parish Church reconstruction, Geilenkirchen-Hunshofen, near Aachen, West Germany

Catholic Parish Church reconstruction, Geldern, West Germany (project)

Catholic Church and Parish Plan, Bruhl, Rheinland, West Germany (project)

Catholic Church, Emsdetten, Westphalia, West Germany (project)

Catholic Church, The Hague, Netherlands (project)

Wallraf-Richartz-Museum, Cologne (project)
1952 St. Anthony's Catholic Parish Church reconstruction, Münster, West Germany

St. Josef's Catholic Parish Church reconstruction, Kalk, Cologne
1953 St. Marien Catholic Parish Church, Ochtrup, Westphalia, West Germany

Corona del Mar Cathedral, San Salvador (competition project)
1954 St. Elisabeth's Catholic Parish Church, Koblenz, West Germany

Catholic Church extensions, Puttlingen an der

Saar, West Germany
Maria-Königin Catholic Church, Marienburg, Cologne
Catholic Church, Getulio, Brazil
1955 St. Veit's Catholic Parish Church, Mayen in der Eifel, West Germany
Catholic Parish Church of the Holy Ghost, Emst, Hagen, West Germany
Catholic Church, Hilgen-Burscheid, West Germany
1956 St. Josef's Catholic Parish Church, Rodenkirchen, Cologne
Catholic Church extensions, Hohenberg, Cologne
St. Anna's Catholic Parish Church reconstruction, Ehrenfeld, Cologne
1957 Catholic Church of the Heart of Jesus, Oberhausen, West Germany (project)
1958 St. Paul's Catholic Parish Church, Beuel/Rhein, West Germany

Publications:

On BÖHM: books—*Dominikus Böhm* by August Hoff, Berlin 1930; *Dominikus Böhm* by August Hoff and J. Habbel, Regensburg, Germany 1943; *Dominikus Böhm: Leben und Werk* by August Hoff, Herbert Muck and Raimund Thoma, Munich and Zürich 1962; *Studien zu Dominikus Böhm* by Gesine Stalling, Bern and Frankfurt 1974; articles— "Dominikus Böhm und sein Werk" by Rudolf Schwarz in *Moderne Bauformen* (Stuttgart), vol. 26, 1927; "Dominikus Böhms eigenes Wohnhaus" in *Moderne Bauformen* (Stuttgart), December 1934; "St. Joseph's Church, Hindenburg, Germany" in *Architectural Forum* (New York), August 1935; "Dominikus Böhm" in *Moderne Bauformen* (Stuttgart), August 1940; "Kirchenbau und planung von Dominikus and Gottfried Böhm" by August Hoff in *Bauen und Wohnen* (Zürich), December 1949; "Dominikus Böhm" by Rudolf Schwarz in *Baukunst und Werkform* (Nuremberg), February 1955; "Brief Biographies of German and Swiss Architects Distinguished for Church Design" in *Bauen und Wohnen* (Zürich), November 1958; "Documents of 20th Century Architecture: Priests' Seminary of the Diocese of Limburg" in *Architekt* (Stuttgart), April 1978; "Dominikus Bohm (1880-1955)" in *Bauwelt* (Berlin), 7 November 1980.

Dominikus Böhm's architecture is virtually confined to churches and ecclesiastical buildings, all of them Roman Catholic. And these may seem semi-traditional in comparison with the daringly innovative structural use of reinforced concrete by his contemporary Auguste Perret in the Church of Notre-Dame at Le Raincy, now acknowledged to be an exemplary masterpiece of twentieth-century architecture. But Böhm's originality lay in his emotional approach, which inspired his bold Expressionist churches of the 1920's. His War Memorial Church of 1927 at Neu-Ulm is a free fantasia on Gothic themes with little feeling of structural reality; it produces a psychological atmosphere similar to that of the strange stylized sets of German silent films of that period. His audacious Church of Christ the King at Mainz-Bischofsheim of 1926 is an early example of the use of paraboloid forms, with the concrete barrel vault of the nave intersected by lower cross-vaults over the bays of the aisles, creating a strong Expressionist-Gothic emotional effect.

Like his contemporary Rudolf Schwarz, Böhm was a pioneer of the one-room, open-plan church interior, in which a significant development was the circular plan. This is strikingly seen in what is usually considered to be the finest of Böhm's earlier churches, St. Engelbert at Cologne-Riehl (1931-32). This circular church is also notable for its very ingenious roof, which is not the expected dome but eight paraboloid vaults, with small circular windows near the apex of each, so that the interior is rather

dark, helping to produce a sense of religious mystery. Others of his churches are experiments in simple rectangular forms. Böhm was in fact fulfilling that fundamental axiom of modern architecture, "form follows function," for one of the purposes of these open-plan churches was to bring the congregation into more active participation in the Mass in accordance with the Liturgical Revival. Architecturally this meant bringing priest and congregation physically closer together around the focal point of the altar. Böhm's church at Ringenberg (1936) was the first modern church in which the altar was placed so that the congregation was on three sides; he used an altar at the centre of the crossing, with the congregation occupying the nave and transepts.

Böhm was not very active during the Nazi period, but after the war, when there was a great resurgence of new church building to replace those destroyed in the bombing, Böhm resumed his career. In his postwar churches he aimed at an even great simplicity of structure, while achieving a spiritual atmosphere in other ways, such as decorative enrichment. A notable example is the Maria Königin Church in Cologne-Marienburg of 1954. The whole south wall of the church is a great curtain wall of stained glass. Its intricate pattern is a stylized leaf design in a limited palette of semi-transparent silver-grey and grey-green, harmonizing with the leaves of the trees in the park outside, with only some fragments of antique glass making accent points which blaze out in full colour: the whole wall of moving light gives a shifting veil-like effect in striking contrast to the severity of the rest of the squarish church with its slender metal supports.

Along with Rudolf Schwarz, Dominikus Böhm is generally acknowledged to be the most original of modern German ecclesiastical architects, a tradition that has been carried on by his son Gottfried. Although Dominikus Böhm was an innovatory and modern architect, his work always arose from his own deep spirituality: "Only what comes from the heart can find the way to the heart."

—Konstantin Bazarov

BÖHM, Gottfried.

German. Born in Offenbach am Main, 23 January 1920; son of the architect Dominikus Böhm, *q.v.* Educated at the Aposteln-Gymnasium, Cologne, graduated 1939; Technische Hochschule, Munich, 1942-46, B.Eng. 1946; Academy of Sculptural Art, Munich, 1947. Served in the German Army, 1938-42. Married Elisabeth Haggenmüller in 1948; children: Stefan, Markus, Peter, and Paul. Worked as an assistant architect in his father's office, Cologne, 1947-50; assistant to the architect Rudolph Schwarz, Cologne, 1950; assistant architect in the office of C. Baumann, New York, 1951; practised with his father, in Cologne, 1952 until his death in 1955. Since 1955, private practice, Cologne. Professor of Architecture, Institute of Technology, Aachen, West Germany, since 1963. Exhibitions: *5 Architekten zeichen für Berlin*, Internationale Design Zentrum, Berlin, 1979; *Transformations in Modern Architecture*, Museum of Modern Art, New York, 1979; *Internationale Bauausstellung*, Berlin, 1984; *The European Iceberg*, Art Gallery of Ontario, Toronto, 1985. Recipient: Gold Medal, Académie d'Architecture, Paris, 1983. Honorary Professor, University of Lima, Peru, 1979; Honorary Fellow, American Institute of Architects, 1983. Member, Akademie der Künste, Berlin, 1968; Member, German Academy for Urban and Regional Planning, 1976. Address: Architekturbüro Böhm, Auf dem Römerberg 25, 5000 Cologne 51 (Marienburg), West Germany.

Works:

1947 New membrane building structure (project)
1949 St. Columba's Church, Cologne
1955 Church in Ching Liau, Formosa
1957 Cathedral, and Chapel, Tubarao, Brazil (project)
Herz Jesu Church, Schildgen, near Cologne
1958 St. Christopher's Church, Oldenburg, West Germany
The Queen of Grace Church, Kassel-Wilhelmschohe, West Germany
1959 Theatre, Bonn
Corpus Christi Parish Centre, Porz-Urbach, near Cologne
St. Joseph Parishioners' Centre, Kierspe, West Germany
1960 Church, Bemkastel, Kues, West Germany (project)
Chapel, Cochem, Mosel, West Germany (project)
City Hall, Cologne (project)
Godesburg Castle renovations, restaurant and hotel, Bad Godesburg, Bonn
1962 Thomas Morus Parishioners' Centre, Gelsenkirchen, West Germany
Church of the Pilgrimages, Neviges, West Germany
Town Hall, Bensberg, West Germany
Housing for the elderly, Garath, Düsseldorf
1963 Children's Village, Refrath, Bensberg, West Germany
Church of the Annunciation, Impekoven, West Germany
The Resurrection Church, Melaten, Cologne
1965 Cultural Centre, Bensberg, West Germany (project)
St. Ludwig Church, Saarlouis, West Germany
Children's Village, near Lake Bracciano, Italy
1966 Dr. Paul Böhm House, Munich
1967 City Hall, Amsterdam (project)
Auditorium Centre, Aachen, West Germany (project)
City Centre Plan for Bensberg, West Germany
1968 University of Dortmund, West Germany (project)
University of Bielefeld, West Germany (project)
City Hall, Wesseling Industrial District, near Cologne (project)
1969 Housing complex, Chorweiler, Cologne
Cathedral restoration, Trier, West Germany
Kauzenburg-Ruine renovation and restaurant, Bad Kreuznach, West Germany
Diocesan Museum, Paderborn, West Germany
Music College, Cologne (project)
Printing Factory, Cologne (project)
State Bureau for Data Processing and Statistics, Düsseldorf
1970/
80 Housing and Commercial Development, Bad Godesberg, Bonn
1971/
80 Reception Centre with Housing, Aachen, Germany (project)
1972 Pilgrimage Church, Wigratzbad, West Germany
1973 Parliament Buildings, Bonn (project)
Housing development, Porz-Zündorf, near Cologne (project)
City Hall and Cultural Centre, Bocholt, West Germany
St. Mathew Parishioners' Centre, Kettwig, Essen, West Germany
1973/
80 Reconstruction Plan, Porz-Zündorf, near Cologne (project)
1974 Residential quarter, Stuckenbroich, West Germany (project)
1975 City Hall, Cologne (project)
Wallraf-Richartz Museum new Buildings, Cologne (project)

Housing for the German Embassy, Moscow (project)

Neckermann Store facade and renovation, Braunschweig am Alstadtmarkt, West Germany

1976 Residential quarter on old factory site, Cologne (project)

1977 Adult Education Boarding School, Kreuzberg, Bonn (project)

Administration Building, Marsdorf, Cologne (project)

Viktria Insurance Building, Düsseldorf (project)

Community Centre, Kettwig, Essen, West Germany

Regional and Federal Government Quarter, Bad Godesberg, Bonn (project)

1977/
80 Municipal Hall, Bergisch-Gladbach, West Germany

Townhouse, Rheinberg, West Germany

Prager Platz Development, Berlin (project)

1978 Friedrichsplatz Development, Kassel, West Germany (competition project)

Castle Area Development, Saarbrücken, West Germany (competition development)

Castle restoration, Saarbrücken, West Germany (project)

Building Complex, Talstrasse, Saarbrücken, West Germany (project)

Housing Block, Spandau, Berlin (project)

1979 Redevelopment Plan, Düsseldorf (project)

Museum rebuilding, Cologne (competition project)

City Centre Development, Dudweiler, Saar, West Germany (project)

Parish Centre with Church and Housing, Bremen, West Germany (project)

City and Suburban Extension Plan, Konz, Saar, West Germany (project)

1979/
80 Judicial Building, Kerpen, West Germany (competition project)

1980 Community Centre extensions, Kettwig, Essen, West Germany (project)

Housing Development, Hasenheide, Berlin (project)

Feuerwache Municipal Centre with Housing and Commercial Buildings, Cologne (project)

Platz Heumarkt reconstruction, Cologne (project)

1981 Single-Family Terraced Housing, Porz-Zündorf, near Cologne

Opera House renovations, Stuttgart (competition project)

1981/
84 Town House, Dudweiler, near Saarbrücken, West Germany

1982/
84 Foyer of the Opera House, Stuttgart

Baufirma Züblin Headquarters Building, Stuttgart

Publications:

By BÖHM: articles—"Die Gewebedecke" in *Neue Baumethoden 1*, edited by H. Hoffmann, Stuttgart 1949; in *Bauwelt* (Berlin), June 1974; in *Kunst und Kirche* (Linz, Austria), October 1975; "Interview with Gottfried Bohm" by H. Klumpp and Egon Schirmbeck in *Bauen und Wohnen* (Zürich), November 1977.

On BÖHM: books—*Der Baumeister Gottfried Böhm*, booklet, Wuppertal, West Germany 1968; *Spazi dell'architettura moderna* by Bruno Zevi, Turin 1973; *Die Architektur des Expressionismus* by Wolf-

Gottfried Böhm: Town Hall, Bensberg, West Germany, 1962.

gang Pehnt, Stuttgart 1973; *Deutsche Kunst seit 1960: Architektur* by Paolo Nestler and Peter M. Bode, Munich 1976; *Die Architektur von Gottfried Böhm*, thesis by Fritz Schwartz, Eidgenossische Technische Hochschule, Zürich 1977; *Die Architektur im 20, Jahrhundert* by Udo Kultermann, Cologne 1977; *Funf Architekten zeichnen für Berlin*, exhibition catalogue, edited by François Burkhardt, Berlin 1979; *Transformations in Modern Architecture, exhibition catalogue*, by Arthur Drexler, New York 1979; *Gottfried Böhm: Bauten und Projekte 1950-1980*, edited by Svetlozar Raev, Cologne 1982; *The European Iceberg*, exhibition catalogue, edited by Germano Celant, Milan 1985; articles— "Vacation Village for Children" in *Architecture francaise* (Paris), January/February 1974; "An Expressionist Presence: Gottfried Böhm" by Giuliano Chelazzi in *L'Architettura* (Rome), April 1974; "Fifteen Hundred Years Revealed in New Glory: Trier Cathedral" in *Deutsche Bauzeitung* (Stuttgart), July 1974; "Oasis in the Desert—Old People's Home in Dusseldorf-Garath" by Max Bacher in *Architekt* (Stuttgart), April 1976; "Observations on the Architectural Work of Gottfried Böhm" by Egon Schirmbeck in *Bauen und Wohnen* (Zürich), November 1977; "Form as an Expression of Technical Function" in *Architektur und Wohnwelt* (Stuttgart), December 1977; special issue of *Architecture + Urbanism* (Tokyo), March 1978; "Der Architekt Gottfried Böhm" by Hans Kump in *Bauen und Wohnen* (Zürich), no. 9, 1980; "Gottfried Böhm" by Charlie Genders in *Architect* (The Hague), no. 11, 1980.

*

The actual career of Gottfried Böhm, a somewhat withdrawn architect, disinclined to sensationalism, started with a bang—with the construction of the Bensberg Town Hall at the end of the 1960s. This concrete edifice is of great dramatic strength and is as unique in its way as are most of Böhm's buildings. One could say that the earlier churches, with their perfunctory dignity, had already shown that Böhm—the son of the highly illustrious master church builder Dominikus Böhm—had freed himself entirely from any dictates of architectural fashion. All his works are thought out in an unusually sculptured way; they are intensely expressive and have a kind of rhythmically animated and joyous spaciousness. They seem to extract from their construction, and their materials, designs that are totally unexpected but in no way forced (as are those of Scharoun). Architecture, according to Böhm, "must eventually achieve its own surrender." Groups of buildings, such as the Children's Village, Bensberg-Refrath, the Housing for the Elderly in Düsseldorf-Garath, or the Housing Complex at Cologne-Chorweiler, are characterized by an "organic" municipal layout that reminds one of the work of Häring. Their arrangement follows the landscape and the topography of the district and conveys the desired social effect.

In the works of Böhm—which have avoided the International Style from the beginning—one can distinguish until recently three more or less different phases: The first involves the recognizable traits of the 1950s. The second, to which the above-mentioned Town Hall, Children's Village, and Housing for the Elderly belong, identified itself through an inward plasticity; it is externally marked in its use of brick, concrete, and coloured wood. This phase reaches its climax in the Church of the Pilgrimages, Neviges, an enormous concrete cathedral that puts the name of Böhm on a par with that of Brunelleschi or Gaudí. In the third, the steel and glass phase, everything that is ponderous is replaced with simplicity and transparency; noteworthy examples are the State Bureau for Data Processing and Statistics, Düsseldorf, and the Diocesan Museum at Paderborn, which illustrates the exceptionally courageous, and very tensely held, symbiosis of a neighbourhood architecture that is both contemporary and historical. The most original and most elegant example of this phase is the civic

building of the small city of Rheinberg; here, Böhm built the town hall around a rectangular, almost cubic hall. For its radiant entrance, there is a three-storey lobby covered with three saddle roofs of steel and glass, creating a loggia that endeavors to symbolize democracy.

Since then, a new period seems to have begun in Böhm's work, with an individual mixture of playfulness and monumentality. Now, he tries to give the concrete, so often misused, color and relief by building with industrially produced finished parts. The most characteristic example is the new administration building of the Züblin construction firm in Stuttgart. Here, we find two high rectangular structures with a load-carrying concrete façade; the decor is developed from manufacturing technique and construction methods. The tall inner court has a glass saddle roof and is closed with glass walls.

—Manfred Sack

BONATZ, Paul Michael Nikolaus.

German. Born in Solgne, Lorraine, 6 December 1877. Educated at the Humanistische Gymnasium, Hagenau, Germany, 1896; Technische Hochschule, Munich, Dip. Arch. 1900. Married Helene Frohlich in 1902; daughter: Susanne. Assistant to Theodor Fischer 1902-06, and Professor, from 1907, at the Technische Hochschule, Stuttgart; in private practice, with F. E. Scholer, Stuttgart, 1913-27. Consultant to the Neckar Canal Authority, Germany, 1929-36; Consultant to the Inspector-General of Highways, Germany, 1935-40; Consultant Architect, City of Ankara, Turkey, 1943-46; Professor at the Technical University of Istanbul, 1946-54; returned to private practice, Stuttgart, 1954-56. Recipient: First Prize, Stuttgart Central Railway Station Competition, 1911. *Died* (in Stuttgart) *20 December 1956*.

Works:

1909 Henkell Warehouses, Biebricher, Wiesbaden, Germany

Library, University of Tübingen, Germany

1912 School, Feuerbach, near Stuttgart

Bonatz House, Stuttgart

1913 German Embassy, Washington, D.C. (project)

Bridge, near Ulm, Germany

Roser House, Stuttgart

Country house, Marienburg, Cologne

1914 Hospital, Strasbourg (with Karl Bonatz)

Municipal Hall, Corviniusplatz, Hannover, Germany

1915 Municipal Hall, Stettin, Germany (project)

Monument to the War Dead (2 projects)

1916 Assembly Building, Oldenburg, Germany

Zeppelindorf Workers' Housing Development, Friedrichshafen, Germany (with F. E. Scholer)

General Lotterer Monument, Ludwigshafen, Germany

Turkish-German Hall of Friendship, Istanbul (competition project)

1917 Hartmannsweilerkopf Monument (project)

Commemorative Hall (project)

1922 Office Building, Königsberg, Germany (project)

Heymarkt Building, Cologne (project)

Kriegerfriedhof Monument, Waldfriedhof, Stuttgart

1924 Scheibler House, Marienburg, Cologne

Arntzen House, Marienburg, Cologne

1925 Hornschmich House, Mainleus, near Kulmbach, Germany (with F. E. Scholer)

Am Bismarckturm Housing Development, Stuttgart

Bonatz House, Stuttgart (destroyed, 1944)

Trade Fair Building, Hamburg (2 projects)

1926 Buhler House, Goppinger, Germany (with F. E. Scholer)

Dyke Project, Ladenburg bei Mannheim, Germany (project)

Palace of the League of Nations, Geneva (competition project; with F. E. Scholer)

1927 Jeweller's Hall, Domplatz, Cologne

Municipal Hall, Sports Hall and Museum (competition project)

Gymnasium, Aalen, Germany

1928 Baer House, Stuttgart

Central Railway Station, Stuttgart (with F. E. Scholer)

1929 Unterturkheim Swimming Baths, Stuttgart

Radio Broadcasting Building, Berlin (project)

Hotel Graf Zeppelin, Station Square, Stuttgart (with F. E. Scholer)

House, Dortmund, Germany

House, Bochum, Germany

1930 Cathedral Terrace/Plaza, Cologne (project)

1933 House, Gertingen, near Stuttgart

Roser House, Stuttgart

Vorster House, Cologne

Strenger House, Cologne

Muller House, Cologne

Flag Tower, *Turnfestival*, Stuttgart

1935 Stumm Company Building, Düsseldorf (with F. E. Scholer)

Water Tower, Kornwestheim, near Stuttgart

Reichsnahrstandes Buildings, Goslar, Germany (project; with K. Dubbers)

1936 Locks, bridges, and weirs on the Neckar Canal, Heidelberg, Rockenau, Hirschhorn and Oberesslingen, Germany

Kunstmuseum, Basel, Switzerland (with Rudolf Christ)

Memorial Chapel to the War Dead, Heilbronn, Germany

Offender Rundbau Monument (project with K. Dubbers)

1939/
42 Main Railway Station, Munich (project)

1939/
43 Naval High Command, Berlin (project)

1941 Bridges for the Autobahn: over the Waschmuhltal near Kaiserslauten; Saale near Lehesten; Donau near Leipheim (Ulm); Elbe near Hohenwarthe (Magdeburg); Elbe near Dessau; Rhine near Frankenthal (Mannheim)

Suspension bridges at Cologne and Hamburg

1943 Stuttgart Corporation Buildings (project)

1946 Schukru-Saracogu Housing Development, Ankara, Turkey

1948 State Opera House, Ankara, Turkey

Imperial Palace, Addis Ababa, Ethiopia (competition project)

1949 Old barracks renovations, Technical University, Istanbul

1949/
50 Bonatz House extension, Am Bismarckturm, Stuttgart (with Erich Fritz)

1950 Plaza with obelisk, Istanbul (project)

1950/
51 Traffic and Road Plan, Stuttgart (project; with D. Christoskoff)

1951 Bosphorus suspension bridge, Istanbul (project; with Krupp Firm)

Concert Hall, Darmstadt, West Germany (project)

Domplatz layout plan, Paderborn, West Germany (project)

Herrenhausen Castle Hotel, Hannover, West Germany (project)

1951/
52 Elementary School and Local Museum, Hohen Ufer, Hannover, West Germany (project)

1952 Administration Building, Goslar, West Germany (competition project)

Hotel, Heidelberg, West Germany (competition project)

City Hall extension, Hannover, West Germany (project)

Schlossplatz and Theatre conservation plan, Stuttgart (project)

1954/
55 Suren house, Istanbul

Opera House, Düsseldorf (with Schultze-Frohlinde und Huhn)

1954/
56 Hotel, Izmir, Turkey (project)

1955/
56 Ozar House, Istanbul (project)

Central Giro Office (Zeppelin-Building) extension, Stuttgart (with Karl Ellsasser)

Regional Land Planning Office, Stuttgart (competition project)

1956 Art Building extensions, Stuttgart (with Walter Kruspe)

Schlossplatz redevelopment plan, Stuttgart (project)

Publications:

By BONATZ: books—*Leben und Bauen*, Stuttgart 1950, 4th edition 1958; *Brücken*, with Fritz Leonhardt, Königstein, West Germany 1951; articles—"Hochhauser von Paul Bonatz und F. E. Scholer teils in Gemeinschaft mit Karl Bonatz" in *Moderne Bauformen* (Stuttgart), June 1926; "The Madrid Conference" in *Revista Nacional de Arquitectura* (Madrid), November 1943.

On BONATZ: books—*Paul Bonatz und seine Schüler*, edited by G. Graubner, Stuttgart 1930; *Paul Bonatz Arbeiten aus den Jahren 1907 bis 1937*, edited by Friedrich Tamms, Stuttgart 1937; *Neue Deutsche Baukunst* by Albert Speer, Berlin 1941; *Architecture and Politics in Germany 1918-1945* by Barbara Miller Lane, Cambridge, Massachusetts 1968; *Paul Bonatz 1877-1956* by Norbert Bongartz, Peter Dübbers and Frank Werner, Stuttgart 1977; articles—"Neue Bauten von Paul Bonatz und F. E. Scholer" by Julius Baum in *Moderne Bauformen* (Stuttgart), December 1913; "Zu neueren arbeiten von Paul Bonatz" by G.K. in *Moderne Bauformen* (Stuttgart), January 1919; "Paul Bonatz" by Julius Posener in *L'Architecture d'Aujourd'hui* (Paris), June/July 1932; "Architecture of the Nazis" in *Architectural Review* (London), October 1933; "Paul Bonatz" by Karl Bonatz in *Neue Bauwelt* (Berlin), no. 49, 1948; "A Minor Master" by Julius Posener in *Architectural Review* (London), July 1951; "Paul Bonatz 1877-1956" by Nieto and Bellmunt in *Arquitectura* (Madrid), March 1977.

Paul Bonatz, born in 1877, belongs to that important and not uncontroversial group of architects known as the German Pre-Moderns. After studying architecture at the Munich Technische Hochschule, he became assistant to Theodor Fischer at the Technische Hochschule in Stuttgart; during that period, he was totally influenced by Fischer who, in contrast to the movement toward an international style, was continually looking for a "regionalism" specific to place. In 1907 Bonatz succeeded Fischer as Professor at Stuttgart, and from 1913 to 1927 he maintained his own architectural practice in Stuttgart with F. E. Scholer. Important early works were the Henkell Warehouses and the Library of the University of Tübingen.

He achieved his first real breakthrough when in 1911 he won first prize in the competition for the rebuilding of Stuttgart's main railway station. With the exception of some of Peter Behrens's large buildings, this construction is perhaps the most important monument of German Pre-Modernism. Bonatz succeeded not only in giving a clear, function-related expression to the various technical and transport problems but also in formulating the arrangement of the masses in such a way that he largely determined the expansion of the surrounding area during the twentieth century. The Stuttgart Station thus became the first "Space-Time-Architecture" in Germany. Although the building was not completed until 1928, it never really came within an International Style sphere of influence. Strongly reminiscent of Eliel Saarinen's Helsinki Railway Station in its general arrangement, the Stuttgart Station reveals an abundance of eclectic details. Nevertheless, its basic expression is matter-of-fact to a hitherto unknown degree—that is to say, it is function-oriented.

During the period from the end of World War I until about 1930, Bonatz was admittedly divided in his stylistic expression. While he turned almost exclusively to the German Biedermeier and the so called "Heimatstil" motives for single-family houses and villas, his public buildings obeyed New Building principles. But, by 1928, Bonatz was one of those architects who were strongly folk-orientated and who at the time of the Weissenhof Estate in Stuttgart made a radical departure from New Building. He was one of the signatories to the so-called "Block Manifesto," which attempted to establish "the attitudes to life of our own people." The first and only National Socialist architectural program emerged from the circle of signatories to this manifesto. In 1933 Bonatz took part in the project for the Kochenhof Estate in Stuttgart, which would later achieve sad renown as the "Anti-Weissenhof."

A further interest in his work was civil engineering. From 1929-36 Bonatz was a consultant to the Neckar Canal Authority, and as such he executed an impressive collection of locks, sluices, bridges, etc. that are among the most important engineering achievements of the time. Later, after the National Socialist seizure of power, it became increasingly difficult for so unpretentious an architect as Bonatz to build anything. In 1935, Dr. Fritz Todt, the Inspector-General of German Road Buildings, appointed him as his personal adviser. In this capacity, up until World War II, Bonatz, was, at least, able to plan and executive a number of outstanding bridges.

Torn between protest at and loyalty to National Socialism, Bonatz tried to create works for the regime's leaders in Berlin. He produced gigantic and megalomaniacal projects—the Main Railway Station in Munich and the Naval High Command in Berlin—which could not be built. Like Kreis and others, he was now regarded as an elder architect, and, thus, despite his previous work for the state, of little use to the National Socialist Culture and Construction Policy.

For that reason, among others, Bonatz decided to emigrate; he went to Ankara, where the Turkish Government appointed him consultant to the City Architect. In 1946 he became Professor at the Technical University of Istanbul. In Turkey Bonatz developed a moderately antique style that, in many ways, is reminiscent of the work of Auguste Perret. In 1954 he returned to Stuttgart where, until his death, he occupied himself chiefly with the reconstruction of his own war-damaged buildings.

Bonatz's chief accomplishment—apart from his pioneer work in the German Pre-Modern style—is that over the decades at the Technische Hochschule he gathered around him a circle of architectural teachers, known as the "Stuttgart School," who were internationally acknowledged and esteemed. And he was one of the most important teachers of that time in Germany to preach the abolition of the separation between civil engineering and architecture. But he did not achieve his main ambition, which was to create a regional architecture that would be a real alternative to the New Building.

—Frank Werner

Pep Bonet: House in Argentona, Barcelona, 1982-83.

BONET Bertran, Pep.

Spanish. Born in Barcelona, 19 November 1941. Educated at the Escuela Tecnica Superior de Arquitectura, Barcelona, under Federico Correa, 1958-65, Dip.Arch. 1965. Served in the Spanish Army, in Castillejos (Tarragona) and Gerona: Lieutenant. Married Marta Monne Corbero in 1964; Children: Sebas, Sara, and Elias. Formed the partnership, Studio PER, with Cristian Cirici, *q.v.,* Luis Clotet, *q.v.,* and Oscar Tusquets, *q.v.,* Barcelona, 1965. Professor, EINA, Barcelona, 1969-70. Professor, Escuela Tecnica Superior de Arquitectura, Barcelona, since 1976. Exhibitions: *Arquitectura del Studio PER,* Lerida, 1971; *Triennale,* Milan, 1973; *Arquitectura y Lagrimas,* Sala Vincon, Barcelona, 1975; *Centenario de la Escuela Tecnica Superior de Arquitectura de Barcelona,* Palacio National, Barcelona, 1977; *Festival of Films about Architecture,* Centre Georges Pompidou, Paris, 1978; *The Presence of the Past,* at the *Biennale,* Venice, 1980. Address: Studio PER, Caspe 151, Barcelona 13, Spain.

Works:

1968 Design of the *Miro Otro* exhibition, Barcelona (with Cristian Cirici, Luis Clotet, and Oscar Tusquets)
1972 Llambes Offices, Barcelona (with Cristian Cirici)
1973 Profitos Factory, Polinya, Barcelona (with Cristian Cirici)
1974 C./Tokio Housing Block, Barcelona (with Cristian Cirici)
1976 Aguila House, Llavaneras, Barcelona (with Cristian Cirici)
      Bricall House, Vilasar, Barcelona (with Cristian Cirici)
      Pep Bonet House, Vilamajor, Barcelona (with Cristian Cirici)

1977 Francés House, Menorca (with Cristian Cirici)
1978 Housing Complex, Gran Via, Barcelona (with Cristian Cirici, Lluis Clotet and Oscar Tusquets)
1979/
80 Casa Thomas restoration and B.D. Shop interiors, Calle Mallorca, Barcelona (with Critian Cirici, Lluis Clotet and Oscar Tusquets)
1979/
81 House at Sant Feliu de Codines, Barcelona (with Cristian Cirici)
1982/
83 Row-houses (8), San Antonio de Vilamajor, Barcelona
     House at Argentona, Barcelona
1984/
85 Plaza Universo Exhibition Complex and Square, Barcelona
     Social Assistance Centre, Parets del Vallés, Barcelona

Publications:

By BONET: articles—"Architect's House in the Country" in *Cuadernos de Arquitectura* (Barcelona), May 1976; "El año II" in *Cuadernos de Arquitectura* (Barcelona), 1985.

On BONET: articles—"Studio PER" in *Architecture + Urbanism* (Tokyo), no. 4, 1977 "Arquitectura con Ventanas" by Xavier Sust in *Arquitecturas Bis* (Barcelona), September 1977; 'Per, Uno per uno, tutti per tutti" by Alessandro Mendini in *Modo* (Milan), November 1977; "On Architecture: report from Barcelona" in *Bauen und Wohnen* (Zurich), January 1978; "National Award for restoration and rehabilitation" in *Arquitectos* (Madrid), July/August 1980; "Studio PER" by Masayuki Matsuzake in *Space Design* (Tokyo), August 1980;

"House in Sant Feliu de Codines" in *Quaderns* (Barcelona), March/April 1981; "Un sillón intelligente" in *Dediseño* (Barcelona), no. 1, 1985.

Once in Japan I saw a Spanish juggler who impressed me a lot. He carried through his performance with just a teaspoon. He put it over his shoe, threw it up into the air, turning it over and over, and with an incredible precision made it stand vertically over his forehead. He didn't do anything else, but I found it wonderful. With such a simple performance he gave the exact measure of his great capacity to solve this or any other problem of equilibrium, and the audience applauded him, appreciating the difficulty of his work and his precise execution.

Something very different happens to architects like us. For a long time we don't know who is to be our audience, and it is with great pain that we obtain a teaspoon with which to perform. And if we pretend to do it with more spectacular contraptions, we must try to achieve equilibrium long before going on to the stage—and this is tiring.

And when we are finally able to perform, nobody understands anything or applauds us. And that is that apart from achieving equilibrium, we would like to convince the rare remaining audience that it isn't the teaspoon that they should wish to have; it's the cup of tea. Above all, we are pedants.

And meanwhile the Spanish juggler I saw in Japan is turning up all over the world, very much in demand. And we are not.

—Pep Bonet

Studio PER is four architects in related practices in one office. Apart from administrative convenience, what really binds them together is that they share the same approach to architecture in valuing positively its cultural objectives. Their architecture is essentially intellectual. They are eager to discuss, argue, and defend their work against all criticism in order to explore all the rich possibilities available to their avant-garde position. This makes their buildings, and their explanation, often contradictory—but that is the price of an open mind—adventure and doubt. But this attitude, which is almost literary rather than visual, would be of little interest if it was not backed up by secure professional ability, compositional control, and a sensitive feeling for proportions.

Pep Bonet and Cristian Cirici present one side of the practice; they share with their partners, Lluis Clotet and Oscar Tusquets, an invigorating concern for industrial design. Between them they have a large list of products on the market. Their attention to minute detail, and the production problems involved, is reflected in the care they take in designing architectural details. Their drawings and perspectives are explicative.

Bonet and Cirici are more conservative than their partners in their architecture; they fall more clearly within the mainstream of modern architecture—as in their Profitos Factory, the C./Tokio luxury flats in Barcelona, and the social housing unit, Besos, Barcelona. But perhaps their most significant work is Bonet's own house in Vilamajor, where the directness of industrial architecture has inspired the conception of the house. The skeleton of two parallel naves made of block columns and pre-cast concrete beams generate two related open spaces, one partially occupied by the main body of the dwelling and the other by a studio. Details are reduced to a minimum, to the area where industrial and rural architecture meet. This voluntary simplification of architecture to the bare necessities follows Mies van der Rohe in an unsophisticated and relaxed manner.

The common freshness and professional skill of Bonet and Cirici, and that of their associates in Studio PER, together with their sensitive alertness to current architectural fashion, enable them to translate new concepts quickly into the local Catalan cultural context. It is a task that is needed if the modern movement is to take root geographically.

—David Mackay

BOTTA, Mario.

Swiss. Born in Mendrisio, 1 April 1943. Educated at primary school in Genestrerio, Ticino, and secondary school in Mendrisio, until 1957; apprentice building draughtsman, office of Carloni and Camenisch, Lugano, 1958-61; studied at the Liceo Artistico, Milan, 1961-64; under Carlo Scarpa and Giuseppe Mazzariol, Istituto Universitario di Architettura, Venice, 1964-69, Dip.Arch. 1969. Assistant in the office of Le Corbusier, in Venice and Paris, 1965. Since 1969, in private practice, Lugano. Visiting Professor, 1976, 1980, 1982, and Full Professor since 1983, Ecole Polytechnique Federale, Lausanne. Member of the Swiss Federal Commision for Fine Arts, from 1982. Exhibitions: *Tendenzen—Neuere Architektur im Tessin*, Eidgenössische Technische Hochschule, Zurich, 1975; *Mario Botta: works and projects*, Technische Universitat, Vienna, 1977 (toured Europe and the United States); *Topologia e morfogenesi*, at the *Biennale*, Venice, 1978; *10 Tessiner Architekten*, Technische Hogeschool, Delft, Netherlands, 1979; *Transformations in Modern Architecture*, Museum of Modern Art, New York, 1979; *La Arquitectura de Mario Botta*, Centro de Arte y Comunicacion, Buenos Aires, 1980 (toured Brazil and Hungary); *Architecture 70/80 in Switzerland*, Kunsthalle, Basle, 1981 (travelled to Vienna, Rome, Padua, Montreal and Turin); *Un cilindro da abitare: Casa Medici a Stabio di Mario Botta*, Studio Marconi, Milan, 1981; *Maquettes d'architectes*, Centre d'Art Contemporain, Geneva, 1982 (travelled to Lyon-Villeurbanne, France); *Prima e Seconda: Due sedie di Mario Botta*, Studio Marconi, Milan, 1982; *Ten New Buildings*, Institute of Contemporary Arts, London, 1983; *Mario Botta: Dans le paysage comme un poing sur la table*, Musée Savoisien, Chambery, France, 1983; *Mario Botta*, Sala del Rettorato, Ancona, Italy, 1983; *Mario Botta 1961-1982*, Historisches Archiv, Cologne, 1983; *Mario Botta, architecte*, Musée d'Art et d'Histoire, Fribourg, Switzerland, 1984; *Preliminary Studies: Mario Botta*, GA Gallery, Tokyo, 1985 (travelled to Stuttgart); *Nouveaux plaisirs d'architectures*, Centres Georges Pompidou, Paris, 1985; *Mario Botta: Architetture 1960-1985*, Scuola di San Giovanni Evangelista, Venice, 1985. Recipient: Beton Architecture Prize, 1985. Honorary Fellow, Bund Deutscher Architekten, 1983, and American Institute of Architects, 1984. Member, Federation of Swiss Architects (FAS), 1978. Addresses (office): Via Lavizzari 10, 6900 Lugano, Switzerland; (home): 6835 Morbio Superiore, Ticino, Switzerland.

Works:

1961/
63 Rectory, Genestrerio, Switzerland (with T. Carloni)
1965/
67 Single-family House, Stabio, Switzerland
1966 Chapel in the Convent of Bigorio, Switzerland (with T. Carloni)
1969 District Redevelopment Plan, Venice (degree project)
1970 Lausanne Polytechnic School Master Plan, Lausanne, Switzerland (project; with T. Carloni, A. Galgetti, F. Ruchat and L. Snozzi)
District Restructuring Plan, Lugano, Switzerland (competition project)
School, Locarno, Switzerland (competition project)
1970/
71 Single-family House, Cadenazzo, Switzerland
1971 New Administration Centre, Perugia, Italy (competition project; with L. Snozzi and I. Gianola)
1972 House, Vacallo, Switzerland (project; with E. Ostinelli)
Administration Building, Chiasso, Switzerland (competition project)
Children's Home, Stabio, Switzerland (competition project)

1972/
73 Single-family House, Riva San Vitale, Switzerland (with S. Cantoni)
1972/
77 Secondary School, Morbio Inferiore, Ticino, Switzerland (with E. Bernegger, R. Hunziker and L. Tami)
1973 Single-family House, Caslano, Switzerland (project)
Library of the Capuchin Convent, Lugano, Switzerland (project)
Meeting-Hall conversion in the Capuchin Convent, Lugano, Switzerland
1974
Secondary School, Colderico, Switzerland (competition project)
Housing Estate near Mendrisio, Switzerland (competition project; with L. Snozzi)
Multifunctional Development, Samedan, Switzerland (competition project; with R. Hunziker)
1975 Single-family House, Manno, Switzerland (project)
1975/
76 Single-family House, Ligornetto, Switzerland (with M. Boesch)
1975/
77 Single-family House, Maggia, Switzerland
1976/
77 Housing conversion, Lugano-Rivigliana, Switzerland
1976/
78 Municipal Gymnasium, Balerna, Switzerland
1976/
79 Library of the Capuchin Convent, Lugano, Switzerland (with R. Hunziker)
1977/
78 Farmhouse conversion, Lugignano, Chiasso, Switzerland (with R. Leuzinger)
1977/
78 Housing conversion, Riva San Vitale, Switzerland
1977/
79 Craft Centre, Balerna, Switzerland (with R. Leuzinger)
1977/
81 State Bank, Fribourg, Switzerland (with E. Hutter and T. Urfer)
1978 Rail Station extensions, Zurich (competition project; with L. Snozzi and M. Boesch)
1979 Single-family House, Pregassona, Switzerland (with R. Hunziker)
Area Restructuring Plan, Basle, Switzerland (competition project; with R. Leuzinger)
Terraced Housing, Riva San Vitale, Switzerland (project)
Artisans' Centre, Balerna, Switzerland (project)
1980 Administration and Reception Building, Bruhl, West Germany (competition project)
Clinic, Agra, Switzerland (project)
Lakeside Recreational Development, Lugano, Switzerland (project)
Science Centre, West Berlin (competition project)
City Centre Re-Integration Plan, Stuttgart (competition project)
1981 Guernica Museum, Guernica, Spain (project)
Administration and Commercial Building, Lugano, Switzerland
Casa Rotonda single-family House, Stabio, Switzerland
1982 Andre Malraux House of Culture, Chambery, France
Bank of Gothard Offices, Lugano, Switzerland
Building on the TGV Station Square, Lyon, France (project)
1983 Siemens Headquarters Building, Munich (competition project)
1983/
84 Single-family House, Morbio Superiore, Switzerland

1984 Library, Villeurbanne, France (competition project)
Single-family House, Breganzona, Italy (project)
Carlo Scarpa 1906-1978 exhibition layouts, Gallerie dell'Accademia, Venice (with B. Podrecca)
1985 Campo di Marte restructuring, Giudecca, Venice (competition project)
Administration Building with Laboratories, Geneva (project)
Office Building, West Berlin (project)
Housing Development, Turin, Italy (project)

Publications:

By BOTTA: articles—"Architecture and Environment" in *Architecture + Urbanism* (Tokyo), no. 105, 1979; "Swiss Transmission and Exaggerations", interview with Livio Dimitriu, in *Skyline* (New York), vol. 2, no. 8, 1980; "Une Maison Familiale Encore!" in *Werk, Bauen und Wohnen* (Zurich), no. 5, 1980; "An Interview with Mario Botta" in *Q* (Barcelona), February 1981; "Ein Raum for Guernika" in *Werk, Bauen und Wohnen* (Zurich), no. 11, 1981; "L'albero come eccezione" in *Lotus* (Venice), no. 31, 1982; "Casa a Stabio" in *Rivista Tecnica* (Bellinzona, Switzerland), no. 2, 1982; "Architecture Means Giving Form to History", interview, in *Arkkitehti* (Helsinki), vol. 79, no. 4/5, 1982; "Interview with Emilio Ambasz", with A. Mendini in *Domus* (Milan), May 1983; "The Neo-Rationalists Are Coming", interview with Stanley Abercrombie, in *Interior Design* (New York), June 1983; "Architecture and Morality", interview, in *Perspecta* (New Haven, Connecticut), no. 20, 1983; "Il teatro e la città", interview with Mirko Zardini, in *Casabella* (Milan), November 1983; "Una visita al nuovo Lingotto", interview with Mirko Zardini, in *Casabella* (Milan), May 1984.

On BOTTA: books—*Mario Botta: Architecture and Projects in the 70s*, edited by Italo Rota, Milan 1979, London 1981; *Mario Botta—La Casa Rotonda* by Eduardo Sanguineti, Alberto Sartoris, Pierluigi Nicolin and others, Milan 1982; *Mario Botta: Buildings and Projects 1961-1982* by Pierluigi Nicolin, New York 1984; *GA Architect 3: Mario Botta*, edited by Yukio Futagawa, Tokyo 1984; *Mario Botta: Architetture 1960-1985* by Francesco Dal Co, Milan 1985; articles—"Una casa nel Ticino" by Bruno Alfieri in *Lotus* (Venice), no. 5, 1978; "Einfamilienhauser—Ferienhauser", special issue of *Werk* (Zurich), January 1969; "Habitation à Cadenazzo, Ticino" in *L'Architecture d'Aujourd'hui* (Paris), August/September 1972; "Mario Botta—Works and Projects" in *Casabella* (Milan), June 1976; "Two Projects by Mario Botta" by Joseph Rykwert in *Lotus* (Venice), no. 11, 1976; "Projects by Mario Botta" in *Lotus* (Venice), June 1977; "The Houses of Mario Botta" in *Archives d'Architecture Moderne* (Brussels), November 1977; "Meet the Architect: Mario Botta" in *GA Houses* (Tokyo), December 1977; "Mario Botta and the School of Ticino" in *Oppositions* (New York), Fall 1978; "Mario Botta—One of the Ticino Architects" by Jord den Hollander in *De Architect* (The Hague), June 1979; "Contemporary Architects 14: Mario Botta" in *Architecture + Urbanism* (Tokyo), June 1979; "Mario Botta: recherche patiente" in *Archithese* (Niederteufen, Switzerland), no. 1, 1980; "Mario Botta: il passato come un amico" in *Werk, Bauen und Wohnen* (Zurich), no. 3, 1980; "Botta's Walls" in *Forum* (Hilversum, Netherlands), May 1980; "Mario Botta—architetto ticinese" in *Ottagono* (Milan), September 1980; "Visit by Mario Botta" by Michael Hedgepeth in *Archetype* (San Francisco), no. 4, 1980; "Mario Botta: S'il vous plait dessine-moi une maison" by Jean-Paul Rayon in *Techniques et Architecture* (Paris), no. 332, 1980; "Intellectual Tradition—Mario Botta" in *Space Design* (Tokyo), no. 3, 1981; "Botta" by Lance Knobel in *Architec-*

Mario Botta: Single-family house (Casa Rotonda), Stabio, Switzerland, 1981.

tural Review (London), July 1981; "Mario Botta—
A Portrait" in *Domus* (Milan), September 1981;
"Mario Botta" by Gyorgy Keves in *Muveszet*
(Budapest), February 1982; "Mario Botta—Tran-
salpine Rationalist" by Peter Arnell in *Architectural
Record* (New York), June 1982; "Mario Botta: o
passado como amigo" by Jorge Glusberg in *Modulo*
(Rio de Janeiro), no. 71, 1982; "Mario Botta:
Critique" in *Progressive Architecture* (New York),
July 1982; "Mario Botta: parpaings et chocolat" by
Francois Lamarre in *Architecture* (Paris), December
1982; "Mario Botta", special issue of *Werk, Bauen
und Wohnen* (Zurich), January/February 1983;
"Mario Botta: Portrait of an Architect in Ticino" by
R. F. Strzala in *Yorkshire Architect* (Sunderland),
January/February 1983; "Three Houses by Mario
Botta" in *Architectural Review* (London), April
1983; "Mario Botta Talks on Recent Works" by A.
Pelissier and K. Morita in *Architecture + Urbanism*
(Tokyo), April 1983; "Botta in the City" by Lance
Knobel in *Architectural Review* (London), May
1983; "Botta on Botta's Chair" by Pilar Viladas in
Progressive Architecture (New York), May 1983;
"Mario Botta and the New Tuscanism" by Charles
Jencks in *Architectural Design* (London), vol. 53,
no. 9/10, 1983; "Botta: Themes and Variations" by
M. McTeague in *Architecture South Africa* (Cape
Town), January/February 1984; "Mario Botta: The
Spartan Classicist" by Charles Jencks in *Connois-
seur* (London), April 1984; "Die Grossen Architek-
ten 13: Mario Botta" in *Hauser* (Hamburg), no. 2,
1984; "Mario Botta", special issue of *Space Design*
(Tokyo), August 1984; "On the Architectural
Drawings by Mario Botta" by Alberto Sartoris in
GA Gallery (Tokyo), September 1984.

This text deals with a number of matters that have a
direct effect upon my work as an architect. The
observations it contains are made, therefore, by

someone who is directly involved in the field and not
by a critic or an historian. They are observations
that have matured within the empirical researchers
which both feed and restrain my whole approach to
architecture. The activity they concern is actually in
progress and should be treated as heterogeneous
and anecdotic, as are the research and operative
work of an architect today.

This is why it is difficult for me to appraise the
intentions and perspectives of my work beyond
certain lines developed in connection with particular
objects and experiments, and to arrive at a more
general critical synthesis which might permit and
warrant some possible theory. So it will be best to
interpret these few remarks as notes on recurrent
themes in the work I am engaged in at present.

Despite this I feel that some useful purpose may
be served by talking about certain of my experiences.

I believe that we architects can legitimately and
hence not too ambitiously discuss these problems
even on the basis of our own limited individual
experiences. In this way ambiguities and a lot of
musunderstandings can be cleared up. This more
forthright discussion will have the merit of being
overtly "biased", as befits a prevalently creative
profession.

In this case relations between architecture and its
"environment", and our search for the meanings
which they convey today, will provide a pretext for
talking about what I think at this time and about my
feelings today as regards certain aspects of the
discipline. In order better to understand the sense of
the remarks which follow it may perhaps be useful
to clarify the difference between the two possible
interpretations I have mentioned.

My view of architecture is a compound of ideas
and thoughts forming the theoretic foundations in
my mind today and in which I distinguish among the
broad spectrum of theories put forward by the

architectural discipline. This is all that the information and culture of my time can offer me. In a sense,
it represents the collective cultural heritage passed
down to us by earlier generations. These are the
thoughts and interpretations which have moulded
and helped to feed my basic training. They constitute the theoretic condition of being an architect
today, of being directly or indirectly heir to what
previous architecture has produced.

So what I think is made up of sufficiently rational
and describable aspects of the social and collective
values of our discipline—those values around which
a reasoned critical evaluation can be propounded.

What I feel on the other hand about architecture
embraces the more subjective and autobiographical
and, in a sense, secret aspects which together
constitute one's irrational motivations (at times
hard to describe) but which also come into the
process of appraisal and of choosing, which characterizes the act of design.

It is in the light of these two alternate phases
(collective and private, rational and irrational) that
these notes should be situated.

Each work of architecture has its own "environment", which, for the sake of convenience, may be
defined as its territory. Between architecture and
territory a constant mutual dependency is established right from the earliest stages of the design.

The first thing to be done when creating a piece of
architecture is to get to know its territory. Interpretation and reading take place through the
verifications and the relations defined with the
architectural design choices made.

The relation between architecture and territory is
not a fixed one; it is dynamic and continuous,
specified through the design's progress and consolidated in a fresh new balance when the architecture is built. Then, this relation goes to its dynamic
state and starts once again to define continually
changing relations with that architectural work. In a
way, the territory could be described as conversing
continually with its own architecture, in a dialogue
similar to the changing of time and history.

The exact definition of the architecture occurs
with its being proposed as the model for a habitat,
and precisely when the new meanings in its context
are consolidated.

Between architecture and "environnement" (built
or natural, it doesn't matter which) a real exchange
(give and take) takes place, which is reciprocal and
continuous.

I believe that the quality of any architectural
endeavour directly hinges upon the intensity of this
exchange.

What I love in architecture is not the object but
the spatial, emotive and suchlike relations which
that object manages to set up with its "environment".

It is this relationship and the need to seize its
significations which take priority in my concept and
interpretation of architecture.

The evaluation of these relations is always uppermost in my mind when I look at or interpret a work
of architecture today.

In order better to grasp the nature and the
meaning of these relations I think it is worth while
making one or two remarks about some serious
misunderstandings that are still widespread convictions today and which, I feel, are harmful to our
proper understanding of the subject.

One such misunderstanding that periodically
crops up in the assessment of the relations between
architecture and "environnement" stems from the
idea that all new architecture is subordinate to the
presumed superiority of the existing values of the
context in which it is to be built.

This theory holds that the territory, the "environnement", is a value to be protected against aggression and destruction by new works. The attitude is
extremely common and it accounts for the
numerous societies and committees for the protec-

tion of the landscape, the environment, etc. It interprets the existing context and the equilibrium of its setting as a static factor, laden with values and testimonies that on most occasions (and let this not be said in irony) emerge or are rediscovered in the imminence of, and are prompted by, future dangers identified in the proposed action itself.

This widely held view also conditions the thinking of a large number of architects. I believe that this attitude, far from expressing sensitivity and attention to existing values, betokens instead a fear and mistrust of all new expression. On most occasions, it does not express the desire for conservation so much as a reactionary sentiment.

This conception of the relations between architecture and its surroundings has directly influenced the majority of our existing building regulations and has also conditioned plain common sense to quite an extent, without however so much as scratching, and indeed for the most part merely abetting, the bulk of the speculative building being done today.

In this outlook we notice that the protection of landscape, environmental and other such "values" is often entrusted not so much to rational motivations as to the most perverse aesthetic senses (of adjustment, inclusion, etc.) displayed by the innumerable commissions and associations for protection and preservation, where the cultural corruption of these trade pundits really seems—judging by what has been produced in recent years—to have no limits.

Contrary to this attitude, I think that more simply the evidence of the facts must be accepted and that, once the legitimacy of the project has been recognized, it should be seen to be the fulcrum of a new transformation. In this case the architecture is enhanced as the tool for constructing a new balance where the existing values (natural or constructed) will be adopted not to be defended or protected but, rather, to be interpreted and projected as qualities within the newly established needs.

One must therefore talk not of protection, but of the promotion of the landscape's values and testimonies. In this way a great many misunderstandings can be dispelled. The delusions and phantoms of an impossible conservation can make way for a more disenchanted, a more deeply committed, appreciation in establishing a new balance between man and his environnement.

In presenting some of my works I shall now try to explain in what measure the relations between architecture and "environment" have affected the projects.

The relations that I have talked about certainly constitute one of the major features of my own relation to the project. This "reading" is intended not so much as an outline of the various projects as an analysis which tends to highlight those relations, to try to understand their purposes and to check to what extent my interpretation of the territory has contributed towards, or directly influenced, the typology, spaces and actual stuctures of the designs.

From an analysis of the relations and of the meanings which are defined between architecture and "environment", I believe that three aspects arise as a constant in the evaluation and comparison stage of the project process.

First of all: the reading and interpretation of the "environnement", as a physical datum.

The territory is seen therefore as a place, as a special "site", as something like a "unicum" closely tied up with the geography and morphology of the context in which the project is to be carried out.

This physical datum makes it necessary to comprehend and to define the identity of the place, its meanings and its most distinguishing features, to be taken as elements of reference and of continuous dialogue with the architecture datum.

A plain, a wood, a lake, a hill or a village are, then, real elements of the new project, the meeting place between natural and artificial. Thus every "territory" has its own character, a thickness and a structure of its own, a law of its own, to be understood and assumed as a sometimes secret, but

profound, parameter for the intended new architecture.

Water and piles, rock and stone walls, clay and brick walls, are a series of binomials which to this day hide the most profound sense of the contact and possession established between man and his land.

The second aspect is the interpretation of the "environnement", as a testimony of history and of memory. This aspect embaces everything that reaches beyond the physical data.

So it is the symbolic aspects, the ancestral toil, the unknown struggles hidden in the soil, which fall as memory data under every new project. They are presences and values that belong to us not as nostalgic projections of a past, but as data in a real tissue, as the signs of the work, or rather, of the fatigue of that work, which has brought us to our own reality. The "environnement" is also and primarily the evidence of this presence of men and generations that are gone but can still give meaning and courage to our work.

A third aspect present in the relations between architecture and "environnement" is the notion of time.

Architecture, it has been said, makes a place different today to what it was yesterday. It is perhaps the tangible expression of the relating of man's labours (artificial) to his nature.

It is in this way that architecture alters and is transformed in synchrony with its time.

The periodical relating to the laws of nature (the seasonal cycle, the passing of the day, and so forth) situates architecture as a continuous and dynamic moment of reference to the "cosmic" values of our living.

I believe that it is in the comparison and in the awareness of these data that the architectural event today can be fed by its context. In this way architecture as the formal expression of history can be the active witness to the aspirations, uneasiness and hopes of our culture.

—Mario Botta

Mario Botta has built almost exclusively in Ticino, the Italian canton of Switzerland. His built works date from 1961, and his contribution to the current architectural debate continues to develop. He is identified with the Italian Neo-Rationalist movement, the Tendenza, whose philosophies—although manifested mainly in unbuilt projects—address the issue of reconciling traditional architectural symbolism with the severe but rational codes of modern movement ideology. Botta, who along with Aldo Rossi has made eminent buildings while others have made ideas, is situated centrally in the context of the other Ticinese architects. Constant collaboration with contemporaries such as Rudy Hunziker and Luigi Snozzi has resulted in local architectural statements with a much wider message.

The single-family house at Stabio (La Casa Rotonda, 1981) illustrates aspects of this message. Built of concrete blocks, this great drum is cut away sharply to reveal cavernous openings. Botta's fluency with his materials, crisply economic as they are, achieve richness, for example, in the layering of the windows behind the primary structure. Unlike its neighbours of more conventional form, this house interrelates with the surrounding natural world by means of openness within the general solidity of the structure.

Some thirty years earlier, Philip Johnson had opened the house to the external environment in his Glass House of 1949, in contrast to Le Corbusier's placing of primary forms in the landscape, as in the Villa Savoye of 1923. Corresponding, but more ancient, historical models may be found in Japanese architecture and in the mediaeval fortresses of Europe.

Botta emphasizes that "the quality of any architectural dendeavour hinges upon the intensity of this exchange" (between the built work and its spatial environment). La Casa Rotonda is at once a

fortress of great strength, alluding in a giant way to Italian classical precedent, and a coliseum—a theatre, in which natural light and the stark rationalist poise of the internal elements create a dynamic that contrasts with the tough concrete exterior.

Kenneth Frampton has noted that Botta "builds the site". The primary shapes of the Casa Rotonda plant it firmly in the ground and link it to nature; it contains illusions—the tree-trunk standing sentinel, and the opening to a deep, protective cave. The message here at Stabio is of a craft-oriented discipline and of a spatial awareness that embraces the site and the furthest horizon. Botta believes that regressive environmental contextualism, found commonly today, where the site and its surroundings are considered superior to any new spatial dynamic, must be overcome.

On an urban site, Botta's projected design for the enlargement of the main railway terminus at Zurich (1978) confronts a major contemporary problem, namely the restructuring of the urban fabric. He has designed a giant bridge across the rails, linking two sides of a city divided since the railway's original incursion. The bridge is a galleria, its concourse linking four levels of shops and restaurants. The project also places a large parking slab adjacent to the bridge structure over the rail tracks, with a rhythmically powerful row of buildings parallel to the rails alongside the station, the great frontage of which addresses the neighboring district. The aim of the development is to re-establish urban links, and to enliven the city by direct controntation. Here, as at Stabio, Botta builds the site. Seen as part of the Tendenza, this project avoids the rigid urban masterplan attitude that helped Le Corbusier develop his Plan Voisin for Paris (1925), and stresses the requirement for an evolving response in all urban intervention.

Botta's intention to set up taut but flixible relationships between buildings and their spatial environment enables both the Casa Rotonda and the Zurich station project to be seen as achievements at a technical and cultural level which advance and enrich our understanding of the true nature of functionalism. The task is wider and takes in issues of the total environment, where, as Alberto Sartoris has said of Botta, "intuition precedes reason".

—Darius Gilmont

BOURGEOIS, Victor.

Belgian. Born in Charleroi, 29 August 1897. Educated at the Académie Royale des Beaux-Arts, Brussels, 1914-19. Married to Jeanne Goos. In private practice, Brussels, 1920 until his death in 1962. Technical Consultant, Ministry of Public Health, Brussels, 1937-40; Technical Consultant, Société des Habitations à Bon Marché, Brussels, 1938-40; Technical Counsellor to the Town Planning Administration, Province of Hainaut, Belgium, 1945-47. Professor, École Nationale Supérieure d'Architecture, Brussels; Professor, Université du Travail Paul Pasteur, Charleroi. Editor or Co-Editor, Au Volant, Brussels, 1919; Le Geste, Brussels, 1920; Sept Arts, Brussels, 1922-28, 1948; Bruxelles, 1932-33. Vice-President, CIAM (Congrès Internationaux d'Architecture Moderne), 1928-40; President, Belgian Society of Modernist Town Planners and Architects, 1936-39. Exhibition: Victor Bourgeois 1897-1962, École Nationale Supérieure d'Architecture, Brussels, 1971. Recipient: Hainaut Architecture Prize, Belgium, 1960. Member, Free Academy of Belgium. Died (in Brussels) 24 July 1962.

Works:

1922 Multiple housing development, rue du Cubisme, Brussels

1922/
25 Cité Moderne (300 houses and town plan), Berchem-Sainte-Agathe, Brussels
1923 Town plan for Cité de Flenu, Mons, Belgium
1924 Sept Arts-L'Equerre Display, *Exposition de Lanterne Sourd,* Palais d'Egmont, Brussels
1925 Victor Bourgeois House, 103 Avenue Seghers, Koekelberg, Brussels
Housing complex, rue Robert Scott, Uccle, Brussels
1927 Maison Belge, Weissenhof Estate, Stuttgart
1928 L'Urbaneum (Museum of Town Planning), Brussels (project)
La Maison Blanche (Buchet House), Loth, Belgium (project)
Jespers House and Sculpture Studio, Avenue du Prince Heritier, Woluwe, Brussels
Apartment block, Avenue Franklin Roosevelt, Brussels
1929 Central air, rail and road transport stations, Brussels (project)
1930 House alterations and extensions, 263 Avenue Rogier, Schaerbaek, Brussels
La Nouveau Bruxelles (city expansion plan; project)
1931 Plan for *Mont des Arts* Exhibition Terraces, Brussels (project)
House, Wuthier-Braine, Brabant, Belgium
Nord-Midi International Train Station, Brussels (project)
Maison du Livre Belge display, Brussels
1932 Cité Mondiale (new town), Tervueren, Brussels (project)
House, Avenue Marianne, Uccle, Brussels
Villa in a park, Anderlecht, Belgium
1933 Director's House, Avenue Prekelinden, Woluwe, Brussels
1934 Victor Bourgeois House alterations, 103 Avenue Seghers, Koekelberg, Brussels
1935 Leopold II Restaurant, and Ruwenzori Pavillion Display, World's Fair, Brussels
Nouveau Frameries Development, Hainaut, Belgium
1936 La Jeannerie villa, Rhode-Saint-Genese, Belgium
Continental Cinema, Etterbeek, Belgium
1937 School of La Chapelle, Hornu, Belgium
1937/
49 Central Post Office, Brussels
1938 House, Avenue de l'Uruguay, Brussels (with gardens by Caneel-Claes)
Old people's housing, Kessel-Loo, Belgium
Leisure and Games Complex, Hornu, Belgium
Vacation and leisure centres plans, Congrès International de l'Habitation et de l'Urbanisme, Mexico (projects)
1938/
40 Hofstade Beach Development, Belgium (with Ministry of Public Health)
1939 Belgian Pavilion, World's Fair, New York
Pavilions, *Exposition de Liège,* Belgium
1939/
40 Housing and workers' facilities buildings, for Thy-le-Chateau Iron and Steelworks, Marcinelle, Belgium
Housing and office complex for Braine-le-Comte Factories, Belgium
1940/
41 City centre plan for Nivelles, Belgium (project; with G. Pepermans, V. Lichtert and H. Barigand)
1946 City and regional plan for Charleroi, Belgium (with Renée de Coomans)
Housing and workers' facilities buildings, for Saint-Roch Factories and Foundries, Couvin, Belgium
1947 Gustave Boel Offices, La Louviere, Belgium
1947/
48 Baume et Marpent Offices and Shop, Haine-Saint-Pierre, Belgium
1948 Housing and workers' facilities buildings, for Belge d'Azote Company, Renory-Ougree (Liège), Belgium

1948/
49 Hainaut Women's Technical School, Saint-Ghislain, Belgium
1950 Nos Caiaux Society Housing, La Borinage, Belgium
1953 Charleroi District Social Services Offices, Courcelles, Belgium
Sportsground, Jumet, Belgium (project)
Old people's home, Kessel-Loo, Belgium
1954 New Town Hall, Ostend, Belgium
New Saint-Camille Hospital, Namur, Belgium
Le-Foyer Montagnard (housing estate), Cité Selestat, Montigny-sur-Sambre, Belgium
1955 Medical Centre, Charleroi, Belgium
1955/
57 Francois Bovesse Cultural Centre, Namur, Belgium (with J. Ledoux, G. Lambeau, and J. Colin)
1957 Monument to the War Dead, Jemappes, Belgium (with Frans Lamberechts)
1958 Flats, Cité Moderne, Berchem-Sainte-Agathe, Brussels
Eternit Tower and Germinal Pavilion, World's Fair, Brussels
1959 Grandstand, Sportsground, Kessel-Loo, Belgium
1962 Le Rayon de Soleil Hospital Centre, Montignies, Charleroi, Belgium
1966 City centre development plan for Ixelles, Belgium

Publications:

By BOURGEOIS: books—*Rationelle Bebauungsweisen,* with Cor Van Eesteren and Sigfried Giedion, Frankfurt 1931; *Charleroi: Terre d'Urbanisme,* with Renée de Cooman, Brussels 1946; *De l'Architecture au Temps d'Erasme à l'Humanisme Social de Notre Temps,* with Renée de Cooman, Brussels and Paris 1949; *L'Architecte et Son Espace,* Brussels 1955; article—"La Cité Moderne" in *L'Habitation à bon marché* (Brussels), October 1923.

On BOURGEOIS: books—*Die Wohnung für das Existenzminimum,* Frankfurt 1930; *Neuzeitlicher Verkehrsbau* by H. Gescheit and K. Wittmann, Potsdam, Germany 1931; *Gli elementi dell'architettura funzionale* by Alberto Sartoris, Milan 1932; *International Architecture 1924-1934,* London 1934; *Victor Bourgeois: Architecture 1922-1952* by Pierre-Louis Flouquet, Brussels 1952; *Victor Bourgeois* by Georges Linze, Brussels 1959; *Victor Bourgeois 1897-1962,* exhibition catalogue, by R. Delevoy, M. Culot and Pierre Bourgeois, Brussels 1971; *Victor Bourgeois, Architect* by Maurice Coulot and others, New York 1980; articles—"Junge Kunst in Belgien" by Hannes Meyer in *Werk* (Zürich), September 1925; "La Cité moderne" by Pierre Bourgeois in *L'Habitation à bon marché* (Brussels), October 1925; "Un Musée d'urbanisme" in *Arlequin* (Brussels) no. 22, 1929; "Victor Bourgeois: Studio House for Oscar Jespers, and two Villas for Herman Terlinck" in *Archives d'architecture moderne* (Brussels), no. 16, 1979.

*

Victor Bourgeois was one of the most important figures of twentieth-century architecture in Belgium. For most of his professional life, he visualized architecture as the mirror of society, and because of his social concern, he specialized in public housing early in his career. Bourgeois claimed his primary influence was Berlage, who, with Frank Lloyd Wright, had made a deep impression on the students at the Académie Royale des Beaux-Arts in the Belgian capital, where he himself had studied.

His most celebrated work was the municipal housing scheme known as the Cité Moderne at Berchem-Ste-Agathe outside Brussels. In it, he created a variation in the appearance of terrace housing by the articulation of blocks and by the introduction of highly organized relationships between solids and voids, creating strong façades that were classics of their type. Indeed, Bourgeois attempted to give the elevations of his buildings a new language as tightly refined and controlled as that of classicism itself. Not for him was the free abstraction of shapes that were chaotically unrelated to each other. It is in these façades that the influence of the great American architect is paramount. Courtyards and squares added interest to the planning of the estates as a whole. Unquestionably, if Wright was the primary influence on the relationships between solids and voids (though he would not have approved of the hard materials), the ideas behind the layout came from Tony Garnier's Cité Industrielle and from other ideal schemes derived from French rather than from English Garden-City sources. The flat roofs, projecting flat balcony roofs, and plain, flat walls were very much in the severely formal mode of the period and might, with some adaptation, have sprung back into the Garnier scheme.

Bourgeois also designed schools and public buildings, as well as housing estates. He was also a town planner who became influenced by English ideas and by developments in the Netherlands and in Germany. He was a member of the Congrès Internationaux d'Architecture Moderne, and, through his offices, the third congress was held in Brussels in 1930. The theme was land-use planning and rational methods of site organization. The result was the publication of a report entitled *Rationelle Bebauungsweisen* which, like so many CIAM documents, mixed prolix dogma with sound sense.

He was invited to contribute designs for the Weissenhof Housing Settlement in Stuttgart in 1927; they were distinguished in their genre but were perhaps overshadowed by the more famous and supremely elegant block by Ludwig Mies van der Rohe.

—James Stevens Curl

BOYD, Robin Gerard Penleigh.

Australian. Born in Melbourne, Victoria, 3 January 1919. Educated at the Malvern Church of England Grammar School, Melbourne, 1926-36; served articles with the architect Kingsley A. Henderson, Melbourne, 1936-40, and concurrently attended evening classes at the Royal Melbourne College, 1936-39, and University of Melbourne Architectural Atelier, 1939-40 and 1945-46 (Editor, *Smudges,* 1939-42); registered architect, 1946; awarded Haddon Travelling Scholarship, 1947. Served as a Warrant Officer Class II in the 3rd Field Survey Company of the Australian Imperial Forces, in New Guinea, 1941-45. Married Dorothea Patricia Madden in 1943; children: Carolyn, Penleigh, and Suzy. In private practice, Melbourne, 1946-52; Partner, with Roy Grounds and Frederick Romberg, Grounds, Romberg and Boyd, Melbourne, 1952-62; returned to private practice, Melbourne, 1962 until his death in 1971. Part-time Lecturer in Design and Architectural History, University of Melbourne, 1948-56; Visiting Bemish Professor of Architecture, Massachusetts Institute of Technology, Cambridge, 1956-57. Member, Industrial Design Council of Australia, 1965-70; Trustee, National Gallery of Victoria, 1965-71; Member, National Capital Planning Committee, Canberra, 1968-71; Member, Melbourne Underground Rail Loop Authority, 1970-71; President, Victorian Chapter, Royal Australian Institute of Architects, 1970-71. Recipient: Gold Medal, Royal Australian Institute of Architects, 1970; Architecture Critic's Medal, American Institute of Architects, 1973. D.Litt.: University of New England, Armidale, New South Wales, 1967. Fellow, Royal Australian Institute of Architects, and

Robin Boyd: Menzies College Student Housing, La Trobe University, Melbourne, 1968.

Royal Society of Arts, London. Honorary Fellow, American Institute of Architects, 1960. C.B.E. (Commander, Order of the British Empire), 1971. *Died* (in Melbourne) *16 October 1971.*

Works:

1947 Boyd House, Camberwell, Victoria
1948 White House, Mentone, Victoria
1949 *House of Tomorrow* exhibition, Melbourne
1950 Gillison House, Balwyn, Victoria
1951 Darbyshire House, Templestowe, Victoria
      Miss Elizabeth Wade House, Mount Eliza, Victoria
1953 Professor Manning Clark House, Canberra
      Finlay House, Warrandyte, Victoria
      John Boyd House, North Balwyn, Victoria
      Professor Frank Fenner House, Canberra
1954 Ctesiphon House and Shop, Jordanville, Victoria
      Bridgford House, Black Rock, Victoria
      Richardson House, Blackfriars Close, Toorak, Victoria
      Blott House, Lilydale, Victoria
1955 Troedel House, Wheeler's Hill, Victoria
      Stegbar Windowall factories in Melbourne, Sydney, and Brisbane
1956 C. W. P. Wilson House, Kew, Victoria
      Kenneth Myer "Pelican" House, Mount

Eliza, Victoria
      Gavin Walkley House, North Adelaide, South Australia
      Foy House, Beaumaris, Victoria
1957 Holford House, Ivanhoe, Victoria
      Haughton-James House, Kew, Victoria
      McManamny House, Beaumaris, Victoria
      Peninsula House (project)
1959 Professor Zelman Cowen House, Kew, Victoria
      Boyd House II, Walsh Street, South Yarra, Victoria
1960 Clemson House, Kew, Victoria
      Southgate Fountain, Snowden Gardens, Melbourne
      Lloyd House, Brighton, Victoria
1961 Black Dolphin Motel, Merimbula, New South Wales
1962 Phillip, Blakers, and Griffin Houses, Canberra
      McNicoll House, South Yarra, Victoria
      Handfield House, Eltham, Victoria
      Richardson House, Barwon Heads, Victoria
      Domain Park Flats, South Yarra, Victoria
1963 Wright House, Warrandyte, Victoria
      Burgess House, Ivanhoe, Victoria
1965 Baker House, Bacchus Marsh, Victoria
      Kaye House, Frankston, Victoria
      Shelmerdine House, Mornington, Victoria
      Verge House, Canberra

Simon House, Narre Warren, Victoria
      Moysey House, Echuca, Victoria
      Blackwell House, Echuca, Victoria
      Moore House, Wheeler's Hill, Victoria
      John Balman Motor Inn, Queen's Road, Melbourne
1967 Apple Tree Project Houses, Wheeler's Hill, Victoria
      McCaughey Court Student Housing, University of Melbourne
      Fletcher House, Brighton, Victoria
      Lyons House, Dolan's Bay, near Sydney
      President Motor Inn, Queen's Road, Melbourne
      Australian Pavilion interiors, *Expo '67,* Montreal
      Purves House, Kew, Victoria
      Lawrence Flats, Kew, Victoria
      Featherston-Currey House, Ivanhoe, Victoria
1968 Tower Hill Natural History Museum, Warrnambool, Victoria
      Menzies College Student Housing, La Trobe University, Melbourne
      Farfor Holiday Houses, Portsea, Victoria
      Eltringham House, Aranda, A.C.T.
1970 Australian Pavilion interiors, *Expo '70,* Osaka, Japan
1971 Hegatty House, Ringwood, Victoria
      Ian Crawford House, Canterbury, Victoria
      Churchill Memorial Trust House, Canberra

Publications:

By BOYD: books—*Victorian Modern,* Melbourne 1947; *Australia's Home: Its Origins, Builders and Occupiers,* Melbourne 1952; *The Australian Ugliness,* Melbourne 1960; *Kenzo Tange,* London and New York 1962; *The Walls Around Us: The Story of Australian Architecture,* Melbourne 1962; *The New Architecture,* Melbourne 1963; *The Puzzle of Architecture,* Melbourne, London and New York, 1965; *The Book of Melbourne and Canberra,* with Harold Freedman and Charles Troedel, Adelaide, South Australia 1965; *New Directions in Japanese Architecture,* London and New York 1968, Barcelona 1969; *Living in Australia,* with Mark Strizic, Sydney 1970; *The Great, Great Australian Dream,* Sydney 1972; articles—"A New Eclecticism" in *Architectural Review* (London), September 1951; "The Functional Neurosis" in *Architectural Review* (London), February 1958; "The Engineering of Excitement" in *Architectural Review* (London), November 1958; "The Sad End of the New Brutalism" in Architectural Review (London), July 1967; "Anti-Architecture" in *Architectural Forum* (New York), November 1968; "A Glimpse of the Future" in *Architectural Record* (New York), March 1970; "Expo '70" in *Architectural Review* (London), August 1970.

On BOYD: articles—afterword by David Saunders to Boyd's book *Living in Australia,* Sydney 1970; "Retrospective Robin Boyd" by David Saunders in *Architecture in Australia* (Sydney), February 1972; "Peter Crone Adds to Robin Boyd" by Ian McDougall in *Transition* (St. Kilda, Victoria), March 1981; "Anger and New Order—Some Aspects of Robin Boyd's Career" by Conrad Hamann and Chris Hamann in *Transition* (St. Kilda, Victoria), September/December 1981.

*

Robin Boyd began practice at a time when the Modern Movement was gaining foothold in Australia. His contribution was not to its establishment but to its maturity. He edited a student broadsheet, *Smudges,* from 1939 to 1942, in which he attacked not only the still prevalent historicist design but the crude limitations of functional forms as well. Boyd played a great part in focussing Australian interest on American modern regional movements such as the Bay Region style. He wrote the first study of modern architecture in Australia, *Victorian Modern,* in 1946, and later, from it, developed a history, *Australia's Home,* in 1952. After 1950, regionalism see-sawed with internationalism in Boyd's architecture. He came to be drawn to the International Style. In particular, he became interested in the use of the cantilevered structure, the open plan, and crisp, simple forms.

In the practice of Grounds, Romberg and Boyd, he produced numerous house designs. All were marked by open planning, the extension of a functional element to a major formal theme, and the reflection of site conditions in structure. These themes found their most complete expression in his own house of 1959 and in his Featherston-Currey house of 1967. The second was a simple oblong space, where platforms replaced rooms and gardens formed part of the internal flooring. The roof lines corresponded to the slopes of their sites.

His architecture clearly took the problem-solving approach. Faced with a large roof area in his own house, he simply suspended the roof on cables. Over a creek-bed site, he suspended another house from two bridge arches. His work was highly conceptual, and a whole series of his designs adapted basic geometric forms for the ground plans—the crescent and semi-ellipse in particular. These interests were reflected elsewhere in contemporary designs but seldom with such purity of concepts and form. In many instances, Boyd led what became popular planning solutions. He saw himself as defending the functionalism of the militant Modern Movement.

His defence against its opponents was that functionalism was being discarded before it had been adequately tested. True to this principle, he constantly introduced new materials and detailing in his work.

It is not surprising that Boyd became one of the earliest critics to study new Japanese architecture, where he saw architects defending functionalism in their work. He wrote the first monograph on Kenzo Tange in 1962 and followed it with the seminal *New Directions in Japanese Architecture* in 1968. He was fascinated by the promise that advanced technology held for architects and was interested in the way the Japanese and Archigram were giving leads in this area. He felt that the greatest field for the new technology was in large-scale design and entered this field for ten years before his death.

His position moved from the defence of functionalism to that of an interested observer of new trends. This stance can be seen in some of his articles for *Architectural Review.* He also expressed his views through radio and television broadcasts for the Australian Broadcasting Commission.

—Dorothea Boyd

*

Robin Boyd made a twofold contribution to Australian architecture—as a distinguished practising architect and as a critic and writer. And although he undoubtedly thought of his architecture as being more important than his writing, it was his writing about architecture, and about the lifestyle of Australia, that has had the greater influence. Boyd was the first Australian writer on architecture to adopt the role of social commentator. His approach led to a more critical appraisal of Australian buildings and a protracted campaign against Australian visual traditions and cultural deficiencies. The chief defect of Australian architecture, Boyd contended, was that buildings lacked a single strong idea and were instead an "assortment of little ideas which are shaken up together to make a building; typically, the 'Featuremarket' with its many loud, stale ideas mixed together."

Boyd's writing and architecture were not separate and unrelated; rather, they express, in different ways, his deep involvement with people and buildings. His dual interest in architectural criticism and housing were first expressed in the student publication *Smudges* of the University of Melbourne. In 1950 he founded the Small Homes Service operated by the Victorian Institute of Architects. A few years later, he designed Australia's first project house—Peninsula House—for Contemporary Homes Ltd. This concept was later to be developed in Sydney by Ken Woolley and Michael Dysart in their project homes for Lend Lease (1961) and Pettit and Sevitt. At about this time, Boyd designed a stock "window-wall" system with various options for the Stegbar company. But his principal achievement is in the area of domestic architecture—he built about 100 houses in all. It was not until 1968 that a major commission, Menzies College, La Trobe University, in a 1960's Brutalism idiom, was offered to Boyd. Of his houses, "Pelican," the Kenneth Myer House (1956), Robin Boyd's own house at South Yarra (1959), the Lloyd House (1960), the Lyons House, Dolan's Bay, near Sydney (1967), a group of holiday houses, Portsea, Victoria (1968), and the Featherstone House, Ivanhoe, Victoria (1967) are some of his best works.

The intentional crudeness of the thick gumtree trunks which serve as columns in the Black Dolphin Motel, Merimbula (1961) marks a new rustic bush phase in Australian architecture and, at the same time, reflects Boyd's growing disenchantment with the machine-made appearance of the International Style. His penchant for social comment was well suited to one of his last important projects, the design of the exhibits in the space tunnel of the Australian Pavilion at *Expo '70,* Osaka.

Boyd disapproved of style up to a point and believed that architectural form should be the product of the directness with which functional problems are solved with inventive structures. His

architectural approach was essentially pragmatic; he liked to describe it as "realism." And while Boyd displayed a consistency in his buildings, he regarded each new problem as something unique and special, with the result that there is no recognizable Boyd style. One feature of his buildings, which is not much commented on, is his use of the tent. His own house at South Yarra had a simply suspended roof, and the Myer House has a parasol roof standing proud of the living components.

Boyd wrote some eleven books between 1947 and 1971, of which *The Australian Ugliness* is perhaps the best known, though *The Puzzle of Architecture* is probably his most important book. His writings mark the beginning of a new self-consciousness in architecture, an important first step in establishing a coherent relationship with architectural history.

—Philip Drew

*

BRAWNE, Michael.
British. Born in Vienna, Austria, 5 May 1925. Educated at the University of Edinburgh, 1942-43; Architectural Association School, London, 1948-53, Dip.A.A. 1953; Massachusetts Institute of Technology, Cambridge, 1953-54 (Smith-Mundt Fellow), M.Arch. 1954. Served as a Sergeant Meteorologist in the Royal Air Force, 1944-47. Married Rhoda Dupler in 1954; children: Peter, Alison, and Nicholas; married the architect Charlotte Baden-Powell in 1983. Worked for the Soullee Steel Company, San Francisco, 1954-56, Architects' Co-Partnership, q.v., London, 1956-59, British Transport Commission, 1959-61, and Denys Lasdun q.v., and Partners, London, 1961-64. Since 1964, Principal, Michael Brawne and Associates, London and Bath, Avon. Instructor in Architecture, Cambridge University, England, 1964-78; Professor of Architecture, University of Bath, Avon, since 1978. Director, Architectural Association/Royal Institute of British Architects Seminar on University Planning, University of Sussex, Brighton, 1964; Royal Institute of British Architects Representative, Illuminating Engineering Society panel on museum lighting, 1966-69; British Council Lecturer in India, 1968; Member, Advisory Panel, Centre for Advanced Studies in Environment, Architectural Association, London, 1969; Member, International Colloquium on the Technical Equipment of Central Libraries, Prague, 1974. Member of the Consultative Committee, Thames Polytechnic School of Architecture, London, 1974-77; Trustee, Holburne of Menstruie Museum, Bath, Avon, since 1978. Honorary M.A.: University of Cambridge, England, 1977. Associate, 1954, and Fellow, 1969, Royal Institute of British Architects. Address: Michael Brawne and Associates, 15 Northampton Street, Bath BA1 2SN, England.

Works:

1954/
56 Wall system and door units for Soullee Steel Company, San Francisco
1956/
59 House, Enugu, Nigeria (at Architects' Co-Partnership)
Esso Oil Terminal, Apapa, Nigeria (at Architects' Co-Partnership)
1959/
61 Power Signal Box, British Railways, Manchester (at British Transport Commission)
Power Signal Box, British Railways, Edge Hill, Liverpool (at British Transport Commission)
Marshalling Yard and Amenity Buildings, British Railways, Carlisle (at British Transport Commission)

1961 House, 31 South Hill Park, London
    Trinity College Library, Dublin (competition project)
1966 Housing study for Bovis Holdings Ltd., London
1967 House, Fisher's Pond, Hampshire
1968 Bettwys Comprehensive School, Newport, Monmouthshire (competition project)
    Oxford Gallery, Oxford, England
1969 Agricultural Research Council Maintenance Workshop, Babraham, Cambridgeshire
1969/
71 Horne Brothers Shop, 4 Oxford Street, London
1970 Agricultural Research Council Animal Research Laboratories, Babraham, Cambridgeshire
    Agricultural Research Council Biochemistry Laboratory, Babraham, Cambridgeshire (with Colin St John Wilson)
1971 Dorset County Museum extension, Dorchester
    Indoor swimming pool, Bosham, Sussex
1972 Gimpel Fils Art Gallery, London
1972/
73 Consumer Association Testing and Research Laboratory, stage I and II, Harpenden, Hertfordshire
1974 Costume Gallery, Royal Courts of Justice, London (with Colin St. John Wilson)
    Physics Building, Royal Holloway College, Egham, Surrey
1977 Arts Centre, Cambridgeshire, England (project)
    Central Art Gallery conversion, Rochdale, Lancashire (with the Borough Architect)
    National Museum and Archive, Oman (project)
1978 Cooper Art Gallery, Barnsley, Yorkshire
    National Gallery renovation, London (as consultant)
    National Library, Colombo, Sri Lanka (with Chief Government Architect)
    Library for Rare Books and Manuscripts, San'a, Yemen (as consultant)
1979 National Archaeological Museum, Citadel Amman, Jordan (project)
1980 Institute for Scientific and Technological Information, Beijing, China (as consultant)
1981 International Data Bank for Non-Aligned Countries, Colombo, Sri Lanka (as consultant)
    Jamiah Naleemiah Library, Beruwela, Sri Lanka
1983 Physics Research Laboratory, Royal Holloway and Bedford Colleges, Egham, Surrey
1984 Students' Union Building, Royal Holloway and Bedford Colleges, Egham, Surrey

Exhibition Designs: *Gauguin and the Pont-Aven Group,* Tate Gallery, London, 1966; *Naum Gabo,* Tate Gallery, London, 1966; *Jean Dubuffet,* Tate Gallery, London, 1966; *Marcel Duchamp,* Tate Gallery, London, 1966; *Rouault,* Tate Gallery, London, 1966; *David Smith,* Tate Gallery, London, 1966; *L. S. Lowry,* Tate Gallery, London, 1966; *Bomberg/Zoltan Kemeny,* Tate Gallery, London 1966; *Great Britain/U.S.S.R,* Victoria and Albert Museum, London, 1967; *Picasso Sculpture, Ceramics and Graphics,* Tate Gallery, London, 1967; *Cubist Art from Czechoslovakia,* Tate Gallery, London, 1967; *Derain,* Royal Academy, London, 1967; *Turkish Art,* Victoria and Albert Museum, London, 1967; *Ancient Art from Afghanistan,* Royal Academy, London, 1967; *Marzotto Prize,* Tate Gallery, London, 1967; *Alfred Wallis/Peter Lanyon,* Tate Gallery, London, 1968; *Henry Moore,* Tate Gallery, London, 1968; *Balthus,* Tate Gallery, London, 1968; *Roy Lichtenstein,* Tate Gallery, London, 1968; *Barbara Hepworth,* Tate Gallery, London, 1968; *Hungarian Art Treasures,* Victoria and Albert Museum, London, 1968; *Willem de Kooning,* Tate Gallery, London, 1969; *Magritte,* Tate Gallery, London, 1969; *Art of the Real,* Tate Gallery, London, 1969; *Pop Art,* Hayward Gallery, London, 1969; *Claes Oldenburg,* Tate Gallery, London, 1970; *Multiple Art,* Whitechapel Art Gallery, London, 1970; *Richard Hamilton,* Tate Gallery, London, 1970; *Cambridge Festival,* Corn Exchange, Cambridge, England, 1970; *Early Celtic Art,* Hayward Gallery, London, 1971; *Art in Revolution,* Hayward Gallery, London, 1971; *Ceramic Art of China,* Victoria and Albert Museum, London, 1971; *Victorian Church Art,* Victoria and Albert Museum, London, 1971; *Amiet and Giacometti,* Kettle's Yard Gallery, Cambridge, England, 1971; *Gerrit Rietveld,* Hayward Gallery, London, 1972; *French Symbolists,* Hayward Gallery, London, 1972; *The Age of Neo-Classicism,* Royal Academy, London, 1972; *The King's Arcadia: Inigo Jones and the Stuart Court,* Banqueting House, London, 1973; *Treasures from the European Community,* Victoria and Albert Museum, London, 1973; *Man and Beast: The Work of Elisabeth Frink,* Kettle's Yard Gallery, Cambridge, England, 1973; *The Art of Woodcarving in West Africa and New Guinea,* Kettle's Yard Gallery, Cambridge, England, 1975; *The Arts of Islam,* Hayward Gallery, London, 1976; *John Constable Bicentenary,* British Council, London, 1977 (toured overseas); multi-screen presentation at *Islam dans les Collections Nationales,* Grand Palais, Paris, 1977; multi-screen presentation at *Architecture in the Lands of Islam,* State Museum, Dahlem, Berlin, 1981.

Publications:

By BRAWNE: books—*the New Museum: Architecture and Display,* Stuttgart and London 1965; *University Planning and Design: A Symposium,* editor, London 1967; *Libraries: Architecture and Equipment,* Stuttgart and London 1970; entries on architecture and town planning in *A Dictionary of Modern Thought,* edited by Alan Bullock and Oliver Stallybrass, London 1977; entry on museums in *The Macmillan Encyclopaedia of Architecture and Technological Change,* edited by Pedro Guedes, London 1979; *The Museum Interior: Temporary and Permanent Display Techniques,* London and Stuttgart 1982, Milan 1983; *Arup Associates: The Biography of an Architectural Practice,* London 1983; articles—"Project in Steel: A House in Berkeley" in *Arts and Architecture* (Los Angeles), January 1956; "The Production of Shelter: A System of Prefabrication" in *Arts and Architecture* (Los Angeles), September 1956; "Walls off the Peg: The Curtain Wall" in *Architectural Review* (London), September 1957; "Geometry of Shade" in *Architectural Review* (London), June 1958; "Looking Up: Suspended Ceilings as an Element in Interior Design" in *Architectural Review* (London), September 1958; "Le Corbusier: A Symposium" in *Architectural Association Journal* (London), May 1959; "The Picture Wall: An Analysis of Art Gallery Design" in *Architectural Review* (London), May 1959; "Object on View: An Analysis of Museum Design" in *Architectural Review* (London), November 1959; "Polyester Fibreglass" in *Architectural Review* (London), December 1959; "Parking Terminals" in *Architectural Review* (London), August 1960; "Libraries: Communicating with Individuals" in *Architectural Review* (London), October 1961; "Airport Passenger Buildings" in *Architectural Review* (London), November 1962; "Commonwealth Institute, South Kensington: Critical Appraisal" in *Architectural Review* (London), April 1963; "Student Living: Approaches to Residential Planning" in *Architectural Review* (London), October 1963; "University Planning" in *Architectural Association Journal* (London), January 1965; "University of York: Critical Appraisal" in *Architectural Review* (London), December 1965; "The Wit of Technology: The Works of Charles Eames" in *Architectural Design* (London), September 1966; "The New Whitney: The Building: A Critical Appraisal" in *Artforum* (Los Angeles), November 1966; "Museum Design for Conservation" in *London Conference on Museum Climatology,* London 1967; "Library Planning" in *Better Library Buildings,* London 1969; "The New Universities," editor, a special issue of *Architectural Review* (London), April 1970; "Off the Shelf: A Review of the Library at Redcar" in *Architectural Review* (London), July 1971; "A Museum and Some Problems of Tradition: A Review of the North Jutland Museum of Arts" in *Architectural Review* (London), March 1973; "Briefing: Museums" in *Architectural Design* (London), October 1973; "Wolfson College, Oxford: An Appraisal" in *Architectural Review* (London), October 1974; "What Is Wrong with Eclecticism?" in *Gottfried Semper und die Mitte des 19 Jahrhunderts,* Basel and Stuttgart, 1976; "Museum of London: An Appraisal" in *Architectural Review* (London), July 1977; "Art Gallery Extensions" in *Architects' Journal* (London), 30 November 1977; "Geoffrey Bawa: An Appraisal" in *Architectural Review* (London), April 1978; "Milton Keynes Central Library" in *Architects' Journal* (London), 30 September 1981; "Some Recent Trends in Museum Design" in *International Journal of Museum Management and Curatorship* (Guildford, Surrey), September 1983; "The Burrell" in *Architects' Journal* (London), 9 October 1983; "Education in Practice: Counting the Cost" in *Architects' Journal* (London), 9 November 1983; "Museums: Mirrors of Their Time?" in *Architectural Review* (London), February 1984.

On BRAWNE: books—*New Architecture of London* by Sam Lambert, London 1963; *Maisons de vacances en Europe* by Bernard Wolgensiger, Fribourg, Switzerland 1968; *Zodiac 18: Great Britain,* Milan 1968; *50 Ville de nostro tempo* by Roberto Aloi, Milan 1970; *Modern Houses in Town and Country* by Joyce Lowrie, London 1974; *House Conversion and Renewal* by Peter Collymore, London 1975; *Architectural Guide to Cambridge and East Anglia since 1920* by Charles McKean, London 1982; article—"50 Noteworthy World Architects" in *Nas Dom* (Maribor, Yugoslavia), June 1984.

All statements of architectural intent are difficult and risky since the correspondence between such verbal statements and the architectural end product is invariably shadowy. To say therefore that I believe it important to create an architecture of complex simplicity may not be very helpful or, in the end, accurate, even given a certain amount of explanation. Its reverse, simple complexity (to make a negative statement, which is often easier), is either the inability to resolve the enmeshed nature of all architectural problems or just an accumulation of elements for their own sake; in the end a kind of fussiness. Attempts to enrich architecture consciously but without much thought often produce just such simple complexity.

By complex simplicity, I mean a kind of order which has arisen out of a set of unique circumstances, modified always of course by one's own visual likes and dislikes; an order which is intelligible to others and, hopefully, not so banal that it is boring or so weak that it has failed to deal with the important problems. This is not a matter of decoration but of the way in which all aspects are handled, including those that show how a building is put together. Perhaps it has something to do with the density of visual information.

I have, as an architect, found myself involved with a limited number of building types: houses, laboratories, museums, and libraries. It could be argued that the kind of attitude towards complexity which I am advocating is particularly appropriate to these buildings. I do not believe this to be the case. First, the types are sufficiently dissimilar in their characteristics, and second, twenty years of teaching have persuaded me that the attitude can be extended over a wide range of architectural tasks. The limited palette was also, of course, by no means self-imposed but a matter of circumstance which has become self-perpetuating. The need to test these assumptions actively on other problems is thus one of the drives that makes an involvement in practice continuously necessary and hopeful.

Architecture as both a practical and academic activity I find totally absorbing and believe it moreover to be important. Not simply because I find it enjoyable but because I am convinced that buildings, quite apart from sheltering so much of our life, can give great pleasure and security to most of us. It would be hard to think of a civilised world without architecture; not just great architecture, but any.

—Michael Brawne

Much of the flavour of Michael Brawne's architecture can be surmised from the tone and method of his writings—cool, intellectual, self-conscious, raising interesting questions about the nature of architecture, not without a mannered charm.

Very much a part of a certain Cambridge circle (though he now holds the chair at the University of Bath, leaving his frequent collaborator, Colin St. John Wilson, as professor in the fens), Brawne has had his major influence through his words, as a critic in the *Architectural Review,* and as a teacher, in the studio of the architecture department at Cambridge University. Nor, even as a designer, has his public impact been through his occasional series of finely ordered buildings. For nearly twenty years, Brawne has produced, with great skill, a large number of major art exhibitions of a staggeringly catholic range, usually for one of the leading U.K. public galleries. With the touch of a fine accompanist, he has managed consistently to enhance both the material and its setting, whilst remaining unobtrusive himself—a point well illustrated in the Hayward Gallery's *Art in Revolution* in 1971 (the major Constructivist show, with its banners and agit-prop streaming from the presses) and in *The Age of Neo-Classicism,* an equally important but utterly contrasting event the following year in the very different setting of the Royal Academy.

Brawne's buildings—research laboratories clad in russet steel, museum and library, the occasional houses—all bear the stamp of his sense of order, immaculate yet informal. Apart from an occasional heaviness of frame (which is almost ungainly), there is, in his work, from the Fisher's Pond House of 1967 to the National Library of Sri Lanka of 1978, no family pattern in image or in form-generator. (His recurring interest in the diagonal never becomes a trademark.)

His own house in Hampstead (1961) expresses the man. The stair had to be a certain width; the window module was less. And so, with complex simplicity, Brawne created a cranked internal wall, the return leg fully glazed into the stair well. The architecture would have been less had the glazing bar been moved, the wall angled, or the planning simply changed. He said, "The need to accommodate the difference between the width of stairs and the module of the external glazing created the opportunity for an unusual internal window...." Too far, perhaps. Brawne's civility, nevertheless, remains a precious quality.

—J.M. McKean

BREUER, Marcel Lajos.
American. Born in Pécs, Hungary, 22 May 1902; emigrated to the United States, 1937; naturalized, 1944. Educated at the Allami Föreáiskola, Pécs, 1912-20; Bauhaus, Weimar, Germany, 1920-24, graduated 1924. Married Martha Erps in 1926; Constance Crocker Leighton in 1940; children: Thomas and Francesca. Master of the Bauhaus, in Weimar, 1924, and Dessau, Germany, 1925-28;

architect and planner in Dessau, 1925-28, Berlin, 1928-31, and London (in partnership with F.R.S. Yorke, *q.v.*), 1935-36; Associate Professor, Harvard University School of Design, Cambridge, Massachusetts, 1937-46; Principal, Marcel Breuer and Associates, Cambridge, 1937-46, and New York City, 1946 until his retirement in 1976. Member, National Council of Architectural Registration Boards, 1947. Exhibitions: *Werkbund Exhibition,* Grand Palais, Paris, 1930; *Bauausstellung,* Berlin, 1931; *Bauhaus 1919-1928,* New York, 1938; Museum of Modern Art, New York (individual), 1949; Metropolitan Museum of Art, New York (individual), 1972; Musée du Louvre, Paris (individual), 1973; Bauhaus Archives, Berlin, 1974; *Boston: Forty Years of Modern Architecture,* Institute of Contemporary Art, Boston, 1980; Museum of Modern Art, New York (retrospective), 1981. Recipient: First Prize, International Aluminum Competition, 1930, 1933; Medal of Honor, 1965, Gold Medal, 1968, Award for Excellence, 1970, Honor Award, 1970, 1972, 1973, and Education Award, 1981, American Institute of Architects; New York State Council on the Arts Award, 1967; Bard Award, City Club of New York, 1968; Thomas Jefferson Foundation Medal, University of Virginia, Charlottesville, 1968; Metropolitan Washington Board of Trade Award, 1969; Grande Medaille d'Or, French Academy of Architecture, 1976. Honorary doctorates: Pratt Institute, Brooklyn, New York, 1950; University of Budapest, 1957; University of Notre Dame, Indiana, 1968; Harvard University, Cambridge, Massachusetts, 1970. Fellow, American Institute of Architects. Member, National Institute of Arts and Letters. Honorary Member, Association of Argentine Architects, 1947, and Association of Architects of Colombia, 1947. *Died* (in New York City) *1 July 1981.*

Works:

1924/
28 Prototype steel furniture and interchangeable cabinet units
1930 Fuld Factory, Frankfurt (project)
1932 Harnischmacher House I, Wiesbaden, Germany
1936 Doldertal Apartments, Zürich (with A. and E. Roth)
Isokon Laminated Furniture
Gane's Stone Exhibition Pavilion, Bristol, England
Civic Centre of the Future, London (project; with F. R. S. Yorke)
1938 Haggerty House, Cohasset, Machachusetts (with Walter Gropius)
Wheaton College Art Center, Norton, Massachusetts (with Walter Gropius)
1939 Breuer House I, Lincoln, Massachusetts
1940 Chamberlin Cottage, Wayland, Massachusetts (with Walter Gropius)
1942 South Boston Redevelopment (project)
Prefabricated houses, Cambridge, Massachusetts (project)
1945 Servicemen's Memorial, Cambridge, Massachusetts (project; with L. Andersen)
Tompkins House, Hewlett Harbor, New York
Geller House, Lawrence, Long Island, New York
1947 Breuer House II, New Canaan, Connecticut
Robinson House, Williamstown, Massachusetts
1948 Breuer Cottage, Wellfleet, Massachusetts
1949 Wolfson House, Pleasant Valley, New York
Clark House, Orange, Connecticut
1950 Co-operative Dormitory, Vassar College, Poughkeepsie, New York
Stillman House I, Litchfield, Connecticut
1951 Breuer House III, New Canaan, Connecticut
1952 Art Center, Sarah Lawrence College, Bronxville, New York
Caesar Cottage, Lakeville, Connecticut

1953 Torin Corporation Building, Oakville, Ontario
1953/
70 St. John's Abbey and University, Collegeville, Minnesota (with H. Smith)
1954 Grieco House, Andover, Massachusetts
1954/
57 Institute for Advanced Study Housing, Princeton, New Jersey (with R. F. Gatje)
1956 Litchfield High School, Connecticut (with O'Connor and Killham)
1956/
61 New York University, University Heights, New York (with H. Smith and R. F. Gatje)
1957 De Bijenkorf Department Store, Rotterdam (with A. Elzas)
Laaff House, Andover, Massachusetts (with H. Beck- hard)
1958 Unesco Headquarters, Paris (with Pier Luigi Nervi and Bernard Zehrfuss)
United States Embassy, The Hague
Stachelin House, Feldmeilen, Switzerland (with H. Beckhard)
Van Leer Headquarters, Amstelveen, Netherlands
El Recreo Urban Centre, Caracas (project; with E. Fuenmeyer and H. Beckhard)
Resort Development Apartments, Tanaguarena, Venezuela (project; with H. Beckhard)
1959 Convent of the Annunciation, Bismarck, North Dakota (with H. Smith)
Hunter College Library, New York (with R. F. Gatje)
Hanson House, Huntington, Long Island, New York
Ustinov House, Vevey, Switzerland (project; with R. F. Gatje)
1960 Charles Center, Baltimore, Maryland (project; with H. Smith)
1960 Flaine Ski Resort, Haute Savoie, France (with R.F. Gatje)
1961 IBM Research Center, La Gaude, Var, France (with R. F. Gatje)
Temple B'nai Jeshurun, Short Hills, New Jersey (with H. Beckhard)
1962 Torin Corporation Machine Building, Torrington, Connecticut (with R. F. Gatje)
1963/
68 United States Department of Housing and Urban Development Headquarters, Washington, D.C. (with H. Beckhard)
1963/
70 ZUP Development, Bayonne, France (with R. F. Gatje)
1964 Torin Manufacturing Plant, Nivelles, Belgium (with H. Smith)
Van der Wal House, Amsterdam (project; with H. Smith)
New England Merchant's Bank, Boston (project; with H. Beckhard)
1965 New York University Dormitory, Bronx, New York (project)
1965/
68 Laboratories Sarget, Bordeaux, France (with R. F. Gatje and Daurel)
1965/
69 University of Massachusetts Campus Center and Garage, Amherst (with H. Beckhard)
1966 Whitney Museum of American Art, New York (with H. Smith)
Stillman House II, Litchfield, Connecticut (with H. Beckhard)
Torin Corporation Adminstration Building, Torrington, Connecticut (with H. Beckhard)
Franklin D. Roosevelt Memorial, Washington, D.C. (project; with H. Beckhard)
1967 St. Francis de Sales Church, Muskegon, Michigan (with H. Beckhard)
Interama, Miami, Florida (project; with H. Beckhard)
Kent School Girls' Chapel, Connecticut (project; with R. F. Gatje)

Flushing Meadow Sports Park, New York (project; with Beckhard, Tange, and Halprin)

1968   175 Park Avenue Office Building, New York (project; with H. Beckhard)

Parish Church, Olgiata, Rome (project; with M. Jossa)

1968/
77   Third Power Plant and Visitor's Center, Grand Coulee Dam, Washington State (with H. Smith)

1969   New York University Technology Building II, Bronx, New York (with H. Smith)

Armstrong Rubber Company Headquarters, West Haven, Connecticut (with R. F. Gatje)

Yale University Engineering Building, New Haven, Connecticut (with H. Smith)

Convent, Baldegg, Switzerland (with Jordi and Gatje)

Soriano House, Greenwich, Connecticut (with T. Papachristou)

Office Building, Syracuse, New York (project; with H. Beckhard)

1970   Cleveland Museum of Art, Ohio (with H. Smith)

1971   Cleveland Trust Headquarters, Ohio (with H. Smith)

1975   Stillman House III, Litchfield, Connecticut (with T. Papachristou)

Australian Embassy, Paris (with Harry Seidler and M. Jossa)

Gagarin House II, Litchfield, Connecticut (with T. Papachristou)

1977   Hubert Humphrey Building, Washington, D.C. (with H. Beckhard)

Roxbury High School, Boston (with T. Papachristou)

IBM Complex, Boca Raton, Florida (with R. F. Gatje)

Central Library, Atlanta, Georgia (with Smith, Stevens, and Wilkinson)

Federal Courthouse and Office Building, Columbia, South Carolina (with H. Beckhard, David and Floyd, and J. Hemphill)

Publications:

By BREUER: books—*Sun and Shadow: The Philosophy of an Architect,* edited by Peter Blake, New York and London 1956; *Marcel Breuer 1921-62,* Stuttgart 1962; articles—"Die Möbelabteilung des staatlichen Bauhauses zu Weimar," in *Fachblatt für Holzarbeiter* (Weimar), 1925; "Metallmöbel" in *Deutscher Werkbund* (Stuttgart), 1928; "Metallmöbel und moderne Raumlichkeit" in *Das Neue Frankfurt,* January 1928; "Beitrage zur Frage des Hochhauses" in *Die Form* (Opladen Germany), no. 5, 1930; "Das Innere de Hauses" in *Bauwelt* (Berlin), May 1931; "Aus einem Vortrag...gehalten im Kunstgewerbemuseum, Zürich" in *Werk* (Zürich), no. 19, 1932; "Where Do We Stand?" in *Architectural Review* (London), April 1935; "Architecture and Material" in *Circle: International Survey of Constructive Art* (London), 1937; "What Is Modern Architecture?" in *Museum of Modern Art Bulletin* (New York), Spring 1948.

On BREUER: books—*Staatliches Bauhaus in Weimar,* Weimar/Munich 1923; *Bauhaus 1919-1928,* exhibition catalogue. New York 1938; *Marcel Breuer and the American Tradition in Architecture* by Henry Russell Hitchcock, Cambridge, Massachusetts 1938; *Marcel Breuer: Architect,* exhibition catalogue, New York 1949; *Marcel Breuer 1921-1962* by Cranston Jones, London 1962; *Marcel Breuer: New Buildings and Projects* by Tician Papachristou, New York 1970; *GA 5: Marcel Breuer—Koerfer House, Tessin, Switzerland; Stillman House III, Litchfield, Connecticut,* with text by Stanley Abercrombie, Tokyo 1977; *Boston: Forty Years of Modern Architecture,* exhibition catalogue, by William J. R. Curtis, Boston 1980; *Marcel Breuer: Furniture and Interiors* by

Christopher Wilk, London 1981; *Visionary Architecture of the 20th Century* by Vittorio Magnago Lampugnani, Stuttgart and London 1982; *The Decorated Diagram: Harvard Architecture and the Failure of the Bauhaus Legacy* by Klaus Herdeg, Cambridge, Massachusetts 1984; articles—"El Arquitecto Marcel Breuer" by Siegfried Giedion in *Arquitectura* (Madrid), no. 3, 1932; "Carattere dell'opera di Marcello Breuer" by A. Podesta in *Domus* (Milan), no. 86, 1935; "A View of Marcel Breuer" by Richard G. Stein in *Metropolitan Museum of Art Exhibition Guide* (New York), 1972; "Breuer wins AIA Education Award" in *Progressive Architecture* (New York), April 1981; "Marcel Breuer as Interior Designer" by Stanley Abercrombie in *AIA Journal* (Washington, D.C.), July 1981; "Obituary: Marcel Breuer—Architect Who Designed Tubular Steel Furniture" in *The Times* (London), 4 July 1981; "Marcel Breuer" in *The Architects' Journal* (London), 8 July 1981; "Marcel Breuer 1902-1981" in *Building* (London), 10 July 1981; "Marcel Lajos Breuer as He Is Remembered" in *AIA Journal* (Washington, D.C.), August 1981; "Marcel Breuer 1902-81" in *Architectural Record* (New York), August 1981; "Obituary: Marcel Breuer" by Deyan Sudjic in *Design* (London), August 1981; "Marcel Breuer 1902-1981" by Christopher Wilk in *Progressive Architecture* (New York), August 1981; "MBA: the Legacy of Marcel Breuer," special issue of *Process: Architecture* (Tokyo), September 1982.

Bibliographies—*Marcel L. Breuer: Architect and Designer* by Lamia Doumato, Monticello, Illinois 1979; *The Architecture of Marcel Lajos Breuer* by Robert B. Harmon, Monticello, Illinois 1980.

*

Shall we attempt to condense the central issue facing architecture today into one sentence?

In search of a precise formulation, I wrote my first and only poem (of a sort):

Colors which you can hear with ears;
Sounds to see with eyes;
The void you touch with your elbows;
The taste of space on your tongue;
The fragrance of dimensions;
The juice of stone.

—Marcel Breuer (1980)

*

There can be doubt that Marcel Breuer was one of the most important architects of our era. The extent and lasting validity of his contribution for well over half a century have no equal. And yet, in contrast to other "form givers" of our time, Breuer defies classification: any attempt to label his contribution in simple terms is virtually impossible.

Breuer's unique and independently creative gifts came out early in his career, and much has been written on the subject of his origins in a provincial Hungarian town, his meteoric rise as one of the architectural "stars," the dynamic center of the Bauhaus image, his early work in Europe and England, to the period of his teaching at Harvard. My first encounter with him was when I was a student at Harvard in 1945. He gave the impression of being not that much older than his students. He exuded a warm spirit of comradeship, a yearning, searching spirit, a delight in finding satisying solutions to design problems. We all knew his early work from books, but what made the greatest possible impression on us were the built images emanating from his Cambridge, Massachusetts office. The pilgrimages to his house at Lincoln, to the Haggerty House at Cohasset, the Chamberlin Cottage at Wayland, the Geller and Tompkins houses near New York, were absolutely shattering experiences to his students who, after all, had not seen or experienced any truly modern architecture in North America at that time, certainly none that had the air of authenticity, that generated such a sense of well-being and aesthetic joy.

Of all the teachers at Harvard at that time, it was Breuer who was the taste-setter. He combined

diverse and normally irreconcilable tendencies: an almost lyrically romantic spatial aesthetic (and use of material) with disarmingly simple, uncanny "Gordian Knot" solutions to planning and structural problems. He stimulated in his students the development of designs that were at once essentially rational devices yet also deliberate, visually tantalizing compositions.

Later, when working with him in New York in 1946-48, I became intimately involved with his methodology. Every building design had as its theme a single strong idea. Plans were always basically direct in organization and resulted in beautifully related and sculptured masses. In house designs, there was usually a spatially powerful living area with horizontal and often verticaly interplay; sleeping areas were organized separately and were more compartmentalized. Detailing was direct and completely consequential: it was always universally applicable to the limited varieties of intersections that evolved from a design. The resulting technical systems were constantly refined and carried over from one project to another. Visual tension was generated in the juxtaposition of materials as much as in elevational compositions: synthetic smooth materials to natural rough stone, natural timber against manufactured white masonry blocks. This pulling of forces also existed strongly in his Mondrianesque glass wall subdivisions and in the relationship of solids to voids. Structural devices were exploited expressively: thin, steel-cable tension members held up visually heavy masses; walls, stair and ramp balustrades fulfilled their function but were also sculptural forms as well as logically shaped supporting elements. Breuer always had an instinctive concern with sun control—which also aided his aesthetic aims toward deeply textured exteriors.

In the great amount of his executed work from the 1950s to the 1970s a continuing clear direction and logical development is evident. Each Breuer project consistently grew from the visual and technical experience of those preceding it (in contrast to the wild gyrations in form language of other celebrated—but now largely forgotten—practitioners of that time). The housing designs he developed have become the essence of prototypes throughout the world. The concrete technology he developed both in prefabricated and pour-in-place forms has been emulated everywhere—but none of the imitations have that instantly warm emotional appeal or rationally satisfying quality of his work.

The consistency of Breuer's work can best be illustrated by noting that themes developed in a seminal design concept of 1936, the Civic Centre of the Future, continued to recur—in the double Y-shaped office designs of Unesco in Paris, in the IBM Research Center at La Gaude, France, in the HUD Building in Washington, and in many other buildings.

No other modern architect's work has remained as valid visually and technically for fifty years and more as has Breuer's. His earliest, as much as his latest, building exude that unique and characteristic warmth and give the visitor a feeling of well-being. It took half a century for the world to rediscover the magnificent qualities of his Wassily and Cesca chairs. In our shallow era of short-lived thrills of appearance, it may take as long again for the world to fully appreciate and rediscover the great genius inherent in all the wealth of his architecture.

—Harry Seidler

BRINKMAN, Johannes Andreas.
Dutch. Born in Rotterdam, 22 March 1902. Educated at the Technische Hochschule, Delft. Worked in the office of his father, Michiel Brinkman, Rotterdam, 1921-25; in partnership with L. C. van

der Vlugt, Rotterdam, 1925-36; with Johannes van den Broek, *q.v.,* Rotterdam, 1937 until he retired, 1948. Exhibitions: *Building for an Open City,* Boymans Museum, Rotterdam, 1963, toured the Netherlands, Germany, Austria, and Italy; *Het Nieuwe Bouwen in Rotterdam 1920-1960,* Museum Boymans-van Beuningen, Rotterdam, 1982. *Died* (in Rotterdam) *6 May 1949.*

Works:

1925/
26 Theosophical Union Meeting Hall and Administration Building, Tolstraat, Amsterdam

1925/
27 Van Nelle Tobacco Company Offices, Aalmarkt, Leiden

1926 Theosophical Union Building, Ommen, Netherlands
Van Nelle Company Boilerhouse, van Nelleweg 1, Rotterdam

1926/
27 Public housing, Mathenesserweg, Rotterdam

1926/
29 Van Nelle Tobacco Company Factory, van Nelleweg 1, Rotterdam

1928/
29 Van der Leeuw Villa, Kralingseplaslaan, Rotterdam

1929 Tennis Club, Delftshavensee Schie, Rotterdam
Internationale Crediet en Handelsvereiniging Headquarters extensions, Wolfshoek, Rotterdam

1929/
31 Grain silos, Maashaven, Rotterdam

1930 Mees and Zoonen Bank Building, Beursplein, Rotterdam (project)
Van der Leeuw holiday house, Rockanje, Netherlands
De Maas Steam Mills extensions, Maashaven, Rotterdam

1930/
31 De Bruyn Villa, Ary Prinslaan, Schiedam, Netherlands
Mees and Zoonen Bank Building, 's-Gravendijkwal, Rotterdam

1930/
32 Van Stolk and Zn. Office Building, Abraham van Stolkweg, Rotterdam

1931 Concert Hall and Cultural Centre, Coolsingel, Rotterdam (project)

1931/
32 Graansilo N.V. Offices and Housing, Maashaven, Rotterdam
Van Ommeren N.V. Travel Bureau rebuilding, rue Auber, Paris
Maas Millworks Office Building, Canteen and Porter's House, Brielselaan, Rotterdam
Prototype telephone booth, Rotterdam

1932 University buildings, Rotterdam (project)

1932/
33 Sonneveld Villa, Jongkindstraat, Rotterdam

1932/
34 Boeve Villa, Mathenesserlaan, Rotterdam

1932/
38 Van der Leeuw holiday house, Ommen, Netherlands

1933 Van Hoey-Smith weekend house, Rockanje, Netherlands (project)
Golf Club, Kralingseweg, Rotterdam

1933/
34 Rotterdamse Kunstkring rebuilding, Witte de Withstraat, Rotterdam

1933/
35 Steel Skyscraper Block, Bergpolder, Rotterdam (with Willem van Tijen)
Maas Grain and Coal Silos, Brielselaan, Rotterdam

1934 Zoological Gardens, Rotterdam (project)

Diaconessenhuis/Schwesternheim Clinic, Westersingel, Rotterdam (project)
Holland-America Lines Ticket Offices, rue Scribe, Paris
Low-cost housing, Amsterdam (competition project)

1934/
35 Zuid Navigational Union Station, Vierhavenstraat, Rotterdam

1934/
36 Vaes Villa, Kortekade, Rotterdam

1935 University Extension Buildings, Westzeedijk, Rotterdam (project)
van der Vlugt holiday house, Noordwijk aan Zee, Netherlands

1935/
36 Feijenoord Stadium, Olympiaweg, Rotterdam
Airport Reception Building, Ypenburg, Netherlands
Tennis Club, Rotterdam

1936/
37 Muntz Country House, de Koog, Texel, Netherlands

1936/
38 Diaconessenhuis Clinic extensions, Westersingel, Rotterdam

1937 Hoogendijk Villa, Holyweg, Vlaardingen-Ambacht, Netherlands
Hospital, Terneuzen, Netherlands (project)
Plate holiday house, Rockanje, Netherlands (project)
Backx holiday house, Rockanje, Netherlands (project)

1937/
38 Holland-America Lines Departure Hall, Wilhelminakade, Rotterdam
Ten Horst-Vogel House, Vierhouten, Netherlands
Niehuis-van den Berg Office extensions, Pastoriestraat, Rotterdam

1937/
39 Snoek House, C.N.A. Looslaan, Hillergersberg, Rotterdam

1937/
40 Van Ommeren N.V. Office Building, Antwerp

1938 House of Art and Science, Rotterdam (project)
Nygh House, Rotterdam (project)

1938/
39 Gestel House, Bentincklaan, Rotterdam
Arend Central Club House, Rotterdam
Public housing, Bentincklaan, Rotterdam

1938/
40 Low-cost housing, Tarwebuurt, Rotterdam-Sud

1939 Mass Exhibition Hall of 1941, Rotterdam (project)
Public housing, Statensingel, Rotterdam (project)

1940/
41 Workers' housing, Rotterdam
Temporary shops, Mathenesserlaan, Rotterdam

1941 Garden Housing Estate, Wilgenplas, Rotterdam (project)
Blaak Development Plan, Rotterdam (competition project)

1941/
43 Tollens and Company Dye and Lacquer Factory, Overschieseweg, Overschie, Netherlands
Public housing, Rotterdam-Sud

1941/
45 Gispen N.V. Factory and Office Building extensions, Stationsweg, Culemborg, Netherlands

1941/
48 Strijp I Terrace Housing, Strijp, Eindhoven, Netherlands

1942 Development plan for the Hofplein, Rotterdam (competition project)
Engels N.V. Slaughterhouse, Garage and Canteen, Landsmeer, Netherlands (project)

1942/
43 Van Nelle Company Warehouse extensions, van Nelleweg, Rotterdam

1943 Reconstruction plan for Schiedamsesingel-Binnenweg, Rotterdam (project)
Post-war public housing, Rotterdam (project; with the Woning-Architectuur Group)
Maritime Centre, Vasteland, Rotterdam (project)

1944 Slaughterhouse and cattle-market, Rotte, Rotterdam (project)

1945 Wevers Circus, Blijdorp, Rotterdam (project)
Parish Centre, Rotterdam-Sud (project)

1945/
49 Ardath Tobacco Company extensions, Spuiweg, Dordrecht, Netherlands

1946 Reform Church, Kralingen, Rotterdam (project)

1946/
47 Nederlandse Agrarische Industrie Factory rebuilding, Poeldijk, Netherlands

1946/
48 Aircraft Hangar reconstruction, Ypenburg, Netherlands

1946/
49 Holland-America Lines Warehouse and Office Building, Wilhelminahaven, Rotterdam
Thomsen's Havenbedrif Harbour Building, Lekhaven, Rotterdam

1947 Main Hall, Volksuniversiteit, Diergaardesingel, Rotterdam (project)
Single-family housing (project)
Terraced housing, Hook of Holland (project)

1947/
50 Strijp II Terrace Housing, Strijp, Eindhoven, Netherlands
Holland-America Lines Harbour Building, Rijnhaven, Rotterdam

1947/
51 Lamers and Indemans N.V. Factory, Parallelweg, 's Hertogenbosch, Netherlands

1948 Church Community Centre, Charlois, Rotterdam (project)

Publications:

By BRINKMAN: book—*Woonmogelijkheden in het nieuwe Rotterdam,* with Willem van Tijen, Huig A. Maaskant, and J. H. van den Broek, Rotterdam 1941.

On BRINKMAN: books—*Nuova Architettura nel Mondo* by A. Pica, Milan 1938; *Geschichte der Moderne Architektur* by Jürgen Joedicke, Stuttgart 1963; *Building for an Open City,* exhibition catalogue, Rotterdam 1963; *Amsterdamse Bouwen 1880-1980,* edited by Ids Haagsma and others, Utrecht and Antwerp 1981; *Het Nieuwe Bouwen in Rotterdam 1920-1960* by Wim Beeren, Rob Dettingmeijer, Frank Kauffman and others, Delft, Netherlands 1982; articles—"Usines de Tabac, Rotterdam" in *Cahiers d'Art* (Paris), vol. 4, 1929; "La nuova architettura olandese" by Leo Lionni in *Casabella* (Milan), May 1934; "Twee Woonhuizen te Rotterdam van de Architecten Brinkman en van der Vlugt" by B. Merkelbach in *De 8 en Opbouw* (Amsterdam), no. 11/12, 1934; "Casa popolare a Rotterdam" by R. Rothschild in *Casabella* (Milan), December 1934; "Brinkman e van der Vlugt, architetti" by Edoardo Persico and Leo Lionni in *Casabella* (Milan), March 1935; special issue of *De 8 en Opbouw* (Amsterdam), October 1936; "House van der Leeuw, Rotterdam" in *Architectural Record* (New York) October 1950; "van der Broek und Bakema: A Contribution to the History of Architecture" by Franz Fueg in *Bauen und Wohnen* (Zürich), October 1959; "Brinkman, Brinkman, van der Vlugt, van den Broek, Bakema" by B. Housden, special issue of *Architectural Association Journal* (London), December 1960; "Van Nelle Factory in Rotterdam" in *Architecture* (Paris), April 1975; "A New Social and Cultural Centre—Cinema Becomes a Library" by Hilde de Haan and Ids Haagsma in *De Architect* (The Hague), no. 6, 1981.

Unquestionably the greatest work of Johannes Brinkman's partnership with L.C. van der Vlugt is the Van Nelle Tobacco Factory near Rotterdam (to the design of which Mart Stam also contributed). This famous modern building, dating from 1929, is one of the most important of all twentieth-century industrial buildings, and one of the most elegant. It consists of a large, eight-storey block with an attic, the staircases being expressed; curved wings of three storeys over basements, with attics; tall chimneys; and freely expressed ramped corridor-connections with lower industrial buildings. The cladding is one of the best examples of a fully developed curtain-wall system, while the treatment of the massing of blocks, relationships of solids to voids, and disposition of elements, is masterly.

Brinkman and van der Vlugt collaborated with Willem van Tijen on the design of the slab-shaped Bergpolder high-rise block in Rotterdam of 1933-34, one of the earliest buildings on the *piloti* base made fashionable by Le Corbusier.

Upon the death of van der Vlugt in 1936, Brinkman entered into another fruitful partnership with J.H. van den Broek, who was to join up with Jacob B. Bakema in 1948 when Brinkman retired. These architects took up a philosophical stance that was derived from the theories of De Stijl, and so was seen to be functionalist and materialist by the devotees of Granpré Molière of Delft. The Professor at Delft Technical College encouraged the traditions of craftsmanship that had been a part of Berlage's work, which had followers in many countries. Brinkman and van der Vlugt were opposed to the traditionalists; they favoured a functionalism that was anathema to Granpré Molière. The office that harboured men such as Mart Stam remained radically committed to industrialized, non-craft techniques of design, and so remained out of favour with mainstream architectural thought in the Netherlands during the late 1930s and 1940s. When van den Broek himself was appointed professor at Delft in 1948, he and Bakema attacked the traditionalists of the Delft School and rallied support from the survivors of De Stijl.

—James Stevens Curl

BRODY, Samuel.
American. Born in Plainfield, New Jersey, 9 August 1926. Educated at Dartmouth College, Hanover, New Hampshire, B.A. Graduate School of Design, Harvard University, Cambridge, Massachusetts, M.Arch. Married to Sally Brody; children: David, Elizabeth and Daniel. Architect, Kelly and Gruzen, New York, 1950-53. Since 1953, Partner, with Lewis Davis, *q.v.*, Davis Brody and Associates, New York. Adjunct Professor, Cooper Union School of Architecture, New York, since 1959. Davenport Professor of Architecture, Yale University, New Haven, Connecticut, 1974. Chairman, Selection Jury for the New York City Mayor's Panel, 1969; Chairman of the Housing Committee, 1971. Chairman of the Committee on Fellows, 1971-72, Vice-President, 1971-73, and Chairman of the Committee on Ethics, 1973, American Institute of Architects, New York Chapter; Vice-President, Harvard Graduate School of Design Council, 1975. Recipient: Design Award, *Progressive Architecture*, 1954, 1955, 1958, 1961 (twice), 1962, 1966, 1982; Honor Award, American Institute of Architects, Potomac Valley, Maryland, Chapter, 1958; Design Award, Church Architectural Guild of America, 1958; Certificate of Merit, New York City Department of Commerce, 1958; Certificate of Merit, 1958, 1963, and Award, 1973, 1974,

New York State Association of Architects; Award of Merit, *House and Home*, 1960; United States Department of Health, Education and Welfare Award, 1966; Honor Award, AIA, New England Regional Council, 1966; Higher Education Facilities Design Award, 1966, Honor Award, 1968, 1971 (twice), 1976, and Architectural Firm Award, 1975, national AIA; Bard Award, City Club of New York, 1969, 1973, 1975; Certificate of Merit, Municipal Arts Society, New York, 1969, 1972, 1973 (twice); Concrete Industries Award, 1969; Staten Island Chamber of Commerce Award, New York, 1970; Golden Triangle Award, National Society of Interior Designers, 1970; International Design Award, American Institute of Design, 1970; Bartlett Award, 1971, 1976; Homes for Better Living Award, 1971; Award of Honor, New York Society of Architects, 1972, 1973, 1974; Medal of Honor, AIA, New York Chapter, 1973; Mayor of New York's Citation for Distinguished Service, 1973; Brunner Award, National Institute of Arts and Letters, 1975; Louis Sullivan Award, 1977; Landscape Award, American Association of Nurserymen, 1981; Thomas Award, 1981, and New York Chapter Award, 1983, American Institute of Architects; Delaware County Planning Commission Award, 1981; Industrial Research and Development Lab of the Year Award, 1982; New Jersey Society of Architects Award, 1982; Reliance Development Group Award, 1982; Interiors Award, 1983. Fellow, American Institute of Architects, 1969. Address: Davis, Brody and Associates, 100 East 42nd Street, New York, New York 10017, U.S.A.

See DAVIS, Lewis

BRUBAKER, Charles William.
American. Born in South Bend, Indiana, 28 September 1926. Educated at Purdue University, West Lafayette, Indiana, 1945; University of Texas at Austin, 1947-50, B.Arch. 1950. Served in the United States Navy, 1945-46. Married Elizabeth Allen Rogers in 1955; children: William, Elizabeth, and Robert. Designer, Project Manager, Partner, and Vice-President, 1950-68, President, 1968-74, and since 1974, Senior Vice-President, Perkins and Will, Chicago, with offices in New York and Washington, D.C. Member of the Board, Society for College and University Planning, 1968-70. Currently: Member, National Urban Planning and Design Committee, City Planning Committee of the Chicago Association of Commerce and Industry, Board of Directors of the Metropolitan Housing and Planning Council of Chicago, and Council of Educational Facility Planners; Vice-President, Chicago Architecture Foundation; President, Elu chapter, Lambda Alpha. Fellow, American Institute of Architects, 1968. Address: Perkins and Will Architects, 2 North LaSalle Street, Chicago, Illinois 60602, U.S.A.

Works:

1963 National College of Agriculture, Chapingo, Mexico (with Alvarez and Carral)
Eckerd College, St. Petersburg, Florida
1964 Cairo-American College, Cairo, Egypt (with Salah Zietoun)
1965 First National Bank, Chicago (with C. F. Murphy Associates)
1966 New Trier West High School, Winnetka, Illinois (with The Architects Collaborative)
School of Technology, Southern Illinois University, Carbondale
1967 Sandhill College, Southern Pines, North Carolina (with Hayes-Howell)

1968 First National Bank Plaza, Chicago (with C. F. Murphy Associates)
Orchard Ridge College, Farmington, Michigan (with Giffels and Rossetti)
1970 Richland College, Dallas, Texas (with The Oglesby Group)
College of Alameda, near San Francisco (with Stone, Maracini and Patterson)
1972 Disney Magnet School, Chicago
1974 Whitney Young High School, Chicago
1976 Arvada Center, Arvada, Colorado (with Seracuse and Lawler)
Fort Hayes Career Center, Columbus, Ohio (with Dan Carmichael)
1978 Robert Morgan Technical-Vocational Institute, Miami
Oakton Community College, Des Plaines, Illinois
Augustana College Center, Rock Island, Illinois (with Parkhurst, Appier, Marolf)
Lake County Public Library, Merrillville, Indiana (with George Hall)
Grand Rapids Junior College, Michigan (with WBDC)
1981 Woodbridge High School, Irvine, California
1983 Youngstown State University Master Plan, Ohio
1984 Santa Fe High School, New Mexico (with Mimbres, Inc.)
Convention Center, Fort Myers, Florida (with Parker-Mudgett)

Publications:

By BRUBAKER: books—*Schools for America,* with others, Washington, D.C. 1967; *The Schoolhouse in the City,* with others, New York 1968; *Planning Flexible Learning Spaces,* New York 1977; articles—"Space for Individual Learning" in *School Executive* (Chicago), February 1959; "Planning the Community College" in *College and University Business* (Chicago), October 1967; "How to Create Territory for Learning in the Secondary School" in *Nation's Schools* (Chicago), March 1968; "Urban Design and National Policy for Urban Growth" in *AIA Journal* (Washington, D.C.), October 1969; "The Three-Generation Neighborhood" in *Interiors* (New York), November 1970; "Long Island: 2001" in *Newsday* (Long Island, New York), 24 June 1973; "The Corridor" in *Architectural Forum* (New York), February 1974; "Tomorrow's Malls" in *Chain Store Age Executive* (New York), September 1975; "Ten Decades of Chicago Architecture" in *Commerce* (Chicago), October 1977; "Chicago's New Downtown" in *Chicago Daily News,* 4 December 1977; "New Trends in Building Design" in *Dodge Construction News* (Chicago), 19 December 1977; "New Life for Chicago's Central Business District" in *Union League Men and Events* (Chicago), May 1978.

On BRUBAKER: books—*Open Space Schools* by American Association of School Administrators, Washington, D.C. 1971; *The New Downtowns* by Louis G. Redstone, New York 1976; *Human Response to Tall Buildings* by Donald J. Conway, Stroudsburg, Pennsylvania 1977; articles—"Chicago," special issue of *Architectural Forum* (New York), January/February 1974; "In Progress: Nationwide Plaza" in *Progressive Architecture* (New York), October 1975.

Architecture for education has been, is, and will continue to be a most important component in the design of communities. The school has become the principal community center, and the college has become the principal cultural center.

Children and adults are influenced by the learning environment. Schools and colleges give each of us rich experiences that profoundly affect our lives. In the future, more people will be life-long learners, schools will be community centers, and colleges will

Charles Brubaker: Woodbridge High School, Irvine, California, 1981.

serve a broader spectrum of people. Therefore, in the future, architecture for education will be even more important.

My work and interests are primarily in the design of educational facilities. I am particularly concerned with the creation of schools and colleges that are pleasant and humane, capable of responding to both the current and changing future needs of people.

The successful design of educational facilities depends on the ability to analyze needs and to create spaces that make learning effective. I have found this experience to be valuable in the design of other kinds of buildings which are primarily created for people.

—Charles William Brubaker

Though Charles William Brubaker is best known for the First National Bank Building and Plaza in Chicago, the focus of his career has been in designing buildings for educational institutions. The sweeping, tapered form of the First National Bank Building (designed with C. F. Murphy Associates) grew out of the differing needs of the occupants. The public banking area on the ground floors required large amounts of open space, while the bank offices on higher floors needed less area. To enhance the sense of unobstructed interior space, Brubaker used twin elevator cores at two ends of the building, rather than the traditional central core.

The glass and gray granite of the bank serve as backdrop for the sunken plaza (also designed with C. F. Murphy Associates). In the tree-lined plaza, Brubaker and Murphy play off square and rectangular shapes; at the center is a fountain composed of nine squares within a square. The spacious open areas of the plaza provide a space which Chicago's office workers and shoppers use during good weather months to enjoy either entertainment programs or the plaza's most famous feature, Marc Chagall's mural Four Seasons.

Brubaker has designed buildings for numerous educational institutions, from primary schools through colleges. In many of them, he uses the conventional Bauhaus style: the buildings are clean, open, and sparse in architectural detail.

Brubaker fights the horizontality of the school buildings with vertical detail. At New Trier West High School in Winnetka, Illinois, there are echoes of Greek temple design with pseudo-pilasters instead of columns. In the Walt Disney Magnet School in Chicago Brubaker uses free-standing white columns to divide the dark curtain wall into three segments. The vertical line is enhanced by the site, which is at the top of a slight slope.

Brubaker has taken different directions in his designs for Richland College in Dallas and Alameda Community College near San Francisco. For Richland, Brubaker's design juxtaposes interlocking geometric forms. The Performance Hall is a central hexagon; from it, other buildings for Art and Music radiate at sharp angles. The effect of the angles is softened by the adjacent tree-lined lake, the open arcade supported by graceful T-shaped columns, and the clerestory windows used to light the artists's studios.

At Alameda College, Brubaker has again used contrasting shapes and interlocking lines. Here he has taken the shape of the amphitheatre and in it has played with the relationship of space and solid object. By putting staircases on the outside of the buildings and thus eliminating interior corridors, Brubaker has enabled the college to cut energy costs substantially. Since rooms get natural light and cross-ventilation, there is minimum cost for electricity and no need for air-conditioning.

In journals, articles, Brubaker has proposed radical changes in access to educational institutions and in the interior design of primary and secondary schools. For example, he has suggested that community colleges be combined with shopping malls,

thus creating community centers which integrate culture and commerce.

Brubaker's proposals for redesigning the interiors of secondary schools would provide more flexibility in the learning process. Each student would share a space of 144 square feet with four other students plus the equipment needed for the special programs in which they might be involved. Faculty members would have individual studio areas or work as a team in the center of twenty student spaces. Studenst could thus work individually or in groups of varying size.

Whether in designing bank buildings, plazas, or educational institutions, Brubaker has employed the conventions of modern architecture, but he has softened and humanized them.

—Mary Elizabeth Devine

BRYGGMAN, Erik William.

Finnish. Born in Turku, 7 February 1891. Educated at the Turku School of Art, 1906-09; Öbo Svenska Klassiska Lyceum, Turku, 1910; Institute of Technology, Helsinki, graduated 1916. Married Agda Grönberg in 1918; daughter: Carin. Worked in the office of architect Valter Jung, Helsinki, 1916-23; in private practice, Turku, 1923 until his death in 1955. Exhibitions (individual) Turku Art Museum, 1967; Museum of Finnish Architecture, Helsinki, 1968. Honorary Professor of Architecture, Finland, 1948; Honorary Member, Royal Academy of Art, Denmark, 1954, and Royal Academy of Art, Sweden, 1955; Honorary Member, Association of Finnish Architects, 1955. Died (in Turku) 21 December 1955.

Works:

1913 *Otava* Magazine Prototype Villa (competiton project)

1917 Town plan for Kuopio, Finland (competition project)
Agricola Memorial, Turku, Finland (competition project; with E. Ilkka)

1918 War Memorial, Keuruu, Finland (competition project; with E. Ilkka)
Tomb Memorial, Old Church Park, Helsinki (with E. Ilkka)

1919 Memorial of Liberty, Alimaalahti, Finland
Petrelius Fountain, Turku, Finland (competition project; with H. Linden)
Vaasa Theatre, Vaasa, Finland (competition project; with H. Ekelund and M. Valikangas)
Burial Grounds and Chapel, Tammisto, Viborg, Finland (competition project)
Sellgren's Department Store, Viborg, Finland (competiton project)
Crematorium, Helsinki (competition project)

1920 Memorial of Liberty, Oulu, Finland (with I. Saxelin)

1921 Town Hall, Iisalmi, Finland (competition project)
Town plan for Lahti, Finland (competition project)

1922 Boman furniture prototypes (competition project)
Memorial of Estonian Liberty (competition project; with E. Rautala)

1923 Hotel Hamburger Börs, Turku, Finland (project)
Hospital for Rheumatics, Heinola, Finland (competition project)
Church, Sveaborg, Finland (competition project)
Medieval Cathedral Restoration, Turku, Finland (with Armas Lindgren)

1924 Suomen Sokeri Oy Employees' and Workmen's Housing, Turku, Finland
Marketplace Stands, Turku, Finland (project)
Residential block, Brahenkatu 9, Turku, Finland
Savings Bank, Kemiö, Finland
Skogsböle Farmhouse, Kemiö, Finland
House of the Diet, Helsinki (competition project)

1925 Haartman Villa, Naantali, Finland
Kellonsoittaja Residential Block, Turku, Finland

1926 Olympia Cinema interiors, Turku, Finland
Power Station, Imatra, Finland (competition project)

1927 Länsi-Suomen Pankki (Western Bank of Finland) interiors, Turku, Finland
Arts Museum Grounds Plan, Turku, Finland (with W. Aaltonen)
Atrium Residential Block, Turku, Finland
Lounais-Suomen Sähkö Oy (Southwestern Electricity Ltd.) Workers' Housing, Turku, Finland
Atlas Bank Interiors, Turku, Finland
M. Solin Villa, Turku, Finland
Lounais-Suomen Maalaisten Talo (Southwestern Farmers' House), Turku, Finland (competition project)

1928 Pharmacy interiors, Humalistonkatu 7, Turku, Finland
Hotel Seurahuone-Societetshuset, Turku, Finland (with I. Ahonen)
Erstan Villa, Kakskerta, Finland
Aitta Magazine Villa Prototype (competition project)
Business block, Vaasa, Finland (competition project)
Suomi Insurance Company Office Building, Helsinki (competition project)
Kotkan Rauta Office Building, Kotka, Finland (competition project)

1929 Design of *7th Centenary of Turku* exhibition Turku, Finland (with Alvar Aalto)

Tuorla Manor renovation plan, Piikkiö, Finland (project)
Hotel Hospits Betel, Turku, Finland
E. Solin Villa, Hirvensalo, Finland
Sanatorium, Paimio, Finland (competition project)
South-Carelian Sanatorium, Joutseno, Finland (competition project)
Puijo Tourist Hotel and Restaurant, Kuopio, Finland (competition project)
Columbus Lighthouse, Santo Domingo (competition project; with H. Fürst)
Thonet-Mundus furniture prototype (competition project)
Church, Sortavala, Finland (competition project)

1930 Burial chapel, Parainen, Finland
Finnish Pavilion, World's Fair. Antwerp, Belgium
Exhibition Department, *Design Industry Exhibition,* Helsinki
Student Association Building, Ös, Norway (competition project; with H. Fürst)
Water supply plant, Turku, Finland (competition project)
Royal Summer Residence Annex, Oslo, Norway (competition project; with H. Fürst)
Central Library, Helsinki (competition project)
Stadium, Helsinki (first competition project)
Tehtaanpuisto Church, Helsinki (first competition project)

1931 Sauna for the Sports Institute, Vierumäki, Finland
T. Ylipohja Sauna, Hirvensalo, Finland
Church interiors, Luhanka, Finland
Town Hall, Kotka, Finland (competition project)
Lallukka Artists' Home, Helsinki (competition project)
St. Martin's Church, Turku, Finland (competition project)

1932 Sports Institute Residential Building, Vierumäki, Finland
Tehtaanpuisto Church, Helsinki (second competition project)
Enso-Gutzeit Holiday House (competition project)
Insulite Company Villa (competition project)
Special Construction Houses, Scandinavian Building Congress (competition project)

1933 Warén Villa, Ruissalo, Finland
Ekman Villa, Hirvensalo, Finland
Communal Hall, Korppoo, Finland (project)
J. J. Wecksell Statue Plan, Turku, Finland (project)
Railway Station, Tampere, Finland (competition project)
Temppelinaukio Church, Helsinki (competition project)
Stadium, Helsinki (second competition project)

1934 Mattsson Villa, Salo, Finland
Olympic Games Sauna, Döberitz, Germany
Exposition Hall, Helsinki (competition project)

1935 Öbo Akademi Library Book Tower, Turku, Finland
Pharmacy, Sauvo, Finland
Kaino Villa, Kakskerta, Finland
Köhler Sauna, Kuusisto, Finland

1936 Sports Institute, Vierumäki, Finland
Kinopalatsi Cinema, Turku, Finland
Öbo Akademi Student Association Building, Turku, Finland
Pharmacy, Forssa, Finland (project)
Church, Varkaus, Finland (competition project)

1937 Kansallis-Osake-pankki Bank renovations, Turku, Finland (project)
Öbo Akademi Dormitories, Turku, Finland (project)
Cemetery enlargement, Turku, Finland (competition project)

1938 Kiva Cinema, Salo, Finland
Sampo Insurance Company Office Building, Turku, Finland
Café Lehtinen interiors, Turku, Finland

1939 Power plant, Harjavalta, Finland
Power plant engineers' housing, Harjavalta, Finland (project)
Oy Vilen Factory, Turku, Finland
Jaatinen Villa, Vessölandet, Finland
Salainen Manor renovation, Halikko, Finland (project)
Ministry of Social Affairs Single-Family House (competition project)

1940 Church restoration, Kakskerta, Finland
Cinema and residential building, Mariehamn, Finland (project)
War cemetery, Kotka, Finland (with E. Filén)

1941 Resurrection Chapel (Turku Cemetery Chapel), Turku, Finland
War Memorial, Parainen, Finland
Schleutker Villa, Parainen, Finland (project)
Paavola and Muuramá Single-Family Houses, Turku, Finland
Porin Puuvilla Oy (Pori Cotton Factory) Workers' Housing, Pori, Finland (project)
Provincial theatre, Kotka, Finland (project)
Molin Villa, Hirvensalo, Finland (project)
University College of Commercial Sciences, Helsinki (competition project)
Pinella Restaurant, Turku, Finland (project)

1942 Joutsen Pharmacy interiors, Turku, Finland (with Carin Bryggman)
Sharpshooters' Chapel restoration, Turku Cathedral, Finland (project)
Ginstrom Villa and Sauna, Dragsfjärd, Finland (project)
Keppo Manor conversion, Jepua, Finland (project)
Turun Asunto Oy Residential Block (competition project)

1943 Värtsilä Kone (Värtsilä Machinery) Catering Barracks, Turku, Finland
Church interiors, Naantali, Finland
Cinema, Hanko, Finland (project)
Children's Hospital, Hogsand, Finland (project)
Town centre plan for Tollered, Sweden (competition project)
Church, Sakkola, Finland (competition project)

1944 Oy W. Schauman Ab Catering Barracks, Joensuu, Finland
War Memorial, Dragsfjärd, Finland
War Memorial, Mietoinen, Finland
Kupittaa Folk Park, Turku, Finland (project)

1945 Schmandt Oy Bakery, Turku, Finland (project)
Elementary school, Mariehamn, Finland (competition project)
Savings Bank Residential Block, Turku, Finland (competition project)

1946 Vuoksenniska Oy Workers' and Foremen's Housing, Turku, Finland
Vasaramäki Congregation Hall, Turku, Finland
Grandell Villa, Parainen, Finland
Staffans Villa, Kakskerta, Finland
Uusimaa Central Hospital, Helsinki (project)
National Anthem Memorial, Kumpula, Finland (competition project)
Finnish Women's Welfare Foundation Collective House, Helsinki (competition project; with Sirkka Tarumaa)
University Library, Turku, Finland (competition project)

1947 Jaatinen Sauna, Vessölandet, Finland
Staffans Sauna, Kakskerta, Finland
Laivateollisuus Oy (Ship Industry) Residential Developement, Turku, Finland
Hotel Maakunta interiors, Turku, Finland (with Carin Bryggman)

Erik Bryggman: Resurrection Chapel, Turku, Finland, 1941.

Erik Julin Statue Plan, Turku, Finland
(project)
Town Hall and Hotel, Tammisaari, Finland
(project)
War Memorial, Kakskerta, Finland
Congregational Hall, Järvenpää, Finland
(competition project)
1948 Laivateollisuus Oy (Ship Industry) Engineers'
Housing, Turku, Finland
Salon Seudun Sanomat Office Building, Salo,
Finland
Blumenthal Villa, Parainen, Finland
Grandell Sauna, Parainen, Finland
National Anthem Memorial, Kumpula,
Finland
Crematorium, Varberg, Sweden (competition
project)
1949 Nuuttila Villa, Kuusisto, Finland
Itämeri Restaurant interiors, Turku, Finland
(with Carin Bryggman)
Elementary school, Hanko, Finland (project)
Children's hospital, Turku, Finland (project)
Aleksis Kivi Statue Plan, Turku, Finland
(project)
Residential block development, Läntinen
Rantakatu, Turku, Finland (project)
1950 Öbo Akademi Student Association Building
and Dormitory, Turku, Finland
Children's Day-Home, Oy Finlayson-Forssa
Ab Residential Area, Tampere, Finland
Arvonen House restoration, Turku, Finland
(project)
War Memorial, Mänttä, Finland
War Memorial, Noormarkku, Finland
Town Hall, Kajaani, Finland (competition
project)
1951 Öbo Akademi Chemical Laboratory, Turku,
Finland
House, Läntinen Rantakatu 21, Turku,
Finland
Nuuttila Sauna, Kuusisto, Finland
District Hospital, Mänttä, Finland
War Memorial, Turku, Finland
Turku University (competition project)
1952 Water supply plant, Riihimäki, Finland
Football Stadium, Turku, Finland
Western Uusimaa Hospital, Tammisaari,
Finland
University Student Association Building,
Turku, Finland
War Memorial, Lassila, Finland
Residential Buildings II, Oy Finlayson-Forssa
Ab Residential Area, Tampere, Finland
1953 Central Elementary School, Parainen,
Finland
University Student Association Building II,
Turku, Finland
Palmroth Villa I, Partola, Tampere, Finland
Finnish Savings Bank interiors, Turku, Fin-
land (with Carin Bryggman)
War Memorial, Kemiö, Finland
Burial chapel, Nokia, Finland (project)
Burial chapel, Loviisa, Finland (project)
Congregational Office Building, Turku, Fin-
land (competition project)
Kopenen Villa, Rymättylä, Finland
1954 Turunmaa Hospital, Turku, Finland
Swimming hall, Vierumäki, Finland (project)
Burial chapel, Lohja, Finland (completed by
others)
Burial chapel, Lappeenranta, Finland (com-
pleted by others)
Turku Castle restoration, Finland (with Carin
Bryggman)
1955 Elementary school, Mariehamn, Finland
Honkanummi Burial Chapel, Puistola, Fin-
land (completed by others)
Residential Buildings III, Oy Finlayson-
Forssa Ab Residential Area, Tampere,
Finland
Sharpshooters' Chapel interiors, Turku Cath-
edral, Finland (project)
Palmroth Villa II, Partola, Tampere, Finland
University Student Association Building III,

Turku, Finland
Municipal Theatre, Turku, Finland (competition project; with O. Kestilä)

Publications:

By BRYGGMAN: book—*Turun siunauskappeli*,
Turun, Finland 1948.

On BRYGGMAN: books—*Erik Bryggman* by
Anna-Lisa Stigell, Ekenäs 1965; *Erik Bryggman*,
exhibition catalogue, by Esa Piironen, Turku,
Finland 1967; articles—"Finnische Landhauser" in
Monatshefte für Baukunst und Städtebau (Berlin), no.
10, 1936; "Geschäftshaus Sampo in Turku" and
"Sportakademie Vierumäki" in *Werk* (Zürich), no.
3/4, 1940; "Chapel at Öbo" in *Architectural Review*
(London), no. 617, 1948; "Mortuary Chapel,
Turku" in *Architectural Design* (London), no. 7,
1948; "L'opera di Erik Bryggman nella storia
dell'architettura finlandese" by Leonardo Mosso in
Atti SJA (Turin), December 1958; "Architect Erik
Bryggman, 1891-1955" in *Architektura CSR*
(Prague), no. 2, 1977; "The Last 100 Years—The
Masters" by Luciano Rubino in *Ville giardini*
(Milan), June 1979.

When Erik Bryggman completed his architectural
studies in 1916, political conditions in Finland were
unsettled; the achievement of independence from
Russia in the following year and the ensuing civil war
hardly offered the young architect an inspiring start.
In architecture, too, it was a time of change. The
vigorous National Romantic period of the early part
of the century had passed. It was succeeded by a
return in part to a more rigid, monumental classicism
and to ponderous architecture inspired by the
Swedish Vasa Renaissance. As soon as contacts with
other countries were resumed after the war, Italy,
with Sweden and Denmark, became the focal point
for young Finnish architects, and this interest is easy
to understand, for architecture as taught at the
Institute of Technology stressed a thorough knowledge of Italian Renaissance and Baroque architecture. On his journey to Italy in 1920, Bryggman made
numerous sketches, concentrating, in addition to
Renaissance architecture, on anonymous peasant
architecture and the relationship of buildings to their
surroundings. The influence of Italian architecture
was later visible in Bryggman's works, not only in his
obviously classical buildings of the 1920s, the best
examples of which are the Atrium Housing Block
and the Hotel Hospits Betel complex, but also,
throughout his career, in his sensitive approach to
building and concern for setting.

Bryggman's first work was completed in the
offices of older colleagues, and, because of the
postwar recession, part of it involved renovation of
old buildings. He took part in the restoration of
Turku's Medieval Cathedral as an assistant to his
teacher Armas Lindgren, who had won his reputation early in the century as a member of the famous
Gesellius-Lindgren-Saarinen team. Work with Lindgren and a thorough grounding in historical architecture apparently helped Bryggman to learn to value
old cultural milieus (a concern that was not very
common amongst architects from the 1930s to the
1960s). The cathedral project also brought him back
to his home town of Turku, where he settled and
thereafter secured most of his planning commissions.

Towards the end of the 1920s, Bryggman became
friends with Alvar Aalto, who moved to Turku in
1927 after his success in the competition for the
Farmers Hall in Southwestern Finland. At about this
time, both men became interested in Functionalism
and began introducing it to Finland in late 1927. In
the summer of 1928, Bryggman visited the Weissenhof Siedlung in Stuttgart, the residential districts of
Frankfurt under the direction of Ernst May, and the
Bauhaus at Dessau, where he met Walter Gropius.
Aalto introduced the ideas of Le Corbusier and the

Dutch modernists to Turku at about the same time.
The changeover to Functionalism was immediately
visible in Bryggman's architecture. The Hotel Hospits Betel, which had been a straightforward classical
work during the design stage, was relieved of all
ornamentation during construction and emerged in
the simple forms of Functionalism. The Öbo
Akademi Library (1935) and the Vierumäki Sports
Institute (1936) are among the purest examples of
Functionalism in Bryggman's architecture. In these
buildings, he also retained the architectural sensitivity and lightness so characteristic of his personality.

In the late 1930s there was a widespread attempt to
rid architecture of the over-simplified style of
Functionalism, and Bryggman's Resurrection
Chapel at Turku (1941) clearly reflects this shift to a
more romantic architecture. Although the curved
concrete ceiling and the colonnade of the chapel
interior clearly still suggest functionalist/ structuralist forms, the details, such as the ornamental door
handles, the carefully placed vines, and the use of
slate on the outside walls and paths, indicate a trend
in a more decorative direction.

In the 1950s, Bryggman received many commissions, ranging from summer villas and schools to
hospitals and power plants. The influences of the
1920s are apparent in the Nuuttila Villa (1949), the
water supply plant at Riihimäki (1952), and the
student dormitories at Öbo Akademi (1950) and the
University of Turku (1952). Yet, his buildings also
became increasingly dry and matter of fact, with their
dark, plastered facades and pitched roofs, features
typical of contemporary Swedish architecture.

Bryggman's last works included reconstruction of
Turku Castle, which had been damaged during the
war. Bryggman restored the castle to its former state
in part, yet he also adapted it for his own era by
including modern congress and restaurant facilities.
This achievement serves as a fine end to an
architectural career that had begun with the renovation of another Turku monument, the Cathedral.
—Raija-Liisa Heinonen

BUNSHAFT, Gordon.
American. Born in Buffalo, New York, 9 May 1909.
Educated at Lafayette High School, Buffalo, 1924-
28; Massachusetts Institute of Technology, Cambridge, 1929-35, B.Arch. 1933, M.Arch. 1935;
awarded M.I.T. Honorary Travelling Fellowship,
1935, and Rotch Travelling Fellowship, for study in
Europe and North Africa, 1935-37. Served in the
United States Army Corps of Engineers, 1942-46:
Major. Married Nina Elizabeth Wayler in 1943.
Chief Designer, New York office, 1937-42 and 1946-
49, and Partner since 1949, Skidmore, Owings and
Merrill, *q.v.* Visiting Critic, Massachusetts Institute
of Technology, 1940-42, Harvard University, Cam-
bridge, Massachusetts, 1954-60, and Yale Univers-
ity, New Haven, Connecticut, 1959-62. Member of
the President's Commission on the Fine Arts, 1963-
72. Trustee, Museum of Modern Art, New York,
since 1975, and Carnegie-Mellon University,
Pittsburgh, Pennsylvania, since 1977. Exhibition:
Three Skyscrapers, Museum of Modern Art, New
York, 1983. Recipient: Brunner Award, National
Institute of Arts and Letters, 1955; Medal of Honor,
New York Chapter of the American Institute of
Architects, 1961; Chancellor Norton Medal, Univer-
sity of Buffalo, 1969; Gold Medal, American
Academy and Institute of Arts and Letters, 1984.
D.F.A.: University of Buffalo, Buffalo, New York,
1962. Honorary Member, Buffalo Fine Arts Acad-
emy, Buffalo, New York, 1962; Honorary Professor,
Universidad Nacional Federico Villareal, Lima,
Peru, 1977. Academician, National Academy of
Design; Fellow, American Institute of Architects,
and American Academy of Arts and Sciences.
Addresses: (home) 200 East 66th Street, New York,

Gordon Bunshaft: Lyndon Baines Johnson Library, University of Texas at Austin, 1971.

New York 10021, U.S.A.; (office) Skidmore, Owings and Merrill, 220 East 42nd Street, New York, New York 10017, U.S.A.

Works (as Partner-in-Charge of Design, Skidmore, Owings and Merrill):

1943 Hostess House, Great Lakes Naval Training Center, Illinois

1952 Lever House Corporate Headquarters, Park Avenue, New York
H. J. Heinz Company Vinegar Plant, Pittsburgh, Pennsylvania
United States Consular Housing, Bremen, West Germany

1954 Manufacturers Hanover Trust Bank Branch Headquarters, Fifth Avenue, New York
United States Consulate, Düsseldorf

1955 Hilton Hotel, Istanbul

1957 Connecticut General Life Insurance Company Office Building, Bloomfield
Karl Taylor Compton Laboratories, Massachusetts Institute of Technology, Cambridge

1958 Reynolds Metals Company Building, Richmond, Virginia

1960 PepsiCo Inc., Building, New York

1961 First National City Bank, Houston, Texas
Chase Manhattan Bank, New York
Union Carbide Corporation Building, New York

1962 Albright-Knox Art Gallery addition, Buffalo, New York

1963 Emhart Corporation Building, Bloomfield, Connecticut
Beinecke Rare Book and Manuscript Library, Yale University, New Haven, Connecticut

1965 Banque Lambert Office Building and Bank, Brussels
H. J. Heinz and Company Ltd. Headquarters and Research Buildings, Hayes Park, Middlesex (with Matthews, Ryan, and Simpson)
American Republic Insurance Company Building, Des Moines, Iowa

1967 Marine Midland Building, 140 Broadway, New York

1968 No. 1 Main Place, Dallas, Texas

1970 American Can Company Suburban Corporate Headquarters, Greenwich, Connecticut

1971 Lyndon Baines Johnson Library and Sid W. Richardson Hall, University of Texas at Austin (with Brooks, Barr, Graeber, and White)

1973 W. R. Grace Building, 1114 Avenue of the Americas, New York

1974 Office Building, 9 West 57th Street, New York
Hirshhorn Museum and Sculpture Garden, Washington, D.C.
Philip Morris Cigarette Manufacturing Plant, Richmond, Virginia

1975/
85 Jeddah International Airport, Saudi Arabia (SOM Partner-in-Charge of design of the Haj Terminal, Administration Building, RSAF, and Quarantine Building; Design Coordinator of the total project)

1983 National Commercial Bank, Jeddah, Saudi Arabia

Publications:

By BUNSHAFT: article—"25-year Award Goes to Lever House" in *AIA Journal* (Washington, D.C.), March 1980.

On BUNSHAFT: books—*Masters of Modern Architecture* by John Peter, New York 1958; *Architecture of Today and Tomorrow* by Cranston Jones, New York 1961; *Architecture of Skidmore, Owings and Merrill 1950-62,* introduced by Henry-Russell Hitchcock, Stuttgart 1962; *Architects on Architecture,* edited by Paul Heyer, New York 1966, London 1967; *Great Libraries* by Anthony Hobson, New York 1970; *Vacation Houses,* New York 1970; *Will They Ever Finish Bruckner Boulevard?* by Ada Louise Huxtable, New York 1970; *Architecture of Skidmore, Owings and Merrill 1963-1973,* introduced by Arthur Drexler, Stuttgart 1974; *Who's Who in Architecture from 1400 to the Present* by J. M. Richards, London and New York, 1977; articles—"Gordon Bunshaft: The Establishment's Architect—Plus" by David Jacobs in *New York Times Magazine,* 23 July 1972; "Art Gallery and Sculpture Garden, Washington, D.C." in *Architect and Builder* (Cape Town, South Africa), March 1975; "Making It on Tobacco Road" in *Progressive Architecture* (New York), June 1976; "Bunshaft and Noguchi" in *AIA Journal* (Washington, D.C.), October 1976; "Three Distinct Approaches to Skyscraper Design" by Paul Goldberger in the *New York Times,* 30 January 1983; "Lever's Landmark Status Upheld" in *AIA Journal* (Washington, D.C.), April 1983; "Lever House Gets Landmark Status" in *Building Design* (London), 8 April 1983; "New York's Lever House Landmark Is Sold and Saved" in *Building Design* (London), 21 October 1983.

To describe properly my approach to architecture would require me to be a professional writer, which I am not. I am an architect. I express what I believe through the buildings I have done over the past thirty years. They are the language I use—not the written word.

—Gordon Bunshaft

The names Gordon Bunshaft and Skidmore, Owings and Merrill are all but synonymous. Bunshaft has been associated with the New York office, but he has had a strong formulative influence over the work of the branches. Bunshaft's reputation and contribution rests on his pioneering influence on American corporate and industrial architecture. It is no small achievement. He was able to persuade the community of American corporations that contemporary American architecture could serve them as a signature.

The work that established this notion was the headquarters for the Lever Brothers Corporation in New York City. While not the first example of "glass box" architecture, it affirmed the role of open space and efficient geometric enclosure as a theme for housing large office organizations.

But to say that the strictly geometric enclosure is Bunshaft's hallmark is as inaccurate as to say that his work is limited to the architectural needs of corporate America. It is more accurate to describe Bunshaft's philosophy as a disciplined contemporary classicism. He has avoided aberrant fashions; his preference is for a reasoned and always crisply-disciplined functional solution. At the same time, his designs have always had a careful and steady wholeness. On occasion, they have also been innovative.

With Lever House, he set a glass box on a raised glass base. For the Manufacturers Hanover Trust Company Branch Headquarters on Fifth Avenue, New York, he revolutionized bank design; it is entirely enclosed in glass, and a vault is put on full public display at ground level. For the Beinecke Rare Book and Manuscript Library at Yale, he set a translucent marble block on a series of base piers; its interior light envelopes the books in a hallowing glow. For the Albright-Knox Art Gallery addition in Buffalo, New York, Bunshaft posed a serene glass box against a neo-classical predecessor. The two complement each other in scale, delicacy, and refinement—each mirroring its age and architectural atttitudes. The Banque Lambert in Brussels is a box-like building of classicial proportion, its facade an articulation of horizontal and vertical thrusts of force. The Connecticut General Life Insurance Company Office Building is a serene, horizontal mass set in a quietly rolling landscape. In this work Bunshaft utilized a familiar theme—a clear geometric form set on a larger terrace, the building form itself punctuated by courtyards.

His urban office architecture is all but his signature, an outstanding example being the Chase Manhattan Bank in lower Manhattan. Here, again, a tower is set on a supporting base, the base's top, in this case, being a terrace.

Bunshaft—and S.O.M.—have always established a strong identity for their clients through architecture. It is at once identifiable and respectful. And it is realized with equal success in work for the corporate as well as for the institutional client. It also succeeds in work of a monumental nature, as in the Lyndon Baines Johnson Memorial Library at the University of Texas at Austin.

A particular emphasis in his work is the incorporation of embellishing sculpture. He has utilized freestanding works, such as those by Isamu Noguchi, as well as sculptural screens, such as those of Harry Bertoia. Painstakingly careful interior design and furnishing is also a characteristic of his work.

Bunshaft's development has extended into an interval of somewhat frantic if not scattered search for new principles and forms in American architecture. While not participating adventurously in that search, he has not remained static or aloof; his recent buildings have employed more daring and adventuresome forms and structures. The Hirshhorn Museum and Sculpture Garden in Washington, D.C. is a case in point. The museum, a circle in form, still remains classic in its balanced repose. The sculpture garden is a masterpiece of the placement of sculpture in space, all but unrivalled. Bunshaft's contribution has been to be squarely at the front of his time, yet classical in his reasoned compositions.

—Paul Spreiregen

BURGEE, John Henry.

American. Born in Chicago, Illinois, 28 August 1933. Studied architecture, University of Notre Dame, Indiana, B.Arch. 1956. Served in the U.S. Army, 1956-58. Married Gwendolyn Mary Heinson in 1956; son: John Gerard. Head of Construction, Holabird and Root, Chicago, 1955-56; Project Manager, Naess and Murphy, Chicago, 1958-61; Design Administrator and Project Architect, 1961-65, Associate Partner, 1965-67, and Partner, 1967, C. F. Murphy Associates, Chicago; Associate, Philip Johnson Architects, New York, 1967-68; Partner, Johnson/Burgee Architects, New York, 1968-82. Since 1983, Partner, John Burgee Architects with Philip Johnson, New York. President, Chicago Near North Montessori School Board, 1962-63; Chairman, Building Material Section, Metropolitan Crusade of Mercy, Chicago, 1966-67; Chairman, Architectural Review Board, Bronxville, New York, 1974-75; Co-Chairman, Architecture Committee, Statue of Liberty/Ellis Island Commission, New York, since 1983; Chairman and President, Institute for Architecture and Urban Studies, New York, 1984-85; Advisory Board Member, University of Notre Dame, Indiana, since 1982. Recipient: Honor Award, 1975, 1976, and Chicago Architecture Award, 1984, American Institute of Architects; Reynolds Prize, 1978. D.Ing.: University of Notre Dame, Indiana, 1983. Fellow, American Institute of Architects, 1976. Address: John Burgee Architects with Philip Johnson, 375 Park Avenue, New York, New York 10152, U.S.A.

Works:

1962 O'Hare International Airport, Chicago
1965 Chicago Civic Center, Chicago
1967 First National Bank, Chicago
1970 J. Edgar Hoover FBI Building, Washington, D.C.
1972 Art Museum of South Texas, Corpus Christi
       Neuberger Museum, State University of New York at Purchase
       Burden Hall, Harvard University, Cambridge, Massachusetts
1973 IDS Center, Minneapolis, Minnesota
1974 Convention Center, Niagara Falls, New York
1976 Pennzoil Place, Houston, Texas
1977 Century Center, South Bend, Indiana
1980 National Center for the Perfoming Arts, Bombay, India
       Garden Grove Community Church, California
1983 101 California Street Office Building, San Francisco
       Republic Bank Center, Houston, Texas
1984 American Telephone and Telegraph Headquarters, New York
       PPG Building, Pittsburgh, Pennsylvania
       Transco Tower, Houston, Texas
       United Bank Center, Denver, Colorado
       580 California Street Office Building, San Francisco

1985 53rd at Third Office Building, New York
       Tycon Towers, Tyson's Corner, Virginia
       Fort Hill Square, Boston
1985- Times Square Redevelopment, New York
1986- Momentum Place, Dallas, Texas
       500 Boylston Street Office Building, Boston
       190 South LaSalle Office Building, Chicago
       Atlantic Center, Atlanta, Georgia

Publications:

On BURGEE: books—*Johnson/Burgee Architects*, with text by Nory Miller, New York and London 1980; articles—"Philip Johnson and John Burgee: Avery Fisher Hall" in *Interiors* (New York), February 1977; "Three designs by Johnson/Burgee" in *Architectural Record* (New York), July 1978; "Two works by Philip Johnson and John Burgee" in *Industria delle Costruzioni* (Rome), October 1978; "Pennzoil Place, Houston" in *Informes de la Construccion* (Madrid), January/February 1979; "It's the real thing" in *Building Design* (London), 14 March 1980; "New Crystal Palace" in *Progressive Architecture* (New York), December 1980; "Johnson/Burgee", special issue of *Progressive Architecture* (New York), February 1984.

See JOHNSON, Philip

BURLE MARX, Roberto.

Brazilian. Born in São Paulo, 4 August 1909. Educated in Rio de Janeiro, from 1914; studied music, Rio de Janeiro; studied painting in a private studio, Berlin, and studied Brazilian flora, privately, at the Dahlen Botanical Gardens, Berlin 1928-29; studied at the Escola Nacional de Belas Artes, Rio de Janeiro (gold medal for painting); took a course in ecology, Botanical Garden, Rio de Janeiro; self-taught in landscape design. Director of Parks, Recife, Brazil, 1935-37. Since 1937, in private practice as a landscape architect, Rio de Janeiro; has discovered and cultivated numerous plants that now bear his name; has also worked as a painter, as well as a designer of jewellery, tapestries, stage scenery, sculptural reliefs, and fabric panels. Exhibitions (landscape design, paintings, tapestries, sculptures, fabric panels): individual—Palace Hotel, Rio de Janeiro, 1941; Galeria Itapetininga, São Paulo, 1946; Museum of Art, São Paulo, 1952; Museum of Modern Art, Rio de Janeiro, 1956; Institute of Contemporary Arts, London, 1956; Stedelijk Museum, Amsterdam, 1957 (toured Europe); *Bienal*, São Paulo, 1959; National Museum of Art, Buenos Aires, 1961; University of Montevideo Faculty of Architecture, 1962; Museum of Modern Art, Rio de Janeiro, 1963; Galeria Bonino, Rio de Janeiro, 1967; A Galeria, São Paulo, 1968; Gallery of the Banco Nacional de Minas Gerais, São Paulo, 1968; *Biennale*, Venice, 1970; Galeria Bancipe, Recife, Brazil, 1971; Belo Horizonte Museum of Art, Brazil, 1972; Galeria do Instituto Brasil-Estados Unidos, Rio de Janeiro, 1972; Gulbenkian Foundation, Lisbon, 1973; Musée Galerie, Paris, 1973; Galeria Bonino, Rio de Janeiro, 1974; Museum of Modern Art, São Paulo, 1974; Museum of Contemporary Art, Curitiba, Brazil, 1974; Teatro Castro Alves, Salvador, Brazil, 1974; Cultural Foundation, Brasilia, 1975; Hotel Ambassador, Porto Allegre, Brazil, 1976; Oficina d'Arte, Rio de Janeiro, 1976; Atelier Noth und Hauer, Berlin, 1976; Case de Olinda, Recife, Brazil, 1977; Museum of Contemporary Art, Caracas, 1977; Bolsa de Arte, Rio de Janeiro, 1978; Fine Arts Center/Contemporary Art Museum,

John Burgee and Philip Johnson: AT & T Corporate Headquarters, New York, 1984.

Caracas, 1978; Atelier Internacional, Buenos Aires, 1978; Galeria AKI, São Paulo, 1978; Galeria Guignard, Belo Horizonte, Brazil, 1978; Fine Arts Museum, Rio de Janeiro, 1978; group—*20 Brazilian Artists,* Provincial Museum, Buenos Aires, 1945; *Modern Brazilian Painting,* Royal Academy, London, 1945; *Biennale,* Venice, 1947; *Bienal,* São Paulo, 1953; *Landscape Architecture,* Institute of Contemporary Art, Boston, 1955; *Brasilien baut,* Leverkusen Museum, West Germany, 1956; *International Flower Show,* Paris, 1957, Trieste, 1960; *Bienal,* São Paulo, 1963; *International Garden Show,* Hamburg, West Germany, 1963; *Biennale,* Venice, 1978. Collection: Sitio Santo Antonio da Bica, Guanabara State, Brazil. Recipient: Gold Medal, Escola Nacional de Belas Artes, Rio de Janeiro, 1941; First Prize, *Bienal,* São Paulo, 1953; First Prize, *International Flower Show,* Paris, 1957; Gold Medal, *International Flower Show,* Trieste, Italy, 1960; First Prize, *International Garden Show,* Hamburg, West Germany, 1963; Santos Dumont Medal, Brazil, 1963; Fine Arts Medal, American Institute of Architects, 1965; Personality of the Year Award, Institute of Architects of Brazil, 1969; Museum of Image and Sound Trophy, Rio de Janeiro, 1970; Alfonso de Souza Cultural Medal, PHAN: Patrimonio Historico e Artistico da Nacao, São Paulo, 1975; Medal of Honor, Belo Horizonte, Brazil, 1976; Great Gold Medal, Royal Horticultural Society, London, 1982; Gold Medal, French Academy of Architects, Paris, 1982; Greenfelder Medal, Missouri Botanical Garden, 1983. Honorary Member, National Society of Interior Designers, New York, 1959; Institute of Landscape Architects, London, 1968; British Columbia Society of Landscape Architects, 1968; and American Academy of Arts and Letters, 1979.

Commander, Order of the Rio Branco, Brazil, 1971. Honorary doctorates: Royal College of Art, London, 1982; Royal Academy of Art, the Hague, 1982. Chevalier, Order of the Couronne, Belgium, 1959; Commander, Order of Merit, Chile, 1962, and Nicaragua, 1970; Member, Andres Bello Order, Venezuela, 1977. Address: Cardosso Junior 95, Laranjeiras, Rio de Janeiro, Brazil.

Works (landscape architecture):

1932   Schwarz House, Rio de Janeiro
1934   Public Gardens, Recife, Brazil
1938   Ministry of Education and Health, Rio de Janeiro
      Santos Dumont Airport, Rio de Janeiro
      ABI Building terraces, Rio de Janeiro
1939   IRB Building, Rio de Janeiro
      Solon de Lucena Park, Joao Pessoa, Brazil
1942   Yacht Club Restaurant, Pampulha, Belo Horizonte, Brazil
      Francisco Inacio Peizoto House, Cataguazes, Minas Gerais, Brazil
1943   Araxa Park, Minas Gerais, Brazil (with Henrique Lahmeyer de Mello Barreto)
1948   Odette Monteiro House, Correias, Brazil
      Samambaia Farm, Petropolis, Brazil
      Diego Cisneiros House, Caracas
      Burton Tremaine House, Santa Barbara, California
1950   Parahyba Textile Factory, Sao Jose dos Campos, São Paulo State, Brazil
      Olivo Gomes House, São Jose do Campos, São Paulo State, Brazil

      Hotel Amazonas, Manaus, Brazil
      Hotel da Bahia, Salvador, Brazil
1951   PDF Building, Rio de Janeiro
      Teatro Popular de Marechal Hermes, Rio de Janeiro
      Galeao Airport, Rio de Janeiro
      Nossa Senhora da Conceicau da Jaqueira Church Courtyard, Recife, Brazil
      Roche Laboratories, Rio de Janeiro
      Cassiano Ribeiro Coutinho, Joao Pessoa, Brazil (project)
1952   Independence Square, Joao Pessoa, Brazil (project)
      Cathedral Precinct, Salvador, Brazil (project)
      Carlos Somlo House, Vale da Boa Esperanca, Terezopolis, Brazil (project)
1953   University of Rio de Janeiro (project)
      Ibirapuera Park, São Paulo (project)
      Pampulha Airport, Belo Horizonte, Brazil (project)
      American Embassy, Rio de Janeiro (project)
1954   Promenade at Botafogo Beach, Rio de Janeiro (project)
      Museum of Modern Art, Rio de Janeiro
      Machado Lagoon, Rio de Janeiro
      Fourth Centenary Exhibition, São Paulo (project)
      Ernesto Waller House, Barra da Tijuca, Brazil
      Edmundo Cavanellas House, Pedro do Rio, Petropolis, Brazil
1955   Labor Temple Planting Project, Los Angeles
      South America Hospital, Rio de Janeiro (project)
      Alberto Kronsforth House, Terezopolis, Brazil
      Dr. Miranda House, Rio de Janeiro

Roberto Burle Marx: Garden for Petro-Bras Building, Rio de Janeiro, 1972.

Sergio Correia da Costa House, Rio de Janeiro
Imperial Museum, Petropolis, Brazil
1956   East and West Parks, Caracas
Canal Development, Caracas
El Castano Apartment Building, Caracas
Club Playa Azul, Caracas
Inocente Palacios House, Caracas
Diego Cisneros House, Caracas
Henrique Delfino House, Caracas
Eduardo Rahn House, Caracas
Carlos Alberto Punceles House, Caracas
Ernesto Valenilla House, Caracas
Luiz Carias House, Caracas
Hacienda Monte Sacro, Valencia, Spain
Lindoia Park, São Paulo State, Brazil
1957   Guararapes Airport, Recife, Brazil
Schulthess House, Havana, Cuba
1958   Olivetti Sports Ground, Buenos Aires
(project)
1961   Flamengo Park, Rio de Janeiro
Monumental Axis, Brasilia (project)
Zoo/Botanical Park, Brasilia (project)
Botanical Gardens, São Paulo (project)
1962   Park of the Americas, Santiago, Chile
(project)
1963   Unesco Building, Paris (project)
National Gardens, Vienna (project; with Karl
Mang)
Brazilian Pavilion, International Fair, Tokyo
1965   Ministry of Foreign Affairs, Brasilia (project)
Fernandez Concha House, Lima, Peru
(project)
Biological Reserve, Jacarepagua, Guanabara,
Brazil
Morro da Viuva Restaurant, Rio de Janeiro
(project)
Irmaos Gomes House, Ubatuba, Brazil
(project)
1966   Sousa Hospital, Rio de Janeiro
Civic Center, Curitiba, Brazil
Manchete Building, Rio de Janeiro
North Park, San Isidro, Argentina (project)
Dorado Hilton Hotel, San Juan, Puerto Rico
(project)
Siqueira Campos Park, São Paulo (project)
Ponte Alta Farm, Barra do Pirai, Rio de
Janeiro State, Brazil (project)
Candido Guinle de Paula Machado House,
Rio de Janeiro (project)
1967   Civic Center, Santo Andre, Brazil (project)
United States Embassy, Brasilia (project)
Santa Barbara Development, San Juan,
Puerto Rico (project)
Tribunal Federal de Recursos Building,
Brasilia
1968   Leoes Palace, Sao Luiz, Brazil (project)
Anhembi Park, São Paulo
Sao Judas Tadeu Square, Santo Andre, Brazil
Cathedral Square, Rio de Janeiro (project)
German Embassy, Brasilia (project)
Santuario de Jesus do Matosinhos, Congon-
has do Camp, Minas Gerais, Brazil
Benedito Dias Macedo House, Fortaleza,
Brazil
Clemente Gomes House, São Paulo
Gravata Condominium, São Paulo (project)
Brazilian Embassy, Washington, D.C.
Condominium Araucaria, São Paulo
National Gardens, Recife, Brazil (project)
1969   Federal University of Santa Catarina Cam-
pus, Florianopolis, Brazil (project)
National-Rio Hotel, São Conrado, Rio de
Janeiro (project)
Bloch Building, Rio de Janeiro
Petrobras Headquarters, Rio de Janeiro
Flamengo Park Aquarium, Rio de Janeiro
(project)
SESI/FIESP/DIESP Building, São Paulo
(project)
Telepar Headquarters, Curitiba, Brazil
Santuario Dom Bosco, Brasilia (project)
1970   Botanical Garden, Federal University of
Minas Gerais, Belo Horizonte, Brazil
(initial project; for further development by

students)
Federal University of Paraiba, Joao Pessoa,
Brazil
Copacabana Promenade (with beach widen-
ing), Rio de Janeiro
Ministry of Justice, Brasilia
Esporte Clube Sirio, São Paulo
Hilton Hotel, São Paulo (project)
Lodrina City Park, Parana, Brazil
Central Park, Caracas (project)
1971   Urban renovation plan for Zone 1a of Buenos
Aires
Chacra Saavedra Sport and Leisure Center,
Buenos Aires (project)
Estadual de Torres Park, Porto Alegre, Brazil
(project)
City Park and Zoo/Botanical Gardens, Bari-
gui, Curitiba, Brazil (project)
São Lourenco Park, Curitiba, Brazil (project)
Community Park, Santo Andre, Brazil
(project)
Jundiai Housing Complex, São Paulo
Iranian Embassy, Brasilia
Hotel Belneario Laguna, Santa Catarina,
Brazil (project)
DNER Residence, Brasilia
Belgian Embassy, Brasilia (project)
Urbanization plan for Patamares, Salvador,
Brazil
1972   Federal University of Pernambuco, Recife,
Brazil (project)
Karnak Palace, Teresina, Piaui State, Brazil
(project)
Planalto Palace, Brasilia
American Embassy, Brasilia (project)
Peru Square, Buenos Aires (project)
SUDENE Headquarters, Recife, Brazil
(project)
Concert Hall, Caracas (project)
Brasilia Square, Quito, Ecuador
Club Vale Verde, Campinas, São Paulo
Merck Factory, Rio de Janeiro
Plan for the city of Ouro Preto, Brazil (as
consultant)
Ministry of Development, Brasilia
Petrobras Building and Terminal, Santa Ter-
esa, Rio de Janeiro
1973   Teatro Jose de Alencar, Fortaleza, Brazil
(project)
Cemetery, Recife, Brazil (project)
Jornal do Brasil Building, Rio de Janeiro
(project)
East-West Avenue, Fortaleza, Brazil (project)
Glasner de Barros House, Recife, Brazil
(project)
Municipal Prefecture, Fortaleza, Brazil
(project)
Administrative Center, Salvador, Brazil
(project)
Milton Campos Square, Belo Horizonte,
Brazil (project)
Banco Nacional do Desenvolvimento Econo-
mico, Brasilia (project)
Sports Center, Cuiaba, Brazil (project)
Guarapirange Park, São Paulo (project)
Realdo Santos Guglielmi House, Criciuma,
Brazil (project)
United Nations Avenue Junction, São Paulo
(project)
1974   Governor's Palace, Alagoas, Brazil (project)
Electricity Company of Pernambuco, Recife,
Brazil (project)
Comercial do Piquero Building, Tatuape, São
Paulo (project)
Edgars Stores, South Africa (project)
Swagershoek Farm, Lydenberg District,
Transvaal, South Africa (project)
Ermirio Pereira de Moraes House, São Paulo
(project)
Juqueri Reservoir, São Paulo (project)
Administrative Center, São Paulo (project)
Jaragua Tourist Development Plan, Atibaia,
São Paulo (project)
Olga Cunha Bueno Ferreira House, São Paulo

(project)
Augusto Esteves de Lima Jr. House, São Paulo
Banco Nacional do Desenvolvimento Eco-
nomico Building, Rio de Janeiro (project)
Hering Textile Factory, Santa Catarina,
Brazil (project)
Rogerio Pithon Serejo Farias Recreational
Park, Brasilia (project)
Maria do Carmo Nabucco de Magalhaes Lins
House, Rio de Janeiro (project)
1975   Vice-President's House, Brasilia (project)
Bloch Building, São Paulo (project)
Hans Broos House, São Paulo (project)
Bicalho Goulart Park, Belo Horizonte, Brazil
(project)
Da Costa and Silva Square, Piaui, Brazil
(project)
Monumental Axis, Brasilia (project)
Inconfidencia Square, Belo Horizonte, Brazil
Abbey of Santa Maria, São Paulo (project)
Residential development, Avenida Sernambe-
tiba, Rio de Janeiro (project)
Alberto Kronsforth House, Angra dos Reis,
Brazil (project)
Rodrigo de Freitas Lagoon, Rio de Janeiro
(project)
Elie Douer House, São Paulo (project)
Kurt Waissman House, São Paulo (project)
Wimbledon Park Building, Avenida das
Americas, Rio de Janeiro (project)
1976   Plan for the center of Vivencia de Guarapari,
Espirito Santo, Brazil
Pedro Biagi Building, São Paulo (project)
Riviera dei Fiore Buildings, Rio de Janeiro
(project)
Enrique Delfino House, Caracas (project)
Rua Coronel Agostinho, Campo Grande, Rio
de Janeiro (project)
Teatro Nacional, Brasilia (project)
River Tiete Ecological Park, São Paulo
(project)
Gilberto Canuki Daccache House, São Paulo
(project)
Campos do Jordao Convention Center, São
Paulo (project)
Celso Gerbassi Ramos House, Rio de Janeiro
(project)
Ipanema Farm, Sorocaba, São Paulo (project)
Viana Wood, São Paulo (project)
Joao Borges de Assis House, Aracatuba, São
Paulo (project)
Abbey of Santa Maria, São Paulo
Marina, Rio de Janeiro (project)
Le Corbusier Building, Recife, Brazil (project)
Oscar Niemeyer Building, Recife, Brazil
(project)
Restaurant, Conservatory and Recreational
Park, Brasilia
Bangu Prison, Rio de Janeiro (project)
Fernando Conde Lorenzo House, Itacoatiara,
Rio de Janeiro (project)
Renato de Toledo e Silva House, São Paulo
(project)
Luiz Lucio Constabile Izzo House, São Paulo
(project)
Wimbledon Park Building, São Paulo
(project)
Juan les Pins Building, Rio de Janeiro (project)
Fernando Magalhaes Pinto House, Rio de
Janeiro (project)
Emilio Maya Omena House, Maceio, Brazil
(project)
Sotave Nordeste Industria e Comercio Build-
ing, Recife, Brazil (project)
Romildo de Carvalho Coutinho House,
Paraiba, Brazil (project)
OMPI Headquarters, Rio de Janeiro (project)
1977   South Beach reclamation, Santa Catarina,
Brazil (project)
Edgar Hargreaves House, Rio de Janeiro
(project)
São Luiz Square, Terezopolis, Brazil (project)
Civic Center, Curitiba, Brazil
Roberto Malzoni House, São Paulo (project)

Linneo de Paulo Machado House, Rio de Janeiro (project)

Exhibition and Convention Center, Recife, Brazil (project)

Magaly Cannizaro-Miranda House, Caracas (project)

Artemio Furlan Filho House, São Paulo (project)

El Hatillo House, Caracas (project)

Pedregal Building, Caracas (project)

John Machado Urbina House, Caracas (project)

COMIND Central Administration Building, Barueri, São Paulo (project)

1978 Itarare Beach, São Vicente, São Paulo (project)

Glaucio Carneiro Leao House, Recife, Brazil (project)

SESC Amphitheatre, Rio de Janeiro (project)

Cerro del Vigia Development, Puerto la Cruz, Brazil (project)

International Airport, Rio de Janeiro (project)

Banco Boavista, Rio de Janeiro (project)

Walter Clark House, Rio de Janeiro (project)

Servino Y.R.S. Ortiz Building, Buenos Aires (project)

Publications:

By BURLE MARX: book—*Rino Levi,* with Nestor Goulart Reis Filho, Milan 1974; articles—"Gardens and Ecology: A Personal View" in *Plan* (Johannesburg), no. 10, 1973; "Landscape Gardening" in *Arts and Architecture* (Los Angeles), July 1954; recording—*A Garden Is Like a Poem,* tape cassette and slides, London 1982.

On BURLE MARX: books—*The Tropical Gardens of Burle Marx* by Pietro Maria Bardi and M. Gautherot, London 1964; *Roberto Burle Marx e a nova visao da paisagem* by Flavio L. Motta, São Paulo 1984; articles—"The Gardens of Roberto Burle Marx" in *Royal Architectural Institute of Canada Journal* (Toronto), February 1952; "Burle Marx et le jardin contemporain" in *L'Architecture d'aujourd'hui* (Paris), August 1952; "Roberto Burle Marx und das Problem der gartengestaltung" in *Werk* (Zürich), August 1953; "Jardins de l'Aéroport de Rio" in *L'Architecture d'aujourd'hui* (Paris), February 1954; "A Garden Style in Brazil to Meet Contemporary Needs" in *Landscape Architecture* (Louisville, Kentucky), July 1954; "Roberto Burle Marx: Art and the Landscape" in *Architectural Record* (New York), October 1954; "Musée d'Art Moderne à Rio de Janeiro" in *L'Architecture d'aujourd'hui* (Paris), October 1956; "Brazilianische Garten von Roberto Burle Marx" in *Baukunst und Werkform* (Nuremberg), no. 9, 1956; "Roberto Burle Marx y sus jardines" in *Arquitectura* (Mexico City), June 1957; "Roberto Burle Marx: pittore di giardini" in *Zodiac* (Milan), no. 6, 1960; "Appraisal of a Master Artist" by Anthony Walmsley in *Landscape Architecture* (Louisville, Kentucky), July 1963; "The Versatility of Burle Marx" by Guy Playfair in *Architectural Review* (London), November 1964; "Roberto Burle Marx of Brazil" by Alice Graeme Korff in *AIA Journal* (Washington, D.C.), May 1965; "Robert Burle Marx: Parks, Gardens, Towns, Squares, Beaches" by Miguel Thomas Kerner in *L'Architettura* (Rome), April 1976; "Roberto Burle Marx" by M. Emanuel in *Landscape Design* (London), August 1979; "Roberto Burle Marx—The One-Man Extravaganza" by F. L. Gregory in *Landscape Architecture* (Louisville, Kentucky), May 1981; "Brazilian Brilliance" by C. Glasspoole in *Building Design* (London), 19 March 1982; "Wasteland" by A. Best in *Architects' Journal* (London), 24 March 1982.

The most important thing for me is the link with existing nature: a garden cannot be artificial when you are dealing with natural elements. I do admit to principles, but I hate formulas. A garden is not a painting, and a painting is not a garden, but the two have an interwoven theme. When I create a garden, I speak an art language. You must have form, starting from what is there; and if it is a cleared space, then form must be based on what is to be seen around that space. Indiscriminate planting makes a salad—it does not create a work of art. Perhaps this sounds chauvinistic, but with 5,000 trees and 50,000 plants to choose from in Brazil, why should I import plants from abroad?

—Roberto Burle Marx

The revolution of ideas created by Le Corbusier in mathematical architecture called for its complement in biological landscape. Roberto Burle Marx was the first landscape designer to evolve such an art. Painter, designer of fabrics and jewellery, stage designer, and animator of fêtes and festivals, he channelled all these qualities into the single art of landscape design. The task he undertook was the translation of abstract art into reality, using his living plant materials much as a painter uses the colour and texture of paint. Although his practice now extends all over South America and beyond, he will probably be best remembered for the pioneer gardens made among the mountains round his home town of Rio de Janeiro.

The spirit behind these gardens is his personal vision and interpretation of the Brazilian forests and their rivers. In using only indigenous plants he was influenced by William Robinson, whom he admired; but in the *manner* of using them, he is quite different. His gardens are organized as baroque gardens of movement; the sweeping and beautiful curves seem like water eddies and currents against their background of mountains. The flower beds have been described as cloud shadows passing over the landscape. To steady this movement, Burle Marx introduces geometry on plan that may originally have been inspired by that of Le Corbusier, for whose Ministry of Education and Health in Rio he made one of his most spectacular roof gardens.

Burle Marx breathes originality in all he creates, from his own home outside Rio, where he grows and experiments with plants, to such inventions as a chequered lawn of two grasses kept apart by metal strips concealed below the surface. Above all, his work is stamped as the creation of an artist of many accomplishments and wide vision, an artist who first raised modern garden design to an international plane of art.

—Geoffrey Jellicoe

BUSZKO AND FRANTA.

Partnership; established, Katowice, Poland, 1950, by Henryk Buszko (born 1924) and Aleksander Franta (born 1925). Architects to the City Architectural Office (Miastoprojekt), Katowice, 1950-58. Since 1958, Senior Architects, Architectural Office of General Construction, Katowice. Exhibitions: group—Warsaw, 1951-54; Katowice, 1951-73; *Exposition international d'urbanisme,* Paris, 1963; *International Union of Architects Exhibition,* Prague, 1967, Buenos Aires, 1969, Madrid, 1975, and Warsaw and Katowice, Poland, 1981; *Polish Architecture Exhibition,* Moscow, 1974-75; *Regional Architecture Exposition,* Katowice, 1979, 1981, 1984; *Terra 2,* Wroclaw, 1981; partnership—SARP, Warsaw, 1975; Historical Museum, Koszalin, Poland, 1975; SARP, Gdansk, Poland, 1976; Architectural Museum, Wroclaw, Poland, 1976; *Buszko and Franta: 25 Years,* Katowice, Poland, 1983. Recipient: Town Planning and Architecture Committee Prize, 1959, 1961, and 1962; Ministry of Construction Prize, 1964, 1969, and 1973; SARP Medal, Katowice, Poland, 1972; Supreme Technical Organization (NOT) Prize, 1972; Ministry of Science and Technology Prize, 1973; Honorary Award, Polish Architects Association, 1975; Regional Art Award, Katowice, Poland, 1981. Address: Pracownia Projektowa Budownictwa Ogolnego, ul. Marchlewskiego 19, Katowice, Poland.

Works:

1950/
54 Trade Unions Centre, Katowice, Poland (with J. Gottfreid)

1951 Malapanew Steelworks Social Centre, Ozimek, near Opole, Poland (with J. Gottfreid)

Baildon Steelworks Technical College, Katowice, Poland (with J. Gottfreid)

Ministry of Mining Stand, Home Trade Fair, Poznan, Poland (with T. Mroszezak and B. Gorecki)

1954 Zgoda Steelworks Social Centre, Katowice, Poland (with J. Gottfreid)

1955/
58 Transport Union Holiday Hotel, Olszowka-Mikuszowice, near Bielsko, Poland (with J. Gottfreid)

1956 Ministry of Mining Stand, Home Trade Fair, Poznan, Poland (with T. Mroszczak and B. Gorecki)

1956/
57 Torkat Winter Stadium with Ice Rink, Bankowa Street, Katowice, Poland (with J. Gottfreid)

1956/
58 Regional Theatre, Rybnik, Poland (with J. Gottfreid)

1957 Ministry of Mining Stand, Home Trade Fair, Poznan, Poland (with T. Mroszczak and B. Gorecki)

1958 Apartments, Reymonta Street, Katowice, Poland (with J. Gottfreid)

Terrace housing, Norwida Street, Tychy, Poland (with J. Gottfreid)

Terrace housing, Karolinki Street, Gliwice, Poland (with J, Gottfreid)

1958/
60 Mostostalu Workers' Apartment Building, Zabrze, Poland

1958/
62 Wujek Coal Mine Housing Estate, Katowice, Poland

1958/
78 "1,000 Year" Urban Housing Development, Katowice, Poland: housing blocks with service buildings, five schools, health centre, four shopping and restaurant units, Centrum Department Store, social centre, church, sports centre

1959 Buszko and Franta Architectural Office Building, Marchlewskiego Street, Katowice, Poland

1959/
60 Wedding-Palace Building, Chorzow, Poland

1959/
62 Gornik Sanatorium, Szczawnica, Poland

1960 Teachers' Holiday Centre, Jaszowiec Health Resort, Ustron, Poland

Parkland Tourist Hotel, Chorzow, Poland

1960/
61 Baildon Steelworks Social Centre conversion, Katowice, Poland

1961 Miners' Seaside Holiday Centre, Leba, Poland

Apartment building, Strzelcow Bytomskich Street, Bytom, Poland

1962 Agricultural Bank Office Building, Katowice, Poland

Wedding Palace Building, Sosnowiec, Poland

1963/
65 Exhibition Stand Design, Brno, Czechoslovakia

Buszko and Franta: Roman Catholic Church in the 1,000-Year Settlement, Katowice, Poland, 1978-79.

1964 Ministry of Mining Stand, Home Trade Fair, Poznan, Poland (with T. Mroszczak and B. Gorecki)

1964/
65 Polish Workers Party Office Building, Armii Czerwonej Street, Katowice, Poland
Building Industry Workers Health Centre, PCK Street, Katowice, Poland

1966/
67 Academy Teachers' Terrace Housing, Brynow, Katowice, Poland (with T. Czewczyk)

1968 Ministry of Mining Stand, Home Trade Fair, Poznan, Poland (with T. Mroszczak and B. Gorecki)

1968/
78 Ustron-Zawodzie Mountain Health Resort, Ustron, near Bielsko, Poland (with T. Dzewczyk, D. Korczyk, and I. N. Lazowski): sanatorium, natural therapy centre, eighteen holiday hotels, three shopping and restaurant sub-centres, resort medical staff housing estate, management office building

Rozdzienski Housing Settlement, Katowice, Poland (with T. Szewczyk, D. Korczyk, J. Kielski, and L. Baron): seven housing blocks, with integral nurseries, kindergartens, and ancillary buildings; school; shopping centre with cafe and restaurant

1969 Parks Department Office Building, Chorzow, Poland
Zeto Computer Centre, Owocowa Street, Katowice, Poland (with T. Czewczyk)

1970/
72 Twelve-storey prototype apartment block, "1,000 Year" Urban Housing Development, Katowice, Poland

1973 Gornictwa Mine Engineering Works Training Centre, Rolna Street, Katowice, Poland

1974/
77 Single-family housing, Katowice and Ustron, Poland

1977 Prototype prefabricated single-family housing, Stalowa Wola, Poland

1978 Health Resort Social Centre, Ustron-Zawodzie, Poland (project)

1978/
79 Lubin Holiday Centre, Swieradow, Poland
"1,000-Year" Commercial Centre, Katowice, Poland
Roman Catholic Church, in the "1,000-Year" development, Katowice, Poland
RETA Housing Settlement, Mikotow, Poland

1980/
81 Polish Catholic Church, Jasnogorska Street, Czestochowa, Poland

1983/
84 Roman Catholic Chapel, in the "1,000-Year" development, Katowice, Poland

The Buszko and Franta partnership has also worked on more than two dozen competition projects, residential planning schemes, and furniture and interior designs.

Publications:

By BUSZKO/FRANTA: book—*My Meditations About Housing* by Henryk Buszko, Warsaw 1982; articles—"The Source of Justifiable Pride: Railway Station in Katowice" by Aleksander Franta in *Architektura* (Warsaw), October 1973; and numerous articles by Buszko and Franta in publications of the Polish Academy of Sciences in Krakow, Katowice, and Warsaw, 1975-83.

On BUSZKO/FRANTA: books—*Modern Architecture in Poland* by Bohdan Lisowski, Warsaw 1968; *Nowa Architektura Polski Diariusz lat 1966-1970* by Przemyslaw Szafer, Warsaw 1971; *Polska Architektura Wspolczesna* by Przemyslaw Szafer, Warsaw 1977; *Nowa Architektura Polska, diariusz lat 1971-1975* by T. Przemyslaw Szafer, Warsaw 1979; *Nowa Architektura Polska, diariusz lat 1976-1980* by T. Przemyslaw Szafer, Warsaw 1981; articles—"Dom Metalowca" by Z. Rzepecki in *Architektura* (Warsaw), no. 5, 1955; "Architecture of Buszko and Franta" by W. Geppert in *Architektura* (Warsaw), no. 3, 1964; "Architecture of the 1,000 Year Housing Settlement" by J. Brzozowski in *Architektura* (Warsaw), no. 10, 1964; "Bederowiec" by A. Ligocki in *Poglady* (Warsaw), no. 19, 1964; "Review of the 1,000 Year Housing Settlement in Katowice" by A. Wojda in *Architektura* (Warsaw), no. 1, 1971; "The Art of the Background" by T. Barucki in *Projekt* (Warsaw), no. 2, 1971; "Honorowa Nagroda SARP" in *Architektura* (Warsaw), no. 9/10, 1975.

Architecture is planned environmental conditioning, and the architect's task is to design space for human needs—biological, functional, and psychological. Architecture emerges and develops under conditions determined by time, place, and function. As a result, insight is needed in understanding man and his needs—an awareness of his psyche, his social background, his history and culture, and his environment. Also needed is the ability to work in different scales, from furniture and interior design to district, town and regional planning. And a wide range of technology must be mastered, from the crafts to industrial production. The building industry, with its technology and organization, is the tool to realize architecture.

We regard the process of architectural creativity as operating in a cultural sequence; it is a search for the characteristic spatial features of a particular place and a search for the individual image of settlement, town, or country. Architecture conceived at a specific time is also a function of the past and determines the conditions of life in the future. Therefore, it should perhaps have a high degree of adaptability, particularly at the present time when the future is difficult to define.

We believe that the architect is a specialist, designing space for man in accordance with nature. We believe, too, that the architect, as specialist, is a social tool through which—with the help of his relatively autonomous creativity—society expresses its culture in environmental form. From this awareness results a responsibility for one's work and a sense that one is performing a service to the community; it also helps to create modesty, strength of purpose, and a desire for positive and courageous reasoning within one's professional activity. We consider such an attitude to be a necessary condition for the practice of our profession—if we aim to achieve as high a quality of architecture as possible.

Architecture of the highest order can exist at any stage in technological development, provided that all the technical potential of that stage is used. Each building process results in new architecture—new space for human life. Each spatial pattern influences man and his psyche. Architecture of high quality influences positively; bad architecture influences negatively: it deforms, reduces sensitivity, weakens receptivity. Generally, man surrenders unconsciously to its influence and does not understand the implications of its quality. It is difficult to find architecture of high quality even in highly developed societies. We believe that every man has the right to architecture of high quality and that space shared in common should be employed for the good of the community.

The primary condition for creating such architecture is a high proficiency in making spatial decisions, for which only the architect is qualified. We believe in the future, and we believe in the human intellect and in man's abilities and his good will. Therefore, we believe in the significance of our profession. We believe that future architecture will be diverse, as varied as man and his culture, and that everywhere it will be of higher quality. To achieve this goal, the work must be done by architects, the best educated ones possible, working in the right professional relationship with contractors and investors. The discovery of effective working arrangements—and appropriate means of funding—to promote a generally high standard of architecture, is the central issue in the future of architecture.

—Henryk Buszko and Aleksander Franta

Henryk Buszko and Aleksander Franta regard architectural work as creating the art of the "background," the background to human life.

Unlike painting and sculpture, which are arts of the object, architecture should not play a striking role but should organize the subtle framework within which human actions gain their meaning and significance. The basic medium of architecture is building, but as Buszko and Franta realize, a number of other relationships determining the quality of human environment have to be considered. The most important is preservation of the balance between nature and built form, a homeostasis regarded as essential for human life, both technologically and psychologically.

The work of the Buszko and Franta practice ranges from furniture and interior design, in a variety of different types of buildings, to housing developments, holiday villages, and other large-scale town planning projects. Both Buszko and Franta are lecturers at the Gliwice School of Architecture, and both are active members of the Polish Architects Association (Buszko was its President for several years) and the UIA (International Architects Association—in which Franta is a consultant to the General Secretary). Their work has won several architectural awards, and Buszko has been made a honorary member of both the American Institute of Architects and the Mexican Architects Association.

—Teresa Czaplinska-Archer

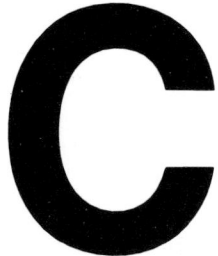

CALLISTER, Charles Warren.
American. Born in Rochester, New York, in 1917. Studied architecture and fine arts, University of Texas, Austin, 1935-41, B.A. 1941. Served in the United States Army Corps of Engineers and the United States Air Force, 1941-45. In private practice, San Francisco, 1946-55; Partner, with John M. Payne and J. Martin Rosse, Callister, Payne and Rosse, Tiburon, California, 1955-69, Callister and Payne, 1969-72, with Payne and James Bischoff, Callister, Payne and Bischoff, 1972-81, and since 1981, with Bischoff and David K. Gately, Callister, Gately and Bischoff; established second office in Amherst, Massachusetts, 1968. Lecturer in Architecture, Stanford University, California, since 1961; Visiting Lecturer in Architecture, Syracuse University, New York, 1962, 1965, Columbia University, New York, 1962, University of Colorado, Boulder, 1963, University of British Columbia, Vancouver, 1964, the universities of California, Texas, and Oregon, the California Polytechnic Institute, and East-West Center of the University of Hawaii, 1966, University of Massachusetts, Amherst, 1973. Exhibition: *A View of California Architecture 1960-1976*, San Francisco Museum of Modern Art, 1976. Recipient: Award of Excellence, Urban Land Institute, 1982; Award of Honor, San Francisco Art Commission, 1983. Addresses: Callister, Gately and Bischoff, 1865 Mar West, Box 377, Tiburon, California 94920, U.S.A.; and, 6 Main Street, Amherst, Massachusetts 01002, U.S.A.

Works:

1947 House, 405 Goodhill Road, Kentfield, California (with Jack Hilmer)
1948 Upper Lake Union High School additions, Upper Lake, California
      Kelseyville High School additions, Kelseyville, California
1948/
   52 Exhibition Buildings, 49th District Agricultural Fairground, Lakeport, California
1949 House, 106 Diablo Drive, Kentfield, California
      Clear Lake Presbyterian Church, Kelseyville, California
      Lakeport Grammar School additions, Lakeport, California
1950 Kelseyville Grammar School additions, Kelseyville, California
      Lower Lake Grammar School additions, Lower Lake, California
      Grandstand, 44th District Agricultural Fairground, Clousa, California
1951 First Church of Christ Scientist, San Raphael Avenue, Tiburon, California
      East Lake Grammar School additions, Clear Lake Park, California
      Clear Lake Union High School additions, Lakeport, California
1952 House, 3456 Dwight Way, Berkeley, California

Clear Lake Oaks Grammar School additions, Clear Lake Oaks, California
1953 House, 250 Curry Lane, Sausalito, California
1955 Portola School, 765 Portola Road, Woodside, California (with additions, 1957, 1964)
      First Church of Christ Scientist, Pleasant Hill, California
1958 House, 2637 Rose Street, Berkeley, California
      Corte Madera School, Portola Valley, California
1959 Bel Air School additions, 259 Karen Way, Tiburon, California
      House, 176 Palo Alto Avenue, Twin Peaks, San Francisco
      House, 2625 Rose Street, Berkeley, California
1960 Maybridge Cluster, Belvedere, California
      O'Connell House, Elk, California
      Steinhart House, Belvedere, California
1960/
   65 Rossmoor Leisure World Community Development, Walnut Creek, California
1961 Benson House, Clear Lake, California
      Johnson House, Alameda, California
      Deutscher House, Pleasant Hill, California
      Hill House, Tiburon, California
1961/
   62 Lagunitas School additions, Lagunitas, California
1961/
   64 Del Mar Middle School, Tiburon, California
1962 Cove Apartments, Belvedere, California
      Duncan House, San Francisco
      Miller House, Mill Valley, California
      Haviland Hall remodelling, University of California, Berkeley
1963 Albrecht House, Los Gatos, California
      Reed School addition, Tiburon, California
1964 Callister House, Belvedere, California
      Gordon House, San Francisco
      Silva House, Oakland, California
      Portola Valley School additions, Portola Valley, California
      U.S. Ambassador's Residence, Manila, Philippines
      Rossmoor Leisure World Shopping Center, Walnut Creek, California
1964/
   65 Field House and Playing Fields, University of California, Santa Cruz
      Hiller Highlands Community Development, Oakland, California
1964/
   66 Valencia New Town Plan, near Los Angeles
1965 Granada Community School, Tiburon, California
      First Church of Christ Scientist, Mill Valley, California
      Harvey's Ranch House Restaurant, State Highway 99, Valencia, California
      Red Hill Intermediate School, San Anselmo, California
      Ross Grammar School additions, Ross, California
      Sierra Tahoe Incline Village, Lake Tahoe, California

Downtown Plan, Tiburon, California
Unitarian Church, San Mateo, California (project)
Valencia Golf Clubhouse, State Highway 99, Valencia, California
Neighborhood Rehabilitation Project, St. Louis, Missouri
1965/
   66 Campus Commons Community Development, Sacramento, California
1965/
   67 Sycamore Community Development, Danville, California
      Diaz Ranch Community Development, Marin County, California
1965 Heritage Village Development, Southbury, Connecticut
1966 Hidden Valley School additions, San Anselmo, California
1966/
   67 Enclosed Handball Courts, University of California, Santa Cruz
1966/
   68 Exhibition Buildings, *California Exposition and Fair*, Sacramento, California
1967 Myers House, 455 Belvedere Avenue, Belvedere, California
      Chapel, Mills College, Oakland, California
      Sonoma Student Barns, Sonoma County, California (project)
      Sparta Mountain Planning Study, New Jersey
1967/
   68 Social Sciences and Humanities Building, University of California, Davis
      Heritage Apartments Development, Simsbury, Connecticut
1967/
   69 Woodmoor Community Development, Monument, Colorado
1968 Maloney House, Lucas Valley, California
      First Unitarian Church, Franklin and Geary Streets, San Francisco
      Bahia Community Development Master Plan, Marin County, California
1968/
   70 Heritage Village Green, Southbury, Connecticut
      Hollywood Hills Hotel, California
1968 Talcott Village Development, Farmington, Connecticut
      Heritage Woods Community Development, Avon, Connecticut
1969 Pacifica Condominiums, Pacifica, California (project)
1969/
   70 Amherst Apartments Development, Buffalo, New York
      North Parking Facilities, California State University, San Jose
1970 Ark Apartments, Belvedere, California
      Administration Buildings and School, First Unitarian Church, San Francisco
      The Mill Community Development, Stowe, Vermont

Charles Warren Callister: House in Tiburon, California, 1978.

Bucks Corner Development, Glastonbury, Connecticut

1970/
71 Harrison House, Heritage Village, Southbury, Connecticut
Peachtree City Master Plan, Georgia

1970/
72 Snapfinger Woods Community Development, De Kalb County, Georgia

1971/
73 Exchange Building, Talcott Village, Farmington, Connecticut
Vineyards of Saratoga Community Development, Saratoga, California

1971 Tinsley Mill Village, Peachtree City, Georgia
Crown Colony Community Development, Kingsport, Tennessee

1972 Living and Learning Center, Amherst, Massachusetts
Living and Learning Center, Farmington, Connecticut
Kingsmill Adult Housing, near Williamsburg, Virginia
Cordelia New Community, Cordelia, California

1972/
73 Hampshire College, Amherst, Massachusetts

Toyon Farm Community Development, Los Altos, California

1972 Village Center, De Kalb County, Georgia
Amherst Field Commercial Development, Massachusetts
Suburban Community Master Plans for New York, New Jersey and Connecticut
Northville Commons Community Development, Wayne County, Michigan
Old Yorktown Village, Mohegan Lake, New York
Dennison Land/Vest Project Community Development, Framingham, Massachusetts
Fairington Community Development, De Kalb County, Georgia
Eatons Neck Community Development, Long Island, New York
Buckland Community Development, Manchester, Connecticut

1973 Highlands Community Development, Cobb County, Georgia
Southhaven Community Development, Brookhaven, New York
Shaker Farms Country Club Village, Westfield and Southwick, Massachusetts
Foxledge Corporation Community Development, Poughkeepsie, New York

Glenlochen Community Development, Glastonburuy, Connecticut
Castle Mountain Community Development, Athens, New York
Kingsmill Hotel, Williamsburg, Virginia
Talcott Village Inn, Farmington, Connecticut
Buckland Commercial and Hotel Development, Manchester and South Windsor, Connecticut
Bucks Corner Village, Glastonbury, Connecticut

1974 Riverside Community Development, San Jose, California
Solarium Restaurant, Tucson, Arizona

1974/
75 Golf Clubhouse, Kingsmill, Virginia
Ski Lodge, Shawnee, Pennsylvania

1974/
76 U.S. Post Office, Amherst, Massachusetts

1974/
78 Landmark Corporation Community Development, Shawnee, Pennsylvania

1975 The Villages Master Plan, San Jose, California
Pancho's Restaurant, Manhattan Beach, California (project)

1975/
76 Woodlands Community Development, Houston, Texas

Tattersall Community Plan, Loudoun County, Virginia

1975/
77 Boltwood Walk Community Development, Amherst, Massachusetts

1975/
78 Treelake Community Development, Placer County, California

1976 Davidson House, Aptos, California

1976/
77 Pond Place Community Development, Avon, Connecticut

1976/
78 All Saints Church Parish House, Pasadena, California

1977 Foley-Corsano House, Santa Cruz, California
Jones House, Tiburon, California
Powder Forest Community Development, Simsbury, Connecticut

1978 House, Tiburon, California
Paparazzo Associates Community Development, Danbury, Connecticut
Canal Place Community Development, Avon, Connecticut
Downtown Community Development, Pittsburg, California
Howard Lorton Furniture Showroom, Denver, Colorado
Airport 2000 Master Plan, Sonoma, California

1979 Carleton House Hotel, Dallas, Texas

1979/
80 Portola Highlands Community Development, Livermore, California
Stratton Forest Community Development, Simsbury, Connecticut
Red Oak Housing Development, Farmington, Connecticut
Embarcadero Beach Community Development, Santa Barbara, California

1980 Indian Harbor Community Development, Indian River Shores, Florida
Old Farms Forest Community Development, Woodbury, Connecticut
River Bend Community Master Plan, Sacramento, California
St. Johns Riverfront Development, Portland, Oregon
Castle Pines Condominium, Denver, Colorado
Levi's Plaza Condominium Development, San Francisco

1981/
83 Ridge Community Development, Castle Rock, Colorado
Sterling Pines Community Development, Tuxedo, New York

1982 Cibola Community and Spa Development, Carefree, Arizona
Pancho Magee's Bar and Restaurant, West Hartford, Connecticut

1982/
83 Regatta Square Office Building, Richmond, California
Grist Mill Restaurant, Simsbury, Connecticut
BT II Restaurant, West Hartford, Connecticut
R. and A. Moran Vacation House, Stinson Beach, California
Pond Place House, Castle Rock, Colorado

1983 Lakecrest Community Development, Pittsfield, Massachusetts
Island Woods Development Plan, Columbia, Connecticut
Powder Forest Office Building, Simsbury, Connecticut
J. and M. Mudd House renovations, Kentfield, California
Belvedere Court House, Castle Rock, Colorado

Publications:

On CALLISTER: books—*Architects on Architecture*, edited by Paul Heyer, London 1967; *Bay Area Houses* by Sally Woodbridge, New York 1976; *A View of Caifornia Architecture 1960-1976*, exhibition catalogue, by David Gebhard and Susan King, San Francisco 1976; articles—"The Bold Approach in a Magnificent New House" in *House Beautiful* (New York), February 1962; "Profiles in Design: Warren Callister" in *House and Home* (New York), July 1962; "Northern California and the Tradition of Wood Design" in *House and Home* (New York), May 1969; "Tent Pavilion for Flower Show at State Fair" in *Architectural Record* (New York), May 1970; "Wild about Wood" by Roger Yee in *Progressive Architecture* (New York), September 1974; "Green Mansion", in *Progressive Architecture* (New York), October 1975; "Record Houses of 1976" in *Architectural Record* (New York), May 1976; "From a top housing innovator … a new package for first-time buyers" in *Housing* (New York), January 1978; "Modern Houses in America", special issue of *Process: Architecture* (Tokyo), no. 7, 1978; "Old buildings for work put to new use" in *Abitare* (Milan), November 1979; "Building Types Study 568: Hotels" in *Architectural Record* (New York), December 1981.

Bibliography: *Community Planning and the Architecture of Charles Warren Callister: An Introductory Bibliography*, Monticello, Illinois 1984.

I was born in the Northeast, schooled in the Southwest, survived a war, began a family and commenced the art of architecture in San Francisco. From that beginning to today, after four decades of working with many others, I find myself still within the enjoyment of the consensual art of architecture.

Today we call our group Callister, Gately and Bischoff. This architectural venture, together with our several colleagues, is only the reality of the moment within a longer tradition. There have been many contributors, many colleagues, clients, friends, and families working together which have generated and persuaded the very nature of our manner of working together.

Our studio is of a size that is no larger than an agreeable number of guests one might invite to lunch. It is a family, it is a community, it is the doing of architecture. We join with our clients in their endeavors and dreams as friends, extending to them an artfulness which is the aesthetic of our approach to architecture. We think of architecture as an art more than as a profession or business.

Quite simply architecture is one of the most collective endeavors in the realm of the cultural arts, and for me it is a joy to participate in this very social art. Doing architecture, I imagine, is much like making a film; many roles are to be played, there are many creative minds involved, it is a group effort. Architecture in its process is the collecting and the development of ideas emanating from the many participants: from the client, from the investors, from the community, from the engineers, from the architects, from the builders, from the landscape architects, and from the interior designers. And from these many people emerges the architectural form and the building of a structure, and then commences the life within.

Architecture is an ongoing experience when built. The devotion and delight of those many people who created a beautiful work is clearly visible and most enjoyable even by those who need not understand the ambiance of such a process and such art.

Although we involve ourselves in many parts of the country, we search out and respond to the best of their regional history, culture and traditions; and yet we seem to bring a romantic interpretation transported from here to there, which is often in much demand and most always highly regarded. It is not very profound, it seems to me, to respond to critic or editor or to temporal fashion when there is greater regional, cultural and environmental motif. There is little reason to search the world for form when regional culture and environment can form a definitive architecture.

—Charles Warren Callister

Charles Warren Callister has retained a remarkable sensitivity to siting and detail while moving from small-scale designs to major community developments. He began practice in San Francisco in 1946 with designs for private houses that combined motifs from New England and Japan with the so-called Bay Area regional style. By the mid-1950s he had begun to take on bigger commissions, including schools, university buildings, and the large-scale community planning and housing projects for which he is now well known.

The influence of Frank Lloyd Wright, clearly visible in his Kentfield house of 1949, gave way to a lighter, more Japanese style. The Dwight Way house, on a steep site in the Berkeley hills, is perched on concrete piers with floor and roof beams projecting in a lively rhythm. The Oriental effect is heightened by window treatment reminiscent of shoji screens.

His Field House for the new University of California campus at Santa Cruz shows Callister's typical sensitivity to siting. Set on a gentle hill leading up to the central college clusters, the building is tucked discreetly into the slope so as not to interfere with the ocean view from the entry road or the campus above. A lower level of reinforced concrete, with narrow openings for light, supports a copper-clad hexagonal roof that blends well with the surrounding brown hills. He achieves additional visual compactness by having the roof of the locker and shower extension double as a grandstand for the playing fields below.

The Chapel at Mills College is again a circular building—but in a woodsy setting. Entry is through a low, earth-bound vestibule leading into the great round nave that acts as a compression ring for a burst of complex wood vaulting, a structural metaphor for the exultation of worship.

An unusual commission, for the Floriculture Pavilion at the *California Exposition and Fair* in the scorching Sacramento Valley, caused Callister to produce an uncharacteristically flamboyant structure. Triangular trusses of open-web steel, recalling the Snowdon/Price Aviary at London Zoo, combined with sail-like tensile surfaces create an airy oasis of color and greenery over a covered walkway and meandering stream connected to a nearby lake. The canvas panels can be removed completely or partially for different effects and purposes.

Callister's entry into large-scale housing and community planning necessitated fundamental changes in his work methods: he had to deal with the unpredictable tastes and lifestyles of a wide audience, to say nothing of developers' demands. Rossmoor Leisure World in California, built for a projected population of 18,000, has a 2,200 acre site of which one third was left in its natural state. Garden villas and condominium apartments are grouped in clusters to lend a sense of intimacy and to blend in with the existing terrain. Facilities include a medical center, golf courses, swimming pools, art studios, and a shopping center; all utilities are under ground.

Hiller Highlands, another California development, was built in a former rock quarry with most of the site on a 2.1 incline. Callister turned this potential disadvantage to advantage by giving each townhouse a spectacular view.

East Coast developments of the 1970's—such as Amherst Fields in Massachusetts—show increased simplification of form (with structural elements bearing full aesthetic weight) and an increased reliance on factory-made pre-fabricated parts. But the general level of design and siting indicates that Callister's sensibility has survived concessions to the mass market.

—Lucinda Hawkins

CAMBRIDGE SEVEN ASSOCIATES.

Partnership; established by the architects Louis J. Bakanowsky, Peter Chermayeff, Alden B. Christie, Paul E. Dietrich, and Terry Rankine, and the graphic designers Ivan Chermayeff and Thomas Geismar, in Cambridge, Massachusetts, and New York City, 1962; additional partner since 1970, Charles Redmon. Recipient: Design Award, American Institute of Architects, 1967; Design Award, *Progressive Architecture,* 1967 and 1979; United States Department of Housing and Urban Development Award, 1968; American Institute of Architects/American Library Association Award, 1970. Addresses: 1050 Massachusetts Avenue, Cambridge, Massachusetts 02138, U.S.A.; 15 East 26th Street, New York, New York 10010, U.S.A.

Works:

1962 New England Aquarium, Boston
1963 Washington Park Shopping Center, Roxbury, Massachusetts
1964 United States Pavilion, *Expo '67,* Montreal
1965 Pittsfield Cooperative Bank, Massachusetts
     School study, Weston, Massachusetts
1965/
   70 Arlington Station prototype modernization, Massachusetts Bay Transportation Authority, and development plan for the entire rapid transit system
1966 Knapp Shoes Office and Distribution Center, Brockton, Massachusetts
1967 Design of DC-10 airplane interiors for Douglas Aircraft
1968 Consumer Value Stores, Boston
     Allendale School, Rochester, New York
     Studies for industrialized and rationalized traditional housing

Boston Police Station, District 11
Visitors' Center, Children's Museum, Boston
1968/
   72 Harvard University Observatory, Cambridge, Massachusetts
1969 Weston Junior High School, Massachusetts
     Library, Pomfret School, Connecticut
     Arthur D. Little Inc. Office Building, Cambridge, Massachusetts
     Student Union, Syracuse University, Syracuse, New York (project)
1970 1050 Massachusetts Avenue Office Building (Cambridge Seven Offices), Cambridge, Massachusetts
1971 Graphics and urban furniture for the new town of Lysander, Massachusetts
     Robinson Hall renovation, Harvard University, Cambridge, Massachusetts
     North Carolina Marine Science Center, Wilmington, North Carolina
     Chermayeff House, Concord, Massachusetts
     Eighth Street Station modernization, Philadelphia
1972 Graphics for Market Street East, Philadelphia
     Study for a World's Fair, for the Bicentennial Commission, Philadelphia
1973 Solar Energy Study
     College 2, University of Massachusetts, Columbia Point, Boston
     Mabel Brady Garven Exhibit of American Arts, Yale University, New Haven, Connecticut
1974 Library, Smith College, Northampton, Massachusetts
     Theatre/Auditorium, New Bedford Whaling Museum, Massachusetts
     Wellesley Senior High School modernization, Massachusetts
     Graphics for the British Terminal of the English Channel Tunnel

Solar Energy Building, Massachusetts Audubon Society, Boston (project)
1975 Music Facility, Williams College, Willamstown, Massachusetts
     Where's Boston? Pavilion, Prudential Center, Boston
     Beltway Stations, North East Rail Corridor, Boston-Washington, D.C. (prototypes)
1976 Porter Square Red Line Station extension, Massachusetts Bay Transportation Authority
     Layout for *Solar Energy Exhibit.* United States Energy Resource Development Agency, Washington, D.C.
     Wellesley Elementary Schools, Massachusetts
1977 Master plan for the IBM Corporation Complex, Essex Junction, Vermont
1978 MCI Corrections Institute, Concord, Massachusetts
     Resource Planning Associates, Cambridge, Massachusetts
     Lonestar Brewery/San Antonio Museum of Art Conversion, Texas
     Displays for the Meldisco Shoe Company
     Boston Safe Deposit Company interiors
     Master plan for the IBM Corporation Complex, Endicott, New York
     The Talbots Inc. Office Distribution Center, Hingham, Massachusetts
     Library, Whaling Museum, New Bedford, Massachusetts
1979 Digital Equipment Corporation Office Building, Nashua, New Hampshire
     Library addition and renovation, Trinity College, Hartford, Connecticut
1980/
   81 National Aquarium, Baltimore, Maryland
1982/
   84 Charles Square Complex, Cambridge, Massachusetts

Cambridge Seven Associates: National Aquarium, Baltimore, 1980-81.

1984/
85 Design Center, Houston, Texas
1985/
87 Com/Energy Building, Riverfront Office Park, Cambridge, Massachusetts

Publications:

On CAMBRIDGE SEVEN ASSOCIATES: articles—"Museum" in *Architectural Record* (New York), October 1974; "No Kitsch Kitchen" in *Interiors* (New York), January 1975; "Some Projects by Cambridge Seven Associates" in *Domus* (Milan), January 1975; "Air Offices..." in *Architectural Review* (London), May 1977; "Cambridge Seven Associates" by N. Asihara in *Space Design* (Tokyo), May 1977; "Old Brewery Complex Will Become Art and Transportation Museum" in *Progressive Architecture* (New York), January 1979; "The Fine Art of Brewing" in *Building* (London), 15 May 1981; "Museum of Art in San Antonio" in *Baumeister* (Munich), October 1981; "Another Powerful Harborside Attraction" in *AIA Journal* (Washington, D.C.), May 1982; "Look What's Brewing in San Antonio" in *Historic Preservation* (Washington, D.C.), September/October 1982; "National Aquarium in Baltimore" in *Alam Albena* (Heliopolis, Egypt), June 1983; "Preservation and Renewal of Architecture and Urban Spaces," special issue of *Space Design* (Tokyo), October 1983; "Houston Design Center Puts Its Architectural Foot Forward" by Ann Holmes in *Houston Chronicle*, 18 March 1984; "Charles Square—A Triumph of Good Design" by Robert Campbell in *The Boston Globe*, 27 March 1985; "Second Building at Riverfront" by Anthony J. Yudis in *Boston Sunday Globe*, 14 April 1985.

*

In addition to sharing the concerns of my partners in Cambridge Seven Associates in the design of a physical environment which provides a context for deeper and more meaningful human experience, I am particularly interested in the integration of all the visual arts with architecture. I feel that a more thorough incorporation of the visual arts into architecture will provide the designer with a richly expanded environmental palette. This will be facilitated through a relational, space-field approach to architecture, rather than a consideration of isolated buildings.

—Louis J. Bakanowsky

*

My work as an architect has been for the most part collaboration with a group of designers and others committed, without stylistic or other formal preconceptions to finding fresh solutions to diverse problems—rationally in all cases, and dramatically where appropiate.

—Peter Chermayeff

*

A strong interest in all aspects of designs led to my involvement in the formation of Cambridge Seven Associates. My work with my fellow principals and other designers has expanded that interest and provided the opportunity to achieve design solutions that attempt to extend beyond normal expectations and to improve the quality of our environment.

—Paul E. Dietrich

*

Although I have been responsible for the design of many individual buildings since the founding of Cambridge Seven Associates, I have felt that my most important contribution has been to help in the establishment, the development, and the continuing ability of the group practice to produce excellence in design. At Cambridge Seven Associates we share the design experience and help each other in the design process. We have built an organization that can, with great effect, produce design for buildings, exhibits, urban, multi-media events, large developments, and transportation systems. We intended this at the outset, and I feel that I and all of the other principals have fashioned an effective team to achieve these goals.

—Terry Rankine

*

Cambridge Seven Associates was founded in 1962 by seven young men, all of whom had only recently graduated from schools of architecture or design. Six of the founders are still principals of the firm: Louis Bakanowski, Peter Chermayeff, Paul E. Dietrich and Terry Rankine in its Cambridge office; Ivan Chermayeff and Thomas Geismar in its New York office. Charles Redmon, in Cambridge, is the seventh principal, replacing one of the founding partners.

From the beginning these talented designers decided not to limit themselves to the design of buildings. They aspired to design everything that could be designed, as did most architects before our present era of specialization. (The eclipse of the Art Nouveau, Bauhaus, and Art Deco periods marked the end of the architect's preception of himself as a universal designer, confidently engaged in as many of the arts and crafts as he had time for, including the design of furniture, fabrics, ornament, and typography.

Deciding to be as many-sided as today's world would allow, the Cambridge Seven became filmmakers, graphic designers and creators of exhibitions and interiors as well as buildings. Like the late Charles Eames, who had a similar vision, the Cambridge Seven have excelled in exhibition design, most notably at *Expo '67* in Montreal. In collaboration with Buckminster Fuller, who invented the geodesic dome in which it was housed, they devised a brilliant exhibit designed to tell the world of the scientific and cultural achievements of the United States.

Unlike Eames, however, who did more exhibitions, furniture, and films than buildings, the Cambridge Seven have built aquariums, galleries, museums, display pavilions of all kinds, park visitor centers, theatres and performing arts centers. Their work includes mixed-use developments, housing, retail, office, and hotel space, a police station, subway station, and school and college buildings. They are also restoring important buildings of the past and adapting them for re-use. They still, however, pursue the ideal of diversity with which they began. Other non-architectural work includes the design of a bookplate, a Harvard-Yale trophy, and all the graphics for Boston's subway system.

The work they have completed is almost too heterogenous to be appraised as a whole. The volume accomplished is uneven in quality, but that is inevitable. Since the firm appears not to turn down jobs that must be done quickly and cheaply, some of their work reflects this circumstance. Projects with adequate budgets and time schedules are carefully designed and meticulously constructed. The work of the Cambridge Seven that has been done under favourable circumstances is comparable with the best of its type done everywhere.

The Cambridge Seven have developed no design style of their own. Their buildings are indistinguishable from others built throughout the United States by leading American firms. But the Cambridge Seven, in the scope of their work, have sustained a vital idea—the concept of the architect as an all-encompassing artist. In today's world of ever increasing specialization, that is a major accomplishment.

—Mildred F. Schmertz

CANDELA Outeriño, Felix

American. Born in Madrid, Spain, 27 January 1910; emigrated to Mexico in 1939: naturalized, 1941; emigrated to the United States, 1971: naturalized, 1978. Educated at the Escuela Superior de Arquitectura, Madrid, 1927-35, Dip.Arch. 1935; Academia de Bellas Artes de San Fernando, Spain, 1936; study fellowship in Germany, 1936. Served as a Lieutenant in the Spanish Army Artillery, 1935, and as a Captain of Engineers in the Spanish Republican Army, 1936-39. Married Eladia Martin in 1940 (died, 1963); Dorothy Davies in 1967; children: Antonia, Jane, Manolita, Teresa, and Pilar. Worked as an architect in the Agricultural Colony, Chihuahua, Mexico, 1939-40; Partner, Candela and Bringas, Acapulco, Mexico, 1940-41; Assistant Architect, Jesus Marti and Associates, Mexico City, 1941-44; in private architectural practice, Mexico City, 1944-49; Founder-President, Cubiertas ALA S.A., design and construction company, Mexico City, 1950-69; Associate Architect, Praeger-Kavanagh-Waterbury, New York, 1969-71. In private practice, Chicago, 1971-79, and in Madrid, Spain, since 1980. Consultant Architect, Project Planning Association, Toronto, since 1977, and IDEA Center, Athens, Greece, since 1978. Professor of Architecture, National University, Mexico City, 1953-70; Professor of Architecture, 1971-78, and since 1978 Professor Emeritus, University of Illinois at Chicago Circle. Charles Eliot Norton Professor of Poetry, Harvard University, Cambridge, Massachusetts, 1961-62; Jefferson Memorial Professor, University of Virginia, Charlottesville, 1966; Andrew D. White Professor-at-Large, Cornell University, Ithaca, New York, 1969-74; Honorary Professor, Escuela Tecnica Superior de Arquitectura, Madrid, 1969; William Hoffman Wood Professor of Architecture, University of Leeds, Yorkshire, 1974-77; Honorary Professor, Universidad Nacional Federico Villareal, Lima, Peru, 1977. Exhibitions: University of Southern California, Los Angeles, 1957; Harvard University, and United States tour, 1961; McNair Museum, San Antonio, and Museum of Modern Art, Houston, Texas, 1966. Recipient: Institute of Structural Engineers Gold Medal, London, 1961; Auguste Perret Prize, International Union of Architects, 1961; Plomada de Oro, Sociedad de Arquitectos Mexicanos, 1963; Alfred E. Lindau Award, American Concrete Institute, 1965. D.F.A.: University of New Mexico, Albuquerque, 1964; D.Eng.: Universidad de Santa Maria, Caracas, Venezuela, 1968. Fellow, American Concrete Institute. Honorary Member, Sociedad Colombiana de Arquitectos, Sociedad de Arquitectos Venezolanos, American Institute of Architects, International Association for Shell Structures, Royal Institute of British Architects, Church Architectural Guild of America, Associacion Costarricense de Arquitectos, Colegio de Arquitectos del Peru, and Sociedad Bolivariana de Arquitectos. Address: Avenida America 14, Madrid - 09, Spain.

Works:

1939 Two small villages, Chihuaha Sierra, Mexico
1940 Apartment house, Acapulco, Mexico
1943 Hotel and cinema, Guamuchil, Mexico
1945 Apartment block, Mexico City
     Hotel Catedral, Mexico City
1948 Houses, Mexico City
1949 Experimental Funicular Vaults, San Bartolo, Mexico City
     Rural school, Ciudad Victoria, Tamaulipas, Mexico
1950 Fernández Factory, San Bartolo, Mexico City
     Pinedo Factory, Nativitas, Mexico City
     Boliches Marsella, Juarez, Mexico City
1951 Pisa Warehouse, San Bartolo, Mexico City
1952 Junior Club, Escandon, Mexico City
     Cosmic Ray Pavilion, Ciudad Universitaria, Mexico City

Romero House, El Pedregal, Mexico City
Ras Martín Flower Shop, Chapultepec, Mexico City
Lechería Ceinsa, Tlalnepantla, Mexico
Nash Automobile Agency, Anzures, Mexico City
Almada House, El Pedregal, Mexico City
Umbrella prototype, Tecamachalco, Mexico City
Las Aduanas Warehouse, Vallejo, Mexico City

1953 Five houses for Novedades, El Pedregal, Mexico City
Madaria Warehouse, Ciudad Victoria, Tamaulipas, Mexico
Hidalgo School, Unidad Modelo, Mexico City
Convent school, Guerrero, Mexico City
Monte Alpes School, Lomas de Chapultepec, Mexico City
Chemical Sciences Auditorium, Ciudad Universitaria, Mexico City
Centro Gallego, Roma, Mexico City
Ciba Laboratories, Churubusco, Mexico City
Church of the Miraculous Virgin, Navarte, Mexico City

1954 Río Warehouse, Linda Vista, Mexico City
Sedas Parasinas Warehouse, Xochimanca, Mexico
La Jacaranda Cabaret, Juarez, Mexico City

1955 Lederle Laboratories, Coapa, Mexico City
Herdez Warehouse, San Bartolo, Mexico City
Bicardi Distillery, Matamoros, Puebla, Mexico
Civic Center Auditorium, Ciudad Sahagun, Hidalgo, Mexico
High Life Factory, Coyoacan, Mexico City
Acabados Finos Factory, Puente de Vigas, Mexico
Coyoacán Market, Mexico City
Dock de la Tolteca, Vallejo, Mexico City
Rastro de Pollos, Vallejo, Mexico City
Remington Rand Factory, Vallejo, Mexico City
Celestino Warehouse, Vallejo, Mexico City
Cabero Warehouse, Vallejo, Mexico City
Jamaica Wholesale Market, Mexico City
Banco Núñez, Havana, Cuba
Presidential Palace, Havana, Cuba (project)
Low-cost housing, Monterrey, Nuevo Leon, Mexico
Cross Roads Restaurant, Great Southwest District, Texas
Insignia of the Great Southwest District, Texas
Stock Exchange Hall, Mexico City (with Enrique de la Mora)
El Altillo Chapel, Santo Angel, Mexico City (with Enrique de la Mora)
Rivetex Treadmill, Cuernavaca, Mexico
La Fama Factory, Tlalpan, Mexico City
Aceros de México Factory, Monterrey, Mexico
Cafés de México Factory, Santa Clara, Mexico
Toyoda Factory Canteen, Ciudad Sahagun, Hidalgo, Mexico
Belron Factory, Ixtapalapa, Mexico
Swimming pool, Lomas de Chapultepec, Mexico City
Church of Santa Teresa del Niño Jesús, Monterrey, Mexico
Champagnac Church, Las Charcas, Guatemala
Television transmitting tower, Mexico City
El Léon Confectionery, Vallejo, Mexico City
Borges House, Havana, Cuba
Mexican Travel Association, Juarez, Mexico
Lederle Laboratories Boiler House, Coapa, Mexico City
Oratory, Havana, Cuba
Beach Club, Playa Azul, Venezuela
Synagogue, Guatemala City

Lederle Laboratories Entrance Pavilion, Coapa, Mexico City (with Alejandro Prieto)

1956 Band shell, Santa Fé, Mexico City (with Mario Pani)
Church of San Antonio de las Huertas, Tacuba, Mexico City (with Enrique de la Mora)

1957 Sign Post, Tequesquitengo, Mexico
Plaza de los Abanicos, Lomas de Cuernavaca, Mexico
Bazaar, Lomas de Cuernavaca, Mexico
La Jacaranda Night Club, Acapulco, Mexico (with J. Sordo Madaleno)
Texas Instruments Factory, Dallas (with O'Neil Ford and Associates)
Entrance Monument, Cuernavaca, Mexico (with Guillermo Rossell)

1958 Centro Electrónico, Ciudad Universitaria, Mexico City
Restaurant, Xochimilco, Mexico City (with J. Alvarez Ordonez)
Auditorium and restaurant, Casino de la Selva, Cuernavaca, Mexico

1959 Open chapel, Lomas de Cuernavaca, Mexico (with Guillermo Rossell)
Church of San José Obrero, Monterrey, Mexico (with Enrique de la Mora)

1960 Chapel of San Vicente de Paul, Coyoacan, Mexico City (with Enrique de la Mora)
Bacardi Bottling Plant, Carretera Mexico, Queretaro, Tlalnepantla, Mexico
Sales office, Guadalajara, Jalisco, Mexico

1963 John Lewis Warehouse, Stevenage, Hertfordshire, England (with Yorke, Rosenberg and Mardall)

1964 Aztec Stadium, Mexico City (project)

1968 Mexican Olympic Sports Palace, Mexico City (with E. Castaneda and A. Peyri)

1969 Brown University Sports Complex, Providence, Rhode Island (project; with Praeger-Kavanagh-Waterbury)
City for Sports, Kuwait (competition project)

1975 Bernabeu Stadium, Madrid (project)

1977 King Abdulaziz University, Jeddah, Saudi Arabia (consultant; with Project Planning Associates)

Publications:

By CANDELA: book—foreword to *Frei Otto: Spannweiten* by Conrad Roland, Berlin, Frankfurt and Vienna, 1965; articles—"Cubierta Prismática de Hormigón en la Ciudad de México" in *Revista Nacional de Arquitectura* (Mexico City), March

Felix Candela: Church of the Miraculous Virgin, Navarte, Mexico City, 1953.

1950; "Simple Concrete Shell Structures" in *American Concrete Institute Journal* (Detroit), December 1951; "Structural Digressions on Style" in *Espacio* (Mexico City), May 1953; "The Shell as Space Encloser" in *Arts and Architecture* (Los Angeles), January 1955; "A New Way to Span Space" in *Architectural Forum* (New York), November 1955; "Construction en Voiles Minces, au Méxique" in *Techniques et Architecture* (Paris), January 1956; "Shell Concrete Construction in Mexico" in *Municipal Journal* (London), March 1956; "Lezione di Modestia di Felix Candela" in *L'Architettura* (Rome), August 1957; "Hyperbolic Paraboloids" in *Conferencia* (Chicago), 11 December 1957; "Understanding the Hyberbolic Paraboloids" in *Architectural Record* (New York), July 1958; "Felix Candela" in *Arquitectura* (Madrid), October 1959; "Planta Embotelladora Bacardi en México" in *Nuestra Arquitectura* (Buenos Aires), March 1961; "Design and Construction in Mexico: Shell Construction" in *Industrial Building* (New York), September 1961; "Une Suele Conscience pour l'Oeuvre à Créer" in *Architecture d'Aujourd'hui* (Paris), December 1961/January 1962; "Comprender il Paraboloide Iperbolico" in *Casabella* (Milan), October 1965; "Architettura e Strutturalismo" in *Casabella* (Milan), no. 306, 1966; "Shell Structure Development" in *Canadian Architect* (Toronto), January 1967; "The Heritage of Maillart" in *Archithese* (Niedertaufen), no. 6, 1973; etc.

On CANDELA: books—*Candela: The Shell Builder* by Colin Faber, New York and London 1963; *Builders in the Sun: Five Mexican Architects* by Clive B. Smith, New York 1967; articles—"Una Casa de Ensueno" in *Novedades* (Mexico City), 1 June 1951; "The New University City of Mexico" by Esther McCoy in *Arts and Architecture* (Los Angeles), September 1953; "Shell Concrete Today" in *Architectural Forum* (New York), August 1954; "The Work of Felix Candela" in *Progressive Architecture* (New York), July 1955; "Folded-Slab Church" in *Architectural Review* (London), January 1956; "Incontro con Felix Candela" by Manfredi Nicoletti in *L'Architettura* (Rome), February 1957; "Felix Candela" in *Concrete Quarterly* (London), April/June 1957; "Fyller, Candela, Headline AIA Convention" in *Architectural Record* (New York), December 1957; "Felix Candela: Architect of Shells" in *Time* (New York), 8 September 1958; "Engineering of Excitement" by Robin Boyd in *Architectural Review* (London), November 1958; "Wizard of the Shells" in *Architectural Forum* (New York), November 1959; "Enrique de la Mora y Palomar—Felix Candela—Deux Eglises au Mexique" in *Architecture d'Aujourd'hui* (Paris), September/November 1960; "Felix Candela" by Betty Campbell in *The Guilds' Engineer* (London), no. 13, 1962; "Felix Candela at the A.A." in *Architectural Association Journal* (London), vo. 80, no. 883, 1964; "Casing the Olympics" in *AIA Journal* (Washington, D.C.), December 1967; "Mexico and the Olympics—The Daring Design" in *Saturday Review* (New York), 22 June 1968; "Candela: Recent Works" in *Zodiac* (Milan), October 1973; "Modern Mexican Architecture," special issue of *Process: Architecture* (Tokyo), July 1983.

Like Prouvé in France and Nervi in Italy, Felix Candela is both builder and designer, and he shares with them the advantages and disadvantages of this situation. The advantages are a close relationship between design and construction and an interest in the formal possibilities of building very cheaply. The chief disadvantage is that the work is often carried out for indifferent architects, so that Candela has himself confessed to preferring many of his buildings half finished—"before the architecture is added."

Candela has made himself effective by narrowing the range of what he has to offer and by being uninterested in problems—like multi-storey buildings—that do not readily lend themselves to his chosen form of construction. Candela's achievement has been in the field of thin shell vaulting in concrete reinforced with mild steel, and for this a Spanish upbringing and a Mexican practice could not be bettered. In the Madrid of the 1930's, the young Candela witnessed the construction of the vaults of the Zarzuela race track and the Fronton Recoletos, two of the first masterpieces of thin concrete shell design, and he could learn from their designer Eduardo Torroja that a great engineer is a poet, one who uses imagination and intuition as much as he uses calculation. However, war-torn Europe could not offer Candela the chance to build, and the USA, that magnet for European emigrés, could not offer the low labour costs required to make shell vaulting an economical way to roof buildings. Mexico, with its post-war building boom combined with cheap labour, gave Candela his opportunity.

Candela built his first shell structure in the summer of 1949. It was a development of the war-time British Cresiphon system where the vault is rippled to give greater rigidity to a thin shell. As a contractor, Candela was concerned to simplify the form-work into which the concrete was poured, and to this end he evolved shells whose geometry was such that the forms could be entirely constructed of straight timbers. The roof of the Fernandez factory uses conoids to this end, but the really dramatic breakthrough came with the use of hyperbolic paraboloids, a form that became almost a Candela trademark, and the economy of construction was such that he was able to win many contracts on cost alone.

In the early 1950's the vast campus of Mexico University was built. The scientists wanted a small building for research into cosmic rays, and they needed a concrete structure no more than 15mm thick to admit the rays to the interior. This was Candela's opportunity, and he seized it with both hands. The Cosmic Ray Pavilion is a delightful structure, with its undulating shell vaulted building standing on slender arches. From being an unknown contractor Candela was catapulted to the forefront of the design world, and his practice grew in size and importance.

The period following the completion of the Cosmic Ray Pavilion was the most productive of Candela's career. Concrete columns supporting an umbrella consisting of four hyperbolic parabloids became his norm for factory and warehouse building, sometimes used in a straightforward way as in the warehouses at Linda Vista in Mexico and Stevenage, England, and sometimes distorted to enable light to enter between the shells, as at the Coyoacan High Life Factory. Warping of the hyperbolic parabloid form was taken further in the Church of the Miraculous Virgin, where concrete, 37mm thick, twists and bends to give a Gaudi-like spookiness without ever losing its structural logic. Other churches followed—the exteriors were often kitsch in the extreme, but the logic of the structure usually created an interior of real quality. The roofs were beautiful, but the walls spoilt the magic, and in the early 1960's Candela found himself in the same dilemma as Buckminster Fuller. Both had evolved structural systems that were sane, logical and beautiful, but in each case the clarity of the structure was marred when incorporated into a real building. However, both Fuller and Candela were so widely admired that they were commissioned to design and build structures that remained structures—beautiful sculptures without the enclosures that destroyed their charm. Candela built a whole series of shells that are really playful demonstrations of what shells can do; the entrance to the Lederle laboratory complex, the Bandshell at Santa Fé, and especially the bird at Lake Tequesquitengo can be regarded as pure sculpture, with form the only aim.

Shells as sculpture were fun, but Candela is essentially a builder. After the tours-de-force he was content to turn his mind back to buildings, and a second constructive period begins with the three 30 metre square groined vaults that he built for Bacardi Rum in Mexico City. This last building stands next to an office building by Mies van der Rohe, two very different buildings but both by designers who believed that form comes from structure, in one case concrete, in the other steel.

—John Winter

CANDILIS, Georges.

French. Born in Baku, Azerbaidzhan, U.S.S.R., 11 April 1913; emigrated to France, 1945: naturalized, 1946. Educated at the Athens Polytechnic, Dip. Arch. 1936. Served as a First Lieutenant in the Greek Army, 1940-42: awarded Order of St. George. Married Christiane Richard in 1959; children: Alexis, Alexandrine, and Panaghyote. Architect, Greek Ministry of Aviation, Athens, 1937-40; worked in the office of Le Corbusier, *q.v.,* Paris, 1945-48, and Marseille, 1948-50; in partnership with Shadrach Woods, *q.v.,* and Vladimir Bodianky, *q.v.,* in ATBAT-Afrique, Casablanca, Morocco, 1951-54; in partnership with Woods and Alexis Josic, *q.v.,* as Candilis-Josic-Woods, Paris, 1955-63. In private practice, Paris, since 1963. Assistant Professor of Architecture, Athens Polytechnic, 1936-40; Professor, Greek National School for Building Techniques. Athens, 1940-45. Since 1959, Professor of Architecture, Ecole Nationale Supérieure des Beaux-Arts, Paris. Member, CIAM (Congrès Internationaux d'Architecture Moderne), and of Team 10. Member of the Council for Cultural Development, Paris, 1971-73. Recipient: First Prize, Marseille Housing Competition, 1959; First Prize, Toulouse-le-Mirail New Town Competition, 1960; Grand Prize for Urban Development, New Town of Bagnols-sur-Cèze, 1961; First Prize, Free University of Berlin Competition, 1963. Honorary Fellow, American Institute of Architects. Chevalier, Légion d'Honneur. Address (office): 17/5 rue Campagne Première, 75014 Paris, France.

Works:

1946/
52 Unité d'Habitation (Cité Radieuse), 280 Boulevard Michelut, Marseille (with Le Corbusier and others)
1949 Chalets, Megève, St. Gervais, France
1951/
55 Musulman Collective Housing Development, Casablanca (with Vladimir Bodiansky and Shadrach Woods)
1952/
54 Master plan for the City of Casablanca (with Vladimir Bodiansky and Shadrach Woods)
1953/
56 Apartment buildings, Algiers
1954 Housing for Tropical Countries (competition project)
Tobacco Factory, Lebanon (competition project)
1954/
55 Opération Million: 3,600 housing units, France, particularly the Paris suburbs (with Shadrach Woods and Alexis Josic)
1955 Elementary and secondary schools, French Guiana
1956 Low-cost housing, Nicaragua (project)
1956/
59 Housing complex for oil company employees, Abadan, Iran (project)
1956/
61 Plan and housing for the new town of Bagnols-sur-Cèze, France (with Shadrach Woods and Alexis Josic)
1957 Low-cost housing, Panama (project; with Jean Prouvé)

1958 Plan for tourist development in New Caledonia
Hotel, San Juan, Puerto Rico (project)
1959 Caribbean Hotel (project) Housing (4,000 units), Marseille (with Shadrach Woods and Alexis Josic)
1959/
62 Tropical housing, Martinique (with local firms)
1960 Urban pre-fabricated houses, Algeria (competition project; with Shadrach Woods and Alexis Josic)
Master plan for the new town of Toulouse-le-Mirail, France (with Shadrach Woods and Alexis Josic)
1961 French Secondary School, Geneva
New town of 30,000 inhabitants, Caen, France (competition project; with Shadrach Woods and Alexis Josic)
New town of 10,000 inhabitants, Hamburg, West Germany (competition project; with Shadrach Woods and Alexis Josic)
1962 University for 2,000 students, Bochum, West Germany (competition project; with Shadrach Woods and Alexis Josic)
Hotel Complex and Leisure Center, Phalere Bay, Greece (project)
Plan for tourist development, Spetsai, Greece
Plan for hotel accommodation, New Caledonia
1962/
63 Schools, Fort-de-France, Martinique (with local firms)
1962/
65 Apartment buildings, Paris
1963 Plan for the center of Frankfurt (with Shadrach Woods and Alexis Josic)
Master plan of Fort Lamy, Chad, Africa (with Shadrach Woods and Alexis Josic)
Master plan for the Free University of Berlin (with Shadrach Woods and Alexis Josic)

Leisure Center and Harbour, Beirut (project; with El Khoury)
Hotel, Tahiti (project)
Hotel, Guadeloupe (project)
Cultural and Sports Center, Bagnols-sur-Cèze, France
Gypsy Settlement, Avignon
1963/
65 Apartment buildings and maisonettes, Aix-en-Provence, France
1964 Apartment buildings, Marseille and Nîmes, France
1964/
65 Ski Resort, Vallée de Belleville, France (with Shadrach Woods and Jean Prouvé)
Apartment buildings, Lyon, France (with others)
Cité Artisanale (Workshop Center for Artisans), Sèvres, France (with Shadrach Woods and Alexis Josic)
1964/
67 Tourist Development, Languedoc-Roussillon, France (project; with others)
1965/
75 Leisure Center of Barcarès-Leucate, Languedoc-Roussillon, France
1966 Tourist Development, Tahiti
Steilshoop Regional Center, Hamburg, West Germany (with Shadrach Woods)
Hotel, Cesarea, Israel
1966/
67 Water Treatment Plant, Toulouse-le-Mirail, France (with Alexis Josic)
1966/
68 Faculty of Literature, Restaurant, Administration Building, and Sports Facilities, University of Toulouse-le-Mirail, France (with Alexis Josic)
Tourist Development, Corsica (project)
1966/
69 Three apartment buildings, Paris

1967 Experimental housing, stage I, Fort Lamy, Chad, Africa (project)
Plan for the city of Athens
University of Zürich (competition project)
1967/
77 New town of Toulouse-le-Mirail, France
Free University of Berlin
1968 Covered Market, Toulouse
Technical Offie Building, Toulouse
Garage, Toulouse
Master plan for Plovdiv, Bulgaria (competition project)
Leisure housing development, Cap Martin, France
1968/
72 Low-cost apartments, Paris
1969 University of Madrid (competition project)
Master plan of the Old City of Kuwait (competition project)
Marina-type housing, with harbor facilities, St. Raphael and Deauville, France (project)
1969/
70 Housing (10,000 low-cost units), Lima, Peru (competition project; with Alexis Josic)
1970 Hilton Hotel, Lahore, Pakistan (with Alexis Josic)
Leisure housing development, Cannes, France (with others)
1970/
79 Luxury apartment buildings, Le Havre, France
1971 Tourism facilities for the Peninsula of Lavrotto, Monaco (competition project; with Alexis Josic)
1972 Plans for the residential areas of the Old City of Kuwait
1972/
74 Residentail complexes, Jeddah, Al Khobar, and Dammam, Saudi Arabia (with R. H. Sanbar)

Georges Candilis: Project for the Cultural Centre, Athens, 1981-83.

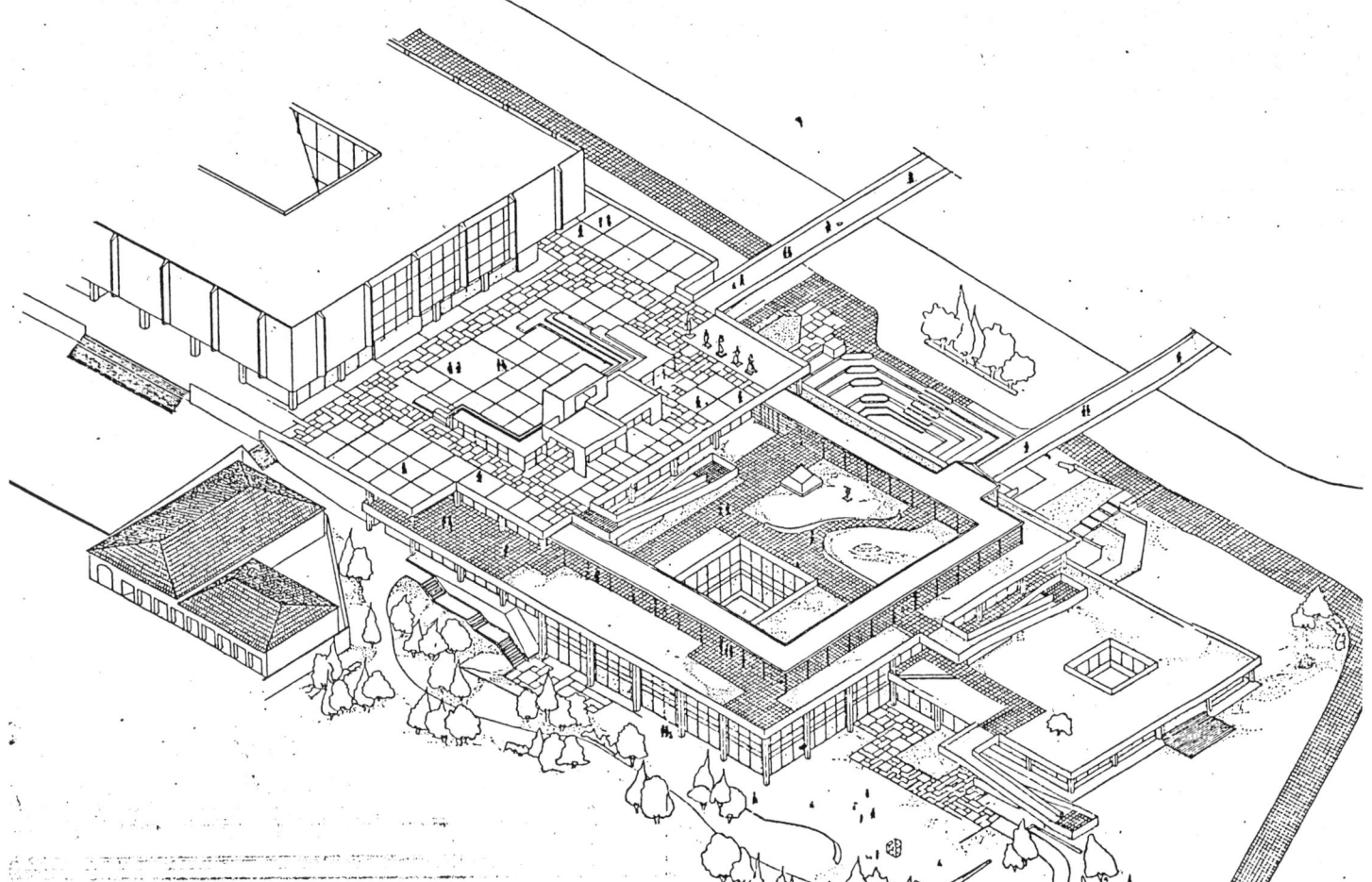

1973 University of Lattakia, Syria (competition project)

1973/
75 Master plan and design by Bu Ali Sina University, Hamadan, Iran (with the Mandala Collaborative)

Luxury residential complex, Kuwait (with the Kuwaiti Engineering Office)

1973/
76 Master plans for the cities of Dammam, Al Khobar, Qatif, Al Ahsa, and Al Jubayl, Saudi Arabi (projects; with the Metra Consulting Group)

1974 NIRT Employees Apartment Buildings, Tehran (project)

1974/
78 Housing development, Dohar, Qatar

Plans for residential areas in Jeddah, Al Khobar, Medina, and Mecca, Saudi Arabia

1975 Qatar Embassy renovation, Paris

1976/
77 Academic Buildings, Dormitories, and Administration Housing, Bu Ali Sina University, Hamadan, Iran (with the Mandala Collaborative)

1976/
78 Plan for naming and numbering city streets and buildings, Dammam, Saudi Arabia (with Denco)

1976/
79 Eastern Province Corniche, Saudi Arabia (project; with Denco)

1977/
78 Bus Terminal, Depot, Garage, and transport system plan, Dammam, Saudi Arabia (with Denco)

1977 Umm Said Residential Area, phase I, Qatar (with R. H. Sanbar)

1981/
83 Cultural Centre, Athens, Greece

Publications:

By CANDILIS: books—*Planning and Design for Leisure*, Stuttgart 1972; *Toulouse le Mirail: Birth of a New Towm*, with Alexis Josic and Shadrach Woods, Stuttgart 1975; *Habitat Bill of Rights*, with Nader Ardalan, Balkrishna Doshi, Moshe Safdie, and Josep Lluis Sert, Tehran 1976; *Bâtir la vie*, Paris 1978; articles—"Problème d'une ville: Barcelone" in *L'Architecture d'aujourd'hui* (Paris), March 1960; "New Town in France: Bagnols-sur-Cèze" in *Architectural Association Journal* (London), April 1960; "Le Corbusier et nôtre epoque," "1918-1930; Le Moment héroique de l'architecture moderne en U.R.S.S." and "De Stijl, Hollande, 1920-1930, et le Bauhaus, Allemangne, 1922-1933" in *L'Architecture d'aujourd'hui* (Paris), April/May 1964; "Problèmes d'urbanisme" in *L'Architecture d'aujourd'hui* (Paris), December 1964/February 1965; "Le Corbusier" in *L'Architecture d'aujourd'hui* (Paris), June/July 1965; "La Formation de l'architecte" in *Architecture: formes et fonctions* (Lausanne), vol. 12, 1965-66; "Le Mythe de l'habitat individuel" in *L'Architecture d'aujourd'hui* (Paris), February/March 1968; "A la réchèrche d'un sens nouveau au mot l'architecte" in *Architecture: formes et fonctions* (Lausanne), vol. 15, 1969; "Ideas" in *Architecture: formes et fonctions* (Lausanne), vol. 16, 1971.

On CANDILIS: books—*Candilis, Josic, Woods* by Jürgen Joedicke, Stuttgart 1968; *Guide d'architecture contemporaine en France* by D. Amouroux, M. Crettol and J. P. Monnet, Paris, 1974; *Guide de l'art dans la rue au XXe siecle—Paris et sa Banlieue* by Bernard Marrey, Paris 1974; articles—"Habitat Collectif: Morocain Etude ATBAT-Afrique" in *L'Architecture d'aujourd'hui* (Paris), February/March 1953; "New Apartment Houses in Rabat and Casablanca" in *L'Architecture d'aujourd'hui* (Paris), December 1954; "L'Architecte Georges Candilis" in *L'Architettura* (Rome), July 1958; "Low-Cost Housing in Blanc Mesnil" in *Architectural Design* (London), May 1959; "Bagnols-sur-Cèze" in *Architectural Design* (London), May 1960; "Candilis, Josic, Woods" in *Cimaise* (Paris), January/February 1961; "Recherches: Candilis-Josic-Woods" in *L'Architecture d'aujourd'hui* (Paris), June/July 1964; "Riviera Wall: Vast Candilis Scheme" in *Architectural Review* (London), November 1964; "Atelier Candilis, Josic, Woods" in *Architectural Design* (London), January 1965; "Freie Universität Berlin" in *Deutsche Architektur* (East Berlin), July 1967; "Toulouse-le-Mirail" by Peter Smithson in *Architectural Design* (London), October 1971; "Georges Candilis: Research on the Architecture of leisure" by Piergiorgio Tosoni in *L'Ingegnere* (Rome), March 1974; "Bu Ali Sina University, Hamadan" in *L'Architecture d'aujourd'hui* (Paris), February 1978; "Team 10," special issue of *Deutsche Bauzeitung* (Stuttgart), November 1978; "New Greek Architecture" by Emile Chlimintzos and others in *Wonen-TA/BK* (Heerlen, Netherlands), October 1981; "Buildings as Structures" by Wim J. van Heuvel in *Polytechnisch Tijdschrift* (The Hague), November 1981; "Twenty Years On: A Forgotten Mirage—Le Mirail" by Carine Lenfant in *Architecture* (Paris), January 1982.

More than ever before, our society needs architects. But we have to define which society and which architects.

Man's habitat, the habitat of all men, expresses the focal spirit of our society. These men, omnipotent by their number, make up the Society of the Greatest Number. The Greatest Number, an idea without limit, has its own way of thinking. Numbers disappear and are replaced by facts: white, black, yellow; cold, temperature, hot; poor, rich. We must not confuse Number with the Greater Number. A Number has limits; the Greatest Number has none. The spirit of the Greatest Number sets conditions for everyone—whereas yesterday's problem was that of only a few.

Enormous technical progress, social struggles, and the century's wars have upset completely the order of values: limits, frontiers, distances lose their importance and indeed all significance. Growth is universal; the same needs, rights, and duties occur at the same time in China, Africa, Russia, and America. Today man occupies more and more of the earth's surface. In order to live, the man of tomorrow will need more and more square kilometers, more and more kilowatt hours. Villages will turn into towns; towns will become regions. Under the pressure of the Greatest Number, sooner or later, architecture, urbanism, technique, and the technology of construction will change completely.

In our time, architects and town planners have unconsciously become experts in the "organization of disorder" and in confusion. Town planning programs conform to a so-called efficacy. In reality, they advocate an appalling and artificial vision of our future—tentacular motorways, fathomless underground parking areas, super-hyper markets, vertiginous skyscrapers and other towers of Babel where everything is provided for except the presence of a child. Now, today, only the poet can shout out this truth: No child, no town! How can we establish the relationship of town, vehicle, and child? Who can really achieve this? Who can be made responsible?

Everything changes, everything grows, everything becomes more complicated. Man alone is out of date. So man alone will inevitably be replaced by a team. But, in order for that to happen, we have to train men who can work as a team and who will speak the same language while contributing their complementary disciplines. The presence of the architect—or, rather, the architectural point of view—must be assured at all levels within the team, which will bring together engineers, sociologists, economists, biologists, lawyers, politicians, artists, and—poets.

First, teams of programmers will effectively interpret the country's politico-economic program and create an executive program. Then, teams of normalizers will be entrusted with making things "normal," that is, with establishing the normalization of needs first and of objects thereafter. In this way, we will achieve real standards for serial production and the creation of urban industry, and we will achieve quality and prices that will allow us to avoid penury, excess, and waste. The programmers and normalizers will clear the way for the executors—architects, town planners, engineers, entrepreneurs and industrialists who will carry out the functional, useful, and necessary work truly expressive of our age.

Whether we like it or not, we live in a consumer society. There is nothing wrong with that as long as the consumption is controlled. Consumption implies change, elimination, and renewal. It leads and encourages us to think of a house as an impermanent object. And, indeed, it is absurd to think that because a building now exists, it must necessarily continue to exist. The "machine for living" should not have to survive the family for which it was conceived. Kafka, visiting an abandoned and derelict house, described, in a novel, the family that had lived there: "No family, no house!" It is the family that creates the house.

The crinolines and wigs of the marchionesses determined Louis XV's architecture. Our grandmothers' and our great-grandmothers' corsets influenced nineteenth-century bourgeois architecture. The couturier Paul Poiret, in dispensing with "bonework," liberated women and inspired the modern movement in architecture. Today, more than ever before, men and women, young and old, wear jeans. Jeans are not only clothing; they are also the expression of an attitude that sooner or later must provoke an upheaval and give rise to a truer, younger, and more candid architecture. Jeans architecture? Why not?

But to be truer, younger, and more candid, the act of building must also and above all be an act of love. As, in the creation by Paul Valéry of the words of the architect Eupalinos: "This little temple that I have built for Hermes a few steps from here—if you knew what it means to me! The passer-by sees only an elegant chapel. It is nothing—just four columns, a very simple style. I have put into it the memory of a bright day in my life. Oh gentle transformation. This delicate temple, though no one knows it, is the mathematical image of a girl from Corinth whom I dearly loved..."

—Georges Candilis

Among those who worked for a long time for Le Corbusier, it was perhaps Georges Candilis who first learned how to free himself from the influence of the master in order to assert his own personality. His temperament—the opposite of that of his patron—prompted him to the break. Born in the capital of Azerbaidzhan of a Greek family, he studied in Athens and immediately after the war, on arriving in Paris, joined the studio of Le Corbusier in the rue de Sèvres. Responsible for representing Corbu during the construction of l'Unité d'Habitation in Marseille, Candilis then directed the Moroccan offshoot of ATBAT created by Le Corbusier, whose only real contribution to the enterprise was that he succeeded in encouraging, in a rather autonomous manner, his young protegé. Returning to France, Candilis set up on his own account, and thanks to a very happy choice of associates—Josic the Yugoslav and Woods the American—he created in the rue Dauphine a studio whose style was soon recognized, and a research center whose achievements were soon known, throughout the world.

Candilis has always remained a Mediterranean. He is interested in man before he is interested in form; he is guided by his heart rather than by his head; his intelligence is supple, his approach infused with warmth. He possesses to the highest degree what we call the "human touch." He has all the necessary qualities to be an excellent actor—he "goes over well," as one says in the jargon of that profession. That is what makes him so popular, particularly with the young.

Though nothing that comes out of his studio is unimportant, and though the average level of its production is distinctly superior to that of most of the architectural practices in France, the interest and merit of the projects and achieved works is variable. There are some that I consider frankly poor, such as the project for the creation of a very dense property development on the site of a navy yard in Le Havre. Among the non-successes, I would also cite the Free University of Berlin, a Mediterranean conception that is lost on the banks of the Spree—but it seduced a competition jury and inspired, more or less happily, many student architects. The buildings give the impression of an immense, abandoned military camp.

Yet, the accomplishments are great too. The hotel built for Rothschild at Cesarea in Israel is a small jewel. The sector of the Languedoc-Roussillon coast development entrusted to Candilis is, without question, the most successful. And at the summit of his achievement is the Mirail district of Toulouse. The project was remarkable. If, since the completion of the first phase, Candilis has had to make concessions, the result is still indisputably one of the best urban complexes built in France since the beginning of this century, a complete justification of an architectural vision.

—Pierre Vago

CANELLA, Guido.

Italian. Born in Bucharest, Rumania, of Italian parents, 19 January 1931. Educated at the Liceo Parini, Milan, until 1948; studied architecture, under Ernesto N. Rogers, Milan Polytechnic, 1953-58, Dip.Arch. 1959. Served in the Italian Army, Bergamo, 1958-60. Married Laura Testori in 1960; children: Maria, Riccardo, Gentucca and Tito. Worked on research projects, associating with Ernesto N. Rogers' *Casabella-Continuita* magazine, Milan, 1957-64; in private practice, working with the architects Michele Achilli and Daniele Brigidini, Milan, since 1959. Assistant to Giuseppe Samona, 1960-63, Professor of Architectural Composition, 1968-70, Istituto Universitario di Architettura, Venice; Assistant to Ernesto N. Rogers, 1962-70, Professor of the Elements of Architectural Composition from 1970, Director of the Institute of Architectural Composition, 1974-79, Director of the Department or Design, 1979-81, and Director of Degree Studies in Architectural Design since 1982, Milan Polytechnic. Organizer, with Vittorio Gregotti, *New Designs for Italian Furniture* exhibition, Milan, 1960; Director of the Architectural Section, *Triennale*, Milan, 1978-82. Editor, *Architettura e città* series of books for Dedalo publishers, Bari, Italy, 1966, and *Hinterland* magazine, Milan, from 1978. Exhibitions: *New Designs for Italian Furniture*, L'Osservatore delle arti industriali, Milan, 1960; *Alternative attuali*, Castello Cinquecentesco dell' Aquila, Italy, 1962; *Aspetti dell'arte contemporanea*, Castello Cinquecentesco dell'Aquila, Italy, 1963; *Prima Triennale itinerante d'architettura italiana contemporanea*, toured Italy and abroad, 1965; *Guido Canella: disegni e opere*, Centro Arte Viva, Trieste, Italy, 1967; *Giovane Architettura Italiana*, toured Europe, 1968; *Premi Nazionali IN/ARCH 1968*, Palazzo Taverna, Rome, 1971; *Immagine per la città*, Palazzo Reale and Palazzo dell'Accademia, Genoa, Italy, 1972; *Milano 70/70*, Museo Poldi Pezzoli, Milan, 1972; *Young Italian Architecture*, toured Europe, 1972; *Triennale*, Milan, 1973, 1979; *Art et Architecture*, Galerie Daniel Gervis, Paris, 1976; *Immaginazione Megastrutturale*, at the *Biennale*, Venice, 1978; *28/78 Architettura*, Palazzo delle Stelline, Milan, 1979; *Un'idea di teatro*, Galleria

Architettura Arte Moderna, Rome, 1980; *Progetti di Citta*, Collegio delle Stelline, Milan, 1980; *Cento progetti da ricordare*, Galleria Iannone, Milan, 1980; *Architetture italiane degli anni '70*, Galleria Nazionale d'Arte Moderna, Rome, 1981; *La Modernité—un projet inachevé*, at the Festival d'Automne, Paris, 1982; *Futurama*, Teatro Nuovo, Turin, 1983; *Parole e linguaggio dell'architettura religiosa*, Villa Reale, Monza, Italy, 1983; *Das Abenteuer der Ideen*, Neue Nationalgalerie, Berlin, 1984; *Guido Canella: opere recenti*, Galleria Civica, Modena, Italy, 1984; *Guido Canella*, Centro Civico, Pieve Emanuele, Milan, 1984; *Vu de l'interieur ou la raison de l'architecture*, at the *Biennale*, Paris, 1985; *L'Avventura delle idee nell'architettura 1750-1980*, at the *Triennale*, Milan, 1985. Recipient: IN/ARCH Prize, Rome, 1969. Address: Via Revere 7, 20123 Milan, Italy.

Works:

1959 *Corriere dei Piccoli* display, at the *Salone del Bambino*, Palazzo dell'Arte, Milan (with M. Achilli and D. Brigidini)
   Corriere della Sera display, at the *GEC Exhibition*, Fiera Campionaria, Milan (with M. Achilli, D. Brigidini and S. Rizzi)

1960 *New Designs for Italian Furniture* exhibition layouts, Osservatore delle Arti Industriali, Milan (with V. Gregotti and G. Aulenti)
   Business Centre, Padua, Italy (competition project; with M. Achilli, D. Brigidini and V. Vercelloni)
   Savings Bank Headquarters, Modena, Italy (competition project; with M. Achilli, G. Aulenti and D. Brigidini)
   Savings Bank Headquarters, Lecco, Italy (competition project; with M. Achilli, D. Brigidini and L. Ferrari)
   Palazzo dell'Economia, Brescia, Italy (competition project; with M. Achilli, G. Aulenti and D. Brigidini)

1961 Offices and Warehouses, Arona, Novara, Italy (with M. Achilli and D. Brigidini)
   Houses at Lisanza di Sesto Calende, Varese, Italy (with M. Achilli and D. Brigidini)
   House at Lentate sul Seveso, Milan, Italy (with M. Achilli and D. Brigidini)

1962 Business Centre, Turin (competition project; with M. Achilli, L. S. D'Angiolini and V. Vercelloni)
   Nursery School at Settala, Milan, Italy (with M. Achilli and D. Brigidini)
   Elementary School, Segrate Milan, Italy (with M. Achilli and D. Brigidini)

1963 International Theoretical Section, at the *XIII Triennale*, Milan (project; with E. Mantero and L. Semerani)
   Bowling Alley, Monza, Milan, Italy (with M. Achilli and D. Brigidini)
   Segrate Town Hall, Milan, Italy (with M. Achilli, D. Brigidini and L. Lazzari)

1964 Tronchetto Inlet Development, Venice (competition project; with M. Achilli, L. S. D'Angiolini and L. Lazzari)
   New Town Hall, Novara, Italy (competition project; with M. Achilli, L. S. D'Angiolini, L. Gallarini, L. Lazzari and C. Ravarelli)
   Zanardi-Bonfiglio Barracks conversion, Voghera, Pavia, Italy (competition project; with M. Achilli, L.S. D'Angiolini and L. Lazzari)

1965 Theatre Network prototype studies, Milan (projects)

1966 Nursery School at Novegro, Segrate, Milan (with M. Achilli and D. Brigidini)

1967 Fondazione Arnaboldi Hospital extensions, Broni, Pavia, Italy (with M. Achilli and D. Brigidini)

1968 Piazza Roma/Piazza Carducci Pedestrian Zone, Monza, Milan (with M. Achilli and D. Brigidini)
   Central Services Piazza at the INCIS Village, Pieve Emanuele, Milan (with M. Achilli

and D. Brigidini)
   Elementary School at the INCIS Village, Pieve Emanuele, Milan (with M. Achilli and D. Brigidini)

1969 Elementary and Secondary School Service Structures, Sesto San Giovanni, Milan (project; with M. Achilli and D. Brigidini)
   Don Zeno Santini Nursery School at the INCIS Village, Pieve Emanuele, Milan (with M. Achilli and D. Brigidini)

1970 Shopping Centre at the INCIS Village, Pieve Emanuele, Milan (with M. Achilli and D. Brigidini)

1971 Manufacturing, Research and Service Facility on the Northern Industrial Park, Milan (project; with M. Achilli and D. Brigidini)
   Civic Centre with Town Hall, Secondary School and Sports Ground, Pieve Emanuele, Milan (with M. Achilli and D. Brigidini)

1972 Paolo VI Parish Centre at the INCIS Village, Pieve Emanuele, Milan (with M. Achilli and D. Brigidini)
   Emilio Alessandrini Nursery School and Day Nursery, Zerbo di Opera, Milan (with M. Achilli and D. Brigidini)
   Day Nursery, Gennara di Abbiategrasso, Milan (with M. Achilli and D. Brigidini)
   Secondary School, Viale Santuario, Saronno, Varese, Italy (competition project; with A. Christofellis and G. Fiorese)

1973 University of Calabria, Montalto Uffugo, Cosenza, Italy (competition project; with C. Bono, A. Christofellis, G. Di Maio, G. Fiorese, V. Parmiani and G. P. Semino)
   Multi-Purpose Building at the INCIS Village, Pieve Emanuele, Milan (with M. Achilli and D. Brigidini)
   House near Meina, Novara, Italy (with A. Valenti)

1974 Regional Goverment Offices, Trieste, Italy (competition project; with A. Acuto, R. Busolini, A. Christofellis, G. Di Maio, G. Fiorese, R. Schnabl, E. Segatti and M. Suttora)
   IACP Reseidential Complex, Bollate, Milan (with A. Maresca)
   Fratelli Cervi Elementary School, Nursery School and Sports Ground at the Mirasole Village, Noverasco di Opera, Milan (with M. Achilli and D. Brigidini)
   Senior Secondary School reorganization studies, Milan Polytechnic (projects)
   Zone 7 Pedestrian Area Redevelopment Plan, Milan (project; with A. Acuto, A. Christofellis, G. Di Maio and G. Fiorese)
   GESCAL Housing prototypes for Zones 11 and 12 of Metropolitan Milan (projects; with A. Acuto and L. Cansella)

1975 Secondary School with Public Areas, Monaca di Cesano Boscone, Milan (with M. Achilli)
   Law Courts redevelopment, Ancona, Italy (with F. Clemente)

1976 Civic Centre with Town Hall, Residential, Commercial and Sports Facilities, Seggiano di Pioltello, Milan (project; with M. Achilli)
   Town Hall, Seggiano di Pioltello, Milan (with M. Achilli)
   Indoor Swimming Pool, Seggiano di Pioltello, Milan (with M. Achilli and D. Brigidini)

1978 New Piazza in the area of the former Ancona Bakery, Ancona, Italy (competition project; with A. Acuto, A. Maresca, A. Monti, V. Paci, M. Russi and A. Ubezio)
   Museum-Tower by the Civic Gates, Milan (prototype study)

1979 Senior Secondary School, San Martino-Cascine d'Agnona di Borgosesia, Vercelli, Italy (competition project; with A. Acuto, P. Bonaretti, D. Gaggetti, V. Garatti, P. Godio, E. Mezzetti, G. P. Semino and K. Suzuki)

Guido Canella: Pieve Emanuele Civic Centre, Milan, 1971.

Zone 2 Redevelopment (Isola Garibaldi), Milan (project for *Casabella* magazine)

1980 School Centres in Abbiategrasso and Pioltello, Milan (competition projects; with L. Fiori)

Municipal Office and Theatre Courtyard, in the Zanardi-Bonfiglio Barracks Redevelopment, via Fratelli Rosselli, Voghera, Pavia, Italy (project; with M. Calzavara)

Legal, Finance and Municipal Offices, Legnano, Italy (competition project; with A. Acuto, E. Bordogna, A. Ferre, P. Godio, E. Mezzetti, P. Paganini, G. P. Semino and K. Suzuki)

Calusco-to-Paderno d'Adda road and rail crossings over the River Adda, Italy (competition project; with M. Achilli, and A. Acuto)

1981 School Centre, Albino, Bergamo, Italy (competition project; with A. Acuto and L. Fiori)

Municipal Offices, Monaca di Cesano Boscone, Milan (project; with M. Achilli)

1982 Legal, Finance and Municipal Offices, Legnano, Italy (project 2; with A. Acuto, G. Morano and F. Rozza)

Public Housing Development, San Marino, Italy (project; with M. Achilli)

Cemetery refurbishment, Gallarate, Varese, Italy (competition project; with A. Acuto, G. Clementi, A. Colombo, L. Colombo, A. Ferre, E. Mezzetti and C. Rossetti)

Cemetery reorganization and extension, Arnate di Gallarate, Varese, Italy (competition project; with A. Acuto, G. Clementi, A. Colombo, L. Colombo, A. Ferre, E. Mezzetti and C. Rossetti)

1983 IACP Residential Quarter and Service Area between Bettola and Zeloforamagno di Peschiera Borromeo, Milan (project; with M. Achilli)

Nursery School with Social and Health Services Complex, between Bettola and Zeloforamagno di Peschiera Borromeo, Milan (project; with M. Achilli)

New Central Station and Rail Junction reorganization, Bologna, Italy (competition project; with A. Acuto, V. Garatti and C. Quintelli)

Civic, Commercial and Business Centre, Mezzano, Brescia, Italy (competition project; with A. Acuto, A. Ferre, A. Imperadori, E. Mezzetti and V. Vitali)

Office and Social Complex in the Via Nono Pedestrian Zone, Milan (project; with A. Balzani and U. Pierini)

Opera of the Bastille, Paris (competition project; with A. Acuto, E. Bordogna, A. Colombo, A. Cortesi, M. Ferrari, A. Ferre, V. Garatti, E. Mezzetti, C. Quintelli and G. P. Semino)

Town Hall, Avellino, Italy (competition project; with A. Ferre)

1984 Service Centre Piazza at the Monte d'Ago 2 Quarter, Passo di Varano, Ancona, Italy (project; with M. Achilli)

Publications:

By CANELLA: books—*Caratteri dell'architettura romantica milanese da Carlo Amati alla Torre Velasca*, thesis, Milan Polytechnic 1959; *Sulle trasformazioni tipologiche degli organismi architettonice*, Milan 1965; *Il sistema teatrale a Milano*, Bari, Italy 1966; *Teoria della progettazione architettonica*, Bari Italy 1968; *Universita: ragione, contesto, tipo*, Bari, Italy 1975; *Documento costitutivo del Dipartimento di progettazione dell'architettura*, Milan Polytechnic 1979; articles—"La tradizione in architettura", in *Casabella* (Milan) July/August 1955; "Architecture d'un capitole", in *L'Architecture d'Aujourd'hui* (Paris) December 1967/January 1968; "Un'architettura di architetture", in *Lotus* (Venice) October 1970; "Piazza of the INCIS development, Pieve Emanuele", in *Casabella* (Milan) November 1974; "Altezza e falsa conscienza", in *Hinterland* (Milan) March/April 1978; "For a metropolitan museum", in *Hinterland* (Milan) July/August 1978; "L'architettura del ferro e del mattone", in *Casabella* (Milan) October/November 1979; "Triennale 'in progress'", in *Hinterland* (Milan) September/December 1979; "Designing with the aid of history", in *Hinterland* (Milan) July/December 1980; "Scuola e paesaggio: un'occasione perduta?", in *Hinterland* (Milan) January/March 1981; "The city of alternative futures", in *Hinterland* (Milan) September 1981; "Town, country and industrialization", in *Hinterland* (Milan) December 1981; "Milan and its museums", in *Hinterland* (Milan) March/June 1982; "Bergamo, arca di Lombardia", in *Hinterland* (Milan) January/March 1983; "Ricostruzione, ancora . . .", interview with E. Valeriani, in *Controspazio* (Bari, Italy) January/June 1983; "A school in Bisceglie and a water tower in Naples", in *Casabella* (Milan) May 1983; "Mors construens", in *Hinterland* (Milan) January/June 1984; etc.

On CANELLA: books—*Esposizioni, architetture, allestimenti* by R. Aloi, Milan 1960; *New Directions in Italian Architecture* by V. Gregotti, New York 1968, Milan 1969; *Citta, museo e architettura* by E. Bonfanti and M. Porta, Florence 1973; *Progetti per una citta* by L. Semerani, Milan 1980; *Architecture italiane degli anni '70* by E. Valeriani, Rome 1981; *Postmodern: l'architettura nella societa post-industriale* by P. Portoghesi, Milan 1982; *La Modernité—un projet inachévé*, exhibition catalogue by J. P. Chimot, K. Frampton, B. Lubetkin and others, Paris 1982; *Architettura italiana contemporanea: Gli anni '70* by A. Acocella, Florence 1983; *Guido Canella*, edited by K. Suzuki, Bologna 1983; *Guido Canella: opere recenti*, exhibition catalogue by V. Savi, Modena, Italy 1984; *Il Progetto di Architettura: Guido Canella*, exhibition catalogue by M. de Micheli and others, Milan 1984; *Annali dell'architettura italiana contemporanea 1984*, edited by M. Casciato and G. Muratore, Rome 1985; *Vue de l'intérieur ou la raison de l'architecture*, exhibition catalogue, Paris 1985; articles—"Il nuovo centro civico di Segrate", in *Architettura* (Rome), January 1968; "La generation de l'incertitude" in *L'Architecture d'Aujourd'hui* (Paris) September/October 1975; "Nursery schools as houses of the people" in *Architettura* (Rome), October 1976; "Guido Canella: towards an archaeology for the city of the future" in *Architecture + Urbanism* (Tokyo), May 1978; "Municipio di Pieve Emanuele" in *Casabella* (Milan), May/June 1979; "Architect at work: Guido Canella" in *Architecture + Urbanism* (Tokyo), November 1980; "Guido Canella: Housing for residents of Bollate" in *Architecture + Urbanism* (Tokyo), May 1981; "Canella: concrete constructor" in *Architectural Review* (London), October 1982; "Monumenti alla periferia" in *Domus* (Milan), January 1983; "L'illuminismo contaminato" in *Parametro* (Bologna), November 1984; "Guido Canella, opere recenti" in *Controspazio* (Bari, Italy), October/December 1984; "Guido Canella, Centro Civico di Pieve Emanuele" in *Casabella* (Milan), March 1985.

I conceive everything I plan in such a way that it will last. And this is not because I place a particularly high value on what I build but because, unlike the designer, interior decorator, or set designer, for the architect it should be impossible to conceive architecture in terms of the perishable or the ephemeral. Together with this innate inclination to stability, research and the construction of opportunities for employment also play their part, as they condition decisively the possibility of stating a poetic. So it is not by chance, you see, that, bypassing a conventional rapport with private enterprise on the urban chessboard, I found myself designing for competitions or, commissioned by local authorities, for the Milanese concentric, where the job to be done was to give a stable shape to an amorphous and as yet indeterminate landscape. Every project, whether it is implemented or whether it remains on paper unexecuted, can do no other than be conceived and bear within itself the responsibility of a monument, but, particularly in the desolate landscape where I have chosen to work, a piece of work presents itself as a sole existing exemplar *unicum* non-repeatable and, destined to survive.

To build a scenario for the social life of the community, a tool moreover for changing and improving the quality of life is another aspect and another constant of my work, which operates—so to speak—on two distinct fronts, a figurative world, a veritable artificial landscape, perceptible through the sequences that follow one upon the other in the intricate interior of the building, with a plot of its own. But also with precise obligations, which the planner has to observe, of putting through a given programme of tasks to be performed, and an external representative world, only partly an expression of the internal world which interprets evocatively, epically, and which at all events emerges with an autonomy all of its own on the surrounding territory, drawing attention to the historical landscape much more than to the geographic landscape, to the structural precendents, much

more than to the environmental aspects. This is possibly the reason why it is said that my poetic is difficult to decipher.

—Guido Canella

Criticised, paradoxically, for being both "decorative" and "stark", Guido Canella is one of the most controversial of modern Italian architects.

He was born in Bucharest where his father, a hydraulic engineer, had been appointed as an advisor to the Rumanian Government for a series of projects connected with the water system. His father's family, of Venetian origin, boasts generations of engineers, architects and painters. Among these were Giuseppe and Carlo, brothers who worked in Venice, Milan and Paris, and prolonged until the mid-nineteenth century the tradition of the Lombardy-Venetian veduta painting genre; Guido's cousin, Renzo, the author of manuals on styles of architecture and professor of architectural design at the Padua Faculty of Engineering; his uncle Carlo who, as Chief Engineer, designed the new city centre of Lower Bergamo in 1906; his brother Luciano who took a degree in architecture at the Milan Politecnico in 1942 and was active even during his student days in the Milanese Rationalist movement before the war, in the circle of Giuseppe Pagano.

Within his family circle, and particularly from his brother, Canella received a natural initiation into avant-garde culture and modern architecture. In 1943 he met Ernest Rogers who was to become his tutor at the Milan Politecnico ten years later.

But Canella was to find that, apart from Roger's teaching, the Faculty of Architecture in Milan had little to offer him. Against opposition from within the school and outside it, he chose to reveal a commitment to historicize the poetic of the Modern Movement, rejecting the schematic significance attributed then to the International Style. Taking the form of critical contributions and projects, this commitment led to him being accused of nostalgia for columns, of returning to Art Nouveau or to the classicism of Marcello Piacentini.

From the mid-1950s right through the 1960s, following study tours in Europe, Canella published a series of essays on national schools of architecture that Rational historians had tended to exclude or to regard as marginal in the concept of the Modern Movement (for example, the Amsterdam School, Soviet Constructivism, Eclecticism and Milanese Novecento). Alongside these, he conducted a series of studies refuting functionalist determinism through the concept of system (education, management, theatre, prisons, trade, museums) where he found the authentic path of activities within the framework of the built environment. Canella chose to link the function and representation of architecture not by a linear and monotonously deductive rapport, but by a much more structurally and allusively complex one.

Having completed his military service, Canella began his university career: from 1960 at the Istituto Universitario, Venice, with Giuseppe Samona (who called on him later to take his place for the course of Architectural Composition from 1968 to 1970); from 1962 at the Milan Faculty with Ernest Rogers (with whom he worked from 1965 at the course of Elements of Composition, and from whom he took over the chair in 1970).

He had already done design work with Michele Achilli and Daniele Brigidini on furniture and decor in their student days, and after they had taken their degrees they collaborated on a series of competitions, including the business centres of Padua and Turin, the new inlet of Tronchetto, Venice, the new Town Hall, Novara, and the re-utilization of the barracks at Voghera. The first project implemented was a one-family residence at Lentate sul Seveso (1961) in that Milanese hinterland where Canella's constructed work was destined almost exclusively to be. In 1963 he designed the Town Hall, Segrate,

which in 1969 was awarded the national prize, IN/ARCH.

As a result of events in the Italian University at the end of the 1960s, and of the experiments made at the Faculty of Architecture at the Milan Politecnico, Canella was suspended with the other seven members of the Council of the Faculty, and reinstated in 1974 without any judgement being passed. During this period he travelled in Japan, China and South America, devoting himself to a further series of papers, in which he made an indepth analysis of the typological characteristics of architecture in the Milanese context. Since 1978 Canella's research has been brought to public notice in the periodical *Hinterland*.

However, none of this should lead us to conclude that Canella is chiefly notable as an iconaclastic theoretician. Despite his academic commitments, Canella is a prolific designer, building as much as most Italian architects draw. His practical application of his theories mark out his work as an intense, almost aggressive pursuit of a suburban architecture with real form, force and vitality.

The most striking demonstration of this in his recent work is the civic centre at Pieve Emmanuele (1971-81). This complex, which unites town hall, school, library, gymnasium and playing fields, is almost a town in itself. It is here that one can most readily observe Canella's preoccupation with defence, protection and history translated into an architectural concept. Although it is constructed in various blocks, it is made compact by a supple interplay of internal and external walkways which guide the passageway from the base of the playing field to the higher level, where a terrace with pictorial decoration seals the uppermost roof. The variety of forms, together with the differences in level and their arrangement in assymetrically counterpoised blocks, abound in cultural references and motifs. The prime contribution to this can be found in the use of materials: bare rough concrete and red brick facing outwards, glazed walls and metal components giving a vivid chromatic effect, all these serve as much to articulate the various parts as to create their relationships. Canella nevertheless maintains the architectural tension of the complex, allowing himself to recall cultural refences to the monumental precedents of the area. These, equally isolated and highly distinctive, are the fortified sixteenth-century framstead at Tolcinasco, and the Baroque parish church of Sant'Alessandro. These powerful historic links underline the sense of permanence which characterises the Pieve Emmanuele centre.

In discussing the Pieve Emmanuele, Canella said: "On the historic route that links Milan to Vigevano, I thought of its Piazza Ducale, but also of the citadels constructed over the Roman amphitheatres . . ." And so it is that the complex resembles nothing so much as a castle, a fortification in neo-brutalist style, with a view across the sports field from the administrative block which is a lot like looking down into one of the arenas of imperial Rome. Canella has given us further clues to his method of synthesising tradition with modernity by quoting other inspirations: Le Corbusier's cantilever roof for the Cité de Refuge in Paris, which dates from the end of the 1920s; the decoration of the covered passageway under the terrace of Parque Güell in Barcelona, created by Gaudi; typological research of the early Russian constructivism: all these elements taken not as "references" but rather as part of one vital identity.

Canella's visual language is that of heroic Brutalism, with close affinities to that of Kenzo Tange's Tokyo. Indeed, the Japanese magazines have been keenest of all to publish his work and one of his senior partners, Katuyuki Suzuki, is Japanese.

For some, his work is simply too powerful, too uncompromising in the magisterial manner in which it seems to bypass the considerations of those for

Douglas Cardinal: St. Mary's Church, Red Deer, Alberta, 1968.

whom it is intended. Canella is seen to lack human delicacy and humility, but, as a man who is profoundly concious of his artisitic heritage (and who wrote, at the age of fourteen: "I am destined to become an architect") he is being closely watched for signs of his response to the challenges of the 1980s. The future of this skilled and impressive form-giver promises to be an exciting one

—Paul Ryan

CARDINAL, Douglas Joseph.

Canadian. born in Calgary, Alberta, 7 March 1934. Educated at the University of British Columbia, Vancouver, 1953-54; University of Texas, Austin, 1956-63, B.Arch. 1963. Married Marilyn Gale Zamar in 1973; children: Lisa, Nancy, Guy, Bret, and Jean Marc. Design Architect, Bissell and Holman, Red Deer, Alberta, 1963-67. Principal, Douglas J. Cardinal Architect, Red Deer, Alberta, 1964-67, and Edmonton, Alberta 1967-76, and Douglas J. Cardinal Architect Ltd., Edmonton, Alberta, since 1976. Exhibitions: University of Alberta, Edmonton, 1978; Burnaby Art Gallery, British Columbia, 1978; *Transformatons in Modern Architecture,* Museum of Modern Art, New York, 1979. Recipient: Honor Award, Alberta Association of Architects, 1968; Honour Award 1969, and Award of Excellence, 1978, City of Red Deer, Alberta; Award of Excellence, *Canadian Architect,* 1972; Achievement of Excellence Award in Architecture, Province of

Alberta, 1974. Member, Royal Canadian Academy of Arts, 1974; Fellow, Royal Architectural Institute of Canada, 1983. Address: Douglas J. Cardinal Architect Ltd., 10160 112th Street, Edmonton, Alberta T5K 2L6, Canada.

Works:

1967 Guloien House, Sylvan Lake, Alberta
1968 St. Mary's Church, Red Deer, Alberta
1970 Master plan for the Alberta Indian Education Centre, Edmonton
1971 Stettler Municipal Hospital, Alberta
1972 Hay River High School, North West Territories
      Provost Provincial Building, Alberta
      St. Michael's School, Bow Island, Alberta
1975 Kehewen School, Alberta
1976 Ile à La Crosse School, Alberta
      Bonnyville Rehabilitation Centre, Alberta
      Grande Prairie Regional College and Theatre, Alberta
1977 La Ronge Elementary School, Saskatchewan
      Alberta Government Services Centre, Ponoka
1978 Slave Lake Senior Citizens Residence, Alberta
      Slave Lake Drop-In Centre, Alberta
1978 Community Development Studies (James Smith, Onion Lake, Thunderchild, Saddle Lake, and Cold Lake)
1979 Grotski House, Edmonton, Alberta
1980 Spruce Grove Composite High School, Alberta
1981 Spruce Grove Multi-Use Building, Alberta

1983 Churchill High School, Manitoba
      Space Sciences Centre, Edmonton, Alberta
1984 Holy Trinity Catholic High School, Edmonton, Alberta
      St. Albert Place
      Leighton Colony, Banff, Alberta
1985 National Museum of Man, Hull, Quebec

Publications:

By CARDINAL: book— *Of the Spirit: Writings by Douglas Cardinal,* Edmonton, Alberta 1977; article— "In Harmony with the Land" in *Habitat* (Ottawa), no. 3/4, 1977.

On CARDINAL: books— *A Decade of Canadian Architecture* by Carol Moore Ede, Toronto 1971; *Explore Canada* by George Ronald, Toronto 1974; *Building with Words: Canadian Architects on Architecture,* with introduction by W. Bernstein and R. Cawker, Toronto 1981; articles— "Alberta Indian Education Centre" by R. Gretton in *Canadian Architect* (Toronto), September 1970; "The Work of Douglas Cardinal" by Abraham Rogatnick and A. Balkind in *Artscanada* (Toronto), October 1976; "Two Buildings by Douglas Cardinal" in *Canadian Architect* (Toronto), February 1978; "Doug Cardinal" by Suzanne Zwarun in *En Route* (Weston, Ontario), November 1983; "Preview: National Gallery and Museum of Man" in *Canadian Architect* (Toronto), February 1984; "The Cardinal Rule" by Lynda Ashley in *Alberta Construction* (Edmonton), March/April 1984.

In my profession and in my daily living, I have always maintained that the endeavours of all Canadians should be towards a betterment of the human condition. Therefore, in my role as a planner and architect, as the coordinator of technologists, I see tremendous opportunity to petition the needs of the individual and to reinstate our humanness as the most important element in all our efforts.

Learn from your body. Solve the problem organically. You have a brain, a stomach, a mouth, a heart, a pair of lungs. You think, eat, talk, feel, breathe. Build around what you are and want to be. I have found that placing the needs of the human being before the systems created by modern man ensures that man is indeed served by these systems rather than becoming a slave to them.

—Douglas Cardinal

Douglas Cardinal's aim has been to give architectural expression to a synthesis of the indigenous culture of the Indians of North America with that of the dominating Euro-American culture. Although his ancestry is largely Indian, he has had to take deliberate steps in his adulthood to learn and absorb Indian lore and philosophy, an effort that, coming after his study of architecture, inexorably influenced his philosophy of architecture as profoundly as it influenced his philosophy of life.

It is mainly the culture of the Plains Indians of Central Canada and the North-Central United States that Cardinal has studied and, to a considerable extent, practices. Since the Plains Indians are not noted for a strong building tradition, the impression of their culture on the work of an architect would be assumed to be slight. However, in Cardinal's case, the lack of dominating structural techniques or architectural stylistic details as base ingredients for an eclectic porridge has been both unmissed and irrelevant. It is the Indian attitude toward life, toward nature, toward man, and toward collective and private functions that Cardinal is most interested in utilizing, expressing, and practicing. Formal influences do indeed enter, however, since Cardinal believes that the Indian way is based on certain spatial conceptions that pervade Indian thought, which, when taken into account, result in superior architectural solutions, as well as superior solutions to the problems of life itself.

Thus, the emphasis on the circle and on curvilinearity, which, in Cardinal's view, tend to facilitate the most natural physical as well as symbolic functions of man. The circle symbolizes, but also facilitates, the double function of face-to-face group contact, as well as the communication, radiation, and dissemination of ideas from a central point, and of the double need of the individual to face toward the company of society and also to face away into the loneliness of the wider world.

Cardinal's emphasis on curvilinearity is inspired on the one hand by a positive response to the notion of man and his works as constituting an integral part of nature, a nature that seems to favour curvilinear forms flowing easily and felicitously in and out and from and to every direction at once. On the other hand, there is also a kind of negative defiance in Cardinal's use of curves which, in his mind, contradicts the rectilinearity, the rigid sequential thinking, the strait lacedness of the culture that he feels the Europeans brought to and imposed upon the western hemisphere with an arrogant and erroneous conviction of its superiority over the indigenous ones.

In his efforts to educate and to impress the non–Indian world with what he feels are quite practical and non-romantic expressions of his philosophy, Cardinal makes a special point of using the most sophisticated methods of design and construction in order to execute the unusual shapes of his buildings. This was probably best illustrated in the construction of the suspended, reinforced-concrete roof of St. Mary's Church in Red Deer, Alberta, for which computerized calculations furnished the structural

solution. Since then, Cardinal has continued to increase computer assistance to his practice, boasting one of the first architectural offices to use computer graphics and to utilize computers for "complex dimensioning systems, equipment coordination and fast-track construction." The most recent projects to benefit from these innovations have been the Edmonton Space Sciences Centre (1981) and the large and complex National Museum of Man near Ottawa (1985.)

According to Cardinal, the Indian approach has deeply affected every aspect of his architectural practice, and he prides himself on having successfully handled client-architect relations in new and satisfactory ways, placing great emphasis on patiently fostering group decision-making on the part of the client and on an open-minded, honest response to these decisions on the part of the architect.

—Abraham Rogatnick

CASSON, Hugh Maxwell.

British. Born in London, 23 May 1910. Studied at Eastbourne College, Sussex, 1924-27; St. John's College, Cambridge, 1929-31, M.A. 1931; Bartlett School of Architecture, University College, London, 1931-32; architecture, British School, Athens, 1933. Served as a camouflage officer, Air Ministry, London, 1940-44, and as a technical officer, Ministry of Town and Country Planning, London, 1944-46. Married the architect Margaret MacDonald Troup in 1938; daughters: Carola, Nicola, and Dinah. In partnership with Christopher Nicholson, London, 1937-39; in private practice, London, 1946-52. Since 1952, Senior Partner, with Neville Conder, Casson Conder Partnership, q.v., London. Professor of Environmental Design, Royal College of Art, London, 1953-75. Architectural Editor, *Arts and Technics*, London, 1947-50; Editorial Board Member, *Architectural Review*, London, 1948-65. Member, Royal Fine Arts Commission, 1960-83; Royal Mint Advisory Committee, since 1972; Greater London Historical Buildings Board, since 1975; British Rail Development Panel, since 1977; Council Member and Executive Board Member of the National Trust, since 1965; President, Greater London Arts Association, 1974-76; President, Royal Academy of Arts, London, 1975-84; Trustee, National Portrait Gallery, 1976-84, and British Museum of Natural History, London, since 1976. Exhibitions of paintings: annual individual shows at the Workshop Gallery, London; regular exhibitor at the Royal Academy Summer Exhibitions, London; also at the New Art Centre, London; Bohun Gallery, Henley-on-Thames, Oxfordshire; and at galleries in Birmingham, King's Lynn, Bath, Windsor, and Glasgow. Recipient: Honorary Doctorates: Royal College of Art, London, 1975; University of Southampton, Hampshire, 1977; University of Birmingham, England, 1977; Loughborough University, Leicestershire, 1979; University of Glasgow, 1980. Fellow, Royal Institute of British Architects, and the Society of Industrial Artists and Designers. Royal Designer for Industry, Royal Society of Arts, 1951 (Master of the Faculty, 1969-71); Royal Academician, 1960. Honorary Member, Royal Danish Academy, 1954; Honorary Associate, American Institute of Architects, 1968. Knighted, 1952; KCVO (Knight Commander, Royal Victorian Order), 1978; Italian Order of Merit, 1980; Companion of Honour, 1985. Addresses: (home) 60 Elgin Crescent, London W11 2JJ, England; (office) Casson Conder Partnership, 35 Thurloe Place, London SW7 2HJ, England.

Publications:

By CASSON: books—*New Sights of London*, London 1937; *Bombed Churches*, London 1946; *Houses by the Million: An Account of the Housing Achievement in the USA 1940-1945*, London 1947; *Houses; Permanence and Prefabrication*, with Anthony Chitty, London 1947; *An Introduction to Victorian Architecture*, London 1948; *Red Lacquer Days*, London 1956; *The Unseeing Eye*, London 1958; *Bridges*, editor, text by E. M. Hatt, London 1963; *Follies*, editor, text by E. M. Hatt, London 1963; *Monuments*, editor, text by E. M. Hatt, London 1963; *Sailing Tours: Solent*, editor, text by E. M. Hatt, London 1964; *Sailing Tours: Thames and S. E.*, editor, text by E. M. Hatt, London 1964; *Museums*, editor, London 1964; *Inscape: The Design of Interiors*, editor, London 1968; *Nanny Says*, with Joyce Grenfell, London 1972; *Sketchbook*, London 1975; *Diary*, London 1981; *Hugh Casson's London*, London 1983.

Sir Hugh Casson is a complete and well-rounded person with as many facets as the working head of a golf-ball typewriter. He is, above all, an artist combining the skills of architect, environmentalist, conservationist, interior designer, industrial designer, water colourist, author, illustrator, teacher, public speaker, star performer on the media, supporter of good causes, inveterate writer to *The Times*—and many other things besides.

Casson is the senior partner of a well-known firm of architects and as such has been concerned over the years with a steady output of buildings of many kinds. It is not easy to pick out those with which he has been most closely concerned, but it is comparatively easy to see where he has added a touch, often a magic touch, to a scheme. The work of the firm, which is never less than distinguished, is usually given a good send-off with one of his inimitable perspective sketches, which have the remarkable quality of accurately suggesting what the finished building will look like, presented with a masterful economy of line and colour. His photographically accurate memory enables him to produce in a trice a drawing of a building in its true setting. It is the same with his architecture, and in this particular skill he resembles Eric Mendelsohn whose miniature sketches from the trenches of World War I so closely resemble his later completed buildings.

Casson seems to design by intuition. The whole building is contained in the first sketch, but there may be many sketches; designing may stop only with the last coat of paint. A Casson building must fit its environment; it may be placed there firmly, but it will never be obtrusive and, above all, it will be friendly to its neighbours. Sometimes it may suffer from an over-keen awareness of both sides of a problem and thereby fall between two stools, but very gently and without hurt. Excessive interest in high technology and structure are not to be found in the Casson armoury, but choice of materials, colour, and every aspect of interior design are among his sharpest weapons.

Casson first showed his flair and lightness of touch in his layout of the South Bank Exhibition in London in 1951. His flow of good ideas has continued unabated and supported him admirably when he held the highly influential position of President of the Royal Academy of Arts.

—Gontran Goulden

See CASSON CONDER PARTNERSHIP

CASSON CONDER PARTNERSHIP.

Founded by Sir Hugh Casson, q.v., and Neville Conder (born 1922), in London, 1952. Current partners: Hugh Casson, Neville Conder, Ronald Green (born 1927, partner since 1960), Michael Cain (born 1930, partner since 1960), David Ramsay (born 1929, partner since 1969), Montague Turland

Hugh Casson: Elephant House, London Zoo, 1964.

(born 1929, partner since 1969), Stuart Taylor (born 1932, partner since 1969), Kenneth Price (born 1937, partner since 1981), Edwin Bulley (born 1942, partner since 1982), and Anthony Tugwell (born 1947, partner since 1982). Exhibition: Monks Hall Museum, Eccles, Lancashire, 1966. Recipient: First Prizes in the competitions—University of Cambridge Arts Faculty Site, England, 1952; New Telephone Kiosk for the General Post Office, London, 1958; National Westminster Bank Regional Headquarters, Manchester, Lancashire, 1965; Derby Assembly Rooms, England, 1970. Civic Trust Awards, London, 1961, 1964, 1969, 1972, and 1981; Royal Institute of British Architects Awards, 1966, 1971, and 1972; Quigley Award, London, 1969; Heritage Year Award, London, 1975; Tonbridge Civic Society Award, Kent, 1982. Address: 35 Thurloe Place, London SW7 2HJ, England.

Casson Conder Partnership: The Assembly Rooms, Derby, 1977.

Work

1952 Arts Faculty Site Development Plan, University of Cambridge, England

1956/
84 State and Royal Apartment alterations, at Windsor Castle, Berkshire, and at Buckingham Palace, London

1958 Site Development Plan, University of Birmingham, Warwickshire

1959 King George VI Memorial Youth Hostel, London

1960 General Dental Council Headquarters, Wimpole Street, London

Martin's Bank Branch Offices in Garrick Street and Castrol House, London

1961 Academic and Residential Site Development Plan, University of Birmingham, Warwickshire

S.S. Canberra first-class accommodation and public areas, for P. & O. Orient Lines

1962 Development Plan for Pestalozzi Children's Village, Sussex

Residential Building and Warden's House, Pestalozzi Children's Village, Sussex

Royal College of Art, Kensington Gore, London (with H. T. Cadbury-Brown and R. Y. Goodden)

Students' Refectory and Staff Club, University of Birmingham, Warwickshire

1963 Residential Building, Worcester College, Oxford, England

Rooftop Restaurant and Bar, Hilton Hotel, Park Lane, London

Elephant and Rhinoceros Pavilion, Zoological Gardens, Regent's Park, London

1964 Faculty of Modern and Mediaeval Languages, English and Moral Science, University of Cambridge, England

Westfield College Development Plan, University of London

Martin's Bank, Regent's Circus, Swindon, Wiltshire

Shops, offices, and flats, Winchester, Hampshire

1965 Department of Economics and Politics, University of Cambridge, England

Civic Centre Development Plan, Swindon, Wiltshire

1966 Lady Mitchell Hall and Little Hall, University of Cambridge, England

Parking Structure, University of Birmingham, Warwickshire

Structures Laboratory and Offices for the Cement and Concrete Association, London

St. James' Club new accommodation, Manchester, Lancashire

1968 Odeon Cinema, St. Martin's Lane, London

1969 Department of Oriental Studies, University of Cambridge, England

1970 Library Building, Badminton Girls' School, Bristol, Avon

Director's Offices, Australia and New Zealand Banking Group, Cornhill, London

1971 RSPB Vane Farm Conservation Centre, Loch Leven, Scotland

1972 School of Education, University of Birmingham, Warwickshire

National Westminster Bank Regional Headquarters, Manchester, Lancashire

Pulteney Weir and Landscaping, Bath, Avon

1975 Computer Centre, University of Birmingham, Warwickshire

Wyvern Theatre and Arts Centre, Swindon, Wiltshire

Pavilion Bar and Bird's Nest discotheque, Swindon, Wiltshire

1976 Caroline Skeel Library, Westfield College, University of London

Zoo Study Centre, Zoological Gardens, Regent's Park, London

Information Centre, Witley Common, Surrey

1977 Sixth Form Residential Building, Badminton Girls' School, Bristol, Avon

Assembly Rooms multi-purpose centre, Derby, England

1978 Bridge and Summerhouse, Savill Garden, Windsor Great Park, Berkshire

Information Centre, Queen Elizabeth Country Park, Hampshire

1979 Halls of Residence, Westfield College, University of London

Development Plan, Millfield School, Somerset (consultancy)

W. H. Smith Head Office Building, New Fetter Lane, London

Plunkett Memorial, Windsor Great Park, Berkshire

1980 Suffolk Street and Hobhouse Court new urban courtyard, London

1982 Music School, Badminton Girls' School, Bristol, Avon

Benn Brothers Head Office, Tonbridge, Kent

1983 Aga Khan Trust Stud Farm, Sheshoon, County Kildare, Ireland

Sutton Place restoration and alterations, Guildford, Surrey

1984 Faculty of Classics and Museum of Classical Archaeology, University of Cambridge, England

Ismaili Centre, London

Benn Brothers Headquarters extensions, Tonbridge, Kent

Building extension and refurbishment, 78 Pall Mall, London

1985 Gower Street frontage completion, University College, London

Publications

By CASSON/CONDER: book—*New Parliamentary Building, Bridge Street: Feasibility Study,* London 1979.

On CASSON/CONDER: articles—"Padiglione per uno zoo" in *Casabella* (Milan), December 1965; "Dei edifici di Casson Conder and Partners" in *Architettura* (Rome), March 1966; "Two by Two" in *Building Design* (London), 27 February 1976; "Food for Thought" in *Interior Design* (New York), July 1977; "Interiors: W. H. Smith Headquarters" in *Design* (London), December 1977; "Civic Pride" in *Architects' Journal* (London), 7 December 1977; "Ismaili Religious and Cultural Centre" in *RIBA Journal* (London), April 1978; "Information Centre, Witley Common, Surrey" in *Architectural Review* (London), May 1978; "Mini Profile: Casson Conder and Partners" in *Building* (London), 25 August 1978; "Finely Mixed" in *Building Design* (London), 28 September 1979; "Two-Day Wonder of Parliament" in *Building Design* (London), 14 December 1979; "New Parliamentary Building" in *Architects' Journal* (London), 19 December 1979; "Hobhouse Court, near Leicester Square" in *Progressive Architecture* (New York), June 1980; "Reflections of Islam in the Cromwell Road" in *Landscape International* (London), January/February 1984; "Ismaili Centre" in *Building* (London), 24 February 1984; "Ismaili Centre in London" in *Baumeister* (Munich), May 1984.

The Casson Conder Partnership is a London based practice which has gained a wide experience in most types of architectural and related design over a period of more than twenty-five years. The partnership has tended to attract commissions for projects that are specially tailored to particular sites or circumstances rather than for the "programme architecture" of housing or schools. While most of the buildings have been realised within modest budgets established by local authorities or the University Grants Committee, the firm has also established a reputation for its work in fine materials in connection with such projects as the Ismaili Centre, its work for banks, and in the refurbishment of historic buildings.

We regard ourselves primarily as modern architects building new buildings for the age in which we live. Several of our commissions have, however, been on sensitive sites or alongside noted historic buildings. Development plans have formed an important part of our work, as have landscape work, interior design, and industrial design related to the building industry.

—Casson Conder Partnership

See CASSON, Hugh Maxwell

CATALANO, Eduardo.

American. Born in Buenos Aires, Argentina, 1 December 1917; emigrated to the United States, 1951: naturalized, 1963. Educated at the University of Buenos Aires, 1940; University of Pennsylvania, Philadelphia, 1944, M.Arch. 1944; Harvard University, Cambridge, Massachusetts, 1944-45 (Institute of International Education/United States Depart-ment of State Scholarship), M.Arch. 1945. Children: Alejandrina and Adrian. Since 1958, Principal, Eduardo Catalano, Architects and Engineers, Cambridge, Massachusetts. Visiting Professor of Architecture, Architectural Association School, London, 1950-51; Professor of Architecture, University of North Carolina, Raleigh, 1951-56, and Massachusetts Institute of Technology, Cambridge, 1956-77. Exhibition: *Eduardo Catalano,* toured European cities, 1978. Recipient: First Prize, Carrier Company National Competition, 1953; First Prize, Ferro-Enamel National Competition, 1954; First Prize, Health Center Competition, Philadelphia, 1954; Award, American Institute of Architects, North Carolina Chapter, 1956; Award, *Progressive Architecture,* 1969. Address: Eduardo Catalano, Architects and Engineers, 300 Franklin Street, Cambridge, Massachusetts 02139, U.S.A.

Works:

1954 Raleigh House, Raleigh, North Carolina

1961 Master plan for the campus of the University of Buenos Aires (with H. Caminos and E. Sacriste)

Burton-Connor Dining Room, Massachusetts Institute of Technology, Cambridge (with W. Brown)

1962 Science Building, University of Buenos Aires (with H. Caminos)

1963 Student Center, Massachusetts Institute of Technology, Cambridge

1965 Architecture Building, University of Buenos Aires (with H. Caminos)

Married Student Housing and Polaroid Building, Massachusetts Institute of Technology, Cambridge

1968 Juilliard School of Music, Lincoln Center for the Performing Arts, New York (with Pietro Belluschi and Helge Westermann)

Central Plaza, Cambridge, Massachusetts

1969 Civic Center, Springfield, Massachusetts

Bay State West Urban Complex, Springfield, Massachusetts

Charlestown Library, Boston

1970 Governmental Center, Greensboro, North Carolina

1971 Washington Mall, Boston

1973 Hall of Justice, Springfield, Massachusetts

1974 United States Embassy, Buenos Aires

1975 Civic Center, Portland, Maine

1976 Cambridge High School, Massachusetts

La Guardia High School, New York

1977 Superior Court Building, Springfield, Massachusetts

District Court Building, Holyoke, Massachusetts

1978 Office Building, Burlington, Massachusetts

1981 Cambridge Park office complex, Cambridge, Massachusetts

1982 Computer Center, Dammam, Saudi Arabia

1983 Office Building, Burlington, Massachusetts

1984 Cranberry Hill Office Building, Lexington, Massachusetts (with Eugene Hayes)

Cambridge Park Two office building, Cambridge, Massachusetts

Publications:

By CATALANO: books—*Teoria de las sombras y tratados de perspectiva,* with Oscar Crivelli and Rene Nery, Buenos Aires 1940; *Structures of Warped Surfaces,* Raleigh, North Carolina 1958, as *Estructuras de superficies alabeadas,* Buenos Aires 1962; articles—"Un Concurso de Arquitectura en U.S.A." and "Auditorium Ciudad de Buenos Aires" in *Nuestra arquitectura* (Buenos Aires), July 1946; "From the Crystal Palace to the 1951 Exhibition" in *Nuestra arquitectura* (Buenos Aires), July 1951;

Eduardo Catalano: Office building for an international organization, 1984 (project).

bility for growth and change. We cannot aspire to work as individuals, producing individual solutions to satisfy individual whims and needs through custom-made construction and, at the same time, pretend to be part of a generation that is searching for an architectural alternative of social and technological dimensions.

The scale of our collective unsatisfied needs is too great to satisfy them through small "museum pieces" and isolated individual efforts, infested with personal mannerisms and romantic techniques. The art gallery of yesterday has been replaced today by the entire city.

The origin of a system is life and its capability to adapt itself to changing human physical environments. They are not sterile patterns but topological networks in constant transformation. In 1851 Joseph Paxton proved that systems could become the means to structure a poetic thought. After Paxton, there has not been continuity in research and development.

—Eduardo Catalano

The Argentine Eduardo Catalano believes that contemporary architects must abandon individualistic design and turn to the paths opened by science and technology and industrialization to develop a systems architecture responsive to the ever-expanding population, increasing governmental control of urban construction, and introduction of new materials.

Architecture is presently moving but not advancing when compared to the achievements of science and technology. And because the population, legislation, economics, energy consumption, etc, have expanded all known proportions, so too must architecture abandon the isolated individual building as we see it today, and respond with new systematized urban complexes of a new proportion and scale.

Catalano suggests that the future of architecture rests in the hands of the students of this new approach who can combine the advances of industry and science with the designing of space. But, so far, architecture schools have not taken their share of the responsibility to develop this alliance. They should participate more in the research and development of new construction materials and processes. And teachers should encourage the study of total systems of urban design, rather than dabble with little single solutions to individual buildings that are responsive only to a limited user population.

His own designs exhibit an underlying and visible expression of pure form, often pure geometry in their structural systems. His buildings make bold statements. Several of his houses employ the simplest of structure, for example, the hyperbolic paraboloid. All of the inside spaces and functions are subservient to the powerful geometric shape. The Student Center at MIT, with its simple horizontality of large cantilevers, resists gravity and declares its structural integrity in an expression of unilateral boldness.

Both a city and a house have a pattern of behavior that comes from spatial and structural systems that overlap and interplay to create shelter as a main theme. The architect designs and builds systems and subsystems. Like a city with its layers of circulation paths from limited access highways to the neighborhood alleys, the form changes as the shapes and scales change, but all exist in a cohesive network exclusive of construction inconsistencies or random moods. Architecture is the three-dimensional event that consistutes growth and change according to a pattern of behavior and construction.

In his teachings and in his designs, Catalano expresses architecture as a system responsive to technological and behavioral order generated from a purity of geometry and structure. A building is an offering to this order of nature, following the norms of organization, responding to a value far above the constraints imposed by individual sites or individual clients or individual programs.

—Stephen P. Hamilton

"Three Stadiums" in *Nuestra arquitectura* (Buenos Aires), December 1952; "Two Warped Surfaces" in *Student Publication of the School of Design* (University of North Carolina, Raleigh), no. 1, 1955; "A Talk to Students" in *Northwest Architect* (Minneapolis, Minnesota), July/August 1966; "Por una arquitectura de sistemas" in *La Prensa* (Buenos Aires), 23 March 1969; "A Case for Systems" in *Progessive Architecture* (New York), November 1969; "A New Scale for Architecture Through Systems" in *Systems Building News* (Chicago), July 1970; "On Rhynoceros and Architecture" in *North Carolina Architect*, July 1984.

On CATALANO: books—*A Decade of New Architecture* by Sigfried Giedion, Zurich 1951; *Eduardo Catalano* by Gazaneo Scarone, Buenos Aires 1956; *Aluminum in Modern Architecture* by John Peter, New York 1956; *Architecture, You and Me* by Sigfried Giedion, Cambridge, Massachusetts, 1958; *Structures in Art and in Science* by Gyorgy Kepes, New York 1965; *Architects on Architecture*, edited by Paul Heyer, New York 1966, London 1967; *Eduardo Catalano: Buildings and Projects*, edited by Camillo Gubitosi and Alberto Izzo, Rome 1978; articles— "The State of Contemporary Architecture" by Sigfried Giedion in *Architectural Record* (New York), February 1954; "Raleigh House" in *Progressive Architecture* (New York), September 1955; "A New Way to Span Space" in *Architectural Forum* (New York), November 1955; "Structure of Hyperbolic Paraboloids" in *Architectural Review* (London), November 1958; "Structures of Warped Surfaces" in *Arts and Architecture* (Los Angeles), December 1963; "MIT Student Center: Eduardo Catalano Starts with Systems and Creates Architecture" in *Architectural Record* (New York), March 1966; "Sobre una obra de Eduardo Catalano" by Fernando Alvarado in *La Prensa* (Buenos Aires), 18 September 1966; "Prefabricated Housing System— Ledgewood" in *Progressive Architecture* (New York), January 1970; "La arquitectura actual segun Eduardo Catalano" by Fernando Alvarado in *La Prensa* (Buenos Aires), 9 August 1970; "Baystate West Shopping Mall" in *Architectural Record* (New York), April 1974; "Greensboro Governmental Center" in *Architectural Record* (New York), June 1974; "Como nacio la arquitectura moderna" by Peter Blake in *La Nacion* (Buenos Aires), 5 November 1975; North Carolina Governmental Center" in *L'Industria italiana del cemento* (Rome), December 1978; "Building Types Study 548: Four Schools with Thought" in *Architectural Record* (New York), August 1980; "Linked Schools in Cambridge" in *Industria delle costruzioni* (Rome), September 1981; "Three Works by Eduardo Catalano" in *Industria delle costruzioni* (Rome), November 1983; "The Conceptual Key of Eduardo Catalano's House" in *La Prensa* (Buenos Aires), January 1984.

Like politics, architecture has changed only its face through the use of new visual slogans. Buildings of the last decades, considered outstanding examples of architecture, are merely archaeological resurrections disguised by short-lived visual slogans. We have made no attempt to find the common denominators of human behavior and needs to formulate the few buildings constants from which a systematized design and construction process evolves to achieve flexible and long-lasting buildings.

The emphasis on an architecture to satisfy individuals and temporary needs has wrongly led to the construction of frozen structures without flexi-

CAUDILL, William Wayne.

American. Born in Hobart, Oklahoma, 25 May 1914. Educated at Oklahoma State University, Stillwater, 1933-37, B.Arch. 1937; Massachusetts Institute of Technology, Cambridge, 1937-39, M.Arch. 1939. Served in the United States Navy during World War II. Married Edith Rosellel Woodman in 1940; children: Susan and William Jr.; married Aleen Plumer Harrison in 1974. Principal of Caudill Rowlett Scott, Houston, Texas, 1946 until his death in 1983: Chairman of the Board, CRS Inc., from 1950; firm became CRS Sirrine upon merger with J.E. Sirrine, 1983. Professor of Design, 1939-42 and 1946-49, and Research Architect, Texas Engineering Experiment Station, 1946-49, Texas A and M University, College Station; Director of the School of Architecture, 1961-69, and William Ward Watkin Professor of Architecture, 1969-71, Rice University, Houston. Chairman of the National School Committee, 1956-59, and Member of the Research Committee, 1963-66, American Institute of Architects; Director, Association of College Schools of Architecture, 1965-66; Member of the Advisory Committee for New Educational Media, United States Department of Health, Education and Welfare, 1966-68; Member of the Advisory Panel on Architectural Services, United States General Services Administration, 1966-69; Director, Council of Educational Facility Planners, 1968-69; Member of the Advisory Panel for Building Research, United States Academy of Sciences, 1969-71; Architectural Consultant to the United States Department of State on Foreign Buildings, 1974-77. Member, United States Energy Research and Development Ad Hoc Advisory Committee, 1977-83. Recipient: College of Engineering Hall of Fame Award, 1964, and University Hall of Fame Award, 1973, Oklahoma State University; Planner of the Year Award, Council of Educational Facilities Planners, 1970; Dean's Council Award, University of California at Los Angeles, 1976; Gold Medal, Tau Sigma Delta Fraternity, 1978; Gold Medal, Association of Collegiate Schools of Architecture, 1978; Llewelyn W. Pitts Award, Texas Society of Architects, 1980; LL.D.: Eastern Michigan University, Ypsilanti, 1947. Fellow, American Institute of Architects, 1962. Founding Member, Academy of Texas, 1969. Member, Oklahoma Hall of Fame, 1983. *Died* (in Houston, Texas) *25 June 1983*.

Works:

1969 CRS Office Building, Houston, Texas
1970 First Hutchins-Sealy National Bank, 2200 Market Street, Galveston, Texas
      Four-College Science Center, Claremont, California
      Rehabilitation Building, Manhattan Psychiatric Center, Wards Island, New York
1973 Desert Samaritan Hospital, Phoenix, Arizona
      Fodrea Community School, Columbus, Indiana
1974 State and Mapleton Banking Center, 301 Washington, Columbus, Indiana
      Hyatt Regency Hotel, Houston, Texas
      Salanter-Akiba Riverdale Academy, 655 West 254th Street, Bronx, New York
      Houston National Bank, Texas
1975 Thomas E. Leavey Student Activity Center, University of California at Santa Clara
1975 University of Petroleum and Minerals, Dhahran, Saudi Arabia
1976 County Office Building, 1555 Berger Drive, Santa Clara, California
1976 Mass Seating and Natatorium, Gainesville, Florida
1977 Tulane University Hospital and Teaching Center, 1430 Tulane Avenue, New Orleans
      Rochester General Hospital, Rochester, New York
      Public School/Intermediate School 229, Bronx, New York
1978 Bahrain Monetary Building, Manama
      University for Girls, Riyadh, Saudi Arabia
1979 IBM Office Building, Riverway, Houston, Texas
      Albert Thomas Convention Center, Houston, Texas
      Federal Youth Center, Bastrop, Texas

Publications:

By CAUDILL: books—*Space for Teaching*, College Station, Texas 1942; *Your Schools: An Approach to Long Range Planning*, College Station, Texas 1950; *Toward Better School Design*, Chicago 1953; *In Education the Most Important Number Is One*,

Houston 1964; *Memos from Russia*, Boston 1969; *Architecture by Team*, New York 1971; *A Bucket of Oil: The Humanistic Approach to Building Design for Energy Conservation*, with Frank Lawyer and Thomas A. Bullock, Boston 1975; *Problem Seeking: An Architectural Programming Primer*, with William M. Pena and John Focke, Boston 1977; *From Infancy to Infinity*, with Charles Schorre and Jeffrey Conroy, Houston 1977; *Architecture and You: How to Experience and Enjoy Buildings*, with Paul Kennon and William M. Pena, New York 1978; *Memos from Indonesia*, 1983; articles—"William W. Caudill on Lawrence B. Anderson" in *AIA Journal* (Washington, D.C.), July 1978; "Interview" with Nathan Good in *Crit* (Washington, D.C.), Winter 1983; and numerous other articles and technical reports.

On CAUDILL: articles—"An Image for Technology" by Sharon Lee Ryder in *Progressive Architecture* (New York), May 1974; "Houston's Hyatt Regency: Coherent Expression of Multi-Use Space" in *Architectural Record* (New York), May 1974; "I'm an Architecture: Fodrea Elementary School" by Sharon Lee Ryder in *Progressive Architecture* (New York), May 1974; "How to Work with the Health Client" by James Falick in *Progressive Architecture* (New York), July 1974; "Rust City" by Jonathan King in *Architectural Design* (London), June 1975; "Productive Elegance for Industry" by Charles Hoyt in *Architectural Record* (New York), July 1975; "Bank Transparency: A Visual Come-on: The Houston National Bank" in *Interiors* (New York), August 1975; "Tilt to the River: S.A.R. Academy, New York" by Jack W. Smith in *Progressive Architecture* (New York), December 1975; "Joint Ventures and Associations" by C. A. Carlson and Wallie E. Scott, Jr. in *AIA Journal* (Washington, D.C.), June 1976; "Evaluations" by Jonathan King in *AIA Journal* (Washington, D.C.), August 1976; "Money-Changers in the Temple of Architecture" by Roger Yee in *Interiors* (New York), November 1976; "Construction Management, in a Miami Test" in *Architectural Record* (New York), January 1977; "The Corporate Architect" by James Murphy in *Progressive Architecture* (New York), May 1977; "Organization of Architecture: CRS," special issue of *Space Design* (Tokyo), March 1980; "Games in CRS" by Charles e. Estes in *Summarios*

William Wayne Caudill: CRS Office Building, Houston, Texas, 1969.

(Rio de Janeiro), March 1980; "Works: Caudill Rowlett Scott" in *Architecture + Urbanism* (Tokyo), May 1983; "William W. Caudill, Founder and Spiritual Leader of CRS" by Allen Freeman in *Architecture* (Washington, D.C.), August 1983.

I am a professor/architect involved in theory and practice since 1947, committed to the team concept of practice. The practice is international. CRS Inc. has grown from two members in 1947 to more than 1,000 employees, including those of affiliate companies. Probably I am best known for innovations in educational architecture and management procedures, although the firm of CRS has received literally hundreds of awards.

—William W. Caudill (1980)

William Caudill was the founder of Caudill Rowlett Scott of Houston, Texas. The company has been in existence for almost forty years; during that time, it has grown enormously, has been a pioneer in the development of management techniques, and has been a leader in technological advance in architecture. Perhaps most important, it has become a highly influential model for other American architectural firms in its concept of architecture by team.

Caudill was a firm believer in the team—a team comprising not only architects but the client as well. His vision proved highly successful. A team of architects, other specialists, and client(s), often on site, quickly devise design objectives, work together during the process of design refinement, execution, and completion of a project, then, post-occupancy, come together to discuss success or failure. A simple questionnaire for the client includes such questions as: Are the materials withstanding wear? Has the building merged well with its environment? What do you consider to be the building's assets and its problems? In Caudill's own words:

We believe that many people should be involved in the design process, particularly if they are the users of the building.... The key to this approach is communication. But communication must have a broad meaning. It is being direct and frank with people. And when you can successfully do that, you have a good chance to produce a direct and frank architecture. The quality of ruggedness found in this approach is also reflected in our buildings—no namby-pamby architecture. From the beginning of Caudill-Rowlett-Scott, we have not been able to separate our *process* from our *architecture*.

Such directness (and prompting of frank criticism) has produced considerable respect and prestige from clients, from potential clients, and from within the architectureal profession.

Caudill also maintained that a designer sitting in his Houston office is not going to be able to assess the environmental requirements in, say, the Bronx or the Colorado mountains with just a couple of hurried site visits. Far better to send a team to the spot. A good example of this attitude in practice is the CRS work on Saudi Arabia's University of Petroleum and Minerals. To accomplish this huge project, CRS sent top people and a carefully chosen crew of builders and engineers to the site, established stringent quality control, worked closely with the local client, and produced a showplace for Saudi Arabia. Caudill again:

Our "formula" for a building is this: take a client, teach him to speak architecture and make him a part of your team. Add technologists as well as designers to the team. Condition the reflexes of each of the members to absorb and accept ideas. Then go directly to the site and mix them up in a group. We feel that if, after programming is completed, we have not educated our clients and raised their aspirations for a better physical environment, then we have not done our professional job.

This is not to suggest, however, that the firm produces design-by-vote. All group action is led by a strong designer of outstanding abilities in leadership, quality control, and creativity, and, indeed, many well-known designers, not least Caudill himself, have emerged from within the company. It would probably be fair to say that the firm strives for diversity through team effort, a diversity to match the requirements of the varying environments of different American states and different foreign countries—yet assures design excellence by always remembering that creativity is still the province of the individual. As usual, Caudill puts it better:

There must be strong leadership, plus plenty of imagination, as well as competence and skill, to pull off one of these things. And even more important, there must be the freedom of choice for using analyzed elements which seem capable of giving architecture a strong art form. Again, it is people involvement, but with strong architectural leadership....

Architecture is more than a reflective art of civilization. It is a regenerative force—the force that is created through group dynamics. We believe that architecture must reflect the excitement of life found in our democratic society, which respects the individual. We believe in the individual over the team, and that architecture is for everybody, not just the privileged few.

—Colin Naylor

CETTO, Max Ludwig.

Mexican. Born in Coblenz, Germany, 20 February 1903; emigrated to the United States, 1938, then to Mexico, 1939; naturalized, 1947. Educated at the Technical Universities of Darmstadt and Munich, 1921-23, Technical University of Berlin, under Hans Poelzig, 1923-26, Dip.Ing. 1926. Married Gertrude Catherine Kramis in 1940; children: Veronica, Ana Maria, and Bettina. Designer, City Planning and Building Office, Frankfurt, 1926-31; Supervisor of industrial construction in various parts of Germany, 1932-38; worked with Richard Neutra, *q.v.,* in San Francisco, 1938; worked as a designer for various architects in Mexico City, 1939-45. In private practice, Mexico City, 1945 until his death in 1980. Professor, School of Architecture, Universidad Nacional Autonoma, Mexico City, 1965-79. Visiting Professor, School of Architecture, University of Texas, Austin, 1960-61; School of Architecture, Clemson University, South Carolina, 1962 and 1967; School of Arts, Auburn University, Alabama, 1965. Founder-Member, CIAM (Congrès Internationaux d'Architecture Moderne), 1928. *Died* (in Mexico City) *5 April 1980.*

Works:

1926/
30 Various works, including park pavilions, university dental clinic, teachers' seminary, old people's asylum, electrical generating/transforming plants, etc., for the Frankfurt Building Office
1927 League of Nations Building, Geneva (competition project; with Wolfgang Bangert)
1939 Hotel, San José Purrua, Mexico (with Jorge Rubio)
1945 Wolfgang Paalen Studio, San Angel, Mexico City
1946 Señor House, Gen. Cano, Tacubaya, Mexico City
1947 Quintana Weekend House, Lago de Tequesquitengo, Morelos, Mexico
1948 Hill House, Guerrero 10, San Angel, Mexico City (with John McAndrew)
1949 Tamayo House, Leibnitz 248, Col. Anzures, Mexico City
Max Cetto House, Auga 130, Pedregal, Mexico City

1950 Pedregal Show House, Fuentes 130, Mexico City (with Luis Barragán)
1951 Berdecio House, Fuentes 140, Mexico City (with Luis Barragán)
1952 Friedeberg House, Agua 330, Mexico City
1953 Boehm House, Agua 737, Mexico City
1954 Kirk House, Creston 232, Mexico City
1955 Deutsch Weekend House, Tepozotlan, Morelos, Mexico
Reforma Office Building, Reforma 134, Mexico City
1956 Deutsch House, San Jeronimo, Mexico City
1957 Krupenski House, Pirules 106, Mexico City
1959 Vetter House, Picacho 239, Mexico City
1960 Ehni House, Fuente de Diana 45, Tecamachalco, Mexico
1961 Cold Rolled Company Workshop, Calz. del Moral 186, Ixtapalapa, Mexico
1962 Novick House, Avenida 3, 43, Las Aguilas, Mexico City
1963 Kirchhoff House, Juarez 18, Tlacopac., Mexico City
1964 Crevenna House, Av. San Jeronimo 136, Mexico City
1965 Ezquerro House, Cerro del Tesoro, Coyoacan, Mexico City
1966 Sevilla House, Santiago 258, San Jeronimo, Mexico City
Moore House, Genung Road, Ithaca, New York
National Gallery, Berlin (competition project)
1967/
68 Morelos Tanning Company, Cuautla, Morelos, Mexico
1968/
71 Office Building, Obrero Mundial 629, Mexico City
1970/
79 German Club of Mexico, Aldama 153, Tepepan, Mexico
1974 Strötgen House, San Diego de los Padres 51, Club de Golf Hacienda, Mexico
1975 Cold Rolled Company Office Building, Calz. del Moral 186, Ixtapalapa, Mexico
1977 Frenk Weekend House, Jiutepec, Morelos, Mexico
1979 Brody House, Cerro del Agua 43, Mexico City

Publications:

By CETTO: books—*Moderne Architektur in Mexico,* Stuttgart 1960, as *Modern Architecture in Mexico,* New York 1961; *Knaurs Lexikon der modernen Architektur,* with others, Munich 1963; *Candela und seine Schalen,* translation into German of *Candela, The Shell Builder* by Colin Faber, Munich 1965; *Latin America in its Architecture,* with others, edited by Roberto Segre, London and New York 1981; articles—"External Influences and the Importance of Tradition" in *American latina en su arquitectura,* Unesco, Mexico City 1975; "Architecture mexicaine" in *Techniques et architecture* (Paris), June/July 1978; interview, in *Testimonios vivos/20 arquitectos,* Mexico City 1981.

On CETTO: books—*18 Homes of Mexican Architects* by E. Yanex, Mexico City 1951; *Mexico's Modern Architecture* by I. E. Myers, Mexico City 1952; *Encyclopédie de l'architecture nouvelle* by Alberto Sartoris, Milan 1954; *Latin American Architecture since 1945* by Henry-Russell Hitchcock, New York 1955.
Bibliography—*Max Cetto: A Bibliography and Building List* by Edward M. Teague, Monticello, Illinois 1984.

A generation ago, the term ecology was used only by biologists and was widely unknown to the general public, including architects. For me, it always meant, and goes on meaning, the most important auxiliary

Max Cetto: Cetto House, Pedregal, Mexico City, 1949.

science in planning the humans "habitat." That does not mean that other, humanistic or technological, aspects should be neglected. The following is a quotation from an article that I wrote twenty-eight years ago (in *Arts and Architecture,* Los Angeles, 1951) that is still valid today, despite the fact that in the meantime building procedures have been more and more mechanized in Mexico:

Because of the lack of qualified personnel with sufficient intermediate technical knowledge, houses cannot be built by simply providing a complete set of drawings and specifications.... If the architect cares to see the building finished according to his concepts, he has to supervise the work every day, playing the part of a general contractor himself. Knowing that even the most careful preparation on the drawing board would not free him from spending at least half his time to put them through on the job, he very often prefers to rely on sketches and oral directions.

This method is not as bad as one would imagine. What is lost in efficient preparation is gained the directness of approach, new suggestions coming out of the work in progress, and a flexibility that allows one to make improvements on a moment's notice.

Under such circumstances it seems considerably wiser to renounce certain ideals of mechanical perfection, which we adored in the first years of functional architecture, and accept the blessings of a rather rustic, handmade, and more human touch, which is probably the most adequate expression of the natural and spiritual resources of this country.

Obviously the remantic working habits of an architect, as described above, will not last any longer than the underdevelopment of any given population of which he is a part.

—Max Cetto (1980)

In 1939, when Max Cetto came to Mexico, fundamental changes were occurring in the politics of the country, changes that were having repercussions in the field of architecture. Private capital was regaining the power it had lost during the period of revolution and was once again becoming a powerful patron. During the 1930s, Mexican architecture had been characterized by an open struggle between, on the one hand, a young generation fighting to establish functionalism in a purely technical sense as the means of resolving social need and, on the other, the traditionalists, with their concept of beauty and culture, defending the styles and fashions of the past. After 1940, the political climate favored functionalism, a potentially lucrative international idiom that would achieve maximum gain at minimum cost. This was the sad fact that Cetto, having fled from European fascism, and hoping to live in a socialist country, had to accept upon his arrival in Mexico.

His career had begun—after his studies under the great master Hans Poelzig—in the Frankfurt City Planning and Building Office. There, he was responsible for several impressive municipal works, but it was his competition entry for the League of Nations

Building in Geneva that brought him to public notice and earned him a place in CIAM at the early age of twenty-four. The fascist escalation in Germany halted what promised to be a brilliant career, and finally, in 1938, Cetto abandoned Germany and went to the United States, where he worked for a year with Richard Neutra. A year later he established himself in Mexico.

Cetto's first important Mexican project, built in collaboration with Jorge Rubio, was the Hotel at San José Purrua. With this building, Cetto established the basis of an integral functionalism of a kind different from that which had formerly been practised in the country. As the site—around an area of natural springs—was rugged and uneven, Cetto actually sketched his plan on the earth with chalk. He wanted to make the best use of the topographical variations and to incorporate views of the countryside as well as its rocks and trees; he studied the various surrounding elements in order to utilize them to best advantage or, alternatively, to avoid them. His method showed that his was an architecture that arose out of nature and was inextricably bound up with it. Three years later, after visiting the hotel, Walter Gropius wrote to him: "The work at San José appeals to me very much indeed. One needs imagination to implant a building among the rocks. The concept of different levels is carried out in a masterly fashion. The details may be a little rough, but the line of the whole, its 'elan,' stands out above everything."

By 1949 Cetto had become famous in Mexico and was known affectionately as "Le Hombre del Pedregal." He had built and now lived in the first house in Pedregal, an area of Mexico City devastated during two millenia by volcanic eruption and again threatened by a large and new split in the earth. The rough ground, formed of volcanic lava, with its strange vegetation and colouring, was a challenge to the imagination of the architect, and the complete and successful way in which he overcame the problems, humanizing a hitherto purely technical functionalism in order to solve the psychological problem involved, became a great example to contemporary architects. It might even be claimed, without exaggeration, that without this work, Mexican residential architecture would have taken a different road. The use of natural materials—lava stone, mosaic, wood—created the feeling of a construction sown among the natural folds of the earth, integrating the internal and external vistas. The house was a revelation, the basis of a new kind of construction.

The other dwellings that Cetto built in the same volcanic zone of El Pedregal—either alone or in collaboration—are equally successful and beautiful variations of this architectural theme. He applied the same principles when building the Morelos Tanning Factory in the torrid Valle de Cuautla, where he dispensed with the hitherto indispensable international-style window and inserted open tile shutters to create currents of air. He employed a similar solution for the Quintana Weekend House in the tropical region of Tequesquitengo by taking advantage of the cool freshness provided by a nearby lake.

Cetto has also been interested in the history of architecture, in criticism, and in practical teaching. Part of his role as craftsman has been to devise a method of teaching, the result of which can be of service to rural and outlying communities. He has shown his students the uselessness of working in an office in a kind of conceptual vacuum. Creation, according to Cetto, is the product of contact, study, and the appraisal of the reality of a situation in all its aspects. Only an exact but loving comprehension of reality can transform it in the service of man—a truth that Cetto never stopped preaching: to students, whom he has taken to deprived villages in order to study economic, social, and building problems at first hand; to architects, the "visionaries of the future," to whom he has spoken out, cautioning them against faith in technology as a solution to social problems; and, as it were, to architecture itself, in the example of his own work. The problem that preoccupied him is that of alienation and conflict—between nature and man, the individual and society, pure materialism and pure aesthetics. The struggle and commitment of his life was to bring about the harmony of man with the world in which he lives.

—Ida Rodriguez

CHADIRJI, Rifat.

Iraqi. Born in Baghdad, in December 1926. Studied at the Hammersmith School of Arts and Crafts, London, under Arthur Korn, *q.v.,* 1946-52, Dip.Arch. 1952. Married Balkis Sharara in 1954. Since 1952, Founder, Senior Partner, and Director, Iraq Consult, Baghdad. Building Department Section Head, Waqaf Organization, Baghdad, 1954-57; Director-General of Housing, Ministry of Planning, Baghdad, 1958-65; Head of the Planning Committee, Ministry of Housing, Baghdad, 1959-63; returned to full-time private practice with Iraq Consult, 1965. Member of the Mayor's Council, Baghdad, 1958-61; Member of the Iraqi Government Tourist Board, 1970-75. Exhibitions: Beirut, 1966; Madrid, 1966; Sudan, 1967; Ghana, 1967;

Tunisia, 1967; Kuwait, 1967; Ankara, 1968; Baghdad, 1972; Damascus, 1973; Kuwait, 1975; Tunisia, 1975; *Modern Arab Architecture,* London, 1978. Recipient: First Prize, Mortgage Bank Building Competition, Baghdad, 1956; First Prize, Al-Pasha Al-Sajheer Building Competition, Baghdad, 1961; First Prize, Tobacco Monopoly Administration and Stores Building, Baghdad, 1965; Honors Prize, Ministry of Municipalities Competition, Baghdad, 1965; Bronze Medal, International Interior Architecture and Design Competition, Madrid, 1966; First Prize, Commercial Bank of Iraq Competition, 1967; Co-First Prize, Kuwait Parliament Complex Competition, 1971; First Prize, Council of Ministers Building, Baghdad, 1975; First Prize, National Theatre Competition, Abu Dhabi, United Arab Emirates, 1977. Honorary Fellow, Royal Institute of British Architects, 1982. Address: Iraq Consult, Hasib Saleh Building, Nidhaj Street, Post Office Box 2291, Alwiyah, Baghdad, Iraq.

Works:

1957	Munir Abbass Building, Iraq
1959	Unknown Soldier Monument, Baghdad
1960	National Insurance Company Building, Baghdad
1961	Tobacco Monopoly Offices, Baghdad
1962	Al Azzawi House, Baghdad
1964	Rifidain Bank, Sinak, Baghdad
	Veterinary hospital, Baghdad
1965	Waqaf Office Building, North Gate, Baghdad
	Tobacco Monopoly Headquarters Building, Baghdad
	M. Othman Villa, Baghdad
	Yasoob Rafiq Villa, Baghdad
1966	Tobacco Monopoly Office II, Baghdad
	Iraqi Federation of Industries Building, Baghdad
	National Insurance Offices, Mosul, Iraq
	Commercial Bank, Mansoor, Iraq
1967	Al Hamad Villa, Kuwait
	Veterinary college, Baghdad
1968	Iraqi Scientific Academy, Baghdad
	Hawalli Residential Complex, Kuwait (with Pan Arab Consultants)
1969	Monument for the workers' housing scheme, Baghdad
	Kufa Cement Factory, Iraq (with N. Fetto and P. Nacy)
	Central Communication Building, Baghdad (with Henry Svoboda)
	Waqaf Building, Alwiyah, Iraq
	Orphanage, Dohuk, Iraq
	Orphange, Arbil, Iraq
	Medical Auxiliary Training Institute, Baghdad
	Andulus Cinema, Manama, Bahrain
	Housing complex, Salimiya, Kuwait
1970	Office building, Bahrain
	Sheikh Khalifa Building, Bahrain
	Gali Ali Beg Sector Development Study, Iraq
1972	Qatar Cinema Complex, Doha
	Kurdish Scientific Academy Building, Baghdad
	H. H. Hmood Villa, Baghdad
1973	Gate of Arbil fortress Conservation, Iraq
	General Federation of Trade Unions Assembly Hall, Baghdad
1975	Reinsurance Company Building, Baghdad
1976	Cabinet of Ministers Building, United Arab Emirates
1977	National Theatre, Abu Dhabi, United Arab Emirates
	Al Ain Public Library, United Arab Emirates

Publications:

By CHADIRJI: articles—"Rifat Chadirji," interview, by M. Ali in *Domus* (Milan), December 1983;

"The Identification of Architectural Needs in the Middle East" in *RIBA Transactions* (London), no. 2, 1983; "Regenerative Approaches to Mosque Design" in *Mimar* (Cambridge, Massachusetts), January/March 1984.

On CHADIRJI: book—*Architekten der Dritten Welt* by Udo Kultermann, Cologne 1980; articles—"Modern Arab Architecture" by W. Mason in *Building Design* (London), 21 April 1978; *Arts Review* (London), 12 May 1978; *Al-Watan Al-Arabi* (London), 20-26 May 1978; *Al Dastor* (London), 22-28 May 1978; "Modern Arab Architecture" by Konstantin Bazarov in *Art and Artists* (London), June 1978; "Contemporary Arab Architecture: The Architects of Iraq" by Udo Kultermann in *Mimar* (Cambridge, Massachusetts), July 1982; "Lessons from the East" in *Building Design* (London), 14 January 1983; "Middle Eastern Realities at RIBA" in *Architects' Journal* (London), 19 January 1983; "Architect of Baghdad: Rifat Chadirji" in *Middle East Construction* (Sutton, Surrey), January 1984.

Since 1952, I have been concerned to find an appropriate path for a modern Arab architecture. The point of departure in this search was intensive discussion between architects, painters, sculptors, and thinkers in Baghdad in the 1950s. The question was whether contemporary art and architecture should continue to be a by product of European ideas or whether it could be influenced by local environment, tradition, and materials.

I set out to learn from traditional architecture and to achieve a synthesis between traditional forms and the inevitable advent of modern technology. My aim was to create an architecture which at once acknowledges the place in which it is built, yet which sacrifices nothing to modern technical capability. At the same time I was concerned to understand analytically the reasoning behind traditional devices of environmental control such as courtyards, screen walls, natural ventilation, and reflected light.

Until 1965, my work on understanding traditional elements of Iraqi architecture led to an idiosyncratic regional modern architecture. The roots of inspiration were clearly apparent in the buildings, and yet they continued to subscribe to the European functionalist concept of form being determined by structural considerations.

Only later, in the early 1970s, again through close study of traditional buildings, did I reach the view that this connection between form and structure is not inevitable. This realization has led to increased freedom of composition and an increase in the plastic possibilities of building form.

Within the context of Arab architecture generally, I can say that my earlier search for understanding of traditional elements has had some influence on the younger generation of architects who have seen the buildings themselves or published projects.

My more recent concern is to develop further the abstraction of national and regional traditional forms—their aesthetic values—independent of the structural concept of the building. This endeavour is essential, I believe, if we are to escape the possibility that by the end of the century the whole world will be covered by a uniformly mediocre travesty of some European ideas that are now half a century old.

—Rifat Chadirji

Cities in various parts of the world used to be radically different in character, not merely because they arose out of distinctive artistic traditions but also because they were constructed out of quite different local materials. But the growing internationalism in the arts and the triumph of functionalistic modernism in architecture has meant that many once beautiful cities have had their own unique cultural identity swamped in a sea of indifferent International Style architecture. The Iraqi architect

Rifat Chadirji, since returning to his native Baghdad after studying in England, has faced this crucial dilemma of our time by gradually rediscovering the cultural and social traditions of his own country—but always in the context of the need to keep abreast of the realities of modern technology and rapid technological change. His work shows a development from the early European influence of Le Corbusier and Mies van der Rohe to his gradual rediscovery of the qualities of Iraqi traditional architecture and so to an individual style that aims to reconcile the need to use modern building technology with the cultural traditions of Iraq.

In the earliest phase of his work, from 1952 to 1962, when he was mainly designing private houses, he was still heavily under European influence, but he was already concerned with the central issue of whether contemporary art in Iraq should continue to be a byproduct of European art and how far it should respond to local environment and tradition. He was exploring those traditional approaches to environmental control, insulation, ventilation, and cool courtyards that have been highly developed in the extreme climates of the Middle East. Thus, in his Wahab residence of 1953 he exploited the possibilites of filtered light through screens and environmental control through the use of air corridors. He was also experimenting with Islamic decorative patterns and with traditional Arab architectural features such as doors, windows, balconies, and screens, to determine whether they could become elements of composition in a new modern architecture.

Chadirji's understanding of Arab tradition was greatly enhanced when from 1954 to 1957 he was head of the Building Department of Waqaf, the government body responsible for the maintenance of mosques, khans, and old houses throughout Iraq. During the 1960s he used this experience of traditional architecture to develop his own style in public buildings such as the National Insurance Company offices at Mosul, with its almost baroque use of traditional forms to make the building a sculptural entity. At this time, he was still holding to the basic functionalist doctrine of expressing the building's structure in its form. But by the 1970s he had realized, through studying the Yemeni capital city of San'aa, Iraqi village architecture, and the ancient buildings of Baghdad itself, that this doctrine of form expressing the underlying structure did not necessarily apply in traditional Arab architecture, where the sculptural treatment of volumes and surfaces is a more important factor in determining form. He has thus, since 1975, been freeing himself from functionalist dogma, a freedom that brings with it the need for a rich vocabulary of symbolic forms with which to develop a "post modern" architecture.

Chadirji's work has been a major influence on other young Arab architects from Iraq and the Gulf States, because it does explore alternatives to the standardized International Style architecture that has proliferated in the Middle East, moving towards renewed diversity and variety. And in its acknowledgement of the importance of searching beyond the bald and often brutal statements of functionalism, his work is an interesting contribution to the debate about the path recent contemporary architecture has been taking.

—Konstantin Bazarov

CHAMBERLIN POWELL AND BON.

Partnership; established, London, 1952, by Peter Chamberlin (born 1919; died 1978), Geoffrey Powell (born 1920), and Christoph Bon (born 1921); additional partner, Frank Woods. Associate company: Chamberlin, Powell and Bon (Barbican), London, established 1960; additional partner, Charles Greenburg. Recipient: Bronze Medal, Royal Institute of British Architects, 1956, 1957; Ministry of Housing and Local Government Medal, 1965; Civic Trust Commendation, 1973; RIBA Architecture Award, 1973, 1974; Concrete Society Award, London, 1983. Address: 1 Lamont Road Passage, Kings Road, London SW10 OHW, England.

Works

1955 Cooper Taber Factory, Witham, Essex
1956 Bousefield Primary School, South Kensington, London
1957 Rossdale House, 30a Hendon Avenue, London N.3
       Golden Lane Estate, Finsbury, London
1960 Two Saints Primary School, London
1962 Goswell Road Extension, London
1963 Shipley Salt Grammar School, Shipley, Yorkshire
       Henry Price Buildings, University of Leeds
1965 Vanbrugh Park Housing, Greenwich, London
       New Hall Residential College, Cambridge
1966 Physical Education Centre, University of Birmingham
       Physical Education Centre, stage II, University of Leeds
       New Hall College, phase II, Cambridge
1966/
80 The Barbican, City of London
1967 Squash Courts, New Hall College, Phase IIa, Cambridge
       Mathematics Building and Senior Common Room, University of Leeds
       Charles Morris Hall of Residence, University of Leeds
       Cheltenham Grammar School, Gloucestershire
1968 Television Centre, University of Leeds
1969 Biology Multipurpose Building, University of Leeds
       Biophysics Building, University of Leeds
       Physics Building, University of Leeds
       St. George's Fields Garden, University of Leeds
       Students Union Extension, University of Leeds
1970 Lecture Theatre Block, University of Leeds
       J. Sainsbury Shop, Folkestone, Kent
       Moravian Corner, Chelsea, London
1971 Welfare Insurance Company Building, The Leas, Folkestone, Kent
       Computer Laboratory Extension, University of Leeds
       Medical Multipurpose Building, University of Leeds
1972 Library Building, University of Leeds
       Chancellor's Court, University of Leeds
       Flats and maisonettes, 9-15 The Leas, Folkestone, Kent
1973 Offices, 69 Sandgate Road, Folkestone, Kent
1974 General Electric Technical Marketing Centre, Warrington, Lancashire,
       Physics Education Centre and School of Physiotherapy, University of Leeds
       Arts Block, University of Leeds
       Flats and maisonettes, 5-6 The Leas, Folkestone, Kent
       Houses and maisonettes, 35-37 Earls Avenue, Folkestone, Kent
1975 Undergraduate Library, University of Leeds
       Block 19, University of Leeds
1981 Napp Pharmaceutical Laboratories, Cambridge, (competition project)

Also designed modular furniture for the University of Leeds Complex, 1964-75.

Publications:

By CHAMBERLIN POWELL AND BON: reports—*Residential Development within the Barbican Area* by Peter Chamberlin and others, London 1956; *Barbican Redevelopment 1959* by Peter Chamberlin and others, London 1959; *University of Leeds Development Plan*, Leeds 1960; *Proposals for the redevelopment of central Weston-Super-Mare* by Peter Chamberlin and others, London 1961; *University of Leeds Development Plan Review 1963* by Peter Chamberlin and others, Leeds 1963; *Barbican Arts Centre 1968*, London 1968.

On CHAMBERLIN POWELL AND BON: articles—"Barbican: Metropolitan Neighbourhood" in *Bauen und Wohnen* (Zurich), April 1974; "Barbican: London's Domestic Fortress" by Will Howie in *New Civil Engineer* (London), August 1975; "New Towns: English Encampments" by Barbara Goldstein in *Progressive Architecture* (New York), July 1977; "The Right Note: Guildhall School of Music and Drama" by Joseph Boys in *Building Design* (London), November 1977; "The final stage - Barbican Arts Centre" by Brian Waters in *Building* (London), 16 June 1978; "Lecture Theatre block—University of Leeds" in *Architecture + Urbanism* (Tokyo), September 1979; "Great White Hope—Barbican Arts Centre" in *Building* (London), 29 February 1980; "Tough and Talented" by Maurice Cooper in *Building Design* (London), 19 June 1981; "Blending in at the Barbican" in *Design* (London), September 1981; "Double Allusion" by Janet Abrams in *Building Design* (London), 11 September 1981; "New Billingsgate Scheme is Unveiled" in *London Architect* (London), March 1982; "City Showpiece" by Dennis Sharp in *Building* (London), 5 March 1982.

The practice started in 1952, and from the first one of our principal interests has been the creation of places—not just buildings. With a romantic enthusiasm for the cities of Italy and the colleges of Oxford and Cambridge, we have been concerned to bring together buildings and related elements to make places with strong identities of their own. If the greater part of our work has been on large projects, this has been partly accidental; our approach is to avoid specialisation as we welcome and enjoy fresh opportunities of any size and type. In a difficult period culturally and economically we believe that architecture is still far more than a technology and that some buildings have a magic that others conspicuously lack.

—Chamberlin Powell and Bon

Urban architecture is a continuous source of disenchantment between the end user, urban man, and the creator of his environment, the architect. In winning the Barbican development Plan competition in the early 1950's, the partners of a practice that on the strength of their success became known as Chamberlin Powell and Bon, made sure of their own positive contribution of the dialogue.

Peter Chamberlin was quoted as saying of their work "that architects have to somehow pin down the aspects of living" and that "the fundamental element an architect deals with is space."

But it is in very development of wholesale areas of living, sleeping and working space by deliberate design, rather than by softer mellowing of time and change on established city settlements, that so many architects fail to appreciate the importance people place on their need to identify with their environment. High-rise urban dwellings seen from a distance at sunset may well appear aesthetically satisfying and maximize the use of space, but they fail dramatically for the old age pensioner on the sixth floor attempting to use a vandalised lift. Successful identification in urban housing must include the territory outside the immediate unit of shelter.

The Barbican is now a reality, and the innovation and excitement of the original proposal can be seen in perspective with other and later developments on a similar scale. The development will continue to be a classic example of how a particular generation dealt with the problem of urban renewal. The strength and sense of identity of the project will continue to be in its honest approach to the almost insoluble problem of creating wholesale areas of urban environment that provide areas of living space for people, rather than mere units of shelter.

—T.Q. Battle

CHAREAU, Pierre.

French. Born in Bordeaux, 3 August 1883. Studied painting, music, and architecture at the Ecole des Beaux-Arts, Paris, 1900-08. Served in the French Army, 1914-18. Married. Worked as an apprentice at Warings and Gillow Furnishings, Paris, 1908-13; in private practice as an architect and designer, Paris, 1918-40: worked with Bernard Bijvoet, 1925-35; emigrated to the United States and settled in East Hampton, Long Island, New York, 1940; practiced in New York, 1940 until his death in 1950. Founder Member, with Mallet-Stevens, Barbe, Herbst, Jourdain and Perriand, Union des Artistes Modernes, Paris, 1929. Exhibitions: *Salon d'automne*, Paris, 1919; *Salon des arts décoratifs*, Paris, 1925. *Died* (in New York) *in 1950.*

Works:

1918/
19 Dalsace Apartment interiors, rue Saint-Germain, Paris
1925 Embassy Office interiors, *Salon des arts décoratifs*, Paris
1927 Gold Club, Beauvallon, France (with Bernard Bijvoet)
1928 Hotel interiors, Tours, France
1928/
31 Dalsace House (Maison de Verre), rue St. Guillaume, Paris (with Bijvoet and Dalbet)
1931/
32 Compagnie du Téléphone Offices, Paris
1937 Djemel Anik Country House, near Paris
     Office interiors, Ministry of Foreign Affairs, Paris
     Union des Artistes Modernes Pavilion, International Exposition, Paris (with others)
1939 Soldat Colonial Foyer, Grand Palais, Paris
1940/
50 Exhibition layouts for the French Cultural Center, New York
     Library interiors, French Cultural Center, New York
     Robert Motherwell House, near New York
     "La Colline" (Monteux-Laughlin House) alterations, New York
     Chareau House, East Hampton, Long Island, New York

Publications:

By CHAREAU: book—*Meubles,* Paris 1929; article—"La Création artisique et l'imitation commerciale" in *L'Architecture d'aujourd'hui* (Paris), September 1935.

On CHAREAU: books—*Art d'Aujourd'hui,* Paris 1928; *Pierre Chareau* by René Herbst, Paris 1954; *Global Architecture 46: Maison Dalsace* by Yukio Futagawa and Fernando Montes, Tokyo 1977; articles—"A House of Glass in Paris—Architect Pierre Chareau" in *Architect and Building News* (London), 13 April 1934; "Maison d'été pour un peintre à Long-Island" in *L'Architecture d'aujourd'hui* (Paris), July 1950; "Maison de Verre" in *Werk* (Zürich), February 1965; "Maison de Verre" by Kenneth Frampton in *Arena* (London), April 1966; "La casa di verro di Pierre Chareau" by Richard Rogers in *Domus* (Milan), October 1966; "Modern Antiques: 20th Century Landmarks" by Cervin Robinson in *Architectural Forum* (New York), June 1967; "Maison de Verre" by Kenneth Frampton in *Perspecta* (New Haven, Connecticut), vol. 12, 1969; "The 1929 Paris House of Glass" in *House and Garden* (London), October 1973; "Le Corbusier, Mallet-Stevens, Chareau and Some Others" by Michel Lugnier in *Architecture française* (Paris), October 1975; "The Empty House—A Tale of Architecture" by Cecilia Polidori and Pierluigi Nicolin in *Modo* (Milan), April 1979; "A Look at Pierre Chareau—Inside the Maison de Verre" by Odile Fillion in *Architecture-Interieure-Créé* (Paris), April/May 1983; "Pierre Chareau and the Glass House" by Paolo Melis in *Domus* (Milan), June 1983; recording—*Pierre Chareau, Maison de Verre,* tape cassette by Tim Benton, Milton Keynes, Buckinghamshire 1977.

*

Like many others of his generation, Pierre Chareau had a difficult start in life. His career was interrupted in 1914 by the war; later, the economic crisis of 1929 prevented him forever from finding his own place as an architect. From then on, his field of activity was almost entirely restricted to interior decoration and furniture design. The label "decorator" attached itself and remained with him. In 1940 he emigrated to the United States, where he worked with the French Embassy, concerned more with cultural programs than with architecture. He arranged exhibitions and interiors and—unusually—built two small houses.

Chareau passed for an eccentric, but in fact his reserved and timid character hid an honest man, intransigent and totally incapable of coming to terms with error. His own curiosity was the basis of his education and of his knowledge of materials. He mastered them as if by magic. With a good team of workmen he was capable of turning iron into gold: indeed, this was the result he achieved with the Maison de Verre. For Chareau all materials were worthy of attention, as if each were rare and precious. Each detail of his construction became an object in itself which he linked with the environment, creating a space proper to itself.

As he worked primarily in the late 1920's and 1930's, Chareau remains connected with Art Deco, yet his interiors and furniture do not reveal the formalist or decadent approach characteristic of this period. We may eventually discover that the origin of his method of working and his conception of objects is to be found in the masters of Art Nouveau; this would also explain his almost instinctive ease with architecture. For Chareau, the arrangement of an interior or an exhibition, the creation of a piece of furniture or of architectonic space, comes from the same approach. All of his works result from mastery, invention, and precision that very often produce poetry.

A man of his time, Chareau admitted no compromises. Even among the group of artists with whom he was linked and worked, the Union des Artistes Modernes, Chareau remained fundamentally isolated, respected by his contemporaries but as often feared. The impression made by his Maison de Verre remained an isolated event in the French cultural debate of the 1930's: it was a period in which architects confused style with architecture. Apart from his most intimate friends—Jourdain, Paul Nelson, Herbst—the only person to have realized the value of his contribution to modern architecture was Le Corbusier, who is said to have often visited the site in the rue Guillaume.

Even the most recent criticism portrays Chareau as an "enigmatic" personality. Apart from the rediscovery of his now famous house, a rediscovery linked with a revival of interest in the years 1920-30, he has still not been given his rightful place in the history of architecture. This neglect may have something to do with the lack of a *History of Modern French Architecture,* and the "Chareau case" can, in effect, be studied as a example of the constraints upon French architectural culture in those years.

—Luciana Miotto-Muret

CHARNEY, Melvin.

Canadian. Born in Montreal, Quebec, 28 August 1935. Educated at the McGill University School of Architecture, Montreal, 1952-58 (C.P.I. Design Scholarship; A. F. Dunlop Travelling Scholarship), B.Arch. 1958; Yale University School of Architecture, New Haven, Connecticut, under Louis I. Kahn, *q.v.,* 1958-59 (W. S. McCay Fellowship), M.Arch. 1959. Married Ann Korsower in 1960; daughter: Dara. Worked for John M. Johansen, New York, 1959-61, Guillaume Gillet, Paris, 1961-62, and Victor Prus, *q.v.,* 1962-63. Since 1964, Principal of Melvin Charney, Architect, Montreal. Assistant, then Associate Professor, 1964-72, Director of the Graduate Program, 1966-70, and since 1972, Professor of Architecture, University of Montreal School of Architecture. Visiting Critic in Design, Graduate Program, University of Toronto Department of Architecture, 1968-70. Member, Architects Committee, American Academy of Arts and Sciences, 1968-69; Director, Canadian Government Task Force on the Production and Adequacy of Low-Income Housing, 1970-71. Exhibitions: *Montréal... plus ou moins,* Museum of Fine Arts, Montreal, 1972; *Canada trajectoires—'73,* Musée d'Art Moderne de la ville de Paris, 1973; *Triennale,* Milan, 1973; *Quebec '75,* National Museums of Canada, 1975; Graduate School of Design, Harvard University, Cambridge, Massachusetts, 1977; Art Gallery of Ontario, Toronto, 1978; *Melvin Charney, 1970-79,* Musée d'Art Contemporain, Montreal, 1979; P.S.1, Institute for Art and Urban Resources, New York, 1979; John Weber Gallery, New York 1979; Max Protetch Gallery, Washington, D.C., 1979; *Architectural Sculpture,* Los Angeles Institute of Contemporary Art, 1980; *Architectural References,* Vancouver Art Gallery, British Columbia, 1980; *Biennale de Paris,* Pompidou Center, Paris, 1980; *Art et société, 1975-80,* Musée du Québec, 1981; *Citysite Sculpture,* Visual Arts Ontario, Toronto, 1982; Museum of Contemporary Art, Chicago, 1982; Akademie der Künste, Berlin, 1982; *Documenta-Urbana,* Kassel, West Germany, 1982; Richard Gray Gallery, Chicago, 1982; 49th Parallel Gallery, New York, 1982; Würtembergischer Kunstverein, Stuttgart, 1983; Chicago Sculpture International, 1983; Agnes Etherington Art Center, Queen's University, Kingston, Ontario, 1983; *The Villas of Pliny,* Montreal Museum of Fine Arts, 1983; *Festarchitektur,* Nordrhein-Westfalen Akademie, Düsseldorf, West Germany, 1984; *IBA—Idee, Process, Ergebnis,* Martin Gropius Bau, Berlin, 1984. Collections: National Gallery of Canada, Ottawa; Canada Council Art Bank, Ottawa; Art Gallery of Ontario, Toronto; Agnes Etherington Art Center, Queen's University, Kingston, Ontario; Musée d'Art Contemporain, Montreal; Musée du Québec; Museum of Contemporary Art, Chicago; Recipient: Deutscher Akademischer Austauschdienst, Berliner Künstler Programm Award, 1982. Member, Royal Architectural Institute of Canada, 1963-74; Ordre des architectes du Québec, 1974; Royal Canadian Academy of Arts, 1981. Address (office): 3620 Marlowe Avenue, Montreal, Quebec H4A 3L7, Canada.

Works:

1964 Ecole Notre-Dame des Laurentides, Lac Beauport, Quebec
1967 Canadian Pavilion, *Expo '70,* Osaka, Japan (project; with J. Baracs and H. Parnass)
1969 Canadian Air Force Museum, Trenton, Ontario (project)
1976 *Corridart* (five-mile long museum-in-the-Street), 21st Olympiade, Montreal
 Les Maisons de la rue Sherbrooke, Montreal
1978 *Streetwork,* Art Gallery of Ontario, Toronto
1979 *Edifice,* Musée d'Art Contemporain, Montreal
1982 *A Chicago Construction,* Museum of Contemporary Art, Chicago
 A Toronto Construction, Visual Arts Ontario, Toronto
1983 *A Kingston Construction,* Agnes Etherington Art Centre, Queen's University, Kingston, Ontario
 Pliny on my Mind, No. 1 and No. 2, Montreal Museum of Fine Arts

Melvin Charney: Les Maisons de la rue Sherbrooke, Montreal, 1976 (exhibition project).

Publications:

By CHARNEY: books—*Pour une définition de l'architecture au Québec,* Montreal 1971; *The Adequacy and Production of Low Income Housing in Canada,* Ottawa 1972; *Melvin Charney, Oeuvres 1970-79,* exhibition catalogue, Montreal 1979; *Melvin Charney, 1981-83,* exhibition catalogue, Kingston, Ontario 1983; articles—"A Journal of Istanbul: Notes on Islamic Architecture" in *Journal of the Royal Architectural Institute of Canada* (Toronto), June 1962; "Troglai: Rock Cut Architecture" in *Landscape* (Sante Fe, New Mexico), no. 3, 1963, reprinted in *La Vie des arts* (Montreal), no. 34, 1964, and (in part) in *Caves of God* by Spiro Kostof, Cambridge, Massachusetts 1972; "The Trulli of Southern Italy" in *Landscape* (Sante Fe, New Mexico), no. 1. 1965, reprinted in *La Vie des arts* (Montreal), no. 38, 1965; "Environmental Chemistry: Design Application of Plastics Technology" in *Journal of the Royal Architectural Institute of Canada* (Toronto), May 1966; "Environmental Conjecture: In the Jungle of the Grand Prediction" in *Landscape* (Santa Fe, New Mexico), no. 3, 1967, reprinted in *Planning for Diversity and Choice,* edited by Stanford Anderson, Cambridge, Massachusetts 1969; "An Environment for Education" in *Canadian Architect* (Toronto), March 1967; "Grain Elevators Revisited" in *Architectural Design* (London), July 1967; "Naissance d'une architecture" in *Cimaise* (Paris), July 1967; "Beyond Flexibility: A Study of Education Environments" in *Architecture Canada* (Toronto), March 1968; "Concrete: A Material, a System, an Environment" in *Architecture Canada* (Toronto), June 1968; "A Self-Erecting Exhibit System" in *Architecture Canada* (Toronto), March 1969; "Experimental Strategies: Notes for Environmental Design" in *Perspecta 12* (New Haven, Connecticut), March 1969, reprinted in *Deutsche Bauzeitung* (Stuttgart), August 1969, and in Formalism, Realism, Contextualism, edited by Hajime Yatsuka, Tokyo 1979; "Memo Series: On the Liberation of Architecture" in *Artforum* (New York), May 1971; "Learning from the Wire Services" in *Architectural Design* (London), April 1974; "Understanding Montreal" in *Exploring Montreal,* edited by Pierre Beaupré and Annabel Slaight, Toronto 1974; "Dead-End Choices: Housing in Canada" in *Architectural Design* (London), April 1975; "Other Monuments: Four Works 1970-76" in *Vanguard* (Vancouver, British Columbia), March 1977; "Art as Urban Activism" in *Architectural Design* (London), July/August 1977; "Modern Movements in French Canadian Architecture" in *Process: Architecture* (Tokyo/Pittsburgh), March 1978; "Monuments Now: On Contemporary Architecture and the Avant-Garde" in *Avant-Garde: A*

History of Innovation and Invention in Architecture, Eindhoven, Netherlands 1978; "The Montrealness of Montreal: Formations and Formalities in Urban Architecture" in *Architectural Review* (London), May 1980; "Interview Two: Melvin Charney" in *Transition* (St. Kilda, Victoria), June 1981; "The City within the City" in *Domus* (Milan), July/August 1981; "On Architecture: A Statement about Statments" in *Building with Words,* edited by William Bernstein and Ruth Cawker, Toronto 1981; "A qui de droit: au sujet de l'architecture contemporaine au Québec in *Architecture/Québec* (Montreal), January/February 1982; "A Chicago Construction" in *Melvin Charney,* exhibition catalogue, by Mary Jane Jacob, Chicago 1982; "Of Temples and Sheds" in *Architecture/Québec* (Montreal), October 1983; "Signs of Recognition, Ciphers of Deception" in *Parachute* (Montreal), September 1984.

On CHARNEY: books—*The Future of Canadian Architecture* by Anthony Jackson, Halifax, Nova Scotia, 1979; *Building with Words: Canadian Architects on Architecture* by W. Bernstein and R. Cawker, Toronto 1981; *Citysite Sculpture,* exhibition catalogue, by Heather Hatch, Toronto 1982; articles—"Progretto canadese per Osaka '70" in *L'Architettura* (Rome), December 1967; "The Real Housing Report" by Sara Berger in *Canadian Dimension* (Toronto), 1972; "Melvin Charney" by Normand Thériault in *Québec '75,* Montreal 1975; "Megacity Montreal" in *Megastructures: Urban Futures of the Recent Past* by Reyner Banham, New York 1976; "Corridart: Instant Archeology in Montreal" by Dale McConathy in *Artscanada* (Toronto), July/August 1976; "Les Maisons de la rue Sherbrooke" in *Process: Architecture* (Tokyo/Pittsburgh), March 1978; "Melvin Charney" by Chantal Pontbriand in *Parachute* (Montreal), December 1978; "Art: The New Work" by John Russell in the *New York Times,* 8 June 1979; "Melvin Charney ou l'illusion de la preuve" by Johanne Lamoureux in *Parachute* (Montreal), Winter 1979; "Melvin Charney: Constructs and Concepts" by Gerald Needham in *Artscanada* (Toronto), April/May 1980; "Melvin Charney ou les traces d'une mémoire collective" by Claudette Hould in *Vie des arts* (Montreal), Spring 1980; "AR Canada," special issue of *Architectural Review* (London), May 1980; "The Inside Picture from the Outside" by Lucy Lippard in *Architectural Sculpture,* exhibition catalogue, Los Angeles 1980; "Melvin Charney" by Lucius Burkhardt in *Werk und Zeit* (Berlin), April

1981; "Form Follows Form—Pictures by Architects" by Babs Shapiro in *Trace 1, 2* (Toronto), April 1981; "Melvin Charney" by Ian McDougall and Kathy Peake in *Transition 2* (Melbourne), June 1981; "Contro l'International Style" by Eugenio Battisti in *Casa del libro* (Rome), January 1982; "Architecture in Canada," special issue of *Bauwelt* (Berlin), 3 December 1982; "Corridart, Montreal" by William Bernstein and Ruth Cawker in *Contemporary Canadian Architecture,* Toronto 1982; "To Build a House in Paradise" by Bill Hutchison in *Whig-Standard Magazine* (Toronto), 16 March 1983; "Melvin Charney—Architectural Sculpture" by Virginia Nixon in *Canadian Forum* (Toronto), May 1983; "Melvin Charney" by Bruce Grenville in *Parachute* (Montreal), November 1983; "Contradictions of Preservation and Destruction" by Kurt W. Forster in *Architext* (Cambridge, Massachusetts), December 1983.

The kind of architecture I do is involved in two areas of activity outside the sphere of traditional "office" practice. The first is the creation of autonomous works of architecture which delve into experimentation with the iconography of built form and with the symbolic nature of architecture. This work has evolved from projects based on the use of ready-made parts of buildings and found typologies; to the use of images found in the popular press in the creation of "monuments"; to the creation of constructions and drawings which are sited in and intervene upon urban and historic situations, so as to engage both the underlying structure of built objects found in these situations and the figural representations of potential archetypal constructs. Much of this work is published and exhibited. The second and complementary aspect of the work is the research, teaching, and writing on critical themes in contemporary architecture, particularly on formative processes in the representation of buildings and of the city as architecture, and on the relationship of built form to social processes.

—Melvin Charney

The general territory of contemporary Canadian architecture may be seen to be limited by two extreme forms of professional practice. On the one extreme, one finds a mode of commercial practice that raises programmatic expediency to a very high order; the practitioners now find themselves in demand from a commercial clientele not only in Canada but also around the world. On the other extreme, one finds a poetic—sometimes even mystical—mode of practice, the adherents of which are elevated to the rank of acclaimed national gurus by the media of this country. Needless to say, most architectural activity in Canada proceeds within the vast territory that lies between these two extremes, but the majority of practitioners who occupy that middle ground continue to find themselves less successful than their more commercially oriented fellow-practitioners and less well recognized than the celebrated poets of the media. What is perhaps less evident to the world at large is that the sad tendency of Canadian architecture to polarize in this fashion has prevented much architecture of world rank from being created in Canada in recent years.

No one has challenged the resultant poverty of architectural praxis in this country with more acumen than has the Montreal architect, artist, and theorist Melvin Charney. In 1970, Charney challenged the assumptions of the architectural establishment in his submission to the competition for an Air Force Memorial for Trenton, Ontario. Refusing to meet the programme requirement for a "Memorial Hall of History," Charney proposed instead to organize a decentralized cross-Canada network of existing buildings and objects, many of which have played a crucial role in the training of personnel and in the development of machinery for flight. Since 1970, Charney has moved further and further away from any address to the norms of conventional architectural practice, turning instead to a new role in which his chief forums for intervention have been the art gallery and the street. In 1973, for example, he organized the exhibition *Montréal . . . plus ou moins* at the Montreal Museum of Fine Arts, incorporating within the walls of the museum for the first time a vast array of heterogeneous—often almost dada—fragments of "everyday life" in Montreal. In 1978 Charney showed "Six Other Monuments" at the Art Gallery of Ontario. The two most significant of these were *Le Trésor de Trois Rivières* and *Streetwork*. The first is a modest, but highly charged house facade which Charney had admired, which had been subsequently demolished, and which Charney reconstituted in an extensive series of modes—photographs, drawings, and models. The second, created especially for the Toronto show, consisted of a "wall," which in an arrested process of erection/dismantling figuratively penetrated the gallery from outside to inside.

By far the most important of Charney's recent interventions occurred in the street. This was *Corridart*, the collective work he organized along five miles of Sherbrooke Street in Montreal during the 1976 Olympics. *Corridart* constituted a striking transformation of this major street into an instant history of itself and into a series of appropriations of its contemporary reality. Large metal scaffoldings displayed historical episodes of the street's history, giant hands pointed to elements of major but unappreciated significance along its length. Some dozen other artists contributed a range of icons of Sherbrooke Street's contemporary reality to its overall sequence of street events. Perhaps as a reward for Charney's all-too-acute perception of the reality of architectural praxis in Canada, *Corridart* was destroyed in its entirety by orders of the Mayor of the City of Monreal.

Some of Charney's admirers have been concerned, in the wake of the 1978 show, by what appears to be a discernible new tendency in his activities, a tendency that might be characterized as a retreat to the gallery and, within the gallery, as a retreat from forms to texts. But it has to be said that this perceived "retreat" must be viewed reciprocally with the territory of feasible architectural praxis in Canada today. To the extent that Charney's recent "retreat" is a real one, it mirrors the difficulties encountered by any practitioner making any primary commitment to architecture as cultural praxis in this country.

—George Baird

CHERMAYEFF, Serge Ivan.

American. Born in Grosny Azerbaijan, Caucasus, Russia, 8 October 1900; emigrated to England, 1910: naturalized, 1928; emigrated to the United States, 1939: naturalized, 1946. Educated privately in Moscow; at Peterborough Lodge Preparatory School, Hampstead, London, 1910-13; Royal Drawing Society School, London, 1910-13; Harrow School, 1914-17 (scholarship; Yates Thompson Prizes); studied art and architecture at various schools in Germany, Austria, France, and the Netherlands, 1922-25. Married Barbara Maitland in 1928; sons: the graphic artist Ivan Chermayeff and the architect Peter Chermayeff (*See* CAMBRIDGE SEVEN ASSOCIATES). Worked as a journalist for the Amalgamated Press, London, 1918-23; Chief Designer for the decorators E. Williams Ltd., London, 1924-27; Director of the Modern Art Development, Waring and Gillow, London, 1928-29; in private architectural practice, London, 1930-32; in partnership with Eric Mendelsohn, *q.v.,* London, 1933-36; in private practice, London, 1937-39, San Francisco, 1940-41, and in New York, 1942-46; Professor of Architecture and Chairman of the Department of Design, Brooklyn College, New York, 1942-46; President and Director of the Institute of Design, Chicago, 1946-51; Lecturer, Massachusetts Institute of Technology, Cambridge, 1951-52; Professor of Architecture, Harvard Graduate School of Design, Cambridge, Massachusetts, 1953-62; Professor of Architecture, 1962-71, and since 1971 Emeritus Professor, Yale University School of Architecture, New Haven, Connecticut; Gropius Lecturer, Harvard University, Cambridge, Massachusetts, 1974. Consultant on Planning, Architecture and Industrial Design, Museum of Modern Art, New York, 1942-47; Member, Editorial Board, American Federation of Art, 1942-47; Consultant, Chicago Plan Commission, 1946-48. Founder, 1942, and Member of the Executive Council, 1942-47, American Society of Planners and Architects. Exhibitions: *First London Exhibition of Art,* 1929; *White City Exhibition,* London, 1936; *Whiteley's Housing Exhibition,* London, 1936; *Tommorrow's Small House,* Museum of Modern Art, New York, 1945; *Chicago Planning Exhibition,* 1949. Recipient: Gold Medal, Royal Canadian Institute of Architects, 1974. D.F.A.: MacMurray College, Jacksonville, Illinois, 1946; Washington University, St. Louis, 1964. Fellow, Royal Institute of British Architects, Royal Society of Arts, London, and the American Institute of Architects. Address: Box NN, Wellfleet, Massachusetts 02667, U.S.A.

Works:

1929 Ambrose Wilson Ltd. office interiors, Vauxhall Bridge Road, London
1930 Chermayeff House interiors, London
       Chermayeff Office interiors, 173 Oxford Street, London
       Cambridge Theatre interiors, Seven Dials, London (with Wimperis, Simpson and Guthric)
1931 Venesta Plywood Company Exhibition Stand, *Building Trades Exhibition,* Olympia, London (competition project)
1932 British Broadcasting Corporation interiors, Broadcasting House, London
       English Country House (project)
       A. G. Gibbons Grinling Flat interiors, London
1933 "Kernal" House Prototypes and Exercise Court, *British Industrial Art Exhibtion,* Dorland Hall, London
1934 House in reinforced concrete, Rugby, Warwickshire
       Living Room, *Contemporary Industrial Design in the Home* exhibition, Dorland Hall, London
       British Broadcasting Corporation interiors,

Broadcasting House, Birmingham, England
       Corset showrooms, Regent Street, London
1935 Workingmen's flats (competition project; with Helsby-Hamann-Samuely, and Cyril Sweet and J. Stinton-James)
       House, Chalfont St. Giles, Buckinghamshire (with Eric Mendelsohn)
       Flat interiors, 42 Upper Brook Street, London
       Hotel, Southsea, Hampshire (project; with Eric Mendelsohn)
       de la Warr Pavilion, Bexhill-on-Sea, Sussex (with Eric Mendelsohn)
1936 House, Frinton Park, Essex (with Eric Mendelsohn)
       White City Housing Development, London (project; with Eric Mendelsohn)
       House, 64 Old Church Street, Chelsea, London (with Eric Mendelsohn)
       Music Room, *Piano Exhibition,* Dorland Hall, London
1937 Gilbey House Office Building, James Street and Oval Road, Camden Town, London
       Flat interiors, Connaught Place, London
1938 Chermayeff House, Bentley, near Halland, Sussex
       Imperial Chemical Industries Research Laboratories, Blackley, Manchester
       Imperial Chemical Industries Offices and Works Canteen, Huddersfield, Yorkshire (project)
       Ciro Jewelry Shop, 48 Old Bond Street, London
1939 Government evacuation camps, England (with others)
1941 Walter Horn House, Richmond, California
       Park-Type Apartments, New York (exhibition project; with Black and Sorensen, and Fletcher and Hebbeln)
       Revere Copper and Brass Company Nursery School (project)
1945 Neighborhood Development and Community Buildings, *Tomorrow's Small House* exhibition, Museum of Modern Art, New York (with others)
1946 House, Piedmont, California
       Duplex flat interiors, New York
       Studio, New York (with Konrad Wachsmann)
1947 House, Redwood, California
1948 Ciro of Bond Street Store, San Francisco (with Raphael Soriano)
1950 British Railways Offices, Rockefeller Center, New York (with Ketchum, Gina and Sharpe)
1952 Chermayeff Studio, Wellfleet, Massachusetts
       Cottage interior renovations, Chermayeff Compcund, Wellfleet, Massachusetts
1953 Sigerson Cottage, Wellfleet, Massachusetts
       Herbert Payson, Jr. House, Portland, Maine
1954 Wilkinson Cottage, Wellfleet, Massachusetts
       Cape Codder Newspaper Plant, Orleans, Massachusetts
1956 Weekend House, Flato, Massachusetts (with Heyward Cutting)
       Edwin O'Connor House, Wellfleet, Massachusetts
1957 Harvard Prototype Houses, Cambridge, Massachusetts (project)
1962 Chermayeff House, 28 Lincoln Street, New Haven, Connecticut
1963/
64 Courtyard House, New Haven, Connecticut (project; with Christopher Alexander)
1972 Chermayeff Studio II, Wellfleet, Massachusetts

Numerous exhibition and furniture designs, 1928-49

Publications:

By CHERMAYEFF: books—*Colour and its Application to Modern Building* (pamphlet), London 1936;

Serge Chermayeff: Chermayeff House, Bentley, near Halland, Sussex, 1938.

Plan for A.R.P.: A Practical Policy (pamphlet), London 1939; *Report on the Future Development of Diamond K. Ranch,* Cambridge, Massachusetts 1955; *The Shape of Privacy,* Cambridge, Massachusetts 1961; *Community and Privacy;* with Christopher Alexander, New York 1963, Tokyo and London 1966, Buenos Aires 1967, Paris and Stuttgart 1972; *Advanced Studies in Urban Environments,* with Alexander Tzonis, New Haven, Connecticut 1967; *Synopsis of Conclusions and Record of Progress: The Chermayeff Studio,* edited by W. Mitchell, New Haven, Connecticut 1969; *The Shape of Community,* with Alexander Tzonis, New York 1970, London 1971; *Verse of Anger and Affection, 1957-1973* Orleans, Massachusetts 1973; *Design and the Public Good: Selected Writings 1930-1970,* edited by Richard Plunz, Cambridge, Massachusetts 1982; articles—"A New Spirit and Idealism" in *Architects' Journal* (London), 4 November 1931; "Film Shots in Germany with Notes on the Film" in *Architectural Review* (London), November 1931; "The Modern Approach to Architecture and its Equipment" in *Architects' Journal* (London), 8 March 1933; "The Grammar of Groundwork" in *Architectural Review* (London), October 1933; "A Hundred Years Ahead: Forecasting the Coming Century" in *Architects' Journal* (London), 10 January 1935; "Modern Art and Architecture" in *RIBA Journal* (London), 9 January 1937; "Circulation: Design: Display" in *Architectural Record* (New York), September 1937; "Telesis: The Birth of a Group" in *Pencil Points* (New York), July 1942; "Art and the Industrial

Designer" in *Magazine of Art* (New York), February 1945; "Structure and the Esthetic Experience" in *Magazine of Art* (New York), May 1946; "Education for Modern Design" in *College Art Journal* (New York), no. 3, 1947; "L'Architecture au 'Bauhause' de Chicago" in *Architecture d'aujourd'hui* (Paris), February 1950; "How Designers See Themselves" in *Print* (New York), January 1967; "Thinking Before Acting" in *AIA Journal* (Washington, D.C), April 1980; recording—*Environmental Design Is Our Task,* tape cassette and slides, London 1980.

On CHERMAYEFF: books—*20th Century Houses* by Raymond McGrath, London 1934; *The House: A Machine for Living In* by Anthony Bertram, London 1935; *New Research Laboratories, Manchester* (ICI pamphlet), London 1938; *Projects and Theories of Serge Chermayeff* by Richard Plunz, Cambridge, Massachusetts 1972; *Thirties: British Art and Design Before the War,* exhibition catalogue, by A. J. P. Taylor, Ian Jeffrey and others, London 1979; *Contemporary Designers,* edited by Ann Lee Morgan, New York and London 1984; articles—"Bexhill Entertainment Hall Competition" in *Builder* (London), 9 February 1934; "Working Details: BBC Studios, Birmingham" in *Architects' Journal* (London), 23 February 1934; "House at Rugby Designed by Serge Chermayeff" in *Architects' Journal* (London), 19 April 1934; "House at Chalfont St. Giles" in *Architectural Review* (London), November 1935; "The de la Warr Pavilion, Bexhill" in *Builder*

(London), 20 December 1935; "Leisure at the Seaside" in *Architectural Review* (London), July 1936; "Two Houses in Church Street, Chelsea" in *Architects' Journal* (London), 24 December 1936; "Gilbey House, Camden Town" in *Architectural Review* (London), July 1937; "Research Laboratories, Manchester" in *RIBA Journal* (London), 7 March 1938; "Offices and Factories" in *Architectural Design and Construction* (London), June 1938; "House near Halland, Sussex" in *Architects' Journal* (London), 16 February 1939; "Trends in Shop Construction" in *Architectural Design* (London), May 1939; "Profile: Serge Chermayeff" in *Aufbau* (Vienna), September 1957; "Time and Chermayeff" in *Architectural Review* (London), June 1960; "Perspective: In Hampstead in the 30s" in *Building Design* (London), 17 January 1975; "Technology in the 1930's" by Alvin Howard in *Building Design* (London), 8 October 1976; "Chermayeff Wins Memorial Medal" in *Architects' Journal* (London), 1 October 1980; "Chermayeff: Ahead of His Time" in *Architects' Journal* (London), 15 October 1980; "Serge Chermayeff" in *The Designer* (London) December 1980.

*

During my lifetime, entirely and precisely of this century, I have witnessed a series of events in my chosen field announcing profound change. I have seen Eclectic Architecture respectfully buried. I have observed, with some pleasure, that the mythical beast "International Style" did not rise from the ashes of

World War II. I have seen with deep chagrin the anarchic, fashionable western shapes confront the dull paraphernalia of western commerce in cities, and even in remote islands, all over the world. Embassies, universities, hospitals, housing, offices, and factories—Western Buildings without rhyme or reason, interlopers in cultures, places, economies, and climates unable to accommodate them.

I hope that our "Shape-Makers" will, like old soldiers or the Cheshire Cat, fade away along with their "creations". I hope to see these replaced by "Problem-Solvers." I hope to see an "International Space Agency" established for here below. I continue to believe that artistic independence is not a myth. I am therefore confident that the beauty of nature and art will join the elegance of science in a new amalgam. And I feel that once this is achieved, this new excellence will be recognized.

—Serge Chermayeff

Serge Chermayeff, born in Russia in 1900, emigrated to England at the age of ten and received his formal education in architecture in that country. Notable among his first achievements in the profession were the projects designed in collaboration with Eric Mendelsohn between 1933 and 1936. Chermayeff's work in England was at the forefront of modern architecture in the 1920s and 1930s and gave the country some of its first International Style buildings. In 1939 Chermayeff and his family moved to America where his interests expanded more deeply into the field of education. In addition to an active professional practice, Chermayeff has taught and/or served as director at Brooklyn College, the Institute of Design in chicago, Harvard University, The Massachusetts Institute of Technology, and Yale University—a total of twenty-nine years of active involvement with architectural education in this country.

Chermayeff is also known for his writings. In 1963 he wrote *Community and Privacy* with Christopher Alexander. As a response to their concerns over basic social problems in architecture, the book proposed criteria for urban housing generated from a necessary balance of public and private spaces. Chermayeff's concern involves a broad range of levels from urban to a domestic scale, all based on the assumption that a more meaningful architecture can be created through utilizing the contrast inherent in the public/private dichotomy, a balance between individual privacy and the possibilities for communal interaction.

The same theme is again addressed in *The Shape of Community*, written with Alexander Tzonis in 1970. The focus of this book is the problem of urban design, and the authors provide a theoretical model for contemporary and future urban planning. Again, the basic premise concerns the social and formal need for public gathering places to be provided in conjunction with elements of privacy. The movement between spaces in an urban environment is given great emphasis as the basis for communication. In any concept of "community," communication by definition becomes one of the dominating features of urban life. Chermayeff considers an understanding of, and the design potential in, these communication networks to be a prime issue in architecture and planning on an urban scale.

His philosophy, however, is applicable to small-scale projects as well. In 1962 Chermayeff built his own house in New Haven as a prototypical example of his ideas about residential living. The house is arranged as a series of one-storey pavilions and courtyards. This pattern of open and closed spaces is an attempt to provide a physical separation between private and communal functions in the house. As a prototype, the house provides an economical solution to domestic programs.

Chermayeff's own studio and guest house on Cape Cod (1952) is another example of his interest in simple, contexual architectural forms. The design

was developed on a modular geometry, for ease of construction. The materials and architectural elements are borrowed from the vernacular of traditional New England architecture. The sense of order created by this type of construction is very similar to that of the repetitive structure and bay system so integral to the International Style and to the work of Mies van der Rohe in particular.

It could be said the Chermayeff's work and attitudes are a direct result of his belief in functional planning and of his sense of social responsibility.

—S. Fiske Crowell, Jr.

CHURCH, Thomas Dolliver.

American. Born in Boston, Massachusetts, 27 April 1902. Educated at Berkeley High School, California, 1914-18; University of California, Berkeley, 1918-23, B.A. Landscape Arch. 1923; Harvard Graduate School of Landscape Architecture, Cambridge, Massachusetts, 1924-26, M.S. 1926; awarded Sheldon Travel Scholarship, 1926-27. Married Elizabeth Roberts in 1930; daughters: Judith and Belinda. Assistant Professor of Landscape Architecture, Ohio State University, Columbus, 1927-29, and University of California, Berkeley, 1929-30; Landscape Architect for Pasatiempo Estates, Santa Cruz, California, 1930-32; Principal of Thomas D. Church and Associates, San Francisco, 1933 until his death in 1978. Consultant Landscape Architect, Stanford University, Palo Alto, 1957-77, and University of California at Berkeley and Santa Cruz, 1959-77. Recipient: Fine Arts Medal, American Institute of Architects, 1951; Oakleigh Thorne Medal, Garden Club of America, 1969; Honor Award, 1971, and Gold Medal, 1976, American Society of Landscape Architects; Citation for Outstanding Contributions, American Horticultural Society, 1974. Honorary Fellow, American Institute of Interior Designers, 1970; Fellow, American Academy of Arts and Sciences, 1978. *Died* (in San Francisco) *30 August 1978.*

Works:

Approximately 2,000 private gardens throughout the United States, 1930-77, and landscape design for:
1935 War Memorial Opera House Garden Court, San Francisco
1941/
50 Park Merced, San Francisco
1945 General Motors Research Center, Detroit
1946 El Panama Hotel, Panama City
Des Moines Art Center, Iowa
1958 Stanford Medical Center, Palo Alto, California
Stuart Pharmaceutical Company, Pasadena, California
1961 Master plan for the University of California, Berkeley
1963 *Sunset Magazine* Gardens, Menlo Park, California
Master plan for the University of California at Santa Cruz
Strybing Arboretum Home Demonstration Gardens, Golden Gate Park, San Francisco
Master plan for Harvey Mudd College, Claremont, California
1964 Caterpillar Tractor Company, Peoria, Illinois
1965 Master plan for Stanford University, Palo Alto, California
1969 Master plan for Scripps College, Claremont, California

Publications:

By CHURCH: books—*Gardens Are for People*, New York 1955; *Your Private World; A Study of Intimate Gardens*, San Francisco 1969; articles—in *Arts and Architecture* (Los Angeles), May 1932, May 1933, April 1934, June 1935; in *House Beautiful* (New York), July 1944, January 1948, July 1948, October 1948, January 1949, October 1952, April 1955, September 1955, May 1957; in the *New York Times*, 9 January 1966; in *Horticulture* (Boston), October 1967; numerous articles in *Bonanza*, Sunday magazine of the *San Francisco Chronicle* from the late 1950s to the early 1960s.

On CHURCH: books—*Landscape Gardening* by James Underwood Crockett, New York 1971; *Designs on the Land* by Norman T. Newton, Cambridge, Massachusetts 1971; *A History of Landscape Architecture* by G. B. Tobey, New York 1973; *The Art of Thomas Dolliver Church*, thesis by Pam-Anela Messenger, University of California, Berkeley 1976; *80 Years of Ideas and Pleasure from House and Garden*, edited by Mary Jane Pool, New York 1980; articles—in *Sunset* (Menlo Park, California), April 1935, February 1937, June 1941, May 1942, June 1946; in *Pencil Points* (New York), May 1941, January 1944, June 1944; in *House Beautiful* (New York), March 1948, May 1961, February 1964, November 1967, September 1969; in *Better Homes and Gardens* (Des Moines, Iowa), April 1948; in *Architectural Forum* (New York), April 1951; in *Landscape Design and Construction* (Elm Grove, Wisconsin), March 1964; "Thomas Church and the Evolution of the California Garden" by Michael Laurie in *Landscape Design* (London), February 1973; "Thomas D. Church: His Role in American Landscape Architecture" by P. A. Messenger in *Landscape Architecture* (Louisville, Kentucky), March 1977; "Thomas Church" in *San Francisco Chronicle* (San Francisco), 1 September 1978; "University of California, Santa Cruz" in *AIA Journal* (Washington, D.C.), August 1979; "Reflections on Tommy church and His Gardens" by Joseph E. Howland in *Landscape Architecture* (Louisville, Kentucky), July 1981.

Bibliographies—*Thomas D. Church, Landscape Architect* by Mary Vance, Monticello, Illinois 1980; *Bibliography: Thomas Dolliver Church* by Pam-Anela Messenger, Monticello, Illinois 1981.

Gardens are for people. In every case, they should please and serve the people who live in them.

The only limit to your garden is at the boundaries of your imagination.

Your entrance should say "Welcome," and the steps should be an invitation.

Landscaping is not a complex and difficult art to be practised only by high priests. It is logical, down-to-earth, and aimed at making your plot of ground produce exactly what you want and need from it.

The site may be a garden in the true sense of providing trees and flowers, fruits and vegetables; it should be a place where man can recapture his affinity with the soil, if only on Saturday afternoons. It must be a green oasis where memories of his bumper-to-bumper ride from work will be erased.

The direction in which to move will be determined by the desires of the people who expect to find happiness in their gardens. Happiness will come by adding as much beauty and by eliminating as many irritations as possible within the limits of the problem. The limits of the problem will be the restrictions and opportunities of the site and the ability of the owner and designer to overcome or make use of them.

No definite style of gardening from the past will answer all the needs ot today's small garden. Many old gardens do help us, however, to understand the underlying principles of building gardens for maximum enjoyment. There were the smart town gardens

Thomas Church: Wagner Garden, Tacoma, Washington, 1967.

of Pompeii, the courtyards of Spain, the walled flower gardens of Queen Elizabeth and Henry VIII. They all contribute to our knowledge of scale and livability as applied to the areas surrounding the house. This is a new era in garden-making because, while many things have entered our life to make the problem complex, our ideas and requirements tend toward simplicity of solution.

To weigh, advise, interpret, integrate, and come up with some answers beyond the ability and imagination of the layman is the role of the landscape architect.

—Thomas D. Church (1978)

Thomas D. Church began his professional career in San Francisco in the 1930s after conventional Beaux Arts training at the University of California at Berkeley and the Harvard Graduate School of Design. The timing coincided with a rapidly changing social context in California and a revolution in art and architecture on an international scale. By the 1950s, Church had become one of the leading landscape architects in the United States, working on large commercial and institutional projects with eminent architects of the modern movement, including Eero Saarinen and Edward Durell Stone. But the bulk of his practice was at the domestic scale, and it was on garden design that his reputation was based.

His sensitivity to historical precedent, the environ-

ment of California, the changing lifestyle and values of his clients, together with a mind receptive to new concepts in art and architecture, brought to his early work unique forms and new spatial qualities. His best gardens seem to be natural products of time and place and reflect the changes in taste and attitude already growing and requiring to be given form. These gardens not only fall into the realm of fine art but also represent an important milestone in the evolution of the modern garden and landscape architecture.

Locally, Church associated with young modern architects of the Bay Area (William Wurster, Gardener Daily, Ernest Born and others) and together, for adventurous clients, they produced integrated houses and gardens based on the new aesthetic and designed for California living. The ratio of house to garden was frequently high, and the automobile further contributed to a reduction of useable garden space for the average home owner.

Church's designs to accommodate the increasing use of small gardens by families and the need to reduce maintenance included hard surfaces and ground cover planting, screens to separate areas and provide privacy, techniques and illusions to increase apparent size, and shapes suited to topography, function, and upkeep. The combination of this relatively new design problem, the small garden, with the new approach to form resulted in a major breakthrough for landscape architecture. While

satisfying all practical criteria, the central axis was abandoned in favor of a multiplicity of viewpoints. Simple planes and flowing lines, texture and color, space and form, were manipulated in a manner reminiscent of the cubist painters. Not only did the gardens that Church designed in the late 1930s look different, they also represented a new and improved way of dealing with landscape design at any scale. Each design derived form and uniqueness from careful appraisal and analysis of the site, from the architecture of the house, and from the client's personality and preferences.

Historical precedent was not rejected by Church. In fact, his work drew strength from an appreciation of good design of whatever age and an understanding of the present as it evolves out of the past. Church had an exceptional ability to translate a client's requirements into a logical and intelligent plan, which at the same time derived specific quality from the surrounding environment. His deep understanding of the California landscape, its tradition and history, and of the life style and values of his clients, makes his work, albeit for a small section of society, a logical part in its evolution.

Church had an enormous influence on modern landscape architecture as it evolved in the postwar years in the United States, and his office nurtured many young landscape architects who are now leaders in the profession.

—Michael Laurie

CIAMPI, Mario Joseph.

American. Born in San Francisco, California, 27 April 1907. Educated at the Night College of the San Francisco Architectural Club, 1927-29; Harvard University Graduate School of Design, Cambridge, Massachusetts, 1930-32; Beaux-Arts Institute of Design, Paris, summers 1932-33. Married Loretta Keane in 1939 (died, 1972). Draftsman, office of Alexander Cantin and Dodge A. Riedy, San Francisco, 1927-29; Associate Architect, office of Dodge A. Riedy, San Francisco, 1932-38. Since 1945, Principal, Mario J. Ciampi and Associates, San Francisco. Design Critic, San Francisco Architectural Club, 1935-40. Urban Design Consultant, San Francisco Market Street Development Plan, since 1963, and San Francisco Yerba Buena Project, since 1971. Member of the Board of Trustees, San Francisco Art Institute; Member of the Board of Regents, St. Mary's College, Moraga, California; Member of the Board of Directors, Museo Italiano, San Francisco Art Academy. Recipient: Collaborative Medal of Honor, Architectural League of New York, 1960; First Prize, University of California Arts Center Competition, 1965; Albert John Evers Environmental Award, 1972; Supervisors Award, County and City of San Francisco, 1973; San Francisco Art Festival Award, 1974. D.F.A.: California School of Arts and Crafts, Oakland, 1980. Fellow, American Institute of Architects. Address: Mario J. Ciampi and Associates, 617 Front Street, San Francisco, California 94111, U.S.A.

Works:

1950 War Memorial Community Center, 6655 Mission Street, Daly City, California
1953 Vista Grande Elementary School, Wyandotte Avenue and Thiers Street, Daly City, California
1954 Olympia Primary School, 200 Northgate Avenue, Daly City, California
1955 Westlake Elementary School, Daly City, California
1956 Garden Village Elementary School, 208 Garden Lane, Daly City, California
      House, 760 Chiltern Road, Hillsborough, California (with Germano Milano)
1957 Pauline Margaret Brown Elementary School, 305 Eastmoor Avenue, Daly City, California
      Olympia Primary School addition, 200 Northgate Avenue, Daly City, California
1958 Westmoor High School, 131 Westmoor Avenue, Daly City, California
1959 Vista Mar Elementary School, 725 Southgate Avenue, Daly City, California
1960 Fernando Riviera Elementary School, 101 Lake Merced Boulevard, Daly City, California
1962 Master plan for downtown San Francisco
1963 Embarcadero Plaza, phase I, San Francisco (with Lawrence Halprin and John S. Bolles)
1964 Oceana High School, Pacifica, California
      Jefferson High School District Master Plan, for Pacifica, Brisbane, and Daly City, California
      St. Peter's Roman Catholic Church, 700 Oddstad Way, Pacifica, California
1965 Development plan for St. Mary's College, Moraga, California
1966 Study of the Panhandle and Golden Gate Freeway, San Francisco (as urban consultant)
1967 Newman Center and Chapel, University of California, Berkeley
1967/
74 Site selection study, for the State College of San Mateo/Santa Clara Counties, California
1968 Market Street Development Plan, San Francisco (with John Carl Warnecke and Associates)

Humanities Complex, San Francisco State College
1970 University Art Museum, University of California, Berkeley
1971 Menlo Circus Club, Atherton, California (project)
      Ferry Park, San Francisco (phase II of the Embarcadero Plaza)
1971/
74 Market Street reconstruction, San Francisco (with Lawrence Halprin and John Carl Warnecke)
1972 Tennis Center, Olympic Club, San Francisco (project)
1973 Powell Plaza, Powell, Eddy, and Market Streets, San Francisco (with Lawrence Halprin and John Carl Warnecke)
      Office Building Complex, West San Mateo, California (project)
1974 Seton Provincial House, Los Altos Hills, California
      Development plan for Pier 45, Fisherman's Wharf, San Francisco
      Master plan for Parking Center, Embarcadero Park, San Francisco
1975 Performing Arts Theatre, San Francisco (project)
1980 North Waterfront Port Commission Plan, San Francisco

Publications:

On CIAMPI: articles—"University Arts Center" in *Arts and Architecture* (Los Angeles), October 1965; "UC Shows Art Center Plans" by Alexander Fried in *San Francisco Examiner*, 5 January 1966; "Three New Museums" by Peter Selz and Spiro Kostof in *Art in America* (New York), January/February 1968; "The Great Museum Debate" by C. Ray Smith in *Progressive Architecture* (New York), December 1969; "An Art Museum Designed for the Campus" in *Architectural Record* (New York), July 1972; "Embarcadero Plaza, San Francisco" in *Architecture + Urbanism* (Tokyo), August 1973; "Barley to Blueprints" in *Interiors* (New York), September 1973.

*

By the early 1950s, California's post war expansion was in full flood: the state's population was increasing by 5,000 people a week, mostly accommodated in the new suburbs of the San Francisco Bay Area and the Los Angeles Basin. Bay Area Region architecture had achieved recognition as an identifiable style, continuing the material and craft traditions of half a century earlier but reinterpreting forms and spaces for the culture of the 1950s. Brilliantly successful in responding to and forming the lifestyle of the Bay Area's cultured upper middle class, the style—and its creators—struggled to find as comfortable an expression for its institutions, its schools, universities, and city halls. Where these works could be interpreted at the residential scale, there were some successes, but, as state expansion continued, the size of building programs destroyed the fiction that such works could be designed as if they were houses.

During this period, Mario Ciampi executed a series of public buildings that put the San Francisco suburbs of Daly City and Pacifica on the architectural tour map. As architect for the local school district, Ciampi designed—and, more remarkable, had built—a series of schools that replaced the current idiom of wood frame and pink stucco with one of bright hard materials—steel and ceramic tile—and forms such as concrete folded plates that, at the time, were more familiar in Europe and Brazil than in San Francisco.

These buildings showed promise of a sophistication and world reference that were missing in a Bay Area architecture already become cozy and self satisfied with small-scale triumphs. Westmoor High School in Daly City was a cheerful version of a 2,000-

student loft-plan high school, a huge one-story warehouse penetrated by courts, its gymnasium roofed with a rippling shell, its walls enlivened by bright paint and ceramic color. Oceana High School in Pacifica opposed a square space framed gymnasium by a huge crescent of concrete and glass classrooms. St. Peter's Roman Catholic Church, also in Pacifica, brought a whiff of Brasilia to this raw and foggy oceanside suburb.

This flurry of activity and hope lasted about fifteen years. Ciampi's attempt to insert color and excitement into the local school environment failed, stifled by the grim humourlessness of the educational establishment, and he was replaced by an anonymous hack. Ciampi went on to execute one other work of great interest, the Art Museum of the University of California in Berkeley. This monolithic concrete building, with its linked, fan-shaped galleries stepping up to form a single exhibition space of great vitality, unfortunately shows the weakness of an exterior that is allowed to happen as a result of the interior.

In fact, Ciampi's work must be evaluated as placed uncomfortably in a middle range: too sophisticated for his clients, yet too casual and glib in its acceptance of fashionable forms and materials to have the staying power of the work of the more meticulous craftsmen of his generation. But his work cheered us up a lot in its time, and, as the Bay Area style never did find a way to do public buildings, Ciampi's defects weigh light against his accomplishments.

—Christopher Arnold

CIRICI Alomar, Cristián.

Spanish. Born in Barcelona, 26 September 1941. Educated at the Escuela Tecnica Superior de Arquitectura, Barcelona, under Federico Correa, 1958-65, Dip.Arch. 1965. Served in the Spanish Army, in Castillejos, Tarragona, 1961, 1962, 1965: Lieutenant. Married Ana Bricall Orellana in 1967; children: Carla, Marc, and Iu. Formed the partnership, Studio PER, with Pep Bonet, *q.v.,* Luis Clotet, *q.v.,* and Oscar Tusquets, *q.v.,* Barcelona, 1965. Professor, EINA, Barcelona, 1969-70; Professor at the Escuela Tecnica Superior de Arquitectura, Barcelona, 1976-78; Visiting Architect, Washington University, St. Louis, Missouri, 1981, and University of New Mexico, Santa Fe, 1983. Member of the Board of Governors, Collegi Oficial d'Arquitectes de Catalunya, Barcelona, 1976-78. President of the Board, ADI/FAD industrial design association, Barcelona, 1980-82. Exhibitions: *Arquitectura del Studio PER,* Lérida, 1971; *Triennale,* Milan, 1973; *Arquitectura y Lágrimas,* Sala Vincon, Barcelona, 1975; *Centenario de la Escuela Tecnica Superior de Arquitectura de Barcelona* , Palacio Nacional, Barcelona, 1977; *Festival of Films about Architecture,* Centre Georges Pompidou, Paris, 1978; *Biennale,* Venice, 1980. Address: Studio PER, Caspe 151, Barcelona 08013, Spain.

Works:

1968 *Miró Otro* exhibition plan, Barcelona (with Pep Bonet, Luis Clotet, and Oscar Tusquets)
1972 Llambes Office, Barcelona (with Pep Bonet)
1973 Profitos Factory, Polinya, Barcelona (with Pep Bonet)
      Housing, Queralbs, Gerona, Spain (with Santi Loperena)
1974 C./Tokio Housing Block, Barcelona (with Pep Bonet)
1976 Aguila House, Llavaneras, Barcelona (with Pep Bonet)

Cristian Cirici: Diaz-Morera House, Santa Elena d'Agell, Barcelona, 1981.

I remember that in 1965, when we were students of architecture in Barcelona, we used to get together in order to speak about our future as professionals. We specially debated the sociological, political and moral circumstances under which we would accept future commissions.

During the following ten years, in the practice of my profession, I never got the opportunity of that debate and in order to keep myself in training, expecting the *great opportunity*, I accepted almost any commission, which taught me various things. It may be a long time before my expectations are realized, and now, just in case, I have gone back to school to explain to others younger than I the most exciting and subtle things I learned in my training.

Some may reach the great opportunity and others may go back to school as professors.

—Cristián Cirici

See BONET, Pep

Studio PER is four architects in related practices in one office. Apart from administrative convenience, what really binds them together is that they share the same approach to architecture in valuing positively its cultural objectives. Their architecture is essentially intellectual. The are eager to discuss, argue, and defend their work against all criticism in order to explore all the rich possibilities available to their avant-garde position. This makes their buildings, and their explanations, often contradictory—but that is the price of an open mind—adventure and doubt. But this attitude, which is almost literary rather than visual, would be of little interest if it was not backed up by secure professional ability, compositional control, and a sensitive feeling for proportions.

Pep Bonet and Cristian Cirici present one side of the practice; they share with their partners, Lluis Clotet and Oscar Tusquets, an invigorating concern for industrial design. Between them they have a large list of products on the market. Their attention to minute detail, and the production problems involved, is reflected in the care they take in designing architectural details. Their drawings and perspectives are explicative.

Bonet and Cirici are more conservative than their partners in their architecture; they fall more clearly within the mainstream of modern architecture—as in their Profitos Factory, the C./Tokio luxury flats in Barcelona, and the social housing unit, Besos, Barcelona. But perhaps their most significant work is Bonet's own house in Vilamajor, where the directness of industrial architecture has inspired the conception of the house. The skeleton of two parallel naves made of block columns and pre-cast concrete beams generate two related open spaces, one partially occupied by the main body of the dwelling and the other by a studio. Details are reduced to a minimum, to the area where industrial and rural architecture meet. This voluntary simplication of architecture to the bare necessities follows Mies van der Rohe in a unsophisticated and relaxed manner.

Cirici has brought his detailed design skills not only to significant restoration work, like the Casa Thomas by the turn-of-the-century architect Domenech i Montaner, and the rebuilding of the Barcelona pavilion by Mies van der Rohe, but also to the motorway service buildings at the entrance to the Cadi tunnel near Puigcerda.

The common freshness and professional skill of Bonet and Cirici, and that of their associates in Studio PER, together with their sensitive alertness to current architectural fashion, enable them to translate new concepts quickly into the local Catalan cultural context. It is a task that is needed if the modern movement is to take root geographically.

—David Mackay

Bricall House, Vilasar, Barcelona (with Pep Bonet)
Pep Bonet House, Vilamajor, Barcelona (with Pep Bonet)
1977 Francés House, Menorca (with Pep Bonet)
1978 Kuijlaars House, Castelldefels, Barcelona (with Pep Bonet)
    Housing Complex, Gran Via, Barcelona (with Pep Bonet, Lluis Clotet and Oscar Tusquets)
1979 Casa Thomas restoration and B.D. showroom, calle Mallorca, Barcelona (with Pep Bonet, Lluis Clotet and Oscar Tusquets)
1981 Diaz-Morera House, Santa Elena d'Agell, Barcelona (with Pep Bonet)
    Housing Complex, calle Selva, Barcelona (with Pep Bonet)
1982 Museu de Zoologia restoration and extension, Barcelona (with Pep Bonet)
1983 Industrial and Commercial Buildings, Area del Cadí, Cerdanya, Spain (with Pep Bonet)

Also numerous furniture designs for B.D. Ediciones de Diseño, Barcelona, from 1972.

Publications:

By CIRICI: articles—"El Plan que Sale del Armario" in *Destino* (Barcelona), 2 December 1967; "Popularidad del Diseño?" in *Destino* (Barcelona), 23 February 1968; "En el Proceso de Consumo" in *Destino* (Barcelona), 22 March 1968; "La Arquitectura de Vanguardia" in *Destino* (Barcelona), 20 April 1968; "Una Banca Catalana" in *Destino* (Barcelona), 18 May 1968; "Vivir en Barcelona" in *Destino* (Barcelona), 7 June 1968; "Premios FAD 1967" in *Destino* (Barcelona), 13 July 1968; "El Boom del Turismo de Verano" in *Destino* (Barcelona), 10 August 1968; "En Torno a la Parcelacion de un Area de Spot" in *Destino* (Barcelona), 7 March 1967; "En la Muerte de Ernesto Rogers" in *Destino* (Barcelona), 15 September 1969; "Revestimientos" in *Nuevo Ambiente* (Barcelona), no. 17, 1969; "El Esqui, Juego de Sociedad de los anos 70" in *Cuadernos de Arquitectura* (Barcelona), no. 95, 1973; "Una Historia de Oficinas" in *Nuevo Ambiente* (Barcelona), no. 24, 1974; "Les obres de Carlo Scarpa al museu de Castelvechio a Verona" in *Cuaderns* (Barcelona), no. 158, 1983.

On CIRICI: articles—"Studio PER" in *Architecture + Urbanism* (Tokyo), no. 4, 1977; "Arquitecturas con Ventanas" by Xavier Sust in *Arquitectura Bis* (Barcelona), September 1977; "Per, uno per uno, tutti per tutti" by Alessandro Mendini in *Modo Milano* (Milan), November 1977; "On Architecture: report from Barcelona" in *Bauen und Wohnen* (Zurich), January 1978; "National awards for restoration and rehabilitation" in *Arquitectos* (Madrid), July/August 1980; "Studio PER" by Masayuki Matsuzake in *Space Design* (Tokyo), August 1980; "House in Sant Feliu de Codines" in *Quaderns* (Barcelona), March/April 1981; "House in Santa Elena d'Agell, Barcelona" in *Quaderns* (Barcelona), no. 156, 1983; "Progetto Climatico" in *Casa Vogue* (Milan), no. 141, 1983; "Studio PER" in *El Croquis* (Madrid), August/October 1983; "Cristián Cirici" in *L'Uomo Vogue* (Milan), no. 133, 1984.

CLOTET Ballus, Lluis.

Spanish. Born in Barcelona, 31 July 1941. Educated at the Escuela Pías, Barcelona, 1951-57; Escuela Tecnica Superior de Arquitectura, Barcelona, 1958-65: studied with Federico Correa Ruiz. Married Nuria Bohigas in 1966. Formed the partnership, Studio PER, with Cristian Cirici, *q.v.*, Pep Bonet, *q.v.*, and Oscar Tusquets, *q.v.*, Barcelona, 1965. Exhibitions: *Arquitectura del Studio PER*, Lérida, 1971; *Triennale*, Milan, 1973; *Arquitectura y Lágrimas*, Sala Vincon, Barcelona, 1975; *Centenario de la Escuela Tecnica Superior de Arquitectura de Barcelona*, Palacio Nacional, Barcelona, 1977; *Festival of Films about Architecture*, Centre Georges Pompidou, Paris, 1978; *Transformations in Modern Architecture*, Museum of Modern Art, New York, 1979; *Forum Design*, Linz, Austria, 1980; *Biennale*, Venice, 1980; *The House as Image*, Louisiana Museum, Humlebaek, Denmark, 1981; *La presence du passe*, Paris, 1981; *The Presence of the Past*, San Francisco, 1982; *Ten New Buildings*, Institute of Contemporary Arts, London, 1983. Recipient: Premio F.A.D., 1965, 1972, 1978, 1979, 1980; Premio Nacional de la Restauracion Madrid, 1980; First Prize, Faculty of Medicine Competition, Barcelona, 1980; Delat de Oro industrial design prize, Madrid, 1974, 1979, 1980; Kunstmuseum Prize, Frankfurt, 1983. Address: Studio PER, Caspe 151, Barcelona 08013, Spain.

Works:

1963 Colegio Mayor San Raimundo de Peñafort, Barcelona (with Oscar Tusquets)
1965 Editorial Lumen Offices, Barcelona (with Oscar Tusquets)
　　 Emilio Blay House interiors, Barcelona (with Oscar Tusquets)
　　 Apartment Block I, Cadaqués, Gerona, Spain (with Oscar Tusquets and Xavier Carulla)
　　 Sonor Hi-Fi shop and studio, Barcelona (with Oscar Tusquets and Xavier Carulla)
1968 Gremio Vidrieros Building, Barcelona (with Oscar Tusquets and Xavier Carulla)
　　 Maspons-Ubiña Studio, Barcelona (with Oscar Tusquets and Xavier Carulla)
　　 Fonda Sala Restaurant, Olost de Llusanes, Barcelona (with Oscar Tusquets and Xavier Carulla)
　　 Ibars Offices, Barcelona (with Oscar Tusquets and Xavier Carulla)
　　 Casa Fullá apartment building, Barcelona (with Oscar Tusquets and Santiago Loperena)
　　 Single-family housing, La Atmella del Vallés, Barcelona (with Oscar Tusquets and Xavier Carulla)
　　 Solitari Apartments, Cadaqués, Gerona, Spain (with Oscar Tusquets and Xavier Carulla)
　　 El Colomer Apartment Complex, Cadaqués, Gerona, Spain (with Oscar Tusquets, Santiago Loperena, and Anna Bohigas)
　　 Casa Penina (house), Cardedeu, Barcelona (with Oscar Tusquets, Santiago Loperena, and Anna Bohigas)
　　 Ancla Roja Apartments, Salou, Tarragona, Spain (with Oscar Tusquets and Anna Bohigas)
　　 Miró Otro exhibition plan, Barcelona (with Oscar Tusquets, Pep Bonet, and Cristian Cirici)
1970 Gil Sala residential additons, Barcelona (with Oscar Tustquets, Santiago Loperena, and Anna Bohigas)
1971 Casa Regás (house), Llofriu, Gerona, Spain (with Oscar Tusquets, Santiago Loperena, and Anna Bohigas)
　　 Puig and Cadafalch Housing Block, Mataró, Barcelona (with Oscar Tusquets, Santiago Loperena, and Anna Bohigas)
　　 Unión Lloyd Travel Agency Building, Barcelona (with Oscar Tusquets, Santiago Loperena, and Anna Bohigas)
1972 Aerojet Travel Offices, Barcelona (with Oscar Tusquets, Santiago Loperena, and Anna Bohigas)
　　 Belvedere Georgina (house), Llofriu, Gerona, Spain (with Oscar Tusquets, Santiago Loperena, and Anna Bohigas)
1973 Mozart-Fortuny Apartments, Sant Cugat del Valles, Barcelona (with Oscar Tusquets, Santiago Loperena, and Anna Bohigas)
　　 Aerojet Travel Offices, Palma, Majorca (with Oscar Tusquets and Santiago Loperena)
　　 Alpes Building, Hospitalet, Barcelona (with Oscar Tusquets, Santiago Loperena, and Anna Bohigas)
1974 Tusquets Family Apartment alterations, Barcelona (with Oscar Tusquets, Santiago Loperena, and Anna Bohigas)
　　 Casa Vittoria (house), Pantelleria, Italy (with Oscar Tusquets)
　　 Stephanie Apartment, Barcelona (With Oscar Tusquets, Santiago Loperena, and Anna Bohigas)
　　 Sahatuje Studio, Barcelona (with Oscar Tusquets, Santiago Loperena, and Anna Bohigas)
1975 Jacob Levy Apartment, Barcelona (with Oscar Tusquets, Santiago Loperena, and Anna Bohigas)
　　 Editorial Lumen Offices, Barcelona (with Santiago Loperena)
　　 Feria Textiles Exhibition Stand, Valencia (with Oscar Tusquets)
1976 Housing group, Sardanola, Barcelona (with Oscar Tusquets, Santiago Loperena, and Anna Bohigas)
　　 Gloria Rognoni House, Sant Cugat del Valles, Barcelona (with Santiago Loperena)
1977 Ramirez House, Alella, Barcelona (with Santiago Loperena)
1978 Casa Simon house conversion, Sant Cugat del

Lluis Clotet: **Casa Vittoria single-family house, Pantelleria, Italy, 1974.**

Valles, Barcelona (with M. Riera)

Santa Maria de Gallecs redevelopment plan, Mollet del Valles, Barcelona (with O. Tusquets and X. Sust)

Housing in the Gran Via, Barcelona (with Studio PER partners)

La Balsa Restaurant, Barcelona (with O. Tusquets)

1979 Casa Verdura house conversion, Sant Cugat del Valles, Barcelona (with M. Riera)

Fortuny Swimming-pool, Sant Cugat del Valles, Barcelona

B.D. Ediciones de Diseno awning and frontage (conversion of Casa Thomas), Barcelona (with Studio PER partners)

Faculty of Medicine alterations and extensions, Barcelona (competition project; with O. Tusquets, C. Diaz and F. Basso)

1980 Liceo al Seminario plan for the Raval district, Barcelona (with O. Tusquets)

1981 House by a Lake, Sant Cugat de Valles, Barcelona (project)

Palau de la Musica Catalana remodelling, Barcelona (with O. Tusquets, I. Paricio and C. Diaz)

1982 Banco de Epsana building, Gerona, Spain (project; with O. Tusquets and I. Paricio)

Casa Guiu house conversion, Sant Cugat del Valles, Barcelona (with M. Riera)

1983 Modern Art Museum, Frankfurt (competition project; with O. Tusquets)

Publications:

By CLOTET: books—*Arquitectura Modernista,* with Oscar Tusquets, Barcelona 1968; *Arquitectura Gótica Catalana,* with Oscar Tusquets, Barcelona 1968; *Arquitectura y Lágrimas,* with Oscar Tusquets, Barcelona 1975; *Vivir en el Campo,* Barcelona 1976; articles, with Oscar Tusquets—"Acondicionamento sala estar y comedor" in *Cuadernos Arquitectura* (Barcelona), no. 4, 1965; "Viviendas en Hospitalet de Llobregat" in *Hogar y Arquitectura* (Madrid), October 1968; "Casa Regás" in *Cuadernos Arquitectura* (Barcelona), July/August 1972; "El chalet masia" in *Mobelart* (Barcelona), October 1972; "Belvedere Georgina casita unifamiliar" in *Cuadernos Arquitectura* (Barcelona), September/October 1973; "Mi Terraza, Studio PER en el Industrial Design de la Triennales de Milan" in *Hogares Modernos* (Barcelona), November 1973; "Biblioscala de un piso en Barcelona" in *Nuevo Ambiente* (Barcelona), March/April 1974; "Manzana Puig i Cadafalch" in *Cuadernos de Arquitectura Anuario* (Barcelona), no. 109, 1975; "Viviendas en Sant Cugat" in *Cuadernos de Arquitectura Anuario* (Barcelona), no. 110, 1975.

On CLOTET: books—*Casa Vittoria, Pantelleria* by the Habitat editors, Barcelona 1976; *El Studio PER o los confines de la Arquitectura actual* by J. Muntañola, Barcelona 1976; *Arquitecturas Catalanas* by Helio Piñón, Barcelona 1977; *Eclecticismo y Vanguardia* by Ignacio Solà Morales, Barcelona 1982; *Nacionalism i Modernitat en l'Arquitectura Catalana Contemporania* by Helio Piñón, Barcelona 1982; *Clotet, Tusquets* by Claudia Mann, with introduction by Alessandro Mendini, Barcelona 1983; *Spanish Contemporary Architecture* by E. Bru and J. L. Mateo, Barcelona 1984; articles—"Los Premios FAD" by Oriol Bohigas in *Serra d'Or* (Barcelona), January 1967; "Canaletas Neighbourhood" by David Mackay in *World Architecture,* London 1968; "Uma lonja em Barcelona" in *Arquitectura* (Lisbon), July 1968; "Chalet en una ciudad jard." in *Nuevo Ambiente* (Barcelona), no. 15, 1969; "Exposición Miró Otro" in *Summa* (Buenos Aires), 20 November 1969; "Vivre dehors: Autour de patios-terrasses" in *Maison Francaise* (Paris), June 1971; "Obras de Clotet-Tusquets," special issue of *Hogar y Ar-*

quitectura (Madrid), July 1971; "Los Premios de interiorismo FAD 1971" in *Hogares Modernos* (Barcelona), January 1972; "Allestimento a Barcelona" in *Domus* (Milan), October 1972; "Nuevas Tendencias de la Arquitectura española" in *Arquitectura* (Madrid), May 1972; "Belvedere Georgina" in *Nuevo Ambiente* (Barcelona), September 1973; "Casa Regas Llofriu" in *Nuevo Ambiente* (Barcelona), November 1973; "Casa Georgina" in *Toshi Yutaku* (Tokyo), November 1973; "Introducir una vivienda functional en un Belvedere Palladiano" in *Domus* (Milan), no. 522, 1973; "Opiniones sobre el Belvedere" by Correa, Sust, and Flores in *Jano Arquitectura* (Barcelona), December 1973; "Agencia Viajes Aerojet" in *Nuevo Ambiente* (Barcelona), March 1974; "Gil Sala Building" in *Toshi Yutaku* (Tokyo), no. 8, 1975; "Casa Vittoria en la isla de Pantelleria" in *Arquitecturas Bis* (Barcelona), May/June 1976; "Anarchist's Guide" by Chris Fawcett in *Architectural Association Quarterly* (London), Vol. 7, no. 3, 1976; "C'e un designer sul trapezio" by Bruno Zevi in *Espresso* (Milan), 23 July 1977; "Studio PER," special issue of *Architecture + Urbanism* (Tokyo), April 1977; "Per, uno per uno, tutti per tutti" by Alessandro Mendini in *Modo Milano* (Milan), November 1977; "Apartamentos Mozart, Fortuny, Manzana Puig i Cadafalch" in *Summa* (Buenos Aires), no. 125, 1978; "Casa Rognoni" in *Arquitecturas Bis* (Barcelona), no. 27, 1979; "Casa Rognoni" in *L'Architecture d'Aujourd'hui* (Paris), "Casa Rognoni" in *Werk/Archithese* (Zurich), no. 35, 1979; "Belvedere Georgina" in *Controspazio* (Bari, Italy), 1979; "Clotet/Tusquets" in *Architectural Design* (London), no. 51, 1981; "Piscina Mozart, Fortuny" in *Arquitectura* (Madrid), no. 230, 1981; "Apartamentos en Cerdanyola" in *Arquitectura* (Madrid), no. 231, 1981; "Casa Simon, Casa Verdura" in *Cuadernos d'Arquitectura* (Barcelona), no. 148, 1981; "Del Liceo al Seminario" in *Arquitectura* (Madrid), no. 232, 1981; "Remodelacion del Palau de la Musica Catalana" in *Arquitectura* (Madrid), no. 238, 1982; "Studio PER", special issue of *El Croquis* (Madrid), August/October 1984.

It was the first woman's bottom I saw in my Life. I was five and looked at her while she was dressing herself. My cousin and I slept in the same bed.

She still lives in that village, and now I am putting her house in order.

Arturo, the best centre-halfback the team has ever had, is the bricklayer. The plumber is the only guy I ever fight with.

There are no estimates, no permissions, no discussions; everything is as plain and simple as it should be. And the pies and sausages they give me for my work are delicious.

—Lluis Clotet

Studio PER is four architects in related practices in one office. Apart from administrative convenience, what really binds them together is that they share the same approach to architecture in valuing positively its cultural objectives. Their architecture is essentially intellectual. They are eager to discuss, argue, and defend their work against all criticism in order to explore all the rich possibilities available to their avant-garde position. This makes their buildings, and their explanations, often contradictory—but that is the price of an open mind—adventure and doubt. But this attitude, which is almost literary rather than visual, would be of little interest if it were not backed up by secure professional ability, compositional control, and a sensitive feeling for proportions.

Lluis Clotet and Oscar Tusquets have, until recently, been one practice. From the beginning they were immersed in the neorealist, historically-based, so-called Barcelona School of Architecture that achieved a coherent local style during the 1960's and 1970's. It was based on program analysis, environ-

mental integration, economic use of materials, and constructional detailing as a basis for decoration. Their apartment building Casa Fullá in Barcelona and the private house Casa Penina are the most representative of this period.

The small week-end house, "Belvedere Georgina," in Llofriu, is so ironic in poking fun at the modern movement and so dexterous in its use of historical vocabulary that at first it seems to be just a brilliant example of pop art in architecture. The house is conceived as a garden pavilion in the form of a temple in homage to the motor-car, which makes the week-end house possible. The car is parked under a classical pergola, and one enters the house down through the pit. Part of the pavilion is cut away to form a sheltered court, and the missing section is painted on the walls. The window shutters are designed and placed according to the proportions and rules of classical composition, allowing the real windows to be placed haphazardly behind, according to the dictates of the interior function. Though the image of the house is an irrelevant exercise in pop history, it has given the authors the freedom to extend the frontiers of architectural composition in its own right to give a cultured solution to the building so that it reads well in the landscape and allows the exterior and interior design to overlap independently.

It is through this "second reading" of their architecture that one finds the common denominator that runs through their buildings—be it the outside rooms defined by concrete columns in the Vittoria house on the Island of Pantelleria or the split-level row housing in Sant Cugat.

Clotet has recently been able to concentrate his professional skills and extraordinary sensitivity to the new urban design for the historic centre of Barcelona, El Raval – which includes the restoration of the Convent dels Angels.

The common freshness and professional skill of Clotet and Tusquets, and that of their associates in Studio PER, together with their sensitive alertness to current architectural fashion, enable them to translate new concepts quickly into the local Catalan cultural context. It is a task that is needed if the modern movement is to take root geographically.

—David Mackay

COATES, Wells Wintemute.

Canadian. Born in Tokyo, Japan, of Canadian parents, 17 December 1895. Educated privately in Tokyo; at the University of British Columbia, Vancouver, 1914-16, 1919-21, B.S. in engineering 1921; University of London, 1922-24, Ph.D. in engineering 1924. Lieutenant in the Canadian Infantry, in France and Belgium, 1915-17; served as a pilot in the Royal Navy Air Services and the Royal Air Force, in Italy, 1917-18; Technical Staff Officer, with rank of Wing Commander, Royal Air Force, 1939-45. Married Marion Grove in 1927 (separated, 1935); daughter: Laura. Worked as a journalist for the *Daily Express* in London and Paris, 1923-26; worked in the office of Adams and Thompson, with Maxell Fry, *q.v.,* London, 1924; Engineer/Architect, Chrysede Textiles Company, London and Cornwall, 1927-28 in private practice as designer and architect, London, 1929-39, 1945-52: in partnership with David Pleydell-Bouverie, 1933-34, with Patrick Gwynne, *q.v.,* 1935-39, with Jacqueline Tyrwhitt, 1949-52, and with Michael Lyell, 1954-56; Architect and Planner for Iroquois New Town, Ontario, Canada, 1952-54; Visiting Professor, Harvard University, Cambridge, Massachusetts, 1955-56; returned to private practice in London, 1956 until his death in 1958. Design Consultant, Cresta Silks Shops, London, 1929-33; consultant, De Havilland Aircraft Company, 1946, and EMI Electrical Industries, London, 1952. Member, Executive Council, Twentieth Century Group, London, 1930-31; Founder Member, Modern Architectural, Research Group (MARS), London, from 1933; Member, Unit One, London, 1933-35. Exhibitions: *Hampstead in the Thirties,* London 1974; PEL, London 1977; *The Wireless Show!,* London 1977; *Tendenzen der Zwanziger Jahre,* Nationalgalerie, West Berlin, 1977; *Thirties,* Hayward Gallery, London, 1979; *Wells Coates—Architect and Designer 1895-1958,* Museum of Modern Art, Oxford, 1979. Fellow, Royal Institute of British Architects; Member, Royal Architectural Institute of Canada. Associate, Royal Society of Arts, 1944; Royal Designer for Industry, 1944: Master of the Faculty of Design for Industry, 1951-53. O.B.E. (Officer, Order of the British Empire), 1944. *Died* (in London) *17 June 1958.*

Works:

1928 Chrysede Silk Shop, Cambridge
1929 Cresta Silks Factory interiors, Welwyn Garden City, Hertfordshire
      Cresta Silks Shop, Brompton Road, London
      Cresta Silks Shop, Bournemouth
1930 Cresta Silks Shop, Brighton
      Cresta Silks Shop, Bromley, Kent
      Two linked houses, Lawn Road, Hampstead, London (project)
1931 Cresta Silks Shop II, Brompton Road, London
      British Broadcasting Corporation Studios, Broadcasting House, London
      House conversion, 1 Kensington Palace Gardens, London
      Flat conversion, 34 Gordon Square, Bloomsbury, London
      Venesta Plywood, *Empire Trade Exhibition,* Manchester
      Venesta Plywood Display, *Empire Trade Exhibition,* Buenos Aires
      Venesta Plywood Display, *Brewers' Exhibition,* London
      Venesta Plywood Display, *Commercial Motor Exhibition,* Olympia, London
      Isotype House (project)
1932 British Broadcasting Corporation Studios, Newcastle
      Airport (project)
      Cresta Silks Shop, Baker Street, London
      Cresta Silks Shop, Bond Street, London
      Office conversion, Elizabeth Street, London
      Venesta Plywood Display, *Empire Trade Exhibition,* Olympia, London
1933 Lawn Road Flats, Hampstead, London
      Minimum Flat, *British Industrial Art Exhibition.* Dorland Hall, London
      House conversions, 78 Addiscombe Road, Croydon, Surrey (with David Pleydell Bouverie)
      Layout for *Artists of Today* exhibition, Zwemmer Gallery, Litchfield Street, London (with David Pleydell-Bouverie)
      Second Feathers Club, Norland Gardens, London (with David Pleydell-Bouverie)
      Venesta Plywood Display, *Building Trades Exhibition,* Olympia, London
      Permanent stage set for the 1933-34 season, Old Vic Theatre, Waterloo, London
1934 Sunspan House, *Ideal Home Exhibition,* Olympia, London (with David Pleydell-Bouverie)
      MARS Group Display, *Building Exhibition,* Olympia, London (with David Pleydell-Bouverie)
      Embassy Court Flats, Brighton
1935 Sunspan Single-Storey House, Welwyn Garden City, Hertfordshire
      Studio flat, 18 Yeoman's Row, Knightsbridge, London

Wells Coates: Lawn Road Flats, Hampstead, London, 1933.

      School camp, Ogmore, Glamorgan, Wales (with Elizabeth Denby)
      Flats, Sleepy Hollow, Hove, Sussex (project)
      Venesta Plywood Display, *Building Trades Exhibition,* Olympia, London
1935/
38 Sunspan House, Angmering, Sussex
      Sunspan House, Portsdown Hill, Hampshire
      Sunspan House, Wentworth Close, Ditton Hill, Kent
      Three Sunspan Houses, Surbiton, Surrey
      Two Sunspan Houses, Avondale Avenue, Esther, Surrey
      Two Sunspan Houses, Southwood Gardens, Esher, Surrey
      Three Sunspan Houses, Woodlands Avenue, New Malden, Surrey
1936 Ekco Factory, Southend-on-Sea, Essex
      Hampden Nursery School, Holland Park, London
      Flat conversion, 2 Devonshire Street, London
      Hairdressing salon, Canterbury, Kent (with Edric Neel)
      Flats, Durdham Park, Bristol (project)
1937 Flats, 10 Palace Gate, Kensington, London
      House, Benfleet, Essex

      SCS Slum Clearance, Bethnal Green, London (project)
      News Chronicle School (competition project; with Denys Lasdun)
1938 The Homewood (house), Esher, Surrey (with Patrick Gwynne)
      Layouts for the *MARS Group Exhibition,* New Burlington Galleries, London
1944 Share Farm alterations and additions, Horsmonden, Kent (project)
1945 AIROH Aluminium House (project)
1946 St. Lawrence Cliffs Hotel conversion and additions, Isle of Thanet, Kent (project)
1947 BOAC Aircraft interiors
      A. W. Hawksley Display, and Thomas French and Sons Display, *Building Trades Exhibition,* Olympia, London
1949 James Clark and Eaton Display, *Building Trades Exhibition.* Olympia, London
1950 British Broadcasting Corporation Television Studio, *Festival of Britain.* London (project)
      Telekinema, *Festival of Britain,* South Bank, London (with Peter Bender)
      Television Pavilion, *Festival of Britain.* South Bank, London (with Peter Bender and Denys Hinton)

1951 James Clark and Eaton Display, *Building Trades Exhibition*, Olympia, London
1953 Master plan for Iroquis New Town, Ontario
1954 Toronto Island Development Plan (project: with J. B. Parkin)
1955 Flats, The Drive, Hove, Sussex (project; with Michael Lyell)
       Prince's Gardens Development, Kensington, London (project; with Michael Lyell)
1956 House, Thames Ditton, Surrey (with Michael Lyell)
       Hope Brothers Shop, Regent Street, London (with Michael Lyell)
       House, West Wittering, Sussex (with Michael Lyell)
       Flats, Ottawa, Ontario (project)
1957 Flats, Vancouver, British Columbia (project)
       Project 58, Vancouver, British Columbia (project; with Arthur Erickson, Geoffrey Massey, Peter Oberlander and E. J. Watkins)
       Mass Rapid Transit System (project)

       Designs: numerous items of furniture and fitments for incorporation into his building projects, as well as commissioned projects for radio and television sets and boats, 1928-55.

Publications:

By COATES: articles—"Critics: A Reader's Way to Reconcile Their Unfriendliness" in *The Architects Journal* (London), 11 February 1931; "Inspiration from Japan" and "Material for Architecture" in *The Architects' Journal* (London), 4 November 1931; "Furniture Today—Furniture Tomorrow" in *Architectural Review* (London), July 1932; "Response to Tradition" in *Architectural Review* (London), November 1932; "Modern Shops and Modern Materials" in *Building* (London), December 1932; "Wells Coates: Interview," with J. Craven, in *Advertisers' Weekly* (London), March 1933; "Design in Modern Life: Modern Dwellings for Modern Needs," with Geoffrey Boumphrey, in *The Listener* (London), 24 May 1933; "Planning in Section" in *Architectural Review* (London), August 1937; "The Conditions for an Architecture of Today" in *Architectural Association Journal* (London), April 1938; "Planning the Festival of Britain Telekinema" in *British Kinematography* (London), April 1951; "The Cine-Theatre Today and Tomorrow" in *Atti e rassegna tecnica della società degli ingegnieri e degli architetti* (Turin), December 1952; "The Fiilm Theatre of the Future" in *Ideal Kinema* (London), 26 May 1953; "Graduation Banquet Address" in *Royal Architectural Institute of Canada Journal* (Toronto), June 1959.

On COATES: books—*Unit One: The Modern Movement in English Architecture, Painting and Sculpture,* edited by Herbert Read, London 1934; *Interior Decorating* by Duncan Miller, London 1937; *The Modern Flat* by F.R.S. Yorke and Frederick Gibberd, London 1950; *The Politics of Architecture: A History of Modern Architecture in Britain* by Anthony Jackson, London 1970; *Hampstead in the Thirties,* exhibition catalogue, edited by Michael Collins, London 1974; *PEL,* exhibition catalogue, edited by Dennis Sharp, Tim Benton and Barbie Campbell Cole, London 1977; *The Wireless Show!,* exhibition catalogue, edited by Carol Hogben, London 1977; *Wells Coates* by Sherban Cantacuzino, London 1978; *Wells Coates: architect and designer 1895-1958,* exhibition catalogue, Oxford 1979; articles—"The Year's Work" by C.H. Reilly in *The Architects' Journal* (London), 10 January 1935; "The Year's Work at Home" by C.H. Reilly in *The Architects' Journal* (London), 16 January 1936; "The Designers: Wells Coates" by Geoffrey Boumphrey in *Architectural Review* (London), January 1936; "The

Year's Work" by C.H. Reilly in *The Architects' Journal* (London), 18 January 1940; "Broadcasting Comes of Age: The Radio Cabinet 1919-1949" by Nikolaus Pevsner in *Architectural Review* (London), May 1940; "Isokon Flats" by Reyner Banham in *Architectural Review* (London), July 1955; "English Architecture from the Thirties" by E. Maxwell Fry in *The Architect's Year-book 8,* London 1957; "Wells Coates 1895-1958" by J.M. Richards in *Architectural Review* (London), December 1958; "The Complete Coates—Exhibition at the Museum of Modern Art in Oxford" by Corin Hughes Stanton in *Building Design* (London), 13 July 1979; "Frontiersman of the Heroic Age" by Andrew Ozanne in *RIBA Journal* (London), September 1979; "The Double Tragedy of Architect Wells Coates" in *House and Garden* (London), September 1980.

Wells Coates was one of the small group of cosmopolitans who were the spearhead of the modern movement during the 1930's in England. Born in Japan in 1895 of Canadian parents who were missionaries, he was educated in Canada and at the University of London, from which he obtained a doctorate in engineering in 1924. By the time he focussed fully on architecture in the late 1920s he had had a versatile career as war-time pilot, research student, journalist, and exhibition display designer. Between 1929 and 1932 he established himself at the forefront of English modern tendencies with a series of designs for Cresta shops and with the planning of the BBC Special Effects studios.

Coates' formation as an architect corresponded with the "heroic phase" of the European Modern Movement. His innate sense of abstract form had already received stimulus from the controlled proportions and clean forms of Japanese architecture, and he was naturally attracted to abstract art of the 1920s and to the stripped shapes of the International Style. Moreover, Coates' engineering sensibility was in sympathy with Le Corbusier's machine aesthetic, and he was also attracted to the quality of dynamic expression in the work of Eric Mendelsohn.

These disparate influences and attitudes were synthesised in Coates' first major work, Lawn Road Flats in Hampstead (1933), designed for Jack Pritchard. Here, the rationally arranged apartments have been packed into a tight oblong form from which the access balconies have been cantilevered and to which a block containing vertical circulation and garages has been attached. The result is a disciplined communal statement and a demonstration of the potentials of reinforced concrete: it is entirely fitting that the flats should have been the temporary home of such a cosmopolitan emigré as Walter Gropius, who fled Nazi oppression by coming to England. Lawn Road embodied a manifesto for a new way of life in the English context.

Coates was involved with the political and propaganda activities surrounding the formation of English modern architecture during this period and took part in such avant-garde manifestations as the Twentieth Century Group, Unit One, and The Modern Architectural Research Group (MARS), the English wing of the Congrès Internationaux d'Architecture Moderne (CIAM). His personality was well suited to liaison with foreign architects, as he delighted in demonstrating his broad range of knowledge of foreign cultures and cut an elegant figure in his reticent but immaculate clothes and his Ronald Colman moustache. It was entirely consistent with Coates' persona that he should have driven a flamboyant Lancia Lambda sports car and that his flat in Kensington should have contained a radio set of his own design with a transparent front. But beneath this self-consiousness and theatricality, there was a passionate character of great intergity: Coates' architectural activities were rooted in aesthetic and moral principles and in the quest for a new social ethos.

Coates' other major work of the 1930s, the flats at Palace Gate, Kensington, resulted from an attempt

at synthesising this social vision with new forms and techniques. The architect here combined the plan arrangements of Le Corbusier's Pavillon Suisse with an ingenious, space-saving 3/2 section derived from Russian Collectivist dwellings of the late 1920s. Whatever the sources, the result is uniquely Coates' own and, along with Lubetkin and Tecton's High Point Flats at Highgate, must rank as one of the clearest statements of the highrise urbanistic principle before the Second World War in England.

Coates applied his mind to a broad range of architectural problems: the creation of house prototypes (the "Sunspan" house of 1934), the study of urban problems (studies for Bethnal Green slum clearance, 1937), even the design of catamarans and radio sets (his EKCO wireless cabinet of 1934 is a classic of the period). But in the broad context, his output must be seen as of secondary importance alongside the original thinkers who created the modern movement. Moreover, Coates' extremely individualistic temperament was better suited to the atmosphere of the battlegrounds for modern architecture of the 1930's than to the more complacent postwar years, and his later development did not lead to the fulfilment of the early promise. His last years, up until his death in 1958, were spent mostly in Canada working on urban schemes and teaching.

Coates was a complex man who impressed most who met him with the quality of his high ideals and with a certain sadness. The historian Sigfried Giedion perhaps spoke the truth when he suggested that Coates was "never completely at home in architecture or in life."

—William J. R. Curtis

CODERCH y de Sentmenat, José Antonio

Spanish. Born in Barcelona, 25 November 1913. Educated at the Escuela Tecnica Superior de Arquitectura, Barcelona, under José Maria Jujol y Gibert, José Rafols, and Professor Florensa, 1929-36, 1939-40, Dr.Arch. 1940; influenced by the work of the Madrid architect Secundino Zuazu and by popular Mediterranean achitecture. Served as a Lieutenant in the Spanish Civil War, 1936-39; Cruz de Guerra al mérito en Campana; Cruz Roja al mérito militar. Married Ana Maria Giménez Ramos in 1943; children: José Antonio, Ana Maria, Gustavo, and Elvira. Worked in the offices of the Director-General of Architecture, Madrid, 1940-42, offices of the City Architect, Sitges, Spain, 1942-45, Obra Sindical del Hogar, Barcelona, 1944-52, and at the Naval Institute, Barcelona, 1949-52. In private architectural practice, Barcelona, 1947 until his death, 1984 (partner from 1947: J. Sanz Luengo; partners from 1967: G. Coderch Giménez; J.A. Coderch Giménez). Professor, Escuela Tecnica Superior de Arquitectura, Barcelona, 1965-68. Member of Team 10, 1961. Exhibitions: National Architecture Congress, Barcelona, 1949; *Triennale,* Milan, 1951; *National Fine Art Exhibition,* Madrid, 1960; Centre Pompidou, Paris, 1978; *Transformations in Modern Architecture,* Museum of Modern Art, New York, 1979. Recipient: Gold Medal and Grand Prize, *Triennale,* Milan, 1951; Gold Medal, *National Fine Art Exhibition,* Madrid, 1960; Gold Delta, ADIFAD, Barcelona, 1962, 1964; Obelisk Prize, *Domus,* 1963; National Design Prize, Argentina, 1964; Professional Merit Medal, FAD, Barcelona, 1977. Academician of the Real Academia Catalana de Bellas Artes de San Jorge, Barcelona, 1977. *Died* (in Barcelona) 6 November 1984.

Works:

1945 Las Forcas Urban Plan, Sitges, Spain (project)
1946 Ferrer Vidal House, Cala d'Or, Majorca

José A. Coderch: Trade Office Building, Barcelona, 1965.

1971 Guell House, Barcelona
      Gran Kursaal House, San Sebastian (competition project)
      Fermina Coderch House, Sant Feliu de Codines, Barcelona
      Mercedes Belango House, Sant Feliu de Codines, Barcelona
1972 French Institute Building, Barcelona
1973 SEAT Technical Centre, Martorell, Spain
1976 Housing block, Madrid (competition project)
      Lacua House, Vittoria, Spain (competition project)
1978 School of Architecture additions, Barcelona (project)

Publications:

By CODERCH: books— *Espiritualidad de la Arquitectura*, Barcelona 1977; *José Antonio Coderch de Sentmenat: conversaciones*, interviews with Enric Soria Badia, Barcelona 1979; articles— "No son genios lo que necesitamos ahora" in *Arquitectura* (Madrid), February 1962; "Un proyecto de viviendas" in *Arquitectura* (Madrid), June 1972; "Conjunto de viviendas, Barcelona" in *Informes de la Construccion* (Madrid), September 1975; "Enlargement of the School of Architecture of Barcelona" in *Arquitecturas Bis* (Barcelona), January/April 1980.

On CODERCH: books— *Arquitecturas Catalanas* by Helio Piñon, Barcelona 1977; *José Antonio Coderch, 1945-76* by Anton Capitel, Madrid 1978; *Bouwen in Barcelona* by Cornelis van de Ven, Amsterdam 1980; *Nacionalisme i Modernitat en l'Arquitectura Catalana Contemporania* by Helio Piñon, Barcelona 1980; articles— "Proyecto de viviendas maritimas en Sitges" in *Arte y Hogar* (Madrid), December 1945; "Due ville à Sitges" in *Domus* (Milan), November 1949; "La nueva arquitectura rural" by Alberto Sartoris in *Revista Nacional de Arquitectura* (Madrid), December 1949; "Deux Villas a Sitges" in *L'Architecture d'Aujourd'hui* (Paris), July 1950; "Giro d'orizzonte alla T9" by Marco Valsecchi in *Edilizia Moderna* (Milan), December 1951; "Casa a Majorca" in *Domus* (Milan), November 1952; "Per i pescatori di Tarragona" in *Domus* (Milan), September 1952; "Villa en Caldetas" in *Revista Nacional de Arquitectura (Madrid), December 1953*; "Casa a Barcelona" *in Domus* (Milan), May 1955; "Jose Coderch y Manuel Valls" by Juan Teixidor in *Zodiac 5* (Milan), October 1957; "L'Architecture de Coderch et Valls Verges" by Alberto Sartoris in *Architecture: Formes et Fonctions* (Lausanne), no. 4, 1957; "Real Club de Golf del Prat, Barcelona" in *Cuadernos de Arquitectura* (Barcelona), no. 31, 1958; "Hotel and Apartments at Torre Valentina" in *Architectural Design* (London), May 1960; "Casa a Camprodón" in *Domus* (Milan), December 1960; "Hotel und Apartmenthauser en Torre Valentina, Costa Brava" in *D.B.Z.* (Gutersloh), February 1961; "Casa per vacanze in Spagna" in *Edilizia Moderna* (Milan), December 1961; "Maison Coderch" in *L'Oeil* (Lausanne), April 1962; "Luxury Flats, Barcelona" in *Architect and Building News* (London), July 1962; "Village de Vacances sur la Costa Brava" in *Réalités* (Paris), April 1963; "Conversacion con José A. Coderch" by Rafael Marquina in *Clima* (Madrid), 1964; "José Antonio Coderch, Manuel Valls" in *Arquitectura* (Madrid), December 1965; "Zwei Wohnhauser in Spanien" in *Baumeister* (Munich), May 1966; "New Ideas Revive an Ancient House" in *House Beautiful* (London), August 1966; "Une parfaite maison de vacances" in *Maison Francaise* (Paris), April 1968; "Tutta Bianca sul Mare" in *Ville-Giardini* (Milan), January 1970; "Dernier grand maître solitaire de l'architecture espagnole" in *L'Architecture d'Aujourd'hui* (Paris), January/ February 1975; "J.A. Coderch," special issue of *Architecture + Urbanism* (Tokyo), February 1976; "Institut francais à Barcelona" in *L'Architecture d'Aujourd'hui* (Paris), October 1977;

"The Dilemma of Coderch" by Toshiaku Tange in *Architecture + Urbanism* (Tokyo), April 1978; "Six works by José A. Coderch y de Sentmenat", special issue of *Informes de la Construccion* (Madrid), June 1978; "50 Years in Barcelona", special issue of *Wonen-TA/BK* (Heerlen, Netherlands), April 1979; "Ugalde House revisited" by Emili Donato and others in *Quaderns* (Barcelona), January/February 1981.

An old and famous American architect said to another who was very much younger and was asking for his advice: "Open wide your eyes and look; it is much easier than you think." He also said to him: "Behind every building that you see there is a man that you don't see." A man, he said. He did not mention whether he was an architect or not.

No, I do not think that it is miracles or geniuses that we need at this time. I believe genius is an occurrence that is an Act of God, not a goal or an end. Nor do we need High Priests or dubious Prophets of Architecture or great doctrinaires. There is something of a living tradition that is still within our reach, and there are also many ancient moral doctrines concerning our trade or profession (and I use these terms in their best traditional sense) of architect. We need to take advantage of what little there is left of the constructive tradition and, above all, the moral tradition in this epoch when the most beautiful of our words have practically lost their real and true meaning.

The thousands and thousands of architects in the world should think less about Architecture (with a capital A), about money or about cities of the year 2000, and more about their trade as architects. Let them work tied by a leg so that they cannot stray too far from the earth in which they have their roots or from men they know best; let them always clutch a firm foundation based on dedication, good will and honour.

I am convinced that any present-day architect moderately endowed and developed or formed who is able to understand this, is easily capable of producing truly living work. This is, for me, the most important, more important than any consideration or end that only *apparently* takes precedence.

I believe that it is from works, possibly of the greatest diversity, carried out with a sound knowledge of the fundamentals and also great conscientiousness, without worrying about the final result (which, fortunately anyway, escapes us and is not an end but a consequence) that an authentic, live new tradition will be born.

To bring this about, I believe that we must first rid ourselves of many ideas which appear clear but are false, of many hollow words, and work, each and every one of us, with that good will that is translated into one's work and teaching rather than with a mere concentration on doctrinairism. I think that the best teaching is that which teaches our trade, teaches us to work with great faith, or, in short, that which teaches us to be architects, knowing, at the same time, as we must, that we can all make mistakes. It is also the example of working, continuously watching in order not to confuse human frailty, the right to be mistaken (a cloak which if wrongly used can cover a multitude of sins), with inconstancy of will, immorality or the cold calculation of the climber or "getter-on."

I imagine society as a sort of pyramid, with, at the peak, the best and least numerous and at the wide base, the masses. There is an intermediate zone where may be found people of all sorts who are aware of some superior values and have decided to act accordingly. These people are aristocrats and on them everything depends. They enrich society upwards towards the peak with words and deeds, and downwards towards the base by example, as the masses are enriched only through respect and mimicry. Today this aristocracy hardly exists, swallowed by materialism, the philosophy of success, State technocracy and bureaucracy, incompatible with liberty and creative initiative, with what is holy.

My parents used to tell me that a gentleman, an aristocrat, is the person who finds himself unable to do certain things which even the law, the Church and the majority approve or permit. Each one of us, if we aware, must try to form a new aristocracy. This is an urgent problem. We must begin soon, and then go on without losing heart. The main thing is to begin to work, and then, and only then, can we talk about it.

We must pit ourselves against money, against the vanity of success, against excess of property or earnings, against inconstancy or haste, and against the lack of spiritual life and conscience; we must put instead dedication, craftsmanship, good will, time, the bread we need for every day and, above all, love, which is acceptance and giving, not possession and domination— all these must be taken hold of and clung to, for these are the true values.

Seeing and knowing more or less profoundly the works or forms (the exterior signs of spiritual richness) of the great masters is considered to be culture or architectural formation. The same means of classification are applied to our craft or profession as are used (exterior signs of economic richness) in our materialistic society. And then we complain or lament because there are no great architects now, that the majority of architects are bad, that the new urbanization is anti-human almost without exception through the world, that our towns and villages are destroyed, and houses and towns are built like film sets along the length of our beautiful Mediterranean coasts.

The value, merit and acclaim bestowed upon the great masters, who are not within our reach, contrast vividly with the silence, indifference or even ignorance concerning their moral values or their attitude to their work, which is, let it be clearly said, something we can aspire to. Is it not curious that people write and talk of their weakness and frailty as an attractive oddity or a tit-bit for gossip or just as being mistaken, and at the same time conceal as a forbidden subject or as an anecdote their attitude to life or to their work? Is it not also strange that we have here, very near to us, Gaudi (I myself have known people who worked with him), and so much is said about his work and so little about his moral position and his dedication?

Almost the same thing happens with the great masters of our time; their works are admired, or rather the shapes of their works, and nothing else. There is no attempt to go deeper and discover what there is within, the most valuable, which is, after all, exactly that which is within our reach. Of course it is clear that this would mean accepting our own limitations, which is not possible when one wishes to be a Le Corbusier or make a great deal of money.

The real spiritual culture of our profession has always belonged to a few. The circumstances that enable nearly anyone to have the possibility of access to this culture is the heritage of nearly all, and is one that is not generally taken. Neither, unfortunately, do we accept cultural behavior which should be obligatory and in the consciousness of us all.

In ancient times architects had a certain solid support. Many things existed that were accepted by the majority as good or, at any rate, inevitable, and the organization of society, as much in its social problems as in its economic, religious and political ideas, was stable or evolved slowly. On the other hand, there was greater faith, more dedication, less false pride and a living tradition on which to lean. With all their defects, the upper classes had a clear idea of their duty and seldom did they err in their choice of the best architect or artist, so spiritual culture was naturally propagated. The little cities grew like plants in different ways, but slowly, and gathering together the common life of the people. Seldom was there sloth, improvisation or irresponsibility. Works of all sorts were created which had a human value seldom found today. Sometimes, but not often, there were growth problems to overcome, but without that feeling, inevitable today, that the evolution of the cities is extremely rapid and, except in the short term, difficult to plan for.

Nowadays, the ruling classes have lost their sense of mission, and all, including the aristocracy of the blood, of money, of intelligence, of politics and the Church or Churches, with only a few and personal exceptions, serve to contribute decisively to the chaos of present-day architecture by their uselessness, their money-grabbing souls, their cowardice, their love of power and lack of any sort of consideration for their responsibilities.

On the other hand, the circumstances on which we have to base our work vary continually. There are religious, moral, social and economic problems; those of education, the family and energy sources, which can all play a part in changing, unsuspectingly, the face and structure of our society. Brutal changes whose meanings are lost to us are also possible, but their existence can impede honest long-range planning.

As I've said before, a live tradition is not clear to us, a tradition that to the majority of us is essential. That which has so far been done (a great deal in certain cases, of course) is not sufficient to light the necessary path the great majority of architects must follow. Lacking this live tradition, our solution is at best looked for in formalism, in the application of fashionable methodology or in routine and the topic of some of the great and old masters of modern architecture, forgetting their mistakes and leaving out their spirit, their circumstances and, above all, carefully hiding with magnificent words our great irresponsibility (which is often only lack of thought), our ambition and our inconstancy.

It is ingenious to think, as is thought, that the ideal and the practice of our profession may be condensed into slogans such as the sun, light, air, greenness; the social, the political and so many others. A formalistic base, dogmatic, above all if it is only partial, is in itself bad, save in exceptional and catastrophic circumstances. From all this I deduce that among the different paths that each thinking architect will choose to follow, there must be some common factor, something which must be in all of us, without forgetting history and its ancient wisdom.

Goethe, as an old man, said: "The true subject of world history and humanity, the only and most profound subject to which all the rest are subordinate, is the conflict between faith and incredulity. All the periods of history marked by faith, regardless of the form in which it appears, are brilliant, lift the soul and bear fruit in the present and in the future. On the other hand, all periods when incredulity, in whatever guise, has gained its sad victory, even when it happens to shine for a time with false brilliance, disappear from view for posterity, because there is nobody willing to take the trouble to know what has not borne fruit."

A sentence of Einstein's hung in our office for many years: "The most beautiful thing to be felt by man is the mysterious side of life. There is the cradle of Art and real Science."

Note : The text is practically the same as a letter I wrote to my good friend the architect Bakema, secretary of the Team 10, concerning my joining this team of architects in 1961, so that they should know my beliefs before admitting me. In this version I have made slight changes in order to make the text clearer.
—José A. Coderch (1980)

José A. Coderch's work has been a consistent stabilizing force in post-Civil War Catalan architecture. His extraordinarily sensitive designs spring from a profound love for the art and science of his profession and the reality of human nature. The cultural content of his work, though never absent, takes second place to the human problems involved. His buildings are always disarmingly pure, often reducing complex problems to incredible simplicity. There is always great care taken with the proportions of his buildings and their elements, not only with form but also with materials, allowing large expanses of blind walls to induce a constant note of tranquility. This urge to simplicity is applied to every detail and

joint in the building. His work is not just rooted in the observation of popular Mediterranean architecture but also in the great static spaces of the Catalan civic and religious medieval architectural tradition. It is this quality that makes his work transcend the purely local arena and makes it relevant to the wider sphere of the modern movement in architecture.

Although he was a recluse, Coderch's isolation is only apparent. His work responds not to the whims of fashion but to the strong cultural currents of a turbulent 20th century architecture. It is this that has made him a constantly young architect whose work, whatever year it was built, remains a fresh reminder that the craft of architecture still exists.

Because of the Civil War Coderch qualified late as an architect. He was 27 years old in 1940, and after a brief encounter with official work in Madrid, close to the mentality of dictatorship, he moved back to the Mediterranean as municipal architect to the seaside resort of Sitges. Here he made his first attempt at popular architecture—Las Forcas, a housing estate that was never built. It consisted of a series of aggregated volumes for each function, extended over the sites, forming outside courts that were designed as extensions of the living space. The style was clearly Ibizan, the same popular architecture from the island that had inspired the rationalist architects in the 1930's. Although official architecture, when not concerned with the imperial image of Escorial, was bent on the revival of rural architecture as the true "blood and earth" response to nationalism, Coderch's Mediterranean model was more cubic than stylistic. As an abstraction from this model, and as a rupture from the cultural vacuum of the dictatorship, Coderch took refuge in surrealism in his Ugalde House in Caldetas: orthogonal planning is destroyed; cubes explode into bent and curved forms to gather in the external views and immediate countryside. Although he was never to repeat this exercise—his feeling for reality was too strong—this flight beyond realism to destroy rigidly-contained spaces is present in all of his buildings. It is immediately apparent in the plan of his Pescadores Housing Block in Barceloneta, where the splayed walls increase the richness of the space by making it flow slightly beyond immediate comprehension, thus releasing the restrictive feeling of a tiny flat. These flats are contained within a double facade, which acts as a climatic filter, that is almost diagramatically simple, alternating splayed tiles and louvered vertical strips slightly cantilevered over the street from the first floor upwards. This concern to contain a complex plan within a simple envelope is another of Coderch's recurring themes.

For many years his work lay mostly in the design of private houses for which he evolved an almost standard single-storey, L-shaped plan with rows of parallel walls set back to contain balcony windows between them. This system of fenestration is another personal feature of Coderch's work. We find it in the Hotel de Mar in Majorca and in the Cocheras Flats in Sarria, Barcelona (though in the Cocheras he combines this composition with corner windows).

Two non-residential buildings of note—The Trade Office Building, Barcelona, obviously inspired by Mies van der Rohe's glass skyscraper project of 1921, and the French Institute, Barcelona—demonstrate Coderch's ability to sheathe his buildings with simple skins.

However, his design of urban spaces rests more on complexity rejecting the usual approach of an ordered street front. The jagged plan and broken facade of the Cocheras Flats, and his project for housing in Vittoria, may be ingenious in removing the obligatory enclosed light and ventilation wells for deep plans, but the monotony of constant movement is a wearing experience, even when mitigated by an elegance in design details and careful paving and gardening around the base of the buildings. Is this perhaps Coderch's substitution of an urban city for a rural one?

What is certain is that the example of Coderch remains a living force not only in Catalan architec-

ture but also in the modern movement as a whole. His last design, for the extension to the Barcelona School of Architecture, demonstrated his everlasting capacity to break fresh ground with ordinary problems. His lifelong passion for simplicity, light, and spatial movement are all resumed in this extraordinary building. He died, after a long illness, in 1984—unable to see the school's completion.
—David Mackay

COLQUHOUN AND MILLER

Partnership; established in London, 1961, by Alan Colquhoun (born 1921) and John Harmsworth Miller (born 1930); additional partner since 1975, Richard J. Brearley (born 1944). Exhibitions: University of Architecture, Palermo, Sicily, 1974; Royal College of Art, London, 1974; *Bienal*, Santiago, Chile, 1981; Housing Awards Exhibition, London, 1983; *Art and Architecture* Institute of Contemporary Arts, London, 1983; *Biennale*, Paris, 1983; *Summer Exhibition*, Royal Academy of Art, London, 1984. Recipient: Royal Institute of British Architects Awards, 1974, 1975, 1983, 1984. Address: 23 Neal Street, London WC2H 9PU, England.

Works:

1965 Forest Gate High School, West Ham, London
1969 Weinreb and Douwma Print Shop and Offices, 22 Bloomsbury Street, London
    Hotel du Cap, Antibes, France (project)
    Library, Eaton Square, London, S.W.1 (project)
    Derby Civic Centre (project)
1970 Chemistry Building, Royal Holloway College, Englefield Green, Surrey
1972 Canon Lee School, Clifton, North Yorkshire
1973 Holiday chalets, Aviemore, Scotland (project)
1974 Pillwood House, Feock, Cornwall
    Melrose Avenue, Activity Centre, Bletchley, Buckinghamshire
1975 Private house, Feock, Cornwall (project)
    Colnaghi Gallery conversion, Bond Street, London W.1 (project)
    U.K. Canning Plant for Coca Cola Export Corporation (project)
1977 Two Mile Ash (housing), Milton Keynes, Buckinghamshire (project)
    2 community centres, Welbourne and Tenterden Road, Haringey, London
    Milbank Housing, London (project)
1978 West Green Road Old People's Home, Haringey, London
    Exhibition layout for *Dada and Surrealism Reviewed*, Hayward Gallery, London
    Housing, Gaisford Street, Camden Town, London
    Infill housing, Fenny Stratford, Buckinghamshire
    Single person flats, Hornsey Lane, London N.6
1979 Whitechapel Art Gallery renovation and extension, London (project)
    Royal Holloway College Theatre Workshop, Englefield Green, Surrey (project)
    150 rental houses, Central Milton Keynes, Buckinghamshire (project)
    Royal Holloway College Theatre Workshop, Englefield Green Surrey (project)
1979 Whitechapel Art Gallery renovation and extension, London
1980 Single-person Flats, Hornsey Lane, London N.6.
1981 *Picasso's Picassos* exhibition design, Hayward Gallery, London
1982 *10 Modern Houses* travelling exhibition design, Britain

Colquhoun and Miller: Oldbrook II Housing, Milton Keynes, Buckinghamshire, 1983.

1983 Housing, Oldbrook, Milton Keynes, Buckinghamshire
Wren Exhibition design, Whitechapel Art Gallery, London
1984 Housing, Church Crescent, Hackney, London
Housing in Albion, Brownlow and Shrubland Roads, Hackney, London
Housing, Two Mile Ash, Milton Keynes, Buckinghamshire

Publications:

By COLQUHOUN: book—*Essays in Architectural Criticism*, Cambridge, Massachussetts and London 1981.

On COLQUHOUN/MILLER: book—*British Buildings 1960-1964* by Douglas Stephen, Kenneth Frampton and Michael Carapetian, London 1965; articles—"From theory to practice: architects Colquhoun and Miller" in *L'Architecture d'Aujourd'hui* (Paris), November/December 1974; "Colquhoun and Miller: chemistry building, Royal Holloway College" in *Parametro* (Bologna), February 1975; 'Self critic of the Modern Movement: Alan Colquhoun" by Helion Pinon in *Arquitecturas* (Barcelona), March 1975; "Pillwood House" in *Architectural Design* (London), March 1975; "Works and projects of Colquhoun and Miller" in *Casabella* (Milan), May 1976; "Greenhouse to live in" in *Ville Giardini* (Milan), January 1977; "Millbank competition, London"in *L'Architecture d'aujourd'hui* (Paris), 1978; "Picture Palace", in *Building Design* (London) 17 August 1979; "Housing Links" in *The Architects' Journal* (London), 9 September 1981; "Public Housing" in *Architecture + Urbanism* (Tokyo),

April 1982; "Flats in Kentish Town, London" in *Baumeister* (Munich), November 1982; "Three of a Kind" in *The Architects' Journal* (London), 9 February 1983.

The architectural problem presents itself as the need to satisfy the demands of distribution, environment, site, construction, etc.

But the designer would be unable to decide on a distributive scheme unless he already had a certain ideal configuration in his mind. This is the constant against which possible solutions are measured.

The design process would seem to be more dialectical than deductive. It is similar to what in the context of painting Gombrich calls "making and matching."

Since one no longer designs according to a set of rules, as was the case with the Beaux-Arts, the guiding principles are eclectic. They are extracted from one's experience of existing architecture. The "programme" itself is formless. It does not suggest an architectural solution until it has been subjected to classification and has become generic rather than particular. The value of typology is that it shows the result of this classification. There are a limited number of possible architectural forms.

What Levi-Strauss says of structuralism applies to architecture: "A resolutely intellectual approach, a bias in favour of systematic arrangements, a mistrust of mechanistic and empirical solutions."

Our work, like that of many other architects, discloses the existence of a conflict between functionalism and older typologies.

The old avant-garde functionalism, which was associated with a unique vision of society, is no longer possible.

The symbolism of the plan as "a machine at rest" is

constantly challenged by more static forms of order. (The dialectic was already present in the 1920's and 30's in the work of Le Corbusier.) But it is not possible simply to turn one's back on functionalism and try to outflank history by treating historical forms as belonging to a kind of specious present.

Functionalism intervenes between us and the past, and modifies anything we take from it.

—Colquhoun and Miller

Shying away from the architecture-of-leftovers which "participation" and the supposed demystification of the environment proposed by Kroll, Alexander and others has inevitably led to, and similarly not impressed by the architecture-of-decomposition that litters the city, and certainly uninterested in architecture as a conflux of not too clear images based on very slender conceptions of democracy, Colquhoun and Miller hone in on a more classicizing skeleton of possibility: their work is a stereometric distribution of almost glacial tectonics, within which invitations, vistas, fissures and stops are framed and architecturalized.

Their aim, as Colquhoun puts it, is the fabrication of a non-dispersed, centralized Renaissance whole, with sufficient autonomy to be able to take on the kind of semantic role expected of a building by its context—but with sufficient gaps at its perimeter to meet the social expectations as well. This image is best exemplified in their Forest Gate High School, which features a porous threshold connecting with a more consolidated focus by means of "annular rings of innerness." The red brick finish typifies their earlier primitivism with regard to materials (earth-affirming echoes of Louis Kahn) and was employed in the struggle against dispersion.

Colquhoun and Miller are not afraid of the "institution"; neither are they afraid of giving it expression through their work. The Chemistry Building of Royal Holloway College is a good example of their cool, unflinching, institutional-typology; each of their projects involves a similar act of assembling elements most typical of the programme in hand. The civic face of the building, fronting a communications spine, has all the symmetrical sense of purpose and frontality of Isozaki's museum at Gumma; but from behind it turns into a more dynamic projectile that could for all the world be the Katsura Palace refurbished by Craig Ellwood—it bolts down the sloping section at a superb A-B-A rhythm, and would break away completely, making for the surrounding parkland land, if it weren't for the facade tethering it to its location.

The Chemistry Building impresses us with its turns and ways: we feel intuitively that the architects responsible must have entered into a pact with the sublime; one feels sure that "what they know is worth knowing." This contrasts with the vicarious dignity of so many buildings that are merely the product of the bickerings and jealousies of the ethics of commerce. Colquhoun and Miller prefer to construct an architecture that waits for the time when it will come into its own, rather than accept an architecture that assumes any guise the marketplace might demand—Palladian one moment, Venturian the next, its thousand masks as unpredictable as the thousand eyes of a primitive deity, with vague historical epochs coming forward in turn, as though auditioning. In place of this kind of transient Rent-a-Style plurality, which at worst can be a blundering disruption of the events and sequences that existence insists on, Colquhoun and Miller prefer a more unwavering and penetrating solution.

—Chris Fawcett

COLVIN, Brenda.

British. Born in Simla, India, 8 June 1897. Educated in Paris; studied at the Swanley Horticultural College, c.1920; privately with Madeline Agar. Worked as site assistant for Madeline Agar on War Memorial Garden, Wimbledon, 1921-22. In private practice, as landscape architect, England, 1922-69. Senior Partner, with Hal Moggridge, Colvin and Moggridge, landscape consultants, in London, and Filkins, Gloucestershire, 1969, until her death in 1981. Landscape Consultant to the East Kilbride Development Corporation, 1950. Lecturer, Department of Architecture, Regent Street Polytechnic, London, 1937, and Architectural Association School, London, 1937. Founder-Member, 1929, Honorary Secretary, 1941-48, Vice-President, 1949-50, President, 1951-53, and Trustee 1968-81, Institute of Landscape Architects, London. Founder Member, International Federation of Landscape Architects. Exhibition: Gardens Section, *Royal Horticultural Society Show,* London, 1928. C.B.E. (Commander, Order of the British Empire), 1973. *Died* (at Filkins, near Lechlade, Gloucestershire) *27 January 1981.*

Works: (landscape architecture):

1935 West Stowell House, near Marlborough, Wiltshire
1937 Chateau Zywiec, Poland
1948 Sutton Courtenay Manor Gardens, Oxfordshire
     Garden for the Port of London Authority, Tower Hill, London
1953 Compton Beauchamp Estate, Oxfordshire
1956 Salisbury Crematorium, Wiltshire
1958 Shotton Steelworks, Cheshire
1959 Queen Elizabeth Gardens, Wiltshire
     Drakelow Power Station, Burton-on-Trent, Staffordshire (grounds layout)
1961 Eggborough Power Station, Yorkshire
     Halls of Residence, Queen's University of Belfast
1962 Rugeley Power Station, Staffordshire (grounds layout; with Rendel, Palmer and Tritton)
     Trimpley Reservoir, Worcestershire (with Binne and Partners)
1962 Ash Disposal Scheme, Gale Common, Eggborough, Yorkshire
1971 Lower Farm, Coombe, Berkshire
     Numerous private and public gardens and parks

Publications:

By COLVIN: books—*Trees for Town and Country,* with Jacqueline Tyrwhitt, London 1947, 3rd edition 1972; *Land and Landscape,* London 1947, 1970; articles—"Planting Design" in *Landscape Design* (London), March 1951; "Presidential Address" in *Landscape Design* (London), November 1951; "Garden Architecture" in *Country Life* (London), September 1952; "Planting as a Medium of Design" in *Landscape Design* (London), August 1961; "Landscape Maintenance of Large Industrial Sites" in *Landscape Design* (London), November 1968; "Of Time and Trees: What the Eye Will See, the Imagination Foresees" in *Landscape Design* (London), February 1974; "Power Station, Didcot, Berkshire" and "Potash Mine, Boulby, Yorkshire" in *Architectural Review* (London), August 1974; "Beginnings" in *Landscape Design* (London), February 1979.

On COLVIN: articles—"Gale Common, Eggborough, Yorkshire" in *Landscape Design* (London), November 1968; "Ideas into Landscape" by David Streatfield in *Landscape Architecture* (Louisville, Kentucky), January 1972; "Brenda Colvin Dies Aged 83" in *Building* (London), 6 February 1981; "Brenda Colvin: Obituary" by Jane Wood in *Landscape Design* (London), May 1981.

I have had some part in the development of the profession of landscape architecture and am a founder member of the Institute of Landscape Architects and of the International Federation of Landscape Architects. I think the profession has an important role in the future. Its value will gain increasing recognition if it continues to be non-political and if it emphasizes that landscape design is essentially a problem of long-term issues rather than immediate, short-term policy. Landscape design differs from architectural design in fundamental aspects of both time and space.

Most landscape design projects take far longer to mature than those of architecture, and they are far more vulnerable to short-term destruction or inadvertent neglect. The time required for the successful establishment of major landscapes is related to, and must influence, the initial design from the outset of operations. Long-term management in harmony with the intention of the design is essential if the intention is to reach maturity; flexibility and the possibility of change must be built into the design.

Spatially, landscape covers larger areas than architecture. Agriculture, forestry, reservoirs, and other land uses form an important element of many major landscape projects. In many cases, architectural features may be absent or of secondary importance, although where they are in themselves of importance, man-made artifacts form the focus of attention.

The basis of landscape design is biological rather than geometrical: the laws of nature remain dominant over human fashion and convention.

—Brenda Colvin (1980)

One of the pioneers of modern landscape design, Brenda Colvin was throughout her life dedicated to her profession. She became highly respected both for her work and her writings, but perhaps, above all, her place in history is assured by her unstinted efforts to help create an independent landscape profession in a country previously dominated by gifted laymen. A founder member of the Institute of Landscape Architects, later President and Trustee, she encouraged younger members in every way open to an established practioner. Before schools of landscape design were created, Miss Colvin's office was one of the few that were in a position to take in students. Later, when students were leaving school and seeking practical experience, her office was foremost in taking on the idealistic but immature assistant. There are many practioneers today who remember their office experience with her with affection and gratitude.

Like others of her generation, Brenda Colvin had no formal education in landscape architecture, for there was none to have. She emerged from horticulture, virtually teaching herself the elements of design. Prior to World War II, the employment of landscape designers, slight as it was, was confined almost entirely to private gardens. With an immense experience of such works behind her, Miss Colvin played an invaluable part when the clientele changed from private to public. Her experience, technical skill, good judgment, and increasing wisdom made her advice acceptable to committees who chiefly relied on the reputation of the professional involved. Although her work for the War Office at Aldershot was probably her largest contract, the most spectacular was the proposal for disposing of fly-ash from the Central Electricity Generating Board's power station at Gale Common, Eggborough, Yorkshire. Here, she proposed a new, undulating, agricultural countryside made out of waste, presenting her scheme in the manner of Humphrey Repton's Red Books, with photo-montage of "before" and "after."

Although Brenda Colvin early published an invaluable technical guide to forest trees, gave many lectures and contributed countless articles to the landscape press, her literary claim to fame rests on one work, *Land and Landscape.* Known and read throughout the English-speaking world, respected in Europe and translated into Japanese, it has become a standard work on good landscape practice.

Today, her practice continues from her charming house in the Cotswold village of Filkins under the direction of her former partner Hal Moggeridge, the recently appointed Professor of Landscape Architecture in the University of Sheffield.

—Geoffrey Jellicoe

CONNELL, Amyas Douglas.

New Zealander. Born in Eltham, 23 June 1901; emigrated to England, 1924. Educated at the Stratford High School, New Zealand, 1912-16, and studied painting with his father; articled to the architect Stanley Fearn, Wellington, 1919-24; studied at the Bartlett School of Architecture, University of London, 1924-26, Dip.Arch. 1926; British School, Rome, 1926-29 (Rome Scholarship). Served in the British Army as a Garrison Engineer, Royal Engineers, Aldershot, Hampshire, 1939-43, and as Architect to the Ministry of Works, London, 1943-45. Married Maud Hargroves in 1930; Margret Stroud in 1957; children: James, Graham, Diane, and Katharine. In private practice, London, 1929-

Amyas Connell: New Farm, Grayswood, Surrey, 1933.

31; in partnership with Basil R. Ward, London, 1932-33; Partner, with Ward and Colin Lucas, *q.v.,* Connell, Ward and Lucas, London, 1933-39; in private practice, Tanganyika and Kenya, 1947-77. Founder-Director, TRIAD Architects and Engineers, Nairobi, Kenya, 1967; Consultant to TRIAD Architects and Planners, London 1975 until his death in 1980. Founder-Member, MARS (Modern Architecture Research) Group, London, 1931. Served as President, Kenya Institute of Architects, Nairobi. Exhibitions: *Contemporary Industrial Design in the Home* Dorland Hall, London, 1934; *Exhibition of Drawings of Blocks of Working Class Flats in Reinforced Concrete,* Imperial Institute, London, 1935; *Contemporary Industrial Design,* London, 1935; Musuem of Modern Art, New York, 1939. Recipient: Bronze Medal, Royal Institute of British Architects, 1960. Fellow, Royal Institute of British Architects, 1964. *Died* (in London) *in May 1980*

Works:

1928 "High and Over" (Professor Bernard Ashmole House), Amersham, Buckinghamshire

1929 "Noah's House," Bourne End, Buckinghamshire (destroyed)
Trent Park garden design
Lyme Park garden design

1932/
33 "New Farm" (Sir Arthur Lowes Dickenson House), Grayswood, Surrey (with Basil Ward)

1933 "The Hop Field" (house), St. Marys Platt, Wrotham, Kent (with Basil Ward and Colin Lucas)

1934 "The Saltings" (Dr. R. D. Lawrence House), Sinah Lane, Hayling Island, Hampshire (restored, 1977)
Three houses, Wiclands Avenue, Saltdean, Sussex (destroyed)
Four houses, High and Over Estate, Amersham, Buckinghamshire (with Basil Ward and Colin Lucas)

1935 Kent House Flats, Ferdinand Street, Chalk Farm, London (with Basil Ward and Colin Lucas)
Two pairs of semi-detached houses, Parkwood Estate, Ruislip, Middlesex (with Basil Ward and Colin Lucas)
"The Firs" (house), Brighton Road, Redhill, Surrey (with Basil Ward and Colin Lucas)
Hertford County Buildings (competition project; with Basil Ward and Colin Lucas)

1936 Individual Health Centre (project)
"Dragons" (house), Woodmancote, Sussex (with Basil Ward and Colin Lucas)
"Concrete House" (Ronald Gunn House), The Ridgeway, Westbury-on-Trym, Bristol (with Basil Ward and Colin Lucas)
Civic Buildings, Newport, Monmouthshire (competition project; with Basil Ward and Colin Lucas)

1937 House, Wentworth, Virginia Water, Surrey (with Basil Ward and Colin Lucas)
Geoffrey Walford House, 66 Frognal, Hampstead, London (with Basil Ward and Colin Lucas)

House, Worcester Park, Surrey (with Basil Ward and Colin Lucas)
Sound City Film Studios, Shepperton, Middlesex (with Basil Ward and Colin Lucas)

1937/
38 Tarburn House, 6 Temple Gardens, Moor Park, Hertfordshire (with Basil Ward and Colin Lucas)

1938 "Potcraft" (Dr. Thomas House), Sutton, Surrey (with Basil Ward and Colin Lucas)

1938/
39 Major Proudman House, 26 Bessborough Gardens, Roehampton, London (with Basil Ward and Colin Lucas)

1939 Lords Court (apartment building and shops), 32 St. John's Wood Road, London (partially built with Basil Ward and Colin Lucas)
Edith Edwards Preventorium, Papworth Village Settlement, Cambridgeshire (project)

1941 Cathedral, Auckland (competition project)

1948 Executive Houses, Tanga, Tanganyika
Cinema, Tanga, Tanganyika
Dalgety Office Building, with shops, Tanga, Tanganyika
Tzambourakis Office Building, Tanga, Tanganyika

1949 Village development (with mosque, hospital, market, and church), Kangri, Tanganyika

1955 Kenya Legislative Council Building, Nairobi (with H. Thornley Dyer)

1959 Aga Khan Platinum Jubilee Hospital, Nairobi
Out-Patients Clinic, King George VI Hospital, Nairobi

1960 Crown Law Offices, Nairobi

1963 Parliament Buildings, Nairobi

Publications:

By CONNELL: articles—"For and Against Modern Architecture," with Sir Reginald Blomfield, in *The Listener* (London), 28 November 1934; "Heroes of the Modern Movement: Amyas Connell Talks about the Problems of Modern Architects in the 30's," interview with Walter Menzies, in *Building Design* (London), 27 February 1976; "Basil Ward 1902-1976" in *RIBA Journal* (London), October 1976.

On CONNELL: articles—"Auckland Cathedral" in *The Architects' Journal* (London), 27 February 1941; "Parliament Buildings for the Government of Kenya at Nairobi" in *The Architects' Journal* (London), 13 January 1955; "Connell, Ward and Lucas 1927-1939," special issue of *Architectural Association Journal* (London), November 1956; "Connell, Ward and Lucas" by Peter Smithson in *Architectural Association Journal* (London), December 1956; "Aga Khan Platinum Jubilee Hospital, Nairobi" in *Architect and Building News* (London), 18 February 1959; "Side View of 66 Frognal" and "Block of Flats, Ferdinand Street, Designed in 1936 by Connell, Ward and Lucas" in *Design* (London), December 1974; "Connell, Ward and Lucas" in *RIBA Journal* (London), March 1976; "Architect's Approach to Architecture: Connell, Ward and Lucas" in *The Architects' Journal* (London), 10 March 1976; "Mending the Modern Movement: Restoration of The Saltings, Hayling Island" in *The Architects' Journal* (London), 30 March 1977; "A Tribute to Amyas Connell" in *Build Kenya* (Nairobi), May 1980; "Amyas Connell, 1901-1980" by Dennis Sharp in *RIBA Journal* (London), June 1980; and "High and Over Revisited" by Robert Maxwell and Celia Scott in *Architectural Design* (London), no. 6/7, 1981.

*

From inception to completion, each building for which I, as the architect, have been responsible has been the best that I could do. I have looked on each project as a projection of my past experience, and, on completion, it becomes the prime subject for exercising my critical faculty.

I have travelled widely and have learned that the understanding of the timeless quality of a great work of art begins with the analytical study of social history related to the aesthetic expression of its creator and grows with the realization that those moments of delight and joy felt when one is in the presence of a great work of art are indelibly implanted in one's memory. Consciously or unconsciously, they become part of one's aesthetic expression.

So, a target is set for achievement, and the core of my critical faculty was established.

—Amyas Connell (1980)

*

English architecture had its heroic period in the 1930's, and the most memorable buildings of that period were private houses. The finest of the private houses were designed by the firm of Connell, Ward and Lucas, the star of which was Amyas Connell.

New Zealand, the Bartlett School of Architecture, and the British School in Rome does not sound like the background for a major innovative architect. Nor does the ex-director of the British School in Rome sound like the sort of client who would commission an architect who had not built anything to design his house. Yet that is what happened. "High and Over" at Amersham, built in 1928 for Professor Bernard Ashmole, is the most inventive English house of the 1920's. It stands on a bluff, commanding a view over a beautiful valley. The plan, a three-pointed star, has a sense of classical ordering that might be expected with both architect and client fresh from the British School in Rome. But the concrete is frankly a reinforced concrete frame, with a formal language taken from a villa that André Lurçat had just completed overlooking the Parc Montsouris in Paris. The result was both inventive and spectacular, and the widespread publicity was enough to make modern architecture a "cause."

In "New Farm" at Grayswood, Surrey, Connell finally abandoned the classical approach to planning: the house is expressed as a series of cubes fanning out from the circulation area. He turned to Le Corbusier's Maison Domino for the structural parti, with the columns placed internally and continuous strip windows used to demonstrate that the walls contained no structure. In his "Concrete House" at Bristol, Connell reversed the idea and pulled the columns outside the skin, as in Le Corbusier's Villa at Carthage.

Connell formed a partnership with Basil Ward in 1932 and Colin Lucas joined them in 1933 to form Connell, Ward and Lucas, a team that continued throughout the 1930's to build houses of increasing clarity and formal confidence, culminating in the magnificent Tarburn House at Moor Park and Walford House in Frognal, Hampstead. Increasing clarity and formal confidence yes, because the partners obviously worked well together, but the work is maybe duller than Connell's early houses—as if group discussion had killed off the more outlandish formal inventiveness of the Grayswood and Amersham houses.

Connell, Ward and Lucas gave credit to the individual partner responsible for each of their houses, and it cannot be said that those attributed to Connell are amongst the firm's best works; however, they were a team, and Connell remained the spokesman for the practice.

After the war Connell developed a practice in East Africa, and he built on a far larger scale than his pre-war English houses. The work, however, did not again reach such high standards of quality.

—John Winter

COOK, Peter Frederic Chester.

British. Born in Southend, Essex, 22 October 1936. Educated at Stoneygate School, Leicester, Ipswich School, Suffolk, and Bournemouth School, Hampshire, until 1953; Bournemouth College of Art Department of Architecture, under Ronald Sims, 1953-58; Architectural Association School, London, under James Gowan, John Killick and Peter Smithson, 1958-60, Dip.A.A. 1960. Married the painter Hazel Fennell in 1960. Architectural Assistant, Jackson and Greenen, Bournemouth, 1956-58, and James Cubitt and Partners, London, 1960-62; Founder Member, with Ron Herron, Dennis Crompton, Warren Chalk, Mike Webb and David Greene, Archigram Group, London, 1960, and Co-Editor of *Archigram* magazine, 1961-70; Assistant Architect, Taylor Woodrow Design Group, London, under Theo Crosby, 1962-64; Partner, with Ron Herron and Dennis Crompton, Archigram Architects, London, 1969-75; Director, Institute of Contemporary Arts, London, 1973-74. Director, Art Net, London, since 1974 (Editor of *Net* magazine, 1974-78); Partner, with Christine Hawley, Cook-Hawley Architects, London, since 1978. Assistant 5th Year Master, 1964-66, 5th Year Master, 1966-70, Head of the Diploma School, 1970-72, and since 1973 Unit Master, Architectural Association School, London; Professor of Architecture, Staatliche Hochschule für Bildende Kunste/Stadelschule, Frankfurt, since 1984. Visiting Critic, University of California at Los Angeles, 1968-69; Visiting Fellow, Institute of Architecture and Urban Studies, New York, 1975; Visiting Critic, Rhode Island School of Design, Providence 1976; Visiting Professor, School of Architecture, University of Strasbourg, 1978, School of Architecture, Oslo, 1981, and University of Queensland School of Architecture, Brisbane, 1983. Exhibitions: *Living City*, Institute of Contemporary Arts, London 1963; *New Designers*, Woollands, London, 1965; *Summer Show*, Royal Academy, London, 1965, 1976, 1977; *Biennale*, Paris, 1967; *Triennale*, Milan, 1968, 1984; *Expo '70*, Osaka, Japan, 1970; *Monte Carlo Casinos*, Victoria and Albert Museum, London, 1972-73; toured Europe; *Archigram*, Institute of Contemporary Arts, London, 1973; *New Work: Peter Cook*, London, 1976; *40 London Architects*, Art Net Gallery, London, 1977, toured Europe; *Ron Herron and Peter Cook*, London, and New York, 1978; *Peter Cook and Christine Hawley*, International Design Zentrum, Berlin, and Stadelschule, Frankfurt, 1979; *Peter Cook and Christine Hawley*, Tokyo, 1980, toured Japan; *Herron, Hawley and Cook*, Aedes Gallery, Berlin, 1981; *New Work: Peter Cook*, Southern California Institute of Architecture, Los Angeles, 1982; *Follies*, Leo Castelli Gallery, New York, Corcoran Gallery, Los Angeles, and State Architecture Museum, Madrid, 1983-84; *Peter Cook: tower projects*, Hughes Gallery, Brisbane, Queensland, 1984; *21 Years: 21 Ideas*, Architectural Association, London, 1985; *New Tech*, Deutsches Architekturmuseum, Frankfurt, 1985; *International Urbanism*, Sao Paulo, Brazil, 1985. Recipient: First Prize, Gas Council Old People's Housing Competition, London, 1962; First Prize, Monte Carlo Entertainment Centre Competition, 1970; Graham Foundation Award, Chicago, 1970; Japan Foundation Award, Tokyo, 1977; First Prize (with Christine Hawley), Experimental Solar House Competition, Landstuhl, Germany, 1980. Associate of the Royal Institute of British Architects, 1968; Fellow, Royal Society of Arts, London, 1974. Addresses: 12 Ladbroke Square, London W11 3NA, England; Dürerstrasse 10, Frankfurt-am-Main, West Germany.

Works:

1956   Furniture for Kinson Congregational Church, Bournemouth

1956/
58   Detailing for various buildings, Bournemouth

1960/
62   Detailing for various buildings, London

1962   Euston Station Detail Plans, London (project)
        Berkshire County Offices, Reading (project; with David Greene)

1963   Design of the *Living City* exhibition, Institute of Contemporary Arts, London (with others)
        Shopping Centre, Nottingham (project; with David Greene)

1964   Fulham Housing Study, London
        Plug-in City (project)

1965   Plug-in University (project)

1965/
66   Plug and Clip Room, Woollands, London

1966   Plug and Clip Housing (project)

1967   Control and Choice House, *Biennale*, Paris (exhibition project; with Dennis Crompton and Ron Herron)
        Plug-in City (project model)

1968/
69   Electric Car for Plug-in Projects (project; with Hornsey College of Art students, London)

1969   Monte Carlo Entertainments Centre (project; with C. Fournier)

1969/
70   Archigram Capsule, *Expo '70*, Osaka, Japan (with Archigram Group)
        Instant City (project; with Ron Herron and Dennis Crompton)

1970   Bournemouth "Steps" (project; with Archigram Group)

1971   Cheek-by-Jowl (project)
        "Addhox" Urban Housing (project)
        Foulness Airport City alternatives, Essex (project)

1971/
73   Development plans for the Monte Carlo Entertainments Centre

1972 "Urban Mark" (project)
      Hedgerow Village (project)
      Monte Carlo Casino (competition project; with B. Tschumi and D. Jowsey)
1973 "Lump" (project)
1974 "Prepared Landscape" (project)
      Riverside Housing (competition project; with D. Jowsey)
1975 "Sponge" (project)
      Roosevelt Island Housing, New York (project; with others)
1976 Shinkenchiku House (House on the Via Appia) (competition project; with Christine Hawley)
1976/
  77 Trondheim Library, Norway (competition project; with Christine Hawley)
1977/
  78 "Arcadia" Housing and Town Plan (project)
1978 "Mesh" Projects (with Christine Hawley)
      Antique Exchange, London (project; with Christine Hawley)
1979 Landstuhl Solar House, West Germany (competition project; with Christine Hawley)
1980 Geschwindigkeit and Information Pavilion, Linz Exhibition, Austria (with Christine Hawley)
      Karmeliter Museum, Frankfurt (project; with Christine Hawley)
1981 Shadow House (project; with Christine Hawley)
      Layer City urban plan (project)
1982 Triangletomten, Oslo (project; as consultant to F. S. Platou A/S)
      Peak Plan, Hong Kong (competition project; with Christine Hawley)
1983 Bloch City theoretical plan (project)
      Lantern in Secret Blue (Folly project)
1983/
  84 Garden Tower, London (project)
      Lantern Tower, Oslo (project)
      Studio Tower, Frankfurt (project)
1984 South London Lagoon (project)
      His-and-Hers Room exhibit, *Triennale*, Milan

Publications:

By COOK: books—*Fulham Study* (report), London 1964; *Architecture: Action and Plan*, London and New York 1967; *Experimental Architecture*, London and New York 1970; *Archigram*, London and New York 1974; *Melting Architecture*, exhibition catalogue, London 1976; *The Arcadian City* (pamphlet), London 1978; *21 Years —21 Ideas*, exhibition catalogue, London 1985; *Arcadias*, London 1985; articles—"Living City" in *Living Arts* (London), 1963; "Plug-in City" in *The Sunday Times* (London), October 1964; "Instant City" in *Architectural Design* (London), November 1970; article in *The Japan Architect* (Tokyo), December 1976/January 1977; "Unbuilt England," editor and contributor, special issue of *Architecture + Urbanism* (Tokyo), September 1977; article in *The Japan Architect* (Tokyo), December 1977/January 1978.

On COOK: articles—"Archigram" by Claude Parent in *L'Architecture d'Aujourd'hui* (Paris), 1965; "Monte Carlo" by Reyner Banham in *The Architects' Journal* (London), 1970; "The Work of Archigram" in *Russian Architect* (Leningrad), 1972; "A Green-Obsessed Architect" by Arata Isozaki in *Space Design* (Tokyo), 1977; "Arcadias" by F. Bernard in *L'Architecture d'Aujourd'hui* (Paris), 1977; article by Deyan Sudjic in *The Architects' Journal* (London), 12 July 1978; "The Work of Cook and Hawley", special issue of *Architecture + Urbanism* (Tokyo), February 1980; "British Architecture", special issue of *Architectural Design* (London), Autumn 1981; "Cook's chef-d'oeuvre" in *Architectural Review* (London), March 1984; "Tower Projects" in *Architectural Design* (London), March 1984.

Peter Cook: Tower of Studios, Sachsenhausen, Frankfurt, 1984 (project).

I was a founder member of the "Archigram Group." I am the author of many projects that have been published all over the world. I am also a teacher, and I lecture all over the world. My projects are much discussed by *other architects*. But I consider myself a designer rather than a theoretician.

My work in the mid 1960's was inspired by the possibilities of technology: by the possibility that architecture could break out of its narrow-mindedness if it acquired elements (a vocabulary of form) from outside itself.

Towards the end of the 1960's I began to break down the notions of "definite subject:" a moving and robot-like architecture that conceptually dismembered "the city," "the university," "the house," etc. As well as physically dismembering it, Plug-in City was a "throw-away" city—with expendable parts. The Control-and-Choice House was a home like a robot—made up of apparatus that could flex and respond to the individual members of the family.

Towards the early 1970's the notion of "metamorphosis"—implicit in the earlier work—could be explored more as a romantic and simbiotic study, so that the "urban mark" could take a prognosis of urban form: form the earlier, more rigid, more "architectural" state to the final state whereby the landscape had taken over. (The straight-forward functional demands of the Monte Carlo Building were meanwhile developing one's physical design abilities.)

During the 1970's the idea of incorporating natural, and quasi-natural, elements has re-asserted one's basic desire to break architecture out of its narrow limits, particularly those of its formal vocabulary, so the "Lump" and "Sponge" projects suggest an architecture where high technology and nature are mixed together, the overall form being often "melted" together, rather than formally composed.

In the most recent work, the combination of "sleek" or highly-tailored architectural elements with free-form and vegetal architecture has composed itself around a "back-front" format (as in the Roosevelt Island Housing and some of the "Arcadia" housing. Or in a smooth exterior containing a disintegrative or "Gothic" internal architecture (as in the Trondheim Library). This is allied to a developing interest in the idea of a matrix (or grid) as the point of departure: overlaid and "eaten into" so that the final building is a dismembering or "melting" of the matrix. The Shinkenchiku House of 1976, designed with my partner, Christine Hawley (who has even more extreme abilities with "melting" aesthetic), is the prototype project for most of the recent output.

—Peter Cook

Speaking of England, in an article in the Japanese magazine *A + U*, Peter Cook says "in the country at large, architecture is discussed in pragmatic terms. Style is mistrusted, unless it is in the traditional style of the area. Innovation occurs more frequently in plan or in section, the dimensions that cannot be understood by a layman." It is an interesting observation, and it is probably true. In matters of building, art is best kept as a secret activity that does not obtrude on the simple and dominant processes of reasoning and selection.

In the late 1950's Peter Cook came to the Architectural Association from Bournemouth to complete his studies, and, happily, an aspect of that south-coast background remains uppermost in his thoughts. Holidays, when the whole family relaxes and behaves less formally and predictably; the pier and its fun and amusements; childish foods, ice-cream, candy floss, and lemonade. Several of his early projects—or I should say Archigram's, because much of his work has been done with that group—harness this mood and its licence too. Fairs, circuses, arriving by air and bombarding the sleepy inhabitants with noise and excitement. Like that of the clowns in a Continental movie who embarrass staid folk with their antics and advances, this is a most theatrical view of what life might be. It is also a very abrasive artistic gesture—small wonder that this vision of play and pleasure has been met with reserve and even the antagonism of main-stream architects. In another context, Peter Cook gives one a clue to his stance when he says, "Pragmatism can only be fought (and fortified) by bouts of wild optimism. Dreams and fancies undermine the Puritan instincts and rekindle the Romantic." Perhaps it would not be unfair to remind him of "invention can be piled upon invention until the resultant beast resembles a monster."

Speaking of English design he says, directly and not without justification, that it "comes from the strongest area of English art, the compositions and observations of rural painters such as Constable, the suggestiveness of the watercolour tradition, and from the gardeners of the 18th century who combine an instinct for the picturesque with the reality of diminutive undulation that is the raw material of the English countryside. All of this is soft, Romantic, episodic." It is clear that he does not rate trivial and small-scale incident too highly. Elsewhere he says of English conversation that it is "discussive rather than polemical; mood is a substitute for form."

From this particular selection of quotations it would seem that Peter Cook's work is addressed critically to two streams of traditional architectural thought, the formal and the picturesque, and (at the risk of oversimplification) the former is represented as dull and the latter petty. Necessarily, he engages these established cultures with grand Utopian gestures, and, much in the spirit of the 19th century French visionaries, his canvases are larger and their ramifications panoramic. His is a formidable commitment, but he brings into this field of the imagination a skill and attack that are a match for it.

—James Gowan

CORREA, Charles Mark.
Indian. Born in Hyderabad, 1 September 1930. Educated at St. Xavier's College, Bombay, 1946-48; University of Michigan, Ann Arbor, under Buckminster Fuller, *q.v.*, and Walter Sanders, 1949-53, B.Arch. 1953; Massachusetts Institute of Technology, Cambridge, under Buckminster Fuller and Lawrence Anderson, 1953-55, M.Arch. 1955. Married Monika Sequeira Kamat in 1961; children: Nondita and Nakul. Partner, G. M. Bhuta and Associates, Bombay, 1956-58. Since 1958, in private practice, Bombay. Chief Architect, City and Industrial Development Corporation, Government of Maharashtra, 1971-74. Visiting Critic, Graduate School of Design, Harvard, University, Cambridge, Massachusetts, 1974; University of Bombay, 1976 and 1977; Massachusetts Institute of Technology, Cambridge 1981: University of Pennsylvania, Philadelphia, 1982; and Columbia University, New York, 1984. Albert Bemis Professor, Massachusetts Insitute of Technology, Cambridge, 1962; Bannister Fletcher Professor, University College, London, 1974; Arthur Davis Visiting Professor, Tulane University, New Orleans, Louisiana, 1979. Member of the Council, Indian Institute of Architects, since 1964; Member of the Western Board, Reserve Bank of India, since 1973; Member, Council of Architecture, India, since 1974; Member, Steering Committee, Aga Khan Architecture Awards, Paris, since 1977; Consultant to U.N. University, Tokyo, 1982-83. Exhibition: *Contemporary Architecture in India*, Boston, 1975 (toured the United States); *Charles Correa*, at the *Biennale*, Venice, 1982; *Correa*, British Council, India, 1984. Recipient: First Prize, Gujarat Low-Cost Housing Competition, 1962; Padma Shri Award, Government of India, 1972; Prize for the Improvement in the Quality of Human Settlements, International Union of Architects (presented at the World Congress in Cairo), 1985. Fellow of the Indian Institute of Architects, 1964; Honorary Fellow, American Institute of Architects, 1979; Honorary Doctorate, University of Michigan, Ann Arbor, 1980; Gold Medal, Royal Institute of British Architects, 1984. Address: 9 Mathew Road, Bombay 400 004, India.

Works:

1958 Handloom pavilion, Industrial Fair, Delhi
1959 Vallabh Vidyanagar University new campus buildings, Gujerat, India
      Merchant Houses, Bhavnagar, India
      Lalbhai House, Ahmedabad, India
      Sen House, Calcutta
1960 Gun House Office Building, Ahmedabad, India
      Plutonium plant, Bombay
      Cricket Stadium and Sports Complex, Ahmedabad, India
1961 Suhrid-Geigy Laboratory and Workshop, Bombay
      Lever Pavilion, All-India Fair, Delhi
      Workshop, Ahmedabad Municipal Transport Service, India
1962 Futehally House, Bandra, Bombay
      Mahtama Ghandi Memorial Museum, Ahmedabad, India
1963 Ramkrishna House, Ahmedabad, India
      Sonmarg Apartments, Bombay
1964 Catering Institute, Bombay
      Planning Proposals for Bombay (with P. Mehta and S. Patel)
1965 Mascarenhas House, Bangalore, India
      Kasturba Ghandi Memorial, Poona, India
      Dutta House, Delhi
1967 Cablenagar Township, Kota, India
      Parikh House, Ahmedabad, India
      ECIL Offices, Hyderabad, India
1969 Gandhi Darshan Museum, Delhi
      Union Carbide Factory, Hyderabad, India
      Heredia House, Bombay
      Patwardhan Houses, Poona, India
1970 SNDT Campus, Juhu, Bombay
      EMD Plant, Bombay
      Previ Housing, Lima, Peru
      Jeevan Bima Nagar Township, Borivli, India
      Mazumdar House, Delhi
1971/
74 Plan for New Bombay (as Chief Architect of CIDCO)
1972 Group Housing, Ahmedabad, India
1974 Kovalam Beach Resort, Trivandrum, India
      Planning Proposals for Bangalore, India
1976 Steel Township Master Plan, Libya
      Salvacao Church, Bombay
1978 Tara Group Housing, Delhi (with M. Raj and J. Sawhney)
      Cyclone Victims Housing, Guntur, India
      Watsa Foundation Village Clinic, Alibag, India
1980 Malabar Cements Township, Kerala, India
      HHEC Garment Factory, Madras, India
      Kanchanjunga Apartments, Bombay
1981 Bay Island Hotel, Andaman, India
      Bharat Bhavan, Bhopal, India
1982 Cidade de Goa, Dona Paula
      ONGC Township Master Plan, New Bombay
1983 Gymkhana Bar, Bombay
1984 Kala Academy, Goa
      L & T Housing, Awarpur, India
      Low-income housing, Nerul, New Bombay
1985 New International Airport, Delhi
      Barapani Tourist Resort, Meghalaya, India
      MSEB Offices, Shillong, India
      LIC Centre, Delhi
      Verem Houses, Goa
      Tata Press, New Bombay

Publications:

By CORREA: articles—"Fatehpur Sikri" in *Architectural Forum* (New York), November 1963; "Corbusier in Chandigarh" in *Architectural Review* (London), June 1964; "Our Cities" in *Seminar* (Delhi), March 1965; "Planning for "Bombay" in *Marg* (Bombay), June 1965; "Architecture and Climate" in *Architectural Design* (London), March 1970; "On Urban Planning" in *Science Today* (Bombay), May 1971; "India Today: Programmes and Priorities" in *Architectural Review* (London), December 1971; "Self-Help City: The International Organisation" in *United Nations Bulletin* (Stockholm), August 1973; "Mass Transport" in *Seminar* (Delhi), November 1973; "La Citta che si fa da se" in *Lotus* (Milan), September 1974; "Urban Pollution" in *Times of India Annual,* Bombay 1974; "Space as a Resource" in *Ekistics* (Athens), January 1976; "India: The Urban Scene" in *The Guardian* (London), November 1977; "Functional and Spatial Planning in Low-Cost Housing" in *International Journal for Housing Science* (Oxford, England), December 1977; "Housing for All" and "Towards the New Landscape" in *Urbanisation: 2001,* Paris 1977; "Architects in the Third World" in *Aga Khan Award for Architecture Proceedings,* Geneva 1979; "Urban Strategies for the Third World" in *Habitat International,* London 1980; "Urban Housing in the Third World" in *Openhouse* (Eindhoven, Netherlands), no. 2, 1981; "Open-to-Sky Space" in *Mimar* (Singapore), July-September 1982; "Cidade de Goa" in *Inside Outside* (Bombay), October/November 1982; "Chandigarh: The View from Benares" in *Le Corbusier Archive,* New York 1983; "Comment: of Frogs, Well-Done" in *India Magazine* (Delhi), April 1983; "A Place in the Sun" in *Places,* Cambridge, Massachusetts 1983; "Conflict" in *Architect* (Melbourne), December 1983; recordings—*Form Follows Climate,* tape cassette and slides, London 1980; *Sun and Shadow,* BBC radio interview with Stephen Games, 1984.

On CORREA: books—*New Buildings in the Commonwealth,* edited by J. M. Richards, London 1961; *World Architecture,* vol. 3, edited by John Donat, London 1965; *Architecture in Dry, Hot Climates* by Balwant Saini, Melbourne 1973; *Architects of the Third World* by Udo Kultermann, Cologne 1980; *Charles Correa* by Sherban Cantacuzino, London and Singapore 1984; articles—in *Architectural Review* (London), July 1960, December 1971; *Architectural Design* (London), April 1960; *Architectural Forum* (New York), September 1982; 1962; *Marg* (Bombay), December 1963; *Architecture d'aujourd'hui* (Paris), September 1969; *Daily Telegraph Magazine* (London), 28 September 1973; *Architecture Plus* (New York), March/April 1974; *Design and Environment* (New York), Spring 1976; *Arts et techniques* (Paris), December 1976; *L'Architettura* (Rome), March 1977; *Art and Architecture* (Tehran), April 1978; "A Report from India: Current Work of Charles M. Correa" in *Architectural Record* (New York), July 1980; "Contemporary Asian Architecture," special issue of *Process: Architecture* (Tokyo), November 1980; *Spazio e società* (Milan), December 1981; *Casabella* (Milan), December 1981; *Skyline* (New York), July 1982; *Mimar* (Singapore), July-September 1982; *Asiaweek* (Hong Kong), 3 September 1982; "Open the Box" in *Progressive Architecture* (New York), October 1982; "Mediterranean Metaphors" in *Architectural Record* (New York), April 1983; "Charles Correa: A Profile" in *RIBA Journal* (London), February 1984; "Charles Correa—Royal Gold Medallist 1984" in *Building* (London), 10 February 1984; "British Gold Medal to Indian Architect Correa" in *Architecture* (Washington, D.C.), March 1984; "Correa Comes to Town" in *Building Design* (London), 18 May 1984; "Indian Gold" in *Building* (London), 25 May 1984; "Reaching for the Sky: Charles Correa" in *India Today* (New Delhi), 15 June 1984.

For the architects of the Third World there are four issues of decisive importance. The first has to do with living patterns in a warm climate; the second, with energy conservation; the third, with urbanization; and the fourth, with the nature of change.

1. LIVING PATTERNS: In a warm climate, people have a very different relationship to built form. One needs but a minimal amount of protection, such as a *chatri* (i.e., an overhead canopy), during the day; in the early morning and at night, the best place to be is of course outdoors, under the open sky. Thus, in Asia, the symbol of enlightenment has never been the school building, but rather the guru sitting under a banyan tree; and the monumental temples of south India are experienced not just as gopurams and shrines, but as a movement through the great open-to-sky spaces that lie between them. This movement—which is unknown in a cold climate—has always been a decisive factor in the spatial and functional organization in Indian architecture (from Fatehpur-sikri to Shrirangam).

2. ENERGY-PASSIVE: In a Third World coun-

Charles Correa: Mahatma Gandhi Museum, Ahmedabad, India, 1963.

try such as India, we simply can't afford to squander the kind of energy required to construct—and aircondition—a glass tower in a tropical climate. And this, of course, is an advantage; for it means that the building must itself, through its very form, create the "controls" that the user needs. Such a response necessitates much more than just sun angles and louvres; its needs must involve the section, the plan, the shape—in short, the very heart of the building.

To cross a desert and enter a house around a courtyard is a pleasure beyond mere photogenic image-making; it is the quality of light, and the ambiance of moving air, that forms the essence of our experience. Architecture as a mechanism for dealing with the elements (truly a machine for living!), this is the great challenge—and opportunity—of out Third World.

3. URBANIZATION: The rural migrants pour into our cities. They are looking not merely for houses, but for jobs, education, opportunity. Is the architect, with his highly specialised skills, of any relevance to them? This will remain the central issue of our profession for the next three decades. To find how, where, and when he can be useful is the only way the architect can stretch the boundaries of his vision beyond the succession of middle- and upper-income commissions that encapsulate the profession in Asia.

THE NATURE OF CHANGE: We live in countries of great cultural heritage, countries that wear their past as easily as a woman drapes her sari. But in understanding and using this past, let us never forget the actual living conditions of many of the peoples of Asia and their desperate struggle to shape a better future. Only a decadent architecture looks obsessively backward ("I have seen the past, and it works"). At its most vital, architecture is an agent of change; to invent tomorrow: that is its finest function.

—Charles Correa

Like most of his contemporaries, Charles Correa is one of the post-World War II generation of Indian architects who acquired their professional training in the West and who returned to their homeland to revive the profession of architecture which lay dormant during the 150 years of colonial rule. After years of absence abroad, these architects have shown little sensitivity to local conditions, and many, to this day, continue to inappropriately transplant European forms of building in what is essentially a tropical Indian setting. Correa is an exception. His record to date clearly indicates that he realized the folly of this approach and set about systematically familiarizing himself with the local environment and developing solutions that show sensitivity to and awareness of the local culture.

To achieve this, he did not look to ancient monuments of the past; rather, he sought inspiration from the humble peasant buildings of the land. Some of Correa's best work, such as the Ghandi Memorial Museum in Ahmedabad, is low-cost, utterly simple in concept, and utilizes materials and techniques widely employed in the villages of Goa on the west coast of India where his roots lie. He has used white washed stucco walls and red clay tiled roofs, which remind one of the thousands of villages that blend happily with their environment, as they lay scattered throughout the southern Indian landscape.

In recent years, he has extended his vocabulary by using applied colours and textures as positive elements of his architecture. A spectacular example of this approach can be seen in the Cidada de Goa Hotel, where rich colour compositions dominate the structure itself and thus add a refreshing touch of freedom and flamboyance to the building.

Correa's early work mostly involved architecture in a limited sense, the design of individual buildings, ranging from housing to buildings for tourism, education, commerce, and industry. These projects still continue to form an important part of his work. In fact, his output has expanded both in range and complexity ever since he established his multi-disciplinary professional practice.

During the past decade, Correa has also increasingly concerned himself with the plight of homeless people who are the victims of urbanization in the Third World countries. His theories and solutions to these urgent problems are pragmatic and are based on his own work as planner of New Bombay, a settlement of two million people across the harbour from the existing city. These solutions have attracted worldwide attention because they get to the source of the problem and have relevance to similar situations faced by governments in many developing regions of Africa, Asia, and Latin America.

Correa suggests that in order to build reasonable living environments for the maximum number of people, governments should not concentrate on building houses but should leave this to the resources of the people themselves. In proposing this solution Correa is, of course, fully aware that self-help housing has been most successful in rural areas where people have access to building materials and sufficient spare time on their hands to construct their own shelter. It is much more difficult to accomplish this task in urban areas, and here lies the challenge for planners and architects to use their expertise and innovative abilities to generate low-cost building activity.

This is a refreshing view, particularly since it emanates from a representative of a profession that has always been preoccupied with building forms. He believes the main effort of housing authorities should be directed to the provision of an infrastructure of basic services, that the problem is not one of low-cost housing but of proper land-use planning. Correa's major contribution in this area lies in developing planning proposals that can lend themselves to high densities in order to reduce development costs of land, yet ensure adequate community facilities.

Correa has already proved himself as a thinker and pacesetter in pointing the way in which architects may possibly contribute to solve the enormous problems of urban environmental crises, particularly in the Third World.

—B. S. Saini

CORRIGAN, Peter Russell.

Australian. Born in Daylesford, Victoria, 6 May 1941. Educated at the University of Melbourne, 1959-65, B.Arch. 1966; Yale University, New Haven, Connecticut, 1967-69, M.Environmental Design 1969. Design draftsman, Godfrey and Spowers Pty. Ltd., Melbourne, 1964, and Best Overend Pty. Ltd., Melbourne, 1965-66; draftsman, Mockridge, Stahle and Mitchell, Melbourne, 1966; draftsman/theatrical engineer, George Izenour and Associates, New Haven, 1967; Senior Urban Planner, New Haven Redevelopment Agency, 1967-68; worked in the Design Department of Roche Dinkeloo (q.v.: Kevin Roche and John Dinkeloo) and Associates, Hamden, Connecticut, 1969; Design Architect for Paul Rudolph, q.v. ,New York,1971; Programme Architect, Ulrich Franzen (q.v .) and Associates, New York, 1971-73; worked in the Design Group, Gruen (q.v. Victor Gruen) Associates, New York, 1973-74; Design Architect, Johnson and Burgee, q.v. Philip Johnson and John Burgee, New York, 1974. Since 1975, Partner, with Maggie Edmond, Edmond and Corrigan, Architects and Planners, Melbourne. Tutor, Yale University, 1968-69; Guest Critic, City University of New York, 1971-73; Guest Lecturer in Stage Design, University of Melbourne, 1976; Guest Professor, Harvard University Graduate School of Design, Cambridge, Massachusetts, 1983-84. Lecturer in Design Theory and Design Studio, Royal Melbourne Institute of Technology, since 1973. Member, Australian Performing Group, Melbourne, since 1974. Member, Education Service Board, Royal Australian Institute of Architects, Victoria Chapter, since 1976. Exhibition: *Four Melbourne Architects*, Powell Street Art Gallery, Melbourne, 1979; *The Pleasures of Architecture*, New South Wales Institute of Technology, Sydney, 1980; *Australian Perspecta 81*, Art Gallery of New South Wales, Sydney, 1981; *Seven in the Seventies*, Visual Arts Gallery, Monash University, Melbourne, 1981; *Australian and British Stage Design*, at the Adelaide Festival, South Australia (toured Australia), 1982; *La Modernité* , at the *Biennale*, Paris, 1982; *Architecture as Idea*, R.M.I.T. Gallery, Melbourne, 1984; International Organization of Scenographers and Theatre Technicians Exhibition, Tokyo, 1984. Recipient: Bronze Medal, 1979, Citation Awards, 1981 (twice) and 1982, Merit Award, 1982 and 1983, and National Award, 1982, Royal Australian Institute of Architects. Address: Edmond and Corrigan, 40 Little Latrobe Street, Melbourne, Victoria 3000, Australia.

Works:

1965 Mercovich House, Burwood, Victoria
     McCarthy House, Lillydale, Victoria
1966 Schmidt House, Eltham, Victoria
     Hosking House, Donvale, Victoria
1974 Resurrection Parish Centre, Keysborough, Victoria
     St. Colman's Church, Mortlake, Victoria
1975 Resurrection Church, Keysborough, Victoria
     Resurrection School, stage 1, Keysborough, Victoria
     Amenities Block, Nagambie, Victoria
     City Square, Melbourne (competition project)
     Freedom Club Kindergarten, Keysborough, Victoria
1976 St. Joseph's Chapel, Surrey Hills, Victoria
     Resurrection School, stage II, Keysborough, Victoria
1977 Wonthaggi Arts Activity Centre, Wonthaggi, Victoria
     Housing for the elderly, Keysborough, Victoria
     Sister Nance's Studio, Keysborough, Victoria
     Union Theatre renovations, University of Melbourne
1978 Westcott House, Burwood, Victoria
     Last Laugh Restaurant, Collingwood, Victoria
     Barber House, Carlton, Victoria
     Industrial park and high-rise development, for McIvor Village, Footscray, Victoria
1979 Performing Arts Centre, Sale, Victoria
     National Archives, Canberra (competition project)
     Football Club, Sale, Victoria
     Community Centre, Sale, Victoria
1980 Wurruk Industrial Park, Sale, Victoria
     Hamad Factory, Sale, Victoria
     Dog Pound, Sale, Victoria
     Cemetery Gates, Sale, Victoria
     Low-energy housing prototypes, Sale, Victoria
     Macartney House, Camberwell, Victoria
1981 Mercovich House, Doncaster, Victoria
     Newcastle Foreshore Development, New South Wales (competition project)
     Sculpture Park, Melbourne
     Wodonga Housing, Victoria
     Portland Housing, Victoria
     Kay Street housing, Melbourne
1982 St. Francis Xavier Presbytery, Frankston, Victoria
     Australian pavilion, at the *Biennale*, Venice, Italy
     Lygon Street Action Plan
1982 Calnin House, Korumburra, Victoria
     Newman House, Sherbrook, Victoria
1983 St. Francis Xavier Primary School, Frankston, Victoria

Peter Corrigan: Macartney House, Camberwell, Victoria, 1980.

Bato Reid Merchant Bank Tenancy, Melbourne
Charman House extension, Melbourne
Clock Tower, Sale, Victoria
1984 Batman Park, Yarra River, Melbourne
Australian Naval Memorial, Canberra,
Knox Gardens Primary School, Melbourne
Service Centre, National Sports Institute, Canberra
Buckland Hill Study, Fremantle, Western Australia

Theatre: sets and costumes for 14 student productions, University of Melbourne, 1963-66; sets and costumes for *Don Giovanni*, Sydney Opera House,1974; stage designs since 1974—9 Australian performing Group productions, Pram Factory, Carlton, Victoria; 7 Melbourne Theatre Company productions St. Martin's Theatre, Melbourne; 7 Last laugh Theatre Restaurant productions, Collingwood, Victoria; 4 Adelaide Arts Centre productions; 2 Grant Street Theatre productions, Melbourne; 1 Victorian Opera Company touring production (children's opera); 1 Australian Performing Group touring productions, Bergamo, Italy; 2 Night Shift Company busking productions, Melbourne; 13 Hoopla Theatre Company productions, Playbox Theatre, Melbourne, and Nimrod Theatre, Sydney; 1 Art Nouveau Theatre productions, South Melbourne; 2 La Mama Theatre productions, Carlton, Victoria.

Publications:

By CORRIGAN: articles—"Featurism and Our Spire" in *Farrago* (Melbourne), 5 May 1961; 'Smudges' in *Melbourne University Architecture School Broadsheet*, November 1961; "Stage Space" in *Theatre* (Melbourne), July 1962; "Church Architecture" (lecture), published by the Newman Society, Melbourne University 1964; "2 Houses at Burwood and Croydon" in *Cross-Section* (Melbourne), February 1967; "Life in the Plug-In Age" in the *Herald* (Melbourne), 3 April 1967; "Reflections on a New North American Architecture—The Venturis" in *Architecture in Australia* (Sydney), February 1972; "Inside the Third Reich" in *Architecture in Australia* (Sydney), December 1972; "On Non-Architecture" in *Architecture in Australia* (Sydney), December 1973; "Education Hobart" in *Architecture in Australia* (Sydney), February 1974; "Workbook of an Unsuccessful Architect" in *Architecture in Australia* (Sydney), June 1974; "Architecture's Changing Role" in *The Age* (Melbourne), 14 October 1974; "Bronze Medal and Brute Steel" in *Meanjin Quarterly* (Melbourne), no. 1, 1976; "Molnar House, Glen Waverley" in *Architect* (Melbourne), September 1976; "Passion in the Suburbs" in *Architecture in Australia* (Sydney), February/March 1977; "Church News" in *Architect* (Melbourne), May 1977; "Carlton Designs" in *Theatre Australia* (Newcastle, New South Wales), August 1977; "Australian Architecture and the stage" in *Architecture Australia* (Melbourne), September 1979; "An Interview" with Betsy Brenan in *Vogue Living* (Sydney), October 1984.

On CORRIGAN: books—*Housing 82*, Melbourne 1981; *La Modernité ou l'esprit du temps* , exhibition catalogue with texts by Georges Boudaille, Jean-Pierre Dupont and others, Paris 1982; *Australian Art Review 1982*, edited by Leon Paroissien, Sydney 1982; *Housing 83*, Melbourne 1983; *Old Continent—New Building*, edited by Leon Paroissien and Michael Griggs, Sydney 1983; articles—"Civic Square Competition" in *Architecture in Australia* (Sydney), September 1976; "Exorcism of the Modernist Spirit" by Norman Day in *The Age* (Melbourne), 23 May 1978; "The Australian Eleven " by Philip Drew in *Architecture + Urbanism* (Tokyo), August 1978; "Suburban Manifesto" by Cathy Peake in *The National Times* (Sydney), 10 February 1979; "Peter Corrigan: Architetto australiano" in *Domus* (Milan), April 1980; "Peter Corrigan's Architecture: A Kind of Exposition" by Greg Missingham in *Transition* (St. Kilda, Victoria), March 1981; "Edmond and Corrigan and Poor Architecture" in *Pol* (Sydney), March 1981; "In Focus: Edmond and Corrigan, Melbourne" in *Architecture + Urbanism* (Tokyo), April 1981; "Suburban passion" by Jennifer Taylor in *Architecture Australia* (Melbourne), November 1981; "Corrigan's Magical Island" by Stephen Downes in *The Age* (Melbourne), 4 September 1984.

This office's search for form is conducted as a search for both content and value for money. It is intended as a fruitful interplay between the traditions of architecture and the social philosophies of our time. Mind you, there is now an emerging Australian urban culture, and it would be a serious blue to miss the tram.

—Peter Corrigan

Peter Corrigan studied architecture at the University of Melbourne, then completed a post-graduate degree in Environmental Design at Yale and worked for five years in the United States. As a student and since graduation, Corrigan has been active as a designer of sets and costumes for numerous theatrical productions, most of which have had to be carried out with little money. This experience of "poor theatre" in off-Broadway companies and in Melbourne has exerted a strong influence on his ideas concerning architecture. Much as in the theatre, Corrigan improvises his architecture; he uses cheap, ordinary materials in a decorative, entertaining manner.

In the direct intervention of the architect in the building process, in the decorative use of brickwork, and in the exploitation of local building motifs, Corrigan's architecture closely resembles that of the Amsterdam Expressionist Michel de Klerk. The inspiration for the decorative ideas in Corrigan's buildings is the common and ugly buildings of the new suburbs—he prefers to describe his architecture as "poor architecture." The form and structure of these buildings as opposed to the imagery, is far from unsophisticated, having benefited from Corrigan's studies with Venturi.

Corrigan's creation of a unique style based on local suburban motifs is an impressive achievement. It has not been easy, and some of Corrigan's buildings, such as the Parish Centre, Keysborough, and St. Joseph's Chapel, Surrey Hills, testify to the struggle, while others, notably the Resurrection School, Keysborough, are far more successful in relating all the individual themes in a coherent whole.

In the early 1980s, Corrigan's architecture was the subject of both Australian and international critical acclaim, which applauded his adventurous appropriation of motifs drawn from the vulgar Australian suburb. Of the three principal environments—the bush, the suburb, and the city—Corrigan chose to explore the suburb for evidence of the Australian character, Amongst his most recent works, the Macartney house (1980), Kay Street housing (1981), and the Calnin (Korumburra, 1982), and Newman (Sherbrook, 1982) houses point most clearly to new tendencies. Whereas the earlier works were self-conscious assemblies of such common suburban elements as verandahs, parapets, porches, bay windows, etc., brought together in pivoting, colliding, or dangerously skidding plans that frequently shocked with their very fragmented composition and multivalent exhibitionism, in these more recent works there is a strengthened interest in type and the assembly of the building group from an assortment of building types drawn from sources that are now no longer restricted to the suburban milieu.

The question raised by Corrigan's architecture is whether an authentic expression of an Australian national sentiment can be distilled from the dissection of the vulgar Australian suburb or whether, as in the example of a contemporary, Glenn Murcutt, it is the inspiration of the Australian landscape and flora that will lead to a new form that is authentic and true Australian places. What is incontrovertible is that Corrigan has broken with the vision of Australia as a "New Britannia" in the southern hemisphere and has succeeded in suitably honouring Australian experiences.

Corrigan's architecture is rich and complex, so it is not easy to come to a concise assesment of its full import. His buildings ignore the taboo against ornamentation and introduce a rich decoration of patterned brickwork. They are open and inclusive, rather than closed and exclusive. And instead of seeking to correct and improve on Australian visual traditions as Robin Boyd wanted to, Corrigan exploits these traditions in much the same fashion as, in another genre, Barry Humphries does, by employing them within a strong artistic framework. Corrigan's architecture will not satisfy those who demand an architecture of equilibrium, poise and harmony. His architecture, after all, is true to life.

—Philip Drew

COSTA, Lúcio.

Brazilian. Born in Toulon, France, of Brazilian parents, 27 February 1902. Educated at the Royal Grammar School, Newcastle, England, 1911-13; Collège National de Montreux, Switzerland, 1914-16; National School of Fine Arts, Rio de Janeiro, 1917-22, Dip.Arch. 1924. Served in the Brazilian Army, 1920. Married Julieta Guimaraes in 1928 (died, 1954); children: Maria Elisa and Helena. In private practice, Rio de Janeiro, since 1924 (collaborated with Gregori Warchavchik, 1931-33). Director, National School of Fine Arts, Rio de Janeiro, 1930-31. Since 1937, Consultant Architect, IPHAN: Instituto do Patrimonio Historico e Artistico Nacional, Rio de Janeiro. D.F.A.: Harvard University, Cambridge, Massachusetts, 1960. Honorary Member, Royal Institute of British Architects, American Institute of Architects, and the Académie d'Architecture, France. Commandeur, Légion d'Honneur, France. Address: Avenida Delfim Moreira 1212, Leblon, Rio de Janeiro, Brazil.

Works:

1932   Alfredo Schwartz House, Rio de Janeiro (with Gregori Warchavchik)
        San Miguel Church restoration, Rio Grande Do Sul, Brazil
1937/
  43   Ministry of Education and Health, Rio de Janeiro (with Le Corbusier, Oscar Niemeyer, Affonso Eduardo Reidy, Jorge Machado Moreira; now the Palace of Culture)
1939   Brazilian Pavilion, World's Fair, New York (with Oscar Niemeyer)
1942   Hungria Machado House, Rio de Janeiro
1943   Saavedra House, Correias, Brazil
1944   Park Hotel, Friburgo, Brazil
1948/
  54   Guinle Park Apartments, Rio de Janeiro
1957- Master plan for Brasilia
1969   Master plan for Baixada de Jacarepagua, Rio de Janeiro

Publications:

By COSTA: books—*Arquitectura Carioca,* Rio de Janeiro 1952; *The Architect and Contemporary Society,* Venice 1952; *About My Work in Brazil,* Rio de Janeiro 1958; *Scientific and Technological Humanism,* Cambridge, Massachusetts 1961; *Biblioteca Educacion y Cultura, vol. 10: Arquitectura,* Rio de Janeiro 1980; articles—"A Necessary Documentation" in *Revista do Servico do Patrimonio historico Artistico* (Rio de Janeiro), no. 1, 1938; "Portuguese-Brazilian Furniture" in *Revista do Servico do Patrimonio Historico Artistico* (Rio de Janeiro), no. 3, 1940; "Jesuit Architecture in Brazil" in *Revista do Servico do Patrimonio Historico* (Rio de Janeiro), no. 5, 1941; "L'Urbaniste Défend sa Capitale" in

Lúcio Costa: Park Hotel, Friburgo, Brazil, 1944.

Architecture: Formes et Fonctions (Lausanne), no. 14, 1968; "Manifestation Normale de Vie" in *Architecture: Formes et Fonctions* (Lausanne), no. 15, 1969; "Lucio Costa por ele mesmo" in *Jornal do Brasil* (Rio de Janeiro), 27 February 1982.

On COSTA: books—*Modern Architecture in Brazil* by Henrique Mindlin, Rio de Janeiro and Amsterdam, 1956; *Lúcio Costa* by J. O. Gazenco and M. M. Scarone, Buenos Aires 1959; *Doorway to Brasilia* by A. Magalhaes and E. Feldman, Philadelphia 1959; article—"Individualidades na historia da atual arquitectura no Brasil" by G. Ferraz in *Habitat* (Sao Paulo), October 1956; "Lucio Costa – Brazilian town planner" in *Metropolis* (Paris), November/December 1974; "Lucio Costa: notes for a revolutionary biography" in *Summa* (Buenos Aires), April 1983.

Lúcio Costa established himself as a leader of the avant-garde in Brazil after the revolution in 1930. He worked in partnership with Gregori Warchavchik who had brought new Cubist ideas from Europe to developing Brazil. Costa himself was appointed Director of the School of Fine Arts in Rio de Janeiro (which embraced architectural studies), and so was able to influence subsequent generations of architects in the ideals of the modern movement.

One of the most significant of his buildings was the Ministry of Education and Health in Rio de Janeiro, 1937-43, for which Le Corbusier acted as consultant. This huge slab building was erected to the designs of a team led by Costa which included Niemeyer. The *brise-sôleil* and the *pilotis,* trademarks of Le Corbusier, were ideal for the Brazilian climate, and the architecture was enthusiastically hailed by Brazilians. Costa's next building was the Brazilian Pavilion for the New York *World's Fair* of 1939, again designed in collaboration with Oscar Niemeyer.

Costa has always been devoted to the study and conservation of historic buildings in Brazil; as well, he has been a perceptive discoverer of architectural and innovatory talent. His early championing of Niemeyer ensured the rise of that architect to the singular position he later held for many years.

Following the Second World War, Costa designed the Guinle Park Apartments in Rio de Janeiro. His most famous work, however, is his design for the new capital of Brasilia. The master plan has a shape rather like a crossbow that recalls the geometrical simplicity of Renaissance and classical town plans. Significantly, Costa's extremely pellucid plan serves as a framework for the great number of buildings erected to designs by Oscar Niemeyer.

—James Stevens Curl

COTTIER, Keith Eric.
Australian. Born in Sydney, New South Wales, 27 May 1938. Educated at the Sydney Technical College; 1954-60 (Board of Architects Travelling Scholarship, 1960). Married Elizabeth Wickham Barrett in 1962; children: Sarah, Benjamin, and Hugo. Travelled in Europe for two years, and worked with Ian Fraser and Associates, London, for two years, 1960-64; returned to Australia to work with John Allen and Russell C. Jack, 1964. Since 1965, Partner, Allen, Jack and Cottier, architects, Paddington, Sydney. Recipient: Blacket Award, 1967 and 1970, and New South Wales Merit Award, 1971 and 1976, Royal Australian Institute of Architects; ACI-St. Regis Travelling Scholarship,1972. Fellow of the Royal Australian Institute of Architects, 1975. Address: Allen, Jack and Cottier, 6a Liverpool Street, Paddington, New South Wales 2021, Australia.

Works (with Allen, Jack and Cottier):

1965 House, 99 Riverview Road, Clareville, Sydney
1967 Clubbe Hall, Frensham School, Mittagong, New South Wales
1969 Bryant House school dormitory, Frensham School, Mittagong, New South Wales

Keith Cottier: Swimming Pool of Knox Grammar School, Wahroonga, Sydney, 1982.

1970 Library, Frensham School, Mittagong, New South Wales

Rothbury Winery, stage 1, Pokolbin, New South Wales

1971 Kuringai College of Advanced Education, Lindfield, New South Wales (with the New South Wales Department of Public Works)

1972 Rothbury Winery, stage II, Pokolbin, New South Wales

1974 Swimming Pool Complex, Mount Druitt, New South Wales

1975 Seymour Centre for the Performing Arts, University of Sydney

1980 New Teaching Building, Knox Grammer School, Wahroonga, Sydney

1982 Music Centre, Physical Education Centre and Car Park/Playing Fields, Knox Grammer School, Wahroonga, Sydney

Macquarie Galleries, and Magnus Nankervis & Carl advertising agency (conversion of Masonic Temple building), 204 Clarence Street, Sydney

1983 Stratford Hall houses/apartments conversion, Darling Point, Sydney

Cottier House, Paddington, Sydney

1984 Residential and Administrative Buildings, Bruce National Institute of Sport, Canberra

Publications

By COTTIER: book—*Sydney Faces Special Places*, editor, Sydney 1983; articles—"Holiday residence for Mr. Lochhead at Paradise Beach, Sydney" in *Nuove Ville—New Villas*, edited by Robert Aloi, Milan 1970; "Paddington, New South Wales" in *Historic Places of Australia, vol. 2* , Sydney 1979.

On COTTIER: books—*Architecture in Australia* by J.M. Freeland, Melbourne 1968; *Towards an Australian Architecture* by Harry Sowden, Sydney 1968.

Much of my work has been concerned with relatively low-cost buildings, often using quite traditional materials and construction techniques. The architecture is seen as a direct response to the demands of both the existing environment or "place" and the functional needs of the users. The resultant character of the built forms may therefore differ considerably from one project to another, "appropriateness" to the particular problem being the guiding principle. Whilst the functional needs are becoming increasingly complex and technical, underlying all my work is an attempt to maintain human scale and to produce a relaxed, easily-understood organization of spaces.

—Keith E. Cottier

Keith Cottier's work falls within the style of what has become to be known as the Sydney School, an idiom of brick and timber construction, appropriately within the capacity of available expertise of the traditional Australian builder (applied as it was mainly to domestic work) but using a new approach towards traditional materials. Cottier's approach to design is, in his own words, pragmatic. His initial concentration is on planning, the relationship of building to environment, the sequence of internal spaces, and, finally, the influence of the subsequent forms on the three-dimensional qualities of the design.

One of his earlier works is a house in the beach suburb of Clareville. It is set on a steep site, amongst trees, overlooking the water. It is of timber construction, with the frame pulled out from the wall surface, creating what is almost a cage of timber members to relate to the surrounding trees.

His work at Frensham School, Mittagong, includes the multi-purpose Clubbe Hall, Bryant House dormitory, and a Library. The Hall, in addition to its school function, provides a well-used and much-needed venue in a country town for visiting musical

and dramatic groups. Cottier's realization of the importance of spaces external to a building is shown in his design of the Library: by careful siting of the Library, he turned existing spaces into protected external courtyards that have proved to be a major social congregation point for the school.

In 1970 he completed stage I of the Rothbury Winery (stage II was completed in 1972), which he feels to be his most satisfying project. It provides accommodation not only for wine making and storage but in addition for a large banqueting hall used for promotion. This was an ambitious building programme for a new winery, and in part the programme was responsible for creating "image." The clients were a group of wine makers and connoisseurs whose tastes are somewhat romantic: that attitude influenced the establishment of atmosphere. The building's form, enclosing as it does the paraphernalia of wine making, needed to be a blend of factory and traditional Australian country style. Cottier was influenced by the classic Australian woolshed, with its strong timber detailing and simple forms, and the site provided few constraints.

The Seymour Centre for the Performing Arts at the University of Sydney best exemplifies Cottier's concentration on external spaces between buildings, the need to have good working spaces internally, and the growth of forms from these work points. The site is surrounded by a multiplicity of buildings and interspersed by services that constrained the physical limits of planning. Three theatres provide venues for drama, chamber music, and experimental theatre. The complex thus provides for a wide variety of users, a necessity that influenced him in his selection of materials, both simple and sophisticated. There was no client in the form of a resident company, and Cottier was required to make many of the decisions that normally would have been made by such a client. His overriding determination was to provide workable, flexible theatres.

Cottier regards the psychological analysis of the client's needs, immediate and future, as a paramount influence. He sees every job as an individual problem in which there is always a need to recognize, isolate, and solve the problem at the core of the situation. When it has been grasped, all other decisions—in planning, massing, and detailing—will fall within the pattern prescribed. Each building needs to work on many different levels, and the greatest test is whether it stands the test of time.

—Diane Kell

COX, Philip Sutton.

Australian. Born in Sydney, New South Wales, 10 September 1939. Educated at the Church of England Grammar School, Sydney, 1949-55; University of Sydney, 1956-62 and 1969-71 (Royal Australian Institute of Architects Silver Medal, 1962), B.Arch. (honours) 1962, and Diploma in Town and Country Planning 1971. Married Louise Gowing in 1973; daughter: Charlotte. Worked with S.P. Higgins, New Guinea, 1962, Bruce Rickard, Sydney, 1962-63, and Ian McKay, Sydney, 1963-66. Since 1967, Principal, Philip Cox and Partners, Sydney (practice divided into three separate parts, 1974; Philip Cox and Partners, architectural services; Cox, Tanner, architectural conservation and publishing; Cox and Corkill, environmental planning). Tutor, University of Sydney, 1963-70, and University of New South Wales, Sydney, 1971-73; Visiting Professor, University of New South Wales, Sydney, 1980. Chairman, Historic Buildings Committee, Royal Australian Institute of Architects, 1971-76; Member, Historic Buildings Committee, National Trust, New South Wales, 1971-78; Member, 1979, and Vice-Chairman, 1980, Architecture and Design Panel, Visual Art Board of Australia; Councillor, 1979, and Member of the Board of Architectural Education, 1982-83, New South Wales Chapter, Royal Australian In-

stitute of Architects; Design Arts Committee Member, Australia Council, 1982-83. Exhibition: *Sydney Young Contemporaries*, Blaxland Galleries, Sydney, 1966. Recipient: Silver Medal, 1963, and Merit Award, 1973, 1976 (twice), and 1977 (twice), 1978 (twice), 1979 (twice), 1980, and 1981 (twice), Urban and Community Design Award, 1977, Conservation Award, 1983, and Canberra Medallion, 1983, and Urban and Community Design Award, 1977, Royal Australian Institute of Architects; Sir John Sulman Medal, with Ian McKay, 1964, 1966; Wilkinson Award, 1970; ACI St. Regis Travelling Scholarship and Institute of Valuers Prize, University of Sydney, 1971; Gray and Mulroney Award, with Louise Gowing, 1975; Canberra Medallion for Architectural Merit, 1978; C.S. Daley Medal, 1979; New South Wales Permanent Building Society Award, 1980; Sir Robert Metthew Award, Commonwealth Association of Architects, 1983. Address: Philip Cox and Partners, 2 McManus Street, McMahon's Point, New South Wales 2060, Australia.

Works:

1964 St. Andrews Presbyterian Preparatory College, Leppington, New South Wales (with Ian McKay)

1966 C.B. Alexander Presbyterian Agricultural College, stage I, Paterson, New South Wales (with Ian McKay)

Yarrawarra Boys Home, Kurri Kurri, New South Wales (with Ian McKay)

1968 Ferguson House, Palm Beach, New South Wales

1969 Hawkins House, Cheltenham, New South Wales

1971 Hotel, Minto, New South Wales

1971/
81 Norfolk Island restoration, Kingston, Norfolk Island

1972 Hotel, Leppington, New South Wales

1974 Union Building, stages II and III, Macquarie University, Sydney

1975 Non-Collegiate Student Housing, Macquarie University, Sydney

Special Education Centre, Macquarie University, Sydney

Denham Court restoration, Ingleburn, New South Wales

Admiralty House restoration, Kirribilli, New South Wales

Housing development, McMahon's Point, Sydney (with Louise Gowing)

Doctor's House, Kellyville, New South Wales

Embassy for the Republic of Ireland, Canberra

Jerilderie Court, Reid, A.C.T.

1976 C.B. Alexander Presbyterian Agricultural College, stage II, Paterson, New South Wales

Burrundulla, Homestead restoration, Mudgee, New South Wales

Report on official residences' grounds, Sydney and Canberra

Yarramlumla Building, Canberra, A.C.T.

Narooma High School, Narooma, New South Wales

Moore House, McMahons Point, New South Wales

Supreme Courts restoration, Sydney, New South Wales

Old Canberra Brickworks commercial development, Canberra, A.C.T.

Parameadows Special Purpose School, Wollongong, New South Wales

1977 Dalwood House restaurant conversion, Branxton, Hunter Valley, New South Wales

National Sports Stadium, Bruce, Canberra,

Kambah Health Centre, Canberra

Conservation study: Braidwood, New South Wales

Resource Centre and Student Amenities Building, Hawkesbury College, Richmond, New South Wales

1978 Reid Medium Density Housing, Canberra

Akuna Bay Marina, Coal and Candle Creek, New South Wales

Family Court and Australian Capital Territory Juvenile Court, Canberra

Woolloomooloo Housing Development, Woolloomooloo, New South Wales

1979 Brougham Street Housing, Woolloomooloo, New South Wales

Golden Grove Street Housing, Newtown, New South Wales

Lindgren Holdings factory and offices, Brisbane, Queensland

National Indoor Sports and Training Centre, Bruce, A.C.T.

1980 Hawkesbury Agricultural College, Richmond, New South Wales

Mudgee Shire Council Chambers, Mudgee, New South Wales

Villawood Housing Commission Development, Villawood, New South Wales

New South Wales Institute of Technology Market 3 Development, Sydney

1981 Garden Island Refit Berth Facility, New South Wales

Senior School extensions, Barker College, Hornsby, New South Wales

Specialist Gymnastic Facility, Canberra

Smiths Hill High School, New South Wales

1982 Armidale Civic Centre, New South Wales

Hambrett House, Dural, New South Wales

Garden Island Naval Stores conversion, New South Wales

Kent Street Housing, Millers Point, New South Wales

National Council of Independent Schools Building, Deakin, A.C.T.

Resort Centre, Ayers Rock, Northern Territory

Malaysian Hospital Buildings, Telok Intan, Malaysia

1983 Academic Building, Nepean College of Advanced Education, Kingswood, New South Wales

Tivoli Gardens, National Conference Centre and Hotel, Canberra

Wittenoom Township Development, Pilbra, Western Australia

Sydney Cricket Ground, New South Wales

1984 Junior School extension, Barker College, Hornsby, New South Wales

World Cup Athletics 1985 staging, Canberra

Publications:

By COX: books—*Rude Timber Buildings in Australia*, with J.M. Freeland and Wesley Stacey, London 1969; *Building Norfolk Island*, with Wesley Stacey, Melbourne 1970; *The Australian Homestead*, with Wesley Stacey, Melbourne 1972; *Historic Towns of Australia*, with Wesley Stacey, Melbourne 1973; *Restoring Old Australian Houses and Buildings*, with Howard Tanner, Melbourne 1975; *Colonial Architecture of Australia*, with Clive Lucas and Wesley Stacey, Melbourne 1978; *South Coast of New South Wales*, Melbourne 1978; *Hunter Valley of New South Wales*, with Howard Tanner and Meredith Walker, South Melbourne 1978; *Functional Vernacular, with David Moore, 1980; An Australian Architecture—architecture of the new world*, 1982; *The Work of Philip Cox and Partners, 1963-83: A Chronological Survey of Major Architectural Works*, Sydney 1983; articles—"Housing over the Past Ten Years" in *Architecture in Australia* (Sydney), October 1973; "Belltrees, Scone, N.S.W." in *Architecture in Australia* (Sydney), 1976; "Collapse of the Suburban Dream" in *Medium Density Housing in Australia*, edited by John Dean and Bruce Judd, Sydney 1983.

On COX: books—*Towards an Australian Architecture* by Harry Sowden, Sydney 1968; *Architecture in Australia* by J.M. Freeland, Melbourne 1968; *Australian Housing in the Seventies* by Howard Tanner, Sydney 1976; *Australian Architects No. 1: Philip Cox*, Sydney 1984; articles—"Tocal": C.B. Alexander Presbyterian Agricultural College in *Architecture in Australia* (Sydney), September 1966; "Special Education Centre, Macquarie University" and "Doctor's House, Kellyville" in *Architecture Australia* (Sydney), October/November 1976; "Special Education Centre, Macquarie University, Ryde, N.S.W." in *Builder NSW* (Sydney), March 1977; "Architecture as Spatial Enclosures" by Neville Couten in *Architecture Australia* (Sydney), April/May 1977; "House, Castle Hill, N.S.W." and "National Athletics Stadium, Bruce, A.C.T." in *Architecture Australia* (Sydney), January 1978; "National Athletics Stadium" in *Architecture + Urbanism* (Tokyo), September 1978.

The architecture of Philip Cox and Partners is not the creation of one person alone. It is the collective aspiration and philosophy of a group of people dedicated in their ambition to create an architecture relevant to Australia.

Our first buildings were designed with a passion of Australia. "Emerald Hill" was our first commission. This school for delinquent children consisted of an old homestead with a split timber settler's hut at the rear. The house was a typical vernacular homestead of the 1880s and had little architectural pretension. The buildings emerged unconsciously accepting the same vocabulary of verandahs and covered ways. The architecture that emerged was the basis for all future work—that is, an architecture pays that respect for its immediate environment, essentially horizontal and punctuated by simple massing, and one that integrates the outdoors with indoors. This architecture acknowledges the Australian climate by the use of sun-shading devices such as breezeways, verandahs, pergolas, and lattice and by these means achieves passive energy efficiency as does most Australian vernacular architecture. The buildings built in this first period had a restricted vocabulary of materials, such as natural brick, unglazed tiles, rough timber, and glass. The restriction was necessary to get back to the genesis of things, as a potter might do when dealing with raw clay rather than relying on glaze or ornament.

Philip Cox: National Sports Stadium, Bruce, Canberra, 1977.

The architecture was sincere in its belief that it was a "bare bones" architecture displaying its entire skeletal anatomy. It related completely to the cathedrals of the Australian Bush—the woolsheds, incredibly beautiful buildings where structure delights and inspires. Here, there is no division between architecture and structural engineering, and this axiom follows our thinking even to the present.

We would like to think we are less influenced than others by fashionable scrimmages of the architectural world. We would like to think we are dealing with fundamental issues and basic concepts of architecture, such as mass, form, space, colour, and textures, whilst recognising social, political, and economic values.

—Philip Cox

During Philip Cox's student years, a natural skill at drawing and an interest in architectural history were broadened by employment with Bruce Rickard and travels in New Guinea. Rickard has studied landscape architecture with Ian McHarg in Pennsylvania and had experienced Frank Lloyd Wright's architecture firsthand; he was endeavouring to integrate these influences with a human-scaled architecture appropriate to the Sydney region. New Guinea revealed a rich variety of vernacular architecture and provided an abiding interest in abstract and primitive forms of art.

At twenty-three, Cox was presented with his first major design commission by the Presbyterian Church. A bequest of one C.B. Alexander, grazier of "Tocal," Paterson, New South Wales, sought to establish a private agricultural college the architecture of which would reflect the traditions and materials embodied in Tocal homestead. The scope of the project was beyond the capabilities of a recent graduate, so Cox began an association with Ian McKay, an older architect with a range of practical experience and a similar design direction. For a "test run," the Presbyterian Church commissioned the new practice to undertake St. Andrews Home for Boys, centred around an old verandahed farmhouse at Leppington to the southwest of Sydney. New pitch-roofed and verandahed buildings formed courtyard spaces and extended the vernacular tradition of the homestead group. During this time, the scheme for Tocal developed—a great range of buildings set on a hilltop in countryside of extraordinary beauty. The spired chapel was the central pivot, with planes of roof defining the other functions. Timber, brick, and tile, of local origin, combined in massive walls, trusses, and roofscapes to make an impressive organic composition. The association with McKay produced as well a range of sensitively detailed brick and timber houses, forming a significant portion of the "Sydney School" of domestic architecture of the 1960s—informal houses of rustic materials nestled in bushland settings.

Cox set up practice on his own in 1967 and commenced an involvement in architectural education and publishing; his interest in architectural history provided the basis for several books. One outgrowth of these books was involvement in architectural restoration—for example the military building at Kingston, Norfolk Island and the Old Supreme Court in Sydney). During this period, his commissions were generally domestic, and Cox experimented with massed form in the landscape, emphasizing pitched roofs, chimney stacks, and angled glazing. Two houses, Ferguson at Palm Beach, New South Wales and Hawkins at Cheltenham, New South Wales, best show this trend.

Cox now sought grander opportunities, and the practice went through a difficult transition into larger-scale work. In Canberra, the national capital, medium-density housing (1976) at Reid explored stepped planes of walls and roofs around landscaped courtyards and terraces. These themes were further pursued in the Family Law Courts building (1977), where intimate scale and the use of a translucent roofing system sought to establish a calm environment. Both works are innovative but somewhat confused in their junctions and adoption of new technology.

The culminating work of this phase was the National Sports Stadium, completed in 1977. Here, the site was carefully modelled to provide graded surrounds to the arenas and to emphasize the existing forest landscape towards Black Mountain. The cable-suspended roof structure provides a distinctive focus for the site. The neighbouring Indoor Sports Hall (1979) also exploits cable-suspended, column-free technology, and both structures have a geometric abraction new in Cox's work. In part, they reflect the involvement of engineers Bond, James, Laron.

Cox has written extensively of the ethos of the Australian environment and his response to it. The long, low-lying, verandahed homestead placed in a scorched landscape set with primeval forest and hills and the romantic street profiles of Victorian and Edwardian Sydney provide the themes of his best work. A doctor's residence at Kellyville (1971) is a clever modern interpretation of the Australian homestead—the forms are traditional, the details, modern. The Akuna Bay marina and boating complex (1975) in Kuringai Chas National Park, built mainly of western red cedar shingle, board and batten, integrates well with the bushland and waterfront. It can be linked to the great rural sheds of the outback, and also American West Coast architecture.

Gradually, all references to history have been abstracted, and the mood lightened by the use of modern technology. Curving steel frames have replaced timber trusses, latticed and slatted screens have replaced solid verabdahs. These refinements are seen in the Hambrett house (1982) at Dural, a series of delicate sheds set straight on pavements level with the ground and dominated by gabled roofs and bull-nosed verandahs in corrugated steel. The Yulara tourist resort (1983) in Central Australia is the most extensive demonstratioon of this approach. Its colours—ochres, pinks, terracottas, browns—derive from the desert and reflect the input of design consultant Janne Faulkiner. A delicate grid of fabric canopies shelter central courtyard areas. The use of advanced solar technology has effectively tempered the harsh environmental conditions.

The urban infill architecture has been equally successful, initiated by the Forbes Street, Woolloomooloo (Sydney) redevelopment (1977), where a shallow, yet varied facade accepts the render, balconies, arched windows, and parapets of the Victorian neightbours without prejudicing individuality. Close by in Brougham Street, bracketed tubular-steel balconies and a rhythm of roofs accented by chimneys amplifies the qualities of the adjoining historic townscape. The attempts at neo-Classical and Edwardian infill have been less successful. In the Blaxland house (1982), the New South Wales Institute of Technology (1983), and the Garden Island Dockyard Amenities Building (1984), Cox's exuberance is out of step with the mix of strength and discretion evident in John Verge's Camden Park (1830) or the circa 1900 "blood and bandage" facades.

Since 1980, Philip Cox and Partners has become one of Australia's largest architectural practices. Cox remains its pivotal figure, engrossed in design and the entrepreneurial side of the office. The constructional realities of the past decade reflect the efforts of his partners, particularly Philip Taylor and John Richardson. The work is increasingly eclectic, and on a large commercial scale. Its magnificence lives in giant, abstract geometries—the minutae is of little interest to Philip Cox. Current work includes the Macarthur Institute at Campbelltown, the Canberra National Convention Centre, the Northern Territory Parliament House, hospitals in Malaysia, and stadiums at Sydney Cricket Ground and Parramatta Park.

—Howard Tanner

COX, Warren Jacob.

American. Born in New York City, 28 August 1935. Educated at the Hill School, Pottstown, Pennsylvania, graduated 1953; Yale University, New Haven, Connecticut, 1953-57 (History of Art Prize), B.A. (magna cum laude) 1957, and Yale University School of Architecture, 1957-61 (Editor of *Perspecta: The Yale Architectural Journal*, 1961; American Institute of Architects Prize, 1961), M.Arch. 1961. Married Susan Elizabeth Shifley in 1966 (divorced, 1974); married Claire A. Christie-Miller in 1975. Worked for BBPR, *q.v.*, Milan, summers 1954 and 1958; Technology Editor, *Architectural Forum*, New York, 1961-62; Designer and Draftsman, Keyes, Lethbridge and Condon, architects, Washington, D.C., 1962-65. Since 1965, Partner, with George E. Hartman, *q.v.*, Hartman-Cox Architects, Washington, D.C. Lecturer on Architecture, Washington Gallery of Modern Art, 1965; Visiting Design Critic, 1966, and Lecturer on Architecture, 1972, Yale University; Visiting Design Critic, Catholic University of America, Washington, D.C., 1966-67; Visiting Professor of Architecture, University of Virginia, Charlottesville, 1976. Chairman of the Jury, Louis Sullivan Award, 1975, and AIA/ *House and Home* Awards Program, 1978. Exhibitions: *The Work of Hartman-Cox*, University of Virginia, Charlottesville, 1973; *Recent Work of Hartman-Cox*, University of Maryland, College Park, 1974; *Award Winning Architecture by Yale Graduates*, Yale University School of Architecture, 1976. Collections: Museum of Modern Art Archives, New York. Recipient: Potomac Valley Chapter Awards, 1968, 1970, 1972, 1974, and 1976, National Honor Awards, 1970, 1971, 1981, and 1983, Homes for Better Living Awards, 1976 and 1981, and twenty-three Washington Metropolitan Chapter Awards, 1977-84, American Institute of Architects; Louis Sullivan Prize, 1972; Honor Award, AIA/Concrete Reinforcing Steel Institute, 1977. Fellow, American Institute of Architects, 1977. Address: Hartman-Cox Architects, 1071 Thomas Jefferson Street N.W., Washington, D.C. 20007, U.S.A.

Works (with George E. Hartman):

1964   Office for Cox, Langford and Brown, New Hampshire Avenue, Washington, D.C.
1965   Symington House additions, stage I, Washington, D.C.
1966   Tager House additions, Bethesda, Maryland
       Office for James Symington, 19th Street, Washington, D.C.
       Ballroom addition, Saudi Arabia Embassy, Washington, D.C.
1967   Long-range development plan for Mount Vernon College, Washington, D.C.
1968   Walinsky House, McLean, Virginia
       Phillips-Brewer House, Connecticut Avenue, Chevy Chase, Maryland
       Symington House additions, stage II, Washington, D.C.
       Fairfax Village Recreational Centre, National Park Service, Washington, D.C.
1969   St. Alban's Tennis Club, Mount St. Alban's, Washington, D.C.
       Chapel and Gate House, Mount Vernon College, Washington, D.C.
       Leventhal House additions, Washington, D.C.
1970   Dormitory, Mount Vernon College, Washington, D.C.
       Stable for the National Park Service, Rock Creek Park, Washington, D.C.
       Offices for the Washington Chapter of the American Institute of Architects, Washington, D.C.
1971   Euram Building, Dupont Circle, Washington, D.C.
       Carmichael House, Annapolis, Maryland
       Watts House additions, Washington, D.C.
       Tennis stadium, Washington, D.C.

1972 Kenney House additions, Washington, D.C.
Student Lounge, St. Alban's School, Washington, D.C.
New Chancery, French Embassy, Washington, D.C. (project)

1973 Saltonstall Farm, Rappahannock County, Virginia
Carousel Shelter Study for the Smithsonian Institution, Washington, D.C.
Visitors' Center, Washington Monument, Washington, D.C.

1974 Walker House, St. Mary's County, Maryland
Preservation plan for the urban core of New Hanover County, Wilmington, North Carolina

1976 Conant House, Potomac, Maryland
National Bookstore, National Visitors' Center, Washington, D.C.
Swimming pool, Brown House, Washington, D.C.
Resort hotel complex, Williamsburg, Virginia (project)
Recreation Centers, Department of the Army, Washington, D.C. (project)
Study of public places for the National Archives, Washington, D.C.

1977 Dodge Center, Wisconsin Avenue, Washington, D.C.
National Permanent Building, Pennsylvania Avenue, Washington, D.C.
Office building for the Arnold and Porter law firm, Washington, D.C. (project)
Long-range development plan for the National Humanities Center, Raleigh, North Carolina

1978 Stable, Saltonstall Farm, Rappahannock County, Virginia
Law Enforcement Center, Wilmington, North Carolina (with V. J. Ballard, McKim and Sawyer)
Headquarters Building, Maryland National Capitol Park and Planning Commission, Silver Spring, Maryland
National Humanities Center, Raleigh, North Carolina
Folger Shakespeare Library additions and remodelling, Capitol Street, Washington, D.C.
Medical Office Building, Warrenton, Virginia

1979 Gallery Row renovation and additions, Washington, D.C.
Freer Gallery of Art Study Center, Washington, D.C.
Foster House, McLean, Virginia

1980 Apex Building renovation and additions, Washington, D.C.
Building, 1001 Pennsylvania Avenue, Washington, D.C.
Immanuel Presbyterian Church, McLean, Virginia

1981 United States Embassy Office Building, Kuala Lumpur, Malaysia
Van Ness Center, Washington, D.C.
Music Conservatory Study, Kennedy Center for the Performing Arts, Washington, D.C.

1982 Monroe Hall addition, University of Virginia, Charlottesville
Dumbarton Oaks renovation, Washington, D.C.
St. Patrick's Church and Day School, Washington, D.C.

1983 HEB Grocery Company Headquarters, San Antonio, Texas
Chrysler Museum additions, Norfolk, Virginia
Sumner School Project, Washington, D.C.

Interiors:

Symington House, Washington, D.C., 1968; Leventhal House, Washington, D.C., 1969; Chapel, Mount Vernon College, Washington, D.C., 1969;

Warren Cox: Folger Shakespeare Library, Washington, D.C., 1983.

offices, Washington Chapter, American Institute of Architects, 1970; Gate House, Mount Vernon College, Washington, D.C., 1970; Dormitory, Mount Vernon College, 1971; offices, Euram Corporation, Washington, D.C., 1971; offices, Cox, Langford and Brown, Washington, D.C., 1972; residence rooms, Cosmos Club, Washington, D.C., 1973; Robert House, Washington, D.C., 1973; offices, Koteen and Burt, Washington, D.C., 1976; offices, Financial General Bankshares Inc., Washington, D.C., 1976; Research Center, National Humanities Center, Raleigh, North Carolina, 1977.

Publications:

By COX: book—*AIA Guide to the Architecture of Washington, D.C.*, editor with others, Washington, D.C. 1965, 1974; article—in *Architectural Forum* (New York), May 1965.

On HARTMAN/COX: book—*Houses Architects Live In* by Barbara Plumb, New York 1977; articles—"Brewer Residence" in *House and Garden* (New York), April 1969; "Chapel for Mount Vernon College" in *Architectural Forum* (New York), March 1971; "Hartman-Cox Wins First Sullivan Award" in *AIA Journal* (Washington, D.C.), October 1972; "The Euram Building" in *Architectural Forum* (New York), October 1972; "Dormitory and Plan for Mount Vernon College" in *Progressive Architecture* (New York), June 1972; "Brewer House/Leventhal Remodelling" in *Architecture + Urbanism* (Tokyo), November 1973; "Mount Vernon College Dormitory" in *Architecture Plus* (New York), December 1973; "Cox Residence" in *House and Garden* (New York), June 1974; "Conant Residence" in the *New York Times*, 6 June 1976; "Evaluation: Euram Building" in *AIA Journal* (Washington, D.C.), September 1976; "Forty under Forty" in *Architecture + Urbanism* (Tokyo), January 1977; "In Washington—A Serious Design" by Paul Goldberger in the *New York Times*, 9 February 1977; "Conant Residence" in *Architectural Record* (New York), May 1977; "National Permanent Building" in *Progressive Architecture* (New York), December 1977; "National Humanities Center" in *Architecture* (Washington, D.C.), May 1979; "U.S. Embassy Office Building, Kuala Lumpur" in *Architectural Record* (New York), December 1980; "Immanuel Presbyterian Church" in *Architecture* (Washington,

D.C.), May 1981; "Church in McLean, Virginia" in *Baumeister* (Munich), October 1982; "Foster House" in *Architecture* (Washington, D.C.), October 1983; "Folger Shakespeare Library" in *Architecture* (Washington, D.C.), November 1983; "Van Ness Station" in *Architecture* (Washington, D.C.), December 1983; "Folger Shakespeare Library" by Paul Goldberger in the *New York Times*, 5 February 1983; "Folger Shakespeare Library" in *Progressive Architecture* (New York), July 1983.

film—*Architects/Architecture*, International Masonry Institute, 1977.

One hopes that the work of Hartman-Cox is marked by a lack of recognizable office style and by a variety of response. Most of our work has been in the quite unique environment of Washington, D.C. and its surrounds, usually on difficult, prominent, and very particular sites. This has been coupled with an unusually wide variety of commissions, ranging from libraries to houses, jails to stables. We have attempted to honor these situations and programs rather than ignore or oppose them.

In principle, therefore, the buildings vary in design (or "style") the one from the other, based on the premises that each combination of site, program, and client is unique and deserves treatment specific to its particular demands and that the use of the same aesthetic or design vocabulary on quite different and unrelated projects is not only likely to be counter to that end but is irresponsible.

This should not be confused with the hopefully discredited 1950s approach of a new, spectacular "concept" for each job, usually, if not invariably, unrelated to or dominating its environment. On the contrary, we assume that the old is as valid as the "new" and, for example, that the level of assertiveness of a building or its scale should be a rational choice based on its context, not predicated on an abstract design prejudice.

I suppose we are proposing a mixture of eclecticism and contextualism for want of better terms. We aspire to a level of design professionalism where one is able to work in a wide variety of styles or aesthetics (as was the case in past eras), as required.

—Warren J. Cox

George E. Hartman and Warren J. Cox, working in the quasi-isolation of the small Washington, D.C. architectural community and without a conscious polemic, were among the early defectors from the Modern Movement in the United States. "We were just never convinced that Modern was the answer," they say and trace this attitude to their schooling—both took degrees in art history before attending professional schools (Hartman at Princeton and Cox at Yale)—and to their early practice, which in conservative Washington consisted of dozens of remodelings, giving them an appreciation for older architecture. Further, Hartman's professional education at Princeton was under Jean Labatut, one of the America's last remaining believers in Ecole des Beaux-Arts training, and, for a short time, Louis Kahn.

The design of Hartman-Cox is purposefully eclectic and widely varied from one project to another. Primary is an effort to relate each building to its particular site, for instance the horseshoe plan of their Euram Building as a way of fronting on a traffic circle. The stepped pyramid is their frequent response to sitting on a hill. For their dormitory at Mt. Vernon College, they not only used a variation of this form to deal with the sloped landscape but also distinguished between its various facades, turning a quiet brick face to the neo-Georgian campus and a dramatic chiaroscuro elevation away from it.

The whole point of their design repertory has been to avoid the minimalism of their elders. "Modern architecture," Cox says, "gives you five shapes and tells you they will solve all problems. But you can't get there from here. You need more pieces." For years, one of the pieces was the angle, a formal tool exploited not only by them but also by an entire generation to such an extent that it has become a cliché of the 1960s. Today, the firm is more likely to turn to an historical or contemporary quotation to enrich a building's vocabulary and modulate its scale. Their National Permanent Building superimposes huge concrete columns, a reference to a French Second Empire landmark nearby, on a grid of black pipes, inspired by Piano and Rogers's high-tech Beaubourg Center. The glass bays are derived admittedly from Alder and Sullivan's Guaranty Building.

In keeping with their attitudes toward site and scale, Hartman and Cox prefer molded spaces to free-flowing ones, which they call "ill-defined." Their Conant House, with its octagonal library, or Folger Library, with its barrel-vaulted spine, simultaneously disregard the Modern concepts of planes in space and interior form reading through on the exterior.

Yet Hartman-Cox does not consider itself—nor is it considered by the propagators of the term—postmodern. The firm enjoys an impressive local reputation and a growing national one, but has eschewed identification with any architectural group or theoretical position.

—Nory Miller

CRANE, David Alford.

American. Born in Mutoto, Belgian Congo, now Zaire, of American parents, 25 January 1927. Educated at lower schools in the Belgian Congo, 1932-40; Tuscaloosa Senior High School, Alabama, 1941-43; Davidson College, North Carolina, 1943-44 and 1946-47; Georgia Institute of Technology, Atlanta, 1947-50, B.S. and B.Arch. 1950; Harvard Graduate School of Design, Cambridge, Massachusetts, under Walter Gropius, *q.v.*, and G. Holmes Perkins, 1950-52 (Lehman Fellow: Rumrill Scholar), M.City Planning 1952. Served in the United States Navy, in the Pacific, 1944-46: Quartermaster 2nd Class; and as a Reserve Officer in the United States Corps of Engineers, 1950-57: First Lieutenant. Married Bonnie Beth Loyd in 1954; children: Melinda, Matthew, and Lauren. Assistant Director, Tampa, Florida Housing Authority, 1951; Designer, IBEC Housing Corporation, New York, 1952-53; Draftsman, Marcel Breuer *q.v.*, Associates, New York, 1953-54, and Wiener and Sert, *q.v.*: Josep Lluis Sert, Associates, New York, 1954; Planner, Mayer and Whittlesey Associates, New York, 1954-55; Designer, Carl Koch, *q.v.*, Associates, Cambridge, Massachusetts, and Research Associate, Massachusetts Institute of Technology School of Architecture and Planning, Cambridge, 1955-57; Assistant Professor of Architecture and Planning, Graduate School of Fine Arts, University of Pennsylvania, Philadelphia, 1957-61; Director of Design and Planning Administrator, Boston Redevelopment Authority, 1961-65; Professor of Architecture and Chairman of the Urban Design Program, Graduate School of Fine Arts, University of Pennsylvania, 1965-72. Since 1966, Founding Partner, David A. Crane and Partners, and Chairman of the Board, DACP Inc., Philadelphia, Boston, and Cairo, Egypt. Dean and Distinguished Professor of Architecture, Rice University School of Architecture, Houston, Texas, 1972-77, and Founder, Chairman of the Board, and Chief Executive Officer, Rice Center for Community Design and Research, Houston, Texas, 1973-77; Program Director, Sadat City Development Group, Cairo, Egypt, 1978-79. Member, National Architectural Accrediting Board, 1968-71; Special Consultant to the United States Department of Housing and Urban Development for the Urban Development Action Grants, 1977. Exhibitions: *For Lincoln New Town*, Corcoran Gallery, Washington, D.C., 1969; *New York State Urban Development Corporation Projects*, Whitney Museum, New York, 1972. Recipient: Young Engineer of the Year Award, Tau Beta Pi Engineering Society, 1950; Italian Government Travelling Fellowship, 1955; Award, *Progressive Architecture*, 1969 and 1970; Award, American Institute of Architects, Philadelphia Chapter, 1969 and 1970; Award, Texas Society of Architects, with W. T. Cannady, 1974.

Works:

1952/
53 Low-cost housing systems designs for Cuba, Puerto Rico, Venezuela, etc. (with IBEC Housing Corporation)

1953/
54 Houses and schools projects (with Marcel Breuer Associates)

1954 Urban design projects for Latin American countries (with Wiener and Sert Associates)

1954/
55 Master plan for Krobo New Town, Ghana (with Mayer and Whittlesey Associates)

1955/
57 Housing designs and hotel projects in various American cities (with Carl Koch Associates: F. Day)
"Image of the City," Los Angeles, Boston, and Jersey City (M.I.T. research project; with Kevin Lynch)

1958/
61 Urban renewal design plans and site designs, Philadelphia, Washington, D.C., and Pennsylvania and Delaware towns (with various collaborators)

1961/
65 General plan for Boston and the Boston Regional Core
Ten general neighborhood renewal plans, Boston
Urban renewal project design plans for: Government Center; Water-Front-Faneuil Hall; Washington Park; South End; Charlestown; South Cove; Central Business District; Back Bay—all Boston
Project briefs and design review management for Boston redevelopment projects: City Hall and other Government Center buildings; Washington Park housing, commercial, and public facilities; Water-front Aquarium; etc.

1966 "Planning and Design in New York" (policy study for the Mayor of New York; with Edward J. Longue)

1966/
67 Master plan for the Main Street Campus of the State University of New York, Buffalo
Area renewal plan for Bedford-Stuyvesant, Brooklyn, New York (with E. J. Logue, I. M. Pei Associates, and Raymond and May Associates)

1967 Multi-User Center, for Food Fair Inc. and Horn and Hardart Inc., Philadelphia

1967/
68 Master plan for the in town new town of Spring Creek-East New York, New York City (with S. W. Killinger)
Education Park prototypes, for the Corde Corporation
North Philadelphia School Facilities Systems Design
Buffalo-Amherst Corrior Development Plan and Transport Systems Concept Design, Buffalo, New York (with S. W. Killinger)

1968/
69 Master plan for Ft. Lincoln New Town, Washington, D.C. (with Keyes, Lethbridge and Condon)

David Crane: Radisson New Town, near Syracuse, New York, 1974 (model).

"Applications of New Technology in Developing New Communities," Washington, D.C. (development study for the United States Department of Housing and Urban Development; with Keyes, Lethbridge and Condon)

1968/
70 Plan for the 1976 *Philadelphia Bicentennial Exposition* (with S. W. Killinger and others)

1969/
70 "Quality in Environment" (policy study of public design processes in Albuquerque, New Mexico)

Campus master plan for the Université Libre de Congo, Kisangani (with J. Lane and others)

South Central Corridor Transport Design and Impact Study, Philadelphia (with A. M. Voorhees and Associates, and J. Lane)

1969/
73 Master plan, demonstration building systems coordination, and architectural designs for Total Energy Plant, School, and Commercial Structure, United States Department of Housing and Urban Development "Operation Breakthrough" Project, Jersey City, New Jersey

1969/
74 Master plan for Radisson New Town, formerly Lysander New Town, near Syracuse, New York (with J. N. Kise, R. Glaser, P. Franks, J. Straw and others)

1970/
72 Building systems development and architectural designs, Université Libre de Congo, Kisangani: Proto Classroom Building; Proto Dormitory; Proto Lecture Hall; Library; Chapel/Socio-Cultural Center; Dining Commons; Central Kitchen (with J. Lane and others)

Industrialized housing systems, for various clients, U.S.A.

New town feasibility studies for Tennessee Valley Authority, Illinois Housing Development Authority, etc.

1972/
73 Village center and subdivision design, Flower Mound New Town, Texas (with J. V. Thomas)

Crane House, Houston (with W. T. Connaly)

1973/
75 Bedford-Pine in town new town, and other renewal projects for Atlanta, Georgia (with S. W. Killinger, P. Franks and others)

1974 City master plan revision and Glenloch Village design plan, Peachtree City, Georgia (with J. V. Thomas and others)

1974/
77 Project designs and strategy services for developers in Houston, Dallas, and El Paso, Texas, and Atlanta, Georgia

1975/
77 Oklahoma City Plan for Growth Management and Community Development (with

RERC, Haines, Luudberg and Waehler, and Marshall Kaplan, Gans and Kahn)

1976/
79 Master plan for Sadat City, Egypt (with J. N. Kise and S. W. Killinger, Parons Brinckerhoff, Marcel Breuer Associates, and Sabbour Associates)

1977 Design plan for the Capital Gateway Community, Washington, D.C. (with Gibbs and Hill, and P. Franks)

1978/
79 Nasr City Center, Cairo (with S. Heikin, Marcel Breuer Associates, and Sabbour Associates)

Publications:

By CRANE: books—*Philadelphia Tomorrow* (AIA Guidebook), Philadelphia 1961; *Planning and Design in New York: A Study of Problems and Processes of the Physical Environment Developing New Communities,* with Keyes, Lethbridge and Condon, New York 1966, Washington, D.C. 1968; articles—"The Vital City: The Gift of America Unchallenged" in the *Daily Pennsylvania* (Philadelphia), March 1959; "The Dynamic City" in *Architectural Design* (London), April 1960; "Chandigarh Reconsidered" in *AIA Journal* (Washington, D.C.), May 1960; "The City Symbolic" in *Journal of the American Institute of Planners* (Washington, D.C.), Fall 1960; "Alternative to Futility: Design in the Boston Redevelopment

Authority" in *The Architect and the City* (seminar proceedings), Cranbrook, Michigan 1962, reprinted in *AIA Journal* (Washington, D.C.), November 1962; "Education for City Form Makers, Not Cosmeticians" in *Education for Urban Design*, St. Louis 1962; "The Public Art of City Building" in *Annals of the American Academy of Political and Social Science* (Philadelphia), March 1964; "Design and Urban Renewal in Boston" in *The Role of Government in the Form and Animation of the Urban Core* (conference report), Cambridge, Massachusetts 1964; "Architecture and the Urban Revolution" in *Connection* (Cambridge, Massachusetts), Winter 1966; "Achieving Quality in Environment," with George Rolfe, in *Proceedings of the Institute of Planning, Zoning and Eminent Domain*, New York 1971; "Responsiveness in the Design of Transportation and Environment" in *Transportation* (Boston Architectural Center Proceedings), 1971; "In Search of 'New' New Towns" in *New Towns in America*, edited by James Bailey, New York 1973; "Back to the City: Atlanta Points Toward New Housing Options" in *Real Estate Atlanta* (Georgia), no. 1, 1976; "Energy and Urban Living" in *Energy and the Quality of Life* (proceedings of a conference in Houston), 1976.

On CRANE: articles—"Design Awards" in *Progressive Architecture* (New York), January 1969, January 1970; "Awards" in *Texas Society of Architects Journal* (Austin), Spring 1975; "Houston Architects" in *Inland Architect* (Chicago), July 1977; "New Sadat City Hopes To House Half a Million" in *Architectural Record* (New York), September 1978; "Lowell National Cultural Park" in *Architectural Record* (New York), September 1979.

David Crane is one of the architects who has pioneered in the development of effective urban design techniques, and the firm he founded is one of the leading practitioners of urban design and planning. Crane is also well-known as an educator, particularly for his contributions to urban design education.

A major professional opportunity opened up for Crane in 1961, when Edward J. Logue, the administrator of the Boston Redevelopment Authority, made Crane, in effect, the director of planning for the City of Boston. Under the centralized system of administration created by Logue in Boston, the planning administrator had less autonomy than is customary in such positions but, in exchange, became part of an exceptionally effective implementation process. While he was with the Boston Redevelopment Authority, Crane was responsible for a number of specific development plans, but his major work was the production of the General Plan for Boston and the Boston Regional Core. This plan was unusual for a number of reasons: it was one of the few detailed, comprehensive plans to be adopted in a major American city; it went beyond the official boundaries of the city to consider Boston's role in the metropolitan region; it was not solely a physical plan (although the emphasis was certainly on physical planning); and—most unusual of all—large parts of it have actually been carried out. In this plan Crane developed the concept that he calls "The Capital Web," using government capital expenditure strategically to achieve larger objectives.

In 1965 Crane returned to the University of Pennsylvania as a professor and chairman of the Graduate Program in Civic Design. With several younger associates, he opened the office now called David A. Crane and Partners. This office is best known for its work with large-scale urban design plans, including the new communities of Lysander (now called Radisson), near Syracuse, New York, and Fort Lincoln in Washington, D.C. These plans have distinctive urban design elements, notably the use of a grid pattern with a strong diagonal emphasis, that mark them as the work of the Crane office and show a kinship to the distinctive approach to architecture developed at the School of the Fine Arts at the University of Pennsylvania in the years when Louis I. Kahn was its leading figure.

From 1972 through 1977, Crane was the Dean of the School of Architecture at Rice University in Houston, Texas, a move that necessarily cut down his involvement with David A. Crane & Partners in Philadelphia. Crane's most significant achievement at Rice was the creation of a research center, supported in part by the Houston business community, that investigates large-scale planning and community design issues. In Houston, noted for its laissez-faire attitude towards planning, the creation of such a center was a major achievement.

After returning to his firm for the design of Sadat City, which is to be the keystone of Egyptian national planning policies, Crane has opened a new office in Boston, where he continues to practice urban design.

—Jonathan Barnett

CROSBY, Theo.

British. Born in Mafeking, South Africa, 3 April 1925; settled in England, 1947. Educated at the University of the Witwatersrand, Johannesburg, 1940-47, B.Arch. 1947: influenced by R. D. Martienssen; Sir John Cass School, Central School of Art, and St. Martin's School of Art, all London, 1947-56. Served in the British Army in the 6th South Africa Armoured Division, 1944-46: Signaller. Married Anne Buchanan in 1960 (separated, 1977); children: Dido and Matthew. Worked in the office of Maxwell Fry, *q.v*., and Jane Drew, *q.v*., London, 1947-52; Technical Editor, *Architectural Design*, London, 1953-62; Founder-Partner, with Alan Fletcher and Colin Forbes, Crosby/Fletcher/Forbes, London, 1965-72. Since 1972, Partner, with Fletcher, Forbes, Mervyn Kurlansky, and Kenneth Grange, Pentagram Design, London (current additional partners: John McConnell, since 1974; David Hillman, since 1978; Peter Harrison, since 1979; David Pelham, since 1983). Exhibition: Sculpture, ICA Gallery, London, 1960. Recipient: Grand Prize, *Triennale*, Milan, 1963; two Architectural Heritage Year Awards, 1973. Associate, Royal Institute of British Architects, 1944; Fellow, Society of Industrial Design, 1963; Member, Akademie der Künste, Berlin, 1978; Associate, Royal Academy of Art, London, 1983. Address: Pentagram Design, 11 Needham Road, London W11 2RP, England.

Works:

1961 Design of the *International Union of Architects Exhibitions*, South Bank, London

1962/
64 Euston Station reconstruction, London (as supervising architect for Taylor Woodrow)

1963 Design of the British Section, *Triennale*, Milan

1964 "Twilight Areas" Study, Fulham, London (for Taylor Woodrow)

1967 Industry Section of the British Pavilion, *Expo '67*, Montreal

1968 "The Lookout" (observation lounge), *Queen Elizabeth II*

1969 Design of the Cape Universal Buildings Products display, *International Building Exhibition*, Olympia, London
Rowe Rudd office interiors, 63 Moorgate, London

1971/
73 Ulster Terrace reconstruction, Regent's Park, London (with Edward Armitage).
Chalcot house renovation and conversion, Westbury, Wiltshire

1972 Boase Massimi Pollit Advertising Agency conversion and interiors, Paddington, London

1972/
73 Cherry Garden Pier development, Bermondsey, London (project; with others)

1973 Design of *The Environment Game* exhibition, Hayward Gallery, London

1975 Malaysia House conversion and interiors, London
Geers Gross Advertising Agency interiors, London

1976 Design of the *British Genius* exhibitions, Battersea Park, London

1978/
83 Unilever House refurbishment, London

1979 Boase Massimi Pollit Advertising Agency further conversion and interiors, Paddington, London

1982 Globe Theatre reconstruction and museum complex, South Bank, London(project)

1984 Geers Gross Advertising Agency II, London
Design of *Festival of Architecture* exhibition, London Docklands

1984 Nederlandse Middelstande Bank interiors, Amsterdam

Publications:

By CROSBY: books—*This Is Tomorrow*, exhibition catalogue, London 1956; *Le Corbusier*, exhibition catalogue, London 1959; *An Anthology of House*, with Monica Pidgeon, London 1960; *The Architecture of Technology*, editor, London 1961; *Architecture: City Sense*, London and New York 1965; *The Necessary Monument*, London 1970; *A Sign Systems Manual*, with Alan Fletcher and Colin Forbes, London 1970; *Pentagram: The Work of Five Designers*, with Pentagram Partners, London 1972; *How to play the Environment Game*, London 1973; *Living by Design*, with Pentagram Partners, edited by Peter Gorb, London and New York 1978; articles—editor, with John Bodley, of five issues of *Uppercase* (London), 1958-61; editor of three issues of *Living Arts* (London), 1962; "The Modern Movement" in *RIBA Journal* (London), February 1974; "Arup Museum" in *Architectural Review* (London), February 1974; "Another World!," with Idris Watts, in *Building Design* (London), 5 July 1974; "Docklands Feedback" in *Architectural Design* (London), April 1975; "Johannesburg Revisited" in *RIBA Journal* (London), February 1976; "Architect's Approach to Architecture" in *Architects' Journal* (London), 11 February 1976; "Port Sunlight: The First and Only Good Housing Estate in England" in *RIBA Journal* (London), July 1978; "The Modern Movement" in *RIBA Journal* (London), January 1979; "Bomarzo" in *Architectural Design* (London), no. 1/2, 1980; "Patrons of the arts" in *Architects' Journal* (London), 18 January 1984; recording—*The Integration of the Arts*, tape cassette and slides, London 1979.

On CROSBY: Books—*Art without boundaries 1950-1970*, edited by Gerald Woods, Philip Thompson and John Williams, London 1972; *Contemporary Designers*, edited by Ann Lee Morgan, New York and London 1984. articles—"Exhibition Design" in *Architectural Review* (London), January 1974; "Six Design Offices in Europe" by Gilles de Bure and Gerard Negreaunu in *Crée* (Paris), May 1974; "Nash Conversion with Imagination" in *House and Garden* (London), October 1975; "Living by Design" in *RIBA Journal* (London), February 1976; "Pentagram: Style and Content" in *Building* (London), 13 February 1976; "A Return to Ornament?" in *Architectural Review* (London), October 1976; "Technology in the 1930's" by A. Howard in *Building Design* (London), 8 October 1976; "Advertising Agency" in *RIBA Journal* (London), November 1976; "Corridor Street Life Detail" in *Design* (London), January 1977; "Tentative Genius" in *Building Design* (London), 3 June 1977; "Globe

Theatre Replica for South Bank" in *Building* (London), 20 November 1981; "Inner Light" by Gavin Stamp in *Architects' Journal* (London), 10 February 1982; "Advertising Standard" in *RIBA Journal* (London), March 1982; "The Executive as Emperor" in *Design* (London), April 1982; "Art Deco Renewed in London" by Monica Pidgeon in *Progressive Architecture* (New York), November 1982.

Pentagram is a partnership which explores a great variety of problems. Its strength is in its self-limiting organization, which places total responsibility on the partner. Each partner has a small, young team. There is no pyramidal structure but an association of determined equals.

With regard to my own work, I am concerned with the extensioin of the barren and commercially worn language of modern architecture, not in the direction of an ever more streamlined technology but through the involvement of other disciplines.

Designers and artist can add a dimension to architecture, a way of mediating between architect and the public. Nothing new in this. It was the normal mode in building until the 1950s, before our puritan masters changed the rules.

For a new, and responsive, architecture, and a decent environment, we need more intelligent input at every level. Thus, I am concerned with public art, monuments, and monumentality, with decoration, with the sensuous use of material. It has also become clear that my training has quite, unfitted me for this task, though it is very enjoyable, if painful, trying to rediscover skills that were common to every nineteenth-century draftsman.

—Theo Crosby

When Theo Crosby arrived in England from South Africa in 1947, he was just in time to experience the mixture of optimistic euphoria about the possibilities of modern architecture in postwar Britain and the reality of economic depression, a mixture exemplified by the *Britain Can Make It* exhibition at the Victoria and Albert Museum in 1946 and by the Festival of Britain five years later. Crosby's first job was with the Fry/Drew partnership where he could have been expected to absorb the traditional and received truths about modernism as they were defined before 1939. He went on to the influential journal, *Architectural Design*, and, later, to found Pentagram.

Crosby is the only qualified architect in the Pentagram group, which makes it a speciality to offer a wide range of design services in diverse fields, services defined by the group as those that are "not quite architecture," including signs, posters, exhibitions, and shopping centres. The Lewisham Shopping Centre (architects: Bernard Eagle Partnership) is one recent example of Pentagram's work in shaping the whole environment: the possibilities of the shopping arcade included integrating graphics into the fabric of the building. The Arts Council Shop in Sackville Street, London, is another popular example of Pentagram's environmental design. The group has also been very influential in the fashionable areas of design, including the Art Nouveau revival (which began with Pentagram's logo for the Biba Department Store) and extending to corporate identity programmes for large companies such as BP, Reuters and St. Ivel.

In 1976 Crosby, together with his partners Fletcher and Forbes, addressed the Royal Institute of British Architects in the popular "Architect's Approach to Architecture" series of lectures. The lecture gave the only architect in a prominent design partnership an opportunity to define and clarify his views. Crosby offered a view of architecture that stressed the importance of visual complexity and compound symbolism. He complained of architectural imaginations being dessicated by imposed economies and, reversing Mies's awesome *diktat* (rather as Robert Venturi had already done), maintained that "less is not more, it is actually less."

Pentagram's most famous building is the complex remodelling of a part of Nash's Ulster Terrace in Regent's Park, where the architectural effect depends on elaborate brickwork and fine detailing. Crosby is opposed to the monopoly that architects have over the appearance of our environment and maintains, as one might expect from an architect who spends most of his time with professional designers, that "good building is rich with the work of many men."

—Stephen Bayley

CROWE, Sylvia.

British. Born in Banbury, Oxfordshire, 15 September 1901. Educated at the Berkhamsted Girl's School, Hertfordshire, 1908-12; Swanley Horticultural College, Kent, 1920-22; pupil of the landscape architect Edward White, London, 1926. Served as a Volunteer Ambulance Driver with the Polish Army in France, 1940; with Motor Transport Companies in the Auxiliary Territorial Service, in the U.K., 1940-45: Sergeant. Garden Designer for Cutbush Nurseries, Barnet, Hertfordshire, 1939. In private practice as a landscape architect, London, since 1945. Consultant to Harlow and Basildon New Town, 1948-58, Central Electricity Generating Board, 1948-68, Essex County Council, 1957, Forestry Commission, 1964-76, and since 1969 to the Southern and South West Water Authorities. Founder-Honorary Secretary, 1948-58, and Vice-President, 1958-70, International Federation of Landscape Architects; President, Institute of Landscape Architects, London, 1957-61. Recipient: Woman of the Year Award, *Architects' Journal*, London, 1960; John Bracken Medal, University of Pennsylvania, 1984. D.Litt.: University of Newcastle, 1976; Heriot-Watt University, Edinburgh, 1976; LL.D.: University of Sussex, Brighton, 1978. Honorary Fellow, Royal Institute of British Architects, 1969, Royal Town Planning Institute, 1970, and Institute of Chartered Foresters, 1984. Corresponding member, American Society of Landscape Architects; Honorary Fellow, Australian Institute of Landscape Architects C.B.E. (Commander, Order of the British Empire), 1967; D.B.E. (Dame Commander, Order of the British Empire), 1973. Address: 59 Ladbroke Grove, London W11 3AT, England.

Works (landscape architecture):

1927/
39 Numerous private gardens
1946 Public gardens, Mable Thorpe, Lincolnshire (destroyed by floods, 1953)
1948/
68 Harlow and Basildon New Towns, Essex (as consultant)
Nuclear power stations, Trawsfynydd and Wylfa, Wales
Power line routing in southern England (as consultant)
Coastal reclamation and restoration of the public gardens, Mable Thorpe, Lincolnshire
Coastal reclamation, Sutton-on-Sea, Lincolnshire
1950 St. Mary's Churchyard, Banbury, Oxfordshire
Quadrangles, University College, Oxford
Rose Garden, Magdelen College, Oxford
Neville Hall Hospital, Abergavenny, Wales
Housing for the United States Air Force in Britain
Friern Barnet Hospital, London
1957 Nuclear power station, Bradwell, Essex (as consultant)
Landscape master plan for Washington New Town, County Durham
Landscape master plan for Warrington New Town, Lancashire
Knaresborough Churchyard, Yorkshire
County Hall and Colleges, Bedford
Teachers' Training College, Norham Gardens, Oxford
Cement and Concrete Association Research Station, Wexham Springs, Buckinghamshire (roof garden moved to Edinburgh, 1978)
1966 Master plan for the Commonwealth Gardens, Canberra, A.C.T.
1976 Scottish Widows Fund and Life Assurance Society Office Building, Edinburgh
Bewl Bridge Reservoir (as consultant)
Bough Beech Reservoir (as consultant)
Empingham Pumping Station, Rutland Water (as consultant)
Wimbleball Reservoir (as consultant)
Imperial College, South Kensington, London (as consultant)
Cumberland Basin and Ashton Park Parkway, Bristol
1976/
84 Colliford Reservoir, South Western Water Authority, Cornwall
Planting, Eton College Playing Fields, Buckinghamshire (as consultant)
Haily House garden plan, Benson, Oxfordshire
Grove Farm planting plan, Harwell, Berkshire
Landscaping Master Plan, Warrington New Town, Lancashire
North Stainley Hall garden plans, near Ripon, Yorkshire
1983/
84 British Pavilion and Garden, Liverpool International Garden Festival, Merseyside

Publications

By CROWE: books—*Tomorrow's Landscape*, London 1956; *Garden Design*, London 1958, Chichester, Sussex 1981; *The Landscape of Power*, London 1958; *The Landscape of Roads*, London 1960; *Space for Living*, editor, Amsterdam 1961; *Shaping Tomorrow's Landscape*, with Zvi Miller, Amsterdam 1964; *Forestry in the Landcape*, London 1966; *The Gardens of Mughul India*, with others, London 1972; *Landscape of Forests and Woods*, London 1978; articles—"Garden Design" in *Country Life* (London), 1958; "Roads in the Landscape" in *Landscape Design* (London), November 1967; "Landscape of Unity and Surprise: The Wye Valley" in *Country Life* (London), May 1977; "International Scene" in *Landscape Design* (London), February 1979.

On CROWE: articles—"Power and the Landscape" and "Making the Landscape Plan" in *Landscape Design* (London), November 1960; "Upland Catchment Management" in *Landscape Design* (London), February 1969; "Empingham Pumped Storage Project" in *Architecture East Midlands* (Lincoln), November/December 1976; "Pumping Stations in the Landscape" in *Concrete Quarterly* (London), April/June 1977; "New Head Office for the Scottish Widows Fund Life Assurance Society" by David Colley in *Arup Journal* (London), December 1977; "Scottish Widows Fund and Life Assurance Society Office Building, Edinburgh" in *Landscape Design* (London), May 1978; "In Person: Lady in the Landscape" by Sally Festing in *New Scientist* (London), January 1979.
Bibliography—*Dame Sylvia Crowe: A Bibliography* by Mary Vance, Monticello, Illinois 1982.

Theo Crosby: Ulster Terrace, Regent's Park, London, 1973.

The object of my work and writing is to reconcile the needs and aspirations of men with the welfare of the natural order and to create beauty out of the fusion of the human spirit and the workings of nature, I try to enter into the spirit of each landscape and to express its individual character.

—Sylvia Crowe

Sylvia Crowe was first recognised as a sensitive designer for her exhibition garden at the *Chelsea Flower Show* shortly before the war. Her more important career, however, was to lie outside domestic gardens. While still an officer in the ATS during the war, and while stationed in Kent, she made a landscape plan for the Isle of Sheppey during her spare time. The combination of horticultural knowledge and planning instinct at that time made her unique, and postwar architects and town planners employed her to fill a vacuum in their knowledge. Particularly valuable were her pioneer landscape survey reports on the new towns and, later, her detailed designs, under Sir Frederick Gibberd, for Harlow New Town. From the 1950s, her practice developed with ever-widening scope. One recalls with pleasure her little fountain garden at the Cement and Concrete Association Research Station at Wexham Springs, her original treatment of the centre of a roundabout at Basildon, or a more recent Edinburgh roof garden, designed to merge with the surrounding landscape. But her greatest ambition, as she herself has said, was fulfilled when she was appointed landscape consultant to the Forestry Commission—an assignment that called for all her wide vision, ecological knowledge, and aesthetic sense.

Apart from her own practice, Sylvia Crowe (like her colleague Brenda Colvin, with whom for a long time she shared a London office) has been dedicated to the interests of landscape as a whole. Her various books were written at a time when the information was sorely needed. She has been a continuous and highly respected supporter of the professional body, now the Landscape Institute. As founder Honorary Secretary of the International Federation of Landscape Architects she worked unsparingly for its development. Behind a singularly charming manner lies an ordered and acute mind that can penetrate unhesitatingly to the root of a problem. Factors on all sides are weighed, seen to be weighed, and presented to committee or lecture audience with eloquence and clarity.

—Geoffrey Jellicoe

CUBITT, James William Archibald.
British. Born in Melbourne, Victoria, Australia, 1 May 1914. Educated at the Harrow School, Middlesex, 1928-32; Brasenose College, Oxford, 1932-35, B.A. (honours) 1935; part-time student at Ruskin School, of Art, Oxford; studied at the Architectural Association School, London, 1935-40, A.A. Diploma (honours) 1940. Served with the Royal Engineers, in West Africa, India, and Burma, 1940-46; Major; commanded the 5th West African Field Company; M.B.E. (Member, Order of the British Empire), 1945. Married Ann Tooth in 1939 (divorced, 1947); Constance Anne Sitwell in 1950 (divorced, 1972); Eleni Alkmene Kiortsis in 1973; children: Jennifer, Benjamin, and Francis. Studio Master, Department of Architecture, Kingston School of Art, Surrey, 1946-48. Senior Partner, James Cubitt and Partners, London 1949 until his death in 1983 (as James Cubitt Fello Atkinson and Partners from 1967—partners: Cubitt, Atkinson, John Baker, and Alan Craig), with branches in Ghana, 1951-55, Burma, 1954-58, Malaysia, 1955-70, Nigeria, from

1956, and Libya, from 1965. Architectural Correspondent, *Westminster Review,* London, 1957-61. Member of the Council, 1959-66, President, 1965-66, and Trustee of the Development Fund, 1969-83, Architectural Association, London. Chairman, Mortimer and Burghfield local Labour Party, Berkshire, 1974-82. Exhibitions: Royal Academy of Art, London, 1959; Eastern Region House of Assembly, Enugu, Nigeria, 1959; Heinz Gallery, Royal Institute of British Architects, London, 1983. Also a sculptor, from 1957; one-person shows at the John Whibley Gallery, London, 1962, Burgos Gallery, New York, 1966, and Anthony Mould Gallery, London, 1985. Associate, 1940, and Fellow, 1955, Royal Institute of British Architects. *Died* (in London) *16 December 1983* .

Works:

1949/
51 minor works, including airline offices, London (with Stefan Buzas and R. M. Maitland)
1950/
57 Office group, Accra, Ghana (with Cubitt, Scott and Partners)
1951/
54 Teacher training college, Berekum, Ghana (with Cubitt, Scott and Partners)
Teacher training college, Secondi, Ghana (with Cubitt, Scott and Partners)
Teacher training college, Jasikan, Ghana (with Cubitt, Scott and Partners)
Secondary School, Jasikan, Ghana (with Cubitt, Scott and Partners
College of Technology, Kumasi, Ghana (with R. M. Maitland)
1952/
54 Technical Institute, Accra, Ghana (with Cubitt, Scott and Partners)
Technical Institute, Kumasi, Ghana (with Cubitt, Scott and Partners)
1954/
57 Ryburn Secondary School, Sowerby Bridge, Yorkshire (with Gerry Richards and Don Lee)
Carleton Primary School, Pontefract, Yorkshire (with Stefan Buzas)
1954/
58 Pharmaceutical factory, Rangoon, Burma (with R. M. Maitland)
1957/
59 First development, University of Nigeria, Nsukka (not completed; with John Baker and Keith Banks)
1958 Nsukka New Town, Nigeria (project; with Keith Banks and Otto Koenigsberger)
1958/
61 Paramount Hotel, Freetown, Sierra Leone (with Henry Smith and Keith Banks)
1958/
62 Elder Dempster Shipping Offices, Freetown, Sierra Leone (with Keith Banks)
Elder Dempster Shipping Offices, Lagos, Nigeria (with Keith Banks)
1959 Churchill College, Cambridge (project; with Keith Banks)
1960/
62 Two schools for delicate and handicapped children, Putney, London (with Dennis Marshall)
1961 St. Anthony's College, Oxford (project; with Keith Banks)
1961/
65 Flats and houses, Harlow New Town, Essex (with Dennis Marshall)
1962/
67 Old people's home, Islington, London (with Peter Gray)
Old people's home, Stoke Newington, London (with Peter Gray)

Faculty of Medicine and Teaching Hospital, Kuala Lumpur, Malaysia (with J. L. Middleton and Alan Craig)
1964/
66 Secondary modern school, Highbury, London (with Peter Gray)
1966/
74 Academic and Administrative Buildings, University of Garyounis, Benghazi, Libya, master plan phase I (with Alan Craig, Keith Banks, and Ward Koss)
1971 Redevelopment of the University of Nigeria Campus, Nsukka (with Keith Banks)
1974/
78 University of Garyounis, Benghazi, Libya, phases II and III (with Craig and Grant)
1977 University of Garyounis, Benghazi, Libya, phase IV

Publications:

By CUBITT: articles—in the bi-monthly *Westminster Review* (London), 1958-60; "University of Malaya Medical Centre, Kuala Lumpur" in *Hospital Management Planning and Equipment* (Sevenoaks, Kent), November 1964; "The Need for Self Awareness" in *Arena* (London), January 1966.

On CUBITT: articles—"70 Piccadilly" in *Art News and Review* (London), October 1950; "The Work of James Cubitt and Partners" in *Architect and Building News* (London), April 1957; "B.P.I. Burma" in *International Monthly Journal for Prefabrication and New Building Techniques* (London), May 1957; "James Cubitt and Partners: Work in Ghana" in *Architectural Forum* (New York), July 1957; "University of Nigeria" in *Architectural Review* (London), February 1959; "Sowerby Bridge School" in *Architectural Design* (London), July 1959; "Special School" in *Interbuild* (London), April 1961; "I.D.C. Group, Accra" in *West African Builder and Architect* (Lagos), 1961; "University of Garyounis, Benghazi" in *The Times* (London), 6 March 1968; "Medical Centre, Kuala Lumpur" in *Architectural Review* (London), July 1968; "University of Garyounis" in the *Architectural Association Quarterly* (London), vols. 3-4, 1974; "University of Garyounis, Benghazi" in *L'Archittetura* (Rome), April 1975; "Garyounis University" in *The Observer* (London), 13 June 1976; "Fond Remembrance" in *Building Design* (London), 22 May 1981; "Saving Islington's Grandest Chapel" in *Country Life* (London), 18 February 1982; "Cubitt at Work in Libya" in *RIBA Journal* (London), March 1983; "James Cubitt: Obituary" by Stefan Buzas in *Architects' Journal* (London), 4-11 January 1984; "Mr. James Cubitt" in *The Times* (London), 11 January 1984; "James Cubitt, 1914-1983" in *Building* (London), 13 January 1984; "Obituary: James Cubitt, 1914-1983" in *RIBA Journal* (London), February 1984.

My architectural qualification is dated 1940, From then until 1950 my contribution to architecture was a bamboo officers' mess in the jungle south of Chittagong. The war took ten vital years in exchange for an intimate knowledge of the tropics and, in 1951, the commission for a large education programme in Ghana, part of which was carried out. In 1957 I started sculpture "to improve my architecture and for itself if successful," returning to early passions rendered impossible in the lost years. Sculpture played a part in forming my own leanings, beliefs and wishes in architecture, bits and pieces of which began to emerge in the late 1950's. The context was seldom right for me until abundant opportunity came in 1966 with the start of design for the University of Garyounis at Benghazi, leading to the completion, so far, of three phases.

A new and mature period starts about 1967/68

James Cubitt: University of Garyounis, Benghazi, Libya, 1978.

when I felt liberated in architecture, in sculpture, and in my personal life. By then I had many years' knowledge of different peoples, customs and cultures outside Europe. Certainly, I have never looked on architecture abroad as an export product, like a car or a radio, more or less suitable to greatly differing physical and cultural conditions. On the contrary, architecture is significant only in its response to specific needs. It is the response that creates the formal values: the architect's concern with the interaction of people, place, climate, and function brings everything together as "architecture," a highly-formal art having its own discipline of volume, scale and materials, as other arts have theirs.
—James Cubitt (1980)

When I met James Cubitt in the mid-1950s and watched him at work giving shape, conherence, and sense to the groups of buildings destined for the University of Nigeria, I was reminded of a remark made by my teacher Hans Poelzig in 1930 in an address to architecture students in Berlin. Poelzig warned his audience not to rely too much on the certainty than "form would follow from function." "Buildings," he asserted, "Tend to outlive their functions. You work your fingers to the bone to meet your client's brief, you invoke science and technology or even sociology to make your building perfectly functional and give your client good value for his money—only to find, thirty years later, that few people remember the reasons for your virtuous thrift and the special circumstances that governed your efforts at the time of designing. All that future generations will see will be the forms you have created, and it is by these that you will be judged." These were bold worlds at a time when Hannes Meyer at the Bauhaus could declare "ornament is

crime" and progressives, especially students, considered "form" a dirty word. A quarter of a century later, the pendulum had only just begun to swing back, and Cubitt's unashamed concern with the art of architecture was still viewed with suspicion by a generation of professionals who preferred to consider themselves scientists, artisans, technologists, economists—anything rather than artists.

Cubitt would have been a man after Poelzig's heart. Not that he was a formalist; on the contrary, his great University of Garyounis at Benghazi is the result of more than fifteen years of intensive study of university building and university design. This preoccupation with the physical background of academic life began when he became architect for the University of Science and Technology in Kumasi and several teachers' training colleges in Ghana in the 1950s. In 1957 he was commissioned by Dr. Nnamdi Azikiwe, Premier of the Eastern Region of Nigeria, to plan the University of Nigeria at Nsukka. University work in West Africa was followed by the Churchill College competition in Cambridge in 1958/59, a design for St. Anthony's College, Oxford, in 1961, the Medical Centre (Faculty of Medicine and University Teaching Hospital) at Kuala Lumpur, in 1963/67, the start in 1966 of design at Benghazi, and the return in 1971 to the University of Nigeria at Nsukka.

What is essential in the context of Poelzig's remarks is that Cubitt's involvement with university life and university buildings coincided with an intensive preoccupation with drawing and sculpture. This was no accident. Cubitt was fully conscious of the importance of his work as a sculptor for his own architectural development. He made this clear in his presidential address to the Architectural Association in October 1965: "Compared with painting and sculpture, very few buildings have survived for more than a few centuries. Yet these, which have obviously

far outlived their creators' purposes, can still be judged—are *always* judged—by their formal/ spiritual qualities. To know much beyond their general purpose and historical context is irrelevant to this judgement: our response is much too direct. Of course, this process is happening today too. In fact, today change is so rapid in some fields—hospitals, factories—that the functional edge is blurred even before the contractor moves out and the client in." In keeping with this philosophy, Cubitt's buildings are not only the results of long and painstaking involvement with his clients' life and needs, but they are also deliberate and positive statements in the language of colour and shape.

Architects in Northern Europe, particularly in England, are trained to fit their buildings into a friendly, man-made landscape which is often of great beauty. The people who live or work in these buildings want to look out onto this landscape and enjoy the reassuring effect of familiar meadows, hedgerows, and trees. Well-designed buildings in England are outward looking and liked best if they are so in harmony with their surroundings that they appear a natural part of the countryside. The situation is different in the Libyan desert. The desert climate is not friendly, but severe. Desert scenery can be dramatic and exciting, but it is seldom restful; it can be terrifying in its stark contrasts. Human beings who are exposed to it for long periods feel the need for refuge and protection among the man-made surroundings of towns and buildings. It is no accident that the best architects have used geometrical forms in arid climates, thereby emphasizing the contrast between an orderly built environment and a hostile outer world. Good desert buildings have few outside windows and look inward to small but carefully-controlled and tended courtyards or gardens. Some of the famous historical buildings of the arid world meet this psychological need perfectly.

The palaces of Shush and Persepolis, the desert cities of north Africa, and the great mosques of Isfahan or Kairuan are well-known examples.

The University of Garyounis at Benghazi shows that Cubitt and his partners learned to speak the language of desert architecture and, I believe, produced something that future generations will value as a powerful statement in this language. The strength of the architecture of the University of Benghazi will help it to satisfy another function that was often overlooked by the pioneers of the modern movement of the 1920s and 1930s; that is, the essential role of public buildings in providing a city or country with an image or point of identification. Libya, one of the youngest among the new countries, needs emotional rallying points and images, features that visitors and natives alike remember as characteristic of their country or city. Even if this were not specifically mentioned in his brief, Cubitt was clearly meant to create at Benghazi a memorable image for a newly awakened nation that was proud of putting a large part of its resources into a peaceful endeavour—the creation of a large central university. I believe he has achieved this and found an architectural language that will be understood even after the oil wells have run dry and life on the north coast of Africa has assumed a character that cannot be predicted or visualized today.

One can imagine future visitors admiring the boldness of placing this monumental group of buildings in a barren, windswept, and treeless plain by the sea. One can imagine their excitement at meeting strong colours and shapes in the glaring sunlight and their surprise and pleasure on entering the courtyards and spaces between university buildings with their sense of protection, calm, and even gentleness.

—Otto Koenigsberger

CULLINAN, Edward.

British. Born in London, 17 July 1931. Educated at Ampleforth College, Yorkshire, 1944-49; Cambridge University (Anderson and Webb Scholarship), 1951-54, B.A. (first-class honours) 1954; Architectural Association School, London, under Arthur Korn, John Killick, Denys Lasdun, and Peter Smithson, 1954-56; University of California, Berkeley (George VI Memorial Fellowship), 1956-57. Served in the British Army, 1949-51. Married Rosalind Yates in 1961; children: Emma, Kate, and Tom. In private architectural practice, London, since 1957. Second-Year master, Cambridge University, 1968-73; Visiting Critic, University of Toronto, 1973-78, 1981-83, and University of Cincinnati, 1977-78; Tutor, Polytechnic of the South Bank, London 1977-78; Bannister Fletcher Professor, Bartlett School of Architecture, University College, London, 1978-79; Visiting Critic and External Examiner at the Architectural Association, London, Royal College of Art, London, Hull College of Art, Yorkshire, Ulster Polytechnic, Belfast, Leicester Polytechnic, Cambridge University, Technical University of Nova Scotia, and Oslo University. Exhibitions: British Olivetti Ltd., London, 1970; Architectural Association, London, 1973; *British Architecture Exhibition*, Tehan, 1977; Royal Academy, London, 1982, 1983; *British Architecture Now*, London, 1982; *Continuity in Architecture*, London, 1983; *Association of Consultant Architects*, Royal Academy, London, 1984; *Festival of Architecture*, Royal Institute of British Architects, London, 1984; *Edward Cullinan, Architects*, Royal Institute of British Architects, London, 1984. Recipient: Industrial Architecture Award, *Financial Times*, 1973; Heritage Year Award, Civic Trust, 1975; *Architectural Design* Project Awards, London, 1981, 1983. Address: Edward Cullinan Architects, 57d Jamestown Road, London N.W.1, England.

Works:

1958 Bell Tout Lighthouse, Birling Gap, Eastbourne, Sussex
1960 Horder House, Ashford Chase, Petersfield, Hampshire
Marvin House, Panoramic Boulevard, Stinson Beach, California
1964 Knox House I, New Maltings, Nayland, Suffolk
1965 Cullinan House, Camden Mews, London
Kawecki House, Bartholomew Villas, London
Church (project)
1966 Garrett House, Greenholm Road, London
Garage and filling station, Nayland, Suffolk
Surgery, Church Road, Ashford, Kent
1967 Warehouse and printshop, Stepfield, Witham, Essex (with Julyan Wickham)
Morrison House (project)
Houses at Wilmslow, Cheshire (project)
1968 House and barns, Little London Farm, Oakley, Aylesbury, Buckinghamshire (with Julyan Wickham)
1969 Conference and study centre, Minster Lovell Mill, Oxfordshire (with Julyan Wickham and Julian Bicknell)
Knox House II, New Maltings, Nayland, Suffolk (with Julyan Wickham)
1971 Olivetti Offices and Workshops, Dundee, Scotland, Belfast, Derby and Carlisle (with Julyan Wickham, Julian Bicknell, Michael Chassay, and Giles Oliver)
1972 Residential Wing, Olivetti Training Centre, Haslemere, Surrey (with Julyan Wickham, Julian Bicknell, Michael Chassay, and Anthony Peake)
Apartment conversion, Powis Terrace, London (with Michael Chassay)
Olivetti Training Centre, stage II, Haslemere, Surrey (project)
Olivetti Branch Offices, Edinburgh (project)
North End Road Development, London (project)
Houses and apartments, Montpelier Estate, London (project)
Olivetti office conversions, Cardiff, Coventry, Thornton Heath (Surrey), Hove (Sussex), and Bootle (Merseyside)
Trojan Factory, Stonebroom Industrial Estate, Chesterfield, Derbyshire (with Michael Chassay)
House conversion, Gilston Road, London (with Philip Tabor)
1974 Village Hall, Mildenhall, Wiltshire (with Mark Beedle)
1975 House conversion, Cambridge Gardens, London (with Brendan Woods and Michael Chassay)
Maisonettes, Selhurst Road, South Norwood, London (with Anthony Peake)
The Orchard Development, Nassington Road, Hampstead, London (project)
1976 Studio, Powis Terrace, London (with Michael Chassay)
Old people's apartments, Roy Road, Northwood, Middlesex (with Philip Tabor)
1977 Housing estate, Highgrove, Ruislip, Middlesex (with Michael Chassay, Mark Beedle, Anthony Peake, Brendan Woods, and Philip Tabor)
1978 Housing estate and house conversions, Chester Road and Green Lane, Northwood, Middlesex (with Anthony Peake, Philip Tabor, and Michael Chassay)
1979 Flats and maisonettes, Westmoreland Road, Bromley, Kent (with Brendan Woods and Sunand Prasad)
Flats, Leighton Crescent, North London (with Philip Tabor, Michael Chassay and Mark Beedle)
Houses and shops, Bradwell Common, Milton Keynes, Buckinghamshire (with Anthony Peake and Giles Oliver)
Designers' offices conversion, Central London (with Michael Chassay)
1980 Workshop for the Mentally Handicapped, Westoning Manor, Bedfordshire (with Michael Chassay and Robin Nicholson)
Adventure Playground and Building, Kennington Park, South London (with Sunand Prasad and Mungo Smith)
1981 Conference Centre, High Wycombe, Buckinghamshire (with Anthony Peake and Mark Beedle)
Swan Hotel extension, Bedford (project; with Sunand Prasad)
1982 Parish Church of St. Mary Barnes rebuilding, South London (with Mark Beedle and Alan Short)
Theatre/Workshop conversion, Winchester College, Hampshire (with Anthony Peake)
1983 Residence for the Mentally Handicapped, Westoning Manor, Bedfordshire (with Michael Chassay, Robin Nicholson and Gregory Penoyre)
Community Care Centre, Lambeth Hospital, London (with Robin Nicholson and Mungo Smith)
Single-People's Hostel, Basingstoke, Hampshire (with Sunand Prasad, Gregory Penoyre and Frances Holliss)
Calthorpe Park School additions and alterations, Hampshire (with Alan Short)
1984 Arts Centre conversion, Winchester College, Hampshire (with Anthony Peake)
Elderly Persons' Day Care Centre, South London (with Robin Nicholson and Mungo Smith)
Category 2 Sheltered Flatlets for the Elderly, Ealing, London (with Alan Short and Gregory Penoyre)
Residences, Farm, Moot Hall, Bakery and Shop for the Mentally Handicapped, Milton Keynes, Buckinghamshire (with Mark Beedle and Frances Holliss)

Publications:

By CULLINAN: articles—"British Architecture" in *Architectural Design* (London), September/October 1977; "Materials in Use—The Roofs of Highgrove" in *RIBA Journal* (London), November 1977; "Cullinan and Hillingdon," with Thurston Williams, in *RIBA Journal* (London), February 1978; "A Question of Style" in *Spazio e Società* (Milan), January 1982; "Oriental Museum, Durham" in *Architectural Review* (London), February 1984; "Morris, Architecture and Art" in *William Morris Today*, London 1984; "The Morris Papers" in *Architectural Review* (London), March 1984.

On CULLINAN: books—*World Architecture One*, edited by John Donat, London 1964; *British Architecture: Arts and Leisure*, edited by Sherban Cantacuzino, London 1977; *Architectural Association Annual Review*, London 1977; articles—"A Studio Near Petersfield" in *House and Garden* (London), May 1963; "Non Profit Architektur" in *Baumeister* (Munich), April 1969; "AR Preview—Olivetti Edinburgh" by Peter Collymore in *Architectural Review* (London), January 1973; "Architect's Work" in *Architectural Association Quarterly* (London), Spring 1973; "Olivetti's New Branches in England" in *Architectural Design* (London), April 1973; "Houses for Tomorrow—Hunters Hill, Wilmslow" in *The Architects' Journal* (London), May 1973; "Four Olivetti Offices" by Mark Girouard in *The Architects' Journal* (London), June 1973; "Olivetti's New Branches" in *Architecture + Urbanism* (Tokyo), February 1974; "Two for Olivetti" by Reyner Banham in *Architectural Review*

Edward Cullinan: Parish Church of St. Mary, Barnes, South London, 1982.

(London), April 1974; "Pick of the Projects" in *Architectural Design* (London), May 1974; "Study Centre, Minster Lovell, Oxfordshire" by Sherban Cantacuzino and Anthony Ambrose in *Architectural Review* (London), July 1976; "Interior Architecture—Artist's Flat" by Gordon Bowyer in *RIBA Journal* (London), November 1976; "Olivetti Aujourd'hui" in *L'Architecture d'Aujourd'hui* (Paris), December 1976; "Building Study—Highgrove Housing" by David Wild in *The Architects' Journal* (London), July 1977; "British Architecture—Edward Cullinan Architects 1959-1977" by David Wild in *Architectural Design* (London), September/October 1977; "Radical Alternatives—Cullinan's Co-op" by Tom Woolley in *The Architects' Journal* (London), October 1977; "MK Two Housing" in *Building* (London), March 1980; "London: post modern architecture new house in Leighton Crescent" in *Abitare* (Milan), July/August 1981; "St. Mary Barnes" in *Spazio e Societa* (Milan), January 1982; "Beautiful Barnes" in *Architects' Journal* (London), March 1982; "Two Projects by Edward Cullinan Architects" in *Architects' Journal* (London), June 1982; "Gymnastic Conversions" in *Architects' Journal* (London), March 1983; "Adventure Playground in London", and "Workshops for the Handicapped at Westoning" in *Baumeister* (Munich), August 1983; "The Cullinan Phenomenon – the act and art of building"

in *Architectural Review* (London), September 1983; "Reformation of the Church at Barnes" in *Architects' Journal* (London), April 1984; "Barnes Continuity" by Peter Cook and John Whale in *Architectural Review* (London), May 1984; "Royal Opera House Competition" in *Architects' Journal* (London), July 1984; "Down at Uplands" in *Architects' Journal* (London), August 1984; "Show for architect who won royal praise" by Charles Knevitt in *The Times* (London), 12 September 1984.

I started at the beginning; I encourage my friends to build houses, studios and conversions, however small: we sometimes built them ourselves.

Minster Lovell, a place for conferences in the Cotswold National Park, followed: I designed it with Julian Bicknell and Julyan Wickham as a series of new buildings that connected old ones and made useful an existing graceful garden.

We were joined by Michael Chassay and Giles Oliver to make new branch offices for Olivetti. We made each one as it if were a home for its fifty occupants, gathered round a partial courtyard, designed to expand to complete it.

With Mark Beedle, we designed a group of a hundred low-lying, relaxed, wide frontage houses at Highgrove in the North West London suburbs—laid out as a series of paths, hedges, houses, trees and bushes; formally like an Elizabethan garden, they deliberately embrace and progress a suburban ideal.

At Chester Green with Anthony Peake, the same ideals were carried forward to embrace both new houses and modifications to existing ones; intermeshed and supporting one another.

Our latest schemes of houses move from the country and suburb into the city, and with Anthony Peake, Brendan Woods, Sunand Prasad and Philip Tabor, we have enjoyed devising houses that support the city fabric that understand the street, the close and the square as rooms with the sky for a ceiling, whose walls are the public fronts of the buildings through which doorways lead to a more personal world beyond.

From this background we have moved to the design of more complex buildings in the city; an hospital, a church, and buildings for the old and disabled, and schools and conference buildings in the country buildings that make more of "the place" than strict necessity demands. Our practice has now grown to include the architects Mungo Smith, Alan Short, Frances Holliss, Gregory Penoyre and Alex Freemantle, and together we propose a future that joyfully accepts the materials and methods of our time to support and enhance the rural, suburban or urban context we find, to make an art of Architecture in the service of our shared humanity.

—Edward Cullinan

The clarity of the thinking that underlies each of Edward Cullinan's designs is immediately apparent in the building's sections and its plans: each drawing reads almost like a diagram of an idea. Invariably, it is the section that most eloquently expresses this idea, a key section that acts as a sort of three-dimensional template from which the more complex forms of the building may then develop, not one by which they are restrained. Cullinan is forced to rationalize and order the relationships within the building in order to achieve this key section, but he does so for two reasons, firstly because it will facilitate a modular, repetitive system of construction, and secondly because it will plant the seed from which a variety of spatial inter-relationships may then begin to grow.

This fascination on the one hand for the use of new constructional systems and, on the other, for the intricate manipulation of space, points to Cullinan's firm roots in the architectural philosophies of the Modern Movement. But, to Cullinan, as important as the philosophies themselves was the force of the social responsibility and concern that accompanied them, a view reflected in his personal commitment to the design of low-cost housing, to maximizing the physical return to be gained from very limited financial resources. (It is interesting to note that Cullinan's own office is run as a cooperative.) Where Cullinan has moved beyond the Modern Movement is in his particular response to the need for simplicity and economy. His interest has been in simplicity of technique rather than simplicity of form. He has adopted straight-forward and additive, rather than refined and reductive, methods of construction, partly because of his own experience of self-building, but also because he believes that it is through the manifestation of its construction that a building gains its particular meaning. Cullinan retains a conventional masonry structure at the base of his buildings, but the solidity and permanence of this part of the construction then gives way to a lighter, more flexible structure towards the roof. Paradoxically, it is the base of the building which is formally most fluid and relaxed while the lightweight structure above is very rigidly defined and ordered; ultimate flexibility necessitates preliminary restraint.

These primary elements, base, wall, roof, then receive an accretion of secondary elements, decks, entrances, porches, planting boxes, rainwater butts, balustrades, modulating and ormamenting the facade

Each building has one, or sometimes two, facades, consistent, linear and open-ended. The facade commands the external space before it in the rather formal relationship of building to landscape, house to garden. These traditional relationships Cullinan respects, as he does the conventional values of the prospective tenants of his houses. But while endeavouring to embody these traditional relationships and conventional values, Cullinan is equally committed to experimentation, invention, to the search for new ways of building. His own work is continually evolving, lessons are always being learnt. But the ideas and the principles originally expressed in the design of his first, small, private house are those that he still carries with him today.

—Bob Allies

D

DAHINDEN, Justus.

Swiss. Born in Zürich, 18 May 1925. Educated at the Federal Institute of Technology, Zürich, 1945-49, Dip.Arch. 1949, D.Sc.Tech. 1956. Married Marta Arquint in 1950; children: Zeno, Ivo, and Delia. In private practice, Zürich, since 1955. Professor of Architecture, and Director of the Institute for Design, Technical University, Vienna, since 1973. Member, International Congress of Religion, Architecture, and the Visual Arts, New York/Montreal, 1967, Brussels, 1970, and Jerusalem, 1973. Member of the Groupe International d'Architecture Prospective, Paris, since 1968. Exhibitions: Paris, 1967; Salzburg, 1968; Munich, 1968; Moscow, 1969; London, 1969; St. Louis, 1969; New York, 1973; Lyon, 1973; Zürich, 1974; Poland, 1975; Lausanne, 1976; Moscow, 1978; Musée des Arts Décoratifs, Paris, 1981; University of Texas, Austin, 1981; Dallas City Hall, Texas, 1981; University of Texas, San Antonio, 1981; Rhode Island School of Design, Providence, 1982; Virginia Polytechnic Institute, Blacksburg, 1982; *Quadriennale d'Arte*, Rome, 1984; *Man and Architectural Space*, International Research Centre, Vienna, 1984; Centro de Arte y Comunicacion, Buenos Aires, 1985; *Interarch 85*, Sofia, 1985. Recipient: three awards for excellence in design, Guild for Religious Architecture, 1969; two awards for achievement in interior design, *Institutions Magazine*, 1969; Grand Prix International d'Urbanisme et d'Architecture, 1970; Grand Prix d'Architecture, Cercle d'Etudes Architecturales, Paris, 1981; City of Nantes Award and Bronze Medal, 1981, National Peace Committee Award and Silver Medal, 1983, World Biennale of Architecture, Sofia. Honorary Fellow, American Institute of Architects, 1973; Honorary President, International Society of Christian Artists, 1976. Address (office): Kienastenwiesweg 38, 8053 Zürich, Switzerland.

Works:

1962 St. Paulus Catholic Church, Dielsdorf, Switzerland
Bosco della Bella Holiday Village, Fornasette, Switzerland
Primary School, Weggis, Switzerland
1963 St. Franziskus Catholic Church, Huttwilen, Switzerland
1964 St. Batholomeus Catholic Church, Rielasingen, West Germany
Ventilator AG Administrative Building, Stafa, Switzerland
1965 St. Stefan Catholic Church, Arlen, Germany
Maria Kronung Swiss Academy and Parish Centre, Witikon, Zürich
Herz-Jesu Catholic Church, Buchs, Switzerland
Hotel Continental, Lausanne
1966 Craftsmen School and Church, Taitung, Formosa
1967 Dominican Monastery, Kinshasa, Zaire
Hostellerie Rigi Hotel Centre, Rigi-Kaltbad, Switzerland

1968 Swiss Fair Restaurants and Shopping Centre, London
1969 Doldertal Trigon Village, Zürich
1970 St. Antonius Catholic Church and Parish Centre, Wildegg, Switzerland
Ferrolegeringar Pyramidal Administrative Building, Zürich
1971 St. Antonius Catholic Church and Parish Centre, Kleindottingen, Switzerland
1972 Martyrs' Shrine, Church, Convent, School, and Social Centre, Mityana, Uganda
Tantris Restaurant, Munich
Hotel Aarauerhof, Aarau, Switzerland
Ratia Shopping Centre, Davos, Switzerland
1973 Hotel Alpha Palmiers, Lausanne
Trigon Village, Cala en Bosc, Menorca, Spain
Justus Dahinden House, Kienastenwiesweg 41, Zürich
1974 Bruder Klaus Catholic Church and Community Centre, Spiez, Switzerland
Schwab ylon Leisure City, Munich
1975 Catholic Cathedral and Martyrs' National Shrine, Namugongo, Uganda
1976 San Giuseppe Catholic Church and Community Centre, Monza, Italy
1977 Zur Gottlichen Vorsehung Catholic Church and Community Centre, Königsbrunn, near Augsburg, West Germany
St. Michael Catholic Church and Community Centre, Vettelschoss, West Germany
Heilig Geist Catholic Church and Parish Centre, Weingarten, West Germany
Trottenhof Historic Residential Building, Weggis, Switzerland
Villa on Lake Geneva, Villette, Switzerland
Family houses, Rotzenbuhlstrasse, Oberwil, Switzerland
Residential area for elderly people, Königsbrunn, West Germany
1978 St. Josef Catholic Church and Community Centre, Dotzheim, Wiesbaden, West Germany
1979 St. Jakobus Catholic Church and Civic Centre, Limburg-Lindenholzhausen, West Germany
St. Elisabeth Catholic Church and Community Centre, Wiesbaden, West Germany
Catholic Church and Community Centre, Ingelheim-West, West Germany
Waidburg Restaurant, Zürich
Hotel Zentrum Gaggenau, Gaggenau, West Germany
Pearl-of-Cairo Floating Hotel, Egypt
Ivoirexpo African International Exhibition, Abidjan, Ivory Coast
1980 Makurdi International Hotel, Nigeria
1981 Twannberg Swiss Holiday Village and Recreation Centre, near Biel, Switzerland
Moghan East Village Town Plan and Bubble low-cost housing Iran
1982 Parkhotel, Bad Mergentheim, West Germany
Zur Gass Village, Gaggenau, West Germany
Haus zum Erker residential building, Zürich
1984 Technical University Library, Vienna
Derksen private high-school, Munich

Riviera Arcade multifunctional settlement, Tel Aviv

Research: Floating structures, such as Pearl-of-Cairo Floating Hotel, Egypt, and "Floating Theatre on the Lake of Zürich;" Urban structural system TRIGON for housing, schools, offices, hotels; Town planning system AKROPOLIS; housing systems—BUBBLE system for low cost housing; TUBBY system for housing; CUBO system for low-cost housing.

Publications:

By DAHINDEN: books—*Standortbestimmung der Gegenwartsarchitektur*, Zürich 1956; *New Trends in Church Architecture*, New York 1968; *Urban Structures for the Future*, London 1971; *Urbanisme*, Brussels 1972; *Thinking—Feeling—Acting*, Stuttgart 1973; *Leisure Cities*, Stuttgart 1974.

On DAHINDEN: books—*The Church of the Future*, New York 1970; *Buildings for Hospitality*, Zürich 1968; articles—"Contemporary Catholic Church Building" in *Building and Home* (Zürich), 1963; "New Trends in International Hotel Building" in *Building and Home* (Zürich), 1964; "Holiday Hotels for the Future" in *Building and Home* (Zürich), 1965; "La cita di domani" in *Chiesa e Quartiere* (Milan), 1967; "Architecture?"in *Arch* (Stuttgart), no. 3, 1968; "Prospective Environmental Design" in *Baumeister* (Munich), no. 4, 1968; "Leisure Society and Leisure City" in *Transparent* (Vienna), no., 7/8, 1971; "The Visual Environment" in *Kunst and Kirche* (Linz, Austria), 1971; "Animation by Holiday Architecture" in *Building and Home* (Zürich), 1976; "Acculturation in Architecture" in *Schweizerische Bauzeitung* (Zürich), 1978; "Architectural Education" in *DBZ Deutsche Bauzeitung* (Gütersloh, West Germany), no. 4, 1978; A New Face for Gaggenau" by Gunter Mader in *Deutsche Bauzeitung* (Stuttgart), November 1979; "Twannberg Holiday Village in Switzerland" in *Baumeister* (Munich), March 1981; "Parish Church in Limburg" in *Deutsche Bauzeitung* (Stuttgart), April 1981; "Dahinden in Lindenholzhausen" in *Architectural Review* (London), August 1981.

My recent research concerns the relationship between MAN and Architectural SPACE. Architecture's central problem is the formation of SPACE, designed to assure and maintain physical and mental health. It is the fundamental task of architecture to establish equilibrium, even full of dissonances, between MAN and SPACE. To do this requires a global approach to fulfillment of practical needs, as well as a sense-oriented medium and the manifestation of unconscious wishes and desires ultimately performing the transcendental functions of the human psyche. Too often, during the

Justus Dahinden: House of the Oriels, Zurich, 1983.

development of the Modern Age, this holistic service of SPACE and MAN has been lost. It is implied in the basic principles of architecture, but it must be regained every day.

To regain it, I use *LAW OF THREE* in Architecture. This law, which appears suitable as a foundation for a new convention defining architectural qualities, is basically rooted in the law of evolution and creation of all esoteric traditions. It states that the dualism between two opposing forces must always lead to a third force, which is independent of the two original forces and which manifests itself in the spiritual realm beyond the reality of perception. For architecture as an integral part of creation and evolution, the two opposing forces of this holistic law are represented by the concepts of "Structure" and "Gestalt"; they are transcended by the third or "Spiritual" force. In his spatial dependency (Domosphere), MAN becomes the focal point of a threefold force field, the sources of which can be described as follows:

STRUCTURE consists of the architectural manifestation in its natural and artificial aspects. Its structural-biological efficiency depends on the extent to which the methods and materials employed serve man's well-being. Besides its protective function, space must provide environmental compatibility. In the larger ecological frame, architecture therefore assumes the role of another skin for man.

GESTALT is perceived by our senses. According to Walter Gropius, perceived GESTALT leads to inner sensations and feelings. Architecture mobilizes feelings and creates emotional dependencies. GESTALT determines whether a particular segment of space accepts or rejects Man, whether it leaves us warm or cold. GESTALT is, furthermore, information; it communicates the meaning of a structure. Beauty dignifies its appearance.

SPIRIT transcends architecture; it is beyond structural efficacy and perceived GESTALT. While the rational mind and the senses cannot provide more than limited perception, the human Spirit aspires towards grander images and more comprehensive associations. This stimulates the Trans-life. Included are myth and ritual, both of which have impressed themselves on first-rate structures throughout the ages. We are in need of such buildings. MAN and his effigy, SPACE, are made

complete in the spiritual realm. Only there can Man achieve his highest aspiration of realizing himself, and only this realm can create and maintain the necessary cosmological consensus on a socio-cultural level.

The LAW OF THREE in architecture is based on the ecological dictates from the new universal consciousness. This consciousness excludes any one-sideness, as developed within the decades. It is such one-sidedness that disables architecture again and again and that leads to short-lived trends and to uncertainty about the cultural status of architecture. It is our task to create an environment encompassing the totality of MAN's needs and uses. As we become aware of the anthropological quality of architecture as a holistic service for MAN, the LAW OF THREE can lead us to a new consensus on architectural qualities.

—Justus Dahinden

Switzerland has made a notable contribution to European architectural culture since the war, and the Zürich Polytechnic, with its great traditions linked with the Mosers, Haefeli, Hubacher, and Roth, has been the standard-bearer of new architectural trends. Justus Dahinden, a native of Zürich, has been one of its most illustrious graduates.

Dahinden decided very early in life to be an architect. His study of the work of Frank Lloyd Wright expanded his vision as well as created a sound professional ethic; his contact with Gaudí's extraordinary structures galvanized his lively imagination and enabled him to achieve an ideal balance between radical design and sound method. In an effort to continually excel himself, he began, in his works, to work to the limits of his intuition, beyond the goals he had earlier set himself. The Catholic Church also played a part in his development because he is himself a Christian and because the Church provided his first commissions. His analyses of religious complexes became the basis of his first theories on urban complexes.

Dahinden has also been influenced by the avant-garde projects of the Archigram group and by the theories of the Metabolist Group in Japan. He has developed a vocabulary for devising and testing his

works: *biotectonics,* covering the totality of life in its evolutionary processes; *geometrics,* the ordered and disciplined expression of original forms: Psychologics, the inter-related processes that affect the environment; and *cosmics,* the superior force able to overwhelm human constructs. The unit of measurement of his modular constructional system is the *trigon,* a triangular prism made stable by angular columns. Among his achievements in the trigon mode are the village in Cala en Bosc, Menorca, and the village at Doldertal in Zürich.

In Dahinden's work on "urbanotopia," he seeks an alternative to the dehumanization of the megalopolis, a new orientation in the use of leisure as an integral part of individual life and behaviour and as a pattern of socio-economic structure. Schwabylon Leisure City, Munich, was one effort in that direction, but the "precociousness" of the contents proved fatal to the functioning of the complex and condemned it to early demolition. The floating town centres, based on the same principle, and planned for the Aegean and on the Nile, reached a successful execution in a new lagoon city on the Ivory Coat. What Dahinden has achieved is a projection of the integrated urbanistic system of the "fantascientific" design of Radio City.

The wealth of his imagination can also be seen in smaller, individual works, such as his houses. The Villa on Lake Geneva is a successful demonstration of the articulation of surroundings centred on a vacation or holiday: the villa is the centre of activities and communications and its space is extended down to the lake by terracing. The roof is made to conform, also descending through inclined planes down to the quay.

On a larger scale, Dahinden's religious centres are designed according to the same principle—an open flexible church integrated with the social and urban texture. His work on these complexes clearly demonstrates that normally "immobile structures" can be rendered in dynamic, flexible forms, forms that closely relate to, and participate in, their surroundings. One of his most significant achievements of this kind is to be found a Mityana, a centre of pilgrimage in Uganda, where Dahinden masterfully integrates indigenous tribal forms with secular surroundings as the key to his architectural solution.

—Giuliano Chelazzi

DALTON, John.

Australian. Born in Leeds, Yorkshire, England, 30 December 1972; emigrated to Australia, 1950: naturalized, 1960. Educated at the Adel School, Leeds, 1939; Leeds Technical College, 1940-45; Queensland University, Brisbane, under R. P. Cummings, 1952-58, Dip.Arch. 1958. Served in the Royal Air Force, 1946-48. Married Sheila Harvey in 1952; Suzanne Elizabeth Crozier in 1970; children: Penelope and Amanda. Since 1958, Principal of John Dalton Architect and Associates, Brisbane. Part-time Lecturer in Design, Faculty of Architecture, 1963-71, and since 1969, Member of the Faculty Board of Architecture, Queensland University. Executive Member of the Council for the Queensland Art Gallery Society, Brisbane, 1960-74; Chairman of the Publications Committee, 1962-71, and Member of the Council of the Queensland Chapter, 1966-70, Royal Australian Institute of Architects; Executive Member of the Contemporary Art Society of Australia, 1965-74. Exhibitions: Australian Pavilion, Lausanne Fair, Switzerland, 1959; Qantas Australian Architecture Exhibition, London, 1962; Australian Pavilion, *Expo '67,* Montreal, 1967; Australian Pavilion, *Expo '70,* Osaka, Japan, 1970; *Brisbane Telegraph* Design Exhibition, Brisbane, 1972; *Australian Design,* toured Australia, 1983; *Australian Architecture,* London, Paris, Bonn, Ghent, and New York, 1983. Recipient: First Prize, Queensland Plywood Competition, 1956; *Arts and Architecture* (Brisbane) Award, 1960, 1961, 1962; First Prize, Brick Manufacturers of Queensland Competition, 1962; Bronze Medallion, Queensland Chapter of the Australian Institute of Architects, 1964, 1967, 1972, 1975; Timber Development Association Award, South Australia, 1971; Merit Award, 1977, and Bronze Medals, 1978 and 1982, Royal Australian Institute of Architects. Fellow, Royal Institute of British Architects; Life Fellow, Royal Australian Institute of Architects, 1982. Address: John Dalton Architect and Associates, 38 Sylvan Road, Toowong, Brisbane, Queensland 4066, Australia.

Works:

1956 Spinks House, Quentin Street, Indooroopilly, Brisbane
      Head House, Fleming Road, Chapel Hill, Brisbane
1957 Young House, Frost Street, Mount Gravatt, Brisbane
1960 Battersby Flats, Quinton Street, Kangaroo Point, Brisbane
      Dalton House, Fig Tree Pocket, Brisbane
      Farbach House, Moordale Street, Indooroopilly, Brisbane
      Henricks House, Homestead, Roma, Queensland
      Masters House, Sophia Street, Kenmore, Brisbane
      Tennett Town Houses, Terrace Street, Toowong, Brisbane
      Professor Whitehead House, Kirkdale Street, Chapel Hill, Brisbane
1961 Mayo House, Kroshanne Street, Aspley, Brisbane
1962 Brick Manufacturers House, Ipswich Road, Brisbane
      Clayton House, Retreat Road, Aspley, Brisbane
      Collier House, Equinox Street, Kenmore, Brisbane
      Leverington House, Kenmore Road, Kenmore, Brisbane
1963 Arts Theatre, Petrie Terrace, Brisbane
      Burke House, Waterworks Road, Ashgrove, Brisbane
      Hinstedt Town Houses, East Brisbane
      Magee House, Woodfield Road, Kenmore, Brisbane
      Morrocco Homestead, St. George, West Queensland
      Pickworth Town Houses, Waterloo Road, East Brisbane
      Stirling House, Moggill Road, Moggill, Brisbane
      Wipple Homestead, St. George, West Queensland
1964 Deignan House, Hoya Street, Holland Park, Brisbane
      Stoneham House, Kenmore Road, Kenmore, Brisbane
      Watson House, Deerhurst Road, Brookfield, Brisbane
      Wareham House, Kenmore Road, Kenmore, Brisbane
      Wilson House, Mount Coot-tha Road, Brisbane
1965 Belligoi House, Munro Street, Indooroopilly, Brisbane
      Davidson House, Ardell Street, Kenmore, Brisbane
      Quilpie Memorial Pool, Western Queensland
      Dr. Whitfield House, Cadiz Street, Indooroopilly, Brisbane
1966 Barrett House, Kingussie Street, Kenmore, Brisbane
      Buckley House, Fontayne Street, Aspley, Brisbane
      Graham House, Gower Street, Indooropilly, Brisbane
1967 Kaeshagen House, Musgrave Street, Kenmore, Brisbane
1968 Barclay House, Indus Street, Whites Hill, Brisbane
      Bucknell House, Sutton Street, Chelmer, Brisbane
      Clark House, Prospect Street, Sherwood, Brisbane
      Dr. Douglas House, Hill Crescent, Gladstone, Queensland
      Crozier House, Woodfield Road, Brookfield, Brisbane
      Gamin House, Skyline Drive, Burleigh Heads, Queensland
      Hodges House, Clontarf Beach, Redcliffe, Queensland
      Hollingsworth House, Helse Street, Bardon, Brisbane
      Krebs House, Ventura Street, Mermaid Beach, Queensland
      Leitch House, Sunset Road, Kenmore, Brisbane
      McDonald House, Banbury Street, Carina, Brisbane
      Professor Neale House, Roseberry Street, Chelmer, Brisbane
      Rabaa House, Kimba Street, Indooroopilly, Brisbane
      Swan House, Lois Street, Kenmore, Brisbane
1969 Bolton Holiday Units, Attunga Heights Road, Noosa Heads, Queensland
      Bowers House, Castile Street, Indooroopilly, Brisbane
      C.H.I. House, Mimosa Downs, Mount Gravatt, Brisbane
      Ebzery House, Tallaro Street, Jindalee, Brisbane
      Hughes House, Brookfield Road, Kenmore, Brisbane
      Jamieson House, Kenmore Road, Kenmore, Brisbane
      King House, Castile Street, Indooroopilly, Brisbane
      McGregor House, Musgrave Street, Kenmore, Brisbane
      Nell House, Queenscroft Street, Chelmer, Brisbane
      Smith House, Brookfield Road, Brookfield, Brisbane
1970 Cameron House, Bycroft Street and Heron Road, Pullenvale, Brisbane
      Griffin House, Long Road, Mount Tamborine, Queensland
      Handicrafts of Asia Shop, Lennons Plaza, Brisbane
      Meek House, Haven Road, Brisbane
      Robinson House, Luckins Street, Aspley, Brisbane

John Dalton: Peden Farm, Moggill, Brisbane, 1975.

1971 Read House, Lavereigh Street, Indooroopilly, Brisbane

Roberts House, Orme Road, Buderim, Queensland

1972 Myers House, Wonalee Street, Kenmore, Brisbane

Salter House, Fig Tree Pocket Road, Fig Tree Pocket, Brisbane

Strugnell House, Grandview Road, Brookfield, Brisbane

Vice-Chancellor's Residence, University of Queensland, Brisbane

1973 Musgrave House, Roseberry Street, Chelmer, Brisbane

Rosenblum House, Kneele Street, Holland Park, Brisbane

1974 Arts, Crafts and Music Centre, Darling Downs Institute of Technology, Toowoomba, Queensland

1975 Anderson House, Kruger Road, Carbrook, Queensland

Covacevich House, Cairns, North Queensland

Dunlop House, Jesmond Street, Indooroopilly, Brisbane

Louis House, Alton Estate, The Gap, Brisbane

Peden Farm, Waroolba A.I.S. Stud, Moggill, Brisbane

University House, Griffith University, Nathan, Brisbane

1976 MacFarlane House, Repton Street, Pullenvale, Brisbane

Bardon Professional Development Centre, Bardon, Brisbane

1977 Hall of Residence, College of Technical Education, Kelvin Grove, Brisbane

1978 Lambtail Cottage restoration, Allora, Darling Downs, Queensland

1979 Boundy House, Mandalay Street, Fig Tree Pocket, Brisbane

1981 Dunlop House 2, Creswick Street, Clayfield, Brisbane

1982 Mount Manning Homestead, Darling Downs, Queensland

1984 Mobinbry Homestead, Bogga Billa, New South Wales

Morahan House, The Esplanade, Manly, Queensland

Publications:

By DALTON: books—*The Wise House,* Perth, Western Australia 1978; *Old Continent: New Building,* Sydney 1983; articles—"Australia—Brisbane," special issue of *Architectural Review* (London), September 1978; "Detailing" in *UIA: International Architect* (London), no. 4, 1984.

On DALTON: books—*Best Australian Homes* by Neil Clerehen, Melbourne 1961; *Towards an Australian Architecture* by Harry Sowden, Sydney 1968; *Architecture in Australia* by J.M. Freeland, Sydney 1968; *Architecture in Tropical Australia* by Balwant Singh Saini, London 1970; *Living and Partly Living: Housing in Australia* by Ian McKay and others, Melbourne 1971; *The Visual Arts* by M. Symonds, Brisbane 1972; *Understanding Art* by B. Churcher, Adelaide, South Australia 1973; *Australian Housing in the 70's* by Howard Tanner, Sydney 1976; articles—"We Should Build to Suit the Climate" in *Courier Mail* (Brisbane) 21 July 1965; "Architect of Sun and Shadow" by Babette Hayes in *Belle* (Sydney), July/August 1977.

Design for climate is the simple solution for all our architectural endeavour in Queensland. It is the mainspring for all the magical qualities that add up to a vital architecture. The broad verandahs and the cool, serene arcades found in our early architecture are qualities that we recognize and unconsciously delight in. The delicate tracery of shadow on a simple light-washed wall reveal the ever-changing character of buildings in the sun. We instinctively love these patterns of climate, as they are part of our experience, and we have every right to expect them in contemporary design. Our delight is to build in the sun and gather our poetic inspiration from the sunlight, shade, and shadow that is our heritage.

—John Dalton

John Dalton belongs to a small band of English architects who migrated to Australia after World War II. Most of them chose to live and work in the comparatively temperate cities of Melbourne, Adelaide and Sydney, but Dalton decided to settle in the sub-tropical environment of Brisbane, where he extended his earlier training in building and finally qualified as an architect. Dalton's early practice was confined to domestic building, mainly single houses, and it was in this kind of work that he built his reputation as a highly senstive and skilful designer. During the 1970s, however, his work has considerably expanded, and it now includes a number of larger projects—educational, professional, and student residential buildings.

Dalton built houses at a time when many of the existing large, old, colonial timber houses with high ceilings and generous rooms and verandahs were being pulled down and replaced by more compact brick and brick-veneer houses popular in the more temperate zones of south and east Australia. His buildings offered a refreshing contrast. He adapted quickly to his new humid, sub-tropical surroundings and realized that the main problem in building design lay in control of the sun, provision of cross ventialtion, and reduction of glare. The roots of Dalton's earlier buildings, however, did not lie in the traditional Queensland vernacular, though he did make occasional gestures to the local domestic building tradition by adding wood lattice work between verandah posts, louvres, and horizontal lattice blinds. His earlier solutions were more in tune with the prevalent domestic architecture of Richard Neutra, William Wurster, and others who were busy on the west coast of the United States.

Over the years Dalton has absorbed some of the casual, semi-outdoor lifestyle of Queenslanders, and his recent houses reflect this influence. The rooms are planned to suit the specific needs of the owners, and the verandahs and terraces are generous and cantilevered well beyond the houses to reach out to nature. They have resulted in a highly personalized style that has been born out of his use of white, masonry walls, natural timbers and sloping roofs admirably suited to steep sites typically found in some of the outer areas of Brisbane.

Dalton is thorough, meticulous in detail, and extremely sensitive to the needs of his client. He has already established himself as an important designer and, judging by his recent work, should continue to make significant contributions to architecture in tropical Australia.

—B. S. Saini

DANNATT, (James) Trevor.

British. Born in London, 15 January 1920. Educated at Colfe's School, London; Regent Street Polytechnic, London, Dip.Arch. 1942. Married Joan Howell Davies in 1953; children: Clare and Adrian. Studio Assistant, School of Architecture, Regent Street Polytechnic, 1942-43; Assistant Architect, office of Jane B. Drew, *q.v.,* London, 1943-44, office of E. Maxwell Fry*q.v.,* and Jane B. Drew, London, 1944-48, and London County Council Architects' Department, Royal Festival Hall Group, 1948-52. Since 1952, in private practice London: formed Trevor Dannat and Partners, 1972 (with Colin Dollimore and Ronald Paxton; currently, with Colin Dollimore). Instructor, Central School of Arts and Crafts, London, 1952-54; Chair of Architecture (part time), University of Manchester, England, 1975; Visiting Professor, Washington University School of Architecture, St. Louis, 1976. Editor, 1945-46, and Joint Editor, with Jane B. Drew, 1946-62, *Architects Yearbook,* London. Secretary, MARS Group, London, 1948-54. Exhibitions: *British Architecture,* Arts Council, London, 1955; *Architecture Today,* with Alan Irvine, Arts Council, London, 1961. Recipient: First Prize, Conference Centre and Hotel Competition, Riyadh, Saudi Arabia, 1968. Honorary M.A.: University of Manchester, England, 1979. Associate, 1943, and Fellow, 1961, Royal Institute of British Architects;Associate of the Royal Academy, 1977, and Royal Academician, 1984. Address: Trevor Dannatt and Partners, 115 Crawford Street, London W1, England.

Works:

1957 Congregational Church, Blackheath, London
1958 Dobbs House, Hampstead, London
      Laslett House, Cambridge, England
1960 Plante House, Hampstead, London
      College Hall Student Residence, University of Leicester, England (with Leslie Martin)
1962 Vaughan College and Museum, Leicester, England
1963 Interiors and reconstruction, 40 Berkeley Square, London
      Needler Hall, University of Hull, Humberside
      Fellows Social Building, Trinity Hall, Cambridge, England
1965 Library and Council Chamber, University of Leicester, England
      Gymnasium and Science Building, Rosa Bassett School, London
1966 Assembly Hall, Botham School, York, England
      House, Colinsburgh, Fife, Scotland
      Housing, Poplar High Stret, London
1969 Classroom Building, Eltham Hill School, London
      Old people's home, Cedars Road, London
1971 Children's Reception Home, Davey Street, London
      Old people's home, Sumner Road, London (with John Shaw)
1972 Meeting halls, Acorn Estate, and Sceaux Gardens, Southwark, London
      Friends' Meeting House, Blackheath, London
      Trevor Dannatt and Partners:
1974 Conference Centre, Riyadh, Saudi Arabia
      Intercontinental Hotel, Riyadh, Saudi Arabia (with Colin Dollimore and Ronald Paxton)
      Mosque and villas, Riyadh, Saudi Arabia (with Colin Dollimore and Ronald Paxton)
      Housing, Charminster Road, Mottingham, London (with Colin Dollimore)
      Building society offices, Greenwich, London (with Colin Dollimore)
1975 Housing, Union Road, Lambeth, London (with Colin Dollimore)
      Welfare home, Union Road, Lambeth, London (with Colin Dollimore)
1976 Playground, Greenwich Park, London (with Colin Dolimore)
      Meeting hall, Warwick Estate, London (with Colin Dolimore)
1977 Housing, Langton Way, London (with John Shaw)
      Playground, Lilestone Estate, London (with Colin Dollimore)
      Sheltered Housing Extension, Whittington College, Felbridge, Surrey (with Colin Dollimore)

Trevor Dannatt: King Feisal Hall, Riyadh, Saudi Arabia, 1974.

It is not the size of what we build but the quality of thought and the task evaluation that matters. There is a time to be noble and a time to be modest—which doesn't mean relaxing thought but possibly intensifying it to decide what can be discarded and what is appropriate.

Where does design start? At the conscious level, no doubt, the functional/practical—but at the same time maybe with a vision, the idea of a space or form, or perhaps with a magic image of a conjunction of materials and light. The clarificaton of the problems, the accomodation/site equation determine the generating line. Sometimes an idea does spring out of the side of a problem, unsought, and development in one way is explored and then stopped or redirected for this or that severely practical reason, or because of one's inner censor. The process is one of continuous-fusion, sometimes clear, sometimes mysterious.

We extend from the practical field of circulation and function, structure, services, and economy, to consideration of wellbeing—pyshological as well as physical needs. In certain areas, we cannot just refer to intuitions but need to support them with more informed knowledge; thus, it is "not only thought, not only intuitions, but a terrrible amount of disciplined labour"—at the level of the task (the function/folk equation) and then at the level of a building design (the means/milieu equation) and its realization.

We *may* start with a "concept" along with the analysis and consideration of parts, the latter a necessary study, albeit crude, a design process that sorts out basic accommodation and makes an arrangement serving convenience, economy—securing appropriate advantages to each part while considering structure and services. Such a *synthetic* result is a reassuring standby but one which should be taken apart immediately for recreation as an *Organic* entity. For, that deeper structuring, however we may start, is the essential basis of architecture, the organizational/spatial pattern which should pervade a building in all dimensions, transmuting the utilitarian into significant order to produce "the architectural totality, the building task realized within a characteristic formal organization," and through this we are concerned with *ambience,* something to which we respond beyond convenience, a milieu whichconnects us to the poetry of living, heightening our awareness of today as part of yesterday and the day before yesterday. This is the *organic* architecture for which we strive.

—Trevor Dannatt

1980 Arkendale Housing, Whittington College, Felbridge, Surrey
  Housing for the Disabled, King Henry's Walk, London
  Colet Court Centenary Building, St. Paul's School, Lonsdale Road, Barnes, London
1981 Thames Polytechnic additions and alterations, Woolwich, London, and Dartford, Kent
1982 Science Lecture Theatre, St. Paul's School, Lonsdale Road, Barnes, London
1983 Chapel alterations, St. Paul's School, Lonsdale Road, Barnes, London
1984 Arts/Lecture Building, Colfe's School, Lewisham, London
1985 Diplomatic Staff Housing, British Embassy, Riyadh, Saudi Arabia

Designs:

interior for Richard Church, Curtisden Green, Kent, 1950; tea bar, *Festival of Britain,* South Bank, London, 1951; Spry Cooking Centre, London, 1954; reception area, Lund Humphries, publishers, Bradford, 1955, and London, 1958.

Development Studies:

Hatcliffe Charity, 1965; London University Precinct, with Leslie Martin, 1965; Trinity Hall, Cambridge, 1966; Trinity College, Cambridge, 1967; Bootham School, York, 1969; Parcorm Estate, Beirut, 1972; Society of Friends Euston Road Building, London, 1973.

Publications:

By DANNATT: books—*Architects Yearbook,* editor, nos. 1-2, joint editor, with Jane B. Drew, nos.3-10, London 1946-62; *Modern Architecture in Britain,* London 1959; articles—"The Architect's Approach to Architecture" in *RIBA Journal* (London), March 1969; foreword to *Ideas and Buildings 1933-1983, from the Studio of Leslie Martin,* London 1983.

On DANNATT: book—*Trevor Dannatt: Buildings and Interiors 1951-72,* introduced by Theo Crosby, London 1972; articles—in *Architectural Design* (London), May 1963, and *Architectural Review* (London), March 1967, April 1973, and April 1975.

Trevor Dannatt is an eminent example of dedicated professional whose maturity came about in the immediate postwar years. His work bears the stamp of deep consideration for the user, combined with a strongly disciplined aesthetic sensibility. No seeker for huge commissions and someone who would not wish to approach the "executive" role as the ruler over a large commercial practice, Dannatt keeps his finger on the design process throughout, with the result that the whole range of his considerable achievement is utterly consistent.

There is a modesty and tolerance in his approach that is exemplified in his own words: "I am amazed at the certainty with which others speak about matters that to my mind can be seen in at least two ways." For this reason, perhaps, Dannatt, although producing work of the greatest significance, cannot be regarded as an "influence" in the sense that he has turned the direction of architectural design by his own example, a task that in any case demands a single-minded obstinacy. Such a tremendous steering of a whole generation of the profession, however, has two sides to be considered: it may powerfully influence design towards a new aesthetic, but it equally engenders a following of enthusiasts many of whom misinterpret and vulgarize it, often with a self-destructive result.

Even his largest work—an hotel, conference centre, and mosque, won in an international competition—is unlikely to influence work in his own country, for it is in Riyadh, Saudi Arabia; nevertheless, it might well influence the emergent architects of the Middle East.

The most important aspect of Dannatt's widely diverse practice is that the results stand as examples to be digested by any student and to those in the profession who can bring themselves to study the work of their contemporaries, for in Dannatt's work can always be detected the absolute dedication of the man both in his control of form and in the smallest detail of design, with the proper and logical use of materials, the reaching back as well as forward to uphold the essential continuity of architectural development. He has expressed his antipathy to "the idea of archtecture as business, and the fallacy of size, the thought that we might solve our problems by making them bigger....I believe we should aspire to relieve the anthill of society and technology rather than the apostles of the brave new world."

Architecture is fortunate in having amongst its practitioners such a pure professional whose example, both practical and aesthetic, has been expressed in such permanent ways and whose strength of character shows nothing of the arrogance that is so often the accompaniment of great gifts.
—H.A.N. Brockman (1980)

da ROZA, Gustavo.

Canadian. Born in Hong Kong, of Portuguese nationality, 24 February 1933; emigrated to Canada, 1960: naturalized, 1966. Educated at the School of Architecture, University of Hong Kong, under R. Gordon Brown, 1950-55, B.Arch. (first class honours) 1955. Married Gloria Go in 1961; children: Guia, Gabriella, Gina, Gustavo III, and Gil. Assistant Architect to R. Gordon Brown, Hong Kong, 1955-56; Designer, The Architects Collaborative, *q.v.,* Cambridge, Massachusetts, summer 1959, and office of E. Lloyd Flood, San Francisco, 1959-61. Since 1961, Principal, da Roza Architects, Winnipeg, and since 1982, Camac and Da Roza Inc., Harlingen, Texas. Instructor in Architecture, University of Hong Kong, 1956-58, and University of California, Berkeley, 1958-60. Assistant Professor, 1960-65, Associate Professor, 1965-71, and, since 1971, Professor in Architecture, University of Manitoba, Winnipeg. Chairman, Canadian Housing Design Council, 1975-77. Honorary Consul of Portugal in Winnipeg since 1970. Exhibitions: Royal Academy, London, 1956, 1958, *Indianapolis Home Show*, Indiana, 1959, 1960; *Os Portugueses e o Mundo,* Porto, Portugal, 1985. Recipient: First Prize, with others, Winter Olympic Games Project Competition, Banff, Alberta, 1963; First Prize, Canadian Lumbermen's Association National House Design Competition, 1965; First Prize, Winnipeg, Winnipeg Art Gallery Competition, 1967; House Design Award, Canadian Housing Design Council, 1967; Special Arts Award, 1967, and Senior Arts Award, 1975, Canada Council. Fellow, Royal Architectural Institute of Canada, 1973; Academician, Royal Canadian Academy of Arts, 1973. Knight Commander, Order of Prince Henry, Portugal, 1985. Address: da Roza Architects, 515 Shaftesbury Boulevard, Winnipeg, Manitoba R3P OM3, Canada.

Works:

1955 F. Remedios House, 10 Kent Road, Kowloon, Hong Kong
1957 Wan Yan College Chapel, Waterloo Road, Kowloon, Hong Kong (design only)
1958 P. Remedios House, Clear Water Bay Road, New Territories, Hong Kong
 Chiap Hua Clock Factory, Matauwei Road, Kowloon, Hong Kong

1962 da Roza House, 23 Waterford Bay, Fort Garry, Manitoba
1963 Speers House, 3304 Assiniboine Avenue, Assiniboia, Manitoba
 Scalena House, 3276 Assiniboine Avenue, Assiniboia, Manitoba
1964 Hutcheson House, Rover Road, Selkirk, Manitoba (with A. J. Donahue)
 Kalef House, 403 Boreham Boulevard, Tuxedo, Manitoba
 Sokolov House, 413 Shaftesbury Boulevard, Tuxedo, Manitoba
 Bergman House renovations, 209 Yale Avenue, Winnipeg
1965 Pitcairn House, 516 Laidlaw Boulevard, Tuxedo, Manitoba
 Four houses, Cuthbertson Avenue, Tuxedo, Manitoba
1966 Lockhead House, 634 Kilkenny Drive, Fort Garry, Manitoba
 C. Smith House, 3354 Assiniboine Avenue, Assiniboia, Manitoba
 "Man and His Home" Pavilion, *Expo '67,* Montreal
1967 da Roza House II, 515 Shaftesbury Boulevard, Tuxedo, Manitoba
 Ferguson House renovations, 78 Thatcher Drive, Fort Garry, Manitoba
 Fingold House renovations, 236 Victoria Crescent, St. Vital, Manitoba
1968 Nitikman House, 519 Shaftesbury Boulevard, Tuxedo, Manitoba
 Walder House, 513 Shaftesbury Boulevard, Tuxedo, Manitoba
 Frame House, 3348 Assiniboine Avenue, Assiniboia, Manitoba
1969 Burstein House, 455 Park Boulevard East, Tuxedo, Manitoba
 Yip House, 14 Paradise Bay, Charleswood, Manitoba
 Bihler House, 507 Shaftesbury Boulevard, Tuxedo, Manitoba
 Merchanical consultants Western Ltd. office interiors, Winnipeg
1970 Standing House, 14 King's Drive, Fort Garry, Manitoba
 R. Smith House, Southboine Avenue, Charleswood, Manitoba
 Schwartz House additions, Thatcher Drive, Fort Garry, Manitoba
 Decorations for the Royal Visit, Manitoba Centennial Celebrations, Winnipeg
 Decoration of the National Arts Centre, Manitoba Centennial, Ottawa
1971 Winnipeg Art Gallery, Memorial Boulevard, Winnipeg (with Number Ten Architectural Group)
 Vincent Weekend House, Victoria Beach, Manitoba
 WAG System Furniture, for Krug Furniture, Kitchener, Ontario
1972 Ringers Drug Store renovations, 1151 Pembina Highway, Fort Garry, Manitoba
 Wong House, 2 Paradise Bay, Charleswood, Manitoba
 Owens Art Gallery, Mt. Allison, Sackville, New Brunswick (with Brown, Brisley and Brown)
1973 Bank of Montreal Branch, Mountain and McGregor, Winnipeg
 Wittman House additions, 516 Laidlaw Boulevard, Tuxedo, Manitoba
 Berkowitz House additions, 23 Carmarthen Boulevard, Tuxedo, Manitoba
 YIP Orthodontic Clinic, 1887 Portage Avenue, St. James, Manitoba
 Feasibility study: Little Grindstone Development Proposal, Manitoba
1974 Summer Cabins for Provincial Parks, Hecla Island, Manitoba
 Art Bank, for the Canada Council, Ottawa
 Thomas Art Gallery, River and Osborne, Winnipeg

Venture Manitoba Tours Convention Centre interiors, Winnipeg
 Feasibility study for the redevelopment of Chinatown in Winnipeg
 Functional program for the Consulate General Residence of Japan, Winnipeg
1975 Apartments (45 units), 727 Nassau Street South, Winnipeg
 Ferguson Week-end House, Clytie Bay, Ontario
1976 Asper House renovations, 1063 Wellington Crescent, Winnipeg
 Stephens House additions, 1536 McCreary Road, Charleswood, Manitoba
 Len Steingarten office interiors, Winnipeg
 Functional program for the Vancouver Art Gallery
1977 Gull Harbour Resort Hotel, Hecla Island, Manitoba (also furniture for the hotel)
 Tadman Hornstein Kalef and Company office interiors, Winnipeg
 Nassau Square Townhouses (95 units), Winnipeg
 Ringer Week-end House, Falcon Lake, Manitoba
1978 Payne House, Lot 1, Headingley, Manitoba
 Sellers House, Lot 218, Riverbend Farms, St. Francois Xavier, Manitoba
1979 Church of the Immaculate Conception, 181 Austin Street, Winnipeg
 Loewen House, 75 Elmvale Crescent, Charleswood, Manitoba
1980 St. Viator Church Tower, Dauphin, Manitoba
 Schwartz Condominium Apartment, Winnipeg
 Commercial Development, Calgary, Alberta (project)
1981 Calgary City Hall and Municipal Building Competition Program, Alberta
 Anchorage Club Resort Development, South Padre Island, Texas
1982 Gull Harbour Resort Hotel addition, Heclas Island, Manitoba
 Camac and Da Roza Office, Harlingen, Texas
1983 McCullough Law Office, Harlingen, Texas
 Beach Homes Condominiums, Runaway Bay, Antigua, West Indies
 Thirty MHRC Infill Houses, Winnipeg
1984 Laguna del Sol Resort Condominiums, South Padre Island, Texas
 Landfall Tower Resort Condominiums, South Padre Island, Texas
 Fainman House renovations, St. Vital, Manitoba
 Vaucluse Village Housing, Fort Worth, Texas (project)
 Movie Village interiors, Winnipeg
1985 Hulen Bend Heights Housing Development, Fort Worth, Texas (project)
 Harlingen Cultural Center, Texas
 Gull Harbour Townhouses, Port Mansfield, Texas
 Gomes House addition, Belmont, California
 N. Da Roza House, Oxford, Mississippi
 Portuguese Cultural Centre, Winnipeg

Publications:

On da ROZA: book—*Winnipeg* by Mitchell and Benham, Winnipeg 1974; articles—in *Architect and Building News* (London), 10 May 1956; *Star Weekly* (Toronto), 3 September 1966; *Canadian Builder* (Toronto), April 1967; *Chatelaine* (Toronto), May 1967; *Artscanada* (Toronto), April 1968, and February/March 1971; "Branch Bank, Winnipeg" in *Canadian Architect* (Toronto), June 1971; "Winnipeg Art Gallery" in *Canadian Architect* (Toronto), July 1972; Canadian issue of *Progressive Architec-*

Gustavo da Roza: Winnipeg Art Gallery, Manitoba, 1971.

ture (New York), September 1972; *Kenchiku Bunka* (Tokyo), January 1973; *Asian Architect and Builder* (Hong Kong), April 1973; "A Perspective of Modern Canadian Architecture" in *Process: Architecture* (Tokyo/Pittsburgh), no. 5, 1978.

Architecture is the art of resolving our needs for physical shelter harmoniously with the environment, while responding to visual aspirations, thus contributing to our cultural heritage.

Architecture is more than sound building. It must meet ALL design determinants: functional requirements, environmental conditions, technical and economic limitations, and visual aspirations.

Architecture is a continuous and dynamic challenge to contribute positively to society in spite of difficulties of contradictions, of time, of place, and of personalities. It is a pragmatic art requiring dedicated application of knowledge and principles, thus adding to the fountain of ideas, experience, and experiments, and contributions made by the profession through history to date.

—Gustavo da Roza

Gustavo da Roza in an exotic plant in an alien environment in which he not only flourishes unexpectedly but also provides unique fruits to enrich his new land. Fundamental to da Roza's architectural style is the belief that the natural environment must be accepted and not fought. Working primarily on the great prairie of Canada, he must cope with powerful forces: the extreme flatness of the land and the limited color in the plant life it supports; the dominant horizontality that is reinforced by the great sky and its abundant sunshine; above all, the snow and ice of the long winters, which da Roza loves for the constantly changing sun-washed tints and frigid purity. In response, da Roza's buildings invariably hug the ground and present solid faces to the winds; openings are few and judiciously placed for visual and functional reasons. His palette is restricted to whites, browns, and grays, though he orchestrates these to enhance space and defeat monotony; when strong color appears, such as a red door, it is as a definite statement of function and never as ornament.

Da Roza's most celebrated building is the Winnipeg Art Gallery, a triangular mass on an urban site that dictated the ground plan. The gallery is virtually windowless and the form is simple; its austere silhouette is low; it is faced with an off-white local limestone that resembles frozen oatmeal. Yet, the modulations to the austerity are telling: a simple cutout from the roof line reveals the walled outdoor roof sculpture gallery and allows the eye to pierce deeply into an important sheltered function otherwise hidden; a wedge protruding from the main mass announces the entrance, and a grid of clear glass lamps intensifies the event of arrival without disturbing the monochromatic whole. Inside, the gentle gradations of warm grays, whites, and browns provide a muted background for art and comfortable spaces for viewing. It is a building that responds perfectly to the environment according to its designer's beliefs, and the response is intensely cerebral without the inhumanity of mere singleminded restraint.

But da Roza is not primarily a designer of monuments. For one thing, his practice is intentionally limited; he is primarily an architectural teacher. One of his great interests is housing, and he has expressed his ideas through the design of numerous houses. On the whole, these tend to be small, introverted, and practical, with interest provided by the same subtle techniques of light and form manipulation used in the art gallery. His designs provide a rich yet simple backdrop for family living and do not intrude.

Da Roza has built a solid reputation on this solid approach to his art. The oriental delicacy of his sensitivity and the clarity of his intellectual approach to design have produced works of peaceful dignity not usual for a designer so comparatively young. In this era of bravura exhibitionism and mass-produced extrusions, his sweet reasonableness is welcome.

—Kent Hurley

DAVIDSON, Julius Ralph.

American. Born in Berlin, Germany, 7 February 1889, emigrated to the United States, 1924: naturalized, 1938. Educated at preparatory college in Posen, now Poznan, Poland, and at gymnasium, Berlin, until 1907. Served in the Engineer Corps of the German Army, on the French and Russian Fronts, 1915-19. Married Greta Wollstein in 1914; son: Ralph Thomas. Worked as a delineator for the architect Moritz Hirschler, Berlin, 1908-09; detailer and designer for the architect Frank Stuart Murray, London, 1910-12; part-time designer, with Fred Osborn, Paris, 1912-13; designer for architects Paul and Alfred Dumas, Paris, 1913-14; in private practice as an architect, Berlin, 1919-23; detailer and designer for the architect David Farquhar, Los Angeles, 1924-25; set designer for Cecil B. DeMille, Los Angeles, 1925; in private practice, Los Angeles, 1926 until he retired to Ojai, California in 1972. Exhibitions: *Modern Architecture,* University of California, Los Angeles, 1930; *L.A. in the Thirties,* University of California, Los Angeles, 1975. Recipient: First Award, Pittsburgh Glass Institute, 1939; *Progressive Architecture* Award, 1946; Special Award, California Council of the American Institute of Architects, 1977. *Died* (in Ojai, California) 2 May 1977.

Works:

1919 Pfeifferling House facade and interiors, Grunewald, Berlin
1920 Dupont Apartment interiors, Charlottenburg, Berlin
1920/
  21 Davidson Penthouse remodelling, Schöneberg Park, Berlin
1921 House in Saxony, Germany
      Hans Feigen House on the Rhine, Bonn
1922 Three shops for Stiller Shoes, Berlin
1923 Hupfeld Piano Showroom and Auditorium, Berlin
1927/
  29 Office building with shops and restaurant, Wilshire Boulevard, Los Angeles
1932/
  35 Knickerbocker Hotel alterations, Chicago
      Shoreland Hotel alterations, Chicago
      Pearson Hotel alterations, Chicago
1937 Maitland House, 230 Strada Corta, Bel Air, Los Angeles
      Stothart House, 2501 La Mesa Drive, Santa Monica, California (altered in 1984)
1940 Gretna Green Apartment Building, 12201 Dunoon Lane, Los Angeles
      Sabsay House, 2351 Silver Ridge, Silver Lake, Los Angeles
1941 Medical building, 6222 Wilshire Boulevard, Los Angeles
      Thomas Mann House, 1550 San Remo Drive, Pacific Palisades, California
      Vigeveno House, Ojai, California
1945 Cron House, 540 South Barrington Avenue, Los Angeles (razed)
      Kingsley Houses, 1620 and 1630 Amalfi Drive, Pacific Palisades, California
      Davidson House, 560 South Barrington Avenue, Los Angeles (razed)

Crosby-Furniss House, 473 Denslow Avenue, Los Angeles (with addition, 1954)
1948 McFadden House, 1052 Toluca Lake Avenue, North Hollywood, California
      Case Study House, 4756 Lasheart Drive, La Canada, California
1949 Osherenko House, 1005 North Alpine Drive, Beverly Hills, California
      Schapiro House, Waverlyand Maxwell Streets, Los Angeles
1951 Dann House, 1369 Londonderry Place, Los Angeles
1957 Dr. Egeberg House, 6918 Oporto Drive, Los Angeles
      Dr. Fenichel House, Tigertail Road, Los Angeles
      Dr. Munk House, 290 Westgate Avenue, Los Angeles
      Dr. Rabinowitz House, 2262 Stradella Road, Los Angeles
1958 Dr. Jokl House, 563 North Bundy Drive, Los Angeles
1966 Westgate Apartment Building, Westgate and Darlington, Brentwood, Los Angeles

Publications:

On DAVIDSON: books—*Tomorrow's House* by George Nelson and Henry Wright, New York 1945; *Houses* by Thomas Creighton, New York 1947; *The American House Today* by Thomas Creighton, New York 1951; *Contemporary Houses* by Thomas Creighton, New York 1961; *Modern California Houses* by Esther McCoy, New York 1962; *The Architecture of the Well-Tempered Environment* by Reyner Banham, Chicago 1969; *Los Angeles* by Reyner Banham, New York 1971; *L.A. in the Thirties, 1931-1941* by David Gebhard and Harriette von Breton, Salt Lake City, Utah 1975; *The Second Generation* by Esther McCoy, Salt Lake City, Utah 1984; articles—"30 Distinguished Houses and Plans" in *House and Garden* (New York), November 1939; "Villa a Santa Monica" in *Casabella* (Milan), December 1940; "Small House on a Hill" in *Arts and Architecture* (Los Angeles), October 1941; "Interiors by J. R. Davidson" in *Arts and Architecture* (Los Angeles), June 1944; "40 Houses," special issue of *Architectural Forum* (New York), May 1948; "Sixteen Southern Californian Architects Exhibit Contemporary Trends" in *Arts and Architecture* (Los Angeles), April 1950; "Arts and Architecture Case Study Houses" by Esther McCoy in *Perspecta* (New Haven, Connecticut), no. 15, 1975; "J. R. Davidson" by Esther McCoy in *L.A. Architect* (Los Angeles), May 1977; "J.R. Davidson, 1889–1977" by Esther McCoy in *Progressive Architecture* (New York), September 1977.

J.R. Davidson was essentially a designer of interiors, and these were so carefully studied in terms of plan, circulation, storage spaces and human use that eventually the exterior form was little more than a loose envelope around a complex plan. His early work was mainly in the design of shops. His Stiller bootery shops and Hupfeld piano showroom and auditorium in Berlin were notable for the elegant use of metals, glass, flush surfaces, ingenious storage spaces, experiments in indirect lighting, and the discreet introduction of *fauve* colors. His first work in Los Angeles, a group which included a two-story office building, a restaurant, and shops brought into harmony a collage of materials and colors; his remodellings of three Chicago hotels included what were to become prototypes of the post-Prohibition intimate cocktail lounge.

In 1937 he turned to the design of houses, and from then on his commissions were mainly residential. He adapted for his houses many of the practices for shops, especially indirect lighting and the glass screen wall—in the Stothart house they are used to separate entrance hall from living room, and bedroom from dressing room. In his experiments in floor planning, he minimized halls or pressed them into a dual use (Cron house); in his "gallery" plan, used in most of his later houses, he broadened and lengthened the entrance hall to connect with the bedroom and service wings, and placed a glass screen above built-in cabinets between the gallery and living room. His skill in the design of storage units came from his three years in London as a detailer and designer of interiors of ocean liners and yachts for Frank Stuart Murray, while his sensitivity to colors and fabrics was heightened during the pre-Art Deco period in Paris.

His early houses and flats (Gretna Green Apartments) fell into the International Style, but he never strictly obeyed its tenets. By the end of the 1940s, many of his roofs were sloped and no module was respected; walls were often of plywood, and a combined ceiling/roof surface of wood planking replaced plastered surfaces.

Davidson's most complex plans came in the late style; most successful among them were ones for psychiatrists whose offices were attached to the house (Dr. Jokl house, Dr. Fenichel house).

—Esther McCoy

DAVIS, Lewis

American. Born in New York City, 31 July 1927. Educated at the University of Pennsylvania, Philadelphia, B.Arch.,M.Arch. Served in the United States Air Force, 1942-45. Married to Anne Davis; children: Steven, Michael, Peter, and Ariel. Architect, Kelly and Gruzen, q.v.; Barnett Gruzen, New York, 1948-51, Mayer and Whittlesey, New York, 1951-52, and Samuel Juster, New York, 1952. Since 1953, Partner, with Samuel Brody, q.v.,Davis, Brody and Associates, New York. Adjunct Professor, Cooper Union School of Architecture, New York, since 1958. Davenport Professor of Architecture, Yale University School of Architecture, New Haven, Connecticut, 1947. Member, Mayor's Advisory Committee on Housing in New York, 1965; Member of the Executive Committee, 1965-69, Vice-President, 1969, and Chairman of the Housing Committee, 1972, American Institute of Architects, New York Chapter; Member, National Commission on Urban Problems, 1967-69; Chairman, Progressive Architecture Design Awards Jury, 1968; Member, Task Force Advisory Council, United States Department of Housing and Urban Development, 1973; Board Member, Municipal Art Society, New York, since 1975; Architectural Advisor and Member of the Board of Overseers, University of Pennsylvania, Philadelphia, since 1975; Director, Landmarks Conservancy, New York, 1976-83. Recipient: Design Award, *Progressive Architecture,* 1954, 1955, 1958, 1961 (twice), 1962, 1966, and 1982; Honor Award, American Institute of Architects, Potomac Valley, Maryland Chapter, 1958; Design Award, Church Architectural Guild of America, 1958; Certificate of Merit, New York City Department of Commerce, 1958; Certificate of Merit, 1958 and 1963, and Award, 1973 and 1974, New York State Association of Architects; Award of Merit, *House and Home,* 1960; United States Department of Health, Education and Welfare Award, 1966; Honor Award, New England Regional Council, American Institute of Architects, 1966; Higher Education Facilities Design Award, 1966; Honor Award, 1968, 1971 (twice), and 1976, Architectural Firm Award, 1975, and Thomas Award, 1981, American Institute of Architects; Bard Award, City Club of New York, 1969, 1973, and 1975; Certificate of Merit, Municipal Arts Society, New York, 1969, 1972, and 1973 (twice); Concrete Industries Award, 1969; Staten Island Chamber of Commerce Award, New York, 1970; Golden Triangle Award, National Society of Interior Designers, 1970; International Design Award, American Institute of Design, 1970; Bartlett Award, 1971 and 1976; Homes for Better Living Award, 1971; Award of Honor, New York Society of Architects, 1972, 1973, and 1974; Medalof Honor, 1973, and Award, 1983 New York Chapter, American Institute of Architects; Mayor of New York's Citation for Distinguished Service, 1973; Brunner Award, National Institute of Arts and Letters, 1975; Louis Sullivan Award, 1977; Landscape Award, American Association of Nurserymen, 1981; Delaware County Planning Commission Award, 1981; Industrial Research and Development Lab of the Year Award, 1982; New Jersey Society of Architects Award, 1982; Reliance Development Group Award, 1982; *Interiors* Award, New York, 1983. Fellow, American Institute of Architects. Address: Davis, Brody and Associates, 100 East 42nd Street, New York, New York 10017, U.S.A.

Works (with Samuel Brody):

1963 Waterside (apartments), New York
     Riverbend (apartments), New York
     East Midtown Housing, New York
     Science Building, State University of New York, New Paltz
     Esté e Lauder Cosmetics Plant, Melville, New York (with Richard Dattner)
     Library, Cooper Union, New York
     Social Science Building, Long Island University, Brooklyn, New York (with Hordwitz/Chan)
1965 Bronx Park South Housing, Bronx, New York
1966 Brody House, Brooklyn, New York
     Westport Office Building, Connecticut
     River Park Towers, New York
     Science Building, State University of New York, Binghamton
     Lambert Houses (apartments), Bronx, New York
1967 United States Pavilion, *Expo '70,* Osaka, Japan
     Sachs Furniture Stores, New York
     Boston Road Apartments, Bronx, New York
1968 100 William Street Office Building, New York (with Emery Roth and Sons)
     Dormitories and Dining Halls, State University of New York, Buffalo
     Group Residence, Children's Aid Society, Staten Island, New York
     Library, Long Island University, Brooklyn, New York (with Horowitz/Chan)
1969 Interiors of the State University of New York, Binghamton
     Central Refrigeration Plant, State University of New York, Buffalo
1971 Cathedral Parkway Housing, New York
1972 Robert Crown Athletic and Recreation Centre, Hampshire College, Amherst, Massachusetts
     Coney Island Housing, Brooklyn, New York
     Waterside Health Club and Pool, New York
1973 St. Lawrence State Hospital, Ogdensburg, New York
1974 Quadrangle renovation, University of Pennsylvania, Philadelphia
     Brooklyn College of Pharmacy, Brooklyn, New York (with Horowitz/Chan)
1975 Athletic facilities for Massachusetts Institute of Technology, Cambridge
     Estée Lauder Cosmetics Plant, Switzerland (with Richard Dattner)
     Federal Correctional Institution, Otisville, New York (with Large/Moger)
     Office Building rehabilitation, for American Airlines, Hartford, Connecticut (with Associated Architects)
     Allan Harvey House, Vermont
1976 Biochemistry Building, Princeton University, New Jersey
     Town Hall, Huntington, Long Island, New York
1977 Corning Glass Works Building, Corning, New York
     Yale/New Haven Medical Center, New Haven, Connecticut (with Russo and Sonder)
     Atlantic-Richfield Research Building, Newtown Square, Pennsylvania (with Llewelyn-Davies Associates)
     Intercontinental Hotel, Isfahan, Iran (with DAZ)
1978 Acro Chemical Corporation Research and Development Center, New Town Square, Pennsylvania (with Jaquelin Robertson)
     Time Inc. Auditorium and Conference Center, New York
     Philip Morris U.S.A. Operations Center, Richmond, Virginia
     American Stock Exchange Headquarters, New York
     United States Consulate Housing, Hong Kong
1979 Cambridge Center Office Building, Cambridge, Massachusetts
     Loral Electronic Research laboratory, Yonkers, New York
     Library for the Blind and Handicapped, Trenton, New Jersey (with Mahoney and Zvosec Associates)
     Hudson Tower, Battery Park City, New York
1980 Geology/Chemistry Laboratory, Brown University, Providence, Rhode Island (with Russo + Sonder)
     2000 Broadway Condominiums, New York
     Brooklyn Botanic Garden New Exhibition Greenhouses, New York
     Delmonico Plaza Office Building, New York
     Esté e Lauder Research Park, Melville, New York (with Richard Dattner and Associates)
1981 Science Building, Queens College, New York
     Bio-Technia International Research Laboratory, Cambridge, Massachusetts
     Yorkville Gardens Housing for the Elderly, New York
     New York Public Library restoration study, New York
     Museum of Broadcasting, New York
1982 130 Fifth Avenue renovation, New York
     IBM Research Facility, Manassas, Virginia
     IBM Interior Design Master Plan, Poughkeepsie, New York
     Riverwalk Development, New York
     Mount Sinai Medical Center Resident Facility, New York
     Gottesman Exhibition Gallery, New York Public Library, New York
     Estée Lauder Executive Offices, New York (with Richard Dattner and Associates)
     Carnegie Park Apartments, New York
     Rockefeller Foundation Executive Offices, New York
     University of Virginia Medical Center, Charlottesville (with Russo + Sonder, and Metcalf and Associates)
1983 Research Library, New York Polytechnic Institute, Brooklyn, New York
     Science Complex, Bryn Mawr College, Pennsylvania
     Athletic Complex, University of Pennsylvania, Philadelphia
     Hallmark Inc. Technology and Innovation Center, Kansas City, Missouri
     Union Square Redevlopment, New York
     Memorial Sloan Kettering Cancer Center, New York (with Russo + Sonder)
     Guggenheim Hall renovation, Mount Sinai Medical Center, New York
1984 Veterinarian School, Cornell University, Ithaca, New York (with Russo + Sonder)
     American Telephone and Telegraph Research Laboratory, Lehigh Valley, Pennsylvania

Lincoln Center Residential Tower, New York (with Abramovitz, Harris, Kingsland)

Student Townhouses, Brown University, Providence, Rhode Island

Columbus Circle Development, New York

Publications:

On DAVIS/BRODY: books—*Religious Buildings for Today* by John Knox Shear, New York 1957; *Schoolhouse* by Walter McQuade, New York 1958; *Architecture of Monuments* by Thomas Creighton, New York 1962; *Architectural Design Preview U.S.A.* by John Dixon, New York 1962; *New Directions in American Architecture* by Robert A.M. Stern, New York 1969; *Will They Ever Finish Bruckner Boulevard?* by Ada Louise Huxtable, New York 1970; *Principles of Pneumatic Architecture* by Roger Dent, London 1971; *Industrial Buildings and Factories* by Oswald Grube, London 1971; articles— "10 Project" in *Kenchikubunka* (Tokyo), August 1970; "Work of Davis, Brody and Associates" in *Architecture d'aujord'hui* (Paris), August 1971; "The Work of Davis, Brody and Associates" in *Architecture + Urbanism* (Tokyo), December 1972; "Davis, Brody and Associates" in *AIA Journal* (Washington, D.C.), May 1975; "Waterside" in *Architectural Record* (New York), March 1976; "Air Offices..." in *Architectural Review* (London), May 1977; "Order from Chaos" in *Contract Interiors* (New York), August 1978; "To Save a Landmark" in *Architectural Record* (New York), January 1980; "New Focus on Princeton Campus" in *Architectural Record* (New York), March 1980; "United States Consulate Staff Housing, Hong Kong" in *Architectural Record* (New York), December 1980; "New Landmark for MIT" in *Architectural Record* (New York), February 1981; "A Meeting of Minds at Corning" in *Architectural Record* (New York), September 1981; "The Meadows: A Sylvan Campus for ARCO" in *Architectural Record* (New York), April 1982; "Architecture and the Information Revolution" in *AIA Journal* (Washington, D.C.), July 1982; "Davis, Brody and Associates" in *Architecture + Urbanism* (Tokyo), August 1982; "Efficiency Enriched and Enlivened" in *Architectural Record* (New York), March 1983; "New MIT Sports Centre" in *Industria delle costruzioni* (Rome), April 1983; "Work by Davis, Brody and Associates" in *Architettura* (Rome), May 1983; "Building Types Study 591: Libraries" in *Architectural Record* (New York), August 1983; "Works: Davis, Brody and Associates" in *Architecture + Urbanism* (Tokyo), November 1983; "Battery Park's Grand Design" in *Progressive Architecture* (New York), December 1983; "5th Annual Interiors Awards" in *Interiors* (New York), January 1984.

In more than twenty-five years of partnership, Lewis Davis and Sam Brody have consistently produced architecture of outstanding quality. Their buildings are handsome and carefully detailed, but, far more important, they are unpretentious examples of a rational, humanistic approach to architecture that displays uncommon integrity and conscientiousness.

Their work has been remarkably varied; they have completed major commercial, industrial, educational, and residential projects. Without doubt, though, their most significant contribution has been in the field of public housing, which thay have almost single handedly revolutionized. Rejecting the pattern of Pruitt-Igoe, which continued to be a model for low-income residential development in America well into the 1960s, Davis and Brody have created projects that are highy economical, offer up-to-date facilities, and yet, unlike earlier projects, still

Lewis Davis and Samuel Brody: W. C. Decker Building, Corning Glass Works, New York, 1981.

preserve human identity and existing urban patterns.

The Key to their success has been sophisticated architectural maneuvers, accomplished not at the expense of contextual and human concerns but in support of them. Unusual massing gives many of the buildings a sculptural quality: inhabitants sense individuality in them, and they have therefore become sources of inspiration—a change from the dreary mediocrity to which residents are usually condemned. Any extra expense incurred by formal manipulation, though, has been more than recovered by Davis and Brody's efficient planning and careful choice and application of materials.

Most of the projects employ standard masonry construction because it is inexpensive, allows great planning flexibility, and is resistant to the "urban vandal's ultimate weapon—the spray paint gun." At Lambert Houses, an urban renewal project for New York City's decayed South Bronx, a special brick was developed by Davis and Brody that was larger (requiring fewer courses of brick), extruded with horizontal cavities (for lighter weight), and finished with a handle (for easier laying). Estimates suggest that the man-hours saved as a result of this innovation cut more than half a million dollars off the total project budget.

In other projects, Davis and Brody have been given opportunities to design with less restrictive budgets, but one still never senses any sort of wastefulness, and their concern for creating dynamic spaces for people has remained unfaltering. In an office building in New York's commerical district, for example, the architects have presented the public with an eighty-foot high passage from one street to another. The huge galleria is lined with shops and suggests a visual connection with an existing plaza across the street, thus extending the site, conceptually, in that direction. They developed a new Science Building Complex for the State University of New York Center at Binghamton only after completing a remarkably elaborate user- requirement study, further demonstrating their genuine concern with user- satisfaction over formal architectural statement.

Nevertheless, their work is visually excellent, and Davis and Brody cannot be accused of aesthetic insensitivity. They are masters who have skillfully used their ability to mold space for the benefit of those people who most frequently are abused by architects. Not only have they created institutions that maintain human scale and propriety, but they have also offered decent, pleasant, and gaily exciting housing to the people of the city of New York. The residents of that city ought to be deeply grateful, and we, as architects, ought to take great heed of the lessons Davis and Brody have, through their work, offered us.

—Mitchell B. Rouda

DE CARLO, Giancarlo.

Italian. Born in Genoa, 12 December 1919. Educated at the Polytechnic, Milan, Dip.Ing. 1942; Institute of Architecture, Venice, 1945-49, Dip.Arch. 1949. In private practice, Milan, since 1950. Professor of Urban Design, Institute of Architecture, Venice, since 1955; Visiting Professor, Yale University, Massachusetts Institute of Technology, Cornell University, and the University of California. Member, Team 10; Member of the Italian group of CIAM (Congres Internationaux d'architecture Moderne), 1952-60. Editorial Committee Member, *Parametro*, Bologna; Director, *Spazio e societa*, Milan. Director, ILAUD: International Laboratory of Architecture and Urban Design. Exhibitions: *Utopia e crisi dell'antinatura*, at the *Biennale*, Venice, 1978; *Fotografia e immagine dell'architettura*, Galleria d'Arte Moderna, Bologna, 1980; *Architetture italiane degli*

Anni '70, Galleria Nazionale d'Arte Moderna, Rome, 1981. Recipient: INA-Casa National Prize, 1949; National Prize, Urban Development Competition, Aldisio, Italy, 1953; First Prize, Housing Development Competition, Matera, Italy, 1954; Firstprize, Urban Development Competition, Donoratico, Italy 1957; First Prize, with others, Master Plan for the City Centre of Padua Competition, 1960; Edoardo Caracciolo Prize 1963; Sir Patrick Abercrombie Prize, International Union of Architects, 1967; First Prize, General Hospital Competition, Milan, 1967; First Prize, Community Education Centre Competition, Perugia, 1976. Honorary Member, American Academy of Arts and Sciences and American Institute of Architects; Honorary Fellow, Royal Institute of British Architects, 1981. Member, National Academy of San Luca, Rome. Address (office): Via Mascheroni 18, 20145 Milan, Italy.

Works:

1946 Small houses for ex-servicemen, Quarter T.8, Milan (competition project; with others)

1947 Youth Hostel, Quarter T.8, Milan (competition project; with others)

Standardization and Industrialization Display, *Triennale*, Milan

1948 Master plan for Reggio Emilia, Italy (with Franco Albini)

Public housing development, Sicily (competition project; with others)

1949 Workers' housing development, Varese, Italy

1950 Master plan for Tortona, Italy (competition project)

Spontaneous Architecture Display, *Triennale*, Milan

INA-Casa Housing Development, Sesto S. Giovanni, Italy

1951 Flight of steps, Viale delle Palme, Nervi, Italy (project)

INA-Casa Apartment Buildings, Arona, Baveno, and Stresa, Italy

1952/
60 Free University reconstruction, Urbino

1953 Cesate Residential Centre, Varese, Italy (competition project)

1954 Structural frame for the *Santa Lucia* cargo boat, constructed at Pietra Ligure, Italy

Residential development, Matera, Italy

Urbanism Exhibition, *Triennale*, Milan

1955 Student Housing, Free University, Urbino

Congress House, Stresa, Italy (competition project)

Cassa del Mezzogiorno Housing Developments (3), Metera Italy

Two urban plans for the Canton Vesco Quarter, Ivrea Italy

1956/
57 Apartment building, Matera, Italy

Pineta Costiera di Donoratico Urban Development, Livorno (competition project)

INA-Casa Apartment Building, Villanuova sul Clisi, Italy

1957 Farmhouse, Colbordolo, Urbino (project)

Elementary school, Pievebovigliani, Italy

1957/
59 Cedas e Santi Co-operative Apartment Building, Urbino

School, Fiastra, Italy

1958 Zigiaina House, Cervignano del Fiuli, Italy

Urban plan for the Feltre Quarter of Milan (with others)

1958/
64 Master plan for the City of Urbino

1959 School Campione d'Italia, Italy (competition project)

Italian/Swiss Education Centre Children's Home, Rimini, Italy

Children's Mountain Resort (project)

Giancarlo De Carlo: Faculty of Education, Free University of Urbino, Italy, 1976.

1960/
68 School for Humanities restoration, Milan
   Plan for the centre of Padua (competition project, with others)
1961 Apartment and shop building, Feltre Quarter, Milan (project)
   Marcello Ceccarelli House, Bologna
   Residential Zone, Marbella, Spain (competition project)
   Master plan for Volterra, Italy (competition project; with others)
1961/
63 SIP Children's Colony, Riccione, Italy (with Armando Barp)
1961/
64 Marine Colony, Classe, Ravenna (project)
1961/
66 High school, Feltre Quarter Milan
   Azienda Trasporti Holiday Home, Bordighera, Italy

1962 SIP Recreational Centre, Viverone Lake, Italy
   Lavagine Quarter, Urbino (enquiry/reclamation project)
   Master plan for the Commune of Ameglia, Italy (with Paolo Ceccarelli)
1962/
65 Residential Development for 25,000 Inhabitants, Assago, South Milan (project)
1962/
66 Faculty buildings, Free University, Urbino
1963 Apartment buildings, Assago, South Milan
   Palazzo degli Anziani restoration and re-constructrion, for the Faculty of Economics and Commerce, Free University of Urbino at Ancona
   Children's Library, School of Humanities, Milan
1964 University of Dublin (competition project; with Armando Barp)
   Houses for journalists, Anzano del Parco,

Milan (project)
   Master plan for the Commune of Sarzana, Italy (with others)
1965 Italian/Swiss Education Centre, Rimini, Italy
1965/
66 School for the Disabled, Bologna (project)
   Open-Air School and Heliotherapy Centre, Bologna
1965/
68 Giovanni Santi Co-operative Apartment Building, Urbino
1966 Plan for the Piansevero zone of Urbino (with others)
   Re-organization of the Free University buildings within the master plan of the City of Urbino (with others)
   Cultural Centre, Riyadh, Saudi Arabia (competition project)

1966/
68 XVII Century Convent restoration and re-construction, for the Faculty of Law, Free University, Urbino
1967 Faculty of Economics and Commerce, University College, Ancona, Italy (project)
Livio Sichirollo House, Cavallino, Urbino
General Hospital, Mirano, Italy (competition project)
Town Hall, Amsterdam (competition project; with Armando Barp and George Solms)
Plan for the Petriccio zone of Urbino
1967/
69 La Pineta Residential Complex, Urbino
1968 Plan for the Cesane area, Urbino (with others)
Plan for the reconstruction of the centre of Plovdiv, Bulgaria (competition project; with F. Spirito and P. de Brerleville)
Development plan for the coastline between Antignano and Quercianella, Livorno (with others)
Commercial Centre reconstruction, Urbino (project)
1968/
76 XV Century Convent restoration and re-construction, for the Faculty of Education, Free University, Urbino
1969 International Pavilion, *Expo '70*, Osaka
Matteotti Quarter reconstruction, Terni, Italy (project)
"Casa dei Ragazzi," Urbino (project)
Oil company headquarters, Garbagnate, Milan (project)
1969/
72 Underground carpark, Commercial Centre, Urbino
1970 Plan to re-site the "Orto dell'Abbondanza," Urbino (project)
Underground Terminal, Colle delle Vigne, Urbino (project)
1970/
72 Plan for the centre of Rimini, Italy
1970/
77 Restoration of the ramp of Francesco di Giorgio and re-opening of a passage under the Theatre Sanzio, Urbino
1970/
79 Theatre Sanzio reconstruction, Urbino
1971/
74 Matteotti New Village, phase I, Terni, Italy
1972/
75 Development plan for the University of Pavia, Italy
1972/
80 Institute of Art, Urbino
1974/
76 CNR Laboratories, and Faculty of Engineering, University of Pavia, Italy
1976 Institute of Genetics, University of Pavia, Italy
Community Education Centre, Perugia (competition project; with others)
1976/
79 Development plan for the San Miniato area and the Lizza area, Siena (with others)
1977 United Nations Environment Program Headquarters, Nairobi (with others)
1977/
80 Buia Elementary School, Friuli, Italy
Osoppo Elementary and Middle School, Italy
1979 Novafeltria Theatre, Marche, Italy (project)
Plan for the reconstruction of the Vigne e dell'Orto degli Scalzi area, Urbino
Hospital of Mirano, stage I, Venice
Historical Town Centre reconstruction, Palermo, Sicily, (as consultant)
Development Plan, Mazzorbo, Venice
1980 Town Centre Plan and School, San Pietro in Verzolo, Pavia Italy (project)
Piazzale della Pace redevelopment, Parma, Italy (project)
1981 San Cassiano Complex redevelopment plan, Urbino, Italy (project)

Publications:

By DE CARLO: books—*Le Corbusier*, Milan 1945; *William Morris*, Milan 1947; *Questioni di Architettura e Urbanistica*, Urbino, Italy 1965; *Proposal for a University Structure*, Venice 1965; *Urbino: La Storia di Una Cittàe il Piano della sua Evoluzione Urbanistica*, Padua 1966, Cambridge, Massachusetts 1970; *Pianificazione e Disegno della Università*, Venice 1968; *La piramide rovesciata,*, Bari, Italy 1968; *An Architecture of Participation*, Melbourne 1972, Milan 1973; articles—"L'Ensegnamento di F. L. Wright" in *Domus*(Milan), no. 207, 1946; "William Morris: Pioniere dell'Arte Sociale" in *Domus*(Milan), no. 211, 1947; "Formalismo, Continuitàdell'Accademismo" in *Casabella*(Milan), no. 199, 1954; "Discussione sulla Valutazione Storica dell'Architettura e sulla Misura Umana" in *Casabella*(Milan), no. 210 1956; "Una Precisazione" in *Casabella*(Milan), no. 214, 1957; "Il Contributo degli Architetti Italiani alla Cultura Internazionale" in *L'Architettura*(Rome), no. 33, 1958; "Furniture, Exhibition and Industrial Design in Contemporary Italian Architecture" in *The Architects Yearbook*, London 1958; "The Situation of Contempary Architecture: CLAM 1959" in *Dokumente der Modernen Architekur*, Stuttgart 1959; "I Piani Paesistici e il Codice dell'Urbanistca" in *Urbanistica* (Turin), no. 33, 1961; "Programmi di Sviluppo Economico e Pianificazione Urbanistica: Proposte Operative" in *Casabella* (Milan), no. 270, 1962, reprinted in *Urbanistica* (Turin), no. 38, 1963; "Why/How to build School Buildings" in *Harvard Educational Review* (Cambridge, Massachusets), no. 4, 1969; "Il Publico dell'Architettura" in *Parametro* (Bologna), no. 5, 1971; "Architecture Between Self and System" in *Parametro* (Bologna), March 1975; "Rimini: A Plan for Today and Tomorrow" in *Parametro* (Bologna), September/October 1975; "Giancarlo De Carlo, Architect, " interview with P. Korose-Serfaty, in *Neuf* (Brussels),September/ October 1975; "Team X at Royaumont, 1962, in *Architectural Design* (London), November 1975; "Further Notes on Participation" in *Parametro* (Bologna), January/February 1977; "Reflections on the Present State of Architecture" in *Architectural Association Quarterly* (London), no. 2, 1978; "La non cultura della città" in *Spazio e Società* (Milan), no. 6, 1979; "Giancarlo de Carlo in Urbino", interview with Judy Loach, in *Architectural Review* (London), no. 986, 1979; "Il fascino discreto del riuso" in *Spazio e Scocieta*(Milan), no. 10, 1980; "Sharon Temple e la purezza" in *Spazio e Società*(Milan), no. 11, 1980; "An architecture of participation" in *Perspecta* (New Haven, Connecticut), no. 17,1980.

On DE CARLO: book—*Giancarlo De Carlo* by C. Colombo, Milan 1964; *Architettura di riuso in citta italiane*, Milan 1980; *Complessi residenziali nell'Italia degli anni '70* by Alfonso Acocella, Florence 1981; *Giancarlo de Carlo* by Fabrizio Brunetti and Fabrizio Gesi, Florence 1981; *Modern Architecture since 1900* by William J.R. Curtis, London 1982; articles—"University College in Urbino" by Aldo van Eyck in *Zodiac* (Milan), no. 16, 1960; "De Carlo" in *Architectural Review* (London), October 1970; "Counterpoint in Concrete" in *Architectural Forum* (New York), May 1972; "Works by Giancarlo De Carlo" in *Architecture + Urbanism* (Tokyo), July 1974; "Giancarlo De Carlo; La Réconciliation de l'Architecture et de la Politique" in *L'Architecture d'Aujourd'hui* (Paris), January/February 1975; "Monastery, Urbino; Convent, Urbino; Orto dell'Abbondanza, Urbino" in *New Uses for Old Buildings*, edited by Sherban Cantacuzino, London 1975; "Matteotti Housing Development" by Naomi Miller in *Progressive Architecture* (New York), December 1976; "The Work of Giancarlo De Carlo" in *Architect and Builder* (Cape Town), November 1977; "Urbino: A Story Which Continues" by Pier Carlo Santini in *Ottagono* (Milan), September 1978; "Urbino Outlook" by Judy Loach in *Architectural Review* (London), April 1979; "Faculty of Education, Urbino", special issue of *GA Document* (Tokyo), summer 1980; "Urbino - historic hill town" by Mark Mares in *AIA Journal* (Washington, D.C.), April 1981; "Giancarlo de Carlo in Urbino" by J.M. McKean in *Building Design* (London), 24 February, and 2 March 1984.

Against a background of constant political change and cultural turmoil, Giancarlo De Carlo has remained committed to his fundamental belief in the inevitability of Sopcialism. It is with this atitude firmly in mind that his contribution to the evolution of the new architecture of Italy must be considered. In every sense he is an architect of social commitment; he believes that what he builds is but a facet of the total human, social, and, often unpredictable, economic situation.

The history of post-war Italian architecture is ridled with movement and counter-movement, and that history, coupled with a traditional enmity between North and South, between Milan and Rome, has made it extremely difficult for an Italian architect to arrive at any coherent formal plan. Like other Italians, De Carlo has had to learn to live with the splendours of the past; he has had to make a very deliberate attempt to blend the best of traditional methods and accomplishments with what he realizes are the vital necessities of the present. He is constantly looking for new ways and, more important, new forms with which to answer today's problems. He is a realist; he knows what he is up against.

An intellectual in the true Italian sense, De Carlo has proposed changes not only in the building process but also, at the very earliest stages, in committee procedures. Constantly frustated by the ever changing pattern of local authority polotics and by uninformed public opinion, he has become one of the most articulate polemicists in the whole of Western Europe. He realizes the need to maintain contact with the general public in order to enlist sympathy and interest: he wants to build for the individual so as to give him a sense of value in his everyday existence. Those who are to live and work in his buildings are given every possible say in the initial design, and his concept of architecture is truly democratic.

De Carlo is internationally respected for his work on the Free University in Urbino, one of the most teraditional of all Italian cities, where he has built what ammounts to a 'cartoon' of a hill-top town: it is at once physically unlike anything that has been built before, yet in essence it is highly familiar. His ability to keep the balance between past and present is remarkable.

A regular member ot Team 10 in recent years, De Carlo has also become one of the dominant personalties of the 1970's, with a particular appeal for the younger generation. He is an inspiring teacher. His avowed distrust of an 'expressionist' answer to a possible anti-formalist method makes him one of the men of the moment, and his contribution to the new architecture of the future is awaited with interest by all those concerned with the steady evolution of the Modern Movement.

—John Furse

DEILMANN, Harald.
German. Born in Gladbeck, Westphalia, 30 August 1920. Educated at the J. C. Schlaun Gymnasium, Münster, graduated 1938; Technische Hochschule, Stuttgart, under Richard Döcker, *q.v.*, Gunter Wilhelm, Hans Volkart, and Rolf Gutbrod, *q.v.*, 1946-48, Dip.Ing. Arch. 1948. Served in the German Army, 1938-46. Married Elsbeth Schole in 1949;

children: Thomas, Andreas, and Cordula. Lecturer, Technische Hochschule, Sturrgart, 1949-51; Partner, with H. Bartmann, Bartmann and Deilmann, Münster, West Germany, 1951-53; Partner, with Max von Hausen, Ortwin Rave, and Werner Ruhnau, Architektenteam, Münster, West Germany; 1953-55. Since 1955, in private practice, Münster, West Germany; offices established in Dortmund, 1969, and Düsseldorf, 1973. Professor, Technische Hochschule, Stuttgart, 1963-69, and Director of the Institute for Building Studies, University of Stuttgart, 1964-69. Since 1969, Professor at the University of Dortmund, West Germany. Exhibitions: *Christliche Kunst,* Schloss Corvey, Germany, 1972; *Kirchenbau in der Diskussion,* Stadtmuseum, Munich, 1973; *Vorbildliche Bauten Nordrhein-Westfalen,* Tonhalle, Düsseldorf, 1979; *Somerakademie Venedig,* University of Dortmund, 1982, 1983; *Das Dortmunder Modell Bauwesen,* Museum am Ostwall, Dortmund, 1984. Recipient: First Prize in the competitions: Housing Block, Neuss, 1978; City Plan, Versmold, 1979; Finance Office, Bochum, 1979; Volksbank, Ibbenbüren, 1979; City Wall Development, Ruthen, 1980; Karstadt Development, Berlin-Tempelhof, 1981; St. Josefshaus, Essen-Kettwig, 1981; Lambertusplatz Development, Castrop-Rauxel, 1981. North Rhine-Westphalia Prize, 1962, 1979 (twice), and 1984 (twice); Federal Distinguished Service Medal, 1977; Grand Federal Cross for Distinguished Service, 1978; Bund Deutscher Architekten Prize, 1980; Beton Award, Düsseldorf, 1983. Member, Akademie der Künste, Berlin, 1967; Member, Akademie für Städtebau und Landesplanung, 1970. Address (office): Prinzipalmarkt 13, 4400 Münster, West Germany.

Works:

1954/
56 Municipal Theatre, Münster, West Germany (with Max von Hausen, Ortwin Rave, and Werner Ruhnau)
1955 Wustener Strasse Treatment Clinic, Bad Salzuflen, West Germany
    Fraling Weaving Mill, Bahnhofstrasse 41-43, Norwalde, West Germany
1956 Tuberculosis Sanatorium, Engelskirchen, West Germany
    Heerde College, Münster, West Germany
1957 Vocational Training School, Bockum-Hovel/Ludinghausen, West Germany (competition project)
    Vocational Training School, Bielefeld, West Germany (competition project)
    High School, Marl, West Germany (competition project)
    Town Hall, Dillingen/Saar, West Germany (competition project)
    Central Regional Bank, Düsseldorf (competition project)
    Guildhall, Nordwalde, West Germany
1958 School Hospital, Sendenhorst, West Germany (competition project)
    Religious Seminary, Essen, West Germany (competition project)
    Norwest-Lotto Office Building and Administration Centre, Münster, West Germany
1959 Concert Hall, Saarbrucken, West Germany (competition project)
    Boys' Vocational School, Münster, West Germany (competition project)
    Eye Clinic, Essen, West Germany (competition project)
    Vicarage, Kindergarten and Library, Stromberg, West Germany
1960 District Administration Centre, Münster, West Germany, (competition project)
    Hospital, Lintfort, West Germany (competition project)
    Public Health Department and Administrative Savings Bank School, Münster, West

Germany (competition project)
    Heuting-Esch Community Centre, Bocholt, West Germany (competition project)
    Natural Sciences Faculty, University of Münster, West Germany (competition project)
    Student Hostel, Essen, West Germany (competition project)
    Sanatorium, Bad Driburg, West Germany
    Agricultural Centre, Münster, West Germany (project)
1961 C. and F. Fraling Needlework Establishment, Saerbeck, West Germany
    Engineering School, Cologne (competition project)
    Secondary school, Dorsten, West Germany
    Metalwork school, Gelsenkirchen, West Germany
    Martin Luther Primary School, Bielefeld, West Germany
1962 District Council Centre, Ludgeriplatz, Münster, West Germany
    DRK Centre, Münster, West Germany (competition project)
    Theatre Square, Gelsenkirchen, West Germany (competition project)
    City Hospital and Staff Housing, Siegburg, West Germany
    Pötterhoek Primary School, Münster, West Germany (competition project)
    Deutsche Bank, Alter Fischmarkt/Vossgasse, Münster, West Germany
    Special school, Gescher, West Germany
    Concert Hall, Bochum, West Germany (project)
    High School, Oelde, West Germany (competition project)
    Primary and secondary schools, Versmold, West Germany
    Student Centre, Stuttgart (competition project)
1963 Agricultural Insurance Association, Münster, West Germany (competition project)
    Clinics, University of Münster, West Germany, (competition project)
    Sanatorium, Bad Lippspringe, West Germany (competition project)
    Electricity Works, Hamburg, West Germany (competition project)
1964 Council Building, Leverkusen, West Germany (3 projects)
    State Library, Berlin (competition project)
    Market/Church Square restoration, Lubbeck (project)
    Primary School, Hürth, West Germany (competition project)
    Modern School, Senden, West Germany (competition project)
    Professional School, Altena-Lüdenscheid, West Germany (competition project)
    City and District Hospital, Herford, West Germany (competition project)
    Hospital, Waldbröl, West Germany (competition project)
    SOS Children's Village, Materborn, West Germany
1965 Modern school, Lemgo, West Germany
    Church of St. Michael, Gievenbeck, Münster, West Germany
    Plan for the restoration of Moers, West Germany (project)
    Tourist Hotel, Bamberg, West Germany (competition project)
    Primary School, Selm, West Germany (project)
    Max-Planck Institute for Child Nutrition, Dortmund, West Germany (competition project)
    Rehabilitation Centre, Dortmund, West Germany (competition project)
    Cathedral Square, Münster, West Germany (competition project)
    Herz-Jesu Church, Bad Homburg, Frankfurt
    Montessori School Centre, Cologne (compe-

tition project)
    Church of St. Joseph, Mülheim-Ruhr, West Germany (competition project)
    Parish Church, Coesfeld-Goxel, West Germany (competition project)
    Hospital, Itzehoe, West Germany (competition project)
    Plan for the restoration of Beckum, West Germany (project)
    J. F. Kennedy School, Zehlendorf, Berlin
    Space utilization plan for Warendorf, West Germany (project)
    German Legation, Vatican City (competition project)
    Agricultural Building, Stuttgart (project)
    High School, Brandenburg Quarter, Reinickendorf, Berlin (competition project)
1966 Institute for the Promotion of Housing Construction, Düsseldorf (competition project)
    Hospital, Freudenstadt, West Germany (competition project)
    Urban District Administration Building, Cologne (competition project)
    Tegel Airport, Berlin (competition project)
    Robert Bosch Hospital, Stuttgart (competition project)
    Hürth District Administration Building, Cologne (competition project)
    Town Library and Adult Education Centre, Gelsenkirchen, West Germany
    District Administration Centre, Halle, West Germany (competition project)
    Max Planck Institute, Göttingen, West Germany, (competition project)
    Town restoration plan for Emmerich, West Germany (project)
    Regional Savings Bank, Aegidiiplatz, Münster, West Germany (project)
    District Administration Centre, Warendorf, West Germany (project)
    Plan for restoration and slum clearance of Ibbenbüren, West Germany (project)
    Secondary School with Sports Centre, Emsdetten, West Germany (competition project)
    Vocational Training School, Coesfeld, West Germany (competition project)
    Town restoration plan for Warendorf, West Germany (project)
    School Centre, Ochtrup, West Germany (competition project)
    Cathedral Academy, Schwerte, West Germany
    Max Planck Institute for Biochemistry, Martinsried, Munich (competition project)
    Max Planck Institute, Berlin (competition project)
    St. Anna Cathedral Church Centre, Mecklenbeck, Münster, West Germany
1967 Hospital, Göppingen, West Germany (competition project)
    District Hospital, Donaueschingen, West Germany (competition project)
    Technical College Centre, Aachen, West Germany (competition project)
    District Administration Centre, Schwelm, West Germany (competition project)
    St. Joseph Church Centre, Oelde, West Germany (competition project)
    Swimming Centre, Lake Zürich (competition project)
    Matriculation Institute, Paderborn, West Germany (competition project)
    Children's Home, Gutersloh, West Germany (competition project)
    Accountancy Department, Administrative Centre, Hibernia, Herne, West Germany
    Day Centre Gymnasium, Osterburken, West Germany (competition project)
    Vocational School, Gutersloh, West Germany (competition project)
    Gymnasium, Marl, West Germany (competition project)

Harald Deilmann: Trade Fair Building, Frankfurt, 1984 (model).

Administration and Exhibition Building, Hochdahl, West Germany (competition project)

Town Hall, Münster, West Germany (competition project)

Hotel by the Zoo, Münster, West Germany (project)

Westdeutsche Landesbank, Münster, West Germany

Administration and Bank Building, Heilbronn Street, Stuttgart

District Administration Centre, Büren, West Germany (competition project)

Slum clearance plan for Lemgo, Altstadt, West Germany (project)

1968 Regional Vocational School, Wiedembrück, West Germany (competition project)

High School, Barmen, Wuppertal, West Germany (competition project)

Bergisch-Gladbach School, Paffrath, West Germany (competition project)

Haus Hall School for the Mentally Handicapped, Gescher, West Germany

Commerzbank, Münster, West Germany

Laurentianum High School, Warendorf, West Germany

Social Welfare Building, Dortmund, West Germany

Regional Vocational School, Wiedenbrück, West Germany (competition project)

University of Dortmund, West Germany (competition project)

University of Bremen, West Germany (competition project)

Allianz Administration Building, Stuttgart

University of Bielefeld, West Germany (competition project)

Haus Hall Clinical Centre, Gescher, West Germany (project)

Gymnasium and Swimming Hall, Secondary School, Lemgo, West Germany

High School Hall and Sports Centre, Ochtrup, West Germany (competition project)

West German District Bank, Dortmund, West Germany

Teaching Workshops, for the Apostolic Governing Body, Sibolga (project)

1969 Administration/Research Centre, Siemens-Perlach, Munich (competition project)

All-Weather Zoo, Münster, West Germany

Capuchin Monastery Mission Headquarters, Münster, West Germany

Town Savings Bank, Erkelenz, West Germany (competition project)

High School, Rheda, West Germany (competition project)

Zimmerman Villa, Kinderhaus, Münster, West Germany (project)

Aula Theatre, Menden, West Germany (competition project)

Plan for Perlach Urban Building Development, Munich (competition project)

Town Savings Bank, Düsseldorf (competition project)

Town Hall, Gronau, West Germany

Guildhall, Gronau, West Germany (competition project)

Guildhall and Adult Education Centre, Porz, West Germany (project)

Rhineland Savings Banks Administration

Centre and Central Clearing House, Düsseldorf

St. Barbara Hospital, Gladbeck, West Germany (project)

Provincial Insurance Building, Münster, West Germany (competition project)

Germany Radio Building, Cologne (competition project)

School Centre, Oerlinghausen, West Germany (competition project)

1970 Diocesan Museum, Paderborn, West Germany (competition project)

Cultural Centre, Herne, West Germany (competition project)

Guildhall, Iserlohn, West Germany (competition project)

Hospital Nurses' Home, Gladbeck, West Germany

Ostermann and Schweiwe Plastics Factory, Münster, West Germany

Hospital, Osnabrück, West Germany (competition project)

School and Sports Centre, Kreuztal, West Germany (competition project)

Factory, Buer, Gelsenkirchen, West Germany (competition project)

Old Peoples' Home, Amrum, Norddorf, West Germany (project)

German Savings Bank Training Centre, Bad Godesberg, West Germany (competition project)

Postal Headquarters, Bremen, West Germany (competition project)

Caroline Hospital, Neheim/Husten, West Germany (competition project)

School Centre, Soest, West Germany (competition project)

1971 Guildhall, Wanne Eickel, West Germany (project)

Guildhall and Adult Education Centre, Wesel, West Germany (competition project)

Clemens Sels Museum, Neuss, West Germany

Service Centre, Langenberg, West Germany (competition project)

Rhine Province State Insurance Organization Building, Düsseldorf

Bus Station, Ibbenbüren, West Germany

House restoration, Turmhof Porz, Cologne (project)

Town Hall and Park, Schwelm, West Germany (project)

Town Savings Bank, Schwelm, West Germany

District Leisure Park, Karkortsee/- Hengstaysee, Hagen, West Germany (project)

Finance Bureau, Aachen, West Germany (project)

Finance Bureau, Düsseldorf (project)

1972 Town Hall, Paderborn, West Germany (competition project)

Administration Centre, Government Quarter, Düsseldorf (competition project)

Postal Headquarters, Dortmund, West Germany (competition project)

Market Place rebuilding, Staelen, West Germany

1973 "Flexible Living" Housing Development, Barop, Dortmund, West Germany

Town Savings Bank, Bad Honnef, West Germany (competition project)

German Legation, Rome (competition project)

Sports School of the Armed Forces, Warendorf, West Germany (competition project)

Guildhall, Menden, West Germany (competition project)

Old Peoples' Centre, Porz-Urbach, Cologne

Central Law Courts, Münster, West Germany

School Centre, Altena, West Germany (competition project)

Town Savings Bank, Oberhausen, West Germany (competition project)

Colonia Insurance Building, Hamburg, West Germany (competition project)

Hospital Ibbenbüren, West Germany (competition project)

1974 Cultural Centre, Lingen, West Germany (competition project)

Guildhall, Minden, West Germany

Business Centre, Neumarkt, Cologne (competition project)

Dresdner Bank, Kampstrasse, Dortmund, West Germany

Casino, New Health Farm, Aachen, West Germany

Leisure Pool, Wulfen, West Germany (competition project)

Hospital, Reinickendorf, Berlin (competition project)

Clinic, Bohlmke, Dortmund, West Germany

Kudamm Karree Casino, Berlin (project)

Karstadt Department Store, Münster, West Germany (project)

German Student Foundation Headquarters, Würzburg, West Germany (competition project)

North Rhine-Westphalia Provincial Diet, Düsseldorf (competition project)

Old Peoples' Home, Boelerheide, Hagen, West Germany (competition project)

1975 Banking Hall, Westdeutsche Landesbank, London

Plan for an integrated city centre extension, Dülmen, West Germany (competition project)

Open-Air Baths, Elmsdetten, West Germany (competition project)

District Council Centre, Osnabrück, West

Germany (competition Project)

District Council Centre, Recklinghausen, West Germany (competition project)

Guildhall, Montabaur, West Germany (project)

1976 Financial Training Centre, Münster, West Germany (competition project)

Health Guest House, Stattsbad, Salzüflen, West Germany (competition project)

Warendorf District Vocational School Centre, Beckum, West Germany (competition project)

Old Peoples' Centre, Emmerich, West Germany (competition project)

Krupp Headquarters remodelling and conversion, Essen, West Germany

Mannesmann Headquarters, Ratingen-Lintorf, West Germany

Banking Hall, Westdeutsche Landesbank, New York

Westdeutsche Landesbank Branch, Luxembourg

Westdeutsche Landesbank Branch, Frankfurt

Westdeutsche Landesbank Headquarters, Düsseldorf

Communications Centre, Dortmund-North, West Germany (competition project)

Pilgrims' Centre, Kappellenplatz, Kevelaer, West Germany (project)

Musselmann Estate, Hygstetten/Donau, West Germany

1977 Gelsenwasser AG Laboratory Buildings, Gelsenkirchen, West Germany

Federal Academy, Brühl, West Germany (competition project)

Youth and Sports Centre, Gronau, West Germany (competition project)

Communications Centre, Gladbeck, West Germany (competition project)

Nigerian Legation, Bad Godesberg, Bonn (project)

Covered and Open-Air Baths, Lüdenscheid, West Germany (competition project)

Ministry of Food, Agriculture and Environment, Stuttgart (competition project)

Casino, Bottcherstrasse, Bremen, West Germany (project)

Restroom, United Nations Building, New York (project)

1978 Flight Simulator, for Lufthansa, Frankfurt

National Library, Tehran (competition project)

Television Tower, Düsseldorf (project)

Restaurant and Bistro, in the Casino, Aachen, West Germany

Guildhall and Adult Education Centre, Porz, Cologne

Hotel Malek-Shar, Iran (project)

Casino, Bad Oeynhausen, West Germany (project)

Mosque, Malek-Shar, Iran (project)

Multi-Purpose Hall, Malek-Sharr, Iran (project)

Garniran New Town, for the Tehran Housing Development Corporation, Iran (competition project)

Rehabilitation and Leisure Centre, Wilgertswiesen, West Germany (project)

Housing Block, Neuss, West Germany

Petrikirchplatz Plan, Dortmund, West Germany (project)

Neuer Markt Plan, Dortmund, West Germany (project)

Library, Ochtrup, West Germany (project)

Old LVA Building alterations, Düsseldorf

Westdeutscher Landesbank alterations, Essen, West Germany

Legal Administration and Outer-City Finance Office, Bonn (competition project)

Borkhauser Feld Housing Development, Solingen-Ohligs, West Germany (competition project)

City Plan Study, Ahaus, West Germany

Kerneplatz City Plan Study, Stuttgart (competition project)

City Planning Scheme, Warstein, West Germany (competition project)

Greve House, Münster, West Germany

Volksbank Building, Münster, West Germany (competition project)

Northern Inner-City Pedestrian Zone, Lüdenscheid, West Germany

City Hall alterations and extensions, Düsseldorf

Office and Commercial Building, Mutter-Ey-Strasse, Düsseldorf (project)

Town Hall extensions, Emmerich, West Germany (competition project)

Grutholz Building Development, Castrop-Rauxel, West Germany

Seeland Aquarium Room Plans, Cologne and Bonn (projects)

Regional Administration Building, Leer, West Germany (competition project)

Spielbank Building, Bad Oeynhausen, West Germany

Federal Ministry of Trade Building, Bonn (competition project)

Schole Residential and Commercial Building, Lüdinghausen, West Germany

Town Hall, Oldenburg, West Germany (competition project)

New High School and Sports Facilities, Ochtrup, West Germany (competition project)

BRBS City Building Study, Fulda, West Germany (project)

1979 Gerberviertel district development, Bochum, West Germany (competitionproject)

New Hotel Building, Bad Oeynhausen, West Germany (project)

Landeszentralbank Hessen building, Frankfurt (competition project)

Town Square, Montabaur, West Germany

Gürzenich Town Hall, Cologne (competition project)

City Plan, Versmold, West Germany

Savings Bank extensions, Ochtrup, West Germany

Finance Office Building, Bochum, West Germany (competition project)

Volksbank Building, Ibbenbüren, West Germany (competition project)

Town Hall, Rheine, West Germany (competition project)

Hallenfreibad Study, Herne, West Germany (competition project)

Judicial Offices, Solingen, West Germany (competition project)

Salzhof Building, Bad Salzuflen, West Germany (competition project)

Judicial Authority Building, Dortmund, West Germany (competition project)

Town Hall, Attendorn, West Germany (competition project)

Petersberg Study, Bonn (competition project)

City Centre Plan, Hamm, West Germany (competition project)

City Suburb Housing, Bielefeld, West Germany (competition project)

School Centre, Dortmund-Huckarde, West Germany (competition project)

City Hall/Town Hall Complex Studies, Höxter, West Germany

District Offices extension, Soest, West Germany (competition project)

District Office, Borken, West Germany (competition project)

Building Development Plans 52 and 53, Emsdetten, West Germany

Realschule at the School Centre, Borken, West Germany (competition project)

Realschule Building, Dülmen, West Germany (competition project)

District Government Building, Gelsenkirchen, West Germany (competition project)

Krupp Administration Building Study, Essen, West Germany (competition project)

Dr. Schumacher Office Building, Münster, West Germany

Stuhlmarker Building Facade, Prinzipalmarkt, Münster, West Germany

Fraulandshügel Development, Borghorst, West Germany (competition project)

Housing Park, Dortmund-Menglinghausen, West Germany

Town Hall, Dortmund, West Germany (competition project)

Hospital, Aschaffenburg, West Germany (competition project)

BMA and BML Building, Bonn (competition project)

1980 Pedestrian Zone Study, Sendenhorst, West Germany (competition project)

Schönwälder Family House, Münster, West Germany

Lindenhof Development, Münster, West Germany (competition project)

Romerberg Development, Frankfurt (competition project)

Main-Taunus District Plan, Hofheim, West Germany (competition project)

District Administration Building, Meschede, West Germany (competition project)

Sell House, Düsseldorf-Unterbach, West Germany

Knickelmann Restaurant, Münster, West Germany

Gambling Machine Room in the Spielcasino, Bremen, West Germany

"Bezirkstelle" branch office prototype, for Nordwestlotto

Colonia Insurance Company Headquarters, Cologne (competition project)

Residential and Commercial Building, Bochum-Stiepel, West Germany (project)

Neumarkt Development, Ibbenbüren, West Germany (competition project)

City Hall, Telgete, West Germany (competition project)

City Hall, Bielefeld, West Germany (competition project)

Wechloy Development for Uni, Oldenburg, West Germany (competition project)

Town Hall and Concert Hall, Oldenburg, West Germany (competition project)

Town Hall extensions, Delmenhorst, West Germany (competition project)

Landtag Development, Düsseldorf (competition project)

Marktplatz Development, Hildesheim, West Germany (competition project)

Alrajhi Bank Study, Riyadh, Saudi Arabia (competition project)

Town Hall extensions, Schwerte, West Germany (competition project)

Börsenplatz Development, Wilhelmshaven, West Germany (competition project)

Trade School Centre, Lüdinghausen, West Germany (competition project)

Marktplatz City Buildings Study, Gescher, West Germany (competition project)

Muhler Kopf Building Development, Hagen, West Germany

City Wall Development, Rüthen, West Germany (competition project)

Sports and Recreation Centre, Fürstenau, West Germany (project)

Sports and Recreation Centre, Bitburg, West Germany (project)

Housing Development, Dortmund-Lücklemberg, West Germany

Tee-Store System Plan

Tee-Treff store prototype, Oberhausen, West Germany

Tee-Treff store, Krefeld, West Germany

Tee-Treff store, Bonn

Aldruper Weg Development, Greven, West Germany

City Savings Bank Study, Bad Oeynhausen, West Germany (competition project)

Central Hotel alterations, Münster, West Germany

Technical University, Hamburg-Harburg, West Germany (competition project)

Nachtigallenweg Building Development Plan II, Ochtrup, West Germany

1981 Federal Ministry of Post and Telecommunications, Bonn (competition project)

City Library, Gütersloh, West Germany (competition project)

Town Hall, Dormagen, West Germany (competition project)

City and Festival Hall, Ludwigsburg, West Germany (competition project)

Professor Kollhosser Family House, Münster, West Germany

School Centre, Dortmund-Dostfeld, West Germany (competition project)

Enery Museum Study, Essen, West Germany (competition project)

Spielbank Building, Dortmund Hohensyburg, West Germany

Truxhof Housing Development, Dortmund, West Germany

Mallinkrodt-Gymnasium, Dortmund, West Germany (competition project)

Natural History Museum, Bielefeld, West Germany (competition project)

Northside Marktplatz layout, Ahlen, West Germany

P. J. Schmetz Housing Development, Kleve, West Germany (project)

Berliner Platz Development, Mülheim, West Germany (competition project)

Karstadt Development, Berlin-Tempelhof (competition project)

Housing, Cultural Centre and Nationalgalerie extension, Berlin (competition project)

Town Hall extensions, Wilhelmshaven, West Germany (competition project)

Judicial Training School, Recklinghausen, West Germany (competition project)

Altenheim rebuilding and development, West Germany (competition project)

St. Josefshaus, Essen-Kettwig, West Germany

Petrol Service Station, Saudi Arabia

Community Centre, Sennestadt, West Germany (competition project)

Lambertusplatz Development, Castrop-Rauxel, West Germany

Michels Housing and Commercial Building, Von-Kluck-Strasse, Münster, West Germany

City Building Study, Minden-Weingarten, West Germany (competition project)

German Library, Frankfurt (competition project)

Rail Station Forecourt Development, Düsseldorf

Municipal Theatre, Essen, West Germany

Prozessionsweg Building Development, Appelhülsen, West Germany

Obere Munsterstrasse Development, Castrop-Rauxel, West Germany

District Authority Offices, Starnberg, West Germany (competition project)

Multiple-Family House, Eupener Weg 11, Münster, West Germany

1982 Development Plan, Remscheid-Lüttringhausen, West Germany (competition project)

Development Plan, Altstadt Kaiserslautern, West Germany (competition project)

Gambling Machine Hall, Bremerhaven, West Germany

Schlömag-Siemag Headquarters Study, Düsseldorf (competition project)

Rail Station, Kassel-Wilhelmshohe, West Germany (competition project)

Town Hall Study, Olsberg, West Germany (competition project)

Am Markt Development, Nordhorn, West Germany (competition project)

Landesmuseum fur Technik und Arbeit, and Süddeutscher Rundfunk Studios, Mannheim, West Germany (competition project)

Cost- and Space-Saving Buildings, Essen-Vogelheim, West Germany (competition project)

Brauereigelände Development, Paderborn, West Germany (competition project)

Altstadtring/Denkmalstrasse Study, Castrop-Rauxel, West Germany (competition project)

Schötmar Rail Station, Bad Salzuflen, West Germany (competition project)

Scharn Pedestrian Zone, Minden, West Germany (competition project)

Western Area Development, Altstadt Warendorf, West Germany (competition project)

Neues Lurgi-Haus Study, Frankfurt (competition project)

Kennedyplatz Development, Essen, West Germany (competition project)

Daimler-Benz Headquarters Building, Stuttgart (competition project)

Viehmarktplatz Development, Essen, West Germany (competition project)

Marktzentrum Development, Rheda-Wiedenbrück, West Germany (competition project)

PPM Office Building, Telgte, West Germany (project)

Town Hall/Raiffeisenbank alterations and annex, Schöllkrippen, West Germany (competition project)

Tete Defense Plan, La Defense, Paris (competition project)

1983 Youth and Cultural Centre, Bergkamen, West Germany (competition project)

Housing Development, Wittbräucker Strasse, Dortmund, West Germany

Capuchin Mission Hall, Gunungsitoli, Nias, Indonesia

Apartment Building, Mondstrasse 28, Münster, West Germany

Deilmann-Haniel Headquarters Building Study, Dortmund, West Germany (competition project)

District and City Library Study, Erkelenz, West Germany (competition project)

Dr. Bröker House, Tecklenburg, West Germany

Old City Quarter Development, Hoxter, West Germany (competition project)

Hebel-haus prototype plans

Town Hall extensions, Neuss, West Germany (competition project)

Rail Station Forecourt, Meppen, West Germany (competition project)

Opera de Paris Development, Paris (competition project)

Sports Museum (conversion of harbour warehouses), Cologne (project)

Povel Housing Development, Nordhorn, West Germany (project)

House alterations, Prinzipalmarkt 36, Münster, West Germany

Klosterkaserne Housing Development, Konstanz, West Germany (competition project)

Development Plan, Siegen-Seelbach, West Germany (competition project)

1984 Trade Fair Study, Frankfurt (competition project)

Regional Garden Show 1988, Rheda-Wiedenbruck, West Germany (competition project)

Tormin Bridge Study, Münster, West Germany (competition project)

Herrenberg Building Development Study, Bad Bentheim, West Germany (competition project)

Berliner Platz Development, Mülheim, West Germany (competition project)

Publications:

By DEILMANN: books—*30 junge Deutsche,* with others, exhibition catalogue, Leverkusen, West Germany 1961; *Zehn Jahre Grosser Kunstpreis des Landes Nordrhein/Westfalen,* with others, exhibition catalogue, Düsseldorf 1962; *Einfamilenhaus für morgen,* with Einar Ridderström, Stuttgart and Bern 1967; *Umstrukurierung historischer Stadtgebiete* with K. F. Gehse and B. Jensen, Dortmund, West Germany and Stuttgart 1970; *Schulbauten: Planungsgrundlagen für allgemeinbildende Schulen,* Gütersloh, West Germany 1971; *Lerne Wohnen,* with others, exhibition catalogue, Düsseldorf 1971; *Menschlich Bauen,* with others, exhibition catalogue, Düsseldorf 1972; *Bauten des Gesundheitswesen: Planungsgrundlagen für allgemeine Krankenhäser,* Gütersloh, West Germany, 1972; *System der Gebäudeerschliessung und ihre Auswirkung auf die Baukosten und den Nutzwert der Wohnungen,* with Herbert Pfieffer, Dortmund, West Germany 1972; *Bebauungssysteme I: Wohnungsbau,* Dortmund 1972; *Stadt in Test,* with others, exhibition catalogue, Düsseldorf 1973; *Wohnungsbau/The Dwelling/L'Habitat,* with Jörg C. Kirschenmann and Herbert Pfieffer, Stuttgart 1973; *Wohnsysteme Anwendungsbeispiele,* Dortmund, West Germany 1973; *Bebauungssysteme II, volume 1, Anlagen für Bildung und Kultur,* with K. H. Merkel, volume 2, *Anlagen für Gesundheit, Soziales und Sport,* with K. H. Merkel, and volume 3, *Anlagen für Handel, Gewerbe und Verwaltung,* with H. Brettschneider and K. H. Merkel, Dortmund, West Germany 1974; *Umstrukturierung historischer Stadtbegiete: Kriterien, Methoden, Beispiele,* with others, Dortmund, West Germany 1974; *Bau- und Wohnforschung,* Bonn 1974; *Die Eignung des Grossraumbüros für die kommuunale Verwaltung,* Bonn 1975; *Dokumentation: Bauplanung und Städtebau,* Münster, 1975; *Werkbericht 1976: Bauplanung und Städtebau,* Münster, West Germany 1976; *Wohnbereiche, Wohnquartiere,* with Gerhard Bickenbach and Herbert Pfeiffer, Stuttgart 1977; *Versicherungsgebäude, Banken, Sparkassen,* with Thomas Deilmann, Stuttgart 1978; *Gebaude für die öffentliche Verwaltung,* with Andreas Deilmann, Stuttgart 1979; *Werkbericht 77/78: Bauplanung und Städtebau,* Münster, West Germany 1979; *Werkbericht 79/80: Bauplanung und Städtebau,* Münster, West Germany 1980; *Werkbericht 1981–1983: Bauplanung und Städtebau,* Münster, West Germany 1983; *Wohnungebietsplanung,* Dortmund, West Germany 1984; articles—"Post War Architects," with others, in *Zodiac* (Milan), February 1956; "Für Architektur," with others," in *Bauwelt* (Berlin), January 1974; "Thus They Project" in *Proceedings of the World Congress of the International Union of Architects,* Madrid 1975.

On DEILMANN: books—*Das Haus in dem wir wohnen* by H. W. Theil, Stuttgart 1978; *Wo Wohnen, wie Bauen?,* Düsseldorf 1978; *Architekturkonzepte der Gegenwart* by Peter Schweger, Wolfgang Schneider and Wilhelm Meyer, Stuttgart 1983; *Harald Deilmann: Ausgewahlte Projekte,* Dortmund, West Germany 1984; articles—"Porträt Harald Deilmann" by Udo Kultermann in *Deutsche Bauzeitung* (Stuttgart), April 1961; "Dem Menschen und dem Material gerecht" by Hannelore Schubert in *Die Welt* (Hamburg), 3 May 1965; "Harald Deilmann: Werkbericht 1955-1965" by Jürgen Joedicke in *Deutsche Bauzeitung* (Stuttgart), August 1965; "Werkbericht Harald Deilmann' in *Die Ziegelindustrie* (Wiesbaden, West Germany) no. 24, 1967; "Harald Deilmann" in *Japan Interior Design* (Tokyo), February 1975.

Architecture is mainly a question of overcoming certain practical problems. Solutions must be found for the many different projects arising out of human needs, and these solutions must take into account physical as well as psychological facts. This, in a nutshell, is the formula that these days seems so difficult for us to achieve. But the deplorable deterioration of the three dimensional imagination is due not only to an unsympathetic and materialistically oriented world but also to a hostility towards architects and to the lack of an educated clientele.

For when it comes to artistic production of any kind, including architecture, the question is not one of individual taste but of absolute values that can be established by anyone with the requisite understanding. There are certain forces underlying every perception, for which every epoch has its own collective sensibility. The architect, looking for original solutions to present-day problems, must be familiar with current forces in order to integrate them in the dialogue, as it were, to be expressed.

A change of form, resulting from a change in awareness—a coming to terms with the spiritual and social currents of the day—must not be seen as short-lived modernism. Intrinsic expression of contemporary conditions can only originate from a fundamental reference to the spiritual issues that have developed. My ambition in my work is to satisfy both those factors that are unique to time and place and those that relate to a universal validity and are archetypal and timeless. This creative symbiosis of present and unique elements with those that are universal and timeless is the only identifiable common characteristic of the works for which I have taken responsibility. I concern myself with the greatest variety of forms and modes of expression possible for each individual assignment, rather than adhere to any consistent and uniform style or set of rules.

It was Walter Gropius who said that "specialists are people who always repeat the same mistakes." I do not feel that his warning applies to me: I constantly make new mistakes, but I hope thereby to make my own contribution to the development of architecture.

My work method is this: If architectural planning is seen as the solving of problems for new and unique assignments, then it follows that one must look for solutions that derive from an ever-changing technology. The reason that stereotyped plans and buildings fail so disastrously is that there has been a neglect of the dimension of time—in the sense of historical development. With the fast-moving advances of our day, any restriction to previous plans creates anachronism. Because building systems are various and flexible does not mean that no further thought is necessary: one must plan ahead, taking decisions that will not become obsolete too quickly.

As far as my design methodology is concerned, I can best describe it by describing the day to day running of my practice, which deals with all kinds of commissions connected with the human environment. First, we sift the basic information regarding the task to be carried out—such factors as its special requirements, programming of work, surface ground conditions, intended function of the building, and local building regulations. All are thoroughly analyzed and studied. Of the greatest importance, however, is the search for an Idea: the essence of the task and its unique formula must be formed into a comprehensive unity that takes account of all the given circumstances. In the first phase, the integration of functional requirements with architectural image must be so fused that one can no longer conceive of the one without the other. There is no hard and fast rule about the method of this conceptual form-finding stage, and it will vary according to the situation and the frame of reference. One cannot repeat past experience exactly, and yet the knowledge gained in previous situations will play a role in solving the new problems. The design conception may occur spontaneously, through the working of the imagination in relation to the job content, or through an inspiration provoked by the setting, tradition, or visual suggestion.

It is this Idea that is the foundation of design and sets off the work process, the process of harmonizing the various technical and creative details. The final outcome must be a compatible interpretation of planning in three-dimensional or even four-dimensional spatial reality, so as to enrich the human environment.

The various necessary work proecesses—plans, building regulation procedures, and actual realization of the project with all its technical details—are all processes that also vary from task to task; there is very little point, therefore, in trying to systematize. In an experience practice, all these duties are discharged as a matter of routine, naturally, with the help of modern planning aids and computerized cost- and time-planning.

The creative process itself cannot be rationalized, but with increased experience it can be better guided and directed. In order to synthesize the details of production, one must make both quantitative and qualitative analyses, within the terms of reference of the limited possibilities of the particular task. It is more difficult to analyze the process of designing than to analyze the design itself, and this problem may explain the many unfruitful attempts to make attractive and appealing so much that was previously better lost to sight.

—Harald Deilmann

Harald Deilmann was only in his thirties when, in collaboration, he built the Municipal Theatre at Münster. Prior to this first work, he had been a lecturer at the Technische Hochschule in Stuttgart where many of the postwar architects of the Federal Republic had connections. Deilmann started practice firmly in the modern camp, and he seems to have eschewed constantly any thought or any sense of formality in his designs. Even the Münster theatre is almost self-consciously informal, as though its authers were deliberately going out of their way to make the building as un-grand as possible. This informality is accentuated by the setting back of the structure diagonally on the site, thus creating a restless and uneasy sense of gaiety. The curved upper works around the foyer area combine with the flytower to give the building a centre of gravity. Paradoxically, Deilmann and his colleagues integrated a neoclassical ruin into the scheme, which remains a brilliant essay in refined understatement. The tendency to an informal approach is peculiar to the post-1945 German architects who were concerned to reject the neoclassical planning of so much work produced during the era of the Third Reich.

Deilmann's subsequent work includes hospitals, cultural buildings, and many office blocks. The Nordwest-Lotto building at Münster is perhaps his best-known office structure, but all his work reveals the same careful, intellectual approach, an approach that has led him into academic life as well as professional practice. In general, Deilmann's oeuvre inspires a quiet admiration for its intellectual rigour and for the refinement of his detailing. He did much to re-establish the pre-eminence of Germany architecture in its European context in the difficult years after the war.

—James Stevens Curl

DE LA SOTA Martinez, Alejandro.

Spanish. Born in Pontevedra, 20 October 1913. Educated at the Escuela de Madrid, Dip.Arch. 1941. Designer, Institute Nacional de Colonización, Madrid, 1942-49. In private practice, Madrid, since 1950. Professor of Design, Escuela de Madrid, 1956-63, 1965-66, 1969-71. Recipient: First Prize, Treasury Office Competition, Tarragona, 1954; First Prize, Housing Competition, La Coruna, Spain, 1956; First Prize, Civilian Government Building Competition, Tarragona, 1957; National Prize for Architecture, 1974. Address (office): Breton de los Herreros 66 (3), Madrid, Spain.

Works:

1942/
49 Housing development, Gimenells, Spain
Rural housing development, Valuengo, Spain
Rural housing development, La Bazana, Spain
Rural housing development, Jerez de los Caballeros, Spain

1948/
52 Rural housing development, Esquivel, Spain

1954 Local Treasury Office, Tarragona
Chalet, calle Doctor Arce, Madrid

1956 Housing development, La Coruna, Spain

1956/
59 Commercial and residential development, Zamora, Spain

1957 Civilian Government Building, Tarragona

1958 TABSA Workshops Building, Barajas Highway, near Madrid

1959 Workers' Children's Center, Miraflores de la Sierra, Madrid (with J. A. Corrales and R. Vasquez Molezun)
Alejandro de la Sota House, Avenida le los Toreros, Madrid

1959/
65 Clesa Diary Works, Madrid

1960 Residential development, Salamanca, Spain

1964 Chalet, Villalba, Madrid

1965 Gymnasium, Maravillas College, Madrid

1966 Sports Club, Pontevedra, Spain
Alejandro de la Sota House, Avenida de America, Madrid

1970 Cesar Carlos High School, Madrid
Faculty of Law Building, University of Granada, Spain

1973/
74 Post Office Bank and Accounts Centre, Avenida de Betanzos, Madrid

1974 Lecture Hall Pavilion, University of Seville
Guzman House, Santo Domingo Development, Madrid

1975 Aviaco Headquarters Building, Madrid (competition project)

1980 Dominguez House, La Caeyra, Pontevedra, Spain

1980 Post Office Communications Building, Leon, Spain (with Carlos Sidro)

Publications:

On DE LA SOTA: book—*Arquitecture Española Contemporanea* by Luis Domenech Girbau, Barcelona 1968; articles—"Vividena Agrupada—Pueblo de Gimenells" in *Revista National de Arquitectura* (Madrid), November 1948; "El Nuevo Pueblo des Esquivel" in *Revista Nacional de Arquitectura* (Madrid), January 1953; "Alejandro de la Sota", special issue of *Nueva Forma* (Madrid), December 1974; "Seven Masters of Madrid and 7 + 7 Young Architects" by Alberto Campo Baeza in *Architecture + Urbanism* (Tokyo), March 1978; "Casa Dominguez in La Caeyra, Pontevedra" in *Arquitectura* (Madrid), January/February 1981; "Alejandro de la Sota: an incomplete anthology", special issue of *Arquitectura* (Madrid), November/December 1981; "Alejandro de la Sota" by J. L. Mateo in *Quaderns* (Barcelona), May/June 1982.

In the isolationist climate of the first post-war years in Spain, Alejandro de la Sota began his career as a designer in the Instituto Nacional de Colonizacion in Madrid. During those years—1942-49—he worked on a series of new rural developments, works in which he allowed patterns similar to those of the modern tradition to act as the foundation for a style that accepts the inheritance of vernacular elements and uses them as plastic means. During the 1950's, after the isolated experience of the Instituto, de la Sota quickly accepted the ideal of modernism and

Alejandro de la Sota: Commercial and residential development, Zamora, Spain, 1959.

thereafter remained faithful to it, making function and technique the criteria of architecture. But the plastic/aesthetic considerations that informed his first designs did not disappear; they continued to impregnate his work; and some of his most successful buildings have been those in which his impulses took over, making use of technical means to create a plastic medium, an architectural language. At the same time his evolution as an architect has involved an increasingly restricted language, a purism that suggests both Mies and the rationalism typical of Italy in the 1930's.

In the early 1950's, de la Sota joined the modernists with some works that share the informal plasticity of the International Style of that period. Examples are the Local Treasury Office in Tarragona, the housing development at La Coruna, and the "chalet" in c. Doctor Acre, Madrid. But, by 1957, in his Civillian Government Building in Tarragona, he had begun to suggest the nature of his future career, the works of his maturity. The loyalty is still to modernism, but to a less informal modernism; there is now an interest in something more plain, unadorned, purist. The striving is for a sparkling quality, for the kind of rationalist style fathered by Terragni—a quest for formal radiance, simple and perfected, which alone can be the expression of functional and spatial rationality. Thereafter, de la Sota's work is pervaded with that neo-Platonism implicit in so many works of

the modern movement, especially those that took technology as guiding star and linguistic medium.

dela Sota's buildings, then, are more or less inclined to convert the functional and the technical into an architectural language. Besides the Civilian Government Building, such buildings include the commercial and residential development at Zamora, the residential development at Salamanca, the Gymnasium at Maravillas College, Madrid, the Cesar Carlos High School, Madrid and the Faculty of Law at the University of Granada. More decidedly inclined towards the technical, and prone therefore to the ambiguity associated with much of the avant garde architecture of Europe in the 1960's, are the Clesa Dairy Works in Madrid and the Sports Club at Pontevedra.

Like Miers, de la Sota feels that architecture, in spite of appearances, is not determined by technology but adopts connotations of order, smoothness, simplicity, purity—the synonyms of technology for some of the modernists. The demands of the technical elements may be great, but the architect, consciously or unconsciously, turns technology into language.

Whatever the validity of these premises. Alejandro de la Sota has created works of such high standards as to make him one of the giants of contemporary Spanish architecture.

—Anton Capitel

de la TOUR d'AUVERGNE, Bernard.

French. Born in Maisons-Lafitte, 9 September 1923. Educated at the Ecole Nationale Supérieure des Beaux-Arts, Paris; Ecole Spécial d'Architecture, Paris, graduated 1948. Served as a volunteer in the Royal Air Force, in North Africa, 1940-44. Worked in the offices of Palmer Krissel, Los Angeles, Philip Johnson, *q.v.*, New York, and Eugène Beaudouin, *q.v.*, Paris, 1948-55. In private practice, Paris, 1955 until his death in 1976. Professor, Ecoles d'Art Américaines, Fontainebleau, 1960-61; Professor and Studio Master, Ecole Spécial d'Architecture, Paris, 1961-68; Professor, California Polytechnic University, San Luis Obispo, 1968-71; Director, Ecoles d'Art Américaines, Fontainebleau, 1972-75. Recipient: Bronze Medal, Society for the Encouragement of Arts and Industry. Member, Order of Architects, France, 1951. *Died* (in Paris) *8 October 1976.*

Works:

1952 House, Cuernavaca, Mexico

1955 Museum, Aleppo, Syria (competition project; with J. Lauffroy)

1957 City Centre, West Berlin (competition project; with M. Tournon Branly, P. Devinoy, J. Faugeron Associates, and M. Schlote)

Mausoleum, Quay Azam Jinnah, Karachi, Pakistan (competition project; with M. Andrault, P. Parat and M. Calka)

Palace of Justice, Lille, France (competition project; with M. Calka)

1958 Automobile Museum and Congress Hall, Le Mans, France (project; with M. Andrault and P. Parat)

1959 S.C.I.C. Housing Development, Gonesse, France (competition project; with M. Andrault and P. Parat)

1960 Tourist Centre, Saut-du-Doubs, France (project; with M. Tournon Branly)

Club Martini, Champs Elysées, Paris (with M. Tournon Branly, M. Pechere and M. Calka)

1961 Civic and Cultural Centre, Cape Town, South Africa (project; with E. Beaudouin, A. Fournier, and A. Laprade)

ZUP Housing Development, Caen-Herouville, France (competition project)

1962 Housing development, Limeil-Brevannes, France (project; with J. Viallefond)

Mehringplatz Redevelopment, West Berlin (project; with M. Tournon Branly)

1963 Housing development, Chilly-Mazarin, France (project)

1964 National School of Taxes, with Residences, Clermont-Ferrand, France (with E. Beaudouin)

1965 Housing, Limeil, France (project; with P. Lacroix)

1966 Institut Européen d'Administration des Affaires, Fontainebleau, France (with R. Cidrac)

1967 Pavilions, Parc de Chambly, France (project; with P. Lacroix)

Town Hall, Amsterdam (competition project)

Air and Space Museum, Paris (competition project)

1968 Fiat Planning Centre, Trappes, France (project)

Winter sports centre, Vallée de Chasse, France (project)

Housing and leisure complex, Vallée de Risle, France (project)

1969 Centre Européen d'Education Permanente, Fontainebleau, France

1970 Tourist centre, Caicos Island, Bahamas (project)

S.C.I.C. Cultural Centre, Maffliers, France (project)

ARCS 2000 Winter Sports Centre, Mont Pourri, France (project; with B. G. Huidobro)

Bernard de la Tour d'Auvergne: Centre Européen d'Education Permanente, Fontainbleau, France, 1969.

1971 Small tourist complex, Megeve, France (project; with P. Lacroix)

1972 French Embassy, Beijing (project)

Institute of Management, Front de Seine, Paris (project; with E. Duhart and M. Le Caisne)

L'Oréal Headquarters and Laboratories, Clichy, France (project; with A. Bailly)

S.C.I.C. Planning Centre, Menucourt, France (project)

1973 National School of Treasury Services, Marne-la-Vallée, France (with C. Costantini)

Tourist complex, Port-de-l'Orb, Languedoc-Roussillon, France (project; with C. Costantini and M. Regembal)

Pavilions, La-Queue-les-Yvelines, France (project; with M. Regembal)

ELF Conference Rooms and Museum of Gabon, Libreville (competition project)

Saint-Germain Market redevelopment, Paris (competition project; with C. Costantini, G. Hoym de Marien, and M. Regembal)

Plateau de Vanves renovation, Vanves, France (competition project; with C. Costantini and M. Regembal)

1974 Four Seasons Hotel, Les Halles, Paris (project; with the Webb Zerafka Menkes Housden Partnership)

Redevelopment plan for Les Halles, Paris (project)

Educational complexes for Tehran, Shiraz and Isfahan, Iran (projects; with C. Costantini and M. Regembal)

Tax Centre (competition project; with C. Costantini and M. Regembal)

Damascus Public Library, Syria (competition project; with D. Harding)

Museum of Prehistory of the Ile de France, Nemours (competition project)

1975 Village of the West (tourist complex), Leucate-Barcares, France (project)

Redevelopment plan for Les Halles, Paris (2nd project; with others)

Hotel complex, Moulin de Paillas, Les Combes, France (project)

Publications:

On de la TOUR d'AUVERGNE: book—*Bernard de la Tour d'Auvergne,* with a preface by Eugène Beaudouin, Paris 1975; article—"The National School for Treasury Services" in *Mur vivant* (Paris), no. 51, 1979.

During his twenty-five years of activity Bernard de la Tour d'Auvergne was motivated by a desire to protect the sensitivity of other people, to respond to the human need for equilibrium and harmony, and to accomplish the modest but essential task of creating an architectural object that could be experienced with discreet-exaltation, then looked upon with joy. Because of these goals, one finds in his work a coherence both in the process of creation and in the direction of his research.

This coherence has principally to do with the relationship of contents to container and with the articulation of volumes, each responding to its own function but intimately linked with each other according to a subtle hierarchy implying a progression towards the fundamental element, the heart of the composition. The variety of these volumes is expressed not only by their forms and their siting but also by the choice and use of materials employed. Contrasts, counterpoint, and rhythm are created that visually express the "elements" of the architecture in an undisguised, open manner. For example, one can cite two particularly characteristic studies: the Centre Européen d'Education Permanente at Fontainebleau and the National School of Treasury Services at Marne-la-Vallée.

At the Centre Européen d'Education Permanente a large, transparent volume on an orthogonal plane has as its centre a vast cylinder containing four amphitheatres, and alongside the two facades there are eight towers comprising sixteen chambers, little "oratories" for group work. For the cylinder and the towers, de la Tour d'Auvergne designed massive walls in a warm tinted brick, to contrast with the light, polished steel skeleton and curtain facade of the overall structure.

The National School of Treasury Services is defined as a curved, linear building sliding between cylindrical masses of the amphitheatres. All the activities of the school converge on the areas essential to study and reflection, and the contrast is emphasized in a differentiation of construction principles: unclad brick for the interior and exterior of the amphitheatres, bronze-coloured steel skeleton and tinted glass for the linear building.

These principles of contrast and relation are, in fact, to be found in all of his work, whether in the Club Martini in Paris or in some of his projects for the many competitions in which he took part—the Palace of Justice in Lille, the Amsterdam City Hall, the Museum of the Prehistory of the Ile de France, or the study he was asked to complete of a Social Centre for l'Oréal.

His principal work could have been the architectural complex he conceived for the development of the Les Halles area of Paris; it included a five-acre garden designed to set off that marvellous jewel, the Church of St. Eustache, and, in counterpoint to the Bourse du Commerce, volumes of resolutely contemporary architecture sited around a vast "crater" and bringing together very varied activities. It is greatly to be regretted that his premature death prevented him from defending his project and achieving at least part of it.

De la Tour d'Auvergne was an aesthete, a cultured man who had travelled a great deal; he loved travel, and in his youth he had been strongly influenced by Egypt and by Greece, countries to which he liked to return. He was very interested in the United States of America, and he had close contacts with young American architects. He devoted himself to his task as Professor and then Director of the Ecoles d'Art Américaines, in Fontainebleau, where he was joined and then succeeded by Marion Tournon Branly.

Finally, one must not forget his origins. He belonged to one of the great families of France. His uncle was Emilio Terry, a gifted creator with a powerful imagination, who encouraged him, while very young, to reflect upon architecture and to develop his knowledge and sensitivity; perhaps as a reaction to this early influence, he later devoted himself to a search for austerity and rigour. Apparently retiring but in reality remote and vulnerable, de la Tour d'Auvergne gave all of his strength to his work.

—Renée Diamant-Berger

del MORAL, Enrique.

Mexican. Born in Irapuato, Guanajuato, 20 January 1905. Educated at the Instituto Franco Ingles, Mexico City, 1913-22; Universidad Nacional Autonoma, Mexico City, at the National School of Architecture, under José Villagrán García, q.v., and Carlos Obregón Santacilia, 1923-27, Dip. Arch. 1928, and at the School of Philosophy and Letters, under José Gaos, 1943-46. Married Elisa Madrid in 1940. Worked in the studio of Carlos Obregón Santacilia, Mexico City, 1928-35. Since 1935, in private practice, Mexico City. Member, Federal School Construction Administration Committee, Guanajuato, 1944-46; Member, Medical Center Construction Committee, Mexico City, 1945-46; Architectural Coordinator and Director, Ciudad Universitaria, Mexico City, 1947-54; Executive Member, National Commission of Hospitals, 1954-58. Professor of Architectural Drawing, 1934, Adjunct Professor of Architectural Composition, 1934-36, Professor of Architectural Composition, 1938-50, Member of the Technical Council, 1940-44, and Director, 1944-49, National School of Architecture, Universidad Nacional Autonoma, Mexico City; Advisor to the School of Architecture, Universidad Iberoamericana, Mexico City, 1958-62. Secretary, 1967 and 1973, and Treasurer, 1972 and 1973, Academy of Arts, Mexico; President, Seminar on Mexican Culture, 1968 and 1969; President, Sociedad de Arquitectos de Mexico, 1972-73, 1974, and 1975, Recipient: Monterrey Prize, 1972; National Architecture Prize, 1978; Grand Prize, Sociedad de Arquitectos de Mexico, 1982. Member, Sociedad de Arquitectos de Mexico, Colegio de Arquitectos de Mexico, and Association of Mexican Art Critics; Founder-Member, Mexican Academy of Arts. Honorary Member, Sociedad Bolivarianna de Arquitectos, Caracas, Venezuela, Address (office): Calle General Francisco Ramirez 5, Mexico 18, D.F., Mexico.

Works:

1936 Ten workers' houses, Irapuato, Mexico (with M. Gutierrez Camarena)
1937 R. E. Calles House, Pirineos 519, Mexico City (with M. Gutierrez Camarena)
1938 Four rental houses, for R. E. Calles, Monte Altai 215, Mexico City (with M. Gutierrez Camerena)
 Palomino House reconstruction, Tabasco y Valladolid, Mexico (with M. Gutierrez Camerena)
 Banco Capitalizador de Ahorros Building conversion, Calle de las Cruces, Mexico City (with M. Gutierrez Camarena)
1939 Juan Gallardo Moreno House, Paseo de la Reforma 1115, Mexico City (with M. Gutierrez Camarena)
 J. Gama Apartment Building, Abraham Gonzalez 123, Mexico City (with M. Gutierrez Camarena)
 Andre Guieu House, Cuernavaca, Mexico
 Saenz House, Paseo de la Reforma 414, Mexico City
1940 Palomino Apartment Building, Calle del Panuco, Mexico City
 General P.E. Calles Apartment Building, Plaza Meclhor, Ocampo 64, Mexico City
1940/
 41 J. Gama Apartment Building, Zacatecas y Cordova, Mexico
 Three rental houses, for Gallardo Moreno, Cuernavaca, Mexico
1941 Four rental houses, Sierra Nevada 315, Mexico City
1941/
 42 Apartment/Office Building, for J. Gama, Independencia 67, Mexico City
1942 Seven rental houses, Monte Altai 215, Mexico City
 R.E. Calles Apartment Building, Plaza Melechor, Ocampo 56, Mexico City
 L. Avalos House, Playo de Rivera 240, Mexico City
1942/
 43 C. Palomino Apartment Building, Tigris, Mexico
 Palomino House alterations, Tabasco y Valladolid, Mexico

1943 Carlos Tejeda House, Aida y Cedros, Mexico City
 V. Gama House, Tlacopac, San Angel, Mexico
1943/
 46 General Hospital, San Luis Potosi, Mexico
1944 Alteration of two houses for J. Gama, General Farias 41, Mexico City
 José Iturbi House, Acapulco
 Fregoso House, Avenida Pirineos, Mexico City
 Zumpano Apartment Building, Sinaloa 75, Mexico City
1944/
 46 Fifteen schools, Jefe de Zona, Guanajuanto, Mexico
1945 R. E. Calles House, Cajema, Mexico
 Flavio Borquez House, Cajeme, Mexico
1945/
 46 J. and V. Gama Apartment Hotel, Farias 39, Mexico City
 Nursery School, Colonia Buenos Aires, Mexico City
1946 José Iturbi House, San Angel, Mexico City
1947/
 54 Master plan for Ciudad Universitaria (University City), Mexico City (with Mario Pani)
1948/
 49 del Moral House, Francisco Ramirez 5, Mexico City
1950 Coghlan House, Puebla, Mexico
 Office building, Avenida 5 de Mayo, Mexico City (with José Villagrán García)
 Alterations to four shops, Avenida 5 de Mayo and Condesa, Mexico City (with José Villagrán Garcia)
 Hydraulic Resources Secretariat Building, Paseo de la Reforma-Artes, Mexico City (with Mario Pani)
 Sports Fields, Ciudad Universiataria (University City), Mexico City (with Mario Pani)
 Men's Bathing and Changing Rooms, Ciudad Universitaria (University City), Mexico City (with Mario Pani)
 Five houses, Costera M. Aleman 36-44, Acapulco, Mexico (with Mario Pani)
 Apartment building, Hamburgo 5, Mexico City (with Mario Pani)
1951 Sierra de Fernandez House, Tennyson 117, Mexico City (with Mario Pani)
 Flores Zavala House, Calle de Andre Dumas, Mexico City (with Mario Pani)
 Raya Manrique Rental Bungalows, Acapulco (with Mario Pani)
1951/
 52 Miguel Arias House, Acapulco (with Mario Pani)
 Hotel Pozo del Rey, Acapulco (with Mario Pani)
 Hotel Posada de los 7 Mares, Acapulco (with Mario Pani)
 Hotel Villas Monte Mar, Pinzona 126, Acapulco (with Mario Pani)
 Mexico Golf Club Building, Tlalpan, Mexico City (with Mario Pani)
1951/
 53 Reaseguros Alianza Building, Insurgentes and Hamburgo Streets, Mexico City
 Arturo Pani House, Mexico City (with Mario Pani)
1952 Club de Pesca, Puente Hotel, Acapulco (with Mario Pani)
 Airport Building, Laguna Tres Palos, Acapulco (with Mario Pani)
 A.L. de Rabell House, Acapulco (with Mario Pani)
1952/
 53 Gallardo Moreno House, Mexico City
 Gallardo Moreno Rental House, Caucaso, Mexico
1953 Bullfight Ring, Acapulco (with Mario Pani)
 Luis R. Montes House, Acapulco (with Mario Pani)

Enrique del Moral: La Merced Market Hall, Mexico City, 1957.

1954/
55 Bernardo Quintana House, Pedregal San Angel, Mexico City
   R. de la Roziere House, Colonel Flores Magon, Mexico City
   Kaye House, Pedregal San Angel, Mexico City
1955/
58 Federal Medical Center Emergency Hospital, Central Laundry Building, and Laboratory Building, Mexico City
1956 Children's Hospital, Villahermkosa, Tabasco, Mexico
1956/
57 La Merced Market Hall, Mexico City
1958 Chemical Industry Building, Atenas y Versalles, Mexico City
1958/
60 Hirsch House, Lipodromo Edo, Mexico City
1959/
60 Attorney General's Office Building, Mexico City
1960/
61 Secondary school, Postal, Mexico City
1961/
62 Federal Penal Court Building, Mexico City
1962 House renovation, Jonacatepec, Mexico
1962/
63 Federal Treasury Building, Mexico City Sears Roebuck Department Store, Mexico City

1964 Federal Employees Social and Security Institute Nurses' School and Medical Investigation Center, Mexico City
   Federal Employees Social and Security Institute Hospital and Clinic, Monterrey, Mexico
1964/
65 Federal Employees Social and Security Institute Hospital and Clinic, Tampico, Mexico
1966/
67 Gildred Fountain Geriatric Hospital, Lindavista, Mexico City
1966/
68 Mexican Social Security Institute Hospital and Clinic, Ciudad Obregon, Sonora, Mexico
1967 Mexican Social Security Institute Hospital and Clinic, Cuautla, Mexico
1967/
68 Subways stations, Tlalpan, Mexico City
1968 Mexican Social Security Institute Medical Center, Olympic Village, Mexico City
1969 Federico Sanchez, Fogarty Picture Gallery and Studio, Nepantla, Morelos, Mexico
1969/
74 Mexican Social Security Institute Complex (Gynaecological Clinic, Branch Office Building, Laundry Building, and Hospital and Clinic), Monterrey, Mexico

1972 Mexican Social Security Institute Hospital and Clinic, Nogales, Sonora, Mexico
1973/
74 Mexican Social Security Institute Psychiatric Hospital, Mexico City
1975/
77 Bernardo Quintana Apartment Building Acapulco
1979 Constitution Plaza, Mexico City (competition project; with Mario Schejtnan)

Publications:

By del MORAL: books—*The Style—The Plastic Integration,* Mexico City 1966; *Protection and Conservation of Cities and Monumental Urban Units,* Mexico City 1977; *Man and Architecture: Essays and Testimonies,* with an introduction by Alberto Gonzalez Pozo, Mexico City 1983.

On del MORAL: books—*Mexico's Modern Architecture* by I.E. Myers, New York 1952; *Modern Architecture in Mexico* by Max Cetto, Stuttgart and London 1961; *The Work of Enrique del Moral* by Salvador Pinocelly, Mexico City 1983; *Enrique del Moral; Chosen Work and Images* by Louise Noelle, Mexico City 1984; article—special issue of *Architecture and Society* (Mexico City), no. 25, 1983.

It is indispensable, if we are to talk about Style, to consider the two forces involved: first, the one that both confirms and defines it by determining the "general" tone of the epoch which is established by just a few countries; and second, the one that represents the "particular features" of other nations within the same period of time.

Considering the above in terms of architecture, there are in Mexico two positions that coexist; they are neither opposed one to the other nor contradictory, and they can be defined more or less clearly. One of them, "internationalism," is the position wherein forms are born as a product of the dominant ideas in the world architecture; this position involves pretending, although it is not completely possible, not to consider local features or ways of being. The formal expessions that derive from this posture are characterized by their lack of regional identity, their internationalism.

The other posture, the "regionalist"one, is also a response to dominant architecture ideologies, but as well it takes into account particular regional conditions of all kinds, integrally and with all the complexities involved; it is concerned, too, with cultural, psychological, physical, and economic factors, as well as others of an atavistic nature. Thatis, attention is paid to differences; the architect struggles towards the goal that his creations be not "transplanted," that they show clearly they belong to Mexico, being within our scope and circumstances.

Undoubtedly, communications nowadays create a link with other countries and make, available to us not only the ideas but also the products, systems, and methods of building of other countries. But it is also true that this modern world, which we did not invent, which has been "manufactured" and "supplied" to us by nations whose ideas are sometimes contrary to our ways of thinking, is—at least in part—difficult for us to understand and to swallow.

Those things that may distinguish us will be more outstanding in solutions to programs in which man appears as a differentiated being—for instance, in residences, either individual or collective. I think too that, on some occasions, it might happen that the expression of our particularity could reflect a lack of resplendent modernity due to the fact that Mexico is not a characteristic or outstanding country in terms of modernism.

—Enrique del Moral

During the late 1920s and through the 1930s, Enrique del Moral, along with Villagrán García and O'Gorman, played a leading role in a movement among Mexican architects to construct severely functional buildings—mostly pure white boxes that looked as if ornament were to be regarded as some sympton of mental poverty. Concurrently with this "anti-ornament" feeling there was a belief that the new architecture had a propagandistic social role to play and that somehow the work of the most talented Mexicans was not fulfilling that role. On the international scene, "integration of the arts" was fashionable currency, and many architects collaborated with painters such as Orozco, Siqueiros, and Rivera, whose murals filled the interior (and sometimes exterior) surfaces of their buildings with distinct accents of social protest. The movement, either through lack of energy andreal direction or the political climate, petered out in the early 1950s. The lessons gained from these experiences were not lost on del Moral, however, and traces of the search for a truly "national" Mexican architecture remain in his work today.

Consequently, we find in one of del Moral's best known works, the La Merced Market Hall complex in Mexico City, a rigorous practicality. Large prestressed concrete shells span the open-plan layouts of the twenty acres of main halls; the produce from the extensive agricultural regions around Mexico City flows freely through the bays where up to 140 trucks can be unloaded at a time; clean concrete walls and a high roof contribute to the cool airness of the building in the height of the summer. And, as in many public buildings throughout Mexico, the market is also a social centre, containing an auditorium, 300 public baths, and eight day nurseries that can cope with approximately 1500 children. Despite the complexity such a description suggests, the formalsimplicity and social awareness del Moral brought to La Merced's design and construction meant it was built in a record time of eight months.

An earlier work, the rural school at Casacuran, eschews the use of high technology in its construction but, nonetheless, is of a sophisticated standard in its amenities. Here, del Moral displays his concern for the social needs of the area, creating simple, open classrooms, each with its own kitchen, bathroom, and sleeping quarters, often necessary in ruralareas. Local materials are employed throughout, both as a practical and environmental consideration; peeled logs are used as columns supporting the shady patio roof overhang, native tiles cover the surface of the roof itself, local brick and stone for the walls—all blending with the existing village buildings. The school for 200 students, set a high standard even by today's criteria for rural amenities on a severely limited budget.

Nor does del Moral, for all his strict adherance to functional concerns, lose sight of the "aesthetics" of the environment for which he is building. In an apartment house in Mexico City, designed in 1952 in collaboration with Mario Pani, the somewhat stark character of the neighborhood is relieved by his skilful handling of everyday materials. The ground floor is shaded by a perforated screen of hollow cement brick, concrete has a hammered texture and is painted in earth colours, a discreet glass mosaic on the facade delineates each level of the building, and the basically simple structure is "off-set" from the street by a long low trough planted with native Mexican cacti and succulents.

Again, in a 1951 house in Polanco, Mexico City, del Moral made successful use of difficult terrain. The confined site is bounded by a retaining wall in warm buff-coloured stone, and the upper floors of the house, with their plain, deep terracotta walls and white trim, actually project beyond the retaining wall, whilst its spacious upper terrace looks inward over the private garden. Its pleasing combination of carefully chosen colours, volumes, and proportions prevent the somewhat "daring" structure from overwhelming the observer.

—Colin Naylor

DeMARS, Vernon Armand.
American. Born in San Francisco, California, 26 February 1908. Educated at the University of California, Berkeley, 1925-31, B. Arch. 1931. Served in the United States Navy, 1944-45, as Lieutenant Junior Grade and Navigator on the U.S.S. Yakona, later as Lieutenant and Naval Aide to the Governor of Puerto Rico. Married Betty Bates in 1940. Member, Monument Valley-Rainbow Bridge Expedition, Arizona, 1934; Architectural Draftsman, United States Resettlement Administration, 1936; District Architect, for the Western States, United States Farm Security Administration, 1937-43; Founder, with Burton Cairns, Joseph McCarthy, Garrett Eckbo, T. J. Kent Jr. and Francis Violich, of TELESIS (city and regional planning organization), San Francisco, 1939; Chief of the Housing Standards Section, Technical Division, National Housing Agency, Washington, D.C., 1943-44; Visiting Professor in Architecture, Massachusetts Institute of Technology, Cambridge, 1947-49; Partner, with Donald Reay, DeMars and Reay, Berkeley, California, 1950-65. Since 1965, Principal, with John Wells, DeMars and Wells, Berkeley, California. Lecturer in Architecture, 1951-52, Professor of Architecture, 1953-75, and Chairman of the Department of Architecture, 1959-62, University of California, Berkeley. Exhibitions: *TELESIS*, San Francisco Museum of Art, 1940; *Built in U.S.A. 1932-1944*, Museum of Modern Art, New York, 1944; *Homes for Tomorrow*, Museum of Modern Art, New York 1944; *10 Buildings in America's Future*, American Institute of Architects, Washington, D.C., 1957 (toured the U.S.S.R., 1958). Recipient: Parker Medal, with others, Boston, 1951; Regional Award of Merit, 1957, and Merit Award, 1963, American Institute of Architects; First Prize, Student Center Competition, University of California, Berkeley, 1957; First Prize, Capitol Towers Competition, Sacramento, California, 1958; Design Award, 1958, and First Design Award, 1959 and 1960, *Progressive Architecture;* Special Award, *Sunset Magazine,* 1959; First Prize, Golden Gateway Competition, San Francisco, 1959; First Prize, The Plaza Redevelopment Competition, Richmond, California, 1959; First Prize, Marin City Urban Renewal Competition, California, 1960; Award of Merit, AIA/*House and Home/Life,* 1960; First Honor Award, with others, Urban Renewal Administration, 1964; First Honor Award, Community Facilities Administration, 1964; California Governor's Design Award, 1966 (twice); Award of Merit, 1967, and First Honor Award, 1978, Northern California Chapter, American Institute of Architects; United States Department of Housing and Urban Development Award, 1968; American Society of Landscape Architects Award, 1971; San Francisco Planning and Urban Renewal Award, 1972; Association of American Universities Award, 1974; "The Berkeley Citation," University of California, 1975. Fellow, American Institute of Architects, 1964. Address: 240 The Uplands, Berkeley, California 94705, U.S.A.

Works:

1937/
43   Forty Farm Workers' Communities in the western United States, including the Farm Workers' Centre at Yuba City, California, Cooperative Farm and Workers' Housing at Chandler, Arizona, and the Woodville Farm Workers' Center near Porterville, California
1949   Bannockburn Cooperative Houses, Washington, D.C. (with Rhees Burket and Joseph Neufeld).
1950   Eastgate Apartments (for the Massachusetts Institute of Technology faculty), 100 Memorial Drive, Cambridge, Massachusetts (with Brown, Kennedy, Rapson and Koch)
1951   DeMars House, 240 The Uplands, Berkeley, California
1954   Easter Hill Village (public housing development), Richmond, California (with Donald Hardison)
1955   Cathedral Precinct, Cologne (competition project)
1956   Residence Halls, University of California, Berkeley (competition project)
1957   Sydney Opera House (competition project)
1958/
65   Marin City Redevelopment, near San Francisco
Capitol Towers (four-block apartment development), Sacramento, California (with Wurster, Bernardi and Emmons, and Edward Larrabee Barnes)
1959/
66   The Golden Gateway (high-density redevelopment project), San Francisco (with Wurster, Bernardi and Emmons)
1960/
69   Student Center: Sproul Plaza, Student Union, Dining Commons, Eshleman Hall (office

Vernon DeMars: Student Center, University of California, Berkeley, 1969.

building for student activities), and Zellerbach Hall (Auditorium, Concert Hall, and Playhouse), University of California, Berkeley (with Donald Hardison, Donald Reay, and John Wells)

1960/
73 Master plan for the Walnut Creek Civic Center, California

1961 Ocean Park (urban renewal: high-rise and terrace apartments), Santa Monica, California (competition project)

1962 Master Plan for Mililani New Town, Oahu, Hawaii (with Livingston and Blayney, and Lawrence Halprin)
Columbia Plaza, Washington, D.C. (with Keyes, Lethbridge and Condon)
Lawrence Hall of Science, University of California, Berkeley (competition project)

1963 Master plan for the redevelopment of the Historic Old Sacramento Waterfront, California (with Candeub, Fleissig and Associates)

1965 Wurster Hall (College of Environmental Design), University of California, Berkeley (with Joseph Esherick and Donald Olsen)
Wells Fargo Bank, El Cerrito, California
Master Plan for Hamilton New Town, near San Jose, California (with Livingston and Blayney, and Lawrence Halprin)

1966 Housing designs for Mililani New Town, Oahu, Hawaii

1968 701 Projects (urban design guide), Oakland, California (with Jack T. Sidener)
Urban design plan for the Historic Old

Sacramento Waterfront, California (with Robert D. Hill)
Library and Classroom Buildings, California College of Arts and Crafts, Oakland (with Donald Reay)

1969/
75 San Francisco Performing Arts Centre (preliminary planning and design)

1970 Library, Mount Angel Abbey, Oregon (with Alvar Aalto)

1971 Grattan Elementary School, San Francisco
Cutting and Fairmont Stations, in El Cerrito, California, for the San Francisco Bay Area Rapid Transit District

1973 Wheeler Hall Auditorium reconstruction, University of California, Berkeley

1974 Aster Park (moderate-income housing), Sunnyvale, California

1975 Student Union, California State University, Sacramento

Publications:

By DeMARS: articles—"Look Homeward, Housing" in *Architectural Record* (New York), April 1946; "Design Awards Seminar" in *Progressive Architecture* (New York), December 1958; "Urban Design and the Great Exhibitions" in *Daily Pacific Builder* (for the AIA Convention), San Diego 1967.

On DeMARS: books—*The New Architeture* by Alfred Roth, Zürich 1940; *The People's Architects,* edited by Harry Ransom, Chicago and London 1964; *Architects on Architecture,* edited by Paul Heyer, New York 1966, London 1967; articles— "Farm Security Administration" in *Architectural Forum* (New York) January 1941; "Farm Security Architecture" by Talbot Hamlin in *Pencil Points* (New York), November 1941; "War Housing Dormitories, Vallejo, California" in *Arts and Architecture* (Los Angeles), June 1943; "Eastgate Apartments" in *Architectural Record* (New York), February 1949; "Bostons Builds Balconies" in *Magazine of Building* (New York), May 1951; "Easter Hill Village" in *House and Home* (New York), July 1955; "Redevelopment of Marin City, California" in *Progressive Architeture* (New York), January 1960; "Golden Gateway Redevelopment" in *Arts and Architecture* (Los Angeles), November 1960; "Planned Chaos on the Piazza" by Allan Temko in *Architectural Forum* (New York), October 1961; "Neues Wohngebiet in Santa Monica, Kalifornien" in *Baumeister* (Munich), June 1962; "La Wurster Hall della Universitàdi California a Berkeley" in *Industrie italiano del cimento* (Rome), November 1970; "Center of Action" by Robert Montgomery in *Architectural Forum* (New York), reprinted in *Cities Fit to Live In,* edited by Walter McQuade, New York 1971; "Sproul Plaza and Sather Gate Mall, University of California at Berkeley" in *Architecture + Urbanism* (Tokyo), August 1973; "A Much-Praised Housing Project Becomes the West Coast's Pruitt-Igoe" in *AIA Journal* (Washington, D.C.), August 1976.

I have always approached my architecture as a *setting* for life's events and people's activities. As in theatre, "the play's the thing"—not the setting. This should not lower the architect's aspirations to provide as rewarding a total experience as possible—in usefulness, stability, and esthetic satisfaction—the Vetruvian components. But it does raise a danger signal against unheeding, often arrogant pursuit of novelty or of art for art's sake alone.

I have never held that mere honest problem-solving would automatically yield a soul-uplifting result, but I did expect that the basic tenets of Modern architecture, thoughtfully and sensitively pursued, would produce a more satisfactory total environment than now seems to be the case.

The strong, simple forms of the New Architecture in the hands of the pioneering masters had an exciting initial impact when set amid the typical complex tapestry of older street and cityscapes. Now, complete street scenes of Modern buildings, whether in New York, Rotterdam, or Berlin, are often uninteresting, bland, and monotonous. The man in the street has long held this to be so. The architect is beginning to agree with him.

The collective architecture of the city needs a richer complexity than the limited vocabulary of Modern architecture now seems to produce. The vernacular urban architecture of the nineteenth century, even in the hands of lesser talents than the masters of the time, added needed texture to the urban scene. A conscious search for its equivalent should be a prime concern for our time.

I have been fortunate in having had the experience of so many problems for which there were few, if any, satisfactory precedents. For the migratory farm workers' communities of the West, there were only pitiful, unsatisfactory examples to draw upon for guidance. This experience in the provision of modest dwellings for low-income families led to both my interest and opportunities in a wider range of housing problems in more normal communities. Easter Hill Village attempted to bring individuality and personal identification to each dwelling of a low-income housing development. The Golden Gateway pioneered a high-density, inner-city housing solution which fully accommodates the automobile in storage as well as movement. The Berkeley Student Center provided the rare opportunity to plan and to execute, over a period of years, a contemporary version of the medieval town square and its important buildings.

—Vernon DeMars

Working mainly as a designer of "contained streetscapes," Vernon DeMars denegrates the sterility of uniformity and Miesian formalism. As one of America's strongest advocates of the need for variety in modern design, he stresses in his work the "accidental" or semi-planned urban situation. His spaces, instilled with a sense of the familiar and a variety of forms, elevations, and materials, handsomely succeed in evoking an easily related to, human-scale environment.

From his experience as the Farm Security Association's district architect for the western states from 1937 to 1943, DeMars recognized the tendency of uniformity to lack of vitality. During this period, he suggested the creation of mixed neighborhoods in government projects, to include highrise apartments, townhouses, duplexes, and single-family dwellings. He has successfully carried out this concept in several of his designs including the Marin City redevelopment project, the Golden Gateway project, and the Santa Monica Ocean Park project. The last is indicative of his approach. Confronted with the need to provide as much outdoor recreation space as possible, DeMars designed seven highrise, tower apartments that rise from multi-level parking garages. The sloping exteriors of the garages are given over to townhouse-like, terraced apartments with flora-covered patios. This arrangement provided for a fifty-fifty ratio between high-and low-rise dwellings, which this community a desirable population

diversity, as well as providing large open recreational spaces.

The Student Center at the University of California, Berkeley, well demonstrates DeMars's "planned chaos" ideology. Perhaps his most successful and certainly his most controversial undertaking, the Student Center consists of four buildings placed on each side of a sunken central square with a plaza serving as a transition area for the remainder of the campus. The four buildings, the student union, the dining commons, the two thousand seat Zellerbach auditorium, and the eight-story office tower, Eshleman Hall, are individual entities with distinct styles, scales, and characters. No one structure can be considered an architectural masterpiece, but taken as a whole they compliment one another and contribute enormously to the patina of the square. Such a diversity exudes visual excitement and allows a vibrant tension to exist between the structures that in turn enhances the dynamics of the open space.

The buildings, which are in scale with their surroundings, do not obtrude on the spatial freedom of the square, the main attraction of the Student Center. The square's openness, coupled with the eclectic employment of such familiar elements as the fountain on the plaza, Maybeck-inspired trellises in the dining commons and as a cornice on the student union, kiosks that serve as bulletin boards, trees and street furniture, provides a casual, rather European, and extremely viable human space. With a mixture of modern and familiar forms, open and private spaces, multi-level pedestrian pathways, and a diversity of materials, the Student Center provides a pleasingly provocative campus streetscape.

By recognizing a community's need for diversity in building types, and by an intermixing of the traditional and modern, DeMars has taken a large step towards combating the critical assertions leveled against the sterility of much of modern architecture. He has developed a workable synthesis that incorporates traditional haphazard urban planning and design with modern architecture's preoccupation with rationality and order.

—Don J. Hibbard

DIAMOND, Abel Joseph.
Canadian. Born in Piet Retief, South Africa, 8 November 1932; emigrated to Canada, 1964: naturalized, 1965. Educated at the University of Cape Town, South Africa, 1951-56 (Thornton White Prize, 1952), B.Arch. (distinction) 1956; Oxford University, England, 1956-58, M.A. 1958; University of Pennsylvania, Philadelphia, 1961-62 (Marley Scholarship, 1961; Italian State Bursary, 1961; Graham Foundations Scholarship, 1962), M.Arch. 1962. Married Gillian Mary Huggins in 1959; children: Andrew and Alison. Assistant Professor, University of Pennsylvania, 1962-64; Associate Professor, University of Toronto, 1964-69; Professor, York, University, Toronto, 1969-73; part-time tutor, School of Architecture, University of Toronto, 1980-81; Adjunct Professor of Architecture, University of Texas at Arlington, 1980-81. In private practice, as A.J. Diamond Architect, Toronto, 1965-69; Partner, with Barton Myers, *q.v.,* Diamond and Myers, Toronto, 1969-74; Principal, A.J. Diamond Associates, and President, A.J. Diamond Planner Ltd., Toronto, 1975-83. Since 1983, Senior Partner, A.J. Diamond and Partners, and A.J. Diamond Planners Ltd., Toronto (partners: Don Schmitt, Paul Syme; and Kevin Garland), branch office in Ottawa. Member, Registration Board, Ontario Association of Architects, 1974-78; Chairman of the Visiting Committee, Ontario Schools of Architecture, 1977-78. Exhibition: *This City Now;* Art Gallery of Ontario, Toronto, 1969. Recipient: Canada Council Grant, 1967. Fellow, Royal Architectural Institute of Canada; Associate, Royal Institute of British Architects. Address: A.J. Diamond and Partners, Architect and Planners, 2 Berkeley Street, Toronto, Ontario M5A 2W3, Canada.

Works:

1967 Eedee Chair for the Canadian Federal Government (project)
1969 York Square (restaurant/shops complex), Yorkville, Toronto (with Barton Myers)
Housing/Union Building, University of Alberta, Edmonton (with Barton Myers)
Alcan Executive Headquarters interiors, Toronto (with Barton Myers)
Long range development plan for the University of Alberta, Edmonton (with Barton Myers)
Vidal Sassoon Salon interiors, Toronto (with Barton Myers)
1970 Roy Foss Motors Building, Toronto
Ontario Medical Association Headquarters, Toronto (with Barton Myers)
1971 Dofasco/Ibis Steel Manufacturers Housing, Hamilton, Ontario
Warehouse to office conversion, 322 King Street West, Toronto
1973 Union Facilities, University of Maryland, Baltimore (project; with Barton Myers)
1974 Pickering Airport Impact Study, Toronto
Rideau Street Mall, Ottawa, Ontario
Union Station Feasibility Study, Toronto
1975 Innis College, University of Toronto
1976 Student housing, Queen's University, Kingston, Ontario (partly complete)
Citadel Theatre, Edmonton, Alberta (with Barton Myers and R.L. Wilkin)
Dundas/Sherbourne Housing, Toronto (with Barton Myers)
1977 Beverley Place: Hydro Low-Rise, High-Density Housing Block, Toronto
Gerrard Library, Toronto
Le Breton Flats, Ottawa (project)
Downtown revitalization plans for St. Mary's, Barrie, Perth, Dundas, and Prescott, Ontario
1978 Rail relocation plan for Sudbury, Ontario
Victoria Park Infill Housing, London, Ontario
St. Michael's Lands Multiple Housing, Forest Hill, Toronto
Alcan Aluminium Corporation Executive Offices, Cleveland, Ohio
1979 Public Library and Art Gallery renovation, Woodstock, Ontario
Church Street School, Aurora, Ontario
University of Alberta Long-range Plan, Edmonton
1980 Stage Training Facility, National Ballet School, Toronto
Burns Building renovation, Calgary, Alberta
Metropolitan Toronto Central YMCA
Urban Study, Calgary, Alberta
Town Centre Development, Malvern, Ontario
1981 St. Lawrence Housing Study, Toronto
Solar Zoning Study
St. Michaels's Lands Housing, Phase 2, Forest Hill, Toronto
1984 Natural Resource Center, University of Toronto
Japan Restaurant Centre, Toronto
Arcadia cooperative Housing, Toronto
CFCSC Curtis Hall extension, Toronto

Publications:

By DIAMOND: articles—"Eye Witness—Cranbrook" in *AIA Journal* (Washington, D.C.), December 1962; "Critique of the UBC Student

A. J. Diamond: Metropolitan Central YMCA Building, Toronto, 1984.

Centre" in *Royal Architectural Institute of Canada Journal* (Toronto), October 1964; "Expo" in *AIA Journal* (Washington, D.C.), February 1967; "Shopping Centres—New Urban Nucleii" in *Toronto Daily Star*, 3 February 1968; "There Are Solutions to the Housing Crisis" in *Toronto Daily Star*, 2 March 1968; "Residential Density and Housing Form" in *Journal of Architectural Education* (Washington, D.C.), February 1976; "Big City Trends Eroding the Quality of Life in Small Centres" in the *Globe and Mail* (Toronto), 29 July 1976; "Taking Risks out of Design" in the *Globe and Mail* (Toronto), 28 December 1977; "On Sleeping with an Elephant" in *Process Architecture* (Tokyo/ Pittsburgh), March 1978.

On DIAMOND: book—*Building with Words: Canadian Architects on Architecture*, with introduc- tion by W. Bernstein and R.Cawker, Toronto 1981; articles—"The Diamond Residence" in *Canadian Homes* (Toronto), August 1968; "Mobile Homes" in *Canadian Homes* (Toronto), April 1969; "York Square" in *Canadian Architect* (Toronto), June 1969; "Long Range Development Plan, University of Alberta" in *Canadian Architect* (Toronto), July/August 1969; "Long Range Plan—Alberta" in *Architecture Canada* (Toronto), July/August 1969; "York Square" in *Progressive Architecture* (New York), September 1969; "York Square" in *Byggen- kunst* (Oslo), September 1969; "York Square" in *Canadian Architect* (Toronto) April 1970; "York Square and Student Union House, Alberta" in *Architecture Canada* (Toronto), April 1970; York Square" in *Abitare* (Milan), October 1970; "Alcan Interiors" in *Canadian Architect* (Toronto), March 1971; "Ontario Medical Association" in *Canadian Architect* (Toronto), June 1971; "Vidal Sassoon

Salon" in *Architectural Record* (New York), August 1971; "Ontario Medical Association" in *Archi- tectural Record* (New York), September 1971; "York Square" in *Architecture + Urbanism* (Tokyo), November 1971; "Alcan Interiors" in *Architectural Record* (New York), March 1972; "Work of Diamond and Myers" in *Architecture + Urbanism* (Tokyo), May 1972; "Dofasco Steel Housing" in *Chatelaine* (Toronto), May 1972; "The Campus as a Lesson in Urban Form—Students' Union Housing" in *Progressive Architecture* (New York), September 1972; "York Square in Toronto" in *Baumeister* (Munich), October 1972; "Old Is New in Office Space" in *Executive* (Toronto), November 1972; "The Low Rise Alternative Urban Recycling" in *Time* (New York), 16 April 1973; "To Save a Fabric" in *Progressive Architecture* (New York), May 1973; "Student Street" in *Progressive Architecture* (New York), February 1974; "La Cantinetta Restaurant" in *Interiors* (New York), June 1974; "Students' Union Housing, University of Alberta" in *Architec- ture + Urbanism* (Tokyo), December 1974; "Diamond amd Myers: The Form of Reform" in *City Magazine* (Toronto), August 1975; "999 Queen Street West" in *City Magazine* (Toronto), Summer 1976; "The Democratization of Canadian Architec- ture" in *Library of Canadian Architecture*, Halifax, Nova Scotia 1978; "A Hybrid Rival to High-Rise Has Character" in the *Globe and Mail* (Toronto), 15 March 1978; "Hydro Block" in *Toronto Star*, 18 March 1978; "In Downtown Toronto" in *Domus* (Milan), September 1979; "Gerrard Branch Library, Toronto" in *Baumeister* (Munich), October 1979; "Hydro Block in Toronto" in *Baumeister* (Munich), May 1980; "Alcan Corporate Headquarters, Montreal" in *Canadian Architect* (Toronto), Sep- tember 1980; "Hydro Block" in *Architecture + Urbanism* (Tokyo), November 1980; "Graceful Stylization" in *Progressive Architecture* (New York), December 1980; "Innis College, University of Toronto" in *Baumeister* (Munich), August 1981; "1982 Awards of Excellence" in *Canadian Architect* (Toronto), December 1982; "Architecture in Canada," special issue of *Bauwelt* (Berlin), 3 December 1982; "Dundas Sherbourne Infill Hous- ing, Toronto in *Industria delle costruzioni* (Rome), no. 124, 1982; "Alcan Aluminium Office, Montreal" in *Industria delle costruzioni* (Rome), January 1983; "From Mies to Metaphors" in *Canadian Architect* (Toronto), May 1983; "Cullinan-Diamond-Rogers" in *Architects' Journal* (London), 25 July 1984.

There are several characteristics to my work. The first is the range of scales of projects, from urban planning (for example, the towns of Sudbury, Barrie, Dundas, Perth, and Ottawa, Ontario) to building interior (executive offices and residential projects).

The second is the conviction that existing con- ditions must be seen as a resource to be utilized in new development. Examples of this aspect of my work are infill housing, re-using of existing buildings for new purposes, and using alternatives to highrise in existing neighbourhoods.

The third characteristic is a concern for the social content and impact of architecture—that architec- ture is not merely a set of formal physical consider- ations: the *user's* needs and satisfactions are paramount.

Finally, I am concerned with scale and historical precedent.

—A.J. Diamond

Doubtless what sticks in the public mind as most exemplary of A.J. Diamond's work was his de- monstration, by turning an architectural model on its end, that high-density lowrise was no more than highrise on a human scale. At Beverley Place, the Hydro Site project in Toronto, he went on to put into action just this principle, thereby saving some fine old houses and providing a liveable high-density project that interestingly combines new and old.

Diamond brings to his architecture his career as a designer and his care for intimate space. In 1969 he first demonstrated this (with Barton Myers) in the creation of York Square, a complex of shops and restaurants around a tree-shaded square behind a set of old houses. That the tree was preserved and is central to the attractiveness of the square was a pleasant feature uncharacteristic of much other "development" in Toronto at that time. More recently, at Innis College, he has similarly preserved old houses in conjunction with a new building.In spite of economies in the project and the use of an unattractive brick, the complex as a whole works better than many more expensive and attractive academic buildings. The use of exposed ductwork in this complex and in Diamond's conversion of 322 King Street West, a bow to trendy functionalism, is less successful. In the latter offices, however, there is a skilful use of exposed brick and lightwells that gives what was an unprepossessing building a surprising grace. This is especially obvious in La Cantinetta, the restaurant on the ground floor of the building, where the Diamond-Myers Partnership succeeded in combining intimacy with an airy lightness.

Diamond's participation (with Barton Myers) in the long-range development plan for the University of Alberta, as well as his own more recent Le Breton Flats in Ottawa, show his capacity for large-scale planning. And this is borne out too in his numerous ambitious plans for the renovation of a number of small urban centres in Ontario. Indeed, when his career as a whole comes to be assessed, it seems likely that his concern for "urban recycling" by conversion and adaptation will be seen as his major achievement.

—D.D.C. Chambers

DIBA, Kamran Tabatabai.

Iranian. Born in Teheran, 5 March 1937. Educated at Alborz, Teheran, 1947-55; studied architecture, 1958-64, and sociology, 1964-65, Howard University, Washington, D.C. In private practice, since 1966: Founder-President and Partner, with Ahmad Amir-Rezvani, Farzin Sadeghi, Ahmad Kashanijo, and Parviz Rezagholizadeh, DAZ Consulting Architects and Engineers, Teheran, 1969-80. Since 1980, Architect in joint venture with Plaseied and Associates, Vienna, Virginia. Director, Museum of Contemporary Art, Teheran, 1976-78. Exhibitions: La Modernité—un projet inachévé, at the Festival d'Automne, Paris, 1982; Biennale, Venice, 1982. Addresses: 78 rue des Archives, 75003 Paris, France; Plaseied and Associates, 380 Maple Avenue West, Suite L-3, Vienna, Virginia 22180, U.S.A.

Works:

1966/
69 Garden of Yousef-abad Community Centre, Teheran (with Boduhi and T. Tabatabai)
    Children's Village, Shahsavar, Caspian Coast, Iran (with Baduhi and P. Varjavand)

1967/
68 Javadiyeh Playground, Teheran (with P. Varjavand)

1967/
76 Museum of Contemporary Art, Teheran (with N. Ardalan and A. J. Major)

1968 Army Museum, Teheran (project; with P. Jalayer)
    Shrine of Shah Cheragh, Shiraz, Iran (with P. Jalayer and A. Shaterian)

1968/
71 Children's Day Care Centre prototypes, Teheran (with P. Gupta)

Jondi-Shapour University Master Plan, Ahwaz, Iran (with N. Beyzavi)

1969/
72 Student Union Building, Jondi-Shapour University, Ahwaz, Iran (with N. Beyzavi)
    Faculty Housing phase I, Jondi-Shapour University, Ahwaz, Iran (with N. Beyzavi)

1969/
73 University Mosque, Jondi-Shapour University, Ahwaz, Iran (with A. Frouhi)
    Garden of Delgosha, Shiraz, Iran (with P. Gupta)

1970/
72 Shahbanou Farah Dam Monument, Sefid Rood, Iran (with P. Gupta)

1970/
73 Women's Social Centre prototypes, Teheran (project; with P. Gupta)

1970/
78 Garden of Niavaran Cultural Centre, Teheran (with A. Major and P. Gupta)

1970/
79 Empress Farah's Secretariat Building, Garden of Niavaran, Teheran (with A. Major and P. Gupta)

1972 Summer Resort, Mahmoud-abad, Caspian Coast, Iran (with F. Esfandiari and F. Hessamian)

1972/
76 Gymnasium Building, Jondi-Shapour University, Ahwaz, Iran (with A. Shaterian and A. Frouhi)
    Administration Building, Jondi-Shapour University, Ahwaz, Iran (with N. Beyzavi and A. Shaterian)

1973 Astara Resort, Caspian Coast, Iran (project; with Fathali Behnam)
    Government and Civic Centre, Isfahan, Iran (project; with P. Rezagholizadeh and R. Amirian)

1973/
76 Valiahd High School extensions, Teheran (with P. Gupta)

1974 Maidan-e-Shahr City Square Development, Shushtar New Town, Iran (with C. A. Kondylis and S. Sen)
    Institute for Intellectual Development Offices, Teheran (with R. Amirian and P. Pezeshki)

1974/
77 Faculty Housing phase II, Jondi-Shapour University, Ahwaz, Iran (with N. Beyzavi, A. Shaterian and S. Maghen)

1974/
78 Neighborhood Housing phase I, Shushtar New Town, Iran (with C. P. Saberwal)
    Neighborhood Mosque, Shushtar New Town, Iran
    Neighborhood Plaza, Shushtar New Town, Iran
    Public Buildings, Shushtar New Town, Iran
    Maidan-e-Shahr Town Square, Shushtar New Town, Iran
    Housing phase III, Shushtar New Town, Iran

1975 Intercontinental Hotel, Isfahan, Iran (project; with C. A. Kondylis and T. Berezowski)
    School of Human Sciences, Isfahan University, Iran (with R. Amirian and S. Sen)
    Bazaar of Farahzad, Teheran (with R. Amirian and S. Sen)

1976 Schools, Shushtar New Town, Iran (with Fathali Behnam)

1976/
79 Cheshmeh Housing, Teheran (with S. Maghen)

1977 Public Park, Tabriz, Iran (project; with S. Maghen and S. H. Bagley)
    Lavizan Housing, Teheran (project; with C. A. Kondylis)
    Friday Mosque, Shushtar New Town, Iran (project; with M. T. Behrouzian)
    Elahiyeh Garden Apartments, Teheran (project; with C. A. Kondylis and T. Berezowski)

1977/
78 Earth Sculpture, Garden of Niavaran, Teheran

1978 Sculpture Plaza, Farha Park, Teheran (project; with T. Berezowski)
    Zur-khaneh Exercise Building, Jondi-Shapour University, Ahwaz, Iran (project; with P. Pezeshki)

1981/
85 Monticello of Tysons townhouse cluster, Vienna, Virginia (with Plaseied and Associates)

1984 Valewood Church of the Nazarene, Fairfax, Virginia (project; with Plaseied and Associates)

1985 Guaranty Bank and Trust Building, Arlington, Virginia (project; with Plaseied and Associates)
    Twenty Luxury Houses, Great Falls, Virginia (project; with Plaseied and Associates)

Publications:

By DIBA: book—Kamran Diba: Buildings and Projects, with preface by Max Bill, Stuttgart 1981.

On DIBA: books—La Modernité—un projet inachévé, exhibition catalogue by J. P. Chimot, K. Frampton, B. Lubetkin and others, Paris 1982; Architettura nei paesi Islamici, exhibition catalogue, Venice 1982; articles—"Resort at Mahmoodabad" in Art and Architecture (Teheran), April/July 1976; "Iran—University" in Architectural Review (London), July 1977; "Museum of Contemporary Art, Teheran" in L'Architecture d'Aujourd'hui (Paris), February 1978; "Contemporary Art Museum in Iran" by Pierre Restany in Domus (Milan), February 1978; "Cultural Hybrid—Teheran Museum of Contemporary Art" in Progressive Architecture (New York), May 1978; "The New Town of Shushtar", and "Jondi Shapur University" in L'Architecture d'Aujourd'hui (Paris), October 1979; "Traditional Weave—Housing in Shushtar, Iran" by J. M. Dixon in Progressive Architecture (New York), October 1979; "Shushtar New Town" in Domus (Milan), February 1981; "Shushtar New Town—A Company Town in Persia" in Lotus (Venice), no. 36, 1982; "Ville Nouvelle de Shushtar, Iran" in Techniques et Architecture (Paris), December 1982/January 1983; "Gardens and Landscapes: Smile of Paradise" by Brian Brace Taylor in Mimar (Singapore), April/June 1983.

My main concern in architecture has its roots in sociology. I always try to take into account the nature of human activity and interaction in architecture and urban environment. This objective is achieved by a conscious effort of organizing, programming and planning prior to, or simultaneously with, the design process.

The result is setting the stage for influencing human movement, interaction and behaviour. Long ago I discovered that buildings have personality and character. They could be serious and patronizing or friendly and humble. Then I tried to have an impact on the personality of my own buildings which would naturally depend on the pattern of human activity and the physical character of the environment. I am also influenced and inspired by vernacular architecture and try to fit and maintain a relationship to the existing architecture or cityscape.

—Kamran Diba

Iranian architect Kamran Diba is principally noted for his work in the preservation of traditional Persian culture—a culture threatened until recent years by rapid Western-style industrialization and technology. As much a sociologist as an architect, Diba has been concerned with the integration of vernacular architecture and the demands of a modern urban society. Inspired by traditional urban structures, such as the Italian piazza, he perceived that their historical dimension accented architecture of different eras through underlying social and artistic attitudes. To Diba, they symbolised a continuity, linking our past to a functional present. In the introduction to a recent book on his work in Iran, Diba wrote: "My interest in architecture has always transcended its physical dimensions. One of my obsessions was to influence and intensify human interaction and activity . . . I believe that the mode of human interaction which creates particular patterns of activity within an architectural space is of utmost importance (and) I deliberately attempt to build an environment which multiplies and enhances this quality of interaction." Diba understands that the architect, conscious of these patterns of activity and interaction, behaves much like a theatre director, setting that stage and motivating certain human situations. This conviction is clearly illustrated by the urban renewal projects begun in Iran in 1966.

The new town of Shushtar, planned to accommodate 30,000 people in a satellite of an ancient Persian city, owes its successful vernacular style to Diba's application of traditional construction patterns—despite administrative efforts toward current Western-style town planning. The quality of the city depends on the preservation of harmony between the problem-solving process and the aesthetic vision evolved from functional and cultural demands. Prominent features of this ambitious development include building types derived from traditional models, but with a contemporary urban logic; multi-faceted pedestrian boulevards embellished with gardens, bazaars, and seating areas to encourage community life; numerous cul-de-sacs to maintain an atmosphere of privacy and identity. Throughout, the housing units rejected the Western pattern of assigned rooms, and favoured fewer but larger, adaptable spaces to accommodate different daily functions.

In the new campus of Jondi-Shapour University (1968-78), located near the Karoun River on barren, flat land next to a lush botanical garden, Diba's contributions include stadium, student union, faculty housing, mosque, gymnasium, administration and Zur-khaneh exercise buildings. Particularly striking is the University's mosque, built of wheat-coloured brick and exploiting the potential of traditional Persian masonry. Here, Diba created a structure reminiscent of a monolithic environment, enhanced by a vertical turquoise-glazed minaret and traditional mosaic tiles. Nevertheless, its minimal use of colour, coupled with gently curved corners to avoid sharp shadows created by the intense sunlight, conveys a feeling of softness, intimacy and humility.

Unexpectedly resuscitated from plans shelved ten years earlier, the 1977 Teheran Museum of Art houses a national and international collection of post-Impressionist, Modernist and contemporary paintings and sculptures, with photographs, prints and architectural drawings. A semi-underground construction built into an artificial turfed hill which ends in a sculpture garden, it is among the most fascinating and functional museum buildings of recent decades. Diba's complex boasts a playful quality in undulating and volumetric vernacular roofscapes open to pedestrian use, and owes its uniqueness to a cosmopolitan architect's willingness to learn from and adapt a local past.

—Carolyn Cole

DIESTE, Eladio.

Uruguayan. Born in Artigas, 1 December 1917. Educated at the Faculty of Engineering of the Universidad de la Republica, Montevideo, Dip.Ing. 1943. Married Elizabeth Friedheim Utke in 1944;

children: Juan, Esteban, Eduardo, Antonio, Marta, Teresa, Bernardo, Pedro, Tomás, Inés, and Isabel. Engineer, Ministry of Public Works, Montevideo, 1943-45; Engineer, Represa Rincon del Bonete, Montevideo, 1945-46; Chief Engineer, Head Architectural Technical Office, Ministry of Public Works, Montevideo, 1946-48; Chief Engineer, Viermond S.A., Montevideo, 1948-55. Since 1955, Founder and Chief Engineer, with Eugenio R. Montañez, Dieste and Montañez, Montevideo. Consultant Engineer for the Salto Grande and Palmer Dams, Uruguay, since 1973. Professor of Engineering, Universidad de la Republica, Montevideo, 1943-73. Visiting Professor and Lecturer, University of Buenos Aires, since 1959. Member, Academia Nacional de Ingenieria del Uruguay, 1966. Address (office): Carlos Roxlo 1606, Montevideo, Uruguay.

Works:

1957 Ceramic Shell Garage, for the Insurance Bank, Avenida Rondeau, Montevideo (with Eugenio R. Montañez)
1958 TEM S.A. Industrial Plant, Cno. Carrasco 5975, Montevideo (with Eugenio R. Montañez)
   Church, Atlántida Station, Canelones, Uruguay
1968 CALNU Industrial Plant, Bella Union, Artigas, Uruguay (with Eugenio R. Montañez)
1969 St. Peter's Church, Durazno, Uruguay (with A. Casto and A. Romero)
1971 Caputto Orange Packing Plant, Salto, Uruguay (with Eugenio R. Montañez)
   Central Market, Porto Alegre, Brazil (with C. M. Fayet and C. Araujo)
1972 Brick Shell Bus Station, Salto, Uruguay
   Market Building, Maceió, Brazil
1975 Agro-Industrial Complex, Vergara, Treinta y Tres, Uruguay
1977 Massaro S.A. Industrial Plant, Joanico, Canelones, Uruguay
   Agro-Industrial Complex, Young, Rio Negro, Uruguay
1978 Port of Montevideo Industrial Building
   Refrescos del Norte S.A. (Coca-Cola Export) Industrial Plant, Salto, Uruguay (with E. Dieste)

Eladio Dieste: Brick shell bus station, Salto, Uruguay, 1972.

Industrial building for construction company, Avenida Italia 3656, Montevideo
1980/
   82 Central Woolen Warehouse, Uruguay
1983/
   84 Shopping center, Montevideo

Publications:

By DIESTE: monographs—*Problems of the Foundations of Turbo-Alternators*, Montevideo 1969; *Buckling of Double Curvature Shells*, Montevideo 1970; *The Action of Wind over Long-Span Industrial Buildings*, Montevideo 1972; *Reinforced Ceramic Hollow Towers*, Montevideo 1972; articles— "Atlántida Church" in *Informes de la construccion* (Madrid), no. 127, 1961; "Reinforced Ceramic Structures" in *Ingenieria* (Montevideo), nos. 657/660, 1963; "Double Curvature Shells of Reinforced Ceramic" in *Proceedings of the World Conference on Shell Structures*, Washington, D.C. 1964; "About Reinforced Brick Constructions," "Technique and Underdevelopment," and "St. Peter's Church" in *Summa* (Buenos Aires), no. 70, 1973; "About Reinforced Brick Construction" in *Summa* (Buenos Aires), no. 85, 1975.

On DIESTE: books—*Eladio Dieste* by Juan P. Bonta, Buenos Aires 1963; *New Directions in Latin American Architecture* by Francisco Bullrich, New York 1969; *The Changing Shape of Latin American Architecture* by D. Bayon and P. Gasparini, Chichester, Sussex 1979; articles—"Eglise paroissiale d'Atlántida" in *L'Architecture d'aujourd'hui* (Paris), June 1961; "Atlántida Paris Church" in *Architectural Review* (London), September 1961; "Brick Shell Construction" in *Progressive Architecture* (New York), April 1962; "Architecture in Uruguay" in *Summa* (Buenos Aires), no. 27, 1970; Eladio Dieste—Master of Brick," special issue of *Summarios* (Buenos Aires), July 1980; "Building in the Present, Respectful of the Past: The Work of Eladio Dieste" in *Projecto* (Sáo Paulo), April 1982.

I was trained as a civil engineer. I graduated in 1943, and my initial work was in the areas of pilings, foundations, bridges, construction machinery, and

the design of big structures. In 1948 I made my first reinforced ceramic shells.

My purpose has been to create rational and economical structures, and I have, gradually, refined the shapes that I have created. Both aims—technical rationality and aesthetic worth—are, in fact, different aspects of the same attitude. I am pleased that architects are now very interested in our work.

I believe that the techniques that we have developed provide the beginnings of a new kind of construction, one that really works. Despite current opinions about reinforced ceramics (based on the fact that both the material cost and the labor cost are low), I do not believe that the techniques need be restricted to underdeveloped countries.

—Eladio Dieste

For thousands of years, man used such materials as brick, stone, or wood for construction and created buildings based on processes of trail and error. History has taught us that the architecture of the past was the result of the very experience of building. But in the last two centuries this situation has changed. New structural materials—iron, concrete—have created new technologies, and the science of engineering has been so refined as to allow us to project construction and to forecast its behaviour. Roman or Gothic architecture were the result of techniques learned in the actual process of construction, without pre-planning. In our century, very few architects work in that way; in a highly technical age we can hardly conceive of an architecture that does not involve elaborate prior controls. The advantages of the new materials and technologies are obvious; architecture has been rationalized, industrialized, internationalized. But there are disadvantages too; in the process, architects have been drawn away from a direct experience and intimate contact with construction, and this withdrawal has, in turn, brought about an impoverishment of forms, a lessening in creativity. Eladio Dieste is an exception to these generalizations. He attempts to rescue the experience of artisan labor; he believes in the value of actual involvement in the building process and in the environment in which buildings are created. Dieste does not subscribe to the tenets of international, rational, industrialized architecture: he believes that most of such architecture is inhuman. His country, Uruguay, is not in a period of industrialization, so Dieste has been able to pursue his goals of rescuing the traditional values of intimate contact with material and of "living with" construction as a creative process. He uses the same material used by the workmen of Mesopotamia thousands of years ago—brick, the fundamental element in his work.

A quarter of a century ago, Dieste, in association with Eugenio Montañez, began to construct vaults made of brick (though, then, he strengthened his structures with an iron frame able to withstand traction stresses), and from that time, with the vaults, he has created a constructive language, which, given his formal sensibility, has been inevitably transformed into an architectural language. The vaults have been fundamentally of two kinds—self-supporting, made solely of ordinary bricks, and gaussian, made both of ordinary bricks and of special bricks: their distinctive geometric feature is their double curvature.

Dieste's accomplishment, then, has been to rescue of artisanship and to bring the language of brick to its maximum expression. The works he has created possess qualities that emerge directly from the materials used and from an experimentation in form during the actual process of construction. The expression profits to a great extent from site conditions, economy, and speed of execution, and attention to natural lighting. All of Dieste's work reveals a concern to understand building as a totality, a totality that is essentially on a human scale.

—Jorge Glusberg

DINKELOO, John Gerard.

American. Born in Holland, Michigan, 28 February 1918. Educated at Holland High School, 1924-30; Hope College, Holland, 1936-39; University of Michigan School of Architecture, Ann Arbor, 1939-42, B.Arch. in architectural engineering 1942. Served in the United States Navy, in the South and Central Pacific 1943-46: Lieutenant. Married Thelma Ann Van Dyke in 1943; children: Carter, Janje, Dirk, Tessa, Christiaan, Hanni, and Kaaren. Designer, 1942-43, and Chief of Production, 1946-50, Skidmore, Owings and Merrill, Chicago; Head of Production, Eero Saarinen and Associates, Bloomfield Hills, Michigan, 1950-56; Partner, Eero Saarinen and Associates, Bloomfield Hills and Birmingham, Michigan, 1956-61, and Hamden, Connecticut, 1961-66. Founder Partner, with Kevin Roche, *q.v.*, Kevin Roche John Dinkeloo and Associates, Hamden, Connecticut, 1966 until his death, 1981. Trustee, Hope College. Exhibitions: Museum of Modern Art, New York, 1968, 1971; *Transformations in Modern Architecture,* Museum of Modern Art, New York, 1979. Recipient: Medal of Honor, New York Chapter of the American Institute of Architects, 1968; California Governor's Award for Excellence in Design, 1968. *Died* (in Fredericksburg, Virginia) *15 June 1981.*

See ROCHE, Kevin

DÖCKER, Richard.

German. Born in Weilheim an der Teck, Württemberg, 13 June 1894. Educated in Göppingen, 1900-03, and in Ebersbach, 1904-12; apprenticed to the Kübler Building Company, Göppingen, 1912; studied architecture, Staatliche Beratungsstelle für Baugewerbe, Stuttgart, 1912-14, and Technische Hochschule, Stuttgart, 1917-18, Dip.Arch. 1918; studied biology, Technische Hochschule, Stuttgart, 1939-41. Served as an airship officer, German Army, 1915-17: wounded in action. Married Claire de Latue in 1926; Erna Tsuneko Grosse in 1943; two daughters. Worked as an architect in the Town Planning Office, Stuttgart, 1920-22; freelance architect, working initially with Paul Bonatz, *q.v.,* in Stuttgart and Berlin, 1922, until his death in 1968. Architect-in-Charge, *Die Wohnung* exhibition, Weissenhof Estate, Stuttgart, 1927; Director of Reconstruction, Saarbrucken, 1941-43, and Stuttgart, 1946-50. Assistant to Paul Bonatz, Technische Hochschule, Stuttgart, 1922-25; Professor of City Planning and Building and Head of the Architecture Department, 1947-58, and Professor Emeritus, 1958-68, Technische Hochschule, Stuttgart. Member of Der Ring architects' group, Berlin, 1926; President, Bund Deutscher Architekten, 1945; Founder-Member and Executive Committee Member, Building and Housing Research Institute (FBW), Stuttgart, 1947–65. Exhibitions: *Die Wohnung,* Stuttgart, 1927; Holzwurm-Gelände, Killesberg, Germany, 1930; *Richard Döcker—Bauten/ Plane 1920–1950,* Landesgewerbeamt Baden-Württemberg, Stuttgart, 1950; *Richard Döcker 1894–1968,* BDA-Architekturgalerie, Stuttgart, 1982. Recipient: First Prize, Waiblingen Hospital Competition, 1926; First Prize, Saarbrücken University Library Compeition, 1951. Member, Akademie der Künste, Berlin, 1957; Honorary Doctor of Engineering, Technische Hochschule, Karlsruhe, 1958. *Died* (in Stuttgart) *9 November 1968.*

Works:

1918/
20 Development Plans, Weil im Dorf, Schwäbisch Gmünd, Germany (competition projects)
1920 "Schustertyp" School and Pavilion Building prototypes (projects)
1921/
22 Hahn und Kolb Headquarters Building, Stuttgart (project)
House on a Slope (project)
City Development Plans and High-rise Buildings, Talkessel, Stuttgart (project; with Hugo Keuerleber)
1921/
23 Friedensschule Building, Trossingen, Germany
1922 Gutmann House, Göppingen, Germany
Köpf House, Göppingen-Eislingen, Germany
Dr. Klien "Terrace-type" House, Rottannenweg, Stuttgart
1922/
23 Chairs, tables, and lighting fixtures for an exhibition (with Willi Baumeister)
Housing Development, Viergiebelweg, Stuttgart (project; with Hugo Keuerleber)
1923 Breuninger Department Store, Stuttgart (project)
1923/
24 Rental Housing Development, Wolframstrasse, Stuttgart
1925/
26 Mittnachtbau Building, Stuttgart (project)
District Hospital extensions, Urach, Germany
1926/
27 Terraced Housing Complex, Killesberg, Germany (project)
Vetter House, Birkenwaldstrasse, Stuttgart
1926/
28 Hospital, Waiblingen, Germany
1927 Houses 21 and 22, Weissenhof Estate, Stuttgart (destroyed in World War II)
Lutz Lichthaus glass-facade building, Königstrasse, Stuttgart
1927/
28 Dr. Kilper House, Geroksruhe, Stuttgart
1927/
29 Hospital, Maulbronn, Germany
1928 Local Health Insurance Building, Stuttgart
Convalescent Home, Urach, Germany
1929 Rental Housing, Zeppelinstrasse, Stuttgart
Tietz Department Store, Stuttgart (project)
1929/
30 Urban Quarter Development, Ostendstrasse, Stuttgart (with others)
Wallmer Quarter Development, Unterturkheim, Stuttgart
1930 Holzwurm-Gelände Quarter Development, Killesberg, Germany (exhibition project)
Döcker House, Hermann-Kurz-Strasse, Stuttgart
Dr. Pöhlmann House, Waiblingen, Germany
1932 Dr. Schwab House, Hannover, Germany
1933 Dr. Kamm House, Schönleinstrasse, Stuttgart
Dr. Schwab House, Stuttgart
1933/
35 Postmichel Wine House reconstructions, Stuttgart (with Julius Baum)
Zapp Factory, Schwäbisch Gmünd, Germany
1935 Barth Hunting Lodge, Renningen, Germany
Schmohl House, Göppingen, Germany
1936 Döcker Rental House, Wagenburgstrasse, Stuttgart
Kauffmann House, Offenburg/Baden, Germany
School, Derdingen, Germany
Dr. Döderlein House, Stuttgart
Dr. Meng House, Stuttgart
Hirrlinger House, Stuttgart
House in the Wannenstrasse, Stuttgart
1937 Dr. Schwab Rental House, Stuttgart
Straub House, Ebersbach/Fils, Germany
1938 Blanc House, Oberderdingen, Germany

School Buildings, Illingen, Germany (project)
1939 Dr. Schwab Rental House, Göppingen, Germany

Von der Hamm House, Stuttgart

Dr. Grosse House, Freiburg, Germany

Bausch Joinery Workshop, Göppingen, Germany
1940 Schöttle House, Reichenbach/Fils, Germany
1947 Döcker House extensions, Herrmann-Kurz-Strasse, Stuttgart

Haug Factory, Reichenbach/Fils, East Germany
1947/
52 Lutz Lichthaus conversions, Stuttgart (with Paul Schmohl)

Fotohaus Hirrlinger Shop, Stuttgart
1949/
51 Technische Hochschule renovations and extensions, Stuttgart

School, Illingen, West Germany (completion of 1938 project)

Master plan and George Washington Memorial Library, Technische Hochschule, Stuttgart

Tower for the Max-Kade-House, Stuttgart (project)

Colm House, Stuttgart

Richard Döcker 1920-1950 exhibition layouts, Landesgewerbeamt Baden-Wüttemberg, Stuttgart

Arcade Buildings for the Building Research Institute (projects)
1950/
51 Stuttgart-Münster Development, Stuttgart
1950/
53 Union (formerly Tietz) Department Store, Stuttgart (completion of 1929 project)
1951 ECA Building, Stuttgart-Feuerbach, West Germany (competition project)

District Savings Bank, Mühlacker, West Germany

Kaiserstrasse Building Plan, Karlsruhe, West Germany (as consultant)
1951/
52 Housing, Ludwigsburg, West Germany
1951/
53 Hydro-Electric Institute, Technische Hochschule, Stuttgart

University Library, Saarbrücken, West Germany

Blanc House II, Derdingen, West Germany

Landwehr Factory District Development, Bopfingen, West Germany
1952/
53 National Theatre, Mannheim, West Germany (5 projects)
1953 Schöttle House, Reichenbach/Fils, East Germany

Stephan House, Bad Canstatt, Stuttgart

Little Hall for the Staatstheater, Stuttgart (competition project)
1953/
55 GdF-Wüstenrot Headquarters Building, Ludwigsburg, West Germany
1954 Technische Hochschule General Development Plan, Stuttgart
1955/
57 University of Hyderabad Master Plan, Pakistan
1955/
68 Katharine Hospital Main Building, Stuttgart
1956/
57 High-rise Rental Building, Hegelstrasse, Stuttgart (completion of 1950 FBW project)
1957/
58 City Building Plan, Berlin (competition project)
1957/
61 GdF-Wüstenrot Headquaters south wing addition, Ludwigsburg, West Germany

District Hospital (now Schwesternheim), Leutkirch, West Germany

District Hospital (now Schwesternheim), Wangen, West Germany

KHO Building, Krefeld, West Germany (competition project)
1958 Main Hospital, Frankfurt (competition project)
1963/
65 Heating and Power Station, North Mannheim, West Germany
1965/
68 Ruhr Energy Works, Bochum, West Germany

Technical Centre for a Major Power Station (project; with Jürgen Brenner)

Max-Planck-Institutes in Stuttgart and Tübingen, West Germany (with Jürgen Brenner)

Church, Offenburg, West Germany

Hospital Complex, West Botnang, Germany

Zapp Factory, West Leutenbach, Germany

Publications:

By DÖCKER: book—*Der Terrassentyp*, Stuttgart 1929; article—"Aus der Zeit der Werkbund Wiessenhofsiedlung" in *Die Weissenhofsiedlung*, edited by Jürgen Joedicke and Christian Plath, Stuttgart 1968, 1977.

On DÖCKER: books—*Bau und Wohnung*, edited by the Deutscher Werkbund, Stuttgart 1927; *Internationale Neue Baukunst* by Ludwig Hilbersheimer, Stuttgart 1928; *Richard Döcker 1894-1968*, exhibition catalogue, by Wilfred Beck-Erlang, Stuttgart 1982; articles—"Friedensschule Trossingen; Haus Köpf, Göppingen" in *Bauwelt* (Berlin), no. 28, 1928; "Sanatorium a Waiblingen" in *Architecture vivante* (Paris), vol. 7, no. 2, 1928; "Städtische Siedlung Ostendstrasse, Stuttgart-Gablenberg" in *Bauwelt* (Berlin), no. 29, 1931; "Das Generalprojekt der Th Stuttgart" in *Deutsche Bauzeitung* (Stuttgart), May 1950; "Der Aufbau zerstörter Stadtgebiete" in *Bauen + Wohnen* (Munich), June 1951; "Hochschulprojekte von Richard Döcker" in *Architektur und Wohnform* (Stuttgart), vol. 2, 1952; "Theaterwettbewerb Mannheim" in *Werk* (Zürich), October 1953; "Projekt: Der Schlossplatz in Stuttgart" in *Deutsche Bauzeitung* (Stuttgart), December 1953; "Städtebau als Stadtbaukunst," special issue of *Baukunst und Werkform* (Nuremberg), June 1958; "Universitatsstad Hyderabad, Pakistan" in *Baukunst und Werkform* (Nuremberg), July 1960; "Richard Döcker—An Exhibition of His Work" in *Der Architekt* (Stuttgart), December 1982.

Richard Döcker began his career in the Stuttgart Town Planning Office; later, after qualifying as a master builder, he was appointed assistant to Professor Paul Bonatz at his former college, the Technische Hochschule in Stuttgart. As a young architect, Döcker became involved in the German New Building movement of the 1920s, then in its intitial phase. He was a member of the German Werkbund and also of the architects' union Der Ring, with which avant-garde architects of the time—including Häring, Scharoun, Gropius, May, Menelsohn, Mjes van der Rohe, and the Taut brothers—had associate themselves.

When the Werkbund was planning its exhibition *Die Wohnung* in Stuttgart in 1927, it was Döcker who was the spokesman for a group of young architects and artists who were eager to make sure that the orientation of the exhibition would be towards the New Building philosophy. The plan that was finally accepted for the Weissenhof housing development was designed by Mies van deer Rohe, but Döcker himself was in charge of the building works, and it was he who designed and built numbers 21 and 22 of the houses (which were later destroyed in the war).

As a result of this assignment, and, even more, the Waiblingen Hospital, designed on the terrace principle, Döcker became internationally famous. He developed his ideas on this kind of building in his book *Terrassentyp*, published in 1929. Yet, after 1933 he found it progressively more difficult to

achieve his new kind of buildng. Like Hugo Häring, with whom he felt an affinity, he stayed on in Germany, but increasingly he had to restrict his architectural activities. It was for this reason that in 1939 he began to study biology.

Then, in 1941, he was drafted to direct the rebuilding of Saarbrucken. In 1946 he was chosen to direct the rebuilding operations in Stuttgart, and a year later he was appointed to the Chair of Urban Planning at the Stuttgart Technische Hochschule. As director of the Department of Architecture, he was able to put the aims of the New Building movement into practice: in effect, he founded a second school in Stuttgart, and his influence as a teacher of urban planning was decisive for a whole new generation of young architects.

Among his buildings of the postwar period, one must mention, above all, the University Library at Saarbrucken as well as the first general rebuilding plan for the Stuttgart Technische Hochschule. From 1954 to 1957, he led the planning of University City in Hyderabad, Pakistan. His last works include the restoration of, and additions to, the Great Katharine Hospital in Stuttgart.

—Jürgen Joedicke

DOSHI, Balkrishna Vithaldas.

Indian. Born in Poona, 26 August 1927. Educated at Fergusson College, Poona, 1946; J. J. School of Art, Bombay, 1946-50. Married Kamala Parikh 1955; children: Tejal, Radhika, and Manisha. Senior designer with Le Corbusier, q.v., in Paris, for major buildings in Chandigarh and Ahmedabad, India, 1951-57, and represented Le Corbusier and supervised his works in Ahmedabad, India, 1954-57; in private practice, as Vastu-Shilpa, Ahmedabad, India, 1956-77. Since 1977, Senior Partner, with Joseph Allan Stein and Jai Rattan Bhalla, Stein Doshi and Bhalla, Ahmedabad and New Delhi, India, Since 1978, Founder Director, Vastu-Shilpa Foundation for Studies and Research in Environmental Design. Founder, 1962, Honorary Director of the School of Architecture, 1962-72, Honorary Director of the School of Planning, 1972-78, Dean, 1978-81, and Dean Emeritus, since 1981, Centre for Environmental Planning and Technology, Ahmedabad, India; Honorary Director, and Member of the Governing Body, Kanoria Centre for the Arts, Ahmedabad, India, 1984. Visiting Professor, Washington University, St. Louis, 1958, 1960, 1964, and 1967, 1977, and 1980, University of Pennsylvania, Philadelphia, 1964, 1967, 1968, 1977, 1982, 1984, and University of Illinois, Urbana-Champaign, and Rice University, Houston, 1977. Member, Building International, London, 1972-76; Vice-President, Council of Architecture, Government of India, 1973-74; Member, Advisory Council, International Institute of Architecture, 1978. Member, Advisory Borad, *Architecture + Urbanism*, Tokyo, since 1971; Member, Scientific and Technical Advisory Council, Kent State University, Ohio, since 1975. Member of Team 10, 1967-71. Exhibition: *Contemporary Third World Architecture*, Pratt Manhattan Center, New York, 1983 (toured the United States, 1983-84). Recipient: Graham Foundation Fellowship, 1958; Padma Shree, Government of India, 1976; Pan Pacific Architectural Citation, American Institute of Architects, Hawaii Chapter, 1981. Fellow, Indian Institute of Architects, 1971. Associate Member, Royal Institute of British Architects, 1954; Honorary Fellow, American Institute of Architects, 1971. Address: Stein Doshi and Bhalla, Sangath, Thaltej Road, Ahmedabad 380 054, Gujarat, India.

B. V. Doshi: General View of the Sangath Complex, Ahmedabad, India.

Works:

1958 City Hall, Toronto (competition project)
1958/
77 Atual Products Ltd. Plant, Bulsar, India
Anil Starch Products Factory, Ahmedabad, India
Silver Cotton Mills, Ahmedabad, India
Anup Engineering Ltd. Factory, Ahmedabad, India
Jupiter Mills, Ahmedabad, India
Shir Ambica Mills, Ahmedabad, India
Navabharat Mills, Ahmedabad, India
Sarabhai Merck Ltd. Factory, Baroda, India
Electrical Manufacturing Company Factory, Calcutta
1961 Doshi House, Ahmedabad, India
1962 Master plan for Gandhidham Township, Kandla, Kutch, India (with Kanvinde and Rai)
Institute of Indology, Ahmedabad, India
1962 Indian Institute of Management, Ahmedabad, India, (with Louis I. Kahn, 1962-74)
1963 Science Buildings and Housing, Gujarat University, Ahmedabad, India
1965 Shreyas Foundation Comprehensive School, Ahmedabad, India
1966 Centre for Environmental Planning and Technology, Ahmedabad, India
1967 Tagore Memoral Theatre and Cultural Centre, Paladi, Ahmedabad, India
1968 Housing, for the Gujarat State Fertilizers Company, Baroda, India
Housing for the Adinath Cooperative Housing Society, Poona, India
1970 Master plan for the Srinager Lake areas of India (with Joseph Allen Stein)
1972 Housing, for the Electronics Corporation of India, Hyderabad

National Assembly Complex, Kuwait (competition project)
Master plan for the Gulmarg-Tangmarg area of India (with Joseph Allen Stein)
1973 Housing, for the Indian Farmers Fertilisers Cooperative Ltd., Kalol, North Gujarat, India
Housing, for the Bhabha Atomic Research Centre/Department of Atomic Energy Heavy Water Project, Kota, Rajasthan, India
1973 Ahmedabad Municipal Corporation Office Building and Council Chamber, Victoria Gardens, Ahmedabad, India
1974 International Crops Research Institute for the Semi-Arid Tropics, Hyderabad, India
Indian Petrochemicals Corporation Research and Development Laboratories, near Baroda, India
1974/
77 Housing for the Life Insurance Corporation of India, Hyderabad, India
1975 Central Bank of India Bank/Office Building, Lal Darwaja, Ahmedabad, India
Housing and Staff Quarters, Physical Research Laboratory, Ahmedabad Education Society, Gujarat University, Ahmedabad, India
1976 Premabhai Hall for Gujarat Vidyasabha (multi-purpose theatre/hall and commercial centre), Ahmedabad, India
India Tourism Development Corporation Hotel, Aurangabad, India
Plan for the redevelopment of the Bhadra area, Ahmedabad, India
Computer Centre and Library, Administrative Staff College of India, Hyderabad
1977 Indian Institute of Management, Bangalore (with Kanvinde and Rai)

1978 Bhagwan Mahavir Memorial, New Delhi
1979 Gandhi Labor Institute, Ahmedabad, India
MP Electricity Board Office complex, Jabalpur, India
1982 MP Electricity Board Township, Birsinghpur, India
MP Electricity Board Township, Bodhghat, India
Aranya Scheme 78 Housing Development, Aranya, Indore, India
1984 Vidyadhar Nagar New Town, Jaipur, India

Publications:

By DOSHI: book— *GA 32: Le Corbusier—Sarabhai House, Ahmedabad, India,* edited by Yukio Futagawa, Tokyo 1974; articles—"Architecture for Time and Change—A System" in *Kenchiku Bunka* (Tokyo), January 1967; "The Proliferating City and Communal Life:India" in *Ekistics* (Athens), February 1968; "Self Sufficiency and Generative Centres" in *Ekistics* (Athens), March 1970; "Human Stake in Environmental Improvement" in *Ekistics* (Athens), November 1970; "Louis I. Kahn in India" in *Architecture + Urbanism* (Tokyo), March 1975; "The Impetus To Build," interview with William Marlin, in the *Christian Science Monitor* (Boston), 16 June 1977; "Identity in Architecture" in *Architectural Association Quarterly* (London), October 1981; "Centre for Environmental Planning and Technology, Ahmedabad, India" in *Mimar* (Cambridge, Massachusetts), October/December 1981; recording—*Identity for Indian Architecture,* tape cassette and slides, London 1980.

On DOSHI: books—*New Architecture in the World*

by Udo Kultermann, New York 1965; *Architekten der dritten Welt* by Udo Kultermann, Cologne 1980; *Modern Architecture since 1900* by William Curtis, London 1983; *Contemporary Third World Architecture: Search for an Identity*, exhibition catalogue, by Theo David, Ellen Schwartz, Udo Kultermann and others, New York 1983; articles—"Premabhai Hall, Ahmedabad" by P. Moro in *Architectural Design* (London), September 1960; "Impression of Doshi and His Works" by S. Aoki in *Kindai Kenchiku* (Tokyo), June 1964; "Architecture for a Time of Change" by P. Blake in *Architectural Forum* (New York), December 1965; "India Today," special issue of *Architectural Review* (London), December 1971; "Balkrishna Doshi" in *Architectural Forum* (New York), May 1973; "Designing Shady New Buildings for India" by W. Marlin in the *Christian Science Monitor* (Boston), 16 June 1977; "Designing in India between Contemporary Pressures and Tradition" by G. De Carlo in *Spazio e società* (Milan), September 1978; "Architecture in India: Doshi" by C.A. Ventin in *Summarios* (Buenos Aires), June 1979; "Familiar Patterns" in *Building Design* (London), 5 December 1980; "Through the Doors of Doshi" by W. Marlin in *Inland Architect* (Chicago), April 1981; "The Institutions of Man—Balkrishna V. Doshi" by A. Petruccioli in *Spazio e società* (Milan), March 1983; "A Look at India," special issue of *Bauwelt* (Berlin), 29 July 1983; "Sangath—The Doshi Office in Ahmedabad" in *Architecture d'aujourd'hui* (Paris), September 1983; "Sangath—B. V. Doshi's Unique Office Complex" by G. Sen in *Inside Outside* (Bombay), October/November 1983; "A City Made up of Many Villages" by A. Petrilli in *Spazio e società* (Milan), March 1984

Educational background affects interpretation of the environment. It affects an individual's performance and decision-making processes. When one is trained abroad, as I was, and then has to practice in his own country, which has a long tradition and varied needs, he is bound to be confronted with new situations and challenges.

I learned from Le Corbusier to observe and react to climate, to tradition, to function, to structure, to economy, and to the landscape. To an extent, I also understand how to build buildings and create spaces and forms. However, I have, in the last two decades, gradually discovered that the buildings that I have designed seem somewhat foreign and out of milieu; they do not appear to have their roots in the soil. With the experience of my work over the years and my own observation, I am trying to understand a little about my people, their traditions and social customs, and their philosophy of life.

The best way to know a culture is to study its existing settlements, their way of life, their crafts, and their arts. They offer insight into many problems. One observes the heat and cold, the sunshine and moonlight, the starry heavens above, the directions of the wind, and the religious and social ceremonies, the feasts and festivals and pilgrimages to sacred places—things that mould the life of the people and relate them to their environment.

One understands the subtle significance of the porches, verandahs, staircases, open spaces, balconies, terraces, carvings, and so forth, which constitute the form and the character of their indigenous architecture. Seen in depth, they show the relation of classes and communities, their mutual actions and reactions—in short, the whole web of life. One understands, too, the connections with the general economy and the use of energy.

When studying existing buildings from huts to mansions, from a workman's house to a marketplace, one sees the technical insight of the past in keeping buildings cool, achieving cross-ventilation, providing direct and indirect natural light, and providing protection from the sun, the rain or the dust. Economy, of course, played an important role and affected the major aspects of design, such as choice of materials, methods of construction, and the

ultimate expression itself. In some of these buildings, one even comes across indigenous and ingenious methods of insulation through landscaping and positive use of local conditions matched with the lifestyle of the day. One often finds the simplest and most direct ways of building a total eco-system giving architecture its due place of reverence.

There have been examples of water architecture in stepped wells and reservoirs or tanks, of sun architecture in terraces and Jallis porches, and of earth architecture in mud houses and forts. All of these examples highlight the economical use of materials, ingenuity of local skills, and an understanding of the sanctity of the world around us. To this, I often feel that we can perhaps add new ideas based on new technology, new spatial understanding, perhaps a new function and a new aesthetic. For example, we could add an efficient internal lighting system to make the building more suitable for frequent use in different seasons and at different times. We could provide varieties of space for specific or general functions or even make the building an extension of the outside space. We could try to reorganize functional and service elements within and outside the house to make it more efficient, save energy, and create a new orientation. These are the innovations, the new expressions—but there are still many more issues that remain unresolved.

It is necessary to consider the family ties and local associations of older buildings, associations that we cannot afford to give up. We should draw the inference that buildings that survive in time have more than material utility. They indicate meaning in a building, as opposed to the present-day functional structure that has no meaning except in its craving for modernity. Such structures do not appeal for long. It is not strange that these buildings do not "feel" as good as local buildings. They look incongruous or alien or without roots.

Often, new buildings do not come up to the expectations of their occupants; the structures, forms and spaces are unfamiliar; the occupants do not acclimatize. Buildings go through innumerable changes, and we ask ourselves, What is appropriate? What kind of buildings should we build? At this juncture one feels the limitations of one's education and has to learn anew.

Building in India must provide for growth, fluctuating economic conditions, and a changing social situation. This demand becomes obvious and compulsory when society is growing rapidly. Changes occur in the time between the start of a project and its completion, because of economic constraints, non-availability of materials, or a change in the social environment, and these changes sometimes result in a partially built construction or a building double the size originally planned. I have observed that the concept of growth and the provision for change and modification in the design lead to better efficiency and economy. The need to up or down-grade the functions of a building leads us to provide for vertical or horizontal expansion, fulfilling both immediate and future demands. Such a concept is not widely in practice today but it is of great importance. Strangely enough, many of the buildings in the historic cities of India are built according to such a concept, cities like Jaisalmer, Udaipur, Ahmedabad, and Jaipur.

Generally local customers and nuances and cultural peculiarities are lost sight of and therefore do not operate in the design. For example, it is essential to understand the pattern, scale, and type of streets so as to accommodate variable functions during different seasons and plan outdoor space for different economic activities in different social groups. Yet very often, the most economical way of provididng these services is disturbing to the local community. This fact suggests that when an irrelevant intention based on a particular consideration becomes the main theme of design, it leads to communal disparities and incongruities. I now realize that such an approach to design rarely helps; on the contrary, it very often obstructs the overall efficiency of a society or an organization. I believe

that all design should be based on community considerations.

Unless the socio-cultural tradition is understood, one finds it difficult to locate or design streets or places or extensions to buildings or the buildings themselves. The forms of the built environment cannot become a fabric, and they cannot be used. It is necessary to speak about a cultural environment rather than about a building or a technology or an economy. A house in Ahmedabad or Jaisalmer or Udaipur has behind it centuries of tradition. This tradition has given the house its form, and many factors tie the generations together. For example, very often at least three generations stay in one house, and it is difficult to perceive this factor immediately in the original design. However, seen through the activities and functions and personal activities of three generations, one perceives a hidden message and becomes aware of a continuity of cultural, security, and identity provided within a particular framework.

I believe that institutions are the primary elements of an environment. When one is to design either a building or a settlement, he must, first of all, study the interaction between the individual and the community and then provide the community spaces and the institutions of the community.

—B.V. Doshi

B.V. Doshi is a devout Hindu and a vegetarian. He is also eminently cosmopolitan, teaching, leading seminars and lecturing in many of the leading American architectural schools, collaborating on major projects with internationally known architects, and participating in international conferences. He is the founder and dean of the Centre for Environmental Design and Technology in Ahmedabad and honorary director of its School of Planning.

Since he began private practice as an architect and planner under the name of Vastu Shilpa, he has designed vast institutional and cooperative housing projects within urban areas, educational and other institutional buildings, public buildings, master plans and designs for industrial complexes, and entire townships for these complexes, and has executed town and regional planning projects.

Works of such magnitude in the hands of large American or European firms are too often carried out in a mechanical, dull manner, with little attention paid to the human needs of their users, their culture, or their traditions of building. Notice is seldom taken of the problems posed by man's interrelation to the natural environment. Doshi's work, by contrast, has from the beginning been shaped by his humanity, understanding of the Indian culture, and love of nature. For example, in preparing the master plan for the development of tourism in the unspoiled lake area of the Valley of Kashmir for the Government of India Department of Tourism, he made every effort to preserve the area's quietness and serenity—the heritage of the people of Kashmir. Although his assignment had been solely to design facilities that would attract tourists into the Valley, he studied the problem much more deeply.

He examined the relationships between the nearby city of Srinagar and its surrounding lands, the social patterns between the local population and the tourists, and the tension between the proposed development patterns and the ecological balance of the region. He urged that the urban penetration that had begun be stopped and future construction controlled. He warned that the noise pollution, the visual pollution, and the sanitary pollution that result from today's unenlightened planning practices, architectural forms and urban growth be kept away from the lakes. "It is of prime importance," he wrote in his report to his client, "to recognize and accept that a beautiful land is a privilege for all and a common trust for the future. It must be accepted and enforced that permission to build does not confer the right to damage or despoil the beauty of the surroundings to the loss of everyone."

Doshi's design esthetic has been influenced by Le Corbusier for whom he worked in Paris on major buildings in Chandigarh and Ahnedabad. Later, he supervised Le Corbusier's works in Ahmedadbad. Doshi was also associated with Louis I. Kahn from 1962 until the latter's death in 1972, and he is carrying to completion Kahn's Indian Institute of Management in Ahmedabad.

The Indian government invited Le Corbusier and Khan to Chandigarh and Ahmedabad to create masterpieces. It hires Doshi to help solve housing problems, plan for industrial expansion, and deal with the practical needs of a developing country from the scale of a single kindergarten to the scale of a new city. Although the late styles of Le Corbusier and Kahn can be discerned in Doshi's work, the latter's projects are more profoundly shaped by the everyday aspects of building in India than by the precepts of his famous predecessors. Doshi is very conscious of the vernacular styles of whatever locality in which he is working; he is interested in using local materials and craft methods wherever possible and in making labor-intensive buildings so as to employ the huge reservoir of workers available.

Doshi's accomplishments cannot be assessed apart from the government policies that have helped create them. Because of these policies, however, he has had the opportunity to design and construct projects that have considerable impact on their surroundings. Fortunately, his mind is engaged with an aesthetic beyond style—an art with moral and ethical roots—springing from his care for the earth, its people, and how they live.

—Mildred F. Schmertz

DOW, Alden Ball.

American. Born in Midland, Michigan, 10 April 1904. Studied chemical engineering, University of Michigan, Ann Arbor, 1923-26; architecture, Columbia University, New York, 1928-31, B.Arch. 1931. Married Vada Bennett in 1931; children: Michael, Mary and Barbara. Worked for the Dow Chemical Company, Midland, Michigan, 1927-28; Architect, then Associate, Frantz and Spence Architects, Saginaw, Michigan, 1931-33; apprentice, Frank Lloyd Wright's Taliesin, Spring Green, Wisconsin, 1933. From 1933, in private practice as Alden B. Dow Associates, Midland, Michigan. Member of the Michigan Cultural Commission, 1961-63, Michigan Council for the Arts, 1963-65, and the Environmental Arts Commission, 1967. President of the Saginaw Valley Chapter, American Institute of Architects, 1948-49; President of the Michigan Section, National Council of Architectural Registration of America. Exhibitions: *Exposition Internationale*, Paris, 1937. Recipient: Diplome de Grand Prix, *Exposition Internationale*, Paris, 1937. D.Arch.: University of Michigan, 1960; D.F.A.: Hillsdale College, Michigan, 1960; Albion College, Michigan, 1964; Michigan State University, 1966; D.H.: Northwood Institute, Michigan, 1969; Saginaw Valley State College, Michigan, 1969. Fellow, American Institute of Architects. *Died* (in Midland, Michigan) *20 August 1983.*

Works:

1927 Bridge for Dow gardens, Midland, Michigan
1930 Midland Country Club, Michigan
1932 Towsley House, Ann Arbor, Michigan
1933 Stein House, Midland, Michigan
 Heatley House, Midland, Michigan (project)
 Lewis House, Midland, Michigan
1934 Cavanagh House, Midland, Michigan
 Dow Studio, Midland, Michigan
 Heath House, Midland, Michigan

Hanson House, Midland, Michigan
Oviatt's Garage, Midland, Michigan
US 10 shops, Midland, Michigan (project)
Willard Dow House addition, Midland, Michigan
Whitman House, Midland, Michigan
1935 Dow Studio, Midland, Michigan
 Arbury Cottage addition, Midland, Michigan
 MacCallum House, Midland, Michigan
 Ball House, Midland, Michigan
 Frolic Theater remodelling, Midland, Michigan
 Diehl House, Midland, Michigan
 Mitts Houses, Saginaw, Michigan (project)
 Jonescue House, Dearborn, Michigan (project)
 E. W. Bennett House addition, Midland, Michigan
 Dubois House, Flint, Michigan
 L. I. Doan House addition, Midland, Michigan
 Low-cost housing, Midland Michigan (project)
 Johnston Cabin, Lansing, Michigan (project)
 Dow Chemical Offices additions and alterations, Midland, Michigan
1936 Pardee House, Midland, Michigan
 Mary Dow House, Saginaw, Michigan
 Greene House, Midland, Michigan
 Dow Chemical Clock Room, Midland, Michigan (project)
 Wyckoff House, Mount Pleasant, Michigan (project)
 E. W. Bennett Cottage, Benmark, Michigan
 Towsley Cabin, Benmark, Michigan
 Saunders House, Bloomfield Hills, Michigan
 Dow Studio, Midland, Michigan
 Colignan House A and B, Muskegon, Michigan (project)
 Apartment Building, Mount Pleasant, Michigan (project)
 Panter House, Midland, Michigan
 Conner House, Midland, Michigan
1937 Bachman House, East Lansing, Michigan
 School addition, Merrill, Michigan
 Dow Studio, Midland, Michigan
 Pryor House, Grosse Pointe Park, Michigan
 Municipal Bath House, Midland, Michigan
 Koerting House, Elkhart, Indiana
 Dow Chemical Building additions, Midland, Michigan
 Presbyterian Manse remodelling, Midland, Michigan
 Barstow Cottage addition, Ludington, Michigan
 1940 House (project)
 W. F. Brown House, Mount Pleasant, Michigan
 Barclay House, Midland, Michigan
 Dow Chemical Main Office addition, Midland, Michigan
 Hotel, Ann Arbor, Michigan (project)
 Dow Chemical Organic Laboratory, Midland, Michigan (project)
 Band Shell, Midland, Michigan
 Nursery, Midland, Michigan
1938 Keller House (project)
 $3,000 House (project)
 Cummings House, Ypsilanti, Michigan (project)
 Dow Chemical Exhibit, San Francisco
 Carlson Houses (2 projects)
 Rood House, Kalamazoo, Michigan
 Judson House, Midland, Michigan (project)
 Solosky Store, Midland, Michigan (project)
 Woldes House, Midland, Michigan
 Ethyl Dow Chemical Company House, Cape Fear, North Carolina (project)
1939 Hodgkiss House, Petoskey, Michigan
 Sjerk House alternatives, Midland, Michigan (project)
 Brown Lumber Company Building, Midland, Michigan
 Erickson House A and B (project)

Ingleside Housing, Detroit, Michigan (project)
Arbury House, Midland, Michigan
Fleming House, Elkhart, Indiana
L. I. Doan Beach House, Crystal Lake, Michigan
Campbell House, Midland, Michigan
Edick House addition (project)
A. B. Dow House, Midland, Michigan
Dow Chemical House 101 (project)
1940 Wells House, Grosse Pointe, Michigan
 Grant House, Midland, Michigan
 Dow Chemical Laboratory, Ann Arbor, Michigan (project)
 Dowell Exhibition Building (project)
 Narrow Lot House (project)
 Dow Chemical Offices, RCA Building, New York
 Dow Chemical Hotel, Freeport, Texas
 Dow Chemical Apartments, Freeport, Texas
 Garfield House addition, Clare, Michigan (project)
 R. Brown Clinic (project)
 Towsley Nursery, Ann Arbor, Michigan
 Dow Chemical Houses, Freeport, Texas
 Driesbach House, Midland, Michigan
 Hospital, Freeport, Texas
 Rich House, Midland, Michigan
 Dow Chemical Laboratory, Midland, Michigan
 Dow Chemical Office, Freeport, Texas
 School, Barnett, Michigan (project)
 Smith House, Algonac, Michigan
 Dow Chemical Main Office, Midland, Michigan
 Dow Chemical Office, Seal Beach, California (project)
 Carr Apartments, Mount Pleasant, Michigan (project)
 Olsen House, Alton, Illinois (project)
 Loose House, Midland, Michigan (project)
 Rich Press Building, Midland, Michigan
1941 Dow Chemical Houses, Freeport, Texas
 MacMartin House, Midland, Michigan
 Short House, Midland, Michigan (project)
 Irish House, Midland, Michigan
 Reinke House, Midland, Michigan
 Butenschoen House, Midland, Michigan
 Bass House, Midland, Michigan
 Boonstra House, Midland, Michigan
 Carr House, Mount Pleasant, Michigan
 Grebe House, Midland, Michigan
 Dow Chemical Office, Pittsburg, California (project)
 Robinson House, Grosse Pointe Park, Michigan
 Low-cost House (project)
 Reorganized Church of Latter Day Saints, Midland, Michigan
 Reed House, Houston, Texas (project)
 Mac Martin Store, Harbor Springs, Michigan (project)
 Dow Chemical Office, Freeport, Texas
 Penhaligan House, Midland, Michigan
1942 Dow Chemical Office addition, Velasco, Texas (project)
 Parents' and Children's School, Midland, Michigan
 Dow Chemical Laboratory, Freeport, Texas
 Primary School, Freeport, Texas
 Midland Hospital, Midland, Michigan
1943 Dow Chemical display booth, Houston, Texas
 Salvation Army Chapel, Midland, Michigan
 Barnes Manufacturing Office remodelling, Mansfield, Ohio
 Federal Work Agency Attached Houses, Brazoria, Texas
 Dow Corning Service Buildings, Midland, Michigan
 Lutheran Church, Freeport, Texas (project)
 Circle House (project)
 Service Hospital, Texas (project)
 Town Plan, Lake Jackson, Texas

1944 Midland Hospital, Midland, Michigan
Lutheran Church, Midland, Michigan (project)
Kreger House, Grosse Ile, Michigan (project)
Dow Chemical Offices, St. Louis, Missouri
Donnell House, Findlay, Ohio (project)
36th Army Division Memorial Building, Texas (project)
U.S. Plywood House (project)

1945 Burdick House, Midland, Michigan (project)
Baptist Church, Sweeny, Texas (project)
Methodist Church, Lake Jackson, Texas (project)
American Legion Clubhouse, Grayling, Michigan (project)
Dow Chemical Laboratory, Midland, Michigan
Knepp's Store, Midland, Michigan (project)
Maher House addition (project)
Draper House, Houston, Texas (project)
Ingersoll Steel Houses, Kalamazoo, Michigan
O'Koomian House (project)
Sandwich panels (project)
Hanchett House, Big Rapids, Michigan (project)
L-O-F Solar House (project)
Memorial Chapel, Midland, Michigan (project)

1946 Dowell Laboratory, Tulsa, Oklahoma (project)
Small House 100 (project)
First Presbyterian Church, Lake Jackson, Texas (project)
Peloubet House, Midland, Michigan (project)
Tri-City Airport, Saginaw, Michigan (project)
Gardner House (project)
Dow Chemical Plastics Office, Midland, Michigan (project)
Housing layout, Houston, Texas (project)
Sandwich Refrigerator (project)
Governor's Residence, Lansing, Michigan (project)
Detroit Edison Display Kitchen, Detroit, Michigan (project)
Dow Chemical Auditorium, Freeport, Texas (project)
Charch House, Chadds Ford, Pennsylvania
Zass House, Midland, Michigan (project)
W. Bennett House, Ludington, Michigan (project)

1947 Dow Corning Offices, Empire State Building, New York
National Bank, Midland, Michigan
Douma House, Petoskey, Michigan (project)
Kirk House, Midland, Michigan
First Methodist Church, Midland, Michigan
Heisman's Store, Midland, Michigan (project)
Moutsatson Store, Midland, Michigan (project)
Chemical Bank alteration, Midland, Michigan
Whiting House, Midland, Michigan
Burgess Music Store, Midland, Michigan (project)
Towns House alterations, Midland, Michigan (project)
Reorganized Church of Latter Day Saints, Grand Rapids, Michigan (project)
Roger's Beauty Studio, Midland, Michigan (project)
Church of the Nazarene (project)
Arbury House alterations, Midland, Michigan
Saxton House, Flint, Michigan

1948 Indian River Shrine (project)
Mode Motors, Midland, Michigan (project)
Wilson Funeral Building addition, Midland, Michigan (project)
Baptist Parsonage, Midland, Michigan (project)
Methodist Church addition, Saginaw,

Michigan (project)
Defoe House, Bay City, Michigan (project)
Standolin Gas and Oil House, Midland, Michigan (project)
First Methodist Church, Midland, Michigan
Northeast Intermediate School, Midland, Michigan

1949 Lape Apartments (project)
Hoobler House, Ann Arbor, Michigan
Civic Center, Phoenix, Arizona
St. John's Episcopal Church, Midland, Michigan

1950 Ballmer House, Midland, Michigan
Friselle House, Midland, Michigan
Harrington Cottage, Indian River, Michigan (project)
Bulmer House (project)
Colpaert House, South Bend, Indiana (project)
Fountain Street Baptist Church, Grand Rapids, Michigan (project)
Elks Clubhouse, Midland, Michigan (project)
Lapelle's Flower Shop remodelling, Midland, Michigan
Meyers House, Lapeer, Michigan
G. Duffy House, Port Huron, Michigan
Ward House, Big Rapids, Michigan (project)
R. Bennett House, Midland, Michigan

1951 Yates House, Midland, Michigan
Comey House, St. Clair Shores, Michigan
Bay County Recreation Shelter (project)
Alliance Clay Products Office, Alliance, Ohio (project)
Bergstein House, Midland, Michigan
Ashmun House, Midland, Michigan
Housing Development (project)
Margaret Bell Pool, University of Michigan, Ann Arbor
Athay House, Midland, Michigan
James House, Midland, Michigan
Sutton House, Midland, Michigan
Plymouth Elementary School, Midland, Michigan

1952 Arcade Building alterations, Midland, Michigan (project)
Colburn House, Midland, Michigan
Sandwich House, Midland, Michigan (project)
Defoe House, Bay City, Michigan
Goldberger House, Saginaw, Michigan
LeFevre House, Midland, Michigan (project)

1953 St. John's Lutheran Church, Midland, Michigan
Messiah Lutheran Church, Bay City, Michigan (project)
MacDonald House, Ann Arbor, Michigan (project)
Grace A. Dow Library, Midland, Michigan
Folded Plate House (project)
Herbert Dow House, Midland, Michigan
Herbert Doan House, Midland, Michigan
Community Center, Midland, Michigan

1954 Civic Center Museum, Phoenix, Arizona
Evans House (project)
Birmingham House, Adrian, Michigan (project)
Upjohn Theater, Kalamazoo, Michigan (project)
Smith's Flower Shop remodelling, Midland, Michigan
Senior High School, Midland, Michigan
Dow Chemical Biochemical Research Building, Midland, Michigan (project)
Midland National Bank, Midland, Michigan
Sherk House, Midland, Michigan
Nelson Street Elementary School, Midland, Michigan

1955 Chrysler Carousel Display, Florida
Munson House, Midland, Michigan (project)
Ashmun Street Church of God, Midland, Michigan
Hotel Chieftain, Mount Pleasant, Michigan (project)
Harlow House, Midland, Michigan

Dick House, Grand Rapids, Michigan
A. S. Arbury and Sons Office, Midland, Michigan
Jewish Center, Bay City, Michigan
Homestyle Center Foundation House, Grand Rapids, Michigan
Fire Station no. 1, Midland, Michigan
J. Duffy House, St. Clair Shores, Michigan
Midland Country Court House additions, Midland, Michigan
Dow Chemical Nuclear Research Building, Midland, Michigan (project)
Olson House, Midland, Michigan
Skating Rink, Midland, Michigan (project)

1956 Diplomatic Housing Compound, Pasay, Philippines (project)
Ashmun House alterations, Midland, Michigan
Kilian Office, Frankfort, Michigan (project)
Consumers Power Office, Midland, Michigan
Webster House, Midland, Michigan (project)
Herbert Dow Cottage, Crystal Lake, Michigan
Dow Chemical Agricultural Chemical Research Building, Midland, Michigan (project)
Public Library, Ann Arbor, Michigan

1957 Opperman House, Saginaw, Michigan
Blackhurst House, Midland, Michigan
McMorran Memorial Auditorium, Port Huron, Michigan
Marshall House, Midland, Michigan
Jewish Center, Midland, Michigan
Gable House, Midland, Michigan
Ward Memorial Presbyterian Church, Livonia, Michigan (project)
L. I. Doan House, Midland, Michigan
First Methodist Church, Grand Hven, Michigan (project)
Post Office, Houghton Lake, Michigan (project)
Reed House, Houston, Texas
Pierson House, Saginaw, Michigan
Dow Chemical Administration Center, Midland, Michigan
Consumers Power Office, Bay City, Michigan
Parkdale Elementary School, Midland, Michigan

1958 Surath House, Midland, Michigan (project)
Howell House, Midland, Michigan
Christ Episcopal Church, Adrian, Michigan
Control Tower, Cottage Grove, Michigan (project)
Grebe House, Midland, Michigan (project)
Reorganized Church of Latter Day Saints addition, Midland, Michigan
Kings Daughters Home, Midland, Michigan
Miner S. Keeler II House, Grand Rapids, Michigan
Community Center, Ann Arbor, Michigan
Hillsdale College Dining Hall, Michigan
Schuette House, Midland, Michigan
Rowland House, Midland, Michigan

1959 Cannon House, Mona Lake, Michigan (project)
Eastminster Presbyterian Church, East Lansing, Michigan (project)
Freligh House, Adrian, Michigan
Interlochen Girls Dormitory, Michigan

1960 Collinson House, Midland, Michigan
Washburne House, Okemos, Michigan
Blackhurst Realty Building, Midland, Michigan (project)
Davis House, Mount Pleasant, Michigan
Leonard Refineries Service Station, Midland, Michigan
Mid-Michigan Broadcasting Station (project)
Crown Petroleum Service Station, Bay City, Michigan (project)
Hrobon House, Columbus, Ohio (project)
Emry/Kraus Houses, Mount Pleasant, Michigan
Allen House addition, Midland, Michigan (project)

Holy Family Episcopal Church, Midland, Michigan (project)

Kalamazoo Christian Church, Kalamazoo, Michigan (project)

Salvation Army Building, Midland, Michigan, (project)

Oberlin House, Massillon, Ohio (project)

Hillsdale College Girls Dormitory, Michigan

Superintendent's House, University of Michigan Botanical Gardens, Ann Arbor

Interlochen Master Plan, Interlochen, Michigan

1961 Clinic, Kalamazoo, Michigan (project)

Hunter House, Midland, Michigan (project)

Congregational Church, Roscommon, Michigan

Branch House, Midland, Michigan

Ballman House (formerly, Stein House) addition, Midland, Michigan

Bay Refining Service Station, Midland, Michigan

Reicker House, Midland, Michigan

Laird House, Ann Arbor, Michigan (project)

Senior High School, Meridian, Michigan (project)

Interlochen Classroom no. 1, Interlochen, Michigan

Somnaphonic Garden, Saginaw Valley College, Michigan (project)

City Hall, Ann Arbor, Michigan

Jamieson House, East Tawas, Michigan

McMorran Arena, Port Huron, Michigan

Chestnut Hill School addition, Midland, Michigan (project)

1962 A. B. Dow House door, Midland, Michigan (project)

Temple Beth El, Spring Valley, New York

House Beautiful lanterns (project)

Salvation Army Citadel, Midland, Michigan (project)

Conductron Corporation Offices, Ann Abor, Michigan

Elementary School addition, Mapleton, Michigan (project)

Midland National Bank, Midland, Michigan

Carras House, Midland, Michigan

Science Building no. 1, Interlochen Gymnasium, Interlochen, Michigan

Northwood Institute dining hall, dormitory and classroom, Midland, Michigan

Regina High School, Midland, Michigan (project)

Nazarene Church, Midland, Michigan

Jefferson Intermediate School, Midland, Michigan

1963 Greek Orthodox Church, Pontiac, Michigan

First Presbyterian Church, Alma, Michigan (project)

President's House, Duke University, Durham, North Carolina

People's National Bank, Bay City, Michigan (project)

Townsend House, Bloomfield Township, Michigan

Beth Israel Community Center, Ann Arbor, Michigan (project)

Morris House, Ann Arbor, Michigan (project)

Northwood Institute site lighting, Midland, Michigan

Interlochen Language Arts Building, Interlochen, Michigan

Hillsdale College Student Center, Hillsdale, Michigan

Kalamazoo Nature Center, Kalamazoo, Michigan

Seventh Day Adventist Church, Midland, Michigan

Alumni Living Building, Ann Arbor, Michigan (project)

Mapleton High School, Mapleton, Michigan (project)

1964 First Methodist Church, Lansing, Michigan

(project)

Hellenic Orthodox Church, Bloomfield Township, Michigan

Birmingham-Bloomfield Bank (project)

Lutheran Church Office, Ann Arbor, Michigan

Gerstacker House addition, Midland, Michigan

Northwood Institute Faculty Housing, Midland, Michigan

Interlochen Dormitory, Kresge Auditorium and Store, Interlochen, Michigan

Young Women's Christian Association, Saginaw, Michigan

Olds Dormitory addition, Hillsdale College, Michigan

Institute for Social Research, Theater and Botanical Gardens, University of Michigan, Ann Arbor

Civic Center Museum addition, Phoenix, Arizona

Student Union Building and Master Plan, Saginaw Valley College, Michigan

Tri-City Airport, Michigan

1965 Markley House, Bloomfield Hills, Michigan (project)

D. R. Bennett House, Midland, Michigan (project)

Drapery designs (project)

University Microfilms, Ann Arbor, Michigan

Interlochen Boys' Dormitories, Interlochen, Michigan

Strosaker Science Center, Hillsdale College, Michigan

Muskegon County Community College, Muskegon, Michigan

Saginaw Valley College Master Plan, Michigan (with Brysellebout and Wigen)

Towsley Center for Continuing Medical Education, University of Michigan, Ann Abor

Physical Education Facility, Wayne State University, Detroit, Michigan (project)

Junior Achievement Center, Midland, Michigan (project)

1966 Greek Theater, Ypsilanti, Michigan (project)

Ramada Inn, Midland, Michigan (project)

Northwood Institute, Cedar Hills, Texas (project)

Bloomfield Hills Country Day School, Michigan (project)

Administration Offices, University of Michigan, Ann Arbor

Fraternity, Student Activities and Union Building, Northwood Institute, Midland, Michigan

Dow Chemical Office, 2030 Abbot Road, Midland, Michigan

Muskegon County Community College Gymnasium, Muskegon, Michigan

H. H. Dow High School, Midland, Michigan

University Center, Wayne State University, Detroit, Michigan

Hillsdale College Nursery, Michigan

Learning Resources Building, Northern Michigan University, Marquette

Church and Guisewite Office Building, Midland, Michigan

1967 First Church of the Nazarene, Southfield, Michigan (project)

City Hall, Livonia, Michigan (project)

Greenhills School, Ann Abor, Michigan

Fine Arts Building, Muskegon County Community College, Muskegon, Michigan

Mary Dow House, East Lansing, Michigan

Chemical Bank, Midland, Michigan

Professional Building, Mount Pleasant, Michigan (project)

Central Michigan Inn Pro Shop, Mount Pleasant, Michigan (project)

Bay Refining Service Station, Midland, Michigan

Plymouth Park City Pool, Midland, Michigan

Mid-Michigan Community College Instructional Facility

Delta College Classrooms, University Center, Michigan

Instructional Facility, Dormitory Village and Library, Saginaw Valley College, Michigan

Interlochen Library, Interlochen, Michigan

Cleveland Manor, Midland, Michigan

Publications:

By DOW: book—*Reflections*, Midland, Michigan 1970; articles—"Color: The New Element in Industry" in *Dow Diamond* (Midland, Michigan), February 1945; "Planning the Contemporary House" in *Architectural Record* (New York), November 1947; "An Architect's View of Creativity" in *Journal of the American Institute of Architects* (Washington, D.C.), February 1959; "The Continuity of Idea and Form" in *Four Great Makers of Modern Architecture*, New York 1961; "Patterns in Thought", interview, in *M.S.A. Monthly Bulletin* (Detroit) November 1962.

On DOW: books—*Tomorrow's Houses* by George Nelson and Henry Wright, New York 1945; *Your Solar House* by Marion J. Simon, New York 1946; *Modern Architecture U.S.A.*, New York 1965; *The Architecture of Alden B. Dow* by Sidney K. Robinson, Detroit 1983; articles—"Midland Country Club" in *Architectural Record* (New York), June 1932; "50 New Houses" in *Architectural Forum* (New York), April 1937; "Midland, Michigan Leads the Way in Private Housing" in *Life* (New York), 15 November 1937; "The Modern House in America" in *Architectural Forum* (New York), July 1939; "Plastics and Architecture" in *Architectural Record* (New York), July 1940; "The Architect and House" by Talbot Hamlin in *Pencil Points* (New York), May 1942; "The Town a Test Tube Built" by Mary Ellen Green and Mark Murphy in *Saturday Evening Post* (Philadelphia), 1 May 1943; "Acoustic of Music Shells" in *Pencil Points* (New York), September 1945; "Architecture: Alden Dow" in *Life* (New York), 15 March 1948; "The Work of Alden B. Dow" by Talbot Hamlin in *Nuestra Arquitectura* (Buenos Aires), November 1948; "The Architect and his Community in *Progressive Architecture* (New York), February 1955; "Your Legacy from Frank Lloyd Wright" in *House Beautiful* (New York), October 1959; "Five Buildings by Alden B. Dow" in *Architectural Record* (New York), September 1967.

Writing about the architecture of Alden B. Dow is discomfiting because Dow's work defies some of the most basic assumptions of current architectural criticism and theory. These are buildings that genuinely do not "speak for themselves." These are buildings that are connected to the life, status, and identity of their designer. These are buildings that demand attention as much because of who designed them as because of "what they are."

Dow's architecture has to be seen in three segments: pre-Frank Lloyd Wright, under the tutelage of Wright, and rejecting Wright. The fact that Dow was the first Taliesin Fellow to enter private practice is critical to an understanding of the significance of his architecture. This challenges one of the basic assumptions both of contemporary architecture and of architectural theory: that buildings have a formal integrity such that historical data surrounding them serve as an embellishment of the "facts" provided by the built form.

The Midland Country Club, predating formal contact with Wright; his own studio, very much under the influence of Wright; and the Center for the Arts, Midland, conceived after the personal and professional break with Wright, exemplify these three phases of Dow's work. The forms themselves are so fundamentally different that they can only be understood in terms of Dow's life-politics. They have to be taken as the touchstones of Wright's influence on a disciple. Their variety resists a "new critic's" approach.

Just as it is impossible to ignore the relationship to Wright in discussing Dow's architecture, so is it impossible to ignore his position as the second son of the founder of the Dow Chemical Company. The three works mentioned above relate the company to the home community and Dow to his home community. They are the Dow family holding a colloquy with Midland. They are in (but not on) and of Main Street. The sites are not random—they are part of the significance of the work—and they claim relevance to an artist's status and forbears in evaluating his work. But our very concept of art denies the importance of the artist's background and elevates "artistic genius" above class or even education.

In the Country Club, Dow celebrates leisure as the basis of the elite of an "egalitarian" society. It is a "room for one's own class" in a "classless" society. He celebrates relation of himself and his family as chieftains of this leisured class—and celebrates the virtues provided by leisure.

In his studio, Dow shows how Wright's romantic, domestic Jeffersonianism can endow an aristocratic "work"-space with "cosmic" significance, distinction, class, and taste. Built on Dow family land, it is a demonstration of the worthiness of inherited wealth for the privileges it affords its unselected beneficiaries. The worthiness comes from the act of choice, benefited from breeding (born a Dow) and good education (contact with Wright), where these can and do provide cultivation of the senses.

The Center for the Arts turns its back to Wright and Domestic Virtues. This is Dow speaking. An enormous Jack-in-the-box, it patronizes its users and gingerly exposes them to the fringes of high culture in a shopping-center-like setting. Better *they* spend their time watching Live Theater than go bowling. No Wrightian romance here: this building is about making money off culture—and patronizing it at the same time. It is yet another act of defiance of the dictates of High Culture and the priestly class of Critics. For "what it is," it is an utterly wretched building; for "what it says," it is a statement whose significance should be neither belittled nor ignored.

—Joseph Juhasz

DOWNS, Barry Vance.

Canadian. Born in Vancouver, British Columbia, 19 June 1930. Educated at Lord Byng High School, Vancouver, 1941-47; University of Washington, Seattle, 1949-54, B.Arch. 1954. Married Mary Hunter in 1955; children: William and Elizabeth. Architect/Draftsman/Designer, Thompson Berwick Pratt and Partners, Vancouver, 1954-63; Partner, with Fred Hollingsworth, Hollingsworth and Downs, West Vancouver, 1963-67; in private practice, Vancouver, 1967-69. Since 1969, Partner, with Richard B. Archambault, Downs/Archambault Architects, Vancouver. Visiting Lecturer, University of British Columbia, Vancouver, 1960-63. Member, Vancouver Civic Design Panel, 1967-68; Member, Housing Design Council of Canada, 1969-73; Member, Heritage Advisory Committee, Vancouver, 1974-76. Member, City of Vancouver Historical Advisory board, since 1971. Recipient: First Prize, Canada Art Gallery Competition, 1957; Massey Medal, Canada, 1964; First Award, Canadian Wood Design Awards, 1965; Canadian Housing Design Award, 1967, 1969,1974, 1976, and 1981; Award of Excellence, *Canadian Architect,* 1969, 1971, 1974, and 1981; Canadian Education Showplace Award, 1973; Award, Royal Architectural Institute of Canada, 1980; Award, Architectural Institute of British Columbia, 1983 and 1984. Member, Architectural Institute of British Columbia; Fellow, Royal Architectural Institute of Canada. Member, Royal Canadian Academy of Art, Address: Downs/Archambault, 1272 Richards Street, Vancouver, British Columbia V6B 3G2, Canada.

Works:

1960 Winnipeg City Hall (competition project)
1961 Ladner Public Library, Ladner, British Columbia (with Richard Archambault)
1964 Rayer House, West Vancouver
1966 Cocking House, West Vancouver
1967 Smith House, West Vancouver
1968 Canadian Pavilion, *Expo '70,* Osaka, Japan (competition project)
    Toy Ski Cabin, Whistler, British Columbia
    Bowker House, West Vancouver
1969 Prettie House, Bowen Island, British Columbia
    Strathcona Girls' School, Shawnigan Lake, British Coumbia (with Ian Davidson)
1970 Guerin House, Point Roberts, Washington
    Lamont House, Langley, British Columbia
1971 Sedgewick Building, University of Victoria, British Columbia
    Botanical Gardens, University of British Columbia, Vancouver
1972 McNairn House, Salt Spring Island, British Columbia
    Caine House, West Vancouver
1973 Lions Paraplegic Lodge, Vancouver FP.18 (public housing development), Vancouver
1973/
75 North Vancouver Civic Centre
    Britannia Community Services Centre, Vancouver
1974 Murphy House, Hernando Isand, British Columbia
    Master plan for Champlain Heights, Vancouver
    Single women's apartments, Vancouver
    MacInnes Place (courtyard housing), Burnaby, British Columbia
1974/
77 Lester Pearson College of the Pacific, Peddar Bay, Vancouver Island (with Ron Thom)
1975 Burke Mountain Enviroment Planning Study, Coquitlam, British Columbia (with others)
1976 Multi-Purpose Complex, Simon Fraser University, Burnaby, British Columbia
1977 RCMP Building, Prince Rupert, British Columbia
    R.C. Macdonald Elementary School, Coquitlam, British Columbia
    False Creek Housing, Vancouver
1978 Chinese Cultural Centre, Vancouver (competition project)
    Public Library, New Westminster, British Columbia
    Carnegie Building Community Centre, Vancouver
1979 Patio Houses, Champlain, Vancouver
    Gymnasium/Arts Building, York House School, Vancouver
    Arts Club Theatre, Granville Island, Vancouver
    Alder Bay Co-op Housing, Vancouver (with Davidson/Johnson)
    Spruce Townhouses, Vancover
1980 Office Building, 541 Howe Street, Vancouver
1981 Mountain Inn, Whistler, British Columbia
1982 Simon Fraser University Club, Vancouver
    Surrey Centennial Centre, British Columbia
1983 Tumbler Ridge Town Hall, Royal Canadian Mounted Police Headquarters, and Firehall, British Columbia
    White Rock Royal Canadian Mounted Police Detachment, British Columbia
    Langara Student Building, Vancouver
1984 St. Pius X Church, North Vancouver
    Songhees Point Master Plan, Victoria, British Columbia

Publications:

By DOWNS: book—*Sacred Places: British Columbia's Early Churches,* Vancouver 1980; articles—"Vancouver" in *Canadian Architect* (Toronto), October 1963; "A Plea for What Counts" in *Western Homes and Living* (Vancouver), January/February 1970; "Focus on British Columbia" in *Architecture Canada* (Toronto), 22 May 1972; "The Royal Engineers in British Columbia" in *Canadian Collector* (Toronto), May/June 1976; "Dawson City: A Tour of Heritage Town" in *Western Living* (Vancouver), September 1976; "A Richness of Form, Space and Books" in *Canadian Architect* (Toronto) January 1978.

On DOWNS: books—*Canadian Architecture 1960-70,* Toronto 1970; *Building with Words: Canadian Architects on Architecture.* with introduction by W. Bernstein and R. Cawker, Toronto 1981; articles—"This Is a Factory Built House?" in *Plywood World* (Vancouver), January-April 1968; "Projects: Barry Downs" in *Canadian Architect* (Toronto), August 1968; "Faculty Club" in the *Canadian Architect Yearbook,* Toronto 1971; "A House Built Open to Nature" in *House and Garden* (New York), July 1973; "Community Effort to Make Allies of Education and Leisure" in *Architectural Record*(New York), May 1975; "Vancouver's Land Shortage Gets Citizens into the Design Process" in *Landscape Architecture* (Louisville, Kentucky), March 1976; "Britannia Community Services Centre, Vancouver" and "North Vancouver City Centre" in *Canadian Architect* (Toronto), June 1977; "Strandhaus am Pazifik" in *Baumeister* (Munich), January 1978; "Downs Residence, West Vancouver" in *Wood World* (Vancouver), no. 1, 1980; "Homemaking at Harborside" in *Progressive Architecture* (New York), August 1980; "Participatory Planning," in *Architects' Journal* (London), 13 August 1980; "Clement Residence, Vancouver" in *Canadian Architect* (Toronto), December 1981; "Heritage and Harmony" in *Canadian Architect* (Toronto), August 1983; "Idea into Form" in *Vanguard* (Vancouver), September 1983.

Architecture cannot divorce itself from social and humanistic needs. In our practice, it has been possible to include these major considerations in a planning process where user and client play a major part in shaping the building or master plan. We often act as a catalyst in this process and supply background material; talk out psychic, social, and physical needs helps establish design criteria, and provide a full range of design alternatives. In so doing, our work remains consistently flexible, although always concerned with human scale, the use of natural materials, and appropriateness of building to site (and/or street), and embodies all the design elements so essential in the North-West, including the harnessing of natural light and the insuring of a strong sense of shelter.

Through design, architectural styles are explored as the program and client demand, yet an underlying language prevails. A building's aesthetic results, which is at once familiar, sometimes unique, often romantic or borrowed from history. All this is fused to its urban or natural setting, which in the end acts as the primary force at work.

—Barry Downs

Now that the functional concerns of modern architecture have been broadened to include the psycho-social needs of its users, some architects have realized that cultural values differ between groups and yet are equally valid. Under our educational system, the architect's taste is usually shaped away from that of the people for whom he designs, and a number of approaches have been evolved to somehow bridge this gap: for example, limiting the architect's role to the provision of basic frameworks

Barry Downs: Church of Pius X, North Vancouver, 1984.

on which users may imprint their personalities; do-it-yourself kits; feeding sociological norms into the computer. Barry Downs has favoured another approach, that of bringing the users into the design process instead of restricting client participation to owners and administrators.

Down's method has been to determine the key elements of design, such as entrances or lighting effects, then with the users to work out appropriate environmental responses, thereby establishing a range of patterns to be later organized into a building solution. Citizen participation in this sense is a feedback mechanism that reacts to the architect's design proposals; the user does not initiate those proposals. The resultant architecture, while looking as if it has responded to its users' concerns, is therefore likely to be really a modified projection of the architect's own beliefs concerning the sort of architecture that is socially relevant. For instance, while some widley popular buildings take advantage of their bigness to create dramaticeffects, Downs's buildings are small in scale even when they are large in size, a refelction of his own design philosophy. Similarly, the domestic range of materials with which he works is of the West Coast residential idiom rather than of the internationalism of industrial technology.

Small is beautiful, a homely style, citizen participation: that these are what the majority believes or wants is difficult to prove. The West Coast style is different in character from the sort of homes and furnishings that are generally sold on the open market. Conversely the West Coast style was admired by certain architects and their middle-class clients long before it was associated with other virtues. In this context, Downs's work does not reach the highest qualitative level. On the other hand, unlike most of his comtemporaries, he has sucessfully extended his philosophy into the public realm, seemingly reducing the architectural schism between

small-scale and large-scale environments. The virtue of his work is that it accommodates a humane way of life without pretentiousness, and in its time and place, this achievement is sufficiently rare to warrant notice and respect.

—Anthony Jackson

DOWSON, Philip Manning.

British. Born in Johannesburg, South Africa, 16 August 1924. Educated at Gresham's School, England, 1937-42; studied mathematics at University College, Oxford, 1942-43, and fine arts at Clare College, Cambridge, 1947-50, M.A. 1950; studied at the Architectural Association School, London, 1950-53, Dip.A.A. 1953; influenced by Arthur Korn, *q.v.*, Ernesto Rogers, *q.v.*, and Eduardo Catalano, *q.v.* Served in the Royal Navy, in the North Atlantic, Mediterranean, and Far East, 1943-47; Lieutenant in the Royal Navy Volunteer Reserve. Married Sarah Crewdson in 1950; children: Anna, Charles, and Katherine. Worked as an architect with Ove Arup, *q.v.*, and Partners, London, 1953-63; Architectural Founder Partner, Arup Associates, London, since 1963 (group practice: with Ove Arup, Ronald Hobbs, and Derek Sugden, engineers); Senior Partner, Ove Arup Partnership, London, since 1969. Member of the Crafts Advisory Committee, London, 1971-75; Governor, St. Martin's School of Art, London, 1975-80. External Examiner for Cambridge University, since 1965; Member, Royal Fine Art Commission, since 1971; Trustee, Thomas Cubitt Trust, London, since 1978; Council Member, Royal Academy of of Arts, London, since 1981; Trustee,

Royal Botanical Gardens, Kew, and The Armouries of the Tower of London, since 1983. Exhibitions: Lyon, France, 1966; *Arup Associates,* Architectural Association, London, 1973; *Models,* Sheffield Society of Architects, 1974; *Summer Exhibition,* Royal Academy of Arts, London, 1975, 1976, 1977, 1978, 1979, 1981, 1982, and 1983; Munich, 1977; Association of Consulting Architects Salon, Royal Academy of Arts, London, 1978, 1979, 1982, and 1984; British Council, Tehran, 1978; Parma, Italy, 1979; *Biennale,* Venice, 1982; *Arup Associates,* Edinburgh and Dundee, Scotland, 1984; *Architecture Now,* Royal Institute of British Architects, London, 1984; *The Art of Architecture,* Royal Institute of British Architects, London, 1984. Recipient: Civic Trust Awards, 1965, 1968, 1972, 1980, and 1984; Architecture Awards, 1966, 1972, 1979, 1980, 1981, and 1983, and Gold Medal, 1981, Royal Institute of British Architects; Concrete Society Awards, 1969, and 1976; Structural Steel Design Awards, 1970, 1977, and 1984; *Financial Times* Architecture Awards, 1972, 1973, and 1983; Business and Industry Awards, 1976, 1978, 1979, and 1982. Associate, Royal Academy of Arts, London, 1979; Fellow, Society of Industrial Artists and Designers, London, 1981. CBE(Commander, Order of the British Empire), 1969; Knighthood, 1980. Address: Arup Associates, 2-4 Dean Street, London W1V 5RN, England.

Works:

1954/
  64 Ciba (ARL) Ltd. plants, offices and laboratories, Duxford, Cambridgeshire
1958/
  62 Vaughan Building, Somerville College, Oxford

Philip Dowson: International Garden Festival Building, Liverpool, 1982-84.

1959/
64 Point Royal Flats, Bracknell, Berkshire
1960/
71 Department of Nuclear Physics, Oxford
1961/
64 Leckhampton House, Corpus Christi College, Cambridge
1962/
64 Long Wall House, Long Melford, Suffolk
1964/
66 Department of Metallurgy and Mining, University of Birmingham
1964/
70 Department of Arts and Social Sciences, University of Leicester
1964/
71 New Museums Building, Department of Zoology, Metallurgy, and Computer Science, Cambridge
1965/
66 Old Addenbrooke's Area Development Plan, Cambridge
1965/
67 The Maltings Concert Hall, Snape, Suffolk
1965/
69 House, 2a Drax Avenue, Wimbledon, London
1965/
71 *Oxford Mail and Times* Headquarters and Printing Works, Oxford
1966/
68 Graduate and Undergraduate Accommodation, Trinity Hall, Cambridge
Penguin Books Offices and Warehouse, Harmondsworth, Middlesex
1966/
72 IBM Process Assembly Plant, Warehouse, Offices, and Computer Centre, Havant, Hampshire
1967/
74 Married Students Community Development, University College, Oxford

1968/
71 Horizon Factory, John Player and Sons Ltd.,
1969/
71 Development plan, stage II, University of Sheffield, Yorkshire
1969/
75 IBM Headquarters, Johannesburg, South Africa
1970/
73 Department of Music and Music School, University of East Anglia, Norwich
1970/
76 Sir Thomas White Building, St. John's College, Oxford
1970/
82 IBM Headquarters, North Harbour, Portsmouth, Hampshire
1971/
78 Dock and support buildings, Portsmouth Dockyard, Hampshire
1972/
76 Trumans Ltd. Brewery Headquarters, Brick Lane, London
1973/
76 Wiggins Teape Headquarters, Basingstoke, Hampshire
1973/
78 Lloyd's Administrative Headquarters, Chatham, Kent
Central Electricity Generating Board South-West Regional Headquarters, Bristol
1977/
82 Babergh District Council Offices, Hadleigh, Suffolk
1978/
83 Leslie and Godwin Ltd. Offices, Farnborough, Kent
1979/
81 Bedford School, Bedfordshire
Digital Equipment Company computer assembly plant and offices, Reading,

Berkshire
1981 Bab Al Sheikh city centre redevelopment, Baghdad, Iraq
Sports Centre for the Diplomatic Quarter, Riyadh, Saudi Arabia
1982/
84 International Garden Festival Building, Liverpool, Merseyside
Eton College Science Laboratories, Buckinghamshire
1983/
84 London Docklands Light Railway Study, London
1983 BBC Broadcating Centre, Edinburgh, Scotland
1984 Building renovation, 416 Dundas Street, Toronto
Guild Hall Building, Toronto (project)
All Saints' Hospital, Springhill, Nova Scotia (project)
Maple Leaf Key West Building (project)
1985 Life Sciences and Environmental Studies Building, York University, Toronto
Reininger House, Newmarket, Ontario

Publications:

By DOWSON: articles—"The Architect's Approach to Architecture" in *RIBA Journal* (London), March 1966; "Building for Science" in *Architectural Design* (London), April 1967; "A Room of One's Own" in *Architectural Design* (London), April 1968; "Architecture and Professional Integration" in *Public Works Congress Report,* London 1972; "Integration—Disintegration?" in *JLO Conference Report,* York 1973; "Complex Yet Humane Architecture" in *The Times* (London), 7 May 1975; "Offices" in *Arup Journal* (London), December 1977; "Some Personal Thoughts During European Architectural Heritage Year, 1976" in *Architecture*

+ *Urbanism* (Tokyo), December 1977; "Commodity, Fitness and Harmony," interview in *Concrete Quarterly* (London), April/July 1981; "Discourse at the RIBA Gold Medal Presentation" in *Arup Journal* (London), March 1981; "Architecture: In Crisis?" in *RIBA Transactions* (London), no. 1, 1982.

On DOWSON: books—*Precast Concrete in Architecture* by A. E. J. Morris, London 1978; *Arup Associates: The Biography of an Architectural Practice* by Michael Brawne, London 1983; articles—"Arup Associates" in *Architecture + Urbanism* (Tokyo), December 1977; "Arup Associates and the Group Practice Experience" by M. O'Hare in *Progressive Architecture* (New York), no. 4, 1971.

*

Architecture requires us constantly to re-interpret and revalue technology in human and social terms. The conviction that close-knit, interdisciplinary design teams are necessary to confront the scale and complexity of modern buildings for the survival of an architecture that embodies humane ideas led directly to the creation of Arup Association.

However, whilst method and analysis can never substitute for an architecture that helps to enrich and not diminish our lives and surroundings, nevertheless, in considering means and ends, the "ends" have become so complex that it has become necessary to design new ways of designing buildings, if an architecture is to be derived from all the sources that can nourish it.

We are faced with a daunting problem of creating an environment for mass need that will not itself be despoiled by the very measures designed to meet the need. The teachings of Gropius and the example of the Bauhaus have perhaps been the main influence.

—Philip Dowson

*

It is exceptional for a distinguished architect to be a member of a firm of structural engineers, but Philip Dowson almost uniquely spans the gap that exists today between science and the arts. Ove Arup and Partners have acquired an international reputation not only for their own pure structural form but also for their interpretation of an architect's idea, such as the Sydney Opera House, imaginatively if vaguely designed by the Danish architect JØrn Utzon. With the head of the firm so sensitive to architecture himself, it is not surprising that he should have encouraged architecture as one of the multi-disciplines within his organization.

Since architects usually employ engineers rather than the other way round, the architectural profession felt some concern over what was described as a "package deal." It is to Dowson's credit that he has risen above any criticism that he is making the arts subservient. On the contrary, in all the work that he has designed under the firm's name (with full acknowledgement to himself personally), he seems never to have been anything other than an artist working freely and without restraint in a medium that he thoroughly understands and can control.

Dowson's work is clearly inspired and enriched by the closeness to his varied colleagues and by the constant interchange of ideas that is only possible in a multi-purpose and friendly office. This reversal of the normal relationship between architect and engineer has probably called for a special approach. Usually, an architect expands outwards, as it were, from the creative artist within himself, and his early ideas of form may later be modified by the engineer; in the process his building may lose some of its original humanity. The evidence suggests that Dowson begins from the functional and structural angle and afterwards gives it warmth and humanity as only an artist can. Certainly, all his work has an element of classicism in its pure geometry and in the charm that it holds for the layman so easily overwhelmed by bigness, hostility of material, and inelegance.

—Geoffrey Jellicoe

DOXIADIS, Constantinos Apostolos.

Greek. Born in Stenimachos, 14 May 1913. Studied architecture and engineering, Technical University, Athens, Dip.Arch.Ing. 1935; engineering, Berlin-Charlottenburg University, Dr.Ing. 1936. Served in the artillery of the Greek Army, 1940-41, 1944-45, and as Head of the Hephaestus National Resistance Group, 1941-44: Captain; Greek Military Cross. Married Emma Scheepers in 1940; children: Evanthia, Calliope, Euphrosyne, and Apostolos. Chief Town Planning Officer of the Greater Athens Area, Athens, 1937-39; Head of the Department of Regional and Town Planning, Ministry of Public Works, Athens, 1939-45; Under-Secretary and Director General, Ministry of Housing and Reconstruction, Athens, 1945-48; Under-Secretary and Co-ordinator of the Greek Recovery Programme, Ministry of Co-ordination, Athens, 1948-51; Founder-president, 1951-72, and Chairman, 1973 until his death, 1975, Doxiadis Associates International, Athens: established Washington, D.C., office, 1959. Lecturer and Acting Professor of Town Planning, Technical University, Athens, 1939-43; also Visiting Lecturer at University of Chicago, University of Dublin, Harvard University, University of Michigan, New York University, Oxford University, Princeton University, Massachusetts Institute of Technology, Yale University, University of Massachusetts, Georgia Institute of Technology, and Swarthmore College. Chairman of the Board of Directors, and Founder of the Center of Ekistics, Athens Technical Organization, from 1958. Member of the International Federation for Housing and Planning; Society for International Development; American Management Association; American Institute of Planners; American Society of Planning Officials; International Committee of the Institute on Man and Science. Recipient: Sir Patrick Abercrombie Prize, International Union of Architects, 1963; Cali de Oro Award, Society of Mexican Architects, 1963; Award of Excellence, Industrial Designers of America, 1965; Humanities Award, Aspen Institute of Humanistic Studies, Colorado, 1966; Gold Medal, Royal Architectural Institute of Canada, 1976. Honorary LL.D.: Swarthmore College , 1962; Mills College, 1964; University of Michigan, 1967; Tulane University, 1978; Kalamazoo College, 1968; D.H.: Wayne State University, 1964; L.H.D.: Northern Michigan University, 1965; Case Western Reserve University, 1969; D.Sc.: Detroit Institute of Technology, 1966; University of Pittsburgh, 1967; Marietta College, 1969; D.F.A.: University of Rhode Island, 1966. Honorary Member, Industrial Designers of America; Honorary Corresponding Member, Royal Incorporation of Architects of Scotland; Town Planning Institute of Great Britain; Deutsche Akademie fur Stadtebau und Landesplanung. O.B.E. (Order of the British Empire), 1945; Order of the Cedar, Lebanon, 1958; Royal Order of the Phoenix, Greece, 1960; Order of the Flag, Yugoslavia, 1966. *Died* (in Athens) *28 June 1975.*

Works:

1947/
  60 City Development Plan, Islamabad, Pakistan
1955 National Housing Programme, Iraq
1958 National Housing Programme, Lebanon
     University of the Panjab, Pakistan
1965/
  70 Urban Development Plan, Detroit, Michigan
1966 Kafue Town Development Plan, Zambia
1972/
  75 University of Patra Master Plan, Greece
     (completed by others, 1985)
1974/
  75 Housing Development, Apollonion, Greece
     (completed by others, 1976)
  Ongoing projects include—Regional Plans for: State of Guanabara, Brazil; Mediterranean Region, France; Accra-Tema-Akosombo, Ghana; Athens, Greece; Mainland Greece; Greater Mussayib, Iraq; Cyrenaica, Libya; Lagos State, Nigeria; Bendel Midwestern State, Nigeria; Central Region, Saudi Arabia; Northern Region, Saudi Arabia; Province of Guipuzcoa, Spain; Island of Tenerife, Canary Islands; Province of Barcelona, Spain; Province of Gerona, Spain; Province of Lerida, Spain; Greater Cleveland, Ohio; Greater Detroit, Michigan; Great Lakes Megalopolis, U.S.A.; Province of Lusaka, Zambia; Urban Master Plans for: Limassol, Cyprus; Accra-Tema, Ghana; Akosombo, Ghana; Tema, Ghana; Arta, Greece; Aspra Spitia, Greece; Igoumenitsa, Greece; Ioannina, Greece; Patmos, Greece; Preveza, Greece; Rhodos, Greece; Serres, Greece; Baghdad, Iraq; 25 towns (50,000 hectares), Iraq; Kirkuk, Iraq; Otranto, Italy; South Aqaba, Jordan; Beida, Libya; Marsa al Bregah, Libya; major urban centres (342,000 hectares), Nigeria; Black Arts Festival Village, Lagos, Nigeria; Ilorin, Nigeria; Jos-Bukuru, Benue Plateau, Nigeria; 4 towns in the South-Eastern State, Nigeria; Islamabad, Pakistan; Korangi, Pakistan; Riyadh, Saudi Arabia; 5 towns in the Central Region, Saudi Arabia; Leon, Spain; Zumarraga, Spain; Chiclana de la Frontera, Spain; Playa de las Americas, Tenerife, Canary Islands; Capdepera, Majorca, Spain; La Orotava, Spain; Puerto de la Cruz, Spain; La Guardia, Pontevedra, Spain; Tuy, Pontevedra, Spain; Khartoum, Sudan, Sudan; Port Sudan; Homs, Hama and Selemiyah, Syria; Eastwick, Pennsylvania; Skopje, Yugoslavia; Chipata, Zambia; Kafue, Zambia; Lusaka, Zambia; Mongu, Zambia; 16 rural townships, Zambia.

Publications:

By DOXIADIS: books—*Raumordnung in griechischen Stadtebau*, Berlin and Heidelberg 1937, as *Architectural Space in Ancient Greece*, Cambridge, Massachusetts 1972; *A Simple Story*, Athens 1945; *Ekistic Analysis*, Athens 1946; *Destruction of Towns and Villages in Greece*, Athens 1946; *A Plan for the Survival of the Greek People*, 2 vols., with others, Athens 1947; *Ekistic Policies for the Reconstruction of the Country with a 20-year Programme*, Athens 1947; *Dodecanese*, 2 vols., with others, Athens 1950; *March of the People*, Athens 1949; *Our Capital and its Future*, Athens 1960; *Architecture in Transition*, London and New York 1963; *The New World of Urban Man*, with T. B. Douglass, Philadelphia and Boston 1965; *Urban Renewal and the Future of the American City*, Chicago 1966; *Between Dystopia and Utopia*, Hartford, Connecticut 1966; *Emergence and Growth of an Urban Region: the Developing Urban Detroit Area*, 3 vols., Detroit 1966-70; *Ecumenopolis: The Settlement of the Future*, Athens 1967; *Campus Planning in an Urban Area: A Master Plan for Rensselaer Polytechnic Institute*, New York 1971; *The Two-Headed Eagle: From the Past to the Future of Human Settlements*, Athens 1972; *The Great Urban Crimes We Permit by Law*, Athens 1973; *Anthropopolis: City for Human Development*, Athens 1974; *Building Entopia*, Athens 1975; *Action for Human Settlements*, Athens 1976; *Ecology and Ekistics*, edited by Gerald Dix, London 1977.

On DOXIADIS: articles—"Konstantinos Apostolu Doxiadis" in *Der Aufbau* (Vienna), no 12, 1958; "Dr. C. A. Doxiadis und die 'Oekistik'" by M. Wegenstein in *Schweizerische Bauzeitung* (Zurich), 20 August 1959; "Doxiadis Associates" by L. K. Watson in *RIBA Journal* (London), October 1960; "The Remarkable Dr. Doxiadis" by E. Ehrenkrantz and O. Tanner in *Architectural Forum* (New York), May 1961; "Doxiadis' contribution to the pedestrian view of the city" by Roland Wedgwood in *Architects Year Book*, London 1965; "Doxiadis' Anthropocosmos" in *Ekistics* (Athens), November 1967; "Emanation from Athens" by Joseph Watterson in *AIA Journal* (Washington, D.C.), May 1968; "Obituary: Prof. Konstaninos Doxiadis" in *Building* (London), 4 July 1975; "Constantinos Doxiadis, City Planner" in *Architectural Record* (New York), August 1975; "Constantinos A. Doxiadis, 1913-

Jane Drew: Torbay Hospital Operating Theatres, Devon, 1973.

1975: pursuit of an attainable ideal", special issue of *Ekistics* (Athens), June 1976; "Constantinos A. Doxiadis: projects and writings", special issue of *Space Design* (Tokyo), July 1976; "Doxiadis: the man and his ideas" by James R. Stewart in *Majallah Akitek* (Kuala Lumpur), March 1977; "Background to Constantinos A. Doxiadis' Ecology and Ekistics" by J. Tyrwhitt in *Ekistics* (Athens), January 1978.

It was chiefly as an original urban planner that Constantinos Doxiadis acquired his world-wide reputation. He founded in Athens the organisation known as Doxiadis Associates, which was responsible for urban projects in many countries. But it was mainly for his theories, applied in several plans, that Doxiadis exerted so extensive an influence. He coined several new words to explain his theories, words such as "Ekistics," "Dynapolis," and "Ecumenopolis," The most important was the general term "Ekistics," which is defined as the Science of Human Settlements. He established in Athens an Ekistics Centre and issued a periodical called *Ekistics*.

He was actuated in his theories by the desire to provide the best possible living conditions for people, which has been extremely difficult because of the pressure on space, often resulting in congestion and slums, which too frequently occur with the rapid increases of world population. The spread of cities has often been haphazard and unplanned, with the disastrous result of overcrowding with all its evils. His contention was that the rapid growth of population should be accommodated by careful planning on the basis of well-thought-out principles. To do this, he evolved the idea of the dynamic city, which meant expansion not by a concentric growth in the surrounding country as had been done in the past, but by creation of new centres along an axis, thus linearly and in one direction, each forming a limited concentric growth, a process he called Dynapolis. It can thus be seen that a chain of cities, with open country on either side, is created. When the first city reaches a maximum size, another is created in one direction, and when this second city approaches a maximum population, a third city is started, and so on. He was influenced to some extent in his theories by the Spanish planner, Arturo Soria, who planned a small linear city near Madrid about 1882. This was based mainly on transport—a

tramway spine. Although transport is an important factor, this was not the main consideration for Doxiadis, who was rather more concerned with accommodation of a fast-growing population in a spacious manner and giving a high quality of life to its inhabitants.

Doxiadis was able to apply some of his theories in actual projects. With his partners and assistants, he prepared plans for Islamabad, the new capital of Pakistan, for the city of Tema in Ghana, Kafue in Zambia, and Beida in Libya. In addition, he produced several urban renewal plans, not only in his own country of Greece, but in the United States, including those for Detroit, Washington D.C., Eastwick in Philadelphia, and Hampton, Virginia.

It should be emphasised, as previously indicated, the purpose of these theories and plans is to replace laissez-faire development and its evil consequences with a planned and systematic development according to well-thought-out principles based on extensive social research and thus provide populations with satisfactory living conditions. It is a purpose similar to that of dispersal by means of satellite towns, each surrounded by a green belt, although the method is different. Doxiadis deserves to be remembered as one of the imaginative planning theorists of the century.

—Arnold Whittick

DREW, Jane Beverley.

British. Born in Thornton Heath, Surrey, 24 March 1911. Educated at Croydon High School, Surrey, 1917-23; Architectural Association School, London, 1924-29, Dip. A.A. Married the architect James Thomas Alliston in 1937; the architect E. Maxwell Fry, *q.v.*, in 1942; children: Jennifer and Sarah. Assistant to architect Joseph Hill, London, 1938-39; Partner, with James Alliston, Alliston and Drew, London, 1939; Principal, Office of Jane B. Drew, London, 1940-45: Consultant to the British Commercial Gas Corporation, 1941-43, and Assistant Town Planning Adviser to the Resident Minister for the West African Colonies, 1944-46. Founder-Partner, with E. Maxwell Fry, of Fry, Drew and

Partners, London (including Fry, Drew, Drake, and Lasdun, 1951-58), 1946-73, and Fry, Drew, Knight and Creamer (with Frank S. Knight and Norman Creamer), London, since 1973. Senior Architect to the Punjab Government, India, 1952-54. Beamis Professor, Massachusetts Institute of Technology, Cambridge, 1961; Visiting Professor of Architecture, Harvard University, Cambridge, Massachusetts, 1970; Bicentennial Professor, University of Utah, Salt Lake City, 1976. Joint Editor, with Trevor Dannatt, *Architects Yearbook*, London, 1946-62. President, Architectural Association, London, 1969. Member of the Council, Royal Institute of British Architects. Exhibitions: *Kitchen Planning*, Dorland Hall, London, 1941; *Britain Can Make It*, Olympia, London, 1942; *Rebuilding Britain*, National Gallery, London, 1943; *South Bank Exhibition*, Festival of Britain, London, 1951; *Suffragettes and Suffragists*, St. James Hall, Westminster, London, 1978. LL.D.: University of Ibadan, Nigeria, 1966; Open University, Milton Keynes, Buckinghamshire, 1973. Fellow, Royal Institute of British Architects, Institute of Arbitrators, and the Society of Industrial Artists. Associate, Indian Institute of Architects; Honorary Fellow, American Institute of Architects, 1978. Address: Fry, Drew, Knight and Creamer, The Chantry, 19 High Street, Sevenoaks, Kent TN14 6HG, England.

Works:

1940 Walton Yacht Works, London
1946 Prempeh College, Kumasi, Ghana
      Adisadel College, Ghana (with E. Maxwell Fry)
      Amedzofe Teacher Training College, Togoland (with E. Maxwell Fry)
1947 Wesley Girls School, Cape Coast, Ghana
1949/
  51 Hospital buildings, Kuwait Oil Company
1950 Passfields (flats), Lewisham, London (with E. Maxwell Fry)
1951 Waterloo Bridge Entrance and Harbour Bar, *South Bank Exhibition*, Festival of Britain, London (with E. Maxwell Fry)
1953 Flats, Whitefoot Lane, Lewisham, London (with E. Maxwell Fry)

1953/
  59 Ibadan University College, Nigeria (with E. Maxwell Fry)
1954/
  56 New Capital City, Chandigarh, India (with E. Maxwell Fry, Le Corbusier, and Pierre Jeanneret)
1957/
  59 Housing, health, and amenity buildings, Iran Oil Company, Tehran
1959 Gach Saran New Town, Iran
       Co-operative Bank Offices and Shop, Lagos, Nigeria
       Co-operative Bank Assembly Hall and Maiso-nettes, Ibadan, Nigeria
       Gulf House, Gulf Oil Company, London
1960 Lionel de Wint Art Centre, Ceylon
1964 Apowa Training Centre, Ghana
       Institute of Contemporary Arts, London
       Housing, Hatfield, Hertfordshire
       Housing, Mark Hall Neighbourhood, Har-low, Essex
       Housing, Welwyn, Hertfordshire
1965 Kaduna Olympic Stadium and Swimming Pool, Nigeria
       Hotel, Colombo, Ceylon
1968 School for the Deaf, Herne Hill, London
1969/
  77 Open University, Milton Keynes, Bucking-hamshire
1970 Carlton House Terrace and Art Gallery, London
1973 Torbay Hospital and Nurses' Residence, Devon
1976 Gestetner Building, Stirling, Scotland
1977 Institute of Education, Mauritius
1978 Science Block, St. Paul's Girls' School, London

Publications:

By DREW: books—*Kitchen Planning*, London 1945; *Architects Yearbook*, editor, 14 numbers, 1946-62; books, with E. Maxwell Fry—*Architecture for Children*, London 1944, re-issued as *Architecture and the Environment*, London 1976; *Village Housing in the Tropics*, with Harry L. Ford, London 1947; *Tropical Architecture in the Humid Zone*, London 1956; *Tropical Architecture in the Dry and Humid Zones*, London 1964; article—"Some Work by Women Architects" in *Architectural Design* (London), August 1975.

On DREW: book—*Fry, Drew, Knight and Creamer: Architecture*, edited by Stephen Hitchins, with introduction by H. A. N. Brockman, London 1978; article—"Nigeria Today" by Noel Moffett in *RIBA Journal* (London), June 1977.

My work has ranged from specialist studies on kitchen planning when I was a consultant to the British Commercial Gas Corporation during the War, to large-scale town planning work first in West Africa and later in India and Iran. A major part of my work is in West Africa and India, but there is some in Ceylon, France, Mauritius, Kuwait and some in England.

I have been a friend of artists and very interested in contemporary artists' work. My friendships have included Ben Nicholson, Henry Moore, Barbara Hepworth, Eduardo Paolozzi, Lynn Chadwick, Graham Sutherland, Victor Pasmore, Le Corbusier and Gropius, Burle Marx and, above all, my husband Maxwell Fry. These friendships have much influenced me, including the work of Denys Lasdun who was our partner, and the work of the CIAM Group and the MARS Group. The support of staff and partners has been invaluable to me; more and more do I agree with Professor Lethaby who said that a good building is many men thick.

I have liked to be concerned with buildings where the purpose of the building itself is a challenge—such as the first university in West Africa, Ibadan University, or the School for Deaf Children at Herne Hill or the Open University or, perhaps most of all, the Institute of Contemporary Arts. When working on hospitals, I have tried to make them friendly, not frightening, whilst remaining efficient. I love good colour and find it lacking in most contemporary work. Luckily, our overseas practice has given us good opportunity to use colour—which is less important than material and form but which can compliment both. I think scale is the most difficult problem in architecture and regret that teaching about it is negligible now. Le Corbusier, Lutyens, and Louis Kahn all considered it an essential ingredient in good architecture.

—Jane B. Drew

That the designing of buildings starts with human needs and climatic conditions and the most efficient methods to satisfy them is perhaps obvious, but the methods and the success vary. Much of Jane Drew's architectural work has been in tropical countries, chiefly Ghana, Nigeria, India, and Ceylon, and the study of climatic conditions (very different from those in northern Europe) and their effects on buildings have been a paramount consideration. By residing in these countries and studying how modern building technology could best answer these needs, she has created some outstanding work—what might be called a functional adaptation of the modern idiom to tropical building. Some of her best earlier work has been in Chandigarh (1954-56) with Le Corbusier, Pierre Jeanneret, and Maxwell Fry, where each was responsible for various buildings.

Drew's consisted of government and private housing, shops and shopping areas, health centres, schools, and colleges. In speaking of her work in Chandigarh she said that a house there is essentially a shade and shelter from the sun. She realized that it is also necessary to consider established customs and taboos, to respect them, and to combine them with modern, efficient structural methods. She con-cluded, however, that tradition was not important except where it followed the climate and habits of living—determining factors for the architect.

The government housing with its minimum accommodation and economy hardly gave scope for notable design, with long low blocks and plain walls, yet she was able to introduce attractive features in the passageways between houses with lintel and post entrances. More scope was provided by the larger private housing, where an early experience in kitchen planning prompted some very practical designs. In the exteriors of these houses, she appears as a designer on geometric principles probably much influenced by Le Corbusier whom she greatly admires. The pale walls and nicely calculated relations of volumes with sun-protecting canopies and deep, shadowed recesses are often impressive. In the designs of long rows of shops with flats above, in the schools and colleges, hospitals and health centres, the sun is a determinant in the character of the geometric design. Canopies, recesses, and egg-crate walls often result in a fascinating decorative appearance.

Among her best work in England is some housing in the Mark Hall neighbourhood of Harlow consist-ing mainly of long, terraced units and four-storey blocks of flats. The general effect in terrace housing depends much on the excellence or otherwise of the repeated unit; and here it is well proportioned with a mono-pitched roof. The contrasting squarish blocks of flats provide a varied note, resulting in a very satisfactory ensemble in a spacious setting.

Among Drew's most notable later work are the buildings for the Open University at Milton Keynes. The necessity of harmonizing with the existing late Georgian Walton Hall, which is a centre of the complex, may have been an inhibiting influence, resulting in very restrained architecture, but it has been tastefully designed with windows between

broad vertical slabs. Starting from scratch is always an advantage in this kind of grouping.

Actuated in much of her work by geometric precision, she sometimes achieved in her designs the kind of aesthetic satisfaction that one derives from a typical painting of Ben Nicholson. She is an imaginative architect, rich in ideas that often had interesting fruition. For example, she suggested to Le Corbusier that he should set up in the heart of the capital of Chandigarh the symbols of his philosophy governing his conception of city design. From this suggestion arose the idea of the great esplanade where the signs of the modulor, the harmonic spiral, and the open hand are displayed on a generous scale.

—Arnold Whittick

DuBOIS, Macy.

Canadian. Born in Baltimore, Maryland, 20 De-cember 1929; emigrated to Canada, 1958. Educated at the Baltimore Polytechnic Institute, 1943-47; Tufts University, Medford, Massachusetts, 1947-51 B.S. Eng. (cum laude) 1951; Graduate School of Design, Harvard University, Cambridge, Massa-chusetts, under Sigfried Giedion, 1954-58, M.Arch. 1958. Served in the United States Navy, as a Lieutenant Junior Grade, in the Mediterranean area, 1951-52, and in the Pacific area and Korea, 1952-54; Korean Service Medal; United Nations Battle Star. Married Sarah Buchanan in 1957; children: Mark and Lindsay; married Helga Plumb in 1975. Archi-tectural Designer, John B. Parkin, *q.v.* and Associ-ates, Toronto, 1958-59; Architectural Designer, Rounthwaite and Fairfield, Toronto, 1959-60; As-sociate in charge of Design, Robert Fairfield Associates, Toronto, 1960-62; Partner in Charge of Design, Fairfield + DuBois, Toronto, 1962-75. Since 1975, Principal, DuBois + Associates, Toronto, Exhibitions: group shows—*Plan for Toronto*, Art Gallery of Ontario, Toronto 1963; *Bienal*, Sao Paulo 1965; individual shows—University of Toronto, 1970, 1978; University of Waterloo, Ontario, 1970, 1978; Carleton University, Ottawa, 1978; Harvard University, Cambridge, Massachusetts, 1978; Toronto Dominion Centre, 1978; Ontario College of Art, Toronto 1979. Fellow, Royal Architectural Institute of Canada; Academician, Royal Canadian Academy of the Arts. Address: DuBois + Associates, 76 Richmond Street East, Toronto, Ontario M5C 1P1, Canada.

Works:

1958 City Hall, Toronto (competition project; with John Andrews, William Morgan, and Bryon Ireland)
1960 Oxford University Press, Don Mill, Ontario
       Canadian Ambassador's Residence, Ankara, Turkey
1961 Smyth Road Housing, Ottawa (competition project)
       Central Technical School Art Centre, Toronto
       Residence, New College, University of Toronto
1964 45 Charles Street East Office Building, Toronto
       Dow Corning Silicones Ltd. Office Building, North York, Ontario
       Ontario Government Pavilion, *Expo '67*, Montreal
1965 Master plan and various buildings, Lakehead University, Thunder Bay, Ontario
       ECE Group Office Building, Don Mills, Ontario
       Ithaca Festival Theatre, Ithaca, New York (project)
       York Regional School of Nursing, North York, Ontario (project)

1966 Hamilton Civic Theatre, Ontario (project)
Tecumseh Senior Public School, Scarborough, Ontario
1968 Albert Campbell District Library, Scarborough, Ontario
Fischbach and Moore Office Building, Etobicoke, Ontario
City Hall Amsterdam (competition project)
1969 Greenwood Vocational School, Toronto
Consumer's Gas Company Office Building Toronto
Casa Loma Campus of the George Brown College of Applied Arts and Technology, Toronto
Rogers Public School, Newmarket, Ontario
1970 Residences, and the Academic and Student building, Otonabee College, Trent University, Peterborough, Ontario
1971 Sarnia Opera House, Ontario (project)
Garrison Motor Inn, Fort Erie, Ontario
1972 Ontario Police College, Aylmer
Foxboro Senior Elementary School, Belleville, Ontario (project)
1973 House of Parliament, London, England (competition project)
Joseph Shepard Building (Government of Canada Office Building) North York, Ontario
Baha'i National Offices, North York Ontario
1974 Bloor Park Squash Club interiors, Toronto
1975 Grand River Cable TV Company Office and Studio, Kitchener, Ontario
Master plan and several buildings, Lakefield College School, Ontario
1978 The Oaklands (housing development), Toronto
Ambulance Services Headquarters Services for Metropolitan Toronto, North York, Ontario
Bell Canada Alness Street Street Bar X Building, North York, Ontario
The Longboat Junior Public School, Scarborough, Ontario
1979 Canadian Embassy, Beijing
Cricket, Skating and Curling Club renovations, Toronto
Scaramouche Restaurant interiors, Toronto
1980 Camp Hill Medical Centre, Halifax, Nova Scotia (project)
De la Salle Building extension, Toronto
1981 Harbourfront Parcel E Project, Toronto
Labour Council Development Foundation Housing, Toronto (project)
Windsong Galleries renovations, Toronto
1982 Apartment Building, Wellington Street and University Avenue, Toronto (project)
Darlington Nuclear Power Station Information Centre, Ontario Hydro, Toronto
Office Building, King and York Streets, Toronto (project)
Harbour Towers Apartment Building, Toronto (project)
Bookstore interiors, George Brown College, Toronto
1983 Tannery Bay Housing Project, Kingston, Ontario
St. Andrews-by-the-Lake Anglican Church renovations, Centre Island, Toronto
St. James campus Feasibility Study, George Brown College, Toronto
Canada Realities Office interiors, Toronto
Mclean House, Toronto (project)
Science laboratory Building, York University, Toronto (project)
Grace Maternity Hospital and Isaak Walton Killam Hospital Master Plan, Halifax, Nova Scotia

Publications

By DuBOIS: books—*Exploring Toronto,* with others, Toronto 1972, 1973, 1974; articles—"The Impact of Size: Reflections of a Seasoned Traveler"

Macy DuBois: The Oaklands Condominiums, Toronto, 1978.

in *Canadian Architect* (Toronto), May 1967; "Toronto Dominion Centre: A Critique" in *Canadian Architect* (Toronto), November 1967; "Winnipeg Art Gallery Competition" in *Canadian Architect* (Toronto) February 1968; "Critique Towards a New Prose Architecture" in *Canadian Architect* (Toronto), November 1968, "New College II: Straight Line and Curve" in *Canadian Architect* (Toronto), May 1970; "The Sixties: A Decade of Innovation?," with others in *Canadian Architect* (Toronto), July 1971; "A Protestant Work of Architecture" in *Canadian Architect* (Toronto), January 1973; "Two Schools" in *Canadian Architect* (Toronto), April 1973; "Book Review: 'The Prairie School: Frank Lloyd Wright and His Midwest Contemporaries' by H. Allen Brooks" in *Architecture Plus* (New York), September 1973; "Architectural Concepts; George Brown College of Applied Arts and Technology, Toronto" in *Canadian Architect* (Toronto), March 1974; "Erickson" in *Canadian Architect* (Toronto), November 1974; "Commentary: Otonabee College, Trent University, Peterborough Ontario" in *Canadian Architect* (Toronto), July 1975; "Otonabee College" and "Fort Erie Motel" in *Canadian Interiors* (Toronto), August 1976; "Casa loma Campus, George Brown College" in *Contract Interiors* (New York), October 1977; "Ontario Police College" in *Canadian Interiors* (Toronto), November/December 1978; "Focus on a

Federal Building" in *Canadian Architect* (Toronto), March 1979; "Trees Grow in Glass Domed Interior Walkway" in *Toronto Star*, 17 May 1980; "Plans picked for Embassy in China" in *Globe and Mail* (Toronto), 30 March 1981; "Scaramouche Restaurant" in *Canadian Architect* (Toronto), September 1981; "Apartments with Inner Streets" in *Canadian Architect* (Toronto), January 1982; "Stylistic School" in *Canadian Architect* (Toronto), May 1982.

On DuBOIS: book—*Building with Words: Canadian Architects on Architecture*, with introduction by W. Bernstein and R. Cawker, Toronto 1981; articles—"Portfolio: Fairfield and DuBois" in *Canadian Architecture* (Toronto), May 1965; "George Brown in Toronto" in *Architectural Review* (London), June 1976; "Three Public Schools", and "Albert Campbell Library" in *Modern Canadian Architecture*, Edmonton, Alberta 1983.

Architecture can resolve the problems posed in building for the use of people, yet so much stands in the way of lucidity. Past solutions are powerful preconditioners. The architect must start from the first principles of the program itself. He must truly understand the social context and the psychological impact of his architecture. He must use logical construction responding to time and place. What evolves must be devoid of current, fashionable affection. The design itself is the style.

Architecture must evolve like nature, eliminating the inutile and reaffirming the utile. Nature is always structurally responsive, climatically correct, and functionally rational. By contrast, I have seen buildings conceived in southern climates struggling to survive our northern winters. On the other hand, I have seen buildings in Beijing and Kuala Lumpur looking like buildings in Boston in an attempt to be technically up-to-date but looking rather lost and illogical. There is something totally irrational in non-Westerners, with strong architectural traditions, building Western – style buildings developed by architects largely ignorant of non-Western architectural history.

Not only do we have to see our own time with clear eyes, but we must become more aware of worldwide architectural experience. Knowing about other architecture and understanding its conceptual rationale should lead to a richer new architecture more responsive to environment, less preconceived, and better able to reflect the demands of utility.

It is the architect's role to proselytize for real architecture, to underline for society the verities of social impact and physical reality, to make clear the choices and to supply our countries with models of how the environment can be shaped to enhance human pleasure and facility. We have a responsibility to the larger community of builders to show the way and make signposts.

We architects examine how people work, relax, and respond to size, colour, light, texture, sound, and materials. We analyze to evolve a logical assembly of our buildings. We look at social relationships. We respond to cultural images and historic patterns. We do not imitate, we invent. We are society's eyes, ears, and hands attempting to create without enervating preconceptions.

We want our buildings to be powerful without being overpowering. We try to be low where possible and long where practical, so that the relationship to the ground is not lost. Because of our prehistory, plant material is essential to human wellbeing. Falling snow and rain create their own responses in the human mind. Highrises are increasingly anarchistic, encouraging the uncaring in our societies. We must build so that people care about where they are and understand collective responsibilities.

People are defined by their culture. We understand how we feel about ourselves by what we build. Never believe what a society says, believe what it does. Architecture is a physical manifestation of people doing. Highrise office blocks for a city hall or a bank or apartments are symbolic of authoritarian logic. Cities planned with the car all-dominant are communities devoid of comprehension of low speed, individual delight. Views from the fortieth floor or from high-speed car windows are absent of detail.

Architects have a committed mission to bring people to see the miraculous world around them. To love the play of light on surfaces, the fall of rain on their surroundings, the whirl of snow coming down, the texture and heft of materials, the response of temperatures on skin, and the sounds and smells of the world. Our buildings make that happen if we are skillful. This is why architecture is such a trying but heady experience.

—Macy DuBois

While some of the images of modern architecture could be seen in earlier Canadian buildings, the underlying principles of the style were not at first consistently applied except in the work of John B. Parkin Associates. Quickly passing from a Gropius idiom to that of Mies, the office endeavoured to maintain its lead into the 1960s by hiring talented new designers, one of whom was Macy DuBois.

At this time, although very little good modern architecture existed in Canada, in the United States, there had already been a reaction to the first phase of actual building based on the example of the European prewar leaders who now resided there. This reaction showed itself in a greater freedom of form, a wider choice of materials, and a more decorative treatment of facades. The even more basic difference in approach taken by Eero Saarinen, who returned to the use of metaphorical form, also underlay the Finnish architect Viljo Revell's winning competition design for the Toronto City Hall, which inaugurated the effective spread of modern architecture in that city.

The work of DuBois, which matured during this later period, has been based on the accepted credo of the early modern movement, which stressed rational planning, structural order, and a straightforward attitude to design; that is, a belief in honesty of expression that came down from Gothic Revival theory and a functionalist concern for measurable space rather than its psychological qualities.

At the same time DuBois has enlarged his architectural vocabulary both from other sources and his own. Different building problems have suggested different precedents. He has exploited the current interest in large multi-storey interior spaces as well as the breaking up of large exterior masses into smaller cubic units so as to produce a more human scale and interest. Similarly, with the recent broadening of functional expressionism, he has exposed mechanical services. Elsewhere, the influence of Aalto is apparent in an undulating facade or ceiling and also in the sensitive handling of brick and other masonry. This attention to detail distinguishes the work of DuBois, and his intelligent resolution of constructional situations gives it an overall consistency of design. His own contribution to the enrichment of a working vocabulary includes distinctive elements such as the architectural use of standard commercial siding and a collaboration with artists that adds a symbolic dimension to his work, which, as part of what may be categorized as the extended modern style, has integrity and a pervasive seriousness.

—Anthony Jackson

DUDOK, Willem Marinus.

Dutch. Born in Amsterdam, 6 July 1884. Educated at the Cadet School, Alkmaar, Netherlands, 1899-1902; Royal Military Academy, Breda, Netherlands, 1902-05. Served as a telegraphist and engineer in the Dutch Army, in Utrecht and Purmerend, 1905-13, and in the Engineering Corps, 1914-15: Lieutenant. In private practice, Leiden, 1913-14, and Hilversum, Netherlands, from 1915. Acting Municipal Engineer, Leiden, 1913-14; Director of Municipal Works, Hilversum, 1915-27; Municipal Architect, Hilversum, from 1927. Exhibitions: *Funzione e senso: architettura-casa-città olanda, 1870-1940*, Museo Archeologico Nazionale, Naples, 1980; *Willem Dudok 1884-1974*, Cultureel Centrum De Vaart, Hilversum, Technische Hochschule, Eindhoven, Bouwcentrum, Rotterdam, Raadhuis, Velsen, and Technische Hochschule, Delft, all Netherlands and Architectuurinstitut Sint Lukas, Ghent, Belgium, 1981-82. Recipient: Gold Medal, Royal Institute of British Architects, 1935; Gold Medal, Municipality of Hilversum, 1949; Gold Medal, Municipality of The Hague, 1949; Gold Medal, American Institute of Architects, 1955. Honorary Member: Koninklijke Maatschappij der Bouwmeesters, Antwerp; Academic Corps, Koninklijke voor Schone Kunsten, Antwerp; Zentralvereinigung der Architekten Österreichs, Austria; Bund Deutscher Architekten; Vereinigung Bildender Künstler Wiener Secession, Vienna; Société Centrale des Architectes, Paris; Académie d'Architecture, Paris; Sindicato Nacional dos Arquitectos, Lisbon; Architectural Association, London; American Institute of Architects. Officer, Order of the Oranje Nassau, Netherlands; Knight of the Order of the Nederlandse Leeuw. Officer, Order of the Crown of Belgium. *Died* (in Hilversum, Netherlands) *6 April 1974*.

Works:

1916	Secondary school, Leiden, Netherlands
1917	*Leidse Dagblad* Offices, Leiden, Netherlands
1918	Residential development, 1st Municipal Quarter, Hilversum, Netherlands
1920	Rembrandt School, Hilversum, Netherlands
	"Huize Sevensteijn," Zorgvliet Park, The Hague
1921	Residential development, Naarden, Netherlands
	Municipal Baths, Hilversum, Netherlands
	Dr. H. Bavinck School, Hilversum, Netherlands
	Residential development, 4th Municipal Quarter, Hilversum, Netherlands
	Netherlands
1922	Oranje Primary School, 5th Municipal Quarter, Hilversum, Netherlands
1923	Slaughterhouse, Hilversum, Netherlands
1925	Jan van der Heyden School, Hilversum, Netherlands
	Minckelers School, Hilversum, Netherlands
	Manager's office and dressing rooms, Sports Ground, Hilversum, Netherlands
1926	Juliana School, Hilversum, Netherlands
	Fabritius School, Hilversum, Netherlands
	Columbarium, at the Crematorium, Westerhaven, Netherlands
	Dudok House, Hilversum, Netherlands
1927	Van Heutsz Monument, Gambir, Indonesia
1928	Netherlands House, Cité Universitaire, Paris
	Ruysdael School, Hilversum, Netherlands
	Nassau School, Hilversum, Netherlands
1928/30	Town Hall, Hilversum, Netherlands
1929	Vondel School, Hilversum, Netherlands
	De Bijenkorf Department Store, Rotterdam (destroyed in World War II)
	Noorder Cemetery, Hilversum, Netherlands
1930	Multatuli School, Hilversum, Netherlands
	Johannes Calvijn School, Hilversum, Netherlands
	Valerius School, Hilversum, Netherlands
	Marnix School, Hilversum, Netherlands
1931	Snellius School, Hilversum, Netherlands
1932	Town Hall, The Hague (project)
1933	Monument on the Zuyderzee Dike, Netherlands
1934/35	H.A.V. Bank, Schiedam, Netherlands
1936	Aquatic Sports Pavilion, Hilversum, Netherlands
	Garden Theatre and Lighthouse Cinema, Calcutta, India
1937	Harbour Master's Office, Hilversum, Netherlands
1938	De Burgh Garden City, Eindhoven, Netherlands
	Town Hall, Amsterdam (project)
1939	Bridge over the River Vecht, near Vreeland, Netherlands
	Erasmushuis Office and Apartment Building, Rotterdam
	Office building, Dam Square, Amsterdam (project)
	De Nederlanden van 1845 Office Building, Arnhem, Netherlands
1940	Reception and office building, Crematorium, Westerveld, Netherlands
1941	Municipal Theatre, Utrecht, Netherlands
1943	Plan for the redevelopment of the town centre of Alkmaar, Netherlands
1945	Plan for the reconstruction of The Hague
1947	Residential development, 19th Municipal Quarter, Hilversum, Netherlands
	Protestant church, Schiedam, Netherlands (project)
	Cultural Centre, Soest, Netherlands (project)

Willem Dudok: Town Hall, Hilversum, Netherlands, 1930.

1948 Royal Dutch Steelworks Offices, Velsen, Netherlands
1951 House, Oegstgeest, Netherlands
1952 De Nederlanden van 1845 Office and Apartment Building, Rotterdam
Old people's flats, Amsterdam (project)
1953 Race course grandstand, Sports Ground, Hilversum, Netherlands
Park Flats, Bussum, Netherlands
Bungalow, Jacobus Pennweg, Hilversum, Netherlands
Residential development, Jacobus van Campenlaan, Hilversum, Netherlands
Esso Service Stations, Netherlands
1954/
55 Quatre-Bras apartments, 's-Gravelandseweg, Hilversum, Netherlands
1954/
60 Kom van Biegel apartment block, Gooilandseweg and Parklaan, Bussum, Netherlands
1955 Cultural Centre, Alkmaar, Netherlands (project)
Bieshaar residential building, Groenekanseweg and Dr. Letteplein, De Biet, Netherlands
Julianaflat building, Julianalaan, Bilthoven, Netherlands
Laboratory Building, Wenckebachstraat, Velsen, Netherlands (project)
Gallery-housing, Voorburg, Netherlands (project)
1955/
57 HEMA Shopping Centre with housing, Vlietlaan and Veerstraat, Bussum, Netherlands

1956 CBS Office Building, Voorburg, Netherlands (project)
1957 Apartment housing, Keizer Karelweg, Amstelveen, Netherlands
Nederlandse Bank Building, Oude Turfmarkt, Amsterdam (project)
Zeewijk Development Plan, Velsen, Netherlands
1957/
63 Civic Centre, Palace of Justice and Police Headquarters, Baghdad, Iraq (project)
1957/
64 Housing Block, Boshuizenstraat, Amsterdam
Zuiderhof Building, Korhornsweg, Hilversum, Netherlands
1959 Four shops with housing, Kerbrink, Hilversum,
1959/
61 C. de Boer Jr. NV Printing Works, Zeverijnstraat, Hilversum, Netherlands
1959/
63 Westerveld Auditorium and Meeting-Plaza, Driehuis/Velsen, Netherlands
1959/
64 Kamrad Housing Block, Kamerlingh Onnesweg, Hilversum, Netherlands
1960 MAHUKO Amsterdam Finance Company Bank building, Weteringschans, Amsterdam (project)
Philips Recording Studio, Schuttetsweg, Hilversum, Netherlands (project)
1960/
64 Police Headquarters, Langestraat, Hilversum, Netherlands (project)

1961 Albert Heijn Supermarket, Marsdiepstraat, Den Helder, Netherlands (project)
1961/
62 Motel and Bowling Centre, Soestdijkerstraatweg, Hilversum, Netherlands (project)
1961/
63 Lindelaan/Meerweg/Graaf Wichmanlaan/ Nieuwe 's-Gravelandseweg redevelopment, Bussum, Netherlands (project)
1961/
67 Cultural Centre, Witte Hullweg, Hilversum, Netherlands (project)
1962 Singel and Brinklaan redevelopment, Bussum, Netherlands (project)
C & A Building, Kerkstraat, Hilversum, Netherlands
's-Gravenhof and Hortensiusstraat redevelopment, Naarden, Netherlands (project)
1962/
64 Zaanstad Office Building, Coentunneltrace, Amsterdam
Lindenheuvel redevelopment, Bloemendaal, Netherlands (project)
1963 Housing Block, Konigslaan and Breedelaan, Bussum, Netherlands (project)
Shopping Centre, Diemen, Netherlands
1963/
64 Duinpark redevelopment, Noordwijk, Netherlands (project)
1963/
66 Voss Fashion Store, Kerkstraat, Hilversum, Netherlands
1967 Technical Administration Offices, Oude Enghweg, Hilversum, Netherlands (project)

Publications:

By DUDOK: articles—"Foreword" in *Hilversum: A Short Introduction to the Recent Plans of Extension*, Hilversum, Netherlands 1924; texts in *Moderne Bouwkunst in Nederland*, edited by H. P. Berlage, J. Gratema and others, 20 vols., Rotterdam 1932-35; lectures in *Willem M. Dudok* by G. Stuiveling, F. Bakker-Schut and others, Amsterdam 1954.

On DUDOK: books—*W. M. Dudok* by G. Friedhoff, Amsterdam 1930; *Willem M. Dudok* by G. Stuiveling, F. Bakker-Schut and others, Amsterdam 1954; *75 maal Dudok*, brochure, Hilversum, Netherlands 1977; *Funzione e senso, architettura-casa-cittàolanda, 1870-1940*, exhibition brochure by M. Nunziata and others, Naples 1980; *Willem M. Dudok, 1884-1974* by Max Cramer, Hans van Grieken and Heleen Pronk, Amsterdam 1980; *GA 58: Willem Dudok – Town Hall, Hilversum, Netherlands 1928-1931*, edited by Yukio Futagawa, with text by Wilhelm Holzbauer, Tokyo 1981; *Amsterdamse Bouwen, 1880-1980*, edited by Ids Haagsma and others, Utrecht, Netherlands and Antwerp 1981; articles—"La nuova architettura olandese" by Leo Lionni in *Casabella* (Milan), May 1934; "Baukunst des Auslandes: Holland" in *Deutsche Bauzeitung* (Stuttgart), April 1937; "Willem Marinus Dudok" by Jan de Meyer in *Bouwkundig Weekblad* (The Hague), 23 November 1940; "Dudok and the Repercussions of His European Influence" by R. F. Jordan in *Architectural Review* (London), April 1954; "Forty Years of Hilversum" in *Town and Country Planning* (London), November 1955; "Willem Marinus Dudok: In Memoriam" by Gert Jonker in *Bouw* (Rotterdam), 20 April 1974; "Willem Dudok 1884-1974" by Richard Padovan in *Architectural Review* (London), June 1974; "The Architectural History of a Department Store—'The Palace of the Queen Bee'" by Hilde de Haan in *De Architect* (The Hague), September 1980; "Exhibition of the Work of Architect Dudok" in *Polytechnisch Tijdschrift* (The Hague), May 1981; "Hilversum Town Hall" in *Architecture + Urbanism* (Tokyo), May 1982; "Willem Dudok—Modernist But Not Mainstream" by Richard Guy Wilson in *AIA Journal* (Washington, D.C.), August 1982; "Berlage, Dudok and Weeber" in special issue of *Wonen-TA/BK* (Heerlen, Netherlands), January 1983.

Willem Dudok was remarkable in a number of ways. As city architect of a provincial Dutch town, Hilversum, and after training to be an army engineer, he produced and fully developed a personal style in little more than ten years. Although he designed some distinguished buildings here and there outside Hilversum, the greatbulk of his work was done within the city boundary. His style was attractive and much imitated outside Holland, though never really successfully. Popular though it was, it left no permanent mark in the development of modern architecture, and he had no successors.

The main features of Dudok's work were the dramatic massing of asymmetrical blocks of plain, high-quality brickwork, often with deeply-raked, horizontal joints; ranges of continuous, low, deep-set horizontal windows set under projecting concrete hoods; deep-set, semi-circular-headed entrance doors; and skilfully managed corner treatments between blocks, often incorporating large windows and towers. His details were always very carefully worked out, and the general effect of his buildings was handsomely comfortable. All these features can be found in the Vondel School, Hilversum.

Dudok's most important building was the Hilversum Town Hall, where the pale yellow brick masses are dominated by a tower in a setting of formal pools and gardens. The carefully chosen materials look as fresh today as they did when they were first used. Internally, the building holds the attention by the skilful use of differing ceiling heights.

Besides a number of schools, Dudok's other important buildings in Hilversum include the abattoir and the public baths. Outside Hilversum, his most important building was the Bijenkorf Department Store in Rotterdam, destroyed in World War II. Large areas of glass were contrasted with mass brickwork without ornament but with strongly-marked, horizontal projecting balconies and a well-managed corner tower.

—Gontran Goulden

DÜTTMANN, Werner.

German. Born in Berlin, 6 March 1921. Educated at high school in Berlin, 1939-42, and at the Technical University of Berlin, 1947-48, Dip-Arch. 1948; Town and Country Planning Institute, King's College, University of Durham, England, 1950-51. Served in the German Army, 1942-46. Married Martina Schneider in 1979; children: Hans-Werner and Katharina. Architect with the Planning Board, Kreuzberg, Berlin, 1949; architect in the design office of the Public Buildings Administration, Berlin, 1951-56; freelance architect, Berlin, 1956-60; City Architect and City Planner of Berlin, 1960-66. Honorary Professor from 1963, and Ordinary Professor, 1966-70, Technical University of Berlin. President, Akademie der Künste, Berlin, 1971-83; Recipient: Bildende Kunst Prize, Association of German Critics, 1959-60; Berliner Kunstpreis, 1964. Honorary Fellow, American Institute of Architects, 1971. *Died* (in Berlin) *26 January 1983*.

Works:

1953 Old People's Home, Wedding, Berlin
1954 Youth Center, Zehlendorf, Berlin
1956 Congress Hall, Tiergarten, Berlin (as associate architect to Hugh Stubbins)
1957 District Library and Metro Entrance, Tiergarten, Berlin
1960 Academy of Arts (Akademie der Künste), Tiergarten, Berlin
1961 Edinburg House (hotel), Charlottenburg, Berlin
1964 Salzenbrodt House, Wachstrasse, Tegel, Berlin
1965 Dr. Dienst House, Bismarckallee, Grunewald, Berlin
1966 Dr. Menne House, Zingerleweg, Kladow, Berlin
     Plan for Märkisches Viertel Satellite Town, Wittenau, Berlin (with Georg Heinrichs and Hans Christian Müller)
1967 St. Agnes Church and Community Center, Kreuzberg, Berlin
     An der Urania Office Building, Schöneberg, Berlin
     Mensa, Technical University, Charlottenburg, Berlin
     Brücke-Museum, Dahlem, Berlin
1970 Apartment buildings, Märkisches Viertel, Wittenau, Berlin
1971 Apartment buildings, Heerstrasse, Spandau, Berlin
1972 Kudamm-Eck Shipping Center, Charlottenburg, Berlin
1973 Office building extension, Ernst-Reuter-Platz, Charlottenburg, Berlin
1974 Apartment buildings, Mehringplatz, Kreuzberg, Berlin
     Rodenkirchen-Sürth Housing Estate, Cologne
1975 Urb an renewal apartment housing, Ritterstrasse, Friedrichstrasse, and Putkamer Strasse, Kreuzberg, Berlin
     St. Martin's Church, Kindergarten, Old People's Home and Community Center, Märkisches Viertel, Wittenau, Berlin
     Kleiner Wannsee Housing Estate, Wannsee, Berlin
     Hotel Schweizer Hof extension, Schöneberg, Berlin
     Low-density housing, Heiligensee, Berlin
1975/
82 Kunsthalle extension, Bremen, West Germany
1976 Schiepe House, Griegstrasse, Dahlem, Berlin
1977 Lentzealle Housing Estate, Dahlem, Berlin
     Youth Hostel, Schöneberg, Berlin
     Dohnenstieg Housing Estate, Dahlem, Berlin (project)
     Apartment building, Markgrafenstrasse, Kreuzberg, Berlin (project)
     Apartment building, Klausener Platz, Charlottenburg, Berlin (project)
1980/
82 Archaeological Museum, Samos, Greece

Publications:

By DÜTTMANN: book— *Berlin ist viele Städte*, with others, Berlin 1984; article—"Berlin Freie Universität: Nine Evaluations," with others, in *Architecture Plus* (New York), January/February 1974.

On DÜTTMANN: books—*Modern Architecture in Germany*, with introduction by Ulrich Conrads, Stuttgart and London 1962; *The Voice of the Phoenix: Postwar Architecture in Germany* by John Burchard, London and Cambridge, Massachusetts 1966; *Architecture in Germany* by Alfred Simon, Essen, West Germany 1969; *German Architecture: 1960-1970* by Wolfgang Pehnt, London and Stuttgart 1970; *Deutsche Kunst seit 1960, Teil IV: Architektur* by Paolo Nestler and Peter M. Bode, Munich 1976; *Architektur in Deutschland* by H. and M. Bofinger, J. Paul and H. Klotz, Stuttgart 1979; articles—"Europe 5: Housing in Berlin" in *The Architect* (London), May 1974; "Die Brücke Museum in Berlin" by Leopold Reidemeister in *Du* (Zürich), March 1975; "Extension to the Art Museum in Bremen" in *Baumeister* (Munich), October 1982; "Werner Düttmann, 1921-1983" in *Bauwelt* (Berlin), 4 February 1983.

I hope that my architecture will be recognizable and understandable and livable in without any comment. I think that if interpretation becomes necessary, architecture may have failed.

—Werner Düttmann (1980)

Werner Düttmann was City Architect of Berlin during the 1960s, and it was his judgment and his work that created the image of the city during this period of its reconstruction and redevelopment. He invented concepts as contradictory as the "Märkisches Viertel" and the movement "Rettet den Stuck" (Save the Stucco—of the nineteenth century facades). And it was he who persuaded Mies van der Rohe to come back to Berlin to realize his last work, the National-galerie.

Düttmann was then, for more than ten years, President of the Academy of Arts, and his efforts remained the same, gathering to Berlin creative people from all over the world to maintain the city's liveliness, cultural activity, and meaning. He always was a *Zeitgenosse*, a person who devotes himself and his work totally to the ideas and people of his time, observing, encouraging, criticizing, somebody with a severe power of judgment, somebody who would humbly set his work as a frame of reality for the dreams of others. Düttmann's work is concentrated in Berlin, and the new Berlin would have been very different without him.

Comprehensive and strong in judgment, he created architecture that is lively, amorous, and

Werner Düttmann: Brücke-Museum, Dahlem, West Berlin, 1967.

warm. It is "architecture for people," and he did not rely on any individual formal language to express his goal. In some ways, his buildings are a reflection of the different styles and dreams that architecture has lived through during the past thirty years. His works look simple, almost incidental, from the outside, but they are welcoming within. The proportioning of space, the hidden order of wide and narrow, of dark and light, of intimate and generous, make his buildings livable, easy to use, and accommodating.

His Academy of Arts, completed in 1960, is still the centre of cultural life in Berlin, and on Sunday mornings, when the exhibitions open, it buzzes with activity; it is a place that people like to go.

During this period of search for meaning in architecture—when solutions range from a new formal expressionism to re-evaluation of the forms of the past—one is almost relieved to find so simple a quality in architecture as that which one discovers in Düttmann's work. It makes you feel good.

—Martina Düttmann

EAMES, Charles.

American. Born in St. Louis, Missouri, 17 June 1907. Educated at the Washington University School of Architecture, St. Louis, 1924-26. Married Ray Kaiser in 1941; daughter by previous marriage: Lucia. Worked for the architectural firm of Trueblood and Graf, St. Louis, 1925-27; in private practice, St. Louis, 1930-34; travelled and worked in Mexico, 1934; returned to private practice, St. Louis, 1935-36; Fellow, 1936, and Head of the Department of Experimental Design, Cranbrook Academy, Bloomfield Hills, Michigan, 1937-40; worked in the Art Department of Metro-Goldwyn-Mayer, Los Angeles, while experimenting in molding plywood, 1941; began development laboratory, with John Entenza, Gregory Ain, q.v., Margaret Harris, and Griswald Raetz, Los Angeles, 1942-45; in partnership with wife Ray Eames, Los Angeles, subsequently Venice, California, 1944 until his death in 1978: formed Molded Plywood Division of Evans Products Company, Los Angeles, 1944; Consulting Designer, Herman Miller Inc., Los Angeles, 1946. Lecturer, California Institute of Technology, Pasadena, 1953-56. Charles Eliot Norton Professor of Poetry, Harvard University, Cambridge, Massachusetts, 1970. Member, National Council on the Arts, 1970-78. Exhibitions: Museum of Modern Art, New York, 1946; *Triennale*, Milan, 1954 and 1957; Museum of Modern Art, New York, 1973; Walker Art Center, Minneapolis, Minnesota, 1972; Frederick S. Wight Gallery, University of California, Los, Angeles, 1976; Sainsbury Centre, East Anglia University, Norwich, England, 1978; *Design in America: The Cranbrook Vision 1925-50*, toured the United States and Europe, 1983-84; *Socialites and Satellites*, Ronald Feldman Fine Arts, New York, 1984. Collections: Museum of Modern Art, New York; Philadelphia Museum of Art. Recipient: First Prize, with Eero Saarinen, Organic Design Chair Competition, Museum of Modern Art, New York, 1940; National Award, Industrial Designers Institute, 1951; Gold Medal, *Triennale*, Milan, 1954; Grand Prize, *Triennale*, Milan, 1957; Gold Medal, 1957, Industrial Arts Medal, 1972, and, with Ray Eames, Distinguished Service Citation, 1974, American Institute of Architects; Kauffmann International Design Award, with Ray Eames, 1960; Honor Award, with Eero Saarinen, American Institute of Architects, New York Chapter, 1964; Honor Award, American Institute of Architects, Los Angeles Chapter, 1967; Design Medal, Society of Industrial Artists and Designers, London, 1967; Elsie de Wolfe Award, with Ray Eames, American Society of Interior Designers, 1975; Royal Gold Medal, Royal Institute of British Architects, 1979. D.F.A.: Kansas City Art Institute, 1955; California College of Arts and Crafts, Oakland, 1962; Pratt Institute, Brooklyn, New York, 1964; D.Art: Washington University, St. Louis, 1970. Fellow, Royal College of Art, London, 1960. Member, American Academy of Arts and Sciences. *Died* (in St. Louis) *21 August 1978.*

Works:

1940 Molded Plywood Chair (competition project; with Eero Saarinen)
1942 Molded Plywood Leg Spring, for the United States Navy
1944 Child's Chair, for the Evans Projects Company, Los Angeles
1946 Molded Plywood Chair
     Molded Plywood Folding Screen
1947 Folding Dining Table
1948 ETR (Eames Table Rod) Table
1949 Fiberglass Chair
     Eames House, 203 Chautauqua, Pacific Palisades, California
     John Entenza House, 205 Chautauqua, Pacific Palisades, California
     Herman Miller Showroom, 8806 Beverly, Los Angeles
1950 Eames Storage Units
     Good Design Show, Musum of Modern Art, New York
1951 LTR (Low Table Rod) Table
     Wire Chair
     The Toy, for Tigrett Enterprises, Chicago
1952 House of Cards, for Tigrett Enterprises, Chicago
     The Little Toy, for Tigrett Enterprises, Chicago
1953 Upholstered Fiberglass Chair
     Giant House of Cards, for Tigrett Enterprises, Chicago
1954 Sofa Compact
1955 Stacking Fiberglass Chair
1956 Lounge Chair and Ottoman
1957 Solar Toy, for Alcoa Aluminium, Pittsburgh, Pennsylvania
1958 Aluminium Group
1959 *American National Exhibition*, Moscow (with George Nelson)
1960 La Fonda Chair
     Time/Life Chair
1961 Eames Contract Storage
     Mathematica exhibition, for IBM, California Museum of Science and Industry, Los Angeles
1962 Tandem Sling Seating
     Stock Certificate, for the Herman Miller Company, Los Angeles
     House of Science, *Century 21*, Seattle
1964 IBM Exhibit, World's Fair, New York
1965 *Nehru: His Life and His India* exhibition, Ahmedabad, India (toured New York, London, Washington, D.C., and Los Angeles; with Alexander Girard)
1968 Billy Wilder Chaise
     Photography and the City exhibition, Smithsonian Institution, Washington, D.C.
1969 Soft Pad Chair
1971 Loose Cushion Chair
     A Computer Perspective exhibition, IBM Exhibition Center, New York
1972 Executive Oval Table
     Wallace Eckert: Celestial Mechanic exhibition, IBM Exhibition Center, New York
     Fibonacci: Growth and Form exhibition, IBM Exhibition Center, New York
     Nicholas Copernicus: An Exhibition in Celebration of His 500th Anniversary, IBM Exhibition Center, New York
1973 *Movable Feasts and Changing Calendars* exhibition, IBM Exhibition Center, New York
     The Shoulders of Giants exhibition, IBM Exhibition Center, New York
     Isaac Newton exhibition, IBM Exhibition Center, New York
1975/
76 *The World of Franklin and Jefferson* exhibition, for the American Revolution Bicentennial Administration (toured the Grand Palais, Paris; National Museum, Warsaw; British Museum, London; Metropolitan Museum of Art, New York; Art Institute of Chicago; and the Los Angeles County Museum of Art)

Films: with Ray Eames—*Traveling Boy*, 1950; *Parade; or, Here they Come Down the Street*, 1952; *Blacktop*, 1952; *Bread*, 1953; *Calligraphy*, 1953; *Communications Primer*, 1953; *Sofa Compact*, 1954; *Two Baroque Churches in Germany*, 1955; *House*, 1955; *Textiles and Ornamental Arts of India*, 1955; *Eames Lounge Chair*, 1956; *The Spirit of St. Louis* (aerial sequences only), 1956; *Day of the Dead*, 1957; *Tocatta for Toy Trains*, 1957; *Information Machine*, 1957; *Expanding Airport*, 1958; *Herman Miller at the Brussels Fair*, 1958; *DeGaulle Sketch*, 1959; *Climpses of the U.S.A.*, 1959; *Jazz Chair*, 1960; *Introduction to Feedback*, 1960; *Fabulous Fifties* (sequences in CBS-TV Special), 1960; *IBM Mathematics Peep Show*, 1961; *Kaleidoscope*, 1961; *Kaleidoscope Shop*, 1961; *ECS*, 1962; *House of Science*, 1962; *Before the Fair*, 1962; *The Good Years* (sequences in CBS-TV Special), 1962; *Think*, 1964; *Think* (revised version), 1965; *IBM at the Fair*, 1965; *Westinghouse ABC*, 1965; *The Smithsonian Institution*, 1965; *The Smithsonian Newsreel*, 1965; *Horizontes*, 1966; *Boeing: The Leading Edge*, 1966; *IBM Museum*, 1967; *A Computer Glossary*, 1967; *National Aquarium Presentation*, 1967; *Schuetz Machine*, 1967; *Lick Observatory*, 1968; *Babbage*, 1968; *Powers of Ten*, 1968; *Photography and the City*, 1969; *Tops*, 1969; *The U.N. Information Center*, 1970; *Man's View of Himself*, 1970; *Memory*, 1970; *The Perry Expedition*, 1970.

Publications:

By EAMES: books—*A Computer Perspective*, Cambridge, Massachusetts 1973; *The World of Franklin and Jefferson*, exhibition catalogue, Los Angeles 1976; articles—"Design Today" in *Arts and Architecture* (Los Angeles), September 1941; "Organic Design" in *Arts and Architecture* (Los Angeles), December 1941; "General Motors Revisited" in *Architectural Forum* (New York), June 1971; "A Conversation with Charles Eames," interview, with Owen Gingerich in *The American Scholar* (Washington, D.C.), Summer 1977.

On EAMES: books—*Charles Eames,* exhibition catalogue, by Arthur Drexler, New York 1973; *Connections: the work of Charles and Ray Eames,* exhibition catalogue, by Ralph Caplan and Philip Morrison, Los Angeles 1976; *Ray and Charles Eames: il collectivo della fantasia* by Luciano Rubino, Rome 1981; *Design in America: The Cranbrook Vision 1925-1950,* exhibition catalogue, by Robert Judson Clark and others, New York 1983; *Contemporary Designers,* edited by Ann Lee Morgan, New York and London 1984; articles— "Charles Eames" by Eliot Noyes in *Arts and Architecture* (Los Angeles), September 1946; "Three Chairs/Three Records of the Design Process' in *Interiors* (New York), April 1958; "Some Thoughts about Eames" by Jane McCullough in *Zodiac* (Milan), no. 8, 1961; "Mathematica" by J. R. Miller in *Industrial Design* (New York), May 1961; "Design in America: The Last 25 Years" by George Nelson in *Interiors* (New York), November 1965; "Eames Celebration," special issue of *Architectural Design* (London), September 1966; "Poetry of Ideas: The Films of Charles Eames" by Paul Schrader in *Film Quarterly* (Berkeley, California), Spring 1970; "Eames Perspective" by Esther McCoy in the *New York Times Magazine,* 15 April 1973; "At the Modern Museum: The Thoughts of Chairman Eames" by Paul Goldberger in *Art News* (New York), Summer 1973; "An Affection for Objects" by Esther McCoy in *Progressive Architecture* (New York), August 1973; "Charles Eames Isn't Resting on His Chair" by Walter McQuade in *Fortune* (New York), February 1975; "Charles Eames" by John Winter in *Architectural Review* (London), October 1978; "The Keen and Loving Eye of Charles Eames" by Paul Goldberger in *Art News* (New York), October 1978; "Charles Eames 1907-1978" by Olga Guelft in *Interiors* (New York), October 1978; "Charles Eames, A Personal Memoir" by Esther McCoy in *Progressive Architecture* (New York), January 1979; "Golden Connections" in *Building* (London), 6 April 1979; "Charles Eames— Scholar and Architect" in *MD:Moebel Interior Design* (Stuttgart), September 1980; "An Eames Celebration" in *Architecture South Africa,* (Cape Town), Summer 1980; "Form and Its Double" by Daniele Baroni in *Ottagono* (Milan) June 1981; "Eames' Epitaph" by Mike Hill in *Building Design* (London), 11 February 1983; "The Eames House" in *Arts and Architecture* (Los Angeles), no. 2, 1983.

Charles Eames occupied a unique position in the design world from 1940 when he and Eero Saarinen won the competition for the design of a chair sponsored by the Museum of Modern Art in New York. But it is not just for his designs that he is important. Eames and his wife and partner Ray Eames achieved something much more rare: they caused a shift in the way that we look at everything. Bright and cheerful objects that are commonplace in one culture or another, be they tin trains or carved Indian animals, were placed to form a montage of images that spread from the Eameses' own living room to those of designers around the world. No money was needed, just a good eye.

Part of the secret of Eames's success was that the items that he picked for display were never from the world of high art. Normal, commercially-made objects, often not highly regarded in their place of origin, were combined with natural objects to make a kaleidoscopic collection of bric-a-brac that is cheerful and fascinating, pleases the senses, and makes no moral or political point. Perhaps only Los Angeles, with its free-wheeling cultural ambience and its questioning of European values, could have nurtured and sustained such a frankly hedonistic approach to design. The rest of the world is still too serious about art.

Eames designed exhibitions and showrooms, made films, invented toys, and spread his skills over the whole field of design, but the artifacts that have made the greatest impact on architects are his chairs and the house that he built for himself in Pacific

Charles Eames: Eames House, Pacific Palisades, California, 1949.

Palisades, California. The house was sponsored by the magazine *Arts and Architecture* as one of its series of "Case Study Houses," surely one of architectural journalism's most adventurous and rewarding notions (it also brought Raphael Soriano and Pierre Koenig to fame). Eames' House is on a beautiful site: a steep bank with eucalyptus trees along one side. When the steel framing members were already fabricated, Eames completely changed the design, from a bridge house spanning between two supports to a ground-hugging house tucked into the bank, a demonstration of his calm flexibility of approach—

most architects are very uptight about making changes once the project has reached a certain point. The steel frame, cleverly detailed to emphasize its lightness, has a skin that is typically Eames— windows and panels just as found in the catalogue. Like his toys and bric-a-brac, the house is designed on the select-and-arrange technique, not on the I-must-design-it-all-myself approach.

Equalling the house in importance are the series of chairs he designed over a period of thirty years. As Eames grew older, so his chairs became less stark, more comfortable, and more expensive, as if he were always designing for his own age group. In retrospect, it is the youthful inventiveness of the early chairs that appeals, those shells of formed plywood or fibreglass on light metal supports that may well strike the antique collector of the future as the noblest product of the 1940s.

The story of modern design has been a very sombre one, deadly serious about its responsibilities and totally lacking in any sense of fun. Eames added a touch of whimsy, or lightness and delicacy. He could get away with it because he combined these characteristics with superlative technical know-how and a sharp, discerning eye for colour and form.

—John Winter

EATON, Norman.

South African. Born in Pretoria, in October 1902. Educated at the Diocesan College, Cape Town, 1915-21; University of the Witwatersrand, Johannesburg, under G. E. Pearse, Dip.Arch. 1928; articled to Gordon Leith, Johannesburg and Pretoria, 1927-28; studied at the British School of Architecture, Rome (Herbert Baker Scholarship), 1930-32. In private practice, Pretoria, 1933 until his death in 1966: in partnership with T. J. Louw, as Norman Eaton and Louw, from the mid-1950s. Recipient: Gold Medal, Suid-Afrikaanse Akademie vir Wetenskap en Kuns, 1960; Posthumous Gold Medal of Honour, Institute of South African Architects, 1968. Honorary Member, Suid-Afrikaanse Akademie vir Wetenskap en Kuns. *Died* (in Pretoria) *in November 1966.*

Works (all South Africa):

1933/
34 Boyes House, Pretoria
1935 Nicolson House, Pretoria
1937/
38 Van Wouw House, Pretoria
De Loor House, Pretoria
1940 Land Bank Building, Potchefstroom, Transvaal
Children's Art Centre, Pretoria
1940/
41 Van der Merwe House, near Pretoria
1941/
43 Land Bank Building, Pietermaritzburg, Natal
1943/
44 Land Bank Building, Kroonstad, Orange Free State
1944/
48 Ministry of Transport Building, Pretoria (project; with R. Cole-Bowen and A. L. Meiring)
1946/
53 Netherlands Bank Building, Pretoria (with A. L. Meiring)
1949/
50 Anderssen House, near Pretoria
1949/
51 Greenwood House, near Pretoria
1954/
56 Holsboer House, Pretoria
1955/
60 Wachthuis Building, Pretoria
1961/
62 Moolman House, Pretoria
1961/
65 Netherlands Bank Building, Durban
1964 Van den Berg House, Pretoria

Publications:

By EATON: articles—"Pretoria of the Future" in *Journal of the Society of Old Pretoria,* August 1958; "The Architect Today" in *South African Architectural Record* (Johannesburg), June 1964; "Aims and Procedures in the Preservation and Restoration of Historic Buildings" in *Preservation and Restoration of Historic Buildings in South Africa,* edited by R. F. M. Immelmann and G. D. Quinn, Cape Town 1968.

On EATON: book— *Norman Eaton: Architect* by Clinton Harrop-Allin, Cape Town and Johannesburg 1975; article—"The ISAA National Congress of April 1983", special issue of *Architecture South Africa* (Cape Town), July-August 1983.

Norman Eaton's training and early experience prepared him for the rôle of an architect whose work

Norman Eaton: Wachthuis Building, Pretoria, 1960.

was to be based upon historical themes and precedents. He nevertheless emerged, during the 1940s and 1950s, as one of South Africa's foremost modern architects, merging in his work the traditional and the contemporary. Although his plans were as modern as anything produced by his contemporaries who followed the precepts of the International Style, Eaton's work showed from the outset a regional emphasis.

His success in establishing a special relevance and harmony of building and environment springs from a more profound faculty than the mere ability to reproduce traditional detailing or the satisfaction of regional demands of climate, techniques and materials. His evocation of locality does not rest upon an exploitation of the picturesque, and the emotions it evokes are far removed from mere sentimentality. In his striving for a harmony between building and place, or in the suggestion through detailing of an African touch, there is also a realization that this could only be done with success if it could be brought into the context of his own time and society and the basic problems of function and structure with which he was involved. The evocation of the regional and the indigenous thus occurs at a level which precludes any suggestion of a vernacular character. With Eaton, the creative process was intuitively subjected to a refinement determined by his deep feeling for the landscape, climate, materials and crafts of Africa. The result is a capturing of a regional ethos: the intangibles of mood, atmosphere and tradition and, in the last analysis, a sense of belonging.

He concentrated largely upon traditional and indigenous materials, exploiting their inherent qualities, extending their possibilities, and showing that modern architecture can attain a richness and warmth without compromising its principles. In the handling of stone, wood, terra-cotta and above all the simple brick, no other South African architect can be compared to Norman Eaton for inventiveness and creative originality.

Finally, through his study of architectural history, including South Africa's own Cape Dutch heritage, Eaton became convinced that the achievements of the past held vital lessons of continuing applicability. This study and this conviction enabled him to rise above the constricting precepts of styles and movements. His work is significant in the development of a modern architecture in South Africa because of, not in spite of, the fact that he was steeped in tradition and man's architectural accomplishments over the ages. His best work is that of an artist who did not stand in awe of conventions, either of his own day or of the past. He understood the meaning of tradition. He grasped its spirit. His work is part of it, and, within the considerable powers at his command, an extension of it.

—Clinton Harrop-Allin

ECKBO, Garrett.

American. Born in Cooperstown, New York, 28 November 1910; raised in California. Educated at Marin Junior College, now College of Marin, California, 1930-31; University of California, Berkeley, under H.L. Vaughan, 1932-35, B.S. in Landscape Design 1935; Harvard University Graduate School of Design, Cambridge, Massachusetts, under Walter Chambers, 1936-38, M.L.A. 1938. Married Arline Williams in 1937; daughters: Marilyn and Alison. Worked at Armstrong Nurseries, Ontario, California, 1935-36; worked for Kastner and Berla, architects, Washington, D.C., United States Housing Authority, Washington, and the designer Norman Bel Geddes, New York, 1938; Landscape Architect, Farm Security Administration, San Francisco, 1939-42; Partner, Eckbo and

Williams, San Francisco, 1942-45, Eckbo, Royston and Williams, San Francisco, 1945, Los Angeles, 1946-58, Eckbo, Dean and Williams, Los Angeles, 1958-64, and Eckbo, Dean, Austin and Williams, San Francisco, 1964-68; Principal, Eckbo, Dean, Austin and Williams Inc., San Francisco, Los Angeles, Honolulu, and Minneapolis, 1968-73. Principal, Garrett Eckbo and Associates, San Francisco, since 1973, and Eckbo-Kay Associates, San Francisco, 1979-82. Lecturer, then Associate Professor, University of Southern California, Los Angeles, 1948-56. Professor, College of Environmental Design, 1965-78, Chairman of the Department of Landscape Architecture, 1965-69, and, since 1978, Professor Emeritus, University of California, Berkeley. Visiting Lecturer, University of Osaka Prefecture, 1969, and the University of New South Wales, Sydney, and University of Queensland, Brisbane, 1974. Recipient: Award of Merit, Homes for Better Living, American Institute of Architects/*House and Home/Sunset Magazine,* 1956; Award of Merit, American Institute of Architects/*Sunset Magazine,* 1961-62; First Honor Award, 1962, Honor Award, 1966 and 1978, Merit Award, 1970 (twice), 1972, and 1976, Bradford Williams Award, 1963, Medal of Honor, 1975, Special Honor Award, 1978, and Outstanding Contribution Award, 1981, American Society of Landscape Architects; California Govenor's Design Award, 1966; Merit Award, United States Department of Housing and Urban Development, 1968; Achievement Award, California Landscape Contractors Association, 1968; Certificate of Merit, American Association of Nurserymen, 1971; Grand Award, Council of Engineering Consultants, 1972; Certificate of Achievement, Department of Landscape Architecture, Harvard University, 1976; Business and Industry Award, Los Angeles Beautiful Inc., 1979; Design Arts Fellowship, National Endowment for the Arts, 1979; California Council Special Award, American Institute of Architects, 1980; Richard Neutra Award, California State Polytechnic University, 1983. Fellow, American Society of Landscape Architects; Member, American Inistitute of Planners, and International Federation of Landscape Architects; Associate, National Academy of Design. Honorary Fellow, American Institute of Interior Designers. Address: 1006 Cragmont Avenue, Berkeley, California 94708, U.S.A.

Works:

1939 General Motors Building, World's Fair, New York (project)
Federal Building, International Exposition, San Francisco (project)
1939/
42 Site planning and landscape development for 50 rural housing/camp developments in the Western United States, for the Farm Security Administration, San Francisco
1940 Plan for a cooperative housing development at Ladera, California
Weltner House garden, Woodside, California
Fisk House garden, Atherton, California
Bagley House garden, San Francisco
1942/
45 Plans for 50 war and public housing developments in northern California
1947 Park Planned Homes landscaping, Altadena, California
1948 Mar Vista Homes landscaping, West Los Angeles
1950 Olivet Memorial Park (cemetery), Colma, California (project)
Plan for cooperative housing development at Reseda, California (project)
Rich's Department Store landscaping, Knoxville, Tennessee
Mankowski Homes landscaping, Azusa, California
Central Quadrangle, Long Beach City College, California

Campus development plan for Orange Coast College, Costa Mesa, California
1952 Campus development plan for Occidental College, Los Angeles
1953 S. A. Camp Company landscaping, Shafter, California
1954 Aeronautical District Lodge 727 landscaping, Burbank, California
1955 Plan for parks and recreation spaces for Lakewood, California
Lucky Lager Brewery landscaping, Azusa, California
Neighborhood plan for Wonderland Park, Los Angeles
Sunset Capri Apartments landscaping, Los Angeles
City Hall Plaza and Gardens, Civic Center, Whittier, California
1955/
60 Designs for power generating plant landscapes at Point Arena, Oxnard, and Huntington Beach, California, and Agua Fria, Arizona
1955/
65 Campus development plan for Ambassador College, Pasadena, California
School ground development plans for 6 high schools, 7 intermediate schools, and 53 elementary schools, throughout southern California
Gardens for Frank House, Holmby Hills, California; Johnson-McFie Houses, Los Angeles; Duke House, Benedict Canyon, Los Angeles; Cooper House, Holmby Hills, California; Sudarsky House, Bakersfield, California; Geman House, Bakersfield, California; Cameron House, Beverly Hills, California; Frik House, Arvin, California; Karlen House, Thunderbird Ranch, Palm Springs, California; Keatinge House, San Marino, California; Mayer House, Bel Air, California; LeRoy House, Bel Air, California; Koolish House, Bel Air, California; May House, Beverly Hills, California; Mandel House, Beverly Hills, California; Prinzmetal House, Holmby Hills, California; Goetz House, Holmby Hills, California; Goldstone House, Beverly Hills, California; Hartman House, Beverly Hills, California
1956 El Caballero Country Club landscaping, Tarzana, California
Longwood Redevelopment landscaping, Cleveland, Ohio
Douglas Aircraft Company landscaping, Long Beach, California
Churchill Apartments landscaping, West Los Angeles
Design plans for Live Oak Cemetery, Monrovia, California
Plan for cooperative housing development at Kenter Canyon, West Los Angeles
Collins Radio Inc. landscaping, Newport Beach, California
Campus development plan for Loyola University, Los Angeles
Neighborhood Church landscaping, Pasadena, California
1956/
58 Mayfair, Jese San Martin, Jese del Valle, and Simon Bolivar Parks, Lakewood, California
1957 Plan for parks and recreation spaces for Casper, Wyoming
Farnsworth and Chambers Office Building landscaping, Houston
Parkway systems, Lakewood, California
Bellehurst Country Club landscaping, Buena Park/Fullerton, California
Bel-Air Lanai Apartments landscaping, Los Angeles
1958 Great Lakes Carbon Corporation Land Reclamation Plan, Palos Verdes, California
Bellehurst Community Development landscaping, Buena Park/Fullerton, California

Garrett Eckbo: Student Union Square, University of New Mexico, Albuquerque 1977.

Neighborhood plan for Nichols Canyon, Los Angeles

Twenty-eighth Church of Christ Scientist landscaping, Westwood, California

Eagle Rock Park, Los Angeles

Civic Center landscaping, El Monte, California

La Canada Country Club landscaping, La Canada, California

Design study for the Hipodromo Nacional, Caracas, Venezuela

Alcoa Forecast Garden, Los Angeles

Design plans for Crestlawn Memorial Park (cemetery), Norco, California

Los Angeles All-City Outdoor Art Festival

Communities Facilities Planners Offices landscaping, South Pasadena, California

Dow Chemical Company Administrative Center landscaping, Freeport, Texas

1958/
65 Campus development plan for Ambassador College, Bricket Wood, England

1959 Central park, lake, and waterfall, California City

Wilderness Park, Arcadia, California

1960 Harper Humanities Garden, University of Denver, Colorado

Fifth Church of Christ Scientist landscaping, Hollywood, California

Special playground, City of Hope, Duarte, California

Waterside Promenade, Newport Beach, California

1960/
62 Campus development plan for St. John's College, Santa Fe, New Mexico

1961 Mt. Sinai Hospital Playground, Los Angeles

Long Beach Community Hospital landscaping, Long Beach, California

1962 Design study for the Golden Pagoda Hotel, Hilo, Hawaii

House of the Book landscaping, Brandeis Camp Institute, Brandeis, California

1962/
67 Campus development pan for Monterey Peninsula College, Monterey, California

1962/
78 Open spaces master plan for the University of New Mexico, Albuquerque (and consultancy since 1978)

1963 Downtown pedestrian mall, Fresno, California

Housing for the elderly landscaping, Las Vegas, California

Temple Mt.Sinai landscaping, El Paso, Texas

Urban design study for El Centro, California

El Paso International Airport landscaping, Texas

1963/
65 Campus development plan for California State College, San Barnardino

1964 Union Bank Square, Los Angeles

1965 Urban-Metropolitan Area Open Space Study, Southern Section, State of California

Mission Bay Park, San Diego, California

1966 Old Monterey Plaza, Monterey, California

Plan for City/County Civic Center, Santa Ana, California

Campus development plan for Leeward Oahu Community College, Honolulu

1968 Plan for the Sausalito Waterfront, California

Science-Engineering Mall, University of California at Davis

Land-use plan for Redwood Shores, Redwood City, California

Master plan for Lodi Park, New Delhi

Downtown pedestrian mall, Sacramento, California

Ford Foundation Headquarters landscaping, New Delhi

1969 Plans for service facilities relocation, Yosemite National Park, California

Critique of environmental and urban design proposals for the State Foundation for Culture and the Arts, Hawaii

1970 Master plan for the river channel, Mississippi River at St. Paul, Minnestoa

Right-of-way and station design studies, San Francisco Municipal Railway

Urban design study for Hayward, California

The Villages (housing), San Jose, California

Design plan for Community Center Park, Castro Valley, California

McKeon House garden, Hillsborough, California

Design plan for a downtown pedestrian mall, Sunnyvale, California

Tuscon Community Center, Arizona

Quail Hill landscaping, Terra Linda, Marin County, California

1971 Expressway location and design, Minneapolis

P.G. & E. Building landscaping, San Francisco

Bechtel Corporation Office Building landscaping, San Francisco

1972 Master plan for the Berkeley Waterfront, California

Yosemite Village Mall, Yosemite Valley, California (design only)

Design plan for Horse Ranch Park, Cupertino, California

Freeway location and design, Dubuque, Iowa

1973 Freeway location and design, Duluth, Minnesota

Plan for the Civic Center, Mountain View, California

Denver Botanic Garden, Colorado

Housing rehabilitation study for the Navajo Nation, Arizona-New Mexico

Park/parkway system review and rehabilitation plan, Minneapolis

1974 Public Safety Building landscaping, Mill Valley, California

North Country Coach Terminal landscaping, San Jose, California

Plan for parks, recreation areas and open spaces, Ojai, California

Comparative study of Sydney/San Francisco Bays

American Falls International Board, Niagara Falls, New York/Ontario

1974/
75 Plans for Penasquitos Canyon Regional Park, San Diego, California

1974/
76 Plan for urban squares, malls, and plazas, University of California, Berkeley

1974/
78 Bayhill Office Building landscaping, San Bruno, California (with Kenneth Kay)

1975 Plan and program for the public use of Shelby Farms, Memphis, Tennessee

1976 Central Park, University of New Mexico, Albuquerque

Land-use, circulation, and vegetation management plan for Strawberry Canyon, University of California, Berkeley

Plan for the Esplanade/Great Highway Corridor, San Francisco

Study for the California State Parks and Recreation Commission (with Sydney Williams)

Cypress Lawn Cemetery, Colma, California (as consultant)

New master plan for the Botanic Garden, Memphis, Tennessee

Tri-Cultural Fountain, College of Santa Fe, New Mexico (with Kenneth Kay)

Plans for the Living History Center, Novato/Black Point, California (with Kenneth Kay)

1976/
78 Kaiser Medical Clinics landscaping, Santa Clara, California

1977 Plan for radio communication facilities, Mt. Diablo, California

Plan for solar access for residential commmunities (with Living Systems)

Church of the Winding Way landscaping, Sacramento, California (project)

Black's Beach Access Trail, San Diego, California (project)

1978 Capital improvement development plan for Garin Regional Park, Hayward, California

Galvez Mall, Stanford University, California

Sand Bay Village Condominiums landscaping, Discovery Bay/Byron, California

Buena Vista Park path and stairway system, San Francisco

California Shakespearean Festival, Visalia/Three Rivers, California (as consultant)

Oakmead Office Building landscaping, Sunnyvale, California

Plans for Puerto Azul Resort Community, Ternate, Cavite, Philippines

Hellinger House garden, Pacific Palisades, California

1978 Master plan for Baylands, Palo Alto, California (with Kenneth Kay)

1979/
84 Moffet Field Naval Air Station, Sunnyvale, California

Lasuen Mall and Braun Music Center, Stanford University, California

Byxbee Park Master Plan, Palo Alto, California

SRI International Complex, Menlo Park, California

Blood Bank, Burlingame, California

Columbus Square Monument to Joseph Con-

rad, San Francisco

Waterfront Plan, Sausalito, California

Lake Merritt Channel Park and Sculpture Garden, Oakland, California

Naval Weapons Station, Concord, California

Radio Communications Facilities Plan, Mount Diablo, California

Naval Air Station, Fallon, Nevada

Addis House, Malibu, California

Bolles House, Santa Rosa, California

Bolton High School, Memphis, Tennessee

Riverside Promenade, Jacksonville, Florida

Maiden Lane renewal, San Francisco

Pebble Beach Lodge, Monterey Peninsula, California

Richmond Hilltop Fire Station, Richmond, California

Salvation Army Senior Center, San Francisco

Shelby Farms Agricenter, Memphis, Tennessee

Recreation Facilities, Lake Sonoma, California

Willwerth House, Los Altos Hills, California

1984/
85 Fourth District Urban Design Plan, San Diego, California (with Southeast Urban Design Group)

Landscape Garden Show Master Plan, San Francisco

Fort Canning Park, Singapore (with Robert Royston)

Publications:

By ECKBO: books—*Landscape for Living,* New York 1950; *Urban Landscape Design,* New York 1964, Tokyo 1970; *The Art of Home Landscaping,* New York 1965, revised edition as *Home Landscape,* New York 1977; *The Landscape We See,* New York 1969, Tokyo 1972; *Environment and Design,* Tokyo 1971; *Public Landscape,* Berkeley, California 1977; articles—"Small Gardens in the City" in *Pencil Points* (New York), September 1937; "Sculpture and Landscape Design" in *Magazine of Art* (New York), April 1938; "Landscape Design in: The Urban Environment; The Rural Environment; The Primeval," three articles with James Rose and Daniel Urban Kiley, in *Architectural Record* (New York), May and August 1939 and February 1940; "Outdoors and In" in *Magazine of Art* (New York), October 1941; "Site Planning" in *Architectural Forum* (New York), May 1942; "Landscape Gardening," two articles in *Architectural Forum* (New York), February and March 1946; "Land Planning Knits House and Site Together" in *Sunset Magazine* (Menlo Park, California), May 1946; "Landscape Architecture: A Professional Adventure" in *Architect and Engineer* (San Francisco), September 1946; "Planning and Design Today" in *Parks and Recreation* (Washington, D.C.), March 1948; "Urban Landscape" in *Journal of the Town Planning Institute* (London), February 1950; "Landscape Design in the Pacific Southwest Today" in *Architectural Record* (New York), January 1953; "Living with Gardens" in *California Garden* (Berkeley), Spring 1956; "Converging Forces on Design" in *Journal of Architectural Education* (Washington, D.C.), Autumn 1956; "The Urban Landscape" in *Synthesis* (Cambridge, Massachusetts), April 1957; "A Splendid View of Mission Bay" in *San Diego Magazine,* February 1960; "Longwood: Antidote for Pomposity" in *Landscape Architecture* (Louisville, Kentucky), Spring 1960; "Landscape Design Potentials for Education" in *American School and University Yearbook,* New York 1960-61; "Is It Possible to Design a City?" in *Landscaping* (Washington, D.C.), February 1961; "Urban Design: A Definition" in *AIA Journal* (Washington, D.C.), September 1963; "Design and Criticism" in *AIA Journal* (Washington, D.C.), September 1964; "Architecture and the Landscape" in *Arts and Architecture* (Los Angeles), October 1964; "Landscape and Garden in Japan" in *Garten und Landschaft* (Stuttgart), October 1964;

"Creative Design of the Landscape" in *Landscape Architecture* (Louisville, Kentucky), January 1965; "Planning the Gross Society" in *Landscape Architecture* (Louisville, Kentucky), July 1965; "The Personalized Landscape" in *AIA Journal* (Washington, D.C.), May 1965; "Campus Landscape" in *American School and University* (New York), April 1966; "The Mission of the Department of landscape Architecture" in *Journal of Environmental Design* (Berkeley, California), May 1966; "Design and Landscape Character" in *Landscape and Human Life,* edited by Cru Tandy Diambatan, Amsterdam 1966; "The Decision-Making Totem Pole" in *AIA Journal* (Washington, D.C.), July 1966; "The Quality of Urbanization" in *Centennial Review* (East Lansing, Michigan), no.3, 1966; "Defining the Cultural Environment" in *Landscapes* (Santa Fe, New Mexico), Autumn 1966; "Parklands in the Urban Desert" in *Cry California* (Sacramento), Winter 1966; "People in Landscape Space" in *Mountain States Architecture* (Denver), September/October 1966, reprinted in *New Mexico Architecture* (Alburquerque), November/December 1966; "Commentary on Qualification of Professional School Graduates" in *Grounds Maintenance Magazine* (Kansas city), May 1968; "Garden or Jungle?" in *American Institute of Landscape Architects Journal* (Los Angeles), June 1969; "The Landscape of Tourism" in *Landscape* (Santa Fe, New Mexico), Spring/Summer 1969; "Too Much Analysis or Designer's Fantasy?: An Eckbo-Porterfield Interchange" in *Landscape Architecture* (Louisville, Kentucky), April 1970; "K Street Mall, Sacramento" in *Design and Environment* (New York), June 1970; "Green Land in Japan" in *Landscape Architecture* (Louisville, Kentucky), April 1971; "Ecology and Design" in *Journal of Soil and Water Conservation* (Washington, D.C.), July/August 1971; "Shopping in Gardens" in *Year-Book of the United States Department of Agriculture,* Washington, D.C. 1972; "Open Space and Land Use" in *Land Use and Landscape Planning,* edited by Derek Lovejoy, London 1973; "Sculpture in the Garden—Wood" in *House and Garden Guide,* New York 1973; "Garden and Landscape Design" in *Encyclopedia Britannica,* Chicago 1974; "Landscape Architecture" in *Landscape Australia* (Mont Albert, Victoria), July 1979; "Is Landscape Architecture?" in *Landscape Architecture* (Louisville, Kentucky), May/June 1983; "Man and Nature at Levi Strauss" in *Landscape Architecture* (Louisville, Kentucky), November/December 1983; "People, nature and design in the West" in *Space Design* (Tokyo), April 1984.

On ECKBO: articles—"Landscape Design in the U.S.A." in *Architectural Review* (London), January 1949; "The Landscape We See" by D. Streatfield in *Landscape Architecture* (Louisville, Kentucky), January 1972; "Northstar" by Henrik Bull in *Architectural Record* (New York), January 1974; "Nine Landscaping Projects in America" in *Building Ideas* (Sydney), November 1974; "Garret Eckbo—The Early Years" by Esther McCoy in *Arts and Architecture* (Los Angeles) no. 4, 1982.

Bibliography: *Garrett Eckbo: A Bibliography* by Mary Vance, Monticello, Illinois 1980.

I am a planner and designer of outdoor environments, particulary where qualitive experience is important. That is, or should be, everywhere that people will see rather than only where the well-to-do and discriminating live.

Outdoor environments begin just outside all of the doors and windows of every building and extend to the next visual or movement block—or other structure, land, or water form or vegetation mass. Outdoor environments therefore begin in everyone's back or front yard and extend around the world. At individual and/or urban scale, buildings dominate outdoors; at regional or large scale, outdoors dominates buildings, even cities. Small towns and suburbs fall between.

Outdoors is where people and society meet nature or the existing landscape as a composite of structural and natural elements. Construction (architecture, engineering) is the representative technology of society in the landscape. Agriculture and horticulture are the intermediate technologies which remodel nature without losing its vitality.

Planning sets policy for land use, change, and developed character in general terms. Design establishes specific forms for change and development when they are to occur. Outdoor design begins with situations as they exist and with programs for change as they are presented. It functions as intermediary between people and nature or, more specifically and qualitatively, between architecture and ecology.

The most traditional product of outdoor design is the agricultural landscape, followed by gardens, parks, malls, plazas, and planned/designed communities and urban sectors in which there is a symbiotic relationship between indoor and outdoor development. Qualitative standards for form and space, scale and proportion, rhythm and balance, with unstable or incomplete equilibrium as the ultimate goal, are as demanding and compelling as in any of the other fine/social arts. Ultimate success will come from a balance of social, ecological, and qualitative design standards.

—Garrett Eckbo

Garrett Eckbo has been in the forefront of those trying to articulate the need for a contemporary expression of American ideals in the urban landscape. He has severely criticized the undemocratic, exploitative, and mechanical aspects of the rapid urbanization that has taken place in the United States during and since World War II. In response, he has formulated a design philosophy for gardens, parks, and the urban landscape based on equality, sharing, and humanism. This philosophy stresses rural-centered values of maximum interpenetration of natural with made elements in urban and suburban settings. The stress is on keeping urbanized individuals and communities in touch with their own non-urban roots throgh maximum use of accessible social areas based on aesthetic and variable landscaping. He thus stands opposed both the helter-skelter suburbanization (private development for maximum profit) and to high-density urban cores with their stress on totally human-made forms. He stands for the essentially romantic mainstream of American aesthetics: preservation and cultivation of values and technologies tying the industrial and post-industrial environment to its agrarian past.

In terms of his professional practice, Eckbo is perhaps the individual most responsible for the "Quality California Look" in American landscape design. Although he viewed his solutions as prototypic to any urban or suburban environment, the distinct regional climate of California overcame even the most technologically sophisticated attempts at a homogeneous American aesthetic of landscape design. His work out of state tends to look either out-of-place or out-of-phase with the bulk of his work which is located in California.

His 1941 Garden in Oakland (Figures 15-20 in *Landscape for Living*) serves as an illustration of this look for a private garden. It presents an idealized California landscape, totally removed from the visual and auditory urban fabric and stressing leisure living on outside patios surrounded by trees and screens. Communication with neighbors would involve the telephone, a car trip, or a detour around the front gate. The illusion of country-in-the-city is as near-perfect as can be accomplished on a small lot.

José del Valle Park (Lakewood, California) demonstrates these same principles on the scale of a neighborhood park. A strong separation is achieved from the displeasing visual forms of the city by surrounding the park with screens, berms, and tress. The internal environment intersperses small paved areas and leisure activity centers with nodes of plantings. The philosophy of interpenetration works out in practice to be a quasi-rural retreat in what is perceived as an urban wasteland.

The grounds of the Polytechnic High School, Long Beach, operate on the level of a building cluster. Here the plantings are more formal and less introverted than on the garden or park scale design. The rural clumps of trees and meadows in the center of an educational complex again reach for a nature-culture interpenetration.

In theory and practice, Eckbo has made a great contribution to the improvement of the American landscape. From today's perspective, the main weaknesses of his approach, both in theory and practice, seem to be an excessive fragmentation of experience from the realities of contemporary life and a mannered aesthetism not directly related to the ecology of the region, area, or the particular site. The main strengths are a genuine concern for the welfare of users rather than clients alone and an ability to relax the severity of the contemporary urban landscape.

—Joseph B. Juhasz

ECOCHARD, Michel Marie Leon.
French. Born in Paris, 11 March 1905. Married; has five children. Town Planner in Syria, 1932-45; Director of Town Planning and Architecture, Morocco, 1946-53. In private practice, Paris, since 1953. Member of the High Council for Civic Buildings, Paris, since 1962; Chief Architect of Civic Buildings and National Palaces, France, since 1962. Exhibitions: *Biennale,* Venice, 1982; Kunstmuseum, Bochum, West Germany, 1983. Recipient: First Prize, Kuwait National Museum Competition, 1960; Grand Prix d'Architecture, Cercle d'Etudes Architecturales, Paris, 1964; Gold Medal, Société d'Encouragement à l'Art et à l'Industrie, Paris, 1967; Aga Khan Prize, 1982. Address (office): 55 Boulevard du Montparnasse, 75006 Paris, France.

Works:

1931 Antioch Museum, Turkey
1936 Damascus Museum
French Institute, Damascus
Master plan for Damascus
1943 Master plan for Beirut
1946/
53 Master plans for Casablanca, Fez, Rabat, and Meknes, Morocco
1955 French Protestant School for Girls, Beirut (with Le Coeur)
Kindergarten, Beirut
1955/
58 University of Karachi (with Riboulet and Thurnauer)
1958 Mohenjo-Daro Museum, Pakistan
City plan for Sabende, Guinea
1959 Marist Brothers School, Saida, Lebanon (with Amine Bezri)
Master plan for Conakry, Guinea
Master plans for Jounieh and Byblos, Lebanon
1959/
60 Secondary school, Beirut (with Faez Ahdab)
1960 Kuwait National Museum (competition project)
Antonine Fathers Boys' College and Seminary, Baabda, Lebanon (with Gabriel Tabet)
1961 Sisters of Charity Hospital, Beirut (with Henri Edde and ATBAT)
Sisters of Charity School, Church and Convent, Tripoli
Governmental city plan for Beirut

Plan for a summer resort, Coti-Chiavari, Corsica
1962/
78 University of the Ivory Coast, Abidjan
Master plan for Satellite City, near Marseille
Master plan for the city and suburbs of Beirut
Plan for an express highways network, Lebanon
1963 College of Further Education, Brazzaville, Congo
University of the Federation of the Cameroons, Yaounde
Social Security Training Center, Lyon (project)
Master plan for Dakar, Senegal
City Center Plan, Beirut
Satellite City, Beirut
1964 Primary School, Martigues, France
Master plan for Damascus
Mohenjo-Daro Museum, Pakistan (project)
1967 House of Culture, Nanterre, France
Master plan for Tabriz, Iran
1969 University Center for the Health Sciences, Yaounde, Cameroons
Center for African Studies, British Foundation, and Open Amphitheatre, Yaounde, Cameroons
French Embassy, Yaounde, Cameroons
General plan for Corsica
1971 City Center Plan, Mashhad, Iran
1972 Museum, Bahrain (project)
University of Yaounde Polytechnic School, Cameroons
1973 University of Yaounde Amphitheatre, Cameroons
Master plan for a new capital city, Sultanate of Oman
1977 Farabi Arts University, Karadj, near Tehran (with Lombard and Vakili)
Kuwait National Museum
1978 Study of the city center of Tehran

Publications:

By ECOCHARD: books—*Les Monuments ayyoubides de Damas,* 3 vols., with Jean Sauvaget, Damascus 1938-48; *Les Bains de Damas, monographies architecturales,* 2 vols., with Claude Le Coeur, Paris 1943; *Casablanca, le roman d'une ville,* Paris 1955; *Filiation des monuments grecs, byzantins et islamiques,* Paris 1978; articles—"L'Urbanisme au Levant" in *L'Architecture d'aujourd'hui* (Paris), September/October 1945; "Problèmes de l'urbanisme au Maroc" in *L'Architecture d'aujourd'hui* (Paris), May 1951; "Menace pour nos villes: la speculation foncière", in *Critique* (Paris), July 1955; "Une mythe: le plan de la région parisienne' in *L'Architecture d'aujourd'hui* (Paris), December 1955/January 1956; "Point de vue sur l'urbanisme" in *La Nouvelle Critique* (Paris), November 1960; "Des Villes qui explosent" in *Cahiers de la république* (Paris), February 1961; "Habitat musulman au Maroc" in *L'Architecture d'aujourd'hui* (Paris), June 1965; "Kritik des Strukturplanes für die Entwicklung von Paris bis zue Jahr 2000" in *Baumeister* (Munich), June 1966; "Une lettre de Michel Ecochard à propos de l'aménagement des Halles" in *Techniques et architecture* (Paris), no. 303, 1975.

On ECOCHARD: books—*Karachi: The New University,* with introduction by S. M. Sharif, Paris 1956; *La Nouvelle Architecture française* by Maurice Besset, Teufen, Switzerland 1967; *Sixty Years of Planning in Morocco* by Jean Dethier, Princeton, New Jersey 1970; *Histoire mondiale de l'architecture moderne et de l'urbanisme* by Michel Ragon, Paris 1972; *The Arab City, Its Character, and Islamic and Cultural Heritage,* edited by Imail Serazeldin, Arlington, Virginia 1982; articles—"Transformation of the Centre of Mashhad" and "Damascus Centre Renewal" in *L'Architecture d'aujourd'hui* (Paris),

Michel Ecochard: City Centre Plan, Mashad, Iran, 1971.

September/October 1973; "The Mohenjo-Daro Museum" by Mohammed Ishtiaq Khan in *Museum* (Paris), no. 2/3, 1977; "Casablanca" by Jean-Claude Delorme and others in *Architecture, mouvement, continuité* (Paris), June 1977.

The major part of Michel Ecochard's career as a town planner and architect has been spent abroad—from 1932 to 1945 in Syria, then in Morocco where he was in charge of the Department of Town Planning and Architecture. A man of rare integrity, he necessarily found himself in conflict with speculators and opportunists. The probity of his character and the firmness of his convictions made him an inconvenience to an administration subject to many kinds of pressures and predisposed to compromise.

As a government servant he was "transferred" to France and condemned to an inactivity that weighed heavily on him. A mission to Pakistan got him out of the way. There he drew up very fine plans for a university that were rejected thanks to a change of generals at the head of the government. He had to begin again. The project as finally executed has indisputable qualities, but unfortunately it does not stand comparison with the initial project.

Looking over Ecochard's list of works, one is impressed by the number of plans, proposals, and town planning studies that resulted in little or nothing! It is a story of difficult struggles that were rarely crowned with success—that is to say, with execution. Ecochard's work—and he was a town planner in the fullest sense of the words—poses serious questions. His works in the architectural sphere are less characteristic of Ecochard the man; however, they reveal a certain strength in idea, a sobriety in form, and honesty in conception tempered by a profound sense of humanity.

Ecochard continued his struggles in the Near East and in Black Africa, always enthusiastic, always ready to fight for idealistic and progressive solutions for towns and their populations. Many futile struggles, many disappointments, and a great deal of travelling have worn him down. It is a great pity that our society has not known how to make better use of a person of such professional and moral worth.

—Pierre Vago

EHRENKRANTZ, Ezra David.

American. Born in Newark, New Jersey, 20 February 1932. Educated at the Massachusetts Institute of Technology, Cambridge, 1950-54, B.Arch. 1954; University of Liverpool, 1955-56 (Ford Fellow), M.Arch. 1956; Building Research Station, England (Fulbright Fellow), 1957-58. Served as a Lieutenant in the United States Navy. Since 1966, President, The Ehrenkrantz Group, New York. Associate Professor of Architecture, University of California, Berkeley, 1967-70. Member: Presidential Task Force on Cities, 1966; National Committee on Urban Problems, 1966-68; Technological Advancement Board, and the Construction Affairs Committee, United States Chamber of Commerce, 1968-69; National Committee on Architectural Education, 1968-70, and the National Committee on Research in Architecture, 1969, American Institute of Architects. Recipient: Innovation in Building Award, *American Builder*, 1965; Service to the Building Industry Award, 1966; Construction Man of the Year Award, *Engineering News Record*, 1968; Quarter Century Award, Building Research Advisory Council, 1977. Address: The Ehrenkrantz Group, 19 West 44th Street, New York, New York 10036, U.S.A.

Works:

1964 School Construction Systems Development (SCSD) Pilot Unit, 770 Pampas Lane, Stanford, California (now the Stanford Employees Credit Union)

1966 DeLaveaga Elementary School, Santa Cruz, California

1969 Silvercreek High School, San Jose, California

1974 Canaday Hall, Harvard University, Cambridge, Massachusetts

1976 Interdisciplinary Resource Center, Pratt Institute, Brooklyn, New York (with Daniel Tully)

1978 Aaron Davis Hall, City College of the City University of New York, Convent Avenue and West 135th Street, New York (with Abraham Geller)

Publications:

By EHRENKRANTZ: books—*The Modular Number Pattern: Flexibility Through Standardization*, London 1956; *British Prefabricated School Construction*, Stanford, California 1962; articles— "Flexibility Through Standardization" in *Progressive Architecture* (New York), July 1957; "How to Make Things Fit Together" in *Architectural Forum* (New York), August 1960; "The Remarkable Dr. Doxiadis" in *Architectural Forum* (New York), May 1961; "Modular Materials and Design Flexibility" in *Arts and Architecture* (Los Angeles), April 1967; "The System to Systems" in *AIA Journal* (Washington, D.C.), May 1970; "Systems Building" in *Ekistics* (Athens), February 1971; "BSD Building Systems Development" in *Architectural Design* (London), November 1971.

On EHRENKRANTZ: articles—"Architecture by the Carload" in *Architectural Forum* (New York), April 1965; "SCSD Project, U.S.A.: School Construction Systems Development" in *Architectural Design* (London), July 1965; "School Construction Systems Development Program" in *Arts and Architecture* (Los Angeles), April 1967; "R and D Takes a Sea Change" by Michael Hacker in *Architects' Journal* (London), November 1967; "Pratt's Athletic Facility Opens" in *Progressive Architecture* (New York), January 1976; "Evaluation: A Look Back at the 60s' Sexiest System—SCSD", in *AIA Journal* (Washington, D.C.), April 1979; "Aaron Davis Hall" in *Architectural Record* (New York), June 1980.

Ezra Ehrenkrantz first attracted national attention with his plan to use standardized components to assemble low-cost school buildings with flexible interiors that retained architectural integrity. The pilot unit for the School Construction Systems Development (SCSD), built at Stanford, California in 1964, was hailed as a "jewel-like pavilion," and it was quickly followed by DeLaveaga Elementary School at Santa Cruz and Silvercreek High School at San Jose. The choice of non-systematized outer walls meant that the schools were quite different in external appearance, and users could modify the interiors to suit their changing needs.

Building Systems Development Inc., Ehrenkrantz's firm, pursued this approach, designing self-perpetuation building systems such as those for University of California residences and for academic buildings there and at the University of Indiana.

Ehrenkrantz went on to design such notable works as Aaron Davis Hall at the City College of New York and the Interdisciplinary Center at the Pratt Institute, Brooklyn. Davis Hall is an intricate building that expresses the complexity of its task, to house three separate theatres and serve an open-air amphitheatre. The Interdisciplinary Resource Center is dominated by an enormous hyperbolic paraboloid roof that results from the upward curve of two diagonally opposite corners of the square and the downward curve of the other two corners. The huge clear span of the upper level houses the gymnasium, with athletic offices and dance studios on the mezzanine and other offices and laboratories under ground. The need for expensive air-conditioning was circumvented by an ingenious system of wells and pumps, using water from an underground stream (aquifer) with a constant temperature of fifty-four degrees to cool the structure.

—Lucinda Hawkins

EIERMANN, Egon.

German. Born in Neuendorf, near Berlin, 29 September 1904. Educated at the Technische Hochschule, Charlottenburg, Berlin, Under Hans Poelzig, 1923-27. Married Brigitte Feyerabendt in 1954; children: Andreas (from previous marriage) and Julie Anna. Worked in the architectural office of the Rudolf Karstadt Company, Hamburg, 1927-28, and for BEWAG, Berlin, 1928-30; in private practice, Berlin, 1934-45, and Karlsruhe, West Germany 1947 until his death in 1970. Dean of the Faculty of Architecture, University of Karlsruhe, 1947-70. Chairman, Olympic Buildings Jury, Munich, 1968. Recipient: Good Design Award, Museum of Modern Art, New York, 1953; Architecture Prize, Cercle d'Etudes Architecturales, Paris, 1959; Berlin Art Prize, 1962; Best Building Award, *Architectural Forum*, 1963; Hessen Landspreis, Wiesbaden, 1965; Architectural Award of Excellence, American Institute of Steel Construction, 1965; Architecture Prize, Board of Trade, Washington, D.C., 1965; Institutional Landscaping Award, Washington, D.C., 1967; Nordrhein/Westfalen State Prize, 1965; Cross of Merit, German Federal Republic, 1968; Grand Prize, Bund Deutscher Architekten, 1968. D.Eng.: Technical University, Berlin, 1965. Honorary Member, Zentralvereinigung der Architekten Österreichs, Vienna, 1960; Honorary Corresponding Member, Royal Institute of British Architects, London, 1963. Member, Akademie der Künste, Berlin, 1955; Member, German Order of Merit for Science and Art, 1970. Member, Order of Leopold, Belgium, 1958. *Died* (in Baden-Baden, West Germany) *19 July 1970.*

Works:

1929/
30 Berlin Electricity Company Transformer Station

1930 Central Justice Building, Berlin (competition project: preliminary sketches; with Fritz Jaenecke)

1930/
31 Price-controlled, modern, self-contained private house (competition project; with Fritz Jaenecke)

1931/
32 "The Growing House," Berlin (with Fritz Jaenecke)

1931/
33 Hesse House, Berlin (with Fritz Jaenecke)

1934/
35 Bolle House, Berlin

1934/
37 Grieneisen Undertakers' Quarters, Berlin

1935 Friedrich Theatre, Dessau, Germany (competition project; with Fritz Jaenecke and Gunther Andretzke)

1935/
36 Dienstbach House, Berlin
Mathies House, Babelsberg, near Berlin

1936/
37 Steingroever House, Berlin
Display and Cinema for the *Gebt mit 4 Jahre Zeit* exhibition, Berlin

1936/
39 Foerstner and Company's Totalwerke alterations and extensions, Apolda, Germany

1937/
39 Dega-AG-Auergesellschaft Production and Administration Buildings, Berlin

1938/
42 Vollberg House, Berlin (with Rudolf Büchner)

1939/
41 Märkische Metallbau GmbH Factory Administration Building, Canteen, Boiler House and Porter's Lodge, Oranienburg, Germany

1942/
43 Plan for town of 20,000 inhabitants with an aircraft repair works, Udetfeld, Germany (project)

1946/
48 Community estate, Hettingen, Germany
Community estate, Buchen, Germany

1947 Airline Terminal and Hotel, Frankfurt (competition project; with Robert Hilgers)

1947/
48 Textile/Leather Goods Factory, Hassmersheim, Germany (project; with Robert Hilgers)

1948/
51 Südd.-Rundfunk Broadcast and Administration Building, Stuttgart (competition project)

1948/
52 Ciba AG Administration and Factory Buildings, Wehr, Germany (with Robert Hilgers)

1949/
51 Handkerchief Weaving Mill and Boiler House, Blumberg, Germany (with Robert Hilgers)

1950/
53 Vereinigten Seidenweberei AG Administration Building, Krefeld, West Germany (with Robert Hilgers)

1951 Merkur Store, Heilbronn, West Germany (with Robert Hilgers)
Textile Engineering School, Krefeld, West Germany (competition project)

1951/
52 University of Saarbrucken extension, West Germany (competition project; with Robert Hilgers)

1951/
60 Merkur Store, Stuttgart (with Robert Hilgers)

1951/
65 Experimental Generating Station, Technische

Hochschule, Karlsruhe, West Germany (with Robert Hilgers)

1952 Chemical/Pharmaceutical Institute reconstruction, University of Munich (competition project; with Robert Hilgers)

Merkur Store, Reutlingen, West Germany (with Robert Hilgers)

1952/
53 Small Hall reconstruction, Württemberg State Theatre, Stuttgart (competition project)

1952/
56 Matthäus Church, Pforzheim, West Germany (with Robert Hilgers)

1953 German House, Cité Universitaire, Paris (competition project)

St. Nikolai Church redevelopment, Hamburg, West Germany (competition project)

1953/
54 Evangelical Church with Community Centre, Baden-Baden, West Germany (competition project)

1953/
55 Burda-Moden Depot, Offenburg, West Germany (with Robert Hilgers)

1954 German Section, *Triennale*, Milan

Main Fruit and Vegetable Market, Hamburg, West Germany (competition project)

Lecture Hall extension, University of Freiburg, West Germany (competition project)

1955/
57 Volkshilfe-Lebensversicherungs AG Office Building, Cologne (with Robert Hilgers)

1956 Theatre, Recklinghausen, West Germany (competition project)

1956/
60 Essener Steinkohlenbergwerke AG Administration Building, Essen, West Germany (with Robert Hilgers)

1956/
62 Mannheimer Lebensversicherungsgesellschaft AG Headquarters, Mannheim, West Germany (project)

1957 "Object 13," *International Building Exhibition*, Berlin (with Robert Hilgers)

1957/
63 Kaiser-Wilhelm Memorial Church, Berlin

1958 German Pavilion, World's Fair, Brussels (with Sep Ruf)

1958/
60 Horten Store, Heidelberg, West Germany (with Robert Hilgers)

Hardenberg House, Baden-Baden, West Germany (with Georg Pollich)

1958/
61 Steel Works Administration Building, Offenburg, West Germany (with Robert Hilgers)

Josef Neckermann KG Dispatch Building, Frankfurt (with Robert Hilgers)

1958/
64 Chancery, German Embassy, Washington, D.C. (with Eberhard Brandl)

1959 Red Sand Artificial Island Lighthouse, Outer Weser, Bremerhaven, West Germany (competition project)

1959/
60 Baden State Theatre, Karlsruhe, West Germany (competition project)

1959/
62 Egon Eiermann House, Baden-Baden, West Germany

1960 Johannis Church and Community Center, Mulheim/Ruhr, West Germany (competition project)

1961/
63 Dea-Scholven GmbH Refinery, Karlsruhe, West Germany (with Robert Hilgers)

1962 Town Hall, Essen, West Germany (competition project)

1962/
67 Hotel Prinz Carl extension, Buchen, West Germany

1963/
64 Housing, South Backenberg Sector, Wulfen

Egon Eiermann: Olivetti Headquarters, Frankfurt, 1972.

New Town, West Germany (competition project)

1964 Office building, Frankfurt (project; with Theo Ambos)

1964/
65 Prefabricated atrium houses, Offenbach, West Germany

1964/
66 Fichtel & Sachs AG Administration Building, Schweinfurt, West Germany (project)

1965/
66 Town Centre, Castrop-Rauxel, West Germany (competition project)

IBM Administration Building, Böblingen, West Germany (project: planning study)

1965/
69 Members Building, Bundestag, Bonn (design and artistic direction; with Georg Pollich)

1966 Biochemical Centre, Max Planck Institute, Martinsried, near Munich (competition project)

1966/
68 Hochtief AG Office Building, stage I, Frankfurt

1967/
72 IBM-Germany Headquarters, Vaihingen, Stuttgart

1968/
72 Olivetti-Germany Administration and Development/Training Centre, Frankfurt

1972/
74 Hochtief AG Office Building, stage II, Frankfurt

Publications:

By EIERMANN: book—*Planungsstudie Verwaltungsgebaude: am Beispiel für die IBM-Deutschland*, with Heinz Kuhlmann, Stuttgart 1967; articles— "Das Theater in Dessau und die Baukunst von

heute" in *Monatshefte für Baukunst und Städtebau* (Berlin), no. 19, 1935; "Hans Poelzig unserem lehrer" in *Bauwelt* (Berlin), no. 27, 1936; "Einige Bermerkungen über Technik und Bauform" in *Baukunst und Werkform* (Frankfurt), no. 1, 1947; "Der arbeitende Mensch und die Technik" in *Baukunst und Werkform* (Frankfurt), no. 4, 1951; "Der Neubau des Versandhauses der Josef Neckermann KG" in *Baukunst und Werkform (Nuremberg)*, no. 14, 1961; "Wohnhaus der Familie des Grafen Hardenberg in Baden-Baden" in *Baukunst und Werkform* (Nuremberg), no. 15, 1962; "Taufschale und Orgel der neuen Kaiser-Wilhelm-Gedächtniskirche in Berlin" and "Raffinerie Dea-Scholven GmbH, Karlsruhe" in *Architektur und Wohnform* (Stuttgart), no. 73, 1965; "Neubau der Kanzlei der Deutschen Botschaft in Washington, D.C." in *Architektur und Wohnform* (Stuttgart), no. 74, 1966.

On EIERMANN: book—*Landhäuser* by H. J. Zechlin, Tübingen, West Germany 1951; *Egon Eiermann, 1904-1970: Bauten und Projekte*, edited by Wulf Schirmer, Stuttgart 1984; articles— "Wohnhaus H. in Lankwitz" in *Bauwelt* (Berlin), no. 24, 1933; "Ein Fabrikbau im Norden Berlins" in *Bauwelt* (Berlin), no. 29, 1938; "Erweiterung und Umbau der "Total"-Werke Foerstner & Co." in *Moderne Bauformen* (Stuttgart), no. 38, 1939; "Ein Wohnhaus im Grunewald" in *Moderne Bauformen* (Stuttgart), no. XLI, 1942; "Vom Sauerteig des Künstlerischen: Zu den Arbeiten von Professor Egon Eiermann" by Alfons Leitl in *Baukunst und Werkform* (Heidelberg), April 1951; "Kaufhaus Merkur in Heilbronn der Kaufhaus Merkur AG in Nürnberg" in *Bauen und Wohnen* (Zürich), no. 7, 1952; "St. Nicolai Kirche in Hamburg" in *Architekturwettbewerbe* (Stuttgart), October 1956; "Ein verlorener Beitrag zur Bauaustellung: Hansaviertel-Projekte von Egon Eiermann, Karlsruhe" in

Baukunst und Werkform (Heidelberg), no. 10, 1957; "Deux Projets récents" in *L'Architecture d'aujourd'hui* (Paris), September/October 1960; "Verwaltungsgebäude eines Stahlbauwerkes in Offenburg" in *Bauwelt* (Berlin), September 1961; "Steel Company Offices, Offenburg" in *Architectural Design* (London), June 1963; "Haus und Nebenhaus in Baden-Baden" in *Architektur und Wohnform* (Stuttgart), No. 71, 1963; "West German Chancery: Bauhaus Precision Overlooking the Potomac" in *Interiors* (New York), May 1965; "Deutsche Botschaft in Washington" in *Bauen und Wohnen* (Zürich), January 1966; "One, Two, Three" in *Architectural Forum* (New York), March 1966; "Obituary: Professor Egon Eiermann" in *The Times* (London), 22 July 1970; "Egon Eiermann (1904-1970)" in *Bauwelt* (Berlin), 12 October 1970; "Egon Eiermann 1904-1970" in *Architektur und Wohnwelt* (Stuttgart), 12 October 1970; "Egon Eiermann 1904-1970" by H. Werner Rosenthal in *RIBA Journal* (London), January 1971; "Das Abgeordneten-Hochhaus in Bonn" in *Deutsche Bauzeitschrift* (Stuttgart), September 1972; "Hauptverwaltung IBM Deutschland GmbH, Stuttgart-Vaihingen" in *Bauen und Wohnen* (Zürich), March 1973; "Egon Eiermann" in *Architecture Plus* (New York), September 1973; "Headquarters of Olivetti-Germany" and "Headquarters of IBM-Germany" in *Architecture + Urbanism* (Tokyo), June 1974.

One of the vices of postwar architectural criticism has been that of returning too often and too readily to categories that were already showing signs of wear in the 1930s. Such an attitude risks doing less than justice to those personalities in architecture who have developed mainly since the war. A good example is Egon Eiermann: his widely publicized support of rationalism has caused him to be placed in that critical "category" occupied by Mies van der Rohe, Gropius, the Bauhaus. And, to a certain extent, it was because of that identification that Eiermann received some of his most important commissions: Olivetti, a firm always careful and particular in its choice of architects and designers, chose him to design its Administration Center in Frankfurt; the American Government, for the German Embassy in Washington, also chose this "awkward" architect, veteran of outstanding work on the German Pavilion at the 1958 Brussels World's Fair and the Kaiser Wilhelm Memorial Church in Berlin, two works that attracted both enthusiasm and criticism.

Yet, looking at these four works and trying to compare them, we can deduce everything but a common denominator—i.e., the rationalist constant. And when we go on to look at his other work, we recognize Eiermann's creative breadth and variety.

With the thirty-story building for members of the Bundestag in Bonn, Eiermann copes admirably with the problems of the skyscraper: he achieves a lightness by arranging the glazed surfaces horizontally and an elegance by emphasizing the fixed sunscreens in wavy fibre, varying them in height from sector to sector. The marked "gap" half way up also lightens the upper bulk of the building, and the cooling towers are a screened prism. Two of these features figure prominently in Eiermann's work—the fixed sun-screen; the technical facilities in a compact form placed at the margin of the architectural complex.

The Washington scheme quite rightly reminds one of Frank Lloyd Wright's organic creed, not so much in its actual architectural effect (though some of the structural elements do recall well-known features of Wright's work), as in Eiermann's architectural attitude. For Mies, the technical treatment came to determine design to such an extent that many of his works simply repeat themselves, often losing contact with environmental conditions that might well have suggested a different treatment. In his Washington design, Eiermann offers an alternative that seems to have disappeared since Wright's time: he rejects showy, expensive materials in favor of a more "human" choice—brick walls both inside and outside, tiled floors, lighting by ordinary electric light bulbs. The building earned him high praise throughout America.

This more "human" quality is always found in Eiermann's work, and the master's last works should perhaps be looked at from this perspective. Of course, a certain rigidity of approach is evident, but most of all, there is a plastic power and an elegance unique in Germany, achieved by a brilliant architectural self-control together with an exceptional attention to detail that extends down to the smallest particular. In the Essener Steinkohlenbergwerke Administration Building in Essen or the more recent IBM Building at Stuttgart, every structural point is given a fascination of its own by the ease and lightness with which the problem involved has been solved. No one travelling on the Autobahn in the area of Vaihingen can miss the IBM Building: it creates a profound impression, as does the Olivetti Building (which can be seen along the Autobahn from Frankfurt to Kassel), with its graceful shape of sixteen stories, nine of them visible, tapering at the base to form an inverted pyramid, the windows in the shade brightened by the fixed sun-screens.

—Giuliano Chelazzi

EISENMAN, Peter D.
American. Born in Newark, New Jersey, 11 August 1932. Educated at Cornell University, Ithaca, New York, 1951-55 (Charles G. Sands Memorial Medal for Senior Thesis, 1955), B.Arch. 1955; Columbia University, New York, 1959-60 (William Kinne Fellowship, 1960-61), M.S.Arch. 1960; Cambridge University, England, 1960-63, M.A. in theory of design 1962, Ph.D. in theory of design 1963. Married to Elizabeth Henderson; children: Nicholas and Julia. Worked for Percival Goodman, New York, 1957-58, and The Architects Collaborative, *q.v.*, Cambridge, Massachusetts, 1959; Assistant Lecturer, 1960-61, Assistant First Year Master, 1960-61, and First Year Master, 1962-63, Cambridge University, England; Assistant Professor, 1963-67, and Third Year Master, 1965-66, Princeton University, New Jersey. Lecturer, 1967-75, and Adjunct Professor, since 1975, Cooper Union, New York. Architect-in-Residence, American Academy in Rome, 1976; Kea Professor, University of Maryland, College Park, 1978, Founder-Director, Institute for Architecture and Urban Studies, New York, 1967-82; Editor, *Oppositions* magazine, New York, 1973-82. Co-Founder of CASE (Conference of Architects for the Study of the Environment), 1964; Vice-President, Architectural League of New York, 1970. Exhibitions: *40 under 40*, Architectural League of New York, 1966; *The New City: Architecture and Urban Renewal*, Museum of Modern Art, New York, 1967; *Architecture of Museums*, Museum of Modern Art, New York, 1968; *Another Chance for Housing*, Museum of Modern Art, New York, 1973; *Architettura razionale*, *Triennale*, Milan 1973; *Contemporanea*, Rome, 1973-74; *Five Architects*, Princeton University, New Jersey, and the University of Texas, Austin, 1974; *Five Architects*, Castel Nuovo, Naples, 1975; *The New York Five*, Art Net, London, 1975; *Biennale*, Venice, 1976; *Two Hundred Years of American Architectural Drawing*, Cooper-Hewitt Museum, New York, 1977 (toured the United States); *Abraham, Eisenman, Hedjuk, Rossi*, New York, 1977; *House X*, Princeton University, New Jersey, 1977; *Numerals*, Yale University, New Haven, Connecticut, 1978; *Assenza-Presenza*, Bologna, 1978; *10 Immagini per Venezia: mostra dei progetti per Cannaregio ovest*, Ala Napoleonica, Venice, 1980. Recipient: Graham Foundation Fellowship, 1966; Guggenheim Fellowship, 1976; Brunner Prize, American Academy and Institute of Arts and Letters, 1984. Address: Eisenman Robertson Architects, 560 Fifth Avenue, New York, New York 10036, U.S.A.

Works:

1960 Liverpool Cathedral (competition project)
1961 Boston City Hall (competition project; with Anthony Eardley)
1963 Boston Architectural Center (competition project; with Michael Graves)
1964 American Institute of Architects Headquarters, Washington, D.C. (competition project; with Michael Graves)
1964/
65 Jersey Corridor Study (New York/Philadelphia urban corridor) (project; with Michael Graves and Anthony Eardley)
1965 University of California Arts Center, Berkeley (competition project; with Michael Graves)
1966 The Manhattan Waterfront, New York (project; with Michael Graves)
1967/
68 House I: Barenholtz House, Princeton, New Jersey
1968 Townhouses, Princeton, New Jersey (project)
1969/
70 House II: Falk House, Hardwick, Vermont
House III: Miller House, Lakeville, Connecticut
1971 House IV, Falls Village, Connecticut (project)
1972 House VI: Frank House, Cornwall, Connecticut
1973 Lowrise, high-density housing, Fox Hills, Staten Island, New York (project)
1975 Roosevelt Island Housing, New York (competition project)
House X: Aronoff House, Bloomfield Hills, Michigan (project)
1978 House 11a: Forster House, Palo Alto, California (project)

Publications:

By. EISENMAN: books—*Giuseppe Terragni*, Cambridge, Massachusetts 1985; *House of Cards*, New York 1985; articles—"Towards an Understanding of Form in Architecture" in *Architectural Design* (London), October 1963; "The Big Little Magazine: Perspecta 12 and the Future of the Architectural Past" in *Architectural Forum* (New York), October 1969, reprinted in *Casabella* (Milan), January 1970; "Notes on Conceptual Architecture I" in *Design Quarterly* (Minneapolis), no. 78/79, 1970, reprinted in *Casabella* (Milan), December 1971; "Ordinariness and Light" in *Architectural Forum* (New York), May 1971; "Meier's Smith House: Letter to the Editor" in *Architectural Design* (London), August 1971; "The City as Artifact," editor, special issue of *Casabella* (Milan), December 1971; "From Object to Relationship II: Guiseppe Terragni" in *Perspecta* (New Haven, Connecticut), no. 13/14, 1972; "From Golden Lane to Robin Hood Gardens; or, If You Follow the Yellow Brick Road You May Not Get To Golders Green" in *Architectural Design* (London), September 1972, reprinted in *Oppositions* (New York), September 1973; "Notes on Conceptual Architecture II" in *Arquitectura: historia y teoria de los signos*, Barcelona 1973; "Notes on Conceptual Architecture II A" in *Environmental Design Research* (Stroudsburg, Pennsylvania), vol. II, 1973; "Cardboard Architecture" in *Casabella* (Milan), February 1973; "From Adolf Loos to Bertold Brecht" in *Progressive Architecture* (New York), May 1974; "Real and English: Destruction of the Box I" in *Oppositions* (New York), October 1974; "Post Functionalism" in *Oppositions* (New York), Fall 1976; "Behind the Mirror: On the Writings of Philip Johnson" in *Oppositions* (New York), Fall 1977; "Three Texts for Venice" in *Domus* (Milan), November 1980; "Interview: Peter Eisenman" in *Archetype* (San Francisco), Winter 1980; "Aspects of Modernism" in *Cahiers de la recherche architecturale* (Roquevaire, France), November 1982.

On EISENMAN: books—*The New City: Architecture and Urban Renewal, exhibition catalogue, New York 1967; New Urban Settlements: Analytical Phase, New York 1971; Five Architects by Kenneth Frampton and Colin Rowe, New York 1972; Another Chance for Housing, exhibition catalogue, New York 1973; Five Architects, New York, edited by Camillo Gubitosi and Alberto Izzo, Rome 1976; Europa/America, edited by Franco Raggi, Venice 1978; Judith Turner Photographs Five Architects, with introduction by John Hejduk, London and New York 1980; Houses for Sale, with introduction by B.J. Archer, New York 1980; 10 Immagini per Venezia: mostra dei progetti per Cannaregio ovest, exhibition catalogue, by Francesco Dal Co and Ennio Concina, Rome 1980; Follies: Architecture for the Late-Twentieth-Century Landscape by B.J. Archer and A. Vidler, New York 1983; Abstract Representation edited by Charles Jencks, New York 1984; articles—"On Reading Architecture" by Mario Gandelsonas in Progressive Architecture (New York), March 1972; "European Graffiti" in Oppositions (New York), Summer 1976; "Peter Eisenman and the longing for classical reason" in Wonen-TA/BK (Heerlen, Netherlands), February 1977; "Peter Eisenman: House VI" in Architectural Design (London), January 1978; "Peter Eisenman", special issue of Architecture + Urbanism (Tokyo), January 1980; "Architect as Non-Hero" in Architects' Journal (London), 5 March 1980; "Eisenman/Hejduk," special issue of Wonen-TA/BK (Heerlen, Netherlands), November 1980; "Houses for Sale" in Architecture + Urbanism (Tokyo), December 1980; "Modern Greek Dramas" in Building Design (London), 28 January 1983; "Architecture in Progress" in Architectural Design (London), no. 1/2, 1983; "From Object Art to Living Space" in Domus (Milan), April 1983; "Polyrationalism at the RIBA" in Building Design (London), 17 June 1983; "New York Five" in Arkitektur (Stockholm), November 1983; "Contrasting Concepts of Harmony in Architecture" in Lotus International (New York), no. 40, 1983.

Bibliography: Peter D. Eisenman, 1932-, by Lamia Doumato, Monticello, Illinois 1982.

The critical establishment within architecture has told us that we have entered the era of "post-modernism." The tone with which this news is delivered is invariably one of relief, similar to that which accompanies the advice that one is no longer an adolescent. Two indices of this supposed change are the quite different manifestations of the Architettura razionale exhibition at the Milan Triennale of 1973 and the Ecole des Beaux Arts exhibition at The Museum of Modern Art in 1975. The former, going on the assumption that modern architecture was an outmoded functionalism, declared that architecture can be generated only through a return to itself as an autonomous or pure discipline. The latter, seeing modern architecture as an obessional formalism, made itself into an implicit statement that the future lies paradoxically in the past, within the peculiar response to function that characterized the nineteenth century's eclectic command of historical styles.

What is interesting is not the mutually exclusive character of these two diagnoses and hence of their solutions, but rather the fact that both of these views enclose the very project of architecture within the same definition: the terms continue to be function (or program) and form (or type). In so doing, an attitude toward architecture is maintained that differs in no significant way from that of the five hundred-year-old tradition of humanism.

The various theories of architecture that properly can be called "humanist" are characterized by a dialectical opposition: an oscillation between a concern for internal accommodation—the program and the way it is materialized—and a concern for articulation of ideal themes in form—for example, as manifested in the configurational significance of the plan. These concerns were understood as two poles of a single, continuous experience. Within pre-industrial, humanist practice, a balance between them could be maintained because both type and function were invested with idealist views of man's relationship to his object world. In a comparison first suggested by Colin Rowe of a French Parisian hôtel and an English country house, both buildings from the early nineteenth century, one sees this opposition

Peter Eisenman: House VI (Frank House), Cornwall, Connecticut, 1972.

manifested in the interplay between a concern for expression of an ideal type and a concern for programmatic statement, although the concerns in each case are differently weighted. The French *hôtel* displays rooms of an elaborate sequence and a spatial variety born of internal necessity, masked by a rigorous, well-proportioned external facçade. The English country house has a formal internal arrangement of rooms that gives way to a picturesque external massing of elements. The former bows to program on the interior and type on the facçade; the latter reverses these considerations.

With the rise of industrialization, this balance seems to have been fundamentally disrupted. In that it had of necessity to come to terms with problems of a more complex functional nature, particularly with respect to the accommodation of a mass client, architecture became increasingly a social or programmatic art. And as the functions became more complex, the ability to manifest the pure type-form eroded. One has only to compare William Kent's competition entry for the Houses of Parliament, where the form of a Palladian Villa does not sustain the intricate program, with Charles Barry's solution, where the type-form defers to program and where one sees an early example of what was to become known as the *promenade architecturale*. Thus, in the nineteenth century, and continuing on into the twentieth, as the program grew in complexity, the type-form became diminished as a realizable concern, and the balance thought to be fundamental to all theory was weakened. (Perhaps only Le Corbusier in recent history has successfully combined an ideal grid with the architectural promenade as an embodiment of the original interaction.)

This shift in balance has produced a situation whereby, for the past fifty years, architects have understood design as the product of some oversimplified form-follows-function formula. This situation even persisted during the years immediately following World War II, when one might have expected it would be radically altered. And as late as the end of the 1960's, it was still thought that the polemics and theories of the early Modern Movement could sustain architecture. The major thesis of this attitude was articulated in what could be called the English Revisionist Functionalism of Reyner Banham, Cedric Price, and Archigram. This neo-functionalist attitude, with its idealization of technology, was invested with the same ethical positivism and aesthetic neutrality of the prewar polemic. However, the continued substitution of moral criteria for those of a more formal nature produced a situation that now can be seen to have created a functionalist predicament, precisely because the primary theoretical justification given to formal arrangements was a *moral* imperative that is no longer operative within contemporary experience. This sense of displaced positivism characterizes certain current perceptions of the failure of humananism within a broader cultural context.

There is also another, more complex, aspect to this predicament. Not only can functionalism indeed be recognized as a species of positivism, but also, like positivism, it now can be seen to issue from within the terms of an idealist view of reality. For functionalism, no matter what its pretense, continued the idealist ambition of creating architecture as a kind of ethically constituted form-giving. Because it clothed this idealist ambition in the radically stripped froms of technological production, it has seemed to represent a break with the pre-industrial past. But, in fact, functionalism is really no more than a late phase of humanism, rather than an alternative to it. And in this sense, it cannot continue to be taken as a direct manifestation of that which has been called "the modernist sensibility."

Both the *Triennale* and the Beaux Arts exhibitions suggest, however, that the problem is thought to be somewhere else—not so much with functionalism *per se* as with the nature of this so-called modernist sensibility. Hence, the implied revival of neo-classicism and Beaux Arts academicism as replacements for a continuing, if poorly understood, modernism. It is true that sometime in the nineteenth century, there was indeed a crucial shift within Western consciousness, one that can be characterized as a shift from humanism to modernism. But, for the most part, architecture, in its dogged adherence to the principles of function, did not participate in or understand the fundamental aspects of that change. It is the potential difference in the nature of modernist and humanist theory that seems to have gone unnoticed by those people who today speak of eclecticism, post-modernism, or neo-functionalism. And they have failed to notice it precisely because they conceive of modernism as merely a stylistic manifestation of funtionalism, and functionalism itself as a basic theoretical proposition in architecture. in fact, the idea of modernism has driven a wedge into these attitudes. It has revealed that the dialectic form and function is culturally based.

In brief, the modernist sensibility has to do with a changed mental attitude toward the artifacts of the physical world. This change has not only been manifested aesthetically, but also socially, philosophically, and technologically—in sum, it has been manifested in a new cultural attitude. This shift away from the dominant attitudes of humanism, which were pervasive in Western societies for some four hundred years, took place at various times in the nineteenth century in such disparate disciplines as mathematics, music, painting, literature, film, and photography. It is displayed in the non-objective abstract painting of Malevich and Mondrian; in the non-narrative, atemporal writing of Joyce and Apollinaire; in the atonal and polytonal compositions of Schönberg and Webern; in the non-narrative films of Richter and Eggeling.

Abstraction, atonality, and atemporality, however, are merely stylistic manifestations of modernism, not its essential nature. Although this is not the place to elaborate a theory of modernism, or indeed to represent those aspects of such a theory which have already found their way into the literature of the other humanist disciplines, it can simply be said that the symptoms to which one has just pointed suggest a displacement of man away from the center of his world. He is no longer viewed as an *originating agent*. Objects are seen as ideas independent of man. In this context, man is a discursive function among complex and already-formed systems of language, which he witnesses but does not constitute. As Levi-Strauss has said, "Language, an unreflecting totalization, is human reason which has its reason and of which man knows nothing." It is this condition of displacement which gives rise to design in which authorship can no longer either account for a linear development that has a "beginning" and an "end"—hence the rise of the atemporal—or account for the invention of form—hence the abstract as a mediation between pre-existent sign systems.

Modernism, as a sensibility based on the fundamental displacement of man, represents what Michel Foucault would specify as a new *épistème*. Deriving from a non-humanistic attitude toward the relationship of an individual to his physical environment, it breaks with the historical past, both with the ways of viewing man as subject and, as we have lsaid, with the ethical positivism of form and function. Thus, it cannot be related to functionalism. It is probably for this reason that modernism has not up to now been elaborated in architecture.

But there is clearly a present need for a theoretical investigation of the basic implications of modernism (as opposed to modern style) in architecture. in his editorial "Neo-Functionalism," in *Oppositions 5*, Mario Gandelsonas acknowledges such a need. However, he says merely that the "complex contradictions" inherent in functionalism—such as neo-realism and neo-rationalism—make a form of neo-functionalism necessary to any new theoretical dialectic. This proposition continues to refuse to recognize that the form/function opposition is not ;necessarily inherent to any architectural theory and so fails to recognize the crucial difference between modernism and dhumanism. In contrast, what is being called post-functionalism begins as an attitude that recognizes modernism as a new and distinct sensibility. It can best be understood in architecture in terms of a theoretical base that is concerned with what might be called a modernist *dialectic*, as opposed to the old humanist (i.e., functionalist) opposition of form and function.

This new theoretical base changes the humanist balance of form/function to a dialectical relationship within the evolution of form itself. The dialectic can best be described as the potential coexistence within any form of two non-corroborating and non-sequential tendencies. One tendency is to presume architectural form to be a recognizable transformation from some pre-existent geometric or platonic solid. In this case, form is usually understood through a series of registrations designed to recall a more simple geometric condition. This tendency is certainly a relic of humanist theory. However, to this is added a second tendency that sees architectural form in an atemporal, decompositional mode, as something simplified from some pre-existent set of non-specific spatial entities. Here, form is understood as a series of fragments—signs without meaning dependent upon, and without reference to, a more basic condition. The former tendency, when taken by itself, is a reductivist attitude and assumes some primary unity as both an ethical and an aesthetic basis for all creation. The latter, by itself, assumes a basic condition of fragmentation and multiplicity from which the resultant form is a state of simplificiation. Both tendencies, however, when taken together, constitute the essence of this new, modern dialectic. They begin to define the inherent nature of the object in and of itself and its capacity to be represented. They begin to suggest that the theoretical assumptions of functionalism are in fact cultural rather than universal.

Post-functionalism, thus, is a term of absence. In its negation of functionalism it suggests certain positive theoretical alternatives—existing fragments of thought that, when examined, might serve as a framework for the development of a larger theoretical structure—but it does not, in and of itself, propose to supply a label for such a new consciousness in architecture as I believe is potentially upon us.

—Peter D. Eisenman

Peter Eisenman has been more active as an educator than as a builder of architecture, and it is as an educator, author, critic, and publisher that he has been most influential. As the founder of New York City's Institute for Architecture and Urban Studies in 1967, he provided a forum for discussion among the profession and with students and laymen that has made that organization the most public and polemic voice of architecture in New York, perhaps on the east coast. To the lecture platform, exhibition walls, and published pages of the Institute have come virtually every distinguished practitioner, thinker, author, and critic in today's architecture world. Eisenman's aim is to "bridge the gap between architecture and contemporary culture." His espousal of aestheticians' latinate complexity of language hardly facilitates his progress, however.

As architect of some dozen house designs, Eisenman also is a polemicist. He feels that "mechanization, prefabrication, repetition, and standardization have made our existence merely routine, and that the role of art is to alienate and disclocate man from his environment so that he is jolted into seeing what it is again." In his house designs, therefore, Eisenman abrasively jars and jabs, tricks and stuns the occupants into seeing architecture—their environment—in a new way. Stairs have no railings; columns do not touch the ground but hang obviously suspended; the functional requirements of kitchens and baths are denied; air conditioning is needed on the north side. He wants us to break through the habits of seeing and hearing and to experience new insights into reality

In his House VI for Suzanne and Richard Frank, a stair is too low for one to descend without ducking; a door is too narrow for one to enter without turning sideways; a column comes down between the chairs on one side of the dining table. Eisenman wants to force people to see their new dinner partner—architecture. For him physical hardship or readjustment is the elected eye-opener. For him architecture is a kind of shock therapy.

He aims to make us see architecture "through creating a climate that accepts architecture as necessary," and to understand that "the actual tactile sensation of space as an independent object is necessary." That may not be the most winning way to lure back to architecture a public that has been alienated by abstraction for fifty years, but is a way to make architecture unavoidable.

At a larger scale, Eisenman's architecture is concerned with a further abstraction of Miesian structural play clothed in Corbusian forms. He is concerned with a basic grid to which he makes reductive and additive variations. He has professed an interest in constructing architecture as if it were a language composed of columns, beams and walls—like words, sentences, and paragraphs. In his houses, the structural grid is left exposed as much as possible, and the overlapping of columns and beams is often treated as the joint of a Chinese puzzle. Where elements are not articulated by separation or reveals, they are often distinguished by color. It is an architecture that is highly photogenic, cubistic and volumetric, interlocking and ambiguous, perhaps mythic in its expression of the protean elements of construction. It is also purely intellectual, coldly alienating, maddeningly non-functional, and as maddeningly impossible to ignore. By espousing neither *utile dulci* nor firmness, commodity, and delight, Eisenman strikes out as a polemical iconoclast of forceful influence.

—C. Ray Smith

ELLIOTT, Julian Arnold.

South African. Born in Cathcart, 27 August 1928. Educated at the University of Cape Town, 1948-53, B.Arch. 1953. Married Helene Joubert in 1953; children: Paul and Mary. Assistant Architect, with Fry, *q.v.*: Maxwell Fry, Drew, *q.v.*: Jane Drew, and Partners, London, 1951 and with Frederick Gibberd, *q.v.,* and Partners, London, 1953-54; Partner, with Philippe Charbonnier, Charbonnier and Elliott, Lubumbashi, Congo, 1955-58; in private practice, Ndola, Zambia, 1959-68. Since 1969, in private practice, Newlands, South Africa. Visiting Lecturer, University of Cape Town, 1967, and University of Natal, South Africa, 1968 and 1969. Director, University of Cape Town Planning Unit, since 1969. Recipient: Bronze Medal, for religious, community, and domestic buildings, Zambian Institute of Architects, 1967; Ernest Oppenheimer Study Grant, 1969; First Prize, Catholic Church Competition, Constantia, South Africa, 1973; University of Cape Town travel grant, 1977; First Prize, University of the Witwatersrand Sciences Building Competition, Johannesburg (with Neil Grobbelaar and Montgomerie, Oldfield & Kirby), 1978; Merit Award, Institute of South African Architects (with Hallen, Theron & Partners), 1984. Associate of the Royal Institute of British Architects, 1955; Member, South African Institute of Architects, 1969, and South African Council for Architects, 1971. Address: 5 Pembroke Lane, Newlands 7700, South Africa.

Works:

1956 Bocskay Flats, Lubumbashi, Congo (with Philippe Charbonnier)

1958 Border Motors Building, Kitwe, Zambia (with Philippe Charbonnier)
1959 Attala House, Ndola, Zambia (with Gluckman, de Beer, and Peters)
1960 Border Motors Building, Kabwe, Zambia (with Neil Grobbelaar)
1961 Bracaire Shop, Ndola, Zambia (with Neil Grobbelaar)
    Groenewald House, Ndola, Zambia (with Neil Grobbelaar)
1962 Llewelyn High School, Zambia (with Neil Grobbelaar)
1963 Chifubu Community Hall, Ndola, Zambia
    Ndola Library, Zambia (project)
1964 Kasama Cathedral, Zambia
1964/
  68 University of Zambia, Lusaka (with Anthony Chitty, Douglas Yetton, and Munnik, Visser and Black)
1965 Pilcher House, Ndola, Zambia
    Ndola Museum, Zambia (project)
1966 Allen House, Ndola, Zambia
1971 Schuurmans House, Cape Town
1972 Huyghe House, Cape Town
1974 Elliott House, Cape Town
1975 Middle Campus, University of Cape Town (with Neil Grobbelaar)
1977 Catholic Church, Constantia, South Africa
1979 Krone House, Tulbagh, South Africa
    Mangosuthu Technikon, Umlazi, South Africa (with Hallen, Theron & Partners)
1981 Education Faculty Building, University of Cape Town (with Neil Grobbelaar and Revel Fox & Partners)
1984/
  86 New Middle Campus, phase 1, University of Cape Town

Julian Elliott: New Middle Campus, University of Cape Town, 1984-86 (model).

Publications:

By ELLIOTT: articles—"Zambian Architecture" in *Edilizia Moderna* (Milan), 89-90, 1968; "University Planning" in *Architectural Review* (London), April 1970; "University of Cape Town Campus, 1918-81—A Case Study in University Planning" in *Architecture South Africa* (Cape Town), October 1981.

On ELLIOTT: books—*New Architecture of Africa* by Udo Kultermann, London 1963; *Pianificazione e disegno dell'Università* by Giancarlo De Carlo, Venice 1968; *New Directions in African Architecture* by Udo Kultermann, London 1969; *The Phenomenon of Architecture in Cultures of Change* by David Oakley, Oxford 1970; articles—"Commonwealth Architecture" in *Architectural Review* (London), June 1961; "University of Zambia" in *Architectural Review* (London), January 1967; "Kasama Cathedral" in *Architect and Builder* (Salisbury, Rhodesia), February 1968; article in *Bauen und Wohnen* (Zürich), November 1969; "Kasama Cathedral" in *Architectural Review* (London), July 1971.

*   *   *

The projects and completed works to date have all been undertaken on the African sub-continent and are the direct result of four architectural understandings:

First, that architecture is a lived environment; that form/container, space/contained, and observer/experience are locked together into a single reality.

Second that there are timeless ways of building which have evolved organically over time and that the relevance of these patterns, structures, and processes is always travelling with us into contemporary time.

The third factor follows directly from this, in that the African timeless way has had a particular influence. One aspect of this is the African idea of space, whereby buildings are placed within external open space (*lapas*), and it is these external "courtyards" with their sense of protection, order, and repose that are the dominant architectural element. This idea is best experienced in the Zimbabwe ruins in Zimbabwe and the Ndabele villages in the Transvaal, South Africa. It has particular relevance in the domestic architecture of Africa.

Finally, most of the work has been concerned with developing generic building types: families of houses, libraries, churches, and, most importantly, a family of university building types. It is the range of university building types which has provided the most interesting research in appropriate assembly of space and structure in order to make buildings that accommodate a diverse range of activities, some highly specialized, and that readily respond to change in use and user over time.

—Julian Elliott

*   *   *

Julian Elliott's best-known project has been the coordination and development of the design for the University of Zambia, which, when it was produced, was in the forefront of thinking about new universities. The careful control of open space, the creation of linking elements between buildings, an ingenious linear plan which allowed for growth, and the meticulous approach to the programming of the project are its most impressive characteristics. There is a sure attitude to form in all of Elliott's work; for example, his use in the Kasama Cathedral and in several houses of brick barrel vaults together with crisp detailing of voids and openings gives the buildings a sharp and characacteristic form. There is also in his work an appealing empathy with older traditions in South Africa.

The number of Elliott's works is not vast, but their quality has had a considerable influence upon his colleagues. Although the works are for the most part "one-off," they seek to be generic solutions. His recent projects—for example, the University of Cape

Town Middle Campus—reveal a concern for the organization of buildings within a suitable geometry. Further, Elliott is concerned to find an appropriate density of site usage that allows for simple pedestrian movement and access and for a humane relationship in scale between open space and building.

Elliott is an incisive thinker on architectural problems and an excellent architectural critic. Although one at first gains the impression of strong links with the early era of the modern movement, there is in his work a much more personally developed vocabulary of ideas; these are best seen in Kasama Cathedral, the Pilcher House, and his own house in Cape Town.

Working for much of his career in Central Africa in an area with little urban building tradition either in cultural values or technology, Elliott has been able to develop both, as well as managing to build structures appropriate to climate and social setting. These are rare qualities.

—Hans Hallen

ELLWOOD, Craig.
American. Born in Clarendon, Texas, 22 April 1922. Studied structural engineering at night classes at the University of California at Los Angeles Extension Division, 1949-54. Served in the United States Air Force, 1942-46. Married Gloria McInery in 1949 (divorced, 1976); children: Jeffrey, Erin, and Adam; married Anita Gail Eubank in 1978 (divorced). Worked for a construction company, Los Angeles, 1946-48; Principal, Craig Ellwood Associates, Los Angeles, 1948-76. Since 1976, has devoted himself to painting and sculpture. Visiting Lecturer, Yale University, New Haven, Connecticut, 1959 and 1960, Cornell University, Ithaca, New York, 1960, and Syracuse University, Syracuse, New York, 1961. Exhibitions: architecture—*International Exhibition of Architecture*, São Paulo, 1953, 1957; *Craig Ellwood*, Sioux Falls Art Museum, South Dakota, 1955; *Three Young Architects*, Long Beach Art Museum, California, 1956; *The Architecture of Steel*, Architectural League of New York, 1962; *The Twentieth Century House*, Museum of Modern Art, New York, 1962; painting—Anhalt-Barnes Gallery, Los Angeles, 1979; Art Center College of Design, Pasadena, California, 1979; Mirage Gallery, Santa Monica, California, 1980; Lorenzelli Arte, Milan, 1981, 1985; Trimarchi Galleria, Bologna, Italy, 1985. Recipient: First Prize, Collective Dwelling Category, *International Exhibition of Architecture*, São Paulo, 1953; Governor's Design Award, California, 1966; American Institute of Architects Award, 1967; Los Angeles Beautiful Award, 1972 and 1975; Fellowship, National Endowment for the Arts, 1973; Pasadena Beautiful Award, 1976; Design Award, *Progressive Architecture*, 1976; Fellowship, Graham Foundation, 1978. Honorary doctorate: University of Mexico, 1966. Address: Casanovalta, Pergine/-Valdarno, 52020 Arezzo, Italy.

Works:

1948 Lappin House, Cheviot Hills, California
1949 Epstein House, 401 North Cliffwood, Brentwood, Los Angeles
       Broughton House, 909 North Beverly Glen Boulevard, Bel Air, Los Angeles
1949/
50 Hale House, 9618 Yoakum Drive, Beverly Hills, California
       Zimmerman House, 400 North Carmlina Avenue, Brentwood, Los Angeles
1950 Brown House, 902 North Roxbury Drive, Beverly Hills, California

Anderson House, 656 Hightree Road, Pacific Palisades, California
       Unity Church, Santa Monica, California (project)
1951 Elton House, Pacific Palisades, California
       Case Study House 16, Los Angeles (for *Arts and Architecture*)
1952 Courtyard Apartments, 1570 Labaig Avenue, Hollywood, California
1953 Pierson House, Malibu Beach Road, Malibu, California
1954 Case Study House 17, Los Angeles (for *Arts and Architecture*)
1955 Smith House, Crestwood Drive, West Los Angeles
       Case Study House 18, Los Angeles (for *Arts and Architecture*)
1955/
56 South Bay Bank, Manhattan Beach, California
1957 Hunt House, 24514 Malibu Beach Road, Malibu, California
1957/
58 Westchester Post Office, California
1958 Carson-Roberts Building, 8233 Beverly, West Hollywood, California (now rental office building)
1960 Daphne House, 20 Madrone Place, Hillsborough, California
1960/
61 Acme-Arcadia Building, Los Angeles (project)
1961 Pierson House, 32320 Pacific Coast Highway, Malibu, California (destroyed by fire)
       Rosen House, 910 Oakmont Drive, Brentwood, Los Angeles
1962 Office Building, Los Angeles (project)
       Carson-Roberts Square, Los Angeles (project)
1962/
63 Two factories for Litton Systems, New York (project)
       Chamorro House, Los Angeles (project)
1964 Moore House, 4791 Bonvue, East Hollywood, California
       Kubly House, 215 La Vereda, Pasadena, California
       Courtyard House (project)
1965/
66 Craig Ellwood Associates Office Building remodelling, 1107 South Robertson Boulevard, Los Angeles
1966 Scientific Data Systems Building, 555 South Aviation Boulevard, El Segundo, California (now Zerox Building)
1967 Scientific Data Systems Buildings 2 and 3, El Segundo, California
       Weekend house, San Luis Obispo, California
       Craig Ellwood Associates Building Annex remodelling, 1111 South Robertson Boulevard, Los Angeles
1967/
68 Goldman House, Beverly Hills, California
1968 Scientific Data Systems PCM Building, Pomona, California
       Bridge House (project)
       Kawahara House, Rolling Hills Estates, California
       Design of "Knockdown" Computer Exhibit, for Scientific Data Systems Company
       Airport Business Center, Irvine, California
1968/
69 Palevsky House, 1021 Cielo Drive, Palm Springs, California
1969 Master plan for the Rand Corporation, Santa Monica, California
       Security Pacific Place, Wilshire and Bedford, Beverly Hills, California
1970/
75 Art Center College of Design, Pasadena, California
1972 Performing Arts Building, Immaculate Heart College, Los Angeles (project)

1972/
73 Joy Manufacturing Company, 4565 Colorado, Glendale, California

Security Pacific National Bank, 1811 North Western, East Hollywood, California

1973 Xerox Computer and Data Processing Center, Culver City, California (project)

1974 GF Furniture Showroom, Pacific Design Center, Los Angeles (subsequently altered)

1978 Fifteenth-century farmhouse restoration, Tuscany, Italy

Publications:

By ELLWOOD: book—*Architects on Architecture,* edited by Paul Heyer, New York 1966, London 1967; articles—"Form, Function and Architecture" in *Architecture d'aujourd'hui* (Paris), April 1955; "On Prefabrication and the Product House" in *Arts and Architecture* (Los Angeles), February 1956; "Non-sensualism" in *Bauen und Wohnen* (Zürich), April 1962; interviews with Thomas Vreeland in *L.A. Architect,* December 1975 and March 1978; "The Search for Post-modern Architecture" in *Crit* (Washington, D.C.), Fall 1978.

On ELLWOOD: books—*Quality Budget Houses* by Katherine Morrow Ford and Thomas H. Creighton, New York 1954; *Aluminium in Modern Architecture* by John Peter, 2 volumes, New York 1956; *Craig Ellwood: Architecture* by Esther McCoy, New York 1968; *12 Los Angeles Architects,* edited by N. Charles Slert and James R. Harter, Pomona, California 1978. articles—"Designers of Change: Craig Ellwood" by Olga Gueft in *Interiors* (New York), November 1970; special issue of *Bauen und Wohnen* (Zürich), December 1971; "Triangular Bank in Los Angeles" in *Domus* (Milan), October 1974; "Tradition Imposes Obligation" in *Bauen und Wohnen* (Zürich), December 1975; "Art Center College of Design, Pasadena" in *Progressive Architecture* (New York), January 1976; "And Then There Were 12" in *Architectural Record* (New York), August 1976; "Abstraction of the House" in *Ville Giardini* (Milan), November 1978; "On the Mies Edge" in *Domus* (Milan), February 1981.

*   *   *

The essence of architecture is the interrelation and interaction of mass, space, plane, and line. The purpose of architecture is to enrich the joy and drama of living. The spirit of architecture is its truthfulness to itself: its clarity and logic with respect to its materials and structure.

Building comes of age when it expresses its epoch. The constant change in technology demands a continuously maturing expression of itself. When technology reaches its fulfilment in perfect equilibrium with function, there is a transcendence into architecture.

The consciousness of truth is not static but ever progressively unfolding. We must strive for intrinsic solution, not extrinisc effect. The moment form becomes arbitrary, it becomes novelty or style—it becomes something other than architecture. Materials and methods will certainly change, but the basic laws of nature finally make everything timeless.

Architecture, by its own nature, must certainly be more than an expression of an idea. Art in architecture is not arbitrary stylism or ethereal symbolism but rather the extent to which a building can transcend form the measurable into the immeasurable. The extent to which a building can evoke profound emotion. The extent to which a building can spiritually uplift and inspire man while simultaneously reflecting the logic of the technique which alone can convey its validity to exist.

—Craig Ellwood

*   *   *

In an age when architects are expected to spend years at university learning their craft, what can one make of the builder's cost estimator who leaves his employer and set up practice as a designer and, within a few years, is acclaimed as one of the most sensitive and sophisticated architects in the world? The earlier Los Angeles architects, Neutra and Soriano, had come to the machine very much as to an aesthetic idea. Craig Ellwood learnt about building in steel and plastic sheet before he owned up to any aesthetic theories, and this gave him a fluency and ease with steel construction that his contemporaries from architectural schools could never acquire.

Hale House, one of his first independent commissions, is very much a builder's house in steel, although the use of "flash-gap" detailing shows a thoughtful, craftsmanly mind at work in the relationship of material to material. His third Case Study House for the magazine *Arts and Arhitecture* moves some way to exploiting the elegance of steel with its thin columns, but the eight-foot spans do not exploit the spanning potential of steel with the confidence of contemporary houses in Chicago.

In 1953 came the first real breakthrough; a group of four dwellings, Courtyard Apartments in Hollywood, won the world's top architecture award. Of beautiful and simple elegance, the structure introduces what was to become one of Ellwood's favourite structural devices—the exposed warren truss, using small members to span big distances. In the Courtyard Apartments, the trusses just span the width of an apartment under the first floor windows, but they are a portent of what was to become a dominant motif in his work.

In the early 1960s, the world of architectural fashion swung against the hard, pristine style of Mies van der Rohe. The decorative and crumbly manner was all the rage. Yet it was at this moment that the full impact of the work of Mies hit Ellwood, and his Daphne House and his Rosen House take the Miesian parti to unequalled heights of elegance and luxury. In the Rosen House, in particular, architecture reaches near to perfection.

But Ellwood was, in many ways, a Los Angeles man and thus closer to the light-steel cage of Charles Eames tham to the structured formalism of Mies van der Rohe. Ellwood loved his exposed trusses, and in the Scientific Data Systems plant at El Segundo he got his chance to build on a big scale—a spreading factory with glorious trusses clearly expressed externally: the columns, and hence the beam ends, are pulled well outside the skin. The El Segundo factory was designed and built very quickly—Ellwood had the advantage of having a lifetime's work on one idea behind the design.

In a more fanciful mood, Ellwod proposed storey-high trusses enclosing the living area of a house; the entire building becomes a beam spanning its length, glazed on the long sides so that the diagonals of the warren truss can be seem from within. The first of these designs, the Chamorro House, was never realized, but, due largely to Jerry Horn's seductively beautifuly perspectives, the idea caught on, and students at the California State Polytechnic College built a slightly smaller version spanning a modest ravine.

Craig Ellwood: Arts Center, Pasadena College of Design, California, 1975.

Trusses are fascinating for small houses, but the idea really demands size. In the Arts Centre College of Design in Pasadena, Ellwood got his chance. Here a linear building, gently Miesian in form, lays on the landscape and suddenly leaps across a valley with four parallel warren trusses, starkly exposed inside and out—a permanent exemplar to the students within of the importance of structure in the design of buildings.

—John Winter

ENGLAND, Richard.

Maltese. Born in Sliema, 3 October 1937. Educated at St. Edward's College, Malta, 1947-53; Royal University of Malta, 1954-61, B.Arch. (Architecture and Civil Engineering) 1961; Polytechnic, Milan (studied interior design), 1960-61. Married Myriam Borg Manduca in 1962; children: Sandra and Marc. Student Architect, Studio Ponti, Fornaroli and Rosselli, Milan, 1960-62. Formed the company, England + England, Malta, 1961; Partner/Director and Head of the Design Section of Architectural Plus Engineering Services Limited (now Richard England and Partners Ltd.), Malta, since 1976. Visiting Lecturer, Architectural Association, London, the University of Liverpool and the University of Manchester, 1974, Sheffield Polytechnic, 1957, and Yale University, New Haven, Connecticut, the University of Pennsylvania, Philadelphia, and the University of Florida, Gainesville, 1977. Exhibitions: *Art from Malta,* Richard Demarco Gallery, Edinburgh, 1970; *Malta Now,* St. George's Park, Malta, 1970; Grand Hotel Ambasciatori, Turin, 1971; *Henraux Collection,* Palazzo dei Diamanti, Ferrara, Italy, 1972; *Mostra Internazionale del Marmo,* Carrara, Italy, 1972; *Form Is My Language,* Phoenicia Hotel, Floriana, Malta, 1973; Richard Demarco Gallery, Edinburgh, 1974; University of Manchester School of Architecture, 1974; *Sculpture and Maquettes,* Architectural Association, London, 1974; University of Liverpool School of Architecture, 1974; *Terra I,* Wroclaw, Poland, 1975; *Threads of Stone,* Commonwealth Art Gallery, London, 1975; Bund Deutscher Architekten exhibition, Oldenburg, West Germany, 1976; University of Florida School of Architecture, 1977; *Images of an Island,* National Museum of Fine Arts, Malta, 1980; *Incontro con Richard England,* Italian Cultural Institute, Malta, 1980; *World Biennale of Architecture,* Sofia, Bulgaria, 1981 and 1983; *Richard England—Recent Architecture,* Building Centre, London, 1984; *The Spirit of Place,* Museum of Architecture, Wroclaw, Poland, 1984; *The Architecture of Richard England,* Sofia, Bulgaria, 1984. Recipient: First Prize, Yorkton International Film Festival, Canada, 1973; Gold Medal, Malta Society of Arts, 1984. Fellow of the Institute of Professional Designers, London, 1977. Addresses: Richard England, Oleander Street, The Gardens, St Julian's, Malta; England + England, 26 Merchants Street, Valletta, Malta.

Works:

1964 Paradise Bay Hotel, Marfa, Malta
Ramla Bay Hotel, Marfa, Malta
Mid Med Bank, formerly Barclays Bank, Sliema, Malta
Bank of Valletta, formerly Tagliaferro Bank, St. John Square, Valletta, Malta
1965 Dolphin Court Apartments, Ta'Xbiex, Malta
1966 Joinwell Furniture Showrooms, Sliema, Malta
Mid Med Bank, formerly Barclays Bank, Spinola, Malta

Villa Girna, Naxxar, Malta (project)
Villa Calypso, Gozo Island, Malta (project)
1967 Dolmen Hotel, St Paul's Bay, Malta
Hyperion Hotel, St. Paul's Bay, Malta
Mariners Court Apartments, St. Paul's Bay, Malta
Haro Fashion Boutique, Valletta, Malta
Villa "La Maltija," Naxxar, Malta
1968 Villa "Brockland," St Julian's, Malta
Cavalieri Hotel, St Julian's, Malta
Malta Hilton Hotel, Spinola, Malta (with Thomas E. Stanley and Associates)
Leroy Hotel, Sliema, Malta
1969 Cavalli Marini Apartments, St. Paul's Bay, Malta
St. George's Park Apartments, Spinola, Malta
Salina Bay Hotel, Salina, Malta
Trilithon Court Apartments, St. Paul's Bay, Malta
1970 Tower Palace Hotel, Sliema, Malta
Dinmore Court Apartments, Sliema, Malta
Bahar-ic-Caghaq Studio Apartments, Salina, Malta
Joinwell Furniture Factory, Qormi, Malta
Edwin England Sant Fournier Office Block, Spinola, Malta
1971 Edrichton Court Apartments, St. Paul's Bay, Malta
Central Bank of Malta, Valletta, Malta
Ta' Monita Apartments, Marsascala, Malta
Malta Development Corporation office interiors, Floriana, Malta
Printex Limited Factory, Qormi, Malta
Mid Med Bank, formerly Barclays Bank, Floriana, Malta
Mid Med Bank, formerly Barclays Bank, St. Paul's Bay, Malta
1972 Villa complex, St. Julian's, Malta
Mid Med Bank, formerly Barclays Bank, Msida, Malta
Bank of Valletta (Tagliaferro Centre), Sliema, Malta
Aragon Court Apartments, Marsascala, Malta
Villa "Gascan," Naxxar, Malta
Twin villas, St Julian's, Malta
Villa "The Blessings," Ta'Xbiex, Malta
1973 American Embassy Offices, Floriana, Malta
Mid Med Bank, formerly Barclays Bank Computer Centre, Qormi, Malta
Philips Pavilion, *Malta Trade Fair,* Naxxar
1974 Church of St. Joseph, Manikata, Malta
Chapel, Addolorata Cemetery, Malta
Mid Med Bank, formerly Barclays Bank, Rabat, Gozo, Malta
Mid Med Bank, formerly Barclays Bank, Valletta, Malta
1975 Villa "It-Tina l-Helwa," Naxxar, Malta
Il-Piazzetta Offices and Apartments, Sliema, Malta
1976 Stones Boutique, Sliema, Malta
Villa "La Saracena," Marsascala, Malta
House of Representatives, Valletta, Malta (with Uhlin and Malm)
1977 Dragonara Court Apartments, Spinola, Malta
American Ambassador's Residence, Lija, Malta
1978 Mid Med Bank, formerly Barclays Bank, extension, Spinola, Malta
Mid Med Bank, formerly Barclays Bank, Mosta, Malta
Museum Chapel, Naxxar, Malta
Penthouse, Sliema, Malta
Malta Exhibition Stand, Commonwealth Institute, London
H.R.H. Prince Mohammed Ibn Fahd Guest House, Jeddah, Saudi Arabia
Conference Centre, Sports City, Riyadh, Saudi Arabia (with Suter and Suter)
Villa Abdul Aziz al Malik Al Sheikh, Riyadh, Saudi Arabia
Royal Summer Palace, Jeddah, Saudi Arabia (project)

Redec Villa complex, Jeddah, Saudi Arabia (project)
Riofines Residential Complex, Jeddah, Saudi Arabia (project)
1979 Private Chapel, Addolorata Cemetery, Malta (project)
Gozo Hotel, Gozo Island, Malta (project)
Land's End Apartments, Tigne, Malta
Perellos Apartments, Spinola, Malta
Islamic Cultural Centre, Madrid (competition project)
Grand Master's Pub, Perellos, Spinola, Malta
1980 Festival Tourist Village, Mellieha, Malta
White Rocks Holiday Complex, St. Andrew's, Malta
Marina San Gorg Apartments, St. George's Bay, Malta
Incontro con Richard England exhibition layouts, Italian Cultural Centre, Valletta, Malta
Air Malta Offices, London
1981 National Library, Riyadh, Saudi Arabia (competition project)
Tower Mansions, Sliema, Malta
Air Malta Offices, Valletta, Malta
Mid Med Bank, formerly Barclay's Bank, Mellieha, Malta
Il-Fortizza interior designs, Sliema, Malta
Mid Med Bank, formerly Barclay's Bank, Balzan, Malta
Haifa Street Apartments, part 4, Baghdad, Iraq
1982 Galleria Building, Bab Al Sheikh Zone 4.1, Baghdad, Iraq
Office Block, Bab Al Sheikh Zone 4.1, Baghdad, Iraq
Housing, Bab Al Sheikh Zone 4.1, Baghdad, Iraq
Housing, Bab Al Sheikh Zone 4.2, Baghdad, Iraq
The Peak Club House, Hong Kong (competition project)
Garden for Myriam, St. Julian's, Malta
Mid Med Bank, formerly Barclay's Bank, Bugibba, Malta
1983 Office Building, Khulafa Street, Baghdad, Iraq
Aquasun Lido, Spinola, Malta
Mid Med Bank, formerly Barclay's Bank, Valletta, Malta
Private Villa, Ta'Xbiex, Malta (project)
1984 Mid Med Bank Office extensions, Valletta, Malta
Mid Med Bank new offices at computer centre, Qormi, Malta
Richard England— Recent Architecture exhibition layouts, Building Centre, London
Dun Gorg Chapel, Blata I-Bajda, Malta
Old People's Home, Qormi, Malta

Publications:

By ENGLAND: books—*Walls of Malta* (photoprose poem), Malta 1973; *White Is White* (poems and epigrams), Malta 1973; *Contemporary Art in Malta,* editor, Malta 1974; *Carrier-Citadel Metamorphosis,* Malta 1974; *Island— A Poem for Seeing,* Malta 1980; *Uncaged Reflections—Selected Writings, 1965-80,* Malta 1980; *In Search of Silent Spaces,* Malta 1980; articles—"L'Architettura di Malta" in *L'Ingegnere* (Rome), March 1968; "Cinque progetti a Malta"in *L'Ingegnere* (Rome) January 1969; "Contemporary Architecture in Malta" in *Architectural Review* (London), June 1969; "The Architecture of the Maltese Islands" in *Architectural Association Quarterly* (London), April 1970; "Notes on the Maltese Vernacular" in *Richard England. Architect in Malta* by Emile Henvaux, Brussels 1970; "Internal Pressures" in *Architectural Conservation in Europe,* London 1975; "Foreword" to *Megalithic Monuments of Malta* by G. Formosa, Vancouver 1975; "Mdina" in *European Heritage* (London), October

1975; Design Methodology" in *Cards on the Table,* Malta 1980, 1983; "Foreword" in *Designs for Holidays and Tourism,* London 1983; "Tourism and Architecture" in *International Social Science Journal* (Paris), vol. 32, no. 1, 1980; "Malta—Monuments in Peril" in *UNESCO Campaign for the Restoration of Historic Monuments in Malta,* Paris 1981; "Foreword" in *Norbert Attard—Artist in Malta,* Malta 1983; "Turismo y arquitectura" in *Tiempo Argentino* (Buenos Aires), 11 July 1983; "Forms Borrowed from the Summer of My Childhood" in *Sunday Times* (Malta), 7 August 1983; also numerous articles in the *Sunday Times of Malta* and Maltese daily newspapers; other—graphic offset litho sets in limited editions, Malta, 1972-76.

On ENGLAND: books—*Richard England, Architect in Malta* by Emile Henvaux, Brussels 1970; *Contemporary Art in Malta,* Malta 1974; *Manikata: The Making of a Church* by Charles Knevitt, Malta 1980; *Cards on the Table: Concept Drawings by Richard England* by Maelee Thomson Foster, Malta 1980, 1983; *Connections: The Architecture of Richard England* by Charles Knevitt, London 1984; *Fifty Outstanding Architects of the World* by Ivan Mladjenovic, Belgrade 1984; articles—"Modern Vernacular in Malta" in *Architectural Review* (London), August 1965; "Travaux de l'architecte Richard England" in *La Maison* (Brussels), February 1966; "The Maltese Fashion" in *Progressive Architecture* (New York), June 1966; "Richard England el gran arquitecto actual de la isla de Malta" in *Obras* (Madrid), October 1966; "Richard England nel avant-guardia d'arquitectura de Malta" in *Obras* (Madrid), February 1967; "La Maltija" in *L'Architettura* (Rome), March 1967; "Recherches et travaux de l'architecte Richard England" by Emile Hanvaux in *La Maison* (Brussels), July 1967; "Malta—Rebirth or Death of an Island" by Eric Ambrose in *Ideal Home* (London), May 1968; "England in Malta" in *Concrete Quarterly* (London), October 1968; "The England Look Is So Maltese" by Robert Langton in *Evening News* (London), 23 September 1969; "Explosie op Malta" by R. Blijstra in *Plan* (The Hague), no. 6, 1970; "Malta: Richard England's Visionary View" by Richard England in *Malta News,* 14 October 1973; "The Architect as Artist" by P. Serracino Inglott in *Times of Malta,* 7 December 1973; "Richard England's Exhibition" by A. C. Sewter in *Royal Society of Arts Journal* (London), February 1974; "Richard England, Architect, Sculptor and Poet of Malta" by Mitzi Cunliffe in *Sunday Times of Malta,* 22 December 1974; "A Bit of England" by Charles Knevitt in *Building Design* (London), 19 March 1976; "There Are Some Corners of Foreign Lands" by Charles Knevitt in *Building Design* (London), 4 July 1980; "Church of St. Joseph" in *Architecture + Urbanism* (Tokyo), October 1981; "An Architect's Garden of Personal Symbols" in *House and Garden* (London), August 1983; "Baghdad Restaurant" by Sherban Cantacuzino in *Mimar* (Singapore), no. 6, 1982; "A Garden for Myriam" in *Architecture + Urbanism* (Tokyo), January 1983; "The Art of England" by Ian Latham in *Building Design (London), 17 February 1984;* "Richard England: un buscador de espacios" by Jorge Glusberg in *Clarin Arquitectura* (Buenos Aires), 24 February 1984; "England's Achievement" by Colin Amery in *Financial Times* (London), 27 February 1984; "Modern in Malta" by David Atwell in *Building* (London), 1 March 1984; "England in Malta" by Nicholas Bagnall in *Sunday Telegraph* (London), 4 March 1984; "In Praise of England" in *What's New in Building* (London), April 1984; "Richard England" by Ingrid Herting in *Danske Praktiserende Arkitekter* (Copenhagen), no. 6, 1984; "Richard England" in *Architektura* (Warsaw), no. 1, 1985.

Voices of a Site
The Site constitutes the land within its boundaries
And Yet it extends Beyond.
The Site is the hill, the valley, the rocks,
The very earth itself.
The Site is the climate, the sun, the rain, the wind,
The lights and shadows which fall on it.
The Site is the sum of the very materials which constitute it:
Materialistic and etheric.
The Site is the tradition: the background, the past, the present
The whole totality of that particular place: visible and invisible.
The Site is the place
The Site is totality
The Site is environment.
An environment which sends out vibrations
Vibrations of esoteric waves
Impregnating and pulsating through the enveloping surrounding air
The very air which belongs to and limits that environment.
For that environment has its own personality
Not only material but also spiritual
Not only visual but also aural.
It is here that the role of the architect

Richard England: Aquasun Lido, Spinola, Malta, 1983.

As an intruder to this harmony is paramount.
He must first of all look
Then he must listen
But most of all he must understand
He must discover the tuning in and switching off
distance of the Site.
In other words he must understand what is included
in
And what is excluded from the environment.
Its aural and visual, spiritual and materialistic
boundaries and limitations.
It is a moment of pause and reflection
It is a moment of silence and contemplation
A moment of almost mystical expectation
Before man and site, man and environment
reciprocate
And establish the right wave lengths and vibrations
It is an almost frightening moment of soundless
silence,
Of loneliness and nothingness
Then suddenly contact is established:
The voices are heard . . .
The voice of the land
The voice of the hill
The voice of the rocks
The voice of the earth, sky, sun and winds,
The voice of totality.
The totality of that site
The totality of that environment.

These are the voices which in a moment of mystic rare
faery-like contact will reveal the traces and images of
the solution required. Voices that will tell the
architect (if he is a sensitive one) whether the
environment is weak and this in turn requires him to
be strong and dominant; or they will tell him perhaps
that the environment is strong, and that he, in turn,
should be docile and servient.
The architect must now listen . . . listen
. . . listen . . . listen . . .
Only after this spiritual contact has been established can the mechanical, materialistic wheels of
the rest of the architectural creative process continue,
then and only then is one able to produce a truly
inspired architecture: an architecture of *evolution*, an
architecture of *place*, an architecture of *environment*.
—Richard England

The work of Richard England in Malta shows up one
of the paradoxes of modern architecture since World
War II. The most easily recognized distinguishing
feature of most design derived from the European
Modern Movement is its anonymity and internationalism, despite the fact that figures such as Le
Corbusier, Mies van der Rohe, Alvar Aalto, and
many others were individual artists whose work was
instantly recognizable. But they did not create
architecture that was rooted in a particular place and
its qualities. Their idioms and ideas were exported all
over the world and copied without discrimination,
and the assumption has been that this is an
unavoidable and inevitable result of industrialization, ease of travel, and communication. But when a
body of work as large and consistent as that of
Richard England seems to contradict this tendency,
one has to question the inevitability of the process.
In a way, the cicumstances in Malta contributed:
an island with a very restricted range of available
materials; a local, traditional vernacular that had
developed undisturbed by industrial or cultural
revolutions for centuries; an economy that suddenly
boomed as a result of tourist development in the
Mediterranean, creating a demand for new building
that was catastrophic. But in these circumstances,
where so many other architects failed to produce
anything worthwhile, England succeeded in making
a subtle synthesis of local, traditional forms and
materials, the possibilities inherent in newer
materials such as reinforced concrete, and the new
visual expectations of his generation.
Beginning as soon as he went into his father's
established architectural practice in Malta, he has

been extraordinarily prolific in his architectural
output and has also found time for making sculpture,
drawings, and photographs and for writing poetry,
criticism, and essays on the Maltese townscape and
landscape. He is sensitive to the qualities of a site to a
degree and in a way that was preached (but not
always practised) by Frank Llyod Wright. The
geometry and massing of his buildings and sculpture
are organic in the true sense of the word. Some, like
the Manikata Church, seem to have grown out of the
landscape—to have been formed with it. On a
sundrenched land without much natural vegetation,
dominated by the angular forms of natural limestone
formations, organic expression in buildings, as
shown by the vernacular, will be angular, cubic,
geometric, full of contrast of light and shadow and
emphatic in massing. England's work also shows a
deeply felt response to the history of Malta, going
right back to the mysteriously impressive megalithic
remains there. It never copies but comments in a
completely contemporary way, sometimes with
subtle irony.
But the paradox is that such a deep-rooted
architecture cannot be exported, and as his work
becomes quite deservedly internationally well
known, its genesis may be obscured and give rise to
imitations in inappropriate places. The hope is that
England himself, exercising his skill, sensitivity, and
analysis in new environments, will demonstrate that
connection that should exist between a place and its
architecture.

—Cedric Green

ERICKSON, Arthur Charles.

Canadian. Born in Vancouver, British Columbia, 14
June 1924. Educated at the University of British
Columbia, Vancouver, 1942-45; McGill University,
Montreal, 1946-50 (Lieutenant-Governor's Bronze
Medal), B.Arch. (honours) 1950; awarded
McLennan Travelling Scholarship, for architectural
research in the Middle East and Europe, 1950-53.
Served in the Canadian Army, 1943-45: Captain,
Canadian Intelligence Corps in India, Ceylon, and
Malaya, 1945. In private practice, Vancouver, 1953-
62; Partner, with Geoffrey Massey,
Erickson/Massey Architects, Vancouver, 1963-72.
Since 1972, Principal, Arthur Erickson architects,
Vancouver, Los Angeles, and Toronto; since 1977,
President, Arthur Erickson Associates, Vancouver,
Toronto, Kuwait, and Jeddah, Saudi Arabia. Assist-
ant Professor, University of Oregon, Eugene, 1955-
56; Instructor, 1956-57, Assistant Professor, 1958-
60, and Associate Professor, 1961-64, University of
British Columbia, Vancouver. Broadcaster,
Canadian Broadcasting Corporation, 1956-62.
Exhibitions: *The Architecture of Arthur Erickson*,
Vancouver Art Gallery, 1966; *Art in Architecture—
Arthur Erickson*, University of Calgary, Alberta,
1976; *Arthur Erickson: Recent Work*, University of
Toronto, 1977; *Transformations in Modern Architec-
ture*, Museum of Modern Art, New York, 1979; *Six
Architectural Offices in Toronto: Arthur Erickson
Architects*, Canada House, London, 1984. Recipi-
ent: Massey Medal, 1955, 1958, 1967 (3 times), and
1970 (3 times); Canada Council Fellowship, 1961;
Pan-Pacific Citation, American Institute of Architects, Hawaii Chapter, 1963; First Prize, Simon
Fraser University Competition, Burnaby, British
Columbia 1963; Tokyo International Trade Fair
Award, 1965; Vancouver Citation Award, Architectural Institute of British Columbia, 1965; Pre-
stressed Concrete Institute Award, 1966, 1967, and
1972; Molson Prize, Canada Council, 1967; Centennial Design Award, National Housing Design
Council, 1967; Design Award, Architectural Institute of British Columbia, Vancouver Chapter,
1967 (twice) and 1968 (twice); Award of Merit,

Canadian Architect, 1968; House Award, *Archi-
tectural Record*, 1969; Architectural Institute of
Japan Award, 1970; Triangle Award, National
Society of Interior Designers, 1970; First Prize,
Elementary School Competition, Southeast Sector
of Vancouver, 1970; Award of Excellence, *Canadian
Architect Yearbook*, 1970 and 1977; Royal Bank of
Canada Award, 1971; First Line Award, 1971, and
Residential Design Award, 1975, Canadian Housing
Design Council; Man of the Year Award, Greater
Vancouver Visitors and Convention Bureau, 1972;
Gold Medal, Tau Sigma Delta, 1973; Auguste Perret
Award, International Union of Architects, 1974;
President's Award of Excellence, American Society
of Landscape Architects, 1979; four Honour
Awards, 1980, and Gold Medal, 1984, Royal
Architectural Institute of Canada; Chicago Archi-
tecture Award, 1984; Gold Medal, French Academy
of Architecture, 1984. D.Eng.: Nova Scotia Techn-
ical College, Halifax, 1971; LL.D.: Simon Fraser
University Burnaby, British Columbia, 1973;
McGill University, Montreal, 1975; University of
Manitoba, Winnipeg, 1978; University of Lethbrid-
ge, Alberta, 1981. Fellow, Royal Architectural
Institute of Canada, 1953; Academician, Royal
Canadian Academy of Arts, 1953. Honorary Fellow,
American Institute of Architects, 1978. Companion,
Order of Canada, 1981. Address: Arthur Erickson
Architects, 2412 Laurel Street, Vancouver, British
Columbia V5Z 3T2, Canada.

Works:

1958 Filberg House, Comox, British Columbia
1962 Graham House, West Vancouver
1963 Simon Fraser University, Burnaby, British
Columbia
1964 Lloyd House, Vancouver
Danto House, Vancouver
Bayles House, Vancouver
Smith House, West Vancouver
1965 Pavilion for the International Trade Fair,
Tokyo
1966 Development study of the downtown core of
Vancouver
Townhouses, Point Grey Road, Vancouver
1967 Craig House, Kelowna, British Columbia
Catton House, West Vancouver
Theme Building, *Expo '67*, Montreal
Campus development plan for the University
of Victoria, British Columbia
Transportation study of Vancouver
1968 Faculty Club, University of British Columbia,
Vancouver
Snauq Harbour, Vancouver
Marathon Realty M-3 Development, Montreal
(with David Boulva Cleve)
1969 Married Student Housing, Simon Fraser
University, Burnaby, British Columbia
MacMillan Bloedel Office Tower Block,
Vancouver
Cité des Terrasses (housing development),
Montreal (with David Boulva Cleve)
Campus development plan for the University
of Lethbridge, Alberta
Development study for the Bank of Canada,
Ottawa
West Seattle Freeway
1970 Sikh Temple, Vancouver
Canadian Pavilion, Expo '70, Osaka, Japan
Biological Sciences Building, University of
Victoria, British Columbia
1971 Nelson Towers (housing), Vancouver
Centre Beaubourg, Paris (competition
project)
University of Lethbridge, Alberta
Bank of Canada, Ottawa (with Marani,
Rounthwaite, and Dick)
Village Lake Louise, Alberta
1971/
77 Museum of Anthropology, University of Brit-
ish Columbia, Vancouver

Arthur Erickson: Government Offices and Courthouse Complex, Vancouver, 1979 (project).

1972 Queen's University Centre, Vancouver
Home Lumber Company, Saanich, British Columbia
Study of downtown Vancouver
1973 Shannon Mews (housing), Vancouver
Oppenheimer Lodge, Vancouver
Christ Church Cathedral, Vancouver
Elementary school, Vancouver
Canadian Pacific Hotel, Vancouver
Intermediate Transit Demonstration project, for the Government of Ontario

Inner Harbour, Victoria, British Columbia
False Creek East End Lake, Vacouver
Area plan for Langley, British Columbia
Traffic study for the University of British Columbia at Fort Camp
1973/
79 Blocks 51-56-71 Project (government offices and courthouse complex), Vancouver
1974 Arthur Erickson House, Vancouver
Hilborn House, Cambridge, Ontario
Eppich House, West Vancouver

1975 Ghajere Ski Condominiums, Tehran
Kanata Recreation Plan, Ottawa
Development plan for East End Lake, Vancouver
Expansion study for British Columbia Hydro and Power Authority Head Office, Vancouver
Midtown Terrace, Toronto
1976 Sawaber Housing Development, Kuwait
Habitat Pavilion, Vancouver
British Columbia Medical Centre, Vancouver

Downtown West (commercial development)
and City Park, Toronto (with Mathers and
Haldenby)
Hornby-Smithe Development, Vancouver
Office building, Abbotsford, Ontario
Centro Simon Bolivar, Caracas, Venezuela
1976/
80 Roy Thomson Hall, Toronto
1977 Islamic Centre, Richmond, Ontario
National Gallery of Canada, Ottawa
Eglinton West Subway Station, Toronto
Yorkdale Rapid Transit Station, Toronto
1978 Performing Arts Centre, Calgary, Alberta
Hotel/Convention Center, Victoria, British
Columbia
Federal Office Building, Vancouver
Ministy of Foreign Affairs Interim Headquar-
ters, Jeddah, Saudi Arabia
1979 Wright House, Seattle, Washington
Town Centre, Fintas, Kuwait
Condominiums, Reno, Nevada
Keevils Bunkhouse addition, Kamloops, Brit-
ish Columbia
Beron House, Woodside, California
Wilson Bradley House, Carpinteria,
California
Laxton Office interiors, Vancouver
King Faisal Air Academy, Jeddah, Saudi
Arabia
1980 Mall extension, University of San Francisco
Laxton House renovation, Vancouver
Grant House II, Vancouver
Teck Mining Office, Toronto
Teck Mining Office, Vancouver
Harbor Properties Development, Vancouver
Ministry of Foreign Affairs Building, Jeddah,
Saudia Arabia
Caulfield Plateau Development, British
Columbia
Boz Scaggs House, Cappie's Island, British
Columbia
Marathon Development, Montreal (project)
Museum of Anthropology landscape,
Vancouver
Bene House, Carmel Valley, California
Dr. Hwang House, Vancouver
Brentwood College, Mill Bay, Vancouver
Island
Shelter Island Marina, Richmond, British
Columbia
Museum of Anthropology extension,
Vancouver
Stamford Atrium redesign, Toronto
Sun Life Head Office Building, Toronto
Air Defence Headquarters, Jeddah, Saudi
Arabia
Caledon Housing, Toronto
King Abdul Aziz University Master Plan,
Jeddah, Saudi Arabia
1981 Songhees Provincial Government Develop-
ment, Victoria, Vancouver Island
Marathon Residential and Office Block,
Montreal
University Village, University of San
Francisco
Sunkin House, Malibu, California
Laxton House interiors, Vancouver
Red Deer and Regional Art Centre, Alberta
Saudi Arabian National Centre for Science
and Technology, Jeddah
Georgian Court Hotel, Vancouver
Waterfront Centre, Vancouver
Academic extension, University of San
Francisco
Harbourplace Square Development, Balti-
more, Maryland
Harbourfront/Spadina Quay Development,
Toronto
Harbourfront Development, Dartmouth,
Nova Scotia
Canadian Chancery Building, Washington,
D.C.
1982 Fairfax County and Government Centre,
Washington, D.C.

Saudi Arabian Embassy, Ottawa
Pedersen House, Toronto
National Gallery of Canada, Ottawa (compe-
tition project)
West Mall Complex, University of San
Francisco
Landscaping, University of San Francisco
Mont Bre Housing, Toronto (project)
Riverbend Houses, Edmonton, Alberta
Office Complex, Anchorage, Alaska
B.C. Place Master Plan and Development,
Vancouver
Hernando Island House (Keevil House),
British Columbia
B.C. Place Apex Site Development,
Vancouver
Red Deer Arts Centre interiors, Alberta
Marathon Waterfront Centre Site Study,
Montreal
1983 Saudi Arabian Embassy Residence, Ottawa,
Ontario
King Faisal Air Force Academy Mosque
redesign, Jeddah, Saudi Arabia
Trump Tower Development, New York
Office Building, 60 Wall Street, New York
Canada Place Development, Edmonton,
Alberta
Medina University, Saudi Arabia
East Boston Harborfront Master Plan,
Boston
Ohio State University Visual Arts Centre,
Columbus (competition project)
Tanjun Batu Coastal Reserve Master Plan,
Borneo, Indonesia
Islamic University, Medina, Saudi Arabia
Kuwait Insurance Company Offices, Kuwait
City
Commercial and Residential Development,
Dubai, United Arab Emirates
Red Deer Arts Centre addition, Alberta
B.C. Place Park, Vancouver
Falah Trust School, Jeddah, Saudi Arabia
(competition project)
Arts, Sciences and Technology Centre,
Vancouver
Lipkland Housing, Malaysia
B.C. Place pavilion, Vancouver
Vista Hotel, Seattle, Washington
1984 Datuk Dr. Chen House, Kuala Lumpur,
Malaysia
Bukit Ceylon Condominium and Hotel,
Kuala Lumpur, Malaysia
City Hospital, Saskatoon, Saskatchewan
Lim House, Kuala Lumpur, Malaysia
Laxton Office Building, Vancouver
McLaughlin Gallery extensions, Alberta

Publications:

By ERICKSON: book—*The Architecture of Arthur
Erickson*, Montreal 1975; articles—"The Weight of
Heaven" in *Canadian Architect* (Toronto), March
1964; "The Roots" and "A Tendency Towards
Formalism" in *Canadian Architect* (Toronto), De-
cember 1966; "The University; The New Visual
Environment" in *Canadian Architect* (Toronto),
January 1968; "Architecture, Urban Development,
and Industrialisation" in *Canadian Architect* (Tor-
onto), January 1975; "The Context for Urbanization
and Industrialization" in *Towards a Quality of Life:
The Role of Industrialization in the Architecture and
Urban Planning of Developing Countries*, Teheran
1976; "Ideation as a Source of Creativity" in *A
Political Art*, edited by W.H. New, Vancouver 1978.

On ERICKSON: books—*Lotus 5: The Language of
Erickson* by Giuseppe Mazzariol, Venice 1970; *The
Architecture of Arthur Erickson*, Montreal 1975; *By
Their Own Design*, edited by Abby Suckle, New York
and St. Albans, Hertfordshire 1980; *Building with
Words: Canadian Architects on Architecture*, with
introduction by W. Bernstein and R. Cawker,

Toronto 1981; *Seven Stones: A Portrait of Arthur
Erickson* by Edith Iglauer, Vancouver 1981;
articles—"The Design of a House" in *Canadian Art*
(Toronto), November 1960; article in the *New York
Times Sunday Magazine*, 20 November 1961; article
in *Architecturel Design* (London), March 1962;
article in *Design* (Bombay), January 1965; article in
Time (New York), 25 August 1967; "Canadian
Architect Arthur Erickson Gets Major Award for
His Expo '70 Pavilion" in *Design* (Bombay), October
1971; article in *Progressive Architecture* (New York),
September 1972; article in *Architecture Plus* (New
York), February 1973; "Erickson" by Macy DuBois
in *Canadian Architect* (Toronto), November 1974;
"Design for Transit" in *Canadian Architect* (Tor-
onto), May 1976; "Architecture as Cultural Ex-
pression" in *Arts Canada* (Toronto), October/
November 1976; "Meet the Architect: Arthur
Erickson" in *Global Architecture Houses*, Tokyo
1977; "The Architect as Artist" in *Illustrated London
News*, January 1978; "Sawaber Project, Kuwait" in
Canadian Architect (Toronto), no. 8, 1979; "Arthur
Erickson vs. the All-Stars" in *Trace* (Toronto),
July/September 1981; "Simple Elegance" in
Canadian Architect (Toronto), March 1984:

Bibliography: *Arthur C. Erickson* by Lamia
Doumato, Monticello, Illinois 1984.

I like to think of building design not as the product of
an architect's imagination but as the inevitable result
of the two conditions of its being: its purpose and its
context. These, in my view, become like two opposite
forces, one pushing out the form through the
programmatic pressures from within and the other
molding it through the environmental pressures
from without.

I probably don't differ from other contemporaries
in this stance, except perhaps that these become equal
sources of inspiration. The context or site, in the
broadest sense of site, pervades the design so
irrevocably that the building form is meaningless
without it. The program goes beyond the definition
of building requirements to the redefinition of
purpose in the context of the society and the culture
at that particular time and place. This is the real
source of innovation—not the forms themselves, nor
the structure or materials—and from it a building
injects into its culture a fresh response to its
traditions. All my building forms can be traced to
these sources.

Of course, the matter of personal taste must play a
role. My preference is for the horizontal line and for
simple forms and materials that are uncomplicated,
if not austere. Surfaces are unadorned to the extent of
rejecting ornament of any kind—even board formwork. I abhor subterfuge or disguise, crave
frankness, especially in exposing and featuring
structure, though structure never determines the
form but rather is the result of it. Things should be
themselves above all, which is sometimes difficult in
this age of the artificial. Life is rich, always changing,
always challenging, and we architects have the task
of transmitting it into wood, concrete, glass, and
steel, of transforming human aspirations into habitable and meaningful space.

—Arthur Erickson

"The greatest architect in Canada, and maybe the
greatest on this continent," according to Philip
Johnbson (quoted by Edith Iglauer in *The New
Yorker*, 4 June 1979), Arthur Erickson gained
international recognition for his (and Geoffrey
Massey's) plan and covered mall for Simon Fraser
University in 1963. This striking conception extended a linear university plan across the two high
points of a low mountain. The saddle between the
peaks accommodates a vehicular underpass and
terminal for entry to the pedestrian campus above.
Individual buildings were awarded to the competition finalists; Erickson chose to build the huge

covered mall which created a central, weather-protected gathering place adjacent to the point of arrival, stretching between the university library and theatre. The mall roof itself, a composite wood, steel, and glass space-frame spanning forty by ninety medtres, was designed by the structural specialist Jeffrey Lindsay.

Simon Fraser suggests a key to Erickson's particular interests and abilities; his essential contribution was more in the orchestration of space and movement than a matter of detailed physical design. The same fascination with movement, with place, route, and destination, appears in other major structures such as the Museum of Anthropology and the Provincial Government Offices and Courthouse in Vancouver.

Not preoccupied with particular forms, materials, and technologies, Erickson pursues effects, appropriate to the place and program; architecture is seen as performance, with physical structure, users, and landscape or urban context as actors. Though the forms of his buildings are often striking, his materials and colours tend to neutral tones, lending unity to the overall shapes and creating a background for people and planting. Conflicts arise, however, between the large-scale gesture, as at the two universities (Simon Fraser, spanning its mountain tops; Lethbridge, damming a coulee) and the internal environments—in these examples overextended, attenuated.

A variety of techniques and memorable images characterize Erickson's other buildings: the visually dominating horizontal timber beams in the Smith House, the deeply recessed in-situ concrete openings of the massive moated MacMillan Bloedel Office Tower, the glittering faceted mirror-glass canopy over Roy Thomson Hall in Toronto. The concern for the dramatic—in form, use, and setting—is a unifying constant.

One architectonic theme that runs through many of Erickson's buildings is trabeation—massive horizontal beams on vertical piers or columns—used to define and frame volumes and vistas. The governing discipline is Picturesque rather than Renaissance, however, and "functional" rather than classical. Little sympathy with revived Beaux Arts formalism appears, for example, in his adaption of Rattenbury's 1906-12 Court House as the new Vancouver Art Gallery.

The picturesque use of such classical elements appears powerfully vindicated in the project for the new Canadian Embassy in Washington on a Pennsylvania Avenue site with strict guidelines for colour, height, and continuity. The design appears to meet all requirements with an impressive presence: the assertive formality of the framing facades, then a welcoming flow within the frame through the courtyard to lobby, gallery, theatre, and offices. This project shows Erickson continuing to develop, as a designer in full control of his material, masterfully shaping the effects at his command to each occasion.

—Michael McMordie

ERSKINE, Ralph.
British. Born in Mill Hill, London, 24 February 1914; moved to Sweden, 1939. Educated at the Friends School, Saffron Walden, Essex, 1920-32; Regent Street Polytechnic, London, 1932-37, Dip.Arch. 1937; Royal Academy of Arts, Stockholm, 1944-45. Married Ruth Monica Francis in 1939; children: Jane, Karin, and Patrick. Since 1946, in private practice, Drottningholm, Sweden: now in partnership with Aage Rossenvold; acquired Thames barge Verona, sailed it to Drottningholm, and converted it to offices, 1956-63; established branch office on the Byker Estate, Newcastle, England, 1968. Guest Professor, Eidgenössische

Technische Hochschule, Zürich, 1964-65, and McGill University, Montreal, 1967-68. Member, Team 10, since 1959. Exhibitions: *Architecture in Cold Climates,* Cornell University, Ithaca, New York, 1959; *The Climate,* Tokyo, 1960; *Ralph Erskine/Ilhan Koman,* Schindler Gallery, Bern, 1962; *Ralph Erskine,* travelling exhibition Sweden and Canada, 1963; *Architecture Overseas,* Guildhall Art Gallery, London, 1984. Recipient: Architecture Medal, Swedish Ski and Recreation Association, 1943; Golden Pyramid Award, *Domus* magazine, Milan 1963; Kasper Salin Prize, Sweden, 1970 and 1980; Ytong Prize, with Höjer and Ljungqvist, Sweden, 1974; Ambrose Congreve Architecture Award, 1979; Civic Trust Award, Britain, 1979; Britain in Bloom Prize, 1979 (twice); Eternit and UIA (International Union of Architects) International Prize, 1980; Litteris et Artibus Royal Gold Medal, Sweden, 1980; Gold Medal, Royal Architectural Institute of Canada, 1982; PaStan Award, Stockholm, 1983; Wolf Foundation Prize, Israel, 1984; Fritz Schumacher Medal and Prize, 1984; Expressens Miljö Diploma, Sweden, 1984. Dr. Tech.: University of Lund, Sweden, 1975; D. Litt.: Heriot-Watt University, Edinburgh, 1982. Associate, Royal Institute of British Architects, 1937; Member, Royal Town Planning Institute 1938; Member, Swedish Arkiteks' Riksforbund, 1965. Honorary Fellow, American Institute of Architects, 1966; Foreign Member, Swedish Royal Academy of Arts, 1972. C.B.E. (Commander, Order of the British Empire), 1978. Address: Ralph Erskines Arkitektkontor, Gustav III's väg 4, 170 11 Drottningholm, Sweden.

Works:

1941/
42 Erskine House, Lissma, near Stockholm
von Platen House, Djupdalen, near Stockholm
1942/
43 Skiing Hotel/Centre, Lida Friluftsgard, Stockholm (with Birch-Lindgren)
1945/
55 Housing development for workers, Gyttorp, Sweden
1946/
47 Town plan and housing, Storviks-Hammarby, Sweden
1947 Molin House, Lidingö, near Stockholm
1947/
48 G. Erskine House, Lewes, Sussex, England
Nilsson House, Storviks-Hammarby, Sweden
Mattress Factory, Köping, Sweden
1947/
49 Wooden Chapel, Borgafjäll, Sweden
1948/
49 Nilsson House, Saltsjö-Duvnäs, Stockholm
1948/
50 Skiing Hotel/Centre, Borgafjäll, Sweden
1949 Bžge Weekend House, near Stockholm
1949/
62 Erskine Summer Studio, Ragö, Sweden
1950 Factory and offices, Gnesta, Sweden
Offices and warehouse, Uppsala, Sweden
1950/
53 Cardboard Manufacturing Factory, Fors, near Avesta, Sweden
1951 Workers' housing, Jädražs, near Sandviken, Sweden
1951/
53 Enequist, Holme and Company Offices and Factory, Stockholm
1953 Paper-pulp Facotry, Storviks-Hammarby, Sweden
Scouts' Hut, Lovö, near Drottningholm, Sweden
Monument to the Unknown Political Prisoner (competition project; with E. Möller-Nielsen)
1953/
54 Oestermans Truck Building Plant, Södertälje,

Sweden
1954 House, Skövde, Sweden
Shopping Centre, Lulež, Sweden
Apartment buildings, Växjö, Sweden
1955/
56 Engström House, Sorunda, Isle of Lisö, near Nynäshamn, Sweden
Möller and Company Offices and Warehouse, Stockholm
1956 Verona barge conversion to Erskine offices, Drottningholm, Sweden
1957/
58 Offices, laboratory and warehouse, Sollentuna, Stockholm
1958 Ideal Subarctic Town, Lappland, Sweden (project)
Recreation Centre, Västerzs, Sweden (project)
1959/
67 Brittgžrden Housing Estate, Tibro, Sweden
1960 Church, Segato, North Africa (project)
1961 Primary school, Gyttorp, Sweden
Gadelius House, Lidingö, near Stockholm
Ström House, Stocksund, Stockholm
1961/
62 Ortdrivaren Housing Development, Kiruna, Sweden
1962 Nordmark House, near Södertälje, Sweden
Redevelopment plan for the centre of Cambridge, England (project)
1962/
72 Barberaren Housing Estate, Sandviken, Sweden
1963 LKAB Staff Housing, Svappavaara, Sweden
Erskine House and Studio, Drottningholm, Sweden
1965 Town Hall and Administration Building, Tibro, Sweden (project)
1965/
66 Development plan for South Sergels Torg, Stockholm (competition project; with L. Geisendorf and A. Tengbom)
1966 Development plan for the centre of Ashdod, Israel (competition project)
Hotel and Ski Resort Complex, Crosets, Switzerland (project)
1967/
69 Post-Graduate College, Clare Hall, Cambridge, England
1969 Pžgens Bakery Headquarters, Malmö, Sweden
1969/
70 Esperanza Housing Development, Landskrona, Sweden
1969/
72 Killingworth Housing Estate, near Newcastle upon Tyne, England
1969- Byker Housing Estate, Newcastle upon Tyne, England
1970/
76 Studlands Park Housing Estate, Newmarket, Suffolk, England
1971 Development plan for the Hansta Urban District, Jarvafaltet, Stockholm (project; with L. Geisendorf and A. Tengbom)
1972 Development plan for the Marsta Residential District, Stockholm (project)
1972/
73 Church and Parish Community Centre, Bodafors, Sweden
1973/
74 Plan for the development of the Old City, Resolute Bay, Northwest Territories, Canada
1973/
77 Eaglestone Housing Estate, Milton Keynes, Buckinghamshire, England
1973/
78 Bruket Housing Estate, Sandviken, Sweden
1974/
82 Library and Student Centre, Frescati University, Stockholm
1975 Commercial Centre, Resolute Bay, Northwest Territories, Canada (project)
Town plan for Rissne, Stockholm

1975/
77 Housing Myrstugeberget, Huddings, Sweden
    (project)
    Holiday Village, Härjedalen, Sweden (project)
1976 Multiple Staff Housing, Resolute Bay, North-
    west Territories, Canada
    Fermont New Town, Canada (project; as
    consultant)
1976/
77 Vallhov Housing, Sandviken, Sweden (pro-
    ject)
1977 Planning Study, Ekerö Mälarstad, Sweden
    (project)
    Rissne Housing, Sundyberg, Sweden (project)
    IOGT Centre, Nya Bruket, Sandviken,
    Sweden
    Holiday Village, Lindö Säteri, Vallentuna,
    Sweden (project)
1978 Town plan for Lina, Södertälje, Sweden
    Town Plan for Ekerö, near Stockholm
1979 Hotel, Jochberg, Austria (project)
    Housing, Tyresö, Sweden (project)
1980 Health centre, housing, and offices, Tapetse-
    raren, Sandviken, Sweden
    Housing, Malminkartano, Helsinki, Finland
    (project)
    Moliets-et-Maa Village, Côte d'Aquitaine,
    France (project)
    Library, Uppsala, Sweden (competition
    project)
    Temporary Exhibition '80, Kungsträdgards-
    gatan, Stockholm
    Planning Study, South Stockholm (project)
    Housing, Wolfen Neustadt, West Germany
    (competition project)
    Conference and Sports Centre, Docksta,
    Kramfors, Sweden (project)
    Tegel Harbour Plan, West Berlin (competition
    project)
    Parish Hall, Färentuna, Sweden
1981 Office Building, Cologne, West Germany
    (competition project)
    Infill Building, Utkiken, South Stockholm
    (project)
    Öbacka Housing, Umea, Sweden (project)
    Sports Hall, Frescati, Stockholm (project)

Publications:

By ERSKINE: articles—"Town Planning in the
Swedish Subarctic" in *Habitat* (Ottawa),
November/December 1960; "The Challenge of the
High Latitudes" and "Community Design for
Production, for Publication, or for People" in *Royal
Architectural Institute of Canada Journal* (Toronto),
1964; "Construire dans le nord" in *L'Architecture
d'aujourd'hui* (Paris), no. 134, 1967; "Architecture
and Town Planning in the North" in *Polar Record*
(Cambridge), no. 89, 1968; "Climate" in *Werk*
(Zürich), no. 4, 1969; "8 Riposte a 8 domande" in
L'Architettura (Rome), November 1974; "Ralph
Erskine Talks to AJ" in *Architects' Journal* (Lon-
don), 3 March 1976; "Working on Projects Abroad"
and "Byker," with J. Sjostrom, in *Arkitektur* (Stock-
holm), October 1976; "On the Situation of the
Architect," special issue of *Bauen und Wohnen*
(Zürich), January 1977; "Byker: New Building Best
Solution" in *Arkitektur* (Stockholm), February
1977; "Nya Bruket: Daynursery in Sandviken" in
Arkitektur (Stockholm), August 1977; "The Loyal
Architecture" in *Arkitektur* (Stockholm), June 1979;
"Architecture in a Cold Climate" in *RIBA Journal*
(London), October 1980; "Democratic Architec-
ture" in *RSA Journal* (London), September 1982.

On ERSKINE: books—*GA 55: The Byker Redevelopment,* edited by Yukio Futagawa, with text by
Mats Egelius, Tokyo 1980; *The Architecture of Ralph
Erskine* by Peter Collymore, London 1982; *Recent
Developments in Swedish Architecture: A Reappraisal*
by Mats Egelius, Gunilla Lundahl, Eva Rudberg and
others, Stockholm 1983; *Ornamentalism: The New*
Decorativeness in Architecture and Design by Robert
Jensen and Patricia Conway, New York 1984;
articles—"Individual Houses in Sweden" in *Re-
cherche et architecture* (Paris), no. 19, 1974; special
issue of *L'Architettura* (Rome), November 1974;
"Byker by Erskine" by Colin Amery in *Architectural
Review* (London), December 1974; "Byker: Archi-
tect Ralph Erskine" by Diana Rowntree in *Archi-
tectural Design* (London), June 1975; "Housing—
Still More New Ideas?" by John McKean in
Architects' Journal (London), 2 July 1975; "The
Village Lives!" by G. Darley in *Building Design*
(London), 14 November 1975; "Ralph Erskine" by
M. Corominas and I. Castineira in *Jano arquitectura*
(Barcelona), March 1976; "Byker in Newcastle" by
J. Gomez Morata in *Arquitectura* (Madrid),
March/April 1976; "Romantic Pragmatism and
Lyric Continuity" in *L'Architecture d'aujourd'hui*
(Paris), October 1976; special issue of *Bauen und
Wohnen* (Zürich), January 1977; "Ralph Erskine,
The Human Architect" by M. Egelius in *Archi-
tectural Design* (London), November/December
1977; "Children's Day Centre in Sandviken" in
Baumeister (Munich), January 1978; "In
Newcastle—Byker" in *Abitare* (Milan), December
1978; "Ralph Erskine," special issue of *Arkitektur*
(Stockholm), September 1981; "Erskine's Allhus"
by Peter Collymore in *Architectural Review* (Lon-
don), November 1981; "The Way Leads to Ralph
Erskine" by Julius Posener in *Der Architekt* (Stuttgart), October 1982; "Erskine" by John Maule
McKean in *Architects' Journal* (London), 6 October
1982; "Ralph Erskine," special issue of *Deutsche
Bauzeitung* (Stuttgart), no. 3, 1983.

After studying architecture at the Regent Street
Polytechnic in London, Ralph Erskine moved to
Sweden just before the war started in 1939. Sweden
represented the idea of the new welfare state, with a
new architecture to go with it, and was the Mecca for
many architects at that time.
    The culture shock of moving to Sweden and,
perhaps, the physical shock of the northern climate
formed Erskine's architectural philosophy, based on
a functional response to climate and related to social
and political requirements. Erskine felt that "modern" architecture paid only lip-service to these
fundamental ideals of the movement and had got
side-tracked by aesthetic and formal considerations.
Face to face with the problems of building in Sweden,
Erskine, in his arctic studies, attracted interest from
countries with similar problems such as Canada and
the U.S.S.R. He evolved building types to take
advantage of what sun there was, to keep out the
arctic winds, and to control snowdrifts.
    The northern perimeter of his sketch for an arctic
town became a continuous wall-building, turning its
back on the cold winds and opening out to the south.
This wall-building has appeared in many of his
projects since then, principally at Svappavaara in the
Swedish north, Byker in the English north at
Newcastle, in the Canadian township for Eskimoes
and white Canadians at Resolute Bay, and to a lesser
extent in other schemes. Apart from their functional
appropriateness, these wall-buildings have given
Erskine an opportunity to exercise his romantic
inclinations—to have gateways through the wall and
to decorate it on its northern face, where there are few
windows, with brick murals as at Byker or bright
coloured stained boarding as at Resolute Bay.
    Too much emphasis should not be placed on the
wall-buildings, however. Erskine has built tower
blocks at Kiruna and Växjö, courtyard housing,
factories, and single houses, and he has designed
many town planning projects. The town plans have a
casual, intimate, and informal atmosphere on the
ground, but, when examined, often reveal a strong
backbone of geometrical regularity—planned
groups with informal spaces between them.
    One of Erskine's strongest held ideals is that of
participation with the people who will use or live in
his buildings. This goes beyond dealing with the
client; it has been extended to making direct contact

with the potential inhabitants of his housing
schemes. Erskine feels that the professions have
distanced themselves from the people they purport to
serve and have erected barriers through using special
professional language when plain language would be
more sensible. Thus at the Byker housing scheme at
Newcastle, Erskine set up his English office in a
disused building in the middle of the housing area
where tenants go to raise points about their
accommodation and future tenants can see their
housing being designed, after previous open-
discussion meetings. The Byker office has become
something of a communal centre as well as being
Erskine's office. Byker is only one example of this
principle at work. Erskine tries to make this special
contact in all his work.
    Erskine has designed some eighty projects, most of
which have been built in collaboration with his
partner Aage Rosenvold. Principal among these
many, varied buildings are the village at Storviks-
Hammarby (1947) houses at Lisö (a dome house),
Lidingö, Södertälje, and Drottningholm; factories at
Hammarby and Fors; housing schemes at Kiruna
and Svappavaara (in sub-arctic Sweden), Tibro, and
Sandviken, Sweden, and Newcastle-upon-Tyne,
Newmarket, and Milton Keynes in England; a
school at Gyttorp; a postgraduate college at Cambridge; a housing township in north Canada at
Resolute bay; a ski hotel at Borgafjäll, as well as an
enclosed shopping centre at Lulea, both in north
Sweden. Recently, Erskine has completed a large
library, sports hall, and students' centre at Stockholm Unviersity. Overall, these buildings show an
early eclecticism and the development of a personal
style, taking ideas from traditional building in
Britain and Sweden but very much related also to the
mainstream modern movement, a relationship sustained through Erskine's meetings with CIAM and
Team 10.

—Peter Collymore

ERVI, Aarne Adrian.
Finnish. Born Aarne Adrian Elers in Forssa, 19 May
1910; adopted the surname Ervi, 1935. Educated at
the Helsingin Suomalainen Yhteiskoulu, Helsinki,
1930; Technical University of Helsinki, 1930-35,
Dip.Arch. 1935. Married Naemi Inkeri Hanninen in
1935 (divorced, 1957); Rauni Maria Erika Luoma in
1957; children: Heikki, Heidi, and Matti. Assistant
Architect, City Building Office, Helsinki, 1934;
worked in the office of Alvar Aalto, *q.v.*, Helsinki,
1935, and Toivo Paatela, Helsinki, 1937; in private
practice, Helsinki, 1938 until his death in 1977.
Worked in the Standardization Department, Finnish Rebuilding Office, Helsinki, 1942-44; Director,
Standardization Institute, Association of Finnish
Architects (SAFA), 1942-45; Director, City Plann-
ing Office, Helsinki, 1965-68. Special Instructor,
Central School of Arts and Crafts, Helsinki, 1937-38;
Instructor, Technical University of Helsinki, 1943-
46. Assistant Editor, *Arkkitehti,* Helsinki, 1937-43.
Exhibition: *Finnish Building,* Helsinki, 1953. Recipi-
ent: First Prize, University of Helsinki Library
Extension Competition, 1937; First Prize, University
of Helsinki Building Institute Competition, 1949;
First Prize, Tapiola Garden City Town Centre
Competition, 1954. D.Tech.: Technische Hochs-
chule, Stuttgart, 1966; Honorary Professor, Finland,
1967. Honorary Fellow, American Institute of
Architects, 1966. *Died* (in Helsinki) *26 September
1977.*

Works:

1931 Student Union Building alterations, Technical
    University, Helsinki (competition project;
    with Erkki Taimi)

Aarne Ervi: Library, Turku University, Finland, 1952.

1936 Temppeliaukio Church, Helsinki (competition project; with Toivo Paatela)
     Plan for the centre of Tampere, Finland
1937 Heinolan Liike Oy Office Building, Heinola, Finland
     Library extension, University of Helsinki
1938 Apartment building, Lauttasaarentie 9, Helsinki
     Design of the *International Air Exhibition*, Helsinki
     Cap factory, Kurikka, Finland
     Karjala Insurance Company, Viipuri, Finland (competition project)
1939 Private house, Harjavalta, Finland
     Kupittaa Park, Turku, Finland (competition project)
     Small house design, for the Finnish Ministry of Agriculture
     Church, Härmälä, Finland (competition project)
1940 Berger House, Inkoo, Finland
1941 Institute of Economics, Helsinki
1942/
  46 Oulujoki Oy Power Plants, and their housing areas, at Pyhäkoski, Jylhämä, Nuojua, and Pälli, Finland
1944 Rikkihappo Oy Housing Development, Harjavatta, Finland
1945 Secondary school, Kurikka, Finland
     Secondary school, Kauniainen, Finland
1945/
  49 Regional master plan for Oulu, Finland (with Otto Meurman)
1947 Finland House (store and restaurant), New York
1947/
  53 Voimatalo Commercial and Office Building, Helsinki (with Tapani Nironen)
1949 Parish Centre, Lohja, Finland
     City development plan for Helsinki (competition project)
1950 Ervi House, Kuusisaari, Helsinki
     KOP Casino, Otaniemi, Espoo, Finland
1950/
  57 Helsinki University Institute, Porthania, Helsinki
1952 Secondary school, Lohja, Finland
     Secondary school, Somero, Finland

1952/
  56 Library, Main Building, and Institute of Natural Sciences, Turku University, Finland
1952/
  64 Town centre, houses, apartments, and row housing, Tapiola Garden City, Espoo, Finland
1954 Himberg House, Helsinki
1955 Office building, Ruoholahdenkatu 8, Helsinki
1956 Hotel Management School, Helsinki
     Keri Oy Stocking Manufacturing Company, Tornio, Finland
     Secondary school, Urjala, Finland
1957 Furniture prototypes for the Merivaara Company, Finland
1958 Mannerheimintie Secondary School, Helsinki
1959 Secondary school, Voikka, Finland
     Secondary school, Salo, Finland
     Office building, Eerikinkatu 27, Helsinki
1960 Town Hall extension, Tampere, Finland
     Cafe Töölönranta, Helsinki
1961 Atelier Ervi (extension to Ervi House), Kuusisaari, Helsinki
     Apartment building, Mylltie 3, Helsinki
     Rikkihappo Oy Chemical Factory, Kokkola, Finland
     Oulujoki Oy Power Plant, Seitenoikea, Finland
     Merivaara Factory, Kerava, Finland
     Secondary school, Messukylä, Finland
     Kauppa-Häme Commercial Building, Tampere, Finland
1962 Swimming Hall, Tapiola Garden City, Espoo, Finland
     Apartment building, Vantaanpuisto, Vantaa, Finland
1963 Town Hall extension, Kemi, Finland
     Terrace houses, Itaranta, Tapiola, Finland (with Heikki Koskeloand and Markus Tavio)
     Rikkihappo Oy Chemical Factory, Uusikaupunki, Finland
1964 Swimming Hall, Kemi, Finland
     M/S Finnhansa interiors, Helsinki
1965 *M/S Finnpartner* interiors, Helsinki
     Heikintori Department Store, Tapiola Garden City, Espoo, Finland

1966 Municipal Office Building, Tampere, Finland
1967 Institute of Natural Sciences Building II, Turku University, Finland
1968 Töölö Library, Helsinki
1969 Kaleva Insurance Company Offices, Espoo, Finland
1970 Imatran Voima Oy Thermal Power Plant extension, Finland
1971 Housing development, Stuttgart (competition project)
     Plan for Hanko Island, Uusikaupunki, Finland
1973 Swimming Hall, Salo, Finland
1974 Tapiola Garden Hotel, Espoo, Finland

Publications:

On ERVI: books—*Finnish Building*, exhibition catalogue, Helsinki 1953; *Modern Finland* by Pirkka Saivo, Helsinki 1956; *Esempi di pianificiazione edilizia in Finlandia* by H. J. Becker and W. Schlote, Milan 1960; *New Finnish Architecture* by Egon Tempel, London 1968; *Aarne Ervi arkkitehtuuria* by Pentti Solla, Helsinki 1970 (includes bibliography); articles—"Nouveau Bâtiments de l'Université de Turku" in *L'Architecture d'aujourd'hui* (Paris), no. 93, 1960/61; "Centre de Tapiola, cité satellite d'Helsinki" in *L'Architecture d'aujourd'hui* (Paris), no. 101, 1962; "Terassenhaus, Tapiola" in *Architektur und Wohnform* (Stuttgart), no. 4, 1967; "Aarne Ervi: Ein Ritter der alten Schule" by Pentti Solla in *Deutsche Bauzeitung* (Stuttgart), no. 9, 1968; "Libraries in Finland" in *Architektura* (Munich), August 1975; "Aarne Ervi in Memoriam" by Timo Penttila and Heikki von Hertzen in *Arkkitehti* (Helsinki), no. 7, 1977.

Among the small countries (in terms of population), Finland has made one of the richest contributions to the evolution of modern architecture and town planning, and Aarne Ervi, with Aalto and a few others, can be regarded as one of the authors of this achievement. He has designed power stations and industrial and university buildings, but his crowning achievement has been as planner and architect at Tapiola.

Among his earlier works the University Library at Turku is distinctive. It is a long, squarish, four-storey building with the two lower floors housing the book stacks and the two upper floors, the reading rooms, with vertical services to provide rapid supply of books. It is a reinforced concrete structure, and the broad, simple massing, with ample fenestration of the upper floors, makes a very effective exterior.

Tapiola Garden City is one of the most beautiful small new towns in Europe. Ervi won the competition for its over-all plan and also for the design of its town centre. The site is a forest by the sea, seven miles west of Helsinki. Its flat centre is surrounded by low hills, while in the forest there are large granite protuberances. Ervi took full advantage of these natural features in planning the town. He placed the centre in flattish land, and built three neighbourhoods to the east, north, and west. These neighbourhoods, separated from the centre by forest belts, are mixed developments of tower and slab blocks of flats with family houses, and all are grouped round gardens and children's playgrounds. Particularly successful is the western neighbourhood. It is approached from the town centre by a short, paved footpath through the forest. The path rises on a rocky hill, and at the summit are tall, white tower blocks among the dark pines, as if the granite protrusions were continued upwards. A little beyond, slab blocks enclose extensive gardens and children's playgrounds. Many of the granite boulders are used as garden features and as bases for sculpture.

Ervi was responsible for the design of the centre and of many of its buildings. In the middle of the area, there was an old gravel pit, and it was converted to a two-and-one-half-acre square pool surrounded by buildings and gardens. Adjacent is the shopping centre, which is a complete pedestrian precinct approached by a broad flight of steps and enclosed on three sides by arcaded shops with a garden with trees in the centre. To the right of the approach is a tall thirteen-storey block; it gives a note of contrast to the general horizontality. A restaurant at the top provides views of the lovely surrounding country. This centre has a Greek-like quiescence that conveys a happy sense of peace.

Tapiola is necessarily a product of team work, but Ervi was the main planner and architect of its centre, and he necessarily set the style for much of the architecture of this lovely town. In the integration of architecture with scenery and natural features, Tapiola and the work of Ervi are unsurpassed.

—Arnold Whittick

ESHERICK, Joseph.

American. Born in Philadelphia, Pennsylvania, 28 December 1914. Educated at the University of Pennsylvania, Philadelphia, 1933-37, B.Arch. 1937. Served in the United States Navy, 1943-46. Married Rebecca Wood in 1939; children: Lisa, Joseph, and Peter; married Ann Rowe in 1953; children: Maria and Julia. In private architectural practice, San Francisco, 1946-53; President, Joseph Esherick and Associates, San Francisco, 1953-72. Since 1972, President, Esherick Homsey Dodge and Davis, architects and planners, San Francisco (partners: George Homsey, Peter Dodge, and Charles Davis). Instructor, 1952-56, Associate Professor, 1956-58, Professor of Architecture, since 1958, and Chairman of the Department of Architecture, since 1977, University of California, Berkeley. Secretary, Northern California Chapter, American Institute of Architects, 1959-60; Member, San Francisco Art Commission, 1959-69; Member, Architectural Advisory Committee, San Francisco Housing Authority, 1965; Jury Chairman, Nebraska Honor Awards,

American Institute of Architects, 1975; Architectural Consultant to the United States Department of State on Foreign Buildings Operations, 1975-78; Member, Architectural Consultant to the United States Department of State on Foreign Buildings Operations, 1975-78; Member, Architectural Review Panel, United States Federal Reserve System, 1976-79. Recipient: American Institute of Architects Award, 1953, 1965, 1966, 1970, and 1973; Graham Foundation Fellowship, 1962; Bay Area Honor Award, 1967; Homes for Better Living Award, 1966; *Progressive Architecture* Award, 1974; AIA/ACSA Award of Excellence, 1982. Honorary Fellow, Adlai E. Stevenson College, University of California at Santa Cruz, 1968. Fellow, American Institute of Architects, 1965; Associate, National Academy of Design, 1976. Address: Esherick Homsey Dodge and Davis, 2789 25th Street, San Francisco, California 94110, U.S.A.

Works:

1940 Esherick House, Ross, California
1946 Holt House, Stockton, California
      Guide Dogs for the Blind School, Marin County, California
      Grill House, Oakland, California
      Campbell House, Sacramento, California
      Cahill House, San Francisco
      Lewis House, Belvedere, California
1947 Smith House, Orinda, California
1948 Walker Summer House, Lake Tahoe, California
      Revere Quality House Institute House, San Bruno, California
      Metcalf Summer House, Lake Tahoe, California
      McCoy House, Kentwoodlands, California
      Kelham Summer House, Lake Tahoe, California
      Huish House, Contra Costa County, California
      Harrington House, San Joaquin County, California
      Frohlick House, San Rafael, California
      Bradley Summer House, Lake Tahoe, California
1949 Wiper House I, Sausalito, California
      Smith House, Piedmont, California
      Norton House, San Rafael, California
      MacChesney House, San Rafael, California
      Campbell House, Palo Alto, California
      Brown House, Stockton, California
      Albert Field Recreation Center, San Rafael, California
1950 Squaw Valley Ski Lodge and Facilities, Sun Valley, Idaho
      Women's Athletic Club alterations, San Francisco
      Rose House, Sausalito, California
      Perry House, Sausalito, California
      Wiper House II, Sausalito, California
      Kimball House, Kentwoodlands, California
      Gassman House, Palo Alto, California
      American Home Company Houses, Sacramento, California
      Alden House, Woodside, California
1951 Summers House, Hillsborough, California
      Smith House, Orinda, California
      San Rafael Fire Depatment alterations, California
      Jurs House, Contra Costa County, California
      Hellyer House, San Francisco
      Goldman House, San Francisco
      Gibson House, Sacramento, California
      Dern House, San Mateo, California
1952 Starr House, Mission San Jose, California
      Smith House, Happy Valley, California
      W. N. Breeze Commercial Building, San Bruno, California
      Borregard House, Oakland, California
      Beardslee House, Stockton, California

1953 Pike House, San Mateo, California
      Medical office building, San Francisco
      Lezin House, Woodside, California
      Eastman House, Woodside, California
      Daly House, Eureka, California
      Bewley House, San Joaquin, California
1954 Tobin House, Hillsborough, California
      Pan American Airways Sales Office, Oakland, California
      Bergin House, Kentwoodlands, California
      Belvedere Land Co. Houses, Belvedere, California
1955 Wiley House, Belvedere, California
      Weigel House, Bolinas, California
      Teigland House, Orinda, California
      Pan American Airways Sales Office, San Francisco
      Pacific Overseas Showroom, San Francisco
      Kelham House, San Francisco
      Franck House, Woodside, California
      Ecker House, Greenbrae, California
      Buck Summer House, Lake Tahoe, California
      Burman House, Kentfield, California
      Atwater House, Sausalito, California
      Ackerman House, Berkeley, California
1956 Svend Wohlert Showroom, San Francisco
      Pelican Building, University of California, Berkeley
      Gallo House, Livingstone, California
      Fisher-Harlow Company Houses, Atherton, California
      Bridge House, Belvedere, California
1957 Wieser House, Kentfield, California
      Walker House, San Francisco
      Hubbard House, Dover, Massachusetts
      Holt Guest House, Stockton, California
      Fisher House, Berkeley, California
      Cappeller House, Woodland, California
      Best House, Woodland, California
      Baum House, San Francisco
1958 Lyon House, Berkeley, California
      Kibbey House, Sacramento, California
      Grant House, Hillsborough, California
1959 Martin House, Ross, California
1960 Y.M.C.A., Berkeley, California
      Mantegani House, Belvedere, California
1961 Thompson House, Modesto, California
      McIntyre House, Hillsborough, California
      Heller House, Atherton, California
      Hartzell House, Sonoma, California
      Hamilton House, Atherton, California
      Child Study Center, Berkeley, California
      Cary House, Mill Valley, California
1962 Pan American Airways Ticket Office, San Francisco
      McLeod House, Belvedere, California
      Lowe House, San Francisco
      Lehman House, San Francisco
      Larson House, San Francisco
      Dennis House, Woodside, California
1963 Wheary House, San Francisco
      Steffanides House, Piedmont, California
      Roth House, Hawaii
      Kesten House, Inverness, California
      Joseph Esherick and Associates Office Building alterations, San Francisco
      Four Townhouses, Culebra Terrace, San Francisco
      Burr House, Sunol, California
      Botsford Office, San Francisco
      Bermak House, Oakland, California
      Bacci House, San Anselmo, California
1964 Management Science Laboratory, University of California, Berkeley
1965 Seven demonstration houses, general store/restaurant and entry marker, Sea Ranch, California
      Kylling House, Live Oak, California
      Wurster Hall: College of Environmental Design, University of California, Berkeley (with Vernon DeMars and Donald Olsen)
1966 Romano House, Kentwoodlands, California
      Carlson House, Sea Ranch, California
      Oestreicher House, Sausalito, California

Joseph Esherick: Maslack House, California.

Longyear House, Sacramento, California
Hewlett House, Berkeley, California
Church of Christ the Saviour, San Francisco
1967 Very Very Terry Jerry Dress Shop, Cannery, San Francisco
Splendiferous Dress Shop, Cannery, San Francisco
Palo Alto Unitarian Church additions, California
1968 Cahill House, Woodside, California
Cannery, San Francisco
Mini-Mod I and II, Sea Ranch, California
1973 Rounds House, Sea Ranch, California
Botsford House, Los Altos Hills, California
Roscoe House, Walnut Creek, California
Coblentz House, Pajaro Dunes, California
Family Development Center, San Francisco
1975 Willoughby Vacation House, Sugar Bowl, California
1977 New Exhibits, San Francisco Zoological Gardens
Gallo House, Modesto, California
1978 Garfield Elementary School, San Francisco
Fremont High School additions, Oakland,
California
1979 World Savings and Loan Association Office, Santa Cruz, California
United States Embassy, La Paz, Bolivia

Publications:

By ESHERICK: books—*Hollein Peichl Architektur: Work in Progress*, exhibition catalogue, Vienna 1963; contributor to *Color in Architecture* by Tom Porter, New York 1976; *The Architect: Chapters in the History of the Profession*, with others, edited by Spiro Kostof, New York 1977; articles—"Graduate Programs, I: The University of California," with others, in *AIA Journal* (Washington, D.C.), September 1963; "Management Teamwork Ensures Better Design" in *Pacific Factory* (San Francisco), May 1965; "Some Notes on Wood Frame" in *Architecture Canada* (Toronto), December 1965; "Realités et significations de l'architecture" in *Aujourd'hui: art et architecture* (Paris), January 1967; "A Laboratory to Facilitate Computer-Controlled Behavioral Experi-

ments," with others, in *Administrative Science Quarterly*, (New York), June 1969; "A Planned Campus: The University of California Santa Cruz Experiment" in *Architecture Canada* (Toronto), June/July 1969; "Highlands of American Architecture 1776-1976," with others, in *AIA Journal* (Washington, D.C.), July 1976; "The Beaux-Arts Experience" in *Architectural Education* (London), no. 1, 1983.

On ESHERICK: books—*Architects on Architecture* by Paul Heyer, New York 1966, London 1967; *Global Interiors I*, edited by Yukio Futagawa, Tokyo 1971; *Observations on American Architecture* by Ivan Chermayeff, New York 1972; *Adhocism* by Charles Jencks and Nathan Silver, New York 1973; *The Place of Houses* by Charles Moore and others, New York 1974; *Dimensions* by Charles Moore, New York 1976; *Bay Area Houses*, edited by Sally Woodbridge, New York 1976; *Supermannerism: New Attitudes in Post Modern Architecture* by C. Ray Smith, New York 1977; articles—"Joseph Esherick: Theory and Practice" in *Western Architect and*

Engineer (Portland, Oregon), December 1961; "Form Is What Things Are" in *Progressive Architecture* (New York), May 1964; "World Architects: Joseph Esherick" in *Japan Architect* (Tokyo), March 1965; "A Building for People" in *California Monthly* (Berkeley), November 1965; "Aujourd'hui USA" in *Aujourd'hui: art et architecture* (Paris), January 1967; "The Use of Human Use" by Nathan Silver in *The Nation* (New York), 15 May 1967; "What the Architect Tried to Do" in *Architectural Forum* (New York), June 1968; "Focus: Grass Roots in American Architecture II" in *Toshi-Jutaku* (Tokyo), November 1968; "World Famous Architects: Joseph Esherick" in *Nikkei Architecture* (Tokyo), 21 March 1977; "A View of Contemporary World Architects" in *Architecture + Urbanism* (Tokyo), December 1977; "Evaluation: A Class Recycling after 11 Years" by James Burns in *AIA Journal* (Washington, D.C.), July 1978; "Expedition Houses for American Archaeologists at Karnak" in *Progressive Architecture* (New York), January 1979; "House near Kentfield, California" in *Baumeister* (Munich), March 1980; "Addition to a Hotel, San Francisco" in *Baumeister* (Munich), July 1980; "Building Types Study 553: Embassies and Consulates" in *Architectural Record* (New York), December 1980; "Elementary School in San Francisco" in *Baumeister* (Munich), March 1981.

Bibliography: *Joseph Esherick* by Lamia Doumato, Monticello, Illinois 1983.

In architecture today, a multitude of small voices is being raised to tell us that we are not on the right track, that we must go this way or that way. For the most part, they are subjective and trivial because they are concerned only with esthetics. They are part of a new cult of beauty for beauty's sake, at all costs and no matter how arrived at.

Beauty is a consequential thing, a byproduct of solving problems correctly. It is unreal as the goal. Preoccupation with esthetics leads to arbitrary design, to buildings which take a certain form because the designer "likes the way it looks." No successful architecture can be formulated on a generalized system of esthetics; it must be based on a way of life. We must decide what is alive and vital in our culture and approach each problem with this in mind. By approaching things subjectively and in a materialistic way we will never learn what things are. We need to know what things are, and what they are for. We need to discover realities and meanings.

Architecture is a process, a way of bringing together spoken and unspoken needs in relation to reality. I think we have been confusing the process with the end product. We have been thinking of the building instead of man living in space and using space. We have been concerning ourselves with expressions instead of realitites.

Consider the often stated relationship between functionalism and the industrial process. The prewar buildings of the Bauhaus group and the postwar functionalist buildings in this country—Lever House, the Seagram Building, Crown Zellerbach in San Francisco—are claimed to be expressions of the industrial approach, but in fact they represent merely a handcraft approach, the only change being that machines are used to do what otherwise would have been done by hand; a machine esthetic has been constructed, and while this has transient importance in indicating future possibilities, it is still an esthetic system and therefore a limiting thing.

The industrial process, for example, has nothing built into it that suggests a modular system. There are modular systems in certain related activities such as cataloging, distribution, shipping, and warehousing, but the industrial process itself can be as fluid as we want it to be. I would suggest a radically different concept of its application to architecture. Conceive the implications of an enormous, completely automatic factory that never produces the same thing twice. Today this is possible. If we will look beyond esthetics, we will find that tools are available to deal with particularity that did not previously exist.

I would suggest that a few sentences in the internal revenue code have far more effect today on the general physical form of our communities than all the architects in the country. The reason may be that we have lost sight of the total impact of our work. We have run out of steam on the big problems like urban ghettos, which can be created either by abandonment or by construction.

A scientific and systematic approach to the process of architecture has one radical difference from the majority of classical systems: it does not depend on broad general laws, but on the particular nature of each individual problem, so that everything can be considered for what it is and nothing need be relegated to arbitrary categories. With this it should be possible to move on to a plastic, free approach where our primary media are space, light, and time—where the building itself disappears and we sense only space, light, and time.

—Joseph Esherick

In an attempt to break with "dogmatic" tradition, including the formalism of the Bauhaus, Joseph Esherick claims to have reverted to a utilitarian approach to design. Rejecting formal aesthetics and concepts of beauty, he pragmatically believes a building should not be judged by any arbitrary standards but only as good or bad in relation to its specific purpose. He rules out the associative functions of architecture as insignificant; he attempts to discover unique solutions to the problems of form and function.

Although sounding very mechanistic, Esherick retains a semblance of humanism and recognizes the need for ambiguity in architecture. The Cannery project in San Francisco, which gutted and transformed a Del Monte cannery into a large mall, well demonstrates Esherick's desire to create a rationalized irrationality. Its three-storey interior and roof plaza feature a stimulating and delightful pedestrian space of many turns, zigzags and corners, which offers the hint of a maze. While it is possible to go through the mall in a clear and obvious way, the option of "getting lost" also presents itself to the consumer. Ten means of vertical circulation, of which the most dramatic is a free-standing, glass-encased elevator, further contribute to the spatial experience.

Even the extremely brutalistic Wurster Hall, the environmental design building at the University of California, Berkeley, attempts to retain a sense of ambiguity. The utterly utilitarian building was described by *Architectural Forum* as a "wonderland of perhaps premeditated but evidently uncensored mechanical happenings." The plumbing, ventilation, and electrical conduits remain exposed and the walls are either of dense, smooth concrete or resawn redwood plywood panels which serve as bulletin boards. Little effort seems to have been expended to meld the various shapes and forms, including a ten-storey tower, into a coherent entity. The exterior window-sill heights vary to accommodate the lighting needs of the rooms without reference to massing or alignment with adjoining windows. As such, the building stands a testimony to Esherick's belief that architecture should not attempt a series of compromises to resolve conflict but rather should preserve oppositions and tensions.

The majority of Esherick's residential designs tend to be simple and rather stark, vertically elongated, two-storey boxes. Several are distinguished by pergola-like sun-shading devices that project out above each window. This innovation supplants the function of the traditional roof with overhanging eaves. One of the more exciting dwellings designed by Esherick is the McIntyre House, which features a central living space covered by a skylight. The concrete beams that support the glass roof also serve as gutters in rainy weather. This solarium-like room opens on a terraced garden court with rectilinear pools and waterways. The house itself, which is extremely compartmental to provide privacy for the various family members, displays very sleek lines which evoke a Spanish mission spirit and unite the varying roofline elevations.

Esherick's work displays an enormous diversity, as well it should if he has indeed forsaken the dictates of any universal laws of taste. Yet the vocabulary of Esherick's diversity remains very much tied to the functional postulates that have been in vogue for the past four decades. As such, much of his work's theoretical underpinning appears to make a virtue out of a commonly accepted artistic premise—that is, that every project presents distinct problems that require special solutions which are handled within the constraints of accepted form. Perhaps, as in Wurster Hall, Esherick's solutions are slightly more extreme and exaggerated than those of other function-oriented architects, but without a doubt, he remains fully ensconced within the dogmatic confines of the modern movement.

—Don J. Hibbard

FATHY, Hassan.

Egyptian. Born in Alexandria, 23 March 1900. Studied architecture, School of Engineering, Giza, Cairo, Dip.Arch. 1926. Worked at the Department of Municipal Affairs, Cairo, 1926-30. Since 1930, in private practice, Cairo: designed first mud-brick structures, 1940. Director of the School Building Department, Ministry of Education, Cairo, 1949-52; Consultant to the United Nations Relief and Works Agency, 1950; Consultant Architect, with Doxiadis Associates, Athens, 1957-62; Director of Pilot Projects for Housing, Ministry of Scientific Research, Cairo, 1963-65; Consultant to the Minister of Tourism, Cairo, 1963-65; Founder-Director, International Institute for Appropriate Technology, Cairo, since 1977. Instructor, 1930-46 and 1953-57, and Head of the Architectural Department from 1954, Faculty of Fine Arts, Cairo; Lecturer on Climate and Architecture, Athens Technical Institute, 1957-62; Lecturer on Philisophy and Aesthetics, Department of Town Planning and Architecture, al-Azhar University, Cairo, 1966; Lecturer on Rural Housing, Faculty of Agriculture, Cairo University, 1975-77. Member of the Steering Committee, Aga Khan Awards for Architecture, 1977-80. Exhibition: *Hassan Fathy*, Technische Universität, Vienna, 1980. Recipient: Chairman's Prize, Aga Khan Awards for Architecture, 1980; Gold Medal, International Union of Architects, 1985. Fellow, Adlai Stevenson Institute of International Affairs, Chicago; Honorary Fellow, American Institute of Architects; Fellow, American Research Centre of Cairo; Member, High Council of Arts and Letters, Egypt. Address: 4 Darb el Labbana, Citadel, Cairo, Egypt.

Works:

1940/
41 Experimental Housing for the Royal Society of Agriculture, Bahtim, Egypt
1942/
45 Hamed Said House, Marg Plain, near Cairo
1946/
53 New Gourna Village, near Luxor, Egypt
1954 Village rebuilding, Mit-el-Nasara, Egypt
1963/
65 High Institute of Social Anthropology and Folk Art, Cairo (project)
Bariz Village, Kharga Oasis, Egypt (project)
1966 Prototype Rural Housing Development, El Dareeya, Saudi Arabia
1970/
80 Series of private residences, Egypt
1974 Mansion for a V.I.P., Jeddah, Saudi Arabia (project)
1980 Dar el Islam Mosque Complex, Albiquiu, New Mexico

Publications:

By FATHY: books—*Gourna: A Tale of Two Villages*, Cairo 1969, as *Architecture for the Poor: An Experiment in Rural Egypt*, Chicago and London 1973; *The Arab House in the Urban Setting: Past, Present and Future*, London 1972; articles—"Le pays d'utopie" in *La Revue du Caire* (Cairo), November 1949; "La Voute dans l'architecture egyptienne" in *La Revue du Caire* (Cairo), May 1951; "Rural Self-Help Housing" in *Ekistics* (Athens), June 1962; "Planning and Building in the Arab Tradition: The Village Experiment at Gourna" in *The New Metropolis in the Arab World*, edited by Morroe Berger, New Delhi 1963; "An Ekistic Approach to the Problem of Roofing in Peasant House-Building" in *Ekistics* (Athens), June 1964; "Model Houses for El Dareeya, Saudi Arabia" in *Ekistics* (Athens), March 1966; "Constancy, Transposition and Change in the Arab City" in *Madina to Metropolis*, edited by L. Carl Brown, Princeton, New Jersey 1973; "Beyond the Human Scale," interview, with Yorick Blumenfeld in *Architectural Association Quarterly* (London), no. 3/4, 1974; "Self-Help Mud Building,

Hassan Fathy: Market Place, Gourna Village, Egypt, 1945-48.

Egypt" in *Architectural Design* (London), October 1976; "Gourna—Peasant Houses" in *L'Architecture d'aujourd'hui* (Paris), February 1978; "De l'implicite en architecture" in *Le M'Zab, une leçon d'architecture*, edited by André Ravereau, Paris 1981.

On FATHY: books—*Hassan Fathy*, exhibition catalogue, Vienna 1980; *Architecture and Community: Building in the Islamic World Today*, edited by Renata Holod and Darl Rastorfer, Millerton, New York 1983; *Hassan Fathy* by J.M. Richards, I. Serageldis and D. Rastorfer, London 1985; articles—"Le Nouveau Village de Gourna" in *Architecture française* (Paris), no. 73/74, 1947; "Gourna, ein architektonische Experiment in Aegypten" by Jakob Schilling in *Deutsche Bauzeitung* (Stuttgart), January 1965; "Nouveau Village de Gourna" in *L'Architecture d'aujourd'hui* (Paris), October/November 1968; "Gourna: A Lesson in Basic Architecture" by J.M. Richards in *Architectural Review* (London), February 1970; "An Architect Whose Clients are Peasants" in the *Christian Science Monitor* (Boston), 5 December 1974; "Hassan Fathy: The Logical Building Material Is What the Peasants Dig Out of the Ground" by Ursula Cliff in *Design and Environment* (New York), Spring 1976; "Hassan Fathy" by Jean-Pierre Cousin in *L'Architecture d'aujourd'hui* (Paris), February 1978; "A Billion Clients: Hassan Fathy" in *Inside Outside* (Bombay), February/March 1980; "Hassan Fathy," special issue of *Summarios* (Buenos Aires), November 1980; "Hassan Fathy Demonstrates Ancient Construction Methods in New Mexico" by Simone Swan in *Architectural Record* (New York), December 1980; "Egypt's Prophet of Appropriate Technology" by R.B. Marquis in *AIA Journal* (Washington, D.C.), December 1980; "Arab Architecture—Between Locality and University" by A. Ibrahim in *Alam Albena* (Heliopolis, Egypt), May 1982; "Tracking Down the Poet of Raw Bricks" by Attilio Petruccioli in *Spazio e società* (Milan), no. 5, 1982; "A Mosque for Albiquiu" by D. Dillon in *Progressive Architecture* (New York), June 1983.

Hassan Fathy has devoted himself to the task of housing the poor in developing nations. His work in a particular village in Egypt deserves the closest study by anyone involved in rural improvement.

The essence of his work and his approach in directing architectural planning to the needs of the poor are seen in the rural village of New Gourna, Egypt. It is located near Thebes and Luxor, on the eastern side of the Nile River near the famous Colossus of Memnon. The objective of New Gourna was to create an indigenous environment at a minimal cost, and in so doing to improve the economy and the standard of living in a rural area. Fathy planned a complete village in all its parts, using the familiar forms of Egyptian village design. He also planned the construction method of these buildings; it, too, corresponded to local tradition. The main materials were to be mud brick formed on site—in exactly the same way that brick had been made since ancient times. The forms of the structures also derived from ancient experience: thick, dense walls to absorb heat in daytime and to release it at night, and courtyards affording utility, openess, and privacy to both houses and communal buildings. Fathy also planned for the revival of ancient crafts.

In short, he devised a system for bring together ancient design methods by using modern organizational skills. In so doing he integrated a knowledge of the socio-economic composition of rural Egyptian society, of ancient architectural and town design techniques, of climate, of public health considerations, and of ancient craft skills. Fathy saw New Gourna not as an end in itself but as an experiment whose lessons could inform a national rural redevelopment program.

New Gourna was built, but numerous problems, including a sluggish if not resistant bureaucracy, prevented full success. But, as built, in three construction seasons, from 1945 to 1948, it was a strikingly beautiful architectural and urban ensemble.

—Paul Spreiregen

FEHLING, Hermann.

German. Born in Hyeres, France, of German parents, 10 September 1909. Educated in Lübeck and Hamburg, Germany; apprentice carpenter, Hamburg; studied architecture, Baugewerkschule, Hamburg. Served in the German Army, 1939-45. Married Dora Fränkel in 1954. Assistant in the studio of Erich Mendelsohn, *q.v.*, Berlin, 1929-30; worked on industrial building with Werner Issel, Berlin, 1931-37; in private architectural practice, Berlin, 1945-53; Partner, with Daniel Gogel, *q.v.*, Fehling + Gogel Architects, Berlin, since 1953. Exhibition: *Fehling + Gogel: Architekturen von 1947-1980*, Internationale Design Zentrum, Berlin, 1981. Recipient: First Prize in the competitions—Volksbühne Theatre, Berlin, 1948; Berlin Pavilion, at *Interbau*, 1956; Glass Industry Pavilion, at *Interbau*, 1956; Paulus Parish Centre, Mainz, West Germany, 1965; Max Planck Institute, Berlin, 1965; French School, Berlin, 1966; Zeli-Eck Housing Complex, Berlin, 1975; Max Planck Institute, Garching, West Germany, 1975; Technical University Auditorium, Berlin, 1978. Berlin Arts Prize, 1965. Honorary Professor, Technical University of Berlin, 1966. Member, Akademie der Künste, Berlin, 1961. Address: Margartenstrasse 4, 1000 West Berlin 33, Germany.

Works:

1943 House of Fragments, Berlin (project; with Sobottka and Müller)
1948 Volksbühne theatre, Berlin (competition project; with Sobottka and Müller)
1952 Studio/Capitol Cinemas (rebuilding of Mendelsohn's UFA-Palast), Lehniner Platz, Berlin
 Main Auditorium of the Free University, Berlin (with P. Pfankuch)
1954 Haas & Son Enamel Works Annex and Exhibition Stand, Sinn/Dillkreis, Germany
1955 Haas & Son bachelor apartment, Sinn/Dillkreis, Germany
With Daniel Gogel:
1953/
73 Four Schoeller Bookshops, Berlin
1955 Rhine Steelworks Headquarters Offices, Essen, West Germany (project)
1956/
57 Berlin Pavilion, *Interbau* exhibition, Berlin
 Glass Industry Pavilion, *Interbau* exhibition, Berlin
1956/
59 Student Residential Complex for the Free University, Nikolassee, Berlin
1957 Berlin Philharmonic Concert Hall, Berlin (competition project)
 Kolmar House, Blankensee, Hamburg, West Germany (project)
1957/
59 Platte House, Dahlem, Berlin
1958 Krüger House, Dahlem, Berlin (project)
1960/
63 Paul Gerhardt Church and Parish Centre, Schoneberg, Berlin
1961 Haas & Son Headquarters Offices, Sinn/Dillkreis, West Germany
1963 Kühlis-Gerber House, Berlin
1964 Koch House additions, Sinn/Dillkreis, West Germany
 Donges House, Sinn/Dillkreis, West Germany
1964/
66 Dr. Prawitz House, Gelnhausen, West Germany
1965 Dr. Krey House, Herborn/Dillkreis, West Germany (project)
 Workers' Housing Estate for Haas & Son, Sinn/Dillkreis, West Germany (project)
1965/
66 Alt-Schöneberg Parish Church and Community Centre, Berlin
1965/
67 Paulus Parish Centre, Mainz, West Germany (competition project)
1965/
68 Schatz House, Baden-Baden, West Germany
1965/
74 Max Planck Institute for Educational Research, Dahlem, Berlin
1966 Berliner Disconto Bank, Berlin (competition project)
 French School, Berlin (competition project)
1966/
74 Institute for Hygiene and Medical Microbiology, Free University, Lichterfelde, Berlin
1967 Schiller Archive extensions, Marbach, West Germany (competition project)
1968 Halleschen Ufer housing complex, Kreuzberg, Berlin
1968/
73 Funeral Chapel, Tegel, Berlin
1971 Centre for the Handicapped, Bofingen, Ulm, West Germany (competition project)
 Commercial and Business Offices, Kreuzberg, Berlin (competition project)
1973 Südlicher Tiergarten development, Berlin (competition project)
1974/
80 Housing Development on the Hindenburgdamm, Lichterfelde, Berlin
1975 Main Auditorium additions, Free University, Berlin
1975/
80 Zeli-Eck housing complex, Zehlendorf, Berlin (competition project)
 Max Planck Institute for Astrophysics, Garching, near Munich
1976/
80 European Southern Observatory, Garching, near Munich
1976/
81 Kleinen Messel housing complex, Berlin
1978 *Anonymes Design* exhibition layouts for Modus, Berlin
 Main Auditorium, Technical University, Berlin
 Hotel Berlin, Budapesterstrasse, Berlin (competition project)
 Institute for Meteorology, Free University, Berlin (project)
1979 Institute for Philosophy, Free University, Berlin (competition project)
1980 Tegeler Hafen housing and community development, Berlin (competition project)

Publications:

By FEHLING/GOGEL: articles—"Max Planck Institute" in *Bauwelt* (Berlin), 14 March 1980, and in *Deutsche Bauzeitung* (Stuttgart), January 1982.

On FEHLING/GOGEL: books—*The Voice of the Phoenix: Postwar Architecture in Germany* by John Burchard, London and Cambridge, Massachusetts 1966; *German Architecture 1960-1970* by Wolfgang Pehnt, Stuttgart and London 1970; *Der Kirchenbau des 20. Jahrhunderts in Deutschland* by Hugo Schnell, Munich and Zürich 1973; *Deutsche Kunst seit 1960: Architektur* by Paolo Nestler and Peter M. Bode, Munich 1976; *Bauen der 70er Jahre in Berlin* by Rolf Rave, Hans-Joachim Rave and Jan Rave, Berlin 1980; *Hermann Fehling + Daniel Gogel*, exhibition

Hermann Fehling and Daniel Gogel: Max Planck Institute for Educational Research, Dahlem, West Berlin, 1974.

distinct personality; there is no trace of "international" match-making.

The apparently free forms of their architecture show slight traces of the potent graphics of Le Corbusier's white architecture, of the Luckhardt brothers, of the playful visions of Bruno Taut, and the "organic functionalism" of Hugo Häring. Superficially, therefore, Fehling and Gogel could be placed in a line of descent from Scharoun—I say "superficially" because their work is unmistakably their own and free from any fashionable or inherited attitudes.

Fehling and Gogel develop their designs principally from the ground plan. Because a building for them in a body that (like that of man) is not square as a matter of course and because they feel that a building should have a face, an expression of its destiny, they arrive at impressive, plastic, extremely rhythmic spatial compositions. The buildings achieve their logic by means of a distinct, well-composed, functional structure.

In two of their most expressive buildings—the Max Planck Institute for Educational Research and the Institute of Hygiene, both in Berlin—the distinct order achieves harmony by the musicality of the free but not arbitrary spatial forms. It could be said that Fehling and Gogel's informing principle in these two buildings was this: "A building must be a pleasure to its users. When they are at work there, they should feel at home."

—Manfred Sack

catalogue edited by Ulrich Conrads and Manfred Sack, Berlin and Braunschweig, West Germany 1981; *L'Architettura di Fehling e Gogel: vitalita dell'espressionismo* by Piergiacomo Bucciarelli, Bari, Italy 1981; articles—"Fehling et Gogel: projects récentes" in *L'Architecture d'aujourd'hui* (Paris), October 1967; "Max Planck Institute for Educational Research" in *Bauwelt* (Berlin), 14 October 1974; "Institute for Hygiene and Medical Microbiology" in *Bauwelt* (Berlin), 14 March 1975; "A Work of Art for Science" by Gerhard Ullmann in *Bouw* (The Hague), 5 June 1976; "The Max Planck Institute" by Hans Moldenschardt in *Der Architekt* (Stuttgart), June 1977; "Institute for Astophysics in Garching, near Munich" in *Baumeister* (Munich), February 1978; "Contemporary Architects: Her-

mann Fehling and Daniel Gogel" in *Architecture + Urbanism* (Tokyo, August 1978, "State Library, Berlin" in *L'Architecture d'aujourd'hui* (Paris), April 1980; "The Staatsbibliothek in Berlin" in *Architettura* (Rome), November 1980; "Centrifugal Expressionism" by François Burkhardt in *Modo* (Milan), November 1981; "Works by Hermann Fehling and Daniel Gogel at Garching, Munich" in *Architettura* (Rome), January 1982.

The list of the buildings by Hermann Fehling and Daniel Gogel is not long. For, in their joint practice, each work is personally designed and drawn down to the smallest detail with a devotion and patience worthy of a medieval craftsman. Each work has a

---

FEHN, Sverre.

Norwegian. Born in Kongsberg, 14 August 1924. Educated at the Tønsberg Gymnasium; Oslo School of Architecture, Dip Arch. 1948. Married Ingrid Løvberg Pettersen in 1952; son: Guy. In private practice, Oslo, since 1949. Professor, Oslo School of Architecture, since 1970. Exhibitions: CIAM (Congrès Internationaux d'Architecture Moderne), Aix-en-Provence, France, 1953; *Bienal,* São Paulo, 1957; Vasa University, Finland, 1964; Galerie des Beaux-Arts, Paris, 1965; Museum of Modern Art, New York, 1968; Munch Museum, Oslo, 1973; Galleri Palladio, Oslo, 1981; Bergen Festival, Norway, 1982; Architectural Association of Minneapolis, Minnesota, 1983; Palazzo Paverna, Rome, 1984; Convent of St. Maria de Castello, Genoa, Italy, 1984; Reykjavik, Iceland, 1984. Recipient: First Prize, Norwegian Pavilion Competition, for the World's Fair, Brussels, 1956; First Prize, Nordic Pavilion Competition, for the *Biennale,* Venice, 1958; Anton Christian Hougens Award, Federation of Norwegian Architects, 1961 and 1975; First Prize, Church of Cap Nord Competition, 1965; First Prize, Tønsberg Housing Competition, 1967; Wood Prize, Norwegian Concrete Association/Council for Tree Information, 1973; Concrete Prize, Federation of Norwegian Architects/Norwegian Concrete Association, 1976; Prince Eugen Medal, Stockholm, 1982. Carnegie Distinguished Professor of Architecture, New York, 1980. Member, Order of Leopold, Belgium. Address: Havna Allé 15, Oslo 3, Norway.

Works:

1953 Handicraft Museum, Lillehammer, Norway (with Geir Grung)
1955 Økern Home for Elderly People, Oslo (with Geir Grung)
1958 Norwegian Pavilion, World's Fair, Brussels
1962 Nordic Pavilion, *Biennale,* Venice
1964 Villa Schreiner, Langmyrgrenda 79, Oslo Villa Norrkøping, Sweden

1966 Villa Arne Sejersted Bødtker, Setra vei 18, Oslo
1967 Villa Carl Sejersted Bødtker, Setra vei 16, Oslo
1970 Bøler Community Centre, Oslo
     Bøler Library, Oslo
1973 Archeological Museum, Hamar, Norway
1974 School for Deaf Children, Skådalsveien 33, Oslo
1980 Permanent Mediaeval Exhibition layouts, Ethnographic Museum, Oslo
1985 Villa Carl Sejersted Bødtker 2, Oslo

Publications:

By FEHN: articles—in *Byggekunst* (Oslo), March 1950, October 1951, May 1952, June 1952, April 1956, April 1958, April 1962, June 1962, May 1964, July 1968, August 1968, February 1971, April 1973, March 1975, and June 1978; *Arkitekten* (Helsinki), September 1954, August 1956, July 1966, and August 1966; *Byggmerstaren* (Stockholm), August 1958; *Architectural Design* (London), August 1958 and October 1963; *Domus* (Milan), no. 345, 1958, no. 424, 1965, no. 409, 1963, no. 461, 1968, and no. 481, 1969; *L'Architecture d'aujourd'hui* (Paris), no. 27, 1960, no. 38, 1962, and no. 49, 1964; *Werk* (Zürich), July 1961; *Forum* (Amsterdam), November 1962; *Bauen und Wohnen* (Zürich), December 1964; *Deutsche Bauzeitung* (Stuttgart), January 1965; "The Tree and the Horizon" in *Spazio e societa* (Milan), no. 11, 1980; "The School of Silence" in *Spazio e Società* (Milan) no. 13, 1980; "A Journey in a Forgotten World" in *Spazio e Società* (Milan), no. 17, 1980.

On FEHN: books—*Esposizioni esempi* by Roberto Aloi, Milan 1960; *The New Architecture of Europe* by G. E. Kidder-Smith, New York and London 1961; *Musei Architectura Technica* by Roberto Aloi, Milan 1962; *Intentions in Architecture* by C. Norberg Schulz, London 1963; *World Architecture I* and *II,* edited by John Donat, London 1964, 1965; *Decorative Art and Modern Interiors,* London 1979; *Sverre Fehn; The Thought of Construction* by Per Olaf Fjeld, New York 1983; articles—"Skådalen school" in *Byggekunst* (Oslo), no. 6, 1973; "Archaeological Museum in Stormhamarlaven, Hamar" in *Byggekunst* (Oslo), no. 3, 1975; "Preservation in Norway: Museum at Hamar" in *Domus* (Milan), October 1975; "C. Seiersted Bodtken House, Oslo, Norway, 1965-67", in *GA Houses* (Tokyo), April 1977; "Skådalen School (1969-1975)" in *Byggekunst* (Oslo), no. 6, 1978; "Library in Trondheim" in *Byggekunst* (Oslo), no. 1, 1979; "Skådalen School for the Deaf, Oslo" by Per Olaf Fjeld in *Arkitektur DK* (Copenhagen), no. 1, 1980; "Origins and History: Norway in Modern Architecture" by Christian Norberg-Schulz in *Parametro* (Bologna), March 1980; "Unappreciated Architects: The Architecture of Sverre Fehn" by Peter Cook in *Architectural Review* (London), August 1981; "Projects by Sverre Fehn" in *Byggekunst* (Oslo), no. 1, 1984.

*

By walking through the wood, you made a path. The rhythm of your footprints are marks for the column's base. The path, indicating your adventures, is architecture written on earth. In this image, we are all architects.

The materialized construction is the language of architecture, born by poetic thought. When constructions meet the earth, dimensions are born and the room is created.

No constructions have ever been more beautiful and great than those made around death—poems of life after death.

—Sverre Fehn

Sverre Fehn was one of the postwar generation of architects who emerged from the Oslo School with Norberg-Schulz, Grung, Mjelva, and Vesterlid. The influence of this generation on the postwar architecture in Norway was of the greatest importance. This group created a new architecture that was clearly based on the Modern Movement, but was expressed in a regional form both in the choice and use of materials and in the formal language. This renewal was essential to overcome the nationalistic tendencies of the immediate pre- and post-war periods which had resulted in an enfeebled aesthetic. The group was closely involved with CIAM, *Carré Bleu,* and Team 10. While Norberg-Schulz is the outstanding theoretician, Fehn is without doubt the most gifted practitioner in the group.

The Handicraft Museum at Lillehammer of 1953 was a major event in Norwegian architecture. It

Sverre Fehn: Nordic Pavilion, Venice Biennale, 1962.

established the new language. It was characterised by great clarity in form, organisation, and the use of materials. Twenty-five years later it is still an outstanding museum building.

Fehn has never been a dogmatist; his buildings have always had a human and poetic quality beyond and transforming the clear Modern Movement statement. This quality is perhaps most clearly revealed in his Nordic Pavilion at the Venice *Biennale* of 1962: the building, of the greatest simplicity, has also poetic qualities of light and subtleties of form.

Fehn has also explored the ideas of Japanese architecture in some deceptively simple timber houses. In the planning of these houses, he demonstrates a great sensitivity to the needs of the client, resulting in a refreshing freedom from the conventional plan. His more recent work at Hamar (an archaeological museum) and in Oslo (a school for deaf children) continues to exhibit his bold and firm grasp of form and materials at the same time as he continues to explore new architectural language.

—Michael Lloyd

FEILDEN, Bernard Melchior.

British. Born in London, 11 September 1919. Educated at Bedford School, 1927-37; worked in the office of O. P. Milne, architect, London, 1937-38; studied at the Bartlett School of Architecture, London (exhibitioner), 1938, and the Architectural Association School, London, 1946-49, Dip.A.A. (honours) 1949; awarded Bratt Colbram Travelling Scholarship, 1949. Served in the Royal Engineers, in India, the Middle East, and Italy, 1940-46: Captain. Married Ruth Bainbridge in 1949; children: Henry, Harriet, Mary, and Francis. Assistant in the office of J. Douglas Matthews, London, 1949-50, and E. Boardman and Son, Norwich, Norfolk, 1950-54; in private practice, Norwich, Norfolk, 1954-56; Partner, with David Mawson, Feilden and Mawson, Norwich, Norfolk, 1956-77; in private practice, Wells-next-the-Sea, Norfolk, since 1981. Architect, Norwich Cathedral, Norfolk, 1963-77; Surveyor to the Fabric, York Minster, England, 1965-77; Surveyor to St. Paul's Cathedral, London, 1969-77; Consultant Architect to the University of East Anglia, Norwich, Norfolk, 1969-77. Hoffman Wood Professor of Architecture, University of Leeds, West Yorkshire, 1973-74. Director of the International Centre for Conservation, Rome, 1977-81. Member of the Council, Royal Institute of British Architects, 1972-77; President, Ecclesiastical Architects and Surveyors Association, 1975-77, and Guild of Surveyors, 1976-77; U.K. Chairman, International Council on Monuments and Sites, Cathedrals National Advisory Commission, and the Council for the Care of Churches, since 1981; Executive Committee Member, Council for the Protection of Rural England, since 1981. Member of the Ancient Monuments Board of England. Recipient: Civic Trust Award, 1960 and 1968; Architectural Heritage Year Award, and Royal Institute of Chartered Surveyors Conservation Award, 1975. Honorary doctor of the University of York, England, 1973. Associate, 1949, and Fellow, 1968, Royal Institute of British Architects; Fellow of the Society of Antiquaries, 1969, and of the Royal Society of Arts, 1973; Honorary Fellow, University College, London, 1982. O.B.E. (Officer, Order of the British Empire), 1969; C.B.E. (Commander, Order of the British Empire), 1976. Address: Stiffkey Old Hall, Wells-next-the-Sea, Norfolk NR23 1QJ, England.

Works:

1954 Trinity Presbyterian Church, Norwich, Norfolk

1955 North Transept Roof, Norwich Cathedral, Norfolk (Conservation)
1956 Feilden and Mawson Offices, The Close, Norwich, Norfolk
1957 May and Baker Chemical Warehouse, Norwich, Norfolk
     F.W. Harmer Warehouse, Norwich, Norfolk
     Civic Trust Scheme, Magdalen Street, Norwich, Norfolk (project)
1958 May and Baker Warehouse, Dagenham, Essex
1959 Ambulatory Roof, Norwich Cathedral, Norfolk (conservation)
1960 South Transept Roof, Norwich Cathedral, Norfolk (conservation)
     Ethelberg Gateway, Norwich, Norfolk (conservation)
1961 Aylsham Scheme, Norfolk (project)
1962 Heslington Hall and Kings Manor, University of York, England (conservation)
1963 Spire, Norwich Cathedral, England (conservation)
     The Village, University of East Anglia, Norwich, Norfolk with David Luckhurst)
1964 Wessex Hotel, Winchester, Hampshire (with consultant Lord Esher)
     Raynham Hall, Norfolk (conservation)
1967 Tower and Bells, Wymonham Abbey, Norfolk (conservation)
1968 Tower, Norwich Cathedral, Norfolk (conservation)
     St. Paul's School, Barnes, London (with Ray Thompson and Graham Keith)
     Bauchim Chapel Screen, Norwich Cathedral, Norfolk
     Bauchim Chapel Ceiling, Norwich Cathedral, Norfolk (conservation)
     Bishop's Throne, Norwich Cathedral, Norfolk
     Bell Hotel, Thetford, Norfolk (conservation and extension; with Mary Reader)
1969 Feilden and Mawson Offices, Riverside Road, Norwich, Norfolk (with Malcolm Rose)
1970 Nave Roof, Norwich Cathedral, Norfolk (conservation)
     Teaching Hall, University of East Anglia, Norwich, Norfolk (with David Luckhurst)
     Dining Halls, University of East Anglia, Norwich, Norfolk (with Geoffrey Mitchell)

Bernard Feilden: New Treasury, York Minster, 1967-77.

Chapel, University of East Anglia, Norwich, Norfolk (with Simon Crosse)
     Registry and Senate, University of East Anglia, Norwich, Norfolk (with David Luckhurst)
     The Square, University of East Anglia, Norwich, Norfolk (with Geoffrey Mitchell)
     The Broad, University of East Anglia, Norwich, Norfolk (with Rosamunde Reich)
     University of East Anglia Master Plan and Landscaping, Norwich, Norfolk (with Maldwyn Morgan)
     Science Block, Greshams School, Holt, Norfolk (with Graham Keith)
     Barclays Bank, Swaffham, Norfolk (with Charles Carus)
1972 Watney Mann Brewery, Norwich, Norfolk (with Graham Keith)
     Dining Halls, Greshams School, Holt, Norfolk (with Graham Keith)
1973 York Minster, England (conservation)
     Nave Aisles, Norwich Cathedral, Norfolk
1975 Welcoming Area, Norwich Cathedral, Norfolk
1976 Chesterfield Town Centre Conservation Plan, Derbyshire (project)
1977 West Tower, St. Paul's Cathedral, London (restoration)
     Doors, organ rebuilding, lighting and choir cleaning, St. Paul's Cathedral, London (restoration)
     West Front and Upper Close, Norwich Cathedral, Norfolk (landscaping)
     Hyde Park Estate, London (as consultant)
     St. Giles Cathedral, Edinburgh (as consultant)
     Kitchens, Buckingham Palace, London (with Graham Keith)

Publications:

By FEILDEN: books—*The Wonder of York Minster* York 1976; *Conservation of Historic Buildings*, London 1978, 1982; articles—"Training for Restoration" in *Architectural Review* (London), November 1970; "Saving York Minster" in *International Nickel* (London), 1970; "The Restoration of York Minster" in *Chartered Surveyor* (London), August 1974;

"Vibration from Motor Traffic" in *European Heritage* (London), no. 2, 1974; "Training for Conservation: A European View," with Derek Linstrum, in *Architectural Review* (London), January 1975; "Craftsmen for Conservation"in *Quantity Surveyor* (London), January 1975; "The Storehouse of Tradition" in *Architectural Association Quarterly* (London), January/March 1975; "The Care of Cathedrals and Churches" in *Royal Society of Arts Journal* (London), March 1975; "Feasibility Study for Setting Up Training Schools for Craftsmen in Venice" in *Council of Europe Pro Venetia Report*, Strasbourg, France 1977; "An Introduction to Conservation," report for Unesco, Paris 1978; "Conservation of the Architectural Heritage" in *Council of Europe Bulletin* (Strasbourg, France), no. 17, 1981; "Dialogues: Museums," with G. Schichilone, in *Museum* (Paris), no. 1, 1982; "The Case for Conservation" in *International Architect* (London), no. 5, 1984.

On FIELDEN: articles—"The Road to Rome: Bernard Feilden Takes Over as Director of the International Centre for the Preservation and Restoration of Culture Property" by Vic Tapner in *Building Design* (London), July 1977; "The Conservation Brotherhood" by Vic Tapner in *Building Design* (London), October 1977; "Diagnosis for Decay" by Penny McGuire in *Building Design* (London), 26 January 1979; "Feilden Faces the Prospect of the World's Crumbling Buildings" in *Building Design* (London), 30 November 1979; "Conservation Profile 4: Bernard Feilden" by Vic Tapner in *Building Refurbishment and Maintenance* (London), April 1980.

*

I have believed in architecture but learned that it can be both good and bad. Architecture enables man to become human and should, therefore, be humane and not totalitarian. Architects should define what they mean by the word *architecture*. Through architecture, man is enabled to fulfill his needs for living, working, leisure, and social, cultural, and spritual activities. Architecture includes, by extension, town or city, the whole built environment. I have learned much from my work with amenity societies.

Architecture must be structurally stable, weatherproof, able to moderate the external climate to give internal comfort, economical in scarce materials and metals, and durable, with low maintenance costs. Design should be for long life, flexibility, and low energy consumption. All this may seem simple common sense, but, with the exception of stability, modern technology in the last twenty-five years has not been outstandingly successful in solving the above problems, nor have designers understood buildings as unified spatial environmental systems. Historic buildings are a laboratory of experience. I would suggest that architectural students should be taught how to evaluate buildings and make intelligible criticism; they should also be taught the causes of decay in buildings and the importance of designing for maintenance.

I believe that to produce human architecture, the architect must have a deep-rooted empathy with the users of his buildings, a fellow feeling for their fears and hopes, and a responsible attitude to possible dangers. The practice of architecture is not for self-expression and nothing is less original than trying to be original. Design must have unity if the architect is to be an effective artist, and the skilled men who carries out his work must have an appreciation of the artist's aims as well as job satisfaction in its execution—hence my deep interest in the state of the building craftsman, my writings on the subject, and my gratitude to them.

Conservation of historic buildings and a modern practice go hand in hand, as the latter proposes new techniques and the former teaches humility and old lessons if the building is understood as a spatial environmental system. In this work, the architect

must accept responsibility and not be afraid of decisions—some of which must be made quickly if men's lives are at stake, as I found in my work on the Spire at Norwich or in ordering the evacuation of San Michele twelve hours before a part fell. In conservation, the architect is like a conductor—with the building as the musical score and the building team as the orchestra.

To produce humane architecture that looks better ten years after it has been built has been the policy of my partnership who have nobly supporated my in my major works of conservation, at Norwich, York, and St. Paul's.

—Bernard Feilden

*

Bernard Feilden's English architectural practice was devoted to both new building and conservation, reflecting his own interests and capabilities. To a much greater extent than in most other countries, British architecture in the 1960s and 1970s particularly centred on problems of combining new with old and making the best of the old (in the long run this attitude may produce one of the most interesting national architectures of the time). Feilden has been a leader in this movement.

Infill buildings in Norwich and on the Hyde Park Estate, London, are among the subtle works he directed. At the end of a terrace of historic houses, a new Feilden building might be a facsimile done with integrity, or a complementary contemporary one: he has ample self-confidence to rely on his personal judgement above rulebook principles to determine which course to follow, not unlike the bold eclectics of years ago. In conservation matters he recognizes that taste and discretion must combine with historical knowledge. That attitude makes a difference from the hack conservationism sometimes practised by official planners and design controllers; Feilden has had his battles with these experts but has usually won.

An able scholar and charismatic teacher, Feilden nevertheless deserves consideration mainly on the basis of his practice. His reliance upon judgement augmented with advanced scientific capability is like that of an updated Viollet-le-Duc. As appreciation of the useful life of historical architecture continues to grow, our pains to preserve the existing stock of buildings will have to increase, and we are probably only at the beginning of an endless interest in architectural conservation: any idea about continuity in the man-made world that excludes conservation is inconceivable. The kind of skill and insight Feilden has demonstrated is fundamental to architecture's immediate future. He must be reckoned a crucial exemplar in both national and international spheres.

—Nathan Silver

FIGINI, Luigi.

Italian. Born in Milan, 27 January 1903. Educated at the Liceo Leone XIII, Milan; School of Architecture, Milan Polytechnic, 1921-26, Dip.Arch. 1926. Served in the Italian Army, 1928. Married Teresa Bottinelli in 1935. Founder-Member, with Guido Frette, Sebastiano Larco, Adalberto Libera, Gino Pollini, *q.v.,* Carlo Enrico Rava and Giuseppe Terragni, *q.v.,* Gruppo 7, Milan, 1927-29. In partnership with Gino Pollini, Milan, 1929 until his death in 1984. Member, MIAR (Movimento Italiano per l'Architettura Razionale), 1930-32, and Quadrante, Milan, 1933-35. Member of CIAM (Congrès Internationaux d'Architecture Moderne). Contributor to the magazines *Natura, Quadrante, Comunità,* and *Chiesa e quartiere,* Milan. Exhibitions: Rationalist Architecture Exhibition, *Biennale,* Monza, Italy, 1927; *Triennale,* Monza, 1930; Modern Architecture Exhi-

bition, Museum of Modern Art, New York, 1931; Union des Artistes Modernes, Paris, 1932; IV CIAM, Athens, 1933; CIAM Pavilion, *Triennale,* Milan, 1933; *Italian Aeronautical Exhibition,* Milan, 1934; *Triennale,* Milan, 1936; VII CIAM, Bergamo, Italy, 1949; *Italian Architecture,* London, 1952 (toured the United Kingdom); *The Modern Movement in Italy: Architecture and Design,* Museum of Modern Art, New York, 1953 (toured the United States); *Triennale,* Milan, 1954; *Mostra documentaria dell' architecturea sacra italiana del dopoguerra,* Bologna, Italy 1955; *Triennale, Milan,* 1960; *Milano 70-70,* Museo Poldi Pezzoli, Milan, 1971; *Domus: 45 anni dell'architettura,* Louvre, Paris, 1973; *Il razionalismo e l'architettura italiana durante il fascismo,* Venice, 1976; *Utopia e crisi dell'antinatura,* at the *Biennale,* Venice, 1978; *Design Process—Olivetti 1908-78,* University of California, Los Angeles, 1979; *28/78 Architettura,* Palazzo delle Stelline, Milan, 1979; *Figini e Pollini: architetti,* Padiglione d'Arte Contemporanea, Milan, 1980; *F. Melotti/L. Figini e G. Pollini/R. Melotti,* Rovereto, Italy, 1984. Member, Accademia di San Luca, and the Accademia Tiberina. *Died* (in Milan) *15 March 1984.*

Works:

1927 Garage (project; with Gruppo 7)
      Casa del Dopolavoro (project; with Gruppo 7)
1930 Electric House, *Triennale,* Monza, Italy (with Gruppo 7)
1931 De Angeli-Frua Offices, Milan (with Gino Pollini and Luciano Baldessari)
      Bar Craja, Milan (with Gino Pollini and Luciano Baldessari)
1933 Artist's House and Studio, *Triennale,* Milan (with Gino Pollini)
1934 Sala dei Precursori, *Italian Aeronautical Exhibition,* Milan (with Gino Pollini)
      Figini House, Villaggio dei Giornalisti, Milan
      Palazzo del Littorio, *Mostra della rivoluzione fascista,* Rome (competition project; with Gino Pollini, BBPR, and Luigi Danusso)
1934/
57   Olivetti Factory, Nursery School, Workers' Housing, and Social Services Centre, Ivrea, Italy (with Gino Pollini)
1935 Plan for the New Town of Ivrea, Italy (with Gino Pollini)
1936 Living Room and Roof Garden, *Triennale,* Milan (with Gino Pollini)
      Brera Academy, Milan (with Gino Pollini, Pietro Lingeri, and Giuseppe Terragni)
      Master plan for the Val d'Aosta (with Gino Pollini, BBPR, Piero Bottoni, and other)
1939 Sala del Volo, Milan (exhibition project; with Gino Pollini)
1942 Villa Manusardi, Cartabbia, Italy (with Gino Pollini)
1946 Master plan for the centre of Milan (with Gino Pollini, BBPR, Piero Bottoni, Franco Albini, and others)
1948 Apartment and Office Building, Via Broletto, Milan (with Gino Pollini)
1951 INA-CASA Housing Estate, Via Harar, Milan (with Gino Pollini and Gio Ponti)
1952 Plan for the Borgo Porto Conte, Sardinia, Italy (with Gino Pollini)
1954 Church of the Madonna of the Poor, Milan (with Gino Pollini)
1957 Apartment building, Via Circo, Milan (with Gino Pollini)
      Hoepli Building, Milan (with Gino Pollini)
1963 Pozzi Ceramic Factory Industrial Complex, Sparanise, near Caserta, Italy (with Gino Pollini)
      Church for the CEP Housing Scheme, near Bergamo, Italy (project; with Gino Pollini)
      Hotel Largo Augusta, Milan (with Gino Pollini and C. Blasi)
1974 Villa Guida, Guanzate, Italy (with Gino Pollini)

1976 IACP Housing Development, S. Giuliano Milanese, Italy (with Gino Pollini and G. Marini)
1977 Church of Master Ecclesiae, Rome (project; with Gino Pollini and G. Marini)
1983/
84 Church of the Madonna of the Poor extensions, Milan (project)

Publications:

By FIGINI: books—*Il piano regolatore della Valle d'Aosta,* with Gino Pollini, BBPR, Piero Bottoni and others, Ivrea, Italy 1943; *L'Elemento verde e l'abitazione,* Milan 1950; articles—"Architectura," with Gruppo 7, in *Rassegna italiana* (Rome), December 1926; "Gli stranieri," with Gruppo 7, in *Rassegna italiana* (Rome), February 1927; "Impreparazione, incomprensione, pregiudizi," with Gruppo 7, in *Rassegna Italiana* (Rome), March 1927; "Una nuova epoca arcaica," with Gruppo 7, in *Rassegna Italiana* (Rome), May 1927; "Un Programma di architettura," with Gino Pollini and others in *Quadrante* (Milan), May 1933; "Realazione al progetto del Palazzo del Littorio," with Gino Pollini, BBPR, and Luigi Danusso, in *Quadrante* (Milan), August/September 1934; "Appunti per una casa" in *Quadrante* (Milan), no. 33, 1936; "Diario illustrato di Ibiza, isla blanca" in *Domus* (Milan), November 1951; "Origines de l'architecture moderne en Italie," with Gino Pollini, in *L'Architecture d'aujourd'hui* (Paris), June 1952; "Comunicazione al Congresso Nazionale di Architettura Sacra" in *Dieci Anni di Architettura Sacra in Italia,* Bologna, Italy 1956; "Intervista con gli architetti Figini e Pollini" in *Edilizia popolare* (Milan), November/December 1959.

On FIGINI: books—*Figini e Pollini* by Eugenio Gentili, Milan 1959; *Figini e Pollini* by Cesare Blasi, Milan 1963 (includes bibliography); *New Italian Architecture* by Alberto Galardi, Stuttgart and London 1967; *La cultura architettonica in Italia tra le due guerre* by Cesare De Seta, Rome 1972, 1983; *CIAM:Dokumente 1928-1939,* edited by Martin Steinman, Basel and Stuttgart 1979; *Design Process—Olivetti 1908-1978,* exhibition catalogue, by Nathan H. Shapira, Los Angeles 1979; *Luigi Figini e Gino Pollini: architetti,* exhibition catalogue, edited by Vittorio Savi, Milan 1980; *La casa elettrica di Figini e Pollini* by Giacomo Polin, Rome 1982; *F. Melotti, L. Figini e G. Pollini, R. Melotti,* exhibition catalogue, by C. Melograni, Rovereto, Italy 1984; articles—"Luigi Figini's House" in *Interiors* (New York), July 1950; "Luigi Figini e Gino Pollini" in *Epoca* (Milan), December 1956; "L'architecte et sa maison" in *Architecture* (Paris), July 1957; "Figini e Pollini" by S. Tintori in *Casabella-Continuita* (Milan), October 1959; "Figini e Pollini" by Pier Carlo Santini in *Comunita* (Milan), no. 76, 1960; "Figini e Pollini" by Joseph Rkywert in *Architectural Design* (London), August 1967; "Bottoni, Figini, Pollini and BBPR and the Valle d'Aosta Plan" by Ezio Bonfanti in *Controspazio* (Bari, Italy), October 1973; "House by Luigi Figini, 1934-35" by S. Nagao and Y. Tominaga in *Space Design* (Tokyo), September 1977; " 1935: Home of an Architect" in *Abitare* (Milan), September 1978; "Luigi Figini 1903-1984: la bontà dell'architettura" by Giacomo Polin in *Casabella* (Milan), May 1984.

Luigi Figini and Gino Pollini, exact contemporaries, both trained at the Polytechnic in Milan. With their junior by one year, Giuseppe Terragni, and four others, they founded the Gruppo 7, with which Italian "modern" or "rational" architecture begins in 1927, and showed a project in the first exhibition of Rationalist architecture at the Monza *Biennale* of that year. Their first important commission was the Electric House for the Monza *Triennale* of 1930,

followed, in 1931, by their first industrial building, the De Angeli Frua Offices in Milan (with Luciano Baldessari). For the *V Triennale* in Milan in 1933 they designed an Artist's House and Studio; the studio looked on Marino Marini's first large horsemen. Like most Italian architects, in 1934 they entered the competition for the Palazzo Littorio in Rome (with Luigi Danusso and BBPR). They went on to design the new Brera Academy, with Pietro Lingeri and Giuseppe Terragni. Although by 1935 they were doing much domestic and exhibition work, as well as furniture, their most important next step was their collaboration with Adriano Olivetti for whom they designed the new Olivetti factory in Ivrea (first stage, 1934-35; second stage, 1939-41; third stage, with Annibale Fiocchi, 1947-49; fourth stage, 1956-57). They also designed the nursery school there (1939-41), workers' housing (1940), projected (unbuilt) cafeteria (1940), and built the social services centre (1954-57).

Olivetti also promoted the regional development plan for the Valle d'Aosta, which Figini and Pollini ambitiously prepared with Piero Bottoni and BBPR in 1936. Its publication during the war was seen as a harbinger of postwar ideas. This was not the case, and Olivetti's campaign for regional development in Italy has had little effect.

After the wartime hiatus, their first important building was the flat/office block in the Via Broletto, Milan, a return to the prewar elegance of their geometrical refinements. But perhaps their most influential single building is the small Church of the Madonna of the Poor in an industrial suburb of Milan: it transforms the geometries developed in industrial and office building to the needs of a suburban parish, in a new translation of the early Christian basilica. Another church, for the CEP Housing Scheme near Bergamo, adopts this approach less successfully to a much larger scale.

The general loss of direction Italian architecture suffered in the 1950s is reflected by their INACASA Housing Estate in Milan (with Gio Ponti) and in some other less happy housing blocks. The large ceramic factory for Pozzi at Sparanise near Caserta (Naples) has, however, much of the earlier assurance and inventiveness. In the last fifteen years, before Figini's death, most of the partnership's work was in housing and office building in Milan.

—Joseph Rykwert

FILGUÉIRAS Lima, João.
Brazilian. Born in Rio de Janeiro, 10 January 1932. Educated at the Colegio Santa Catarina, Rio de Janeiro, 1939-43; Colegio Militar, Rio de Janeiro, 1943-49; Escola Militar, Aqulhas Negras, 1949; National Faculty of Architecture, University of Rio de Janeiro, 1950-55, Dip.Arch. 1955. Married Alda Rabello Cunha in 1960; children: Luciana, Adriana, and Sonia. Worked as a clerk in the Naval Ministry, Rio de Janeiro, 1949-50; Technical Designer, Arquitec Ltda., Rio de Janeiro, 1950-52; Technical Designer, 1952-55, and Architect, 1955-58, 1961-62, IAPB (Institute of Retirement and Pensions of Bankers), Rio de Janeiro; Managing Architect, Constructions Ltda., Brasilia, 1958-60; Executive Secretary, with Oscar Niemeyer, *q.v.,* Planning Centre, University of Brasilia, 1962-65; worked in collaboration with Oscar Niemeyer, Brasilia, 1962-70; Head Architect, Department of Architecture, Projectum Ltda., Brasilia, 1970-71. Since 1971, in private practice, Brasilia. Coordinator of the Post-Graduate Course, Faculty of Architecture, University of Brasilia, 1962-65. Architectural Consultant, Hospital Foundation, Brasilia, 1969-72. Exhibitions: *Architecture Bienal,* Brasilia, 1969; *Bienal,* São Paulo, 1974. Address: SCRN Q-714, Block G-1 17/19, W-3-N Brasilia, Brazil.

Works:

1958 Temporary residence for IAPS employees, Brasilia
1960 Cesar Prates House, SHI, S-QL-1, Brasilia
1962 Staff Residence, University of Brasilia
General Services Building, University of Brasilia
Colina Housing Complex, University of Brasilia
1963 Faculty of Sciences, University of Brasilia (with Oscar Niemeyer)
1965 Volkswagen Factory, Brasilia
Disbrave Headquarters, Brasilia
1966 Waldir Fonseca House, SHI, S-QL-1/8, Brasilia
1967 Public Libraries, Brasilia (with Oscar Niemeyer)
Cultural Centre, Brasilia (with Oscar Niemeyer)
1968 Taguatinga Hospital, Brasilia
National Congress Annex 1, Brasilia (with Oscar Niemeyer)
1969 Aloysio Campos da Paz House, ML-1, Brasilia
1970 Ministry of Defence, Brasilia (with Oscar Niemeyer)
1971 Residence of the Minister of Planning, Brasilia
Rabello Construction Building, Brasilia
1972 Tennis Academy, Brasilia
Museum, Brasilia (with Oscar Niemeyer)
National Congress Annex 11, Brasilia (with Oscar Niemeyer)
Assembly Hall, House of Deputies, Brasilia (with Oscar Niemeyer)
João Machado House, Est. Tres Rios-Jacarepagua, Rio de Janeiro
1973 Rogério Ulissea House, SH1, S-QL-3, Brasilia
Portobras Building, Brasilia
Engine Rebuilding Plant, Brasilia
DASP Training Centre, Brasilia
Mercedes-Benz Factory, Brasilia
Ford-Planalto Factory, Brasilia
1974 Church of Ascensão do Senhor, Salvador, Brazil
Commercial Federation of Brasilia Headquarters, Brasilia
Comargo Correa Complex, Brasilia
Disbrave Building, Brasilia
Salvador Administration Centre Secretariat, Salvador, Brazil
Exhibition Centre, Salvador, Brazil
1975 José da Silva Netto House, S-1, Brasilia
Codipe Building, Public Utility Sector, Brasilia
Nivaldo Borges House, Mansion Sector, Brasilia
1976- Hospital for Locomotor Diseases, Brasilia
1977 DAHER Surgical Clinic, Brasilia
Filgueiras Studio, SCRN 714, BGL 17/19, Brasilia
1979 Research Centre for the Cerrado Regions, Brasilia
Mario Kertesz House, Pituba Beach, Salvador, Brazil
Eduardo Kertz House, Mansion Sector Lake, Brasilia
Secretariat of Finance, for the Government of Bahia, Salvador, Brazil

Publications:

By FILGUÉIRAS: articles—"Block of Flats for the Teachers of the Univeristy of Brasilia" and "General Services Building of the Univeristy of Brasilia" in *Modulo* (Rio de Janeiro), no. 28, 1963; "Disbrave: Volkswagen Workshop" in *L'Oeil* (Lausanne, Switzerland), no. 184, 1970; "Church for the Administration Centre of Salvador, Exhibition Centre of Salvador, and Secretariat of the Administration Centre of Salvador" in *Architecture Review* (Rio de Janeiro), no. 7, 1974; "Church for the Centre of

Salvador, Exhibition Centre of Salvador, and Centre of Administration of Salvador" in *Modulo* (Rio de Janeiro), no. 40, 1975; "Residence of José da Silva Netto" in *Modulo* (Rio de Janeiro), no. 43, 1976; "Hospital of Taguatinga" in *Modulo* (Rio de Janeiro), no. 44, 1976; "Hospital Planning" in *Modulo* (Rio de Janeiro), no. 45, 1977; "Research Centre for the Cerrado Regions" in *Modulo* (Rio de Janeiro), no. 48, 1977; "Headquarters of Portobras" in *Modulo* (Rio de Janeiro), no. 52, 1978.

On FILGUÉIRAS: articles—"Les Progrès de Brasilia" by Francois Loyer in *L'Oeil* (Lausanne, Switzerland), no. 184, 1970; "A Arquitetura Brasileira ate hoje" by Italo Campofiorito in *Modulo* (Rio de Janeiro), no. 42, 1976; "Taguatinga District Hospital" in *Modulo* (Rio de Janeiro), March/April 1977; "Corrados Cattle Raising Research Centre" in *Modulo* (Rio de Janeiro), April/May 1978; "Official Residence for the Minister of State, Brasilia" in *Modulo* (Rio de Janeiro), June/July 1978; "Headquarters of Portobras, Brasilia" in *Modulo* (Rio de Janeiro), December 1978/January 1979; "Bahia Administrative Centre, Salvador" in *Summa* (Buenos Aires), October 1979; "Daher Clinic, Brasilia" in *Modulo* (Rio de Janeiro), November/December 1979; "João Filgueiras Lima, Architect" in *Modulo* (Rio de Janeiro), February 1980; "The Central Administration of Bahia Church, Salvador, Brazil" in *Summa* (Buenos Aires), May 1980; "Modern Brazilian Architecture", special issue of *Process: Architecture* (Tokyo), August 1980.

*

One of the essential factors which enables me to exercise the liberty of creation and to guarantee a result that is architecturally valid is the comprehension of the process of construction from the initial phase of conception.

This does not simply mean that I must go into the chosen techniques in depth and that I must also search for the sources of material and labour beyond those available. What is demanded, above all, is a realization of the fact that the construction starts from a constant critical awareness of the social and technological context and the will to confront the distorted, unjust, and predatory structures that man has instituted.

—João Filgueiras Lima

*

João Filgueiras Lima's work is of two coexisting kinds, differentiated from each other by the nature of the building methods employed. The first, of traditional construction, is marked by a strong expression of structural concrete and results in massive-looking architectural objects with compact and unitary volumes. Examples are the Exhibition Centre in Salvador, the Portobras Building in Brasilia, and the houses for the Minister of Planning and José da Silva Netto, both in Brasilia. A certain reference to Oscar Niemeyer's latest work can be detected, the architect having collaborated with Niemeyer for quite a long time at the beginning of his career. However, unlike the master, it is not when employing free-flowing forms but when relying on the disciplinary support of the constructive units, which characterizes his second manner, that Filgueiras Lima is most successful. This second manner is important for its use and improvement of prefabrication methods. Prefabrication is not a common practice in Brazil, but Filgueiras Lima has obtained outstanding results with the formal and spatial qualities of his buildings.

At an early stage, he worked on a concrete prefabrication system reminiscent of wood construction—as in the General Services Building and, much more sophisticated, in the charming Colina Housing Complex at the University of Brasilia. Precise technology is vigorously displayed inside the flats as well as on the facades, and the very long spans, which give the buildings their lightness, are "conquered" by pre-stressed concrete beams

attached to the pillars by steel pins.

More recently, Filgueiras Lima has been using a system of structural concrete boxes that form the load-bearing facades that support the floor-slabs. Despite the restrictions of such a repetitive vocabulary, the resulting mass, which expresses the demands of the different functions, has quite a variegated profile and suggests a discreet organic tendency. Two very important examples are the Taguatinga Hospital, near Brasilia, and the Salvador Administration Centre.

Because it stretches flatly over a large area, Taguatinga Hospital emphasizes the gentle slope of the site on which it is built and reaches out to the vast horizon in a way that is so typical of Brasilia. The building is composed of two blocks, tied together by towers for vertical circulation. The wards are in a long and echeloned building of structural concrete boxes. The ambulatory areas, surgical centre, and other services are located in a low-lying construction, lighted and ventilated by a "shed" roof of concrete "Y" beams. Both blocks can be extended at will without interfering with existing activities and without disrupting the appearance of the whole. Such "open-ended" aesthetics, clearly readable in the complex articulation of the mass, plus the subtle relationship of the building to the surrounding countryside, and the high quality of the technical solutions, make Taguatinga Hospital one of the most important recent projects on the Brazilian architectural scene.

The Salvador Administration Centre is placed on very uneven ground: it can only be reached "from the top." Respecting the existing topography, Filgueiras Lima designed seven long and narrow buildings that are mounted on "bridges" that follow the winding contour of the hillside. This system of construction on "bridges" is the same as that used for the ward block at Taguatinga; vertical circulation, audi-

toriums, cafeterias, and other special functions are enclosed in individual volumes attached to the office-block spines.

Filgueiras Lima's more recent Hospital for Locomotor Diseases in Brasilia, is distinguished by the use of Virendeel trusses, with octagonal openings that support and enclose the floors, which are in turn supported by eight powerful pylons containing the stairs and lifts. The functional solution is carefully thought out—Filgueiras Lima is a specialist in hospital building—and the wards, which open on two sides onto double-height "loggias" (reminiscent in disposition and elevation of Le Corbusier's first project for a house in Carthage), provide the patients with generous amounts of light, sun, and greenery.

—Jorge Czajkowski

*

FINTA, József.

Hungarian. Born in Kolozsvár (now Cluj, Rumania), 12 June 1935. Studied at the Faculty of Architecture, Budapest Technical University, graduated 1958; Master School of the Union of Hungarian Architects, Budapest, 1958-60. Married Zsuzsa Zarka in 1963. Architect, then Chief Architect, Lakóterv housing design and public buildings company, Budapest, since 1958. Associate Professor, Budapest Technical University, 1979. Recipient: First Prize, Salgótarján City Centre Plan Competition, 1963; Ybl Miklós Prize, Budapest, 1965, 1972; First Prize, Danube Bank Competition, Budapest, 1966; Hungarian State Prize, 1970; Pro Urbe Award, Budapest, 1983. Czechoslovakian Order of Labour, 1974; Hungarian Order of Labour, 1983; Doctor of

József Finta: Hotel Forum, Budapest, 1981.

the Hungarian Academy of Sciences, 1984. Address: Lágymányosi u. 16.1.5, 1111 Budapest XI, Hungary.

Works:

1963 Master Plan for Salgótarján, Hungary
1966 Shopping Centre, Salgótarján, Hungary
       Plan for reconstruction of hotels on the Danube-bank, Budapest
1969 Hotel Duna intercontinental, Budapest
1971 Hotel Volga, Budapest
1972 Housing, Salgótarján, Hungary
1974 Hotel Bratislava, Pozsony, Czechoslovakia
1979 Hotel Voronyezs, Brno, Czechoslovakia
1981 Hotel Forum, Budapest
       Students' Hostel, Budapest
1982 Hotel Novotel, Budapest
       Hotel Penta, Budapest
1984 Zentral Wechsel–und Creditbank, Vienna
       Hotel Hungaria, Vienna (with Egyed and Hohenegger)
1984/
85   Congress Centre, Budapest
1985 Hotel Taverna, Budapest

Publications:

By FINTA: books—*Blocks of Buildings*, Budapest 1970; *Hungarian Architecture*, with Jenö Szendröi, Budapest 1972; *Neue Architektur in Ungarn*, Budapest and Munich 1978; *Plans-Troubles-Thoughts*, Budapest 1978; *Fine Arts and Architecture*, lecture paper, Budapest 1981; *About our Architecture*, Budapest 1982; article—"Where is the Architecture?" in *Magyar Epitómüvészet* (Budapest), no. 2, 1976.

On FINTA: books—*Modern Architecture* by Ferenc Vámossy, Budapest 1974; *József Finta* by Irén Lipták, Budapest 1978; *Encyclopaedia of Modern Architecture* by Mihály Kubinsky, Budapest 1978; articles—"Uferverbauung für Panoramablick" in *Baumeister* (Munich), no. 12, 1970; "The architecture of József Finta" in *Projekt* (Bratislava), no. 9, 1974; "Architekt József Finta" in *Projekt* (Bratislava), no. 4, 1981; "Hotel Forum" in *Der Aufbau* (Vienna), no. 9/10, 1982; "The architectural work of József Finta" in *Architektura SSSR* (Moscow), no. 11, 1983; "Hotel Forum, Hotel Novotel, Hotel Penta" in *Bauforum* (Vienna), no. 90/100, 1983; "Hotel of Austrian construction in Budapest" in *Bauforum* (Vienna), no. 98/100, 1983; "Hotel Hungaria" in *Der Aufbau* (Vienna), no. 2/3, 1984.

Although still in the era of functionalism's decline, I declare myself – in a rather anachronistic way – a functionalist: not a proponent of the formal flatness of functionalism, but more a modest seeker of the purpose behind the task itself. More plainly, I am a "romantic" or "emotional" functionalist.
The current irresponsible tendency of present architecture is to give attention only to the surface of the problem, to matters of form, forgetting the more important questions of unresolved socio-political-economic concerns and demands of the programme. Ultimately, I believe in the future of the architect's profession, and build with a view to the long-term. Architecture is science, craft and play at the same time, the sort of play that should be acted out with a child's sincerity and imagination.

—József Finta.

Although Finta continues to be involved with the plans for Salgótótarján, he has since 1966, that is since the commission of the Hotel Duna Intercontinental, been primarily involved with hotel planning. In 1970 he completed the plans for the Budapest Hotel Volga, a building with 700 rooms, constructed with concrete panels. This task turned his attention

in a new direction and to a new set of problems; namely, the analysis of the contradictory relations between prefabricated construction based on standardized production and a construction based on compliance with special, functional and formal demands. The Hotel Volga, the Hotel Bratislava and, most recently, the Hotel Voronyezs have all been built from prefabricated ferro-concrete panels. With their chiselled exteriors and exciting interior construction, these buildings effectively contradict the belief that buildings constructed of such materials can only be monotonous and boring.

—Anonymous

FISKER, Kay.
Danish. Born in Frederiksberg, 14 January 1893. Educated at Gustav Vermehren's School of Art, Copenhagen, 1909, and School of Architecture of the Academy of Fine Arts, Copenhagen, 1909-20, Dip.Arch. 1920; studied English housing legislation, London, 1919; travelled and studied in Italy, France, India, China, and Japan, 1920-22. Editor, *Arkitekten* magazine, Copenhagen, 1919; Assistant to Edvard Thomsen, Academy of Fine Arts, Copenhagen, 1919-20; in private practice, Copenhagen, 1920-30; in partnership with C. F. Møller, Copenhagen, 1930-43; returned to private practice, 1944 until his death in 1965. Visiting Lecturer, Technical School, Helsinki, 1928; Professor of Architecture, Academy of Fine Arts, Copenhagen, from 1936, and Dean of the Architectural School, from 1941; Visiting Professor, Harvard Graduate School of Design, and Massachusetts Institute of Technology, Cambridge, 1952; Visiting Lecturer, Tulane University, New Orleans, and Georgia Institute of Technology, Atlanta, 1952; Visiting Lecturer, Royal Technical School, Stockholm, 1954; Visiting Professor, Massachusetts Institute of Technology, 1957. Chairman, Academic Architects Society, Copenhagen, 1937-42; Chairman of the School Committee, Academy of Fine Arts, Copenhagen, 1940; Member of the Council, State Building Research Institute, Copenhagen, 1946; Member of the Council, Society for Architectural History, Copenhagen, 1947; Member of the Council, Danish Architects National Association, 1952; Vice-President, Academic Council, Copenhagen, 1959. Exhibitions: Charlottenborg, Denmark, 1934 (individual); Charlottenborg and Aarhus, Denmark, 1954 (individual); *Interbau Exhibition,* Berlin, 1956. Recipient: City Council Prize, Copenhagen, 1923, 1927, 1928, 1929, 1934, 1941, 1942, 1953, 1960; Eckersberg Medal, Academy of Fine Arts, Copenhagen, 1928; First Prize, Aarhus University Competition, 1932; City Council Prize, Lyngby-Taarbaek, Denmark, 1946; C. F. Hansen Medal, Copenhagen, 1947. Member, Royal Academy for the Liberal Arts, Stockholm, 1936; Honorary Corresponding Member, Royal Institute of British Architects, 1946; Member, Royal Society of Arts, London, 1948; Extraordinary Member, Heinrich Tessenow Gesellschaft, Berlin, 1948; Honorary Member, Architectural League of New York, 1952; Honorary Fellow, American Institute of Architects, 1955; Extraordinary Member, Society of Architectural Historians, Philadelphia, 1960; Extraordinary Member, Akademie der Künste, Berlin, 1960. *Died* (in Copenhagen) *21 June 1965.*

Works:

1915 Railway stations, Almindingen-Gudhjem Railway, Denmark (with Aage Rafn)
1918 F. W. Friis House, Rønnebarallé, Snekkersten, Denmark
       Exhibition layouts for the Society for Art and Design, Liljevalchs Konsthall, Stockholm

       Kristiana Tivoli Circus Building, Oslo (project; with Carl Petersen)
1918/
21   Cooperative Building Society Housing, Borups Allé and Stefansgade, Copenhagen
1919 Race-course, Amager, Denmark (project)
1920 Holiday hotel, Solrød Strand, Denmark (project)
1920/
22   Hornbaekhus Co-operative Society Housing, Borups Allé, Aagade and Hornbaekgade, Copenhagen
1921 Handelsbanken Building, Rønne, Denmark
       Jantzens Hotel extension, Gudhjem, Denmark (project)
1922 Two single-family houses, Lundeskovvej, Hellerup, Denmark
1924 Jagtgaarden Housing, Jagtvejen, Copenhagen (with Christian Holst)
1924/
26   Amagerbo Housing, Englandsvej and Østerdalsgade, Copenhagen (with S. C. Larsen)
1925 Danish Exhibition Stands, World's Fair, Paris
1925/
27   Glaenøgaard Housing, Vognmandsmarken, Copenhagen
1926/
27   Brigadegaarden Housing, Brigadevej, Copenhagen (with S. C. Larsen)
1927 Gullofshus Housing, Artillerivej and Gullofsgade, Copenhagen
1928 Richard von Hauen House, Hellebak, Denmark
1929/
32   Østergaarden Housing, Vognmandsmarken, Copenhagen
1930 Housing, Herman Triers Plads, Copenhagen
       Single-family house, Egehøj 4, Ordrup, Denmark
       Single-family house, Exnersvej 44, Ordrup, Denmark
       Single-family house, Schimmelmannsvej 47, Klampenborg, Denmark
       Jarner Summer House, Jonstrup Hegn, Hellerup, Denmark
       Single-family house, Damstien 27, Vanløse, Denmark
       Single-family house, Frølichsveg 17, Ordrup, Denmark
       Housing, Vodroffsvej 2-4, Copenhagen
1930/
32   Housing, Aaboulevarden and Rosenørns Allé, Copenhagen
1931 Nürnberggaarden Housing, Nürnberggade, Copenhagen
       Single-family house, Bispebjerg Parkallé 29, Copenhagen
       Tagensgaard Housing, Tagensvej, Copenhagen
1932 District Hospital, Aarhus, Denmark
       Radium Centre, Aarhus, Denmark
1932/
45   Aarhus University, Denmark (with Pøul Stegmann until 1937; with C. F. Møller until 1945)
1933 Housing, Grøndals Parkvej and Gudenaavej, Copenhagen
       Fisker Summer House, Udsholt Strand, Denmark
       Single-family house conversion, Kildeskovvej 50, Hellerup, Denmark
       Single-family house, Fyrrehøj 11, Gentofte, Denmark
       Single-family house, Skolevangen, Aarhus, Denmark
       Single-family house, Gardevej, Aarhus, Denmark
       Housing, Marselis Boulevard, Aarhus, Denmark
       Commemorative Park Buildings, Aarhus, Denmark
       Corn-Silo, Vejle Harbour, Aarhus, Denmark
1934 Housing, Godthaabsvej and Grøndals Parkvej, Copenhagen

Kay Fisker: Aarhus University, Denmark, 1932-45.

Otto Summer House, Ramløse Strand, Frederiksvaerk, Denmark
Radium Centre, Strandboulevarden, Copenhagen
Sandberg Summer House, Løkken, Aarhus, Denmark
Natural History Museum, Aarhus University, Denmark
Summer House, Vejlby Fed, Aarhus, Denmark
Housing, Skovvej, Aarhus, Denmark
A/S Jernkontoret Office Building, Aarhus, Denmark
Housing, Aalborggade, Aarhus, Denmark
1935 State School, Vordingborg, Denmark (project)
Golf Clubhouse, Skaade Bakker, Aarhus, Denmark
Summer House, Abeltoft Vig, Mols, Denmark
Kolding Amts og Bys Sygehus Hospital conversion and extensions, Copenhagen (with Ernst Petersen)
Jutland Trade and Agricultural Bank, Riisskov, Aarhus, Denmark
Finsen Institute conversion and extensions, Strandboulevarden, Copenhagen
Single-family house, Skovgaardsvej 11, Charlottenlund, Denmark
Vestersøhus I Housing, Vester Søgade, Copenhagen
1936 M/S Hammershus ship interiors
Hotel, Rønne, Denmark (project)
Vintersbølle Children's Sanatorium, Vordingborg, Denmark
Albani Hotel, Odense, Denmark (project; with Viggo Jacobsen)
M/S Kronprins Olav ship interiors
Ship interiors for the East Asiatic Company (projects)
1937 Hegnshusene Terraced Housing, Brønshøjvej, Copenhagen (with Erik Jensen)
M/S Frem ship interiors

1938 M/S Hans Broge ship interiors
M/S C. F. Tietgen ship interiors
Vestersøhus II Housing, Vester Søgade, Copenhagen
1939 Hotel Richmond, Copenhagen (project)
M/S Rotna ship interiors
Housing, Griffenfeldsgade 37-39, Copenhagen (with Eske Kristensen)
Vestersøhus III Office Building, Vester Søgade, Copenhagen (project)
Hillerødsholm Housing, Hillerød, Denmark
Town Hall conversion, Mariager, Denmark
M/S Kronprins Frederik ship interiors
1939/
44 Stefansgaarden Housing, Stefansgade, Copenhagen (with Eske Kristensen)
1941 Movable pre-fabricated houses
State Youth Camp, Avdebo, Denmark
Monastery Work-Supervisors' Housing, Vitskol, Denmark
State Youth Camp Work-Supervisors' Housing, Asserbo, Denmark
Shipbuilding Works extensions and conversions, Helsingør, Denmark
1941/
56 Ny Søndergaard Apartment Blocks and Terraced Housing, Vangedevej, Copenhagen (with Eske Kristensen)
1942 Housing, Dronningens Tvaergade and Adelgade, Copenhagen (with Eske Kristensen)
Doctor's House, Helsinge, Denmark
1943 Vintersbølle Children's Sanatorium extensions I and II, Vordingborg, Denmark
Egeparken Terraced Housing, Bredevej and Lindevangen, Lyngby, Denmark
Book designs for Nyt Nordisk Forlag, Copenhagen
Fogedgaarden Old People's Housing, Copenhagen
Sandmose Camp, Denmark (project)
Housing, Lystoftevej, Lyngby, Denmark (with Viggo Møller-Jensen)

Broparken Housing, Lyngvyvej and Brogaardsvej, Gentofte, Denmark
1944 Housing, Aaboulevarden and Blaagaardsgade, Copenhagen (project)
Brøndbyøster Town Plan, Denmark (with M. Askjar Ravn)
Svanholm Estate Farmworkers' Housing, Hornsherred, Denmark
Beringparken Housing, Køgevej, Copenhagen
1945 Hotel, Køge, Denmark (project)
Lundehøjgaard Soldiers' Home, Høvelte Camp, Denmark
Voldparken Housing and School, Husum, Denmark
1946 Villa Højstrup conversion and extension, Strandvejen 257, Copenhagen (project)
1947 Single-family house conversion, Nyelandsvej 115, Copenhagen
M/S Kronprinsesse Ingrid ship interiors
M/S Kronprins Frederik ship interior conversion
1948 Plan for the pedestal and installation of King Christian X Statue, Bispetorvet, Aarhus, Denmark
1949 Catholic Grammar School, Strandvejen, Copenhagen (project)
Lundehøjgaard Soldiers' Home II, Høvelte Camp, Denmark
1950 M/S Kongedybet ship interiors
1951 Nygaardsparken Housing and Shopping Centre, Brøndbyøster, Denmark
Praestekaershave Housing, Frederikssundsvej and Praestekaersvej, Copenhagen
Scho Factory conversion and extensions, Copenhagen
1954 Housing, Dronningens Tvaergade, Copenhagen (with Eske Kristensen)
M/S C. F. Tietgen ship interiors
M/S Hans Broge ship interiors
Brondbyoster School, Brondbyerne, Denmark

1955 National Council for Unmarried Mothers Administration Building and Home, Strandboulevarden, Copenhagen

Housing, Dronningens Tvaergade and Borgergade, Copenhagen (with Eske Kristensen)

1956/
57 Interbau Housing, Hansaviertel, Berlin

Mogens Schubart House, Solbakken 17, Virum, Denmark

1957 Soldiers' Home, Troldevej, Fredericia, Denmark

1958 Hans Buus House, Skovmindevej 1, Holte, Denmark

Egmontgaarden College for Single Mothers, Faaborggade, Copenhagen (with Robert Duelund Mortensen)

1959 Nygaard School, Roskildevej, Brøndbyøster, Denmark (with Robert Duelund Mortensen)

Nygaardsparken Children's Home, Brøndbyøster, Denmark (with Robert Duelund Mortensen)

Commercial and Residential Building, Østervold, Randers, Denmark (with Robert Duelund Mortensen)

1960 Beringgaarden Housing Development and Shopping Centre, Køgevej, Copenhagen (with Robert Duelund Mortensen)

Multi-storey development, Backa, Göteborg, Denmark (with Robert Duelund Mortensen)

Publications:

By FISKER: books—*Modern Danish Architecture*, with F. R. Yerbury, London 1927; *Kobenhavnske Boligtyper*, with others, Copenhagen 1936; *Danish Architectural Drawings of All Periods*, with others, Copenhagen 1947; *Den Funktionelle Tradition*, Copenhagen 1950; *Danske Arkitekturstromninger 1850-1950*, Copenhagen 1951; *Danish Architectural Drawings*, with C. Elling, Copenhagen 1961; articles—numerous in *Arkitekten* (Copenhagen), 1917-60; "The Danish House" in *Berlingske Tidende* (Copenhagen), no. 1, 1942; "Better Dwellings" in *Berlingske Tidende* (Copenhagen), no. 3, 1942; "Gunnar Asplund and Scandinavian Architecture" in *Svenska Dagbladet* (Stockholm), no. 9, 1942; "The History of Domestic Architecture in Denmark" in *Architectural Review* (London), November 1948; "The Development of Architecture in Denmark" in *L'Architecture d'aujourd'hui* (Paris), June 1949; "The Moral of Functionalism" in *Magazine of Art* (New York), February 1950.

On FISKER: books—*The New Architecture* by Gregor Paulsson, Copenhagen 1920; *Nordic Calendar*, Copenhagen 1934; *Denmark's Building Culture* by Harald Langberg, Copenhagen 1955; *Arkitekten Kay Fisker* by Hans Erling Langkilde, Copenhagen 1960; articles—numerous in *Arkitekten* (Copenhagen) from 1915; "U.S.A. Exhibition" in *AIA Journal* (Washington, D.C.), June 1958; "Bay Region—stilens ophavsmaend" in *Arkitekten* (Copenhagen), January 1962; "Kay Fisker—70 Years," special issue of *Arkitekten* (Copenhagen), February 1963; "Den Klintske Skole," special issue of *Arkitekten* (Copenhagen), April 1963; "Station Buildings at Bornholm" in *Arkitekten* (Copenhagen), 24 June 1980; "A Danish Building Story in Rome" by Kjeld de Fine Licht in *Architectura* (Munich), no. 3, 1981.

Kay Fisker was a traditionalist who resolutely refused to be drawn into the Modern Movement and even, in his early days, set up a group in opposition to it. Afterwards, he took the lead in establishing the high standards of modern Danish housing which became the admiration of the world. Having worked in the offices of Asplund and Lewerentz, he had an approach that was essentially human, and he was a keen follower of Voysey, Baillie-Scott, and the English planners.

In partnership with Pøul Stegmann and C. F. Møller, Fisker won the competition for Aarhus University. The partnership broke up, and Møller completed the project alone. Fisker, however, was responsible for the large Institute of Chemistry, Physics and Anatomy. Here, the architects demonstrated their opposition to the "new efficiency" of functionalism by designing a building that was a frank development of mediaeval brick tradition. Strong material unity combines with simplicity and clarity. The university site is in undulating parkland, and the whole conception is devoid of pomposity or even formality. Unity of composition is maintained by siting all primary building groups to run north-south and secondary groups east-west. Added cohesion is provided by maintaining the same steep angle of the tiled roofs which are designed without eaves. Many of the details of these buildings became part of the grammar of late modern Danish architecture.

Fisker was largely responsible for the introduction of projecting but partly recessed balconies, coupled with informal fenestration, in Danish housing. These features are illustrated in the main facade of the Vestersøhus Flats in Copenhagen, built with C. F. Møller in 1935-39. The Vestersøhus, completed in two stages, has 264 flats; a third stage was abandoned because of the war.

Another large development, Voldparken, at Husum, near Copenhagen, includes a notable school with classrooms giving on to courtyards. The Voldparken flats include six seven-storey blocks, but the majority of the blocks are three-storey with lower buildings for shops, garages, and a recreation centre. The tiled roofs with projecting eaves are rather heavy. The layout of the blocks shows the beginning of the fashion of dividing very large residential districts into smaller groups of blocks, which, with varying design in the blocks themselves, helps to avoid monotony. There are, in all, 1075 flats.

Fisker also designed a number of distinguished ship interiors. Outstanding among them was that of the DFDS Company's *Kronprinsesse Ingrid* (1947) for the Harwich-Esbjerg service.

—Gontran Goulden

FORD, O'Neil.

American. Born in Pink Hill, Texas, 3 December 1905. Educated at North Texas State University, Denton, 1924-26. Served in the United States Army Air Force, 1942-45. Married Wanda Graham in 1940; children: Wanda, Michael, John, and Linda. Draftsman, David R. Williams, Dallas, Texas, 1926-32; in private practice, Dallas, Texas, 1932-34; Chief Architect, Rural Rehabilitation Association, in East Texas and Georgia, 1934-36; Partner, with A.B. Swank, Ford and Swank, Dallas, Texas, 1936-39, and with Jerry Rogers, Ford and Rogers, San Antonio, Texas, 1939-53; Principal, O'Neil Ford and Associates, San Antonio, Texas, 1953-65. Partner, with Boone Powell and Chris Carson, Ford, Powell and Carson, San Antonio, Texas, 1965 until his death in 1982. Consultant to the United States Corps of Engineers, 1967-82. Visiting Professor, Harvard University, Cambridge, Massachusetts, 1953; Ward-Lucas Lecturer, Carleton College, Northfield, Minnesota, 1971; Visiting Professor, University of Texas at Austin, 1974. Member, National Council on the Arts, 1968-74. Recipient: Thomas Jefferson Award, University of Virginia, Charlottesville, 1967; Pitts Award, Texas Society of Architects, 1978. D.F.A.: Trinity University, San Antonio, Texas, 1968; Skidmore College, Saratoga Springs, New York, 1978; D.H.L.: Southern Methodist University, Dallas, Texas, 1970; University of Dallas, Texas, 1976. Fellow, American Institute of Architects, 1960. Honorary Fellow, Sociedad Arquitectos Mexicano, 1975. *Died* (in San Antonio, Texas) *20 July 1982.*

Works:

1949 Trinity University, San Antonio, Texas (with Bartlett Cocke and Associates)

1956/
59 Library, Science Building, Planetarium, and Gymnasium, St. Mark's School, Dallas, Texas

1956 Pan American School, Kingsville, Texas

1959 Texas Instruments Laboratory and Plant, Houston, Texas with Colley and Tamminga)

1960 Texas Instruments Factory, Bedford, England (with Richard Colley)

1960/
65 Science Building, Dining Hall, and Library, Greenhill School, Dallas, Texas

1962 New campus of Skidmore College, Saratoga Springs, New York

1963 Carter House, Tulsa, Oklahoma

Commercial development plan for San Antonio, Texas (with Allison B. Peery)

Science and Mathematics Quadrangle, St. Mark's School, Dallas, Texas (with Sam Zisman)

1964/
76 Selwyn School, Denton, Texas

1965 Design of *Hemisfair*, San Antonio, Texas

1965/
72 New Graduate Center, Lecture Hall, College Tower, Gymnasium, and College Center, University of Dallas, Texas (with Duane Landry Associates)

1966 Printing plant, St. Gallen, Switzerland

1966/
69 St. Mary's Hall (school), San Antonio, Texas (with Bartlett Cocke Associates)

1967 Steves House, San Antonio, Texas

1967/
68 Tower of the Americas, San Antonio, Texas

1967 Holland Hall school, Tulsa, Oklahoma (with H. B. Bernard)

1968 Texas Instruments Building, Dallas, Texas (with Richard Colley)

1970 Hotel, Lima, Peru

1970/
74 Master plan, Humanities Building, Art Building, Science Building, Library, and Field House, University of Texas at San Antonio (with Bartlett Cocke Associates)

1977 Information center and office buildings, Riyadh, Saudi Arabia

Oakwell Farms (housing, offices, shops), San Antonio, Texas

Plaza Nacional Hotel, San Antonio, Texas

Hyatt Regency Hotel, San Antonio, Texas

1978 Texas House, Mission Trace, San Antonio, Texas

1978 Chamber Music Hall, Vienna, Virginia

Bexar County Office Building, San Antonio, Texas

Glen Lakes Center (hotel, office buildings, shops), Dallas, Texas

San Fernando Cathedral restoration, San Antonio, Texas

Wulff House restoration, San Antonio, Texas

Moody Building restoration and additions, Galveston, Texas

Blum Building restoration, Galveston, Texas

Whiteside House restoration, Galveston, Texas

St. Paul's Square (neighborhood commercial buildings) restoration, San Antonio, Texas

Hicks House restoration ad additions, Bandera, Texas

O'Neil Ford: Laurie Auditorium, Trinity University, San Antonio, Texas, 1949.

Alamo National Bank rehabilitation, San Antonio, Texas
Stockman's Restaurant rehabilitation and additions, San Antonio, Texas

Publications:

By FORD: article—"Interview: O'Neil Ford" by Larry Paul Fuller in *Texas Architect* (Austin), May/June 1978.

On FORD: articles—"Laurie Auditorium, Trinity University: Art for Art's Sake" in *Texas Architect* (Austin), September/October 1973; "'Landmark' Ford: Nation's Leading Architect" by Wolf Von Eckardt in the *Washington Post*, 24 April 1976; article in *Building Design* (London), 5 November 1976; "Doing What Comes Naturally" by Michael Ennis in *Texas Monthly* (Austin), June 1978; "Built Especially for Texas" by Philip Morris in *Southern Living* (Birmingham, Alabama), November 1978; "O'Neil Ford: Musings of a National Landmark" by W. Marlin in *Architectural Record* (New York), December 1979; "O'Neil Ford, 1905-1982" by David Dillon in *Progressive Architecture* (New York), September 1982; "Architecture Loses Three Very Different Leaders: O'Neil Ford, Bruce Goff and George E. Kassabaum" in *AIA Journal* (Washington, D.C.), September 1982.

Bibliography—*O'Neil Ford, Architect* by Carol Cable, Monticello, Illinois 1981.

Fame, international acclaim, and an influential architecture were concerns that occupied the least of O'Neil Ford's time. Yet he had a good deal of public exposure for *Hemisfair* in 1965 and for his work at Trinity University, both in San Antonio, Texas. Various articles have sung his praises as one of the nation's best unknown architects. And, until his last years, his schedule was filled with lectures to various organizations across the country. Why, then, isn't he better known?

The answer can be found in his architecture. It could be called vernacular, and America does not aspire to vernacular architecture. Though the problems of energy shortages are changing this situation, most architects are still seekers after the avant-garde. Ford did not even join the competition. Nor was he interested. As well, his work doesn't cry out for attention, which is what it would have to do to be heard above the noise in America today. It is, instead, quiet, low key, and comfortable. Most often his interiors are detailed by craftsmen—up until his death, by Ford's brother Lynn. Ford's willingness to consider as many ideas and opinions as possible reflected his effort to achieve a total design, not unlike that of Eliel Saarinen. And—as, for example, at Skidmore College in New York—the user's needs and the environmental requirements are successfully resolved in a humane, unpretentious design.

Bricks, glass (in moderate amounts), wood, and stone were Ford's principal building materials. Rooted in the requirements of a region of America known for its torrid summers and miserable, cold winters, his designs have one attribute above all others—good common sense. Few people can claim such simplicity of approach, and few can claim to have adhered to such a credo and succeeded. It is simplicity that returned San Fernando Cathedral, in San Antonio, to its original elegance.

Ford also made important contributions in planning and preservation. Preservation, which was an unheard of endeavor until lately, was one of Ford's priorities. His exemplary work in Texas helped to make preservation/restoration a viable alternative to the destructiveness of "urban renewal."

Ford was around for fifty years, and he continued until his death to practice "common sense architecture." (He would preach it too, with a brash Texas charm.) Many people have missed and will continue to overlook his accomplishments by labelling his work as "regional" or "vernacular" or merely "Texana." And the American public, and many of its architects, are quick, too quick, to criticize when the architect doesn't shine, shout and/or intellectualize. Ford was too modest and too busy to bother defending himself. But there is no need to be hesitant about making firm predictions about his reputation in the future. Ford will be known and admired in ever growing circles, both within the United States and without.

—Logan Cravens

FOSTER, Norman Robert.
British. Born in Manchester, 1 June 1935. Educated at the University of Manchester School of Architecture and Department of Town and Country Planning, 1956-61 (Builders' Association Scholarship; Royal Institute of British Architects Silver Medal; Heywood Medal; Manchester Society of Architects Bronze Medal), Diploma in Architecture and Certificate of Town Planning 1961; Yale University School of Architecture, New Haven, Connecticut, 1961-62 (Henry Fellowship), M.Arch. 1962. Served in the Royal Air Force, 1953-55. Married Wendy Cheeseman in 1964; children: Ti and Cal. Partner, with Wendy Foster and Richard Rogers, Team 4, London, 1963-67. Since 1967, Partner, Foster Associates, London (associates: Loren Butt, Chubby S. Chaabra, Spencer de Grey, Roy Fleetwood, Birkin Haward, James Meller, Frank Peacock, Graham Phillips, and Mark Robertson). Exhibitions: *Foster Associates*, Colegio des Arquitectos, Barcelona, 1976; *Foster Associates: Original Drawings*, Royal Institute of British Architects Heinz Gallery, London, 1978; *Hammersmith Centre Project*, Riverside Studios, London, 1979; *Transformations in Modern Architecture*, Museum of Modern Art, New York, 1979; *Foster Associates*, University of Hong Kong, 1980; *Foster Associates*, Singapore, 1981; *Foster Associates: Architecture 1967-83*, Studio Marconi, Milan, 1983; *Three Skyscrapers*, Museum of Modern Art, New York, 1983; *Model Futures*, Institute for Architecture and Urban Studies, New York, 1983; *Foster Associates*, Gainsborough House, Sudbury, 1983; *Norman Foster: Selected Works 1962/84*, Whitworth Art Gallery, Manchester, England, 1984. Recipient: Project Award, *Architectural Design*, 1964, 1965, 1966, and 1969; Industrial Architecture Award, *Financial Times*, 1967 and 1974; Royal Institute of British Architects Award, 1969, 1972, 1977, and 1978, and Gold Medal, 1983; Structural Steel Award, 1972 and 1978; Business and Industry Award, 1976; International Prize for Architecture, 1976; Reynolds Memorial Award, American Institute of Architects, 1976 and 1979; British Tourist Board Award 1979; 6th International Prize for Architecture, Brussels, 1980; Ambrose Congreve Award, 1980; Museum of the Year Award, 1980; Premier Architectural Award, Royal Academy, London, 1983. Fellow of the Society of Industrial Architects; Associate of the Royal Institute of British Architects. Address: Foster Associates, 172-182 Great Portland Street, London W1N 5TB, England.

Works:

1965 Mews Houses, Camden, London
1966 Creek Vean House, Feock, Cornwall
       Skybreak House, Radlett, Hertfordshire
       Reliance Controls Factory, Swindon, Wiltshire
1971 Fred Olsen Passenger Terminal and Operations Centre, Millwall, London
       Computer Technology, Hemel Hempstead, Hertfordshire
       Foster Associates Studio, Fitzroy Street, London
       IBM Advance Head Office, Cosham, Hampshire
1973 Modern Art Glass Warehouse, Thamesmead, Kent
       Spastics Society Special Care Unit, Hackney, London
       Orange Hand Shops, London, Nottingham, Brighton, and Reading, England
1974 Fred Olsen Showroom, Regent Street, London
1975 Bean Hill Rental Housing, Milton Keynes, Buckinghamshire
       Palmerston Special School, Bellvale, Liverpool
       Willis Faber Country Head Office, Ipswich, Suffolk
1977 SAPA Aluminium Extrusion Plant, Tibshelf, Derbyshire
1978 IBM Technical Park, Greenford, Middlesex
       Sainsbury Centre for the Visual Arts, University of East Anglia, Norwich
1979 IBM Technical Park, phase II, Greenford, Middlesex
       Norman and Wendy Foster House, Cannon Place, Hampstead, London
       Joseph Shop, Sloane Street, London
1979/
  85 Hong Kong and Shanghai Banking Corporation Headquarters, Hong Kong
1979/
  86 Hammersmith Centre, London
1980 Student Union Building, University College, London (project)
       Billingsgate Fish Market Development, London (project)
       Statue Square Development, Hong Kong (project)
1980 Third London Airport Stansted Feasibility Studies (project)
1981 Foster Associates Office interiors and furniture, London
1981 National Indoor Athletics Stadium, Frank-

Norman Foster: Sainsbury Centre for the Visual Arts, University of East Anglia, Norwich, 1978.

furt (project)
1982 Humana Headquarters, Louisville, Kentucky (project)
Autonomous House, U.S.A. (project; with Buckminster Fuller)
1983 Renault UK Parts Distribution Centre, Swindon, Wiltshire
1983 BBC New Broadcasting Centre, London (project)
1984 IBM Technical Park new master plan, Greenford, Middlesex (project)
IBM Headquarters refitting, Cosham, Hampshire (project)
Mediathèque, Nîmes, France (project)

Publications:

By FOSTER: articles—"How to Design Low-Cost Flexible Quick-Build Buildings" in *Building Design* (London), October 1973; "Alvar Aalto 1898-1976" in *RIBA Journal* (London), July 1976; "Foster Associates: Buildings and Projects" in *Architectural Design* (London), September/October 1977; "Fostering Good Relations," interview, in *Building* (London), 7 May 1982; recording—*Norman Foster: More with Less*, tape cassette and slides, London 1979.

On FOSTER: books—*Principles of Pneumatic Architecture* by Roger N. Dent, London 1971; *New British Architecture* by Robert Maxwell, London 1972; *Design and Planning of Retail Systems* by David Gosling and Barry Maitland, London 1976; *Foster Associates*, with introduction by Reyner Banham, London 1979; *The State of British Architecture* by Sutherland Lyall, London 1980; *Late-Modern Architecture* by Charles Jencks, London 1980; *Modern Architecture since 1900* by William J.R. Curtis, London 1982; *The Story of Architecture* by Patrick Nuttgens, Oxford, England 1983; *Model Futures*, exhibition catalogue, by Bob Allies, New York 1983; *Norman Foster: Architect—Selected Works 1962/84*, exhibition catalogue, with introduction by C. R. Dodwell, Manchester, England 1984; articles—"Foster Associates' Recent Work" in *Architectural Design* (London), May 1970; "Architect's Approach to Architecture" in *RIBA Journal* (London), June 1970; "Foster Associates: Assembly Without Composition" in *Casabella* (Milan), March 1973; "Orange Hand: The Shops for Boys" in *Architecture + Urbanism* (Tokyo), September 1973; "Teamwork" in *L'Architecture d'aujourd'hui* (Paris), November/December 1973; "Perspective" in *Building Design* (London), March 1974; "Fred Olsen Operations—Amenity Building" in *Byggekunst* (Oslo), April 1974; "Orange Hand Shops" in *Baumeister* (Munich), August 1974; "Orange Hand: The Image of a Children's Clothing Shop" in *Domus* (Milan), August 1974; "Foster Associates—IBM UK, Cosham" by Roberto Collova in *Parametro* (Bologna), February 1975; "Foster Associates" in *Architecture + Urbanism* (Tokyo), September 1975; "High-tech to Appropriate: A View of Foster Associates' Approach to Appropriate Technology" in *Architectural Design* (London), March 1976; "Engineering Design and Foster Associates" in *Northern Architect* (Sunderland, England), April 1976; "Low-Profile School" in *Architectural Review* (London), November 1976; "Palmerston Special School in London" in *Bauen und Wohnen* (Zürich), May 1977; "Unbuilt England" by Peter Cook in *Architecture + Urbanism* (Tokyo), October 1977; "Preview 78: Distribution Centre, Greenford, Middlesex" in *Architectural Review* (London), January 1978; "Stretching Glass" and "Roundabout" by Stephanie Williams in *Building Design* (London), February 1978; "Fostering the Arts" in *Architects' Journal* (London), April 1978; "Art Shed" by Martin Spring in *Building* (London), April 1978; "East Anglia Arts Centre" in *Architectural Review* (London), December 1978; "Eternit Hat Trick" in *Building* (London), 25 April 1980;

"Foster's Other Side" in *Architects' Journal* (London), 21 May 1980; "Method on a Macro Scale" in *Design* (London), March 1981; "Is There Life after Norman?" in *Building* (London), 3 April 1981; "Foster Associates: The Architecture of the Near Future," special issue of *Space Design* (Tokyo), March 1982; "BBC Choose Foster" in *Architects' Journal* (London), 22 December 1982; "Three Distinct Approaches to Skyscraper Design" by Paul Goldberger in the *New York Times*, 30 January 1983; "Foster To Receive 83 RIBA Gold Medal" in *Building Design* (London), 4 February 1983.

*

Design can be many things to many people. To us, as an office, it is a means of integrating and resolving conflicts, to avoid an either/or situation, to recognise needs which might be spiritual as well as material, and to recognise that beautiful things can and should be reconciled with moving through the maze of cost, time and quality control. We really do not see why "art" and "business" have to be put into separate pigeonholes. If you break down the conflict between private and public, the individual and the community, and between short and long-term requirements, this raises the whole issue of multi-use and flexible building—flexibility for choice, change, and growth, and the problems of flexibility as well as the bonuses. In the end, it means resolving and integrating many conflicting requirements

High technology is not an end in itself, but rather a means to social goals and wider possibilities. High-technology buildings are hand-crafted with the same care as bricks and mortar or timber. Hand-crafted care is the factor that makes a building loved by its users and by those who look at it. However, materials have changed, and quality control no longer comes from site-based crafts.

—Norman Foster

*

By the mid-1960s, the architectural scene in England was sliding into chaos. Many leading architects were disillusioned, and it became normal for the architectural magazines to attack the modern movement without knowing what to put in its place. Into this vacuum came many theorists for a postmodern architecture, but they, too, had neither images to convince nor ideas to hold the imagination. Throughout this period of turmoil, the work of Norman Foster has steadily and consistently developed. Far more advanced in concepts than the apologists for "postmodernism" could imagine, it yet remained rooted in one wing of the modern movement.

Stripped of the formal ideas put forward by various of its practitioners, the architecture of the modern movement basically rested on two ideas. The first was that the architecture of our time was to be founded on a serious, objective study of the needs of the client; the second was that the new buildings would not only be built by machines but also that they would celebrate their origins by being light, shiny, and orderly. It is an amusing historical irony that the modern movement in England first achieved these ideals in Foster's work just at the moment when the magazines and the writers had given up hope. The result is that the *Architectural Review*, for example, writes of Foster's work with incomprehension and bewilderment.

Foster first achieved fame as a partner of Team 4 when they completed a low industrial building at Swindon for Reliance Controls. This little building relied for much of its quality on an elegant structure, beautifully expressed externally with cantilever beams all round, indicating the possibility of extension. Such a strong, horizontally proportioned structure made up of rolled sections clearly owed much to the work of Skidmore, Owings and Merrill, and in fact one of the partners in Team 4, Richard Rogers, had work in their office. With the break up of Team 4 and the departure of Rogers, structure ceased to play such a strong formal role in Foster's buildings.

In Foster's work of the 1970s, the structure is retained as an ordering device, but it is played down externally and interest is concentrated on a minimal skin that pushes glazing technology to the limit. Earlier glassy buildings had retained top rails, had kept a demonstration of floors and structures; Foster dispensed with all this, and his first mature work, the Olsen building at Millwall, is surely more minimal than any building had every been before—and with its calm proportions, its reflections, and its top melting into the sky, it is a beautiful building to see. "This line of development can obviously go no further," said the critics. Foster spent the next eight years taking it further, and saved English architecture from dying of boredom.

Millwall was followed by a series of industrial buildings. Here, the architectural requirement was low key, and the Foster approach worked well. His housing at Milton Keynes suffered somewhat from tenants used to tougher buildings; it serves to show that there is far to go before this kind of minimum, hi-tech building is appropriate for low-cost housing.

The completion of the Willis Faber office building at Ipswich and the Sainsbury Centre for the Visual Arts in Norwich showed Foster to be an architect of world stature. The Ipswich building, externally reflecting the surrounding buildings and following the old street pattern, is internally planned around an escalator bank that must be one of the few great spaces in a modern office building. The Norwich building is of great constructional originality, with its curtain walling being carried over the roof and its clear glazed ends. This building shows both the glories and the limitations of the open, flexible plan (restaurant, offices, senior common room, and art gallery share one great room), for the scale and the calm atmosphere is magnificent, but the noise of one vacuum cleaner can disturb the entire building.

The 1978 design for Hammersmith Centre showed Foster's skill expanding from isolated buildings to an urban complex, with buildings surrounding a city-scale square under a lightweight roof. Back to a single building again for the Renault Warehouse in Swindon, finished in 1982—there, a large roof is supported by numerous bright yellow masts, adding a love of complexity which was absent from the earlier buildings. New commissions for the BBC in London's Langham Place and at Nîmes in France are testing Foster's skill at placing modern buildings in historic settings. During the early 1980s, Foster's Hong Kong and Shanghai Bank rose on the Hong Kong waterfront. The most exciting high-rise building of the decade, the bank with its bold structure, great spaces in the air, and immaculate detailing set a new world standard for the modern office building—the first time this has ever been achieved outside America.

—John Winter

FOX, Revel Albert Ellis.
South African. Born in Durban, 20 September 1924. Educated at the University of Cape Town School of Architecture, 1942-44 and 1946-48, B.Arch. 1948; University of Cape Town Department of Urban and Regional Planning, 1966-69, M.Urban and Regional Planning (with distinction) 1969. Served in the Union Defence Force, in the Special Service Battalion, 6th Armoured Division, in Italy, 1944-46. Married Suzanne Hermine Krige in 1948; children: Grethe-Maria, Revel, and Justin. Assistant and Associate, Ayers, Wilson and Parker, Bulawayo and Gwelo, Rhodesia, 1948-51; Assistant in the studio of Ivar, *q.v.*, and Anders Tengbom, Stockholm, 1951-52; in private practice in Worcester, Cape Province, South Africa, 1953-56; Partner, Revel Fox and George Krige, Worcester and Cape Town, 1957-62; in private practice, Cape Town, 1962-66. Since 1966, Principal, Revel Fox and Partners, Cape Town

(partners: William Ritchie, Bruce Milne, Peter Puttick, John Wilmot, Kathryn Lochner, and Quinton Lawson). Regional Editor, *South African Architectural Record*, Cape Town, 1959-60. Studio Master, School of Architecture, University of Cape Town, 1959-63; Visiting Lecturer/Critic, University of the Witwatersrand, Johannesburg, 1962, University of Pretoria, 1963, Yale University School of Art and Architecture, New Haven, Connecticut, 1964, and the University of Natal, South Africa, 1965, 1966, and 1967. Member of the Central Council, 1966-70, Chairman of the Board of Education, 1970, Member of the National Board, 1971-75, and Member of the Executive Committee of the National Board, 1974, Institute of South African Architects; Chairman of the Educational Advisory Committee, 1971-75, and Chairman of the Visiting Board, 1972-75, South African Council for Architects; Chairman, National Architectural Education Conference, Cape Town, 1972; President, Cape Provincial Institute of Architects, 1974-75, and Representative of the Institute on the Environmental Advisory Board of the Cape Town City Council, 1975-76. Chairman of the Architectural Heritage Committee of the Cape Provincial Institute of Architects, since 1975, and Housing Research Steering Committee of the National Building Research Institute, since 1978. Exhibitions: *Architecture as We See It*, University of Cape Town, 1969; *The Work of Revel Fox*, Institute of South African Architects, Cape Town, 1977; *ISAA Models and Drawings*, Johannesburg and Pretoria, 1981; *Festival of Architecture*, Royal Institute of British Architects, London, 1984. Recipient: Ernest Oppenheimer Memorial Trust Fund Grant, 1963; Carnegie Travel Grant, 1964; Cape Provincial Institute of Architects Medal, 1968, 1969, and 1973; South African Institute of Architects Travel Grant, 1970 and 1983, Gold Medal, 1977, and Award of Merit, 1981; IBM International Fellowship, 1981; *Cape Times* Centenary Medal, 1983; Fulton Award, Concrete Society, 1983. Honorary Curator, South African National Monuments Council, 1982. Associate of the Royal Institute of British Architects, 1951; Member of the Institute of South African Architects, 1953, and of the South African Council for Architects, 1971. Address: Revel Fox and Partners, 117 Waterkant, Cape Town 8001, South Africa.

Works:

1954 Courtyard House, Worcester, Cape Province
1955 Fox and Ross houses, Worcester, Cape Province
        Droomer House, Worcester, Cape Province
1956 Hill House, Worcester, Cape Province
1959 Giannellos House, Camps Bay, Cape Province
        High school and school hall buildings, De Doorns, Cape Province
        Meerlust Homestead restoration, Faure, Cape Province
1960 Deanery, Cathedral Church of St. George, Cape Town
1961 Rust en Vreugd Town House restoration, Cape Town
        Esselen Park High School, Worcester, Cape Province
        La Cock House, Higgovale, Cape Town
1962 Le Roux House, Llandudno, Cape Province
        Robinson House, Higgovale, Cape Town
        Theunissen House, Klipvlei, Philadelphia, Cape Province
        Ballet School, stage 1, University of Cape Town
1963 Odes House, Clifton, Cape Province
        Vlok House, Bishopscourt, Cape Province
1964 Municipal Market, Worcester, Cape Province
        Municipal Workshop, Worcester, Cape Province
        Faure House, Rondebosch, Cape Province
        Ballet School, stage II, University of Cape Town

Revel Fox: Cape Provincial Administration Building, Cape Town, 1984.

1967 Faure House, Bloubergstrand, Cape Province
        Fischer House, Milnerton, Cape Province
        Shell and British Petroleum Properties Development Report (project)
        Housing development, Claremont, Cape Province (project)
        Housing development, Pinelands, Cape Province (project)
1968 Montebello Apartments, Newlands, Cape Province
        Van Lennep House, Monterey, Wynberg, Cape Province
        Zaaiman House, Hout Bay, Cape Province
        Moses Beach Development Study (project; with E.W.N. Mallows and Julian Beinart)
        Port Elizabeth Civic Centre Development Plan (project; with E.W.N. Mallows and Julian Beinart)
        Scott House, Constantia, Cape Province
1969 Post Office Development Report (project; with E.W.N. Mallows and Julian Beinart)
        Faculty of Education, university of Cape Town
        Eoan Group Cultural Centre and Joseph Stone Auditorium, Athlone, Cape Province
        Shell Company experimental open office layouts, Port Elizabeth

1970 Worcester Library, Cape Provenice (project)
        School for Botanical Studies, Kirstenbosch, Cape Province (with Lindsay Falck)
        Revel Fox and Partners Offices and Studios conversion, Cape Town
1971 Krige House restoration and museum conversion, Worcester, Cape Province (with Henry Villet)
1972 Early Learning Centre, Athlone, Cape Province
        Rhenish Parsonage restoration, Stellenbosch, Cape Province (with Henry Villet)
1973 BP Centre, Cape Town
        Crematorium extension, Maitland, Cape Province
        Tafelberg Petrol Service Station, Cape Town
        Entokozweni Early Learing Centre, Moletsane, Soweto
        Kanetvlei Homestead renovation, Sandhills, Cape Province
        Devon Valley Development, Stellenbosch, Cape Province (with A. and A. de Souza Santos)
        Ballet School, stage III, University of Cape Town
1974 Demonstration houses, Marina da Gama, Muizenberg, Cape Province

Nieuwenhuizen House, Somerset West, Cape Province

Geustyn House, Camps Bay, Cape Province (project)

1975 Hunyani Early Learning Centre, Salisbury, Rhodesia

Port Zimbali Resort Town, Natal, South Africa (project; with Wilhelm O. Meyer and Partners)

Urban and dwelling unit plan for a sector of Mitchell's Plain, near Cape Town (project; with Lowe, Simpson and Associates, Louis Karol, and Peter Land)

1976 Maria van Riebeeck Domestic Science High School, Riebeek West, Cape Province

Cullinan Holdings Administration Building, Olifansfontein, Transvaal, South Africa

Hertford Estate Farm Village Community (project)

Lion's Kloof cluster housing development (project)

1977 Geustyn House, Stellenbosch, Cape Province

Gamsberg Zinc Township Development, Cape Province (project)

1978 Leeusig Telephone Exchange, Cape Town

Mitchell's Plain Urban and Dwelling Unit Plan, near Cape Town (with Lowe, Simpson and Associates, and Louis Karol)

Shelter Housing Schemes: Expandable Starter Units, Valhalla Park, Cape Province

Family house conversions, Lange, Cape Province

Emergency Relief Housing, Kensington, Cape Province (project)

1979 Franschoek School Hostel, Cape Province

Middelman House, Marina da Gama, Cape Province

Parker House, Hermanus, Cape Province

Houses of Parliament gatehouse, Cape Town

Reformed Presbyterian Church Lay Training Centre and Henderson Memorial Church, Lovedale, Cape Province (project)

Archer House, Welgemoed, Cape Province

Jonkershuis restoration, Morgenster, Somerset West, Cape Province

City Hall rebuilding, Port Elizabeth, South Africa (as consultant)

1980 Federal Theological Seminary, Edendale, Natal, South Africa

St. George's Cathedral extensions, Cape Town

1980 Moravian Mission Station Community Hall, Wupperthal, Cape Province

Houses of Parliament extensions, Cape Town

Stepping Stones Nursery School, Paarl, Cape Province

Our Little People Nursery School, Paarl, Cape Province

Grobler House, Kenilworth, Cape Province

Black House, Bishopscourt, Cape Province (project)

Ons Speelnessie Nursery School, Sir Lowry's Pass Village, Cape Province (project)

1981 O'OKiep Copper Company housing and urban development, Nababeep, Cape Province (project)

Retat House, Clifton, Cape Province (project)

Ashbey's Galleries townhouse conversion, 43 Church Street, Cape Town

Nasionale Pers Centre office conversion, Cape Town

1982 Tuynhuis underground parking and area remodelling, Stalplein, Cape Town

McMillan House, Hermanus, Cape Province

Crossroads self-help housing and business development, Cape Province (as consultant)

Middelpos farm house restoration, Riebeeck West, Cape Province

Barn/house conversion, Morgenster, Somerset West, Cape Province

Fleur du Cap Manor House additions, Somerset West, Cape Province

Lorraine Homestead restoration, Rawson-

ville, Cape Province

The Lodge office building conversion, Rondebosch, Cape Province

Wavecrest house restoration, Kalk Bay, Cape Province

All Saints Church restoration and extensions, Durbanville, Cape Province

Moroka Community Centre, Soweto, Transvaal, South Africa (project)

Uluntu Utility Company student accommodation, Malunga Park, Cape Province

Paarl-East Town Centre development, Paarl, Cape Province

Uluntu Housing, Cape Province

St. John's Church housing, Wynberg, Cape Province (project)

Nasionale Boekwinkels bookshop, Cape Town

"The Star" house, Lone Hill, Sandton, Transvaal, South Africa (project)

1982/
84 Beach and City Development Plan, Durban (as consultant)

1983 Anderson House renovation, Simonstown, Cape Province

North Pine Housing, Pinelands, Cape Province

Townhouse/Offices conversion, 72 Loop Street, Cape Town

Fernandas House, Loewenstein, Cape Province

Sauerman Bungalow, Clifton, Cape Province

Gordon's Bay urban development plan, Cape Province (as consultant)

Annette se Speelkring early learning centre, Wellington, Cape Province

Women's Peace Movement study centre, Langa, Cape Province (project)

Retat House, Camps Bay, Cape Province (project)

Fabig House, Camps Bay, Cape Province (project)

Eikenfort Housing, Stellenbosch, Cape Province (project)

Malherbe House, Constantia, Cape Province (project)

1984 Provincial Administration Building, Long Street, Cape Town

Bertram House restoration, Cape Town

New Faculty of Education, Middle Campus, University of Cape Town (with Julian Elliott and Neil Grobbelaar)

Town Centre Plan, Botshabelo, Orange Free State, South Africa (project)

Maitland Cottage Homes hospital extension, Cape Province

Townhouse/Offices restoration, 71 Hout Street, Cape Town

The Residency magistrates court/museum conversion, Simonstown, Cape Province

Posts and Telecomunications construction and maintenance yards, Mitchell's Plain, near Cape Town (with Sikkel, Hansen and Koper)

Seatides Housing, Tongaat, Natal, South Africa

Siseko Early Learning Centre, Guguletu, Cape Province

Tannery Park office development, Rondebosch, Cape Province

Maturation Cellars, Meerlust, Cape Province

Whale Rock Apartments, Clifton, Cape Province

False Bay Yacht Club new clubhouse, Simon's Town, Cape Province

Vlok House, Hermanus, Cape Province

Robertson House, Hermanus, Cape Province

Princess Marina Housing, Cape Province

Harbour and Urban Plan, Mossel Bay, Cape Province (as consultant)

Fabian House, Marina da Gama, Cape Province

Noyce House, Hillcrest, Natal, South Africa

Laphumilanga Housing, Ciskei

Mount Nelson Hotel room refurbishing, Cape Province

Urban Development Plan, Simons Town, Cape Province (as consultant)

Good Shepherd Church rectory building, Kensington, Cape Province (project)

General Purposes Building, University of the Western Cape, Bellville (project)

Westtidge Child Care Centre, Mitchell's Plain, Cape Provine (project)

Myburgh House, Hermanus, Cape Province

Administration Employees Housing, Bisho, Ciskei (project)

Faculty of Education/Faculty of Law conversion, University of Cape Town (project)

Lady Buxton Child Care Centre, Cape Town (project)

Publications:

By FOX:books—*The Preservation and Restoration of Historic Buildings in South Africa,* with others, Cape Town 1968; *The Buildings of Central Cape Town,* 3 vols., with others, Cape Town 1978-84; articles—"Investigation into the Use of Plastics in architecture" in *South African Architectural Record* (Johannesburg), August 1962; "The Squares of Cape Town" in *South African Architectural Record* (Johannesburg), February 1963 "Cape Town: The Old and the New in a Changing Environment" in *Cape Town Times,* 24 September 1965, reprinted in *South African Architectural Record* (Johannesburg), February 1966; "Serendipity as Education" in *Architectural Education Symposium,* Johannesburg 1969; "The Education of the Disadvantaged Pre-School Coloured Child at the Cape of Good Hope" and "Proposals for an Experimental Pre-School Centre at Athlone," with others in *Plan* (Johannesburg), December 1969; "Conservation in Cities" in *Plan* (Johannesburg), December 1972; "Strategies to Solve Urban Dilemmas" in *Society for the Protection of the Environment Newsletter* (Stellenbosch, South Africa), no. 1, 1973; "Traffic and People" in *Cape Times,* 29 March 1973; "Those Who Care Must Organize" in *Cape Times,* 12 March 1974; "Conservation in the City, the Historical Process, Conservation of Urban Artifacts: The Methods and the Results" in *Metropolitan Dialogue,* Cape Town 1974; "Urban Design as an Aid to Conservation" in *Plan* (Durban, South Africa), December 1974; "Housing Objectives in Southern Africa" in *Housing People,* edited by Michael Lazenby, Johannesburg 1977; "The Role of the Quantity Surveyor as Seen by an Architect" and "Architects Speak" in *Institute of South African Architects and Association of South African Quantity Surveyors' Golden Jubilee Congress Report,* Johannesburg 1977; "The Residential Component: Conservation and Rehabilitation of the Existing Housing Stock" in *Urban Revitalisation: New Life for Our Cities,* Johannesburg 1978; "Guest Column" in *Architecture South Africa* (Cape Town), March 1979; "Housing" in *Cape Town—An Open City in an Open Society,* edited by Douglas Walker, Cape Town 1980; "The Chief Executive and the City" in *Leadership* SA (Johannesburg), February 1982; "Housing Alternatives in Southern Africa" in *Affordable Housing in the Eighties and Nineties,* edited by Franco Frescura, Johannesburg 1983; "Improvements to Durban's Central District" in *Town and Regional Planning* (Stellenbosch, South Africa), March 1984.

On FOX: articles—"The Small House in Modern South African Architecture" by Alan Lipman in *Lantern* (Pretoria), December 1962; "The House" by Michael Munnik and Dirk Visser in *South African Architectural Record* (Johannesburg), June 1965; "The Work of Revel Fox" by Danie Theron in *Credo* (Pretoria), April 1967; "Architecture as We See It" in *Architect and Builder* (Cape Town), no. 11, 1969; "Visitors' Guide to Cape Town" by Paul Righini in

Credo (Pretoria), April 1973; "Letter from Cape Town" by James D. Morgan in *Architecture Plus* (New York), March/April 1974; "The Institute Gold Medal Award" in *Institute of South African Architects Newsletter* (Johannesburg), no. 1, 1976; "Institute's Gold Medal Awards" in *Architect and Builder* (Cape Town), May 1977; "Architects Gold Medal Award" in *Planning and Building Developments* (Braamfontein, South Africa), May 1977; "Thoughts of a Committed Architect" in *Financial Mail* (Johannesburg) 5 May 1978; "Revel Fox—A Profile of the Architect, and a Review of His Work" in *Architecture South Africa* (Cape Town), Summer 1979; "Profile: Revel Fox …Giving Shelter" in *Fair Lady* (Cape Town), 4 November 1981; "Cape Times Awards Medals" in *Cape Times* (Cape Town), 27 August 1983; "Two Architects" in *RIBA Journal* (London), September 1984; film—*Revel-Fox: Third World Architect,* SATV film, 1982.

After training at the University of Cape Town under L. Thorton White and working in 1951-52 with Ivar and Anders Tengbom in Sweden, Revel Fox quickly established a reputation as an avant-garde architect of outstanding sensitivity and skill in detailing, in the small country town of Worcester in the Cape province. His courtyard house for the Wilson family (1954) and the Fox and Ross houses (1955) exerted great influence on a generation of young architects, who often travelled great distances to study them.

Although primarily interested in the development of a new and personal domestic architecture, Fox was too responsive to the continuity of tradition not to be influenced by the past. His houses shared with those of the eighteenth century a concern with the articulating of light-coloured surfaces and the use of openings to make precise punctuations related to internal and external volumes. The appreciation shown in his work for the essential qualities of Dutch colonial architecture was soon sensed by the more perceptive among the public, with the result that he was chosen as architect for the most important restoration projects of the 1950s and early 1960s, Meerlust and Rust en Vreugd. This field has continued to involve him deeply throughout his career.

After moving the centre of his activities to Cape Town, Fox exerted a much more direct influence on students through his association with the University, and this association also resulted in several of the most important of his buildings, the new Ballet School (1962) and the Eoan Group Cultural Centre and Joseph Stone Auditorium (1969).

Meanwhile, his concern with domestic architecture had taken him into the field of multiple housing, in which he first came to the attention of the general public with his award-winning Montebello Apartments in Newlands and subsequently with demonstration housing at Marina da Gama, Muizenberg. Increasing social involvement, together with a more favourable investment situation, enabled him to apply his standards of design to low-cost housing in the Mitchell's Plain development of 5000 dwellings and in projects for Shelter focusing on the provision of emergency and minimum shelter, using self-help expansion and upgrading.

The growth of his reputation and practice resulted in his being given the commission for a number of large commercial buildings, each one of which exhibits his tireless concerns with the search for orginal solutions and the polished detailing of every element; the most notable is the BP Centre. These commisions were paralleled by an increasing involvement in large-scale planning projects, such as those for parts of Port Elizabeth and the development of a new mining township in the North West Cape.

Fox has earned a reputation of commitment to design integrity even at the sacrifice of remunerative commissions. Public acknowledgement of his achievement led to a number of awards for specific buildings, culminating in the Gold Medal of the South African Institute of Architects in 1977.

—Ronald Lewcock

FRANZEN, Ulrich.

American. Born in Düsseldorf, Germany, 15 January 1921; emigrated to the United States, 1936: naturalized, 1943. Educated at Williams College, Williamstown, Massachusetts, 1938-42, B.A. 1942; Graduate School of Design, Harvard University, Cambridge, Massachusetts, 1944-48, M.A. 1948. Served in the United States Army, 1942-44: Bronze Star; Croix de Guerre. Married to Josephine Burgess; children: Peter, David, and April. Worked for I. M. Pei, *q.v.,* and Partners, New York, 1950-55. Since 1955, Principal, Ulrich Franzen and Associates, New York. President, Architectural League of New York, 1966. Exhibitions: *Boston Arts Festival,* 1961; *Transformations in Modern Architecture,* Museum of Modern Art, New York, 1979. Recipient: Excellence in Design Award, *Architectural Record,* 1956, 1957, 1959, 1960, 1963, 1964, 1965, 1966, 1967, and 1968; Arnold Brunner Prize, National Institute of Arts and Letters, 1962; Award of Merit, 1962 and 1964, Homes for Better Living Award, 1966, and Honor Award, 1971 and 1972, American Institute of Architects; Award Citation, 1964, and Medal of Honor, 1972, New York Chapter, American Institute of Architects; Louis Sullivan Award, American Institute of Architects/Bricklayers International Union, 1970; Thomas Jefferson Award, University of Virginia, Charlottesville, D.H.L.: Williams College, Williamstown, Massachusetts, 1972; Postgraduate Center for Mental Health, New York, 1978. Fellow, American Institute of Architects. Address: Ulrich Franzen and Associates, 228 East 45th Street, New York, New York 10017, U.S.A.

Works:

1950 Cook House, Palo Alto, California (project)
1955 Bejan House, Katonah, New York (project)
1956 Franzen House, Rye, New York
1958 Weissman House, Rye, New York
      Barkin Levin Factory, New York
1959 Beattie House, Great Neck, Long Island, New York
      Scheinman House, York, Pennsylvania (project)
1961 Miller House, Brewster, New York
      Franklin Delano Roosevelt Tidal Basin Project, Washington, D.C. (competition project)
      Philip Morris Research Center I, Richmond, Virginia
      Bernstein House, Great Neck, Long Island, New York
1962 Elliot House, Pound Ridge, New York
      Hubbard House addition, Greenwich, Connecticut
      Tenafly Cluster Housing, New Jersey
      Philip Morris Power Plant, Richmond, Virginia
      Helen Whiting Dress Factory, Pleasantville, New York
1963 Dana House, New Canaan, Connecticut
      Philip Morris Operations Center, Richmond, Virginia
      Fleschner House, Westport, Connecticut
      Castle House, New London, Connecticut
      Towers House, Essex, Connecticut
1963/
64 MVR Hall, Cornell University, Ithaca, New York
1964 Buttenwieser House, Mamaroneck, New York
      Growth Chamber Laboratories, Cornell University, Ithaca, New York
1965 United States Consulate, Montreal (project)
      Bloedel Guest House, Williamstown, Massachusetts
1966 Jefferson Memorial, Birmingham, Alabama (competition project)
      Motel, Westhampton Beach, Long Island, New York (project)

      Weathersfield Motor Inn, Westport, Connecticut (project)
1966/
69 Residence Hall, University of New Hampshire, Durham
1967 Elk Grove Presbyterian Church, Illinois (project)
1968 Bronx State School, New York (project)
      House, Pound Ridge, New York (project)
      Alley Theatre, Houston, Texas
      Agronomy Building, Cornell University, Ithaca, New York
      Forest Hills Public Housing, New York (project)
1969 Dormitory and Classroom Building, Watchtower Bible and Tract Society, Brooklyn Heights, New York
      Astor Place Building, Cooper Union, New York (project)
      Harpers Ferry Center, Harpers Ferry, Virginia
      Torrington Housing, Torrington, Connecticut
1970 Urban Development Corporation Housing, Binghampton, New York (project)
      First Unitarian Church, Richmond, Virginia
      Kennedy Plaza Apartments, Utica, New York
      Paraphernalia (boutiques), Lexington Avenue, New York
      Dining Hall, University of New Hampshire, Durham
1971 Philip Morris Research Center II, Richmond, Virginia
      The Evolving City (service megastructure), New York (project)
1972/
77 English and Modern Languages Building, New York State University, Amherst
1973 First City National Bank, Binghamton, New York
      Mono Rail Station at Interstate Highway, New York (project)
      Urban design plan for Ossining, New York (project)
      Library, Wesleyan University, Middletown, Connecticut
1973/
75 William Street Housing, Wesleyan University, Middletown, Connecticut
1974 Plymouth Street College, University of New Hampshire, Plymouth
      Research Tower, College of Vetinary Medicine, Cornell University, Ithaca, New York
1975 Undergraduate Library, University of Virginia, Charlottesville
      Residential Community in Southern California (project)
      Hunter College, New York
1977 Harlem School of the Arts, 645 St. Nicholas Avenue, New York
1978 E. Krauss House, Old Westbury, Long Island, New York
      Visitors Center, Miller Brewing Company, Eden, North Carolina
      Miller Brewing Company Headquarters, Milwaukee
      Franzen House, Bridgehampton, New York
      800 Fifth Avenue (housing), New York
1978/
80 Music Building, State University of New York, Amherst
      Champion International Headquarters, Stamford, Connecticut
1979 A. Krauss House, Old Westbury, Long Island, New York
      Boyce Thompson Institute, Cornell University, Ithaca, New York
      Student Center, University of Michigan, Flint
1979/
81 Philip Morris Headquarters Building, New York
1981/
83 Torrington Housing for the Elderly II, Torrington, Connecticut

Forest Hills Tower, Queens, New York
1982/
84 New Academic Facilities, Hunter College,
New York

Publications:

By FRANZEN: book—*The Evolving City*, with Paul
Rudolph, New York 1974; articles—"Bravado with
Brick," with Sharon Lee Ryder, in *Progressive
Architecture* (New York), September 1974; "A
Weekend Place in Bridgehampton" in *GA Houses*
(Tokyo) no. 6, 1979.

On FRANZEN: books—*The New House for Family
Living* (Treasury of Contemporary Living), New
York 1956; *Architecture U.S.A.*, London 1959;
Observations on American Architecture by Ivan
Chermayeff, New York 1972; *The Current Situation
in Architecture* by Paul Heyer, New York 1978; *A
Tower for Louisville*, edited by Peter Arnell and Ted
Bickford, New York 1982; articles—"Five New
Projects by Ulrich Franzen" in *Architectural Record*
(New York), February 1969; "Four Current Projects
by Ulrich Franzen" in *Architectural Record* (New
York), July 1971; "Ulrich Franzen" in *Architec-
ture + Urbanism* (Tokyo), June 1973; "Multi-Cat's
Vetinary Lab" by Peter Blake in *Architecture Plus*
(New York), May 1974; "Studenthauser Universität
von New Hampshire" in *Baumeister* (Munich),
August 1974; "Ulrich Franzen," special issue of
Architecture + Urbanism (Tokyo), May 1975;
"Changing Design Solutions for a Changing Era" in
Architectural Record (New York), September 1975;
"A View of Contemporary World Architects,"
special issue of *Shinkenchiku* (Tokyo), October
1975; "Philip Morris Plans Tower at 42nd Street" in
the *New York Times*, 4 December 1978; "Ulrich
Franzen" in *Process Architecture* (Tokyo/Pitts-
burgh), May 1979; "Project for Philip Morris
Headquarters, New York City" in *Architecture
d'aujourd'hui* (Paris), April 1980; "Building Types
Study 565: New Priorities in College Building" in
Architectural Record (New York), September 1981;
"Corporate Culture" in *Architects' Journal* (Lon-
don), 20 July 1983; "Philip Morris Headquarters" in
Building Stone Magazine (New York), November/
December 1983; "Die neuen Wolkenkratzer in den
USA" in *Baumeister* (Munich), February 1984.

In the last few years, the idea of modern architecture
as the puritanical uniform of political as well as
social reform has finally expired. The current
architectural situation offers no mainstream but
many contending positions of validity. Thus, there is
neither the crutch of socio-political salvation nor a
correct aesthetic system to lean on. The most
important aspect, therefore, of the serious
architect's approach today and in the future is a
philosophical frame of reference, a sensitive understanding of the relationship of idea systems and a
particular cultural situation. While we are, now,
decrying the anti-historical and anti-intellectual
stance of the so-called "modern movement," we fail
to recognise that the reformist zeal of the modern
movement was nurtured within the cultural ideas of
Marxism, Futurism, and even Fascism. The formal
solutions of that era were emblems of a "brave new
world," and their alienation from any context was,
in fact, perceived as witness of ideological correctness and therefore, architectural importance. Now
that the folly of "brave new world" attitudes is
recognized not only by broad numbers of architects
but also, more importantly, by society, a cultural
situation is arising as a precondition for an architecture which is generous where "modern" architecture
was didactic. What flows from this are design
notions not based on holistic systems but on combinations of idea systems, often unresolved within a
single scheme, but related nonetheless as sysmbols
of our delight in the often perverse but always
intriguing multiplicity of ideas that sustain man.

Perhaps this explains why there is in my work,
today, a preoccupation to fuse into a single concept
both abstract ordering devices as well as easily
recognized fragments of reality. In the same vein, but
of a different tune, are those buildings. I have
recently designed which combine within a single
broad solution more than one organizing idea, as
well as several architectural vocabularies corresponding to the different organizing geometrics. Just
as our conceptual thinking today must stem from a
full knowledge of architectural history and become a
commentary to it, in the same spirit, our form
language will become more eclectic. The effort is then
to make buildings that are assemblages or "combines" of parts and ideas, evoking a multi-faceted
present and past. I see architecture, today, as creating
bridges for valid formal elements of the past and
present, including aspects of modernism, to move

into fresh compositional systems.

—Ulrich Franzen

The work of Ulrich Franzen has been constant in its
variety of experimentation. This variety stems
perhaps from Franzen's knowledgeability about the
work of his peers, but also perhaps equally from his
sensitivity to the social context within which he and
they work. In either case, the significance of
Franzen's work strongly rests on his responsiveness
to the social context.

He has said, "Architecture is the servant of its time
and significant designs are experiments of an era. The
buildings that are designed become footprints of our
own socio-cultural hisotry, reflections of the ideas
and concerns of an era, and not those of an
individual." Indeed, Franzen's work reflects much of
what modern architecture has been atempting in its
search for directions.

Influences on Franzen were varied, and he was
certainly affected by the time and place in which he
studied, under Marcel Breuer and Walter Gropius at
Harvard's Graduate School of Design in the 1940s.
In many ways, their effect was negative, however,
and Franzen's own inclinations in his earliest
independent work were towards the only other
available model (one that would have been somewhat less acceptable to the GSD faculty at that time),
Mies van der Rohe. This may have been partly due to
a mildly rebellious streak in a young architect, but it
must have been due as well to a strong natural
affinity.

Particularly, Franzen adopted Mies's characteristic hardness, and his designs were also dominated
by materials that are physically tough, permanent,
and precise. As this Miesian respect for permanent
materials (without Mies's penchant for luxurious
materials) has pervaded Franzen's work, so also was
his earliest work pervaded by Miesian plan compositions. One characteristic of this type that Franzen
has used repeatedly are free planes: walls which
almost intercept each other but slip past, never quite
touching, and extending into the landscape.
Franzen's use of symmetry can also be traced,
however indirectly, to Miesian themes. Although
most of Mies's smaller buildings were dramatically
asymmetrical, he experimented with symmetry at a
larger scale, and Johnson's variation on Mies's work,
at a residential scale, provided a link that extended to
Franzen.

Ulrich Franzen: Alley Theater, Houston, Texas, 1968.

Angularity and the frequent use of modules also characterized Franzen's earliest work, and many of his more recent designs continue to exhibit these traits as well. Additionally, a preoccupation with the qualities of collage, or juxtaposition of parts, has been periodically evident in his architecture.

Despite the formal nature of many of these properties, Franzen has linked them together through a careful and consistent analysis and response to *Zeitgeist* and social conditions. Franzen has always attempted to integrate "form and reality," and his formal designs are responsive not merely to physical reality but also to the realities of attitude, fashion, and spirit. To whatever extent a cohesive *Zeitgeist* exists, Franzen senses it. In this sense of form yielding to "cultural context," his Paraphernalia shops of 1970 are a perfect case in point, responding to the multi-media, audiovisual craze of that time. None of the merchandise was directly displayed; images of the stock were flashed continuously on screens around the walls.

More recently, his desings have reflected current trends towards social responsiveness as well as conscientious planning of movement within space. Context, established as a primary concern in Franzen's work of the late 1960s, remains important in all of his later designs. Even Franzen's recent formal preoccupation with juxtaposition, and the dynamism created by many parts that are combined but not quite unified, often stems from a study of context. His display of natural conflict between polar forces is often one that arises in response to site conditions.

The sense of diversity within his buildings that arises from his combination of strictly ordered spaces with parts that fragment that order is further responsive to social climate, because it appropriately reflects the pluralism of American culture today. Art that invites us to recognize and take pleasure in surprising combinations may prepare us to enjoy the contradictions of a society that can be both violent and sentimental, both conventional and permissive, and both idealistic and intensely pragmatic.

—Stanley Abercrombie

FREYSSINET, Eugène.

French. Born in Objat, Corrèze, 13 July 1879. Educated at primary school in the Rue des Ecluses-Saint-Martin, Paris, 1886-90; Collège Chaptal, Paris, 1891-97; studied engineering, under J. Resal, P. Sejourne, and C. Rabut, Ecole des Ponts et Chaussées, Paris, 1899-1904. Served in the 7th Regiment, Avignon Engineers, French Army, 1900: Captain; as engineer in the French Army, Grenoble and Moulins, 1914-18. Married Jeanne Martin-Cheutin in 1916. Rural Services Engineer (roads and bridges), in Moulins, Vichy, and Lapalisse, 1905-13; Technical Manager, Mercier, Limousin et Cie, engineers, in Moulins and Paris, 1914 and 1916-18; Partner, with Claude Limousin, Société Limousin et Cie, Procédés Freyssinet, Paris, 1918-28; in private practice as architect and engineer of reinforced and pre-stressed concrete structures, working with the FORCLUM factories, in Montagis and Bezon, France, 1929-33; Chief architect and Engineer, with Edme Camperon, Camperon-Bernard building company, Paris, 1935 until his retirement in 1954. President, International Federation of Pre-Stressed Concrete, 1952-58. Honorary Member, Académie d'Architecture, France, 1916; Commandeur, Légion d'Honneur, France, 1950; Honorary Inspector-General of Bridges and Roads, France, 1951; Honorary Doctor of Science, University of Leeds, Yorkshire, 1953. *Died* (in Saint-Martin-Vesubie, France) *8 June 1962.*

Works:

In reinforced concrete:
1906/
09 Railway bridge, Ferrières-sur-Sichon, France
Single-span bridge, over the River Jolan, France
Bridge at Dompierre-sur-Besbre, France
Arch over the River Sioule, France
Four-span bridge over the River Jolan, France

Bridge at Les Malavaux, France
Bridge over the River Jolan, Cusset, France
1907 Bridge at Praireal-sur-Besbre, France
Test arch at Moulins, France
1910 Suspension bridge over the River Allier, Le Veurdre, France (destroyed, 1940)
1912 Suspension bridge over the River Allier, Boutiron, France
1913 Viaduct over the Bernard, France
1914/
18 Hauts Fourneaux industrial buildings, La Chasse, Isère, France
1914/
19 Bridge at Villeneuve-sur-Lot, France
Bridge over the River Garonne, Tonneins, France
1914/
20 National Radiator Company workshops and buildings, Dôle, France
Loire Mining Company workshops and buildings, Saint-Etienne, France
1915/
17 Verreries du Centre glassworks, Montluçon, France
1916 Arms factory, Saint-Etienne, France
Munitions depot, Port-Set, Bourges, France
Central Pyrotechnic School, Bourges, France
Aircraft hangars(8), Avord, near Bourges, France
Hauts Fourneaux towers, silos, and reservoirs, in Rouen and La Chasse, France
1916/
17 Gunpowder factory, Bergerac, France
Quayside workshops, Montluçon, France
1916/
18 Gunpowder factory, Toulouse, France
Schneider factory, Le Creusot, France
Quayside workshops, Moulins, France
Normandy Metal Company gas pipelines and concrete coverings, Caen, France
1916/
19 Building workshops, Bourges, France
1917/
19 Aircraft hangars(31), Istres, France

Eugène Freyssinet: Airship hangars at Orly Airport, Paris, 1924.

1917/
20 General Locomotive Construction Company, Nantes, France
1918/
21 Reinforced concrete boats, built at Rouen, France
Northern Railway bridges, St. Quentin-to-Guise line, France
Northern Railway bridges(14), Becherel-to-Lille line, France
Northern Railway bridges(6), Valenciennes-to-Aulnoye line, France
Northern Railway bridges(15), Cambrai-to-Dour line, France
Northern Railway bridges(9), Valenciennes-to-Douzies line, France
Northern Railway bridges(11), Valenciennes-to-le Cateau line, France
1920 Franco-Belgian Railway Material Company workshops, Raismes(Nord), France
1920/
21 Glass factory, Follembray, Aisne, France
1921 Cardboard factory, Venizel, Aisne, France
Candelier railway bridge over the River Sambre, Belgium (destroyed, 1940; rebuilt, 1945)
1921/
23 Twin airship hangars, Orly, France (destroyed, 1944)
1922 Gorcy Metal Company wireworks reconstruction
Forge Company of Chatillon-Commentry and Neuves-Maisons machine and cauldron halls, mine tower, and buildings, Noyant, France
Chatillonais Factory hangars, Sainte-Colombe, Côte-d'Or, France
1923 Loire Metal Company electric steelworks, Saint-Etienne, France
Glass factory and chemical products factory, Saint-Gobain, Oise, France
Bridge over the River Seine, Saint-Pierre-du-Vauvray, France
1924 Commercial building, 28 rue Saint-Joseph, Saint-Etienne, France
Commercial building, 20 rue Vernier, Paris
Telephone Exchange, Boulogne-sur-Seine, France
Ericson Company buildings, Colombes, France
1924/
25 Two aircraft hangars, Villacoublay, France
1924/
30 Plougastel bridge (Pont Albert Louppe), Elorn Estuary, near Brest, France (destroyed, 1944; rebuilt)
1925 Raised silo (11,000m³), Bordeaux, France
1926 Hangars, Polyvestre, France
Railway suspension bridge, Laon, France
Bridge at La Corde, France
1927 Sunken reservoir (6,000m³), France
Paris Metro workshop roofs, at Choisy, Montrouge, Fontenay-sous-Bois, and Bagneux, France
1928 National Radiator Company factory, Dammarie-les-Lys, France (now Ideal Standard factory)
1929 National Radiator Company factory, Aulnay-sous-Bois, France
Austerlitz Railway Station despatch bay halls, Paris
1930 Railway station passenger hall, Rheims, France

In pre-stressed concrete:
1934 Transatlantic Marine Terminal consolidation, Le Havre, France
1935/
39 Works on the Oued-Fodda Dam, Algeria
Port foundation caissons, Brest, France
1937/
39 Dam at Beni-Bahdel, Algeria
1938 Bridge over the Reichsautobahn, Oelde, Germany

1941/
46 Bridge over the River Marne, Luzancy, France
1942 Bridge over the River Andelle, Elbeuf-sur-Andelle, France
1943 Bridge at Longroy, France
1944 Pedestrian walkway over railway, Bully-Grenay, France
1945/
48 Five slab bridges, Territory of Belfort, France
Bridge with eleven-metre span, Flaugeac, France
1945/
49 Bridge over the River Boule, Bouleterniere, near Prades, France
Bridge over the River Tet, Ille, near Perpignan, France
Bridge over the River Tech, Arles, near La Junquera, France
Bridge over the River Isère, Fontaine, Grenoble, France
Bridge over the River Romanche, Bourg-d'Oisans, Isre, France
Bridge over the Eau-d'Olle, La Vigne, Fonderie-d'Allemont, France
Bridge over the River Arc, Hermillon, Savoie, France
Bridge over the River Arc, La Denise, France
Bridge at Neufchatel-en-Bray, France
1946 Wind Tunnel, Toulouse, France
1947 Landing strips, Orly Airport, France
1947/
51 Five bridges over the River Marne, at Annet, Trilbardon, Esbly, Ussy, and Changis Saint-Jean, France
1948 Water reservoir (7,000m³), Orléans, France
Sevres-Achères outlet tunnels, under the River Seine, at Frette and Montesson, France
Covered tunnel bridge, Rouen, France
1949 Galion Bridge, Rio de Janeiro, Brazil
1950 Lighthouse, Breck, France
1951 France dock works rebuilding, Cherbourg, France
Racetrack bridge, Lille, France
1951/
53 Three La Guaira-to-Caracas motorway viaducts, Venezuela
1955 Radio Transmitter repairs and reinforcements, Felsberg
1956/
58 Saint Pius X underground basilica, Lourdes, France (with Pierre Vago)
1958 Number 10 motorway bridge over the Autoroute du Sud, Orly, France
1959/
62 Saint-Michel Bridge over the River Garonne, Toulouse, France

Publications:

By FREYSSINET: books—*Limousin et Cie: Reinforced Concrete, Public Works, Compressed Air*, with others, Paris 1922; *Le Pont Candelier*, Paris 1923; *Les Grandes Constructions*, Paris 1930; *Ponts en beton preconstrait*, lecture paper, Liège 1948; articles—"Les Hangars d'Orly" in *Le Génie civil* (Paris), September 1923; "Les Ponts en beton armée de très grande portée" in *Architecture vivante* (Paris), Spring/Summer 1931; "Preface" in *Architecture d'aujourd'hui* (Paris), November 1936; "Une revolution dans l'art de bâtir" in *Travaux* (Paris), November 1941; "Prefabrication et bâtiment" in *Bâtir* (Paris), January 1953; "Three Monumental Bridges Built in Venezuela" in *Civil Engineering* (London), March 1953; "The Birth of Pre-Stressed Concrete and the Prospects for Its Future Use" in *Travaux* (Paris), June/August 1954.

On FREYSSINET: books—*Baukunst der neuester Zeit* by G. A. Platz, Berlin 1927, 1930; *Concrete: The Vision of a New Architecture* by P. Collins, New York

and London 1959; *Eugene Freyssinet* by Jose A. Fernandez Ordonez, Barcelona 1978, 1979; articles—"Les Hangars à dirigeables de l'aeroport d'Orly par Eugène Freyssinet" by Jean Badovici in *Architecture vivante* (Paris), no. 2, 1924; "Les Hangars d'avions de palyvestre près de Toulon" by Charles Dantin in *Le Génie Civil* (Paris), 27 August 1927; "Le Pont en beton armé Albert Louppe" by A. Coyre in *Le Génie civil* (Paris), 4 October 1930; "Eugène Freyssinet" by Jean Badovici in *Architecture vivante* (Paris), Spring/Summer 1931; "The Freyssinet Process of Pre-Stressing Concrete" by Archibald Kirkwood Dodds in *Architect and Building News* (London), 26 June 1942; "El Puente de Luzancy" by Eduardo Torroja, in *Revista de obras publicas* (Madrid) March 1947; "The Basilica of St. Pius" in *Architectural Design* (London), June 1959; "Adieu à Eugène Freyssinet" by Albert Laprade in *Bulletin SADPG* (Paris), June 1962; "Obituary: M. Eugène Freyssinet" in *The Times* (London), 9 June 1962; "Souvenir d'Eugène Freyssinet" by Urbain Cassan in *Bulletin d'academie d'architecture* (Paris), no. 37, 1962; "Eugène Freyssinet (1899)—A Great Builder" by Albert Caquot in *Le Jaune et le rouge* (Paris), December 1962; "Eugène Freyssinet" by J. R. Robinson in *Annales de ponts et chaussées* (Paris), July/August 1963; "Freyssinet: A Revolution in the Art of Construction" by Jose A. Fernandez Ordonez in *2C Construction de la ciudad* (Barcelona), June 1978.

It is to Eugène Freyssinet that we owe some of the most beautiful architectural works in reinforced concrete. The most beautiful—the hangars for airships at Orly Airport, Paris—were unfortunately destroyed during World War II. The "father of pre-stressed concrete" had many achievements to his credit. He did not consider himself as an architect, but architecture interested him. He hoped for collaboration with architects, but few such opportunities arose.

I had the good fortune to live through one of these valuable experiments at the time of the conception of the subterranean Basilica at Lourdes. It was an exemplary experiment in real collaboration, in a patient search for a common language. It resulted in the free expression of a rigorously logical purity put at the disposition of a spatial will but accepting all the constraints imposed by technique and economy.

—Pierre Vago

FRIEDBERG, Marvin Paul.

American. Born in Brooklyn, New York, 11 October 1931. Educated at Cornell University, Ithaca, New York, 1950-54, B.S. in horticulture 1954; Art Students League, New York, 1959; New School for Social Research, New York, 1962. Served as a Lieutenant in the United States Army, 1954-56. Married Ester Louise Hidary in 1962 (died, 1982); children: Mark and Jeffrey. Landscape Architect, with Arthur Hoffman, Hartford, Connecticut, 1954, and with Joseph Gangemi, New York, 1956-58. Since 1958, Principal, M. Paul Friedberg and Partners (landscape architecture and urban design), New York. Founder-Director, Urban Landscape Program, City College, City University of New York, since 1971. Member, Board of Directors, Municipal Arts Society, New York, 1968-71; Vice-President, Architectural League of New York, 1969-70; Member, Art Commission of the City of New York, 1971-72; Chairman/Designer, *Not Too Late* exhibition, Guild Hall, New York, 1972; Vice-President, American Society of Landscape Architects, 1973. Member of the Board, 1975-78, Chairman of the 1976 Conference "Exploring Change," and, since 1978, Member of the Advisory Board, International Design Conference at Aspen,

Colorado; Trustee, American Academy in Rome, since 1978. Recipient: Commercial Landscape Design Award, 1962, World's Fair Award, 1964, Merit Award, 1970, 1971 and 1974, and Certificate of Merit, 1977, 1979 and 1982, American Association of Nurserymen; Client Award, 1964, Certificate of Merit, 1970, and Excellence in Design Award, 1973, New York State Association of Architects; Commendation, New York Park Association, 1965 (twice); Albert S. Bard Award, City Club of New York, 1965 and 1967; Honor Award, 1965 (three times), 1968, and 1970, Merit Award, 1965 (twice), 1967 (three times), 1968, 1969, 1971 (three times), 1974 (three times), 1975, and 1982, and Special Award, 1978, American Society of Landscape Architects; Honor Award and Merit Award, United States Department of Housing and Urban Development, 1966; New York Council of the Arts Award, 1967; Merit Award, 1967, and Bronze Plaque, 1967 and 1974, New York Municipal Arts Society; Honor Award, 1967, and Award Citation, 1969, American Institute of Architects; Special Citation, American Association of School Administrators, 1970; Residential Design Award, National Landscape Association, 1971; Mayor's Medal, New York City Diamond Jubilee, 1973; Excellence in Enviromental Design Award, *Industrial Design*, 1973; Award of Merit, Concrete Industry Board of New York, 1974; Design in Steel Citation, American Steel Institute, 1975; Award, *Progressive Architecture*, 1977; Certificate of Excellence, Urban Awards Program, 1978; Merit Award, New York State Council of Landscape Architects, 1979; I.D.E.A. Downtown Achievement Award, New York, 1979; Building Stone Institute Award, New York, 1982; New York City Art Commission Annual Award, 1983. Fellow, American Society of Landscape Architects, 1979. LL.D.: Ball State University, Muncie, Indiana, 1983. Address: M. Paul Friedberg and Partners, 4 West 62nd Street, New York, New York 10023, U.S.A.

Works (landscape and urban design):

1965 Bay Ridge Air Rights, New York
Carver Houses, New York
Chatham Towers, New York
Commodore John Rogers School Number 27, Baltimore, Maryland
Israel Senior Citizens Housing, New York
Ittelson Center, New York
Jacob Riis Houses and Jacob Riis Plaza, New York
Leesburg Prison, New Jersey
1966 Bridgeport Courthouse Plaza, Connecticut
Dag Hammarskjold Plaza, New York
Lancaster Public Square, Pennsylvania
Letchworth Village, Haverstraw, New York
1967 Bedford-Stuyvesant Superblock, New York
Playground, Buchanan School, Washington, D.C.
Buttenweiser House, Mamaroneck, New York
Capper Plaza Urban Renewal, New York
Madison Public Library, New Jersey
New York Institute of Technology, Westbury
Ottumwa Central Business District, Iowa
Temple B'nai Jeshurun, Short Hills, New Jersey
Wilton State School, Wilton, New York
Woodlawn Park, Buffalo, New York
1968 Essex Community College, Newark, New Jersey
Fall River Housing, Massachusetts
Gottesman Plaza, New York
Master plan for the Harlem River State Park, Bronx, New York
Humboldt School, Boston
Kent General Hospital, Easton, Pennsylvania
Nassau County Civic and Social Services Center, Mineola, Long Island, New York
Site evaluation: New York University at Sterling Forest

Paerdegat Housing, New York
Parks improvement plan for Poughkeepsie, New York
Peachtree Center, Atlanta
Public School 166, New York
Queens College, New York
Temple B'nai Abraham, South Orange, New Jersey
Vest Pocket Parks, New York
Wilson College, Chicago
Worcester Center Development, Massachusetts
Central Park Police Stable, New York
1969 Beef Island Enviromental Study, British Virgin Islands
Canadian Jewish Congress, Montreal
Chelsea Park, New York
Creedmore State Hospital, Queens, New York
IBM, Burlington, Vermont
Jeanette Plaza, New York
Kaufman Campgrounds, Sullivan County, New York
Mid-Westchester YM-YWHA, Scarsdale, New York
Roberto Clemente State Park, Bronx, New York
Schaefer Brewery, Scranton, Pennsylvania
Seton Park, Riverdale, New York
State University of New York, at Brockport, Buffalo, Delhi, New Paltz, and Stony Brook
Stevens Institute, Hoboken, New Jersey
Wall Street Park, Staten Island, New York
Washington Street Urban Renewal, New York
Model Cities Open Space Study: Waterbury, Connecticut
1970 Cadman Plaza Urban Renewal, New York
Consolidated Edison Indian Point Project, Westchester County, New York
Open Space Study, East Hampton, New York
East Orange Housing, New Jersey
Easton Hospital, Pennsylvania
Ellicot Neighborhood Facility, Buffalo, New York
Lindsay Bushwick Housing, New York
Lindsay Park, New York
Marcus Garvey Park Village, New York
Nassau Community College, Long Island, New York
Newark Vest Pocket Parks, New Jersey
New Jersey Housing Authority, Morristown
New York City Housing Authority Developments: Allen Stanton, Amherst Houses, Amsterdam Houses, Coney Island Site 13, East Houston, First Avenue and 10th Street, Mermaid Avenue, Penn Wortmann, and Warren Street
Operation Breakthrough, Wilmington, Delaware
Townland Housing Systems, Operation Breakthrough, Newark, New Jersey
Model Cities Training Program, New York
Twenty-four Forty Boston Road, Bronx, New York
29th Street Park, New York
University Towers, New York
Urban Development Corporation Mobile Home Project, Brooklyn, New York
Urban Nature Study, New York
Watertown East New Town, Massachusetts
West Side Urban Renewal (five sites), New York
1971 AT & T Long Lines Headquarters, Bedminster, New Jersey
Clinton Towers, New York
Kings County State School, New York
Kingsborough Community College, Queens, New York
Dr. Martin Luther King Boulevard, Miami
Nielsen Building, Chicago
Rochester Recreational Parks, Rochester, New York
Rome State School, Rome, New York
Smithbridge Towers, New York

South East Loop Housing, Rochester, New York
South Hall Housing, Albany, New York
Village Mall, Queens, New York
1972 Harlem River Houses, New York
Metropark/Tri-State Regional Planning Commission, New York
Middletown Urban Development Corporation, Midletown, New York
Oakley Oval, Jersey City, New Jersey
Pearl Ridge Shopping Center, Honolulu
Recreational facilities, Pittsburgh, Pennsylvania
River Plaza, New York
Stevenson Commons, New York
Summer Street Plaza, Boston
Synthetic Land: Ford Foundation, New York
1973 Bergdorf-Goodman Store, White Plains, New York
College Point, Queens, New York
Cook County Hospital, Chicago
East Boston Housing
First of Denver Plaza
Fitzgerald Park, Beckley, West Virginia
Site development impact study: Leonia Golf Course, New Jersey
Minneapolis Orchestra Hall
Urban beautification: Yonkers, New York
Village Green, Staten Island, New York
Washington Market Urban Renewal, New York
1974 Cité Concordia, Montreal
Fordham Medical and Mental Hospital, Bronx, New York
Model Cities Open Space Plan for Harlem, New York
Hancock/Saratoga Housing, New York
Hofstra University, Hempstead, New York
Kemper Williams Park, Patterson, Louisiana
Loring Park Development, Minneapolis
Melrose Housing, Bronx, New York
Menorah Park Home for the Aged, Beechwood, Ohio
Police Plaza, New York
Rainbow Center Mall/Winter Garden, Niagara Falls, New York
Social Security Administration, Metro West, Baltimore, Maryland
Staten Island Theme Park, New York
State Street Mall and Capitol Concourse, Madison, Wisconsin
1975 African Square Park, Miami
Ayra Sheraton Hotel, Tehran
Farahzad Housing, Tehran
Home Furnishing Center, Auroa, Illinois
Department of Housing and Urban Development Beautification Demonstration: Ten Demountable Parks, New York
Jamaica "El" Study, New York
Plan for Main Street, Poughkeepsie, New York
Moscow World Trade Center
State Street South Operations Center, Quincy, Massachusetts
1976 Jersey City State College, New Jersey
John F. Kennedy Plaza and Civic Center, Lowell, Massachusetts
Junior High School 320, New York
Kissena Park and Park Corridor, Queens, New York
Lafayette Boynton Housing, New York
Monroe Center, Grand Rapids, Michigan
1977 Bowling Green Park restoration, New York
Alaska State Capital Competition Plan, Willow, Alaska (with Jonathan Barnett and Benjamin Thompson)
1978 Baychester Housing, New York
Campau Square, Grand Rapids, Michigan
Peavey Plaza, Minneapolis
1979 Fort Lincoln New-Town In-Town, Washington, D.C.
Garden Court Apartments, New York
Poughkeepsie Central Business District Redevelopment, Poughkeepsie, New York

1980 Great Wall Hotel, Beijing
Hurt Park, Roanoke, Virginia
Comprehensive Open Space Plan, Roanoke, Virginia
Broward Detention Center, Fort Lauderdale, Florida
Fort Worth Cultural District, Texas
Riverwalk Development, New York
County Justice Complex, Hamilton, Ontario
Social Security Administrative Building, Baltimore, Maryland
Dravo Building, Pittsburgh, Pennsylvania
1981 World Financial Center, Battery Park City, New York
Riverfront West, Detroit, Michigan
67th Street Park Playground, New York
Dag Hammarskjold Tower, New York
Sommerville Parks Master Plan, Sommerville, Massachusetts
Pershing Park, Washington, D.C.
1982 Center at Purchase, New York
Fifth Avenue restoration, New York
Eagle Ridge, Steamboat Springs, Colorado
Jeanette Park Plaza, New York
1983 New York City Grand Prix, Flushing, New York
James Center, Richmond, Virginia
Bank of America, New York
Continental Tower, New York
First Stamford Place, Stamford, Connecticut
1984 40-41st Street Plaza, New York
Transpotomac Canal Center, Alexandria, Virginia

Hall of Science, Flushing Meadow Park, New York
Society Hill Sheraton Hotel, Philadelphia, Pennsylvania
Old Stone Square, Providence, Rhode Island
Veterans' Administration Medical Center, Castle Point, New York
Springs School, East Hampton, Long Island, New York
Barclays Bank, New York

Publications:

By FRIEDBERG: books—graphics and captions in *Planning for Parks and Recreation in Urban Areas* by Elinor Guggenheimer, New York 1968; *Playgrounds for City Children,* Washinton, D.C. 1969; *Creative Play Areas,* Portland, Oregon 1970; *Play and Interplay,* New York 1970; *Handcrafted Playgrounds,* New York 1975; articles—"In Search of Eden" in *Interiors* (New York), July 1963; "Patios for Parlous Suburbia" in *Landscape Architecture* (Louisville, Kentucky), January 1964; "Programming Play" in *Schoolhouse in the City,* edited by Alvin Toffler, New York 1968; "Manhattan Protest" in *Landscape Architecture* (Louisville, Kentucky), October 1968; "Systems for Play" in *Small Urban Spaces,* edited by Whitney North Seymour Jr., New York 1969; "Sharing the Spaces, Sharing the Yields" in *AIA Journal* (Washington D.C.), March 1969; "Dealing with Public Agencies" in *Journal of the*

Industrial Designers Society of America (Washington D.C.), June 1969; "Roofscapes" in *Architectural and Engineering News* (Philadelphia), September 1969; "A Further Proposal" in *The New York Society of Architects Annual Report,* 1970; "Projects for Urban Spaces" in *Design Quarterly* (Minneapolis), Spring 1970; "What is an Adventure Playground" in *New York Planning Review,* Fall 1970; "Is This Our Utopia?" in *The Social Impact of Urban Design,* Chicago 1971; "Park Power" in *Parks and Recreation* (Arlington, Virginia), July 1971; "Clustering Is for Sharing" in the *New York Times,* 12 March 1972; "Plazas" in *Site* (New York), August 1973; "Where Have All the People Gone?" in *The Designer* (New York), September 1973; "Community Renewal: A Position Paper" in *Proceedings of the ASLA National Growth Task Force,* Washington, D.C. 1974; "Performance as Energy (in Public Spaces)" in *Site* (New York), Fall 1974; "How to Develop New Open Space Inside Our Cities" in *Inland Architect* (Chicago), January 1975; "Urban strollways", in *Urban Open Spaces,* edited by the Cooper-Hewitt Museum, New York 1979; "Focus on what people need" in *Where is downtown going?,* New York 1979; "Gardens on the inside" in *Landscape Architecture* (Louisville, Kentucky), January 1980; "Interview with the World's Front Line Architect—M. Paul Friedberg" by F. Shaik in *Nikkei Architecture* (Tokyo), January 1980; "People, Places and Plants" in *Urban Design* (Purchase, New York), Spring 1980; "Juvenile Play Areas" and "Decorative Pools and Fountains" in *Handbook of Specialty Elements in Architecture,* edited by Andrew

M. Paul Friedberg: Peavey Plaza, Minneapolis, 1978.

Alpern, New York 1981; "Twentiety Century Park" in *Casabella* (Milan), June 1983; slide film—*Nine by Nine for Downtown*, New York 1979.

On FRIEDBERG: books—*Design on the Land* by Norman T. Newton, Cambridge, Massachusetts 1971; *Alive in the City* by August Heckscher, New York 1974; articles—"Parks Are Not for Planners" by J. C. Ely in *Progressive Architecture* (New York), March 1966; "Riis Houses Replanned Open Space, New York City; Capper Plaza and Buchanan School Playground, Washington, D.C." in *Architectural Record* (New York), December 1966; "Parc de loisirs de l'ensemble Jacob Riis" in *Architecture d'aujourd'hui* (Paris), April 1967; "His Work" in *Architectural and Engineering News* (Philadelphia), September 1967; "Designing the Spaces in Between" in *Architectural Record* (New York), March 1968; "Playgrounds in Temporary Vacant Lots, New York" and "Play Space Any Space" in *Architectural Forum* (New York), November 1968; "Bedford-Stuyvesant Superblock" in *Architecture d'aujourd'hui* (Paris), February 1971; "Designing the Urban Landscape: New Projects by M. Paul Friedberg" by Mildred F. Schmertz in *Architectural Record* (New York), March 1972; "M. Paul Friedberg: Designer of Spaces for City People" by Ursula Cliff in *Design and Environment* (New York), Winter 1973/74; "M. Paul Friedberg" in *Kenchiku Bunka* (Tokyo), March 1974; "Towering Urban Garden Under Glass" in *Life* (New York), December 1978; "The Greening of Offices" by P. Viladas in *Interiors* (New York), June 1979; "See you in Cincinnati" by P. Viladas in *Interiors* (New York), May 1980; "Monroe Mall Gets Ready" by J. Blaich in *West Michigan* (Detroit), July 1980; "Loring Greenway: Another Urban Intervention" in *Architecture Minnesota* (Minneapolis), September/October 1980; "The Washington Landscape: Recent Works" in *Landscape Architecture* (Louisville, Kentucky), November 1981.

Bibliography: *M. Paul Friedberg: A Bibliography* by Mary Vance, Monticello, Illinois 1980.

The actual process of design is a mystery to me. I have no notion of where ideas come from. Like most people in creative fields, I work by a trial-and-error process. I try an idea, and if I like it, I pursue it; if I don't, I discard it or hold it in abeyance.

Design for me is an intuitive process by which I attempt to solve the problem of transferring a verbal, intellectually conceived idea into three-dimensional form. It's my wish to be sensitive to the client and his needs, so that I might satisfy him in a manner that is not only understandable and functional but also will provide him with new insights and an expanded view of the world. I don't believe it is necessary to put myself in the place of a client in order to provide him with a fulfilling environmental experience.

Design is the interplay of form or aesthetics with function. The dynamic poles from both sides of this polarized arrangement create the tension that gives drama to the process of designing. I seek solutions which are open-ended, if not in form, then in interpretation. In this way the design can be both dynamic and offer opportunites for participation in a fixed environment.

One of the joys of working with plants is that, like all living things, they are always in a state of change—growing and responding to climatic changes of light, wind, and other environmental forces. I seek to simulate this state of flux and motion in my designs. I provide environments that are stage settings in which all of us become actors and spectators. Spontaneity, interaction, and involvement are the script and scenario; the drama is provided by our encounters and the ways in which we see each other. Both the stage and the seats are fluid, depending upon the activity taking place. I design to provide a choice, a chance for participation and interpretation in a wide variety of experiences—without this, my designs have no meaning. That is why I enjoy design problems ranging from playgrounds, which challenge and allow children to display the unplumbed depths of their imagination, to plazas which serve as outdoor rooms, to parks which are spaces for encounters with the natural environment.

Because we change, environments change; therefore, there is no one solution which allows my work to provide constant challenge and interest. There is always room for new ideas, new experiments and adventures. For me, design is a hands-on exercise in which we talk to one another. Through the vocabulary of form, we provide the opportunity for understanding and participation in our environment.

—M. Paul Friedberg

The large volume of work produced by M. Paul Friedberg and his staff of thirty-five landscape architects, architects, engineers, planners, urban designers, and graphic and product designers is broad in scope. It includes open space and recreational analysis and programming; comprehensive master planning; development of site and landscape designs; civil engineering; environmental surveying and analysis; research and technology; as well as services patterned for community participaton.

Early in his career, Friedberg developed a landscape design formula to which he remains faithful. It is highly successful with owners and is essentially what each client who hires him hopes he will produce. Friedberg takes the area with which he is working, whatever its size, and breaks it down into spaces of a more human scale by means of steps, platforms, occasional clusters of regularly spaced trees, other trees or flagpoles in rows, play sculpture, playing grounds for particular sports, cantilevered terraces, trellises of heavy lumber, wading pools, fountains, waterfalls, amphitheatres, yacht basins, bollards, kiosks, benches, tables, lighting fixtures, and specially designed trash cans. Almost all surfaces are hard and consist of bricks, concrete slabs or granite setts. His larger spaces do not encourage biking, jogging, or cross-country skiing because they have few paths which are not interrupted by flights of steps or sudden changes of pattern. His urban landscapes have no sylvan glens, little juxtaposition of soft greenery against asphalt streets and brick facades, no relief from the tough unyielding textures of the city—only more of the same. Friedberg's work bears no resemblance to the urban parks and squares built in the United Stated in the nineteenth centry, which are still leafy, filled with birds and squirrels, and restful.

It is true that today these lovely places are wearing out through over-use, neglect, and lack of money for maintenance. But for graffiti and the fragility of trees (always used sparingly by Friedberg not only because of their initial cost but also because of the expense of pruning and care), his landscapes are virtually indestructable. He doesn't use grass because it wears out, nor earth because it is complicated to drain and gets muddy. Shady glens invite mugging and worse. Friedberg's urban landscapes may be the best we in the United States can do today, and this may be why they are to be found everywhere at every scale from small mid-block playgrounds to cheer a city slum to a grand cadenced plazas to enhance the importance of proud new civic monuments.

—Mildred F. Schmertz

FRIEDMAN, Yona

French. Born in Budapest, Hungary, 5 June 1923; emigrated to France 1957; naturalized, 1966. Educated at the Technical University, Budapest, 1943; The Technion, Haifa, Israel, Dip. Arch. 1948. Married Denise Charven in 1960; children: Anat and Marianne. Worked as a free-lance architect, 1949-57; has worked on theoretical projects and concepts since 1956; settled in Paris, 1958; Founder-Member, GEAM (Group d'Etude d'Architecture Mobile), Paris, 1958; published the manifesto *Architecture Mobile,* 1958; Founder, Communication Centre of Scientific Knowledge for Self-Reliance, at the United Nations University, Paris, 1982. Visiting Lecturer, Massachusetts Insitute of Technology, Cambridge, University of California at Los Angeles, Harvard University, Cambridge, Massachusetts, University of Michigan, Ann Arbor, Rutgers University, New Brunswick, New Jersey, and Princeton University, New Jersey, 1958-74. Exhibitions: French Exhibition, Moscow, 1960; *Une Utopie Réalisée,* Musée d'art Moderne de la ville de Paris, 1975, toured South America. Recipient: Grand Prize, *Venice Film Festival,* 1962; Grand Prix de Récherches et Formes de Demain, Paris, 1967; Architecture Prize, Academy of Arts and Sciences, Berlin, 1972. Honorary Member, Royal Academy of Fine Arts, Amsterdam; Honorary Fellow, Academy of the Hague, 1976. Address: 42 Boulevard Pasteur, 75015 Paris, France.

Works:

1953/
58 Cylindrical Shelters
1957/
58 Span-over Blocks
1958 Cabins for the Sahara
      Stacked Concrete Boxes
1958/
59 Spatial Town (including Tunis Spatial, Paris Spatial, etc.)
1959 The Venice of Monaco
      African Proposals
1963 Bridge-Town over the English Channel
1964 American Projects
      Headquarters of the SNCF (French National Railways) and Neighbourhood Centre over the marshalling yards of the Gare St Lazare, Paris
1969 Venice
      The Flatwriter
1971 Alternative plan for the Place Beaubourg, Paris
1972 The Manuals
1974 Architecture by Yourself
1976 CDC Headquarters, Ivry, France
      Self-help Housing for Slum Dwellers (project)
1978 Lycée David, Angers, France ·
1980 "Green" Church (project)
1981 Museum of Basic Technology, Madras, India (project)

Publications:

By FRIEDMAN: books—*L'Architecture Mobile,* Paris and Tournai, Belgium, 1970; *Pour Une Architecture Scientifique,* Paris 1971, Cambridge, Massachusetts 1975; *Les Mécanismes Urbains,* Brussels, 1968; *La Planification Urbain,* Brussels 1968; *Société-Environment,* Brussels 1972; *Meine Fiebel,* Dusseldorf 1974; *Comment vivre entre les autres,* Paris 1974; *It's Your Town—Know How to Protect It,* Strasbourg, France 1975; *Utopies Réalisables,* Paris, 1975; *Une Utopie Réalisée* (catalogue: Musee d'Art Moderne de la ville de Paris), Paris 1975; *Les Pictogrammes de la Genèse,* Paris 1975; *Comment habiter la terre,* Paris 1976; *L'Architecture de Survie,* Tournai, Belgium 1978; *Où Commence la Ville?,* Paris 1978; *Better Life in Cities,* Strasbourg, France 1980; *Alternatives Energetiques,* Paris 1980; articles—more than 500 articles in periodicals throughout the world.

Yona Friedman: Project for a Spatial Town, 1959.

On FRIEDMAN: article—"Yona Friedman: An Appreciation" by Anthony Hill in *RIBA Journal* (London), March 1976.

From 1956 on I have believed that architectural objects should be determined and designed not by the architect but by their future users—the inhabitants. Obviously this does not exclude, for the architect, a technician's role. My research, my publications, my books, all had this basic statement as their starting point.

It is evident that, as a consequence, I had to endure unfriendly reactions from various professional bodies. My first book, *Mobile Architecture* appeared in print twelve years after its first photocopied publication.

I was trying to develop the possibility of implementation of my thesis; I had many difficulties. In the first years (1957-62) I developed the principle of "infrastucture," a skeleton in which the effectively used space-defining elements (walls, floors, partitions, etc.) could be "mobile" and thus be manipulated by the inhabitant. The next step (1962-65) was to demonstrate the enormous combinatory range resulting by such manipulation, and only after 1966 did I start to present these ideas (and some simple methods to help the inhabitant to become master of his own design) to a public of architects rather than to laymen (who are professional inhabitants). I worked for a long time to refine these methods for laymen (using cartoons for explanations—as in the "manuals" distributed in many countries by U.N. agencies, endeavouring to improve conditions in shantytowns).

The first occasion to implement "Mobile Architecture" (in the sense explained before) was at the project C.D.C. in Ivry, near Paris, where 300 people working in a firm conceived for themselves their own future premises, after having had an introductory courso based on the "manual," The project was finished in 1976, but the building could not be realized because of C.D.C'S being absorbed by another company. Actually, other similar implementations are in progress.

Most of my projects prior to 1974 were conceived of as demonstrations of the feasibility of my theses, and many of them influenced architects in many countries, if not to follow the idea, at least to become inspired by the forms and organization of space visualized in my projects.

The Lycee David d'Angers was conceived by the future users, demonstrating that the method implemented for the CDC building is viable for public buildings too. The school, finished 1980, is very well considered by it present users.

From 1976 on I worked on transposing my methods and principles into the context of developing countries. "Food and roof" was the program I presented at the Habitat Conference in Vancouver, in the form of a manual (reported in The Vancouver Sun, and in many professional magazines).

From 1977 on, experience proved that program viable, and that information necessary for implementing it can be made accessible for most disfavoured people through inexpensive communication techniques like the "manuals" (wall-journals).

In 1982 the United nations University commissioned me to start a Communication Centre, whose task should be the transposition into the form of my "manuals" all the scientific results which can be useful and affective for poorest people (no-cash techniques in the fields of food, water management, land rehabilitation, self-help housing, energy, health and environment. Presently about 150 such manuals are ready and a large part of them is implemented.

The architect's task might be to make environment livable for people, livable in any sense . . .

—Yona Friedman

Yona Friedman is considered to be more a theoretician than a practicing architect, but he holds an accepted place in twentieth-century architecture, and his projects and concepts are valued by the profession.

Mobiltiy is his theme, and Friedman himself could be described as mobile. He left his native Hungary for France as a young man of twenty-two, and, after completing his architectural studies in Israel during the War of Independence, he returned to Paris. He has since made numerous journeys to the United States and Canada, Brazil, Great Britain, and Germany, where he has presented papers at conferences and lectured at universities and architectural schools.

It was at CIAM in Dubrovnik in 1956 that he realized that his ideas on the mobility of architecture were still largely unexplored. He began his search for young architects throughout Europe with ideas similar to his own, and formed his Group d'Etude

d'Architecture Mobile (GEAM) in 1958. By "mobility" Friedman suggests that the functional planning of a building must involve the ultimate user/owner: he must make the planning decisions; he must also be able to alter them again and again as situations change over a period of time. The purpose of GEAM was to research the possibilities of implementing changes for any possible use without having to demolish a building or any part of it. His concept of a non-determined infrastructure and the technique of "spanning over" a clear ground level allow the self-planner to design or redesign his space as he needs to use it.

Friedman's ideas were very slow to gather interest, but in the 1960s his first projects were published in Japan with the encouragement and help of Kenzo Tange. Interest in his work appeared across a wide spectrum of the profession, from the young student, Moshe Safdie, who used the subject for his master's thesis, to the wise and experienced Buckminster Fuller.

Despite his success and the interest now shown in his concepts, Friedman has remained a theoretician, not a builder, yet he derives enormous satisfaction from seeing his ideas implemented in the work of other architects and planners. He is also interested in putting into simple language, understood by the layman, the necessary instructions for the self-planner. This goal involves more than simple "do-it-yourself" planning instructions. Friedman's theories—to involve the occupant/worker/user in his surroundings, to allow him to plan them, to allow him the possibility of change to suit his routine and to facilitate his day-to-day work—require continual reassessment and refinement. He spends his time re-researching and reformulating his original ideas and working out what he sees as faults in his own proposals.

His book, *Towards a Scientific Architecture*, has been compared to Le Corbusier's *Towards a New Architecture*, and it is considered by some to contain deeper and more innovative architectural thought.

—Muriel Emanuel

FRY, E(dwin) Maxwell.
British. Born in Wallasey, Cheshire, 2 August 1899. Educated at the Liverpool Institute, 1910-17; School of Architecture, University of Liverpool, under Charles Reilly, 1920-23. Served in the King's Regiment, 1918-20: Lieutenant; served with the Royal Engineers in the Department of Fortifications and Works, War Office, London, 1939-42; Staff Captain/Major; Deputy Commandant, Royal Engineers, Gold Coast, West Africa, 1942-44. Married Ethel Speakman in 1927 (divorced, 1942); the architect Jane B. Drew, *q.v.*, in 1942; daughter: Ann. Assistant to the architects Adams and Thompson, London, 1925-27; Chief Assistant, Architects Department, Southern Railway, London, 1927-30; Partner, with Thomas Adams and Longstreth Thompson, Adams, Thompson and Fry, London, 1930-34; Partner, with Walter Gropius, Gropius and Fry, London, 1934-36, and continued alone until 1939; Town Planning Advisor to the Resident Minister, West Africa, 1944-46; Founder Partner, with Jane B. Drew, Fry, Drew and Partners, London (including Fry, Drew, Drake, and Lasdun, 1951-58), 1946-73, and Fry, Drew, Knight and Creamer (with Frank S. Knight and Norman Creamer), London, since 1973: now retired. Senior Architect for the New Capital, Chandigarh, Punjab, India, 1951-54. Vice-President, Royal Institute of British Architects, 1961-62. Exhibition: Drian Gallery, 1974 (paintings and drawings). Recipient: Royal Gold Medal for Architecture, Royal Institute of British Architects, 1964. LL.D.: University of Ibadan, Nigeria, 1966. Fellow of the Royal Institute of British Architects, and of the Royal Town Planning Institute; Associate

of the Royal Academy, 1966, and Royal Academician, 1972. Honorary Fellow, American Institute of Architects, 1973. C.B.E. (Commander, Order of the British Empire), 1953. Address: Fry, Drew, Knight and Creamer, The Chantry, 19 High Street, Sevenoaks, Kent TN14 6HG, England.

Works:

1933 Showroom for Westminster Electricity Supply Corporation, Victoria Street, London (demolished)
1934 "Little Winch" (house), Chipperfield, Hertfordshire
1935 The Sun House, Frognal Way, Hampstead, London
R. E. Sassoon House, St. Mary's Road, Peckham, London
Apartments, St. Leonard's Hill, Windsor, Berkshire (project; with Walter Gropius)
1936 Kensal House, Ladbroke Grove, London
House, 66 Old Church Street, Chelsea, London (with Walter Gropius)
Impington Village College, Cambridgeshire (with Walter Gropius)
The Wood House, Skipbourne, near Sevenoaks, Kent (with Walter Gropius)
Papworth Sanatorium School, Cambridgeshire (project; with Walter Gropius)
Histon School, Cambridgeshire (with Walter Gropius)
London Film Productions Worshops, Denham, Hertfordshire (with Walter Gropius)
Donaldson Houe, Sussex (with Walter Gropius)
1937 "Miramonte" (house), Coombe, near Kingston, Surrey
1938 Electricity showrooms, Regent Street, London
Flats, Ladbroke Grove, London
1940 Homerton College Nursery School, Cambridge
Cecil House (girls hostel), Gower Street, London
1946 Aburi School and College, Ghana
Adisadel College, Ghana (with Jane Drew)
Accra Community College, Ghana
Amedzofe Teacher Training College, Togoland (with Jane Drew)
1948 Broadcasting House, Nigerian Broadcasting Company, Kaduna
1949 The Tea Centre, London
1950 Passfields (flats), Lewisham, London (with Jane Drew)
Cooperative Bank of Western Nigeria, Ibadan
Ashanti Secondary School for Boys, Kumasi, Ghana
Royal Exchange Assurance Company Ltd., Ibadan, Nigeria
1951 Waterloo Bridge Entrance and Harbour Bar, *South Bank Exhibition*, Festival of Britain, London (with Jane Drew)
1953 Flats, Whitefoot Lane, Lewisham, London (with Jane Drew)
Flats, Bromley Road, Lewisham, London
1954 Oriental Insurance Company Office Block, Calcutta
1956 New Capital City, Chandigarh, India (with Jane Drew, Le Corbusier, and Pierre Jeanneret)
1958 Teacher Training Centre, Wudil, Nigeria
Women's Teachers Training College, Kano, Nigeria
1959 University College, Ibadan, Nigeria (with Jane Drew)
1960 Holy Cross School, Lagos, Nigeria
St. Matthias School, Lagos, Nigeria
St. Patrick's School, Lagos, Nigeria
College of Engineering, and Veterinary Science Buildings, University of Liverpool
Dow Agro Chemicals Ltd. Plant and Offices, King's Lynn, Norfolk

1961 British Petroleum Company Offices, Lagos, Nigeria
Housing, Lagos, Nigeria
Offices for Longmans Green, publishers, Lagos, Nigeria
1963 Wates Ltd. Head Office, Norbury, London
Plan for the University of Sheffield, Yorkshire
1964 Isle of Thorns College, Chelwood Gate, Sussex
1965 Chelwood House, Gloucester Square, London
1966 Legislative Assembly, Port Louis, Mauritius
1967 Kingston House, Hull
Macintosh Square Development, Gibraltar
1969 Mid-Glamorgan Crematorium
1972 Redevelopment of Hatfield Old Town, Hertfordshire
Garage, Old Hatfield, Hertfordshire
Shop Block A, Hatfield, Hertfordshire
1973 A1 Trunk Road Development Study
1974 Flats, Portchester Terrace, London
1975 Breakspear Crematorium, Northwood, London
1977 Institute of Education, Le Reduit, Mauritius

Publications:

By FRY: books—*The Need for Planning Town and Countryside* (pamphlet), with John Gloag, London 1933; *English Town Hall Architecture*, London 1934; *Fine Building*, London 1944; *The Bauhaus and the Modern Movement*, London 1968; *Art in a Machine Age*, London 1969; *Maxwell Fry: Autobiographical Sketches*, London 1975; books with Jane B. Drew— *Architecture for Children*, London 1944, revised edition as *Architecture and the Environment*, London 1976; *Village Housing in the Tropics*, in collaboration with Harry L. Ford, London 1947; *Tropical Architecture in the Humid Zone*, London 1956; *Tropical Architecture in the Dry and Humid Zones*, London 1964; articles—in *The Architects' Journal*, *RIBA Journal*, *Building*, *Contemporary Review*, etc.

On FRY: book—*Fry, Drew, Knight, Creamer: Architecture*, edited by Stephen Hitchins, introduction by H.A.N. Brockman, London 1978; articles— "Max Fry Remembers" by Maurice Cooper in *Building Design* (London), 24 January 1975; "The Origins of Impington" by Jack Pritchard and Alan Moody in *Northern Architect* (Sunderland), April 1975; "Modern Architecture in England" by Miguel Corominas in *Arquitectura* (Madrid), May 1975; "Max Fry" by A. E. J. Morris and Cornelius Murphy in *Building* (London), 31 October 1975; "Nigeria Today" by Noel Moffett in *RIBA Journal* (London), June 1977.

I entered architecture sufficiently versed in medieval architecture to win a history essay prize soon after joining the Liverpool School of Architecture. By the time I set my real course in architecture I had immersed myself in its classical interpretation of which I could value its detailed modulations as I could its larger modellings.

It was my appreciation of its excellence *in itself* that justified me in finding no place for it in a technocratic world and renouncing it. It was the prompting of my moral as of my reasoning nature that decided me in favour of a clean sweep of historical and associational references and that brought me at once to the centre of the Modern Architectural Movement, but without the widespread but foolish revolutionary gesture of condemning all that came before me.

In the hey-day of the Movement I found all the warmth and humanity I needed, for it freely encompassed what we have now, unwisely, I think, separated into the pseudo-science of sociology, into the amorphous pursuit of an environment, into a vain and vapid historicism, and into town-planning divorced from its roots in architecture.

The basic principles of the Movement enabled me

to analyse the human and climatic conditions of the humid West African tropics and to harmonise them in a manner that remained valid over a respectable period of time in any but the centres of high technology, money and nationalism.

A devastating war bringing in its wake vast increases in mechanical reproduction and instrumentation, together with an intensification of both commercialism and bureaucracy, prevented modern architecture from a gradual diversification in various materials at the expense of reinforced concrete as the sole means of expression, though not of support. I have never used it in its "brut" state on account of its manifest inability to weather in any but the dryest climates.

For all my working life I have been an independent individual for whom work has been the greatest pleasure. I believe that art is a celebration of life and is so recognised by those who value life. In my old age I paint, which is the next best thing.

—E. Maxwell Fry

E. Maxwell Fry can be rightly regarded as the father of the Modern Movement in architecture in Britain. Born near Liverpool, he trained at the University School of Architecture under Professor Charles Reilly and joined the London town planning practice of Adams and Thompson in the mid 1930s. One of the first examples in London of Fry's work was the showroom for the then Westminster Electricity Supply Corporation in Victoria Street. The building has since been destroyed in the redevelopment of Victoria Street, but it was one of the outstanding examples of shop design in Europe. By the use of a large non-reflecting window set back from the pavement, Fry united interior and exterior of the showroom. The interior fittings and furniture were all designed with great care and set a standard for shop design than has seldom been equalled.

In the 1930s, much of Maxwell Fry's work was concerned with individual houses, many of which were built only after prolonged battles with planning authorities and local objectors. Fortunately, several still survive and today, more than 40 years later, it is difficult to understand the heated debate caused by "Little Winch" at Chipperfield, Hertfordshire, a flat roofed, brick house with a weather-boarded studio, and the Sun House, Frognal Way, Hampstead, a concrete house on a south facing steeply sloping site with splendid views over London.

The problem of low rental housing was one to which Fry devoted much attention and research at a time when local authority housing was universally conceived in "mock Georgian" style. The block of flats built in Peckham and known as R. E. Sassoon House was unique. Admittedly, the size of the scheme was modest by today's standards—twenty flats on five floors with balcony access and no lift— but each flat had a large balcony and generously sized rooms, fitted kitchen and a separate bathroom. This latter feature was a novelty in "working class" dwellings where the norm was a bath under a tabletop in the kitchen. By careful standardization of details and repetition throughout, Fry built the flats of in-situ concrete at an average cost of 362 per flat (including professional fees), just over 50 pence per square foot; they were let at economic rents of little more than 50 pence per week. Kensal House, a second low-cost housing project, was built on the site of an abandoned gas-holder in Ladbrook Grove. The scheme, which was sponsored by the Gas Light and Coke Company to demonstrate the use of coal gas, consisted of 68 flats and included a social club, tenants' recreation room, shops, and a nursery school and playground. Like Sassoon House, Kensal House was limited to five floors without lifts, but staircase access was provided to each pair of flats instead of the common gallery approach. The flats were spacious and well planned, and each had both sitting and drying balconies; once again the structure was in-situ reinforced concrete, and Fry paid great attention to detail and to standardization. Rents at Kensal House also averaged 50 pence per week. Few

modern housing projects can compare favourably with these schemes both in overall conception and detailed design: after 40 years Kensal House is still a model of its kind. Maxwell Fry's early housing work set the standard, influenced by the Gropius's housing work of the early 1930s, by which all subsequent housing must be judged.

Fry himself admits that his pre-war work was influence by Mies van der Rohe, and both The Sun House and Miramonte show that influence clearly in the horizontal window pattern, the white walls and the projecting balcony roofs, all reminiscent of Mies' Tugendhat House of 1930. Walter Gropius joined Fry in London from 1934 to 1936, having left Germany as a refugee from the Nazi regime; but during his resident in Britain little advantage was taken of the presence of such a distinguished educationalist and designer. A number of interesting projects were produced with Fry, but they were often rejected because they were too modern. The most important building actually erected by the Fry-Gropius partnership was the Impington Village College. This building, small by present-day school standards, was a landmark in school design in its integration of building and site; the simple internal spatial arrangements and human scale resulted in a complex that caused a contemporary critic to describe it as "one of the finest sets of school buildings in the country."

During the war years Maxwell Fry spent part of his period of war service in West Africa and later advised on village planning in Nigeria. This led to the establishment of a practice with Jane Drew which was responsible for large scale planning and building work in that country. It was typical of the Fry approach to architecture that a great deal of basic research was carried out on tropical architecture, and the book by Fry and Drew on the subject soon became the standard textbook for architects involved in building in the tropics. Much of the work of the practice was concerned with school and university building. In the immediate post-war years Maxwell Fry was one of the first British architects to become involved in overseas work, and his distinctive style of building, using local materials combined with careful detailing intended to reduce the impact of the climatic extremes, resulted in a series of buildings, such as the University of Ibadan, which demonstrate Fry's role as a pioneer.

In 1951 Le Corbusier invited Maxwell Fry to join the team at Chandigarh, the new capital of the Punjab in India. Fry, with Jane Drew, took on the task of translating Le Corbusier's design for a new city in the arid plains of Noth India into a reality. They were particularly concerned with the housing zones of the project, and it is in these areas that Chandigarh is most successful, in spite of the rigid road grid established by Le Corbusier's master plan. The architectural achievements of the new capital were largely due to the influence of Maxwell Fry and his concern not only for good buildings but also for the people who would use them.

Throughout his professional career Maxwell Fry has always been a pioneer. Attention to detail, the understanding of basic needs, and his insistence on the importance of a building in its environment has earned him a place in the history of twentieth century architecture.

—Edward D. Mills

FUCHS, Bohuslav.

Czechoslovakian. Born in Všechovice, Bystřice pod Hostýnem, 24 March 1895. Educated under Jaroslav Syřišté, Technical School, Brno, 1910-14; under Jan Kotěra, Academy of Arts, Prague, 1916-19. Married. Worked in the architectural office of Jan Kotěra, Prague, 1919-21; shared studio with the architect Josef Štěpánek, Prague, 1921-23; architect. City Building and Planning Department, Brno, 1923-29; also in private practice, Brno, 1923, until his death, 1972. Lecturer, School of Art, Gottwaldov, Czechoslovakia, in the 1930s; Lecturer, 1945-47, and Professor of Architecture, 1947-58, Technical University of Brno. Member, Left Front, Czechoslovakia, 1930; member of the Czech group from 1930, and Czech delegate 1953, CIAM (Congres Internationaux d'Architecture Moderne). Honorary Deputy Chairman, International Federation of Housing and Town Planning, The Hague, 1948-60. Recipient: Brno Prize, 1955; Gottfried von Herder Prize, Vienna, 1969. Honorary Corresponding Member, Royal Institute of British Architects, 1937; Member, Czech Academy of Arts and Science, 1940; Honorary Doctor of Technical Science, Czechoslovakia, 1956; Artist of Merit, Czechoslovakia, 1966; National Artist, Czechoslovakia, 1968. *Died* (in Brno) *18 September 1972.*

Works:

1920 Malá Strana Master Plan, Prague (competition project)
Letná Master Plan, Prague (competition project; with J. Štěpánek and A. Moudry)
City Centre Master Plan, Prostejov, Czechoslovakia (competition project; with J. Štěpánek)
Masaryk Chalet, Serlich, Orlické hory, Czechoslovakia
Klostermann Chalet, Modrava, Sumava, Czechoslovakia
1923 Single-family housing, Mickova Street, Husovice, Brno
Single-family houses, Mahenova Street/ Barvičova Street, Lerchov, Brno
River Training Works, Klarow Bridgehead, Malá Strana, Prague (project)
Administration Building, Bystřice pod Hostýnem, Czechoslovakia
1923/
24 Single-family housing, Dolnopoloi Street, Brno
1924 Meat Exchange Building, Masná Street, Brno
Summer School, Lelekovice, Czechoslovakia
Elementary School, Maloměřice, Brno
1925 Ceremonial Hall, Central Cemetery, Brno (with J. Polášek)
Zeman Café, Brno
Nursery School, Husovice, Brno
1926 Municipal housing, Nováčkova Street, Husovice, Brno
Elementary and Secondary School, Křídlovická Street, Brno (completed by J. Polášek, 1932)
1926/
27 City Centre Master Plan, Brno (Competition project)
1927 Open-air swimming pool reconstruction, Brno (project)
Rudolf Kropáče Sanatorium, Brno
Viola and Radum Boarding Houses, Brno
1927/
28 Triple-house, 6-10 Petřvaldská Street, Brno (for the *New Housing Exhibition*)
Hotel Avion, 20 Česka Street, Brno
Fuchs House, 2 Hvězdárenká Street, Brno
Brno Pavilion, *Exhibition of Contemporary Culture,* Brno
1928 Spa Centre reconstruction, Luhačovice, Czechoslovakia (competition project)
Elementary School additions, Židenice, Brno
Elementary School, Jiráskova čtvrt, Brno
1928/
30 VESNA Women's Vocational School, 18 Lípová Street, Brno (with J. Polášek)
1929 Bohemian-Moravian Printing Company Offices, Brno (competition project)
Trade and Commercial Schools Complex, Brno (competition project)

Display installations, *Modern Trade Exhibition,* Brno
Dagma Children's Hospice, Zeleného Street, Brno
Workers' Colony, Lyskov u Frydu-Kistek, Czechoslovakia
1929/
30 Municipal Swimming Pool, 25 Kimentova Street, Zábrdovice, Brno
Eliška Machová Boarding-house, 16 Lípová Street, Brno
Masaryk Students' Hostel, 21 Cihlářská Street, Brno
Moravian Bank, 21 Svobody Square, Brno (with A. Wiesner)
1930/
31 Morava Convalescent Home, Tatranská Lamnica, Czechoslovakia
1931 Municipal Savings Bank, Třebič, Czechoslovakia
Sokol Cinema reconstruction, Lipník nad Bečvou, Czechoslovakia (project)
1932 Pešat Department Store, Moravská Ostrava, Czechoslovakia
1933 Velké District Communications and Economic Master Plan, Brno (competition project)
Hamalčík Sanatorium, Starý Smokovec, Czechoslovakia (project)
Family house with picture-gallery, Židenice, Brno (project)
1935 Apartment Building, Bratislava, Czechoslovakia
Fuchs weekend house, Dolni Loučky, Czechoslovakia
1935/
36 Zelena Zaba (Green Frog) Thermal Swimming Pool and Restaurant, Tenčianské Teplice, Czechoslovakia
1936 Petrák Villa, 4 M. Pujmannové Street, Brno
ALDA Company Administration Building, 34 Mencova Street, Brno
Family house, Heřmanův Městec, Czechoslovakia
Czech Pavilion, *Exposition Internationale,* Paris (competition project)
Single-family house, Brno
1937 Tesař Villa, 18 Hroznová Street, Brno
Provincial Military Headquarters Building, 73/75 Leninova Street, Brno
Family house, Mokrá Hora, near Brno
Czech Pavilion, *World's Fair,* New York (competition project)
1938 Railway Station Post Office, 7 Czech Army Square, Brno
1939 Family houses, Skryje, near Tišnov, Czechoslovakia
House of Culture, Moravaská Ostrava, Czechoslovakia (project)
1940/
46 Hotel Vicina, Frenštát pod Radhoštěm, Czechoslovakia
1942 Water Power Plant, Skryje, near Tišnov, Czechoslovakia
1943 Western District Reconstruction Plan, Zlín, near Gottwaldov, Czechoslovakia
1948/
49 Bus Terminal Building, Brno (partially constructed)
1951 City Centre Master Plan, Košice, Czechoslovakia
1952/
54 City Master Plan, Velká Nitra, Czechoslovakia
1954 City Centre Clearance Plan, Brno
1957 City Hall and Square, Toronto, Ontario (competition project)
1959/
60 City and Regional Traffic Plan, Prague
1961 Ethnographic Collection installations, Moravian Museum, Brno
1962/
64 National Theatre Area Development Plan, Prague

Publications:

On FUCHS: books—*Architekt Bohuslav Fuchs: 1919-1929* by Zdeněk Rossmann, Basle 1930; *Bohuslav Fuchs* by Zdeněk Kudělka, Prague 1966; *Bohuslav Fuchs: Architectural Works in Brno* by František Kalidova, Brno 1970; articles—"Die Neue Frauenschule in Brunn" and "Das Brunner Studenthaus" in *Wasmuth's Monatshefte für Baukunst* (Berlin), vol. 15, 1931; "Das Haus der Mahrischen Bank in Bruno" in *Wasmuth's Monatshefte für Baukunst* (Berlin), vol. 16, 1932; "Das Stadische Bad in Brunn" by Wilhelm Bisom in *Wasmuth's Monatshefte für Baukunst* (Berlin), vol. 17, 1933; "A Swimming Pool in Czechoslovakia" in *Architect and Building News* (London), 23 September 1938; "Piscine Thermale en Plein Air à Trencianske Teplice, Tchechoslovaquie" in *L'Architecture d'Aujourd'hui* (Paris), October 1938; "Bathing Pool, Czechoslovakia" in *The Architects' Journal* (London), 16 March 1939; "Piscina en Checoslovaquia" in *Arquitectura* (Madrid), July 1943; Bohuslav Fuchs, 1895-1972" in *Bauwelt* (Berlin), 13 November 1972; "Obituary: Bohuslav Fuchs" in *RIBA Journal* (London), January 1973; "Bohuslav Fuchs" by Frank Ameil Walker in *The Architects' Journal* (London), 7 November 1973; "Bohuslav Fuchs" in *Parametro* (Bologna), March 1983.

Bohuslav Fuchs was 23 years of age in 1918 when the Czechoslovak Republic came into being. He was then a student at the Academy of Arts in Prague under Professor Jan Kotěra in whose celebrated School of Architecture a number of leading Czechoslovak architects were trained, among them Gočár, Chochol and Janák. Fuchs inevitably caught the enthusiasm and optimism that swept through the new independent Republic, an ideal social and cultural climate for the development of a highly-gifted architect who had already had a thorough technical training before becoming Kotěra's pupil.

As early as 1920 Fuchs, while working as an assistant in Kotěra's studio, was among the prize winners in two town planning competitions for the Malá Strana district of Prague and the new City of Prostějov.

During the formative years of the early 1920's, which were of great importance in the evolution of modern architecture there was a struggle to break from the already sterile but still prevailing formalism of the past and to find a new visual and functional expression of the rapidly changing social and political conditions. Fuchs' first buildings of this period—the Administrative offices in Bystřice and the Meat Exchange in Brno—vividly illustrate this struggle. They are a mixture of Dutch influence (Dudok), Behrens' monumentality and the starkness of Adolf Loos, but Fuchs' planning already shows the clarity and functional logic which would mark his later work.

His 1925 buildings in Brno—the Ceremonial Hall for the City Cemetery and the Cafe Zeman—marked the next step towards a definitive breakthrough, which came two years later with the Hotel Avion and the housing estate Nový Dum. Mies van der Rohe, in a lecture at the Technical University in Brno in 1930, said that the Hotel Avion was one of the most important buildings in the modern international movement. It stands on a very narrow and deep site in a small street in the centre of the city and is a little masterpiece of spatial and functional design. The progression of interlocking spaces, both in plan and section, is perfectly handled and visually exciting. The Vitrolite-clad elevation has a crispness and precision that could only have been achieved by the new industrial technology. Fuchs repeated it on his Moravian Bank in Brno, and the cladding was subsequently widely used by other architects.

The International Trade Fair and Exhibition Hall, bold in conception, with a daring reinforced concrete structure, gave Fuchs an opportunity to take his understanding of space a step further. On a visit to Prague in 1938 Le Corbusier commented: "It is

instructive for me to see architecture on this scale in actual reality. I, who have so far built only a few relatively small buildings, understand now how I must design big buildings."

In the foothills of the Carpathian Mountains in a beautiful thickly wooded valley, Fuchs built the Zelená Žaba (Green Forg Open Air Swimming Pool, Café and Restaurant. This light and airy building, its long curving balconies and terraces following the contours of the hills, belongs in its setting as if it had grown up with the trees. It was his last major work before the Second World War.

After the War Fuchs devoted most of his time to town planning and teaching at the Technical University of Brno. Town planning—then a purely statistical and technical problem, the exclusive domain of the civil engineer—was for Fuchs an integral part of architecture. To clear logic, strict discipline in functional planning, thorough understanding of structure and an appreciation of existing social conditions, he added a feeling for form and composition that gave his work an added dimension.

Fuchs' contribution to the shaping of modern architecture in the 1920's and '30's in Czechoslovakia and in Europe as a whole was very considerable, but he was, perhaps, less well known abroad than some of his contemporaries. This may to some extent have been due to the fact that he lived and worked not in the capital Prague but in Brno, Moravia, the second city of Czechoslovakia.

—Eugene Rosenberg

FUJII, Hiromi.

Japanese. Born in Tokyo, 23 August 1935. Studied at the Waseda University School of Architecture, Tokyo, 1958; studied and worked in Professor M. Take's studio at Waseda University, 1958-64. Married Hiroko Todoroki in 1968; child: Yuri. Worked for Angelo Mangiarotti, Milan, 1964-66, with Peter Smithson, London, 1966, and for Yorke, Rosenberg, Mardall, London, 1967. Since 1968, Principal, Hiromi Fujii Architect and Associates, Tokyo. Lecturer, 1968, and Associate Professor, 1973, Shibaura Institute of Technology, Tokyo; Visiting Critic, Waseda University School of Architecture, 1978. Exhibitions: *Matwya Exhibition*, Tokyo, 1978; *New Wave of Japanese Architecture*, toured the United States, 1978. Address (office): Room 402, 37-4 Toya-ma-cho, Shinjuku-ku, Tokyo, Japan.

Works:

1971 Suzuki House, Tokyo
  Suzuki Apartment, Tokyo
  Project C (house)
  Project E (house)
  Project S (house)
  Project L (house)
  Project for Mr. Y (house)
  Project for Mr. A. (house)
1972 Snack 7 (restaurant), Tokyo
1973 Miyajima House, Tokyo
1975 Todoroki House, Ichikawa, Chiba Prefecture, Japan
  Project: Similar, Connotation (house)
  Project: Continuity (house)
  Project: Similar, Symmetry (house)
  Project: Congruity, Symmetry (house)
  Project: Similar, Connotation, Junction (house)
1976 Marutake Doll Company Office Building, Saitama, Japan
1980 House/Pharmacy, Chofu, Tokyo
1985 Ushimado International Arts Centre, Japan

Publications:

By FUJII: articles—"Architectural Senses of Anonymity" in *Toshijutaku* (Tokyo), January 1969; "On Negativity" in *Space Design* (Tokyo), February 1969; "A Note on the Negativity of Materialism" in *Architecture + Urbanism* (Tokyo), February, April and July 1971; "Architecture of Negativeness" in *Toshijutaku* (Tokyo), October 1971; "Now What Are We Asking of Architecture" in *Space Design* (Tokyo), March 1972; "Articulation" in *Toshijutaku* (Tokyo), June 1972; "Indication of the Visual Point of Absence" in *Space Design* (Tokyo), August 1972; "The Meaning of Negativeness" in *The Japan Architect* (Tokyo), July 1973; "Sympathy for the Solid" in *Architecture + Urbanism* (Tokyo), December 1973; "Reflection and Transparency" in *Architecture + Urbanism* (Tokyo), June 1974; "Aspects of Intimacy to Objects" in *Toshijutaku* (Tokyo), June 1974; "On Deep Structure" in *Kenchikubunka* (Tokyo), April 1975; "The Castle of Cards" in *The Japan Architect* (Tokyo), July 1975; "Expression for Itself" in *Kenchikubunka* (Tokyo), November 1975; "Zero Degree of Recognition" in *The Japan Architect* (Tokyo), June 1976; "Liberation from Existence" in *The Japan Architect* (Tokyo), February 1977, "Casa del Fascio, Italy" in *Space Design* (Tokyo), March 1979; "Hiromi Fujii's vision-reversing machine", with Hajime Yatsuka, in *Oppositions* (New York), Fall 1980; "Architectural Metamorphology" in *The Japan Architect* (Tokyo), November/December 1980.

On FUJII: book—*New Wave of Japanese Architecture*, exhibition catalogue, by Kenneth Frampton, New York 1978; articles—"Hiromi Fujii" by Veda Makoto in *Mizue* (Tokyo), July 1975; "The Game of Intellectual Matter" by Kazuyuki Honda in *The Japan Architect* (Tokyo), August 1975; "Intension to Architectural Language" by Masahiko Mineo in *Shotenkenchiku* (Tokyo), August 1975; "The Work of Hiromi Fujii" by David Stewart in *Architecture + Urbanism* (Tokyo), September 1975; "An Anarchist's Guide to Modern Architecture" by Chris Fawcett in *Architectural Association Quarterly* (London), no. 3, 1975; "The Post Metabolists" in *Arquitectura* (Madrid), January/February 1979; "Thirty controversial houses", special issue of *l'Architecture d'Aujourd'hui* (Paris), April 1983.

It happened several years ago. I used to pass in front of an old building near my office that was being pulled down. On that particular day, as it was already late in the evening, I could see no one working on the building. Several stories of the old building had been demolished, leaving only a few concrete pillars and the first and second floors.

The buildings nearby were already lit up; neon lights were beginning to brighten; people were hurrying for their homes. The thick, clouded sky echoed commotion and the noises of the town. Yet, in spite of the clamour of the town, I felt a different atmosphere, as if of a completely different time and space, over the block of the demolished building. Inside and outside of the building there were lumps of stone, concrete and iron scattered about: there was no space to put a foot.

At the one corner retaining some of its original shape, the thick concrete wall's section produced irregular geometrical patterns. They dispersed so much they looked almost beautiful. Surrounded by these bare "objects," which seemed lurid and frightful, I was more impressed with the grave importance of existence than with magnificent town buildings. "Is our meaningless and useless existence untrue—or are you who grasp it only in that way mistaken?" This encounter with objects was one of the few experiences that appealed to my inner life. A ruin is, fundamentally speaking, a place which is bare or useless. The real shape or phase of objects can be visible here, whereas in our daily life it is difficult to face up to the reality of a structure because of its effective value, or the terms we artificially believe. But ruins no longer flatter us, they are no longer subordinate to men. They recover their real expression, and this existence itself appeals exactly to our inner life. From the ordinary point of view, this bare object, after effacing its effectiveness or its ordinary affectation, can be described as simply meaningless or "negative." On the other hand, from a spiritual point of view, it can be described as "positive." But I dare to name it a "negative object" because of its daily occurrence, and also name the process effacing its usual meaning as "negativeness."

Putting aside the question of whether this negative object can be recognized as architecture, I convey my new encounter between the mind and the object in a concept of "negativeness." Moreover, it is not only this bare object in the ruins that can be called a "negative object;" we are also able to find unexpected objects when we enlarge the encounter between man and objects.

Even now, I am struck from time to time by the old encounter with the space abruptly seen at the corner of the town where there are splendid buildings and colorful displays in shop windows.

A previous encounter with space was in a tunnel, an encounter I still remember as of blank geometric patterns stretching straighforwardly. Nothing in particular appealed to me there. I saw nothing but grey color fading away between the boundaries of the walls, ceiling, floor and a straight edge stretching to the infinity of the grey square box. It was as if I was under an hallucination, absorbed by the infinity of the tunnel. I felt a certain response: I thought of the scene as beautiful. Surrounded by these objects, I was more comfortable in the complete silence than in the noises of the town, deeply impressed more by the existence of the grey color than by the bright colors of the outside world. It is possible to explain exactly about this tunnel? Of course, it is correct to say that it is an underground communication road from one place to another—but that is not the point: an explanation of function does not explain my experience in the tunnel. The only explanation of the experience of the tunnel is that it involved blank, square geometrical patterns and grey color; the reason of my partiality for the tunnel is that it refused every usual significance. It is an ultimate shape without any banal explanation, without any meaning in our everyday life. This ultimate shape is the very form of the blank geometrical patterns and the grey color which I have been repeating, over and over again. This form can also be said to be a negative object. When I stand in front of this negativeness I am aware of the uselessness of expression, of the terms which I have learned in order to explain. There, negative form and color is so neutral that we have to create its meaning as we like. It may also be said that this negative object is absolute existence, which is impartial, neither objective nor subjective, neither rational nor irrational.

I have been explaining my experiences of these encounters with the object at great length—but I have been trying to show that my new theory is on the same lines as that of something as material as a manhole cover and something as abstract as the color grey. It is difficult to generalize or to formulate a logical theory here and now. At the moment, on one hand, I am trying to put the theory of the manhole cover and the color grey into a logical pattern, but, on the other hand, I am searching for a pattern more practical and more radical to replace it.

—Hiromi Fujii

The information immediately available to us before one of Hiromi Fujii's houses is both slender and rich. He feels no need to inform. He wants to express nothing, consequently his buildings are without the burden of language. He presents us with an objective denial of any representation. By expressing nothing he is acting in accordance with his perception of what he calls the encompassing "emptiness." This expression of nothing is the paradoxical basis of his work, for one of his buildings is quite clearly a threat

Hiromi Fujii: Todoroki House, Chiba, Japan, 1975.

to the emptiness. His designs, therefore, have a way of simultaneously portraying and effectively diminishing the emptiness, and through this dialectical process we come to envisage the limits within which architecture can be found. Imagining and understanding aren't so very different.

Fujii is appraising architecture on a time scale far removed from our usual reckoning. The past that he faces could be said to be our future, and this is how the menacing aspect enters in. It's the fellowship of the marvellous and the ominous: his designs don't fit current facts but are more predictive, probing into what others shun. Can we say we learn enough from one of his designs to guide us through our surroundings? What we can recognize there apart from architecture itself? Faces have two eyes, and only one needs to be seen for a face to be identified. If a head, one can guarantee a body and a pair of legs. In much the same way we can make great sense of a house by just glimpsing its pitched roof, and through a chain of associated images readily picture it. This isn't the case with a house by Fujii, and identification of its function is impeded by its form, scale and materials, so that its setting in a residential context only serves to exaggerate the ambiguity, i.e. the richness of conflicting associations. Are we being urged to help salvage architecture from the twentieth century? Or is it beyond assistance, does it need something more?

To see one of Fujii's buildings is to see the whole of architecture on trial, and in this way he can be considered the watching institution of Japanese

architecture, tackling many problems not only overlooked by architects, but also more generally ignored. He goes directly to the authentic processes of architecture, while ignoring what seems to be the actual components. He does not begin with a site and derive from it some particular values; instead, at the outset, he has an a priori formulation, which he doesn't so much apply to the site as apply to the whole world. Everything must be compatible with the real world, and his buildings are no exception, despite the rigorous standard he pursues in his own way. Seeing Fujii's work is one way of seeing more than I have ever seen before.

His constructs, then, could be said to be building towards the *mu no basho* (the place of nothingness), central to the theory of Kyoto school philosopher Kitaro Nishida. This is as true for his earlier work (take the negating absence of the Suzuki House, 1971) as it is for his middle period (such as his Marutake Building, 1976, which involves conditions of ellipsis, proportional opposition, link-like layering, shearing...) as it is for his later work (his Ushimado International Arts Centre, 1985, which he devotes to a variety of transformations rst he transformed a barn on the site, which was then transformed into a white office, which was then transformed into the coffee shop...) Whatever the specific form or method, they are all substantial annexes to his place or nothingness. He helps us to see what otherwise we wouldn't want to.

—Chris Fawcett

FULLER, Richard Buckminster.

American. Born in Milton, Massachusetts, 12 July 1895. Educated at Milton Academy, 1904-13; Harvard University, Cambridge, Massachusetts, 1913-15; United States Naval Academy, Annapolis, Maryland, 1917. Served in the United States Navy, 1917-19: Lieutenant. Married Anne Hewlett in 1917; children: Alexandra (died) and Allegra. Assistant Export Manager, Armour and Company, New York, 1919-21; National Accounts Sales Manager, Kelly-Springfield Truck Company, 1922; President, Stockdale Building System, Chicago, 1922-27; Founder and President, 4D Company, Chicago, 1927-32; Editor and Publisher, *Shelter* magazine, Philadelphia, 1930-32; Founder, Director, and Chief Engineer, Dymaxion Corporation, Bridgeport, Connecticut, 1932-36; Assistant to the Director of Research and Development, Phelps Dodge Corporation, New York, 1936-38; Technical Consultant on the staff of *Fortune* magazine, New York, 1938-40; Vice-President and Chief Engineer, Dymaxion Company Inc., Delaware, 1940-50; Chief Mechanical Engineer, United States Board of Economic Warfare, Washington, D.C., 1942-44, and Special Assistant to the Deputy Director of the United States Foreign Economic Administration, Washington, 1944; Chairman and Chief Engineer, Dymaxion Dwelling Machine Corporation, Wichita, Kansas, 1944-46; Chairman, Fuller Research Foundation, Wichita, 1946-54; President, Synergetics Inc., Raleigh, North Carolina, 1954-59. President of Geodesics Inc., Forest Hills, New York, 1949 until his death in 1983; President of Plydomes Inc., Des Moines, Iowa, 1957-83; Chairman, Tetrahelix Corporation, Hamilton, Ohio, 1959-83; Senior Partner, Fuller and Sadao, Long Island City, New York, 1979-83; Chairman of the Board, R. Buckminster Fuller, Sadao and Zung Architects, Cleveland, Ohio, 1979-83; Senior Partner, Buckminster Fuller Associates, London, 1979-83. Research Professor, 1959-68, University Professor, 1968-75, Distinguished University Professor, 1972-75, and University Professor Emeritus, 1975-83, Southern Illinois University, Carbondale. Charles Eliot Norton Professor of Poetry, Harvard University, 1962-63; Harvey Cushing Orator, American Association of Neuro-Surgeons, 1967; Nehru Lecturer, New Delhi, 1969; Hoyt Fellow, Yale University, New Haven, Connecticut, 1969; Fellow, St. Peter's College, Oxford, 1970; World Fellow in Residence, consortium of the University of Pennsylvania, Haverford College, Swarthmore College, Bryn Mawr College, and the University City Science Center, Philadelphia, and Consultant to the Design Science Institute, Philadelphia, 1972-83; Tutor in Design Science, International Community College, Los Angeles, 1975, Editor-at-Large, *World Magazine*, New York, 1972-75; President, Triton Foundation, Cambridge, Massachusetts, 1967; International President, MENSA, Paris, 1975, and World Society for Ekistics, Athens, 1975; Consultant to Architects Team 3, Penang, Malaysia, 1974-83. Exhibitions: Dymaxion House, Harvard University, 1929, and American Institute of Architects, Washington, D.C., 1930; Dymaxion Automobile, Worlds Fair, Chicago, 1933; Dymaxion Bathroom, Museum of Modern Art, New York, 1937; Dymaxion Deployment Unit, Museum of Modern Art, New York, 1940; Dymaxion World Map, Museum of Modern Art, New York, 1943; outdoor garden exhibit, Museum of Modern Art, New York, 1959; United States Embassy, London (individual), 1962; Spoleto Festival, Italy (individual), 1967; Dymaxion Car No. 2, Museum of Modern Art, New York, 1968; Museum of Science and Industry, Chicago (retrospective), 1973 (toured the United States); Tetraschroll, Museum of Modern Art, New York, and Museum of Art, Philadelphia, 1977; *50 Years of Buckminster Fuller*, Ronald Feldman Gallery, New York, 1977; Carl Solway Gallery, Cincinnati, Ohio, and New York, 1977; *Jitterbug—A Sculpture*, Protetch McIntosh Gallery, Washington, D.C., 1977; *Toward a Fuller Future*, Van Wezel Performing Arts Center, Sarasota, Florida, 1978; *Inventions*, Getler Pall Gallery, New

R. Buckminster Fuller with geodesic dome at *Expo 67*, Montreal, 1967.

York, and Carl Solway Gallery, Cincinnati, Ohio, 1981, De Cordova Museum, Lincoln, Massachusetts, Fendrick Gallery, Washington, D.C., and Watari Gallery, Tokyo, 1982; *Creativity*, Pacific Science Center, Seattle, Washington, 1983. Collections: Art Institute of Chicago; Baltimore Museum of Art, Maryland; University of California, Los Angeles; Fogg Museum, Harvard University, Cambridge, Massachusetts; Metropolitan Museum of Art, New York; Museum of Modern Art, New York; Philadelphia Museum of Art; Seattle Art Museum, Washington; Staatliche Museum, Berlin; Victoria and Albert Museum, London. Recipient: Award of Merit, American Institute of Architects, New York Chapter, 1952; Grand Prize, *Triennale*, Milan, 1954 and 1957; Award of Merit, United States Marine Corps, 1955; Gold Medal, Scarab: National Architectural Society, 1958; Gold Medal, Philadelphia Chapter, American Institute of Architects, 1960; Frank P. Brown Medal, Franklin Institute, Phildelphia, 1962; Allied Professions Gold Medal, 1963, Architectural Design Award, 1968, and Gold Medal, 1970, American Institute of Architects; Plomado de Oro Award, Society of Mexican Architects, 1963; Delta Phi Delta Gold Key, 1964; Creative Achievement Award, Brandeis University, Waltham, Massachusetts, 1965; First Award of Excellence, Industrial Designers Society of America, 1966; Order of Lincoln Medal, Lincoln Academy, Illinois, 1967; Gold Medal for Architecture, National Institute of Arts and Letters, 1968; Royal Gold Medal for Architecture, Royal Institute of British Architects, 1968; Citation of Excellence, National Institute of Steel Construction, 1969; Humanist of the Year Award, American Association of Humanists, 1969; McGraw-Hill Master Designer in Product Engineering Award, 1969; Alpha Rhio Chi Master Architect Life Award, 1970; President's Award, University of Detroit, 1971; Salmagundi Medal, Salmagundi

Club, New York, 1971; Annual Award of Merit, Philadelphia Art Alliance, 1973; Honorary Citizenship Award, City of Philadelphia, 1973; Service Award, Southern Illinois University, 1976; Gold Medal, National Arts Club, U.S.A., 1976; Architectural Achievement Award, Samsonite Corporation, 1977; Engineering and Science Award, Drexel University, Philadelphia, 1977; Henry Townley Heald Award, Illinois Institute of Technology, Chicago, 1977; Honor Award, Stevens Institute of Technology, Hoboken, New Jersey, 1977; Quest Medal, St. Edward's University, Austin, Texas, 1979; Lifelong Learning Award, Metropolitan State University, 1979; Raymond A. Dart Award, United Steelworkers Association, 1979; John Scott Award, City of Philadelphia, 1979; Dean's Award, Buffalo Architectural School, Buffalo, New York, 1980; President's Fellow Award, Rhode Island School of Design, Providence, 1982; Distinguished Service Award, World Future Society, 1982; Medal of Freedom, U.S.A., 1983. Doctor of Design: North Carolina State University, Raleigh, 1954; Doctor of Arts: University of Michigan, Ann Arbor, 1955; Southern Illinois University, Carbondale, 1959; D.Sc.: Washington University, St. Louis, 1957; University of Colorado, Boulder, 1964; Bates College, Lewiston, Maine, 1969; University of Maine, Orono, 1972; Pratt Institute, Brooklyn, New York, 1974; McGill University, Montreal, 1974; Hahnemann Medical College, 1978; D.H.L.: Rollins College, Winter Park, Florida, 1960; Monmouth College, West Long Branch, New Jersey, 1965; California State Colleges, 1966; Long Island University, Greenvale, New York, 1966; Dartmouth College, Hanover, New Hampshire, 1968; University of Rhode Island, Kingston, 1968; New England College, Henniker, New Hampshire, 1968; Brandeis University, Waltham, Massachusetts, 1970; Columbia College, Chicago, 1970; St. Joseph's

College, Philadelphia, 1974; University of Pennsylvania, Philadelphia, 1974; Hobart and William Smith Colleges, Geneva, New York, 1975; Southern Illinois University, Carbondale, 1979; Alaska Pacific University, 1979; Roosevelt University, Chicago, 1980; Newport University, 1980; D.L.: Clemson University, South Carolina, 1964; Park College, Parkville, Missouri, 1970; Grinnell College, Iowa, 1972; Emerson College, Boston, 1972; Nasson College, Springvale, Maine, 1973; International College, 1979; D.F.A.: University of New Mexico, Albuquerque, 1964; California State College of Arts and Crafts, Oakland, 1966; Ripon College, Wisconsin, 1968; Boston College, 1969; Minneapolis School of Art, 1970; Rensselaer Polytechnic Institute, Troy, New York, 1973; D.Eng.: Clarkson College of Technology, Potsdam, New York, 1967; University of Notre Dame, Indiana, 1974; D.Arch.Eng.: University of Wisconsin, Madison, 1969; Doctor of Science and Humane Letters: Wilberforce University, Ohio, 1970; Doctor of Fine and Applied Arts: Southeastern Massachusetts University, North Dartmouth, 1971; D.Lit.: Beaver College, Glenside, Pennsylvania, 1973; D.Hum.: Georgian Court College, Lakewood, New Jersey, 1980; Texas Wesleyan University, Fort Worth, 1981. Member, National Academy of Design; Fellow, American Institute of Architects, and of the Building Research Institute of the National Academy of Sciences; Life Fellow, American Association for the Advacement of Science. Member, National Institute of Arts and Letters; Fellow, American Academy of Arts and Sciences. R. Buckminster Fuller Chair of Architecture established at the University of Detroit, 1970. Member, Mexican Institute of Architects; Honorary Member, Society of Venezuelan Architects, Israel Institute of Engineers and Architects, Zentralvereiningung der Architekten Österreichs, Royal Society of Siamese Architects, and Royal Architectural Institute of Canada; Benjamin Franklin Fellow, Royal Society of Arts; Honorary Fellow, Royal Institute of British Architects, and Royal Academy of Fine Art, Netherlands. *Died* (in Los Angeles) *1 July 1983.*

Works:

Geodesic domes (there are now more than 300,000 domes in more than half the countries of the world), including:

1954 United States Air Force Early Warning System Domes, in the Arctic
1958 Union Tank Car Company quarter sphere, Baton Rouge, Louisiana, and Wood River, Illinois
1959 United States Pavilion, Sokolniki Park, Moscow
Palais de Sports, Paris
1960 Climatron botanical garden, St. Louis
1963 Cinerama Theatre, Hollywood, California
1964 Yomiuri "Star" Golf Club Field House, Tokyo
1966 County Administration Headquarters, Placer County, California
1967 United States Pavilion, *Expo '67*, Montreal
1969 Airplane Museum, Skipoel Airport, Amsterdam
1972 United States Research Station, Antarctica
1973 Weather Radome, Mt. Fuji, Japan
1979 Archaeological Site Dome, Ban Chiang, Thailand
1981 Fly's Eye Information Center, Los Angeles
1982 Spruce Goose Airplane Hangar, Long Beach California
Spaceship Earth Dome, Walt Disney World, Orlando, Florida
Home of the Future Cathedralite Dome, Worlds Fair, Knoxville, Tennessee

Patents: Stockade (building structure), 1927; Stockade (pneumatic forming process), 1927; 4D House, 1928; Dymaxion Car, 1937; Dymaxion Bath, 1940; Dymaxion Deployment Unit, 1944; Dymaxion Airocean World, 1946; Fuller House, 1946; Geodesic Dome, 1954; Paperboard Frame, 1959; Plydome, 1959; Catenary, 1959; Octertruss, 1961; Tensegrity, 1962; Submarisle, 1963; Aspension, 1964; Monohex, 1965; Laminar Dome, 1965; Octa Spinner, 1965; Star Tensegrity, 1967; Rowing Device, 1970; Tensegrity Dome with Spaced Lesser Circles, 1973; Geodesic Hexa Pent, with Shoji Sadao, 1974; Floating Breakwater, 1975; Non-symmetrical Tension-integrity Structures, 1975; Floating Breakwater, 1979.

Publications:

By FULLER: books—*4D Timelock*, Chicago 1928; *Nine Chains to the Moon*, New York 1963; *The Dymaxion World of Buckminster Fuller*, with Robert W. Marks, New York 1960; *Untitled Epic Poem on the History of Industrialization*, New York 1962; *Education Automation*, New York 1963; *Ideas and Integrities*, Englewood Cliffs, New Jersey 1963; *No More Secondhand God*, New York 1963; *World Design Decade Documents*, with others, 1965-75; *Operating Manual for Spaceship Earth*, New York 1968; *What I Have Learned*, with others, New York 1968; *Utopia of Oblivion*, New York 1969; *The Buckminster Fuller Reader*, edited by James Meller, London 1970; *I Seem To Be a Verb*, with Jerome Agel and Quentin Fiore, New York 1970; *Intuition*, New York 1971; *Buckminster Fuller to Children of Earth*, New York 1972; *Earth Inc.*, New York 1973; *Synergetic Explorations in the Geometry of Thinking*, with E. J. Applewhite, New York 1975; *Tetrascroll*, New York 1975, 1976, 1985; *Pass, Not to Stay*, New York 1977; *Synergetics 2: Further Explorations in the Geometry of Thinking*, with E.J. Applewhite, New York 1979; *R. Buckminster Fuller on Education*, edited by Robert Khan and Peter Wagschal, Amherst, Massachusetts 1979; *Synergetics Folio*, privately printed 1979; *Buckminster Fuller Sketchbook*, Philadelphia 1980; *Critical Path*, with Kiyoshi Kuromiya, New York 1980; *Grunch of Giants*, New York 1983; articles—"The Case for a Domed City" in the *St. Louis Post Dispatch*, 26 September 1965; "City of the Future" in *Playboy* (Chicago), January 1968; "The Earthian's Critical Moment" in the *New York Times*, 11 December 1970; "Ethics" in the *Saturday Review* (New York), 6 November 1973; "Energy Through Wind Power" in the *New York Times*, 17 January 1974; "Time Present" in *Harper's Magazine* (New York), March 1975; and numerous others.

On FULLER: books—*R. Buckminster Fuller* by John McHale, New York 1962; *Wizard of the Dome—R. Buckminster Fuller, Designer for the Future* by Sidney Rosen, Boston 1969; *Bucky: A Guided Tour of Buckminster Fuller* by Hugh Kenner, New York 1973; *Mind's Eye of Buckminster Fuller* by Donald W. Robertson, New York 1974; *Buckminster Fuller at Home in the Universe* by Alden Hatch, New York 1974; *Cosmic Fishing: An Account of Writing Synergetics with Buckminster Fuller* by E.J. Applewhite, New York and London 1977; *Pilot for Spaceship Earth* by Athena V. Lord, New York 1978; *Robert Buckminster Fuller: uno spazio per la technologia* by Pier Angelo Cetica, Padua, Italy 1979; *Buckminster Fuller: An Autobiographical Monologue/Scenario* by Robert Snyder, New York 1980; *Synergetic Stew: Explorations in Dymaxion Dining*, Philadelphia 1982; articles—"The Dymaxion American" in *Time* (New York), 10 January 1964; "Profile" by Calvin Tomkins in *New Yorker*, 8 January 1966; "Meet Bucky Fuller, Ambassador from Tomorrow" in the *Reader's Digest* (New York), November 1969; "A Buckminster Fuller Survival Kit" in *Queen* (London), May 1970; "Relax—Bucky Fuller Says It's Going To Be All Right" by Hal Aigner in *Rolling Stone* (San Francisco), 10 June 1971; "The World of Buckminster Fuller" in *Architectural Forum* (New York), January/February 1972; "Whole Earth Man" by Tony Lang in the *Cincinnati Enquirer* (Ohio), 11 November 1973; "Bucky Fuller and the Final Exam" by Hugh Kenner in the *New York Times Magazine*, 6 July 1975; "Richard Buckminster Fuller: A Life Spent Redesigning the Planet" by Gianni Pettena in *Modo* (Milan), June 1978; "Buckminster Fuller" by Robert MacBride in *Interview* (New York), April 1979; "Dr. Buckminster Fuller" by Radu Varia in *Vogue* (Paris), November 1979; "Planetary Planner: in Orbit with Buckminster Fuller" by Bob Baker in *Los Angeles Times* (Los Angeles), 26 February 1981; "Richard Buckminster Fuller" by Daniele Baroni and Antoni D'Auria in *Ottagono* (Milan), September 1982; "Obituary: Dr. R. Buckminster Fuller—Philosopher of a Technological Future" in *The Times* (London), 4 July 1983; "R. Buckminster Fuller, Futurist Inventor, Dies at 87" in the *New York Times* (New York), 4 July 1983; "A Man Who Believed in Mankind" in *Time* (New York), 11 July 1983; "21st Century Man" by Martin Pawley in *Architects' Journal* (London), 15 February 1984.

Bibliography—*Richard Buckminster Fuller: A Bibliography* by Mary Vance, Monticello, Illinois 1980.

Although "Bucky" Fuller was long ago recognized and embraced by the architectural community and while he identified himself as an architect, he was much more: an author, inventor, cartographer, mathematician, engineer, futurist, philosopher, poet, teacher, and resource expert. He was as much of a universal man as our century can produce. His work embraces the principal issues of the twentieth century, and his thinking points to the future with a sense of constructive reason.

Born in Milton, Massachusetts, in 1895, Richard Buckminster Fuller attended Harvard for two years, leaving to hold a variety of jobs in industry, interrupted by two years of service in the United States Navy. His experience in industry, in several capacities, established an insight into technical processes and the relation between materials and manufacturing. Similarly, his experience in the Navy afforded him a sense of the wholeness and interrelatedness of complex but integral systems. In future lectures, he was, often, to comment on the self-sufficiency of modern warships and on the knowledge required of a ship's captain of the resources of the ports to which he had access. He was to enlarge on this theme, later, in reference to the conduct of nations and, indeed, "spaceship earth."

The death of one of his two children while still an infant imbued a seriousness in Fuller. A sense of moral purpose in the sharing of the world's resource bounty, including knowledge and technique, was at the root of his work thereafter.

His efforts to design for a more judicious apportionment began with housing and automobiles. He sought to apply new industrial techniques to housing in particular, but he also experimented with automobile transportation. The broad researches he made in the 1920s and 1930s included examinations of world resources for *Fortune* magazine in the late 1930s. During the war, he worked on problems of economic welfare and foreign economies.

After the war, Fuller developed the Dymaxion House, a circular structure supported on a central mast. He also developed insights into the mathematics of highly efficient structures. His particular emphasis was to make the most appropriate use of each material. He also probed the nature of efficiency in structural form. These investigations led to the work that all but characterizes Fuller—the Geodesic Dome. It was a configuration of structural members forming a dome, the intersection points being equipoised, spherical great circles.

Fuller espoused a philosophy of resource-sharing made possible by the application of a technology of efficiency. This moral attitude, as well as his frequent criticism of inefficient techniques and the obsolete institutions that both stem from them and support them, made him a favorite of schools of architecture. Many are the students, worldwide, who have had the benefit of hours with him.

His dome concept is applicable to small-scale, domestic as well as large-scale, industrial usage. It has been used in hundreds, if not thousands, of applications, short, however, of covering an entire city. The essential purpose of his domes is to achieve a maximum of structural rigidity and strength with a minimum of materials. Thus, a maximum of space and useful surface area is enclosed by a minimum of materials.

Among his other innovations are the concept of a geodesic world map. Using "geodesic" geometry, he developed a map in which the continents and ocean masses can be portrayed flat or in three dimensions without great distortion. A further application was the construction of a huge electronic version of his map. Computerized, it could be used to play world resources relationship games or "World Games." A further structural innovation was his concept of discontinuous compression. With this compression, forces were translated into series of short tension increments. In applications, this created lighter compression members.

A remark that Fuller once made about thinking and doing characterizes his life. He said: "You can't re-order the world by talking to it."

—Paul Spreiregen

FULTON, Don Hendry.

Australian. Born in Melbourne, Victoria, 30 January 1925. Educated at the Royal Melbourne Institute of Technology, 1942, 1946-47 (Illuminating Engineering Society Award for Lighting Design in Architecture, 1946, 1947), Dip.Arch. 1947; University of Melbourne, under Sir Roy Grounds, 1948-50 (Picton Hopkins Award), B.Arch. 1950; University of Calforna, Berkeley, under William Wurster, *q.v.*, Catherine Bauer, Vernon De Mars, *q.v.*, Joseph Esherick, *q.v.*, Charles Eames, *q.v.*, and John Carl Warnecke, *q.v.*, 1953-54 (Fulbright grant; Skidmore, Owings and Merrill Fellow in Architecture), M.Arch. 1954. Served as a cartographer in the Royal Australian Air Force, 1943-45. Married Joane Thorne Goss in 1954 (divorced, 1975); children: Simon, Joel, and Mathew; married Helen Elizabeth Fraser in 1978; daughter: Sara. Architect, office of Brian Lewis and Roy Grounds, Melbourne, 1950, Mussen, Mackay, Potter and Grounds, Melbourne, 1951-53, and Mussen, Mackay and Potter, Melbourne, 1955; Principal Partner, E.E.Milston and Don Fulton, Melbourne, 1956. Since 1956, Principal, Don Hendry Fulton Pty. Ltd., Melbourne; established new practice partnership with Charles Stuart Arnold, Fulton & Arnold Pty. Ltd., in Melbourne, Brisbane, Queensland, and Townsville, Queensland, 1984. Councillor, Historic Buildings Council, Victoria, 1974-78. Councillor, Royal Australian Institute of Architects, Victoria Chapter, since 1972. Exhibition: Abstract Graphics, International Art Fair, Düsseldorf, 1973. Recipient: Bronze Medal, Royal Australian Institute of Architects, Victorian Chapter, 1966; Bronze Award, Illuminating Engineers Association of Australia, 1976. Fellow, Royal Australian Institute of Architects, 1967. Address: Don H. Fulton Pty Ltd., 439 King Street, Melbourne, Victoria 3000, Australia.

Works:

1955 Mary Kathleen Township (new uranium mining township for Conzinc Riotinto), Central Queensland (with E.E. Milston)

1960 Weipa Township (new bauxite mining township for Colmalco), Northern Queensland
1962 Studio 9, General Television Corporation, Richmond, Victoria
1963 Ministry of Education and Fine Arts, for the Royal Cambodian Government and the Australian Government, Phnom Phen, Cambodia (project)
1966 Administrative Centre, BP Refinery, Westernport, Victoria
1970 St. Kilda Marina. Victoria
1972 Australian and New Zealand Banking Group Regional Bank, Darwin, Northern Territory
1976 Municipal Offices, Flinders Civic Centre, Rosebud, Victoria
1978 Robertson Township, Narracan, Victoria
1980/
83 State Forensic Science Laboratories, Macleod, Victoria (as Principal Consultant to the Victoria public Works Department)
1984 Australian Antarctic Scientific Buildings, Antarctica (as Consultant Architect and Committee Member to the Ministry of Science and Technology)
1985 General Television Corporation Earth Satellite Station(GTV9), Melbourne

Publications:

By FULTON: articles—"Philosophy and Design Approach to Weipa Township in Tropical Australia" in *Australian Mining Journal*(Sydney), May 1967; "This Is Munich" in the Saturday Review Magazine of *The Age*(Melbourne), 26 August 1972; "Ein australischer Architekt sieht Ulm" in *Ulmer Forum* (Ulm, West Germany), Winter 1972/73.

An early confrontation with the images of Angkor: I think this propelled the dream/need to become an architect. And I'm sure that the vital elements of ancient Asian architecture—rhythmically structured, strongly shaped, sheltering—have had an important influence on founding a particular aesthetic mechanism.

We all begin with the urge to push forward the conceptual frontiers, to considerably influence the shape of buildings in one's own time—fortunately for all, a few of the talented and tough manage to do so and make the marks of history. But from the threshold of the school to that of one's own practice—indeed, that now seems a great leap by the unknowing into the unknown—the dreamer perforce becomes legally and financially accountable—called 'responsible,'

Who was it said "I don't want to be interesting, I want to be good?" Mies, I think. Well, to me, architecture necessarily is all about *buildings that are both good and interesting*. It's about the good and interesting shapes and forms of buildings and the spaces within and between them. And of course, it's also about the proper functioning of systems and equipment in buildings and how properly buildings use energy, modify the climate, andd fit their sites.

If, in the course of time and well beyond its first purpose, a building is somehow still good and interesting, then perhaps it's touched that quality of art called style that sets certain manmade things apart, whether buildings sculpture, music, tools, or toys.

But isn't our involvement in architecture essentially about the whole built fabric working well and looking good in our time? I think this 'overview' attitude leads to architecture of the overall, to townplanning.

Indeed, fortunately, it has led us to the planning of small, new, self-contained townships associated with Australia's developing mining industries and major civil works, in remote areas of the country. From the development 'go' point to that of people moving in, in layout, systems, and building, they are usually

towns "in a hurry." The challenge is to help make them good and interesting to work and live in.

Acceleration of international tourism and commerce in Queensland (Australia's California) and background of planning there for the minerals-mining industries (uranium and bauxite) have allowed expansion of the practice to cover Australia's East Coast.

The technological thrust of our time invites the 'imagineering' architect's participation in shaping the built works associated with major and complex technical undertaking: design of advanced laboratories for the conduct of forensic science in society's fight against sophisticated crime; design of prefabricated, modular building concepts container-shipped to the Antarctic to speed Australia's major scientific role and management of that remote territory's international developmental future, prospectively for hydro-carbons; design of satellite stations in an international chain linking global communications via television networks.

For today's new purposes, architects and engineers integrate new techniques, use new materials, develop new skills, and gain new know-how from those who have pioneered modern design in the transportation modes of containerisation, in the vehicles of the aero-space industry, and in the rigs accommodating the technics and the teams for oil exploration.

—Don Hendry Fulton

Against stiff competition from large and expensive city buildings, a small, economical, out-of-the-way administration block at an oil refinery won the top architectural award for any building in the state of Victoria in the years 1963-66. This modest building is typical of architect Don Hendry Fulton's work: austere, rational, and elegant. At first sight, it appears to owe much to the temple form of United States embassies built during the 1950s (notably by The Architects' Collaborative in Athens, and John Carl Warnecke in Hawaii). But this building is not a simple exercise in the International style. It results from a careful study of functional requirements, climatic conditions, and socio-cultural influences. These determinants of form are the raw material from which the architect must seek the underlying order and derive the appropriate style

For Fulton, who was strongly influenced by American architecture during his studies for Master of Architecture at the University of Calforna in Berkeley, style is of major importance, for he sees architecture as an art, and style as the mediator between art and mere building. In the refinery administration block, the style is uncompromisingly classic; a tetrastyle peripheral temple form with wide, overhanging eaves is poised delicately around a symmetrical but direct response to a complex brief. To one side is a small gatehouse, the roof of which is visually accommodated by a slight inflection of the ground floor walls of the main building. The two-storey columns are slender, square-section shafts, necked and splayed to give visual strength to the base. They are topped with a steel capital that passes through a slot in the eaves soffit, so that the roof appears to float. The same separation and articulation of parts and the careful attention to detail are apparent throughout the building.

Besides a number of buildings with a high technical component, such as radio and television studios, the major part of Fulton's practice has been the planning layout and building design of a number of 'company' towns for large civil engineering projects in remote areas all around Australia, from Robertson in Victoria in the south to Weipa in Queensland in the north. In each case, his design approach is as direct as possible. The elements of vernacular buildings are the basic forms from which the architectural style and planning geometry are derived. The resulting buildings are simple, elegant, and formal; above all, they are experienced as familiar places.

—David Watson

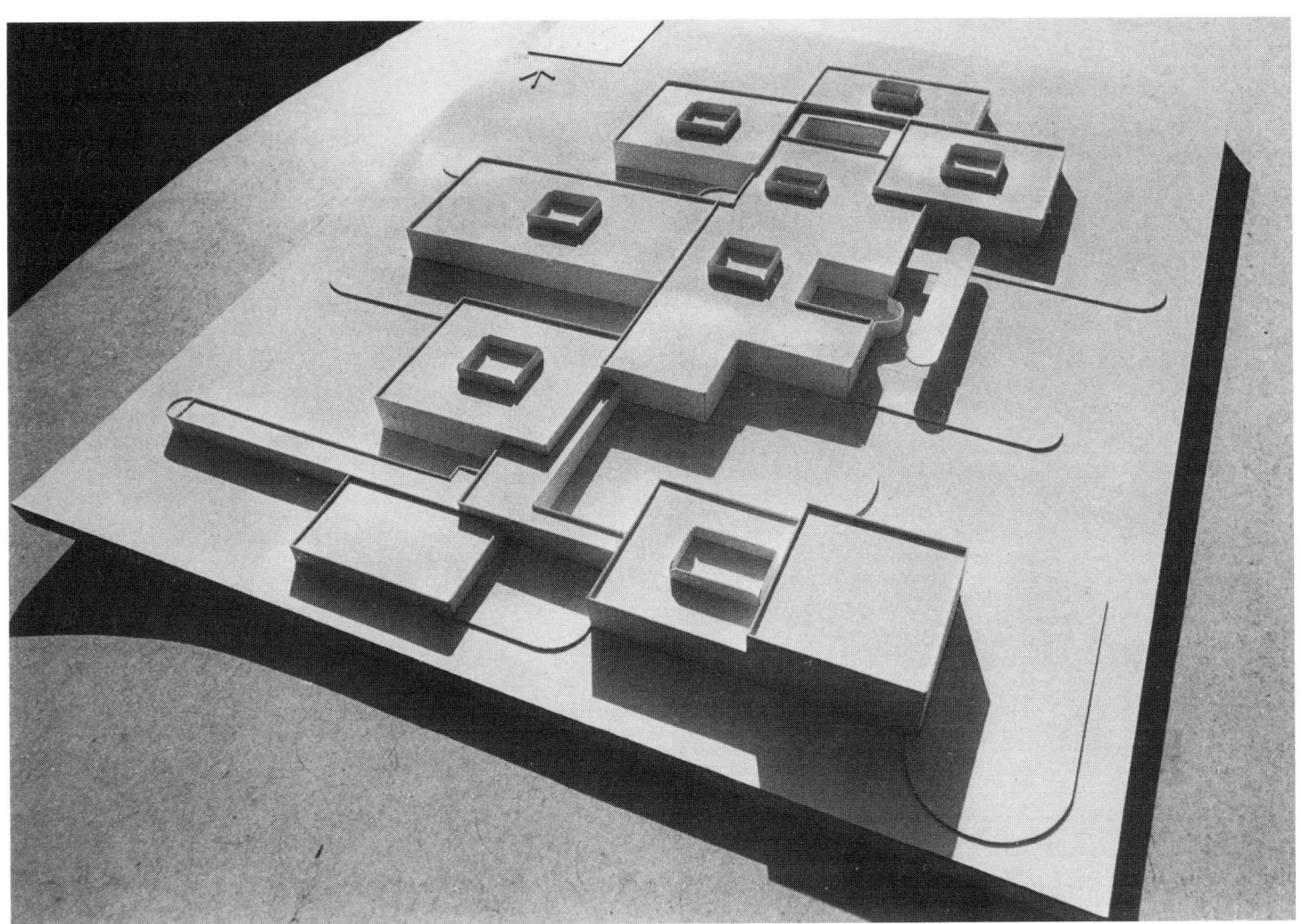

Don Fulton: State Forensic Laboratories, Macleod, Victoria, 1980-83 (model).

G

GARDELLA, Ignazio.

Italian. Born in Milan in 1905. Studied architecture with his father Arnaldo Gardella, Milan; studied civil engineering, Milan Polytechnic, Dip.Ing. 1930; studied architecture, Istituto Universitario di Architettura, Venice, Dip.Arch. 1949; also made study-trips to Germany, 1931, and to Finland, Sweden, and Norway, 1939. Since 1931, in private practice, Milan; associated with G. Pagano's *Casabella* group of architects, Milan, 1931-49; in partnership with Anna Castelli-Ferrieri, Milan, 1959-73. Ordinary Professor, 1949-52, Professor of Architectural Composition, 1952-62, and Professor of the Elements of Composition, 1962-75, Istituto Universitario di Architettura, Venice. Member, Joint Executive Committee, *Triennale*, Milan, 1959; Member, CIAM (Congrès Internationaux d'Architecture Moderne); Istituto Nazionale di Urbanistica. Exhibitions: *Ten Italian Architects*, Los Angeles, 1967; *Utopia e crisi dell'antinatura*, at the *Biennale*, Venice, 1978; *Architetture italiane degli anni '70*, Galleria Nazionale d'Arte Moderna, Rome, 1981. Recipient: Olivetti National Prize, Milan, 1955. Address: Via Marchiondi 7, 20122 Milan, Italy.

Works:

1932 Venzahi Apartment alterations, Piazza Italia 3, Milan
 Caruso Dairy and Stables, Retorato, Arquata Scrivia, Italy
1933 Calvi Cottage, San Vito, Italy
1934 Bell Tower, Piazza del Duomo, Milan (project)
 Theatre restoration, Busto Arsizio, Italy
 Hospital Isolation Unit, Busto Arsizio, Italy (1st project)
1935/
 36 Villa Borletti extensins and alterations, Milan
1936 Chapel-Altar, Varinella, Arquata Scrivia, Italy (project)
1936/
 37 Hospital Isolation Unit, Busto Arsizio, Italy (second project)
1936/
 38 Anti-Tuberculosis Dispensary, Alessandria, Italy (with L. Martini)
 Milano Verde: City Plan for Milan (project: with others)
1937 Gardella Apartment interiors, Milan
1937/
 39 Provincial Laboratory for Hygiene, Alessandria, Italy
1938 Cattle Market Building, Alessandria, Italy (competition project)
 Hotel for the E.42 Development, Rome (project; with others)
 Palazzo della Civiltà Italiana Building, E.42 Development, Rome (project; with others)
1939 Palace of Water and Light, E.42 Development, Rome (project; with others)
1940/
 41 Pirovano Shrine, Municipal Cemetery, Missaglia, Italy
1942 CNASA Employees Apartment Building, Marina Carrara, Italy (not completed)
1942/
 47 la Fergan Housing Block, via Severino Boezio, Milan (not completed)
1946 Apartment building, Castana, Italy
 Borsalino Company Exhibit, Trade Fair, Milan
1947 Redevelopment plan for the Angeli Quarter, Genoa (project; with others)
 Redevelopment plan for the Balzaretti and Modigliani Glassworkers' Quarter, Livorno, Itay (project; with Alberto Menghi)
1947/
 48 Apartment House by the Park, Piazza Castello, Milan
1948 Redevelopment plan for Turin (competition project)
1950 Regina Isabella Spa Building, Lacco Ameno, Isle of Ischia (with Elena Balsari Berrone)
1951 Condominium Apartments, Milan (with Anna Castelli Ferrieri and Alberto Menghi)
 Italian Chairs Exhibition, *Triennale*, Milan
1951/
 53 Borsalino Employees' Block of Flats, Corso Teresio Borsalino, Alessandria, Italy
1952 Villa Baletti, Lesa, Lake Maggiore, Italy
 Terrace apartment houses, INA-CASA Quarter, Cesate, Milan
1953 Gallery of Modern Art, Giardini della Villa Reale, Milan
1953/
 59 Olivetti Recreation Centre Complex, Ivrea, near Turin
1955 Columbus House and Museum, Genoa
1956 Fabric-Cutting Building, Borsaino Factory, Alessandria, Italy
 New Exhibition Rooms, Uffizi Gallery, Florence
1957 New Building, Cesar Arrigo Children's Hospital, Alessandria, Italy
 Brick Church, Cesate, Milan
 Alle Zattere Apartment Building, Grand Canal, Venice
 Edizioni Paoline Bookstore, Piazza del Duomo, Milan
 Thermo-Electric Plant, Ravenna, Italy
1958 Grassi Collectin Rooms, Villa Belgioioso, Milan
 Hotel Punta San Martino, near Genoa (with Marco Zanuso)
1959 C.P.E. Pilot Residential Development, Vicenza, Italy (with Anna Castelli Ferieri, Plinio Marconi, Valeriano Pastor, and Guido Pravato)
1960 Alitalia DC-8 aircraft interiors
1960/
 61 Piazza with Shops and Housing, Arenzano Pineta, Capo San Martino, Italy
1960/
 62 Villa, Arenzano, Capo san Martino, Italy (with Anna Castelli Ferrieri)
1961 Agricultural Pavilion, Fiera Campionaria, Milan
1961/
 62 Olivetti Showrooms and Offices, Königsallee, Düsseldorf
1962/
 63 Einaudi Bookstore, via Veneto, Rome (with Luigi Parisi)
1963 Elementary school, Alessandria, Italy
1964 San Enrico Church, Metanopoli, near Milan
1966/
 68 IBM Offices, Vimercate, near Milan
 Kartell Factory and Offices, Binasco, Italy
 Porto di Punta Ala Residential Development, Grosseto, Italy (with Alberto Mazzoni, Diego Guicciardi, and Vito Sonzongni)
1968 Parish Church, Forlanini Quarter, Milan
1970 Theatre, Vicenza, Italy (competition project)
 House, via Marina, Milan
1970/
 72 Alfa Romeo Technical Offices, Arese, Milan
1970 Plan for the restoration of the centre of Genoa (with Daniele Vitale and others)
1972 IACP Quarter Plan, Turin (competition project)
1973 Tourist-Residential Centre, Campo Felice, Rocca di Cambio, Italy (project)
1973/
 76 Kartell Offices (Centrokappa), Noviglio, Milan (with Anna Castelli-Ferrieri)
1974 Shahrestenak Winter Tourist Resort, near Tehran (project)
1976 University Building, San Donato and San Silvestro, Genoa
1977/
 81 Plan 167 experimental development, Genoa
1980 Monument to Fallen Partisans, Piazza della Loggia, Brescia, Italy (competition project)
1981 Genoa Quarto Plan variations
1981/
 83 Carlo Felice Theatre reconstruction, Genoa

Numerous designs for furniture and light fittings, especially for the Azucena Company of Milan, 1947-51.

Publications:

By GARDELLA: articles—"Arredamento" in *Pirelli* (Milan), March 1949; "Scuole di archittettura" in *Venezia architettura* (Venice), no.1, 1952; "Problemi della prefabbricazione" in *Casabella-Continuità* (Milan), November/December 1954; "Opinioni sulla architettura italiana" in *Casabella-Continuità* (Milan), April/May 1955; "Quindici anni di architettura italiana" in *Casabella-Continuità* (Milan), May 1961; "La ricerca progettuale" in *Controspazio* (Bari, Italy), May/June 1972; "Interview in *L'Architettura oggi*, edited by J.A. Dols, Novara, Italy 1977; "Una forma primaria" in *Lotus* (Venice), no. 25, 1979; "Rationalism and figurative regeneration" in *Hinterland* (Milan), January/June 1980; recordings—*La casa nella città*, radio broadcast, Rome 1945; *Funzioni della città*, radio broadcast, Rome 1946.

On GARDELLA: books—*Ignazio Gardella* by Giulio Carlo Argan, Milan 1959; *New Italian Architecture* by Alberto Galardi, Stuttgart and London 1967; *La cultura architettonica in italia tra le due guerre* by Cesare De Seta, Rome 1972, 1983; *Architetture italiane degli anni '70*, exhibition catalogue, edited by Giovanna De Feo and Enrico Valeriani, Rome 1981; *Ignazio Gardella e il professionismo italiano* by Alberto Samona, Rome 1981; articles—"Concorso per i mercato bestiame di Alessandria" in *Casabella* (Milan), April 1939; "Espressione di Gardella, espressione di Rouault" in *Domus* (Milan), June 1954; "Ignazio Gardella" by Giulio Carlo Argan in *Architects Yearbook*, London 1956; "Casa di abitazione in condominio" and "Galleria d'Arte Moderna" in *Forum* (Amsterdam), October 1957; "Umanesimo di Gardella" by Giuseppe Mazzariol in *Zodiac* (Milan), no. 2, 1958; "Progetto per il quartiere pilota C.P.E. a Vicenza" in *Casabella* (Milan), August 1959; "Appunti sulla progettazione di Gardella" and "La Mensa Olivetti a Ivrea" in *Casabella* (Milan), January 1960; "Nel centro residenziale di Arenzano Pineta, sul Capo San Martino: La Piazza" in *Domus* (Milan), August 1960; "Negozio Olivetti a Dusseldorf" in *L'Architettura* (Rome), December 1961; "A Roma, una libreria in via Veneto" in *Domus* (Milan), November 1969; "Ingnazio Gardella" by Aldo Rossi in *Architecture + Urbanism* (Tokyo), December 1976; "Incontri con i protagonisti: Ignazio Gardella" by Pier Carlo Santini in *Ottagono* (Milan), September 1977; "The theatre of Gardella" by Giulio Carlo Argan in *Lotus* (Venice), no. 25, 1979; "Origins of a Professional: Ignazio Gardella" by Federico Correa in *Arquitecturas bis* (Barcelona), January/March 1981; "The Alfa Romeo Offices in Arese" in *Architettura* (Rome), January 1983.

Although Ignazio Gardella's career has coincided with the often tortuous development of modern architecture in Italy, which has been accompanied by lively controversy and fierce commitment, Gardella himself has never been committed to any social or aesthetic ideology. Indeed, his famous Zattere Apartment House, on the Grand Canal in Venice, has been something of an embarrassment to modernist extremists: nobody can deny that it is not supremely functional, yet so far from having the ugly brutality too often associated with functionalism, this witty variation on modern and vernacular themes fits in perfectly with its environment.

Gardella has in fact always shown great sensitivity to the demands of the environment. Many of his works have indeed been whole environments rather than single buildings. For instance, the Hotel Punta SanMartino of 1958, which he designed with Marco Zanuso, is splendidly set on the cliffs of the gulf of Genoa as part of a whole Gardella plan for Arezano, to develop this stretch of coastline without allowing it to be ruined by speculators (as, in fact, to some extent it unfortunately has been).

Many of his most important works have been at Alessandria, an important market town and communications centre between Milan and Genoa. His first work there was the splendid Anti-Tuberculosis Dispensary, an outstanding early example of modern Italian architecture. It already suggests the lines along which Gardella was to develop; it shows his respect for the traditional environment in its use of techniques and materials drawn directly from the local tradition. For though this a reinforced concrete building, and its windows and plane surfaces are all clearly modern, its facing of grillwork in the local coloured bricks not only gives it a lively surface but also helps it blend harmoniously with the local architecture. His many other works in Alessandria include the Provincial Laboratory for Hygiene, the Children's Hospital, and the block of flats built for the Borsalino workers, which has been called "bourgeois neoclassicism" yet is a highly original building with such unusual features as its deeply overhanging eaves.

Gardella has also created some interesting furnishings. He bagan his career with interior decoration and rebuilding schemes, such as the renovation of the theatre at Busto Arsizio in 1934. But his most distinctive contribution to architecture has been his remarkable ability to use the formal vocabulary of Italian rationalism or modernism while at the same time reinterpreting regional and traditional elements in a modern key—as in his block of flats at Castana. Similarly his work in the Cesate district of Milan involves a subtle geometric layout very much in the contemporary spirit, yet it also includes a brick-built church with historic overtones. As used by Gardella, such traditional elements can never be accused of being merely fancy-dress architecture, for they embody his characteristically thoughtful and critical attitude to the landscape and environment.

—Konstantin Bazarov

GEDDES, Robert.

American. Born in Philadelphia, Pennsylavania, 7 December 1923. Educated at Yale University, New Haven, Connecticut, 1941-42 and 1945; Graduate School of Design, Harvard University, Cambridge, Massachusetts, 1946-50, M.Arch. 1950. Served in the United States Army, 1942-45. Married Evelyn Basse in 1947; children: David and Ann. Since 1954, Principal, Geddes Brecher Qualls Cunningham, architects, Princeton, New Jersey, and Philadelphia. Professor of Architecture and Civic Design, University of Pennsylavania, Philadelphia, 1951-65; Dean of the School of Architecture, 1965-82, and Kenan Professor of Architecture, since 1968, Princeton University, New Jersey. Board Member, Manville Corporation, since 1970, and Butler Manufacturing Company, since 1971. Exhibitions: *Modern Architecture*, Museum of Modern Art, New York, 1963; *Two Buildings*, Boston Architectural Center, 1978; *Transformations in Modern Architecture*, Museum of Modern Art, New York, 1979; *Two Centuries and Beyond*, University of Pennsylvania, Philadelphia, 1979; *Geddes Brecher Qualls Cunningham*, American Institute of Architects Convention, Kansas City, Missouri, 1979; *Liberty State Park: The Master Plan*, Museum of Modern Art, New York, 1979 (travelled to the New Jersey State Museum, Trenton, 1980); *The Forest Edge*, AIA Gallery, Philadelphia, 1982; *New American Art Museums*, Whitney Museum, New York, 1982. Recipient: National Honor Award, 1960 and 1976, Architectural Firm Award, 1979, First Honor Award, 1980, and four Philadelphia Chapter Gold Medals, American Institute of Architects; First Design Award, *Progressive Architecture* magazine, New York, 1960 and 1980; First Honor Award, U.S. Department of Housing and Urban Development, 1963; Excellence in Architectural Education Award, Association of Collegiate Schools/American Institute of Architects, 1984; five Silver Medals, Pennsylvania Society of Architects; eight Design Awards, New Jersey Society of Architects; First Prizes in the competitions: Vienna-South Town Plan, 1972; New Jersey Housing for the Elderly, 1978; Alabama Power Company Headquarters, 19681. Member, National Academy of Design, 1967. Fellow, American Institute of Architects, 1967. Address: Geddes Brecher Qualls Cunningham, 120 Alexander Street, Princeton, New Jersey 08540, U.S.A.

Works:

1954 Fotteral Square, Philadelphia
Geddes House, Radnor, Pennsylvania
1955 Lawncrest Center, Philadelphia
1956 Wister Playground, Philadelphia
Beachcomber Swim Club, Gwynedd, Pennsylvania

Alter House, Brockton, Massachusetts
Bentman House, Lancaster, Pennsylvania
Scaeffer House, Rydal, Pennsylvania
1957 Roosevelt Playground, Philadelphia
Bulk Zoning Controls Study, Philadelphia
Eastwick New House, Philadelphia (project)
1957/
65 Tarkin Playground, stages I and II, Philadelphia
1958 Dolphin Swim Club, Lower Bucks County, Pennsylvania
Urban renewal plan for the North Marshall Street Shopping Mall, Philadelphia
Pender Laboratory, Moore School of Electrical Engineering, University of Pennsylvania, Philadelphia
1959 Development proposal for Eastwick Urban Renewal Area, Philadelphia
1960 F.J. Cooper Jewelry Shop, Philadelphia
Plan for undergraduate men's housing, University of Pennsylvania, Philadelphia
1962 Police Headquarters, Phildelphia
Huntington Laboratories, Lansdale, Pennsylvania
1963 Northeast Regional Library, Philadelphia
Temple Beth Sholom, Manchester, Connecticut
Master plan for Penn's Landing Philadelphia
1963/
64 Land plan for the Southern Sector of Reston, Virginia
1964 Master plan for the University City Science Center, Philadelphia
Development plan for the Community College of Philadelphia
1965 Pine Street Row Houses, Philadelphia
Development plan for cluster housing and recreational facilities, Reston, Virginia
Master plan for the Peddie School, Hightstown, New Jersey
Master plan for the Center City YM-YWHA, Philadelphia
1966 Community College of Philadelphia Department Store remodeling
Unitarian Church of Delaware County, Springfield, Pennsylvania
Geddes House, Princeton, New Jersey
Master plan for the town center of Rockville, Maryland
Bernards Street Housing, West Chester, Pennsylvania
1966/
68 Theatre and Fine Arts Complex, Beaver College, Glenside, Pennsylvania
1967 Residence and Dining Halls University of Delaware, Newark
Graduate Research Center, Moore School of Electrical Engineering, University of Pennsylvania, Philadelphia
Proposal for Kukui Redevelopment Area, Honolulu
1968 Middle-income housing, Princeton, New Jersey (project)
Holmcrest Houses, Philadelphia
Master plan for the central campus of Southern Illinois University, Carbondale
1968/
72 Study/Dining Hall and Academic Buildings, Institute for Advanced Study, Princeton, New Jersey
1969 Development plan for Beaver College, Glenside, Pennsylvania
1970 Classroom/Office Building, Rutgers University, Newark, New Jersey
Research Laboratories, Academy of Natural Sciences, Philadelphia (project)
Library, Southern Illinois University, Carbondale (project)
1971 Science/Academic Building, Beaver College, Glenside, Pennsylvania
Pickett Middle School, Philadelphia
Fine Arts Building, Goucher College, Towson, Maryland (project)
Master plan for the Haile Selassie I University,

Addis Ababa, Ethiopia

Plan for the Vienna South New Community, Austria (competition project)

1971/
76 Stockton State College, Pomona, New Jersey

1972 Downing renewal plan for the Corning, New York

Stauffer Dormitory and Dining Hall, University of Pennsylvania, Philadelphia

IBM Branch Office Building, Bethlehem, Pennsylvania

Master plan for a new town at Ken-Caryl Ranch, Colorado

Design of public works for the town center of Rockvile, Maryland

Urban design study of the center of Trenton, New Jersey

1973 Coatesville Public Housing, Coatesville, Pennsylvania

Plan for a proposed new community in Readington Township, New Jersey

Study of the Spring Garden Street Campus, Community College of Philadelphia

Building systems research for the Johns-Manville Corporation, Denver

Urban design study of the Henderson Street Urban Renewal Area, Jersey City, New Jersey

1974 Psychology Building, Rutgers, University, New Brunswick, New Jersey

United States Mint renovation, Philadelphia

1975 Humanities and Social Sciences Center, Southern Illinois University, Carbondale

Trenton Commons Garage, Trenton, New Jersey

1976 Dock Street Theatres and Shops, Philadelphia

1977 Master plan for Howell Farm, Mercer County, New Jersey

1977 Hospital Master Plan and Buildings, University of Pennsylvania, Philadelphia

1978 Master Plan, New Gallery, Chapel, and renovations, Trinity Church, Princeton, New Jersey

United States Navy Recreation Facility, Sandy Hook Bay, New Jersey

Master plan for the Columbian Mutual Life Insurance Company, Binghampton, New York

School of Medicine, Medical Education Building, and Hamilton Walk Development, University of Pennsylvania, Philadephia

1979 Housing for the elderly, West Orange, New Jersey

Housing for the elderly, Trenton, New Jersey

Columbian Mutual Life Insurance Company Office Building, Binghampton, New York

Flint Riverfront Center, Flint, Michigan

1979/
85 Liberty State Park, JerseyCity, New Jersey

1980 Master plan of the Downtown Government Center, Miami

1981 General Motors Building, Valley Forge, Pennsylvania

Downtown Hotel and Plaza, Kansas City, Missouri (project)

1981/
85 Alabama Power Company Headquarters, Birmingham

1982 Student Center and Housing, Stockton College, Pomona, New Jersey

Pioneer Square, Portland, Oregon (competition project)

School of Law, University of Missouri, Columbia (competition project)

1982/
85 Livingston College Student Center, Rutgers State University, Piscataway, New Jersey

State Commerce Building, Trenton, New Jersey

1982 St. David's Center, Radmor, Pennsylvania

1983 Environmental and Health Science Laboratory, Mobil Oil Corporation, Hopewell, New Jersey

South Wing, J.B. Speed Art Museum, Louisville, Kentucky

1983 Campus Commercial Development, University of Pennsylvania, Philadelphia

Children's Seashore House rehabilitation center, Philadelphia

Robert Geddes: J. B. Speed Art Museum, Louisville, Kentucky, 1983.

1984 Delaware River Basin Marine Safety Office, Philadelphia (project)

Central Research Division, Mobil Oil Corporation, Hopewell, New Jersey

Lehigh Valley Laboratories, American Telephone and Telegraph Company, Pennsylvania

1984/
85 Mount Vernon College Library, Washington, D.C.

1984 New Laboratory, American Telephone and Telegraph Company, New York

1985 Commercial Development, 34th and Walnut Street, Philadelphia Office Building and Hotel, Harrisburg, Pennsylvania

Hillel House, University of Pennsylvania, Philadelphia

Public Safety Building, White Plains, New York

Dormitories, McGuire Air Force Base, New Jersey

Publications:

By GEDDES: articles—"Theory in Practice: The Dual Values of Teacher and Practitioner" in *Architectural Forum* (New York), September and October 1972; "The Nature of the Built Enviroment" in *Progressive Architecture* (New York), June 1974; "The Responsibilities (and Joy) of Architecture," interview with Diane Hempel, in *University Magazine: A Princeton Quartely,* Summer 1974; annual review of architecture and civil engineering in *Encyclopaedia Britannica Yearbook,* Chicago 1976, 1977, 1978; "Possibilities in Architecture" in *Architectural Record* (New York), November 1977; "Three Associations: Archtecture in the Public Realm" in *Inlond Architect* (Chicago), April 1981; "The Forest Edge" in *Architectural Design* (London), no 11/12, 1982; "Architecture: Compositions for Living" in *OZ* (Manhattan, Kansas), vol. 41, 1982; "Architecture and Landscape" in *Architecture New Jersey* (East Orange), July/September 1982; "The Common Ground" in *Landscape Architecture* (Louisville, Kentucky), May/June 1983.

On GEDDES: articles—"Interiors as an Integral Part of Practice" by Andrea Dean in *AIA Journal* (Washington D.C.), July 1975; "Kind of Uptown—Concert Hall in Jefferson Civic Center" by David Morton in *Progressive Architecture* (New York), November 1975; "The Home Towns Come Back" in *Architectural Record* (New York), December 1976; "Faner Hall at Southern Illinois University" by John Morris Dixon in *Progressive Architecture* (New York), December 1976; "It's Back to School for the Systems Approach: Stockton State College" by William Marlin in *Architectural Record* (New York), May 1977; "Humanities and Social Sciences Building, Southern Illinois University" by Mary E. Osman in *AIA Journal* (Washington D.C.), May 1977; "USA Universitas" in *Architectural Review (London), October 1978; "Profile: the 1979 Firm Award Winner"* in *AIA Journal* (Washington, D.C.), February 1979; "Liberty State Park" in *Architecture + Urbanism* (Tokyo), May 1980; "Completion for Longevity" in *Progressive Architecture* (New York), August 1981; "Response to Opposition: Robert Geddes" by David Epstein in *Portfolio* (Knoxville, Tennessee), Spring 1982; "Architecture at Princeton: Reflecting on Seventeen Years at Princeton" in *Princeton Weekly Bulletin,* 29 March 1982; "A Museum Masterpiece" in *Horizon* (New York), January/February 1984; "ACSA honors Robert Geddes for Excellence in Education in *Architecture* (Washington, D.C.), March 1984; "A Special Kind of Classicism" by Robert Campbell in *Architecture* (Washington, D.C.), October 1984.

*

Architecture arises out of our need to shelter the human animal in a spatial environment and to enclose the social animal in a group space. In this sense, architecture serves our institutions and expresses the values of our culture.

Architecture is a public art, not a private expression of a single person. The production of architecture involves historical and cultural factors, social and behavioral factors, economic and political factors

Architecture is the expression of institutions, their purposes, activities, and qualities. While the architecture of an institution should provide for future change and growth, it must also be responsive to the immediate satisfactions of the users and community.

Architecture should be both coherent and complex in form. It should be colorful and stimulating to the senses, yet modest and economical in its use of resources. It is an "enabling" mechanism, which makes possible, but does not determine, the achievement of individual and social goals. In the construction of its spaces, its walkways and rooms, its landscapes, architecture participates in creating a framework for living.

—Robert Geddes

*

Robert Geddes is an architect who would disagree with Oscar Wilde that "Art never expresses anything but itself." Geddes believes that the art of architecture expresses the nature of institutions—the family, church, school, state—and that it communicates emotion and ideals. He is convinced that architecture can inprove society and influence character and that the aesthetics of architecture cannot be separated from moral and ethical purpose. For him, both are "two parts of a unity; to emphasize either at the expense of the other is improper. The social responsibility of the architect is to be aesthetic. His total responsibility is to bring the two together. When he does, there is great joy in architecture."

Geddes the philosopher translates these articles of faith into his everyday practice of architecture by accepting commissions which he deems to be of the most social importance to a community and its individuals—housing, educational buildings, and urban design projects. He believes housing to be one of the most important social and aesthetic responsibilities of our time. It is his credo that school buildings by the nature of their forms instruct the young, in and out of the classroom. As an urban designer, he contends with all the forces that continually transform the city in his effort to create new physical patterns that will enable people to lead better lives.

Geddes's building as sculptural forms are influenced by the works of Le Corbusier in the master's pre-Brutalist, 1920s period. Geddes develops complex, interlocking volumes by means of alternatingly curving or flat thin planes which, in combination with transparent glass, dramatically advance and recede. In most of his projects, he articulates rather than conceals structure. His completed works are precise and elegent solutions of technical as well as social problems.

Geddes believes that buildings should be constructed to last, and, if they do, that their functions will change through time, as those of today's valuable old structures usually have. He therefore designs flexible, adaptable structures because, as he has said, "the fit between form and function should not always be close." He hopes that each of his buildings will have second and third lives after their first use is past. Such meticulously conceived and executed works deserve the future he hopes for them.

—Mildred F. Schmertz

GEHRY, Frank O.

American. Born in Toronto, Ontario, Canada, 28 February 1929. Educated at the University of Southern California, Los Angeles, 1949-51 and 1954, B.Arch. 1954; Graduate School of Design, Harvard University, Cambridge, Massachusetts, 1956-57. Served in the Special Services Division of the United States Army, 1955-56. Architectural Designer, Victor Gruen, *q.v.*, Associates, Los Angeles, 1953-54; Planner and Designer, Robert and Company, architects, Atlanta, 1955-56; Architectural Designer and Planner, Hideo Sasaki, *q.v.*, Associates, Boston, 1957; Architectural Designer, Pereira, *q.v.*: William Pereira, and Luckman, Los Angeles, 1957-58; worked in planning, design, and project direction for Victor Gruen Associates, Los Angeles, 1958-61; Project Designer and Planner, André Remondet, Paris, 1961. Since 1962, Principal, Frank O. Gehry and Associates, Los Angeles. Assistant Professor, University of Southern California, 1972-73; Visiting Critic, University of California at Los Angeles, 1977 and 1979; William Bishop Professor, 1979, and Charlotte Davenport Professor of Architecture, 1982, Yale University, New Haven, Connecticut; Eliot Noyes Professor, Harvard University, Cambridge, Massachusetts, 1984. Member, Los Angeles 12. Exhibitions: *International Design: New Attitudes, New Forms,* Contemporary Arts Museum, Houston, Texas, 1972; *45 Years of Architectural Design,* Musée des Arts Décoratifs, Paris, 1973; *Innovations: Contemporary Home Environs,* La Jolla Museum of Contemporary Art, California, 1974; *Drawings of American Architects,* Cooper-Hewitt Museum, New York, 1977; *Collaboration: artists and architects,* Architectural League, New York 1981; *Window Room, Furniture,* Cooper Union, New York, 1981-82; *Ten New Buildings,* Institute of Contemporary Arts, London, 1983. Recipient: Special Award, American Institute of Architects/*Sunset Magazine,* 1975; Honor Award, 1975 (twice), 1976, and 1978, and Merit Award, 1975 and 1977, Southern California Chapter, American Institute of Architects; Honor Award, American Institute of Architects, 1977; Award of Excellence, American Institute of Steel Construction, 1977; Architectural Design Award, 1981, and Special Merit Award, 1983, California Coastal Commission; California Chapter Honor Award, 1982, Los Angeles Chapter Honor Award, 1983 and 1984, American Institute of Architects; Arnold W. Brunner Memorial Prize, American Academy and Institute of Arts and Letters, 1983. Fellow, American Institute of Architects. Address: Frank O. Gehry and Associates Inc., 11 Brooks Avenue, Venice, California 90291, U.S.A.

Works:

1963 Kay Jewellers Office Building, Los Angeles

1964 Faith Plating Company, Los Angeles

1965 Danziger Studio/House, 7001 Melrose Avenue, West Hollywood, California

Design of the *Art Treasures from Japan* exhibition, Los Angeles County Museum of Art

1967 Merriweather Post Pavilion of Music, Columbia, Maryland

Feasibility study of the central business district of Hermosa Beach, California

O'Niel Hay Barn, San Juan Capistrano, California

1968 Joseph Magnin Store, South Coast Plaza, Costa Mesa, California

Joseph Magnin Store, Almaden Fashion Plaza, San Jose, California

Bixby Garden Townhouses, Garden Grove, California (with Walsh and O'Malley)

Design of the *Billy Al Bengston* exhibition, Los Angeles County Museum of Art

1970 University Park Apartments, Irvine Ranch, California

Vernon-Central Redevelopment Plan, Los Angeles

Temporary acoustical shell for the Hollywood Bowl, Los Angeles

1972 Ron Davis Studio/House, 29715 West Cuthbert Road, Malibu, California
Easy Edges Cardboard Furniture
1973 Cochiti Indian Reservation Commercial Center, Cochiti, New Mexico
1974 Westinghouse Office Building, Los Angeles
Larkspur Center, Larkspur, California
Janss House, West Los Angeles
Rouse Company Headquarters, Columbia, Maryland
1975 Concord Pavilion, Performing Arts Center, Concord, California
1976 Gemini G.E.L. Lithography Shop and Gallery remodelling, 8365 West Melrose, Hollywood, California
Norton Simon House, Malibu, California
Santa Monica Pier renovation, Santa Monica, California
Harper House Condominiums, Village of Cross Keys, Baltimore
Hollywood Bowl Shell, phase I, Los Angeles
1977 Ron Davis Studio/House interior additions, 29715 West Cuthbert Road, Malibu, California
Rudge and Guenzel "The Atrium," Lincoln, Nebraska
Berger, Berger, Kahn and Shafton Law Offices, Los Angeles
Cheviot Hills House remodelling, Los Angeles
Design of the *Tutankhamun* Exhibition, Los Angeles County Museum of Art
Design of the *Heeramaeneck Exhibition*, Los Angeles County Museum of Art
1978 Mid-Atlantic Toyota Distributorship (warehouse and offices), Glen Burnie, Maryland
1979 Cabrillo Marine Museum, San Pedro, California
Santa Monica Place (mall and parking structures), Santa Monica, California
DeMenil Townhouse, New York
Frank O. Gehry House, Santa Monica, California
Spiller House, Venice, California
Los Angeles Children's Museum
1980 Indiana Avenue Project (three artists' studios), Venice, Los Angeles
Strada Novissima, at the *Biennale*, Venice (exhibition project)
World Savings and Loan Association Offices, North Hollywood, California
1981 House for a Filmmaker, Santa Monica Canyon, California
Law School Building, Loyola University, Los Angeles
Smith House, Los Angeles
Lafayette Street Project, New York
Avant-Garde in Russia exhibition layouts, Los Angeles County Museum of Art
House, Beverly Hills, California
Central Business District Feasibility Study, Kalamazoo, Michigan
1982 Benson House, Calabasas, California
Los Angeles Aerospace Museum, Los Angeles
Civic Center, Beverly Hills, California (competition project)
Amphitheatre for the World's Exposition, New Orleans, Louisiana
1983 *Available Light* performance installation, Museum of Contemporary Art, Los Angeles (with choreographer Lucinda Childs and composer John Adams)
Temporary Quarters for the Museum of Contemporary Art, Los Angeles
Winton House, Wayzata, Minnesota
Frances Howard Goldwyn Regional Branch Library, Hollywood, California
1984 Sirmai-Peterson House, Thousand Oaks, California
Médiathéque, Centre d'Art Contemporain, Nîmes, France
Fish and Snake lamps
Borman House, Malibu, California

Publications:

By GEHRY: articles—"Interview: Frank Gehry" with William Ted Georgis in *Archetype* (San Francisco), Summer 1979; "Loyola Law School," interview, with John Mutlow in *LA Architect* (California), January 1982; "Interview: Frank Gehry" in *Transition* (St. Kilda, Victoria), February 1983; "Today We Have a Kind of Free-for-All Architecture," interview, in *U.S. News and World Report* (Washington, D.C.), 30 May 1983; recording—*Counter Statements*, tape cassette and slides, London 1981.

On GEHRY: books—*Innovations: Contemporary Home Environs*, exhibition catalogue, La Jolla, Los Angeles 1973; *12 California Architects*, edited by N. Charles Slert and James R. Harter, Pomona, Los Angeles 1978; *American Architecture Now*, edited by Barbaralee Diamonstein, New York 1980; *Gehry, Site, Tigerman: trois portraits de l'artiste en architecte* by Olivier Boissière, Paris 1981; *Collaboration: Artists and Architects* by Barbaralee Diamonstein, New York 1981; *Window, Room, Furniture*, exhibition catalogue, New York 1981; *Follies: Architecture for the Late-Twentieth-Century Landscape* by B. J. Archer and A. Vidler, New York 1983; articles—"The Quiet Townhouse" in *House and Home* (New York), December 1968; "Alfresco Spectacular" by Arthur C. Risser in *AIA Journal* (Washington, D.C.), August 1969; "Innovations: Easy Edges Does It" in *Architectural Forum* (New York), April 1972; "Ready-to-Go Zest: Cardboard Furniture" in *House and Garden* (New York), August 1972; "Report from the Malibu Hills" by Esther McCoy in *Progressive Architecture* (New York), December 1974; "Studied Slapdash" by Paul Goldberger in the *New York Times Magazine*, 18 January 1976; "Frank Gehry: The Search for 'No Rules' Architecture" by Janet Nairn in *Architectural Record* (New York), June 1976; "And Then There Were Twelve: The California 12" in *Architectural Record* (New York), August 1976; "Law Offices, California" and "Offices and Warehouse, near Baltimore" in *Architectural Review* (London), May 1979; "Gehry Residence in Santa Monica" in *GA Houses* (Tokyo), no. 6, 1979; "Ten Los Angeles Architects: Frank Gehry" by Olivier Boissière in *Domus* (Milan), March 1980; "Frank O. Gehry and Associates" by Suzanne Stephens in *Progressive Architecture* (New York), March 1980; "Frank Gehry" in *Architectural Review* (London) July 1980; "A New Wave in American Architecture: Frank O. Gehry" in *Space Design* (Tokyo) July 1980; "Frank Gehry's House" in *De Architect* (The Hague), March 1981; "Eccentric Space Architect: Frank Gehry" in *New Zealand Architect* (Wellington), no. 4, 1981; "Charles Eames, Frank O. Gehry—la maison manifeste" by Jean-Louis Cohen in *Architecture mouvement continuité* (Paris), June/September 1981; "Collision Architecture" in *Arkitekten* (Copenhagen), 11 August 1981; "The Play of Roles" in *Domus* (Milan), September 1981; "Frank O. Gehry's California Framework" by Frank Israel in *Gentlemen's Quarterly* (New York), December 1981; "Frank O. Gehry and Associates" in *GA Document* (Tokyo), no. 5, 1982; "Cabrillo Marine Museum" in *Architecture interieure créé* (Paris), April/May 1982; "The Gehry Style" by Joseph Morgenstern in the *New York Times Magazine*, 16 May 1982; "The Gehry Intersection" by Maria Luisa Scalvini in *Domus* (Milan), September 1982; "Gehry's Urbanism" by Martin Filler in *Skyline* (New York), October 1982; "MOCA Builds" in *Arts and Architecture* (Los Angeles), no. 1, 1983; "The Ten New Buildings Exhibition at the ICA" in *Building Design* (London), 28 January 1983; "Obsession of an Architect with Fish on a Grand Scale" by Joe Morgenstern in *Los Angeles Herald Examiner*, 4 March 1983; "A Minimalist Architecture of Allusion: Current Projects of Frank Gehry" by Lindsay Stamm Shapiro in *Architectural Record* (New York), June 1983; "Gehry as Goth" in *Architectural Review* (London), June 1983; "Frank Gehry: Understanding the Urban Campus" by Roger Kempler in the *Loyola Reporter* (Los Angeles), March 1984; "Genius or Eccentric?" by Paul Goldberger in the *New York Times Magazine*, 15 April 1984; "Mixed Metaphors: the New Orleans Fair" in *Progressive Architecture* (New York), May 1984; "Reality Squeezes Out Fantasy in Louisana Fair's Architecture" by Paul Goldberger in the *New York Times*, 13 May 1984; "Frank Gehry's Buildings Invent Their Own Order" by Leon Whiteson in *Los Angeles Herald Examiner*, 29 July 1984; "Frank Gehry" by Ulrike Jehle-Schulte Strathaus in *Werk, Bauen und Wohnen* (Zurich), July/August 1984; "Norton House, Venice, California" in *Architectural Record* (New York), mid-April 1985; film—*Beyond Utopia: Changing Attitudes in American Architecture* by Michael Blackwood, 1983.

*

I am interested in finishing work, but I am interested in the work's not appearing finished, with every hair in place, every piece of furniture in its spot ready for photographs. I prefer the sketch quality, the tentativeness, the messiness if you will, the appearance of "in progress" rather than the presumption of total resolution and finality. The paintings of Cézanne, Monet, deKooning, Rauschenberg, to name a few, compared to the hard-edge painters, Albers, Kelly, et al.—perhaps that comparison makes my point more explicit.

I have been searching for a personal vocabulary. This search has been far-ranging, from childlike exploration of my fantasies—a fascination with incoherent and seemingly illogical systems—to a questioning of orderliness and functionality. If you try to understand my work on the basis of fugal order, strtuctural integrity, and formalized definitions of beauty, you are apt to be totally confused.

A client's programs are interesting to me but are not the driving force in creating his building. I approach each building as a sculptural object, a spatial container, a space with light and air, a response to context and appropriateness of feeling and spirit. To this container, this sculpture, the user brings his baggage, his program, and interacts with it to accommodate his needs. If he can't do that, I've failed.

The manipulation of the inside of the container is for me an independent, sculptural problem and no less interesting than the design of the container itself. This manipulation tests the adaptability of the space for a program that by now can have changed several times. In my work, the perception of the object is primary. The imagery is real and not abstract, using distortion and juxtaposition of cheap materials to create surrealistic compositions.

All in the pursuit of firmness, commodity, and delight.

—Frank O. Gehry

*

Frank O. Gehry practices in an avant-garden manner. His design concepts have to do with creating architecture as pure art and sculpture. He has concentrated on flexibility and economy as expressed in angular forms and an unusual use of materials.

One of his goals is that of minimal construction: he strongly defines the outer walls, forcing the user to totally define the interior space. He is also acutely aware of building economics—what he refers to in his own work as "cheapscape architecture"—and his structures are clad in materials that have been stereotypically relegated to other building types. In particular, he has explored the use of corrugated metal panels, chain link fence, and exposed structural trusswork, to give the effect of industrial structures, in both commercial and residential work.

Gehry's artistic panache is obvious in such works as the warehouse and office for Toyota in Maryland. The metal supports and bridges form patterns against the corrugated background of the roof and the colorful partitions, which vary in height and width. The horizontal is interrupted at times by diagonals, forming triangles. There are panels of metal caging, and the divisions meet and cross at different levels, sometimes right through the middle of a paneless window or a doorless entrance. The shapes created for such purposes are irregular, and the whole effect is that of a Mondrian painting.

The exposed service transmitters are another example of Gehry's creation of abstract sculptural effects, and add further interest to the structures of this original designer.

—Janet Nairn

GIBBERD, Frederick.

British. Born in Coventry, 7 January 1908. Educated at the King Henry VIII School, Coventry, 1913-25; studied architecture in the office of Crouch, Butter and Savage, Birmingham, and at the Birmingham School of Architecture, 1925-29. Married Dorothy Philips in 1938 (died, 1970); children: Geoffrey, Kate, and Sophie; married Patricia Fox Edwards in 1972. In private practice, London, 1930 until his death in 1984: Principal, Frederick Gibberd and Partners, London 1950-78, and consultant, 1978-84; firm re-named Frederick Gibberd, Coombes and Partners in 1983. Retired, to concentrate on his own sculpture garden and landscaping projects, Harlow, Essex, 1978. Principal, Architectural Association School, London, 1942-44; Architect-Planner, Harlow New Town, Essex, 1946-72. Member, Royal Fine Art Commission, 1950-70; Member of the Council, Royal Institute of British Architects, 1951-70; President, Building Centre, London, 1959-76. Exhibitions: MARS Group, London, 1936; Museum of Modern Art, New York, 1936; Playhouse Gallery, Harlow, 1978. Recipient: Festival of Britain Award, 1951 (three times); Civic Trust Award, nine times; Bronze Medal, Royal Institute of British Architects, 1955; European Architectural Heritage Award, 1975 (twice); Housing Medal, three times; Gold Medal, Royal Town Planning Institute, 1978. Honorary Professor of Architecture, National Engineering University, Peru, 1965; LL.D.: University of Liverpool, 1969. Fellow, Royal Institute of British Architects, 1939, Society of Industrial Artists, 1943, Royal Town Planning Institute, 1948, and the Institute of Landscape Architects, 1956. Associate of the Royal Academy, 1961, and Royal Academician, 1969. C.B.E. (Commander, Order of the British Empire), 1954; Knighted, 1967. *Died* (in Harlow, Essex) *9 January 1984.*

Works:

1933   Pullman Court, Streatham, London
1935   Park Court, Crystal Palace, London
1936   Ellington Court, Southgate, London
1937   Macclesfield Nurses Home, Cheshire
1943   Howard Pre-Fabricated House (project)
        British Iron and Steel Federation Pre-Fabricated House
1945   Somerford Estate, Hackney, London
1946   Cladwell and Marston Estates, Nuneaton, Warwickshire
        Nuneaton Town Centre, Warwickshire
        Master plan for Harlow, Essex
1947   Steel rolling mill, Scunthorpe, Lincolnshire
        Civic Centre, Harlow, Essex
1948   Demps ter Court, Town Centre, Nuneaton, Warwickshire
        Beecholme Housing Estate, Prout Road, Hackney, London
        Cofton Common School, Worcestershire
1949   Lansbury Market, London
        Stow Shopping Centre, Harlow, Essex
        The Lawns, Harlow, Essex

1950/
  69   Terminal Buildings, London Airport
1951   Hull College of Technology, Yorkshire
        College of Further Education, Kidderminster, Worcestershire
        Westcliffe Secondary School, Scunthorpe, Lincolnshire
        Foley College of Technology, Stourbridge, Worcestershire
        Guinness Trust Flats, Cadogan Street, Chelsea, London
1952   Orchard Croft Housing Estate, Harlow, Essex
        Oakside Housing, Rutland Road, Hackney, London
        Market Square, Harlow, Essex
        National Dock Labour Board Office, Albert Embankment, London
1953   Ulster Hospital, Belfast
1955   Hancock House Office Block, Vincent Square, London
        Shell Research Centre, Thornton, Cheshire
        College of Technology, Huddersfield, Yorkshire
        Hill County Secondary School, Upton-on-Severn, Somerset
        High School, Henley-in-Arden, Warwickshire
        Hinkley Point Nuclear Power Station, Somerset
1956   The Beckers Estate, Rectory Road, Hackney, London
        Sion Hill Secondary School, Kidderminster, Worcestershire
        ICI Offices, Runcorn, Cheshire
        Kingsgate Estate, Tottenham Road, Hackney, London
        Bath Technical College, Somerset
        Civic Centre, St. Albans, Hertfordshire
1957   Kennedy Square, Leamington Spa, Warwickshire
        Redditch Secondary School, Worcestershire
1958   Shell Agricultural Research Centre, Sittingbourne, Kent
        St. Neots Bridge, Huntingdon
        Derwent Reservoir, Durham and Northumberland
1959   Alconbury Bridges, A1 Trunk Road, Huntingdon
        Fulwell Cross Library and Swimming Pool, Ilford, Essex
        Roseberry Square Neighbourhood Centre, Redcar, Yorkshire
        The Lakes Estate, Redcar, Yorkshire
        Llyn Celyn Reservoir, Merioneth, Wales
        Nuneaton Library, Warwickshire
        Corn Exchange Development, Stratford-upon-Avon
        Civic Centre, Doncaster, Yorkshire
1960   Roman Catholic Cathedral, Liverpool
        Colonnade Shopping Precinct, Birmingham
        Hopwood Hall Chapel, Middleton, Lancashire
        Old Harlow Redevelopment, Essex
1961   Barclays Bank, Bletchley, Buckinghamshire
1962   Douai Abbey, Berkshire
        South East Highgate Housing, Kendal, Westmorland
        Lowfellside Housing, Kendal, Westmorland
        Northumberland Court, Leamington Spa, Warwickshire
        Sydenham Farm Neighbourhood and Housing, Leamington Spa, Warwickshire
        Catholic Chaplaincy, University of Liverpool
        Leamington Spa Courthouse, Warwickshire
        Hull Youth Centre, Yorkshire
1964   St. George's Chapel, London Airport
        Didcot Power Station, Berkshire
1965   The Royal Spa Centre, Leamington Spa, Warwickshire
        Newbold Comyn Park, Leamington Spa, Warwickshire
        Crown Offices, Leamington Spa, Warwickshire
        Longman House, Harlow, Essex
1966   Arundel Great Court, The Strand, London

        Grays South Redevelopment Grays, Essex
        The Howard Hotel, Temple Place, London
1967   Cleveland Potash Mine, Yorkshire
1968   Inter-Continental Hotel, Hyde Park Corner, London
        York House, The Parade, Leamington Spa, Warwickshire
        Godfrey Holmes Offices, Lincoln
        Memorial University of Newfoundland, St. John's
        Town Centre, Haverhill, Suffolk
        Bell Court Shopping Centre, Stratford-upon-Avon
1969   The Harpur Centre Shopping Centre, Bedford
        Coutts Bank, The Strand, London
        London Central Mosque, Regent's Park, London
        Kielder Reservoir, Northumberland
        Thomas Cooper Memorial Chapel, Lincoln
1970   Dinorwic Pump Storage Power Station, Snowdonia, Wales
1971   Lion Walk Shopping Centre, Colchester, Essex
        Castle Centre Shopping Centre, Banbury, Oxfordshire
1973   Environmental Centre, Llanberis, Caernarvon, Wales
        Harvey Shopping Centre, Harlow, Essex

Publications:

By GIBBERD: books—*The Modern Flat*, with F. R. S. Yorke, London, 1937; *The Architecture of England*, London, 1938, 5th edition 1965; *Harlow New Town*, Harlow, Essex 1947, 1952, 1973; *Report of the Oxford University Drama Commission: Supplementary Architectural Report*, Oxford, 1948; *Town Design*, London 1953, 4th enlarged edition 1962; *Design in Town and Village*, with others, London 1953; *Architecture in the New Towns*, London 1963; *Metropolitan Cathedral of Christ the King*, London 1968; *Sculpture in Harlow*, Harlow, Essex 1973; *Harlow Expansion 1974*, Harlow, Essex 1974; *A Tonic for the Nation—Lansbury*, London 1976; *The Design of Harlow*, Harlow, Essex 1980; *Harlow: The Story of a New Town*, with others, Stevenage, Hertfordshire 1980; articles—"Wall Textures" in *Architectural Review* (London), July 1940; "The Schools and Practice" in *Architectural Review* (London), November 1943; "Landscaping a New Town" in *Architectural Review* (London), March 1948; "Three Dimensional Aspects of Housing Layout" in *RIBA Journal* (London), August 1948; "Detail in Civic Design" in *Town Planning Institute Journal* (London), March 1951; "Expression in Modern Architecture" in *RIBA Journal* (London), January 1952; "High Flats in Medium Sized Towns" in *RIBA Journal* (London), February 1955; "Mark Hall Neighbourhood" in *Architectural Review* (London), May 1955; "Ten Years After" in *The Sunday Times* (London), 19 May 1957; "Designing a New Town" in *Far and Wide* (London), Winter 1957/58; "The Landscape of Reservoirs" in *Journal of the Institute of Water Engineers* (London), March 1961; "New Towns in Britain" in *AIA Journal* (Washington, D.C.), March 1961; "Reflections on Architecture, 1965" in *The Builder* (London), December 1964; "The Landscaping of Reservoirs" in *Architectural Review* (London), July 1966; "Environmental Aspects of Boulby Mine" in *Minerals and the Environment* (London), June 1974; "A New Lake for Northumbria" in *Country Life* (London), December 1974; "Sculpture in the Landscape: The Private Garden" in *Journal of the Institute of Landscape Architects* (London), February 1978; "An Environmental Centre of the Year 2000" in *BEE/Bulletin of Environmental Education* (London), January 1979; "Harlow—The Design of a New Town" in *Town Planning Review* (London), January 1982; "On Making a Garden" in *RIBA Transactions* (London), no. 1, 1982; "Public Parks" in *Landscape Design* (London), August 1982; "Further Stages in the

Making of a notable garden" in *House and Garden* (London), December 1982.

On GIBBERD: book—*Designs of Frederick Gibberd,* exhibition catalogue, Harlow, Essex 1978; articles—"A 50 ft. Living Room" in *House and Garden* (London), June 1966; "Hotel, Hyde Park Corner" by Lance Wright in *Architectural Review* (London), December 1975; "London Central Mosque" in *RIBA Journal* (London), June 1976; "The Making of Harlow" by Stephanie Williams in *Building Design* (London), 27 August 1976; "Arundel Great Court, Strand" by Sutherland Lyall in *The Architects' Journal* (London), 3 November 1976; "Harpur Centre, Bedford" by James Madge in *The Architects' Journal* (London), 24 November 1976; "The Gibberd Touch" by Tony Aldous in *The Architects' Journal* (London), 11 January 1978; "Reservoir, Harrow on the Hill" in *Landscape Design* (London), February 1980; "Colchester Camouflage" by Dan Cruickshank in *Architects' Journal* (London), 27 August 1980; "Landscape Creation of the Present" by Anthony Huxley in *Country Life* (London), 18 December 1980; "Sir Frederick Gibberd, 1908-1984" by Michael Coombes in *Building Design* (London), 13 January 1984; "Sir Frederick Gibberd (1908-1984)" in *Building* (London), 13 January 1984; "Sir Frederick Gibberd: Obituary" by Philip Powell in *Architects' Journal* (London), 18 January 1984; "Death of Sir Frederick Gibberd" in *RIBA Journal* (London), February 1984.

*

My interest is in design. I have spent most of my life at the drawing board and have never been interested in a professional career as such. I do not produce imaginative sketch designs and leave them to others to work out. To me design is a long and laborious process, and I am involved until it is finally settled. I have avoided specialising because the more varied the design problems, the more interesting life is.

Unlike most architects, I practice Landscape Architecture and Town Planning. My imagination is probably at its best when I am able to combine these three arts into a complete environment.

I came to town planning from architecture because, apart from the design problems being more complex, it enabled me to determine the environment for my buildings and to relate buildings to each other and to the landscape to make urban spaces. The English landscape has had a strong influence on my work. Harlow is based on the land form, and large-scale industrial projects like Didcot Power Station and the Cleveland Potash Mine were fundamentally landscape problems.

I am told that I have a reputation for being sensitive to the character of English towns and villages. I received European Architectural Heritage Awards for the village of Old Harlow and Lowfellside housing in Kendal and design awards for Lansbury Market and schemes at Stratford-upon-Avon, Bedford, and elsewhere.

I have a capacity for realising my designs (I swallow my pride and do not resign) with the consequence that I remained with Harlow until its completion, and at places such as Leamington Spa and Nuneaton, I carried out a whole series of designs over long periods.

My concern for the environment has been a strong influence on my architecture: Liverpool Cathedral has a tower to give, with the Catholic Cathedral, two crowns to the urban composition; the Inter-Continental Hotel is designed to terminate the long frontage of Piccadilly, leaving Aspley House as a pavillion in the park; and Arundel Great Court in the Strand has given London a new landscaped court.

—Frederick Gibberd (1980)

*

Although, as the list of his works demonstrates, Sir Frederick Gibberd has designed a wide variety of buildings, it is possible to discern definite and persistent characteristics that pervade most of his work. In his concepts, whether in individual structures, groups of buildings or town planning schemes, he has been socially progressive in answering human needs, he has been anxious to conserve and introduce amenities, and in doing this, he has kept abreast of technical developments so as more efficiently to satisfy needs. Aesthetically, simplicity and restraint, with a few exceptions, have generally prevailed in his designs.

Throughout most of his work Gibberd has been a designer in rectangles, with a studied adjustment of their relations, of the parts to each other and of the parts to the whole, so that the appearance of most of his buildings might be described as a rectangular massing of the parts, with variety secured by various textures of wall and patterning of fenestration, with projections and recessions giving light and shade. Occasionally there is a horizontal emphasis, but it is rarely sufficient to disturb a general sense of repose. These qualities are seen in Pullman Court, Streatham, one of his earliest buildings, where the large rectangular blocks arranged round a court have well spaced windows and balconies which give variety. A simpler treatment is seen in the three-storey blocks at Park Court, Crystal Palace, where the flatnes of square windows on plain walls is saved perhaps from dullness by the integration with an attractive landscape setting. In his tall, square blocks of flats at Harlow, the good effect depends on the slightly curved facades, on the vertical recessions, the well-proportioned window spacing, and the landscape setting. The rectangular motif controls much of Gibberd's planning of many town centres, of which that for Harlow is a conspicuous example, where Gibberd started from scratch. This centre, looked at on plan, is a rectangular pattern and the buildings—the shops, offices and those surrounding the market square—have this same characteristic with occasional horizontal emphasis. It is seen too in the water gardens, south of the centre, with long, straight pools and rectangular flower beds, while the

Frederick Gibberd: Harlow New Town, Essex, 1946-72.

theme is continued horizontally and vertically in the adjacent tower hall. The consciousness of this square, formal massing is strong because of the simplicity and the restrained articulations. At its best, it achieves a Greek-like serenity, and dignity; when it is less successful, as in some of the extremely simple terrace housing and blocks of flats, it is dull, monotonous and cold, where regularly spaced, squarish windows on smooth, plain pale walls wait for shrubs and trees to grow nearby to make them aesthetically effective.

One of Gibberd's best works in the idiom is the Civic Hall, St. Albans, the principal building in the Civic Centre that he planned. It is very broadly and effectively treated. A broad canopy projects above the ground floor, which has extensive glazed areas, while on the first floor the extensive fenestration at the corners of the block relate very well to the plain walls. The building is in sunken area from the main approach ways, and thus the broad massing can be well seen.

Gibberd is probably best known for Harlow New Town, Heathrow Airport terminal buildings, and the Liverpool Roman Catholic Cathedral. The best of the airport buildings is the last, which represents an advance in fuctional design with its two main levels for arriving and departing passengers and two-level road access. It is the most dramatic in appearance of the group—a long rectangular building with the horizontal bands of wall and fenestration giving a more dynamic emphasis than is usual in his work.

Gibberd's designing for human needs is seen both in his work as a town planner and in his housing. The visit of a resident to a town centre may include a dozen calls to shops, bank, post office, library, etc. located there; it is a great advantage if these are concentrated to minimize movement from one to the other. In Harlow town centre, Gibberd has achieved this concentration and has grouped his buildings round squares and pedestrian ways. Gibberd must also be accounted one of the pioneers of pedestrianization, and good examples are seen in his many designs for town centres. That at Nuneaton, designed at the end of World War II, is a good example, and here Gibberd made use of the natural feature of the river Anker that runs through the centre to introduce the amenities of a park and tree planting while retaining some of the old features, such as flour mills, achieving a happy blending of old and new, something that he also achieved at St. Albans and in the old town, or rather village, of Harlow, where the narrow High Street was bypassed and converted into a pedestrian way, with some new modern buildings in excellent harmony in scale and massing.

In designing for human needs, Gibberd has always been ready to use and develop modern materials and methods of construction. During World War II, he designed the Howard House, which structurally had a light steel frame with panels of suitable weatherproof and insulating materials and a kitchen made in the factory and transported complete to the site. With other designs of the period, it was a useful contribution to prefabrication. A valuable factor in the design of the house was a service unit consisting of kitchen, utility room on the ground floor, and bathroom on the first, kept separate from the living and sleeping sections and ingeniously arranged to come together in terrace housing. A further example is the structural innovation in his design for the Liverpool Cathedral, which is rather a departure from Gibberd's other work. With its circular plan and central altar (following the modern liturgical movement), it is of tent-like form similar to the old bell tent of the British Army, surmounted by a tower and culminating in a crown of thorns. The construction is of reinforced and pre-stressed concrete with a careful calculation of compression and tension, making possible an economy of bulk and material. But the conical roof coming low on the cylindrical wall hardly gives the spatial feeling that is desirable in a church of his size. It is not typical of Gibberd's best work, which resides more in the attractive and often ingenious variations of rectangular massing.

—Arnold Whittick

GIBSON, Robin.

Australian. Born Robert Findlay Gibson in Brisbane, Queensland, 15 May 1930. Educated at the University of Queensland, Brisbane, 1948-54, Dip.Arch. 1954. Married Moorea Roach in 1957 (died, 1977); children: Kristina and Nicholas. Student Architect, City Architect's Department, Brisbane, 1948, office of Frank Cullen, Brisbane, 1949, Hayes and Scott, Brisbane, 1950, and Theo Thynne, Brisbane, 1951-54; Architect, James Cubitt and Partners, London, 1955, and Sir Hugh Casson and Neville Conder, London, 1955. Since 1957, Principal of Robin Gibson and Partners, Brisbane. Exhibitions: Queensland Art Gallery, Brisbane, 1974; Australian Pavilion, Spokane, 1976. Recipient: First Prize, Queensland Art Gallery Competition, 1973; Bronze Medal for Meritorious Architecture, Royal Australian Institute of Architects, Queensland Chapter, 1973 and 1976. Life Fellow, Royal Australian Institute of Architects, 1981. Address: Robin Gibson and Partners, 130 Mary Street, Brisbane, Queensland 4000, Australia.

Works:

1961 Miss Shirley's Shop, Brisbane
1963 Perrins House, Ascot, Brisbane
      Wallace Bishop Store, Fortitude Valley, Brisbane
1964 Shirley Shoes and Players, Surfers Paradise, Queensland
      British Overseas Airways Corporation, Brisbane
1965 Qantas House, Brisbane
1966 Mocatta House, Yeronga, Brisbane
1968 Kenmore Presbyterian Church, Brisbane
      Robinson's Sports Store, Queen Street, Brisbane
      Wallace Bishops' Store, Toombul Shopping Town, Brisbane
1969 Commonwealth Industrial Gases Office Building and Stores, Brisbane
      Commonwealth Industrial Gases Research Centre, Sydney
1970 I.A.C. House, Brisbane
1972 Office building, 40 Queen Street, Brisbane

1973 Mayne Hall, University of Queensland, Brisbane
      Central Library, University of Queensland, Brisbane
      Mathers Shoes Warehouse, Brisbane
1974 Administration and Psychology Building, Mount Gravatt Teachers College, Brisbane
1975 Library and Humanities Complex, Griffith University, Brisbane
      Mathers Shoes Retail Premises, Townsville, Queensland
1975/
78 Queensland Cultural Center, Brisbane: Art Gallery; Performing Arts Complex; Museum; and State Library
1976 Library/Arts and Crafts and Music Students Union, Mount Gravatt Teachers College, Brisbane
1977 State Control Centre, Queensland Electricity Generating Board, Brisbane
1982 Queensland Art Gallery, Brisbane

Publications:

On GIBSON: books—*Towards an Australian Architecture* by Harry Sowden, Sydney 1968; *University Library Buildings in South East Asia,* University of Singapore Library, 1976; *Old Continent—New Building: Contemporary Australian Architecture,* edited by Leon Paroissien and Michael Griggs, Darlinghurst, New South Wales 1983; article— "Three on the Campus" in *Architecture Australia* (Melbourne), September 1978.

Architecture is the truthfulness of creating spaces effective for their use and enjoyable to the user in the answering of those usages.

"In the beginning" are magical works, and the opportunity to create and bring into being a tangible reality is the joy of architecture. The processes to achieve it are a complex matrix based on a continuing assessment of applied techniques overlaid with modern technological advances.

Problems to be solved are analysed and abstracted to the minimal elemental bases so that the end result

Robin Gibson: Mayne Hall, University of Queensland, Brisbane, 1973.

is the essence of the problem. From this base, architecture is created with an emotional and subjective but, above all else, an imaginative input. An architecture which is on-going with previous experiences and examples is the basis for development.

Architecture that relies on the purity of material use, the clarity of structural solutions, and the objectivity of planning solutions as the language creates a poetry which is known and seen as a personal architecture. The built result is seen as a place which is in context with its use, brings joy and happiness to the user, and contributes to the improvement of the total environment.

—Robin Gibson

Robin Gibson practices architecture in Queensland, which is the only part of the world where five generations of Europeans have lived and worked in what is largely a hot, humid, tropical climate. These families successfully adapted themselves to an environment different from that of their historical experience. They also developed a distinctive vernacular buildingtradition that extensively used light, durable, low-cost materials, such as timber and tin. This tradition is unique to Queensland, and it has also substantially helped to establish what is considered by many as a transitory environment.

In sheer contrast to this tradition, Gibson's buildings are solid, carefully detailed, and permanent enough to give the impression that they are likely to stay there for some time. In a region where fortunes are quickly made and lost, Gibson's buildings continue to provide a sense of stability and order.

Gibson's projects are associated with cultural, civic, and educational institutions. His design approach has its links with the Bauhaus which reached Australia via the United States, particularly the Californian west coast, where the climate is not unlike that of Queensland. His style is tightly controlled in the Miesian tradition, with judicious use of concrete—mainly precast—and glass and steel. The details are meticulous and highly refined. However, unlike Mies van der Rohe's architecture, Gibson's buildings are open-ended and can be extended to satisfy the changing requirements.

Since most of Gibson's buildings are air-conditioned, climate, as a basis of design, plays only a minor role. He uses large glass areas and extensive terraces that lend themselves to enjoyment of the outdoors.

Gibson has made a major contribution to changing the face of Brisbane, Queensland's capital city of one million people. He has designed a number of important buildings in the city centre and set a high standard in a State which, until recently, largely remained outside the mainstream of architectural development.

One of his most recent projects is a large cultural centre complex on the Brisbane River's southern banks. The complex incorporates buildings for the performing arts, a museum, an art gallery, restaurants, an auditorium, and the State library. One of the most ambitious projects ever undertaken by the Government of Queensland, its design includes the best elements of Gibson's approach and indicates a high level of sensitivity for its unique location. These buildings have firmly established their designer as one of the most significant contributors to the architectural heritage of the State.

—B.S. Saini

GINSBERG, Jean Ernest.
French. Born in Czestochowa, Poland, 20 April 1905; emigrated to France, 1924: naturalized, 1939. Educated at the Technical College, Warsaw, B.A. 1922; Berlin University, 1923; Ecole Spéciale d'Architecture, Paris, 1924-29, Dip.Arch. 1929. Married Olga de Krassilnikoff (divorced); May d'Ornhjelm in 1954; children: Corrine and Christiane. In private practice, Paris, 1929 until his death in 1983; Principal, Jean Ginsberg & Associes, Paris, from 1932. Permanent Member, Housing Committee of the International Union of Architects. Recipient: First Prize, Academy of Architecture,

Jean Ginsberg: Les Speluges Complex, Monte Carlo, 1977.

Paris, 1962; First Prize, Ashdod Harbour Competition, Israel, 1966; First Prize, Beauty of Paris Competition, 1967; First Prize, National Housing Program Consultation, Paris, 1967; First Prize, Ministry of Equipment Housing Competition, Paris, 1969 and 1973; First Prize, Center of the New Town of Evry, France, Competition, 1972. Member: Academy of Architecture, Paris; French Society of Town Planning; Cercle d'Etudes Architecturales; Industrial Aesthetic Institute; and Franco-British Union of Architects. Chevalier of the Légion d'Honneur, 1974, and of the National Order of Merit, 1980; Chevalier de Saint Charles, Monaco, 1960. *Died* (in Paris) *14 May 1983.*

Works:

1927   Apartment building, 25 Avenue de Versailles, Paris (with Bertold Lubetkin)
1930/
   72   Group of 2,000 flats, Meaux, France
      Group of flats, Meudon, France
      Group of 275 flats, Massy, France
      Group of 220 flats, Montrouge, France
      Group of 360 flats, Courbevoie, France
      Group of 300 flats, Gif-sur-Yvette, near Paris
      Group of 320 flats, Poissy, France
      Building, Boulogne sur Seine, near Paris
      Group of 1200 flats, Argenteuil, France
      Group of 2080 flats, Le Mureaux, France
      Building, Saint Cloud, near Paris
      Embassy of Finland, Paris
      O.E.C.D. (Organisation for Economic Co-operation and Development) Offices, Paris
      Administrative Offices, Orly Airport, Paris
      General Secretary's Office, Civil Aviation Board, Paris
      Government Administration Buildings, Monaco
      Holiday centres at Biarritz and Lacanau, France
      Holiday centre at Ibiza, Spain
1972   Centre of the new town of Evry, France (competition project)
1975   Gif-sur-Yvette Commercial Centre, near Paris
      City Centre of the new town of Vitrolles, near Marseille
1975/
   77   Technical University, Libreville, Gabon (with others)
      Les Speluges Complex, Monte Carlo: Palais Heracles; Mille Fiori Tower, Las Palmeras Building; Monte Carlo Star Building; Loew's Hotel and Casino; and International Convention Centre and Auditorium
      The Regina apartment and shop complex, Monte Carlo

Publications:

On GINSBERG: articles—"A Different Kind of Building Complex: Les Speluges at Monte Carlo" by Abel Blanc in *La Construction moderne* (Paris), September/December 1974; "Residential Complex, Marly-le-Roi" in *Bauen und Wohnen* (Zürich), September 1975; "Les Speluges Complex in Monte Carlo" in *Recherche et architecture* (Paris), no. 28, 1976; "Luxury Hotel with Convention Hall and Flats on the Mediterranean" in *Bauen und Wohnen* (Zürich), May 1976; "Technical High School at Libreville for 3,000 Pupils" in *Mur vivant* (Paris), no. 48, 1978; "Convention Centre Architects Win Top Monaco Award in Monte Carlo" in *Building Design* (London), 9 February 1979; "Hommage: Jean Ginsberg" by Charles Rambert in *Architectes* (Paris), July 1983.

Jean Ginsberg's practice, in association successively with Lubetkin, Heep, and others, shows a continuity in architectural ideas, a search for imaginative solutions, an attention to detail, and a quality in the completed work that clearly bear the stamp of this excellent architect's personalilty.

His first-class organising ability and business competence do not detract from this excellence. Fate has made of him an architect chiefly concerned with property developments for various clients whose main concern is profitablity. He has given them satisfaction without sacrifice of architectural quality. Nor does he bow to fashion; Ginsberg remains faithfull to "line" and develops it wherever possible.

We do not choose our clients, and to a certain extent they fashion us. It is to Ginsberg's great credit that he has always known how to please his clients and yet produce good architecture—as every architect knows, not always an easy task.

—Pierre Vago

GISEL, Ernst.
Swiss. Born in Adliswil, near Zurich, 8 June 1922. Educated at primary and secondary schools, in Adliswil, 1928-32, and Zurich-Wollishofen, 1932-37; apprentice draughtsman, architectural studio of Vogelsanger and Maurer, Zurich, 1938-40; studied interior design, under Wilhelm Kienzle, Kunstgewerbeschule, Zurich, and at the ETH: Eidgenossische Technische Hochschule, Zurich, 1940-42. Served in the Swiss Army, 1942-45. Married the art historian Marianne Sessler in 1946; children: Anna, Georg, Eva, and Helen. Worked in the architectural studio of Alfred Roth, *q.v.*, Zurich 1942-44. Since 1945, in private practice, Zurich: in partnership with Ernst Schauer, 1945-48, and with Louis Plüss, 1964-67; established second studio in West Berlin, 1966-71. Member of the Building Board, Zurich, 1962-75. Visiting Professor, ETH: Eidgenossische Technische Hochschule, Zurich, 1968-69; Guest Professor, Technische Universität, Karlsruhe, West Germany, 1969-71. Exhibitions: *Scuole*, at the *Triennale*, Milan, 1960; *Ernst Gisel: Bauten und Projekte*, Bund Deutscher Architekten, Stuttgart, 1966 (toured West Germany, 1966-67); *Architettura Razionale*, at the *Triennale*, Milan, 1973; *Museumsbauten: Entwürfe und Projekte seit 1945*, Museum am Ostwall, Dortmund, West Germany, 1979; *Architecture 70/80 in Switzerland*, Kunsthalle, Basel, Switzerland, 1982 (toured Europe). Recipient: Good Building Prize, Zurich, 1957, 1961, 1965, 1973, 1981, and 1985; Paul Bonatz Prize, Stuttgart, 1967. Honorary Member, Bund Deutscher Architekten, 1966; Member, Akademie der Künste, West Berlin, 1968. Member, Schweizer Werkbund, 1948, and Bund Schweizer Architekten, 1952. Address (office): Streulistrasse 74A, 8032 Zurich, Switzerland.

Works:

1941   Rotschuo Youth Hostel (competition project)
1943   ABZ Housing Development, Zurich (with Ernst Schaer)
1944   Im Gut School, Zurich (competition project)
1945   Housing Project for War-damaged Countries (project)
      Rebhügel School, Zurich (competition project; with Ernst Schaer)
1945/
   47   ABZ Herrlig Housing Development, Zurich (with Ernst Schaer)
1946   Steig Church, Schaffhausen, Switzerland (competition project; with Ernst Schaer)
      Hospital, Zurich (competition project)
      Kügeliloo School, Zurich (competition project; with Ernst Schaer)
      Otterstall Open-air Swimming Facilities, Neuhausen, Switzerland (competition project)
1947   Studio House, Solduno, Switzerland

1947/
   48   Maag Farmstead, Bachenbülach, Switzerland (with Ernst Schaer)
      Aeschbach Studio House, Zumikon, near Zurich
1947/
   52   Recken School, Thayngen, Switzerland
1948   Nestlé Company collapsible sales stand, Zurich
      Artists' Colony, Zurich (project)
1949   Artists' Colony, Zurich (second project)
      Apartments, Zurich (project)
      Oesterleden Development, Stockholm (competition project)
      Hall Structure, Romont, Switzerland (competition project)
1949/
   55   Garden Park Theatre, Grenchen, Switzerland
1950   Kolbenacker School, Zurich (competition project)
      Werkbund Exhibition designs, Museum of Applied Arts, Zurich
      Protestant Church, Witikon, Zurich (competition project)
1951   Trade School, Schaffhausen, Switzerland (competition project)
      Matzinger Holiday House, Braunwald, Switzerland
      Theatre, Delsberg, Switzerland (project)
      Herzogenmühle School, Zurich (competition project)
1951/
   53   Hauser-Bucher House, Niederweningen, Switzerland
1952   Fratelli Caflisch Establishment, Catania, Italy (project)
      Hospital with Nurses' Housing, Zurich (competition project)
      Untermoos School, Zurich (competition project)
1952/
   53   Pfäffli House, Zweisimmen, Switzerland
1953   Church and Community Centre, Zofingen, Switzerland (competition project)
      Employees' Housing, Niederweningen, Switzerland (project)
      School, Eschlikon, Switzerland (project)
1953/
   54   Three Studio Houses (including Gisel House) and Artists' Cooperative Housing, Wuhrstrasse, Zurich
1953/
   56   Letzi School, Zurich
1954   Freudenberg School, Zurich (competition project)
      Chriesiweg School, Zurich (competition project)
1954/
   55   Paul Speck Studio House, Tegna, Switzerland
1955   Krauer House and Zuppinger House, Reinach, Switzerland (projects)
      Open-air Swimming Facilities, Horgen, Switzerland (competition project)
      Bucher-Guyer Exhibition Hall and Factory Buildings, Niederweningen, Switzerland
      Youth Hostel, Zurich (project)
      Gemeindewiese School, Neuhausen, Switzerland (competition project)
1955/
   58   Auhof School and Open-air Swimming Facilities, Zurich
      School and Community Centre, Würenlos, Switzerland
1956   Administration Building with Swimming Pool, Biel, Switzerland
      Grob House and Schweizer House, Hedinger, Switzerland
      Hauriweg Parish Centre, Zurich (competition project)
1956/
   61   Protestant Church, Effretikon, Zurich
1957   Workers' Monument, Helvetiaplatz, Zurich (competition project; with sculptor H. J. Meyer)

Triemli City Hospital, Zurich (competition project)

Heuried Recreation Centre and Swimming Pool, Zurich (competition project)

Open-air Swimming Facilities, Zollikon, near Zurich (competition project)

1958 Trade School, Schaffhausen, Switzerland (competition project)

1958/
59 Gisel Holiday House, Rigi-Kaltbad, Switzerland

Zweidler House rebuilding, Zurich

1958/
60 Apartment Building, Hegibachstrasse, Zurich

1959 Congress Centre, Geneva (competition project)

Letzi School garden and changing-rooms, Zurich

1959/
60 Hechtplatz Theatre, Zurich

A. and R. Zürcher Studio House, Maur, near Zurich

1959/
63 Protestant Church, Reinach, Switzerland

Sports Complex and Congress Centre, Davos, Switzerland (competition project)

1959/
66 J. Sessler Factory rebuilding and extension, Hedingen, Switzerland

1960 Opera House, Zurich (competition project)

1960/
61 Apartment Building, Clausiusstrasse, Zurich

J. Leutert House, Aurorastrasse, Zurich

1960/
62 Alpha Apartment House, Davos, Switzerland (project; completed by others)

1960/
63 Protestant Church on the Rigi Mountain, Rigi-Kaltbad, Switzerland

1960/
64 Protestant Church, Oberglatt, Switzerland

Erachfeld Open-air Swimming Facilities, Bülach, Switzerland

1960/
66 Youth Hotel, Mutschellenstrasse, Zurich

Fire-Brigade Station, Zumikon, near Zurich

1961/
62 Congress Centre, Ascona, Switzerland (competition project)

Dr. Köppel House, Gossau, Switzerland

1961/
67 School and Kindergarten, Engelberg, Switzerland

1962 Protestant Church and Parson's House, Luterbach, Switzerland (competition project)

Open-air Swimming Facilities, Zollikon, near Zurich (second competition project)

1962/
63 Parson's House, Parish of Altstetten, Zurich

Ch. Schmid Holiday House, Splügen, Switzerland

1962/
64 F. Schaer and W. Reinle Holiday House, Rigi-Kaltbad, Switzerland

W. Keller House, Zollikon, near Zurich

1962/
65 Indoor Swimming Pool near the Congress Centre, Davos, Switzerland

1962/
69 Congress Centre, Davos, Switzerland

1962/
72 Breite Open-air Swimming Facilities, Indoor Pool, and Skating Rink, Schaffhausen, Switzerland (competition project)

1963 Assembly Hall and Gymnasium, Thayngen, Switzerland (completed by others)

Student Village, Enschede, Netherlands (competition project)

1963/
64 Ecumenical Church and Exhibition Hall, *Expo 64*, Lausanne, Switzerland (with Hans Howald)

1963/
66 Protestant Church and Parish Centre, Sonnenberg, Stuttgart

1964 W. Keller Holiday House, Eggberge, Switzerland (project)

Cemetery Development, Albisgütli, Zurich (competition project)

1964/
67 Hamme School, Thayngen, Switzerland

1964/
69 Märkisches Viertel Housing Development, West Berlin

Protestant Students' Community Centre, Mainz, West Germany

1966 Protestant Church, Wil-Dübendorf, near Zurich (competition project)

Neue Pinakothek Art Gallery, Munich (competition project)

French High School, West Berlin (competition project)

Open-air Swimming Facilities, Frauenfeld, Switzerland (competition project)

1966/
67 Gisel Studio House, Zumikon, near Zurich

1966/
71 Friesenberghalde Housing, Studios and Kindergarten, Zurich

1967 Theatre, Vaduz, Liechtenstein (project)

1967/
68 Ecumenical Chapel at Pestalozzi Children's Village, Trogen, Switzerland

St. Etienne Catholic Church, Lausanne-La Sallaz, Switzerland (competition project)

1968 University Sports Facilities, Regensburg, West Germany (competition project)

Stalder and Howald Houses, Zumikon, near Zurich

Thermal Baths, Bad Ragaz, Switzerland (competition project)

Clock Museum, La Chaux-de-Fonds, Switzerland (competition project)

Indoor Swimming Pool, Winterthur, Switzerland (competition project)

1968/
70 Protestant Community Centre, Kobylisy, Prague

1968/
71 Skating Rink, Davos, Switzerland (project)

1968/
73 High School, Vaduz, Liechtenstein

1968/
78 Ch. Baumann House, Schönenberg, Switzerland

1969 Protestant Church, Hüntwangen-Wil, Switzerland (competition project)

1969/
70 H. U. Hauser House, Niederweningen, Switzerland

1969/
72 Monastery High School and Boarding House, Engelberg, Switzerland (competition project)

Housing and Studios, Perlach, West Germany

1970 College of Music, Freiburg, West Germany (competition project)

Town Hall and Theatre, Bocholt, West Germany (competition project)

1970/
73 Gisel Studio, Streulistrasse 74A, Zurich

1971 Gymnasium and School extension, Schaffhausen, Switzerland (competition project)

1971/
72 Congress/Exhibition Centre and Housing, Oerlikon, Zurich (competition project)

1971/
76 Zurich State Archives, Zurich (project)

1972 Theatre rebuilding, Schaan, Liechtenstein

Ernst Gisel: Church and Community Centre, Steinhausen, Switzerland, 1976-81.

Catholic Church, Lengnau-Endingen, Switzerland (competition project)

1972/
75 Wenaweser House, Schalunstrasse, Vaduz, Liechtenstein

1973 Guggach Trade School with Sports Facilities, Zurich (competition project)

Old People's Home and Indoor Swimming Pool, Männedorf, Switzerland (competition project)

1973/
74 Parson's House for the Anglican Church, Zurich

1973/
75 A. Streiff House, Küsnacht, near Zurich

Lehni Factory Building, Dübendorf, Switzerland

1974 Administration Building, Dübendorf, Switzerland (competition project)

Allmend School, Horgen, Switzerland (competition project)

Housing Development, Rousseaustrasse, Zurich (competition project)

1974/
78 Allmend School and Indoor Swimming Pool, Meilen, Switzerland (competition project; pool built)

1975 Swiss Federal Railways Training Centre, Löwenberg, Murten, Switzerland (competition project)

Catholic Parish Centre, Zollikon, near Zurich (competition project)

Im Wiesli Old People's Home, Schaffhausen, Switzerland (competition project)

Housing Development near the Oerlikon Cycling-Track, Zurich (project)

1975/
76 Dr. Köppel House, Zumikon, near Zurich

1975/
81 Community Centre, Wetzikon, Switzerland (completed by others)

1976 Kranichstein Ecumenical Community Centre, Darmstadt, West Germany (competition project)

Contraves AG Building, Zurich (project)

Schwarztor/Güterhof City Plan, Schaffhausen, Switzerland (competition project)

1976/
77 Obstmarkt Centre Plan, Herisau, Switzerland (competition project)

1976/
78 City Plan and Milchbuch Tunnel Entrance, Zurich (project)

1976/
80 Steinboden School, Eglisau, Switzerland

1976/
81 Two Churches and Community Centre, Steinhausen, Switzerland

1977 Museum, Vaduz, Liechtenstein (competition project)

Marktplatz Office Building and Shops, Gaggenau, West Germany (competition project)

1977/
79 Wettingerwies Housing Development, Zurich

1977/
84 Cantonal Bank, Herisau, Switzerland

1978 Rämi Post Office Building, Zurich (competition project)

Old People's Home, near the Milchbuch Tunnel Entrance, Zurich

1978/
79 Palais Ephraim Development, West Berlin (project)

1978/
83 Traffic Control Building and Ventilator Tower, Milchbuch Tunnel, Zurich

1979 Lietzensee Roof Superstructures, Dernburgstrasse, West Berlin (project)

1979/
82 Housing Development, Waldemarstrasse, West Berlin

1979/
86 Town Hall, Fellbach, West Germany

1980 Apartment Building, Prinzenallee, West Berlin

Stock Exchange Building, Zurich (competition project)

1980/
83 Stadelhofer Passage Apartments, Offices, Shops and Studios, Zurich

1980/
84 Housing and Community Development, Hasenheide, West Berlin (completed by others)

1981/
82 Berlin Museum extension, Lindenstrasse, West Berlin (project)

1981/
83 Museum and Library, Chur, Switzerland (competition project)

1981/
84 City Hall, Dübendorf, near Zurich (project)

1981 Rotillon Housing and Business Development, Lausanne, Switzerland (project)

Schloss-Platz Development, Stuttgart (competition project)

Grünau Protestant Church, Switzerland (competition project)

1982 High School extension, Vaduz, Liechtenstein

Community Centre, Oberglatt, near Zurich (competition project)

Mühlenareal Development, Thun, Switzerland (competition project)

1982/
83 Ramspeck House, Zumikon, near Zurich

1982 University rebuilding, Zurich

1983 Stadelhofen Rail Station, Zurich (competition project)

Opéra de la Bastille Development, Paris (competition project; with Marx Lévy)

1983- Schwarztor Housing and Business Development, Schaffhausen, Switzerland (competition project)

1984 Cantonal Bank, Appenzell, Switzerland (competition project)

1985 City Plan and Administration Building, Frankfurt-am-Main (competition project)

Housing Development, Brünnerstrasse, Vienna (project)

High School extension, Vaduz, Liechtenstein

Publications:

By GISEL: articles—"Ueber das Dach", with Marianne Gisel, in *Forum*(Hilversum, Netherlands), no. 1, 1954; "Zur Integration der Kunste" in *Werk*(Zurich), August 1960; "Der Backstein in der Schweiz" in *Element*(Zurich), no. 1, 1960; "Churches", editor of special issue of *Werk*(Zurich), December 1961; "Moderner Kirchenbau" in *Baumeister*(Munich), December 1965; "Badenweiler Spa", with Marianne Gisel, in *Der Architekt* (Stuttgart), November 1977.

On GISEL: books—*Moderne Schulbauten* by E. Brödner and J. Kroeker, Munich 1953; *Modernes Wohnen* by E. Brödner, Munich 1954; *Das neue Schulhaus* by Alfred Roth, Zurich 1957; *Das Haus des Architekten* by Robert Winkler, Zurich 1957; *Architettura per lo spettacolo* by R. Aloi, Milan 1958; *Kleinsthäuser, Ferienhäuser, Bungalows* by Martin Mittag, Gütersloh, West Germany 1959; *Scuole* by R. Aloi, Milan 1960; *Neue Schweizer Architektur* by Alfred Altherr, Teufen, Switzerland 1965; *Bauen mit Holz* by Kurt Hoffmann, Stuttgart 1966; *L'Architettura in Svizzera oggi* by Benito De Sivo, Naples 1968; *New Directions in Swiss Architecture* by Jul Bachmann and Stanislaus von Moos, New York 1969; *Neue Deutsche Architektur III* by Wolfgang Pehnt, Teufen, Switzerland 1970; *Museumsbauten: Entwürfe und Projekte seit 1945*, exhibition catalogue edited by Josef Paul Kleihues, Dortmund, West Germany 1979; *Architektur und Städtebau des 20. Jahrhunderts* by Vittorio Magnago Lampugnani, Stuttgart 1980; *Architecture 70/80 in Switzerland* by Werner Blaser, Basel, Boston and Stuttgart 1982; articles—"Atelierhaus in Zumikon-Zurich" in *Werk*(Zurich), May 1950; "Maison des vacances, Suisse" in *Architecture Francaise*(Paris), vol. 15, no. 147/148, 1954; "Un teatro nel parco" in *Architettura*(Rome), August 1956; "Swiss Revival" by Ian Nairn in *Architectural Review*(London), March 1959; "Atelierhaus eines Bildhauers in Tegna" in *Werk*(Zurich), May 1960; "Einfamilienhaus am Sonnenberg in Zurich" in *Werk*(Zurich), January 1962; "Jugendherberge der Stadt Zurich" in *Baumeister*(Munich), July 1966; "Evangelische Gemeinde Zentrum in Stuttgart-Sonnenberg" in *Bauwelt*(West Berlin), February 1968; "Wohnhaus und Atelier des Architekten Ernst Gisel in Zumikon/Zurich" in *Bauwelt*(West Berlin), 25 November 1968; "Bauen in den Alpen: Ein Panorama" in *Werk*(Zurich), April 1969; "Private House in Schonenberg" in *AC: International Asbestos Cement Review*(Zurich), April 1975; "Theater am Kirchplatz, Schaar" by U. Rellstab in *Werk*(Zurich), August 1975; "New School Compound for the Former Grammar School in Liechtenstein" in *Moebel Interior Design*(Stuttgart), December 1975; "Artist's Studio in Zurich" in *Werk*(Zurich), January 1976; "Heuried Estate in Zurich-Wiedikon" in *Werk*(Zurich), December 1976; "The Architect's Own Practice in Zurich: Ernst Gisel" in *AC: International Asbestos Cement Review*(Zurich), July 1977; "The Blue Studio-House" in *Moebel Interior Design*(Stuttgart), November 1977; "Ideas Competition for Bahnhofstrasse in Dubendorf" in *Aktuelles Bauen*(Zurich), November 1978; "A Row of Five Houses in Vaduz" in *AC: International Asbestos Cement Review*(Zurich), July 1979; "Town Hall Project at Fellbach" in *Deutsche Bauzeitung* (Stuttgart), February 1981; "Steinhalde Schoolhouse in Eglisau" in *Werk, Bauen und Wohnen*(Zurich), April 1981; "Terraced Family Housing in Vaduz" in *Archithese*(Niederteufen, Switzerland), November/December 1981; "Observations on the Work of Ernst Gisel", special issue of *Werk, Bauen und Wohnen*(Zurich), July/August 1982.

Some fifteen years ago I attended a lecture given to architects by Ernst Bloch in Berlin. He said at the time— and I recall it with pleasure— the architect should just leave philosophising to him and design a chair instead. Since then, the guild of architects has been divided. Bloch would perhaps tell us now that we had better take the part of those— myself one of them— who want to bless mankind with a chair that is realized instead of just publishing dream designs in a philosophical context.

The commitment claimed by the stage of realization is situated beyond the artist's area of seclusion:in a battlefield, where we depend on the skilled and creative assistance of others who make our objective their own. Most of our work is obtained by competition— a problematic procedure, yet in democratic Switzerland the clean way to get interesting work. Competition projects— up to now more than a hundred, a quarter of them successful— are thus the adventurous part of my work. Yet as soon as a project wins us the first prize and is likely to be built, I am no longer able to believe wholeheartedly in its initial significance. It turns out to be just an impulse setting off the process of realization: the fascination with a beautiful design might prevent me from using the chance of a longer gestation period.

We always try to do our work as if it were for the first time and without copying our own archives. For years, I have kept the number of draughtsmen and architects collaborating in the studio about constant, approximately twenty. None of them is specialized and each deals, if possible, with one and the same job from start to finish, almost daily escorted by myself. Until the very last moment, we leave our design open with regard to the uniqueness of a site, of its people, its topography, its climate, its natural and built environment.

In this way, it should be possible to bring the external

aspect of a building and its contents up to the innermost detail into line with its surroundings, without constraint and in a spirit of democratic candour, a free juxtaposition of various autonomous values.
—Ernst Gisel.

Ernst Gisel is one of the most distinguished Swiss architects of the second half of the twentieth century. Not only is he an innovator, but very versatile, for he has been the architect of a wide variety of buildings—churches, schools, houses, and buildings to serve cultural and recreational purposes. His work is essentially functional; he studies the purpose of a building, then designs a structure which logically emanates from that purpose. He is conspicuous for logical analysis and owes very little to traditional styles but thinks out the most suitable forms from scratch with the result that new and unusual shapes emerge. A notable example of this is the Reformed Church at Effretikon, near Zürich, where unusual forms emanate from Gisel's interpretation of the most effective way of meeting the needs of the building. The west side has a stepped, pitched roof which provides a series of sloping lights to the interior. At the southeast corner is a square framed concrete tower with exposed bells. Adjacent to the nave are two rooms for meetings, for the church is designed to accommodate various purposes: meetings, concerts, and drama. An original structure, with the dramatic impact of strange new shapes in its situation at the top of a hill, it has been likened to abstract sculpture with good attention to light and shadow.

Among his early works is the Park Theatre at Grenchen, a small town near Zürich. It demonstrates Gisel's ability to design for the utmost flexibility in a building, and for this purpose he takes advantage of modern technology. From being a theatre, the building can be transformed for other uses and can be adjusted in size by the use of folding partitions; it can be used for receptions and exhibitions, while it also includes a restaurant, council room, and hotel. Its exterior grows out of these uses and is an effective composition of triangles and rectangles.

Among his buildings for education is the large, functionally conceived Letzi Secondary School at Zürich for 800 pupils. A courtyard is enclosed by three two-storey classroom strips on the south, east, and west sides. The separate buildings of the complex are linked by pergolas. For the classroom strips, cross-ventilation is secured by windows on opposite walls. In the centre of the courtyard is a two-storey building, almost square on plan, with music and lecture rooms on the ground floor and an art room on the upper floor. The construction is of reinforced concrete with flat roofs. The group of buildings has a quiescent effect which gives a Greek-like serenity.

Another large school, designed in collaboration with Christian Zweifel, is that in Liechtenstein; here, several diverse blocks integrate into an orderly composition. The buildings are of various heights: a curved block of five storeys adjoins two rectangular blocks of two and three storeys, all growing out of function yet composing a unity.

A particularly ambitious scheme for which Gisel was mainly responsible, although collaborating with Harry Moor and Leo Schweitzer, is the town hall and centre at Fellbach near Stuttgart. Here again, a variety of uses spells flexibility, yet the whole is organised into an effective unity. One feature repeated in several buildings is the variety of roofs: flat, doubled mono-pitched, and triangular, all of which are integrated into a satisfactory whole.

Gisel's individually designed houses are also notable. One that is particularly attractive is a house at Sonnenberg, Zürich.
The internal organisation for a specific family stems from an imaginative interpretation of domestic needs. Part of it is open-planned, which encourages an impression of spaciousness, while the exterior, with white concrete rectangular and triangular forms, contrasts effectively with a copper roof. From his functional designs, Gisel has arrived at arresting compositions of original and unusual forms.
—Arnold Whittick

GIURGOLA, Romaldo.
American. Born in Rome, Italy, 2 September 1920; emigrated to the United States, 1954: naturalized, 1959. Educated at the School of Architecture of the University of Rome, 1945-49, B.Arch. (honors) 1949; Columbia University, New York, 1949-51, M.Arch. 1951. Married Adelaide F. Bercivenga in 1952; daughter: Paola. Since 1958, Partner, with Ehrman B. Mitchell, *q.v.*, Mitchell/Giurgola Architects, Philadelphia; office established in New York, 1966. Assistant Professor of Architecture, Cornell University, Ithaca, New York, 1952-54; Professor of Architecture, University of Pennsylvania, Philadelphia, 1954-66. Chairman of the Department of Architecture, 1966-71, and since 1971, Ware Professor of Architecture, Columbia University, New York. Architect-in-Residence, American Academy in Rome, Autumn 1977. Member of the Advisory Council, School of Architecture, Princeton University, New Jersey, 1975-77; Member, Architectural Review Board, Charles Center/Inner Harbor, Baltimore, Maryland, 1975-77. Exhibitions: University of Pennsylvania Museum, Philadelphia, 1965; Pennsylvania Academy of Fine Arts, Philadelphia, 1975; Columbia University, New York, 1977; *200 Years of American Architectural Drawing*, American Federation of Arts travelling exhibition, 1977-78; *Drawing Toward a More Modern Architecture*, Drawing Center, New York, 1977, and Otis Art Institute Gallery, Los Angeles, 1978; *Roma interrotta*, Rome, 1978; *City Segments*, Walker Art Center, Minneapolis, 1980 (toured the United States, 1980-81); *Parliament House Competition, Canberra, Australia*, Architectural League, New York, 1980; *Parliament House, Australia—Formative Sketches*, Max Protetch Gallery, New York, 1981; *New American Art Museums*, Whitney Museum, New York, 1982; *American Architecture: Innovation and Tradition*, Temple Hoyne Buell Center, Columbia University, New York, 1983; *Honor and Intimacy: Architectural Drawings 1907-1983*, American Institute of Architects travelling exhibition, 1984-85. Recipient: First Award, 1961, Gold Medal, 1964 and 1982, Honor Award, 1974, 1975, 1977, and 1985, Architectural Firm Award, 1976, and Award of Merit, 1978, American Institute of Architects; Gold Medal, Philadelphia Chapter, American Institute of Architects, 1961, 1964, 1972, 1974, 1977; Silver Medal, 1965, 1974, 1975, and 1977, Distinguished Building Award, 1971, 1975, and 1977, and First Honor Award, 1977, Pennsylvania Society of Architects; Gold Medal, Artists Guild of Philadelphia, 1966; Arnold Brunner Award, National Institute of Arts and Letters, 1966; First Prize, Wainwright State Office Complex Competition, St. Louis, 1974; Medal of Honor, New York City Chapter, American Institute of Architects, 1975; Bard Award, City Club of New York, 1978; Design Award, *Urban Design*, 1978. D.Sc.: Ball State University, Muncie, Indiana, 1983; D.H.L.: Long Island University, Greenvale, New York, 1984; D.F.A.: Parsons School of Design, New York, 1984. Fellow, American Institute of Architects, 1975; Fellow, Royal Australian Institute of Architects, 1983; Institute Member, American Academy and Institute of Arts and Letters, 1977. Commendatore, Republic of Italy, 1972. Member, Accademia Nazionale di San Luca, Rome, 1980. Address: Mitchell/Giurgola Architects, 170 West 97th Street, New York, New York 10025, U.S.A.

Works (with Ehrman B. Mitchell):
1958 Crockett House, Corning, New York
      Mitchell House, Lafayette Hill, Pennsylvania
      Far East Asia Development (project; with Wright and Mitarachi)

1959 Stine House, Bryan, Ohio
      Public Health Center 9, 13 East Cheltan Avenue, Philadelphia
1960 Evansville Petroleum Club interiors, 420 Main Street, Evansville, Indiana
      Wright Brothers Memorial Visitors Center, Kill Devil Hills, North Carolina
1961 Mednick House, Philadelphia
      Lumberyard Town House Development, Philadelphia (project)
      Franklin Delano Roosevelt Memorial, Washington, D.C. (competition project)
      Huebner Hall: American College of Life Underwriters National Headquarters, Bryn Mawr, Pennsylvania
1962 Philadelphia Life Insurance Company Office Building addition, Philadelphia
      Boston City Hall (competition project)
      Campus Plan, and Dormitory, Academy of the New Church, Bryn Athyn, Pennsylvania
      Market Street East Development, Philadelphia
1963 White House, Chestnut Hill, Pennsylvania
      Patzau House, Philadelphia (project)
      Andale Company Office Building, Lansdale, Pennsylvania
      Frankford Arsenal Metrology Laboratories, Philadelphia
      Administration Building, Academy of the New Church, Bryn Athyn, Pennsylvania
      Maintenance Building, Academy of the New Church, Bryn Athyn, Pennsylvania (project)
      Parking Garage I, University of Pennsylvania, Philadelphia
      Classroom and Laboratory renovation, University of Pennsylvania, (project)
1964 Bethlehem Steel Company Office Building, Philadelphia (project)
1965 International House, Philadelphia (competition project)
      Headquarters Building, Acadia National Park, Bar Harbor, Maine (project)
      Newman Center, University of Kentucky, Lexington (project)
      Swarthmore Presbyterian Church and School, Swarthmore, Pennsylvania (project)
      American Institute of Architects National Headquarters, Washington, D.C. (competition project)
      Myrick Pavilion, American College, Bryn Mawr, Pennsylvania
1966 Five Cents Savings Bank, Boston
      Campus plan for American College, Bryn Mawr, Pennsylvania
1967 Hotel and Office Building, Wilmington, Delaware (project)
      William Jeanes Memorial Library, Whitemarsh, Pennsylvania (project)
      Parking Garage, State University of New York, Oneonta (project)
      Plan for the central business district of Wilkes Barre, Pennsylvania
1968 Zebooker House, Philadelphia
      Roberts House, Philadelphia
      Rockefeller Center Theatre, New York (project)
      United States Embassy, Bogota Colombia (project)
      Interim facilities for the United Nations International School, New York
1969 United Nations International School, New York (project)
1970 Dayton House, Wayzata, Minnesota
      Parking Garage II, University of Pennsylvania, Philadelphia
      Women's Physical Education Facility, Swarthmore College, Swarthmore, Pennsylvania (project)

Romaldo Giurgola and Ehrmann Mitchell: Liberty Bell Pavilion and Penn Mutual Tower, Philadelphia, 1975.

Master plan for the 30th Street Site, Philadelphia (with David A. Crane)

Campus plan for Swarthmore College, Swarthmore, Pennsylvania

1971   United Fund Headquarters, Philadelphia
South End Branch Public Library, Boston
Subway Concourse Entrance, Market and Eighth Street, Philadelphia
University Museum Academic Wing, University of Pennsylvania, Philadelphia
Apartment Building, Welfare Island, New York (project)

1972   Peacock Hill Redevelopment, Williamsburg, Virginia (project)
Bok Tower, Mountain Lake Sanctuary, Lake Wales, Florida
Mission Park Residential Houses, Williams College, Williamstown, Massachusetts
Adult Learning Research Laboratory, MDRT Foundation Hall, The American College, Bryn Mawr, Pennsylvania
Master plan for the Eastwick Site, Philadelphia plan (with others)
Convention Center, Philadelphia (project)
Twin Parks East Apartment Building, Bronx, New York (project)

1973   Administrative Office interiors, N and G Buildings, Westminghouse Electric Corporation, Lester, Pennsylvania
Worship Assembly Building, Benedictine Society of St. Bede, Peru, Illinois
Lang Music Building, Swarthmore College, Swarthmore, Pennsylvania
Columbus High School, Columbus, Indiana
Undergraduate Housing, Yale University, New Haven, Connecticut

1974   Central Service Building, Westinghouse Electric Corporation, Lester, Pennsylvania
Student Union, State University College of New York, Plattsburgh
Casa Thomas Jefferson (United States Information Agency/Thomas Jefferson Cultural Center), Brasilia
Master plan for the Springhouse Research Center, Rohm and Haas Corporation, Springhouse, Pennsylvania

1975   William Penn High School, Philadelphia
Condon Hall: School of Law, University of Washington, Seattle
Indian Point Energy Education Center, Buchanan, New York
Penn Mutual Tower, Philadelphia
Liberty Bell Pavilion, Philadelphia
Two INA Plaza (office building), Philadelphia
Feasibilit y study for the Philadelphia College of Art
Master plan for the Volvo Manufacturing Plant, Chesapeake, Virginia
University City Science Center office interiors, Philadelphia

1976   Philadelphia College of Art renovation and alterations
Volvo of America Office and Assembly Building, and Power House, Chesapeake, Virginia
Girard Bank main office renovation, Philadelphia
Living History Center, *Philadelphia '76*
Tredyffrin Public Library, Tredyffrin Township, Strafford, Pennsylvania
St. Joseph's Village for Senior Citizens, Brookhaven, New York (competition project)

1977   Benjamin F. Feinberg Library, State University College of New York at Plattsburgh
Sherman Fairchild Center for the Life Sciences, Columbia University, New York
Master plan for Harbor Plaza (office/parking/hotel complex), Stamford, Connecticut
Master plan for the future development of the United States Capitol, Washington D.C. (design consultant; with Wallace, McHarg, Roberts and Todd)

1978   Harbor Plaza, Stamford, Connecticut
Hardie A. Beloff Nursing Home, West Goshen, Pennsylvania (project)
Development plan for the East Campus, Massachusetts Institute of Technology, Cambridge (with Gruzen and Partners)
Bershad House kitchen addition, Philadelphia
DeCordova Museum renovation and addition, Lincoln, Massachusetts

1979   Beni Stabili Apartment/Retail Complex, Houston (competition project)
South Central Bell Telephone Company Regional Headquarters, Nashville, Tennessee (competition project; with Gassner, Nathan and Partners)
Newman House, Bedford, New York
Harristown Key Block, phase I, Harrisburg, Pennsylvania (with Lawrie and Green)
Physical Activities Building, Swarthmore College, Swarthmore, Pennsylvania
Administrative Resources Center, Lukens Steel Company, Coatesville, Pennsylvania
General Services Building, American College, Bryn Mawr, Pennsylvania
Ten Stamford Forum (office building/parking garage), Stamford, Connecticut
Master plan for the Art Museum, Princeton University, New Jersey
Central Chilled Water Plant, Massachusetts Institute of Technology, Cambridge (project; with Gruzen and Partners)
Blank, Rome, Comisky and McCauley office interiors, Philadelphia
Kasperson House, Conestoga, Pennsylvania

1980   Geology Library renovation and addition, Princeton University, New Jersey
Bookstore and Lounge, Union Theological Seminary, New York
Men's Shelter feasibility study, New York

1981   Technical High School, Maniago, Italy
Elementary School, Aviano, Italy
Student Housing, San Pietro al Natisone, Italy
Concert Theatre renovation and reconstruction, C. W. Post Center, Long Island University, Greenvale, New York
Battery Park City Commercial Centre Development, New York (competition project)
General Office Building, Olympia, Washington (project; with Joyce/Nordfors and Associates)
Lincoln West Hotel and Apartment Complex, New York (project)
Wunsch Arts Center renovation, Glen Cove, New York
Westlake Park museum, retail, and parking complex, Seattle, Washington (project)
Winwright State Office Complex, St Louis, Missouri (with Hastings and Chivetta
Maintenance Facility, Independence Park, Philadelphia
Graduate Center, American College, Bryn Mawr, Pennsylvania

1982   Los Palos Grandes office and retail complex, Caracas, Venezuela (with W. James Alcock)
Cell Biology Research Center renovation, New York University
Library renovation, Union Theological Seminary, New York
Student Center, Bryn Mawr College, Bryn Mawr, Pennsylvania
Knoll International Manufacturing Facility Master Plan, East Greenville, Pennsylvania
College of Health Sciences Technology and Management Building, and Health Services Building, Massachusetts Institute of Technology, Cambridge (with Gruzen and Partners)

1983   Pennsylvania Avenue hotel, office, retail, and parking complex, Washington, D.C. (with Frank Schlesinger)
Schlechter Group Building, New York
Knoll International Assembly and Shipping Facility, phase I, East Greenville, Pennsylvania

Walter Royal Davis Library, University of North Carolina at Chapel Hill (with Leslie N. Boney)
Lafayette Place hotel, retail, and parking complex, Boston

1984   Anchorage Historical and Fine Arts Museum, Anchorage, Alaska (with Maynard and Partch)
AB Volvo Corporate Headquarters, Göteborg, Sweden
Annenberg School of Communications addition and renovation, University of Pennsylvania, Philadelphia
Princeton University Art Museum, New Jersey

1985   300 Atlantic Office Building, Stamford, Connecticut
Kershaw House, Montgomery, Alabama

1986   Center for Industrial Innovation, Rensselaer Polytechnic Institute, Troy, New York

1988   Parliament House of Australia, Canberra (Mitchell/Giurgola and Thorp) Convention Center, San Jose, California

Publications:

By GIURGOLA: book—*Louis I. Kahn*, with Jaimini Mehta, Zürich and Boulder, Colorado 1975; articles—"Eric Mendelsohn 1887-1953" in *Interiors* (New York), December 1953; "Architecture in Change" in *Journal of Architectural Education* (Washington, D.C.), November/December 1962; "Reflections on Buildings and the City: The Realism of the Partial Vision" in *Perspecta* (New Haven, Connecticut), no. 9/10, 1965; "Aldo Giurgola" in *Arts and Architecture* (Los Angeles), April 1965; "On Louis Kahn" in *Zodiac* (Milan), no. 17, 1967; "Five on Five," with others, in *Architectural Forum* (New York), May 1973; "Louis I. Kahn 1901-1974" in *Progressive Architecture* (New York), May 1974; article in *Space Design* (Tokyo), December 1975; article in *Christian Science Monitor* (Boston), 21 April 1977; interview with Kenneth Frampton in *Controspazio* (Bari, Italy), July/August 1977; "Roma Interrota" in *Architectural Design* (London), no. 3/4, 1979; "Forces Shaping Current Design" in *AIA Journal* (Washington, D.C.), May 1979; "The Producing Moment" in *Inland Architect* (Chicago), January/February 1981; "Notes on Buildings and Their Parts" in *Harvard Architectural Review* (Cambridge, Massachusetts), Spring 1981; "Giurgola on Kahn" in *AIA Journal* (Washington, D.C.), August 1982; "Reflections on the Order of the City and the Order of the Land" in *Architect* (Melbourne), December 1983.

MITCHELL/GIURGOLA: books—*Three Architects at Williams College*, exhibition catalogue, by John Stamper, Williamstown, Massachusetts 1976; *New Directions in American Architecture* by Robert Stern, New York 1977; *City Segments*, exhibition catalogue, edited by Mildred S. Friedman, Minneapolis 1980; *Guide to U.S. Architecture 1940-1980* by Barbara Goldstein and Esther McCoy, Santa Monica, California 1981; *Mitchell/Giurgola Architects*, New York 1983; articles—"Conscious Contrasts" in *Progressive Architecture* (New York), May 1965; "Should Anyone Care about the 'New York Five' or about Their Critics, the 'Five on Five'" by Paul Goldberger in *Architectural Record* (New York), February 1974; "Mitchell/Giurgola" in *Architecture + Urbanism* (Tokyo), December 1975; "On Trying to Understand the Significance of Mitchell/Giurgola" by William Marlin in *Architectural Record* (New York), April 1976; "Profile of Mitchell/Giurgola" by Andrea O. Dean in *AIA Journal* (Washington, D.C.), April 1976; "Structures with a Social Value" by William Marlin in *Christian Science Monitor* (Boston), 21 April 1977; "Mitchell/Giurgola," special issue of *Process: Archi-*

tecture (Tokyo/Pittsburgh), July 1977; "Mitchell/-Giurgola," special issue of *Process: Architecture* (Tokyo), October 1977; "A View of Contemporary World Architects; Ehrman Mitchell, Jr., and Romaldo Giurgola" in *Shinkenchiku* (Tokyo), December 1977; "Unity and Aesthetics of Incompletion in Architecture" by David Bell in *Architectural Design* (London), July 1979; "International Houses Competition, Philadelphia" in Harvard Architectural Review (Cambridge, Massachusetts), Spring 1981; "Giurgola Selected as AIA's 43rd Gold Medallist" in *AIA Journal* (Washington, D.C.), January 1982; "Giurgola in Friuli" in *Architectural Review* (London), August 1982.

Bibliographies: *The Firm of Mitchell/Giurgola, 1958* by Lamia Doumato, Monticello, Illinois 1980; *The Architecture of Reality in the Work of Romaldo Giurgola: A Selected Bibliography* by Robert B. Harmon, Monticello, Illinois 1981.

Arts were begot by Chance and Observation, nurtured by Use and Experience, and improved and perfected by Reason and Study—Alberti

Our buildings are reflections of aspects of life, expressing continuity, history, and the desire of a future. They are manifestations of projects for life that people everywhere pursue. In them all is design, from the texture of a wall to the caliber of a space. They aspire to be architecture.

—Romaldo Giurgola

The work of Romaldo Giugola and Ehrman B. Mitchell continually exhibits strong consistency in design—but with a flavor all its own. At a time clouded with rhetoric and doctrine, Mitchell/Giurgola Architects have produced singular buildings, relying on new perceptions of design criteria. They have worked to develop new directions, expressions, and alternatives, in order to give form to a place. This approach has emerged from Giurgola's concern with reality—reality, in all its aspects, is what makes Mitchell/Giurgola distinct from other firms.

Their buildings do not participate in the profession's preoccupation with intra-architectural arguments; instead, they emerge from a clear synthesis of external constraints. Much thought is applied to the nature of functional relationships and visual implications, but, most importantly, architecture is always seen in context. The product is not an individual monument; it is part of both a social and an architectural environment.

Theory is important, nevertheless, and Giurgola is an academician trained in Europe and reared in the tradition of the Beaux-Arts. He maintains an acute interest in tradition and history, and he sees architecture as a continuous progression. It is because of this temporally conscious view that he shies away from fashion or what he calls "perennial eclecticism," preferring an expression of more meaningful connections with change and the "dynamics of life." His buildings establish a sense of propriety free from style or time.

Giurgola's notions of order are reflective of his deep debt to his teacher Louis Kahn, but the ideas have been modified and adapted to suit Giurgola's environmentalist approach. He loves Kahn's work, not for shape but for the sudden discoveries or "realizations," as Kahn used to say. He refers to Kahn's architecture as deriving from "the architecture of the past and tangentially the Beaux-Arts connection." He respects Kahn's approach to place and sympathizes with the value of conceptual operations in design.

Modern technology makes of our society fasttrack representatives of a particular event. "Forget the past and create the new present," we say. But while many people enjoy instant happenings, Mitchell/Giurgola continues to fight for the importance of the process. Process not only represents a contemporary idea of architecture but also reflects the past in combination with the dynamics of the present.

This methodological concern, coupled with Giurgola's conviction that architecture's major task is in giving form to a place, reflects a desire to go far beyond functional satisfaction. His architecture becomes the realization of his own personal sense of place, accomplished skilfully and rationally.

—Ching-Yu Chang

GOERITZ, Mathias.

German. Born in Danzig, Germany (now Gdansk, Poland), 4 April 1915; moved to Mexico, 1949. Educated at the Kaiserin-Augusta-Gymnasium, Charlottenburg, Berlin, 1924-34. Friedrich-Wilhelms-Universität, Berlin, 1934-40, Ph.D. 1940; Kunstgewerbeschule, Charlottenburg, Berlin, 1937-39. Married Marianne Gast in 1942 (died, 1958); Ida Rodriguez Prampolini in 1960; son: Daniel. Professor, Centro de Estudios Marroquies, Tetuan, Spanish Morocco, 1940-44; worked as a painter in Granada, Spain, 1945-47, and Madrid, 1947-49; Professor of Visual Education and Design, Escuela de Arquitectura, Universidad de Guadalajara, Jalisco, Mexico, 1949-54. Since 1953, painter, sculptor, and architect in Mexico City, and Founder/Professor, Department of Basic Design, Universidad Nacional Autónoma de Mexico, Mexico City. Founder/Director, Escuela de Artes Plasticas y Escuela de Diseño Industrial, Universidad Iboamericana, Mexico City, 1957-60; Artist-in-Residence, Aspen Institute for Humanistic Studies, Aspen, Colorado, 1970-72. Editor, Art Section, Arquitectura Mexico, Mexico City, since 1958. Founder, La Escuela de Altamira movement, Santillana del Mar, Santander, Spain, 1948 and Los Hartos movement, with José Luis Cuevas, Pedro Friedeberg, Jesus Reyes Ferreira, and others, Mexico City, 1961. Member of GIAP (Groupe International d'Architecture Prospective), since 1965. Exhibitions: individual—Sala Clan, Madrid, 1946; Salon Alerta, Santander, Spain, 1948; Galeria Palma, Madrid, 1949; Galeria Camaraux, Guadalajara, 1950; Galeria Clardecor, Mexico City, 1950; Galeria Jardin, Barcelona, 1952; Galeria de Arte Mexicano, Mexico City, 1952; Galeria Proteo, Mexico City, 1955; Carstairs Gallery, New York, 1956; Galeria de Arte Mexicano, Mexico City (retrospective), 1959; Carstairs Gallery, New York, 1960; Galerie Iris Clert, Paris, 1960; Galeria de Antonio Souza, Mexico City, 1960; Galeria de Arte Mexicano, Mexico City, 1961; Carstairs Gallery, New York,1962; group—*New Media-New Forms*, Martha Jackson Gallery, New York, 1960; *Aspects de la sculpture américaine*, Galerie Claude Bernard, Paris, 1960; *New Europeans*, Contemporary Arts Museum, Houston, Texas, 1960; *Art of Assemblage*, Museum of Modern Art, New York, 1961. Collections: Museum of Modern Art, New York; Museo de Arte Moderno, Mexico City; Israel Museum, Jerusalem. Member, Akademie der Künste, Berlin, 1973; Honorary Fellow, Royal Academy of The Hague, 1976; Honorary Academician Emeritus, Academia Nacional de Arquitectura de la Sociedad de Arquitectos Mexicanos, 1983. Address: Apartado 20-390, Mexico 20, D.F. 01000, Mexico.

Works:

1952/
53   El Eco Experimental Museum, Calle Sullivan 43, Mexico City (now altered)

1957 Open Chapel, Guadalajara (with Luis Barragán; unfinished)
      Towers, Satellite City, near Mexico City (with Luis Barragán and Mario Pani)

1959/
61   Studio, Avenida Hidalgo Temixco, Morelos, Mexico

1964 Automex Towers, near Toluca, Mexico (with Ricardo Legorreta)

1966 House, Calle Dr. Manuel Mazari 112, Cuernavaca, Morelos, Mexico

1975 Jerusalem Labyrinth: Community Center Alejandro and Lilly Saltiel, Jerusalem (with Arthur Spector and Micha Amisar)

1977/
78   Belfry of the Instituto Technologico, Monterrey, Mexico (with Team Gocadiguse)

Mathias Goeritz: El Eco Experimental Museum, Mexico City, 1953.

Publications:

By GOERITZ: books—*Manifesto of the School of Altamira*, Santander, Spain 1948; *Manifesto: Estoy harto*, Mexico City 1960; *Manifesto: Estamos hartos*, Mexico City 1961; articles—"Manifesto: Arquitectura emocional" in *Cuadernos de arquitectura* (Guadalajara), no. 1, 1954; "Statement" in the catalog for his individual show, Carstairs Gallery, New York 1962.

On GOERITZ: books—*Encyclopédie de l'architecture nouvelle* by Alberto Sartoris, Milan 1954; *Mathias Goeritz* by Olivia Zúñiga, Mexico City 1963; *Encyclopaedia of Modern Architecture* by Max Cetto, London 1963; *Art in Latin American Architecture* by Paul F. Damaz, New York 1963; *Arquitectura contemporanea mexicana* by Israel Katzman, Mexico City 1964; *Bouwmeesters van morgen* by J. J. Beljon, Amsterdam 1964; *El arte contemporaneo* by Ida Rodriguez Prampolini, Mexico City 1964; *Les Cités de l'avenir* by Michel Ragon, Paris 1966; *Builders in the Sun* by Clive B. Smith, New York 1967; *The Aesthetics of Contemporary Architecture* by Michel Ragon, Neuchâtel, Switzerland 1968; *A History of Latin American Art and Architecture* by Leopoldo Castedo, New York 1969; *Histoire mondiale de l'architecture et de l'urbanisme modernes* by Michel Ragon, Paris 1972; *Mathias Goeritz—Architectural Sculpture* by Michael Levin, Jerusalem 1980; *Mathias Goeritz* by Frederico Morais, Mexico City 1982; *Mathias Goeritz—Arquitectura emocional*, Mexico City 1984; articles—"El Eco: Ein Experimental-Museum in Mexiko" in *Baukunst und Werkform* (Frankfurt), no. 4, 1954; "Architektur in Mexiko" by Helmuth Borcherdt in *Baumeister* (Munich), November 1959; "Mathias Goeritz" by Michel Ragon in *Cimaise* (Paris), no. 106, 1972; "Mathias Goeritz—Une éthique de l'architecture" by David Miller in *Art Press International* (Paris), no. 7, 1977.

*

Art in general (and naturally also architecture) reflects man's spiritual state. But the impression exists that modern architects, too individualistic and intellectual—Perhaps because they have lost their close ties with the community—emphasize the rational side of architecture. As a result, the twentieth century man feels crushed by the exaggerated "functionalism," logic, and usefulness of modern architecture.

He looks for a solution, but neither exterior aesthetics defined as "formalism," nor organic regionalism, have adequately faced the problem of the common man of our times—creative or receptive—who aspires to something more than a pretty, pleasant, and comfortable house. He asks—or will one day ask—that architecture with its modern means and materials give him a spiritual lift or—said in a simpler way—move him, as did in its time the architecture of the pyramid, the Greek temple, the Romanesque or Gothic cathedral, or even that of the Baroque palace. When architecture causes an emotive response in man, he will again consider it an art.

—Mathias Goeritz

*

Functionalism claims to have invented an environment in which architecture would adopt as its aesthetic principle the new technology of mechanics and engineering. Thus, for more than three decades—between 1920 and 1950—and even today, the landscape of many of the cities of Europe, the United States, and Latin America has been invaded by monotonous units of construction whose square outlines and glass walls give the impression of space planned with a utilitarian aim in mind. Mathias Goeritz, painter, sculptor, and architect, who was born in Germany but settled in Mexico, questions both the plastic and the spiritual values of Functionalism. His attitude is obviously not an isolated one. The horrors of World War II implanted in the

Western mentality a mistrust of reason and caused a revaluation of subjectivity and emotion as valid means and forms of knowledge and understanding of the world.

In 1952, the time of the triumph of Functionalism, Goeritz chose to construct the El Eco Experimental Museum, a work accompanied by a manifesto in which he developed his idea of an emotional architecture; he used the building as an example of a kind of architecture whose principal function is to arouse emotion. The modern architect, according to Goeritz, is out of touch with man and society, and as a result, he has created constructions that are merely "decorative, pleasant and adequate." As far as Goeritz is concerned, however, as artist-philosopher the architect, with his new methods and materials, must be able to create works that invoke a spiritual response: "Only when architecture inspires real emotions can it again be regarded as an art."

The aim of the experimental museum was not merely to make good use of space; the architectural features—walls of between seven and eleven metres in length, corridors, open and enclosed spaces—were arranged in such a way as to involve man and awaken in him the emotion that at one time he was able to feel when confronted by the Greek temple, the pyramids, or a Gothic cathedral—before the onset of a modern architecture of indifference.

The importance of El Eco is in its integrated plasticity—the way in which paintings and sculptures are not superimposed but grow naturally with the walls of the building. It has become a living example of "collective artistic production," combining experience in music, literature, the theatre, and the cinema.

In the years that followed, Goeritz created monumental sculpture. The gigantic Towers of Satellite City are symbols of the town, as medieval cathedrals once were. In this way, sculpture and architecture unite. Sculpture fulfils the symbolic functions of architecture, and in return, architecture makes sculpture inhabitable—as for example in the house that Goeritz built at Cuernavaca in 1966.

Goeritz has been concerned to articulate a philosophy of need for an aesthetic based on a new morality that leaves out the self complacency of much of contemporary art. The inability of society and its artists to produce structures and images of significance is more and more apparent. Art has become tepid—on the one hand because everyone is competing to produce the most brilliant gesture, on the other because of an increasing assimilation with the mentality of technology. Goeritz replies with spectacular forms, pure and monumental, which throw down a challenge to the ugliness of towns, the products of growing industrialization, and the gratuitous gestures of so many contemporary experimentalists.

—Rita Eder

GOFF, Bruce Alonzo.

American. Born in Alton, Kansas, 8 June 1904. Educated at Lincoln Public School, Tulsa, Oklahoma, 1914-22; apprenticed to the firm of Rush, Endacott and Rush, Tulsa, Oklahoma, 1916. Served in a United States Navy Construction Batallion, in the Aleutian Islands and California, 1942-45. Married Evelyn Hall in 1926 (divorced, 1926). Worked for Rush, Endacott and Rush, Tulsa, Oklahoma, 1916-30; Partner, Endacott and Goff, Tulsa, Oklahoma, 1930-33; worked for the industrial products design firm of Alfonso Iannelli, Chicago, 1934; in private practice in the Chicago suburb of Park Ridge, 1935; Teacher of Art Composition, Chicago Academy of Fine Arts, 1935; Director of Design, Libbey-Owens-Ford Glass Company, Toledo, Ohio, 1935-36; in private practice, Chicago, 1936-42, and Berkeley, California, 1945-56; Professor, 1947-55,

and Head of the School of Architecture, 1948-55, University of Oklahoma, Norman; in private practice, Bartlesville, Oaklahoma, 1956-64, Kansas City, Missouri, 1964-69, and Tyler, Texas, 1970, until his death in 1982. Exhibitions: Architectural League, New York, 1970; Yellowstone Art Center, Billings, Montana, 1978; *New American Art Museums*, Whitney Museum, New York, 1982. Collection: Columbia University, New York. *Died* (in Tyler, Texas) *4 August 1982.*

Works:

1918 Indiana Limestone Residence (project)
Stucco House and Reflecting Pool (project)
Frame House with Four-Way Fireplace (project)
1920 A Modern House of the Midwest Type (project)
Mausoleum for Grant McCullough, Tulsa, Oklahoma (project)
Way House, Tulsa, Oklahoma
Consolidated Cut Stone Company Offices, Tulsa, Oklahoma
McClure House, Tulsa, Oklahoma
Graves Summer House, Los Angeles
Marquee for the Lorton Building, Tulsa, Oklahoma
1921 Hansen House, Tulsa, Oklahoma
Police Station, Tulsa, Oklahoma (competition project)
1922 Directors' Dining Room, First National Bank, Tulsa, Oklahoma
Concrete and Glass Hill House, Tulsa, Oklahoma (project)
Stucco and Shingle Tile House, Tulsa, Oklahoma
Concrete Auditorium, Tulsa, Oklahoma (project)
1923 Tulsa Building, Tulsa, Oklahoma
Atlas Office Building, Tulsa, Oklahoma (project)
Hodgson House, Tulsa, Oklahoma (project)
1924 Robinson Studio, Tulsa, Oklahoma
1925 Medical Arts Building, Tulsa, Oklahoma (project)
1926 Boston Avenue Methodist Episcopal Church, Tulsa, Oklahoma
Cole Commercial Building, Tulsa, Oklahoma
1927 Page Warehouse, Tulsa, Oklahoma
1928 Genett Furniture Store, Tulsa, Oklahoma (project)
Guaranty Laundry, Tulsa, Oklahoma
Riverside Music Studio, Tulsa, Oklahoma
1929 Indian Memorial, Tulsa, Oklahoma
Gas Company Building, Tulsa, Oklahoma (project)
Tulsan Athletic Club, Tulsa, Oklahoma (project)
Memorial Hospital, Tulsa, Oklahoma (project)
Children's Pre-School, Tulsa, Oklahoma (project)
City Market, Tulsa, Oklahoma (project)
Glass House, Tulsa, Oklahoma (project)
Tulsa Convention Hall interior remodelling, Tulsa, Oklahoma
1930 Merchants Exhibit Building, Fair Grounds, Tulsa, Oklahoma
Phi Beta Delta Fraternity House, University of Oklahoma, Norman (project)
East Methodist Church, Tulsa, Oklahoma (project)
Catholic Cathedral, Oklahoma City (project)
Baptismal font, side altars, mosaics, bishop's throne and priest's bench in Christ the King Church, Tulsa, Oklahoma
Lathan House, Tulsa, Oklahoma
Higgins House additions, Tulsa, Oklahoma
Skelly Building additions, Tulsa, Oklahoma
1931 Pittsburgh Equitable Meter Company Warehouse, Sand Springs, Oklahoma

Parental Home, Tulsa, Oklahoma (project)
Railway Passenger Station, Sand Springs, Oklahoma (project)
Chicago War Memorial (competition project; with Alfonso Iannelli)
1935 Cole House, Park Ridge, Illinois
Badlands Hotel, South Dakota (project; with Alfonso Iannelli)
Turzak House, Edison Park, Chicago
1936 Rant House, Northfield, Illinois
Elin House, Northfield, Illinois
1937 Colmorgen House, Glenview, Illinois
Showroom for Libbey-Owens-Ford Glass Company, Toledo, Ohio
Advertising designs for Libbey-Owens-Ford Glass Company, Toledo, Ohio
1938 Theobald House, Chicago (project)
Langdon House, Chicago (project)
Burt House, LaGrange, Illinois (project)
1939 Unseth House I, Park Ridge, Illinois (project)
1940 Unseth House II, Park Ridge, Illinois
Triaero Vacation House, Fern Creek, Kentucky
1942/
43 United States Navy Seabee Base Complex, Camp Parks, California
1944 Chapel, United States Navy Seabee Aleutian Base Facilities, Adak, Attu
Durfee House, Birmingham, Alabama (project)
Wold House, Altadena, California (project)
Ennis House, Coronado, California (project)
1945 Leidig House, Hayward, California (project)
1946 San Jule House, Sausalito, California (project)
Patri Studio, Sausalito, California (project)
Warren House, Orinda, California (project)
1947 Giganto House, San Francisco (project)
Butley Packing Company Executive Offices, Oakland, California
Riley House, Oakland, California (project)
Kozak House, Marin City, California (project)
Hudson House, Oakland, California (project)
Gillis House, Bend, Oregon (project)
Church of Jesus Christ of Latter Day Saints, Cody, Wyoming (project)
Ledbetter House, Norman, Oklahoma
Family Circle House, Midwest City, Oklahoma (project)
Ledbetter Summer Lodge, Texoma Lake, Oklahoma (project)
1948 Garden City Apartments, Norman, Oklahoma (project)
Cox House, Boise City, Oklahoma
Bachman House alterations and additions, Chicago
Kinkaid Apartment, Oklahoma City (project)
1949 Ford House, Aurora, Illinois
Newton House, Bradenton, Florida (project)
Crystal Chapel and Student Religious Center, University of Oklahoma, Norman (project)
1950 Blakely House, Dallas, Texas (project)
Goodman House, Norman, Oklahoma (project)
Key House, Norman, Oklahoma
R. Goff House, Norman, Oklahoma (project)
Reece House, Norman, Oklahoma (project)
Whitaker House, Norman, Oklahoma (project)
Angelina House, Norman, Oklahoma (project)
Bavinger House, Norman, Oklahoma
Magyness House, Norman, Oklahoma (not completed)
Plan for the Wetzler Subdivision, Norman, Oklahoma
Concrete Block House, Norman, Oklahoma (project)
Wilson House, Perdido Bay, Pensacola, Florida
1951 Stulman House, Baltimore, Maryland (project)
Blakely House, Dallas, Texas (2nd project)
1952 Garvey House, Urbana, Illinois (project)

Hopewell Baptist Church, near Edmond, Oklahoma
1953 Murdoch House, Midwest City, Oklahoma (project)
Perez House, Caracas, Venezuela (two projects)
Corsaw House, Norman, Oklahoma
1954 Cunningham House, Lawton, Oklahoma (project)
Garvey House, Urbana, Illinois (second project)
Allen House, Tulsa, Oklahoma (project)
1955 Frank House, Sapullpa, Oklahoma
Barnes House, Canyon, California (project)
Pi Lambda Phi Fraternity House, University of Oklahoma, Norman
Trinity Baptist Church, Duncan, Oklahoma (project)
1956 Bass House, Tulsa, Oklahoma (project)
Circle Tower (project)
McCullough House, Wichita Falls, Texas
Comer House, Dewey, Oklahoma
Circle Center Development, Bartlesville, Oklahoma (project)
Tele-Movies Theatre, Bartlesville, Oklahoma (project)
Space Study Institute (project)
Price House, Bartlesville, Oklahoma
1957 Dord Fitz Studio-School, Amarillo, Texas (project)
Dewlen Aparature, Amarillo, Texas (project)
Grain Bin House (project)
Motsenbocker House, Bartlesville, Oklahoma (two projects)
Van Dall House, Bartlesville, Oklahoma (project)
Price Studio, Bartlesville, Oklahoma
1958 Pollock House, Oklahoma City
Darling House, El Dorado, Kansas (project)
Snyder House, El Dorado, Kansas (project)
Kennedy House, Bartlesville, Oklahoma (project)
White House, Bartlesville, Oklahoma
Adams House, Vinita, Oklahoma (project)
Stull House, Dewey, Oklahoma (project)
Gutman House, Gulfport, Mississippi
Allen House, Bartlesville, Oklahoma (project)
Durst House, Houston, Texas
Deutsch House, Jacksonville, Florida (project)
J. and S. Foundry, Dewey, Oklahoma (project)
Jones House, Bartlesville, Oklahoma (two projects)
Rudd House, Portola Valley, California (project)
Collins House, Bartlesville, Oklahoma (two projects)

1959 Freeman House, Joplin, Missouri (three projects)
Swambt House, Michigan City, Indiana (project)
Venus Soft Drinks Bar, Wichita, Kansas (project)
Tolff House, Lake Koshkonong, Wisconsin (project)
Gelbman House, Jacksonville, Florida (two projects)
Kennedy House, Bartlesville, Oklahoma (second project)
Daphne House, Hillsborough, California (project)
Allen House, Bartlesville, Oklahoma (second project)
Rudd Store remodelling, San Francisco
Akright House alterations and additions, Bartlesville, Oklahoma
Education Building, Redeemer Lutheran Church, Bartlesville, Oklahoma
Plan for the development of Redeemer Lutheran Church, Bartlesville, Oklahoma
McBryde House, Kansas City, Missouri (project)

1960 Daphne House, Hillsborough, California (second project)
Beal House, Wichita, Kansas (project)
Darling House, El Dorado, Kansas (second project)
Gryder House, Ocean Springs, Mississippi
Flora 1 Hills Memorial Park, Las Vegas, Nevada (project)
Cowboy Hall of Fame (competition project)
1961 Viva Hotel and Casino, Las Vegas, Nevada (project)
Rodin House, Libertyville, Illinois (project)
Blackbear Motor Lodge, Jackson Hole, Wyoming (project)
Giacomo Motor Lodge, McAlester, Oklahoma (project)
Blackwell Clinic, Dallas, Texas (project)
Fitchette House, Bartlesville, Oklahoma
Grady House, Casa Grande, Arizona (project)
Unitarian Fellowship Hall, Bartlesville, Oklahoma (project)
Plan for the Baxter Subdivision, Quincy, Illinois
Rudd House, Portola Valley, California (project)
1962 Quail Valley Country Club, Rogers, Arkansas (project)
H. and B. Goff House, Tulsa, Oklahoma (two projects)
Barby House, Beaver, Oklahoma (two projects)
Rudd House, Portola Valley, California (second project)
Entrance for the Woodland Hills Subdivision, Roland, Oklahoma (project)
Miller House, Kennedy Mountain, Harrison, Arkansas (project)
Phi Sigma Epsilon Fraternity House, Tahlequah, Oklahoma (project)
Slater House, Roland, Oklahoma (project)
1963 Giacomo Motor Lodge, McAlester, Oklahoma (second project)
Loosen Lodge, Okarche, Oklahoma (project)
Butler Mortuary, Tulsa, Oklahoma (project)
Stewart House, Tulsa, Oklahoma (two projects)
Playtower and Moebius Strip Crawler, Sooner Park, Bartlesville, Oklahoma
Seventh Day Adventist Church, Bartlesville, Oklahoma (project)
Apartment building, Tyler, Texas (project)
Fitzgerald Realty Office, Tyler, Texas
1964 Van Doll House, Bartlesville, Oklahoma (project)
Bird Rehabilitation Center, Kansas City, Kansas (project)
Dace House, Beaver, Oklahoma
Briar Associates Doctors Building, Kansas City, Missouri
Housing, for Briar Associates, Kansas City, Missouri (project)
Vacation cabins, for Briar Associates, Kansas City, Missouri
Haven House Nursing Home, Las Vegas, Nevada (project)
1965 Combs Farmhouse, Gower, Missouri
Van Doll House, Bartlesville, Oklahoma (second project)
Hyde House, Kansas City, Kansas
Riddle House, Kansas City, Kansas (project)
Hollander House additions and alterations, Missouri City, Kansas (project)
Phi Kappa Tau Fraternity House, Kansas State University, Lawrence (project)
Price House, Lake Tahoe, California (project)
Duncan House, Cobden, Illinois
Jacquart House, Sublette, Kansas
Ski Lodge, Crested Butte, Colorado
1966 Searing House, Kansas City, Kansas (three projects)
Yockey House, Tonganoxie, Kansas (project)
Nichol House, Kansas City, Missouri (four projects)

Youngstrom House, Lake Quivira, Missouri (project)
Heft House, Racine, Wisconsin (project)
Plunkett House, Tyler, Texas (project)
Plunkett Apartment Building, Tyler, Texas (project)
Price House additions and alterations, Bartlesville, Oklahoma
1967 Mercedes-Benz Sales and Shops Building, Atlanta
Youngstrom House, Lake Quivira, Kansas (second project)
Abraham House, Kansas City, Kansas (project)
Heft House, Racine, Wisconsin (second project)
1968 Mitchell House, Dodge City, Missouri
Britton House, Warrensburg, Missouri (project)
Nichol House, Warrensburg, Missouri (project)
Youngstrom House, Lake Quivira, Kansas (third project)
Heft House, Racine, Wisconsin (third project)
Searing House additions, Kansas City, Kansas
Ford House additions, Aurora, Illinois
Jones House I additions, Bartlesville, Oklahoma (project)
Wynes House, Butler, Missouri (project)
First National Bank alterations, Independence, Missouri (project)
1969/
70 Jones House II, Bartlesville, Oklahoma (two projects)
1970 Main Entrance Feature, Lake Village, Tyler, Texas (project 1)
Shelter pavilion, Lake Village, Tyler, Texas (project)
Plunkett House, Lake Village, Tyler, Texas
Glen Harder House, near Mountain Lake, Minnesota
1971 Jacob Harder House, Mountain Lake, Minnesota
First parade of Homes House, Lake Village, Tyler, Texas
Stables and Shops, Lake Village, Tyler, Texas (projects)
Pacific Coast Estate Development (project)
Wakil House, Houston, Texas (two projects)
Pool Bath house, Lake Village, Tyler, Texas
1972 Eddy Road Entrance Features, Lake Village, Tyler, Texas
First Independence Bank alterations, Independence, Missouri (project)
Three speculative housing types, Lake Village, Tyler, Texas
Double House, Lake Village, Tyler, Texas
Water Tower, Lake Village, Tyler, Texas (two projects)
Love Animal Clinic alterations, Tyler, Texas (project)
Plunkett Guest House, "Lakescape," Lake Village, Tyler, Texas (project)
Durst House additions, Houston, Texas
1973 Frank Memorial Chapel, Tulsa, Oklahoma (project)
Caddo Inn, Lake Village, Tyler, Texas (project)
Pollock House addition, Oklahoma City (project)
Scofinato Clubhouse, near Milwaukee, Wisconsin (project)
Stark House, Austin, Texas (project)
Barby House II, Colorado (project)
1974 Price House additions, Bartlesville, Oklahoma
Barby House, Tucson, Arizona
McCleary House, Fort Worth, Texas (project)
Community Center, Mineola, Texas (project)
Woodside Lodge, near Scranton, Pennsylvania (project)
1975 Taylor House alterations, Seattle, Washington

Fleming House, Dallas, Texas (project)
Gordon House, Dallas, Texas (project)
Harvey House, Jackson, Missouri (project)
Jones House II, Bartlesville, Oklahoma (project 3)
Mason House, Lake Village, Tyler, Texas (project)
1976 Durst House additions II, Houston, Texas
Plunkett House alterations, Tyler, Texas
John Bass House, Amarillo, Texas (project)
Garzio House, Manhattan, Kansas (project)
Innis House II, Washington, D.C. (project)
Kinsey Clinic alterations, Linsdale, Texas (project)
Nicol House II, Kansas City, Missouri (project)
Pensacola Chapel, Pensacola, Florida (project)
Peter and Suzie Plunkett House, Lake Village, Tyler, Texas (project)
Price Studio alterations, Bartlesville, Oklahoma (project)
Prost Studio, Oak Park, Illinois (project)
Robins Gambling Casino, Las Vegas, Nevada (project)
1977 Japanese Galleries, Metropolitan Museum of Art, New York (project)
Blair House alterations, Cody, Wyoming (project)
1978 Shin'Enkan Museum of Japanese Art, for Los Angeles County Museum of Art (completed by Bart Prince, 1985)
Dr. Melaragno Clinic, Charlotte, North Carolina (two projects)
Goff Studio (conversion of Starview Barn), Bartlesville, Oklahoma (project)
1979 Justice House, Tyler, Texas (project)
1980 Stuckus House, Woodland Hills, near Los Angeles
Pollock House alterations, Oklahoma City, Oklahoma (project)
1981 First City Bank of Olathe, Kansas (project)

Publications:

By GOFF: portfolio—*Bruce Goff, Architect,* Chicago 1978; articles—"A Declaration for Independence" in *Western Architect* (Los Angeles), January 1930; "Notes on Architecture" in *Bauwelt* (Berlin), January 1958; "Absolute Architecture" in *L'Architecture d'aujourd'hui* (Paris), June/July 1962; "Architecture as Art" in *Progressive Architecture* (New York), December 1962; "Frank Lloyd Wright: le roi des étoiles" in *L'Architecture d'aujourd'hui* (Paris), April/May 1964; "Originality and Architecture" in *Bruce Goff in Architecture* by Takenobu Mohri, Tokyo 1970.

On GOFF: books—*Utopian Architecture* by Ulrich Conrads, New York 1963; *An Architectural Biography of Bruce Goff* by John A. Zaluski (student paper: Columbia University, New York), 1965; *Bruce Goff: A Portfolio of the Work of Bruce Goff,* compiled by William Murphy and Lois Muller, New York 1970; *Bruce Goff in Architecture* by Takenobu Mohri, Tokyo 1970; *Bruce Goff: Bavinger House and Price House* by Yukio Futagawa, Tokyo 1975; *The Architecture of Bruce Goff: Buildings and Projects 1916-1974* by David DeLong, London and New York 1977; *The Architecture of Bruce Goff* by Jeffrey Cook, London and New York 1978; *Late-Modern Architecture* by Charles Jencks, London 1980; *New American Art Museums,* exhibition catalogue, by Helen Searing, New York 1982; articles—"Bruce Goff: Architecture Without Style" by G. S. Thomas in *Baukunst und Werkform* (Nuremberg), July 1953; "Bruce Goff" in *Wisconsin Architect* (Madison), January 1956; "Bruce Goff" by Ben Allan Park in *Architectural Design* (London), May 1957; "Bruce Goff" by Ian McCallum in *Architectural Review* (London), May 1957; "Bruce Goff's Architecture"

by H. Waichter in *AIA Journal* (Washington, D.C.), December 1959; "The Master Builder" by Ian Nairn in *Punch* (London), 1 June 1960; "Pavilions on the Prairie" by John Canady in *Horizon* (New York), November 1961; "Portrait" in *Architectural Forum* (New York), July 1962; "Goff Rides Again" in *Architectural Review* (London), March 1963; "The Serious American" by Alan Pryce-Jones in *Harpers* (New York), September 1963; "Principles of Design: A Seminar with Bruce Goff" by Linda Troxel and Julian Ominski in *Kansas Engineer* (Lawrence), March 1964; special issue of *Kentiku* (Tokyo), March 1969; "A View of Contemporary World Architecture" in *Japan Architect* (Tokyo), July 1970; special issue of *Architectural Design* (London), October 1978; "The Diversity of Bruce Goff" by Sutherland Lyall in *Building Design* (London), 13 October 1978; "Bruce Goff," special issue of *Inland Architect* (Chicago), December 1979; "Bruce Goff, 1904-1982" by David De Long in *Progressive Architecture* (New York), September 1982; "Architecture Loses Three Very Different Leaders: O'Neil Ford, Bruce Goff and George E. Kassabaum" in *AIA Journal* (Washington, D.C.), September 1982; "The Loner" by J. Cook and H. Alan in *Inland Architect* (Chicago), September/December 1982; "Goodbye to Bruce Goff, The Geometric Eclectic" by John Sergeant in *Building Design* (London), 28 October 1982; "Shin'Enkan: Project for a Museum of Japanese Art" in *Techniques et architecture* (Paris), November 1982; "Bruce Goff" by Esther McCoy in *Arts and Architecture* (Los Angeles), no. 3, 1983; "Bruce Goff," special issue of *L'Architecture d'aujourd'hui* (Paris), June 1983; film—*The Architecture of Bruce Goff,* BBC television film directed by Charles Chabot, 1984.

Bibliography—*Bruce Goff, Architect: Writings 1918 to 1978* by Patrick Joseph Meehan, Monticello, Illinois 1979.

For well over half of the twentieth century, Bruce Goff generated a world architectural presence based almost exclusively on isolated, idiosyncratic and inaccessible one-family houses scattered through rural and suburban American locations of the Great Plains and neighboring states. Without urban or rural theories and without apparent connection with current tastes and trends, Goff's work simultaneously epitomizes the vagaries of the century and some of its most creative variants.

Goff was born on the thirty-seventh birthday of Frank Lloyd Wright in the heartland of the United States. Apprenticed at twelve, he had major buildings to his credit before he left high school. At twenty-two, he designed the Boston Avenue Methodist Episcopal Church, Tulsa, Oklahoma, the international publication of which brought attention to Goff before he was twenty-five. An early imitator and lifelong friend of Frank Lloyd Wright, Goff quickly established his own much more pluralistic approach in which each building program was regarded as unique and particular.

Goff's designs for the Seabees during World War II examined the free use of "as found" and "ad hoc" materials. His most exploratory designs followed during his teaching years. His professional office years (1956-1969) produced work that was increasingly regular and polished both technically and aesthetically. Goff's mature work extended his skill with materials, space, and structure.

Although his polychromatic originality seems unfettered by academic discipline, Goff was among the most informed architects of his time—his personal library, both in twentieth century architecture and in post-classical musical recordings, is probably unparalleled. His homespun, broadly-based leadership of the school at the University of Oklahoma (1948-1955) established it as one of the most stimulating and distinctive architectural curricula. Since then, a series of apprentices have always assisted in his small office.

Goff's creative method of free association and subconscious techniques pushed certain architectural explorations well beyond most expectations. Anthracite walls, goose-feather ceilings, and carpeted roofs are among his protagonist architectural inventions that have challenged his inclusion in many contemporary surveys. He freely used the word "beauty" and persisted in designing sometimes lavishly ornamental buildings. But structural clarity and material integrity are also characteristic of his richly tactile spatial compositions.

In spite of the regularity and even symmetry of his plans, there is no institution, style, movement, or association that represents Goff. The individuality of his designs and the profusion of potential sources defy attempts at classification.

Goff has explored virtually every geometry and most construction materials and structural techniques; handmade and mass-produced components; Woolworth ashtrays and suspension cables; sequins and plastic rain; disposable pie plates and boiler tubing; stencils and glass culletts—these abound to frustrate all attempts at categorizing his "place."

From abroad, Goff's apparent exuberance is assumed to be characteristically American; at home, he has been regarded as an irrelevent eccentric. Indeed, the settings and ultimate quietude of many of his houses, together with the richness of his craft, suggest that Goff is left over from the nineteenth century of some other place. But TV antennae and all kinds of cars are especially compatible with Goff houses. Goff can be associated with the "organic" not only in his esteem for that triumvirate, Richardson, Sullivan, and Wright, but also in his intimate considerations of function and site, client and climate. Goff's sensitive client-response has produced a succession of "client" styles unparalleled in architecture. The "transcendental" label identifies Goff's sense of the natural world and man's perception of its harmonies—a subliminal Emerson influence on many native-born Americans. But "visionary" and "fantastic" are adjectives that hardly apply to an architect who has built almost one-third of everything he has ever designed. "Expressionistic" themes often seem evident, but they have a colorful wit and whimsey never allowed the obsessive, monochromatic German and Dutch Expressionism of the 1920s. Goff's architectural expressions are generated abstractly, without the narrative or subjective allusions often applied by critics.

Goff's dramatic approaches are also personal and unpredictable; he imitates neither himself nor others. Perhaps Goff's most published work is the owner-built Bavinger house, with its spiral plan and floating saucers suspended from a central mast. The succession of house designs and additions for Joe Price, built from 1956 to 1978, is the most complex, rich, and elegant summary of his later work. The unbuilt Dewlin Aparture was both apartment and departure in its playful, animistic, and amorphous imagery. But the teepee-clustered Nicol House, the Harder House with its farmhouse working elegance, the crystalline Gutman House, and the Ford House with its interlocking spheroids are among many that represent great maturity in Goff's distinctive and uniquely imaginative buildings. Goff's work is living and entertaining proof that the artistic potentials of the twentieth century are continuously realizable.

—Jeffrey Cook

GOGEL, Daniel.

German. Born in Berlin, 20 March 1927. Educated at a gymnasium, Berlin; studied architecture under Max Taut, q.v., and Georg Niedenberger, Hochschule für bildende Künste, Berlin, Dip.Arch. 1950. Served in the German Marine Corps, 1943-45. Worked as a bricklayer, Berlin, 1945-46, and as a docker in a shipyard, 1946-48; in private practice, working with Ludwig Leo, q.v., and Hans Müller as part of an architectural cooperative, Berlin, 1950-53; Partner, with Herman Fehling, q.v., Fehling + Gogel Architects, Berlin, since 1953. Guest Lecturer, Technical University of Berlin, 1975-76. Exhibition: *Fehling + Gogel: Architecturen von 1947-1980*, Internationale Design Zentrum, Berlin, 1981. Recipient: First Prize in the competitions—Berlin Pavilion, at *Interbau*, 1956; Glass industry Pavilion, at *Interbau*, 1956; Paulus Parish Centre, Mainz, West Germany, 1965; Max Planck Institute, Berlin, 1965; French School, Berlin, 1966; Zeli-Eck Housing Complex, Berlin, 1975; Max Planck Institute, Garching, West Germany, 1975; Technical University Auditorium, Berlin, 1978. Address: Margartenstrasse 4, 1000 West Berlin 33, Germany.

See FEHLING, Hermann

GOLDBERG, Bertrand.

American. Born in Chicago, Illinois, 17 July 1913. Educated at Harvard College, Cambridge, Massachusetts, 1930-32; Bauhaus, Berlin, 1932-33 (worked in the office of Mies van de Rohe, Berlin, 1932); Armour Institute of Technology, now Illinois Institute of Technology, Chicago, 1933-34. Married Nancy S. Florsheim in 1946; Children: Nan, Lisa, and Geoffrey. Since 1937, Principal of Bertrand Goldberg Associates, architects and engineers, Chicago; branch office established in Boston, 1964; also Director of the subsidiary companies (all Chicago) of Computer Service Inc., since 1969, Environmental, Engineering, Corporation, since 1974, and Copy Corporation, since 1975. Exhibitions: *Sculpture in Architecture*, Paris, 1967; Museum of Modern Art, New York, 1968; *Bauhaus Travelling Exhibition*, 1970; Glessner Foundation, Chicago (individual), 1972; *Bauhaus Archives Exhibition*, Germany, 1974; *100 Years of Architecture in Chicago*, Museum of Contemporary Art, Chicago, 1976; *Chicago Architects Design*, Art Institute of Chicago, 1982; *A Bertrand Goldberg Retrospective: 1937-1983*, Archicenter of the Chicago Architectural Foundation, 1984; *150 Years of Chicago Architecture*, Paris Art Center and Ecole des Beaux Arts, Paris 1984. Recipient: *Architectural Forum* Award, 1945 and 1951; Apartment Project Award, *Progressive Architecture*, 1954; First and Second Awards, Fine Hardwoods Association, 1956; Apartment Project Award, American Institute of Architects/Chicago Chamber of Commerce, 1959; Chicagoan of the Year Award, in architecture, Chicago Junior Association of Commerce and Industry, 1965; Silver Medal, Architectural League of New York, 1965; Distinguished Building Award, American Institute of Architects, Chicago Chapter, 1967; Award for Concrete Shell Structures, *Engineering News Record*, 1975; Design Excellence Award, Society of American Registered Architects, 1978; Award of Merit, Society of American Registered Architects, 1982; Excellence in Concrete Award, Arizona Rock Products Association, Phoenix, 1982. Fellow, American Institute of Architects, 1966. Address: Bertrand Goldberg Associates, Marina City, Chicago, Illinois 60610, U.S.A.

Works:

1937/
44 Prefabricated houses and industrial units for the United States Government
Town of Suitland, Maryland (prefabricated housing)
1938 Prefabricated housing, Lafayette, Indiana
1939 Prefabricated housing, Indian Head, Maryland
1945/
48 Stanfab prefabricated unit bathroom
1948 Master plan for Calumet New Town, Calumet City, Illinois
1949 Unicel Plastic Freight Car for the Pressed Steel Car Company
1950 Unishelter Prefabricated Unit Houses for the Pressed Steel Car Company
1955 Michael Todd Theatre, Chicago
Michael Todd Theatre, Paris
1957 Drexel Town and Garden Apartments, Chicago
1959 Marina City, Chicago
The Happy Medium Theatre, Chicago
Astor Tower Hotel, Chicago
1960 Joseph Brennenmann School, Chicago
1962 Civic Auditorium, West Palm Beach, Florida
Elgin State Hospital, Illinois
1963 Raymond Hilliard Center, Chicago
1965 Squantum Point, Squantum, Massachusetts
Outpatients Clinic, Menninger Foundation, Topeka, Kansas
1966 Burns-Jackson Center, Dayton, Ohio
1967 Biology Building, State University of New York, Stony Brook
Stanford University Medical Center and Stanford University Master Plan, Palo Alto, California
1968 La Trinidad Medical University and Health Center Campus, Caracas, Venezuela
Health Services Center, State University of New York, Stony Brook (with Abam Engineers and Seifert, Forbes and Berry)
1969 St. Joseph Hospital, Tacoma, Washington
Sidney Farber Cancer Center, Boston
1970 Prentice Women's Hospital and Maternity Center, and Institute of Psychiatry, Northwestern Memorial Hospital, Chicago
1972 St. Mary's Hospital, Milwaukee
1974 University of Illinois Replacement Hospital, Chicago (with A. Epstein and Sons, and Schmidt, Garden and Erickson)
Basic Science Research Building, State University of New York, Stony Brook
1976 Affiliated Hospitals Center, Boston
Good Samaritan Hospital, Phoenix, Arizona (with Associated Samaritan Architect)
1982 Metroplaza, Samaritan Health Services, Phoenix, Arizona
Providence Hospital, Mobile, Alabama
1985 River City, Chicago

Publications:

On GOLDBERG: books—*Architects on Architecture*, edited by Paul Heyer, New York 1966, London 1967; *Conversations with Architects* by John Cook and Heinrich Klotz, New York 1973; *The New Architecture of Bertrand Goldberg* by Linda Legner, Chicago 1974; *A View of Contemporary World Architects*, Tokyo 1977; *Gestaltung einer neuen Umwelt* by Heinrich Klotz, Frankfurt 1978; *Architecture de Chicago*, edited by Ante Glibota, Paris 1983; articles—"Marina City Architect is Still Throwing Curves" by Rita Tatum in *Building Design and Construction* (Chicago), March 1974; "Towers' Cores Implanted Idea for Cantilevered, High-Rise Shell" in *Engineering News Record* (New York) July 1974; "Bertrand Goldberg" in *Architecture + Urbanism* (Tokyo), July 1975; "The Goldberg Variations" by Gregg W. Downey in *Modern Healthcare* (New York), March 1976; "The Goldberg Effect" in *Architectural Record* (New York), July 1976; "L'Ospedale St. Joseph a Tacoma" by Federico Zabo in *Industria italiana del cemento* (Milan), November 1977; "St. Mary's Hospital, Milwaukee" in *Informes de la construccion* (Madrid), July/August 1978; "Saint Joseph Health Care Centre" in *Industria delle costruzioni* (Rome), July/August 1979; "Local Authority Housing in

Bertrand Goldberg: Prentice Women's Hospital and Maternity Center, Northwestern University, Chicago, 1970.

Chicago" in *Industria delle costruzioni* (Rome), April 1980; "River City" in *Inland Architect* (Chicago), May/June 1983.

Both contemporary architecture and modern physics have their roots in similar Victorian concepts of duality. As the nineteenth century closed, that sibling relationship between neutron and proton was matched by the incest of form and function. Continuing investigation by scientists in this century has shown the neutron-proton to have developed a family of quarks, pies, and mesons, while the architects have only discovered that life with form and function was a void.

Why were form and function so sterile? Why didn't we do as well as the physicists? The world of the physicist was what they had started off with in the Victorian days—it has never changed, and they are finding what is there. The world of the architect is a changing world wherein form and function no longer can play their role as a lovely couple.

Form is no longer *the form*, the perfect Ur-form in a simple Miesian world of columns and beams produced by the universal machine administered by a Faustian Speer. Form is whatever we can think. We

have reached that moment of freedom for the first time in the history of man where we almost can economically produce whatever we can imagine. Form no longer is a box made by columns and beams, but spaces made by tubes, shells, and even by air. Material is not brick, steel and glass, but poly, moly, and ium.

Function is no longer the knee-jerk function of the Victorian mass man controlled by a latter-day Hitler. Function is rather that aspiration, that spirit given action that identifies each individual emerging from and merging with neighborhood and society. These new social changes demand new forms to shelter them. The box is not the universal package for functions of living in contemporary society.

Will the architect study himself? Will the architect make new promises to a new humanism? For the first time in the history of the world, we now can build whatever we think. What shall we build for people?

—Bertrand Goldberg

Bertrand Goldberg's early work was a direct outgrowth of his training at the Bauhaus and his years with Mies van der Rohe's office in Germany. Throughout his career, Goldberg has continued to

show this influence, regarding the task of architecture to be one of finding new structural solutions and improving social and psychological conditions through building design. But, with time, Goldberg has broken with Mies. He rebelled against what he calls "the engineer's module applied to society," "the anonymous development of space as yardgoods." He considers rectilinear shapes antithetical to much human activity and espouses instead nuclear forms. Activity revolves around focal points, he says, so circular buildings serve activity better and help to create a sense of community in anonymous situations such as hospitals and large apartment buildings. In addition, he claims that circular buildings provide more efficient wind resistance, more direct mechanical distribution and, frequently, more usable interior square footage. "Industrialization has developed beyond straight line objects," says Goldbergs, lamenting that, "architects continue to use concrete as if it were wooden logs." His towers represent a line of experimentation in concrete shell structure.

Most famous of these towers, however, is still the first one, Marina City, famous also as the first American government-sponsored downtown housing and among the first multi-use projects in the United States, public or private. Marina City, which has long been nicknamed "The Corncobs" because of the shape of its two towers, provides apartments, parking, movie theaters, a marina, shops, restaurants, and office space. It was with Marina City that Goldberg developed his theory of kinetic space. Nonparallel walls, he believes, give the illusion of expanded room size because the space is set in motion—a further rationale.

Goldberg is often heralded as proof of a continuing Chicago School of Architecture, a label he denies. Ignoring here the question of whether such a continuing school can be postulated, it is probably sufficient, and more to the point, to see Goldgberg as a true student of the principles, if not the forms, of the German Bauhaus. Though widely published and well-known, he has operated virtually in a vacuum and his utopian ideas have not, as yet at least, developed what could be called a following.

—Nory Miller

GOLDFINGER, Ernö.

British. Born in Budapest, Hungary, 11 September 1902; emigrated to England, 1934: naturalized, 1945. Educated at the Gymnasium, Budapest, 1912-19; Le Rosay School, Gstaad, Switzerland, 1919-20; Ecole National et Supérieure des Beaux-Arts, Paris, 1923, DPLG 1931; co-founder of the breakaway Beaux-Arts "Atelier Auguste Perret," 1924; Ecole d'Urbanisme, La Sorbonne, Paris, 1927-28. Married Ursula Ruth Blackwell in 1933; children: Peter, Elisabeth, and Michael. In private practice, Paris, 1924-34, and London, 1934 until he retired in 1979. Correspondent for Great Britain, *Architecture d'aujourd'hui*, Paris, 1934-74. Honorary Member, Association of Building Technicians, 1937; Member, Foreign Relations Committee, Royal Institute of British Architects, 1937-45; Member of the Council, Architects Registration Council of the U.K., 1941-50; Honorary Organizing Secretary, International Union of Architects, 1946; Member of the Council, Architectural Association, London, 1960-63 and 1965-68, Council of Industrial Design, 1961-65, and the Royal Academy, 1974. Member of CIAM (Congrès Internationaux d'Architecture Moderne), 1928-59: Honorary Secretary, French Section, Athens Congress, 1933; also, Member of the MARS Group (U.K. Section of CIAM), 1935-60. Exhibitions: *CIAM Exhibition*, Athens, 1934; *Housing Exhibition*, Grand Palais, Paris, 1934, and Olympia, London, 1935; *MARS Group Exhibition*, Burlington Gallery, London, 1938; *CIAM Exhibition*, Aix-en-Provence, France, 1952; *This is Tomorrow*, Whitechapel Art Gallery, London, 1955; *UIA Sports*

Buildings Commission Exhibition, Moscow, 1968; *Thirties,* Hayward Gallery, London, 1979; *Works 1: Ernö Goldfinger,* Architectural Association, London, 1983. Collection: Royal Institute of British Architects Drawings Collection, London. Fellow, Royal Institute of British Architects, 1966; Fellow, Royal Society of Arts, 1968; Associate of Royal Academy, 1971, and Royal Academician, 1975. Honorary Member, Association of Hungarian Architects, 1963. Address: 2 Willow Road, London NW3 1TH, England.

Works:

1926 Library (Aghion), in Aghion House (designed by Auguste Perret), Alexandria, Egypt
Helena Rubinstein Beauty Salon, 24 Grafton Street, London
1927 Central European Express, rue Godot de Mauroy, Paris
1928 La Portique (picture gallery), Boulevard Raspail, Paris
Cheftel Apartment furniture and interiors, 6 rue d'Astorg, Paris
Grossman Apartment furniture and interiors, 6 rue d'Astorg, Paris
Alpina Exhibition Stand, *Foire de Paris*
Alpina Exhibition Stand, *British Industries Fair,* Olympia, London
1929 Luteaux Monument, Jardin d'Acclimatation, Algiers
Hotel, Philippeville, Algeria (project)
Housing Philippeville, Algeria (project)
Nursery School, Vitry-Seine, near Paris (with Pierre Forestier)
1930 Hollender Apartment interiors, Paris
Susanne Blum Offices and Apartment, 53 rue de Varenne, Paris
Dick Wyndham Studio interiors, rue Froidevaux, Paris
1931 Ernö Goldfinger Studio and Apartments interiors, 3 rue de la Cité Universitaire, Paris
Entas Steel Stacking Chairs, Paris
Aero Club (project)
1932 Heliometer (scientific instrument for measuring isolation)
1933 15-Storey Apartment Building (exhibition project)
P. and M. Abbatt Toy Showroom, Endsleigh Street, London
Lahousse House and Studio, near Le Touquet, France
1934 Abbatt Apartment, Tavistock Square, London
1935 S. Weiss Shop, Golders Green, London
"Easiwork" Toys and Furniture, for P. and M. Abbatt Company, London
1936 P. and M. Abbatt Toy Shop, Wimpole Street, London
1937 House, Broxted, Essex (with Gerald Flower)
Children's Section, British Pavilion, World's Fair, Paris
Three terrace houses, including Goldfinger House, 1-2-3 Willow Road, London
1938 ICI Exhibition Stand, *British Industries Fair,* Olympia, London
Children's Section, *MARS Group Exhibition,* Burlington Gallery, London
Benroy Apartment, Hendon, London
Wordsworth House, 13 Westhill, London
1939/
45 Education exhibitions for the British Army, Royal Navy, and Royal Air Force
1940 Air Raid Shelter, Bedales School, Petersfield, Hampshire
Blastproof Housing (competition project)
1945 Planetarium for Hyde Park, London (project)
1947 Newspaper Office and Printing Press, 75 Farringdon Road, London
1949 Fletcher Hardware Company Warehouse and Offices, Pershore Street, Birmingham, England

Fletcher House, Henley-in-Arden, Warwickshire
1950 Brandlehow Road Primary School, Wandsworth, London
Westville Road Primary School, Hammersmith, London
Dairy farm, Ibstone, Buckinghamshire
House with two apartments, 74 Avenue des Chênes, Uccle, Brussels
1951 S. Weiss Shop, Shaftesbury Avenue, London (with Lilian Ladlow)
Kiosks, *Festival of Britain,* South Bank, London
1952 Four houses, Broadstairs, Kent
1954 Block of flats, 10 Regent's Park Road, London
1955 Carr and Company Offices, Shirley, West Midlands
1956 Albemarle Street Office Building, 45-46 Albemarle Street, London
Taylor Woods Showrooms, 45-46 Albemarle Street, London
Design of the *This Is Tomorrow* exhibition, Whitechapel Art Gallery, London (with Victor Pasmore and Helen Phillips)

Ernö Goldfinger: Alexander Fleming House, London, 1966.

1957 Wallis House, Amersham, Buckinghamshire
1957/
60 Hille Factory, 134 St. Albans Road, Watford, Hertfordshire
1958 Abbotts Langley Housing, Hertfordshire
French Government Tourist Office, 66 Haymarket, London (with Charlotte Perriand; now Belgium Tourist Office)
1959 Elephant and Castle Development, London (competition project)
1960 Hille House (offices and showroom), 134 St. Albans Road, Watford, Hertfordshire
1962 Player House, Coombe Hill Road, Coombe Hill, Surrey
Westminster Bank, Elephant and Castle, London
1962/
66 Alexander Fleming House (Ministry of Health), in two phases, Elephant and Castle, London
1963 French Government Tourist Office, 177 Piccadilly, London (with Charlotte Perriand)
1965 Motz House, 16 Bedford Street, Oxford, England

1966 Odeon Cinema, Old Kent Road, Elephant and Castle, London

1966/
78 Rowlett Street Housing, in three phases, St. Leonard's Road, London

1967 Martins Bank, Wigmore Street, London (now Barclays Bank)

French Government Tourist Office and SNCF (French Railways) Office, 127 Avenue des Champs Elysées, Paris (with Pierre Forestier)

1968 Teesdale (Perry House), Westwood Road, Windlesham, Surrey

Haggerston Comprehensive School, Queensbridge Road, London

1968/
69 Edenham Street Housing, in two phases, Cheltenham Estate, Golborne Road, London

1971 Office conversion, South Hill Park, London (project)

1972 Hille Factory, phase III, St. Albans Road, Watford, Hertfordshire (project)

1974 Hille House extension, St. Albans Road, Watford, Hertfordshire (project)

1976 Dr. Silva Surgery Conversion, Edenham Street, London (project)

Publications:

By GOLDFINGER: books—*County of London Plan Explained*, with E. J. Carter, London 1945; *British Furniture Today*, London 1951; articles—"Der neue Baustil" in *Pester Lloyd* (Budapest), 8 August 1925; "Der Baumeister Unserer Lieben Frau" in *Pester Lloyd* (Budapest), 30 December 1925; articles in *L'Organisation ménagère* (Paris), 1928-1929; "Heliometer" in *L'Architecture d'aujourd'hui* (Paris), March 1934; "MARS Group Exhibition" in *L'Architecture d'aujourd'hui* (Paris), July 1938; "Art of Enclosing Space" in *Architectural Review* (London). November and December 1941 and January 1942; "Town and Country Planning Conference" in *Architects' Journal* (London), April 1942; "Standardisation" in *Architect and Building News* (London), 15 January 1943; "Organisation of Science in *Architects' Journal* (London), 11 March 1943; editor, *MARS News* (London), July 1944, February 1945 and July 1945; "Building Research in Great Britain" in *Werk* (Zürich), April 1947; "Problèmes du logement en Grande Bretagne" in *L'Architecture d'aujourd'hui* (Paris), September 1950; special issue on Great Britain of *L'Architecture d'aujourd'hui* (Paris), February 1952; "Perret" in *Architectural Review* (London, May 1954; "Aesthetic Control" and "France Rebuilds" in *Architectural Design* (London), July 1954; "André Sive" in *The Times* (London), 25 September 1958; "Londres et sa region" in *L'Architecture d'aujourd'hui* (Paris), February/March 1960; "Corbusier at Pessac" in *RIBA Journal* (London), September 1969; "Auguste Perret: The Last of the Master Builders" in *Building Design* (London), 7 March 1975; "Serge Chermayeff" in *Architects' Journal* (London), 15 October 1980; "A Conversation with Ernö Goldfinger" by Gavin Stamp in *Thirties Society Journal* (London), no. 2, 1982.

On GOLDFINGER: books—*Junge französische. Architektur* by Roger Ginsburger, Geneva and Ghent, Belgium 1930; *Shops* by Brian and Norman Westwood, London 1937; *Modern Houses in England* by F.R.S. Yorke, London 1944; *Houses for the People*, London 1946; *Architects' Homes* by Robert Winkler, Zürich, 1955; *Public Interiors* by Misha Black, London 1960; *Exterior Space in Architecture* by Yoshinobu Ashihara, Tokyo 1962; *Office Building* by Leonard Manasseh, London 1962; *Glass* by Raymond McGrath, London 1967; *Ernö Goldfinger* by Mate Major, Budapest 1970; *Works 1: Ernö Goldfinger*, compiled by James Dunnett and Gavin Stamp, London 1983; *Contemporary Designers* edited by Ann Lee Morgan, New York and London 1984; articles—"Ernö Goldfinger," special issue of *Architectural Design* (London) January 1963; "Elephant and Castle" by Kenneth Frampton in *Architectural Design* (London), October 1967; "Ernö Goldfinger—A Tribute" by John Winter and James Dunnett in *RIBA Transactions* (London), no. 2, 1982; "The Architect as Constructor" by James Dunnett in *Architectural Review* (London), April 1983.

ARCHITECTURE THE ART OF ENCLOSING SPACE

A particle is snatched from space, rhythmically modulated by membranes dividing it from surrounding chaos: that is Architecture.

There is other enclosed space, not modulated, not rhythmic, but that is not Architecture.

The "sensation of space" is to Architecture what looking at a picture is to painting, moving around and touching to sculpture, or listening to music. But "sensation of space" is a subconscious phenomenon; to undergo its effect it is not necessary to be aware of it

To undergo the effects of Architecture you have to be in it; you need not contemplate it or be conscious of it. If you shut your eyes, the painting disappears. If you stop your ears, the music no longer exists. But as long as you are inside "the rhythmically enclosed space" of Architecture, you undergo its effects.

You cannot see Architecture; you can only be in it, as in music (what you see are the real or imaginary membranes which divide space).

You can move through Architecture, and when doing so, the spatial sensation becomes four-dimensional.

It is the Architect who, when he identifies with the anticipated user, creates a "thing" which has never existed before. While creating this "thing," he undergoes an emotion (call it an artistic or creative inspiration, if you will), which then is transmitted to the subconsciousness of the "user."

Whenever "space" is enclosed, "spatial sensation" will automatically result for the person within this "space"; it is therefore axiomatic that the creator of Architecture must be an artist, and Town Planning and Building is not merely the work of the Sociologue, the Drain-layer, the Statistician, the Health Inspector, or the Politician.

Politics, Statistics, Social Relations, Economics, Transport, Hygiene—are all part of it, but it is the artist who comprehends and identifies with the SOCIAL REQUIREMENTS of his time and is able to integrate them with the TECHNICAL POTENTIALITIES to create the shape of the SPACES OF THE FUTURE—ARCHITECTURE.

—Ernö Goldfinger

The 1930s was the great period for modern English domestic architecture. At the beginning of the decade, a few local architects were taking tentative steps in the new direction, but it was the arrival of the European emigres, including Ernö Goldfinger, that gave real quality and a sense of confidence to the nascent movement. As years went by, some of the distinguished emigrants departed, mainly to the United States, and some retired; by the 1970s, Goldfinger was one of very few who remained.

As a man, Goldfinger's total commitment to architecture, his unshakeable integrity of outlook, and his indifference to passing fashions earned him the respect of younger architects; however, he was not an easy person to work with, and he had no long-term collaborators, so his work, at times, ploughed a lonely furrow. This isolation of ideas can be seen in the mid-1970s when he seemed the only person left who believed in high-rise flats.

As an architect, there are two high points in his English career. The first was undoubtedly in the late 1930s. The completion of his Willow Road houses just before World War II summed up the English modern movement at that time: the white cube period was over and bricks were again acceptable but with the underlying concrete structure made plain on the highly-modelled facades. After the extremes of a few years previously, a quiet sanity now reigned supreme, and Goldfinger summarized this at Willow Road with a design that is thoughtful and gives evidence of common sense at every turn. Moreover, there was concern for urbanistic problems; Goldfinger, as a European, was very impressed with the English eighteenth and early nineteenth century town building tradition of Bath and Bloomsbury, and he designed his houses as a prototype urban terrace, publishing elevations to show how the design might be extended. These proposed extensions to his Willow Road houses had a profound influence ten years later when, in coarsened form, they formed the basis of such design as Gibberd's work at Harlow New Town.

The second high point occurred some twenty years after the first. Goldfinger's Albemarle Street Office Building is one of the very few successful examples of urban infill in London, a demonstration that a calm, modern building of quality can fit well into a distinguished traditional street. The Carr and Company Office Building at Shirley, near Birmingham, showed similar quality in a free-standing structure, unfortunately marred in this case by poor surroundings and lack of landscaping. A few years later, on a suburban site at Coombe Hill, the Player House shows Goldfinger at his best—in a clear, clean building for an upper-middle-class lifestyle.

—John Winter

GOLDSMITH, Myron.

American. Born in Chicago, Illinois, 15 September 1918. Educated at the Armour Institute of Technology, Chicago, 1935-39, B.S. in Architecture 1939; Illinois Institute of Technology, Chicago, under Mies van der Rohe, 1939-40, 1947-53, M.S. in Architecture 1953; University of Rome (Fulbright Fellow), under Pier Luigi Nervi, 1953-55. Served as a Staff Sergeant in the United States of Army Corps of Engineers, Fort Belvoir, Virginia, 1944-46. Married Robin W. Squier in 1962; children: Marc and Chandra.
Worked as a structural engineer in various offices, 1939-44; Architect and structural Engineer, Office of Ludwig Mies van der Rohe, Chicago, 1946-53. Joined Skidmore, Owings and Merrill, 1955: Chief Structural Engineer, Skidmore, Owings and Merrill, San Francisco, 1955-58; Associate Partner and Senior Designer, 1958-67, General Partner, 1967-80, and Consulting Partner, 1980-83, Skidmore, Owings and Merrill, Chicago; retired, 1983. Professor of Architecture, Illinois Institute of Technology Graduate School of Architecture, since 1961; Eliot Noyes Visiting Professor of Architecture, Harvard Graduate School of Design, Cambridge, Massachusetts, 1982-83. Chairman, Friends of Mies van der Rohe Archive, Museum of Modern Art, New York, 1972; President, Chicago Architectural Club, 1983-84. Exhibitions: *Twentieth Century Engineering*, Museum of Modern Art, New York, 1964; *100 Years of Architecture in Chicago*, Museum of Contemporary Art, Chicago, 1976; *The Work of Myron Goldsmith*, Harvard Graduate School of Design, Cambridge, Massachusetts, 1982; *Myron Goldsmith* (retrospective), Illinois Institute of Technology, Chicago, 1983 (travelled to New York, Tempe, Arizona, and Albuquerque, New Mexico); *150 Years of Chicago Architecture 1833-1983*, Paris Art Center, Paris, 1983. Collection: Art Institute of Chicago. Recipient: Honor Award, 1963, 1970, 1977, Citation of Merit, 1966, and Distinguished Building Award, 1969 (twice), 1970, 1971, 1978, American Institute of Architects, Chicago Chapter, and Chicago Association of Commerce and Industry; Architectural Award of Excellence, American

Institute of Steel Construction, 1963, 1964, 1971; Award of Merit, American Society of Civil Engineers, 1967; Honor Award, AIA, Northern California Chapter, 1967; James F. Lincoln Arc Welding Foundation Award, 1970; 4th Biennial Award for Design Excellence, United States Department of Housing and Urban Development, 1970; Citation of Excellence for Design of Low-Rise Construction, American Iron and Steel Institute, 1973; Honour Award, National AIA, 1975; Excellence in Masonry Award, 1976, and Gold Medal, 1980, Metropolitan Chicago Masonry Council; Architectural Merit Award, Association of School Business Officials, 1976 (twice); Award of Merit, Chicago Lighting Institute, 1976; First Award, *Progressive Architecture* magazine, New York, 1979; Distinguished Alumni Award, Illinois Institute of Technology, Chicago, 1984. Fellow of the American Institute of Architects, 1972. Address: 503 Central Avenue, Wilmette, Illinois 60091, U.S.A.

Works:

1959 Norton Office Building, Seattle, Washington
1960 United Air Lines Hangars and FlightKitchen Complex, San Francisco
1962 United Air Lines Headquarters Building and Stewardess Training School, Chicago
Solar Telescope, Kitt Peak, Arizona
1964 Home News Enterprises Building, Franklin, Indiana
1965 Brunswick Office Building, Chicago
De Witt-Chestnut Apartments, Chicago
1966 Life Science Building, Illinois Institute of Technology, Chicago
1967 Gymnasium, Illinois Institute of Technology, Chicago
Ultra High Energy Cosmic Ray Physics Facility feasibility study, Mount Evans, Colorado (project)
Inland Steel Research Laboratory, East Chicago, Indiana
Engineering Building No. 1, Illinois Institute of Technology, Chicago
Spectrum Arena, Philadelphia
1968 Oakland-Alameda County Coliseum, Oakland, California
1969 Central business district plan for Columbus, Indiana
1970 Central business district plan for Elkhart, Indiana
1971 *The Republic* Newspaper Plant, Columbus, Indiana

1972 Stellar Telescope, Kitt Peak, Arizona
Management Building, Illinois Institute of Technology, Chicago
Rapid Transit Stations for the Kennedy Expressway and Dan Ryan Expressway, Chicago
Crosstown Expressway, Chicago (project)
1973 Diamond Shamrock Building, Cleveland
Arthur Andersen Center, St. Charles, Illinois
1974 St. Joseph Valley Bank Headquarters, Downtown Drive-In Branch, and Concord Mall Branch, Elkhart, Indiana
The Royal Gazette Newspaper Plant, Hamilton, Bermuda
1975 Illinois Tool Works Deltar Plant, Chicago
Percy L. Julian High School, Chicago
George Henry Corliss High School, Chicago
Equibank Building, 2 Oliver Plaza, Pittsburgh
1976 Europoint II and III Office Buildings and Parking Garage, Rotterdam
1978 Tropic World of Primates, Chicago, Zoological Park, Brookfield, Illinois
Fort Dearborn Station Post Office, Chicago
Europoint IV Office Building, Rotterdam
1979 National City Bank Building, Cleveland
1980 Jefferson Park Rail/Rapid Transit Station Parking Structure, Chicago (project)
Ruck-a-Chucky Bridge, Auburn, California (as consultant)
International Museum of Photography, George Eastman House, Rochester, New York (project)
New Jeddah International Airport Master Plan, Jeddah, Saudi Arabia
1981 Ten Penn Center Office Building, Philadelphia
298 Large Mammal Complex, Lincoln Park Zoo, Chicago
Harlem Station Complex, Chicago
Office Building, 875 Third Avenue, New York (as consultant)
1983 Central Business District Master Plan Update, Columbus, Indiana
Birds of Prey Flight Cage, Lincoln Park Zoo, Chicago

Publications

By GOLDSMITH: articles—"Triumph and failure of the Skyscraper," with others, in *Casabella* (Milan), October 1976; "The Effects of Scale" in *AIA Journal* (Washington, D.C.), October 1980.

On GOLDSMITH: books—*100 Years of Architecture in Chicago*, exhibition catalogue by Oswald W. Grube, Peter C. Pran and Franz Schulze, Chicago 1976; *150 Years of Chicago Architecture 1833-1983*, exhibition catalogue by Frederic Edelmann and Ante Glibota, Paris 1983; articles—"Dimensione e Struttura" in *Architettura* (Rome), July/August 1955; "Three Projects by Myron Goldsmith and James D. Ferris" in *Arts and Architecture* (Los Angeles), August 1958; "Pre-stressed Concrete: The Big Stretch" in *Architectural Forum* (New York), March 1959; "Punctured Pre-stressed Beams Frame West Coast Skyscraper" in *Architectural Forum* (New York), March 1960; "Jet Age Hangars" in *Architectural Forum* (New York), March 1961; "A Dream of Splendor for Oakland" by Allan Temko in *San Francisco Chronicle*, 30 April 1962; "Goldsmith: Chicago's New Structural Poet" by Allan Temko in *Architectural Forum* (New York), May 1962; "Structer Studien aus der Meisterklasse von Professor Myron Goldsmith am Illinois Institute of Technologie" in *Bauwelt* (Berlin), October 1962; "Air Lines Offices, Des Plaines, Illinois" in *Architectural Design* (London), April 1984; "A Diagonally-Braced Tall Office Building" by Mikio Sasaki in *Column* (Tokyo), June 1965; "Annual Discourse" in *RIBA Journal* (London), June 1966; "Brunswick Building" in *Kenchiku Bunka* (Tokyo), November 1966; "Daily Journal" in *Vitrum* (Milan), July/August 1976; "Solar Telescope, Kitt Peak" in *Bauen und Wohnen* (Zurich), December 1969; "Urban University" by Dorman D. Anderson in *Column* (Tokyo), January 1970; "Large, Clear Span Structures" by Peter Pran in *Byggekunst* (Oslo), January 1971; "Follow Mies" in *Architectural Review* (London), July 1973; "Chicago Architektur" by Peter Pran in *Byggekunst* (Oslo), September/October 1974; "Mantled Printing Plant" in *Bauen und Wohnen* (Zurich), December 1974; "Prairie Showplace" by Paul Goldberger in the *New York Times*, 4 April 1976; "Structure, Scale and Architecture" in *Casabella* (Milan), October 1976; "Engineering Marvels Spanning the Ages" by Paul Weingarten in the *Chicago Tribune*, 1 December 1977; "E una ragnatela? No, e un ponte" in *L'Espresso* (Milan), March 1978; "The Ruck-A-Chucky Bridge, Auburn, California" in *Progressive Architecture* (New York), January 1979; "Spans to Set Spirits Soaring" in *Newsweek* (New York), 30 July 1979; "Myron Goldsmith appointed Noyes Visiting Professor of Architecture," in *HGSD News* (Cambridge, Massachusetts), January/February 1983; "Mountain of Modern Icons" in *Architecture* (Washington, D.C.), March 1984.

Myron Goldsmith: Solar Telescope, Kitts Peak, Arizona, 1962.

The spreading organisation of Skidmore, Owings and Merrill has acted as an umbrella for many architects of talent, amongst whom are a few of world stature—Gordon Bunshaft, Walter Netsch, Charles Bassett, Myron Goldsmith. These men are essentially members of a team, and Myron Goldsmith has collaborated closely with many others, notably James Ferris in the early days and Bruce J. Graham more recently; but, though much credit must be shared with his colleagues, a number of buildings can be discussed as being, in large part, his own creation. The key to Myron Goldsmith's approach is to be found in Mies van der Rohe and Pier Luigi Nervi, each of whom regarded Goldsmith as his protegé. Mies the architect and Nervi the engineer both believed that structure is the basis of architecture, and Goldsmith, who is both an architect and an engineer, combines the concept of structural purity of Mies with Nervi's concern for shaping the structure to enjoy and to explain the forces within. During his years of apprenticeship with Mies and with Nervi, Goldsmith produced a series of designs which have proved to be the basis of his subsequent work with Skidmore, Owings and Merrill. From his studies under Mies emerged the design for a high-rise building with its skeleton boldly expressed and with beams chamfering into columns to resist sheer forces; from these days also date studies of towers with horizontal forces taken by boldly expressed diagonals. From his period in Rome with Nervi there are designs for sports arenas and a bridge with every member profiled in sinuous curves to correspond to and to demonstrate the stresses within.

Myron Goldsmith's hangars for San Francisco airport, his first job within S.O.M., owe much to Nervi's recently completed Palace of Labour at Turin. For the main hangar there are steel roof beams on concrete columns, all tapering and profiled to explain the stresses in a very large structure. For a smaller wash hangar, tapered steel plate portals create an exceptionally economical structure which is quite delicious as an object; it's so unforced as to seem calm, natural, almost sweet, and it is clear that Goldsmith had been building up skills for many years that made his first builtwork a modest masterpiece.

In the years around 1960 the concepts of the formative years one by one achieved reality in various S.O.M. buildings, but the going was never easy and there were false starts and abandoned schemes along the way. The multi-storey frame chamfering to respond to the nature of the forces within was first proposed by Goldsmith when a student of Mies, and later within S.O.M. for a hotel in Chicago: the latter project was abandoned, but the idea realized, not very elegantly, in the firm's Hartford Building in Chicago. The diagonally braced tower, which similarly dates from Goldsmith's days with Mies, was first proposed within S.O.M. by Goldsmith for the Norton Building in Seattle: the idea stayed and was incorporated by other S.O.M. designers in San Francisco's Alcoa Building and Chicago's John Hancock Center. The sports arenas Goldsmith had designed for Nervi were the basis for his subsequent designs within S.O.M., first for Portland, Oregon, where his design was discarded, and then for Oakland, where the concept was realized by others.

The arrival of Goldsmith into the Chicago office in 1958 had an effect far beyond those schemes for which he was personally responsible. His input of ideas based on the poetry of a rational, structural architecture was just what part of that office was looking for, and he became a kind of guru from whom ideas circulated, often to be executed by others with varying degrees for skill and understanding. In terms of architectural quality, the smaller buildings which Goldsmith could control himself show the true measure of the man. He has become known as a prime theorist of the Chicago school of thought, which is fascinated by the nature of truly giant structures, but the more modestly scaled buildings show his skill as a sensitive architect for more normal requirements. His newspaper office building for *The*

Republic in Columbus, Indiana, has a lightness and a delicacy that is new to the Mies tradition. It has no special features; it isits sense of calm, effortless quality that makes it architecturally significant, whilst historically it is important as a link building from Mies to those English architects like Norman Foster who are seeking to lighten the Chicago inheritance.

—John Winter

GOLLINS, MELVIN, WARD.

Partnership; established, London, 1947, by Frank Gollins, James Melvin and Edmund Ward; branch office established, Berkhamsted, Hertfordshire, 1965; GMW International Europe established, in Brussels, 1976; GMW International Middle East Architects established, Jersey, Channel Islands, 1975; HOK + 4 established in Riyadh, Saudi Arabia, 1975. Current partners: W. Robert Headley; Brian Mayes; Robert Smith; Anthony Gregson; Julian Ryder Richardson; Neil Southam; M.G. Carr; P. Chambers; R.M. Kimble; G.P. Pueschel; L. Edwards; K.A. Uttley; D.S. Broadbent; A.E. Ozveren; J.D.W. Bevan; T.G. Brown; with Frank Gollins, James Melvin and Edmund Ward consultants to the practice. Exhibitions: *New Development in Historic Towns*, Hobhouse Court, London, and Gewerbe Museum, Basle, 1983; *Arab Architecture—past and present*, Royal Institute of British Architects, London, 1984; *CLAWSA Members' Exhibition*, The Barbican, London, 1984. Recipient: Concrete Society Award, London, 1970; Civic Trust Award, London, 1970; Special Structural Steel Design Award, London, 1970, 1974; Concrete Industry Board Award, New York, 1971; Bronze Medal, New York Borough of Queens, 1971; *Financial Times* Industrial Architecture Award, London, 1975; Civic Society Conservation Award, Tunbridge Wells, Kent, 1980; Design Awards (2), Dubai Municipality, 1983. Address: GMW Partnership, 18 Manchester Square, London W1M 6AY; and Castle Mill, Berkhamsted, Hertfordshire, England; GMW International Europe, Avenue Moliere 206, 1060 Brussels, Belgium; GMW International Middle East Architects, Wellington House, 17 Union Street, St. Helier, Jersey, Channel Islands; HOK + 4, P.O. Box 5921, Riyadh 11432, Saudi Arabia.

Works:

1947 Trades Union Congress Memorial Building, London (competition project)
1948 Leigham Court Road Residential Development, Streatham, London (competition project)
1950 Infant and junior school, Oxhey, Hertfordshire
1951 Infant and junior school, Little Furze, Hertfordshire
1952 Secondary modern school, St. Julians, St. Albans, Hertfordshire
1953 Master plan for the central redevelopment of the University of Sheffield, Yorkshire
1956 Secondary school, Southborough, Kent
1957 Office buildings, 93-97, 118-126 New Cavendish Street, London
1959 Library and Arts Tower, University of Sheffield, Yorkshire
       Fracture Clinic and Rehabilitation Centre, St. Mary's Hospital, Praed Street, London W.2
       Grammar and modern school, Stokesley, Yorkshire
       Home for Aged Seamen, Belvedere, Erith, Kent
1960 Classrooms and Assembly Hall, Radley College, Berkshire

Castrol House (office building), 174-204 Marylebone Road, London
       E.M.I. House (including GMW Offices), Manchester Square, London W.1
1961 Technical College, Scarborough, Yorkshire
       Department of Pharmacy extension, Oxford University
       Civic Centre, Lincoln (competition project)
1962 University House, University of Sheffield, Yorkshire
       Spencer Steel Works, Newport, Monmouthshire (with Sir Percy Thomas and Son)
1964 Regional Hospital Administration Offices, Headington, Oxford
       District General Hospital, stage I, Kettering, Northamptonshire
       Secondary School, Ecclesfield, Yorkshire
       Residential development, Hermitage Lane, Hampstead, London N.W.2
       Pavilion, West Hendon Playing Fields, London
1965 College of Education, Loughborough, Leicestershire
       Women's Royal Army Corps College, Camberley, Surrey
       Outpatients' and Maternity Departments, Sevenoaks Hospital, Kent
       Arts, Economics and Social Studies Buildings, University of Sheffield, Yorkshire
1966 District General Hospital, Hillingdon, Middlesex
       Equitable Life Assurance Society Headquarters Offices, Coleman Street, London E.C.
       Grammar School, Lutterworth, Leicestershire
       Residential development, St. George-in-the-East, Stepney, London
1967 Boadicea House Computer Building, London Airport, Heathrow
       Rawlins Grammar School, Quorn, Leicestershire
       Holophane Ltd. Factory and Offices, Bletchley, Buckinghamshire
1968 Royal Military College of Science, Shrivenham, Wiltshire
       South Wales Electricity Board Headquarters Offices, St. Mellons, Monmouthshire
       P and O Tower Offices, Leadenhall Street, London
       Administrative Offices, Eponer Steel Works, Newport, Monmouthshire (project)
       British Airways Flight Catering Centre, London Airport, Heathrow (project)
       Chemistry Building, University of Sheffield, Yorkshire
       Samuel Fox and Company Canteen and Dining Rooms, Stockbridge, Derbyshire
1969 Commercial Union Tower Offices, Leadenhall Street, London
       House, Campden Hill, London W.8
       British Airways Freight Terminal, London Airport, Heathrow
1970 The Polytechnic, Sheffield, Yorkshire
       Post Office Savings Department, Durham (with P.O. Directorate of Works)
       HMS Caledonia Naval Barracks, stage I, Rosyth, Scotland
       Royal Air Force Residential Accommodation, West Drayton, Middlesex
       Royal Military Academy, Sandhurst, Camberley, Surrey
       Upper School, Desford, Leicestershire
       British Airways/Air Canada International Airport Terminal, J.F. Kennedy Airport, New York
       Air Canada Services Building, London Airport, Heathrow
       Hoverlloyd Hoverport, Weymouth, Dorset (project)
       Master plan for the District General Hospital, Barnet, Hertfordshire
1971 HMS Caledonia Naval Barracks, stage II, Rosyth, Scotland
       Upper School, Syston, Leicestershire

Gollins, Melvin, Ward: Mobil Court Offices, London, 1983.

Biological Sciences Building, University of Sheffield, Yorkshire

Library extension, Cambridge University, Grange Road, Cambridge

Teaching hospital, Goldhawk Road, Hammersmith, London (project)

1972 Teacher training college, Portsmouth, Hampshire

District General Hospital, Harold Wood, Essex

1973 Manufacturers Life Insurance Company Headquarters Offices, Stevenage, Hertfordshire

Woking Centre Swimming Pool, Surrey

District General Hospital, stage II, Kettering, Northamptonshire

1974 Junior mixed and infant school, Chipperfield, Hertfordshire

Department of Drama Building, Portsmouth College of Education, Hampshire

Lennox Estate, stage I, Wandsworth, London

1975 Equitable Life House, Walton Street, Aylesbury, Buckinghamshire

Kingfisher House Office Building, Aylesbury, Buckinghamshire

Centre Halls, Woking, Surrey

New Covent Garden Market, Nine Elms, London S.W.8

Central Fish Market, Djeddah, Saudi Arabia (competition project)

Town Hall, Medina, Saudi Arabia (competition project)

District General Hospital, stage III, Kettering, Northamptonshire

Michelin Tyre Company Headquarters Offices, Fulham Road, London S.W.3

Feasibility study for the Munich 2 Airport

Holiday resort and hotel, Cesme Peninsula, Turkey (with Transport and Tourism Technicians Ltd.)

Westminster City School, Nine Elms, London S.W.8 (project)

Royal Opera House additions, Covent Garden, London W.C.2

1978 Mombasa Airport Development, Kenya

American Express International Banking Corporation Headquarters Offices, Brighton, Sussex (with Peter Wood and Partners)

Banque Belge, London

Zurich House, Portsmouth, Hampshire

Crown House, Woking, Surrey

Housing renovations, 2 and 4 Calthorpe Street, London W.C.1

Mamos Garage Site, Stanmore, Middlesex

1979 Pedestrian Zone, Barrett Street, London W.1

1982 Shell Centre new entrance, York Road, London S.E.1

National Westminster Bank refurbishment, Southwark, London

CIBC Building alterations, 55 Bishopsgate, London E.C.2

1982 Equitable/Life Insurance Headquarters, 154-156 Fenchurch Street, London E.C.3

Standard Telephones and Cables semiconductor factory, Foots Cray, Kent

1983 Second Airport Master Plan Study, Hong Kong (project)

Mobil Headquarters Offices, Aldwych, London

Equitable/Life Insurance Company Headquarters, Aylesbury, Buckinghamshire

Stafford House Office Headquarters, King William Street, London E.C.4

Shell Centre restaurant and kitchen refurbishment, York Road, London S.E.1

Shell Mex building refurbishment, The Strand, London W.C.2

Townsend Thoresen Office Headquarters, Dover, Kent

New Development in Historic Towns exhibition layouts, Gewerbe Museum, Basle, Switzerland

Arab Architecture exhibition layouts, Royal Institute of British Architects, London

1983- BOC Headquarters, Windlesham, Surrey

Municipal Swimming Pool, Exmouth, Devon

1984 *CLAWSA Exhibition* layouts, The Barbican Centre, London

Publications:

By GMW PARTNERSHIP: book—*Architecture of the Gollins Melvin Ward Partnership*, with an introduction by Tony Aldous, London 1974.

On GMW PARTNERSHIP: articles—"Imaginative Approach to New Market Development" in *Asian Building and Construction* (Hong Kong), November 1973; "Perspective: In the Swim" in *Building Design* (London), November 1973; "Two Office Buildings in the City of London" in *Bauen und Wohnen* (Zurich), January 1974; "Spring Start on 5M. Portsmouth Offices" in *Building* (London), January 1974; "Insurers Cut Their Ground Risks" in *Contract Journal* (London), March 1974; "Woking Pool" in *Surveyor* (London), May 1974; "Contract Awarded for Zurich Insurance Headquarters at Portsmouth" in *Building* (London), November 1974;

"Business as Usual, or Almost, at the New Covent Garden Market" in *The Architect* (London), December 1974; "Flower Power Relies on Steel" in *Design* (London), January 1975; "New Covent Garden Market, Nine Elms, London" in *Bauwelt* (Berlin), January 1975; "Architect's Approach to Architecture" in *The Architects' Journal* (London), February 1975; "Good Gollins" by Maurice Cooper in *Building Design* (London), February 1975; "A 30-year-old Practice Looking at Architecture" by David Crawford in *Building* (London), February 1975; "Woking Centre Pool" in *The Architects' Journal* (London), May 1975; "Woking's New Swimming Pool" in *Concrete Quarterly* (London), October/December 1975; "VIP Treatment for BSC's Computer House" in *Building* (London), December 1975; "Design Confidence in Assurance Offices" in *Interior Design* (London), September 1976; "A Tale of Two City Banks" in *Building Design* (London), March 1978; "Shades of Steel" in *The Architects' Journal* (London), 26 April 1978; "All things bright and beautiful" in *Building* (London), 2 June 1978; "Roehampton goes trad" in *Building Design* (London), 30 June 1978; "American Express builds on the English Channel in gleaming white plastic" in *Architectural Record* (New York), August 1978; "An Appraisal of Banque Belge, Leadenhall Street, London" in *Interior Design* (New York), October 1978; "Brash but Effective" in *Building Design* (London), 4 December 1981; "Mainstream Design Flows On" in *Building* (London), 18 February 1983; "Project that takes passive energy seriously" in *Architectural Record* (New York), June 1983; "Aus dem Lot Geraten" in *MD: Moebel Interior Design* (Leinfelden, Germany), 6 June 1983; "Opera House Extension", in *Concrete Quarterly* (London), July-September 1983; "Building for Quality", in *Building* (London), 14 October 1983; "King-Size Commission" in *Building* (London), 4 November 1983.

In 1947 when the Gollins Melvin Ward Partnership was formed and when the partnership's work was confined to the re-habilitation of bomb destroyed dwellings for the London boroughs the partners realized that only by combining all of their resources and skills and eschewing the cult of personality could design and technical abilities be developed sufficiently to face the demands and challenges of the 1950's and 1960's. These skills stood the partnership in good stead, for as the new generation grew up, the demands in the field of education, first for primary and secondary schools then technical colleges and universities as well as colleges for teachers' training and further education, increased immensely. Simultaneously with this ever increasing programme went the need for the construction and extension of buildings for the National Health Service, admission units, clinics, general and specialized hospitals and post-graduate teaching facilities.

Parallel with this local authority government and corporation work, the partners developed also the commercial side of the partnership, starting with comparatively restricted office schemes in London. The scope of this division gradually increased to include high-rise developments in the city of London, many for the headquarters the leading insurance and banking firms.

The Partnership now has, in addition to 15 partners, 9 associates and 1 consultant and an average total staff of 150. The practice has experience in most aspects of building—educational, medical, commercial, residential—and has developed specialist groups with detailed knowledge of user requirements and an awareness of the complexities of present day and future construction and environmental technology. The principle determining the character of the organization is that each of the specialist groups be headed by a partner or partners supported by an associate and project architect who provide the basic link with the client during the life of the project. The policy remains that a partner or partners are always readily available for discussion with the client on all matters of policy and administration, and are actively involved in the progress of each project through its various phases. Computer techniques are used for accounting, job costing, budgeting, forward planning and pre-contract and contract programmes, architectural design, architectural drafting and services coordination. The differing age groups of the partners has allowed the structure of the practice to be so developed that there is a continuing process of growth, ensuring in particular that clients with long-term development schemes can rely on a sequence of service.

There are separate sections concerned with graphic design and printing, model making and interior design, working in close liaison with the architectural teams, specializing in the selection of furnishings, fittings and materials together with the preparation of detailed schemes in all types of interiors. There is also a separate section concerned with landscape design in all its aspects, both in the UK and abroad. Considerable experience has also been gained abroad on research and development studies, particularly in relation to the design of airports, shopping centres, offices, hotels, holiday resorts and hospitals. With overseas projects the policy is normally to collaborate with local architects by setting up a joint overseas office. Overseas offices are located in Belgium and Riyadh, Saudi Arabia.

—Anthony Gregson

GONZÁLEZ de LEÓN, Teodoro.

Mexican. Born in Mexico City, 29 May 1926. Educated at the Universidad Nacional Autonoma, National School of Architecture, Mexico City, 1942-47, Dip.Arch. 1947. Married Ulalume Ibañez in 1948; children: Berenice, Diego, and Sofia. Worked in the architectural studio of Le Corbusier, Paris, 1948-49. In private practice, Mexico City, since 1949: in partnership with Abraham Zabludovsky, *q.v.*, since 1968. Director of Rural Housing, National Housing Institute, 1956-58; Technical Director, Council of Economic and Social Planning, Mexico City, 1958; Adviser, Operating and Banking Discount Fund for Housing, Mexico City, 1966-70, and Public Works Department, Mexico City, 1970-76. Adviser to the Ministry of Public Education, Mexico City, 1978-82. Visiting Professor, Pratt Institute, New York, 1982, 1983. Exhibitions: *XX Centuries of Mexican Architecture*. El Colegio de México, Mexico City, 1965, and toured Mexico; Colegio Nacional de Arquitectos, Mexico City, 1969; *Arquitectura Contemporánea Mexicana*, Galeria Misrachi, Mexico City, 1969; *The Photography of Architecture and Design*, Los Angeles, 1977; *Mexican Architecture* Mexico City, 1978; *Transformations in Modern Architecture*, Museum of Modern Art, New York, 1979; *Modern Architecture: Mexico*, SCI-ARC Architecture Gallery, Los Angeles, 1981; *Latinamerica 82*, Berlin, 1982; *Contemporary Third World Architecture*, Pratt Manhattan Center Gallery, New York, 1983 (toured the United States). Recipient: First Prize, with Abraham Zabludovsky, El Colegio de México Competition, Mexico City, 1973; Premio Nacional de Ciencia y Artes (with Abraham Zabludovsky), Mexico City, 1982. Emeritus Member, Sociedad de Arquitectos Mexicanos, 1978; Honorary Fellow, American Institute of Architects, 1983. Member of the Colegio de Arquitectos de Mexico, 1966; Academia de Artes, Mexico City, 1984. Address: Avenida Mexico 99 B, 06100 Mexico, D.F., Mexico.

Works:

1953 Catan House, Reforma 2135, Mexico City (with Armando Franco)

1957 Orozco Housing Estate, Guadalajara, Jalisco, Mexico
1957/
58 Rural towns research project, Mexico (with Luis Lesur)
1958 Plan for Barra de Navidad, Jalisco, Mexico
1962 Sahagun Housing Estate, Hidalgo, Mexico
1962/
64 Urban research project, Mexico (with Luis Lesur)
1964 IMSS Housing Estate, Toluca, Mexico
1965 Bodega Dina Building, Sahagun, Hidalgo, Mexico
1966 Sears Roebuck Building, Guadalajara, Mexico
     School of Law, University of Tamaulipas, Tampico, Mexico
1969 Gonzáles de León House, Galeana 107, Mexico City
1972 Office building, Leibnitz 20, Mexico City
1973 Weekend house, Cocoyoc, Morelos, Mexico
1978 Ex-Hacienda de Emmedio (1150 units), Mexico City
1981 Town House, Guadalquivir 82, Mexico City
1984 Nacional Financiera Computer Center, Mexico City (with Francisco Serrano)
     Administrative Center, Villahermosa, Tobasco, Mexico (with Francisco Serrano)
     Garrido Park remodelling, Villahermosa, Tabasco, Mexico (with Francisco Serrano and Aurelio Nuño)

The following works are with Abraham Zabludovsky:

1963/
77 Eight planning surveys for various Mexican cities
1968 José Luis Cuevas House, Galeana 109, Mexico City
1969/
70 Office building, Nuevo León and Campeche Street, Mexico City
   Office building, Campos Eliseos 169, Mexico City
   Office building, Presidente Masarik 191, Mexico City
1969/
71 Mixcoac Towers, Mixcoac-Lomas de Plateros, Mexico City
1970/
73 Vallejo-La Patera (1418 apartments), Avenida Vallejo/Torres/de los Cien Metros/Margarita M. de Juárez, Mexico City (with Armando Franco)
1971 Apartment buildings (2), Avenida de las Fuentes and Fuente de la Templanza, Tecamachalco, Mexico City
1972 Apartment buildings (2), Victoria 34, Echegaray, Mexico
   Sports and Civic Center (public square; movie theatre, library; club; gymnasium; swimming pool; etc.), Sor Juan Inés de la Cruz 45, Tlainepantla, Mexico
1972/
73 Cuauhtemoc District Municipal Building, Mexico City (with Luis Antonio Zapiain and Jaime Ortiz Monasterio)
   Apartment buildings (2), Fuente de las Pirámides 20 and 22, Tecamachalco, Mexico City (with Rosemberg)
1973 Conasupo Branch Stores, throughout Mexico INFONAVIT Building (administrative offices for workers' housing development), Mexico City
1973/
75 Mexican Embassy, Brasilia (with J. Francisco Serrano)
1974/
75 El Colegio de México (library; seminar rooms;

Teodoro González de Léon and Abraham Zabludovsky: El Colegio de Mexico, Mexico City, 1975.

computer center; offices; auditorium; cafeteria; parking), Mexico City

1975 25-story apartment building, Tecamachalco, Mexico City

1979 National Pedagogical University, Mexico City

1981 Tamayo Museum Complex, Chapultepec Park, Mexico City

1982 Office Tower Block, Avenida Palmas, Mexico City

1984 Cultural and Services Building, Chichen-Itza, Yucatan, Mexico

Publications:

By GONZÁLEZ de LEÓN: books—*Barra de Navidad: Survey of an Area,* Mexico City 1958; *Housing in Mexico,* Mexico City 1960; *Research on Housing in Eleven Mexican Cities,* 3 volumes, Mexico City 1966; *Catalogue of Cartograms,* compiler, Mexico City 1969; *Arquitectura Contemporanea Mexicana: Obras de Teodoro Gonzalez de Leon y Abraham Zabludovsky,* Mexico City 1971; *Ocho Conjuntos de Habitacion,* with Abraham Zabludovsky, Mexico City 1976; articles—"Problems of Sunlight and Control of Temperature in the Work of Le Corbusier" in *Espacios* (Mexico City), 1949; "Le Corbusier" in *Dialogos* (Mexico City), January 1966; "The Twentieth Century Stone" in *Concrete International* (Detroit), January 1984.

Although every artist tends to emphasize those aspects of his work which he feels owe least to other people, an unprejudiced analysis will often reveal that—as T.S. Eliot once suggested—not only the best but also the most individual part of a work of art may well consist in the recreation of what is *given*. In architecture each local and personal recreation enriches the current formal language on an International plane, provides a universal patrimony. That is why, from among the varied elements that come together in our work, I should like to draw attention to the presence of two constants in which I feel that the *given* is transformed in precisely this way into something creative. These two constants are the patio and the special concrete finish to our buildings.

The patio, with its age-old history, is an important element in Mexico's architectural tradition. We inherited it from the two civilizations that converged to give us the culture we have today: on the one hand, the pre-Hispanic; and on the other, the Spanish, with its own version of Mediterranean architecture. In the Toltec, Zapotec, Mayan and Aztec cultures the more complex structures were all organized around patios. The same was true of the majority of the Renaissance, Baroque and Neo-Classical buildings— monasteries, hospitals, palaces and houses— constructed in Mexico from the Conquest onwards (countless examples of these buildings still exist, despite the systematic destruction they have suffered over the years). In the present day the patio continues to offer the most natural way of articulating space in complex-program buildings. The task of integrating the patio into our work involved "translating" it into personal and contemporary terms. The syntax of this new language varies, of course, according to the specific purpose that is to be given to the building under construction. We have designed patios of different sizes and shapes: square, rectangular and trapezoidal; open, semi-covered and completely covered. But in everycase we have given them a use analogous to their traditional one: not that of a void designed to be contemplated (of the sort that we find, for example, in some of Mies van der Rohe's projects), but that of a central space in which people circulate and which at the same time organizes the distributions of the rest of the building. The patio in this way becomes the most significant element in the whole construction: an area of encounter, exchange and coexistence; a symbol of the institution that the building houses. Mention should also be made at this point of the experience of spatial perception that the patio makes possible. Whoever crosses it, percieves *from inside it* the totality of the mass that has been constructed; appreciates its distribution and its scale; and also captures the changing profile of the enclosure, which, breaking the visual monotony, alters with every step one takes. All this necessarily happens every time one goes from one part of the building to another, whilst it is quite impossible in a building conceived of as a block; neither the space available in an elevator nor the short time it takes to go up or come down in it encourage human and interdisciplinary relations between people on different floors; each floor is an island. Furthermore, the totality and scale of such buildings can only be appreciated from the outside..

The other constant in our work, the finish to the buildings, is the fruit of long years of experimentation. It came about as a result of an attempt not only to provide an alternative to the monotonous appearance of the usual concrete finish, but also to invent a type of technology that could make the most of a labor force as deficient as ours. The finish that we elaborated represented an innovation in the field and has since been adopted by others. It involves a process of deep chiselling to expose the marble chips used as an aggregate in the cement. The result is a warm, craft-like texture akin to that of natural stones, reflecting the fact that human hands have been at work on it. In addition, this material offers important financial advantages since it means that low-cost wood forms can be used; also, unlike the usual exposed concrete, it can be repaired. Finally, it resists the passage of time—which is a basic requirement of all architecture—living up to Le Corbusier's definition of concrete as "the stone of the 20th century".

This brief analysis of two constants in our work once again poses the question of where creation really begins (and not only in architecture, but in the other artistic spheres as well). Complete novelty would seem to be an impossible goal without that total destruction of language proposed in a different context by the Dadaists. For language "speaks us": it determines in part what we produce, by providing us wth the tools that make thought and communication pssible. But there can be no art without language and history teaches us that the languages of art, far from being a dead weight, are susceptible of infinite transformations. Furthermore, a completely new conception would imply the negation of everything "spoken" by architects from other countries or from other periods in time. And here history shows us that the great styles—from the Gothic, the Renaissance and the Baroque through to the modern movement—embody the spirit of the time and therefore have no regard for geographical frontiers; and that, similarly, no temporal frontiers are ever closed for good, since a style can always be revived. In short, the new in art is the "translation" into contemporary, vernacular terms of a language used at other times and in other places. There is novelty not only because this translation in the work of an individual who is unique, but also because the artist is an individual who uses an additional element in his explorations: an innate gift, a sense of surprise. Once the new has been born, the circle begins again. The creative element will cross frontiers and will be the object of local translations, will survive its owntime and be transformed into languages whose syntax is still unknown to us.

—Teodoro González de León.

See ZABLUDOVSKY, Abraham

GOODY, Joan Edelman.

American. Born Joan Edelman in New York City, 1 December 1935. Studied at the University of Paris, France, 1954-55; Cornell University, Ithaca, New York, B.A. 1956; Harvard Graduate School of Design, Cambridge, Massachusetts, M.Arch. 1960. Married the architect Marvin E. Goody in 1960 (died, 1980); Peter Davison in 1984. Since 1961, Principal, Goody, Clancy and Associates, Inc., Boston. Instructor, 1961-66, Board Member, 1975-80, Boston Architectural Center; Assistant Professor, 1973-76, Design Critic, 1976-80, and Eliot Noyes Visiting Critic, 1985, Harvard Graduate School of Design, Cambridge, Massachusetts. Member of the Boston Landmarks Commission, since 1976; Board Member, Boston Society of Architects, 1983-85. Recipient: First Prize, Winthrop Housing for the Elderly Competition, Massachusetts, 1974, and Eagle Ridge Ski Resort Competition, Colorado, 1981; Housing Award, Boston Society of Architects, 1978, 1979, 1981; Award of Merit, 1978, North East Regional Council Award, 1979, and National Honor Award, 1980, American Institute of Architects; Record Houses Award, *Architectural Record,* 1979; Merit Award, 1982, and Performance Award, 1985 (three), Associated General Contractors, Massachusetts; Owens-Corning Fiberglass Energy Conservation Award, 1983; Urban Planning Award, *Progressive Architecture,* 1983; Outstanding Planning Program Award, American Planning Association, 1983. Honorary Member, Boston Architectural Center, 1982. Address: Goody, Clancy and Associates, Inc., 334 Boylston Street, Boston, Massachusetts 02116, U.S.A.

Works:

1961 Field House, Camp Kenwood, Potter Place, New Hampshire

1968 Byron Street Townhouses, Boston

1970 Jewish Family and Children's Service Building, Boston

1970/
75 Papoose Pond Development, Norway, Maine

1971 Burton-Conner Apartments, Massachusetts Institute of Technology, Cambridge

1974 Faculty Club, Massachusetts Institute of Technology, Cambridge

Administration Building, University of Massachusetts, Boston Harbor

1977 Heritage Gardens Housing for the Elderly, Winthrop, Massachusetts

1978 Student Housing, Bridgewater State College, Massachusetts

Main Academic Building Master Plan, Simmons College, Boston

Heaton Court Housing, Stockbridge, Massachusetts

1980 Summer Street Housing for the Elderly, Hyde Park, Massachusetts

Latin Way Housing, Tufts University, Medford, Massachusetts

Wood Ridge Housing, North Andover, Massachusetts

1981 Hillside Housing, Tufts University, Medford, Massachusetts

Atwater Kent Laboratories, Worcester Polytechnic Institute, Massachusetts

Eagleridge Resort Community, Steamboat Springs, Colorado (competition project)

1982 Agassiz House and Hemenway Gym renovations, Radcliffe College, Cambridge, Massachusetts

1983 Village at Fawcett's Pond, Hyannis, Massachusetts

State Transportation Building, Boston

1984 Paine Webber Building, 265 Franklin Street, Boston

Whitehead Institute for Biomedical Research, Cambridge, Massachusetts

1985 West Broadway Comprehensive Renewal Program, South Boston

1986 HCW Building, 99 Sumer Street, Boston
      Faunce House renovations, Brown University, Providence, Rhode Island
1989 Harbor Point Housing, Columbia Point, Boston

Publications:

By GOODY: book—*New Architecture in Boston*, Cambridge, Massachusetts 1965; articles—"Special Design and Specification Problems in Rehabilitation and Re-use", with others, in *Architectural Record* (New York), December 1982; "A Rare and Rich Response to Context: Keio University Library, Tokyo" in *Architectural Record* (New York), May 1983; "New Directions" in *Architecture* (Washington, D.C.), May 1985.

On GOODY: articles—"The Conquest of Space" in *House and Garden* (New York), May 1968; "River Street Townhouse" in *House Beautiful* (New York), Spring/Summer 1972; "University of Massachusetts Administration Building" in *Architecture Plus* (New York), 4 March 1974; "Multis for the Elderly" in *Housing* (New York), July 1978; "Winthrop Housing" in *Architectural Record* (New York), March 1979; "Building Types Study 531: Record Apartments" in *Architectural Record* (New York), mid-May 1979; "Calm Excellence in a Retirement Housing Complex" in *AIA Journal* (Washington, D.C.), May 1980; "Housing for the Elderly" in *Architektur und Wettbewerbe* (Stuttgart), March 1981; "Eagleridge Design Competition" in *Architectural Record* (New York), February 1982; "West Broadway Comprehensive Renewal, Boston" in *Progressive Architecture* (New York), January 1983; "Radcliffe College Renovations" in *Interior Design* (New York), October 1983; "The Village at Fawcett's Pond" in *Architectural Record* (New York), February 1985; "State Transportation Building" in *Progressive Architecture* (New York), April 1985.

*

As a principal of an architectural firm working in one of America's oldest cities, my buildings are usually set in an established architectural context, although a continuously changing one. I see our work adding its particular theme to those already present (and those which will follow) in the composition of the urban whole. Travels abroad to even older cities, and out West to newer ones, convince me that a place which reflects a variety of incremental changes over many years is usually richer, more humane and more interesting than anything created at one time and maintained in its pure, original form.

The major issue in building today is the scale at which we can—and often are asked—to build. We can dig deeper, climb higher, span further by far than former generations could do. Our programs often call for an agglomeration of space far greater than the scales of anything around them: government entities are bigger, as are corporate offices and shopping centers. We are in danger of overwhelming if not obliterating our past.

The creation itself—particularly when it is a larger scale building or complex—is the product of many, whether acknowledged or not. As principal-in-charge of a particular project, I am ultimately responsible for the decisions and the work expresses my goals and philosophy. But contributions range from the informal consultation with partners and associates to the creative suggestions of many other team members. Beyond that, many of those who will be affected by the project (as owners, users, neighbors, financers or governmental regulators) have a strong, and potentially beneficial influence. If integrated properly, the reflection of their diverse views can also enrich the building as well as make it better suited to its time and place. As the architect I try to create the theme that will unite these many lines in harmony, try to find the order that will support their diversity, both current and future.

Whether a major new construction (such as one of our downtown office buildings), the renovation of an older building or a combination of both, the available means and materials of construction are always a major determinant of the possible expression. Building in New England, with its construction traditions and harsh climate, certain materials and forms reappear frequently among the reasonable choices. Thus our work typically is clad in a continuous skin (be it clapboard, brick or granite) more often obscuring structure than expressing it. Pitched roofs are frequently used in our small scale residential construction and the warm colors of local brickyards are often our selection for exterior use in this chilly climate. Where possible, covered spaces (or protected, south facing exterior ones) are formed where groups may want to gather. The old town square (or Commons) often becomes an atrium in our large buildings, the well (or pump) a waterfall among planters. But the organization of space to provide a place where the community (of residents or worker) may meet and gather remains a goal in all of our projects.

—Joan E. Goody

Joan E. Goody: Paine Webber Building, Boston, 1984.

"The organization of space to provide a place where the community (of residents or workers) may meet and gather remains a goal in all our projects." The words of architect Joan Goody reverberate around New England, testified by her twenty-four years of work in the area. Though herself a native New Yorker, Goody has been sensitive to the construction traditions and the harsh climate of the northern states, perhaps influenced by her husband and partner Marvin Goody of Boston. Her buildings are typically clad in a continuous skin of clapboard, brick or granite, with pitched roofs and warmly-coloured bricks to offset the chilly climate. Goody also favours protected or covered spaces facing south to encourage public congregation; the old town square (or Commons) becomes an atrium in her large buildings.

Yet Goody's emphasis on spatial organization that fosters a sense of community earned her reputation. She rejects the role of the modern Western architect whose tasks often demand an agglomeration of space far greater than the scale of anything around it. In an era when shopping centers, corporate offices and government entities are overwhelming, her objective is to conserve the spatial proportions so vital to that community heritage. Her regard for those who will be affected by the project has brought her distinction. Creating themes that integrate the diverse views harmoniously and anticipating both current and future needs, Goody behaves much like a diplomat and a sociologist.

A housing complex for the elderly in Stockbridge, Massachusettes, designed by Goody, Clancy and Associates, Inc. in 1978, is demonstrative of her ambitions. Once a rambling resort hotel, this low-income, government-subsidized complex is noted for its delightfully planned courtyard, careful detailing of traditional forms and materials, simple shapes rich in texture and subtle integration into the landscape. Nostalgic amenities such as rocking chairs on long porches, too, make it reminiscent of the once-enjoyed leisure hotel. Goody's concern for the project's efficiency is evidenced by the two exposures within each unit, creating cross ventilation and eliminating the need for air conditioning.

Much of Goody's work has reinforced the value of contextualism. Among the most notable is the 1983 Massachusetts Department of Transportation Building in Boston, whose form, appearance and very operation respond to its physical and social surroundings. The eight-storey structure with its irregular perimeter and brick cladding resembles the architecture of neighboring buildings. A convex frame maintains the curving street line. Its features similarly respond to its social context. To revitalize the neighborhood and stimulate street-level activity, a retail-space is situated on the ground floor and an atrium available for community meetings or cultural events lies at the base. But the building is reputed for its method of conserving energy, a contextualism of a political and economic kind. In typical Goody fashion, the project contains centralized variable air volume heat pumps capable of recycling heat lost from people, lights and equipment. Solar panels on the roof furnish the building with 82 per cent of its hot water needs. A cooling system designed to reduce the amount of mechanical refrigeration from 2000 to 1200 tons is also included in the Goody/Clancy strategy to construct a neighborly building able to heat and cool itself. The project has been criticized, however, for its lack of aesthetic appeal; too self-effacing with awkward and unresolved fenestration, some claim. But what the building lacks in visual aesthetics, it makes up for in its functional accomplishments.

A housing project in South Boston illustrates another construction in which her spatial demands are executed. The development consisted of 27 identical three-storey walk-up buildings arranged in a once vandalized superblock with no through traffic, housing a thousand veterans and their families. But the complex will soon become more livable and reintegrated into the neighborhood by Goody's strategy to eliminate the existing superblock configuration. A new "Main Street" will link community facilities and courtyards, and the creation of seven "villages," each with its own design identity, will decentralize the project. The number of units will be reduced by enlarging some of the apartments, many in duplex configurations with their own front and back doors, and by demolishing sections of existing buildings to mitigate the institutional character. Tenants will finally retain their privacy when the courtyards are converted to individual backyards.

Goody is not only an effective architect, she is also an educator. A lecturer in residential design, her buildings, too, metaphorically profess the cultural insistence on retaining individual space and privacy. In doing so, paradoxically, they enhance the community. Functional, practical and inviting, conveying an aura of the traditional, Goody's work adapts to modern society and supports the diversity of the community at large.

—Carolyn Cole

GOWAN, James.

British. Born in Glasgow, Scotland, 18 October 1923. Educated at the Glasgow School of Art, Department of Architecture, 1940-42; Kingston School of Art, Surrey, with tutors Philip Powell, *q.v.*, James Cubitt, *q.v.*, and Peter Chamberlin, *q.v.*: *Chamberlin Powell and Bon,* 1946-48. Served as a radar instructor in the Royal Air Force, 1942-46. Married Margaret Aileen Barry in 1946; children: Lindy and Joanna. Worked as an occasional assistant to architect Brian O'Rorke, London, 1946-50; architect with Powell and Moya, London, 1950-51, with the New Town Corporation, Stevenage, Hertfordshire, 1952-53, and with Lyons, Israel and Ellis, *q.v.*: *Lyons, Israel, Ellis and Gray,* London, 1954-56; Partner, firm of James Stirling, *q.v.*, and James Gowan, London, 1956-63. Since 1964, in private practice, London. Tutor at the Architectural Association School, London, 1958-60, 1970-72; Visiting Professor, Princeton University, New Jersey, 1965; Banister Fletcher Professor, University College, London, 1975; Visiting Professor, Simon Bolivar University, Caracas, Venezuela, 1982; Senior Tutor in Environmental Design, Royal College of Art, London, since 1983. Member of the Council of the Architectural Association, 1963-64. Exhibitions: Architectural Association, London, 1978. *Triennale,* Milan, 1973; Architectural Association, London, 1978. Recipient: Reynolds Memorial Award, Leicester, 1965. Associate of the Royal Institute of British Architects, 1950. Address: 2 Linden Gardens, London W2, England.

Works:

1957 Expandable House (project: with James Stirling)
1958 Private house, Baring Road, Cowes, Isle of Wight (with James Stirling)
 Low-rise flats, Ham Common, Richmond, London (with James Stirling)
1960 Private house, Grenville Place, London (with James Stirling)
 Churchill College, Cambridge (project; with James Stirling)
1961 Low-rise houses and flats, Preston, Lancashire (with James Stirling)
 Selwyn College, Cambridge (project; with James Stirling)
1963 Dining Hall, Brunswick Park Primary School, London (with James Stirling)
 Engineering Department, University of Leicester (with James Stirling)
1964 Old people's dwellings, Blackheath, London (with James Stirling)
 Children's home, Frogmore, Wandsworth, London (with James Stirling)
 Private house, West Heath Road, Hampstead, London (with Frank Newby)
1965 Furniture warehouse, Birkbeck Mews, London (project; with Stephen Revess)
1967 Private house, St. Davids, Wales
 City Hall, Amsterdam (project; with Brian Richards)
 Low-rise housing, Creek Road, Greenwich, London (with Stephen Revess)
1968 Swimming pool, West Heath Road, Hampstead, London (with Frank Newby)
 Neighbourhood housing, Runcorn, Cheshire (project)
 Old people's dwellings, Byfleet, Surrey (project)
 Low-rise housing, Trafalgar Road, Greenwich, London (with Stephen Revess)
 Laminated timber furniture (with C. S. Schreiber)
1969 Luxury flat, Fountain House, Mayfair, London
1970 Unit warehouses, Pages Walk, London (with Stephen Revess)
1971 Unit warehouses, Crimscott Street, London (with Stephen Revess)

1972 Rural housing, Bembridge, Isle of Wight (with Stephen Revess)
 Nelson House restoration, Rotherhithe Street, London (with Jampel and Partners)
 Redevelopment, Oban, Argyll, Scotland (project)
1973 Warehouse and offices, Evelyn Street, London
1974 Unit warehouses, Blackhorse Road, London (with Jampel and Partners)
 Family health clinic, Polygon Road, London (project)
 Rural housing, East Hanningfield, Essex
1978 Rural Housing II, East Hanningfield, Essex
1980 Chester Villa, Cheshire
1982 Sainsbury D.I.Y. Centre, Bromley, Kent (project; With Tony McIntyre)
 Templewood Avenue Housing, Hampstead, London (project)
1984 Temple Hill House, Hampstead, London

Publications:

By GOWAN: books—*Projects: Architectural Association 1946-71,* London 1972; *A Continuing Experiment: Learning and Teaching at the Architectural Association,* London 1975; articles—"Le Corbusier Exhibition in London" in *Architect and Building News* (London), February 1959; "Architectural Association: Review of the Annual Exhibition" in *Architectural Association Journal* (London), June 1959; "Curriculum: A Structure for Teaching Architecture" in *Architectural Review* (London), December 1959; "Notes on American Architecture" in *Prospecta* (New Haven, Connecticut), no. 7, 1963; "British Ministry of Works Exhibition" in *The Architects Journal* (London), January 1964; "Le Corbusier" in *RIBA Journal* (London), October 1965; "Architectural Education and Its Technical Aspects" in *The Architects' Journal* (London), November 1970; "AA Architects" in *Architectural Association Quarterly* (London), Spring 1973; "Five Architects: Review of the New York Five" in *The Architects' Journal* (London), May 1975; "Millbank Exhibition: Sketches and Comments" in *Architectural Design* (London), Autumn 1977; "No. 13, Lincoln's Inn Fields" in *Architecture + Urbanism* (Tokyo), April 1980; "The MacGlurglen Phenomenon" in *The Architects' Journal* (London), 28 January 1981; "East Hanningfield" in *Architectural Design* (London), March/April 1981; "Chester Villa" in *International Architect* (London), no. 1, 1982; "Preface" in *Mike Gold,* exhibition catalogue, London 1982; "Introduction" in *Model Futures,* exhibition catalogue, London 1983; "Design and circumstance" and "A Place for Propriety" in *Architectural Design* (London), December 1983.

On GOWAN: books—*New English Architecture* by Robert Maxwell, Stuttgart 1972; *Multiple Family Housing* by David Mackay, London 1977; *James Gowan, Architectural Monographs 3,* edited by David Dunster, London 1978; *British Buildings* by Anthony McIntyre, London 1984; *The Modern House* by David Mackay, Barcelona 1984; articles—in *Casabella* (Milan), October 1972; in *Arquitecturas Bis* (Barcelona), July 1974; "Unbuilt England" by Peter Cook in *Architecture + Urbanism* (Tokyo), October 1977; "East Hanningfield" in *Architectural Review* (London), January 1978; "East Hanningfield" in *L'Architecture d'aujourd'hui* (Paris), June 1979; "East Hanningfield" in *Spazio e società* (Milan), September 1979; "Chester Villa" in *Architectural Review* (London), January 1980; "Chester Villa" in *The Architects' Journal* (London), February 1981; "Chester Villa" by Anthony McIntyre in *Spazio e società* (Milan), March 1982; "Chester Villa" by David Gray in *The Architects' Journal* (London), January 1983; "Chester Villa" by Peter Buchanan in *Architectural Review* (London), February 1983;

James Gowan: Chester Villa, Cheshire, 1980.

"Chester Villa" by Alain Pelissier in *Techniques et architecture* (Paris), September 1983; "Temple Hill House" in *Architectural Review* (London), January 1984; film—*Two Architects: James Stirling and James Gowan,* British Aluminium 1965.

Some years back I wrote a programme for the Architectural Association Diploma School: the domestic refurbishment of the room I worked in ... large, bay-windowed, scruffy. Unusually so, there was a big response; the projects filled several rooms and were restless with ideas and complications. One project was different and, I thought then, a little facile, but the image has stayed with me. It is an ink-line drawing of the room, empty, and as it was when new: clean, with the ornamental plasterwork perfect and precise. There was a second drawing which was a repeat of the first, except for an open suitcase in the middle of the floor. This was crammed and neatly compartmented with everything one needed: a heater, bedding, books ... all trimmed down to essentials.

The drawings and their implications have needled me occasionally since. Though, I regard myself as observant in architectural matters, I had never seen my room as a fresh, fine space ... only as a room in transition, genteelly fighting off seediness. Secondly, the drawings arrested or questioned my thoughts on architecture ... the grand spread of design and action that was unlikely ever to be realized. And the possibility that architecture of the future would have more to do with a shrinking compass of events, the room, significantly, and perhaps its enrichment with

cultural symbols and gestures not attainable by any other means. There are signs enough that the promise for many may be no better than a slice of old building stock, andour nearest visual experience of what this might be is through photographs and films of the immediate post-revolutionary Russia ... stark rooms and stripped, shared establishments. In such a condition, the architect's role, if it continued to exist at all, could shrink to advising on the most simple requirements—where best to place a precious nail in the wall.

—James Gowan

James Gowan is remembered by many architects as the co-designer with James Stirling of what was perhaps the most startlingly original work of architecture to be built in Britain since the war—the Engineering Department at the University of Leicester, completed in 1963. This was a milestone in British architecture for a number of reasons: it exemplified a new and expressive use of materials—particularly patent glazing which had previously had only industrial uses; a new and bold formal articulation that was much limited in subsequent years; and, perhaps most significantly, a departure from the influence of Le Corbusier which had until then dominated British architecture.

The Leicester building was the last major work on which Stirling and Gowan worked together, and it represents the summit of their mutual achievement: neither architect has since produced its equal. Since the partnership split up, Stirling has enjoyed great

public acclaim, producing a series of brillantly inventive though often controversial works which unfortunately seem to lack the intellectual rigour of those produced by the partnership. Gowan, meanwhile, has worked mainly on small projects, remaining renowned within the profession but without much public recognition. Some call him an "architect's architect," meaning that his work is better appreciated by fellow professionals than by laymen, but he might more justly be called a client's architect, for he leaves in his wake a train of satisfied clients, many of whom have returned to him with further commissions. He is careful on every occasion to produce a design appropriate to its purpose and surroundings, so that his work is varied in style, somewaht unpredictable, and often baffling to critics. It reflects well his personal modesty, his reluctance to attach himself to any one movement or design philosophy, and his considerable historical knowledge. In recent years, he has been involved in some extremely lowcost projects, such as East End warehousing at three pounds per square foot, and has proved his ability to make a silk purse out of a sow's ear, never relaxing his strict attention to detail no matter how humble the task. His reputation for efficiency and thoroughness in the execution of his works is legendary.

Gowan also taught for some years at the Architectural Association and more recently at the Royal College of Art. He has a high reputation as a teacher, widely respected for his penetrating judgment, and also for his infectious and sometimes rather reckless wit.

—Peter Blundell Jones

GRAHAM, Bruce John.

American. Born in LaCumbre, Bogota, Colombia, of American parents, 1 December 1925. Educated at the University of Dayton, Ohio, 1942-43; Case School of Applied Sciences, Cleveland, Ohio, 1943-44 and 1946; University of Pennsylvania, Philadelphia, 1946-48, B.Arch. 1948. Served in the United States Navy, 1943-45. Married Jane Johnson in 1960; children: George, Lisa, and Mara. Worked in the offices of Holabird, Roche and Burgee, now Holabird and Root, Chicago, 1949-51. Chief of Design, 1951-60, and, since 1960, Partner, Skidmore, Owings and Merrill, *q.v.*, Chicago. President, Society for Contemporary American Art, Art Institute of Chicago, 1968-69; President, Chicago Central Area Committee; Trustee, Museum of Contemporary Art, Chichago, and University of Pennsylvania, Philadelphia. Exhibition: *Architecture of Chicago,* Museum of Contemporary Art, Chicago, 1976. Fellow, American Institute of Architects, 1966. Honorary Member, Institute of Urbanism and Planning of Peru, Royal Architectural Institute of Canada, and Royal Institute of British Architects. Address: Skidmore, Owings and Merrill, 33 West Monroe Street, Chicago, Illinois 60603, U.S.A.

Works:

1957   United States Navy Service School, Great Lakes, Illinois
1958   Inland Steel Company Headquarters, Chicago
    Standard Oil Company Technical Service Buildings, Whiting, Indiana
1960   Parke Davis and Company Offices and Research Laboratories, Ann Arbor, Michigan
1961   Upjohn Company Corporate Headquarters, Kalamazoo, Michigan
1962   Central Motor Bank, Jefferson City, Missouri
1964   Business Men's Assurance Company of America Corporate Headquarters, Chicago
1965   Brunswick Office Building, Chicago
    Civic Center, Chicago
    Equitable Life Assurance Society of the United States Office Building Chicago
1968   Boots Pure Drug Company Ltd. Corporate Headquarters, Nottingham, England
1969   One Marine Midland Plaza Bank and Office Building, Rochester, New York
1970   John Hancock Center, Chicago
    International Bank for Reconstruction and Development, Washington, D.C.
    Eastman Kodak Company Marketing Education Center, Henrietta, New York
1971   One Shell Plaza Office Building, Houston, Texas
    Bond Court Office Building, Cleveland
    Office Building, 1010 Common Street, New Orleans
    Hartford Fire Insurance Company Building, Chicago
    Trans World Airlines Office Building, Kansas City, Missouri
1972   Two Shell Plaza Office Building, Houston, Texas
    One Shell Square Office Building, New Orleans
    Gateway III Office Building, Chicago
    Office building, O'Hare Plaza, Chicago
    Central area study, Milwaukee, Wisconsin
1973   National Life and Accident Insurance Company Headquarters, Nashville, Tennessee
    MGIC Plaza Office Building, Madison, Wisconsin
    Chicago 21 Plan
    Woodfield 76 Office and Commercial Development, Schaumburg, Illinois
1974   First Wisconsin Center Bank and Office Building, Milwaukee, Wisconsin
    First Wisconsin Plaza Bank and Office Building, Madison, Wisconsin
    Fourth Financial Center Bank and Office Building, Wichita, Kansas
    Sears Tower, Chicago
    W. D. and H. O. Wills Corporate Headquarters and Tobacco Processing Facility, Bristol, England
1975   Baxter Travenol Laboratories Inc. Corporate Headquarters, Deerfield, Illinois
    Harris Trust and Savings Bank, Chicago
    Marathon Realty Development Office and Commercial Complex, Montreal (project)
1976   Ohio National Bank Building, Columbus
    Charles Stark Draper Laboratory, Cambridge, Massachusetts
    Central Bank of Iran, Tehran (project)
1977   Office building, 60 State Street, Boston
    Apparel Mart and Holiday Inn Hotel, Wolf Point, Chicago
    Master plan for the Chicago Dock and Canal Trust
    Master plan for Dearborn Park, Chicago
    Group Alfa Corporate Headquarters, Monterrey, Mexico (project)
    Khaneh Center Multi-Use Complex, Tehran
1978   New World Center Multi-Use Complex, Hong Kong
    Hyatt International Hotel, Surabaya, Indonesia
    Hyatt International Hotel and Cultural Center, Kuwait City
1979   Banco de Occidente Building, Guatemala City
    Central Trust Center Bank and Office Building, Cincinnati, Ohio
1980   Office Building, 33 West Monroe, Chicago
    King Abdul Aziz University, phase 1-A and 1-B, Makkah, Saudi Arabia
1981   Office Building, Three First National Plaza, Chicago
1982   *Chicago Tribune* Freedom Center Printing Plant, Chicago
    Office Building, Madison Plaza, Chicago
1983   One Magnificent Mile multi-use complex, Michigan Avenue, Chicago
    McCormick Place expansion, Chicago
1984   Hyatt International Hotel, Lima, Peru
    Perimeter Center Office Building, Atlanta, Georgia
1985   Office Complex, Phase 1, Citicorp Plaza, Los Angeles
    Federal Inspection Services relocation, O'Hare International Airport, Chicago
1986   Lucky Building Corporate Headquarters, Seoul, Korea
1987   Asian Development Bank Headquarters, Manila, Philippines
    Dearborn Center Office Building, Chicago
    World Trade Centre multi-use complex, Cairo
1988   Hyatt International Hotel, Cairo

Publications:

By GRAHAM: article—"The Architecture of Skidmore, Owings and Merrill" in *RIBA Transactions* (London), no. 2, 1983.

On GRAHAM: articles—"Bruce Graham of SOM" in *Building Design* (London), 28 September 1973; "A Consistent Bank Landscape" in *Interiors* (New York), February 1975; "Bruce Graham" in *Arquitecto peruano* (Lima, Peru), March/June 1977; "SOM Superstar Bruce Graham" in *Building Design* (London), 11 June 1982; "Minister for the Exterior" in *Building Design* (London), 20 May 1983; "PR for SOM at RIBA" in *Architects' Journal* (London), 25 May 1983.

*

In Architecture, as in many other arts, it should be unnecessary to explain the work's existence within the certain time and special relationship. To discover and understand this position is the role of the Architect. To function within that framework, to understand the transitory quality, and to place the work within this context and then be sure of its validity is the satisfaction of an Architect. Recognition is not to be expected for this labor, as it is not the produce of life, but of a whole sequence of lives. We judge not a building; but, rather, let an architectural vocabulary illuminate an Age.

We are, at this particular time, in an Age of discovery of a new Civilization. We have the technical tools as well as the crude consciousness of a new Age. I feel very much that this time is a beginning; and this being the case, our buildings must be clear, free of fashion, and simple statements of the truth.

—Bruce J. Graham

*

Bruce J. Graham is one of the leading American designers of highrise buildings. After graduating from the University of Pennsylvania, he moved to Chicago, where he has lived and worked ever since. Following a tour of duty with the firm of Holabird, Root and Burgee, he accepted a position in the Chicago office of Skidmore, Owings and Merrill, and nine years later, in 1960, he became a general partner. By that time, he had already begun to specialize in the design of large commercial structures. He played a leading role in the design of the Inland Steel Building, one of the most important works in the recent history of Chicago architecture. Inland was the first major building to be erected in the Loop after World War II, as well as the first to incorporate clearly the principles and the lean, directly structural look of Miesian building. For about fifteen years following Inland, Chicago commercial architecture, like that of most of the United States, was in debt to the Miesian manner, and Graham—though he never studied with Mies—became one of the ablest and most enthusiastic practitioners of the genre.

In 1965 three of the best known skyscrapers of the "Second Chicago School" were completed: the Brunswick Building, the Civic Center, and the Equitable Building. Graham played a significant role in the planning of all three. His reputation took on international luster in the later 1960s and early 1970s when, together with the brilliant Bangladesh-born engineer Fazlur Khan, he designed a number of towering skyscrapers utilizing the revolutionary tubular frame principle: the John Hancock Center, Chicago; the First Wisconsin Center, Milwaukee; One Shell Plaza, Houston; and the Sears Tower, Chicago. The last of these, composed of nine bundled tubes, the tallest of which rises 1,454 feet from the ground, is the world's loftiest building.

Graham and SOM have continued to build on the large urban scale; in locales as far flung as Hong Kong (the New World Center, a multi-use complex) and Cairo (the Arab International Bank, another multi-use facility). As the popularity of the classical Miesian look has waned, Graham has often grown consciously more lyrical and complex, as in the imaginatively prismatic First Wisconsin Plaza in Madison.

—Franz Schulze

GRASSI, Giorgio.

Italian. Born in Milan, 1935. Studied architecture, Milan Polytechnic, 1955-60, Dip.Arch. 1960. Since 1960, in private practice, Milan: established own studio, Milan, 1965. Editorial Board Member, *Casabella-Continuita* magazine, Milan, 1961-64. Instructor, University of Pescara, Italy, from 1965; Instructor, then Professor of Architectural Composition, Milan Polytechnic, since 1965. Exhibitions:

Italian Architecture of the Sixties, Rome, 1972 (and world tour); *Nouveaux Plaisirs d'Architecture*, Centre de Création Industrielle, Paris, 1985; *Architekturgraphik Originalzeichnungen*, Architekturgalerie H + H Haffner, Munich 1985. Address: Via A. Saffi 15, 20123 Milan, Italy.

Works:

1961 Apartment Block, Via Tibaldi, Milan (competition project; with others)
Housing Block, Via Leopardi, Milan (with G. Gavazzeni)
1962 Sea-coast Urban Development, Roseto degli Abruzzi, Italy (with G. Gavazzeni, L. Patteta and G. Spalla)
House by a Lake (project; with G. Gavazzeni)
House on Lake Iseo, Italy (with G. Gavazzeni)
School in a Park, Monza, Italy (competition project; with G. Gavazzeni, L. Meda and A. Rossi)
1963 Hotel in a Mountain Pass, Croce Comelico, Italy (with G. Gavazzeni and A. Rossi)
Housing Distribution Code for District 16, ·Milan (with others)
1964 New Secondary School Complex, Bologna, Italy (competition project; with G. Gavazzeni and G. Spalla)
1965 Monument to the Resistance, Brescia, Italy (competition project; with L. Meda)
ISES High- and Low-rise Residential Developments, Naples (competition project; with A. Rossi)
1966 San Rocco Housing Development, Monza, Italy (competition project; with A. Rossi)
Monumental Building renovations and alterations, Pavia, Italy (project)
1968 Biological Research Equipment Workshops, Paullo, Italy
1969 Main Hall/Congress Auditorium conversion, Castle of Abbiategrasso, Italy (project)
Secondary School, San Sabba, Trieste, Italy (with R. Agosto, A. Rossi and F. Tentori)
1970 Castle/Town Hall conversion, Abbiategrasso, Italy
1970/
72 Housing and Street Redevelopment, Pavia, Italy (project)
1970/
73 Housing Block on the Rio and Borgo Ticino, Milan (project)
1972 Housing Block, Abbiategrasso, Italy
1974 Regional Government Building, Trieste, Italy (competition project; with A. Monestiroli)
1975 Secondary School in the Tollo Region, Italy (with A. Monestiroli)
Regional Government Building at the Municipal Centre, Milan (project)
1976 Student Centre, Chieti, Italy (competition project; with A. Monestiroli)
1977 Elementary School, Bergoro, Fagnano Olona, Italy (competition project; with R. Campagnola and E. Guazzoni)
1981 Town Redevelopment Plan, Teora, Italy

Publications:

By GRASSI: books—*La Costruzione Logica dell'Architettura*, Padua, Italy 1967; *Das Neue Frankfurt 1926-1931*, editor, Bari, Italy 1975; *L'Architettura come mestiere e altri scritti*, Milan 1980; articles—"Immagine di Berlage" in *Casabella-Continuita*(Milan), March 1961; "Un piano per Tokio" in *Casabella-Continuita*(Milan), December 1961; "L'Edilizia Scolastica in Svizzera" in *Casabella-Continuita*(Milan), August 1962; "An Opinion on drawing and two projects" in *Arquitectura*(Madrid), July/August 1980; "Avantgarde and continuity" in *Oppositions*(New York), Summer 1981.

On GRASSI: book—*Italian Architecture of the Sixties*, exhibition catalogue by Ludovico Quaroni, Paolo Angeletti, Alessandra Muntoni and others, Rome 1972; articles—"Students' hostel at Chieti" in *Lotus*(Venice), June 1977; "Giorgio Grassi", special issue of *2C Construccion de la Ciudad*(Barcelona), December 1977; "Small scale projects and works", special issue of *Lotus*(Venice), no. 22, 1979; "AD Profile 41: Classicism is not a style" in *Architectural Design*(London), vol. 52, no. 5/6, 1982; "Dismayed; scurf from iron; unforgivable" by P. Bayerer in *Bauwelt*(Berlin), 1 June 1984.

Giorgio Grassi was born in 1935 in Milan. He graduated with the award of Diploma in Architecture from the Polytechnic of Milan in 1960, after which he worked for some time on the magazine *Casabella*. Since 1965 he has practised and lived in his native city and has been particularly concerned with the problems of designing dwellings, notably in large blocks or as part of a major urban context. His work rises above the petty clichés of fashionable architects and, indeed, eschews the kind of private language that architects seem to have tried to develop particularly at the expense of homogeneity, serenity, and continuity of scale.

The search to recover the values of architecture has led Grassi to a number of sources from which he finds inspiration. The first of these is the work of Heinrich Tessenow, the great German architect and teacher, particularly in its ethical contribution and sheer inventiveness. The second is in the towns designed by Ernst May, with their roots in the Garden City movement in England and in a German vernacular language of architecture.

In some of Grassi's recent designs, the influence of neoclassicism is strong; the Student Accommodation for Chieti in southern Italy, for example, owes much to the work of Friedrich Weinbrenner (the early nineteenth-century German neoclassicist), with its gigantic order of a plain, square colonnade uniting the whole range of apartments. Grassi's project for the small town of Teora of the early 1980s demonstrates his search for a neutral, elemental, timeless architecture that has its roots firmly within a European tradition. The destruction of Teora in an earthquake did not suggest to Grassi that a clean sweep should be made (as would have been the case with the Modern Movement architects of 1920-70). He sought the reconstruction of the basic form of the town and proposed rows of houses on the hillsides consisting of blocky structures with rigidly controlled and formalised fenestration. The influences were Mediterranean vernacular clusters of dwellings and a stripped-down neoclassical language of architecture that derives partly from German exemplars and partly from Italy's own experiments with simplified neoclassicism during the Mussolini era. The continuity with the past was to be emphasised by a reconstruction of the blocky masses of the church and castle at Teora.

As a draughtsman, Grassi relies on the purest line and on a pellucid clarity of watercolour for some of his best effects, and his graphics recall some German neoclassical work of the last century, although much of the richness of the German masters' designs is absent from his architecture, which tends to starkness in its inexorable search for purity of line and expression.

—James Stevens Curl

GRAVES, Michael.

American. Born in Indianapolis, Indiana, 9 July 1934. Educated at the University of Cincinnati, Ohio, 1954-58, B.Arch. 1958; Harvard University, Cambridge, Massachusetts, 1958-59, M.Arch. 1959;

American Academy, Rome, 1960-62 (Prix de Rome; Brunner Fellowship). Divorced; children: Sarah and Adam; step-children: Anne and Elizabeth. Since 1964, Principal, Michael Graves, Architect, Princeton, New Jersey. Lecturer, 1962-63, Assistant Professor, 1963-67, Associate Professor, 1967-72, and, since 1972, Professor of Architecture, Princeton University, New Jersey. Visiting Fellow, Institute for Architecture and Urban Studies, New York, 1971-72; Visiting Professor, University of Texas at Austin, 1973 and 1974, University of Houston, Texas, 1974 and 1978, New School for Social Research, New York, 1975, and the University of California at Los Angeles, 1977. Exhibitions: *40 Under 40*, Architectural League, New York, 1966; *The New City: Architecture and Urban Renewal*, Museum of Modern Art, New York, 1967; *Union County Nature and Science Museum*, Princeton University, New Jersey, 1967; *Architecture of Museums*, Museum of Modern Art, New York, 1968; *Birch Burdette Long Memorial Drawing Exhibition*, Architectural League, New York, 1973; *Triennale*, Milan, 1973; *Due architetti*, USIS Gallery, Milan, 1974; *Five Architects*, Princeton University, and University of Texas, Austin, 1974; *Architectural Drawing*, Institute for Architecture and Urban Studies, New York, 1974, and Carnegie Mellon University, Pittsburgh, Pennsylvania, 1974; *Architectural Studies and Projects*, Museum of Modern Art, New York, 1975; *The New York Five*, Art Net, London, 1975; *Five Architects*, Castel Nuovo, Naples, 1975; *1975 AIA Honor Awards*, Kimbell Art Museum, Fort Worth, Texas, 1976; *Michael Graves: Projects, 1967-1976*, Columbia University, New York, 1976 (toured the United States); *Two Hundred Years of American Architectural Drawing*, Cooper-Hewitt Museum, New York, 1977 (toured the United States); *Drawing Toward a More Modern Architecture*, Drawing Center, New York, and Otis Art Institute, Los Angeles, 1977; *Beyond the Modern Movement*, Harvard University, Cambridge, Massachusetts, 1977; *Artists' Postcards*, Drawing Center, New York, 1977 (toured the United States); *Grafica 80—Architettura*, Milan, 1977; *Architecture: Service, Craft, Art*, Rosa Esman Gallery, New York, 1978 (toured the United States); *Collage*, Goddard-Riverside Community Center, New York, 1978; *Roma interotta*, Rome, 1978 (toured internationally); Max Protetch Gallery, New York (group show), 1978; *Ornament in the Twentieth Century*, Cooper-Hewitt Museum, New York, 1978; *Trends in Contemporary Architecture*, New Gallery of Contemporary Art, Cleveland, Ohio, 1978; *Speaking a New Classicism: American Architecture Now*, Smith College Museum of Art, Northampton, Massachusetts, 1981; *Intuition and the Block Print*, John Nichols Printmakers and Publishers, New York, 1984. Recipient: Design Award, *Progressive Architecture*, 1970, 1976, 1977, 1978 (twice), and 1979; National Honor Award, 1975, and Design Award, 1985, American Institute of Architects Fellow, Society for the Arts, Religion and Culture. Address: Michael Graves, Architect, 34 Witherspoon Street, Princeton, New Jersey 08540, U.S.A.

Works:

1963 Boston Architectural Center (competition project; with Peter Eisenman)
1964 American Institute of Architects Headquarters, Washington, D.C. (competition project; with Peter Eisenman)
1964/
65 Jersey Corridor Study (New York/ Philadelphia urban corridor) (project; with Peter Eisenman and Anthony Eardley)
1965 University of California Arts Center, Berkeley (competition project; with Peter Eisenman)
1966/
68 Urban design plan for Oyster Bay, Long Island, New York (project)
1967 Hanselmann House, Fort Wayne, Indiana
Urban County Nature and Science Museum,

Mountainside, New Jersey

Upper West Side of Manhattan Urban Design Plan (exhibition project; with Peter Eisenman)

1967/
68 Low-income and elderly people's housing, Coatsville, Pennsylvania (with Geddes, Brecher, Qualls and Cunningham)

1967/
71 Rehabilitation housing for N.E.S.T., Trenton, New Jersey

1968 Middle-income housing, Newark, New Jersey (project)

Master plan for the Newark Museum, New Jersey (project)

1969 Benacerraf House, Princeton, New Jersey

Rockefeller House, Pocantico Hills, New York (project)

1970 Drezner House, Princeton, New Jersey (project)

1971 Ear, Nose and Throat Associates Medical Office, Fort Wayne, Indiana

1971/
73 Alexander House, Princeton, New Jersey

1972 Gunwyn Ventures Investment Office, Princeton, New Jersey

Keeley Guest House, Princeton, New Jersey (project)

Snyderman House, Fort Wayne, Indiana

1973 Mezzo House, Princeton, New Jersey (project)

Sklute House, Bucks County, Pennsylvania (project)

Mural, *Triennale*, Milan

1974 Three murals, Transammonia Inc. Offices, New York

Mural, School of Architecture, University of Texas, Austin

Claghorn House, Princeton, New Jersey

Wageman House, Princeton, New Jersey (project)

1975 Housing for the elderly, Trenton, New Jersey (competition project)

Newark Museum Carriage House renovation, Newark, New Jersey (project)

Newark Museum Art School renovation, Newark, New Jersey

1976 Crooks House, Fort Wayne, Indiana

Schulman House, Princeton, New Jersey

1977 Chem-Fleur Inc. factory addition and renovation, Newark, New Jersey (project)

Warehouse/house conversion, Princeton, New Jersey

Plocek House, Warren Township, New Jersey

Abrahams Dance Studio, Princeton, New Jersey

Fargo-Moorhead Cultural Center Bridge between Fargo, North Dakota and Moorhead, Minnesota

1978 Railroad station conversion and office building, Millburn, New Jersey

Mural, John Witherspoon School, Princeton, New Jersey

Porta Maggiore, *Roma interotta*, Rome (exhibition project)

Kalko House, Green Brook, New Jersey

Newark Museum Children's Museum, Newark, New Jersey

House, Aspen, Colorado (project)

Furniture Demonstration Center, E. F. Hauserman Corporation, New York

Furniture Showroom and Offices, E. F. Hauserman Corporation, Cleveland

1983 San Juan Capistrano Regional Library, California

1983/
84 Civic Center, Portland, Oregon

1983 Humana Corporation headquarters, Louisville, Kentucky

1984 Diane Von Furstenberg boutique, Fifth Avenue, New York

1985 Highrise building, Columbus Circle, New York (Project; with Gruzen Partnership)

1985 Whitney Museum of American Art addition, New York

Publications:

By GRAVES: book—*Michael Graves: Buildings and Projects 1966-1981*, New York 1982; articles—"The Swedish Connection" in *Journal of Architectural Education* (Washington, D.C.), Fall 1975; "Elusive Outcome, Mental Mise-en-scene" in *Progressive Architecture* (New York), May 1977; "The Necessity of Drawing: Tangible Speculation" in *Architectural Design* (London), June 1977; "Snyderman House," with M. Perkins, in *GA Houses 2*, Tokyo, 1977; "Porta Maggiore" in *Roma interotta*, exhibition catalogue, Rome 1978, "Three Architects, Three Approaches to Color Use" in *AIA Journal* (Washington, D.C.), October 1978; "Thought Models" in *Publication of the School of Design* (North Carolina State University, Raleigh), 1978; "Referential Drawings" in *Journal of Architectural Education* (Washington, D.C.), Fall 1978; "The Necessity of Drawing" in *Arquitectura* (Madrid), January/February 1979; "An Interview with Michael Graves" in *Via* (Cambridge, Massachusetts), vol. 4, 1980; introduction to *Selected Drawings by Le Corbusier*, London 1981; "Michael Graves: An Interview" in *Architecture South Africa* (Cape Town), August 1981; "Interview with Michael Grave" in *Architecture + Urbanism* (Tokyo), December 1982; "Michael Graves Talks on His Works" in *Architecture + Urbanism* (Tokyo), December 1983; "Architecture in Question," interview, with Philip Jodidio in *Connaissance des arts* (Paris), March 1984; recording—*The Sense of Boundary in Architecture*, tape cassette and slides, London 1982.

On GRAVES: books—*Five Architects: Eisenman, Graves, Gwathmey, Hejduk, Meier* by Kenneth Frampton and Colin Rowe, New York 1972; *Architettura razionale* by E. Bonfanti and others, Milan 1973; *Five Architects NY*, Rome 1976; *The Language of Post-Modern Architecture* by Charles Jencks, London 1977; *200 Years of American Architectural Drawing* by David Gebhard and Deborah Nevins, New York 1977; *New Directions in American Architecture* by Robert A. M. Stern, New York 1977; *Architectural Monographs 5: Michael Graves* by Alan Colquhoun and others, London 1979; *American Architecture Now*, edited by Barbaralee Diamonstein, New York 1980; *Collaboration: Artists and Architects* by Barbaralee Diamonstein, New York 1981; *Speaking a New Classicism: American Architecture Now*, exhibition catalogue, by Helen Searing and Henry Hope Reed, Northampton, Massachusetts 1981; *A Tower for Louisville*, edited by Peter Arnell and Ted Bickford, New York 1982; *Follies: Architecture for the Late-Twentieth-Century Landscape* by B. J. Archer and A. Vidler, New York 1983; *Abstract Representation*, edited by Charles Jencks, New York 1984; articles—"Private Residence, Pocantino Hills, New York" in *Progressive Architecture* (New York), January 1970; "On Reading Architecture: Eisenman and Graves: An Analysis" by Mario Gandelsonas in *Progressive Architecture* (New York), March 1972; "Michael Graves: Doctor's House" in *Architecture + Urbanism* (Tokyo), November 1972; "Towards a Pluralist Architecture" by Peter Carl in *Progressive Architecture* (New York), February 1973; "Five on Five" by Robert A. M. Stern, Jaquelin Robertson, Charles Moore, Allan Greenberg and Romaldo Giurgola in *Architectural Forum* (New York), May 1973; "Architecture's '5' Make Their Ideas Felt" by Paul Goldberger in *New York Times*, 26 November 1973; "Should Anyone Care about the New York Five...?" by Paul Goldberger in *Architectural Record* (New York), February 1974; "Rockefeller House and Keeley Guest House" and "About Michael Graves" by Takeo Hatae in *Architecture + Urbanism* (Tokyo), March 1974; "Five Architects" by Kenneth Frampton in *Lotus 9* (Venice), February 1975; "The Architect as Intellectual Artist" by John McKean in *Building Design* (London), 10 October

1975; "Les Cendres de Jefferson" by Manfredo Tafuri, and "Michael Graves: Maison Snyderman" in *Architecture d'aujourd'hui* (Paris), August/September 1976; "Living in a Work of Art" by Suzanne Stephens in *Progressive Architecture* (New York), March 1978; "Michael Graves: Evolving a Language" in *Fifth Column* (Montreal), Fall 1980; "Graves Wins Library Competition" in *Progressive Architecture* (New York), March 1981; "Graves, Koolhaas and Baird in Australia" in *International Architect* (London), no. 4, 1981; "Graves New World" in *Fifth Column* (Montreal), Fall 1981; "Graves Commission" in *Architectural Review* (London), July 1982; "Graves Deco" in *Architectural Review* (London), November 1982; "Michael Graves," special issue of *Space Design* (Tokyo), April 1983; "Graves' Elegy" in *Architects' Journal* (London), 18 May 1983; "Three by Graves" in *Building Design* (London), 17 June 1983; "Encore Graves" in *Progressive Architecture* (New York), July 1983; "The Question of Representative Form" in *Archithèse* (Niederteufen, Switzerland), July/August 1983; "Portland Civic Center" in *Architecture interieure créé* (Paris), August/September 1983; "Robert Stern and Michael Graves" in *Fifth Column* (Montreal), Fall 1983; "New York Five" in *Arkitektur* (Stockholm), November 1983; "The Price of Fame: Michael Graves" in *Blueprint* (London), March 1984; "The Enigma of Michael Graves" in *Architects' Journal* (London), 14 March 1984; "Whitney Addition Is Planned" in *New York Times*, 22 May 1985.

Bibliographies: *Michael Graves* by Lamia Doumato, Monticello, Illinois 1980; *Building with Symbols—The Architectural Work of Michael Graves: A Selected Bibliography* by Robert B. Harmon, Monticello, Illinois 1981.

*   *   *

There appear to be two major positions in current architectural thought. Although they are not mutually exclusive, these two attitudes can be seen in opposition to each other.

The first can be characterized as constituting a part of symbolic and mythic representations of the culture. One assumes that there is a correspondence between cultural values and physical artifacts, and that these physical artifacts provide representations both of symbolic objects and of ritual participation. This position, by its nature, relies on the literal, often familiar characteristics of form which are thought of as respresentational.

The second position is primarily abstract in nature, having been derived from an early-twentieth-century, self-conscious rejection of historical precedent in favor of an interest in machine technology and its symbolism. The building is seen as a technical artifact whose abstract geometric devices are generally unadorned and read as minimal. The loss of those figurative elements thought to be derived from classical analogies of man and nature leads to a sense of alienation or a lack of association with the architecture.

If we are to increase the participation in and identification with architecture by the culture at large, we must begin to re-establish the former, somewhat classical, mode of thinking which is capable of representing in physical form the symbolic and mythic aspirations of that culture.

—Michael Graves

*   *   *

By the time he had been in practice for fifteen years—in the late 1970s—the Princeton, New Jersey-based Michael Graves was one of the most inspirational and influential American architects for the younger generation that was exploring the poetry—allusion and metaphor—and the meanings—semiology—in architecture. His work is in the realm of built architecture, as well as in the form of murals, paintings, and drawings, which are among the most persuasive and appealing by today's architects. In addition, Graves is an educator—teaching at Princeton University and lecturing across the country — with great popularity. He is one of the most cerebral theorists and exciting aestheticians of architecture today.

The principal feature of his work is a cubist simultaneity of images, meanings, and inspirations or derivations. He is concerned with multiple layers of space, structure, and symbolism. In his early work, the forms and images were those of the Cubists themselves, especially Juan Gris, and of the early Le Corbusier—fragments, overlay and superimposition, multiple perspective, and the juxtaposition of the grid against such unexpected shapes as the violin curve. In more recent work, the inspirations or derivations have been ever more far-reaching into forgotten or rejected history—to Ingres and Poussin, to Ledoux and Boullée, to early-nineteenth-century English landscape painting, and constantly to classical Greece and Rome. Always these forms and images are overlaid to produce a new language of almost polyphonic simultaneity.

Questions about contextual continuity—the relationship of his architecture to its physical site and its cultural background—are the primary concerns of Graves and place him in the forefront of those architects dealing with historicism or historical allusion. His is architectural storytelling. Questions about the relationship of architecture to the site bring him to statements about the relationship of his work to nature. He relates foreground, middleground, and background or ground, horizon, and sky to base, wall, and roof; or he relates foot, body, and head to base, wall, and cornice. It is anthropomorphic rather than machine symbolism. It rejects abstraction in favor of the representational, the humanistic, the communicative.

Most accessible of Graves's architectural metaphors of nature is his use of color—a much wider and fuller use of color and patterned color than most of his contemporaries—to create "metaphorical landscapes." The landscape of Graves's mind believes that it is part of our cultural heritage to make a simile, if not to equate, blue with sky and water, green with plants and leaves, yellow with sunlight, and red with wall. He believes we have an inherent tradition—long felt, if for a while forgotten by the Modern movement—that red, since the time of the Etruscans, has meant wall. So he locates his colors high or low in his architecture as they are located in nature. This makes or tells special meanings: blue on the ceiling means sky; on the floor it might symbolize pool; yellow on a pipe signifies a streak of sunlight; green on a floor can connote grass, on a wall can mean a bush or a hedge, or on an overhead duct can say, "leaves of trees."

But that is not enough for Graves. He compounds his work with multiple images and multiple meanings for each. Blue on the floor, in the Claghorn kitchen, means the reflection of the sky through the window—and the shadow of a muntin should tell us so. And there, too, brown on the exterior base relates not only to the ground but also to the stone base of the original house; dark green not only connotes leaves but also reiterates the shutters on the existing house. Forms of architecture can serve the same double purpose. The *tabula rasa* and the mountain are mythic images for him that convey both their own meanings and their prototypical messages as structure, space, and extension—especially in the House in Aspen project.

With ever more delicate and sophisticated colorings and poetic allusions therefrom, and with ever more abstruse and interrelated historical inspirations or derivations, Graves's work is among the most lively mosaics of overlaid grids and diaper patterns, of classicism and neo-classicism, of high art and late pop, of delicacy and boldness, of functional circulation and historical memory, and it reflects one of the most complete aesthetic mythologies at work in architecture today.

—C. Ray Smith

GRAY, Eileen.

Irish. Born at Brownswood, Enniscorthy, County Wexford, Ireland, 9 August 1879. Educated at the Slade School of Art, London, 1898-1902; studied lacquerwork, D. Charles furniture workshops, Soho, London, 1900-02; drawing, Académie Colarossi and Académie Julian, Paris, 1902-05; studied furniture-making and lacquerwork with Sugawara in Paris, 1907-14. Served as an ambulance driver in the French Army, 1914-15. Proprietor of a lacquerwork/furniture studio and workshop, with Sugawara, in London, 1915-17, and Paris, 1917-22; Proprietor of the Galerie Jean Désert, Paris, 1922-30; first architectural projects, with Jean Badovici, Roquebrune, France, 1926; worked in Castellar, France, 1939-45, and Paris, 1945 until her death in 1976. Exhibitions: *Exposition des Artistes Décorateurs,* 1913, 1922; World's Fair, Paris, 1937; Heinz Gallery, Royal Institute of British Architects, London, 1973; *1925,* Musée des Arts Décoratifs, Paris, 1976; *Eileen Gray: Designer 1879-1976,* Victoria and Albert Museum, London, and Museum of Modern Art, New York, 1979. Honorary Royal Designer for Industry, Royal Society of Arts, London, 1972; Fellow, Royal Institute of Irish Architects, Dublin, 1973. *Died* (in Paris) *28 November 1976.*

Works:

1919/
22 Suzanne Talbot (Madame Mathieu-Lévy) Apartment interiors, Rue de Lota, Paris
1923 Monte Carlo Boudoir (exhibition project)
1925/
28 Eileen Gray Apartment interiors, 21 Rue Bonaparte, Paris
1926 House for an Engineer (project)
1927/
29 E-1027 (Eileen Gray House), Roquebrune, Cap Martin, France (with Jean Badovici)
1930 Jean Badovici Studio/Apartment interiors, rue Châteaubriand, Champs Elysées, Paris
1932/
34 Tempe à Pailla (Eileen Gray House), Castellar, near Menton, France
1933 House for Two Sculptors (project)
1937 Tube House (project)
  Centre des Vacances (project; exhibited at the World's Fair, at Le Corbusier's Pavillon des Temps Nouveaux, 1937)
1939 Eileen Gray Apartment interiors, St. Tropez, France (destroyed, 1944)
1946/
49 Cultural and Social Centre (project)

Publications:

By GRAY: article—"La Maison minimum," with Jean Badovici, in *L'Architecture d'Aujourd'hui* (Paris), no. 1, 1930.

On GRAY: books—*Gli elementi dell'architettura funzionale* by Alberto Sartoris, Milan 1932; *Des Canons, des munitions? Mercie! Des logis...* by Le Corbusier, Paris 1938; *Eileen Gray: Designer 1879-1976,* exhibition catalogue, by Stewart Johnson, London 1979; articles—"Salon des Artistes Décorateurs" in *Art et décoration* (Paris), March 1913; "Lacquer Walls and Furniture Displace Old Gods in Paris and London" in *Harper's Bazaar* (New York), September 1920; "Les Lacques de Miss Eileen Gray" by E. de Clermont-Tonnerre in *Feuillets d'art* (Paris), February/March 1922; article by Jan Wils and Jean Badovici in *Wendingen* ((Amsterdam), no. 6, 1924; "Maison en bord de mer" by Jean Badovici in *Architecture vivante* (Paris), 1929; "Projet centre culturel" in *L'Architecture d'aujourd'hui* (Paris), no. 82, 1949; "Un imaggio di Eileen Gray" by Joseph

Eileen Gray: Dressing cupboard E-1027, at the Gray House, Roquebrune, France, 1928.

Rykwert in *Domus* (Milan), December 1968; "Eileen Gray: The Houses and an Interior" by Joseph Rykwert in *Perspecta* (New Haven, Connecticut), no. 13, 1971; "Eileen Gray: Pioneer of Design" by Joseph Rykwert in *Architectural Review* (London), August 1972; "The Complete Designer" in *Design* (London), January 1973; "Eileen Gray" in *RIBA Journal* (London), February 1973; "Eileen Gray" in *The Sunday Times Magazine* (London), 22 June 1975; "Eileen Gray Lives" by Richard Carr in *Building Design* (London), 30 June 1978; "Eileen Gray" by Joseph Rykwert in *Architecture + Urbanism* (Tokyo), August 1978; "Shades of Gray" by Corin Hughes Stanton in *Building Design* (London), 9 February 1979; "MOMA shows the 20s Avant-Garde Work of Eileen Gray" in *Architectural Record* (New York), March 1980; "Eileen Gray: Architect Designer" by Cynthia Weese in *Inland Architect* (Chicago), May 1980; "A Soft Rationalism by a Great Woman Designer" by Claudia Dona in *Modo* (Milan), May 1980; "Eileen Gray, 1879-1968" by Jean Paul Rayon and Brigitte Loye in *Casabella* (Milan), May 1982.

Bibliography—*Eileen Gray, 1879-1976* by Lamia Doumato, Monticello, Illinois 1981.

Overshadowed as she was by the giants of her era, Eileen Gray is a comparatively little known exponent of the modern movement. Unlike many of her contemporaries, she intensely disliked self-publicity, and that attitude contributed to her neglect by clients and critics alike. Her total output is two houses, some interiors and unexecuted projects—her work nevertheless displays a full and original understanding of the language of that style.

It is difficult to categorize Gray's work, falling as it does between the over-ornamentation of Art Deco and the purely functional of the machine aesthetic. Some critics have associated her with the De Stijl group, and parallels can be found, but she rejected the group's intellectual austerity, reasoning that "Man is not purely Spirit." She was essentially an individualist, believing that her creations, whilst reflecting her artistic outlook, should first and foremost be practical.

The one European whose philosophy attracted Gray was her friend Le Corbusier. They were in many ways kindred spirits. Neither had been subjected to a recognized architectural training, and they were able to view the world with unblinkered eyes. Both had a clear vision of the way ahead for modern design in the "New World" that was emerging. Yet—whilst agreeing in principal with ideas expressed in his contributions to *L'ésprit Nouveau* in 1920-26—she nevertheless revolted against the over-mechanisation of things to the exclusion of emotion.

Apart from Rietveld's Schroeder house in Utrecht, completed in 1924, and Adolph Loos's house for Tristan Tzara in 1926, there were few precedents for such completeness of design as displayed in Gray's first building begun in 1927 at Roquebrune in collaboration with the Rumanian architect Jean Badovici. The spaces are furnished with floor coverings, light fittings, murals, furniture of absolute appropriateness, all designed and made to specification in her Paris workshop. She pioneered the use of a variety of the "new" materials—cork, aluminium, tubular steel, suede, leather, perforated metal sheeting, always sensitive to the nature of the material. A fusion of formal invention with craftsman's skills, which received a fully articulated expression only in the work of the early Bauhaus masters, is very evident in her creations.

Her houses and interiors are a celebration of Corbusier's *machine à hâbiter* ideal in its true sense but with an entirely humanistic approach. "In the limited confines of domestic space," she said, "everything must be made to adjust—to be adaptable." Thus she initiated folding windows, sliding screens and blinds, false ceilings concealing storage space, staircases hidden in cupboards or under seating, adjustable skylights, extending wardrobes, all things functioning with the maximum of ease, every detail adjusting to form part of a larger and potentially variable spatial composition, the exterior spaces becoming an extension of the interior.

In retrospect, Gray's work can be seen to be a product of its time, but it was her feeling that artists should "be of their era"—should live in their own epoch and express it with honesty. "The beautiful work of art is more real than the artist" must surely be her epitaph.

—Elizabeth Murphy

GREENBERG, Allan.

American. Born in Johannesburg, South Africa, 7 September 1938; emigrated to the United States, 1964: naturalized, 1973. Educated at King Edward School, Johannesburg, until 1955; studied architecture, University of the Witwatersrand, Johannesburg, B.Arch., 1961; Yale University, New Haven, Connecticut, M.Arch., 1965. Worked in the offices of Jorn Utzon, Denmark, 1962, Viljo Revell, Helsinki, 1963, Ahlsens Arketekt, Stockholm, 1964, and the New Haven Redevelopment Agency, Connecticut, 1965-67. Since 1967, in private practice, New Haven, Connecticut. Architectural Consultant to the Chief Court Administrator, Supreme Court, State of Connecticut, 1964-79. Visiting Critic in

Architectural Design, Yale University, New Haven, Connecticut, 1968-73; Lecturer, Yale Law School, New Haven, Connecticut, 1974; Associate Professor of Architecture, University of Pennsylvania, Philadelphia, 1975-78; Visiting Professor, Temple University, Philadelphia, 1980-81, and University of Illinois, Chicago, 1982; Visiting Associate Professor, Columbia University, New York, 1983-84. Board Member, Society of Architectural Historians, 1983-87. Exhibitions: *Architectural Drawings*, Otis Institute, Los Angeles, and Drawing Center, New York, 1977; *Park Design for Rockefeller Center*, Museum of Modern Art, New York, 1979; Linz Festival, Austria, 1980; *Best Products*, Museum of Modern Art, New York, 1980; *Presence of the Past*, at the *Biennale*, Venice, 1980 (travelled to Paris, ,1981, and San Francisco, 1982); *Speaking a New Classicism*, Smith College, Northampton, Massachusetts, 1981 (travelled to Houston Museum of Art, Texas, 1982, and the Smithsonian Institution, Washington, D.C., 1983). Collections: Museum of Modern Art, New York; National Building Museum, Washington, D.C.; U.S. Secretary of State Collection, Washington, D.C. Recipient: First Prize, Art Center Competition, Thibodeaux, Louisiana, 1982. Address: 31 High Street, New Haven, Connecticut 06510, U.S.A.

Works:

1968/
74 State Library and Supreme Court additions, Hartford, Connecticut (with Jeter and Cook)

1970 Hartford County Courthouse addition, Hartford, Connecticut (project; with Russell Gibson von Dohlen)

1975 Memorial Flagpole, Valley Forge, Pennsylvania (project)

1975/
78 Courthouse and Office Site Plan, Alexandria, Virginia

1978 House renovation and addition, Guilford, Connecticut

1979 Court of Common Pleas renovation study, New Haven, Connecticut

1979/
80 Manchester Courthouse, Manchester, Connecticut

1979/
81 Juvenile Detention Building renovations and alterations, New Haven, Connecticut

1979/
83 Farmhouse, White Birch Farm, Greenwich, Connecticut

Allan Greenberg: George C. Marshall Reception Room, U.S. Department of State, Washington, D.C., 1984.

1980 Rockefeller Center Midblock Park Project, New York
1982 Naval War Memorial and 8th Street Redevelopment, Washington, D.C. (project)
Library, Theater and Arts Center, Thibodeaux, Louisiana (competition project)
1983 Park Avenue Apartment House, New York (project)
Bergdorf Goodman Store facade, Fifth Avenue, New York
1984 Holocaust Memorial (project)
New Offices for the Secretary of State, State Department Building, Washington D.C.
Office Building addition, Greenwich, Connecticut (project)
1984/
85 *Antiques Magazine* and *Art in America* Offices, New York
1985 Manor House additions and restoration, Conyers Farm, Greenwich, Connecticut (project)
House, Conyers Farm, Greenwich, Connecticut (project)
Hyundai Automobile Dealership (project)
Riggs Bank renovation and restoration, Georgetown, Connecticut (project)
House, Southampton, Long Island, New York (project)
Trellis Room, The White House, Washington, D.C. (project)

Publications:

By GREENBERG: books—*Courthouse Design: A Handbook for Judges and Court Administrators*, Chicago 1975; *Standard Facilities for Juvenile Justice*, Chicago 1979; articles—"Lutyens' Architecture Restudied" in *Perspecta* (New Haven, Connecticut), no. 12, 1969; "The Lurking American Legacy" in *Architectural Forum* (New York), February 1973; "Introductory Guidelines to Planning a Modern Courthouse" in *Architectural Record* (New York), June 1973; "Symbolism in Courthouse Design" in *Judicature* (Chicago), April 1976; "Raising Temples of Justice" in *Judicature* (Chicago), May 1976; "Symbolism in Architecture: A Case Study" in *Architectural Record* (New York), May 1979; "Sir Edwin Lutyens—Tigborne Court" in *Architectural Digest* (Los Angeles), September 1980; introduction to *Monograph of the Work of McKim, Mead and White*, New York 1981; "A Sense of the Past" in *Chicago Architectural Journal* (Chicago), vol. 1, 1981; "David Adler: House for William McCormick Blair" in *Architectural Digest* (Los Angeles), January 1984.

On GREENBERG: articles—"Courthouse, Alexandria, Virginia" in *Architectural Review* (London), February 1979; "American Architecture—After Modernism" in *Architecture + Urbanism* (Tokyo), March 1981; "Good, ordinary, classical, modern" in *Progressive Architecture* (New York), October 1981.

*

The meaning of our architectural past is more complicated than simply duplicating or distorting the forms bequeathed to us by history. As a tradition, it is the vehicle through which we embody our systems of social, political, and religious norms. This is accomplished by means of typologies of buildings which are continuously modified, as circumstances in society change. These building types provide a range of expressive and functional solutions to architectural problems.

It is the role of the architect to aid in the realization of society's aspirations by designing buildings which express the meaning and significance of the institutions they house. Architectural forms should facilitate, therefore, both the communication and the expression of these meanings. The most highly developed language of form available to us for this purpose is the classical language of architecture. Since antiquity, generations of architects have worked with the elements, grammar and meanings of classical architecture and adapted it to the needs of widely differing cultures, and functions.

The use of precedent enabled both the architect and the client to incorporate the aesthetic and functional experience of the past into new solutions. For the great architects, this was liberating as it enabled them to master and expand the boundaries of the tradition; for the average practitioner, it provides a canon to design competent buildings, such as the great Georgian squares of London, Edinburgh and Boston. The buildings should complement, rather than contrast, with the extant architectural tradition.

In the United States classical architecture is the architecture of our revolution. Our legacy of architecture from the seventeenth-century to 1940 challenges us to create a fitting architecture for our times.

—Allan Greenberg

*

Allan Greenberg has sustained a fascination with the creation of American courthouses, judicial and public buildings throughout his career as teacher and architect. Born in South Africa and naturalized as an American citizen in 1973, he embarked on twenty-four major projects after receiving his Masters Degree in architecture from Yale University in 1965. These projects include the Connecticut State Library and Supreme Court, the Naval War Memorial and 8th Street redevelopment plans in Washington, D.C., juvenile detention building, and courthouses in Alexandria, Virginia, and Manchester, Connecticut.

Greenberg's designs are markedly influenced by the work of Sir Edwin Lutyens (1869-1944), whose most significant achievement was to raise English domestic architecture from the vernacular to the palatial. Lutyens' own architecture was an original interpretation of European styles of the Renaissance, and from this interpretation he bridged the centuries by a new presentation of traditional development. The first major Lutyenesque revival to appear in America was Greenberg's project for the new courthouse of Alexandria, Virginia. Noted for its immediately recognizable 'public' quality, the building is based on Classical styles, evidenced by its applied system of orders and discipline of proportion. Helped by the long crystallization of use, the classical approach still acts as a kind of architectural Esperanto, while the building's formal plan and legal use allows the expression of a certain grandeur reinforced by the generous use of fine materials.

Whereas Lutyens remained chiefly style-conscious, however, Greenberg focuses on the role of symbolism and expressed meaning through architecture, explaining thus: "Symbolism plays an important role in planning the setting for the judicial system, and the design of courtrooms and courthouses offers a provocative case study for the assessment of its crucial features in architecture."

In Manchester, Connecticut, the courthouse he designed in association with Peter Kosinski Associates in 1979/80 exemplifies symbolic architecture. An expression of Classical style, this modest civic building communicates clarity and the dignity of the legal process. With a strong and silent facade, the design embodies a polemic about contemporary architectural styles whose demands are less simplistic. Set on the foundations of an older structure—a 1962 supermarket—the planning and building method was cost effective, but somewhat limited Greenberg's creative licence—which was already restricted by a degraded area and difficult contours of the site. He neutralized these effects, however, by rejuvenating the landscape surround and embellishing the interior with taste and simplicity. Greenberg notes: "The exterior articulation of a courthouse and the relationship of the building to its surroundings expresses our concept of the role of law in our society. Similarly, the building's internal arrangement reflects the relative importance assigned to transactions and the roles of various groups using the building."

Three courtrooms occupy almost the whole width of the building, each varying in size and importance. The entrance in the centre opens into a broad lobby, the most public part of the courthouse. "The grand public space and elaborate design found in older courthouses still convey an aura of dignity and, despite current overcrowding and obsolescence, continue to provide a sense of order, orientation and hierarchical importance of destinations", remarked the architect. Private rooms are tucked away behind and in front of the lobby, metaphorically suggesting both the law's disposal and inaccessibility to the general public. The implications of Classical style are present in the lobby, the terrazzo floor of which is composed of alternating squares of light and dark, while the doors of each courtroom, with their Tuscan columns and pilasters, recall the tradition and imperatives of the events that take place behind them.

The classical vocabulary is still current in America, particularly as it relates so well to the constitutional origins of the buildings that support American public life. In Greenberg's designs, the processional public spaces, the fine materials and functional planning put him in the forefront of the new traditionalists.

—Carolyn Cole

GREENE, Charles Sumner.
American. Born in Brighton, Ohio, 12 October 1868; brother of the architect Henry Mather Greene, *q.v.* Educated at the Manual Training High School of Washington University, St. Louis, 1886-88; Massachusetts Institute of Technology School of Architecture, Cambridge, 1888-91. Married Alice Gordon White in 1901; had five children. Worked for Winslow and Weatherall and other Boston architects, 1891-94; Partner, with Henry Mather Greene, Greene and Greene, Pasadena, Calfornia, 1894-1903, Los Angeles, 1903-06, and Pasadena, 1906-22; practised independently, in Carmel, Calfornia, from 1922. Recipient: Certificate of Merit, 1948, and Citation, 1952, American Institute of Architects. *Died* (in Carmel, California) *11 June 1957.*

Works (with Henry Mather Greene; all California unless noted):

1894 John Breiner House, Pasadena
Mrs Martha Fynn House, Pasadena
Conrad A. Covelle House, Pasadena
Pasadena Security Investment Company House, Pasadena
Pasadena Security Investment Company House II, Pasadena
1895 Robert Eason House, Pasadena
Willis M. Eason House, Pasadena
Dr. Thomas J. Rigg House, Pasadena
Charles Eldred House, Pasadena
Pasadena Presbyterian Church additions
Edward s. Crump House, Pasadena
1896 Robert S. Allen House, Pasadena
Minney-Kendall Building, Pasadena
Rollin H. Miller House, Pasadena
Edward B. Hosmer House, Pasadena
Mrs. C. Gartzman House, Pasadena
1897 Theodore P. Gordon House, Pasadena
Dr. Fenyes House, Pasadena (project)
J.J. Neumeister House, Pasadena
Dr. George S. Hull House, Pasadena
Dr. George S. Hull Office, Pasadena

Elizabeth A. McLean House, Pasadena
Howard Longley House, South Pasadena
1898 Dr. W.H. Roberts Office, Pasadena
Winthrop B. Fay House, Pasadena
Wilson School addition, Pasadena (project)
William B. Tomkins House, Pasadena
James Swan House, Pasadena
1899 J.M. Smith House, Pasadena
Charles W. Hollister House, Pasadena
Pasadena Library addition, Pasadena (project)
Dr. William T. Bolton House, Pasadena
George H. Coffin House, Pasadena
1900 Pasadena Ice Company Building, Pasadena
John C. Bentz Building, Pasadena
Mrs. Mary R. Milnor House, Pasadena
Katherine M Duncan House, Pasadena
1901 Mrs. Metilde Phillips House, Pasadena
Mrs. Benjamin C. Brown House, Pasadena
Lorenz P. Hansen House 'A', Pasadena
Lorenz P. Hansen House 'B', Pasadena
James F. Ker House, Pasadena
Dr. John M. Radebaugh House additions, Pasadena
Miss H. Sybil Swett Private School, Pasadena
Charles S. Greene House, Pasadena
1902 George H. Barker House, Pasadena
Mrs. Rose J. Rasey Rooming House, Pasadena
All Saints Episcopal Church Rectory, Pasadena
James A. Culberton House, Pasadena
W.B.T. House, near Pasadena(project)
George G. Guyer House additions and alterations, Altadena
1903 F.J. Martin Studio Apartments, Pasadena
Emma M. Black House, Pasadena
Martha, Violet and Jane White House, Pasadena
Philip L. Autin House, Pasadena
Katherine M. Duncan House additions, Pasadena
Samuel P. Sanborn House and Stable, Pasadena
Arturo Bandini House, Pasadena
Dr. Frances F. Rowland House and Office, Pasadena
Mrs. Mary R. Darling House, Claremount
Dr. Edith J. Claypole House, Pasadena
1904 Mrs. Jennie A. Reeve House, Long Beach
Henry M. Greene House, Pasadena
Charles W. Hollister House, Hollywood
Edgar W. Camp House, Sierra Madre
Mrs. James A. Garfield House, South Pasadena
R. Henry/C. Green House, Vancouver, Britsh Columbia
Adelaide M. Tichenor House, Long Beach
Thomas Palmer House additions, Los Angeles
Rev. Alexander M. Merwin House, Pasadena
Kate A. White House, South Pasadena
Dr. William T. Bolton House alterations, Pasadena
1905 Mrs. William A. Bowen House, Altadena
S. Hazard Halsted House, Pasadena
South Pasadena Realty and Improvement Company Entrance Gates, Fence, and Bridge, South Pasadena
Dr. Arthur A. Libby House, Pasadena
Charles J. Willet House, Pasadena
Lucy E. Wheeler House, Los Angeles
Mrs T. Stewart White House, Santa Barbara (project)
Iwan Serrurier House, Pasadena
A.C. Brandt House, Altadena
Tod Ford House alterations, Pasadena
Henry M. Robinson House, Pasadena
Mrs. L.G. and Marion Porter House, Los Angeles
1906 Mrs. Josephine Van Rossem House additions and alterations, Pasadena
James A. Culbertson House additions and alterations, Pasadena
Tod Ford House additions, Pasadena

Pasadena Ice Company Offices, Pasadena
Pomona Valley Ice Company Offices, Pomona
Mrs. Jennie A. Reeve House, Sierra Madre
Caroline S. DeForest House, Pasadena
Louis K. Hyde House, Plainfield, New Jersey (project)
John B. Phillips House, Pasadena
Robert Pitcairn Jr. House, Pasadena
Dr. William T. Bolton House, Pasadena
Katherine M. Duncan House alterations and additions, Pasadena
John C. Bentz House, Pasadena
John A. Cole House, Pasadena
F.W. Hawks House, Pasadena
Charles S. Greene House alterations and additions, Pasadena
1907 Fred Stahlhuth House, Pasadena
James A. Culbertson House alterations and additions, Pasadena
Mary L. Ranney House, Pasadena
Pasadena Hospital Association Nurses' Home, Pasadena (project)
S. Hazard Halstead House addditions, Pasadena
Charles W. Leffingwell Bunk House, Whittier
Robert R. Blacker House, Pasadena
Freeman A. Ford House, Pasadena
Lon F. Chapin House alterations and additions, Pasadena
William W. Spinks House, Pasadena
Rev. Alexander M. Merwin House additions, Pasadena
John Wadsworth House additions, Pasadena
Theodore Irwin House additions, Pasadena
Tod Ford House additions, Pasadena
Shelter for Viewlovers, Pasadena
1908 David B. Gramble House, Pasadena
Robert R. Blacker House additions, Pasadena
S. Hazard Halsted House alterations, Pasadena
Charles K. Silent House, Glendora (project)
William J. Lawless House, Sierra Madre
James W. Neill House additions, Pasadena
Theodore Irwin House alterations, Pasadena
Armenian Pilgrims Church, Fresno (project)
1909 John B. Phillips House additions, Pasadena
Charles M. Pratt House, Nordhoff
William R. Thorsen House, Berkeley
William W. Spinks Garage, Pasadena
Dr. S.S. Crow House, Pasadena
Earle C. Anthony House, Los Angeles
1910 John G. Neumeister House, Redondo (project)
John Lambert House, Pasadena (project)
John C. Bentz House alterations and additions, Pasadena
James A. Culbertson House additions, Pasadena
Ernest W. Smith House, Pasadena
James W. Neill House alterations, Pasadena
Howard Longley House alterations and additions, South Pasadena
Samuel L Merrill House, Pasadena
Keith Spaulding Bunk House, Fillmore
John C. Bentz Garage, Pasadena
A.C. Drake House, Pasadena (project)
Henry M. Robinson House additions, Pasadena
1911 Alexander M. Drake House, Pasadena (project)
Mortimer Fleishhacker House, Woodside
S. Hazard Halsted House additions, Pasadena
William W. Spinks House alterations, Pasadena
Crow-Crocker Garage additions, Pasadena
Nathan Bentz House, Santa Barbara
Earle C. Anthony Automobile Showroom interiors, Loa Angeles
Henry M. Greene House additions, Pasadena
Cordelia A. Culbertson House, Pasadena
Longfellow School, Pasadena
S.C. Graham House, Los Angeles (project)
Charles P. Wilcox House, Pasadena

Mrs. Charles G. Brown House, Pasadena
Pasadena Ice Company Building alterations, Pasadena
Joseph K. Huston House, Pasadena
1912 Mrs. Parker A. Earle Apartment House, Pasadena
Charles M. Pratt House alterations, Nordhoff
Annie Blacker House, Pasadena
Edwards S. Crocker House, Pasadena
Dr. Frances F. Rowland House moving and alterations, Pasadena
Charles S. Greene House alterations and additions, Pasadena
Frank L. Palmer House, North Pomona (project)
S. Hazard Halsted House alterations and additions, Pasadena
Michael Kew House, San Diego
George A. Gibbs House additions, Pasadena
Vista del Arroyo Hotel east annex and bungalow alterations, Pasadena
Dr. Robert P. McReynolds House alterations, Los Angeles
F.W.Hawks House alterations, Pasadena
J.S. Silverberg House alterations, San Mateo
1913 Henry A. Ware House, Pasadena
Earle C. Anthony House alterations and additions, Los Angeles
Dr. Edward H. Angle House, Pasadena (project)
William M. Ladd House, Nordhoff
Mrs. J. Herbert Ballentine House alterations and additions, Altadena
Sidney D. Gamble House, Escondido (project)
James W. Neill House alterations, Pasadena
1914 James A. Culbertson House additions, Pasadena
Vista del Arroyo Building, Pasadena (project)
Dr. Rosa Englemann House, Pasadena
Cordelia A. Culbertson House additions, Pasadena
Charles S. Greene Garage, Pasadena
Theodore Irwin House additions, Pasadena
Henry A. Ware House additions, Pasadena
Dr. William T. Bolton House additions, Pasadena
1915 John T. Greene House, Sacramento
Dr. Robert P. McReynolds House additions, Los Angeles
Mortimer Fleischhacker House additions, San Francisco
William E. Hamlin House, Pasadena
F.W. Hawks House alterations, Pasadena
Charles M. Pratt House alterations, Nordhoff
Dr. Nathan H. Williams House, Altadena
S. Hazard Halsted House alterations and additions, Pasadena
Dr. Rosa Engelmann House additions, Pasadena
Dr. Arthur A. Libby House additions, Pasadena
Herbert Fleishhacker House alterations, Atherton
Pasadena Ice Company Offices alterations and additions, Pasadena
Pasadena Ice Company Ice Storage Building additions, Pasadena
William E. Hamlin Garage, Pasadena
Dr. Frances F. Rowland House alterations, Pasadena
1916 H.T. Proctor House, Cocoa Nut Beach, Florida (project)
J. Herbert Hall Apartment House alterations and additions, Pasadena
Dr. Robert P. McReynolds House alterations, Los Angeles
Westmoreland Place Portals and Gates, Pasadena
Mortimer Fleishhacker House additions, Woodside
S. Hazard Halsted House additions and garage, Pasadena

Greene and Greene: David B. Gamble House, Pasadena, California, 1908.

1917 Charles H. Stoddard House, Burlingame (project)
Dr. Martha J. Kuznik House, Hollywood (project)
John H. Poole House, Pasadena
Earle C. Anthony House alterations and additions, Los Angeles
Cordelia A. Culbertson House alterations, Pasadena
Henry M. Robinson House alterations and additions, Pasadena
1919 John H. Poole Houise, Pasadena (project)
Hubert F. Krantz Development for Prospect Park, Palm Beach County, Florida (project)
Hubert F. Krantz House, Pasadena (project)

Works (by Charles Sumner Greene only; all California)

1902 W.B.T. House near Pasadena (project)
1918 Daniel L. James House, Carmel Highlands
1920 Charles S. Greene House, Carmel
1921 Thomas C. Greene House, Carmel
Carmel Country Club Clubhouse (project)
1922 Carmel War Memorial
Rudolf Schevill House alterations and addition of Music Studio, Berkeley
1923 Robert Tolmie House andd Music Studio, Piedmont
Mortimer Fleischhacker House additions, Woodside
Charles S. Greene Studio, Carmel
1925 Jessie H. Payne House, Carmel (project)
1926 Mrs. Willis Walker Stable, Pebble Beach
Mrs. Jennie Crocker Whitman House, Pebble Beach (project)

1927 Mortimer Fleishhacker House water garden, Woodside
Violet Campbell House additions, Carmel
1928 Martin Flavin House entry walls and gates, Carmel Highlands
Robert R. Blacker House fountain, Pasadena
Mortimer Fleishhacker Dairy House, Woodside
1929 Ralph C. Lee House garden pergola, Hillsborough (project)
John L. Howard House and Studio, Monterey
Mrs. Frank J. Kelley House alterations and additions, San JosE
Martin Flavin House alterations, Carmel Highlands
Mortimer Fleishhacker House gothic room addition, San Francisco (project)
Violet Campbell House alterations, Carmel
1931 Mrs. Frank J. Kelley House additions, San Jose
Mortimer Fleishhacker House fountain, Woodside
1932 Martin Flavin House alterations, Carmel Highlands
1934 Rinehart House (project)
Martin Flavin House alterations, Carmel Highlands
Mortimer Fleishhacker House alterations and additions, Woodside (project)
1937 Park Abbott House and Offices, Oakland (project)
1938 Adelaide Howard House (project)
1939 Martin Flavin House alterations, Carmel Highlands
1940 Daniel L. James House library addition, Carmel Highlands

See GREENE, Henry Mather

GREENE, Henry Mather.
American. Born in Brighton, Ohio, 23 January 1870; brother of the architect Charles Sumner Greene, *q.v.* Educated at the Manual Training High School of Washington University, St. Louis, Missouri, 1886-88; Massachusetts Institute of Technology School of Architecture, Cambridge, 1888-91. Married Emeline Augusta Dart in 1899; had four children. Worked for Stickney and Austin, then for Shepley, Rutan and Coolidge, Boston 1891-94; Partner, with Charles Sumner Greene, Greene and Greene, Pasadena, 1894-1903, Los Angeles, 1903-06, and Pasadena, 1906-22; practiced independently, in Pasadena, from 1922. Recipient: Certificate of Merit, 1948, and Citation, 1952, American Institute of Architects. *Died* (in Altadena, California) *2 October 1954.*

Works (with Charles Sumner Greene; all in California unless noted):

1894 John Breiner House, Pasadena
Mrs. Martha Fynn House, Pasadena
Conrad A. Covelle House, Pasadena
Pasadena Security Investment Company House, Pasadena
Pasadena Security Investment Company House II, Pasadena
1895 Robert Eason House, Pasadena
Willis M. Eason House, Pasadena
Dr. Thomas J. Rigg House, Pasadena
Charles Eldred House, Pasadena
Pasadena Presbyterian Church additions, Pasadena
Edward S. Crump House, Pasadena
1896 Rober t S. Allen House, Pasadena
Minney-Kendall Building, Pasadena

Robin H. Miller House, Pasadena
Edward B. Hosmer House, Pasadena
Mrs. C. Gartzman House, Pasadena
1897   Theodore P. Gordon House, Pasadena
Dr. Fenyes House, Pasadena (project)
J.J. Neumeister House, Pasadena
Dr. George S. Hull House, Pasadena
Dr. George S. Hull Office, Pasadena
Elizabeth A. McLean House, Pasadena
Howard Longley House, South Pasadena
1898   Dr. W.H. Roberts Office, Pasadena
Winthrop B. Fay House, Pasadena
Wilson School addition, Psadena (project)
William B. Tomkins House, Pasadena
James Swan House, Pasadena
1899   J.M. Smith House, Pasadena
Charles W. Hollister House, Pasadena
Pasadena Library addition, Pasadena (project)
Dr. William T. Bolton House, Pasadena
George H. Coffin House, Pasadena
1900   Pasadena Ice Company Building, Pasadena
John C.Bentz Building, Pasadena
Mrs. Mary R. Milnor House, Pasadena
Katherine M. Duncan House, Pasadena
1901   Mrs. Metilde Phillips House, Pasadena
Mrs. Benjamin C. Brown House, Pasadena
Lorenz P. Hansen House "A", Pasadena
Lorenz P. Hansen House "B", Pasadena
James F. Ker House, Pasadena
Dr. John M. Radebaugh House additions, Pasadena
Miss H. Sybil Swett Private School, Pasadena
Charles S. Greene House, Pasadena
1902   George H. Barker House, Pasadena
Mrs. Rose J. Rasey Rooming House, Pasadena
All Saints Episcopal Church Rectory, Pasadena
James A. Culberton House, Pasadena
George G. Guyer House additions and alterations, Altadena
1903   F. J. Martin Studio Apartments, Pasadena
Emma M. Black House, Pasadena
Martha, Violet and Jane White House, Pasadena
Philip L. Autin House, Pasadena
Katherine M. Duncan House additions, Pasadena
Samuel P. Sanborn House and Stable, Pasadena
Arturo Bandini House, Pasadena
Dr. Frances F. Rowland House and Office, Pasadena
Mrs. Mary R. Darling House, Claremont
Dr. Edith J. Claypole House, Pasadena
1904   Mrs. Jennie A. Reeve House, Long Beach
Henry M. Greene House, Pasadena
Charles W. Hollister House, Hollywood
Edgar W. Camp House, Sierra Madre
Mrs. James A. Garfield House, South Pasadena
R. Henry/C. Green House, Vancouver, BritishColumbia
Adelaide M. Tichenor House, Long Beach
Thomas Palmer House additions, Los Angeles
Rev. Alexander M. Merwin House, Pasadena
Kate A. White House, South Pasadena
Dr. William T. Bolton House alterations, Pasadena
1905   Mrs. William A. Bowen House, Altadena
S. Hazard Halsted House, Pasadena
South Pasadena Realty and Improvement Company Entrance Gates, Fence, and Bridge, South Pasadena
Dr. Arthur A. Libby House, Pasadena
Charles J. Willet House, Pasadena
Lucy E. Wheeler House, Los Angeles
Mrs. T. Stewart White House, Santa Barbara (project)
Iwan Serrurier House, Pasadena
A. C. Brandt House, Altadena
Tod Ford House alterations, Pasadena
Henry M. Robinson House, Pasadena

Mrs. L. G. and Marion Porter House, Los Angeles
1906   Mrs. Josephine Van Rossem House additions and alterations, Pasadena
James A. Culbertson House additions and alterations, Pasadena
Tod Ford House additions, Pasadena
Pasadena Ice Company Offices, Pasadena
Pomona Valley Ice Company Offices, Pomona
Mrs. Jennie A. Reeve House, Sierra Madre
Caroline S. DeForest House, Pasadena
Louis K. Hyde House, Plainfield, New Jersey (project)
John B. Phillips House, Pasadena
Robert Pitcairn Jr. House, Pasadena
Dr. William T. Bolton House, Pasadena
Katherine M. Duncan House alterations and additions, Pasadena
John C.Bentz House, Pasadena
John A. Cole House, Pasadena
F. W. Hawks House, Pasadena
Charles S. Greene House alterations and additions, Pasadena
1907   Fred Stahlhuth House, Pasadena
James A. Culbertson House alterations and additions, Pasadena
Mary L. Ranney House, Pasadena
Pasadena Hospital Association Nurses' Home, Pasadena (project)
S. Hazard Halsted House additions, Pasadena
Charles W. Leffingwell Bunk House, Whittier
Robert R. Blacker House, Pasadena
Freeman A. Ford House, Pasadena
Lon F. Chapin House alterations and additions, Pasadena
William W. Spinks House, Pasadena
Rev. Alexander M. Merwin House additions, Pasadena
John Wadsworth House additions, Pasadena
Theodore Irwin House additions, Pasadena
Tod Ford House Additions, Pasadena
Shelter for Viewlovers, Pasadena
1908   David B. Gamble House, Pasadena
Robert R. Blacker House additions, Pasadena
S. Hazard Halsted House alterations, Pasadena
Charles K. Silent House, Glendora (project)
William J. Lawless House, Sierra Madre
James W. Neill House additions, Pasadena
Theodore Irwin House alterations, Pasadena
Armenian Pilgrims Church, Fresno (project)
1909   John B. Philips House additions, Pasadena
Charles M. Pratt House, Nordhoff
William R. Thorsen House, Berkeley
William W. Spinks Garage, Pasadena
Dr. S. S. Crow House, Pasadena
Earle C. Anthony House, Los Angeles
1910   John G. Neumeister House, Redondo (project)
John Lambert House, Pasadena (project)
John C. Bentz House alterations and additions, Pasadena
James A. Culbertson House additions, Pasadena
Ernest W. Smith House, Pasadena
James W. Neill House alterations, Pasadena
Howard Longley House alterations and additions, South Pasadena
Samuel L. Merrill House, Pasadena
Keith Spaulding Bunk House, Fillmore
John C. Bentz Garage, Pasadena
A.C. Drake House, Pasadena (project)
Henry M. Robinson House additions, Pasadena
1911   Alexander M. Drake House, Pasadena (project)
Mortimer Fleishhacker House, Woodside
S. Hazard Halsted House additions, Pasadena
William W. Spinks House alterations, Pasadena
Crow-Crocker Garage additions, Pasadena
Nathan Bentz House, Santa Barbara

Earle C. Anthony Automobile Showroom interiors, Los Angeles
Henry M. Greene House additions, Pasadena
Cordelia A. Culbertson House, Pasadena
Longfellow School, Pasadena
S.C. Graham House, Los Angeles (project)
Charles P. Wilcox House, Pasadena
Mrs. Charles G. Brown House, Pasadena
Pasadena Ice Company Building alterations, Pasadena
Joseph K. Huston House, Pasadena
1912   Mrs. Parker A. Earle Apartment House, Pasadena
Charles M. Pratt House alterations, Nordhoff
Annie Blacker House, Pasadena
Edward S. Crocker House, Pasadena
Dr. Frances F. Rowland House, moving and alterations, Pasadena
Charles S. Greene House alterations and additions, Pasadena
Frank L. Palmer House, North Pomona (project)
S. Hazard Halsted House alterations and additions, Pasadena
Michael Kew House, San Diego
George A. Gibbs House additions, Pasadena
Vista del Arroyo Hotel east annex and bungalow alterations, Pasadena
Dr. Robert P. McReynolds House alterations, Los Angeles
F.W. Hawkes House alterations, Pasadena
J.S. Silverberg House alterations, San Mateo
1913   Henry A. Ware House, Pasadena
Earle C. Anthony House alterations and additions, Los Angeles
Dr. Edward H. Angle House, Pasadena (project)
William M. Ladd House, Nordhoff
Mrs. J. Herbert Ballentine House alterations and additions, Altadena
Sidney D. Gamble House, Escondido (project)
James W. Neill House alterations, Pasadena
1914   James A. Culbertson House additions, Pasadena
Vista del Arroyo Building, Pasadena (project)
Dr. Rosa Englemann House, Pasadena
Cordelia A. Culbertson House additions, Pasadena
Charles S. Greene Garage, Pasadena
Theodore Irwin House additions, Pasadena
Henry A. Ware House additions, Pasadena
Dr. William T. Bolton House additions, Pasadena
1915   John T. Greene House, Sacramento
Dr. Robert P. McReynolds House additions, Los Angeles
Mortimer Fleischhacker House additions, San Francisco
William E. Hamlin House, Pasadena
F.W. Hawks House alterations, Pasadena
Charles M. Pratt House alterations, Nordhoff
Dr. Nathan H. Williams House, Altadena
S. Hazard Halsted House alterations and additions, Pasadena
Dr. Rosa Englemann House additions, Pasadena
Dr. Arthur A. Libby House additions, Pasadena
Herbert Fleischhacker House alterations, Atherton
Pasadena Ice Company Offices alterations and additions, Pasadena
Pasadena Ice Company Ice Storage Building additions, Pasadena
William E. Hamlin Garage, Pasadena
Dr. Frances F. Rowland House alterations, Pasadena
1916   H.T. Proctor House, Cocoa Nut Beach, Florida (project)
J. Herbert Hall Apartment House alterations and additions, Pasadena
Dr. Robert P. McReynolds House alterations, Los Angeles

Westmoreland Place Portals and Gates, Pasadena
Mortimer Fleischhacker House additions, Woodside
S. Hazard Halsted House additions and garage, Pasadena
1917 Charles H. Stoddard House, Burlingame (project)
Dr. Martha J. Kuznik House, Hollywood (project)
John H. Poole House, Pasadena
Earl C. Anthony House alterations and additions, Los Angeles
Cordelia A. Culbertson House alterations, Pasadena
Henry M. Robinson House alterations and additions, Pasadena
1919 John H. Poole House, Pasadena (project)
Hubert F. Krantz Development for Prospect Park, Palm Beach Country, Florida (project)
Hubert F. Krantz House, Pasadena (project)

Works (by Henry Mather Greene only; all in California unless noted)
1901 All Saints Episcopal Church alterations, Pasadena
1917 Jennie A. Reeve House moving and alterations, Long Beach
Charles S. Witbeck House, Santa Monica
Howard F. Mundorff House, Fresno
Dr. William T. Bolton House alterations, Pasadena
1918 John Whitworth House additions, Altadena
1922 S. Hazard Halsted House alterations, Pasadena
1923 Earle C. Anthony House moving, Beverly Hills
Pasadena Drapery Workshop
1924 Thomas Gould Jr. House, Ventura
Mrs. J.H. Jones House garden plan, Pasadena
Mrs. Datus C. Smith House alterations and garden, Pasadena
Mrs. Kate A. Kelley House, Los Angeles
Mrs. D.G. Wilson House alterations, Los Angeles
Rev. Charles Hibbard House alterations, Pasadena
Mrs. Paran F. Rice House additions, Monrovia
1925 J.H. Huntoon Duplex, Visalia (project)
Earle C. Anthony House garden development, Beverly Hills
Dr. Robert P. McReynolds House alterations, Los Angeles
Haigag H. Khazoyan Store alterations, Pasadena
A.C. Blumenthal Garage, Los Angeles
Walter D. Valentine Garage additions, Altadena
Samuel Z. Mardian Store and Apartment Building, Pasadena
William Thum House, Pasadena
Lloyd E. Morrison House, South Pasadena
"The Dugout," California Institute of Technology, Pasadena
Ernest E. Wennerberg Store alterations, Pasadena
Miss Hatcher House, Pasadena (project)
Arthur Savage Duplex, Pasadena
Mary R. Darling House additions and garage, Claremont
Mary R. Darling House garage, Claremont
James W. Neill House alterations, Pasadena
James Swan House alterations and moving, Pasadena
1926 Mrs. C.P. Daly House, Ventura (project)
Pacific Southwest Trust and Savings Bank alterations, Pasadena
Dr. William T. Bolton House alterations, Pasadena
Dr. Robert P. McReynolds House alterations, Los Angeles

Mrs James E. Saunders House, Pasadena
1927 Crow-Crocker House alterations and additions, Pasadena (project)
Jennie A. Reeve House alterations, additions and second moving, Long Beach
1928 Lucy E. Wheeler House alterations, Los Angeles
1929 Mrs. Edward Strasburg House, Covina
Walter L. Richardson House, Porterville
Whitworth Corporation Building alterations, Pasadena
1930 Frank M. Brininstool House alterations, Pasadena
Mrs. Carrie Whitworth House alterations, Altadena
Mrs. Fred W. Horne House alterations, Pasadena
1931 Emma M. Black House alterations, Pasadena
Cordelia A. Culbertson House potting house addition, Pasadena
1932 George W. Gain House alterations, Pasadena
B.O. Kendall House alterations, Pasadena
1933 George F. Kernaghan House alterations, Pasadena (project)
Carl Mencerberg Shop, Pasadena (project)
William H. Rapp House alterations, Pasadena (project)
James Howard House alterations, Pasadena
1934 William M. Beeson Shop Building, Pasadena (engineering consultant)
1935 Howard K. Brick House, Philadelphia (project)
L.C. Johnson Garage, Altadena
George H. Barker House alterations, Pasadena
William H. Sloane House alterations and additions to garage, South Pasadena
1936 J.M. Ritson House alterations, Pasadena
1938 Cordelia A. Culbertson House alterations, Pasadena
1941 Mrs. Louise Thum House alterations and additions, Glendora
1943 Mrs. James E. Saunders House alterations, Pasadena
1944 William S. Greene House, Pittsburg (project)

Publications:

On the GREENES: books—*Five California Architects* by Esther McCoy, New York 1960; *Greene and Greene: Architects in the Residential Style* by William Current, Fort Worth, Texas 1974; *A Greene and Greene Guide* by Janann Strand, Pasadena, California 1974; *A Guide to the Works of Greene and Greene* by Randell L. Makinson, Salt Lake City 1974; *Greene and Greene Collection in the Avery Library: Inventory and Index* by John K. McAskill, New York 1976; *Greene and Greene* by Randell L. Makinson, volume I: *Architecture as a Fine Art*, volume II: *Furniture and Related Designs*, Salt Lake City, 1977, 1979; *Greene and Greene: David B. Gamble House, Pasadena, California, 1908*, Tokyo 1984; articles— "Greene and Greene" by Jean Murray Bangs in *Architectural Forum* (New York), October 1948; "A obra dos irmaos Greene" by Jean Murray Bangs in *Arquitectura portuguesa* (Lisbon), April/June 1949; "Greene and Greene of Pasadena" by L. Morgan Yost in *AIA Journal* (Washington, D.C.), September 1950; "Prophets Without Honor" by Jean Murray Bangs in *AIA Journal* (Washington, D.C.), July 1952; "Notes on Greene and Greene" by Esther McCoy in *Arts and Architecture* (Los Angeles), July 1953; "California: The Emergence of a Tradition" in *Architectural Record* (New YOrk), May 1956; "Roots of California Contemporary Architecture" by Esther McCoy in *Arts and Architecture* (Los Angeles), October 1956; "Recognizing Our Own Architectural Traditions" in *House Beautiful* (New York), January 1957; 'A Parting Salute to the Fathers of the California Style" in *House and Home* (New York), August 1957; 'Some Sources of Greene and Greene" by Clay Lancaster in *AIA Journal*

(Washington, D.C.), August 1960; "The Gamble House by Greene and Greene" in the *Prairie School Review* (Chicago), no. 4, 1968; "Architecture West" in *Progressive Architecture* (New York), November 1972; "Greene and Greene" by Randell L. Makinson in *Approach* (Tokyo), Spring 1975; "The Brothers Greene" by Harwell Hamilton Harris in *Architectural Record* (New York), November 1975; "Recent Books on Greene and Greene" by Esther McCoy in *Progressive Architecture* (New York), January 1976; "Greene and Greene" by Philip Jodidio in *Connaissance des arts* (Paris), December 1977; "Greene and Greene" in *American Preservation* (Little Rock, Arkansas), April/May 1978; "The Morphology of Los Angeles" in *Architectural Design* (London) no. 8/9, 1981; "Controversy over the Stripping of a Historic Pasadena House" by Joseph Giovannini in the *New York Times*, 6 June 1985.

Bibliographies—*The Greene Brothers* by Lamia Doumato, Monticello, Illinois 1980; *The Firm of Greene and Greene and Its Impact on Californian Domestic Architecture: A Selected Bibliography* by Robert B. Harmon, Monticello, Illinois 1980.

For nearly a decade, the young architects Greene and Greene explored and experimented with a variety of styles in their search for an architectural expression that, in their minds, would represent the natural living patterns and regional characteristics of California. They had been trained in the principles of William Morris, enchanted by the California missions, intrigued by the valley landscapes, fascinated by Oriental art and architecture and by the publication of Swiss chalets and Italian gardens and villas. In 1902 their dramatic shift from traditional styles and their embrace of the concepts of the Arts and Crafts Movemnet was clearly revealed in the James Culbertson house. Although the exterior was reminiscent of the half-timbered construction of English country houses, their use of loval cobblestones and clinker brick, the influence of Japanese timber construction in the interiors, and the selection of Gustav Stickley furnishings suggested a more relaxed life style. The brothers themselves regarded their 1903 bungalow for Arturo Bandini as the turning point in their work. The significance of this design, however, lay in its U-shaped courtyard plan, incorporating the garden into the total living pattern and introducing floor plan concepts into the Greenes' work that were less formal and a synthesis of relationships between indoor and outdoor space.

The elements of true care and craftsmanship appeared in various of their designs during 1902 and 1903, but it was the 1904 house for Jennie A. Reeve that brought together, for thefirst time, the full range of the Greenes' architectural vocabulary and established their California Bungalow style. Here, in this two-story, shingle-clad bungalow were the articulated timber structure, multiple gabled over-hanging roofs, projecting support beams now carefully shaped on the ends, open sleeping porches, vertical slit windows, horizontal bands of casement windows, combinations of cobblestones and brick masonry, leaded stained glass and lantern designs, coordination of landscape, walks, fencing, and gates, and the full development of furniture and interior accessories. Here, as in other unpretentious designs, they demonstrated that modest dwellings could be endowed with grace, dignity, and character.

In the Adelaide Tichenor house, also of 1904, their growing interest in the Orient was reflected throughout the structure, interiors, and gardens. At this time, their own furniture designs began to depart from the four-square directness of Stickley's work. The lines of their designs were more relaxed, and, as their experience and convictions grew, they gracefully combined integrity, craftsmanship, and human personality into their works.

As larger commissions came into the office the Greens, through careful handling, they easily adapted the bungalow philosophies for more sophisticated designs by stretching its flexibility of concept and their personal sensitivities to the fullest. Structure and site became one. In order to relate the larger structures to the landscape, they emphasized and expressed the horizontal line in cantilevered roof lines, broad bands of casement windows, and sleeping porches. Outdoor terraces with wide stairways provided positive transitions to the grounds. The Greenes firmly maintained that a wooden structure should express the integrity and identity of each separate part, each treated as a design element. It was their handling of this concept that produced a symphony of wooden joinery. Wood panelling and trim were fastened with brass screws covered at times with square pegs of ebony, mahogany, and oak. Woodwork was brought together in different planes. Materials other than wood—brick, tile, boulders, metal, and glass—retained their own identities and functions, yet each contributed to the richness of the total composition. No detail was overlooked. Every peg, wedge, downspout, air vent, and fixture was designed into the whole.

At the height of their career, in the elaborate residences designed between 1907 and 1910, the Greenes' meticulous attention todetail, their insistence upon the highest quality of craftsmanship and materials, and the latitude given by clients for the design of nearly all of the interior furnishings developed in the brothers so exalted a set of standards for their work that soon very few people were able to afford their creations. At this same time, public tastes were changing, poor emulation of their work obscured the progressive spirit and integrity of the originals, and thus fewer and fewer commissions came into their offices.Concurrently, the brothers' individual interests again surfaced. Charles in particular wanted time to pursue his painting, photography, writing, and philosophical studies. The brothers' mutual respect allowed each of them to follow an independent path while they continued to work together. In the years that followed, their independent commissions and the clearly identifiable individual input into joint work attest to their unique and varying personal genius.

Today, their reputation as the leading architects of the Arts and Crafts Movement in America presently rests on the incredible craftsmanship and progressive designs for their ultimate bungalows for the Blacker, Ford, Gamble, Pratt, Thorsen, and Culbertson families. Time will, however, focus considerable importance upon the swift evolution and refinements of their works between 1902 and 1906 as well as their independent designs after 1910, where their personal responses to changing attitudes reveals the brothers' sensitivity to each new day, client, and site.

—Randell L. Makinson

Herbert Greene: Prairie House (Greene House), Norman, Oklahoma, 1961.

Information Agency tour of Europe, 1966; *Environment*. Kansas City Art Institute, Missouri, 1967; Florence Duhl Gallery, New York (individual show of architectural drawings), 1977; *An American Architecture*, Milwaukee Art Center, 1977. Also a painter; exhibitions: group—Oklahoma City Art Museum, 1962, *Illinois Biennal*, 1965; individual-Fine Arts Gallery, University of Arkansas, Fayetteville, 1966; Kovler Gallery, Chicago, 1966; Phoenix Gallery, New York, 1970, 1971; University of Kentucky Fine Arts Gallery Lexington 1974; Living Arts and Science Center, Lexington Kentucky, 1975; Louisville Arts Association, Kentucky, 1976. Recipient: Fellowship, 1977, and Senior Fellow, 1982, National Endowment for the Arts. Address: 1218 Queens Road, Berkeley, California 94708, U.S.A.

Works:

1955 Lurie House, Houston (with Joseph Krakower)
Rainey House, Houston (with Joesph Krakower
Gulf Coast Finance Company Office, Houston (with Joseph Krakower)
1956 Long Point Clinic, Houston (with Joseph Krakower)
Folloder House, Houston (with Joseph Krakower)
Houston Typewriter Exchange Building with Joseph Krakower)
Salsman House, Houston (with Joseph Krakower)
Mendel House, Houston (with Joseph Krakower)
1957 Lyne House, Houston
1958 Southwestern Bell Telephone Company Office Building, Houston
Baylor Medical College Research Building, Houston (Project)
1960 Mr. Mrs. John Joyce House, Snyder, Oklahoma
Roosevelt Granite Company Offices, Synder, Oklahoma
Burton's IGA Supermarket, Holdenville, Oklahoma
Northwestern Electric Cooperative Office and Warehouse alterations, Woodward, Oklahoma

1961 Herb and Mary Greene House (Prairie House) Norman Oklahoma
Downtown urban remodelling plan for Norman, Oklahoma
Lyons House and Museum, Holdenville, Oklahoma
1962 Metropolitan pedestrian Overpass System (project)
Theatre-in-the-round (project)
1964 Housing for the Elderly, Paris, Kentucky (with Jim Clark) Low-cost Mountain Housing Reasearch Project, Eastern Kentucky
Dr. and Mrs. Earl Cunningham House, Quail Creed Road, Oklahoma City (with Robert Alan Bowlby)
Unitarian Church, Higbee Mill Road, Lexington, Kentucky
1966 Painting and photography research project, Lexington, Kentucky
Dr. and Mrs. Richard French House, Paynes Mill Road, Versailles, Kentucky
1967 Multi-Use Space for Urban Areas (project; with C.A. Coleman, Jr)
Mr. and Mrs Harry Furchess House, Murray Kentucky
1969 Mr. and Mrs. Philips lovass House, Grimes Mill Road, Lexington, Kentucky
1970 Parking Structure II, University of Kentucky, Lexington (design consultant; with C.A. Coleman, Jr.)
University of Kentucky Academic Facilties Building, Ashland Community College, Ashland, Kentucky (design consultant; with C.A. Coleman, Jr.)
Community Park Shelter, Lexington, Kentucky (with C.A. Coleman, Jr.)
1971 Dr. and Mrs. Will Ward House, 5801 Orion Road, Glenview, Kentucky
Polyurethane foam experimental project, Lexington, Kentucky
1972 Courtyard Housing (project)
1974 Medical Center, Harrodsburg Road, Lexington, Kentucky
Dr. and Mrs. Richard O'Neill House, Evans Mill Road, Lexington, Kentucky
1978 Urban studies and armatures (projects)
Dr. and Mrs. Clinton Cook House, Glenview, Kentucky
1980 Villa Blanca Horse Farm Complex, Lexington, Kentucky
1983 Dr. and Mrs. Richard Dubou House, Lexington, Kentucky

GREENE, Herb(ert)
American. Born in Oneonta, New York, 13 September 1929. Educated at Syacuse University, New York, 1947; University of Oklahoma, Norman under Bruce Goff, *q.v.*1948-52 (First Prize, Indiana Limestone Competition, 1951), B.Arch. 1952. Married Mary Morrison in 1955; children: Tom and Lauren; married Nanine Hilliard in 1977. Worked in the office of John Lautner, *q.v.*Hollywood, California, 1952, Bruce Goff, Norman, Oklahoma, 1950-53, and Wirtz, Calhoun, Tungate and Jackson,Houston Texas, 1954; Associate Architect with Joseph Krakower, Houston, 1955-57. In private practice,. Houston and Norman, 1957-64 in Lexington, Kentucky, 1964-83, and in Berkeley, California, since 1984. Associate Professor, University of Oklahoma, 1957-63; Professor of Architecture, University of Kentucky, Lexington 1963-83. Exhibition: *Modern Architecture U.S.A.*, Museum of Modern Art, New York, 1965; *American Churches*, United States

Publicatons:

By GREENE: books—*Mind and Image: An Essay on Art and Architecture*, Lexington, Kentucky 1976, London 1980; *Building to Last: Architecture as Ongoing Art*, New York 1981; *Herb Greene: Works*, booklet, Lexington, Kentucky 1981; articles—in *Kentucky Architect* (Louisville), October 1966, June 1968, July 1968; "Refining your designs" in *Fine Homebuilding* (Newtown, Connecticut), December 1982/January 1983.

On GREENE: books—*Photography of Architecture* by Julius Shulman, Los Angeles 1964; *Residential Architecture in America* by Helmut Borchartdt, Munich 1965; *Architecture at Rice 15*, Houston 1965; *Architects on Architecture*, edited by Paul Heyer, New York 1966, London 1967; *Photographic History of Modern Architecture* by Dennis Sharp, New York 1972; *Modern Movements in Architecture* by Charles Jencks, New York 1973; *Ad Hocism* by Charles Jencks and Nathan Silver, New York 1973; *The Prairie School Tradition*, edited by Brian A. Spencer, New York 1979; articles—"Greene Residence" in *Architectural Design* (London), May 1957; "Greene Residence" in *Progressive Architecture* (New York), May 1962; "Green Residence" in *Architecture d'aujourd'hui* (Paris), June 1962; "Greene Residence" in *Life* (New York), November 1962; "Joyce Residence" in *Progressive Architecture* (New York), November 1962; "Greene Residence in *Look* (New York), September 1963; "Cunningham Residence" in *Progressive Architecture* (New York), May 1965; "The Unitarian Church of Lexington" in *Progressive Architecture* (New York), March 1966; "A Modern Farmhouse for the Kentucky Blue Grass" in *Kentucky Architect* (Louisville), June 1966; "The Paintings of Herb Greene" in *Arts and Architecture* (Los Angeles), November 1967; "Four House Projects" in *Progressive Architecture* (New York), August 1968; "Shades of Greene" in *Building* (London), May 1979.

I conceive the architectural image as an assemblage to which significant harmonized experience of the user and the audience can be attached. Ideas of shelter, sanctuary, social gathering, valued historic architecture, characteristics of particular sites and climate are primary sources for images, as are feelings and associations from bodily life and memory.

The Prairie House communicates protection by enveloping forms. The soft textures, rhythms, and warm color of the shingles and boards seem human. At the same time, they relate the house to the American shingle style and the exposed prairie site which is left in a natural condition. Ideas such as looking out at the world and bodily sentience are also consciously included. The image contains references ranging from primordial creature to futurist object and represents my interest in creating metaphors of age and the passage of time.

Iam at present developing new forms of urban architecture in which similar aims are expressed in long-lasting frameworks or armatures that can be added to by many participants over generations. Human beings, with our unique ability to remember and anticipate, need to develop an architecture whose primary esthetic impact gives direction to an imaginative mingling of past, present, and future. This architcture, as a built continuum, should be a receptacle for many individualized acts of expression which are symbolic of a democratic society and the diversity and indeterminacy of the world. Orchestrated in an armature whose forms are grounded in long-sanctioned relationships to region and historic form, individualized acts become a mosaic for reverie and a record of social and esthetic comment.

—Herb Greene

Herb Greene is the major prophet of American

vernacular high-art architecture practicing today. His Prairie House of 1961 quicklyestablished him as the primary artistic spokesman for the organicism developed by Bruce Goff from elements of the Frank Lloyd Wright heritage. The continuity with Wright and Goff is evident in the use of native materials, organic forms, comfortable sheltering proportions, and in the integration into the solid earth of the site and the human culture of the region. While the continuity of form is evident, the new departure is both striking and daring. Prairie House, much more than an organic form of bird-pyramid that settled down on the Oklahoma prairie, is a personal talisman or sheltering power-object and transformation place of the Greene family.

Wright's struggles for a contemporary organicism were always in the context of the prototypic rather than the personal solution to the shelter problems if not of the whole world, then at least of America. Goff's fantasy places were indeed unique creations, but they also remained on an impersonal plane of purely formal aestheticism. It is the infusion of the personal statement into the fixed medicine-bag of the abode that transforms this ironic tradition into Greene's talismanic Prairie House. In creating a personal statement, a modern vernacular becomes possible, and the "professionalism" of the architect comes under severe strain.

It is to the tension between the personalism of the truly organic power-object and the universalism of our conception of art that I referred when I said "vernacular high-art architecture." On the face of it, this isa contradiction in terms, a contradiction that has at least in part been responsible for the divergence in Greene's more recent work. The highly personalistic and subjective has become increasingly concentrated into collages, which, hung on a wall, are sharable talismanic objects. The residences and projects have evolved into much more "general" solutions that leave room for personalization by users and inhabitants.

This divergence in Greene's work may be both unfortunate and inevitable. Yet, oneis struck by the enormous influence that Greene's early work has had on self-built housing in the late 1960s and since, particularly in California and in mountainous regions in the United States. Similarly, attempts to "give away" architecture as a profession, as in the populist projects of Christopher Alexander and his group, have radically redefined the role of the architect as professional in an evolution toward a new vernacular folk art in the built environment. Prairie House can be seen as the starting point of both of these trends—a starting point from which Greene has himself retreated perhaps due to a high regard for museum art or the exigencies of professional career, or both.

Alternatively, Greene may have correctly perceived that the exterior shells that house private lives gain their power in and through use rather than throuhh the direct formal reflection of the dreams they shelter. Instead of giving a place, form, and habitation to a dream then, the architectural artist may only make it possible to create a safe place for dreaming.

—Joseph B. Juhasz

GREGOTTI, Vittorio.

Italian. Born in Novara, Italy, 10 August 1927. Educated at the Milan Polytechnic, School of Architecture, 1948-52, Dip.Arch. 1952. Married Marina Mazza in 1975. Partner, with Lodovico Meneghetti and Giotto Stoppino, Architetti Associati, Milan, 1952-67; in private practice, Milan, 1968-74. Since 1974, Partner, with Pierluigi Cerri and Augusto Cagnardi, Gregotti Associati, Milan. Architectural Consultant, La Rinascente Stores

Group, Milan, 1968-71; Director, Visual Arts Section, *Biennale,* Venice, 1974-76. Professor of Architectural Composition, Milan Polytechnic, since 1964, and School of Architecture, Venice, since 1978. Associate Editor, with Ernesto N. Rogers, *Casabella,* Milan, 1952-60; Editor, *Edilizia Moderna* monographs, Milan, 1962-64; Architectural Editor, *Il Verri,* Milan, 1963-65. Co-Editor, *Lotus,* Venice, 1974-82; Director, *Rassegna* magazine, Milan, since 1979, and *Casabella* magazine, Milan, since 1982. Exhibitions: *Triennale,* Milan, since 1951; *28/78 Architettura,* Palazzo delle Stelline, Milan, and Palazzo Grassi, Venice, 1979; *The Project for Calabria University,* Syracuse, New York, 1981; *Architettura Italiana 1970-80,* Rome and Milan, 1981; *Internationale Bauausstellung,* Berlin and Dortmund, West Germany, 1981; *Vittorio Gregotti: progetti,* Palermo, Sicily 1981; *Architecture and Territory,* Paris, 1982; *Maquettes d'architectes,* Centre d'Art Contemporain, Geneva, and Le Nouveau Musée, Lyon-Villeurbanne, France, 1982; *La Modernité,* Paris, 1982; *Architettura nei paesi islamici,* Venice, 1982; *Progetto per il centro ricerche Monedison a Napoli,* Rome, 1983; *Il mestiere di architetto: Botta, Gregotti, Piano,* Ferrara, Italy, 1984; *Vittorio Gregotti,* Harvard University, Cambridge, Massachusetts, 1984; *The European Iceberg,* Art Gallery of Ontario, Toronto, 1985. Recipient: Grand Prize, *Triennale,* Milan, 1963; Compasso d'Oro, Milan, 1968; First Prize, IACP Housing Development Competition, Palermo, 1970; First Prize, University of Florence Competition, 1971; First Prize, University of Calabria Competition, 1973. Address: Gregotti Associati, via Bandello 20, 20123 Milan, Italy.

Works:

1953 Exhibition Pavilion, Market Fair, Novara, Italy
1956 Worker's house, Novara, Italy
1958/
59 Three apartment buildings, Novara, Italy
Istituto di Credito Headquarters, Novara, Italy
1961/
62 Co-operative housing development, Novara, Italy
Cottage on a Slope, near Varese, Italy (project)
Three single-family houses, Lake Maggiore, near Stresa, Italy (project)
1962 Two houses, Portofino, Italy (project)
1962/
67 Co-operative housing development, via Palmanova, Milan
Master plan for the city of Novara, Italy
1964 Entrance Pavilion, *Triennale,* Milan (with Peppo Brivio)
1964/
68 Co-operative housing development, via Desiderio Settignano, Milan
1967 Gregotti Apartment conversion, via Regaldi 2, Milan
1968 Bossi Cotton Mill, Novara, Italy
Istituto di Credito Headquarters, Bra, Italy
1969 La Rinascente Supermarket, Milan
La Rinascente Supermarket II, Milan
La Rinascente Department Store, via Carlo Alberto, Turin (project)
La Rinascente Department Store, via Ruggero Settimo, Palermo, Sicily (project)
1970/
72 Science Department, University of Palermo, Sicily
1970 IACP Zen Housing Development, Cardillo District, Palermo, Sicily
1971/
78 Community Centre, Gibellina, Sicily
1971 New buildings, University of Florence
1972/
74 Gabel's Offices and Warehouse, Como, Italy
1972/
75 New University of Calabria, Cosenza, Italy

1974   Integrated Development Plan for the Adda, Lombardy, Italy

1974/
75   Ricordi Music Store, Milan

1974/
84   Feltrinelli Foundation Headquarters, Milan (project)

1976   Residential Estate Plan, Cefalù, Sicily

1977   Research Centre, Portici, Naples

1977/
83   Single-Family House, Oleggio, Novara, Italy

1978   Girls' School, Jeddah, Saudi Arabia

1979   New Italian Cultural Institute, Tokyo (project)

1980/
81   Shipyards, Giudecca Island, Venice (project)

1980/
83   Isola del Tronchetto Plan, Venice

1980/
84   Housing Development, Lutzowstrasse, West Berlin

Housing Development, Cannareggio, Venice (project)

1981   New Arrival Centre, San Marino, Italy (project)

1981/
83   City Park and Academic Centre, Sassuolo, Modena, Italy (project)

Bossi Offices, Cameri, Novara, Italy

1981/
84   Chemical Research Centre, Alessandria, Italy

1982   Tourist Resort, Riccione, Italy (project)

Office Tower Block, Milan (project)

1982/
83   Single-Family House, Chiasso, Switzerland (project)

Plan for the 1989 World's Fair, Paris (project)

1983   Lingotto Area Development Plan, Turin (as International Consultant)

1983/
84   Mixed-use Housing and Business Complex, Modena, Italy (project)

1984   New Olympic Centre, Barcelona (competition project)

Civic Centre, Arezzo Italy (project)

Publications:

By GREGOTTI: books—*Territorio dell'architettura*, Milan 1966; *New Directions in Italian Architecture*, London 1968, New York 1969; *Il disegno del prodotto industriale*, Milan 1982; articles—"Marco Zanuso, un architetto della seconda generazione" in Casabella (Milan), no. 216, 1957; "Complessità di Max Bill" in *Casabella* (Milan), no. 228, 1959; "Classicità a razionalismo di Auguste Perret" in *Casabella* (Milan), no. 229, 1959; "Peter Behrens 1868-1940" in *Casabella* (Milan), no. 240, 1960; L'Architettura dell'expressionismo" in *Casabella* (Milan), no. 254, 1961; "Facolta del costruire" in *Casabella* (Milan), May 1964; "La ricerca storica in architettura" in *Edilizia moderna* (Milan), no. 86, 1965; "L'Art Nouveau" in *L'Arte Moderna* (Milan), no. 91, 1967; "L'Architettura tedesca dal 1900 al 1930" in *L'Arte Moderna* (Milan), no. 94, 1967; "Les Nouvelles Tendances de l'architecture italienne" in *L'Architecture d'aujourd'hui* (Paris), September 1968; "Italian Design 1945-1971" in *Italy: The New Domestic Landscape*, exhibition catalogue, New York 1972; "ANIACAP/IN/ARCH Competition for Low-Cost Housing" in *Domus* (Milan), October 1973; "Auguste Perret 1874-1974," with Jean Prouvé, in *Domus* (Milan), May 1974; "Per una storia del design italiano" in *Ottagono* (Milan), nos. 32, 33, 34, 36, 1974. "For Which Modern Movement?" in *Parametro* (Bologna), June 1977; "Palermo: The Necessity of Architecture," with Pierluigi Nicolin, in *Casabella* (Milan), September 1977; "Bellinzona: Architecture for the Ancient City" in *Casabella* (Milan), November 1977; "Il filo rosso del razionalismo italiano" in *Casabella* (Milan), no. 440-441, 1978; "Proget-

tazione e una parola" in *Alfabeta* (Milan), June 1979; "L'Università della Calabria" in *Progetto Realizzato*, Venice 1980; "La nozione di contesto" in *Casabella* (Milan), January 1981; "Megasegno in laguna" in *Domus* (Milan), May 1981; "Carlo Scarpa" in *Rassegna* (Milan), July 1981; "Tadao Ando" in *Casabella* (Milan), October 1982; "Giuseppe Terragni" in *Rassegna* (Milan), September 1982; "A Formal Balance" in *Design Furniture from Italy*, Milan 1983; "Die kritische Kontinuat zwischen den Generationen" in *Junge Architekten in Europa*, Stuttgart 1983; "The Place in Time" in *Daidalos* (Berlin), June 1984.

On GREGOTTI: books—*Il progetto per l'Universita delle Calabrie e altre architetture di Vittorio Gregotti*, Milan 1979; *Berlino 1984*, Florence 1982; *Vittorio Gregotti: progetti e architetture* by Manfredo Tafuri, Milan and New York 1982; *Architetture nei paesi islamici*, Venice 1982; *Venti progetti per il futuro del Lingotto*, Milan 1984; *The European Iceberg*, exhibition catalogue, edited by Germano Celant, Milan 1985; articles—"Padiglioni in un parco alla Terza Fiera-Mercato di Novara" in *Domus* (Milan), December 1953; "Case d'Affito a Novara 1958-59" in *Casabella* (Milan), July 1960; "Due case di Portofino 1962" in *Casabella* (Milan), no. 276, 1963; "Architettura italiana 1963," special issue of *Edilizia moderna* (Milan), no. 82/83, 1964; "Contemporary Italian Architects" in *L'Architecture d'aujourd'hui* (Paris), no. 48, 1965; "Apartment in Milan" in *House and Garden* (London), March 1968; "Le cento città d'Italia: Milano" in *Controspazio* (Bari, Italy), September/October 1969; "L'Architettura interrota: tre progetti di Vittorio Gregotti" in *Controspazio* (Bari, Italy), March 1971; "Civile abitazione: complessità di linguaggio per il recupero dell'unità architettonica alla periferia di Milano" in *Casabella* (Milan), April 1972; "Vittorio Gregotti" in *Architecture + Urbanism* (Tokyo), July 1977; "Centro di ricerca a Napoli" in *Casabella* (Milan), September 1979; "Vittorio Gregotti" in *GA Document* (Tokyo), special issue, 1980; "Due proposte per la Giudecca" in *Lotus* (Venice), no. 28, 1980; "Città senza bandiere" in *Domus* (Milan), September 1980; "Variation on a Grid Shape" in *Architectural Record* (New York), May 1981. "Costruire en terra d'Islam" in *L'Architecture d'aujourd'hui* (Paris), September 1981; "Riti di fondazione, Palermo University" in *Domus* (Milan), October 1981; "La generazione dello Zen", in *Lotus* (Venice), no. 36, 1982; "Gregotti Associati" in *Space Design* (Tokyo), April 1982; "Verde pensiero in un'ombre verde" in *Domus* (Milan), May 1982; "Nuovi uffici Bossi a Cemeri" in *Casabella* (Milan) July/August 1983; "Barcelona, Juegos Olimpicos 1992" in *Arquitecturas bis* (Barcelona), January/February 1984; "House in Oleggio" in *GA Houses* (Tokyo), January 1984; "Bossi's Factory Extension" in *GA Document* (Tokyo), February 1984; "La Ville-territoire" in *Techniques et architecture* (Paris), December 1983/January 1984; "Paris, Paris" in *Domus* (Milan), January 1984; "Gregotti Associati 1981-1983" in *Process: Architecture* (Tokyo), June 1984.

Everything around us, our environment or *Umwelt* as Husserl and phenomenology term it, is in my opinion the physical manifestation of its own memory, i.e., of the way in which the various strata of memory and of the decisions to shape the place are superimposed. Environment is nature turned culture, not just in external appearance but, more importantly, in the structural features as the real truths of any place.

Vittorio Gregotti: New Department of Science, University of Palermo, Sicily, 1984.

In contrast to the abstract purity of the idea of space, the concepts of environment and of site always contain a great quantity of physical and historical debris which can become an important source and material for the architectural project, a material which is capable of describing differences and determining the quality of the architectural project. The worst enemy of the architecture of modernity is that conception of space which is concerned only with its economic and technical qualities, remaining completely oblivious of other values a particular place might possess. Seen in this light, geography may be considered to be the description of how the vestiges of history have assumed their particular physical form; thus geography can also provide clues to that which it unshakingly supports. The architectural project faces the task of revealing the true essence of an environment by changing its form.

This environment is by no means a structural whole in which architecture disappears; on the contrary, it is the most important material for developing the architectural design. It is in the concepts of the place and of the principle of settlement that the environment becomes the essence of architectural creation. As a result, new principles and procedures are developed: the relationship between individual objects becomes equally important as the linguistic definition of the object itself; in fact, the linguistic definition of the context is determined by the knowledge of the specific place, and this knowledge is gained through the architectural project.

The origin of architecture lies not in the hut or the cave or even the mythical "house of Adam in Paradise": long before he turned pillar into column and roof into gable, before he placed stone upon stone, man put stones on the ground to mark a place in the middle of an unknown universe and to survey and change it. And just as with any other act of measuring, this process requires a distinct and specific method. When seen in this light, there are but two different ways of establishing a relationship with a place: the first uses mimetic imitation, organic assimilation, and the creation of a conspicuous complexity, while the second relies on measurement, distance, definition, and change within the complexity. We prefer and believe in the second way, for the simple reason that it does not make us strive for the impossible reconciliation of nature and artifice, of the new and the pre-existing; instead, it enables us, with the aid of the particular tools of the craft, to provide it with a new meaning of its own, based on the specific quality of non-coincidence.

This method involves a series of tension-producing subdivisions. One need only think of erecting a wall, building a fence, or marking off a particular area. This results, on one hand, in the creation of a highly articulated interior corresponding with the diversity of human activities; on the other, a simple exterior which serves as a measure for the totality of the great potential of our architectural environment. In this context, "great" does not refer to a spatial dimension but instead denotes the "great" capacity for contextual modification. In order to design a project, it is necessary to establish a rule. In essence, this rule has to do with the tradition of the style and the practice and with their advancement. Yet, what lends truth and architectural reality to the rule is the encounter with the actual site: Only from the experience of the place emerge the characteristic features that pave the way for architecture and determine its form.

—Vittorio Gregotti

Vittorio Gregotti's career spans a wide artistic spectrum. He is well known as an architect and planner; he has also been involved in furniture and industrial design; and he is a prolific writer and an impresario. During the period of his co-editorship with Ernesto N. Rogers of *Casabella*, he became the main apologist of the Art Nouveau revival (Stile Libertà), but his essays have a forthright quality that puts them above the more morbid and extreme exercises in the style.

Gregotti's commitment to historicism was very sophisticated, and he soon passed beyond the limitations that the revival imposed—as may be seen in his section of the *XIII Triennale* in Milan, a radical departure in exhibition design. In his most important book to date, *Territorio dell'Architettura*, he sets out his theoretical position, which owes something to phenomenology and something to the structuralists. It also discusses the planner's almost geographical concern with environment, which has been one of Gregotti's overriding interests, evident in his early plan of Novara and in his more recent planning work, explicitly in the winning schemes for the universities of Florence and Calabria. His architecture, meanwhile, was becoming increasingly stereometric. The Architetti Associati office was dissolved in the late 1960's, and thereafter Gregotti became an independent practitioner, working with a number of different associates. The most considerable of his later works is the Zen Housing Development in Palermo.

His exhibition work and his writings have made Gregotti one of the best-known architects in Italy. Although the volume of his built work to date is not vast, all that he has done has had a great influence. His development has been accompanied by polemics that have elucidated the rationale of every step he has taken, in a way that cannot be paralleled by any other European architect.

—Joseph Rykwert

GROPIUS, Walter Adolf.

American. Born in Berlin, Germany, 18 May 1883; emigrated to England, 1934; emigrated to the United States, 1937. Educated at the Humanistisches Gymnasium, Berlin, 1903; Technische Hochschule, Munich, 1903-04; Technische Hochschule, Charlottenburg, Berlin, 1905-07. Served as an Officer in the German Army, 1904-05, 1914-18: IronCross (first and second class); Bavarian Military Medal; Royal Austrian Decoration. Married Alma Schindler Mahler (widow of the composer) in 1916 (divorced); daughter: Alma; married Ise Frank in 1923; daughter: Beate. Worked in the office of the architects Solf and Wichards, Berlin, 1904; travelled in Europe, 1906-07; Chief Assistant in the office of architect Peter Behrens, *q.v.*, Berlin, 1907-10; in private practice, Berlin, 1910-14; Director, Grand Ducal Academy of Arts, Weimar, Germany, and Grand Ducal Saxon School of Applied Arts, Weimar, Germany, 1915-19: merged the two schools under the name Das Staatliche Bauhaus, 1919: Director of the Bauhaus, at Weimar, Germany, 1919-25, and at Dessau, Germany, 1925-28 (associates: Herbert Bayer, Marcel Breuer, *q.v.*, Josef Albers, László Moholy-Nagy, Wassily Kandinsky, Paul Klee, Lyonel Feininger, Johannes Itten, Gerhard Marcks, Adolf Meyer, Ludwig Mies van der Rohe, *q.v.*, Georg Muche, and Oskar Schlemmer); in private practice, Berlin, 1928-33; in partnership with E. Maxwell Fry, *q.v.*, London, 1934-36, and with Marcel Breuer, Cambridge, Massachusetts, 1937-41; Founder/Partner, with seven associates, TAC: The Architects' Collaborative, *q.v.*, Cambridge, 1945-69. Professor of Architecture, 1937-52, Chairman of the Department of Architecture, 1938-52, and Professor Emeritus, 1952-69, Graduate School of Design, Harvard University, Cambridge. Founder-Member and President, 1928, and Vice-President, 1929-57, CIAM (Congrès Internationaux d'Architecture Moderne); Vice-President, Institute of Sociology, London, 1937. Exhibitions: World's Fair, Ghent, Belgium, 1913; *Deutsche Werkbund*, Cologne, 1914; *Deutsche Werkbund*, Stuttgart, 1927; *Wohnen im Grünen*, Berlin, 1928; *Deutsche Werkbund*, Paris, 1930; *Bund Deutscher Architekten Exhibition*, Berlin, 1931; *The Extendable House*, Berlin, 1932; *German People—German Work*, Berlin, 1934; *Non-Ferrous Metals Exhibition*, Berlin, 1934; *The Bauhaus 1919-1928*, Museum of Modern Art, New York, 1938; World's Fair, New York, 1939; *Bauhaus*, London, 1969; *Walter Gropius: Das Spätwerk*, Bauhaus-Archiv, Darmstadt, West Germany, 1970; *Walter Gropius: Buildings, Plans, Projects, 1906-1969*, toured the United States, 1973; *Boston: Forty Years of Modern Architecture*, Institute of Contemporary Art, Boston, 1980. Recipient; Gold Medal, World's Fair, Ghent, 1913; First Prize, Dammerstock District Development Competition, Karlsruhe, Germany 1928; First Prize, Spandau-Haselhorst Experimental District Competition, Berlin, 1929; Gold Medal of Honor, The Architectural League of New York, 1951; Grand Prix d'Architecture, São Paulo, 1953; Royal Gold Medal, Royal Institute of British Architects, London, 1956; Hanseatic Goethe Prize, University of Hamburg, West Germany 1956; Ernst Reuter Medal, City of Berlin, 1957; Gold Medal, American Institute of Architects, 1959; Grand State Professor of Architecture Award, West Germany, 1960; Prince Albert Gold Medal, Royal Society of Arts, London, 1961; Goethe Prize, Frankfurt, 1961; Kaufmann International Design Award, 1961; Cornelius Gurlitt Medal, Germany Academy for City and Regional Planning, 1962. Dr. Ing.: Technische Hochschule, Hannover, Germany, 1929; M.A.: Harvard University, 1942; D.Sc.: Western Reserve University, Cleveland, Ohio, 1951; University of Sydney, 1954; D.Arts: Harvard University, Cambridge, Massachusetts, 1953; D.Arch.: North Carolina State College, Raleigh, 1953; Dr.: University of Brazil, 1955; D.F.A.: Pratt Institute, Brooklyn New York, 1961; D.H.L.: Columbia University, New York, 1961; Williams College, Williamstown, Massachusetts, 1963; Dr.Phil.: Free University, Berlin, 1963. Fellow, American Institute of Architects, 1954; Member, National Institute of Arts and Letters; Associate, National Academy of Design, 1967. Honorary Member, Royal Institute of British Architects, London, 1937; Honorary Member, Royal Society of Arts, London, 1946; Fellow of the Society of Industrial Artists and Designers, London, 1950; Honorary Senator, Hechschule für Bildende Künste, Berlin, 1962; Honorary Royal Academician, London, 1967. Grand Cross of Merit with Star, West Germany, 1958. *Died* (in Boston) *5 July 1969*.

Works:

1909 Farm-workers' houses, Janikow, near Dramburg, Germany
1911 Fagus Shoe Factory, Alfeld-an-der-Leine, Germany (with Adolf Meyer)
1913 Design of railway car for a factory at Königsberg, Germany
Interior design for the World's Fair, Ghent, Belgium
Single-family houses, Wittemberg, Frankfurt-on-Oder, Germany (with Adolf Meyer)
Plan for the Fitz District, Frankfurt-on-Oder, Germany (with Adolf Meyer)
Hospital, Alfeld, Germany (project; with Adolf Meyer)
Regional Councillor's Office, Rummelsberg, Germany (project)
Savings Bank, Dramburg, Germany (project; with Adolf Meyer)
Shops and regional plan for Posen, Germany (now Poznan, Poland) (project)
House, Semmering, Vienna
Car factory employees' housing, Bernburg, Germany
Shops, Märkisch Friedland, Germany
Kleffel Cotton Factory, Dramburg, Germany (with Adolf Meyer)
Mendel House furniture and interiors, Berlin
Langerfeld House furniture and interiors, Königsberg, Germany
Dr. Herzfeld House furniture and interiors, Hanover, Germany
Rural houses on the von Brockhausen estate, Pomerania, Germany (now Poland)

1914 Industrial complex (administration building, garage compound, and medium-sized factory), *Deutsche Werkbund Exhibition,* Cologne (with Adolf Meyer)
Steel furniture for the warship *Von Hindenburg, Deutsche Werkbund Exhibition,* Cologne (with Adolf Meyer)
Farm-workers' houses and shops, Dramburg, Germany

1921 Sommerfeld House, Dahlem, Berlin
Workers' houses for the Hess Stocking Factory, Erfurt, Germany (competition project; with Adolf Meyer)
Chicago Tribune Tower (competition project; with Adolf Meyer)

1922 War Memorial, Weimar, Germany
Bauhaus Building, Weimar, Germany

1923 Villa Hausmann, Pyrmont, Germany (project; with Adolf Meyer)
State Theatre renovation, Jena, Germany (with Adolf Meyer)

1924 Auerbach House, Jena, Germany (with Adolf Meyer)
Academy of Philosophy, Erlangen, Germany (project; with Adolf Meyer)
Fröbel Institute, Bad Liebenstein, Germany (with Adolf Meyer)
Hanover Paper Mill, Alfeld, Germany (with Adolf Meyer)
von Klitzing Beach House (project with Adolf Meyer)
Engelhard Workshops (project; with Adolf Meyer)
Banqueting Hall, Frankfurt (competition project; with Adolf Meyer)
Reis and Mendel Tombs, Berlin

1925 Kappe Shops, Alfeld, Germany (with Adolf Meyer)
Fagus Shoe Factory Annex, Alfeld-an-der-Leine, Germany (with Adolf Meyer)
Benscheidt House, Alfeld-an-der-Leine, Germany (project)
Benscheidt Jr. House reconstruction, Alfeld-au-der-Leine, Germany
Old people's home, Alfeld-an-der-Leine, Germany (project)
Teachers' Association Headquarters, Dresden (project)
Sanatorium, Thuringia, Germany (project)
Teachers' houses at the Bauhaus, Dessau, Germany

1926 Bauhaus, Dessau, Germany
Miller Factory, Kirchbraach, Germany
Terrace houses, groups I and II, Törten, Dessau, Germany

1927 Terrace houses, group III, Törten, Dessau, Germany
Two prefabricated houses, *Deutsche Werkbund Exhibition,* Stuttgart
Cooperative store, Dresden (project)
Dairy, Törten, Dessau, Germany (project)
Apartment building, Marburg, Germany (project)
Hecke House, Hamburg, Germany (project)
Small houses for the firm of Molling and Company (project)
House for the *Pressa* Exhibition, Cologne (project)
"Totalheater" (project; with Erwin Piscator)
Zuckerkandl House, Jena, Germany
Wooden weekend houses (project)
Town hall, museum and sports grounds, Halle, Germany (competition project)
Biesenhorst District development, Berlin (project)

1928 Municipal Labor Office, Dessau, Germany
Dammerstock District development, Karlsruhe, Germany (competition project; in collaboration)
Lewin House, Zehlendorf, Berlin
Harnischmacher House, Wiesbaden, Germany (project)
Country district development, Wolfen, Dessau, Germany (project)

Co-operative District, Merseburg, Germany (project)
Co-operative Store, Törten, Dessau, Germany
Terrace houses, group IV, Törten, Dessau, Germany
Prefabriacted houses for the Mirsch Copper and Brass Factory, Finow, Germany

1929 Spandau-Haselhorst Experimental District, Berlin (competition project)
Prefabricated furniture for the Feder Shops, Berlin
Houses, Sommerfeld, Berlin (project)
Professional School, Kopenick, Berlin (project)
Engineering School, Hagen, Germany (competition project)
Old people's home, Kassel, Germany (project)
Gagfab District, Lindenbaum, Frankfurt

1930 Bodywork for Adler cars
Siemensstadt District, Berlin (supervising architect; with Bartning, Forbat, Häring, and Scharoun)
Cheap flats and houses for the Reichsforschungsgesellschaft (project)
Deutsche Werkbund Exhibition, Paris (with Herbert Bayer, Marcel Breuer, and László Moholy-Nagy)
House with a steel structure (project)
Law Courts, Berlin (project)
Theatre, Charkov, Russia (competition project)
Houses of recreation and education at the Tiergarten, Berlin (project; with R. Hillebrecht)
School of Physical Education, Schwarzerden, Germany (project)

1931 Meeting room and gymnasium, *Bund Deutscher Architekten Exhibition,* Berlin
Erich Mendelsohn Sanatorium (project)
Bienert Tomb, Dresden
Soviet Headquarters, Moscow (competition project)
Electrical machinery for the Voss Factory, Hanover, Germany
Houses and flats, Wansee, Berlin (project)
Apartment buildings, Nagel, Nuremberg, Germany (project)
Kass House interiors, Zehlendorf, Berlin
Apartment buildings, Paris (project)

1932 Adler Workshops reconstruction, Frankfurt (project)
Club Building, Buenos Aires (project)
Standardized houses, Buenos Aires (project)

1933 Stoves for the Frank Factory
Prefabricated houses, A. Rosa Works, Barcelona (project)
Reichsbank, Berlin (project; with J. Schmidt)
Bahner House, Berlin
Maurer House, Dahlem, Berlin

1935 Apartments, St. Leonard's Hill, Windsor, Berkshire, England (with E. Maxwell Fry)

1936 London Film Productions Workshops, Denham, Buckinghamshire, England (with E. Maxwell Fry)
House, 66 Old Church Street, Chelsea, London (with E. Maxwell Fry)
Donaldson House, Sussex, England (with E. Maxwell Fry)
Impington Village School, Cambridgeshire, England (with E. Maxwell Fry)
Papworth Sanatorium School, Cambridgeshire, England (project; with E. Maxwell Fry)
School, Histon, Cambridgeshire, England (with E. Maxwell Fry)
Christ's College, Cambridge, England (project)

1937 Kindergarten, Cambridge, Massachusetts (project)
Art Center, Wheaton College, Norton, Massachusetts (competition project; with Marcel Breuer)

1938 Gropius House, Lincoln, Massachusetts (with Marcel Breuer)

Breuer House, Lincoln, Massachusetts (with Marcel Breuer)
Professor J. Ford House, Lincoln, Massachusetts (with Marcel Breuer)
Hagerty House, Cohasset, Massachusetts (with Marcel Breuer)

1939 Chamberlain House, Sudbury, Massachusetts (with Marcel Breuer)
Frank House, Pittsburgh, Pennsylvania (with Marcel Breuer)
State of Pennsylvania Pavilion, World's Fair, New York (with Marcel Breuer)
G. House, Lincoln, Massachusetts (with Marcel Breuer)
Black Mountain College, Lake Eden, North Carolina (project; with Marcel Breuer)

1940 Leisure center at Key West, Florida (project; with Konrad Wachsmann)

1941 Dr. Abele House, Framingham, Massachusetts (with Marcel Breuer)

1942 Storrow Land Division, Lincoln, Massachusetts (with Marcel Breuer)
Convalescent home, Key West, Florida (project; with Konrad Wachsmann)

1943 Aluminium City, New Kensington, near Pittsburg, Pennsylvania (with Marcel Breuer)

1943/
45 Packaged House System for the General Panel Corporation (project; with Konrad Wachsmann)

1944 Jeweller's Shop, New York
Factory, Greensboro, North Carolina
Factory, Cali, Colombia

1945 Catholic church, Torreon, Mexico (with J. Gonzales Rejna)

1946 Town planning consultancy, Black Mountain College, North Carolina (with Marcel Breuer)
Ryan House, Cambridge, Massachusetts
Poppleton House, Dayton, Ohio
Lexington Nursery School, Lexington, Massachusetts (project)
Skiing hut, Franconia, New Hampshire (project)
Library, Willimantic, Connecticut (project)
Kaplan House, Newton, Massachusetts
Usiskin House, Long Island, New York (project)

1947 Brockelman House, Worcester, Massachusetts
Neil House, Andover, Massachusetts
Wolfers House, Maine
Peter House, Cape Cod, Massachusetts
Catheron House, Foxboro, Massachusetts
Heywood House reconstruction, Maine
Town plan for Michael Reese Hospital, Chicago

1948 Hua Tung University, Shanghai, China (project)
Peter Thacher Junior High School, Attleboro, Massachusetts
Lawrence House, Lexington, Massachusetts
McMahon House, Lexington, Massachusetts
House, Providence, Rhode Island
England House, Pittsfield, Massachusetts
Howlett House, Belmont, Massachusetts
Elementary school, Sherborn, Massachusetts (project)

1949 Pillsbury House, Rumford, Rhode Island
Field House, Cape Cod, Massachusetts
Graduate Center, Harvard University, Cambridge, Massachusetts (with Brown, Lawford and Forbes)

1950 Park buildings, Lexington, Massachusetts
Apthop House, Concord, Massachusetts
Hechinger House, Washington, D.C.
England House, Washington, D.C.
Napoli House, Concord, Massachusetts
Theatre, New Rochelle, New York (project)
Medical center, Mt. Kisco, New York (project)
Barnes House reconstruction, Belmont, Massachusetts (project)

1951 Business school, Attleboro, Massachusetts
Burncoat Secondary and Senior Schools, Worcester, Massachusetts (with A. Johnson)
Pillsbury House, Milton, Massachusetts
Vischer House furniture, Indiana
Vannah House, Foxboro, Massachusetts
Stichweh House, Hanover, Massachusetts
Elementary and secondary schools, Amesbury, Massachusetts (project)
Donelly Bureau reconstruction, Boston (project)
Bradley House (project)
Housing and Home Finance Agency Headquarters, San Jose, Costa Rica (project)
1952 Wasco Flashing Corporation, Cambridge, Massachusetts (project)
Five Fields Housing Complex, Lexington, Massachusetts
Houses, Lake Bancroft, Falls Church, Virginia
American University Office Building, Washington, D.C. (project)
Mulcahey Elementary School, Taunton, Massachusetts
Pilgrim Park Elementary School, Warwick, Rhode Island
Elementary school, Providence, Rhode Island
Senior school, Concord, New Hampshire
American Association for the Advancement of Science Office Building, Washington, D.C.
Shops, for the Hechinger Company, Falls Church and Alexandria, Virginia
Designs/models for school and college furniture for the Thonet Factory
Cole House, Cambridge, Massachusetts
Baruch House, Newton, Massachusetts
Lang House, Newton, Massachusetts
Elementary school, Cambridge, Massachusetts
Elementary school, Cambridge, Massachusetts
Elementary school, North Adams, Massachusetts
1953 McCormick and Company Office Building, Chicago
Wherry District Housing, for the United States Navy, Rhode Island
Back Bay Center, Boston (with Pietro Belluschi, Carl Koch, Hugh Stubbins, and Walter Bogner)
National Education Association Building (project)
1954 Flag Street Elementary School, Worcester, Massachusetts (with A. Roy)
Shopping center, Saugus, Massachusetts (with Ketchum, Gind and Sharp)
Overholt Thoracic Clinic, Boston
1955 Elementary school, Waltham, Massachusetts
Secondary school, Attleboro, Massachusetts
1956 Elementary school, West Bridgewater, Massachusetts
Housing at Otis Air Force Base, Falmouth, Massachusetts
United States Embassy, Athens
1957 Oheb Shalom Temple, Baltimore
Littleton Junior-Senior High School, Massachusetts
Pioneer Valley Regional High School, Northfield, Massachusetts
1958 William F. Pollard Junior High School, Needham, Massachusetts
Elementary school, Stoughton, Massachusetts
Two dormitories for Phillips Academy, Andover, Massachusetts
Reyim Synagogue, Newton, Massachusetts
Murchison House, Provincetown, Massachusetts
Pan American Building, New York (consultant architect, with Pietro Belluschi, on plan of Emery Roth and Sons)
1959 Elementary school, Acton, Massachusetts

Britz-Buckow-Rudow Settlement, West Berlin (project)
Apartment block, Hansa District, Berlin
Academic Quadrangle, Brandeis University, Waltham, Massachusetts
1960 L. G. Hanscom Field Elementary School, Lincoln, Massachusetts
Elementary School additions, Kingston, Massachusetts
Northeast Elementary School, Waltham, Massachusetts
Gould Hospital, Presque Isle, Maine
Hemoglobin Laboratory alterations, Children's Hospital Medical Center, Boston
1961/
69 Wayland High School, Wayland, Massachusetts
1964 Britz-Buckow-Rudow Center, West Berlin (project)
1965 Rosenthal China Factory, Selb, West Germany
Master plan for a university at Mosul, Iraq
1967 Experimental buildings for a primary and secondary school at Britz-Buckow-Rudow, West Berlin
Huntington Art Gallery addition, San Marino, California
Tower East Óffice and Commercial Building, Shaker Heights, Ohio
Thomas Glassworks, Hamburg, West Germany
Town plan for Selb, West Germany
1968 Kennedy Federal Building, Civic Center, Boston

Publications:

By GROPIUS: books—*Programm des Staatlichen Bauhauses*, Weimar, Germany 1919; *Idee and Aufbau des Staatlichen Bauhauses*, Munich and Weimar, Germany 1923; *Internationale Architektur*, Munich and Weimar, Germany 1925, 1927; *Neue Arbeiten in Bauhauswerkstätten*, editor, Munich 1925; *Bauhausbauten*, Munich and Dessau, Germany 1928; *The New Architecture and the Bauhaus*, London 1935, New York 1936; *Bauhaus 1919-1928*, with Herbert Bayer and Ise Gropius, New York 1938, Stuttgart 1955; *Rebuilding Our Communities*, Chicago 1945; *Architecture and Design in the Age of Science*, New York 1952; *The Scope of Total Architecture*, New York and London 1955, Buenos Aires 1956, Tokyo 1958, Milan 1959; *Architektur: Wege zu optischen Kultur*, Frankfurt and Hamburg, West Germany 1956; *Arquitectura y planeamiento*, Buenos Aires 1958; *Katsura: Tradition and Creation in Japanese Architecture*, with Tange and Ishimoto, New Haven, Connecticut 1960; *The Architects Collaborative, 1945-1965*, editor, with others, New York 1966; *Apollo in the Democracy: The Cultural Obligation of the Architect*, New York 1968; *Vertical City*, Urbana, Illinois 1968; *Walter Gropius: Das Spätwerk*, exhibition catalogue, Darmstadt, West Germany 1970; *Walter Gropius: Buildings, Plans, Projects, 1906-1969*, exhibition catalogue, with introduction by James Marston Fitch, Washington, D.C. 1973; articles—"Die Entwicklung moderner Industriebaukunst" in *Jahrbuch des Deutschen Werkbundes*, Berlin 1913; "Das flache Dach: International Umfrage über die technische Durchführbarkeit horizontal abgedeckter Dächer und Balkone" in *Bauwelt* (Berlin), 25 February, 4 March, 8 and 22 April 1926; "Offset-, Buch-, and Werbekunst" in *Bauhaus* (Leipzig), no. 7, 1926; "Geistige und technische Voraussetzung der neuen Baukunst" in *Umschau* (Frankfurt), no. 31, 1927; "Der Architekt als Organisator der moderner Bauwirtschaft und seine Forderungen an die Industrie," with F. Block, in *Wohnbau* (Potsdam, Germany), no. 1, 1928; "Das Ergebris des Reichsforsehungs—Wettbewerbes" in *Bauwelt* (Berlin), February 1929; "Grossiedlungen" in *Zentralblatt der Bauverwaltung* (Berlin), 26 March 1930; "Flach-, Mittel-, oder Hochbau?" in *Neues Frankfurt*, February 1931; "Arquitectura Funcional" in *Arquitectura* (Madrid), no. 2, 1931; "The Small House of Today" in *Architectural Forum* (New York), March 1931; "Wohnhochhäuser im Grunen: Ein Grosstadtische Wohnform der Zukunft" in *Zentralblatt der Bauverwaltung* (Berlin), no. 49/50, 1931; "The Formal and Technical Problems of Modern Architecture and Planning"in *RIBA Journal* (London), May 1934; "Theaterbau" in *Atti della Reale Accademia d'Italia* (Rome), October 1934; "The Role of Reinforced Concrete in the Development of Modern Constructions" in *The Concrete Way* (Chicago), September/October 1934; "Grandes Polaciones" in *Nuestra Arquitectura* (Buenos Aires), September 1934; "Education Toward Creative Design" in *American Architect* (New York), May 1937; "Architecture at Harvard University" in *Architectural Record* (New York), May 1937; "Essentials for Creative Design" in *The Octagon* (Philadelphia), July 1937; "Background of the New Architecture" in *Civil Engineering* (New York), December 1937; "Towards a Living Architecture" in *American Architect* (New York), January/February 1938; "General Panel System" in *Pencil Points* (New York), April 1943; "A Program for City Reconstruction" in *Architectural Forum* (New York), July 1943; "Field Experience and the Making of an Architect" in *AIA Journal* (Washington, D.C.), November 1945; "A Frank Letter and Its Answer" in *AIA Journal* (Washington, D.C.), April 1947; "Design Topics" in *Magazine of Art* (New York), December 1947; "What Is Happening to Modern Architecture" in *Museum of Modern Art Bulletin* (New York), Spring 1948; "Organic Neighborhood Planning: Housing and Town and Country Planning" in *UN Bulletin* (New York), April 1949; "Plan pour un enseignement de l'architecture"and "Le theâtre total" in *L'Architecture d'aujourd'hui* (Paris), February 1950; "Architecture fonctionnelle" in *L'Architecture française* (Paris), no. 11, 1950; "The Position of Architecture in the Century of Science" in *The Architect and Building News* (London), 19 July 1951; "Not Gothic but Modern for Our Colleges" in *AIA Journal* (Washington, D.C.), April 1952; "Gropius on Gropius: Letter to the Editor" in *Architectural Forum* (New York), August 1952; "Faith in Planning" in *American Society of Planning Officials Journal* (Chicago), October 1952; "Eight Steps Toward a Solid Architecture" in *Architectural Forum* (New York), February 1954; "Is There a Science of Design" in *Journal of the Royal Australian Isntitute of Architects* (Sydney), July/September 1954; "The Necessity of the Artist in a Democratic Society" in *Arts and Architecture* (Los Angeles), December 1955; "Architecture in Japan" in *Perspecta* (New Haven, Connecticut), no. 3, 1955; "Kompass für Architekten" in *Werk* (Zürich), June 1955; "Discorso di Gropius alla inaugurazione della scuola di Ulm" in *Domus* (Milan), February 1956; "The Curse of Conformity" in *Saturday Evening Post* (Philadelphia), 6 June 1958; "Einheit in der Vielfalt: ein Pardox der Kultur" in *Bauen und Wohnen* (Zürich), December 1959; "Una testimonianza diretta" in *Casabella* (Milan), June 1960; "True Architectural Goals Yet toBe Realized" in *Architectural Record* (New York), June 1961; "The Architect in Society" in *Architectural Association Journal* (London), January 1962; "Creative Education: Key to Good Architecture and Design" in *Architectural Record* (New York), November 1963; "Tradition and Continuity in Architecture" in *Architectural Record* (New York), May, June, July 1964; "L'Architetto e la società" in *Casabella* (Milan), October 1965; "Ludwig Mies van der Rohe" in *Bauen und Wohnen* (Zürich), May 1966; "Programm zur Grundüng einer allgemeinen Hausbaugesellschaft auf künstlerisch einheitlicher Grundlage MbH" in *Baumeister* (Munich), April 1969; etc.

On GROPIUS: books—*Walter Gropius* by Siegfried Giedion, Paris 1931; *Walter Gropius e la Bauhaus* by Giulio Carlo Argan, Milan 1951; *Walter Gropius* by

Chikatada Kurata, Tokyo 1953; *Walter Gropius: Work and Teamwork* by Siegfried Giedion, Stuttgart, Paris, London and New York 1954; *Walter Gropius* by Masakazu Koyama, Tokyo 1954; *Walter Gropius: The Man and His Work* by Siegfried Giedion, Milan 1954; *Bauhaus: Weimar, Berlin* by Mityiko and Iwao Yamawaki, Tokyo 1954; *Walter Gropius* by the Centro Estudiantes de Arquitectura, Montevideo 1955; *Gropius in Japan* by the editors of the International House of Japan, Tokyo 1956; Gropius section by Ernesto Rogers of *Universal Encyclopedia of Art*, Rome 1958; *The Synthetic Vision of Walter Gropius* by Gilbert Herbert, Johannesburg 1959; *Walter Gropius* by James Marston Fitch, New York 1960; *Walter Gropius und das Faguswerk* by H. Weber, Munich 1961; Gropius section by Elio Piroddi in *Encyclopaedic Dictionary of Architecture and Town Planning*, Rome 1969; *Four Great Makers of Modern Architecture*, Columbia University, New York 1970; *Gropius* by Alberto Busignani, Florence 1972, London 1973; *Art and Act: On Causes in Art History—Manet, Gropius, Mondrian* by Peter Gay, New York and London 1976; *Masters of Modern Architecture* by Edwin and Joy Hoag, Indianapolis 1977; *Walter Gropius e le Bauhaus* by Giulio Carlo Argan, Paris 1979; *Gropius, Hirsch—The Saga of the Copper Houses* by Gilbert Herbert, Haifa, Israel 1980; *Boston: Forty Years of Modern Architecture*, exhibition catalogue, by William J.R. Curtis, Boston 1980; *Walter Gropius* by Gabor Preisich, Berlin 1982; *Walter Gropius Industriearchitekt* by Karin Wilhelm, Braunschweig, West Germany 1983; *The Dream of the Factory-Made House: Walter Gropius and Konrad Wachsmann* by Gilbert Herbert, Cambridge, Massachusetts 1984; *The Decorated Diagram: Harvard Architecture and the Failure of the Bauhaus Legacy* by Klaus Herdeg, Cambridge, Massachusetts 1984; articles—"Das neue Bauhaus in Weimar" by Dr. Fritz Hoeber in *Der Architekt* (Vienna), no. 22, 1919; "The Work of Walter Gropius" by Herman George Scheffauer in *Architectural Review* (London), August 1924; "Exposition du 'Werkbund' à Stuttgart" in *Cahiers d'art* (Paris), no. 7/8, 1927; "The 'Total-theatre' Proposed by Walter Gropius" in *Architectural Record* (New York) April 1930; "Der deutsche Werkbund in Paris" in *Bauwelt* (Berlin), June 1930; "Bauhaus School" in *Architectural Record* (New York), October 1930; "Walter Gropius" by J. M. Richards in *Architectural Review* (London), August 1935; "Professor Gropius Designs in Glass" in *The Architects' Journal* (London), 4 October 1945; "Le Préfabrication aux Etats Unis" in *L'Architecture d'aujourd'hui* (Paris), January 1946; "Walter Gropius et son école," special issue of *L'Architecture d'aujourd'hui* (Paris), February 1950; "Gropius in Retrospect" in *Architectural Record* (New York), February 1952; "Gropius Symposium" in *Arts and Architecture* (Los Angeles), May 1952; "Gropius, 1952" by William Holford in *Architectural Review* (London), July 1952; "Labatut on Gropius" by Jean Labatut in *Architectural Forum* (New York), August 1952; "Walter Gropius" by E. Maxwell Fry in *Architectural Review* (London), March 1955; "Presentation of the Royal Gold Medal to Dr. Walter Gropius" by Charles Aslin in *RIBA Journal* (London), May 1956; "Gropius and Van de Velde" by Nicholas Pevsner in *Architectural Review* (London), March 1963; "Architectural Details: Walter Gropius" in *Architectural Record* (New York), February 1964; "Gropius, Wright, and the Intentional Fallacy" by Charles Jencks in *Arena: Architectural Association Journal* (London), June 1966; "All Purpose Old Master of Design" by Peter Blake in *Life* (New York), 7 June 1968; "Gropius Throws His Hat in the Ring" in *AIA Journal* (Washington, D.C.), July 1968; "Gropius: Young at His Passing" by Wolf Von Eckardt in the *Washington Post*, 31 July 1969; "Bauhaus Birthday" by Stanley Abercrombie in the *Wall Street Journal* (New York), 16 October 1969; "Meeting Gropius Again" by Walter Segal in *The Architects' Journal* (London), 13 February 1974;"The True Relevance of Walter Gropius" by Stan Scott in *RIBA Journal* (London), March 1974; "Analyzing the Gropius House as Energy-Conscious Design" by Neil Summers in *AIA Journal* (Washington, D.C.), February 1977; "Bauhaus Archive, a New Gropius Design, Opens in Berlin" in *Architectural Record* (New York), October 1979; "Bauhaus Back to Berlin" by Ingebord Flagge in *Architectural Review* (London), December 1979; "TAC—The Heritage of Walter Gropius," special issue of *Process:Architecture* (Tokyo), October 1980; "The Bauhaus Building in Dessau" by Falk Jaeger in *Deutsche Kunst und Denkmalpflege (Munich), no. 2, 1981;* "The Fagus Factory: Contemporary Design Seventy Years Later" by Barclay F. Gordon in *Architectural Record* (New York), July 1981; "The Bauhaus as You've Never Seen It" by John Allen Burns and Deborah Stephen Burns in *AIA Journal* (Washington, D.C.), July 1981; "Gropius in England" by Paolo Berdini in *Controspazio* (Bari, Italy), July/December 1981; "The Lecacy of Walter Gropius" by Richard G. Stein in *Architectural Design* (London), no. 7/8, 1982; "Bauhaus, Dessau" in *Architecture + Urbanism* (Tokyo), October 1982; "Walter Gropius and the Bauhaus," special issue of *Architektur der DDR* (East Berlin), April 1983; "Walter Gropius, 1907-1934," special issue of *Rassegna* (Milan), September 1983; "A Modernist Monument Opening To Public" by Joseph Giovannini in the *New York Times*, 30 May 1985; recording—*Walter Gropius before 1923*, tape cassette by Jacques Paul, Milton Keynes, Buckinghamshire 1977.

Bibliography—*Modern Architectural Vision in the Works of Walter Gropius: A Selected Bibliography* by Robert B. Harmon, Monticello, Illinois 1979.

Walter Gropius deserves to be considered as one of the chief architectural innovators of this century. He was essentially progressive, making full use of new materials and methods of construction made possible by modern technology, and, with Le Corbusier, he contributed much towards the transformation of building from an empirical craft to a science in which precise mathematical calculations are possible. He made the Staatliche Bauhaus, of which he was director from 1919 to 1928, the most vital and influential school of industrial design in Europe. He was an important theorist and teacher, and he advocated and contributed much to the acceptance of standardization, prefabrication, and team work.

His qualities as a progressive designer are first significantly apparent in the Fagus Shoe Factory at Alfeld-an-der-Leine, built in 1911 in collaboration with Adolf Meyer. The structure is a steel frame that supports the floors, while the external walls are glass screens that continue, without interruption of corner supports, round the building. This admits the maximum of light and minimizes the distinction between outer and inner space. It was a design that had far-reaching influence. A building with a similar motif was the administration building at the Deutsche Werkbund Exhibition at Cologne in 1914. Here, continuous fenestration is carried from the circular glass corners on the first floor along the sides and for the entire length of the rear of the building. These circular glass structures enclose spiral staircases, another motif widely adopted in much modern building, especially in departmental stores.

One of the best and most complete examples of the glass screen wall occurs in the workshop that forms part of the Bauhaus building erected at Dessau in 1926. This workshop is of four storeys with a post-and-slab construction; supports are set well back to allow a large, uninterrupted glass screen of the three upper floors to continue without the interruption of any structural supporting member round three walls. This was the most complete utilizationof the glass screen to date, and it was a long time before anything comparable was used.

The main purpose of these buildings by Gropius was to admit the maximum of light, for even today there is no satisfactory substitute for daylight either from an amenity or functional standpoint. This preoccupation with light influenced much of Gropius's domestic architecture. One of the best early examples is the Siemensstadt Development near Berlin of 1929-30, for which Gropius was, as supervising architect, responsible for the general layout. The estate consists mainly of long, fourd five-storey apartment blocks designed by Gropius, Scharoun, and Forbat. In siting these parallel slab blocks, Gropius aimed, within the required densities, to make them of such a height as to provide as much sunlight as possible, at the same time providing for maximum space for lawns and gardens between the blocks. The calculations on which the layout are based are given in his book, *The New Architecture and the Bauhaus*, and this exercise in site planning had much influence at the time.

Siting of domestic buildings for maximum sunlight was always a prime consideration with Gropius. Another notable example is the Aluminum City housing estate near Pittsburgh, designed in collaboration with Marcel Breuer in 1943. A road winds through a hilly wooded site; the blocks of terrace houses are oriented to get maximum sunlight, and thus there is an irregular relation to the road:some face it, some abut its end-wise, and others are away from it, reached by branching service-ways. At the time, this unusual yet functional siting excited controversy.

Gropius was a functionalist and most of his buildings in Germany, England, and America are constructions that aim to be logical interpretations of purpose. This is seen conspicuously in the Impington Village School, designed in collaboration with Maxwell Fry in 1936, and the Harvard Graduate Center of 1949.

All of these works demonstrate that Gropius was very much an experimenter. He was also an experimenter in his projects. Conspicuous among these is his 1927 total-theatre. In this design, three forms are combined:the circus with the central area, the Greek semi-circular shape, and the proscenium stage. The theatre is so arranged that tiers of seats can be revolved in section so that change from one form to another can be effected quickly.

As a progressive architect, Gropius was quick to see the advantages of economy and speed in building and was a strenuous advocate of standardization, prefabrication, and dry assembly, making possible mass production and large, factory-made units. This advocacy of industrilaized building carried with it a belief in teamwork.

Aesthetically, Gropius was a classicist, as his most beautiful buildings prove—such works as the houses built with the Bauhaus in 1925-6, the Harvard Graduate Centre of 1949, the apartment block in the Hansa District of Berlin, 1957-9, and the American Embassy building at Athens 1956. Although in most of these buildings there is a slight horizontal emphasis, it is balanced by verticals that, together with rectangular windows moving towards squares and large areas of plain walls always well proportioned, create a feeling of classic repose and serenity. Almost all his buildings have flat roofs conducive to this feeling of repose. But it was not only aesthetically that he liked the flat roof; he also realized its functional advantage in freedom of planning.

Gropius has sometimes been criticized onaesthetic grounds and for his advocacy of teamwork. For architecture is an art, the creation of individual artistic feeling, and therefore it cannot be the work of equals in a team. It is possible that there is some contradiction here between advocacy and practice:it is difficult to imagine that Gropius was not the determining influence in any design that bore his name.

—Arnold Whittick

GROSSMAN, Irving.

Canadian. Born in Toronto, Ontario, 7 December 1926. Educated at the University of Toronto, 1945-50 (Ontario Association of Architects Scholarship, 1947; Hobbs Glass Prize, 1948; Toronto Brick Prize, 1949; Architectural Guild Medal, 1950; Pilkington Glass Fellowship, 1950), B.Arch. 1950. Married Helena Derwinger in 1971; sons: Adam and Jonas. Assistant in the offices of R.M. Schindler, *q.v.*, California, 1947, Fry, *q.v.*: E. Maxwell Fry, Drew, *q.v.*: Jane Drew, and Partners, London,1950-51, and in the Housing Department of the London County Council, 1952-53.Since 1954, in private practice, Toronto. Teacher at the School of Architecture, University of Toronto, 1954—62; Visiting Professor of Architecture, Nova Scotia Technical College, Halifax, 1984, and University of Toronto, 1985. Exhibitions : School of Architecture, University of Toronto, 1974; Canadian Exhibition, Hungary, 1979. Recipient: Regional Design Award, 1957, and National Design Award, 1962 and 1971, Canadian Housing Design Council; Canada Council Research Award, 1959; Massey Medal, 1967; Design Award, Ontario Association of Architects, 1967; Canadian Centennial Medal, 1967; Design Award of Excellence, *Canadian Architect's Yearbook*, 1970, 1972, and 1978; Ontario Masons Relations Award, 1970 and 1973; Design Award, Scarborough, Ontario Planning Board, 1972; Annual Design Award, *Canadian Architect*, Toronto, 1978. Fellow, Royal Architectural Institute of Canada, 1970; Fellow, Royal Canadian Academy, 1973. Address (office): 7 Sultan Street, Toronto, Ontario M5R 1L6, Canada.

Works:

1955 Winesanker House, 24 Croydon, Toronto
Houzer House, Maple Lane, Ottawa
Workmen's Circle Peretz School, Toronto

1955/
59 Shaarei Tefellah Synagogue, three phases, Toronto
1956 Adath Israel Synagogue, phase I, Toronto
MacPherson House, Bayview Village, Downsview, Ontario
Betal House, 55 York Downs Drive, Downsview, Ontario
Berman House, Hog's Hollow, Toronto
Fogel House, Sandringham Avenue, Toronto
1957 Korn House, Toronto
1958 Ison House, Denmark Crescent, Downsview, Ontario
Klamer House, Wilket Road, Bayview, Ontario
1958/
60 Beth David Synagogue, Toronto (with artist Graham Coughtry)
1959/
65 Flemingdon Park (residential community), Toronto
1960 Morris Winchevsky School, Toronto
Central Library Theatre interiors, Toronto
1961 Isaacs Gallery interiors, Toronto
1961/
64 Temple Emanu-El Synagogue, Toronto
1963 Puppet Theatre, Toronto Island
Yorkdale Fountain, Toronto (with Graham Coughtry)
Somerset Apartments, Toronto
Kiosks, on the Centre Islands, Toronto
1964 Administration and New Building for *Expo '67*, Montreal (with artists Coughtry, Vaillancourt and Comtois)
Tea House, Toronto Islands
Urban Renewal Designs, Elmwood Park, Detroit, Michigan
Beth David Synagogue expansion, Toronto
1964/
73 Edgeley (residential community), Toronto

1965 Cedarbrae Library, Scarborough, Ontario
1966 Condominium Town Houses, Edgeley, Toronto
Shoreham Drive Public School, Edgeley, Toronto
1968 Edgeley in the Village Apartments, Toronto
1969 Student Residence, Elrond College, Kingston, Ontario
1970 YWCA Women's Residence, Toronto
Highlands (residential community), phase I, Ottawa
1976 St. Lawrence (residential community), phase I, Toronto
1983 Senior Citizens' Apartments, Moore Place, Toronto

Publications:

By GROSSMAN: articles—"Mathematics in Architecture" in *Royal Architecture Institute of Canada Journal*(Toronto), February 1956; "Human Patterns" in *Canadian Architect*(Toronto), April 1956; "Seminar on Colour in Architecture" in *Canadian Architect* (Toronto), August 1960; "The Forgotten Image" in*Canadian Architect*(Toronto), September 1960; "In Search of the Lost Street" in *Canadian Arts*(Ottawa), November 1960; "Le Corbusier" in*Architects of Modern Thought*(radio talks), Toronto1962; "The Monstrous Menace," with H. Blumenfeld, in *Ontario Housing*(Toronto), June 1964; "City Hall" in*RAIC Journal*(Toronto), September 1965; "Building the City" in *Ontario '66*, Toronto 1966; "Flemingdon Park (Revisited)" in *Canadian Architect*(Toronto), April 1967; 'Edgeley' in *Canadian Architect* (Toronto), August 1971; "Don Vale Walking Tour" in *Exploring Toronto*, Toronto 1972; "The Environment—What Is and Can Be" in *Habitat '77*, report, Stratford, Ontario 1977.

Irving Grossman: Crombie Park Housing, St. Lawrence, Toronto, 1980.

On GROSSMAN: book—*Multi-Use Architecture in the Urban Context* by Edberhard H. Zeidler, New York 1985; articles—"Betel Residence" in *Arts and Architecture* (Los Angeles), May 1959; "Beth David Synagogue" in *The Face of Toronto*, Toronto 1961; "Flemingdon Park" by M. Hancock in *Plan Canada* (Toronto), May 1961; "Flemingdon Park" in *House and Home* (New York), April 1962; "Flemingdon Park" by G. Ritter in *Architectural Design* (London), May 1962; "Flemingdon Park as an Example of Design for the Car" by William Goulding in *Canadian Art* (Ottawa), February 1962; "Flemingdon Park" in *Architectural Forum* (New York), August 1962; "Flemingdon Park" by Mayer in *American Journal of Housing* (Washington, D.C.), April 1963; "Expo Building" in *Progressive Architecture* (New York), June 1964; "Expo Building" in *Architecture Review* (London), August 1967; 'Edgeley' in *Ontario Housing* Toronto), February 1968; "Alvin Avenue Housing" in *Canadian Architect* (Toronto), January 1979; "Crombie Park: Profile" in *Toronto Star*, 16 September 1979; "Crombie Park" in *Canadian Architect* (Toronto), June 1981.

Over the thirty years of my practice, I have dealt a great deal with the residential environment, trying to capture the human qualities that the best of the great historic cities have offered, at the same time coming to terms with the impact of the automobile—shaping exterior space with the housing forms, as a wilful creative act, yet also trying to inject the arbitrary, the accidents and whimsy that the world of shelter should enjoy—so that it speaks not of architects, but of the richness of the social fabric within.

The austere vocabulary of the modern movement on which I was raised was a problem for me as far back as the 1960s, and I probed in my way to reject the platonic, all-perfect, singular solutions that a rational architect was supposed to repeat all over the landscape. Self-conscious anonymous architecture is a contradiction, however, and poses problems of identity and reference. Along with this involvement in the mass problems of habitation and the developer's world, I have enjoyed my artistic explorations into the sculptural aspects of architecture, believing for years that the artist's imprint on my work would add to the totality, as it has done through the ages around the world.

The recent postmodern and other tendencies are sure demonstrations that the language can be widened, that our tools are limitless—and for me confirm that the age is upon us when the architects will more and more rejoin their painter/sculptor colleagues without feeling threatened and produce integrated works that can stand beside the sculptured temples of India, or Baroque palaces of Europe, as powerful statements with orchestration and depth.

—Irving Grossman

Irving Grossman's contribution to architecture is primarily in the area of housing and community design. His sensitivity to the human scale and to ground-related housing, coupled with his recognition of the wastefulness associated with urban sprawl, has led him to a continuous search for viable housing alternatives. As a result, he was one of the early proponents of medium-density housing when the choice for Canadians was (and to a great extent still is) limited to two extremes, namely the low-density, lowrise, single-family detached house in the suburb or the high-density, highrise apartment block in the city.

Grossman's first accomplishment was the design of the initial stages of Flemingdon Park, a mixed housing development hailed in the early 1960s as a breakthrough. Designed for middle-income groups at a density of eighteen to twenty-five dwelling units per acre, this development received international recognition for its 'linear-attached' concept, which introduced the pratise of vertical traffic seperation to modest housing developments. It suggested a so-lution to the incompatible needs of pedestrian and vehicular traffic in a lowrise residential environment. The solution involved a slightly raised pedestrian deck giving access to the dwellings, while a slightly depressed garage concealed the car and stored it in close proximity to the owner's house. The Flemingdon concept has since emulated by many Canadian architects and has no doubt contributed to the acceptance of the once ill-framed rowhouse, now known as the 'townhouse.'

Edgeley, a suburban medium-density housing development, was envisaged as an integrated community of free-market and subsidized housing linked to each other by a community center. Grossman was commissioned in the late 1960s to design the master plan and the public housing component as well as the public school for this development. The housing of Edgeley is a continuation of the 'linear-attached' housing concept used at Flemingdon Park but with horizental rather than vertical traffic seperation. A thirty-foot-wide pedestrian street links all the houses and, in spite of the budgetary constraints implicit in subsidized housing, a charming and picturesque environment resulted through good design. The traditional rowhouse monotony was avoided by juxtaposing various dwelling unit types next to each other and by individualizing the design of each unit through color, texture, and building materials. In fact, the public housing sector of Edgeley is, in my opinion, as attractive as its freemarket housing counterpart, if not more so.

In early 1970s, Grossman was commissioned to design a large condominium community in Ottawa, The Highlands. Once again, he developed a linear concept, with a pedestrian spine seperating two rows of multiple housing units—one row of six-storey apartments punctuated by point blocks paralleled by a four-storey stacked townhouse row. These linear buildings were superimposed upon a garage substructure and, when all stages are completed, will encircle a large central park and recreational area with some community facilities. Although this development exceeds sixty dwelling units per acre in density, it still retains cross-ventilation and two-sided exposure for most units.

More recently, Grossman designed a high-density sector of the St. Lawrence redevelopment area of downtown Toronto. Featuring mixed land-use and a medium-profile housing development for both low and middle-income families, this development may become a trend-setter for urban housing in Canada. Grossman's sector involves housing accomodation for 210 households in a six-storey linear building incorporating two elementary schools and several commercial and community facilities at sidewalk level.

Of course, Grossman has also designed several private homes as well as non-residential buildings of some renown. A synagogue in North York, highly sculptural, and a community library in Scarborough, consisting of a cluster of skylit pyramids, are just two examples of well-designed community buildings. The three-storey adminstrative office building he designed for *Expo '67* has since become the headquarters of the Harbour Authorities and is still a landmark at the harbour front of Montreal.

—Norbert Schoenauer

GRUEN, Victor David.
American. Born Viktor Grünbaum in Vienna, Austria, 18 July 1903; emigrated to the United States in 1938; naturalized, 1943. Educated at the Architectural School, Vienna, 1918-23, and the Academy of Arts, Vienna, under Peter Behrens, 1924-25; influenced by the work and writings of Le Corbusier. Married Lizzie Kardos in 1930 (divorced, 1941); Elsie Krummeck in 1941 (divorced, 1951); Lazette van Hauten in 1952 (died, 1962); Kemija Salihefendic in 1963; children: Michael and Margaret. Worked as a technician for Melcher and Steiner, Vienna, 1923-32; organizer, author, and actor in "Politische Kabarett," Vienna, 1926-34; in private architectural practice, Vienna, 1932-38; Designer IVEL Corporation, New York, 1938, and in the office of Norman Bel Geddes, New York, 1938; organizer and producer, Viennese Theatre Group, New York, 1938-40; with Elsie Krummeck, formed design partnership, Grünbaum and Krummeck, New York and Los Angeles, 1940-48; in private architectural practice, as Victor Gruen, Los Angeles, 1948-51; Founder and Chief Architect, Victor Gruen Associates, Los Angeles, New York, Washington, and Tehran, 1951-68, and Victor Gruen International, Vienna, Paris, and Los Angeles, 1963-72. President of the Victor Gruen Center for Environmental Planning, Los Angeles, 1968-80; Chief Architect of Victor Gruen AG, Switzerland, Vienna, and Paris, 1969-80; President of the Zentrum für Umweltplanung, Vienna, 1973-80. Exhibitions, 1955-68: National Gallery, Washington, D.C.; *World's Fair*, Brussels; United States Information Service, Washington, D.C.; Architectural League of New York; 8th Pan-American Congress of Architects, Mexico City; American Institute of Architects Exhibition in Moscow; Berlin International Building Exhibition; American Embassy, Paris; Brooklyn Museum, New York. Recipient: Honor Award, American Institute of Architects, Southern California Chapter, 1949, 1951; Avenue of the Americas Association Award, New York, 1953; Gold medal, AIA, Detroit Chapter, 1955; Gold Medal, AIA, Memphis Chapter, 1958; Special Medallion, "Architect of the People," Rice University, Houston, Texas, 1963; Community Architecture Citation, New York State Association of Architects, 1965; *Who's Who in America* Award, 1966; Significant Artistic Achievement Award, City of Vienna, 1972; etc. Honorary doctorate: Pepperdine University, Los Angeles, 1976. Fellow, American Institute of Architects, 1948. *Died* (in Vienna, Austria) *14 February 1980.*

Works:

(Only the most important buildings and projects, as selected by Mr. Gruen, are listed. More than 1,000 works have been executed under Mr. Gruen's direction—including offices, hospitals, hotels, department stores, city plans, and interior design projects.)

1939 Lederer Shop, Fifth Avenue, New York
1939/
  51 Twelve stores for Barton's Bonbonnerie, New York
1940 Altmann and Kuehne Candy Store, Fifth Avenue, New York
1954 Northland Center, Detroit
  Master plan for 5,000 acres, Palos Verdes, California
  Dayton Department Store, Rochester, Minnesota
1955 Revitalization plan for Fort Worth, Texas (project)
1956 Southdale Shopping Center, Minneapolis
1957/
  65 Various office buildings for the Tishman Company
1958 Wilshire Terrace Apartment House, Los Angeles
  Revitalization plan for the city core of Kalamazoo, Michigan
  2500 apartments, Charles River Park, Boston
1958/
  64 Commercial, recreational and civic center project at Redondo Beach, California
1958/
  65 Southdale Medical Building, Minneapolis
1959 World's Fair Plan, Washington, D.C. (project)

City, County and Federal Civic Center, Syracuse, New York

1960 Museum of Arts and Science, Evansville, Indiana

Cherry Hill Center, Camden, New Jersey

Winrock Center, Little Rock, Arkansas

27 acre commercial, residential and institutional complex at Newark, New Jersey

Master plan for Welfare Island Model Town, New York

1960/
66 Nine department stores for the May Company in California

1963 Midtown Plaza, Rochester, New York

Randhurst Shopping Center, Mt. Prospect, Chicago

Doheny Towers Apartment Building, Los Angeles

Marina del Rey, Los Angeles

Redevelopment study of 27 acres, The Rocks, in downtown Sydney

12 block redevelopment project in the central area of Urban, Illinois

1963 Square block central area multi-functional development in Salt Lake City, Utah

Wilshire Comstock Apartment Building, Los Angeles

1963/
66 California Mart, Los Angeles

1964 Leo Baeck Temple, Los Angeles

1965 New satellite town in Valencia, California (in development)

1966 Sea World (marine exhibit), San Diego, California

Business sector revitalization plan, Bostin (in process)

Fox Plaza, San Francisco

1968 City core revitalization plan, Fresno, California

City master plan for Teheran (project)

1969 Harbor and city core revitalization plan for Antwerp (project)

1971 University City plan, Louvain-la-Neuve, Belgium (in process)

City core revitalization plan, Vienna (in process)

1972 City core plans for 7 satellite cities in the Paris region

Publications:

By GRUEN: books:—*How to Live with Your Architect*, New York 1949; *Shopping Towns USA*, with Larry Smith, New York 1960; *Stadsfornyelse i Forenta Staterna*, Stockholm 1963; *Heart of Our Cities*, New York 1964; *The Ideal City*, with others, New York 1964; *The People's Architect*, with others, Chicago 1964; *New Cities USA*, Washington, D.C. 1966; *Who Designs America?*, with others, New York 1966; *The Downfall and Rebirth of City Cores on Both Sides of the Atlantic*, Los Angeles 1972; *Centers for the Urban Environment*, New York 1973; *Das Überleben der Städte*, Vienna 1973; *Die Alte Schuhschachtel*, Vienna 1973; *Die Lebenswerte Stadt*, Munich 1975; *Ist Fortschritt ein Verbrechen?*, Vienna 1975; numerous articles in architectural magazines throughout the world.

On GRUEN: books—*Architecture, You and Me* by Siegfried Giedion, Cambridge, Massachusetts 1948; *Urban Pattern: City Planning and Design* by Arthur B. Gallion, New York 1950; *Shopping Centers* by Geoffrey Baker, New York 1951; *Forms and Functions of 20th Century Architecture* by Talbot Hamlin, New York 1952; *Mixed Blessing: The Motor in Britain* by Colin Buchanan, London 1958; *Shops and Stores* by Morris Ketchum, New York 1958; *Cities in the Motor Age* by Wilfred Owen, New York 1959; *An Introduction to Modern Architecture* by J. M. Richards, London 1960; *Architecture and the Esthetics of Plenty* by James Marston Fitch, New York 1961; *Death and Life of Great American Cities* by Jane Jacobs, New York 1961; *Man-Made America* by Christopher Tunnard, New Haven, 1963; *Urban Landscape Design* by Garrett Eckbo, New York 1964; *1976: Agenda for Tomorrow* by Stewart Udall, New York 1968; *Art in Architecture* by Louis G. Redstone, New York 1968; *Les Villes Nouvelles aux USA* by Nardin, Paris 1968; *Die Ohnmacht des Bürgers* by Theodor Leuenberger and Rudolf Schilling, Frankfurt 1977; *GA 59: Cesar Pelli/Victor Gruen Associates*, edited by Yukio Futagawa, Tokyo 1981; articles—"Victor Gruen Associates" in *Interiors* (New York), July 1960; "Victor Gruen" in *Arts and Architecture* (Los Angeles), October 1964; "The Heart of Gruen's Fresno Plan" in *Progressive Architecture* (New York), January 1965; "Victor Gruen's one-building town" in *Progressive Architecture* (New York), February 1967; "Great Builders of the 1960s" in *The Japan Architect* (Tokyo), July 1970; "Gruen's Vienna" in *Progressive Architecture* (New York), May 1975; "Victor Gruen, FAIA" in *AIA Journal* (Washington, D.C.), March 1980; "Victor Gruen, 1903-1980" in *Building* (London), 21 March 1980; "Victor Gruen: 1903-1980" by Stuart J. Lattman in *L.A. Architect* (Los Angeles), April 1980; "Legacy of a planning legend" by David L. Browning in *Crit* (Washington, D.C.), Winter 1983.

*

I regard architecture as an integrating professional art, which combines all activities which contribute to the shaping of the man-made and man-influenced environment. To these belong, of course, architecture, planning, and engineering, but also ecology and last, but not least, philosophy. I see the architect as a generalist, who knows much about something, namely architecture in the narrower sense, but also something about everything. This striving for the acquisition of multi-disciplinary knowledge and interest has shown itself early, but has become stronger with age. I am, in fact, still a student, and I try to widen my horizon by a steady dialogue with scientists of all disciplines.

As far as the term "architecture" is concerned, I base it on the teachings of Pollio Vitruvius, which—though they are nearly 2,000 years old—seem to me still applicable. He states in his work about architecture, in the volumes devoted to the "true art of building" the following: "Architecture is based on three conditions—firmness, commodity and delight." What I have tried to achieve in my building is the provision of formness in a manner in which the structure does not interfere or impose upon the conditions of commodity and delight. I have always understood the term "commodity" in a very wide sense. Buildings have not just to be useful but commodious in the physical, psychological, and spiritual sense. Delight is to me one of the most important conditions and to create it one of my greatest aims.

With these aims before me, it should not be surprising that I have tried to move in my career from the single structure to the creation of environmental compositions and finally to the rehabilitation of existing cities and the planning of new urban units.

Recognizing the importance of all environmental aspects to every individual personand every individual structure, I have turned my interests increasingly to the task of becoming an environmental planner.

—Victor Gruen (1980)

*

Victor Gruen, like Neutra and Schindler before him, emigrated from Vienna to Los Angeles, but unlike them he is not noted for the design of innovative or beautiful buildings. Gruen said that he saw little value in buildings themselves and that energies should be devoted to improving the environments; but in such pronouncements he was not thinking in baroque terms of architecture on a city scale, for to him formal values are of less importance than providing a comfortable and convenient place for the American life-style.

From his earliest day of practice, both in Vienna and in the U.S.A., Gruen had been concerned with the design of shops, and it is in the design of retailing establishments that he became well known in the decade following World War Two. With the knowledge of traffic and concern for traffic-free zones learnt from shopping centres, he felt emboldened to tackle urban problems and gained a reputation as the planner who would put the automobile in its place.

Gruen's concern that people should have the convenience of cars without letting their lives be destroyed by them was a continuing and constructive thread in his work. He believed that the car is right for individual mobility but wrong for mass transport: we ought to be able to make social life and shopping journeys by car, but office workers in the big cities should use public transport for the journeys to and from work. By the late 1960's, this was conventional thinking in planning circles; in post-war Los Angeles it was heresy. It is perhaps somewhat cruel that Victor Gruen had great success with his shopping centres which encourage the use of cars, yet his planning advice to numerous cities to require greater use of public transport has more often than not fallen on deaf ears.

Soon after the war Gruen designed a department store outside Los Angeles with its image derived from ramps giving access to rooftop parking. This store, besides revealing Gruen's fascination with vehicular movement, was his only memorable piece of architecture until younger partners, like Cesar Pelli, designed for the firm a couple of decades later.

In 1954 Victor Gruen Associates completed the Northland Center, outside Detroit, the first large scale shopping centre designed to serve the motorists of an entire region. As architecture the Northland Center is pleasant if bland; as a circulation system, a series of systems, it demonstrates a clear grasp of the problem. Servicing of the stores is by underground truck route, freeing the ground around the building for the base acreage of shoppers' cars, which are on turn served by a highway net of mammoth proportions which surrounds the site. The actual shopping area of the Northland Center stands in the centre of the sea of cars and is completely traffic free: shoppers can walk and children can play as if the internal combustion engine had never been invented.

When the Northland Center had been completed, the next logical step in pampering the shopper still further was to enclose completely the shopping complex by roofing over the "pedestrian malls." This was accomplished in subsequent shopping centres, such as the Southdale Shopping Center in Minneapolis. The inside space now becomes multi-storey with different shopping levels, and the space itself filled with pools, hanging lamps and a whole paraphernalia of commercial kitsch.

Despite the success of the suburban shopping centres, Victor Gruen was genuinely concerned with the decay of American cities, a decay hastened, perhaps, by the very success of the shopping centres. He was given opportunities to construct shopping centres in the old city cores—his Midtown Plaza in Rochester, New York, for example, covers a quarter of the downtown area.

Buildings like Midtown Plaza did indeed help to revitalize the downtown area, but Gruen had always known that shopping alone could not solve the problem. When he was asked to make proposals for Fort Worth, Texas, he seized the chance to show his ideas for the centre of cities. The Fort Worth plan was never realized, but it remains Gruen's most important work, and there can be few city planners anywhere in the world have not been influenced by it. In Britain, for example, Colin Buchanan's famous report *Traffic in Towns* follows many of the strategies proposed for Fort Worth.

The Fort Worth plan consists, in essence, of ringing the downtown area with a highway and parking garages, and within this area all is pedestrianized except for a gentle public transport system. The concept was clear, and one would have thought appealing, but in the 1950's Texans were not yet in the mood to be told that they could not take their cars wherever they wanted.

The fame of the Fort Worth plan brought Victor Gruen Associates work for various smaller cities and Gruen himself wrote his book *Heart of Our Cities*. He was fascinated by metropolitan scale and on his own initiative prepared a plan for Manhattan that proposed cross-town freeways to divide the island into segments.

In retrospect, it is the Northland Center and Fort Worth that are memorable. Both were optimistic about the possibilities of the good life for Americans. The Northland Center took the squalor of roadtown, made sense of it and gave it an image. The Fort Worth plan took a step on the road to making cars compatible with a great city.

—John Winter

GRUZEN, Barnett Sumner.

American. Born in Dankera, Latvia, 25 July 1903; emigrated to the United States, 1905; naturalized, 1925. Educated at the Massachusetts Institute of Technology, Cambridge, 1921-28, B.Arch. 1926, M.Arch. 1928; Ecole des Beaux-Arts, Paris, 1930-32 (Rotch Travelling Fellowship). Married Ethel Brof in 1930; children: Jordan and Maxson. Worked in the offices of Ritchie, Parsons and Taylor, Guy Lowell, and Perry Shaw and Hepburn, Boston, 1928-30, and Stone and Webster, and Emery Roth, New York, 1930-32; in private practice, Jersey City, New Jersey, 1932-37; Partner, with Hugh Kelly, in Kelly and Gruzen, Jersey City, 1937-41; Chief Executive, Kelly and Gruzen, Jersey City, 1941-46, and New York, 1946 until Kelly's death, 1967; name changed to Gruzen and Partners, 1967; served as Consultant to the Partnership, 1971 until his death, 1974; direction of the firm assumed by son Jordan, 1971. President, American Society for Technion: Israel Institute of Technology, 1936-64; Chairman, Architectural Division, United Jewish Appeal and Federation of Jewish Philanthropies, New York, 1951. Recipient: First Prize, New Jersey State Capitol Competition, 1945; National Honor Award, 1951, 1968, Medal of Honor, 1974, American Institute of Architects; School Design Prize, *School Executive* magazine, 1955; Diamond Jubilee Citation, New York City, 1973. Fellow, American Institute of Architects, 1957. Member, National Council of Architectural Registration Boards; Society of Professional Engineers; New Jersey Society of Architects; New York State Association of Architects; Society of American Military Engineers; Architectural League of New York. *Died* (in New York) *27 September 1974.*

Works:

1955 Milton Steinberg House, Park Avenue Synagogue, East 87th Street, New York
Forchheimer Medical Science Building, Albert Einstein College of Medicine, Bronx, New York

1956 Junior High School 22, and adjoining Hamilton Fish Park Branch of the New York Public Library, Houston Street, New York

1958 Robbins Auditorium, Friedman Lounge, and Gottesman Library, Albert Einstein College of Medicine, Bronx, New York

1961 United States Mission to the United Nations, U.N. Plaza, New York

1962 Chatham Green Apartments, Park Row, New York

1963 Litho City, New York (project)
University Terrace Apartments, Brooklyn, New York

1964 Spanish Pavilion, *World's Fair*, New York
Congregation Knesseth Israel Synagogue, Empire Avenue, Queens, New York

1965 Chatham Towers Apartments, Park Row, New York

1966 Loeb Pavilion, Montefiore Hospital and Medical Center, Bronx, New York

1967 Lindsay Park Houses, Montrose Avenue, Brooklyn, New York

1968 Goldine Pavilion, Hebrew Home for the Aged, Bronx, New York

1969 Bache and Company Headquarters, 100 Gold Street, New York

1970 Southbridge Towers Apartments, Gold, Frankfort, Water and Fulton Streets, New York
Anniel Lichtenhein Pavilion, Montefiore Hospital and Medical Center, Bronx, New York
Kissena II Apartments, 45th Avenue, Flushing, New York

1971 Bronx State Hospital Rehabilitation Center, Waters Place, Bronx, New York
Japan House, East 47th Street, New York (with Junzo Yoshimura)
New Amsterdam Apartments, Amsterdam Avenue at West 95th Street, New York
Reuther Houses (apartments), Seagirt Avenue, Queens, New York

1972 Beekan Downtown Hospital Staff Residence, New York

1974 Police Headquarters Building and Pedestrian Plaza, Park Row, Pearl, Henry and New Streets, New York
United States Courthouse annex and modernization, New York
Beth Israel Medical Center, Newark, New Jersey

1975 Beekman Dowtown Hospital Ambulatory Care Facility, New York
Murray Bergtraum High School, Pearl Street, New York

Publications:

On GRUZEN: articles—"The 1968 AIA Honor Awards" in *AIA Journal* (Washington, D.C.), June 1968; "Age-Old Problem" in *Industrial Design* (New York), July/August, 1969; "Bauen für Kranke Menschen" in *Baumeister* (Munich), September 1970; "Barnett Sumner Gruzen" in *AIA Journal* (Washington, D.C.), November 1974; "Barney Gruzen, FAIA, Dies at 71" in *Architectural Record* (New York), November 1974; "Low-rise housing in America: the suburban scene", special issue of *Process: Architecture* (Tokyo), no. 12, 1980; "The New American Skyscrapers— the fifth generation" by Pierre Lucain in *L'Architecture d'Aujourd'hui* (Paris), April 1982.

*

During Barnett Gruzen's partnership with Hugh A. Kelly he built numerous public housing schemes, hospitals and community centers, and this experience stood him in good stead for his later work. Towards the end of the partnership, Gruzen was responsible for gaining no less than ten separate commissions for developments in downtown Manhattan, and it is for these substantial contributions to that area that he is now best known.

After Kelly's death in 1967, Gruzen reorganized the office into Gruzen and Partners, taking on five new associates, including his son Jordan. The strength of the company during the next five years, before he retired to become a consultant to the firm, lies in Gruzen's political acumen, diplomacy, and almost bulldozing determination. When it came to a complicated civic development involving the sort of long-term wrangles with publicly funded agencies that big-city projects often entail, Gruzen had the patience and stamina to follow through.

A good example is one of the later downtown

Manhattan works (which was finally completed by Jordan Gruzen), the new Police Headquarters Building. Originally commissioned in 1960 and opened in 1974, this project spanned the reign of two mayors, six police commissioners, and nine public works commissioners. During the inevitable and vexing delays, Gruzen and Partners were the only continuing prescence.

The project required the shifting of several approach ramps to the Brooklyn Bridge, which in turn required the co-operation of a spate of city agencies and a helping hand from the Office of Lower Manhattan Development. In spite of fierce opposition from promoters of alternative and temporarily expedient projects, Gruzen helped the city to gain a sound and coherent piece of civic planning in an area where that virtue had been absent for too long.

The building itself, clad in brick, with its echoing grid of regularized deep set windows, towers over its basement car park and open lobby, but it is the use of the irregularly shaped site that is most impressive. A 75 foot wide pedestrian plaza—designed with the landscapists Friedberg and Associates, with whom Gruzen had often collaborated—has been planted with rows of honey locust trees, fitted with benches, with a large steel sculpture placed in the center, creating such a grand and spacious outdoor lounging area that it is difficult for the visitor to realize that he is actually on a bridge with a busy traffic artery—Park Row—cutting beneath it. The Police Department is now physically and symbolically linked both to the residential neighborhood to the South and to the courthouses along Center Street.

New York has sometimes seemed a city intent on bleeding itself to death in fragmented and ad hoc planning decisions. It is to Barnett Gruzen's credit that he never gave up when others did, and that he persevered against what many would regard as formidable odds to create such an intelligently planned addition to the city center.

—Colin Naylor

GUEDES, Amancio d'Alpoim Miranda ("Pancho")

Portuguese. Born in Lisbon, 13 May 1925. Educated at Principe Island, Gulf of Guinea, 1930; São Tomé School, Gulf of Guinea, 1931; in Lisbon, 1932; Manjacaze Primary School, Mozambique, 1932-33; Lourenço Marques (now Maputo) High School, Mozambique, 1934-38; Maritz Brothers College, Johannesburg, South Africa, 1939-44; University of the Witwatersrand, Johannesburg, under Donald Pilcher, 1945-50, B.Arch. 1950. Married Dorothy Ann Phillips in 1947; children: Pedro Paulo, Veronica, Godofredo, and Katarina. In private practice, Lourenço Marques (now Maputo), Mozambique 1949-75, and in Johannesburg, since 1975; worked with engineers Silva Carvalho, Ferrera and Gaddini, 1950, with city-planner F. Mesquita, 1951-52, and with engineer Vitale Moffa, 1952-53. Part-time instructor, Escola Technica, Lourenço Marques (now Maputo), Mozambique, 1955-56. Since 1975, Professor and Head of the Department of Architecture, University of Witwatersrand, Johannesburg. Exhibition: *Bienal,* São Paulo, 1961; *Biennale,* Venice, 1975; Institute for Architecture and Urbanism, New York, 1976; Architectural Association, London, 1980. Recipient: Gold Medal, Institute of South African Architects, 1979. Commander, Order of Santiago e Espada, Portugal, 1979. Address: 17 Ninth Avenue, Melville, Johannesburg, South Africa.

Works:

1950 Saca dura Botte House, Lourenço Marques (now Maputo), Mozambique

Amancio Guedes: Smiling Lion Apartments, Maputo, Mozambique, 1958.

1951/
52 Leite Martins House, Lourenço Marques (now Maputo), Mozambique
Dragão Apartments, Lourenço Marques (now Maputo), Mozambique

1951/
53 Prometheus Apartments, Lourenço Marques (now Maputo), Mozambique
Mendes d'Almeida House, Machava, Mozambique

1952/
53 Hotel and shops, Palmeira, Mozambique
Semi-Detached Houses for Matos Ribeira, Lourenço Marques (now Maputo), Mozambique

1952/
54 Saipal Bakery, Lourenço Marques (now Maputo), Mozambique

1953 Santos Marques e Silva Building, Lourenço Marques (now Maputo), Mozambique

1953/
54 Otto Barbosa Garage and Offices, Lourenço Marques (now Maputo), Mozambique
Co-Op Rowhouses, Lourenço Marques (now Maputo), Mozambique
Eight houses, Avenida Belgarde da Silva, Lourenço Marques (now Maputo), Mozambique

1953/
59 Abreu, Santos e Rocha Building, Lourenço Marques (now Maputo), Mozambique

1954 Nucleo de Arte Art Club, Lourenço Marques (now Maputo), Mozambique
Zambi Restaurant, Lourenço Marques (now Maputo), Mozambique

Exhibition Pavilions, Lourenço Marques (now Maputo), Mozambique

1954/
55 Pylon Cement Factory, Matola, Mozambique
Abreau Family Rowhouses, Lourenço Marques (now Maputo), Mozambique

1954/
56 Mann George Shipping Company Building, Lourenço Marques (now Maputo), Mozambique
Twelve houses, Avenida Miguel Bombarda, Lourenço Marques (now Maputo), Mozambique
Dr. Simoes Ferreira Apartment Block, Lourenço Marques (now Maputo), Mozambique

1954/
57 Tonelli Condominium, Lourenço Marques (now Maputo), Mozambique

1954/
59 Polana Bar, Polana Hotel, Lourenço Marques (now Maputo), Mozambique

1955 Hotel, San Martinho de Bilene, Mozambique

1955/
56 House, Avenida Caldas Xavier, Lourenço Marques (now Maputo), Mozambique

1955/
57 Barclays Bank Building, Lourenço Marques (now Maputo), Mozambique

1956/
57 Engenheiro Gomes Rowhouses, Lourenço Marques (now Maputo), Mozambique

1956/
58 House of the Three Giraffes, Lourenço Marques (now Maputo), Mozambique

Smiling Lion Apartments, Lourenço Marques (now Maputo), Mozambique

1957/
62 Isauro Lopes Building, Lourenço Marques (now Maputo), Mozambique

1958/
60 Saturio Pires House, Lourenço Marques (now Maputo), Mozambique

1958/
61 The Pyramidal Kindergarten, Lourenço Marques (now Maputo), Mozambique

1958/
63 Spence e Lemos Building, Lourenço Marques (now Maputo), Mozambique

1959/
72 Boror Building, Lourenço Marques (now Maputo), Mozambique

1960/
61 Service Station, Komatipoort, South Africa

1960/
63 Motel, Komatipoort, South Africa

1961/
62 Yes House, Lourenço Marques (now Maputo), Mozambique

1962/
64 Sagrada Familia church, Machava, Mozambique

1963 Mayers House, Piet Retief, South Africa
Associacão dos Naturais Building, Lourenço Marques (now Maputo), Mozambique

1963/
65 Church of St. James the Great, Nyamandhlovo, Rhodesia
Casa Salm, Lourenço Marques (now Maputo), Mozambique

1963/
72 Waterford School, Mbabane, Swaziland
1964/
65 Dr. Jose de Costa Building, Lourenço Marques (now Maputo), Mozambique
Primary school, Antioka, Magude, Mozambique
1964/
66 Church of Santa Ana da Munhuana, Lourenço Marques (now Maputo), Mozambique
Casa Almiro do Vale, Lourenço Marques (now Maputo), Mozambique
1965 Enfermagem School, Lourenço Marques (now Maputo), Mozambique
1965/
66 Agricultural Adviser's House, Mavuvulane, Mozambique
1965/
67 Police Widows and Orphans Savings Bank Building, Lourenço Marques (now Maputo), Mozambique
Dr. Lopes da Silva House, Lourenço Marques (now Maputo), Mozambique
1966/
68 San Jose de Lhanguene Convent, Lourenço Marques (now Maputo), Mozambique
Hospital extension, Chicumbane, Gaza, Mozambique
1966/
69 Octavio Lobo Building, Lourenço Marques (now Maputo), Mozambique
1966/
73 Khovolar Hostel, Lourenço Marques (now Maputo), Mozambique
1967 College of Nossa Senhora da Conceicão, Inhambane, Mozambique
1967/
68 Desirello House, Illovo, Johannesburg

1968 Canha St. Andrews House, Johannesburg
1968/
69 Clandestine Nursery School, Canico, Lourenço Marques (now Maputo), Mozambique
Congregational Church, Choupal, Mozambique
1968/
71 The Red House, Lourenço Marques (now Maputo), Mozambique
1969/
71 The House of the Broken Pediment, Lourenço Marques (now Maputo), Mozambique
1970/
72 Standard Totta Bank Director's House, Lourenço Marques (now Maputo), Mozambique
1970/
4 7 Parque Condominium, Lourenço Marques (now Maputo), Mozambique
Nurses' Hostel, Chicumbane, Gaza, Mozambique
Church of San Cipriano do Chamanculo, Lourenço Marques (now Maputo), Mozambique
1971 Church of the Twelve Apostles, Gala Massala, Lourenço Marques (now Maputo), Mozambique (with Pedro Guedes)
1971/
73 Boesch House, Lourenço Marques (now Maputo), Mozambique
Waterford School Girls Hostel, Mbabane, Swaziland (with Pedro Guedes)
1972/
74 Post Office School, Inhambane, Mozambique
1972/
75 Hostel and Farm School, Estevel, Boane, Mozambique
1973 Governor's Palace, Vila Pery, Mozambique
1973/
75 Totta Standard Building, Porto Alexandre, Angola
Hotel, Alto Mahe, Lourenço Marques (now Maputo), Mozambique

1974/
75 Regentes Agricolas School, Vila Pery, Mozambique

Publications:

By GUEDES: book—*Fragments from an Ironic Autobiography*, Johannesburg 1977; *Amancio Guedes*, exhibition catalogue, London 1980; articles—"Les Mapogga" in *Aujourd'hui* (Paris), June 1962; "Amancio guedes: Y aura-t-il une architecture" in *L'Architecture d'aujourd'hui* (Paris), June/July 1962; "Things Are Not What They Seem To Be" in *Proceedings of the First National Congress of African Culture*, Salisbury 1962; "Four Sights and the Whosing of Sakes" in *For Us*, Johannesburg 1963; "The American Egyptian Style" in *World Architecture 1*, edited by John Donat, London 1964; "The Practice of Architecture" in *South African Architectural Record* (Johannesburg), June 1964; "Architects as Magicians, Conjurors, Dealers in Magic Goods, Promises, Potions, Spells—Myself as Witchdoctor" in *World Architecture 2*, edited by John Donat, London 1965; "Buildings Grow Out of Each Other; or, How My Own Sagrada Familia Came To Be" in *World Architecture 4*, London 1967; "The Intuitive Process and Some Other Ideas" in *Architectural Education Symposium*, Johannesburg 1967; "The Language of Sculpture" in *Faculty of Arts Colloquium*, Johannesburg 1975; "Bush Schools" in *RIBA Journal* (London), no. 10, 1976; "On Architecture," interview, in *Architecture South Africa* (Cape Town) March 1979; recording—*Thirteen Architectures*, tape cassette and slides, London 1980.

On GUEDES: books—*New Directions in African Architecture* by Udo Kultermann, London and New York 1969; *Pancho Guedes: The Collective Unconscious of Architecture*, thesis by Timothy Ostler, Sheffield University, 1978; *Architekten Zeichnen*, edited by Claudius Coulin, Stuttgart 1980; articles—"Amancio Guedes, Architect of Lourenço Marques" by Julian Beinart in *Architectural Review* (London), April 1961; "Emergence of a New and Original Figure: Remarkable Work by Amancio Guedes" in *The Times* (London), 17 May 1961; Pancho Amancio d'Alpoim Miranda Guedes: Arquitecto escultor—escultor arquitecto" by Salette Tavares in *Coloquio* (Lisbon), April 1977; "On Amancio d'Alpoim Guedes" by Alison Smith and "Down There on a Visit" by Alan Berman in *Architecture + Urbanism* (Tokyo), no. 6, 1978; "Team 10," special issue of *Deutsche Bauzeitung* (Stuttgart), November 1978; "Guedes in Profile" in *Building Design* (London), 1 December 1978; "The ISAA Gold Medal Awards: Hans Hallen and Prof. Amancio d'Alpoim Guedes" in *Architecture South Africa* (Cape Town), Summer 1979; "Pancho Guedes," special issue of *Architecture South Africa* (Cape Town), May/June 1982.

For twenty-five years, I invented and made enough buildings to make up a city. An imaginary but quite probable city, chaotic and layered with memories, a city of many separate and tiny cases of obsessive regularity.

I am also a painter and sculptor. I cannot tell painting and sculpture apart from architecture. Many of the ideas of my architectue have originated in drawings whichare common to the three. Some of the other ideas are paraphrases or distorted quotations from other architects' works and ideas. I believe that buildings grow out of each other, that each artist invents his own precursors, that there is an incessant dialogue with many pasts. Sometimes I have ridden a track of ideas for a number of years with other ideas interspersed. Often the ideas have crashed and turned into other ideas. I have worked in many styles simultaneously. I have dismissed any

sort of chronology long ago. I have, instead, classified my architectural inventions into twenty-five families and filed them into a catalogue of twenty-five architectures. In that catalogue there is a family of learning machines, some slices of street face, some slabs, some temporary towers, buildings in parts of rings, wedges and circles, a whole neo-colonial revival, some transformations and resurrections, a set of parts of villages, remembering other villages far away in my mother country, many disparate churches, a collection of Euclidian palaces, a few grass houses, a chain of service stations, thirty or forty little blue banks on the east side and ten little black and white ones on the west side, buildings in my arched and somewhat roman manner, the Wrightian works and the earlier Wright houses, a whole industrial zone of factories and warehouses, the clubs and associations, the passages, steps, places and squares of the city, the bargains in a bush style, the bubblies, a number of tents and sails, a couple of box houses, all the works in the American-Egyptian style, the buildings with walls twisting and turning and stilo guedes.

I have always worked at home with the help of a few draughtsmen who, in most cases, I have trained myself. I have always done all the design work myself (and by all I mean all, from the invention to the detail which is as much a part of the invention) except for the few times when I have collaborated with my son, Pedro.

Most of my works now lie dead or wounded, casualties andvictims of four revolutions. I now live in exile. I carry the ideas of all these twenty-five architectures within me. They have become the drawings and photographs I have with me. I have become a teacher. My task is now to explore the borders of architecture, to expand its territories to illuminate the new lands and sign-post them for my students and for myself.

—Amancio Guedes

To summarise the work of Amancio Guedes in just a few hundred words is something of a challenge. Whereas other architects tend to settle fairly soon—after perhaps a little wobbling at the beginning—on a more or less consistent style, Guedes has continued to give the appearance of leaping from one fascination to another throughout his career. Indeed, it is probably this talent for, as he says, "turning on a style at a moment's notice" that is his most characteristic feature.

He has set his face resolutely against the suggestion that there should be any kind of chronological development in an architect's work, with the arch declaration that "all ideas are as good as each other." A Glance through the widely divergent styles of his work, taken even over a short period of time, lends weight to an initial impression that the choice of style for each project is almost a matter of whim. The truth is, however, that each theme derives more from the peculiarities of the site or the brief than from the architect's enthusiasm of the moment. Guedes, unlike many architects, does not spend time trying to force a preconceived architectural ideology on a reluctant brief. He is assisted by a repertoire of form extending right across the historical and stylistic spectrum, from Palladio, Serlio, through Frank Lloyd Wright, Kahn, and Le Corbusier, to Gaudí and Miro—and much more in between. But throughout, there is never any danger that one of Guedes's buildings might be mistaken for the work of someone else.

Over a period dating from soon after qualification to his departure in 1975, Guedes worked profusely from an office in his house in Lourençço Marques, producing well over five hundred works of all kinds. As he puts it, "for about twenty-five years I just did one building after another in a kind of daze." His productivity becomes all the more striking when one considers that he has always insisted being sole author of his buildings. In the light of this, it is remarkable that he managed to keep closely in touch with contemporary developments all over the world, becoming a member of Team 10 in 1962, and formuch of the time subscribing to and avidly reading every architectural magazine of any consequence. During this time, Guedes's spectacular buildings in their sultry location became something of a tourist attraction, and in additional many students from Johannesburg enjoyed a spell in his office during their holidays.

Although a vigorous and outspoken critic of the *ancien régime*, Guedes left Mozambique in 1974, in disgust and disappointment at the actions of the post-revolutionary Frelimo government. Since his departure, he has been freer to lead a less hectic existence, as Professor of Architecture at the University of the Witwatersrand, Johannesburg; although he has produced numerous projects, the quantity of his built work has been relatively small. At the same time, not only are the threads connecting his current designs more apparent, but in addition, they have begun to shed light on the common themes running through his earlier work.

During these last few years, the feeling hehas always had for the historic architecture of Portugal has begun to emerge more clearly in his designs. Having been exposed to them in his childhood, Guedes has always maintained a deep affection for the structures erected by the early Portuguese colonialists. Not long before the change of government, he and his son Pedro (also an architect) were fortunately able to complete a very valuable and comprehensive survey of all the major colonial buildings of northern Mozambique.

Guedes has always considered himself, with some justification, as much a painter and a sculptor as an architect. But the same formal preoccupations haunt him, in no matter what medium he happens to be working. If all his buildings, paintings, and sculpture were photographed, then projected rapidly on a screen, one after the other, the result would be an animated film of some coherence, throbbing with life as first one theme, then another, metamorphosed through all possible combinations. It would also probably be of several hours duration.

—Timothy Ostler

GUEDES, Joaquim.

Brazilian. Born in São Paulo, 18 June 1932. Educated at the University of São Paulo, Faculty of Architecture and Urbanism, 1949-54, Dip.Arch. 1954, D.Arch. 1972. Married Liliana Marsicano in 1953; children: Joaquim José, Maria Clara, Alberto, Francisco, and Tereza Matilde. Since 1955, in private practice, São Paulo. Professor of Building Materials, 1958-59, and, since 1969, Professor of Town Planning, University of São Paulo. Associate Professor, Institute of Architecture and Urbanism, Strasbourg, France, 1970-73. Director, São Paulo Division, 1959-62, and Member of the Council, 1959-69, Brazilian Institute of Architects; Member, International Union of Architects/Unesco Commission on Habitat, Paris, 1963-69. Exhibition: *Salão Paulista de arte moderna*, São Paulo, 1959, 1961, and 1969; *Bienal*, São Paulo, 1965; *Premiacão anual*, Brazilian Institute of Architects, São Paulo, 1969; *Joaquim Guedes*, Centro de Arte y Communicacion, Buenos Aires, 1978. Recipient: Governor's State Prize, São Paulo, 1959 and 1969; *Bienal*, São Paulo, 1965; Rino Levi Prize, Brazilian Institute of Architects, 1969. Address: Joaquim Guedes e Associados, Avenida Paulista 1776, 21st Floor, São Paulo 01310, Brazil.

Works:

1957 J.A. Guedes House, Rua Georgia, São Paulo
1958 Cunha Lima House, Rua Silvio Portugal, São Paulo

1959 Itapira Forum, São Paulo
  Ataliba Nogueira Primary School, Itapira, São Paulo
1961 Costa Neto House, Rua Itapanhau, São Paulo
  São Domingos High School, São Paulo (project)
1962 Toledo House, Rua Samuel Neves, Piracicaba, São Paulo
  Areia Branca Primary School, Taubaté, São Paulo (project)
1963 Mathematics Institute, University of São Paulo (project)
1965 Breyton House, Rua Souza Ramos, São Paulo
  Landiu House, Rua Guilherme Milward, São Paulo
1966 Pereira House, Rua Carangola, São Paulo
  Agricultural School, Lorena, São Paulo
  Campinas Electronics School, São Paulo (project)
  Faculty of Philosphy, Lorena, São Paulo (project)
  Carvalhosa House, Rua Polonia, São Paulo
  Reinach House, Braganca Paulista, São Paulo
1967 São José High School, Sororcaba, São Paulo (project)
  Preparatory institute, Jandira, São Paulo
1968 Apartment building, Al. Ministro Rocha Azevedo, São Paulo (project)
  Vila Galvão State High School, Guarulhos, São Paulo
  Central Library of Bahia, Salvador, Brazil (project)
1969 Urban plan for São Paulo
  Preliminary plan for Campinas, São Paulo
  United Nations Conference Center, Vienna (project; with E.S.Mello)
1970 Monteil House, Itanhaem, São Paulo
  Master plan for the Mogí Guacú, São Paulo
1971 School of Architecture, Strasbourg, France (project; with P. Chemetov and R. Chomel)
1972 Urban plan for Porto Velho, Rondonia, Brazil
  Civic and Cultural Center, Mogí Guacú São Paulo (project)
1973 Urban plan for the Carajás Iron Mines new town project, Pará, Brazil
  Urban plan for Marabá, Pará, Brazil
1974 J. Guedes House, Rua Prof. Luciano Gualberto, São Paulo
  Urban plan for Piracicaba, São Paulo
  Residential complex, Campinas, São Paulo
  Marsicano Factory, Salto, São Paulo
  Plan for the island of Tamandua, São Paulo
  São Bernardo Satellite Town, São Paulo (project)
  Dourado House, Rua Albert Einstein, São Paulo
1975 Convention Center, Foz do Iguaçcu, Paraná, Brazil (project)
  Beer House, Rua Jacupiranga, São Paulo
  Romero House, Campinas, São Paulo
  Monteil House, Avaré, São Paulo
1976 Hotel, Rua Ministro Nelson Hungria, São Paulo
  Urban plan for Taquaral, Piracicaba, São Paulo
  Monteiro Lobato Public Library, São Bernardo, São Paulo (project)
  Urban plan for Caraiba, Bahia, Brazil
1977 Campinas Maternity Hospital, São Paulo (project)
1978 Urban plan for Paiva, Recife, Brazil
  Anna Mariani House, Ibiuna, São Paulo
1979 Urban plan for Barcarena, Belém, Brazil

Publications:

By GUEDES: book—*Arquitectura brasileira após Brasilia/Depoimentos*, Rio de Janeiro 1978; articles—"José Anthero Guedes House" in *Bem Estar* (São Paulo), no. 4, 1957; "Architecture in the VIII Bienal" in *Acrópole* (São Paulo), October 1965; "O exercício da profissao em funcçao da arquitetura

e o meio ambiente," "A integracao do arquiteto no planjamento" and "Arquitetura e planejamento urbano," with J. Wilheim, in *Acrópole* (São Paulo), November 1966; "Concurso para Bilioteca Central de Salvador" in *Acrópole* (São Paulo), November 1968; "The Private Home in Brazilian Tradition and the Problem of the New Generation" in *Global Interiors 2*, Tokyo 1972; "Obras y proyetos del estudio Joaquim Guedes y Associados" in *Revista summa* (Buenos Aires), June 1979; "Caraiba New Town and Other Works" in *Spazio e società* (Milan), no. 7, July 1979.

On GUEDES: books—*New Directions in Latin American Architecture* by Francisco Bullrich, New York 1969, London 1970; *Profile of New Brazilian Art* by P.M. Bardi, São Paulo 1969; *Panoramica de la arquitectura latinoamericana* by P. Gasparini and D. Bayon, Barcelona 1975; *Architekten der Dritten Welt* by Udo Kultermann, Cologne 1980; articles—"Cunha Lima House" in *Kokusai Kentiku* (Tokyo), July 1967; special issue of *Acrópole* (São Paulo), February 1968; "Nouvelle Ecole d'architecture à Strasbourg" in *Architecture d'aujourd'hui* (Paris), September 1971; Works and Projects of Joaquim Guedes and Asociados", special issue of *Summa* (Buenos Aires), June 1979; "A Country House for a Photographer, Ibuna, Sao Paulo" in *AC: International Asbestos Cement Review* (Zurich), April 1980; "Modern Brazilian Archtecture", special issue of *Process: Architecture* (Tokyo), August 1980.

*

All projects are important, even the smallest and most incoherent. They are laboratories allowing one to think about and to work with man and his complex and marvellous needs, with materials, matter, and technologies, with light, economics, ethics, politics. "A house is a small town" (V. Eyck).

For many years, I thought that construction was the most important thing. Architecture was a construction to house a system of activities/spaces organized for man. This way of seeing guided and even differentiated my work. As a result, it was characterized by a certain severity in the analysis of factors andwas, in consequence, severe in its end solutions; it was an architecture opposed to ornament, to decoration, and to traditional national or foreign forms, a point of departure for many projects. I did not know and even denied the importance of beauty.

As time has passed, I have become aware that, even with an aversion to any kind of forcibly preconceived aesthetic, my great desire has always been to create beauty, to produce increasingly beautiful architecture, marked, nevertheless, by a sense of human, social, and anthropocentric destiny. But who, in all conscience, can imagine himself to be in possession of such reserves of beauty as to offer it so prodigally to others? Beyond all the rhetoric—what criteria must be satisfied to produce beauty? What is beauty? How to learn it? How to teach it? How to create it?

Looking into myself, looking for points of reference that have guided me in this quest for beauty, I can identify an analysis of the relationship between habitat and landscape; the perfect siting of a work; its integration into the town from a functional, atmospheric, cultural, and yet formal point of view; a compromise with man, whose needs and sensibilities are the prime reasons for the project (and this compromise involves more than simply and conveniently supposing his participation; it involves guaranteeing his participation, his freedom, in relation to the work; and, finally, a rigorous, coherent and accurate construction, one that realizes and is expressive of these relationships and compromises.

—Joaquim Guedes

Joaquim Guedes is one of a few modern Brazilian architects who have chosen the path of experimentation, and his completed buildings, though hardly numerous, are clearly representative of his proposals and research. At first sight, his works present a deceptively large number of different forms; on closer inspection, they are manifestations of a systematic and coherent work process, a solving of the problems posed by all the factors that go to make upa work of architecture. These factors may be intrinsic and specific, such as the technology, the building program, or the economics; or they may be part of a larger context, factors around which the building will emerge. And a crucial concern for Guedes is that each project is started from scratch—creation in its purest form, abandoning existing notions and earlier premises in favor of a complete return to the drawing board and a fresh start.

This philosophy and method accounts for the predominant organic quality in Guede's architecture; at the same time, his work is characterized by a clear logic that often results in a sensitive rationalism. The dynamic relationship between these two tendecies, coexisting within a single project, creates a special tension.

Guedes' architectural output can be divided into three groups. The first is characterized by importance of the structural system, the element that organizes space. External surfaces and other architectural elements are clearly subservient to the structure, which determines the volume—as in the Cunha Lima House of 1958, the Campinas Electronics School of 1966, and the Guedes House of 1973.

The second group involves works of much greater complexity of form, and here it is that Guedes gives his virtuoso performances. Here, structure loses its importance and becomes subservient to a stronger

organic tendency. The mass is divided into smaller volumes, often with irregular shapes—prismatic surfaces of frameless panes of glass, which break up the dividing line between interior and exterior; overhangs and *Brises-soleil* that give rhythm to the facades. The resulting combination is powerfully dynamic, its cohesion assured by its very logic. Buildings in this group include the Pereira House, Dourado House, the Itapira Forum, and the unbuilt plans for the São José High School, the Central Library of Bahir, and the Mogí Guacçú Cultural and Civic Center.

Of his third group, it can be said that Guedes reverts to the vision of simplicity that existed in Brazilian architecture in the works of Lúcio Costa and a few others, a vision that was abandoned by the end of the 1940s in the wake of the great "Brazilian Style." Without favoring any particular trend (though he was, perhaps, influenced most directly by the works of Alvar Aalto), Guedes rediscovers the human subtleties of his early vision and, in doing so, returns to an option far better suited to the realities of everyday life in Brazil. The Landi House—notable for its subtle use of space, its mass, and its architectural elements, and built by extremely economical means—is a perfect example. Others are the group of architectural projects for the town of Caraiba.

Yet another, fourth group could be made up by linking certain buildings whose structure plays a less important part than in those of the first group and whose appearance is more compact and less elaborate externally than those of the third. Examples are the Toledo House, Beer House, and the project forthe United Nations Center in Vienna. But this

excessive categorization is valid only as a means of explanation in Guede's work as a whole, the most diverse, even contradictory, solutions are merely ways of dealing with certain facets of the total situation within which the architect is working.

Town planning has also been an important part of Guede's career from the beginning. Among the more recent of these plans, Caraiba stands out by virtue of its staying within basic limitations and restricting itself to a simplicity of function and construction that has resulted in the elimination of all superfluity and the consequent minimilization of production costs. It has a modest dignity rare in this kind of work

The new town of Caraiba, in the interior of Bahia, is a "company town" for the 15,000 employed by a mining company. Its conception was based on socio/anthropological research, a facet of town planning that is usually neglected. The plan is based, too, on traditional urban models in theregion and on the study of vehicular and pedestrian circulation patterns. The plan relies on the archetypal solution of the grid pattern but develops it in a way that optimizes urban integration. Social stratification and limitation is avoided by a distribution of dwellings of varying size within the urban area and by creating open spaces within the city for the accommodation of external or neighboring populations that will no doubt be attracted to this economic center. The structure allows for a natural, ordered growth. The existing houses can be altered by their occupiers, and the buildings are endowed with a certain spontaneity.

Guede's architectural projects for Caraiba are simple and in perfect accord with local conditions. They have an irregular plan, resulting from the

Joaquim Guedes: Guedes House, Sao Paulo, 1974.

informal distribution of functions that are, in turn, organized and supplied by means of interlinked circulation axes. The basic module is elaborated and disappears behind the volumes, which play an important part in plastic terms, without losing their entirely functional role and without compromising the rationale and the economy of construction. Guedes deals with the region's severe climatic conditions (semi-desert) by various means—in the urban planning (streets running east-west, buildings oriented north-south), in the architecture (buildings with patios, covered walkways, etc.), and in the building techniques (thick walls of bricks specially made from local clay).

Caraiba illustrates clearly all of Guedes's professional views. It is also one of the most interesting experiments in town planning ever attempted in Brazil.

—Jorge Czajkowski

GUTBROD, (Konrad) Rolf (Dietrich).

German. Born in Stuttgart, 13 September 1910. Educated at the Freie Waldorfschule, Stuttgart, 1919-29; Technical Universities of Berlin and Stuttgart, 1929-35, Dip.Ing. 1935; worked with Professor Güter Wilhelm, in Stuttgart, 1935-36. Married Thekla von Ploetz in 1941 (divorced, 1969); Kari Schwenda in 1982; children: Christiane, Verena, and Ghita. Served on the Government Building Council, 1940-45. In private practice, Stuttgart, since 1946; established offices in Berlin, 1961-78 and Riyadh, Saudi Arabia, 1977-78; consultant to architects Wolfgang Henning, Hermann Kendel and Bernd Riede (HKR), Berlin and Stuttgart, since 1978. Professor, Technical University of Stuttgart, since 1953 (Chair of Interior Decoration and Design since 1961). Guest Professor, Technical University of Istanbul, 1957-59; Walker Ames Professor, University of Washington, Seattle, 1963. Exhibitions: *Von Schinkel bis Mies van der Rohe*, Kunstbibliothek, Berlin, 1974; *Architekturzeichnungen 1479-1979*, Berlin and Cologne, 1979-80; *Bilder vom Menschen*, Nationalgalerie, Berlin, 1980; *Seconda Mostra Internazionale di Architettura*, Venice, 1982; Akademie der Künste, Berlin, 1983. Recipient: First Prize, IBM Administration Building Competition, Berlin 1959; First Prize, Cologne University Centre Competition, 1960; First Prize, Württembergische Bank Competition, Stuttgart, 1963; First Prize, Student Hostel Competition, Stuttgart, 1963; First Prize, Max-Planck-Institut and Dahlem Row Houses Competition, Berlin, 1965; First Prize, Museums of European Art Competition, Berlin, 1966; First Prize, with Frei Otto, Hotel and Conference Centre Competition, Mecca, Saudi Arabia, 1966; Auguste Perret Prize, International Union of Architects, 1968; First Prize, SDR Radio Station Building Competition, Stuttgart, 1968; Paul Bonatz Prize, Stuttgart, 1970 and 1972; First Prize, Sparkassen-Versicherung AG Building Competition, Stuttgart, 1970; Grand Cross of Merit, German Government, 1972; Hugo Häring Award, 1972; Aga Khan Award (with Frei Otto), 1980; Kunstpreis, Berlin, 1983; Architekturpreis Beton (with Billing, Peters and Ruff), 1983. Member, Akademie der Künste, Berlin, 1963; Member, Ordre pour le Mérite, 1971. Address: Büro Gutbrod (Architekten Henning, Kendel, Riede), Ebereschenallee 27, 1000 Berlin 19; or Schoderstrasse 10, 7000 Stuttgart 1, West Germany.

Works:

1954 Chamber of Commerce, Stuttgart (with Rolf Gutbier)
1956 Concert Hall, Berliner Platz, Stuttgart (with Adolf Abel and B. Spring)
1957 SDR Broadcasting Studios, Villa Berg, Stuttgart (with Helmut Weber and Hertha–Maria Witzemann)
1962 IBM Administration Building, Ernst-Reuter-Platz, West Berlin
1965 German Embassy, Metternichgasse, Vienna
SDR Television Studios, Villa Berg, Stuttgart (with Helmut Weber and Hertha-Maria Witzemann)
1966 Advertising Center, Berlin (with Hermann Kiess)
Teachers' College, Freie Waldorfschule, Uhlandshöhe, Stuttgart (with Wolfgang Henning)
Volkswagen Building, Stuttgart
1967 German Pavilion, *Expo '67*, Montreal (with Frei Otto)
Library, University of Cologne
1968 Auditorium Building, University of Cologne
Württembergische Bank, Stuttgart (with Hermann Kiess)
1969 Britz-Buchow-Rudow Housing, Gropiusstadt, Berlin
Student Hostel, Schwerzstrasse, Birkach, Stuttgart (with Hermann Kiess)
1970 Opernplatz Housing, Berlin
1971 Max-Planck-Institut, Dahlem, Berlin
Development plan for the Kurfüstendamm Quarter of Berlin
1972 Row houses, Dahlem, Berlin
1973 Classroom Building, for the Freie Waldorfschule, Uhlandshöhe, Stuttgart (with Wolfgang Henning)

Rolf Gutbrod: Hotel and Conference Centre, Mecca, Saudi Arabia, 1974.

Master plan for the Museums of European Art (Museum of Arts and Crafts; Picture Gallery; Sculpture Gallery; Print Gallery; Art Library), Tiergarten, Berlin

Cultural Center, Abidjan, Ivory Coast (project; with Frei Otto and Ove Arup and Partners)

1974 Hotel and Conference Center, Mecca, Saudi Arabia (with Frei Otto and Ove Arup and Partners)

Spa and Recreation Center, Baden-Baden, West Germany (competition project; with Frei Otto)

ZDF Television Center, Lerchenberg, Mainz, West Germany (competition projects; with Hermann Kiess)

Pilgrims' Accommodation, Muna, Saudi Arabia (competition project)

1974 H.M. The King's Office, Council of Ministers Buildings, and Majlis-al-Shura Building, Riyadh, Saudi Arabia

1976 SDR Radio Station Building, Neckerstrasse, Stuttgart

Sparkassen-Versicherung AG (insurance company) Building, Löwentorstrasse, Stuttgart

Ministry of Industry and Electricity, Riyadh, Saudi Arabia (project; with Frei Otto and Ove Arup and Partners)

Mannesmann Administration Building, Stuttgart (competition projects; with Wolfgang Henning)

1980 Congress Centre and Hotel, Stuttgart (project)

Sports Complex, King Abdul Aziz University, Jeddah, Saudi Arabia (with Frei Otto)

1981 Intercontinental Hotel extension, Riyadh, Saudi Arabia

Ministry of Finance Building refurbishment, Riyadh, Saudi Arabia

Housing, University of Riyadh, Saudi Arabia (with Samkari)

Cultural Centre, Ludenscheid, West Germany (with Billings, Peters, Ruff)

1982 Conference Centre, Abu Dhabi, United Arab Emirates (project)

Cultural Centre, Baghdad, Iraq (project)

1984 Museum of Arts and Crafts, Berlin

Institute of Gene Technology, Berlin

Publications

On GUTBROD: books—*Konzerthaus Stuttgarter Liederhalle* by Dr. Pollert, Stuttgart 1956; *Bibliotheksbauten in der BRD*, Frankfurt 1968; *Funkhaus Stuttgart*, Stuttgart 1976; *Frei Otto* by Philip Drew, Stuttgart 1976; *Deutsche Kunst seit 1960: Architektur* by P. Nestler and P. Bode, Munich 1976; *Stuttgarter Kunst im 20. Jahrhundert,* Stuttgart 1979; *Die vergeudete Moderne* by Frank Werner, Stuttgart 1981; *Die Waldorfschule baut* by Rex Raab, Stuttgart 1982; *Architettura nei paesi islamici,* Venice 1982; *Akademie der Künste, Kunstpreis Berlin 1983*, exhibition catalogue, Berlin 1983; *Bauten für Schulingen, Tagungen, Kongresse* by W. and T. Meyer-Bohe, Leinfelden 1983; articles—"Planung für die Museen am Tiergarten" in *Jahrbuch Preussischer Kulturbesitz 1971*, Berlin 1972; "Die neue Gemaldegalerie" in *Jahrbuch Preussischer Kulturbesitz, Sonderband 1,* Berlin 1983.

*   *   *

If an architect such as Felix Candela, the great inventor of new structures, who was invited to report on his ideas about the "influence of technology on architectural creativity," reveals himself as a non-technologist—being disappointed with the tendencies of today's technology—and if Candela demands an entirely different attitude form us architects, and if he thinks it necessary to stop the "inhuman and bureaucratic production of buildings," and if he invites us to "rediscover the pleasure of creation"—and if, too, Arthur Erickson, speaking about the "influence of ideology on architectural creativity" comes to the conclusion that our ideology today is valid for only a very small part of the world and has to be reflected and revised in view of world wide needs and that all ideology can be valued only in the context in which it has to serve—then it is quite obvious that the high aim of creativity (creativity as understood and hoped for as the salvation of our profession) cannot be achieved simply by combining technology and ideology.

There is a worldwide concern about the changes that have taken place in our surroundings during the last twenty years. Everyone seems shocked about the escalation of needs and about the way in which changes for the worse always happen most quickly.

At the University of Stuttgart, for a few years, our young students were enthusiastic about the scientific approach; they had slogans such as "death to the artist-architect" they were negative about design; they voted against learning to be draftsmen. Now, the great majority seems to realize that his belief in research only and the adoration of the quantifiable is a danger to our built surroundings.

The reports of the Club of Rome have made it clear to everyone where this road leads—and even the stupid now understand that once everyone has a bathroom, a washingmachine and a dishwasher, there will not be enough hot water; and if everyone in the world has a color television set or two, and a car or two, there cannot be enough energy to run them. So a change *must* come, and surely this is not a problem that requires more analysis, more futurology, more perfection, or—worst of all—more production.

We architects will never have the possibilities and means for research as do those groups working for governments or for, say, armaments and mass-production industries, and if we look at what these experst, with all this support, have produced in response to relatively simple problems (as, for instance, the price and availability of crude oil), we cannot hope to come up with better answers for the problems connected with accommodating the fast-growing world population, building in harmony with existing topography and culture, and using more technology without further destroying and polluting our surroundings. So, I think, we have to admit that only a fundamental change in our attitude will give us a chance to meet the challenge.

We must convince ourselves and our clients and the public that the problems cannot be solved with more technology but that we are confronted with a spiritual problem and that we must learn to have confidence in ingenuity, in ideation, in creativity. And it is *our* job to achieve this change.

The more complex our problems became, the more we looked for help—we formed teams, we collaborated with sociologists, ecologists, doctors, psychologists, experts of all kinds; we resigned ourselves to being the leader of the team. But in the public mind, we, the architects and engineers, are responsible for the destruction of existing values, for the dreariness of the newly built environment, for the production of new slums. And—maybe—this serves us right.

As architects, *we* should have known that though our work is becoming more and more specialized and though the problems to be solved are becoming more and more complex and though, naturally, our work today is involved with and is characterized by technology, our profession must remain an art, must allow for spiritual values, must leave room for intuition, must reflect philosophy.

These most valuable notions, inherent in our profession, are not so easily quantifiable as the other elements that influence the construction of buildings and surroundings. But why are we not looking for new methods of integration? We must not allow ourselves to be outmaneuvered. No, I don't want to go back to the old image of the artist-architect as someone wearing a special hat and a funny tie. And, of course, what we need is the well-informed and educated architect who has an excellent knowledge of today's technology or, at least, knows where to find and how to use it. But the more architecture is rationalized, "progressive," and profit-oriented, the more the creative element must balance this development. The important ideas, the creative guidelines, and the solutions for tomorrow cannot be expected to come from the computer.

—Rolf Gutbrod

In 1974 an interesting architectural manifesto was published, a manifesto in open opposition to the renunciatory and classicist tendencies of contemporary architecture. Among the signatories was Rolf Gutbrod who was then, with Frei Otto, putting the finishing touches to the Hotel and Conference Center in Mecca, a work that in itself marks a fundamental stage in the progress of architectural planning in Arab countries.

Gutbrod's career has been a preparation for the manifesto. His Volkswagen Building of 1966, like Scharoun's towers and the elegant houses of Chen Cuen Lee, was one of the most significant buildings completed in Stuttgart in the 1960s. That the irregular ground plan of the Volkswagen Building is derived from Scharoun is easily recognizable in the facades set at different angles. A little later Gutbrod completed the Student Hostel in Birkach; in a way similar to the Volkswagen Building, it burst out from the sides of an acute-angled triangle with the single rooms along the sides directed toward the central nucleus of the service complex.

These designs would lead one to describe Gutbrod as an organic architect, to associate him with Scharoun and German expressionism—but that is perhaps rather too common an exaggeration. His conceptions are in a field and in an epoch that have already emerged from the classical currents of expressionism. Born in Stuttgart, and educated at the Freie Waldorfschule, Gutbrod was raised in a basically humanistic-naturalistic tradition. His work on the Freie Waldorfschule, on the Uhlandshöhe, Stuttgart, completed in 1973, is evidence of Gutbrod's humanistic interests and sensitivity; it is obviously a task in which he cared particularly deeply. And Gutbrod is a Moslem convert: he has shifted the axis of his activities more and more to the Middle East.

Collaboration with Frei Otto has also constituted an important chapter in his life; it has given Gutbrod the opportunity to dedicate himself to a search for associative forms and to work with tensile roofs. This technological instrument has enabled him to broaden his units of measurement and to adapt tensile forms to the requirements of the Arab peoples, who perform their religious devotions mainly in the open air. The German Pavilion at *Expo '67* in Montreal was another stage in his coming to a global view of the concept of community, a concept that he had been developing ever since he won international recognition for his Concert Hall in Stuttgart in 1956.

Gutbrod's recent work, the Museums of European Art Complex in Berlin, of which the Museum of Arts and Crafts is already being built, is also certain to attract international attention. This site is, in fact, the completion of the quadrangle formed by Scharoun's Philharmonie and Library and Mies van der Rohe's National Gallery. To design a complex to stand next to these buildings must have been, for Gutbrod, a delicate task. Yet, he at once rejects any seductive monumental gesture; he has designed a continuous, articulated block surrounding closed and open courts, forming an organic urban texture that contributes to the richness of the architectural landscape, a landscape characterized by blocks that are, in contrast, closed and compact. Once again Gutbrod has given priorirty to the social obligation of architecture—the most significant aspect of his work.

—Giuliano Chelazzi

GWATHMEY, Charles.

American. Born in Charlotte, North Carolina, 19 June 1938. Educated at the Music and Art High School, New York, 1952-56; University of Pennsylvania School of Architecture, Philadelphia, under Louis I. Khan, *q.v.*, Robert Venturi, *q.v.*, and Thomas Vreeland, 1956-59; Yale University School of Architecture, New Haven, Connecticut, under Paul Rudolph, *q.v.*, James Stirling, *q.v.*, and Shadrach Woods, *q.v.*,1959-62, M.Arch. 1962; awarded William Wirt Winchester Travelling Fellowship, 1962; Fulbright Fellow in France, 1962-63. Married Bette Ann Damson in 1974. In private practice, New York, 1964-66; Partner, Gwathmey-Henderson, New York, 1966-70, and Gwathmey-Henderson-Siegel, New York, 1970-71. Since 1971, Partner, with Robert Siegel, Gwathmey Siegel and Associates, Architects, New York. Professor of Architectural Design, Pratt Institute, Brooklyn, New York, 1964-66, Yale University, New Haven, Connecticut, 1966, Princeton University, New Jersey, 1966-69, Harvard University, Cambridge, Massachusetts, 1970-72, Cooper Union, New York, 1971-72, University of California at Los Angeles, 1973-74, Princeton University, 1975-76, and Columbia University, New York, 1976-77; Eliot Noyes Professor of Architecture, Harvard University, Cambridge, Massachusetts, 1985. Trustee; from 1978, and President of the Board of Trustees, 1979-82, Institute for Architecture and Urban Studies, New York. Recipient: New York Chapter Residential Design Award, 1968, 1969, 1971, 1975, 1978, 1979, 1980, and 1981 (five), Distinguished Architecture Award, 1982 and 1984, Medal of Honor, 1983, National Honor Award,

1968, 1976 (twice), and 1984, Connecticut Chapter Design Award, 1976, Los Angeles Chapter Design Award, 1982, and National Firm Award, 1982, American Institute of Architects; House Award, 1968, 1969, 1970, 1973, 1975, 1978, 1979, 1980, 1981, and 1982, and Interiors Award, 1974, 1981, 1982, and 1984, *Architectural Record* magazine,New York; Arnold Brunner Prize, American Academy/Institute of Arts and Letters, 1970; Design Award, New York State Association of Architects, 1973, 1974, 1978, 1979, 1980, and 1984 (twice); Design Award, *Progressive Architecture* magazine, 1973 and 1982 (twice); Honor Award, New York Society of Architects, 1974; Leadership in America Citation, *Time* magazine, New York, 1974; Bartlett Award, 1976; Bard Award, City Club of New York, 1977; United States Plywood Award, 1977; Lumen Council Award, 1977; VFM Award, *Institutions* magazine, 1977; Interior Design Award, Institute of Business Designers, 1980; Product Design Award, 1981; Design Award, *Interiors* magazine, New York, 1983. Member, American Academy/Institute of Arts and Letters, 1976; Fellow, American Institute of Architects, 1981. Address: Gwathmey Siegel and Associates, Architects, 475 Tenth Avenue, New York, New York 10018, U.S.A.

Works:

1964 Miller House, Fire Island, New York
1965 Gwathmey House and Studio, Amagansett, New York (with Henderson)
1966 Straus House, Purchase, New York (with Henderson)
1967 Sedacca House, Easthampton, New York (with Henderson)
    Goldberg House, Manchester, Connecticut (with Henderson)
1968 Cooper House, Orleans, Massachusetts (with Henderson)
    Steel House I, Bridgehampton, New York (with Henderson and Siegel)
    Steel House II, Bridgehampton, New York (with Henderson and Siegel)
    Service Buildings and Heating Plant, State University of New York, Purchase (with Henderson and Siegel)
1969 Brooklyn Friends School, New York (with Henderson and Siegel)
    Dormitory, Dining and Student Union Building, State University of New York, Purchase (with Henderson and Siegel)

as Gwathmey Siegel and Associates:
1970 Eskilson House, Roxbury, Connecticut (project)
    Whig Hall, Princeton University, New Jersey
    Tolan House, Amagansett, New York
1971 Cogan House, East Hampton, New York
    Elia Bash House, Califon, New Jersey
1972 Cohn House, Amagansett, New York
    Whitney Road Housing, Perinton, New York
1973 Gwathmey Barn, Greenwich, Connecticut
    Sagner House, West Orange, New Jersey (project)
    Geffen House, Malibu, California (project)
    St. Casimir Housing, Yonkers, New York (project)

Charles Gwathmey: Francois de Menil House, East Hampton, New York, 1979.

1974 Buettner House, Sloatsburg, New York
Charof House, Montauk, New York
Four Seasons Restaurant, Nagoya, Japan (project)
Kislewitz House, Westhampton, New York
1975 Student Apartment Housing, State University of New York, Purchase
Nassau County Art Center, Roslyn, New York (project)
One Times Square Office Building, New York (project)
Island Walk Cooperative Housing, Reston, Virginia
Evans Partnership Prototype Office Building
Evans Partnership Office Building, Piscataway, New Jersey
Damson Oil Corporation Office Building, Houston, Texas
Northpoint Office Building, Houston, Texas
1976 East Campus Student Housing and Academic Center, Columbia University, New York
Haupt House, Amagansett, New York
Weitz House, Quogue, New York
Thomas and Betts Corporation Office Building, Raritan, New Jersey
Bebenson House, Rye, New York
Hyatt Hotel and Casino, Aruba, Antilles (project)
1977 Crowley House, Greenwich, Connecticut
Belkin Memorial Room, Yeshiva University, New York
Taft House, Cincinnati, Ohio
Northgate Housing, Roosevelt Island, New York (project)
American Telephone and Telegraph Office Building, Parsippany, New Jersey
Evans Partnership Office Building, Parsippany, New Jersey
Evans Partnership Offices, New York
1978 Amax Petroleum Corporation Office Building, Houston, Texas
Knoll International Showroom and Office Building, Boston
Sycamore Place Housing for the Elderly, Columbus, Indiana
Pence Street Family Housing, Columbus, Indiana
1979 Library and Science Building, Westover School, Middlebury, Connecticut
Hines House, Martha's Vineyard, Massachusetts (project)
Triangle Pacific Corporation Office Building, Dallas, Texas
De Menil House, Houston, Texas
De Menil House, East Hampton, New York
Block House, Wilmington, North Carolina (project)
Greenwich Savings Bank, New York
Viereck House, Amagansett, New York
1980 First City Bank Building, Houston, Texas
1981 Evans Partnership Office Building, Montvale, New Jersey
Wick Alumni Center, University of Nebraska, Lincoln
Summit Hotel, New York (project)
Westport Public Library, Connecticut
De Menil House, Santa Monica, California
Gimelstob House, New Vernon, New Jersey
Speculative Office Building, New York (project)
De Menil House, New York (project)
1982 Liberty National Bank Building, Hobbs, New Mexico (project)
Nassau Park Office Building, West Windsor, New Jersey
IBM Prototype Product Center
Evans Partnership Office Building, Paramus, New Jersey
Evans Partnership Office Building, Parsippany, New Jersey
Civic Center, Beverly Hills, California (competition project)
1983 International Design Center Showroom Buildings, Long Island City, New York

Evans Partnership Office Building, Piscataway, New Jersey
New York Public Library Yorkville Branch, New York
Museum of the Moving Image, Astoria, New York
Garey House, Kent, Connecticut
1984 Gymnasium addition and renovation, Dartmouth College, Hanover, New Hampshire
Administration and Classroom Buildings, New York State College of Agriculture and Life Science, Cornell University, Ithaca, New York
1985- Solomon R. Guggenheim Museum addition, New York

Interiors: with Henderson—Herlinger Bristol Ltd., New York, 1966; with Siegel—Dunaway Apartment, New York, 1970; Pearl's Restaurant, New York, 1974; Blum Hellman Gallery, New York, 1974; Transammonia Corporation, New York, 1974; Vidal Sassoon Salons in La Costa, California, New York, Chicago, Atlanta, and Beverly Hills, California, 1974-77; Breslow Apartment, New York, 1975; General Motors Acceptance Corporation, Brooklyn, New York, 1975; U.S. Steakhouse Restaurant, New York, 1976; Shezan Restaurant, New York, 1976; Poster Originals Ltd., New York, 1976; Unger Apartment, New York,1976; Bower and Gardner Law Offices, New York, 1976; Damson Oil Corporation, Houston, Texas, 1976; Lisner/Richelieu Corporation Showroom, New York, 1977; Barber Oil Corporation, New York, 1977; Vidal Sassoon International, Los Angeles, 1977; Vidal Sassoon Inc., New York, 1977; Swirl Inc., New York, 1977; Garey Shirtmakers Inc., New York, 1977; Swid Apartment, New York, 1978; Geffen Apartment, New York, 1978; General Mills Corporation Headquarters, New York, 1978; F.D.M. Productions, New York, 1978; Lincoln Center for the Performing Arts, New York, 1978; Evans Shure Corporation, New York, 1978; Shezan Restaurant, New York, 1979; Giorgio Armani Inc. Offices and Showrooms, New York, 1979; Einstein Moomjy Showrooms, New York, 1980; Reliance Group Holdings Offices, New York 1980; Morton L. Jankow and Associates Offices, New York, 1980; Ally and Gargano Inc. Offices, New York, 1980; Arango Apartment, New York, 1982; Gwathmey Siegel and Associates Offices, New York, 1983; Steinberg Apartment, New York, 1983; IBM Product Center, Albany, New York, 1983; Spielberg Apartment, New York, 1984.

Product designs: with Siegel— Desk and Credenza System for Knoll International, 1979; De Menil Table Series ICF, 1982; V'Soske Tapestry, 1982.

Publications;

On GWATHMEY: books—*The New York Times Book of Interior Design and Decoration,* edited by George O'Brien, New York 1965; *Vacation Houses: An International Survey* by Karl Kaspar, New York 1967; *Young Designs in Living* by Barbara Plumb, New York 1969; *Observations on America Architecture* by Ivan Chermayeff, New York 1972; *Five Architects* by Kenneth Frampton and Colin Rowe, New York 1972; *Great Houses* by Walter F. Wagner, New York 1976; *Five Architects, New York,* edited by Camillo Gubitosi and Alberto Izzo, Rome 1976; *Charles Gwathmey and Robert Siegel: Residential Architecture,* edited by Kay and Paul Breslow, Tokyo 1976, New York 1977; *Five Houses by Gathmey Siegel Architects,* exhibition catalogue with introduction by Kenneth Frampton, New York 1977; *American Architecture Now,* edited by Barbaralee Diamonstein, New York 1980; *Judith Turner Photographs Five Architects,* with introduction by John Hejduk, London 1980; *Gwathmey Siegel* by

Stanley Abercrombie, New York 1981, St. Albans, Hertfordshire 1982; *Styled for Living,* edited by Sherman R. Emery, New York 1983; *Corporate Design: The Interiors Design and Architecture of Corporate America* by Roger Yee and Karen Gustafson, New York 1983; *Furniture by Architects* by Marc Emery and Harry N. Abrams, New York 1983; *Charles Gwathmey and Robert Siegel: Buildings and Projects, 1964-1984,* edited by Peter Arnell and Ted Bickford, New York 1984; articles—"Three projects by Gwathmey Siegel" in *Architectural Review* (London), July 1974; "Works of Gwathmey Siegel" in *Architecture + Urbanism* (Tokyo), October 1974; "European Graffiti" in *Oppositions* (New York), Summer 1976; "Three Interiors by Gwathmey Siegel" in *Architectural Record* (New York), September 1976; "Some Recent Works by the Gwathmey Siegel Office" in *Industria delle costruzioni* (Rome), September 1978; "A Section Through the Thinking of Gwathmey Siegel Architects" in *Architectural Record* (New York), September 1979; "The Boston Knoll Showroom" in *Progressive Architecture* (New York), July 1980; "Residences" in *Architecture + Urbanism* (Tokyo), July 1980; "Gwathmey and Siegel—Distinction in Wood" in *Architect* (The Hague), September 1980; "Long Island Residence, New York" in *GA Document* (Tokyo), no. 4, 1981; "Architects' Furniture" in *RIBA Journal* (London), November 1981; "Gwathmey Siegel—Winner of AIA's 1982 Firm Award" in *AIA Journal* (Washington, D.C.), February 1982; "Five Plus Ten" in *Building Design* (London), 9 July 1982; "Houses," special issue of *GA Houses* (Tokyo), March 1983; "Wick Alumni Center" in *Architecture Nebraska* (Lincoln), vol. 4, 1983; "Columbia University Student Housing and Academic Center" in *Architecture + Urbanism* (Tokyo), May 1983; "East Campus Complex, Columbia Univerity" in *Industria delle costruzioni* (Rome), May 1983; "New Architects' Offices on 10th Avenue, New York" in *Industria dell costruzioni* (Rome), October 1983; "In Praise of Modernism: De Menil Residence at East Hampton" in *Domus* (Milan), February 1984;"AIA Honor Awards: No Duds, No Surprises" in *Progressive Architecture* (New York), May 1984; "A Factory for Living In" in *Connaissance des arts* (Paris), June 1984.

Our approach to design is based upon three propositions that interrelate: 1) There is no aesthetic preconception of form. Every program generates new and different sets of information and constraints. Form is generated by site, orientation, climate, program and technological references. 2) The essential organizational components in any design are circulation, light, and volumetric clarity. 3) All buildings are similar in abstraction, thus the design process for specific programs is similar. This position was clearly stated by Michael Graves as an introduction to our first book:

There appear to be two major positions in current architectural thought. These two attitudes can be seen as opposing orientations although they are mutually exclusive. However in attempting to characterize them as intrinsic modes of thought they are nonetheless generally seen as polar.

The first can be characterized as constituting a part of the symbolic and mythic representations of the culture. This position holds that there is an architectural thought process in the tranferral of cultural values to physical artifacts and a corresponding interpretation of symbolic themes which requires one's perception to make the connection between cultural value and architectural symbol. This architectural position must by its nature rely on somewhat literal characteristics of form which could be thought of as representational.

The second architectural position is primarily abstract in nature, based on the assumption that there is a correspondence between Euclidian geometry and human action; there is a parallel drawn between the cardinal axes of geometry and human movement patterns. This architecture which relies heavily on the counter distinctions of passage and rest is able to capitalize on the natural tension established by these two phenomena. An additional interest of this position is that provided by the possibilities of geometrical overlay or transparencies which contribute toward a spatial interlock developed through plan and section. The abstract geometric devices used to articulate these spatial correspondences are generally unadorned and read as minimal in order to clarify the original assumption of man's action related to geometry.

Without the work of Gwathmey Siegel we would not be able to give precise definition to the latter mode of thinking, as they are significant authors of the genuine ideas embodied in an architecture of abstraction and continue to develop the strengths of that position by the sheer artistry of their compositions.

The transcendence of accommodation is the difference between the art of architecture and building.

—Charles Gwathmey

In the search for an American architecture, Charles Gwathmey has found an appropriately distinctive Northeastern expression. His work imports the sophisticated vocabulary of the International Style as developed by Le Corbusier and builds it—and builds on it—in a distinctly American way. From Le Corbusier, Gwathmey has adopted a family of forms—the cube, the cylinder, the partial cylinder—and a set of details—round columns, ribbon windows, ship railings, and glass block. All these elements are expressed with a decidedly Yankee twang—with spontaneity, exaggeration, and clear-eyed pragmatism.

The neo-Corbusian forms are overlaid, intersected, and telescoped in a neo-cubist time-space simultaneity that suggests the brashness and bustling vitality of American activity. The cube is slashed open, gouged out, interspersed with rotated elements—fragments of cylinders, steep shed roofs, diagonal stripes of stairways in a continuum of inside-outside space. Asymmetrical geometries are caught in collision. Overall, however, there is no confusion of ambiguity in the richness and complexity of detail but a disciplined clarity of parts.

Gwathmey also invests his forms with the exaggeration of American superscale, which is sometimes described as never big enough, sometimes as too big. Perhaps this is due to the forms being sliced off and not ended, suggesting an infinite open-endedness. Perhaps it is due to the emphasis on verticality, both inside and outside, which may be influenced by Paul Rudolph.

Then the forms are sheathed with wood siding, which suggests the rustic New England vernacular and the Shingle Style, the latter surely an influence of Vincent Scully. And the cube is set squarely on the ground, like the sober New England saltbox house—not elevated in a structural pirouette, what Frank Lloyd Wright called "boxes on stilts." Gwathmey's work also shows a craft of construction that sets him apart from other "Cardboard Corbu" architects, perhaps due to the influence of Louis Kahn—another poet of materials—who combined the handcraft of nineteenth-century brickwork with the Modern movement's passion for industrial buildings. Similarly, Gwathmey combines the Corbusian forms and the American vernacular of wood construction, in sleek, smooth, and unarticulated surfaces (despite their wood textures) that suggest the tight-skinned minimalism of Edward Larrabee Barnes.

The most significant achievement of this architect's work, however, is in its volumetric invention and spatial variety. Inside, the exterior geometry seems to be only the framing of continuous spatial juxtaposition, high against low, long against short, flat against curved, and enclosed against the calculated vista. This is a spatial vision that owes greatly, but not entirely, to the process of axonometric presentation. It is experiential, luminescent,

and related to both site and time-space—even the variety of flooring materials form country to city bears this out. In volumetric variety is housed functional appropriateness—good planning that recognizes physical activity patterns as well as orientation for access and view.

This synthesis of European and American influences is strong and robust, sophisticated yet simple, angular and curved, crisp yet cosy, static yet lively, monumental yet in rotated action, seductive and sentimental in its nostalgia for the early 1920s.

Theoretically, Gwathmey's work raises a significant opposition to proponents of representational architecture. Although Gwathmey himself generally abjures aesthetic pronouncements, his work posits a demonstrably attractive kind of abstraction. That abstract geometry, which is itself without reference to other cultural or historical associations—except for the vernacular wood siding—is strong and resolute, iconographic, and perhaps mythic. In this abstraction lies the elegance and the sophisticated achievement of his architecture.

—C. Ray Smith

GWYNNE, Patrick.

British. Born in Porchester, Hampshire, 24 March 1913. Educated at preparatory school, 1923-27; Harrow School, Middlesex, 1927-30; articled pupil, 1930-32. Served as a Squadron Leader in the Royal Air Force, in Britain, Canada, and Europe, 1940-45. Worked as an assistant, then as Associate Architect, in the office of Wells Coates, q.v., London, 1935-37. Since 1946, in private practice, Esher, Surrey. Recipient: First Prize, Furniture Competition, London, 1935; Civic Trust Award, 1968. Address: Office of Patrick Gwynne, The Homewood, Esher, Surrey, England.

Works

1938 The Homewood, Esher, Surrey (with Wells Coates)
1949 EMG Gramophone Showroom, Newman Street, London
1951 Restaurant building, Battersea Park, London
1952 Supreme Radio Shop, Edmonton, London
1953 Freeman-Hardy-Willis Shop, Catford, London
1954 Clifford Curzon Music Studio, Highgate, London
Ox-on-Roof Restaurant, Chelsea, London
1955 House reconstruction, Blackheath, London
1958 House, Spaniard's End, Hampstead, London
Chesnut Lodge House conversion, Cobham, Surrey
Jack Hawkins House, Bournemouth, Hampshire
1959 House, Henley-on-Thames, Oxfordshire
1960 Group of four houses, Kingston, Surrey
1961 House, 4 Beechworth Close, Hampstead, London
1962 Gerald Bentall House, Witley Park, Godalming, Surrey
1963 House, 3 Beechworth Close, Hampstead, London
1964 Serpentine Restaurant, Hyde Park, London
1965 Dell Restaurant, Hyde Park, London
House, Virginia Water, Surrey
1966 Quantity surveyor's offices, Hobart Place, London
1967 Theatre Royal remodelling, York, England
1968 Flats, St. Paul's Bay, Malta
1969 House, Blackheath, London
1970 Doctors' group practice surgery, Henley-on-Thames, Oxfordshire

House, Angmering-on-Sea, Sussex
1971 Pergola Restaurant, Hyde Park, London
Lawrence Harvey House, Hampstead, London
House, Esher, Surrey
1974 M62 Motorway Service Area, Burtonwood, Lancashire
1975 Restaurant building, Dubai, United Arab Emirates
1977 Fairmile Hotel, Cobham, Surrey
1979 House, 22 Park Gate, Blackheath, London
1980 Office Block, Leigh Delamere Service Area, M4 Motorway, Wiltshire
Mews House, Petersham Place, London
1981 Squash Courts, Sutton Place, Guildford, Surrey
1982 Penthouse, Berkeley Square, London
1983 Apartment interior, St, James's Place, London
1984 House at Winterdown, Esher, Surrey
1985 Artist's Studio, Brook Road, Wormley, Surrey

Publication:

On GWYNNE: articles—"Awards: 7 U.K. Entries for Cembureau—Theatre Royal Extension, York" in *Building* (London), 14 February 1975; "Three Theatres—Restored, Extended and Modernized" in *Lighting and Environmental Design* (London), September/October 1975.

Mine is a small practice and the works so far have been mainly divided between private houses of a fairly luxurious standard designed for individual clients and larger works mostly connected with the catering trade. I have been sought out by clients who wanted an unusual solution in the modern manner and where attention to detail was considered important.

Particularly in regard to the houses, I was strongly influenced by my client's views and character and each design would have been completely otherwise, I believe, if the clients had been different people—or if they had gone to another architect. Nevertheless, people seem to recognize my work as being from my hand in spite of the strong influence of client and site in each case.

The larger works—such as the Hyde Park restaurants and the York Theatre—were intended to be showy buildings albeit with the need to fit into the famous park scenery and into the historic centre of York. It has pleased me that these buildings seem to be popular with the ordinary people who see them and use them.

I have also striven through my work to produce buildings which would be reasonably easy to maintain without undue expense and would remain looking in good condition over the years.

—Patrick Gwynne

A happy-go-lucky building with a hop-scotch plan gambolling like a young deer by the waterside: such is Patrick Gwynne's Serpentine Restaurant in Hyde Park, London. Its busy indentations, facetted glazing, sketchy run-through sections would like to have us believe that the Festival of Britain has never quite ended. Its balustrades serve perfectly as footing for the pigeons. The mini-ramps and decks suggest so many things for the children. Its fairy-tale, grotto-like crystalline resolution can be traced, via Taut's Alpine architecture, back into folklore and legends of another, more paradisic world where people live in jewel-like houses—or else the dwellings are made from eagles' feathers, human eyes, fused sand, or a myriad of materials inconceivable to those condemned to mere mortal life on earth. Gwynne's extension to the Theatre Royal at York has this same fabulous touch, as though it had been revealed to him in a reverie.

This fanciful architecture delights with its inno-

Patrick Gwynne: Theatre Royal, York, 1967.

cent language, its rhyming, its exquisite miniaturist flourishes; this is the kind of architecture we can see in Miró's earlier canvases, in Chagall, Rousseau . . . its unflinching love of architecture is akin to the frontal emphasis found in children's art and in that of the naive and primitive artist. The Serpentine Restaurant is given strong outline, and one can imagine the process whereby it was designed and realised as being not altogether different from the way a child would sit down and draw it. Fountains of transparent quartz, alabaster windows, rainbow-tinted pools, a seesaw of black glass—such is the Tolkien-like associational journey one embarks on from the contemplation of the Serpentine Restaurant. The stream-of-consciousness blur of images opens up a world so much closed by this century.

—Chris Fawcett

HABRAKEN, Nicolaas John.

Dutch. Born in Bandung, Indonesia, 29 October
1928; settled in the Netherlands, 1946. Educated at
the Department of Architecture, Technical University, Delft, Netherlands, 1948-55, Bouwkundig Ingenieur 1955. Served in the Royal Dutch Air Force,
1955-57. Married Emmie Marlene Van Hall in 1959;
children: Julie and Gysbert. Instructor, Department
of Architecture, Technical University, Delft, Netherlands, 1958-60; also worked in the office of
architect J. E. Berghoef, Delft, Netherlands, 1958-
60; freelance architect in the Netherlands, 1960-62;
Job Captain, architectural office of Lucas and
Niemeyer, Voorburg, Netherlands, 1962-65; Director, Stichting Architecten Research (SAR), Voorburg, Netherlands, 1965-67, and Eindhoven, Netherlands, 1967-75. Chairman of the Department of
Architecture, 1967-70, and Professor of Architecture
and Urban Design, 1967-75, Technical University,
Eindhoven, Netherlands. Since 1975, Professor and
Head of the Department of Architecture, Massachusetts Institute of Technology, Cambridge. Recipient: David Roell Prize, Amsterdam, 1979.
Address: Department of Architecture, Massachusetts Institute of Technology, 77 Massachusetts
Avenue, Cambridge, Massachusetts 02139, U.S.A.

Works:

1959 Private house, 63 Wildernislaan, Apeldoorn,
      Netherlands
1962 Arntz House, Millingen, Netherlands
1965/
   75 Design method for open-ended systems and
      their evolution; and method for design of
      "urban tissues"
1968 Amsterdam Town Hall (competition project)
1975/
   85 Design theory and method researches for
      architecture and other design disciplines

Publications:

By HABRAKEN: books—*Supports: An Alternative
to Mass Housing,* Amsterdam 1962, London and
New York 1972; *Three R's for Housing,* Amsterdam
1970; *SAR '73: The Methodical Formulation of
Agreements in the Design of Urban Tissues,* with
others, Eindhoven, Netherlands 1973; *Deciding on
Density,* with others, Eindhoven, Netherlands 1974;
Variations; The Systematic Design of Supports, with
J. T. Boekholt, A. P. Thyssen and P. M. J. Dinjens,
Alphen, Netherlands 1974, Cambridge, Massa-
chusetts 1976; *The Grunsfeld Variations,* with others,
Cambridge, Massachusetts 1981; *Transformations of
the Site,* Eindhoven, Netherlands 1983; *The Ap-
pearance of Form,* Cambridge, Massachusetts 1985;
articles—"The Tissue of the Town" in *Forum*
(Amsterdam), no. 1, 1964; "Quality and Quantity:
The Industrialization of Housing" in *Forum*
(Amsterdam), no. 2, 1964; "Supports, Responsi-

bilities and Possibilities" in *Architectural Association
Quarterly* (London), Winter 1968/69; "The Pursuit
of an Idea" in *Plan* (Amsterdam), no. 3, 1970;
"L'Habitat, l'home et l'industrie" in *L'Architecture
d'aujourd'hui* (Paris), February/March 1970; "You
Can't Design the Ordinary" in *Architectural Design*
(London), April 1971; "Support Structure and
Detachable Unit, on the Basis of Industrialization
and Participation" in *Toshi-Jukaku* (Tokyo), Sep-
tember 1972; "Das Ende des Wohnbahnprojektes"
in *Archithese* (Zürich), no. 1, 1972; "Playing Games"
in *Architectural Design* (London), no. 4, 1972;
"Involving People in the Housing Process' in *RIBA
Journal* (London), November 1972; "SAR Design
Method for Housing: Seven Years of Development
in the Real World" in *DMG-DRS Journal for Design
Research and Methods* (San Luis Obispo, Califor-
nia), July/September 1973; "Création architectural
et industrie: intervention au colloque d'Yerres" in
Techniques et architecture (Paris), March 1975;
"Fragments" in *Techniques et architecture* (Paris),
October/November 1976; "The Limits of Pro-
fessionalism" in *Architectural Association Quarterly*
(London), no. 1, 1978; "The Leaves and the
Flowers" in *Via* (Philadelphia), December 1980;
"Interventions: Professionals and User Inputs" in
Openhouse (Eindhoven, Netherlands) no. 4, 1980;
"The Role of Industrial Production," with E.
Dluhosh, in *Ekistics* (Athens), January/February
1980; "The Built Environment and the Limits of
Professional Practice" in *Housing Form and Public
Policy in the U.S.,* edited by R. Plunz, New York
1980; "The Turtle Tissue Project," with Marc
Gross, in *Openhouse* (Eindhoven, Netherlands)
no. 2, 1982; "Viviendas de menor costo por medio
del diseño para adaptabilidad" in *Memoria* congress
report, Mexico City 1983; "Architectural Education
and the Third World," with others, in *Openhouse*
(Eindhoven, Netherlands) no. 2, 1983; "Architecture for Developing Countries" in *Architectural
Education* (London), no. 2, 1983; "On Writing
Form" in *Design Studies* (London), July 1984.

On HABRAKEN: books—*SAR 65* report, Voorburg, Netherlands 1965; *SAR 73* report, Eindhoven,
Netherlands 1973; *N. J. Habraken e il Gruppo SAR:
materiali di ricerca sulla progettazione della residenza*
by Marcello Mamoli and others, Venice 1973;
*Deciding on Density: An Investigation into High
Density Allotment with a View to the Waldeck Area,*
The Hague 1977; *Architectuur en Planning; Neder-
land 1940-1980,* edited by S. Umberto Barbieri,
Rotterdam and Amsterdam 1983; *Habraken,* edited
by the Prins Bernhard Foundation, The Hague 1984;
Alltägliche Architektur by Arnulf Lüchinger, The
Hague 1985; articles—"The Perfect Barracks and the
Support Revolution" by Martin Pawley in *Interbuild
Arena* (London), October 1967; "Mass Housing: The
Desperate Effort of Pre-Industrial Thought to
Achieve the Equivalent of Mass Production" by
Martin Pawley in *Architectural Design* (London),
January 1970; "SAR" by Makato Uyeda in *Toshi-
Jutaku* (Tokyo), September 1972; "Nikolaas Hab-

raken: du règne de la quantité à l'ordre de la qualité?"
by B. B. Taylor in *L'Architecture d'aujourd'hui*
(Paris), July/August 1974; "Involving People in the
Housing Process: The Story of Habraken's Supports
and Detachables" by Eric Dluhosch in *Industrializ-
ation Forum* (Montreal), no. 1, 1976; "Habraken:
SAR 73," special issue of *Parametro* (Bologna,
Italy), June 1982.

Looking back at years of research, writing, teaching,
and consulting, it seems that those efforts reveal
some consistency. What runs through it as a
continuous thread could perhaps be best described as
an attempt to introduce the concepts of time and
change into architectural thinking.

As architects, we still operate in a social role
bestowed on us in the Renaissance. We dream of
monuments and try—by building—to stop time, try
to erect a symbol that transcends everyday life.

Simultaneously, we embrace today the whole built
environment as worthy of our attention or service.
But the built environment is a living thing. Change
within durable patterns is its primary characteristic.
Although one can design for it, it cannot be designed
but wants to becultivated.

Thus, we find ourselves in conflict with our chosen
subject matter. Neither our theories, nor our
methods, nor our education give us the understanding or the tools needed to operate in the broader
realm of the everyday world. Some of us have to sit
and think; the dilemma is as fascinating as its
solution is crucial.

—N. John Habraken

In the early 1960s, international architecture was in a
transitional phase in the sense that fundamental
theories from the 1920s and 1930s were being rejected
and new, partly utopian proposals were emerging.
Criticism was mainly directed against the fundamental concepts for planning a functional town. The
essays of Jane Jacobs who, inter alia, supported
municipal diversity, are well known in this respect.
Aldo van Eyck held similar views when, in 1960, he
suggested replacing the traditional "Space-Time"
concept of Giedion with a "Sense of Place" concept:
"Whatever space and time mean, place and occasion
mean more." Similarly, we can point to the utopian
town planning proposals of the Japanese Metabolists and to the English Archigram projects.

N. John Habraken's utopian town planning
proposals, with their emphasis on codetermination
by the inhabitant, also come from this period. His
ideas appeared in his book *Supports: An Alternative
to Mass Housing,* which was enthusiastically received. In the book, Habraken critized the uniform
character of new housing and its surroundings,
where individual endeavors are unwelcome and
personal initiative undesirable. He starts his argument from the idea that one can identify with one's
surroundings only if one has contributed something
to those surroundings, something for which one is
responsible. The inhabitants should also be able to
take possession of their surroundings. According to

Habraken, possession (which is different from property) is connected with action. Something will belong to us, become part of our lives, only by our own efforts. Because man wants to take possession of his surroundings, he touches them, puts his personal stamp on them.

Habraken distinguishes between two kinds of architecture: the architecture of specific buildings (public buildings, private houses, and so forth) and the architecture of the ordinary environment (for instance, mass housing). He himself is concerned with the latter, and he points out that architects still believe that they can solve the problems of mass housing with the same approach as for specific buildings. He considers that, in comparison with specific buildings, an ordinary environment is built up differently and has different but equally valuable qualities.

Habraken proposes the building of prefabricated housing structures (*terrains artificiels*/artificial sites) which can be individually filled in—like Le Corbusier's project, Fort l'Empereur, designed for Algiers in 1933. He puts forward the idea that dwellings could be assembled like built-in kitchens. The housing structures would belong to the community and would be built to last, while it would have to be expected that the built-in dwelling would be built, altered, and demolished.

On the image of the new town, he comments: "There is one architecture that makes uniform and another that gives form to diversity. With the latter the principle is structure with built-in elements. In this way a form can be designed for a facade of such strength that anything can happen inside without giving a totally chaotic impression on the outside. This will provide an experience of lively diversity."

Fascinated by these ideas, architects from ten well-known practices in Holland decided, in 1964, to form a working party to make a reality of the "support" town. The working party was called SAR (Architects Research Foundation) and was led by Habraken. In the course of time, various mass and support systems appeared which were partly adopted by foreign architects. But, as the SAR made hardly any pronouncements about the form of the structure or about basic town planning concepts, their influence on house building remained on the whole rather insignificant.

Yet, Habraken's original and imaginatively written vision of a town planning utopia still has an influence, and, as he himself expressed it in 1961, it continues to represent "a formidable challenge to the greatest talents in design for living."

—Arnulf Lüchinger

HALLEN, Hans Heyerdahl.
South African. Born in Durban, 31 August 1930. Educated at Durban High School, 1944-48; University of Natal, Durban, under Barrie Bierman and Ronald Lewcock, 1949-53 (Kimberley Scholarship; Government Scholarship), Dip-Arch. 1953. Married June Wendy Meiring in 1955; children: Martin, Andrea, and Michele. Worked in the offices of Frolich and Kass, Durban, 1948-50, and A.B. Adkin, Durban, 1950-53; Architect, London County Council, 1956; associated with O. Pretorius, Durban, 1959. Since 1959 in private practice, Durban: Partner with A.J. Diamond *q.v.*, 1959-62, with M. Dibb, 1963-69, with J. D. Theron, since 1969, with M.J. Speed, since 1970, and with P.H.A. Custers, F.G.C. Emmett, and J.L.H. Smith, since 1980. Lecturer, University of Natal, 1966-78. Member of the Natal Provincial Committee, 1964-77, Member of the National Board, 1968-77, and President-in-Chief, 1974-75, Institute of South African Architects; Member of the Council for Architects, 1970-78, and

Chairman of the Fees Committee of the Council for Architects, 1976-78; Member of the Council, International Union of Architects, 1975-81; Delegate of the Institute of South African Architects to the United Nations "Habitat" Conference, Vancouver, British Columbia, 1976. Consultant to the Urban Foundation, Johannesburg, since 1977. Exhibitions: *The City Is a Walking Place*, Durban, 1964; *Riebeeck Festival*, Cape Town, 1970; *Work of Natal Architects*, Durban, 1983; *Overseas Architects*, Royal Institute of British Architects, London, 1984; *Brenthurst Library*, University of Natal, Durban, 1984. Recipient: First Prize, Voortrekker Monument Competition, Winburg, South Africa, 1964; First Prize, La Lucia Civic Centre Competition, South Africa, 1971; Institute of South African Architects Award of Merit, 1977 and 1983, and Gold Medal, 1980; E. G. Malherbe Award, University of Natal Convocation, Durban, 1981; Corobrik Award, Durban, 1983. Honorary Fellow, American Institute of Architects, 1981. Address: 741 Musgrave Road, Durban 4001, South Africa.

Works:

1959 Eckhoffs Corner, Durban
1960 Hallen House, Nicolai Crescent, Durban
      Norwegian Lutheran Mission Church, Kwa Mashu Umlazi Glebe, South Africa
1961 Bassudey House, Crescent Street, Durban
      Sparks House, Westville, South Africa
      Masojada House, Essenwood Road, Durban
1962 Stellenberg Flats, Essenwood Road, Durban
      Illing House, Kloof, South Africa
      Hattingh House, Kloof, South Africa
      Sculptural reliefs and panels, Marine Terminal Restaurants, Durban (with Warunkiewicz)
      Lutheran Seminary, Zululand, South Africa (project)
1963 Drosdy Flats, Silverton Road, Durban
      Musgrave Mews Flats, Musgrave Road, Durban
      Reed House, Durban
      Maisonettes Zakrzewski, 602 Essenwood Road, Durban
1964 Fouche House, Durban
      Riebeeck Flats, Durban
      Bellevue Flats, Durban
      St. Luke's Church, Chatsworth, South Africa
      Powell House, Westville, South Africa
      Voortrekker Monument, Winburg, South Africa (competition project)
      Ulundi Court, Durban
1964/
66   Residences, University of Natal, Durban
1965 Seedat House, Westville, South Africa
      Lakhi House, Reservoir Hills, South Africa
      Ceza Mission Hospital, Ceza, South Africa
1966 Barker House, Gillets, South Africa
      Dublin Library (competition project; with Danie Theron)
      Hall House, Durban
1967 Thabane Li Mele Arts and Crafts School, Lesotho
      St. Olav's Church, St. Thomas Road, Durban
      Lunn House, Durban
      Umlazi Polyclinic, Durban (project)
      St. John's Convent, Durban
      Reservoir Hills Mosque, Reservoir Hills, South Africa
      Norwegian Seamen's Mission, Durban
1968 Habib Factory, Durban
      Nkonjeni Mission, South Africa
      Shaw House, Lamont Road, Durban
      Ceza Mission, South Africa
1969 Fine Fare Supermarket, Pietermaritzburg, South Africa
      Smit House, Westville, South Africa
      Habib Duplexes, Durban
      Entabeni Hospital redevelopment, Durban (with M. Dibb)
      Little Top Beach Pavilion, Durban

Alleson House, Durban
      Mosque, Chatsworth, South Africa
      Castle Wine and Brandy Factory, Cape Town (with L. Louw and Partners)
      Sacca Ltd. Factory, Durban
      Reform Church, Durban
1970 Rustomjee House, Reservoir Hills, South Africa
      Sacca Ltd. Factory, Kimberley, South Africa
      Golden Hours Centre for Retarded Children, Sherwood, South Africa
      Taikyo Restaurant, Durban
      Jacobson House, La Lucia, South Africa
      Beckerling House, Zinkwazi, South Africa
      Tollman Towers by the Sea, Umhlanga Rocks, South Africa (project)
1971 Civic Centre, La Lucia, South Africa (competition project)
      Beach Offices, Durban
1972 Villa Road Flats, Durban
1972/
77   South African Railways Service Buildings, Durban
1974 Kara House, Westville, South Africa
1974/
76   Huletts Head Office, La Lucia, South Africa
1974/
78   Hospital redevelopment, Wentworth, South Africa
1975 St. John's School, Pietermaritzburg, South Africa
      St. John's Church Hall and Nursery School, Pinetown, South Africa
      Plan for the redevelopment of Tel Aviv (competition project; with Danie Theron)
1976 Catholic Church, Bluff, South Africa
      Technical School, Clairwood, South Africa
1977 Anglican Church, Amanzimtoti, South Africa
      Redevelopment proposals for Durban North Beach
1978 Business and Community Centre, Kwa Mashu, South Africa
      Sacca Ltd. Factory, Cape Town
      Restaurant, President Hotel, Bloemfontein, South Africa
      Mangosuthu College of Technology, Umlazi, South Africa (with Julian Elliott)
      Schmidt House, Kloof, South Africa
1979 Sacca Ltd. Distribution Centre, Johannesburg
      Golden Hours Training Centre for Mentally Retarded Children, Durban North
      Brenthurst Africana Library, for H.F. Oppenheimer, Johannesburg
1980 G. North and Son Factory, Standerton, South Africa
      Umlazi Hotel Complex, Umlazi, South Africa (project)
      Golden Steps Training Centre for Mentally Retarded Children, Verulam, South Africa
1981 Durban-Westville University Dentistry Unit, Westville, South Africa
      Beach Restaurant Complex, Durban
      President Hotel tower block additions, Bloemfontein, South Africa
      Sacca Ltd. Head Office Building, Johannesburg
1982 Durban Old Station restoration, Durban
      Newland Telephone Exchange conversion, Johannesburg
      Mangosuthu Technikon stage 2 development, Umlazi, South Africa
      Singh House, Westville, South Africa
1983 Wentworth Hospital Operating Theatres, Durban
      Water Theme Park Beachfront Development, Durban (project)
      Opera House, Paris (competition project)
      BMW Head Office, Midrand, South Africa
      Small Business Development Corporation Office Building, Westville, South Africa
      Expo '85 exhibition concept design, Durban (as Team Leader)
1984 Station Workshop Speciality Centre, Durban (project; with Bentel and Abramson)

Hans Hallen: Sacca Head Office, Johannesburg, 1981.

Publications:

By HALLEN: books—introduction to *Housing People,* Johannesburg 1977; *Needs and Resources Survey: Durban,* Durban 1977; articles—"Quality of Place" in *ISAA Record* (Johannesburg), July 1965; editor of special issue on Natal in *ISAA Record* (Johannesburg), July 1965; "Voortrekker Monument" in *ISAA Record* (Johannesburg), August 1965; "Greek Islands—Cycladic Architecture" in *ISAA Record* (Johannesburg), March 1966; editor of the Congress issue of *ISAA Record* (Johannesburg), October 1966; "University and Profession" in *Plan* (Johannesburg), July 1970; "Beggar, Borrowers and Fat Colonials" in *New Check* (Johannesburg), October 1970; "Hindu Temples" and "Indian Temples and Mosques" in *Plan* (Johannesburg), June 1973; "Towards the City University" in *Concept Five* (Durban), June 1974; "Architecture and the World Around Us" in *South African Builder* (Johannesburg), November 1974; "Urban Heritage in *Plan* (Johannesburg), 1975; "The Quality of Life and Urban Development" in *Optima* (Johannesburg), April 1976; "Huletts Group Office New Headquarters at La Lucia, Durban" in *Planning and Building Developments* (Johannesburg), March/April 1977; "Mexican Mornings— UIA Conference" in *Architecture South Africa* (Cape Town), June 1979; "Mangosuthu Technikon" in *Planning and Building Developments* (Johannesburg), May/June 1980; "My Friends Want to Leave Poland— This Is Why..." in *Sunday Times* (Johannesburg), July 1981; "George Rhodes-Harrison, 1925-1981" in *Architecture South Africa* (Cape Town), October 1981; "We've Stuck a Faustian Bargain...and We Can't Go Back" in *Sunday Times* (Johannesburg), August 1981; "Durban: 3 Cultures" in *Sunday Times* (Johannesburg), July 1982; "Durban Peri-Urban Housing" in *Architecture South Africa* (Cape Town), January 1983; "Mangosuthu Technikon, Umlazi" in *Architecture South Africa* (Cape Town), February 1983; "Stern Lessons from Graves" in *Natal Provincial Institute of Architects Newsletter* (Durban), February 1983; "Thoughts on Libraries" in *Natal Provincial Institute of Architects Newsletter* (Durban), March 1983; "Durban, Discovered and Re-Invented" in *Lantern* (Pretoria), April 1983; "Temple in the Canefields" in *Architect and Builder* (Cape Town), June 1983; "S.A. Architecture" in *Leadership S.A.* (Johannesburg), July 1983; "Doors of memory— Brenthurst Library" in *Architect and Builder* (Cape Town), October 1983; "1983 Awards of Merit" in *Architecture South Africa* (Cape Town), December 1983; "Sacca Head Office" in *Architect and Builder* (Cape Town), February 1984; "Doors" in *Architecture South Africa* (Cape Town), May 1984.

On HALLEN: articles—"Bassudey, Hallen, Masojada—3 Houses" by B. E. Bierman in *ISAA Record* (Johannesburg), July 1963; "Huletts Building" in *Planning and Building Development* (Johannesburg), April 1971; "Houses of the Sixties" by Danie Theron in *Lantern* (Pretoria), September 1972; "Huletts Head Office" in *Architecture South Africa* (Cape Town), July 1978; "Hans Hallen, Gold Medallist, ISAA 1980" in *Architecture South Africa* (Cape Town), Winter 1981; "Where Function Is a Matter of Form" in *The Office in Southern Africa* (Johannesburg), February 1983; "Sacca Head Office" in *AIA Journal* (Washington, D.C.), Winter 1983; "Hans Hallen, Making It" in *Fair Lady* (Cape Town), July 1983.

The small houses in my first period of practice were white and cube-like experiments in geometry—the houses such as Masojada, Hattingh,Hallen, and Seedat attempted to escape from the prevalent three-bedroomed layout used in Durban and sought in plan and section new and more valid solutions to orientation and ventilation in a subtropical climate with a very direct relationship of the interior and exterior with associated rich planting. Most of this and subsequent work has been done for sloping sites.

The early churches and mosques used a formal geometric shape, cladding around a plan form that uses the new liturgical attitudes of closeness to the focus of worship which emphasise a sense of community. Churches such as St. Olav's, St. John's Convent, and various mission churches, as well as the Reservoir Hill's Mosque, are expressive of this phase.

Some of the earliest experiments with low-rise, high-density housing in this area were done in the early 1960s, using crosswall construction both in brick and concrete with apartments opening onto private and semi-private courts. The early examples were in whitewashed brick, and such buildings as Stellenberg, Drosdy, and Musgrave Mews were typical.

The larger buildings of the mid-1960s, such as the University of Natal Student Residences and competition entries for Dublin and for Tel Aviv (both of these with Danie Theron), focused upon the organisation of pedestrian movement through buildings. These buildings show a concern for the use of changes of level with open and expressed staircases and ramp systems.

Much of the later work, from 1970 on, has been concerned withlarge-span roof structures, where any number of variations of the problems of sheet roofing of various types have been resolved to give new forms, and the series of buildings that include the railway buildings, Huletts Head Office, Wentworth Hospital buildings, and other industrial buildings are typical. They have deeply shaded areas and large, simple volumes. Colourful facades and a degree of overt symbolism has been used in later years.

My work and that of my colleagues (in latter years Danie Theron and Mike Speed) has emphasised close links with site—often with full landscaped and conceived environs, emphasis upon the gentle treatment of changes of level, the creation of buildings that also react to and encourage socially desirable use of buildings both in terms of the movement areas and in the scale of the spaces, nearly always enclosed in clearly expressed structural form.

Low-rise courtyard buildings set in landscaped settings, such as the Mangosuthu Technikon and the new BMW head office building, are recent examples of these qualities, as is the new Africana Library at Brenthurst for Mr. H. F. Oppenheimer.

—Hans Hallen

There are many ways in which an architect can be of service to the public and to his profession. Hans Hallen has explored probably every one and excelled in all. Urging international architectural circles to greater tolerance, his own government and local authorities to greater flexibility, and educationists and fellow practitioners to higher standards, he has had to draw on reserves of talent, energy, and character at the expense of his own practice. Nevertheless, his design work constitutes a remarkable record of achievement of the same restless, probing, catholic nature. A sound apprenticeship in the eclectic design procedures prevailing before the advent of dogmatic modern architecture in the university of schools provided a base from which he could operate with confident independence.

His first contact with architecture beyond local confines came on a visit to the Cape of Good Hope where he was captivated by the humanity and simplicity of the historical style and the rich pictorial quality of its peasant materials—an experience he expanded by visits to the Mediterranean homeland of the Cape style. These cultural forays found expression on his return to Durban in a wide range of building types developing the potential of white modulated surfaces in the local tropical context.

By way of reaction to this "soft" period, there followed an intense investigation of in situ concrete structure and finish of uncompromising angularity but with spatial qualities related to his more humanistic early works. By degrees, he passed on to a somewhat doctrinaire exploitation of the local red brick together with glass and metal in prismatic association. It was an obsession with him to master every material and structural technique, and in the process, he contributed to conventional design problems, a series of new formal solutions, derived from precast concrete, epoxy resins, and the newly available range of non-ferrous metals.

After some fifteen years in practice, versatility fully demonstrated, Hallen was creating designs that reflected increasingly the style of our age, each new project not only engendering its appropriate formal language (form follows function) but also determining the use of specific materials handled in a particular way (technological eclecticism). Since the late 1970s, original murals, sculptures, and etched glasswork evolved in the fabric of his structures by collaboration with a leading artist—Andrew Verster, retained on his staff—serve to mellow the hard edges.

—B.E. Biermann

HALPRIN, Lawrence.

American. Born in New York City, 1 July 1916. Educated at Cornell University, Ithaca, New York, 1935-39, B.S. 1939; University of Wisconsin, Madison, under Professor Aust, 1939-41, M.S. 1941; Harvard University, Cambridge, Massachusetts, under Walter Gropius, q.v., Marcel Breuer, q.v., and Christopher Tunnard, 1941-42, B.Land.Arch. 1942. Served as a Lieutenant Junior Grade in the United States Navy, 1942-45. Married Anna Schuman in 1940; children: Daria and Rana. Senior Associate Architect with Thomas D. Church and Associates, San Francisco, 1945-49; Principal, Lawrence Halprin and Associates, San Francisco, 1949-76; Partner, with Sue Yung Li Ikeda, RoundHouse, San Francisco, 1976-79. Since 1979, in private practice, San Francisco. Design Consultant California Division of Highways, 1963-65; Landscape Architect and Urban Consultant, San Francisco Bay Area Rapid Transit District, 1963-66. Visiting Lecturer, University of British Columbia, Vancouver, 1954, University of North Carolina, Raleigh, 1955, and University of Pennsylvania, Philadelphia, 1956; Lecturer, University of California, Berkeley, 1960-65 and 1978; Director, Halprin Summer Workshop, San Francisco, 1966 and 1968. Exhibitions: San Francisco Museum of Art, 1952, 1960, and 1976; Bolles Gallery, San Francisco (paintings), 1965; Berkeley Museum, California, 1971; Columbia University, New York, 1972; Kennedy Gallery, New York (drawings), 1978; San Francisco Museum of Modern Art, 1986. Recipient: Honor Award 1953, 1957, and 1968 (twice), Merit Award, 1953 (three times), 1956, 1957, 1959, 1966 and 1972, and First Honor Award, 1961, American Institute of Architects; Design Award, 1954, 1958, 1959, 1963 (three times), 1964, 1966, and First Design Award, 1959 and 1960, Progressive Architecture, New York; Special Award for Land Planning, House and Home, 1956; Collaborative Medal of Honor, Architectural League of New York, 1960; Honor Award, Southwest Washington Chapter, American Institute of Architects, 1962; Honor Award, Chicago Chapter, American Institute of Architects, 1963; Honor Award, Federal Housing Authority, 1963; California Governor's Design Award, 1966 (three times); Industrial Design Award of Excellence, Smithsonian Institution, Washington, D.C., 1968 (twice); Certificate of Merit, Municipal Art Society of New York, 1969; Merit Award for Environmental Design Excellence, American Institute of Planner, 1970; Fourth Biennial Award, 1970 (three times), Fifth Biennial Award, 1972, and Design Award, 1974 (three times), United States Department of Housing and Urban Development; Commercial Landscaping Award, 1972, and Municipal Landscaping Award, 1973 and 1974, American Association of Nurserymen; Annual Art Directors Award for Report Design, Art Directors Club of Metropolitan, Washington, 1973; Award of Excellence, Design and Enviroment, 1975 and 1976 (twice); First Place Award, Association of Landscape Contractors of America, 1976; Merit Award, American Society of Landscape Architects, 1977; Thomas Jefferson Award in Architecture, 1979. Fellow, American Society of Landscape Architects; Honorary Fellow, American Institute of Interior Designers. Member, American Academy of Arts and Sciences. Address: 1620 Montgomery Street, San Francisco, California 94111, U.S.A.

Works (landscape architecture):

1949   Schuman House, Bay Area, San Francisco
        Bissinger House, Bay Area, San Francisco
1950   Esherick House, Bay Area, San Francisco
1951   Woerner House, Bay Area, San Francisco
1952   Master plan, University of California, Davis
1953   Halprin House, Kentwoodlands, California

Lawrence Halprin: Lovejoy Plaza, Portland, Oregon, 1961.

1954 Baer House, Berkeley, California
1955 Greenwood Common, Berkeley, California
Halprin House and Dance Deck, Kentfield California
Washington Water Power Company Corporate Headquarters, Spokane, Washington
Old Orchard Shopping Center, Skokie, Illinois
1956 Grant House, Berkeley, California
1957 Stanford Medical Plaza, Palo Alto, California
Sproul Plaza and Student Union, University of California, Berkeley
Married Student Housing, University of California, San Francisco
Public housing, Marin County, California
Master plan for the Seattle Center, Worlds Fair, Seattle
1958 McIntyre House, Bay Area, San Francisco
1959 Navajo Nation Master Development Program, Window Rock, Arizona
Crocker Industrial Park, Brisbane, California
1960 Capitol Towers Housing, Sacramento, California
1961 Lovejoy Plaza, Portland, Oregon
Pettigrove Park, Portland, Oregon
1962 Nicollet Mall, Minneapolis
1963 Stevenson, Cowell, and Crown Colleges, University of California, Santa Cruz
Woodlake Housing, San Mateo, California
Ghirardelli Square, San Francisco
Urban Freeways Study, State of California
St. Francis Square Housing, San Francisco
1965 California State Capital Plan, San Francisco (project)
Customs House Plaza, Monterey, California
Hadassah Medical Center Master Plan, Ein Karem, Israel
1966 BART (Bay Area Rapid Transit) Design Criteria and Open Space Amelioration, San Francisco
Ida Crown Museum Garden, Jerusalem
Halprin House, Sea Ranch, Mendocino County, California
1967 New York New York, Open Space Study
Oakcreek Apartments, Palo Alto, California
Flushing Meadow Sports Park, New York
1968 Enviroment Workshop Studies, San Francisco
Trojan Nuclear Power Plant, Portland, Oregon
Jewish Home for the Aged, San Francisco
Anacostia River Master Plan, Washington, D.C.
Virgin Islands Master Plan
Oatbrook Shopping Center, Illinois
Community Plan, Everett, Washington
Auditorium Forecourt Plaza, Portland, Oregon
Sea Ranch, Mendocino County, California
Foothills Ecological Study, Palo Alto, California
California State Fairgrounds, Sacramento
Trinity River Plan, Fort Worth, Texas
1968 Market Street, San Francisco
1969 Bank of America World Headquarters, San Francisco
1970 State Capital Plan, Olympia, Washington
Embarcadero Plaza, San Francisco
Willemstad Downtown Plan, Curacao
Welfare Island, New York
Urban Design Study, Caracas, Venezuela
1971 Cold Springs New Town, Baltimore, Maryland
Israel National Park, Mount Carmel, Jerusalem
1972 Fox Valley East New Town, near Aurora, Illinois
Willamette Valley: Choices for the Future, Willamette Valley, Oregon
1973 Workshop and Village Plan, Yountville, California
Main Street Mall, Charlottesville, Virginia
Concept for Cleveland and Master Plan, Ohio
1974 Settlers Landing, Cleveland, Ohio

Manhattan Square Park, Rochester, New York
Babi Yar Memorial, Denver, Colarado
1974 Franklin Delano Roosevelt Memorial, Washington, D.C.
Battery City Park, New York
1975 Skyline Park, Denver
1976 Freeway Park, Seattle
Transit Mall, Portland, Oregon
1976 Second Avenue Mall, New York
1978 Levi Strauss Headquarters, San Francisco
1984/
85 Plaza Las Fuentes, Pasadena, California (with others)

Publications:

By HALPRIN: books—*Cities*, New York 1963, revised edition, Cambridge, Massachusetts and London 1972; *Freeways*, New York 1966; *New York New York*, New York 1968; *The Freeway in the City*, with others, Washington, D.C. 1968; *RSVP Cycles: Creative Processes in the Human Environment*, New York 1970; *Notebooks of Lawrence A Workshop Approach to Collective Creativity*, with Jim Burns, Cambridge, Massachusetts 1974; *The Sketchbook of Lawrence Halprin*, Cambridge, Massachusetts 1981; articles—"The Choreography of Gardens" in *Dance* (New York), July 1953; "Dance Deck in the Woods" in *Impulse* (San Francisco), 1956; "The Edge of the Garden" in *Landscape Architecture* (Louisville, Kentucky), Winter 1956/57; "Landscape Between Walls" in *Architectural Forum* (New York), November 1959; "Houses and Landscapes" in *Progressive Architecture* (New York), May 1960; "Israel: The Man-Made Landscape" in *Landscape* (Berkeley, California), Winter 1960; "The Landscape of Israel" in *Landscape Architecture* (Louisville, Kentucky), April 1961; "The Community and the Landscape" in *AIA Journal* (Washington, D.C.), September 1961; "The Gardens of the High Sierra in *Landscape* (Berkeley, California), Winter 1961; "The City Tree" in *Architectural Forum* (New York), October 1961; "Portrait of a Garden" in *Progressive Architecture* (New York), December 1961; "The Shape of Erosion" in *Landscape Architecture* (Louisville, Kentucky), January 1962; "Transportation and the City" in *Architectural Forum* (New York), April 1963; "San Francisco, Panhandle Freeway" in *San Francisco Examiner*, May 1964; "Motation" in *Progressive Architecture* (New York), July 1965; "This is a City" in *Western Building Design* (Los Angeles) 1973; "Jerusalem as Place and Vision" in *AIA Journal* (Washington, D.C.), December 1980; films—*Le Pink Grapefruit*, 1976; *How Sweet It Is!*, with Anna Halprin, 1976; recording—*The Ecology of Form*, tape cassette, London 1982.

On HALPRIN: book—*The Third Generation Architect and Concept* by Ted Itoh, Tokyo 1974; articles—"Riding a Revolution: A Radical Experiment in Reorganization" by Nilo Lindgren in *Innovation* (New York), Februray 1971; "Lawrence Halprin: Humanizing the City Environment" by Elin Schoen in *American Way* (New York), November 1972; "The Halprin Revolutions Revisited" by Nilo Lindgren in *Landscape Architecture* (Louisville, Kentucky), April 1974; "FDR and the Cherry Blossoms: A New Design for a Roosevelt Memorial" in *Horizon* (New York), May 1977; "Lawrence Halprin," special issue of *Process: Architecture* (Tokyo/Pittsburgh), February 1978; "The FDR Memorial" in *Landscape Architecture* (Louisville, Kentucky), January 1979; "The 'Artificial Nature' of Lawrence Halprin" in *Ville giardini* (Milan), May 1980; "Lawrence Halprin in Australia" in *Landscape Australia* (Mont Albert, Victoria), February 1982; "Lawrence Halprin Workshop, Darling Harbour, Sydney" in *Landscape Australia* (Mont Albert, Victoria), May 1982; "Halprin's FDR Memorial

Design Gains Congressional Approval" in *AIA Journal* (Washington, D.C.), August 1982; "Designing for the Christian Brothers" in *AIA Journal* (Washington, D.C.), February 1983; "Evaluation: Park Atop a Freeway" in *AIA Journal* (Washington, D.C.), June 1983; "Halprin riorganizza il suo parco e l'autostrada" in *Architettura* (Milan), March 1984; "Proposal for a Holocaust Memorial" by S.R. Frey in *Landscape Architecture* (Louisville, Kentucky), March/April 1984.

*

I have always felt that design is a total involvement and that it is not purely visual. The process for me has been always inextricably intertwined with the results. This is a hard concept to explain, in a sense, except perhaps through a diagram.

You can view process as a way to arrive at a solution, in which case it is a means towards an end or you can perceive it as important and valid in itself—full of twisting and turning, unknown explorations, reactive to many different inputs and influences along the way and lacking a clear image of what the end product is or should be. What emerges then is, in fact, *part* of the process. This diagram looks more like this:

It is really more like life itself—unforeseen, adventurous, exploratory: with only two fixed points—a beginning and an end but even those linked up with larger changes. It is in this way—a holistic way—that I have designed

For me, too, the progression of problems which I have been solving has been important. I started with issues of personal relationships: gardens and houses—evocative of private family needs, tract houses and gardens after the war. After that, I attempted to link these together: group housing, suburban villages, shopping centers. Gradually these issues have aggregated into larger ones—how people, in regions, can live together in towns and villages without raping the land and destroying the very environment they live in. This led to concerns about transportation, both freeways for cars and mass transporation (BART), with particular concern for how these mammoth constructions could do more than just function as carriers, but go further and become forms of sculpture (as well as sociology) in the landscape.

Eventually—perhaps inevitably—I came into the city whose decaying cores, streets, and ghettos were losing ground yearly. I felt that somehow *cities* could be reconstructed and that many of the lessons we had learned in the new communities could be brought to bear in our older cities—amenities, liveliness, open spaces, pedestrian networks, recycled old buildings—and that if we conceived of cities as places of enjoyment and creativity, they could flower once again.

During this time of working—particularly during the latter part when projects became larger and more and more complex, reaching into whole regions and very large urban complexes—many dedicated and talented young people spent time in my office and contributed profoundly to the projects you see listed here. Lawrence Halprin & Associates was, itself, an example of collective creativity—of the process itself. It exemplified in its best moments the idea that a group can work synergistically and develop more than the sum of its individual components—an organism in itself. We were full of high energy, of boundless enthusiasm, high spirits, and an eager search for new ways of doing things!

In more recent years, in addition to designing actual projects, I have turned to new explorations, trying to dig deeper into the sources of collective creativity. I am concentrating on the issue of people's interactions with their environment both as individuals *and* in groups—both aspects are important. I have been searching for archetypal relationships in workshops which take place primarily in the field. These TAKING PART workshops allow people the opportunity to discover and articulate their own needs and desires for themselves and for their communities. Working with the RSVP cycles, they discover ways of communicating with each other and arriving at creative decisions based on multiple input. Then they can implement what they want with the full support and enthusiasm of the entire group.

We hope to reveal two things—what is the fundamental human environment symbiosis and how people can go about providing it for themselves. It is a hope to a design *with* its inhabitants a human ecosytem biologically and emotionally satisfying.

—Lawrence Halprin

In the annals of landscape architectural history, few individuals have had such an impact on the human environment as Lawrence Halprin. He has responded to current social needs, created imaginative sculptural places for all segments of society, and provided leadership in the related design professions with new design processes.

Following an apprenticeship with Thomas Church, where he helped develop the contemporary California garden concept, Halprin opened his own office in 1949. Continued concern with the private personal space saw him linking them together in suburban villages, shopping centers, and educational facilities. Scattered centers of habitation called for freeways and public transportation, which, in turn, led to problems at the urban core. Perhaps Halprin's career will be best known for his innovative and imaginative response to urban renewal, downtown malls, and recycling of old buildings. Regional planning and very large urban design projects complete the scale cycle.

Design process is as important to Halprin as the end result, and every human activity is as important as the notes in a musician's score. The activities are orchestrated and analyzed to develop diagrams and designs that are translated into organic built spaces.

A greater awareness and concern by the public for the total environment and an infusion of young, enthusiastic, free-thinking designers into his office resulted in Halprin's developing a design methodology involving client and user. Workshops were organized in communities where representatives of different interest groups would come together under the leadership of a professional designer/facilitator. Their dreams, desires, aspirations, and needs were discussed in a creative, collective effort and synthesized by the professional into a final design statement.

To Halprin, the whole of life is design process. Everything we need to know as creative environmental designers can can be observed in nature, from the cascading waters of the Sierras to the freedom seen in the flight of a bird. The organic, free-flowing, romantic people-spaces created by Halprin express these lessons from nature as well as being a response to mid-twentieth-century environmental needs.

—Roger Osbaldeston

HANSEN, Oskar.
Polish. Born in Helsinki, Finland, of Norwegian parents, 12 April 1922; emigrated to Poland, 1922: naturalized, 1926. Educated at the Technical College, Vilnius, Lithuania, 1942, Dip.Ing. 1942; Institute of Technology, Warsaw, under Romuald Gutt, 1946-51; Fernand Léger Studio, Paris (studied painting), 1948-49; CIAM International Summer School of Architecture, London, 1949. Served in the Polish Partisan Army, 1944. Married the achitect Zofia Garlinska in 1950; children: Igor and Alvar. Assistant Architect, Workers Housing Association, Warsaw, 1948; worked in the studio of Pierre Jeanneret, *q.v.,* Paris, 1948-49, and of Jerzy Soltan, Warsaw, 1950-56. Senior Architect, 1958-60, and since 1960 Chief Architect, Housing Cooperative, Warsaw. Assistant, 1950-51, Adjunct Professor and

Chairman of the Studio of Basic Design, 1952-55, Assistant Professor and Chairman of the Visual Structures Studio of the Sculpture Department, 1956-64, and since 1964, Professor and Chairman of the Unit of Sculpture in Architecture, Academy of Fine Arts, Warsaw. Exhibitions: *Oskar Hansen: Architecture, Sculpture, Painting,* Jewish Theatre, Warsaw, 1957; *Oskar Hansen: In Search of Methods of Teaching Art,* Mickiewicz Museum, Warsaw, 1966; *Linear Continuous System Housing Development,* toured Poland, 1976; *Oskar Hansen: Open Form,* at the *Biennale,* Venice, 1977; *Automats Factory Work/Environment Study,* Chocianow, Poland, 1977; *Train Works Environment Study,* Pruszkow, Poland, 1981; *Oskar Hansen L'art de la forme ouverte,* Museum of Architecture, Oslo, 1984; with Zofia Hansen—Rotterdam, 1962; Helsinki, 1962; Delft, Netherlands, 1963; Oslo, 1964; Warsaw, 1967; Zielona Gora, Poland, 1967; Warsaw, 1971. Recipient: CIAM Housing Prize, London, 1949; Polish 10th Anniversary Medal, 1955; Architecture Prize, Warsaw, 1957; Art Prize, Warsaw Journalists Committee, 1958; Silver Medal, *Triennale,* Milan, 1959; Polonia Restituta Cross, 1959; Silver Badge, Housing Cooperatives Union, Poland, 1964; Silver Medal, *Exempla '74,* Munich, 1974. Address (office): ul. Sedziowska 3/4, 02-081 Warsaw, Poland.

Works:

1948 Debiec Housing Estate, near Poznań, Poland
1948/
49 Aluminium Villas, Villeneuve St. Georges, France (with Pierre Jeanneret)
1949 Housing Estate, London (project)
1951/
52 Interior designs, Warsaw and Suzewiec, Poland (with Jerzy Sotan)
1953 Polish Pavilion, Trade Fair, Stockholm (with Stanislaw and Wojciech Zamecznik)
1955 Plan for the *Folk Art Exhibition,* Warsaw (with Jerzy Sotan)
Hansen Apartment interiors, Warsaw (with Zofia Hansen)
1956 Polish Pavilion, Trade Fair, Izmir, Turkey (with Lech Tomaszewski)
1957 Plan for the *National Exhibition of Interior Design,* Warsaw (with Zofia Hansen and J. Meisner)
1958 Polish Pavilion, World's Fair, Brussels (with others)
Rakowiec Housing Estate, Warsaw (with Zofia Hansen, Z. Malicki, M. Szymanowski, and Z. Gurtzman)
Cultural Centre, Montevideo (project; with Zofia Hansen and Lech Tomaszewski
Zacheta Building extension, Warsaw (with Lech Tomaszewski and Stanisaw Zamecznik
1959 Monument, Auschwitz-Birkenau, Poland (project; with Zofia Hansen, Jerzy Jarnuszkiewicz, Julian Paka, and Lechostaw Rosiński
Polish Pavilion, *Bienal,* São Paulo (with Zofia Hansen and Lech Tomaszewski)
1960 Polish Radio Experimental Music Centre, Warsaw (with J. Patkowski
Polish Pavilion, *Triennale,* Milan
1960/
61 Master plan for the Sowacki Housing Estate, Lublin, Poland (with Zofia Hansen and J. Dowgiao)
1961 City Monument, Westerplatte, Poland (with J. Kucz)
1962 Open Form Theatre, Lublin, Poland (with Zofia Hansen and M. Konieczny
Energetyk-Torwar Housing Estate, Warsaw (with Zofia Hansen and B. Ufnalewski)
1963 Przyczoek Grochowski Estate, for the Young Men's Housing Cooperative, Warsaw (with Zofia Hansen, J. Dowgiao, and M. Konieczny

Teacher Training College, Lublin, Poland (with Zofia Hansen, J. Wolski, and M. Konieczny)
1964 Skoczylas Monument, Warsaw (with E. Cieślar)
1965 Sowacki Housing Estate, Lublin, Poland (with Zofia Hansen and Jerzy Dowgiao)
1966 Shopping Centre, Sowacki Housing Estate, Lublin, Poland (with Zofia Hansen)
Linear Continuous System Housing Estate (project; with Zofia Hansen, M. Konieczny, T. Kujawa, G. Marczak, and H. Rzenca
Museum of Modern Art, Skopje, Yugoslavia (with B. Cybulska, Lars Fasting, and Svein Hatløy)
1967 Linear Continuous System Settlement Definition Study (with Zofia Hansen)
1968 Hansen Country House, Szumin, Poland (with Zofia Hansen)
Linear Continuous System Housing Development, Ursynów-Lasy Kabackie, near Warsaw (with others)
1969 Low-cost housing, Lima, Peru (competition project; with Svein Hatløy, J. Dowgiao, and J. Kozierski)
1971 Development plan for the Warta River, Poznań, Poland
1972 Polish Regional Development Forecast Plan (Linear Continuous System study; with Svein Hatløy)
Linear Continuous System Housing Development, near Poznań, Poland (project; with Svein Hatløy)
Studio Theatre modernization, Warsaw
1973 Monument, Lodz, Poland (project; with J. Kucz)
Polish Embassy, Washington, D.C. (with P. Damiecki)
St. George Church/Cultural Centre conversion, Gdansk, Poland (with Zofia Hansen)
1947 Linear Continuous System Housing Development, near Przemyśl, Poland (project; with Zofia Hansen, P. Damiecki, and Svein Hatløy)
Polish Pavilion, *Exempla '74,* Munich
1975 Environmental study of the city centre of Lubin, Poland (with E. Bartman, H. Górka, T. Banovitz, and P. Piwowarczyk)
1976 Linear Continuous System Housing Development, Legnica, Lubin, and Gogow, Poland (project; with E. Bartman and M. Czernicki)
1977 Polish Pavilion, *Biennale,* Venice
1977/
78 Work-environment study for the Automats Factory, Chocianów, Poland (with E. Bartman, H. Górka, E. Kun, and H. Szmalenberg)
1979/
81 Rail Train Factory Work/Environment Study, Pruszkow, Poland (project; with E. Bartman, I. Basskowska, H. Górka, Z. Hansen, and H. Szmalenberg)
1983 Adaptable Furniture System (with M. Filipowicz, H. Górka, A. Hansen, and P. Piwowarczyk)
Electronic Music Studio, State Radio Headquarters, Warsaw (project)
1984 Transformable Pictures with plastic frames and visors (with Z. Hansen)

Publications:

By HANSEN: articles—"Biotechnique" in *Projekt* (Warsaw), no. 5, 1957; "Open Form" in *Przeglad Kulturalny* (Warsaw), no. 355, 1958; "Open Form—The Art of the Great Number," with Zofia Hansen, in *CIAM 1959 Otterlo,* edited by Oscar Newman, Stuttgart 1959; "Auf der Suche nach der offenen Form" in *Bauwelt* (Berlin), no. 37, 1963; "Evolution ou révolution," with Zofia Hansen, in *L'Architecture d'aujourd'hui* (Paris), no. 119, 1965; "Komposis-

Oscar Hansen: Monument at Auschwitz-Birkenau, Poland, 1959-84.

jonsundervisningen ved akademiet i Warszawa" in *Arkitektnytt* (Oslo), no. 14, 1965; "Linear Continuous System" in *Diekorativnoje Isskustwo* (Moscow), no. 9, 1967; "Towards the Architecture for 30 Million Caesars" in *Kenchiku Bunka* (Tokyo), no. 1, 1967; "Dipoli ist Architektur" in *Bauwelt* (Berlin), no. 28, 1968; "Proposition pour un urbanisme lineaire" in *Le Carré bleu* (Paris), no. 2, 1969; "Lima, Peru," with Svein Hatløy, in *Bafnytt* (Bergen), no. 2, 1972; "Pilotsprojektet i Lima" in *Byggekunst* (Oslo), no. 5, 1977; "Un quart du siècle de la forme ouverte" in *Un Cercle d'Otterloo*, Hamburg, West Germany 1983.

On HANSEN: books—*Oskar Hansen: Architecture, Sculpture, Painting,* exhibition catalogue, by Jerzy Sotan, Warsaw 1957; *Oskar Hansen: In Search of Methods of Teaching Art,* exhibition catalogue, Warsaw 1966; *L'Architecture polonaise contemporaine* by B. Lisowski, Warsaw 1968; *Nowa architektura Polska* by P. Szafer, Warsaw 1972; *Przygody Architektury XX weiku* by P. Trzeciak, Warsaw 1974; *Biennale di Venezia: Polonia,* exhibition catalogue, Venice 1976; articles—"Oskar Hansen Exhibition" in *Projekt* (Warsaw), no. 3, 1957; "De Technische en Riumtelijke Experimenten von Oskar Hansen" in *Het Bouwwerk* (The Hague), no. 1, 1961; "Oskar Hansen and His Open Form" by S. Stopczyk in *Projekt* (Warsaw), no. 1, 1962; "The Searches of Oskar Hansen" by A. Oseka in *Poland* (Warsaw), no. 4, 1962; "In Defence of Professor Hansen's Ideas" in *Poland* (Warsaw), no 2, 1967; "Oskar Hansen" by A. Moffet in *Architectural Design* (London), no. 2, 1968; "About Lima, Peru Housing" in *Architectural Design* (London), no. 6/7, 1970; "Hansen—en aporte al diseño de rivienelas colectivas" in *Summa* (Buenos Aires), no. 67, 1973; "Slowacki—Newcastle" by Svein Hatløy in *Bafnytt* (Bergen, Norway), no. 6, 1977; "Modernizacja na miare przyszlosci, czyii studium humanizacji pracy" in *Ochrona Pracy* (Warsaw), no. 6, 1979.

*

The growing discord between man and his physical surroundings and the disharmony between man and man result first of all from the objective organization of space, which I have called the "Closed Form," being the semantically spatial derivative of a consumer life-style. In order to create a balance between man and his natural and technical environments and harmony between men, one ought to realize, the spatial conditions for a different qualitative style of life. The consumer model should be exchanged for a cognitive model—encouraging the growth of the level of life rather than the standard of living, which is merely based on growth in the quantity of goods produced in relation to the number of inhabitants. Achieveing a cognitive model requires us to grasp the problems in a complex and integrated way. In the 1950s these premises promoted the idea of ordering space based on the "Open Form" concept.

The idea of architecture and art based on "Open Form" results from the principles of situational relations. The aim of an architect or an artist should not be to create finished works of art but to provide a background for the user's expression and, in this process, to search for anexpressional synthesis. Life processes and man himself should develop these forms.

The term "Open Form" derives from the fact that works of art created by its conventions are based on the user's intervention; therefore, they are forms that will adapt to the evolutionary process. It may seem that the freedom given to user's by "Open Form" is synonymous with spatial anarchy. But this is not so. The content of "Open Form" revealed, for example, in Housing—a process for evolving the user's consciousness, expressed by an active transformation of space—is expressed through the interpretation of a background of events taking place in accordance with the readability of individual constituent elements. The user is liberated from the rigour with which space has been previously arranged. This type of environment makes it possible to broadly compare the various concepts for organizing living space, and it creates possibilities for development and progress through choice and natural selection.

Regional planning in the context of "Open form" implies that the objective elements—permanent and scientifically defined—would be applied in such a way the the subjective elements—the development processes—would become organic events and constitute the basic wealth and character of the surrounding built forms.

In considering the postulates of "Open Form" in the context of both function and form (or colour) and the architect's or artist's new approach to design, one realizes that there is a need to create new didactic programmes. These programmes should derive from the reality of development processes, not from the reality of static situations. Technical knowledge should be conveyed in the context of a humanist education.

In organizing space in accordance with "Open Form," painting and sculpture lose their consumer character and become integral components of the whole. Their new function, I believe, is to make the events occurring in space more legible, to clarify their spontaneous character, and to articulate the compositional openness of their surroundings. The interpenetration of spontaneous elements with conscious artistic creativity should lead us to an authentic environmental art.

—Oskar Hansen

*

The inspiration of Oskar Hansen's work is a search for a future relationship between man and his surroundings that corresponds to an egalitarian social system and that solves the problems of mass population. Hansen contrasts the old, objective approach to architecture with an architecture created by a series of events—man and nature in a developing process. An absence of events would mean the absence of Hansen's architecture, the architecture of Open Form; that is, in his opinion, his activity only initiates one of the elements of architecture—the organisation of a framework for coming events. Closely related to Hansen are Svein Hatløy, Herman Hertzberger, Lucien Kroll, and Ralph Erskine, who are also searching for a crystallization of the Open Form concept, working inthe much more difficult conditions of a civilization dominated by the myth of consumption and commodity.

Hansen, with his wife Zofia, search for a concept of social space, the creation of certain frameworks in which individual activities—irrespective of personal intentions—will by necessity be in agreement with the spirit of the community, creating a type of community life in which each memeber, while attending to his own minor everyday needs, will contribute to the creation of the whole. This viewis connected with his belief in the necessity for a profound re-evaluation in architecture, the acquisition of new vision and imagination.

The ideas of "Open Form" and the "Art of Great Numbers," defined by Hansen in 1958 and presented at the 11th Congress of CIAM in Otterlo (1959), are attempts to specify the contemporary philosophy of architectural thought, based on an awareness of the role played by social factors in the creation of our environment. The concept of "Closed Form" formerly used by CIAM (which Hansen felt neglected the psychic needs of the individual, did not allow flexibility in lifestyle, and did not solve the problems of mass living) he contrasts with that of Open Form, which accepts the individual in the community as a whole, helping him to identify himself in the building of his own environment. It is a synthesis of impersonal social elements and the subjective elements of the individual.

Using as an analogy the development of Christian ideology, Hansen remarks that in the development of a new social outlook on life and the new forms that result, we also have to pass through a period of "Christian basilicas built of pagan columns." Step by step, we have to break with the present forms of our human environment (and change people's spatial and social imagination), which are the result of the needs of former times—such as the atrophy and disintegration of human settlements on a village scale, the concentric patterns of cities, specialized education based on static values—reflected in the dogmas of Closed Form. The goal of Open Form is to free man from the present comsumptional, objective model of life and to direct his interests towards the development of social conciousness, towards authentic creative interests, and finally towards the needs of his own "nest."

The Open Form concept formed the basis for Hansen's "Linear Continuous System" LCS, which attempts to answer the problems of settlement patterns that lag behind growth processes and the organization of mass living when it is in a state of continuous motion. The Linear Continuous System is a proposal for creating man's environment within a socialist framework, based on the growth of organic structure: a flexible, proportionally correlated interdependence of urban zones ruuning parallel to each other, clearly relating the service zones to those serviced. It is the kind of urban profile whose interpretation depends on the number of inhabitants, their social structure, their technical resources, and so forth. Thus, it is a model with an open and highly flexible character, set of organically linked functional systems, each of which goes through biotechnical evolution both qualitative and quantitative in nature.

LCS proposes coordinated action on the scale of a whole country; it is an attempt to bring together the combined resources of state-owned land, funding, and industry—an attempt to get a "percentage" for the individual from the national economy. LCS defines three linear planning zones on both sides of an axis of major communication routes and rivers. Immediately adjacent is the housing and light industry and an appropriate service infrastructure; beyond this is a zone of open land containing existing historical settlements, woods, and farmland; the outermost zone contains heavy industry appropriate to the available resources. LCS creates a approach to planning different from that of the concentric pattern, and some structural units such as the market place, shopping centre, and residential neighbourhood characteristic of concentric patterns disappear or change their meaning. Instead, new structural units arise, such as housing lines, service lines, lines of communication, and lines of work. The linear concentration of this approach causes a rise in the individual's standard of living, enables closer contact with a less spoilt natural environment, and creates a more balanced relationship between work and recreation. The high standard of living, the variety of local countryside, the scale of the social milieu, this great linear concentration of people, equipped with efficient, rationally used commmunication—these are the advantages of LCS, the attractiveness of which, in Hansen's opinion, will draw people to it, and at the same time will rescue the towns from further pathological expansion.

In LCS an individual has a clear image of relationships, both objective—of a scientifically motivated public area—and subjective—of his own private area. The primary axis consists of a bearing structure together with infrastructure and services—this is a public area. The private houses on the structure—this is a private area. During the developing process, the relationship between public and private areas in LCS form harmonious dependencies that come together at various times, unlike the zonal relationships in a concentric town.

In Hansen's view of human surroundings, there are no inert, indifferent forms. Each spatial activity expresses a certain idea, a philosophy related to man's affairs. Open Form is an activity for the sake of mankind, for those who are creative and conscious, understanding, and prepared to be individuals in the framework of community life.

Two somewhat compromised attempts to put Hansen's LCS idea into practice are the Sowacki Housing Estate in Lublin and Warsaw's Przycoek Grochowski. They are, in Hansen's view, still only objects, individual items, still using the old language but at the same time being experimental vehicles for the Open Form concept.

Hansen agrees that he is a little doctrinaire, with clearly stated views on the essence of his creativity. He consistently accepts only those design commissions in the solution of which he can sense the potential for making the next step forward, for bringing Open Form to fruition. He is often accused of turning the problem of people into the problem of the idea, of preaching the pragmatism of utopia, and of an uncompromising attitude in making judgements. But Hansen believes that the realization of the LCS model will be the expression of an integrated social consciousness, and he is conscious that the LCS model will not be fully realized in his lifetime. This is an idea for many generations to come, an idea that he is trying to implant in his students and the younger generation of architects.

Hansen believes that, now, one must be an *enfant terrible*, must design so-called utopias, and must try to arouse and shape social consciousness, so that tomorrow LCS may become a reality.

—Teresa Czaplinska-Archer

HANSON, Norman Leonard.

South African. Born in Johannesburg, 19 June 1909; resident in England since 1963. Educated at the King Edward VII School, Johannesburg, 1921-24; University of the Witwatersrand School of Architecture, Johannesburg, under G.E. Pearse and A. Stanley Furner, 1925-31, B.Arch. 1932. Married Matle Joyce Frank in 1961; children: Caroline and Roger (Hanson); Natalie and Vivienne (née Frank). Partner, with S. N. Tomkin and N. I. Finkelstein, in Hanson, Tomkin and Finkelstein, later Hanson and Tomkin, Johannesburg, 1932-70; Partner, with Tomkin and latterly C. E. Harris, in S. N. Tomkin, Hanson and Harris, Durban, 1946-78. Development Consultant, New Town of Ashkelon, Israel, 1949-61. Visiting Professor, University of New South Wales, Sydney, 1962. Professor and Director, School of Architecture, 1963-71, and, since 1971, Professor Emeritus, University of Manchester. President, Transvaal Provincial Institute of Architects, 1943, and Institute of South African Architects, 1947; Executive Member of the National Housing and Planning Commission, Founder-Member of the Building Research Advisory Committee of the National Building Research Institute, Founder-Member of the Management Committee of the National Development Fund for the Building Industry, Member of the Board of the Faculty of Architecture of the University of the Witwatersrand, and Member and Chairman of the Board of Education of the Institute of South African Architects, all South Africa, 1946-63. Recipient: Award of Merit, 1948, and Gold Medals, 1959 and 1982, Institute of South African Architects. M.A.: University of Manchester, 1966. Norman Hanson Bursary and Fellowships established by the Institute of South African Architects, Council for Scientific and Industrial Research, Association of South African Quantity Surveyors, and Building Industry Federation of South Africa, 1963. Associate, Royal Institute of British Architects, 1935. Address: 5 Straffan Lodge, Belsize Grove, London NW3 4XE, England.

Principal Works:

1932 Saffer House, Johannesburg (project)
1933 Harris House, Johannesburg
1934 Brookstone House, Johannesburg
     Hotpoint House (showrooms, offices and flats), Johannesburg
1935 Yeoville Flats, Johannesburg (project)
1936 Suzman House, Johannesburg
     Reading Court, Johannesburg
1937 Denstone Court, Johannesburg
1938 Hanson House, Johannesburg
1940 20th Century Cinema, Johannesburg (with Cowin and Ellis)
1948 Medical Centre, Johannesburg
1956 Zionist Centre, Johannesburg (with Cooper and Hellmann)
     Government Offices, Esplanade, Durban (with S. N. Tomkin)
1958 Broadway Building, Foreshore, Cape Town (with Kantorowich and Skacel)
1961/
  66 Medical School and Library, University of the Witwatersrand, Johannesburg (with P. Aneck-Hahn and H. M. J. Prins)
1962 Geology and Mining Engineering Building, University of the Witwatersrand, Johannesburg (with H. M. J. Prins)
1963 Electrical Engineering Building, University of Natal, Durban (with S. N. Tomkin)
1963/
  77 Science Complex, University of Natal, Durban (with S. N. Tomkin)
1970 Architecture and Planning Building, University of Manchester, England (with Roy Kantorowich, M. Schonegevel, and G. Skacel)

Publications:

By HANSON: book—*Zerohour*, editor with Rex Martienssen and Gordon McIntosh, Johannesburg 1933; articles—"Metaphysics of Space" in *South African Architectural Record* (Johannesburg), September 1932; "Architecture and the New Aesthetic" in *South African Architectural Record* (Johannesburg), November 1936; "An Architect's House" in *South African Architectural Record* (Johannesburg), October 1939; "The Twentieth Century Cinema" in *South African Architectural Record* (Johannesburg), August 1940; "Rex Martienssen: In Memoriam" and "The Student and Philosopher of Architecture" in *South African Architectural Record* (Johannesburg), November 1942; "Community Planning" in *South African Architectural Record* (Johannesburg), October 1943; "South Africa—Architecture from 1700 to 1930," special issue of *Architectural Review* (London), October 1944; "The Architect's Dilemma" in *Manchester Literary and Philosophical Society Proceedings 1964-65*, Manchester 1965; "Professional Education" in *Research for Better Building* (Proceedings of the Third South African Building Congress), Durban 1974.

On HANSON: books—*Twentieth Century Houses* by Raymond McGrath, London 1934; *Martienssen and the International Style* by Gilbert Herbert, Cape Town and Rotterdam 1975; articles—"An Experiment in Technique" in *South African Architectural*

Norman Hanson: Architecture and Planning Building, University of Manchester, 1970.

lenges. An introspective review and re-appraisal of past attitudes indicated for me the need to recast my architectural approach. Though valuing the achievements in many respects of the proponents of the modern movement, I nevertheless saw a profound weakness in the technical base of the pre-war work (as well as social shortcomings). As I now believed that sound constructional techniques were the foundation of all good architecture, I re-shaped my approach from first principles and found much common ground with architects and constructors such as Perret and Nervi. Under prevailing immediate postwar conditions, building resources were scarce, the most readily available materials being brick and concrete. I concentrated on these age-old materials and have stayed with them ever since. Developing techniques in factory production and site assembly have transformed the use of concrete, and modern science, applied to building, has improved, and is improving, building standards. For myself, I believe that the mainspring of the creative process may be found in structure, though architecture itself arises from an amalgam of social, functional and constructional factors brought to the level of an art form.

—Norman Hanson

Norman Hanson played a considerable role in the development of modern architecture in South Africa, as a close associate of Rex Martienssen, a leading member of the Transvaal Group, and as the designer of some of the finest examples of modern buildings of the day outside of Europe. After his overwhelming confrontation (together with Martienssen) with the new architecture at Stuttgart in 1930—the Weissenhofsiedlung and Mendelsohn's Schocken Store—Hanson unequivocally accepted the International Style. He was moved by the austere power of its forms and stimulated by the philosophy that informed them. His early papers in the *South African Architectural Record* ("Metaphysics of Space" and "Architecture and the New Aesthetic") indicate the formidable mind of a very capable theoretician; but his principal contribution was to be in the field of architectural practice. In 1932, in Johannesburg, he established the firm of Hanson, Tomkin and Finkelstein, which was the pioneer firm of architects undertaking work only in the contemporary manner; this integrity of purpose ensured an outflow of high quality but, naturally, inhibited the quantity of work produced. The influence of Mies van der Rohe is evident in much of the early work, sometimes explicitly in the plan forms adopted, as in the virtuoso Saffer House project, or the simpler Brookstone House swimming pool—which formed the basis for a polemical article by Martienssen in the *Record* ("An Experiment in Technique"). The less superficial and more enduring effect of the Miesian influence, however, lay in Hanson's respect for the precision of Mies's designs and his emphasis on the primacy of technology as a formgiving force.

In a series of notable houses in the 1930s, Hanson allied this creative use of technology with a growing mastery of the language of the International Style, notably the idioms of Le Corbusier. From the very first realized example, Harris House—the first South African work to receive international recognition, being published in Raymond McGrath's *Twentieth Century House*—there is a consistent use of white wall surfaces and large glazed areas; the frequent juxtaposition of a dominant prismatic architecture with sensuously curved, sculptural forms; spacious exercises in the free flow of the plan; and an overall character of power and strength. To an even greater degree, these characteristics may be seen in his larger buildings: Hotpoint House, a tall building on a narrow centre-city site, with a beautifully modelled facade; the Yeoville flats project, which combines a free-flowing plan with a vigorously plastic external form; and Reading Court, a relatively small building which somehow is almost monumental in scale. In Reading Court, and more explicitly in Denstone

Record (Johannesburg), January 1935; "Formal Problems in Cinema Design" by Monte Bryer in *South African Architectural Record* (Johannesburg), November 1941; "Contemporary Building" by J. Fassler in *Architectural Review* (London), October 1944; "Contemporary Architecture in South Africa" by J. Fassler in *Architectural Design* (London), June 1956; "Le Corbusier and the South African Movement" by Gilbert Herbert in *Architectural Association Quarterly* (London), January/March 1972.

My work as a practising architect over a period of forty-six years has had two distinct phases, the first dominant in the years preceding the war, that is, from 1932 to 1939, and the second, part development and part reorientation, dating from 1946 to the present time.

In the first phase, as a young architect, I participated actively in the evolution of the modern movement in South Africa, itself an offshoot of the architectural revolution in Europe, epitomised in the work, theoretical and practical, of the pioneers, Gropius, Mies van der Rohe and, above all, Le Corbusier. With Le Corbusier a strong link was forged, essentially through the contact made with him by Rex Martienssen, then teaching at the University of the Witwatersrand. The small band of young architects, recently graduated from that University, absorbed and put into practice the principles enunciated by the master and were labelled by him "the Transvaal Group." In spite of some initial public and professional opposition, a considerable body of work was carried out by the group, mainly in the domestic field, but culminating, in my case, in the building of a large project, the 20th Century Cinema in Johannesburg. The history of that period has been written by Gilbert Herbert in his monumental *Martienssen and the International style*.

After the hiatus of the war years (during which Martienssen died while in military training), the problem of re-starting practice brought new chal-

Court, Hanson emphasized the communal aspects of the building—the open spaces, recreation areas, etc.—for the idea of the flat, the communal residential building, had for Hanson, as it had for Gropius, a social basis, an ideological as well as an architectural motivation.

In his last works prior to the war—his own house and the outstanding 20th Century Cinema building—the sensuous, almost baroque elements are still present but in combination with strong forms of geometric precision, taking the architecture beyond the formal limits set by the International Style and presaging the romantic modernism then being evolved, unknown to Hanson, in Brazil.

The outbreak of the war, and the caesura it enforced on building, enabled Hanson to pause and to re-examine the premises upon which he had built his architectural philosophy. He came to question the social validity of Le Corbusier's proposals, the lack of realism which the new aesthetic had imposed upon building technology, the invalidity of the International Style in respect to the South African climate—in effect, the very ethical bases of the architecture he had espoused. He retreated—in such postwar buildings as the Medical Centre and the Zionist Federation Building in Johannesburg—into a conservative mode, sacrificing the exuberance of his earlier buildings to the interests of rational planning and meticulous detailing of constructional elements. The strong controlling hand of Hanson was always evident, but the forms became subdued, austere almost, neo-classical in spirit in their strict modularity. With difficulty, it seemed, a new architecture gradually emerged, of which the Architectural School building at Manchester University (where he had taken up the chair of architecture) is a late flowering.

—Gilbert Herbert

HARA, Hiroshi.

Japanese. Born in Kanagawa Prefecture in 1936. Educated at Nagano Prefectural High School, graduated 1955; Tokyo University, under Kenzo Tange, q.v., and Professor Uchida, 1955-59, Dip.Arch. 1959, D. Arch. 1964. In private practice, Tokyo: Founder/Director, Research Studio for Architecture and Space (RAS). Associate Professor, 1969-82, and Professor since 1982, Institute of Industrial Science, University of Tokyo. Exhibitions: *From Space to Environment*, Tokyo, 1966; *Styrian Autumn* festival of culture, Graz, Austria, 1984; *Tokyo: Form and Spirit*, San Francisco Museum of Modern Art, 1987. Addresses (office): Sakuragaoka High Home no. 701,13-10 Sakuragaoka, Shibuya-ku Tokyo, Japan; (university): 7-22-1, Roppongi, Minato-ku, Tokyo 106, Japan.

Works:

1965   Hotel Yamagishi (project)
1966   Primary School (project)
       Wooden House, Tokyo (project)
1967   Itoh House, Tokyo
1968   Keisho Kindergarten, Machida City, near Tokyo
       Induction House (project
1969   Mountain Lodge, Tanzawa, Tokyo
1970   Hakone International Culture Center, Japan (competition project)
1972   Toba Maritime Museum, Tokyo
       Awazu House, Kawasaki, Kanaga Prefecture, Japan
       Izu Fishing Lodge, Shizuoka, Japan
1974   Hiroshi Hara House, Machida City, near Tokyo
       School Kasumageseki, Japan
1975   Villa Kudo, Nagano, Japan

Hiroshi Hara: Hara House, Machida, Tokyo, 1974.

1977   Kuragaki House, Tokyo
1978   Niramu House, Tokyo
1979   Akita House, Tokyo
       Shokodo Building, Aichi, Japan
1980   Spanish Embassy, Tokyo (project)
1981   Sueda Art Gallery, Oita, Japan
       Tsurukawa Nursery School, Tokyo
       Mori Lithography Workskhop, Nagano, Japan
       Yokozawa House, Tokyo
1982   Hillport Hotel, Tokyo
       The Stage of Dream/Nakatsuka House, Shizouka, Japan
       Parc de la Villette development, Paris (competition project)
1983   Shibukawa Central Area renewal, Gunma, Japan
1984   Araya Housing Project, Akita, Japan

Publications:

By HARA: book—*Global Architecture 4: Kevin Roche, John Dinkeloo and Associates—The Ford Foundations Building, New York 1967; The Oakland Museum, California 1969*, with Yukio Futagawa, Tokyo 1971; articles—"E.N. Rogers, the Critic," with Ken-ichi Karasaki, in *Kokusai Kentiku* (Tokyo), June 1960; "Architecture and Individuality" in *Japan Architect* (Tokyo), June 1966; "Notes Concerning Spatial Concepts" in *Space Design* (Tokyo), no. 96, 1972; "Theory of Dwelling Group", five special issues of *Space Design* (Tokyo), 1973, 1974, 1976, 1978, and 1979; "Okaya Municipal Minato Primary School" in *Japan Architect* (Tokyo), January 1974; "Theory of Homogeneous Space" in *Shiso* (Tokyo), August/September 1975; "House as Culture" in *Kenchiku Bunka* (Tokyo), December 1979; "It Is Impossible to Reconcile Tradition and Modernism" in *Architecture interieure creé* (Paris), July/August 1980; "Mori Lithography Workshop" in *GA Document* (Tokyo), no. 4, 1981; "Tsurukawa Nursery School" in *Japan Architect* (Tokyo), September 1982; "Residential Architecture, Japan: Part II" in *GA Houses* (Tokyo), no. 14, 1983; "Richard Meier and Associates: Hartford Seminary" in *Architecture + Urbanism* (Tokyo), February 1983; "International Competition for La Villette Park" in *Space Design* (Tokyo), July 1983.

On HARA: books—*A New Wave of Japanese Architecture*, with introduction by Kenneth Frampton, New York 1978; *The Japanese House* by Chris Fawcett, London, 1980; *Architecture Today* by Charles Jencks, London 1982; articles—"Japanische enfamiliehuse" by Helle Klint in *Arkitekten* (Copenhagen), no. 10, 1968; "A New Generation of Architects" in *Japan Architect* (Tokyo), June 1968; "Awazu Residence" and Toba Ocean Museum" in *Kenchiku Bunka* (Tokyo), September 1972; "Houses" in *Japan Architect* (Tokyo), November 1972; "House for a Graphic Artist: Awazu Residence, Kawasaki" in *Architecture francaise* (Paris), October 1975; "Villa Kudo" in *Kenchiku Bunka* (Tokyo), January 1977; "Hiroshi Hara: An Introduction" by Chris Fawcett in *Architectural Association Quarterly* (London), no. 4, 1978; "The Post Metabolists" in *Arquitectura* (Madrid), January/February 1979; "Hiroshi Hara: maison Hara, maison Kuragaki, maison Niramu" in *Architecture interieure creé* (Paris), July/August 1980; "Reflection Houses" in *Progressive Architecture* (New York), September 1980; "Japan Through the Looking Glass," special issue of *Domus* (Milan), June 1981; "Japon: 30 maisons manifestes," special issue of *Architecture d'aujourd'hui* (Paris), April 1983; "SD Review 1983," special issue of *Space Design* (Tokyo), December 1983; "Shinkenchiku Design Competition 1984" in *Japan Architect* (Tokyo), March 1984.

*

"The basic nature of architecture is in its holes. The geometric relations between 'open' and 'closed' determine what the piece stands for."

I first saw Hiroshi Hara's own house in the rain, against a copper sky, in Machida City, some kilometres southwest of Tokyo. The self-effacing exterior ran away from the hill, its timber cladding vanished in the site overrun with vegetation—"even in a city, architecture is a device for evoking the natural strengths of location." While the outside was intent on doing a disappearing act, the inside made its presence felt the instant one entered—the levels cascade down, Mediterranean hill-village style, with servant spaces on either side of the processional descent. The extraordinary topography of dwelling is emphasized by the quality of light, fluttering through roof-lights, intermediary translucent perspex membrances, and apertures of various kinds. One had the feeling of standing in the centre of some mysterious mass that had over a period of time been punctured, pierced, tunneled and, through a process of attrition, worn down into a porous, honeycombed space where cavaties and hollows overlapped in a warren of hideaways. The Ninja Yashiki is a pertinent metaphor here, the place of a refuge of the Ninja, a seventeenth century Japanese mercenary: fold-away stairs, secret passageways, one-way views, hidden floors, the very apotheosis of our idea of the flexibility of the Japanese house.

Hara's school at Kasumageseki; the Keisho Kindergarten at Machida City; the Awazu, Itoh and Hara houses—all are characterized by a hollowing out, a concavity, excavation, cave, recess, niche. Internally, his buildings tend to string the concavities together on a linear basis—"to equipmentalize the building so that its spaces participate in the control of the activities of the occupants."

In the 1970s, Hara presented a series of Reflection Houses, where the buildings (largely houses) had symetrically mirror-structured "reflection" plans, reflecting light and sound at the same time. These feactured "anti-traditional devices" aimed at investigating a new tradition. Hara has always had a fascination for primitive/vernacular studies alongside his enthusiasms for the avant-garde, and he is intent on building bridges between the two. The Niramu House (1978) is an example of the reflection house period.

As for now, his latest design-self sees him conjuring "multi-layer structures" packed with miniaturized and internalized cities of fantasy, gobbling whole Kahnian elements, clouds, Art Deco-isms, schematic earth-and skyscapes. The Sueda Art Gallery, Tsurukawa Nursery School, and the Izu Stage of Dreams represent the current preoccupation.

—Chris Fawcett

HARDY, Hugh Gelston.

American. Born in Majorca, Spain, of American parents, 26 July 1932. Educated at Princeton University, New Jersey (D'Amato Prizeman), B.Arch. 1954, M.F.A. 1956. Served in the Engineering Corps of the United States Navy, 1956-58. Married Tiziana Spadea in 1966; children: Sebastian and Penelope. Architectural Assistant to the scenic designer Jo Mielziner, New York, 1958-62; Principal, Hugh Hardy and Associates, New York, 1962-67. Since 1967, Partner, with Malcolm Holzman and Norman Pfeiffer, Hardy Holzman Pfeiffer Associates, New York. Vice-President for Architecture, Architectural League of New York; Vice-President and Member of the Executive Committee, Municipal Art Society of New York (also, Chairman, Committee to Save Grand Central Terminal, and Member of the Advisory Board to its Public Arts Council); Member, Advisory Committee to the National Design Network. Davenport Professor, with partners, Yale University, New Haven, Connecticut, 1976. Exhibitions: *Collaboration: Artists and Architects*, Architectural League, New York, 1981; *New American Art Museums*, Whitney Museum, New York, 1982. Recipient: Design Award Citation, *Progressive Architecture*, New York, 1967; Architectural Award Citation, American Institute of Steel Construction, 1969; Beautifying America Award, *Holiday Magazine*, New York, 1969; Certificate of Merit, 1970, and Citation of Merit, 1978, Municipal Art Society of New York; Bard First Honor Award of Merit, 1977, City Club of New York; First Honor Award, American Institute of Architects/*House and Home*/*American Home*, 1973; Excellence of Design Award, *Industrial Design*, 1974; Brunner Prize, National Institute of Arts and Letters, 1974; Lumen Citation, Illuminating Engineering Society, 1975, 1979, 1980, and 1984; Award for Excellence in Environmental Design, *Design and Environment*,

1975; Honor Award, American Institute of Architects/New York State Association of Architects, 1976 (twice); Bartlett Award, 1977, Honor Award, 1977 and 1983, and Honor Award for Extended Use, 1978, 1979, and 1981, American Institute of Architects; Award of Honor, New York Society of Architects, 1977; Medal of Honor, American Institute of Architects, New York Chapter, 1978; Grand Award, Consulting Engineering Council of Colorado, 1980; Award of Merit, Colorado Masonry Institute, 1980; Award of Excellence, Building Owners and Managers Association of Greater New York, 1983; Land Development Award, Somerset County Planning Board, 1984. Fellow, American Institute of Architects. Address: Hardy Holzman Pfeiffer Associates, 257 Park Avenue South, New York, New York 10010, U.S.A.

Works:

1963/
65 Playhouse in the Park adaptive re-use, Cincinnati, Ohio
1966 Simon's Rock Art Center adaptive re-use, Great Barrington, Massachusetts
Ingersoll House, Sharon, Connecticut (with T. Merrill Prentice, Jr.)
Dobell House, Ottawa, Ontario
1967 Performing Arts Center, University of Toledo, Ohio (project)
Hadley House, Martha's Vineyard, Massachusetts
1968 New Auditorium, for Playhouse in the Park, Cincinnati, Ohio
Aver y Johnson House adaptive re-use, Boston
MUSE (museum) adaptive re-use, Brooklyn, New York
New Lafayette Theatre adaptive re-use, New York
1969 Exeter Assembly Hall adaptive re-use, New Hampshire
Taylor Theatre adaptive re-use, Lockport, New York
Knowlton House adaptive re-use, Sneden's Landing, New York
Newark Community Center of Arts adaptive re-use, New Jersey
1970 Cloisters Condominium, Cincinnati, Ohio, Exeter Theatre, New Hampshire
Community Services Center, Shaw University, Raleigh, North Carolina
1971 Dance Theatre of Harlem School adaptive re-use, New York
1972 Cultural Ethnic Center adaptive re-use, New York
Salisbury School, Maryland
Mt. Healthy School, Columbus, Indiana
Schaefer House (project)
Emelin Theatre, Marmaroneck, New York
Weber Ski House, Straton Mountain, Vermont
Spaeth House, Easthampton, Long Island, New York
1973 American Film Institute Theatre, Washington, D.C.
American Film Institute Headquarters, Washington, D.C.
Occupational Health Center, Columbus, Indiana
1974 Artpark, Lewiston, New York
Orchestra Hall, Minneapolis (with Hammel Green and Abrahamson)
Olmsted Theatre, Adelphi University, Garden City, New York
von Bernuth House, Dobbs Ferry, New York
Pratt House adaptive re-use, Bridgewater, Conecticut
1975 Firemen's Training Center, New York
Agnes deMille Theatre adaptive re-use, Winston-Salem, North Carolina

1976 Baskerville Hall and Wingate Gymnasium adaptive re-use, City College of New York
Terry Dintenfass Gallery adaptive re-use, New York
Cooper-Hewitt Museum adaptive re-use, New York
1977 Brooklyn Children's Museum, New York
Eliot Feld Ballet Studio and Headquarters adaptive re-use, New York
St. Louis Art Museum restoration for extended use
1978 Eye Institute, Pennsylvania College of Optometry, Philadelphia
Boettcher Concert Hall, Denver Center for the Performing Arts
1979 Langworthy House, New York
Best Products Corporate Headquarters, Richmond, Virginia
1980 Civic Center, Madison, Wisconsin
Dance Studio and Music Performance Hall, St. Paul's School, Concord, New Hampshire
1982 Toledo Museum of Art addition, Ohio
Joyce Theater, New York
Hult Center for the Performing Arts, Eugene, Oregon
Currier Gallery of Art, Manchester, New Hampshire
1983 Willard Hotel Master Plan, Washington, D.C.
WCCO-TV Building, Minneapolis
Pingry School and Campus, Bernards Township, New Jersey
1984 Ohio Theatre expansion and Arts Pavilion, Columbus, Ohio
Scholastic Inc. Building, New York
1985 Sports Center, Wellesley College, Massachusetts
Rizzoli Bookstore, New York
IBM Infomart Showroom, Dallas, Texas
West Wing, Virginia Museum of Fine Arts, Richmond

Publications:

By HARDY: report—*Re-Using Railroad Stations,* with Malcolm Holzman and Norman Pfeiffer, Washington D.C. 1974; articles—"Flexible Theatres of Performance" in *Theatre Design and Technology* (New York), Spring 1968; "Designing Random Focus" in *The Drama Review* (New York), Spring 1968; "The Overpermanent Architecture" in *Theatre I* (annual), New York, 1969; "An Architecture of Awareness for the Performing Arts" in *Architectural Record* (New York), March 1969; "An Interview with Hugh Hardy" in *Historic Preservation* (Washington, D.C.), July/September 1972; "Architecture as Environment" in *Design Quarterly* (Minneapolis), Spring 1975; "Music, Architecture and Choice" in *Symphony News* (Vienna, Virginia), August 1975; "Machines, Man and Architecture" in *Architectural Record* (New York), October 1975; "Acts of Conscious Choice" in *Canadian Architect* (Toronto), March 1976; "An Evocative Approach to Adaptive Re-Use," in *AIA Journal* (Washington D.C.), June 1976; "Between Science and Scenery" in *Architectural Record* (New York), Summer 1977; "Inventing a Sixth Order to Honor a Beaux Arts Building", with Mildred Schmertz, in *Architectural Record* (New York), August 1982.

On HARDY: books—*American Architecture Now,* edited by Barbaralee Diamonstein, New York 1980; *Hardy Holzman Pfeiffer* by Michael Sorkin, New York and St. Albans, Hertfordshire 1981; *New American Art Museums,* exhibition catalogue, by Helen Searing, New York 1982; articles— "Supermannerism" by C. Ray Smith in *Progressive Architecture* (New York), October and November 1967; "Design for Learning" in *Architectural Record* (New York), April 1971; "Hardy Holzman Pfeiffer on America" by Stuart E. Cohen in *Progressive*

Architecture (New York), February 1975; "Hardy Holzman Pfeiffer Associates" in *Architecture + Urbanism* (Tokyo), March 1976;"Hardy Holzman Pfeiffer Associates Projects in Re-Use" in *AIA Journal* (Washington, D.C.), June 1976; "Re-using Railroad Stations" in *Domus* (Milan), September 1976; "Hardy Holzman Pfeiffer Associates" in the *New York Times,* 20 February 1977; "Hugh Hardy: Approaches to Color" in *AIA Journal* (New York), October 1978; "The New Madison Civic Center" in *Architectural Record* (New York), July 1980; "Profile: Hardy Holzman Pfeiffer Associates" in *AIA Journal*(Washington, D.C.), February 1981; "LACMA expands" in *Arts and Architecture* (Los Angeles), no. 1, 1983; "Modernism Explodes onto the Streets" in *Building Design* (London), 25 February 1983; "One for the Arts" in *Building Design* (London), 11 March 1983; "Art for Art's Sake" in *Architectural Record* New York), May 1983; "Class Distinctions" in *Progressive Architecture* (New York), August 1983; "Solid and Spare Urban Geometry" in *Architecture* (Washington, D.C.), May 1984; "Indivisible Diversity" in *Interior Design* (New York), May 1984; "Upscale School" in *Progressive Architecture* (New York), August 1984; "For Dancers Exclusively" in *Architectural Record* (New York), November 1984.

The process of collaboration is redundant, sometimes noisy, given to compromise, but essential if architecture is to make structures that are responsive to people. Although there is no reason to believe the urge to build monuments isover, architecture now has more pressing things to do than sentimentalize the past. It must deal with the present, giving us buildings that are responsive to changes, expressive of our pluralistic society, and cognizant of economic and technical realities.

The design of a building passes from abstract to specific and requires conscious choice. The advantage of collaboration is that these choices are externalized thorough a process of continuing pin-up reviews, some informative, some competitive. Competitive pin-ups are used to elicit design ideas that are publicly synthesized into the design intent of each project. Informative pin-ups are conducted by the project architect and provide the design group with an opportunity to assess how well the project is proceeding in relation to its design intent.

Good ideas can come from anywhere. Collaboration solicits them without prejudice from all participants. The idea of an individual creative genius radiating superior instinct over a network of technical drones is at once too monarchistic and too machine-like an image for a people-oriented architecture.

With the year of 1985, our collaboration has survived a twenty-year span of exploration. The results have produced building in a variety of shapes, uses, and locations. This activity has given rise to the series of ideas outlined below:

1) Old and new are of equal importance. There is no present without the past, and putting new life in old structures is as valid as the creation of new buildings. The present includes the past. The future is more of the present, not utopia.

2) A variety of spaces gives flexibility of use for far less cost than moveable walls, ceilings, or floor. (It is easier to make people move than architecture.)

3) Architectural elements need not be unified to provide order. It is possible to have an *order of disparate parts.*

4) Buildings need *not* appear the same from all sides. They can and often *should* appear different from differentvantages.

5)Buildings are *never* complete. They cannot be permanent when the society that surrounds them is in flux. In fact they grow or decline in appearance and importance—without physically changing—and should not be thought of as fixed in time

6) Buildings *should,* therefore, be incomplete

7) Open planning can best be achieved through the inclusion of fixed, enclosed elements, a process called Residual Space Planning.

8) Activites need *not* match space enclosures. Some activities are best housed *both* in and betweeen non-standard enclosure.

9) Standard parts can be combined to make a non-standard enclosure.

10) Architecture is built in the future—not the past—and must be receptive, not coercive.

11)Architecture is a language through which society both expresses and confronts itself. It is made for people, not architects.

12) Architects have the responsibility to consider

Hugh Hardy: WCCO-TV Building, Minneapolis, 1983.

their clients' intent in relation to the overall social well-being, especially in a time of potential environmental disaster.

13) Architecture must resolve the interaction of five kinds of concerns: social purpose, technology, geometry, time, and money.

—Hugh Hardy

Of all the flamboyant young, revolutionary architects of the 1960s, Hugh Hardy and his partners Malcolm Holzman and Norman Pfeiffer have survived the maturing process most successfully and have progressed from houses and other small commissions to generally approved major civic monuments. It has been an unlikely transformation, but not entirely surprising. For additive growth and transformation, or recycling, have been fundamental interests and explorations of the three partners from the beginning in the early 1960s

Even before the firm of Hardy Holzman Pfeiffer Associates (HHPA) was formed, Hardy had defined his interest in the concept of the "additive assemblage" in the Ingersoll house (designed with T. Merrill Prentice, Jr.). And from the first works of the three partners this collage idea was apparent; it was a collage of many parts, with "inclusion"—the early equivalent of the later "pluralism"—as the catchword. HHPA has always posited that architects should include more of the world than the limited range of natural and elegant materials that their predecessors had accepted for the International Style. HHPA expand that architectural vocabulary to include low art as well as high, the old as well as the new, applied decoration as well as integral, tinsel as well as bronze.

Therein lies their growth pattern to maturity and their lifeline to large-scale projects. It is not the witty or scandalizing use of unexpected materials, with which pranksterism they began, that gives them significance, but rather their larger view that sees more of the world, that looks to see the whole environment as it is. With that overview, they came to portray a contemporary America that is both true and harsh, witty and painful, sophisticated and common, sleek and kitsch. For America, like life, is all of those things—accomodating, aspiring, acquisitive, additive, and more. This an overview that is real, and therefore more accessible to the lay public, because it accepts and includes more known objects.

Still, the first thing noticeable about each of the buildings by HHPA is that as a totality each is a work of non-architecture. That is, their buildings are either literally underground, bermed structures, and therefore ostensibly invisible, like the Brooklyn Children's Museum (1977), orthey are virtually formless, non-geometrical, and freeform faceted envelopes, like the Toledo Performing Arts Project (1966-67), that seems to reject any appearance of unified exterior composition. This derived in the beginning from a rejection of architecture as their predecessors made it and from a rejection of monumentality as an inaccurate expression of the tradition, context, and fact of American building. Yet this contextual awareness seems at times antithetical to the individual in relation to itsspecific physical context. A kind of Palladian siting is evident in some HHPA buildings that are not actually underground.

Instead, their self-effacing exterior envelopes are tents for the occupants and for the components of which they are built—for the found objects of our culture, the known fragments with which HHPA composes, like signs on a building. Essentially this is a Pop direction that involves two routes. The most prominent route throughout the twenty-year development of the firm's work isin the industrial image, with its catalogue of prefabricated industrialized components. These the firm uses freely for their functional and economic values as well as leaving them exposed for their aesthetic contributions— structural elements such as steel decking and preassembled stairways; mechanical elements such as ducts and anemostats; and lighting systems with their wiring conduits. Superficially this could be seen as a development into a full-scale aesthetic of Charles Eames's house at Venice, California of 1947-49. Certainly it is a rococo cadenza of the industrial revolution and of man's fascination with the machine. And as certainly it is a romantic revival in representational terms of the classical period of Modern architecture, which used the machine and industry as its pre-eminent abstraction.

The second route in the search for Pop components by HHPA is vernacular building and the roadway culture. Vernacular via Shingle Style is the main source. Objects from the roadway, including the airport runway, are standard building components for these architects—signs, neon, lights of all kinds, and whatever can be used decoratively out of the roadway context. As a sub category of this Pop direction, kitsch and camp objects are also in the expanded HHPA vocabulary—stuffed animal heads, "hideous" theatre and hotel carpeting, and a riot of "ordinary" colors. From what began, seemingly, as pranks and games, inconsequential manipulations and inversions, HHPA have developed a serious and significant architecture.

Also, the partners have always been open to the old as well as the new, to historical artifacts as building components—such as the train kiosk from the Queensborough Bridge that is used as the entry to the Brooklyn Children's Museum—as well as to the preservation of complete old buildings and the adaptation of them to new uses. They were forerunners in the recycling movement, and that activity as well as Hardy's early interest in theatre design has led HHPA into the restoration and recycling of cultural facilities—theatres and museums of large scale, such as Cincinnati's Playhouse in the Park (1965), the Cooper-Hewitt Museum (1976), and the St. Louis Museum (1977). New symphony halls are also a part of their practice—Orchestra Hall in Minneapolis (1974) and Boettcher Concert Hall in Denver (1978).

All of this new vocabulary is assembled or collaged into collisions of form (Hadley House, 1967) or superimpositions of one plan idea on another, as in the parallel banks of stairs rising up both legs of an A-shaped plan (von Bernuth house, 1974) or rising up across a crescent shaped plan (Schaefer house project, 1972). Other collages are shifted grids, sometimes carried to their ultimate completion even if outside the building envelope (Mt. Healthy School, 1972). These superimpositions—an essentially additive process like the firm's early collisions with supergraphics—reflect the use of the diagonal to "break out of the box" of International Style architecture to produce something freer, more informal, and more humanistic.

The questions that the work of HHPA raises, then, are twofold: What is an architecture that is so generally self-effacing on the exterior and primarily concerned with the interior? And how can collage or assemblage be considered a higher achievement than architectural decorating? Furthermore, can any one architecture be representative of all America? Is a synthesis of America with all its regions and diversities ever really possible? And, finally, by including so wide a range of human experience as possible vocabulary for architecture, HHPA includes the possibility of the bad as well as the good. How can that do other than leave critics nonplussed for several years? In their new American statement, HHPA seems to omit one large segment—the formally elegant, the classical, refined, and serene, the world of international diplomacy and protocol, of high society and tact. Only Orchestra Hall in Minneapolis appears to accomodate traditional elegance in a consistent way, and consistency seems almost mutually exclusive from the HHPA collage technique. Instead, the HHPA view of our environment is of a more popularized America—a youthful, democratic, domestic and middle-class common man. This is a sure reality of much of America, perhaps even the majority. But it seems to accept the myth of the classless society, of the one-class democracy, and that is less than total realism. Still, in their ever youthful looks, HHPA has given us an architecture of fun and vitality, of joy and chaos, of additive collage and recycled treasures that is among the realest architecture of our time. Theirs is certainly one valid and illuminating view of American architecture.

—C. Ray Smith

HÄRING, Hugo.

German. Born in Biberach, Württemberg, 22 May 1882. Educated at the Technische Hochschule, Stuttgart, under Theodor Fischer, 1899-1902; Technische Hockschule, Dresden, under Gurlitt, Schumacher and Wallot, 1901-02; studied privately in Stuttgart, 1903. Served in the German Army, 1914-15, 1917-18; Architect for the rebuilding of East Prussia, 1915-16. In private practice, Ulm, 1903-04, Hamburg, 1904-14, Berlin, 1918-43, and Biberach, 1943 until his death, 1958. Director, Reimann School (Kunst und Werk School), Berlin, 1935-43. Member of the Novembergruppe, Berlin, from 1918; Founder Member, Zehner Ring, Berlin, 1924 until it expanded to form Der Ring, 1926: served as Secretary of Der Ring, 1926-33; Founder Member, CIAM (Congrès Internationaux d'Architecture Moderne), 1929, and served as the Vice-Chairman of the German Section. Exhibitions: *Berlin Architectural Exhibition,* 1924; *Werkbund Exhibition,* Vienna, 1932. Honorary doctorate: Technische Hochschule, Stuttgart, 1950. *Died* (in Göttingen, West Germany) *17 May 1958.*

Works:

1907 Main Railway Station, Leipzig (competition project)
1912 Royal Opera House, Berlin (competition project; with Gustav Blohm)
1916/
18 Manor House, Gr'Plauen, East Prussia, Germany
1916/
19 Hans Romer House, New Ulm, Germany
1917 Reimann Shop and Living Quarters, Allenburg, East Prussia, Germany
1921 Reception Building, Main Railway Station, Leipzig (project)
1922 Gaffre Guinle Hospital, Rio de Janeiro
Skyscraper, Friedrichstrasse, Berlin (competition project)
1923 Garkau Complex, near Lubeck
Germania Club rebuilding, Rio de Janeiro
Revenue Office rebuilding, Schöneberg, Berlin
1924 Auction Rooms, Lubeck
Prince Albert Garden alterations, Berlin
1925 Tobacco Goods Factory, Neustadt, Holstein, Germany
1925/
26 Berlin Sezession Building (competition project)
1926 Terrace housing, Zehlendorf, Berlin
1927 Max Voythaler Building, Lankwitz, Berlin
Tiergarten rebuilding, Berlin (competition project)
Reichstag rebuilding, Berlin (competition project)
1928 Art Exhibition Hall, Tattersalle, Berlin
Adler Week-end House, Wannsee Country Club, Berlin
Apartment buildings, Stockholmstrasse and Christianistrasse, Wedding, Berlin
1928/
29 Frentzel House, Elbing, East Prussia, Germany

1929 Plan for Zagreb, Yugoslavia (competition project)
Bin-Copernick Vocational School, Germany (competition project)
Siemenstadt (North) Housing Development, Charlottenburg, Berlin
1930 Behrendt House, Berlin
Karlshorst Housing Development, Treskow-allee, Berlin
Roderstrasse Housing Development, Lichtenberg, Berlin
1930/
31 Beck/Segmehl House, Biberach, Germany
1932 Eichkamp Housing Development, Berlin
Hugo Haring House, Berlin
1933 Design of the *Werkbund Exhibition,* Stuttgart
Kochenhof Housing Development, Stuttgart (project)
Trade Union Housing Development, Vienna (project)
1937/
41 von Prittwitz Building, Tutzing, Germany
1938 Open-air school, Torbole sul Garda, Italy
1942 Kunst and Werk School, Berlin
1947/
48 Housing development, Birkendorf, Germany
1949/
50 Outer harbour, Friedrichshafen, Germany
1949/
52 Outer harbour, Biberach, Germany
Werner Schmitz House, Biberach, Germany
1950 Outer harbour, Aulendorf, Germany
Gert Schmitz House, Biberach, Germany
1951/
54 Outer harbour, Krefeld, Germany

Publications:

By HÄRING: book—*Hugo Häring: Entwürfe, Bauten* by H. Lauterbach and Jürgen Joedicke, Stuttgart 1965; (include writings); monographs— *Vom Neuen Bauen,* Berlin 1952; *Vom Geheimnis der Gestalt,* Berlin 1954; articles—"Probleme des Bauens" in *Der Neubau* (Berlin), September 1924, February 1925; "Wege zur Form" in *Die Form* (Berlin), October 1925; "Geometrie and Organik" in *Baukunst und Werkform* (Nuremberg), no. 9, 1951;"Beispeil einer Wohnung" in *Deutsche Architektur* (East Berlin), July 1967; "Approaches to Form" in *Architectural Association Quarterly* (London), vol. 10, no. 1, 1978; "Two Cities— a study on urban planning problems" in *Daidalos* (Berlin), 15 June 1982.

On HÄRING: book—*Hugo Häring: Schriften, Entwürfe, Bauten* by H. Lauterbach and Jürgen Joedicke, Stuttgart 1965 (includes bibliography); articles—"Häring at Garkau" by Jürgen Joedicke in *Architectural Review* (London), May 1960; "Hugo Häring: Zur Theorie des Organheften Bauen" by Jürgen Joedicke in *Bauen und Wohnen* (Zurich), November 1960; "Hugo Häring" by Jürgen Joedicke in *Arts and Architecture* (Los Angeles), February/March 1966; "Restoration of the co-whouse in Gut Garkau" in *Deutsche Bauzeitung* (Stuttgart), August 1980; "Hugo Haring" by Peter Blundell Jones in *Architectural Review* (London) April 1982; "Hugo Haring, on his 100th birthday" by Adalbert Behr in *Architektur der DDR* (East Berlin), May 1982; "Hugo Haring on his 100th birthday" by Sabine Kremer in *AIT* (Stuttgart), May/June 1982; "A Farm of Organic Logic" by Piergiacomo Bacciarelli in *Modo* (Milan), November 1982.

*

Hugo Häring is an important representative of the "New Building" in Germany. Although he adopted the posture of an outsider, he was one of the few German avant-garde architects who brought a quite unmistakable personal touch to the International Style.

After studying architecture with Theodor Fischer in Stuttgart and Fritz Schumacher in Dresden, Häring set up in private practice in Ulm and then in Hamburg. One of his most important works from this period is undoubtedly his design for the Main Railway Station in Leipzig: Häring broke away from the traditional ground plan and worked his way to flowing, function-related solutions that precipitated a plastic transformation of structure.

During the years following his military service in World War I, after he had settled in Berlin, Häring produced a series of buildings and projects that brought him world renown. In the Prince Albert Garden in Berlin, the Neustadt Tobacco Goods Factory, the Garkau Complex, and his design for the Berlin Sezession Building, Häring used curves to mark out space, and, while maintaining traditional spatial sub-divisions, defined its flowing continuity. Unlike Erich Mendelsohn, for whom architecture was the expression of stasis in movement, Häring tried to show outwardly the function-related movements taking place inside the building.

During this period Häring's credentials in the modernist movement were impeccable. He joined the Novembergruppe in 1918; he exhibited at the *Berlin Architectural Exhibition* of 1924, and the same year (with Hilberseimer, Mendelsohn, Mies van der Rohe and Bruno Taut, among others) he helped to found the Zehner-Ring, the aim of which was to counteract all anti-moderninterpetations of architecture. In 1926 Zehner Ring expanded to form the famous Ring, and Häring was named as its first secretary: in this capacity he took part, in 1929, in the founding of CIAM, which he served as Vice-Chairman of the German Section.

But, from about 1926, Häring's interest began to change; he no longer projected or carried out in his buildings the curved demarcations of space. He began to see form not as "premeditated" fixed masses but, rather, as the result of individual design processes. In the following years his main interest became "basic existence" houses and housing development. He built a terraced housing estate in Zehlendorf, multi-family apartment buildings in Wedding, and the Siemensstadt Housing Development in Charlottenburg—all in Berlin. At the same time, he became interested in the problems of creating rational high-rise buildings and in the requirements of the growing family within a single-family house. With these works, and others, of the late 1920s and early 1930s, and with these interests, Häring had come some way from a simple concern with form. Also, in contrast to the current purist interpretations of white, abstract structure, Häring worked with warm, natural materials—for example, he used bricks for visible masonry, slates for exterior wall cladding. He was also the first avant-garde architect to employ the concrete shell as an architectonic element.

Häring's last designs, prior to the National Socialist period, were the 1933projects for the Trade Union Housing Development in Vienna and the Kochenhof Housing Development in Stuttgart. After the Nazi seizure of power, he was labelled a "degenerate architect," and from then until the end of the war he was able to build very little. In 1935 he became Director of the Reimann School, a private design school in Berlin, and in 1943 he returned to his birthplace, Biberach, where he practiced until his death. Even after 1945, Häring, who had used the enforced idleness of the previous years to clarify and define his architectural theories, was commissioned to build very little.

More than twenty years after his death Hugo Häring is honored, much too one-sidedly, as a protagonist of a formalist, organic architecture. In reality, he was a man to whom form alone signified little. Häring felt a great obligation to the social demands of his profession. His criterion was, first and foremost, the human being with his material needs, his wishes, his movements. Form, as an exterior covering, took second place. Häring's merit lies less in his alleged function as spokesman for organic building than in his search, during the

flowering of the International Style, for consciously more human, warmer variants of architecture.

—Frank Werner

HARRIS, Harwell Hamilton.

American. Born in Redlands, California, 2 July 1903. Educated at San Bernardino High School, California, 1917-21; Pomona College, California, 1921-23; Otis Art Institute, Los Angeles, 1923-26; Frank Wiggins Trade School, Los Angeles, 1928-29. Married the historian Jean Murray Bangs in 1937. Worked as a sculptor, Los Angeles, 1926-28; collaborated with Richard J. Neutra, *q.v.,* Los Angeles, 1928-32; in private practice, Los Angeles, 1933-51, Austin, Texas, 1955-56, Fort Worth, Texas, 1956-58, and Dallas, Texas, 1958-62. Since 1962, in private practice, Raleigh, North Carolina. Lecturer, Chouinard Art Institute, Los Angeles, 1938-39 and 1945-46, University of Southern California, Los Angeles, 1940, 1941, 1945, and 1946, Art Center School, Los Angeles, 1941-45, and Columbia University, New York, 1943-44; Professor and Director, School of Architecture, University of Texas, Austin, 1951-55; Adjunct Professor, Columbia University, 1960-62; Professor of Architecture, School of Design, North Carolina State University, Raleigh, 1962-73. Member of CIAM (Congres Internationaux d'Architecture Moderne), from 1929: Secretary, American Chapter, 1930-32, and Secretary, Relief and Postwar Planning Chapter, 1944-45. Exhibitions: Museum of Modern Art, New York, 1939, 1942, 1943 1945, and 1953; San Francisco Museum of Art, 1940 and 1942; American Federation of Arts, New York, 1947; *Triennale,* Milan, 1957; National Gallery of Art, Washington, D.C., 1957 (toured Europe, Asia, and the United States); International Fair, Moscow, 1959; Olympiad, Munich, 1972; *200 Years of American Architectural Drawing.* Cooper-Hewitt Museum, New York, 1977 (toured Chicago, Fort Worth, Texas, and Jacksonville, Florida, 1978); North Carolina Museum of Art, Raleigh, 1981; Museum of Art, Fayetteville, North Carolina, 1982; University of Texas, Austin, 1985. Collection: University of Texas, Austin (all drawings). Recipient: First Prize, Class 1-A, Pittsburgh Glass Institute Competition, 1937 and 1938; Honor Award, American Institute of Architects, Southern California Chapter, 1938; Honor Award and Merit Award, Texas Society of Architects, 1961; Richard Neutra Medal for Professional Excellence, 1982. Fellow, American Institute of Architects, 1965. Address: 122 Cox Avenue, Raleigh, North Carolina 27605, U.S.A.

Works:

1934 Lowe House, 596 East Punahou, Altadena, California
1935 Fellowship Park House (Harwell Hamilton Harris House), 2311 Fellowship Park Way, Los Angeles
Laing House, 1642 Pleasant Way, Pasadena, California
1936 De Steiguer House, Glen Sumner Road, Pasadena, California
1937 Entenza House, 475 North Mesa Road, Santa Monica, California
Kershner House, Brilliant Way, Los Angeles
1938 Bauer House, 2538 East Glenoaks, Glendale, California
Blair House, 3762 Fredonia Drive, Los Angeles
Clark House, Valley View and 17th, Carmel, California
Granstedt House, Woodrow Wilson Drive, Hollywood, California

Harwell Hamilton Harris: Havens House, Berkeley, California, 1941.

1939 Hawk House, 2421 Silver Ridge, Los Angeles
Harris House, 410 North Avenue 64, Pasadena, California
Pumphrey House, 615 Kingman Avenue, Santa Monica, California
Power House, 5160 La Cañada Boulevard, La Cañada, California
1940 Comstock House, Del Mar, California
Grandview Gardens Restaurant, Los Angeles
McHenry House, 624 South Holmby Avenue, West Los Angeles
Sox House, Ridgeview Drive, Menlo Park
1941 Havens House, 255 Panoramic Way, Berkeley, California
Naylor House, 40 Arden Road, Berkeley, California
Snyder House, 10879 Whipple Street, North Hollywood, California
Treanor House, 343 Greenacres Drive, Hollywood, California
1942 Birtcher House, Sea View Drive, Los Angeles
Lek House, 1600 Mecca Drive, La Jolla, California
Meier House, 2240 Lakeshore, Los Angeles
1945 Fellowship Park Studio, Los Angeles
1946 Calvin House, Sitka, Alaska
Sobieski House, 1420 San Marino Boulevard, San Marino, California
Treanor Equipment Company, Delano, California

1947 Ingersol Demonstration House, Kalamazoo, Michigan
Cruze Studio-House, 2340 West 3rd Street, Los Angeles
Johnson House, 10280 Chrysanthemum, West Los Angeles
Wylie House, 1964 Rancho Drive, Ojai, California
1949 Loeb House, Redding, Connecticut
Mulvihill House, 580 North Hermosa, Sierra Madre, California
1950 Chadwick School, Rolling Hills, Palos Verdes, California
English House, 1260 Lago Vista Drive, Beverly Hills, California
Havens Apartments, Milvia and Blake, Berkeley, California
Ray House, Burma Road, Fallbrook, California
1951 Elliott House, 10443 Woodbridge, North Hollywood, California
Hardy House, Portuguese Bend Club, Palos Verdes, California
1952 Cranfill House, 1901 Cliff Drive, Austin, Texas (with Eugene George)
Harwell Hamilton Harris House, Fallbrook, California
Lang House, 700 Alta Street, San Antonio, Texas
1953 Duhring House, Greenwood Common, Berkeley, California (with Hervey Parke Clark)

House Beautiful Pace-Setter House, Dallas, Texas
National Orange Show Exhibition Building, San Bernardino, California (with Jerome Armstrong)
1954 Barrow House, 4101 Edgemont, Austin, Texas
1956 Antrim House, 6160 North Van Ness, Fresno, California
Johnson House, 1200 Broad, Fort Worth, Texas
Motel-on-the-Mountain, Suffern, New York
St. Mary's Episcopal Church, Big Spring, Texas
Townsend House, 230 Simpson, Paris, Texas
1957 Kirkpatrick House, 457 Harbor Road, Southport, Connecticut
1958 Cranfill Apartments, 1911 Cliff Drive, Austin, Texas
Eisenberg House, 9624 Rockbrook, Dallas, Texas
Security Bank and Trust Company remodeling (Louis Sullivan building), Owatonna, Minnesota (with A. Moorman and Company)
1959 Greenwood Mausoleum, Fort Worth, Texas
Treanor House, 2617 Oldham Road, Abilene, Texas
Talbot House, 1508 Dayton Road, Big Spring, Texas
Woodall House, 808 West 14th Street, Big Spring, Texas

1960 Trade Mart Court, Dallas, Texas
1961 Wright House, 3504 Lexington, Dallas, Texas
1961 First Unitarian Church, Dallas, Texas (with Beran and Shelmire)
Paschal House, 1527 Pinecrest, Durham, North Carolina
1964 Lindahl House, 305 Clayton Road, Chapel Hill, North Carolina
Security Motor Bank, Owatonna, Minnesota
1964 North Country School Cottages, Lake Placid, New York (with Hickey and Little)
Pugh House, Kerr Lake, Virginia
Sweetzer House, Laurel Park, Henderson-ville, North Carolina
1966 Van Alstyne House, 1702 Woodburn, Dur-ham, North Carolina
1967 Sugioka House, 1 Bayberry Drive, Chapel Hill, North Carolina
1968/ Harwell Hamilton Harris Studio and House,
77 122 Cox Avenue, Raleigh, North Carolina
1969 Bryant House, Lake Dam Road, Raleigh, North Carolina
1970 Bennett House, Jones Ferry Road, Chapel Hill, North Carolina
1978 Cullowhee Presbyterian Church, North Carolina

Publications:

By HARRIS: articles—"Ein Amerikanischer Flugh-afen" in Form (Berlin), April 1930; "In Designing the Small House," in California Arts and Architecture (Los Angeles), January 1935; "Wood" in California Arts and Architecture (Los Angeles), May 1939; "What the Architect Can Contribute to the Know-ledge of Tropical Housing" in Proceedings of the Mid-Southwestern Conference on Tropical Housing and Building, Austin, Texas 1952; "Architecture as an Art" in AIA Journal (Washington, D.C.), November 1952; "Rythmic Integration of Panel Elements" in Perspecta 2 (New Haven, Connect-icut), 1953; "Observations on Mexico's University City" in AIA Journal (Washington, D.C.), January 1953; "How a House Can Enrich Life Within" in House Beautiful (New York), May 1953; "Regional-ism and Nationalism" in Texas Quarterly (Austin), no. 1, 1958; "The Architecture" in Dallas Theater Center (brochure), Dallas 1959; "Harwell Hamilton Harris: A Collection of His Writings and Buildings" in Student Publication (School of Design, North Carolina State University, Raleigh), no. 5, 1965; "Design Dimensions" in North Carolina Architect (Raleigh), September 1966; "A Museum Building Is Special," in North Carolina Architect (Raleigh), May/June 1967; "Why Nature?" in North Carolina Architect (Raleigh), June/July 1968; "The Brothers Greene" in Architectural Record (New York), November 1975; "Richard Neutra and the Gold Medal" in North Carolina Architecture (Raleigh), May/June 1977; "Regionalism" in North Carolina Architect (Raleigh), January/February 1978; "An Other View" in Crit (Washington, D.C.), Fall 1978.

On HARRIS: books—Architecture, Ambition and Americans by Wayne Andrews, New York 1955; Masters of Modern Architecture by John Peter, New York 1958; American Art: An Historical Survey by Samuel M. Green, New York 1966; The Second Generation by Esther McCoy, Salt Lake City, Utah 1984. articles—"Houses by Harwell Hamilton Har-ris" in Architectural Forum (New York), March 1940; "Interior Decoration, 1940" by Talbot Hamlin in Pencil Points (New York), July 1940; "Architect Harwell Hamilton Harris" in Kenchiku Sekai (Tokyo), April 1941; "Hillside House for Weston Havens" in Architectural Forum (New York), Sep-tember 1943; "Harwell Hamilton Harris, Arq-uitecto" in Revista de arquitectura (Buenos Aires), August 1944; "Meet Harwell Harris" in House Beautiful (New York), July 1945; "Three California Houses and a Tradition Revitalized" by Douglas Haskell in Magazine of Building (New York), October 1951; "Simple Ideas from a Complex House" by Douglas Haskell in House and Home (New York), January 1953; "Bostadsbygge in Californien" by Gosta Edberg in Byggmastaren (Stockholm), November 1958.

The soil in which these houses are rooted is the same soil that led to the flowering of California architec-ture almost fifty years ago. It is a combination of abundance, love of nature, and unspoiled countryside. Simple as such a combination seems, it has happened but seldom in the world's history. The eventual reward for its cultivation is a spontaneous architecture in tune with democratic aspirations.

This statement was written in 1948 to accompany pictures of my work exhibited in Australia. Of course, other influences have shaped me and so shape my work. Among them are: 1) an early love of sculpture, especially Asiatic sculpture; 2) the discov-ery of Louis Sullivan—his writing before I had seen even a picture of a Sullivan building; 3) the discovery of a Frank Lloyd Wright building before I had even heard Mr. Wright's name—it had everything to do in deciding me to be an architect; and 4) a meeting with R.M. Schindler and Richard Neutra—the men and their buildings: they introduced me to the present and to the particulars of creation.

Though there were other influences, none was as powerful as these are determining my direction. They were made more powerful by the time. It was the time of awakening, and what I had just seen was the birth of the modern spirit, a spirit that had been germinating throughout the whole of the nineteenth century and, with the conclusion of World War I, was bursting ou t everywhere. I had watched painting, sculpture, music, literature and psychology budding. Next it would be architecture, for I had just seen expressiveness in a building. Whether or not these influences appear in my buildings, they nevertheless determined me to be an architect.

—Harwell Hamilton Harris

Harwell Hamilton Harris's sensitivity to site and materials, and his special sympathy with wood, produced a group of buildings, mainly houses, that carried on the tradition of the Greenes of Pasadena and Maybeck of Berkeley. He did not celebrate wood as the Greenes did, using it instead straightfor-wardly as he had little of the willfulness of Maybeck but developed a style uniquely his own—one particularly at home in Southern California, his birthplace. Traces of the vernacular practices of California gave a vigor to his work, and from Neutra came a familiarity with modular practices, which, when applied to wood, carried directly to the source, the Japanese house.

His reputation was established three years after he opened his office, with a small pavilion which had removable walls. The simple platform, capped by a hipped roof with broad eaves, floated above a slope. The house (1935) was for himself and wife, a historian who was the first to rediscover and write about Greene and Greene and Maybeck.

In his houses of the 1930's and 1940's he rarely repeated himself, although his skill in bringing different roof forms into a quiet composition was evident. In his floor planning, to which he was indebted to Wright, there were several variations of the cruciform plan. His many hipped roofs were expressed on the interior; indeed there was a tension between exterior and interior that sprang from his early training as a sculptor; he projected himself into interior forms, and without slighting the exterior gave a sinuosity to interior spaces.

In the Lowe house (1934), there are two minor hipped roofs projecting from a major one; a blunt, wedge-shaped clerestory rises above rooms ranged in a line face the canyon view in the Gransted house (1938); the cruciform plan of the Wylie house (1948) has a major gable rising above a minor trellised gable covering an entrance walk, and a clerestory opposes the two—a measure of Harris's gifts is his ability to order and simplify exterior forms that expand the life within. He could do beautiful little exercises in wood—the scissor truss built up of small framing members for the Johnson house (1948)—but seldom took his mind off the exterior-interior relationship to practice the art.

The most dramatic use of the gable was in the Havens house, Berkeley (1941), in which the inverted gables appear to tie the two-story house into a steeply sloping site facing into the strong winds of the bay. He pushed the house out over the slope to carve out a wind-free garden between house and street.

Work in stucco in California was larger scaled, and the roofs were flat. The Entenza house (1937) was essentially one space, which was extended through a large glazed opening to a deck; the large, cubistic English house (1950) with its emphasis on wall predicted his buildings after 1951, when he went to Texas to head the school of architecture at Austin.

His work in Texas was more compact and had fewer openings; the First Unitarian Church, Dallas (1963), had glass at the perimeter of the roof to bathe the walls in light. Buildings were turned inward to courts as protection against sun and wind; the courts soon evolved from rectangular to more complex shapes—ones to which another leaf or link-up could be added, but which were balanced at all stages. The Greenwood Mausoleum, Fort Worth (1959) has a cruciform court.

Many of his later works have been in North Carolina where he moved in 1962. Here he continued the exploration of negative spaces begun in his courts; in St. Giles Presbyterian Church, Raleigh (1969), the functions of the church were separated into detached buildings, all designed as a family of forms in a family of spaces.

—Esther McCoy

HARRISON, Wallace Kirkman

American. Born in Worcester, Massachusetts, 28 September 1895. Studied at Columbia University, New York, 1916-17; in the atelier of Harvey Corbett, New York, 1916-17, and Gustave Umbdenstock, Paris, 1919-20; awarded Rotch Travelling Fellow-ship, 1922; studied at the Ecole Nationale Superieure des Beaux-Arts, Paris, 1923-24. Served in the United States Navy as a Lieutenant on a submarine chaser, in Greece, 1917-19. Director of the Cultural Rel-ations Division, 1941-44; Deputy coordinator, 1944-45, and Director, 1945-46, Office of Inter-American Affairs, Washington, D.C. Married Ellen Hunt Milton in 1926; daughter: Sarah. Worked as draftsman for Norcross Brothers, Worcester, Mas-sachusetts, 1911-13; worked for Frost and Chamber-lain, Worcester, Massachusetts, 1913-16, McKim, Mead and White, New York, 1916-17 and 1919, and Bertram Goodhue, New York, 1920-21 and 1924, in partnership with Robert Rogers, New York, 1924-25. Associate Architect, New York City Board of Education, 1925-27; Partner, with Harvey Corbett and Frank J. Helmle, Helmle, Corbett and Harrison, New York, 1927-29, and, with Corbett and William H. MacMurray, Corbett, Harrison and MacMurray, 1929-34; in private practice, New York, 1934-35; Partner, with Andre Fouilhoux, Harrison and Fouil-houx, New York, 1935-41, and, with Fouil-houx and Max Abramovitz, Harrison and Abramovitz, 1941-45, and, after Fouilhoux's death, Harrison and Abramovitz, 1945-76. In private practice, New York, 1976, until his

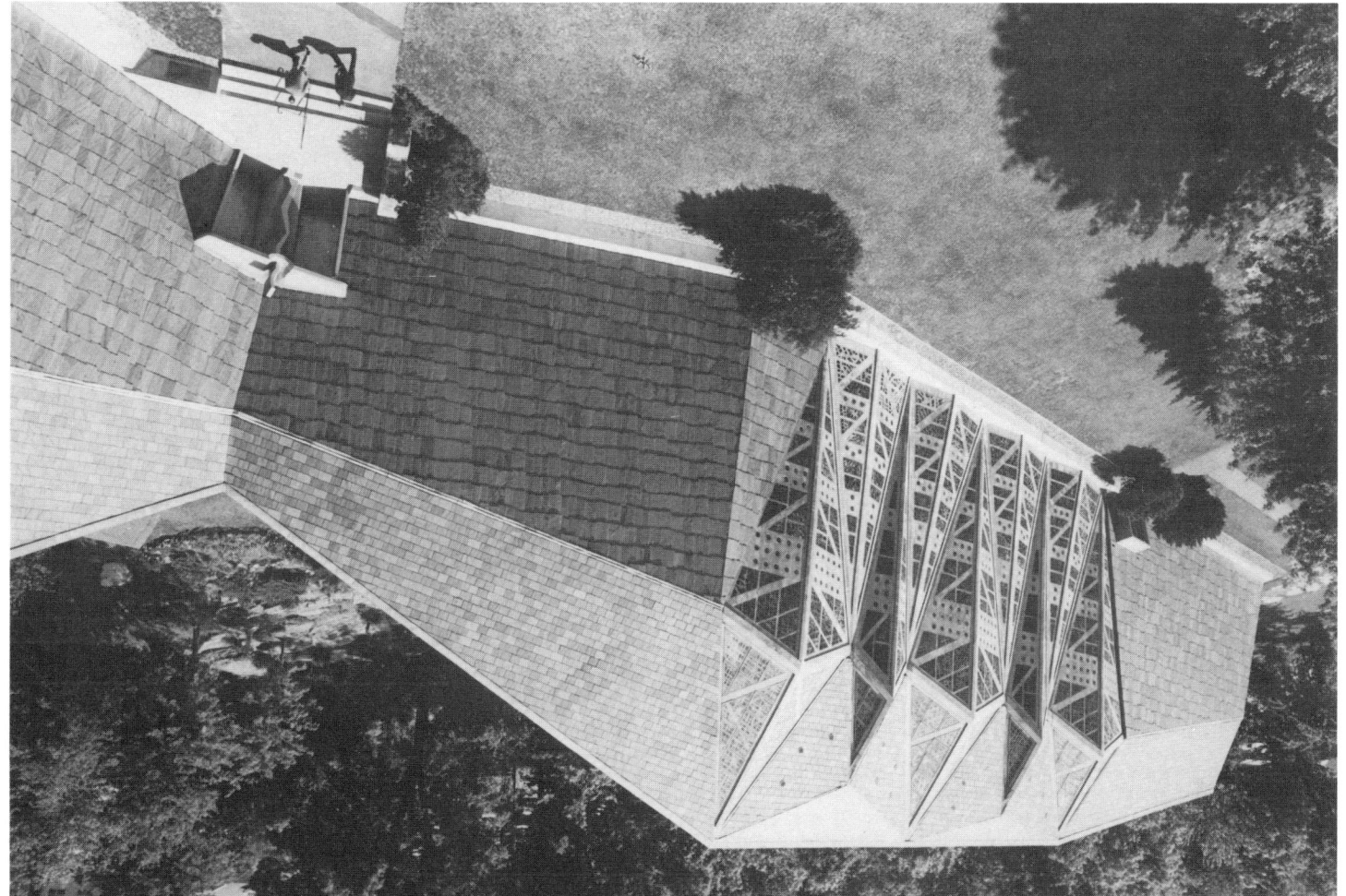

Wallace K. Harrison: First Presbyterian Church, Stamford, Connecticut, 1956.

death in 1981. Member of the Rockefeller Center Architectural Team, New York, 1929-81. Assistant Professor of Design, Columbia University School of Architecture, New York, 1926-27; Associate Professor, and Head of the Department of Design and Urban Planning, Yale University School of Architecture, New Haven, Connecticut, 1938-41. President, Architectural League of New York, 1946-48. Trustee, Museum of Modern Art, New York; Director, New School for Social Research, New York; Member, Art Commission of New York, and Commission on Fine Arts, Washington, D.C. Recipient: Gold Medal, Architectural League of New York, 1936; Gold Medal, 1948 and 1957, and Gold Medal, 1956, and Gold Medal, 1957, Award of Merit, 1954, Annual Massachusetts Chapter Award, 1956, and Gold Medal, 1957, American Institute of Architect, L.H.D.; Dartmouth College, Hanover, New Hampshire, 1950; LL.D.: Harvard University, Cambridge, Massachusetts, 1958; Clark University, Worcester, Massachusetts, 1960; University of Michigan, Ann Arbor, 1968. Honorary Member, Society of Mexican Architects, 1943; Honorary Corresponding Member, Royal Institute of British Architects, 1947; Honorary Member, Philippine Institute of Architects, 1955. Fellow, American Institute of Architects, 1948. Died (in New York City) 2 December 1981.

Works:

1931/ 40 Rockefeller Center, New York (as member of a team of architects including Harvey Corbett and Raymond Hood)
1936 Rockefeller Apartments, 17 West 54th Street, New York (with André Foulihoux)
1937 Avila Hotel, Caracas, Venezuela

1939 The Trylon and Perisphere (theme pavilion), World's Fair, New York
1941 African Plains, Bronx Zoo, New York (with André Foulihoux)
1947/ 53 United Nations Headquarters, First Avenue, New York (as Chairman of the Board of Design and Director of Planning; Max Abramovitz, Deputy Director of Planning; with advisory team of architects, including Le Corbusier, Oscar Niemeyer, and Sven Markelius)
1952 Alcoa Building, Pittsburgh, Pennsylvania
1953 Carnegie Endowment International Center, 345 East 46th Street, New York
1955 Socony-mobil Building, 150 East 42nd Street, New York
       New York Aquarium, West Eighth Street and Boardwalk, Brooklyn, New York
1956 First Presbyterian Church, Stamford, Conecticut
1957 Caspary Auditorium, Rockefeller University, New York
1958 President' s House, Rockefeller University, New York
       Daily News Building addition, 220 East 42nd Street, New York
1962/ 68 Lincoln Center for the Performing Arts, New York (architect of the Metropolitan Opera House; other architect—Max Abramovitz, Philharmonic Hall; Philip Johnson, New York State Theatre; Pietro Belluschi, Juilliard School of Music; Eero Saarinen, Vivian Beaumont Theatre; Gordon Bunshaft, Library)
1962/ 78 New York State Capital, Albany, New York (now known as Nelson A. Rockefeller Plaza; overall architect, and, with Max Abramovitz, responsible for all of the complex except for the Automotive, Justice and Legislative buildings)
1964 Institute of International Education, 809 United Nations Plaza, New York (with Max Abramovitz and Michael M. Harris)
1965 Nurses' Residence, Cornell-New York Hospital School of Nursing, 1320 York Avenue, New York
       Central Terminal and Control Tower, LaGuardia Airport, Queens, New York (later altered by others)
1972 Daily News Gravure Plant, Second Street at Newtown Creek, Queens, New York
1977 Battery Park City, New York
1978 Metropolitan Opera House office alterations, Lincoln Center, New York
       Pershing Memorial design alterations, Washington, D.C.

Publications:

By HARRISON: book—*School Buildings of Today and Tomorrow*, with C.E. Dobbins, New York 1931; articles—"Drafting Room Practice," in *Architectural Forum* (New York), January 1932; "Orientations of Contemporary Architecture," with others, in *Plush* (New York), December 1938-May 1939; "Skyscrapers' in *Forms and Functions of 20th Century Architecture*, edited by Talbot Hamlin, New York 1953.

On HARRISON: articles—"Profile" by Herbert Warren Wind in *New Yorker*, in 3 parts, 20

...November, 27 November, and 4 December 1954; "New York's Biggest Building in 25 Years" in *Architectural Forum* (New York), January 1955; "Architecture for the Arts of Music, Dance and Drama" in *Architectural Record*(New York), November 1969; "Lincoln Center for the Performing Arts, New York" in *Architecture + Urbanism* (Tokyo), August 1973; "A Tale of Two Towers" in *Architecture Plus*(New York), October 1973; "Evaluation: Rockefeller's Two Contrasting Generations of Space" in *AIA Journal*(Washington, D.C.), February 1978; "Halicarnassus on the Hudson" in *Progressive Architecture*(New York), May 1979; "The Gold Medalists," special issue of *AIA Journal*(Washington, D.C.), June 1979; "The Meaning of Albany Mall" in *Domus*(Milan), December 1980; "Cultural Colossi Lincoln Center at 19" in *AIA Journal*(Washington, D.C.), August 1981; "Obituary; Mr. Wallace K. Harrison—Notable Contribution to American Architecture" in *The Times*(London), 4 December 1981; "Wallace K. Harrison, Gold Medalist, Dies" in *Architectural Record*(New York), January 1982.

I have often tried to write about architecture over the years, including the war years 1917-19 and the six years I spent in Washington during World War II with the Office of Inter-American Affairs—but I never had time to write, and, as my friend Nervi once said, "It is hard."

I have worked for more than fifty years on one group of buildings—Rockefeller Center. At the start, it became absolutely clear to me that the only sound approach to architecture is to think in terms of the people who will be using the building—that the function of architecture is to take care of human beings in a pleasant way. The question is, How do I utilize the best principles of design and the advances of modern technology to create the most agreeable atmosphere for the user? When all is said and done, an architect is a designer with a client.

—Wallace K. Harrison(1980)

Until the latter part of the nineteenth century, few American architects had any formal training in their chosen profession. And many of those that did obtained it at the Ecole des Beaux Arts in Paris. Most learned their profession by working in the offices or ateliers of practicing architects and by supplementing that experience with independent study. By the early twentieth century, when Wallace K. Harrison was a young man, university training for architecture had become general, usually in American professional schools, though many young architects still attended the Beaux Arts; a decreasing number learned their profession by working in architectural offices.

After very little formal training as a child and young man, Harrison attended the Beaux Arts for just one year. But before and after that year, he worked in the offices of McKim, Mead and White, of Bertram Goodhue, one of the noted architects of the time, and of Helme and Corbett, with whom he later joined in partnership. Thus, almost all of his training was received by actually working in architectural offices, a feat that had been common in the past but one that had become quite rare by the 1920s.

No one could probably have predicted that Harrison, with so little in the way of formal training, would eventually become one of the most successful architects of his time, make a great reputation, particularly for the design of office and other commercial buildings, and become the leader of several teams of architects who designed great complexes. No one could probably have predicted that he would become possibly the most urbane of American architects of his time and would practice as a principal for more than fifty years.

Although Harrison always said that he preferred his work on single buildings, much of his reputation is derived from his involvement with large complexes. The first was Rockefeller Center, New York City, completed in 1940. Harrison, his partner Harvey Wiley Corbett, and Raymond Hood are acknowledged as the primary designers of this great urban complex. Later, Harrison headed the teams that designed the United Nations Headquarters and the Lincoln Center for the Performing Arts, both in New York City.

For the United Nations, Harrison directed the work of an international team of fifteen architects, including Le Corbusier of France, Oscar Niemeyer of Brazil, and Sven Markelius of Sweden. Buildings at Lincoln Center were designed by Philip Johnson, Pietro Belluschi, Eero Saarinen, and Gordon Bunshaft of Skidmore, Owings and Merrill. Harrison himself designed the Metropolitan Opera House, and his longtime partner, Max Abramovitz, designed Philharmonic Hall.

During his long career, Harrison, mostly in partnership with Abramovitz, designed a very large number of buildings of many types, including apartments, churches, museums, auditoriums, college buildings, and research buildings. But it is the tall, urban office building that he most plainly made his mark on architecture. These buildings are not usually distinguished for innovation or pioneering but for straightforward, functional designs and plans that perform properly and efficiently for their owners and users. For his work, Harrison was awarded, in 1957, the highest honor of his fellow architects, the Gold Medal of an American Institute of Architects. Having received also many other professional honors, he died in 1981 at eighty-six.

—William Dudley Hunt, Jr.

HARTMAN, George Eitel.

American. Born in Fort Hancock, New Jersey, 7 May 1936. Educated at Princeton University, New Jersey, 1953-60, B.A. 1957, M.F.A. 1960. Served in the Field Artillery of the United States Army, at Fort Sill, Oklahoma, 1960: 2nd Lieutenant. Married Ann Burdick in 1965; children Sarah and Joshua. Architect to Princeton University's archaeological excavation in Italy, 1960; Project Manager, Keyes, Lethbridge and Condon, architects, Washington, D.C., 1960-64; in private practice, as George E. Hartman Jr., Architect, Washington, D.C., 1964-65. Since 1965, Partner, with Warren J. Cox, q.v.,

Hartman-Cox Architects, Washington, D.C. Design Critic, Catholic University of America, Washington, D.C., 1964-69; Design Critic, 1972-73, and Kea Distinguished Professor of Architecture, 1973-74, University of Maryland, College Park; Visiting Professor, North Carolina State University, Raleigh, 1977. Director, 1969-71; Treasurer, 1972, Secretary, 1973, and President, 1975, Washington Metropolitan Chapter of the American Institute of Architects; Chairman, AIA National Capital Committee, 1974-76. Member of the National Council of Architectural Registration Boards, since 1965. Member of the AIA Committee on Design, since 1972 (Chairman, 1977); Contributor Editor, *Journal of Architectural Research*, Washington, D.C., since 1975. Exhibitions: *Contemporary Chairs*, Washington Gallery of Modern Art, 1964; *The Work of Hartman-Cox*, University of Virginia, Charlottesville, 1973; *Recent Work of Hartman-Cox*, University of Maryland, College Park, 1974; *Princeton Architectural Drawings*, Institute of Architecture and Urban Studies, New York, 1977; *The Work of Hartman-Cox*, Catholic University of America, Washington, D.C., 1984. Collections: Museum of Modern Art, New York. Recipient: AIA Potomac Valley Chapter Award, 1968, 1970, 1972, 1974, 1976; National Honor Award, AIA, 1970, 1971, 1981, 1983; Louis Sullivan Prize, 1972; Homes for Better Living Award, AIA, 1976; AIA/Concrete Reinforcing Steel Institute Honour Award, 1977; Preservation Award, 1977, 1978, 1980, 1981, 1983, 1984, and Design Award, 1979, 1981, 1982, 1983, AIA Washington Chapter; American Plywood Association Award, 1982; AIA Mid Atlantic Award, 1983; *Interiors* Magazine Award, 1984. Fellow of the American Institute of Architects, 1975, and of the American Academy in Rome, 1977. Address: Hartman-Cox Architects, 1071 Thomas Jefferson Street, N.W., Washington, D.C. 20007, U.S.A.

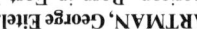

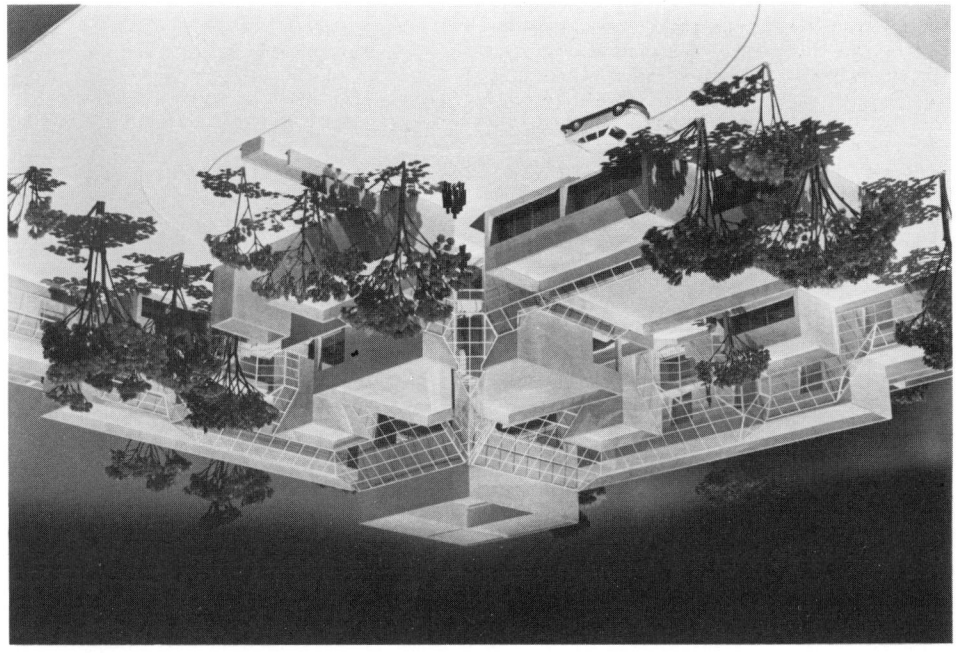

George Hartman and Warren Cox: National Humanities Center, Raleigh, North Carolina, 1978.

Architecture is, as a commissioned art, intended to serve a specific purpose on a given site. The architect's inter-action with the decision to modify an existing order creates most of architecture's unique possibilities as well as many of its problems. The balance between expression, function and context is a tension which at best can neither be resolved nor denied. Architecture emerges as a formal realization of these issues.

—George E. Hartman

See COX, Warren J.

HAVLÍČEK, Josef.
Czechoslovakian. Born in Prague, 5 May 1899. Educated at the Technical High School, Prague, 1916-23, Dip. 1923; Academy of Fine Arts, Prague, 1923-26, Dip. 1926. In partnership with Karel Honzik, Prague, 1928-36; in private practice, Prague, 1936 until his death, 1961. Exhibition: *Exhibition of Contemporary Culture*, Brno, Czechoslovakia, 1928. Recipient: First Prize, State Pensions Institute Headquarters Competition, Prague, 1929. *Died* (in Prague) *30 December 1961.*

Works:

1924/
25 Apartment block, Smichov, Prague
1926/
28 House, Smichov, Prague (with Karel Honzik)
   Dilo Apartment Block, Štěpánská, Prague (with Karel Honzik)
1927 Habich Flats, Offices and Stores Complex, Štěpánská, Prague (with J. Polivka)
   Department store, Danube, Prague (project)
1929/
33 State Pensions Institute Headquarters, Žižkov, Prague (with Karel Honzik)
1931 Koldom Collective Apartment Block, Prague (project; with Karel Honzik)
1936 Sanatorium, Poděbrady, Czechoslovakia
1937 Apartment block, Letná, Prague
1938 Apartment block, Letohradská, Prague
1939 Czechoslovak Red Cross Headquaters, Prague (project)
1940 Žižkov Redevelopment, Prague (project; with E. Hruška)
1942 Regional dairy, Tábor, Czechoslovakia (project)
1943 Car park, Gottwaldov, Czechoslovakia (project)
   Crematorium, Kolin, Czechoslovakia (project)
1944 Crematorium, Prostějov, Czechoslovakia (project)
1945/
50 Town expansion plan for Hradec Králove, Czechoslovakia (project; with F. Bartoš)
1946 Town plan for Záluží u Mostu, Czechoslovakia (project; with F. Pacholik and J. Pokorny)
   Ministry for Post and Telegraph Headquarters, Prague (competition project; with S. Semrád)
1947 Crematorium, Slané, Czechoslovakia (project)
   Crematorium, Havlíčkuv Brod., Czechoslovakia (project)
   University City, Albertov, Prague (project)
   United Nations Housing Scheme, New York (project)
1948/
50 Town plan for Jindřichův Hradec, Czechoslovakia (project; with K. Filsák)
1950 Regional dairy and milk processing plant, Strakovice, Czechoslovakia
   Health and hospital centre, Most, Czechoslovakia (project; with V. Dohnal)
1952 Gottwald Square Redevelopment, Bratislava, Czechoslovakia (project; with K. Filsák)
1952/
58 Vitězného Unora Redevelopment, Kladno, Czechoslovakia (with K. Neuman, V. Hilsky, N. Konerža and E. Kovařik)
1954 Nusle Viaduct and Pankrác Development, Prague (project; with J. Černohorský and Z. Vávra)
   Department store, Bila Labut, Prague (project)
1956 Czechoslovak Embassy Complex, Peking, China (project)
1957/
60 ROH Area Redevelopment, Žižkov, Prague (project; with K. Honzik and J. Sedláček)

Town Hall, Toronto (competition project)
1958 Housing Types Report, Prague (project; with K. Neumann and L. Honeiser)
   Industrialized housing, Prague (competition project; with K. Neumann)
1958/
60 Regional hospital, Jindřichův Hradec, Czechoslovakia (project)
1959 Veletržní Tř. Redevelopment Study, Prague (project; with K. Neumann)
1960 Holešovice-Bubny Redevelopment, Prague (project: with K. Neumann, J. Cila and L. Honeiser)

Publications:

By HAVLÍČEK: articles—"Economy and Architecture," with Karel Honzik, in *Kvart* (Prague), 1935; "High Rise Buildings in Boxframe Construction," with K. Neumann, in *Architekt* (Prague), no. 23, 1958.

On HAVLÍČEK: books—*Maisons d'Habitation*, edited by Morancé, Paris 1926; *Modern Architecture in Czechoslovakia* by J. Krejcar, Prague 1928; *Contemporary International Architecture* by K. Teige, Prague 1929; *The Studio Year Book*, London, 1933; *The Modern House* by F.R.S. Yorke, London 1934; *The Modern Flat* by F.R.S. Yorke and Frederick Gibberd, London 1935; *The New Architecture* by Alfred Roth, Zurich 1940; *An Introduction to Modern Architecture* by J.M. Richards, London 1940; *Gli elementi dell'Architettura funzionale* by Alberto Sartoris, Milan 1941; *A Book about Czech Architecture* by J.E. Koula, Prague 1943; *Skyscrapers* by V. Kolař, Prague 1946; *The New Dictionary of Czechoslovak Artists* by Toman, Prague 1947; *Architecture for Everybody* by Karel Honzik, Prague 1956; *The Road to Socialist Architecture* by Karel Honzik, Prague 1960; *Contemporary World Architecture*, Tokyo 1961; *Josef Havlíček; Projects and Buildings*, Prague 1964; articles—"Josef Havlíček—Oeuvres" in *Cahiers d'Art* (Paris), 1926; "Modern Architecture in Czechoslovakia" by J. Setnicka in *Vedag* (Prague), 1931; "Storia dell'architettura funzionale" by G. Pagano in *Casabella* (Milan), April 1942; "The Question of Monumentality" in *Architekt SIA* (Prague), no. 8, 1944; "The Work of Josef Havlíček" in *Perspective* (Winnipeg), 1948; "The Work of Josef Havlíček" in *Architektura CSR* (Prague), no. 4, 1959; "House at Prague, 1929" by Shigetake Nagao and Yuzuru Tominaga in *Space Design* (Tokyo), May 1977.

*   *   *

Josef Havlíček rejected the national romantic revival that prevailed after the establishment of the Czechoslovak Republic in 1918 and played an active role in the running battle by younger architects and artists against the imitation of past styles. Cubism held a strong attraction for him in the early 1920's, but the transition from Viennese Hoffmann-type Cubism to the new Functionalism was a natural and inevitable process. His deep conviction made him a fighter for what he believed to be of paramount importance. He saw in Functionalism the promise of a solution to the pressing social needs of the time, leading to a new visual expression.

In 1925 at the age of 24 he designed blocks of flats for a Trade Union in Prague. The buildings had flat roofs—then one of the hallmarks of modern architecture—but the Trade Union "boss" had steep pitched roofs added. Characteristically, whenever Havlíček published photographs of the buildings the roofs were left out.

The Habich building in Prague (1927) is a classic example of functional architecture. Behind the street elevation of this comparatively small building are shops, offices and flats. Above the ground floor, with its large plate glass shop windows, are three floors of offices with uninterrupted horizontal windows from

party wall to party wall, topped by three step-back strongly modelled floors with balconies. The different uses are clearly expressed; one can read them. It is a resolved elevation where the individual elements do not compete.

A limited competition for the Headquarters of the State Pensions Institute in Prague was won by Havlíček and his partner Karel Honzik in 1929. The scheme was ferociously attacked from all quarters, and it took a man of Havlíček's determination and staying power to get the project through, but the opposition continued unabated throughout the construction period. Morton Shand called the building "the white cathedral of Prague." It is undoubtedly the best example of "White Architecture" and remains an outstanding contribution to contemporary architecture in Central Europe.

During the lat 1930s, before the Nazi occupation of Czechoslovakia, very few of Havlíček's projectswere realized. He designed a sanatorium in Poděbrady and two blocks of flats in Prague. After the War only two projects were built—a Milk Processing Plant in Strakovice and a development for 8,000 inhabitants in Kladno (1952-58) in which Havlíček was involved as a member of an Architects' Collective.

Soon after the War he was sent by the Czechoslovak Government to New York as a member of the Committee of Architects for the United Nations Building. This was his first visit to the United States and he was strongly influenced by the scale and technology of what he saw. During the last fifteen years if his life the skyscraper in a variety of strongly modelled pyramidal forms dominated his work.

Havlíček was one of a number of gifted architects who came out of the school of Professor Gočar at the Academy of Fine Arts of Prague where, despite the slogans of Functionalism, Rationalism and Constructivism, the emphasis was on the Art of Architecture.

—Eugene Rosenberg

HECKER, Zvi.
Israeli. Born in Cracow, Poland, 31 May 1931 (lived in Siberia, U.S.S.R., 1939-41, and Samarkand, U.S.S.R., 1941-45); emigrated to Israel, 1950. Educated at elementary schools in Cracow and Samarkand, 1937-45; Sobieski Liceum, Cracow, 1945-49; Cracow Polytechnic School of Architecture, 1949-50; Technion: Israel Institute of Technology, Haifa, under Alfred Neumann, 1950-54, B.Arch. 1954; Avni Academy of Art, Tel Aviv, 1954-56. Served in the Corps of Engineers of the Israel Defence Forces, 1955-57. Married Deborah Houchman in 1957; children : Ronnie and Ella. Worked in the office of Arieh Sharon *q.v.*, and Benjamin Idelson, Tel Aviv, 1957-58; in partnership with Eldar Sharon, *q.v.*, Tel Aviv, 1959-65, and with Alfred Neumann, Tel Aviv, 1960-68; Visiting Professor, 1968-69, and Adjunct Professor of Architecture, 1969-72, Laval University, Quebec, Canada; also, Visiting Lecturer and Critic in Architecture, McGill University, Montreal, and University of Pennsylvania, Philadelphia, 1969-72. Since 1972, in private practice, Tel Aviv. Distinguished Foreign Visiting Lecturer, School of Architecture and Environmental Design, University of Texas, Arlington, 1977; Visiting Architect, Washington University, St. Louis, Missouri, 1979; Visiting Professor, Iowa State University, Ames, 1980. Exhibitions: *Today's Form*, Bezalel Museum, Jerusalem, 1963; *Proportion in Architecture*, Carpenter Center, Harvard University, Cambridge, Massachusetts, 1966; *Bienal*, São Paulo, 1969; *Introduction to Design*, Israel Museum, Jerusalem, 1973; *Zvi Hecker: Ployhedral Structures*, Julie M. Gallery, Tel Aviv, 1975, 1980, 1982, and 1985; *Zvi Hecker: Polyhedric Architecture*, Israel Museum, Jerusalem, 1976; *Alternativ Arkitektur*, Louisiana

Zvi Hecker: Ramot Housing, Stage 2, Jerusalem, 1984.

Museum, Humlebaek, Denmark, 1977; *Transformations in Modern Architecture*, Museum of Modern Art, New York, 1979; Mishkan Leomanut Museum of Art, Ein-Harod, Israel, 1980; Vera Biondi Gallery, Florence, Italy, 1981; *The Rational Factor in Works by Israeli Artists*, Haifa Museum of Art, Israel, 1984. Address (office): 22 David Yellin Street, Tel Aviv. 62964, Israel.

Works:

1959/
63   City Hall, Bat-Yam, Israel (with Alfred Neumann and Eldar Sharon)
1960/
61   Club Méditerranée Holiday Village, Arhziv, Northern Israel (with Alfred Neumann and Eldar Sharon)
1961   Arab Village, Ein Raffa, near Jersusalem (with Alfred Neumann and Eldar Sharon)
1961/
63   Dubiner Apartment House, Ramat-Gran, Israel (with Alfred Neumann and Eldar Sharon)
1963/
67   Military Acadamy, Negev Desert, Israel
1964   City Hall, Natania, Israel (project; with Alfred Neumann)
1964/
67   Danciger Hall: Mechanical Engineering Laboratory, Technion: Israel Institute of Technology, Haifa (with Alfred Neumann)

1965   City Centre Plan, Ashdod, Israel (competition project; with Alfred Neumann)
1966/
69   Synagogue, Military Academy Campus, Negev Desert, Israel
1967   City Hall, Amsterdam (competition project)
1969   Dissentshik House, Tel Aviv (project)
1969/
70   Youth Vacation Camp, Beit-Zayit, Jerusalem
1970   Plan for the City Centre of Montreal
1972   Synagogue, Ben-Gurion Airport, Tel Aviv (project)
1972/
78   Ramot Housing, Jerusalem
1974/
76   Marine Restaurant, Coral Beach, Eilat, Israel
1975   Monument, Negev Desert, Israel (project)
1976/
78   Band Shell, Hatikva Park, Tel Aviv
1977   Synagogue, Ramot, Jerusalem (project)
1979/
84   Ramot Housing, stage II, Jerusalem
1983/
85   Spiral Apartment House, Ramat-Gan, Israel
1984   Ramot Housing, stage III, Jerusalem

Publications:

By HECKER: books—*Polyhedric Furniture*, exhibition catalogue, Jerusalem 1973; *Polyhedric Structures*, exhibition catalogue, Tel Aviv 1975; articles—"Gate for Peace" in *B'machane* (Tel Aviv), July 1967;

"A New City Centre for Montreal" in *Architectural Association Quarterly* (London), Winter 1972; "Polyhedric Architecture" in *Architecural Association Quarterly* (London), Summer 1972; "Polyhedra" in *Mussag* (Tel Aviv), no. 12, 1976; "The Geometry of My Polyhedral Sculptures" in *Leonardo* (Oxford), Summer 1977; "Beauty Is the Essence of Architecture" in *Ha'aretz Literary Supplement* (Tel Aviv), 10 September 1977; "Originality and Human Values" in *Ma'ariv Literary Supplement* (Tel-Aviv), 17 July 1981; "Architecture in the Garden of Fools" in *Architectural Association Quarterly* (London), July/December 1982; "The Israeli Art and Moslem Culture" in *Ma'ariv Literary Supplement* (Tel Aviv), 10 December 1982; "Architecture without a Nation" in *Ma'ariv Literary Supplement* (Tel Aviv), 25 January 1985.

On HECKER: book—*Zvi Hecker: Polyhedric Architecture*, exhibition catalogue, by Itzhak Gaon, Jerusalem 1976; articles—"Bat-Yam City Hall" by David Yaarin in *Ha'aretz* (Tel Aviv), 13 September 1963; "A House with a Personality" by Rachel Ramati in *Yediot-Acharonot* (Tel Aviv), 18 March 1966; "Het Stadhuis van Bat-Yam, Israel" by F.E. Rontgen in *Polytechnische Tijdschrift* (The Hague), 17 August 1966; "How to Be an Unsuccessful Architect" by Amos Kenan in *Yediot Acharonot* (Tel Aviv), 21 October 1966; "Honeycomb House on a Hill" by David Rubinger in *Life* (New York), 19February 1968; "Israeli Architecture Spreads Its Influence in Other Areas" by Satish Dhar in *Lively Arts* (Montreal), 27 April 1968; "Geometric Prefabbing" by C. Ray Smith in *Progressive Architecture* (New York), March 1969; "Tinker Toy City Hall in Israel Is 'Spaced Packed'" by Ada Louise Huxtable in the *New York Times*, 5 June 1969; "An Architect Who Break Things" by Evelyn Dumas in *Montreal Star*, 10 October 1970; "Revaloriser Montreal" by Claudette Chauveau in *Culture vivante* (Quebec), June 1971; "The Responsibility of the Architect" by Lesley Hazleton in *Ariel* (Jerusalem), no. 36, 1974; "Das polyedrische Bausystem des Zvi Hecker" by Wulf Brackrock in *Architektur und Wohnen* (Hamburg, West Germany), October 1975; "Hecker's Housing" by Meir Ronen in *Jerusalem Post Magazine*, 23 July 1976; "The Pentagonal Neighborhood of Zvi Hecker" by Menachem Michelson in *Yediot-Acharonot* (Tel Aviv), 3 March 1978; "Geometri på et bjerg ved Jerusalem" by Henrik Sten Moller in *Politiken* (Copenagen), 9 May 1978; "New Angle on Architecture" by Abraham Rabinovich in *Jerusalem Post*, 13 October 1978; "Zvi Hecker in Many-Sided Confrontation" in *International Architect* (London), no. 2, 1979; "Faculty of Mechanic..' Engineering, Haifa" in *Summarios* (Buenos Aires), April 1979; "Work of Hecker: Ramot Housing Estate" in *Architectural Review* (London), June 1979; "Zvi Hecker" by David Diamond in *Nikkei Architecture* (Tokyo), 6 August 1979; "The Architecture of Zvi Hecker" by Anthony C. Antoniades in *Architecture + Urbanism* (Tokyo), November 1980; "Honeycomb Houses" in *Building Design* (London), 5 June 1981; "Enfant Terrible of Israeli Archtecture" by Gree Fay Cashman in *Inside* (Philadelphia), Fall 1981; "Zvi Hecker" by David Palterer in *Casa Vogue* (Milan), October 1981; "Hive of Angular Prefabricated Dwelling Units" by Andrea O. Dean in *AIA Journal* (Washington, D.C.), August 1982; "Neue Kunst aus Israel" by Jürgen Claus in *Kunstwerk* (Baden-Baden, West Germany), October 1982; "Zvi Hecker—An Artist of Two Inspirations" by Yossi Kraiem in *Proza* (Tel Aviv), May 1983; "Zvi Hecker: Oil Paintings" by Tamar Galbetz in *Ha'aretz Weekly* (Tel Aviv), 18 January 1985.

Relieved of the long-standing slogans of modern architecture, we are now in a position to raise questions that have been gradually shaping themselves for the last few decades. We can recognize now that architecture is not merely a self-evident phenomenon and cannot be justified by cause and effect alone. Great architecture never comes into being by absolute necessity. On the contrary, it originates its own demand. Though it records the spirit of the culture to which it belongs, it also casts a lasting image and shapes a symbolic meaning for future generations.

Our growing perception of the complexity of man's environment excludes also the narrow view of architecture as a mere sum of programmatic requirements, even if such requirements can be arranged in orderly functionalistic patterns. Architectural form cannot be derived from function alone but must unfold harmoniously with the confines of an artist's consciousness. He confers meaning on the basic geometric form, which only then becomes architecture.

To express our sense of reality in a more powerful conception of architecture, we must explore and enrich the language of our message: the vocabulary of form and its grammar, the geometry upon which it rests. The deeper our insight and the more profound our mastery of the treasury of form, the greater our freedom of imagination and the greater our chances to avoid stereotyped platitudes, allowing for architectural statements of poetic intensity.

As I see it, the spatial configurations of the ubiquitous cube-form, still predominant in architecture because of inertia, seem particularly exhausted and limited when compared with the vast richness of all the possibilities of polyhedral form, as yet untapped by architecture. Polyhedric Architecture, by assimilating the new-found bounty of polyhedral forms, unfolds, through new possibilities of industrial building techniques, a richness and diversity hitherto unprecedented in architecture.

However, the geometry of polyhedra by itself, inexhaustible and intriguing as it certainly is, must not be confused with the intensity of expression of architectural forms displaying such geometry. Geometry *per se* serves architecture only as an imaginary scaffolding, securing its construction, to be finally removed, its traces only suggested by the created architectural form.

I consider the geometrical principles underlying Polyhedric Architecture to be as much reflections of our ever broadening insights into the structure of matter in space as they are images invoked by the great mathematical and ornamental tradition of the Mediterranean cultural heritage to which I belong.

—Zvi Hecker

Zvi Hecker's contribution to the modern architectural movement is best seen in the contrast between his forms and those of nearly all the other modernists. Firmly rooted in the utilitarian notion "form follows function," classical modernists demand from their architecture economy of materials and construction, pragmatic partis, and flexible, accommodating plans. The forms accordingly should be the logical extension of these demands and should evolve from an unbiased design process generated solely from reason. Hecker's fundamental contribution derives its significance from the architectonic means he uses to satisy these conditions, means quite different from those of the classical modernists, based exclusively on the right-angle geometry.

As a metaphor for his buildings, Hecker uses the crystalline geometry of nature. From his studies in crystallography, he has extracted a myriad of sources for giving organization and form to his architecture. The appropriateness of his model comes from the parallel needs inherent in both the natural and built worlds. Nature's various physical forces present a need for organizing her constituent elements in a fashion extremely efficient in its use of matter, energy, and space. The system which satisfies this need is a spatial close-packing one. Also involved with the spatial ordering of constituent parts, architects are confronted with the need to build with fewer materials, in shorter time, using less space. By carrying the analogy one step further, Hecker employs these extremely flexible close-packing systems in order to develop an architecture responsive to the needs of his time.

Hecker uses the metaphor of crystalline geometry both in his individual building projects and in his plans for the restructuring of major cities. As a source for his synagogue in the Negev Desert, he employed the crystalline structure of a boron and metal compound. The resulting structure is a three dimensional complex of cube-octahedrons, a strikingly unique building. For his Montreal City Center project he used a combination of truncated octahendrons superimposed on a plan grid of regular and semi-regular hexagons as a means of reconciling a growing population and a dwindling of available space. The resulting complex is in many ways similar to the snowflake-patterned utopian city plans of the Renaissance.

Fundamentally, Hecker works with conventional architectural ideas. His planning notions, his handling of a building's programmatic requirements, and his use of the repetitive element as an aesthetic device are all quite common to the modern architect. Hecker's basic building blocks, however, are unique. His three-dimensional polyhedric components and their corresponding two-dimensional planning grids lead him to unusual forms. These forms may indeed be thought of as mere idiosycratic, esoteric, sculptural exercises—or they may be seen as brilliantly utilitarian responses to the mandates of the modern movement.

—Robert B. Nevel

HEJDUK, John Quentin.

American. Born in New York City, 19 July 1929. Educated at the Cooper Union School of Art and Architecture, 1947-50; University of Cincinnati, Ohio, 1950-52, B.Arch. 1952; Graduate School of Design, Harvard University, Cambridge, Massachusetts, 1952-53 (HGSD Scholarship), M.Arch. 1953; University of Rome School of Architecture, 1954 (Fulbright Scholarship). Married Gloria Fiorentino in 1951; children: Renata and Rafael. Worked in various architectural offices, New York, 1947-52, and in the office of I.M. Pei, *q.v.*, and Partners, New York, 1956-58; Chief Designer, A.M. Kinney Associates, New York, 1960. Since 1965, in private practice, New York. Instructor in Architectural Design, University of Texas, Austin, 1954-56; Assistant Professor of Architecture, Cornell University, Ithaca, New York, 1958-60; Critic of Architectural Design, Graduate School of Design, Yale University, New Haven, Connecticut, 1961-64. Professor of Architecture, from 1964, and Dean of the School of Architecture, since 1975, Cooper Union, New York. Exhibitions: *Architectural Projects*, Graham Foundation, Chicago, 1966; *The Diamond in Painting and Architecture*, Architectural League of New York, 1967; *Projects/John Hejduk, Architect*, Le Corbusier Foundation, Paris, 1972; *Architectural Projects*, Eidgenössische Technische Hochschule, Zürich, 1973; *Architectural Projects, Triennale*, Milan, 1973; *Architectural Projects*, Lausanne, Switzerland and Stuttgart, 1974; *Five Architects*, Princeton University, New Jersey, 1974; *Cemetery of the Ashes of Thought*, at the *Biennale*, Venice, 1975 (travelled to Naples and Rome); *The New York Five*, Art Net, London, 1975; *Five Architects, New York*, Naples, Genoa, Zürich, Lausanne, Paris, Brussels, and Helsinki, 1976; *Architectural Projects*, Nova Scotia School of Architecture, Halifax, ; *Cooper Union Foundation Building Renovation*, University of Houston, Texas, 1976; *Hejduk, Rossi, Abraham and Eisenman*, Cooper Union, New York, 1977; *Architectural Projects*, Drawing Center, New York, 1977; *American Drawing*, Cooper Hewitt Museum, New York, 1977; *Architectural Projects*, Oslo Society of Architects, 1978; *Architectural Projects*, Architectural Association, London, 1978; *The Thirteen Watchtowers of Cannareggio*, Venice, 1978-79; *Sculpture and Painting*, Dortmund, West Germany, 1979; *Mind, Child and Architecture*, Newark Museum, New Jersey, 1979; *John Hejduk: 7 Houses*, Institute for Architecture and Urban Studies, New York, 1980; *John Hejduk, Drawings*, Max Protetch Gallery, New York, 1980; *10 Immagini per Venezia: mostra dei progetti per Cannarego ovest*, Ala Napoleonica, Venice 1980; *Window, Room, Furniture*, Cooper Union, New York, 1981; *John Hejduk: Vier Entwürfe*, Eidgenössische Technische Hochschule, Zürich, 1983. Recipient: Graham Foundation grant, 1967; Architectural League of New York grant, 1967; National Endowment for the Arts Award, 1972; Duke Foundation Award, 1973; Municipal Arts Society Award, New York, 1975; New York State Council on the Arts Award, 1975; Graham Foundation/National Endowment for the Arts grant, 1976. Fellow, Royal Society of Arts; American Institute of Architects. Address: 5721 Huxley Avenue, Riverdale, New York 10471, U.S.A.

Works:

1955 Skinner Duplex Apartments, Austin, Texas (project)
1959 Friedlander House, Waverly, New York (project)
1960 Demlin House, Locust Valley, Long Island, New York
1967 Design for Exhibition, Architectural League of New York
1968 Bernstein House, Mamaroneck, New York (project)
1969 Hommel Apartment, New York

1971 Design of the *Education of an Architect* exhibition, Museum of Modern Art, New York

1972 Design of the *Projects/John Hejduk* exhibition, Le Corbusier Foundation, Paris

1973 Bye House, Ridgefield, Connecticut (project)

1975 Foundation Building restoration, Cooper Union, New York

Publications:

By HEJDUK: books—*Three Projects: John Hejduk*, New York, 1968; *Projects/John Hejduk*, exhibition catalogue, Paris 1972; *Fabrications*, New York 1974; articles—"Lockhart, Texas" in *Architectural Record* (New York), March 1957; "Out of Time and Into Space" in *Architecture d'aujourd'hui* (Paris), September 1965; "Me and l'Esprit Nouveau," with others, in *Parametro* (Bologna, Italy), April 1977; introduction to *Judith Turner Photographs Five Architects*, London 1980; "My Favorite Building" in *Architecture + Urbanism* (Tokyo), January 1980; "Cable from Milan" in *Domus* (Milan), April 1980; "John Hejduk and the Criteria of Authenticity in Modern Architecture," interview in *Arkkitehti* (Helsinki), no. 4/5, 1982; "Interview with John Hejduk" in *Domus* (Milan), November 1983.

On HEJDUK: *Five Architects: Eisenman, Graves, Gwathmey, Hejduk, Meier* by Kenneth Frampton and Colin Rowe, New York 1972; *John Hejduk, Architect*, Zürich 1973; *Five Architects, New York* by Manfredo Tafuri, Rome 1976; *Europa/America*, edited by Franco Raggi, Venice 1978; *Judith Turner Photographs Five Architects*, London 1980; *John Hejduk: 7 Houses*, exhibition catalogue, with introduction by Peter Eisenman, New York 1980; *10 Immagini per Venezia: mostra dei progetti per Cannaregio ovest*, exhibition catalogue, by Francesco Dal Co and Ennio Concina, Rome 1980; *Window, Room, Furniture*, exhibition catalogue, New York 1981; *John Hejduk: Vier Entwürfe*, exhibition catalogue, by Thomas Boga, Zürich 1983; articles—in *Architecture + Urbanism* (Tokyo), March and April 1974, May 1975; "Five on Five" in *Architectural Forum* (New York), May 1973; "Architecture's Big Five Elevate Form" by Paul Goldberger in the *New York Times*, 26 November 1973; articles in *Progressive Architecture* (New York), June and July 1974, July 1975; "European Graffiti" by Manfredo Tafuri in *Oppositions 5* (New York), Summer 1976; "New York, New York" in *Architectural Association Quarterly* (London), no. 1, 1978; "Architecture in the American University," special issue of *Lotus* (Venice), no. 27, 1980; "John Hejduk: Constructing in Two Dimensions" in *Architectural Record* (New York), April 1980; "Pictorial Architecture" by Oriol Bohigas in *Domus* (Milan), February 1980; "Ten Architects in Venice" in *Architecture + Urbanism* (Tokyo), October 1980; "Eisenman/Hejduk," special issue of *Wonen-TA/BK* (Heerlen, Netherlands), November 1980; "Medieval Surrealism" in *Inland Architect* (Chicago), March 1981; "Five Plus Ten" in *Building Design* (London), 9 July 1982; "Modern Greek Dramas" in *Building Design* (London), 28 January 1983; "New York Five" in *Arkitektur* (Stockholm), November 1983; "Architectural Querelle: Design of the United States Today" by M. Botero in *Abitare* (Milan), April 1984.

My projects are the result of a twenty-five year effort and search into generating principles of form and space. There is an attempt to understand certain essences in regard to an architectural commitment with the hope of expanding a vocubulary. The discovery of the workings and dictates of an organic development of specific ideas becomes a necessary function of the search. It was from undertaking these projects that I hoped to establish a point of view, a belief—the belief that through self-imposed disci-

pline, through intense contained study, through an aesthetic, a liberation of the mind and hand would be possible, leading to certain visions and transformations of form regarding space.

The realization that profound works in the arts are the embodiment of specific plastic points of view, that the hand and mind are one, working on first principles, and of filling these principles with meaning through juxtaposition of basic relationships such as point, line, plane, and volume opened up the possibility of argumentation. The mind played a most significant part in the support of the creative act. The first gropings were arbitrary; but once the arbitrary beginning was committed, once the initial intuitions were experienced, it was necessary that the organism go through its normal evolution—and whether the evolution of form continued or stopped depended on the use of the intellect, not as an academic tool but as a passionate, living element.

The problems of point-line-plane-volume, the facts of square-circle-triangle, the mysteries of central-peripheral-frontal-oblique-concavity-convexity, of right angle, perpendicular, perspective, the comprehension of sphere-cylinder-pyramid, the questions of structure-construction-organization, the questions of scale, position, the interest in postlintel, wall-slab, vertical-horizontal, the arguments of two-dimensional-three-dimensional space, the extent of a limited field, of an unlimited field, the meaning of plan, of section, of spatial expansion-spatial contraction-spatial compression-spatial tension, the direction of regulating lines, of grids, the meaning of implied extension, the relationships of figure to ground, of number to proportion, of measurement to scale, of symmetry to asymmetry, of diamond to diagonal, the hidden forces, the ideas on configuration, the static with the dynamic—all these begin to take on the form of a vocabularly.

The projects were begun not knowing the above, but knowing that basic orders needed to be searched for, becoming known as the work progressed, as the work was analyzed, as the work was criticized, as the work was formed. In order to have a priori principles meaningful, and to give up and put forth organic relevations, there had to be a given form. The arguments and points of view are within the work, within the drawings; it is hopedthat the conflicts of form will lead to a clarity which can be useful and perhaps transferable.

—John Hejduk

John Hejduk's architecture has evolved through those silent, but complex, exercises in order and disorder which run from the Texas Series House (1954-63) to the Cross House project of 1978. Any symbolic implications these experiments might have contained was carefully eschewed by him. By the 1970s, his studies increasingly suggest emotions which are edited out in the final delineation.

One of the puzzling anomalies of his work during this period is the categorical difference between the hand drawings—vigorous, clumsy, and animated—and the final drawings which became lean, anonymous, and mechanical. It is this distinction between the study drawings and the mechanical drawings that underlies the shifts in his work in recent years, shifts in which the poetic and symbolic character of the freehand drawings become slowly a prime concern. Take for example studies for the Bye House or the Two Family House Project of 1974. In the study drawings, the buildings sit in mystical landscapes and entertain perplexing relationship with the surrounding trees. In the work following, there is increasing confidence in a narrative presence, first fully realized in the Cemetery Of The Ashes Of Thought for the Venice *Biennale* of 1975, and The Thirteen Watchtowers, Cannaregio, in the 1978 *Biennale*. In form, they are rather gentle objects with a filial resemblance to the work of Aldo Rossi; in content, they begin to suggest the relationship between architecture and a specific cultural play.

All comes to a great crescendo in the Berlin Mask

(1980-81) and in the Lancaster Hannover Mask (1983). These are exceptional and significant inventions. Hejduk explains the genesis of the Berlin Mask as being inspired by Calvino; the central concern is the fusion between program and play, between act and stage. In this process, the building becomes anthromorphosized, its form actively participating in the play. In the Berlin set, this fusion of building and actor is only partial.

The buildings are activated, given parts—guest towers, watchtowers, bell towers, wind towers, and so forth—each object consciously displaying the mechanics of its nature. The activated buildings combine with explicit events (book market, maze, reading theater, and house for the oldest inhabitant) to establish the dimensions of the event. Mixed with all this there are examples of a new breed of buildings whose nature is subjective: the Conciliator, the Mask Taker. These directly influence the human player and shape the experience of such elliptical events.

In Lancaster/Hannover mask transformation is complete. All important objects become subjects of the play, actors embodying both in form and content their part in the action, subjects whose character or occupation the architectural form represents in various ways, some literal, some symbolic, and most to some degree anthropomorphic. Among the more intriguing examples are The Keeper of The Time, who inhabits a watch-like Ferris wheel which rotates every twenty-four hours, and The House of the Suicide, from which, in metal welded closed over the body, dead eyes stare at pinpoint openings in conical roofs and turn the day sky into stars. Retired Actor's Place provides both stage and audience. The Retired General lives in a steel-clad armored body. And so they go all sixty-eight, associating and combining into an experience which offers both stage and play of infinite interpretation.

These works herald a new and dramatic presence for architecture—free from stylistic pettiness, reasserting architecture's human nature. This transformation from silent geometrical exercises into a new order seems rather like biological evolution. They have emerged after twenty years in the chrysalis stage into astonishing creatures—beasts of ifinite capacity to speak and gesture and display, to form and tell of fabulous tales, strange, difficult, and provoking, combining the nature of being with the nature of architecture.

Hejduk's one major completed building is the extensive renovation of Cooper Union in New York City. Here, fanciful interests are set aside to produce a convincing rearticulation of this vast Victorian hulk. His solution is clear and simple, and in its strength it possesses the stuff of sheer architecture.

—Alan Balfour

HELLMUTH, George Francis.

American. Born in St. Louis, Missouri, 5 October 1907. Educated at Washington University, St. Louis, B.Arch. 1928, M.Arch. 1930; Ecole des Beaux-Arts, Fontainebleau, France, 1930-31 (Steedman Travelling Fellow), Dip.Arch. 1931. Served in the Reserve Corps of the United States Army, 1930-33. Married Mildred Lee Henning in 1941; children: George, Nicholas, Mary, Theodore, and Daniel. In general practice with his father, George W. Hellmuth, St. Louis, 1935-40; Assistant to the President, Smith, Hinchman and Grylls, Detroit, 1940-49; Partner, with Minoru Yamasaki,*q.v.*, and Joseph Leinweber, Hellmuth, Yamasaki and Leinweber, St. Louis, 1949-55. Since 1955, Principal, with Gyo Obata, *q.v.*, and George Kassabaum, *q.v.*, Hellmuth, Obata and Kassabaum, St. Louis: Chairman of the Board of Hellmuth, Obata and Kassabaum Inc., 1955-78, and of HOK International Inc., St. Louis, since 1978. Chairman, St. Louis Landmarks and Urban Design Commission, 1950-70. Recipient: Outstanding

Alumni Citation, Washington University, St. Louis, 1966; Citation, *Engineering News-Record*, 1977. Fellow, American Institute of Architects. Address: Hellmuth, Obata and Kassabaum Inc., Architects, 100 North Broadway, St. Louis, Missouri 63102, U.S.A.

I came from a family of architects, having a father and uncle who practiced the profession in St. Louis and throughout the Midwest. The tradition is being carried on in the next generation in the persons of my eldest son, George William Hellmuth of Washington, D.C., and my youngest son, Daniel Fox Hellmuth of St. Louis, Missouri, as well as my nephew, William W. Hellmuth of New York City. At the beginning of my professional experience, I realized that the greatest professional satisfaction could be derived from the very highest level of accomplishment. My natural skills—although I have a bachelor's and master's degree in architecture—were in working with people and in understanding the organization of an architectural/engineering practice. In a sense, I have worked with men, rather than with my hands, and the result of this effort has culminated in the vast accomplishments of our organization, Hellmuth, Obata and Kassabaum.

I am convinced that any individual who depends only on himself puts a definite ceiling on his potential accomplishments. However, if he is willing to work with the best men he can find and has enough skill to identify these best men, there can be absolutely no limit to his professional accomplishments.

—George F. Hellmuth

See HELLMUTH, OBATA AND KASSABAUM

HELLMUTH, OBATA AND KASSABAUM.

Partnership; established, St. Louis, 1955, by George F. Hellmuth, *q.v.*, Gyo Obata, *q.v.*, and George Kassabaum, *q.v.* Since 1982, Chairman and President: Gyo Obata; Vice-Chairmen: King Graf (born 1930), and Jerome J. Sincoff (born 1933). Recipient: First Honor Award, 1956, California Council Honor Award, 1981, 1982, American Institute of Architects; Edwin F. Guth Memorial Award, Illuminating Engineering Society of America, 1981. Address: 100 North Broadway, St. Louis, Missouri, 63102, U.S.A.

Works:

1955 United States Military Personnel Records Building, St. Louis County
Pruitt-Igoe public housing, St. Louis, Missouri (destroyed, 1974)
1956 Bristol Primary School, Webster Groves, Missouri
1957 Belleville Memorial Hospital, Illinois
1958 Parkway High School, St. Louis County
KSD-TV Transmitter Building, St. Louis County
St. Louis Five Alarm Headquarters, St. Louis
St. Sylvester'sChurch, Eminence, Missouri
1959 Good Samaritan Home for the Aged, St. Louis
Warson Woods Elementary School, St. Louis County
St. Thomas Aquinas High School, San Fernando Hills, Missouri
Riverview Gardens High School, Bellefontaine Neighbors, Missouri
1960 Kirksville High School, Missouri
Steger Junior High School, Webster Groves, Missouri
Plaza Square Apartments, St. Louis

1961 Blue Cross Building, St. Louis
St. Louis CountyJuvenile Treatment Center
Villa Duchesne Student Activity Building, St. Louis County
1962 Wohl Mental Health Institute, St. Louis
Temple Israel, Ladue, Missouri
Maryland Heights School, St. Louis County
St. Louis Priory School, St. Louis County
United States Naval Reserve Training Center, St. Louis
1963 Berkeley Junior High School, Missouri
McDonnell Planetarium, St. Louis
United States Federal Office Building, Washington, D.C.
1964 IBM Research Center Advanced Systems Development Labs, Los Gatos, California
United States Federal Penitentiary, Marion, Illinois
Psychoanalytic Foundation, St. Louis
Lindell Terrace Apartments, St. Louis
Municipal Ice Rink, Webster Groves, Missouri
1964/
68 Dormitories, Five Dining Halls, School of Fine Art, Mathematics Building, and Social Science Building, University of Missouri, Columbia
1965 American Zinc Building, St. Louis
Student Union, MacMurray College, Jacksonville, Illinois
Conservation Commission Building, Jefferson City, Missouri
Chapel, Mississippi State College for Women, Columbus
Federal Office Building, East St. Louis, Illinois
1966 Dormitory, Science Building, and Library, Hannibal-LaGrange College, Hannibal, Missouri
Wydown Junior High School, Clayton, Missouri
Dormitories, Washington University, St. Louis
Chronic Illness Hospital, St. Louis
Dormitory, Cafeteria, Married Student Housing, Student Union, and Field House, University of Missouri, Rolla
1967 Library, St. Benedict's College, Atchison, Kansas
Apartment Community of Our Lady of the Snows, Belleville, Illinois
Wind Tunnels, Parks Air College, Cahokia, Illinois
United States Embassy, San Salvador, El Salvador
Federal Bureau of Reclamation Building, Denver
Office Building, George Washington University, Washington, D.C.
Office Building, Avenue of the Stars, Los Angeles
Prototype for Canadian Maximum Security Prisons
Dormitories and Fine Arts Building, Maryville College, St. Louis County
Priory Chapel, St. Louis County
1968 Library, Ohio Northern University, Ada
New York Telephone Company Equipment Building, Pearl River, New York
The Galleria, Houston
Neiman-Marcus Store, Houston
Five prototypes for Canadian Medium Security Prisons
Laboratory and Classroom Building, and Mathematics and Languages Building, University of Missouri, St. Louis
1969 Science Building, Women's Physical Education Building, and General Arts Building, Southeast Missouri State College, Cape Girardeau
Library, University of the West Indies, St. Augustine, Trinidad
New York Telephone Company Equipment Building, Elmsford, New York

Technicon Instrument Corporation, Tarrytown, New York
Ralston Purina Corporate Headquarters, St. Louis
Post Oak Tower, Houston, Texas
Salem Memorial Hospital, Missouri
Catholic Seminary Foundation, Indianapolis
1970 Convention Center, Winston-Salem, North Carolina
Y.M.C.A., St. Louis
St. Christopher Church and School, Florissant, Missouri
1971 Emerson Electric Company Building, St. Louis
Equitable Building, St. Louis
New York City Correctional Institution for Women
Hawaii Adult Correctional Training Facility, Pauwela Point
Valancia Community College, Orlando, Florida
Dormitories, Cornell University, Ithaca, New York
Dormitories, Berea College, Kentucky
MAC Building, Scott Air Force Base, Belleville, Illinois
Houston Oaks Hotel, Houston, Texas

1972 Married Student Housing, University of Alaska, Fairbanks
E.R. Squibb World Headquarters, Laurenceville, New Jersey
Kimberley Clark Research and Engineering Center, Menasha, Wisconsin
Sumitoma Bank Building, Pleasant Hill, California
Metropolitan Correctional Facility, San Francisco
1972/
76 Belleville Area College, Illinois
1973 Dallas/Fort Worth Airport, Dallas, Texas
Dupont Company United States Headquarters, Teaneck, New Jersey
Western Union Telegraph Company, Upper Saddle River, New Jersey
IBM Office Building, Columbus, Ohio
Science Building, West Texas State University, Canyon
Bartlett-Begich Junior/Senior High School, Anchorage, Alaska
Penrose Library, University of Denver
Library/Learning Center, University of Wisconsin, Kenosha
Library, University of Alaska, Anchorage
Missouri Botanical Garden, St. Louis
Bent Oak Apartments, Lake St. Louis
Franciscan Sisters Convent, Ferguson, Missouri
Married Student Housing, University of Michigan, Ann Arbor
St. Louis Symphony Pavilion

1974 Singapore International Airport
Quito and Guayaquil Airports, Ecuador
First National Building, Dallas, Texas
Sheraton Park Hotel, Washington, D.C.
Executive Plaza Office Building, Kansas City, Missouri
CAV Building, New York
Blue Cross Office Building, Indianapolis
Lord and Taylor Store, Houston, Texas
South Central Correctional Institution, Eagle River, Alaska
Lake County Junior College, Grayslake, Illinois
Christ Prince of Peace Church, Manchester, Missouri
Community School renovation, Ladue, Missouri
Kodiak High School, Kodiak Island Borough, Alaska
Maryland Gardens Apartments, St. Louis
Central Laundry Facility, Kansas City, Kansas
1975 Kaskaskia Junior College, Centralia, Illinois

Hellmuth, Obata and Kassabaum: Levi's Plaza, San Francisco, 1982.

Southeastern Illinois Junior College, phase I, Harrisburg

Instituto Central, Tegucigalpa, Honduras

Library, Northern Illinois University, De-Kalb

United States Marine Barracks, Washington, D.C.

Murphy-Blair Housing, St. Louis

Western States Bank Card Association Building, San Francisco

Illinois Security Hospital, Chester

St. Edward Community Medical Center, Fort Smith, Arkansas

Incarnate Word Hospital, St. Louis

Health Science Facility, and Pharmacy and Biology Buildings, State University of New York, Buffalo

Xerox Research Center, Palo Alto, California

Greenwich Savings Bank, New York

St. Clair County Courthouse, Belleville, Illinois

West Texas Air Terminal, Lubbock

1976 Boatmen's Tower, St. Louis

Stix, Baer and Fuller Offices, Chesterfield, Missouri

Smithsonian Institution National Air and Space Museum, Washington, D.C.

1977 Mallinckrodt Corporate Center, St. Louis

International River Center, New Orleans

Hilton Hotel International, New Orleans

District of Columbia Courthouse, Washington, D.C.

Medical Center, University of Wisconsin, Madison

1978 Galleria II, Houston, Texas

Library, Vassar College, Poughkeepsie, New York

Science Complex, Butler University, Indianapolis

1979 Olympic Center, Lake Placid, New York

Duke University Hospital, Durham, North Carolina

1980 Graduate Library, Stanford University, Palo Alto, California

Mobil Oil U.S. Division Headquarters, Fairfax, Virginia

Equitable Northeastern Service Center, Milford, Connecticut

1981 Saks Fifth Avenue Store, San Francisco

Moscone Convention Center, San Francisco

McDonnell Douglas Automation Center (McAuto), St. Louis, Missouri

Sony Corporation of America Headquarters, Park Ridge, New Jersey

GTE Corporation Advanced Management Training Center, Norwalk, Connecticut

1982 Levi's Plaza, San Francisco

Owen Graduate School of Management,

Vanderbilt University, Nashville, Tennessee

Ridgway Center, Missouri Botanical Garden, St. Louis

United States Embassy Staff Housing, Cairo

Provident Life Insurance Company Building, Chattanooga, Tennessee

1983 King Khaled International Airport, Riyadh, Saudi Arabia

Galleria, Dallas, Texas

Exxon Research and Engineering Center, Clinton Township, New Jersey

One Oxford Centre Building, Pittsburgh, Pennsylvania

The Forum, San Antonio, Texas

Stanford Cardiovascular Research Center, Palo Alto, California

1984 United States Courthouse and Federal Office Building, San Jose, California

Zale Corporation Complex, phase I, Dallas, Texas

Grumman Aerospace Corporation Office Building, Bethpage, New York

Office Building, 2000 Pennsylvania Avenue, Washington, D.C.

John L. McClellan Memorial Veteran's Hospital, Little Rock, Arkansas

Southwestern Bell Headquarters, St. Louis

King Saud University, Riyadh, Saudi Arabia

1985 Sohio Headquarters, Cleveland, Ohio
     St. Louis Union Station
     Edison Brothers Stores Headquarters, St. Louis
     World Trade Center, Taipei, Taiwan
     Kellogg Headquarters, Battle Creek, Michigan
     Highrise Building, Columbus Circle, New York (project)

Publications:

On HOK: books—*Office Building Design* by Mildred Schmertz, New York 1975; *Mixed-Use Developments: New Ways of Land Use* by E. Robert, Jon P. Abbett and Robert M. Gladstone, Washington, D.C. 1976; *Architecture in America* by G.E. Kidder Smith, New York 1976; *Modern Architecture/America* by Peter Blake and Bernard Quint, Washington, D.C. 1976; *Institutional Buildings* by Louis G. Redstone, New York 1980; *More Places for People* by Charles K. Hoyt, New York 1983; *Corporate Design* by Roger Yee and Karen Gustafson, New York 1983; *Architecture in the Real World: The Work of HOK* by Walter McQuade, New York 1984; articles—"Aéroport de Dallas-Fort Worth" in *Architecture d'aujourd'hui* (Paris), March/April 1974; "Bibliotek, University of Wisconsin" in *Baumeister* (Munich), no. 5, 1974; "The Arabian Building Boom Is Making Construction History" by Walter McQuade in *Fortune* (New York), September 1976; "HOK" in *Space Design* (Tokyo), September 1976; "Saudi Jobs: How HOK + 4 Won a Big One" in *Engineering News-Record* (New York), 11 November 1976; "U.S. Builders Prepare for Superprojects" in *Business Week* (New York), 26 September 1977; "Glass, Concrete Triangles, Roof, Saudi Airport Terminals" in *Engineering News-Record* (New York), 17 November 1977; "Museo Nacional Aerospacial" in *Informes de la construccion* (Madrid), November 1977; "Modules Bloom in the Saudi Desert for $3-Billion University Job" in *Engineering News-Record* (New York), 9 March 1978; "Universidad de Ciencias de Butler" in *Informes de la construccion* (Madrid), March 1978; "Ristrutturazione di complessi ospedalieri in USA" by Denise Lupi Schmid in *Prefabbricare edilizia in evoluzione* (Milan), March/April 1978; "Hellmuth, Obata and Kassabaum et amerikansk arkitektfirma" in *Arkitekten* (Copenhagen), April 1978; "Bibliothek, Vassar College" in *Baumeister* (Munich), November 1978; "Erweiterung einer Bibliotek in Poughkeepsie" in *Deutsche Bauzeitung* (Stuttgart), December 1978; "Works by HOK: D. B. Gale House in Ladue" in *Informes de la construccion* (Madrid), April 1979; "Recent Works of Hellmuth Obata and Kassabaum" in *Space Design* (Tokyo), September 1979; "Winter Olympiad USA 1980" in *AIT* (Stuttgart), January 1980; "Evaluation: The World's Most Popular Museum" in *AIA Journal* (Washington, D.C.), November 1980; "Riyadh's New Airport" in *Middle East Construction* (Sutton, Surrey), August 1981; "Space-Age Imagery for the World's Largest Computer Center" in *Architectural Record* (New York), December 1981; "HOK Office in San Francisco" in *Baumeister* (Munich), January 1982; "Profile of a Giant: Hellmuth, Obata and Kassabaum" in *Interior Design*, (New York), January 1982; "Process of Picking Architects is Getting More Sophisticated" in the *Wall Street Journal* (New York), 13 January 1982; "Three Works by Hellmuth, Obata and Kassabaum" in *Informes de la construccion* (Madrid), January/February 1982; "Hellmuth, Obata and Kassabaum—An American Recipe for Success" in *RIBA Journal* (London), March 1982; "The Odyssey of Levi Strauss" in *Fortune* (New York), 22 March 1982; "HOK's Style" in *Building Design* (London), 2 April 1982; "U.S. Giants" in *Building* (London), 23 April 1982; "Report on the Marketing Methods of the Giant American Group Practice Hellmuth, Obata and Kassabaum" in *Architects' Journal* (London), 28 April 1982; "Computer Centre in St. Louis" in *Architecture d'aujourd'hui* (Paris), December 1982; "Saks Fifth Avenue, San Francisco" in *Architecture + Urbanism* (Tokyo), February 1983; "Moscone Convention Centre in San Francisco" in *Architettura* (Rome), June 1983; "Corporate Headquarters for Levi Strauss, San Francisco" in *Industria delle costruzioni* (Rome), October 1983; "HOK's Gyo Obata, Sculptor of the St. Louis Skyline" in *St. Louis* (St. Louis, Missouri), November 1983; "Affording the Best: The King Khaled International Airport" in *Architectural Record* (New York), March 1984; "Redoing Dulles" in *Progressive Architecture* (New York), April 1984; "KKIA: Riyadh's Royal Airport" in *Airport Forum* (Wiesbaden, West Germany), April 1984; "Airport Fit for a King" in *Building* (London), May 1984.

*

After George Hellmuth completed his architectural education, he did what most young architects do. He went to work for other architects. He spent ten years in various offices but was never completely content as a designer. The longer he practiced, the more aware he became of his abilities to communicate with and motivate people. He also began to develop an idea for the organization of his own firm. Since every architectural commission involves three essential steps—securing the job, creating the design, and executing the building—it seemed only logical to Hellmuth that an architectural office should also be structured along those lines: in essence, one principal would oversee administrative and marketing activities, another would be responsible for design, and a third would supervise production and construction services.

Hellmuth put his idea to the test in 1949 by forming the firm of Hellmuth, Yamasaki and Leinweber. Although this office was dissolved six years later, it had proved to himself and others that a troika approach in architecture was definitely effective. In 1955, with Gyo Obata and George Kassabaum, he founded the now famous partnership on the same efficient principle. Once again Hellmuth took over administration, promotion, and client relations. Obata headed design. Kassabaum directed production

Hellmuth, Obata and Kassabaum has not only remained viable; it has also become one of the most prolific architectural offices in the United States. Designs are diverse and solutions are fresh and practical—yet the quality is always consistently high. Because commissions are varied rather than specialized, the firm has worked on a wide range of projects at various scales—education, health care, criminal justice, transpotation, housing, urban planning, adaptive re-use, and industrial, commercial, and institutional development.

Obata has been the design force in the firm. Although his work is clearly organized and based on sound functionalist principles, Obata's projects do not bear an identifiable signature. Rather, each commission is approached individually, so that the results represent an expression appropriate to the problems involved. His designs are exceptionally diverse and almost always interesting. They tend to reflect the natural features of the site, as well as those of the surrounding area. He takes great care to consider the movement of people, vehicles, and supplies within and around his buildings; that care is one reason why is projects are so successful. And, in most cases, his designs include special interior spaces that seem to have been created purely for drama and enjoyment.

Obata has designed across the broadest spectrum of building types, and he is an experienced urban planner. His projects for HOK have included commisions as large as the complex and innovative Dallas/Fort Worth Airport and as the humane but practical Married Student Housing for the University of Alaska. Other major commissions have included the National Air and Space Museum in Washington, D.C., and the Houston Galleria, which includes two office towers, a hotel, a private club, parking, and America's first enclosed retail mall.

As the partner in charge of project management, Kassabaum oversaw the general administration of all HOK's commissions once they left the design phase and entered the construction process. He was responsible for such critical production services as estimating, scheduling, and the preparation of bid and construction documents. Under his direction, HOK earned a remarkable reputation for completing projects on time and within budget limitations, and, as a result of Kassabaum's inventiveness, the firm is now known as one willing to experiment with new production approaches.

Unlike many professionals who view architecture as a purely creative pursuit, Kassabaum was committed to the concept that architecture is a specialized service that requires precise administrative expertise during the construction process. He was devoted most of his career to this effort and has been recognized throughout the United States for his refined system of cost analysis and control.

—Linda Legner

HENTRICH, Helmut.

German. Born in Krefeld, 17 June 1905. Educated at the University of Freiburg, Germany, 1924; Technical University of Vienna, 1924-25; Technical University of Berlin, 1925-28, Dip.Arch. 1928; Dr.Ing., Technical University of Vienna, 1929. Assistant to the architect Ernö Goldfinger, *q.v.*, Paris, 1930, and to Norman Bel Geddes, New York, 1932-33; in private practice, Düsseldorf, 1933-35; Partner, with Hans Heuser, Dr. Helmut Hentrich-Hans Heuser, Düsseldorf, 1935-53. Since 1953, Partner, with the architectural engineer Hubert Petschnigg, Hentrich and Petschnigg, Düsseldorf (Hentrich-Petschnigg and Partner, 1969; HPP: Hentrich-Petschnigg and Partner KG, since 1972); formed Hentrich-Petschnigg and Partner Planning Company, Düsseldorf, 1971, and IPLA Planning and Consulting AG (as association of Hentrich-Petschnigg and Partner Planning Company and Suter and Suter, architects and engineers, Basel), 1973. Exhibition: *Festival of Architecture,* Royal Institute of British Architects, London, 1984. Recipient: National Prize and Schinkel Medal, 1929, Honorary Professor, National Government of Nordrhein-Westfalen, 1970; Jan Wellem Ring Award, Düsseldorf, 1970; State Medal, Düsseldorf, 1975; IBI Medal, Liechtenstein, 1975; Verdienst Cross of the Bundesrepublik Deutschland, 1976; Europa-Nostra Prize, Düsseldorf, 1979. Member, Academy of Town and Country Planning, Düsseldorf, 1936. Associate of the Royal Institute of British Architects, 1974. Address: HPP: Hentrich-Petschnigg and Partner KG, Heinrich-Heine-Allee 37, 4000 Düsseldorf 1, West Germany.

Works:

1952 Drahthaus, Düsseldorf
1953 Bürohaus Pempelfort, Düsseldorf
1955 Jagerhof Castle, Düsseldorf
1957 BASF Skyscraper, Ludwigshafen, West Germany
1960 Thyssen Building, Düsseldorf
     School, Karl-Muller-Strasse, Düsseldorf
1962 Kaiserhof Office Building, Hamburg, West Germany
     Casino Bayer AG, Uerdingen-Krefeld, West Germany
     British American Tobacco Building, Hamburg, West Germany
     High-rise apartments, Dorotheenstrasse, Hamburg, West Germany

1963 Applied Technology Department of the BASF Company, Ludwigshafen, West Germany
Bayer Skyscraper, Leverkusen, West Germany
Knoll Research Centre, Ludwigshafen, West Germany
Horten Department Store, Neuss, West Germany

1964 Europa Cente, Berlin
Klockner-Humb. Main Administration Building, Deutz, Cologne
Unilever House, Hamburg, West Germany

1965 Family housing estate, Elbchaussee, Hamburg, West Germany
Garath Church, Düsseldrof
Research Building C6 for BASF, Ludwigshafen, West Germany

1966 Finnlandhaus, Hamburg, West Germany
A and M Administration Building, Aachen, West Germany
BASF Laboratory, Ludwigshafen, West Germany

1967 German Africa Lines Building, Hamburg, West Germany

1968 Hoechst Calculating Centre, Frankfurt
Carp-Haus, Düsseldorf
Wayss and Freytag Administration Building, Düsseldorf

1969 Finance Management Building, Münster, West Germany

1970 Procter and Gamble Main Administration Building, Schwalbach, West Germany
WDR Administration Building, Cologne

Engineering School, Düsseldorf
Standard Bank Centre, Johannesburg, South Africa
Horten Department Store, Krefeld, West Germany
Rank Xerox Main Administration Building, Düsseldorf
Ruhr University, Bochum, West Germany

1971 Post Office Headquarters, Hannover

1972 Hillbrow Centre, Johannesburg, South Africa
Sternhaus, Düsseldorf
Thyssen Trade Fair Building, Hannover

1973 Town Hall, Hovel, West Germany
Municipal Savings Bank, Düsseldorf
ERCO Factory, Ludenscheid, West Germany
Post Office, Hannover

1974 VEBA House, Düsseldorf
TUV Main Administration Building, Cologne
A and M Main Administration Building, Frankfurt
Diamond sorting building, Kimberley, South Africa
RWI House, Düsseldorf
Town Hall, Wesel, West Germany
Old Leipzig Administration Building, Oberursel, West Germany
Kapuziner Housing Estate, Cologne

1976 Preussenlektra Administration Building, Hannover
South German Iron and Steel Administration Building, Mainz, West Germany

1977 Klockner Administration and Calculating Centre, Bremen, West Germany

Rhein Braun Main Administration Building, Cologne
West District Telephone Exchange, Cologne

1978 Klockner House, Duisburg, West Germany
Concert Hall, Düsseldorf
German-Japanese Centre, Düsseldorf
IBM Building, Düsseldorf

1979 Landesbank Accounting Centre, Kiel, West Germany

1980 Sempell Administration Building, Korschenbroich, West Germany
Signal Insurance Company Headquarters, Dortmund, West Germany
Nordrhein-Westfalen Ministry of the Interior Building, Düsseldorf

1981 Sheraton Hotel, Essen, West Germany
KHD Accounting Centre, Cologne
Town Hall, Steinfurt, West Germany

1982 HPP-Haus offices, Düsseldorf
Rahe Castle, Aachen, West Germany
Old Rail Station buildings, Bad Homburg, West Germany
Heidelberger Printing Machine Administration Building, Heidelberg, West Germany

1983 KKB-Bank Accounting Centre, Meerbusch, West Germany
Trade Press Building, Düsseldorf
Housing, Limburgstrasse, Düsseldorf
Housing, Hohestrasse, Düsseldorf
Town Hall, Pulheim, West Germany
Ursulines School, Düsseldorf

Helmut Hentrich: Sempel Administration Building, Korsenbroich, West Germany, 1980.

Publications:

By HENTRICH: books—*Buildings 1953-1969,* with Hentrich-Petschnigg and Partners, Düsseldorf, 1969; *Standard Bank, Johannesburg,* Johannesburg 1970; *Buildings 1970-71,* with Hentrich-Petschnigg and Partners, Düsseldorf 1971; *Denkmalpflege 1947-1972,* with Hentrich-Petschnigg and Partners, Düsseldorf 1972; *Buildings 1972-75,* with Hentrich-Petschnigg and Partners, Düsseldorf 1975; *Interior Design,* with Hentrich-Petschnigg and Partners, Düsseldorf 1977; *Entwicklungstendenzen im Verwaltungsbau,* with Hentrich-Petschnigg and Partners, Düsseldorf 1977; *Buildings 1976-1979,* with Hentrich-Petschnigg and Partners, Düsseldorf 1979; *50 Jahre HPP,* with Hentrich-Petschnigg and Partners, Düsseldorf 1983.

On HENTRICH: books—*The BASF Skyscraper,* by BASF editors, Stuttgart 1959; *The Thyssenhaus* by Martin Mittag, Essen, West Germany 1962; *The BASF Laboratory Building* by Martin Mittag, Essen, West Germany 1963; *The Bayer Skyscraper* by Martin Mittag, Essen, West Germany 1963; *Klockner-Humboldt-Deutz* by Paulhans Peters, Munich 1965; *Unilever-Haus, Hamburg,* by Paulhans Peters, Munich 1966; *Finnlandhaus, Hamburg* by Fritz Rafeiner, Munich 1968; *The Hoechst Calculating Centre* by Bruno Krekler, Munich 1970; *The Procter and Gamble Administration Centre* by Bruno Krekler, Munich 1970; *Administration Buildings* by Bruno Krekler, Munich 1973; *Research Laboratories* by Bruno Krekler, Munich 1975; *The New Administration Buildings of Old Leipzig in Oberursel* by the Old Leipzig Administration Editors, Oberursel, West Germany 1975; *Tonhalle Düsseldorf* by Landeshauptstadt editors, Dusseldorf 1978.

*

My guiding principle is from Georges Bernanos: "I do not know whether life loves me but by the Grace of God I love this life through which fools rush without giving themselvews time to look, this life full of amazing mysteries held in readiness for mankind."

—Helmut Hentrich

*

Helmut Hentrich, with his partner Hubert Petschnigg, in the firm now known as HPP: Hentrich-Petschnigg und Partner, became well known mainly for office and adminstration buildings in a style that even today characterizes postwar German architecture. The international Style of Mies van der Rohe or Skidmore, Owings and Merrill did not, in the march of the Americanization of Western Europe, halt at the borders of the Federal Republic. Uniform skyscrapers arose that, unlimited and immoderate, standardized and monotonous, the casual passerby could, in his thoughts, freely recompose.

The best-known example of HPP architecture is the Thyssen Building in Düsseldorf, and the best-known photograph of this edifice is one taken from the nearby Park Lake: it shows two of the three sections in a highly distorted side view. It mirrors the attempt at elegance of a young Federal Republic aspiring at the same time to economic power. Seen from the front, the building, in spite of the different heights of the two visible sections, looks like a monolithic box: the typical German steel-skeleton building totally lacks American luxury in the use of building materials (as in Mies's Seagram Building in New York); in Germany there is additional "frugality" for those who admire the coolness and severity of curtain walling.

HPP's Europa Centre is presented as the first covered shopping centre in Berlin. But violent gusts of wind in the shopping arcades below made stuctural alterations necessary in the 1970s. HPP also developed the first standard facade components for the department store concern Horten AG. They determine today the appearance of all branches in the Federal Republic, whether in a large city or a small town, whatever the characteristics of nearby old or modern architecture. "Identification" of a particular town or city by the forms of its facades or building masses is made increasingly difficult.

HPP have adjusted the facades of their skyscrapers to the fashionable tendencies of the age—from the smooth curtain walling of the 1950s, via the window hatches set into exposed concrete of the 1960s, to the bevelled corners of the 1970s. HPP won the competition for the Ruhr University in Bochum. After a more than ten-year construction period, the building complex was handed over for use to the students; it is a practically structureless example of gigantomachy. The two monotonous rows of the layout, the lack of differentiation in the buildings, the negation of the individuality of the interior courts, and the brutal exposed concrete were all found continually more oppressive by the users. On the other hand, HPP did find inspiration in technical and economic necessity in the Standard Bank Centre in Johannesburg, an office building in three sections, each of nine storeys, which are hung one over the other on a central core. No problem in that: in Johannesburg, buildings may be high so thatthe built-over surface at pedestrian level is limited.

In the postwar period, HPP produced small-format designs for churches and single-family houses, and they have been involved in the restoration and careful rebuilding of historic buildings. They have won more than fifty national and international competitions.

—Christian Borngräber

HERRON, Ronald James.

British. Born in London, 12 August 1930. Educated at various elementary and secondary schools in London, 1934-44; Brixton School of Building, London, 1944-47, and the Brixton School of Building Department of Architecture, evening course, 1950-54; Regent Street Polytechnic, London, evening course, 1954-56. Served in the Royal Air Force, in Germany, 1949-50. Married Patricia Ginn in 1952; children: Andrew and Simon. Architect with the Greater London Council, 1954-61; Founder Member, with Peter Cook, Dennis Crompton, Warren Chalk, Mike Webb and David Greene, Archigram Group, London, 1960, and Co-Editor of *Archigram* magazine, 1960-70; Deputy Architect, Taylor Woodow Construction Ltd., London, 1961-65; Associate, Halpern and Partners, London, 1965-67; Consultant Architect to Colin St. John Wilson, Cambridge, 1967; in private practice, London, 1968; Director of Urban Design, William Pereira and Partners, Los Angeles, 1969-70; Partner, with Cook and Crompton, Archigram Architects, London, 1970-75; in private practice, as Ron Herron, Architect, London, 1975-77; Partner, Pentagram Design, London, 1977-80; Partner, Derek Walker Associates, London and Milton Keynes, Buckinghamshire, 1981-82; Principal, Ron Herron Associates, Architects and Designers, London, since 1982. Tutor, Architectural Association School, London, 1965-68, and since 1970; 2nd Year Master, North London Polytechnic School of Architecture, 1968; Visiting Professor, University of California at Los Angeles, 1968-69, University of Southern California, Los Angeles, 1976, 1977, 1979, and Southern California Institute for Architecture, Los Angeles, 1982; Artist-in-Residence, University of Wisconsin, Madison, 1972; Visiting Lecturer, Universities of New Mexico and Colorado, and Rice University, Houston, 1972, Columbia University, New York, 1972, 1974, University of California, Berkeley, 1972, 1979, Pratt Institute, New York, 1974, Institute for Architecture and Urban Studies, New York, Cornell University, Ithaca, New York, and Massachusetts Institute of Technology, 1975, Universities of Liverpool, Trondheim and Eindhoven, and Institute of Architecture, Barcelona, 1976, Art Net, London, 1976, 1977, 1978, Building Centre, Berlin, 1977, Southern California Institute of Architecture, Los Angeles, 1977, 1978, University of California at Los Angeles, 1977, 1979, Royal Institute of British Architects, London, 1978, Rietveld Academy, Amsterdam, School of Design, Breda, and the Universities of Stockholm, Helsinki and Oslo, 1980. Exhibitions: *Biennale,* Paris, 1967; *Triennale,* Milan, 1968; *Archigram,* Institute of Contemporary Arts, London, 1973; *House for a Superstar,* Art Net Gallery, London, 1975; *40 London Architects,* Art Net Gallery, London, 1977, toured Europe; *Ron Herron: insertions projects,* Art Net Gallery, London, 1977, and Institute for Architecture and Urban Studies, New York, 1978; *Visionary Architecture,* New York, 1979; *Ron Herron: 20 years of drawing,* Architectural Association, London, 1980; *Peter Cook/Ron Herron,* Galerie fur Architektur und Raum, Berlin, 1981; *Cook + Herron,* SCI-ARC Gallery, Los Angeles, 1982; *Architecture et Industrie,* Centre Pompidou, Paris, 1983; *Images et Imaginaires d'Architecture,* Centre Pompidou, Paris, 1984. Recipient: Graham Foundation Fellowship, with Cook and Crompton, 1968; First Prize, with Archigram Group, Monte Carlo Entertainment Centre Competition, 1970. Associate of the Royal Institute of British Architects; Fellow of the Society of Industrial Artists and Designers, and of the Royal Society of Arts, London. Address: Ron Herron Associates, 231 North Gower Street, London NW1 2NS, England.

Works:

1954/
58 Starcross Secondary School, London
Prospect County Secondary School, St. Pancras, London
Student Hostel, Northampton College of Advance Technology
1958/
60 Woolwich Polytechnic extension, London
1963 City Interchange (project; with Warren Chalk)
1964 Study of Twilight areas: Fulham (with Theo Crosby)
"Walking City" (project)
1965 Clarksons Shipping Ltd. Headquarters Building, London (project; with Theo Crosby)
Maternity Wing, Royal Berkshire Hospital, Reading
Gasket House (project; with Warren Chalk)
1966 Free-time Node (project; with Barry Snowden)
Inflatable Dwellings (project; with Barry Snowden)
"Air-Hab" (project; with Barry Snowden)
Shopping Centre, Tredegar, Wales
Shopping Centre, Aberdare, Wales (project)
1967 "House 199-90" (project; with Archigram Group)
"Control and Choice" (project; with Peter Cook and Dennis Crompton)
Amsterdam Town hall (project; with Alex Pike and Barry Snowden)
1968 "Tuned Suburb" (project)
"Oasis" (project)
"Instant City" (project; with Peter Cook and Dennis Crompton)
Housing development at Pacific Palisades, California (project; with Warren Chalk)
1969 Master plan for a new town for the Ford Motor Company at Dearborn, Michigan (project)
"Manzak" (project)
Air terminal at Los Angeles International Airport for Pan American Airlines (project)
1970 Hotel and offices for the Embarcadero Site, San Francisco (project)
Teaching facility for the University of Missouri (project)
"Holographic Scene Setter" (project)

Ron Herron: Demountable rehearsal space for the Lyric Theatre, London, 1982.

Entertainment facility for Monte Carlo (project)

1971 Conference facility and shopping complex at Bournemouth, Hampshire (project)

1972 Casino at Monte Carlo (project; with Archigram Architects)

"Promotional Event Kit" (project; with Barry Snowden)

Development plan for Margate, Kent (project)

1973 Swimming pool and kitchen block for Rod Stewart, Windsor, Berkshire (with Archigram Architects)

"Tuning London" (project; with Diana Jowsey)

Northampton Civic Centre (project; with Archie McNab)

Glasgow river front (project; with Archie McNab)

Offices for the British Oxygen Company, Dublin (project; with Archigram Architects)

1974 Furniture for Cassina, Milan (project; with Archigram Architects)

"Suburban Sets" (project; with Andrew Herron)

Student Centre, Trondheim, Norway (project; with C. Price, P. Kartvedt, T. Dugdale, and Archigram Architects)

1975 Play centre at Calverton End, Milton Keynes (with Archigram Architects)

"Sets Fit for the Queen" (project)

Theatre extension, Trondheim, Norway (project; with Pier Kartvedt)

1976 Government offices, Mineritenplatz, Vienna (project; with Theo Crosby)

Development of the central area of Heathrow Airport, London (project)

1977 Trondheim Library, Norway (project; with Per Kartvedt)

St. Christopher's Place Development, London (with Pentagram)

1978 Bubble Theatre Company inflatable theatre, London (with Pentagram)

Chrysalis Record Offices, London (with Pentagram)

A. T. Kearney Offices, London (with Pentagram)

Cape Products exhibit, at Building Exhibition, Birmingham

1979 Directors' Studio offices and studio, London (with Pentagram)

Boston Consultancy Group offices, London (with Pentagram)

British Telecom new confravision studio and business centre, Bristol, Avon (with Pentagram)

Library, Stavanger, Norway (competition project)

1980 Stromberger Factory site development, Clichy, Paris (project; with Pentagram)

Pentagram exhibit, Linz, Austria (with Alan Fletcher)

Reuters Office, Press Centre, London (with Pentagram)

Swan and Edgar Department Store redevelopment, London (project; with Pentagram)

D.O.M. Office headquarters, Cologne, Germany (competition project; with Peter Cook and Christine Hawley)

Congress Hall inflatable, Berlin (competition project)

Eames House remodelling (competition project; with Donna Brown and Caroline Smith)

1981 Jubail City Business Centre Plan, Saudi Arabia (with Derek Walker Associates)

Urban Sets (competition project; with Andrew and Simon Herron)

Wonderworld theme park, Corby, Northamptonshire (project; with Derek Walker)

1982 L'Oreal offices and hairdressing school, London (with Walker Wright)

Blackrod video production studio and offices, London

Lyric Theatre demountable rehearsal theatre, London

Bankside Power Station entertainment complex conversion, London (feasibility study)

The Peak housing development, Hong Kong (competition project)

The Dolls House, London (competition pro-

ject; with Andrew and Simon Herron)

1983 La Defense development, Paris (competition project; with Warren Chalk)

Battersea Power Station redevelopment, London (projects; with Y.R.M. Architects)

Strategic Planning Associates offices, London

Imagination Ltd. television and sound studios, offices and event spaces, Isle of Dogs, London (project; with Tom Law Associates)

1984 Unity of Man, travelling exhibition layouts, for IBM and the Commonwealth Institute, London (with Richard Leakey)

Gurney Gardens, Penang, Malaysia (project)

Theme Park, Cairo, Egypt (project; with Michael Cassidy Architects)

Imperial Tobacco Company R & D Laboratories, Bristol, Avon

Designs: British Industry section, British Design Exhibition, with Archigram, Paris, 1971; Malaysia Exhibit, Commonwealth Institute, with Archigram, London, 1973; Islamic Art and Architecture Exhibition, Architectural Association, with Dennis Crompton, London, 1976; Frei Otto Exhibition, Architectural Association, London, 1976; Trailer Exhibition, with Pentagram, Milton Keynes, 1978; Pentagram Exhibition, Linz International Fair, with Alan Fletcher, Austria, 1980; Erno Goldfinger Exhibition, with June McGowan, Vicky Wilson and Amanda Innes, Architectural Association, London, 1983; Eduardo Paolozzi Exhibition, Architectural Association, London, 1984.

Publications:

By HERRON: book—Archigram, editor with Peter Cook, London 1973; articles—various projects and writings in Archigram (London), nos. 1-9, 1960-70; "Living City" in Living Arts (London), no. 2, 1963; "Japan's Arata Isozaki" in Lotus (Venice), no. 6, 1969; "Archigram" in Design Quarterly (Minneapolis), no. 74/75, 1969; "Instant City in Progress," with Peter Cook, in *Architectural Design* (London), November 1970; "Trondheim Theatre" in *RIBA Journal* (London), November 1976; "Set Pieces" in *Space Design* (Tokyo), September 1977; "Sets" in *Architecture + Urbanism* (Tokyo), October 1977; "Palace of the League of Nations: An Architectural Competition in Its Social and Historical Context" in *Pentagram Papers* (London), no. 5, December 1977.

On HERRON: books—*British Architecture* by Royston Landau, London 1968; *Experimental Architecture* by Peter Cook, London 1970; *Architecture 2000* by Charles Jencks, London 1971; *The Third Generation* by Philip Drew, London 1972; *Modern Movements in Architecture* by Charles Jencks, London 1973; *Architettura Radicale* by P. Navone, Milan 1974; *Storia dell'Architettura Contemporanea* by Renato de Fusco, Rome 1974; *Korunk Epiteszete* by Vamossy Ferenc, Budapest 1975; *Mega Structures* by Reyner Banham, London 1976; *A Question of Style*, conference catalogue, London 1978; *Visionary Architecture*, exhibition catalogue, New York 1979; *Utvecklingen Mot Strukturalism*, edited by Anders Ekholm, Stockholm 1980; *Architettura Inglese negli Anni 70*, exhibition catalogue, Milan, 1980; *Ron Herron: 20 years of drawing*, exhibition catalogue, London 1980; *Herron + Cook*, exhibition catalogue, Berlin 1981; *Architecture et Industrie*, exhibition catalogue, Paris 1983; articles— "Ron Herron and Warren Chalk" in *Kenchiku Bunka* (Tokyo), February 1968; "Archigram" in *Kenchiku Bunka* (Tokyo), no. 279, 1970; "Walking City" in *IN Magazine* (Milan), no. 2/1, 1971; "Suburban Sets" by Peter Cook in *Casabella* (Milan), no. 398, 1975; "Sets Fit for the Queen" by Arata Isozaki in *The Japan Architect* (Tokyo), February 1976; "Ron Herron" by Sutherland Lyle in *Building Design* (London), 6 May 1977; "Magician of Virtual Images" by Arata Isozaki in *Space Design* (Tokyo), September 1977; "Palace of the League of Nations" by David Pierce in *Building Design* (London), 16 December 1977; "A view of contemporary world architecture" in *Japan Architect* (Tokyo), December 1977; "Ron Herron – insertions" in *Skyline* (New York), August 1978; "Bubble Theatre" in *Building Design* (London), 28 July 1978; "The flight of the Herron" by Sutherland Lyall in *Building Design* (London), November 1980; "Cook + Herron" in *L.A. Architect* (Los Angeles), April 1982; "L'Oreal Hairdressing School" in *Architectural Review* (London), 1982.

I teach at the Architectural Association, London, and have done so for some 18-19 years. I lecture throughout the world on my work and ideas. I was a founder member of the Archigram group. I produce projects, with a heavily theoretical bias, which are widely published. But I am basically a practicing architect. For me, architecture is about: people/ invention/ history/ art/ order/ change/ consistency/ structure/ society/ politics/ movement/ technology/ connectivity/ experience/ beauty/ ingenuity/ response/ flexibility/ place/ pleasure/ needs/ context/ complexity/ imagination/ texture/ comfort/ the banal/ delight/ magic/ inconsistency/ ordinariness/ wit/ the city/ space/ form/ light/ colour/ time/ choice statics/ simplicity/ planning/ the section/ environment/ response/ view/ networks/ sequence/ the weather/ programme/ sound/ ideas/ compatibility/ the present/ the future/ changing the rules........and soon. My own work concerns itself with all these things, and attempts to make architecture by fusing building, technology and art to make something 'special' for the user.

—Ron Herron

Ron Herron is best known as a leading member of Archigram, an organization that has played a prominent role in British architecture during the past two decades. Archigram started as a magazine founded by Peter Cook in 1960. It was brash, exuberant, and very much part of the "Swinging Sixties." From Popculture it borrowed its graphics, its vulgarity and its love of the ephemeral; from the American Space Programme and science fiction its technological imagery. From contemporary architectural thinking came an interest in mobility and prefabrication and a new acceptance of mass-media: "Today we read ads," the Smithsons had written.

Archigram was also part of the new youth culture, a reassertion of identity after the privations of postwar austerity. Like the music of The Beatles and Rolling Stones it was meant to shock older generations, and it succeeded. But of course cultural movements thrive on controversy, and *Archigram* was hungrily read in architectural schools throughout the country. "This is the space age," it asserted. "What are we doing still building with bricks and mortar? Look what we could do with the technology that is already at hand." Seductive images flowed thick and fast, often just about within the bounds of technical possibility but never worked out in detail. Instant City, Walking City, Tuned Suburb, came and went. It was wonderful propaganda, and it paved the way to new applications of technology and to a new kind of non-building, since realized by Piano and Rogers with their Pompidou Centre in Paris and by Cedric Price in his Inter-Action Centre in London.

When the effects of the images had worn off, though, what was left? Archigram was always justly criticised for having no real substance behind its graphics. Would it ever build anything? Ron Herron and Warren Chalk had built when working for the Greater London Council in the early 1960s, and were in fact responsible for the conception of the South Bank Arts Complex, though it was not built as the ambiguous half-buried mound building covered in vegetation that they had originally envisaged but as an unrelenting bunker-like mass of grey concrete. Other Archigram members had built nothing of significance. Their chance to put theory into practice came in 1970 when they were invited to join a limited competition for an entertainments complex in Monte Carlo: they won first prize. This was to be the Archigram *tour de force*, with plenty of high technology in its multi-purpose interior, and no exterior at all—instead, the beloved mound covered with trees and a park. The project was developed over the next three years, but, like so many competition projects, it was eventually dropped, in this case because a developer offered the client a more tempting deal on an adjacent site.

By the mid-1970s Archigram had lost is urgency: its message had either been absorbed or rejected. High technology did not fit in with ecology and conservation or with a new call for craftsmanship. Archigram had had its heyday, and its members moved apart, though remaining close friends. Ron Herron moved to Pentagram, where he became a partner. He builds, albeit at a modest scale, and continues to produce visionary drawings in the evenings. He teaches at the Architectural Association, where one of the essential messages of Archigram still needs to be heard by each generation of students: "When you are looking for a solution to what you are told is an architectural problem— remember, it may not be a building."

—Peter Blundell Jones

HERTZBERGER, Herman.
Dutch. Born in Amsterdam, 6 July 1932. Educated at the Technical University, Delft, Netherlands, graduated 1958. Married Hans van Seters in 1959; children: Akelei, Veronica, and Titus. In private practice, Amsterdam, since 1958. Town Planning Consultant, Deventer, Netherlands, 1969. I\ tor, Academy of Architecture, Amsterdam, 19\ Since 1970, Professor at the University of Lelft, Netherlands. Visiting Professor, Massachusetts Institute of Technology, Cambridge, 1966-67 and 1970, Columbia University, New York, 1968, and the University of Toronto, 1969, 1970, 1971, and 1974. Editor, with Aldo van Eyck, *q.v.*, Jacob Bakema *q.v.*, and others, *Forum*, Amsterdam, 1959-63. Exhibitions: *Biennale des Jeunes*, Paris, 1967; Stedelijk Museum, Amsterdam, 1968; Historical Museum, Amsterdam, 1971; *Biennale*, Venice, 1976; Stichting Wonen, Amsterdam, 1976; Kunsthaus, Hamburg, West Germany, 1980. Recipient: Amsterdam Architectural Award, 1968; Eternit award, 1974; Fritz Schumacher Award, 1974; A. J. van Eck Award, 1980. Address: Architektenburo Herman Hertzberger, Vossiusstraat 3, 1071 AB Amsterdam, Netherlands.

Works:

1959/
66 Students residence, Weesperstraat, Amsterdam
1964 Lin Kij factory extension, Molenwerf, Sloterdijk, Amsterdam
Church in Driebergen, Netherlands (project)
1966 Montessori School, Jacoba van Beierenlaan, Delft, Netherlands
Town Hall in Valkenswaard, Netherlands (project)
1967 House conversion, Laren, Netherlands
Town Hall, Amsterdam (project)
1968 Monogoon housing (project)
1970 Kindergarten and Primary School extension, Jacoba van Beierenlaan, Delft, Netherlands
Neighbourhood Nieuwmarkt, Amsterdam (project)
1971 Eight experimental houses (Diagoon), Gebenlaan, Delft, Netherlands
1972 Renewal plan for the old city of Groningen, Netherlands (project)
Centraal Beheer Office Building, Prins Willem-Alexanderlaan, Apeldoorn, Netherlands (with Lucas and Niemeijer)
1974 De Schalm Community Centre, Dreef, Deventer, Netherlands
De Drie Hoven Old People's Home, Louis Chrispijnstraat 50, Slotervaart, Amsterdam
City centre plan for Eindhoven, Netherlands (project; with Van den Broek and Bakema)
1978 Vredenburg Music Centre, Utrecht, Netherlands
1980 Forty houses, Westbroek, near Utrecht, Netherlands
1982 Haarlemmer Houttuinen City Renewal, Amsterdam
Housing, Kassel, West Germany
1983 Amsterdamsche Montessori School and Willemspark School, Amsterdam
1984 De Overloop Housing for the Elderly, Almere-Haven, Netherlands

Publications:

By HERTZBERGER: book—*Herman Hertzberger: Buildings and Projects 1964-1984*, with Arnulf Lüchinger, The Hague 1985; articles—"Some Notes on Two Works by Schindler" in *Domus* (Milan), September 1967; "Montessori Primary School in Delft" in *Harvard Educational Review: Architecture and Education* (Cambridge, Massachusetts), no. 4, 1969; "Looking for the Beach under the Pavement" in *RIBA Journal* (London), 1971; "Homework for More Hospitable Form," special number of *Forum* (Amsterdam), no. 3, 1973; "A Lesson from St. Peter" in *Spazio e societa* (Milan), September 1980; "The Tradition behind the 'Heroic Period of Modern Architecture' and the New Formalism" in *Spazio e societa*(Milan), March 1981; "The Mechanism of the 20th Century and the Architecture of Aldo van Eyck" in *Aldo van Eyck*, edited by A. van Roijen-Wortman and F. Strauven, Amsterdam 1982.

On HERTZBERGER: books—*Form Viewed as Structure*, thesis by I. W. Bruce, University of Newcastle, England 1976; *The Works of Aldo van Eyck and Herman Hertzberger*, thesis by N. Embleton, University of Newcastle, England 1978; *Amsterdamse Bouwen, 1880-1980*, edited by Ids Haagsma and others, Utrecht, Netherlands and Antwerp, Belgium 1981; articles—"Buildings Designed as Street" by Raymond Lifchez in *Architectural Record* (New York), July 1968; "Young Dutch Architects" by Mette van Regteren Altena in *Arkitekten* (Copenhagen), no. 20, 1972; "Strukturalismus—Architektur als Symbol der Demokratisierung" by Arnulf Lüchingr in *Bauen und Wohnen*(Zürich), May 1974; "Strukturalismus: Eine neue Stromung in der Architektur" by Arnulf Lüchinger in *Bauen und Wohnen* (Zürich), no. 1, 1976; "Herman Hertzberger: Musical Architecture" in *The Architects' Journal* (London), April 1976; "Little Things Mean a Lot: The Philosophy of Herman Hertzberger" by Walter Menzies in *Building Design* (London), April 1976; "Variaciones de Hertzberger sobre temas del team 10" by Oriol Bohigas in *Arquitectura* (Madrid), no. 11, 1976; "Herman Hertsberger, Dutch Architect" by Arnulf Lüchinger in *Architecture + Urbanism* (Tokyo), March 1977; "Herman Hertzberger" by Hans van Dijk in *Dutch Art + Architecture Today* (The Hague), December 1979; "Hertzberger: Music Centre, Utrecht" in *Architectural Review* (London), February 1980; "Man Watching People" by Moyra Doorly in *Building Design* (London), 27 June 1980; "Hertzberger's Variations" in *Progressive Architecture* (New York), July 1980; "Insurance Company Offices in Apeldoorn" in *L'Architecture d'aujourd'hui* (Paris), February 1981; "Herman Hertzberger" by Stefan Schlachta in *Projekt* (Bratislava, Czechoslovakia), May 1981; "Nieuwe Houttuinen Housing," special issue of *Wonen-TA/BK* (Heerlen, Netherlands), September 1982; "Urban Renewal in Amsterdam" in *De Architect* (The Hague), October 1982.

Herman Hertzberger: Montessori/Willemspark School, Amsterdam, 1983.

Designing in such a way that several interpretations are possible should mean not only that the things we make can play several roles, but also that the users themselves are thereby encouraged to play more roles. Not only do we interpret the form, the form simultaneously interprets us, shows us something of who we are.

Thus, user and form begin mutually to interpret each other; their identities are strengthened by each other; each becomes more itself. It is like the actor who interprets his role and is himself interpreted by it at the same time; not only does he manifest something of the play; the play also manifests something of him: actor and play affirm each other.

The more roles the actor plays, the more facets of his identity are expressed; his identity becomes more complete, or is magnified, in the same way as the play, too, through differing interpretations, releases more of its being. Just as the identity of the actor extends as he plays more roles, so our identity will grow as we are drawn into a greater diversity of roles, that is, relationships to others. Thus we have to make things such that it becomes in reality possible for everyone to show as many facets of himself, to be himself in as many ways, as possible.

As the possibilities for interpretation are increased, so the more facets of himself the individual can express are increased, and a greater number of people can simultaneously be drawn into related behavior. Our purpose, then, should be to make as many possibilities for interpretation as possible, in the sense of giving each place its maximum "capacity."

Of essential importance here is that the differences should in fact be qualitative; otherwise, they will all only offer the same thing: it will thus be only a question of pseudo-interpretation, and a new stereotype pattern will be born. Only with a diversity of interpretations that is qualitative will there be a question of choice on which the establishment of a maximally variegated social pattern can be based.

Everything we make must be the catalyst to stimulate the individual to play the roles through which his identity will be enlarged. The aim of architecture is then: to reach the situation where everyone's identity is optimal, and because user and thing manifest each other, affirm each other, make each other more itself, the problem is to find the right conditioning for each thing.

It is a question of the right dimensions, placing, beat, interval, the right articulation, that things and people offer each other. Form makes itself, and that is less a question of invention than of listening well to what person and thing want to be. Form, directed towards a given purpose, functions as an apparatus, where both form and programme are reciprocally evocative; the apparatus evolves into an instrument.

A properly functioning apparatus does the work for which it is programmed, and that is what we expect of it, not less, but also not more. By pressing the right knobs we get the expected result—the same for everybody, constantly the same. An instrument essentially contains as many possibilities as can be drawn out of it; an instrument must be played. Within the range of the instrument, it is up to the player to draw what he can from it, within the limits of his own ability. Thus, instrument and player reveal their ability to complement and fulfil each other. Form as instrument offers the scope for each person to do what he has most at heart, and above all to do it in his own way.

It is because of this that a form must house both private and communal activities, intentions, and associations and, moreover, must be able to suggest different ways in which it can be adjusted constantly to suit the needs of each person. Therefore, the building itself must contain the incentive that provokes each person into making the choices that he feels are most suited to his circumstances at that particular time.

This extraordinary quality of hospitality is the scope a form must provide for people, for their values and dignity, in order to create the conditions that enable everyone to be who he wants to be—whoever that may be. Just as people must put themselves in the place of a form in order to be able to appropriate it, so must form put itself in the place of people to be appropriated. Thus, we could look upon this quality of hospitality of a form as the spatial equivalent of entering into a part.

The architect's task is above all to apply more than cut-to-fit, ready-made solutions and as much as possible to free in the users themselves whatever they think they need, by evoking images in them which can lead to their own personally valid solutions.

What we offer cannot be neutral; it must be the raw material, as it were, containing the "intentions" out of which everyone can make his choice in a particular situation, extracting from it precisely the intention which "resonates" with his intentions—intentions which give the prospect of his doing, or being, whatever will strengthen his ego-ideal. Each user interprets what's offered in such a way that he gets information out of it which is relevant to him and which he can use with relevance.

—Herman Hertzberger

Herman Hertzberger is part of an architectural movement that is essentially different from Machine-Aesthetic, International Style, Brutalism, Mannerism, Rationalism, or Classicism; his architecture has a basis that is broader than the purely aesthetic and formal. He is a descendant of the architectural tradition that had its beginnings at the end of the 1920s in the CIAM movement, a movement that itself diverged into another path at the end of the 1950s. Kenzo Tange speaks of two principal tendencies: Functionalism, from 1920 to 1960, and Structuralism, from 1960 to the present. With the change in direction, there was as well a change in name—from Congrès Internationaux d'Architecture Moderne to Groupe de Recherches des Interrelations Sociales et Plastiques. In the first period (1920-60), importance was attached to the development of a contemporary architectural expression that would replace the stylistic chaos of the nineteenth century. In the second period (1960 to date), there has been an essentially different approach: formalist "isms" now hardly count; the "interrelations sociales et plastiques" are thought to be more valuable. Hertzberger is today the most influential representative of Structuralism in relation to these "interrelations sociales et plastiques," and he has carried out exemplary work both in theory and in practice.

Both Functionalism and Structuralism have political ideologies. The socially committed CIAM Functionalists felt themselves deeply allied with socialist ideology and tried to introduce the scientific materialism of Marxist thought into their architecture. In some ways, Structuralists have a similar attitude. Hertzberger writes: "The architect, as we know, has never been very human: throughout history he has always served the happy few, never the great number. Since buildings cost money, he has always been on the side of money—the wrong side." But the Structuralists totally reject any belief in architecture as a science. With due respect for Marx, they proceed from the fact that he made no competent statements about architecture and art because he had insufficient insight into that sphere of human activity. While Marx can be considered the guru of the CIAM Functionalists, it is Claude Lévi-Strauss, with his structuralism in anthropology, who is spiritual father to the Structuralists. And, while various CIAM Functionalists tried to realize their ideas in Communist Russia, Structuralist architects

have followed the example of Lévi-Strauss and carried out studies in distant lands among primitive peoples, their intention being to learn about archetypal man in his community and to integrate that experience into contemporary architecture.

Team 10, the most active group within CIAM during the 1950s, made a significant contribution to the formation of the theory of Structuralism. Aldovan Eyck, one of the most prominent of the team, exerted great influence, with his theories and in his works, on younger architects, such as Hertzberger and Piet Blom. Influenced as well by John Habraken's book *Supports: An Alternative to Mass Housing,* Hertzberger went on to develop his own major theme—co-determination in architecture. With his nuanced treatises on polyvalent form, identity, structure, infill, etc., he produced theories that compensated for Functionalism's one-sided conception of form.

Hertzberger has always shown a lively interest in the international development of architecture, with the consequent advantage that, in building, he has never copied himself. The influence is perceptible not only of the great masters such as Le Corbusier, Kahn and Tange, but also, among others, of Duiker, Chareau, Bofill, and the architects of other cultures. Hertzberger creates ideas (to borrow from Malraux) from the *musée imaginaire.* He has a special affection for the Dutch architect Duiker. One of the least understood and therefore most underestimated Dutch architects of the 1920s, Duiker had anticipated an important principle of later Structuralism, the legitimate possibility of extension. Further, Duiker's poetic Concrete Constructivism offers many more possibilities for the realization of co-determination (structure and infill) than the modern architecture of the pure cube. Duiker was a musician as well as an architect. So is Hertzberger.

But, finally, it has only been of secondary importance to Hertzberger to function as a theorist. His prime intention has always been to translate into reality the social theories that he and others have developed. As a builder, he has proved to be an unsurpassed master. Four examples from the 1970s will suffice:

Diagoon Houses, Delft, 1971—eight terraced, single-family houses. A test case for co-determination in house building—in the inside, the facade, and the environment. Hertzberger regards the houses as "half-works" (though certainly not neutral works), to be completed by the occupants.

Centraal Beheer Office Building in Apeldoorn, 1972—for an insurance company with 1,000 employees. A statement from Hertzberger, from 1965, is relevant: "A building must be essentially antimonumental in the sense that monumentality is connected with power. A building must be essentially monumental in the sense that monumentality is connected with democracy." The basis of the design is a work island for each group of sixteen exployees, and the building is composed of cubic building components that are connected by a gridiron plan. It is a classic example of co-determination at the place of work, whereby the identity of each employee can be expressed.

De Drie Hoven Old People's Home, Amsterdam, 1974—a variable structure with vertical communications units. Hertzberger pays special attention to the "spaces between"—that is, he creates contact-promoting access areas between the dwellings (seating areas, stable-type doors, interior windows, etc.). There is a smooth transition from the public to the private realm. The building is a demonstration of the goal of "sense of place," and the central image is that of the village square.

Vredenburg Music Centre, Utrecht, 1978—a structure with construction units. Within an amorphous whole that relates to its surroundings, Hertzberger has crystallized ordered, symmetric forms—the main hall block, the other halls and foyers—and the play of free and ordered forms is very exciting. There is also a symmetrically formed main facade: this symbolic interior form is no longer typically Structuralist but is, rather, related to

Expressionism. If one compares Centraal Beheer Office Building, the De Drie Hoven Old People's Home, and the Music Centre, a development of the total form from basic structure to symbolic form is apparent. Ideologically, the Music Centre (with passages, shops, restaurants, information desk, etc.) involves the opposite of the well-known separation of functions in Functionalism. It is more appropriate to talk about "osmotic" achitecture with "semi-permeable" openings. There are fluent transitions—Foyer/Hall and Foyer/Public Passages—in which the view from the public to the private realm strengthens the "osmotic" effect. This effect is perceptible even in the perforated parapet details, the edges of the glass projecting roofs, and even in the lamps, which Hertzberger designed himself, as the architects of the 1920s designed their furniture. He considers lighting an important component of space arrangement.

Hertzberger is an excellent theoretician, of the intellectual level of van Eyck, yet his greatest strength lies in his translation of new social ideas into reality. He has artistic talent, a wealth of ideas, and a tremendous creative capacity. He works roughly on a level comparable to that of Duiker, van der Vlugt, and van Eyck—which is to say, he must be numbered among the most important of avant-garde architects.

—Arnulf Lüchinger

HILBERSEIMER, Ludwig Karl.

American. Born in Karlsruhe, Germany, 14 September 1885; emigrated to the United States, 1938: naturalized 1944. Educated at the Technische Hochschule, Karlsruhe, 1906-11. Architect and planner in various European cities, mainly Berlin, 1918-38; in private practice as a town planner, Chicago, 1938 until his death in 1967. Founder and Director of the City Planning Department at the Bauhaus, Dessau, Germany, 1929-32; Professor and Director of the Department of City and Regional Planning, 1938-57, and Professor Emeritus, 1957-67, Illinois Institute of Technology, Chicago. European Architectural Correspondent, *Chicago Tribune,* 1925; Member, Advisory Board, Burnham Library, Art Institute of Chicago, 1938-60: organized the Town Planning Exhibition at the Art Institute, 1944. Member, Novembergruppe, Berlin, 1919, Der Sturm artist's group, Berlin, 1925, Der Ring, Berlin, 1927, and CIAM (Congrès Internationaux d'Architecture Moderne), from 1928; served as a Director of the Deutsche Werkbund from 1931. LL.D.: Western Reserve University, Cleveland, 1962; D.Eng.: Technical University of Berlin, 1963. Fellow, American Institute of Architects. Member, Akademie der Künste, Berlin. *Died* (in Chicago) *6 May 1967.*

Works:

1911 Opera House, Berlin (project)
1919/
  24 "Minimal Standards" City Planning Studies, Berlin (projects)
1924 Skyscraper City, Berlin (project)
1924/
  27 Housing Studies, Berlin (projects)
1926 Rheinlandhaus Building, Berlin
1927 Werkbund Exhibition House, Weissenhof Estate, Stuggart
    Central Rail Station, Berlin (project)
    Hallesches Gate, Berlin (project)
1929 House, Dahlem, Berlin
1930 Two furnished apartments, *Die Wohnung* exhibition, Berlin (demolished)
1931 Town Hall, Nuremberg (project)
1932 Housing, Zehlendorf Estate, Berlin
    City Development Plan, Dessau, Germany (project)

1935 "Minimal Standards" Housing Studies, Berlin (projects)
Lakeshore Development Plan, Zürich (project)
1936 Housing, Rupendorn Estate, Berlin
Housing, Fichteberg Estate, Berlin
University of Berlin Development Plan (project)
1937 Rental Housing, Kantstrasse, Berlin (project)
Rental Housing, Emserstrasse, Berlin (project)
1938/
45 Evergreen I City Redevelopment Plan, Chicago (project)
City Plan for Montreal (project)
1939 Small City Plan, Wisconsin (project)
1944 Illinois Institute of Technology Development Plan, Chicago (project)
1947 City Plan for Maui, Hawaii (project)
1948/
50 Evergreen II City Redevelopment Plan, Chicago (project)
1955 Lafayette Park Development Plan, Detroit
1956 Hyde Park Development Plan, Chicago
1957 City Plan, Seattle (project)
1958 State Street Plan, Chicago (project)
1959 Lafayette Park Development, Stage 1, Detroit
1961/
63 Revised City Development Plan, Chicago (project)

Publications:

By HILBERSEIMER: books—*Grossstadtbauten*, Hannover, Germany 1925; *Grosstadt Architektur*, Stuttgart 1927; *Beton als Gestalter*, with Julius Vischer, Stuttgart 1928; *Internationale neue Baukunst*, Stuttgart 1928; *Hallenbauten*, Leipzig, Germany 1931; *The New City: Principles of Planning*, Chicago 1944; *The New Regional Pattern*, Chicago 1949; *The Nature of Cities*, Chicago 1955; *Mies van der Rohe*, Chicago 1956; *Entfaltung einer Planungsidee*, Berlin 1963; *Contemporary Architecture: Its Roots and Trends*, Chicago 1964; *Berliner Architektur der 20 Jahre*, Mainz, West Germany and Berlin 1967; articles—"Reichstagerweiterung und Platz der Republik" in *Form* (Berlin), 1 July 1930; "Neue Literatur über Städtebau" in *Form* (Berlin), 15 October 1930; "Vorschlag zur city Bebauung" in *Form* (Berlin), 15 December 1930; "Die Wohnung unserer Zeit" in *Form* (Berlin), 15 July 1931; "Die Bewohner des Hauses Tugendhat aussern sich..." in *Form* (Berlin), 15 November 1931; Reflections on a Greek Journey" in *Inland Architect* (Chicago), February 1967.

On HILBERSEIMER: book—*Bauen seit 1900 in Berlin* by Rolf Rave and Hans-Joachim Knöfel, Berlin 1968; *Visionary Architecture of the 20th Century* by Vittorio Magnago Lampugnani, Stuttgart and London 1982; articles—"Entwurf für die Stadthalle Nürnberg in *Form* (Berlin), 15 October 1931; "Haus Dr. B. in Berlin-Zehlendorf" in *Form* (Berlin), 15 November 1932; *"The New City:* Social Planning Is a Social Task" by Jan Reiner in *Architect and Engineer* (New York), June 1945; "Plan d'urbanisme de Chicago" in *Architecture: formes et fonctions* (Lausanne, Switzerland), 1957; "Profile: Ludwig Hilberseimer" in *Aufbau* (Vienna), March 1959; "Seidlung Lafayette Park, Detroit" in *Bauen und Wohnen* (Zürich), November 1960; "Modern Proposals for the Physical Decentralization of Community" by Henry Winthrop in *Land Economics* (Madison, Wisconsin), February 1967; "Elementos de la nueva ciudad: la obra de Ludwig Hilberseimer" by Reginald F. Malcolmson in *Hogar y arquitectura* (Madrid), May/June 1968; "The Development of the Weissenhof Estate in Stuttgart" by Bodo Rasch in *Deutsche Bauzeitung* (Stuttgart), November 1977.

Bibliography—*Ludwig Karl Hilberseimer: An Annotated Bibliography and Chronology* by David Spaeth, New York and London 1981.

*

Ludwig Hilberseimer was one of the leaders of that singular generation of central European designers born in the 1880s (Gropius, Mies van der Rohe, and Mendelsohn were others) who revolutionized building in Germany during the 1920s, then emigrated to the United States during the following two decades and contributed equally to the reconstitution of architecture in that country.

After taking his training at the Technische Hochschule in Karlsruhe, Hilberseimer settled in Berlin, where he practiced for nearly two decades and where his abiding architectural philosophy was shaped. That outlook was uncompromisingly modernist. Hilberseimer became devoted to the direct structural expression of technological elements in building; he has been called one of the founders of the International Style. As early as 1911, he saw and was impressed by the work of Frank Lloyd Wright, and he later formed a lifelong friendship with Ludwig Mies van der Rohe. He was an early member (in 1919) of the Novembergruppe in Germany and a contributor to the magazine *G*, both radical instruments of the modern movement in art and architecture. He was the first architect to show in the *Der Sturm* exhibitions in Berlin, and in 1927 he became a member of yet another organization of major German vanguard architects, Der Ring.

By this time, Hilberseimer had earned a reputation not only as a designer but also as a writer and city planner. His book *Grossstadbauten* appeared in 1925, and two years later he contributed the design of a house to the Weissenhof Estate project in Stuttgart. In 1929 he became the Founder/Director of the City Planning Department of the Dessau Bauhaus.

Hilberseimer spent most of the 1930s, bleak years for the modern arts in Germany, in his homeland. He was elected to the directorate of the Deutsche Werkbund in 1931, the same year his book Hallenbauten was published. He meanwhile designed housing in Berlin, in Aldershof, Zehlendorf, Rupenhorn, and Fichteberg.

Hilberseimer's career took an important turn in 1938, when he accepted the post of Director of the Department of City and Regional Planning of the School of Archtecture of the Illinois Institute of Technology (then the Armour Institute) in Chicago. There, he and his countryman Walter Peterhans joined the School's newly appointed director Mies van der Rohe in a full-scale reorganization of the architecture curriculum. The modern structuralist principles that the three men had espoused in their European years were communicated to several generations of younger designers who in turn did much to engender the skin-and-bones look of American commercial architecture during the 1950s.
—Franz Schulze

HO, Tao.
British. Born in Shanghai, China, 17 July 1936; emigrated to Hong Kong, 1949; British subject, 1976. Educated at Pui Ching Middle High School, Kowloon, Hong Kong, 1950-56; Williams College, Williamstown, Massachusetts, 1956-60 (Bowdwin Scholarship; Hutchinson Prize, 1960), B.A. 1960; Graduate School of Design, Harvard University, Cambridge, Massachusetts, under Josep Lluis Sert, *q.v.*, and Siegfried Giedion, 1960-64 (Arthur Lehman Fellowship), M.Arch. 1964. Married Chi-Ping Lu in 1960 (divorced, 1978); children: Suenn, Shu, Dien; married Irene Lo in 1978; daughter: Noelle. Research Assistant, Albright-Knox Art Gallery, Buf-

falo, New York, Summer 1959; Architectural Assistant, Harvard University Planning Office, Cambridge, Massachusetts, 1961, Boston Redevelopment Authority, 1962, and The Architects Collaborative, *q.v.*, Cambridge, Massachusetts, 1963-64; architect with various firms in Hong Kong, 1964-68. Since 1968, Principal of TAOHO Design, architects and designers, Hong Kong. Core Member, with Fumihiko Maki, *q.v.*, and Koichi Nagashima of Tokyo, William S.M. Lim, *q.v.*, of Singapore, and Sumet Jumsai, *q.v.*, of Bangkok, APAC (Asian Planning and Architectural Consultants Ltd.), since 1975; Founder-Director, *Vision* magazine, Hong Kong, since 1981. Visiting Lecturer, Fine Arts Department, Chinese University of Hong Kong, 1965-67; Visiting Critic, Harvard University Graduate School of Design, 1975; Part-time Lecturer, 1977-79, and Honorary Lecturer since 1979, School of Architecture, University of Hong Kong; Honorary Lecturer, Department of Fine Arts, University of Hong Kong, since 1982; Visiting Fellow, Hong Kong Macau Study Centre, Zhongshan University, Guangzhou, China, since 1984; Visiting Design Critic, Department of Architecture, National University of Singapore, 1984. Chairman, Visual Arts Committee, Hong Kong Arts Centre, 1972-77 (organized twenty-five art exhibitions at the Centre); President, Harvard Club of Hong Kong, 1975-77; Member, EROPH (Eastern Regional Organization for Planning and Housing), 1975-76; Honorary Advisor, Hong Kong Museum of Art, since 1981; Chairman, Hong Kong Designers Association, since 1981; Design Advisory Committee member, Hong Kong Polytechnic, since 1982; Member of the Hong Kong Technical Education Board, since 1983. Exhibitions (paintings): Museum of Art, Springfield, Massachusetts, 1959; Hong Kong Museum of Art, 1959; Boston Art Festival, 1960; Hong Kong Museum of Art, 1969. Collections (graphics): Art Museum, Lawrence, Massachusetts. Recipient: Design Award, Trade Development Council of Hong Kong, 1969; Silver Medal, 1978, and Design Excellence Award, 1982, Hong Kong Institute of Architects; Silver Award, Hong Kong Designers Association, 1978. Fellow of Robert Black College, University of Hong Kong; D.H.L.: Williams College, Williamstown, Massachusetts, 1979. Member, Hong Kong Institute of Architects, 1971, World Society of Ekistics, 1973, American Institute of Graphic Arts, 1973, and Singapore Board of Architects, 1981; Associate, Chartered Institute of Arbitrators, 1979. Address: TAOHO Design Architects, 33 Leighton Road, 22nd floor penthouse, Causeway Bay, Hong Kong.

Works:

1968 Olivetti Pavilion, *C.M.A. Exhibition*, Hunghom, Hong Kong
1969 Hong Kong Government Pavilion, *C.M.A. Exhibition*, Hunghom, Hong Kong
1971 Rediffusion Pavilion, *C.M.A. Exhibition*, Wanchai, Hong Kong
1973 Feasibility study of village planning policy for New Territories, Hong Kong (as consultant architect to Wilbur Smith and Associates)
1975 Elementary Section, Hong Kong International School, Repulse Bay, Hong Kong (with Wong and Ouyang Associates)
1976 Project Office, Mass Transit Railway Corporation, Admiralty, Queensway, Hong Kong
1977 Hua Hsia Building, Gloucester Road, Hong Kong
Hong Kong Arts Centre
1979 K. S. Lo Residential Development, Shouson Hill, Hong Kong (with K. C. Lye)
H. K. Lee House, Black's Link, Hong Kong
Master Plan, Special Studies Building, and Gymnasium, St. Stephen's College, Stanley, Hong Kong

Tao Ho: Hong Kong Arts Centre, 1977.

1982 Mass Transit Tsuen Wan Depot, Hong Kong
(with Ove Arup and Partners)
Tai Mei Tuk Outdoor Activities Centre, Hong
Kong
1983 Apartment, 6A Bowen Road, Hong Kong

Interiors:

Foreign Correspondents' Club, Sutherland House, Hong Kong, 1968; Johnson, Stokes and Master, Hong Kong and Shanghai Bank Building, Hong Kong, 1969; Merrill Lynch, Pierce, Fenner and Smith, St. George's Building, Hong Kong, 1969; United States Information Service Libraries, Hong Kong, Bangkok, and Taipei, 1969; Hong Kong branches of the Far East Bank Ltd., 1969-72; The Shell Company of Hong Kong, Hong Kong and Shanghai Bank Building, Kowloon, 1969-73; Munichre Service Ltd., Connaught Centre, Hong Kong, 1972; Vickers da Costa and Company, Connaught Centre, Hong Kong, 1972; Union Insurance Society of Canton Ltd., Swire House, Hong Kong, 1972; Coca-Cola Export Corporation, Connaught Centre, Hong Kong, 1973; Marubeni Corporation, Connaught Centre, Hong Kong, 1973; Sing Tao Newspaper Ltd., News Building, Hong Kong, 1973; Hong Kong Stock Exchange, Edinburgh House and Hutchinson House, 1973-76; Charles Fulton (Hong Kong) Ltd., Sincere Insurance Building, Tai Seng Building, Hong Kong, 1973-78; Duty Free Shoppers Ltd., Hayatt Regency Hotel, J. Hotung House, Kai Tak Airport, Kowloon, 1973-78; Lufthansa head office and ticket offices, Pedder Building, Prince's Building, Peninsula Hotel, 1974; Italian Consulate, Hutchison House, Hong Kong, 1975; Nan Fung Textiles Ltd., Central Building, Hong Kong,1975; Hong Kong Institute of Architects, Cheong Sun Building, Hong Kong, 1975; International Maritime Carriers, Connaught Centre, Hong Kong, 1975; Barberlines (Hong Kong) Ltd., Melbourne Plaza, Hong Kong, 1975-77; Slaughter and May, Connaught Centre, Hong Kong, 1976; Zim Isreal Navigation Company Ltd., Alexandra House, Hong Kong, 1976; Austin Centre public space and lobbies, Austin Avenue, Kowloon, 1976; SGV-Sun Hung Kai Ltd., Alexandra House, Hong Kong, 1976; Rigoletto Ristorante Italiano, East Town Building, Hong Kong, 1976; China Engineering Ltd., Ching Lung Tau Facility, Texaco Road, Tsuen Wan, New Territories, Hong Kong, 1976; Longines Hong Kong Ltd., Ocean Centre, Kowloon, 1977; Hambro Pacific, Connaught Centre, Hong Kong, 1977; Li Residence, Mt. Cameron Road, Hong Kong, 1977-78; Sumitomo Bank, Hong Kong, 1978; Exxon Chemical East Pacific Ltd., Connaught Centre, Hong Kong, 1978; Grindlay's Bank Ltd., China Building, Hong Kong; IBM World Trade Corporation, Bank of Canton Building, Hong Kong, 1978; Hong Kong Tourist Association, Connaught Centre, Hong Kong, 1978; Duty Free Shop, Hong Kong International Airport, 1978; Crocodile Garmet Store, Hong Kong, 1978; W. T. Partnership Offices, Hong Kong, 1979; Orchid Palace Hotel, Jakarta, Indonesia, 1979; Japan Airlines Offices, Gloucester Tower, Hong Kong, 1980; China Light and Power Company Ltd., Tsim Sha Tsui Centre, Hong Kong, 1981; Ogilvy and Mather Ltd. Offices, Mount Parker House, Hong Kong, 1982; IBM World Trade Corporation, Sunning Plaza, Hong Kong, 1982; Saab Showroom, Sunning Plaza, Hong Kong, 1982; Arnhold and Company Showroom, Hong Kong, 1982; IBM Computer Centre, Great Eagle Centre, Hong Kong, 1983; Jat Min Chueng Youth Centre, Hong Kong, 1983; Irene Lo Children's Art Centre, Hong Kong, 1983; IBM SEAR Training Centre, New World Centre, Hong Kong, 1984; Hong Kong Trade Development Council, Great Eagle Centre, Hong Kong, 1984; Austrian Trade Commission, Hong Kong, 1984; Duty Free Shop, Kowloon Canton Railway Station, Hong Kong, 1984.

Publications:

By HO: articles/monographs—"Chinese Paintings and Paul Cezanne: A Comparison" in *Williams Review* (Williamstown, Massachusetts), May 1960; "Chinese Architecture and Town Planning, B.C. 1500-A.D. 1911" in *Landscape Architecture* (Louisville, Kentucky), July 1963; "Hong Kong Waterfront Development" in *Ekistics* (Athens), June 1964; "Some Thoughts on the Theory and Technique of Art" in *Art Review of New Asia College* (Hong Kong), September 1966; "A Chinese Architectural Spirit" in *Ekistics* (Athens), November 1965; *Graphic Art in Germany Today: A Brief Development of Art from 1907-1973.* TAOHO Design Publication, Hong Kong 1973; "Design Criteria for Human High-Density Housing" in *Ekistics* (Athens), June 1975; "Hong Kong: A City Prospers Without a Plan" in *City Planning Review* (Tokyo), August 1976; "The Hong Kong Arts Centre—A Piece of Functional Sculpture" in *Hong Kong Exporter and Fat Eastern Importer* (HongKong), Winter 1977/78; *Music in Architecture*, TAOHO Design Publication, Hong Kong 1978; *German Expressionism.* TAOHO Design Publication, Hong Kong 1978; *The Colour of Monet, The Sound of Debussy, and The Spiritual Realm of Huang Pin-Hung*, TAOHO Design Publication, Hong Kong 1978; "Hong Kong—An Architectural Zoo" in *Asian Wall Street Journal* (Hong Kong), February 1980; "Order in Chaos" in *Macao ou jourer différence*, exhibition catalogue, Paris 1983; "Search for an Orderly Chaos" in *Vision* (Hong Kong), no. 8, 1983; *Heaven, Earth and Man*, lecture paper, Singapore 1984; *Asian Metropolis: Hong Kong, Singapore and Beijing*, lecture paper, Washington, D.C. 1984; *Tall Buildings: A Humanistic Appraisal*, lecture paper, Hong Kong 1984; introductions for Hong Kong Arts Centre exhibition catalogues, 1972-77.

On HO: books—*Delos Symposium 1974*, Athens 1974; *The Architecture of Self-help Communities* by Michael Seelig, New York 1978; *Unesco School Furniture* by Bo Fritzell, Paris 1978; *Architecture in the Seventies* by Udo Kultermann, London 1980; *Architekten der dritten Welt* by Udo Kultermann, Cologne 1980; *Fifty Outstanding Architects of the World* by Ivica Meadjenovic, Belgrade 1983; articles—"Tao Ho Sees Great Things Ahead for Arts Centre" by Sheila Wyndham in *South China Morning Post* (Hong Kong), 28 September 1971; "Hong Kong Arts Centre" in *Architecture and Planning* (Taipei Taiwan), December 1972; "An Interview with Mr. Tao Ho" by Ioh Lee in *Grove Magazine* (Hong Kong), 1 January 1973; "11th Delos Symposium 1974" in *Ekistics* (Athens), December 1974; "Stimulating Environment for Learning" by Peter Leung in *Building Materials and Equipment in Hong Kong* (Hong Kong), October 1975; "Hong Kong Arts Centre: Simple, Compact and Functional" by Peter Leung in *Building Journal* (Hong Kong), May 1976; "Arts Centre—Intricate, Economical, Imaginative Design" in *Asian Architect and Builder* (Hong Kong), November 1976; "A Place of Their Own" in *Asia-week* (Hong Kong), 28 October 1977; "Asian Planning and Architectural Consultants" in *Nikkei Architecture* (Tokyo), 14 November 1977; "Hong Kong's Oasis' by Lesley Nelson in *Peninsula Group Magazine* (Hong Kong), April 1978; "Hong Kong Arts Centre" by Michael Outhwaite in *Tabs* (London), Spring 1978; "Design Portfolio: Tao Ho" in *Asian Building and Construction* (Hong Kong), June 1969; "Hong Kong Arts Centre" in *Architecture + Urbanism* (Tokyo), August 1979; "Tao Ho Tower" in *Architectural Review* (London), December 1979; "Contemporaty Asian Architecture," special issue of *Process: Architecture* (Tokyo), November 1980.

The history of civilization is the cycle of man's continuous effort to shape and to reshape his enviroment. During this process, the architect has played a very important role.

It is perhaps, historically inevitable that achitecture will become more and more complicated because of the increasingly complex nature of our society. We have also reached a point in history where, for the first time, almost any conceivable structure can be built in a technical sense. Whether this is a blessing to mankind remains to be judged. The test of the architect in this respect seems to me to be one of his attitude towards the future of humanity.

In order to humanize our future world, which we shoulddo if we do not wish to be ruled by mechanization, an architect must possess both social and spatial imagination. The former is the amorphous ideal of improving our life pattern while the latter is the formal representation of that ideal in terms of better spatial organization for our activities.

An architect, therefore, must be able to penetrate the superficial, the chaotic, and the transitory social phenomena in order to formulate a new dynamic and inspiring social order for tomorrow. At the same time, an architect must have innovative design ability to create functionally and economically whilst aesthetically and poetically expressing his social ideals by means of well articulated and integrated forms in space.

Good architecture is like a piece of beautifully composed music crystallized in space that elevates our spirits beyond the limitation of time.

The Hong Kong Arts Centre is an example of my belief. In addition to being the architect, nine years ago I was one of the initiators who promoted and fought for the idea of providing a people's cultural oasis in the higly commercially oriented city of Hong Kong. It is a very small building on a tiny Thirty-by-Thirty metre site. But it symbolizes a vision. I hope this vision will help to shape the future.

—Tao Ho

Tao Ho is probably the only architect in Hong Kong who is fearlessly committed to the art of making spaces in a city thoroughly committed to commerical imperatives. His background is an interesting one; he is a cosmopolitan Chinese well versed in art and literature of the East and the West. His early work at Harvard exhibited a degree of formalism that was probably generated by his Knowledge of disciplines surrounding Chinese architecture—a frame of mind not dissimilar to Beaux Arts attitudes. But his exposure to Le Corbusier relevant contradictions that have allowed him as an architect to recognize the worth of formalism with all its constraints and positive attributes. Like Sert, he has acquired the ability to externally and internally decompose formalism to an extent that permits his architecture the possibility of indeterminancy within a whole.

Ho is, perhaps, the only one among a small band of young architects in Hong Kong who has remained a constant source of irritation to the establishment, whose preference is for Honky-Tonk Han (Bloodsworth) on the one hand and the Puerile-Virle Pop on the other. It can be said that it is ultimately the Baroqueness of Ho's work that makes him controversial, much discussed, and never a source of boredom. His architecture always delights or frightens, depending on the viewer's frame of mind. He is a cheeky architect and a perfect gentleman—am I describing an English public school boy up to some mischief at the vicar's party in a country churchyard?

—K.C. Lye

HOFFMANN, Josef Franz Maria.
Austrian. Born in Pirnitz, Moravia, now Brtnice, Czechoslovakia, 15 December 1870. Studied architecture at the Academy of Art, Vienna, under Carl von Hasenauer and Otto Wagner, 1892-95; awarded the Rome Prize, 1895. Married Anna Hladik in 1903,

and Karla Schmatz in 1925; son: Wolfgang. Worked with Joseph Olbrich in the studio of Otto Wagner, Vienna, 1896-97. In private practice, Vienna, 1898 until his death in 1956. Professor, Vienna School (now Academy) of Applied Arts, 1899-1936. Founder Member, Sezession Group, Vienna, 1897; Founder, with Kolo Moser and Fritz Wärndorfer, Wiener Werkstätte, 1903; Director, with Gustav Klimt, Kunstschau (secession from the Sezession), Vienna, 1908-09; Co-Founder and Director, Austrian Werkbund, Vienna, 1910; Director, Künstlerwerkstätte, Vienna, 1943-56. Exhibitions: *Josef Hoffmann: 60th Birthday Retrospective,* Vienna, 1930; *Triennale,* Milan, 1933 (retrospective); *Josef Hoffmann,* Vienna, 1950; *Josef Hoffmann,* Galerie Würthle, Vienna, 1960, 1970; *Josef Hoffmann: Drawings* Austrian Institute, New York, 1975; *Josef Hoffmann 1870-1956: Architect and Designer,* Fischer Fine Art Gallery, London, 1977; *Frühes Industriedesign: Wien 1900-1908,* Galerie Nächst St. Stephan, Vienna, 1977; *Josef Hoffmann: architect and designer, 1870-1956,* Galerie Metropol, Vienna, 1981; *Josef Hoffmann: design classics,* Fort Worth Art Museum, Texas, 1983. Recipient: Honor Award, City of Vienna, 1950. Honorary doctorates: Technische Hochschule, Dresden, Berlin, and Vienna. Honorary Member, Akademie der Künste, Vienna and Berlin. Commander, Légion d'Honneur, France, 1926. *Died* (in Vienna) *8 May 1956.*

Works:

1898 Ver Sacrum Salon, *Sezession Exhibition,* Gartenbaugesellschaft Palace, Vienna
Secretariat, Sezession Building, Vienna (building by Joseph Olbrich)
Pollak House interiors, Atzgersdorf, Lower Austria
1899 Wooden Exhibition Pavilion, in the courtyard of the Austrian Museum for Art and Industry, Vienna
Kurzweil Studio interior, Vienna
Apollo Candle Shop, Vienna
Brix Office interiors, Vienna
P. Wittgenstein Hunting Lodge, Bergerhöhe, Lower Austria
1899/
1902 Exhibition designs for the Sezession, Vienna
1900 Mahogany dining-room, World's Fair, Paris
1900/
01 Wittgenstein Foresters' Office and Housing, Hohenberg, Lower Austria
1901/
03 Kolo Moser House, Hohe Warte, Vienna
Karl Moll House, Hohe Warte, Vienna
Henneberg House, Hohe Warte, Vienna
Spitzer House, Hohe Warte, Vienna
1902 Klinger Salon, *XIV Sezession Exhibition,* Vienna
Sezession Room, *Art Exhibition,* Düsseldorf
Poldihütte Steelworkers' Hostel, Kladno, Bohemia (now Czechoslovakia)
Hochstätter House interiors, Vienna
Mauthner Apartment interiors, Vienna
Wärndorfer House interiors, Vienna
Biach Apartment interiors, Vienna
Koller House interiors, Vienna
1903 Church, Hohenberg, Lower Austria
Knips House, Seeboden, Kärnten, Austria
Wiener Werkstätte Headquarters interiors, Neustiftgasse, Vienna
Design of the *Wiener Werkstätte Exhibition,* Vienna (with Kolo Moser)
1904 Design of the *Wiener Werkstätte Exhibition,* Hirschwald Applied Arts House, Berlin
1904/
06 Sanatorium, Purkersdorf, Lower Austria
1905/
06 Beer-Hofmann House, Vienna
1905/
11 Stoclet House, Brussels
1906 Kohn Tomb, Vienna

1906/
07 Wittgenstein Hunting Lodge, Hochreith, near Hohenberg, Lower Austria
1907 Hochstätter House, Hohe Warte, Vienna
Hamburger Apartment interiors, Vienna
Fledermaus Theatre/Cabaret, Vienna
Johann Strauss Tomb, Vienna (project)
Music Pavilion on the River Danube, Vienna (project)
Wiener Werkstätte Shop, Graben, Vienna
Building Complex for the 1908 Austrian Applied Arts Jubilee, Vienna (project)
1908 Pavilion for the Emperor's Jubilee (project)
Temporary building for the *Kunstschau,* Vienna
1909 Sales Room, State Printing House, Vienna
Pickler House alterations and interiors, Budapest
Knips Apartment interiors, Vienna
H. Böhler Apartment interiors, Vienna
H. Böhler House remodelling and interiors, Baden, Lower Austria
C. Böhler House, Kapfenberg, Austria
Moll House II, Vienna
1910 Böhler Company Theatre, Kapfenberg, Austria (project)
Legler House, Döbling, Vienna
1910/
11 Ast House, Hohe Warte, Vienna
1911 Austrian Pavilion, *International Art Exhibition,* Rome
Hanak Salon, *Dresden Art Exhibition*
Stoclet Tomb, Brussels
Marlow Apartment interiors, Vienna
Steckelberg Apartment interiors, Vienna
1912 Graben Coffee House, Vienna
Austrian Pavilion, *Art Exhibition,* Venice (project)
Ast Tomb, Vienna
Zuckerkandl Apartment interiors, Vienna
Josef Hoffmann House renovations and interiors, Pirnitz, Moravia (now Brtnice, Czechoslovakia)
Böhler Tomb, Kapfenberg, Austria
Cellar Bar, Hotel Pitter, Salzburg, Austria
Koller House renovations, Oberwaltersdorf, Lower Austria
Koller House interiors, Vienna
1912/
14 Poldihütte Steelworks Office remodelling, Vienna
Bernatzik House, Hohe Warte, Vienna
Wellesz House, Kaasgraben, Vienna
Botstieber House, Kaasgraben, Vienna
Vetter House, Kaasgraben, Vienna
Yella Herzka House, Kaasgraben, Vienna
Küper House, Kaasgraben, Vienna
Drucker House, Kaasgraben, Vienna
Hodler Apartment interiors, Geneva
Gallia Apartment interiors, Vienna
Förster Tomb, Vienna
1913/
14 Günther Wagner Company Building, Vienna (project)
Design of the *Bugra Graphic Arts Exhibition,* Leipzig, Germany
Primavesi Bank renovations, Olmütz, Moravia (now Olomouc, Czechoslovakia)
Austrian Pavilion, *Werkbund Exhibition,* Cologne
1913/
15 Skywa (Panzer) House, Heitzing, Vienna
Primavesi House, Winkelsdorf, Moravia (now Kouty, Czechoslovakia)
1915 H. Böhler House interiors, Munich
Gödl-Olajossy Apartment interiors, Linz, Austria
1916 Knips Apartment interiors, Vienna
Zuckerkandl Apartment interiors, Vienna
P. Wittgenstein Apartment interiors, Vienna
1916/
17 Salesroom, Fashion Department, Wiener Werkstätte, Vienna
1917 Böhler Studio, Vienna

Display cases for porcelain, for P. Wittgenstein Jr., Vienna
Exhibitions for Copenhagen and Stockholm (projects)
Palace of World Peace, Stockholm (project)
1917/
18 E. Böhler Apartment interiors, Vienna
Town Hall reconstruction, Ortelsburg (now Czczytno), Poland (project)
1917/
19 Poldihütte Steelworks Buildings corrections, Komotau and Kladno, Bohemia (now Czechoslovakia)
1918 Primavesi Apartment interiors, Vienna
Berstel Apartment interiors, Wiener Neustadt, Vienna
Steiner Tomb, Vienna
Displays, *Trade Fair,* Leipzig, Germany
Pazzani Palace, Vienna
1919 Hamburger Tomb, Freudenthal (now Bruntal), Czechoslovakia
Knips House, Vienna (project)
1919/
20 Knips Tomb, Vienna
1920 Convalescent Home remodelling, Gross-Ullersdorf, Moravia (now Velke Losiny, Czechoslovakia)
Gamekeeper's Cottage for Dr. Pazzani, Admont, Austria (project)
Hostel and Bank, Novi-Sad, Serbia, Yugoslavia (project)
Cafe/Restaurant, Laxenburg, Austria (project)
1920/
22 Pazzani House alterations, Pichl, Steiermark, Austria
Berl House, Freudenthal (now Bruntal), Czechoslovakia
F. Grohmann House, Würbenthal (now Vrbno pod Praded), Czechoslovakia
Bernatzik Apartment interiors, in the Ast House, Hohe Warte, Vienna
Gallia Apartment interiors, Vienna
1921 Hotel, Zagreb, Yugoslavia (project)
1922 K. Grohmann House interiors, Pochmühl, Silesia (now Czechoslovakia)
G. Nebehay Building Entrance Doors and Shop, Vienna
1922/
23 Dunckel House, Budapest
Baru Apartment interiors, Vienna
1923 Grohmann Company Offices, Würbenthal (now Vrbno pod Praded), Czechoslovakia
Josef Hoffmann Apartment interiors, Vienna
Baron Bachofen-Echt House, Vienna (project)
Heller House, Vienna (project)
Grohmann Company Workers' Housing, Würbenthal (now Vrbno pod Praded), Czechoslovakia
1923/
24 Ast House, Velden on the Wörthersee, Austria
1924/
25 Knips House, Döbling, Vienna
1925 Public housing, Felix Mottl Strasse, Vienna
Public housing, Stromstrasse, Vienna
Austrian Pavilion, *Exposition des Arts Décoratifs,* Paris
1928 Design of the *Viennese Applied Arts Jubilee Exhibition*
Sarmej Office Building, Cluj, Rumania
Altmann and Kühne Pastry Shop, Vienna
Record shop, Vienna
Sanatorium, Salzburg, Austria (project)
Pre-fabricated house in steel, Vienna
1929 Design of the *Austrian Werkbund Exhibition,* Vienna
1929/
30 Grand Palace of Art, Karlplatz, Vienna (project)
1930 Lengyel House interiors, Bratislava, Czechoslovakia
Central Room and Coffee Terrace, *Werkbund Exhibition,* Vienna

Austrian Section, *International Exhibition,* Stockholm

Graben Cafe/Restaurant remodelling, Vienna

Railway carriage interiors for Austrian Railways

Otto Wagner Monument, Vienna

1932 Four low-cost terraced houses, Werkbund Estate, Vienna

Public housing, Laxenburgerstrasse, Vienna

1934 Austrian Pavilion, *Biennale,* Venice

1935 Austrian Pavilion, World's Fair, Brussels (project)

1936 Austrian Pavilion, World's Fair, Paris (project)

1937 Boudoir for a Great Actress, World's Fair, Paris

1938 Hanak Museum, Augarten, Vienna (project)

1939/
  44 German Officers' Club, Vienna

1940 Reinforced concrete monumental bridges across the Danube Canal, Vienna (projects)

1945 Low-cost terraced housing (project)

Low-cost housing in circular layout (project)

1950 Public housing, Blechturmgasse, Vienna

1952 Public housing, Silbergasse, Vienna (with Josef Kalbac)

1954 Public housing, Heiligenstätterstrasse, Vienna (with Josef Kalbac)

Publications:

On HOFFMANN: books—*Josef Hoffmann* by Leopold Kleiner, Berlin, Leipzig and Vienna 1927; *Josef Hoffmann* by Armand Weiser, Geneva 1930; *Josef Hoffmann zum 60. Geburtstag,* edited by the Austrian Werkbund, Vienna 1930; *Josef Hoffmann* by L. W. Rochowanski, Vienna 1950; *Josef Hoffmann* by Giulia Veronesi, Milan 1956; *Josef Hoffmann 1870-1956: Architect and Designer, exhibition catalogue, by Eduard F. Sekler and Robert Judson Clark, London 1977; Frühes Industriedesign: Wien 1900-1908,* exhibition catalogue, by O. Oberhuber and J. Hummel, Vienna 1977; *Josef Hoffmann e la Wiener Werkstatte* by Daniele Baroni, Milan 1981; *Josef Hoffmann: Architect and Designer, 1870-1956,* edited by Christian Meyer, Vienna and New York 1981; *Josef Hoffmann,* edited by Giuliano Greslieri, Bologna 1981; *Josef Hoffmann: das architektonische Werk* by Eduard F. Sekler, Salzburg, Austria 1982; *Josef Hoffmann: tempo e geometria* by Franco Borsi and Alessandra Perizzi, Rome 1982; *Josef Hoffmann: Design Classics,* exhibition catalogue by David Gebhard, Fort Worth, Texas 1983; articles—"Josef Hoffmann 1870-1920" by Max Eisler in *Wendingen* (Amsterdam), nos. 8/9, 1920; "The Work of Josef Hoffmann" by Peter Behrens in *Architecture* (London), no. 2, 1923; "Josef Hoffmann und seine Schule" in *Moderne Bauformen* (Stuttgart), no. 26, 1927; "Josef Hoffmann, maestro dimenticato" by Vittoria Girardi in *L'Architettura* (Rome), October 1956; "Josef Hoffmann und die Wiener Werkstätte" by Günther Feuerstein in *Der Aufbau* (Vienna), April/May 1964; "Josef Hoffmann 1938-1945" by Othmar Birkner in *Werk* (Zürich), October 1967; special issue of *Alte und Moderne Kunst* (Vienna), November/December 1970; "Gli schizzi del viaggio in Italia di Josef Hoffmann" by Eduard F. Sekler in *Artisti austriaci a Roma,* exhibition catalogue, Rome 1972; "Little Square Hoffmann" by Peter Vero in *Architectural Review* (London), December 1977; "Josef Hoffmann Revisited" by Pilar Viladas in *Interiors* (New York), September 1979; "Hoffmann at Liberty" by Jose Manser in *Building Design* (London), 26 October 1979; "Josef Hoffmann—Palais Stoclet, 1905" in *Architectural Design* (London), no. 1-2, 1980; "Furnishings: Josef Hoffmann" by Nora Richter Greer in *AIA Journal* (Washington, D.C.), April 1983.

For many readers, it will be a surprise to discover that half a century ago a critic could write "No recent architect has influenced Europe more comprehensively than Hoffmann" (*Architectural Forum,* November 1928). In the meantime, many of his buildings have been drastically altered or pulled down, and little has been written about the historic significance of his contribution as a prodigious inventor of forms. There are personal, doctrinal, and typological reasons for this neglect.

As a person, Josef Hoffmann was full of inhibitions and distrustful of the intellectual approach to the arts. He disliked discussions about architecture and did not formulate a body of theory to go with his works; in this respect he differed from his teacher Otto Wagner or his more articulate and aggressive contemporary and competitor Adolf Loos. As far as types of buildings are concerned, he built none that were in the public eye or the focus of public discussion except for some short-lived exhibition pavilions such as those at Rome (1911), Cologne (1914), and Paris (1925). Instead, he designed primarily houses and their furnishings for artistically inclined clients who valued privacy more than publicity. His largest commission was the sumptuous and much admired Stoclet House in Brussels. As far as architectural doctrine is concerned, Hoffmann's oeuvre did not fit easily into any of the great movements of the period, from Bauhaus to CIAM; the Secession movement to which he belonged at the outset of his career remained a local development and moreover soon had run its course.

Much of Hoffmann's creative energy over almost thirty years went into running the Wiener Werkstätte, the workshops for artistic craftsmanship he had helped to found in 1903. But to some critics, his unfaltering belief in artistic craftsmanship seemed anachronistic in an age of rapid industrialisation. Moreover, he mostly worked for a vanishing stratum of Austrian society: the rich, liberal, often Jewish, haute bourgeoisie. Thus his temporary eclipse becomes understandable.

Hoffmann's architectural activity can be divided into at least five periods. After a brief initial infatuation with curvilinear Art Nouveau, which found expression in such works as the Bergerhöhe interiors and the Apollo candle shop, he evolved a mode of expression more truly his own and created a more restrained architecture based on rectilinearity, a predilection for the square, and a preference for white and black, against which a few accents of ornament and chromatic color were set off to greatest advantage. The Purkersdorf Sanatorium best illustrates this phase. In tune with developments in the rest of Central Europe, Hoffmann then turned to a reformulation of classicist and folkloristic themes and at the same time relied on increasingly rich schemes of decoration by means of a very personal kind of ornament, as in the Ast, Primavesi (at Winkelsdorf), Berl, and Knips Houses.

Then the impact of the Modern Movement in its "classic phase" was duly felt in a number of designs from the late 1920s and early 1930s, some of them, such as the Altmann and Kühne shop, joint designs with his chief assistant and head of office, Oswald Härdtl. Finally, during Hoffmann's old age, there is a last phase with a few designs done during the Nazi regime and with a few postwar housing schemes done in partnership with others. During the later periods Hoffmann built comparatively little, but he never ceased to pour out highly decorative designs for textiles, wallpapers, ceramics, tableware, and furniture, even when there was no actual commission.

Hoffmann's best creations are characterized by an unfailing sense of form and color and often by a delightful playfulness and ease of presence, which, however, turns out to be perfectly compatible with great restraint and, at times, puristic severity and with a directness of formal and functional solution that may impart a deceptive air of simplicity. As an architectural draftsman, Hoffmann was a master, especially when it came to making small, dramatically foreshortened perspective sketches that convincingly summed up a building's three-dimensional characteristics.

From 1899 till 1936 Hoffmann was professor at the Vienna School (now Academy) of Applied Arts, and there as well as in his private office, he made it a point to encourage and promote young talents— among them Charles Edouard Jeanneret to whom he offered a position. "Les oeuvres de Hoffmann étaient pour moi l'expression la plus lumineuse de l'évolution architecturale," Le Corbusier remembered in 1928. Fifty years later, many others are beginning to rediscover Hoffmann. Forms of his architecture seem to reverberate in recent Italian designs, patterns from the Wiener Werkstätte turn up in modern fashion design, Hoffmann furniture fetches high prices in the art market, and some pieces are back in production as facsimiles. Considering the abundance of Hoffmann's formal invention and the sensuous appeal of his colors, textures, and forms, it was almost inevitable that he would be rediscovered by the leading architects of today with their renewed interest in the pursuit of pure form.

—Eduard F. Sekler

HOLDEN, Charles Henry.

British. Born in Bolton, Lancashire, 12 May 1875. Educated at a small boys' school, Bolton; studied at Manchester Institute of Technology, Lancashire, 1893-96; articled to E. W. Leeson, Manchester, and attended Manchester School of Art, 1896-97; articled to C. R. Ashbee, London, 1898; studied at the Royal Academy Architecture School, London, 1898-99. Served as a commisioned Lieutenant, Dragoon Guards and Engineers, British Army, 1917-18; Major, 1918. Married Margaret Macdonald in 1913 (died, 1954). Assistant in the office of architect Jonathan Simpson, Bolton, 1896; entered the office of architect H. Percy Adams, London, 1899: Partner, 1907-60 (the firm, known as Adams, Holden and (J.L.)Pearson from 1913, continues at 90/92 Parkway, Regent's Park Road, London NW1 7AN). Town Planning Consultant, City of Canterbury, Kent, 1941-44, and, with W. G. Holford, City of London, 1944-54. Member, War Graves Commission, 1918-22; Member, Royal Fine Arts Commission, 1933-47. Vice-President, Architectural Association, 1933-34, Design and Industries Association, 1935, and the Royal Institute of British Architects, 1935-37. Recipient: Soane Medal, 1896; Godwin Bursary, 1913; Bronze Medal, 1929, and Gold Medal, 1936, Royal Institute of British Architects. D.Litt.: University of Manchester, 1936; University of London, 1946. Associate, 1906, and Fellow, 1921, of the Royal Institute of British Architects; Royal Designer for Industry, Royal Society of Arts, London, 1943. Member, Town Planning Institute, London. *Died* (in London) *1 May 1960.*

Works:

1903 Oakley House, Bury Street, Bloomsbury, London

British Seamen's Hospital, Istanbul

Belgrave Hospital for Children, Kennington, London

1904 Law Society Library Block, Chancery Lane, London

Norwich House, 127-129 High Holborn, London

General Hospital, Tunbridge Wells, Kent

1905 Central Reference Library, Bristol, Avon

1906 King Edward VII Sanatorium, Midhurst, Sussex

1907/
  08 British Medical Association, 429 Strand, London (now Zimbabwe House)

1908 Women's Hospital, Soho Square, London
1910 Evelyn House, 62 Oxford Street, London
　　Institute of Electrical Engineers reconstruction, Savoy Place, London
1911 Royal Infirmary, Marlborough Hill, Bristol, Avon
1912 Sutton Valence School and Chapel, Kent
1914 King's College of Household and Social Science, Kensington, London (now Queen Elizabeth College)
1918 War Cemeteries, in Douvencourt, Forceville, Wimereaux, Corbie, and Boulogne East, France
1920 War Memorial, New College, Oxford
1921 Royal Northern Hospital casualty department and nurses' home, Holloway Road, London
1922 Memorial Gateway, Clifton College, Bristol, Avon
　　S.S. Tuscania interiors, for Anchor-Cunard Line
1922/
39 London Underground Stations: 1922, Oval, Westminster, Bond Street, St. Paul's, Mansion House; 1925, Clapham South; 1928, Balham, Piccadilly Circus, Leicester Square, Tooting Bec, Tooting Broadway, Collier's Wood, South Wimbledon, Morden, Ealing Common, Hounslow West; 1932, Sudbury Town, Sudbury Hill, Alperton, Manor House, Turnpike Lane, Bounds Green, Wood Green, Arnos Grove, Southgate; 1934, Oakwood (formerly, Enfield West), Cockfosters, Chiswick Park, Acton Town, Northfields, Boston Manor, Osterley, Rayners Lane, Hammersmith; 1939, East Finchley.
1924 Westminster Hospital reconstruction, Broad Sanctuary, London (demolished, 1958)
1926 Torbay Hospital, Torquay, Devon
1929 London Passenger Transport Board Headquarters, 55 Broadway, London S.W.1.
1929/
36 National Library of Wales extensions, Aberystwyth
1930 Saint Luke's Hospital, Malta
　　Design of the London omnibus
1931 Empire Marketing Board stand, British Industries Fair, London (with C.H. James)
1935/
38 New High Tension Laboratory and Cavendish Research Laboratories, Cambridge University
1936 Sir James Knott Memorial Housing development, Tynemouth, Northumberland
1936/
39 New Westminster Hospital, Saint John's Gardens, London
1936/
40 London University Complex, phase 1, including Senate House (1936), Tower for Bookstacks (1937), and Institute of Education and Historical Research (1938)
1943 City of Canterbury rebuilding plan, Kent (with H. M. Enderby)
1946 Plan for the South Bank, London (project)
　　Plan for the City of London (project; with W. G. Holford)
　　Finchley Power Sub-Station, Archway Road, London
1947 Edinburgh University-George Square Plan, Edinburgh (as consultant)
1948/
55 London University Complex, phase 2
1949 East End redevelopment, Tynemouth, Northumberland (as consultant)
1953 Queen Elizabeth College rebuilding, Kensington, London
1955/
62 English Electric Company offices, Strand, London
1958 Warburg Institute, Woburn Square, London

Publications:

By HOLDEN: papers—*The Conditions Influencing Contemporary Architecture* (London Passenger Transport Board publication), London 1930; *The City of London: A Record of Destruction and Survival*, with William Holford, London 1947.

On HOLDEN: books—*Charles Holden* by D. F. Austin (unpublished thesis), Royal Institute of British Architects, London 1964; *Edwardian Architecture* by A. Service, London 1977; *Charles Holden: Underground Architect* by Gerald Adler (unpublished M.A. thesis), University of Sheffield 1978; *The Architects of London* by Alistair Service, London 1979; articles—"Patient progress: The Life Work of Frank Pick" by Nikolaus Pevsner, in *Architecture Review* (London), September 1942; "Obituary: Dr. Charles Holden— Architect of London" in *The Times* (London), 2 May 1960; "Underground Architect" by Martin Mayer in *Building Design* (London), 11 April 1975; "Singing the Body Electric with Charles Holden" by B. Hanson in *Architectural Review* (London), December 1975; "Charles Holden" by G. Middleton in *Architectural Association Quarterly* (London), vol. 8, no. 2, 1976; "BMA House and its Architects" by Jane Smith in *BMA Journal* (London), 5 July 1982.

Of much significance for the prevailing character of Sir Charles Holden's architectural designs is that he began practice at about the time that the revival of historical styles was coming to an end and serious architects were looking for an architecture that was expressive of contemporary life. One of the somewhat negative manifestations of this trend was a strong movement towards simplicity and a getting rid of the debris of historical ornament before starting afresh. The greater prominence of structural engineering in the media of steel and concrete facilitated this evolution.

In his early years as a student and then as an assistant to H. Percy Adams, Holden was, in some buildings, associated with mediaeval effects of roofs and windows, but these were soon abandoned when he became a responsible partner in the firm: he essayed designs with rectangular massing and a general simplicity sometimes faulted by contemporary critics as being unusually severe. A significant early example is the Royal Infirmary in Bristol. Here the squarish treatment, broad and massive, seemed at the time severe and simple, yet it carried a stylistic reminiscence in the Ionic columns of the upper portions. If the ornament of bases and capitals disappeared in his later buildings, the Greek-like forms of a lintel architecture with the serenity of balanced verticals and horizontals remained and was a dominating character in all of his work. An even better early example is the fine British Medical Association Building in The Strand, London, where the feeling for stone in the exterior design is strong.

Although well known for his simple and effective London Underground stations, Holden is most likely to be chiefly remembered for the important and impressive London Passenger Transport Board Headquarters and for the London University Complex in Bloomsbury. In both these works a classic dignity and even monumental grandeur are apparent, yet Holden always endeavoured to reconcile these attributes with functional building. In the design of the Passenger Transport Board Headquarters, which had to be combined with St. James Station, the convenience of passengers was carefully studied, together with the convenient disposition of offices. The result was a cross-shaped plan which, in his own words, made possible "good light, no interference with neighbour light, short corridors, and a compact centre containing all services, complete with lifts and staircase communicating directly with all four wings." Above the seven storeys the four arms build up a satisfying sequence of diminishing masses to the central tower. A few

accents of sculpture relieve the general simple treatment.

In the London University Complex the central axis of the British Museum was continued northward to form the spine of the various university buildings branching east and west, with the squarish massive blocks of Senate House at the southern end. The great square tower to house the books stacks of the library rises above the spine just north of Senate House. Heavy load bearing walls of stone and brick (of which there is long experience) were employed, as the building is designed to last for hundreds of years. The result is a heavy, massive, monumental building with, in the context of the design, a seemingly unavoidable monotony of windows.

The interior is more effective, for something of the dignity and repose associated with the architecture of ancient Greece has been recaptured, particularly in the ceremonial hall of Senate House. The Greek atmosphere pervades the entrance hall with its coffered ceiling and bronze bowls along the walls, with sconces for indirect lighting at night. The feeling that ancient Greece was the cradle of culture no doubt prompted these visual reminiscences. The question arises whether a heavy monumental building of this kind can so easily be adapted to changes in educational methods as could a more flexible structure. In the work of Charles Holden the massive, static and monumental, often excellent in design, is perpetuated into our era, an era with an accent on change.

—Arnold Whittick

HOLFORD, William Graham.
British. Born in Johannesburg, South Africa, 22 March 1907. Educated at Diocesan College, Johannesburg (also student apprentice in the architectural office of Cowin, Powers and Ellis, Johannesburg), 1920-24; Liverpool School of Architecture, under Charles Reilly and Patrick Abercrombie, 1925-30, B.Arch. (first class honours) 1930; worked in the office of Voorhees, Gmelin and Walker, New York, 1929 (American Society of Arts and Sciences Scholar); attended British School in Rome, 1930-33 (Royal Institute of British Architects Rome Scholar). Married Marjorie Brooks in 1933. In private practice, as architect and town planner, Liverpool, 1933-46, and London, 1946 until his death in 1975. Architect to the North Eastern Trading Estates, England, 1935; Chief Architect for Wartime Hostels, U.K. Ministry of Supply, 1941; Member, Reconstruction Secretariat, U.K. Ministry of Works, 1942; Chief Technical Officer, U.K. Ministry of Town and Country Planning, 1943; Planning Consultant, City of London, 1946-48, University of Liverpool, 1946-55, County of Cambridge, 1948-53, City of Pretoria, South Africa, 1948-49, Corby New Town Development Corporation, Northamptonshire, 1950-54, and the Government of Australia, 1951-57; Architect and Consultant, University College of the Southwest, later University of Exeter, 1954-58; Consultant Architect, Piccadilly Redevelopment, London, 1960, and University of Nottingham, 1960. Lecturer in Architecture, 1933-36, and Lever Professor of Civic Design, 1936-46, University of Liverpool; Professor of Town Planning, 1947-70, and Professor Emeritus, 1970-75, University College, University of London; Romanes Lecturer, Oxford University, 1969. Member of the Council, 1938-39, Vice-President, 1951-52, and President, 1960-62, Royal Institute of British Architects; Member, Royal Fine Art Commission, 1943-69; Chairman, Advisory Committee on Buildings of Architectural and Historic Interest, 1952-75; President, Royal Town Planning Institute, 1953-54; Trustee, British Museum, 1969-75; Treasurer, Royal Academy of Arts, 1970-75; Director, Leverhulme

Trust, 1972-75. Recipient: Florence Bursary, 1935, and Gold Medal, 1963, Royal Institute of British Architects; Gold Medal, Royal Town Planning Institute, 1961. D.C.L.: University of Durham, 1960; LL.D.: University of Liverpool, 1961; D.Litt.: Oxford University, 1964; University of Exeter, 1968; Honorary Fellow, University College London, 1973. Associate, 1932, and Fellow, 1948, Royal Institute of British Architects; Fellow, Institute of Landscape Architects, and Royal Town Planning Institute; Associate of the Royal Academy, 1961, and Royal Academician, 1968. Knight Bachelor, 1953; Life Peer, 1965. *Died* (in London) *17 October 1975.*

Works:

1939 Royal Ordnance Factory, Kirby, Lancashire
1941 Wartime hostels for the U.K. Ministry of Supply
1941/
   45 Team Valley Industrial Estate, near Newcastle upon Tyne
1946/
   47 Development plans for the City of London
1949 Development plan for the University of Liverpool
      City plan for Pretoria, South Africa
      Liverpool Playhouse Theatre interiors
      War Memorial, Eton College, Buckinghamshire
1950 Regional plan for Cambridgeshire
      Courtyard, Kings College, Cambridge
      Bodley's Building Extension, Kings College, Cambridge
1950/
   60 House conversions, Eton College, Buckinghamshire
1951 Plan for Corby New Town, Northamptonshire
1952 Town centre plan for Corby New Town, Northamptonshire
1953 Nuclear Physics Complex, University of Liverpool
1954 Revised development plan for the University of Liverpool
      Market Square and Housing, Corby New Town, Northamptonshire
1955/
   56 Foundation Buildings restoration, Eton College, Buckinghamshire
1955/
   75 Development plan for the University of Exeter, Devon
1956 Study of St. Paul's Cathedral Precinct, London
1957 Development plan for Canberra
1958 Science Schools, Eton College, Buckinghamshire
      Queen's Building, Refectory and Union Building, University of Exeter, Devon
      King's Avenue Bridge, Commonwealth Avenue Bridge, and Central Parkway, Canberra (with W. H. Maunsell and Partners)
      Plan for the University of Kent, Canterbury
1960/
   70 Administration and Senate Chamber Buildings, University of Exeter
      Jeremiah Ambler Factory, Peterlee, Durham
      Woolworth Building, Cornmarket, Oxford
      Farrer House, Eton College, Buckinghamshire
      High-rise flats and maisonettes, Kensal New Town, London
      Villiers House, Eton College, Buckinghamshire
      Barclays Bank, Maidstone, Kent
      Wholesale Market, Sheffield
      Housing, Gidea Park, Icklesham, Sussex
      Courtyards, King's College, Cambridge
      Viaduct and Queenhill Bridge, Gloucestershire

      Narrows Bridge, Perth, Western Australia (with W. H. Maunsell and Partners)
1961 Redevelopment plan for Piccadilly Circus, London
      Government Offices, Bridge Street, Westminster, London (project)
      Science Buildings, Oxford University (project)
      Chapel Ceiling, Eton College, Bukinghamshire
1962 Library, Tonbridge School, Kent
      Memorial Cloister, Overbury, Gloucestershire
1964/
   67 Conversion of four houses in Carlton House Terrace, London, for the Royal Society of Arts
1969/
   75 Buildings for Lloyds Register of Shipping, City of London
1970 Royal Liverpool Hospital

Publications:

By HOLFORD: books—*The Future of Merseyside,* with W. A. Eden, Liverpool 1937; *The City of London: A Record of Destruction and Survival,* with C. H. Holden, London 1947; *Cambridge Planning Proposals,* Cambridge 1950; *Design in Town and Village,* with Frederick Gibberd and Thomas Sharp, London 1953; *The Future of Canberra,* Canberra 1958; *Land Use in an Urban Environment,* with others, Liverpool 1961; *Our Heritage of Landscape and Building,* Bristol 1975.

On HOLFORD: articles—"Sir William Holford" in *Architects' Journal* (London), 17 January 1957; "Man at the Hub of the Circus" by Robert Harling in *The Sunday Times* (London), 8 October 1961; "Sir William Holford Answers Six Questions" in *Official Architecture and Planning* (London), January 1962; "Profile '67: Lord Holford: To Hell with Talking" by Ivor Herbert in the *Evening News* (London), 19 January 1967; "Anatomy of an Architect" by Leslie Jerman in *The Scotsman* (Edinburgh), 19 January 1968; "Obituary" by John Summerson and others in *Building Design* (London), 24 October 1975; "Obituary" by Bernard Collins in *The Planner* (London), December 1975; "Obituary" by Lord Esher in *RIBA Journal* (London), January 1976; "London to Get Britain's First Mies van der Rohe" in *Building Design* (London), 8 January 1982.

*   *   *

William Holford was born in South Africa and trained as an architect under the noted Professor Charles Reilly at the School of Architecture, Liverpool. He was a brilliant student: he obtained a first class honours degree and won the Rome Scholarship in Architecture in 1930. In 1933 he commenced his long teaching career, first at Liverpool as Lever Professor and later, in 1947, as Professor of Town Planning at University College London.

During the war years, Holford was instrumental, with Lord Silkin, in laying down the framework of British town planning legislation and administration, which has since been followed by many other countries throughout the world. His wartime architectural work included the vast Team Valley Industrial Estate near Newcastle upon Tyne; it was the first major, large-scale industrial scheme and became the model for many subsequent industrial estates.

Holford was closely associated with Abercrombie's County and Greater London Plans; he also prepared plans for the City of London, Cambridge, and Corby New Town, as well as special reports on St. Paul's precinct and Piccadilly Circus. His planning work extended to Australia (where he replanned the capital, Canberra), South Africa, Brazil, and other parts of the world. He was particularly interested in university planning, and his

development plan for the University of Liverpool in 1949 was the first of its kind in Britain and became the prototype for university campus design throughout the world. As an architect, he was able to put his plans into practice at the University of Exeter and at the new University of Kent in Canterbury.

He was an early exponent of modular design, and his fourteen-storey block of flats at Kensal, London, was the first large-scale modular building.

Holford's skill as an adviser and administrator in all matters concerning art, architecture, and town planning was always in great demand, and his involvement in professional affairs took much of his time and energy. He held the Presidency of both the Royal Institute of British Architects and the Royal Town Planning Institute and received the Gold Medals of both institutions. The many honours and awards, both in Britain and overseas, which marked his career in architecture and town planning, culminated in the award of a life peerage in 1965.

It has been said that Holford "came as near as the modern world permits to being one of the artist-craftsmen of the Renaissance who tried to master all branches of knowledge." He was a brilliant speaker, a convincing writer, a gifted administrator, and a skilful draughtsman (he originally intended to be a professional artist); he was even a good amateur actor. With his death in 1975 at the age of sixty-eight, the world of architecture and town planning lost a practical pioneer who had, by his personal tact, charm, and brilliance, established standards and guidelines that have left a mark on the cities of the world and have helped to make that world a more pleasant place in which to live and work. Holford was, in every sense, a great man.

—Edward D. Mills

HOLLEIN, Hans.

Austrian. Born in Vienna, 30 March 1934. Educated at the Department of Civil Engineering, Bundesgewerbeschule, Vienna, 1949-53; School of Architecture, Academy of Fine Arts, Vienna, 1953-56, Dip. 1956; studied architecture and planning, Illinois Institute of Technology, Chicago, 1958-59; College of Environmental Design, University of California, Berkeley, 1959-60, M.Arch. 1960. Worked in various architectural offices in the United States, Sweden, and Germany, 1960-64. Since 1964, in private practice, Vienna; consultant designer for numerous firms, including Herman Miller (U.S.A.), American Optical Corporation (U.S.A.), Franz Wittmann KG (Austria), Cleto Munari (Italy), Alessi (Italy), Memphis (Italy), M.I.D. (Austria), Poltronova (Italy), Knoll International (France), Yamagiwa (Japan), and Baleri (Italy), since 1966. Visiting Professor, Washington University, St. Louis, Missouri, 1963-64 and 1966; Professor of Architecture, Academy of Fine Arts, Düsseldorf, since 1967; Head of the School and Institute of Design, since 1976, and Leader of the Master Class in Architecture, since 1979, Academy of Applied Arts, Vienna; also Visiting Professor, Yale University, New Haven, Connecticut. Editor, *Bau* magazine, Vienna, 1965-70. Member of the Austrian State Commission for the *Biennale,* Venice, 1978, 1980, 1982, 1984, and 1986; Vice-President, Austrian Architects' Association, 1965. Exhibitions: *Architektur,* Vienna, 1963 (with Walter Pichler); Stockholm, 1965; *Idea,* Folkestone, Kent, 1967; *Macrostructures,* Richard Feigen Gallery, New York, 1967; Toronto, 1967; Museum of Modern Art, New York, 1967; Musée d'Art Moderne, Paris, 1968; Konsthall, Lund, Sweden, 1968; *Triennale,* Milan, 1968 and 1979; Feigen Gallery, Chicago, 1969; Museum, Mönchengladbach, West Germany, 1970, 1975, and 1984; *Trigon,* Graz, Austria, 1970; *Biennale,* Venice, 1972, 1978, 1980, 1982, and 1984; Museum Folkwang, Essen, West Germany, 1972; Barcelona, 1975; *Dortmunder*

Hans Hollein: Städtisches Museum, Mönchengladbach, West Germany, 1972-82.

Architekturausstellung, Museum am Ostwall, Dortmund, West Germany, 1976 and 1978; Padiglione d'Arte Contemporanea, Milan, 1979; Drawing Center, New York, 1979; Galerie Ulysses, Vienna, 1979; Florence, 1980; Paris, 1981; San Francisco, 1982; New York, 1983. Recipient: Reynolds Memorial Award, U.S.A., 1966 and 1984; National Committee Prize, *Biennale,* Brno, Czechoslovakia, 1968; Austrian State Award, 1968 and 1983; Bard Award, New York, 1970; *Japan Architect* Award, Tokyo, 1970; Rosenthal Studio Prize, Frankfurt, 1973; City of Vienna Prize, 1974; *Industrial Design* Award of Excellence, New York, 1977; German Architecture Award, 1983; *Sunday Times Magazine* Award, London, 1984; Pritzker Prize, 1985. HonoraryFellow, American Institute of Architects, 1981. Member, Austrian Chamber of Architects; German Chamber of Architects (AKNW); League of German Architects (BDA). Address: Argentinierstrasse 36, 1040 Vienna 4, Austria.

Works:

1964/
65 Retti Candle Shop, Vienna
1966 Experimental Gallery, City Art Museum, St. Louis, Missouri (project)
   Savings Bank, Florisdorf, Vienna (project)
   Selection 66 exhibition layouts, Museum für Angewandte Kunst, Vienna
1966/
67 Christa Metek Boutique, Vienna
1967/
69 Richard L. Feigen Gallery, New York
1968 *Austriennale* exhibit layouts, *XIV Triennale,* Milan
1970 Siemens Museum for the History of Electro-Technology, Munich (as consultant)

Death exhibition layouts, Städtisches Museum, Mönchengladbach, West Germany
1970/
71 Restaurant and Staff Dining Facilities, Siemens AG, Munich
1970/
72 Carl Friedrich von Siemens Foundation, Nymphenburg, Munich
1970/
75 Siemens Headquarters Building, Munich
1971/
72 Section N interior furnishing shop, Vienna
   Media-Lines, Olympic Village, Munich
1971/
73 Wollzeile-Landstrasse Urban Study, Vienna
1971 Rathausplatz Development, Vienna
1972 *Paper* exhibition layouts, Austrian Design Centre, Vienna
1972/
73 Mönchengladbach-Abteiberg Urban Study, West Germany
1972/
74 Schullin Jewellery Shop I, Vienna
   Press and Cultural Section, United States Embassy, Moscow
1972/
82 Städtisches Museum, Abteiberg, Mönchengladbach, West Germany
1973 Uecker Exhibition temporary gallery, Studio Rosenthal, Frankfurt
1973 Museum of Modern Art, Villa Strozzi, Florence
1974 Josef Hoffman displays, Furniture Fair, Cologne and Milan
   Principal Room, Sigmund Freud Museum, Vienna (project)
1974/
76 *Man Transforms* exhibition layouts, Cooper-Hewitt Museum, New York
1974 Ecumenical Church, Turracher Hohe, Austria

1975 Nordrhein-Westfalen Art Collection, Landesgalerie, Düsseldorf (competition project)
   Wallraf-Richartz Museum temporary extension, Cologne (project)
1975/
76 Town Hall reconstruction, Perchtoldsdorf, Austria
1976/
77 Miners' Housing revitalization, Grullbad, Recklinghausen, West Germany (as consultant)
1976/
79 Austrian Tourist Bureau Central Branch Office and three Branch Offices, Vienna
1977/
78 Museum of Glass and Ceramics, Tehran
1977 Single-Family House, Vienna
1978 Museum of Arts and Crafts, Berlin (as consultant)
1979 Alessi display, *Triennale,* Milan
1979/
80 Stage design, Burgtheater, Vienna
1979 City of Vienna Public School, Kohlergasse, Vienna
1980 Museum of Arts and Crafts, Frankfurt (competition project)
   Catholic Centre, Mainz-Lerchenberg, West Germany (competition project)
   Strada Novissima exhibition layouts, at the *Biennale,* Venice
   Umanesimo, Disumanesimo exhibition layouts, Palazzo Pazzi, Florence
1981/
82 Schullin Jewellery Shop II, Vienna
1981/
83 Beck Shop at Trump Tower, New York
1981 Beck Department Store, Munich
   Museum of Energy, Essen, West Germany
   Museum of Applied Art extension, Vienna
1982/
83 Paulskirche Urban Scheme, Frankfurt
   Museum of Postal Services, Frankfurt (competition project)
   Museum of Modern Art, Frankfurt (competition project)
   Die Turken vor Wien exhibition layouts, Vienna
1983 Fiat Museum of Industrial Development, Lingotto Area, Turin (project)
   Cultural Forum, Berlin (competition project)
1983 Apartment House, Berlin
   National Museum of Egyptian Civilization, Cairo
1984 *Dream and Reality: Vienna 1870-1930,* exhibition layouts, Künstlerhaus, Vienna

Work as an industrial designer, from 1966, includes sunglasses, furniture, lighting, and household appliances, as well as the visual corporate image of the Deutsche Bank (1973), the Austrian Tourist Bureau (1976/78), and the Erste Austrian Savings Bank (1979).

Publications:

By HOLLEIN: book—*GA 47: Otto Wagner,* edited by Yukio Futagawa, Tokyo 1978; articles— "Rudolph M. Schindler—ein Wiener Architekt in Kalifornien" in *Der Aufbau* (Vienna), March 1961; "Transformations" in *Arts and Architecture* (Los Angeles), May 1966; "Architecture" in *Aujourd'hui art et architecture* (Paris), May/June 1966; "Edifices publics" in *Architecture d'aujourd'hui* (Paris), December 1967/January 1968; "Alles ist Architektur" in *Bau* (Vienna), no. 1, 1968; "Neue Konzeptionen aus Wien" in *Bau* (Vienna), no. 2/3, 1969; "All is Architecture" in *Architectural Design* (London), February 1970; "Hans Hollein: A Biographic Interview," with Federico Correa, in *Arquitecturas bis* (Barcelona), November 1975; "Position and Move" in *Space Design* (Tokyo), April 1976; "Messages" in

Japan Architect (Tokyo), June 1976; "Church in the Mountains at Turracher Hohe" in *Kunst und Kirche* (Linz, Austria), February 1977; "A Gallery in New York" in *Bauwelt* (Berlin), 11 July 1980.

On HOLLEIN: books—*Hans Hollein/Walter Pichler, Architektur*, exhibition catalogue, by Joseph Esherick, Vienna 1963; *Hans Hollein: Work and Behavior, Life and Death, Everyday Situations*, exhibition catalogue, Vienna 1972; *Hans Hollein*, booklet by Christoph Mackler, Aachen, West Germany 1978; *Architektur in Deutschland* by H. and M. Bofinger, J. Paul and H. Klotz, Stuttgart 1979; *Architektur aus Österreich seit 1960* by Peter M. Bode and Gustav Peichl, Salzburg, Austria 1980; *Late-Modern Architecture* by Charles Jencks, London 1980; *Visionary Architecture of the 20th Century* by Vittorio Magnago Lampugnani, Stuttgart and London 1982; *Bauen in Österreich*, Vienna 1983; *GA 8: Schullin Jewellery Shop, Vienna*, edited by Yukio Futagawa, Tokyo 1984; *Sechs Architekten vom Schillerplatz*, Vienna 1984; *Moderne und Postmoderne* by Heinrich Klotz, Braunschweig, West Germany 1984; *Die Revision der Moderne: Postmoderne Architektur 1960-1980*, Frankfurt 1984; *Architektur in Deutschland '83*, edited by Jürgen Joedicke, Stuttgart 1984; *Ornamentalism* by Robert Jensen and Patricia Conway, New York 1984; *Abstract Representation*, edited by Charles Jencks, New York 1984; articles—"Forms and Design by Hans Hollein and Walter Pichler" by Joseph Esherick in *Arts and Architecture* (Los Angeles), August 1963; "Candleshop by Hans Hollein" in *Arts and Architecture* (Los Angeles), April 1966; "Austriennale" in *Architectural Forum* (New York), September 1968; "Architectural Fabergé" by Don Raney in *Progressive Architecture* (New York), February 1970; "A View of Contemporary World Architecture: Hans Hollein" in *Japan Architect* (Tokyo), July 1970; "Hans Hollein" in *Space Design* (Tokyo), May 1973; "Critique: Derniers travaux de Hans Hollein" by Claude Franck in *Architecture d'aujourd'hui* (Paris), July/August 1975; "A New York: un musée vivant" in *Crée* (Paris), December 1976; "Reconversion: Kavaliershaus—Fondation Siemens" in *Techniques et architecture* (Paris), December 1978; "Hans Hollein: Austrian Travel Agency, Vienna" in *Architecture + Urbanism* (Tokyo), January 1979; "Extracting and Recombining Elements" by Mark Mack in *Progressive Architecture* (New York), December 1979; "Hans Hollein—ein Porträt" by Holger Schnitgerhaus in *Architektur und Wohnen* (Hamburg, West Germany), January 1980; "Hans Hollein's 'architecture parlante'" in *Architectural Review* (London), October 1980; "Hollein in Munich" by Peter Davey in *Architectural Review* (London), June 1981; "Projects of Hans Hollein" in *Werk, Bauen und Wohnen* (Zürich), January/February 1982; "Hollein Fragmenta 1972-82" in *Domus* (Milan), October 1982; "Stirling and Hollein" by Peter Cook in *Architectural Review* (London), December 1982; "Hans Hollein—portrait" in *Architecture intérieure* (Paris), April/May 1983; "Eine Kleine Castle: Shop for Ludwig Beck of Munich, New York City" in *Architectural Record* (New York), March 1984; "Homage to Hans Hollein" by Gustav Peichl in *Domus* (Milan) June 1984.

Bibliography—*Hans Hollein: A Bibliography of Books and Articles* by Carol Cable, Monticello, Illinois 1983.

Hans Hollein is one of the few Vienna-born architects who have successfully derived a dialectical creative advantage from a combination of detachment from, and an intimate knowledge of, the city's culture. Although experience of Amercian plurality of style and the almost uncontrolled treatment of architectonic phenomena were certainly of importance to Hollein's development, his work would

be inconceivable without reference to the aesthetic precision and the semantic spectrum of Viennese historicism and the Secession.

At the beginning of the 1960s, Hollein, together with Walter Pichler, began actively criticizing Functionalism, not only verbally but also with sketches and projects that brought about a broader and more comprehensive understanding of architectonic and extra-architectonic phenomena. The theoretically untenable, almost tautological, extension of the architectural idea—"everything is architecture"—nevertheless proved to be a useful vehicle with which to get away from the trap of Functionalism and to discover a crucial theme for his subsequent works. The success of the small Retti Candle Shop consisted not only in its aesthetic complexity but also, and more precisely, in its new interpretation of a functional problem. It is an apparent paradox of his methods that Hollein's works arrive at a sort of Super-Functionalism, modified by a complex view of the building problem and an aesthetic demonstration of its contents.

From a Viennese standpoint, it is difficult to be fair to Hollein. There is, in Vienna, too much experience of, and too developed a sensibility for, substitutes for reality. Since the Baroque era, possibly because of the Hapsburg's firm suppression of literature, the ambivalence of music or architecture has been favored for the staging of semblances of reality, extending even to the reflection of individual or collective psychic states. The funeral cortèges and festive processions of the Hapsburgs were forerunners of the "staging of the downfall" of the aristocratic-bourgeois world, prior to World War I, accomplished primarily within the Secession. Vienna has its tradition of aesthetizing and equalizing realities—a kind of domestic repression. Assembly, collage, and the alteration of old meanings through new relationships are cultivated in media other than just language.

Hollein seems not only to personify this tradition but, as well, to exaggeratedly express it. Otto Wagner, Sigmund Freud, Adolf Loos, and Ludwig Wittgenstein have not altered the situation—they are merely new figures in the game of ambiguity. This background seems visible again in Hollein's works, and he also possesses the technical skill with which to depict it.

—Friedrich Achleitner

HOLZBAUER, Wilhelm.

Austrian. Born in Salzburg, 3 September 1930. Educated at the Technical College, Salzburg, 1946-50; Academy of Fine Arts, Vienna, under Clemens Holzmeister, *q.v.*, 1950-53 (Golden Füger Medal, 1952; Austrian State Student Prize, 1953), Dip.Arch. 1953; Massachusetts Institute of Technology, Cambridge, 1956-57. Married Ursula Mattes in 1966; children: Svilena, Boris and Philipp. In Partnership with F. Kurrent and J. Spalt, Vienna, 1952-56; Partner, Arbeitsgruppe 4, Vienna, 1959-64. Since 1964, in private practice, Vienna; office established in Amsterdam, 1970. Visiting Critic/Professor, University of Manitoba, Winnipeg, 1958, Yale University, New Haven, Connecticut, 1959 and 1965, University of Illinois at Chicago Circle, 1967 and 1968, and Technische Hochschule, Graz, Austria, 1974-76. Professor of Architecture, Academy of Applied Arts, Vienna, since 1976. Exhibitions: Salzburg, Austria, 1968; Graz, Austria, 1968; New Haven, Connecticut, 1968; Vienna, 1976; Stuttgart, 1977; Moscow, 1977; Salzburg, Austria, 1980; Oslo, 1981; Düsseldorf, 1981; Vienna, 1984; Washington, D.C., 1984. Recipient: Theodor-Körner Prize, Austria, 1954; Austrian State Prize, 1960; City of Kapfenberg Prize, 1967; First Prize, Amsterdam Town Hall Competition, 1967; City of Vienna Prize for Architecture, 1971; Gold Medal, Vienna, 1978; Reynolds Memorial Prize, U.S.A., 1983. Address: Wilhelm Holzbauer, Architect, Franziskanerplatz 3, 1010 Vienna, Austria; or, Staalkade 4, Amsterdam C, Netherlands.

Works:

1953/
56 Parish Church, Parsch, Salzburg, Austria (With F. Kurrent and J. Spalt)
1960/
64 St. Jospeh Seminary, Aigen, Salzburg, Austria (with F. Kurrent and J. Spalt)
1965/
66 Residenz Publishing House, Salzburg, Austria
1966/
73 St. Vitalis Parish Center, Salzburg, Austria
1966/
76 St. Virgil Educational and Cultural Center, Salzburg, Austria
1967 Bettelheim House, Vienna
City Hall, Amsterdam (competition project)
1970/
82 31 stations of Vienna Underground System (with Marschalek, Ladstätter and Gantar)
1971 Urban renewal plan for Salzburg, Austria
1973 Austrian Cultural Institute, Budapest (project)
1975 Stifter House, Ottensheim, Austria
1976/
79 Living Tomorrow Municipal Housing, Vienna
1976/
80 Provincial Government Building, Bregenz, Austria (with Rapf, Mätzler and Schweitzer)
1977 Residenz Publishing House New Quarters, Salzburg, Austria
1978 Conference Center, Abu Dhabi (project)
1978/
82 De Bijenkorf Department Store, Utrecht, Netherlands
1979 Dichand House, Vienna
1979/
86 City Hall and Opera, Amsterdam (with Cees Dam)
1980/
86 Faculty of Natural Sciences, University of Salzburg, Austria (with Ekhart, Hubner, Ladstatter and Marschalek)
1982/
84 IBA Municipal Housing, Berlin-Kreuzberg
1982/
86 ALRT Stations, Vancouver, British Columbia (with A. Parker, Marschalek, Ladstatter und Gantar)

Publications:

By HOLZBAUER: book—*GA 58: Dudok—Town Hall, Hilversum, 1928-31*, edited by Yukio Futagawa, Tokyo 1981.

On HOLZBAUER: books—*Neue Architektur in Österreich 1945-1970*, Vienna 1971; *Österreichische Architektur 1960-70*, Vienna 1972; *Wilhelm Holzbauer: Porträt eines Architekten* by Heinrich Hübl, Vienna 1977; *Sechs Architekten vom Schillerplatz*, Vienna 1977; *Three Viennese Architects: Wilhelm Holzbauer, Gustav Peichl, Roland Rainer*, exhibition catalogue, Vienna 1984; *Wilhelm Holzbauer: Bauten und Projekte 1953-1985*, with foreword by Friedrich Achleitner, Salzburg, Austria 1985; articles—"Design for the New Amsterdam Town Hall" by Sokratis Dimitriou in *Bauforum* (Vienna), January/February 1974; "New City Hall for Amster-

Wilhelm Holzbauer: Housing Project, Berlin-Kreuzberg, 1982-84.

dam" in *Parametro* (Bologna, Italy), July 1974; "Wilhelm Holzbauer" by Naisu Akashi in *Architecture + Urbanism* (Tokyo), October 1976; "St. Virgil Centre for Continuing Education in Salzburg-Aigen," "The Church of St. Vitalis in Salzburg" and "St. Joseph's College in Salzburg-Aigen" in *Art d'eglise* (Ottignies, Belgium), January/March 1977; "Religious Centre in Salzburg" in *Kunst und Kirche* (Linz, Austria), February 1977; "Study and Meditation Centre in Salzburg" in *Domus* (Milan), May 1977; "St. Virgil Institute, Salzburg" in *Bauen und Wohnen* (Zürich), April 1978; "Studio/House for a Painter" in *Domus* (Milan), October 1979; "The Amsterdam Opera House/Town Hall" in *Bouw* (Rotterdam), 19 January 1980; "Painter's House near Linz" in *Baumeister* (Munich), March 1980; "Housing Estate, 15 Bezirk, Vienna" in *Baumeister* (Munich), May 1980; "Social Housing 'Wohnen Morgen', Vienna" in *GA Document* (Tokyo), Autumn 1980; "A City's Memory" in *Domus* (Milan), March 1981; "Experimental Housing in Wenen" in *Architect* (The Hague), October 1981; "The New Vorarlberger Landhaus" in *Bauforum* (Vienna), December 1981; "Town Hall in Amsterdam" in *Plan* (Amsterdam), March 1982.

I adhere to an architecture, the roots of which are based on a pragmatic attitude and not on an ideological, dogmatic one. Whereas the nature of a pragmatic attitude in solving a particular building task is to be seen in the interpretation of the task itself—the transformation of a building program while taking into account external circumstances such as site conditions, urban and geographical relationships, questions of scale, and so forth—an ideological attitude is an intellectual one, the interpretation of a dogmatic thought in a building. A pragmatic architecture then is an architecture of "feeling," of the "nerves," versus an architecture of the intellect. Each of my projects therefore has a basic theme, a *Leitmotiv*, whose characteristics apply only to the particular project and are not and should not be, of universality.

The question of the relation of architecture and representation, the "self-presentation" of a part of society embodied in a building, is taken up in the building for the Provincial Government of Vorarlberg, one of the nine provinces of Austria. The architectural language is modest, complex and yet restrained. Precious and durable materials reflect the importance and dignity the building ought to convey.

The theme of the house, of housing, is shown in three examples showing the extensive scope and variety of this theme, from social housing as a nucleus of a new urbanity in an otherwise drab cityscape, to the small simple house, built partly in cooperation with the owner, to the palatial villa, both mansion and small museum for an extensive art collection.

Planning the buildings for the new Vienna Underground was part of an extremely complex technical and organizational process. The application of overall design principles of the stations of one line – the visual variations of the different stations reflecting only the differences in the urban settings and fuctional layouts – has a unique tradition in Vienna since the Stadtbahn of Otto Wagner, built around the turn of the century. The range of the different stations – 31 altogether – reaches from the complete restoration of existing stations to the restoration of existing entrance pavilions with new platform areas and to the construction of completely new stations, both underground and elevated ones.

The buildings for the Faculty of Natural Sciences of the University of Salzburg will be completed in the spring of 1986. The concept takes into account the specific character of the architecture of Salzburg, an architecture with its roots in the area of transition of Renaissance and baroque, the area of mannerism. The architectural language of the design is specific, not universal; the plan is integrated in the particular-

ities of the site and thus not interchangeable. The formal vocabulary is manneristic and *pittoresque* – functions define the form, yet are not functionally interpreted but subordinated to the formal concept in a pragmatic manner. The plans for the Opera Buildings in Paris and Amsterdam are typical for the process of "reacting" to the specifics and urban characteristics of both cities. The facade taking up the entire length of one side of Place de la République has an important role in developing the architectural concept of the Paris Opera project. The project for Amsterdam – to be completed in 1986 – takes its particularities of the combination of two important buildings – City Hall and Opera House – in one urban complex whose architectural expression has to take into account the peripheral conditions of the site, whereby the building reacts differently to the river, the canal, the market place, and the traffic surrounding the complex on four sides.

A pragmatic approach in developing conceptual thinking in architecture attempts to occupy a position independent of rapidly changing "isms" in architecture, an architecture in the mainstream of historical development.

—Wilhelm Holzbauer

Wilhelm Holzbauer is one of those Holzmeister students who have stayed close to their master in their attitude towards architecture. This has nothing to do with architectural vocabulary, as it were, but above all concerns the art of developing a construction out of all of the given circumstances, seeing architecture both as historic phenomenon and as autonomous medium.

Looking at it superficially, Holzbauer's conception of architecture is nonpolitical and not particularly given to reform. His works show no easily labelled tendencies. Their underlying theories are hidden, and theory is replaced by a stance which gives priority to the traditional values of architecture. Holzbauer does not bow to any system; there are no obvious fundamental premises that can easily be identified. It is more that the philosophy somehow develops itself in the course of the realizaton of the task in hand and within its unique historical setting. Quality is understood on the one hand as the repeated reflection of the complexity of the assignment and on the other as the interpretation of its optimum possibility.

Holzbauer is more likely than not to be uncritical of his commissions. He is interested less in the "what" than in the "how." He wants to change neither his client nor society in general; rather, he tries to interpret their thoughts and wishes. In this, he finds himself entirely in the Viennese tradition of "therapeutic Nihilism" and "Aestheticism" (in the manner of William M. Johnston). That is to say, he has more of an interest in the factual, the great variety of reflections and relationships, than in alteration or in therapy. With this attitude, one might easily underrate the realism of the architectural medium or its possibilities and effects. Holzbauer sees architecture as having the power to incluence life, making it better or more beautiful; but he is skeptical about the greater power that some claim for it, to change society.

This realism of Holzbauer's, which is not necessarily solely skeptical, is above all noticeable in the balance of his materials. His structures often show a good comprehensible and functional concept of space. Materials are used fundamentally where they can make a definite contribution, not merely for their own sake, as their statement can be made only in a structurally coherent relationship. His inclination is therefore towards synthesis, beginning with an acceptance of the commitment to the client's specification. This, however, does not mean that the architectural and spatial resources relate only to themselves and one another. They develop, one might say, a dialectic of reactions, a mannered relativity of form, that makes the building come alive quite independently of its actual function. So, perhaps one could say that his Cultural Center in

Salzburg stands over and above its orginal conception as a dialogue with the Salzburg mannerist-baroque tradition and setting, without having recourse to collage or quotation. Holzbauer avoids the literary or psychological; his manner remains within the frame of pure architecture. For him, architecture is itself a medium of fascination.

—Friedrich Achleitner

HOLZMEISTER, Clemens.

Austrian. Born in Fulpmes, Tyrol, 27 March 1886. Educated at the Volksschule Muhlau and the Volksschule St. Niklaus, Innsbruck, Austria 1893-98; Realschule, Innsbruck, 1899-1906; studied architecture, under Max von Ferstel, Ludwig Simony, and Carl Koenig, Technische Hochschule, Vienna, 1907-13. Married Judith Bridarolli-Guggenberger in 1914 (divorced, 1939); children: Guido and Judith; married Gunda Lexer in 1939; daughter: Barbara. Assistant to the architect Max von Ferstel, Vienna, 1913-19; in private practice, in Vienna, 1919-38, in Tarabya and Istanbul, Turkey, 1939-49, in Vienna, 1949-74, and in Salzburg, Austria, 1975 until his death in 1983. Instructor in architecture, Staatsgewerbeschule (now Höhere Technische Lehrund Versuchsanstalt), Innsbruck, Austria, 1919-24; Professor, Technische Hockschule, Vienna, 1924-38, and at the Akademie, Düsseldorf, 1928-32; Rector and Professor, 1931-38 and 1950-57, and Emeritus, 1957-83, Akademie der bildenden Künste, Vienna; Professor, Technical High School, Istanbul, 1940-49. President, General German Catholic Assembly, 1933; Art Senate of Austria, 1954; Association of Austrian Foreign Works (A.O.W.), 1955. Artistic Council Member, Salzburg Festival, 1955; Chairman, Panel of Awards in Arts and Sciences, Vienna, 1965. Exhibitions: *Clemens Holzmeister—Peter Behrens*, Steiermerkischer Kunstverein, Graz, Austria, 1929; *Das Werk Prof. Holzmeisters*, Museum Ferdinandeum, Innsbruck, Austria, 1956; *Clemens Holzmeister und sein Werk*, Kunstschule, Linz, Austria and Residenz, Salzburg, Austria, 1956; *Clemens Holzmeister—das Lebenswerk*, Akademie der bildenden Künste, Vienna, 1956; *Clemens Holzmeister—75, Lebensjahres*, Kunstschule, Linz, Austria, 1961; *Zeichnungen von Clemens Holzmeister*, Kunst-pavilion, Innsbruck, Austria, 1962; *Clemens Holzmeister*, Galleria del Duomo, Bolzano, Italy, and Residenz, Salzburg, Austria, 1966; *Clemens Holzmeister—Aufzeichen von seinen Reisen*, Graphische Sammlung Albertina, Vienna, 1967; *Clemens Holzmeister zum 85. Geburtstag*, Bauzentrum, in Vienna, Graz, Austria, and Innsbruck, Austria, 1971; *Clemens Holzmeister—Aquarelle, Zeichnungen*, Hypobank, Linz, Austria, 1973; *Clemens Holzmeister—Theaterbauten und Buhnenbilder*, Schloss Arenberg, Salzburg, Austria, 1976; *Clemens Holzmeister*, Bayerische Akademie, Munich, 1978; *Architekt, Zeichner, Maler*, Durnstein, 1979; *Antike Theater—Berg Sinai, Cosmograf*, Landerbank, Salzburg, Austria, 1980; *Clemens Holmeister—Aquarelle, Zeichnungen, Skizzen*, Castello Maresch, Bolzano, Italy, 1981; *Clemens Holzmeister—retrospective*, Akademie der bildenden Künste, Vienna, 1982. Collections: Atelier Holzmeister, Brunnhausgasse 14A, Salzburg, Austria; Graphische Sammlung Albertina, Vienna. Recipient: State Gold Medal, Austria, 1926; Grand Award of Honour, Republic of Austria, 1934; Royal Swedish Order of the North Star, 1951; Josef Hoffmann Prize, Vienna, 1953; Gold Medallion, Austrian Chamber of Architects and Engineers, 1955; Honour Award, Architects' Ring of the Tyrol, 1956, City of Vienna, 1956, Salzburg Region, Austria, 1960, City of Salzburg, Austria, 1966; Award of Arts and Sciences, Vienna, 1957; City of Vienna Prize, 1957; Grand Cross of Merit with Star, Government of West Germany, 1958; Honour

Diploma, Mountain Towns of Pozuzo, Peru, 1963; Gold Diploma for Engineering, Technische Hochschule, Vienna, 1963; Cross of Honour, Austrian Union of Berlin, 1964; Honour Diploma of Volders, Austria, 1965; Medal with Crest, Region of Salzburg, Austria, 1966; Cross with Star, Order of Pope Sylvester, 1976; Grand Order of Honour with Star, Republic of Austria, 1981; Grand Cross of Honour, Salzburg, Austria, 1981. Honoured Citizen, Fulpmes, 1934, City of Durnstein, 1971, City of Vienna, 1971, and Regional Capital of Salzburg, 1976; Honorary President, Central Union of Austrian Architects, 1958, and Association of Friends of the Vienna Theatres, 1971; Honorary Council Member, Dutch Research Commission, 1935; Honorary Member, Church Building Union of Vienna-Mauer, 1936, Akademie der bildenden Künste, Vienna, 1931, 1961, Bavarian Academy of Fine Arts, 1941, South Tyrol Artists Federation, 1955, Union of Austrian Architects, 1967, Vienna Rotary Clubs, 1972, and the Burgenland Community, 1973. Honorary Doctorates: Technische Hochschule, Graz, Austria, 1952; Technical High School, Istanbul, 1963; Technische Hochschule, Vienna, 1965; Building Department of Innsbruck University, Austria, 1971. *Died* (in Salzburg, Austria) *12 June 1983.*

Works:

1913/
14 Elementary School and Teachers' Housing, Marbach, Austria
1914 Cinema, Krohuletzplatz, Eggenburg, Austria
1915 Youth Probationary Institution, Marbach, Austria
1918 Wooden Bridge, Schwaz, Austria
1918/
21 Funeral Chapel and Cemetery, Breitenfurt West, Austria
1919 Post Hotel, Sesto, Italy
1920 Colosseum Complex, Exhibition Park, Innsbruck
   Roter Adler hotel, office and commercial building, Sellergasse, Innsbruck
1921 Kleisel House (now Luftner House), Kufstein/Hintersteinsee, Austria
1921/
22 Crematorium I, Simmeringer Hauptstrasse, Vienna
1921/
23 Parish Church, Batschuns/Rankweil, Austria
1922 Underground works for the Austrian Railways, Roppen/Tyrol, Austria
1922/
23 Sanatorium, Bregenz-Mehrerau, Austria
1922/
26 Bismarckplatz (now Landhausplatz) rebuilding study, Innsbruck, Austria
1923 Ralser House (conversion of old miners' housing), Colle Isarco, Italy
   Demetz House, Ortisei, Italy
   Community House and Meeting Rooms, Sesto, Italy
1923/
25 Hotel Steinbock, Bundesstrasse, Steinach, Austria
1924 Alt-Innsprung Restaurant and Bar, Maria-Theresien-Strasse, Innsbruck
   Hofgarten Cafe, Innsbruck, Austria
   Imperial Chapel, Tummelplatz, Innsbruck, Austria
1924/
25 Ludwig House, Arlbergstrasse, Bregenz, Austria
   Klostergrund Neighborhood Development, Via Armando Diaz, Bolzano, Italy
   Industrial Association Presidential Rooms, Adamgasse, Innsbruck
   Meisel Confectionery Shop, Stadtgraben, Hall, Austria
   Public Housing Block, Rottstrasse, Vienna

1924/
27 Hotel Hospiz, Ahornboden, Innsbruck, Austria
1924/
31 Maria Hilf Parish Church, Mariahilferstrasse, Bregenz-Vorkloster, Austria
1924/
32 St. Judas Thaddaus in der Krim Church, Budinskystrasse, Vienna
1925 Railway Employees' Housing, Ora, Italy
   Mission House Youth Hostel, Kleinholz, Kufstein/Zell, Austria
   Alpenrose Guesthouse, St. Anton, Austria
1925/
26 Hotel Aquila, Ortisei, Italy
1925/
29 Innbrucke Bridge, Schwaz, Austria
1926 Alpenrose Guesthouse, Bahnstrasse, Fulpmes, Austria
   Memorial Chapel, Nauders, Austria
   Theatre I, Hofstallgasse, Salzburg, Austria
   Bernardi House, Ortisei, Italy
   Hotel Tre Cime, Sesto, Italy
1926/
27 Drinking and Changing Halls, Kurpromenade, Bad Hall, Austria
   Dr. August Hermann House (now Hausner-Stollhofen House), Im Schiffeln, Langenzersdorf, Austria
   St. Martin Parish Hall, Grolandstrasse, Nuremberg, Germany
1926/
28 Pretz-Amon Settlement, Bolzano, Italy
   Merciful Sisters of the Holy Cross girls' school and boarding facilities, Stockhofstrasse, Linz, Austria
1926/
35 St. Martin Parish Centre Development, Grolandstrasse, Nuremberg, Gemany
1927 Dr. Wittmann House, Brucknerstrasse, Bad Ischl, Austria
1927/
28 Hans Holzmeister House, Holzgasse, Innsbruck, Austria
   Elementary and Grammar School, Sudtirolerplatz, Jenbach, Austria
   Hotel Post, St. Anton, Austria
   Eichmann country house, with boatd bathhouse, Litzelberg, Seewalchen, Austria
   Ledigenheim Student Hostel, Michaelerstrasse, Vienna
1927/
29 Grammar School, Educational and Mesmer Institute, Schulhausplatz, Landeck, Austria
1927/
30 Regional Ministry of Defence Building, Ankara, Turkey
   Albert Murr House, St. Anton, Austria
1927/
31 Health Cure Centre, Bahnhofstrasse, Bad Ischl, Austria
1928 Community Hall and Cinema, Sudtirolerplatz, Jenbach, Austria
   Elementary and Grammar School, Nova Levante, Italy
   Well-House, Bad Hofhastein, Austria
1928/
29 Grammar School, Imst-Oberstadt, Austria
   Parish Church, Merchingen, Germany
1928/
30 General Staff Building, Ankara, Turkey
1928/
33 St. Peter's Parish Church, Nicodemstrasse, Mönchengladbach, Germany
1929/
30 Maria-Grun Parish Church, Schenefelderlandstrasse, Hamburg, Germany
1929/
31 Franciscan Monastery, Hermsekeil, Germany
1929/
32 Foundation Building, Burggraben, Innsbruck, Austria
1929/
34 Ministry of Labour, Ankara, Turkey

1929/
35 Parliament Buildings Redevelopment Plan, Ankara, Turkey
1930 Clemens Holzmeister Mountain Lodge, Kitzbühel, Austria
1930/
31 New Land-School, Alfred-Wegner-Gasse, Vienna
1930/
32 Two small houses, Werkbund Exhibition Development, Vienna/Lainz, Austria
   Church of the Redeemer, Weikersdorferstrasse, Vienna-Neustadt, Austria
1930/
33 Officers' Casino (Ordu Evi), Ankara, Turkey
   Church of St. Adalbert, Liniemstrasse, Berlin
1930/
35 War School, Ankara, Turkey
   Government Quarter Planning Study, Ankara, Turkey
1930/
36 Church of Christ the King, Merano, Italy
1931 Professor Strieder House, Garmisch-Partenkirchen, Germany
   Ataturk Palace, Cankaya, Ankara, Turkey
1931/
33 Merkezbank State Bank, Ankara, Turkey
1932 Hotel Pera Palace, Istanbul
1932/
33 Trebitsch House, Dubrovnik-Ragusa, Yugoslavia
   Fauststadt Open-Air Theatre with arcades, Salzburg, Austria
   St. Clement's Church, Tasovice/Hodonice, Czechoslovakia
   Cardinal Piffl Student Hostel, Pfeilgasse, Vienna
1932/
34 Victory Avenue and Park layouts, Ankara, Turkey
   Ministry of the Interior, Ankara, Turkey
   Cardinal Piffl Church II, Gloggnitz, Austria
   St. Elisabeth's Church of Christ the King, Lindenallee, Kleve, Germany
   Dr. Seipel and Dr. Dollfuss Memorial Church, Vogelweidplatz, Vienna
1933 Falih Rifki Bey House, Istanbul
1933/
34 Emlakbank Mortgage Bank, Ankara, Turkey
   Supreme Court of Justice, Ankara, Turkey
1933/
35 Austrian Embassy, Ankara, Turkey
   Ministry of the Treasury Building, Ankara, Turkey
   Vilayet Square, Ankara, Turkey
1934 Eisner House, Kitzbühel, Austria
1934/
35 Church of Christ Transfigured, Rueppgasse, Vienna
1935 Anny Schmelling-Ondra House, Berlin-Saarow, Germany
   Bertha Kunz Wine Bar, Albertinaplatz, Vienna
   Luis Trenker Ski Hostel, Saieseralm, Italy
1935/
36 Dr. Atzwanger House, Arzlerstrasse, Innsbruck, Austria
   O. Boeller Company Building Development, Rechte Wienzelle, Vienna
1935/
39 RAVAG Radio Station, Argentinierstrasse, Vienna
1936/
37 St. John's Chapel, Schottenkirche, Vienna
1937 Galzig Railway valley and mountain stations, St. Anton, Austria
   House of the Front, Ballhausplatz, Vienna
   Customs House II, Rennweg, Innsbruck, Austria
1938 Reichsbrucke Bridge, Vienna
1938/
63 Parliament Buildings, Ankara, Turkey
1939 Cathedral, Praca do Cruseiro, Belo Horizonte, Brazil

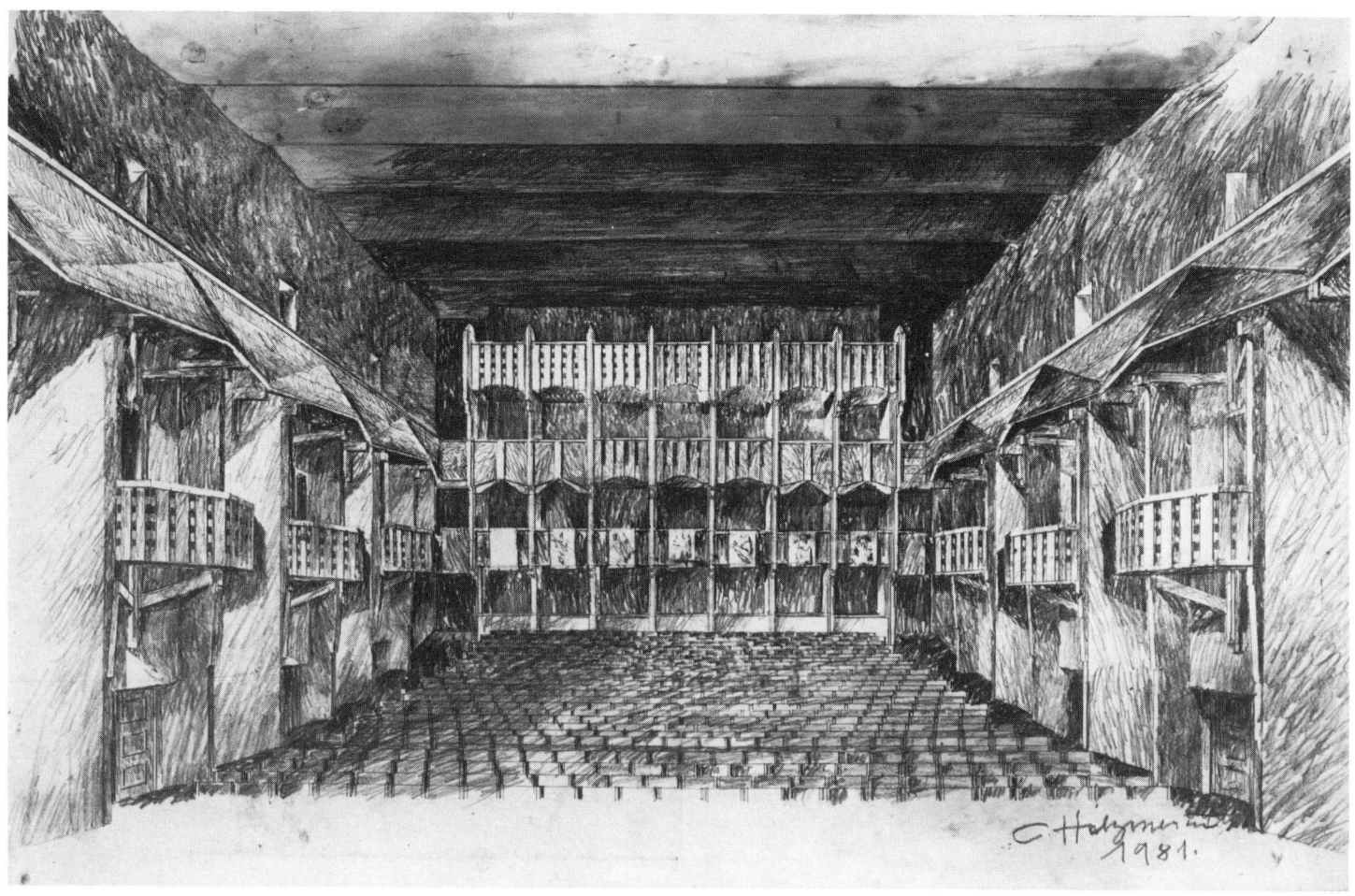

Clemens Holzmeister: Drawing for the interior of the Little Theatre, Salzburg, 1981.

1940 Parish Church of Our Lady Fatima, Tijuca, Brazil
Our Mother of Aparesida Pilgrim's Church, Rio de Janeiro
1943 Eckert-Emirgan House, Istanbul
1947/
50 Judith Holzmeister-Jurgens House, Ginzinger Hauptstrasse, Vienna
1952/
62 Clemens Holzmeister House, Brunnhausgasee, Salzburg, Austria
1953/
56 Kammerspiele Theatre, Promenade, Linz, Austria
1953/
58 Landestheater, Promenade, Linz, Austria
1954/
57 Parish Church, Erpfendorf, Austria
1954/
58 Factory Association Building, Riehlstrasse, Fulpmes, Austria
1955/
60 New Festival Theatre, Hofstallgasse, Salzburg, Austria
1956 Judith Holzmeister-Bridarolli House, Mahlerstrasse, Vienna
1956/
62 Church of Christ the King II, Gloggnitz, Austria
1957/
58 Rollinger House, Espanstrasse, Nuremberg, West Germany
1957/
59 Chapel of the Guardian Angel, Fulpmes/Schlick, Austria
1958/
60 Church of St. Ulrich, Walchensee, West Germany
1958/
64 Chapel, Hochsolden/Gaislach, Austria
Chapel of St. Bernard, Kitzbühel, Austria

1959/
63 Council Offices, Trade Buildings and Museum Development, Hallstatt, Austria
1960/
62 Luise Wolf House, Ischl, Austria
Evangelical Church, Hornbahn, Kitzbühel, Austria
1960/
65 St. George's Parish Church with Kindergarten, Innsbruck, Austria
1961/
62 Mario Retti House, Oberperflus, Austria
1961/
70 Twelve Apostles Parish Church with Hostel, Augsburg, West Germany
1962 Unterrainer Garage, Erpfendorf, Austria
1962/
70 Church of St. Boniface, Breitenfurt, Austria
1963/
66 K.A.V. Norica Club House, Strozzigasse, Vienna
1963/
72 Salesian School Hostel, Fulpmes, Austria
1964/
66 Chapel of St. Pontianus, Telfs, Austria
Parish Church of the Holy Family, with Parish House, and Youth Hostel, Puchsbaumplatz, Vienna
1965/
67 Parish Church of the Holy Trinity, Zwolfaxing, Austria
1966 Sepp Dangl House, Kitzbühel, Austria
1966/
67 Parish Church of St. Christopher, Navis, Austria
1966/
70 Parish Church of the Holy Trinity, Pertisau, Austria
1966/
71 Elementary School, Grafstein, Austria
1967 Funeral Chapel, Navis, Austria

1968/
69 Erich Striegl Bar, Breitenfurter Strasse, Vienna
1968/
75 Three-Rampart Chapel, Bad Garstein, Austria
1970/
72 Leopoldau Parish Church, Vienna
1971 Parish Church, Bruckhaus/Kirchberg, Austria
1972 Consecration Hall, Dollach, Austria
1972/
75 O.N.J. Youth Hostel, Apetlon, Austria
Dr. Hans Holzmeister House, Steinach, Austria
1973/
76 Parish Church of St. John the Baptist, Klosterle, Austria
1977/
81 Elementary School Gymnastics Hall, Himmelberg, Austria
1978/
83 Branch Church, Holzhausen, Austria
1979/
81 Chapel of Mary, Klagenfurt, Austria
1980 Music School, Salzburg, Austria

Also numerous memorials, monuments, interior and stage designs, and additions to existing building.

Publications:

By HOLZMEISTER: books—*Clemens Holzmeister: Entwurfe und Zeichnungen*, Vienna 1927; *Clemens Holzmeister: Bauten, Entwurfe und Handzeichnungen*, Salzburg, Austria, and Leipzig, Germany 1937; *Kirchenbau ewig neu*, Innsbruck, Austria 1951; *Clemens Holzmeister: Werke für das Theater*, edited by Joseph Gregor, Vienna 1953; *Bilder aus Anatolien*, with Gunda Holzmeister and Rudolf Fahrner, Vienna 1954; *Selbstbiographie*, Innsbruck, Austria 1956; *34 Faksimile nach Aquarellen und Zeichnungen*, Vienna 1966; *Salzburg, Lob eines schönen Landes*, with Eligius Scheibl, Salzburg, Austria 1970; Clemens Holzmeister—Architekt in der Zeitenwende, 2 vols., with texts by Herbert Muck, Georg Mladek and Wolfgang Greisenegger, Salzburg, Austria, Stuttgart and Zürich 1976; *Clemens Holzmeister— Kuppelbauten*, Salzburg, Austria, Stuttgart and Zürich 1981.

On HOLZMEISTER: books—*Das neue Festspiel- haus Salzburg*, Salzburg, Austria 1960; *Clemens Holzmeister und Salzburg* by Paul Becker, Salzburg, Austria 1966; *Clemens Holzmeister—Das archi- tektonische Werk*, dissertation by Monika J. Knof- fer, Innsbruck, Austria 1976; *Clemens Holzmeister*, exhibition catalogue, by Friedrich Achleitner, Wil- helm Holzbauer and Herbert Muck, Vienna 1982; articles—"Clemens Holzmeister" in *Casabella* (Milan), July 1934; "Alcuni ultimi lavori di Clemens Holzmeister" by Luigi Lenzi in *Architettura* (Rome), August 1934; "Clemens Holzmeister als Raum- gestalter" in *Innendekoration* (Darmstadt, Ger- many), March 1936; "L'Eglise commemorative de Vienne" in *Construction moderne* (Paris), 9 May 1937; "Clemens Holzmeisters Bauten in der Turkei" by Hans Henniger in *Deutsche Bauzeitung* (Stu- ttgart), June 1938; "Clemens Holzmeister" in *Aufbau* (Vienna), March 1957; "Autriche: nouveau theatre du Festival de Salzbourg" in *Techniques et architec- ture* (Paris), September 1957; "Das neue und das alte Festspielhaus" in *Aufbau* (Vienna), November/ December 1961; "Clemens Holzmeister" by Fried- rich Achleitner in *Bau* (Zürich), no. 1/2, 1966; films— *Zu Gast bei Clemens Holzmeister*, television film by Otto Kamm, 1972; *Portrait: Clemens Holzmeister*, television film by Angelica Bäumer, 1979.

It was certainly no accident that Clemens Holz- meister, teacher of three generations of Austrian architects at the Vienna Academy of Fine Arts, should have continued a master class tradition that included the work of Friedrich von Schmidt, Viktor Luntz and Friedrich Ohmann, rather than the tradition of Theophil Hansen, Karl von Hasenauer and Otto Wagner (the tradition of the "gothic" and later the romanticized-baroque, the classicism of Hansen leading to the functionalism of Wagner). Holzmeister regarded himself as part of the former tradition; it presents itself less as a formal school than as a principle of design in which the thematic, or graphically developed, or that which emanates from one point and proceeds to relate to a definite situation—that is to say, the anti-rational, emo- tional, and sensual—plays an important part.

Holzmeister's theoretical world remains intact. The old, established hierarchies still stand; cult, monument, and signs have all retained their content and significance. His baroque theory of life, with its "triad of the fine arts," and his feeling for stage management—not only of his architecture but also of his way of life—left room in his work for elements that did not necessarily represent his main interest. Thus, for example, the typological elements in his structures are not there as part of an intellectual exercise, but simply because newly worked out formulae required the adaptation, reinterpretation and transformation of traditional space design. His very striking graphic work sets up a strong colloquy with the existing building substance, and his work is, in fact, a constant dialogue with the medium of space. If these terms suggest the theatre, that is appropriate; "theatre" is the key to his temperament.

But, though Holzmeister's training was of the old school of Viennese historical emphasis, and though throughout his life, he designed and theorized from a background of historical awareness, it would never- theless be untrue to say that he was historically oriented in the sense of being an architect who worked strictly within historical forms. In the euphoria of Expressionism, and the realism that followed, Holzmeister learned to transform historic forms, to distance them from their traditions, and so to give them a breath of new life.

Holzmeister designed and built for more than seventy years, yet stagnation never set in. Rather, in his late work there was a new freedom in his use of materials. His work is enjoying a new recognition after a long period of disparagement during the time of Viennese Positivism. Of course, his architecture does involve a playing back of only one side of the Austrian "soul"—but it is one that is too easily described as "barock-kulinarisch," not taking into account its contemplative, basically Liebnitzian, world view. Holzmeister's spiritual and cultural background was Alpine Catholicism, with its existentialist dialectic between reality and make- believe, between realism and mysticism. It is not surprising that the Tyrolean Holzmeister finally made himself at home not in Vienna but in Salzburg.

—Friedrich Achleitner

HORIGUCHI, Sutemi.

Japanese. Born in Mushiroda Village, Gifu Prefec- ture, 6 January 1895. Educated at the Sixth Higher School, Okayama, until 1914; studied architecture, University of Tokyo, under Chyuta Ito, 1916-20, B.Arch. 1920, Dr.Arch. 1944. Married Suzuko Suzumura in 1922; children: Masako, Keiko, Ohi, and Yoshiko. Since 1920, in private practice, Tokyo. Professor, Teikoku University of Art, 1932-38; Lecturer, Tokyo Women's Normal High School, 1938-46; Lecturer, University of Tokyo, 1946-55; Professor, 1949-65, Head of the Engineering Depart- ment, 1952-70, and Lecturer, 1965-70, Meiji Univer- sity, Tokyo. Founder-Member, Secession Group, Tokyo, 1920; Founder-Member, Japan Construc- tion Culture League, 1936 (issued the magazine *Contemporary Architecture*); Director and Trustee, Japan Garden Society, and Japan Ceramics Society, since 1938; Organizer, Symposium on the Culture of the Tea Ceremony, Tokyo, 1943. Exhibitions: *Japan New Tea Ceremony Exhibition*, Matsuzakaya De- partment Store, Ueno, Tokyo, 1951; Kindai Art Gallery, Kyobashi, Tokyo, 1955. Recipient: Kita- mura Tokoku Award, 1941; Award, 1950, and 1951, and Grand Prix, 1969, Architectural Institute of Japan; Mainichi Publications Award, 1953; Art Academy Award, 1957; Medal of Honor, 1963, and Third Class Order of the Sacred Treasure, 1966, Japanese Government; First Chubu Architectural Award, 1969. Address (office): 4-6-5 Sanno, Ota-Ku, Tokyo 143, Japan.

Works:

1922 Four Pavilions, *Tokyo Exhibition* Makita House, Koishikawa, Japan
1926 Shien-So (Purple Smoke Cottage), Warabi, Saitama Prefecture, Japan (destroyed by fire)
1927 Soshokyo House, Koishikawa, Tokyo
1928 Makita Building, Nihonbashi, Tokyo
1930 Kikkawa House, Meguro, Tokyo
1931 Tokugawa House, Koishikawa, Tokyo
1932 Fukuoka Meteorological Observatory, Fukuoka, Japan
1934 Okada House, Omori, Tokyo
1935 Arao House, Tokyo
Mito Weather Station, Ibaragi Prefecture, Japan
1936 Nakanishi House, Tokyo
Toride Racecourse, Ibaraghi Prefecture, Japan

1937 Villa Chokin-Ryo, Yamanaka Lakeside, Yamanashi Prefecture, Japan
1938 Yamakawa House, Nishinomiyashi, Hyogo Prefecture, Japan
Kobe Marine Observatory
Oshima Weather Station, Oshima Ialand, Tokyo
1940 Wakasa House, Shibuya, Tokyo
1950 Emperor's Room, Hotel Hasshokan, Nagoya, Japan
1951 Bijikyo Tearoom (and four other tearooms), *Japan New Tea Ceremony Exhibition*, Mat- suzakaya Department Store, Ueno, Tokyo
Hiyoshigaoka High School, Kyoto
1953 Bath Room, Hotel Hassokan, Nagoya, Japan "Nakamise," Hotel Hasshokan, Nagoya, Japan (destroyed by fire, 1965; rebuilt, 1967)
1954 Okayama Branch of the Fuso Sogo Bank
Japan Pavilion, *Bienal*, São Paulo
1955 Lecture Hall, Meiji University, Tokyo
Number 8 Building, Meiji University, Tokyo
Mannyo Park, with Exhibition Pavilion and Tea Ceremony Pavilion, Yugawara, Kana- gawa Prefecture, Japan
Koraku Hotel, Misasa Hot Springs, Tottori Prefecture Japan
Uemura Restaurant, Tokyo
1956 "A Small House in Omori," 4-6-5 Sanno, Ota- Ku, Tokyo
Izumi Gymnasium, Meiji University, Tokyo
1957 Lecture Hall and Gymnasium, Futaba Gakuen (girls' junior and senior high school), Shizuoka, Japan
Iwanami House, Bunkyo-ku, Tokyo
1958 Sakura Room and Kiku Room, Hotel Hassh- okan, Nagoya, Japan
Otokiki Golf Clubhouse, Hotel Hasshokan, Nagoya, Japan
Number 6 Building and Number 7 Building, Meiji University, Tokyo
1959 Library, Meiji University, Tokyo
1960 Izumi Lecture Hall, Meiji University, Tokyo
Student Union, Meiji University, Tokyo
1961 Tokoname Ceramic Art Research Center, Aichi Prefecture, Japan
1962 St. Maur Abbey, Shizuoka, Japan
1964 Shirakawa House, Setagaya, Tokyo
Number 4 Building, Faculty of Engineering, Meiji University, Kawasaki Kanagawa Pre- fecture, Japan
Number 1 Building, Faculty of Engineering, Meiji University, Kawasaki, Kanagawa Prefecture, Japan
1965 Number 2 Building and Number 3 Building, Faculty of Engineering, Meiji University, Kawasaki, Kanagawa Prefecture, Japan
Kankyo Tea Ceremony Room, Minato-Ku, Tokyo
1968 Ohara Sanso (mountain villa), 238 Ueno- machi, Ohara, Sakyku, Kyoto
1971/
72 Uraku-En (Tea Ceremony Room, relocated from Oiso, Kanagawa Prefecture), with garden, Inuyama, Aichi Prefecture, Japan
1973 Seikeian Tea Ceremony House, Saga-shi, Saga, Japan

Publications:

By HORIGUCHI: books—*Complete Study of the Tea Ceremony*, editor, 15 volumes, Tokyo 1935-37; *The Katsura Imperial Villa*, Tokyo 1952 (included in *The Complete Works*); *Collected Cubic Plans of the Japanese Tea Ceremony Room*, supervising editor, 12 volumes, Tokyo 1963-67; *The Complete Works of Sutemi Horiguchi*, in 7 volumes: volume 1, *The Tradition of Japanese Gardens and Space Construc- tion, Tokyo 1965; volume II, Tea Ceremony Rooms by Rikyu*, Tokyo 1968, 1984; volume III, *The Study of Tea Ceremony Rooms*, Tokyo 1969; volume IV, *Tea Ceremony by Rikyu*, Tokyo 1970, 1984; volume V,

Works of Sutemi Horiguchi Space Construction of Houses and Gardens, Tokyo 1974; volume VI, *Collected Papers on Architecture*, Tokyo 1978; volume VII, *Study of the Shoin-Zukuri and the Sukiya-Zukuri*, Tokyo 1978; *Kusaniwa*, Tokyo 1968 (included in *The Complete Works); Ise Jingu*, Tokyo 1973; *Kashu: A collection of Poems with Essays and Memoirs*, Tokyo 1980; articles—"The Growth of the Japanese Garden" in *Bunkazai* (Tokyo), November 1963; "Gardens in the Asuka and the Nara Era" in *Bunkazai* (Tokyo), August 1965; "The Origin of the Japanese Concept of Beauty," discussion with Kiyonori Kikutake, in *Approach* (Tokyo), Autumn 1972; "Tea Ceremony Rooms," editor, in *Japanese Art* (Tokyo), 15 April 1973.

On HORIGUCHI: books—*History of Modern Architectural Design* by Ryuichi Hamaguchi, Tokyo 1962; *Sutemi Horiguchi* (in Contemporary Japanese Architects series), edited by Isamu Kurita, Tokyo 1971; *Eight Japanese Architects: Witnesses of Modern European Architecture*, edited by Hiroshi Sasaki, Tokyo 1977; articles—"A University Is Circulation" in *Architectural Review* (London), June 1959; "On the Gardens of Sutemi Horiguchi and Masayuki Nagare" by Hiroshi Ohe and Yuichiro Kojiro in *Space Design* (Tokyo), March 1973; "Sutemi Horiguchi," special issue of *Space Design* (Tokyo), January 1982.

Japan was opened to the West when eclecticism was still supreme. Thus, the adaptation of the Western building art meant learning the styles. The man who through his roles as teacher and architect exerted the greatest influence on the first generation of modern Japanese architects, Josiah Conder, came from England in 1877. Within a year of his arrival, he had three buildings of his design under construction, one Romanesque, another Indian-Islamic, and the third Venetian Gothic. The greatest achievement of this initial period of modernization was perhaps the Akasaka Palace (architect: Tokuma Katayama), modelled after Versailles and the Louvre. Ironically, Japan caught up with the West just when eclecticism was being overthrown. One of the first to take a stand for the Modern Movement in Japan was Sutemi Horiguchi, who with fellow students formed the Secession Group in 1920. Having thrown off the older styles, the members of the group experimented with a number of newer styles, notably Expressionism, then current in Europe.

At the same time, however, Horiguchi became increasingly attracted to Japanese traditional architecture. As a scholar, he made important contributions to the study of the tea-ceremony rooms. In his domestic architecture, Horiguchi was very conscious of these two opposite tendencies toward modernism and tradition, even as he deprecated the duality that remained unresolved in some of his own designs. He wrote of the Okada House, with its mixture of styles, that "although inevitable, it is by no means an architecture that ought to be." He labelled it "a house of a transitional period."

In his first house, the Shien-so of 1926, the ground floor Western-style rooms and the upper floor Japanese-style room are in a sense pulled together by the bold thatched roof, reminiscent of contemporary Dutch architecture. This pastoral design might be said to express his youthful optimism for the eventual reconciliation of the two modes.

Horiguchi was from the start concerned with bringing the house and the garden into active relationship. Here, a geometricized stretch of space—a terrace and a pond—is created between the house proper and an auxiliary building.

In the Okada House of 1934, the two modes are more frankly expressed. The house is divided into a front Japanese-style section and a back Western-style section. Though the two parts may be integrated in plan by the central courtyard, the *sukiya*—style Japanese section and the International Style Western section abut in elevation in an awkward, unresolved manner. (In the Meiji Period it was not uncommon for a member of the oligarchy to build two houses for himself, one in front in the Western style in which to receive guests and an adjacent one in the Japanese style in which to actually live. In Horiguchi's scheme the order has been reversed.) The garden, too, is divided into two distinct parts, their only mediation a narrow channel of water. It is as if Horiguchi had decided to admit that the two modes could not be so easily reconciled.

The Wakasa House of 1940 is outwardly completely Western: a white International Style structure. Yet, this may be his most trenchant comment on the state of modern Japanese society. The heart of the house is the two-storey living room located half a floor above the garden. Looking out from the living room, one sees the long, narrow pool which divides the garden in two and which seemingly continues under the house. The apparently serene dwelling is in reality standing precariously atop a fault in the earth, just as Japanese society, superficially successful in adapting to the West, was being threatened by contradictory tendencies.

The state of inner conflict could not be long sustained. Horiguchi's prewar houses, full of tension, gave way eventually to highly refined *sukiya*—style architecture (as in Hasshokan) of impeccable details—of air conditioning intakes and outlets neatly hidden behind beautifully designed "traditional" grills—from which all impure and disharmonious elements have been excised. Horiguchi's scholarly background perhaps accounts for the "correctness" that marks his work in contrast to the oeuvre of Isoya Yoshida and Togo Murano, two other major practitioners of the *sukiya* style.

The path of initial Westernization and eventual

Sutemi Horiguchi: Izumi Lecture Hall, Meiji University, Tokyo, 1960.

return to native traditions is one taken by many Japanese of Horiguchi's generation. It is, however, his prewar work, which attempted to give form to the essential cultural conflict in himself and in Japanese society, that is most interesting today to the postmodernist who finds value in the expression of contradiction and ambivalence.

—Hiroshi Watanabe

HOWE, George.

American. Born in Worcester, Massachusetts, 17 June 1886. Educated at schools in Switzerland and New England 1896-1904: Groton School, Connecticut, 1900-04; Harvard University, Cambridge, Massachusetts, 1904-07, graduated 1907; Ecole des Beaux-Arts, Paris, 1908-12, graduated 1912. Served as a Lieutenant in the Corps of Interpreters, United States Army, as Assistant Military Attaché at Bern, Switzerland, 1917-19. Married Maritje Patterson in 1907; children: Anne and Helen. Practiced in Philadelphia: worked for the firm of Furness, Evans and Company, 1914-16; Partner, with Walter Mellor and Arthur I. Meigs, in Mellor, Meigs and Howe, 1916-28; in private practice, 1928-29; Partner, with William Lescaze, q.v., Howe and Lescaze, 1929-34; in private practice, 1935-40; in partnership with Louis I. Kahn, q.v., 1941, and with Kahn and Oscar Stonorov, q.v., 1942-43; Supervising Architect, 1942-44, and Deputy Commissioner for Design and Construction, 1944-45, Public Buildings Administration, Federal Works Agency; in private pracice, 1945-48; in partnership with Robert Montgomery Brown, 1949 until his death in 1955. Chairman of the Department of Architecture, Yale University, New Haven, Connecticut, 1950-54. Exhibition: *Modern Architecture International Exhiition*, Museum of Modern Art, New York, 1932. Collections: Avery Library, Columbia University, New York; Athenaeum Architectural Archives, Philadelphia. Recipient: Gold Medal, American Institute of Architects, 1922 and 1939. Fellow, American Institute of Architects. *Died* (in Cambridge, Massachusetts) *16 April 1955.*

Works:

1913 George Howe House I renovation, Chestnut Hill, Philadelphia
1914 Kermit Roosevelt House additions and renovation, Oyster Bay, Long Island, New York
1914/
16 High Hollow (George Howe House II), 101 West Hampton, Chestnut Hill, Philadelphia (garage added, 1923; swimming pool, 1928; now the Paley Conference Center of the University of Pennsylvania)
1921 Four-house development, Germantown Avenue, Chestnut Hill, Philadelphia (with Walter Mellor and Arthur I. Meigs)
Leeds Farm Buildings, Clonmell, Pennsylvania (with Walter Mellor and Arthur I. Meigs)
Howe-Fraley House, 10 West Chestnut Hill Avenue, Chestnut Hill, Philadelphia
1921/
23 Stikeman House, West Hampton, Chestnut Hill, Philadelphia
1921/
24 Newbold Estate, Laverock, Pennsylvania (with Arthur I. Meigs; swimming pool added, 1928)
1922 Illoway House, Bell's Mill Road, Chestnut Hill, Philadelphia
1924 Willowbrook Farms (Page House), Paoli, Pennsylvania (with Walter Mellor and Arthur I. Meigs)

Philadelphia Saving Fund Society Main Office renovation, Seventh and Walnut Streets, Philadelphia (with Walter Mellor and Arthur I. Meigs)
Philadelphia Saving Fund Society Branch Office, Eleventh Street and Lehigh Avenue, Philadelphia
Philadelphia Saving Fund Society Branch Office, Broad and McKean Streets, Philadelphia
McManus House, Germantown, Philadelphia (with extensions, 1930)
1924/
28 United States Coast Guard Memorial, Arlington National Cemetery, Virginia (with the sculptor Gaston Lachaise)
1925 Siebecker House, Bethlehem, Pennsylvania
Open-air auditorium, Fairmount Park, Philadelphia (project; with Walter Mellor and Arthur I. Meigs)
1926 Philadelphia Saving Fund Society Branch Office, 52nd and Ludlow Streets, Philadelphia
Philadelphia Saving Fund Society Branch Office, Broad and Ruscomb Streets, Philadelphia
1927 Baker House, Harrisburg, Pennsylvania (with Walter Mellor and Arthur I. Meigs)
Oxmoor (Bullitt House), Fort Washington, Pennsylvania
Holden House, Haverford, Pennsylvania
McLean House, Whitemarsh Valley, Pennsylvania (with Arthur I. Meigs)
Magill House, Germantown, Philadelphia (with Arthur I. Meigs and Walter Mellor)
Philadelphia Saving Fund Society Temporary Banking Offices, 8 South twelfth Street, Philadelphia
1928 George Howe House III renovation, Bell's Mill Road, Chestnut Hill, Philadelphia
Sinkler House, Sugartown and Goshen Roads, Westchester, Pennsylvania
Tyler House renovation, Elkins Park, Pennsylvania
Airport, Camden, New Jersey (project)
Christopher Columbus Memorial Lighthouse, Dominican Republic (competition project)
War Memorial, Somme American Cemetery, Bony, Aisne, France
Wasserman House I, Whitemarsh, Pennsylvania (project)
1929 Howe and Lescaze Offices, Philadelphia (with William Lescaze)
Ingersoll Museum, Pennlyn, Montgomery County, Pennsylvania (project; with William Lescaze)
Monument in Honor of the 27th and 30th Divisions, Kemmels, near Vierstataelt, Ypres, Belgium (with the sculptor Sidney Waugh)
Philadelphia Saving Fund Society Main Building renovation, seventh and Walnut Streets, Philadelphia
William Stix Wasserman Offices, Philadelphia (with William Lescaze)
Wasserman House II, Whitemarsh, Pennsylvania (project; with William Lescaze)
1930/
31 Museum of Modern Art, New York (project: preliminary designs; with William Lescaze)
1931 Hessian Hills School, Mt. Airy Road, Croton-on-Hudson, New York (with William Lescaze; later remodelled; now part of a synagogue complex)
Philadelphia Saving Fund Society Building, Twelfth and Market Streets, Philadelphia (with William Lescaze)
Stikeman Cottage, Sennerville, near Montreal
Emigrant Savings Bank and Office Building, East 42nd Street, New York (project; with William Lescaze)
1931/
32 Frederick V. Field House, New Hartford,

Connecticut (with William Lescaze)
Philadelphia Saving Fund Society Garage, twelfth and Filbert Streets, Philadelphia (with William Lescaze)
Housing development, Chrystie-Forsyth Streets, New York (project; with William Lescaze)
1932 Fifty small houses (project; with William Lescaze)
1932/
34 Square Shadows (Wasserman House II), Butler Pike, Whitemarsh, Pennsylvania
1934/
35 Welsh House, Laverock, Pennsylvania
1935 Speiser House, 2005 Delancey Place, Philadelphia
1936/
37 Levy House, Germantown, Philadelphia
1936/
41 *Evening Bulletin Office* renovation, Juniper and Filbert Streets, Philadelphia (with Louis McAllister)
1937 Hale House renovation, Dover, Massachusetts
1937/
39 Fortune Rock (Thomas House), Northeast Harbor Road, Ellsworth, Soames Sound, Mount Desert Island, Maine
1938 Arts Center, Weaton College, Norton, Massachusetts (competition project)
1939 America at Home Exhibit, World's Fair, New York
Children's World Exhibit, World's Fair, New York (with Oscar Stonorov, Herbert Spiegel, and Cornelius Bogert)
House Prototype, for *Life* magazine, Amityville, Long Island, New York (with Robert Montgomery Brown)
1940/
42 Pine Ford Acres (defense housing), Middletown, near Harrisburg, Pennsylvania (with Louis I. Kahn)
1941 Newhall House, Scarsdale, New York (project)
1941/
43 Carver Court Housing, Coatesville, Pennsylvania (with Louis I. Kahn and Oscar Stonorov)
1942 Information Center, Office of War Information, Washington, D.C. (temporary structure; now demolished)
Pennypack Housing, Philadelphia (project; with Louis I. Kahn and Oscar Stonorov)
West Potomac Women's Residence Halls, Public Buildings Administration, Washington, D.C. (as supervising architect; temporary structures; now demolished)
1943 Lincoln Road Housing, Coatesville, Pennsylvania (project; with Louis Kahn and Oscar Stonorov)
Lily Ponds Housing, Washington, D.C. (project; with Louis I. Kahn and Oscar Stonorov)
1947 United States Consulate, Naples (project)
1952 WCAU Television Studio, City Line Avenue, Philadelphia (with Robert Montgomery Brown)
1954/
55 *Evening and Sunday Bulletin* Building, 30th and Market Streets, Philadelphia (with Robert Montgomery Brown)
1955 Wholesale Food Distribution Center (project; with Robert Montgomery Brown)

Publications:

By HOWE: books—*The Work of Mellor, Meigs, and Howe,* New York 1923; *A Modern Museum,* with William Lescaze, Springdale, Connecticut 1930; articles—"Functional Aesthetics and the Social Ideal" in *Pencil Points* (New York), April 1932; article in *Architectural Forum* (New York), April

1940; "Two Architects' Credos: Traditional Versus Modern," with W. A. Delano, in *Magazine of Art* (New York), April 1940; "New York World's Fair" in *Architectural Forum* (New York), July 1940; "The Meaning of Art Today" in *Magazine of Art* (New York), May 1942; "Monuments, Memorials, and Modern Design—An Exchange of Letters" in *Magazine of Art* (New York), October 1944; "Relation of the Architect to Government" in *Michigan Society of Architects Bulletin* (Detroit), 31 July and 7 August 1945; "Master Plans for Master Politicians" in *Magazine of Art* (New York), February 1946, reprinted in *Metron* (Rome), no. 25, 1948; "Statement by George Howe at Princeton University's Bicentennial Celebration" in *Michigan Society of Architects Bulletin* (Detroit), 24 June 1947; "A Lesson from the Jefferson Memorial Competition" in *AIA Journal* (Washington, D.C.), March 1951; "Old Cities and New Frontiers" in *AIA Journal* (Washington, D.C.), January 1952; Training for the practice of Architecture" in *Perspecta* (New Haven, Connecticut), no. 2, 1953.

On HOWE: books—*George Howe, Architect, 1886-1955* by Helen Howe West, Philadelphia 1973; *George Howe* by Robert A.M. Stern, New Haven, Connecticut 1975; *A Study of the Work of Mellor, Meigs and Howe*, thesis by Sandra L. Tatman, University of Oregon 1977; articles—"Howe and Lescaze" by Henry Russell Hitchcock in *Modern Architecture International,* exhibition catalogue, New York 1932; "Low-cost houses" in *Architectural Forum* (New York), November 1942; "George Howe" by Bruno Zevi in *Metron* (Rome), no. 25, 1948; "George Howe: An Aristocratic Architect" by Bruno Zevi in *AIA Journal* (Washington, D.C.), October 1955; "Philadelphia Saving Fund Society Building: Its Development and Its Significance in Modern Architecture" by William Jordy and "Philadelphia Saving Fund Society Building: Beaux Arts Theory and Rational Expressionism" by Robert A.M. Stern in *Journal of the Society of Architectural Historians* (Philadelphia), May 1962; "Philadelphia Saving Fund Society Building" by Henry Wright in *Architectural Forum* (New York), May 1964; "PSFS: A Source for Its Design" by H. Allen Brooks in *Journal of the Society of Architectural Historians* (Philadelphia), December 1968; "Yale 1950-65" by Robert A.M. Stern in *Oppositions* (New York), October 1974; "New Waves in American Architecture," special issue of *GA Houses* (Tokyo), May 1982.

Bibliography—*George Howe, 1886-1955* by Lamia Doumato, Monticello, Illinois 1982.

Although he is known principally for his contributions to the distinguished International Style skyscraper, the Philadelphia Saving Fund Society Building, George Howe encompassed a wide variety of architectural achievements in his career. Born in 1886 into the wealth and position of Philadelphia society, Howe was, both by education and temperament, suited to be the prototypical "gentleman architect." His early career was restricted largely to residential work inPhiladelphia's fashionable suburbs, and as a partner in the firm of Mellor, Meigs and Howe, he contributed to the design of country houses and estates in historical styles. Both picturesque and dignified, the best of these houses include Howe's own High Hollow and the more extensive Newbold Estate. Although they are conventional in plan and overall conception, these houses exhibit a concern for the clear expression of materials and their construction, complementing the building's charm with directness.

By the late 1920s, Howe grew dissatisfied with his successful career: he quit both his firm and many of the architectural precepts that guided it. What he earnestly sought was a modern architecture, the architecture developing in Europe and beginning to

George Howe: Philadelphia Saving Fund Society Building, 1931.

makes its presence felt in America through various publications. As the decade came to a close, Howe received the commission to,design the Philadelphia Saving Fund Society Building (PSFS)—a large bank building conceived, ironically, during the worst years of the financial depression.

In 1929 Howe formed a partnership with the Swiss architect William Lescaze, with whom he was to do the most significant work of his career. Responsibility for the actual design of PSFS has been a topic of considerable dispute. Original contracts show that Howe was responsible primarily for business and administrative matters, while Lescaze took charge of architectural issues. Lescaze was later to claim full credit for PSFS, although early schemes by Howe, dating from before the partnership with Lescaze, indicate that crucial elements of massing and structure were conceived by Howe. Consisting of a commercial ground floor, a spectacular double-story second floor banking room and a twenty-eight story office tower, PSFS was perhaps the first skyscraper in American to be designed according to the structural and aesthetic tenets of the International Style. Historian William Jordy has pointed out the importance of its "composite image created of a diverse mechanomorphology..." and of its machine image as both "container" and "component." In its compositional asymmetry; the curved, sweeping lines of the base; the extraordinary, uninterrupted expanse of glass; the boldness of its huge, juxtaposed forms; and in its sumptuous use of materials—all accomplished under the imperative of "functional architecture"—the PSFS was, and in many ways still is, the standard against which subsequent skyscraper design must be measured.

The seeming adventurousness of the PSFS was significantly never subsumed by Howe's quest for an authentically functional architecture. Fascinated by the modern quest for anti-gravitational effects in building, Howe was also concerned (as he himself later wrote) with the "true sculptural quality of an organic design" arising from "the moulding of interior space and the shaping of the skeleton to contain it. The functional architect delights in the huge torso of a building swaying on tendoned ankles."

Later projects from the office of Howe and Lescaze all contain their special felicities. The Chrystie-Forsyth Housing Development in New York was a concerted attempt at a large-scale scheme designed to alleviate the acute housing shortage during the early years of the Depression. Sharing certain structural principles with the Chrystie-Forsyth scheme was a group of proposals for the new Museum of Modern Art in New York, in which a skeletal frame held structurally independent gallery boxes. Also during the early 1930s, Howe and Lescaze designed several private houses (though remarkably few were actually built). The most famous was the Wasserman House III, Square Shadows, a large, boxy house, which, for all its notoriety, now seems rather clumsy on the outside and too full of stagey effects on the inside.

In 1935, after several disputes, Howe and Lescaze terminated their partnership, and Howe's career thereafter is an odd jumble of some pedestrian projects, one splendid house, Fortune Rock, which is notable for its extravagant, cantilevered decks and vernacular approach to building, and his own gradual transformation into teacher and elder statesman of American architecture. In 1940 Howe hired Louis Kahn, then a novice architect; they were joined by Oscar Stonorov, and the three men worked together on several housing schemes, including the interesting Carver Court at Coatesville, Pennsylvania. After the war, Howe returned to private practice, and in 1949 he was invited to teach at Yale, where from 1950 to 1954 he was the popular and irrepressible chairman of the architecture department.

Noted for his sardonic wit and sartorial flair, Howe abandoned an easy and lucrative career as a fashionable, patrician architect to, instead, attempt to define the shape and direction of modern American architecture. A talented designer in his own right, he had the intelligence and largesse to recognize the talent of others. Most importantly, in the PSFS he contributed to the design of a building that, now divorced from the ideological struggles of fifty years ago, still retains its spirit of vigor, inventiveness, and sheer excellence.

—Richard Lavenstein

HOWELL, KILLICK, PARTRIDGE AND AMIS. Partnership; established, London, 1959, by former London County Council architects William G. Howell (born, 1922; died, 1974), John A. Killick (born, 1924; retired, 1969; died, 1972), and John A. Partridge (born, 1924); joined by Stanley F. Amis (born, 1924) in 1961. Current partners: Partridge, Amis, Stephen Osgood (born, 1937) since 1973, R. J. Murphy (born, 1932) since 1976, and Paddy J. Lawlor (born, 1942) since 1982; associates: A. H. Miller, L. Goodchild, W. Hodge, and P. Schmitt. Exhibition: *Howell Killick Partridge and Amis: Architecture*, RIBA Heinz Gallery, London, and Puck Building, New York, 1983. Recipient: Civic Trust Award, 1965, 1966, 1968, 1969, 1970, 1971, 1978, 1979, and 1981; Architecture Award, Royal Institute of British Architects, 1966, 1970, 1971 (twice), 1975, 1978, 1980, and 1984; House Design Award, Ministry of Housing and Local Government, 1968; Concrete Society Award, 1968, 1969, 1970, 1971, and 1980; Camden Society of Architects Award, 1969; First Prize, RIBA/*Building Design* Jubilee Competition, 1976; Popular Architecture Award, RIBA Plymouth Branch, 1978; First Prize, Hall of Justice Competition, Trinidad, 1978 (with Anthony C. Lewis Partnership). Address: 20 Old Pye Street, Westminster, London SW1P 2DG, England.

Works:

1951/
60 Roehampton Lane Housing, London (with London County Council Architect's Department)
1954/
55 Terrace houses, Hampstead, London
1958/
60 Timber framed house, Bromley, Kent
1960/
64 Faculty of Commerce and Social Science, University of Birmingham, England
1960/
65 Wolfson Residential Building, St. Anne's College, Oxford, England
1961/
63 Metal Box Company Offices and Computer Centre, Worcester, England
1961/
66 Acland Burghley School, London
1962/
63 Planning study of Mill Lane, Cambridge, England
1962/
66 Furniture Industry Research Association Headquarters, Stevenage, Hertfordshire
Graduate Flats at Summertown House, Oxford University
1963/
67 University Centre, Cambridge, England
1963/
69 Weston Rise Housing, Islington, London
1964/
65 Ramsay Rae House extension, Little Wakestone, Sussex
1964/
66 Old Merchant Taylors' Society Squash Courts, London
Gatehouse Building, St. Anne's College, Oxford, England
1964/
68 Old people's housing, Stonegrove, Harrow, Middlesex
1964/
69 Residential Building, Sidney Sussex College, Cambridge, England
1964/
70 Hall and Residential Building, Darwin College, Cambridge, England
1965 Lenham School, Kent
Planning study of Heythrop College, Oxfordshire

1965/
69 Rayne Residential Building, St. Anne's College, Oxford, England
1965/
70 Combination Room, Hall and Kitchens, Downing College, Cambridge, England
1966/
69 House of Studies for Philosophers, House of Studies for Theologians, Astro Physics Out-Station, and House of Studies for Nuns of the Holy Child, Heythrop College, Oxfordshire (projects)
Alton Road Housing, Roehampton, London
1966/
71 New Hall and Common Rooms, St. Antony's College, Oxford, England
1967/
70 Houses for visiting mathematicians, University of Warwick, England
1968/
71 Young Vic Theatre, Waterloo, London
1968/
73 College of Estate Management Faculty Building, University of Reading, Berkshire
Hall of Residence, University of Reading, Berkshire
1969/
71 Children's Playground, Roehampton, London
1970/
71 Development studies for teaching, music, sports, and study bedrooms, for the Merchant Taylors' School, London
1970/
72 Convent Building conversion, St. Antony's College, Oxford, England
1970/
74 Arts Centre, Christ's Hospital School, Horsham, Sussex
The Grove Old People's Housing, Haringey, London
1971 Children's Reception Home, Kent (project)
Redevelopment Area Housing, Russell Road, Haringey, London
1971/
72 Harris and Sutherland Engineering Office conversion, Whitfield Street, London
1971/
80 Fleet Maintenance Base and Submarine Refit Complex, H.M. Dockyard, Devonport, Devon
1972 Arts Based Building, University of Reading, Berkshire (project)
Cement and Concrete Association Office Building, Wexham Springs, Buckinghamshire (project)
Faculty of Art and Design, phase II, Middlesex Polytechnic, Enfield, London
1972/
73 Teaching Block, Music School, and Swimming Pool, Merchant Taylors' School, Northwood, Middlesex (project)
1972/
74 Squash Courts, Merchant Taylors' School, Northwood, Middlesex
1972/
75 New Auditorium, Open Air Theatre, Regent's Park, London
1972/
79 Magistrates Courthouse, Chatham, Kent
1973/
75 Farmhouse and outbuildings conversion, Saltash, Cornwall
1973/
76 Development studies of Great Scotland Yard and Whitehall, London
1973/
78 Redevelopment Area Housing, Somerville Road, Lewisham, London

1974 New housing and rehabilitation, Trewsbury Road, Lewisham Road (project)
Development study of Ilford High Road, Essex

Howell, Killick, Partridge and Amis: The Albany Community Centre, Deptford, London, 1977-81.

1974/
76 Regency Cottage (John Partridge house) restoration, Cudham, Kent
  Old People's Housing, Haringey, London
1976/
77 Box Office, Scenery Workshop, Dressing and Administration Rooms, Open-Air Theatre, Regent's Park, London
  New Kitchens, Farnborough Hospital, Kent
1977 Wilsdon House, St. Dominick, Cornwall (project)
1977/
79 Sorensen House extensions, Great Trevollard, Saltash, Cornwall
  Coach House/Music Room conversion, St. Anne's College, Oxford, England
  New Boiler House, Farnborough Hospital, Kent
1977/
80 Office and Shops restoration and conversions, Whitehall, London
1977/
81 Community Centre and Theatre, the Albany, Deptford, London
1978 Housing Feasibility Study, St. Budeaux, Cornwall
  IBM Residential Education Centre Feasibility

Study, Stoke D'Abernon, Surrey
Elmfield (Stephen Osgood house) restoration, Bromley Common, Kent
1978/
79 Joyce Shopfitters Joinery Workshop, Farnborough, Kent
  Holiday Development, Cumble Tor Quarry, Saltash, Cornwall
  Buro Happold Office conversion, 17 Portland Square, Bristol, Avon
1978/
80 Brittania Royal Naval College modernization study, Dartmouth, Kent
  Royal Western Yacht Club Feasibility Study, Plymouth, Devon
1978/
82 H. M. Prison, Ranby, Nottinghamshire
  Cement and Concrete Association Training Centre new building project and development plan, Fulmer Grange, Buckinghamshire
1978/
85 Hall of Justice, Port of Spain, Trinidad (with Anthony C. Lewis Partnership)
1979/
80 Brittania Royal Naval College fire precautions, Dartmouth, Kent (project)

Fleet Maintenance Base II Feasibility Study, H. M. Naval Base, Devonport, Devon
1980 Clifton Hill (Stanley Amis house) refurbishment, St. John's Wood, London
1980/
82 H. M. Prison Feasibility Study, Sudbury, Derbyshire
1980 H. M. Prison New Development, Durham, England
  H. M. Prison New Development, Birmingham, Warwickshire
1981/
84 Young Vic Theatre extension and alterations, London
1982 Building refurbishment, 28 Wilton Crescent, Westminster, London
1983 H. M. Prison, Woolwich, London
1984 CEGB Electricity Power Station Development Study, Winfrith, Dorset
  Docklands Office and Industrial Development, Tower Hamlets, London
1985 Metropolitan Police Station Divisional Headquarters, Forest Gate, London
  New Catering Facilities, St. Bartholomew's Hospital, City of London
  King's School Theatre Development Study, Canterbury, Kent

Publications:

On HKPA: books—*Late-Modern Architecture* by Charles Jencks, London 1980; *Howell Killick Partridge and Amis: Architecture*, with introduction by Sherban Cantacuzino, London 1981; articles— "Two Oxford Colleges" in *Aujourd'hui: art et architecture* (Paris), July 1965; "Universitäts-gebaude in England," special issue of *Werk* (Zürich), January 1966; "University Centre, Cambridge" and "Young Vic Theatre, London" in *Architecture + Urbanism* (Tokyo), May 1973; "HKPA Vertebrae" by C. Amery in *Architectural Review* (London), November 1973; "Wells Hall Residential Building, University of Reading" in *Architectural Review* (London), July 1975; "Christ's Hospital Arts Centre" in *RIBA Journal* (London), July/August 1975; "Theatre in the Park" in *Building Design* (London), 25 June 1977; "Young Vic Theatre in London" in *Baumeister* (Munich), February 1978; "Urban Housing Variations" by J. M. McKean in *Building Design* (London), 21 July 1978; "Precast Concrete Walling for a Naval Base" by Stephen Osgood in *Concrete* (London), August 1978; "New Housing: New Cross Area" by Peter Collymore in *Architectural Review* (London), October 1978; "Christ's Hospital Art Centre, Horsham" in *Informes de la construccion* (Madrid), May 1980; "A Shipshape and Handsome Set of Buildings" in *Concrete* (Slough, Buckinghamshire), June 1980; "Design for Law and Order" in *Architects' Journal* (London), 25 June 1980; "Faculty of Art and Design at Cat Hill" in *Industria delle costruzioni* (Rome), February 1981; "Community Centre for Deptford" in *RIBA Journal* (London), March 1981; "Art and Design Faculty of the Middlesex Polytechnic, Cat Hill" in *Baumeister* (Munich), August 1981; "New Albany Community Centre, Deptford" in *Architectural Review* (London), September 1982; "Theatre of Life" in *Building* (London), 8 October 1982; "Through from the Sixties" by Martin Pawley in *Architects' Journal* (London), 29 June 1983.

*

We have no "house style," though no doubt the authorship of our buildings can usually be guessed by those who know our work. However, this is not due to our having any particular formal obsessions or predilection for certain materials or structural methods. We aim to choose materials, structures, and geometrical systems appropriate to the locations, the budgets, and the functions of the buildings. We have designed brick buildings, stone, timber, concrete and steel buildings, and buildings which combine these materials.

We have developed certain themes which can be traced through a series of jobs. From our work at Roehampton, the first large-scale use of pre-cast concrete cladding in this country, we have gone on, particularly in our Oxford College work, to try to achieve richness and quality from this often misused material. This we have done partly by using three-dimensional forms of pre-cast units, which derive from the splayed window units we have developed to introduce light into rooms in a well-modulated way and partly from our research into ways of detailing, surfacing, and assembling pre-cast concrete so that it weathers well and ages gracefully.

Another theme has been the evolution of less boxlike geometry than that which characterizes much of modern building. This rather crude angularity no doubt partly results from most building materials being rectilinear (sheets, blocks, or linear elements such as timber or steel beams). However, we have developed, in a series of buildings, ways of using these materials, which while respecting their inherent geometry and avoiding expensive cutting or bending, build up from them more complex geometrical forms that may well be more suitable to the internal functions or characteristics of the environment in which the building is to go. (Our octagonal dining hall at Darwin College, Cambridge, is an example.) We have also developed an approach to interiors, using "as found" materials, natural timber, bricks,

and blocks (painted or natural), which we feel avoid the bleakness often associated with modern interiors and give a humanity and warmth often hard to achieve, especially in institutional buildings.

In all our work, we attempt to pay particular attention to neighbouring buildings and existing landscape. We prefer to blend, rather than stick out like a sore thumb, and tend to choose materials, colours, textures, and scale of elements that will fit naturally, especially when faced with an existing environment of quality.

—Howell, Killick, Partridge and Amis

*

Bill Howell, who was born in 1922, became Professor of Architecture at Cambridge, and died in a car crash in 1974, was the best known partner of Howell, Killick, Partridge and Amis. In his obituary *The Times* offered an explanation of the significance of HKPA, saying that Howell "belonged to the generation that made British architecture, in the years after the war, respected all over the world." Almost as a model of the whole postwar profession in Britain, HKPA have been concerned with the public sector: they have specialized in housing and schools and have attempted to find an architectural expression of the social responsibilities that have characterized the age.

Howell, Killick, Partridge and Amis was set up in 1959 by architects who had been employed by the London County Council in the immediate postwar years. In a period of economic depression, the offices of Britain's largest local authority provided an opportunity for architectural experimentation that made it one of the centres of the contemporary architectural enlightenment. One of the major schemes produced by the LCC in these years, and one in which Howell and the others were prominent, was the award-winning Roehampton Housing Estate in southwest London. Often reproduced as a symbol of the best in British housing, in reality Roehampton was the superficial vernacular expression in England of the ideas that Le Corbusier had made the everyday stuff of architectural education.

Howell left the LCC in 1956, and in eighteen years of improving and declining economic conditions, he managed to make himself and his firm leading, articulate spokesmen of the conservative best in current British architecture. The architecture of the whole group was heavily influenced by the example of the Smithsons, and each HKPA building concentrates heavily on what older architectural jargon calls "circulation" and what Reyner Banham has called "connectivity." Asked just before his death to cite the partnership's most important buildings, Howell listed St. Anne'S and St. Antony's Colleges, Oxford; Darwin, Downing, and Sidney Sussex Colleges, Cambridge; the University Centre, Cambridge; Young Vic Theatre, London; and the Arts Centre at Christ's Hospital School, Horsham. Of the Roehampton episode, he concisely referred only to "GLC Housing," a suggestion that with maturity the naive expectations and empty rhetoric of the immediate postwar period were best forgotten.

—Stephen Bayley

HUGHES, (Henry) Richard.

British. Born in London, 4 July 1926; emigrated with his parents to East Africa in 1937. Educated at Hilton College, Natal, South Africa, 1940-44; Architectural Association School, London, under R. F. Jordan, Arthur Korn, *q.v.*, Felix Samuely, and Ernesto Rogers, *q.v.*, 1947-50, 1951-53, A.A. Diploma 1953; attended short course in city and regional planning at Massachusetts Institute of Technology, Cambridge, Summer 1954. Corporal in the Kenya Regiment, attached to the Royal Engineers, 1944-46. Married Anne Hill in 1951; children: Bridget, Penelope, and

Mervyn. Assistant Architect to Henry J. Ludorf, Hartford, Connecticut, 1953-55, and to Blackburn and Norburn, Nairobi, Kenya, 1955-57; in private practice, as H. Richard Hughes, Nairobi, 1957-76; Partner, with Brian Arthur Smith, Richard Hughes/Smith Patnership, Nairobi, 1976-78; resumed private practice, Nairobi, 1978. Member of the Council, East African Institute of Architects, 1956-57; Chairman, Kenya Branch, Capricorn Africa Society, 1958-61; Governor, Hospital Hill School, Nairobi, 1962-75; Vice-President, Kenya Arts Society, 1965-73; Chairman, East African Institute of Architects Board of Architectural Education, 1972-74; Governor, Kenya Polytechnic, 1972-75; Chairman, Kenya Museum Society, 1974-75; Consultant to the United Nations Environment Programme on Human Settlements Technology, 1976; Chairman, Environment Liaison Centre, Nairobi, 1976-78; Chairman, Lamu Society, 1977-78. Exhibitions: Overseas League and Imperial Institute, London, 1953; East African Institute of Architects, Nairobi, 1963; Commonwealth Arts Festival, Cardiff, 1965; German Africa Society, Bonn and Berlin, 1966; CAA Conference Exhibition, Nairobi, 1982; *Overseas Architects*, Royal Institute of British Architects, London, 1984. Associate, 1954, and Fellow, 1969, Royal Institute of British Architects. Address: Post Office Box 14390, Nairobi, Kenya.

Works:

1957/	
74	Alliance Girls' High School Chapel and Redevelopment, Kikuyu, Kenya
1957/	
75	Private houses in Nairobi, Mombasa, Gilgil, and Nanyuki, Kenya, and in The Seychelles
1958	Council chamber and offices, Kenya Federation of Labour, Nairobi
1958/	
76	Hospital Hill Primary School Assembly Hall and Classrooms, Nairobi
1960/	
62	University of Nairobi Institute of Adult Studies, Kikuyu, Kenya
1960/	
70	Churches in Embu, Meru, Kilifi, Maralal, Mombasa, Maguga, Masasi, Nairobi, and Nambale, and in Zululand, South Africa
1962	Television Studios, Nairobi
	Egerton Agricultural College redevelopment, Njoro, Kenya
	Kaimosi Teachers' Training College redevelopment, Kenya
1963	Trinity College for the Anglican Church, Nairobi
1964	Makerere University Chapel extensions, Kampala, Uganda
	Town Hall, Bukoba, Tanzania
1964/	
67	Radio studios, control rooms and offices, Nairobi
596	Broadcasting House, Mauritius
1965/	
73	Limuru Girls' School extensions, near Nairobi
1965/	
76	East African Posts and Telecommunications staff housing, Nairobi
1967	Coast Hotel, Watamu Beach, Kenya
	Transmitter Building, Ngong, Kenya
1967/	
73	Student residences, University of Nairobi
1968	Houses, Moi Estate, Nairobi
	Development House (office building), Nairobi
	Lutheran Cathedral, Bukoba, Tanzania
	Industrial and Commercial Development Corporation industrial estate, Nairobi (with Sir Alexander Gibb and Partners
	Kenya Institute of Mass Communication, Nairobi

All-Africa Conference of Churches Radio and TV Training Centre, Nairobi

1968/
72 Tea factory and extension, Mauritius

1969 Makerere University Art Gallery, Kampala, Uganda

VOK Outside Broadcasting and Transport Unit, Nairobi

1970/
78 East African External Telecommunications Company Headquarters Buildings, Nairobi and Kampala, Uganda

1971 Coast Transmitting Station, Mombasa, Kenya

1972 New Stanley Hotel alterations, Nairobi

Block Hotels Office Building extensions, Nairobi

1973 University of Nairobi Senior Staff Houses, Kabete, Kenya

Flats and maisonettes, Nairobi

Katoke Teachers' College redevelopment, Tanzania

Two secondary schools, Bukoba, Tanzania

Norfolk Hotel extensions, Nairobi

1974 Civil servants' housing, Old Racecourse, Nairobi

Murang'a College of Technology, Kenya

Town Hall, Embu, Kenya

1975 Hillcrest Secondary School, Nairobi

1976 Residential estate, near Nairobi

Christian Students Leadership Centre, Nairobi

University of Nairobi Library, Chiromo Campus, Nairobi

1977 Mombasa Airport, Kenya (production drawings and supervision as joint production architects; design by Gollins, Melvin and Ward Partnership)

National Bank of Kenya Headquarters, Nairobi

1978 S. M. Githunguri Office Development, Nairobi

Development House II, Nairobi

Insurance Company of East Africa Office Building, Nairobi

1979/
81 Insurance Company of East Africa office building, Nairobi

1980 Grindlays Bank International branch office, Nairobi

Grindlays Bank International branch office, Mombasa, Kenya

1981 Jubilee Insurance Company office extensions, Nairobi

1982 Insurance Company of East Africa housing development, Nairobi

International Laboratory for Research on Animal Diseases housing and office extensions, Nairobi

1983 Bank of Oman building, Nairobi

Bank of Oman building, Khartoum, Sudan

Kenya Commercial bank buildings(5) and housing in Nairobi, Marsabit, Lodwar, Nandi Hills, and Loitokitok

Kenyatta University College library, Kahawa, Kenya

Airport Freight Facility, Mombasa, Kenya

1984 New Stanley Hotel alterations, Nairobi

Central Bank of Kenya extension, Nairobi

African Medical and Research Foundation headquarters building, Nairobi

African Medical and Research Foundation headquarters building, Dar-es-Salaam, Tanzania

Publications:

By HUGHES: books—*The Habitat Handbook*, with Graham Searle, London 1980; *Kenya Commercial Bank Design Manual*, Nairobi 1983; articles—"East Africa" in *New Buildings in the Commonwealth*, edited by J. M. Richards, London 1951; "Proposals

Richard Hughes: ICEA Building, Nairobi, 1981.

for an Inter-Racial Settlement in Kenya" in *East Africa and Rhodesia* (London), August 1953; "Town Plan to Facilitate Racial Integration" in *New Commonwealth* (London), September 1953; "Continuing Boom in New Construction" in *Manchester Guardian*, 25 April 1956; "Five Church Buildings in Kenya" in *Church Buildings Today* (London), January 1962; "Protestant Churches of Kenya" in *East African Annual*, Nairobi 1964/65; "Development of a Private Practice in Kenya" in *Architects' Journal* (London), October 1969; "Religious Architecture and Planning" in *Kenya Churches Handbook*, edited by D. B. Barrett, Nairobi 1973; "Lamu: A Lesson in Townscape," with U. Ghaidan, in *Architectural Review* (London), November 1973; "Instruments of Creativity" in *Thus They Project*, International Union of Architects, Madrid 1975; "Lamu: A Study in Conservation" in *Azania* (Nairobi), no. XI, 1976; "Planning Policies and Proposed Byelaws for Lamu" in *Lamu: A Study in Conservation*, Nairobi 1976; "The Logic of Geometry" in *Build Kenya* (Nairobi), August 1981.

On HUGHES: books—*East African Institute of Architects Year Book*, Nairobi 1961; *New Architecture in Africa* by Udo Kultermann, London 1963; *East African Institute of Architects Jubilee Handbook*, Nairobi 1963; *Modern Churches of the World* by R. Maguire and K. Murray, London 1965; *University Hostel Research Project* by D. M. Ferguson, London 1968; *New Directions in African Architecture* by Udo Kultermann, London 1969; *The History of the Alliance High School* by J. S. Smith, Nairobi 1973; *Then and Now: The Norfolk Hotel* by Jan Hemsing, Nairobi 1975; articles—editorial comment in *East Africa and Rhodesia* (London), August 1953; "A Nairobi House" in *Trade and Industry* (Nairobi), July 1958; illustrations in *Architectural Review* (London), July 1960; "New Churches" in *Church Buildings Today* (London), 1962; illustrations in *Architects' Journal* (London), October 1969; "New Churches in Kenya" in *Church Buildings Today* (London), October 1969; illustrations in *Architectural Review* (London), February 1970, July 1973; illustrations in *Plan East Africa*

(Nairobi), February 1975; "National Bank Building" in *Build Kenya* (Nairobi), August 1977; "Murang'a College of Technology" in *Build Kenya* (Nairobi), January 1978; "Richard Hughes: A Man for All Reasons" in *Build Kenya* (Nairobi), June 1978; Triangles and Hexicurious corners" in *Build Kenya* (Nairobi), September 1979; "L'edificio della National Bank of Kenia a Nairobi" in *Cemento* (Rome), April 1980; "A Plot of Eucalpytus...23 years later" in *Build Kenya* (Nairobi), June 1980; "A Review of Work by Members of the RIBA Who Live and Work Overseas..." in *RIBA Journal* (London), July 1980; "Architectural Practice in Kenya, Two Kenyan Firms Discuss Their Work" in *RIBA Journal* (London), July 1982.

My design objectives are easily stated but hard to achieve: to meet all the client's requirements, including those he has not thought of or formulated; to reflect the constraints and nature of the site and the environment; to be concerned about all those who will use and be influenced by the building; to have regard for the economic level of the area, regardless of the actual budget; and to create a series of spaces that are coherent and defined. The subconscious synthesis of all these and myriad other inputs to produce a three-dimensional concept requires time to evolve (usually just the period available up to the last minute) and, even more important, time for the rigorous testing of the solution against the requirements, both those that are absolute and those that are negotiable depending on one's judgement of priorities.

Although the external appearance of a building and the materials used are important, they are less so than the clarity of the enclosed spaces, for it is space that distinguishes architecture from the other visual arts, plus the need to meet functional requirements.

The relationship to the local environment, social, economic and physical, is vital, particularly in new countries such as Kenya, if the building is not to seem alien and out of context. Many long-absorbed and unrecorded scraps of information have to be part of the synthesis at the design stage, which is why the developing world suffers from jobs designed overseas by architects who think it sufficient to study the site plan and climatic data and then impose their preconceptions.

It is my belief that the environment, in the broader context, must be a major concern and responsibility of any architect: not only human settlements or "Habitat," but the whole spectrum of energy, water, waste, appropriate technologies, and the fundamental problems of development within environmental constraints.

Seen from the Third World, many of the technologies that are imposed or transferred through sale of equipment and expertise by the industrialized countries on the less developed are inappropriate in scale and in the relation between capital and labour. They often seem wasteful of resources in their country of origin, too.

—Richard Hughes

Nairobi resembles the capital cities of many developing nations in, being young and growing fast. From having been a small administrative and commercial town on the Uganda railway, it has become the principal focus for development, commerce, and communications in Kenya and eastern Africa. Most of Richard Hughes's work has been in East Africa, much of it in Nairobi itself, and his professional practice has spanned the major period of growth in this region and in the city.

The recent expansion of opportunities for architects in Kenya is mirrored in the fact that though many of Hughes' earlier buildings were on a relatively domestic scale, some of his more recent works are very large complexes in the city centre. What is unusual about his work is the consistency of approach in more than twenty years of practice and the exposition of principle that is as evident in a tiny youth hostel chapel as in a vast communication centre. In spite of the changing scale of his buildings over the years, Hughes has continued to express and develop an imaginative but essentially functionalist aesthetic. The most immediately striking features of his buildings are a bold, sometimes almost brutally deliberate, articulation and interplay of volumes and spaces, an equally deliberate parsimony in the number of materials or finishes that go into the fabric, and an unusual sensitivity to the relationship between the needs and activities of people, the numbers likely to use a space, and the modelling and scale of the rooms, halls, and passages they occupy.

Detailing in his buildings is invariably simple and unobtrusive but immaculate.

All too often, fancied needs for pretentious facades, irrelevant gimmicks, or "prestige" have been indulged or pandered to by architects working in developing countries. When I interviewed Hughes for an article in 1961, he remarked "good buildings result from imaginative and honest solutions to the many problems of site, climate, clients, brief, and budget.... I believe that grossly expensive buildings, even if the money happens to be available, are out of place in a country without enough school buildings, housing, or hospitals. The budget dictates standards of finish and workmanship and the architect must design and detail accordingly."

It is significant that Hughes has never departed from these principles, nor have his major clients (government agencies, education authorities, the communications industry, and banks) imposed irrelevant demands. Hughes's special talent for buildings of a social nature has led to numerous commissions from Protestant organizations for cathedrals, churches, chapels, community centres, clinics, and educational complexes.

Hughes has never clad a building in marble or used imported materials in preference to suitable local ones. Wherever budgets have allowed his doing so, he has involved reputable local artists in murals, sculpture, stained glass, and ceramics so that, in addition to his own creative role, he has done more to actively foster the fine arts in East Africa than any other architect.

The arrival of the United Nations Environmental Programme in Nairobi in 1973 stimulated Hughes's sustained concern for architectural principles and channelled his energies and vision into the wider field of human habitat (the subject of a book he has recently written with a colleague).

Hughes believes that architects should not only use technologies that are appropriate to "place" and site, but they must also accept responsibility and be concerned for every aspect of human settlements, particularly the environmental constraints on water supplies, waste disposal, energy sources, and the less tangible social problems of rapid development. In his buildings, in words and in print, Hughes continues to call for greater awareness of our environment and action to save us from the spreading cancer of urban and rural squalor.

—Jonathan Kingdon

ISHII, Kazuhiro.

Japanese. Born in Tokyo, 1 February 1944. Educated at the University of Tokyo, under Arata Isozaki, *q.v.*, B.A. 1968, M.A. 1970: Yale University, New Haven, Connecticut, under Charles Moore, *q.v.*, James Stirling, *q.v.*, and Louis I. Kahn, *q.v.*, M.Ed 1974. Worked for Isozaki, in Tokyo, 1969. Since 1970, in private practice, Tokyo: Principal, Kazuhiro Ishii Architect and Associates, since 1976. Lecturer, Waseda University, Tokyo, 1978; Visiting Professor, University of California at Los Angeles, 1978, Yale University, New Haven Connecticut, 1979, Waseda University and Nihon University, Tokyo, from 1980. Address: Kazuhiro Ishii Architect and Associates, Gable Building 3F, 3-5 Shibadaimon, 1-chome, Minato-ku, Tokyo 105, Japan.

Works:

1970 "Genshu" Tea House, Oizumigakuen, Tokyo
Naoshima Elementary School, Naoshima, Kagawa, Japan
1971 Cyclotron House, Tokorozawa, Saitama, Japan
1972 Ishii Residence, Kokubunji, Tokyo
1974 Naoshima Kindergarten, Naoshima, Kagawa, Japan
1975 "54 Windows" (Soya Clinic and Residence), Hiratsuka, Kanagawa, Japan
1976 "Strawberry" Cafe, Kanda, Tokyo
Naoshima Gymnasium, Naoshima, Kagawa, Japan
1977 Takahashi Residence, Kichijoji, Tokyo
1978 Honda Residence, Aoyhama, Tokyo
Ishii Garden House, Kokubunji, Tokyo
1979 Naoshima Junior High School, Naoshima, Kagawa, Japan
"54 Roofs" (Takebe Nursery School), Takebe, Okayama, Japan
1980 Gable Building, Minato-ku, Tokyo
1982 Moon Rabbit *sukiya*-style House, Tokyo
"Jazzy Baroque" House, Nakano Ward, Tokyo

Publications:

By ISHII: book—*Yale, Architecture, Commuting,* Tokyo 1977; translations of books—*James Stirling* by John Jacobs, Tokyo 1975; *MLTW Houses* by Donlyn Lyndon, Tokyo 1975; *Dimensions* by Charles Moore and Gerald Allen, Tokyo 1978; *Learning from Las Vegas* by Denise Scott Brown, Robert Venturi and Steven Izenour, Tokyo 1978; *Place of Houses* by Charles Moore, Gerald Allen and Donlyn Lyndon, Tokyo 1978; articles—"Analysis of Kohou-an, Daitokuji-Temple" in *Kenchikubunka* (Tokyo), April 1971; "Independence or Isolation" in *Toshijutaku* (Tokyo), May 1972; "Total Institution," editor, in *Toshijutaku* (Tokyo), October 1972; "Los Angeles," editor, in *Architecture + Urbanism* (Tokyo), November 1972; "Documents on Motomachi, Hiroshima" in *Shinkenchiku* (Tokyo), May 1973; "Notes on Open School" in

Space Design (Tokyo), June 1973; "The Column, Culture and the Wall Culture in Japanese Architecture" in *Shinkenchiku* (Tokyo), June 1975; "Notes on Arata Isozaki" in *Space Design* (Tokyo), April 1976; "Post Metabolism" in *Japan Architect* (Tokyo), October/November 1977; "Sukiya Concept" in *GA Houses 3,* Tokyo 1978; "Kisho Kurokawa" in *Shinkenchiku* (Tokyo), March 1978; "Deliberate Regression from Modern Architecture: Eleven Points, The Contribution of Charles Moore" in *Architecture + Urbanism* (Tokyo), May 1978; "Kenji Kawaii and Osamu Ishiyama" in *Shinkenchiku* (Tokyo), May 1978; "Togo Murano" in *Shinkenchiku* (Tokyo), June 1978; "Fumihiko Maki" in *Shinkenchiku* (Tokyo), September 1978; "Junzo Yoshimura" in *Shinkenchiku* (Tokyo), November 1978; "Shin'ichi Okada" in *Japan Architect* (Tokyo), January 1981; 'Astounding: Togo Murano" in *Japan Architect* (Tokyo), June 1981; "Gable Building" in *Japan Architect* (Tokyo), October 1981; "J. P. Getty Museum, Malibu," with Kohbun Itoh, in *Space Design* (Tokyo), September 1982; "Togo Murano" in *Japan Architect* (Tokyo), October 1982.

On ISHII: article—"Reality and Mask" by Koji Taki in *Japan Interior* (Tokyo), November 1977; "Sports Building in Naoshima, Japan" in *Baumeister* (Munich), April 1978; "School Zone in Naoshima" in *Space Design* (Tokyo), July 1979; "Naoshima Junior High School" in *Japan Architect* (Tokyo), November 1979; "AD Profile: Free-Style Classicism" in *Architectural Design* (London), no. 1/2, 1982; "Tokyo Through the Eyes of 12 Young Architects," special issue of *Japan Architect* (Tokyo), April 1982; "Jazzy Baroque" in *Japan Architect* (Tokyo) November/December 1982.

*

Unlike most architectural students who see their projects die in the oblivion of their portfolios, Kazuhiro Ishii has managed to make real some of the products of his students days. Furthermore, in the years of his short but extraordinary career, Ishii has continued to create projects that retain the spark of student freshness; his works are intolerant of conventional professional compromises, yet they are highly disciplined at all levels of their architecture—conceptual, spatial, structural, and functional. So far, there has been no project of Ishii's that cannot be regarded as a unique case study. All of his works, covering a wide range of building types (educational facilities, residential buildings, ceremonial structures), have been studied intensely; he has produced a series of prototypes that other architects will find it difficult to surpass.

Ishii's design method is heavily dependant on history. Although not an historian, he is highly conversant in world and Japanese history of architecture. Observation and hard analysis of historical examples have been his tutors in design, and his exercises in design history have often stimulated his imagination in the creative process. The tea ceremony room, the "54 windows" project, and the curved colonnade of the Naoshima Gymnasium are all results of Ishii's interpretations of historical

examples. His scholasticism is empirical; combined with his socio-worldly concerns and creative drive, it produces projects that are consistent with the theories and circumstances of their making.

An intentional inclusion of conventional symbols and schemata, as well as an appropriate display of occassional subtle "humour," distinguish Ishii's architecture from the mainstream. His humor is reminiscent of Gaudi's (the Gaudi of the non-vertical colonnade of the Park-Güell in Barcelona). Ishii has totally omitted two columns in the curved colonnade of his Naoshima Gymnasium. The Visible Bar reinforcement suggests the two columns that ought to have been there but are not there; it suggests, too, that our current high technology can permit us to play such non-conventional games.

The house in Hiratsuka, known as "54 Windows" or "Tokyo Boogie Woogie," is Ishii's answer to current building practices in today's conventional environment. It demonstrates his concern and offers his answer to contemporary Japanese regionalism, which, in his own words, is characterized by "excess and display." This house—Ishii's masterpiece, in my opinion—offers a diagrammatic intellectual answer to metropolitan alienation. The easily built, thus economic, rigid-frame structure permits the display of abundant information on the elevations by means of clipped window cubicles (54 or 171), each conveying to the outside the varying "meanings" of the inside. "54 Windows" is a symphony of "messages," subordinate to the severe discipline of a low-budget structural system and an efficient functional layout.

Ishii's school buildings (kindergarten, elementary school, gymnasium, etc.) on the Island of Naoshima, all designed in his late twenties and constructed by his early thirties, have already opened new horizons for the architecture of Japanese educational facilities.

Ishii is, in my opinion, the happiest product of Oriental and Western influences. His education at Yale under the guidance and inspiration of Charles Moore, along with his strong concern for meaningful contemporary Japanese regionalism, have produced a most sensitive architecture, unique in Japan and the world.

Tange, Kurokawa, and Isozaki tried to show the world that Japan could do equally well, and perhaps even better, what everybody else was doing architecturally. Tange tried it through structural expressionism and Metabolism, Kurokawa through a multiplicity of expressions, and Isozaki through a Japanese version of often ultra-incomprehensible interpretations of New York "metaphysics." Ishii has gone beyond all that. He belongs to a post-Metabolist, much younger, generation, a down-to-earth but highly dedicated generation in which a claim to immortality can be made even through involvement with trivia.

This young talented architect, also a dedicated scholar and tireless writer, is a model not only in his joyful, pleasing, consistent, and human architecture but also in the way in which he practices architecture as a vocation—an example for architects and architectural students in our complex and demanding era. One of his most successful recent achieve-

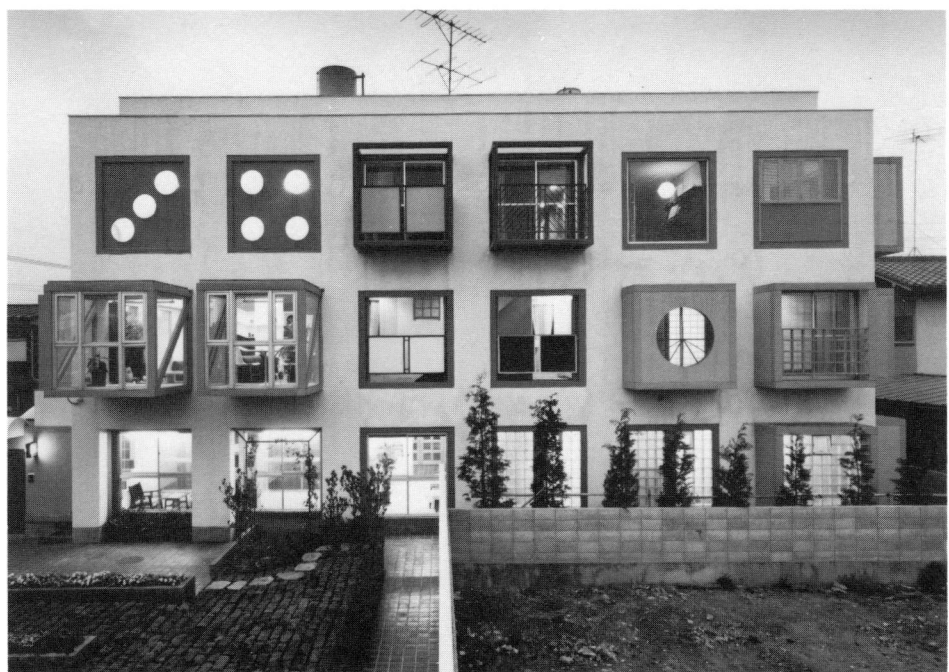

Kazuhiro Ishii: "54 Windows" (Soya Clinic and Residence), Hiratsuka, Kanagawa, Japan, 1975.

ments, an example of his scholarly pursuit of architecture, is the Naoshima City Hall. Its contextually difficult and successful resolution, along with its historically derivative morphology, render it one of the most pleasing samples of the genre. Ishii is still in the forefront of the deeply intellectually inclined yet professionally dedicated avant-garde. He has already become an indispensable member of the Japanese architectural pyramid. Its top is but within easy distance.

—Anthony C. Antoniades

ISOZAKI, Arata.

Japanese. Born in Oita City, 23 July 1931. Educated at the University of Tokyo, Faculty of Architecture, Dip.Arch. 1954. Married the sculptor Aiko Miyawaki in 1972. Worked with Kenzo Tange's, *q.v.*, Team and Urtec, Tokyo, 1954-63. Since 1963, Director of Arata Isozaki and Associates, Tokyo. Visiting Professor, University of California at Los Angeles, 1969, University of Hawaii, Honolulu, 1974, Rhode Island School of Design, Providence, 1976, Columbia University, New York, 1976 and 1979, Harvard University, Cambridge, Massachusetts, 1981, and Yale University, New Haven, Connecticut, 1982. Exhibitions: *Space and Color*, Tokyo, 1966; *From Space Towards Environment*, Tokyo, 1966; *Triennale*, Milan, 1968; *Operation Vesuvius*, Naples, 1972; *Terra-1: International Exhibition of Architecture*, Warsaw, 1975; *Arata Isozaki: Retrospective*, London, 1976; *Dortmunder Architecturausstellung*, Dortmund, West Germany, 1976; *Man TransForms*, Cooper-Hewitt Museum, New York, 1976-77; *Architecture of Quotation and Metaphor* (individual show), Tokyo, Chicago, and Lodz, Poland, 1977; *Assenza/Presenza*, Bologna, Italy, 1977; *Bienal*, São Paulo, 1977; *Numerals: Mathematical Concepts in Contemporary Art*, Leo Castelli Gallery, New York, 1977; *A New Wave of Japanese Architecture*, toured the United States, 1978-79; *MA-Space/-Time in Japan*, at the *Festival d'automne*, Paris, 1978(travelled to New York, Houston, Chicago, Stockholm, and Helsinki, 1979-81); *11th International Biennale of Prints*, Tokyo, 1979; *City Segments*, Walker Art Centre, Minneapolis, 1980; *The Presence of the Past*, at the *Biennale*, Venice,

1980; *Architecture II—Houses for Sale*, Leo Castelli Gallery, New York, 1980; *Architects Make Art*, Spaced Gallery, New York, 1980; *Furniture by Architects*, Massachusetts Institute of Technology, Cambridge, 1980; *Memphis*, Milan, 1981; *Window, Room, Furniture*, Cooper Union, New York, 1981; *La Modernité—un projet inachevé*, at the *Festival d'automne*, Paris, 1982; *Ten New Buildings*, Institute of Contemporary Arts, London, 1983; *Arata Isozaki: Prints*, Philippe Bonnefant Gallery, San Francisco, 1983 (travelled to the Rosa Esman Gallery, New York, and the GA Gallery, Tokyo); *Maki/Isozaki Arhitectural Field Report*, Axis Gallery, Tokyo, 1983; *Architecture III—Follies*, Leo Castelli Gallery, New York, 1983; *ICSID Design '83*, Milan, 1983; *Tokyo: Form and Spirit*, San Francisco Museum of Modern Art, 1987. Recipient: Annual Prize, 1967 and 1975, and Special *Expo '70* Prize, 1970, Architectural Institute of Japan; Annual Prize, *Architectural Year Book*, Japan, 1968; Artist Newcomer Prize, Ministry of Culture, Japan, 1969; Annual Prize, Building Contractors Society of Japan, 1975 and 1984; *Interiors* magazine Award, New York, 1983; Mainichi Art Award, Tokyo, 1983. Honorary Fellow, American Institute of Architects, 1983; Honorary Member, Bund Deutscher Architekten, West Germany, 1983. Member, Accademia Tiberina, Italy, 1978. Address: Arata Isozaki and Associates, 6-14, Akasaka 9-chome, Minato-ku, Tokyo, Japan.

Works:

1959/
60 Oita Medical Hall, Oita City, Japan
1960 Joint Core System for large-scale urban development (project)
Tokyo Plan 1960 (with the Kenzo Tange Team)
1960/
62 Future Dwelling (project)
Process Planning (project)
Ruin Future City (project)
Clusters in the Air (project)
1962/
66 Oita Prefectural Library, Oita City, Japan
1963 Upper Structure, for the Central District of Tokyo (project)
1963/
64 Iwata Girls' High School, Oita City, Japan
1964 Nakayama House, Oita City, Japan

1965 Set designs for the film *The Other Man's Face*
1965/
66 Plan for the reconstruction of Skopje. Yugoslavia (with the Kenzo Tange Team)
1966 Monument for a Poet, Kuju Mountain, Oita, Japan
1966/
67 Oita Branch of the Fukuoka Mutual Bank, Oita City, Japan
1966/
70 *Expo '70*, Osaka: site planning; cybernetic environment for the Festival Plaza; layout of urban trunk facilities; and mechanics of the Festival Plaza
1968/
69 Diamyo Branch of the Fukuoka Mutual Bank, Fukuoka City, Japan
1968/
71 Fukuoka Mutual Bank Head Office, Fukuoka City, Japan
1970/
71 Tokyo Branch of the Fukuoka Mutual Bank (with Kijo Rokkaku)
Computer Aided City (project)
1970/
72 Annex, Oita Medical Hall, Oita City, Japan
1971 Nagazumi and Ropponmatsu Branch of the Fukuoka Mutual Bank, Fukuoka City, Japan
1971/
74 Gunma Prefectural Meseum of Fine Arts, Takasaki City, Japan
1972/
74 Kitakyushu City Museum of Art, Kitakyushu City, Japan
1972/
75 Kitakyushu Central Library, Kitakyushu City, Japan
1973 Saga Branch of the Fukuoka Mutual Bank, Saga City Japan
1973/
74 Fujimi Country Club, Oita City, Japan
1973/
75 Kitakyushu Central Library, Kitakyushu City, Japan
1974 Katsuyama Country Clubhouse (project)
I and T House, Karuisawa, Japan (project)
Cultural Center, Oita City, Japan (project)
1974/
75 Shuko-sha Office Building, Fukuoka City, Japan
1975 Yano House, Takaishi, Tama-ku, Kawasaki City, Japan
Kawarayu Spa Removal (project)
1975/
77 West Japan General Exhibition Center, Kitakyushu City, Japan
Kamioka Town Hall, Gifu Prefecture, Japan
1976 Kaijima House, Honcho, Kichijoji, Musashino City, Tokyo
Information/Cultural Center (project)
1976/
77 Tomb of Ootomo Sorin, Oita City, Japan
1977 Hayashi House, Kozasa, Fukuoka City, Japan
1977/
79 Audio-Visual Center, Oita City, Japan
1978 Sueoka Clinic, Oita City, Japan
Karashima House, Oita City, Japan
1978/
80 Hakubi Kyoto Kimono School, Tokyo
Employees' Service Facilities, Nippon Electric Glass Company, Ootsu City, Kyoto Prefecture, Japan
1978/
83 Tsukuba Center Building, Tsukuba Science City, Ibaragi Prefecture, Japan
1979 Aoki House, Tokyo
Ministry of Foreign Affairs, Riyadh, Saudi Arabia (as consultant)
1980 Waseda Sho-Gekijo Toga Sanbo Theater, Toga Village, Toyama Prefecture, Japan
Tegel Harbor Development, West Berlin (competition project)

1981 Etoh Clinic, Kitsuki City, Oita Prefecture,
        Japan
        Hofu Housing Development (project)
        Historical Museum, Noogata City, Japan
            (project)
1981 Museum of Contemporary Art, Los Angeles
1982 House 2, Housing Block 4, West Berlin
        Houserman Showroom at Merchandise Mart,
            Chicago
        Waseda Shogekijo Toga Sanbo Open-Air
            Theater, Toga Village, Toyama Prefecture,
            Japan
1982/
    84 Okanoyama Graphic Art Museum, Nishiwaki
        City, Hyogo Prefecture, Japan
1983 Nakagami House, Katsuyama City, Fukui
        Prefecture, Japan
        McGrath House, Los Angeles
        Olympic Sports Stadium Complex, Bar-
            celona, Spain (competition project)
1983 Palladium Club, New York
        Glass Art Akasaka Building, Tokyo
        Sports Hall for the 1992 Olympic Games,
            Barcelona, Spain
1984 Shufu-noTomo Office Building, Tokyo
1984 Gymnasium and Dormitory, Iwata High
        School, Oita City, Japan

Publications:

By ISOZAKI: books—*Kukan-e* (collected writings,
1960–69), Tokyo 1971; *Kenchiku-no-kaitai* (monograph on contemporary architecture), Tokyo 1975;
Kenchiku Oyobi Kenchikugal-taki Shiko (dialogue
with other architects and people from various fields),
Tokyo 1976; *Kenchiku-no-1930-nendai* (architecture
of the 1930's: dialogue with other architects), Tokyo
1978; *Shuho-ga* (collected writings, 1969-78), Tokyo
1979; *Kenchiku-no-Shuji* (notes on a counter architecture), Tokyo 1979; *Kenchiku-no-Chiso* (critical
essays), Tokyo 1979; *Architectural Pilgrimage to
World Architecture*, series, with photographs by
Kishin Shinoyama—volume 5, *Abbaye du Thornet*,
Tokyo 1980; volume 10, *Les Salines Royale de
Chaux*, Tokyo 1980; volume 1, *Le Temple d'Amon à
Karnak*, Tokyo 1980; volume 8, *Palazzo Del Tè*,
Tokyo 1980; volume 3, *Villa Adriana*, Tokyo 1981;
volume 6, *Chartres Cathedral*, Tokyo 1983; volume
9, *Chiesa di San Carlo alle Quattro Fontane*, Tokyo
1983; volume 12, *The Chrysler building*, Tokyo 1984;
articles in English—"About My Method" in *Japan
Architect* (Tokyo), August 1972; "The Metaphor for
the Cube" in *Japan Architect* (Tokyo), March 1976;
"A Metaphor Relating with Water" in *Japan
Architect* (Tokyo), March 1978; "Formalism" in
Japan Architect (Tokyo), January 1979, "Ma:
Japanese Space-Time" in *Japan Architect* (Tokyo),
February 1979, "When the King was Killed" in *GA
Document* (Tokyo), August 1980; "A Rethinking of
Space of Darkness" in *Japan Architect* (Tokyo),
March 1981; "The Ledoux Connection" in
Architectural Design (London), January/February
1982; "Interview with Arata Isozaki" in *Modo*
(Milan), January/February 1982; "Interview: Arata
Isozaki" in *Crit* (Washington, D.C.), Winter 1983;
"Of City, Nation and Style" in *Japan Architect*
(Tokyo), January 1984).

On ISOZAKI: books—*New Directions in Japanse
Architecture* by Robin Boyd, London and New York
1968; *Third Generation: The Changing Meaning of
Architecture*, London 1972; *Modern Movements in
Architecture* by Charles Jencks, London 1973;
Decorative Art and Modern Interiors, London 1977;
Beyond Metabolism: The New Japanese Architecture
by Michael Franklin Ross, New York 1978; *A
New Wave of Japanese Architecture*, with introduc-
tion by Kenneth Frampton, New York 1978; *Houses
for Sale*, with introduction by B. J. Archer, New
York 1980; *Late Modern Architecture* by Charles

Arata Isozaki: Tsukuba Center Building, Ibaragi Prefecture, Japan, 1978-83.

Jencks, London 1980; *City Segments*, exhibition
catalogue, edited by Mildred S. Friedman, Minneap-
lis 1980; *The Architecture of Arata Isozaki* by Philip
Drew, New York and London 1982; *Follies: Archi-
tecture for the Late-Twentieth-Century Landscape* by
B. J. Archer and A. Vidler, New York 1983; *Arata
Isozaki; architecture 1959-1982* by Brunilde
Barattucci and Bianca Di Russo, Rome 1983;
articles—"Architecture for the Mini-skirt Age" by
Yoshiaki Tono in *Japan Architect* (Tokyo), May
1968; "Recent Works by Arata Isozaki" in *Japan
Architect* (Tokyo), August 1972; "Die Maniera des
Arata Isozaki" by Jürgen Joedicke in *Bauen und
Wohnen* (Zürich), March 1975; "Arata Isozaki,"
special editions of *Japan Architect* (Tokyo), March
and April 1976; "Position and Move" by Hans
Hollein in *Space Design* (Tokyo), April 1976; "The
Unreal Architecture of Arata Isozaki" by Jennifer
Taylor in *Progressive Architecture* (New York),
September 1976; special issue of *Architectural Design*
(London), January 1977; "Arata Isozaki" by Jen-
nifer Taylor in *Architecture Australia* (Sydney),
September 1977; "The Latest Work of Arata
Isozaki," special issue of *Kenchiku Bunka* (Tokyo),
September 1978; "Arata Isozaki in Paris" in
Architectural Design (London), no. 2, 1979; "Isozaki:
Exploring Form and Experience" in *AIA Journal*
(Washington, D.C.), November 1979; "The

Space/Time of Arata Isozaki" in *Architecture
d'aujord'hui* (Paris), December 1980; "Semiology of
the Architecture of Arata Isozaki" in *Architektura*
(Warsaw), no. 1, 1981; "Iso-Morphism" by Martin
Filler in *Art in America* (New York), February 1981;
"Isozaki: Turning His Back on Japan's Past" by
Henry Scott Stokes and "Houses of Strength and
Serenity by Arata Isozaki" by Paul Goldberger in the
New York Times, 13 April 1981; "Arata Isozaki and
the Japanese Vernacular Tradition" in *HGSD News*
(Cambridge, Massachusetts), Summer 1981; "Arata
in America" in *Building Design* (London), 11 March
1983; "Project by Arata Isozaki for the Museum of
Contemporary Art" in *Casabella* (Milan), May 1983;
"Recent work of Arata Isozaki, Part I" in *Architec-
tural Record* (New York), October 1983; "The
Art of Isozaki" by Martin Filler in *House and Garden*
(New York), October 1983; "Arata Isozaki" in
Architecture interieure créé (Paris), October/
November 1983; "Arata Isozaki 1976-1984," special
issue of *Space Design* (Tokyo), January 1984;
"Recent Work of Arata Isozaki, Part II" in
Architectural Record (New York), May 1984.

Bibliography: *Arata Isozaki: Japanese "Avant
Garde" Architect* by James P. Noffsinger, Monticello, Illinois 1979.

The last twenty-five years of my architectural career manifest two fairly distinct tendencies which coincide with two periods, the 1960s and the 1970s-80s. The transition between these two periods stems from my situation as architect in the stream of social, economic, and cultural events of Japan in these years.

In my work of the 1960s, I attempted to represent the rapid expansion of the Japanese city and the extensive development of technology and economy in Japan by my architectural method. At this same time, in the early 1960s, the Metabolist Movement was begun by a group of young Japanese architects. This architectural movement aimed to express directly the specific development of technical method itself, which could correspond to the changing situation of the city and architecture. Although I was not a member of the Metabloist group, I remained sympathetic but always critical, while trying to find my own method. I sympathized with the Metabolists primarily on the technical and expressive levels. My Joint Core System of 1960, a project working with architectural concepts on an urban scale, and Oita Prefectural Library (1960), the concrete realization of the earlier project, represent this tendency. Later, this tendency was further developed in the Master Plan for *Expo '70* in the idea of the Festival Plaza and, moreover, in the design of mechanical equipment and in the direction of performance at the Festival Plaza in 1970.

My criticism of the Metabolist Movement was directed against what I considered to be their somewhat facile and naive interpretation of modern architecture—the tendency to reduce architecture to simply an answer to utilitarian needs. My objection, in rurely conceptual terms, argued that architecture must posses its own independent form and that this would ultimately secure for architecture an original cultural meaning. This attitude would be kept in my work in the 1970s. My Nakayama House of 1964, based on purely geometric form, is important when seen from this point of view.

In the 1970s, the number and functions of my buildings increased, from private houses to public buildings (The Kitakyushu Central Library, 1975; Gunma Prefectural Museum of Find Arts, 1974),

from the structural development at the West Japan General Exhibition Center of 1977 to the organization of a new-style exhibition, *MA-Space/Time in Japan* (1978-79), introduction the unique and deeply-rooted Japanese concept of *ma* to the west. Through these various works, I have consistently intended to locate architecture in the context of culture, by clarifying conceptualization and method. Such a pursuite may represent a unique point of view, missing not only in Japanese architecture but also in modern architecture in general. Therefore, in my work, I have always regarded architecture as a play of pure forms, simultaneously containing economic, functional, technical, and various other solutions.

In order to synthesize in architecture these posited but undefined dimensions, I have adopted an architectural method, a "Maniere (Maniera)" as a means of critically passing beyond the Modern Movement.

More explicity, in attempting to establish "architecture," my work includes quotations from the whole of our cultural legacy up to the present, bringing forth, hopefully, unique metaphors. This architectural attitute will continue to preoccupy me in the future.

—Arata Isozaki

Arata Isozaki is one of the most prolific and creative personalities in international contemporary architecture. In terms of boldness of design and creative power, he can be compared only with James Stirling, Richard Meier, and Aldo Rossi. Like them, he must be acknowledged as one of the masters of the 1970s and 1980s. Isozaki's early architectural work in his home town of Oita in the south of Japan, his work with the Kenzo Tange Team in Tokyo, his proposals for Clusters in the Air of 1962, and especially his work since 1979 show innovative exploration into the complexity of architectural space and its meaning.

Most characteristic of Isozaki's buildings is their ambiguous nature, an ambiguity that includes a sense of irony and wit. The complexity of meaningful spatial articulations in his work is often hidden by an academic perfection of execution. Yet the basic goal remains the revelation of the autonomous and complicated meaning of spaces. In Isozaki's own terms, "Architecture is a machine for the production of meaning." And he continues, "I attempt to use the simplest possible techniques to embody my methods because I feel that without the intermediary of what I call the traces of human hands, the method itself will be more effective and the range greater. Of course, the method involves the use of the hands, and the traces of their activities only begin to vanish as the result of the virtually automatic process originating with the use of the ruler."

In order to achieve his goals, Isozaki makes the images and quotations of earlier architectual solutions integral parts of the design process; he aism at what could be called "architectural multimedia." Isozaki's term "maniera" designates the re-use or variation of preconceived themes from different periods and places at the same time and in the same work. This method results in a pluralization of elements and a multi-level approach that, in itself, causes a multiplicity of meaning and eclecticism of radical dimensions. The conceptual presence of all historical phases from the past—Greek temples, Shinto shrines, Buddhist temples, Palladio's villas, the buildings of Kenzo Tange, Superstudio design, and technological images in general—makes Isozaki's work one of international, universale synthesis. In 1984, Isozaki wrote, "Anything occurring in the history of architecture—even the history of the world—is open to quotation." As with other contemporary pioneers of an autonomous architecture, Isozaki defends his medium against its exploitation as a language of social comment, cultural or personal expressionsim, and political propaganda.

Isozaki's major buildings include the Saga Branch of the Fukuoka Mutual Bank; Gunma Prefectural Museum of Fine Arts, Takasaki; Fujimi Country Club, Oita; Kamioka Town Hall; Kitakyushu Central Library; and the Yano House in Kawasaki.

—Udo Kultermann

JACKSON, Daryl Sanders.

Australian. Born in Clunes, Victoria, 7 February 1937. Educated at Wesley College, Melbourne, 1950-53; Royal Melbourne Institute of Technology, 1954-56, Dip.Arch. 1956; University of Melbourne, 1957-58, B.Arch. 1958. Married Kay Jackson in 1960; children: Timothy, Sara, Olivia, and Melissa. Assistant, Edwards, Madigan and Torzillo, Sydney, 1959, Don Hendry Fulton, *q.v.*, Melbourne, 1960, Chamberlin, Powell and Bon, *q.v.*, London, 1961-63, Paul Rudolph, *q.v.*, New Haven, Connecticut, 1963-64, and Skidmore, Owings and Merrill, *q.v.*, San Francisco, 1964. Partner, Daryl Jackson/Evan Walker Architects Pty. Ltd., Melbourne, 1965-79; Partner/Director, with Bill Ryan and Bryan Miller, Daryl Jackson Pty. Ltd., Melbourne, since 1979. Exhibition: *Architecture, Drawings and Photographs*, Christine Abrahams Gallery, Melbourne, and Canberra School of Art, 1984. Recipient: Stramit Architectural Research Scholarship, 1969; Victorian Architecture Awards, 1970, 1973, 1976, 1978, and 1982; Australian Capital Territory Awards, 1981 and 1982; Parliament House Competition Prize, Canberra, 1979; Sir Zelman Cowan Award, Canberra School of Art, 1981. Address: Daryl Jackson Pty. Ltd., Brunswick Place, Fitzroy, Victoria 3065, Australia.

Works:

1967/
  69 Special Studies Building and Gymnasium/Music School, Lauriston Girls' School, Malvern, Victoria
1969 E.S. and A. Bank, Hawthorn, Victoria
    Harold Holt Memorial Swimming Centre, Melbourne (with Kevin Borland)
1971 Residential Wing, St. Hilda's College, University of Melbourne
    Science/Humanities Wing, Presbyterian Ladies' College, Burwood, Victoria
    Sports Complex and Kindergarten, Eltham, Victoria
1972 Redevelopment of Wesley College, Prahran, Victoria (with McGlashan and Everist)
    Library/Resource Centre, St. Leonard's College, Brighton, Victoria
    The Hermitage Church of England Girls' Grammar School Education Complex, Highton, Geelong, Victoria
1973 Princes Hill High School Education Complex, Carlton, Victoria
    Resource Centre, Methodist Ladies' College, Kew, Victoria
1973/
  75 Student Union and Student Housing, Ballarat College of Advanced Education, Victoria
1974 New Courts and Clubrooms, Royal Melbourne Tennis Club, Sherwood Street, Richmond, Victoria
    Y.W.C.A., Suva, Fiji
    Tenaden School, Belgrave, Victoria
    Senior Centre, Kingswood College, Box Hill, Victoria

Library/Resource Centre, Mount Scopus Memorial College, Burwood, Victoria
    Australia and New Zealand Bank Building, Kyabram, Victoria
    Queen's College renovations, University of Melbourne, Parkville, Victoria
1974/
  79 St. Paul's School, Woodleigh, Baxter, Victoria
1975 New Music School, Presbyterian Ladies' College, Burwood, Victoria
    Australia and New Zealand Bank Building, Glen Waverley, Victoria
    Art Gallery and Old Physics Building renovation, University of Melbourne
    Resource Centre, St. Patrick's CBC College, Ballarat, Victoria
    Staff Quarters, Government House, Canberra
1976 Junior Library and Art/Craft Building, St. Leonard's College, Brighton, Victoria
    Hall/Synagogue, Mount Scopus Memorial College, Burwood, Victoria
    Yooralla Special Day School, Glenroy, Victoria
    City Edge (high-density housing development), Eastern Road, South Melbourne
    School of Music, Canberra
    Tullamarine Sports Pavilion, Keilor, Victoria
    New Teaching and Library Facilities, St. Alipius Parish School, Ballarat, Victoria
    State Bank of Victoria Building, Richmond, Victoria
1977 Student Housing, University of Melbourne, Cardigan Street, Carlton, Victoria
    New Biology Laboratory, St. Patrick's CBC College, Ballarat, Victoria
    Residential Staff College, State Bank of Victoria, Richmond
    Indoor Swimming Complex, Collingwood, Victoria
    Squash Courts, Dickson Square Centre, Canberra
    Association for Modern Education School, Weston Creek, Canberra
1978 Pre-School Building, Yooralla Special Day School, Glenroy, Victoria
    Boarders' Wine, St. Patrick's CBC College, Ballarat, Victoria
    Camberwell City Council Branch Library, Balwyn, Victoria
    Student Union extensions, Ballarat College of Advanced Education, Victoria
    Staff Housing, Royal Melbourne Hospital, North Melbourne
    Activities Centre, Blackburn South High School, Melbourne
    Synday Primary School, Wesley College, Melbourne (with McGlashan and Everist)
    Collingwood Branch Library, Victoria
    Emu Ridge High Density Housing, Belconnen, Canberra
    Moorabbin Indoor Swimming Pool, Victoria
    Moorabbin Link Shopping Centre, Victoria
    Union and Administration Building, Deakin University, Geelong, Victoria

1979 National Circuit Offices, Canberra
    Ashburton Branch Library, Melbourne
    Lecture Theatre, Deakin University, Geelong, Victoria
    St. Paul's School multi-purpose hall, Woodleigh, Victoria
    Parliament House, Canberra (competition project)
    Eastern Suburbs Geriatric Centre, East Burwood, Victoria
    Discurio-Met Record Shop and Bistro, Melbourne
    Uniting Church of Australia housing for the handicapped, North Essendon, Victoria
    Council of Adult Education building renovations, Melbourne
1980 Walter and Eliza Hall Institute of Medical Research, Parkville, Victoria (with Godfrey Spowers Pty.)
    Box Hill Indoor Recreation Centre, Victoria
    Cox House, Hawthorn, Victoria
    Conference Centre, University of Melbourne, Parkville, Victoria
    Catholic Diocesan Offices, Ballarat, Victoria
    Abrahams House, Brighton, Victoria
1981 Indoor Sports Centre, Australian Defence Forces Academy, Canberra
    City Offices, Canberra
    Jackson House renovations, East Melbourne
    Singapore High Commission, Canberra
    Latchford Barracks Master Plan and buildings, Bonegilla, Victoria
    Southport Nursing Home, South Melbourne
    Isobel Henderson Free Kindergarten, North Fitzroy, Victoria
    Municipal Works Depot, Camberwell, Victoria
    Royal Melbourne Hospital long-term development study, Melbourne
    Commonwealth Bank, Rosanna, Victoria
    South Yarra Project, for Jack Chia Australia Pty., Victoria (with South Yarra Collaborative)
    National Mutual Retail Development Study, Frankston, Victoria
1982 Australian Chancery Complex, Riyadh, Saudi Arabia
    Australian Film and Television School, North Ryde, New South Wales (Daryl Jackson Basil Carter Pty. Ltd.)
    Esprit de Corps Development, Yarra Falls, Collingwood, Victoria
    Swimming Training Halls in the National Sports Centre, Bruce, A.C.T.
    Houses for the Victorian Ministry of Housing, Nelson Road, South Melbourne
    National Mutual Retail Centre redevelopment study, Camberwell, Victoria
1983 National Archives, Canberra (competition project)
    Hotel Canberra, Canberra
    Graduate School of Management, University of Melbourne, Carlton, Victoria
    State Insurance Office Building, Collins

Daryl Jackson: National Sports Centre, Canberra, 1983.

Street, Melbourne (with Godfrey & Spowers)
Office Building, Collins Street, Melbourne (with South Yarra Collaborative)
Sports Training Facilities at the National Sports Centre, Bruce, A.C.T.
Sports Union Building, Deakin University, Geelong, Victoria
Ministry of Housing, Dight Street, Collingwood, Melbourne
Northcote Library, Melbourne

Publications:

By JACKSON: book—*Daryl Jackson: Architecture, Drawings and Photographs*, South Melbourne 1984; articles—"Getting Away from It All" in *Design Australia* (Melbourne), February/March 1973; "Daryl Jackson on Robin Boyd" in *Architecture in Australia* (Sydney), April 1973; "A Show of Hands" in *Architect* (Melbourne), November 1976; "Every Hand Counts" in *Architect* (Melbourne), January 1977; "Where Is Your Hand" in *Architect* (Melbourne), March 1977; "Handing It Up" in *Architect* (Melbourne), May 1977; "Hands Up (Gloves Off)" in *Architect* (Melbourne), July 1977; "Put Your Hands Together" in *Architect* (Melbourne), November 1977; "Lost Chance at the Last Laugh?" in *Architect* (Melbourne), August 1978.

On JACKSON: book—*Modern Houses, Melbourne* by Norman Day, Melbourne 1976; articles— "Princes Hill High School," "M.L.C. Resource Center," and "Y.W.C.A., Suva" in *Constructional Review* (Sydney), June/September 1974; "YWCA Community Resource Centre, Suva, Fiji" in *Architecture in Australia* (Sydney), December 1974; "Daryl Jackson" by Laurie Thomas in *The Most Noble Art of Them All*, St. Lucia, Queensland 1976; "Two Recent Projects by Jackson/Walker" in *Architect* (Melbourne), July 1976; "Scuola in Australia" in *Domus* (Milan), November 1976; "Royal Tennis Club" and "Mt. Scopus College" in *Constructional Review* (Sydney), August 1977; "The Golden Rules of Brutalism" by Norman Day in *The Age* (Melbourne), 30 August 1977; "A Bush Haven for Bank Men" by Norman Day in *The Age* (Melbourne), 13 September 1977; "Pool Plan Still in the Swim" by Norman Day in *The Age* (Melbourne), 25 October 1977; "Three Approaches to Preserving the Past" by Norman Day in *The Age* (Melbourne), 28 November 1977; "Sins to Avoid in Design for the Faith" by Norman Day in *The Age* (Melbourne), 3 January 1978; "Daryl Jackson Designs an End or a Beginning" by Brian Talbot in *Architect* (Melbourne), April 1978; "Terraces for the Seventies" by Norman Day in *The Age* (Melbourne), 25 April 1978; "Calling the Tune in the Schoolyard" by Norman Day in *The Age* (Melbourne), 25 July 1978; "Music School, Canberra" and "St. Paul's School, Woodleigh, Baxter" in *Architectural Review* (London), September 1978.

*

In a democratic society, architecture is, we believe, an essentially social art with a level of accountability/expectation extending well beyond those notions of aesthetic morality which are so closely identified with the development of the Modern Movement.

The act of design, while it remains an intrinsic function of architecture, does so as part of an inclusive life-process, which in itself is a key function of the society for whom things are built.

There are three critical areas: 1) the context of problem-solving; 2) ideas and idea-making; and 3) architectural form, object, and symbol... (out of ideas and into context).

None of these aspects can be ignored; they are fundamentally related or associated. And architecture, if it is to be of value—moral value—can only become so by addressing "the whole" or universal proposition, not merely one of its parts.

Idea-making on behalf of society remains a necessary function of architecture, with architectural form seen in the first instance as a *fertile proposition* against which ideas (of use, shape, and materials utilisation) can be tested and a hierarchical structuring established. Our preference is to develop forms which are not visually constrained and which therefore enable us to hold the proposition "open to verification" for as long as possible.

The substance of our approach to architectural composition and architectural morality can be summarized as follows: 1) *The Social Stance Adopted*—associative understanding, not dissociative method; 2) *Assembly of Parts*—space realms as cues to enabling and facilitating human encounter; exposing the circulation; 3) *Place and Identity*—context determinants as basics for physical expression; 4) *Expressionism and Symbolism*—geometric abstraction; formal complexity; adaptability and changeability; industrial vernacular. We are convinced that architecture is concerned with creative fit, and in the ultimate sense this is the measure of the art.

—Daryl Jackson

Find a nice safe niche, my boy, develop a fashionable style of building, attract all the right sort of clients and then relax—you will enjoy a comfortable practice. Such a philosophy would be poisonous to Daryl Jackson, who has no apparently consistent architectural style and no special group of clients (except perhaps educational ones), and he seldom sits back because he enjoys too much the business of life.

If you like the comfort of labels, you could say that Jackson's work ranges somewhere between vernacular sophistication and a subtle brand of brutalism. A better description would be that he brings an open mind to each project. With a wide range of projects and a mind not closed, he produces results that are seldom predictable. When a client wanted to collect the rays of the sun to heat his bath water, Jackson gave him a bank of solar absorbers and stood them proudly on the roof. If a government authority needs a public swimming pool, he makes it a happy and colourful place, one that opens to the gardens in good weather and withdraws into an exciting shell when the fogs come. In Fiji, he has built with concrete because it is an economic and thermally successful material; in the country, he uses local materials and techniques; in the city he uses materials that will survive the fetid air and grit.

Jackson has developed some sort of a following with school and college buildings and, more recently, with housing groups, but even then the products are as varied as the problems. The working spaces of his buildings are clear expressions of their functions, but because he works from the inside out, he often ends up with unobvious boundaries to the spaces. This is all very confusing to the receiver of his messages. Usually the real mechanics of his designs, and their logical systems, become clear only after trying them out.

The process of design is seldom concealed in a Jackson building. Conflicts and contradictions faced in that process end up as conflicts and contradictions in the building fabric. He can juggle nuts and bolts with one hand and sinuous curves with the other, when many of his fellows would probably have put one set of problems down to polish the act of the other. He would seem to be a disquieting influence in the quiet school of Melbourne architects, yet he can also give a flat street a serene little house or an extensive group of apartments, buildings that sit calmly denying that anything else could ever have been there.

There is a strong connection between the visual variety of his buildings and his quest for a valid role for the architect in society. From Jackson's searches will come one day a better understanding of the essential catholicity of an environmental scientist. In the interim, a whole lot of clients are getting the sort of architecture that is too rarely found, architecture that feels good.

—Roger Pegrum

JACKSON, David.

Australian. Born in Gloucester, England, 12 November 1931; emigrated to Australia, 1958; naturalized, 1976. Educated at the Architectural Association School, London, 1950-55 (5th Year Prize, Dip.A.A. 1955; Yale University of City Planning, New Haven, Connecticut (King George VI Memorial Fellowship), 1955-56. Married Barbara Hansen in 1962; children: Ann, Sophie, Rachel, and Theo. Architectural Adviser, City Planning Commission, New Haven, Connecticut, 1955-56; Architectural Assistant, Norman and Dawbarn, Kingston, Jamaica, 1956-58; Architectural Assistant, subsequently Associate, then Partner, McConnel, Smith and Johnson, Sydney, 1958-71. Since 1971, Director, with J. D. Chesterman, A. L. Teece, and F. D. Willis, Jackson Teece Chesterman Willis Pty. Ltd., Sydney. Chairman, New South Wales Board of Architectural Education, 1972-78; President, New South Wales Chapter, Royal Australian Institute of Architects, 1978-80; President-Elect, Royal Australian Institute of Architects, 1984-85. Exhibitions: *Old Continent— New Buildings*, toured Australia, Europe, and the United States, 1982-84; *Overseas Members' Exhibition*, Royal Institute of British Architects, London, 1984. Recipient: National Illumination Award, Australia, 1976; Civic Design Award, Australia, 1980. Fellow, Royal Institute of British Architects, 1970; Life Fellow, Royal Australian Institute of Architects, 1980. Address: Jackson Teece Chesterman Willis Pty. Ltd., 40 King Street, Sydney, New South Wales 2000, Australia.

Works:

1971 Development Finance Corporation Head Office renovations, Sydney
Guardian Royal Exchange Assurance Office Building, Chatswood, New South Wales
Guardian Royal Exchange Assurance Open Office Plan, Kindersley House, Sydney
1972 Rosemont Gardens Housing, Edgecliff, New South Wales
Public Transport Interchange remodelling and pedestrian tunnel, Railway Square, Sydney (with Rankine and Hill)
Six houses, Armidale, New South Wales
Twenty town houses, William Street, Double Bay, New South Wales
Flookies Boutique interiors, Sydney
Angus and Robertson Bookshop interiors, Elizabeth Street, Melbourne, and Ballarat, Victoria (with Jackson and Walker)
Thirty-five town houses, Bellevue Hill, New South Wales
1973 Chandlers Ltd. Electrical Retail Shop interiors and warehouse, Cairns, Townsville and Rockhampton, Queensland
School of Behavioral Science, Macquarie University, Ryde, New South Wales (with the University Architect)
Medical Centre, Dee Why, New South Wales
Field staff management and organization study for the University of New England, Armidale, New South Wales
Socio-economic study for the preservation of a suburb, Glebe, Forest Lodge, New South Wales
1974 Mass housing plan, East Balmain, New South Wales
Harris House, Simmons Street, Balmain, New South Wales
1975 Ore loader repairs, Darwin, Northern Territory
College of Art Site Planning Study, Ryde, New South Wales
Library extension, Macquarie University, Ryde, New South Wales
College/Community Activity Centre, Wanniassa, A.C.T.
Social and Education Facilities Integration Study, Lanyon, A.C.T.
Warehouse conversion to Science Centre, Clarence Street, Sydney (with Ruth Inall)
1976 New Sydney Stock Exchange, Bond Street
Wabo Dam Town Planning Study, Papua New Guinea
Factory buildings conversion to shops and marina, Birkenhead Point, Drummoyne, New South Wales
Teachers College renovations and landscaping, Carillon Avenue, Sydney
1977 Police College and Services Centre, Weston, A.C.T.
Beach management study, Maroubra, New South Wales
Medibank Head Office, Woden, A.C.T.
Botany Bay Visual Study, Botany Bay, New South Wales

R. Young House, Cherry Road, Warners Bay, Newcastle, New South Wales
Medical Centre Plan, Ryde, New South Wales
1978 Kindersley House renovations, O'Connell Street, Sydney (with L. J. Hooker)
Ski Resorts Development Plan, Kosciusko National Park, New South Wales
Circular Quay and Customs House forecourt, Sydney
Port Macquarie Planning Study, New South Wales
National Archives Building, Canberra (competition project)
1979 New Sydney Stock Exchange, Bond Street, Sydney
Townhouses and flats (Tyrell House conversion), Newcastle, New South Wales
Dixon Library, stage 3, University of New England, Armidale, New South Wales
Philippine Airlines office interiors, Sydney
Power House Museum, stage 1, Sydney (with the New South Wales Government Architect)
Stock Exchange Clearing House, Sydney
Japan/Australia Development Corporation office interiors, Sydney
1980 University of New England Eastern Campus Plan, Armidale, New South Wales
Jackson Securities office interiors, Sydney
Office Building, 26 O'Connell Street, Sydney
Wangi Point landscaping, Lake Macquarie, New South Wales
Paramatta Stadium Environmental Impact Study, New South Wales
Goodooga Energy-Saving Hospital, New South Wales (project)
Attorney General's Office Building, and Old Patent Office restoration, Canberra (with National Capital Development Corporation)
C.S.I.R.O. Laboratory, Ryde, New South Wales (with Department of Housing Construction)
McDougall House, Daleys Point, New South Wales
1981 Glenbawn Dam environmental study, New South Wales
General Post Office facade restoration, Martin Place, Sydney (with Department of Housing Construction)
Duke of Cornwall Hotel, Broken Hill, New South Wales
Blue Cow Ski Resort Plan, Kusciusko, New South Wales
Townhouses, Squizzy Taylor Square, Sydney
Municipal Council Office extensions and renovations, Ku-Ring-Gai, New South Wales
1982 Thiess Contractors Office Building and Workshops, Botany Bay, New South Wales
Community Building (Orion Cinema conversion), Canterbury, New South Wales
Showground Managment Plan, Newcastle, New South Wales
Bank of New Zealand interiors, Sydney
Ferrier Hodgson Office interiors, Sydney
Maria Gillies Barber's Shop, Sydney
Retirement Village, St. Ives, New South Wales
Dalmar Homes property development plan, New South Wales
Arakoon State Park management plan, New South Wales
1983 Showground stables, Canberra
Ocean Shores development plan, New South Wales
Tamworth Music Centre development plan and Tavern, New South Wales
Dalmar Retirement Village, New South Wales
Narabeen Retirement Village, New South Wales
Church Street Mall, Parramatta, New South Wales

David Jackson: Squizzy Taylor's Square inner city housing, Sydney, 1981.

Royal Prince Alfred Hospital development plan, Sydney
1984 Woolloomooloo Naval Housing, Sydney
Australian Institute of Chartered Accountants office interiors, Sydney
University of New England campus master plan, Armidale, New South Wales
Macquarie University GeneralStudies Building, North Ryde, New South Wales
Office Building, Brisbane, Queensland
St. George Hospital development plan, New South Wales
Sydney Eastern Distributor Environmental Impact Study, New South Wales

Publications:

By JACKSON: articles—"Student Teacher Relations at the AA," with Tony Moore, in *Architecture in Australia* (Sydney), September 1961; "Dimensional Co-ordination" in *Building Science Forum*, Sydney 1970; "Costs of Regulations" in *Building Economist* (Sydney), December 1981.

*

My work is my firm's work. We are a group with wide-ranging skills—planners, architects, economists, landscapers, and interior designers—the basic skills essential to the solution of today's complex architectural and planning problems. We like to have our clients as part of the project teams because it is the best way for us to understand their needs and aspirations and for them to develop a full appreciation of their project and its community impact.

We encourage team members to perform as individuals rather than as shadows of the firm. Our design judgements are based on common sense, good looks, economy, and professional performance. We make our buildings good neighbours and part of their context, and eschew flamboyance. The adjacent photograph shows an example a new houses fitting well into a locality of two-storey Victorian dwellings and small warehouses.

The result of this approach is an absence of consistent architectural style. Because we respond to differences in time, context, client, and brief, our products vary considerably. Since 1981, we have been using computers in design and documentation. At first, we thought that they would impose a sameness on our building. The fear was unfounded. Computers give us more time and facility to get each project right in itself.

—David Jackson

*

David Jackson emphasizes the importance of teamwork. He considers that the buildings in whose design he has participated are the work of his firm rather than of himself as an individual. He also disclaims the need for consistency of style in his architecture because each building is designed to respond to the client's requirements and the limitation set by its surroundings. Jackson's work is therefore marked by a quiet competence rather than by flamboyant touches.

This attitude is demonstrated by his pedestrian subway at Railway Square, used daily by many thousands of people. Placed in a part of the city where buildings have been declining for several decades, it provides not merely efficient pedestrian circulation and a pleasant shopping area but also a small oasis of trees at a busy traffic intersection. The Birkenhead Point project is another example of a redevelopment of a declining neighbourhood. This old industrial area is now a major shopping centre and a site for the Sydney Maritime Museum.

Jackson's designs are notable for their wide range and their consistently successful solution of the client's problems. They include several office buildings, among them the Philip Street Office Tower; several residential buildings of which the fifty-unit Rosemont complex in Edgecliff is particularly noteworthy; a number of educational buildings; some renovations, including the highly successful interior of the new Angus and Robertson Bookshop in Melbourne, and the repair of the classical facade of the General Post Office in Sydney; and several town planning projects.

In recent years, Jackson Teece Chesterman Willis and Partners have increasingly provided the construction management as well as the design of their buildings, for example in the complex new headquarters of the Sydney Stock Exchange and in the Canberra Head Office Building of Medibank (the government health insurance).

—Henry J. Cowan

JACOBSEN, Arne.

Danish. Born in Copenhagen, 11 February 1902. Educated at the School of Architecture of the Academy of Arts. Copenhagen, Dip. Arch. 1928. Married; had two sons. Worked in the office of the city architect Paul Holsoe, Copenhagen, 1927-30; in private practice Copenhagen, 1930 until his death, 1971; also designed textiles and furniture from 1943. Professor of Architecture, Academy of Arts, Copenhagen, 1956-71. Exhibitions (one-man): Royal Institute of British Architects, London, 1959; McLellan Galleries, Glasgow, 1968; Ministry of Cultural Affairs, Copenhagen, 1971. Recipient: First Prize, Bellevue Seaside Development Competition, 1932; Eckersberg Gold Medal, Academy of Arts, Copenhagen, 1936; First Prize, Aarhus Town Hall Competition, 1937; First Prize, Søllerød Town Hall Competition, 1939; Grand Prize, *BienaL*, São Paulo, Brazil, 1953. D.Litt.: Oxford University, 1966; LL.D.: Strathclyde University, Glasgow, 1968. Honorary Corresponding Member, Royal Institute of British Architects; Honorary Fellow, American Institute of Architects. *Died* (in Copenhagen) *24 March 1971.*

Works:

1926/
27 C.V.E. House, Knutsvej 9, Copenhagen
House, Knutsvej 11, Copenhagen
1928/
29 Jacobsen House, Gotfred Rodesvej 2, Copenhagen
House, Baunegardsvej 22, Copenhagen
1929 House of the Future, *Danish Building Exhibition*, Copenhagen (exhibition project; with Flemming Lassen)
1930 Rothenborg House, Klampenborgvej 37, Copenhagen
Friss House, Tranegardsvej 25, Copenhagen
Mattsson's Riding School, Bellevuevej 12, Klampenborg, near Copenhagen
1930/
31 House, Ole Olsens Alle 28, Copenhagen
House, Baunegardsvej 81, Copenhagen
House, Hegelsvej 8, Copenhagen
1932 Bellevue Seaside Development, Denmark
Bellevue Tower and Restaurant, Denmark (project)
1933 Brobjerg House, Hegelsvej 18, Copenhagen
Grumstrup House, Vemmetofte Alle 10, Copenhagen
Povl Munck House, Hegelsvej 17, Copenhagen
Bellavista Housing Estate, Klampenborg, near Copenhagen
1934 Steinthal House, Hegelsvej 9, Copenhagen
Erik Dugdale House, Kratvaenget 9, Copenhagen
Erhardt House, Hegelsvej 3, Copenhagen
Seaside Bathing Complex, Dragor, Denmark (demolished)
1934/
35 Novo Therapeutic Laboratories, Fuglebakkevej, Copenhagen
1935 Juncker's Tennis Hall, Malthegardsvej, Gentofte, Denmark
1936 Landmandsbanken, Norrebrogade 160, Copenhagen
1936/
42 Gentofte Stadium, Jaegersborg, Gentofte, Denmark
1937 Christensen House, Skovvangen 17, Copenhagen
Bellevue Theatre and Gammel Bellevue Restaurant, Copenhagen
Hellerup Idraetsklub Tennis Hall, Hartmannsvej 37, Gentofte, Copenhagen
Jacobsen Country House, Gudmindrup Lyng, Denmark
1937/
38 Stelling House, Gammel Torv 6, Copenhagen

1937/
42 Town Hall, Aarhus, Denmark (with Erik Møller)
1938 Pedersen House, Kongehojen 3, Copenhagen
1939 Housing Estate, Jaegersborg Alle, Annettevej, Copenhagen
1939/
42 Town Hall, Søllerød, near Copenhagen (with Flemming Lassen)
1940 Ibstrupparken I Housing Estate, Horsholmvej, Jaegorsborg, Gentofte, Denmark
1943 Smoke House, Oddenhavn, Denmark
Terraced housing, Ellebaekvej, Copenhagen
1944/
45 Ebbe Munck Country House, Arild, Sweden
1946 Ibstrupparken II Housing Estate, Smakkegardsvej, Jaegersborg, Gentofte, Denmark
1947 Young People's Housing, Gentofte, Denmark
1948 Paulsen and Company Building interiors, Frederiksgade 19, Copenhagen
1949 Creche and Kindergarten, Bornevenneme, Copenhagen (project)
Yacht Harbour, Vejle, Denmark (project)
1950 Søholm Terraced Housing, Strandvejen, Klampenborg, near Copenhagen
1951 Islevvaenge Terraced Housing, Rødovre, Denmark

C.A. Møller House, Vedbaek, Denmark
Harby Central School and Teachers' Housing, Funen, Denmark
1952 Allehusene Housing Estate, Jaegersborg Alle, Gentofte, Denmark
Massey-Harris Showroom and Spares Depot, Roskilde Landevej 183, Copenhagen
1952/
56 Munkegaard School, Vangedevej, Gentofte, Denmark
1953/
58 Town Hall, Glostrup, Denmark
1954 Upton Hansen House, Kalundborg, Denmark
Henning Simony House, Geelsvej 10, Copenhagen
1955 Town Hall, Rødovre, Denmark
Jespersen and Son Office Building, Copenhagen
1956 Ruthwen Jurgensen House, Vedbaek, Denmark
Kokfelt Summer Cottage, Tisvilde, Denmark
1957 Lan dskrona Sports Hall (project)
Circular House, Odden, Denmark
Atrium Houses, Hansaviertel, Berlin
Terraced housing, Ornegardsvej, Jaegersborg, Gentofte, Denmark

Arne Jacobsen: Town Hall, Rodøvre, Denmark, 1955

Carl Christensen Factory, Aalborg, Denmark
Town Hall, Marl, Germany (project)
Atrium Houses, Carlsminde, Søllerød, near Copenhagen (project)
1958 Town Hall extensions, Cologne (project)
1958/
  59 Nov Industri A/S Factory, Gladsaxe, Denmark (project)
1958/
  60 SAS Royal Hotel and Air Terminal, Vesterbrogade, Copenhagen
1959 Erik Siesby House ("Sorgenfri"), Prinsessestien, Lyngby, Denmark
  School, Rødovre, Denmark (project)
  Orderinges Headquarters Building, The Hague (project)
1960 Edwin Jensen House, Mosehojvej, Ordrup, Denmark
  Housing block, Rødovre, Denmark
  St. Catherine's College, Oxford
  World Health Organization Headquarters, Geneva (project)
  Bellevue Bay Housing Estate, Klampenborg, near Copenhagen
1961 Gertie Wandel House, Ordrup, Denmark
  Library, Rødovre, Denmark (project)
  Ovo Industri A/S Factory, Hillerogade, Copenhagen
  National Bank and Bill Printing Plant, Copenhagen (project)
  Tom's Chocolate Factory, Ballerup, Copenhagen
1962 Electricity Company Headquarters, Hamburg, Germany (with Otto Weitling)
  Parliament Building, Islamabad, Pakistan (project)
  Landskrona Sports Hall II (project)
  Town Hall, Essen, Germany (competition project)
1966/
  77 Town Centre, Castrop-Rauxel, Germany (with Otto Weitling)
1969/
  70 Novo Factory, Mainz, Germany
  Novo Factory, Chartres, France
1970 HEW Offices, Hamburg
  Hotel, Newcastle, England (project)
1970/
  73 Modular Cubic House Type (with Otto Weitling)
1970/
  74 Town Hall, Mainz, Germany (with Otto Weitling)
1970/
  75 Holiday Resort Development, Fehmarn Island, Germany (with Otto Weitling)
1970/
  77 Danish Embassy, Sloane Street, London (with Dissing/Weitling)
1971 National Bank of Kuwait (project)
  Danish National Bank, Copenhagen

Publications:

On JACOBSEN: books—*Arkitekten Arne Jacobsen* by J. Pedersen, Copenhagen 1954; *Arne Jacobsen: Architecture, Applied Art,* exhibition catalogue Poul Erik Shriver, London 1959; *Arne Jacobsen* by T. Faber, London 1964; *Arne Jacobsen at the McLellan Galleries, Glasgow,* exhibition catalogue, Glasgow 1968; *Arne Jacobsen* by Jorgen Kastholm, Copenhagen 1968; *Arne Jacobsen: A Danish Architect* by Poul Erik Shriver, Copenhagen 1972; *Arne Jacobsen* by Poul Erik Shriver and Ellen Waade, Copenhagen 1976; *Arne Jacobsen: opera completa, 1909-1971* by Luciano Rubino, Rome 1980; articles—"Evoluzione di Jacobsen nella Moderne Architetura Danese" by E. Gentili in *Casabella* (Milan), September/October 1956; "Regent Buildings by Arne Jacobsen" in *Zodiac* (Milan), no. 5, 1959; "L'Oeuvre d'Arne Jacobsen" by Poul Erik Shriver in *L'Architecture d'Aujourd'hui* (Paris), December 1960/January 1961; "Obituary: Arne Jacobsen" in *The Times* (London), 26 March 1971; "A Furniture Artist: Arne Jacobsen's last series of chairs" by Magnus Stephensen in *Mobilia* (Snekkersten, Denmark), May 1971; "Obituary: Arne Jacobsen" in *Design* (London), May 1971; "Arne Jacobsen: architecture and fine art" by R. Hackney in *Leonardo* (Oxford), Autumn 1972; "Danish Embassy in London" in *Deutsche Bauzeitschrift* (Gutersloh), July 1980; "The New House of Industry in Copenhagen" in *Arkitekten DK* (Copenhagen), February 1981; "Arne Jacobsen's Saint Catherines" in *Arkitekten DK* (Copenhagen), April 1982.

Arne Jacobsen was the leading exponent of the International School in Denmark in the middle of the 20th century. Combining the comfortable humanity of Gunnar Asplund, a close friend of his early professional days, and the absolute and uncompromising precision of Mies van der Rohe, Jacobsen reached in his work a zenith of perfection in the Rødovre Town Hall of 1955. Devoid of all showmanship and gimmickry, he had a sureness of touch that was also reflected in the domestic industrial design in which he also excelled. Nevertheless, his work was more highly revered abroad than in his own country.

Jacobsen was first noticed at a Danish building exhibition in 1929, the year before Asplund's famous exhibition in Stockholm. There, with Flemming Lassen, he built a revolutionary circular show house that broke entirely with tradition. At that time Danish architecture was still narrowly neo-classical. Much of his early work consisted of private houses that combined the best of traditional techniques and materials with a growing sense of functionalism and fitness for purpose. His ability to find simple and logical solutions to problems made him a successful competitor in many architectural competitions. His first real chance came in 1932 when he won the competition for a seaside development at Bellevue, north of Copenhagen. The open planning and carefree atmosphere which his skill in architecture and landscaping gave to this scheme made a deep impression on the thousands of holiday makers who used it and enormously helped its general acceptance. Jacobsen returned to add other buildings to this development on several more occasions: it became a record of the development of his domestic architecture.

One of his first commercial buildings was Stelling House in old Copenhagen on a site surrounded by plain neo-classical domestic apartment houses. Jacobsen's was the first modern building to be built in the area and produced violent protests because of its "inconsiderate" treatment of the old civic environment. Today it is accepted as a fine example of the considerable adjustment of a modern design to surroundings of an earlier and different style. The building is a parallel to Gunnar Asplund's skilful additions to the law courts at Gothenburg, which were much admired by Jacobsen.

Immediately before the Second World War Jacobsen won two important town hall competitions—the first, in partnership with Erik Møller, at Aarhus in Jutland; the second, with Flemming Lassen, at Søllerød, north of Copenhagen. Both designs owe much to the influence of Asplund.

In 1943 Jacobsen took refuge from the Germans in Sweden. There, in collaboration with his wife Jonna, a textile printer, he produced some distinguished designs for floral furnishings fabrics based on his watercolour studies of Danish flora. These designs were much imitated.

He returned to Denmark immediately after the war, and once again a competition win took him back to the site near Belle Vista. It was a small development known as Søholm. Terraced and linked in echelon, these houses aroused tremendous interest internationally. Admirably sited among old trees and beautifully planted, Søholm is a masterpiece of small scale domestic architecture. It is not surprising that Jacobsen chose to live there himself, continuing to do so even after he became rich and famous. "We have never lived grandly or in style," he said in an interview published in 1971, the year of his death, "and one reason for that is that, although at times I may have made money, I have always had the feeling that you can't go on doing it, and so why should you have the upset of having a high standard of living reduced to a more sensible one?" You can feel this kind of sensible reasoning in his work.

His next important work was the Munkegaard School at Gentofte, north of Copenhagen. In a single-storied building of formal and rigid layout the class rooms are arranged around individual internal courtyards, each differently planted and laid out. Good lighting and a pleasant outlook make the rooms excellent for work; each has the feeling of an individual summer house.

Although a master in the use of traditional materials and techniques, Jacobsen was interested in industrialized buildings and the introduction of new materials and techniques. In Rødovre Town Hall the reinforced concrete skeleton has centrally placed vertical members, the lightweight curtain walling being suspended from the floor slabs. Many of the components are factory made. Externally the building is as severe as ruled paper, but internally, where Jacobsen designed all the furniture and fittings, it is as light and delicate as a cobweb. The rod-suspended staircase and the council chamber are specially notable. Jacobsen's other major exercise in industrialized building was the SAS Royal Hotel in Copenhagen. One of that city's only tall buildings, eighteen stories high, it is very much less bulky than it might be because of the skilful way in which Jacobsen used the glass of his curtain walling to reflect the passing cloud patterns. The heavier design of the lower stories housing the air-terminal forms a solid base for the much lighter looking tower. Jacobsen designed everything in this building down to the ashtrays, and the result is unique and very satisfactory. Much of the furniture was made available to the general market and has become famous in its own right, like that of Alvar Aalto.

Jacobsen's industrial building followed the same distinguished pattern of simplicity, good proportion and fitness for purpose. To these qualities he added the discipline of standardized, factory-made building components. A factory at Aalborg for Carl Christensen, in 1957, and Tom's Chocolate Factory, 1961, are both outstanding by the highest standards.

Arne Jacobsen built a lot abroad in the last ten years of his life, his most important commissions being St. Catherine's College, Oxford, where he managed to combine something of the traditional college quadrangle with his own classical quality and simplicity of design. Speaking of the buildings, Alan Bullock, the master, said: "The longer I live in them, the more I find they delight and satisfy me."

—Gontran Goulden

JACOBSEN, Hugh Newell.

American. Born in Grand Rapids, Michigan, 11 March 1929. Educated at the University of Maryland, College Park, B.A. 1951; Architectural Association School, London, Dip.A.A. 1954; Yale University, New Haven, Connecticut, B.Arch. 1955. Served in the United States Air Force, at the Headquarters of the Tactical Air Command, 1955-57: Lieutenant. Married Robin Kearney in 1952; children: John Matthew and Simon. Architect/Draftsman in the office of Philip Johnson, *q.v.*, New Canaan, Connecticut, 1955, and Keyes, Lethbridge and Condon, Washington, D.C., 1957-58. Since 1958, in private practice, Washington, D.C. Visiting Professor for the Arts and Humanities, University of Cairo, Egypt, 1970; John Fitzgerald Kennedy Memorial Fellow, New Zealand, 1971. Trustee, Washington Gallery of Modern Art, 1965-69; Trustee, Washington Theatre Club, 1965-72; Member of the Board of Governors, 1968-73, and Trustee, 1973-81, Corcoran Gallery of Art, Washington; Member of the Joint Committee on Landmarks, Commission of Fine Arts and the National Capital Planning Commission, Washington, D.C., 1976-82. Recipient: National Honor Award, American Institute of Architects, 1969, 1974, 1978, 1980, and 1985; Excellence in House Design Awards, *Architectural Record*, 1964-71, 1973, 1975-82, and 1984; Tau Sigma Delta Silver Medal, Clemson University, South Carolina, 1981; and more than fifty other design awards. D.H.L.: Gettysburg College, Pennsylvania, 1974. Fellow, American Institute of Architects, 1971. Address(office): 2529 P Street, NW, Washington, D.C. 20007, U.S.A.

Works:

1959 Christopher Thoron House, Baltimore, Maryland
1960 Robert E. Lee House, Q Street NW, Washington, D.C.
1961 Alan Naftalin House, Riva, Maryland
1962 Robert Shorb House, Montgomery County, Maryland
1963 Benjamin Thoron House, Martha's Vineyard, Massachusetts
 William Shaw House, New York
1964 Woods/Vest Guest House, 28th Street NW, Washington, D.C.
 Calvin Cafritz House, Cambridge Place NW, Washington, D.C.
1965 Ronald Gainer House, McLean, Virginia
1966 Stephen Millett House, Poppasquash Road, Bristol, Rhode Island
 Robert Newmyer House, Washington, D.C.
1967 Bolton Square Townhouses, Baltimore, Maryland
1968 Stephen Trentman House, 27th Street NW, Washington, D.C.
1969 Gerald Smernoff House, Montgomery County, Maryland
 Hugh Jacobsen House, P Street NW, Washington, D.C.
1970 Stuart Land House, North Shores, Rehoboth Beach, Delaware
 Clyde's Bar, Georgetown, Washington, D.C.
 King of the Road Motor Inn, Nashville, Tennessee
 Tidesfall Lake Townhouses, Columbia, Maryland
 Dr. Proctor Harvey House, McLean, Virginia
 Edward Echeverria House remodelling, Olive Street NW, Washington D.C.
 Arthur Hartman House additions and swimming pool, McKinley Street NW, Washington, D.C.
 Cord Meyer House remodelling, 33rd Street NW, Washington, D.C.
 Mrs. V. V. King Vacation House, Springs, Long Island, New York
1971 Alexander Blumenthal House, Easton, Maryland
 Washington Theatre Club (church conversion), Washington, D.C.
 Miller and Smith Detached Houses, Fairfax County, Virginia
 C. Woods Vest House, St. Croix, Virgin Islands
1972 Renwick Gallery interior restoration, Smithsonian Institution, Washington, D.C.
 Ralph Schwaikert House, Salisbury, Connecticut
 Robert Porter House, Newark Street NW, Washington, D.C.
 Guggenheim Products Inc. Office remodelling, South Street NW, Washington, D.C.

 Alfred Moses Houses, Georgetown Pike, McLean, Virginia
 James Kemper House, 57th Street, Kansas City, Missouri
1973 Berton Korman House, Philadelphia
 Burton Reiner House, Chevy Chase, Maryland
 Mr. and Mrs. Peter Peterson Apartment remodelling, 10 Gracie Square, New York
 Sam Korman Apartment remodelling, Philadelphia
1974 Joseph Baker House, Frederick County, Maryland
 Housing, Pennsylvania Avenue Development, Washington, D.C.
1975 Hugh Jacobsen House, 28th Street NW, Washington, D.C.
 Half Moon Bay Hotel and Golf Club additions, Antigua, West Indies
1976 Michael Straight House remodelling, Montgomery County, Maryland
 Mr. and Mrs. Robert Burling House additions, 29th Street NW, Washington, D.C.
 Mr. and Mrs. Edwin Stetson House swimming poolhouse, Montgomery County, Maryland
 Arts and Industries Building restoration, Smithsonian Institution, Washington, D.C.
1977 Bricklayers and Allied Craftsmen Office design, 15th Street NW, Washington, D.C.
 Calvin Cafritz House, R Street NW, Washington, D.C.
 Robert Elliot House, Bethesda, Maryland
1978 Master plan and feasibility study for Gallaudet College, Washington, D.C.
 Library, Deree-Pierce Colleges, Athens
 Gymnasium, Anatolia College, Thessaloniki, Greece
 Library, Harvard University, Dumbarton Oaks, Washington, D.C. (project)
 Private House, Wayzata, Minnesota
1979 Mr. and Mrs. John Kingdon House addition, Chevy Chase, Maryland
 Private House, Noroton, Connecticut
 Private House in central Pennsylvania
1980 Private House in eastern Pennsylvania
 Pool House, Upperville, Virginia
 National Defense University Library Study, Fort Lesley J. McNair, Washington, D.C.
 General Services Administration Office Building, Savannah, Georgia(competition project)
1981 Gymnasium/Auditorium, Deree-Pierce Colleges, Athens
 Old Gymnasium restoration, Gallaudet College, Washington, D.C.
 Garden for the Handicapped, Smithsonian Institution, Washington, D.C.
 Gettysburg College Library, Pennsylvania
 New Academic Building Study, National War College, Washington, D.C.
 Private House, Eastern Shore, Maryland
1982 Athens College Theatre, Athens
 Library, American University, Cairo
 National Defense University Alternative Extension Site Study, Washington, D.C.
 Alumni Center, University of Michigan, Ann Arbor
 Private House, McLean, Virginia
1983 Private House, Maryland Tidewater Region
 Bricklayers and Allied Craftsmen Office design, 15th Street, NW, Washington, D.C.
1984 Hotel Talleyrand restoration and rehabilitation, American Embassy, Paris
 Guardhouse Building, American Embassy, Paris
 Village B Student Housing, Georgetown University, Washington, D.C.
 Brice House restoration, Annapolis, Maryland
 International Masonry Institute Regional Training Centers (project)
 International Masonry Institute National Training Center (project)

Private House, Nelson County, Virginia
Private House, Bowling Green, Ohio
Private House, Lima, Ohio
Private House, Athens

Publications:

By JACOBSEN: book—*A Guide to the Architecture of Washington D.C.*, editor, New York 1964; article—"Hugh Newell Jacobsen in Cairo" in *Architectural Digest* (New York), March 1984.

On JACOBSEN: books—*A Place to Live* by Wolf Von Eckardt, New York 1967; *Great Houses* by Walter Wagner, New York 1976; *Kicked a Building Lately?* by Ada Louise Huxtable, New York 1976; *Recycling Buildings* by Elizabeth Kendall Thompson, New York 1977; *Contextual Architecture* by Ray Keith, New York 1980; *Architecture 1970-1980: A Decade of Change* by Jeanne Davern, New York 1980; *Neues Wohnen in alten Hausern*, with introduction by Frank Werner, Stuttgart 1981; *25 Years of Record Houses* by Herbert L. Smith, Jr., New York 1981; *The Architecture of the United States*, vol. 1 by G. E. Kidder Smith, New York 1981; *New Life for Old Buildings* by Mildred Schmertz, New York 1982; *Wohnen unter schragem Dach* by Annemarie Mutsch-Engel, Stuttgart 1982; *White by Design* by Bo Niles, New York 1984; articles—"Naftalin and Newmyer Residences" in *Architecture d'aujourd'hui* (Paris), January 1967; "Naftalin, Newmyer and Millett Residences" in *Tochi-Jutaku* (Tokyo), January 1967; "Bolton Commons" in *Detail* (Munich), no. 5, 1968; "Vest Residence, St. Croix" in *Casa Vogue* (Milan), July/August 1972; "Tidesfall, Columbia, Maryland" in *Architecture + Urbanism* (Tokyo), October 1973; "Hugh Jacobsen" in *Architecture + Urbanism* (Tokyo), November 1973; "Five Current Projects from the Office of Hugh Jacobsen" in *Architectural Record* (New York), May 1974; "Eichholz Residence" in *Casa Vogue* (Milan), October 1974; "Pennsylvania Avenue" in *Baumeister* (Munich), December 1974; "Hartman House" in *House and Garden* (London), July/August 1977; "Search for a Broadening Design Expression: Hugh Newell Jacobsen" in *Architectural Record*(New York), November 1978; "Design House" in *Casa Vogue*(Milan), March 1979; "Arts and Industries Museum Restoration" in *AIA Journal* (Washington, D.C.), May 1980; "Modern Wooden House," special issue of *Process:Architecture*(Tokyo), August 1980; "Record Houses of 1981" in *Architectural Record* (New York), May 1981; "Johnson House" in *Haus*(Stuttgart), November 1981; "Gettysburg College Library" in *AIA Journal*(Washington, D.C.), May 1982; "Maryland Eastern Shore House" in *Nikkei Architecture*(Tokyo), August 1982; "The Gentle Art of Abstraction: Six Recent Projects by Hugh Newell Jacobsen" in *Architectural Record*(New York), September 1982; "Houses That Work" in *Architectural Digest*(Los Angeles), November 1982; "Alumni Center, University of Michigan" in *Architectural Record*(New York), April 1983; "Buckwalter House" in *Hauser*(Hamburg West Germany), January 1984; "The Telling Detail" in *Architectural Record*(New York), February and March 1984; "Hugh Newell Jacobsen" by Barbara Gamarekian in the *New York Times*, 31 May 1984; "Maryland Tidewater Area Residence" in *House and Garden*(New York), July 1984; "La Grande Parure de l'Hôtel Talleyrand" in *Figaro*(Paris), 11 September 1984.

Bibliography: *Hugh Newell Jacobsen: A Bibliography* by Mary Vance, Monticello, Illinois 1982.

All an architect does is make spaces. It is the quiet and thoughtful arrangement of these spaces that makes houses, neighborhoods, streets, and environments. Good architecture never shouts. It is like a well-

Hugh Jacobsen: Alumni Center, University of Michigan, Ann Arbor, 1982.

mannered lady that is polite to its neighbors. The order and progression of the street is more important than the individual building. In looking back over my work for the past twenty years, it seems I have been obsessed with the quality of light. I am still learning.

—Hugh Newell Jacobsen

Hugh Newell Jacobsen has spent a career upholding the tradition of the gentleman architect. He has upheld it in the face of utopian architects, corporate architects, radical architects, and avante-garde architects. He is none of these. Jacobsen is concerned primarily with the sensory aspects of design. He talks about buildings in terms of how they will be experienced. How they look from far away and how they look close up. How the light comes through the windows in the morning and how it moves through the building during the day. How space is gathered up in one place and how linked. Formally, there are certain tendencies—pavilion arrangements, pyramid and prism shapes, flat arches, plans with elements slipped back and forth to break up masses. But there are not consistent stylistic mannerisms nor rigorous intellectual underpinning. Jacobsen's houses—he has done other buildings but many houses—are designs that have their moments. They show taste and judgment and erudition. And they are carefully attuned to their practical requirements. In one sense, Jacobsen is more a client's than an architect's architect.

He has emerged as well as one of the few American architects capable of truly sensitive restorations. His Renwick Gallery and Smithsonian Arts and Industries Building stand as examples of how to integrate contemporary service technologies delicately within the shadows. Jacobsen has as well tackled the difficult problem of building new construction in the midst of harmonious older buildings. His taste in architecture is catholic—"there are no bad periods, only bad buildings"—and he has drawn freely on historic motifs for both "loaded" sites and in isolation.

—Nory Miller

JAHN, Helmut.

German. Born in Nuremberg, 4 January 1940; moved to the United States, 1966. Educated at the Technische Hochschule, Munich, 1960-65, Dip.Ing./Arch. 1965; Illinois Institute of Technology, Chicago, under Myron Goldsmith, *q.v.*, and Fazlur Khan, *q.v.*, 1966-67. Married Deborah Ann Lampe in 1970; son: Evan. Worked with P. C. von Seidlein, Munich, 1965-66. Joined C. F. Murphy Associates, Chicago, 1967: Assistant to Gene Summers, 1967-73; Partner, Director in charge of Planning and Design, and Executive Vice-President, 1973-81; Principal, from 1981, President, since 1982, and Chief Executive Officer, since 1983, Murphy/Jahn Associates, Chicago. Teacher, University of Illinois, Chicago, 1981; Eliot Noyes Visiting Design Critic, Harvard University, Cambridge, Massachusetts, 1981; Davenport Visiting Professor of Architectural Design, Yale University, New Haven, Connecticut, 1983. Member, Chicago 7, since 1977. Exhibitions: *Exquisite Corpse,* Walter Kelly Gallery, Chicago, 1978; *Townhouses,* Walker Art Center, Minneapolis, 1978; *City Segments,* Walker Art Center, Minneapolis, 1980; *The Presence of the Past,* at the *Biennale,* Venice, 1980; *Chicago Architectural Drawing,* Frumkin/Struve Gallery, Chicago, 1981; *Architecture as Synthesis,* Harvard University, Cambridge, Massachusetts, 1981; *Chicago Architects Design,* Art Institute of Chicago, 1982; *150 Years of Chicago Architecture,* Paris Art Center, Paris, 1983; *Helmut Jahn,* Ballenford Architectural Books, Toronto, 1984; *Chicago and New York: Architectural Interactions,* Art Institute of Chicago, 1984 (travelled to Washington, D.C., Houston, Texas, and New York). Collection: Deutsches Architekturmuseum, Frankfurt. Recipient: Bartlett Award, 1975; National Honor Award, American Institute of Architects, 1975, 1978, 1979, 1980, 1982, 1983, and 1984; AISC Award, 1975, 1978, 1979, and 1983; *Progressive Architecture* Award, 1976, 1977, and 1978; Owens-Corning Fiberglass Energy Conservation Award, 1979; Ashrae Energy Award, 1981, 1982; Arnold W. Brunner

Memorial Prize, 1982; Reliance Development Group Annual Award, 1982; Distinguished Building Award, Chicago Chapter, American Institute of Architects, 1984. D.F.A.: St. Mary's College, Notre Dame, Indiana, 1979. Address: Murphy/Jahn Associates, 35 East Wacker Drive, Chicago, Illinois 60611, U.S.A.

Works:

1970 McCormick Place (convention Center), Chicago
1972 Grant Park Bandshell, Chicago (project)
1974 Kemper Arena, Kansas City, Missouri
1975 Auraria Library (learning center), Denver
1976 Fourth District Courts Building, Maywood, Illinois
     John Marshall Courts Building Richmond, Virginia (with Wright/Jones/Wilkerson)
     Kansas City Convention Center, Missouri (with Seligson Associates, and Horner, Blessing, Howard, Needles, Tammen, and Bergendoff)
     Conference City, Abu Dhabi (project)
     One Exchange Place, Chicago (project)
     Minnesota II, St. Paul (competition project)
1977 Michigan City Library, Indiana
     Athletic Facility, St. Mary's College, Notre Dame, Indiana
     Monroe Garage (parking facility), Chicago
1978 Springfield Garage (parking facility), Springfield, Illinois
     Glenbrook Professional Building, Northbrook, Illinois
     La Lumiere Gymnasium, La Porte, Indiana
     Rust-Oleum Corporate Headquarters, Vernon Hills, Illinois
     Pahlavi National Library, Tehran (competition project)
     St. Paul Convention Center, Minnesota (project)
     Plan for the redevelopment of the North Loop, Chicago (project)
1979 W. W. Grainger Corporate Headquarters, Skokie, Illinois
1980 Xerox Center, Chicago
1981 De La Garza Career Center, East Chicago, Indiana
     Post Office, Oak Brook, Illinois
     Commonwealth Edison District Headquarters, Downers Grove, Illinois
     Area 2 Police Headquarters, Chicago
1982 Support Facility, Argonne National Laboratory, Illinois
     First Source Center, South Bend, Indiana
     Private House, Eagle River, Wisconsin
     One South Wacker office building, Chicago
     Board of Trade addition, Chicago
1983 Mercy Hospital addition, Chicago
     Office Building, 11 Diagonal Street, Johannesburg, South Africa
1984 Agricultural Engineering Science Building, University of Illinois, Champaign
     Learning Resource Center, College of Du Page, Glen Elly, Illinois
     Plaza East, Milwaukee, Wisconsin
     Shand Morahan Corporate Headquarters, Evanston, Illinois
     Office Building, 701 Fourth Avenue South, Minneapolis
     O'Hare Rapid Transit Station, Chicago
1985 State of Illinois Center, Chicago
     Park Avenue Tower, New York
     Highrise building, Columbus Circle, New York (project)
1986 North Western Rail Terminal, Chicago
     Office Building, 120 North La Salle Street, Chicago

Helmut Jahn: One South Wacker Drive office building, Chicago, 1984.

1986 Greyhound Bus Terminal, Chicago
     O'Hare Airport expansion, Chicago
     Southwest Center, Houston, Texas
     Office Building, 362 West Street, Durban, South Africa
     Wilshire/Midvale Office Building, Los Angeles
     Unifirst Center, Jackson, Mississippi
     Office Building, 425 Lexington Avenue, New York
     City Center Building, New York
     Two Energy Center Building, Naperville, Illinois
     Frankfurter Messe Convention Center, Frankfurt
     Hyatt Hotel, Frankfurt
     Office Building, 1650 Market Street, Philadelphia
     Housing Development, Parktown, Johannesburg, South Africa
     North Loop Office and Commercial Block 16, Chicago
     North Loop Office and Commercial Block 37, Chicago
     Von Aken Office Building, Shaker Heights, Ohio
     Houston Esplanade, Houston, Texas
     Minnesota Convention Center, Minneapolis
     Office Building, 600 California Street, San Francisco
     Naiman Company Sporting Club, Chicago
     Naiman Company Sporting Club, Atlanta, Georgia
     One Hennepin Center, Minneapolis
     Office Building, 750 Lexington Avenue, New York
     Office Building, Second Avenue at 85th Street, New York

Publications:

By JAHN: articles—"Architectural Form," with James Gottsch, in *Bauen und Wohnen* (Zürich), December 1975; "Romantic Hi-Tech," interview, in *Planning and Building Developments* (Braamfontein, South Africa), March/April 1983.

On JAHN: books—*After Mies* by Werner Blaser, New York 1977; *Late Modern Architecture* by Charles Jencks, London and New York 1980; *The Skyscraper* by Paul Goldberger, New York 1981; *New Chicago Architecture* by Maurizio Casari and Vincenzo Pavan, New York 1981; *Southwest Center: The Houston Competition,* edited by Peter Arnell and Ted Bickford, New York 1982; *A Tower for Louisville,* edited by Peter Arnell and Ted Bickford, New York 1982; *Atrium Buildings— Development and Design* by Richard G. Saxon, London 1983; *Postmodern: The Architecture of the Postindustrial Society* by Paolo Portoghesi, New York 1984; *Moderne und Postmoderne* by Heinrich Klotz, Braunschweig, West Germany 1984; articles— "Analysis of Planned and Completed Projects by C. F. Murphy Associates" in *Bauen und Wohnen* (Zürich), September 1974; "Kemper Arena" in *Domus* (Milan), April 1976; "Grand Structures" in *Techniques et architecture* (Paris), May 1976; "Abu Dhabi Conference City" in *Progressive Architecture* (New York), January 1977; "CFMA Portfolio" in *Architettura* (Rome), December 1977; "Design Directions: Looking for What Is Missing" in *AIA Journal* (Washington, D.C.), May 1978; "The Chicago Seven" in *Architecture + Urbanism* (Tokyo), June 1978; "Contemporary Architects: Helmut Jahn" in *Architecture + Urbanism* (Tokyo), July 1978; "Chicago on the Drawing Boards" in *Horizon* (New York), September 1978; "Minnesota II" in *Progressive Architecture* (New York), January 1979; "St. Mary's Athletic Facility" in *Industria delle costruzioni* (Rome), February 1979; "Kansas City Convention Center" in *Domus* (Milan), February

1979; "Missing Mies" by William Marlin in *Architectural Record* (New York), July 1979; "The Building of the Year 2,000" in *Inland Architect* (Chicago), May 1980; "One South Wacker, Chicago" in *GA Document* (Tokyo), Summer 1980; "Chicago, Chicago" in *Building Design* (London), 25 July 1980; "Facade at Right Angles" in *Progressive Architecture* (New York), December 1980; "Panoply of Images: State of Illinois Center, Chicago" in *Progressive Architecture* (New York), February 1981; "Jahn Wacker" in *Architectural Review* (London), April 1981; "Helmut Jahn/Murphy Associates" in *Controspazio* (Bari, Italy), April/June 1981; "Three Designs by Murphy Jahn" in *Architectural Record* (New York), December 1981; "Helmut Jahn Topples the Box" in *Architect and Builder* (Cape Town, South Africa), June 1982; "Works: Helmut Jahn of Murphy Jahn" in *Architecture + Urbanism* (Tokyo), November 1983; "Building Types Study 598: Office Interiors" in *Architectural Record* (New York), March 1984; "Architecture: Helmut Jahn" by Nory Miller in *Architectural Digest* (Los Angeles), March 1984; "High Tech Expansion: United Airlines Terminal 1 Complex, O'Hare International Airport and O'Hare Rapid Transit Extension Station, Chicago, Illinois" in *Architectural Record* (New York), May 1985.

Bibliographies: *Chicago Seven* by Lamia Doumato, Monticello, Illinois 1982; *The Architecture of Helmut Jahn: An Introductory Bibliography,* Monticello, Illinois 1983.

*

Our approach to design is both rational and intuitive; it attempts to give each building its own philosophical and intellectual base and establishes an opportunity to exploit its particular elements to achieve a visual and communicative statement. The rational part deals with the realities of a problem, consciously analyzing the many discrete but related planning and technical aspects of a design problem and synthesizing them along functionalist construction principles. The intuitive aspect deals with the theoretical, intellectual aspects, a subconscious ability to sense the intrinsic structure of a problem and establish priorities for the elements of design which deal with space, form, light, color, and materials, and the way architecture communicates through symbol and meaning of architectural language.

There is a strong relationship between the problem and the way that architecture articulates it. It may come with the conditions of the site, the program, the circulation and general organization of the plan, with the structure, with the enclosure, with the technical systems, or with the effect of light, reflections and transparency, the creation of space or form, and the expression of symbol or meaning through communicative associations. Such attitudes free our skills to practice architecture beyond a mere problem solving, functionalist methodology, resulting in a pluralism, which is multi-directional, less restrictive and less dogmatic, characterized by a loss of conviction as to exclusivist principles and more communicative and user-oriented. It may contain much of the past or present. It doesn't always contain something new, but it is based on idea content.

—Helmut Jahn

*

Helmut Jahn's architectural career at C. F. Murphy Associates in Chicago has been a parallel of the recent history of international movement in architecture known as Rationalist Functionalism. The shadow of Mies van der Rohe was long and apparently all-pervasive.

Jahn began as a strict believer in functionalism; design was a matter of problem-solving according to firmly rational and theoretically "correct" principles and, as such, was a purely "objective" process. Critics have characterized this attitude to design as "exclusivist" or "reductive," and questioned the value of a conceptual grid that yielded so many icy, if elegant, edges. Today, it is clear that many architects *were* boxed in—more by their acceptance of the austerity and apparent "ease" of the style than by any real understanding of Mies's concept of functionalism. (Far from being a dogma which hemmed architecture in, the concept made room for adventure. Moreover, it has actually made that adventure inevitable.) In the fifteen years since the master's death, Jahn has been changing the strictly "Miesian" character of the output at C. F. Murphy Associates.

The difference now, as Jahn perceives it, is that the postmodernist sees architecture more as a social art, and he uses many codes to signal the building's relationship to context, history, or the popular vernacular of its own, or some other, time, creating an architecture that—aided by the latest developments in technology—is engineered rather than designed. He stresses the intuitive nature of creative rationalism, which in the design process becomes a conscious assignment of priority to the expressive power of space, form, light, colour, and material within a framework of cultural and human references. Such an attitude frees the architect to develop an approach that is multi-directional, less restrictive, and less dogmatic.

In appearance, Jahn's designs, from before about 1980, don't seem to make any radical departure from those of the Mies period. For instance, his First Bank Center complex in South Bend, Indiana, looks to be a mere geometrical permutation of the box; the Energy Conservation Offices for the Argonne National Laboratories is also rigidly "geometric"—regular ridges of building across a circular format; the Rust-Oleum Headquarters at Vernon Hills, Illinois, is a bright, white, floating box, split lengthwise by a skylit circulation spine. All make extensive use of glass sheathing to achieve that quality of lightness so characteristic of late Mies. Observers of the "strange" doings at C. F. Murphy Associates focus on details like a pediment or organically curved edge to explain their notions of what is different about Jahn's approach. And, indeed, there is the odd neo-Georgian facade (Agricultural Engineering Building at the University of Illinois) or Art Deco outline (Board of Trade Building extension, Chicago).

But the difference doesn't lie in "geometric" instead of "organic" form, or decorative elements or the lack of them, or pedimented platform or clean cantilever. It isn't really in the outward appearance of his buildings that Jahn is radically different; what is important is the way the buildings work.

The First Bank Center design isn't merely of two angled building blocks with a dramatic glasshouse section slicing downwards between them; the whole complex becomes a metaphor for city life itself. The central glass section functions as a public plaza with retail shopping areas leading to a hotel block and the bank offices themselves, the big space relating symbolically to the pattern of the surrounding streets.

Similarly, the interior spaces of the University of Illinois Agriculture Building, devised on a linear plan as demanded by the site, has a long, wide spine running its entire length, with tall single-storey workshops on one side and smaller laboratories on three levels on the other. Effectively, the spine becomes a sunny "street," illuminated from outside during the day by virtue of glass-block panel walls and skylights.

The Rust-Oleum central circulation spine also splits the complex lengthwise, its lofty single-storey avenue sheathed in glass with ramped pathways encouraging movement through the various levels of the building, whilst the openness of its plan links the green landscape outside to the interior flow of space.

The State of Illinois Center in Chicago, completed in 1985 and already hailed as the "first building of the year 2,000", demonstrates another, and perhaps more theatrical, turn to Jahn's fast-moving repertoire. Occupying a previously cramped and deteriorating area bounded by the business district of LaSalle, Clark, Lake and Randolph Streets, the massive blue-glass structure looks like an outsized version of E.T.'s space ship. Here, Jahn has eschewed

the conventional high-rise tower that might have been built out of interchangeable parts by any private developer, and opted for a stunning central rotunda capped with a lacelike net of glass and structural steel. Most controversial is the functional emphasis on the 80,000-square-foot retail space within this government building – a feature which enlivens Chicago's Loop area in the manner of Renaissance Italian piazzas, and confounds those critics who describe the complex as "totally unrelated to anything else in the whole history of Western civilization."

This attention to performance rather than just appearance is combined in Jahn's work with context, with metaphor and symbol, and visual and physical richness—a true synthesis of many viable pathways to postmodernist architecture.

—Colin Naylor

JAIN, Uttam Chand.

Indian. Born in Malwara, 15 January 1934. Educated at Sardar High School, Jodhpur, India, 1948-51; Jaswant College, Jodhpur, 1951-53; Indian Institute of Technology, Kharagpur, 1953-58 (Merit Scholarship) B.Arch. (first class honours) 1958; National University of Tucuman, Argentina, 1958-59 (Advanced Study Scholarship). Married Rasila Shah in 1953; children: Chirag, Leela, Neena, Seema, and Maya. Travelled abroad, 1959-60. Since 1961, in private practice, as Uttam C. Jain, Architects and Planners, Bombay. Visiting Lecturer, University of Roorkee, 1962-63, 1965-67, and 1983-84, Academy of Architecture, Bombay, 1965-66, 1972-73, and 1975-76, the J. J. College of Architecture, University of Bombay, 1973-77, 1982-84, Ahmedabad School of Architecture, India, 1974-76, 1982-84, and Punjab University, Chandigarh, India, 1981-84. Member of the Public Affairs Board, 1972-73, and Member of the Council, 1973-77, Indian Institute of Architects, and Editor of the Institute's Journal, 1975-77, and since 1983; Member of the Board of School Inspectors, Indian Council of Architecture, 1979-80, 1982, and 1983; Member of the Architectural Course Committee, Perarignar Anna University, Madras, India, since 1980; Member of the Commonwealth Educational Panel, London, since 1980; Member of the Board of Studies, School of Planning and Architecture, New Delhi, since 1983. Exhibition: *Contemporary Third World Architecture: Search for Identity*, Pratt Manhattan Center Gallery, New York, 1983(toured the United States, 1983-84). Recipient: First Prize, Contemporary Indian Architecture Essay Competition, Commonwealth Association of Architects, London, 1969; First Prize, Goa Memorial Competition, India, 1973; First Prize, College of Engineering Competition, Kota, India, 1984. Fellow, Indian Institute of Architects, and Institute of Valuers, New Delhi. Addresses: Uttam C. Jain, Architects and Planners, 408 Regent Chambers, 208 Nariman Point, Bombay 400 021, India; and 59 Bombay Samachar Marg, Sonawala Building, Bombay 400 023, India.

Works (all in India):

1960 Rural school at Kuha, Ahmedabad
Girls school, Bhavnagar
1961 High school at Bhayli, Baroda
Warden's Residence, Boys Hostel, Malwara
1962 Bright Tubes Corporation Plant for lightweight steel components, Bombay
1965 Nayan Co-op Society Residential Flats, Bombay
Urvashi Co-op Society Flats, Bombay (with Romesh Pathare)

Sanjog Co-op Society Flats, Bombay (with Romesh Pathare)
Guest house for Raisil India, Juhu Lane, Bombay
1966 Themis Pharmaceuticals Ltd. Vitamin B-12 Producing Plant, Vapi
Modern Water Proof Paper Manufacturing Company Plant, Thana
1968 Chamosyn Ltd. Plant, Vapi
Pre-cast, pre-stressed housing project, Surat
Amich and Bungalow, Surat
Kirtibhai Bungalow, Surat
Main Gate, University of Jodhpur
1969 Pump Houses, University of Jodhpur
Zoology Experimental Field Station, University of Jodhpur
1970 Printing Plant, University of Jodhpur
1971 Junior Staff Housing, University of Jodhpur
1972 Lecture Theatre Complex, University of Jodhpur
Amphitheatre, University of Jodhpur
1973 Department of Botany, University of Jodhpur
Department of Zoology, University of Jodhpur
Boys' Hostels, University of Udaipur
1974 Residences for the deputy and assistant registrars, University of Jodhpur
Oil and Gas Plant, University of Jodhpur
Memorial to the Chief Minister, Miramar, Panaji, Goa
Flour mill plant, Thana
1975 Faculty Residences (four variations), University of Jodhpur
Vice-Chancellor's Residence, University of Jodhpur
Boys' Hostel, University of Udaipur, Jobner
Faculty of Parasitology, Bikaner Veterinary College
Students' Cafeteria, Bikaner Veterinary College
Ambika Electrolytic Capacitators Ltd. Factory, Jodhpur
1976 Student dormitory, University of Jodhpur
Faculty of Surgery and Radiology, Bikaner Veterinary College
Home Science College, University of Udaipur
Faculty of Agronomy and Soil Sciences, University of Udaipur
Block of flats for Mrs. Sarlabahen Vyas, Bombay
1977 Week-end cottage, Lonawla
Resort hotel, Colva, Margoa, Goa
1978 Tradewinds Resort Hotel, Bogmalo Beach, Goa
Central Library, University of Jodhpur
Gymnasium, University of Jodhpur
1979 Faculty of Arts, Education and Social Science, University of Jodhpur
1980 Health Centre, University of Jodhpur
Faculty of Geology, University of Jodhpur
Yatri Nivas Building, Sevagram, Wardha
1981 Olympic Swimming Pool, Kota
1982 Sports Complex, Jodhpur
Incremental Housing, Indore
Motel, Indore
1983 Balotra City Hall, Rajasthan
Neelam Cinema, Balotra, Rajasthan
1984 Engineering College Campux Complex, Kota

Publications:

By JAIN: articles—"Turning Point in Architecture" in *Indian Builder* (New Delhi), September 1965; "Obituary of a Poetic Genius" in *Architects' Trade Journal* (Bombay), May 1974; "Anonymous Architecture and Naive Art in Western India" in *Architecture + Urbanism* (Tokyo), June 1975; "Sturdy Town of Chitogarh" in *Architecture + Urbanism* (Tokyo), October 1978; "Balance sheet of Chandigarh" in *Architecture + Urbanism* (Tokyo), May 1979; "Jodhpur— A City in Sandstone" in *Architecture + Urbanism* (Tokyo), June 1979.

Uttam Jain: Lecture Theatre Complex, University of Jodhpur, 1972.

On JAIN: books—*New Architecture in the World* by Udo Kultermann, London 1966; *Building Environment* by B. S. Saini, Sydney 1973; *Architekten der dritten Welt* by Udo Kultermann, Cologne 1980; *Contemporary Third World Architecture: Search for Identity*, exhibition catalogue, by Theo David, Ellen Schwarz, Udo Kultermann and others, New York 1983; articles—"Indian Prints" in *Architectural Forum* (New York), October 1971; "Jain's Clusters" in *Architectural Review* (London), December 1973; "Jain at Jodhpur" in *Architectural Review* (London), February 1976; "Uttam C. Jain" in *Architecture + Urbanism* (Tokyo), October 1977; "The Third World: Continuity of the Modern Style among Native Architects" in *Bauen und Wohnen* (Zürich), October 1977; "A View of Contemporary World Architects" in *Japan Architect* (Tokyo), December 1977; "Architect in India: Uttam C. Jain" in *Bauen und Wohnen* (Zürich), September 1978; "Contemporary Houses of the World" in *Architecture + Urbanism* (Tokyo), February 1979; "Uttam Jain: Third World Architect" in *Architectural Review* (London), August 1981.

The word "modern" in India acquires a different connotation than in the advanced communities in the West. Modern India is unable to modify her texture because of a lack of a rapid rolling culture and remains untouched by super-industrialism as well. Seventy per cent of her population dwells in a rural setting, primarily under thatched shelters.

Social landscape having a rural tinge and high technology remaining a distant drum-beat, India is at the intermediate level of technology. Manpower is a factor to reckon with at all levels of national planning.

As an architect, I am involved in creating physical environments for two universities in western India— the University of Jodhpur and the University of Udaipur. Jodhpur and Udaipur have their origins in mediaeval India. Their architectural heritage is so intense that its streaking into the new town's fabric is natural. The present practice of producing buildings in these towns retains its favour for indigenous building materials locally available.

Experience through observations here focussed on two principles. First, creation of many architectural objects over centuries enabled craftsmen to master the art of controlling rigours of extreme climate and rugged terrain. Second, the intensive use of local stone through structural permutations and combinations improved economics of building at the regional level. Universities funded by the public exchequer could ill afford consumption of factory products, when local materials, coupled with high craftsmanship, could be the logical answer. Besides, this adaptation (not imitation) permitted a sense of historical linkage in these towns.

Again, in seeking answers to climatic problems, the accepted process seemed simpler—smaller openings, over-scaled walls, bare exteriors, stone-textured faces, weighty roofs, and the emphasized narrow lanes with still shorter distances became parameters for my works.

At the grassroots level, I observed and assimilated what was authentic. I also became aware of confining my architectural indulgence at different levels of micro-detailing. This way I strived to enhance the physical ambient without playing a discordant note on the cultural wave-lengths of the towns. My concern was that preservation and progress should go hand in hand.

—Uttam C. Jain

The work of the Indian architect Uttam C. Jain is directed toward harmony with the traditional values of India and the specific requirements of the contemporary situation in that country. His buildings for the universities at Jodhpur and Udaipur parallel the steps taken in other countries that question the doctrines of the Modern Movement.

Jain advocates learning from the works of Le Corbusier and Louis I. Kahn in India as well as from old architecture of Indian cities such as Rajasthan. Both lines of tradition have to be integrated into a new Indian architecture. Jain's historical studies into Indian cities and buildings thus blend with the recent trends in international developments which aim at a more realistic understanding of the local situation. Jain says: "Architecture is a social activity and must not leave any aspect of human life untouched."

Materials of traditional and local character dominate Jain's buildings in Jodhpur, Udaipur, Goa, and Bombay. Landscape and climate, the Indian tradition, and modern technology merge into a new vocabulary with which Jain attempts to create a new level of architecture in India, to "manifest the creative mind of the simple people in rural India as an organic part of human existence."

—Udo Kultermann

JEANNERET, (Arnold André) Pierre.

Swiss. Born in Geneva, 22 March 1896; cousin of the architect Charles-Edouard Jeanneret (Le Corbusier, *q.v.*). Studied at the Ecole des Beaux-Arts, Geneva, 1913-15, 1918-21 (Architecture, Sculpture and Painting Prizes, 1915). Served in the Army, 1915-18. Worked in the studio of Auguste and Gustave Perret, Paris, 1921-22; in partnership with Le Corbusier, Paris, 1922-40; worked with Charlotte Perriand, *q.v.*, Jean Prouvé, *q.v.*, G. Blanchon and A. Masson, in the French Pyrenees, 1940, with G. Pollak, and in the studio of Jean Prouvé, Nancy, 1941, and in the Bureau Central de Construction (Atelier BCC), Grenoble, 1941-44; collaborated with G. Blanchon, Grenoble, 1941-44, Paris, 1944-49; in private practice, Paris, 1944-51; joined Le Corbusier at Chandigarh, India, 1951-55; Director, School of Architecture, University of Chandigarh, 1955-65; Architect-in-Chief and City Planner, State of Punjab, India, 1955-65. Founder-Member, CIAM (Congres Internationaux d'Architecture Moderne), 1928; Union des Artistes Moderne, Paris, 1929. Exhibitions: *Salon d'Automne*, Paris, 1929; *Union des ArtistesModerne*, Musée des Arts Décoratifs, Paris, 1930; *La Machine à s'asseoir: Le Corbusier, Charlotte Perriand, Pierre Jeanneret*, Palazzo dei Convegni, Rome, 1976. Recipient: First Prize, with Le Corbusier, League of Nations Competition, Geneva, 1927. *Died* (in Geneva) *11 December 1967.*

Works:

(Major buildings and projects only; much of Jeanneret's work was produced in collaboration with Le Corbusier, especially during the periods 1922-40 and 1950-65. For a full list of works and projects, *see* the entry on LE CORBUSIER.)

1925 Pavillon de l'Esprit Nouveau, *Exposition des arts décoratifs*, Paris
House, Pessac, France
Voisin Plan for Paris (project)
1926 Salvation Army Dormitory (Palais du Peuple), 29 rue des Cordelières, Paris
1927 House, Weissenhoff Estate, Stuttgart
Plainex House, 24 bis Boulevard Massena, Paris
League of Nations Headquarters, Parc Mon Repos, Geneva (competition project)
1929 "Mundaneum" World Museum, Geneva (project)
Loucher Housing (project)
1929/
31 "Les Heures Claires" (or "Villa Savoye"), 82 chemin de Villiers, Poissy, France
1929/
33 Centrosoyus Building, Kirova Ulitsa, Moscow (now altered)
Salvation Army Hotel (Cité de Refuge), 12 rue Cantagrel, Paris (now altered)
1930 City Plan for Algiers
1930/
31 Mandrot House, Le Pradet, near Toulon, France
1930/
32 Swiss Students'Hostel, Cité Universitaire, Paris (now altered)
"Clarte", 2 rue Saint-Laurent, Geneva
1931 Palace of the Soviets, Moscow (competition project)
1933 City Plan for Stockholm
Durand Housing, Oued-Ouchaia, Algeria (project)
1935 "Cartesian" Tower (project)
1936 University, Rio de Janeiro (project; with Lucio Costa and Oscar Niemeyer)
"Paris 37" Plan (project)
"Ilot Insalubre no. 6" Plan, Paris (project)
National Sports Centre, Bois de Vincennes, Paris (project)
1936/
45 Ministry of National Education and Public

Health, rua Araujo, Porto Alegre, Rio de Janeiro (with Costa, Niemeyer, Reidy, Moreira, Leao and Vasconcelos)
1937 Jaoul Weekend House (project)
1939 Museum of Endless Growth, Philippeville, Algeria (project)
Research Laboratory, Roscoff, France (project)
Prefabricated Housing (project; with Perriand, Prouvé, Blanchon and Masson)
Prefabricated Housing for the Péchiney and Aluminium Francais companies, at Issoire, Saint-Auban, Gardanne, Salindres, Brignoles, Lunel, and Bedarieux, France
1945/
46 Military School, Uriage, France
1947 City Plan for Puteaux, France (project; with G. Blanchon)
Apartment Building, Puteaux, France (project)
1948/
49 House, Ile de Breham, Brittany, France
1949/
50 Technical Centre, Béziers, France (with Escorsat)
Town Development Plan for Montpellier, France (project)
1951/
65 University Campus, Chandigarh, India
Housing, Schools and Hospitals, Chandigarh, India
City Plan for Chandigarh, India
Gandhi Memorial, Bhawan, India
City Plan for Pandoh, India
City Plan for Sundernagar, India
City Plan for Slapper, India
City Plan for Ahmedabad, India
1964/
65 City Development Plan for Talwara, India

Publications:

By JEANNERET: book—introduction to *Conversations with Painters* by N. Barber, London 1964.

On JEANNERET: books—*Zwei Wohnhauser von Le Corbusier und Pierre Jeanneret* by Alfred Roth, Stuttgart 1927; *Le Corbusier: Complete Works*, 7 vols., edited by Willy Boesiger, Zurich, subsequently London and New York 1929-65; *Le Corbusier and Pierre Jeanneret* by Francois de Pierrefeu, Paris 1932; *La Machine à s'asseoir: Le Corbusier, Charlotte Perriand, Pierre Jeanneret*, exhibition catalogue by M. di Puolo, M. Fagiolo and M. L. Madonna, Rome 1976; articles—"The French System of Prefabrication", in *The Architects' Journal* (London) 27 June 1946; "Pierre Jeanneret of Chandigarh" in *Design* (Bombay) September 1964; "Sur la collaboration entre Le Corbusier et Pierre Jeanneret", in *Werk* (Zürich) November 1966; "Homage to Pierre Jeanneret", in *Design* (Bombay) December 1967; "Pierre Jeanneret 1896-1967", in *L'Architecture d'Aujourd'hui* (Paris) February/March 1968; "Hommage à Pierre Jeanneret" by C. Petit and others in *Werk* (Zurich) June 1968; "Pierre Jeanneret, 22 Mars 1896 – 4 Decembre 1967" by G. Barbey in *Architecture Formes et Fonctions* (Lausanne) vol. 15, 1969: "Charles Edouard and Pierre", in *Building* (London) 8 November 1972; "Beistegui penthouse of Le Corbusier and Pierre Jeanneret, Paris, 1930-31" by Paolo Melis in *Controspazio* (Bari, Italy) September 1977; "Dialogue in tradition – and reality" by Bruno Reichlin in *Archithese* (Niederteufen, Switzerland) January/February 1981.

Arnold André Pierre Jeanneret-Gris (1896-1967) was born in Geneva, the cousin of Charles Édouard Jeanneret (known as Le Corbusier). His early education was obtained at the École des Beaux Arts in the Swiss city, after which he joined the architects Auguste and Gustave Perret in Paris, where he had a sound grounding in modern and experimental building techniques.

From 1921 to 1940 Jeanneret was in partnership with Le Corbusier in Paris, producing architectural designs, town-planning projects, and many examples of modern furniture proposals. The office rapidly attracted young architects from several countries, not only for the many important texts of modernist polemic signed by both cousins that were written there, but for the steady flow of designs for small and experimental houses in which simple forms and smooth surfaces were well to the fore. The villa at Vaucresson of 1922 is one of the earliest of these schemes, but the influential *Pavillon de L'Esprit Nouveau* at the 1925 Paris Exhibition achieved notoriety and much acclaim. Houses for the Weissenhof Siedlung at Stuttgart followed in 1927, in which year the partnership won the international competition for the design of the League of Nations building at Geneva, a project that was not realised. A succession of celebrated designs followed: the *Maison Stein* at Garches (1927-9); the *Villa Savoie* at Poissy (1928-31; the Co-operative building in Moscow (1928); the Salvation Army hostel in Paris (1929-31); and the *Maison Suisse* at the *Cité Universitaire* in Paris (1930-3). The latter structure was the first to employ *pilotis*, although the concept had existed for several years previously. The apartment house Clarté in Geneva (1930-2) can be said to complete the major works of the first era of co-operation between the cousins that ended in 1940.

Jeanneret was closely involved in the founding of C.I.A.M. and often spoke at the proceedings of that body. He was more interested in rationalism and in the problems of industrialisation than was Le Corbusier, whose concerns with the machine age appear to have been more symbolic than practical. The two men held patents of designs for frames for horizontal sliding windows (used on several of their seminal buildings of the 1920s) dating from 1926, for a chaise of 1929, and for sanitary appliances of 1930. Following the collapse of France in 1940 Jeanneret and Le Corbusier parted company. Jeanneret set up in Grenoble, where he designed housing and prefabricated systems for factories and other buildings. In 1944 he returned to Paris where he produced a proposal in 1946 for a large apartment-block that was a pre-echo of the *Unite d'Habitation* with which Le Corbusier's name is so closely associated. Although Jeanneret's design was not realised, there is too much of a similarity for the work of the two men to be seen as individual ideas. Jeanneret's block has rather more ingenious internal planning, emphasising his concern for the control of natural phenomena such as sunlight penetration. It seems likely that Le Corbusier's Unites owe more to Jeanneret than has been conceded so far, although there was not any official collaboration between the two men at that time.

Jeanneret went to the United States in that late 1940s where he designed furniture and had a considerable (and fashionable) success. In 1951 he joined the Corbusian team (that included Maxwell Fry and Jane Drew) to work on the designs for the new capital city of the Punjab at Chandigarh in India. Jeanneret himself was director of the office responsible for the major public buildings designed by Le Corbusier, including the Supreme Court complex. He remained in India after 1954 and was responsible for the design of hospitals, schools, shops, housing, office buildings, the State Library, the City Hall, the palace for the Governor, and many others. He was the architect for the University of Punjab, and oversaw the construction of many buildings at Chandigarh. His practice extended to several other centres in India, and he prepared town-planning schemes for Talwara and elsewhere. He was involved in architectural education in the Punjab, where he was able to pursue his ideas for non-mechanical methods of controlling the elements, sun penetration, and ventilation. He also experimented with rough brickwork, stone walls, and smooth rendered techniques for walls. He did not neglect his earlier concerns with lightweight furniture, prefabricated components, and industrialised building methods, all of which he attempted to adapt to the peculiar circumstances of the Punjab climate and economy. He returned briefly to France, went back to Chandigarh, and finally departed from India in 1965, although after his death his remains were scattered at the city he had helped to create.

Pierre Jeanneret's name has been somewhat overshadowed by that of his more charismatic cousin, yet there can be no doubt of his importance in creating many of the buildings with which Le Corbusier's name alone is associated in the popular mind. The latter himself paid tribute to Jeanneret when he said that his work only existed because of the teamwork between the two men. The part played by Jeanneret not only at Chandigarh (where his contribution was immense) but in the classic houses of the 1920s must be stressed and given true emphasis in the interests of justice.

—James Stevens Curl

JELLICOE, Geoffrey Alan.

British. Born in London, 8 October 1900. Educated at Cheltenham College, Gloucestersire 1915-18; Architectural Association School, London, under Howard Robertson, *q.v.*, 1919-23 (Bernard Webb Scholarship, Neale Bursary), Dip.A.A. 1923. Married Ursula Pares in 1936. Partner, with J. C. Shepherd, Shepherd and Jellicoe, London, 1925-31; Principal, G. A. Jellicoe, London, 1931-38; Senior Partner, with Russell Page and Richard Wilson, Jellicoe, Page and Wilson, London, 1938-39; Principal, G. A. Jellicoe, London, 1939-58; Senior Partner, with Alan Ballantyne and Francis Coleridge, Jellicoe, Ballantyne and Coleridge, 1958-64; Senior Partner, Jellicoe and Coleridge, London, 1964-73. Since 1973, Consultant to Jellicoe, Coleridge and Wynn, Pershore, Worcestershire. Studio Master, 1929-34, and Principal, 1939-42, Architectural Association School, London. Founder Member, 1929, and President, 1939-49, Institute of Landscape Architects; Founder President, 1948-54, and Honorary Life President since 1954, International Federation of Landscape Architects; Member, Royal Fine Arts Commission, 1954-68; Trustee, Tate Gallery, London, 1967-74. Exhibition: Sutton Place, Guildford, Surrey (permanent exhibition of drawings). Recipient: American Society of Landscape Architects medal, 1981; John R. Bracken Medal, Pennsylvania State University, 1982; City key, Galveston, Texas, 1984. Associate, Royal Institute of British Architects. Honorary Corresponding Member, American Society of Landscape Architects, and Venezuelan Society of Landscape Architects. C.B.E. (Commander, Order of the British Empire), 1963; Knighted, 1979. Address: 19 Grove Terrace, London NW5 1PH, England.

Works:

1929 Gordon Russell Ltd. Workshops, Broadway, Worcestershire
1933 Advisory plan for Broadway, Worcestershire
1934 Development plan for Goldsmiths' Company Estates, Acton, London
1934/
36 Caveman Restaurant, Cheddar Gorge, Somerset (with Russell Page)
1935/
36 House, Stanmore, Middlesex (with Russell Page)
1935/
39 Ditchley Park gardens, Oxfordshire
1936/
37 Gordon Russell Showrooms, Wigmore Street, London
Gordon Russell Factory, Park Royal, London
1936/
39 Royal Lodge gardens, Windsor, Berkshire
Kelmarsh Hall gardens, Northamptonshire
The Holme gardens, Regent's Park, London
Pusey House gardens, Faringdon, Oxfordshire
Hever Castle gardens, Kent
Mottisfont Abbey gardens, Hampshire
Overbury House gardens, Gloucestershire
Cottesbrook gardens, Northamptonshire
St. Paul's gardens, Walden Bury, Hertfordshire
1938/
40 Calverton Colliery Buildings, Bestwood, Nottinghamshire (with Richard Wilson)
Calverton Village and Landscaping, Bestwood, Nottinghamshire
1939/
43 Housing for the U.K. Ministry of Supply, in Theale, Berkshire; Hereford; Newport, Monmouthshire; Cardiff; Worcester; and Poole, Dorset
1942 Landscape plan for Earle's Cement Works, Hope Valley, Derbyshire
1943 *Motorways for Britain* exhibition, British Road Federation, London
1944 Landscape plan for Pistone Cement Works, Buckinghamshire
1945 Landscape plan for Imperial Chemical Industries, Wilton, Yorkshire
Town and country plan for Wolverton, Buckinghamshire
Outline plan for Guildford, Surrey
1945/
53 Mulgrave Castle garden, Whitby, Yorkshire
1946 Outline plan for Wellington, Shropshire
Foreshore development plan for Mabelthorpe

Geoffrey Jellicoe: Kennedy Memorial, Runnymede, Berkshire, 1965.

and Sutton-on-Sea, Lincolnshire
1947 Sandringham House garden, Norfolk
New town plan for Hemel Hempstead, Hertfordshire
1947/
50 Livingstone Airport, Zambia (with Ronald Rutherford)
Broken Hill Hospital, Zambia (with Ronald Rutherford)
Schools in the Copper Belt, Zambia (with Ronald Rutherford)
1949/
52 Gardens and housing, Church Hill Memorial Landscape, Walsall, West Midlands
1950 Town plan for Lusaka, Zambia
1951 Lansbury Neighborhood Housing, Poplar, London
Ashmore, Benson and Pease Engineering Works and Offices, Stockton-on-Tees, Cleveland
Palladian House, Heron's Beach, Barbados
Cement works, Shoreham-by-Sea, Sussex
1951/
52 Ridgeway Hotel, Lusaka, Zambia (wth Denis Lennon)
1952/
53 Bennett's End Housing, Hemel Hempstead, Hertfordshire
1954 Landscaping for Cadbury Brothers Factory, Moreton, Cheshire
Housing at Levylsdene, Merrow, Surrey (with F. S. Coleridge)
Pilkington Brothers "Glass Age" Project, Soho, London
1955 Landscape development plan for the University of Nottingham
Landscape plan for St. Margaret's Bay, Kent
Landscape design for the Volta River Project, Ghana
1955/
56 Sylvania-Thorn Colour Television Laboratories, Enfield, Middlesex (with Alan Ballantyne)
1956 Landscape design for the Barry foreshore, South Wales
Housing, Basildon New Town, Essex (with F. S. Coleridge)
1956/
57 Harvey's Department Store, Guildford, Surrey (with F. S. Coleridge)
Harvey's Deparment Store Roof Garden, Guildford, Surrey
1957 Civic and Market Hall, Totnes, Devon
1957/
58 Pilkington Brothers Sports Pavilion and Recreation Ground, Ruskin Drive, St. Helen's, Lancashire
1957/
59 Water Gardens, Hemel Hempstead, Hertfordshire
1957/
62 Civic Centre and Great Square, Plymouth, Devon (with Alan Ballantyne)
1959 Gardens, Cement and Concrete Association Research Centre, Wexham Springs, Slough, Berkshire
Motopia: Pilkington Brothers "Glass Age" Project
Artifical hills for Guinness, Park Royal, London
Redevelopment plan for Digbeth Street, Walsall, West Midlands
1960 Artificial hills for Rutherford High Energy Laboratory, Harwell, Berkshire
Landscape plan for the Nuclear Power Station, Oldbury-on-Severn, Gloucestershire (with John Ingleby)
1960/
63 Landscape for the Queen Elizabeth II Hospital, Welwyn, Hertfordshire
1961 Crystal 61: Pikington "Glass Age" Project (with Hal Moggridge)
Cornwall County Hall, Truro (as consultant; with F. K. Hicklin)

Comprehensive plan for the centre of Gloucester (with Hal Moggridge)
1961/
64 Civic Centre, Chertsey, Surrey (with F. S. Coleridge)
1962 Garden at Cliveden, Buckinghamshire
1963 Proposals for Christchurch Meadow inner relief road, Oxford
Crystal Span: Pilkington "Glass Age" Project (with Hal Moggridge)
1964 Report on the M4 Motorway, Berkshire
1964/
65 Kennedy Memorial, Runnymede, Berkshire
1965 Outline scheme for the redevelopment of the Tollcross area, Edinburgh (with C. Davidson)
Westcliff Estate Flats, Scunthorpe, Humberside (with F. S. Coleridge)
Landscape charter for the Isles of Scilly
Garden, Horsted Place, Uckfield, Sussex
1966 Report on the Oaklands Development, Nassau, Bahamas
Report on a Height of Buildings Policy for cathedral and other historic English cities
1966/
67 Crematorium, Grantham, Lincolnshire (with F. S. Coleridge)
1967 Landscape plan for Sark, Channel Islands
Landscape plan for Armagh Cathedral, Northern Ireland
1968 Sea City: Pilkington "Glass Age" Project (with Hal Moggridge)
Control Building and Office Block for the Central Electricity Generating Board at Durley Park, Keynsham, Avon (with F. S. Coleridge)
1968/
71 Landscape plan, with swimming baths, for Pittville, Cheltenham, Gloucestershire (with F. S. Coleridge)
1970/
78 Garden at Shute House, Donhead St. Mary, Dorset
1971 Report on urban road through Cardiff
1971/
72 Pools at the Royal Horticultural Society Gardens, Wisley, Surrey
1971/
74 Country park at Fish Hill, Broadway, Herefordshire and Worcestershire
1971/
75 Landscape plan for the river area, Stratford upon Avon
Gardens, Hilton Hotel, Stratford upon Avon
1972 Landscape for bypass, Warwick
Landscape advisory plan for the Chequers Estate, Buckinghamshire
Landscape plan for Chevening, Kent
1972/
75 Landscape for Delta Metal Works, West Bromwich, Staffordshire
Landscape for New Palace Yard, Westminster, London (not completed)
1972/
77 Landscape for Fitzroy Square, London W.1
1973 Landscaping of roads in central area, Leicester Terrace and general landscape at Stratfield Saye, Berkshire
1974 Landscape development plan for oil platform construction works, Kishorn, Wester Ross, Scotland
Processional way, Exeter Cathedral, Devon
Garden at Everton Park, Sandy, Bedfordshire
1975 Garden at Northington, Hampshire
1976 Garden and landscape at Dewlish House, Dorset
1977/
78 Landscape development plan at Buckenham Broad, Norfolk
1979 Gardens at Luntley Court, Hertfordshire
1980/
84 Landscape for Sutton Place, Guildford, Surrey
Civic Landscape for Modena, Italy

1982 Gardens for Wilverley, Hampshire
1983 Estate Park, Brescia, Italy
1984 Moody Foundation Botanical Gardens, Galveston, Texas

Publications:

By JELLICOE: books—*Italian Gardens of the Renaissance*, with J. C. Shepherd, London 1925; *Gardens and Design*, with J. C. Shepherd, London 1927; *Baroque Gardens of Austria*, London 1932; *Garden Decoration and Ornament*, London 1936; *Gardens of Europe*, London and Glasgow 1937; *Conurbation: Report for the West Midland Group on Post-War Reconstruction and Planning*, London 1948; *Motorways: Their Landscaping, Design and Appearance*, London 1958; *Studies in Landscape Design*, 3 volumes, 1960-70; *Motopia*, London 1961; *Modern Private Gardens*, with Susan Jellicoe, London, Toronto and Paris 1968; *L'Architettura del Paesaggio*, Milan 1969; *Water: The Use of Water in Landscape Architecture*, with Susan Jellicoe, London and New York 1971; *The Landscape of Man*, with Susan Jellicoe, London and New York 1975; *The Guelph Lectures on Landscape Design*, Guelph, Ontario 1984; articles in *Architectural Review* (London); *Country Life* (London); *Landscape Design* (London); etc.; recording—*Abstract Art into Landscape*, tape cassette and slides, London 1982.

On JELLICOE: articles—"Landscape Knight" in *Building Design* (London), 7 September 1979; "A Garden through six reigns" by Tony Venison in *Country Life* (London), 19 June 1980; "2m pounds landscape for Sutton Place" in *Building Design* (London), 26 June 1981; "Sir Geoffrey conducts grand opera" in *Building Design* (London), 11 September 1981; "Garden Culture" by Stephen Rettig in *The Architects' Journal* (London), 28 July 1982; "Conservation without tears" in *Chartered Surveyor Weekly* (London), 4 November 1982.

*   *   *

Post-student research into the classical Italian garden (with fellow student J. C. Shepherd—published in 1925 as *Italian Gardens of the Renaissance* and still the standard work) convinced me unhesitatingly that architecture was part of the environment and therefore incomplete when considered in isolation. This timeless idea has always remained the basis of the thought, design and execution of my work.

—Geoffrey Jellicoe

*   *   *

Geoffrey Jellicoe is widely known for his influence on the profession of landscape architecture, which has been profound and worldwide. His practice as an architect led him to see the importance of the setting—the relationship of buildings to their context. He studied gardens and garden design, and his books on these subjects have inspired a whole generation of designers and will remain as outstanding classics of this period.

The Institute of Landscape Architects had begun rather unsteadily in 1929, just before he joined it, and would probabky have collapsed but for the support he brought it from the architectural world and for his continuing support through the years of World War II, when he provided secretarial and office accommodation in his Gower Street office. Other distinguished architects and town planners who shared his views on the relationship of buildings to landscape follwed his example and brought further recognition to the art of landscape design which, though it had been described as a "new art" in the eighteenth century, had languished in a sort of doldrums (at least in Britain) since the days of Kent, Repton and Brown.

Soon after the war, heavy correspondence from

other countries on the subject of landscape design proved that there was a revival of interest and showed that the time had come to launch an International Federation of Landscape Architects. Earlier meetings held in Paris and elsewhere in Europe had not foreseen this brave possibility, but Jellicoe saw the matter in its broadest light as a common interest capable, if suitably focussed, of healing wartime antagonisms and containing perhaps some seeds of peaceful international co-operation in the future. He used the resources of his office to organize an international conference to be held in Cambridge; he was elected first President and then Life President of Honour of IFLA and has been constantly in touch with its development: since then it has greatly outgrown—at least in numbers—the Institute of Landscape Architects, its parent body.

During that time several important books by Jellicoe appeared, all concerned with garden or landscape matters. In particular his three volumes of *Studies in Landscape Design* and his important work *The Landscape of Man* (written jointly with his wife Susan) have expanded the basis of his wide philosophic thinking on the subject, and these books have exerted untold influence on public appreciation of the growing art wherever it has been practiced. His keen realization of the links between the arts of painting and sculpture and that of landscape design is a main characteristic of his approach. He had also fully understood the limitations imposed on landscape design by the laws of nature—the inevitable ecological necessities and the land sciences that must govern landscape design far more stringently than they do the visual arts.

He was among the first landscape architects to be consulted by a major industry on the setting of its works. His report and plans for Earle's Cement Works in Derbyshire set an example and precedent for the treatment of open-cast mining and quarrying to prevent disfigurement of the landscape and showed how multiple land use, properly balanced, could create fine new landscapes. This recognition of the function of landscape design has since become generally adopted by industry and planners. On a smaller scale Jellicoe showed a different aspect of his design in the little park at Hemel Hempstead, making delightful gardens in an area of disused urban space.

His work and his writings constantly emphasise the role of each individual site. The spirit of place, "genius loci," is a main inspiration of every serious landscape project, but whereas many buildings have been designed on the drawing board with little reference to the individuality of the site, Jellicoe has underlined the designer's need to draw inspiration from the existing conditions of every site—an approach tending to counteract the risk of monotony which seems to be a bane of the architecture and town planning of this age throughout the world.

A summary of his views and his influence on contemporary thought may be found in his own words from *The Landscape of Man:*
The world is moving into a phase when landscape design may well be recognized as the most comprehensive of the arts. Man creates around him an environment that is a projection into nature of his abstract ideas. It is only in the present century that the collective landscape has emerged as a social necessity. We are promoting a landscape art on a scale never conceived of in history.

Brenda Colvin (1980)

JOHANSEN, John MacLane.
American. Born in New York City, 29 June 1916. Educated at Harvard University, Cambridge, Massachusetts, 1935-39, B.S. (cum laude) 1939; Harvard Graduate School of Design, Cambridge, 1939-42. Married Mary Lee Longscope in 1946 (divorced, 1954); Mary Ellen Goode in 1959 (divorced 1967); daughters: Deborah and Christen. Worked as a draftsman for Marcel Breuer, *q.v.*, Cambridge, 1942; Researcher, National Housing Agency, Washington, D.C., 1943-45; Designer, Skidmore, Owings and Merrill, *q.v.*, New York, 1945-48; in private practice, New Canaan, Connecticut, 1948-70. Since 1970, partner, with Ashok M. Bhavnani, Johansen and Bhavnani, New York. Professor of Architecture, Yale University School of Arhiteture, New Haven, Connecticut, 1955-58, and Columbia University, New York 1964-66; lectured in Italy, 1974; Architect-in-Residence, American Academy in Rome, 1975. Professor of Architecture at the Pratt Institute, New York, since 1976. Exhibitions: *Built in U.S.A.: Post-War Architecture,* Museum of Modern Art, New York, 1952; *International Exhibition of Architecture,* Berlin, 1962; *Selected Works of American Architects,* Moscow, 1965; *Architecture U.S.A.,* United States Pavilion, World's Fair, Osaka, 1970; *Exhibition U.S.A.,* Katowice, Wroclaw, Posnan and Warsaw, Poland, 1970; *Architecture in America,* United States Information Agency tour, 1976; *Transformations in Modern Architecture,* Museum of Modern Art, New York, 1979. Recipient: Record House Award, *Architectural Record,* 1956, 1958, 1977, 1978; Award of Merit, 1963, and Honor Award, 1972, American Institute of Architects, AIA, Connecticut Chapter, 1964; Honor Award, Indiana Association of Architects, 1965; Honor Award, Connecticut Association of Architects, 1965, 1966; First Award, Florida Society of Architects, 1966; Award of Merit, United States Department of Health, Education and Welfare/AIA, 1966; First Honor Award, Baltimore Chamber of Commerce/AIA Baltimore Chapter, 1967; First Honor Award, AIA, Mid-Atlantic Region, 1968; Brunner Award, American Academy and Institute of Arts and Letters, 1968; Award of Merit: Library Buildings, AIA, 1970; Honor Award, American Concrete Association, Florida Chapter, 1971; Medal of Honor, AIA, New York Chapter, 1976; Bard Award, City Club of New York, 1977. D.F.A.: Maryland Institute, Baltimore, 1965; Clark University, Worcester, Massachusetts, 1970. Fellow, American Institute of Architects, 1969. Member, American Academy and Institute of Arts and Letters. Address: Johansen and Bhavnani, 401 East 37th Street, New York, New York 10016, U.S.A.

Works:

1948 Coggeshal House, Schenectady, New York
1949 Langenwalter House, Schenectady, New York
     Bengst House, Schenectady, New York
1950 Johansen House I, New Canaan, Connecticut
1951 Barlow House, New Canaan, Connecticut
1952 Dunham House, New Canaan, Connecticut
     Lake Dwellers House (project)
1953 Huvelle House, Litchfield, Connecticut
     Campbell House, New Canaan, Connecticut
     Goode House, New Canaan, Connecticut
1954 Dickenson House, New Canaan, Canaan, Connecticut
1955 Sprayform Houses I and II (projects)
     McNiff House, Stockbridge, Massachusetts
     Stillman House, Newburgh, New York
1956 Goodyear House, Darien, Connecticut
     Sprayform United States Pavilion, Zagreb, Yugoslavia
1957 Warner House, New Canaan, Connecticut
     Sprayform Church, Norwich, Connecticut (project)
     Sprayform Restaurant, Mount Kisco, New York (project)
1958 Roe House, Greenwich, Connecticut
1959 Durst House, Mount Kisco, New York
1960 Franklin Delano Roosevelt Memorial, Washington, D.C. (competition project; with John McVitty)
1961 Museum of Art, Science and Industry, Bridgeport, Connecticut
1962 Church, Norwich, Connecticut
1963 Schwarzenbach House I, Norwalk, Connecticut
     Simon House, Bedford, New York (project)
     Clowes Hall, Indianapolis, Indiana
1964 United States Embassy, Dublin
1965 Florence Virtue Housing (120 units), New Haven, Connecticut
     Helen Grant Elementary School, Dixwell Renewal Area, New Haven, Connecticut
     Theatre, Vassar College, Poughkeepsie, New York (project)
     Cultural Center, Wallingford, Connecticut (project)
1966 Taylor House, Westport, Connecticut
     Public Library, Orlando, Florida
     Leapfrog City, New York (project)
     Master plan of the new campus for the State University of New York at Old Westbury, Long Island (with Alexander Kouzmanoff and Victor Christ-Janer)
1967 Morris Mechanic Theatre, Baltimore, Maryland
     Leapfrog Housing, New York (project)
1968 Ritts House, Greenwich, Connecticut
     Goddard Library, Clark University, Worcester, Massachusetts
     Junior High School, Litchfield, Connecticut
1969 Dixwell Avenue Congregational Church, New Haven, Connecticut
     KQED TV Studio, San Francisco (project; with George Rockwise)
     Twin Parks Housing, Bronx, New York (project)
     Car Body Office Building, Baltimore, Maryland (project; with Ashok Bhavnani)
     L. Francis Smith School, Columbus, Indiana
1970 Oklahoma Theatre Center, Oklahoma City
     Western Connecticut State College, Danbury (project; with Ashok Bhavnani)
     Guest House, Fishers Island, Connecticut (project)
     Foster and Company Corporate Headquarters and Plant, Hanover Park, New Jersey
1971 High school, New York (project; with Ashok Bhavnani)
1972 State University of New York Campus Plan and College, at Old Westbury, Long Island
1974 Johansen House II, Stanfordville, New York
1975 Library and TV Resource Center, Staten Island Community College, New York (project; with Ashok Bhavnani)
1976 Roosevelt Island Neighborhood, New York (with Ashok Bhavnani)
     Ellsworth House, Salisbury, Connecticut
1977 Pope House, Salisbury, Connecticut
1978 Schwarzenbach House II, Vieques, Puerto Rico
     Kinetic House (project)
1979 Barna House, Bedford, New York
1982 Resort Hotel (project)
1983 Fiat-Lingotto Plant Redevlopment, Turin, Italy (competition project)

Publications:

By JOHANSEN: book—*The New Urban Aesthetic,* New York 1972; articles—"Johansen Declares Himself" in *Architectural Forum* (New York), January 1966; "An Architecture for the Electronic Age" in *American Scholar* (Washington, D.C.), 1966, reprinted in *McLuhan, Hot and Cool,* New York 1967; "New Town" in *Architectural Forum* (New York), September 1967; "The Mummers Theatre, A Fragment, Not a Building" in *Architectural Forum* (New York), May 1968; introduction to *Islamic Architecture,* Milan 1971; article in *On Philosophies of Construction,* compiled by Abby Suckle, New York 1979; "Architecture: three imperatives" in *Architecture* (Washington, D.C.), March 1984.

On JOHANSEN: books—*Built in U.S.A.: Postwar Architecture* by Stephen Mahony, New York 1952; *Architecture USA,* edited by Ian McCallum, London 1959; *Architects on Architecture,* edited by Paul Heyer, London 1967; *By Their Own Design,* edited by Abby Suckle, New York, and St. Albans, Hertfordshire 1980; articles—"A Platform Raised Above a Field: House in New Canaan, Connecticut" in *Architectural Forum* (New York), July 1951; "Textbook House, New Canaan, Connecticut" in *House and Home* (New York), May 1952; "Genetrix: Personal Contributions to American Architecture" in *Architectural Review* (London), May 1957; "Jeunes Architectes aux Etats Unis" in *L'Architecture d'Aujourd'hui* (Paris), September 1957; "The New House of 1958" in *Architectural Record* (New York), May 1958; "Embassy with a New Twist" in *Architects' Journal* (London), August 1958; "Sculpting with Sprayed Concrete" in *Architectural Forum* (New York), October 1959; "Design for the Architect's Own House, New Canaan, Connecticut, and U.S. Embassy Office Building, Dublin" in *Art in America* (New York), vol. 49, no. 1, 1961; "Architecture of Ideas: The Romantic House" in *House and Home* (New York), March 1962; "Labyrinthian Environs: Residence, Westport, Connecticut" in *Progressive Architecture* (New York), May 1962; "Architectural Changes Forecast New Adventures in Living: House at Westport, Connecticut" in *House and Garden* (New York), October 1962; "Theatre Block, Charles Center, Baltimore, Maryland" and "U.S. Embassy Office Dublin" in *Architectural Design* (London), November 1964; "Theatres and Auditoriums" in *Architectural Record* (New York), December 1964; "College Buildings" in *Architectural Record* (New York), June 1965; "Anti-Architecture" by Robin Boyd in *Architectural Forum* (New York), November 1968; "A View of Contemporary World Architecture," special issue of *The Japan Architect* (Tokyo), July 1970; "The Mummers Theatre" by Peter Blake in *Architectural Forum* (New York), March 1971; "Towards a New Slang" by Robert Hughes in *Time* (New York), 31 May 1971; "Rigged House" in *Architecture Plus* (New York), December 1974; "A Model City Within a City" in *U.S. News and World Report* (Washington, D.C.), December 1977/January 1978; "Mechanic Theatre" in *AIA Journal* (Washington, D.C.), February 1978; "Private House" in *Architectural Record* (New York), May 1978; "Around a greenhouse in Connecticut" in *Ville Giardini* (Milan), February 1979; "Rigged House, Stanfordville, New York" in *GA Houses* (Tokyo), December 1979; "Rebuilding a modern house" in *Fine Homebuilding* (Newtown, Connecticut), June/July 1981; "Two recent projects by John M. Johansen" in *Architettura* (Rome), August/September 1983.

John Johansen: Oklahoma Theater Center, Oklahoma City, 1970.

After a rather nonsequential search in my early career, I have more recently come to see buildings and building complexes in terms of their parts—i.e., individuation. for some time I have considered the most essential elements in architecture to be enclosures, generalized or specific, to accommodate function. These functions were seen to be "static" and contained, as opposed to elements which served as access to static elements in the kinetic function of moving people and mechanical services. The third category of elements were structural, which held it all up in some sort of mutually agreeable disposition. In concept and procedure I saw it to be as simple as 1) "place it," ie., the enclosures; 2) "support it," i.e., hold it together structurally; and 3) "connect it," i.e., provide access. However the sequence might be in reverse: Starting with a structural frame to which are attached enclosures later to be connected. Or, starting with a circulation system, add structure and then enclosures.

Still another "dimension," as it were, is kinetics. We are now able to satisfy the basic fascination with movement, not by illusion, as in the baroque period, but with the technology we now command, producing buildings which, in part, do indeed move. As the history of architecture bears out, most innovations are drawn from either humble or crude and vulgar utilitarian origins. The barrel vault and arch were known to the Egyptians and Greeks who used them only for underground sewage, whereas the Romans and those for centuries later got, as we might say, a "lot of mileage" out of them. Hidden steel tension structures used to hold Renaissance domes from collapsing, and have now come to be commonly exposed. Kinetic devices first appeared in industrial buildings in the form of attached hoists, overhead conveyors, power scaffolding, pneumatic tube intercom, trackage, self-erecting cranes, etc. Now when an improved service is performed, sooner or later an architect will make it somehow publicly acceptable on an aesthetic level. Increasingly there appear kinetic devices, vividly expressed, in airports, supermarkets and flashy hotels. Kinetics is here; to perform greater service, and to delight in.

Except for the most usual moving elements such as elevations, I have not yet designed a kinetic building. Yet following the sequence of my works, and with my continuing interest in an architecture of parts, it is with kinetics that I now come face to face. And as the house, as building type, is always a good proving ground, I sketched, in 1960, a house of parts, assembling and disassembling themselves on railroad trackage. A central element containing the entrance, living room, kitchen, bath, power source, etc., had other parts, i.e. master bedroom, guestroom, studio and a "folly" or "mood room," grouped around it. For the practicabilities of domestic life, or for reason of pure whim, this house could change its functional grouping. From an aesthetic point of view, this house is never a static composition, but enters that field of experience now limited to kinetic sculpture.

I believe kinetics is more and more a part of our lives. The fusion of transportation and the building, people-moving devices, theatre technology, museum and exposition display, and opening and closing of solar heated buildings—all these current developments confirm the functional justification of moveable parts, while the public's delight in the exposed machinery of theRoosevelt Island cable car system, or the exposed elevator cabs of the Portman hotels, or the scenic railroad entering the hotel lobby in Orlando's Disney World, and now the "Super-Mannerists'" growing involvement with changeable facades and changeable "room liners" confirms the aesthetic acceptance of kinetics as well.

My philosophy of construction, then, would develop around "the part." The part appears first in analysis of the program, then in synthesis, in the typing of parts, then the grouping of parts, assembly, interchange, reshuffling, and finally in movement. This seems to be the basis of my "ordering devices" or "organizing ideas." The vivid expression, articulation, detailed connections and couplings are the "poetic touches" I give in the design process, thereby making of problem solving and building technology possibly something more. And if I add to this my other concerns—our sense of life, our basic psychological motivations, newly awakened perception of the impact of our electronic age, and our historic derivations—I hope I may come up with something which can be called architecture.

—John M. Johansen

John Johansen's is a punchy, loose-limbed architecture, full of solidified desire: his designs don't get bogged down in the quagmire of impulsive forms; they embody a surprisingly wide strain of social factors, though without for a single moment ever denying that, when all is said and done, they nonetheless owe something to form too. But in his case the forms are strong and roughly woven shapes going out to greet function. His Mechanic Theatre in Baltimore, the result more of thrust than intention, comprises brute contrete embracing the fuctional parameters in a dizzy architectural rewriting of Léger's Ballet Mechanique. His "Leapfrog City" project takes off in multi-determinate axes, like trails of smoke from a team of aerobatic aircraft.

His starting point is, how to make a human but unpredictable project? It must be the product of an enormous argument between everyone concerned, resulting in an agglutinative whole, alive with associations and suggestions. It is the way his buildings have obviously been argued through into their final form that prevents them from succumbing to that no-go area between architecture and sculpture: the reference-point established by means of the argument guarantees that only a few responsibilities and obligations at the most are lost in the formation process. Under such conditions, real, hard-headed "content" is very much on the cards.

The danger facing the designer today is that his

-parameters are all moving along similiar lines and that one criteria has come to be as good as another. Johansen instead insists on a provocative hierarchy of conditions as the only way of trying to get to the end of a sentence: this pugnacious vocabulary is what saves him from the spatial fixations and mechanical obsessions of the megastructure: he manages to come up with a language half given, half shared . . .fighting against the ghost seriality of the ultimate cliches.

His buildings, through their considerations of the social and anthropological, and through their lucid expression of the urban, seem to magnify one's whole being: the charitable gesture that characterizes his buildings is an index of the way they give themselves not just to ourselves but to the whole of the world—this might seem ludicrous only because of our current notions of selfishness. He recognizes that architecture can be a candidate for another dimension. Having admitted the power architecture commands over the elements, he has sworn not to abuse his own powers as architect. Architecture is something we ought to chase after, although we seldom do—we are led from it by personal foibles, mad impulses, eccentric codes of conduct: Johansen tries to reverse this, inviting us back directly to architecture. In order to do this, his buildings must boast many points of fusion with one's mind, which they do. He is afraid that the architect today could best be compared to an old woman who considers she is a lover of flowers when she presses them in a book instead of planting them.

—Chris Fawcett

JOHNSON, Philip Cortelyou

American. Born in Cleveland, Ohio, 8 July 1906. Educated at Harvard University, Cambridge, Massachusetts, 1923-30. A.B. (cum laude) 1930; Harvard Graduate School of Design, 1940-43, B.Arch. 1943. Director, Department of Architecture, Museum of Modern Art, New York, 1930-36; practised architecture in Cambridge, Massachusetts, 1942-46; again served as Director, Department of Architecture, Museum of Modern Art, 1946-54; returned to private practice in New York, 1954-64; Partner, with Richard Foster, Philip Johnson and Richard Foster, New York, 1964-67; Partner, with John Burgee, Johnson/Burgee Architects, New York, 1967-83, and John Burgee Architects with Philip Johnson, New York, since 1983. Trustee of the Museum of Modern Art since 1958. Recipient: Silver Medal of Honor, Architectural League of New York, 1950; First Prize, *Bienal*, Sao Paulo, 1954; Grand Festival Award, Boston Arts Festival, 1955; Merit Award, 1956, First Honor Award, 1956, 1961 (twice), Twenty-Five Year Award, 1975, and Gold Medal, 1978, American Institute of Architects; Award of Excellence, *Architectural Record*, 1957, 1962; Gold Medal of Honor, with Mies van der Rohe, Architectural League of New York, 1960; Best New Institutional Building, Fifth Avenue Association, New York 1962; Design Award, *Progressive Architecture,* 1964; First Honor Award, City Club of New York, 1966; Louis Sullivan Award; Bricklayers, Masons, and Plasterers International Union of America, 1975; R. S. Reynolds Memorial Award, 1978; Thomas Jefferson Medal, University of Virginia, Charlottesville, 1978; Bronze Medallion, City of New York, 1978; Pritzker Architecture Prize, Hyatt Foundation, 1979. D.F.A.: Pratt Institute, Brooklyn, New York, 1962. Fellow, American Institute of Architects, and American Academy of Arts and Letters. Address: Johnson/Burgee Architects, 375 Park Avenue, New York, New York 10152, U.S.A.

Works:

1942 Philip Johnson House, Cambridge, Massachusetts
1944 Townsend Farms Barn, New London, Ohio
1947 Farney House, Sagaponack, Long Island, New York
1949 Philip Johnson House, New Canaan, Connecticut
1950 Annex, Museum of Modern Art, New York
John D. Rockefeller III Guest House, New York
1951 Hodgson House, New Canaan, Connecticut (with Landes Gores)
Oneto House, Irvington, New York (with Landes Gores)
1952 Davis House, Wayzata, Minnesota
Schlumberger Administration Building, Ridgefield, Connecticut
1953 Alice Ball House, New Canaan, Connecticut
Rockefeller Sculpture Garden, Museum of Modern Art, New York (with James Fanning)
Wiley House, New Canaan, Connecticut
1956 Boissonnas House, New Canaan, Connecticut
Kneses Tifereth Israel Synagogue, Port Chester, New York
Leonhardt House, Lloyd's Neck, Long Island, New York
1957 Auditorium and Classroom Buildings, University of St. Thomas, Houston (with Howard Barnstone and Partners)
1958 Seagram Building, 375 Park Avenue, New York (with Mies van der Rohe and Kahn and Jacobs)
1959 Asia House, New York
1960 Museum Building, Munson-Williams-Proctor Institute, Utica, New York
Nuclear reactor, Rehovot, Israel
Roofless Church, New Harmony, Indiana
Dormitories, Sarah Lawrence College, Bronxville, New York
1961 Amon Carter Museum of Modern Art, Fort Worth, Texas
Computing Center, Brown University, Providence, Rhode Island
1962 Pavilion, Philip Johnson House, New Canaan, Connecticut
1963 Museum for Pre-Columbian Art, Dumbarton Oaks, Washington, D.C.
Sheldon Memorial Art Gallery, University of Nebraska, Lincoln
1964 Boissonnas House, Cap Benat, France
Kline Geology Laboratory, Yale University, New Haven, Connecticut (with Richard Foster)
East and Garden Wings, Museum of Modern Art, New York
New York State Theatre, Lincoln Center, New York (with Richard Foster)
New York State Pavilion, *Worlds Fair,* New York (with Richard Foster)
1965 Epidemiology and Public Health Building, Yale University, New Haven, Connecticut (with the Office of Douglas Orr)
Geier House, Indian Hills, Ohio
Painting Gallery, Philip Johnson House, New Canaan, Connecticut
Kline Science Center, Yale University, New Haven, Connecticut (with Richard Foster)
Henry L. Moses Institute, Montefiore Hospital, Bronx, New York
Hendrix College Library, Conway, Arkansas (with Wittenberg, Delony, and Davidson)
1968 Bielefeld Art Gallery, West Germany (with Cäsar Pinnau)
WRVA Radio Station, Richmond, Virginia (with Rudia and Freeman)
Kreeger House, Washington, D.C. (with Richard Foster)
1970 Sculpture Gallery, Philip Johnson House, New Canaan, Connecticut
John F. Kennedy Memorial, Dallas
1971 List Art Building, Brown University, Providence, Rhode Island
1972 Art Museum of South Texas, Corpus Christi (with John Burgee, and Barnstone and Aubry)
Burden Hall, Harvard University, Cambridge, Massachusetts (with John Burgee)
Neuberger Museum, State University of New York at Purchase (with John Burgee)
1973 Elmer Holmes Bobst Library, New York University, New York (with Richard Foster)
Hagop Kevorkian Center for Near East Studies, New York University, New York (with Richard Foster)
I.D.S. Center, Minneapolis (with John Burgee, and Edward F. Baker Associates)
Boston Public Library addition (with John Burgee, and Architects Design Group)
1974 Convention Center, Niagara Falls, New York (with John Burgee)
1975 Water Garden, Fort Worth, Texas (with John Burgee)
Morningside House, Bronx, New York (with John Burgee)
1976 Pennzoil Place, Houston (with John Burgee, and Wilson, Morris, Crain and Anderson)
Post Oak Central 1, Houston (with John Burgee, and Wilson, Morris, Crain and Anderson)
Avery Fisher Hall interiors, Lincoln Center, New York (with John Burgee)
1977 Muhlenberg College Fine Arts Center, Allentown, Pennsylvania (with John Burgee, and Coston, Wallace and Watson)
General American Life Insurance Company, St. Louis (with John Burgee)
Thanks-Giving Square, Dallas (with John Burgee)
1979 Garden Grove Community Church, California (with John Burgee)
American Telephone and Telegraph Corporate Headquarters, New York (with John Burgee)
1980 Office Building, 101 California Street, San Francisco (with John Burgee)
Dade County Cultural Center, Miami, Florida (with John Burgee)
1981 PPG Building, Pittsburgh, Pennsylvania (with John Burgee)
Transco Tower, Houston, Texas (with John Burgee)
Republic Bank Center, Houston, Texas (with John Burgee)
United Bank Center, Denver, Colorado (with John Burgee)
1983 Office Building, 580 California Street, San Francisco (with John Burgee)
Office Building, 53rd Street at Third Avenue, New York (with John Burgee)
1984 Times Square Redevelopment, New York (with John Burgee)
Mercantile Bank, Dallas, Texas (with John Burgee)
Fort Hill Square, Boston (with John Burgee)
New England Life Building, Boston (with John Burgee)
Tycon Towers, Tyson's Corner, Virginia (with John Burgee)

Publications:

By JOHNSON: books—*Modern Architects,* with others, New York 1932; *The International Style,* with Henry-Russell Hitchcock, New York 1932, 1966; *Machine Art,* New York 1934; *Mies van der Rohe,* New York 1947, 1953; *Selected Writings,* Tokyo 1975; *Philip Johnson: Writings,* edited by Robert A.M. Stern, New York 1978; *Writings of Philip Johnson,* with introduction by Peter Eisenman, New York 1979; articles—"Interview with Philip Johnson" in *Summa* (Buenos Aires), November 1982; "Interview with Philip Johnson" in *Archetype* (San

Francisco), Winter 1983; recording—*Philip Johnson: Annual Discourse, 1979, at the Royal Institute of British Architects,* tape cassette, London 1979.

On JOHNSON: books—*Philip Johnson* by John Jacobus, Jr., New York 1962; *Philip Johnson: Architecture 1949-1965* by Henry-Russell Hitchcock, New York and London 1966; *Philip Johnson* by Charles Noble, Tokyo 1968, London 1972; *Johnson House, New Canaan, Connecticut,* edited by Yukio Futagawa, text by Bryan Robertson, Tokyo 1972; *Conversations with Architects,* edited by John W. Cook and Heinrich Klotz, New York and London 1973; *New Directions in American Architecture* by Robert Stern, New York 1977; *Philip Johnson: Processes,* exhibition catalogue with preface by Craig Owens, New York 1978; *Inside New York's Art World* by Barbaralee Diamonstein, New York 1979; *Late-Modern Architecture* by Charles Jencks, London 1980; *Johnson/Burgee: architecture,* with text by Nory Miller, London 1980; articles—"Profile: Philip Johnson forms under light" in *The New Yorker,* 23 May 1977; "The New Age of Philip Johnson" by Paul Goldberger in the *New York Times Magazine,* 14 May 1978; "Three designs by Johnson/Burgee" in *Architectural Record* (New York), July 1978; "The man who designed a Chippendale skyscraper" by Paul Goldberger in *The Observer Magazine* (London), 17 December 1978; "Philip Johnson," special issue of *Architecture + Urbanism* (Tokyo), no. 6, 1979; "The tastemakers: Philip Johnson" in *Building Design* (London), 20 April 1979; "Philip Johnson; rediscoverer of architecture" by W. Marlin in the *Christian Science Monitor* (Boston), 30 July 1979; "Philip Johnson on Philip Johnson" by Wayne Fujii in *GA Document* (Tokyo), Summer 1980; "Philip Johnson: modern or post-modern?" in *Casabella* (Milan), April 1981; "Johnson's Polish" in *Building Design* (London), 20 May 1983; "California Trio", special issue of *Building Design* (London), 17 February 1984; "MOMA Gallery Opens in Honour of Johnson" in *Building Design* (London), 20 April 1984.

Bibliography: "Writings by and about Philip C. Johnson," compiled by William B. O'Neal, in the *American Association of Architectural Bibliographers Papers,* vol. I, 1965, vol. II, 1966; *Philip Johnson and American Architecture: A Selected Bibliography* by Robert B. Harmon, Monticello, Illinois 1979.

Philip Johnson occupies a unique position in the architectural world. A man of unequalled taste and sensibility, but one with no consistent idea of the kind of buildings that he should be building, he has left a trail of admiration and confusion. Most of the admiration is centred on the period of his work in the decade after the war when, briefly, he settled on a Miesian direction: if it were not for the buildings of this period, he would certainly not be regarded as a major architect.

It is significant that Philip Johnson came to designing buildings comparatively late in life, after a period as client, critic, author, and museum director. It was in pursuing these activities that he found his real training, and it was these capacities that he became an important figure in the American East Coast architectural scene of the 1930's. He organized the first visits of both Mies van der Rohe and Le Corbusier to America. An affluent young man, he commissioned Mies to design his New York apartment for him in 1930, then found Mies his next American client; subsequently he wrote a book on Mies (based on the catalogue he had written for the New York Museum of modern Art exhibition he had organized), which still remains the best of many books on its subject. Most important, in the years before and after the war he was the Director of the Department of Architecture at the Museum of Modern Art, a post he used forcefully to promote the causes in which he believed.

Johnson was a key propagandist for the Modern Movement in architecture, and the subsequent history of modern architecture in the U.S.A. is in many respects influenced by its having been brought to the country by Johnson, with his particular set of values. In Europe, the modern movement in architecture was closely related to social problems: it involved a belief that the good life must be for everyone, and working class housing was considered a major building type. Philip Johnson, the hedonist, filtered out these notions of social responsibility and sold America the new architecture as a new style. From Le Corbusier he gave them Poissy, but not the Ilot Insalubre, with the result that the movement had a very different history in America from, say, England, where architecture and welfare were seen as closely related.

Johnson's apprenticeship was long and thorough, and when, at the age of 43, he built his first significant building, the result was a knock-out. The Glass House (Johnson House) at New Canaan states his position well: it is a historian's modern building. At a time when history was anathema to architects, Johnson published his house and illustrated some of the many sources of his design, not only Mies van der Rohe but also Schinkel, Choisy, Ledoux and Ben Nicholson. The modern movement had lost the innocence of its notion of a clean sweep of history. Yet, however clever the polemic that surrounded the completion of the Glass House, it would have remained an intellectual game had it not been for the manifest quality of the building itself. This was not the work of a mere critic but of a designer of the first rank. The building can be enjoyed for its historical allusions or for the quality of its materials. It can be appreciated for the clarity of its structure or for the elegance of its siting. Most of all, it must be admired as one of architecture's magic spaces, with the play of reflections and transparency of glass: thanks to the genius of Richard Kelly, the lighting consultant, the space at night is a veritable wonderland, as glass walls disappear and grass and trees are illuminated.

Johnson never again matched the memorability of the Glass House, but in the years following its completion he designed and built a series of middle-class family houses, often on modest budgets, that take much of the formalism and the quality of the Glass House and make it work in load-bearing brickwork for a plan with separate bedrooms. The Hodgson House and the Oneto House are particularly successful in this respect and must rate as amongst the most habitable family houses yet designed—one of the many curious twists to be found in Johnson's work is that he castigates architects who over-emphasise the functional basis for architecture, yet his own builings often function superlatively well, while those of supposedly functionalist architects prove impracticable.

But by the mid-1950's Johnson was becoming bored with the limitations imposed by the Miesian world. Mies had worried about the disorder apparent in cities, but Johnson welcomed chaos as preferable to order. "It's chaos and I love it," he said of the architectural situation in New York. First he turned to Louis Kahn, and Johnson's Boissonnas house of 1956 had brick piers and a rambling plan in the manner of Kahn's Adler and de Vore houses. The Boissonnas house was a lovely building, but Johnson did not feel that he had gone far enough. He wanted to overthrow not just Mies but the whole modern movemnet. The sheer architectural quality of his houses, and his prestige as Mies's colleague on the Seagram Building, meant that Johnson was an architect who had to be taken seriously, but from 1960 onwards he devoted his energies and his talents to twisting the tail of the modern movement.

In his design for Asia House, New York, Johnson published "alternative elevations": one involved sensuous curves, devoid of structural meaning, and these he employed in the Sheldon Memorial Art Gallery at the University of Nebraska. Later buildings, such as the theatre at Lincoln Center, often had the overblown banality of Mussolini's buildings, while others, such as the Moses Institute

for Montefiore Hospital, New York, are just plain dull. A dull building is something Johnson himself would not wish for, and his recent project for an office building on a Chippendale cabinet parti can be seen as an effort to maintain interest almost at any price.

Whatever we may take of his flamboyant later buildings, consistent qualities remain. A certain exquisiteness, an instinctive understanding for quality in artificial lighting, and a sure sense of the way a building is walked through—the professional route that has fascinated him for thirty years, ever since he placed his glass house at the end of an elaborate route from the highway.

—John Winter

JOHNSON, Richard Norman.
Also known as Peter Johnson. Australian. Born in Armadale, Victoria, 15 December 1923. Educated at Sydney Boys' High School, 1936-40; University of Sydney, 1946-50, B.Arch. (honours) 1951. Served as a Flight Lieutenant in the Royal Australian Air Force, in Australia, Canada, the United Kindgom, and France, 1942-45. Married Jane Margaret Adria Meade-Waldo in 1944; children: Christopher, Timothy, and Simon. Partner, McConnel Smith & Johnson, architects and planners, Sydney, 1955-71, and since 1971, Director, McConnel Smith & Johnson Pty. Ltd., Sydney; since 1974, Director, MSJ Keys Young Planners Pty. Ltd., Sydney. Director, YRM + MSJ Pty. Ltd. (Architects), Sydney, 1971-78. Professor of Architecture, since 1967, and Dean of the Faculty of Architecture, since 1968, University of Sydney. Foundation Chairman, The Architectural Society, Sydney, 1960-65; President, New South Wales Chapter, Royal Australian Institute of Architects, 1968-70; Member of the Senate, University of Sydney, 1968-72; Member of the Commonwealth Board of Architectural Education, 1971-77; Chairman, 1973-77, Member of the Executive, 1976-77, 1979-82, and President, 1982-85, Commonwealth Association of Architects; Member of the Council, New South Wales Branch, National Trust of Australia, 1972-77. Member, Board of Architects of New South Wales, since 1966; Member of the Council, since 1967, and Deputy Chancellor, since 1981, New South Wales Institute of Technology; Member of the Advisory Council, Sydney Building Information Centre, since 1970; Federal Councillor, 1977-84, and President, 1982-83, Royal Australian Institute of Architects; Councillor, since 1982, and Vice-President, 1983, Australian Council of Professions. Recipient: Canberra Medallion, 1961; Royal Australian Institute of Architects Wilkinson Award, 1964, and Merit Awards, 1971, 1977, and 1978 (twice); City of Sydney Architectural Award, 1971 and 1972, and Commendation Award, 1977. Life Fellow, Royal Australian Institute of Architects, 1970; Honorary Fellow, Royal Architecutral Institute of Canada, 1983, and American Institute of Architects, 1985. Member, Royal Institute of British Architects. Officer, Order of Australia, 1979. Address: McConnel Smith & Johnson Pty. Ltd., 35 Richards Avenue, Surry Hills, Sydney, New South Wales, Australia.

Works (with McConnel Smith & Johnson):

1952 Chatswood West Kindergarten, Chatswood, New South Wales
1957 Neuchatel Asphalt Company Offices, Sydney
1960 Western Assurance Company Building, Sydney
1961 Kindersley House, Sydney
1963 R. N. Johnson House, Chatswood, New South Wales

R. N. Johnson: Benjamin Government Offices, Belconnen, Canberra, 1978-79.

1964 Riker Pharmaceutical Factory and Offices, Thornleigh, New South Wales
Swire House, Sydney
1965 Sydney Water Board Building, Sydney
1969 Law School, University of Sydney
Northbourne House, Canberra
St. Andrew's Residential College, University of Sydney
1970 CSIRO Headquarters, Canberra
1970/
76 Qantas Flight Operations Training Centre, Mascot, New South Wales
1971 St. Luke's Hospital Operating Theatre Complex, Darlinghurst, New South Wales
Workers' Compensation Courts, Sydney
1972 War Veterans' Home Nursing Unit, Narrabeen, New South Wales
1973 War Veterans' Home Rehabilitation Centre, Narrabeen, New South Wales
Patrick House, Sydney (with Ancher Mortlock Murray & Woolley)
1974 West Street Offices, North Sydney
1976 National Press Club, Canberra
Canberra Club, Canberra
Adult Deaf Society Welfare Centre and Offices, Stanmore, New South Wales
Warilla Community Centre, Shellharbour, New South Wales
1977 New South Wales Club Offices and restoration, Sydney
Commonwealth/State Law Courts, Queens Square, Sydney
1978 Hampstead Housing, Five Dock, New South Wales
1978/
79 Benjamin Government Offices, Belconnen, Canberra
1983 Royal Prince Alfred Hospital New Wing, Camperdown, New South Wales
New South Wales Housing Commission Housing, Woolloomooloo, Sydney
1984 Mechanical and Electrical Engineering Building, Australian Defence Force Academy, Canberra

Publications:

By JOHNSON: books—*Architectural Education: A Survey of Schools,* with S. Clarke, Sydney 1979; *Leslie Wilkinson,* with others, Sydney 1982; articles—"Annual Review of Architecture in Australia" in *Sydney Morning Herald,* 1963-70; "Suggestions for a Course in Architecture," with others, in *Architecture in Australia* (Sydney), June 1963; "Architect's Own House" in *Architecture in Australia* (Sydney), December 1963; "Internal Use of Plastics in Buildings" in *Architectural Science Review* (Sydney), March 1964; "The Board's Head Office Building" in *Sydney Water Board Journal,* July 1964; "No, Architects Do Not Have Their Heads in the Sand" in *Australian Financial Review* (Sydney), August 1969; "Five Buildings Tight or Loose: Contrasting Approaches to Design" in *Art and Australia* (Sydney), September 1969; "Joseph Fowell" in *Architecture in Australia* (Sydney), August 1970; "Does Town Planning Retard Development?" in *Builder NSW* (Sydney), November 1972;

"Emeritus Professor Leslie Wilkinson" in *Architecture in Australia* (Sydney), December 1973; "Leslie Wilkinson and His Architecture" in *Art and Australia* (Sydney), July/September 1974; "Sydney Opera House Since Utzon" in *Current Affairs Bulletin* (University of Sydney), August 1974; "Community Attitudes: New Respectability for an Ancient Custom" in *The Building Economist* (Sydney), December 1976; "Commonwealth State Law Courts, Sydney" in *Architecture Australia* (Melbourne), May 1978; "(Professional Responsibility) Is There a Solution?" in *The Building Economist* (Sydney), June 1978; "Government Contracts Part I" in *Architecture Australia* (Melbourne), September 1979; "RAIA:Energy and Buildings" in *Architecture Australia* (Melbourne), April/May 1980; "CAA Problems Recede" in *RIBA Journal* (London), October 1982.

On JOHNSON: books—*Towards an Australian Architecture* by Harry Sowden, Sydney 1968; *Australian Art and Artists in the Making* by Craig McGregor, Melbourne 1969; *Modern Architecture since 1900* by William J. R. Curtis, London 1982; articles—"World" in *Architectural Review* (London), February 1964; "Commonwealth State Law Courts, Sydney" in *Architecture Australia* (Melbourne), January 1978; "Commonwealth State Law Courts Building, Sydney" in *Architectural Review* (London), September 1978; "Modern Australian Architecture," special issue of *Process:Architecture* (Tokyo), March 1981; "Benjamin Offices" in *Architecture Australia* (Melbourne), March 1981.

Society has made increasingly insistent demands on architects that their buildings should meet social and economic needs while still contributing to the quality of the built environment as art. McConnel Smith & Johnson accept that, in architecture, serving society comes before the pursuit of personal artistic goals. For us, architecture is a social art in which we aim to meet the shelter needs of the people who use the spaces we design in a way which evokes a positive response. We believe that architects must consider all the information available about the needs of those for whom they design and, whenever possible, share with them the experience of developing the design.

Architecture takes place in context—an organisational context, a physical context, and a cultural context. We believe that the inspiration for architectural form should be drawn from the functional need for which the building exists, from the physical location, whether natural or man-made, and from the historical tradition of the community.

For us, architecture is a social art in another sense—today it is rarely the product of one man. We believe in working together as a team so that not only those in the architects' office but also the specialist consultants and the builder and his artisans should have a sense of involvement and be able to contribute actively to the nature and the quality of the final work. As a consequence, we have always thought of our buildings as products of the firm as a whole and not as the products of particular individuals.

Architects now working in Australia do not have the long, local traditions which surround architects working in other, older, countries. They are, however, aware of the influences brought to Australia by migrants during its relatively short history and, in this century, of the pervasive influence of the ideas of the modern movement.

An Australian tradition will grow as the Australian culture itself becomes more mature and more self-assured. Its beginnings can be seen in a response in architecture to the strong sun and clear light and the need for shade. The country itself has a sense of space; it is big and varied and still uncluttered.

We hope that we will contribute to the development of an Australian architecture which will have a character responding to the nature of the people and the country, growing out of, expressing, and contributing to Australian traditions.

—R. N. Johnson

The characteristic feature of R. N. (Peter) Johnson's building is the rationality of their design. The needs of the people who are going to use the buildings, not merely the needs of the client organization, are carefully studied, and the design revolves around the satisfaction of those needs. This is apparent in his three best-known buildings, the head office of the Sydney Water Board, the high-rise building housing the Federal/State Law Courts in Sydney, and the Benjamin Government Offices in Belconnen, Canberra.

For the Water Board Building, the study of the needs of the occupants was relatively simple, as they consisted of the staff of the Board. For the Law Courts, it was necessary to ascertain not merely the view of judges, administrators, and lawyers, but also of the members of the public who would use the courts as jurors and as litigants. This was done by interviews and questionaires, with advice from psychologists in a process that took almost two years. Models were used extensively to explain the layout to various user-groups. The result is an environment that is exceptionally humane without sacrificing the dignity appropriate to a court of law. Several of the courts are octagonal; this shape provoked discussion in the conservative legal profession, but it has proved to be successful. The law courts require three circulation systems that must be kept separate: one for the judges, one for the prisoners, and one for the public.

The Benjamin Offices were designed for government departments as yet unspecified, so flexibility was needed. Johnson avoided the anonymity often

associated with a "flexible" layout by using a hexagonal plan, which fitted the site, gave fine views over the lake on one side, and provided favourable orientation to the sun. The hexagons created some interesting interior spaces that counteracted the blandness of the office atmosphere. Each block has a distinctive colour to give identity to the building and to aid the visitor to find his way. The colours, initially conceived as an aid to circulation, are well chosen and constitute an important visual element.

Johnson has attached particular importance to the space between the inside and the outside of his buildings, occupied by a verandah or balcony in traditional Australian architecture. He devoted a great deal of attention to sun control and energy conservation long before they became fashionable. In his office buildings "the space between the inside and outside" becomes a neutral zone occupied by sunshades and sun screens, which are accurately designed in accordance with solar altitute and azimuth. The visual character of the buildings owes a great deal to this aspect of his design.

Although Johnson has a good understanding of structure, he never uses it purely for show. In the Water Board Building, exceptionally long spans produce large spaces uninterrupted by supports, but generally his structures are the simplest and most economical that will serve the purpose. His buildings therefore lack the demonstrative elements evident in the work of some other Australian architects. Johnson admits that it is sometimes necessary to rearrange the interior spaces to satisfy the aesthetic needs of the facade, but essentially the buildings are designed to serve a purpose and to satisfy human needs.

In the most recent work of the office, for example in the Mechanical and Electrical Engineering Buildings for the Australian Defence Force Academy in Canberra (1984), there is evidence of a search for a richer architectural vocabulary making reference to cultural and social context, in this case to the Australian tradition of military buildings. It is an extension of a rational approach developing further concern for human emotional response to building form.

—Henry Cowan

JONES, A(rchibald) Quincy.

American. Born in Kansas City, Missouri, 29 April 1913. Educated at the University of Washington, Seattle, 1931-36, B.Arch. 1936. Served in the United States Navy, 1945. Married Ruth E. Schneider in 1937 (divorced, 1942); married Anne B. Austin in 1943 (divorced, 1961); children: Michael, Hilary, and Timothy; married Elaine Kollins Sewell in 1962. In private practice, Los Angeles, from 1937: in partnership with Frederick E. Emmons, 1950-69. Professor of Architecture, University of Southern California, Los Angeles, 1951-67. President, 1960, Member of the Housing Committee, 1963-64 and 1969-79, and Member of the International Relations Committee, 1969-79, American Institute of Architects, Southern California Chapter. Recipient: First Honor Award, 1950, and Award of Merit, 1952, 1955, and 1957, American Institute of Architects. Fellow, American Institute of Archtects. *Died* (in Los Angeles) *3 August 1979.*

Works (all in California, except as noted):

1938 Jones House and Studio, 8661 Nash, West Hollywood, Los Angeles
1948 Nordlinger House, 11492 Thurston Circle, Bel Air, Los Angeles
1949 Fuller House, 3068 Chevy Chase, Glendale

Griffith Park Girls' Camp, Griffith Park Boulevard, Hollywood (with Smith and Contini)
1950 Mutual Housing Association Development, Los Angeles (with Smith and Contini)
Hvistendahl House, San Diego
1951 Campbell Hall School, 4717 Laurel Canyon, North Hollywood
1952 House, Bienveneda and Marquette Streets, Pacific Palisades
1953 Greenmeadows Subdivision, Palo Alto (with Anshen and Allen, and Claude Oakland)
St. Matthew's Episcopal Church, Pacific Palisades
1954 Emmons House, 661 Brooktree, Pacific Palidsades
1955 Jones House, 1223 Tigertail Road, Los Angeles (destroyed by fire)
Research Village, Barrington, Illinois
1959 Biological Sciences Building, University of California at Santa Barbara
1960 Faculty Center, University of Southern California, Los Angeles
1963 Shorecliff Tower Apartments, 535 Ocean Avenue, Santa Monica
1964 Joseph Eichler Housing Development, Granada Hills
University Research Library, unit 1, University of California at Los Angeles
Laguna/O'Farrell Apartments, 66 Cleary Court, San Francisco
Joseph Eichler Housing Development, Thousand Oaks
1965 The Barn, 10300 Santa Monica, Westwood
Library (unit 1), Crawford Hall, Steinhaus Hall, and the Humanities-Social Sciences Building, University of California at Irvine (with William L. Pereira, and Blurock and Ellerbrock)
1966 Carillon Tower, University of California at Riverside (competition project)
1967 Chemistry Building, Unversity of California at Riverside
1969 Medical Unit, I and II, University of California at Riverside
Library, unit II, University of California at Irvine
1971 University Research Library, unit II, University of California at Los Angeles
1972 Educational Resources Center, State University of California at Dominguez Hills
1975 Mandeville Center for the Arts, University of California at San Diego, La Jolla
Warner Brothers Records Office Building, Burbank
1976 Annenberg School of Communications, unit I, University of Southern California, Los Angeles
1979 Annenberg School of Communications, unit II, University of Southern California, Los Angeles

Publications:

On JONES: articles—"Pushbutton Paradise in California" in *House and Garden* (New York), April 1953; "Escape for City Children" in *Progressive Architecture* (New York), March 1954; "Research Village" in *Arts and Architecture* (Los Angeles), April 1955; "Four Offices of Distinction" in *Architectural Forum* (New York), November 1956; "Genetrix: Personal Contributions to American Architecture" in *Architectural Review* (London), May 1957; article in *Arts and Architecture* (Los Angeles), May 1966; "Modular Project for More Flexible Hospitals" in *Progressive Architecture* (New York), September 1971; "School of Communications, University of Southern California" in *Progressive Architecture* (New York), May 1977; "Getting It All Together" by Martin Filler in *Progressive Architecture* (New York), December 1977; "A. Quincy Jones 1913-1979" by Esther McCoy in *L.A.*

A. Quincy Jones: Annenberg School of Communications, University of Southern California, Los Angeles, 1976.

Architect (Los Angeles), September 1979; "A. Quincy Jones, FAIA" in *AIA Journal* (Washington, D.C.), October 1979; "A. Quincy Jones 1913-1979" in *Progressive Architecture* (New York), October 1979; "The Morphology of Los Angeles" in Architectural Design (London), no. 8/9, 1981.

Much of A. Quincy Jones's work from the 1960s to the present has been in the design of buildings for university campuses and of office buildings, but he first gained recognition in residential work in the postwar era when the need for housing was acute. His houses set standards of excellence that affected all house design of the period, especially the tract house, to which he was one of the few to give architectural consideration. A characteristic of these small houses was the simplified structural system which allowed for spatial diversity, in contrast to the usual static box.

Typical of his early planning was Mutual Housing (with Smith and Contini), a development of 100 houses, in which the houses were adjusted to a hilly terrain with little disturbance of the contours. He was not opposed to changing the natural terrain, however, when it served environmental purposes, as in his unique proposal in 1962 to contour a flat building tract for 260 houses in order to create sight and sound barriers between houses.

Certain characteristics of Jones's large-scale work grew out of his solutions for residences, particularly in siting and in the development of flexible structural systems, although in his larger building, his experiments were aimed at the intergration of mechanical systems; previous to his researches, each system was treated as a separate element, and their haphazard installation reduced their efficiency and retrievable space. The aesthetic of the Jones buildings emerges very often from structural or mechanical simplification: the 1959 Biological Sciences Building on the Santa Barbara campus and the 1967 Chemistry Building on the Riverside campus of the University of California are visually dominated by a heavy continuous cap which houses an integrated mechanical system, and it is expressed on the interiors by a prefabricated coffered ceiling of concrete which carries conduits in the channel.

Jones never hesitated to mix heavy and delicate scale, often with great success, as in the University Research Library at UCLA (Unit I, 1964; Unit II 1971), in this case the delicate almost Gothic scale deriving from the structural expression of narrow study carrels.

With the University Research Library, he initiated a planning practice that effectively minimized the height and simplified circulation by depressing the ground story somewhat below grade and placing the entrance at the second level. The ground level

workrooms and offices are naturally lighted by windows facing a terrace which ends in a landscaped gentle upslope to grade level. The main entrance is reached by a series of stairs which are interrupted by plazas at two levels, the plazas serving as meeting places for students, with one extended to a protected patio furnished with tables. This scheme was adapted for the 1972 Educational Resources Center for the State University of California at Dominguez Hills, Units I and II (1976, 1979) of the Annenberg School of Communications at University of Southern California, the Mandeville Center for the Arts at the University of California at San Diego, and for a woodsheathed office building for Warner Brothers Records. The latter, planned around interior patios, is in the spirit of many of Jones's large houses, although even in his university buildings there are definite traces of the residential scale—a friendly scale which, combined with the exercises in simplification, created warm and principled buildings.

—Esther McCoy

JOSIC, Alexis.

French. Born in Stari Becej, Yugoslavia, 24 May 1921; emigrated to France, 1953; naturalized, 1964. Studied painting at the National Fine Art School, Belgrade, 1940-46, graduated 1946, and at the Josic Fine Art School, Belgrade (founded by his father Mladen Josic), 1940-46; studied architecture at the Grate Technical School, Belgrade, 1940-48, Dip.Arch. 1948. Served in the Yugoslav Army, 1951-52. Married Douchanka Ivanovic in 1961; children: Jovan and Marko. Architect, Ministry of Construction, Belgrade, 1945-47; Professor of Painting, Josic Fine Art School, Belgrade, 1946-47; Scenographist, National Movie Industry, Belgrade, 1948-50; Architect, ATBAT (Atelier des Bâtisseurs), Paris, 1953-54; Partner, with Georges Candilis, *q.v.,* and Shadrach Woods, *q.v.,* Atelier Candilis-Josic-Woods, Paris, 1953-63. In private practice, Sèvres, France, since 1963. Professor of Architecture, Fine Arts School of Paris (Atelier Candilis-Josic), 1961-64, and Faculty of Architecture of the Unité Pédagogique 5, Paris, 1971-74. Recipient: First Prize, Marseille Housing Competition, 1959; French Government Prize in Town Planning, 1959; First Prize, Toulouse-le-Mirail New Town Competition, 1960; First Prize, Free University of Berlin Competition, 1963; First Prize, Hilton Hotel Competition, Dakar, Senegal, 1972; First Prize, Lille-Est New Town Competition, 1972; Gold Medal for Architecture, Society for the Encouragement of Arts and Industry, France, 1974. Member, l'Ordre des Architectes Francçais, 1963. Address: Alexis Josic—Architecte, 5 rue Carle Vernet, 92310 Sèvres, France.

Works:

1953/
54 Housing for the North Pole (project; with ATBAT)
Operation Emmaus (low-cost housing), France (competition project; with ATBAT)
1954/
55 Opération Million: 3,600 housing units, France, particularly the paris suburbs (with George Candilis and Shadrach Woods)
1956/
61 Plan and housing for the new town of Bagnols-sur-Cèze, France (with Georges Candilis and Shadrach Woods)
1959 Housing (4,000 units), Marseille (with George Candilis and Shadrach Woods)
1960 Urban pre-fabricated houses, Algeria (competition project; with George Candilis and Shadrach Woods)

Master plan for the new town of Toulouse-le-Mirail, France (with George Candilis and Shadrach Woods)

1961 New town of 30,000 inhabitants, Caen, France (competition project; with Georges Candilis and Shadrach Woods)

New town of 10,000 inhabitants, Hamburg, West Germany (competition project; with Georges Candilis and Shadrach Woods)

1962 University for 2,000 students, Bochum, West Germany (competition project; with Georges Candilis and Shadrach Woods)

1963 Plan for the centre of Frankfurt (project; with Georges Candilis and Shadrach Woods)

Master plan of Fort Lamy, Chad, Africa (with Georges Candilis and Shadrach Woods)

Master plan for the Free University of Berlin (with Georges Candilis and Shadrach Woods)

1964/
65 Cité Artisanale (Workshop Centre for Artisans), Sèvres, France (with George Candilis and Shadrach Woods)

1965/
66 Housing (2,000 units), Morangis, France (project)

1965/
67 Regional plan for the development of tourism, Aveyron, France

1965/
72 Master plan for the centre of Sèvres, France

1966/
67 Water Treatment Plant, Toulouse-le-Mirail, France (with George Candilis)

1966/
68 Faculty of Literature, Restaurant, Administration Building, and Sports Facilities, University of Toulouse-le-Mirail, France (with Georges Candilis)

1967 Rural plan for Brittany (competition project)

Housing for a holiday resort, Collioure, France (project)

1968 Thermo-Electric Building, Toulouse-le-Mirail, France

Plan for Chamarande, France

1969/
70 Commercial Centre and Housing, Sèvres, France

Plan for a neighborhood of Limoges, France

Housing (10,000 low-cost units), Lima, Peru (competition project; with Georges Candilis)

1970 Hilton Hotel, Lahore, Pakistan (with Georges Candilis)

1971 Tourism facilities for the peninsula of Lavrotto, Monaco (competition project; with Georges Candilis)

1972 Water Treatment Plant, Neuilly-sur-Marne, France

Hilton Hotel, Dakar, Senegal (competition project)

1972/
78 New town of Lille-Est, France (with François Calsat)

1973 Plan for the redevelopment of Vanves, near Paris

1974 Administrative Centre, Besançon, France (competition project)

Department of Sciences, University of Isfahan, Iran (competition project; with Fereydoun Davarpanah)

1974/
78 Les Passage District, Evry New Town, France: master plan; dwellings; university department of technology; commercial art and workshop centre; international youth hotel

1977/
78 Fine Art School, Mashad, Iran (with Fereydoun Davarpanah)

Cité Artisanale Development (offices), Sèvres, France

1978/
79 Petit House, Magny-en-Vexin, France

Balland House, Chalon-sur-Sâone, France

City Centre Redevelopment, Angers, France (competition project)

1979/
81 Commercial Centre and Residential Complex, rue Jean-Jaurès, Vanves, Paris

1982/
84 Municipal Complex with Sports Centre, Hotel, Shops, and Offices (project)

Residential, Professional, and Parking Complex, Vanves, Paris

Reservoir and Water-Pumping Works extensions, Neuilly-sur-Marne, France

1984 Housing (90 units), Vanves, Paris

Publications:

By JOSIC: book—*Toulouse le Mirail: Birth of a New Town,* with Georges Candilis and Shadrach Woods, Stuttgart 1975; article—"Incertitudes et doctines" in *Cahiers de la recherche architecturale* (Paris), October 1980.

On JOSIC: books—*CIAM 59 in Otterlo* by Oscar Newman, Stuttgart 1961; *Architecture and the Phenomenon of Transition* by Siegfried Giedion, Cambridge Massachusetts 1967; *Candilis, Josic, Woods* by Jürgen Joedicke, Stuttgart 1968; *Architektur in Deutschland* by H. and M. Bofinger, J. Paul and H. Klotz, Stuttgart 1979; *Guide de l'architecture dans les villes nouvelles de la region Parisienne,* with introduction by J. E. Roullier and G. Salmon-Legagneur, Paris 1979; *Modern Architecture since 1900* by William J. R. Curtis, London 1982; *Guide: architecture en France 1945-1983* by Marc Emery and Patrice Goulet, Paris 1983; articles—"Candilis, Josic, Woods" in *Cimaise* (Paris), January/February 1961; "Atelier Candilis, Josic, Woods" in Architectural Design (London), January 1965; "The Work of the Architect Josic" in *Arhitektura-Urbanizam* (Belgrade), no. 58, 1969; "Free University, Berlin, West Germany" in *Techniques et architecture* (Paris), November 1973; "Berlin Free University" in *Architectural Design* (London), January 1974; "New Buildings for the Free University, Berlin-Dahlem" in *Deutsche Bauzeitschrift* (Gütersloh, West Germany), March 1974.

Alexis Josic: New Town of Lille-Est, France, 1978.

The continuously increasing, explosive, and un-controllable population growth, together with the reduction in space available for the life of the individual, provoke a deep and universal anxiety, and a search for additional space becomes mankind's obsession. The lack of vital space obliges mankind to use all of its resources to recover lost space, distribute and reorganize the space still available, and create new physical environments where the man of tomorrow can live.

The organization of life for the "mass" is the fundamental problem facing contemporary civilization. The vast increase in our numbers leads to a violent break with tradition and hastens the world towards an unavoidable transformation and change in scale. The scale of man? The scale of many men. The "mass." That is the point of reference for our world today.

The policy of "land usage" provides one of the fundamental answers to the problem of coexistence with the "mass," and town planning provides the most adequate methods of organization for the sites of collective life, the towns.

We have carried out our studies in this sphere by research into the idea of a town as an environment; we have been guided by methods of perception of architectural space. In consequence, the research has been related to the elaboration of urban systems. The prime objective of the research was to establish a system that created a vast structure that would favour the relationship of man with his environment, a reception site for the sum of man's activities, and a suitable environment for social activity. The pre-established system (mental approach) must be perceived physically (in reality) as a sum of spaces built with continuity. It is brought into being by a spatial structure that includes and organizes the "full" and the "empty" space.

In the structure that is advocated, the act of building is twofold: it creates simultaneously "full" and "empty" space; it makes them interdependent and complementary. It creates a totality of modulated and differentiated spaces, assigned to programmed functions, thus eliminating insignificant and superfluous residual space from the urban structure.

Man inhabits the empty space that is defined, articulated, and organized by the constructed area (the house, the street, the square). The house is an inhabited, contained space, defined by the "constructed area" (walls), but it is itself also the limit of an empty space on a superior scale (the street, the square). Man inhabits the total system: he lives in his dwelling, his street, his district, his town, his world. The structure must provide the idea of a spatial hierarchy that will arouse the feeling of belonging to the largest unit employed by man—the town.

This goal calls for the voluntary abandonment of a contained and definitive architecture, an architecture of objects that separate human activities, for an open and continuous architectural web that unites human activities and favours the perception of the town as an entity. The modulated geometric grid is an integral part of the structure and serves only as a language for the architecture that results. Such an architecture does not impose its specific character by architectural form. It is an open architecture, the form of which is never definitive but always developing, an architecture in waiting, of which one dimension is time.

—Alexis Josic

Alexis Josic's architectural personality is fully expressed in his Cité Artisanale (Workshop Centre for Artisans) in Sèvres, conceived and built in 1965, where he has now set up his practice: five interlocking levels of open-plan spaces overlooking a wood, with a team of young architects, his architect-wife at his side, large-scale plans on the walls, on the drawing tables paper cut-outs for studying planning modules, proportions, volumetric relationships, colours, rhythms. . . .

His architecture is based essentially on the three-dimensional modular system. That is the tool, the methodology, and the process by which he is able to organize his space into constructed and open areas, the filled-in and the unoccupied, allowing him to define and integrate different themes without "leftover" areas. The constructed masses, together with the streets and squares, form an entity that ensures a relationship between dwelling and town, domestic space and public space, and environment and provides for continuity and the possibility of growth. It was with this research into modular space in mind that he devised Cité Artisanale. The continual process of growth and evolution in time is clearly visible in the built form of the upper stories added when and where necessary without destroying the unity of the original conception—a form awaiting change, the antithesis of an object architecture that is in essence definitive.

Josic arrived at this language, this modular system, which he uses in very diverse programs, not as a matter of improvisation but as the result of long experience and deliberation. From his earliest youth, he was aware of space, of the significance of volume, and of "ambience." His father, Mladen Josic, was a well-known Yugoslav painter who founded an art school that rapidly became a centre of creative encounter and exchange of ideas. He created an exciting atmosphere, and he instilled in his son the value of "approach" and "method." Josic grew up and studied while immersed in this stimulating atmosphere. Through painting, he mastered volume; from his researches, he constructed a working method; through a constant feedback from intuition to verification, he arrived, beyond a simple response to function, at "something indefinable that touches the heart—architecture" (Le Corbusier).

Josic arrived in Paris in 1953. He settled quickly into ATBAT (Atelier des Bâtisseurs), then into partnership with Georges Candilis and Shadrach Woods. This association was decisive for each of them. The project Opération Million placed the team in the forefront of research into economical habitat, and in two years they built more than 3,600 dwellings in France. Then there were ten years of strenuous work, of prize-winning in national and international competitions, of executed works, and, above all, of research that would give birth to an ideaology. They proposed an "organization of space" instead of the "juxtaposition" of buildings and "spirit of composition." They developed the idea of "spatial continuity," where the object disappears to the benefit of the whole, creating a bond between all things, and the polyvalent urban system is the basis of architectural language. Each work was a step in the process of the doctrine—from Bagnols-sur-Cèze to the new town at Toulouse-le-Mirail, from Bochum University to the Free University of Berlin.

In 1963 Josic established his own studio, and since then he has independently created a number of works, worked again with Candilis (Faculty of Literature at the University of Toulouse-le-Mirail), and, on a completely different scale, produced a theoretical study for the Aveyron, an important development in the search for a grid plan for the development of regional tourism. In 1972 he won the important national competition for the new town of Lille-Est. It gave him the opportunity to develop and to apply his theories on "filled" and "empty" spaces to achieve spatial continuity, to create a sense of belonging to a structure greater than that of the simple dwelling. It was also an open door to constructive research toward a flexible system that would lead to a personalized architecture. This period was marked by a very fruitful collaboration with François Calsat, who died, unfortunately, in 1976.

Since then, there has been a succession of projects: master plan for a district of Vanves (2,000 dwellings along the Paris Ring Road) and the execution of 300 dwellings; the Les Passages district in Evry New Town; continuation of Lille-Est; the competition for the University of Isfahan; and the Fine Art School at Mashad in Iran. Recently, he has worked on a study of a workers' town of 30,000 inhabitants, in the desert, near a steelworks, not far from Isfahan. In principle, it is a linear town comprising two superimposed urban structures: one fulfills the need for a traditional habitat, a closely-woven structure freely interlaced with small streets and little squares; the other responds to another tradition of habitat that is typically Iranian, terraced buildings around areas of water, creating a landscape, conferring on the town its own silhouette. In this project, Josic was able to give free rein to his abilities, form a synthesis of his experience, and realize his most profound aspirations as an architect, a man, and a creator.

Today, Josic, in full possession of his powers and certain of his convictions, is an international architect of whom we can still expect a great deal.

—Renée Diamant-Berger

JUJOL i GIBERT, Josep Maria.

Spanish. Born in Tarragona, 16 September 1879. Educated at primary school in Taragona, 1885-88; De Gracia Elementary School, Barcelona, 1888-91; Provincial Institute of Higher Education, Barcelona, 1891-96; School of Architecture and Engineering, University of Barcelona, 1897-1906, Dip. Arch. 1906. Married Teresa Gilbert Mosella in 1927; son: Josep Maria, Jr. Worked in the studio of the architect Gallissà, in Barcelona, 1901-03, and in the studio of Font i Gumá, Barcelona, 1903-06; collaborated with Antoni Gaudí, Barcelona, 1906-10: first furniture designs, 1908; in private practice, Barcelona, 1907 until his death, 1949. Auxiliary Municipal Architect, Sant Joan Despí, Barcelona, from 1926. Exhibitions: *Furniture Exhibition,* Barcelona, 1923; World's Fair, Barcelona, 1929. Recipient: Architecture Prize, Fiesta de la Virtud y el Trabajo, Barcelona, 1905. *Died* (in Barcelona) *5 May 1949.*

Works:

1902 Merced Festival street decorations, Calle Fernando, Barcelona (with Gallissà)
    Gallissà House architectural graphics and staircase, Barcelona
    Cloister decorations, Barcelona (project)
    Doorway, Ensanche, Barcelona (project)
1903 House, Calle Valencia 339, Barcelona (with Gallissà)
    Altar, Church of the Holy Trinity, Santa María del Mar, Spain (with Font i Gumá)
    Watchman's cabin, gates and fences, Municipal Park, Barcelona (project)
1904 Ateneo Redevelopment Plan, Barcelona (with Font i Gumá)
    Palace with Museum (project)
    Country Palace (project)
    Historical Archives Building, Barcelona (project)
1905 Mosaics for the Basilica of Our Father, Jerusalem (with Font i Gumá)
    Amusement Park, Barcelona (project)
    Church of St. Eulalia, Barcelona (project)
    Tower (project)
    Street decorations, Calle Cos del Bou, Tarragona (project)
1906 Monument of the 1905 African War (project)
    Health Spa (project)
    Casa Batllo remodelling ("Casa de los Huesos"), 43 Paseo de Gracia, Barcelona (assisted Antoni Gaudi)
    Gallissà House entrance architectural graphics, Barcelona
1907 Casa Milá ("La Pedrera") Apartment Building, 92 Paseo de Gracia, Barcelona (assisted Antoni Gaudi)
    Apartment building, Poble Sec, Barcelona
    Alcover Church and Square temporary decorations, Tarragona
    Theatre of Patronato del Obrero, Tarragona

1909   Torre San Salvador (house), Paseo de Nuestra Senora del Coll, Barcelona
Farinera Teixidor Building, Gerona, Spain (project)

1910   Casa Escofet Mosaics, Barcelona (project)
Gibert-Romeu Tombstone, Barcelona
Cathedral of Palma, Majorca interior alterations (assisted Antoni Gaudi)

1911   Casa de Familia, Calle del Carmen, Barcelona (destroyed)
Manach Store, Calle Fernando 57, Barcelona (destroyed)
Manach Workshop alterations, Calle de Barbara 9, Barcelona (destroyed)

1912   Designs for the roof of the Cathedral, Tarragona (projects)

1913   Cases dels Periodistes, Barcelona (project)
Urban development plan for Les Corts, Barcelona (project)
Apartment building alterations, Calle Sant Oleguer, Barcelona (project)
Lift/Elevator in the Casa Iglesias, calle Mallorca 284, Barcelona
Slaughterhouse, Sant Feliu del Llobregat, Spain (project)
Torre de la Creu (house), Calle Canalias 12, Sant Joan Despí, Barcelona

1913/
   15   Baptistry and presbytery in Constanti, Tarragona

1914   Casa Ximenis, Paseo de Saavedra 17, Tarragona
Casa Befarull, Els Pallaresos, Tarragona
Apartment building, Poble Sec, Barcelona
Chapel, La Secuita Cemetery, Tarragona (project)
Gate for the main square, Montferri, Tarragona (project)

1915   Agua Radial Mines Building, 98 Paseo Nuestra Senora del Coll, Barcelona
Apartment building alterations, Calle Masens, Barcelona
Casa Negre extensions and alterations, Torrent del Negre 37, Sant Joan Despí, Barcelona

1916   Tower, Calle de las Torres, Barcelona
Manach Workhouses, Riera de Sant Miguel 39, Barcelona
Coro de Flora Tower, Calle Falanga, Sant Joan Despí, Barcelona
Apartment building, Calle del Oro, Gracia, Barcelona

1917   Queralt Tower, Calle Pineda 1, Barcelona
Casa Xatruc extensions, La Canonja, Tarragona
Church Bell-Tower, Creixell de Mar, Tarragona
La Budallera Country House alterations, Tarragona
Estate Buildings, Calle Alcolea, Barcelona
Planells Family Tombstone, Barcelona
Parish church baptistry, Alforja, Tarragona (project)

1917/
   20   Schools, Els Pallaresos, Tarragona

1918   House, Calle Verge del Pilar 24, Barcelona
Casa Iglesias, Tarragona (project)
Del Carmen Chapel, Tarragona
San Salvador Family Tombstone, Barcelona
Vda. Casanovas Factory alterations, Barcelona
Convent of the Carmelitas de Badalona, Barcelona (project)
House extensions, Plaza de la Concordia, Barcelona

1918/
   23   Vistabella Church, Tarragona

1920   Casa Malaquer alterations, Sant Joan Despí, Barcelona
Town Hall, Els Pallaresos, Tarragona
Casa Andreu, Plaza de la Iglesia, Els Pallaresos, Tarragona
City Theatre, Barcelona (project)
Gozos de San Silverio (project)

1921   Sisters Oblatas de Bellesguard Building alterations, Barcelona
Senoras Tangenelli Tower, Vallcarca, Barcelona

1922   House, Calle de la Independencia, Barcelona
Samontá (Negre Estate) Development Plan, Sant Joan Despí, Barcelona (project)
Apartment building, Calle del Bruc, Barcelona
Tower, Calle Sicilia, Barcelona (project)
House, Calle Sant Benet, Barcelona
Hospital Espanol, Mexico (competition project)
Public Library (competition project)
Tower, Calle Verdaguer 9, Sant Joan Despí, Barcelona

1924   Casa Planells, Avenida Diagonal 332, Barcelona
Apartment building, Calle San Salvador, Barcelona
Apartment building, Calle de Sant Benet 20, Barcelona
Jujol House, Paseo de Canalias, Sant Joan Despí, Barcelona (project)
Tombstones, Municipal Cemetery, Tarragona

1925   Camprubi Family Vault (project)
Ermita del Roser interior decoration, Vallmoll, Tarragona
Marble Tombstones, Municipal Cemetery, Tarragona (with Arana)

1926   Casa Manach Store electric sign, Barcelona
Ermita de Lloret alterations, Renau, Tarragona
Llobregat Cinema, Sant Joan Despí, Barcelona
Sant Francesc Chapel, Rambla Sant Carles, Tarragona
Reconstruction and development plan for the Roman Amphitheatre, Tarragona (project)
Shrine, Montserrat, Montferri, Tarragona
Casa Rovita architectural graphics and alterations, Calle Mossen Cinto Verdaguer 41, Sant Joan Despí, Barcelona
Lloret Shrine Fountain, Bràfim, Tarragona (later altered)
Ermita del Roser floors, Vallmoll, Tarragona
Casa Joaquim oratory, Sant Joan Despí, Barcelona
Apartment building extensions, calle Libertat, Barcelona
Blessed Sacrament Chapel, Parish Church, Sant Joan Despí, Barcelona (destroyed)
Escuela del Trabajo Arches, Barcelona
Casa Solé window-grille, Els Pallaresos, Tarragona

1927   Esperanza Xaux House extensions, Calle Verdaguer, Sant Joan Despí, Barcelona

1927/
   29   Palacio del Vestido, World's Fair, Plaza de Espana, Barcelona (with Calzada; later altered)

1928   Town Hall alterations, Montferri, Tarragona (project)
Samontá (Negre Estate) Development Plan II, Sant Joan Despí, Barcelona (Project)
Church of Sant Joan Despí garden development, Barcelona
Torre Dot extensions and alterations, Sant Joan Despí, Barcelona (destroyed)
Torre Campubri, between Sant Joan Despí and Cornellà de Llobregat, Barcelona

1928/
   29   Fountain, World's Fair, Plaza de Espana, Barcelona

1929   Land development plan for Sant Joan Despí, Barcelona (project)

1930   Commemorative gravestones, Tarragona (with Arana)

1931   Rectory renovations, Bisbal del Penedès, Tarragona

1932   Torre Jujol (house), Calle Mossèn Cinto Verdaguer 45, Sant Joan Despí, Barcelona

1933   Baptistry windows and chapel renovations, Parish Church, Sant Joan Despí, Barcelona (destroyed)
Fomento Sindicato Agrícola Theatre, Sant Joan Despí, Barcelona (later altered)
Pacual-Carrera House oratory, Barcelona (destroyed)
Casa Pujol facade, Vallmoll, Tarragona (project)

1934/
   35   Presbytery windows, floors and furnishings, Parish Church, Roda de Barà, Tarragona

1935   Mas Carreras renovations, Roda de Barà, Tarragona
New Rectory, Sant Joan Despí, Barcelona (project)

1939   New Parish Church, Sant Joan Despí, Barcelona (project)
Lloret Shrine Presbytery, Bràfim, Tarragona (project)
Monument to the Fallen, Fosos de Santa Elena, Castillo de Montjuic, Barcelona (project)
Apartment building renovations, Calle del Arco del Teatro, Barcelona
House extensions, Sant Joan Despí, Barcelona
Parish Church renovation, Roda de Barà, Tarragona (project)
Parish Church renovation, Campins, Barcelona (partially destroyed)
Carmelitas de la Caridad Convent School alterations, Tarragona
House extensions, Calle Augusto 7, Sant Feliu de Llobregat, Barcelona
Parish Church of Santa Mónica, Barcelona (project)

1940   Monument to the Holy Assumption (project)
Classroom and work archives alterations, School of Architecture, Barcelona
Presbytery and altar, Guimerà, Lerida, Spain
"Gremi de Pagesos" Church alterations, Placa Sant Llorenc, Tarragona
Presbytery floors and altar, El Vendrell, Tarragona

1941   Holy Week Float (project)
Monument to the Fallen, Placa del Marcat, San Joan Despí, Barcelona

1941/
   45   Bonastre Church restoration, Tarragona

1942   Rose Window and Santa Vedrina Memorial Stone, Baptistry of the Basilica del Pino, Barcelona
Casa Solé alterations, Els Pallaresos, Tarragona
Bonastre Baptistry, Tarragona
Blessed Sacrament Altar, El Vendrell, Tarragona

1943   Carmelitas de la Caridad Convent extensions, Calle Agusta 7, Tarragona
"Old Custodia" Guard-House reconstruction, Belltall, Tarragona
Carmelitas de la Caridad Convent, Gerona, Spain (project)
Parish Church interiors, Sant Joan Despí, Barcelona
Casa de l'Abadessa alterations, Tarragona
Pulpit and confessionals, Blessed Sacrament Chapel, El Vendrell, Tarragona
Presbytery, Bonastre Church, Tarragona

1943/
   48   Colonia Güell Church altar, Barcelona

1943/
   49   Torre Codina alterations, del Canyet, Badalona, Barcelona

1944   Emilia Fortuny House alterations, Els Pallaresos, Tarragona
Chapel of Mas Carreras alterations and renovation, Roda de Barà, Tarragona
Samontá (Negre Estate) Development Plan III, Sant Joan Despí, Barcelona (project)
Shrine, Bonastre Church, Tarragona
San José Altar, El Vendrell, Tarragona

1945   Parish Church of Pobla de Claramunt alterations, Barcelona

1945/
47 Side altars, Church of Els Pallaresos, Tarragona
1945/
49 Parish Church of Capellades alterations, Barcelona
1946 Sanctuary, Church of the Hospital at Capellades, Barcelona
1947 Parish Church of San Antonio windows, Vilanova i la Geltrú, Barcelona
"Casa de Amparo" presbytery and main altar, Vilanova i la Geltrú, Barcelona
Pared Delgada Hermitage, Le Selva del Camp, Tarragona, Spain (project)
Parish Church facade and main altar, La Selva del Camp, Tarragona
Utilitarian Bungalows (projects)
Chapel of the Sacrament, La Bisbal del Penedès, Tarragona (project)
Dominicas de la Annunciata Convent extensions, Calle Doctor Dou, Barcelona
1948 Parish Church of Sant Colomba de Gramenet alterations, Barcelona
Blessed Heart Altar, Parish Church of Sant Antoni, Vilanova i la Geltrú, Barcelona (unfinished)
1949 Carmelitas de la Caridad Convent extensions, Vinalesa, Valencia
Bank Agency Building, Sant Joan Despí, Barcelona (destroyed)
Samontá (Negre Estate) Development Plan, Sant Joan Despí, Barcelona (final project)

Publications:

By JUJOL: articles—in *Catalunya Nova* (Barcelona), 2 February 1908; "Necrologia de Concepcion Mallafre" in *La Veu de Catalunya* (Barcelona), 5 July 1922; "L'Esglesia Primera de Vistabella" in *Lo Missatger del Sagrat Cor de Jesus* (Barcelona), March 1923; "Necrologia de Angel Bru" in *Tarragona*, 29 April 1924; "El Nuevo Pendon" in *La Cruz* (Tarragona), 18 November 1925; "Fiestas Centenarias C. de la C." in *Tarragona*, 30 May 1926; "Necrologia de Casimir Llobel" in *La Veu de Catalunya* (Barcelona), 24 January 1929; "El Palacio del Vestido" in *El Iman* (Barcelona), December 1929.

On JUJOL: books—*El Arte Modernista Catalan* by A. Cirici Pellicer, Barcelona 1951; *Arte Religioso Actual en Cataluña* by J. Ferrando Roig, Barcelona 1952; *Barcelona, entre el Pla Cerda i el Barraquisme* by Oriol Bohigas, Barcelona 1963; *Arquitectura Modernista* by Oriol Bohigas, Barcelona 1968; *La Arquitectura de Josep María Jujol* by Josep María Jujol Jr., J. F. Ràfols and C. Flores, Barcelona 1974; *J. M. Jujol, Architect* by R. Saarista and V. Ligtelijn, New York 1980; *Gaudi, Jujol y el modernismo catalan* by Carlos Flores, with prologue by George Collins, Madrid 1982.

The force that pushed Josep María Jujol to the limits of architectural creativity has left us with an astounding lesson in design. His works are characterized by their ability to solve the problems created by the interaction of his two methods of artistic creation—a juxtaposition of different geometrical systems and an independent pictorial composition applied to the resulting form. He was no doubt a precursor of Dada and Surrealism, working from both the cultural freedom of the Catalan Modernisme movement and the discipline of the Noucentist cultural reaction.

The juxtaposition of different geomerical systems can be clearly observed in his Casa Planells, with the curvilinear facade added on to the regular plan, and in his Torre de la Creu, where the merging of five cylinders is regulated by the clean cut of the party wall and the other orthogonal divisions. The unity of the cylindric composition destroys the semi-detached function, which in turn is set against the curvilinear space inside. This tense double-game is one of the great creative characteristics of Jujol's work that sets it apart from, and to some extent above, the work of Antoni Gaudí.

Jujol's most satisfying work is his country parish church in Vistabella. It is essentially a building within a building. The spire, in the centre, consists of a pyramid formed by four columns, which in turn support the vaults that rise over the main space. Wrapped around this space is an aisle, the roof of which spirals up, supporting steps that can take the visitor from the ground to the belfry without his having to enter the church. The plan, which is square, is composed axially along the diagonal, with the entrance at one point and the altar at the other. This tendecey to introduce the diagonal in his compositions is found not only in the planning of major elements but also in the design of details, like the fences that surround several of his small houses, from Torre San Salvador to the Torre Jujol in Sant Joan Despí.

Jujol's other characteristic method is one of architectural graphics, a technique *(esgrafiats* in Catalan) of coloured "stucco," a favourite decorative element used by most Modernist architects on facades. The highly original "calligraphic" style of Jujol is unmistakable, be it a severe, classic rectangular composition or one of baroque lyricism. This graphic ornamentation follows its own internal design structure independent of the architecture that supports it. Independent, but not separate, as Jujol drew lines of colour casually linking a window to a door or a ceiling. Venturi's suggestion that architecture also consists of decorated sheds is a particularly happy phrase to describe this essential part of Jujol's work. Jujol's metalwork is also essentially graphic, with hatched bars contrasting with thin plate strips— best seen in the balcony railings of the Casa Milà, designed in collaboration with Gaudí. Once one has observed Jujol on his own, it is easy to identify his work when collaborating with Gaudí—for example, the "sea-weed" balconies and plaster ceilings of the Casa Milà or the alterations to the Cathedral in Palma.

Jujol took form and pattern and destroyed their normal limis so that they emerged together to produce anarchitecture that is still extraordinarily stimulating and relevant to the twentieth century.

—David Mackay

JUMSAI, Sumet.

Thai. Born in Bangkok, 30 March 1939. Educated at Cambridge University, England (Brancusi Travelling Fund Award, 1963; Breezewood Foundation Scholarship, 1965; JDR III Scholarship, 1965), B.A. 1961, M.A. 1963, Dip. Arch. 1963, and Ph.D. in architectural studies 1967. Married Suthini Jumsai in 1970; children: Siriprapha and Prisdha. Architect, and Assistant to the Chief of the Division of Comprehensive Planning, Thailand Department of Town and Country Planning, Bangkok, 1965-69; Principal, DEC Consultants, Bangkok, 1970-72, and Sumet Likit Tri and Associates, Bangkok, 1972-75. Since 1975, Managing Director, Sumet Jumsai Associates Co. Ltd., Bangkok. Executive Director, APAC (Asian Planning and Architectural Consultants), Hong Kong, since 1969. Guest Lecturer and Visiting Critic, Faculty of Architecture, Silpakorn University, Bangkok, 1967-69, and Chulalongkorn University, Bangkok, since 1970. Member, Government Committee for the Conservation and Registration of Historic Monuments, Bangkok, 1972-75; Chairman, Arts Committee of the Siam Society, Bangkok, 1975. Member, National Board of Environment, Bangkok, since 1976. Exhibitions: Museum of Modern Art, New York, 1979. Member, Association of Siamese Architects under Royal Patronage; Member, World Society of Ekistics. Address: Sumet Jumsai Associates, 106/1 Sukhumvit 53, Bangkok 110110, Thailand.

Works:

1969 Office for the Private Properties of H.M. The King, Bangkok
1970 Nava Nakorn Satellite Town, Pathumthani District, near Bangkok (with Likit Hongladarom and David A. Bailey)
British Council Building, Bangkok
1971 Dr. Pierra Foundation Children's Canteen, Bangkok
Residence for the President of Siam Motors, Sukhumvit 55, Bangkok
1972 Siam Country Club, Pattaya, Thailand Daikin Showroom/Offices, Bangkok
School for the Blind, Bangkok
1973 Guest House, Siam Country Club, Pattaya, Thailand (with Vunchai Nitisophon)
Siam Motors Showroom, Ubol, Thailand
Siam Motors Showroom, Nakorn Pathom, Thailand
Apartments and architect's office, Bangkok
1974 Refrigerator plant, Bangna-Trad Highway, Thailand
1975 Car air-conditioner factory, Bangna-Trad Highway, Thailand
Ambassador Cinema, Bangkok
Private museum/library, Bangkok
1976 Bank of Asia Branch Office, Bang Pakong, Thailand
Bank of Asia Branch Office, Cholburi, Thailand
Bank of Asia Warin Branch Office, Ubol, Thailand (with Somboon Skoolisariyaporn)
1977 Science Museum, Bangkok (with Tri Devakul and Mrs. Kwanchai Laksanakorn)
Siam Motors Industrial Estate, Bagna-Trad Highway, Thailand
Nissan Car Assembly Plant, Bangna-Trad Highway, Thailand (with Sawan Imarom)
Nissan Car Assembly Plant Canteen, Bangna-Trad Highway, Thailand (with Sawan Imarom)
Yamaha Motocycle Factory, Bangna-Trad Highway, Thailand
Low-cost housing, Nava Nakorn Satellite Town, Pathumthani District, near Bangkok
Engineer's studio house, 1/46 Patanawate 10, Sukhumvit 71, Bangkok
1978 Indoor Stadium, Siam Motors Industrial Estate, Bangna-Trad Highway, Thailand (with Jarin Kamklai)
Car inspection plant, Bangna-Trad Highway, Thailand
Industrial showroom/office, Banga-Trad Highway, Thailand
Bus assembly factory, Banga-Trad Highway, Thailand
Bottle factory, Rangsit, Bangkok
Bank of Asia Branch Office, Chiangmai, Thailand (with Pong Wibhvanuwong)
Bank of Asia Branch Office, Phuket, Thailand (with Somboon Skoolisariyaporn)
Bank of Asia Head Office, Bangkok (project)
Advance factories, Nava Nakorn Satellite Town, Pathumthani District, near Bangkok (with Praphont Thanakul)
Siam Motors Head Office, Bangkok (with Kwanchai Laksanakorn)
Bank of Asia Branch Office, Namphong, Khonkaen, Thailand (with Somboon S. Isriyaporn)
1979 Bangkok Glass Industry Housing Complex, Rangsit, Greater Bangkok
1981 Shell House, Bangkok (with Rat Rattanayama and William Lim)

Energy Technology Building I and Science Demonstration Park, Asian Institute of Technology, Greater Bangkok (with Kusol Imerbsin)

Bangkok Mass Transit System (with others)

1982 Science Museum phase II, Bangkok (with Kwanchai Laksanakorn and Vichai Chittseri)

1983 Bang Saray Resort, Cholburi, Thailand (with Kwanchai Laksanakorn and T. Chaivuthikornvanich)

1984 Energy Technology Building II, Asian Institute of Technology, Greater Bangkok (with Sawan lmarom)

New Thammasat University Campus at Rangsit, Greater Bangkok (with Kwanchai Laksanakorn)

Bank of Asia Head Office, Bangkok (with Vichai Chittseri)

Publications:

By JUMSAI: books—*Seen: Architectural Forms of Northern Siam and Old Siamese Fortifications*, Bangkok 1970; editor and translator of *Six Hundred Years of Work by Thai Artists and Architects* by Joti Kalyanamitra, Bangkok 1977; articles—"Some Comparative Aspects of Angkor Thom and Ayutya" in *Journal of the Association of Siamese Architects* (Bangkok), no. 2, 1965; "Bangkok Plan: Technological Changes versus Historical and Geographical Factors" in *Bangkok World*, 9 February 1965; "Some Recollections and a Tribute to Le Corbusier, 1887-1965" in *Bangkok World*, 31 August 1965; "Ayutya. Venice of South Asia" in *Unesco Courier* (Paris), October 1966; "City Plan Thwarted" in *The Times* (London), 3 September 1970; "Sexual Connotations in Urban Symbolism" in *Nation* (Bangkok), 6 and 13 August 1972; "The Proposed Town and Country Planning Act: Towards Urban Dynamics or Standstill?" in *Nation* (Bangkok), 17 November 1974; "Polycentric Plan: Answer to the City's Problem" in *Nation* (Bangkok), 29 July 1975; "Mountain and Water: How Cities Strove for Harmony by Being Macrocosmically Planned" in *Ekistics* (Athens), September 1975; "Urbanization on Low Technology: A Strategy of Majority Survival into an Exponential World" in *City Planning Review* (Tokyo), July/August 1976; "Strategy to Combat World Urbanization" in *Bangkok Post*, August 1976; "Cartography and Beyond" in *Nation* (Bangkok), 26 March 1978; "The World of Buckminster Fuller" in *Nation* (Bangkok), 19 March 1978; "Water and Mountain" in *Ekistics* (Athens), September 1979.

On JUMSAI: books—*Architecture of the Seventies* by Udo Kultermann, London 1979; *Architekten der dritten Welt* Udo Kultermann, Cologne 1980; *Colour Outside* by Tom Porter, London 1982; *Fifty Outstanding Architects of the World* by Ivica Mladjenovic, Belgrade 1984; Articles—"Thai Design for the English" in *Progressive Architecture* (New York), October 1970; "But the Ladies Hate It" by Charles Correa in *Architecture Plus* (New York), November 1973; "Siam Country Club" in *Asian Architect and Builder* (Hong Kong), February 1974; "Bangkok's British Beatnik Building" in *South China Morning Post* (Hong Kong), 3 May 1974; "Apartments and Architect's Office/Private Library" in *Architecture + Urbanism* (Tokyo), October 1976; "A Bangkok Colori: 18 Apartments + 1 Atelier" in *Domus* (Milan), March 1977; "Per le scienze in Thailandia" in *Domus* (Milan), July 1977; "Wissenschaftliches Museum" in *Bauen und Wohnen* (Zürich), October 1977; "Science Museum" in *Architecture + Urbanism* (Tokyo), November 1977; "APAC" in *Nikkei Architecture* (Tokyo), November 1977; "Letter from Bangkok" by Harry Rolnick in *Far Eastern Economic Review* (Hong Kong), 10 February 1978; "Ein Thailhaus im Bambusgarten" in *Architektur und Wohnen* (Hamburg, West Germany), March 1980; "Sumet Jumsai—Profil eines jungen Architekten aus Thailand" in *Architektur Aktuell* (Vienna), April 1980; "Contemporary Asian Architecture," special issue of *Process: Architecture* (Tokyo), November 1980; "Reaching for a Dream: Asian Architecture— Vision or Myth?" in *Asia Week* (Hong Kong), September 1982; "Energy Technology Complex, Asian Institute of Technology" in *Architecture + Urbanism* (Tokyo), January 1983; "Design" in *Asia Magazine* (Hong Kong), May 1984.

Sumet Jumsai: Bank of Asia Head Office, Bangkok, 1985-86.

Postmodern Classicism fits in nicely with a period when an architectural epoque has come to an end. Like Mannerism, it can only exist briefly, lest the initial clever twist in the intellectual game become increasingly twisted and stale. Postmodernism in general has created many useful grammars, but these can only be useful if they help to forge new directions farther afield, and not to fossilize cleverness. Fossilizing itself in a comfortable niche, postmodern *Western* Classicism in particular has become a refuge for many who cannot design, whose business is indeed not in buildable designs, and whose pursuits only reflect an intellectual bankruptcy.

High Tech, too, cannot have its life extended (beyond Centre Pompidou). It has served its time well, and it has left behind many useful grammars. Both postmodernism and High Tech must now be digested and help to smooth the passage of our end-of-century architecture into one for the twenty-first.

While postmodernism has had the effect of a peppill to make architects artificially brave in design, and High Tech has been a potent formula to make technology a thing of beauty, time has arrived to use the licence of the former to open wider the design horizon and to link the latter, not only to abstract beauty, but also to man in his image and aspiration.

If design knows no bound (nor cultural boundary in tomorrow's world), then the robot represents a breakthrough out of such a licence and a breakthrough from the now dated High Tech. The robot is, of course, a human invention and, as such, technological. But it has become more than machinery; already it has become semi-human. Today, especially in Japan, it has become our worker, domestic help and friend, very much like a fellow human. For children, who are much more instinctive than we, it has become a personal companion and a dream and reality at the same time. In its human likeness it proclaims: I am not just machine; I am your extension, and I am your extention forward in point of time. Which is to say that "Robot Architecture," appearance aside, stands for an amalgam between man and machine. The latter no longer stands for itself or for its own aesthetics; rather it is completely humanised by and becomes an automatic part of its creator. The twenty-first century will demand this relationship.

—Sumet Jumsai

Sumet Jumsai's own remarks accurately reflect his architecture and need no further elaboration. He studied under Martin at Cambridge, and to a considerable extent, especially early in his career, a Corbusier/Martin duality can be recognized in his works. Thai sensitivity in the size and delicacy of materials that he chooses to envelope his buildings also creates vernacular spaces that can be thoroughly appreciated, even if they are somewhat Western-looking.

One of his later works is much too *Domus*-esque— a Lamborghini may look fine on an Italian auto-strada but it is totally surrealistic and even frightening in the context of the boats on the Klongs of Bangkok.

Jumsai is perhaps the most intellectual architect in Southeast Asia, but while this intellectualism is acceptable at the Architectural Association or in Cambridge, it does not sit easily with the Southeast Asian businessmen and politicians who have just "made it" or, for that matter, with the masses aspiring toward only the understandable.

Jumsai is intelligent enoughto have observed this difficulty, and I suppose he must live with and through these contradictions if he is to find an Architecture of Thailand. If a new Thai architecture does develop, he will be at the forefront.

—K. C. Lye

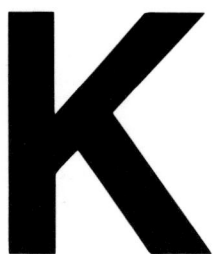

K

KAHN, Ely Jacques.
American. Born in New York City, 1 June 1884.
Studied at Columbia University, New York, B.A.
1903, B.Arch. 1907; Ecole des Beaux-Arts, Paris,
DPLG 1911. Married Elsie Paut in 1913; Beatrice
Sulzberger in 1939; Liselotte Hirshman in 1964;
children: Ely Jacques Jr., Joan and Olivia. Worked in
several architectural offices in Paris and New York,
1911-17; Architect, Buchman and Fox, New York,
1917-19; Partner, Buchman and Kahn, New York,
1919-29; in private practice, New York, 1930-40:
worked with Robert Allan Jacobs, from 1938; in
partnership with Robert Allan Jacobs, Kahn and
Jacobs, New York, 1940 until his death in 1972.
Professor of Design, Cornell University, New York,
1915; Lecturer in Architecture, Metropolitan
Museum of Art, New York, 1929-34; Director of the
Department of Architecture, Beaux Arts Institute of
Design, New York, 1931; Instructor in Design, New
York University, 1932. Member of the Committee
for Decorative Art Exhibitions, Metropolitan
Museum of Art, New York, 1929-34; Chief of the
Industrial Arts Section, *Centennial Fair,* Chicago,
1932-33; President, Municipal Art Society, New
York, 1942-45; Chairman of the Advisory Com-
mission, School of Industrial Design, New York,
1944; Consultant, U.S. Government Housing Pro-
jects, 1944-46; President, Architectural League of
New York; President, Peter Minuit Corporation,
New York; Teasurer, Eray Securities Corporation,
New York. Exhibitions: *American Industrial Art,*
Metropolitan Museum of Art, New York, 1929;
Centennial Fair, Chicago, 1933; *World's Fair,* Flush-
ing Meadow, New York, 1939; *Built in U.S.A. 1932-
1944,* Museum of Modern Art, New York, 1944.
Recipient: Painting Award, Salon des Artistes
Français, Paris, 1910; Prix Labarre, Ecole des Beaux-
Arts, Paris, 1911; Gold Medal, Fifth Avenue
Association, New York, 1921; Carnegie Corpor-
ation Study Grant, New York, 1933. Benjamin
Franklin Fellow, Royal Society of Arts, London;
Fellow, American Institute of Architects; Honorary
Member, Bund Deutscher Architekten. *Died* (in New
York City) *5 September 1972.*

Works:

1918 Ely Jacques Kahn House, Elmsford, New
York
1919 Joseph Plant Garage, Elmsford, New York
Herman Younker Garage, Elmsford, New
York
Thomas Cusack Company Building, Fifth
Avenue at 25th Street, New York
1921 Jay-Thorpe Company Building, 24 West 57th
Street, New York
1924 Quaker Ridge Golf and Country Club, New
York
1925 Hospital for Joint Dieases, Madison Avenue
at 123rd Street, New York
Arsenal Building, Seventh Avenue at 35th
Street, New York
Office Building, 550 Seventh Avenue, New
York

Office Building, Sixth Avenue at 39th Street,
New York
1926 Furniture Exchange Building, Lexington
Avenue at 32nd Street, New York
Office Building, Sixth Avenue at 37th Street,
New York
Office Building, 625 Sixth Avenue, New York
1927 Rutley's Restaurant, Broadway at 40th Street,
New York
Court Square Building, New York
Commercial Building, 247 West 35th Street,
New York
Ed Pinaud Factory, 214 East 21st Street, New
York
Insurance Center Building, 80 John Street,
New York
International Telephone and Telegraph Build-
ing, Broad and Beaver Streets, New York
Office Building, 2 Park Avenue, New York
Commercial Building, Fifth Avenue at 57th
and 58th Streets, New York
Office Building, Broadway at 37th Street, New
York
1928 Office Building, Seventh Avenue at 26th
Street, New York
Office Building, 42-44 West 39th Street, New
York
U.S. Appraisers Building, Varick, King and
Houston Streets, New York
Main Exhibition Hall, *Lord and Taylor Mod-
ern Exposition,* New York
Federation Building, 67-71 West 47th Street,
New York
1929 Jay-Thorpe Company Building 56th Street
addition, New York
Film Center Building, Ninth Avenue at 44th
Street, New York
Furniture and interiors, *Exhibition of In-
dustrial Art,* Metropolitan Museum of Art,
New York
Office Building, Broadway and 41st Street,
New York
Mrs. Alfred L. Rose Apartment, New York
Insurance Building, III John Street, New York
Glen Oaks Country Club, Great Neck, Long
Island, New York
Office Building, 530 Seventh Avenue, New
York
Yardley and Company Offices, 452 Fifth
Avenue, New York
Allied Arts Building, 304 East 45th Street,
New York
Van Cleef and Arpels Jewellery Shop, 671
Fifth Avenue, New York
1930 Office Building, 120 Wall Street, New York
Holland Plaza Building, Canal, Varick and
Watts Streets, New York
C. J. Lieberman Apartment, New York
Squibb Building, Fifth Avenue at 58th Street,
New York
Mrs. M. S. Benjamin Apartment, New York
Bonwit Teller Store, Fifth Avenue at 56th
Street, New York
1931 Buildings at 1400 and 1410 Broadway, New
York

Paramount Publik Warehouse, 521 West 43rd
Street, New York
Continental Building, Broadway at 41st
Street, New York
Richard Hudnut Building, 693 Fifth Avenue,
New York (with Eliel Saarinen)
Office Building, Lexington Avenue at 57th
Street, New York
Leron Speciality Shop, 745 Fifth Avenue, New
York
Commerce Building, Third Avenue at 44th
Street, New York
1939 Marine Building and Ballantine Restaurant,
World's Fair, Flushing, New York
1941 United Service Organization Clubhouse pro-
totypes (projects)
1944 Fort Greene Houses, Section 2, Brooklyn,
New York
Petrol Service Station prototype, New York
(project)
Municipal Asphalt Plant, East River Drive
and 91st Street, New York
1945 Savings and Loan Office prototypes (projects)
New York State Agricultural and Industrial
School, Industry, New York (project)
1947 Universal Pictures Building, 445 Park Avenue,
New York
1955 Mile High Center Building, Denver, Colorado
(with I. M. Pei and Associates)
1969 One Astor Plaza Building, New York

Publications:

By KAHN: books—*Design in Art and Industry,* New
York 1935; *Tall Buildings in New York,* lecture paper,
London 1960; *A Building Goes Up,* New York 1969;
articles—"Do Architects Want Criticism?", in
American Architect (New York) April 1930; "Con-
temporary Design in Architecture", in *AIA Journal*
(Washington, D.C.) April 1948; "American Office
Practice", in *The Architect and Building News*
(London) 15 August 1957; "Tall Buildings in New
York", in *RIBA Journal* (London) October 1960.

On KAHN: books—*American Architecture* by Fiske
Kemball, Indianapolis and New York 1928; *The
Logic of Modern Architecture: Exteriors and Inter-
iors of Modern American Buildings* by R. W. Sexton,
New York 1929; *Ely Jacques Kahn,* with foreword by
Arthur Tappan North, New York and London 1931;
Built in U.S.A. 1932-1944, exhibition catalogue
edited by Elizabeth Mock, New York 1944; *Four
Walking Tours of Modern Architecture in New York
City* by Ada Louise Huxtable, New York 1961; *Mid-
Century Architecture in America,* edited by Wolf von
Eckardt, Baltimore, Maryland 1961; articles—
"American industrial art exhibited at the Metropo-
litan Museum of Art" in *American Architect* (New
York), 3 March 1929; "Designing the Bonwit Teller
Store" in *Architectural Forum* (New York), Novem-
ber 1930; "Office Building, 120 Wall Street, New
York City" in *Architectural Record* (New York),
April 1931; "A Musical modern decor" by A.

Clairbonne in *Arts and Decoration* (New York), November 1936; "Modern Fireplaces" in *Pencil Points* (New York), October 1938; "Pix Theatre" in *Interiors* (New York), December 1940; "Cultural Centers, a building types study" in *Architectural Record* (New York), September 1941; "Service Station" in *Pencil Points* (New York), August 1944; "Home Loan Headquarters" in *Architectural Record* (New York), January 1945; "Obituary: Ely Jacques Kahn" in *The New York Times* (New York), 6 September 1972; "Getting it right the first time" by Martin Filler in *Progressive Architecture* (New York), June 1978.

Ely Jacques Kahn spent five years at the Ecole des Beaux Arts in Paris, receiving his Architecte Diplôme par le Gouvernement Français in 1911. On his return to his native America, he became Professor of Design at Cornell University and held a number of architectural teaching appointments.

He commenced practice in New York in the 1920s at the beginning of the development of high buildings in New York and laid the foundations of a very successful commercial architectural practice that is today still one of the major influences in this field of architecture. During a long and ever-expanding architectural career, he developed a unique understanding of the problems of high buildings for commercial use, and much of the modern technique of construction management and site organisation has developed from his pioneer work in New York in the 1920s and 1930s.

His approach to the architecture of the commercial skyscraper owed much to his early Beaux-Arts training. His early buildings, steel framed and clad in stone, before the days of lightweight cladding and curtain walling, set the standards for the modern skyscraper. These buildings designed by Kahn were not only practical and economically viable but were highly organised and technically very competent. His many commercial clients were impressed by the fact that these buildings not only fulfilled their intended purpose but were sound financial developments.

Many of his early writings which set out his architectural approach were considerably in advance of their time and were later widely accepted into current practice in the United States and elsewhere. His lectures in London at the Royal Institute of British Architects and elsewhere more than thirty fiveyears ago on the subject of "Tall Buildings in New York" and "American Office Practice" were received with considerable interest and were of great value to architects facing what was to them the new problem of high buildings in London and other cities of the United Kingdom.

Robert Jacobs joined the Kahn office in 1938, and the partnership of Kahn and Jacobs was formed in 1942. The practice has been responsible for an enormous output of very large buildings, mainly for commercial and industrial purposes, with a strong emphasis on tall office blocks in New York.

Kahn's work was strongly influenced by his life-long interest in all aspects of architecture and the allied arts and particularly the craftmanship of metals, glass, textiles, and related materials which sprang from his connection with the European Arts and Crafts movement. His early domestic work owned much to the influence of Voysey, Lutyens, and other English architects, and the decorative details of many of his early skyscrapers were devised from the Art Deco movement of Europe. This influence was very clearly apparent in his interior designs for restaurants and similar interiors which were fine examples of Art Deco design.

In many ways, Kahn was a pioneer in a new field of development, one he mastered completely and for which he laid foundations for later generations of architects. He was basically a modest man, cultured, widely read in several languages, a gifted painter, and held in friendly regard and respect by his contemporaries.

—Edward D. Mills

KAHN, Louis Isadore.

American. Born on the Island of Saarama, Estonia, now U.S.S.R., 20 February 1901; emigrated to the United States, to Philadelphia, 1905: naturalized, 1915. Educated at the Central High School and Pennsylvania Academy of Fine Arts, Philadelphia, 1912-20; Graphic Sketch Club, Fleisher Memorial Art School, and the Public Industrial Art School, Philadelphia, 1916-20 (Pennsylvania Academy of Fine Arts Prize, 1920); University of Pennsylvania, Philadelphia, 1920-24, B.Arch. 1924. Married Esther Virginia Israeli in 1930; daughter: Sue Ann. Draftsman with the architects Hofman and Henan, Philadelphia, 1921, and with Hewitt and Ash, Philadelphia, 1922; Teaching Assistant, University of Pennsylvania, 1923-24; Senior Draftsman, 1924-27, and Chief of Design for the *Sesqui-Centennial Exhibition*, 1925-26, City Architect's Department,

Philadelphia; studied and travelled in Europe, 1928-29; Designer, office of Paul Cret, Philadelphia, 1929-30, and Zantziger, Borie and Medary, Philadelphia, 1930-32; Organizer and Director, Architectural Research Group, Philadelphia, 1932-33; Squad Head in charge of Housing Studies, City Planning Commission, for the W.P.A. (Works Progress Administration), Philadelphia, 1933-35; Assistant Principal Architect, office of Alfred Kastner and Partner, Philadelphia, 1935-37; in private practice, Philadelphia, 1937 until his death, 1974: in association with George Howe, *q.v.*, 1941-42, with Howe and OscarStonorov, *q.v.*, 1942-43, and with Stonorov, 1943-48. Consultant Architect, Philadelphia Housing Authority, 1937, and United States Housing Authority, 1939; Consultant Architect to the Philadelphia City Planning Commission, 1946-52, 1961-62; Consultant Architect, Philadelphia Rede-

Louis I. Kahn: Richards Medical Research Building, University of Pennsylvania, Philadelphia, 1964.

velopment Authority, 1951-54. Chief Critic in Architectural Design and Professor of Architecture, Yale University, New Haven, Connecticut, 1948-57; Resident Architect, American Academy, Rome, 1950-51; Albert Farwell Bemis Professor, School of Architecture and Planning, Massachusetts Institute of Technology, Cambridge, 1956; Professor of Architecture, 1957-66, Paul Cret Professor, 1966-71, and Emeritus Professor, 1971-74, University of Pennsylvania. Member, Team 10. Exhibitions: Pennsylvania Academy of Fine Arts, Philadelphia (drawings and paintings), 1930, 1933; *Architecture in Government Housing*, Museum of Modern Art, New York, 1936; *Houses and Housing*, Museum of Modern Art, New York, 1939; *Better Philadelphia Exhibition*, Philadelphia, 1947; *The Works of Louis I. Kahn*, La Jolla Museum of Art, California, 1965; *Louis I. Kahn*, Museum of Modern Art, New York, 1966; *Louis I. Kahn*, ETH: Swiss Federal Institute of Technology, Zurich, 1969, and toured Europe; *Louis I. Kahn: Drawings*, Pennsylvania Academy of Fine Arts, Philadelphia, and toured the United States, 1978. Collections: University of Pennsylvania, Philadelphia; Museum of Modern Art, New York. Recipient: Arnold Brunner Prize, National Institute of Arts and Letters, 1960; Graham Foundation Fellowship, 1961; Philadelphia Art Alliance Medal, 1962; Frank P. Brown Medal, Franklin Institute, Philadelphia, 1964; Medal of Honor, Danish Architects Association, 1965; Annual Award, Philadelphia Sketch Club, 1966; International Silver Medal, University of Connecticut, Storrs, 1969; Centennial Gold Medal, American Institute of Architects, Philadelphia Chapter, 1969; Gold Medal of Honor, AIA, New York Chapter, 1970; Gold Medal, national AIA, 1971; Philadelphia Book Award, 1971; Creative Arts Medal, Brandeis University, Waltham, Massachusetts, 1972; Royal Gold Medal, Royal Institute of British Architects, 1972; Gold Medal, National Institute of Arts and Letters, 1973. H.H.D.: University of North Carolina, Raleigh, 1964; D.Arch.: Polytechnic, Milan, 1964; D.F.A.: Yale University, 1965; Maryland Institute College of Art, Baltimore, 1968; Bard College, Annandale-on-Hudson, New York, 1970; University of Pennsylvania, 1971; LL.D.: LaSalle College, Philadelphia, 1967; D.L.: Tulane University, New Orleans, 1972; D.H.L.: Columbia University, New York, 1974. Fellow, American Institute of Architects, 1953. Member, National Institute of Arts and Letters, 1964, American Academy of Arts and Sciences, 1968, and American Academy of Arts and Letters, 1973. Honorary Member, Royal Swedish Academy of Fine Arts, 1966, and College of Architects of Peru, 1967; Fellow, Royal Society of Arts, London, 1970. *Died* (in New York City) *17 March 1974.*

Works:

1920/
24 Entrance, United States Veterans Hospital, Philadelphia (competition project)
Shopping Center, United States Army Post, Philadelphia (competition project)
1924/
26 Buildings for the *Sesqui-Centennial Exhibition*, Philadelphia
1926/
27 Municipal Building, Philadelphia (project)
City planning studies for Philadelphia
1929/
30 Buildings for the 1933 Chicago World's Fair (project)
1929/
32 Folger Library, Washington, D.C. (with Paul Cret)
1930/
32 Department of Justice Building, Washington, D.C. (project)
1933 Slum block reclamation, Philadelphia (project)

1933/
35 Housing studies for the Philadelphia Planning Commission
1935/
39 Ahavath Israel Synagogue, Philadelphia
Homesteads Development, Hightstown, New Jersey (project)
1939 Rational City (exhibition project)
1940 Jesse Oser House, 688 Stetson Road, Melrose Park, Pennsylvania
1941/
42 Pine Ford Housing, Middletown, Pennsylvania (with George Howe)
1941/
43 Carver Court Housing, Coatesville, Pennsylvania (with George Howe and Oscar Stonorov)
1942 Pennypack Housing, Philadelphia (project; with George Howe and Oscar Stonorov)
Stanton Road Housing, Washington, D.C. (project; with George Howe)
1943 Lincoln Road Housing, Coatesville, Pennsylvania (project; with George Howe and Oscar Stonorov)
Lily Ponds Housing, Washington, D.C. (project; with George Howe and Oscar Stonorov)
Willow Run Housing, Detroit (project; with Oscar Stonorov)
194X Hotel, Philadelphia (competition project; with Oscar Stonorov)
1944 Pennypack Buildings, Philadelphia (project; with Oscar Stonorov)
1944/
45 Health Clinic extension and alterations, 22nd and Locust Streets, Philadelphia (with Oscar Stonorov)
1944/
46 Psychiatric Hospital, Monument Avenue, Philadelphia (project; with Oscar Stonorov)
1945/
49 Philip Roche House, Harts Lane, Whitemarsh Township, Pennsylvania
1946/
54 Mill Creek Redevelopment, Philadelphia (project; with Kenneth Day, Louis McAllister and Anne Tyng)
1947 Offices and Cafeteria, Container Corporation of America, Philadelphia (project; with Oscar Stonorov)
1947/
48 Plan for the Midtown City Center, Philadelphia (exhibition project)
1947/
49 Winslow Tompkins House, Apalogan Road and School House Lane, Germantown, Philadelphia (project)
1948 Jefferson Memorial, St. Louis (competition project)
Radbill Oil Company Office interiors, 1724 Chestnut Street, Philadelphia (project)
1948/
49 Morton Weiss House, Norristown, Pennsylvania
1949 Coward Glass Front Shoe Store, Philadelphia (with Oscar Stonorov)
Samuel Genel House, Lancaster Avenue and Indian Creek Drive, Lower Merion Township, Pennsylvania
1949/
50 Pincus Therapy Building, Psychiatric Hospital, Ford and Monument Roads, Philadelphia (with Isadore Rosenfeld)
1950 St. Luke's Hospital alterations, Philadelphia (project)
Jacob Sherman House, 414 Sycamore Avenue, Lower Merion Township, Pennsylvania
1950/
53 Radbill Psychiatric Hospital, Philadelphia (with Isadore Rosenfeld)
Temple and Poplar Public Housing, Philadelphia (project; with Kennedy Day, Louis McAllister and Anne Tyng)

1951/
53 Yale Art Gallery, New Haven, Connecticut (with Douglas Orr)
1952/
53 Midtown-Penn Center, Philadelphia (project)
1952/
57 City Tower Municipal Building, Philadelphia (project; with Anne Tyng)
1952/
62 Mill Creek Public Housing, 46th Street and Fairmount Avenue, Philadelphia (with Kenneth Day, Louis McAllister and Anne Tyng)
1953 Ralph Roberts House, School House Lane, Germantown, Philadelphia
1954 Adath Jeshurun Synagogue, Elkins Park, Pennsylvania (project)
Weber de Vore House, Montgomery Avenue, Springfield Township, Pennsylvania (project)
Francis Adler House, Davidson Road, Germantown, Philadelphia (project)
1954/
56 Medical Service Building, AFL-CIO, Philadelphia (demolished, 1973)
1954/
59 Bath House, and Master Plan, Jewish Community Center, Lower Ferry Road, Trenton, New Jersey
1955/
57 Martin Research Institute, Fort Meade, Maryland (project)
1956 Library, Washington University, St. Louis (competition project)
1956/
57 Midtown City Center Forum, Philadelphia (project)
Enrico Fermi Memorial, Chicago (competition project)
1957/
59 Irving Shaw House additions and alterations, 2129 Cypress Street, Philadelphia
1957/
61 Fred Clever House, Hunt Tract, Delaware Township, Pennsylvania
1957/
64 Richards Medical Research Building, University of Pennsylvania, Philadelphia
1958 Lawrence Morris House, Mount Kisco, New York (project)
1958/
61 *Tribune Review* Building, Greensburg, Pennsylvania
1959 Robert Fleisher House, Woodland Glen, Elkins Park, Pennsylvania (project)
Morton Goldenberg House, Rydal, Pennsylvania (project)
1959/
61 Esherick House, Chestnut Hill, Pennsylvania
Bernard Shapiro House, Hidden River Road, Penn Valley, Narberth, Pennsylvania
United States Consulate, Luanda, Angola (project)
1959/
62 Mill Creek Community Center, 46th and Aspen Streets, Philadelphia
1959/
65 Laboratory Buildings for the Salk Institute, La Jolla, California
1959/
67 Unitarian Church and School Building, Rochester, New York
1960 Norman Fisher House, Mill Road, Hatboro, Philadelphia
Municipal Building, Mill Creek and Bath Road, Levittown, Bristol, Pennsylvania (project)
1960/
61 Franklin D. Roosevelt Memorial, Washington, D.C. (competition project)
1960/
65 Erdman Hall Dormitories, Bryn Mawr College, Pennsylvania
1961 Thames Barge, London, for the American

Wind Symphony Orchestra, Pittsburgh
Carborundum Co. Warehouse and Sales Office, Niagara Falls, New York (project)
General Motors Exhibition Building, for the 1964 World's Fair, New York (project)
Plymouth Swim Club Building, Pennsylvania (project)
Chemistry Building, University of Virginia, Charlottesville (project)
Shapero Hall of Pharmacy, Wayne State University, Detroit (project)

1961/
62 Mid-town/Market Street East Development, Philadelphia (project)

1961/
64 Levy Memorial Playground, Riverside Park, New York (project; with Isamu Noguchi)

1961/
70 Mikveh Israel Synagogue, Philadelphia (project)

1962/
74 Sher-E-Banglanagar: New Capital of Bangladesh, Dacca: Citadel of Assembly; National Assembly; Prayer Hall; Hostels; Ayub Hospital
Institute of Management, Ahmedabad, India (with B. V. Doshi and A. D. Raje)

1963 President's Estate, Islamabad, Pakistan (project)

1963/
64 Master plan for the Gandhinagar Capital City, Gujarat, India

1964/
67 Philadelphia College of Art (project)
Interama/Pan American Center, Miami (project)

1964/
72 Jewish Martyrs' Memorial, Battery Park, New York (project)

1965/
68 Dominican Sisters Convent, Media, Pennsylvania (project)

1965/
74 Theatre of the Performing Arts, Fine Arts Center, Fort Wayne, Indiana

1966 St. Andrew's Priory, Valyermo, California (project)
Stern House, Washington, D.C. (project)

1966/
70 Olivetti-Und erwood Factory, Harrisburg, Pennsylvania

1966/
72 Kimbell Art Museum, Will Rogers Road West, Fort Worth, Texas (with Preston M. Gerne and Associates)
Temple Beth-El Synagogue, Chappaqua, New York

1966/
73 Kansas Office Building, Kansas City (project)

1967/
68 Broadway Church of Christ Church and Office Building, New York (project)

1967/
72 Library and Dining Hall, Phillips Exeter Academy, New Hampshire

1968 Delaware Valley Family Living Mental Therapy Building, New Britain, Pennsylvania (project)

1968/
73 Hill Central Area Redevelopment, Columbus and Washington Avenues, New Haven, Connecticut (project)

1968/
74 Hurva Synagogue, Jerusalem (project)
Congress Hall, Venice (project)
Wolfson Center, University of Tel Aviv, Israel (project)

1969/
74 Center for British Art and Studies, Yale University, New Haven, Connecticut

1970 Dual Movie Theatre, Sansom Street, Philadelphia (project)

1970/
74 Family Planning Center, Khatmandu, Nepal

1971/
73 Inner Harbor, Baltimore (project)

1971/
74 Design for the 1976 *Bi-centennial Exposition,* Philadelphia

1972/
74 Independence Mall Area Development, for the 1976 *Bi-centennial Exposition,* Philadelphia (project)
Hotel, Government Hill Development, Jerusalem (project)

1973/
74 Theological Library, University of California, Berkeley (project)
Roosevelt Memorial, Roosevelt Island, New York (project)
Pocono Arts Center, Luzerne County, Pennsylvania (project)

1974 Abbasabad Development, Government Complex, Tehran (project; with Kenzo Tange)
Korman House, Whitemarsh Township, Pennsylvania

Publications:

By KAHN: books—*Why City Planning Is Your Responsibility,* with Oscar Stonorov, New York 1942; *You and Your Neighborhood,* with Oscar Stonorov, New York 1944; *The Notebooks and Drawings of Louis I. Kahn,* edited by Richard Saul Wurman and Eugene Feldman, Philadelphia 1962, 2nd edition, Cambridge, Massachusetts 1973; *Louis I. Kahn: Talks with Students,* Houston, Texas 1969; *Light Is the Theme: Louis I. Kahn and the Kimbell Art Museum* (commentary by Kahn), compiled by Nell E. Johnson, Fort Worth, Texas 1975; *Louis I. Kahn: Sketches for the Kimbell Art Museum,* with text by Marshall D. Meyers, Fort Worth, Texas 1978; articles—"Monumentality" in *New Architecture and City Planning,* edited by Paul Zucker, New York 1944; "Toward a Plan for Midtown Philadelphia" in *Perspecta* (New Haven, Connecticut), no. 2, 1953; "Architecture Is the Thoughtful Making of Spaces" in *Perspecta* (New Haven, Connecticut), no. 4, 1957; "Form and Design" in *Architectural Design* (London), April 1961; "A Statement" in *Arts and Architecture* (Los Angeles), May 1964; "Remarks" in *Perspecta* (New Haven, Connecticut), no. 9/10, 1965; "Structure and Form" in *Royal Architectural Institute of Canada Journal* (Toronto), November 1965; "Louis Kahn: Statements and Architecture" in *Zodiac* (Milan), vol. 17, 1967; "Architecture: Silence and Light" in *On the Future of Art* by Arnold Toynbee and others, New York 1970; "Not for the Faint-Hearted" in *AIA Journal* (Washington, D.C.), June 1971; "The Room, The Street, and Human Agreement" in *AIA Journal* (Washington, D.C.), September 1971; "Louis I. Kahn: Royal Gold Medallist" in *RIBA Journal* (London), August 1972; "The Invisible City: An Architect Speaks His Mind: Louis Kahn Talks . . ." in *House and Garden* (New York), October 1972; "Room, Window and Sun" in *Canadian Architect* (Toronto), June 1973; "L'Accord de l'homme et l'architecture: une conference de Louis Kahn" in *La Construction Moderne* (Paris), July/August 1973; "Clearing: Interview with Louis Kahn" in *Via* (Philadelphia), vol. 2; 1973; "Harmony Between Man and Architecture" in *Design* (Bombay), March 1974; "1973: Brooklyn, New York" in *Perspecta* (New Haven, Connecticut), no. 19, 1982.

On KAHN: books—*Louis I. Kahn* by Vincent Scully Jr., New York 1962 (includes bibliography); *Man Made Philadelphia* by Richard Saul Wurman, Philadelphia 1972; *Modern Movements in Architecture* by Charles Jencks, London 1973; *Louis I. Kahn* by Romaldo Giurgola and Jaimini Mehta, Zurich and Boulder, Colorado 1975; *Eighteen Years with Architect Louis I. Kahn* by August Komendant, Englewood, New Jersey 1975; *Louis I. Kahn* by A + U Editors, Tokyo 1975; *Global Architecture: Louis I.*

Kahn, edited by Yukio Futagawa, Tokyo 1975; *GA 38: Louis I. Kahn – Yale University Art Gallery; Kimbell Art Museum, Fort Worth,* edited by Yukio Futagawa, Tokyo 1976; *GA 5: Louis I. Kahn – Richards Medical Research Building, Pennsylvania; Salk Institute for Biological Studies, California,* edited by Yukio Futagawa, Tokyo 1977; *Louis I. Kahn: The Complete Works 1935-1974* by Heinz Ronner, Sharad Jhaveri and Alessandro Vesella, Basle, Stuttgart, and Boulder, Colorado 1977 (includes bibliography); *Between Silence and Light: Spirit in the Architecture of Louis I. Kahn* by John Lobel, Boulder, Colorado 1979; *Louis I. Kahn: idea e immagine* by Christian Norberg-Schulz, Rome 1980; articles—"The Philadelphia Cure" in *Architectural Forum* (New York), April 1952; "Les Reseux à Trois Dimensions" by Robert Le Ricolais in *L'Architecture d'Aujourd'hui* (Paris), September 1954; "The New Brutalism" by Reyner Banham in *Architectural Review* (London), December 1955; "Architect Louis I. Kahn and His Strong-Boned Structures" by Walter McQuade in *Architectural Forum* (New York), October 1957; "Louis Kahn" by E. and R. Katan in *L'Architecture d'Aujourd'hui* (Paris), no. 105, 1962/63; "Louis Kahn" in *Zodiac* (Milan), October 1967; "Louis I. Kahn," special issue of *L'Architecture d'Aujourd'hui* (Paris), February/March 1969; "Louis I. Kahn," special issue of *Architectural Forum* (New York), July/August 1972; "Louis I. Kahn," special issue of *Architecture + Urbanism* (Tokyo), January 1973; "Review of Recent Work: Louis Kahn" by Alison Smithson in *Architectural Design* (London), August 1973; "Within the Folds of Construction" by William Marlin in *Architectural Forum* (New York), October 1973; "Homage to Louis Kahn," special issue of *Werk* (Zurich), July 1974; "Yale Center for British Art" by Vincent Scully Jr. in *Architectural Record* (New York), June 1977; "Kahn at Yale" by William Jordy in *Architectural Review* (London), July 1977; Masters of Light: Louis Kahn" by Marshall Meyers in *AIA Journal* (Washington, D.C.), September 1979; Louis Kahn and the French Connection" by Kenneth Frampton in *Oppositions* (New York), Fall 1980; "Louis Kahn's last work" in *Architettura* (Rome), January 1981; "Louis Kahn in India" by B. K. Doshi in *Architectural Association Quarterly* (London), October 1981; "Louis Kahn", special issue of *Arquitecturas Bis* (Barcelona), January/February 1982; "Kahn and Yale" by William S. Huff in *Journal of Architectural Education* (Washington, D.C.), Spring 1982; "Giurgola on Kahn" by Romaldo Giurgola in *AIA Journal* (Washington, D.C.), August 1982; "Kahn's Warehouse of Art" by Reyner Banham in *New Society* (London), 18 November 1982.

Bibliography—*Louis I. Kahn Bibliography* by Gloria W. Close, Monticello, Illinois 1980.

Louis I. Kahn has become a legend of modern architecture. The architecture he produced, and the philosophy he professed, have had an absolutely monumental impact on the development and re-directioning of progressive design. Apart from his importance as leader of the most dramatic shift in architectural thought since the dawn of modern architecture in the 1920s, the sheer talent that Kahn possessed compelled him to create several of the most sensitive, beautiful and thrilling buildings erected in this century.

Kahn's major work spans barely fifteen years, but it documents a change in architectural perception that, although only recently identified, has certainly become the most salient trend of the 1970s and 1980s. When Kahn's work first gained recognition at the end of the 1950s, the western world was still mesmerized by the advancements of rapid industrialization, and the new construction techniques and materials technology offered. Kahn identified this as blind idolatry, and rejected the uniformity of design response that had made most modern architecture at that time nameless, faceless, and crude. Instead, he espoused individuality, sensitivity, and freedom to respond in unique ways to the particular constraints of each building's program. He never rebelled against the new technology, materials, and aesthetics that had come to characterize contemporary building, but he insisted on reworking the process of design to allow the inclusion of both greater personal artistic statement and occupant concern. What is more, he developed and preached certain formal organizational maneuvers, claimed to be demanded by the integrity of the created pieces themselves, that suggested an architectural order more strict than any imposed since the classicism of antiquity.

While teaching at the University of Pennsylvania in Philadelphia, Kahn had a chance to fully develop his concepts, which he labeled with a unique vocabulary of names that have since become catchwords of architectural rhetoric. "Servant and served space," for example, described formal zoning differentiation between the primary spaces of a building and the portions of a structure reserved for mechanical equipment and ancillary use. "Silence and light" was a more spiritual analogy of the same concept of duality expressed in the physical distinction of servant and served spaces. Kahn's concern with expressing the contrasts of duality are repeatedly evident; his juxtaposition of the "light" of expression against the "silence" of the pre-inspirational void, his interest in the physical modulation of light against darkness, and his insistence on clear distinction between zones of use and zones of service all reflect a similar focus on exposing and identifying opposing forces. These concepts, together with his affinity for geometrical systems of organization in plan (perhaps a vestige of his Beaux-Arts training), account for the most marked features of Lou Kahn's architecture.

Kahn's design process was labeled with a different set of jargon. He used the word "Form" to describe the pure, ideal existence of an architectural program. "Order" was used to refer to architectural maneuvers, including geometry, linearity, symmetry, asymmetry, etc., that could create physical, architectural entities. "Design" was the attempt to approach perfect Form through the imposition of Order.

"Searching for what a material wants to be" was another favorite expression of Kahn's. It implies the importance of using materials in ways that most effectively capitalize on their physical attributes. A "society of rooms" was also an important phrase. It was used to connote a plan that contains dramatic, active architectural response between one area and another, so that there is a level of interactive resonance in the communication of the spaces.

Although Kahn's words often seem cryptic (and he consistently expressed dissatisfaction with his own ability to express himself verbally, even while others lauded him as a poet), his buildings shine through as gems of bursting creativity and instantaneous accomplishment. Each clearly displays the excitement of truly inspirational production, and never is there any evidence of labored attempts to fulfill academic prescriptions. Often his buildings do appear to be full of conflict and doubt, but the tension arises far more from conflict of artistic and expressive intent than from any stifling effort to follow formula.

Kahn's work was inconsistent, sporadic, and frantic, and only a few of his buildings were completely successful. Even those obscured by many unresolved problems, however, still display massive creative effort and the stroke of a hand more artistically impulsive than analytical.

In the Richards Medical Research Laboratories built on the University of Pennsylvania's campus in 1964, for example, Kahn appears to express servant and served space with a clarity not achieved in his later projects. The viewer does not sense this to be the primary issue, though. Instead, one is absorbed with the romantic display of stairtowers and ventilation ducts as futuristic monuments of ascension and simplicity, reminiscent of Sant'Elia's drawings from before the First World War.

The Salk Laboratory, in La Jolla, California, is clearly a continuation of the same exploration for Form, since the programs for the two projects are very much the same. Here, servant and served space is distinguished vertically, and an intermediate storey houses both the structure (huge Veerendell Trusses) and the mechanical facilities. The artistic thrust here is also not on the resolution of servant/served organization, however, but on the creation of a spiritual environment for meditation, conducive to the spontaneous emergence of ideas. The starkness of the interior court, livened only by a thin stream of water analogous to Life Force, makes the site awesome and rich despite the minimalism of the environment.

Several projects in the late sixties, most notably the library of the Phillips Exeter Academy (a prestigious New England preparatory school), evidenced growing interest in material richness and volumetric complexity. In three outstanding projects in South Asia, the Institute of Management in Ahmedabad, India, and the Ayub Hospital and National Capital of Bangladesh, both in Dacca, Kahn used simpler materials (bcick and concrete spandrels) but with equally perfect placement and execution. His masterful use of arches and structural brick remains unequalled, and the powerful forms created by using the material the way it wants to be ("A brick wants to be an arch," he used to say) are compelling, stark, and monumental.

Kahn's work often failed, economically, because, of his unwillingness to compromise his artistic and social goals. Many of his buildings were more costly and more time-consuming than originally planned, and he himself suffered great financial difficulties because he revised plans long after he had expended all of the money he received from commissions.

Kahn's efforts seem so terribly significant, not because of the successes or failures of his particular projects, nor the validity or invalidity of his architectural proposals, but because of his sincere effort to reassign the role of architecture as supplying spiritual values and inspiration to those that use it. This is what made Kahn such a powerful figure. The fact that his talent matched his fine intentions, and his pure sense of beauty was remarkably sharp, elevated his work still highter, far above the class of noble effort, to the level of those few divenely inspired geniuses who occasionally rise above the mundanity of most architectural production.

—Mitchell B. Rouda

KALLMANN, Gerhard Michael.

American. Born in Berlin, Germany, 13 February 1915; lived in England, 1936-49; emigrated to the United States, 1949: naturalized, 1962. Educated at the Architectural Association School, London, 1936-41, Dip.A.A. 1941. Assistant Editor, *Architectural Review*, London, 1945-49; Assistant Professor, Institute of Design, Chicago, 1949-51; Lecturer, Cooper Union, New York, 1951-55; Associate Professor, Columbia University, New York, 1958-62. Since 1962, Professor of Architecture, Graduate School of Design, Harvard University, Cambridge, Massachusetts, and Partner, with Noel Michael McKinnell, *q.v.*, and Henry Wood, Kallmann, McKinnell and Wood, Architects, Inc., Boston. Bemis Professor, Massachusetts Institute of Technology, Cambridge, 1963-64; Bishop Professor, Yale University, New Haven, Connecticut, 1976. Exhibitions: Museum of Fine Arts, Boston, 1962; Metropolitan Museum of Art, New York, 1970; De Cordova Museum, Lincoln, Massachusetts, 1974. Recipient: Honor Award, American Institute of Architects, 1969; Precast Concrete Institute Award, 1969; Bartlett Award, 1969; Harleston Parker Medal, 1970 and 1975; Award of Merit, Concrete Industry Board, 1974; Bard Award, City Club of New York, 1977. Address: Kallmann, McKinnell and Wood, Architects, Inc., 127 Tremont Street, Boston, Massachusetts 02108, U.S.A.

Works (with Noel Michael McKinnell):

1968 City Hall, Boston
1970 City Hall Plaza, Boston
    Government Center Garage, Boston
    Phillips Exeter Academy Athletics Facilities, New Hampshire
1972 Boston Five Cents Savings Bank
    Master plan for Harvard University athletic facilities, Cambridge, Massachusetts
1973 West Bank Student Union, University of Minnesota, Minneapolis
1975 Government Center open spaces, Boston
    Roosevelt Island Motorgate, New York
1976 Dudley Street Library, Boston
1977 Woodhull Medical and Mental Health Center, Brooklyn, New York
    Cardinal Cushing Park, Boston
1980/
81 American Academy of Arts and Sciences, Cambridge, Massachusetts
1982 Back Bay Station, Boston
1983 School of Business, Washington University, St. Louis, Missouri
1983/
86 Becton Dickinson Corporate Headquarters, Franklin Lakes, New Jersey
1983/
88 Hynes Auditorium expansion, Boston
1983 Daresco Commercial Center, Damman, Saudi Arabia (project)
1984 United States Chancery, Dacca, Bangladesh
    Psychology Building, Washington University, St. Louis, Missouri
    School of Law, Columbia University, New York
    Asian Export Wing, Peabody Museum, Cambridge, Massachusetts
1985 Performing Arts Center, Milton Academy, Milton, Massachusetts (project)
    Anthony's Pier 4, Boston (project)

Publications:

By KALLMANN: book—*Houses of Parliament Extension: A Competition Entry*, with Noel Michael McKinnell, Cambridge, Massachusetts 1978; articles—editor of a special issue on the reconstruction of London in *Architectural Review* (London), June 1945; "Structural Trends in Contemporary City Planning" in *Architectural Review* (London), 1946; "Design," with Ian McCallum, in *Physical Planning*, London 1947; "The Way of Technology," special issue of *Architectural Review* (London), December 1950; "Reflections on Design Education" in *Transformation* (New York), March 1952; "Theatres" in *Interiors* (New York), September 1956; "New Tower in Milan" in *Architectural Forum* (New York), February 1958; "Lessons of the Bauhaus for the Second Machine Age" in *Four Great Makers of Modern Architecture*, New York 1963; "Action Architecture of a New Generation" in *Architectural Forum* (New York), October 1969; "Movement Systems as Generators of Built Form," with Noel Michael McKinnell, in *Architectural Review* (New York), November 1975.

On KALLMANN/McKINNELL: book—*A Competition to Select an Architect for the New City Hall in the Government Center of the City of Boston*, Boston 1961; *Architects on Architecture*, edited by Paul Heyer, London 1967; articles—"Boston City Hall Design Finalists Announced" in *Architectural Re-*

Kallmann, McKinnell and Wood: American Academy of Arts and Sciences, Cambridge, Massachusetts, 1980-81.

cord (New York), March 1962; "End of the Glass Box?" in *Time* (New York), 25 May 1962; "La Tourette Comes to Boston: Boston City Hall" in *Architects' Journal* (London) July 1962; "Toughness Before Gentility Wins in Boston" by Walter McQuade in *Architectural Forum* (New York), August 1962; "Boston City Hall" in *Arkitekten* (Copenhagen), no. 26, 1963; "Boston City Hall" in *Casabella* (Milan), January 1963; "Ein Projekt für die Boston City Hall" by J. G. Mertz in *Werk* (Zürich), February 1963; "Projet pour l'Hotel de Ville de Boston, Etats Unis" in *Architecture d'aujourd'hui* (Paris), February 1963; "A Great Plaza for Boston's Government Center" in *Architectural Record* (New York), March 1964; "Office Buildings Sprout in New Hybrids" in *Fortune* (New York), April 1965; "The Boston Government Center: A Study in Urban Design" by Paul Spreiregen in *Arts and Architecture* (Los Angeles), October 1965; "Boston's Emerging Architectural Monument" in *Architectural Forum* (New York), November 1966; "Bold Bastion" in *Time* (New York), 29 December 1967; "Facade: Boston City Hall" in *Architects' Journal* (London), January 1969; "Boston's City Hall: It Binds the Past to Its Future" by Sibyl Moholy-Nagy in *Architectural Forum* (New York), January/February 1969; "You Can Fight City Hall" by David L. Shirey in *Newsweek* (New York), 1 July 1969; "An Airy Fortress" in *Time* (New York), 21 February 1969; "Boston: Where Old and New Meet Graciously" by Alexander Roll in *Cue* (New York), 11 April 1970; "A Prep School Athletics Building— Controlled, Concentrated, Balanced and Alive with Distilled Energy" by Mildred F. Schmertz in *Architectural Record* (New York), June 1971; "The Saving Grace" in *Architectural Forum* (New York), March 1973; "Bank Statement" in *Building Design* (London), 30 April 1974; "U.S. Bank and Gym by Kallman/McKinnell", in *Architectural Review* (London) February 1976; "Arcadian Academy" in *Architectural Review* (London), October 1981; "American Academy of Arts and Sciences" in *Architecture + Urbanism* (Tokyo), August 1982; "American Academy of Arts and Sciences, Cambridge, Massachusetts" in *Detail* (Munich), March/April 1983; "Kallman McKinnell and Wood Receives AIA's Firm Award" in *Architecture* (Washington, D.C.), March 1984.

The architecture of Gerhard M. Kallmann and Noel Michael McKinnell is rooted in two aesthetic movements of the 1950s: the "New Brutalist" and the "Compositional Rigorist" canons of design. The style which came to be called New Brutalism first appeared in the late work of Le Corbusier. Louis I. Kahn led the Compositional Rigorists. Brutalist work can be dramatic, eccentric, aggressive, and anti-rational; Rigorist work has an inner coherence and logic shaped by structural and mechanical systems but also ordered by patterns of movement and the concept of space as either serving or served.

These contradictory approaches overlap in Kallmann and McKinnell's work, most notably in their masterpiece, the Boston City Hall. The power of this building to celebrate the idea of government, to dramatize the concept of citizen participation, to heighten the sense of meaning in the activities of ordinary life stems from the Brutalist canon. Like all Brutalist architecture, the building is without small elegances and refinements. Kallmann, in a speech given in 1959, pointed out that he and other architects of like mind were "contemptuous of agreeable and acceptable aesthetic effect. [The new trends] are expressive only of the process of their genesis; they communicate fundamentally only the manner of their own making, and they do not declare themselves in terms other than those of architectural actuality.... It appears [that thus is ending] a phase of overmuch gratification of the desire to please, and than an architecture more stern and less sensorially directed is in the making."

As a Compositional Rigorist building, Boston City Hall is ordered by a geometry that controls its paths of movement, sequences of space, and its structural and mechanical parts. It is the movement system which is the foundation of this order. The visitor moves across a great square, up broad steps, and into and through magnificent public space and then beyond toward Boston's historic Faneuil

Market district. This movement system links the Boston City Hall to the venerable network of the old city with a degree of style and authority which is seldom seen.

Movement systems are of particular interest to Kallmann and McKinnell who describe them as "generators of built form." Another important work, the athletics facility at the Phillips Exeter Academy in New Hampshire, like the Boston City Hall, consists of spaces supported by an armature of circulation. If Boston CityHall celebrates government and public participation, the Exeter gym dramatizes sport. Swimming, skating, basketball, squash, and gymnastics are totally visible to visitors and athletes as they move through the building's circulation system. For Exeter, as for the Boston City Hall, these paths are the ordering device of the design.

A well-planned movement system makes a building a legible, comprehensible assemblage of functions. As the permanent elements in a building's organization, these routes become the arteries and veins along which other permanent building elements are set. Columns and piers are placed along the movement system instead of within the spaces served by the system. Such great circulation networks become the best place for social interaction within a building. To make them memorable, Kallmann and McKinnell attenuate their heights and introduce light by means of skylights, thus using sky time and weather to connect the user with the world outside. These networks are open ended and can link up later additions to a building or tie into existing or proposed networks beyond the site.

Kallmann and McKinnell use the structural system as well as the movement system to communicate visual information about a building, paying attention to joinery and expressing the multiplication of parts. Thus four principal themes characterize their architecture—dramatization, compositional rigor, the primacy of movement, and the expression of structure. These are the keys which open the mind to an understanding of their distinguished work.

—Mildred F. Schmertz

KARMI, Dov.

Israeli. Born in Odessa, Russia, in 1905; emigrated to Palestine, 1921; Israeli citizen, 1948. Educated at the Harali High School, Haifa, graduated 1923; Bezalel School of Painting and Sculpture, Jerusalem, 1923-26, graduated 1926; University of Ghent, Belgium, 1926-30, Dip.Arch.Ing. 1930 Married Haya Maklev in 1929; children: the architects Ram Karmi, q.v., and Ada Karmi-Melamede. Partner, Karmi and Barak, Jerusalem, 1931-36; in private practice, Tel Aviv, 1936-50; Principal, Dov Karmi Collaborative, Tel Aviv, 1950-56; Partner, with his son Ram and Z. Melzer, Karmi-Melzer-Karmi, Tel Aviv, 1956 until his death in 1962. Visiting Teacher of Architecture, Technion: Israel Institute of Technology, Haifa. President, Association of Israeli Architects, 1952-56. Exhibitions: *The 1920s in Israeli Art*, Tel Aviv Museum, 1982; *White City*, Tel Aviv Museum, 1984. Recipient: National Prize for Architecture, Israel, 1960. *Died* (in Tel Aviv) *14 May 1962*.

Works:

1930/
  39 Feller House, Jerusalem
      Hairdressing salon interiors, Jerusalem
      Zlotopolsky Apartment Building, Tel Aviv
      Simkin Apartment Building, Tel Aviv
      Idelson Apartment Building, Tel Aviv
      Hershkovitch Apartment Building, Tel Aviv
      Armenian Monastery School, Jaffa

Dov Karmi: El Al Office Building, Tel Aviv, 1962.

1940/
  49 Bezzerano House, Tel Benjamin, Israel
      Frumchenko Apartment Building, Tel Aviv
      Mazur Apartment Building, Tel Aviv
      Goldman Apartment Building, Tel Aviv
      Arnon Apartment Building, Tel Aviv
      Allenby Passage (commercial building), Tel Aviv
      Biderman Apartment Buildings, Tel Aviv
      Fellman Apartment Buildings, Tel Aviv

1950/
  56 Histadrut Headquarters, Tel Aviv
      Town Center of Ashkelon, Israel
      Institute of Building Materials, Technion, Haifa
      Yaron Cinema, Tel Aviv
      Bar Shira, Lautman, Frumchenko and Katz Apartment Buildings, Tel Aviv

      Zaks Villa, Tel Aviv
      Klir Villa, Tel Aviv

1956/
  62 Administration Building, and Weiss Auditorium, Hebrew University of Jerusalem (with Ram Karmi)
      Mann Auditorium, Jerusalem (with Jacob Rechter and Ram Karmi)
      Parliament House, Sierra Leone (with Ram Karmi)
      Foreign Trade Bank, Tel Aviv
      Zim Navigation Company Building, Tel Aviv (with Ram Karmi)
      ORT Vocational School, Tel Aviv
      El Al Office Building, Tel Aviv (with Ram Karmi)
      Commercial/Residential Center, Beer Sheva, Israel

Publications:

On KARMI book—*New Israeli Architecture* by Amiram Harlap, London and East Brunswick, New Jersey 1982; articles—"Bureau de la Fédération du Travail, Tel Aviv" in *L'Architecture d'aujourd'hui* (Paris), December 1956/January 1957; "Histadrut" and "University Campus" in *Werk* (Zürich), April 1958; "Dov Karmi 1905-1962" in *L'Architecture d'aujourd'hui* (Paris), February/March 1963; "Palazzo per uffici del'El Al" in *L'Architettura* (Rome), March 1965.

Dov Karmi, born in Russia but educated in Israel, must be regarded as one of the founding fathers of the modern movement in architecture in Israel. After graduating from the Bezalel Academy of Art in Jerusalem, he went overseas to continue his professional studies, receiving his diploma in architecture and engineering from the University of Ghent in 1930. On his return to Eretz, Israel, he set up an office in Jerusalem (in association with the architect Barak) and a few years later moved to Tel Aviv, where the bulk of his early work is located.

Two very different examples of his work of the 1930s indicate his approach as an architect and give evidence of his great ability. The school of the Armenian Monastery in Jaffa is a stone building of cut ashlar blocks, with triple round-headed windows and a bold, arched entrance on the ground floor, and a row of well-proportioned French windows set deep and opening on to elegant shallow balconies above. A block of flats in Tel Aviv, of the same period, is a simple, white, cubic structure, with windows and recessed balconies banded together to form shadow-filled horizontal slits. In architectural style, the Armenian school is timeless, almost vernacular (albeit an architect-designed and most subtle vernacular); on the other hand, the apartment building is uncompromisingly modern, as Gropius or Mendelsohn might have built it. But despite the apparent differences, the two buildings are remarkably similar in architectural approach: both emphasize the cubic form, the clipped roof-line, the dominance of simple unadorned wall surfaces, the boldness of deep-set fenestration, and the overriding importance of sunlight and shadow.

Throughout the productive years that followed, many of these qualities still obtained in Karmi's work. In the large commercial and institutional projects of the 1950-56 period (the Karmi Collaborative) and the subsequent partnership with Z. Melzer and son Rami Karmi, the architecture of necessity became more complex. The famed Mann Auditorium of Tel Aviv (in association with Rechter) has a magnificent interior, and together with the associated buildings of the cultural centre forms a monumental group of tremendous civic presence. In the commercial and office buildings, the expression of structure becomes more dominant, and the modular nature of the facade is indicative both of the constructive imperatives of pre-cast concrete and the planning imperatives of repetitive, cellular space divisions. One sees fine examples of this approach in the Histadrut Building in Tel Aviv, in the Administration Building of the Hebrew University in Jerusalem, and in the Zim Navigation Company headquarters in Tel Aviv.

All these examples of the 1950s show the strength, discipline, and restraint of a master architect thoroughly in control, in buildings that may not aspire to the highest levels of architectural poetry but are never prosaic. The last in this series of excellent buildings, the El Al Building in Tel Aviv, is something of a departure and perhaps indicates the growing influence of the young Ram Karmi in the design office: the vigour of the curved facade, the bravura sculptural effect of the exposed spiral staircase, and the greater textural richness of the facade all point to new directions, to be explored by Ram Karmi in the 1960s, following the death of his father.

The design talents of the son are his own, and highly individual. The standard of excellence to which he aspires was set for him, as it was for a whole generation of Israeli architects, by pioneers such as Dov Karmi.

—Gilbert Herbert

KARMI, Ram.

Israeli. Born in Jerusalem in 1931; son of the architect Dov Karmi, *q.v.* Educated at the Tichon Hadash High School, Tel Aviv, graduated 1947; Technion: Israel Institute of Technology, Haifa, 1949-50; Architectural Association School, London, 1950-55, Dip.A.A. 1955. Partner, with his father and Z. Melzer, Karmi-Melzer-Karmi, Tel Aviv, 1956 until his father's death in 1962; Principal, with his sister Ada Karmi-Melamede (born, 1936), Karmi Associates, Tel Aviv, from 1962; established branch office in New York, 1972. Chief Architect, Israel Ministry of Housing, Tel Aviv, 1975-79. Adjunct Teaching Fellow in Architecture, subsequently Holder of the Special Chair in Architecture, Technion, Haifa, 1968-85. Visiting Lecturer and Critic, Columbia University, New York, 1969, Princeton University, New Jersey, 1969, Massachusetts Institute of Technology, Cambridge, 1972, the University of Houston, Texas, 1972, Stuttgart University, West Germany, 1979-81, Architectural Association School, London, 1983, and Innsbruck University, Austria, 1983. Recipient: Rokach Prize, Tel Aviv, 1965, 1970; Rechter Prize, Tel Aviv, 1967; Reinholds Prize, Tel Aviv, 1969. Associate, Royal Institute of British Architects, 1973. Address: Karmi Associates, Ben Zion Boulevard 5, Tel Aviv, Israel.

Works:

1956	Zim Navigation Company Building, Tel Aviv (with Dov Karmi)
1957	Weiss Auditorium and Administration Building, Hebrew University, Givat Ram Campus, Jerusalem (with Dov Karmi)
1960	Negev Centre Commercial and Housing Development, Beer Sheva, Israel
1962	Parliament Building, Sierre Leone (with Dov Karmi)
1963	El-Al Office Building, Tel Aviv (with Dov Karmi)
1964	Hadar Dafna Office Buildings, Tel Aviv
1968/73	Central Bus Station, phase I, Tel Aviv
1972	Argaman Textile Factory, Yavneh, Israel
1974	Lady Davies Amal Vocational and Technical High School, Tel Aviv
1976	Student Dormitory, phase I, Ben Gurion University of the Negev, Beer Sheva, Israel
1977	Hulda Kibbutz Master Plan and Housing, Israel
1978	Department of the Humanities, Hebrew University, Mount Scopus Campus, Jerusalem
1978	Special Housing Clusters I and II, Herzlia, Israel
1979	South Acre Housing and Waterfront Development Plan, Tel Aviv
	Ramat Razim Housing Plan, Safed, Israel
	Giloh Housing, phase I, near Jerusalem
1981	Civic Centre with Town Hall and Housing, Herzlia, Israel
	Giloh Housing, phase II, near Jerusalem
1981	Housing Development, Mevaseret Zion, Israel
	Giloh Housing, phase III, near Jerusalem
1982	Student Dormitory, phase II, Ben Gurion University of the Negev, Beer Sheva, Israel
1984	Riviera Apartment Hotel and Commercial Centre, Tel Aviv
1985	Central Bus Station, phase II, Tel Aviv
	Netania Housing Master Plan, Israel

Publications:

On KARMI: books—*Architecture in Israel*, exhibition catalogue, Jerusalem 1968; *New Israeli Architecture, Tel Aviv 1982; Monumental Architecture in Jerusalem*, Tel Aviv 1984; *Synagogues in Israel from the Ancient to the Modern*, Tel Aviv 1985; articles— "Palazzo per uffici del'El Al" in *Architettura* (Rome), March 1965; "Architektur: Kunst and Planung in Israel" in *Werk* (Zürich), January 1973; "Student Residences, Negev University" in *Architecture Plus* (New York), June 1973; "An Israeli School Shaped for Community" in *Architecture Plus* (New York), December 1973; "Les murailles de Jericho" in *Architecture d'aujourd'hui* (Paris), July/August 1974; "Lady Davies Amal Vocational School, Tel Aviv" in *Architecture + Urbanism* (Tokyo), December 1974; "Second Avenue Study" in *Progressive Architecture* (New York), January 1975; "Cultural Centre, Beersheba" in *Architecture in Israel* (Tel Aviv), 1978; "Lady Davies Amal Technical School, Tel Aviv" in *Architecture in Israel* (Tel Aviv), 1979; "Giloh Housing Schemes" in *AIA Journal* (Washington, D.C.), August 1982; "Contemporary Israeli Architecture" in *Process: Architecture* (Tokyo), no. 44, 1984; "Jerusalem: ein Bericht" in *Baumeister* (Munich), March 1985.

After qualifying at the Architectural Association School of Architecture, Ram Karmi worked in association with his father, the well-known Israeli architect Dov Karmi, in the firm of Karmi, Melzer and Karmi. During the 1950s, this firm was responsible for several fine buildings in Israel, including the Administration Building at the Hebrew University of Jerusalem, the Zim Building in Tel Aviv, and the striking El Al Building, perhaps Tel Aviv's most handsome structure of that period. All these buildings are in reinforced concrete, which is handled—both in precast and in situ form—with skill and sensitivity; the resultant architecture is both spirited and ordered, the strict modularity imposing an insistent discipline.

In later years, when head of his own architectural office, Ram Karmi remained faithful to the medium of reinforced concrete but used it with much greater virtuosity and freedom. The series of buildings which then came from his office are monuments to a creative talent that delights in strong complexes of sculptured but geometric form, with intricate silhouettes and boldly modelled surfaces, sparkling in the bright Israeli sunshine. The commercial centre at Beersheva, the Hadar-Dafna Office Complex in Tel Aviv, both of the 1960s, and the Lady Davis Amal School, all indicate a mastery of form, as well as interplay of mass and space, that first catch, and then maintain, the interest. Internal public spaces—the roof-lit atrium in the Negev centre, the lobby and sweeping staircase of Hadar-Dafna, the amphitheatral courtyard of the Amal School—are often breathtaking, always memorable. One may sometimes question the programmatic aspects of Karmi's design, or the aptness of the architectural character for the function served—the school is, in my view, too aggressive and abrasive an environment in which to nurture the young learning mind—but its formal strength is undeniable.

More recently, as in the student dormitories for the Ben Gurion University of the Negev, of the 1970s, or the housing clusters at Giloh, near Jerusalem, one senses a growing interest in the round form and the perforated wall surface as elements that, through bold penetrations and the use of strong primary colour, develop a layering of space, an envelope subtly unfolding to reveal the inner planes of the building's form. The influence of Le Corbusier, present ever since the 1950s, is here brought into fusion with that of Louis Kahn—and especially the

Ram Karmi: Giloh 2 Housing Development, Jerusalem, 1981.

later work of Kahn at Dacca. There are some affinities, too, between the formal approach of Karmi and that of John Andrews, especially Andrews's Scarborough College.

Despite the monumentality of these powerful buildings, Karmi's philosophy of housing tends towards the humane and the romantic. He seeks, through the paradigm of Mediterranean vernacular, the intimate scale of the small dwelling cluster, of which image and sense of place derive from the judicious design of pathway, staircase, entrance. In the pursuance of this vision—and in an unprecedented move for a creatively successful architect—he for a time gave up private practice to become director of the Design Department of the Israel Ministry of Housing.

—Gilbert Herbert

KASSABAUM, George Edward.

American. Born in Atchison, Kansas, 5 December 1920. Educated at Taft Junior High School, Oklahoma City, 1932-35; Classen Senior High School, Oklahoma City, 1935-38; Washington University, St. Louis, 1938-42, 1946-47, B.Arch. 1947. Served in the United States Air Force, 1945-46: Sergeant. Married Marjory Verser in 1949; chidlren: Douglas, Anne and Karen. Worked at the Boeing Aircraft Company, Wichita, Kansas, 1942-45; Instructor, Washington University, 1947-51; Architect, with Hellmuth, Yamasaki, *q.v.*: Minoru Yamasaki, and Leinweber, St. Louis, 1951-55. Principal, with George Hellmuth, *q.v.,* and Gyo Obata, *q.v.,*

Hellmuth, Obata and Kassabaum, St. Louis, 1955 until his death, 1982. Director, Tower Grove Bank, St. Louis, 1973-82. President, 1968-69, and Chancellor of the College of Fellows, 1977-78, American Institute of Architects. Director, Metropolitan St. Louis Y.M.C.A., 1970-82, and Downtown St. Louis Inc., 1974-82; Trustee, Washington University, 1975-82. Recipient: Alumni Citation, Washington University, 1972; Missouri Architect of the Year Award, 1978. Fellow, American Institute of Architects, 1967. Honorary Fellow, Royal Architectural Institute of Canada, and La Sociedad de Arquitectos Mexicanos; Honorary Member, Sociedad Colombiana de Arquitectos. *Died* (in St. Louis, Missouri) *15 August 1982.*

See HELLMUTH, OBATA AND KASSABAUM

KATSELAS, Tasso.

American. Born in Pittsburgh, Pennsylvania, 15 July 1927. Educated at the Carnegie Institute of Technology, now Carnegie Mellon University, Pittsburgh, Pennsylvania, 1946-50 and 1952-54, B.Arch. 1950, M.Arch. 1954. Served in the United States Navy, 1945-46. Married Jane Banning in 1951; children: Dana and Lisa. Since 1956, in private practice, Pittsburgh, Pennsylvania. Exhibitions: *Gold Medal Exhibition*, New York, 1960; *New Form in Concrete*, New York, 1961. Recipient: Architectural Design Award, *Progressive Architecture*, 1961; Architectural Award, Dow Corporation, 1964;

Award of Design Excellence, 1964 and 1970, House Award, 1974, and Apartments of the Year Award, 1974, *Architectural Record;* Architectural Award, *College and University,* 1970. Address (office): 4951 Centre Avenue, Pittsburgh, Pennsylvania 15213, U.S.A.

Works:

1955 Katselas House, Churchill Sector, Pittsburgh
1958 Evanson House, Pittsburgh
1959 Medical building, Pittsburgh
     Neville House Apartments, Pittsburgh
1960 O'Hara Parking Plaza, Pittsburgh
     Berman House, Pittsburgh
     Rich House, Pittsburgh
1961 410 Craig Street Medical Building, Pittsburgh
     Berger House, Pittsburgh
1962 Katselas House II, Fox Chapel Chapel Sector, Pittsburgh
1963 City and Moon Township Campus, Robert Morris College, Pittsburgh
     Highland House, Pittsburgh
1964 Forbes Pavilion Nursing Home, Pittsburgh
1965 Pennley Park North Apartments, Pittsburgh
     Cree House, Corapolis, Pennsylvania
1966 Schenley House Apartments, Pittsburgh
     Cavender House, Pittsburgh
     Penthouse Apartments, Pittsburgh
1967 American Institutes for Research, Pittsburgh
     The Edge Restaurant/Motel, Pittsburgh
     Pennley Park South Apartments, Pittsburgh
     St. Vincent Monastery, Latrobe, Pennsylvania
     Zion Evangelical Lutheran Church, Bridgeville, Pennsylvania

Roberts House, Pittsburgh
1968 Greek Orthodox Church, Poughkeepsie, New York
1969 Berkeley School, White Plains, New Jersey
Centre Towne Mall, Johnstown, Pennsylvania
Johnstown Savings Bank, Johnstown, Pennsylvania
Masterwork Paint Company, Pittsburgh
Pressley Street Highrise Apartments, Pittsburgh
St. Vincent Science Building, Latrobe, Pennsylvania
Rogal House, Pittsburgh
1970 McKeesport Highrise Apartments, McKeesport, Pennsylvania
McKeesport Garden Apartments, McKeesport, Pennsylvania
Penn Circle Tower Apartments, Pittsburgh
1971 East Mall Apartments, Pittsburgh
St. Nicholas Serbian Orthodox Church, Monroeville, Pennsylvania
Winthrop Square I and II, New London, Connecticut
1972 East Hills Highrise Apartments, Pittsburgh
East Hills Housing, phase I and II, Pittsburgh
East Hills Elementary School, Pittsburgh
Rovida House, Pittsburgh
Dining Hall, Indiana University, Pennsylvania
Oakmont North (housing complex), Norfolk, Virginia
1973 Allegheny Commons Housing, Pittsburgh
Community College of Allegheny County, Pittsburgh
Schneirov House, Pittsburgh
1974 Allegheny Airlines Components Overhaul Building, Pittsburgh
American Institutes for Research, Washington, D.C.
Mahoning East Civic Center, Punxsutawney, Pennsylvania
Kamin House, Pittsburgh
1975 City Towers Highrise Apartments, Harrisburg, Pennsylvania
Greater Pittsburgh International Airport
1975/
77 Wimmerton (Mini-City), Latrobe, Pennsylvania
1976 Highpoint Towers Apartments, Erie, Pennsylvania
Mid-City Towers Apartments, Erie, Pennsylvania
Midtown Plaza, McKeesport, Pennsylvania
1977 Court Street Apartments, Reading, Pennsylvania
St. Vincent Mental Health Facility, Erie, Pennsylvania
Hirsch House, Pittsburgh
1977 Bidwell United Presbyterian Church, Pittsburgh
Budget Rent-a-Car, Pittsburgh
YIKC Monroeville Camp, Monroeville, Pennsylvania
1978 St. Vincent Community Center, Latrobe, Pennsylvania
The Pennsylvania Apartments, Erie, Pennsylvania
Neuberg House, Pittsburgh
Katselas House III, Pittsburgh
1979 Addison Place, Corning, New York
Dayspring II, Corning, New York
Montani Towers, Wheeling, West Virginia
Salvator Restaurant, Pittsburgh
Webster Hall Garage, Pittsburgh
1980 Benetwood Housing, Erie, Pennsylvania
Beaver Congregate Housing, Beaver County, Pennsylvania
Olympia Place, Latrobe, Pennsylvania
Village Green, Harrison Township, Pennsylvania
1981 Platt House, Pittsburgh
Webster Hall Apartments, Pittsburgh
Beaver Congregate Housing, Beaver, Pennsylvania

1982 Belvedere Acres, Canton Township, Pennsylvania
Benetwood Congregate Housing, Erie, Pennsylvania
Huntingdon Village, New Stanton, Pennsylvania
Second Federal Bank, Mount Lebanon, Pennsylvania
1983 Coleman Towers, Somerset, Pennsylvania
Juniata Village, Petersburg, Pennsylvania
Mellon Bak, Mount Lebanon, Pennsylvania
Mini-Kane Hospital, McKeesport, Pennsylvania
Rolling Woods, North Versailles, Pennsylvania
Tandem Townhouses, Erie, Pennsylvania
Village Green, Natrona Heights, Pennsylvania
Washington Square Complex, Mount Lebanon, Pennsylvania
Wine Restaurant, Pittsburgh
1984 Allegheny Dwellings, Pittsburgh
Beacon Place, Pittsburgh
McAteer Village, Houtsdale, Pennsylvania
Program Building for Female Offenders, Pittsburgh
St. Regis Housing for the Elderly, Pittsburgh
Development Office, St. Vincent College, Latrobe, Pennsylvania
Penn Group Office Tower, Pittsburgh

Publications:

By KATSELAS: book—writings/speeches in *Tasso Katselas, Architect Planner*, Pittsburgh, Pennsylvania 1969; articles—"The Architects: A Chance for Greatness" in *Fortune* (New York), January 1966; letter in *Architectural Record* (New York), September 1966.

On KATSELAS: books—*Tasso Katselas, Architect Planner*, Pittsburgh, Pennsylvania 1969; *A Continuum 1970/1980*, Boston 1980; articles—"Campus in Motion: Tasso Katselas' New Campus for the Robert Morris Junior College" in *Progressive Architecture* (New York), February 1966; "Community and Privacy for Benedictines at Latrobe" in *Architectural Record* (New York), November 1967; "A New Benedictine Monastery in Pennsylvania" in *Art d'eglise* (Brussels), January/March 1968; "Pittsburgh's Poet in Concrete" by M. Carlin in *Pittsburgh Press Roto*, 9 September 1969; "Architectural Analogy: New Science Center, St. Vincent Archabbey and College" in *Architectural Record* (New York), May 1970; "Greater Pittsburgh Airport Remodels and Expands with Interim Facilities" in *Architectural Record* (New York), October 1972; "Pittsburgh Architect Tasso Katselas: The Architect and His City" in *Space Design* (Tokyo), June 1975; "Tasso Katselas' Architecture" in *Technodomika* (Athens), October 1976; "Two Pittsburgh Houses by Tasso Katselas" in *Architectural Record* (New York), November 1979; "Low-Rise Housing in America," special issue of *Process: Architecture* (Tokyo), April 1980; "New Pittsburgh International Airport" in *Architectural Record* (New York), February 1982; "Pittsburgh's New Terminal Takes Shape" in *Airports International* (London), March 1982; "Journal of Urban Housing" in *Toshi Jutaku* (Tokyo), July 1983.

*

Current architectural trends indicate a general withdrawal from the commitment to values that require direct response to people's needs; instead, we find more and more architecture produced as abstract, personal/private art. This betrays an urge for novelty and performance to camouflage the insecurity of coping with the real economic, technical, political, and social issues which must dominate if we care to improve the man-made environment.

It is destructive and dangerous when arbitrary visual and decorative historic elements become the primary generators of a building's form. This is a visual game, sometimes acceptable in "Display and World's Fair Exhibit Architecture" where whim, humor, and desire to shock may be forgiven. Architecture, however, is not temporary, and one must, therefore, be prepared to take responsibility for one's actions. Materials, process, place, and use are informative delights that should determine the right solution and its ultimate expression. Ignorance cannot override this form-making process with whimsy. The initial smile of amusement that accompanies current architectural frivolities quickly gives way to tears of realization as the search for variety becomes desperate. The diverse entertainment of cut-outs, pop-up classicism, and superficial decoration offers fashion-plate solutions which may titillate but fail miserably in recognizing scale, structure, place, use, and movement as the real architectural elements from which expression develops.

The question is: Are we able to produce buildings that will not succumb to obsolescence and thus avoid the desperate search for variety?

Life in architecture is a call to share in the world's making. It is a chance to intervene, to contribute, to enhance what exists by the sheer power of one's presence and activity. I believe that human life must know ecstasy. I am young enough to hope for a world where this is possible, where the ugly will no longer be tolerated, where intense beauty is liberation. I am old enough to know that the words *economy* and *profit* in architecture are not ugly words but necessary ones that may limit the vocabulary of the engineer, the technician, the builder, but not the poet. I am optimistic enough to see our era as one teeming with lyric possibilities.

My hope is that we can combine practical wisdom and philosophy with our art. The architect's job must be redefined as taking care of the living. Men are difficult, troublesome, but nevertheless, valuable creatures. The creative care of man is an artful and beautiful task. The skills of the architect, the creation and inspiration of which he is capable must be brought fully into life as consequential beauty. We can no longer obscure the issue of quality with neoclassical jests and naked fashion covered with words.

The architect must be involved totally in the character of the activity; design is an activity the content of which is anticipated in space. Design is determined space—through it, architecture has the power to structure environment. Architecture is declaring where use limits, yet provokes, develops, and chooses content. This is where our magic lies— the ability to choose content. Choice is significantly the act of recognition-composition-design. Architecture is the fact and effect of such activity where form and content occur simultaneously.

—Tasso Katselas

*

Like most architects, Tasso Katselas sometimes invents, sometimes adapts. But for him, design is primarily a challenge to his geometrical and spatial skills. And yet his architecture is also a form of self expression and pure creativity emerging from his psyche. These two contradictory aspects of design challenge Katselas's powers of synthesis, and the achievement of such a synthesis has become the principal preoccupation of his life as an artist. The success of each of his works can be measured in part by the degree to which he has solved this basic problem that he has set himself.

As in every art, and as with all architecture that aspires to art, Katselas's buildings are rooted in the architecture of others. He is strongly influenced by Frank Lloyd Wright and by the Le Corbusier of the Jaoul houses. Both these progenitors themselves struggled to achieve the very synthesis that Katselas seeks. Sharing their ambition, he has learned from them, but it is their attitude toward design, rather than their specific geometrical and structural solutions, that informs his work.

Katselas began his practice in the late 1950s and has never had a partner. He has always worked with a small team of never more than eight people, and he exercises complete control over design. His small force has developed designs for almost every building type, including housing, office buildings, schools, churches, shopping centers, college buildings, medical facilities, industrial buildings, airport structures and recreational facilities. The greatest amount of work has been in housing, but his finest design is to be found in his campus work. Such a varied practice, which includes so many buildings the purpose of which is mainly commercial, does not permit Katselas to treat each project as an opportunity for the heroic endeavour that interests him most. He is at his best, however, when he is so engaged, as proved by his finest achievements—the monastery and college for St. Vincent in Latrobe and the Community College of Allegheny County.

—Mildred F. Schmertz

KECK, George Fred.

American. Born in Watertown, Wisconsin, 17 May 1895. Educated at the University of Wisconsin, Madison, 1914-15; University of Illinois, Urbana, 1915-20, B.S. 1920. Served in the United States Coastal Artillery, 1917-18: 2nd Lieutenant. Married Lucile Liebermann in 1921. Worked as a designer in various architectural offices in Chicago, 1920-26. In private architectural practice, Chicago, 1926 until his death in 1980: in partnership with his brother William Keck (born, 1908), as Keck and Keck, Chicago, from 1946 (firm continues at 612 North Michigan Avenue, Chicago, Illinois 60611). Instructor in Design, University of Illinois, Urbana, 1923-24; Head of the Department of Architecture, Institute of Design, Chicago, 1938-44. Exhibitions: *Built in USA, 1932-1944*, Museum of Modern Art, New York, 1944; *Homes for Tomorrow*, toured the United States, 1945; *Keck on Architecture*, Taylor Museum of the Colorado Springs Fine Arts Center, 1947, toured American universities; *Thirties and Forties Modern in Chicago*, Chicago School of Architecture Foundation, 1975; *Chicago Architects*, Cooper Union, New York, 1976, and toured the United States; *100 Years of Architecture in Chicago: Continuity of Structure and Form*, Museum of Contemporary Art, Chicago, 1976, and toured the United States; *Keck and Keck, architects*, Elvehjem Museum of Art, University of Wisconsin, Madison, 1980. Also a painter in watercolors: exhibitions— Katharine Kuh Gallery, Chicago; Baldwin-Kingery Gallery, Chicago; Colorado Springs Fine Arts Center; Feingarten Gallery, Chicago; Feingarten Gallery, San Francisco; Lawrence University, Appleton, Wisconsin; Syracuse University, New York; University of Minnesota, Minneapolis; University of Kansas; Elgin Academy, Illinois; Circle Gallery, New Orleans; Art Institute of Chicago; Main Street Gallery, Chicago; University of Illinois, Chicago. Recipient: Honor Award, 1953, 1958, 1959, 1964, 1967, Citation of Merit, 1957, 1958, 1961, 1964, and Distinguished Service Award, 1980, American Institute of Architects, Chicago Chapter; Award of Merit, national AIA, 1955; Annual Award, Fine Hardwoods Association, 1956; Award of Merit, AIA/*Life*/*House and Home*, 1958; Award, *Architectural Record*, 1958, 1962, 1963, 1967; Award, Chicago Beautiful Committee, 1972; Architecture Medal (with William Keck), University of Illinois, Urbana-Champaign, 1981. *Died* (in Chicago) *21 November 1980*.

Works:

1927 Newton B. Lauren House, Flossmoor, Illinois
1929 "Miralago" (nightclub), Wilmette, Illinois

1933/
34 House of Tomorrow, *Century of Progress Exposition*, Chicago (now Miller House, Beverly Shores, Indiana)
1934 Crystal House, *Century of Progress Exposition*, Chicago (demolished)
1935/
36 Herbert Bruning House, 2716 Blackhawk Road, Wilmette, Illinois
1936/
37 Edward Morehouse House, Ely Place, Madison, Wisconsin
       Bertram J. Cahn House, 270 South Western Avenue, Lake Forest, Illinois
1936/
38 William H. Fricker House, Case Street, Whitewater, Wisconsin
1937 Keck-Gottschalk-Keck Co-op Apartment Building, 5551 University Avenue, Chicago
1939 William Kellett House, Winnefox Point, Menasha, Wisconsin
       Dr. J. R. Buchbinder House, Fish Creek, Wisconsin
1940 Dr. Maurice Rice House, Stevens Point, Wisconsin
1941 Hugh D. Duncan House, 1612 Sylvan Street, Flossmoor, Illinois (now Foertsch house)
       John Bennett House, Cuba Road, Barrington, Illinois

Pete Keck House, 5713 North Lake Road, Oconomowoc, Wisconsin
       Richard E. Pulliam House, 825 East Morningside Drive, Sunset Hills Estate, Lake Forest, Illinois (now Mathews House)
       Dr. Emile Quenneville House, Grandy, Quebec, Canada
1942 Green's Ready-Built Prefabricated Homes, Rockford, Illinois and Lake Geneva, Wisconsin
1946 Thaddeus Stevens Shopping Center, Altgeld Gardens, South Ellis Avenue, Chicago
       Charles Huckins House, 541 West Grant Street, Hinsdale, Illinois
1946/
47 Joseph D. Krueger House, 23 Lake View Terrace, Highland Park, Illinois
1947/
49 Dr. Anne Benjamin House, Dune Acres, Indiana
1948 Howard A. DeMyer House, Indiana Avenue, LaPorte, Indiana
       Abel E. Fagen House, 1581 Old Mill Road, Lake Forest, Illinois
1949 Ezra Levin House, Elmwood and University Avenue, Champaign, Illinois
       Pioneer Co-operative Housing, 5400 South Dorchester Avenue, Chicago
       Avery Craven House, Dune Acres, Indiana

George Keck: Keck-Gottschalk-Keck Co-op Apartment Building, Chicago, 1937.

1949/
52 Harold Friedman House, Lincoln Street, Glencoe, Illinois
1950 Prairie Avenue Courts (public housing), Chicago
Manuel Fink House, 573 Longwood Avenue, Glencoe, illinois (now Knight House)
Hyde Park Neighborhood Center, 5480 Kenwood Avenue, Chicago
1951 Dr. Jacques Olivier House, Sherbrooke, Quebec, Canada
Marshall Goldman House, 430 South Evanslawn Avenue, Aurora, Illinois (now Snell House)
Herman Grossman House, 815 Tostenabe Lane, North Muskegon, Michigan
Sigmund Kunstadter House, 1436 Waverly Road, Highland Park, Illinois
Art Gordon House, 240 Country Club Road, Chicago Heights, Illinois (now Berg House)
1951/
52 Don McNeill House, Dundee, Illinois
1952 Robert Feldman House, Miami Road, Benton Harbor, Michigan
1952/
53 Edwin C. Tukey House, 222 Otis Road, Barrington, Illinois
1953 Edward McCormick Blair House, Lake Bluff, Illinois
1954 Walter Gray House, 7 Graymoor Lane, Olympia Fields, Illinois
1955 Harold E. Levin House, Olympia Fields, Illinois
Robert D. Misch House, 151 Maple Avenue, Highland Park, Illinois
1955/
56 Walter Placko House, Dune Acres, Indiana
1955/
59 Ben Marcus House, Bear Lake, North Muskegon, Michigan
1957 Donald Buser house, Riverdale, Iowa
1957/
58 John S. Patton House, Deep Creek, Maryland
Dr. and Mrs. Robert Hohf House, 303 Sheridan Road, Kenilworth, Illinois
1958 Mortimer M. Bortin House, Mequon, Ozaukee County, Wisconsin
1959 Frank E. Payne House, Box 398, Springtown, Bucks County, Pennsylvania
Dr. Edward Isaacson House, 2747 Ridge Road, Highland Park, Illinois
Dr. Robert Bloom House, North Muskegon, Michigan
1959/
61 Chicago Child Care Society Building, 5467 University Avenue, Chicago
1960 Eugene F. LaBorde House, 103 Idlewild Street, Kaukauna, Wisconsin
Thomas Florsheim House, 730 Redwood Lane, Glencoe, Illinois
Gerald Lindquist House, 19239 North Shore Drive, Grand Haven, Michigan
1960/
61 Joe Weix Jr. House, Beggs Isle, Oconomowoc, Wisconsin
1961 T. M. Koenig House, 2887 Blackthorne Road, Riverwoods, Deerfield, Illinois
1961/
62 Norman Weinrib House, Highland Park, Illinois
1962 Jack Teplinsky House, Highland Park, Illinois
1962/
63 Julian Levi House, Door County, Wisconsin
1964 Roy Golze House, Bloomfield Township, Michigan
James Schramm House, Burlington, Iowa
1964/
65 Peerless Confectionery Co. Warehouse additions, 1250 W. Schubert Avenue, Chicago
Norman Karlin House, 5812 South Blackstone Avenue, Chicago
Edwin Rothschild House, Ellison Bay, Door County, Wisconsin

1965/
66 Lewis Weinberg House, Fisher Lane, Winnetka, Illinois
Ben Marcus House II, 3985 Scenic Drive, Whitehall, Michigan
1967 George Wiss House, 28WO21 Marion, Winfield, Illinois
1967/
72 Harper Square (cooperative housing complex), 4800 Lake Park Avenue, Chicago
1970 Dr. Kyung Ahn House, 1901 Mirmar Road, Munster, Indiana
1972 Cyrus C. DeCoster House, 17 Martha Lane, Evanston, Illinois
Dr. Edward A. Wolpert House, Troy Village, Route 1, Sauk County, Spring Green, Wisconsin
1973 Dr. Robert A. Wolf House, 1447 Oak Park Drive, Munster, Indiana
1975 Dr. Andrew J. Griffin House, Lake Front Drive, Beverly Shores, Indiana
1980 Dr. Dong Kyu Lee House, 15 Graymoor Lane, Olympia Fields, Illinois

Publications:

By KECK: book—*Keck on Architecture*, exhibition catalog, Colorado Springs 1947; articles—"Housing Standards", in *Architectural Forum* (New York) September 1942; "Three Houses for the Postwar World", in *Architectural Record* (New York) December 1944; "The House of Tomorrow May Be on Wheels," interview with William C. Wertz, in the *Washington Post*, 29 May 1977.

On KECK: books—*Built in USA, 1932-1944, exhibition catalogue* edited by Elizabeth Mock, New York 1944; *Chicago's Famous Buildings* by Arthur Siegel, Chicago 1965; *Chicago: Growth of a Metropolis* by Harold M. Mayer and Richard C. Wade, Chicago 1969; *Chicago, 1930-70: Building, Planning and Urban Technology* by Carl W. Condit, Chicago 1974; *Historic Wisconsin Architecture* by Richard W. E. Perrin, Gordon D. Orr and Jeffrey M. Dean, Milwaukee 1976; *Chicago Architects*, exhibition catalogue by Stuart E. Cohen and Stanley Tigerman, Chicago 1976; *Keck and Keck, architects*, exhibition catalogue by Narciso G. Menocal, Madison, Wisconsin 1980; articles—"Keck and Keck, Architects," special issue of *Inland Architect* (Chicago), June 1965; "Child Care Society of Chicago" in *Vitrum* (Milan), July/August 1967; "Architect Specializes in Design of Homes" in the *Chicago Tribune*, 7 April 1968; "The Crystal House of 1934" by Thomas M. Slade in *Journal of the Society of Architectural Historians* (Philadelphia), December 1970; "Chicago Child Care Society and Harper Square Housing Project" in *Architectural Review* (London), November 1973; "Let the Sun Keep You Warm" in *Chicago Sun-Times*, 17 February 1974; "A New Look at Chicago Architecture" by Paul Goldberger in the *New York Times*, 4 March 1976; "Chicago Architects: The New Show in New York" by Nory Miller in the *Chicago Daily News*, 6/7 March 1976; "Rediscovering Chicago Architecture" by Ada Louise Huxtable in the *New York Times*, 14 March 1976; "Report from Chicago—Architecture City: Two Views" by Franz Schulze in *Art in America* (New York), March 1976; "The Makers of the Chicago School—Keck and Keck" by Don Klimovich in *Chicago Magazine*, April 1976; "New York Looks at Chicago Architecture" by Carol Diehl in *New Art Examiner* (Chicago), May 1976; "Battle of the Buildings" by Douglas Davis in *Newsweek* (New York), 21 June 1976; "City of Towers Exposed—Two Architecture Shows" by Jane Allen and Derek Guthrie in *New Art Examiner* (Chicago), June 1976; "A Window on Chicago Architects" by John Dreyfus in *Los Angeles Times*, 26 April 1977; "House of Tomorrow, Herbert Bruning House and B. J. Cahn House" in *Architecture + Urbanism* (Tokyo),

September 1977; "Passive solar concepts" by Allen Freeman in *AIA Journal* (Washington, D.C.) December 1979; "The watercolors of George Fred Keck" by C. W. Kaha in *Inland Architect* (Chicago) June 1980; "George Fred Keck, 1895-1980", in *AIA Journal* (Washington, D.C.) January 1981; "George Fred Keck" by Stuart Cohen and Stanley Tigerman in *Chicago Architectural Journal* (Chicago) vol. 1, 1981; "Climate, nature and house", special issue of *Process: Architecture* (Tokyo) May 1982.

Bibliography—*Keck and Keck: a bibliography* by James Christopher, Monticello, Illinois 1984.

As its most important function, architecture gives an expression in form to the needs and requirements of the day and age in which it is created. Aesthetic expression in the form of any structure develops directly from the need. Such a form arrives instinctively and grows from the requirements of the plan. Its appearance derives from the nature of the materials available at any given time, and, when there is a choice, the selection should be dictated by that material which best fits the particular need.

How that is achieved is the function of the living, contemporary architect who must work with the materials at hand and available, with understanding workmen who can turn architectural ideas and plans into reality. In the last analysis, contemporary architecture is democratic art expressing the needs, requirements and desires of many people in its accomplishment.

—George Fred Keck (1980)

George Fred Keck was one of the pioneer architects of the modern movement in Chicago. He has only lately received his fair share of honor, having long stood in the shadow of Mies van der Rohe, popularly and somewhat inaccurately presumed to be the bringer of modernism to Chicago.

After graduating from the University of Illinois in 1920, Keck worked for several Chicago architectural firms, then opened his own office in 1926. One of his earliest independent works was the Newton B. Lauren House in Flossmoor, Illinois, a curious though fetching mixture of Beaux-Arts and modern manners, which suggested Keck's will toward simplicity of form held in check by the more conservative tastes of his client. In 1929 he completed the strikingly avant-garde "Miralago," a night club in Wilmette, Illinois, whose sleek white exterior prefigured the International Style in America. Its interior contained some of the most elegant Art Deco ever designed by a Chicago architect.

Keck's contributions to the 1933-34 *Century of Progress Exposition* in Chicago were even more forward-looking. His House of Tomorrow, a dodecagonal vitreous box in two levels, the upper set back from the lower, was uncompromising in its abstraction. It included a hangar for a small airplane, a feature evidently suggestive of early 1930s visions of future American transportation habits. Still more startling in its departure from tradition was the Crystal House, a ruthlessly stripped-down structure in which all-glass walls were hung behind a steel exoskeleton.

In 1938 Keck was named head of the architecture department of the Institute of Design, a progressive art school which Laszlo Moholy-Nagy had opened in Chicago a year earlier as a revival of the Bauhaus. Keck retained that position until 1944, then devoted his time more fully to his practice, since 1946 in partnership with his brother William. In those years, Keck produced several of his most accomplished works, mostly residences. Notable among these are the Herbert Bruning House in Wilmette and the Bertram J. Cahn House in Lake Forest, Illinois.

In the years since World War II, Keck gradually slipped from sight, as the Miesian influence spread, as the big commercial firms took command of Chicago building in the 1950s and 1960s, and finallyas postmodernist taste came to dominate in the late 1970s. It is nonetheless this last development that has reawakened interest in Keck's ground-breaking early efforts.

—Franz Schulze

KÉVÉS, György.

Hungarian. Born in Ösi, Veszprem district, 20 March 1935. Educated at Szechenyi Grammar School, Sopron, 1950-54; studied at the Technical University School of Architecture, Budapest, 1954-59, M.A.(Arch) 1959. Married Éva Földvári in 1966. Architect in the Agroterv and ELITI planning offices, Budapest, 1959-61; architect, and subsequently Head of the Architectural Department, Ipaterv, Budapest, 1961-83; also in private practice, with Éva Földvári, Budapest, since 1964; Founder/Director, Studio R architectural planning office, Budapest, since 1983. Visiting Lecturer, Technical Unviersity, Budapest, 1963-76; Chief Architect, Masterschool young architects' postgraduate master course, Budapest, since 1974; lecturer and exhibitor, Washington University School of Architecture, St. Louis, Missouri, 1983. Exhibition: Washington University School of Architecture, St. Louis, Missouri, 1983. Recipient: First Prize, Szentháromság Square Townhouse Competition, Budapest, 1963; Békés County Townhouse Competition, 1974; Sports Hall Competition, Budapest, 1975; Széchenyi Bath Reconstruction Competition, Budapest, 1978; Orsolya Square Competition, Sopron, 1978; Shopping Centre Competition, Rákoskeresztur, 1979; OKH Office Competition, Budapest, 1980; Sports and Resort Centre Competition, Sopron, 1981; Airplane Museum Competition, Nyiregyháza, 1982. Ybl Miklós Architecture Award, Budapest, 1973; Organization of Hungarian Architects Award, 1976. Leading Member, Organization of Hungarian Architects. Address: Melinda Street 21, 1121 Budapest XII, Hungary.

Works:

1964 Ministry of Metallurgy and Machine Industry, Budapest
1965 Block of flats, Meredek Street, Budapest
1967 Block of flats, Hernánd Street, Budapest
 Cultural House, Esztergom, Hungary
1969 Block of flats, Alsó Törökvész Street, Budapest
1970 School, Budapest
 Block of flats, Zólyomi Street, Budapest
1971 Vocational Secondary School of the Catering Trade, Budapest
 Block of flats, Nárcisz Street, Budapest
1972 Block of flats, Pajsz Street, Budapest
 Block of flats, Bimbó Street, Budapest
 Block of flats, Fodor Street, Budapest
 Nursery for children of employees of the Hungarian Radio and Television Authority, Budapest
1973 Vocational School of the Printing and Textile Industry, Budapest
 Block of flats, Hegyteró Street, Budapest
1974 Youth House, Budapest
1975 Block of flats, Dobsina Street, Budapest
 Siemens Computer Centre, Budapest
1977 Haematology Laboratory, Karolina Street, Budapest
1979 Elementary School, Budencz Street, Budapest
1980 Terraced Housing, K. I. Pipiske Street, Budapest
1981 Resort Centre, Sopron, Hungary
 Twin Houses, Vág Street, Budapest

Gyorgy Keves: Terrace House, Somloi Street, Budapest, 1982.

1982 Terraced HOuse, Pethényi Street, Budapest
 Terraced House, Somlói Street, Budapest
 Terraced House, Pusztaszeri Street, Budapest
 Twin House, Rákosmezei Street, Budapest
1983 Orthodox Synagogue reconstruction, Sopron, Hungary
 Townhouse, St. György and Uj Streets, Sopron, Hungary
 Terraced House, 21 Melinda Street, Budapest
 Family House, Aszu Street, Budapest
1983/
84 High School, Majakowski Street, Budapest

Publications:

By KÉVÉS: book—*Architecture of Wilhelm Holzbauer and Gustav Peichl*, exhibition catalogue, Budapest 1983; articles—"Post-Modern Architecture in" *Muvészet* (Budapest), no. 8, 1981; "Architecture of Mario Botta" in *Muvészet* (Budapest), no. 11, 1982; "Today's Chicago" in *Muvészet* (Budapest), no. 7, 1983.

On KÉVÉS: books—*Hungarian Architecture 1945-1970* by J. Szendröi, Budapest 1972; *Die Architektur im 20. Jahrhundert* by Udo Kultermann, Cologne 1980; *Architecture in the Seventies* by Udo Kultermann, London 1980; *Architectural Works of Kévés*, exhibition catalogue by Udo Kultermann, Sopron 1982; *György Kévés, Architect*, exhibition catalogue by Udo Kultermann, St. Louis, Missouri 1983; articles—"Kindergarten in Budapest" in *Deutsche Bauzeitschrift* (Gutersloh, Germany), no. 2, 1977; "Terrace House and Kindergarten in Budapest" in *Bauwelt* (Berlin), no. 110, 1978; "Shopping Centre in Rákoskeresztúr" by K. Nagy in *Magyar Épitömüveszet* (Budapest), no. 2, 1980; "Internationalism or local tradition: architecture of Kévés" by Udo Kultermann in *Interpress Grafik* (Budapest), no. 1, 1983.

In the 1930s the pioneers of modern Hungarian architecture planned numerous family houses in the Buda mountains of the capital. After the Second World War—because of new social conditions—the need in the area was for flats rather than single family houses, but talented architects avoided planning and constructing these flats: they felt this kind of work was "beneath their dignity." Consequently, standards became extremely low. At the beginning of the 1960s György Kéves planned a whole series of terraced houses on the mountains of Buda, harmoniously appropriate to the character of the city and surrounding scenery. Approximately 30 blocks of flats have now been built according to his plans. By this example he has succeeded in raising this kind of architectural planning to a high standard and making it, as well, a sought-after commission.

Since the beginning of the 1970s there has been a new architectural demand in Hungary—for steel-structure construction to satisfy increased need for public housing. In 1970, with his planning team, Kéves constructed a steel-framed, light-structured architectural system called I + F, with which he has now realized several important public buildings, especially educational institutions. These buildings are outstanding examples of current Hungarian architecture with their clear structural systems and rational accomplishment of ground plans.

—Anonymous

KHAN, Fazlur Rahman.

American. Born in Dacca, India, now Bangladesh, 3 April 1929; emigrated to the United States, 1952: naturalized, 1967. Educated at the University of Dacca, 1946-50, B.Eng. 1950; University of Illinois, Urbana, 1952-55 (Fulbright Scholar), M.Sc. in structural engineering 1952, M.Sc. in theoretical and applied mechanics 1955, and Ph.D. in structural engineering 1955. Married Liselotte Lurba in 1959; daughter: Yasmin. Lecturer, University of Dacca, 1950-52. Joined Skidmore, Owings and Merrill, Chicago, 1955: General Partner, 1970 until his death, 1982. Adjunct Professor of Architecture, Illinois Institute of Technology, Chicago, 1966-82. Exhibition: *Architecture of Chicago,* Museum of Contemporary Art, Chicago, 1976. Recipient: Construction Men of the Year Award, 1966, 1969, 1971, and Man of the Year Award, 1972, *Engineering News-Record;* Chicagoan of the Year in Architecture and Engineering, 1970; Wason Medal, American Concrete Institute, 1970; Special Citation, American Institute of Steel Construction, 1971; Chicago Civil Engineer of the Year, 1972, Middlebrooks Award, 1972, Howard Award, 1977, and Earnest Award, 1979, American Society of Civil Engineers; Alumni Honor Award, University of Illinois, 1972; Faber Medal, Institute of Structural Engineers, London, 1973; American National Academy of Engineers Award, 1973; Illinois State Service Award, American Institute of Architects, 1977; *Progressive Architecture* Award, 1981. D.Sc.: Lehigh University, Bethlehem, Pennsylvania; Northwestern University, Illinois; Eidgenossische Technische Hochschule, Zurich. Fellow, American Concrete Institute, and American Society of Civil Engineers. Member, National Academy of Engineering, 1973. *Died* (in Saudi Arabia) *27 March 1982.*

Works:

1961 Hartford Fire Insurance Building, Chicago
1962 United Airlines Administration and Training Center, Elk Grove Village, Illinois
United States Air Force Academy, Colorado Springs
Solar Telescope Mount, Kitt Peak Observatory, Arizona
1964 DeWitt Chestnut Apartment Building, Chicago
1965 University of Illinois at Chicago Circle
Brunswick Building, Chicago

1968 500 North Michigan Avenue Building, Chicago
1969 Marine Midland Bank Building, Rochester, New York
1970 John Hancock Center, Chicago
1971 One Shell Plaza Building, Houston
Latter and Meltzer Building, New Orleans
Hartford Fire Insurance Building II, Chicago
Control Data Center, Houston
1972 Two Shell Plaza Building, Houston
One Shell Square, New Orleans
1974 First Wisconsin Center Bank and Office Building, Milwaukee
Imperial Tobacco Company, Bristol, England
Sears Tower, Chicago
1976/
80 Bu Ali Sina University, Hamadan, Iran
1975 Baxter Travenol Laboratories, Corporate Headquarters, Deerfield, Illinois
Bandar Shahpur New Town, Iran
1976 Jeddah International Airport, Saudi Arabia
1977 National Life Building, Nashville, Tennessee
1977/
78 King Abdul Aziz University, Makkah, Saudi Arabia
1978 Hyatt International Hotel, Kuwait City, Kuwait
1980 Edmonton Centre, Alberta, Canada
1981 University Kehangsaan Sabah Kampus, Kota Kinabalu, Malaysia
1982 Hubert H. Humphrey Metrodome, Minneapolis, Minnesota
One Magnificient Mile Building, Chicago

Publications

By KHAN: monographs—*A Study of Tests on Prestressed Concrete Beams,* Urbana, Illinois 1974; *Analytical Studies of Relations Among Various Design Criteria for Prestressed Concrete Beams,* with N. Khachaturian and C.P. Siess, Urbana, Illinois 1955; articles—"Gantries Set Prestressed Bridge Beams," with A.J. Brown, in *Engineering News-Record* (New York), January 1958; "Load Test of 120 Foot Precast, Prestressed Bridge Girder," with A.J. Brown, in *American Concrete Institute Journal* (Detroit), July 1958; "Proposed Revision of Building Code Requirements for Reinforced Concrete" in *American Concrete Institute Journal* (Detroit), November 1962; "Proposed Recommended Practice for Concrete Formwork" in *American Concrete Institute Journal* (Detroit), March 1963; "Interaction of Shear Walls and Frames," with J.A. Sbarounis, in *Journal of the American Society of Civil Engineers* (New York), June 1964; "Effects of Column Exposure in Tall Structures: Temperature Variations and Their Effects," with Mark Fintel, in *American Concrete Institute Journal* (Detroit), December 1965; "Effect of Column Exposure in Tall Structures," with Mark Fintel, in *American Concrete Institute Journal* (Detroit) August 1966; "The Bearing Wall" in *Architectural and Engineering News* (Philadelphia), September 1966; "Computer Design of the 100-Story John Hancock Center," with S.H. Iyengar and J.P. Colaco, in *Journal of the American Society of Civil Engineers* (New York), December 1966; "Voies Nouvelles dans la Conception des Ossatures Metalliques de Bâtiments" in *Journal Construction Metallique* (Paris), December 1966; "The Nature of High-Rise Buildings" In *Indian Builder* (Bombay), June 1967, reprinted in *Inland Architect* (Chicago), July 1967; "The John Hancock Center" in *Civil Engineering* (New York), October 1967; "Effects of Column Exposure in Tall Structures," with Mark Fintel, in *American Concrete Institute Journal* (Detroit), February 1968; "Office Tower Design Cuts Framing Costs" In *Engineering News-Record* (New York), 15 February 1968; "Shock-Absorbing Soft Story Concept for Multi-Story Earthquake Structures" in *American Concrete Institute Journal* (Detroit), March 1968; "Analysis and Design of the 100-Story John Hancock Center in Chicago," with S. H.

Iyengar and J. P. Colaco, in *Acier Stahl Steel* (Brussels), June 1968; "The Bearing Wall Comes of Age" in *Architectural and Engineering News* (Philadelphia), October 1968; "The Chicago School Grows Up" in *Architectural and Engineering News* (Philadelphia), April 1969; "Temperature Effects on Tall Steel Framed Buildings," with Anthony F. Nassetta, in *Engineering Journal* (New York), October 1970; "Response of Buildings to Lateral Forces," with others, in *Amercian Concrete Institute Journal* (Detroit), February 1971; "Buildings" in the *Mcgraw-Hill Yearbook of Science and Technology,* New York 1972; "The Future of High Rise in America" in *Progressive Architecture* (New York), October 1972; "The Changing Scale of the Cities" in *Consulting Engineer* (New York), April 1974; 'Megastructure' in *Actual Specifying Engineer* (Dayton, Ohio), September 1974; "Tabular Structures for Tall Buildings" in *Handbook of Concrete Engineering,* edited by Mark Fintel, New York 1974.

On KHAN: articles—"Hancock Center Represents Breakthru for Construction" by Alvin Nagelberg in the *Chicago Tribune,* 5 May 1968; "Building Design Reduces Steel with Concrete-Tube Wind Bracing" in *Engineering News-Record* (New York), June 1971: "Fazlur Khan – obituary", In *Building Design* (London) 2 April 1982; "Profile Fazlur R. Khan", in *Mimar* (Singapore) April/June 1982; "Fazlur R. Khan, general partner of Skidmore, Owings and Merrill", in *Architectural Record* (New York) May 1982.

*

The 110-story Sears Tower is the world's tallest building at 1454 feet. It uses the bundled tube concept. This concept makes it possible to build supertall buildings without any cost premium for height.

—Fazlur Khan(1980)

*

Fazlur Rahman Khan, one of America's leading structural engineers, was born in 1929 in Dacca. Following completion of the engineering curriculum at the University of Dacca in 1950, he lectured at that institution for two years before emigrating in 1952 to the United States. Most of his subsequent professional training was at the University of Illinois in Urbana, where he was awarded a Ph.D. in structural engineering in 1955. His first professional connection, with the Chicago office of Skidmore, Owings and Merrill, was formed in 1955, and he has remained with the firm ever since; he became a general partner in 1970. In 1966 he was appointed Adjunct Professor of Architecture at the Illinois Institute of Technology.

Khan's academic appointment suggests something of the eminence he enjoyed in architecture as well as engineering. In Chicago—where a strong structural tradition can be traced back to the metalframe skyscrapers of the 1880s and 1890s—architecture and engineering have been historically allied, and the relationship was never more pronounced than during the 1950s and 1960s, when Mies van der Rohe was the leading spirit in building art in the city. During the 1960s Khan and his I.I.T. and S.O.M. colleague Myron Goldsmith, a former student of Mies, advanced several new theories about the construction of very tall buildings.

Amongst the most important results of these studies was the tubular frame, a construction system that facilitates the building of tall, wind-resistant structures, with a minimum of interior bracing and exterior cladding. Khan and Bruce Graham, another general partner at S.O.M.'s Chicago office, have worked as a team to produce a remarkable group of such buildings in Chicago, including the DeWitt Chestnut Apartments, the John Hancock Center, a 100-story multi-use complex, and Sears Tower, at 1454 feet the world's tallest building. Khan and Graham also played major roles in the design of the

Central Facilities Building of the Baxter Travenol Laboratories Corporate Headquarters in Deerfield, Illinois. This structure features a 288-foot-long cable suspension roof, which at the time of its completion was the longest such structure in the world.

During the late 1970's Khan devoted most of his energies, adminstrative as well as architectural, to several vast building complexes in Saudi Arabia. Most notable are the King Abdul Aziz University in Makkah and the Jeddah International Airport.

—Franz Schulze

KIESLER, Frederick John.

American. Born in Vienna, Austria, 22 September 1890; emigrated to the United States, 1926: naturalized, 1936. Educated at the Akademie der Bildenden Künste, Vienna, 1911-12; Technische Hochschule, Vienna, 1912-14. Served in the Austrian Army, 1914-17. Married Steffie Fritsch in 1919. Worked with Adolf Loos on the first slum clearance and rehousing project in Vienna, 1920; began designing theatre sets/decor, Vienna, in the early 1920s; joined the de Stijl group, with Van Doesburg, J. P. Oud and Mondrian, Leyden, Netherlands, 1923; first endless form/continuous space projects, Vienna, 1923; Artistic Director and Architect, *International Exhibition of New Theatre Technique*, Konzerthaus, Vienna (devised suspension method of exhibition), 1924; Architect/Director, Austrian Section, *Exposition international des arts décoratifs et industriels modernes*, Grand Palais, Paris, 1925; in partnership with Harvey Wiley Corbett, New York, 1926-28; Consulting Architect, National Public Housing Conference, 1931-32; Director of Scenic Design, Juilliard School of Music, New York, 1934-47; Director, Laboratory for Design Correlation, School of Architecture, Columbia University, New York, 1936-42; began association with the Surrealists, 1939: directed installation of the *Exposition International du Surréalisme*, Paris, 1947; in partnership with Armand Bartos, as Kiesler and Bartos, New York, 1957 until his death, 1965. Member, Advisory Board for Advancement of Science and Art, Cooper Union, New York. Exhibitions: *International Theatre Exposition*, Steinway Building, New York, 1926; *Cubism and Abstract Art*, Musem of Modern Art, New York, 1936; *Ten Years of American Opera Design 1931-1941*, New York Public Library, 1941; *Bloodflames 1947*, Hugo Gallery, New York, 1947; *Exposition International du Surréalisme*, Galerie Maeght, Paris, 1947; *The Muralist and the Modern Architect*, Kootz Gallery, New York, 1950; *De Stijl*, Stedelijk Museum, Amsterdam, 1951; *Fifteen Americans*, Museum of Modern Art, New York, 1952; *Two Houses: New Ways to Build*, Museum of Modern Art, New York, 1952; *De Stijl 1917-1928*, Museum of Modern Art, New York, 1952-53; *Galaxies by Kiesler*, Sidney Janis Gallery, New York, 1954; *Beck, Cage, Kiesler, Rexroth*, Great Jones Gallery, New York, 1960; *Visionary Architecture*, Museum of Modern Art, New York, 1960; *Shell Sculptures and Galaxies by Kiesler*, Leo Castelli Gallery, New York, 1961; *The Ideal Theatre: Eight Concepts*, Museum of Contemporary Crafts, New York, 1962; *Frederick Kiesler: Environmental Sculpture*, Guggenheim Museum, New York, 1964; Howard Wise Gallery, New York, 1969; *Frederick Kiesler*, Galerie Nächst St. Stephan, Vienna, 1975; André Emmerich Galleries, New York, 1978-79. Collections: Centre Georges Pompidou, Paris; Museum of Modern Art, New York; Guggenheim Museum, New York. Recipient: First Prize, Community Center/ Playhouse Competition, Woodstock, New York, 1928; Best Store Design Award, City of Buffalo, 1936; Honour Award, American Institute of Architects (posthumous), 1966. *Died* (in New York) *27 December 1965*.

Fazlur Khan: Sears Tower, Chicago, 1974.

Works:

1920 Slum clearance and rehousing project, Vienna (with Adolf Loos)
1923 Endless House (project; and subsequent revisions)
         Production design of *R.U.R.*, Theater am Kurfürstendamm, Berlin
         "Space Stage" for production of *The Emperor Jones*, Berlin
1924 Endless Theatre (project)
1925 Austrian Pavilion, *Exposition international des arts décoratifs et industriels modernes*, Grand Palais, Paris
         Optophon: A "Neoplastic" Building (project)
1927/
28 Museum for the Société Anonyme (project)
1929 Eighth Street Playhouse, New York
1930 Film Guild Cinema, New York
1933 The Universal Theatre, Woodstock, New York
1934 Space House (project)
1934/
47 Sets for productions of the Juilliard School and the Metropolitan Opera, New York
1936 Store, Buffalo, New York
1937/
39 Exhibition Hall, School of Architecture, Columbia University, New York
1942 Art of This Century Gallery for Peggy Guggenheim, New York
1945/
65 Environmental Sculptures
1946 Stage design for *No Exit*, New York
1949 Stage design for *Angélique*, New York
1955 Festival Theatre, Ellenville, New York
1956 John Jacob Astor House extension, West Palm Beach, Florida (project)
1957 World House Gallery, New York (with Armand Bartos)
         Javitts House, Greenwich, Connecticut (project; with Armand Bartos)
         Robbins House, West Palm Beach, Florida (project; with Armand Bartos)
1958 Venetian Theatre ("Caramoor"), Katonah, New York
1959 Hospital section of the Albert Einstein Medical Center, New York (project; with Armand Bartos)
         Ullman Research Center, Albert Einstein Medical Center, New York (with Armand Bartos)
         Kamer Gallery, New York (with Armand Bartos)
         Shrine of the Book, Hebrew University of Jerusalem (with Armand Bartos)
1960 Endless House (expanded model; exhibition project)
1961 Universal (Ideal) Theatre, New York (project; for the Ford Foundation)
1963 Grotto for the New Being, New Harmony, Indiana (project)

Publications:

By KIESLER: books—*International Exhibition of New Theatre Technique*, exhibition catalogue, Vienna 1924; *International Theatre Exposition*, catalogue, New York 1926; *Contemporary Art Applied to the Store and Its Display*, London 1930; *Ten Years of American Opera Design 1931-1941*, exhibition catalogue, New York 1941; *Environmental Sculpture*, New York 1964; *Inside the Endless House*, New York 1966; articles—"Erneuerung des Theaters" in *De Stijl* (Leyden), no. 75/76, 1926; "Eintritt 75 cents" in *G: Zeitschrift für elementare Gestaltung* (Berlin), April 1926; "L'Architecture élementarisée" in *De Stijl* (Leyden) no. 79/84, 1927; "Notes d'Amérique" in *Cahiers d'Art* (Paris), March 1931; "Homage to Theo van Doesburg" in *De Stijl* (Leyden), January 1932; "Notes on Architecture: The Space House: Annotations at Random" in

Hound and Horn (Camden, New Jersey), January/March 1934; "Notes on Improving Theatre Design" in *Theatre Arts Monthly* (New York), September 1934; "Murals Without Walls: Relating to Gorky's Newark Project" in *Art Front* (New York), December 1936; "The Architect in Search of . . . Design Correlation" in *Architectural Record* (New York), February 1937; "Design Correlation" in *Architectural Record* (New York), April, May, June, July and August 1937; "On Correalism and Biotechnique: A Definition and Test of a New Approach to Building Design" in *Architectural Record* (New York), September 1939; "Design Correlation as an Approach to Architectural Planning" in *VVV* (New York), March 1943; "Les Larves d'Imagerie d'Henri Robert Marcel Duchamp" in *View* (New York), March 1945; "Art and Architecture: Notes" and "Trends in Exhibitions" in *Partisan Review* (New York), Winter 1946; "Pseudo-functionalism in Modern Architecture" in *Partisan Review* (New York), July 1949; "Endless House and Its Psychological Lighting" in *Interiors* (New York), 4 November 1950; "A Symposium on How to Combine Architecture, Painting and Sculpture" in *Interiors* (New York), May 1951; "Design in Continuity" in *Architectural Forum* (New York), October 1957; "The Art of Architecture for Art" in *Art News* (New York), October 1957; "Is Today's Artist with or Against the Past?" in *Art News* (New York), September 1958; "Art Is the Teaching of Resistance" in *College Art Journal* (New York), Spring 1959; "Frank Lloyd Wright" in *It Is* (New York), Autumn 1959; "Hazard and the Endless House" in *Art News* (New York), November 1960; "Kiesler's Pursuit of an Idea" (interview) in *Progressive Architecture* (New York), July 1961; "Breaking the Strait Jacket" in *Show* (New York), March 1964; "Keisler by Kiesler" in *Architectural Forum* (New York), September 1965; "The Future: Notes on Architecture as Sculpture" in *Art in America* (New York), May/June 1966.

On KIESLER: books—*Frederick Kiesler: Environmental Sculpture*, exhibition catalogue, New York 1964; *Frederick Kiesler*, exhibition catalogue, Innsbruck 1975; *Frederick Kiesler (1890-1965): Visionary Architecture, Drawings and Models, Galaxies and Paintings*, exhibition catalogue by Cynthia Goodman, New York 1978; *Dortmunder Architekturhefte 15: Museumsbauten – Entwurfe und Projekte seit 1945*, edited by Josef Paul Kleihues, Dortmund 1979; *Endless Innovations: Frederick Kiesler's Theory and Scenic Design* by R. L. Held, Ann Arbor, Michigan 1982; articles—"New Theatre Architecture in Europe" by K. Lönberg-Holm in *Architectural Record* (New York), May 1930; "Space House by Frederick Kiesler" in *Architectural Record* (New York), January 1934; "New Display Techniques for Art of This Century, Designed by Frederick Kiesler" in *Architectural Forum* (New York), February 1943; "Design's Bad Boy" in *Architectural Forum* (New York), February 1947; "The Endless House: Frederick Kiesler, Architect" in *Architectural Forum* (New York), November 1950; "Frederick Kiesler's Theaterprojekte" in *Bauen und Wohnen* (Zurich), November 1951; "Greatest Non-Building Architect of Our Time Expounds His Ideas" by Ada Louise Huxtable in the *New York Times*, 27 March 1960; "The Ideal Theatre: Eight Concepts" in *Progressive Architecture* (New York), December 1961; "Kiesler: Exhibition of His Work in Vienna" by Joseph Rykwert in *Domus* (Milan), May 1975; "Frederick Kiesler's Endless Search" by Cynthia Goodman in *Artsmagazine* (New York), September 1979.

Frederick Kiesler was a visionary architect, sculptor, and theatre designer whose fundamental genius was in the time-space continuum. Yet he was always one step away from whatever vantage point he took to look at the continuum. From the time-space of the Cubists to the De-Stijl group to the Surrealists to the

Space Age of outer space, he was always ahead of each period or art group with which he identified himself. He was always able to add just one more dimension, to flip the coin one more time, to do the opposite, the contrary, the different, the revealingly but not always appealingly new. His interests and energy were seemingly endless, like the continuum to which he related virtually all of his work.

In 1923 his stage setting for Karel Chapek's *R.U.R.* in Berlin included, for the first time, a motion picture as a backdrop to live actors. His setting for the subsequent production in Berlin of O'Neill's *The Emperor Jones* demonstrated the time-space idea by means of revolving flats and drops and a stage flowing continually with light, color, and kinetic scenery that reinforced the increasing drumheartbeats of the play. Kiesler called it "multiple mobility," constant change," and "continuous tension."

In 1925, for the *Exposition international des arts décoratifs* in Paris, Kiesler designed and built an exhibition of intersecting and overlapping columns, beams, and panels that was an epitome of the goals of De Stijl and of the articulated architecture that was to be called The International Style. But Kiesler went one step further; his City in Space exhibition was entirely suspended—a floating, orbiting, time-space satellite that anticipated the grade-level open parkland of Le Corbusier's Voisin Plan and that was not to be fully realized until the Space Age began in the late 1950s.

And in 1924 when he first designed his "Endless" as a theater, he included a continuous intertwining ramp and elevators for both actors and audience that prefigured both Walter Gropius's multi-form Total Theater project and Frank Lloyd Wright's spiral Guggenheim Museum design.

But at a time when Modern design was preoccupied with the grid and the rectangle, with the flat plane and with structural clarity, Kiesler was offering curved corners, continuous wall-and-ceiling planes with no beginning and no end—a three-dimensional, live-in, act-in, Moebius strip. "The time was not ripe," he mused later; yet he had continued to work out these early themes for the rest of his long life.

Then when the Kootz Gallery in 1950 and the Museum of Modern Art in 1952 exhibited his later Endless House model—a smooth egg shape on a rough pedestal surrounded by fern fronds—Eero Saarinen was designing his hockey rink for Yale and his TWA Terminal at JFK Airport. It was clear that the times had changed. Still, Kiesler got to build little. He had continued to design time-space stage settings of astonishing invention for the Juilliard School of Music for fifteen years; he had joined the Surrealists and built in a surrealist vein at Peggy Guggenheim's Art of This Century Gallery in 1942; he had designed and built walk-in or "environmental sculpture" from the mid 1940s to the mid 1960s. And he redesigned his Endless Theater concept for the Ford Foundation's exploration of the Ideal Theater in 1962, having a great egg-shaped theater model cast in gleaming polished aluminium with a movable multi-form stage. It was a lifeline of continuity.

His verse and enthusiasm, his joie de vivre and seemingly endless inventions were an influence on all who came in contact with him or his work. He was a perfectionist of the most demanding character that was sometimes exasperating: toward the end of his life he could not let go his personal control; he could not let anything out of his own hands but continually had to rework it to make it better and better in his view—but never finished. So he built little permanent architecture. His World House Gallery of 1957 may have been the best demonstration of his Endless interior concept. Only his Shrine of the Book in 1959—the sanctuary for the Dead Sea Scrolls in Jerusalem, with Armand Bartos—approaches the full realization of his pursuit of an expression of the continuum of architecture, art, and life.

—C. Ray Smith

KIKUTAKE, Kiyonori.

Japanese. Born in Kurume City, Fukuoka Prefecture, 1 April 1928. Educated at Waseda University, Tokyo, under Kenji Imai, Takeo Sato, Tachu Naito, Motoo Take and Saburo Soshiroda, 1946-50 (Graduate Design Prize, 1950), B.Arch. 1950. Married Norie Sasaki in 1953; children: Yuki, Kasumi and Mitsunori. Since 1953, Principal of Kiyonori Kikutake and Associates, Tokyo. Director of the Urban Industry Company, Tokyo, since 1965. Lecturer at Waseda University, Tokyo, since 1959. Director, Architectural Institute of Japan, 1972-74. Director, Japan Architects Association, since 1974, Association of Tokyo Architectural Design Supervision, since 1974, and Japan Society of Future Research, since 1974; Executive Director, Tokyo Y.M.C.A. Institute of Design, since 1978. Exhibitions: *Japanese Ancient Art Jomon Exhibition*, Tokyo, 1960; *View of Today from Primitive Arts*, Tokyo, 1960; *New Module of Living*, Tokyo, 1961; *Metabolism Exhibition*, Tokyo, 1962; *Kiyonori Kikutake*, Honolulu, 1964; *Modern Japanese Architecture*, Florence, 1964; *Future Garden City Planning of Tama Exhibition*, Tokyo, 1965; *Today's Exhibition*, Tokyo, 1977; *Visual Architecture*, New York, 1978. Recipient: First Prize, Shimonoseki City Hall Competition, 1951; First Prize, Low-Cost Housing Competition, Ministry of Construction, Japan, 1952; Award of Excellence, Japanese Ministry of Construction, 1963; Arts Award, Japanese Ministry of Education, 1964; Pan Pacific Architecture Citation, American Institute of Architects, Hawaii Chapter, 1964; Architectural Institute of Japan Award, 1964, and Special Award, 1970; Building Constructors Society Award, 1965; Low-Cost Housing Competition Prize, Lima, Peru, 1969; Gold Medal, 1972, and Silver Medal, 1973, Sign Design Association, Tokyo; Tokyo Metropolitan Governor's Special Award, 1972; Cultural Merit Award, Kurume City, 1975; Auguste Perret Award, International Union of Architects, 1978; Mainichi Art Award, Tokyo, 1979. Honorary Fellow, American Institute of Architects, 1971. Address: 1-11-15 Otsuka, Bunkyo-ku, Tokyo 112, Japan

Works:

1956 Tonogaya Apartment House, Yokohama
1958 Sky House (Kikutake House), Tokyo
     Tower Shaped City (project)
1959 Shimane Prefectural Museum, Matsue, Japan
     Marine City (project)
1960 Factory and employees' apartment house, Tokyo
     Metabolism Floating City (project)
1961 Indoor gymnasium, Hitosubashi Junior High School, Tokyo
1963 Izumo Shrine Administration Building, Izumo, Japan
     Floating City (project)
     City Hall, Tatebayashi, Japan
     International Conference Hall, Kyoto (competition project)
1964 Tokoen Hotel, Yonago, Japan
     Dining Hall, Olympic Village, Tokyo
1965 Iwate Education Hall, Morioka, Japan
     Tokyo Channel Development (project)
1966 Civic Center, Miyakonojo, Japan
     Pacific Hotel, Chigasaki, Japan
1967 Sado Grand Hotel, Ryozu, Japan
1968 Iwate Prefectural Library, Morioka, Japan
     Shimane Prefectural Library, Matsue, Japan
     Civic Center, Hagi, Japan
1969 Civic Center, Kurume, Japan
     United Nations Low-Cost Housing, Lima, Peru (competition project)
1970 Tower for *Expo '70*, Osaka
     Martial Arts Hall, Matsue, Japan
1971 Suruga Bank Computer Center, Numazu, Japan
     Floating City, Hawaii (project)

Toto Pavilion, Ginza, Tokyo
     Mass Housing (project)
     Kyoto Community Bank Shukagumi Branch Office, Kyoto
1972 Tokoen Hotel extension, Yonago, Japan
     Ube Kosan Factory, Matsuyama, Japan
     Kyoto Community Bank Enmachi Branch Office, Kyoto
     Gymnasium, City University, Shimonoseki, Japan
1973 Tokyo Bay Floating Project (project)
1974 Porsche Showroom, Tokyo
     City Hall, Hagi, Japan
     Pasadena Heights Housing, Mishima, Japan
1975 Aquapolis, *International Ocean Exposition*, Okinawa
     Nikkei Aluminium Factory, Funabashi, Japan
     City Center Redevelopment, Yamaga, Japan
1976 Biwako Shopping Center, Otsu, Japan
     Floating Hotel (project)
     KIC Floating Platform (project)
1977 Floating Cassette System (project)
     Kyoto Community Bank Kisshoin Branch Office, Kyoto
     Kyoto Community Bank Mukoh Branch Office, Kyoto
1978 Junior and Senior High School Buildings, Gakushuin, Japan
1979 Tanabe Museum, Matsue, Shimane, Japan
     Kyoto Community Bank Fushimi Branch Office, Kyoto
1980 Seibu Store, Darumay, Japan
     Kyoto Community Bank Nishiyamashina Branch Office, Kyoto
     Kyoto Community Bank Rakusai Branch Office, Kyoto
1980/
81 TK Museum, Karuizawa, near Tokyo

Publications:

By KIKUTAKE: books—*Architecture Textbook no. 1: Drawing*, Tokyo 1955; *Architecture Textbook no. 6: Planning and Design*, Tokyo 1957; *Metabolism*, Tokyo 1960; *Metabolic Architecture*, Tokyo 1968; *Wooden Culture, The Japanese Language* (high school Textbook), Tokyo 1969; *Human Architecture*, Tokyo 1970; *A Human City*, Tokyo 1970; *Essence of Architecture*, Tokyo 1973; *Kiyonori Kikutake: Works and Methods 1956-1970*, Tokyo 1973; *Floating City*, Tokyo 1973; *Ideology of Design*, Tokyo 1974; *Environment of Design*, Tokyo 1974; *Creation of Design*, Tokyo 1974; *Field of Design*, Tokyo 1974; *Method of Design*, Tokyo 1974; *Future of Design*, Tokyo 1974; *Community and Man*, Tokyo 1975; *Community and Civilization*, Tokyo 1975; *Kiyonori Kikutake: Concepts and Planning*, Tokyo 1978; article—"Humanity and Architecture", with Teijiro Muramatsu, in *The Japan Architect* (Tokyo) March 1975.

On KIKUTAKE: books—*This Is Japan* by Noboru Kawazoe, Tokyo 1962; *World Architecture 4*, London 1967; *New Directions in Japanese Architecture* by Robert Boyd, London and New York 1968, Barcelona 1969; *The Third Generation* by Philip Drew, London 1972; articles—"The Kikutake House" in *The Japan Architect* (Tokyo), January/February 1959; "1963 Pan Pacific Citation Awarded to Japan's Kikutake" in *Architectural Record* (New York), March 1964; "The Approach of Kiyonori Kikutake" by Günter Nitschke in *Architectural Design* (London), October 1964; "Hotel Tokoen, Yonago, Japan" in *Baumeister* (Munich), February 1966; "Suruga Bank Lakeside Lodge" in *L'Architecture d'Aujourd'hui* (Paris), April 1966; "The Morioka Grand Hotel" in *The Japan Architect* (Tokyo), July 1966; "The Miyakonojo City Hall" in *The Japan Architect* (Tokyo), October 1966; "A Profile of Kiyonori Kikutake" by Hiroki Onobayashi in *The*

Kiyonori Kikutake: Aquapolis at the *International Ocean Exposition*, Okinawa, 1975.

architecture such as eternality, completion and unity. Especially, when it comes to modern architectural problems, I define the period after 1950 as the equipment/technological age, brought about by highly-developed equipmental technology such as artificial lighting, elevators, air conditioning, communication, computers, electronics, etc. I believe that the situation calls for the creation of a new type of architecture, one that is entirely different from the structural/technological architecture of the past.

Such ideas of mine towards architecture as well lie behind traditional Japanese architecture and they exist in Japanese culture. My ideas are derived from them. My ideas are characterized by the three-step methodology, in which Image and Form are brought freely into the open by placing Kata (Prototype) as the axis: I consider this the distinctive feature.

—Kiyonori Kikutake

When Metabolism was launched in 1960 at the time of the World Design Conference, Kiyonori Kikutake was already known for his Sky House. Supported on tall wall columns, it is essentially a single room marked off by storage units, with the services located on the periphery to facilitate later change of models. Additional rooms for children were to be suspended underneath the floor slab. Thus he anticipated the Metabolist philosophy of change and growth, despite the deceptively orthodox vocabulary of the design.

Throughout the 1960s, Kikutake was a member of the Metabolism Group, which emphasized the cyclical, organic character of cities, and he himself contributed utopian proposals for cities builtout on water. Yet despite this association, Kikutake never tied himself to any single style or doctrine, and his output during the decade is characterized by great variety.

In the Izumo Shrine Office Building and the Tokoen Hotel, for example, he tried to reconcile historical and modern forms, reflecting the "Tradition Debate" that was most active in the 1950s (and that produced, among other buildings, Tange's Kagawa Prefectural Government Office). Izumo, with its slanted screen-like walls, is meant to recall the way rice is left to dry out in the fields, and Tokoen employs traditional wood structural details (in concrete) and a shell roof for the restaurant on top, which gives the hotel a "traditional" silhouette.

Though the two buildings are different in spirit, they both reveal the architect's preoccupation with structure. Like Tange, Kikutake deliberately sets himself challenging structural problems to be solved for each project: at Izumo there is a 40 meter span cleared by prestressed beams, and in Tokoen the fifth and sixth floor hotel rooms are suspended from above.

But he is unlike Tange in one respect: whereas Tange integrates the design into a tightly-knit whole, Kikutake is often content to let the parts remain individuated—hence the little parabolic explosion in the otherwise monolithic Izumo building or the exuberant articulation of functions in Tokoen.

Perhaps the work that best reveals Kikutake's structural and traditional concerns is the one that was never built, his entry for the Kyoto International Conference Hall competition. Cruciform in plan, it had a central core of elevators to the conference halls at the top level. The building expanded in volume as it went up, and its precast, prestressed beams were staggered to create a structural expression recalling Buddhist temple construction. The jury, though strongly attracted to the project, finally rejected it on the grounds that the placement of the halls on top made the circulation too difficult. (The Conference Hall was built eventually on the basis of Sachio Otani's design.)

Though Metabolism has come to be identified with a futuristic image, Kikutake rarely resorts to the more obvious devices such as capsules in his actual buildings. The Pacific Hotel, with its bathroom units cantilevered out, is one exception and can stand comparison with Kurokawa's later more awkward

Japan Architect (Tokyo), March 1967; "Kritische Anmerkungen" by Manfred Speidel in *Bauen und Wohnen* (Zurich), July 1967; "Wettbewerbsentwürfe für die International Kongresshalle, Kyoto" by Manfred Speidel in *Bauen und Wohnen* (Zurich), July 1967; "Children's Land School in a Grove" in *The Japan Architect* (Tokyo), November 1967; "The Iwate Prefectural Library" in *The Japan Architect* (Tokyo), November 1968; "Shimane Prefectural Library" by Shigeru Furukawa in *Approach* (Osaka), March 1969; "Expo Tower" in *The Japan Architect* (Tokyo), May/June 1970; "New Developments in Japanese Architecture" by Mildred F. Schmertz in *Architectural* Record (New York), September 1970; "Pragmatischer Metabolists: Kurume City Hall" in *Baumeister* (Munich), December 1970; "Pasadena Heights, Tagata", in *The Japan Architect* (Tokyo) June 1975; "Seibu Otsu shopping centre in *The Japan Architect* (Tokyo) March 1977; "Metabolist Kiyonori Kikutake", special issue of *Space Design* (Tokyo) October 1980; "Japanese signs", special issue of *Process: Architecture* (Tokyo) December 1983.

Bibliography: *Kiyonori Kikutake: New Wave Architect of Japan* by James P. Noffsinger, Monticello, Illinois 1979.

My design method involves three steps. These are: 1) ka (image); 2) kata (prototype); and 3) katachi (form). Above all, I consider the problems of metabolism within the prototype stage. That is to say, I pursue a "replacement system" through the fields of city planning, architecture, equipment, tools and details. The reason is that I tend to believe that it creates a more favorable environmental system for man. These ideas have been realized in projects such as a marine city and a mouvenette and in other movable systems and flexible and changeable systems that I have proposed.

Furthermore, I believe that it is necessary to create a favorable environment for man by expanding the alternatives of his life activities. I'm trying to introduce a multi-channel system. This means that I advocate a finiteness, fluidity and co-existence of architecture as opposed to the historical concepts of

Nakagin Building. Rather, Kikutake's work is most striking precisely when he has applied Metabolist ideas to conventional programs.

He has developed over the years proposals for floating cities as a means of expansion for land-starved societies. The Aquapolis, a pavilion built for the Exposition in Okinawa, is a partial realization of these ideas. This is the most futuristic of his buildings, yet it may also be one of his least successful. The architect has lost control in this almost purely engineering enterprise, and the interior with its curiously banal hotel-lobby atmosphere is disappointing.

Like Tange's OsakaExposition Theme Pavilion, the Aquapolis marked the end of an era of rapid economic growth and uncritical worship of technology in Japan. Kikutake's recent work indicates a new direction, but his past accomplishments already assure him a place among the most imaginative architects of his generation.

—Hiroshi Watanabe

KILEY, Daniel Urban.

American. Born in Boston, Massachusetts, 2 September 1912. Educated at the Graduate School of Design, Harvard University, Cambridge, Massachusetts, 1936-38. Served in the United States Corps of Engineers, 1942-45: Chief of Design Presentation Branch, Office of Strategic Services; awarded Office of the United States Chief of Council Legion of Merit for design and construction of the Nuremberg Courtroom Internal Trials, 1945. Married Anne Lothrop Sturges in 1942; children: Kathleen, Kor, Christopher, Antonia, Gracie, Timothy, Aaron and Caleb. Draftsman, Warren H. Manning, Cambridge, 1932-38; Apprentice Associate Draftsman, Landscape Design and Regional Planning, National Park Service, Concord, New Hampshire, 1939; Associate Town Planning Architect, United States Housing Authority, Washington, D.C., 1939-40; President,

Office of Dan Kiley, Washington, D.C., and Middleburg, Virginia, 1940-41, and Franconia, New Hampshire, 1940-51; President, Dan Kiley and Partners, Charlotte, Vermont, 1951-74; President, Kiley/Tyndall/Walker, Charlotte, 1974-79. Since 1979, President, Dan Kiley/Peter Ker Walker, Landscape Architect/Planning Architect, Charlotte. Member: Board of Design, University of Minnesota, Minneapolis, 1960; President Kennedy's Advisory Council for Pennsylvania Avenue, 1962-65; Board of Design, University Circle, Cleveland, 1965-68; Boston Redevelopment Authority Board of Design, 1966-67; Architectural Registration Board, Vermont, 1967; Board of Design, Redevelopment Land Agency, Washington, D.C., 1967-69; Cambridge, Massachusetts Redevelopment Authority, 1968-82; Vermont Governor's Committee of Manufacturing/Housing, 1969-70, and Technical Review Committee for State Planning, 1973; Vermont Council for the Arts, 1974. Member, Minnesota Capitol Area Architectural and Planning Commission, 1968-79. Graham Foundation Lecturer, Chicago, 1975; Landscape-Architect-in-Residence, American Academy in Rome, 1975-76. Exhibitions: *Architects under 45*, Architectural League, New York, 1958 (toured the United States, 1958-62); Museum of Modern Art, New York, 1960; National Academy of Design, New York, 1968; Iowa State University, Ames 1968; Ball State University, Muncie, Indiana, 1972; Metropolitan Museum of Art, New York, 1972; Harvard Graduate School of Design, Cambridge, Massachusetts (retrospective), 1980; *Built Landscapes*, Harvard Graduate School of Design, Cambridge, Massachusetts, 1984 (toured the United States). Recipient: First Prize, with Eero Saarinen, Jefferson Memorial National Competition, St. Louis, 1948; First Prize, with Ron Gourlay, Student Union Competition, University of New Hampshire, Durham, 1951; Residential Design Award, American Society of Landscape Architects 1962; Allied Professions Medal, 1971, Collaborative Achievement in Architecture Award, 1972, and Honor Award, 1973, American Institute of Architects; Residential Design Award, National Landscape Association, 1973; Environmental Award, U.S. Federal Highway Administration, 1977; Out-

standing Contribution to Landscape Architecture Award, American Horticultural Society, 1983. Associate Member, National Academy of Design. Address: Kiley/Walker, East Farm, Charlotte, Vermont 05445, U.S.A.

Works (landscape design and planning):

1940 Collier House, Leesburg Pike, Washington, D.C.
1942 Willow Run Housing, Michigan (with Louis I. Kahn)
Lily Ponds Housing, Washington, D.C.
Penny Pack Woods (housing), Philadelphia
Coatesville Housing, Pennsylvania
1945 Nuremberg Internal Trials, Germany (as architect)
1947/
48 Jefferson Memorial, St. Louis (competition project; with Eero Saarinen)
1951 New Town Aluminium Ltd., Kitimat, British Columbia, Canada
Student Union, University of New Hampshire, Durham (competition project)
Mill Creek housing, Philadelphia (with Louis I. Kahn)
Baker House, Greenwich, Connecticut (with Minoru Yamasaki)
Federal Reserve Bank, Detroit
1953 Miller House, Columbus, Indiana (with Eero Saarinen)
1955 Concordia Junior College, Fort Wayne, Indiana (with Eero Saarinen)
1956 IBM Building, Rochester, Minnesota (with Eero Saarinen)
Union Carbide and Carbine Company, Eastview, New York (with Gordon Bunshaft)
United States Air Force Academy, Colorado Springs (with Walter Netsch)
Reynolds Metals Building, Richmond, Virginia (with Gordon Bunshaft)
1957 Chicago Filtration Plant
1958 Law Library, University of Chicago (with Skidmore, Owings and Merrill)

Dan Kiley: Oakland Museum, California, 1962.

Dulles International Airport, Chantilly, Virginia (with Eero Saarinen)
1959 Third Block, Independence Mall, Philadelphia
1960 North Court, Lincoln Center, New York
1962 Stanley McCormick Court, Art Institute of Chicago
Oakland Museum, California (with Kevin Roche)
Design of Pennsylvania Avenue, Washington, D.C.
Burr Memorial, Hartford, Connecticut
1963 Stiles and Morse Colleges, Yale University, New Haven, Connecticut (with Eero Saarinen)
1964 Irwin Union Bank and Trust Company, Columbus, Indiana (with Eero Saarinen)
IBM Building, Milwaukee (with Harry Weese)
Rochester Institute of Technology, New York (with Kevin Roche, Harry Weese and Edward L. Barnes)
1965 Study of the Washington Mall and Tidal Basin, Washington, D.C. (with Skidmore, Owings and Merrill)
Fredonia College, New York (with I. M. Pei)
Kenwood-Hyde Park Housing, Chicago (with Harry Weese)
1966 New Haven Parks, Connecticut
Snowbird Ski Resort, Alta, Utah
Tenth Street Overlook, Washington, D.C.
Tufts University, Medford, Massachusetts
University of Lagos, Nigeria
1967 Ottauquechee River Basin, Vermont
Calgary Place, Alberta
1968 Cummins Engine Company, Columbus, Indiana
1969 Chicago Inland Regional Parks
Squibb Corporate Headquarters, Lawrenceville, New Jersey
1970 Rockefeller University, New York
Mall and Plazas for Dalle Centrale, La Defense Paris
Miami River Corridor, Dayton, Ohio
1971 National Gallery of Art, Washington, D.C.
Blackwell Park, Roosevelt Island, New York
1972 Baltimore Inner Harbor
1973 Fort Lawton Park, Seattle
McLean Hospital, Belmont, Massachusetts
McLean Hospital, Boston
1974 South Court, Smithsonian Institution Washington, D.C.
Minnesota State Capitol, St. Paul
Riverfront development, Springfield, Massachusetts
1975 Washington Cathedral
Woodruff Plaza, Atlanta, Georgia
Detroit Art Institute
1977 Gallaudet College, Washington, D.C.
Conservatory surround, New York Botanical Gardens
1978 Urban renewal development plan for Winooski, Vermont
East Shore Park, New Haven, Connecticut
Cummins Engine Company, Brussels
Chace Mill Hydro-Electric Dam, Burlington, Vermont
Amalgamated Transit Union, Bethesda, Maryland
Coca Cola Corporate Offices, Atlanta, Georgia
Riverfront Park, Springfield, Massachusetts
Nuclear Use Systems Corporate Headquarters, Rockville, Maryland (with Hellmuth, Obata and Kassabaum)
Kentucky Courts Justice and Law Complex, Frankfort, Kentucky
Kensico Plaza, Vallhalla, New York
Kennedy Library, Columbia Point, Dorchester, Massachusetts (with I. M. Pei)
Kendall Square Redevelopment, Cambridge, Massachusetts (with Design Advisory Group and Moshe Safdie)
1979 Detroit Institute of Art Galleries and Grounds, Detroit, Michigan

London Standard Bank interiors, London
Dallas Art Museum, Dallas, Texas (with Edward L. Barnes)
1980 Mint Museum, Charlotte, North Carolina (with Harry Wolfe)
Cummins Engines Components Plant, Madison, Indiana (with Eisenman/Robertson)
1981 Bank of Korea, Seoul
Carma Towers, Seattle, Washington (with McKinley Architects)
Sedgwick/Gardiner's Corner Offices and Plaza, London (with Fitzroy Robinson Partnership)
Lincoln West, New York (with Gruzen and Partners)
Liverpool Street Station Redevelopment, London (with Fitzroy Robinson Partnership)
1982 Campeau/Criswell Project, Dallas, Texas (with I. M. Pei and Harry Weese)
Mud Island North Resort Development, Memphis, Tennessee (with Walk Jones and Francis Mah)
Villa Philbrook, Tulsa, Oklahoma
1983 Steiren Sculpture Court, Trinity University, San Antonio, Texas
National Sculpture Garden, Washington, D.C. (with Skidmore, Owings and Merrill)
Stamford Atrium interiors, Stamford, Connecticut (with Moshe Safdie)
Candlestick Point Park, San Francisco
Marine World Executive Park, San Francisco (with Gensler and Associates)
1984 Middlebury College, Vermont
Christian Theological Seminary Housing, Indianapolis, Indiana (with Edward L. Barnes)
Gregory Reynolds House, Peecham, Vermont
Offices, 333 Bush Street, San Francisco (with Skidmore, Owings and Merrill)
1985 Dulles Airport Terminal, Washington, D.C. (with Davis Buckley)
East Shore Park phase III, New Haven, Connecticut
Field House, Miami, Florida
Fountain Place, Dallas, Texas (with I. M. Pei, H. Cobb and Harry Weese)
Gregory House, Wayzata, Minnesota (with Eisenman/Robertson)
Shelburne Museum, Vermont
Topnotch at Stowe, Stowe, Vermont
Two Bellevue Center, Seattle, Washington (with McKinely Architects)

Publications:

By KILEY: articles—"Landscape Design in Urban, Rural and Primeval Environments," with Garrett Eckbo and James C. Rose in *Architectural Record* (New York), May 1939; "Site Planning: The Modern Way to Expand Your Living" in *Better Homes and Gardens* (Des Moines, Iowa), 1951; "Three Landscape Architects Look Ahead" in the *New York Times*, 5 January 1959; "Nature; The Source of All Design" in *Landscape Architecture* (Louisville, Kentucky), January 1963; "A Man Is Nature: Thoughtful Planning" in *Echo Vermont* (Thetford Center), January 1963.

On KILEY: articles—"Dan Kiley" by Clemens Kalischer in *Vermont Life* (Montpelier), Summer 1967; "Renowned Landscape Architect Here to Give View on Moving Monument" in *Lancaster News Era* (Pennsylvania), 23 June 1970; "Landscaping the Urban Jungle" by Henry Mitchell in the *Washington Post*, 10 October 1971; "Co-ordination and restraint", in *Country Life* (London), March 1981; "Landscape Design: Works of Dan Kiley", special issue of *Process:Architecture* (Tokyo), October 1982; "Step lightly on this earth" in *Inland Arch-*

itect (Chicago) March/April 1983; "The Work of Dan Kiley", in *Annual Symposium of Landscape Architecture* (Charlottesville, Virginia), February 1984; "Kiley Shares Memoirs of His Education and Development as a Landscape Architect" in *HGSD News* (Cambridge, Massachusetts), May/June 1984; "Return to Columbus" in *AIA Journal* (Washington, D.C.), June 1984.

*

My approach to design is like my approach to life. I seek wholeness in life and therefore in design. Today there is a new cosmic awareness that man and his environment are inseparable; not man and nature but man as nature. Through landscape architecture I seek to express this connectedness with the universe; a thorough analysis of each problem, with up-to-date technical knowledge and an always expanding awareness of nature, yields a solution which is appropriate to the extent that it sensitively expresses the client's needs and the site. The form is the result. Design describes that process of discovery through which the form becomes known. It is unique for each problem; each problem is different and requires fresh insight. I find direct and simple expressions of function and site to be most potent. In many cases, though not all, this has led me to design using classic geometrics to order spaces that are related in a continuous spatial system that indicates connections beyond itself, ultimately with the universe.

I grew up in the heart of Boston, with its maze of backyards and alleys. I experienced space that was predominately architectural, manmade. Summers spent on my grandparents' farm in New Hampshire; I grew aware of a living space moving and changing among the trees, expanding in the fields between the mountains and growing smaller in the dark woods. Simplifying and living close to nature has always been important in my life since then. By increasing knowledge and sensitivity to nature, I attempt to reconnect myself and others with man's ecological source. I gained practical experience in landscape architecture early. Working in the office of Warren Manning after I got out of high school in 1932, design was real life problems, not the academic exercises I found at Harvard School of Design in 1936-38. From my early experience stems my conviction that design aims to solve functional problems not create forms and patterns which are ends in themselves. Greater influence in my approach to design came from the works of world philosophers; Emerson, Thoreau, Goethe, Herodotus, Jung rather than formal education.

My education of the landscape consists importantly of knowledge and experience of historical gardens and places; which continually expose creative and beautiful ways human needs have been accommodated, e.g. Villandry etc.

A great designer faces his problem directly and solves it with the most economical means. He simplifies the problem and finds, through his creative imagination, ways of solving problems in a more economical higher way. This principle, I believe, is the basis for all art. Art is the simple functional utensils of primitive people that we display in our museums.

Though undeniably beautiful, the Japanese garden is highly sculptural. It is the Japanese house which excites me and influences my design with its ordering or continuous, interpenetrating spaces into a serviceable and unified whole.

During the time I was at Harvard I grew aware (through publications mainly) of the development of the modern movement in architecture. Space was now the medium for design, flowing throughout the building freed from traditional structural constraints. This freedom, this design in three dimensions (four including time) must also be expressed in landscape design (Miller House) I was convinced.

I do not believe in checklists and formulas for design. Each problem and site is unique and must be approached with an open mind. Design should not be imposed but *elicited* from the people, the site and the conditions that surround each problem. The designer must first project the ideal solution; i.e. the highest possibility for the place, then modify this ideal projection only as necessary for a realistic solution. The design is incomplete; it is the skeleton for further growth and development. One sets the design in motion and it makes its own growth; and organism continually in a state of dynamic equilibrium trying to find its place in the universe.

In landscape architecture projects of all scales, the objective is the integration of man and nature into one. Obviously the problem becomes increasingly complex moving from small scale (house) to middle scale (multi-use, commercial etc.) to large scale (malls, parks, cities etc.). Keeping in mind wholeness, in any case, the consistent parts of the design must be related one to another and to their surroundings inside and outside.

As situations become increasingly urban, open space and the connections between them become crucial. Open space and green space, as integral not additional parts of the urban fabric can provide relief from urban pressures and a connectedness beyond the city. Without denying the intensely urban character of a place.

The technological revolution has alienated man from nature. I hope we might think about and try to regain the ability, impaired by the selfish pursuit of material wealth, to treat the environment with the respect man had when dependent on it for his livelihood. I am excited by the possibilities of open space and structural interplay as a continuous modulating system relevant to our understanding of the universe today. Despite everything, life should be joyful and there should be a sense of fun and excitement in what you are doing. I believe design can raise people's level of consciousness and heighten awareness of the unity of nature, truth, beauty and ourselves.

—Dan Kiley

Dan Kiley is a pioneer of modern landscape architecture. His education at Harvard Graduate School of Design in the late 1930s exposed him to the transitional period in that school's curriculum, from the Beaux Arts tradition to architectural modernism. Walter Gropius had not yet arrived at Harvard, but the seeds of the modern style were already planted, and Kiley and his contemporaries were searching for expression in landscape design to compliment the new architectural modernism.

At first, Kiley was interested in the development of form as a pure art rather than in the development of solutions to problems from a functional viewpoint. In his early work, his preoccupation with design form led him to ignore the functional aspects, to exploit the ground and design idea, and to use too little restraint.

The great designers, Kiley believes, analyze all the conditions and specific aspects of a problem, and go through all the analyses and processes of design. Then, almost automatically, a larger view presents itself. Although seemingly disconnected, this emergence of understanding develops the solution by itself and transcends conditions and requirements.

Form does not come by searching for it. It comes as a byproduct of solving problems with functional solutions. Form should be forgotten in the process of design and it becomes a reality by way of the solution. Beauty, excitement and possibility come from addressing the simple need, as tools of a primitive culture, whose forms we celebrate in museums, are but objects created to solve a simple need.

Kiley believes each problem requires a new set of investigations, endeavors and values. Design values which are carried from place to place, from problem to problem, are dangerous if they are preconceived. Often a grave task of the designer is to dispel the client's preconceived impressions based on solutions he has seen elsewhere but which do not apply to his problem. The conditions and requirements of each problem are very different, and the designer must approach each problem in a new light. The designer should work to enlighten people of the variety of the possibilities of solutions open to them. He should be looking at the overall idea first and not be thinking of making little designs in space out of reference to any other part.

Many of Kiley's works are not landscape designs surrounding buildings, but works where buildings surround his landscapes. His collaborations with architects are numerous, and his landscape projects, integrally related to buildings, show a genius of design harmony of landscape and building.

The education of the designer should include the knowledge of his materials, his tools, plant materials, structure, drainage, details, and so forth. The broader the background, the more potent the designer. But Kiley believes his greatest inspiration has come from the great, broad philosophers, who have waded through the specific and individual ideas and solutions, and have emerged to a world of overviews and general insight. The strength of a design depends on the sensitivity in working out the functional aspects, to become released from them, and to become connected to the Universe in the broadest, poetical sense.

—Stephen P. Hamilton

KILLINGSWORTH, Edward Abel

American. Born in Taft, California, 4 November 1917. Educated at the University of Southern California, College of Architecture, Los Angeles, 1935-40 (Newcomb Prize, 1940), B.Arch. 1940. Served in the United States Army Engineers, in Europe, 1941-45 (Bronze Star, 1944): Captain. Married Laura Catherine Baird in 1943; children: Gregor and Kim. Associate, office of Kenneth S. Wing, Long Beach, California, 1945-53; Partner, with Jules Brady and Waugh Smith, Killingsworth, Brady, Smith and Associates, Long Beach, 1953-67; President, Killingsworth, Brady and Associates, Long Beach, 1967-82. Since 1982, President, Killingsworth, Stricker, Lindgren, Wilson and Associates, Inc., Long Beach; since 1970, Vice-President, Killingsworth, Brady and (Fred) Sutter, Honolulu. Professor of Architectural Design, University of Southern California, 1963-68. Chairman, American Institute of Architects Fellowship Jury, 1976. Exhibition: *Olympic 84/84 Architects*, Los Angeles, 1984. Recipient: First Prize, *Bienal*, Sao Paulo, 1961; California Governor's Award, 1966. Fellow, American Institute of Architects, 1962. Address: Killingsworth, Stricker, Lindgren, Wilson and Associates, Inc., 3833 Long Beach Boulevard, Long Beach, California 90807, U.S.A.

Works:

1957 Clock-Waestman-Clock Attorneys Offices, Long Beach, California
1958 Hertz Auto Rentals Offices, Pasadena, California
Opdahl House, Long Beach, California
1959 Cambridge Office Building, Long Beach, California
1961 Community Bank, Huntington Park, California
Shell Chemical Laboratory, Torrance, California
Reef, Oakland, California
Hancock House, Long Beach, California
Case Study Triad, for *Arts and Architecture* magazine, La Jolla, California
Alondra Junior High School, Paramount, California
1961 Master plan for the California State University at Long Beach
1962 Montecito Park Apartments, Glendale, California

DeBell Country Club and Facilities, Burbank, California
Case Study House No. 25, for *Arts and Architecture* magazine, Naples, California
1963 Duffield Lincoln-Mercury Showroom, Long Beach, California
Peninsula Shopping Center, Palos Verdes, California
Buffums Peninsula (store), Palos Verdes, California
1964 Kahala Hilton Hotel, Honolulu
1965 Buffums Lakewood (store), Lakewood, California
Coyote Point Restaurant, San Mateo, California
1966 Religious Center, University of Southern California, Los Angeles
Virginia Country Club additions and alterations, Long Beach, California
Atlantic Research Corporation, Costa Mesa, California
Van Luit and Company Offices, Glendale, California
Hof's Hut Restaurant, Long Beach, California (with Eldredge Combs)
1967 Student Union, University of California at Riverside
Dining Facilities, Pitzer College, Claremont, California
1964 Buffums (store), La Habra, California
Kahala Beach Condominiums, Honolulu
Marina Pacifica Condominiums, Long Beach, California
Riviera Methodist Church, Redondo Beach, California
1969 Buffums Fashion Valley (store), San Diego, California
Plaza Inn, Rancho, California
Castaway Restaurant, Burbank, California
Marina, Berkeley, California
Lutheran Church, Newport Harbor, California
1970 Brady House, Long Beach, California
Killingsworth House, Long Beach, California
Roberts House, Laguna Beach, California
1971 Plaza and Access Ways for the *Queen Mary*, Long Beach, California
1972 Married Student Housing, University of California at Santa Barbara
College Union, California State University at Long Beach
Terminal Island Federal Correctional Institution, California
Seaport Village, Long Beach, California
Janss House, Sun Valley, Idaho
1973 Hollywood Park Hotel, Inglewood, California
Halekulani Hotel, Honolulu
Al Khobar Hilton Hotel, Saudi Arabia
Al Jubail Hilton Hotel, Saudi Arabia
Sun Valley Inn, Sun Valley, Idaho
College of Architecture and Fine Arts, University of Southern California, Los Angeles (with Sam Hurst)
Buffums Laguna (store), Laguna Hills, California
Navy Cafeteria, Naval Shipyard, Long Beach, California
Women's Housing, Terminal Island Federal Correctional Institution, California
Harbor Square Condominiums, Honolulu
Dominguez Water Corporation, Long Beach, California
1974 Oceangate Building, Long Beach, California
Buffums Westminster (store), Westminster, California
Buffums Santa Anita Fashion Park, Arcadia, California
Mercedes-Benz Sales and Service Building, Hollywood, California
Honolulu Medical Group Building
Center for Continuing Education, Long Beach Memorial Hospital, California
Elkhorn Condominiums, Sun Valley, Idaho

Edward Killingsworth: Boca Beach Club and Cabanas, Boca Raton, Florida, 1978.

1975 Ascuaga's Nugget Gambling Casino remodel-
ling, Reno, Nevada
1976 Jakarta Hilton Hotel, Indonesia (with Raglan
Squire)
Headquarters Building, California State Uni-
versity at Long Beach (with Deasy and
Bolling)
1977 Marina Pacifica Shopping Center and Village,
Long Beach, California
1978 Korea Hilton Hotel, Seoul
Kapalua Bay Hotel, Maui, Hawaii
Boca Beach Club Hotel and Cabanas, Boca
Raton, Florida
Pacific Terrace Convention Center, Long
Beach, California (with Architects Assoc-
iates)
City Hall and Main Library, Long Beach,
California (with Allied Architects)
Los Angeles County Sheriff's Administration
Building and Crime Laboratory, Los
Angeles
Kapalua Bay Shopping Center, Maui, Hawaii
1979 Postal Facility, Long Beach, California
Patisserie, Kahala Hilton Hotel, Hawaii
1981 Jakarta Hilton Hotel additions, Indonesia
1982 Kuching Hilton Hotel, Sarawak, Malaysia
1983 Mauna Lani Bay Hotel, Hawaii
Aspen Lodge, Colorado
Sheraton Hotel, Redondo Beach, Florida
Mauna Lani Pointe Condominiums, Hawaii
Marriott Resort and Spa, Desert Springs,
California
1984 Crescent Hotel, Phoenix, Arizona
Tucson Inn, Tucson, Arizona
Marriott Hotel, Long Beach Airport,
California
Hyatt Regency Hotel, Grand Cypress, Florida
Emerald Hotel, Anaheim, California
1985 Vista International Hotel, Vista, California
Phoenician Hotel, Scottsdale, Arizona

Publications:

On KILLINGSWORTH: Books—*Photographing
Architecture and Interiors* by Julius Shulman, New
York 1960; *Contemporary Houses Evaluated By
Their Owners* by Thomas H. Creighton and Kath-
erine M. Ford, New York 1961; *Mid-Century*
Architecture in America, edited by Wolf Von
Eckardt, Baltimore 1961; *Modern California Houses*
by Esther McCoy, New York 1962; *Beautiful Homes
and Gardens in California* by Herbert Weisskamp,
New York 1964; *Architects on Architecture,* edited by
Paul Heyer, New York 1966, London 1967; *Intern-
ational Private Houses* by Werner Weidert, Stuttgart
1967; *Art in Architecture* by Louis G. Redstone, New
York 1968; *Hotels: An International Survey* by
Herbert Weisskamp, New York 1968; *The Illustrated
Guide to the Houses of America* by Richard M.
Ballinger and Herman York, New York 1971; *They
Chose to Be Different: Unusual California Homes* by
Chuck Crandall, San Francisco 1972; *Los Angeles:
The Architecture of Four Ecologies* by Reyner
Banham, London 1973; *Houses Architects Design for
Themselves* by Walter F. Wagner Jr. and Karin
Schlegel, New York 1974; *Santa Barbara Architec-
ture* by Herb Andree and Noel Young, Santa
Barbara, California 1975; *Case Study Houses 1945-
1962* by Esther McCoy, Los Angeles 1977; *A Guide to
Architecture in Los Angeles and Southern California*
by David Gebhard and Robert Winter, Santa
Barbara, California and Salt Lake City, Utah 1977;
The Photography of Architecture and Design by
Julius Shulman, London 1977; *Architects' Own
Houses of the World,* Tokyo 1983; articles—
"Elkhorn" in *Architectural Record* (New York),
January 1974; "Elkhorn Holiday Town, Idaho" in
Baumeister (Munich), June 1976; "An Artist in
Architecture" in the *Los Angeles Times,* 1 May 1983;
"Halekulani Hotel" in *Honolulu Magazine* (Hawaii),
August 1983; 'Architects' Work from Here to
Borneo" in *Long Beach Press Telegram* (Long
Beach, California), 9 April 1984; "Hyatt Regency at
Grand Cypress" in *Building Design and Construction*
(Chicago), August 1984; "Grandest Tour of All
Hawaii's Five Finest Hotels" in *Los Angeles Times
Magazine,* 7 October 1984.

It is difficult to say what really punched the button,
turning me to architecture. I'm not sure that I know I
suspect that I am a classicist at heart, and what I liked
most about architecture is to be found in its rich past.
I love balance, a clear and compelling axis, careful
proportion, respect for tradition. What does this love
of classical characteristics have to do with my own
work? Well, I suspect that, somehow, in my way, I
have been trying to recapture what was done so well
in the past, although in an idiom consistent with the
materials and needs of our own time. This is
especially true of our "Case Study" work for that
powerful editor, John Entenza, when he was running
Arts and Architecture. I was searching for an elusive
something in residential design which gave me a
feeling deep down, absolutely true to myself, of
serenity, simplicity and, perhaps because of these,
significance.

It was with those 'Case Study Houses" that I
started my search for good spaces. High ceilings,
rooms flowing into one another without walls, tall
doors—in fact, if I have a 'trademark," it must be
those tall doors. But this is important only in that a
tall door points up the importance of space. It is so
good to be in a space where the spirit can soar, and,
with all of this, it must soar with the sense of balance
and proportion set up by the spaces we create. What
better goals in life can there be? To create a condition
in which you can really *see* the spirit soar?

My original goal was not toward architecture but
toward painting and sculpture; once, I would rather
paint than eat. Although this love has since been
transfused into building, it does say a lot about my
roots as an architect.

Probabaly this love is the main reason I have such a
respect for indigenous architecture, no matter where
it may be. And this is also probably why I have
gradually developed an approach to design which I
call "the architect as collector." Every work is a
collection of, and a sorting out of, a variety of
influences and circumstances that swirl about the
process of design. It is an especially vital perception
when building in other lands, as we are doing in Bali
and Jakarta, where the elements of indigenous
culture are so worthy of respect and can be used as
sources of design. As a "collector," I develop,
through design, the basic parameters and planning
concepts and, into this framework, we bring the local
experts and artisans and craftsmen to "do their own
thing" which, as in Bali or Jakarta, has been a great
tradition for hundreds of years. This is much more
than a plasticized pasting on of old images and
symbols, which is why so many "authentic" buildings, set into *really* authentic locales, come off as
travesties of the very traditions the architecture is
trying to emulate. At our Bali Hilton, for example,
we are working with the craftsmen to create a great
piece of Balinese architecture that will *incidentally* be
a hotel. Here sculptors will work for five to ten years,

as part of the hotel staff, embellishing themes that have been used over and over through time.

My major quarrel with "modern architecture" is that so many building designers seem to be searching for what they think is new rather than for what is good. Most modern buildings make bad neighbors—to me an unforgivable sin. For many years now there has been a theoretical permissiveness about this, as though originality at any cost is all right. This is why, after the similarity of the machine-like structures of the early modernist period, you see so many strange, forced, contrived forms passing for "innovation" and "expressiveness." This has to do with another major quarrel of mine—that too many architects would rather "do their own thing" than respect the character and scale of the locale or district or street in which they are building. Why can't more of us architects be good neighbors?

Then there is one more quarrel. This has to do with the architect's relationship with his client. Architecture as an outgrowth of ego is an imposition on the needs to be served, the people to be accommodated, the community which will have to live with the building, and certainly it is an imposition on the man paying the bills. Not that an architect should bow down and pander to the mediocre, just to get a job. But I feel that an architect can, by identifying himself with the problems and values of his client, help that client to become part of the creative process and, in doing so, instill a sense of quality that might not have been there before. The highest praise that I can have is when the client identifies so much with his *building* that he forgets I ever existed.

—Edward A. Killingsworth

Edward A. Killingsworth's approach to architecture is consistent with a quiet but rich variety. His simple wood post-and-beam construction is carefully detailed to overcome the problem of shrinking and twisting. The entrances to his buildings are frequently through a garden overlooked from the interior spaces surrounding it. Fountains and reflection pools are often employed to utilize the spatial feeling of the intimately scaled proportions. The landscaping becomes an integral part of the whole, with soft textures and irregular outlines contrasting with the refined dimensions of the precise structures.

His award-winning Opdahl House, built in Long Beach in 1958 on a small 30' x 80' lot, was oriented to the courtyard and reflection pool for a sense of spaciousness. Stepping stones across the pool lead to a two-story-high living room with glass from floor to ceiling. The success of this residence influenced his commercial design. His own office is approached over a shallow pool with round pebble-concrete stepping stones stopping at a blank crimson-colored wall before turning left to a tall entrance door flanked by fixed glass. The parking lot, in front, is beautifully landscaped with trees and vines. Elements of his residential design appear in his Duffield Lincoln-Mercury Agency, also in Long Beach—high ceilings with plate glass walls framed in white timber post and beam construction.

In the early 1960s, the magazine *Arts and Architecture* commissioned him to design several case study houses, among them a triad in La Jolla. Here he was allowed to be innovative, expressing all of his fresh, new ideas—seventeen-foot high entrance doors leading into a two-story atrium surrounded by plate glass. The interplay of light and shadow from the trellises he designed for these houses influenced his future work.

The publication of his architectural genius attracted the attention of Hilton Hotels who were looking for an architect for their hotel in Hawaii, one who could reflect the quiet and casual elegance of the islands in a romantic setting. Killingsworth's design for the Kahala Hilton Hotel, at Waikiki, met all their requirements. His aim was an unobtrusive environment in the natural setting of a lagoon, embellished with waterfalls. The main ten-story structure, in the shape of two rectangles raised above the ground, is approached through a grand thirty-foot high lobby.

The trellises of precast, pre-stressed concrete, covered with flowering vines, support the lanai balconies of the guestroom wings. From each window there are framed views of the gardens, which have been laid out according to traditional principles of the Italian Renaissance. Double rows of palms line the entrance driveway. While the structure of the hotel is a work of art, the guests are influenced to remember only the gracious rooms, the lush gardens, and the elegant informality.

Because of the wide publicity given to the Kahala Hilton, the firm of Killingsworth, Brady and Associates was also commissioned to design hotels in Saudi Arabia, Indonesia, Bali, Korea, Tahiti, Noumea New Caledonia, Fiji, and Florida. Their luxurious Kapalua Bay Hotel and shopping center in Maui, Hawaii is thought by many people to surpass even the beauty of the Kahala Hilton.

Killingsworth has also been active in his home city of Long Beach, where he designed the Civic Center, which includes a City Hall tower of concrete spires, separated by smooth planes of glass, reaching toward the sky, the city library, an underground parking structure, and public parks graced with weeping willow trees. Close to the Civic Center is his Pacific Terrace Convention Center. The main form is a large glass structure, topped with a massive concrete cornice, set on a multi-level concrete structure. The fifty-foot high lobby, with its cantilevered grand staircase, takes full advantage of the spectacular view of the Pacific Ocean surrounding it. The interior is simple, devoid of ornament, so as not to distract from the natural setting.

Although Killingsworth sums up his architectural philosophy by saying, "I'm not looking for new principles in architecture, only good principles," he has created a style of his own that is not just "good," but unique in its graceful, delicate simplicity.

—Peggy Cochrane

KIRBY, Ronald Hubert.

British. Born in Lusaka, Northern Rhodesia, now Zambia, 3 January 1936. Educated at Lusaka Convent, 1940-44; Muir College, Uitenhage, South Africa, 1945-52; University of Cape Town, South Africa, 1953-59 (Muir College Bursary; Northern Rhodesia Government Bursary), B.Arch. 1959. Married Rosemary Longridge in 1964; daughter: Jane. Joined the architectural firm of Montgomerie and Oldfield, Salisbury, Rhodesia (now Harare, Zimbabwe), 1960: Partner, with H. G. (Nick) Montgomerie and Peter Oldfield, Montgomerie, Oldfield, Kirby, Salisbury, and Lusaka, Zambia, since 1962, and with Michael Denn and Neil Grobbelaar, Montgomerie, Oldfield, Kirby, Denn, Grobbelaar (MOKDG), in Johannesburg, since 1979; Partner, in association with Denis Clarke-Hall, Montgomerie, Oldfield, Kirby, London, 1964-68; established branch offices of Montgomerie, Oldfield, Kirby, in Blantyre, Malawi, 1966, in London (in association with APT International), 1975, and in Cape Town (in association with Elliott, Grobbelaar), 1977. Founder, Zambia Institute of Architects Board of Education, 1968-71; President, Zambia Institute of Architects, 1970-72; Chairman, Commonwealth Association of Architects Africa Region Meeting, 1971; Chairman, Zambian Southern Planning Authority, 1972-77; Registrar, Architects and Quantity Surveyors Registration Board of Zambia, 1972-78; Zambia Representative, Commonwealth Association of Architects Board of Education, 1977. Chairman, Council for the Construction Industry, Zambia, since 1973. Exhibition: *Studio Kirby*, Johannesburg, 1984. Recipient: Bronze Medal, Royal Institute of British Architects, 1962; Industrial Architecture Award and Commercial Architecture Award, 1964, Commercial Architecture Award and Civic Architecture Award, 1968, Institutional Architecture Award, 1971, 1973 (twice), and Domestic Architecture Award, 1978, Zambia Institute of Architects; First Prize, Central Medical Stores Complex Competition, Lusaka, 1973; First Prize, New Central Ministerial Headquarters Competition, Lusaka, 1975; First Prize, Ndola Civic Centre Competition, Zambia, 1975; First prize, United Arab Emirates National Assembly Complex Competition, Abu Dhabi, 1976; First Prize, New Life Sciences Complex Competition, University of the Witwatersrand, Johannesburg, 1977; International Habitation Space Award, Zambia, 1981; Merit Award, Institute of South African Architects, 1983. Address: Montgomerie, Oldfield, Kirby, Denn, Grobbelaar, Architects and Planners, 12 Clamart Road, Richmond, 2092 Johannesburg, South Africa.

Works:

1963 Queen Victoria Memorial Library, Salisbury (with Peter Oldfield and Andrew Stein)

1964 Refined Oil Products Factory and Offices, Lusaka (with Nick Montgomerie)
John Sisk Headquarters, Lusaka (with Nick Montgomerie)

1965 Development plan for the Evelyn Home College of Further Education, Lusaka (with Nick Montgomerie)

1966 Zambia National Assembly Complex, Lusaka (with Nick Montgomerie and Bob Anderson)

1968 African Farming Equipment Showrooms and Offices, Lusaka (with Nick Montgomerie and Bob Anderson)
National Housing Board Headquarters, Lusaka (with Nick Montgomerie and Bernard Gouveia)
International Air Terminal Buildings, Ndola, Zambia (project; with Nick Montgomerie)

1969 Lochinvar Game Camp, Zambia (project; with Nick Montgomerie)

1971 Lukashya Trades Training Institute, Kasama, Zambia (with Nick Montgomerie and Bob Anderson)
Mansa Trades Training Institute, Mansa, Zambia (with Paul Andrew and Richard Martin)
Development planning study of the Central Government Office Area, Lusaka (with Nick Montgomerie and Paul Andrew)
Prototypical office block for the Central Government Office Area, Lusaka (project; with Nick Montgomerie and Bob Anderson)
Bank of Zambia Town House Complex, Lusaka (with Peter McGurn and Craig Wilson)
Department of Lands and Surveys Headquarters, Lusaka (project)

1972 Development and planning study of Naperi Farm, Blantyre, Malawi (with Mike Denn and Craig Wilson)
Professorial Department, Lusaka Teaching Hospital (with Nick Montgomerie)

1973 Town planning and architectural design for a new Mine Town, Kansanshi, Zambia (with Bob Anderson)
U.S.S.R. Embassy, Lusaka (with Derek Simpson and Nick Montgomerie)

1974 Teaching Block, Evelyn Home College of Further Education, Lusaka (with Bob Anderson)
British High Commission Residence, Lusaka (project; with APT Partnership and David Wager)
Development feasibility studies for Mining Administrative Headquarters, Kankola and Chingola, Zambia (with Bob Anderson)
Development and redevelopment studies for the Lusaka Hotel (with Francis Ndilila)

Ron Kirby: Ravenna Town House, Lusaka, 1977.

Mines Trust Schools, Kankola, Chingola, and Kitwe, Zambia (with Ken Barnes)

1975 Government Ministerial Complex, Lusaka (competition project; with Lewis Construction, Nick Montgomerie, Bob Anderson, Walter Dobkins, and Mick Pilcher)

International School Media Centre, Lusaka (with Bob Anderson)

Ndola Civic Centre, Ndola, Zambia (with Nick Montgomerie and Bob Anderson)

1976 Cathedral Centre, Pietermaritzburg, South Africa (competition project; with Peter Oldfield and Peter Boer)

Federal Headquarters, University of Zambia, Lusaka (project)

Intercity Bus Terminus, Lusaka (with Peter Jackson)

National Assembly Members Motel, Lusaka (with Tony Logan)

1977 National Assembly Speakers Lodge, Lusaka (with Ken Barnes)

Radford House, Leopard's Hill Road, Lusaka (with Tony Logan)

United Arab Emirates National Assembly Complex, Abu Dhabi (competition project; with APT Partnership and David Wager)

Work Bank Student Hostels, Evelyn Home College of Further Education, Lusaka (with Nick Montgomerie and Peter Jackson)

Ravenna Town House, Lusaka (prototype; with Roy MacLachlan)

National Medical Stores Complex, Lusaka (with Lewis Construction and Nick Montgomerie)

Clinic, University of Zambia, Lusaka (with Roy MacLachlan)

1978 Life Sciences Complex, University of the Witwatersrand, Johannesburg (with Julian Elliott and Neil Grobbelaar)

Lonrho Headquarters, Lusaka

1982 University of Bophuthatswana Master Plan and Design, Taung, South Africa (with Neil Grobbelaar)

1983 University of Bophuthatswana Master Plan, Odi, South Africa (with Neil Grobbelaar)

1984 University of Zambia Master Plan, Ndola (with Nick Montgomerie)

Publications:

By KIRBY: articles—"A Review of Educational and Related Problems in Small Developing Countries" in *Insitu* (Lusaka), April 1969; "The Role of the Architect in Development Planning in Africa" in *Insitu* (Lusaka), May 1971; "The Challenge of the Next Two Years" in *Times of Zambia Building Supplement* (Lusaka), October 1971; "Education of the Architect to Meet His Role in Africa" in *Insitu* (Lusaka), no. 18, 1972; "Civil Service Housing in Zambia" in *Insitu* (Lusaka), July 1977; "Science and Technology in the Construction Industry" in *Insitu* (Lusaka), July 1978.

On KIRBY: books—*Economic Housing in Africa* by R. Jährling (United Nations Economic Commission for Africa Publication), Addis Ababa 1976; *Architecture in the Seventies* by Udo Kultermann, London 1980; articles—by Jim Morrison and Ian Whittaker in *Insitu* (Lusaka), July 1969; in *Z Magazine* (Lusaka), April 1973; in *Insitu* (Lusaka), no. 23, 1974; in *Insitu* (Lusaka), no. 24, 1975; in *Insitu* (Lusaka), April 1977; by Alex Brown in *Insitu* (Lusaka), July 1977; by Alex Brown in *Insitu* (Lusaka), December 1977; "Bank of Zambia Maisonettes" in *RIBA Journal* (London), July 1980; "House Ravenna, Lusaka" in *Zimbabwe Environment and Design* (Harare), September 1982; "University of Bophuthatswana at Taung" in *Architecture South Africa* (Cape Town), November/December 1982; "Unibo at Taung – the 'Red Earth' University" in *South African Construction World* (Johannesburg), December 1982; "New Life Sciences Complex, University of Witwatersrand" in *Architect and Builder* (Cape Town), January 1983; "Studio Kirby" in *Architecture South Africa* (Cape Town), November/December 1983.

Architecture is, at any given time, an expressive bridge between man's neophilic desires and neophobic concerns, given context by place, programme and culture. It is a rich language, inherently multivalent with international, national, provincial, parochial and fashionable values. As with all languages, it has a structure, a grammer; it has syntax, verbs and nouns, adjectives and adverbs and it uses characters and symbols as its visual means of communication.

The modern architecture of the thirties through the halcyon sixties, was founded in the rejection of the social, political and artistic values of the previous two decades. Its drive, motivation and relevance was its socio-political aptness in an age when we, in the Third World, were still optimistically termed the New World. A liberal and euphoric age of new values, new dimensions and new opportunities, in which "modern" was a compulsive, glamorous and indeed hopeful architectural banner to which many of us rallied. The best of the architecture in Southern Africa through that period expressed the ebullience and liberal evocations of that time.

Post-sixties realities, the cummulative tyrannies of place, poverty and circumstances of the third world peoples, forced a re-think. We, in Southern Africa, are now concerned with bridging between powerfully driven socio/political desires, with few exceptions neophilic and nacent cultural understandings, always neophobic. To effect this bridge it will be necessary for architects to devise an inclusive design process, in order to structure a relevant African design language as we move to the turn of the century. To quote the poet Robert Graves:

"Assemble, first, all casual bits and scraps
That may shake down into a world perhaps....
Sigh then, or frown, but leave (as in despair)
Motive and end and moral in the air;
Nice contradiction between fact and fact
Will make the whole human and exact".

—Ron Kirby

The architectural work of Ron Kirby is built firmly on the foundation laid by his partners, Nick Montgomerie and Peter Oldfield. Oldfield, a postwar graduate of the Liverpool School, and Montgomerie, from the London office of Denis Clarke-Hall, started practice in Salisbury after winning the Peterhouse School competition in the early 1950s—the first of many competition successes that the firm was to enjoy in the future. A characteristic of the firm's work has been the analytical clarity of problem definition, together with direct and efficient problem solution in the modern idiom. To this, Ron Kirby, who was born in Zambia, has added regional concerns and understandings that include the central as well as the southern and western parts of the African continent. He has also added architectural skills and enthusiasms, as well as administrative involvement, of remarkable dimensions.

Kirby's Zambian work is prolific and consistent. The range of commissions includes important state and civic buildings, a large range of educational buildings, commercial and industrial developments, as well as individual and group housing.

The early work is characterized by a simple palette of materials, mainly unplastered brick with wall dominated edges incorporating adaptive shading devices and flat roofs (African Farming Equipment Offices). At the same time a recurrent built form model has been the low-rise, fat-bodied building with large top lighted and ventilated internal spaces (National Housing Board Headquarters; Department of Land and Surveys Headquarters (project); and the Evelyn Home College of Further Education). The latest work reflects a similar built form model but a different and more appropriate architectural image, a large roof-dominated structure with free standing polychrome walls—as in the Clinic for the University of Zambia.

Any review of the work of Ron Kirby must note his impressive involvement in the affairs of architecture, particularly education, at a local professional, national and international level.

—Julian Elliott

KLEIHUES, Josef Paul.

German. Born in Rheine, Westphalia, 11 June 1933. Educated at the Gymnasium Dionysianum, Rheine, graduated 1955; Technical University, Stuttgart, 1955-57, and Berlin, 1957-59, Dip.Ing. 1959; Ecole Nationale Supérieur des Beaux-Arts, Paris, 1959-60. Married Sigrid Müller in 1961; children: Jan, Hein, Jo, and Anna. In private practice, as architect and town planner, Berlin, since 1962 (in partnership with H.H. Moldenschardt, 1962-67). Professor of Design and Architectural Theory, University of Dortmund, since 1973. Initiator and Director, "Life and Work on the Ruhr" Industrial Environmental Study Project, 1975-78. Initiator and Director, Dortmund Architecture Days, since 1975, and Dortmund Architecture Exhibitions, since 1976; Editor and Publisher, *Dortmunder Architekturhefte*, since 1975; Planning Director, 1984 Internationale Bauausstellung, Berlin, 1979-84; Consultant to the Senate for Housing and Construction, Berlin, since 1983. Exhibitions: *Tendenzen*, toured Germany and Switzerland, 1976; *Wohnen im Revier*, toured Germany

and France, 1978; *Museen*, Dortmund, 1979; *La Modernité – un project inachevé*, Centre Georges Pompidou, Paris, 1982; *Ten New Buildings*, Institute of Contemporary Arts, London, 1983; *The European Iceberg*, Art Gallery of Ontario, Toronto, 1985. Recipient: Young Generation Art Prize, Berlin, 1967; Building in Brick Prize, 1968; Sandstone Building Prize, 1971; Concrete Building Prize, 1975; First Prize, Museum of Ancient History Competition, Frankfurt, 1980. Address (office): Holsterbrink 1, 4408 Dülmen-Rorup; or Schlickweg 4, 1000 Berlin 38, West Germany.

Works:

1960/
66 Kopfklinik Westend Mental Hospital, Berlin (with Peter Poelzig)
1963/
66 Housing, Fussgängerstrasse, Gropiusstadt, Berlin (with H.H. Moldenschardt)
1965 German Embassy, Vatican City (competition project)
Housing, Titusweg, Berlin (project; with H.H. Moldenschardt)
1966 Housing, Ruhwald, Berlin (project; with H.H. Moldenschardt)
1966/
67 Old People's Club, Reinickendorf, Berlin (with H.H. Moldenschardt)
1967/
68 Housing II, Ruhwald, Berlin (project; with H.H. Moldenschardt, O.M. Ungers, and others)
Hospital, Göppingen, Germany (competition project)

Plan for housing and development of the town center of Perlach, Munich (competition project; with H. Goepfert)
1967/
71 "Open Hand" Housing, Gropiusstadt, Berlin (with H.H. Moldenschardt)
1968 Congress Center, Berlin (project)
1968/
69 University of Bielefeld, Germany (competition project; with H. Goepfert)
1968/
74 Kleihues Studio, Schlachtensee, Berlin
1969/
70 Hospital, Ingolstadt, Germany (competition project)
1969/
73 Main Workshops, phase I, Municipal Refuse Collection Depot, Berlin (with W. Stepp)
Lewis-Ham Towers Housing Development, Charlottenburg, Berlin (project; with Leon Krier)
1972 Lamp in Oxidized Aluminum
Sprengel Museum, Hanover (competition project)
House for Georg Baselitz with fractured basis (project)
House for Friedrich Meckseper (project)
1972/
75 Housing Block (600 units) by the Water, Charlottenburg Sluice, Berlin (project; with M. Kausch, Leon Krier, and B. Tonon)
1972/
76 Block 270 Housing Development, Vineta Plaza, Wedding, Berlin (with M. Schonlau)
1973/
81 Neukölln Hospital, Berlin (with J. König)
1974/
75 School, Borken, Germany (competition pro-

Joseph Paul Kleihues: Municipal Refuse Collection Depot, West Berlin, 1979.

ject; with U. Falke)

1975 Reconstruction plan for Dinslaken, Germany (with U. Falke and R. Hauser)

Berliner Ring Redevelopment, Berlin (competition project; with W. Stepp)

Dusseldorf Museum (competition project; with U. Falke and R. Hauser)

Town Center, Dulmen, Germany (project; with U. Falke and R. Hauser)

1975/
78 Dahlhauser Heide Workers' Housing Development, Bochum, Germany (with R. Hauser)

1975/
79 Main Workshops, phase II, Municipal Refuse Collection Depot, Berlin (with W. Stepp)

1975/
80 Town Center Housing and Commercial Development, Wulfen New Town, Germany (with U. Falke)

1976 Financial Administration Building and School, Munster (competition project; with G. Schumann)

Exhibition Pavilion, *Documenta*, Kassel, Germany (project)

St. Martin Oratory, Kevelaer, Germany (project; with U. Falke and R. Hauser)

1976/
81 Museum, Blankenheim, Germany (with R. Hauser)

1977 Park Lenné Inner-City Housing (project; with M. Baum, U. Falke, and R. Hauser)

1978 Dr. Sluka House, Munster, Germany (with M. Baum)

Ephraim Palais (Jewish Museum), Berlin (with M. Baum, U. Falke, and R. Hauser)

Hotel, Budapester Strasse, Berlin (competition project)

Joachimstaler Platz Development, Berlin (project)

1978/
82 German Steel Museum, Solingen (with M. Baum)

1979/
82 Gerleve Monastery extensions, Coesfeld, Germany (with Eggers and U. Falke)

1980/
84 Museum of Ancient History in the old Carmelite Church, Frankfurt

1981/
82 Covered Shopping Centre, Wulfen New Town, Germany

1981/
85 Museum Complex (Bergische Galerie, City Archives, Klingenmuseum, and Grafrather Church Treasury), Solingen, near Dusseldorf

Publications:

By KLEIHUES: books—*Berlinatlas zu Stadtbild und Stadtraum*, Berlin 1974; *Park Lenné: Eine innerstädtische Wohnform*, Berlin 1977; articles—"Siedlung Dahlhauser Heide," with Spiegel and Boennighausen, in *Dortmunder Architekturhefte*, no. 12, 1978; "Building in Berlin" in *Domus* (Milan), June 1980; "Architecture needs to be cared for by all of us" in *Bauen-Wohnen* (Munich), January/February 1981; "German Federal Republic" in Architectural Review (London, June 1981; "1984: the Berlin Exhibition" in *Architectural Association Quarterly* (London), January/June 1982; "Kleihues, Walker and Ungers talk about their work at AIR" in *De Architect* (The Hague), March 1982.

On KLEIHUES: books—*Wohnungsbau/The Dwelling/L'Habitat* by Harald Deilmann, Jörg C. Kirschenmann and Herbert Pfeiffer, Stuttgart 1973; *Architektur in Deutschland* by H. and M. Bofinger, J. Paul and H. Klotz, Stuttgart 1979; *Bauen der 70er Jahre in Berlin* by Rolf Rave, Hans-Joachim Rave,

and Jan Rave, Berlin 1980; *Josef Paul Kleihues*, edited by John O'Regan, Dublin 1983; articles—"Junge Berliner Architekten" in *Deutsche Bauzeitung* (Stuttgart), no. 8, 1968; "Milieu, Surrogat einer besseren Welt" in *Der Architekt* (Stuttgart), no/ 9, 1975; "Architekturzeichnungen heute" in *Bauwelt* (Berlin), no. 19, 1975; "Landesgalerie Düsseldorf" in *Domus* (Milan), no. 4, 1976; "J.P. Kleihues," special issue of *2C Construccion de la Ciudad* (Barcelona), June/September 1977; "Gestörte Form" by Feuerstein in *Transparent* (Vienna), no. 11/12. 1977; "Hauptwerkstatt der Berliner Stadtreinigung" in *Bauwelt* (Berlin), no. 40, 1977; "Work by J.P. Kleihues" in *Space Design* (Tokyo), no. 10, 1977; "Block 270, Geschichte der Blockbebauung" in *Baumeister* (Munich), no. 12, 1977; "J.P. Kleihues: Recent Work" in *Lotus International* (Venice), no. 15, 1977; "Apologie für die Architektur als Kunst…" in *Bauwelt* (Berlin), no. 1, 1978; "5 Arbeitersiedlungen im Revier" in *Bauwelt* (Berlin), no. 14, 1978; "Park Lenné and Block 270" in *Lotus International* (Venice), no. 19, 1978; "Architektur in Deutschland" by H. Bofinger and H. Klotz in *Das Kunstwerk* (Baden Baden), no. 4/6, 1979; "Blankenheim Museum" in *Baumeister* (Munich), January 1979; "Kleihues complexities" by Lance Knobel in *Architectural Review* (London), July 1981; "The Museum of Ancient History in Frankfurt" in *Casabella* (Milan), June 1982; "Shopping Centres in Wulfen and Saarlouis" in *Bauwelt* (Berlin), 4 March 1983; "Kleihues: lining up with the Berliners" in *Building Design* (London), 17 June 1983.

Expecting nothing,
Mostly humourless,
At times angry as well,
Architecture will be talked into nothingness
The Word will, with indifferent agreement, be spoken against architecture.
Architecture is rare:
Architecture as encouragement in an increasingly organized world in which client and architect absolve themselves from responsibility and involvement.
Architecture as opposition
To political technicity and an instrumental way of thinking that reduce to routine planning and construction.
Architecture as example
Against pre-formed belief in experience and function that negates any poetry.
Architecture as poetry
Against the blind arrangement of expedient arrogance.
Architecture looking back
Timid and enchanted.
Architecture as instructive
In classical landscapes, Nepalese mountain villages, and in Las Vegas.
Architecture as renovative
In dialectic with Alberti, Palladio, Schinkel, and all the saints.
Architecture as a potential category of the new
In recognition of ever-similar among ever-changing new hells.
Architecture in search of broader autonomy
Loving planning ahead, collecting attributes,
Set up against the moral terror of pure reason and empiric realities,
Avoiding the market.
Architecture as yearning
Boundlessly.

—Josef Paul Kleihues

"I would describe myself as a rationalist, though not in the Italian sense. . . . I have nothing of the Latin in me." So says Josef Paul Kleihues, who also calls himself a "poetic rationalist" in order to explain his position. This attitude would account for the way in which he incorporates a playful element, based on the given spatial arrangements of a building, into his otherwise strictly "purist" geometrical forms, which

relate to functional purpose with an extraordinarily confident feeling for space.

The roots of Kleihues's characteristically semiotic architecture clearly stretch back as far as the classicism of Schinkel, and the strong feeling for design, combined with a clear humanitarian awareness, as well as a kind of intellectual sense of humor, has led throughout his career to exceptional works of construction. These include the classically oriented workshops of the Berlin Municipal Refuse Collection Depot—a large hall with three nave-like areas in which the collection vehicles are renovated and repaired; the Wohnblock 270, a typical Berlin redbrick town development housing block in Vineta-Platz; the center of Wulfen New Town, consisting of shops and houses; the Neukölln Hospital, Berlin; and several other designs that, *a la* Ledoux, are not more than "thoughts on paper," daydreams.

Kleihues has also gained a reputation as a pedagogue, particularly because of Dortmund Architecture Days, which he founded in 1975. This international symposium on architectural theory is held each year and produces a regular flow of relevant literature.

Together with Hardt-Walltherr Hämer (an excellent architect, who has been much admired for his theaters in Ingolstadt and Wiesbaden, the city hall of Paderborn, and the exemplary modernization of Block 118 in Berlin-Charlottenburg), Kleihues has been occupied with the preparation of the 1987 International Building Exposition in Berlin, an enterprise with hypertrophic features such as the liveliest German city has always loved. It will be the greatest building exposition ever, unusual already for its long-drawn-out development. While Hämer is in charge of the extremely difficult revitalization of Luisenstadt, almost destroyed by planning errors and speculation, in the Kreuzberg district (topic: Urban Renewal), Kleihues is responsible for Southern Friedrichstadt, severely damaged in the war bombing (topic: City Rebuilding). He has won for this cause nearly the entire phalanx of internationally renowned architects of the whole world. Thanks to his engagement, Berlin will be the city in which, as nowhere else, the (civic) architecture of the Late Modern and postmodern is formulated.

Incidentally, Kleihues has realized one of the most brilliant projects that follow his claim to a "poetic rationalism": the continuing education center of the Benedictine Cloister in Gerleve with its imaginatively conceived roof.

—Manfred Sack

KNOWLES, Edward Frank.

American. Born in New York City, 12 August 1929. Educated at Brooklyn Technical High School, 1943-47; Pratt Institute, Brooklyn, New York, 1947-51, B.Arch. 1951. Married Barbara Lee Dupree in 1952; children: Christopher, Sarah, Mary, and Emily. Worked as an assistant to Abraham Geller, New York, 1953-55, to Philip Johnson, *q.v.,* and Mies van der Rohe, *q.v.,* New York, 1955-56, and to Edward Larrabee Barnes, *q.v.,* New York, 1957-58; Instructor, Pratt Institute, 1959-60. In private practice, New York, since 1961. Partner, with Gerhard Kallmann *q.v.,* and Noel McKinnell, *q.v.,* Kallmann, McKinnell and Knowles, Boston, 1963-67; Partner, with John MacFadyen, MacFadyen and Knowles, New York, 1967-68. Professor of Architecture, Cooper Union, New York, 1960-64, and Columbia University, New York, 1965-66. Chairman, LeBrun Scholarship Committee, American Institute of Architects, 1966-67. Recipient: First Prize, New Boston City Hall Competition, with Kallmann and McKinnell, 1962. Address (office): 130 West 56th Street, New York, New York 10019, U.S.A.

Edward F. Knowles: Filene Center for the Performing Arts, Wolf Trap Farm, Virginia, 1971.

Works:

1957 Fairchild Experimental Laboratory, Yonkers, New York
1959 Wiggins Beach House, Ocean Ridge, Fire Island, New York
1960 Knowles Beach House, Davis Park, Fire Island, New York
  Edward Molyneux Townhouse, East 52nd Street, New York
1961 IBM Offices, New York
1962 Fleischmann Shopping Center, Naples, Florida
  Holy Trinity Episcopal Church, Hicksville, New York (with Seth Hiller)
1964 Pine Manor Junior College, Brookline, Massachusetts (with Kump Associates)
1967 Richmond Foundation Housing, New York
  New Boston City Hall (with Kallmann and McKinnell)
  Sachs Department Store, Brooklyn, New York
  Study of American art museums for the National Endowment for the Arts, Washington, D.C.
  Bernbaum Townhouse, East 52nd Street, New York
  Brooklyn Academy of Music Opera House restoration, Brooklyn, New York
1968 Casey's Restaurant, New York
  Forbes House, Briarcliff Manor, New York
1969 Art resources study for the City of San Francisco (with John H. MacFadyen)
  Davis Beach House, Bayberry Dunes, Fire Island, New York

U.S.O. Club, Portsmouth, Virginia
City Center of Music and Drama, New York
Coudert House, Lyme, Connecticut
Stifel House, Short Hills, New Jersey
1970 The LePerc Space (theatre), Brooklyn Academy of Music, New York
  The Chelsea Theatre, New York
  Newhouse Pavilion, Manhattan School of Music, New York (with John H. MacFadyen)
1971 Forstmann House, Montauk, Long Island, New York
  Filene Center for the Performing Arts, Wolf Trap Farm Park, Vienna, Virginia (with John H. MacFadyen)
1973 Richard Lippold Greenhouse, Locust Valley, Long Island, New York
  Music Hall Study, Troy, New York
1974 Birdsall Horse Farm, Southampton, Long Island, New York
  ANTA Theatre Study, New York
  Seattle Opera House
1975 Lowell Nesbitt Studio, New York
  Hubay House, Fishkill, New York
  Blust House, Beacon, New York
  Kislak House, Pound Ridge, New York
1976 Exotic Gardens Greenhouse Complex, Long Island, New York
  Janics House, New York
  The Drawing Center, New York
1977 Friedman-Kien Estate, Garrison, New York
  Bory House, Douglas Manor, New York
  Geoffrey Holder House, New York

Publications:

On KNOWLES: articles—"The New Boston City Hall" by Mildred F. Schmertz in *Architectural Record* (New York), February 1969; "Boston's City Hall" by Sibyl Moholy Nagy in *Architectural Forum* (New York), February 1969; "Boston's City Hall" by Ada Louise Huxtable in the *New York Times*, 8 February 1969; "A Happy Union, A Grand Simplicity" by Wolf Von Eckardt in the *Washington Post*, 23 January 1971; "New Arts Site Near Capitol" by Harold C. Schonberg in the *New York Times*, 1 July 1971; "Washington Joins Showbiz" by Robert J. Landry in *Variety* (New York), 18 August 1971; "Wolf Trap's New Crop" by Phillis Funke in the *Wall Street Journal* (New York), 3 September 1971; "New Boston Center" by Ada Louise Huxtable in the *New York Times*, 11 September 1972; "Mating of Traditional and Modern" by Norma Skurka in the *New York Times*, 1 October 1972; "High, Dry and Handsome" by Richard W. Langer in *New York Magazine*, 10 March 1975; "A 'Bare Bones' Pavilion" in *Architectural Record* (New York), November 1975; "Sculptor of Space" in *MD* (New York), October 1976; "Background for an Artist" by Peter Carlsen in *Architectural Digest* (Los Angeles), April 1977; "Just One Room Can Do It All" in *House and Garden* (New York), Spring 1978; "An Artist's House for all Seasons in New York's Greenwich Village" in *House and Garden* (London), February 1984.

My designs are generated inductively as the result of the interplay of the requirements of the project.

Significant architecture must express the emotional factors of the problem in addition to the obvious requirements of program, site, budget, and structure, or it ceases to be an art form. The rejection of any of the phenomena that are experienced at any point in history is short sighted. Historical references, popular idioms, avant garde statements, sculptural and painterly concepts all have a potential role in the design of buildings.

Any Academic approach to architecture is arbitrary and limiting. We are in an era that is a tornado of ideas. Our architecture should be no less.

—Edward F. Knowles

In 1962 Edward F. Knowles of New York, with Gerhard Kallmann and Noel McKinnell of Boston, won the national competition for the new Boston City Hall. The jury decided that the three young architects had solved the problem of designing an open, accessible structure through which the life of the city could pass—the result of the "rich expressive form" and sensitively scaled interior space. Since its opening, the reinforced concrete City Hall has been acclaimed as "magnificently monumental" without being austere or forbidding. The building doesn't merely *stand* on its sloping, trapezoid site; it is rooted to it, as if growing from the brick-faced gradient, two of its lower floors being partially buried in the mound, the outer staircases echoing the angled incline of the hill. Almost classically detailed, the concrete pillars and cross-members recall archaic Greek temples, but the building clearly forges a link between past and future. Inside, broad concourses are interconnected by escalator ramps and stairs for the 5,000 people who do business there every day. The main offices are built around an open, upper courtyard, through which light shafts illuminate the spacious inner public courts below—and all of these public areas, open night and day, allow the citizens to walk through and be part of City Hall without once having to open a door.

Since the City Hall competition in 1962, Knowles has also become known for his houses and, particularly, for his work on buildings for the arts. He is noted, too, for his skill in conversions and for his sensitivity in handling materials, especially wood.

Knowles' Fire Island beach houses are notable for their maximum utilization of space and their handling of wood and glass. Even more impressive is his conversion of an abandoned New York police stables building into a studio-home for the painter Lowell Nesbitt: it demonstrates both Knowles' genius for moulding space into elegant, functional forms and his ability to harmoniously combine conservation and innovation. A skylight greenhouse roof floods the old building with sunlight, so that details like the well-crafted old timber beams are highlighted by being presented in their new context. Another striking conversion is in upstate New York, where Knowles created a series of dwelling units for a physician from eight old farm buildings and an ice house. The farm's greenhouse was revived to its original splendor, and a cottage was raised on jacks and rebuilt from the bottom to form two apartments. Wherever possible, Knowles retained the original timbers, beamed ceilings and fine old masonry.

Apart from Boston City Hall, the Knowles commission that received the most publicity is the Filene Center Auditorium at Wolf Trap Farm Park in Virginia. It deserves its fame. Sheathed in red cedar for minimal environmental impact and maximum acoustical efficiency, the structure is set in a natural, grassy amphitheatre, so that both those inside the building and those out on its front lawn all sit on the natural slope of the ground with a clear view of the performers.

All of his designs for the musical arts are noteworthy. His work at Brooklyn Academy of Music reveals great care in the refurbished mosaic floors, lobby chandeliers, and re-designed interior spaces. For the Newhouse Pavilion of the Manhattan School of Music he created additional lounge and dining spaces, and shafts of natural light were introduced to a dark old locker room that he converted to a center of student activity.

In contrast to many contemporary architects, whose works are cold and impersonal steel and glass boxes, Knowles has built, converted and restored for people, for their human needs and activities. He follows the dictates of the environment and produces structures that are appropriate to their surroundings yet clearly state their purpose through the use of well-conceived forms and textures.

—Colin Naylor

KNUTSEN, Knut.

Norwegian. Born in Oslo, 4 December 1903. Educated at the State School of Arts and Crafts, Oslo, 1920-25. Married Hjørdis Christiansen in 1930; son: the architect Bengt Espen Knutsen. In private practice, Oslo, from 1933. Design Teacher, State School of Arts and Crafts, 1937-47; Instructor, 1956-66, and Professor, 1966-69, Oslo School of Architecture. Chairman, Oslo Architects' Association, 1952. Exhibitions: *Knut Knutsen/Arne Korsmo,* Henie-Onstad Kunstsenter, Høvikodden, Norway, 1972. Recipient: Henrichsens Fellowship, 1930; Egers Fellowship, 1948; First Prize, Norwegian Embassy for Stockholm Competition, 1952; Treprisen (Wood Architecture Award), 1961; Houens Fond Prize, 1961; Sundts Prize, 1962. *Died* (in Portør, Norway) *9 July 1969.*

Works:

1930 Salicath House, Lillevannsveien 61, Oslo
1936 Nølke House, Holmenkollen, Oslo
1937 Norwegian Pavilion, World's Fair, Paris (with Arne Korsmo and Ole Lind Schistad)
Office building, Munchsgate 5b, Oslo
Office building, Møllergaten, Oslo
Summer cottage, Ildjernet, Nesodden, Norway
Tåsen Home for the Elderly, Oslo
1938 Folk High School, Sørmarka, Norway
Design of the *Vi Kan* exhibition, Oslo (with Arne Korsmo)
Norwegian Pavilion, World's Fair, New York (project)
1939 Knutsen House, Lillevannsveien 8, Holmenhollen, Oslo
1941 Staff House (project)
Pfeiffer Summer House, Kragerø, Norway
1942 Bjørum Summer House, Jomfruland, Norway
Hauen House (project)
1944 Natvig House, Østhorn, Oslo
1946 Church, Snarøya, Norway (project)
Bergman House (project)
Borgan House (project)
Strand Hotel, Gjøvik, Norway

Fossen House, Blommenholm, Baerum, Norway
1948 Knutsen Summer House, Portør, Norway
1949 Housing development, Borstad, Norway (with Rolf Prag)
Forest cottage, Bjørum, Norway
Viking Hotel, Oslo
Town Hall, Vågå, Norway
Villa Rynning, Larvik, Norway
1952 Norwegian Embassy, Stockholm
Sjøfartsmuseet (maritime museum), Bygdøy, Oslo (project)
1953 Sundt House, Holmenkollen, Oslo
1955 Venstres Hus (office building), Møllergaten 16, Oslo
1956 Strand Cinema, Gjøvik, Norway
1958 Wathne House, Sarbuvollveien 11b, Høvik, Norway
Town Hall, Askim, Norway (project)
Lie House, Pans vei 6, Ulvøya, Oslo (with Bengt Knutsen)
Lionaes House, Pans vei 8, Ulvøya, Oslo (with Bengt Knutsen)
1959 Romsdal Vocational School (project)
Folkets Hus (Labor Movement Headquarters), Youngsgate 11, Oslo
Home for the Elderly, Erling Skjalgssonsgate 25, Oslo
Eckhoff House, Lyder Sagens gate 6, Oslo (with Bengt Knutsen)
1960 Bergendal Summer House, Tjøme, Norway
Brumund dal Church (project; with Bengt Knutsen)
1961 Thorkildsen Summer House, Portør, Norway
1962 Landasen Church, Bergen, Norway (project)
1963 Henie-Onstad Art Center, Høvikodden, Norway (project; with Bengt Knutsen)
Sollid House, Dalsveien 21, Oslo
Aasgaard House, Smestad, Oslo
1964 Town Hall, Mo I Rana, Norway (project; with Bengt Knutsen)
1965 Sundt House II, Bygdøy, Oslo
Holmen Church, Asker, Norway
Minister's House, for the Holmen Church, Asker, Norway
Grieghallen (Grieg Concert Hall), Bergen, Norway (project: with Bengt Knutsen)
1966 Cranner Summer House, Tjøme, Norway
1967 Rydning House, Besserud, Oslo
1968 Täby Church, Sweden (project)
Kontorhus (office building), Oslo (project)
Sørkedalen Residential Development, Oslo (project)

Publications:

By KNUTSEN: articles—"Samtidens billigste massemøbler" in *Byggekunst* (Oslo), no. 1, 1934; "Norges paviljong på Verdensutstillingen i Paris" in *Byggekunst* (Oslo), no. 1, 1938; "Om arkitektkurset" in *Byggekunst* (Oslo), no. 9, 1949; "Arkitektur eller pynt" in *Byggekunst* (Oslo), no. 10, 1951; "Forslag til undervisningsplan for avdeling Bygg og Statens

Knut Knutsen: Knutsen Summer House, Portor, Norway, 1948.

arkitektkurs ved SHKS" in *Byggekunst* (Oslo), no. 3, 1958; "Mennesket i sentrum" in *Byggekunst* (Oslo), no. 4, 1961; "En mesterarkitekt i Norden" in *Byggekunst* (Oslo), no. 3, 1963.

On KNUTSEN: books—*Treprisen 1961, 1962, 1964, 1966: Four Norwegian Prize-Winning Architects*, with introduction by Christian Norberg-Schulz, Oslo c. 1967; *Knut Knutsen/Arne Korsmo*, exhibition catalogue, by Per Cappelen and Christian Norberg-Schulz, Høvikodden, Norway 1972; articles—"Norvège" in *L'Architecture d'aujourd'hui* (Paris), May/June 1954; "House in Oslo" in Architectural Design (London), October 1961; "Knut Knutsen 1903-1969" by Per Cappelen in Arkitektnytt (Oslo), no. 12, 1969; "Arne Korsmo/Knut Knutsen: Arkitekturutstilling, Henie-Onstad Kunstsenter" in *Byggekunst* (Oslo), no. 6, 1972.

Knut Knutsen believed that buildings have always been used to publicize their individual owners. He thought that "things" should be made unimportant. Mankind was what mattered. He felt, too, that "nature is the most valuable and greatest source of inspiration. We are never bored with nature, but we are with buildings. We must preserve nature, and we can best do this by seeking harmony with it and making our buildings subservient to it." In an article he called his own house "the unimportant house," and his winning entry in the competition for the Stockholm Embassy was titled "The Considerate."

Knutsen was an opponent of the Modern Movement as it was understood in the immediate pred post-war periods; he also rejected the concept of style and all style-based architecture. His belief that buildings could express freedom, poetry, and harmony with nature suggests the ideas of Frank Lloyd Wright, but Knutsen shows no signs of having been stylistically influenced by Wright. Ideally, Knutsen felt, a building should be invisible, and he very nearly achieved his goal in his own summer house at Portør. This spontaneous design looks like an accidental pile of planks, hidden amongst the rocks.

His buildings demonstrate his evolving ability to embody his concepts. His pre-war Folk High School at Sørmarka is a rather conventional building and, to a high degree, so is his Tåsen Home for the Elderly. But after these works, his formal language becomes less constrained. His own house on Holmenhollen is an assemblage of small units staggered one to another. He added elements to two-storey houses to make the basic shape less clear. Windows seem to be placed where they will, without order in shape and size. But in the Stockholm Embassy, these ideas are combined with a definite architectural order; it is probably his major work. The ground floor has a very free plan, creating lively spatial relationships both between the rooms and between the interior and exterior, but the facade is contained in a clear structural framework. The upper floor uses larger and simpler forms to unite the whole, and walls and terraces tie the building to its site. The Viking Hotel in Oslo and the Strand Hotel in Gjøvik are works from the same period. The Viking Hotel has an irregular plan that relates well to its site; the Strandhas a simple form enriched by the varied use of forms and materials in the facade panels within the structural frame. The later Folkets Hus is a more conventional office building, but Knutsen's later houses continue to involve the theme of disintegration into elements and the use of rustic materials.

Knutsen's influence on the postwar generation that he taught was considerable. His work gave them positive and constructive ideas without resort to nationalistic or romantic precedents, and his ideas have continued to be an influence on several outstanding Norwegian architects who are now themselves teachers.

—Michael Lloyd

KOCH, (Albert) Carl.

American. Born in Milwaukee, Wisconsin, 11 May 1912. Educated at Harvard College, Cambridge, Massachusetts, 1930-34, B.A. (cum laude) 1934; Harvard University, Cambridge, Massachusetts, 1934-37, M.Arch. 1937; awarded Bacon Traveling Fellowship, 1938-39. Served as a Lieutenant in the United States Navy, 1944-46. Married Persis White in 1934 (divorced, 1949); children: Cyrus, Otto, Molly, and Carl, Jr.; married Jean Emery in 1951; children: David, Samuel, and Elizabeth. Worked with Sven Markelius, *q.v.,* Sweden, 1937, and with Walter Gropius, *q.v.,* and Marcel Breuer, *q.v.,* Cambridge Massachusetts, 1938; President, Carl Koch and Associates, Cambridge and Boston, Massachusetts, 1939-78: Senior Architect, United States National Housing Agency, 1942-44. Since 1978, in private practice, as Carl Koch, Architect, Boston. President, Techcrete Inc., since 1971. Exhibition: De Cordova Museum, Lincoln, Massachusetts, 1965. Recipient: Honor Award, 1949, and Industrial Arts Medal, 1969, American Institute of Architects; Bronze Medal, American Institute of Architects, Philadelphia, 1951; Gold Medal, Architectural League of New York, 1953; *Parents Magazine* Award 1954; Award of Merit, AIA/American Library Association, 1956; Boston Arts Festival Award, 1963; Frank P. Brown Medal, Franklin Institute, 1967; Quarter Century Citation, Builders Research Advisory Board, 1977. Fellow, American Institute of Architects. Address (office): 54 Lewis Wharf, Boston, Massachusetts 02110, U.S.A.

Works:

1940/
46 Snake Hill Cooperative Housing Community, Belmont, Massachusetts
1948 Design of Lustron Panelized System Houses
1949/
51 Conantum (community development), Concord, Massachusetts
1952/
63 Techbuilt Houses and Furniture (prototypes)
1953 Back Bay Center, Boston (with Pietro Belluschi, The Architects Collaborative, Hugh Stubbins, and Walter Bogner)
1954/
57 Master plans for Pease Air Force Base, Portsmouth, New Hampshire,; Dow Air Force Base, Bangor, Maine; Westover Air Force Base, Springfield, Massachusetts; Hanscom Air Force Base, Bedford, Massachusetts; and Kindley Air Force Base, Bermuda
1954/
58 Urban renewal planning studies for Webb and Knapp: Laurel Richmond Community and Kenyon Barr Community, Cincinnati; Airport Project, Camden, New Jersey; River Park, Hartford, Connecticut; Seneca Square, Buffalo, New York; Thompson Townsite, Manitoba.
1956/
59 Acorn Prefabricated Houses
1957/
59 Residential construction research project for National Steel
1958 Fiberglas bathroom for Owens-Corning
1959 Design of air conditioning for residential construction for the Carrier Corporation
1959/
60 Basic panels for the Ferro House (research house)
1960 East Hills, Pittsburgh, Pennsylvania (with the Architects Collaborative and Sert, Jackson)
1960/
61 Adaptation and development of new products for housing for Armco Steel
Lane Apartments, Antioch College, Yellow Springs, Ohio

1961/
62 College Dormitory Research Project for the Alcoa Corporation
1962 Downtown renewal plan for Louisville, Kentucky (with Constantinos Doxiades)
1963 Research project for moderate income housing, Boston
1964 Relocatable House, for the United States Air Force
Urban planning study for a new satellite community, for the Union Carbide Corporation
Academy Homes I, Boston
1964/
71 Techcrete Modular Building System
1965 USAHOME Pre-Fabricated Buildings, for the United States Department of Defense
1966/
67 Scotia Square, Halifax, Nova Scotia
1966/
72 Lewis Wharf, Boston
1967 Military housing research and development program, for the United States Department of Defense
Academy Homes II, Boston
Westminster Court, Boston
1968 Cambridge School, Weston, Massachusetts
1969 Stowe House Motor Lodge, Brunswick, Maine
1969/
72 Elmwood Park, Detroit
1970 Housing for the elderly, Lewiston, Maine
1970/
71 Tarlton, Piermont, New Hampshire
1970/
72 Arverne, New York
1971 Housing for the elderly, Brunswick, Maine
1971/
72 Madison Park North, Baltimore
1974 Elmswood Park, stage II, Detroit
1975 Lewis Wharf, stage II, Boston
Arverne, stage II, New York
1976 Madison Park North, stage II, Baltimore
1978 Housing for the elderly, Waterville, Maine

Publications:

By KOCH: book—*At Home with Tomorrow,* with Andy Lewis, New York 1958.

On KOCH: book—*Architecture USA*, edited by Ian McCallum, London 1959; articles—"Rehab Creates an Inner-City PUD" by Michael J. Robinson in *House and Home* (New York), February 1974; "Wharf into Village" in *Architecture Plus* (New York), March/April 1974.

Carl Koch and Associates are working toward an architecture consistent with both the changing tools and materials of today's exploding technology and also those human aspirations which remain unchanged.

This, we think, involves continually fresh thinking without straining for novelty. We believe that cities, buildings, and their smallest parts achieve beauty only if they function well. Good architecture must express primary concern for the people it serves—the individual and the community.

We have long believed that response to the critical problems of speed, economy and quality-control must include design of new building systems using twentieth-century industrial techniques, without sacrificing the flexibility vital to individual expression and modes of living. Close collaboration with business, industry, and government is essential in this process.

We believe in conserving the best elements of the past in our cities and in trying to reflect in new construction a sympathy with this heritage. Our principal commitment is toward improving the

Carl Koch: Lewis Wharf, Boston, 1972.

quality of life through design—to achieve vitality and enrichment of the total living environment.

—Carl Koch

Carl Koch was a pioneer of industrial housing. After spending the beginning of his architectural career designing handsome, single houses for handsome budgets, he realized that since eighty-fivepercent of all houses built come from little or no architectural design, the traditional architect is misdirecting his efforts. Koch saw the need to simplify and modularize multiple housing by using the advantages of industrialization to create sensible and comfortable housing for the increasingly mobile and concentrated, fast-growing population.

Koch, trained at Harvard in the late 1930s when the Beaux-Arts tradition was being pushed out by modernism, was struggling for direction. At this time of architectural confusion, he felt his contemporaries also lacked direction, and he packed himself off to Europe to see for himself what modernism and the International Style were all about. He went to work with Sven Markelius in Sweden, where he gained a great and long lasting reverence for the simple, clean, uncluttered houses of Scandinavia.

The new architecture for Koch lay in the successful combining of the advances of factory production of building component parts with the aesthetics of spatial and material arrangement. Working closely with the modular parts industry, he developed the "Techbuilt" house, an industrialized structure which was cheaper than the one-off singly designed house, yet more individualized than the mobile home. It included a set of prefabricated, stressed skin plywood panels arranged and connected in a simple rectilinear plan. Each set of standardized parts could be arranged with some variety and uniqueness to fit an individual client's needs.

The architect, Koch feels, must design the architectural means, not the architectural answers. He must relinquish the heavy-handedness which often leads to over-design. The architectural elements of buildings must be left to stand on their own. The architect is, in a sense, the moderator of a dialogue between the functional components of construction and the spatial needs of the client. Koch admits he initially thought that the remedy to the housing problem was in the building of more and more systems housing, but later realized that in his overwhelming concern for the construction process, he slighted the resident's humanistic needs. The success of Koch's later efforts was due to his ability to make industrialized commercial housing personally livable.

Koch's houses have a spatial and structural simplicity based on the logical and straightforward process of construction, allowing for individuality of expression in the variety of component arrangement.

—Stephen P. Hamilton

KOENIG, Pierre.

American. Born in San Francisco, California, 17 October 1925. Educated at the University of Utah, School of Engineering, Salt Lake City, 1943; Pasadena City College, California, 1946-48; University of Southern California, Los Angeles, 1948-52, B.Arch. 1952. Served in the United States Army, in Europe, 1943-46: Corporal. Married Merry Sue Thompson in 1953 (divorced, 1959); Gaile Elodie Carson in 1960 (divorced, 1975); children: Randall and Jean. Draftsman in the office of Raphael Soriano, Hollywood, California, and Kistner, Wright and Wright, Los Angeles, 1952. In private practice, Los Angeles, since 1952 (worked as a Draftsman for Jones and Emmons, Los Angeles, 1956). Instructor, Architectural Design Studio, 1961-69, Associate Professor, Institute of Building Technology, 1970-71, and since 1970 Associate Professor of Architecture, University of Southern California, Los Angeles (Director, Chemehuevi Planning Program, 1971-76). Visiting Critic and Lecturer, Yale University, New Haven, Connecticut, 1963; VisitingLecturer, Pratt Institute, New York, 1963, Arizona State University, Tempe, 1964, and University of California at San Luis Obispo, 1965; Participant, Cranbrook Seminar, Illinois, 1965; Guest Lecturer, Architectural Panel, Los Angeles, 1966. Exhibitions: *Bienal,* Sao Paulo, Brazil, 1957; Architectural League of New York, 1957; American Federation of Arts Traveling Exhibition, 1958-59;

Bethlehem Steel Traveling Architectural Exhibit, 1963; *Environment U.S.A.,* Los Angeles, 1964; *Architecture in Southern California,* Los Angeles County Museum, 1965. Recipient: Award, *Bienal,* Sao Paulo, 1957; Award, American Institute of Architects/*House and Home,* 1957, 1960, 1962, 1963; Award, Architectural League of New York, 1957; Honor Award, 1959, and Award, 1961/62, AIA/*Sunset Magazine;* Award, Architectural Institute of Southern California, 1963; Best Exhibition Building Award, Portland, Oregon, 1964; Los Angeles Grand Prix Award, 1967. Fellow, American Institute of Architects, 1971. Address (office): 12221 Dorothy Street, Los Angeles, California 90049, U.S.A.

Works:

1950 Koenig Exposed Steel House, Glendale, California
1953 Lamel Exposed Steel House, Glendale, California
1954 Squiare Exposed Steel House, LaCanada, California
1955 Scott Exposed Steel House, Tujunga, California
1957 Burwash Exposed Steel House, Sunland, California

1958 Case Study House 21, for *Arts and Architecture* magazine, Hollywood, California
Radio Station KYOR, Blythe, California
Western Saw Works, Los Angeles
1960 Case Study House 22, for *Arts and Architecture* magazine, Hollywood, California
1961 Seidel Beach House, Malibu, California
Pre-fabricated Steel Tract, Quebec, Canada
1962 Seidel Exposed Steel House, West Los Angeles
Johnson Exposed Steel House, Carmel, California
1963 Oberman Exposed Steel House, Palos Verdes, California
Mosque, Los Angeles
Willheim Wood House, West Los Angeles
Exhibition Pavilion, *Bethlehem Steel Traveling Architectural Exhibit*
Beagles Steel House, Pacific Palisades, California
1966 Factory, El Segundo, California
1968 Iwata House, Monterey Park, California
1971 Television station, Cypress, Florida
1971/
77 Chemehuevi Indian Reservation, Lake Havasu, California
1972 West Exposed Steel House, Vallejo, California
1978 Burton House, Malibu, California
1980 Gantert House, Hollywood, California
1982 Rollé House, Los Angeles
1984 Koenig House, Los Angeles
1985 Stuermer House, Hawaii

Publications:

By KOENIG: books—*The Chemehuevi Project,* with P. Rodemier and K.H. Grey, Los Angeles 1971; *The Chemehuevi Future,* Los Angeles 1973; *This Is Our Land,* Los Angeles 1974; *Remaking the Homeland,* Los Angeles 1975; *The Chemehuevi Today,* Los Angeles 1976; *Graphic Communication,* Los Angeles 1977.

On KOENIG: books—*Einfamilienhauser in den U.S.A.,* Munich 1963; *Modern California Houses* by Esther McCoy, New York 1962, 1978; *Hauser und Garten in Kalifornien,* Stuttgart 1965; *Los Angeles* by Reyner Banham, London 1971; *Drawings by American Architects* by Alfred Kemper, New York 1973; articles—"Steel and Concrete Hillside House" in *Arts and Architecture* (Los Angeles), January 1959; "Case Study House 21" in *Arts and Architecture* (Los Angeles), February 1959; "Pierre Koenig" by Esther McCoy in *Zodiac* (Milan), no. 5, 1959; "Wasser, Stahl und Glas" in *Bauen und Wohnen* (Zurich), December 1960; "Steel House by Koenig" in *Arts and Architecture* (Los Angeles), April 1961; "Steel House" in *Arts and Architecture* (Los Angeles), September 1962; "Maison Oberman, Los Angeles" in *L'Architecture d'Aujourd'hui* (Paris), September 1965; "Arts and Architecture Case Study Houses" in *Perspecta* (New Haven, Connecticut), no. 15, 1975; "On the Mies Edge" in *Domus* (Milan), February 1981; "University of Southern California—Faculty

Pierre Koenig: Electronic Enclosures Inc. Factory (now Wylie Laboratories), El Segundo, California, 1966.

Members' Projects" in *Architectural Design* (London), vol 52, no. 3/4, 1982.

Bibliography: *The Steel Frame in the Architecture of Pierre Koenig: A Selected Bibliography*, Monticello, Illinois 1984.

I became interested in modern technology and mass production as applied to housing early in my career. In 1950, while still a student at the University of Southern California, I designed and built my first exposed steel and glass house as an extra-curricular project. The house had exposed steel columns, wide flange beams and a steel roof deck, with the underside of the decking working as the ceiling. Sliding glass doors, industrial windows and metal siding completed the shell. Rather than for style, my search was for a new aesthetic based on simplicity and economy.

From this start I went on to design many houses with these systems, refining and extending ideas as new materials and processes became available. Although the houses were custom designed for private clients, each of them was a prototype for mass production.

Notable among the many steel and glass buildings over the years are the Case Study Houses 21 and 22, sponsored by *Arts and Architecture* magazine. John Entenza, editor of *Arts and Architecture*, called Case Study House 21 "some of the cleanest and most immaculate thinking in the development of the small contemporary house."

I have expanded my basic ideas into large-scale projects: factories, commercial buildings such as radio and tv stations, and medical facilities, all of which require unique solutions.

My designs include mass-produced housing for two extreme climatic conditions, one for the near-arctic (Pre-fabricated Steel Tract, Quebec) and one for the desert (Chemehuevi Indian Reservation). The first project dealt with temperatures of -40←F and the other with + 120←F. Both projects represented climatic extremes, yet each problem was solved with similar advanced technological means, using pre-fabricated combination steel and wood panels and steel frames. For the arctic houses the frames were separate and on the inside of the envelope. For the desert houses the separate frames were outside the envelope.

Believing that conservation and ecological balance starts at the land planning level, I spent six years planning the 28,000 acre Chemehuevi Indian Reservation, with the help of a Department of Housing and Urban Development grant for the design of the residential and commercial installations.

While carrying on a professional practice, at the University of Southern California I am currently involved in researching the effects of natural forces on architectural forms. My emphasis is on technology and adaptive architecture, and my research has included an investigation of the relationship between sun and form as well as experimental work with a wind tunnel which I designed and built with the help of my students.

—Pierre Koenig

The lucidity of the steel frame, utilizing industrial methods of technology, is the basis of Pierre Koenig's architectural style. Koenig is a perfectionist who believes that truth in architecture lies in the natural expression of materials, devoid of ornamentation, fakery or fad. His approach is straightfoward simplicity based on economy—not just of cost, but economy of means and of methods of energy conservation. For example, he shuns air conditioning in favour of cross-ventilation; even his buildings in the desert are air-cooled by means of evaporative coolers rather than by refrigeration. In spite of opposition by loan companies, building departments, and contractors, Koenig has remained dedicated to his own unique style.

When the magazine *Arts and Architecture* was seeking inventive architects for its case study houses, it chose Koenig to design two of them. His first house utilized the monoplanar wall together with glass curtain walls and exposed steel beams, with ceilings of steel decking. By orienting the glass walls toward the north and south, he achieved a minimum of heat gain. The house was cooled, in summer, by pumping the water from the reflection pool onto the roof. The striking color scheme of black structural elements contrasting with smooth white planes was achieved by spray painting with a machine.

The site for his second case study house was on the edge of a canyon with a sweeping view of the city lights below. The factor of the design was a ten-foot cantilever to extend the living space and allow for a swimming pool on the same level. Large, flat concrete slab bridges connect the house with the garden.

Both case study houses emerged as pure pavilions with flat roofs and wide overhangs. Industrial materials were handled with unusual spareness to obtain noble perspective. The crispness of the steel frame was accompanied by an inventiveness of plan and detail, combined with a sensitivity of proportion. In both schemes water became an integral part of the floor plan.

These houses, and others he designed for private clients, became prototypes for Koenig's large-scale projects—the 28,000 acres Chemehuevi Indian Reservation on Lake Havasu in California and a housing project near the Arctic Circle in Canada.

Koenig believes that many floor plans can be evolved from the structuralplan, and that the simple multiplication of standard structural parts can produce even more variations. This is one reason why he chooses steel, rather than wood—for economy of mass production.

—Peggy Cochrane

KONSTANTINIDIS, Aris.

Greek. Born in Athens, 4 March 1913. Educated at the Varvakion Model School, Athens, 1926-30; Technical University Architectural School, Munich, 1931-36, Dip.Ing.Arch. 1936. Served in the Greek Army, 1937-38, 1940-41, 1945-47. Married Natalia Melas in 1951; children: Dimitri and Alexandra. In private practice, Athens, since 1938. Architect, Town Planning Department, Athens, 1938-40, and Ministry of Public Works, Athens, 1942-53; Director of the Design Department, Organization of Labour Housing, Athens, 1955-57, and Greek National Tourist Organization, Athens, 1957-67. Since 1975, Special Adviser for Architecture and Environment, Greek National Tourist Organization. Guest Professor in Architectural Design, Polytechnic School (ETH), Zürich, 1967-70. Exhibitions: *Greek Anonymous Architecture* (photographs and drawings by Konstantinidis), Athens, 1967; *The Work of Aris Konstantinidis: Buildings 1938-1966*, University of Stuttgart, 1967, Polytechnic, Zürich, 1967, Architectural Association, London, 1968, Bauzentrum, Vienna, 1968, School of Architecture, Aarhaus, Denmark, 1969, and the Art Academy of Copenhagen, 1969; *Aris Konstantinidis: Drawings*, Desmos Gallery, Athens, 1975. Also a photographer; exhibitions—Athens, 1951; *Greece by Eleven Greek Photographers*, Art Institute of Chicago, 1957; *Two Greek Photographers*, with Harissiadis, Underground Gallery, New York, 1967; *Aris Konstantinidis: Photographs*, Desmos Gallery, Athens, 1976. Honorary doctorate: University of Thessaloniki, 1978. Address: Aris Konstantinidis, Architect, 24 Rigillis Street, 106 74 Athens, Greece.

Works:

1938   Country residence, Eleusis, near Athens
1939   Garden exhibition, Kifissia, near Athens
1940   Cine-News Cinema, Athens
1951   House, Vasil. Sofias Street 4, Athens
        Week-end house, Sikia, near Corinth, Greece
1952   Exhibition pavilion, Thessalonica, Greece
1955   Housing development, Athens
1956   Housing development, Pyrgos, Greece
        Housing development, Thessalonica, Greece
        Housing development, Serres, Greece
        Housing development, Piraeus, Greece
1957   Housing development, Iraklion, Crete
1958   Theatre Dressing Rooms Building, Epidauros, Greece
        Hotel Triton, Andros, Greece
1959   Motel Xenia, Igoumenitsa, Greece
        Motel Xenia, Larissa, Greece
        Exhibition pavilion, Thessalonica, Greece
1960   Hotel Xenia, Mykonos, Greece
        Hotel pavilions, Epidauros, Greece
        Motel Xenia, Kalambaka, Greece
1961   House, Kleitomachou Street, Athens
        House, Pholothei, near Athens
        House, Vouliagmeni, near Athens
1962   Week-end house, Anavyssos, near Athens
        Hotel pavilions, Epidauros, Greece
        Motel Xenia, Paliouri/Calkidiki, Greece
1963   House, Spetses, Greece
        Motel Xenia, Olympia, Greece
        Motel Xenia, Iraklion, Crete
1964   Hotel Xenia, Poros, Greece
1965   Museum, Ioannina, Greece
1966   House, Spetses, Greece
1967   Museum, Komotini, Greece
1971   Four flat building, Philiothei, near Athens
1974   House, Penteli, near Athens
1975   House and studio, Agina, Greece
        Weekend house, Agina, Greece

Publications:

By KONSTANTINIDIS: books—*Two Villages of Mykonos*, Athens 1947; *Old Athenian Houses*, Athens 1951, 1983; *Chapels of Mykonos*, Athens 1953; *Elements for Self-Knowledge: Towards a True Architecture*, Athens 1975; *True Contemporary Architecture*, Athens 1978; *Projects and Buildings: Aris Konstantinidis*, Athens 1981; articles—"Die Zukunft des Architektenberufs" in *Detail* (Munich), no. 5, 1961; "Jedes alte Bauwerk hat Bezug zu unseren eigenen Problemen" in *Detail* (Munich), no. 1, 1964; "Architecture" in *Architectural Design* (London), May 1964; "Heutige Architektur und anonymes Bauen" in *Baumeister* (Munich), no. 4, 1965; "Summer House, Anavysso" in *World Architecture 2*, London 1965; "Architecture of the Xenia Hotels" in *World Architecture 3*, London 1966; "Le Toit avant les fondations," interview, in *Le Monde* (Paris), 12 November 1981.

On KONSTANTINIDIS: books—*The New Architecture of Europe* by G. E. Kidder Smith, New York 1961; *One-Family Houses* by Pfau and Zietzchmann, Zürich 1964; *World Architecture*, vols. 1-3, edited by John Donat, London 1964-66; *Histoire mondiale de l'architecture*, vol. 2, by Michel Ragon, Paris 1972; *Geometry and Spatial Organization: A Syntax of Architecture* by Dimitris A. Fatouros, Athens 1979; *Arisz Konsztantinidisz* by Szilagyi Istvan, Budapest 1982; articles—"The Work of Konstantinidis" in *Architectural Design* (London), May 1964; "Aris Konstantinidis" in *Arquitectura* (Madrid), October 1965; "Aris Konstantinidis" by Josef Krawina in *Domov* (Prague), no. 1, 1966; "Aris Konstantinidis" by S. Dimitrou in *Bauforum* (Vienna), No. 5/6, 1968; "Aris Konstantinidis" by Szilagyi Istvan in *Hungarian Architecture* (Budapest), no. 3, 1975.

Aris Konstantinidis: Weekend House, Anavyssos, near Athens, 1962.

True architecture rises above the ephemeral and the transient and evokes in man the deepest psychological feelings and emotions, according to the conditions existing in every period and to the intellectual climate in each country.

There is always a construction problem that must be solved in harmony with sociological aims, artistic standards, and the economy. Above all, the problem of architecture is a problem of intellectual perception. Architecture reflects not only the technique of the time but also, and most important, the spirit of the time, the social life, the manners and customs, and the deepest personal emotions of man. Inasmuch as each building might be contemporary to its time from the point of view of technique (economy, hygiene, construction, etc.), it is as much a monument from the point of view of its artistic merit.

The purpose to which the architect dedicates himself is to create throughout the medium of his work the framework of a comfortable and pleasant life for the good of all—in otherwords, the architect works for one good and standard way of life, one that will be common to everyone. In this effort to achieve the universal panacea, the architect envisages the perfection of form. This will be based on the perfection of construction. Perfect construction means the research into a "typical construction," because "type" (the ancient Doric temple is a typical form; it is the perfection of a typical form, a *type* of a construction and of a form) is the result of the good and the perfect. With this type of construction and form we serve the common needs for a good and productive social life.

Good architecture starts always with efficient construction. Without construction there is no architecture. Construction embodies material and its use according to its properties, that is to say stone imposes a different method of construction from iron or concrete. I believe that we can create contemporary architecture with all materials—with any material as long as we use it correctly according to its properties. In areas where we can find nothing but stone, we should build with that local stone. We will create contemporary architecture just as we would have done with any other material because the important things will be the spirit of construction and the flexibility of our outlook and not a constructional whim foreign to the site.

I also believe that true architectural work cannot exist without a finite location just as it cannot be created without the people who live in each environment (country, area, etc.) The finite location, the climate, the topography, and the materials available in each area determine the constructional method, the functional disposition, and finally the form. Architecture cannot exist without landscape, climate, soil, and manners and customs. This is the reason why we sometimes see old buildings looking contemporary, and for the same reason, we build today contemporary buildings which could have been built in the past. Since man, from time immemorial to this day, has always lived, moved about, and breathed in the same way, perhaps nothing in our way of life has basically changed.

If something today has changed, it is the techniques of new material and the new constructional possibilities which enable us to build in a different way from our ancestors. What we build is not entirely original or new, for if our ancestors could have had our materials and techniques, they would have created the architecture of our time! However, today, we do have something different from them. It is the way in which we come into contact with our natural surroundings, with nature and landscape. Today we love landscape and nature in a different way, for when we endeavour to live more healthily, when playing sports, we are confronted with nature and landscape not as an image but as a living space. We live with nature, in nature, as we live indoors. So, the new element in contemporary architecture (and this is entirely new) is that we aim to link the interior and exterior as *one* harmonious unit. Interior and exterior space (the natural surroundings, the landscape) become an organic entity with various aesthetic results. This is always in relation to the climate of the country, the nature of the country, and the landscape. Thus, building and landscape combine to create harmony. Architects today organize the landscape as an architectural space—we work differently today because as architects we organize the natural landscape, integrating the exterior and interior into one space.

There are cases when the form of the landscape imposes the use of a material which varies according to area. The first object of care in good and true architecture is to relate the construction harmoniously with the landscape. The form of the building (in texture, colour, and quality) originates from the material as much as from its method of treatment. There comes a moment when the landscape will indicate the material and the method of construction when, in spite of having both concrete and iron, we shall build only in stone. Otherwise, we will be out of character with the landscape and out of step with its organic qualities.

I can build with the most modern materials (iron, concrete, and with the *artificial* materials of contemporary building construction) a building which will be related harmoniously with the character of the landscape. I shall do this frequently in order to challenge my architectural inventiveness, and this I must do in order to be able to prove that true architecture can be created in any place with any material. But I cannot ignore a sentimental factor, which we must reveal in our construction; otherwise, we will be stagnant and inhuman ... we must choose our material not only according to the standards of economy and pure science but also with the spirit of emotional freedom and artistic imagination. Architecture finally stands beyond pure purpose, higher than the achievements of logic and cold calculation.

If the architect is primarily a builder, he becomes finally an inspired organizer of life who designs spaces and creates forms with meaning, liveliness, and character. In the end, when his work exists as a living organism, the individual who lives in it must be able to appreciate it and to let it become a part of himself.

—Aris Konstantinidis

Aris Konstandinidis has created a wise, austere, and consistent kind of architecture, one that is particularly instructive for his contemporaries. His work, at any point in time or space, is a strict application of his socio-spatial philosophy that architecture is a "container of life." This attitude is firmly based on the Greek spatial tradition, which means, for Konstandinidis, that architecture should be organized with a network of communications, should involve well-defined orientations, simple construction materials and methods, and orthogonal geometric elements, and should be in harmony with, or be in dialectic contrast but not contradiction to, the geometry and light of the landscape.

More particularly, these basic principles can be detected in his work: 1) a strict organization based on a rectangular grid; 2) simple methods of construction and simple materials used in their natural state; 3) a persistent effort to relate the architectural work to the natural environment and to the psychological and physical scale of man; 4) space distribution, mainly through absolute and not intermediate limits: "contour" and variants in size—as well as, in particular cases, a series of columns in front of semi-covered spaces—act as transitional elements; and 5) a consistent application of these principles—yet though he strictly follows his organization and construction principles, even to the most minute details, he does not simply repeat himself: by using different materials and because of different environmental conditions, he creates architecture of the same theme but with many variations.

The Xenia Hotel on Mykonos and the tourist hotel complex at Epidaurus are two examples of his method; Konstandinidis uses a simple and clear code of conceptualization and distribution of his space and succeeds in creating solutions of a multivariant quality, appropriate for particular (and different) conditions and needs, yet with a common spatial and geometric organization.

The systematic grid geometry is used everywhere, in interior and exterior spaces, in open and semi-openair situations. The geometry moves up and down and is sensitive to contact with various materials, openings, walls, and the void. It is integrated into the natural and manmade landscape without losing its character. In this way, the geometry becomes a complex semantic system which signifies the space and obeys it as well. In most instances of Kinstantinidis's work, either in small-scale buildings such as the house at Anavyssos or in large-scale complexes such as the Mykonos Hotel, these characteristics create a tenderness, a very personal symbiosis of austerity and tenderness, based on subtle and sensitive relationships and transformations. Thus Konstantinidis lays claim to a personal place in the international scene through work that is difficult to copy.

It is also interesting that his work has developed in the same ways as he developed his relations with his employees and with the authorities. He has insisted in formulating a lifestyle through architecture, and he has defended his propositions against any intervention.

—Dimitris A. Fatouros

KOOLHAAS, Rem.

Dutch. Born in Rotterdam, 1944. Lived in Indonesia, 1950-56; educated at a Lycee in Amsterdam, 1958-62; studied at the Architectural Association School, London, 1968-72 (Harkness Travel Fellowship, 1972). Married to the architect Madelon Vriesendorp. Worked as a journalist for the *Haagse Post* newspaper, and as a freelance film scriptwriter, The Hague, 1962-67; worked with the architect O. M. Ungers, *q.v.*, at Cornell University, Ithaca, New York, 1972-75. Since 1975, Director-Partner, with Elia Zenghelis, Zoe Zenghelis and Madelon Vriesendorp, Office for Metropolitan Architecture (OMA), in New York, Berlin and London. Visiting Fellow, Institute for Architecture and Urban Studies, New York, from 1973; Instructor, Architectural Association School, London, until 1980. Exhibitions: *OMA: The Sparkling Metropolis* Guggenheim Museum, New York, 1978; *Museumsbauten: Entwurfe und Projekte seit 1945*, Museum am Ostwall, Dortmund, West Germany, 1979; *OMA: Drawings*, Architectural Association, London, 1981; *Maquettes d'Architectes*, Centre d'Art Contemporain, Geneva, 1982. Recipient: First Prize, Dutch Parliament House Competition, The Hague, 1978. Address: 10 Stirling Mansions, Canfield Gardens, London NW6, England.

Works:

1972 Exodus, or the voluntary prisoners of architecture (project; with E. Zenghelis, M. Vriesendorp and Z. Zenghelis)

1974 House, Miami, Florida (project; with Laurinda Spear)

1975 Museum of Photography, Amsterdam (project)
Roosevelt Island Redevelopment, New York (competition project; with E. Zenghelis)

1975/
76 Welfare Island Redevelopment, New York (competition project; with M. Vriesendorp)

1976/
77 Welfare Palace Hotel, New York (project; with M. Vriesendorp)

1978 Dutch Parliament House extension, The Hague (competition project; with Z. Hadid and E. Zenghelis)

1979 Prime Minister's Residence, Dublin, Ireland (competition project; with E. Zenghelis)

1979/
80 Prison renovations, Arnheim, Rotterdam (project; with S. de Martino)

1980 Public Housing Development, Kochstrasse and Friedrichstrasse, West Berlin (competition project; with S. de Martino)

1980/
82 Tower Block on a Barrage with Tower-Bridge, Rotterdam (project; with S. de Martino and K. Christiaanse)

1980/
83 Amsterdam North Residential Quarter Urban Plan, Amsterdam (with J. Voorberg)

1980/
84 National Dance Theatre, Scheveningen, Netherlands (2 projects; with J. Voorberg, S. de Martino, W. J. Neutelings and A. Karssenberg)
National Dance Theatre, The Hague (project; with J. Thomas, W. J. Neutelings, F. Roodbeen, J. van Heest and R. Steiner)

1982/
83 Parc de la Villette Development, Paris (competition project; with E. Zenghelis, K. Christiaanse, S. de Martino, R. Roorda, R. Steiner, A. Wall and J. Voorberg)

1983 East and West Site Plans for the 1989 World's Fair, Paris (competition projects; with E. Zenghelis, K. Christiaanse, S. de Martino, W. J. Neutelings, R. Steiner and A. Wall)
Apartment Buildings Complex, Groningen, Netherlands (with S. de Martino, A. Wall, J. Thomas, P. de Vroom and F. Roodbeen)
Public Housing and interiors, Amsterdam North East Quarter III, Amsterdam (with K. Christiaanse, X. de Geyter and J. Voorberg)
Two Public Housing Blocks and interiors, Amsterdam North East Quarter III, Amsterdam (with K. Christiaanse, X. de Geyter, A. Karssenberg, T. Adam and P. de Vroom)

1983/
84 Amsterdam North Redevelopment Plan, Amsterdam (with J. Voorberg)

1984 National Dance Theatre, The Hague (with J. Thomas, W. J. Neutelings, F. Roodbeen, J. van Heest and R. Steiner)
Office Buildings Complex, Churchillplein, Rotterdam (competition project; with G. Keller, J. Thomas and S. Emetts)
Villa near Paris (project; with X. de Geyter)
Landhoofd Sphere, Rotterdam (project; with G. Keller)
Three Houses with Patio, Rotterdam (project; with J. van Heest and G. Keller)
Museum of Architecture, Rotterdam (project; with J. van Heest, G. Keller and M. Guyer)
Police Station, Almere-Haven, Netherlands (with A. Karssenberg)

Community Centre, North Amsterdam East Quarter III, Amsterdam (with K. Christiaanse)
Primary School, North Amsterdam East Quarter III, Amsterdam (with R. Roorda and F. Roodbeen)

1985 De Koepel Prison renovations, Arnheim, Rotterdam (definitive project; with M. Guyer)

Publications:

By KOOLHAAS: books—*Delirious New York: a retroactive manifesto for Manhattan*, New York and London 1978; *OMA: Volendung des Wiederaufbaus, Entwurf fur ein Wohngebaude in Rotterdam*, West Berlin 1981; articles—"Ivan Leonidov's Dom Narkomtjazprom, Moscow", with G. Oorthuys, in *Oppositions* (New York), January 1974; "A Manifesto of Manhattan" in *Progressive Architecture* (New York), December 1978; "Town Planning and Delirium" in *Modo* (Milan), June 1980; "The Pleasures of Architecture", interview, in *Transition* (St. Kilda, Victoria), November 1980; "Arthur Erickson versus the all-stars", with others, in *Trace* (Toronto), July/September 1981; "Puritan-hedonist", interview with Franco Raggi, in *Modo* (Milan), April 1983.

On KOOLHAAS: books—*Museumsbauten: Entwurfe und Projekte seit 1945*, exhibition catalogue edited by Josef Paul Kleihues, Dortmund, West Germany 1979; *Architectuur en Planning: Nederland 1940-1980*, edited by S. Umberto Barbieri, Rotterdam and Milan 1983; articles—"AD Profile 5: The Office for Metropolitan Architecture in Manhattan", special issue of *Architectural Design* (London), vol. 47, no. 5, 1977; "Bijlmermeer, new suburb of Amsterdam" by G. Oothuys in *Werk/Archithese* (Zurich), May 1977; "Unbuilt England", special issue of *Architecture + Urbanism* (Tokyo), October 1977; "Rem Koolhaas and his new book 'Delirious New York'" in *Wonen-TA/BK* (Heerlen, Netherlands), June 1978; "Residence for the Irish Prime Minister", and "Expansion of the Parliament in The Hague" in *Lotus* (Venice), no. 25, 1979; "Competition for a new Parliament Building in The Hague" in *Bauwelt* (Berlin), 14 December 1979; "On Delirious New York", and "Urban Intervention" in *International Architect* (London), vol. 1, no. 3, 1980; "Koolhaas' design for an extension to the Tweede Kamer" in *De Architect* (The Hague), May 1980; "Graves, Koolhaas and Baird in Australia", and "Competition for the Irish Prime Minister's Residence" in *International Architect* (London), vol. 1, no. 4, 1981; "Interbau Berlin 1984: Koolhaas' Berlin's Pompeii" in *De Architect* (The Hague), June 1981; "The superstars of the Office for Metropolitan Architecture" in *Building Design* (London), 12 June 1981; "Rem Koolhaas—a European without humour" in *Architecture Mouvement Continuité* (Paris), June/September 1981; "Delirious Rotterdam" in *Plan* (Amsterdam), February 1982; "The breakdown of the contract—the work of the Office for Metropolitan Architecture" in *Wonen-TA/BK* (Heerlen, Netherlands), July 1982; "Rem Koolhaas: architectonic scenarios and urban interpretations" in *Dutch Art + Architecture Today* (Amsterdam), December 1982; "OMA", special issue of *L'Architecture d'Aujourd'hui* (Paris), April 1985.

*

The Dutch architectural group OMA (Office for Metropolitan Architecture) was founded in 1975 by Rem Koolhaas and Elia Zenghelis, together with Madelon Vriesendorp and Zoe Zenghelis.

OMA views the metropolis of the twentieth century as the dominant area of experience in contemporary life and perceives modern man's experience of the city in terms of symbol and association, fragmentation and collage. Taking the metaphor of the city as its starting point, the design and architectonic work of OMA is directed towards the collage of fragments of real life experience, enriched with historical references. Surrealists and Dadaists constructed "their" reality at times in a similar manner, and the expressionistic conception of the City is likewise related to OMA's. Koolhaas, who started out as a film-script writer, conceives the metropolis as a constantly self-generating anarchic-archaic system of signs and symbols. In this he comes very close to the theoretical position of Robert Venturi, Denise Scott-Brown/and Steven Izenour, formulated in their famous book *Learning from Las Vegas*. This "metropolitan myth of the twentieth century" OMA sees as most clearly embodied in the city of New York.

In their project "Delirious New York", realized between 1972 and 76 and also published as a book, the group shows how this gigantic melting-pot of mass culture and extremely varied life styles has developed an inner mechanism that is almost biological and which has determined and defined the city's inhabitants through architecture and town planning, advertisement and film, design and art, as well as through the offers of the mass media; nature, on the other hand, merely enters the picture as an alien element that has been adapted to civilization. Koolhaas has described the various elements of this collage of current urban perceptions as follows: "Religion in ruins, architecture in the process of its production, Le Corbusier's 'Plan Voisin', the Cabinet of Dr Caligari, the Waldorf-Astoria Hotel, homage to Mies van der Rohe, Dali's architectonic angelus, Ivan Leonidov's ministry of heavy industry, El Lissitzky's speaker's platform for Lenin, Malevich's architectural model, the RCA Building, the Rockefeller Center, Trylon and homage to the superstudio."

Through the associative power of psychoanalytic methods, an allegorical architectural ensemble is created as a new continuum, which represents the urban phenomenon, with all its neuroses, aspirations and phobias, its expectations and acts of aggression, in terms of a detailed architectural fiction. For Koolhaas, the constant self-renewal of that metropolitan culture functions both as program and vindication of honour; the formula on which it rests is "Manhattanism". Titles such as "The City of the Captive Globe" (1976) or "Dream of Liberty" (1974) or, again, "Welfare Palace Hotel" (1975) optimistically convey, despite their inherent neurosis, a sensitive, almost painful perception of the richness of historical forms.

Lively and varied coloration and stylistic variety of architectonic artifacts convey individualism and faith in the future, within a highly developed industrial society: a critique embodied in drawings, which does not claim to be absolute, but expresses a love of life beyond the physical actuality of the illustrated objects. This is one of the principal reasons why the cycle "Delirious New York" is currently one of the leading aesthetic repertoires of young architects and designers, and of people involved in the worlds of film and advertising, in both Europe and America.

Since the end of the 70s, the group has played an increasingly active part in competitions and realizations. Their project for the prison reconstruction at Arnheim, for example, is well known: here, Koolhaas incorporated inside a classical dome inside the building various street and urban structures from "outside" in the manner of an escapist symbol. In the centre of the rotunda, in a sunken network, the prison warders' quarters are housed. According to Koolhaas, the prisoners thus observe the warders from the galleries in a sort of democratic inversion of the conventional system. Architecture is thereby accorded, in extreme form, the function of a psychic stabilizer, a function which it could just possibly fulfil were such a project to be realized.

It was already apparent from this project that Koolhaas was consciously imbibing the planning and representational aesthetics of the early moderns: De Stijl and Constructivism. In contrast, indeed, to the architectural beliefs that held sway during the first third of this century, OMA stands today for an altered, "second modernism", looking beyond a purely pragmatic functionalism to an architecture charged with references and associations, an architecture defined in a narrative and fictional sense.

In 1980/81, for the Kochstrasse/Friedrichstrasse competition at the international architectural exhibition in Berlin, Koolhaas proposed a similarly "modernistic" variant, this time for an urban restoration scheme. Several-storied houses are grouped so as both to harmonize with the surrounding architecture and, at the same time, to point up bold contrasts with it. The project demonstrated that even "modern" blocks of houses need not necessarily be either freely composed one-offs, or those deplorable terraced rows of the 50s and 60s, which still, unfortunately, linger on in East and West Berlin. The residential blocks which Koolhaas has designed for the area right by the Wall are conceived with imaginative variations in terms both of structure and of interior layout. With a strong inward focus, despite their resemblance to Corbusier-like terraces, these buildings give a strong definition to the surrounding street area, and fulfil the function of a sensitive urban restoration without historical conformity.

Reminiscences of the Bauhaus and De Stijl movements are again apparent in a 1982 design for a residential high-rise in Rotterdam. Although the high-rise is, here too, as traditionally abrupt and solitary a structure as any of the high-rises of the so-called "new building", in contrast to the smooth façades of those classical moderns, the façade here is interrupted, broken up, almost sabotaged by the use of additions, gaps, and corridor-like extensions, which protrude obliquely from the façade. Close by this proposed high-rise in the harbour area, one of the uprights of the suspension bridge over the Maas is surmounted by a look-out tower complete with bar and restaurant. Borrowing from El Lissitzky's speaker's platform for Lenin, or from Tatlin's tower at the Second International Exhibition, this building, conceived as a dialogue to the high-rise, would have made the competition area into a constructivistically adorned stage. Through a retrospective reference to the heroic beginnings of modern architecture and its transformation into a "neo-modernism", Koolhaas has given his solution for the Rotterdam harbour area extended programmatic expression.

The radical reformulation of the basic principles of early modern architecture, which runs throughout Koolhaas's work, is amalgamated, in contrast, for example, to Richard Meier's reception of that heroic phase of modern architecture, with the dominant experience patterns of the present day. Such a way of thinking is post-modern in the very real sense of the word, because it invalidates the traditionally accepted unity of chronological, spatial and biographical experiences. The elements which characterized Koolhaas's early poetic designs—surreal experience of the contemporaneity of the uncontemporaneous, fragmentation and collage-like reconstitution of reality in the individual psyche—preserved over the course of a lengthy career, are here embodied in concrete projects. Koolhaas's oeuvre, which one might situate halfway between the poetic alienations of a Raimund Abraham, on the one hand, and the atomized world picture of a Daniel Liebeskind, on the other, demonstrates that it holds reality and fiction, history and modernism effectively in balance.

—Volker Fischer

KORN, Arthur.

British. Born in Breslau, Germany (now Wroclaw, Poland), 4 June 1891; emigrated to England, 1937. Educated at gymnasium in Berlin; Imperial College of Arts and Crafts, Berlin, graduated 1911. Served in the 5th Grenadier Guards of the German Army, 1914-18: Iron Cross. Married Regina Israel in 1919; children: Eva and Susanna. Worked as an assistant in various architectural offices in Berlin, 1911-14; planner in the Town Planning Department of Greater Berlin, 1914; worked with Erich Mendelsohn, *q.v.*, Berlin, 1919; in partnership with Sigfried Weitzmann, Berlin, 1922-30; in private practice, Berlin, 1930-35; worked in Yugoslavia, 1935-37; practised in London, working with F. R. S. Yorke, *q.v.,*and E. Maxwell Fry, *q.v.,* 1938-41; Teacher, Oxford School of Architecture, 1941-45, and Architectural Association School, London, 1945-65; retired to Austria. Secretary of the November Group, Berlin, 1924; Member, Berlin Ring, 1926; German Delegate, with Walter Gropius, *q.v.,* CIAM (Congrès Internationaux d'Architecture Moderne), London, 1934; Chairman, MARS Town Planning Committee, London, 1938. Fellow, Royal Institute of British Architects. Member, Akademie der Künste, Berlin. *Died* (in a nursing home, near Vienna) *14 November 1978.*

Works:

1922   Goldstein Villa, Grünewald, Berlin (with Sigfried Weitzmann)
1922/
  30   Kopp and Joseph Shops, Berlin (with Sigfried Weitzmann)
      Ullstein Building, Berlin (with Sigfried Weitzmann)
1928   Factory, Friedrichshagen, Germany (with Sigfried Weitzmann)
      Fromm Rubber Factory, Cöpenick, Berlin (with Sigfried Weitzmann)
      Business Centre, Haifa, Israel (competition project; with Sigfried Weitzmann)
1929   Intourist Shop, Unter den Linden, Berlin (with Sigfried Weitzmann)
1930   Master plan for Berlin: "The Town as Hotel and Factory" (with the Collective for Socialist Building)
1940   Eight flats, Lettsom Street, Camberwell, London (with F. R. S. Yorke)
1942   Town plan for Nish, Yugoslavia (competition project)
      Study of London (as Chairman of the MARS Town Planning Committee)

Publications:

By KORN: books—*Glas im Bau und als Gebrauchsgegenstand,* Berlin 1929, Munich 1981, as *Glass in Modern Architecture,* London and New York 1967; *History Builds the Town,* London 1953; articles—"Analytische und utopische Architektur" in *Das Kunstblatt* (Berlin), December 1923; "Factory at Copernick—Berlin, 1928" in *Architects' Journal* (London), September 1934; "1891 to the Present Day" in *Architectural Association Journal* (London), December 1957; "55 Years in the Modern Movement" in *Architectural Association Journal* (London), April 1966.

On KORN: books—*Internationale Architektur* by Walter Gropius, Munich 1925, 1927; *Berlin Architektur der Nachkriegszeit* by E.M. Hajos and L. Zahn, Berlin 1928; articles—"Hinweis auf Arthur Korn" in *Das Kunstblatt* (Berlin), December 1923; "Arthur Korn," special number of *Architectural Association Journal* (London), December 1957; "The Ring and Arthur Korn" in *Architectural Association Journal* (London), February 1958; "Arthur Korn (1891-1978)" in *Bauwelt* (Berlin), 9 February 1979; "The Charisma of Korn" by Dennis Sharp in *Building* (London), 9 February 1979; "Arthur Korn" by Leslie Ginsberg in *Building Design* (London), 23 February 1979; "Arthur Korn (1892-1978)" by Maxwell Fry in *RIBA Journal* (London), March 1979; "Remembering Arthur Korn" by Hubert Hoffmann in *Bauforum* (Vienna), May 1982.

While I first worked as a town planner I discovered an interest in the nature and organization of the community. Ever since then I have asked myself three questions: What is a town? What way is a modern town different from an ancient town? How can we express the uniqueness of modern life, with its industry and transport problems in an adequate art form?

In the beginning of the town planning movement, it was the Russian and German revolutions that released a stream of new thoughts, along with Le Corbusier with his design La Ville Contemporaine and the Constructivists with their new conceptions based on the visual attraction of industrial forms.

In 1928 after preliminary studies of the specific crystal character of individual towns—their morphology—and Law of Evolution, I took up the meaning of the town with greater vigour. Of the many aspects involved, two seemed to stick out: living and working. These two activities have to be linked by transport and supplied with amenities. In this way, the plan for Berlin was evolved conceiving two parallel areas, one for living and one for working, and in between, a spine with a cultural centre, shopping facilities, and a power grid.

In 1938, as a result of this spade-work on Berlin, I wrote to the MARS executive outlining a way to study London. The idea was taken up, and during the war we published our results. Having investigated the growth and changing of London, dependent upon her unique position in the world, we studied the four main components, housing, work, transport, and amenities.

Housing proved to be the most formidable problem. Gradually, a fundamentally new solution emerged which, until now, has not received the recognition it deserved. There is a progression, a hierarchy from the individual and the family to the larger unit which is London and further to the country as a whole.

There is still much hard work to be done in town planning. We must explore the possibility of the town, its physical implications and its artistic and symbolic form, and the way these things will change as our lives change under the impact of technical and industrial innovations. The questions are still in the air and demand an answer.

In the end there is still only ONE task—to establish our world—from the whole region, to the town in all its manifestations, down to the individual cell; and not to fake the issues, either by analysis or any other device, but just to establish our world with all our passion, courage, and integrity.

—Arthur Korn (1978)

The career of Arthur Korn can be divided into three phases. The first phase covers his period as a practicing architect in Berlin during the time of the Weimar Republic; the second is a period of thinking about cities and proposing planning theories and remedies for the ills that beset great cities; and the final phase is of the years after World War II, when Korn was an influential teacher in London.

After World War I, Germany was in chaos, physically and intellectually. It was the vital moment when a new architecture was being born. Walter Gropius, Mies van der Rohe, Bruno Taut, and others were evolving a new architecture in an atmosphere where tradition was equated with defeat and the demand was to forget the old world and build a new. Korn shared an office with the young Richard Neutra, and all his life he remained unswervingly loyal to the Berlin architecture of the 1920s.

There may have been plenty of ideas in the Berlin of the 1920s, but there were not many commissions for architects, and in 1929 Arthur Korn published a book, *Glas im Bau,* which showed the work of his friends and the fascination that glass held for them, both for its connotations as an industrially produced material and for its "it's there and it's not there" quality that could be used to play spatial games on a modest budget. Several designs by Korn and his partner, Sigfried Weitzmann, show this fascination with glass, notably the Kopp and Joseph shop where the entire shop front is of obscure and clear glass.

In 1930, and again in collaboration with Weitzmann, Korn produced his one masterpiece, the Fromm Rubber Factory at Copernick. Largely destroyed during World War II, pathetically little of the building now exists in this East Berlin suburb. At a time when most modern buildings were of smooth white stucco, the Fromm factory was a celebration of steel, clearly expressed and painted bright red. Korn did not develop the idea, but Mies van der Rohe took its image as his starting point for the buildings at the Illinois Institute of Technology.

With the coming of the Nazis, Korn came to England and lived modestly in a small, South London terraced house filled with the memorabilia of the heroic days in Berlin. He became chairman of the group that produced the MARS plan for London, and, although he built one small apartment building in South London, his real interest in that time was city planning; the MARS plan and his book *History Builds the Town* sum up his views. As a Hegelian and a Marxist, Korn took an extreme view of planning, which he regarded as the means of redeeming the world. A later generation, including many of his own students, was to react sharply against his belief in a totally planned enviroment.

For twenty years after World War II, Korn taught at the Architectural Association School in London. His willingness to consider and respond to any proposal, however outrageous, made him a well-loved teacher and a lasting influence on the very many students whose vision of architecture and of planning he had extended.

—John Winter

KORSMO, Arne.

Norwegian. Born in Oslo, 14 August 1900. Educated at the Technical University, Trondheim, 1920-26, Dip.Arch. 1926; toured Europe on a Henrichsens Fellowship, 1928-29. Married Öse Thiis in 1928; Grete Prytzin 1945; Hanne Refsdal in 1965; children: Nora, Anne, and Marie. Worked in the architectural office of Bryn and Ellefsen, Oslo, 1927, and Arneberg and Poulsson, Oslo, 1928; in private practice with Sverre Aasland, Oslo, from 1929; Local Government Architect, Kristiansund, Norway, 1940-41; war fugitive in Sweden, 1941-45; resumed private practice, Oslo, 1945. Teacher, and subsequently Head of the Department of Interior Design, State School of Arts and Crafts, Oslo, 1936-41, 1945-56; Professor of Architecture, Technical University of Trondheim, 1956-68. Founder of the Norwegian section of CIAM (Congrès Internationaux d'Architecture Moderne), 1950, Exhibitions: *Triennale*, Milan, 1954, 1957; *Knut Knutsen/Arne Korsmo*, Henie-Onstad Kunstsenter, Høvikodden, Norway, 1972. Recipient: Sundts Prize, 1933; Grand Prize, *Triennale*, Milan, 1954. Died (in Cuzco, Peru) *29 August 1968.*

Works:

1929 Ten single-family houses and area development plan, Frøen, Oslo (with Sverre Aasland)
Bagatelle Restaurant, Bygdøy Allé, Oslo (with Sverre Aasland)
Shops, Bygdøy Allé 3 and 7, Oslo (with Sverre Assland)

1930 Louis Benjamin Shop, Oslo
Dammann House, Havna Allé 8, Oslo (with Sverre Aasland)
Apartment building, Pavelsgate 6, Oslo (with Sverre Aasland)
1931 Three single-family houses, Apalveien, Oslo (with Sverre Aasland)
1933 Eriksen House, Kristiansand, Norway (with Sverre Aasland)
1935 Hansen House, Tuengen Allé 6b, Oslo
Terrace houses, Apalveien, Oslo (with Sverre Aasland)
Riise House, Hamar, Norway (with Sverre Aasland)
1935/
36 Heyerdahl House, Slemdalsveien, Oslo
Benjamin House, Slemdalsveien, Oslo
1936 Grain Silo, Kristiansand, Norway (with Sverre Aasland)
Design of the Trade Fair, Halden, Norway
1937 Norwegian Pavilion, World's Fair, Paris (with Knut Knutsen and Ole Lind Schistad)
Stenersen House, Tuengen Allé 10c, Oslo
Design of the *Polar Exhibition,* Bergen (project)
1938 Design of the *Vi Kan* exhibition, Oslo (with Knut Knutsen)
1947 Von der Fehr Summer House, Larkollen, Norway
Central Railway Station, Oslo (project; with Jørn Utzon)
1948 School of Commerce, Göteborg, Sweden (project; with Jørn Utzon)
Mountain School (project)
Development plan for the Vestre Vika area, Oslo (project; with Jørn Utzon)
1950 Korsmo Apartment, Bygdøy, Oslo
1951 Alfredheim Pikehjem Home for Girls, Tåsen, Oslo
Atrium Houses (project; with Christian Norberg-Schulz)
1952 Prototype apartments (project)
Development plan for the Skøyen-Oppsal area, Oslo (project; with Jørn Utzon)
Aquarium, Bergen (project; with Christian Norberg-Schulz)
1952/
53 Development plan for the central city, Oslo (project; with Christian Norberg-Schulz)
1952/
55 Three Terrace houses, including Korsmo House, Planetveien, Oslo (with Christian Norberg-Schulz)
1953 Crematorium (project; with Gunnar Gundersen)
Institute of Architecture and Design, Oslo (project)
Tostrupgården Office Building, Oslo (project)
1955 Prytz House (project)
1957 Enviromental Center, Technical University of Trondheim (project)
1958 Displays, *Unesco Exhibition,* Paris
1960 Single-family house, Halden, Norway (with Terje Moe)
1962 Britannia Hotel, Trondheim (with Terje Moe)

Designs: furniture, glassware, cutlery, jewellery, and airline cabin equipment, 1950-64.

Publications:

By KORSMO: articles—"Om butikker" in *Byggekunst* (Oslo), no. 5, 1931; "Romeksperimenter: Innredning av egen leilighet på Bygdøy" in *Byggekunst* (Oslo), no. 3, 1952; "Brukskunsts høstutstilling og hus 'Grete'" in *Byggekunst* (Oslo), no. 8, 1952; "Treavdelingen ved Statens håndverks—og kunst—industriskole" in *Byggekunst* (Oslo), no. 12, 1952; "Konferanse hos Aalto" in *Byggekunst* (Oslo), no. 1, 1954; "Drøm og virkelighet" in *Byggekunst* (Oslo), no. 2, 1954; "Japan og Vestens arkitektur" in

Byggekunst (Oslo), no. 3, 1956; "Arme Student—hvor blir det av ditt arkite sinn?" in *Byggekunst* (Oslo), no. 3, 1958.

On KORSMO: book—*Knut Knutsen/Arne Korsmo*, exhibition catalogue, by Per Cappelen and Christian Norberg-Schulz, Høvikodden, Norway 1972; articles—"Arne Korsmo og den Norske Funktionalisme" by Nils-Ole Lund in *Byggekunst* (Oslo), no. 1, 1966; "Arne Korsmo/Knut Knutsen: Arkitekturutstilling, Henie-Onstad Kunstsenter" in *Byggekunst* (Oslo), no. 6, 1972; "Nordic Day" by Peter Cook in *Architectural Association Events List* (London), no. 7, 1983.

Arne Korsmo was a vital influence on the post-war development of architecture in Norway—by example but especially as a source of ideas and as a teacher. He was the first Norwegian to build from the outset in the style of the Modern Movement, having been inspired by a visit in 1927 to the Stuttgart "Siedlung."

Korsmo's ideas are fully developed in the Dammann House of 1930, even though the influence of Mendelsohn and Dudok is detectable. The lounge, which was designed to contain a painting collection, is $15 \cdot 5 \times 4 \cdot 7 \times 3 \cdot 8$ metres, closed to the south but with gable walls fully glazed. One experiences the great panoramic view in a small semi-circular room of glass attached to the south wall. These rooms thus give a complex set of perceptions between closed and open spaces, changes of scale, and a highly-controlled relationship between the interior and exterior. The main facade uses ramps and a loggia to tie the house to its site and to express a typical vertical versus horizontal theme.

In 1938 Korsmo was responsible for the *Vi-Kan* exhibition where, despite great differences in architectural language, he collaborated with Knut Knutsen. His work in this exhibition underlines his great sensitivity to the form, colour and significance of the designed object. This not only enabled him to mount extremely effective exhibitions; it was also the foundation of his industrial design work, for which he was awarded the Grand Prix in the 1954 Milan *Triennale*.

The same sensitivity made him a master of interior design: his apartment on Bygdøy in 1951 is an outstanding example. In 1951 he also build Tåsen girls' home where, with a freer planning technique, he continued the ideas of the 1930s. At this same time he founded and led the Norwegian CIAM group, and through it, and his teaching as Head of the Department of Interior Design at the Oslo State School of Arts and Crafts, he had a powerful influence on the post-war work of younger architects. This group was responsible for examining most of the critical questions facing architecture in Norway in the 1950s and early 1960s.

In 1955, Korsmo, together with Norberg-Schulz, built a small group of houses that are significant not only for integrating industrial design ideas into building and for the extremely flexible planning made possible by these techniques but also for illuminating new paths that architecture might take.

—Michael Lloyd

KRAEMER, Friedrich Wilhelm.

German. Born in Halberstadt, 10 May 1907. Educated at the Technische Hochschule, Braunschweig, Germany, and Vienna, 1928-29, Dip.Arch. Ing. 1929, Dr Ing. 1945. Married Inge Roedenbeck in 1947; children: Annette, Kaspar, Matthias, and Sabine. In private practice, Braunschweig, since 1935: in partnership as Kraemer, Sieverts und Partner, Braunschweig, since 1962, and Cologne, since 1947. Assistant Lecturer, 1929-35, and Professor (chair in architectural theory and design), 1947-74, Technische Hochschule, Braunschweig. Exhibition: *Friedrich Wilhelm Kraemer: Aus 50 Jahren eines Architekten,* Artothek, Haus Saaleck, Cologne, 1979. Recipient: Peter-Joseph-Krahe Prize, 1955; Laves Medal, 1957; Bund Deutscher Architekten Prize, for Northrhine/Westphalia, 1965, Hesse, 1965, Bremen, 1947, Cologne, 1975, and Lower Saxony, 1976, 1982; Cologne Architecture Prize, 1980; Mies van der Rohe Award, 1981. Address: Kraemer, Sieverts und Partner, Am Romerturm 3, 5000 Cologne 1, West Germany.

Works:

1948 NWDR Radio Station, Hanover
Royal Palace, Addis Ababa, Ethiopia (competition project)
1949 Ministry of Trade Building, Bonn (competition project)
1950 High School, Wolfsburg, Germany
"Constructa" Housing, Hanover
1951 Waterways and Navigation Headquarters, Bremen
School Centre, Misburg, Germany (competition project)
Unterharz Mining and Foundry Works, Goslar, Germany
1952 Intermediate School, Peine, Germany
Golf Club, Braunschweig, Germany (competition Project)
1953 Seaside House, Cuxhaven, Germany (competition project)
Trade School, Heidelberg
1954 Evening School Building, Dortmund
1955 City Savings Bank, Osnabruck, Germany (competition project) State Bank, Salzgitter-Lebenstedt, Germany
1957 Landeszentralbank, Dusseldorf
1958 BASF Building, Tor 7, Ludwigshafen, Germany
City Savings Bank, Dusseldorf
1959 Community Building, Aluminium Rolling Mills, Singen, Germany
1960 Centennial Hall, Dyeworks, Hoechst, Germany
Student Union, University of Kiel
1961 State Chancery, Hanover (competition project)
1963 HEW Building, Hamburg (competition projec)
1964 Town Hall, Essen (competition project)
British Petroleum Headquarters, Hamburg
Constanze Company Headquarters, Hamburg (competition project)
Insurance Buildings Complex, Hanover (competition project)
Savings Bank, Einbeck, Germany
1965 Tiergarten Museum, Berlin (competition project)
School Center, Wolfsburg, Germany (competition project)
1966 Simonbank Building Dusseldorf
DKV Insurance Headquarters, Cologne
Volkswagen Foundation Building, Hanover (competition project
Sports Forum, University of Kiel (competition project)
1968 Vogel Building, Hamburg (competition project)
Grammar School, Burgdorf, Germany (competition project)
1969 Veba-Chemie Headquarters, Dortmund (competition project)
Town Hall, Bonn (competition project)
Bayer Sales Department Building, Leverkusen, Germany (competition project)
1970 Siemens Building, Perlach, Munich (competition project)
Shell Company Headquarters, Hamburg (competition project)
Landeszentralbank, Hamburg (competition project)
1971 Colonia-National Headquarters, Cologne (competition project)
1972 German Embassy, Helsinki (competition project)
1973 Bavarian Insurance Company Headquarters, Munich
Landeszentralbank, Ludwigshafen, Germany (competition project)
1974 Social Democratic Party Headquarters, Bonn (competition project)
School Center, Gifhorn-Ost, Germany
1975 DEVK State Railways Insurance Bank Building, Cologne (competition project)
Neckermann Company Building, Braunschweig, Germany (competition project)
North German and Hamburg-Bremer Insurance Company Building, Hamburg (competition project)
Town Hall, Wuppertal, Germany (competition project)
WDR West German Radio Station, Cologne
1976 Deutsche Bank, Dusseldorf
GEW Headquarters, Cologne
Thyssen Gas Company Building, Duisburg, Germany
United Insurance Group Building, Munich (competition project)
1977 Ministry of Public Works and Housing, Riyadh, Saudi Arabia

Publications:

By KRAEMER: books—*BASF Rechenzentrum,* Stuttgart 1965; *Kraemer, Sieverts, Huth: Grossraumbüros,* Munich 1968, as *Open-Plan Offices,* London 1977; *Kraemer und Meyer: Bürohausgrundrisse,* Stuttgart 1974; *Kraemer, Sieverts und Partner: Grossraumbüros,* Stuttgart 1975.

On KRAEMER: articles—"Library of the Technische Universitat, Braunschweig" in *Deutsche Bauzeitschrift* (Gutersloh), December 1973; "DKV triangle in Cologne" in *Architettura* (Rome), December 1973; "Reconstruction of a mansion in Cologne" in *Baumeister* (Munich), June 1976; "Head Office for the VEW in Dortmund" in *Glasforum* (Schorndorf), March/April 1977; "From Arsenal to Library" in *Bauwelt* (Berlin), 5 May 1978; "Insurance Building in Munich with stone facade" in *Detail* (Munich), July/August 1979; "Office Building for the Gas, Electricity and Water Authorities in Cologne" in *AIT* (Stuttgart), vol. 88, no. 5, 1980; "Local newspaper offices, Braunschweig" and "Open plan passe? Office building for Thyssengas in Duisburg" in *Deutsche Bauzeitung* (Stuttgart), October 1980; "Offices for Thyssengas in Duisburg" in *Glasforum* (Schorndorf), vol. 31, no. 3, 1981; "Friedrich Wilhelm Kraemer 70 Jahre" in *AIT* (Stuttgart), March/April 1982; "Friedrich Wilhelm Kraemer" in *Baumeister* (Munich), May 1982; "Wilhelm Kraemer 75 Jahre" in *Der Architekt* (Stuttgart), May 1982; "Cooling in Cologne" by Francis Duffy in *The Architects' Journal* (London), 3 November 1982.

The course of Friedrich Wilhelm Kraemer's career was interrupted by the Second World War, after which, in 1946, he was appointed to the chair in architectural theory and design at the Technische Hochschule in Braunschweig. Like Hans Scharoun in Berlin, Egon Eiermann in Karlsruhe, and Richard Döcker in Stuttgart, Kraemer was one of those architects of the early days who took up their teaching again as soon as the war was over and went

Friedrich W. Kraemer: VEW Consolidated Electricity Works, Dortmund, 1977.

on to impress their particular stamp on a whole new generation of architects.

Kraemer's main achievement in the 1950s—and one of the monuments of the German architectural scene—was the Unterharz Mining and Foundry Works in Goslar. It is a building that impresses for the clarity of its structural order. Compared with the usual frame buildings of the time, buildings by Kraemer, as a result of a variation in the dimensions of the supporting struts, actually succeed in presenting the technology of their construction. It was this architectural method that informed a large number of the buildings that he designed at this time, including private houses, industrial installations, and schools.

In 1962 Kraemer's practice changed, and all his subsequent works emanated from a new partnership, Kraemer, Sieverts und Partner. At the end of the 1960s be built the DKV Insurance Headquarters in Cologne, which signalled a change in the functional concept of office block construction as a series of cellular subdivisions. Instead of the conventional rectangular arrangement, Kraemer and his partners created a multi-dimensional block in relief, based on the fitting together of a chain of mutually displaced triangles, resulting in a succession of areas that were unconnected but inter-related with one another. This functional shaping and three-dimensional organization of the office areas re-emerges on the exterior of the building, to create an architectural composition of powerful effect.

Kraemer has also made a name for himself as an architectural theorist. The subject of his thesis was the planning and building of the classical theatre, and he has written extensively on the construction of office blocks.

—Jürgen Joedicke

KRAMER, (Carl August Friedrich) Ferdinand.
American. Born in Frankfurt am Main, Germany, 22 January 1898; emigrated to the United States, 1938: naturalized, 1945. Educated at the Oberrealschule, Frankfurt, until 1916; studied under Walter Gropius, *q.v.*, and Adolf Meyer, Staatliche Bauhaus, Weimar, and at the Weimar Polytechnic School, 1919; under Theodor Fischer, Technische Hochschule, Munich, 1919-22, Dip.Ing. 1922. Married Beate Feith in 1930 (divorced, 1960); Lore Koehn in 1961; daughters: Barbara, Anna, and Katharina. In private architectural practice, Frankfurt, 1923-24; worked with Ernst May's *q.v.*, City Planning Office, Frankfurt, and as an industrial designer for several companies, 1925-30; in private practice, Frankfurt, 1930-37: forbidden to work by the Reichskammer der bildenden Künste, 1937; in private practice as architect and designer, New York, 1938-52; Head of Planning and Building Office, Johann - Wolfgang - Goethe - Universität, Frankfurt, 1952-64; in private practice, Frankfurt, 1965 until his death in 1985. Exhibitions: *Die Form*, Stuttgart and Frankfurt, 1924; *Deutsche Photographische Ausstellung*, Haus de Moden, Frankfurt, 1926; *Die Wohnung*, Weissenhofsiedlung, Stuttgart, 1927; *Die kleine Wohnung*, Munich, 1928; *Der Stuhl*, Stuttgart, 1928 (travelled to Frankfurt, 1929); *Typenmobel*, Gewerbemuseum, Basle, Switzerland, 1929; *Wohnbedarf*, Stuttgart, 1932; *Good Design Is Your Business*, Albright Art Gallery, Buffalo, New York, 1947; *Bugholzmobel 1830-1947*, Museum for Kunsthandwerk, Frankfurt, 1974; *Ferdinand Kramer: Architektur und Design*, Bauhaus-Archiv, Berlin, 1982 (travelled to Frankfurt, Stuttgart, and Amsterdam, 1983). Recipient: Goethe Plaque, Province of Hesse, 1958; Honour Plaque, City of Frankfurt am Main, 1963; Honour Prize, Architects' Chamber of Hesse, 1975; Bauhaus Medal, Hochschule fur Architektur und Bauwesen, Weimar, 1979; Wilhelm Leuschner Medal, Province

of Hesse, 1981. Honorary D.Ing.: University of Stuttgart, 1981; Technische Universitat, Munich, 1981. Honoured Citizen, Goethe Universitat, Frankfurt, 1965; Honorary Member, Federation of German Industrial Designers (VDID), 1975. *Died* (in Frankfurt) *4 November 1985.*

Works:

1923 Baron von Waldhausen House, Niederpocking, Starnberg, Germany

1924 Hamburg-Amerika Lines Travel Bureau and Showroom, Frankfurt rail station, Germany

1925 Dr. Feith Apartment alterations, Frankfurt, Germany
Displays at the *Exhibition of Monza*, Italy
Frau von Schauroth and Frau Philipp Holzman Residence alterations, Lindenfels, Odenwald, Germany
City Kindergarten refurbishment, Haligartenstrasse, Frankfurt, Germany

1926 Displays at the *Deutsche Photographische Ausstellung*, Haus der Moden, Frankfurt, Germany (with Leistikow)
Frankfurt Taxicab Company Central Garage, Gutleutstrasse, Frankfurt, Germany

1927 Room interiors at *Die Wohnung* exhibition, Weissenhofsiedlung, Stuttgart, Germany
Schwesternhaus Development and City Hospital interiors, Frankfurt, Germany

1928 Eiermann-Goldschmidt House renovations, Hochstrasse, Frankfurt, Germany
Dr. Forell House interiors, Frankfurt, Germany
Dr. Claasen Office interior, at *Frankfurter Zeitung*, Frankfurt, Germany
Heinrich Cassirer Office interiors, Hamburg, Germany
House for the Banker Merzbach, Frankfurt, Germany (project)
Displays at *Die kleine Wohnung* exhibition, Munich
Displays at *Der Stuhl* exhibition, Stuttgart, Germany
Kindergarten interiors, Burchfeldstrasse, Frankfurt, Germany
Montessori Children's Home, Nuss-Allee, Frankfurt, Germany (project)

1928/
30 Henry and Emma Budge Foundation Old People's Home, Frankfurt, Germany (competition project; with M. Stam and W. Moser)
Dining Hall with Kitchen Annexe, Frankfurt, Germany
Leo Lowenthal Office interiors, Institut fur Sozialforschung, Frankfurt, Germany
Paul Wolf Photo-laboratory reconstruction, Frankfurt, Germany

1929 Cafe Goldschmit renovations, Frankfurt, Germany
Trade Education Institute interiors, Frankfurt, Germany
Children's Library, Sachsenhausen, Frankfurt, Germany
Laundry Ironing-Room interiors, Frankfurt, Germany
Office interiors at the Kunstgewerbemuseum, Frankfurt, Germany
Westhausen Residential Development interiors, Frankfurt, Germany
Apartment Building, Frankfurt, Germany (with E. Blank)

1929/
30 Central Laundry Boiler Rooms of the Westhausen Residential Development, Frankfurt, Germany
Herr Stotz Office at the Deutscher Werkbund, Stuttgart, Germany
Dr. Lotz Office at the Deutscher Werkbund, Berlin

Gas-passage reconstruction for the Burger Iron Works, Frankfurt, Germany (destroyed)
Professor Neumark House interiors, Burchfeldstrasse, Frankfurt, Germany
Opel School, Russelsheim, Germany (competition project)
Georg Cassirer Office interiors, Frankfurt, Germany

1930 Erlenbach House, Hans-Sachs-Strasse 6, Frankfurt, Germany
Thonet Company Building renovations, Kaiserstrasse 77, Frankfurt, Germany (destroyed)
Canoe Club-House on the River Main, Frankfurt, Germany (destroyed)
Bauer Cafe renovations and interiors, Schillerstrasse, Frankfurt, Germany

1931 Hessen-Nassau Insurance Company Building renovations, Paul-Ehrlich-Strasse 57, Frankfurt, Germany
Cabeg Gaming-Room interiors, Schillerstrasse 2, Frankfurt, Germany
Hoffmann House, Gemundener Strasse 38, Frankfurt, Germany (project)
Bauer Shop-Cafe renovations, Schillerstrasse 8, Frankfurt, Germany (destroyed)
Dr. Meyer House interiors, Liebigstrasse 1, Frankfurt, Germany
Stock Exchange Industry and Trade Chamber, Frankfurt, Germany
Dr. Wolf Office interiors at *Frankfurter Zeitung*, Frankfurt, Germany

1932 Rosenblum and Company, and Mosthaf Shop renovations, Bibergasse 2, Frankfurt, Germany (destroyed)
Dr. Freibusch House interiors, Staufenstrasse 46, Frankfurt, Germany
Dr. Gottschalk Mansion renovations, Bohmerstrasse 3, Frankfurt, Germany
Strassburger and Company Office renovations, Bockenheimer Anlage 32, Frankfurt, Germany
C. F. Auerbach House renovations, Palmengartenstrasse 5, Frankfurt, Germany
Dr. Kaiser-Salzer House renovations, Holzhausenstrasse 21, Frankfurt, Germany
Dr. Haas House renovations, Friedberger Anlage 9, Frankfurt, Germany
Dr. H. Traube House renovations, Brentanoplatz 4, Frankfurt, Germany
Herr Zeiman Office renovations and foyer at the Constabulary Watch-House, Zeil 67/69, Frankfurt, Germany
J. S. Hess Office renovations, Beethovenstrasse 11, Frankfurt, Germany
Dr. Simon House renovations, Fellnerstrasse 11, Frankfurt, Germany
Frau Beermann House renovations, Westendstrasse 78, Frankfurt, Germany
Bauer Shop-Cafe renovations, Schillerstrasse 2, Frankfurt, Germany
Dr. Frank and Dr. Golo House alterations, Beethovenplatz 9, Frankfurt, Germany
Epstein Shop interiors, Schillerstrasse 2, Frankfurt, Germany
Dr. Gantner-Dreifuss House interiors, Frankfurt, Germany
Dr. Schotthoger House renovations, Feldbergstrasse 35, Frankfurt, Germany
C. N. Oppenheimer House alterations, Niedenau 56, Frankfurt, Germany

1933 Dr. Wilhelmi/J. S. Hess Shop and Office renovations, Kaiserstrasse 2, Frankfurt, Germany
General Insurance Company Office renovations, Neue Mainzer Strasse 25, Frankfurt, Germany
Housing renovations, Friedenstrasse 8, Frankfurt, Germany
J. S. Hess Office renovations, Thomasstrasse 11, Frankfurt, Germany
J. S. Hess Office renovations, Kieserstrasse 35, Frankfurt, Germany

Ferdinand Kramer: Biological Institute and Botanical Gardens, Frankfurt, 1954.

Rontgen Institute renovations and interiors, Bleichstrasse 72, Frankfurt, Germany

Dr. Rosenmeyer House renovations, Bockenheimer Landstrasse 95, Frankfurt, Germany

Israel Nursery School renovations, Bleichstrasse 8, Frankfurt, Germany

Workshop/Residential conversion, Kuhwaldstrasse 66, Frankfurt, Germany (destroyed)

Housing alterations, Schillerstrasse 1, Frankfurt, Germany

Building renovations, Biebergasse 2, Frankfurt, Germany

Cafe Bauer mezzanine floor, Schillerstrasse 2, Frankfurt, Germany

Levi-Michel Office renovations, Reuterweg 40, Frankfurt, Germany

Display-Cases for Max Abeles, Schillerstrasse 2, Frankfurt, Germany

Paul Sinsheimer House renovations, Mertonstrasse 3, Frankfurt, Germany

Dr. Nathan Rosenthal House renovations, Paul-Ehrlich-Strasse 28, Frankfurt, Germany

Leo Wreschner House renovations, Trutz 13, Frankfurt, Germany

Ludwig Baer House renovations and interiors, Viktoria-Allee 26, Frankfurt, Germany

Herr Franck City Governor's Office renovations, Holzhausenstrasse 65, Frankfurt, Germany

J. J. Weiller House renovations, Bockenheimer Anlage 40, Frankfurt, Germany

Dr. Wachter Office, Schweizer Strasse, Frankfurt, Germany (as consultant)

Villa Celia renovations, Kaiser-Friedrich-Allee 107, Bad Homburg, Germany

Land Planning Scheme, Bad Homburg, Germany

H. Reiss Building, Eysseneckstrasse 22, Frankfurt, Germany (project)

Canoe Club-House 2, Old Bridge, Frankfurt, Germany

Housing interiors, Bockenheimer Anlage 32, Frankfurt, Germany

Housing Development, Bockenheimer Landstrasse 79, Frankfurt, Germany (as consultant)

New Street layouts, Ginnheimer Hohe, Frankfurt, Germany

Hackenbrock House interiors, Untermainkai, Frankfurt, Germany

Rontgen Institute, Frankfurt, Germany

1934 Baron von Mayer House renovations, Rusterstrasse 15, Frankfurt, Germany

Carl Kaufmann House renovations, Beethovenstrasse 3a, Frankfurt, Germany

Victor Schuler House renovations, Schumannstrasse 11, Frankfurt, Germany

J. S. Hess Office interiors, Beethovenstrasse 11, Frankfurt, Germany

Shop renovations and interiors, Biebergasse 2, Frankfurt, Germany

Haak and Albers Office renovations, Schillerstrasse 1, Frankfurt, Germany

Leo Wreschner House renovations, Reingamusstrasse 27, Frankfurt, Germany

Max Kass House renovations, Arndtstrasse 7, Frankfurt, Germany

Hertha Jay House renovations, Niddastrasse 32, Frankfurt, Germany

Dr. Traube House renovations, Brentanoplatz 4, Frankfurt, Germany

Adolf E. Cahn House renovations, Niedenau 55, Frankfurt, Germany

David Sohne House renovations, Neue Mainzer Strasse 39, Frankfurt, Germany

Max Neuhofer Building, Leerbachstrasse 9, Frankfurt, Germany (not completed)

Dr. Cramer Office, Hans-Sachs-Strasse 12, Frankfurt, Germany (destroyed)

Constabulary Watch-House renovations, Zeil 65, Frankfurt, Germany

Constabulary Watch-House renovations, Fahrgasse 119, Frankfurt, Germany

Professor Schwarzenski House interiors, Reineckstrasse 3, Frankfurt, Germany

Baron von Wendland House renovations, Eppsteinerstrasse 4, Frankfurt, Germany

1935 F. Sommerlad Building, Ludolfusstrasse 6, Frankfurt, Germany

Schneider Building, Ludolfusstrasse 8, Frankfurt, Germany

Carl Niemeyer Building, Frauenlobstrasse 20, Frankfurt, Germany

Frau Dr. Jo Oppenheimer House renovations, Beethovenstrasse 44, Frankfurt, Germany

Moritz von Metzler House renovations, Schaumainkai 61, Frankfurt, Germany

Hugo von Metzler House renovations, Savignystrasse 16, Frankfurt, Germany

Jutta von Marx House interiors, Forsthaus-strasse 53, Frankfurt, Germany

Mandel Office renovations, Furstenberger-strasse 141, Frankfurt, Germany

Rossle Office renovations, Annastrasse 7, Frankfurt, Germany

Dr. Alexander von Bernus Office renovations, Schlob-Strasse 20, Frankfurt, Germany

Fabian Office renovations, Reuterweg 36, Frankfurt, Germany

Paul Reinemann House renovations, Bocken-heimer Landstrasse 75, Frankfurt, Germany

Land Development Plan, Gruneberg Park, Frankfurt, Germany

Laboratory renovations and interiors, Myliusstrasse 34, Frankfurt, Germany

Baron von Szilvingyi House interiors, Paul-Ehrlich-Strasse 28, Frankfurt, Germany

1936 German Shoe Manufacturers Company Building, Hohenzollern-Allee 130, Frankfurt, Germany

Garages for Dr. Gramberg, Arndtstrasse 7, Frankfurt, Germany

Herr Nagel Office, Frauenlobstrasse 48, Frankfurt, Germany

Anna David House renovations, Neue Mainzer Strasse 39, Frankfurt, Germany

D'Orville Office renovations, Lindenstrasse 5, Frankfurt, Germany

Dr. Engel House interiors, Grillparzerstrasse 23, Frankfurt, Germany

Frau Henry Seligmann House interiors, Liebigstrasse 33, Frankfurt, Germany

Munstermann House interiors, Schaumain-kai 61, Frankfurt, Germany

Dr. Nurnberg-Goldschmidt House interiors, Gruneburgweg 118, Frankfurt, Germany

Harlacher House interiors, Beethovenstrasse 110, Frankfurt, Germany

Heidingsfelder House interiors, Leebach-strasse 44, Frankfurt, Germany

Von Neuville House, Schaumainkai, Frankfurt, Germany (project)

1937 Brautigan House, Lilienthalallee 23, Frankfurt, Germany

Ceelan House, Lilienthalallee 23, Frankfurt, Germany

Dr. Butow House, August-Siebert-Strasse 17, Frankfurt, Germany (destroyed)

Hahn House renovations, Lindenstrasse 24, Frankfurt, Germany

Morell House renovations, Lindenstrasse 3, Frankfurt, Germany

Von Heyden House renovations, Westend-strasse 8, Frankfurt, Germany

Munstermann House renovations, Land-grafenstrasse 12, Frankfurt, Germany

1939 Cottage prototype, New York (project)

Freedom Pavilion, *World's Fair*, New York (project)

1944 General Panel System Weekend House, New York (project)

1944/
45 House and Room Constructions (project; with C. Coggeshall)

1945 Exhibition Hall with "Visual" display-stands (project)

1947 Aldens Store prototype, Chicago (project)

1952 General Building Plan for the University of Frankfurt am Main, West Germany

1952/
53 Main Entrance and Rectors Building, Johann-Wolfgang-Goethe University, Frankfurt, West Germany

Ferdinand Kramer Residence, Senckenberganlage, Frankfurt, West Germany

1953 Students' Studio-Theatre in the Senckenberg Library Building, Frankfurt, West Germany

Deutsche Bibliothek Building, Zeppelinallee, Frankfurt, West Germany (competition project)

Main Boiler Room and Heating Plant, Johann-Wolfgang-Goethe University, Grafstrasse, Frankfurt, West Germany

1953/
54 English Seminary and American Institute for the University of Frankfurt am Main, Senckenberganlage 15, Frankfurt, West Germany

Geology and Palaentology Institute, University of Frankfurt am Main, Senckenberganlage 32, Frankfurt, West Germany

1954 Biological Institute and Botanical Gardens, Gruneburg Park, Frankfurt, West Germany

1956 Student Housing, Bockenheimer Warte, Frankfurt, West Germany

1957 Institute for Food Chemistry, Pharmaceutical Institute, Georg-Voigt-Strasse, Frankfurt, West Germany

Physical Institute additions, University of Frankfurt am Main, Robert Mayer Strasse, Frankfurt, West Germany

House on a slope, Arnoldshain im Taunus, West Germany

New Student Housing, Marburg-Lahn, West Germany (competition project)

1958 Institute for Particle Physics, Atomic Reactor and Accelerator Buildings, University of Frankfurt am Main, West Germany

Auditorium Building I, University of Frankfurt am Main, Mertonstrassse, Frankfurt, West Germany

1959 Lippmann House, Buchschlag, West Germany

Ruth House, Homburg van der Hohe, West Germany

Philosophy Building, University of Frankfurt am Main, Grafstrasse, Frankfurt, West Germany

Walter Lippman House, Kohlseeweg, Buchschlag, West Germany

1960 Max Planck Institute, Heidelberg, West Germany (competition project)

Max Planck Institute for Brain Research, Gottingen, West Germany (competition project)

Walter Kolb Student Housing, Beethovenplatz, Frankfurt, West Germany

1961 Mathematics Institute I, University of Frankfurt am Main, Robert Mayer Strasse, Frankfurt, West Germany

1961/
64 Development Plan for the University of Frankfurt am Main, West Germany

Mathematics Building II, University of Frankfurt am Main, Grafstrasse, Frankfurt, West Germany

Auditorium Building II, University of Frankfurt am Main, Grafstrasse, Frankfurt, West Germany

1962 Physical Chemistry Institute additions, Robert Mayer Strasse, Frankfurt, West Germany

Werkkunstschule, Mathildenhohe, Darmstadt, West Germany (competition project)

1963 Main Assembly Building, University of Frankfurt am Main, Bockenheimer Landstrasse, 121, Frankfurt, West Germany

1964 Institute for Therapeutic Chemistry, University of Frankfurt am Main, West Germany

Theodor-Stern-Haus additions, University of Frankfurt am Main, West Germany

Geographical Institute, University of Frankfurt am Main, Senckenberganlage, Frankfurt, West Germany

Meteorological Institute, University of Frankfurt am Main, Feldbergstrasse, Frankfurt, West Germany

Guest-House additions and interiors, Schumannstrasse, Frankfurt, West Germany

State Library, West Berlin (competition project)

City and University Library, Bockenheimer

Landstrasse, Frankfurt, West Germany

Gerold House, Astano, Tessin, Switzerland

1967 Maurer House, Bad Homburg, West Germany

1968 Dr. Kollatz House, Wiesbaden, West Germany

Kramer Apartment House, Schaubstrasse, Frankfurt, West Germany

1969 Scheunentheater Theatre Building reconstruction, Wilhelmsbad, Hanau, West Germany

1970 Dr. Volhard House, Homburg von der Hohe, West Germany

1971 Christ House, Lerchesberg, Frankfurt, West Germany

Galerie Meyer-Ellinger, Frankfurt, West Germany

1972 Dr. Dietz House, Bergen-Enkheim, West Germany

(As an industrial designer, Kramer also created numerous items of furniture, lighting fixtures, building equipment and architectural fittings from 1924 for various companies, including Emil Graf, Zimmermann und Holl, the Frankfurt Building Office, Hausrat GmbH, Bunte und Remmler, the Obernzerner Stores, Thonet Furniture, Wagner GmbH, Hugo Bruderus, Alden Stores and R. H. White Company).

Publications:

By KRAMER: articles—"Architekten Le Corbusier und Pierre Jeanneret, Paris" in *Die Form* (Berlin), no. 6, 1929; "Die Wohnung fur das Existenzminimum" in *Die Form* (Berlin), no. 24, 1929; "Die Zweckform" in *Stuttgarter Tagblatt* (Stuttgart), 30 April 1930; "Wohnbedarf" in *Frankfurter Zeitung* (Frankfurt), 21 May 1932; "Visiting Germany" in *Architectural Forum* (New York), no. 1, 1948; "Visual planning, equipment selection—an arrangement for small department stores" in *Progressive Architecture* (New York), no. 5, 1948; "Umbau der Universitat" in *Bauen und Wohnen* (Zurich), no. 9, 1954; "Bauten der Johann-Wolfgang-Goethe-Universitat" in *Bauen und Wohnen* (Zurich), no. 2, 1955; "Wohnen in Studentheim" in *Bauwelt* (Berlin), no. 4, 1959; "Seminargebaude der Universitat Frankfurt am Main" in *Bauwelt* (Berlin), no. 15, 1961; "Hochschulplanung gestern und heute" in *Bauen und Wohnen* (Zurich), no. 8, 1962; "Die biologische Institute der Universitat Frankfurt/Main" in *Bauwelt* (Berlin), no. 8, 1966; "Sozialer Wohnungsbau in Wien/in Frankfurt am Main" with Lore Kramer, in *Werk und Zeit* (Darmstadt), no. 4, 1977; "Das Neue Frankfurt" in *Architectural Association Quarterly* (London), vol. 11, no. 1, 1979; "Kollektiv—Die Entstehung des Budgeheims", with Lore Kramer, in *Archithese* (Niederteufen), 2 March 1980; "Zu diesem Zeitpunkt" in *Bauwelt* (Berlin), no. 14, 1982; "Marginalien zur Ausstellung 'der Stuhl'", with Lore Kramer, in *Adolf G. Schenck, 1883-1971*, exhibition catalogue, Stuttgart 1983; "Grusswort" in *50 Jahre Westhausen*, exhibition catalogue, Stuttgart 1983; "Ein Gelaufe um Anschluss" in *Werk und Zeit* (Darmstadt), no. 2, 1984; "Paul Muller gewidmet, dem jungen, ungarischen Architekten und Bauleiter von J. J. P. Oud" in *Zeitschrift der Hochschule fur Architektur und Bauwesen* (Weimar), 8 May 1985.

On KRAMER: books—*Internationale Neue Baukunst* by Ludwig Hilbersheimer, Stuttgart 1927; *The International Style: Architecture since 1922* by Henry-Russel Hitchcock and Philip Johnson, New York 1932; *Zwischen Glashaus und Wohnfabrik* by Eberhard Schulz, Bremen 1959; *Bibliotheken, Architektur und Einrichtung* by Michael Brawne, Stuttgart 1970; *Bauhaus und Bauhausler*, edited by Eckhard Neumann, Berne and Stuttgart 1971; *Ferdinand Kramer: Architektur und Design*, exhibition catalogue edited by Peter Hahn, Berlin 1982; *Neues Bauen—Neues Gestalten*, with preface by Heinz Hirdinga, Dresden 1984; *Funkionalitat und*

Moderne: das Neue Frankfurt und seine Bauten 1925-1983 by Christoph Mohr and Michael Muller, Cologne 1984; articles—"Zu Arbeiten von Ferdinand Kramer" in *Die Form* (Berlin), no. 10, 1927; "Funf Jahre Wohnungsbau in Frankfurt/Main" by Ernst May in *Das Neue Frankfurt* (Frankfurt), nos. 2/3 and 4/5, 1930; "Freedom Pavilion at Fair Planned to Celebrate the Pre-nazi Culture" in the *New York Times* (New York), 13 January 1939; "A New Line of Folding Weatherproof Outdoor Furniture" in *Architectural Forum* (New York), no. 5, 1945; "Aldens Chicago Store" in *Women's Wear Daily* (New York), 1 September 1947; "Designing Couple Cut Corners" in *Look* (New York), 5 June 1951; "Der Architekt Ferdinand Kramer und die Frankfurter Universitat" in *Neue Presse* (Frankfurt), 19 December 1956; "Architekt Ferdinand Kramer" in *Frankfurter Allgemeine Zeitung* (Frankfurt), 4 March 1957; "Ehrenplakette fur Baudirektor Kramer" in *Frankfurter Rundschau* (Frankfurt), 23 January 1963; "Ferdinand Kramer" by H. Rahms in *Frankfurter Allgemeine Zeitung* (Frankfurt), 30 January 1965; "Ferdinand Kramer antwortet" in *Bauwelt* (Berlin), no. 6, 1978; "Ferdinand Kramer—85 years old" in *Bauwelt* (Berlin), January 1983; "Keiner von den Old Boys aus Dessau: Architektur und Design von Ferdinand Kramer" in *Stuttgarter Zeitung* (Stuttgart), 9 July 1983; "Film uber den Architekten Ferdinand Kramer" in *Frankfurter Allgemeine Zeitung* (Frankfurt), 10 November 1983; "Architect of America and Germany" in *The Stars and Stripes* (Darmstadt), 23 June 1984.

Eighteen years old—still too young to vote—I had to fight in the winter of 1916/17 in the swamps of Russia and later in the trenches of Verdun and in front of the cathedral of Reims. Close to my skin, I lived through the horrors of the murderous first world war and—more or less by accident—I survived. Now I wanted to help in building a new cooperative world—across all separating, national borders.

My teacher at the Technische Hochschule of Munich, Theodor Fischer, sharpened our social consciousness. He showed us architecture in its context and demonstrated to us that it is "the inflexible, clear mirror of mankind." He showed us the clarity of the city planning of the antique Prienne and the quality of grown, medieval cities. He talked to us of the "possible beauty of submitting to mutual interests" and "that nothing should be so important to us (so dear to our hearts) as to recognize clearly the importance of those ideas, which are important to our time". Such thoughts and ideas formed me.

It was always my aim, through architecture and through my designs of objects for daily use, as lamps, furniture, stoves, and so forth, to make life easier for people of all walks of life, physically as well as psychologically: simple, but at the same time useful and beautiful buildings and objects, related to our time, for manifold and creative use.

—Ferdinand Kramer (1985)

Ferdinand Kramer's work serves as a lesson to those who see in 1920s avant-garde architecture only the ideology of a technological era. It is true that his furniture and household equipment designs as well as his architecture always clearly indicate from what material, in which technique, and for what purpose they are made, but Kramer was motivated mainly by social factors. What he designed, planned and built had to be economic, practical, sensible and useful. The aesthetic of his designs is inseparable from their usefulness, orderliness and user-compatibility. "Beauty must not be ashamed of purpose", he said.

Although Kramer nearly always avoided radical gestures, he came closest to them in the rigorous four-storeyed arcaded houses for the Frankfurt-Westhausen estate, designed with Eugen Blank (1929), and in the main portal of Frankfurt University (1953), a huge transparent glazed opening in the old neo-baroque building as a symbol of the new university open to all.

After his return from America in 1952, Kramer erected the twenty-three institute and lecture hall buildings for Frankfurt University. A friend of Kramer's youth, the philosopher and university rector Max Horkheimer, also returning from emigration, had called him back as architect for the university. The buildings are of sober skeletal construction with light brick infill developing naturally within the existing structure, but avoiding standardization. In the city and university library, designed in 1964 after his departure as director of the university building office, he linked for the first time in Germany open accessible shelving space with individual reading positions.

Westhausen, on the other hand, arose in Kramer's early Frankfurt period. In 1923 after studying for a few months at the Weimar Bauhaus and with Theodor Fischer in Munich, he returned to his Frankfurt birthplace where he designed for cabinetmakers and locksmiths, rebuilt a travel bureau at the main railway station, and attracted the attention of Frankfurt's City Building Advisor Ernst May. The low-cost housing in the large suburban centres erected by May as a garland around the city between 1925 and 1930 made Frankfurt a centre for new construction. Kramer took part in this enterprise as designer and architect in charge of the planning and standardization department. He designed built-in and standardized furniture, which was made in the city centre workshop for the unemployed, plywood doors and bentwood chairs, a cast-iron stove which was produced in large quantities, lamps, and space-saving baths. The professions of architect, inventor and designer were, to Kramer, one and the same.

In 1938 when the National Socialists had barred him from working, Kramer, then married to a Jew, went to the U.S.A. He worked there as director of two estate projects, and was inspired by the technical ingenuity of American industrial production methods for standardized, flexible design wares (furniture, exhibition systems, an umbrella made from plastic-coated paper).

It was not only abroad that Kramer encountered exile. Throughout practically his entire professional life he felt himself an outsider even in his homeland—especially during the violent controversy over the experiments of the Ernst May era, and after his return from America. The relaxed professionalism and aptness of his architecture first arose with the restorations of the Adenauer period, but were then replaced by the abuses of functionalism in the early 1960s, and contrast today with everything that Kramer calls, "the boom in a style masquerade."

—Wolfgang Pehnt

KRIER, Léon.

Luxembourger. Born in Luxembourg, 7 April 1946; brother of Rob Krier, *q.v.*; moved to England, 1968. Attended the University of Stuttgart for six months, 1967-68. Assistant to James Stirling, *q.v.*, London, 1968-70 and 1973-74; Project Partner, with J. P. Kleihues, *q.v.*, Berlin, 1971-72. Since 1974, in private practice, London. Lecturer, Architectural Association School, London, 1973-76, Royal College of Art, London, 1977, and Princeton University, New Jersey, 1977; Jefferson Professor of Architecture, University of Virginia, Charlottesville, 1982. Exhibitions: *Triennale*, Milan, 1973; *Rational Architecture* (organizer), Art Net, London, 1975; *Léon Krier: 100 Sketches*, Princeton University, New Jersey, 1976; *40 London Architects*, Art Net, London, 1976; *Léon Krier and Rita Wolff*, Institute for Architecture and Urban Studies, New York, 1978; *Mercati Trajani*, Rome, 1978; *Dessins d'architecture*, Centre Georges Pompidou, Paris, 1978; *Analisi e progetto per la citta di Lussemburgo*, C.L.E.A., Rome, 1979; *50 disegni di Léon Krier*, Biblioteca Civica, Bra, Italy, 1980; *Léon Krier: la ricostruzione della citta europea*, Museo di Castelvecchio, Verona, Italy, 1980; *Biennale*, Venice, 1980; *City Segments*, Walker Art Center, Minneapolis, Minnesota, 1980 (travelled to Chicago; Fort Worth, Texas; Houston, Texas; and Purchase, New York); *Drawings by Léon Krier*, Max Protetch Gallery, New York, 1981; *Graves/Krier/Rossi*, Boston, 1981; *Model Futures*, Institute of Contemporary Arts, London, 1983; *Léon Krier*, Max Protetch Gallery, New York, 1984. Recipient: Architecture Prize (with Rob Krier), City of Berlin, 1975. Address (office): 16 Belsize Park, London NW3, England.

Works:

1966 Marthe Krier House, Hesperange-Luxembourg (project)
     J. P. Mitsch House, Dalein-Luxembourg (project)
1967 Single-family house, Hesperange-Luxembourg (competition project)
     Lake Resort, Heilbronn, West Germany (competition project)
     Town Hall, Amsterdam (competition project; with Rob Krier)
1968 University of Bielefeld, West Germany (competition project)
1969 Siemens Computer Centre, Perlach, Munich (competition project; with James Stirling)
1969/
70   Runcorn housing and Lima housing (as assistant in James Stirling studio)
1969/
73   Lewis-Ham Towers, Charlottenburg, Berlin (project; with J. P. Kleihues)
1969/
74   Rita Wolff house, on the Mediterranean coast (project)
1970 City of Karlsruhe redevelopment plan, West Germany (project)
     Civic Centre, Derby, England (competition project; with James Stirling)
     St. Willibrod Abbey extensions, Echternach, Luxembourg (competition project)
1971 Urban Centre Plan, Leinfelden, Stuttgart (competition project)
1971/
72   Redevelopment Plan for ten City Squares, West Berlin (competition project)
1972 Sprengel Museum, Grand Hotel de Babylone, and Maschsee Lakefront development, Hannover, West Germany (competition project)
     Two housing blocks, Vinetaplatz, Wedding, Berlin (completed, with alterations, by J. P. Kleihues)
1973 Housing complex near the Landwehr Canal and Autobain flyover, Tegel, Berlin (competition project; with J. P. Kleihues)
     Luxembourg redevelopment study and plan (project)
1973/
78   Luxembourg redevelopment plan (revised project)
1974 Housing redevelopment, Royal Mint Square, London (two competition projects)
     Giorgio Meyer House, Bagnano, Italy (project)
1975 Notre Dame Square, Amiens, France (four competition projects)
1975/
76   Postwar Housing redevelopment study, London (project; with Architectural Association School students)
1976 Cerda Plain redevelopment plan, Barcelona (project)

1977 La Villette quarter, Paris (competition project)
Social Centre, Piazza Navona, Rome (project)
Social Centre, Via Corso, Rome (project)
Social Centre, Piazza San Pietro, Rome (project)
City Centre redevelopment plan, West Berlin (competition project)
Blundell Corner reconstruction, Hull, Yorkshire (competition project: with Rita Wolff)
Motorway Intersection Park, Piraeus, Greece (competition project)

1977/
79 School and Recreation Centre, St. Quentin en Yvelines, France (project)

1978/
80 Herrlichkeit Island redevelopment, Bremen, West Germany (competition project)

1979 Urban Quarter redevelopment plan, plateau of Cergy-Puiseaux, France (project)
Les Halles quarter redevelopment plan, Paris (competition project)

1980 Recreation Centre and Urban Quarter, Tegel, Berlin (competition project; with Francisco Sanin)

1980/
83 Central Quarter development, Cergy-Puiseaux, France
Strada Novissima facade, Corderie dell'-Arsenale, Venice

1981 Södermalm redevelopment, Stockholm (project)
Tegel Harbour redevelopment, Berlin (project; with Francisco Sanin)
Südliche-Friedrichstadt redevelopment, Berlin (project; with Maurice Culot)
Tegel City redevelopment plan, Berlin (project; with Francisco Sanin)
Tegel Airport district plan, Berlin (project; with Francisco Sanin)

1982 New Quarter plan, Cergy-Puiseaux, France (project; as consultant, with Maurice Culot, Francisco Sanin, and Lucien Steil)
I. Stillman House, Hilldale-on-Hudson, New York (project)
New City Quarter plan, Baghdad, Iraq (project; as consultant)
Pliny Villa reconstruction, Laurentian Plain, Italy (competition project)

1982/
83 Public Buildings for the New District of Tegel, Berlin (projects)

1983 New Town Plan for Südhausbau GmbH, Bavaria, West Germany (project)
Central Bell-Tower, Sea Side, Florida (project)
City redevelopment plan, Filadelfia, Calabria, Italy (project)
Vacation House, Sea Side, Florida (project)

1984 Promenade Michel Delvaux, Luxembourg (project; with Rita Wolff)
Ager Campus development plan for Fiat and Benetton, Caserta, Italy (project)
South Bank master plan, London (project)

Publications:

By KRIER: books—*Buildings and Projects of James Stirling*, editor, Stuttgart and London 1974; *Projects on the City—Projects of Unit 10 Students, Unit-Master Léon Krier*, exhibition catalogue, London 1975; *The Reconstruction of the European city*, Brussels 1978; *The City within the City*, editor, Rome 1979; *Analisi e progetto per una città in pericolo*, exhibition catalogue, Rome 1979; *Südliche Friedrichstadt*, with Maurice Culot, Boissano, Italy 1981; articles—"Progetti di Leoon Krier, 1968-72" in *Controspazio* (Bari, Italy), no. 10, 1972; "Projects on the City" in *Lotus* (Venice), no. 11, 1976; "The City within the City" in *Architectural Design* (London), March 1977; "Cities within the city" in *Architecture + Urbanism* (Tokyo), November 1977; "The Blind Spot" in *Architectural Design* (London), April 1978; "The Lesson of the Urban Block" in *Lotus* (Venice), no. 18, 1978; "The Fable of the Spoon and the Fork" in *Architectural Design* (London), no. 2, 1979; "Léon Krier Talks," interview, with Colin Davies in *The Architect* (London), January 1980; "A Proposal for the Motorway—Athens/Piraeus", and "The Berlin Tiergarten", in *Lotus* (Venice) no. 31, 1981; "Gesprache mit Léon Krier," interview, by Lucien Steil in *De Keisecker* (Luxembourg), no. 6, 1981; "Classical Architecture and Vernacular Building" in *Architectural Design* (London), no. 52, 1982; "Krier on Speer" in *Architectural Review* (London), February 1983; "The Love of Ruins, the Ruins of Love" in *Modulus* (Charlottesville, Virginia), no. 16, 1983; "Interview with Léon Krier" by Peter Eisenman in *Skyline* (New York), February 1983.

On KRIER: books—*Neuere Architektur* by Udo Kultermann, Stuttgart 1978; *A Question of Style*, symposium transcript edited by Wilfried Lang, London 1978; *The Language of Post-Modern Architecture* by Charles Jencks, London 1978; *Léon Krier: Theory, Practice*, thesis by Susan P. James, Washington University, St. Louis 1978; *Die Stadt als Thema der Architektur* by Gerhard Benz, Nikolaus Kuhnert and others, Aachen, West Germany 1979, Aquisgrana 1980; *Urban Space* by Rob Krier, London 1979; *Opposition zur Modern*, edited by G. Blomeyer and B. Tietze, Braunschweig, West Germany and Wiesbaden, West Germany 1980; *50 disegni di architettura*, exhibition catalogue, by Fulvio Quattroccolo, Bra, Italy 1980; *City Segments*, exhibition catalogue, edited by Mildred S. Friedman, Minneapolis, Minnesota 1980; *Léon Krier, La ricostruzione della città europea*, exhibition catalogue, with texts by Luciso Magagnato, Maurice Culot and Vincenzo Pavan, Verona, Italy 1980; *Architektur und Städtebau des XX. Jahrhunderts* by Vittorio Magnano Lampugnani, Stuttgart 1980; *A Critical History of Modern Architecture* by Kenneth Frampton, London 1980; *Dopo l'architettura post-moderna* by Luigi Ferrario, Boissano, Italy 1981; *Architektur Zeichnungen* by Vittorio Lampugnani, Berlin 1983; *Strade e piazze* by Augusto Cagnardi, Lombardia, Italy 1983; articles—"Projects in a Bottle" by G. K. Koenig in *Casabella* (Milan), November 1972; "Les Freres Krier" by Antoine Grumbach in *L'Architecture d'aujourd'hui* (Paris), July 1975; "Culot-Krier" by Robert Maxwell in *Architectural Design* (London), March 1977; "Léon Krier en Valladolid" by Piluca Meneses in *Arquitectura* (Madrid), no. 212, 1978; "Caro Léon: Porque 22 × 22?" in *Lotus* (Venice), no. 19, 1978; "Léon Krier—byeb og kulturen" by Piotr Choynowski in *Byggekunst* (Oslo) no. 6, 1979; "Léon Krier—la ville dans la ville" in *Déclaration de Bruxelles*, edited by André Barey, Brussels 1980; "Léon Krier in Aaken" by Jenny Rodermond in *De Architect* (The Hague), no. 6, 1980; "Léon Krier e Rob Krier" by Nagy Sandor in *Bercsenyi Melleklet* (Budapest), no. 28/30, 1980; "Léon Krier", special issue of *Architectural Design* (London), September 1984.

My projects are a series of polemical statements. They are not experiments; they are reflections on the specific structures and measures of the European city (the streets, the squares, the urban quarters)—meditations on the true and constant elements of architecture and building and their necessary relationships within the urban and social fabric. For architecture to be an art, building must be a craft. A reconstruction of these cannot be a matter of industry, nor can it be a matter of science; it is a cultural and a political project.

A new generation is now discovering the urban cultures of pre-industrial Europe as documents of intelligence, memory, and pleasure. This leads to a clear conclusion. The necessity is for a global plan of reconstruction to oppose the global destruction of European cultures through industrialization.

—Léon Krier

In line with the ideas of Aldo Rossi, Carlo Aymonino, Oswald Mathias Ungers, James Stirling, and Rob Krier, the architectural concept of Léon Krier involves a basic re-evaluation of the total urban fabric as a medium for change and morphological growth.

A most important part of this concept is the distinct concentration of urban activities in *quartiers* (not separated into artificial zones as advocated by Le Corbusier and still seen as relevant by the majority of modern planners and architects). Krier says: "Dezoning is the first step in an anti-monopolistic and democratic planning policy." He is, in this sense, against the continuation of ideas which, from his point of view, interrupted tradition by means of building codes and anti-human ideas. He is against the architect's being the uncritical servant of the building industry; he wants the architect to be responsible for society and the total human environment. Krier advocates the rediscovery of building typologies and an urban experience based on and directed toward the value system of the individual with emphasis on the "public realm." A place is defined by him as "where the individual identifies himself as abeing with full cultural and political responsibility." His concern is urban form and the integration of its social meaning.

In several of his projects (for example, Royal Mint Square in London, La Villette quarter of Paris, and the school in St. Quentin, France), Krier shows a close affinity to the works of painters and sculptors whose imaginative qualities he tries to integrate into his own urbanistic and architectural work. Subconscious elements often enter his work with direct reference to buildings and images from the past (Boullée, Ledoux, Loos, Le Corbusier). Krier says: "Architecture must be refounded in the intelligence of history. This it must take as its concern, the understanding, adaption and evolution of building types which express human needs and experience."

Through his basic education by his brother Rob Krier and the practical experience in the architectural offices of Josef Paul Kleihues and James Stirling, Léon Krier absorbed a great amount of experience which enabled him to look at architecture with a fresh approach. His lectures in Europe and the United States have stimulated contemporary debate on the architectural profession, while his brilliant drawing technique of imaginative and realistic elements has also been widely influential.

—Udo Kultermann

KRIER, Robert.

Austrian. Born in Grevenmacher, Luxembourg, 10 June 1938; brother of Léon Krier, *q.v.*; settled in Austria, 1975. Educated at the Lycée Classique, Echternach, Luxembourg, 1951-59; Technical University, Munich, 1959-64, Dip.Ing.Arch. 1964. Married Gudrun Schnitzer in 1964; children: Caren and Nadine. Worked in the offices of O. M. Ungers, *q.v.*, in Cologne and Berlin, 1965-66, and of Frei Otto, *q.v.*, in Berlin and Stuttgart, 1967-70; engaged in work on the book *Stadtraum*, 1970-75; Assistant Instructor, University of Stuttgart, 1973-75; Guest Professor, École Polytechnique Fédérale, Lausanne, 1975. Since 1976, in private practice as architect and urban planner, Vienna. Professor, and Head of Design Institute, since 1976, and Dean of Architecture and Interior Design, 1979-81, Technical University, Vienna. Exhibitions: University of Stuttgart, 1968; *Triennale*, Milan, 1973; Kunstverein, Stuttgart, 1975; Technical University, Vienna, 1976; Galleria d'Arte Moderna, Bologna, 1977; Institute for Architecture and Urban Studies, New York, 1977; Architectural Book Store, Los Angeles, 1977; Kunstverein, Freiburg, West Germany, 1977; Stadtplanungsamt, Karlsruhe, West Germany, 1978; Deutscher Werkbund, Darmstadt, West Germany,

Rob Krier: Siemer House, Warmbronn, West Germany, 1968.

1978; Architecture Schools of Strasbourg, France, Nancy, France, and Brussels, 1979; Galleria Iannone, Milan, 1980; *City Segments*, Walker Art Center, Minneapolis, Minnesota, 1980; Galerie Archyv, Hannover, West Germany, 1981; Royal Institute of British Architects, London, 1982; Rizzoli Galleries in New York, Chicago, San Francisco, Pittsburgh, and New Orleans, 1982; Institute for Art History, University of Vienna, 1983; Galerie Partikel, Lucerne, Switzerland, 1983; Wiener Sezession, Vienna, 1984; Deutsches Architekturmuseum, Frankfurt, 1984. Recipient: Architecture Prize (with Léon Krier), City of Berlin, 1975; Architecture Prize, City of Vienna, 1982. Address: Bräunerstrasse 4-6, 1010 Vienna, Austria.

Works:

1968/
70 Siemer House, Warmbronn, Stuttgart
1974/
75 Dickes House, Bridel, Luxembourg
1977/
80 Social Housing, Ritterstrasse, Kreuzberg, Berlin
1977- Social Housing, Schinkelplatz, Berlin
1978/
84 Social Housing, Spandau, Berlin
1980/
84 Social Housing, Wilmersdorf, Berlin
1980/
85 Social Housing, Rauchstrasse, Tiergarten, Berlin
1981 Social Housing, Breitenfurter Strasse, Vienna
1982 Social Housing, Schrankenberggasse, Vienna
Social Housing, Hirschstettenerstrasse, Vienna

Publications:

By KRIER: books—*Stadtraum in Theorie und Praxis*, Stuttgart 1975, Barcelona 1976, London 1979, Tokyo and Brussels 1980; *Notizen am Rande: Sketch Book*, Berlin 1975; *Rob Krier on Architecture*, London 1982; *Urban Projects*, New York 1982; *Architectural Composition*, London 1985; article— "Rob Krier: Interview" in *Stadtbauwelt* (Berlin), December 1983.

On KRIER: book—*Rob Krier*, edited by Kenneth Frampton, New York l articles—"The Work of Rob Krier" in *Nueva Forma* (Madrid), April 1973; "House Siemer" in *Bauen und Wohnen* (Zürich), October 1974; "Royal Mint Housing" in *Casabella* (Milan), no. 396, 1974; "The Work of Rob Krier" in *Nueva Forma* (Madrid), February 1975; "Haus Dickes" in *Bauen und Wohnen* (Zürich), February 1975; "Les Frères Krier" by Antoine Grumbach in *L'Architecture d'aujourd'hui* (Paris), July 1975; "The Work of Rob Krier" in *Architecture + Urbanism* (Tokyo), June 1977; "Rob Krier: Projects" in *Space Design* (Tokyo), October 1978; "Habitation à Berlin" in *L'Architecture d'aujourd'hui* (Paris), December 1978; "Rob Krier: Urban Space" in *Architectural Design* (London), no. 18, 1978/79; "Projekte für die Internationale Bauausstellung Berlin 1984" in *Schriftenreihe zu IBA*, vol. 2, Berlin 1981; "Rob Krier" in *Architektura* (Warsaw), no. 6, 1983; "Schinkelplatz" in *Art* (Hamburg, West Germany), January 1984.

Bibliography—*Rob Krier: A Bibliography* by Carol Cable, Monticello, Illinois 1984.

If you ask a forty-year-old architect what he plans to do with the rest of his professional life, you will soon notice that he stands there like a child counting flower petals: "I love you, I love you not, I love you," and so on.

As an architect I would like to achieve three things:

1) Learn to master the building of a house. I know that that doesn't happen at the first attempt. I would like to build a number of types of houses which are not drawn up according to one-sided criteria but which should, over several generations, be able to gain acceptance as prototype dwellings. That might sound like a touching architect's dream, but I mean, rather, to exclude from the building all fashionable trimmings, to limit myself to a few elements without becoming mean-minded.

2) Put together a few buildings in a town building complex in such a way that they form a street sector or a square which can serve as an area for public life. I should like very much to plan so sensibly and generously that the buildings would last well.

3) Finally, I would like to build a house open to the public, preferably one room devoted to worshipful purposes, and which by virtue of its sublime function can raise a claim to the monumental. I should like to prepare myself at length and patiently for this most difficult of all architect's problems.

—Rob Krier

In the current re-evaluation of urban reality, the work proposals and research analyses of Rob Krier are of fundamental importance. Krier's main goal is the re-establishment of articulated space in cities; architecture and urbanism to be united in creating a realistic basis for contemporary solutions. In his book, *Stadtraum in Theorie und Praxis,* he tries to establish a systematic typology of urban space systems and the basis for further research and alternative creative endeavors.

Krier's theoretical and practical work is a counter-attack against the domination of technological means, not against the means themselves. Zoning laws and the division of functions in cities, as proposed by Le Corbusier and many other orthodox modern planners, are seen as basic evils which excluded the human element and prevent active and harmonious urban life. For Krier, typologies should dominate city space, not constructions for specific functions that are subject to change. For transportation, he postulates a strict separation of car traffic and streets for people, with the latter seen as the relevant element in urban space.

Krier's main concerns are the use of spaces by human beings, new perspectives in the creation of squares, and streets and their humanistic function in the larger fabric of cities. He sees the work of Camillo Sitte from the late nineteenth century in a new perspective, especially in regard to the ideas about urban spaces, in comparison with the much more successful ideas of the Garden City as advocated by Ebenezer Howard. For Krier, it is the complexity of urban space, with its multiple and changing functions, not the limited restriction of space to one function only, that creates life and harmony in cities.

Krier's arguments do not remain theoretical; they are manifested in several concrete proposals for cities such as Stuttgart, Vienna, and Berlin. His building activity as an architect was for many years restricted to two houses, the Siemer House in Warmbronn and the Dickes House in Luxembourg, but recently has been expanded to large-scale housing schemes in the context of the International Building Exhibition in Berlin.

—Udo Kultermann

KROLL, Lucien.

Belgian. Born in Brussels, 17 March 1927. Educated at the Ecole Nationale Supérieure de la Cambre, Brussels, Dip.Arch. 1951; studied city planning at the Institut Supérieur de la Cambre, the Institut Supérieur International d'Urbanisme, Brussels, and at the School of Gaston Bardet, Brussels, 1951. Married Simone Marti in 1965; daughters: Adeline and Marie. In partnership with architect Charles Vandenhove, Brussels, 1951-57. In private practice, Brussels, since 1957; established Atelier Kroll, with Vincent Claus, Daniel de Cooman, Simone Kroll, Edouard Lambin, René Strehler, and Jean-Pierre Couwenberg, in Brussels. Professor of Architecture, Ecole Saint-Luc de St.-Gilles, Brussels, 1970-71; Professor, U.P.A., Grenoble, 1979-81; Visiting Critic, Miami University, Oxford, Ohio, 1980. Founder Member, Institut d'Esthetique Industrielle, Brussels, 1956. Exhibitions: *Triennale*, Milan, 1956; *Architecture Vivante*, Colegio de Arquitectos de Cataluña y Baleares, Barcelona, 1965; Avionpuits and Louvain, Belgium, 1966; University of Louvain, 1966; Museum of Utrecht, Netherlands, 1978; Kunstmuseum, Hannover, 1983; *Architecture et Industrie*, Centre Georges Pompidou, Paris, 1983; *Motifs*, Ecole St. Lukas, Brussels, 1983. Recipient: J. F. Delarue Medal, Academie Francaise d'Architecture, Paris, 1980. Honorary Member, Bund Deutscher Architekten, 1983; Member, Academie Francaise d'Architecture, 1984. Member, Order of Belgian Architects. Address (office): 20 Avenue Louis Berlaimont, Auderghem, 1160 Brussels, Belgium.

Works:

1952/
53 Chapel of Pont-de-Bonne, Modave Highway, Huy, Modave, Belgium (with Charles Vandenhove and G. Watelet)
1953 Parish Hall, La Roche, Tangissart, near Villers-la-Ville, Belgium (with Charles Vandenhove)
1954/
55 House, Avenue des Vallons, Waterloo, Belgium (with Charles Vandenhove)
1955 House, 28 Vijverstraat, Kiewit, Hasselt, Belgium (with Charles Vandenhove)

1956 Design of the *Exposition Esthetique Industrielle,* Liége (with Charles Vandenhove)
1956/
57 Tourist Restaurant, Eupen Dam, Belgium (with R. Bastin and Charles Vandenhove)
1957 Designs for industry (projects; with Charles Vandenhove)
Workshops and Permanent Campsite for the Boy Scouts, Abbey of Maredsous, Belgium
1957/
58 Toussaint House, Uccle, Belgium
1958 House, 6 Avenue des Etangs, Sept Fontaines, Braine l'Alleud, Belgium
1958/
59 House, route de Dinant, Sorinnes, Belgium
1958/
62 Design of the travelling exhibition *Le Signe d'Or Industriel,* Bruges, Ghent, Antwerp, and Brussels
1959 House, 18 rue G. Delincé, Auderghem, Brussels
1960 Monin House, rue de Namur, Dinant, Belgium
1960/
61 Lahaut House, rue Joseph Waregne, Salzinnes, Belgium
1960/
62 Church of Ste.-Marie-le-Haut-Clocher restoration, Chevigny, Libramont, Belgium (with G. Watelet)
1960/
63 't Holleken Church, 6 Boesdalstraat, Linkebeek, Belgium
1961/
62 House, rue Soldat La Rivière, Jodoigne, Belgium
Italian Social Center, rue Beaujean, Seraing, Belgium (with A. Constant)
Chapel, between Rendeux and Marche, Waharday, Belgium
1961/
63 Abbey of Gihindamuyaga, near Butare, Ruanda
House, Nihersant, near Poilvache, Evrehaines, Belgium
1961/
64 Medical Student House, rue Graffe, Namur, Belgium
1961/
65 Housing complex, 20 Avenue Louis Berlaimont, Auderghem, Brussels (with participation of future inhabitants)
1962 Electronic Instruments for MBLE, Belgium (projects)
Belgian Pavilion, *International Fair,* Helsinki
1962/
63 Oury House, Embourg, Liége
1962/
65 Martens House, 180 rue Victor Hugo, Waterloo, Belgium
Benedictine Monastery, Butare, Rwanda
1963/
65 Dom Lambert Bauduin Ecumenical Center, Abbey of Chevetogne, Belgium
1963/
68 IATA Artisans' School, rue de la Montagne, Namur, Belgium
1964 Dominican Chapel, 5 rue Leys, Brussels
Design of the *Lyons Fair*
Design of the *Roger de la Pasture Exhibition,* Cathedral of Tournai, Belgium
1964/
65 Pirotte House, 8 Dreve des Equipages, Watermael-Boitsfort, Belgium
Von Scholz House, 47 Avenue des Faisans, Kraainem, Belgium
Villa, Route de Modave, Pont-de-Bonne, Belgium
1965 "Louiseville" Development, Porte Louise, Brussels (project)
Design of the *Belgian Architecture* exhibition, Colegio de Arquitectos, Barcelona
Design of the *4,000 Years of Craftsmanship in Palestine* exhibition, Brussels

1965/
66 Godet House, 213A rue Haute, Heer-Agimont, Belgium
La Maison Familiale Primary School, 150 Chausée Bara, Braine-l'Alleud, Belgium
Design of the *Cadeaux de Firmes, Le Verre Belge* exhibitions, etc., Design Center, Brussels
1966/
67 University Hospital, Butare, Rwanda
1966/
68 Technical School, Fontaine-l'Evéque, Belgium (with E. Lambin)
1966/
70 Ministry of Commerce, Industry and Mines, and the President's Palace, Kigali, Rwanda
1967/
68 Jam Production Works, Gihindamuyaga, Butare, Ruanda
1967/
69 Toussaint House, 13 Avenue G. Mercator, Wemmel, Belgium
Le Cheval Brun House (farmhouse conversion), Route de Huy, Tihange, Belgium
Argricultural Co-operative Administration Center, Nyabisindu, Ruanda
Crahay House, 11 Avenue de l'Aiglon, Waterloo, Belgium
1967/
70 Filles de Marie Primary School, rue de Bouvy, La Luvière, Belgium
1968/
69 "Orban" Shop, 13 rue de la Station, Jemeppesur-Meuse, Belgium
Vandermensbrugghe House, 58 Bruyningstraat, Kortrijk, Belgium
Church, Biesmeree, Namur, Belgium
1968/
70 House, 1 Avenue de Beau Feuillage, Kraainem, Belgium
Dresse House, 47 Warandeberg, Wezembeek, Belgium
1969 Town plan for Barvaux-sur-Ourthe, Belgium
Parking Garage, rue Hotel des Monnaies, Saint-Gilles, Belgium (project)
Benedictine Monastery, Gihindamuyaga, Ruanda
1969/
70 Witte Burg House, Oostduinkerke, Belgium (with J. L. Franchimont)
1970 Iproma School, Namur, Belgium
1970/
75 Master plan for the new capital city of Kimihurura, Rwanda
1970/
77 Paramedical Faculty Buildings Complex, Catholic University of Louvain, Woluwe, Belgium (partially built)
1973/
74 Student housing, work and lifestyle study, University of Louvain, Belgium (project)
1974/
75 Tourist Villages and Facilities study, L'Eau d'Heure, Belgium (project)
1974/
75 Convent for the Dominican Sisters, rue de Renivaux, Ottignies, Belgium
Fro-Bra cheesemakers' cellars and workshops, Maredsous, Belgium
1975 Dominican House, Froidmont, Rixensart, Belgium
1975/
76 Polomski House, Tervuren, Belgium
Von Scholz House, Madeliefjeslaan 2, Tervuren, Belgium
Verhaegen House, Les Fagnes, near Malmédy, Belgium
Wegner and Smida House, Madeliefjeslaan, Tervuren, Belgium
1975/
77 Carton House, Hastière, Belgium
1975/
78 Sperling House, Nilleveldstraat 6a, Hoeilaert, near Brussels

Lucien Kroll: Alma Metro Station, University of Woluwe, Belgium, 1982.

1976 Group of Buildings, Avenue de la Renaissance, Brussels (project)
Town Hall, Cergy-Pontoise, near Paris (competition project)
1976/
77 Vandermensbrugghe House, Wépion, Namur, Belgium
1976/
78 Antoine House, rue du Try, Ophain, Belgium
1977 Kronenbourg Brewery Study, Sélestat, France (project)
School of Plastic Arts alterations, Woluwé-St.-Lambert, Belgium (project)
1977/
79 Vignes Blanche housing group study, Cergy-Pontoise, near Paris (project)
1978 Coin du Balai and Boulevard du Souverain redevelopment plan, Brussels (project)
New Building Complex, University of Kassel, Germany (competition project)
City Centre redevelopment plan, Witten, Germany (as project consultant)
Van Goethem House, Nassogne, Belgium
Puiseaux Development, Cergy-Pontoise, near Paris (competition project)
1979 Metro Station Study, University of Woluwé, Belgium (project)
User-built Housing, Bernalmont, Liege, Belgium (competition project)
Housing Group, Nieuwegein, Utrecht, Netherlands (project)
Académie d'Expression par le Geste et la Parole alterations, Utrecht, Netherlands
1980 DOM Company Offices, Bruhl, Cologne (project consultant; with others)

Housing Development Study, Emerainville/ Marne-la-Vallée, France (project)
Les Vignes Blanches housing, stages 1 and 2, Cergy-Pontoise, near Paris
1981 Urban Study, Montbrison, France
Housing, Laroche-Clermault, France
CAPIAU House, Lasne, Belgium
1982 Housing and Holiday Lodges, Leiné and Seuille, France (project)
School of Architecture, Lyon, France (competition project)
Station Alma, University of Woluwé, Belgium
Parc Palmer buildings renovation, Bordeaux, France (group project)
Pavilions, Marne-la-Vallée, France (project; with future inhabitants)
Group of 95 dwellings, Haillan-Bordeaux, France (preliminary study)
1983 Housing Group, St.-Germain, Indre et Loire, France (preliminary project)
Schools at Cinais, St.-Germain, France (projects)
Lycée d'Education Technique Industriel, Belfort, France (project)
Primary School alterations, in the University of Woluwe, Belgium (study; with students and teachers)
Académie d'Expression alterations, Utrecht, Netherlands
HLM Buildings renovations, Amiens, France (project)
1984 Two small schools, Chinon, Loire, France
Hotel Saint-George, Burg a Brugge, Belgium (project)

Publications:

By KROLL: book—*Composants*, Brussels 1983; articles—"Le Stand d'Esthétique Industrielle" in *Bouwen en Wonen* (Antwerp), no. 6, 1956; "La Vocation de l'Industrial Designer" in *La Relève* (Brussels), no. 3, 1965; "Réponse Architecturale à une Attitude Non Directive" in *Neuf* (Brussels), no. 8, 1967; "Industrial Design en Grande Bretagne" and "Archigram" in *La Maison* (Brussels), no. 4, 1968; "Reply to Christopher Alexander" in *Architectural Design* (London), no. 7, 1968; "L'Institute de l'Environnement" in *La Maison* (Brussels), no. 3, 1970; "Why I Could Build Woluwe" in *Wonen TA/BK* (Heerlen, Netherlands), June 1977; "Construire et Participer", in *Combat Nature* (Perigeaux, France) no. 34, 1978; "Can architecture be taught?", in *Journal of Architectural Education* (Washington, D.C.) Fall 1981; "La polémique de la Mémé à Louvain-en-Woluwé", in *La Cite* (Paris) 20 December 1979; "Architecture 80: Doctrines et Incertitudes", in *Cahiers de la Recheche Architecturale* (Roquevaire, France) October 1980; "Our Friends the Rationalists", in *Architectural Design* (London) December 1981; "Rehabilitation of Perseigne", in *Architectural Association Quarterly* (London) July/December 1982; "L'architecture et l'usager: pour une démilitarisation de l'acte de bâtir", in *Art Press* (Paris) June/August 1983; "Method and Practice—the Alma Subway station", in *Space Design* (Tokyo) May 1984.

On KROLL: book—*La Construction en Belgique 1945-1970* by Geert Bekaert and Francis Strauven, Brussels 1971; *The Language of Post-Modern*

Architecture by Charles Jencks, London 1978; *Architecture for People* by Byron Mikellides, London 1980; *Kroll at Woluwé-St.-Lambert: a new perspective*, thesis by Geoff A. Miller, University of Newcastle, 1983; *Enfin, l'Architecture* by J.-P. Dantec, Paris 1984; articles—"Quelques Réalisations Religieuse de Lucien Kroll" in *Art d'Eglise* (Ottignies, Belgium), July/September 1970; "Portrait de Lucien Kroll" by Christian Hunziker in *L'Architecture d'Aujourd'hui* (Paris), January/February 1976; "Lucien Kroll" in *Art d'Eglise* (Ottignies, Belgium), January/March 1976; "The Anarchitecture of Lucien Kroll" by Francis Strauven in *Architectural Association Quarterly* (London), no. 2, 1976; "Lucien Kroll: Architecture et Participation" by Nicolas Godebski in *Crée* (Paris), December 1976; "The Ideas of Lucien Kroll" in *Architecture* (Paris), April 1977; "Anarchy and Architecture" by Gerald R. Blomeyer in *Bauwelt* (Berlin), 9 December 1977; "Kroll's Krunch" in *The Architects' Journal* (London), 7 June 1978; "Kroll Rocks the Boat" by Joe Holyoak in *Building Design* (London), 30 June 1978; "Lucien Kroll: The Holiday Is Over, Now Order Rules Again" in *Architekt* (Stuttgart), January 1979; "The Ecological Architecture of Lucien Kroll" by Stephanie Williams in *Architectural Review* (London), February 1979; "Anarchitecture of Lucien Kroll", in *Architecture + Urbanism* (Tokyo) November 1979; "Profil 4: Lucien Kroll", in *Byggekunst* (Oslo) February 1980; "Lucien Kroll and his works" in *Nikkei Architecture* (Tokyo) December 1980; "Bauen und Wohnen: Die Architektur des Lucien Kroll" in *Basler Magazin* (Basle) no. 11, 1982; "Lucien Kroll and participatory design—inhabitants and laborers get involved" by Anna Bochan in *Globe and Mail* (Vancouver) November 1982; "Lucien Kroll" by D. Mladenovic in *Nas Dom* (Belgrade) March 1983; "Die Ruckkehr des Sioux—Die Anarchitektur des belgischen Baumeisters Lucien Kroll" by Wolfgang Pehnt in *Frankfurter Allgemeine Zeitung* (Frankfurt) 29 March 1984.

The fight between Gauls and Roman Legions never ends. Roman military Taylorization had mechanized courage and held heroism and poetry up to ridicule because, on specialized battlefields, guerillas have a low rate of survival. Already, although they did not realize it, bronze weapons had been reduced to naught by the new iron technology. Yet, it is always at a second opportunity that the "Greek miracle" happens, when poetry again finds its path and its purpose, when it coexists with and again beleaguers the rigid prisons of the military. The savage always is defeated by the engineer and then, quietly, he reappears (the return of the Sioux). He survives; the environment spontaneously recreates him: As for the engineer, with difficulty he must fight the entropy which tends to make him disappear.

The great civilizations of dreamers (Celtic, Aztec, Hindu, Scottish, etc) died when faced with the mechanical organization of armed forces, just as the cultured and rustic late eighteenth century died when faced with urban and industrial power, and just as the amiabilities of handicraft production were exhausted by machine-made artificial goods. Yet, urban dwellers find their savage again, and neither the artisan nor the horse has truly disappeared.

Since 1910, architecture has been assaulted by the same military forces, which wanted it to be industrial, prefabricated, standardized; what they made of it, we know. Architects have worked wholehearted at disguising themselves as industrialists, so well that we have become disgusted with the "machine-produced" form, even before the machine has had an opportunity to realize it. For it is only much later that heavy and restrictive prefabricated construction abounded and architecture was strangled, the artisan being ridiculed and the occupant, transformed into a consumer.

How are present-day apartments assembled? The mercenary-conceptualists always specialize a functional space, multiply it, and thread it over conduit systems (water, gas, electricity, waste waters and discharge valves, sidewalks, roadways, urban aesthetics, bureaucratic geometries, etc.). Canalization governs, not the "associative desire" of the elements. This is "sewer urbanism." It is necessary to scrutinize the road system and the various internal and external networks and really understand that it is those elements that determine the pattern, not the image of the occupant.

If a knitting needle were to be run from top to bottom through one of those militarized buildings, at certain hours it would certainly pierce all of the housewives busy with their cooking. Let there be no misunderstanding. We are not criticizing training, not even magisterial training, but only drill and that, only outside of war conditions. Neither technical standards nor administrative regulations create a living architecture (a dead one, yes).

The form of a network is haphazard, the opposite of a tree's; it seems to establish connections where it feels a need for contact, in mysterious manner. The tree is hierarchical: from roots to trunk to branches to twigs to leaves. There can be no short-circuit, just as in the Army. Is human sympathy against nature? Jolting technology, giving it life, making a servant of it, letting families and acivities come together as they will. That would create a landscape instead of a warehouse for spare parts, an inventory of merchandise. The choice here is plain: either the mechanical or the organic. Those trends have taken their turn at ruling.

The contempt in which the Renaissance held the local and spontaneous manifestations of the Middle Ages reappears with the same brutality at each "rational" importation of expedience, of tidying-up, of earnestness, of exotic or ancient misinterpretations. Among them may be included, today, Taylorism, engineering, functional urbanism, the recent rationalists, most industrial objects, etc.

Even though the settings differ in detail, the models for Roman camps and for modern armies produce the same pattern: eradication of previous shapes, geometrical arrangement around the command post, and fortified separation from the environment. A perspicacious architect, Hilbersheimer, published striking pictures of contemporary military camps truly showing how they were the models for urban development and how much he himself strove to emulate them, as did most of the members of his generation. That orderly pattern is so deeply rooted in our minds that it is thought to be normal in numerous fields. With the exception, at times, of a few pre-kindergartens, the entire space devoted to education is military: supervision, rows, identical classrooms, long lines, concentration into large units.

We want to call "landscape" that form produced by countless compatible actions of occupants who continuously weave connections among things and not by grand, arbitrary decisions which produce something monumental, some kind of propaganda. In this sense, a military camp is not a landscape; it is a mechanism. Nor is a calculated, artificial creation a landscape; that is a stage setting. Wilderness does not yet constitute a landscape. The urban virtue, urbanity, is the collective building up of social relations (urbanity also means politeness, civilized relationships) and of the environment that expresses and favors it. Repetition and closure do not maintain relationships, while diversity intensifies them.

We are betting on differences, on organic tectures. The participation of its future occupants is one of the means likely to lead to that landscape which is composed of present differences and which welcomes future differences. That is not the only thing, nor is it absolutely necessary: anything organic proceeds first from an attitude. An architect who is deaf or closed to his surroundings cannot create an organic architecture with nothing but the results of its occupants' initiatives. Architecture should stop representing the power of its mercenaries and, using the most contemporary techniques, should become a mosaic of cooperating intentions.

—Lucien Kroll

From the outset of his independent career Lucien Kroll refused to engage in the semantic competition to which many Belgian architects abandon themselves and instead aspired to a mild neo-vernacular described by one critic as "the denial of architecture." His early work seemed to show no sign of "progressiveness;" rather, it involved a modest and constrained use of basic means and materials employed in a natural and apparently haphazard fashion. None of his walls was built entirely of the same material: concrete blocks were mixed with brick of different sizes and colours, rough stone ran into slate—frequently at the discretion of the bricklayer or eventual occupant. Kroll has always favoured materials that live with the weather, that harbour lush growths of moss, lichen and ivy, so that his buildings look as if they have been there forever, absorbed into the landscape. It is Kroll's way of building organically, of trying to create buildings that do not impose themselves on their occupants, buildings that relate to people.

This interest in people informs his 1961/65 housing complex (including his own house and office) in Auderghem, near Brussels: he created a kind of communal dwelling as an experiment in open form, with highly adaptable living/working/playing areas for friends, acquaintances and strangers—all under one roof. The experiment led him to a deeper involvement with "group participation." Kroll even applied group dynamics to the organization of his own office, aiming at a more personal involvement of his assistants in the design process. To achieve his goals, he found that he had to reduce his authority-as-expert as much as possible in order to involve his clients in a kind of neo-anarchist therapy, refusing institutionalized solutions, moving toward self-consciousness and self-determination.

Probably as a result of these experiences, Kroll's descriptions of the conventional products of the Modern Movement are laced with the adjectives of oppression: the administrators who commission designers are fond of "paramilitary models," the Pruitt-Igoe housing development in St. Louis (and developments like it) are the products of a generation of "somewhat militaristic architects;" the dark glazed windows of contemporary office blocks present a "fascist facade," programmes call for completely regular, separate rooms "like ruled metric paper;" and facades of reflecting glass are "like the sunglasses of American policemen."

With views so much at variance with those of the Establishment, it is not surprising that, despite all his care for those who will use his buildings, Kroll is not widely popular in Belgium. His reputation may have had something to do with his not having been invited by the academic authorities to participate in the design of Louvain-La Neuve, the new university town near Ottignies. It was at the request of the students that in 1969 Kroll was commissioned to design the medical complex at Woluwe. The authorities probably granted the request thinking that "group dynamics" meant only another of that kind of harmless verbal participation by which conflict is often reduced. Kroll, however, was as good as his reputation: he involved the students in design decisions that normally belong to the architect—including a deemphasis of the elitism of Henri Montois' original campus master plan. The new complex was designed in such an open, flexible way that internal walls can be built or taken down to give more or less space, sun can come in at the right places, areas can be communally shared or made into self-contained units, all parts have access to outside balconies or terraces, and living quarters can easily be converted into ordinary dwellings and are great fun to be in. Incorporated into the complex is a primary school that was soon occupied by a nearby school that had to be evacuated for underground works: in fact, it seems as if the whole complex could function as a district centre for the adjacent town suburb of Kapellveld.

At first sight the Woluwe complex looks a complete jumble, like the fragments of an old city, the facades a totally disordered collection of brick, glass, grills, balconies, grey tiles, staircases—the sort of "organic disorder" that Kroll had in mind from the beginning. With its intentional promiscuity of quotes (Aalto, Mies, Le Corbusier, Stirling, SITE), the buildings have been characterized as a collage of "war surplus materials, discarded on the battlefield after the defeat of the avant garde." The authorities disliked it so much that in 1977 they dismissed Kroll as architect, and threatened to tear down the buildings. They have already destroyed the planting that was beginning to climb up the walls (Kroll had commissioned Louis Leroy, a Dutch "anarchist" gardener, to make an ecological garden, intertwining itself with the built structures). Ultimately, Woluwe remains a utopian dream to the extent that the complete participation process has had to remain imaginary—though, whereas classical utopia was always the exclusive work of one enlightened man, this utopia did grow from the involvement of many people.

But that Kroll can indeed bring about a successful ecological marriage between the old and the new, between landscape and "organic" architecture, is illustrated by his Dominican House at Froidment. One occupant, despite some reservations about the materials and details of the building, said, "When we moved in, we felt at home immediately. He did exactly what we wanted—in his completely original way."

—Colin Naylor

KUMP, Ernest Joseph.

American. Born in Bakersfield, California, 29 December 1911. Educated at the University of California, Berkeley, 1928-32, B.A. 1932; Harvard University, Cambridge, Massachusetts, 1932-33, M.Arch. 1933. Married Josephine Clark Miller in 1934; children: Peter Clark and Mondi. Principal, Ernest J. Kump Associates, Bakersfield, Fresno, and San Francisco, California, 1934-45, and Palo Alto, California, 1945-75. Founder, Tekkto Systems Research, New York, 1964-66, Palo Alto, California, 1968-76, and London, 1977-81. Since 1981, Archi-

tectural and Systems Technology Consultant, Brixlegg, Tyrol, Austria. Visiting Lecturer, Harvard University, 1945, University of Michigan, Ann Arbor, 1945, University of Texas at Austin, 1946, and University of Melbourne, 1948; Adjunct Professor and Chairman of Advanced Research, 1961, and Professor of Architecture and Chairman of Advanced Research and Educational Planning, 1962, Columbia University, New York. National Chairman for School Buildings, American Institute of Architects, 1948-49; Member, President Reagan's Task Force for the Arts and Humanities, 1981. Exhibitions: Museum of Modern Art, New York, 1943; *World's Fair*, Brussels, 1958; *World's Fair*, Seattle, 1962; Museum of Modern Art, New York, 1965. Recipient: United States Navy Meritorious Civilian Service Emblem, 1944; *Progressive Architecture* Award, 1947, 1948, 1949, 1957, 1958, 1960; Award of Merit, 1954, Honor Award, 1955, and Architectural Firm Award, 1970, American Institute of Architects. Fellow, American Institute of Architects, 1956; Fellow Royal Society of Arts, London, 1950; Honorary Fellow, Royal Institute of British Architects, 1984. Member, Akademie der Künste, West Berlin, 1968. Address: Ernest J. Kump, Consultants, Schloss Matzen, 6230 Brixlegg, Austria.

Works:

1932/
36   Memorial Auditorium, Fresno and O Streets, Fresno, California (with others)
1933   United States Post Office, Madera, California
1933/
35   Tulare County Welfare Building, 210 North Court, Visalia, California
1936   Reedley Junior College, California
     School Adminstration Building, Fresno, California (with others)
1937/
39   Fowler Elementary School, California
1937/
41   School complex, Shafter, California
1938   Development plan for the Greeley Elementary School District, Bakersfield, California
     Sill Property Company Office and Store, Bakersfield, California
     El Tejon Hotel, Bakersfield, California
     Tollhouse High School, California
     Dinuba Joint Union College, California
1938/
39   School complex, Patterson, California

1938/
41   School complex, Wasco, California
1939   Gymnasium, Raymond, California
     Tollhouse High School classroom addition, California
     Elementary school, Ducor, California
     Sierra Vista Elementary School, Mineral King and Dollner Streets, Visalia, California
1939/
40   School complex, Taft, California
1939/
49   Carmel High School, California
1940   United States Army Engine Repair and Storage Building, McClellan Field, Sacramento, California
     Edison Technical High School, Fresno, California
     Sierra Union High School, 4330 East Garland, Fresno, California
     School Administration Building, Tranquillity, California
     City Hall, Fresno, California
     Commercial building, Chesterand 18th Streets, Bakersfield, California
     Acalanes High School, Lafayette, California
     Exeter Union High School, 820 San Juan, Exeter, California
1941   Defense Housing School and Community Center, Vallejo, California
     Carmel Woods School, Carmel, California
     Housing, San Diego
     United States Army Sierra Ordnance Depot, Lassen County, California
     Kern Mutual Telephone Company Building, Maricopa, California
1942   Chabot Acres (housing development), Vallejo, California
     Runways, hangars and living quarters for the United States Navy at Oakland Municipal Airport, California
     Chabot Terrace School and Community Center, Vallejo, California
1943   Alameda Unified School and Community Center, California
     Dover Street School, San Pablo, California
1944   Development plan for the Antioch/Live Oak Unified School District, California
     Elementary school, Albany, California
     White Oaks School, San Carlos, California (with additions, 1948, 1953)
     United States Army Base Engineers Maintenance Building, Suisun, California
     United States Army Test and Storage Building, McClellan Field, Sacramento, California
1944/
45   School complex, St. Helena, California
1945   Development plan for the Tracy Union High School District, California
     Development plan for the Orinda Union Elementary School District, California
     Healey and Popovich Store and Warehouse, Fresno, California
     United States Navy Ordnance and Optical Shop Building, San Francisco Naval Shipyard
     California Packing Corporation Plant and Warehouse, San Francisco
     "Pre-Bilt" Model House, San Anselmo, California
1945/
50   Hoover Elementary School, Redwood City, California
     Lincoln Elementary School, Redwood City, California
     John Gill School, Redwood City, California
     Beresford Park School, San Mateo, California
     Borel School, San Mateo, California
     College Park School, San Mateo, California
     George W. Hall School, San Mateo, California
     Laurel Elementary School, San Mateo, California
     Lawrence School, San Mateo, California

Ernest Kump: Foothill College, Los Altos Hills, California, 1962.

Shoreview School, San Mateo, California
Sunnybrae School, San Mateo, California
1946 School complex, Santa Clara, California
John Marsh Elementary School, Antioch, California
Tracy High School, California
High school, Antioch, California
Merced Passenger Terminals, Modesto, California
Los Lomitos Elementary School, Atherton, California
San Jose High School, California
Broadway Elementary School, San Jose, California
Asilomar Buildings, Pacific Grove, California
YMCA Conference and Guest Buildings, Asilomar, California
1946/
50 Barstow Union High School, California
Las Lomas High School, Walnut Creek, California
1947 Locker Building, San Mateo, California
Line Street Elementary School, Hollister, California
Aquatic Center, Richland, California
Plan for the long-range building program of San Bernardino City Elementary School District, California
Plan for the long-range building program of the Alameda Unified School District, California
1948 Field House, Tamalpais High School, Larkspur, California
Moorpark School, Campbell, California
San Tomas School, Campbell, California
Eliot School, Gilroy, California
Civic Center, Phoenix, Arizona (project)
1949 Laureola School, San Carlos, California
Richland School, Hanford, Washington (project)
Michele and Pfeffer Shop, San Francisco
1950 Encinal High School, Alameda, California
1950/
53 Franklin Elementary School, Berkeley, California
Jefferson Elementary School, Berkeley, California
1950/
56 North School Complex, Hillsborough, California
1951 Bessie Carmichael School, San Francisco
Richland School, Shafter, California
Christ Episcopal Church additions, Los Altos, California
1951/
57 Rickey's Studio Inn, Palo Alto, California
1952 San Jose High School, California (with addition, 1961)
University Village Houses, Redwood City, California
1953 Columbus Park Elementary School, San Francisco
1955 Portable classrooms, Alameda, California
District plan for the Crestmoor Site, San Bruno, California
Plan for the long-range building program of the San Bruno Park School District, California
Vernon J. Pick Laboratory, Saratoga, California
1955/
56 Rollingwood School, San Bruno, California
New classrooms for the Edgemont School, San Bruno, California
New classrooms for the Parkside School, San Bruno, California
Herbert Hoover Junior High School, San Francisco
1956 Parking study for Palo Alto, California
1957 Halfway House Recreation Center, Hillsborough, California
Woodside High School, Atherton, California
1958 United States Navy and Air Force Housing at Zaragoza and Madrid, Spain

Kump Office Building, Lytton Square, Palo Alto, California
Franklin School additions, Berkeley, California
Jefferson School additions, Berkeley, California
1959 Crestmoor Elementary School, San Bruno, California
Northbrae Elementary School additions, San Bruno, California
Eldorado Country Club, Palm Desert, California
United States Embassy and Staff Residence, Seoul, Korea
1959/
65 William H. Crocker Jr. High School, Hillsborough, California
1960 Civic Center, Los Altos, California
United States Coast Guard Indoor Training Pool, Alameda, California
Youth Center, Los Altos, California
Pioneer Senior High School, San Jose, California
Water Treatment Plant, Santa Cruz, California
John Muir School, San Bruno, California
1961 Master plan for the American University, Beirut
Carl Sandburg School, San Bruno, California
Stowell Manor Shopping Center, Santa Maria, California
Chester F. Awalt High School, Mountain View, California
1962 Carmel Valley Junior High School, Carmel, California
All Saints Church, Watsonville, California
San Lorenzo Plaza Redevelopment, Santa Cruz, California
Conference and Commercial Building, Palo Alto, California
Foothill College, Los Altos Hills, California (with others)
Garden Hotel, Oxnard, California
1962/
64 Santa Clara County Superior Court Building, San Jose, California
1964 California Water Service Company, Civic Center, San Jose, California
1965 Cabrillo College, Aptos, California (with others)
Henry M. Gunn High School, Palo Alto, California
Lucie Stearn Hall, Mills College, Oakland, California
Central Service Building, University of California at Santa Cruz
1966 Civic Center, Concord, California
Isabella Cowell Health Center, Mills College, Oakland, California
1967 Crown College, University of California at Santa Cruz
1968 DeAnza College, Cupertino, California (with others)
1971 Union Bank, 400 University, Palo Alto, California
Walter H. Haas Pavilion, Mills College, Oakland, California
1972 Student Union, San Jose State College, California
1973 San Joaquin Delta College, Stockton, California
Parkland Community College, Urbana, Illinois
1975 Las Colinas Urban Community Plan, Dallas, Texas
1978 Bendigo College of Advanced Education, Geelong, Victoria, Australia (as consultant architect)
1978/
80 Herbert Hoover Federal Memorial Building, Stanford University, Palo Alto, California
1984 Reagan Presidential Library, Stanford University, Palo Alto, California (as consultant architect)

Publications:

By KUMP: books—*Realizing the Modern School Plant*, Fresno, California 1943; *School Planning*, Fresno, California 1947; *A New Architecture for Man*, Palo Alto, California 1957; article—"Architecture for the College Campus" in *AIA Journal* (Washington, D.C.), March 1963.

On KUMP: articles—"Pioneer School" in *Architectural Forum* (New York), October 1949; "Design" in *Architectural Forum* (New York), October 1953; "Finger-Plan School Refined" in *Architectural Forum* (New York), October 1955; "Design Notes" in *Architectural Forum* (New York), September 1956; "Quality of School Design" in *Architectural Record* (New York), April 1957; "The Space Module School" in *Architectural Forum* (New York), December 1957; "Colleges for the Community" in *Architectural Forum* (New York), November 1959; "Architect Ernest Kump" by Georgia Hesse in the *San Francisco Examiner*, 8 April 1962; "An Environmental Grid" in *Architectural Forum* (New York), August 1962; "Education: New Two-Year Colleges" in *Time* (New York), 5 March 1965; "Bendigo College of Advanced Education" by Nick Walter in *Architecture in Australia* (Sydney), September 1978; "Seven Just Fellows" in *The Architects' Journal* (London), 30 March 1983; "Gold Medal Jury Decides on Seven Honorary Fellowships" in *RIBA Journal* (London), April 1983.

*

Architecture, to be relevant in today's world, requires a whole new philosophy—an architecture without buildings! This means essentially that architecture must be intrinsically a total dynamic and living environmental system, in harmony with nature.

It must immediately cease to continue to be merely an art or method for the design and construction of inert static structures known as buildings. As the result of the relentless growth of this false concept of architecture, our environment in its present state bears witness to the unconscionable degree of pollution and soulless decadence in which today's society finds itself immersed.

Building Architecture is dead. This is borne out by the fact that one idea that is emphasized and is also a recurring theme in the world of science is that reality in the universe can only be understood as being intrinsically dynamic in terms of flow and movement, change and transformation, and that the whole of nature is engaged in endless motion and activity resulting in a constant state of ever-becoming form. So must architecture be! Without this vision a hostile, soulless, environmental wasteland will be the ultimate destiny of humanity—and in it "the people will perish."

—Ernest J. Kump

*

Foothill College, in the suburbs of San Francisco, is Ernest J. Kump's masterpiece. It solved a problem in California architecture, that of finding a form for larger institutional suburban buildings that would match the comfortable casualness of the redwood and glass suburban house.

Foothill College provided an immediately successful solution. It did it by a planning method that broke down a huge campus into a large number of smaller—but still clearly institutional rather than residential size—buildings. This method had been used before, but Kump introduced a crucial formal innovation in roof form that is reminiscent of the traditional shapes of rural California redwood farm structures. The combined hip and flat roof was attractive in itself, and the flat top allowed Kump to cover a large space with a wide eave pitched roof that did not need to go so high as to cause a problem of both cost and appearance. And the flat roof served as a perfect concealment area within which the elaborate mechanical system now required by a large public building could be placed.

The romantic imagery of Foothill came as a surprise, for prior to its design Kump had been known and respected for his thoughtful rationalist approach to school design. Kump had investigated and expounded the merits of modular design and construction; in his school work he evolved a refined and economical system of construction using available materials and practices, which he then developed into a space module—a wide span supermodule within which a variety of plans could be accommodated (it formed the basis of the planning of Foothill). Kump also worked on, and promoted, technological inventions such as an integrated ceiling system, and he experimented with and used advanced methods of communication and coordination in the construction document process long before such ideas became a matter of more general professional concern.

Foothill College had instant popular appeal, and the Kump office was flooded with commissions for large-scale projects. None succeeded in equalling the strength and conviction of the original, though nearby DeAnza College comes close. Unfortunately, clients saw and loved only the romantic softness of the Foothill image: later projects of the firm seemed to lose the firm rationality upon which Foothill was based and which gave it the timeless quality of great architecture.

All of Kump's work has an old-fashioned respect for materials and a delight in using them as a small scale design element. Although the success of Foothill almost forced the office into an endless repetition of wood gamesmanship, Kump has, over the years, worked intelligently and sensitively in steel and concrete. His office was also old-fashioned in its management style. California offices are populated not only by Kump's ex-employees but also by his ex-partners. He was known to arrive in the morning and fire, sack or dismiss his entire staff. He keeps still a castle on the Rhine, no small feat for a California-based tycoon. But he created an environment in which first class design work was done for education, an institutional field notable, in architecture, for its mediocrity and compromise.

—Christopher Arnold

KUROKAWA, Kisho Noriaki.

Japanese. Born in Aichi Prefecture, 8 April 1934. Educated at Kyoto University, Department of Architecture, B.Arch. 1957; Tokyo University, Department of Architecture, under Kenzo Tange, M.Arch. 1959, D.Arch. 1964. Married Sumie Tsuchiya in 1959; children: Kako and Mikio; married Ayako Wakao in 1984. Founder, Kisho Kurokawa and Associates, Tokyo, 1962–68. Since 1968, President, Kisho Kurokawa Architect and Associates, Tokyo. Principal, Institute for Social Engineering Inc., Tokyo, since 1969; President, Urban Design Consultants Inc., Tokyo, since 1969; Adviser to the Japanese National Railways, since 1970; Analyst for the Japan Broadcasting Corporation, since 1974; Adviser to the International Design Conference, Aspen, Colorado, since 1974. Exhibitions: World Design Conference, Tokyo, 1960; *Metabolism*, Tokyo, 1962; *Team Ten*, Urbino, Italy, 1964; *Contemporary Japanese Architecture*, Florence 1968; *Capsule Architecture*, Rome, 1973; *Kisho Kurokawa: architecture of symbiosis*, London and Dublin, 1981, Paris, 1982, Sofia, Rome and Pistoia, Italy, 1983, Budapest and Moscow, 1984. Recipient: Takamura Kotaro Design Prize, 1965; First Prize, International Competition for Pilot Low-Cost Housing in Peru, 1969; First Prize, International TANU Headquarters Competition, Tanzania, 1972; First Prize, International Conference City Competition, Abu Dhabi, 1975; Silver and Gold Prizes, Japan Sign Design Association, 1977, 1979, 1980; Building Contractors Society Prize, 1977, 1978, 1979, 1983; Mainichi Art Award, 1978; Sofia Prize for Plastic Art, 1979; First Prize, Bayer AG Centre Competition, 1979; Purchase Prize, Internationale Bauausstellung Competition, Berlin, 1980; First Prize, Sofia Urban Centre Competition, 1983. Honorary Fellow, American Institute of Architects, 1982; Honorary Member, Union of Architects of Bulgaria, 1982; Life Fellow, Royal Society of Arts, London. Address: Kisho Kurokawa Architect and Associates, Aoyama Building, 11F, 1-2-3 Kita-Aoyama, Minato-ku, Tokyo, Japan.

Works:

1962 Mass Production Apartments (project)
      Nishijin Labor Center, Kyoto
1963 Shiga Residence, Tokyo
1964 Head Office and Main Factory, Takeda Riken Company, Yamagata Prefecture, Japan
      Nitto Food Company Factory, Yamaguchi Prefecture, Japan
1965 Yoshimatsu Residence, Tokyo
      Rest Station, National Children's Land, Kanagawa Prefecture, Japan
      Hans Christian Andersen Memorial Museum, Kanagawa Prefecture, Japan
1966 Irako Vacation Village, Aichi Prefecture, Japan
      Hishino New Town, Japan
1967 Irako Vacation Village extension, Aichi Prefecture, Japan
      City Hall, Sagae, Japan
      Resort center, Yamagata Prefecture, Japan
1968 Goshikidai Vacation Village Lodge, Yamagata Prefecture, Japan
      Space Capsule Discotheque, Tokyo
1969 Takeda Riken Factory, Gyoda, Japan
      Service area, Tokyo-Nagoya Highway, Kanagawa Prefecture, Japan
      Otome Toge Drive-In Restaurant, Hakone, Japan
1970 Odakyu Restaurant in Ashinoko, Hakone, Japan
      Capsule House at the Celestial Theme Pavilion, *Expo '70*, Osaka
      Toshiba IHI Pavilion, *Expo '70*, Osaka
      Takara Group Pavilion, *Expo '70*, Osaka
1971 Omori Keisi Department Store, Omori, Japan
      City Hall, Sakura, Japan
      Agricultural Experimental Station, Yamanashi Prefecture, Japan
      Long Beach Bowl, Oiso, Japan
1972 Leisure Capsule LC-30X
      Employees' Dormitory, Prince Hotel, Sapporo, Japan
      Capsule House, K, Karuizawa, Japan
      Prince Hotel, Sapporo, Japan
      Nakagin Capsule Tower Building, Tokyo
1973 Sanpo Construction Company Head Office, Tokyo
      Prince Hotel, Shimoda, Japan
      Prince Hotel, Karuizawa, Japan
      Club House, Guam
1974 Koito Office Building, Tokyo
      Hotel White Town, Gunma Prefecture, Japan
      Azabu no. 1 Town House, Tokyo
      Big Box Seibu recreation center, Tokyo
1975 Conference City, Abu Dhabi, United Arab Emirates
      City Hall, Waki Cho, Japan
      Daido Mutual Life Insurance Building, Sapporo, Japan
      Hotel New Otani, Tottori, Japan
      Fukuoka Bank Head Office, Fukuoka, Japan
1976 Wildlife Protection Center, Yamanashi Prefecture, Japan
      Astronomical Observation Building and Guest Houses, Tadeshina Society Club, Tadeshina, Japan
      Aoyama Bell Commons (multi-use plaza), Tokyo
      Hotel New Otani, Saga, Japan Sony Tower, Osaka
      Fujisawa New Town, Japan
1977 Wataya Villa Annex, Saga Prefecture, Japan
      Cottage on Mt. Kitadake, Yamanashi Prefecture, Japan
      Sakuradai Branch Office, Tokai Bank, Tokyo
      Peace Memorial, Gamagori, Japan
      Japanese Red Cross Society Head Office, Tokyo
      Ishikawa Cultural Center, Kanazawa, Japan
      National Ethnology Museum, Osaka
1978 Daido Insurance Building, Tokyo
      Kumamoto Municipal Museum, Japan
1979 New Otani Vitosha Hotel, Sofia, Bulgaria
      Kyojuso Villa and Ritsumeian Tea Ceremony House, Tokyo
1980 Shoto Club, Tokyo
      Urban Hill Shopping Centre, Matsudo, Japan
1981 Fukuoka Prefectural Museum of Modern Art, Fukuoka, Japan
      Great Japan Exhibition display designs, Royal Academy of Arts, London
1982 Saitama Prefectural Museum of Modern Art, Urawa, Japan
      Suginami Ward Central Library, Tokyo
      Edo furniture series
1983 Kanagawa Building, Yokohama, Japan
      National Bunraku Theatre, Osaka
1984 Wacoal Kojimachi Building, Tokyo
      Roppongi Prince Hotel, Tokyo
      Yasuda Fire Insurance Building, Fukuoka, Japan
1985 Shah Alam Skyscraper, Selangor, Malaysia
      Citicenter Skyscraper, Kuala Lumpur, Malaysia
      Center Point Skyscraper, Kuala Lumpur, Malaysia
      Japanese Studies Institute, Thammasat University, Bangkok, Thailand
      Japanese Cultural Centre, West Berlin
      Haskova Opera House, Bulgaria
      Bayer Plant Protection Research Headquarters, Monheim, West Germany

Publications:

By KUROKAWA: books—*Metabolism '60*, with others, Tokyo 1960; *Prefabricated Houses*, with Noboru Kawazoe, Tokyo 1964; *Urban Design*, Tokyo 1965; *Action Architecture*, Tokyo 1967; *Homo Movens*, Tokyo 1969; translation into Japanese of *The Death and Life of Great American Cities* by Jane Jacobs, Tokyo 1969; *Kisho Kurokawa: Architectural Creation*, Tokyo 1969; *Works of Kisho Kurokawa*, Tokyo 1970; *Creating Contemporary Architecture*, Tokyo 1971; *A Discourse on Modern Society: Lectures in Sociology XIII*, co-author, Tokyo 1972; *The Archipelago of Information: The Future Japan*, Tokyo 1972; *Conception of Metabolism*, Tokyo 1972; *In the Realm of the Future*, Tokyo 1972; *Introduction to Urbanology*, Tokyo 1973; *The World of Kisho Kurokawa*, Tokyo 1975; *Metabolism in Architecture*, London and New York 1977; *Concept of Cities*, Tokyo 1977; *Concept of Space*, Tokyo 1977; *A Culture of Grays*, Tokyo 1977; *Kisho Kurokawa: A Contemporary Japanese Architect*, Tokyo 1979; *Thesis on Architecture: Towards Japanese Space*, Tokyo 1982; *Kisho Kurokawa: architecture et design*, Paris 1982; *Social Commentaries: A Cross Section of Japan*, Tokyo 1983; *Architecture of the Street: Towards Intermediate Space*, Tokyo 1983; articles—"The Japanese Housing Problem: A Personal View" in *The Planner* (London), February 1975; "En-Space" in *Bauen und Wohnen* (Zurich), December 1975; "Sony Tower" in *The Japan Architect* (Tokyo), November 1976; "Head Office of the Japan Red Cross Society", with Yasuhiko Nagata, in *The Japan Architect* (Tokyo), September 1977; "Rikyu Gray" in *The Japan*

Architect (Tokyo), January 1978; "National Museum of Ethnology" in The Japan Architect (Tokyo), April 1978; "A Culture of Grays", "Rikyu Gray and the Art of Ambiguity", and "Notes on Mediating Space" in The Japan Architect (Tokyo), June 1979; "Intermediate Space or the Realization of the Indefinite" in The Japan Architect (Tokyo), March 1982; "Japanese Culture and Post-Modernist Architecture" in The Japan Architect (Tokyo), April 1983; "Le Poetique in Architecture: Beyond Semiotics" in The Japan Architect (Tokyo), May 1984; "Karakuri: The Metaphysical Machine" in Kenchiku Bunka (Tokyo), July 1984.

On KUROKAWA: books—The Third Generation by Philip Drew, London 1972; Beyond Metabolism: The New Japanese Architecture by Michael Franklin Ross, New York 1978; By Their Own Design, edited by Abby Suckle, New York and St. Albans, Hertfordshire 1980; Kisho Kurokawa: Il Futuro nella Tradizione by Lia Papa and Vincenzo Manocchio, Naples 1984; articles—"Kurokawa" by Robert Williams in Building Design (London), 2 November 1973; "Kurokawa" by Yasuo Uesaka in Architecture Plus (New York), January/February 1974; "Team 10 at Royaumont" by Alison Smithson in Architectural Design (London), November 1975; "The Enigma of Kurokawa" by Charles Jencks in Architectural Review (London), March 1976; "Kurokawa and Metabolism" by Agnoldomenico Pica in Domus (Milan), December 1977; "Kisho Kurokawa" by Claude Lévi-Strauss in special issue of Space Design (Tokyo), April 1978; "Kumamoto City Museum" in Building Design (London), 19 May 1978; "Kisho Kurokawa: architecture of grays", special issue of The Japan Architect (Tokyo), June 1979; "Kisho Kurokawa: a study in cultural connections" in Architectural Record (New York), August 1979; "Japan's architectural superstar: Kisho Kurokawa" in Building Design (London), 12 October 1979; "Kisho Kurokawa - unity of engineering and architecture" in AIT (Stuttgart), vol. 88, no. 3, 1980; "Tokyo Metabolism: Kisho Kurokawa" in Architectural Review (London), September 1981; "In the Japanese Manner" by Colin Amery in the Financial Times (London), October 1981; "La puissance et la grace de Kurokawa" by Michele Champenois in Le Monde (Paris), July 1982; "Kisho Kurokawa - grey matter" in Architecture (Paris), August 1982; "Kurokawa – a new internationalism" by Francis Rambert in Architectes (Paris), August/September 1982; "The thought and works in architecture of Kisho Kurokawa" in Chinese Architect (Taipei, Taiwan), August 1983; "On the Creative Concepts of Kisho Kurokawa" by A. Zenkevich in Arkitektura (Warsaw), September/October 1983; "Kisho Kurokawa" by Philip Jodidio, in Connaissance des Arts (Paris), October 1983; "A Special Report" by Deyan Sudjic in The Times (London), July 1984.

Bibliography: Kisho Noriaki Kurokawa: Metabolist Pioneer of Japan by James P. Noffsinger, Monticello, Illinois 1979.

I have been engaging in many creative activities based upon the theory of "Metabolism" which I developed as an architectural movement in the 1960s. This theory of metabolism is best explained in my book Metabolism in Architecture. The following summarizes the major points that I stressed in my book:

1) I consider architecture as part of a space opened to society, rather than as a work of art.

2) I have put into my architecture the elements of growth and change.

3) Architecture should not be a world to be thought of as an end in itself. It should be considered as a theatre stage setting where the leading actors are the people, and to dramatically direct the dialogue between these people and space is the technique of designing.

4) Since architecture is closely connected to the culture of each country, its international quality should be gained by discovering a theory to universalize this cultural characteristic.

5) By abolishing the philosophy of dualism which sees the individual in contrast to society, the part to the whole, art against technology, I intend to postulate a new philosophy—the philosophy of coexistence. This philosophy considers these elements in unification with the whole of what's going on.

—Kisho Kurokawa

Kisho Kurokawa is truly one of the boy-wonders of modern Japanese architecture. Born in Nagoya in 1934, at twenty-six he was the youngest and most precocious member of the original Metabolist Group. In their futurist manifesto, Metabolism 1960, the metabolists called for a new method of urban structuring using large, interlocking megastructures. From his experience in Kenzo Tange's office, working on the Plan for Tokyo 1960, Kurokawa evolved his own Helix City Concept. This extraordinary beginning has been followed by an unending series of innovative and intriguing projects.

Kurokawa's interest in new technology has had various repercussions. He visited the Soviet Union in the early 1960s and wrote a book on Soviet prefab systems. He captured the imagination of the international architectural community with his high-tech pavilions at Expo '70, including the Capsule House at the Celestial Theme Pavilion and the Takara Beautillion. Both projects implied an architecture of tomorrow that would be composed of plug-in modules and clip-on capsules suspended from a structural space-frame.

The hopes inherent in the metabolist dream were not simple, and converting them to reality was equally difficult, but Kurokawa persevered and achieved the Nakagin Capsule Building in 1972. The implications of the capsules suspended from the central towers were awe inspiring. Perhaps the future had finally arrived. Kurokawa continued to pursue the capsule concept whenever it seemed to be appropriate as in the LC-30X Leisure Capsule, the Sony Tower in Osaka completed in 1976, and in his own country retreat at Karuizawa. In the final analysis the capsule concept was limited and had only a finite number of intelligent applications.

As an alternative to the purity of the Metabolist manifesto, Kurokawa has been developing a concept which is parallel to and complements his high-tech imagery. This is the traditional Japanese concept of "en" or in-between space. Every Japanese home has a genkan or foyer as a transition zone, and some more elaborate buildings have the engawa or veranda which is an extension of the interior space while also serving as an introduction to the outdoor space. Kurokawa has attempted to incorporate this concept in his modern architecture. It is most apparent in the Head Office of the Fukuoka Bank, the National Ethnology Museum, and the Waki-Cho City Hall. The Fukuoka Bank is clearly indebted to the Ford Foundation Building by Kevin Roche and John Dinkeloo, and Kurokawa admits that he was influenced by the design but that he has extended the concept and adapted it to the Japanese condition. The en-space is part interior and part exterior and forms one layer of a series of transition zones in the sequence of spaces.

Kurokawa is himself a multi-dimensional architect who has written nearly twenty books, designed half a dozen new towns, and built more than fifty major buildings. He agrees that "some may be puzzled at my work, which sometimes expresses technology and sometimes reflects the tradition of Japanese architecture." However, this combination of the past, the present and the future is the key to understanding Kurokawa's work. He further explains that "my creative practice probes the point of contact between modern architecture and Japanese culture; and it is my pleasure to contribute, if it be but a little, to the world of architecture by presenting a different quality." For this we can all be thankful, for Kurokawa has brought us a variety of work that is stimulating and often beautiful.

—Michael Franklin Ross

Kisho Kurokawa: Saitama Prefectural Museum of Modern Art, Urawa, Japan, 1982.

LACHERT, Bohdan.

Polish. Born in Moscow, of Polish parents, 13 June 1900. Educated at the Technical University, Warsaw, under Professor Swierczynski, 1920-26, Dip.Arch. 1926. Served in the Polish Cavalry, 1918-20: prisoner of war, 1920-21; served in the Polish Resistance, 1939-45. Married Irene Nowakowska in 1922; children: Krzysztof, Rudolf, and Krystyna; married Maria Ceglinska in 1945. In partnership with Jozef Szanajca, Warsaw, 1926-39; Lecturer, Underground Polytechnic, Warsaw, 1940-44; Chairman of the Planning Department, Polish Rebuilding Bureau, Warsaw, 1944; Chairman of the Architectural Department, Capital Rebuilding Bureau, Warsaw, 1945-48; Chairman and Chief Designer, Muranow District Architectural Office, Warsaw, 1948-52. Since 1952, Chairman of the Architectural Programming Team, Home Office, Warsaw. Assistant Professor, 1926-28, Senior Assistant Professor, 1928-29, Adjunct Professor of Civil Engineering, 1929-37, Assistant Professor of Architecture, 1945-48, Associate Professor, 1948-66, Dean of the Faculty of Architecture, 1950-54, Professor, 1966-70, and, since 1970, Professor Emeritus, Technical University, Warsaw. Founder Member, 1926, Chairman of the Warsaw Section, 1937-38, and 1948-50, and National Chairman, 1944-45, Polish Architects Association (SARP), Warsaw; Founder-Member, Praesens avant-garde group, Warsaw, 1926-39; First Secretary, Polish Workers Party at the Technical University, Warsaw, 1947-48 and 1955-61; Member, Scientific Publications Committee, 1950-53, and Central Qualifying Committee, 1953-57, Ministry of Higher Education, Warsaw. Exhibitions: *First Exhibition of Modern Architecture*, Warsaw, 1926; *Architectural Exhibition,* Budapest, 1930; *Constructivism in Poland 1923-1936,* Muzeum Sztuki, Lodz, Poland 1973 (travelled to Essen, West Germany, and Otterlo, Netherlands); *Tendenzen der zwanziger Jahre,* Berlin, 1977; *Bohdan Lachert,* Wroclaw, Poland and Warsaw 1981; *Bohdan Lachert,* Liubliana, Yugoslavia, 1983; *Présences polonaises*, Centre Georges Pompidou, Paris, 1983 (travelled to Cambridge, England, 1984). Collection: Museum of Architecture, Wroclaw, Poland. Recipient: Gold Medal, with Jozef Szanaja, and Grand Prix, *Exposition Internationale,* Paris, 1937; Golden Cross of Merit, Warsaw, 1946 and 1947; State Art Award, Warsaw, 1950; Polish Tenth Anniversary Medal, 1955; President's Prize, City of Warsaw, 1984; Honour Prize, Association of Polish Architects, 1984. Commander, Cross of the Order of Polonia Restituta, Warsaw, 1967. Officer, Légion d'Honneur, Paris, 1946. Address (office): ul. Katowicka 9, 03-932 Warsaw, Poland.

Works:

1924 Mansion House, Ciechanki, Poland
     Hydro-Biological Research Station, Lake Wigry, Poland (with Jozef Szanajca)
1927 League of Nations Building, Geneva (competition project; with Jozef Szanajca and S. Hempel)
1928/
  31 Three houses, 9-13 Katowicka Street, Warsaw (with Jozef Szanajca)
     House, Czeska Street, Warsaw (with Jozef Szanajca)
1929 Officers' Housing Estate, Cracow, Poland (competition project; with Jozef Szanajca and W. Winkler)
     Tabita Mansion House, Skolimov, Poland (with Jozef Szanajca)
     Centrocement Pavilion, Home Trade Fair, Poznań, Poland (with Jozef Szanajca)
     Sanatorium, Ustronie, Poland (competition project; with Jozef Szanajca)
1930 School of Political Science, Warsaw (competition project; with Jozef Szanajca)
1931 Krakowskie Przedmiescie Bank, Lublin, Poland (with Jozef Szanajca)
1932 Hospital, Lagiewniki, Poland (competition project; with Jozef Szanajca)
1932/
  35 Rakowiec Housing Estate, Warsaw (with the Praesens Group)
1933 Ministry of Works Building, Warsaw (competition project; with Jozef Szanajca and W. Winkler)
     Ministry of Social Security Building, Warsaw (competition project; with Jozef Szanajca)
1934 Private house, Wolozyn, Poland (with Jozef Szanajca)
     Saski Place, Warsaw (competition project; with Jozef Szanajca, and S. and B. Brukalski)
     Church, Warsaw (competition project; with Jozef Szanajca)
1935 Post Office Building, Stanislawow, Poland (with Jozef Szanajca)
     Aircraft Hangar (competition project; with Jozef Szanajca and S. Hempel)
     Tuberculosis Sanatorium (competition project; with Jozef Szanajca)
1936 Mokotowski Stadium, Warsaw (competition project; with Jozef Szanajca, and S. and B. Brukalski)

Bohdan Lachert and Josef Szanajca: House on Katowicka Street, Warsaw, 1928-31.

Store, Warsaw (competition project; with Jozef Szanajca)

1937 Polish Pavilion, World's Fair, Paris (with Jozef Szanajca)

Polish Radio Building, Warsaw (competition project; with Jozef Szanajca)

Post Office Building, Warsaw (competition project; with Jozef Szanajca)

1938 Pilsudski Bridge, Warsaw (competition project; with Jozef Szanajca, F. Szelagowski, and Z. Wasiutynski)

Post Office Building, Stalowa Wola, Poland (competition project; with Jozef Szanajca)

1939 Polish Pavilion, World's Fair, New York (competition project; with Jozef Szanajca)

Hospital, Warsaw (competition project; with Jozef Szanajca)

School of Trade, Wilnok, Poland (competition project; with Jozef Szanajca and W. Winkler)

1945 *Polish Word* Newspaper Building, Warsaw (competition project)

1946 Victory Monument, Warsaw (competition project; with J. Knothe)

1947 Office building, Marszalkowska Street 124, Warsaw

Post Office and Telecommunications Building, Targowa Street, Warsaw

PKO Bank Building, Warsaw (competition project)

1948 Polish Workers Party Central Committee Building, Warsaw (competition project)

National Bank Building, Warsaw (competition project)

1948/
52 Muranow District Development, Warsaw (with the Architectural Office Team)

1949 Soviet Army Cemetery, al. Zwirki i Wigury, Warsaw (with Architectural Office Team)

Ministry of Finance Building, Warsaw (competition project)

Ministry of Security Social Home, Warsaw (competition project)

1950 Triumphal Arch, Lublin, Poland (competition project; with J. Jarnuszkiewicz)

1952 Marszalkowska Street Development, Warsaw (competition project)

1959 Heroes' Monument, Warsaw (competition project; with J. Jarnuszkiewicz)

1963 Old People's Home, Warsaw (competition project; with W. Benedek and J. Lucki)

1968 Apartment building, Kazimierz Dolny, Poland

Town Hall, Amsterdam (competition project; with J. Cianciara and H. Dabrowski)

1968/
70 Lowrise housing development, Pulawy, Poland (with the Architectural Office Team)

1969 Museum of Modern Art, Lodz, Poland (competition project)

1976 Railway and Bus Station, Lublin, Poland (competition project; with J. Lubanski and A. Pawlik)

1978 National Library, Tehran (competition project; with W. Szober and J. Lubanski)

1979/
82 Atrium Building Types (projects)

1980/
83 Single-Family Housing Development, Warsaw

Publications:

By LACHERT: articles—"The PKO Building in Warsaw" in *Architektura* (Warsaw), no. 2, 1948; "Experimental Building Methods" and "The Streets of Saka Kepa" in *Architektura* (Warsaw), no. 4, 1948; "Muranow Housing District" in *Architektura* (Warsaw), no. 5, 1948; "Two Currents in Contemporary Polish Architecture" in *The Fight for Building Materials,* Warsaw 1949; "Warsaw Bridges" in *Polish Review* (Warsaw), no. 9, 1949; "Muranow" in *Miasto* (Warsaw), no. 9, 1952; "Reflections and Remarks" in *Przeglad kulturalny* (Warsaw), no. 4, 1955; "Low-Rise Housing District: An Architect's Thoughts" in *Architektura* (Warsaw), no. 4, 1963; "Friends Who Have Gone" in *Architektura* (Warsaw), no. 10, 1964; "Mieczyslaw Szczuka as an Architect" in *Mieczyslaw Szczuka,* edited by Anatol Stern and Mieczyslaw Berman, Warsaw 1965; "Institutes of Architectural Design" in *Warsaw School of Architecture 1915-1965,* Warsaw 1967; "Style or School" in *Architektura* (Warsaw), no. 7, 1969; "Reflections on Some Aspects of Architectonics" in *Architektura* (Warsaw), 1 February 1983.

On LACHERT: books—*Gli elementi dell'architettura funzionale* by Alberto Sartoris, Milan 1932, 1940; *Introduzione all'architettura moderna* by Alberto Sartoris, Milan 1944; *Warsaw: The Destruction and Rebuilding of the Town* by A. Ciborowski, Warsaw 1964; *Polish Avant-Garde Architecture 1918-1939* by I. Wislocka, Warsaw 1968; *Constructivism in Poland 1923-1936,* exhibition catalogue, Lodz, Poland 1973; *William Morris und die socialen Ursprünge der modernen Architektur* by E. Goldzamt, Dresden 1976; *Towards the Theory of the Social Housing Unit* by Helena Syrkus, Warsaw 1976; *Atlas of Warsaw Architecture* by J. Chroscicki and A. Rottermund, Warsaw 1977; *Tendenzen der zwanziger Jahre,* exhibition catalogue, Berlin, 1977; *The Polish Avant-Garde, 1918-39,* Paris 1981; *Presences polonaises (constructivisme—les contemporaines),* exhibition catalogue, Paris 1983.

The designer's vision of an urban development may be considered only in the form of a model which reflects the order of people's existence and the pattern of their movement in the area to be developed.

The designer's vision of an architectural work, evolving as it is designed, is not recognizable a priori.

The vague character of both visions—as I see them—means that, although I took part from the very beginning in the rebuilding of Warsaw after the destruction of World War II, I have never had a firm image of the future capital.

The progressive increase in density of urban built form makes one aware of the futility of anticipating its future image.

The creator of an architectural work ought to possess not the intuition for recreating an original vision but an awareness of the need to subordinate himself to an autogenous end product, a design method for generating the shape of an unknown object; the shape that it progressively arrives at will be the result of the accumulation of random and non-random partial decisions taken by the creator.

The later the vision of a work is crystallized in its shape, the more likely it is to become unique and the less it will reflect solutions for analogous subjects that already exist.

The development process of an architectural design has a certain analogy with the development process of a living organism, and only in this way can one see the reason for calling architecture "organic"—formed organically in a creative process but not having the features of an organism.

—Bohdan Lachert

The work of Bohdan Lachert cannot be discussed without paying a tribute to his inseparable prewar partner, Jozef Szanajca, killed by the Nazis in September 1939. Over seventeen years of fruitful cooperation, Lachert and Szanajca produced numerous projects, many of which were constructed; of their competition projects, fifty-one received awards.

While still at the Warsaw School of Architecture in the 1920s, Lachert's and Szanajca's student works attracted the attention of Szymon Syrkus, and as a result they were both invited to join the newly formed avant-garde group Praesens. Their competition project for the League of Nations Building in Geneva also attracted special attention among the Polish entries. One of the most remarkable of their early projects is the unrealized design for the School of Political Science in Warsaw, characterized by outstanding visual values and extremely modern construction. These young architects were constantly looking for new solutions and experimenting with new building methods and materials. Their house in Katowicka Street in the Saska Kepa district of Warsaw provided a real testing ground for their new ideas. The use of transverse structural walls allowed a horizontal arrangement of windows along the whole facade. The internal division into three dwelling units, with differently treated levels, was reflected in the garden elevation. Lachert and Szanajca's houses for the Warsaw Housing Cooperative and their projects for two tuberculosis sanatoriums are also among their best designs.

Since the war, Lachert has developed his own philosophy for teaching architects, his own "school of thinking." He has been interested in the mystery of creativity. As the physicist Robert Oppenheimer said, "Scientists and artists perpetually live on the edge of mystery, being always surrounded by it."

Lachert is interested in the ontological problems as well as the methodology of architecture, and he regards architectural creativity as worthy of separate study and deeper attention—from four aspects: the juxtaposition of preferences and opinions; the intentional object and visionary image; compromise and the hierarchy of problems; and, lastly, the eidetic determinants of design work. With this rigorous analysis of creativity Lachert undermines the "stability" of architectural opinions, depreciates the authority of the visionary image, and demonstrates his disapproval of compromise solutions. He considers the intellectual qualities of the designer to be of most significance in creative architectural work, for it is the intellect that generates and stores the abstract visions related to the intentional object, the visions motivated by the design subject.

—Teresa Czaplinska-Archer

LAPIDUS, Morris.

American. Born in Odessa, Russia, 25 November 1902; emigrated to the United States, 1903: naturalized, 1914. Educated at New York University, 1921-23; Columbia University School of Architecture, New York, 1923-27, B.Arch. 1927. Married Beatrice Perlman in 1929; sons: Richard and Alan. Junior Draftsman, Warren and Wetmore, New York, 1926-27; Draftsman, Block and Hess, New York, 1927-29; Chief Draftsman, Arthur Weiser, New York, 1929-30; Architect, Ross Frankel, New York, 1930-43; from 1943, Principal, Morris Lapidus Associates, New York and Miami Beach. Retired. Exhibitions: *40 Years of Art and Architecture,* Lowe Gallery, Miami University, 1967; *An Architecture of Joy,* American Federation of Arts, New York, 1970. Recipient: Outstanding Citizen Award, Miami Beach, 1960; Justin P. Alman Award, Wallcovering Wholesalers Association, 1963; Citation for Excellence in Community Architecture, American Institute of Architects, 1965; Outstanding Specifications Award, Gypsum Drywall Contractors, 1968; Variety Children's Hospital Award, 1972; Distinguished Service in the Arts Award, Brandeis University, Waltham, Massachusetts, 1974. Address: 3 Island Avenue, Miami Beach, Florida 33139, U.S.A.

Works:

1943 Martin's Department Store, Brooklyn, New York

Morris Lapidus: Fontainebleau Hotel, Miami Beach, Florida, 1952.

1944 A. S. Beck Shoe Corporation, New York
1945 Namm's Department Store, Brooklyn, New York
Crawford Clothes Shops, various U.S. cities
Bond's Clothing Stores, various U.S. cities
1946 Ludwig Baumann Furniture Store, Jamaica, New York, and various U.S. cities
1948 Columbia Mills Showroom, Syracuse, New York
1950 Fresh Meadow Country Club, Long Island, New York
1951 Jewish Center, Long Island, New York
Ainsley Building, Miami
Biltmore Terrace Hotel, Miami Beach
1952 Laurel in the Pines Hotel, Monticello, New York
Fontainebleau Hotel, Miami Beach
Flagler Hotel, Miami Beach
Hicksville Shopping Center, Long Island, New York
Trump Village Housing, Brooklyn, New York
1953 Ocean Haven Shopping Center, Brooklyn, New York
Shopping center, Jackson Heights, New York
Harrison Country Club, Harrison, New York
Sand and Surf Hotel, West End, New Jersey
DiLido Hotel, Miami Beach
Algiers Hotel, Miami Beach
Shopping center, Pritchard, Alabama
Shopping center, Clearwater, Florida
Shopping center, Bradenton, Florida
Airport hotel, New York
Tamarack Lodge, Greenfield Park, New York
1954 Rainbow-Whitestone Beechurst Shopping Center, Whitestone, New York
Westchester Highway Hotel, Westchester, New York
St. Augustine Store Center, Florida
Nautilus Hotel, Atlantic Beach, New Jersey
Surf Club Hotel, Atlantic Beach, New Jersey
Eden Roc Hotel, Miami Beach
Broadway Maintenance Office Building, Long Island City, New York

1955 Bee Hive Department Store, Patchogue, New York
New Rochelle Country Club, New York
Kutsher's Country Club, Monticello, New York
Aruba Hotel, Netherlands Antilles
1956 American Fore Office, Brooklyn, New York
Arawak Hotel, Jamaica
Charlotte Harbor, Punta Gorda, Florida
Federation of State, County, and Municipal Employees Building, New York
1957 The Saxony (apartments), Jamaica, New York
The Highlander (apartments), Jamaica, New York
Shelbourne Hotel, Miami Beach
Voyager Motel, Miami Beach
North Plaza Shopping Center, St. Petersburg, Florida
Biscayne Terrace Hotel, Miami
Mayfair Apartments alterations, Akron, Ohio
Fort Lauderdale Hotel, Broward, Florida
Sea Isle Hotel, Miami Beach
Executive House (apartment hotel), Chicago
Blauvelt Country Club, Nyack, New York
Lincoln Road Mall, Miami Beach
Continental Restaurant, Monmouth, New Jersey
Bay Harbor Isle Apartment Building, Bay Harbor Isle, Florida
Deauville Hotel, Miami Beach
Sunny Isles Shopping Center, Sunny Isles, Florida
1958 Daytona Beach Hotel, Florida
Mayfair Hotel, Palm Beach, Florida
Concord Hotel, Kiamesha Lake, New York
Lucerne Hotel, Miami Beach
Leisure Lake Hotel, Leisure Lake, Florida
Colonial Plaza Hotel, Orlando, Florida
Massena Hotel, Massena, New York
Chicopee Motel, Chicopee, Massachusetts
Brookhaven Laboratory, Long Island, New York

State Office Building, Fall River, Massachusetts
Harrison Hot Springs Hotel, Vancouver
1959 Lobby of the Blair Towers, Washington, D.C.
Lido Beach Hotel, Lido Beach, New York
Golden Triangle Hotel, Norfolk, Virginia
Clason Houses, New York
New Madison Avenue Office Building, New York
Three Chopt Apartments, Norfolk, Virginia
Syracuse Motel, Syracuse, New York
Stadium Lanes Bowling, New York
The Narrows Shore Road Apartments, Brooklyn, New York
Bank of Miami Beach
Condado West Hotel, San Juan, Puerto Rico
Sheraton Motor Inn, New York
Shaare Zion Temple interiors, Brooklyn, New York
Kansas City Motel, Missouri
Ambassador Hotel, Los Angeles
Newark Motel, New Jersey
Motel/Boatel, New Port Richey, Florida
Shelburne Apartment Hotel, Hartford, Connecticut
International Inn, Tampa, Florida
Fresh Meadows Country Club, Lake Success, New York
New Street Building (office building), Newark, New Jersey
Summit Hotel, New York
Australian House, New York
Murphy Houses, Bronx, New York
1960 Ponce de Leon Hotel, San Juan, Puerto Rico
Duck Key Yacht Club and Lanai, Florida
Golden Triangle International Hotel, Norfolk, Virginia
Kipnis Causeway Motel, Tampa, Florida
Indianapolis Motel
International Inn, Washington, D.C.
Loew's Motor Inn, New York
Loew's Midtown Inn, New York
Hebrew Academy, Miami Beach

Sheraton Hotel, New York
Terrace Towers Apartments, Belle Isle, Florida
Meridian Office Building, Miami Beach
Sterling Gardens Lodge, Tuxedo, New York
1961 Crescent Park (housing development), East Orange, New Jersey
Skyline Motel, Washington, D.C.
Temple Beth Tfiloh, Baltimore
Arlington Office Building, Virginia
Cadman Plaza (housing development), Brooklyn, New York
Richmond Motel, Virginia
White Plains Motel, New York
1962 Kings Bay Yacht Club, Miami
South Harrison Apartments, East Orange, New Jersey
Variety Children's Hospital, Miami
1800 G Street (office building), Washington, D.C.
Fairfield Towers, Brooklyn, New York
Concordia Gardens (apartments), San Juan, Puerto Rico
San Patricio Apartments, San Juan, Puerto Rico
Bay Towers (office building), Miami
Horizon House (apartments), San Juan, Puerto Rico
Professional Staff Apartments, Baltimore
1963 Miramar Towers, San Juan, Puerto Rico
Lobby of Clyde Hall, Brooklyn, New York
Lobby of Ocean Terrace, Brooklyn, New York
Skylake Gardens (apartments), Miami
Grossinger's Hotel, Grossinger, New York
Trump Village Shopping Center, Brooklyn, New York
1965 El San Juan, San Juan, Puerto Rico
Matairie Avenue Apartments, New Orleans
Seacoast Towers East (apartments), Miami Beach
El Conquistador (hotel), San Juan, Puerto Rico
North Meeting Room, Seacoast Towers, Miami Beach
Park Towers (apartments), New Orleans
Fairview Country Club, Greenwich, Connecticut
1966 Paradise Island Hotel, Bahamas
Hilton Hotel, Macon, Georgia
Jr. Chamber International Building, Miami Beach
Skylake Shopping Center, Miami
Municipal Swimming Pool, Brooklyn, New York
Fire Station, Miami Beach
Quality Courts Inc., Memphis, Tennessee
1967 Medical Office Building, Bay Harbor Islands, Florida
Americana of New York, New York
Belle Isle Apartments, Miami Beach
Portman Square Hotel, London
Oceanside Plaza (apartments), Miami Beach
Kensington Apartments, Jade Beach, Florida
Americana Hotel, San Juan, Puerto Rico
Mahoe Bay Hotel, St. Maarten's Isle, West Indies
Penn Wortman Apartments, Brooklyn, New York
1968 Parker Towers (apartments), Hallandale, Florida
Parker Plaza (apartments), Hallandale, Florida
Americana Hotel, Bal Harbour, Miami Beach
Regency Tower Apartments, Miami Beach
Crystal House, Miami Beach
Royal Coast Apartments, Pompano Beach, Florida
Arlen Beach Apartments, Miami Beach
Greater Miami Jewish Federation Office Building, Miami
Lauderdale Seasons Apartments, Fort Lauderdale, Florida
Great Neck Office Building, Great Neck, New York

1969 17 Battery Place (office building), New York
Surfside Royale Apartments, Surfside, Florida
1970 Second National Bank, North Miami
Jacksonville Skycenter (hotel/motel), Jacksonville, Florida
1971 555 Griffin Square (office building), Dallas
Trelawny Beach Hotel, New Falmouth, Jamaica
Rivergate Office Building, Miami
Villa Dorada Complex, Miami
Holiday Springs Complex (housing), Margate, Florida
Bonavista Hi-Rise, Miami
Maurice Gusman Concert Hall, Coral Gables, Florida
Blackstone Office Building, Jacksonville, Florida
Bonavida Hi-Rise, Miami
1122 Connecticut Avenue (office building), Washington, D.C.
1972 Arlen House East (apartments), Miami Beach
Coronado Condominiums, Miami
Office Building, New York Avenue at 13th Street, Washington, D.C.
Citizens Federal Savings and Loan Building, Miami
Oceans Two (apartments), Daytona Beach, Florida
Oceans Three, Five, Seven (apartments), Daytona Beach, Florida
1973 Bal Harbour 101 (apartments), Bal Harbour, Florida
Copa City Office Building, Miami Beach
Theatre of the Performing Arts, Miami Beach
Flamenco (apartments), Miami
South Shore Community Center, Miami Beach
1975 TSS *Carnivala* cruise ship, Dodge Island, Florida
TSS *Mardi Gras* cruise ship, Dodge Island, Florida
Carnival Cruise Lines Terminal Building, Dodge Island, Florida
1976 Ogun State Hotel, Abeokuta, Nigeria
Community College, Key West, Florida (with Carr Smith)
1977 Nueva Casa (apartments), Miami
1978 Grandview at Emerald Hills (apartments), Hollywood, Florida
Lausanne (apartments), Naples, Florida

Publications:

By LAPIDUS: books—*Architecture: A Profession and a Business,* New York 1967; *Time Saver Standards: Hotel Design,* New York 1973; *An Architecture of Joy,* Miami 1979; articles—"Planning Today for the Store of Tomorrow" in *Chain Store Age* (New York), 1944; "Good Architecture Is Good Business" in *Institutions Magazine* (Chicago), 1960; "A Quest for Emotion in Architecture" in *AIA Journal* (Washington, D.C.), 1961; "Living Space in Architecture" in *AIA Journal* (Washington, D.C.), 1962.

On LAPIDUS: books—*Design for Modern Merchandising* by Caleb Horbostel, New York, 1945; *The Specialty Shop* by Jose Fernandez, New York 1950; *Hotels and Motor Hotels* by Henry End, New York 1963; *Hotel Planning and Management* by E. A. Braben, New York 1965; *Hotel Restaurant and Business* by Donald E. Lundberg, Chicago 1970; *Conversations with Architects,* edited by John W. Cook and Heinrich Klotz, New York 1973; *Kicked a Building Lately?* by Ada Louise Huxtable, New York 1976; article—"Bedford Stuyvesant Community Pool" in *Architectural Record* (New York), June 1974.

*

During most of my architectural practice I have been known as a controversial architect. The controversy began when I made a decision that I was not going to follow the precepts set down by Walter Gropius and Mies van der Rohe of the German Bauhaus. I felt that what this school and these architects were advocating was a cold, clinical architecture that lacked an appeal which I felt architecture should always have. I followed my own theories, namely that architecture must first of all solve the problems presented by each project and, more important, that each project should have popular appeal. My work has been pragmatic and eclectic. In 1967, Dr. A. L. Freundlic, the present Dean of Art at Syracuse University, said that "Lapidus is an architect by training, but a mob psychologist through experience. He balances architectural forms and textures as units of design with what will attract public attention and what is, therefore, a sound financial return for the investor. He combines showmanship and shape with dramatic texture and lighting to achieve an effect which seems desirable to the average American. Where a Gropius must seek for elegance through a sparsity of materials and linear elements, Lapidus strives for a joyful feeling of overabundance sometimes referred to as an overspilling of the cornucopia of goodies."

Especially in hotels and to a lesser degree in other types of buildings, I employed all of the elements that Dr. Freundlic speaks of. When my first major hotel, the Fontainebleau in Miami Beach, was completed, it became instantly famous, but it also gave rise to some very acrimonious criticism by some architects and some critics; they felt that I had gone too far. Now, in 1979, I find that I am in rather constant demand as a lecturer because the younger generations of architects, who have embarked on what is called postmodernism in architecture, see things in my work to which they seem to relate.

My basic theory is based on the fact that in earliest prehistoric time, primitive man sought to adorn his cave with phenomenally beautiful wall paintings and to adorn himself with shells, feathers, and flowers. The basic human instinct (the love of adornment) is a part of our genes and has manifested itself throughout history up to the present time. It was only during the period from 1930 until about 1975 that we tried to forget those basic human instincts. Now we are coming back to them. Our architecture of today—or postmodernism—reflects a desire to adorn our buildings and so plan and shape them that once again we are satisfying man's inborn instinct—which the Bauhaus halted but which has become only a passing phase in the history of architecture.

—Morris Lapidus

*

"My convictions are that good architecture and good profit are both possible, if we maintain a happy balance between convictions and compromise." This sentence, from Morris Lapidus's major written work *Architecture: A Profession and a Business,* serves as an excellent summary of his design philosophy. Lapidus's work seems to be a consistent compromise between strivings for what he believes to be design excellence on the one hand ("aesthetics") and what are the requirements for attracting large and profitable commissions on the other ("business").

The working out of these compromises in physical form results in sacral embodiments of the complex and contradictory elements that characterized the high point of American optimism about the possibility of combining Power, Profit, and Fun. The Trinity of Power, Profit, and Fun has perhaps never been more eloquently worshipped than in Lapidus's justly famous hotels such as the Fontainebleau in Miami Beach and the New York or Bal Harbour Americana.

Curving the slab of the Fontainebleau was one of those master strokes that looks simple and logical in retrospect but was imaginative and daring in its time. Here, contemporary design dogma would have demanded the power and honesty of a straight building; Good Business might have called for

Rumple, Bieder, or some other Meyer—the compromise put fun and profit into the power and honesty of post World War II aesthetics. The interiors of the Fontainebleau in fact betray the same compromise, although this may be difficult to see for those who are simply struck by the opulence and vulgarity of its greedy profit-seeking.

The New York Americana transported Miami Beach to Sixth Avenue just as the Fontainebleau had previously transported Sixth Avenue to Miami. That is, Lapidus's approach paved the way for the penetration of the urban form into the resort, and vice versa, an approach which finally came to fruition in Portman's work. This interpenetration of megastructure with beach, and resort ambience with Manhattan, is a kind of ultimate celebration of human ability to totally transform nature, exact a profit from its contemplation, and have fun doing it.

Both the Fontainebleau and the New York Americana share a strong emphasis on the horizontal linearity of the multiple storeys. It is almost as if the highrise profitable verticality were once again being compromised with the humanistic values of equality, visual access, and physical groundedness. The lower property values at Bal Harbour gave Lapidus the opportunity to accent the horizontal integration to an extreme. The highrise human warehouse is tucked behind the beach-level plaza/piazza and meeting rooms almost as an afterthought to the profit motive. The move from here to the 1970s Portman indoor piazza becomes simple and logical.

What appeared to Lapidus to be an architecture of compromise appears in the present as an eclectic celebration of America at the height of its powers. The work of Lapidus, then, has all the power and innocence of "popular culture" at its best and worst.

—Joseph B. Juhasz

LAPRADE, Albert.

French. Born in Buzançais, Indre, 29 November 1883. Educated at the Lycée de Chateauroux, Indre, 1894-1900; Ecole des Beaux-Arts, Paris, 1903-1910. Served in the French Army, 1900-03 and 1914-15; wounded at Ypres. Married Marie-Louise Gaillot in 1914; children: Jacqueline, Claude, and Arlette. Worked in Morocco, under Maréchal Lyautey and for the architect Prost, 1915-20; in private practice, Paris, 1920 until his death in 1978. Inspector, then Inspector-General, Ecole des Beaux-Arts, Paris, 1932-45. Member of the Institut de France from 1959: President, 1965. Recipient: Silver Medal, City of Paris. Member, Syndicate of the Arts Press and Men of Letters, Paris. Honorary Corresponding Member, Royal Institute of British Architects; Member, Royal Academy of Belgium. Commander of the Légion d'Honneur, 1945. *Died* (in Paris) *9 May 1978.*

Works

1915/
20 City Plan for Casablanca, Morocco
Résidence Général, Rabat, Morocco
1920 Private houses and gardens, Paris and Paris region
1925 Design of the *Garden Exhibition,* Paris
1928 Marbeuf Garage: Citroen Showroom, rue Marbeuf, Champs Elysées, Paris
E.D.F. Building, 76 rue de Rennes, Paris
1931 *Exposition coloniale,* Musée des Arts Africans, Paris (with Janniot)
1934 *Echo du nord* Newspaper Offices, Lille, France
1935/
37 French Embassy, Ankara, Turkey

1939/
49 E.D.F. Hydro-Electric Dam, Genissiat-sur-le-Rhone, France
Maison de Cuba, Maison de la France d'Outre Mer, and Maison du Maroc, Cité Universitaire, Paris
Kleber-Colombes Factory, Paris
Central Thermique, Oran, Algeria
1943 Redevelopment Plan for Valenciennes, France
Redevlopment plan for Lille, France
Redevelopment plan for Gourney-en-Bray, France
1944/
58 Old City Quarter Development, Le Mans, France
1950/
62 Schneider Company Buildings, Le Creusot, France (as consultant)
1954 Administration Centre, Lille, France
"Ilot XVI" Development, Paris
Old City Development, Alençon, France
E.D.F. Factories at Seyssel sur le Rhone, La Bathie sur le Rhone, and Villarodin sur le Rhone France

1961/
62 Renault Offices, Champs Elysées, Paris (with Claude Barré)
Hilton Hotel, Orly Airport, near Paris (with Claude Barré)
1962 Maréchal Lyautey Tomb, Les Invalides, Paris
1965 Cité Administrative, Paris

Publications:

By LAPRADE: books—*Carnets de croquis: Le Nord de la France, L'Est, Le Midi, Le Centre, L'Ouest, Paris, Espagne-Portugal-Maroc, L'Italie et L'Asie Mineure,* 8 volumes, Paris 1940-70; *François d'Orbay, architecte de Louis XIV,* Paris 1965; *Conte de la démolition de Paris,* edited by Berger-Leurault, Paris/Nancy 1967; *Architectures de France à travers les croquis d'Albert Laprade,* with introduction by Pierre de Lagarde, Paris 1980; *Les rues de Paris à travers les croquis d'Albert Laprade,* Paris 1980; *Architetture del mediterraneo negli schizzi di Albert Laprade,* Turin 1984.

Albert Laprade: E.D.F. Building, Rue de Rennes, Paris, 1928.

On LAPRADE: book—*La Maison et le jardin arabe au Maroc*, Paris 1926.

Albert Laprade. A strange character! I met him when I was a very young student architect writing some articles of "architectural criticism" for my school magazine. I had been carried away by the Citroen Showroom in Paris, so without further ado, I presented myself at the home of the architect who (with his young associate Bazin) had signed the work. He received me very amicably, in his old-fashioned and very "average French bourgeois" apartment in the rue des Eaux Passy. He did not understand my enthusiasm. He disclaimed authorship of the too audacious window of 400 square metres. In fact it was the work of the engineer Perrin and the "client" who had prescribed it. As for the architects, they had masked the elegant metal framework with "casings" which gave the impression of heavy pillars. With the impudence of my twenty years, my critcism was severe. But at that moment a friendship was born that lasted a lifetime.

Of retiring and modest appearance, Laprade was an able man of great sensitivity. His words and his writings always displayed much delicacy, culture, and common sense. Unfortunately, his achievements regularly contradicted his writings. Let us ignore the works of his youth conceived in Morocco in the shadow of Prost and under the rather disdainful authority of Lyautey. But then later on, the building for the principal newspaper of the north, in Lille, is a lamentable pastiche. The enormous Administrative Centre not far away from it is worse than mediocre; entrusted with "protecting" the site of the Seine, Laprade bears the heavy responsibility for a building that in fact disfigures the site. Less questionable are those buildings in good classical form such as the Museum of the Colonies and the lost opportunity that is the hydroelectric complex at Genissiat on the Rhone. Let us forget the work and keep the memory of a delightful man who loved beauty and appreciated the true qualities of all past architectural creation, from the most monumental to the most humble, and whose wisdom united with a genuine intellectual and an artistic subtlety that did not know how to express itself other than in words.

—Pierre Vago

LASDUN, Denys.

British. Born in London, 8 September 1914. Educated at the Rugby School, 1928-31; Architectural Association School, London, 1931-34. Served as a Major in the Royal Engineers, British 2nd Army, 1939-45: M.B.E. (Member, Order of the British Empire). Married Susan Virginia Bendit in 1954; children: Louisa, James, and William. Worked in association with Wells Coates, *q.v.*, founder of the MARS Group, London, 1935-37; joined Tecton, London (partners: Berthold Lubetkin, *q.v.*, Francis Skinner, and Lindsey Drake), 1937-38; Partner in Tecton, 1946 until the firm was dissolved, 1948; taught at the Architectural Association School, London, 1948-49; in partnership with Lindsey Drake, 1949-59. Since 1960, Principal, Denys Lasdun and Partners (Denys Lasdun Redhouse and Softley, since 1978). Visiting Critic, University of Manchester, 1961; Hoffman Wood Professor of Architecture, University of Leeds, 1962-63; British Council Lecturer in Spain and Portugal, 1964. Member of the Jerusalem Town Planning Committee, 1970. Member of the Advisory Council, Victoria and Albert Museum, London, since 1973; Member of the Council, Architectural Association, since 1974; Trustee of the British Museum, London, since 1975; Member of the Slade Committee, since 1976; Member of the Arts Panel, Arts Council of Great Britain, London, 1980-84. Exhibitions: *Twentieth Century Form*, Whitechapel Art Gallery, London, 1953; *Ten Years of British Architecture 1945-1955*, Arts Council Gallery, London, 1956; *Architecture Today*, British Council Gallery, London, 1961; *National Theatre Exhibition*, Royal Institute of British Architects, London, 1968; *Bienal*, São Paulo, Brazil, 1969; *Singapore Planning and Urban Research Group Exhibition*, Singapore, 1971; *The Architecture of Denys Lasdun and Partners*, Heinz Gallery, Royal Institute of British Architects, London, 1976; *Art and Leisure*, British Council, Iran, 1977-78; *RIBA Drawings Exhibition*, Luxembourg and Germany, 1978; *Transformations in Modern Architecture*, Museum of Modern Art, New York, 1979; *Thirties*, Hayward Gallery, London, 1979; *Everyday Architecture*, Royal Academy, London (travelled to Bristol and Lincoln, England), 1979-80; *British Council Exhibition*, Rome, 1981; *Look, Stranger, at This Island Now*, Architectural Association, London, 1983; *Interarch '83*, Sofia, Bulgaria, 1983; *Venti progetti per il futuro del Lingotto*, Turin, 1984. Recipient: Student Award for design of Students' Hostel, London, 1935; First Prize, Cement and Concrete Association Competition, 1950; London Architecture Bronze Medal, Royal Institute of British Architects, 1960 and 1964; Ambassador Award, for contribution to the London skyline, 1965; Civic Trust Award, Class I, 1967, and Group A, 1969; Special Award, *Bienal*, São Paulo, 1969; Royal Gold Medal for Architecture, Royal Institute of British Architects, 1977; Concrete Society Award, 1977; London Region Award, Royal Institute of British Architects, 1978; Honorary Diploma, World Biennale of Architecture, Sofia, 1981. Honorary Associate, Manchester College of Art and Design, 1966; D.Litt.: University of East Anglia, Norwich, 1974; University of Sheffield, 1978. Fellow, Royal Institute of British Architects, 1945. Honorary Fellow, American Institute of Architects, 1966; Honorary Fellow, Royal College of Physicians, London, 1975; Member, Académie d'Architecture, Paris, 1984; Accademia Nazional di San Luca, Rome, 1984. C.B.E. (Commander, Order of the British Empire), 1965; Knighted, 1976. Address: Denys Lasdun, Redhouse and Softley, 30 Queen Anne Street, London W1M 9LB, England.

Works:

1937/
38 House, 32 Newton Road, Paddington, London
1948 Hallfield Housing Scheme, Paddington, London (with Tecton)
1950 Whitleigh Footbridge, Plymouth, Devon (with Harris and Johns, engineers)
1951 Hallfield Primary School, Paddington, London
1952 Usk Street Cluster Block Housing, Bethnal Green, London
1955 Claredale Street Cluster Block Housing, Bethnal Green, London
1958 Flats, 26 St. James's Place, London
Peter Robinson Store and Offices, Strand, London (now London headquarters of the New South Wales Government)
1959 Fitzwilliam College, Cambridge, England
1960 Royal College of Physicians, Regent's Park, London
Wartski shopfront, Regent Street, London
Metropolitan Cathedral of Christ the King, Liverpool (competition project)
1961 Complex of Science Laboratories, New Museum Site, Cambridge, England (project)
1962 Stamford Hall, University of Leicester, England
New buildings for St. John's College, Cambridge, England (competition project)
Royal Institution of Chartered Surveyors, Parliament Square, London (project)

1962/
68 University of East Anglia, Norwich
1963 Charles Wilson Social Centre, University of Leicester, England
Sports Centre, University of Liverpool
1965 National Theatre and Opera House, Shell Site, London (project)
Comprehensive redevelopment for the University of London: School of Oriental and African Studies; Institute of Education; and Institute of Advanced Legal Studies
1966 Residential building, Christ's College, Cambridge, England
1967/
76 National Theatre, Waterloo Bridge Site, London
1971 Burrell Collection, Glasgow (competition project)
Feasibility study: Broad Sanctuary, Parliament Square, London
1972 Cannock Community Hospital, Staffordshire (project)
1973 European Investment Bank (EEC Headquarters building), Luxembourg
1975 Sotheby and Company Headquarters Building, New Bond Street, London (project)
Plant Protection Division Headquarters Building, Imperial Chemical Industries, Fernhurst, Surrey (project)
1977 Feasibility study: Courtauld Institute, University of London Precinct (project)
1978/
84 IBM Central London Marketing Centre, South Bank, London
1980/
85 City of London Real Property Company Offices, Fenchurch Street, London
1981 Hurva Synagogue rebuilding, Old City of Jerusalem, Israel (project)
Cannock Community Hospital, Staffordshire
1982/
83 Carlo Felice Opera House, Genoa, Italy (competition project)
1983 Lingotto Project for Fiat, Turin, Italy (project; as consultant)

Publications:

By LASDUN: book—*Architecture in an Age of Scepticism*, London 1984; articles—"Housing in London" in *Architects Yearbook* (London), 1951; "Impressions of American Architecture" in *Architectural Association Journal* (London), June 1954; "Le Corbusier's Maison Jaoul" in *Architectural Design* (London), March 1956; "LCC Housing Scheme: Picton Street, Camberwell" in *Architectural Association Journal* (London), June 1956; "Thoughts in Progress," monthly discussions with J.H.V. Davies, in *Architectural Design* (London), December 1956 to December 1958; "MARS Group 1953-57" in *Architects' Yearbook* (London), no. 8, 1957; "Means not Ends" in *RIBA Journal* (London), June 1961; "Process of Continual Cooperation" in *The Financial Times* (London), 2 August 1961; "7 Keys to Good Architecture" in *20th Century* (London), Winter 1962/63; "An Architect's Approach to Architecture" in *RIBA Journal* (London), April 1965; "Le Corbusier" (obituary) in *L'Architecture d'aujourd'hui* (Paris), September/November 1965; "A Sense of Place and Time" (radio broadcast) in *The Listener* (London), 17 February 1966; "The National Theatre" (radio broadcast, with J. M. Richards) in *The Listener* (London), 22 February 1968; interview in the series "The Arts Today" in *The Observer Magazine* (London), 16 September 1973; introduction to *A Language and a Theme: The Architecture of Denys Lasdun and Partners* by William J. R. Curtis, London 1976; edited version of talk between Lasdun and Peter Hall originally televised on "Aquarius" in *The Complete Guide to Britain's National Theatre*, London 1977; statements in special issue on National Theatre of *Architectural*

Denys Lasdun: National Theatre, London, 1976.

Review (London), January 1977; "Random Thoughts on Creativity" in *RIBA Journal* (London), May 1977; transcript of RIBA Royal Gold Medal address in *RIBA Journal* (London), September 1977; "Architectural Aspects of the National Theatre" in *Royal Society of Arts Journal* (London), November 1977; "Architecture, Continuity and Change" In *RIBA Transactions* (London), no. 2, 1982.

On LASDUN: books—*The New Architecture of Europe* by G. E. Kidder Smith, New York and London 1961; *Architecture in Britain Today* by Michael Webb, London 1969; *The Politics of Architecture* by Anthony Jackson, London 1970; *Neue englische Architektur* by Robert Maxwell, Stuttgart 1972; *A Visual History of Twentieth Century Architecture* by Dennis Sharp, London 1972; *Age of the Masters: A Personal View of Modern Architecture* by Reyner Banham, London 1975; *A Language and a Theme: The Work of Denys Lasdun and Partners* by William J. R. Curtis, London 1976; *Who Who's in Architecture*, edited by J. M. Richards, London 1977; *The Architects of London* by Alastair Service, London 1979; *The Larousse Encyclopedia of Modern Art*, Feltham, Middlesex 1981; *Buildings of England*, Harmondsworth, Middlesex 1981; *Modern Architecture since 1960* by William Curtis, London 1982; *Art and Architecture in London* by Anne Saunders, London 1984; articles—introduction by John Summerson to *Ten Years of British Architecture, 1944-1955*, exhibition catalogue, London 1956; "The Anti-Pioneers" by Nikolaus Pevsner in *The Listener* (London), 5 January 1957; "Denys Lasdun: England" by Robert Furneaux Jordan in *Canadian Architect* (Toronto), September 1962; "Evolution of a Style" in *Architectural Review* (London), May 1969; "National Monument" by Reyner Banham in *New Society* (London), 18 March 1976; "Building a Landscape for Figures" by Brian Connell in *The Times* (London), 24 March 1975; "University of East Anglia" by William J. R. Curtis in *Archithese* (Zürich), no. 14, 1975; "Denys Lasdun: A New National Role" by Dennis Sharp and Colin Davies in *Building* (London), 17 September 1976; review by William J. R. Curtis in *Architectural Review* (London), January 1977; article by William J. R. Curtis in *The Complete Guide to Britain's National Theatre*, London, 1977; "New Buildings for London University, Bloomsbury" by Sherban Cantacuzino in *Architectural Review* (London), March 1980; "Lasdun Landmark" by Peter Buchanan in *Architectural Review* (London), November 1981; "Hurva Symbol" by Peter Buchanan in *Architectural Review* (London), May 1983.

*   *   *

Architecture, by its form and language and concern for human scale, can maintain its responsibility to bring the highest insights of which art is capable into the lives of everyone. Architecture is a social art and only makes sense as the promoter and extender of human relations. Architectural creation demands a fresh understanding of physical order and the nature of man and particularly of man in society—the clarification, in fact, of order and diversity. Perhaps this clarification is the key to an architectural language which is in tune with that ordinary people want.

—Denys Lasdun

*   *   *

The architecture of Denys Lasdun provides a rare example of a set of forms based on principle. Each of his buildings represents the gradual clarification of ideas expressed in a vocabulary of standard elements which are limited in number but flexible in scope. At the core is the idea of architecture as "urban landscape:" Lasdun's buildings are composed of vertical towers and horizontal terraces and extended into the urban or natural surroundings, the overall effect of these walkways and promenades, which cascade as horizontal planes and stepped levels inside and outside, is of an artificial landscape of "hills" and "valleys." Indeed, the architect calls the terraces "strata," a word that suggests geological sources of inspiration. The system is seen most clearly in such works of the 1960s and 1970s as the University of East Anglia or the National Theatre. Lasdun explains the principle of the "strata":

Most activities take place on "platforms"—floors, paths, terraces, bridges etc. (see Le Corbusier's pronouncement of 1915: "The actual ground of the town is a sort of raised floor, the streets and pavements as it were bridges. Beneath this floor and directly accessible are places for the main services"). A building can be looked at in the same way, as a matter of platforms and connections and interlocking spaces. Sensitive gradations of levels and heights can be made to respond to site and function, creating an endless variety of rhythms and scales, satisfactory in themselves and adaptable to any existing urban situation, including the architecture of the past.

The vocabulary of strata and towers can be seen evolving gradually in Lasdun's work and is in some respects an extension of the vocabulary and concerns of the architect's predecessors in the history of the modern movement. Lasdun was born in 1914 and entered the mainstream of modern architecture before World War II, when the formative impulses and visions were still fresh and were just beginning to influence the English situation. He worked with both Berthold Lubetkin and Wells Coates before design-

ing a house in Paddington (1938) which shows clearly the impact of Le Corbusier's Maison Cook of 1926. Certain foundations were thus defined early: an interest in the horizontal cantilever in reinforced concrete as a generator of vocabulary; a concern for the unity of town planning and architecture; an ethical conviction that the architect might enhance the quality of life with forms matched to modern functions; and an instinctive feeling for abstract form, initially nurtured on the white geometrics of the International Style, later inspired by works in the classical tradition, particularly the English Baroque.

Lasdun's personal synthesis began to emerge after World War II in works such as the Hallfield Primary School and the Bethnal Green cluster blocks. In each case, the program was broken down into distinct formal elements united by articulated spines of circulation. At Bethnal Green, a critique of the standard modern block was implied. The raised bridges and levels linking the stacked maisonettes represent an attempt at turning the local street type on its end. In the late 1950s, in such works as the St. James's flats and the Royal College of Physicians, the vocabulary of elegantly proportioned horizontals and overhanging soffits becomes clearer. The college, with its neoclassical white shell enclosing the areas of ceremonmial and its sprawling mauve brick hump containing a sunken auditorium, is a rare case of truly honorific modern building. Without resorting to pastiche, the college incorporates within itself a modern re-statement of the urban sequences of Nash's surrounding terraces. To pass into the airy hallway with its receding levels of white balconies linked by steps is to experience features that were to become central to the Lasdun vocabulary.

This is clearly seen in the university schemes designed in the 1960s: The University of East Anglia; Christ's College, Cambridge; and The University of London. At the University of East Anglia, the site was some fields tilting down to the River Yare, and the social problem was to lay down the core of an educational experiment involving the rejection of the collegiate ideal. Accordingly, a basic division was adapted between a flexible "teaching wall" containing a spine of the various teaching disciplines ("schools"), and the residences which were to be sited with maximum use of the astounding views over the landscape. Translated into architectural terms, these priorities led to a linear-plan form disposed around a central landscape space and to the creation of an upper social plane of raised pedestrian streets linking all parts of the university with minimum recourse to lifts. The architect organized the residences into steps, thus breaking down their scale and introducing a strong horizontal, unifying theme. The result is, indeed, an artificial landscape grafted to the previous contours.

In the case of the schemes for the National Theatre and Opera House and the final National Theatre, the urban landscape idea and its central element, the strata, came fully into their own and revealed their relevance to a public building.

Over and above the immensely complex tasks of designing the auditoriums and interiors of the theatre, there was obviously the need to exploit to the full the scenographic possibilities of the riverside site, and to give a suitable image to the institution of a public monument. A plan arrangement was found which registered the hierarchy between the main auditoriums and their flytowers and which disposed the public zones of the building alongside the river and linked them to Waterloo Bridge and the riverside walkways. The strata pass through the building and have internal and external volumes cut out of them to provide here an open-air theatre, here a foyer, here an interior auditorium. When the theatre is in use and people pass over the levels, inside and outside, the building resembles a teeming hill. The strata open out the contents of the building to the public and link the theatre visually with the river and the surrounding vistas of London.

Since the National Theatre was designed, Lasdun's ideas and vocabulary have naturally continued to evolve. The European Investment Bank in Luxembourg (1979) is broken down into four wings of offices around a central public area cut through by a diagonal axis. The strata here elide with the natural contours of the setting. In the projects for the Hurva Synagogue (1980) and for the Genoa Opera House (1982), the complex patterns of historical surroundings have been abstracted in the very forms of the buildings in a subtle contextualism that is still not sqeamish about monumental expression. Lasdun remains committed to the continuation of the humanist values within the modern movement. His work is nourished by tradition but without resorting to a superficial play with references.

—William J.R. Curtis

LAUTNER, John.

American. Born in Marquette, Michigan, 16 July 1911. Educated at high schools in Marquette and New York City; Northern Michigan University, Marquette, A.B. in English 1933; worked under Frank Lloyd Wright, q.v., at Taliesin (Wisconsin and Arizona), 1933-39. Married Mary Lautner in 1934; Elizabeth Lautner in 1950; children: Karol, Michael, Mary, and Judith. Associate in the office of Douglas Honnold, Los Angeles, 1944-46. In private practice, Los Angeles, since 1946. Exhibitions: The Three Worlds of Los Angeles, toured Europe, 1974; A View of California Architecture 1960-76, San Francisco, 1977. Fellow, American Institute of Architects, 1970. Address (office): 7046 Hollywood Boulevard, Los Angeles, California 90028, U.S.A.

Works:

1939 Lautner House, 2007 Micheltorena, Los Angeles
1940 Bell House, 7714 Woodrow Wilson, Los Angeles
1946 Mauer House, 932 Rome, Los Angeles
R. and H. Motors Showroom, 600 Colorado, Los Angeles (now Rayco)
1947 Desert Hot Springs Motel, Desert Hot Springs, Colorado
Gantvoort House, Flintridge, California
Henry's Restaurant, Glendale, California
Polin House, Los Angeles
Carling House, Pacific View and Hockey Trail, Los Angeles
1948 Schaeffer House, Glendale, California (now Wallace House)
Sheats ("L'Horizon") Apartments, 10901-19 Strathmore, Beverly Hills, California
1949 Dahlstrom House, South Pasadena, California
United Productions of America Studios, Burbank, California
1950 Foster House, 4235 Las Cruces, Sherman Oaks, California
Harvey House, Los Angeles
Shusett House, Beverly Hills, California
1953 Bergren House, Los Angeles
1954 Beachwood Market remodelling, Los Angeles
1955 Baldwin House, Los Angeles
1956 Harpel House, Hollywood, California
Speer Contractors' Office Building, Los Angeles (now World Supply Company)
1957 Henry's Restaurant, Pomona, California
Pearlman Mountain Cabin, Idyllwild, California
Zahn House, Hollywood, California
1958 Hatherell House, Sun Valley, Idaho
1959 Ernest Lautner House, Florida
1960 Concannon House, Los Angeles (now Chester House)

Malin House ("Chemosphere"), 776 Torreyson Drive, Los Angeles (now Kuhn House)
Midtown School, Los Angeles
Alto Capistrano Apartments and Shopping Center, San Juan Capistrano, California (project)
1961 Wolff House, Hollywood, California
1962 Garcia House, Mulholland Drive, Los Angeles
1963 Sheats House, Beverly Hills, California (now Goldstein House)
"Silvertop" (house), 2138 Micheltorena, Los Angeles
1966 Alto Capistrano Headquarters, San Juan Capistrano, California
Harpel House, Alaska
1968 Elrod House, 2175 Southridge Drive, Palm Springs, California
Stevens House, Malibu, California
Zimmerman House, Studio City, California
1969 Walstrom House, Beverly Glen, Los Angeles
1971 Familian House, 1011 Cove Way, Beverly Hills, California
1973 Jordan House, Laguna Beach, California
Nature Center, Griffith Park, Los Angeles (project)
1976 Bob Hope House, Southridge Drive, Palm Springs, California (partially destroyed by fire)
Trancas Beach House, Malibu, California
Crippled Children's Society Rehabilitation Center, Rancho del Valle, California
1977 Arango House, Acapulco, Mexico
1980 Segel House, Malibu, California
1982 Rawlins House, Newport Beach, California
1983 Sandy Krause House, Malibu, California
1984 Stanley Beyer House, Malibu, California

Publications:

On LAUTNER: books—Petites Maisons en Amerique du Nord, Paris 1957; Einfamilienhauser in den U.S.A., Munich 1962; Beautiful Homes and Gardens in California by Herbert Weisskamp, New York 1964; Drawings by American Architects by A. M. Kemper, New York 1974; A View of California Architecture 1960-76, exhibition catalogue, by David Gebhard and Susan King, San Francisco 1977; 12 Los Angeles Architects, edited by N. Charles Slert and James R. Harter, Pomona, California 1978; John Lautner: architettura organico-sperimentale by Pierluigi Bonvicini, Bari, Italy 1981; articles—"West Coast Architecture V: John Lautner" by Esther McCoy in Arts and Architecture (Los Angeles), August 1965; "Modern Palace in the Desert" in Architectural Digest (Los Angeles), Spring 1970; "Five Distinctive Houses" in Architectural Record (New York), November 1970; "You've Got to Fight for Good Design" in Los Angeles Times Home Magazine, 14 February 1971; "The Architect's Perspective" in Architectural Digest (Los Angeles), September/October 1971; article in Architecture + Urbanism (Tokyo), no. 40, 1974; "Three California Residences by John Lautner" in Architettura (Rome), May 1975; "And Then There Were 12" in Architectural Record (New York), August 1976; "Record Houses of 1977: Arango House, Acapulco" in Architectural Record (New York), May 1977; "John Lautner: Architect and Iconoclast" in L.A. Architect (Los Angeles), November 1979; "Houses", special issue of Ville Giardini (Milan), June 1981; "John Lautner's Mauer House" in Fine Homebuilding (Newtown, Connecticut), December 1983/ January 1984; "Architecture: John Lautner" by David Gebhard in Architectural Digest (Los Angeles), February 1984.

Architecture, in its truest sense, may not be academically defined. If it is, it becomes a dead, nongrowing entity of style or cliché. I see it as a continuous search for total basic human needs in

John Lautner: Arango House, Acapulco, Mexico, 1977.

shelter; emotional, psychological, etc., as well as mere physical; then it becomes a valid enduring Art. In the business of building, when people become commodities or merchandise, we have facilities to house or shelter, but not Architecture.

—John Lautner

John Lautner's dramatic domestic designs are notable even in Southern California, which is famous for its architectural extravagances. Esther McCoy has called him "a lyrical technologist with a style spanning Frank Lloyd Wright and the year 2,000." He boldly experiments with new industrial processes in what he terms his "continual search to answer total basic human needs—emotional as well as physical— in shelter."

The 1948 apartment building L'Horizon, like much of Lautner's work, shows the influence of his six year fellowship at Taliesin. Visually intriguing and functionally ingenious, his design gives each of the nine units its own deck and outdoor garden. The Pearlman Cabin of 1957 is a successful attempt to integrate a modern building into a wooded site without resorting to "rusticness." The sharply angled glass walls of the house are supported by a circle of peeled log pillars, as if the building simply grew out of the surrounding trees. The result is refreshingly direct but not overly intrusive.

Perhaps Lautner's best known building is Malin House (Chemosphere) of 1960. This flying saucer shape perched on a single concrete column may look like futuristic indulgence, but, as Reyner Banham has pointed out, it is also a very sensible solution for a small steep site. The one column foundation minimized destruction of the existing terrain and obviated the usual bull-dozing and retaining walls of hillside building. The clear span interior of the

hexagonal house leaves 1,300 square feet of uninterrupted living space and offers amazing views of the valley below.

Wolff House is again characteristically bold, made of dressed boulders, concrete and jutting glass, with the carport projecting like a great lip. "Silvertop," with a cantilevered driveway *and* swimming pool, is a cascade of projecting forms: it was several years in the building because of difficulties in obtaining permits for its unorthodox structure.

Another Lautner design with space ship overtones is the Elrod House in Palm Springs. Here, however, the circular form is not on a stalk but fit snugly into the rocky hillside. The immense concrete spokes of the roof provide shade and also frame wedge-shaped windows with views of the distant mountains. The indoor-outdoor effect is increased by rocky intrusions on the interior and by the placement of the pool.

One of Lautner's largest private commissions, a house for the comedian Bob Hope, was sadly nipped in the bud. The swooping concrete roof, reminiscent of Saarinen's TWA Terminal, spanned 25,000 square feet of pools, garden and living space arranged around a central court. Begun in 1972, the house burnt back to its steel skeleton in 1976 and may only be rebuilt in a modified form.

South of the border, the Arango House in Acapulco is Lautner at his most elegant and imaginative. Again a colossal concrete roof covers the whole complex, extending over a vast living terrace bordered by a cantilevered moat, which seems to merge with the bay beyond, giving the house a sense of hovering between sky and sea. A lower level has nine bedrooms with quiet terraces sheltered by the overhanging moat; steps lead down to the main swimming pool. The use of space is daring and inventive—but never at the expense of the human needs central to Lautner's view of architecture.

—Lucinda Hawkins

LE CORBUSIER.

French. Born Charles-Edouard Jeanneret in La Chaux-de-Fonds, Switzerland, 6 October 1887; adopted pseudonym Le Corbusier, 1920; emigrated to France, 1917: naturalized, 1930. Studied engraving at the School of Applied Arts, La Chaux-de-Fonds, under l'Eplattenier, 1900-05. Married Yvonne Gallis in 1930 (died, 1957). Worked in the office of the architect Josef Hoffman, *q.v.*, Vienna, 1907, Auguste Perret, *q.v.*, Paris, and, with Walter Gropius, *q.v.*, and Mies van der Rohe, *q.v.*, in the office of Peter Behrens, *q.v.*, Berlin, 1910; Founder-Director, L'Atelier d'Art Réunis, La Chaux-de-Fonds, 1909-14, and Instructor, l'Eplattenier's Nouvelle Section de l'Ecole d'Art, La Chaux-de-Fonds, 1911-14; also worked as a painter and lithographer from 1912. In private practice as an architect, Paris, 1917 until his death in 1965: in partnership with his cousin Pierre Jeanneret, *q.v.*, 1922-40; collaborated with the architect Charlotte Perriand, 1927-29; practiced as ATBAT (Atelier des Bâtisseurs), from 1942; developed Modulor System, with Hanning and Elisa Mailard, 1943-48. Chief Planner, La Rochelle-Pallice, France, 1945; Architectural adviser, Capital City, Chandigarh, India, 1951-59. Founder-Editor, with Amédée Ozenfant and Paul Dermée, *L'Esprit nouveau*, Paris, 1919-25. Founder Member, CIAM (Congrès Internationaux d'Architecture Moderne), 1928; Founder, ASCORAL (Assemblée de Constructeurs pour une Renovation Architecturale), Paris, 1942. Lectured extensively at universities in Europe and the United States, 1921-56. Exhibitions: group—*Exposition internationale d'art décoratif,* Turin, 1902; *Salon d'automne,* Paris, 1912; *Après le cubisme,* Galerie Thomas, Paris, 1918; *Salon d'automne,* Paris, 1922; *Salon des indépendants,* Paris, 1922; *L'Effort moderne,* Galerie Leonce Rosenberg, Paris, 1923; *Exposition des arts décoratifs,* Paris, 1925; *Salon*

d'automne, Paris, 1929; *L'Art primitif*, Studio Louis Carré, Paris, 1935; World's Fair, Paris, 1937; *Ideal Home Exhibition*, London, 1939; *France d'outremer*, Paris, 1940; *Vienna Exhibition*, 1947; *Exposition de nature morte*, Musée de Saint Etienne, France, 1955; *La Machine à s'asseoir: Le Corbusier, Charlotte Perriand, Pierre Jeanneret*, Palazzo dei Convegni, Rome, 1976; individual—Galerie Drouet, Paris, 1921, John Becker Gallery, New York, 1933; Galerie Louis Carré, Paris, 1938; Kunsthaus, Zürich, 1938; Galerie Boesiger, Zürich, 1941; Radio City, New York, 1945; Stedelijk Museum, Amsterdam, 1947; Institute of Contemporary Art, Boston, 1948; Paul Rosenberg Gallery, New York, 1950; Museum of Modern Art, 1951; Galerie Denise René Paris, 1952; Musée National d'Art Moderne, Paris, 1953 (travelled to the Institute of Contemporary Arts, London, and the Samleven Gallery, Stockholm); Kunsthalle, Bern, 1954; Villa del Olma, Como, Italy, 1954; Pierre Matisse Gallery, New York, 1956; Musée d'Art, Lyon, 1956; Kunsthaus, Zürich, 1957; Neue Galerie, Linz, Austria, 1957; Moderna Museet, Stockholm, 1958; Walker Art Gallery, Liverpool, England, 1958; Musée National d'Art Moderne, Paris, 1961-62; Weber Galerie, Zürich, 1962; Palazzo Strozzi, Florence, 1963; Musée National d'Art Moderne, Paris, 1964; Weber Galerie, Zürich, 1968; Nielson Gallery, Boston, 1976; Galerie Kornfeld, Zürich, 1976; Georgia State University, Atlanta, 1977; Ente Fiera di Bologna, Italy, 1977; Castlenuovo, Naples, 1978; Institute for Architectural and Urban Studies, New York, 1981; Xavier Fourcade Gallery, New York, 1984; Prakapas Gallery, New York, 1984; Gallerie d'Arte Moderna, Bologna, Italy, 1985. Collections: Fondation Le Corbusier, 8-10 Square du Docteur Blanche, Paris 16; Centre Le Corbusier, Hoschgasse 8, Zürich. Recipient: Medal, *Exposition international d'art decoratif*, Turin, 1902; First Prize, with Pierre Jeanneret, League of Nations competition, Geneva, 1927; Gold Medal, Royal Institute of British Architects, 1959. Honorary doctorates: University of Zürich, 1933; Eidgenössische Technische Hochschule, Zürich, 1955; Cambridge University, England, 1959. Chevalier, 1937, Commandeur, 1952, and Grand Officier, 1963, of the Légion d'Honneur. *Died* (at Cap Martin, France) *27 August 1965*.

Works:

1906 Fallet House, 1 Chemin de Pouillerel, La Chaux-de-Fonds, Switzerland
1908 Stotzer House, 6 Chemin de Pouillerel, La Chaux-de-Fonds, Switzerland
　　　Jacquemet House, 8 chemin de Pouillerel, La Chaux-de-Fonds, Switzerland (supervised by Chapallaz)
1910 School of Arts and Crafts, La Chaux-de-Fonds, Switzerland (project)
1912 Favre-Jacot House, rue de la Montagne, Le Locle, near La Chaux-de-Fonds, Switzerland
　　　Jeanneret House, 12 chemin de Pouillerel, La Chaux-de-Fonds, Switzerland
1914 Domino House (project)
　　　Norman Houses, Deauville, France (project)
　　　Felix Klipstein House, Loubach, Switzerland (project)
　　　Bank, Neuenburg, Switzerland (project)
1915 Butin Bridge, near Geneva (competition project)
　　　Building on pilotis (projects)
　　　House, Lons-le-Saunier, France (project)
1916 Scala Cinema, 32 rue de la Serre, La Chaux-de-Fonds, Switzerland (demolished)
　　　Schwob House, 167 rue du Doubs, La Chaux-de-Fonds, Switzerland
　　　Fritz Zbinden House, Erlach, Switzerland (project)
　　　Administrative Building, Le Locle, near La Chaux-de-Fonds, Switzerland (project)
　　　Watch Factory, La Chaux-de-Fonds, Switzerland (project)

1916/
21 Paul Poiret Seaside Villa (various projects)
1917 Water Tower, Les Landes, France
　　　Abbatoir, Challay, France (project)
　　　Abbatoir, Garchizy, France (project)
　　　Workers' housing estate, near Dieppe, France (project)
　　　Dam Ile Jourdain, France (project)
1918 Factory, Saintes, France (project)
1919 Pre-cast concrete houses, Troyes, France (project)
　　　Insitu concrete housing (project)
　　　Monol Housing (project)
　　　Hotel, Rabat, Morocco (project)
　　　Distillery, near Lyon (project)
1920 Citrohan House (1st project)
　　　Painter's studio (project)
1921 Citrohan Seaside House (project)
　　　Garage, Lille, France (project)
1922 Besnos House, La Chataigneraie, 49 Avenue du Chesnay, Vaucresson, Paris (now altered)
　　　Ozenfant House, 53 Avenue de Reille, Paris (now altered)
　　　Contemporary City for three million people, *Salon d'automne*, Paris (exhibition project)
　　　Group of Villas and apartments (projects)
　　　Citrohan House (2nd project)
　　　Artist's house (project)
　　　Workers house (project)
　　　La Roche-Jeanneret Houses, Auteuil, France (1st project)
1923/
25 Villa La Roche-Jeanneret, 8-10 Square du Docteur Blanche, Paris 16 (now Fondation Le Corbusier)
　　　Jeanneret House, 21 Route Lavaux, Corseaux-Vevey, Switzerland
1924 Lipchitz/Miestschannioff House, 9 Allée des Pins, Boulogne, Paris
　　　Tonkin House, Bordeaux
　　　10 houses, Lege, near Bordeaux (now altered)
　　　Weekend house, Rambouillet, France (project)
　　　Prefabricated workers' housing (project)
　　　Pavillon de l'Esprit Nouveau, *Exposition des arts decoratifs*, Paris
　　　Cité Universitaire (project)
　　　Meyer House, Paris (project)
　　　Voisin Plan for Paris (project(
　　　Housing, Cité Audincourt, France (Project)
1925/
26 Cité Fruges Development, Pessac, near Bordeaux (now altered)
1925/
27 Two houses, Weissenhof Estate, Stuttgart
1926 Ternisien House, 5 Allée des Pins, Boulogne, Paris
　　　Cook House, 6 rue Denfert-Rochereau, Boulogne, Paris
　　　Salvation Army Dormitory (Palais du Peuple), 29 rue des Cordelieres, Paris
　　　Guiette House, Antwerp (now altered)
　　　Raspail Garage, Paris (project)
　　　Cardinet Stadium, Paris (project)
　　　Fruges Factory (project)
1927 "Les Terraces," 17 rue du Professeur Victor Pauchet, Garches, Paris (now altered)
　　　Plainex House, 24 bis Boulevard Massena, Paris
　　　League of Nations Headquarters, Geneva (competition project)
1928 Villa Baizau, Carthage, Tunisia (now in grounds of presidential palace)
　　　Church house, Ville-Avray, Paris (demolished)
　　　Wanner Apartment Block Geneva (project)
1929 Salvation Army Floating Dormitory, Pont d'Austerlitz, Paris
　　　Planning study of Montevideo
　　　Planning study of São Paulo
　　　Planning study of Rio de Janeiro
　　　Planning study of Buenos Aires
　　　Plan for Porte Maillot, Paris

　　　"Mundaneum" (world museum), Geneva (project)
　　　Loucher Housing (project)
　　　Draeger Printing Works, Paris (project)
　　　Canneels House, Brussels (project)
1929/
31 "Les Heures Claires" (Villa Savoye), 82 chemin de Villiers, Poissy, France
1929/
33 Centrosoyus Building, Kirova Ulitsa, Moscow (now altered)
　　　Salvation Army Hostel (Cité de Refuge), 12 rue Cantargrel, Paris (now altered)
1930 City plan for Algiers (1st project)
　　　Ville Radieuse (project)
　　　Errazuris House, Chile (project)
1930/
31 Charles de Beistegui Penthouse Apartment, rue de Balzac, Paris
　　　Madrot House, Le Pradet, near Toulon
1930/
32 Swiss Students' Hostels, Cité Universitaire, Paris (now altered)
　　　"Clarte," 2 rue Saint-Laurent, Geneva
1931 Palace of the Soviets, Moscow (competition project)
　　　Museum of Contemporary Art, Paris (project)
1932 Apartment block, Zürichhorn, Zürich (project)
1933 Apartment block, 24 rue Nungesser-et-Coli, Paris
　　　MACIA Plan, Barcelona
　　　Plan for the Right Bank, Geneva
　　　City plan for Stockholm
　　　Plan for the Scheldt Left Bank, Antwerp (with H. Hoste and P. Otlet)
　　　City plan for Algiers (2nd project)
　　　Durrand Housing, Oued-Ouchaia, Algeria (project)
　　　Apartment block, Algiers (project)
　　　Rentenanstalt Building, Zürich (project)
1934 City plan for Nemurs (Jamad-el-Ghazuar), Algeria (with N. Bezard)
　　　Worker's housing, Zürich (project)
　　　Apartment block, Esplande des Invalides, Paris (project)
　　　City plan for Algiers (3rd project)
1935 Ville le Settout, La Tremblade, Les Mathes, near Marennes, France
　　　Weekend House, 85 boulevard de la République, La Celle-Saint-Cloud, Paris
　　　Young man's apartment, *International Exhibition*, Brussels (exhibition project)
　　　Study of New York)
　　　Bata Shoe Factory, Hellocourt, Lorraine, France (project)
　　　Bata Shoe Factory, Zlin, Czechoslovakia (project)
　　　Apartment block, rue Fabert, Paris (project)
　　　Bastion Kellerman, Paris (project)
　　　Apartment block, Nemours (Jamad-el-Ghazuar), Algeria (project)
　　　Swimming pool with wave machine, Badjararah, Algeria (project)
　　　College president's house, near Chicago (project)
　　　Museum, Paris (project)
　　　"Cartesian" Tower (project)
1936 University, Rio de Janeiro (project; with Lúcio Costa and Oscar Niemeyer)
　　　"Ilot Insalubre no. 6" Plan, Paris (project)
　　　"Paris 37" Plan (project)
　　　National Sports Centre, Bois de Vincennes, Paris (project)
　　　Studies for Bata Shops (projects)
1937 Pavillon des Temps Nouveaux, World's Fair, Paris
　　　Monument to Vaillant-Courturier, Villejuif, France, (project)
　　　Jaoul Weekend House (project)
1937/
43 Ministry of Education and Health, Rio de Janeiro (with Lúcio Costa, Oscar Niemeyer, Affonso Eduardo Reidy, and Jorge Ma-

chado Moreira; now the Palace of Culture)
1938 Tower and master plan for the Quartier de la Marine, Algiers (project)
Plan for Pont Saint-Cloud, Boulogne, Paris (project)
City plan for Buenos Aires (project)
Cooperative Village (project)
1939 Exhibition Pavilion (project)
Museum of Endless Growth, Philippeville, Algeria (project)
Pavilion, *Ideal Home, Exhibition,* London (project)
Research Laboratory, Roscoff, France (project)
Clarke Arundell House (project)
Plan for the Main Square, Boulogne, Paris (project)
Sports Centre, Var Valley, France (project)
City plan for Algiers (4th project)
1940 Layout for the *France Outremer* exhibition, Grand Palais, Paris
Murondins Housing (project)
Refugee School (project; with Jean Prouvé)
Pre-fabricated housing housing (project)
Foreman's house (project)
Engineer's house (project)
1941 Plans for the Cure Valley, Vézelay, Asquins, Saint-Père, France (projects)
1942 Peyrissac House, near Cherchel, Algeria (project)
Plan for the Linear Industrial City (project)
Plan 7, Algiers (project)
1945 Unité d'Habitation, Marseille (1st project)
City plan for La Rochelle-Pallice, France (project)
City plan for Saint-Gaudens, France (project)
1946 Duval Factory, 1 Avenue de Robache, Saint-Die, France
Airport (project)
1946/
51 City plan for Saint-Die, France (project)
1946/
52 Unité d'Habitation, 280 Boulevard Michelet, Marseille
1947 Redevelopment plan for the Vieux Port, Marseille
Redevelopment plan for Veyres, Marseille
Two Unités d'Habitation, Antony, France (project)
CIAM Grid (project)
"Sept Voies" (7 V's) Planning Studies
City planning study of Begota, Colombia
1947/
53 United Nations Headquarters, First Avenue, New York (as one of team of international architects—Wallace K. Harrison, Chairman)
1948 Plan for La Sainte Baume, France (with E. Trouin)
City plan for Izmir, Turkey
"Roq" and "Rob" Housing, Cap Martin, France (projects)
1949 Currutchet House, La Plata, Argentina
1950 Holiday huts, Cap Martin, France Fueter House, Lake Constance, Switzerland (project)
Studies for the Museum of Endless Growth
City plan of Bogotá Colombia (with J.L. Sert and P.L. Wiener)
Exhibition Pavilion, *Synthèse des Arts Majeurs,* Porte Maillot, Paris (project)
Delgado Memorial Chapel (project)
1950/
55 Notre-Dame-du-Haut Chapel, Ronchamp, France
1951 Master plan for the capital city at Chandigarh, India
Two Unités d'Habitation and Tower, Strasbourg, France (project)
City plan for Marseille South
1951/
59 High Court, Chandigarh, India
1952 Open Hand Monument, Chandigarh, India (project)

Le Corbusier: Notre-Dame-du-Haut Chapel, Ronchamp, France, 1955.

Workers' houses, Chandigarh, India (project)
1952/
54 Jaoul Houses, 81 rue de Longchamp, Neuilly-sur-Seine, Paris
1952/
55 Unité d'Habitation, Reze-les-Nantes, France
1953 Governor's Palace, Chandigarh, India (project)
1953/
59 Couvent de la Sainte-Marie-de-la-Tourette, Eveux-sur-l'Arbresle, near Lyons
1954/
56 Millowners' Association Building, Ahmedabad, India
1955 Bhakra Dam, Himalaya Mountains, India
1955/
56 Sarabhai House, Ahmedabad, India
1956 Shodham House, Ahmedabad, India
Museum, Ahmedabad, India
Prefabricated houses, Lagny, France (project; with Jean Prouvé)
Hospital, Flers, France (project)
Sports Centre, Baghdad (project; with G. Presente)
1957 Unité d'Habitation, Tiergarten, Charlottenburg, Berlin
Unité d'Habitation, Meaux, France
Unité d'Habitation, Briey-en-Foret, France
Unité de Camping, Cap Martin, France
Five Unités d'Habitation, Meaux, France (project)
1957/
59 Brazilian Students' Hostel, Cité Universitaire, Paris (with Lúcio Costa)
National Museum of Western Art, Tokyo (with Kunio Mayekawa, Takamasa Yosizaka, and Junzo Sakakura)

1958 Philips Pavilion, World's Fair, Brussels
Secretariat Building, Chandigarh, India
City plan for Berlin (competition project)
1959 Prefabricated housing, France (project; with Renault Engineering)
1960 Museum of Knowledge, Chandigarh, India (project)
City plan for Firminy-Vert, France
1961 Conference Centre and Hotel, Quai Anatole France, Paris (project)
1961/
64 Carpenter Center for the Visual Arts, Harvard University, Cambridge, Massachusetts (supervised by J.L. Sert)
Legislative Assembly Building, Chandigarh, India
1962 Ahrenberg Exhibition Pavilion, Stockholm (project)
1962/
65 Church of St.Pierre, Firminy-Vert, France (project)
1963 International Art Centre, Erlenbach, near Frankfurt (project)
Church, Bologna, Italy (project)
Olivetti Computer Centre, Rho-Milan (project)
1964 Club House, Chandigarh, India
Congress Hall, Strasbourg, France (project)
French Embassy, Brasilia (project)
1964/
65 Hospital, Venice (project)
1964/
66 Centre Le Corbusier, Hoschgasse 8, Zürich
1964/
68 Museum and Art Gallery, Chandigarh, India
1965 Youth Centre, Firminy-Vert, France
Stadium, Firminy-Vert, France

Museum of the Twentieth Century, Nanterre, Paris (project)
1965/
68 Unité d'Habitation, Firminy-Vert, France

Publications:

By LE CORBUSIER: books—*Feuille d'avis de La Chaux-de-Fonds*, La Chaux-de-Fonds, Switzerland 1911; *Etude sur le mouvement d'art decoratif en Allemagne*, Paris 1912; *Amédée Ozenfant*, Paris 1918; *Architecture d'epoque machiniste*, with Amédée Ozenfant, Paris 1918; *Vers une architecture*, Paris 1923, revised edition Paris 1924, Stuttgart 1926, London 1927, 2nd revised edition Paris 1928; *Urbanisme*, Paris, 1925, as *The City of Tomorrow and Its Planning*, London 1929; *L'Art décoratif d'aujourd'hui*, Paris 1925, 1959; *La Peinture moderne*, with Amédée Ozenfant, Paris 1925; *Almanach d'architecture moderne*, Paris 1927; *Une Maison—un palais*, Paris 1928; *Précisions sur un etat présent de l'architecture et de l'urbanisme*, Paris 1930; *Croisade; ou, le crépuscule des académies*, Paris 1932; *La Ville radieuse*, Paris and London 1935; *Aircraft*, Paris, London and New York 1935; *Quand les cathédrales etaient blanches*, Paris 1937, as *When the Cathedrals were White*, New York 1947; *Des Canons, des munitions?—Merci! Des Logis . . . S.V.P.!*, Paris 1938; *Le Lyrisme des temps nouveaux et l'urbanisme*, Paris 1939; *Destin de Paris*, Paris 1941; *Sur les quatres routes*, Paris 1941, as *The Four Routes*, London 1947; *Les Constructions Murondins*, Paris 1941; *La Maison des hommes*, with François de Pierrefeu, Paris 1942, as *The Home of Man*, London 1948; *Entretien avec les etudiants des ecoles d'architecture*, Paris 1943, as *Le Corbusier Talks with Students from the Schools of Architecture*, New York 1961; *La Charte d'Athenes*, Paris 1943, 1957; *Les Trois Etablissements humains*, Paris, 1944; *Propos d'urbanisme*, Paris 1946, as *Concerning Town Planning*, London 1947; *La Grille CIAM d'urbanisme*, Paris 1948; *Le Modulor 1948*, Paris 1950, London 1954; *Poésie sur Alger*, Paris 1950; *L'Unité d'Habitation de Marseille*, Paris 1950, as *The Marseilles Block*, London 1950; *Une Petite Maison, 1923*, Paris 1954; *Le Modulor 2*, Paris 1955, London 1958; *Le Poème de l'angle droit*, Paris 1955; *Architecte du bonheur*, Paris 1955; *La Chapelle Notre-Dame-du-Haut à Ronchamp*, Paris 1956, as *The Chapel at Ronchamp*, London 1957; *Les Plans de Le Corbusier de Paris 1922-1956*, Paris 1958; *Le Poème electronique*, with others, Brussels 1958; *L'Atelier de la recherche patiente*, Paris 1960; *Petites Confidences*, Paris 1960; *My Work*, London and Stuttgart 1960; *Gaudi*, Barcelona 1967; *Les Maternelles*, Paris and New York 1968.

On LE CORBUSIER: books—*Zwei Wohnhauser von Le Corbusier* by Alfred Roth Stuttgart 1927; *Le Corbusier: Complete Works*, 7 volumes, edited by W. Boesiger, Zürich, subsequently London and New York, 1929-65; *Le Corbusier and Contemporary Architecture* by Siegfried Giedion, Paris 1930; *La Machino-Latrie de Le Corbusier* by Angel Guido, Rosario, Argentina 1930; *Le Corbusier et Pierre Jeanneret* by François de Pierrefeu, Paris 1932; *Revision der Kunstgeschichte: Prolegomena zu einer Kunstgeschichte aus dem Ceiste de Gegenwart, mit einer Anhang "Semper und Le Corbusier"* by Joseph Ganther, Vienna 1932; *L'Abitardie nell' architettura di Le Corbusier* by Alberto Gatti, Rome 1933, 1953; *Von Ledoux bis Le Corbusier: Ursprung und Entwicklung der autonomen Architektur* by Emil Kaugmann, Vienna and Leipzig 1933; *Le Corbusier; ou, l'architecture au service de l'homme* by Maximilien Gauthier, Paris 1944; *Le Corbusier* by Giancarlo De Carlo, Milan 1945; *Que Repose Le Corbusier* by Jacques Clair, Paris 1946; *Le Corbusier, Architect, Painter* by Stamo Papadaki, New York 1948; *A Critical Review of Le Corbusier/Leitura critica de Le Corbusier* by Pietro Maria Bardi, São Paulo 1950; *Le Corbusier* by Jean Alazard, Florence 1951, New York 1960; *Le Corbusier: Idealistisch Architect* by W.S. van de Erve, Utrecht, Netherlands 1951; *Two Standpoints Towards Modern Architecture: Wright and Le Corbusier* by Carl Berger Troedsson, Göteborg, Sweden 1951; *Eight European Artists* by Felix H. Man, London, Melbourne and Toronto 1953; *Le Corbusier: Dessins* by Maurice Jardot, Paris 1955; *Ronchamp: Le Corbusiers erster Kirchenbau* by Anton Henz, Recklinghausen, West Germany 1956; *Le Corbusier* by Anton Henz, Berlin 1957; *Chapelle Notre-Dame-du-Haut à Ronchamp* by Jean Petit, Paris 1957; *Architecture of Truth* by François Cali, London 1958; *Besuch in Ronchamp* by Karl Anton Rohna, Nuremberg 1958; *Le Corbusier* by Henri Perruchot, Paris 1958; *Le Corbusier's Wohneinbeit "Typ Berlin"* by Frithjof Miller-Beppen, Berlin 1958; *The Philips Pavilion at the 1958 Brussels World's Fair*, London 1959; *The Master Builders* by Peter Blake, New York 1960; *Le Corbusier* by Françoise Choay, New York and London 1960; *La Couvent Sainte Marie de la Tourette, construite par Le Corbusier*, edited by M. François Mathey, Paris 1960; *De La Fenetre au pan de verre dans l'oeuvre de Le Corbusier* by Jean Alazard, Paris 1961; *Un Couvent de Le Corbusier* by Jean Petit, Paris 1961; *Le Tourette: Le Corbusiers erster Klosterbau* by Anton Henz and B. Moorbrugger, Starnberg, West Germany 1963, Paris, Fribourg, Switzerland and New York 1966; *Le Corbusier: Architecture and Form* by Peter Baltimore 1964; *Le Corbusier: presentations choix de textes, bibliography, portraits, facsimiles*, edited by Sophie Daria, Paris 1964; *Le Corbusier* by Henrik Sommerschild, Oslo 1966; *Le Corbusier en la historia* by Leonides Guadarrama, Mexico City 1966; *Le Corbusier* by Vittorio Franchetti Pardo, Florence 1966, Paris 1968, New York and London 1971; *Chandigarh* by Norman Evenson, Berkeley, California 1966; *Le Corbusier parle* by Jean Petit, Paris 1967; *Le Corbusier: oeuvre graphique*, edited by Heidi Weber, Zürich 1967; *Documentation of the Centre Le Corbusier* by Heidi Weber, Jean Prouvé and Albert Jeanneret, Zürich 1967; *Four Compositions of Le Corbusier* by John Petit West, New York 1967; *Pavillion de Vendome: Le Corbusier*, Marseille 1967; *Le Corbusier* by Willy Boesiger and Hans Girsberger, Zürich 1967; *Le Corbusier: Elemente einer Synthese* by Stanislaus von Moos, Frauenfeld, Switzerland 1968; *Les Erreurs de Le Corbusier et Leurs conséquences* by J. Riboud, Paris 1968; *Qui était Le Corbusier?* by Maurice Besset, Geneva and Cleveland, Ohio 1968; *Diskusson über Chandigarh: Antworten zu Fragen Europaischer Archiekten* by M. Sharma, Zürich 1968; *Le Corbusier: Chandigarh, neue Haupstadtes Punjab Indien*, Nuremberg 1969; *Pessac de Le Corbusier* by Philippe Boudon, Paris 1969; *Le Corbusier: The Machine and the Grand Design* by Norman Evenson, New York and London 1969; *Fondation Le Corbusier*, Paris 1970; *Le Corbusier lui-même* by Jean Petit, Geneva 1970, New York 1971; *Ausstellungsgebaude von Le Corbusier in Zürich*, Düsseldorf 1970; *Le Corbusier* by Jean Petit, Lausanne 1970; *Le Corbusier: Artist and Writer* by Marcel Joray, New York 1970; *Le Corbusier* by Martin Pawley, New York 1971; *Le Corbusier and the Articulation of Architectural Elements* by G. H. Baker, Newcastle 1971; *Global Architecture 7: Chappelle Notre-Dame-du-Haut, Ronchamp* by Yukio Futagawa and Takamasa Yosizaka, Tokyo 1971; *Global Architecture 11: Couvent Sainte Marie de la Tourette* by Yukio Futagawa and Arata Isozaki, Tokyo 1971; *Le Corbusier: l'architecte et son mythe* by Stanislaus von Moos, Paris 1971; *Le Livre de Ronchamp: Le Corbusier* by Jean Petit, Paris 1971; *Einige deutsche Vorfahren zu Le Corbusiers Proportionstheorie* by Jaques Paul, Nuremberg 1971; *Briefwechsel Le Corbusier-Karl Ernst Osthaus*, edited by Herta Hesse-Fellinghausen, Hagen 1972; *Le Corbusier* by Robert Furneaux Jordan, New York and London 1971; *Le Corbusier* by Willy Boesiger, Zürich and New York 1972; *Global Architecture 18: Unité d'Habitation, Marseilles; Unité d'Habitation, Berlin* by Yukio Futagawa and Takamasa Yosizaka, Tokyo 1972; *Global Architecture 13: Villa Savoye, Poissy* by Yukio Futagawa and Richard Meier, Tokyo 1972; *Begegnung mit Pionieren* by Alfred Roth, Basel 1973; *Le Corbusier and the Tragic View of Architecture* by Charles Jencks, London and Cambridge, Massachusetts 1973; *Global Architecture 30: Chandigarh* by Yukio Futagawa and Takamasa Yoshizaka, Tokyo 1974; *Global Architecture 32: Sarabhai House, Shodhan, House* by Yukio Futagawa and B. V. Doshi, Tokyo 1974; *Le Corbusier* by Stephen Gardiner, London and New York 1974; *Urbanistica e Mobilità* by P. G. Gerosa, Zürich 1974; *Le Corbusier in Perspective* by Peter Serenyi, New York 1975; *Le Corbusier e 'L'Esprit Nouveau'* by R. Gabetti and C. Olmo, Turin 1975; *Le Corbusier: Evolution of His Architecture* by W. Curtis, London 1975; *Global Architecture 37: Millowners Building; Carpenter Centre* by Yukio Futagawa and Kenneth Frampton, Tokyo 1975; *Le Corbusier in Selbstzeugnissen und Bilddokmenten* by N. Huse, Hamburg, West Germany 1976; *La Machine à s'asseoir: Le Corbusier, Charlotte Perriand, Pierre Jeanneret*, exhibition catalogue, by Maurizio Di Puolo, Marcello Fagiolo and Maria Luisa Madonna, Rome 1976; *The Education of Le Corbusier* by P. V. Turner, New York and London 1977; *Masters of Modern Architecture: Frank Lloyd Wright, Le Corbusier, Mies van der Rohe, and Walter Gropius* by Edwin and Joy Hoag, Indianapolis, Indiana 1977; *The Early Drawings of Charles-Edouard Jeannet* by M. P. M. Sekler, New York and London 1977; *The Open Hand* by Russell Walden, London and Cambridge, Massachusetts 1977; *Le Corbusier* by E. Nagy, Budapest 1977; *50 Disegni di Le Corbusier*, exhibition catalogue, edited by Giuliano Greslieri, Bologna, Italy 1977; *Le Corbusier: Image and Symbol*, exhibition catalogue by Richard A. Moore, Atlanta, Georgia 1977; *Le Corbusier: Designer Furniture, 1929* by Renato De Fusco, Woodbury, New York 1977; *Die funktionelle Stadt: Le Corbusiers Stadtvision* by Thilo Hilpert, Braunschweig 1978; *Le Corbusier at Work: The Genesis of the Carpenter Center for Visual Arts* by Eduard F. Sekler and William Curtis, London and Cambridge, Massachusetts 1978; *La torre d'ombre o l'architettura delle apparenze reali* by Francesco Venezia, Naples 1978; *Le Corbusier: Dessins*, exhibition catalogue, by Alberto Izzo and Camillo Gubitosi, Paris and Rome 1978; *C. E. Jeanneret/Le Corbusier* by Alberto Izzo and Camillo Gubitosi, Rome 1979; *Ginevra 1927* by Ciro Luigi Anzivino and Ezio Godoli, Florence 1979; *Vita e opere di Le Corbusier* by Francesco Tentori, Bari, Italy 1979; *Le Corbusier: Selected drawings*, with an introduction by Michael Graves, London 1981; *Le Corbusier: La Cité de Refuge, Paris* by Brian Brace Taylor, Paris 1981; *Le Corbusier's Firminy Church*, exhibition catalogue, with an introduction by Anthony Eardley, New York 1981; *Im Umgang mit Le Corbusier* by Hans Girsberger, Zürich 1981; *Le Corbusier: carnets, 1914-1964*, 4 vols., with commentary by Francoise de Franclieu, Paris 1981-82; *Arte, artigianato e tecnica nelle poetica die Le Corbusier* by Luisa Martina Colli, Rome 1982; *Le Corbusier Archive*, 32 vols., edited by H. Allen Brooks, New York, London and Paris 1982-84; *Le Corbusier: An Analysis of Form* by Geoffrey H. Baker, New York and London 1984; *Les Villes de Le Corbusier et Pierre Jeanneret, 1920-1930* by Tim Benton, Paris 1984; *The Decorated Design: Harvard Architecture and the Failure of the Bauhaus Legacy* by Klaus Herdeg, Cambridge, Massachusetts 1984.

Le Corbusier (Charles Edouard Jeanneret), architect, painter, author, journalist and lecturer, urbanist, wood sculptor, and designer of furniture, enamels, and tapestry, was during his lifetime the doyen, idealistic conscience, and chief propagandist of modern architecture. He inspired fanatical devotion and exercised a magnetic and often barely rational hold over his followers throughout the world. Ferociously egocentric and difficult to work with, he possessed tremendous vitality, high artistic perception, the deepest feelings, remarkable receptiveness, a sense of drama, and throughout his life he was an outsider in Parisian society.

Intellectually, Le Corbusier was a dualist. He was fundamentally a divided human being, torn between precision and sensibility. His brilliant, intuitive approach to design originated in nature, in the rich and diverse landscape of the Swiss Jura. Because of his Calvinist upbringing and individualistic temperament, he never grew into a benevolent man of peace, propriety, or gentility. Indeed, he became the very reverse. Egotistical, proud, and avid for recognition, he drove himself ruthlessly forward in a lifetime of struggle, of intellectual and professional combat.

Le Corbusier experienced the world in a profoundly emotional way and in so doing exposed the Dionysian-Apollonian polarities of his vision. As an artist-architect his themes were on the tension between the individual—especially the creative artist—and society; the notion of the artist as genius, seer and visionary prophet; the value of spontaneous feeling and expression of emotion, the original as against the traditional in art, values, morality, and social conventions. These themes undeniably suggest the romantic. Yet, the High Romantic in Le Corbusier vied with another facet of his personality—that side of him that preferred Cartesian clarity of thought. This more classical aspect of his personality explains his preoccupation with harmony and his interest in the world of the abstract. In fact, functions of this binomial—space, precision, order, form, machine aesthetic, scale, *béton brut*, mathematics, proportion and the modular—are concepts that appear over and over again in his thinking.

As a product of a late nineteenth-century art education and despite his experiences with Peret and Behrens, the young Jeanneret pitched himself into life's battles in the style of his bedside hero Don Quixote. He never rejected the machine as William Morris had done. In fact, as a young man in Paris, he tried unsuccessfully to become an industrialist. Eventually, he emerged under his new name Le Corbusier, not as a technical director of industrialised building systems but as a purist painter and architect of the white, cubic architecture of the 1920s. His most poetic examples were the Villa La RocheJeanneret (1923-25), Le Pavillon de L'Esprit Nouveau (1925; rebuilt in Bologna, 1977), Les Terraces at Garches (1927), and Les Heures Claires at Poissy (1929-31). In effect, Le Corbusier's answer to the industrialisation of housing was Purism. The fact that all his Purist houses demanded a high degree of craft skills to build them meant that the final result was purely symbolic of first-machine-age architecture.

Architectural practice for Le Corbusier in the 1920s was complicated. He had no technical background. He was no builder. He was not even a good technician. Yet he did have technical ideas, and he wanted desperately to be thought of as a man of the twentieth-century. One has the feeling about Le Corbusier that, as a man of action, he would have been much happier had he been practising in the age of Palladio.

An even more striking example of Le Corbusier's idealistic predicament is provided by his encounter with the City of Paris. It was the testing ground of all his urbanism. Le Corbusier hoped that if he could bring order to the disorder of Paris, the event would trigger an urban revolution; within this new framework the architecture of the new age could arise. Le Corbusier's intuitive capacity to anticipate the urban consequences of the car and the motorway, showed remarkable foresight and imagination. At the same time, his answer to meet the future needs of the inner-city demonstrated that he was not a pure intellectual with a classical mentality, who used logic as the organizing principle *par excellence*. His visions were the mystical product of a man who desired the harmonious solution of Nature as the model for twentiethcentury man. Le Corbusier's desire for harmony was the fundamental goal behind all his work.

Nowhere is Le Corbusier's Achilles heel more painfully exposed than in his plans for Paris. On the basis of a Cartesian-geometrical system, he developed his notorious vision of high-density office towers, motorways, and underpasses, so familiar now to Western man. For all his visionary capacity, he never fully appreciated the effect of excesses in transportation and centralization of *people*. As an experimental model, Le Corbusier took the historic right bank of Paris and autocratically applied his heavenly vision to the Marais quarter. Between 1922 and 1946, Le Corbusier put forward five separate schemes for Paris, and each time he abundantly demonstrated his political naiveté As an urbanist, he always considered that he had observed people's needs, and he thought that he had solved the problem of the ugliness of the suburbs. But it is now quite clear that Le Corbusier never understood other people. He conceived his plans messianically and then wondered why he 'got kicked in the arse for his pains'.

There were other inherent weaknesses in his method of working as an architect. From early in his career, his artistic abilities as an architect greatly exceeded his administrative skills. Moreover, under the puritantical influence of Ozenfant, Le Corbusier's creation was strictly limited within the Purist ideology of *objet-types*. Moreover, he had difficulties with land tenure, technical servicing, and the clinical workability of his Purist houses.

By 1925 Le Corbusier had begun to feel his way beyond the Purist, impersonal condition of his painting, and he finally abandoned it in his architecture in 1929. From that time, he tried to adjust his thinking in urbanism, which widened along with his humanity, though perhaps never enough. He embraced the human condition more confidently and richly. He got married. Through his wife Yvonne Gallis, he made his final and irrevocable conversion to the light of Provence and to the psychological spontaneity of the French Mediterranean temperament. These influences are to be found in his paintings from the 1930s onwards. The liberating effect of the Mediterranean upon his work aesthetically, psychologically, and spiritually cannot be overemphasised. Le Corbusier turned his back on Purism, although he retained the Apollonian desire for visual clarity and harmonic measurement through his modular. Above all it was in the Dionysian sphere of feeling and intuition that Le Corbusier's personal development began to leap forward energentically, and his paintings glory in a rich vocabulary and intensity of curvi-linear form and colour that leave one in no doubt about the influence of women in his life.

By the mid-1950s, Le Corbusier was as complete an artist as he would ever be. His paintings were full of a rich multiplicity of meanings. Even in maturity his artistic psyche was still the principal source of his unwavering strength and rebelliousness. Like a monk, he painted every morning in his apartment above the Rue Nungesser-et-Coli, and from the late 1920s onwards, this discipline of plastic research was the basis of his aethetic leadership. There in his studio, his ideas germinated, were imaginatively sorted and reviewed, readied for admission to his mature architecture.

As far as materials were concerned, all his life Le Corbusier had wanted to build a steel building with exactitude, but in the economic climate of postwar France, he was restricted to working in reinforced concrete and using cheap Algerian labour. But what a success he mad of his stringency. In spite of the often sloppy workmanship his office permited, Le Corbusier did for concrete what Michelangelo had done for marble. His *béton brut* potency marked all his mature work from the Unité d'Habitation, Marseilles (1946-52), Notre-Dame-du-Haut de Ronchamp (1950-52), Couvent de La Sainte-Marie-de-la Tourette at Eveux-sur-l' Arbresslе (1953-59), the High Court at Chandigarh (1951-59), to the Carpenter Centre for the Visual Arts, Harvard University (1961-64).

Amongst all the heroic poetry of his mature work, the Chapel at Ronchamp is his enigmatic masterpiece, "the pearl of my career." This commission came at a fortunate time in Le Corbusier's creative life when he had reached artistic and intellectual maturity. His ideas had been fully developed, and he now unashamedly and passionately responded to nature and her inherent rhythms. The idea of pilgrimage, of worship before the spectacle of nature, was extremely appealing to Le Corbusier's developed notion of the spiritual. Such a programme stimulated and exited his imagination. The Chapel is situated on a high point above the village of Ronchamp in the Haute-Saône, where the surrounding configurations of earth and sky reveal a rare richness—basic and profound. For this reason alone, the Chapel of Ronchamp became one of his most revealing commissions. Unhesitantly, he called forth a powerful response before the drama of nature. For Le Corbusier, Ronchamp is the meeting place of the sense-world and the spiritual. In his nature mysticism, he unrelentingly projected the principle of a free, spontaneous, and creative life as the essence of reality and gave instinctual expression to the whole world of nature, that aspect of creation neglected by Christianity.

Although this isolated programme of pilgrimage practically made Le Corbusier a household name, his spontaneous success on the hill of Bourlémont concealed a variety of problems for modern architecture. In the first place, many thought Le Corbusier had betrayed the rational principles upon which modern architecture was based. Several church architects mistakenly aped Le Corbusier's imagery without realizing the individuality of the Ronchamp programme or the uniqueness of its site. Many more misguided architects thought Ronchamp was the signal enabling their liberation to do anything they wanted. Le Corbusier unwittingly prolonged the life of an ideal, that of the Renaissance architect as a messianic prophet. As far as Le Corbusier himself was concerned, these problems of misrepresentation of his vision did not interest him. Ronchamp for him was a spontaneous moment of ecstasy where, in one day, he defined an idea which captured a higher level of reality than the previous chapel. He said of the experience.

This pilgrim chapel is no baroque pennon
May Ronchamp bear witness,
Five years of work isolated on the hill.
I have never in my life explained a work,
The work may be like or disliked, understood or not,
What difference does that make to me.

At Ronchamp, Le Corbusier was as near to expressing his inner voice as he ever came to doing. In this commission he successfully brought together the ideals and realities of the situation, and for that reason Ronchamp was and still is a masterpiece.

To historians, however, the problem becomes one of interpreting the architect's oeuvre. To understand Le Corbusier, one must discover him creatively. There is no short cut to an understanding of his work. There is, for example, the question of whether Le Corbusier's architecture changed fundamentaly during the course of his career. Although his work of the 1950s is more richly expressive and laden with meanings than his Purist architecture of the 1920s, the differences between the two periods is one of degree, not of kind. During both periods, his work owed allegiance and inspiration to nature and to a form of measurement which varied from *les tracés régulateurs* of the 1920s to the modulor—a proportioning harmonic grid—that underlaid all his mature work from the 1950s onwards. In Le Corbusier's Purist period, his work was under the discipline and exactitude of *objet-types*, yet there was still a strong abstracted link with nature, although that link is sometimes difficult to see. Le Corbuier's mature work has a more obvious and richer affinity with nature, which becomes all the more apparent when one has personally experienced the influence of the Mediterranean. The answer to the question of whether or not Le Corbusier's vision as an architect changed categorically is, therefore, no, but it must be admitted that until he built Ronchamp, his nature-mysticism was not fully visible to the world.

Le Corbusier was a brilliant artist. Yet, as a designer, his artistic autocracy often led him, particularly in urbanism, towards sterility and worse. This contagious condition was part of the thinking of all the pioneers of modern design from William Morris to Gropius. And, indeed, Le Corbusier's personality mirrors all the major problems that have beset the twentieth centrury: authoritarianism, fascism, opportunism, and artistic autocracy. Politically, Le Corbusier's dilemma was that he was a nature mystic operating autocratically in the century of mass democracy. Plagued by this disease, whichever way he turned, he suffered defeats. He was rejected at Vichy by an authoritarian body, but his plans were also rejected by the people of Paris. Le Corbusier's problem was that he acted like a god when he was not one, and therefore the gap between his idealism and the political realities was one that could never be closed. However, when commissions came to which Le Corbusier could respond idealistically as a nature mystic he did create architecture that was original not only with the period in which he worked but also within his own oeuvre. He never stood still artistically, and he never created the same building twice.

As an artist-architect, Le Corbusier could be both devastatingly brilliant and overwhelmingly a tragic figure, depending upon the circumstances. Where the arcitect's mysticism was alien to the sociopolitical programme, there was stalemate. But where the architect's vision coincided with the requirements of the client's situation, he achieved a masterpiece—as at Ronchamp. Le Corbusier shared both the brilliance and the central weakness of his spiritual mentor, Jean-Jacques Rousseau: both men radically distrubed the periods within which they worked, both were nature mystics, both were politically impotent, and both died alone. Nevertheless, whatever influence others had on him, Le Corbusier followed his own path; he was master of his own fate, faithful only to himself, lonely as the sun but one who glowed with much the same intensity.

—Russell Walden

LEGORRETA Vilchis, Ricardo.

Mexican. Born in Mexico City, 7 May 1931. Educated at the Universidad Nacional Autonoma de Mexico, Mexico City, 1948-52, Dip.Arch. 1953. Married Maria Luisa Hernandez in 1956; children: Lucia, Lourdes, Elisa, Luis, Ricardo, and Victor. Worked as a Draftsman, 1948-52, and Project Manager, 1953-55, for José Villagrán García, Mexico City; in partnership with José Villagrán García, 1955-60; in private practice, Mexico City, 1961-63. Since 1963, Principal, Legorreta Arquitectos, Mexico City (partners: Noe Castro, Emilio Guerrero, Michel Leautaud and Gerard Alonso); since 1977, President, Legorreta Arquitectos Diseños, furniture and accessory design, Mexico City. Design Professor, 1959-62, and Chief of the Experimental Architecture Group, 1962-64, Universidad Nacional Autonoma de Mexico. Member of the International Council, Museum of Modern Art, New York, since 1970. Exhibitions: Borrowings and Lendings, University of Wisconsin at Milwaukee, 1977; Mexican Architecture of Today, Mexico City, 1978; Master Builders: The Architecture of Mexico, University of California at Los Angeles, 1979. Recipient: Tau Sigma Delta Honor Award, University of New Mexico, Santa Fe, 1983; Copeeche Cobeepea Quelaconechis Award, Oaxaca School of Architecture, Mexico, 1983. Distinguished Honorary Fellow, Mexican Society of Architects, 1978. Honorary Fellow, American Institute of Architects, 1979. Address: Ricardo Legorreta Arquitectos, Palacio de Versalles 285-A, Col. Lomas Reforma, Mexico 10, D.F., Mexico.

Works:

1963 Fabricas Automex Chrysler Office Building and Warehouse, Mexico City
1963/
64 Smith, Kline and French Laboratories, Mexico City
1963/
69 Fabricas Automex Chrysler Office Building and Engine Plant, Mexico City
1966 Nissan Mexicana Office and Manufacturing Building, Cuernavaca, Mexico
1966/
68 Celanese Mexicana Office and Laboratory Buildings, Mexico City (with Roberto Jean)
1967 Cedros School, Mexico City
1968 Camino Real Hotel, Mexico City
Plunket House, Mexico City
1970 Pedro de Gante School, Tulancingo, Hidalgo, Mexico
1972 Camino Real Hotel, Cabo San Lucas, Baja California, Mexico
Office building, Insurgentes and Algeciras, Mexico City
Palacio de Iturbide restoration, for the Financiera Banamex, Mexico City
Monumental fountain for Lomas Verdes, Mexico City (project; with Luis Barragán)
1973 Houses, Valle de Bravo, Mexico City
1974/
75 IBM Office Building, Mexico City
1975 IBM Factory, Mexico City
Kodak Mexicana "Mexicolor" Laboratories, Mexico City
Camino Real Hotel, Can Cún, Quintana Roo, Mexico
1976 Urban design and architectural coordination of "El Rosario," for Infonavit, Mexico City
Gomez House, Mexico City
1976/
77 Seguros America Banamex Office Building, Mexico City
1977 Pedro de Gante School expansion, Tulancingo, Hidalgo, Mexico
IBM Technical Center, Mexico City
1978 La Estadia Housing Development and Equestrian Club, Mexico City
1979 Camino Real Hotel, Ixtapa, Guerrero, Mexico
Las Brisas Hotel renovation, Acapulco
Camino Real Hotel expansion, Can Cún, Quintana Roo, Mexico
1980 Lomas Sporting Club, Mexico City
IBM Factory expansion, Guadalajara, Jalisco, Mexico
DESC Office Building, Mexico City
1981 Banamex Office Building, Monterrey, Mexico
Kodak Mexicana Office Building and Warehouse, Mexico City (project)
Jurica New Town Master Plan, Mexico
1982 Banco de Mexico Office Building, Mexico City
Renault Engines Plant, Gomez Palacio, Mexico
1983 Mr. and Mrs. Ricardo Montalban House, Los Angeles
Bunker Hill Development Plan, Los Angeles (with others)
1984 Valle de Bravo Master Plan, Mexico
San Augustin Convent restoration, Veracruz, Mexico
Bahias de Huatulco Master Plan, Oaxaca, Mexico

Publications:

On LEGORRETA: articles—"Forma y Funcion: Legorreta Arquitectos" in Arquitectura (Mexico City), March 1966; "Ricardo Legorreta" in Arquitectura (Mexico City), April/July 1968; "Camino Real" by Victor R. Zevallos in Architectural Forum (New York), November 1968; "Hotel Camino Real, Mexico City" in Architecture: Formes et Fonctions (Lausanne), 1969; "Everyman's Mexican Home" in Progressive Architecture (New York), June 1969; "Hotel Camino Real in Mexico City" in Deutsche Bauzeitung (Stuttgart), February 1970; "La Arquitectura Mexicana en la Industria," special issue of Arquitectura (Mexico City), no. 104, 1971; "The Mexican Minimalism of Ricardo Legoretta" by C. Ray Smith in Architectural Record (New York), October 1976; "Ricardo Legorreta" in Technodomika (Athens), March 1977; "Ferienwohnungen in Mexico" in Baumeister (Munich), May 1977; "Ricardo Legorreta: Mexico's Mexican Architect" by Anthony C. Antoniades in Architecture + Urbanism (Tokyo), no. 4, 1978; "Valle de Bravo" in Arquitectura Mexico (Mexico City), September/October 1978; "House in Valle de Bravo, Mexico" in Summa (Buenos Aires), July 1979; "The Color Language Home" in Los Angeles Times, October 1979; "Week-end house in Valle de Bravo", and "Camino Real Hotel in Can Cun, Mexico" in Architecture Contemporaine (Lausanne, Switzerland), 1980; "Ricardo Legorreta: Mexican Architect in Mexico" in Summarios (Buenos Aires), January 1980; "Ricardo Legorreta" in El Arquitecto Mexicano (Mexico City), February 1980; "Thick, rough, malleable: IBM Technical Center, Mexico City" in Progressive Architecture (New York), September 1980; "Cinque Case Unifamiliari: Casa Gomez" in Abitare (Milan), April 1981; "Gomez House" in GA Houses (Tokyo), May 1981; "Modern Mexican Architecture", special issue of Process: Architecture (Tokyo), July 1983.

*

Postwar architecture in Mexico was an assembly of foreign imitations. Versions of International Style thrived. If it were not for the murals by some of Mexico's most famous artists that were incorporated on the elevations, many of the buildings could be taken to belong anywhere on earth but in Mexico. This was an architecture of the "column culture," the Corbusier pilotis, and a concern for proportional appeal in the elevations. The "wall culture" of native architecture had been totally forgotten by contemporary Mexican architects.

Ricardo Legorreta brought back the "wall culture"; he brought Mexico's contemporary architecture back to Mexico. His work, along with that of Luis Barragán (who, however, did some works in International Style at the beginning of his career), has evolved out of the study and understanding of the values of traditional architecture in Mexico. Its language recognizes the "wall" rather than the "column," the supremacy of solids over voids, the importance of three-dimensional continuity, the use of color to enclose wall space, and the preference for privacy that is to be encountered in Mexican cloisters and haciendas. Legorreta does responsive regional architecture but does not indulge in the imitations and set design techniques of that "Mexican-looking" architecture so abundant in Mexico as well as in Southern California.

The architect of a diverse number of building types, Legorreta is mainly known as the creator of the superb series of Camino Real hotels. The Camino Real in Baja California, a semi-underground complex facing the Pacific, is totally integrated with its landscape. It is energy efficient and is distinguished by the superb quality of its interiors as well as by the ingenious treatment of its exterior grounds.

The Camino Real in CanCún, in the Yucatan Peninsula, is like an ocean liner floating in vast seas. Its linear form, its strong cross-section, and the ingeniously planned sequence of its functions, make it a "vessel of life," one of the most relaxing environments on our planet.

The dream of the city dweller can become reality: Legorreta's hotels are opened to a cross-section of the population. The Camino Real in Mexico City, perhaps the most 'homey' hotel on earth, is an outstanding example of a mixture of moderation and grandeur, and rich and poor are both to be found in the various bars and restaurants of this machine of

Ricardo Legoretta: Camino Real Hotel, Cancun, Mexico, 1975.

integration. The hotel is the Mexico City address of the extravagant American conventioneer; it is also the place where the Mexican worker takes his date. Legorreta's hotels are palaces for everyone, not just monuments to the vanity of the rich. Something of his attitude is suggested in his acknowledgement that he has been influenced by Hassan Fathy's book *Architecture for the Poor*. The Camino Real in Mexico City is also distinguished by a most appealing use of color and by the incorporation of other visual arts, painting and sculpture, as integral parts of the architecture. A huge stabile by Calder and some works by Mathias Goeritz complete the hotel environment, one that eventually becomes a total experience.

The introverted plan of the Camino Real in Mexico City, as well as the strong grey wall that defines the property of the IBM Factory in the same city, very clearly express Legorreta's concern for privacy and the hacienda prototype. His other factories and some of his residential projects are also case studies in response to landscape, interior simplicity, and three-dimensional continuity of interior space.

Legorreta achieves what he does through extremely hard work. By constructing very large scale models during the design stage, he exploits completely the space possibilities of his project.

Legorreta's architecture has been consistently good, and it has evolved because, despite the capital-making nature of his major commissions (hotels,

IBM factories, etc.), he has never regarded architecture as from the perspective of a businessman. He has always remained a dedicated artist. Along with perhaps two other Latins, Ricardo Bofill in Barcelona and Luis Barragán in Mexico City, Legorreta occupies the top place in Spanish-descendant architecture in the world. He is certainly Mexico's Mexican architect.

—Anthony C. Antoniades

LEO, Ludwig.

German. Born in Rostock, 2 September 1924. Educated at the Hochschule für Bildende Künste, Berlin, 1948-54, Dip.Arch. 1954. Married Sheila Leo in 1955; children: Miriam and Morag. Worked in the office of Hans and Wassili Luckhardt, *q.v.*, Berlin, 1953-55. Since 1956, in private practice, Berlin, Professor, Hochschule für Bildende Künste, Berlin, since 1975. Recipient: Baukunst Prize, Berlin Senat, 1969. Address: (office): Fasanenstrasse 72, Charlottenburg, Berlin, West Germany.

Works:

1958 Kindergarten, Loschmidstrasse, Berlin
1959 Eichkamp Students Residence, Berlin (with Müller and Heinrichs)
1962/
63 Sports Hall, Charlottenburg, Berlin
1965 Town Centre, Gropiusstadt, Berlin (competition project)
1966 Town Hall extensions, Zehlendorf, Berlin (competition project)
French Lycée, Berlin (competition project)
Sewage Plant, Marienfelde Building, Berlin (project)
Multi-purpose floating station, on the River Havel, Berlin (project)
1967/
70 Märkisches Viertel Development, Berlin
1969/
72 DLRG (Deutsche Lebens Rettungs Gesellschaft) Multi-Purpose Station, Am Pichelsee, Spandau, Berlin
Circulation Tank, Institute for Waterways and Shipbuilding, Tiergarten, Berlin
School Building, Bielefeld, West Germany (prototype)
Lighting plan for the Kurfürstendamm, Berlin
Rudolf Virchow Hospital extensions, Berlin (project)
Autobahn redevelopment, Rehberge, Berlin (project)

1976   Water Experiment Institute for the Technical
University, Landwehr Canal, Berlin

Publications:

On LEO: books—*German Architecture 1960-1970*
by Wolfgang Pehnt, Stuttgart and London 1970;
Architecktur in Deutschland by H. and M. Bofinger,
J. Paul and H. Klotz, Stuttgart 1979; *Bauen der 70er
Jahre in Berlin* by Rolf Rave, Hans-Joachim Rave
and Jan Rave, Berlin 1980; *Architektur 1940-1980* by
Adolf Max Vogt, Berlin, Frankfurt and Vienna 1980;
Visionary Architecture of the 20th Century by
Vittorio Magnango Lampugnani, Stuttgart and
London 1982; *Das Ende der Zuversicht* by Wolfgang
Pehnt, Berlin 1983; *Moderne und Postmoderne:
Architektur der Gegenwart 1960-1980* by Heinrich
Klotz, Braunschweig, West Germany, and Wies-
baden, West Germany 1984; articles—"Serious
Sport" in *Architectural Review* (London), July 1966;
"Progetti di Ludwig Leo a Berlino" by A. Carlini in
Controspazio (Bari, Italy), November/December
1972; "Ludwig Leo: A Most Unusual Architect" by
Peter Cook and Leon Krier in *Net* (London), 1975;
"Two Buildings by Berlin Architect Ludwig Leo" in
GA Document (Tokyo), Summer 1980; "Unappre-
ciated Architects 3: Ludwig Leo" by Peter Cook in
Architectural Review (London), June 1981.

It is a difficult task to write about the architect
Ludwig Leo. Difficult, because there are no auth-
oritative or interpretative studies that explain his
work and because his buildings and projects do not
correspond to any of the current and well-known
architectural tendencies. In effect, there is no
available frame of reference. We can, however, rely
on the evidence of the work itself. Specialized
knowledge and historical memory are unnecessary,
for there is no formal quotation, no aesthetic
reference to a previous style, model, or even to his
own evolution. Leo is radically unconcerned with
history in his work; each building is a new, striking,
and above all individual formal solution to a
particular problem. If one looks more closely, even
the means toward the expression of function seem
novel, and here we discover the real significance of
Leo's buildings: they modify the otherwise over
riding demands of pure function. The aesthetic and
social aims of the artistic programs of the historical
avant-garde of functionalism-the Bauhaus-
floundered because of the priority given to function.

Since then, function has established itself as an
absolute-and it is this problem that Leo addresses in
his work. The fact that, so far, he has been able to
realize very little is evidence that he continues the
struggle of historical functionalism without wishing
to be involved in its later compromises. Beyond the
trappings of convention, prejudice, and sterotype,
his search has been for the essence of the building
task, the true function required by the client.
Paradoxically, it is usually this contemporary search
for social universality by means of a particular
building task that deters clients.

A building such as the DLRG Station was
completed after a long process of engineering,
involving research into construction, materials,
spatial arrangement, and self-expression, but it fails
to conform to urban and formal context by its radical
reference to its own particular function. Yet,
whatever their effect, DLRG Station and Leo's other
buildings are not elitist—just the opposite. The
precision and intelligence of their functionalism and
their visible "usefulness" suggest another kind of
society, not one of hierarchy and oppression but one
of equality and freedom, a dynamically permeable
society in which things also are liberated so that they
may really work in cooperation with people.

Both in his theorizing and in his work, Leo has
furthered an enlightened thinking about the machine
age. He has worked not only against the decline into
vulgar functionalism but also against the fashions of
rationalism and populism that altogether ignore
function and are preoccupied with the aesthetic shell.
Of course, Leo's desperate struggle is naive in a
deeply human sense, and of necessity, he has worked
in isolation, away from the prevailing architectural
milieu of commercial success. But his failure is
important, because it stimulates, it leads forward.
Most of the work of his successful colleagues, during
a time of architectural crisis, achieves only the
opposite.

—Günther Uhlig

LEONHARDT, Fritz.

German. Born in Stuttgart, 11 July 1909. Educated at
the University of Stuttgart, 1927-31, Dip.Ing. 1931,
D.Eng. 1938; Purdue University, West Lafayette,
Indiana, 1932-33. Married Liselotte Klein in 1936;
children: Sabine, Monika, Heidemarie, Hans-Jorg,

and Christine. Bridge Engineer of the Autobhan in
Stuttgart, Berlin, and Cologne, 1934-38. Since 1938,
in private practice, as consulting engineer, Stuttgart:
in partnership with Wolfhart Andrä as Leonhardt
und Andrä, since 1953. Professor and Director of the
Institute for Concrete Structures, 1958-74, and
Rector (President), 1967-69, University of Stuttgart.
Member, Deutsche Akademie für Städtebau und
Landesplanung, since 1952; Vice-President, Comité
Européen du Béton, since 1971. Exhibition: *German
Architecture Today*, Royal Institute of British
Architects, London, 1955. Recipient: Honor Award,
Verein Deutscher Ingenieure, 1953; Paul Bonatz
Prize, Stuttgart, 1959; Fritz Schumacher Prize, 1961;
Gold Medal, Austrian Engineers and Architects
Association, 1965; Wernervon-Siemens-Ring, 1965;
Emil Mörsche Medal, 1967; Gustave Magnel Gold
Medal, Belgium, 1968; First Prize, Straits of Messina
Bridge Competition, 1969; Grashof Medal, Verein
Deutscher Ingenieure, 1973; Freyssinet Medal,
Fédération Internationale de la Précontrainte, 1974;
Distinguished Service Award, Oregon State Univer-
sity, Corvallis, 1974; Gold Medal, Institution of
Structural Engineers, London, 1975; Distinguished
Service Medal, Baden-Württemberg, West Germany
1976; Gold Medal, Associazione Italiana Cemento
Armato e Precompresso, 1977; Honor Award,
Washington Roadside Council, U.S.A., 1978; Struc-
tural Engineering Award, International Association
for Bridges and Structural Engineering, 1981; Grand
Cross of Merit, Federal Republic of Germany, 1980;
Gold Medal of Merit, City of Vienna, 1982. Dr.Ing.:
Technical University, Braunschweig, West Ger-
many, 1972; Dr.Tech.: Technical University of
Denmark, Lyngby, 1974; Dr.Ing.: Purdue Univers-
ity, West Lafayette, Indiana, 1980; Dr.Ing.: Univers-
ity of Liège, Belgium, 1980. Honorary Member of the
Chamber of Architects of Baden-Württemberg,
West Germany 1974. Honorary Member of the
American Concrete Institute, 1972; First Honorary
Member, Comité Euro-International du Béton,
1977; Honorary Member, International Association
for Bridges and Structural Engineering, 1979;
Academy of Sciences, Heidelberg, West Germany,
1982; Foreign Associate, National Academy of
Engineering, United States, 1983. Address: Leon-
hardt und Andrä, Lenzhalde 16, Postfach 742, 7000
Stuttgart 1, West Germany.

Works:

1935   Sulzbach Viaduct, Denkendorf, Germany, for
the Stuttgart-Ulm Autobahn

1938/
41   Cologne-Rodenkirchen Suspension Bridge,
across the River Rhine

1947/
48   Cologne-Deutz Bridge, across the River Rhine

1949   Bridge across the River Elz, on the Freiburg-
Offenburg Highway, near Emmendingen,
Germany

1950/
51   Heilbronn-Böckingen Bridge, across the
River Neckar, West Germany

1952/
53   Untermarchtal Bridge, across the Danube
Valley, West Germany

1952/
56   North Bridge, across the River Rhine,
Düsseldorf

1954   Ziegelhausen Bridge, across the River Neckar,
near Heidelberg, West Germany

1955/
56   Television Tower, Stuttgart
Indoor Swimming Arena, Wuppertal, West
Germany

1955/
59   Five bridges, crossing the Delta of the Rio
Jacui, near Porto Alegre, Brazil
Bridge across the Rio Guaiba, near Porto
Alegre, Brazil

1957   Bridge across the River Rhone, St. Moritz,
Switzerland

Ludwig Leo: Circulation Tank, Institute for Waterways and Shipbuilding, West Berlin, 1972.

1957/
62 Bayer Building, Leverkusen, Germany
Mannesmann Building, Düsseldorf
1959 Suspension bridge, across the River Tejo, Lisbon (project)
1960/
61 BASF Building, Ludwigshafen, West Germany
1960/
62 Elevated highway, Jan-Wellem-Platz, Düsseldorf (with T. Tamms)
1961 Mono-cable suspension bridge, across the River Rhine, Emmerich, West Germany (project)
Bridge, Port Elizabeth, South Africa
1961/
63 Unilever Building, Hamburg, West Germany
1962 Agnashini Bridge, India
Lapinlahti Bridge, Helsinki (project)
Alvsborgsbridge, near Göteborg, Sweden (project)
1963 Bridge across the River Ager, near Attersee, Austria
1964 Bridge across the Rio Caroni, near San Felix, Venezuela
1965/
68 Heinrich Hertz Telecommunications Tower, Hamburg, West Germany
1967 German Pavilion, *Expo '67*, Montreal (with Frei Otto)
1968 Bridge across the River Inn, Kufstein, Austria
1968/
69 Knie Bridge, across the River Rhine, Düsseldorf
Sechslingspforte Indoor Swimming Arena, Hamburg, West Germany
1969 Bridge over the Straits of Messina, Italy (competition project)
Ravi Bridge, near Lahore, Pakistan
1971 Andarax Bridge, Spain
1972 Roofing for the Sports Arenas, Olympic Games, Munich
Guadalimar Bridge, Spain
1972/
77 Two bridges across the River Parana, near Buenos Aires
1973 Viaduct No. 302, Peripheral Highway, Istanbul
Val Restel Bridge, near Trento, Italy
1975 Viaduct, across the Neckar Valley, near Weitingen, West Germany
1975/
76 Düsseldorf-Oberkassel Bridge, across the River Rhine
1978 Columbia River Bridge, Connecting Pasco and Kennewick, Washington
Bridge across the Gronach Valley, Heilbronn-Nuremberg Autobahn
Geislingen Bridge, across the Kocher Valley, Heilbronn-Nuremberg Autobahn
Allgemeine Rentenanstalt Administration Building, Stuttgart
University of the Federal Army, Hamburg, West Germany
Bridge II across the Rio Caroni, near San Felix, Venezuela
Telecommunications Tower, Frankfurt
Cologne-Deutz Bridge, across the River Rhine
Weittingen Bridge for the Stuttgart-Singen Autobahn, across the Neckar Valley
1979 Marktbreit Bridge for the Würzburg-Ulm Autobahn, across the River Main, West Germany
Weir-structures across the River Rhine, Kehl, West Germany
Telecommunications Tower, Cologne
Telecommunications Tower, Nuremberg
1980 East Huntington Bridge, across the Ohio River, West Virginia, Ohio
Klinikum University, Heidelberg, West Germany
IBM Office Building, Möhringen, Stuttgart
Telecommunications Standard Tower FMT

Fritz Leonhardt: Weittingen Autobahn Bridge across the Neckar Valley, West Germany, 1978.

13, Plettenberg, West Germany
1981 Bridge across the Aich Valley, near Stuttgart
Wieland-Werke AG Office Building, Ulm, West Germany
Wieland-Werke SRP/SRW Hall, Ulm, West Germany
Sunshine Skyway Bridge, Tampa, Florida (project)
1982 Railway Bridge across the River Main, Gemünden, West Germany
Bridge across the Schwarzbach Valley, near Pirmasens, West Germany
Railway Bridge, near Zeitlofs, West Germany
IBM Administration Building, Möhringen, Stuttgart
1983 Werra Valley Bridge, Hedemünden, West Germany
Bridge across the Schattenring, Stuttgart
Railway Bridge, Dittenbrunn, West Germany
Telecommunications Tower FMT 12, Lauterstein, West Germany

Development of several pre-stressing methods for pre-stressed concrete, since 1949; development of the Incremental Launching System, since 1959.

Publications:

By LEONHARDT: books—*Die Gestaltung der Brücken*, with K. Schaechterle, Berlin 1938; *Brücken*, with Paul Bonatz, Königstein, West Germany 1951; *Spannbeton für die Praxis*, Berlin 1955, 3rd edition 1973, English translation as *Prestressed Concrete Design and Construction*, Berlin 1964; *Brücken aus Stahlbeton und Spannbeton* by Emil Mörsch, editor with H. Bay and K. Deiniger, Stuttgart 1958; *Vorlesungen über Massivbau*: volume I, *Grundlagen zur Bemessung im Stahlbetonbau*, with E. Mönnig, Berlin 1973; volume II, *Sonderfälle der Bemessung im Stahlbetonbau*, with E. Mönnig, Berlin 1975; volume III, *Grundlagen zum Bewehren im Stahlbetonbau*, with E. Mönnig, Berlin 1974; volume IV, *Nachweis der Gebrauchsfähigkeit*, Berlin 1976, 1978; volume V, *Spannbeton*, Berlin 1979; and volume VI, *Grundlagen des Massivbrückenbaues*, Berlin 1979; *Ingenieurbau-Bauingenieure gestalten die Umwelt*, Darmstadt, West Germany 1974; *Der Bauingeniuer und seine Aufgaben*, Stuttgart 1980; *Brücken: Ästhetik und Gestaltung/Bridges: Aesthetics and Design*, Stuttgart, London and Cambridge, Massachusetts 1982; *Baumeister in einer umwälzenden Zeit*, Stuttgart 1984.

On LEONHARDT: books—*German Autobahn Bridges*, report by W. Henderson, British Intelligence Objectives Sub-Committee, London c. 1947; *Triumph der Spannweiten* by Hans Wittfoht, Düsseldorf 1972; *Steel Box Girder Bridges*, with introduction by A. W. Merrison, London 1973; *Verkehrsbauten: Brücken, Hochstrassen, Tunnel*, edited by Erwin Beyer and Karl Lange, Düsseldorf 1974; *Cable-Stayed Bridges: Theory and Design* by M. S. Troitsky, London 1977; article—"Footbridge at the Federal Garden Show in Stuttgart" in *Deutsche Bauzeitung* (Stuttgart), July 1977.

*

For all the many bridges, towers, halls, and industrial structures that I have designed, I have always struggled for beauty. In my experience, beauty can only be obtained by observing rules that can be traced to the oldest monuments. Such rules are good proportions between all elements; order by restriction to only a few directions of lines, edges, etc. in space; simplicity and clearness of structural systems; no unnecessary additives; harmonious colours; and scale appropriate to surroundings and to the human senses.

Sometimes slenderness, lightness, and keenness of structures can help to enhance good appearance.

The aesthetic qualities of all that we build are more important for the future of mankind than most of us realize; they have influence on the health of our soul and, therefore, on social peace and human welfare.

—Fritz Leonhardt

*

Fritz Leonhardt is one of the most influential engineers in Germany, and his research and development work have had a considerable effect on the building of bridges and other engineering works throughout the world.

Leonhardt's development of lightweight tracks made of cellular steel plates led to the building of steel girder bridges and later to the first steel beams for steel bridges. In order to construct large viaducts—such as the Sulzbach Viaduct at Denkendorf and the Neckar Viaduct at Weitingen—he introduced the use of slender steel supports, and so created transparent and filigree-like valley crossings that could be easily integrated into the landscape according to scale. In 1934, at the start of his career in bridge building, it was customary to use statically-determined single-span beams. It took great strength of conviction and perseverance to replace the multi-span girders with a largely continuous construction that had no expansion joints. It was in the 1950s that Leonhardt's bridge over the Hochstrasse in Dusseldorf spanned thirty eight support openings without a joint; today, these jointless constructions are generally accepted in Germany as well as in many parts of the world.

Leonhardt's research on aerodynamically stable suspension bridges began in 1950. He replaced the gigantic trussed reinforcing girders of the earlier American suspension bridges with slender, aerodynamically-formed carriageway slabs, and achieved wind stability without any bracing struts. These developments were based on experiments carried out in the wind tunnel at the National Physical Laboratory at Teddington, near London. The first pioneering projects for this kind of suspension bridge—such as the Tejo Bridge at Lisbon and the Rhine Bridge at Emmerich—came too early for their time; they were too avant-garde to be adopted. It was left to other engineers, inspired by Leonhardt, to take up his ideas in the suspension bridges across the Severn, the Bosphorus, and the Humber. The knowledge and experience gained thereby led to the development of improved cross sections for slanting cable bridges, and Leonhardt's trials for the Parana bridges resulted in an aerodynamic stability for slanting multi-cable bridges through systematic shock absorption. For the bridge over the Straits of Messina, he suggested and executed a slanting cable bridge of 1500 metre span width.

In his conversation and in his lectures, Leonhard often reminds one of his architect father, whom he talks of as his first teacher and the one who first showed him how to observe. Later guiding spirits were the engineers Freyssinet and Maillart and the architect Paul Bonatz. Architects and engineers alike have influenced his achievements, and it is not surprising that he feels strongly about the need for cooperation between them. He has always passed on to his engineering students a necessary understanding of the work of the architect. It has been his concern to make these two professionally autonomous-groups work as one team. This is not to say that he trained engineers who dabbled in architecture or that he wanted architects to act as if they were engineers. He advocates an arrangement in which the engineer is a specialist with a particular responsibility and the architect is the general practitioner with an overview of the project.

Leonhardt has practiced this concept in his daily work. He was the engineer in charge of the German Pavilion at *expo '67* in Montreal and of the Olympic tent constructions in Munich. His design for television/communications towers have influenced the buildings of such towers throughout the world: the best example of his work is the impressive and original television tower in Stuttgart, the first concrete tower with a revolving restaurant—an entirely convincing structure, due to its genuine and uncluttered form. In high-rise blocks, Leonhardt, at an early stage, used the idea of incorporating lifts and staircases in cores and of regarding them—also from the statistical point of view—as stressed towers with boxed sections restrained in the foundations; examples are the BASF building in Ludwigshafen and the Mannesmann Building in Düsseldorf. The idea inspired engineers and architects in the United States to design the external walls of skyscrapers as hollow boxed sections, as in the World Trade Center in New York and the Hancock Building in Chicago.

Leonhardt is one of the great engineers of his time, continuing the line of such renowned figures as Freyssinet, Maillart, and Pier Luigi Nervi, Franz Dischinger, Felix Candela, and Ulrich Finsterwalder. Broadly educated, Leonhardt has been concerned to approach problems from all aspects—in professional practice, in his teaching, in his writings, in his sense of vocation, and in the breadth of his general knowledge as well as professional expertise. He once said that he feels committed to "well-being and beauty," and that, "just as no teacher, lawyer, or sociologist should do so, so too no engineer should any longer be allowed to go out into his profession without at least having come to certain basic convictions about the worth and existence of beauty and its relation to man."

—Kurt Ackermann

LE PLASTRIER, Richard.

Australian. Born in Melbourne, Victoria, 7 November 1939. Educated at the University of Sydney School of Architecture, under Lloyd Rees, 1958-63 (Board of Architects Fellowship and Prize), B.Arch. 1963; Kyoto University Foreign Students' Group, under Tomoya Masuda, *q.v.*, 1966-67. Architect with Clark, Gazzard and Yeomans, Sydney, 1963-64; Jørn Utzon, *q.v.*, Sydney, 1964-66, Kenzo Tange *q.v.*, and Urtec, Tokyo, 1967-68, and Lobb and Partners, London, 1969-70. Since 1971, in private practice, Sydney. Part-time Architect/Tutor, University of Sydney, 1971-78. Address: "Sitting Pretty," Lovett Bay, via Church Point, New South Wales 2105, Australia.

Works:

1961 Changing shed and toilets, Castlecrag Boatshed, Sydney
1963 Halford House, 26 Corniche Road, Church Point, New South Wales
1969/
70 Motorway Service Areas, Hartshead Moor, Killington, and Membury, England (competition projects; with Brian Leather)
1972/
78 Buddhist Meditation Retreat, Cliff Drive, Katoomba, New South Wales
1973/
74 Spencer House, Lovett Bay, near Sydney
1973/
78 Walker House, 4 The Serpentine, Bilgola Beach, near Sydney
1974 High Court of Australia (competition project; with Lawrence Nield)
1974/
75 Paludan House, Gilwinga Drive, Bayview Heights, near Sydney
1976/
78 Craigie House, Wyong Creek Road, Yarramolong Valley, near Wyong, New South Wales (with David Jacobson)
1978/
79 Hebden House, Lovett Bay, near Syndey (project)
Housing, Bathurst, New South Wales (competition project; with Stephen Wells)
Sussman House, Cammeray, near Sydney (with J. Simpson)
1981 System Built Timber House, Hobart Botanical Gardens, Tasmania (prototype; with H. Brunetts, G. Calgorno, S. Ludyk, G. Methe, and A. Sutherland)
1982 House on Never Never River, Gleniffer via Bellinger, New South Wales (with Henk Mulder)
1983 Craigie House extensions, Wyong Creek Road, Yarramolong Valley, near Wyong, New South Wales (with J. Simpson)
1984 Painting Studio, Never Never House, Bellinger, New South Wales
Twenty-foot sailing boat (with shipwright B. Keir)
Roof Garden and Shade Canopy, Elizabeth Bay, Sydney (with G. Blumer and F. Lindsay)
1985 Worker's Cottage extensions, Paddington, New South Wales
Federation Memorial, Centennial Park, Sydney (competition project; with K. Lambert, P. Stutchbury, and R. Stutchbury)

Publications:

By LE PLASTRIER: article—"Utzon's approach to the Sydney Opera House," with Peter Myers, in *Architect* (Melbourne), June/July 1983.

On LE PLASTRIER: article—"Gateway to More" by Col James in *Architecture Bulletin* (Sydney), no. 1/2, 1982.

*

After graduating from the University of Sydney, Richard Le Plastrier worked with Don Gazzard and then in Jørn Utzon's Sydney office. From 1966 to 1970, he travelled extensively in Southeast Asia, the Middle East, and Europe. He studied with Professor Masuda at Kyoto University and worked in Kenzo Tange's office on the Kuwait Stadium project.

Le Plastrier's architectural language exploits the confrontation of opposites as a means of generating an architectural dialectic and synthesis. Thus, his buildings involve a series of contradictions; they are at once romantic and rational, rich in landscape values and highly engineered, primitive and advan-

Richard Le Plastrier and Henk Mulder: Never Never River House, Bellinger, New South Wales, 1982.

ced, soft and hard, and warm and cold. This pervasive complementarism explains the subtlety, richness, and hidden strength of his formal architectural language. He has also made extensive use of corrugated iron formed into elegant barrel-vault or combined segmental and planar profiles for the roofs of his houses.

Each house by Le Plastrier is important, even when, as in the Paludan House in Bayview Heights, his intentions have not been realized fully, because he invests much time and thought in their design and construction. The Walker House at Bilgola Beach is one of the most significant postwar Australian buildings. It consists of two corrugated, copper barrel-vaulted pavilions connected at the rear by a rammed earth wall and linear circulation/service space, facing onto a magnificent tropical garden.

—Philip Drew

LESCAZE, William.

American. Born in Geneva, Switzerland, 27 March 1896; emigrated to the United States, 1923. Educated at the College de Geneve, 1910-14; Ecole des Beaux-Arts, Geneva, 1914-15; E.T.H: Eldgeñossische Technische Hochschule, Zürich, under Karl Moser, 1915-19, M.A. 1919. Married Mary Hughes; son: Lee Adrian. Worked in the war devastated areas of France, and in the office of Henri Sauvage, Paris, 1919-20; worked for Hubbell and Benes, Cleveland, Ohio, 1921-22, and in the office of Walter R. MacCormack, Cleveland, Ohio, 1922; in private practice, New York, 1923-29; Partner, with George Howe, q.v., Howe and Lescaze, Philadelpia, 1929-34; Principal, William Lescaze and Associates, New York, 1934 until his death, 1969. Member, New York State Building Code Commission, 1949-59. Exhibitions: *Third Annual Decorative Art Exhibition*, Wanamaker's Gallery of Decorative Art, New York, 1925; *Art in Industry*, Macy's Department Store, New York, 1928; *Modern Architecture*, Museum of Modern Art, New York, 1932; *Contemporary American Industrial Art*, Metropolitan Museum of Art, New York, 1934; *Built in U.S.A., 1932-1944*, Museum of Modern Art, New York, 1944; Artictectural Association, London, 1976 (one-man); Institute for Architecture and Urban Studies, New York, and Syracuse University, New York, 1982-83 (one-man). Collection: William Lescaze Archive, Syracuse University, New York. Fellow, American Institute of Architects. *Died* (in New York) *9 February 1969.*

Works:

1919 Theatre, Zürich (thesis project)
      Community House, La Chaux de fonds, Switzerland (project; with Edouard Calanne)

1920 Housing reconstruction, Arras, France
1923 Simeon Ford House additions and renovations, Sutton Square, New York
      Board of Education Warehouse, Cleveland, Ohio
      Willow Garden Restaurant renovations, Brooklyn, New York
1926 Lescaze Apartment interiors, East 42nd Street, New York
1927 Capital Bus Terminal, New York
      Soldiers' and Sailors' Memorial, Providence, Rhode Island (competition project)
      League of Nations Building, Geneva (competition project)
1927/
28 Colfax Phillips Apartment interiors, New York
      Jean de Sieyres Hunting Lodge, Mount Kisco, New York
1928 Maison Bertie Beauty Parlor interiors, Fifth Avenue, New York
      Andrew Geller Shoe Factory Showroom, Brooklyn, New York
      Frederick Loeser company Permanent Exhibit, Broooklyn, New York
      Apartment Building, Park Avenue/72nd Street, New York (project)
      Apartment House and Garage, Broadway/50-51st Streets, New York (project)
      The Future American Country House (project)
      Penthouse Studio, *Macy's International Exhibition of Art in Industry*, New York

President's Room, Amos Parrish and Company, New York
1929 Dreyfus Apartment, New York
Howe and Lescaze Office, Philadelphia (with George Howe)
Ingersoll Museum, Pennlyn, Montgomery County, Pennsylvania (project; with George Howe)
Oak Lane Country Day School, Second Street and Oak Lane Road, Philadelphia (demolished)
William Strix Wasserman Office, Philadelphia (with George Howe)
Wasserman House II, Whitemarsh, Pennsylvania (project; with George Howe)
Mrs. Leopold Stowkowski Apartment, New York
1930 Ben Herzberg Apartment, New York
C. Phillips Apartment, New York
Porter House, Ojai, California
1930/
31 Museum of Modern Art, New York (project: preliminary designs; with George Howe)
1931 Hattie Carnegie Shop, New York
Headmaster's House (Curry House), Dartington Hall, Totnes, Devon, England
Hessian Hills School, Mt. Airy Road, Croton-on-Hudson, New York (with George Howe; later remodelled; now part of a synagogue complex)
Philadelphia Saving Fund Society Office Building, 12th and Market Streets, Philadelphia (with George Howe)
Trans-Lux Theatre, New York
Emigrant Savings Bank and Office Building, East 42nd Street, New York (project; with George Howe)
Peck House, Paoli, Pennyslvania (project)
Wertheim House, Cos Cob, Connecticut (project)
Charles Harding Apartment, New York
1931/
32 Frederick V. Field House, New Hartford, Connecticut (with George Howe)
Philadelphia Saving Fund Society Garage, 12th and Filbert Streets, Philadelphia (with George Howe)
Housing development, Chrystie-Forsyth Streets, New York (project; with George Howe)
1932 Belmont-Lincoln Hotel, Park Avenue and 42nd Street, New York (project)
50 small houses (project; with George Howe)
Storefront, Dorothy Gray, New York (project)
Amos Parrish and Company Office Building, New York (project)
Wilbour Library, Brooklyn Museum, New York
1933 Auditorium, Connecticut college, New London, Connecticut (project)
1934 Lescaze House, 211 East 48th Street, New York
1935 Brooklyn Children's Museum, New York (project)
1936 High School, Ansonia, Connecticut
Brooklyn Children's Museum, New York (revised project)
1937 Administration Building, Kimble Glass Company, Vineland, New Jersey
Williamsburg Houses, Brooklyn, New York (with others)
1938 Cherry Lawn School, Connecticut
CBS Radio Building, Hollywood, California (with E.T. Heitschmid)
1939 Aeronautics Pavilion, World's Fair, New York
Swiss Pavilion, World's Fair, New York
1941 Longfellow Building, Washington, D.C.
House, 124 East 70th Street, New York
1946 Eliott House, New York
1949 Calderone theatre, Hempstead, Long Island, New York
1950 Medical Center, Crosset, Arkansas

Harbor Homes Development, Port Washington, Long Island, New York
Spinney Hill Homes Development, Manhasset, Long Island, New York
1951 India Exchange Ltd. Offices, Calcutta
1954 Dune Deck Hotel, Westhampton Beach, Long Island, New York
1955 Houses, Salamanca, New York (project)
Offices, 711 Third Avenue, New York
1956 Laurel Homes Development, Roslyn, Long Island, New York
1958 Offices, 30 West Broadway, New York
1959 Chancellery, Swiss Embassy, Washington, D.C.
1960 Civil and Municipal Courthouse, Centre Street and White Street, New York (with Matthew Del Gaudio)
Manhattanville Residences, New York
The Churchill Apartments, Los Angeles
1961 School of Art and Design, New York
1963 "Christian Peace" Building and Chapel, United Nations, New York
Offices, 300 East 42nd Street, New York
1964 First National City Bank Pavilion, World's Fair, New York
Offices, 777 Third Avenue, New York
1969 One New York Plaza, Water, Whitehall, South and Broad Streets, New York

Publication:

By LESCAZE books—A Modern Museum, with George Howe, Springdale, Connecticut 1930; Architecture for the New Theatre, with others, edited by Edith J. R. Isaacs, New York 1935; The Intent of the Artist, with others, Princeton, New Jersey 1941; On Being an Architect, New York 1942; A Citizens' Country Club or Leisure Centre, New York 1944; Uplifting the Downtrodden, New York 1944; articles—"The Classic of Tomorrow" in American Architect (New York), December 1935; "A Community Theatre" in Architecture for the New Theatre, New York 1935; "America's Outgrowing Imitation of Greek Architecture" in Architectural Record (New York), August 1937; "The Meaning of Modern Architecture" in North American Review (Cedar Falls, Iowa), Autumn 1937; "Why Modern Architecture" in Royal Architectural Institute of Canada Journal (Toronto), 1937; "Marginal Notes on Architecture" in Virginia Quarterly Review (Charlottesville), Spring 1939; article in Pencil Points (New York), July 1940; "These Documents Called Buildings" in The Intent of the Artist, Princeton, New Jersey 1941; "New York State Building Code Commission: Aims and Accomplishments" in Architectural Record (New York), June 1951; "The Correlation of the Arts" in AIA Journal (Washington, D.C.), November 1952; "Another Look at PSFS" in Architectural Forum (New York), June 1964; "Thoughts on Art and Architecture" in Art International (Zürich), February 1968.

On LESCAZE: books—The New Interior Decoration by Dorothy Todd and Raymond Mortimer, New York 1929; New World Architecture by Sheldon Cheney, New York 1930; Modern Architecture: International Exhibition catalogue by Alfred Barr, Henry Russell Hitchcock and others, New York 1932; Twentieth-Century Houses by Raymond McGrath, London 1934; The Modern House in America by James Ford and Katherine Morrow Ford, New York 1940; Dartington Hall by Victor Bonham-Carter, London 1958; American Buildings and Their Architects, vol 4, by William Jordy, New York 1972; Depression Modern— The Thirties Style in America by Martin Greif, New York 1975; William Lescaze, Architect, thesis by Lorraine Welling Lenmon, University of Delaware 1979; William Lescaze by Christian Hubert and Lindsay Stamm Shapiro, New York 1982; articles—"The Future American Country House" in Architectural Record

(New York), November 1928; "City House of William Lescaze, New York" in Architectural Forum (New York), December 1934; "The Proposed Children's Museum, Brooklyn" in American Architect (New York), December 1935; "CBS Broadcasting Studios, Hollywood, California" in Architectural Forum (New York), June 1938; "Longfellow Building, Washington, D.C." in Architectural Forum (New York), June 1941; "Steel House, Factory-Built in Seven Pieces" in Architectural Forum (New York), December 1949; "Multi-Family Housing" in Architectural Record (New York), June 1954; "Proposed City and Municipal Courts" in Architectural Record (New York), December 1955; "Genetrix: Personal Contributions to American Architecture" in Architectural Review (London), May 1957; "Philadelphia Saving Fund Society Buildng: Its Development and Significance in Modern Architecture" by William Jordy and "Philadelphia Saving Fund Society Building: Beaux Arts Theory and Rational Excpressionism" by Robert A.M. Stern in Journal of the Society of Architectural Historians (Philadelphia), May 1962; "Philadelphia Saving Fund Society Building" by Henry Wright in Architectural Forum (New York), May 1964; "William Lescaze, Architect, Dies" in The New York Times, 10 February 1969; "Obituary: William Lescaze" in Architectural Forum (New York), March 1969; "Lescaze" by Agnoldomenico Pica in Domus (Milan), July 1969; "William Lescaze: sa carriere et son oeuvre de 1915 a 1939" by Gilles Barbey in Werk (Zürich), August 1971; "Lescaze and Dartington Hall" by Lawrence Wodehouse in Architectural Association Quarterly (London), vol. 8, no. 2, 1976; "The sky's the limit" by Lawrence Wodehouse in Building Design (London), 15 October 1976.

Bibliography—William Lescaze, 1896-1969 by Lamia Doumato, Monticello, Illinois 1982.

William Lescaze, born in Geneva, Switzerland in 1896, spent most of his life in the United States, where he is remembered as one of the first Europeans to carry the gospel of the modern movement across the Atlantic. Following general schoolng at the College de Geneve, he took his architectural training at the Technische Hochschule in Zürich, where he worked under Karl Moser, an early advocate of modernism and one of the central forces in Lescaze's life.

In 1919 and 1920 Lescaze worked in areas of France devasted by World War I, and did a tour of duty in the Paris office of another pioneer modernist, Henri Sauvage. Early on he developed a yearning to design monumental architecture, a passion which contributed to his decision to emigrate to America in 1923. Employment proved difficult to find in New York, however, and he moved to Cleveland for what turned out to be no more than a six-month stint with Hubbell and Benes, a firm of conservative tastes. He returned to New York late in 1925.

At that time America as a whole had little sympathy for, and less knowledge of, avant-garde European architecture. Lescaze found himself producing work, mostly commercial and residential interiors, in the electric manners of the day. Following a number of projects done more or less after the Art Deco style, Lescaze designed a strikingly modern and experimental penthouse studio for R.H. Macy Company's International Exhibition of Art in Industry in 1928. The following year he met the Philadelphia architect George Howe, with whom he was destined to do his most important work. Howe was then moving closer and closer to modernism himself, and he wanted to form a partnership with someone who knew and stood for the principles of the International Style. Lescaze seemed to be that man. The firm of Howe and Lescaze was begun in May of 1929.

The most significant fruit of this relationship was the majestic Philadelphia Savings Fund Society Building of 1931, which Howe had sketched out before he met Lescaze but to which Lescaze contributed several important refinements. Howe's plan had been at first symmetrical, influenced by Beaux-Arts tradition; Lescaze changed this to an informal organization more in keeping with modernist ideas. The result has been called the first American sky-scraper in the International Style.

Howe and Lescaze broke up their partnership in 1934, after which Lescaze worked mostly on his own. In his later years he vacillated betwen a form of streamlined moderne (e.g., the CBS Radio Building in Hollywood, California, designed with E.T. Heitschmid, 1937-38) and a manner nearer that of the International Style (e.g., the Longfellow Building, Washington, D.C., 1941). He continued practicing after World War II but ceased to be a figure of prominence, and a little notice was taken of hius death in 1969.

—Franz Schulze

LEVI, Rino.

Brazilian. Born in Sao Paulo, 31 December 1901. Educated at primary and secondary schools in Sao Paulo; Academy of Fine Arts, Milan, 1921-22; School of Architecture, Rome, 1923-26, Dip.Arch. 1926. Married Yvonne Theodora Arié in 1933; daughter: Barbara. In private practice in Sao Paulo from 1927: in partnership with Robert Cerqueira Cesar from 1941 and with L.R. Carvalho Franco from 1952 (firm constituted as Rino Levi Arquitetos Associates Ltda., 1965, and continues under the direction of Cerqueira Cesar and Carvalho Franco). Consultant, Interamerican Centre for Housing, Bogota, Colombia, 1957. Professor of Architecture and Urbanism, University of Sao Paulo, 1954-59; Visiting Professor of Architecture and Urbanism,

University of Caracas, Venezuela, 1959. President, Brazilian Institute of Architects, Sao Paulo, 1954-59. Member of CIAM (Congrès Internationaux d'Architecture Moderne), from 1945. Exhibitions: *Bienal Hispano America*. Madrid 1951; Pan American Congress of Architecture, Mexico City, 1952, Washington, D.C., 1965. Recipient: First Prize, Santo André Civic Centre Competition, 1956; First Prize, Albert Einstein Hospital Competition, Sao Paulo, 1957. Honorary Member, Sociedad Colombiana de Arquitectos, 1957, Sociedad Central de Arquitectos, Argentina, 1958, Sociedad de Arquitectos, Mexico, 1960; Honorary Fellow, American Institute of Architects, 1965. *Died*(in Sao Paulo) *29 September 1965.*

Works:

1932 Columbus Apartment Building, Sao Paulo
1935 Do Chá Viaduct, Sao Paulo
1936 Cine UFA Movie Theatre, Sao Paulo
1938 Porchat Building, Sao Paulo
1939 I.A.P.I. Office Building, Sao Paulo
1941 Hotel Excelsior and Ipiranga Cinema Building, Sao Paulo
      Saedes Sapientiae Girls' School, Sao Paulo
1943 Cultura Artística Theatre, Sao Paulo
      Trussardi Building, Sao Paulo
      Stig Building, Sao Paulo
      Companhia Jardim Coffee Processing Plant, Sao Paulo
1944 Rino Levi House, Sao Paulo
      Prudencia Apartment Building, Sao Paulo
1945 Maternity Hospital, University of Sao Paulo (project; with R. Cesar)
1947 Banco Paulista do Comercio Buildding, Sao Paulo
      Central Institute for Cancer Diseases, Sao Paulo

1948 Sao Paulo Chapter Headquarters of the Brazilian Institute of Architects
1950 Gomes House, Sao Jose dos Campos, Sao Paulo
      Cruzada Pro-Infancia Children's Hospital, Sao Paulo
1951 Milton Guper House, Sao Paulo
1952 Industrial workers' housing, Sao José dos Campos, Sao Paulo
1953 Paulo Hess House, Sao Paulo
1956 Copana Parking Garage, Rio de Janeiro (with Luis Roberto Carvalho Franco)
      America Parking Garage, Sao Paulo
      Electrocloro Engineers' Housing, Rio Grande, Brazil
      Paulista Biological Laboratory, Sao Paulo
      Concordia Office Building, Sao Paulo
1957 Master plan for Brasilia (competition project)
1958 Castor Delgado Perez House, Sao Paulo
      Albert Einstein Hospital, Sao Paulo
1959 R. Monteiro Office Building, Sao Paulo
1961 Plavinil-Elcror Building, Sao Paulo
1962 Social Centre, University of Sao Paulo
      Banco Itau America Building, Sao Paulo
1963 Parahyba Milk Plant, Sao José dos Campos, Sao Paulo
1964 Gravatá Apartment Building, Sao Paulo
1965 Tecelagem Parahyba Hangar, Sao José dos Campos, Sao Paulo
      Araucaria Apartment Building, Sao Paulo
      Civic Centre, Santo André, Brazil

Publications:

By LEVI: articles—"The Parking Problem in Sao Paulo" in *Acropole* (Sao Paulo), no. 207, 1950; "The Via 4th Congress" in *Acropole* (Sao Paulo), no. 203, 1955; "Research in Hospital Planning" in *Acropole* (Sao Paulo), no. 204, 1955; "Architects and Pro-

Rino Levi: Santo Andre Civic Centre, Brazil, 1965.

fessional Regulations" in *Bem Estar* (Sao Paulo), no. 4, 1959; "The Role of Acoustics in Architecture" in *Engenharia Municipal* (Sao Paulo), no. 22, 1961.

On LEVI: books—*The Architectural Record Book of Commercial Buildings*. New York 1953; *Selezione Mondiale di Edilizia Ospedalieri* by Augusto Moral, Turin 1954; *Latin American Architecture since 1945* by Henry-Russell Hitchcock, New York 1955; *Garten und Haus* by Julius Hoffmann, Stuttgart 1956; *Modern Architecture in Brazil* by Henrique Mindlin, Rio de Janeiro and London 1956; *L'Architettura Moderna in Brazile* by Sergio Bracco, Milan 1967; *Diccionario da Arquitectura Brasileira* by E. Corona and C. Lemos, Sao Paulo 1972; *L'Architecture Moderne au Brésil* by Yves Bruand, Lille 1973; *Rino Levi*, Milan 1974; *Diccionario de la Arquitectura* by Gerd Hatje, Barcelona 1975; *Profile of the New Brazilian Art* by Pietro Maria Bardi, Rio de Janeiro 1975; *Arquitetura no Brasil: depoimentos* by Abelardo de Souza, Sao Paulo 1978; article—"Una Nuova Dignidad al Habitat" by Bruno Alfieri in *Zodiac* (Milan), no. 6, 1960; "Modern Brazilian Architecture", special issue of *Process: Architecture* (Tokyo), August 1980.

Throughout his career Rino Levi was particularly concerned to maintain a correct professional attitude within the reality of the milieu in which he worked. His work always maintained its excellence despite the enormous pressures exerted by real estate speculation in Sao Paulo, the city where most of it was built. His constant concern with ecology influenced a generation of younger architects and his work helped to focus the search for integration of inside and outside spaces.

In his first works in the late 1930's—the Columbus Apartment Building, the UFA Movie Theatre, and the Porchat Building—the mass is worked in a manner close to expressionism, opposing full and empty, light and dark, indentations and juttings. (They are all buildings of some excellence, compared to the usual work of that period.) Then, progressively, the mass is simplified, losing this sculpture-like quality, and the surfaces flatten out, as in the Trussardi and Stig buildings of 1943. In the Banco Paulista do Comercio Building of 1947, the pure geometry of the glass tower is subtly broken by the curving of one facade, by the jutting-out of the floor slabs, and by the set-back and the glass-brick wall on the ground floor.

This language is further developed in the Headquarters for the Sao Paulo Chapter of the Brazilain Institute of Architects, in the Concordia Building, and in the Banco Itau Building: it forms one of the distinct currents in Levi's work and is characterized by an apparently meaningless contradiction in the articulation of some architectural elements—a "contradiction" that is the means by which he signals the different functions and the constructive hierarchy of the building.

In the Brazilian Institute of Architects Headquarters the curtain wall is fractioned in the same way as in the Banco do Comercio Building, and the prism is further interrupted by the insertion of the twisted volume of the restaurant on the 2nd and 3rd floors. In the Concordia Building the interplay of the "brise-soleil," the hollowed-out elements, and the glazed areas adds an unexpected depth and ambiguity to the facades, enlivening the box-like volume of the building. Banco Itau, a late work—in a phase that was discreetly brutalistic in other, more typical, cases—is an excellent example of the slab-and-tower typology in the tradition of the Lever Building of Skidmore, Owings and Merrill. Its connection with the syntax is in a contradictory fragility that seems to deny the solidity of the volumes. The blocks seem to hover, the facades barely touching one another, and the kinetic quality of the aluminum "brise-soleil" underlines a certain immateriality of the whole.

Another and parallel current in Rino Levi's work, no less involved in the expression of functions but heavier in aspect, encompasses such distinct works as the Companhia Jardim Coffee Processing Plant, all of his hospitals, the Paulista Biological Laboratory, and the Civic Center of Santo André.

The hospitals are all planned on the same principle of sheltering different activities in separate blocks. The complex relationship of the various units sometimes fails to produce a successful whole, but the technical and functional solutions proposed are always paradigmatic. The Santo André Civic Center is the last and the largest of Rino Levi's works. It comprises three different buildings—the City Hall, the Council Chamber, and the Cultural Center. The architectural language is very simple, plastically defined by the clear and sober design of the exposed concrete structure, and particularized in each instance by the functional distinctions of each building. The horizontal "brise-soleil" reinforce the grid of the structure and create planes of light and shadow that lend depth to the facades.

From the 1940's onwards Rino Levi's work also shows a growing concern for the specific conditions of the environment in which he built. This concern can take the simple form of providing adequate sun protection for an over-exposed facade or it can involve the whole project in a much more profound way. In the Rino Levi, Milton Guper, Paulo Hess, and Delgado Perez houses, the theme of inside/outside integration is developed in such a way as to create some of the most important propositions so far devised in urban domestic architecture for subtropical climates. The gardens, in a determining relationship with the house, either isolate the house from the street by merging it with the public space or they extend it by extending the rooms—shadowed, intimate, protected by walls and pergolas, directly connected to the inside through large openings that allow for a pleasant interflow of space.

In the Sedes Sapientiae Girls School, in addition to the light-modulating devices, there is a careful balance between open and built areas. The undulating marquee surrounding and crossing the garden becomes an intermediary zone and connects the blocks of classrooms, bedrooms, and the auditorium. There is a similar distribution at the Parahyba Milk Plant.

Rino Levi's office is still one of the most important in Brazil, and since his death in 1965 his partners, Roberto Cerqueira Cesar, Luis Roberto Carvalho Franco, and, since 1972, Paulo Julio Valentino Bruna, have continued to turn out large scale projects such as the Industries Federation Building, the Siemens Headquarters, and the Gessy-Lever Cosmetics Plant.

—Jorge Czajkowski

LEWERENTZ, Sigurd.

Swedish. Born at the Sandö Glass Works, Bjärtrå, near Sundsvall, Sweden, 29 July 1885. Educated at the School of Building, Chalmers Technical College, Gothenburg, 1905-08; Academy of Arts, Stockholm, 1910; with six fellow students left the Academy and founded the Free School of Architecture, Stockholm, with Carl Westman, Ragnar Östberg, Ivar Tengbom and Carl Bergsten as teachers, 1910-11. Married Edit Engblad in 1911; children: Per, Ewa and Carl. Worked in the office of Bruno Möhring, Berlin, 1907-08, Theodor Fischer, Munich, 1909, and Richard Riemerschmid, Munich, 1910; in partnership with Torsten Stubelius, Stockholm, 1911-17; in private practice, Stockholm, 1917-43, Eskilstuna, Sweden, 1943-58, Skanör, Sweden, 1958-70, and in Lund, Sweden, 1970 until his death, 1975. Founder Director (with Claës Kreüger, 1928-35), Idesta Metal Window Company, Stockholm, 1928-40, and Eskilstuna, Sweden, 1940-75. Exhibitions: Architecture School, Aarhus, Denmark, 1969; Swedish Museum of Architecture, Stockholm, 1969. Recipient: First Prize, with Gunnar Asplund, Stockholm South (Woodland) Cemetery Competition, 1914; First Prize, with Osvald Almqvist, Jönköping Redevelopment Competition, Sweden 1928. *Died* (in Lund) *29 December 1975*.

Works:

1911 Building plan for the Marma Works, Söderhamn, Sweden (project)

1913 Holiday houses, Kummelnäs, near Stockholm
Chinese Garden Pavilion, Drottningholm, Stockholm

1913/
14 Assembly Rooms, Fare Glassworks, Sibbhult, Sweden (with Torsten Stubelius)

1914 Development plan for Brantevik, Sweden
Chapel, Forsbacka, Sweden (with Torsten Stubelius)
Crematorium, Hälsingborg, Sweden (project: with Torsten Stubelius)
Ahxner House, Djursholms-Ösby, Sweden
Ramen House, Hälsingborg, Sweden
Plan for the Stockholm South (Woodland) Cemetery, Stockholm (with Gunnar Asplund)

1914/
15 Workers housing, Forsbacka, Sweden

1917 Shop, Marma, Sweden (project)
Plan for Götaplasten Square, Gothenburg (competition project)

1917/
18 Eneborg Housing Estate, Hälsingborg, Sweden (with Torsten Stubelius)

1920/
25 Burial Chapel, Valdemarsvik, Sweden

1920/
58 Eastern Cemetery, Malmo

1926 Chapel of the Resurrection, Woodland Cemetery, Stockholm

1928 Plan for the redevelopment of 3 blocks in Jönköping, Sweden (4 competition projects; with Osvald Almqvist)
Katarina Secondary School, Stockholm (competition project; with Osvald Almqvist)

1929 Tombstone, Utterö Island, Stockholm Archipelago

1929/
58 Industrial development, Skoghall, Sweden

1930 House, apartment, small pavilions, furniture, 3 coaches for General Motors, and official exhibition sign and posters, *Stockholm Exhibition*

1931 Filips Tea-Rooms, Regeringsgatan, Stockholm
Town plan for Stockholm (with Osvald Almqvist)
National Insurance Building, Adolf Fredriks Kyrkogata, Stockholm
Burial Chapel, Enhöping, Sweden

1932 Museum, Malmo (competition project; with Osvald Almqvist)
Marabou Shop-front, Gothenburg

1932/
44 Municipal Theatre, Malmo (with D. Hellden and E. Lallerstedt)

1933 Villas, Djursholm, Sweden (project)
Johannesberg Church, Gothenburg (competition project)

1935 Burial Chapel and Crematorium, Djursholm, Sweden (project)

1936 Edstrand House, Falsterbo, Sweden
Karolinska Institutet, Stockholm (competition project)

1938/
45 Chapel, Eastern Cemetery, Malmo

1939 New National Insurance Buildings, Gärdet, Stockholm (project)

1943 Crematorium, Eastern Cemetery, Malmo
Lewerentz Apartment, Eskilstuna, Sweden

1946/
62 Cathedral restoration, Uppsala (competition projects; developed with Peter Celsing)

1956/
   60 St. Mark's Church, Skarpnäck, Stockholm
1958 Lewerentz House/Office conversion, Skanör, Sweden
1966 St. Petri Church, Klippan, Sweden
1969 Service Building, Eastern Cemetery, Malmo (with Bernt Nyberg)
1970/
   71 House of Parliament, Stockholm (competition project; with Bernt Nyberg)

Publications:

On LEWERENTZ: book—*Sweden Builds* by G.E. Kidder Smith, New York and Stockholm 1950, London 1957; articles—"Sigurd Lewerentz" by H. Ahlberg and "Kapel og Krematorium i Malmö" by A. Jacobsen in *Byggmästaren* (Stockholm), no. 19, 1945; "Takvåning for architekt SAR Sigurd Lewerentzi Eskilstuna" in *Byggmästaren* (Stockholm), no. 1, 1948; "Markuskirken i Bjorkhagen" by Kay Fisker in *Arkitektur* (Copenhagen), February 1963; "Bjorkhagen Church, near Stockholm" in *Architectural Design* (London), March 1963; special issue of *Arkitektur* (Stockholm), September 1963; "Kyrka i Klippan" by S. I. Lind in *Arkitektur* (Stockholm), May 1968; "St. Petri Kirke i Klippan" in *Arkitektur* (Copenhagen), October 1968; "Sigurd Lewerentz in Memoriam" in *Arkitekten* (Copenhagen), 10 February 1976; "Sigurd Lewerentz's Last House" by Bernt Nyberg in *Arkitektur* (Stockholm), May 1976; "Sigurd Lewerentz 1885-1975" by J. Codrington in *Architectural Review* (London), April 1976; "Swedish neo-classicism of the 1920s" by Johan Martelius in *Arkitektur* (Stockholm), vol. 82, no. 2, 1982; "Swedish Grace," special issue of *International Architect* (London), vol. 1, no. 8, 1982; "Early Lewerentz" by Janne Ahlin in *Arkitektur* (Stockholm), December 1982.

*   *   *

Sigurd Lewerentz was one of the students who joined the Klara School in reaction against the conservative teaching at the Swedish Academy of Fine Arts. His studies in Germany had introduced him to the *Neue Sachlichkeit* and its exponents Bruno Möhring, Theodor Fischer, and Richard Riemerschmid.

His earliest buildings were designed in collaboration with Torsten Stubelius, notably the simple and dignified housing schemes, but the most celebrated work of this partnership was the project for a crematorium at Hälsingborg that was exhibited in 1914. This beautiful and dignified building, so closely wedded to the landscape proposals, led to the friendship and cooperation with Gunnar Asplund in the Woodland Cemetery competition and a labour of immensely spiritual quality that lasted from 1915 until the deaths of the two protagonists. Lewerentz's contribution to this scheme is often overlooked, but includes the Chapel of the Resurrection and its contiguous landscaping (completed in 1926), an ensemble that is among the most distinguished examples of Swedish Neo-Classicism of the present century. Thus Lewerentz established his reputation with buildings and landscapes associated with death, and indeed his most elegant and successful essays are those where formal and ritualistic requirements are paramount. Among his most successful designs are those for the cemetery at Malmö, on which he worked from the 1920s until his death: the drawings and buildings are strongly influenced by the work of the great Prussian architect, Karl Friedrich Schinkel, and indeed the spirit of Schinkel's genius pervades much of Lewerentz's *oeuvre*. Even his presentation drawings owe not a little to the German Neo-Classicist, notably the scheme for the theatre and concert-hall in Malmö.

Like many architects of his generation, Lewerentz was influenced not only by his immediate mentor contemporaries, but also by the writings and examples of professionals as diverse as the great German, Tessenow, and the Englishmen who followed in the wake of the Arts and Crafts movement. However, the most dominant themes in his output derive from Schinkel and from other Neo-Classical architects until about 1930, when his career changed direction. During the 1920s he had entered a number of competitions, and was responsible for many housing schemes. In 1930 he was co-ordinating designer for the Stockholm Exhibition, and produced the emblems, posters, and graphics as well as layout designs and other aspects of this important event in the development of Swedish architecture.

For the next two decades Lewerentz managed a factory that made steel windowframes, and his output as a designer virtually stopped until the 1950s, when he prepared a scheme for the restoration of Uppsala Cathedral and for several churches including a beautiful essay in brick at Skarpnäck (1960) and Klippan (1966).

Sigurd Lewerentz is one of the most important Swedish architects of the 20th century. With his contemporaries Gunnar Asplund and Osvald Almqvist he helped to change the course of Scandinavian design. Perhaps the drastic move away from the picturesque, delicious eclecticism of his early teacher, Ragnar Östberg, was necessary to purify architectural design, but the return to a stripped-down Classicism and then the rejection of even that for an arid functionalism has not been entirely happy. It is a function of architecture to delight, and Lewerentz's earlier work certainly achieves this aim. The landscape at the Woodland Cemetery is largely the creation of Lewerentz, is of a very high order, and, with the buildings, must be regarded as among his finest works.

Paradoxically, just as Lewerentz had been in the vanguard of a rediscovery of simplified Neo-Classicism, so he led the move away from it in Sweden towards a new functionalism, and in turn rejected that dessicated aberration as well. Eternal architectural verities rather than an hysterical belief in progress prevailed as Lewerentz returned before his death in 1975 to an architecture that respected nature and his native landscape.

—James Stevens Curl

LEWIS, David.
American. Born in Southampton, England, of South African parents, 24 January 1922; emigrated to the United States, 1963. Educated at the University of Cape Town, South Africa, 1939-41; Leeds College of Art, Yorkshire, England (Louis Aaron Fellow, 1961-63), Dip.Arch. (with distinction in thesis) 1963. Served in the South African Navy, 1941-44. Partner, Design Collaborative, London, 1956-61; Senior Architect, City of Leeds, 1961-63. Since 1965, Founder-Partner, UDA Architects (formerly, Urban Design Associates), Pittsburgh (partners: Raymond L. Gindroz, James P. Goldman, and Donald K. Carter). Andrew Mellon Professor of Architecture and Urban Design, Carnegie-Mellon University, Pittsburgh, 1963-68; Visiting Critic in Urban Design, Faculty of Architecture, Yale University, New Haven, Connecticut, 1968-70; William Henry Bishop Visiting Professor of Architectural Design, Yale University, 1975, 1977; Visiting Professor of Urban Design, Ohio State University, Columbus, 1977-78; Visiting Professor of Urban Design, 1982-84, and Andrew Mellon Professor, 1985, Carnegie-Mellon University, Pittsburgh. Member, Board of Directors, Pitsburgh Council for the Arts, and Director, Gallery for Contemporary Arts, Pittsburgh, 1968-70; Member of the Board of Advisors, Institute for Urban Design, since 1977; Vice-Chairman, 1977, and Chairman, 1978, National Urban Design and Planning Committee, American Institute of Architects; Member, Arts Commission of Pittsburgh, since 1978. Trustee, Pittsburgh History and Landmarks Foundation, since 1967. Exhibitions: British Exhibit, International Union of Architects, London, 1958; *This Is Tomorrow*, Whitechapel Gallery, London, 1962; *Confluences*, Pittsburgh, and Cincinnati and Columbus, Ohio, 1976. Recipient: three William C. Bellamy annual awards, National Association of Housing and Redevelopment Officials; *Progressive Architecture* Citation; three National Awards, United States Department of Housing and Urban Development; Celebration of Architecture Award, and four Distinguished Architecture Awards, American Institute of Architects; Pennsylvania Historic Architecture Award; and many local design awards. Associate of the Royal Institute of British Architects; Fellow, Royal Society of Arts, London, 1971; Fellow, American Institute of Architects, 1979. Address: UDA Architects, 1133 Penn Avenue, Pittsburgh, Pennsylvania 15222, U.S.A.

Works:

1968/
   72 Human Resources Center, Pontiac, Michigan
1971/
   73 Master plan for the Methodist Hospital, Brooklyn, New York
1971/
   77 Queensgate II Town Center, Cincinnati, Ohio
1973/
   74 Granada Neighborhood Center, Granada, New York
1974 Master plan for Station Square, Pittsburgh (re-use of P. and L.E. Station and Yards)
      Master plan for the new Indiana University/-Purdue University at Indianapolis (with Woollen Associates)
1976/
   78 Master plan and student housing for the University of Pittsburgh at Johnstown, Pennsylvania
1976 New Court Plaza (offices, apartments, commercial and garage), Pittsburgh
1977 Highland Elementary School, DuBois, Pennsylvania
      Sports Center, University of Pittsburgh at Johnstown, Pennsylvania
1977 Shadyside Estates (condominiums and apartments), Pittsburgh
1978 Phoenix-Hills Shopping Center, Pittsburgh
      Luthersburg Elementary School, Pennsylvania
      Forward/Shady Apartments for the Elderly, Pittsburgh
      Glen Hazel Housing, Pittsburgh
      Ethnic Village, Settler's Cabin Park, Pittsburgh
      Oakland Planning Study, Pittsburgh
      Restoration of Historic York, for the National Register of Historic Places, York, Pennsylvania (with UNIPLAN)
1979 Fuhrer Office Building, Pittsburgh
      Urban Development Study, Youngstown, Ohio
      The Olden Triangle, Pittsburgh
1980 Medical Supply Services Building, Johnstown, Pennsylvania
      Randolph Neighborhood Master Plan, Richmond, Virginia
      North Shore Master Plan, Pittsburgh
      Wall Street District Development, Pittsburgh
      Cumberland Arms Apartments, Cumberland, Maryland
      Emma Kaufmann Campus Master Plan and Cable-stayed Bridge, University of West Virginia, Morgantown
1981 Urban Revitalization Plan, Meadville, Pennsylvania
      Liberty Center Site Plan, Pittsburgh
      Eastwick Park, Youngstown, Ohio
      J. C. Oliver House, Pittsburgh
1982 Urban Master Plan, Warren, Ohio
      Town Square Master Plan, Decatur, Georgia
      Manchester Solar Infill Houses, Pittsburgh

David Lewis: Gananda Neighbourhood Center, New York, 1974.

1983 Building conversion, 429 Boulevard, Pittsburgh
La Roche College Campus Plan, Pittsburgh
Center Wheeling, Wheeling, West Virginia
Urban Development Master Plan, Evansville, Indiana
Continental Square, York, Pennsylvania
Landmark Tavern and Nicholas Coffee facade reconstructions, Market Square, Pittsburgh
Shadyside Village Housing phase I, Pittsburgh
Pattern Book Project, Richmond, Virginia
1984 John Casey Company Master Plan, Pittsburgh
One and Two North Shore Center Buildings, Pittsburgh
Office Building, 1133 Penn Avenue, Pittsburgh
Arts Center, Fitness and Recreation Center, and Academic Building, La Roche College, Pittsburgh
Richmond Parks, Richmond, Virginia
Centre Market restoration, Wheeling, West Virginia
Armstrong Square, Pittsburgh
Youngstown State University Plan, Ohio
Denver Convention Center Urban Design, Denver, Colorado

Columbus Center Master Plan, Virginia Beach, Virginia
Rivertown Master Plan, Raritan, New Jersey
Bellefield Tower, Pittsburgh
Riverfront Development Plan, Warren, Ohio
Shadyside Village Housing phase II, Pittsburgh

Publications:

By LEWIS: books—*End and Beginning,* Johannesburg 1945; *The Naked Eye,* Cape Town 1946; *Piet Mondrian,* London 1956; *Constantin Brancusi,* London 1957, London and New York 1975; *New Housing in Great Britain,* with Hansmartin Bruckmann, London 1961; *The Pedestrian in the City,* editor, London 1966, New York 1967; contributor to *The People Versus the System,* edited by Sol Tax, New York 1968; contributor to *Education and Urban Renaissance,* edited by R. F. Campbell, L. A. Marx and R. L. Nystrand, New York 1968; *Urban Structure,* editor, London and New York 1969; contributor to *Values and the Future,* edited by Kurt Baier and Nicholas Rescher, New York 1969; *The Growth of Cities,* editor, London 1971; *The Olden Triangle,* with Raymond Gindroz, Pittsburgh 1977;

articles—numerous in various professional and academic journals; also, editor, with Jules Gregory, "Community Design: By the People," special issue of *Process: Architecture* (Tokyo), March 1977.

On LEWIS: articles—"The School as Community and Education Centre" in *Bauwelt* (Berlin), 22 April 1974; "Schools That Nurture an Understanding for the Dimensions of Life" in *Architectural Record* (New York), May 1975; "Granada Neighborhood Centre" in *Baumeister* (Munich), November 1975; "The Home Towns Come Back," special issue of *Architectural Record* (New York), December 1976.

Our firm under its original name, Urban Design Associates, is one of the first architectural offices in the nation to design buildings in urban design settings. Our position is that cities are in a process of continuous change, evolving from their historic pasts into a future for which citizens, government leaders, and investors have particular aspirations. Architects have an important role to play in translating these aspirations into the physical vocabulary of buildings.

Our work ranges from individual buildings to the design of comprehensive urban environments. In everything we do, we attempt to find the elements of architectural language in the local context. To do this, we often involve citizens and users in open planning and design processes. As a result, the normal inventory of architectural practice— housing, offices, shops, restaurants, institutional buildings, recreation— become elements of city building, inserting the new to revive and evolve the old.

In recent years, much of our practice, like many others, has become involved in recycling old buildings and in the deep social questions that revolve around gentrification and local subsidy programs to assist inner city revitalization. We offer as illustrations of our work projects which range from the $140-million Liberty Center in Pittsburgh (in collaboration with Burt Hill Kosar Rittelmann Associates and The Architects Collaborative) to comprehensive waterfront developments (North Shore Center), insert new housing (The Village of Shadyside), and the recycling of industrial buildings (Armstrong Square) into multi-usage housing, offices, and food markets.

—David Lewis

In 1965 David Lewis founded Urban Design Associates in Pittsburgh, which has since become one of the leading urban design firms, especially well-known for its identification with community participation in the design and planning process.

Lewis came to the United States in 1963 when he was appointed Andrew Mellon Professor of Architecture and Urban Design at Carnegie-Mellon University in Pittsburgh. A native South African, Lewis had spent his earlier professional career as an architect, educator, and author in Great Britain. Soon after Lewis's arrival, Pittsburgh was to begin a period of reaction against the "Pittsburgh Renaissance," which had made astonishingly successful improvements in pollution abatement and in the development of the downtown and other commercial centers. Controlled, however, by a small group of business and political leaders, the "Renaissance" was perceived as making the overall business climate of the city successful at the expense of individual small property holders and neighborhoods.

Perhaps made sensitive to such issues by the social welfare policies prevailing in British planning (although planning of the time in Great Britain was at least as much *de haut en bas* as it was in Pittsburgh), Lewis became active on behalf of the people of the Hill District, an area of run-down small houses inhabited mainly by blacks that lay just to the east of the central business district. As a consultant, he also worked with the Pittsburgh Board of Education on a new building policy to promote school desegregation and began work on a whole series of proposals for small communities and city neighborhoods, where ordinary people, living in the area, were encouraged to comment and make suggestions during the development of designs and plans.

The best-known example of this work by Lewis's firm is the Queensgate II Town Center in Cincinnati, for which Urban Design Associates were both the planners and the architects. This development fulfills a number of purposes, including providing a safe and pleasant transition between parking spaces and the building housing the Cincinnati Symphony Orchestra, creating a sense of urban place and identity, and bridging two inner-city neighborhoods.

Lewis's architectural and urban design philosophy can perhaps best be summarized by his own statement: "Five hundred years ago Alberti encouraged the architect to be an artist, an intellectual and a noble. Today we encourage him to be a citizen."

—Jonathan Barnett

LIM, William Siew Wai.

Singaporean. Born in Hong Kong, 19 July 1932. Educated at the Architectural Association School, London, under John Killick, Bill Howell, Peter Smithson, Ove Arup and Robert Furneaux, Dip.A.A. 1955; Harvard University Department of City and Regional Planning, Cambridge, Massachusetts, under Jaqueline Tyrwhitt, 1956-57 (Fulbright Fellow). Married Lena U. Wen in 1962; children: Lim Chiwen and Lim Weiwen. Worked for the London County Council, 1955-56, and James Ferries and Partners, Singapore, 1957-60; Partner, Malayan Architects Co-Partnership (MAC), Singapore, 1961-67, and Design Partnership, Singapore, 1967-75. Managing Director, APAC (Asian Planning and Architectural Consultants Ltd.), Hong Kong, since 1970 (core members: Tao Ho, Hong Kong; Fumihiko Maki and Koichi Nagashima, Tokyo; Sumet Jumsai, Bangkok; Charles Correa, Bombay); Chairman, DP Consultant Service Pte. Ltd., Singapore, since 1971; Principal Partner, ABC Akitek, Malaysia, 1974-81; Chairman and Principal Partner, DP Architects, Singapore, 1975-81; also, Chairman, Select Books Ltd., Singapore, since 1977, and Managing Director, Select Management Pte. Ltd., Singapore, since 1981; Director, Solectra Ltd., Singapore, since 1977, and Gallery Asia, Singapore, since 1978. Chairman, Singapore Planning and Urban Research Group, 1966-68; External Lecturer, School of Architecture and Faculty of Law, University of Singapore, 1967-71; Member of the Transport Advisory Board and Chairman of the Working Committee, Ministry of Communications, Singapore, 1968-71; Member, International Advisory Committee, Pacific Asrama, 1974-75; Advisory Board Member, *Mimar* publications, Singapore, since 1980; Editorial Board member, *Habitat International*, London. Member, World Society for Ekistics, Athens, Greece. Address: William Lim Associates, 19 Tanglin Road, suite 06-06, Tanglin Shopping Centre, Singapore 1024, Republic of Singapore.

Works:

1962/
64 Singapore Conference Hall
1966/
67 Two houses, 11 and 11a Mount Rosie Road, Singapore
1967/
69 Four houses, 3 Chancery Hill Road, Singapore
Telephone Board Exchange and Engineering Centre, Singapore
1968/
69 House, 114 Windsor Park Road, Singapore
1969 Conference Centre, Vienna (competition project)
1969/
72 People's Park Shopping Complex, Singapore
1970/
71 House, 9 Frankel Street, Singapore
House, 464 Holland Road, Singapore
1970/
72 Golden Mile Shopping Complex, Singapore
Tanglin Shopping Centre, phase I, Singapore
1971 Jurong Town Hall, Singapore (competition project)
1971/
73 Katong Shopping Centre, Singapore
Ampang Park Shopping Centre, Kuala Lumpur, Malaysia
1972/
73 Plastics factory, Jurong, Singapore
Asia Radio Showroom, Singapore
1972/
76 Housing development, Bartley Road, Singapore
1973/
74 Shops and housing development, East Coast Road/Siglap Road, Singapore

1975 Dagat-Dagatan Low-Cost Housing, Manila, Philippines (competition project)
Dumai Complex, Kuala Lumpur, Malaysia
Ridgewood Condominium, Singapore
1975/
76 House renovation, 5 Victoria Park Close, Singapore
1976 Bandar Park Shopping/Entertainment Centre, Kuala Lumpur, Malaysia
St. Andrew's Junior College, Singapore
1976/
77 Yeo Hiap Seng Factory, Singapore
1977/
78 Yeo Hiap Seng Factory, Johor, Malaysia
Shops and housing development, Jln. Larkin, Johor, Malaysia
1978 Shops, hotel and entertainment centre, Malacca, Malaysia
Shopping centre, Temple Street, Singapore
Low-cost housing development, Kota Tinggi, Johor, Malaysia
Low-cost housing development, Plentong, Johor, Malaysia
Jalan Campbell Shopping Complex, Kuala Lumpur, Malaysia
Jalan Imbi Complex, Kuala Lumpur, Malaysia
Two Houses, Coronation Road West, Singapore
Abu Dhabi Tower, Dubai (competition project)
Prefabricated Housing for the Middle East (project)
Sim Lim Tower, Singapore
1980 Low Keng Huat Offices, Kuala Lumpur, Malaysia
Tanglin Shopping Centre phase II, Singapore
1982 Wilayah Shopping Complex, Kuala Lumpur, Malaysia
Merlin Hotel, Johor Bahru, Malaysia
Singapore River Conservation Project
1982/
84 Three Conservation Houses, Singapore
1982 High Technology Industrial Complex, Singapore
1983 Low-cost Housing, Kuala Lumpur, Malaysia (competition project)
1983 Villa Chancery Condominium Housing, Singapore
1984 Unit 8 Luxury Housing, Singapore

Publications:

By LIM: books—*Equity and Urban Environment in the Third World*, Singapore 1975; *An Alternative Urban Strategy*, Singapore 1980; *Pastel Portraits – Singapore's Architectural Heritage*, co-editor, Singapore 1984; articles—"Urban Transport and Mobility of People: Singapore as a Case Study" in *Singapore: A Decade of Independence*, edited by Charles Ng and T. P. B. Menon, Singapore 1975; "Options for Public Housing in Singapore: Some Policy Implications" in *New Directions* (Singapore), December 1975; "Driving Away Cars" in *The Times* (London), 19 July 1976; "Low Resource Urban Centres, with Special Reference to Asian Countries" in *City Planning Review* (Tokyo), 15 August 1976; foreword to *Questioning Development in Southeast Asia*, edited by Nancy Chng, Singapore 1977; "Money Well Spent" in *Singapore Trade and Industry Yearbook,* Singapore 1977; "Going Public—A Gone Case?" in *New Directions* (Singapore), June 1977; "An Overview of Some Policy Guidelines to Low-Income Urban Housing in Third World Countries" in *International Journal for Housing Science* (New York), no. 1, 1978; "If Buildings Could Speak . . ." in *Business Times* (Singapore), 25 August 1978; "When a City Is Not a Home" in *Business Times* (Singapore), 25 September 1978; "A Case for Low-Rise High-Density Living in Singapore" in *University of Singapore Journal*, January 1979; "China Islamic and Rural Architec-

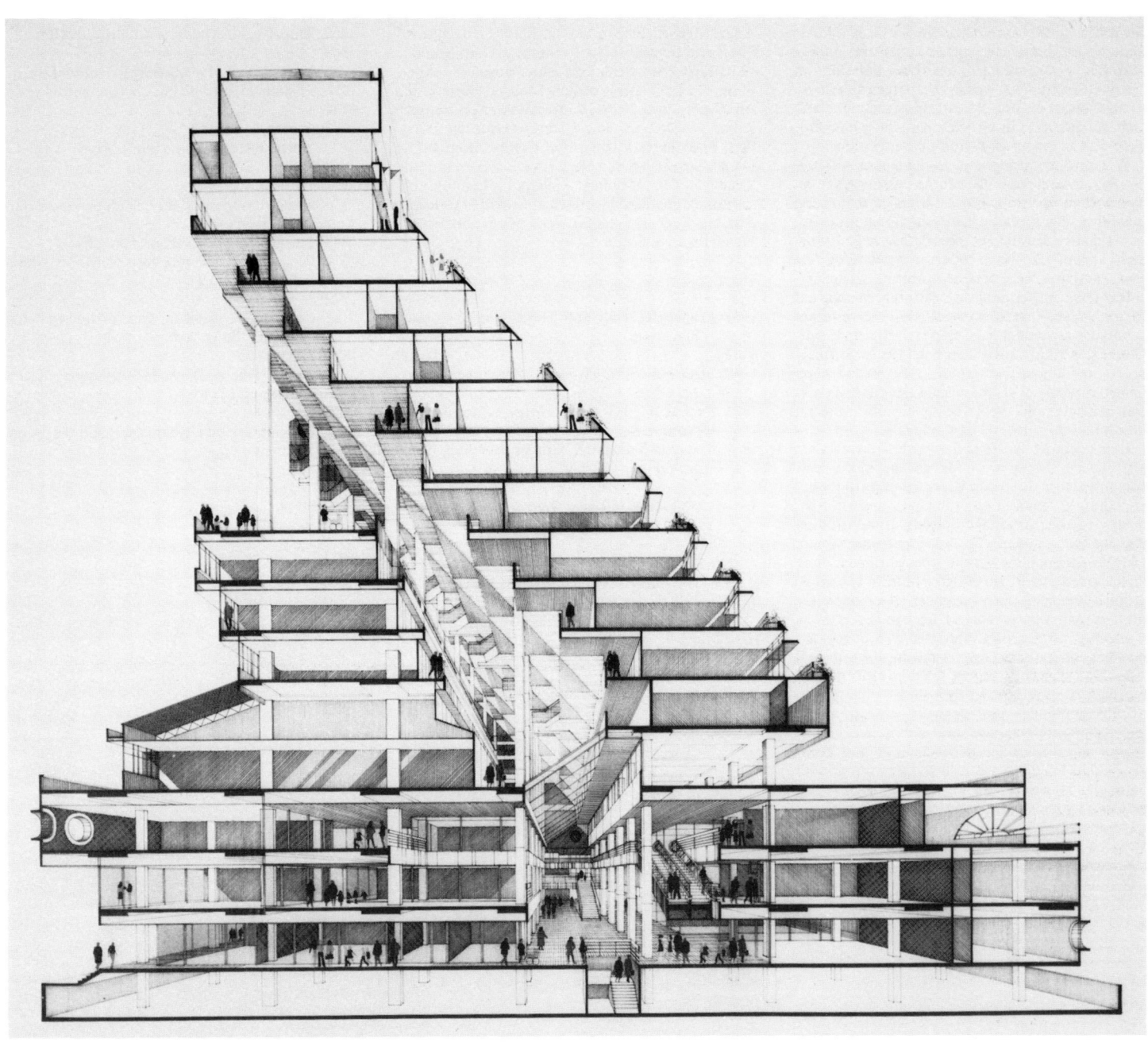

William Lim: Golden Mile Shopping Complex, Singapore, 1972.

ture from Beijing to Kashi," with others, in *Mimar* (Singapore), January/March 1982; "Housing and Community" in *Mimar* (Singapore), January/March 1983; "PAM Annual Discourse on Design," with others, in *Majallah Akitek* (Kuala Lumpur), March 1983.

On LIM books—*Architecture in the Seventies* by Udo Kultermann, London 1979; *Architekten der dritten Welt* by Udo Kultermann, Cologne 1980; articles—"William Lim" by Colin Gibson in *Nikkei Architecture* (Tokyo), no. 3, 1976; "The Ginger Man" by Ilsa Sharp in *Singapore Business*, February 1977; "William Lim" in *Nikkei Architecture* (Tokyo), no. 14, 1977; "Outspoken Architect and Town Planner: William S. W. Lim" in *Asian Building and Construction* (Hong Kong), December 1978; "St. Andrew's Junior College" in *Architecture + Urbanism* (Tokyo), August 1979; "Hotels in Asia: 5-Star Life Style" in *Mimar* (Singapore), January/March 1984.

Values, attitudes, and visual images are changing at an accelerating rate. The speed of these changes is now unprecedented. A talented architect who practices mainly what he learnt during his formal education fifteen or twenty years ago may be financially successful, but he is professionally irrelevant. The master-architect is dead!

In the last decade, we have experimented with group working methods based on a complex blending of group-dynamic theories from the West with traditional practices in Asia. We work with and learn from talented young architects, who are fully integrated into the design team. The group-dynamic process is practiced in the design team to intensify idea-interactions and to generate creativity. This continuous learning process is essential and must include new ideas drawn from other related disciplines. I can honestly state that the design of all of our major buildings was produced through joint, integrated efforts and cannot therefore be claimed by any single member of the team.

Our experience has shown that the team must be relatively small—four to eight persons at most. Team members should be of different ages and with different professional talents. The talent and personality of a single individual must not dominate the team. Common ground—especially relating to architectural theories—must be developed. Personal relationships, trust, and respect must be established. These are essential conditions for effective idea-interactions; so, too, are frank and often heated discussions during design working sessions.

Team members must have common objectives and social values and concern for the improvement of the urban environment for the benefit of the majority. Writings and lectures can be used to articulate complex social and environmental issues. Professional excellence must take absolute precedence over monetary rewards. Recognition by the Establishment can be counter-productive, as it often restrains and discourages new design experimentation. The continuous development and evolution in our approach has often made it impossible for our firm to continue applying certain design idioms, which we have used successfully for five or ten years previously, without being dishonest with ourselves. In the context of the restrictive creative architectural environment of Singapore, we often stand alone professionally, though still unbending and undefeated.

—William S. W. Lim

William Lim combines a busy group practice with jetting about attending conferences and producing a constant stream of papers ranging from "The Impending Urban Crisis" to "The Case Against Tall

Buildings" to "If Concrete Could Speak." He holds frequent forums in his penthouse flat overlooking Singapore Harbour. He has been labelled an "Econut" by the local press, perhaps mainly because of his association with the Singapore Planning and Urban Research Group (SPUR), which has criticized official proposals affecting the environment.

William Lim also leads a young coterie of local, Southeast Asian and international associates in an atelier that has produced a string of interesting buildings; their speciality has been shopping centres in Singapore like the People's Park, Golden Mile, and Tanglin. "We firmly believe in group work," he says, "and we do not believe in a master designer." All professional personnel in the firm are encouraged to initiate and criticize ideas, and the resultant solutions are the combined effort of all participants. Out of this "think tank" approach has surprisingly arisen a recognizable group style, focusing on imaginative use of space, natural materials such as raw concrete, mill timber and plain fibre cement, bold building forms, and simple details.

Lim, of course, has been the coordinator, catalyst and indeed the spur of his group, which feels committed to make a positive contribution to society and the architectural environment—and to comment on public issues like housing, transportation and the environment. The atmosphere he creates provides the bubbling ferment from which his "think tanks" emerge with their design solutions. The whole group is limited to thirty members, ten of whom are professional, twenty technical. Each project is led by a member of the group supported by a consultant member and by others responsible for the technical side of the project. Complete freedom and criticism are required—and apparently it works, while it lasts.

Lim is continually probing the social environment and seeking new architectural alternatives, particularly for the urban environment in the Third World. His buildings are fresh and innovative, with particular attention paid to the division of space, accessibility, movement and circulation. The architectural images he contrives to achieve and has achieved in his group appear to be unified and consistent.

—E.J. Seow

LIM Chong Keat, Datuk.
Malaysian. Born in Penang, 22 December 1930. Educated at the University of Manchester, England, 1951-56 (Hayward Medallist, Royal Manchester Society, 1955), B.Arch. (first-class honours) 1956; Massachusetts Institute of Technology, Cambridge, 1955-57 (Commonwealth Fellow), M.Arch. 1957. Lecturer at the School of Architecture and Building, Singapore Polytechnic, 1959-61; Founder-Partner, Malayan Architects Co-Partnership, Singapore, 1961-67; Founder-Partner, Architects Team 3, Singapore, Kuala Lumpur and Penang, 1967-80. Since 1980, Founder-Partner, Team 3 International, Singapore, Kuala Lumpur, and Penang (with Dato' Hj Baharuddin Abu Kassim and Lim Chin See). Member, Housing and Development Board, Singapore, 1960-69; Governor, Singapore Polytechnic, 1965-67; President, Singapore Institute of Architects, 1966-69; Chairman, Streets Naming Committee, Singapore, 1968-78; Member, United Nations Review Panel for State and City Planning, Singapore, 1969-71; Chairman, Architects Regional Council of Asia (ARCASIA), 1969-74; Member, National Museum Advisory Committee, Singapore, 1974-76. Member, 1972-77, and Chairman, 1977-81, Commonwealth Board of Architectural Education; Member of the Board of Trustees, National Museum of Art of Malaysia, since 1979; Honorary Project Director, Southeast Asian Cultural Research Programme (SEACURP), Institute of Southeast Asian Studies, Singapore, since 1981. Recipient: First Prize, Singapore Conference Hall Competition, 1961; First Prize, Seremban State Mosque Competition, 1962; Federation of Malaya Society of Architects Award, 1964; Bintang Bakti Masharakat Public Service Star, Singapore Government, 1966; First Prize, Jurong Town Hall Competition, 1971; Darjah Setia Pangkuan Negeri Award, Governor of Penang, 1979. Member, Singapore Institute of Architects, and Royal Institute of British Architects. Address: Team 3 International, 211 Upper Bukit Timah Road, Singapore 2158.

Works:

1961 Conference Hall and Trade Union House, Singapore
1962/
  67 Seremban State Mosque, Negri Sembilan, Malaysia
1964 Dr. A. F. H. Aeria House, Cantonment Avenue, Penang
1967 Malaysia-Singapore Airlines Building, Singapore
1969 Bank Negara Malaysia Building, Penang
1969/
  75 Development Bank of Singapore Building
1970 Petaling Jaya Town Hall, Selangor, Malaysia
1971/
  73 Jurong Town Hall, Singapore
      Starpoint Condominium, Pasir Panjang Road, Singapore
1971/
  74 United Overseas Bank Headquarters Building, Singapore
1973 Loh House, Stubbs Road, Hong Kong
1974 Penang Urban Centre/Kompleks Tun Abdul Razak, Penang
1979/
  82 CIAS Flight Kitchen, Changi International Airport, Singapore
1979/
  84 Chung Khiaw Bank Headquarters, Kuala Lumpur, Malaysia
1980/
  84 Bank of Ceylon Headquarters, Colombo, Sri Lanka

Datuk Lim Chong Keat: United Overseas Bank Headquarters, Singapore, 1974.

Publications:

By LIM: articles—"Regeneration of the City: The Planning Crossroads in Singapore" in *Singapore Institute of Architects Journal*, July/August 1969; "Communication and Organization Problems Within Professional Institutes" in *Far East Builder* (Hong Kong), January 1970; "The Role of the Professions in Society" in *Singapore Institute of Architects Journal*, September/October 1971; "Peasant Painters from Bali" in *Asian and Pacific Quarterly* (Seoul), Autumn 1976; "The Role of the Professional Institute in the Development of Architectural Education" in *SIA Journal* (Singapore), July/August 1977; "Peasant Painters of Penestanan, Ubud, Bali" in National Art Gallery exhibition catalogue, Singapore 1983.

On LIM: articles—"MSA Building" in *Singapore Institute of Architects Journal*, March/April 1969; "MSA Building Sets a Pattern" in *Far East Builder* (Hong Kong), May 1969; "Jurong Town Hall Architectural Design Competition" in *Singapore Institute of Architects Journal*, March/April 1970; "Life at the Top—Lim Chong Keat: 'Architects Should Work Together'" by Anthony Ramasamy in *Singapore Trade and Industry*, October 1971; "The Science Centre Design Competition" in *Singapore Institute of Architects Journal*, November/December 1971; "The Man Behind the Face of Singapore" in *Singapore Trade and Industry*, February 1972; "The Public Utilities Board Building" in *Singapore Institute of Architects Journal*, May/June 1972; "Urban Centre Will Bring City Changes into Focus" in *Malaysian Business* (Kuala Lumpur), April 1974; "Penang Urban Centre" in *Asian Architect and Builder* (Hong Kong), May 1974; "UOB Building" in *Building Materials and Equipment* (Singapore), September 1974; "DBS Building" in *Building Materials and Equipment* (Singapore), May 1975; "Huge Multi-Million Dollar Penang Urban Centre" in *Asian Building and Construction* (Hong Kong), September 1975; "Kompleks Tun Abdul Razak: A Mixed Use Project in Penang" in *Building Materials and Equipment* (Singapore), December 1976; "The Causes of Homogeneity Amongst Architects in Urban Areas" in *Majallah Akitek* (Kuala Lumpur), June 1978; "Goodbye, Houses of Tradition" in *Straits Times* (Singapore), 15 November 1983; "Houses Are People" in *New Straits Times Annual* (Malaysia), 1985; "Hotel on the Hill" in the *Straits Times* (Singapore), 15 March 1985.

*

The architect in the developing world has to face a comprehensive range of problems embracing the whole urbanisation process in his country and its cultural evolution in relation to total world change. His work must be conscientious and be free from mimicry, alien concepts or pseudo-folksiness. He has to extend himself in four dimensions: including a time-frame interrelating the past, the present and the future. His general architectural education will not have equipped him for all this, and he has to search and develop extensively and comprehensively so as to be meaningful in his professional work.

—Lim Chong Keat

*

Lim Chong Keat now heads a large practice in Singapore and Malaysia, and his impact on the local architectural scene during the last two decades has been significant.

He began his career as a teacher and had a profound influence on students in the School of Architecture of the Singapore Polytechnic, now part of the University of Singapore. Whilst still a lecturer at the school he won the competition for the design of the Singapore Conference Hall and Trade Union House. The same year, 1961, he formed Malayan Architects Co-Partnership, with William Lim and others; in 1967 he formed Architects Team 3, which continues to develop to the present day with commissions such as the Development Bank, Jurong Town Hall, United Overseas Bank, and other buildings in Singapore and Malaysia.

The Singapore Conference Hall is still perhaps his best major work; it reveals the purity of his architectural approach and individual style, with its imaginative and creative use of space and materials, its disciplined articulation, and the aptness and fluency that he displays not only in his buildings but also in his speeches and writings. His buildings are machine-finished, the concepts well-defined, the details functional and intellectually derived and sometimes playful.

Lim Chong Keat initiates, directs, corrects, attacks, checks, selects, justifies and defends his works like the grand master he is. His interests are wide; he keeps in touch with other architects as well as with architectural education; he continuously searches for models and antecedents for a meaningful architecture; and he is a prolific producer of significant buildings.

—E. J. Seow

LINDE, Horst.

German. Born in Heidelberg in 1912. Educated at primary and secondary schools in Baden-Baden; studied architecture at the Technische Hochschule, Karlsruhe, 1931-36, Dip.Ing. 1936. Served in the German Army, 1939-46; prisoner-of-war. Government Architect, Berlin, 1939; Town Planner, Lahr, Baden, Germany, 1939; worked as an architect for the reconstruction in France, 1941; Director, Office of Reconstruction, University of Freiburg, 1947-49; Director, State Building Administration, South Baden, Germany, 1949-57; Director, State Building Administration, Baden-Württemberg Region of Germany, and Section Head, Finance Ministry, Stuttgart, 1957-72. In private practive, Freiburg, since 1972. Professor, 1961-74, and since 1977 Professor Emeritus, Technische Hochschule, Stuttgart (Director, Institute for University Building, 1969-74). Recipient: Paul Bonatz Prize, Stuttgart, 1961, 1963; Fritz Schumacher Prize, University of Hanover, 1963; Architecture Prize, University of Oulu, Finland, 1967. Honorary doctorate: University of Freiburg, 1957. Member, Akademie der Bildenden Künste, Stuttgart, 1962, and Akademie der Künste, Berlin, 1970; Member, Academy of Town and Country Planning, Berlin, 1970. Honorary Member, Royal Institute of British Architects, Institute of Finnish Architects, and Finnish Academy of Technical Sciences, 1974. Address (office): Schlierbergstrasse 33, 7800 Freiburg, West Germany.

Works:

1928 Timber Houses, Berlin (competition project)
1931 Memorial Tower, Triberg, Black Forest, Germany
1934 Spa Hotel, Bad Dürrheim, Germany (competition project; with Bottling)
1935 Private house, Baden-Baden, Germany
1947 Forest Cafe, Badenweiler, Germany (with Haas)
1947/
 57 Master plan for the reconstruction/redevelopment of the University of Freiburg (with others)
1948 Zoning plan for Badenweiler, Germany (with Haas)
 Vocational School, Gaggenau, Germany
 Plan for the town center of Karlsruhe (competition project; with Diehm)
 Plan for the town center of Frankfurt (competition project)
1949 Commercial and Vocational Trades School, Sackingen, Germany (with W. Müller)
1950 Ludwig Evangelical Church, Freiburg (with Diehm, Hampe and Heine)
 Chapel, at the Catholic Hospital, Freiburg (with Kaufmann, Hasselbacher, and Rolli)
1951 Private houses, Wehr, Freiburg
1952 CIBA Ink Factory, Wehr, Baden, Germany (with Geier and Heinrich)
1953 Spa Hotel, Bad Dürrheim, Germany (with Heid)
 Private houses, Wehr, Baden, Germany
 Markgrafen Baths extension, Badenweiler, Germany (with Geier)
 Weinbrenner City Church reconstruction, Karlsruhe (with Pfeiffer)
 Local Government Administration Building, Freiburg (with Wolf and Heim)
1956 Church of St. John the Evangelist, Bad Dürrheim, Germany (with Heinrich)
 Engineers' School and Clock Museum, Furtwangen, Germany
1957 Plan for the town center of Stuttgart (with Frey and Fecker)
1958 Spa Hotel, Bad Krotzingen, Germany (with Heinrich and Geier)
1961 Design of the *Federal Garden Show*, Stuttgart
1962 Master plan for the University of the Ruhr, Bochum, Germany (competition project; with Conradi and Klose)
 Hotel and Service Station, Freiburg (with Dorr)
1965 St. Michael's Chapel, Ebersteinburg, Germany (with Reichenecker and Schwab)
1967 Design of the *Federal Garden Show*, Karlsruhe
1968 Evangelical Church, Marbach, Black Forest, Germany (with Dorr)
 Deutsche Bank, Schwäbisch Gmünd, Germany (with Markelin)
1969 Max Planck Institute, Freiburg (competition project; with Weber)
1970 Deutsche Bank Headquarters, Frankfurt (with Dionisius)
1973 Development plan for the spa and town of Baden-Baden, Germany (with the Baden-Baden Town Development Study Group)
 Casino extension, Baden-Baden, Germany (with Pfuger, Witzemann, Stadelmaier and Partners)
 Town Hall extensioin, Bad Dürrheim, Germany (with Weber)
1975 Salt Works conversion to Guest House, Bad Dürrheim, Germany (with Weber and Wrangel)
1976 Grand Auditorium and Spa Hotel, Baden-Baden, Germany (with Witzemann, Stadelmaier and Partners)
1977 Master plan for Guilan University, Iran (with Heinle, Wischer and Partners, and Zwirn, Weber, Heinrich and Aminde)

Publicatins:

By LINDE: Books—*Die Eignung Detmolds als Universitätsstandorf*, with W. Rath and others, Stuttgart 1965; *Bremen University*, with others, Berne 1967; *Standortbestimmung einer Universität*, with others, Munster 1967; *Hochschulplanung: Beiträge zur Strukturund Bauplanung*, editor, 4 volumes, Dusseldorf 1969-71; *Tendenzen und Ziele der Hochschulplanung in der Bundesrepublik Deutschland*, Aargau, Germany 1971; *Die Ausbildung des Architekten im Wandel der Zeit*, Stuttgart 1972; *Für Architektur: Ein Manifest*, with others, Stuttgart 1973; *Stadt-und Kurortentwicklung Baden-Baden*, with others, Baden-Württemberg, Germany 1974.

On LINDE: Book—*Horst Linde: Architekt und Hochschullehrer*, edited by the Institut für Hochschulbau, Stuttgart 1977; articles—"Die evangelische Johannis Kirche in Bad Durrheim" by J. Joedicke in

Der Munster (Stuttgart), May/June 1963; "Im Zentrum von Stuttgart" in *Bauwelt* (Berlin), June 1965; "Lesesaal der Württembergischen Landesbibliothek in Stuttgart" in *Detail* (Munich), no. 3, 1972.

Horst Linde studied at the Technische Hochschule, Karlsruhe, where he was influenced by Oscar Ernst Schweizer, an important exponent of the New Building. As with all architects of his age group, Linde had his early professional career interrupted by the war. After his military service, he became, in 1947, Director of the Reconstruction Office at the University of Freiburg, then, in 1949, Director of the State Building Administration for South Baden. It was there and especially after his appointment in 1957 as Director of the State Building Administration for the whole of Baden-Württemberg that he discovered a broad and fruitful field of activity that suited both his personality as an architect and his political philosophy. From then on, Linde directed, influenced and stimulated building activity in an important *land* of the Federal Republic.

Characteristic of his work as Director of Building Administration for both South Baden and Baden-Württemberg is a thorough analysis of problems in the formulation of comprehensive development objectives, and the achievement of those objectives by means of intelligent and clear-sighted policies.

In Freiburg, immediately after the war, Linde directed the reconstruction of the university and completed new buildings that obviously bear his signature as architect. As early as 1950 he built the Chapel at the Catholic Hospital, Freiburg, one of the most important buildings of this period in Germany. In Stuttgart, in the 1960's, he had a significant influence on developments in university building. In 1961 he was appointed a profesor-in-ordinary at the Technische Hochschule, Stuttgart, then in 1963 he founded the central archive for university building and in 1969 the special research facility for university building: he directed both establishments until 1974, creating institutions that could carry out the research and basic work necessary for progress in this field. The results of his work were felt far beyond Germany's borders.

Apart from his obligations—and contributions—as administrator, teacher and researcher, Horst Linde has also been active as an architect. Among his most impressive works are the plan for the town center of Stuttgart, the Church of St. John the Evangelist in Bad Dürrheim, and the Evangelical Church in Marbach.

—Jürgen Joedicke

LLEWELYN-DAVIES, Richard.

British. Born in London, 24 December 1912. Educated privately; at Trinity College, Cambridge, 1931-33, M.A. in engineering 1933; Summer School, Ecole des Beaux-Arts, Paris, 1930-33, Diploma 1933; Architectural Association School, London, 1933-37, Dip.A.A. (honours) 1937. Married Patricia Parry, now Baroness Llewelyn-Davies of Hastoe, in 1943; children: Melissa, Harriet, and Rebecca. Engineering Draughtsman, Sir Alexander Gibb and Partners, London, 1939-42; Architect, London Midland and Scottish Railway Company, London, 1942-48; Director, Investigation into Function and Design of Hospitals, Nuffield Foundation, London, 1948-60. In partnership with John Weeks, *q.v.*, London, 1960 until his death in 1981: Senior Partner of the successor firm, Llewelyn-Davies Weeks. Professor of Architecture, 1960-69, Professor of Urban Planning, 1969-75, Head of the School of Environmental Studies, 1971-75, and Emeritus Professor of Urban Planning, 1976-81, University College, London. Gropius Lecturer, Harvard University, Cambridge,

Massachusetts, 1975. Member, Royal Fine Art Commission, 1961-72; President, World Society for Ekistics, 1965. Chairman, Centre for Environmental Studies, London, 1967-81. Recipient: Bronze Medal, Royal Institute of British Architects, 1957; West Suffolk Award to Architects, 1957. Fellow, Royal Institute of British Architects, 1956, and Royal Town Planning Institute, 1966. Honorary Fellow, American Institute of Architects, 1970, and Sri Lanka Institute of Architects, 1973. Member, Institute for Advanced Study, Princeton, New Jersey, 1980. Created Baron (Life Peer), 1963. *Died* (in London) *27 October 1981.*

Works (all with John Weeks):

1952 Nuffield House, Musgrave Park Hospital, Belfast
1954 Diagnostic Centre, Corby, Northamptonshire
1955 House, Mayford, Surrey
1957 Mignot Memorial Hospital, Alderney, Channel Islands
     Rushbrooke Village Housing, Bury St. Edmunds, Suffolk
1958 *The Times* Newspaper Office Building, London (with Ellis, Clarke and Galleraugh)
1960 Students' Residence and Dining Room, Imperial College of Tropical Agriculture, Trinidad, West Indies (with Colin Laird Associates)
     Meeting halls and laboratories, Zoological Society, London
     Nuffield Institute of Comparative Medicine, London
1961 Stock Exchange redevelopment, London (with Fitzroy Robinson)
     Sun Alliance Insurance Building, London (with Fitzroy Robinson)
     Northwick Park Hospital and Clinical Research Centre, Harrow, Middlesex
1963 Tate Gallery extension, London
     Town Centre Development, phase I, and Sports Centre, Basingstoke, Hampshire (with Ian Fraser Associates)
1966 Barmston Village Housing Project, Washington New Town, County Durham
1968 Experimental Pathology Research Building, St. Mary's Hospital, Paddington, London
     Stantonbury Housing Scheme, Milton Keynes, Buckinghamshire
1970 Youth Treatment Centre, Birmingham
     University Children's Hospital, Louvain, Belgium (with Felix Tanghe and Delarue)
     Medical Centre, Flinders University, Adelaide, South Australia (with the South Australia Department of Public Works)
1971 York District Hospital
     Sciences Laboratories, National Hospital for Nervous Diseases, London
     Salmaniya Medical Centre, Bahrain
1972 Metal Box Company Headquarters Building, Reading, Berkshire
     Singapore General Hospital, Outram Road, Singapore (with INDECO)
     General Hospital, Doha, Qatar
1973 Normanby College Education Centre, King's College Hospital, London
1974 Health Sciences Centre, University of Khon Kaen, Thailand (with Kingston Reynolds Thom and Allardice)
1975 Cancer Research Foundation, Sutton, Surrey
     Rayne Institute Research Laboratories, University College Hospital, London
1975/
78 Shahestan Pahlam, Tehran (with Jaquelin Robertson)
1976 Voluntary Research Trust Research Laboratory Building, King's College Hospital, London
1977 Yale University Teaching Hospital, New Haven, Connecticut

1978 Presbyterian Hospital, Columbia-Presbyterian Medical Center, New York
1979 Arco Research Center, Philadelphia, Pennsylvania
1980 Alexander S. Onassis Memorial Cardiac Surgery Centre, Athens

Publications:

By LLEWELYN-DAVIES: books—*Studies in the Functions and Design of Hospitals,* with others, London 1955; *Building Elements* (textbook), with D. J. Petty, London 1956; *Psychiatric Services and Architecture,* with A. A. Baker and P. Sivadon, Geneva 1959; *Design of Research Laboratories,* with others, London 1961; *Children in Hospital,* with others, London 1963; *Hospital Planning and Administration,* with H. M. C. Macaulay, Geneva 1966; *New Cities—A British Example: Milton Keynes,* Washington, D.C. 1969; foreword to *British Hospitals: Home and Overseas,* 9th edition, London 1973; *The Tuscan Artist: Thought and Action in Design,* Cambridge, Massachusetts 1975; articles—"The Hertfordshire Achievement," with John Weeks, in *Architectural Review* (London), June 1952; "Facilities and Equipment for Health Services—Needed Research" in *Millbank Memorial Fund Quarterly* (New York), no. 3, 1966; "Similarities and Differences in Hospital Design International Trends" in *American Journal of Public Heath* (Washington, D.C.), October 1966; "Town Design" in *Town Planning Review* (Liverpool), October 1966; "Problems and Principles of Synthesis in Planning" in *Ekistics* (Athens), December 1966; "Research for Planning" in *Journal of the Town Planning Institute* (London), June 1967; "Planning to Meet Demand" in *Hospital Administration* (Sydney), October 1967; "New Cities—The British Experience" in *Indiana Architect* (Indianapolis), May 1968; "The Architect in 1988," with Lord Esher, in *RIBA Journal* (London), October 1968; "Educating the Professionals of the Built Environment" in *Architectural Record* (New York), February 1969; "Future of Environmental Studies" in *Architectural Design* (London), March 1969; "The Problems of Design" in *Journal of the Royal Institute of Chartered Surveyors* (London), April 1969; "Modern British Hospital Building" in *Hospital Management* (Sevenoaks, Kent), May 1969; "Villes Nouvelles: l'expérience britannique" in *Revue politique et parlementaire* (Paris, June 1969; "Science and the City," with Peter Cowan, in *Science Journal* (London), October 1969; "Milton Keynes: Goals of the Plan" in *RIBA Journal* (London), July 1970; "How Others See the U.S." in *Daedalus* (Cambridge, Massachusetts), Fall 1972; "The Role of the Social Sciences in Architecture and Planning" in *Anthropology and Society* (Washington, D.C.), 1975; "The Architect as a Planner" in *RIBA Journal* (London), July 1976.

By LLEWELYN-DAVIES WEEKS: reports—*The Plan for Milton Keynes,* 2 vols., London 1970; *Virginia Commonwealth University Master Plan,* 2 vols., New York 1970; *A New Community for Amherst,* 2 vols., New York 1971; *Qatar Development Plan,* London 1974; *Birmingham Inner Area Study,* 6 reports, London and Birmingham 1974-78; *Design Guidance Survey,* London 1976; *Design Tools,* 2 vols., London 1976; *Social Surveys,* London 1976; *Zetland County Structure Plan,* 6 vols., London 1976; *The Menninger Foundation, Planning Analysis and Recommendations,* 2 vols., New York 1977; *Master Plan for Yanbu Town and Sub Region,* Jedda and London 1978.

On LLEWELYN-DAVIES: books—*Changing Ideals in Modern Architecture* by Peter Collins, London 1965; *The New Brutalism* by Reyner Banham, London 1966; *A Broken Wave: The*

Rebuilding of England 1940-1980 by Lionel Esher, London 1981; articles—"To Plan or Not to Plan: Some Interim Thoughts on Milton Keynes" by Hugh Roper in *Journal of the Town Planning Institute* (London), May 1969; "The Plan Is a Beginning: Some Further Thoughts on Milton Keynes" by Hugh Roper in *Journal of the Town Planning Institute* (London), April 1970; "Milton Keynes: L'Etablissement d'un planning en prévision de la Société urbaine des temps futurs" by Jan Tanghe in *Environment* (Brussels), October 1970; "The Shah's New Town" by Miles Chapman in *Harpers & Queen* (London), April 1977; "Llewelyn-Davies—A Profile of his Professional Philosophy" by Susan Braybrooke in *Urban Design International* (New York), January/February 1980; "Obituary: Lord Llewelyn-Davies" in *Building* (London), 6 November 1981; "Richard Llewelyn-Davies" by John Weeks in *Architects' Journal* (London), 11 November 1981; "Richard Llewelyn-Davies (1912-1981)" in *RIBA Journal* (London), December 1981; "Richard Llewelyn-Davies: Obituary" in *AIA Journal* (Washington, D.C.), December 1981.

My work as an architect has been based on belief in the power of human reason. I believe that creative design must be based on real depth of understanding. I believe that an architect has to understand the purpose of his building in a very broad sense, which includes understanding a lot about the society and culture within which he works. I also believe that his technical understanding of the means of building needs to be very complete. I believe that only when he has mastered a design problem in all its rational aspects can he be comfortable with his design. This does not mean that I find that design itself is a deductive process based on a series of steps, one following another. I think that ideas about design come suddenly and unexpectedly in a creative flash, but I think that the result will be shallow and inadequate unless the creative moment comes against a background of deep and wide understanding. I do not think there is a great deal of difference in the creative activity of a designer and that of a scientist. I think both use inspiration on a basis of reason.

—Richard Llewelyn-Davies (1980)

Richard Llewellyn-Davies: Sun Alliance Insurance Building, London, 1961.

Sometimes, but not often, an architect comes along whose interests are so wide-ranging, activities so diversified, and accomplishments so varied that he is difficult, if not impossible, to categorize. Richard Llewelyn-Davies was that kind of architect.

For much of his early career, Lord Llewelyn-Davies was deeply involved in architectural and planning work for various institutions and trusts. As architect for the Nuffield Foundation, he directed and participated in many important research and other studies of hospitals and their functions, design, and planning. The research and studies developed and promoted important new concepts for hospitals and other health-care facilities. From these experiences came an interest in research and teaching; he was Professor of Architecture and Professor of Urban Planning at University College, London. His other interests led him to establish, in 1960, his practice of architecture and planning in London and later to expand the practice internationally.

The Llewelyn-Davies practice developed in a manner unlike that of any other firm that comes to mind. In the first place, it is truly international. In the second, it encompasses work of a scale, completeness, and complexity unknown to most architects. The firm performs architectural services in the usual manner not only for hospitals, a building type in which it is pre-eminent; it is as well noted for housing and shopping centers and for urban design and planning services for new towns, cities, and other urban areas.

Unlike almost any other firm in the world, that of Llewelyn-Davies performs a great variety of other services. These include research, studies, analyses, and consultation of many kinds—social, economic, institutional, strategic, as well as environmental and physical; and the firm continues to perform services for a large number of private and governmental clients in the fields of hospital and health-care planning and facilities.

The firm that Llewelyn-Davies developed produces excellent architecture and planning, along with large-scale programs and plans that are socially, economically, and physically sound, yet creative and pioneering. Since his death, the firm continues such work under the direction of John Weeks.

—William Dudley Hunt, Jr.

LOCSIN, Leandro V.

Filipino. Born in Silay City, 15 August 1928. Educated at De La Salle College High School, graduated 1947; University of Santo Tomas, 1949-53, B.Arch. 1953. Married Maria Cecilia Yulo in 1960; children: Leandro Jr. and Luis. In private practice, Makati, Manila, since 1955; Founder Director, L. V. Locsin and Associates, 1955-78; President, L. V. Locsin and Company Inc., since 1967; President and Manager, L. V. Locsin and Partners, since 1978. Executive Vice-President, Laguna Estates Development Corporation, since 1974; Chairman, LVL-CYL Foundation Inc., since 1974; President, YCLA Sugar Development Corporation, since 1975; President, YNTALCO Investment Corporation, since 1975—all Makati. Vice-President, 1963, and President, 1964-66, Philippine Institute of Architects; Trustee, De La Salle University, 1973-79; Treasurer, 1980, Vice-President, 1981, and President, 1981-83, United Architects of the Philippines. Exhibitions: *Leandro V. Locsin,* University of Hawaii, Honolulu, 1960; *Expo '70,* Osaka, 1970; Fulbright Scholars Exhibition, Cultural Center of the Philippines, Manila, 1978. Recipient: Outstanding Young Man Award, Philippines Junior Chamber of Commerce, 1959; Pan Pacific Architectural Award, American Institute of Architects, Hawaii Chapter, 1960; Rizal Centennial Award for Architecture, Philippines, 1962; Gold Medal, University of Santo Tomas, 1968; Philippine Republic

Cultural Heritage Award, 1970; Philippine Arts and Architecture Award, 1971; Araw ng Maynila Cultural Award, Manila, 1972; Gold Medal, Philippine Institute of Architects, 1978; Professional Award, United Architects of the Philippines, 1978; Architect of the Year Award, Philippines, 1978; Fellow, United Architects of the Philippines, 1978; Honorary Fellow, American Institute of Architects, 1980. Address: Leondro V. Locsin and Partners, 448 E. de los Santos Avenue, Makati, Manila, Philippines.

Works (in the Philippines unless noted):

1955 Chapel of the Holy Sacrifice, University of the Philippines, Quezon City
1957 Monterrey Apartments Ayala Avenue, Makati
1958 Ayala Building I, Ayala Avenue, Makati (now Elizalde Building)
   Marcelo Fernando House, Panay Road, Quezon City
   Fernando Zobel House additions and gardens, Forbes Park, Makati
   G. Yvanovich House, Hidalgo Street, Makati
   José Aldeguer House, Diliman, Quezon City
   Howard Cavender House, Urdaneta Village, Makati
   Robert Ho House, Forbes Park, Makati
1959 Filipinas Life Assurance Company Building, Ayala Avenue, Makati
   Fernando Garcia House, Cubao, Quezon City
   Jaime Zobel de Ayala House, Forbes Park, Makati
   Michael Joseph House, San Lorenzo Village, Makati
   Jaime Lacson House, Makati
1960 Ozamis City Cathedral
   John T. Quimzon House, La Vista, Quezon City
   Angel Heredia House, La Vista, Quezon City
   José Tuason Jr. House, La Vista, Quezon City
   Sergio Montinola House, Forbes Park, Makati
   Residence for the National Life Insurance Company, Urdaneta Village, Makati
   Manuel Escaler House, Wack-Wack, Mandaluyong
   Arturo Rotor House, Urdaneta Village, Makati
1961 Davao Insular Hotel, Davao City
   Commercial Credit Corporation Building, Buendia Avenue, Makati
   Pacita Soriano House, Forbes Park, Makati
   Nicanor Yniguez House, Shaw Boulevard, Mandaluyong
1962 Integrated Realty Building, Buendia Avenue, Makati
   Joaquin de Sequerra House, Urdaneta Village, Makati
   Robert Sy House, Forbes Park, Makati
   José Yulo Sr. House, Forbes Park, Makati
   Ramon Pertierra House, Forbes Park, Makati
   Manuel del Rosario House, Forbes Park, Makati
   René Unson House, Bel-Air Village, Makati
1963 Phil-Am Life Company Building, Cagayan de Oro City
   Enrique Carlos House, Forbes Park, Makati
   Alberto Quiroz del Rio House, Forbes Park, Makati
   Leandro V. Locsin House, Forbes Park, Makati
   Jesus de Veyra House, Greenhills, Mandaluyong
   Johnny de Leon House, Forbes Park, Makati
1964 Emerson CoSeteng House, Marikina
   Domingo Locsin House, Urdaneta Village, Makati
   Henry Moran House, Greenhills, Mandaluyong
   Francisco Tansengco House, Makati
   José San Buenaventura House, Forbes Park, Makati

Ramon Cojuangco House, Forbes Park, Makati
   Salvador de Leon House, Paranaque
1965 Manila Memorial Park Chapel, Paranque
   Sarmiento Office Building, Ayala Avenue, Makati
   American International Underwriters Building, Ayala Avenue, Makati
   Dona Corazon L. Montelibano Memorial Chapel, De La Salle College, Bacolod City
   Mauro Prieto House, Forbes Park, Makati
   Ramon Yulo House, Forbes Park, Makati
1966 Sikatuna Office Building, Ayala Avenue, Makati
   Tuason Building, Ayala Avenue, Makati
   Locsin Office Building, de los Santos Avenue, Makati
   Five executive houses, and pavilion, Central Azucarera, Tarlac
1967 Hyatt Regency Hotel, Roxas Boulevard, Pasay City
   Ricardo Cu Unjeng House, Forbes Park, Makati
   Enrique Zobel House renovations and additions, Forbes Park, Makati
   Antonio Floirendo House, Forbes Park, Makati
   Manolo Lopez House, Wack-Wack, Mandaluyong
1968 Josefa Apartment Building, M. Adriatico, Malate, Manila
   Church of St. Andrew, Bel-Air Village, Makati
   Miguel Yulo House, Forbes Park, Makati
   Florencio Reyes House, Dasmarinas Village, Makati
1969 Filipinas Life Assurance Company Building, Iloilo City
   Manila Intercontinental Hotel, Ayala Avenue, Makati
   First National City Bank Building renovations, Juan Luna, Manila
   Philippine Bank of Commerce, Ayala Avenue, Makati
   Theatre of the Performing Arts, Cultural Center of the Philippines, Manila
   College of Agriculture Dormitories, University of the Philippines, Los Banos, Laguna
   Magnolia Dairy Products Plant, Aurora Boulevard, Quezon City
   Amalgamated Office Building, Makati
   Filipinas Life Assurance Company Building, Mandaue, Cebu
   Holy Cross Memorial Park Chapel, Novaliches, Manila
   Leland Villadolid House, Dasmarinas Village, Makati
   Vicente Paterno House, Paterno Avenue, San Juan, Manila
   Clemente Gatmaitan Jr. House, Dasmarinas Village, Makati
1970 Chapel of St. Alphonsus Liguori, Magallanes Village, Makati
   Union Carbide Office Building, Mandaue, Cebu
   Continuing Education Center of the College of Agriculture, and Student Union Building, University of the Philippines, Los Banos, Laguna
   Filipinas Life Assurance Company Building, Naga City
   David Consunji House, Pasay Road, Makati
   Alejandro Roces House, Forbes Park, Makati
   Cesar Zalamea House, Dasmarinas Village, Makati
   Philippine Pavilion, *Expo '70*, Osaka, Japan
1971 Filipinas Life Assurance Company Building, Cagayan de Oro Coty, Mindanao
   Filipinas Life Executive Center, Mandaue, Cebu
   Church of the Immaculate Heart of Mary Teachers' Village, Diliman, Quezon City
   Auditorium, College of Agriculture, University of the Philippines, Los Banos, Laguna

Hall of Congress renovations, Philippine National Legislative Assembly, Manila
   Romago Office Building, Mandaluyong, Manila
   Filipinas Life Assurance Company Building, Batangas City
   Filipinas Life Assurance Company Building, Dagupan City
   Stock Exchange, Ayala Avenue, Makati
   Luis Maria Guerrero House, Dasmarinas Village, Makati
1972 Cadiz Church
   Filipinas Life Assurance Company Building Annex, Ayala Avenue, Makati
   Session Hall renovations, Congress of the Republic of the Philippines, Taft Avenue, Manila
   Filipinas Life Assurance Company Building, Davao City, Mindanao
   Asian Reinsurance Pool Building, Legaspi Village, Makati
   Terminal Building renovation, Manila International Airport
   Philippine Commercial and Industrial Bank Building, Greenhills, Mandaluyong
   Gregorio Locsin House, Greenhills, Mandaluyong
   José Cruz House, Pasig, Manila
   Ang Maharlika State Guest House restoration, San Miguel, Manila
   Leandro V. Locsin Beach House, Puerto Galera, Oriental Mindoro
1973 Kodak Office Building renovations, Pasong Tamo, Makati
   Edon Yap House, Greenhills, Mandaluyong
   Anton Roxas House, Forbes Park, Makati
   Stephen Zuelling House, Forbes Park, Makati
1974 SEARCA Dormitory, College of Agriculture, University of the Philippines, Los Banos, Laguna
   Ayala Museum, Makati Avenue, Makati
   Design Center, and Folk Arts Theatre, Cultural Center of the Philippines, Roxas Boulevard, Manila
   Population Center, Makati
   Conrado Ocampo House, Dasmarinas Village, Makati
   Ileana Maramag House, Dasmarinas Village, Makati
   Rest house for President Marcos, Olot, Leyte
1975 First National City Bank Building, Paseo de Roxas, Makati
   Nutritional Center of the Philippines, Makati
   Ralph Panganiban House, Dasmarinas Village, Makati
1976 Filipinas Life Assurance Company Building, Tacloban City, Leyte
   Asian Center for Social Welfare Training and Research, Makati
   National Arts Center, Mount Makiling, Los Banos, Laguna
   Philippine International Convention Center, Roxas, Boulevard, Manila
   Philippine Plaza Hotel, Roxas Boulevard, Manila
   Australian Embassy Residence, Forbes Park, Manila
   Manila Hotel renovations and tower addition, Roxas Boulevard, Manila
   Manila Mandarin Hotel, Makati Avenue, Makati
1977 Valle Verde Country Club, Pasig, Metro Manila
1978 Engineering Equipment Inc. Office Building, Pasig, Metro Manila
   Marbella Condominium I, Roxas Boulevard, Manila
   Canlubang Golf and Country Club, Laguna
   Generoso Villanueva House, Tamarind Road, Forbes Park, Makati
1979 Canlubang Sports Complex, Laguna
   Johnny Widjaya House, Djakarta, Indonesia
1980 Philippine Long-Distance Telephone Company Building, Makati

Leandro Locsin: Philippine International Convention Center, Manila, 1976.

Marbella Condominium II, Roxas Boulevard, Manila
1981 Civil Aeronautic and Training Center, MIA Compound, Paranaque
Davao International Airport, Davao City
1982 New Terminal Building, Manila International Airport, Pasay City
Greenbelt Square Commercial Complex, Greenbelt, Legaspi Village, Makati
1983 Vigan Airport Terminal Building, Vigan, Ilocos Sur
Philippine Commercial and Industrial Bank, Makati Avenue, Makati
1984 Istana Nurul Iman—Sultan's Palace, Bandar Seri Begawan, Brunei
Benguet Center, San Miguel Avenue, Mandaluyong

Publications:

By LOCSIN: book—*Oriental Ceramics Discovered in the Philipinnes*, with Cecilia Y. Locsin, Rutland, Vermont 1967 article—"Architecture in the Philippines" in *Pamana Magazine* (Manila), 1970.

On LOCSIN: books—*The Art of the Philippines* by Rodrigo Perez, Manila 1958 *Philippine Contemporary Art* by Manuel Duldalao, Manila 1972; *The Struggle for Philippine Art* by P. Kalaw Ledesma, Manila 1974; *The Philippine Art Scene* by Manuel Duldalao, Manila 1977; *The Architecture of Leandro V. Locsin* by Nicholas Polites, New York and Tokyo 1977; *Philippines* by Richard Chesnoff, New York 1978; *The Manila Hotel* by Beth Day, Manila 1979; *Architekten der dritten Welt* by Udo Kultermann, Cologne 1980; articles—"The Philippine International Convention Center" in *Asian Building and Construction* (Hong Kong), November 1976; "Bold Look for Manila Trade Exhibition Building" in *Asian Building and Construction* (Hong Kong), May 1977; "Site Dictated Design of Manila Mandarin Hotel" in *Asian Building and Construction* (Hong Kong), July 1977; "Contemporary Philippine Architect: Leandro V. Locsin" in *Space Design* (Tokyo), November 1977; "Stately Thriller in Manila" in *Contract Interiors* (New York), April 1978; "Expansion of Manila's International Airport" in *Asian Building and Construction* (Hong Kong), August 1978; "Manila's New Convention center" in *Architectural Record* (New York), October 1978; "Manila Airport Nears Completion" in *Asian Building and Construction* (Hong Kong), October 1980.

*

Equally weighed with considerations of space is the element of time: the past, present and future as seen through the architect's soul, from which emanate his aesthetic perceptions and the strength to transform into architectural conceptualization that which he knows is truth. The process, intuitive or deliberate, represents a synthesis of the designer's personality—the sum total of his experience and his criteria—in dynamic interaction with his understanding of and identification with national traditions, linking generations, periods, epochs, and those traditions which are living, developing, and ever-changing with the demands of the present.

Architecture is not to be experienced in isolation. The architect is ever with his audience: the users, the onlookers, the people. It is, however, left to the architect from his vantage point in the time-continuum to synthesize the arts, beliefs, technology, lifestyles and aspirations of his people; and, by translating these into structures of concrete, stone, wood, or steel, adding one more statement to his country's architectural record by which he, his society, and his times will ultimately be measured.
—Leandro V. Locsin

*

Many western artists have a particularly unfortunate habit of acute ethnocentrism, and rarely if ever look at work produced beyond the Pacific Ocean or the Ural Mountains. For this reason the sensitive and innovative work of Leandro V. Locsin of the Philippines has gone largely unnoticed. That is too bad, because there are many lessons we could learn from Locsin, and much delight we could reap merely from becoming acquainted with his unusual architecture.

Locsin has risen to an extremely difficult challenge, for his work attempts to discover, not in superficial terms, what aspects of his rich tradition retain meaning in a now rapidly changing environment. Although we in the west also face this dilemma of reconciliation between old styles and patterns and contemporary technology, it is an amplified conflict in the Philippines, where many traditional values stand in direct opposition to the current social atmosphere that has been largely imported from the west. Locsin has compounded the struggle still further, by attempting to validate his expression of his heritage through sophisticated abstraction. Had Locsin been a less talented architect than he is, the results could have been chaotic, and in many ways, much of the work of his Asian colleagues has been just that. Locsin's brilliant sense of mass, space, and structure, coupled with a simple and consistent style of personal expression have, though, produced many extremely fine buildings that seem to stand up to these challenges with extraordinary ease.

Locsin's architecture begins with sincere introspection, both of himself and his nation. He is very attuned to Filipino living patterns, and has avidly studied vernacular Filipino building. He frequently incorporates common vernacular spatial qualities into his designs.

His nation's tropical climate, for example, has always exerted considerable influence on architecture produced there, and Locsin responds to the weather in much the same ways as his ancestors. Large open spaces and few ceiling to floor partitions, frequent use of lattices and other partial partitions, and the expression of the roof as the dominant shape, are all qualities of Locsin's work that have been adopted from the vernacular. An exuberant sense of ornament, detail, and architectural intent, contrasted against great simplicity is another characteristic that marks Locsin's buildings, and has been drawn from his own culture.

Locsin is very careful in his adaptations, though. "We must avoid the temptation towards gimicky, carnival architecture," he warns. "The brass tacks are that we *are* using western technology. But we must think of this as an enrichment of our own vocabulary, not an exclusion of it."

Locsin's buildings are fine constructions that are rational, climatically sound, and deftly scaled. They are composed of unusual and carefully selected materials. He uses concrete freely, because of low labor costs, but several of his buildings use earth berms integrally; others use a concrete he devised with a shell aggregate, and his houses are composed of fine wood panels, wood lattice work, masonry, stone, tile, and (as perfectly tangible as all other materials) open air. They are handsome sculptural pieces and demonstrate superb exploration of the expressive potentialities of shade and shadow.

Locsin has been remarkably prolific, and has demonstrated his vitality and truly vibrant creative impulse by completing several very large projects on impossibly tight schedules. Without doubt his biggest project, and to Locsin his greatest honour, has been his virtually single handed execution of the new Cultural Center of the Philippines. The production of four large buildings, two theatres, an exhibition hall, and a convention center, as well as a large, on-site hotel, afforded Locsin the unique opportunity to create variations on principle themes. The result is an exciting, harmonic arrangement of similar shapes, colors, and mass. Locsin exhibits his affection for massive roof shapes, for example, in repeatedly huge, plain cantilevers extending over shaded areas.

The Theatre for the Performing Arts shines as the most outstanding example of Locsin's material restraint informed by spirited, energetic, compositional sense. Today it is becoming a symbol of, and, a monument to, that Filipino spirit so deeply entrenched in Locsin's perceptions. Like all of Locsin's work, it documents a struggle, and a triumph, of a national spirit over the modern world.

—Mitchell B. Rouda

LODS, Marcel Gabriel.

French. Born in Paris, 16 August 1891. Educated at the Ecole Nationale des Arts Décoratifs, Paris; Ecole Nationale Supérieure des Beaux-Arts, Paris, Dip. Arch. 1923. Served in the French Army, 1914-18: Lieutenant; volunteer in 1940. Married Germaine Lucy Empereur Bissonet in 1919; children: Gilbert, Francis, and Denise; married Jacqueline Albert Lambert; children: Martine and Bernard; married Denise Marcelle Martineau. Worked with L. H. Brileau, Paris, 1922-23; in partnership with Eugène Beaudouin, *q.v.*, 1925-40. In private practice, Paris, 1945 until his death in 1978. Studio Master, with André Hermant and Trazzini, Ecole des Beaux-Arts, Paris, 1948-64. Architect-in-Charge of Public Buildings and National Monuments; Architect-in-Charge of the Reconstruction of Sector II of Rouen; City Architect and Urbanist, Sotteville les Rouen, Drancy, and Mayence, France; City Architect to the Government of Guinea. Member of the French Section of CIAM (Congrès Internationaux des Architectes Modernes). Recipient: Reynolds Prize, 1970. Officer of the Légion d'Honneur, of the Order of Merit, and of the Order of Arts and Letters. *Died 9 September 1978.*

Marcel Lods: Open-Air School, Suresnes, France, 1935.

Works:

1933 Palais des Expositions, Paris (with Eugène Beaudouin and Vladimir Bodiansky)

1934 Cité de la Muette, Drancy, France (with Eugène Beaudouin and Vladimir Bodiansky)

1935 Open-Air School, Suresnes, France (with Eugène Beaudouin)

1936 Circular Aircraft Hangar (project; with Vladimir Bodiansky)

1937 Aero-Club, Buc, France (with Eugène Beaudouin and Jean Prouvé; demolished by the Germans during the Occupation, 1940-44)

Design of the World's Fair, Paris (with Eugène Beaudouin)

1938 Dismountable Weekend House, *Exposition Habitation,* Paris (with Eugène Beaudouin)

1939 Maison du Peuple, Clichy, France (with Eugène Beaudouin, Vladimir Bodiansky, and Jean Prouvé)

1945 Retreat House, housing and two school complexes, Sotteville les Rouen, France (with Alexandre, Bloquel, and Yvelin)

1955 Church of Joan of Arc, Belfort, France
      Church of the Cross, Sochaux, France
1955/
  65 Housing, Drancy, France
1956 Air Base, Strasbourg, France (with Arsène
        Henry)
      Air Base, Metz, France
      Housing, Argenteuil, France
1958 Les Grandes Terres Housing Estate, Marly le
        Roi, France (with Honegger)
1960 Five currency-exchange kiosks in Paris depots
      Technical college, Paris
      Supermarket, Sotteville les Rouen, France
        (with Alexandre and Malizard)
      GEAI: La Grand Mare (apartments), Rouen,
        France (with Depondt and Beauclair)
1962/
  63 School, Ivry-sur-Seine, France
      College of Chemistry, Mulhouse, France (with
        Fischbach and Steinmetz)
      University Restaurant, Mulhouse, France
        (with Fischbach and Steinmetz)
      Banque Populaire Offices, Mulhouse, France
        (with Meyer)
1964/
  65 Z.U.P. Housing, Meaux, France (with De-
        pondt and Beauclair)
      Faculty of Sciences Building, University of
        Reims, France (with Durand de Guill-
        arbois)
      Halls of Residence, University of Reims,
        France (with Durand de Guillarbois)
1967 Maison des Sciences de l'Homme, Paris (with
        Depondt and Beauclair)
      French National Printing Works, Douai

Publications:

By LODS: book—*Le Métier d'architecte*, with Hervé
Le Boterf, Paris 1976.

On LODS: articles—"Architecture Between the
Wars: A Conversation with Marcel Lods" in
Architecture mouvement continuité (Paris), March
1974; "Marcel Lods" by Manfred Schiedhelm in
Architectural Design (London), October 1974; "Im-
primerie National Française: New Printing Works
at Douai" by Themis Constantinidis in *Acier Stahl
Steel* (Brussels), January 1975; "Imprimerie Nat-
ionale à Douai" in *Usines d'aujourd'hui* (Paris), no.
127, 1975; "National Printing Works, Douai" in
Informes de la construccion (Madrid), June 1976;
"Grandeur and Misery of a Rationalist Master-
piece" by François Laisney and Ginette Baty-
Tornikian in *L'Architecture d'aujourd'hui* (Paris),
October/November 1976; "The Work of Marcel
Lods (1891-1978)" in *Techniques et architecture*
(Paris), October 1978; "Death of the Fathers" by
François Chaslin in *Macadam* (Paris), 15 November-
1 December 1978; "Marcel Lods—Precursor to the
end" by Jacques Laurent in *Architecture* (Paris),
June/July 1981.

The team of Eugène Beaudouin and Marcel Lods
was remarkable for the complementary qualities of
the two partners. Together they built the first
prefabricated housing schemes, the best known of
which is Cité de la Muette, in Drancy, in the suburbs
of Paris, sadly renowned for its use as a transit centre
for Jewish deportees during the German occupation,
and the excellent open-air school in Suresnes. With
the collaboration of Jean Prouvé, they built the
Maison du Peuple in Clichy, too quickly forgotten in
spite of its indisputable interest and merit.
   Unfortunately, events led to the separation of the
partners. Lods continued in his independent practice
with his strong commitment to industralized architecture. He pleaded for prefabrication with characteristic vigour and with the inner conviction that the
future of architecture depended on the capacity of

architects to infiltrate the industrialization process
and so guide its future development. He had the
opportunity to illustrate his ideas in many important
works, some of them undeniably successful.
   But, after the war, Lods, the enthusiastic and
spirited warrior, really devoted his inexhaustible
energy to another cause—to what has become a
crusade: trying to persuade the political authorities,
the public, and, above all, other architects of the
absolute priority that should be given to land and
town planning. He campaigned tirelessly—in his
writings, in public conferences, in radio
broadcasts—never allowing himself to become discouraged by the feeble echo that his pleadings and
warnings evoked.
   A real force of nature, who visited his sites on a
powerful motorcycle and who liked to pilot his own
aircraft, Lods, with his astonishing youthfulness of
spirit, was and will remain one of the most attractive
figures of twentieth-century French architecture.

—Pierre Vago

LUBETKIN, Berthold.
Russian. Born in Tiflis, Georgia (now U.S.S.R.), 16
December 1901; emigrated to England, 1931.
Educated at the Tenishevskaya Gymnasium, St.
Petersburg, and the Miedvendikoy Gymnasium,
Moscow, 1910-17; studied under A. Rodchenko, V.
Tatlin, and A. Vesnin, at the Vkhutemas, Moscow,
and the Svomas, Petrograd, 1920-22; under Profes-
sor Fleming, Textile Academy, Berlin, and under
Professor Kersten, Building School, Berlin-
Charlottenburg, 1922-23; Warsaw Polytechnic
School of Architecture, 1923-25; Ecole Spéciale
d'Architecture, Paris, 1925; Ecole des Beaux Arts
(Atelier Perret), Paris, 1926-27; Ecole Supérieur de
Béton Armé, Paris, 1927, and the Institut
d'Urbanisme, Sorbonne, Paris, 1927-29. Served as a
Reservist, Red Army, Moscow, 1919-20. Married
Margaret Church in 1931 (died, 1969). Worked
briefly with the architect Bruno Taut, *q.v.*, in Berlin,
1922-23, and with Ernst May, *q.v.*, in Frankfurt,
1924; in private practice as architect and designer,
working for the U.S.S.R. Trades Delegation, Paris,
1926-29, and with the architect Jean Ginsberg, *q.v.*,
Paris, 1928-30; Partner, with Anthony Chitty,
Lindsey Drake, Michael Dugdale, Valentine Harding, Godfrey Samuel, and Francis Skinner, Tecton
Group of architects, London, 1932-48, and with
Skinner and Douglas Bailey, in Skinner Bailey &
Lubetkin, London, 1948-52. Retired from architectural practice to farm in Upper Kilcott, Glouce-
stershire, 1952-69; moved to Clifton, Bristol, Avon,
1969. Editorial Board Member, *L'Architecture
d'aujourd'hui*, Paris, 1930-31. Founder-Member,
MARS (Modern Architecture Research) Group,
London, 1933. Exhibitions: *Lubetkin and Tecton*,
Arnolfini Gallery, Bristol, 1981 (toured Great
Britain); *La Modernité—un projet inachevé*, Centre
Georges Pompidou, Paris, 1982; *Berthold Lubetkin:
un moderne en Angleterre*, Institut Français
d'Architecture, Paris, 1983. Recipient: Royal Gold
Medal, Royal Institute of British Architects, 1982.
Address: 113 Princess Victoria Street, Clifton 8,
Bristol, England.

Works:

1920/
  22 *Dacha* (country retreat), Russia (project)
      Dacha on a sloping site, Russia (project)
      Studio House, Russia (project)
1925 Polytechnic of the Urals, near Sverdlovsk,
        U.S.S.R. (competition project; with C. M.
        Da Costa and L. Ituralde)
1925/
  29 Collective housing, Paris (project)
      Monsieur P. Apartment interiors, Paris
1926/
  29 Dismountable U.S.S.R. Trades Pavilions,
        France
1927/
  28 Club Trapèze Volant (warehouse conversion),
        Rue de Volontaires, Paris
1928 Centrosoyuz Building, Miasnitzkaia, Mos-
        cow (project)
1928/
  31 Apartments, Avenue de Versailles, Paris (with
        Jean Ginsberg)
1930 Harrari House, Hampstead, London (project)
1931 Palace of the Soviets, Moscow (project; with
        Blum and Sigalin)
1932 Tuberculosis Clinic, East Ham, London (pro-
        ject)
1932/
  33 Gorilla House, London Zoo, Regent's Park,
        London
1932/
  34 Houses, Genesta Road, Plumstead, London
        (with Pilichowski)
1933 House, Heath Drive, Hare Street, Gidea Park,
        Essex
1933/
  34 "Beach House," Bay Walk, Aldwick, Bognor,
        Sussex
1933/
  35 Highpoint I flats, North Hill, Highgate,
        London
1933/
  36 Two houses, Whipsnade Zoo Estate, Bed-
        fordshire
1934 Venesta display stand, Building Exhibition,
        Olympia, London
      Penguin Pool, London Zoo, Regent's Park,
        London
1935/
  35 Egypt End house (now Gordonbush), Farn-
        ham Common, Buckinghamshire
      Six Pillars house, Crescentwood, Dulwich,
        London
      Houses, Sunnywood Drive, Haywards Heath,
        Sussex
      Giraffe House, Elephant House, restaurant
        and kiosks, Whipsnade Zoo, Bedfordshire
1935 Working-Class Flats, London (competition
        project)
1935/
  38 Finsbury Health Centre, Pine Street, Fins-
        bury, London
1936/
  37 House alterations, Mill Hill, London
      Refreshment Bar, London Zoo, Regent's
        Park, London
      Dudley Zoo, Dudley Castle, Worcestershire
1936/
  38 Highpoint II flats, North Hill, Highgate,
        London
1937 Studio of Animal Art, London Zoo, Regent's
        Park, London
      News Chronicle School (competition project)
      Elephant House, London Zoo, Regent's Park,
        London (not completed)
1937/
  38 Lubetkin Penthouse in Highpoint II, High-
        gate, London
1937/
  39 Air Raid Shelter Plan, Finsbury, London
1937/
  51 Priory Green Housing Estate, Finsbury, Lon-
        don
1938/
  46 Spa Green Housing Estate, Finsbury, London
1939 "Joldwynds" house (now "The Wilderness"),
        Holmbury St. Mary, Abinger, Surrey
1942 Lenin Memorial, Holford Square, Finsbury,
        London

1947/
55 Hallfield Housing Estate, Bishop's Bridge
Road, Paddington, London (completed by
Lasdun and Drake)
1948/
50 Peterlee New Town Plan, County Durham
(project)
1952 New Docks Development, Karachi, Pakistan
(project)
1953 Lubetkin Farmhouse interiors, Upper Kilcott, Gloucestershire
1954/
56 Holford Square Housing Development, Finsbury, London

Publications:

By LUBETKIN: books—*Opening of Finsbury
Health Centre*, London 1938; *Planned A.R.P.*,
London 1939; *Report to Finsbury Borough Council on
Structural Protection for People Against Aerial
Bombardment*, London 1939; *Spa Green Estate*,
London 1952; *La Modernité—un projet inachevé*,
exhibition catalogue, with others, Paris 1982;
articles—"The Builders," in special Russian issue of
Architectural Review (London), May 1932; "Modern
Architecture in England" in *American Architect*
(New York), Feburary 1937; "Soviet Architecture:
Notes on Developments from 1917-1932" in *Archi-
tectural Association Journal* (London), May 1956;
"Soviet Architecture: Notes on Developments from
1932-1955" in *Architectural Association Journal*
(London), September/October 1956; "Milton
Keynes" in *L'Architecture d'aujourd'hui* (Paris), no.
192, 1977; "Berthold Lubetkin: Royal Gold Medal
Address" in *RIBA Transactions* (London), no. 2,
1982.

On LUBETKIN: books and papers—*Discursive
Notes on Berthold Lubetkin*, thesis by C. W. N.
Mann, University of Liverpool 1975; *Berthold
Lubetkin and Ove Arup: A Study of a Unique
Partnership*, thesis by R. Carroll, University of
Newcastle 1976; *The Rationalists: Theory and Design
in the Modern Movement*, edited by Dennis Sharp,
London 1978; *The Architects of London* by Alastair
Service, London 1979; *Lubetkin and Tecton: the
Modern Architecture of Classicism* by John S. Allan,
London 1981; *A Broken Wave: The Rebuilding of
England 1940-1980* by Lionel Esher, London 1981;
*Lubetkin and Tecton: Architecture and Social Com-
mitment* by Peter Coe and Malcolm Reading,
London and Bristol 1981; *Modern Architecture since
1900* by William J. R. Curtis, London 1982;
Lubetkin—Theory and Practice in Highpoint I and II,
thesis by Tom Diehl, Architectural Association,
London 1982; *Berthold Lubetkin: un moderne en
Angleterre*, exhibition catalogue, by Peter Coe,
Malcolm Reading, Jean-Louis Cohen and others,
Brussels and Liège, Belgium 1983; articles—"Flats
on Spa Green Estate, Finsbury" in *Architects'
Journal* (London), 26 April 1951; "Groupe
d'immeubles Spa Green à Finsbury, Londres" in
Techniques et architecture (Paris), April 1953; "Lub-
etkin" by Robert Furneaux Jordan in *Architectural
Review* (London), July 1955; "Historic Pioneers:
Architects and Clients" by Sam Lambert in *Archi-
tects' Journal* (London), 11 March 1970; "Berthold
Lubetkin on 'Socialist' Architecture in the Dias-
pora" by William J. R. Curtis in *Archithese*
(Niederteufen, Switzerland), no. 12, 1974; "High
Point Flats, Camden" in *Design* (London), De-
cember 1974; "Perspective: Hampstead in the 30's"
in *Building Design* (London), 17 January 1975;
"Apostle of the Concrete Curve" by Stephen
Gardiner in *Observer Magazine* (London), 16 De-
cember 1979; "Good Dreams Gone Wrong" by
Owen Luder in *Building Design* (London), 22 May
1981; "High Points" by Dennis Sharp in *Building*
(London), 5 June 1981; "Lubetkin and Tecton on the
Move" in *The Architects' Journal* (London), 10 June

Berthold Lubetkin: Highpoint II Flats, Highgate, London, 1938.

1981; "Thoroughly Modern Architect" by Sutherland Lyall in *New Society* (London), 14 January
1982; "Lubetkin at Last" by Jonathan Glancey in
Architectural Review (London), April 1982.

In 1930, Berthold Lubetkin, a Russian-born architect, arrived in London from Paris. Although he was
only twenty-nine, his architectural outlook was
already well formed. Lubetkin had been influenced
by the political and cultural upheavals of the Russian
Revolution of 1917 and by the archictectural
transformations that occurred in Paris in the late
1920s, especially the work of Le Corbusier. He had
studied at the atelier Perret in Paris, had learned the
basics of reinforced concrete construction, and had
imbibed something of the classical principles underlying the work of the master.

The young architect who arrived in England in
1930 was well prepared for the building tasks of a
modern society and might well have preferred to
have practised in Russia except that official dogma
there soon turned against modern architecture.
Instead, Lubetkin set up a practice in London with
six Architectural Association graduates, and the
group became known as Tecton. Before his arrival,
Lubetkin had demonstrated the range of his talents
in an apartment building on the Avenue de Versailles
in Paris, but in England his earliest works were for
animals rather than men. The first of these was an
ingenious *machine à habiter* for two Congolese
gorillas in London Zoo. This was built in the form of
an environmentally adaptable cylinder that simu-
lated some of the climatic conditions of the jungle,
while protecting the beasts from germs and providing a circulation route for public viewing. The other
main building, for the same client, was the better
known Penguin Pool of 1933. With its taut,
interlacing ramps and its abstract sculptural quality,
it shows clearly the influence of Russian Constructivists such as Gabo and Pesvner.

High Point I flats in Highgate of 1935 also indicate
Lubetkin's debt to the architecture of the revolutionary avant-garde in Russia, particularly the communal buildings of the OSA group. Thus, despite its
upper-middle-class inhabitants, the building has the
quality of a polemic for a new social order and
contains communal zones on top, on the roof terrace,
and below, in a hallway that is a sort of emblematic

forum. As well as the imagery of socialist architecture, High Point I incorporates a formal vocabulary
and system of concrete construction derived from Le
Corbusier. Indeed Le Corbusier visited the building
and praised it highly, announcing it as "The Vertical
Garden City" of the future. Clearly, he recognized in
it a personal reinterpretation of his own urban
doctrines and utopian fantasies in favor of the
employment of modern technique to create a high-
density communal existence in an idyllic natural
setting.

High Point II, which Lubetkin designed a few
years later, represents an extension of the International Style vocabulary of High Point I so that more
materials and a more complex facade design can be
realized. The later building has a strong neoclassical
quality and contains blatant historical references in
some of its details—for example, the classical
caryatids supporting the cantilevered entrance slab.
The materials and the expensive 2/1 section of High
Point II are luxurious, and it seems in retrospect as if
the polemical quality of the earlier building has been
replaced by superficial stylistic formulae. High Point
II sets the tone for some of the rather mannered
modernistic, curvaceous clichés prevalent in the
1950s.

Lubetkin's sense of social experimentation found
an outlet in the Finsbury Health Centre (1938),
which again indicates some of the architect's deeply
embedded neo-Baroque tendencies. The building is
symmetrical and has clearly arranged hierarchies of
fixed and changeable functions—a formal and
functional strategy to be taken over in the postwar
years by Denys Lasdun, the most gifted of the young
architects to pass through Lubetkin's office.

In the late 1940s Lubetkin was temporarily
involved with design of Peterlee, a new town, which
called for the full range of his social and formal
powers. However, his principles and his clients' were
not in accord, and, strangely, Lubetkin all but ceased
to pratice by the early 1950s. Still, Lubetkin's
influence in England has been considerable. At its
weakest, this has been a matter of a diluted
vocabulary of strip windows, hump-shaped roofs,
colored tiles, and flats on stilts; at its strongest
(particularly via the original talent of Lasdun), it has
been a matter of the extension of basic ideological
and formal messages from early modern
architecture.

—William J. R. Curtis

LUCAS, Colin Anderson.

British. Born in London, 29 December 1906. Educated at Cheltenham College, Gloucestershire, 1919-25; Trinity College, Cambridge (Cambridge University Architectural School), 1925-28. Married Dione Wilson in 1931; Pamela Campbell in 1952; sons: Mark and Peter. Director, Lucas Lloyd and Company, builders, Greenwich, London, 1928-33; Partner, with Amyas Connell, *q.v.*, and Basil Ward, Connell, Ward and Lucas, London, 1933-39; Architect, Ministry of Works, Building Research Station, and Ministry of Home Security, 1941-51, and with the Housing Division, London County Council and Greater London Council, 1951-78; retired, to concentrate on painting, London, 1978 until his death in 1984. Exhibitions: *Contemporary Industrial Design in the Home,* Dorland Hall, London, 1934; Exhibition of drawings of blocks of working-class flats in reinforced concrete, Imperial Institute, London, 1935; *Contemporary Industrial Design,* London, 1935; Museum of Modern Art, New York, 1935; Royal Academy, London, 1938; *Unit one: Spirit of the Thirties,* Mayor Gallery, London, 1985. Fellow, Royal Institute of British Architects, 1939. O.B.E. (Officer, Order of the British Empire), 1972. *Died* (in London) *25 August 1984.*

Works

1927 Silver Birches house, Burghclere, Hampshire
1930 Noah's House (house and boathouse), Spade Oak Reach, Bourne End, Buckinghamshire

1931 Sun House, Chelwood Gate, Ashdown Forest, Sussex
1933 The Hop Field house, St. Marys Platt, Wrotham, Kent (with Amyas Connell and Basil Ward)
1934 Four Houses, High and Over Estate, Amersham, Buckinghamshire (with Amyas Connell and Basil Ward)
1935 Kent House Flats, Ferdinand Street, Chalk Farm, London (with Amyas Connell and Basil Ward)
    Two pairs of semi-detached houses, Parkwood Estate, Ruislip, Middlesex (with Amyas Connell and Basil Ward)
    The Firs house, Brighton Road, Redhill, Surrey (with Amyas Connell and Bail Ward)
    Hertford County Buildings (competition project; with Amyas Connell and Basil Ward)
1936 Dragons house, Woodmancote, Sussex (with Amyas Connell and Basil Ward)
    Concrete House (Ronad Gunn House), The Ridgeway, Westbury-on-Trym, Bristol (with Amyas Connell and Basil Ward)
    Civic Buildings, Newport, Monmouthshire (competition project; with Amyas Connell and Basil Ward)
1937 House, Wentworth, Virginia Water, Surrey (with Amyas Connell and Basil Ward)
    Geoffrey Walford house, 66 Frognal, Hampstead, London (with Amyas Connell and Basil Ward)
    House, Worcester Park, Surrey (with Amyas Connell and Basil Ward)

    Sound City Film Studios, Shepperton, Middlesex (with Amyas Connell and Basil Ward)
1937/
  38 H.Tarburn House, 6 Temple Gardens, Moor Park, Hertfordshire (with Amyas Connell and Basil Ward)
1938 Potcraft (Dr. Thomas House), Sutton, Surrey (with Amyas Connell and Basil Ward)
1938/
  39 Major Proudman house, 26 Bessborough Gardens, Roehampton, London (with Amyas Connell and Basil Ward)
1939 Lords Court (apartment building and shops), 32 St. John's Wood Road, London (partially built with Amyas Connell and Basil Ward)
With Greater London Council Architects Department Housing Division:
1951/
  78 Alton Estate West, Roehampton
    Ackroydon Estate
    Canada Estate
    Somerset Estate
    Westbury Street Estate
    Kidbrooke Estate

Publications:

On LUCAS: book—*Modern Architecture since 1900* by William J.R. Curtis, London 1982; articles—"Heroes of the Modern Movement" by Amyas Connell and Walter Menzies in *Building Design* (London), 27 February 1976; "Building Revisited:

Colin Lucas: The Hopfield House, Wrotham, Kent, 1933.

Alton Estate, Roehampton" by Michael Fleetwood in *Architects' Journal* (London), 30 March 1977; "Obituary: Mr. Colin Lucas" in *The Times* (London), 29 August 1984.

My work as an architect was originally—and is still—inspired by a feeling for the material one is using, and particularly its structural possibilities. This, coupled with the three-dimensional disposition of space dictated by the client's requirements, combines to give the opportunity for the expression of certain proportions in the structure as a whole. Thus, materials, space, and proportion are the three main design elements. Whether the finished building is doomed to be reminiscent of this or that period or style is irrelevant. Ideally, it should have no style other than its own.

—Colin Lucas (1980)

The International Style architecture of Continental Europe was usually constructed of concrete blocks plastered and painted to give the illusion of a building completely constructed of reinforced concrete. That did not worry Le Corbusier, but it did worry the moralizing, puritanical English who felt that if it looked as if it was all made of reinforced concrete, then it should indeed all be made of reinforced concrete. It was Colin Lucas who showed them how to do it.

Lucas felt that the new architecture in England was continually frustrated by the conservatism of builders, so he formed his own building company, Lucas Lloyd and Company, to build unconventional buildings. He evolved a system of building in reinforced concrete, using 100-millimetre walls and 125-millimetre floor and roof slabs, from which he built the first reinforced concrete houses in England. His Noah's House and boathouse at Spade Oak Reach, Bourne End, Buckinghamshire, exploits the potential of reinforced concrete construction; some of the details, such as the curved stair balustrades, seem curiously dated, but the way that the construction allows one whole wall of the living room to be of thin concrete mullions and glass is as fresh today as when it was built. Lucas followed up the success of Noah's House with The Hop Field, St Mary's Platt, Wrotham, Kent, a truly beautiful little building, with a very solid outside staircase tying the house to the ground.

In 1933 Colin Lucas joined Amyas Connell and Basil Ward to form Connell, Ward and Lucas and was able to bring to the firm his unparalleled knowledge of reinforced concrete house-building. For six years, they produced a series of houses that no other contemporary firm could match. They were world class architects.

Connell, Ward and Lucas acted as a team, and Lucas's experience in concrete construction is evident in all the houses built by the firm. However, the individual authorship of the firm's houses is known, and Lucas is seen at his best in the final flowering of the firm just before the war. Lucas's 66 Frognal in London, the firm's most famous house, is inventive, beautifully built, and very habitable; his Roehampton house explores emphasized horizontals and is a response to some of the detailing failures of the earlier houses. Lucas's Potcraft at Sutton is an intriguing tailpiece; built of timber boarding on a timber frame, and with a sloping roof, it shows that the architect had gained sufficient confidence to re-introduce traditional forms and materials.

After the war, Lucas worked in the Architects Department of the London County Council. His role there was largely administrative, but it was the kind of administration that enabled architecture to happen. It was the young architects under Lucas that built the great Roehampton scheme, only a few hundred yards from Connell, Ward and Lucas's last house.

—John Winter

LUCKHARDT, Hans.
German. Born in Berlin, 16 June 1880. Educated at the Technische Hochschule, Karlsruhe. Served in the German Army. In partnership with his brother Wassili Luckhardt, *q.v.,* from 1921, and with Alfons Anker, as Bruder Luckhardt und Anker, Berlin, from 1924 until his death, 1954. Recipient: First Prize, with Wassili Luckhardt, Alexanderplatz Competition, Berlin, 1929. *Died* (in Bad Wiessee, West Germany) *in 1954.*

See LUCKHARDT, Wassili

LUCKHARDT, Wassili.
German. Born in Berlin, 22 July 1889. Educated at the Technische Hochschule, Charlottenburg, Berlin, and Dresden. Served in the German Army. In partnership with his brother Hans Luckhardt, *q.v.,* Berlin, 1921-54, and with Alfons Anker, as Bruder Luckhardt und Anker, Berlin, 1924-54; in private practice, Berlin, 1954 until his death, 1972. Member, Novembergruppe artists' group, Berlin, 1919; Der Ring architects association, Berlin, 1925. Exhibition: *Zeit im Aufriss,* Herkulessaal der Residenz, Munich, 1983. Recipient: First Prize, with Hans Luckhardt, Alexanderplatz Competition, Berlin, 1929; Kunstpreis, Berlin, 1958. D.Eng.: Technische Hochschule, Berlin, 1962. Member, Akademie der Künste, Berlin, 1956. *Died* (in Berlin) *2 December 1972.*

Works:

1919 Glass Banqueting Hall (project)
     Cinema (project)
1920 Private House (project)
1921 Theatre (project)
     Museum of Hygiene (project; with Hans Luckhardt)
1922 Skyscraper, Friedrichstrasse, Berlin (competition project; with Hans Luckhardt)
1923 Private house, Westend, Berlin (with Hans Luckhardt)
     Norma Tool Factory, Berlin (competition project; with Hans Luckhardt)
     Office building conversion, Tauentzienstrasse, Berlin (with Hans Luckhardt)
1924 Housing estate, Dahlem, Berlin (with Hans Luckhardt)
1927 Experimental housing development, Schorlemer Allee, Berlin (with Hans Luckhardt)
     Exhibition Room, Thannhauser Art Gallery, Bellevuestrasse, Berlin (with Hans Luckhardt)
     Office building, Kurfürstendamm, Berlin (with Hans Luckhardt)
1928 Three houses, Rupenhorn, Berlin (with Hans Luckhardt and Alfons Anker)
     Pavilion, *Heim und Technik* exhibition, Munich (with Hans Luckhardt)
1929 Telschow-Haus Department Store, Potsdamer Platz, Berlin (with Hans Luckhardt and Alfons Anker)
     Alexanderplatz redevelopment, Berlin (competition project; with Hans Luckhardt)
     Housing development, Gohlis, Leipzig (project; with Hans Luckhardt)
1930 Berlin House, Potsdamer Platz, Berlin (project; with Hans Luckhardt)
1931 Central Law Courts, Berlin (project; with Hans Luckhardt)
1932 Private house, Velten, near Berlin (with Hans Luckhardt)
     Private house, Lankwitz, Berlin (with Hans Luckhardt)
1933 Pavilion, *Building Exhibition,* Berlin (with Hans Luckhardt)

1946 Building for the University of Jena, Germany (competition project; with Hans Luckhardt)
1948 Bridge, Stockholm (project; with Hans Luckhardt)
1951 Berlin Pavilion, and Terrace House, Constructa Exhibition, Hanover (with Hans Luckhardt)
1952 American Memorial Library, Berlin (competition project; with Hans Luckhardt)
     Institute of Plant Physiology, Free University of Berlin (competition project; with Hans Luckhardt)
     Treasury Building, Steglitz, Berlin (project; with Hans Luckhardt)
1954 German Student Residence, Cité Universitaire, Paris (with Hans Luckhardt)
1956 Apartment building, Kottbusser Tor, Berlin
1957 Social Welfare Administration Centre for Bavaria, Munich (initial design with Hans Luckhardt)
     Berlin Pavilion, *International Building Exhibition,* Berlin (project)
     Town Hall, Bremen, West Germany (competition project)
     Luckhardt House, Dahlem, Berlin
     Apartment building, Hansa District, Berlin (with Hubert Hoffmann)
     City Hall, Toronto (competition project)
1962/
  69 Deputies Assembly Hall, Bremen, West Germany
1962/
  70 Institute for Plant Physiology, Free University of Berlin
1963/
  68 Institute for Veterinary Medicine, Free University of Berlin

Publications:

By LUCKHARDT: books—*Zur neuen Wohnform,* with Hans Luckhardt, Berlin 1930; *Lichtarchitektur,* with Walter Kohler, Berlin 1956; letters in *Die Glaserne Kette,* exhibition catalogue, Berlin 1963; articles—"Gross-Garagenhaus fur tausend Automobile", with Hans Luckhardt and Alfons Anker, in *Architektur und Schaufenster* (Berlin), March 1927; "Das Geschaftslokal im Strassenbild" in *Architektur und Schaufenster* (Berlin), July 1927; "Versuche zur Fortentwicklung des Wohnbaues" in *Bauwelt* (Berlin), no. 31, 1927.

On LUCKHARDT: books—*Wassili und Hans Luckhardt: Bauten und Entwürfe* by Udo Kultermann, Tubingen 1958; *Wassili Luckhardt,* edited by Helga Kliemann, Tubingen 1973; *Deutsche Kunst seit 1960: Architektur* by Paolo Nestler and Peter M. Bode, Munich 1976; *Bauten des Bundes 1965-1980* by Wolfgang Leuschner, Karlsruhe 1980; *Zeit im Aufriss: Architektur in Bayern nach 1945,* exhibition catalogue by Christoph Hackelsberger, Munich 1983; articles—"Die Wohnung unserer Zeit" by Ludwig Hilberseimer in *Die Form* (Berlin), 15 July 1931; "A House Near Berlin by the Brothers Luckhardt" in *Architectural Journal* (London), July 1936; "Wohnhochhausgruppe am Kottbusser Tor in Berlin" in *Bauen und Wohnen* (Zurich), June 1956; "Das Landesversorgungsamt Bayern in Munich" in *Bauen und Wohnen* (Zurich), July 1958; "Das Werk von Wassili und Hans Luckhardt" in *Bauen und Wohnen* (Zurich), February 1959; "Wassili Luckhardt" in *Der Aufbau* (Vienna), June 1959; "Provincial Offices, Munich" in *Architectural Review* (London), September 1960; "Das Haus der Bürgerschaft in Bremen" in *Bauwelt* (Berlin), 13 February 1967; "Pflanzenphysiologisches Institut der Freien Universität Berlin" in *Bauwelt* (Berlin), 10 August 1970; "Obituary: Wassili Luckhardt" in *Architecture Plus* (New York), May 1973; "Farewell to Berlin vanguard architects: Wassili Luckhardt and Hans

Scharoun" by Vladimir Slapeta in *Architektura CSR* (Prague), no. 8, 1973; "Four terraced houses at Schorlemer Allee 12-12C, Berlin-Dahlem (1928)" by Dietrich von Beulwitz in *Der Architekt* (Stuttgart), January 1977.

Wassili Luckhardt worked mainly in collaboration with his younger brother Hans until the latter's death in 1954. Like most of the significant German architects who were active in the 1920s they went through an expressionist phase at a time when, because of a shortage of clients with money, there was little opportunity to construct actual buildings. Those visionary and utopian expressionist architects who were genuinely striving to find new forms for new functions, to provide architecture with a new basis, exchanged ideas and discussed aesthetic questions in their contributions to Bruno Taut's magazine *Frühlicht*, which enabled them to publish designs of projects that were never actually realized. These projects include some highly imaginative designs by Wassili Luckhardt for theatres and cinemas, which would have been as strange in psychological atmosphere as the highly stylized sets of the German silent films of the time—yet these designs have had some influence on younger architects since the Second World War.

In the early 1920s the clients for German housing were largely the building societies; consequently, many housing estates and garden suburbs were built at the time. The Luckhardt brothers designed one of the first modern housing estates in Dahlem, Berlin, in 1924. They showed a marked inclination towards geometrical architecture, retangular and blocky, with a strong emphasis on such motifs as horizontal bands of windows. Despite this concern with the purity of rectangular shapes, they also explored the possibilities of free curved facades, as in the shop frontage of the Telschow-Haus Department Store, or of dynamically-curved blocks divided up by continuous horizontal bands of windows, as in their winning entry for the Berlin Alexanderplatz.

During the same period they built three modern residences on the western outskirts of Berlin at Ruperhorn: the houses take full advantage of the splendid view and other special features of a site where Erich Mendelsohn also chose to build his own house in the same year. The first of these houses to be built is particularly interesting in design, on three floors with a roof garden, full use being made of the steel-frame structure in obtaining the utmost flexibility in the planning of each floor. The first floor living room has six large bays all along its front with large glass panels, alternately fixed and sliding horizontally on rollers, opening out onto a terrace irregularly shaped like half of a tennis-racket, providing maximum opportunity for enjoying the sun and the view throughout the day.

A typical example of the Luckhardt brothers' work after the interruption of the Hitler period and the destruction of the Second World War was the Berlin Pavilion at the *Constructa Exhibition* of 1951 in Hanover. The Pavilion was intended to demonstrate, by a display of drawings and models, Berlin's progress in building since 1945; the construction consisted of a steel frame carrying both roofs and walls, the walls being taken to only half the height of the building, with the intervening spaces entirely glazed with plate glass, producing a partially transparent building: the impression of lightness and floating was heightened by the view of the trees seen through it.

In 1954, before Hans's death, they had produced the final design for the Munich offices of the Social Welfare Administration, which was built in 1957. The special design problem faced here was that since the offices would be regularly visited by many war-disabled and other invalids, it was essential that these visitors should not have to climb stairs—nor did the use of lifts seem practical. The Luckhardts' solution was to situate all the offices to which the public would have access in ground-floor, single storey, pontoon-shaped buildings, while the offices to which the public would not have access are on three floors of a long building that appears to float on pilotis at right angles to the pontoons.

Wassili Luckhardt's apartment building on the Kottbusser Tor, Berlin, shares the propensity to balconies of other German architects of the time, the balconies being built into the structure, shielded by the walls, to produce a flat though indented facade. Even while Hans was alive the brothers had often collaborated with other architects (for example, Alfons Anker), and in 1957 Wassili worked with Hubert Hoffmann in designing a block of flats in the Hansa Quarter, Berlin, consisting of a range of five terrace structures divided longitudinally by staircase towers, with different sizes and plans of flats permitting a wide variety of dwelling types.

In 1958 Wassili Luckhardt was awarded the Kunstpreis of the City of Berlin, where most of his work was built.

—Konstantin Bazarov

LUMSDEN, Anthony.

American. Born (of Australian nationality) in Bournemouth, Hampshire, England, 16 May 1928; emigrated to the United States, 1954. Educated at the University of Sydney School of Architecture, 1947-51, B.Arch. 1951. Married Anne Fowler in 1964; children: John, Thomas, and Fiona. Project Designer, Eero Saarinen *q.v.*, and Associates, Bloomfield Hills, Michigan, 1954-60; Senior Designer, Kevin Roche, *q.v.*, John Dinkeloo, *q.v.*, Hamden, Connecticut, 1962-64. Since 1964, Vice-President and Principal in charge of Design, Daniel, Mann, Johnson and Mendenhall, Los Angeles. Architectural Consultant, United States Department of State, Washington, D.C., 1984-87. Exhibitions: *Three Worlds of Los Angeles*, Brussels, 1974, Paris, 1975; *Los Angeles 12*, Pacific Design Center, Los Angeles, and tour, 1975-76; *California Architects*, Museum of Modern Art, San Francisco, and tour, 1977. Recipient: First Design Award, 1966, and Annual Design Award, 1972, *Progressive Architecture;* Merit Award, United States Department of Housing and Urban Development, 1967; Excellence in Human Factors Design Award, Institute of Human Engineering Sciences, 1967; Architectural Award of Excellence, American Institute of Steel Construction, 1968, 1972; Special Award for Architectural and Engineering Excellence in Design, 1969, and Award of Engineering Excellence, 1973, Portland Cement Association; Award of Honor, 1969, 1975 (twice), 1976, and Award of Merit, 1969, 1973, 1976, American Institute of Architects, Southern California Chapter; Award of Merit, AIA/National Center for Low and Moderate Income Housing/National Urban Coalitation/Urban Design and Development Corporation, 1970; Honor Award, AIA/*House and Home*, 1970; Design Award, 1970, and Honor Award, 1973, AIA, Hawaii Chapter; Award of Merit, National Society of Professional Engineers, 1972; Eminent Conceptor Award, 1972, and Award of Excellence, 1973, Consulting Engineers Association of California. Fellow, American Institute of Architects. Address: DMJM, 3250 Wilshire Boulevard, Los Angeles, California 90010, U.S.A.

Works:

1966 Beverly Hills Jewelry Store, Los Angeles (with Cesar Pelli)
  Sunset Mountain Park, Santa Monica, California (project; with Cesar Pelli)
1967 Los Angeles Rapid Transit
1967/
 68 Third Street Tunnel, Los Angeles (with Cesar Pelli)
1967/
 69 Worldway Post Office, Los Angeles (with Cesar Pelli)
1967/
 70 Kukui Gardens, Honolulu
1967/
 73 Federal Aviation Administration Agency, Lawndale, California
1968 Teledyne Systems Research and Manufacturing Facility, Northridge, California (with Cesar Pelli)
1969 Beneficial Life Building, Los Angeles
  Century City Medical Plaza, Los Angeles (with Cesar Pelli)
  Pacific Ocean Park, Los Angeles
  Lockheed Offices, Sunnyvale, California
1970 Hillrise Apartments, Honolulu (project)
1970/
 72 One Park Plaza, Los Angeles
1971/
 72 Century Bank, Los Angeles
1972 Naval Air Reworks Facility, San Diego, California
  Immobiliaire Apartments, Los Angeles (project)
  Convention Center, Lugano, Switzerland (project)
  Sepulvedra Water Reclamation Plant, Los Angeles (project)
1972/
 75 Marina City, Los Angeles
1972/
 76 Bank Bumi Daya, Jakarta, Indonesia (project)
1973 A La Wai Plaza Skyrise Building, Honolulu
  City Hall, Las Vegas, Nevada
  Sears Warehouse, Los Angeles
  Beverly Hills Hotel, California (project)
  Sepulvedra Bridge, Los Angeles
1974 Holyoke Community College Gymnasium and Natatorium Building, and Student Center, Holyoke, Massachusetts
  El Monte Bus Station, Los Angeles
  Banyan Tree Apartments, Honolulu
  Portland Plaza, Oregon
  Roxbury Plaza, Beverly Hills, California
  Santa Clara Office Building, California
  Van Nuys Housing, Los Angeles
  Kodak Office Building, Whittier, California (project)
  Trident Naval Warehouse, Seattle
1974/
 76 Jacksonville Community College, Jacksonville, Florida (with Reynolds, Smith, and Hills)
  Van Camp Food Processing Factory, San Diego, California
1975 Baltimore Community College
  Ford Office Building, Bethesda, Maryland
  Tempe Mall, Arizona
  University Station, Los Angeles
  Library, Santa Monica Community College, California
  East Los Angeles Medical Clinic
  Plan for the Moda Medical Center, Al Kharj, Saudi Arabia
1976 Northlake Community College, Irving, Texas (with Envirodynamics Inc.)
  Lawrence Laser Laboratories, Livermore, California
  Saudi Youth Evaluation Center, Riyadh, Saudi Arabia
  Detention facility at Peoria, Illinois
  Engine test facility at Tullahoma, Tennessee
  Riyadh New Town, Saudi Arabia
1976/
 77 Pedestrian bridges, Los Angeles
1976/
 81 Business Education/Vocation Building, Santa Monica College, California
1977 Gajah Mada Commercial Complex, Jakarta, Indonesia
  Music Building, Santa Monica Community College, California
  Harapan Plaza, Jakarta, Indonesia

Longview Community College, Kansas City, Missouri

Maplewood Community College, Kansas City, Missouri

Capitol Building, St. Paul, Minnesota (competition project)

Ambassador College Office Building, Pasadena, California

Office building, Anchorage, Alaska

1977/
80 Library and Learning Resource Center, Santa Monica College, California

1978 Los Angeles Valley College, Van Nuys, California

Downtown Moving Pavement, Los Angeles

1979/
81 United States Postal Service General Mail and Maintenance Facility, Long Beach, California

1980/
81 Hertz Corporation Maintenance Facility and Administration Building, Los Angeles International Airport

1980/
82 Bullock's Office Building, Los Angeles

1980/
84 JAL (Japan Airlines) Hotel, Singapore
Meridien Hotel, Singapore
Changi Hotel, Singapore

1981 Ojai Valley Inn, Ojai, California
Overseas Union Bank, Singapore

1981/
82 Hertz Corporation Turnaround Facility, Los Angeles International Airport

1981/
84 American President Lines Administration Building, San Pedro, California

1982 Robin Loh Office Building, Houston, Texas
Knapp Office Building, Los Angeles
San Diego Office Building, San Diego, California
Harborview Complex, San Diego, California
Cheung Office Building, Singapore
Khota Bharu Air Terminal, Malaysia
Golden Triangle Complex, Kuala Lumpur, Malaysia
Bowers Museum, Anaheim, California
Best Products display, Museum of Modern Art, New York

1982/
83 Rockwell Research Laboratory Building, Thousand Oaks, California

1982/
84 Rahardja Centre, Singapore
Encino Terrace Center, Encino, California

1983 Housing for the Elderly, Palos Verdes, California

1983/
84 Capitol Bank of Commerce Center, Sacramento, California

1984 Kent Plaza, Phoenix, Arizona
Makki Office Building, Kuala Lumpur, Malaysia
Kenny Hill Condominiums, Kuala Lumpur, Malaysia
Occupational Education Building, Oxnard Community College, Oxnard, California
San Angeles Little Tokyo Project, Los Angeles

1984/
85 Continental City, Los Angeles
Lockheed Weapons Simulation Center, Rye Canyon, California
Nuccio Office Building, Los Angeles
New California Cuisine Restaurant and Office Building, Encino, California

Publications:

On LUMSDEN: book—*12 Los Angeles Architects*, edited by N. Charles Slert and James R. Harter, Pomona, California 1978; articles—"Anthony Lumsden, DMJM" in *Architecture + Urbanism* (Tokyo),

Anthony Lumsden: Rahardja Centre, Singapore, 1982-84.

March 1975; "The Development of an Esthetic System at DMJM" by Michael Franklin Ross in *Architectural Record* (New York,) May 1975; "Post-Mies: Architetture di Anthony Lumsden" by Esther McCoy in *Domus* (Milan), November 1975; "Images from a Silver Screen" in *Progressive Architecture* (New York), October 1976; "Architecture-Promotion, Architecte-Promoteur" in *Architecture d'Aujourd'hui* (Paris), October 1977; "One Park Plaza in Los Angeles" in *Industria delle costruzioni* (Rome), January 1978; "Bus Stop at Los Angeles" in *Domus* (Milan), July 1978; "St. Vincent Medical Centre, Los Angeles" in *Informes de la construccion* (Madrid), September 1978; "Bridge Connection for a Bus Terminal" in *Informes de la construccion* (Madrid), March 1979; "Anthony Lumsden, DMJM" in *Space Design* (Tokyo), July 1979; "Moveable Grandstand Built for Giant U.S. Stadium" in *Asian Building and Construction* (Hong Kong), January/February 1980; "Best: Exhibition at the Museum of Modern Art" in *Architecture intérieure créé* (Paris), March/April 1980; "Over the Rainbow" in *Domus* (Milan), July/August 1980.

Anthony Lumsden is an architect of polemics, of keen visual awareness, and of bold imagery. His architectural skill is displayed in a large body of work that often breaks from modern precepts to forge new directions and explore previously uncharted waters.

The strength of his convictions can be seen in the powerful images of the Lugano Convention Center, the Beverly Hills Hotel and the Bank Bumi Daya. Lumsden's somewhat unconventional approach to design sometimes leaves the uninitiated and less sophisticated wondering as to the full intent of his work. Careful analysis and patient review of the work reveal a clear, consistent attitude toward the design process, which often manifests itself in diverse and unsuspected exterior forms.

Lumsden is fond of examining the relationship of form and function in nature and applying it to architecture. Any school of fish in the sea or swarm of butterflies clearly indicates a visual diversity that has far more to do with the exterior environment than it has to do with the internal workings of the particular species. Similarly, Lumsden maintains that an architect can solve the internal functions and quite independently develop an exterior that is appropriate to a given environment. The Bevery Hills Hotel, for example, has a dramatic silhouette that steps up along the diagonal in a series of extruded cylinders that enclose a variable-height galleria of terraced shops. By employing a membrane skin enclosure that is not dependent on the structure for its esthetic, Lumsden can allow the rolling surface to respond to variations in site configuration and programmatic requirements. The combination of the sophisticated high-tech membrane enclosure and the extruded, vernacular esthetic was a bold departure for Lumsden that heralded new explorations in the 1970s. The FAA Building, the Sepulvedra Water Reclamation Plant, and the Beverly Hills Hotel, signaled a departure from current architectural preoccupations of the period.

Lumsden's design approach has been applied to both high-rise office towers and horizontal stepping universities and college campuses. The rolling surfaces of Roxbury Plaza, the angled, folded planes of Century Bank Plaza and the extended curved corners of One Park Plaza, headquarters of DMJM, of which Lumsden is Vice President and Principal for Design, form an interesting evolution of the variable surface membrane enclosure as it is applied to commercial office structures.

Perhaps the most successful application of the extrusion esthetic yet to be realized by Lumsden is the Northlake Community College in Irving, Texas. Set on a rolling 276-acre wooded hillside, the new campus is composed of a series of stepping volumes that repeat a similar profile. By employing the extrusion esthetic, Lumsden makes the building step up the hillside in what he describes as, "a series of little buildings like you get in a Japanese village...like vernacular architecture." The use of horizontal planters at grade and cantilevering off the roof is the continuation of an esthetic system that Lumsden first worked on as project architect under Kevin Roche for the Oakland Museum.

The separation of membrane enclosure from structure departs from the trabeated aesthetic of Mies van der Rohe and of his Chicago disciples at Skidmore, Owings and Merrill, but it is not really all that radical. Le Corbusier's Domino House concept and his villas at Vaucresson and at Garches clearly led the way for these more recent explorations. In his *Age of Modern Masters*, Reyner Banham uses Lumsden's Century Bank Plaza and Corbu's Parliament Building at Chandigarh to illustrate his point that,

In a world where art-movements like Pop and Op have evaporated like the morning dew, the style that runs—visually—from Gropius's Fagus factory of 1911 to Le Corbusier's Capitol buildings at Chandigarh and on to the prismatic mirror-glass sky-scrapers being built in the US in the early Seventies, is a style to be reckoned with, durable beyond the expectations of our time.

There is no question that these visual explorations by Lumsden and others will continue. It is interesting to note, looking back over the body of work designed by Tony Lumsden in the last two decades, that his most compelling and original projects have not been built. One can only speculate on the impact a Sepulvedra Water Reclamation Plant, a Beverly Hills Hotel or a Bank Bumi Daya might have had on the profession had they been constructed, and whether future projects will again develop this high level or originality and vision.

—Michael Franklin Ross

LUND, Kjell.

Norwegian. Born in Lillehammer, 18 June 1927. Educated at the Norges Tekniske Høyskole, Trondheim, Dip.Arch. 1950. Married Tove Berg in 1954; children: Martine, Johanne, and Bendik. In private practice, Oslo, 1950-58. In partnership with Nils Slaatto, *q.v.*, Oslo, since 1958. Assistant Editor, *Byggekunst*, Oslo, 1959-70. Exhibitions: *Works of Lund and Slaatto*, Det Kongelige Danske Kunstakademie, Copenhagen, and Det Finske Arkitekurmuseum, Helsinki, 1975, toured universities and architecture schools in Europe and the United Kingdom, 1975-78; *Lund and Slaatto*, Architects' Association, Bergen, Norway, 1981; *Lund og Slaatto—Arkitekter i 25 år*, Norwegian Architecture Museum, Oslo, 1983; *Lund og Slaatto—Skapande Ordning*, Academy of Free Arts, Stockholm, 1984. Recipient: First Prize, Akerhaus County Agricul-

tural School Competition, Årnes, Norway, 1958; The Concrete Award, Federation of Norwegian Architects/Norwegian Concrete Association, 1964, 1977; The Wood Prize, Norwegian Concrete Association/Council for Tree Information, 1966; Sundt's Award, 1972, and Houen's Award, 1976, Federation of Norwegian Architects; First Prize, Norwegian Civil Engineers Main Office Building Competition, Oslo, 1970; First Prize, Eidsvåg Church Competition, Bergen, 1970; First Prize, National Gallery Extension Competition, Oslo, 1972; First Prize, National Theatre Extension Competition, Oslo, 1973; First Prize, Bank of Norway Competition, Oslo, 1973; First Prize, Cultural Centre Competition, Stavanger, 1980; Prize of Honour, Society of Useful Arts, Oslo, 1981. Address: Kjell Lund og Nils Slaatto Arkitekter, Bygdøy Allé 13, Oslo 2, Norway.

Works (with Nils Slaatto):

1958 Sawdust silo, Romedal Almenning, Norway
1958/
   60 Primary school, Vik, Ringerike, Norway
1958/
   63 Town Hall, Asker, Norway
1958/
   66 St. Hallvard Church and Monastery, Oslo
1958/
   68 Akerhaus County Agricultural School, Årnes, Norway
1959/
   61 House, Rostad, Oslo
1961 Bookshop, Gol, Hallingdal, Norway
1961/
   66 Farm, Trones, Verdal, Norway
1961/
   68 Nic Waals Child Psychiatry Institute, Oslo
1961/
   70 Chateau Neuf: Norwegian Student Association Center, Oslo
1962/
   63 Farm, Rua, Hønefoss, Norway
1963 House, Andersen, Lysaker, Norway
1963/
   64 House, Lund, Oslo
      House, Lystrup, Asker, Norway
1964 Henie-Onstad Art Center, Høvikodden, Norway (competition project)
      Radio station, Vardø, Norway
      Employers' Association Study Center, Jevnaker, Norway (competition project)
1966 Pyramiden Mountain Cabin (project)
1967 House, Haraldseid, Gol, Norway
1968 House, Botheim, Oslo
1968/
   69 Farmhouse, Rustad, As, Norway
1968/
   70 House, Kionig, Fredrikstad, Norway
      European Youth Center (Council of Europe), Strasbourg, France
1969 Bekkefaret Church, Stravanger, Norway (project)
1970 Center for Environmental Studies, Interlaken, Switzerland (competition project)
1972 Eidsvåg Church, Bergen (competition project)
      National Gallery extension, Oslo (competition project)
1972/
   74 Høvik Stål Factory and Office Building, Hønefoss, Norway
1972/
   76 Det Norske Veritas Administration/Research Center, Høvik, Norway
1973 National Theatre extension, Oslo (competition project)
      The Bank of Norway, Oslo (competition project)
1974 Plan for the center of Oslo
1974/
   75 Plan for the central park area, Oslo (partially executed, 1975-79)

1976 Farmhouse, Biri, Norway
1976/
   78 Bank building, Bagn, Valdres, Norway
      Andersen Factory, Larvik, Norway
1976/
   79 Police School, Oslo
      Nestlé-Findus Administration Center, Asker, Norway
      Norwegian Civil Engineers Main Office Building, Oslo
1977/
   78 Henrikke Outdoor Restaurant, Oslo
1979/
   80 Paviljongen Outdoor Restaurant, Oslo
1979/
   85 The Bank of Norway, Oslo
1981 Eidsvåg Church, Bergen, Norway
1982/
   84 Det Norske Veritas Administration/Research Center extensions, Høvik, Norway
1983 Pavilion, National Theatre Underground (subway) Station, Oslo (project)
1983/
   84 National Theatre refurbishment, Oslo
1983/
   85 Cultural Centre, Stavanger, Norway
1984 Kreditkasse Bank Head Office, Oslo (project)
      Kreditkasse Bank, Lillehammer, Norway (project)

Publications:

On LUND/SLAATTO: books—*World Architecture 2* and *4* by John Donat, London 1965, 1967; *Lund og Slaatto—Arkitekter i 25 År*, exhibition catalogue by Elisabeth Seip and Nils-Ole Lund, Oslo, 1983; *Skapande ordning—struktur og variasjon i arkitekturen*, exhibition catalogue by Elisabeth Seip, Stockholm 1984; articles—"St. Hallvard" by Nils Ole Lund and Martin Drouzy in *Dansk Arkitektur* (Copenhagen), June 1966; "Works of Lund and Slaatto" by Poul Erik Shriver in *Dansk Arkitektur* (Copenhagen), January 1972; "Modern Scandinavian Architecture," special issue of *Process: Architecture* (Tokyo/Pittsburgh), January 1977; "Veritas Center" by Karen Zahle in *Dansk Arkitektur* (Copenhagen), April 1977; Norges Bank—head offices in Oslo" in *Byggekunst* (Oslo), no. 1, 1979; "Police School" in *Byggekunst* (Oslo), no. 2, 1980; "Nestlé-Findus, Billingstadsletta" in *Byggekunst* (Oslo), no. 3/4, 1980; "Holiday House System in Wood" in *Detail* (Munich), March/April 1980; "Workshop in Larvik" in *Arkitekten* (Copenhagen), 26 August 1980; "Bagn Bank" in *Architectural Review* (London), November 1980; "Open-Air Restaurant in Oslo" in *Detail* (Munich), May/June 1981; "Culture house in Stavanger" in *Arkitekten* (Copenhagen), 20 October 1981; "Lund and Slaatto" by Dag Rognlien in *Arkitektnytt* (Oslo), no. 20, 1983; "Lund and Slaatto" by Elisabeth Seip in *Kunst og Kultur* (Oslo), no. 2, 1984.

At present there is a new wave of formalism in modern architecture. Talented creators of trends and fashions are decking out their mannequin projects with formal elements borrowed from period styles, in the hope that—apart from considering them beautiful—we shall also believe that they possess a soul. I react like a prim old aunt to these trimmings and trappings and the publicity they receive. They affect me like a decadent game for the privileged, an ironical and distasteful playboy architecture.

Flicking through the pages of an architectural periodical is often like looking into an aquarium, where beautiful goldfish, trailing long translucent tails, swim languidly around in an artificially heated and illuminated bowl, protected by invisible glass walls against a malevolent reality in which they would never survive. It's as though the bright boys could conveniently find their souls without bothering to do anything about it. All the same, they have

Kjell Lund and Nils Slaatto: Bank of Norway, Oslo, 1979-85.

our forbearance and understanding: beneath the yoke of rationalism, modern man is looking for a sensible meaning to existence...so why not look in the architectural refuse heap for the cultural remains that generations before us have left behind, so that we can find ourselves—ouridentity. We are more or less all of us suffering from an identity crisis.

One of the solutions emanating from Norwegian ecosophists for meeting the impending crisis is to train *generalists*, people imbued with a large measure of personal complexity, with knowledge from a great many fields, and trained to think along inter-disciplinary lines, accustomed to working with complete systems and capable of conveying all this in a language understood by the majority, that is, the non-academic world. But as a designer the architect must at all times be a specialist. Houses cannot be designed with the help of words. The more knowledgeable one is with regard to the diversity of the means of expression—the language of the architect—the more precisely can one formulate one's ideas through the medium of design.

Structuralism is a grammar to be used in designing houses that ensure generality and flexibility within defined room zones. Structure indicates the way in which something is put together, the internal composition and characteristics. Structure is the skeleton in its aesthetic organization for practical purposes. Within the principle of structuralism there are many organizational patterns for the architecture of the future that have not been thoroughly researched. Nature studies may help us to discover some of them. For this reason, a love-relationship between Structuralism and Spontaneity might be desirable, producing an infant at once young and old, an architectural synthesis of the rational and the irrational, of the prosaic and the poetic.

The Modern Movement still moves, propelled by our curiosity and ambitions. Its fringes spawn such fanciful projects as Buckminster Fuller's idea of a town with several thousand inhabitants housed in a metal capsule—one English mile in diameter—in orbit around the earth, maintaining station because of the difference in temperature between the air outside and inside the metal surface caused by solar heat. But the Movement's moral responsibility must also be extended to include planning housing for the Chinese peasant and the Afghan herdsman. There is every indication that the international development of architecture in the years to come will be fertilised by regional traditions. It is probable that economic stagnation, rising energy prices, growing concern for resources, ecological crisis and greater collective solidarity will compel modern architecture to acknowledge a stronger moral imperative.

—Kjell Lund

Educated in the philosophy of the modern movement, but at the same time steeped in the traditions of timber buildings, Kjell Lund and Nils Slaatto are producing a concrete, tile and glass architecture which, although unashamedly modern, is tempered by a knowledge and understanding of timber construction and by the unavoidable influence of Norway's powerful natural surroundings. The Norwegian people respect nature. Nature is never far away; it is both the scenario and the backdrop for daily life, forcing the Norwegian into an intimate relationship that is essential to the national character. This relationship at once involves submission to and confrontation with the natural processes, and this duality is apparent in the traditional timber buildings. For although the farmsteads and hamlets were clearly man-made and man-arranged, expressing a determination to protect and order existence, yet they were in harmony with the land. And to construct these places, the Norwegian took the materials that nature offered. They devised a simple but highly practicable method of building—placing individual timber components side by side or one above the other. They built by assembly, and while the joints between components were shaped with precision, the surfaces were invariably left untouched. Only the junctions, the corners, consistently provoked more conscious articulation.

The work of Lund and Slaatto clearly expresses this connection with their country's past. Their buildings are assembled piece by piece, and the simple framework produced is brought to life by the detailing of the junctions, of the materials and surfaces and volumes.

Their relationship to the present is also clear, but less conscious and somehow less satisfying. There is a systematic logic in these buildings which, while producing a pleasing coherency, denies incident, spontaneity and fun. This is an architecture with no hierarchy, no hierarchy of forms, spaces or materials. There is no mystery, for order, logic, and equalization defy the existence of the unexpected. These buildings are serious—the occasional flash of a sun blind produces the only light relief. But this is a fair reflection of Norwegian society today, one that is fiercely democratic. Life is ordered, forming a pattern to which everyone is forced to conform, a routine whose only changes are those determined by the passing of the seasons.

The achievement, then, of Lund and Slaatto is to have shown that it is possible today to create an architecture that embodies the aspirations of a contemporary society while maintaining a necessary continuity with the past and a sensitivity to the qualities of place.

—Linda Martin

LUNDY, Victor Alfred.

American. Born in New York City, 1 February 1923. Educated at Harvard University, Cambridge, Massachusetts, 1939-43, 1947-48 (Charles Hayden Scholar, 1939-43, Edward H. Kendall Scholar, 1947-48), B. Arch. 1947, M. Arch. 1948; awarded Rotch Travelling Scholarship in Architecture, 1948-49. Served in the United States Army, 26th Infantry Division, 1943-46. Married to Anstis Burwell; children: Nicholas, Jennifer, and Mark. In private practice, New York, since 1951-80. Since 1980, in partnership with Harwood Taylor, in Taylor, Lundy HKS Architects, Houston, Texas. Visiting Lecturer, Harvard University, 1957, University of California, Berkeley, 1958, University of Florida, Gainesville, 1958, Columbia University, New York, 1963, and Yale University, New Haven, Connecticut, 1964. Recipient: Award of Merit, 1960, 1966, and First Honor Award, 1965, American Institute of Architects. Addresses: Taylor, Lundy HKS Architects, 3000 Post Oak Boulevard, Suite 1550, Houston, Texas, 77056, U.S.A.; 5200 Caroline Street, Houston, Texas 77004, U.S.A.

Works

1956 Venice-Nokomis Presbyterian Church, Venice, Florida
1957 Bee Ridge Presbyterian School, Sarasota, Florida
1958 Warm Mineral Springs Inn, Venice, Florida
      Samuel H. Herron House, Sarasota, Florida
1960 St. Paul's Lutheran Church, Sarasota, Florida
      Elvgren House, Siesta Key, Sarasota, Florida
1961 I. Miller Shoe Salon, 730 Fifth Avenue, New York
      First Unitarian Church, Westport, Connecticut
      Hillspoint Elementary School, Westport, Connecticut
      Ski Center, Lincoln National Forest, Ruidoso, New Mexico
1964 Church of the Resurrection, East Harlem, New York
      IBM Garden State Office Building, Cranford, New Jersey
      United States Embassy, Colombo, Ceylon
1965 Singer Showroom, Rockefeller Center, New York
1970 St. Bernard's School, Gladstone, New Jersey
1972 Intermediate School 53, Nameoke Street, Far Rockaway, Queens, New York
1973 St. Paul's Lutheran Church, Sarasota, Florida
1976 United States Tax Court, Washington, D.C. (with Lyles Bissett Carlisle and Wolff)

Publications:

On LUNDY: articles—"Florida's Parasol Motel" in *Architectural Forum* (New York), May 1958; "Eglise Luthérienne à Sarasota" in *Architecture d' Aujourd'hiu* (Paris), April/May 1960; "Young Architects in the U.S." by Esther McCoy in *Zodiac* (Milan), no. 8, 1961; "New Ideas of Victor A. Lundy" In *Architectural Record* (New York), February 1962; "Victor Lundy: Réalisations et Projects Récents" in *Architecture d'Aujourd'hui* (Paris), February/March 1962; "Victor Lundy et L'Evolution de la Tradition Architecturale Américaine" by H. F. Lenning and P. Simond in *Architecture: Formes et Fonctions*(Lausanne), 1964-65; "Magic Architecture for the Singer Sewing Center" in *Interiors* (New York), August 1965; "Justice on a Pedestal" in *Architectural Forum* (New York), September 1967; "Church under a Great Tent" in *Architectural Forum* (New York), July/August 1970; "Sculpture in Space" in *Architectural Forum* (New York), April 1971; "Sanctuary for St. Paul's Lutheran Church, Sarasota, Florida" in *Architecture + Urbanism* (Tokyo), June 1973; "The Public Schools as Architecture" in *Architecture Plus* (New York), August 1973; "Monumental Suspense" by Stanley Abercrombie in *Progressive Architecture* (New York), July 1976; "U.S. Embassy Office Building, Colombo, Sri Lanka" in *Architectural Record* (New York), December 1980.

Although Victor Lundy's architecture is serene, quiet, delicately balanced and carefully resolved, it is not synthesized from purely intellectural concerns. It is the result of a passionate process that is spontaneous and intuitive. "I strive to make a perfect thing. . . . I seek equilibrium," Lundy claims. Still, he admits, "I am usually in turmoil, agitated and mercurial." Lundy is an intellectual, and his work no doubt reflects the keeness of his mind, but he claims his ultimate strength is drawn not from thinking or discussion, but from what "my own eye sees and tells me, and my own hand does. . . . I do things intuitively, by sheer work, by the act of doing, testing, trying over and over until I get the ultimate irreducible expression of what it is I am after."

Lundy's work reveals an acute concern with pure form. His shapes have been worked out laboriously and joined with great exactitude, and materials and textures are mixed with equal precision. At the same time, though, evidence of his visceral approach is always apparent. His buildings are dramatic, with touches of whimsical artistic action that are not indulgent, but nevertheless clearly express distance from a purely rational approach.

Lundy's new building for the United States Tax Court, constructed in Washington D.C., is a case in point. Clear, careful application of pure geometry and monolithic forms characterize the design, but this sedate approach is broken by a dynamic structural system that allows a 200 foot long slab to cantilever more than fifty feet over the entrance to the building. This feat is accomplished by steel cables mounted to a central structural core. They have been hidden, however, so that the cantilever appears to be floating miraculously.

Steel cables create an unusual roof silhouette at St. Paul's Lutheran Church in Sarasota, Florida. Still, the building was erected within a very restricted budget. Inside, the plan is straightforward, and the congregation faces a barren, concrete wall. The pulpit and chancel are finished cleanly, with severely minimal furnishing and accoutrements. Dramatic contrast between bright light at the ends of the church and relative darkness in the central portion adds more drama to the building, however, contrasting sharply with the starkness of the detailing.

Indeed many of Lundy's buildings have successfully met the challenges imposed by very small budgets, while still providing architectural interest, even excitement. It seems that the difficulty of making an artistic statement with little means has been the catalyst of some of Lundy's finest expressions and attest to the vibrancy of his personality and artistic intent. Lundy also draws, sculpts and paints well; he is one of the few remaining architects still adhering to the Beaux Arts system, which emphasizes the importance of sketching and formal comprehensibility achieved through symmetry.

While never losing sight of the importance of precision and sensibility in plan, Lundy has been able to let other forces emerge more freely. His buildings are not pretentious, but rich in genuine architectural delight.

—Ching-Yu Chang

LURÇAT, André.

French. Born in Bruyères, Vosges, 27 August 1894. Educated at the Ecole Municipale des Beaux-Arts, Nancy, 1911-13; Ecole Nationale Supérieur des Beaux-Arts, Paris, 1913-14 and 1918-23. Served in the Infantry, French Army, 1914-18: military medal and five citations of honor; organized the Architects' National Resistance Front, Paris, 1942; imprisoned, Prison de la Santé, Paris, 1943-45. Married to Renée Michel. In private practice, Paris, 1923-34: Director, Lurçat Atelier, rue Daguerre, Paris, 1932-34; emigrated to Russia: Professor of Town Planning, Institute of Architecture, Moscow, 1934-35; Architect-in-Chief, Commissariat of Public Health of the U.S.S.R., Moscow, 1935-36; returned to France: in private practice, Paris, 1937 until his death in 1970. City Planner and Architect-in-Chief, Saint-Denis, Paris, 1945; Chief City Planner for the Reconstruction of Maubeuge, France, 1945; Consultant Architect, Ministry of Reconstruction and City Planning, Paris, 1945; Member, Commission for the Monnet Modernization Plan, Paris, 1945; Consultant City Planner for the reconstruction of Warsaw, 1946. Appointed Director, Academy of Architecture, Ankara, Turkey, 1939 (declined); Lecturer in Architecture, Ecole des Arts Décoratifs, Paris, 1939-43. Founder-Member, CIAM (Congrès Internationaux d'Architecture Moderne), 1928. Exhibitions: *Salon d'automne*, Paris, 1923, 1924; *Exposition des arts décoratifs*, Paris, 1925; *Arts plastiques en France*, Vienna, 1926; *Architecture internationale*, Nancy, 1926; *Exposition coloniale*, Vincennes, France, 1931; *Triennale*, Milan, 1933 (individual); Atelier Lurçat, Paris, 1934 (individual); Museum of Western Art, Moscow, 1935 (individual); Town Planning and Housing Exhibition, Saint-Denis, France, 1947; *André Lurçat, architecte*, Centre National des Arts et Métiers, Paris, 1967-68, (travelled to Nancy and Vienna); *Het Nieuwe Bouwen Internationaal: CIAM*, Rijksmuseum Kröller-Müller, Otterlo, Netherlands, 1983 (toured the Netherlands). Collection: Conservatoire Nationale des Arts et Métiers, Paris. *Died* (in Sceaux, Hauts-de-Seine), *10 July 1970.*

Works:

1917 Villa, Côte d'Azur, France (project)
1923 Villa by the Sea, *Salon d'automne*, Paris (exhibition project)
    Semi-detached house, *Salon d'automne*, Paris (exhibition project)
1924 Rousset Villa, Eaubonne, Seine-et-Oise, France (demolished)
1924/
  25 Jean Lurçat House, 4 Villa Seurat, Paris
    Quille House, 8 Villa Seurat, Paris
1925 Bertrand Houses, 5 and 9 Villa Seurat, Paris
    Gromaire House, 3 Villa Seurat, Paris
    Townshend House, 1 Villa Seurat, Paris
    Galerie Bignou interiors, Paris (destroyed)
    Galerie Barbazanges interiors, Paris (destroyed)

Galerie Pierre interiors, Paris (destroyed)
Galerie Leonce Rosenberg interiors, Paris (destroyed)
Galerie Bernheim interiors, Paris (destroyed)
Galerie Georges Petit interiors, Paris (destroyed)
1926 Huggler House, Villa Seurat, Paris
    Bomsel House, Versailles, France
    Michel House, rue Georges-Ville, Versailles, France
    Workers' Housing Complex (project)
    Housing Complex for Professional People (project)
    Workers' Housing, Villeneuve-Saint-Georges, France (competition project)
    Myrbor Fashion House Paris
    Group of villas, Parma, Italy (project)
1927 Guggenbuhl House, 14 rue Nansouty, Paris (since altered)
    Housing Complex (project)
    Mediterranean Tourist Hotel (project)
    Apartment building, Bagneux, Seine, France
    Michel House, Bagneux, Seine, France
    Froriep de Salis House, Boulogne, Paris
    Galerie Barbazanges shop-front and interiors, Paris
1928 Workers' Housing, Versailles (two competition projects)
    Luxury hotel, La Baule, France (project)
    Residential quarter development, Paris (project)
    Small apartments complex, Choisy-le-Roi, Paris (project)
    Living room for M. P. David Weill, 1 rue Silvestre de Sacy, Paris
1929 Sanatorium, Durdol, Puy-de-Dome, France (project)
1930 Hotel Nord-Sud, Calvi, Corsica
1931 Tourist Airport on the Seine, Paris (project)
1932 Four Werkbund Exhibition Houses, Lainz, near Vienna
    Hefferlin House, rue de Garches, Ville d'Avray, Seine-et-Oise, France
    Housing development, Villejuif, Seine, France (project)
1933 Karl-Marx School Complex, Villejuif, Seine, France
1934 Metro Engineers' Residential Building, Moscow (project)
1935 Children's Hospital for Contagious Diseases, Moscow (project)
    Institute of Physics and Chemistry, Moscow (project)
    Faculty of Medicine, Moscow (project)
1945/
  50 Reconstruction plan for Maubeuge, France
1946 Karl-Marx School additions, Villejuif, Seine, France
1948 Cité Paul Langevin, Saint-Denis, France
    Cité Fabien, Saint-Denis, France
    Housing, Avenue de la Gare, Maubeuge, France
1949 Boys' and Girls' School, Nevers, France
    André Lurçat House, Sceaux, France
1950 Holiday Village, Meriel, Seine-et-Oise, France
1951 Leduc House, Sceaux, France
1953 Cité Paul Eluard, Saint-Denis, France
    Housing development, Blanc-Mesnil, France
    Michaut House, Sceaux, France
    Hospital Centre additions and alterations, Saint-Denis, France
    School complex, Blanc-Mesnil, France
    Fabien Infants School, Saint-Denis, France
    Holiday house, Franceuil, Indre-et-Loire, France
1954 Cité Paul Semard, Saint-Denis, France
    Cité Auguste Delaune, Saint-Denis, France
    J. Currie School Complex, Saint-Denis, France
    Paul Semard School Complex, Saint-Denis, France
    Cité Daniele Casanova, Blanc-Mesnil, Paris
1957 Henri Barbusse Nursery School, Saint-Denis, France

1958 Paul Vaillant-Couturier School Complex, Villejuif, Seine, France
Church of Saint-Pierre et Saint-Paul, Maubeuge, France
Town Hall, Maubeuge, France
1960 Cité Gabriele Peri, Saint-Denis, France
Square Saint-Livier, Nancy-Saint-Max, France
1962 Palace of Sports, Saint-Denis, France
Paul Langevin School Complex, Ivry-sur-Seine, France
Cité Roger Semat, Saint-Denis, France
Cité Emmaus, Blanc-Mesnil, France
1963 Haut Rivage Development, Nancy-Saint-Max, France
André Lurçat Country House, Sancerre, France
1964 Town Hall, Blanc-Mesnil, France
1965 Cité M. Cachin, Saint-Denis, France
1966 Cité Paul Vaillant-Courturier, Villejuif, Seine, France
1968 Cité Guyemer, Saint-Denis, France

Publications:

By LURÇAT: books—*Architecture*, Paris 1929; *André Lurçat: projets et réalisations*, Paris 1929; *Terrrasses et jardins*, Paris 1929; *Groupe scolaire à Villejuif*, Paris c. 1935; *Urbanisme et architecture*, Paris 1942; *Forms, composition et lois d'harmonie*, 5 volumes, Paris 1953-57; *André Lurçat: oeuvres récentes*, Paris 1961; *Scritti sull'esperienza sovietica*, with E. May and H. Schmidt, edited by M. de Michelis and B. Cassetti, Padua, Italy 1972; articles—in *Architecture internationale*, exhibition catalogue, Nancy, France 1926; "La Formation de l'architecte" in *L'Architecture d'aujourd'hui* (Paris), October/November 1933; "L'Architecture contemporaine en occident" in *Arhitektura SSSR* (Moscow), March 1934; "Retour d'Union Soviétique" in *L'Art vivant* (Paris), March 1934; "Néoclassicisme ou constructivisme" in *Arhitektura SSSR* (Moscow), July 1934; "L'Architecture dans la crise" in *L'Architecture d'aujourd'hui* (Paris), June 1935; "Evolution d'architecture" in *L'Architecture d'aujourd'hui* (Paris), September 1935; "L'Homme, la technique, l'architecture" in *Izvestija* (Moscow), 12 June 1937; "L'Architecture en U.R.S.S." in *Bulletin de l'Union des Architectes* (Paris), February 1938; "Recherche et creation" in *André Lurçat, architecte*, exhibition catalogue, Paris 1967.

On LURÇAT: book—*André Lurçat, architecte*, exhibition catalogue, Paris 1967; *CIAM: Dokumente 1928-1939*, edited by Martin Steinmann, Basel and Stuttgart 1979; *Het Nieuwe Bouwen Internationaal: CIAM—Housing, Town Planning*, exhibition catalogue, by R. D. Oxenaar and A. van der Woud, Delft, Netherlands 1983; articles—"Arbeithauser von André Lurçat" in *Moderne Bauformen* (Stuttgart), vol. 27, 1928; "André Lurçat's Architecture" by P. Morton Shand in *Architects' Journal* (London), 29 April 1931; "André Lurçat" by Edoardo Persico in *Casabella* (Milan), January 1935; "La Reconstruction de Maubeuge" in *Techniques et architecture* (Paris), no. 7/8, 1946; "Reconstruction and Housing in France" in *Techniques et Architecture* (Paris), no 11/12, 1953; "Un'ideologia per la ricostruzione: le opere recenti di André Lurçat" by S. Tintori in *Casabella* (Milan), March 1962; "Omaggio a André Lurçat, ma senza equivoci" by Bruno Zevi in *L'Architettura* (Rome), March 1968; "André Lurçat: 48 ans d'architecture" by J. B. Ache in *La Construction moderne* (Paris), September/October 1970; "Il Municipio di Blanc-Mesnil di André Lurçat" in *L'Architettura* (Rome), October 1970; "André Lurçat in U.R.S.S." by B. Cassetti in *Socialismo, città, architettura U.R.S.S. 1917-1937*, Rome 1971; "Lurçat" by J. L. Cohen and others, in *Architecture mouvement continuité* (Paris), September 1976; "International Werkbund Housing,

Vienna, 1932" by W. Dreibholz in *Bauforum* (Vienna), no. 2, 1977.

The drama of André Lurçat is one of a conflict of loyalties—loyalty to his convictions as an architect, loyalty to his political convictions. At first, the two struggles could run in parallel; they complemented each other. The young member of the revolutionary pacifist student organization was able to follow his path as a modern architect, which, after the house of his brother Jean, built in 1925, led him to that courageous masterpiece, the Karl-Marx School at Villejuif, designed five years later.

Unfortunately, Lurçat's active sympathies led him to Moscow, to the Institute of Architecture and the Health Commissariat, where, from 1934 to 1937, he did his best to defend the architectural "line" of the Bauhaus and CIAM and to justify the system that rejected it. Returning to France, he courageously joined the Resistance, supported the Communist Party despite his disappointments, spent time in prison, and took part in the reconstruction of liberated France. But the purity and impetus of his architectural vision had been destroyed, more by the exhausting ideological struggle from 1934-37 than by any physical ordeals.

Lurçat thereafter was a man who had to accept compromise and the surrender of principles, who built groups of dwellings, schools, a town hall, and other works (none of great importance) and in numerous writings criticized the "capitalist system," incapable of producing a genuine urbanism, and the "cosmopolitan" propositions of Le Corbusier. He praised the middle way in architecture and in urbanism. His experiences nevertheless led the honest man that he had always been to condemn severely in France policies that continued to be rife in the U.S.S.R. and the countries she inspires—the policy of "models," the systematic application of heavy prefabrication, and so forth.

How Lurçat, who always dreamed about the "freedom of creation," must have suffered.

—Pierre Vago

LUZ, Hans.

German. Born in Stuttgart, 10 June 1926. Educated at the Dillmann Real-Gymnasium, Stuttgart, 1936-44, graduated 1944; apprenticed to the landscape architect Adolf Haag, Stuttgart, 1948-50. Served in the Germany Army, and prisoner of war, 1944-47. Married Gretel Reinhardt in 1952; children: Christof, Frieder, Heiner, and Henrike. Landscape Gardener and Site Manager for Adolf Haag, Stuttgart, 1950-52; Landscape Gardener with Otto Valentien, Stuttgart, 1953-55, and Dr. J. Schweizer, Basel, 1955-56. Free-lance landscape gardener since 1956: opened planning office with small nursery, Birkach, Stuttgart, 1958; Principal, Hans Luz und Partner, Birkach, since 1961. Lecturer, 1973, and since 1975 Honorary Professor, Technical University of Stuttgart. Exhibitions: *Bundesgartenschau*, Stuttgart, 1961, Karlsruhe, 1967, Mannheim, 1975, and Stuttgart, 1977. Recipient: Paul Bonatz Prize, in collaboration, 1958, 1959, 1967, 1979; First Prize, Leonberg Cemetery Competition, 1966; First Prize, Höher Odenwald Recreation Center Competition, 1968; First Prize, Leinfelden Cemetery Competition, 1969; Hugo Häring Prize, in collaboration, 1969, 1970; First Prize, Oberboihingen Cemetery Competition, 1972; First Prize, Reichenbach Recreation Center Competition, 1974; First Prize, Bundesgartenschau Competition, Stuttgart, 1974; First Prize, with Dieter Bohnet, Federal Chancellor's Office Competition, Bonn, 1974; Federation of Landscape Architects (BDLA) Prize, 1977; Fritz-Schumacher Prize, 1980. Member, Akademie der

Künste, Berlin, 1975. Address: Hans Luz and Partner, Dinkelstrasse 40, Postfach 72 02 04, 7000 Stuttgart 70 (Birkach), West Germany.

Works (landscape architecture):

1958 Luz House, Birkach, Stuttgart
1960 University of Karlsruhe
1961 *Bundesgartenschau*, Stuttgart
State Parliament House, Stuttgart
1961 University of Stuttgart
1963/
65 ICI Factory, Östingen, Germany
1964/
67 Teachers Training College, Ludwigsburg, Germany
University of Tubingen at Morgenstelle, Germany
1964/
68 Hospital, Leonberg, Germany
1965 Agricultural University of Hohenheim, Stuttgart (with Walter Rossow)
1967 Marwitz House, Sindelfingen, Germany
Bundesgartenschau (25 m² gardens), Karlsruhe
1967/
71 Cemetery, Leonberg, Germany
1967/
73 Asemwald Residential Complex, Stuttgart
1967/
77 Health Resort Park, Wildbad, Germany (with Walter Rossow)
Oberbettringen Residential Complex, Schwäbisch Gmünd, Germany
1968 Beer House, Pflaumloch bei Nördlingen, Germany
1968/
73 Höher Odenwald Recreation Center, Germany
1969/
73 Cemetery, Leinfelden, Germany
1969/
78 Tannenplatz Residential Complex, Ulm, Germany
1970 German Pavilion, *Expo '70*, Osaka, Japan
1970/
72 Central University Sports Complex, Olympia, Munich (with Wolfgang Miller)
1972/
74 Cemetery, Oberboihingen, Germany
Geno House, Stuttgart
1973/
79 Convalescent Centre and Hospital, Bad Šackingen, Germany
1974/
76 Reichenbach Recreation Center, Germany
1975/
76 Federal Chancellor's Office, Bonn (with Dieter Bohnet)
1975/
77 Königstrasse, Stuttgart (competition project)
1977 *Bundesgartenschau*, Stuttgart (with Planungsgruppe 1)
1978/
80 Doctors' House, Möhringen, Stuttgart
1978/
83 City Gardens, Gaggenau, Germany
1979 City Center, Leonberg, Germany
1979/
80 NHS Office interior courtyards, Hamburg
1979/
81 *Landesgartensch au*, Baden-Baden, Germany (with Planungsgruppe LGS)
1979/
82 Hermannshof Shrubbery Exhibition and Visitors' Garden, Bergstrasse, Weinheim, Germany
1979/
84 City Gardens, Schwäbisch Gmund, Germany
1980/
83 Old People's Home, Bietigheim-Bissingen, Germany

Hans Luz: Schwanenplatz layout, Federal Garden Show, Stuttgart, 1977.

1980/
84 Sessions House, Naurod, Germany
1980/
85 Markplatz/Bocksgasse Pedestrian Zone, Schwäbisch Gmund, Germany
1981/
83 Korbmattfelsehof Sanatorium, Baden-Baden, Germany
1981/
85 Augustabad Spa, Baden-Baden, Germany
Allianz Headquarters Roof Garden, Stuttgart
1982/
83 Home and Land Economics School, Herrenberg, Germany
1982/
84 European Cultural Community Offices, Konrnwestheim, Germany
1982/
85 BFG Cultural Centre, Oberursel, Germany
1983 Deacon's Lion Gateway Centre, Stuttgart

Publications:

By LUZ: books—*Stuttgarter Garten:Betrachtungen zur Entwicklung der Gartenkunst von 1900—heute,* Stuttgart 1979; *Garten zwischen Natur und Architektur,* Munich 1984; articles—"Planzung ohne Erdanschluss" in *Gartenamt* (Hanover), June 1973; "Friedhof Leinfelden" in *Garten und Landschaft* (Munich), November 1974; "Beton" in *Garten und Landschaftsbau,* Stuttgart 1977; "Roof Planting—A Necessity" in *Deutsche Bauzeitung* (Stuttgart), April 1979; "Planungs—und Ausfuhrungsprobleme Betonfertigteile" in *Architekt* (Stuttgart) no.,4, 1984; "A year with Dr Johannes Schweizer" in *Anthos* (Zurïch), no. 1, 1984.

On LUZ: articles—"Platz für Garten ist Überall" by Irene Mutz in *Mein schöner Garten* (Offenburg, Germany), April 1977; "In der Luftröhre ein Park" by Manfred Sack in *Garten und Landschaft* (Munich), November 1977; article by K. H. Rucker in *Gartenpraxis* (Stuttgart), March 1979; "New Life for a Stuttgart Park" in *Landscape Australia* (Mont Albert, Victoria), May 1980; "Der Hermannshof" in *Garten und Landschaft* (Munich), no. 6, 1983; "A Living Epidermis for the City", in *Landscape Australia* (Mont Albert, Victoria), no. 4, 1983.

As a practicing landscape architect, I see my task as follows: 1) to make sure that as little harm is done to our landscape as possible (this is unfortunately inevitable at the present time, because of the strain put on the landscape by continual building and other engineering projects); 2) to try to repair the damage caused by these processes; but, above all, 3) to plan and design the new open spaces that should be created with the "genius loci" and the tradition of our predecessors in mind, so that they really become spaces in which we can live.

As a result of my gardening background, vegetation plays an important role in my work. I feel that landscape architects should not forget their creative, imaginative role.

—Hans Luz

Hans Luz has become one of the most prominent garden architects in Southern Germany: he employs a wealth of innovations and new ideas, and he has achieved wide public recognition. He has extended the disciplines of small-scale gardening through domestic projects to the more complex open space systems of community housing and the university campus. He has a reputation for care in detailing—particularly when relating constructional features to planting—which suffuses the whole of his work.

The work of Hans Luz is characterized by a number of clearly definable attributes. He is particularly at ease in dealing with complex level changes. The complicated steps and retainers, often intricately interwoven, that he uses are always subservient to the texture and pattern of the whole design. His enclosures are usually simple (see, for example, his treatment of the ICI Factory at Östingen). He uses natural material when possible, but, when juxtaposed with concrete, both the concrete and the plants echo the form of the construction. The use of natural material, in particular, is always dependent upon a high standard of craftsmanship. As regards concrete, he has developed a number of system blocks that can produce dramatic sculptural effects, e.g. the chevron walling at Dr. Zabel's garden. There is often a strong formality to his designs and a tendency toward pattern making.

There is repeatedly a strong feeling of anti-suggestion—as with, say, cube blocks within school playgrounds. Traditional garden features are frequently translated into a modern vernacular—for example, concrete stools and plant containers. There is always a strong division of elements in his designs, but with little or no duality of purpose. He is masterful at joining different surfaces, often employs Oriental techniques of planting, and is as sparing in his use of water as he is of plant material, a technique that lends great individuality of expression to the species employed.

Among Luz's best-known works may be included a wide of variety of private gardens, notably his own at Stuttgart-Birkach, Garten Marwitz, and Garten Beer, the University of Karlsruhe and the University of Stuttgart-Hohenheim, and various school and municipal projects. His international reputation derives from the *Bundesgartenschau* at Stuttgart in 1961 and Karlsruhe in 1967 and, most notably, from the German Pavilion at *Expo '70* in Osaka.

—Gordon Patterson

LYNDON, Donlyn.

American. Born in California, 1936; son of the architect Maynard Lyndon. Educated at Princeton University, New Jersey, B.Arch. 1959. Partner, MLTW: Moore, Lyndon, Turnbull and Whitaker, Berkeley, California, 1960-65. Principal, Lyndon Associates, Cambridge, Massachusetts, since 1965. Professor at Massachusetts Institute of Technology, Cambridge. Address: Lyndon Associates, 948 Parker Street, Cambridge, Massachusetts 02138, U.S.A.

Works:

1960 Jobson House, Big Sur, California
1961 Bonham House, Boulder Creek, California
1962 Jenkins House, Rutherford, California
Otus House, Berkeley, California
Seaside Professional Building, Seaside, California
West Plaza Condominiums, Coronado, California
1963 Jewell House, Orinda, California
Monte Vista Apartments, Monterey, California

Monte Vista Village, Monterey, California
1964 Hoover-Slater House, Stinson Beach, California
Lone Hill Winery Housing, San Jose, California
Morris-LaForge House, Boulder Creek, California (project)
Speculation II Protype House, Sea Ranch, California
Condominium I, Sea Ranch, California
Sea Ranch Athletic Club I, Sea Ranch, California (with Lawrence Halprin)
Talbert House, Oakland, California
1968/
75 Pembroke Dormitory, Brown University, Providence, Rhode Island
1974/
78 Champy House, Rye Beach, New Hampshire
1978 Housing for the elderly, Marlborough, Massachusetts
Grass House, Hartland, Vermont

Publications:

By LYNDON: books—*The Place of Houses*, with Charles Moore and Gerald Allen, New York 1974; *Houses by MLTW: Moore, Lyndon, Turnbull and Whitaker*, edited by Yukio Futagawa, Tokyo 1975; *The City Observed: Boston*, New York 1982; articles—"Filologia dell'architettura americana" in *Casabella* (Milan), November 1963; "Sea Ranch: The process of Design" in *World Architecture 2*, London 1965; "Seattle: Metamorphosis from Fair into Center" in *Progessive Architecture* (New York), July 1965; "In Canada: The Continent's First Single-Structure Campus" in *Architectural Forum* (New York), December 1965; "Big Happening in Berkeley" in *Architectural Forum* (New York), January/February 1966; "Student Dorms: A University Tries Variety" in *Architectural Forum* (New York), March 1966; "Concrete Cascade in Portland" in *Architectural Forum* (New York), July/August 1966; "The Environment and the Market" in *World Architecture 4*, London 1967; "Sea Ranch: A Second Look," with Charles Moore and Gerald Allen, in *Architectural Record* (New York), November 1974; "Five Ways to People Places" in *Architectural Record* (New York), November 1975; "Commentary" in *Progressive Architecture* (New York), February 1976; "Architectural Education Here" in *Journal of Architectural Education* (Washington, D.C.), February 1978; "Stairs" in *GA Houses* (Tokyo), May 1981; "Design: Inquiry and Implication," with William D. Cooper, in *Journal of Architectural Education* (Washington, D.C.), Spring 1982.

On LYNDON: book—*Immanent Domains*, exhibition catalogue, with introduction by Peter Serenyi, Boston 1971; articles—"Charles W. Moore and His Partners" by Misawa, Ehira and Sugawara in *The Japan Architect* (Tokyo), september 1965; "Lyndon to Move to MIT" in *Progressive Architecture* (New York), February 1967; "Making the Ordinary Extraordinary" in *Progressive Architecture* (New York), February 1976; "Pembroke Dorms" in *Architectural Review* (London), December 1976; "Immanent Domains" in *Architecture + Urbanism* (Tokyo), May 1978; "Pembroke Dormitories, Brown University" in *Architecture + Urbanism* (Tokyo), December 1978; "Four Recent Works by Donlyn Lyndon" in *Parametro* (Bologna, Italy), November 1979; "New Waves in American Architecture," special issue of *GA Houses* (Tokyo), May 1982.

Bibliography: *Living Spaces and the Work of Donlyn Lyndon: A Selected Bibliography* by Robert B. Harmon, Monticello, Illinois 1981.

Donlyn Lyndon is the "L" in MLTW—Moore, Lyndon, Turnbull, and Whitaker—an extraordinary and resilient fraternity, more often apart than together, who first came to prominence as a team with their design of Sea Ranch in 1964. Lyndon's father is a distinguished architect in the California modern manner, and growing up in such an environment was a formative influence. However, it is Princeton and the Class of '59 that established the basis for his architecture: the teaching of Jean Labatut, an anachronism then anticipating the collapse of faith in Modernism because he had never had any, and the stimulus of a shared belief in new possibilities for architecture among fellow students and young faculty, including William Turnbull and Charles Moore. The nature of each individual's contribution to MLTW may be impossible to define. Even for those involved, a shared creative process doesn't have simple boundaries. In judging their independent work, it seems that the genius of the group differs markedly in many ways from the sum of its parts: Turnbull has matured and expanded the innovations of Sea Ranch; Moore has flourished brilliantly; Lyndon has spent most of his time teaching.

Yet, Lyndon has shown limited but significant production. With Moore, he wrote *The Place of Houses*; with great skill and sensitivity they share the lessons and insights from their lives of making houses and experiencing places. The principles underlying the book are wise and robust and have a quiet universality. Essentially, the concern is for poetic contextualism. After the book had been published, Lyndon reviewed his major themes in an article. They were: use elements that suggest the presence of people; emphasize forms that relate to the human body and reveal its functions; create pride of place by continuing care; be open to conflicting claims of use; incorporate what others have built and re-invest their care; give a measured and varied structure to space; make spaces that are contestable and encourage improvised use; make places that nurture celebration and encourage people to pay attention to each other.

These principles were put to the test in Lyndon's major work since Sea Ranch—The Pembroke Dormitory at Brown University in Providence, Rhode Island. Coping with a limited budget, Lyndon has produced a building that is simply and directly made, yet filled with rich and complex invention. With simple means, he creates continuing variation both in the private and public spaces. The individual is left to complete his own celebration of the space given, while the architecture strives to provide a stage for joyous communion. This stage management is most self-conscious in the decorated arches and gateways and in the use of color, particularly on the public street side. The decoration of the arches demands too much and interjects a discordant personality into the internal setting, but the space is strong enough to survive the intrusion. The use of color to modulate the wall surfaces creates a highly effective transformation of mood, which could have been extended.

Lyndon's work is tougher intellectually and less sensual than that of his contemporaries to whom he might be compared. As does his writing, his work, particularly Pembroke, has a didactic quality from which it is possible to learn without merely emulating style.

—Alan Balfour

LYONS, Eric Alfred.
British. Born in London, 2 October 1912. Trained as an articled pupil and part-time student at the Regent Street Polytechnic, London. Married Catherine Joyce Townsend in 1944; children: Richard, Jane, Antony, and Naomi. Worked in the office of Walter Gropius, *q.v.*, and Maxwell Fry, *q.v.*, London, 1936-37; in partnership with G. Paulson Townsend, London, 1945-50; in private practice, London, 1950-63. Partner, with Ivor Cunningham, Eric Lyons Cunningham Partnership, London (Richard Lyons joined partnership, 1972), 1963 until his death in 1980. Member of the Council, 1960-63, Vice President, 1967-68, Senior Vice-President, 1974, and President, 1975-77, Royal Institute of British Architects; Chairman, Association of Consultant Architects, 1973. Recipient: Civic Trust Award, 1961 (twice), 1962, 1964, 1965, and 1967; Ministry of Housing and Local Government Medal, 1961 (3 times), 1963, 1964 (3 times), 1965, 1966, 1967, and 1968; Distinction in Town Planning, 1961, and Eastern region Architecture Award, 1966, Royal Institute of British Architects. Fellow, Royal Institute of British Architects, and Society of Industrial Artists and Designers. Honorary Fellow, American Institute of Architects; Member, Académie d'Architecture, France. C.B.E. (Commander, Order of the British Empire), 1979. *Died* (in Hampton Court, Surrey) *22 February 1980.*

Works:

1951 Box Corner (flats), Twickenham, Midddlesex
1952 Onslow Court (flats), Richmond, Surrey
1954 Cavendish Court (flats), Richmond, Surrey
1955 The Priory (flats), Blackheath, London
1955/
57 Parkleys (flats), Ham Common, Richmond, Surrey
1956 The Hall (flats), Blackheath, London
1957 Flats for the Soviet Trade Delegation, West Hill, Highgate, London
1958 The Cedars (housing), Teddington, Middlesex
1959 Applecourt (flats), Cambridge
Corner Green (housing), Blackheath, London
Howard House (old people's housing), Bognor Regis, Sussex
1960 Fieldend (housing), Twickenham, Middlesex
Hall 2 (housing), Blackheath, London
Highsett (flats), Cambridge, England
Parkgate (flats), Hove, Sussex
1962 Lansdowne Hill (flats, public housing), Southampton, Hampshire
Married soldiers quarters, Pirbright, Surrey
Pitcairn House (public housing), Hackney, London
The Hamlet (old people's housing), Bognor Regis, Sussex
1963 Spangate (flats), Blackheath, London
Southrow (flats), Blackheath, London
The Lane (housing), Blackheath, London
The Padddox (housing), Oxford
1963/
64 Blackheath Park (private housing), Blackheath, London
1964 Albion Primary School, Bermondsey, London
Friar's Primary School, Southwark, London
Highsett II (housing), Cambridge, England
Rayners Road (housing), Putney, London
Templemere (housing), Weybridge, Surrey
1964/
78 World's End Redevelopment (high-density public housing complex), Chelsea, London
1965 Brackley (housing), Weybridge, Surrey
Castle Green (housing), Weybridge, Surrey
Castle House (public housing), Southampton, Hampshire
Hall 4 (housing), Blackheath, London
Highsett III (housing), Cambridge, England
1965/
70 New Ash Green (new village), Kent
1966 Cedar Chase (housing), Taplow, Buckinghamshire
Offices, Holly Road, Hampton Hill, Middlesex
Public housing, Harlow New Town, Essex
Weymede (housing), Byfleet, Surrey

1967 Dryden House (flats), Cambridge, England
     Grasmere (housing), Byfleet, Surrey
     Parkend (housing), Blackheath, London
1969 Westfield (housing), Ashtead, Surrey
1971 Married soldiers quarters, Pirbright, Surrey
     Mayford (public housing), Camden, London
     New Ash Green County Primary School, Kent
1972 Walsingham Lodge (old people's housing),
     Barnes, London
1973 Plan for the central area, and housing and
     shops, Vilamoura, Algarve, Portugal
1974 Plan for the centre redevelopment, and public
     housing and old people's home, Chertsey,
     Surrey
     Wates House (staff common rooms, etc.),
     University of Surrey, Guildford
1977 Master plan for the new village of Aqueduct
     Green, Telford, Shropshire
     Caledonian Estate (public housing), Islington,
     London
     Westbourne Neighbourhood (public housing,
     medical centre, community centre, and old
     people's home), Islington, London
1978 Holm Walk (housing), Blackheath, London
1979 Delhi/Outram Streets (public housing), Isling-
     ton, London
     Fieldend (housing), Telford New Town,
     Shropshire
     Mallard Place (housing), Twickenham, Mid-
     dlesex

Publications:

By LYONS: articles—"Domestic Building and
Speculative Development" in *RIBA Journal* (Lon-
don), May 1958; "Few New Ideas for Homes" in *The
Times* (London), 3 July 1961; "Rebuilding Britain,"
with others, special issue of *Twentieth Century*
(London), Summer 1962; "Criticism of Work
Submitted for RIBA Prizes and Studentships 1963"
in *RIBA Journal* (London), June 1963; "Managing
Without Design?" in *RIBA Journal* (London),
October 1966; "Pushing Hard—But in What Direc-
tion?" in *RIBA Journal* (London), March 1967;
"Why We Want More Competitions" in *RIBA
Journal* (London), January 1968; "Too Often We
Justify Our Ineptitudes by Moral Postures" in *RIBA
Journal* (London), May 1968; "Back to Blackheath"
in *The Architect* (London), July 1971; "I Am Sure It
Will Go Away" in *Architects' Journal* (London), 12
July 1972; "A New Lease for Lyons" in *Building*
(London), 18 October 1974; "Pruning Can Be
Fruitful" in *RIBA Journal* (London), April 1975;
"What Happened to Housing?" in *The Spectator*
(London), 17 May 1975; interview, by Judy Hillman
in *The Times* (London), 28 June 1975; "Eric's
Whistle-Stop Tours" in *RIBA Journal* (London),
February 1976; "The President's Column" in *RIBA
Journal* (London), March 1976; "Eric Lyons Pon-
ders on the Nature of Modern Architecture" in
RIBA Journal (London), April 1976; "Membership
Involvement" in *RIBA Journal* (London), June 1976;
"Aesthetic Control" and "User Involvement in
Housing" in *RIBA Journal* (London), July 1976;
"Mid-Span" interview, by John Donat in *Building*
(London), 16 July 1976; "Habitat Architectural
Competition" in *RIBA Journal* (London), August
1976; "Architects' Pattern Books" in *RIBA Journal*
(London), September 1976; "The Need for an
RIBA" and "Architecture and Place" in *RIBA
Journal* (London), October 1976; "Housing Experi-
ments" in *RIBA Journal* (London), December 1976;
"Building Failures" and "Small Is Beautiful" in
RIBA Journal (London), January 1977; "Growth
Points for the Profession" in *RIBA Journal* (Lon-
don), March 1977; "Not Waving, but Drowning"
and "Death of the Cowboy" in *RIBA Journal*
(London), April 1977; "Private Housing" in *RIBA
Journal* (London), May 1977; "What Is the RIBA
Doing for Its Members?" in *RIBA Journal* (London),
June 1977; "Lyons Untamed," interview, by David
Pearce in *Building Design* (London), 17 August 1979;
"Spanning the Years," interview, by David Pearce in
Building Design (London), 24 August 1979; "Archi-
tects in the Market Place" in *Building* (London), 18
January 1980.

On LYONS: articles—"The Team in the Office" in
Architecture and Building (London), June 1956;
"SPAN" by Robert Furneaux Jordan in *Archi-
tectural Review* (London), February 1959; "The
Man about the Houses" by Richard Findlater in
Punch (London), 17 January 1962; "The Spanman
Cometh" in the *Sunday Times* (London), 10 Novem-
ber 1968; "What We Need Are *Friendly* Homes,"
interview with Rex Grizell, in *Evening News* (Lon-
don), 26 November 1969; "Out of the Strong..." in
The Architect (London), February/March 1975;
"Rus in Urbe" in *Architects' Journal* (London), 9
July 1975; "Building Gardens with Houses in Them"
by Caroline Moorehead in *The Times* (London), 21
July 1975; "Eric Lyons: Architect President" in *The
Architects' Journal* (London), 30 July 1975; "Eric
Lyons and RIBA 1976" in *Building Design* (Lon-
don), 9 june 1976; "Eric Lyons gets CBE" in *Building
Design* (London), 15 January 1979; "Eric Lyons—
fought for good architecture" by Leonard Manasseh
in *Architects' Journal* (London), 27 February 1980;
"Eric Lyons: death of an innovator" in *Building*
(London), 29 February 1980; "Success one Step
Ahead" by David Pearce in *Building Design* (Lon-
don), 29 February 1980; "Eric Lyons" in *Annual
Obituary*, edited by Roland Turner, London and
New York 1981.

From the moment an architect begins his professional education, he is conditioned to geometry
and the T-square. That conditioning is almost
inevitable; mathematics and proportion form his
basic aesthetic. But the more he becomes absorbed in
his art, the further he may lose touch with biological
form. In many schools of architecture, for instance,
the tree is reduced to the mathematical symbol of a
circle, harsh treatment for one of the most expressive
forms in nature. But there have been exceptions, and
Eric Lyons was one who consistently held that
balance between architecture and nature without
which the average human being subconsciously feels
disoriented.

Although Lyons's practice covered a wide field, he
will be remembered mainly for his contribution to
domestic housing, conceived more as landscape
architecture itself. The elegant Span housing he built
for a private company at Petersham, Blackheath,
and Weybridge, mainly for the professional classes
within commuting distance of London, have been a
success speculatively as well as aesthetically. "Good
landscape is good business" was proved right.
Together with his assistant, Ivor Cunningham (who
continues the practice), Lyons evolved a form of
terrace houses enclosing common gardens in a single
total landscape concept—in contrast to the usual
configuration of buildings encircling a space into
which gardens have later been inserted. This unity
was partly achieved by ground modelling, so that, in
contrast to the standard London square, vertical and
horizontal have an agreeable plastic relationship.
There are small private patio gardens, but the
collective gardens are so beautifully and intricately
planted that they have maintained some of the
mystique of nature without being disordered.

In this age of concrete jungles and the mass
production of architecture, the preservation of
human values is vital. This quality in Lyons was
recognized by the profession in Britain when it
elected him its president. He did, in fact, stand astride
the two professions of architecture and landscape
design, and if his endeavours to repeat the success of
Span at New Ash Green in Kent did not succeed, the
fault lay in the market for which his work had to be
designed. A Lyons house—where the sight, touch,
and smell of a plant has as much meaning as a work of
art—is only for the sensitive and the appreciative.

—Geoffrey Jellicoe

LYONS, ISRAEL, ELLIS AND GRAY.

Partnership; established in London, 1947, as Lyons,
Israel and Ellis, by E. D. Lyons (born 1905; retired
1970; died 1983), Lawrence Israel (born 1909; retired
1983), and Tom Ellis (born 1911; retired 1983);
additional partner, David Gray (born 1928), since
1975. Exhibition: *Transformations in Modern Archi-
tecture*, Museum of Modern Art, New York, 1979.
Recipient: First Prize, Falmouth Secondary Modern
School Competition, 1952; First Prize, Finchley
Town Hall Competition, London, 1954; Bronze
Medal, Ministry of Housing, 1958; Architectural
Design Award, 1966 and 1967; Civic Design Award,
1968. Address: 12A Princess Road, London NW1,
England.

Works:

1952 Millbrook Junior School, Southampton,
     Hampshire
     Orpington Infants and Junior School, Kent
1953 Chislehurst Boy's Secondary School, Kent
     Middleton Mixed Secondary School,
     Lancashire
1954 Herne Bay Mixed Secondary School, Kent
1957 Millbrook Infants' School, Southampton,
     Hampshire
     Falmouth Mixed Secondary School, Cornwall
     Hoe Secondary School, Kent
1958 Barnsley Mixed Secondary School, Yorkshire
     Peckham Comprehensive School, London
     Orrell Mixed Secondary School, phase I,
     Lancashire
     Bridgnorth Boy's Secondary School,
     Shropshire
     Hoglands Housing Scheme, Southampton,
     Hampshire
     Vyse Lane Housing Scheme, Southampton,
     Hampshire
1959 Jordanthorpe Girl's Secondary School,
     Sheffield
     Workshop Annex, Old Vic Theatre, London
1960 Weston Park Boy's Secondary School, South-
     ampton, Hampshire
     Northfleet Girl's Secondary School, Kent
     Bridnorth Girl's Secondary School,
     Shropshire
1961 Wolfson Institute, Royal Postgraduate Med-
     ical School, Ducane Road, Hammersmith,
     London
     Workshop Block, Hammersmith Hospital,
     London
     Avenham Estate, Preston, Lancashire
1962 Upholland Mixed Secondary School,
     Lancashire
     Chorley Mixed Grammar School, Lancashire
     Harrow Weald Grammar School extension,
     London
     Bridgenorth Boys' Secondary School exten-
     sion, Shropshire
1963 Urmston Boys' Grammar School, Lancashire
1964 Barnsley College of Technology, Yorkshire
     Parkhouse Mixed Secondary School Sheffield
1965 Windsor Girls' Grammar School, Berkshire
     Wokingham Mixed Secondary School,
     Berkshire
     David Lister High School, Kingston-upon-
     Hull, Yorkshire
1966 Royal Postgraduate Medical School, Ducane
     Road, Hammersmith, London
     Animal Quarters and Animal Kitchen, De-
     partment of Experimental Medicine, 5
     Shaftesbury Road, Cambridge, England
     Wentworth Teachers' Training College, phase
     I, Barnsley, Yorkshire
     Middleton Mixed Secondary School exten-
     sion, phase I, Yorkshire
     National Sea Training School, Gravesend,
     Kent
     Wickersley Mixed Secondary School, phase I,
     West Riding Yorkshire
     Bentley Mixed Secondary School, West Rid-
     ing, Yorkshire

Home for the Aged, Dorinda Street, Islington, London

Town Hall, phase I, Middleton, Lancashire

1967 Dunn Nutritional Laboratories, Milton Road, Cambridge, England

Orpington Junior School, Kent

Hoe Secondary School extension, Kent

1968 Housing, Polthorne Street, Woolwich, London

1969 Housing, Southampton Central Redevelopment Area, Hampshire

1970 College of Engineering and Science, Polytechnic of Central London, New Cavendish Street

Hollybrook Infants' and Junior School, Southampton

Shipping Federation Offices, Tilbury, Essex

1971 Beckenham Girls' Comprehensive School extensions, Bromley, Kent

1972 Queen Elizabeth Hospital for Children, Hackney Road, London

1973 Southampton Retail Trades College, phase I

1974 College of Communication, Polytechnic of Central London, Riding House Street

1975/
76 Medical Research Laboratories, Mill Hill, Middlesex

1978/
81 L Block, Research Laboratories, and Administrative Centre, Royal Postgraduate Medical School, Hammersmith, London

1980/
83 Housing Association rehabilitiation schemes, London

Publications:

By ELLIS: articles—"Symposium on Drawing Office Technique" in *RIBA Journal* (London), March 1957; "Presentation of Gold Medal to Professor Alvar Aalto" in *RIBA Journal* (London), May 1957; "The Disciplines of the Route I" in *Architectural Design* (London), November 1960; "The Disciplines of the Route II" in *Architectural Design* (London), October 1966.

On LYONS/ISRAEL/ELLIS: articles—"The Work of Lyons Israel and Ellis" in *Architectural Design* (London), January 1959; "Scuola Tescobeas a Falmouth" by F. Arichino and G. H. Grima in *Architettura* (Rome), April 1960; "Was ist Brutalismus?" by Wolfgang Pehnt in *Kunstwerk*(Baden-Baden, West Germany), September 1960; "Community in Concrete" by Diana Rowntree in *The Guardian* (London), 7 July 1961; "Wolfson Institute, Hammersmith Hospital" in *Architectural Design* (London), August 1961; "Costume inglese in due opere di Lyons Israel Ellis—Wolfson Institute e Upholland School" in *Architettura* (Rome), March 1962; "Recent Work by Lyons Israel and Ellis" in *Architectural Design* (London), October 1966; "Lesson in Bronze" by D. E. Toner in *Copper Magazine* (London), September 1969; "Polytechnic of Central London" by Sam and Sylvia Webb in *Architectural Design* (London), November 1970; "Certainty and Decision" by Patrick Nuttgens in *Architectural Review* (London), January 1971; "Polytechnique" by Alastair Best in *Design* (London), April 1971; "Hochschulgebaude" in *Deutsche Bauzeitschrift* (Gutersloh, West Germany), May 1971; "Polytechnic of Central London" in *Werk* (Zurich), May 1971; "Polytechnic of Central London" in *Architecture + Urbanism* (Tokyo), June 1971; "Polytechnic of Central London" in *Architettura* (Rome), August 1971; "The Glass of Fashion" by Reyner Banham in *New Society* (London), September 1971; "College of Engineering and Science" in *Arkitekten* (Copenha-

gen), no. 24, 1971; "Southampton Technical College Food Trades Department and Communal Building" in *Architects' Journal* (London), 2 August 1973; "Polytechnickum" in *Die Bauverwaltung* (Hanover, West Germany), December 1973; "Endowment in Concrete—the Queen Elizabeth Hospital for Sick Children, Hackney, London" by Alastair Best in *Design* (London), March 1973; "Das Polytechnickum von Central-London" in *Industrie-bau* (Hannover, West Germany), September 1973; "Central Polytechnickum" in *Glasforum* (Schorndorf, West Germany), September 1973; "Polytechnic of Central London" in *Entwurf und Planung* (Frankfurt), no. 12, 1973; "Polytechnickum" in *Bauwohnen* (Zurich), May 1974.

I have always been a firm believer in the Modern Movement. The ideals and the examples of the pioneers of that movement, Le Corbusier, the Russian Constructivists, Gunnar Asplund, and the early work of Alvar Aalto were the sources for much of my work, and the power of their ideas still has validity for us today. It was from studying the work of Le Corbusier that I developed my theory of the Discipline of the Route as one of the generators of good architecture.

From more than fifty years experience in the practice of architecture, I have learned that to be equipped to take on the responsibility of leading the design team, it is essential for the arcitect to have acquired a thorough knowledge of all aspects of construction and also to have plenty of experience of "dirtying his boots on the site." I would also like to emphasise the importance of the architect's role in the preparation of the brief. In my opinion, he should be deeply involved from the very start in this preparatory phase, which may be so creative that the client may come to realise and to wish for a building that is entirely different from his initial conception.

There are no easy answers. Architecture, like all the arts, reflects the spiritual and aeshetic values of its time. We live in a period of great anxiety and disillusionment and in a society where the educational system seems designed to crush any creative sensibility in its children. All the more reason for the architectural profession to hold fast to the noble ideals of the Modern Movement—the creation of a healthy, socially cohesive, and aesthetically satisfying environment for all our people.

—Tom Ellis

The vigorous expansion of the schools building programme in England in the immediate postwar years gave the young firm of Lyons, Israel and Ellis the opportunity to put into effect soe of the aspirations of the Modern Movement. The movement had had a minimal effect on school design in the established prewar architectural practices—despite a number of outstanding entries in the *News Chronicle* Schools Competition of 1937. The ideas generated in this competition had to wait for the impetus of the 1944 Education Act, and the consequent enlightened administration of the Ministry of Education, before they could be exploited. Lyons, Israel and Ellis built up their practice through their active participation in this programme, for which they built thirty primary, secondary, grammar, technical, and comprehensive schools.

The shortage of building materials and stringent building restrictions stimulated them to a series of imaginative and ingenious solutions. The "handwriting" of their work became evident in the sensitive use of materials, the skillful exploitation of technical solutions as an integral part of the design, and the fastidious attention to detailing. The early schools were all responses to very restrictive briefs from the client as well as some exceptionally difficult sites; they varied in plan from the cross-wall design of the

Upholland School, Lancashire, with the corridor "spine" punched through the classroom block; the volute plan of Jordanthorpe School, Sheffield; the prize-winning linear answer to the shelving site at Falmouth, Cornwall; to the inward-turned "walled town" at the David Lister School, Kingston-upon-Hull.

In the 1960s and 1970s, the firm went on to design technical colleges, laboratories for research units, polytechnics, and hospital and university buildings. Two buildings in particular illustrate their architectural aims:

The Wolfson Institute is a complex of three lecture theatres, common romms, restaurant, and social facilities, built for the Royal Post-Graduate Medical School of London University on the site of the Hammersmith Hospital. The two smaller lecture theatres are slung beneath the counterbalancing large theatre, and this dramatic structure is echoed visually in the stark, clear-cut, white concrete volumes. Around the dominant central fortress of the theatres, the wide corridors, stairs, and social areas flow in a single continuum of space. A remarkable feature of the lecture theatres is their perfect two-way acoustics. Not only can the lecturer be heard in the back row of the 500-seat auditorium without any mechanical aids, but any member of the audience can audibly join in the discussion. The aims, derived from Le Corbusier, were to design a building that would be the symbol of an idea, using a coherent system, a sustained discipline to produce a recognized order in content, route and structure. The most important parts of a building internally to be recognizable externally, the form expressing the inherent use and structure of the various parts. The plan to have a clearly defined route (way in and way out), with the major destinations clearly identifiable.

The College of Engineering of the Polytechnic of Central London is a further attempt to synthesize all these aims. The result is a sophisticated complex, comprising a cranked eight-storey laboratory block, a five-storey tutorial block, and a focal node containing entrance area, two lecture theatres, common rooms, and library. In the basement, there are extensive engineering workshops and garaging. The planning constraints of the cramped, triangular site have been vigorously exploited and turned to advantage, and a feeling of spaciousness has been achieved, particularly in the triple-height entrance hall and the communal areas. Here, students and staff are brought together throughout the day from all the faculties, with no hierarchical segregation.

The floor-to-ceiling glazing on the tutorial block, which is the street facade, provides visual interest and involvement in the life of the Polytechnic for the passerby. It is a building that, very deliberately, does not cut itself off from its immediate environment. It has been designed in white concrete and bronze, and the bronze is used as a unifying element throughout, not only in the windows and spandrel panels but also, inside, on balustrades and door fittings. The bronze may seem costly, but because of its greater structural strength, the architects were able to use much thinner sections (3' x 1/10' extruded) where six-inch thick aluminum sections would otherwise have been necessary to withstand the windloading. Standardization of parts throughout the building also kept the costs down, for, as in all the firm's previous work, a prime consideration was to achieve a building with low operational and maintenance costs. Again the consistent and sustained use of the two-foot bronze module throughout clarifies and makes comprehensible the complex geometry of the building.

Interest in the aims of the partnership over the years have attracted many younger architects to work for the firm. Among them have been James Stirling, James Gowan, Alan Colquhoun and John Miller, Ronald Simpson, Neave Brown, and David Gray, who became a partner in 1975.

—Mary Hayes

Lyons, Israel, Ellis and Gray: College of Engineering and Science, Polytechnic of Central London, 1970.

MACKAY, David John.

British. Born in Eastbourne, Sussex, 25 March 1933; moved to Spain, 1958. Educated at the Northern Polytechnic, London, 1951-58, Dip.Arch. 1958; Escuela Técnica Superior de Arquitectura, Barcelona, 1967-68, Dip.Arch. 1968. Married Roser Jarque in 1957; children: John, Anna, Martha, Sonia, Monica, and Mark. In partnership with Josep Martorell, *q.v.*, and Oriol Bohigas, *q.v.*, Barcelona, since 1962. Professor, Washington University, St. Louis, Missouri, 1981; Director of the Foreign Studies Program, Catholic University of America, Barcelona, 1981-84. Recipient: Essay Prize, Royal Institute of British Architects, 1949-50; Andrew N. Prentice Prize, RIBA, 1960; Puig i Cadafalch Prize, Colegio de Arquitectos de Cataluna y Baleares, 1968; Book of the Year Prize, German Council on Book Art, 1977. Associate, Royal Institute of British Architects, 1959. Address: Martorell, Bohigas, Mackay, Camp 61, Barcelona 6, Spain

Publications:

By MACKAY: books—*World Architecture*, with others, 4 volumes, London 1967; *Contradictions in Living Environment*, London 1971, as *Contradicciones en el Entorno Habitado*, Barcelona 1972; *The Anti-Rationalists*, with others, edited by Nikolaus Pevsner and J. M. Richards, London 1973; *Wohnungsbau im Wandel*, Stuttgart 1977, as *Multiple Family Housing*, London, New York and Toronto 1977, as *Viviendas Plurifamiliares*, Barcelona 1979; *Lexicon der Architektur des 20. Jahrhunderts*, with others, edited by Gerd Hatje, Stuttgart, 1983; *The Modern House*, Barcelona and New York 1984.

See MARTORELL, BOHIGAS, MACKAY

MADIGAN, Colin Frederick.

Australian. Born in Glen Innes, New South Wales, 22 July 1921. Educated at Inverell High School, New South Wales, 1932-37; Sydney Technical High School, 1938-39; Sydney Technical College, 1940, Dip.Arch. 1950. Served as a Sub-Lieutenant in the Royal Australian Navy, 1941-46. Married Ruby Miriam Court-Rice in 1950; son: Guy. Worked with his father, the architect F.J.Madigan, Inverell, 1950-54. Since 1948, in practice with Jack Torzillo and Maurice C. Edwards, in Sydney: as Edwards Madigan and Torzillo, 1954-66, and, with David Briggs, as Edwards Madigan Torzillo and Briggs, 1966-77; Director, Edwards Madigan Torzillo Briggs International, since 1977; office established in Canberra, 1973. Recipient: First Prize, Sydney Rocks Area Competition, 1963; Sulman Medal, 1967 and 1971, and Blackett Award, 1968, Royal Aus-

tralian Institute of Architects; First Prize, Australian National Gallery Competition, Canberra, 1968; First Prize, Town Centre Competition, Mount Druitt, New South Wales, 1970; Firts Prize, High Court of Australia Competition, Canberra, 1973; Gold Medal, Royal Australian Institute of Architects, 1981. Address: Edwards Madigan Torzillo Briggs International Pty. Ltd., 201 Pacific Highway, North Sydney, New South Wales 2060, Australia.

Works (with partners):

1952 Madigan House, Narrabeen, New South Wales

　　　Orange Civic Centre, New South Wales (project)
1956 New South Wales Tourist Bureau, Sydney (with Gordon Andrews)
1967 Warringah Shire Library, Dee Why, New South Wales
1968 Shire Library, Warren, New South Wales

　　　Student Dormitories, Mitchell College of Advanced Education, Bathurst, New South Wales (with New South Wales Government Architect)
1968/
　82 Australian National Gallery, Canberra
1973 Warringah Shire Civic Centre and Administration Offices, Dee Way, New South Wales
1973/
　81 High Court of Australia, Canberra
1979/
　80 Parliament House, Canberra (competition project)
1985 Sports Science and Sports Medicine Building, Canberra

　　　Arts and Mathematics Building, Australian Defence Force Academy, Canberra

　　　Australian Government Offices, Parramatta, New South Wales

Publications:

By MADIGAN: articles—"The New Hero" in *Architecture Australia* (Melbourne), November 1982; "The City Is History, and the Canberra Triangle's Part in It" in *Architecture Australia* (Melbourne),January 1984.

On MADIGAN: books—*Ladenbauten* by Karl Kasper, Stuttgart 1967; *Toward an Australian Architecture* by Harry Sowden, Sydney 1968; *Living and Partly Living: Housing in Australia* by Ian McKay and others, Melbourne 1971; *Old Continent—New Building: Contemporary Australian Architecture*, edited by Leon Paroissien and Michael Griggs, Darlinghurst, New South Wales 1983; articles—"Domestic Architecture in Australia" in *Art and Australia* (Sydney), June 1971; "High Court of Australia" in *Law News* (Canberra), May 1978; "Colin Madigan and the ANG Site", special issue of

Architecture Australis (Melbourne), November 1982; "Capital Idea: Opening of the Australian National Gallery in Canberra" by Jasia Reichardt in *Building Design* (London), 14 January 1983.

It is apparent that new purpose and new functions demand new forms which may even become recognized to be beautiful. By comparison, functionless form denotes atrophy, purposelessness, inertia, a replica of provisional existence, a wasted potential—as we may now consider the effect of much of our built environment.

I tend to think of our architecture—the work I'm involved in—as being 'inclusive' because it reveals its function and purpose readily, allowing each observer to participate in its workings. The design process is from the inside out to achieve this proper 'fit,' and the physical expression reveals this desired intention.

'Exclusive' architecture, so called, can be the opposite to this. In some instances, it develops from a preconceived idea (object or product-oriented) unrelated to the free expression of the function, where the preconception dominates the form, and the programmed requirements are forced into it. The necessary evolution, which at times demands additions or variations to this embalmed architecture, is difficult to formulate.

Participating architecture makes functional space (how it works) its best asset and gives priority to this event over and above what may be considered the conservative "luxury of fine finishes." Instead of the spurious solution by covering up structure that we see so much of in present day building, the nobility of primary materials, such as reinforced concrete, which makes the architecture, must be judged in relation to the spatial forms that it produces, unfolding the sense of a "luxury of space" andd a release from the conservative containment of the box.

The proper and obvious of development theme is 'how' the aesthetic is made relevant and valid. The art of architecture is measured by the exposure of a logical development of theme—and, depending on the degree of exposure, and its degree of consistency, so too can we judge the integrity of that expression.

One can enter a building and see its structure,services, and function expressed. It immediately 'includes' the visitor in the way it works.

—Col Madigan

Col Madigan is one of those blunt 'Australian' Australians that people from other lands sometimes find difficult to understand. He is a pragmatist, but at the same time he is a social philosopher who holds deep convictions as to ideal relationships of man to man and man to buildings. Madigan states that his work is based on his belief in the potential of architecture to extend the freedom of man and to relate man to his context in time and place. He defines his position "as a Romantic one, governed by ideals." Fundamental to the aims of his architecture is the need for a clear communication between the building and those who use it. Consequently,

Col Madigan: Australian National Gallery, Canberra, 1968-82.

Madigan's buildings are articulate (though not always understood), involving, and explicit in their delineation of purpose.

The firm of Edwards, Madigan and Torzillo (and, since 1966, Briggs) was founded in 1954. By Australian standards it is a large firm, employing up to seventy staff members. The work is diversified, but its reputation is based primarily on civic buildings in and around Sydney and on the winning of the two major national competitions held in this country since the war: the Australian National Gallery (1968), and the High Court of Australia (1973), both for Canberra. While in the work of joint partnerships it is often difficult to discern the role of one person, the trademarks of Madigan's hand show clearly on projects with which he was closely involved.

The civic buildings, which include several libraries, are characterized internally by an expansive sense of space arising from the arrangement of particular use areas around a large, central zone and from connections established from room to room and level to level. Spaces are regulated in size and height to fit use, and the functional organization of the buildings show clearly in the planning (which often indicates a potential for expansion).

Madigan employs contemporary technologies in an innovative manner to achieve the sought-after consonance of form and purpose and does not hesitate to combine varied structural systems in one building. Structures and services are commonly left exposed. The confidence shown with structure is also evident in his handling of materials and in the obvious attention to detail and quality throughout the buildings. Organization, structure, and services are further clarified visually by the extensive use of natural light from both high and low sources.

The external forms of the buildings clearly reflect the major design focus on the generation of specific internal spaces. This gives rise to boldly expressive exteriors with complex profiles of skylights, window shades, door canopies, and roof overhangs. The High Court of Australis and the Australian National Gallery stand as focal buildings on adjacent sites on the edge of the lake in the Parliamentary Triangle in Canberra. The High Court is an obvious extension of concepts previously explored but here translated into the monumental language of the angular concrete forms of this imposing structure. With the design for the National Gallery, Madigan adhered to his accustomed organization of internal space, but the freedom accorded previous buildings is disciplined by the imposed order throughout of a three-dimensional geometry based on the equilateral triangle: "the equilateral trangle is the nucleus of the structural code, dictating the dimensions and character of the building." Insitu concrete has allowed for a vigorous, but here a more restrained, modelling of the exterior.

Madigan is a concerned and creative architect who has accepted the challenges posed by his own philosophy. His sometimes controversial architecture has arisen out of his refusal to accept the mediocre and his determination to continually raise consumer expectations of building performance in all respects. Perhaps the highest compliment comes from John Andrews (who worked for the firm in his early years): "Col Madigan taught me what integrity in architecture is all about."

—Jennifer Taylor

MAILLART, Robert.

Swiss. Born in Bern, 6 February 1872. Educated at the Gymnasium, Bern, 1885-89; Eidgenössische Technische Hochschule, Zürich, 1890-94, Dip.Eng. 1894. Married; had two sons, one daughter. Worked for Pümpin and Herzog, Zürich, 1894-97, Städtisches Tiefbauamt, Zürich, 1897-99, and Froté and Westermann, Zürich, 1899-1902; in private practice as Maillart and Company, Zürich, 1902-12; practised in Russia, 1912-14; Principal, Maillart Engineering Office, Geneva, 1919 until his death in 1940; opened branches in Bern and Zürich, 1924. Lecturer, Eidgenössische Technische Hochschule, Zürich, 1911. Honorary Member, Royal Institute of British Architects, 1936; Honorary Member, Special Department for Bridge Builders, Schweizerischer Ingenieur and Architekten-Verein, 1940. Collection: Maillart Archive, Princeton University Library, New Jersey. *Died* (in Geneva) *5 April 1940*.

Works:

1896 Le Veyron Brook Bridge, Pampigny, Switzerland
1899 Sihl River Bridge, Zürich-Staffhausen
1901 Hadlaubstrasse Bridge, Zürich
1903 Steinach Brook Bridge, St. Gallen, Switzerland
      Inn Bridge, Zuoz, Switzerland
1904 Thur Bridge, Billwil-Oberbüren, St. Gallen, Switzerland
1905 Rhine Bridge, Tavanasa, Graubunden, Switzerland (destroyed, 1927)
1907 Railroad Bridge, Aach, Switzerland
1908 Mushroom Structure, Zürich (project)
1909 Thur River Bridge, Wattwil, Switzerland
1910 Warehouse, Giesshübel, Zürich
      Unterwasser Canal Bridge, Wyhlen, Switzerland
1911 Rhine River Bridge, Laufenburg, Switzerland
1912 Grain Depot, Altdorf, Switzerland
      Aare Bridge, Aarburg, Switzerland
      Warehouse, Petrodrad, Russia
      Rhine River Bridge, Augst-Wyhlen, Switzerland
      Rhine River Bridge, Rheinfelden, Switzerland
1913 Muota Bridge, Vorder Ibach, Switzerland
      Shelter, Chiasso, Ticino, Switzerland
1914 Box Factory, Lancey, France
      Cable Factory, Villanueva y Geltrù, Spain
1920 Textile Hall, Sallent, Spain
      Benet Factory, Barcelona
      Arve Bridge, Marignier, France
1924 Rempen Aqueduct, Schwyz, Switzerland
      Schrahbach Bridge, Innerthal, Switzerland
      Flienglibach Bridge, Innerthal, Switzerland
      Ziggenbach Bridge, Waggital, Switzerland
1925 Magazzini Generali S.A., Chiasso, Ticino, Switzerland
      Chatelard Aqueduct, Wallis, Switzerland
      Val-Tschiel Bridge, Donath, Switzerland
1926 Sihl Post Offfice, Zürich
1930 Salginatobel Bridge, Schiers, Switzerland
      Landquart Bridge, Klosters, Switzerland
      Aare River Bridge, Bern
1931 Spital Bridge, Frutigen-Adelboden, Bern
      Ladholz Bridge, Frutigen, Bern
      Hombach Bridge, Schangnau, Bern
      Luterstalden Bridge, Schangnau, Bern
      Aqueduct, Gadmen, Bern
1932 Traubach Bridge, Habkern-Bohl, Bern
      Bohlbach Bridge, Habkern, Bern
      Rossgraben Bridge, near Schwarzenburg, Bern
      Tessin Bridge, Giubiasco-Sementina, Ticino, Switzerland
      Gorge-du-Trent Bridge, Wallis, Switzerland
      Quai Perdonnet, Vevey, Switzerland
1933 Screw Factory, Gerlafingen, Switzerland
      Schwandbach Bridge, Bern
      Thur Bridge, Felsegg, St. Gallen, Switzerland
1934 Viaduct, Sarajevo, Yugoslavia

Robert Maillart: Salginatobel Bridge, Schiers, Switzerland, 1930.

Sitter Bridge, Haggen-Stein, St. Gallen, Switzerland
      Aare Bridge, Innertkirchen, Bern
      Toss Footbridge, Wülflingen-Winterhur, Zürich
1935 Rhine Bridge, Schaffhausen, Switzerland
      Rhine Bridge, near Schaffhausen, Switzerland
      Birs Bridge, Liesberg, Bern
      Aare Bridge, Bern
      Footbridge, Huttwill, Bern
1936 Twannbach Bridge, Twann-Ligerz, Bern
      Aarne Bridge, Vessey, Geneva
      Ticino Footpath, Someo, Ticino, Switzerland
      Quai Turrettini, Geneva
1937 Tara Bridge, Yugoslavia
      Gründlischwand Bridge, Bern
1938 Footbridge, Weissensteinstrasse, Bern
1939 Zementhalle, *Swiss Provinces Exhibition*, Zürich (with Hans Leuzinger)
      Footbridge, Altendorf, Switzerland
      Rhone Bridge, Aire-La-Ville-Peney, Geneva
1940 Simme Bridge, near Laubegg, Bern
      Simme Bridge, Garstatt, Bern
      Footbridge, Lachen, Altendorf, Switzerland
1947 Marchgraben Bridge, Saanenmöser, Bern (completed by others)
1954 Aire Bridge, Lancy, Geneva (completed by others)

Publications:

By MAILLART: book—*Théorie des dalles à champignon*, Paris 1932; articles—"Die Sicherheit der Eisenbeton-bauten" in *Schweizerische Bauzeitung* (Zürich), 27 February 1909; "Zur Brechung der Deckenkonstruktionen" in *Schweizerische Bauzeitung* (Zürich), 1 June 1912; "Ein schweizerische Ausfuhrung der unterzuglosen Decke—Pitz-Decke" in *International Kongress für Bruckenbau und Hockbau*, Zürich 1926; "Die Lorrain-Brucke über die Aare in Bern" in *Schweizerische Bauzeitung* (Zürich), 3 January 1931; "Aktuelle Fragen des Eisenbetonbaues" in *Schweizerische Bauzeitung* (Zürich), 1 January 1938; "Uber Eisenbeton-Brucken mit Rippenbogen unter Mitwikung des Aufbaues" in *Schweizerische Bauzeitung* (Zürich), 10 December 1938.

On MAILLART: books—*Circle* by Herbert Read and Morton Shand, London 1937, 1971; *Maillart Ingenieurbureau: Zürich und Bern*, Zürich and Bern 1938; *Robert Maillart* by M. Ros, Zürich 1940; *Space, Time and Architecture* by Siegfried Giedion, Cambridge, Massachusetts 1941; *Robert Maillart* by Max Bill, Zürich, 1948, 1969; *The World's Great*

Bridges by H. Shirley-Smith, London 1964; *Bridges* by Derrick Beckett, London 1969; *Robert Maillart's Bridges; the Art of Engineering* by David Billington, Princeton, New Jersey 1979; articles—"Robert Maillart: The Architecture of a Great Swiss Engineer" by Morton Shand in *RIBA Journal* (London), September 1938; "Early and Late Works of Robert Maillart" by Siegfried Giedion in *Architect and Building News* (London), January 1948; "Brücken Von Maillart" by Walther Schmidt in *Bauen und Wohnen* (Zürich), no 5, 1949; "En Mémoire de Robert Maillart" by Pierre Tremblet in *Journal de Genève*, April 1965; "Robert Maillart: Pioneer Extraordinary" by Martin Hunt in *Concrete* (London), October 1972; "Robert Maillart," special edition of *Bulletin technique du Suisse romande* (Lausanne, Switzerland), September 1973; "An Example of Structural Art: The Salginatobel Bridge of Robert Maillart" by David P. Billington in *Journal of the Society of Architectural Historians* (Philadelphia), March 1974; "Structural Art and Robert Maillart" by David P. Billington in *Architectural Science Review* (Melbourne), June 1977; "Graceful Span: Robert Maillart's Bridges" by Corin Hughes-Stanton in *Building Design* (London), 11 April 1980.

Robert Maillart was the Swiss engineer who, in a long career spanning the first forty years of this century, brought reinforced concrete design from its crude beginnings to its position as a major engineering material of great aesthetic and structural possibilities. When Maillart was young, reinforced concrete was in the hands of its inventors, men such as Hennebique who made the breakthrough to the new material but could not see its potential except as a substitute for stone. When Maillart died, he was able to hand on the skill of designing beautifully in reinforced concrete to the talented men of the next generation—Nervi, Morandi, Candela, and others.

The discipline of structural engineering can easily lead to codified solutions, with columns calculated separately from beams, and framing members seen as the structure that carries non-load-bearing members. To the tentative design ideas of the earliest reinforced concrete engineers, Maillart brought the power of lateral thinking and the ability to see the problem as a whole. For his multi-storey structures, he invented the mushroom column, so that beams are not required and columns and slabs act together to resist the stresses upon them. In his bridges, he showed that an arch need not support a road deck; the entire structure can act as a whole.

The most memorable images of Maillart's work are his bridges, and in a series of some forty reinforced concrete bridges, plus many abondoned projects, he innovated and refined for forty years. The first mature design is the bridge at Zuoz, built in the first years of this century, in which the box girder is used for the first time, thus changing the structural role of the deck from passive thing to part of the structural whole. Looking at this bridge three-quarters of a century later, one is convinced of its early date only by the incontrovertible documentary evidence, for its image is twenty or thirty years ahead of its time. In the Tavanasa bridge, redundant spandrels to the box girder are omitted, creating triangular openings in the side that separate the arch from the deck—a development that reaches a logical conclusion in Aarburg bridge, where the hollow spandrel has framing members across it, to ensure that deck and arch act together in a bridge that is very open for its size. This schema reaches perfection in the ninety-metre Salginatobel Bridge, set in a beautiful natural landscape. Whereas the earlier bridges had solid, stone-faced abutmentsm, in the Salginatobel Bridge, the row of vertical members under the roadway is continued under the approach spans, so that the entire construction is light; gone are the heavy abutments reminiscent of masonry-arch bridges. Four years later, in the Schwandbach Bridge, the entire plan is curved to suit the U-turn on the road, and at this time Maillart built a series of

bridges that twist, turn, and slope to suit the road engineer's wishes; because the entire bridge structure was in each case working as a single structural element, Maillart was able to wrap and bend it freely. In the Felsegg bridge, he obtained greater structural efficiency by pointing the arch, and in a small bridge over the Simme at Garstatt he abandoned the curved form and made the underside of each half of the bridge a straight line from springing to apex, a solution most enticing in its simplicity.

Although it was bridges that brought him fame, Maillart busied himself with retaining walls, aqueducts, warehouses, and other engineering structures all his working life. His most famous building, the Zementhalle, built for the *Swiss Provinces Exhibition* in Zürich in 1939, is a pioneer shell structure with arches spanning some fifteen metres and shells only sixty millimetres thick cantilevering off the sides of the arches. Beautifully lit at night, the shell was a memorable advertisement for concrete.

Either by natural sympathy or pure chance, Maillart found that his approach to design coincided with that of many of the architects and artists of the Modern Movement. After World War I, Maillart no longer used decoration on his bridges, and ten years later, he abondoned the traditional massive stone-faced approaches, for, he said, engineers had to choose "between mass or quality." The clear forms of his bridges, their understated elegance, and their reinforced concrete construction endeared Maillart to the historians of the Modern Movement both in Europe and the United States; they placed Maillart firmly amongst the great designers of the first half of the twentieth century.

—John Winter

MAKI, Fumihiko.
Japanese. Born in Tokyo, 16 September 1928. Educated in Kenzo Tange's, *q.v.,* Research Laboratory, at the University of Tokyo, 1948-52, B.Arch. 1952; Cranbrook Academy of Art, Bloomfield Hills, Michigan, 1952-53, M.Arch. 1953; Harvard Graduate School of Design, Cambridge, Massachusetts, 1953-54, M.Arch. 1954. Married Misao Matsumoto in 1960; children: Midori and Naomi. Designer, Skidmore, Owings and Merrill, *q.v.,* New York, and Sert *q.v.:* Josep Lluis Sert, Jackson and Associates, Cambridge, 1954-56; Assistant Professor, Washington University, St. Louis, 1956-58; Fellow of the Graham Foundation, Chicago, 1958-60; Associate Professor, Washington University School of Architecture, 1960-62, and Harvard Graduate School of Design, 1962-65. Since 1965, Principal, Maki and Associates, Tokyo. Founder-Member, Metabolist Group, Tokyo. Lecturer, Department of Urban Design, 1965-79, and Professor of Architecture since 1979, University of Tokyo. Visiting Professor, Harvard Graduate School of Design, 1967-68, and University of California, Berkeley, 1970-71; Visiting Lecturer, Columbia University, New York, 1976, 1984, and Technical University of Vienna, 1977; Visiting Critic, University of California at Los Angeles, 1976, and Harvard Graduate School of Design, Cambridge, Massachusetts, 1978-79; Eliot Noyes Visiting Professor, Harvard University, Cambridge, Massachusetts, 1983. Exhibitions: *Late Entries to The Chicago Tribune Tower Competition,* Museum of Contemporary Art, Chicago, 1980; *Architecutre in Place,* Harvard University, Cambridge, Massachusetts, 1983 (toured the United States, 1983-85); *Three Projects in Progress,* Axis Gallery, Tokyo, 1983; *Styrian Autumn,* Graz, Austria, 1984; *Japan Architecture International,* Rotterdam, 1984; *Recent Projects of Fumihiko Maki,* Sony Tower, Osaka, 1985; *Biennale,* Paris, 1985; *Tokyo: Form and Spirit,* San Francisco Museum of Modern Art, 1987. Recipient: Japan Institute of Architects Award,

1963; Joint First Prize, United Nations Low-Cost Housing Competition, Lima, Peru, 1969; Mainichi Art Prize, Tokyo, 1969; 24th Art Prize, Minister of Education, Japan, 1973; 12th Japan Art Prize, Tokyo, 1980. Honorary Fellow, American Institute of Architects, 1980. Member, Japan Institute of Architects. Address: Maki and Associates, 6-2-3-chome Nihonbashi, Chuo-ku, Tokyo 103, Japan.

Works:

1960 Toyoda Memorial Hall, Nagoya University, Nagoya, Japan
 Steinberg Arts Center, Washington University, St. Louis
1962 Memorial Hall, Chiba University, Chiba, Japan
1966 Sakai Sports Park Outdoor Sports Facilities, Sakai, Osaka
1967 Osaka Rinkai Center Building, Sakai, Osaka
 Rissho University, stage I, Kumagaya, Japan
1968 Rissho University, stage II, Kumagaya, Japan
 Hagoromo Station Area and Takaishi City Plan, Osaka
 Korakuen Sports, Recreational and Entertainment Complex redevelopment, Tokyo
1969 Civic Center Building, Senri New Town, Osaka
 Community Center, Mogusa Housing Estate, Tokyo
 Hillside Terrace Apartment Complex, stage I, Tokyo
 Master plan for the Marine Recreational Youth Complex, Tannowa, Osaka
1970 Sirogane Park House, Tokyo
 Archaeological Museum, Senboku New Town, Osaka
 Sumitomo Trading Company Office Feasibility Study, Singapore
 Master plan for Sea Park, Yokohama
1970/
 75 Low-cost experimental housing, Lima, Peru
1971 Kanazawa Ward Office and Community Center, Yokohama
 New town development, Kanazawa, Yokohama
 Development plan for Kotesashi Housing Estate, Saitama, Japan
1972 St. Mary's International School, Tokyo
 Kato Gakuen Elementary School, Numazu, Shizuoka Prefecture, Japan
 Windsor House, Tokyo
 Hiroo Homes, Towers, Apartments and Condominium, Tokyo
 Osaka Prefectural Sports Center, Sakai, Osaka
 Design of the *Japanese Painters Annual Exhibition,* Tokyo
 N.I.R.A. Research Institute (project)
 Development plan for the Yatsugatake Resort Community, Nagano, Japan
1972/
 73 Sennan Residential and Recreation Community Development, Osaka
1972/
 75 Kanazawa Housing Estate Development Plan, Yokohama
1973 Hillside Terrace Apartment Complex, stage II, Tokyo
 Embassy of Japan, Chancellery and Ambassador's Residence, stage I, Brasilia
1974 Center for the School of Art and Physical Education, Tsukuba University, Ibaragi Prefecture, Japan
 Noba Kindergarten, Noba Housing Estate, Yokohama
 Toyota Memorial Museum and Guest Pavilion, Kuragaike, Toyota, Japan
 Irish Embassy Chancellery, Tokyo
 National Institute of Research Advancement Headquarters, Tokyo
 Private research institute main office, Tokyo

1975 Embassy of Japan, Chancellery and Ambassador's Residence, stage II, Brasilia

Marine Life Park, *Expo ı75,* Motobu, Okinawa

Chiba City Development Plan

Master plan for the Kota Kinabalu Sports Complex and Park, Malaysia

Development plan for the Shima Peninsula Resort Complex, Mie Prefecture, Japan

1976 Tsukuba University Center, Ibaragi Prefecture, Japan

School of Art Building, Tsukuba University, Ibaragi Prefecture, Japan

Austrian Embassy, Chancellery and Ambassador's Residence, Tokyo

1978 Hillside Terrace Apartment Complex, stage III, Tokyo

1979 Iwasaki Museum, Kagoshima Prefecture, Japan

Royal Danish Embassy, Tokyo

Municipal Namiki First Primary School phase I, Yokohama

1980 Municipal Kawana Junior High School, Yokohama

1981 New Library, Keio University, Minato Ward, Tokyo

Mitsubishi Bank Hiroo Branch Office, Minato Ward, Tokyo

Toranomon NN Building, Minato Ward, Tokyo

Municipal Namiki First Primary School phase II, Yokohama

1982 Maezawa Garden House/YKK Guest House, Kurobe, Toyama Prefecture, Japan

Old Library renovation, Keio University, Minato Ward, Tokyo

Sabah Sports Centre, Sabah, East Malaysia

1983 Dentsu Advertising Company Offices, Kita Ward, Osaka

1984 Municipal Gymnasium, Fujisawa, Kanagawa Prefecture, Japan

1985 Wacoal Art Center, Minato Ward, Tokyo

1986 National Museum of Modern Art, Kyoto

Publications:

By MAKI: books—*Metabolism 1960,* with others, Tokyo 1960; *Investigations in Collective Form,* St. Louis 1964; *Movement Systems in the City,* Cambridge, Massachusetts 1965; translation of *Communitas* by Paul and Percival Goodman, Tokyo 1967; *What Is Urban Space?* with Kawazoe Noboru, Tokyo 1970; *GA 5: Louis I Kahn chard Medical Research Building, Pennsylvania,* edited by Yukio Futagawa, Tokyo 1971; *The City of the Unseen,* Tokyo 1980; translation of *The Architect: Chapter in the History of the Profession* by Spiro Kostof, Tokyo and New York 1981; articles—"Some Thoughts on Collective Form" in *Structure in Art and Science,* edited by Gyorgy Kepes, New York 1965; "Dialogue On Architecture," with Richard Meier, in *Space Design* (Tokyo), January 1978; "City— within the context of Architecture" in *Reconstruction of Modern Architecture,* Tokyo 1978; "Contemporary Architects: Dolf Schnebli", with Lars Lerup, in *Architecture + Urbanism* (Tokyo), November 1978; "A Different World" in *Japan Architect* (Tokyo), January 1979; "St. Columban's Foreign Mission Society, Tokyo" in *Japan Architect* (Tokyo), September 1979; "The City and Inner Space" in *Ekistics* (Athens), September/October 1979; "Late Entries to the Chicago Tribune Competition," with Stuart Cohen, in *Space Design* (Tokyo), July 1980; "House of Stone and House of Glass" in *Modo* (Milan), July/August 1982; "SD Review 1982," with others, in *Space Design* (Tokyo), December 1982; "Josep Lluis Sert," with others, in *Process: Architecture* (Tokyo), December 1982.

On MAKI: books—*Megastructures: Urban Futures of the Recent Past* by Reyner Banham, New York 1976; *A New Wave of Japanese Architecture,* with introduction by Kenneth Frampton, New York 1978; *Beyond Metabolism: The New Japanese Architecture* by Michael Franklin Ross, New York 1978; *By Their Own Design,* edited by Abby Suckle, New

York and St. Albans, Hertfordshire 1980; *Late Entries to the Chicago Tribune Tower Competition, vol. II,* exhibition catalogue, New York 1980; articles—"Fumihiko Maki" in *Architectural Record* (New York), August 1976; "The growing of grids" in *Architectural Record* (New York), April 1977; "The Post Metabolists" in *Arquitectura* (Madrid), January/February 1979; "Fumihiko Maki," special issue of *Japan Architect* (Tokyo), May 1979; "Fumihiko Maki and Associates," special issue of *Space Design* (Tokyo), June 1979; "Fumihiko Maki," special issue of *Japan Echo* (Tokyo), November 1979; "City House and Country Museum by Fumihiko Mali" in *Architectural Record* (New York), April 1980; "Hillside Terrace Apartments in Daikanyama, Tokyo" in *Industria delle costruzioni* (Rome), May 1980; "Royal Danish Embassy, Tokyo" in *Japan Architect* (Tokyo), June 1980; "Japan:Fumihiko Maki" in *Bauen und Wohnen* (Zurich), June 1980; "Japan Through the Looking Glass," special issue of *Domus* (Milan), June 1981; "Maki Emblems" in *Architectural Review* (London), July 1981; "Architecture in the Urban Desert" in *Oppositions* (New York), Winter 1981; "Fumihiko Maki's Recent Thought" in *Japan Architect* (Tokyo), February 1982; "Fumihiko Maki," special issue of *Japan Architect* (Tokyo), March 1983; "Architects and Builders: The work of Fumihiko Maki and Tadao Ando" in *Japan Architect* (Tokyo), November/December 1983; "Fumihiko Maki," special issue of *Architecture mouvement continuité* (Paris), March 1985.

Bibliographies: *Fumihiko Maki: Japan's Younger Generation Architect* by James P. Noffsinger, Monticello, Illinois 1980; *Fumihiko Maki: A Bibliography* by Carol Cable, Monticello, Illinois 1984.

Fumihiko Maki is a student of two cultures, and the value of his work stems from his successful fusion of both influences. After receiving an undergraduate

Fumihiko Maki: Kato Gakuen Elementary School, Numazu, Japan, 1972.

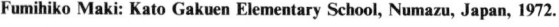

degree from Japan's most prestigious architectural school, Tokyo University, Maki studied in America at Cranbrook and Harvard, and he has since taught at several American universities. He never lost touch with his Japanese acquaintances, however, and in 1960 he helped establish the Metabolism Group.

Along with many other young Japanese designers, Maki has maintained an obsessive interest in new technology and rational design. He uses modular systems in the planning phases and standardized building components in construction. His aesthetic is firmly placed in the modern age, and his favorite materials are metal, glass, and poured concrete. At the same time, however, Maki has not always resorted to the grandiose, monumental expression of either his Japanese or American colleagues. With all of his keen interest in theory and technology, Maki is a populist, and his buildings display a warmth and sense of excitement and surprise that is rarely found in contemporary architecture.

At ground level even his most enormous buildings are scaled appropriately, and his several steelfront designs, notably the Austrian Embassy in Tokyo and his award winning Hillside Terrace Apartments, exhibit carefully manipulated shapes and textures that humanize their total effect. Both buildings are sculptural and plastic, with clean horizontal lines reinforcing the street patterns.

In a different setting, Maki's approach may become entirely different, attesting to his constant concern with contextual response. His design for Tsukuba University is massive, but it is intended to serve as an architectural pivot for the entire campus, to be built on a large, open site. The huge, metalled walls suggest a modern, machine image, but they are carefully reduced, dimensionally, by the relatively small size of the glass blocks that comprise the curtain wall.

At the Toyota Memorial Museum, Maki's concerns are more traditional, and he incorporates directional changes that arise from the intersections of two conflicting grids to express a traditional Japanese spatial property: incompleteness of view. Not only can you not see far ahead or behind you in this very long progression, but although the museum is at the side of a very beautiful lake, only a very limited number of openings reveal views of the outside. Fewer still are directed towards the lake, and the result is that those few have become sacred, and are cherished.

While Maki has rightly gained considerable notoriety as a theoretician, he has clearly not allowed his thinking to become clouded with esoteric ideas. He applies his belief in module, standardized parts and adaptability for change in a very utilitarian, pragmatic way. It is apparent that the thrust of his design attention is not the glorification of these concepts, but the successful employment of them to create inclusive, highly contextual architecture that is in strict accord with human, psychological preferences.

Maki has recently been studying traditional Japanese conceptual notions with increasing depth. Incorporating these ideas into his design work has added even more breadth to his architecture. Far ahead of that of many of his Japanese colleagues who continue to be intrigued solely with pure form, Maki's design work is remarkably mature, not merely in choice of concept, but in terms of compositional sophistication as well.

—Ching-Yu Chang

MAKOVECZ, Imre.

Hungarian. Born in Budapest, 20 November 1935. Educated at the Technical University of Budapest, under Dr. Károly Weichinger, György Szrogh, and György Jánossy, 1954-59, Dip.Arch. 1959. Served in the Hungarian Army, 1955, 1956. Married Marianne Szabó in 1961; children: Benjamin, Anna, and Pál. Architect/Designer in the Bureau of Urban Studies, "Buvati," Budapest, 1959-62, and in SZÖVTERV, Budapest, 1962-71; Chief of the Architectural Studio, VATTI, Budapest, 1971-77. Since 1977, Architect/Designer with the Forestière Organization, Budapest. Member of the Board of the Hungarian Architects Association. Exhibitions: Biennale, Venice, 1973; Hajduszoboszló, 1976; Dombóvar, 1978; Museum of Finnish Architecture, Helsinki, 1981; Stockholm, 1982; Forum Design, Graz, and Innsbruck, Austria, 1983; Munich, 1984. Recipient: Ybl Prize, 1969. Address: Villányi ut. 8, 1114 Budapest, Hungary.

Works: (all Hungary):

1963 Restaurant, Velence
     Restaurant, Balatonszepezd
1965 Hotel, Dombóvar
     Restaurant, Balatonszepezd
1967 Hotel, Sárospatak
     Restaurant, Balatonfured
1968 Restaurant, Tatabánya
     Department store, Letenye
     Department store, Csorna
1971 Department store, Sárospatak
1974/
83 Cultural Centre, Sárospatak
1975 Belvedere, on the River Tisza, Töserdö
     Week-end house, Budapest
     Studio/Apartment, Budapest
1976 Cabana Hoffmann Tourist Hotel and Restaurant, near Budapest
1977 Mortuary Hall, Farkasrét Cemetery, Budapest (with Gábor Mezei)
     Crafts Centre, Szentendre
1978 Collective Housing, Tokaj
     Excursion Centre, Visegrad
1978/
79 Restaurant, Visegrad
     Camp-Site, Visegrad
1979 Ski Lodge, Dobosókö
1980/
85 Cultural Centre, Zalaszentlászo
1982/
84 Cultural Centre, Jászkisén
1982 Apartment Houses in Sárospatak, Budapest and God
1983 Restaurant II, Visegrad

Publications:

By MAKOVECZ: books—*Architectural Forms and Movements'*, privately printed 1970; *The Regulation of Private Competitions*, Budapest 1972, 1974; *Art Almanach*, Budapest 1977, 1978; articles—in *Magyar Épitömüvészet* (Budapest), April 1966; *Magyar Épitömüvészet* (Budapest), January and February 1968; *Magyar Épitömüvészet* (Budapest), January 1969; *DBZ* (Gutersloh, Germany), May 1971; *Magyar Épitömüvészet* (Budapest), June 1971; *Magyar Épitömüvészet* (Budapest), March 1972; *Müveszet* (Budapest), March and April 1972; *Müveszet* (Budapest), June and December 1973; *Müveszet* (Budapest), August 1975; *Art* (Hamburg), 1980; *Arkkitehti* (Helsinki), 1980-83; *Taide* (Helsinki), 1981; *Architectural Review* (London), 1981; *Abitare* (Milan), 1981-82; *Baumeister* (Munich), 1982; *Detail* (Munich), 1983; *Magyar Épitömüvészet* (Budapest), 1984; *Architecture + Urbanism* (Tokyo), 1984.

On MAKOVECZ: books—*Imre Makovecz* by Attila Komjáthy, Budapest 1977; *Imre Makovecz* by János Frank, Budapest 1979; articles—by Ferenc Merényi in *Magyar Épiteszet* (Budapest), 1967; by Ferenc Mendele in *Magyar Épitömüvészet* (Budapest), February 1968; by Mihaly Kubinszky in *Magyar Épitömüvészet* (Budapest), February 1970; by Jenö Szendröi in *Magyar Épiteszet* (Budapest), 1972; by Mihály Kubinszky in *Épiteszeti lexikon* (Budapest), 1978; by J. Glancey in *Architectural Review* (London), 1981; by J. Balint in *Abitare* (Milan), 1981, 1982; by B. Peters in *Baumeister* (Munich), 1982; by R. Pietila in *Arkkitehti* (Helsinki), 1982; by I. Kultermann in *Architecture + Urbanism* (Tokyo), 1984; by B. Botoud in *Architecture + Urbanism* (Tokyo), 1984; by D. Ekler in *Architecture + Urbanism* (Tokyo), 1984.

"Inner man" is spoiled by rapidly-expanding technology and constant anxiety about the threat of all-out war. Celebration and human dignity is doubtful. I am afraid there is no holding an unbalanced mankind from abandoning civilization. A balance can be preserved only by having a relationship between the inner man and lower orders of creation. The Sárospatak House illustrated here represents the formal entry of nature and prehistoric culture into our present day.

—Imre Makovecz

Imre Makovecz: Funeral Chapel, Farkasret Cemetery, Budapest, 1977.

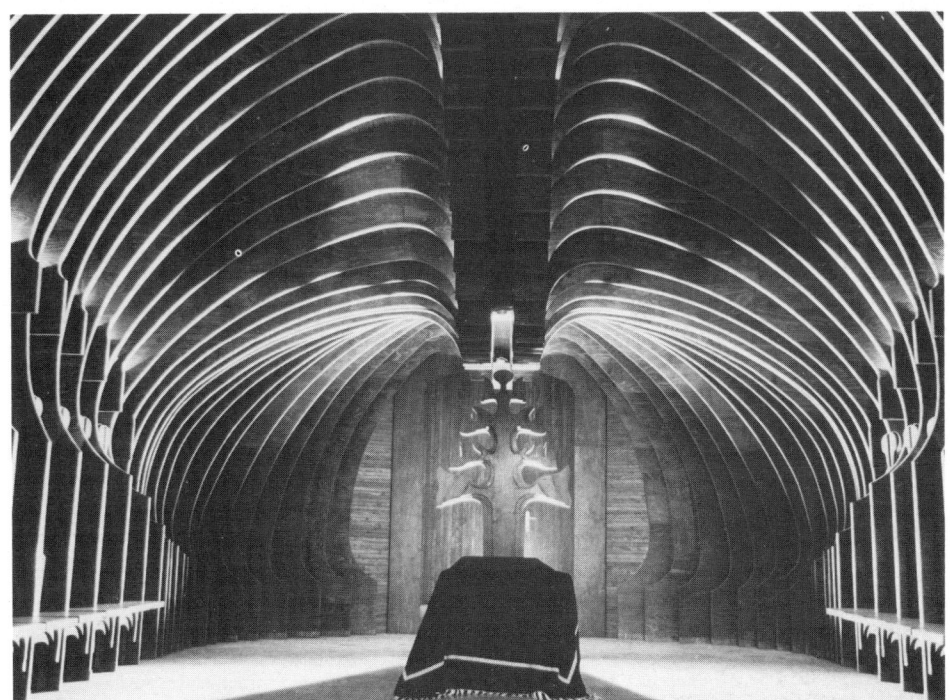

Architecture in a socialist country is subject to demands for a constant raising in the standard of living and to the demands of centralized planning which dictates a whole range of approaches. The work of Imre Makovecz fits only marginally into this framework. Much as he seeks to fulfil general requirements, he searches, equally, for personal solutions to particular circumstances, solutions directly linked to his creed as a creator.

His work is multi-coloured, like a mountain crystal. The facets it shows are as multifarious as the rigorous principals which underlie it. With his passion for the organic architecture of Frank Lloyd Wright and for the anthroposophy of Rudolf Steiner, Makovecz refuses a simple repetition of forms and materials to create, in each of his buildings, a specific work that is at once personal and proper to its site.

Makovecz's architecture resounds with echoes of the Hungarian "pousta," transposing into contemporary terms the traditions of the country (as in the week-end house, Budapest; or the restaurant at Tatabánya). At the same time it remains aesthetically linked to the new physical, economic and political conditions of the country (for example, the Belvedere on the River Tisza).

Makovecz searches for forms that delimit and give character to the interior or exterior space. In this endeavour so much can come into play—from simple building materials to the nature of the direct participation by the users. A good example of this kind of concern is the impressive oak ceiling structure in the Mortuary Hall at the Farkasret Cemetery, Budapest, which creates an exceptional consonance with the vigil of grief.

A designer who is extremely conscientious in his duty to his country and to his people, Markovecz is not afraid to struggle for the sake of his creations, preferring, rather than simply fulfilling quantitative needs, to remain honest with himself and his fundamental principles. His work is a quest for communication between human beings, a communication that can only come about if architecture transcends the realm of the functional and fulfils its psychological and educational obligations.

—Zdravko Natchev

MANGIAROTTI, Angelo.

Italian. Born in Milan, 26 February 1921. Educated at the Milan Polytechnic School of Architecture, 1945-48, Dip.Arch. 1948. Freelance designer and architect, in Milan and Chicago, 1948-55; architect/designer, in partnership with Bruno Morassutti, Milan, 1955-69. In private practice, Milan, since 1960. Consultant to Le Porte Echappement Universal, La Chaux de Fonds, Switzerland, 1955-68, CGE, Milan, 1959, Alfa Romeo, Milan, 1960, and Electrolux, Stockholm, 1961. Editor, *Studi d'architettura* magazine, Milan, 1946. Visiting Professor, Institute of Design, Illinois Institute of Technology, Chicago, 1953-54; Lecturer, Istituto Superiore di Disegno Industriale, Venice, 1963-64; Visiting Professor, University of Hawaii, Honolulu, 1970, Ecole Polytechnique Federale, Lausanne, 1975, University of Adelaide, and South Australian Institute of Technology, Adelaide, 1976, and University of Sao Paulo, 1978; Professor, University of Palermo, Sicily, 1982. Exhibitions: *La Casa Abitata*, Palazzo Strozzi, Florence, 1965; University of Zurich, 1966; Delft, Holland, 1966; *Ten Italian Architects*, Los Angeles County Museum of Art, 1967; *Exposicion Internacional de la Vivienda*, Santiago, Chile, 1972; *28/78 Architettura*, Palazzo delle Stelline, Milan, 1979; Association of Architects of Armenia SSR, Eviran, U.S.S.R., 1979; Galleria Lorenzelli, Milan, 1980; *25th Anniversary of Club 44*, La Chaux de Fonds, Switzerland, 1983; *Matter's*

Tongue, Expo Center, Chicago, 1983; *Industrie et architecture*, Centre Georges Pompidou, Paris, 1983. Recipient: Olimpiadi della Cultura Boys' Club Prize, Milan, 1952; Economic Development Center Prize, Trieste, 1953; *Domus* Prize, 1956; Gold Medal, Villa Comunale dell'Olmo, Como, 1957; Award of Distinction, AITEC (Associazione Italiana Tecnico Economica del Cemento), 1962; IN-ARCH Regional Prize, Lombardy, 1963; Prize for Industrial Design, Nazionale del Golfo de la Spezia, 1963; Associazione Italiana Prefabbricati Prize, 1972; CECM Prix Europeen de la Construction Metallique, 1979; First Prize, *Expo Construccion 80*, Buenos Aires, 1980. Addresses; (office): Via Cappuccio 7, 20123 Milan, Italy; Stradella Valmarana 2, 36100 Vicenza, Italy.

Works:

1953 Master plan for Cervia, Milano Marittima, Ravenna (competition project)

1953 Multi-use furniture in moulded plywood, bronze, and hammered metals; clocks, sewing machines, bronze vases, and other household items

1954 Professional Studio, Perrysburg, Ohio (project)

1955 Skyscraper, Port of Genoa (project; with Bruno Morassutti)
Tomb, Udine

1957 Matris Misericordiae Church, Baranzate, Milan (with Bruno Morassutti)
Three houses, San Martino di Castrozza, Trento, Italy (with Bruno Morassutti)
INA-CASA Housing Development, Feltre, Milan
INA-CASA Housing Development, Ferrara, Italy
Clinic and Nursery, Udine (project, with Bruno Morassutti)
Club 44 interiors, La Chaux de Fonds, Switzerland (with Bruno Morassutti)

1958 Warehouse, Padua (with Bruno Morassutti and Aldo Favini)
Apartment building, Via Fezzan, Milan (project; with Bruno Morassutti)

1959 Apartment building, Via Gavirate, Milan (with Bruno Morassutti)
House restoration, La Chaux de Fonds, Switzerland (with Bruno Morassutti; original building by Le Corbusier, 1914/16)

1960 Apartment building, Via Quadronno, Milan (with Bruno Morassutti)
Sports Stadium, Geneva (competition project; with Bruno Morassutti and Aldo Favini)

1961 Furniture shop, Corsico, Milan
Water Tower and Reservoir, near Rome (project; with Aldo Favini)
Residential complex, Piombino, Livorno

1962 Car Testing Wind Tunnel (project)
SIAG Industrial Complex, with housing, Marcianise, Caserta, Italy
Società Poretti Warehouse, Mestre, Venice
Industrial building, Arese, Italy (project)

1963 Italsider Steel Pavilion, *International Fair of the Sea*, Genoa
Industrial building, Cesena, Forli, Italy (project)

1964 Società Elmag Building, Monza, Milan
School and houses in pre-fabricated metal components (project)

1964/
65 House conversion and interiors, Camogli, Genoa

1965 Policentro Megastructure (project)
Pre-fabricated houses in sheet zinc (project)
Overpass, Piazza della Repubblica, Milan (project)

1966 Industrial building, Rovellasca, Como

1967 CUB 8 Interwall

1968 Pre-fabricated structure in prestressed concrete for a tile factory, Salerno (project)

House, Marina di Pietrasanta, Lucca, Italy
House, Piadena, Cremona, Italy
Commissioner of Automobiles Office, Domegliara, Verona
Design of the *Furniture Exhibition*, Corsico, Milan

1969 Industrial building in prestressed concrete, Alzata Brianza, Como

1971 Villa, Bardolino, Verona
Tourist Center, Murlongo, Verona
Villa, Somma Lombardo, Varese, Italy
Industrial structure in prestressed concrete

1972 Apartment building, Monza, Milan

1973 Pre-fabricated industrial-use structure in reinforced concrete (project)

1975 *Fiera di Padova* Headquarters, Padua (project; with others)

1976 Pre-fabricated industrial-use structure in prestressed concrete

1977 Apartment building, Arosio, Como

1978 Snaidero Industrial Complex, Mayano del Friuli, Udine
Company Building entrance and reception area, Giussano, Milan

1979 Fiat Concessionaire's Building, Bussolengo, Verona

1980 Design of sanitary wares for a company in Palazzolo, Brescia
Design of silver vases and glasses

1982 Milano Rogoeredo, Milano Certosa and Milano Bovisa railway stations, Milan
Garibaldi Vittoria rail station passageways, Milan

Publications:

By MANGIAROTTI: articles—numerous in *Domus* (Milan), 1949-78; *Arts and Architecture* (Los Angeles), 1953-70; *Architecture d'aujourd'hui* (Paris), 1953-73; *Casabella* (Milan), 1955-78; *L'Oeil* (Paris), 1956-72; *Architectural Forum* (New York), 1959-63; *Bauen und Wohnen* (Zürich), 1959-77; *Moebel Interior Design* (Stuttgart), 1960-75; *Industria italiana del cemento* (Rome), 1963-77; *Ottagono* (Milan), 1966-78; *Interni* (Milan), 1967-77; *Casa Vogue* (Milan), 1968-77; etc.; recording—*Expressing Materials and Components*, tape cassette and slides, London 1983.

On MANGIAROTTI: books—*Italian Contemporary Architecture*, London 1952; *New Furniture*, edited by Gerd Hatje, Stuttgart 1952, 1956; *Architettura Moderna in Milano*, Milan 1964; *Angelo Mangiarotti*, Tokyo 1965; *World Architecture, volume 2*, edited by John Donat, London 1965; *Architettura Italiana Contemporanea* by Alberto Galardi, Milan 1967; *Pannelli di Copertura Prefabbricati* by Alberto dal Lago, Milan 1972; *Progettare un Edificio* by Ludovico Quaroni, Milan 1977; *Angelo Mangiarotti: Il Processo del Costruire* by Enrico D. Bona, Milan 1979; *Transformations in Modern Architecture* by Arthur Drexler, New York 1979; *Furniture by Architects: Masterpieces of 20th Century Design and Where to Buy Them*, Tokyo 1982; articles—"Architettura recentissime di Angelo Mangiarotti" by Giulia Veronesi in *Zodiac* (Milan), no. 11, 1963; "The Work of Angelo Mangiarotti and Bruno Morassutti" in *Architectural Design* (London), March 1964; "The 'Avanguardia' di Mangiarotti" by Pier Carlo Santini in *Ottagono* (Milan), March 1971; "Angelo Mangiarotti" in *Architecture + Urbanism* (Tokyo), September 1974; "Expression of Forces—Prefab Project" in *Domus* (Milan), May 1978; "Housing at Monza" in *Architecture + Urbanism* (Tokyo), December 1978; "Office in the Country" in *Domus* (Milan), February 1979; "Recent Works and Manifesto 1980 of Angelo Mangiarotti" in *Space Design* (Tokyo), August 1980; "The Houses of Angelo Mangiarotti," special issue of *Ville-Giardini* (Milan), February 1981; "Recent Works of Angelo Mangiarotti" in *Space Design*

Angelo Mangiarotti: Suspension structure for the State Railway Stations, Milan, 1983.

(Tokyo), February 1982; "Building Complex for Social Services" by E. Bona in *Architettura* (Rome), June 1982.

After a period spent in a progressive search for simplification of the language of the modern architectural tradition—mainly that of rationalism and particularly that of Mies van der Rohe—Angelo Mangiarotti has concentrated on working out a fluid formal language of his own. He has, at the same time, defined articulate modular principles for prefabricated industrial buildings, so constructed that they can be arranged in complex, plastically significant forms.

His research concerns the working out of a construction methodology that is a reflection of his own philosophical program for private and social life, one founded on a search for a new and properly motivated relationship between man and his environment, and this research has constantly moulded the actual design of his architecture: he has tried to form a single, coherent whole in accordance with his basic principles.

Mangiarotti modulates space and surfaces in fluent, almost musical movements—as in the sensitive handling of interior space in his houses, for example the old house at Camogli, in which horizontal and vertical lines create spatial relations of a restful and agreeable clarity.

In his other buildings, too, Mangiarotti makes use of a delicate spatial modulation and employs components from the local countryside, making his architecture almost a scaled-down part of its surroundings. The Steel Pavilion at the entrance to Genoa Harbor, built for the *International Fair of the Sea*, has an open framework, a platform with a hollow-moulded roof of great plastic delicacy supported above it on steel columns. Beneath the exhibition platform, half undergound, there is a hall for film shows, conferences and meetings. The Società Elmag Building is an example of Mangiarotti's total use of pre-fabrication: the three elements (pillar, rafter, roof-tile) are fitted into one another without expansion joints in a structural assembly that is light and organic. The SIAG Industrial Complex, which includes residential buildings, uses as its basic building material the panels produced by SIAG themselves, by a secret process, from a residue (canapulo) of the hemp that is grown locally. The proportions of the buildings depend on the measurements of the panel, in a coherent design that makes use both of the environmental features and of the most advanced experimental research: the solution is simple and extremely flexible and at the same time formally acceptable.

The same methods of working and the same flexibility and delicacy are revealed in his residential buildings, as are the means for almost indefinite practical expansion. Mangiarotti's industrial design shows the same characteristics—simplicity, refinement, flexibility—whether he is designing furniture, interiors, or such useful objects as the clock, in the Section series.

—Lara-Vinca Masini

MANSFELD, Alfred.
Israeli. Born in St. Petersburg, now Leningrad, Russia, 2 March 1912; emigrated to Israel, 1935. Educated at the Technische Hochschule, Berlin, 1931-33, and at the Ecole Spéciale d'Architecture, Paris, under Auguste Perret, *q.v.*, 1933-35. Served as a Second Lieutenant in the Israeli Army, 1948-49. Married Bella Reinin in 1946; children: Michael and Yoel. In private practice, Haifa, since 1938; in partnership with Munio Weinraub, 1951-59. Head, Northern Area Department, Ministry of Building, Tel Aviv, 1949-50. Senior Lecturer, 1949-70, and since 1970 Professor of Architecture, Technion: Israel Institute of Technology, Haifa; also Visiting Lecturer at universities in West Germany, Switzerland, France, Italy and the United States, since 1965. President, Israel Institute of Architects, 1968-70. Exhibitions: *Forms from Israel,* American Federation of Arts, New York, 1958; Museum of Modern Art, Haifa (one-man), 1963; *Architecture in Israel,* Israel Museum, Jerusalem, 1966, and Tel Aviv Museum, 1967; *Architecture of Museums,* Museum of Modern Art, New York, 1968; *Bauhaus,* Musée National d'Art Moderne, Paris, 1969; *The Rational Factor in Works by Israeli Artists,* Haifa Museum of Modern Art, Israel, 1984. Collection: Museum of Modern Art, New York. Recipient: First Prize, Israel Museum Competition, 1959; First Prize, Lod Airport Competition, Tel Aviv, 1962; Israel Prize for Architecture, 1964; First and Second Prizes, Jerusalem Town Hall Competition, 1964; Gold Plaquette for Foreign Architects, Bund Deutscher Archi-

Al Mansfeld: Israel Museum, Jerusalem, 1965.

tekten, 1966; Ratner Architecture Prize, Israel, 1975; Rechter Architecture Prize, Israel, 1979. Member, Akademie der Künste, Berlin, 1970; Honorary Corresponding Member, Académie d'Architecture, Paris, 1983. Address: Al Mansfeld, Architect, 5 Keller Street, Haifa, Israel.

Works:

1951 Cultural Centre, Kiryat Haim, near Haifa (with Munio Weinraub)
      Commemorative monument, Kiryat Haim, near Haifa (with Munio Weinraub)
1953 Housing development, Mount Carmel, Haifa (with Munio Weinraub)
1956 Institute for Hebrew Studies, Hebrew University of Jerusalem (with Munio Weinraub)
      Centre for the Re-education of the Blind, Haifa (with Munio Weinraub)
      Kiryat Eliahu Housing Development, Haifa (with Munio Weinraub)
1957 Hydrotechnical Institute, Technion, Haifa (with Munio Weinraub)
      Mansfeld Residence, Mount Carmel, Haifa
      Ramat Hadar Residential Quarter, Haifa (with Munio Weinraub)
      S. S. Israel and S. S. Theodor Herzl interiors (with Dora Gad)
1960 University of Nigeria, Nsukka (project, partly executed; with Dani Havkin)
      Library, Trinity College, Dublin (competition project; with Dani Havkin and J. Polatsek)
1962 Lod Airport, Tel Aviv (competition project; with Dani Havkin)
      Mausoleum, Rangoon, Burma (project)
1963 Centre for Nuclear Studies, Technion, Haifa
      Israel Pavilion, World's Fair, New York (competition project)
1964 S. S. Shalom interior (with Dora Gad)
1965 Israel Museum, Jerusalem (with Dora Gad)
1972 Mount Carmel Auditorium, Haifa (with Dani Havkin)
1978 Shaar Ha'aliya Housing (250 units), Haifa (with Dani Havkin)
      Kindergarten, Shaar Ha'aliya, Haifa
      Town Hall and Civic Precinct, Jerusalem (with Dani Havkin)
1979 Interfaith Sanctuary, Sinai, Israel (with Pierre Vago and A. El-Rimaly)
      Town Hall and Civic Centre, Jerusalem (3rd and 4th projects)
1980 Two Hundred Houses, French Carmel, Israel
1981 Residential Quarter (four hundred houses), Nazareth, Israel
      Melbourne Landmark, Victoria, Australia (competition project)

Ramat Alon Residential Plan, Haifa
1982 The Peak Development, Hong Kong (competition project)
      Sonol Naveh Shaanan Filling Station, Haifa
1983 Kiryat Ata Residential Town Plan, Israel
      Sonol Filling Station, Jerusalem
      Opera de la Bastille, Paris (competition project)
      Pavilion of Israeli Art, Israel Museum, Jerusalem

Publications:

By MANSFELD: books—*Designing with Open-ended Cumulative Systems*, Haifa 1975; *Designing for Growth and Change*, Haifa 1976; *Sketchbook of Buildings, Projects, Competitions*, Haifa 1980; articles—"Meinungen zu Mies van der Rohe, Al. Mansfeld" in *Baumeister* (Munich), March 1966; "Architecture in Israel—Past and Present" in *Technion Magazine* (Haifa), February 1970; "Building a New Land" in *Tarbut* (New York), Summer 1970; essay in *Design: Umwelt wird in Frage gestellt*, Berlin 1970; "Kann der Designer die Welt retten?" in *Architektur und Wohnen* (Hamburg), no. 2, 1973; "Building a New Land: Architecture in Israel" in *International Technion Diary 1977*, Haifa 1977; "Designing for Growth, Change, Uncertainty" in *Architecture in Israel* (Tel Aviv), 1978; "Structuralistic Design Methods" in *Architecture in Israel* (Tel Aviv), 1980; "Al Mansfeld: Die erst Skizze des Israel Museums" in *Daidalos* (West Berlin), 1982; "A Structuralistic Approach to the Design of Towns and Buildings" in *The Rational Factor in Works by Israeli Artists*, exhibition catalogue, Haifa 1984.

On MANSFELD: books—*Strukturformen der Modernen Architektur* by Curt Siegel, Munich 1960; *Industriebau* by Walter Henn, Munich 1962; *Balkone* by F. Schuster, Stuttgart 1962; *Neues Bauen in der Welt* by Udo Kultermann, Tubingen 1965; *House Plans* by the editors of the Daily Mail, London 1965; *The Aesthetics of Contemporary Architecture* by Michel Ragon, Neuchatel 1967; *Betonkonstruktionen in Hochbau* by P. G. Wieschemann and K. Gatz, Munich 1968; *Mehrzweck-Gebaüde für Gesellschaftliche Funktionen* by Friedeman Wild, Munich 1970; *A History of Building Types* by Nikolaus Pevsner, London 1975; *Public Art: New Directions* by Louis G. Redstone, New York 1981; *New Israeli Architecture* by Amiram Harlap, New York and London 1982; articles—"Centre de Culture à Kiryat Haim" in *Techniques et Architecture* (Paris), January 1951; "S. S. Israel and S. S. Theodor Herzl" in *Architectural Review* (London), September 1957;

"Israel's First Passenger Ship" in *Interiors* (New York), September 1958; "Israeli Culture" in *Architectural Forum* (New York), February 1961; "Dublin University Library Competition" in *Architect and Building News* London), June 1961; "A Visit to Israel" in *Concrete Quarterly* (London), July/September 1963; "L'Art en Israel" in *Les Lettres Francaises* (Paris), August 1963; "Profilo dell'architetto Alfred Mansfeld" in *L'Architettura* (Rome), May 1965; "Israel" by Dore Ashton in *Arts and Architecture* (Los Angeles), October 1965; "The Art That History Shaped—A Report from Israel" by Katharine Kuh in *Saturday Review* (New York), January 1966; "The Planning and Architecture of the Israel Museum" by Willem Sandberg in *Museum* ((Unesco: Paris), January 1966; special issue of *Kokusai-Kentiku* (Tokyo), May 1967; "Architectuur in Israel" in *Cement* (Amsterdam), March 1969; "Various Buildings by Al Mansfeld" in *Kindai-Kenchiku* (Tokyo), April 1970; "Alfred Mansfeld: Tre Opere Communitarie" in *L'Architettura* (Rome), March 1971; "Leisure Centre and Multi-Purpose Auditorium, Mount Carmel" in *Architecture + Urbanism* (Tokyo), May 1976; "Shaar Ha'aliya, Haifa" in *AC: International Asbestos Cement Review* (Zurich), April 1977; "Leisure Centre and Multi-Purpose Auditorium, Haifa", and "Israel Museum, Jerusalem" in *Architecture in Israel* (Tel Aviv), 1978; "Museum of Israel" in *Connaissance des Arts* (Paris), May 1978; "Shaar Ha'aliya and Stella Mans Housing, Haifa" in *Architecture + Urbanism* (Tokyo), December 1978; "Shaar Ha'aliya Residential Quarter, Haifa" in *Architecture in Israel* (Tel Aviv), 1980; "Al Mansfeld: Children's Nursery, Shaar Ha'aliya, Haifa" in *Architecture + Urbanism* (Tokyo), April 1980; "Petrol Station in Haifa" in *AC: International Asbestos Cement Review* (Zurich), May 1982; "Was tun mit Mies – Erweiterung Nationalgalerie Berlin" in *Baumeister* (Munich), July 1982; "Israeli Museum: Filling a Hilltop" in *Landscape Architecture* (Louisville, Kentucky), July/August 1984.

CREDO

I believe in the architect's responsibility towards society, his "ultimate customer" (although the immediate client does not always represent the real needs of society).

I believe that this responsibility results in the conception that design is indivisible, and therefore:

that there is no inherent difference in the act of designing a city, a building, a chair or a spoon, and that the "complete" architect should aspire to universality in this sense;

that in our age of narrow specialization an architect should use his creative forces in order to re-establish the disrupted balance between matter and spirit, and to integrate, humanize and harmonize man's heterogeneous surroundings;

that dreams are the basis of reality and that expediency is not equivalent with practicality;

that true practicality is at the root of any technological development, and that therefore architecture will be decisively influenced by the process of industrialization;

that this development, far from restricting architecture, will produce new systems and values and provide the artist with new tools to create new forms and dimensions;

that an architect should use these tools not only to provide the logical and efficient physical framework for the man of today, but also to create joy and delight in man's visual environment and harmonious space-patterns around him;

that this spatial and plastic order can best be achieved through the use of three-dimensional mathematical elements and systems, and through a combination of a scientist's sobriety and an artist's intuition and vision.

that permanence and transience in architecture are reconcilable twin-phenomena and that our built environment should be structured in such a way that the resulting space-order, in spite of being "complete in itself" should remain open for growth and change;

that such open design-systems are a more appropriate expression of our epoch than architectural "frozen music" compositions.

that the architect's calling is to join, to fit, to create order and to relate, not to separate, to disrupt, to set apart or to cause gaps.

I believe in true team-work, where every member of the team contributes his special knowledge and talent towards a harmonized whole; but I also believe in an undivided responsibility vested in the architect as the leader of the team

I do not believe that the creative tasks and responsibility of the architect can be delegated to committees or "technical offices." I do believe that much good can come out of a close collaboration between the architect and imaginative and enlightened public bodies qualified to formulate the true needs of society.

—Al Mansfeld

Al Mansfeld has practised architecture for the past four decades in Haifa, but he received his formal architectural training in Berlin and Paris, and a touch of European elegance and sophistication has always been evident in his work. This was perhaps to be expected when, in the 1950s, he was in partnership with the late Munio Weinraub, himself a product of the Bauhaus in its Mies van der Rohe phase; but these characteristics carry over into his later association with Israeli-born Dani Havkin, and even to his present-day "Team Mansfeld," a group of young and talented designers—a category he has always attracted to his office, where they found rich opportunities for creative interaction. Mansfeld believes in "true team-work, where every member of the team contributes his special knowledge and talent towards the harmonized whole;" but this is obviously no egalitarian, unstructured team, for he also

believes in the undivided responsibility and leadership of the architect.

While there has been variety and a natural evolution in the character of Mansfeld's output, it has always been marked by distinctiveness, which sets it apart from the general run of contemporary Israeli work. It has, moreover, been characterized in recent years by a certain consistency of architectural approach, which derives not only from Mansfeld's design personality, but also from the discipline of a guiding philosophy. Mansfeld's "Credo" casts the architect in a universalistic role, the "humanizer and harmonizer" of man's surroundings, responding to the needs of society as the "ultimate customer." Lately he has attempted to translate the somewhat lyrical images of this credo into the more hard-edged, precise terms of an architectural theory: this he calls his structuralist approach, utilising open, cumulative design systems as a way of designing for growth, change and uncertainty.

This hierarchical and open-ended approach to design replaced the finiteness of his earlier work: the massive Ramat Hadar flats, with their Corbusian overtones, and the striking Kiryat Eliahu high-rise tower, an exercise in structural formalism. The new approach is first evident in his Israel-prize winning design (with Dora Gad) for the Israel Museum in Jerusalem with its articulated and elegant pavilions; it may also be seen in his multi-purpose auditorium for Haifa, the later development of the Jerusalem town hall project, and the Shaar Ha'aliya housing scheme for Haifa. The theory, as it is here demonstrated, is not a straitjacket but a framework within which ingenious solutions to diverse problems may be postulated, resulting in characterful but essentially modest architectural complexes which seek to enhance rather than to dominate their urban context.

Generally, even the largest projects break down into small-scale units, the picturesque grouping of which is disciplined by the overall structural grid and the insistent morphology. Because of the decomposition of the larger masses, the pictorial quality of surfaces, and the refinement and elegance of detail, the work of the Mansfield office is anti-monumental, but when the need arises, the monumental form is handled convincingly and with great power: the high-rise version of the Jerusalem town hall project, for instance, is a tower of soaring beauty that somehow captures those elusive qualities of grandeur, gravity and grace that one usually associates with an I.M. Pei masterpiece.

—Gilbert Herbert

MANTEOLA, SÁNCHEZ GÓMEZ, SANTOS, SOLSONA, ARCHITECTS.

Partnership; established as Manteola, Petchersky, Sánchez Gómez, Santos, Solsona, Viñoly, in Buenos Aires, 1964, by Flora Manteola (born, 1936), Ignacio Petchersky (died, 1971), Javier Sánchez Gómez (born, 1936), Josefa Santos (born, 1931), Justos Jorge Solsona (born, 1931), and Rafael Viñoly (born, 1944); Associates, since 1974: Carlos Sallaberry and Felipe Tarsitano. Address: Florida 890, 3rd Floor, Buenos Aires 1005, Argentina.

Works:

1960 Church, Venado Tuerto, Argentina (project)
1963 National Library, Buenos Aires (project)
1964 House, La Lucila, Buenos Aires
     Tire (Tyre) sales and warehouse buildings in Buenos Aires, Neuquen, and Santa Fe, Argentina
     Argentine Pavilion, *World's Fair*, New York

1965 Museum and Park, La Plata, Argentina
     Municipal development schemes for Buenos Aires (2 projects)
1966 Hall of Deputies extension, Buenos Aires
     Dental Association Building, Buenos Aires
     Devoto Co-operative Villa, Buenos Aires (with Aftalion, Bischof and Vidal)
     Energy Company Headquarters, Cordoba, Argentina (project)
     Mar del Plata Auditorium, Buenos Aires (competition project)
1967 Housing, Santa Teresita, Buenos Aires
     Tower Restaurant, Buenos Aires
     Teaching Hospital, Cordoba, Argentina (project; with Ernesto Katzenstein)
     City Hall, Amsterdam (competition project)
1968 Bank of the City of Buenos Aires Branch at Casa Matriz, Buenos Aires
     Argentine Industrial Union Building, Buenos Aires
     Hotel, Taormina, Italy
1969 Housing complex, Acoyte, Buenos Aires
     Housing complex, Rioja, Buenos Aires
     Ventas Bank Main Building, Buenos Aires
     Bank of the City of Buenos Aires Branches at Patricios, Barracas, and Liniers, Buenos Aires
     Mental Health Centre, Tucuman, Argentina
     Mental Health Centre, Santiago del Estero, Argentina
     Bialik School, Buenos Aires
     Oks House, Buenos Aires
1970 Hotel Internacional, Buenos Aires
     Bank building, Tucuman, Argentina
     Naval Hospital, Buenos Aires
     Bank building, Chaco, Argentina
     IBM Building, Buenos Aires
     Housing, La Matanza, Buenos Aires
     Bank of the City of Buenos Aires Branches at Villa Urquiza, Flores, Condor, and Retiro, Buenos Aires
     Housing complex, Entre Rios, Argentina
     Argentine Embassy, Brasilia (project)
1971 Durand Hospital, Buenos Aires
     Costanera Avenue Development, Misiones, Argentina
     National Pediatric Hospital, Buenos Aires (project)
     Hospital, Misiones, Argentina (project)
     Hospital, La Rioja, Argentina (project)
     Almirante Brown Hospital, Buenos Aires
1972 Plaza and car park, Buenos Aires
     CGE Office Building, Buenos Aires
     Housing complex, Buenos Aires
     Redevelopment plan for the central area of Santiago, Chile (project; with Bielus, Goldemberg and Wainstein)
     Boating Club House, Buenos Aires
     Auditorium, Buenos Aires (project)
     Goethe School, Buenos Aires
1973 Housing complex, San Isidro, Buenos Aires
     Housing complex, Buenos Aires
1973/
75 Papel Prensa paper factory, San Pedro, Buenos Aires Province
1974 Department of Social Work Headquarters, Buenos Aires (with Sabbatiello and Terzoni)
     Ranelagh Housing Complex, Buenos Aires
     Housing complex, Chubut, Argentina
     Piedrabuena Housing Complex, Buenos Aires
     Housing complex, Chaco, Argentina
1974/
78 Aluar Housing Complex, Puerto Madryn, Chubut Province, Argentina
1975 Urban housing developments (2), Buenos Aires (with Irajtenber, Cano, Lluma and Grennon)
     Sports Centre Complex, Corrientes, Argentina
     Energy Authority Headquarters, Buenos Aires (project)
1976 Aerolineas Argentinas Headquarters, Buenos Aires (project)

Football stadium, Mendoza, Argentina

Football stadium, Rosario, Santa Fe, Argentina (with Pujals and Hope)

Television Production Center, Buenos Aires (with Sadkowska, Trajtenberg, Lluma, Cano and Grennon)

1977 Prourban Office Building, Buenos Aires

Summer holiday housing complex, Punta del Este, Uruguay

Country club house, Buenos Aires

1978 Banco de Italia y Rio de la Plata, Buenos Aires

1978/
   81 Banco de la Provincia de Corrientes Headquarters, Buenos Aires

Publications:

On MANTEOLA/SANCHEZ GOMEZ: book—*Manteola, Sánchez Gómez, Santos, Solsona, Viñoly,* Buenos Aires 1978; articles—"Acerca de la Practica" in *Summa* (Buenos Aires), no. 57, 1972; "Buenos Aires" in *Casabella* (Milan), February 1973; "Piedrabuena Housing Development, Buenos Aires" in *Nuestra arquitectura* (Buenos Aires), no. 500, 1977; "Banco de Italia y Rio de la Plata Headquarters, Buenos Aires" in *Summa* (Buenos Aires), March 1979; "Prototype dwellings for the Province of San Juan" in *Summa* (Buenos Aires), May 1979; "BATV: Buenos Aires Color Television Production Center" in *Progressive Architecture* (New York), July 1979; "House in Belgrano, Buenos Aires" in *Summa* (Buenos Aires), July 1979; "Prourban Building, Avenida de Libertador 498, Buenos Aires" in *Summa* (Buenos Aires), May 1980; "Look South: Modern Architecture is Alive and Well in Argentina" in *Building* (London), 19 September 1980; "The Work of Manteola, Sanchez Gomez, Santos, Solsona, Vinoly" in *Casabella* (Milan), April 1981; "Bank Buildings of the Last Two Decades in Argentina" in *Summa* (Buenos Aires), April 1982; "Color Television Studios in Buenos Aires" in *Summa* (Buenos Aires), April 1983.

In order to write this statement, we have had to try to put into words those motives that underlie all our work, motives that normally remain unspoken. This task would pose problems for anyone, but it does so in our case for a particular reason: we are not in the habit of verbalizing, in any organized sense, those thought processes that form part of our daily routine.

It is now about fifteen years since we began working together, and despite the natural changes in each of us during that time and the irreparable loss of Ignacio Petchersky, we have still managed to retain our original character as a team. The reason for the continuity of this identity, which goes beyond the given eclecticism of our work, seems to us to lie in an almost fanatical attitude towards what we do and in the very real way in which we relate to our projects. Our works have always been, and continue to be, very close to our hearts. Simply as a means of repeating the pleasure we take in seeing the way that the ideas of our sketches become reality, we have always managed to overcome the various obstacles that make it so difficult to set up and maintain an independent practice in a profession as closed as architecture.

Working in architecture in Argentina—as, probably, in many other environments and countries in the world—presents a challenge that resolves itself somewhere between logic and effrontery. To consolidate a coherent style and method, then to attempt a minimum of continuity, and at the same time to remain intellectually faithful to those principles that are generally associated with youthfulness and inexperience—these goals are almost impossible to achieve. Yet we try; even today, each theme provides an exercise that tests the very limits of our capacity for reinterpretation. By adhering to this principle, we believe that we can give the finished objects a certain critical quality; as well, we can fill our daily activity

with cultural significance and contribute something to the language of architecture.

The evolution of our activities has gradually caused us to question our beliefs about the "function of form"—ideologies that we all inherited; we have come to the conclusion, gained as a result of concrete experience, that the essence of architecture is not the reconciling of opposing ends within a forced equilibrium that is always bound to end in instability. Because this idea, enforced with such strictness and authority, has come to seem to us unsatisfactory, it has recently brought us to a serious exercise in self-criticism. This questioning is now the basis of our approach to design, and it seems to us the most legitimate way of dealing with our natural desire to improve or revise our preconceptions.

—Manteola, Sánchez Gómez, Santos, Solsona

The team of Manteola, Sánchez Gómez, Santos, Solsona is undeniably one of the most original and vital contributors to the "making of architecture" in Argentina in recent years. They are the creators of the Television Production Center, one of the best buildings in Buenos Aires in the last decade.

The team approaches each project by a process of analysis and discussion in which each one participates: in this way they interpret the subject, formulate the basic ideas, and define the fundamental generators of the project. The advantage of the method is that it allows the team a "fresh start" with each project; it has also contributed to the enrichment of their repertory of ideas on architecture.

With this method, and given the fact that each member of the team is an individual architect, working and changing with one another for nearly fifteen years, their work ought to reveal an almost casebook eclecticism. And to a certain extent it does. To the extent, that is, that architecture is revealed in forms, and that forms are or are not expressive, and

that the ideas that inform a project are valid only for a particular case, having been conceived as abstract simplifications that solve the problems of manipulation of a complex language—to that extent, their work is eclectic. And, because of their technique and philosophy of working, it *is* difficult to attempt a survey of the studio's style (with the possible exception of the series of banks in Buenos Aires from the period 1967-72, which brought them international fame) for the simple reason that it is difficult to point to formal similarities among their buildings or any givens in their use of architectural elements. Yet a "constant" does run throughout the output of the studio, an insistence on "visuality" and a concern for the relation of the constructed object to the environment. What is obvious, too, is their manifest capacity for creating striking architectural images.

Their management of space in creating and confirming the image of the city is outstanding. High-rise apartments, they have said, "are like bridges, avenues, public squares: they reinforce the urban geography of the neighborhood and transcend the mere fact of containing apartments; they constitute in themselves a modern social and technical phenomenon, that of being able to accommodate 100 dwellings in space at a height of 80 metres. Hence the domestic aspect disappears both in the realization of aesthetics and in the election of materials." This idea, that works of a certain magnitude can both transcend the image of predecessor forms yet simultaneously partake of the established image of their environment, could describe much of their work.

The team's interest in the environment also reveals itself in their propensity to design for flexibility, especially in those works—office buildings, public buildings, hospitals—in which spaces may need to adapt to future changes. The degree of nondetermination is obviously variable, but, mainly, the team attempt to leave "free" the space that is otherwise limited or defined by the outside envelop-

Manteola, Sanchez Gomez, Santos, Solsona: Bank of the City of Buenos Aires, Casa Matriz, 1968.

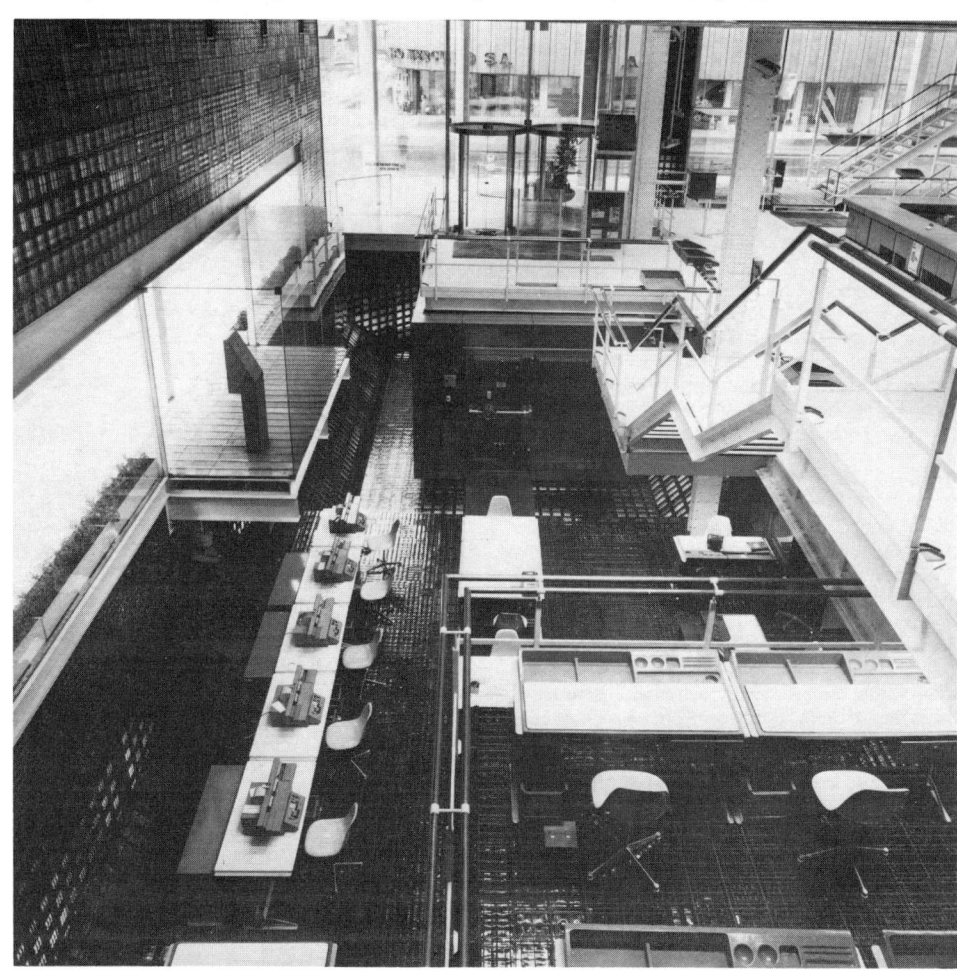

ing line. That may sound like a diffusive kind of architecture, but in their ordering of volumes, in their treatment of structural elements, and in their use of color and light, the team establishes a precise form in each building.

The team's manner of approaching architectural problems is not scientific, and design is not subordinated to technological resources—rather the reverse: such resources are put at the service of space and function (if, at some point, they become manifest, they are being used as communication signs). This attitude allows the team complete freedom with each project, a freedom in which to exercise their critical attitudes, to come up with new solutions. A good example is their headquarters for a bank in Buenos Aires. In place of the usual atmosphere of solemnity the team have created a colorful spectacle in which employees and public both participate, as do (perhaps without even wanting to) the pedestrians on the pavement outside. Thanks to the treatment of space and the technological resources adopted, the passerby is both observer and observed.

Perhaps the most accurate impression one can gain from the work of the team is that they have never stood still. They have stuck to certain principles (a fresh approach to each project; a concern for the visual image and the management of space; a concern for the environment, involving a flexibility in design; a refusal to allow technological means to dominate the expressive goal)—yet, in the course of their practice, they have passed through periods in which they subscribed to various of the architectural concepts of our time—modular coordination, technological purity, anti-stylism, synthesis on ground plan, subdivision of the program into generic categories, softness in formal definition (the cult of additive aesthetics), open forms, growth systems, geometricalization of composition, urban connection, general systems theory, and so forth.

That Manteola, Sánchez Gómez, Santos, Solsona, have seemed to operate as from one of these concepts, then from another, and another, is evidence of nothing more than the sincerity of their critical search. Many of these concepts—and the discipline they impose—have helped the team to create some of their most important work, and, in designing from particular concepts, in changing one for another in a process of continual "testing," the team has really demonstrated the breadth of their vision—that each architectural problem is complex and the instruments of control notoriously precarious.

—Jorge Glusberg

MARDALL, Cyril Sjostrom.

British. Born in Helsinki, Finland, 21 September 1909; emigrated to England, 1927; naturalized, 1928. Educated at the Northern Polytechnic, London; Architectural Association School, London, 1931-32. Served in the Royal Naval Volunteer Reserve, 1940-44: Lieutenant. Married the architect (Hilary) June Park in 1948; children: Georgia and Charles. Year Master, Architectural Association School, 1936-39; Chief of the Shelter Section, UNRRA (United Nations Relief and Rehabilitation Agency), 1944-45; Partner, with F.R.S. Yorke, *q.v.* (died, 1962), and Eugene Rosenberg, *q.v.*, Yorke, Rosenberg and Mardall, 1944 until he retired, 1975. In private practice, with June Park, since 1975. Member of the Council of the Architectural Association, 1950-52. Recipient: Council of Industrial Design Award, 1959; Civic Trust Award, 1961, 1964, 1965, 1966, 1967, 1969; Bronze Medal, Royal Institute of British Architects, 1961, 1966, 1967, 1972; *Financial Times* Award, 1966, 1969. Fellow, Royal Institute of British

Architects. Commander, Order of the Lion of Finland, 1966. Address: 5 Boyne Terrace Mews, London W11 3LR, England.

Works:

1947 Cowley Peachey Housing, Middlesex
1948 Linden Doors Factory, Stowmarket, Suffolk (project)
1949 Temporary Outpatients Department, St. Thomas' Hospital, London
     Shebbear College Boarding School alterations, Devon
     Factories, Dagenham Docks, London (project)
1951 Housing, King's Langley, Hertfordshire
     Susan Lawrence Primary School, London
     Elizabeth Lansbury Nursery School, London
     Housing, Brynmawr, Brecknock, Wales
     Hainault Forest Secondary School, Essex
1952 College of Further Education, Merthyr Tydfil, Glamorgan, Wales
1953 Warren Wood Secondary School, Rochester, Kent
     Upholland Grammar School, Wigan, Lancashire
     West Park Secondary School, Leeds, Yorkshire
     Sheerwater Primary School, Woking, Surrey
     Causeway Green Primary School, Oldbury, Worcestershire
1954 Queensmead Secondary School, Ruislip, Middlesex
1955 Quarles Secondary Modern School, Romford, Essex
     Master plan and stage I of the Leeds Polytechnic, Yorkshire
     Mark Hall Local Authority Housing, Harlow, Essex
     Kingswood School, Essex
1956 Boxgrove Housing Prototypes
     Jack Straw's Lane House, Oxford
     East Anglian Girls School, Bury St. Edmunds, Suffolk
     Bradfield Secondary School, Yorkshire
     Kingswood School extensions, Essex
1957 Southlands College Lecture Block and Dining Room extensions, Wimbledon, London
     Temple Moor Grammar School, Leeds, Yorkshire
     Stanley Outwood Secondary School, Yorkshire
     Oak Park Secondary School, Havant, Hampshire
     Dawley Secondary School, Shropshire
     Master plan for the Bromsgrove Education Centre, Worcestershire
     Timberlog Secondary School, Basildon, Essex
     St. Paul's Secondary School, Addlestone, Surrey
1958 Unilever House, Hamburg (competition project)
     Finnish Seamen's Mission, London
     Chaucer Secondary School, Sheffield
     Leeds Polytechnic, stage II, Yorkshire
1959 Elephant and Castle Development, London (project)
     World Health Organization Offices, Geneva (competition project)
     St. Paul's School Hall alterations, Chertsey, Surrey
     Brays Grove Secondary School, Harlow, Essex
     Upholland Grammar School extensions, Wigan, Lancashire
1960 Rothwell Secondary School, stage II, Yorkshire
     Warslow School, Staffordshire
     United States Embassy, Grosvenor Square, London (with Eero Saarinen Associates)
     Passmores Comprehensive School, Harlow, Essex

Brierly Hill Secondary School, Staffordshire
Rolls Royce Offices, Derby (project)
1961 Royal Masonic School, Ascot, Berkshire (project)
     YRM Offices, Greystoke Place, London
     Kew Bridge Development for British Rail, London (project)
     Kingswood School extensions, stage II, Essex
1962 Elliott Brothers Welfare Building, Rochester, Kent (project)
     Rotameter Factory, Croydon, Surrey (project)
     Library, Cambridge University (project)
     Southlands College: Queensmere Hostels, Lecture Block and Gymnasium, Wimbledon, London
     Barstable Comprehensive School, Basildon, Essex
     College of Further Education extensions, stage II, Merthyr Tydfil, Glamorgan, Wales
     Oak Park Secondary School extensions, Havant, Hampshire
     Timberlog Secondary School extensions, Basildon, Essex
1963 Rolleston Secondary School, Staffordshire
     Rochdale College, Lancashire
     Redevelopment scheme for the Dawley schools, Shropshire
     A. Johnson and Company Factory and Offices, Wokingham, Berkshire
     Harlow Training Centre, Essex
     Bradford Secondary School extensions, Yorkshire
1964 Southlands College Staff Accommodation, Wimbledon, London
     Development plan for the central area of Blackpool, Lancashire
     Blythe Bridge Secondary School, Staffordshire
     Mildmay Secondary School, Aveley, Essex
     Dawley Secondary School extensions, Shropshire
     Chaucer Secondary School extensions, Sheffield
1965 Bakewell Secondary School, Derbyshire
     Simestow Comprehensive School, Tettenhall, Staffordshire
     Romford Technical College, Essex
     Chalvedon Comprehensive School, Basildon, Essex
     German Sailors' Home, London
     Gibbons Road Secondary School, West Willesden, London
     Rochdale College extensions, Lancashire
1966 Local authority housing, Cadell Street, Tower Hamlets, London
     Elliott Brothers Factory extensions, Borehamwood, Hertfordshire
     Westwood Hall and St. Edward's School, Leek, Staffordshire
     Elliott Brothers Factory, Rochester, Kent
     St. Paul's Secondary School extensions, Addlestone, Surrey
     Clements Store extensions, Watford, Hertfordshire
1967 Bacton Street Housing, Tower Hamlets, London
     Ilford Training Centre, Essex
     Sceptre Road Housing, Tower Hamlets, London
     Queensmead Secondary School extensions, Ruislip, Middlesex
     Brays Grove Secondary School extensions, Harlow, Essex
1968 Uxbridge Technical College, London
     Willesden Secondary School, London
     Old Street Concourse, London
     Timberlog Secondary School extensions, stage II, Basildon, Essex
     St. Paul's Secondary School extensions, stage II, Addlestone, Surrey
1969 Kingshold Estate, King Edward's Road, Hackney, London
     Osprey Estate Housing, Bermondsey, London

Chalvedon Comprehensive School extensions, Basildon, Essex
1970 Rochdale College extensions, stage II, Lancashire
Sceptre Road Housing extensions, Tower Hamlets, London
1972 Tomo Estates Factory, Cowley Peachey, Middlesex
Hindrey Place Housing, Hackney, London
High Park School extensions, Stourbridge, Worcestershire
1973/
75 Camden Health Centre, London
Community Centre, King Edward's Road, Hackney, London
Los Llanos Recreational Centre, Costa del Sol, Spain (project)
Library and Community Building, Albion Street, Southwark, London
Brixton Road Development, London
Territorial Army Centre, Camden, London (project)
Tomo Estates Offices, Cowley Peachey, Middlesex
Queensmead School extension, Ruislip, Middlesex
Hillingdon Sports Hall, Ruislip, Middlesex
Residence Hacienda la Mota, Costa del Sol, Spain
1976/
78 Hotel, West Cork, Ireland (with June Park)
Housing and restoration of ruins, St. Maarten, Dutch West Indies (with June Park)
1979 Cultural Centre and Sunday School for Finnish Nationals, Albion Street, London (project; with June Park)
1981/
83 Housing, Dublin, Ireland (project)

Publications:

On MARDALL: book—*The Architecture of Yorke Rosenberg Mardall*, introduction by Reyner Banham, London and New York 1972; articles— "Modern Masters: Yorke Rosenberg Mardall" by Colin Davies in *Building* (London), 20 March 1981; "No more heroes—When is a house style not a house style? When it's a YRM job" by Deyan Sudjic in *Building Design* (London), 8 January 1982; "Miesians move west" by Ted Stevens in *Building Design* (London), 12 March 1982; "Task force from the past" by Martin Pawley in *Building Design* (London), 25 June 1982.

*

I was born in Finland, the son of an architect. It never occurred to me to choose another profession, even had I been talented enough to do so.
The reason I came to England to study architecture was that, after my father's death, my mother opera singer d engagements in Germany and England, and I an only son longer had a home in Finland. I never regretted leaving the country of my birth and becoming a British subject.
The late 'twenties and early 'thirties were exciting years for a young student of architecture. After a brief flirtation with Swedish architecture, as exemplified in the Stockholm Town Hall and later the sensitive creativity of Asplund, I became strongly influenced by Alvar Aalto, who incidentally had worked in my father's office for a short period.
Still later, Frank Lloyd Wright and Le Corbusier became my lodestars. We all felt very strongly about furthering the Modern Movement. I became a member of the MARS Group, and was fortunate in finding work in the office of Gropius and Maxwell Fry. I have never felt the need to depart from these early conceptions, although maturity and experience have had a moderating influence on one's work.
One could contend that, as yet, there is no such thing as post-modern 'Architecture'. Stylistic ornamentation with fussy broken roofscapes does not itself

constitute a change in architectural conception; it merely indicates the lack of creative thought, a lack of understanding of the fundamentals of present-day architecture.

—Cyril Mardall.

*

C.S. Mardall was born in Finland in 1909 and was educated at Northern Polytechnic and at the Architectural Association. His name is most familiar from the partnership with Eugene Rosenberg and F.R.S. Yorke (who died in 1962), which he formed in 1944. All three were associated with the early years of the MARS Group and the foundation of modern architecture in Britain.

YRM, as the partnership is known, has become identified with an uncompromising form of the postwar International Style almost always produced for public sector clients. It was formed in conscious imitation of larger groups like TAC: The Architects Collaborative and has recently established firmer ties still with its trans-Atlantic equivalent, Skidmore, Owings and Merrill. The output of the partnership has been predominately flats, stores, industrial buildings and hospitals. Best known of all, Mardall and his partners have, since 1955, been the architects of Gatwick Airport, an exercise that began in an Anglicised version of Mies' idiom and developed into the partnership's characteristic white-tile-and-Helvetica idiom of the mid-1960s.

YRM has a corporate obsession with detail and claims, popularly, never to have a cut a facing tile, so perfect are the drawings and so well supervised is the execution of each building. The partnership, which is prosperous and successful, is run on hierarchical lines and in a "statement of principles," issued as late as 1966, declared that "a dynamic and developing architectural mainstream, originating from the modern international movement as established in the 1920s and 1930s, is still the correct course to follow." This doctrine compounds the partnership's vaguely leftish sentiments with a sense of social commitment that owes its origins to a belief in "total solutions," an inheritance of the architectural avant-garde from between the wars.
The partnership, the better to advance its austere aesthetic policies, has a "rationalisation section" and prepares its own design manuals for its staff of two hundred.

—Stephen Bayley

MARKELIUS, Sven Gottfrid.

Swedish. Born in Stockholm, 25 October 1889. Educated at the Institute of Technology, Stockholm, graduated 1913; Academy of Fine Arts, Stockholm, graduated 1915. Married Karin Simon in 1938. Worked in the offices of the architects Östberg, Tengbom, Lallerstadt and Grut, Stockholm, 1915; in private practice, Stockholm, from 1915; concentrated on urban planning and building standardization for the Stockholm City Council, 1915-31; Director of the Planning Department, Stockholm Building Institute, 1938-44; Director of the Planning Regulation Office, Stockholm, 1944-54. Assistant, 1919-21, and Professor, 1937-39, Department of Construction Sciences, Stockholm Polytechnic. Visiting Professor, Yale University, New Haven, Connecticut, 1949; Visiting Professor, Massachusetts Institute of Technology, Cambridge, and University of California, Berkeley, 1962. Member, State Committee for Building Technology and Production, Stockholm, 1938-43; Member, Consultants Group for the United Nations Building, New York, 1947; Member, Supervising Committee for the Unesco Buildings, Paris, 1952-58; President, Federation of Swedish Architects, 1953-56; Member,

Unesco Arts Committee, 1954. Exhibitions: *Bygge och Bo*, Lidingo, Sweden, 1925; *Stockholm Exhibition*, 1930; *Standard 1934*, Gallery Liljewalchs, Stockholm, 1934; *House with Collective Services*, Stockholm, 1936; World's Fair, New York, 1939; *Bauen und Wohnen in Schweden 1930-80*, Swedish Architecture Museum, Stockholm, 1976, toured Germany 1977-80; *Nordic Classicism 1910-1930*, Museum of Finnish Architecture, Helsinki, 1982. Recipient: First Prize—Bergastra Building Society Competition, Lidingo, Sweden, 1917; Railway Bridge Competition, Hammarbyleden, Sweden, 1920; Bygge och Bo Town Development Competition, Lidingo, Sweden, 1925; Hälsingborg Concert Hall Competition, 1925; Kristineberg District Urban Redevelopment Plan Competition, Stockholm, 1927; St. Lars Hospital Pavilion Competition, Lund Sweden, 1934; and Association of Constructors Building Competition, Stockholm, 1935; Howland Memorial Prize, Yale University, 1949; St. Erik's Medal, Stockholm, 1959; Federation of Swedish Architects Award, 1961; Prince Eugene Medal, 1961; Patrick Abercrombie Prize, International Union of Architects, 1961; Gold Medal, Royal Institute of British architects, 1962; Statlig Konstnarsbeloning, Stockholm, 1967. Honorary doctorate: Polytechnic of Rheinland/Westphalia, Aachen, 1966. *Died 27 February 1972.*

Works:

1916 Cemetery, Malmo (competition project; with O. Lundgren)
1917 Urban plan for a residential district, Lidingo, Sweden (competition project)
Urban plan for the Graakalbanen Society, near Trondheim, Norway (competition project)
Urban plan for Palsjo Hälsinborg, Sweden (competition project; with O. Lundgren)
1918 Plan for the Central Station, Stockholm (project)
1919 Hotel complex, Saltsjobaden, Sweden (competition project)
1920 Railway bridge, Hammarbyleden, Sweden (competition project; with O. Lundgren)
1923 Redevelopment plan for the Old City, Stockholm (competition project; with E. Sundhal)
1925 Pavilion, and Urban Complex, *Bygge och Bo* exhibition, Lidingo, Sweden
1926 School, Sundsvall, Sweden (competition project)
Ewald Engineering Building, Hälsingborg, Sweden
1927 Urban plan for the Kristineberg District, Stockholm (competition project)
1929 Students Club Building, Stockholm Polytechnic (with U. Ahren)
Apartment building, Berget, Stockholm
Ohman Villa, Salstjo-Duvnas, Sweden
1930 Pavilion, *Stockholm Exhibition*
Hangar, Lindaragnen, Sweden (with Professor Forsel)
Villa, Nockeby, Sweden
Apartment and office block, Sjokatten, Stockholm (project)
1931 Low-cost housing, Graset, Sweden
1932 Engkvist Villa, Eldtomta, Sweden
Liden Villa, Vasteras, Sweden
1933 *Morgonbris* newspaper Editorial Offices, Skolan, Stockholm
Syndicate Headquarters Building, Göteborg, Sweden (project)
Syndicate Headquarters Building, Ilgodset, Stockholm (project)
1934 Concert Hall, Hälsingborg, Sweden
Air Terminal, Bromma, Sweden (project)
House with Collective Services, *Standard 1934* exhibition, Stockholm
Theatre, Malmo (competition project; with V. Goransson)

1935 Office and Cinema Building, Apotekaren 4, Lund, Sweden (project)
Villa, Asen, Lidingo, Sweden (project)
Engkvist Villa expansion and alterations, Eldtomta, Sweden
Blomberg Building, Stocksund, Sweden
Kollektivhus (House with collective Services; apartment building), Fagelbarstradet, Stockholm
Provincial Records Office, Harnosand, Sweden
1936 EPA Building, Sundsvall, Sweden (project)
Commercial Building, Trasket, Stockholm (project)
Industrial building, Morgardshammars, Sweden (project)
ASEA Company Building (project)
1937 Association of Constructors Building, Stockholm
St. Lars Hospital Pavilion, Lund, Sweden
Housing for families with children, at Roda Rummet, Hemsoborna, Kristineberg, Boras, Hasseleholm, Nörrköping, Skara, Karlshamm, and Sala, Sweden
Myrdal Villa, Stockholm
Office building, Sirius, Stockholm (project)
1938 Svenska Flatfabriken Turbine Factory, Humlegarden, Stockholm (project)
1939 Swedish Pavilion, World's Fair, New York
EPA Commercial and Office Buildings, Sweden (projects)
Syndicate Buildings and Urban Renewal Plans, Stockholm (project)
Nynas Petroleum Service Station, Lindköping and Karlstad, Sweden (projects)
1944/
54 Various plans for the city and region of Stockholm
1945 Markelius Villa, Kevinge, Sweden
1947/
52 United Nations Building, New York (with international team of architects, including Le Corbusier and Oscar Niemeyer— Wallace K. Harrison, Chairman)
1952 Syndicate Headquarters, Linköping, Sweden
1958 Munkbrobadet, Stockholm (project)
Hotel, Alvadalen, Sweden (project)
1959 Sailor's House, Lappskon, Stockholm (project)
Theatre Building, Stockholm
Office building, Alvadalen, Sweden
Swedish Forest Industry Offices, Stockholm
Apartment building, Granen, Stockholm
1963 Commercial and office building, Beridarenbanan, Stockholm
Sverigehuset, Stockholm
1965 Apartment building, Reven, Stockholm
New Municipal Theatre, Overkikaren, Stockholm (project)
1966 Burgehaus Cultural and Congress Centre, Giessen, Essen, West Germany
1968 Hotel, Lonnen, Stockholm

Publications:

By MARKELIUS: books—*Acceptera,* with Asplund, Gahn, Paulsson and Sundahl, Stockholm 1930; *Kollektivhuset som bostadsform,* Stockholm 1935; *Det framtida Stockholm,* with Ahlberg, Hofsten and Sidenbladh, Stockholm 1946; *Report on the United Nations Headquarters,* with others, Stockholm 1947; *Vallingby, Stockholm, the new self-supporting neighbourhood,* booklet, Stockholm 1955; articles—"Sverige i New York" in *Byggmarstaren* (Stockholm), no. 33, 1939; "Villa i Kevinge" in *Byggmastaren* (Stockholm), 1945; "Manniskan i centrum?" in *Plan* (Zurich), no. 1/2, 1950; "Nuovi sviluppi urbanistici a Stoccolma" in *Urbanistica* (Turin), no. 10/11, 1952; "Urban Land Policies in Sweden" in *United Nations Housing and Town and Country Planning Bulletin* (New York), no.7, 1953; "Om—och Tillbyggnad av tekniska Hogskolans

Karhus, Stockholm" in *Byggmastaren* (Stockholm), no. 7, 1953; "Hoghus ger Stockholm dess nya stadsbild 2050" in *Byggnadsindustrin* (Stockholm), no. 8, 1955; "Stockholms struktur. Synpunkter pa ett storstadsproblem" in *Byggmastaren* (Stockholm), no. 3, 1956; "Projekt till enfamiljshus" in *Arkitektur* (Stockholm), no. 3, 1959; "Villa pa Lidingo" in *Arkitektur* (Stockholm), no. 8, 1960; "Stockholms Folkets Hus" in *Arkitektur* (Stockholm), no. 11, 1961; "Il Nuovo centro di stoccolma" in *Casabella* (Milan), no. 275, 1963.

On MARKELIUS: books—*Architecture in Sweden* by A. Hahn, Stockholm, 1938; *New Swedish Architecture,* edited by G. Paulsson, Stockholm 1940; *Nordische Baukunst* by S.E. Rasmussen, Berlin 1940; *Ny Arkitektur* by T. Paulsson, Stockholm 1948; *Ten Lessons on Swedish Architecture,* edited by T. P. Jacobson and E. Silow, Stockholm 1949; *Ny Svensk Byggnadskonst* by E. Cornell, Stockholm 1950; *Sweden Builds* by G. E. Kidder Smith, Stockholm and New York 1950, London and New York 1957; *Svensk stad* by G. Paulsson, 3 volumes, Stockholm 1950-53; *Scandinavian Architecture* by T. Paulsson, London 1958; *Ny stad* by T. Paulsson, Stockholm 1958; *International History of City Development, II: The Alpine and Scandinavian Countries* by E. A. Gutkind, New York 1965; *Il Contributo Svedese all'Architettura Contemporanea e l'Opera di Sven Markelius* by Stefano Ray, Rome 1969; *Aufbruch und Krise des Funktionalismus: Bauen und Wohnen in Schweden 1930-80,* exhibition catalogue by Bernt Nyberg, Olof Hultin and others, Stockholm 1976; *Nordic Classicism 1910-1930,* exhibition catalogue edited by Simo Paavilainen, Helsinki 1982; articles— "Vicende dell'urbanistica Svedese" by F. Malusardi in *Quaderni della Societa Generale immobiliare* (Rome), no. 13, 1960; "Building a City and a Metropolis: The Planned Development of Stockholm" by Y. Larsson in *Journal of the American Institute of Planners* (Washington, D.C.), no. 28, 1962; "Il Nuovo centro di Stoccolma" by S. Bracco in *La Cittaterritorio,* Bari, Italy 1964; "Stockholm: A Planned City" by G. Sidenbladh in *Scientific American* (New York), September 1965; "Obituary: Sven Gottfrid Markelius 1889-1972" by T. H. B. Burroughs in *RIBA Journal* (London), June 1972.

One of the outstanding Swedish architects and urban planners of the century, Sven Markelius shows in his work an awareness of most of the modern developments in architectural design and building technology both in Europe and America. He availed himself of these methods whenever they answered requirements, but at the same time he made his own contribution to new and ingenious solutions of problems presented by changing social economic and cultural needs. It could be claimed that his contributions to domestic architecture, concert hall design and urban planning made him to some extent an innovator.

An outstanding early work of domestic architecture is the 1935 Kollektivhus in Stockholm, which was designed to answer the needs of working parents. The flats are mostly one, two and three roomed; they are grouped on each floor with short corridor access, and architecturally attractive and well secluded balconies are provided for the larger flats. There are food lifts, a restaurant, and provision for the collective care of children.

Of the many well designed family houses by Markelius, that which he built for himself at Kevinge (1945) is notable. It is one story in an L-shaped plan; the rooms are in functional sequence, and careful attention has been paid to the best orientation for the various rooms. It is well integrated with its large garden, for full enjoyment of the long summer days.

The building by which Markelius first became famous is the Concert Hall at Hälsingborg of 1934. The design is a new and original departure from traditional halls. It is rectangular with a flat ceiling; the floor rises gently from the orchestra in the front

and then steeply in the rear, and was designed to be removed in sections so that the hall could also be used for banquets and dances. Above the orchestra there is a canopied, well-integrated reflector. Large plain masses, with little ornament, characterize the design, and the interior is reflected in the exterior dispositions of forms which combine with the setting of trees into a pleasing ensemble. A similar original and progressive spirit is seen in Markelius' later Syndicate Headquarters Building, Stockholm, which includes a municipal theatre. The large congress hall is shaped like a Greek theatre, with concentric seating round the orchestra, a foreshadowing of many later theatre and hall designs.

Markelius is best known internationally as planning director in Stockholm, responsible for the planning of the modern city and its surroundings. Markelius' conception was that of a city developed in the centre with a degree of pedestrianization, with several large neighbourhoods or satelite towns planned in the surrounding areas to accommodate the increasing population. Several of these satelites have been built and are distinguised for their imaginative planning. The most famous, Vallingby, has many ingenious features and architectural excellencies, especially in the residential areas on undulating sites. The pedestrian centre built over the railway station has also proved to be very successful. It is significant that Vallingby and also Farsta, another Stockholm satellite in the plan, received the Reynolds Memorial Award for Community Architecture in 1967, the other two so honoured being Cumbernauld and Tapiola.

In all his work Markelius showed the impulses of an artist sensitive to architectural character and proportion, and this artistry distinguished all his original and ingenious utilizations of modern developments in architectural design and building technology.

—Arnold Whittick

MARKSON, Jerome.
Canadian. Born in Toronto, Ontario, 21 March 1929. Educated at the University of Toronto, 1948-53, B.Arch. 1953; Cranbrook Academy of Art, Bloomfield Hills, Michigan, 1952. Married Mayta Ruth in 1953; children: Nancy and Anna. Principal, Jerome Markson Architects, Toronto, since 1955. Vice-Chairman, Toronto Chapter of the Ontario Association of Architects, 1969-70; Member of the Board, 1976, and Vice-President, 1978, Toronto Chapter of the Architectural Conservancy of Ontario. Recipient: Canadian Housing Design Council Award, 1960, 1967, 1969, 1971, 1977, 1980, 1983; Massey Medal for Architecture, 1964; Ontario Association of Architects Award, 1964, 1970, 1977; Canadian Wood Design Award, 1965; Ontario Masons Relations Council Award, 1966, 1973, 1977; *Canadian Architect* Award, 1968, 1970; Design Award, Steel Company of Canada, 1978; Markham Environmental Award, Ontario, 1980. Fellow, Royal Architectural Institute of Canada; Associate, Royal Canadian Academy of the Arts. Member, Ontario Association of Architects, and Ordre des Architectes du Quebec. Address: Jerome Markson Architects, 161 Davenport Road, Toronto, Ontario M5R 1J1, Canada.

Works:

1954 Dawes Road Cemetery Chapel, 3169 St. Clair Avenue East, East York, Ontario
1955 House, 167 Valley Road, North York, Ontario
House, 45 Amelia Street, Hamilton, Ontario

Jerome Markson: Market Square, Toronto, 1980.

1956 House, 16 Monsheen Drive, Woodbridge, Ontario
Dr. Miklos Office Building, Newcastle, Ontario
1957 Woodview Development Houses, Seneca Heights, Woodbridge, Ontario
Stanrock Mines Multiple Housing, Elliott Lake, Ontario
House, 67 Old Park Road, Forest Hill, Ontario
Shops and offices, Elliot Lake, Ontario
House, 79 Amelia Street, Hamilton, Ontario
Whitburn Apartments, Whitburn Avenue, North York, Ontario (with Klein and Sears)
1958 Art Studio and Theatre, Camp Manitou-Wabing, near Parry Sound, Ontario
House I, Winston Avenue, Hamilton, Ontario
1959 House, Mayfair Place, Hamilton, Ontario
House, 125 Amelia Street, Hamilton, Ontario
House, Dixie Road, Mississauga, Ontario
House II, 90 Winston Avenue, Hamilton, Ontario
Ritualarium, Kline Avenue South, Hamilton, Ontario
1960 House, 23 Park Lane Circle, North York, Ontario
Munk House alterations, 63 Woodlawn Avenue, Toronto
House, 32 Saintfield Avenue, North York, Ontario
House alterations, 44 Elm Avenue, Toronto
Architect's house alterations, 15 Poplar Plains Crescent, Toronto
1961 International Woodworkers of America Office Building, 2088 Weston Road, Weston, Ontario
Jewish Home for the Aged, 3560 Bathurst Street, North York, Ontario (with Marani, Routhwaite and Dick)

Cottage at Big Cedar Point, Lake Simcoe, Ontario
Corvette School addition, 30 Corvette Avenue, Scarborough, Ontario
1962 Health Centre, for United Steelworkers of America, 240 McNabb Street, Sault Ste. Marie, Ontario
House, 53 Montressor Drive, North York, Ontario
1963 Chatelaine Houses, Montreal and Brampton, Ontario
1964 House, 63 The Bridle Path Road, North York, Ontario
Clubhouse, Cedarvale Park, East York, Ontario
Dr. Ascah House, Huntsville, Ontario
1965 Alexandra Park Public Housing, Dundas at Spadina, Toronto (with Klein and Sears, Webb, Zerafa, Menkes)
Place Ste. Helene, *Expo '67*, Montreal
Cottage at Kempenfeld Bay, Lake Simcoe, Ontario
1966 Dr. Baida House, Etobicoke, Ontario
Currie House, Claremont, Ontario
1967 Sherman Mine Staff Lodge, Pirates Cove, Lake Timagami, Ontario
Group Health Centre, United Automobile Workers of America, 14 Queen Street, St. Catharines, Ontario
House, 538 Scenic Drive, Hamilton, Ontario
Dylex Diversified Offices and Showroom, Toronto
True Davidson Home for the Aged, 200 Dawes Road, East York, Ontario
1968 Sabre Saw Chain Offices, Hamilton, Ontario
North York Medical Arts Building, 1333 Sheppard Avenue East, North York, Ontario
Country Home, Bolton, Ontario

Housing, Martingrove Road, Etobicoke, Ontario
Six-storey stacked housing, Bramalea, Ontario
1969 Glazier Medical Centre, 136 Simcoe Street North, Oshawa, Ontario
Architect's weekend house, Brock Township, Ontario
105 Maitland Street renovations, Toronto
House, 25 Forest Wood, Toronto
C. A. Pitts Head Office, 30 Commercial Road, Toronto
1970 Nurses' residence, Sioux Lookout, Ontario
1971 Office building, 562 Eglinton Avenue East, Toronto
Jewish Community Centre (including Leah Posluns Theatre and Koffler Centre for the Arts), 4588 Bathurst Street, Willowdale, Ontario
1972 Johnson House, Claremont, Ontario
Community and day care centre, 1386 Victoria Park Avenue, East York, Ontario
Neighbourhood shopping centre, Don Mills and Cliffwood Corners, Don Mills, Ontario
Apartment building, 336 Lakeshore Drive, North Bay, Ontario
Architect's offices, 161 Davenport Road, Toronto
1973 Sherwood Park Manor Nursing Home, Highway 2, Brockville, Ontario
Civic Garden Centre (Edwards Gardens), 777 Lawrence Avenue East, Toronto
Weekend house, near Rosemont, Ontario
Eddie Bauer Shop, 22 Bloor Street West, Toronto
Urban Transportation Development Corporation Offices, 20 Eglinton Avenue West, Toronto
Five Post Office Prototypes, Ontario Region

1974 House, 320 Courtleigh Boulevard, Toronto
Neighbourhood shopping centre, Malvern, Scarborough, Ontario
Parkette for Sefton Memorial, Bay and Hagerman Streets, Toronto
Sherbourne-Pembroke Housing, Toronto
1976 Grace MacInnis Co-op Housing, Church/Gloucester Streets, Toronto
David B. Archer Co-Op Housing, St. Lawrence Project, Toronto
Brantwood Park Housing, Brantford, Ontario
Residential and Commercial Building, 27 Wellesley Street East, Toronto
1977 McDonald's Restaurant, Bayview and Eglinton, Toronto
Barn, Manvers Township, Ontario
House, Parkers Point, Lake Muskoka, Ontario
Cambridge Clothes Offices, 56 York Boulevard, Hamilton, Ontario
1978 House, 4 Cachet Parkway, Markham, Ontario
Shops and Apartments, 200 Avenue Road, Toronto
Lipa Green Jewish Community Services Building, North York, Ontario
Houseboat, near King Bay on Georgian Bay, Ontario
1979 Humber Arboretum, Orientation and Nature Study Centre, Humber College, Rexdale, Ontario
Art Gallery, Koffler Centre of the Arts, North York, Ontario
Southern Pacific Hotels Services Offices, 24/28 Hazelton Avenue, Toronto
1980 Market Square commercial and residential complex, Church and Front Streets, Toronto
Architect's House, 11F Tranby Terrace, Toronto
Holman Productions Offices, 417 Queen's Quay West, Harbourfront, Toronto
Canadian Imperial Bank of Commerce renovations, St. Clair and Dufferin Branch, Toronto
1981 Jones and Morris Photography Laboratories, 24 Carlaw Avenue, Toronto
Canadian Imperial Bank of Commerce, Bloor and Bathurst, Toronto
Boathouse, Munk's Island, Georgian Bay, Ontario
House, 43 Elgin Avenue, Toronto
1982 House renovations, 6 Gibson Avenue, Toronto
Holocaust Memorial, 4600 Bathurst Street, Willowdale, Ontario
Glazier Medical Centre additions, 11 Gibb Street, Oshawa, Ontario
1983 Bathurst Quay Housing, Harbourfront, Toronto (project)
Regent Park Community Centre, 65 Belshaw Place, Toronto (project)
1984 House, 493 St. Clements, Toronto
Enclosed Swimming Pool, 25 Forest Wood, Toronto
Bell Canada AOSS Building, Victoria Park Avenue, Scarborough, Ontario (project)

Publications:

By MARKSON: books—*Exploring Toronto: Its Buildings, People and Places,* Toronto 1972; *Jerome Markson Architects: Twenty-Five Years of Work,* Toronto 1980.

On MARKSON: books—*New Buildings in the Commonwealth* by J. M. Richards, London 1961; *Canadian Architecture* by Carol Moore Ede, Toronto 1971; *Modern Canadian Architecture* by Leon Whiteson, Toronto 1983; articles—"Concept 3: architect Jerome Markson" in *Canadian Architect* (Toronto), February 1973; "Metro House for the Aged, Toronto" in *Canadian Architect* (Toronto), October 1973; "Precise Markson" in *Architectural Review* (London), January 1974; "Pembroke Sherbourne Housing" in *Canadian Architect* (Toronto), May 1979; "Southern Pacific Hotels Services Office, Toronto" in *Canadian Architect* (Toronto), February 1981; "13 Interiors: Canadian Imperial Bank of Commerce, Toronto" in *Canadian Architect* (Toronto), November 1981.

*

Since completing my schooling thirty years ago, I have been struggling to forget the rigid rules gently—and not so gently—imposed. There really aren't any rules other than those of nature—gravity pulling down, water trying to get in and freezing, and so on.

One of the struggles is to break from the ascetic and rigid confines of these teachings and dogmas—the box form and boxed space, the sacred techniques of joining forms and parts together, lightness, separation of the man-made from the natural. Rather, we try to tie a building more easily to its site, to respect a good milieu when it exists, to enhance space and form, to explore better ways of putting things together. Surely it must mean something to the people we serve for architects to respect and, where necessary, to improve upon the past. We attempt to attain a sense of appropriateness and scale in the city or countryside—for our clients, for the users, and for the greater urban context.

To be a sponge, to absorb what we admire in the past and present and adapt it when suitable, to further explore the tendencies we feel developing in our work, to have, however, a sense of realism and to get things built if worthwhile, to free ourselves from the bonds of rigid teachings—these preoccupations and influences are numerous, changing, and, at best, tacit. They are manifested through our buildings which, in turn, are tempered by their physical and social context.

Urban problems in Canada remain our first concern, particularly those of affordable housing. This concern for the form and role of housing in a changing urban setting influences our intentions in architecture. Much of our work lies in this area, and the remainder consists of the special "one-off" problem buildings which seem to revitalize and energize our efforts.

For us, the design and building process seems to be a constant struggle. Like architects everywhere, we are constantly ambushed by innumerable constraints on every project, so that a successful building is something of a wonder.

All we can do is plug away, sometimes succeeding, sometimes not, trying all the while to keep our broader objectives from being overly compromised by bureaucratic requirements and the exigencies of practice, as well as the limitations of our own abilities.

—Jerome Markson

*

In very general terms, the contemporary practice of architecture in Toronto may be viewed as comprising three generations. The first of these—the pre-1950 generation—was led by a group of architects who had mostly grown up and been trained in Toronto and belonged to or were associated with the old, established, Anglo-Saxon families of the city. The second generation, that of the 1950s themselves, also consists largely of architects who grew up and were educated in Toronto, but this generation began for the first time to represent the social and ethnic diversity which has increasingly characterized the life of the city. Jerome Markson is one of a group of young Jewish architects who entered practice at that time, a group which also includes Irving Grossman, Jack Klein, and Henry Sears.

Yet, if he entered practice with that peer group, in the perspective of the past twenty-five years, Markson's career seems increasingly distinct from theirs. Whereas their work has grown increasingly large in scale, his has remained relatively small. Whereas theirs has grown increasingly commercial, his has continued to consist largely of custom-designed, "one-off" works. Whereas they have turned increasingly to planning and research, he has continued to place built projects at the centre of his area of interest.

If Markson cannot now be plausibly seen together with the local peer group of his own circle and generation, neither can he be seen to be one with the varied group of architects who have immigrated to this city since the late 1950s, a third generation. This group includes such well-known figures as Ron Thom, John Andrews, Macy Dubois, A. J. Diamond, and Barton Myers. All of these figures, having been educated elsewhere, brought to Toronto much more clearly articulated design philosophies than it would have been possible for anyone to have gleaned from a Toronto architectural education in the early 1950s. Unlike the members of his own peer group, in his preoccupation with the particularity of individual building tasks, Markson is also uneasy in this circle of notable immigrants to Toronto because of his aversion to their various modes of precocious public theorizing. Instead, Markson has, over the past quarter century of his career, pursued a quite individual course within the territory of Canadian architecture, evidently untheoretical, highly particular and unarticulated.

Given all this, it is predictable that Markson's practice has never grown to a large size; that he has never been awarded a major public commission; that his work lacks a high public profile in this country. From time to time, when his work has come up for more explicit critical consideration, it has often been dismissed as a marginal eclecticism, irrelevant to the main course of Canadian architectural history. Yet notwithstanding a certain apparent plausibility, this simple dismissal fails in the end to take adequate account of the strengths of his work.

One can say that it fails to recognize the implicit psychological qualities that characterize the spatial organization of his projects. It fails to acknowledge the strong consistency—at another level than parti—of the detail and finish of his buildings. Beyond, and I think deeper than both of these, there is also, I think—at least in the best of his works—a characteristic almost unique in contemporary Canadian architecture: a subconscious tactile iconography of the materiality of building, a materiality that is, for me, reminiscent of some aspects of the work of Aalto and Le Corbusier. Albeit an elusive characteristic of any contemporary architecture, this is particularly important in the Canadian context on account of its extreme rarity here. Not only is it usually entirely absent from the work of the large commercial practices, it is often less forceful than one might expect even in the work of such better known architects as Dubois and Thom.

Where this tactile iconography of materials *can* readily be found, of course, is in the vernacular architectures of many parts of the world, and Markson's strong devotion to these other architectures is well-known in his circle of admirers. In the most successful of his projects—I would cite as examples, the Camp Manitou-Wabing Art Studio and Theatre (1958), the renovation to the Munk Residence in Toronto (1960), and the True Davidson Home for the Aged, in Toronto, (1967)—these qualities of intense materiality rank Markson's underrated work with the best that has been accomplished in Canada in the past two decades.

—George Baird

MARTIN, (John) Leslie.
British. Born in Manchester, 17 August 1908. Educated at the University of Manchester School of Architecture, 1927-30 (Royal Institute of British Architects Silver Medallist, 1929; Soane Medallist,

1930), M.A. 1930, Ph.D. 1934. Married the architect Sadie Speight in 1934; children: Susan and Christopher. Assistant Lecturer, University of Manchester School of Architecture, 1930-34; Head of the School of Architecture, University of Hull, Yorkshire, and in private practice in Hull, 1934-39; Principal Assistant Architect, LMS Railway, London, 1939-48; Deputy Architect, 1949-53, and Architect, 1953-56, London County Council. In private practice, Cambridge, since 1956. Consultant to the Universities of Leicester, Hull, and London, 1956-78; Consultant to the Gulbenkian Foundation, Lisbon, 1956-69. Professor of Architecture, 1956-72, and since 1973 Emeritus Professor, Cambridge University; also, Fellow, 1956-73, Honorary Fellow, 1973, and since 1976 Emeritus Fellow, Jesus College, Cambridge. Slade Professor of Fine Art, Oxford University, 1965-66; Gropius Lecturer, Harvard University, Cambridge, Massachusetts, 1966; Ferens Professor of Fine Art, University of Hull, 1967-68; William Henry Bishop Visiting Professor of Architecture, Yale University, New Haven, Connecticut, 1973-74; Lethaby Professor, Royal College of Art, London, 1981. Member of the Council 1952-58, and Vice-President, 1955-57, Royal Institute of British Architects; Member, Royal Fine Art Commission, 1958-72. Exhibitions: *Royal Gold Medal Exhibition*, Royal Institute of British Architects, London, 1973; *Buildings and Ideas 1933-1983*, Gulbenkian Foundation, Lisbon, 1985. Recipient: Bronze Medal, 1954, Distinction in Town Planning, 1956, and the Royal Gold Medal, 1973, Royal Institute of British Architects; Civic Trust Award, 1967; Concrete Society Award, 1972. M.A.: Cambridge University, 1956; Oxford University, 1965; LL.D.: University of Leicester, 1963; University of Hull, 1967; University of Manchester, 1972; D.Univ.: University of Essex, Colchester, 1976. Fellow, Royal Institute of British Architects 1937. Honorary Member, Association of Finnish Architects; Accademico Corrispondente, National Academy of San Lucca, Italy; Commander, Order of Santiago da Espada, Portugal. Knighted, 1957. Address (office): The Kings Mill, Great Shelford, Cambridge CB2 5EN, England.

Works:

1934/
  39 Houses at Ferriby, Yorkshire, and Brampton and Dockray, Cumbria
       Nursery school, Northwich, Cheshire
       Unit Furniture (early models)
1939/
  48 Emergency wartime buildings
1951 Royal Festival Hall, London (with Sir Robert Matthew, Peter Moro and Edwin Williams)
1956 Sports Centre, Crystal Palace, London (project; with others)
1956/
  59 College Hall, Knighton, Leicester (with Trevor Dannatt)
1956/
  58 Martin House, The Mill, Great Shelford, Cambridge
       General layout for the University of Leicester, University of Hull, and Royal Holloway College of the University of London (with Colin St. John Wilson)
       General layout of the University of London (with Trevor Dannatt)
1957/
  58 King's Hostel, Cambridge (with Colin St. John Wilson)
1957/
  62 Harvey Court Residential Building, Gonville and Caius College, Cambridge (with Colin St. John Wilson)
1958 Low-rise housing project, St. Pancras, London (with Colin St. John Wilson)
1959/
  64 Group of library buildings, Manor Road, Oxford (with Colin St. John Wilson)

1960/
  64 William Stone Residential Building, Peterhouse, Cambridge (with Colin St. John Wilson)
       Arts Building and Middleton Hall, University of Hull
1962/
  64 British Museum Library, London (first project; with Colin St. John Wilson)
1964/
  67 Graduate Building, Balliol and St. Anne's Colleges, Oxford
1964/
  70 Zoology/Psychology Building, Oxford University
1968/
  70 Kettle's Yard Gallery, Cambridge (with David Owers)
       General layout of Wellington Square, Oxford (with David Owers)
1970/
  78 Government Centre, Taif, Saudi Arabia (with David Owers)
1972/
  76 Pembroke College Library and St. Ebbe's Building, Oxford (with Colen Lumley)
1972/
  78 Glasgow Cultural Centre (project; with Colen Lumley)
1978 New Music School, Cambridge University (with Colen Lumley and Ivor Richards)
1980/
  84 Kettle's Yard Gallery additions, Cambridge
       New Modern Art Centre, Gulbenkian Foundation, Lisbon (with Ivor Richards)
1981/
  84 Music School additions, Cambridge (with Ivor Richards)
1981 New Building, Royal Scottish Academy of Music and Drama, Glasgow (with Ivor Richards)
1983 Halls and Commercial Development, Glasgow (with Ivor Richards)

Publications:

By MARTIN: books—*Circle*, editor with Ben Nicholson and Naum Gabo, London 1937; *The Flat Book*, editor with Sadie Speight, London 1939; *Whitehall: A Plan for a National and Government Centre*, London 1965; *Urban Space and Structures*, volume I, editor with Lionel March, London 1972; *Fifty Years After Lethaby*, lecture paper, London 1982; *Buildings and Ideas from the Studio of Leslie Martin 1931-1983*, Cambridge 1983; *New Centre for Modern Art, Gulbenkian Foundation, Lisbon*, Lisbon 1984; articles—"Architecture and the Painter" in *Focus*(London), no. 3, 1939; "A Note on Science and Art" in *The Architects Yearbook*(London), 1947; "Design of the Royal Festival Hall" in *RIBA Journal*(London), April 1952; "The Collegiate Plan" in *Architectural Review*(London), July 1959; "Notes on the Study of a Building Type" in *Architectural Design*(London), 1964; "Land Use and Built Forms," with Lionel March, in *Cambridge Research*, April 1966; "An Architect's Approach to Architecture" in *RIBA Journal*(London), May 1967; "Education without Walls" in *RIBA Journal*(London), August 1968; "Education Around Architecture" in *RIBA Journal* (London), September 1970; "Bridges Between Cultures" in *RIBA Journal* (London), June 1973; "Notes on a Developing Architecture" in *Architectural Review* (London), July 1978.

On MARTIN: articles—"Housing Development, St. Pancras" in *Architectural Design* (London), July 1959; "College Hall, Leicester" in *Architectural Review* (London), June 1961; "Harvey Court" in *Architectural Design* (London), November 1962; "Selected Works" in *Architectural Design* (London), September 1965; "The Third Force in English

Architecture" by Thomas Stevens in *Architectural Design* (London), September 1965; "Libraries, University of Oxford" in *Architectural Design* (London), September 1965; "Middleton Hall, University of Hull" in *Architectural Review* (London), October 1967, and in *Baumeister* (Munich), February 1969; "Gold medal Commendation" in *RIBA Journal* (London), February 1973; "Pure Gold" in *Building Design* (London), 2 February 1973; "Architecture's Gold Medallist" in *Financial Times* (London), 3 February 1978; "Appreciation" by Trevor Dannatt in *RIBA Journal* (London), August 1973; "Faculty of Music" in *Architectural Review* (London), July 1978; "Continuing Lines of thought: the work and teaching of Sir Leslie Martin" by Roger Stonehouse, and "New Centre for Modern Art, Lisbon" in *The Architects' Journal* (London), 5 August 1983; "Reasoning into Practice" by Sherban Cantacuzino in *Times Literary Supplement*(London), 13 January 1984.

*

In architecture it seems important to distinguish between external impressions and developing ideas. Superficial form and the imitation of form is fashion. Ideas generate forms, and by consistently developing and elaborating these we build up a language. That language must be effective at the small scale and anonymous level of the vernacular which creates an environment: at the other end of the scale it communicates thorough works which by their nature should be powerfully significant. The development of a language of that range is the basis of a tradition.

—Sir Leslie Martin

*

Sir Leslie Martin's architectural work has always had a firm intellectual basis in an organizing principle. It is achieved thorough the consistent use of a limited range of materials (notably brick, timber or concrete) to explore the potentialities of space and light. Taken as a whole, the work displays an order and control in which all elements are contained within the completeness of a unifying form—a form that marks, as he himself has said, "the end of a process."

This "process" begins with his concept of architecture as not just an isolated activity but as part of a culture. He has consistently spoken for an architecture in which the design activity is build up around contemporary needs and the belief that, as Trevor Dannatt puts it, architects should be concerned "with a whole range of elements in art and science that have to be brought into harmony, and that this constitutes the theme of architecture in our time."

Such ideas, however, are not static, but developing, as can be seen in the range of projects that Sir Leslie and his associates have produced over many years. His work at all scales shows a developing continuity (he calls it a "developing language") which can be seen in the family of forms produced in various schemes for student housing, or in the modulaton within the range of auditoria, or in such university proposals as those to house the departments of Zoology and Psychology at Oxford, where the basic structure plan allows a range of possibilities with each stage of development.

There is a clear link between such an approach and the opportunities, and demands, of education. The stimulus provided by Sir Leslie's attitude to architecture was an essential part of his role as head of the School of Architecture at Cambridge University. Here, principally through the Centre for Land Use and Build Form Studies (now the Martin Centre), he was able to foster the fresh theoretical examination of fundamental architectural issues. The research which he inspired was both challenging and rigorous, as for instance, in the clear demonstration that tall buildings do not make the most effective use of land and that other forms of layout can place the same

Leslie Martin: Calouste Gulbenkian Centre of Modern Art, Lisbon, 1980-84.

floor space on the same land area in one third of the height.

As the citation that accompanied the award of the Royal Gold Medal in 1973 said, "During a most active career, spanning more than 35 years, Sir Leslie Martin has made a truly outstanding contribution to architecture and planning, both through his work in private and public practice and most notably as a leading figure in architectural teaching and research."

—Peter Willis

MARTORELL Codina, Josep (Maria).

Spanish. Born in Barcelona, 21 May 1925. Educated at the Escuela Tecnica Superior de Arquitectura, Barcelona, 1943-51, Dip.Arch. 1951, Dr.Arch. 1963; studied town planning at the Instituto de Estudios de la Administracion Local, Barcelona, 1961. Served in Spanish Army, Campamento de la Granja, Segovia, 1946-47. Married Roser Solanic in 1954. In partnership with Oriol Bohigas, *q.v.*, Barcelona, since 1951, with Bohigas and David Mackay, *q.v.*, Barcelona, since 1962. Worked with Office of the Provincial Commission for Town Planning, Barcelona, 1951-56; President, Cultural Commission of the College of Architecture of Catalunya, Barcelona, 1968-70; Representative, Town Planning and Community Services Commission, Barcelona, 1970-74; President, Architecture Congress of Catalunya, Barcelona, 1980-81; Member of the Architectural Heritage Commission, Barcelona, 1981. Founder-Member, Grupo R, Barcelona, 1951. Recipient: Fundacio Güell Prize, Institut d'Estudis Catalans, Barcelona, 1978. Address: Martorell-Bohigas-Mackay, Camp 61, Barcelona 6, Spain.

Publications:

By MARTORELL: books—*La Inmigracion a Catalunya*, with others, Barcelona 1968; *Guia d'Arquitectura de Menorca*, Barcelona 1978, 1980.

See MARTORELL-BOHIGAS-MACKAY

MARTORELL-BOHIGAS-MACKAY.

Partnership; established, Barcelona, 1962, by Josep Martorell, *q.v.*, Oriol Bohigas, *q.v.*, and David Mackay, *q.v.*, (predecessor firm, Martorell and Bohigas, 1951-62). Exhibitions: *Grupo R.*, Barcelona, 1952-58; *Bienal*, Sao Paulo, 1957; *Biennale*, Venice, 1976; Centro de Arquitectos, Rosario, Argentina, 1977; *Barcelona 1950-77*, Centre Georges Pompidou, Paris, 1978; *Setmanes Catalanes*, Berlin, 1978; Lausanne, 1979; Berlin, Dortmund and London, 1981; Madrid and Bogota, Colombia, 1982. Recipient: First Prize, Ministry of Education Centres of Professional Education Competition, 1954; First Prize, University of Barcelona Colleges Competition, 1956; First Prize, Colegio de Arquitectos de Catalunya Headquarters Competition, 1957, 1958; First Prize, Palacio Municipal Extension Competition, Barcelona, 1958; First Prize, Asociacion Ing. Indus. de Barcelona Housing Competition, 1959; FAD Prize, 1959, 1962, 1966, 1979; Delta de Plata Prize, ADI/FAD, 1966; Garriga Nogues Prize, 1975; Delta de Oro Prize, ADI/FAD, 1976; 2 First Prizes, Prototype Schools Competition, Ministry of Education, Madrid, 1979; Südliche Friedrichstadt Prize, Internationale Bauausstellung, Berlin, 1984. Address: Carrer del Camp 61, Barcelona, Spain.

Works:

Martorell and Bohigas:

1952/
62 Escorial Housing, Calle Escorial 50, Barcelona (with F. Mitjans, M. Ribas, and J. Alemany)

1954/
55 Guardiola House, Argentona, Maresme, Spain

1954/
58 Roger de Flor Housing, Calle Roger de Flor 215, Barcelona

1955/
58 Trade School, Sabinanigo, Huesca, Spain

1955/
59 Mutua Metalurgica de Seguros Clinic, Diagonal 394, Barcelona

1956/
61 Baro de Viver School, Barcelona
1957 Timbaler del Bruc School, Riera d'Horta/ Calle Arnaldo de Oms, Barcelona

1957/
68 Church of the Redeemer, Avenida Mare de Deu de Montserrat 34-40, Barcelona
1958 Provisional Church of St. Sebastian, Via Favencia, Verdum, Barcelona

1958/
59 Housing, Calle Pallars 299-317, Barcelona
1959 Piher Factory, Riera Canado, Badalona, Barcelona

1959/
62 Max Cahner House, Barcelona

Martorell, Bohigas, Mackay:
1957/
64 Via Augusta-Muntaner Housing, Via Augusta 168, Barcelona

1959/
62 Lujan House, Palau de Plegamans, Valles Occidental, Barcelona

1959/
65 Meridiana Housing, Avenue Meridiana 312, Barcelona

1960/
63 Navas de Tolosa Housing, Calle Navas de Tolosa 296, Barcelona

1960/
65 Secretari Coloma Housing, Calle Secretari Coloma 79-89/Providencia 133-35, Barcelona

1960/
68 Sant Sebastian Parish Centre, Calle Viladrosa, Verdum, Barcelona

1961/
62 Orpi House, El Figaro, Valles Oriental, Barcelona
Permit Office, Colegio de Arquitectos de Catalunya, Plaza Nova 5, Barcelona

1961/
64 Casa del Pati Housing, Ronda Guinardo 44, Barcelona

1961/
65 Mas Silvestre Children's Holiday Colony, Canyamars, Maresme, Spain

1962/
64 Milans del Bosch Housing, Calle Sant Adria 196, Barcelona

1962/
65 Can Bordoi House, Llinars del Valles, Valles Oriental, Barcelona
La Vanguardia Newspaper Building, Calle Tallers 52-54, Barcelona

1962/
73 Garbi School, Esplugues de Llobregat, Barcelona

1963/
64 Europalma Housing Development, Costa de la Calma, Majorca

1963/
65 Espar Housing, Calle Milanesado 20-22, Barcelona
Pere IV Industrial Complex, Calle Pere IV 162, Barcelona

1963/
66 Sant Marti Housing, Calle Fluvia 200, Barcelona

1964/
67 Doctor Carulla Housing, Calle Dr. Carulla 53, Barcelona

1964/
70 Xaudiera Housing, Calle Entenca 99-101/Arago 20-22, Barcelona

1965/
67 Destino Publisher's Offices and Warehouse, Riera Canada, Badalona, Spain

1965/
69 Church of the Sagrada Familia, Igualada, Anoia, Spain

1966/
67 Santa Agueda Housing Development, Benicassim, Castello, Spain

1966/
69 Montana House, L'Ametlla del Valles, Valles Oriental, Barcelona
Housing, Calle Casp 114, Barcelona

1967/
68 Heredero House, Tredos, Vall d'Aran, Spain
1967/
69 Sant Jordi School, Calle Mn. Cinto Verdaguer, Pineda, Maresme, Spain
Housing, Calle Buscarons 16, Barcelona

1967/
71 Housing Development, Avenida Dr. Moragas, Santa Maria de Barbera, Valles Occidental, Barcelona

1967/
72 Housing Development, Avenida Angel Sallent Terrassa, Valles Occidental, Barcelona

1968/
69 Housing for Teaching Staff, Calle Mn. Cinto Verdaguer, Pineda, Maresme, Spain

1968/
72 Piher Factory, Avenida San Julian, Granollers, Valles Oriental, Barcelona
M. Serras Shop, Calle Anselm Clave 28, Granollers, Valles Oriental, Barcelona

1968/
75 Augusta Clinic, Calle Madrazo 8-10, Barcelona

1969/
71 Piher Factory II, Riera Canado, Badalona, Barcelona

1969/
72 Giro Hnos Textile Factory, Avenida Navarra, Badalona, Barcelona
Haissa Knitwear Factory, Avenida Marti Pujol 273, Badalona, Barcelona

1969/
73 Crescent de Viladecans Housing Development, Calle del Sol. Viladecans, Baix Llobregat, Spain
Manzana la Salut Housing Development, Calle Ruperto Llado/Riera de la Salud, Sant Feliu de Llobregat, Baix Llobregat, Spain

1970 Sant Cugat Golf Club, Sant Cugat del Valles, Valles Occidental, Barcelona (project)

1970/
73 Bonanova Housing, Plaza de la Bonanova 92, Barcelona
Gubern Footwear Shop, Calle del Mar 54-56, Badalona, Barcelona

1971/
73 Pals Golf Houses, Plays de Pals, Baix Emporda, Spain
Housing, Calle Camp 65, Barcelona

1971/
74 Illuro Department Store, Calle Sant Antoni 82-88, Mataro, El Maresme, Spain

1971/
75 Casa de la Torre Housing Development, Avenida Mossen Cinto Verdaguer, Santa Perpetua de la Moguda, Valles Occidental, Barcelona

1972/
74 Marti House, Sant Jordi d'Alfama, Baix Ebre, Spain

Martorell-Bohigas-Mackay: Primary School, Sant Adria del Besos, Barcelona, 1983.

Cases Bessones Building, Calle Rectoria 36-38, Barcelona
Thau School, Carretera de Esplugues 49-53, Barcelona
1973/
74 Almaina Park Housing Development, Muchamiel, Alacant, Spain (project)
House, Ciutadella, Menorca, Spain
1973/
75 Misser House, Llinars del Valles, Valles Oriental, Barcelona
1973/
79 La Salut Housing, phase 3, Calle Torrent La Salut St. Feliu de Llobregat, Barcelona
1974/
75 El Hacho de Manilva Tourist Development, Manilva, Malaga, Spain (project; with Vittorio Gregotti)
Piher Offices, Tudela, Navarra, Spain
1974/
76 Housing, Calle Angli 32, Barcelona
1974/
77 Housing, Calle La Costa 59-63, Barcelona
1975 Riudellots Housing Development, Riudellots de la Selva, Girones, Spain (project; with Enric Steegman)
1975/
76 Commercial and residential building, Calle Camp 61, Barcelona
Housing Rda. Collsalarca, Sabadell, Barcelona
Housing, Calle Asturias 37, Barcelona
1975/
77 Almirall House, La Garriga Valles Oriental, Barcelona
Otero House, La Garriga, Valles Oriental, Barcelona

Housing, Calle Ossio 45-53, Barcelona
Housing, Calle de Sants 291, Barcelona
1975/
78 Amil House, Sant Vicenc de Montalt, Maresme, Spain
1976 Colegio de Arquitectos Headquarters, Plaza Cristo de Burgos, Seville (project; with Enric Steegman)
1976/
77 Apartments, Santa Agueda, Benicassim, Castellon, Spain
1976/
78 Infant School and Convent, Ciutadella, Menorca, Spain
1977/
78 Garbi School, Esplugues de Llobregat, Barcelona
1977/
79 Housing, Calle Balmes 281, Barcelona
1977/
80 Housing, Calle Caponata/Eduardo Conde, Barcelona
1977/
81 Marti l'Huma Housing, Rambla de Sabadell, Barcelona
1978/
79 Marti House, Sant Jordi d'Alfama, Tarragona, Spain
1978/
80 Bank and Office Building, Rambla de Mataro, Barcelona
Colegio de Arquitectos de Catalunya Headquarters extension, Plaza Nova, Barcelona (project; with Enric Steegman)
1979 Vall-Roig Housing Development, Manzana/ Calle Espana-Roma-Sevilla/Diagonal, Cerdanyola, Barcelona

1979/
81 Serra House, Canovellas, Barcelona
Benejam House, Torrelavit, Barcelona
1981/
82 Housing, Calle Roca i Battle, Barcelona
1983 Primary School, Sant Adria del Besos, Barcelona
Monastery of Santa Cecilia restoration and conversion, Monserrat, Barcelona
Housing, Calle de la Creu, Barcelona
1984 La Catalana Offices restoration and conversion, Plaza de Gracia 2-4, Barcelona (original building by Enric Sagnier, 1890)
Housing, Sant Andreu de la Barca, Barcelona
Camps-Juaneda House, Cala Morell, Ciutadella, Menorca, Spain
Housing, Calle Queralt, Vallvidrera, Barcelona
Parc de la Creueta del Coll, Barcelona
Hortala House, Calle Escoles Pies 120, Barcelona
Nestle Office Building Complex, Esplugues de Llobregat, Barcelona
Primary School, Granollers, Barcelona
Housing, Mollet, Barcelona

Publications:

On MBM: books—*Antologia Espanola de Arte Contemporaneo* by Cesareo Rodriguez-Aguilera, Barcelona 1955; *El Arte en las Artes* by Juan Perucho, Barcelona 1964; *Panorama del Nuevo Arte Espanol* by Vincente Aguilera Cerni, Madrid 1966; *La Otra Cara de Catalunya* by Jose Carlos Clemente, Barcelona and Mexico City 1968; *Los Encuentros* by

Baltasar Porcel, Barcelona 1969; *Temas de Arquitectura Escolar, 1972; Martorell, Bohigas, Mackay* by José Corredor Matheos, Barcelona 1973; *Martorell, Bohigas, Mackay: Arquitectura 1951-1972* by Juan Daniel Fullaondo, Barcelona and Madrid 1974; *Arquitecturas Catalanas* by Helio Pinon, Barcelona 1978; *Martorell-Bohigas-Mackay: Arquitectura 1953-1978* by Helio Pinon and Charles Jencks, Madrid 1979; articles—"Interview mit Josep Maria Martorell, Oriol Bohigas und David Mackay" by Joaquin Gili in *Moebel Interior Design* (Leinfelden, Germany), January 1967; "Testimonianze di Martorell, Bohigas e Mackay" by José Corredor Matheos in *L'Architettura* (Rome), August 1968; "Aportaciones de la Culture Arquitectonica Catalana: Equipo Martorell, Bohigas, Mackay" by Antonio Fernandez Alba in *Nueva Forma* (Madrid), March 1973; "Martorell, Bohigas, Mackay et l'Architecture du Logement a Barcelone" by Ignasi Sola Morales in *L'Architecture d'Aujourd'hui* (Paris), January/February 1975; "MBM and the Barcelona School" by Charles Jencks in *Architectural Review* (London), March 1977; "Martorell Bohigas Mackay" in *Architect and Builder* (Cape Town), September 1978; "50 years in Barcelona", special issue of *Wonen-TA/BK* (Heerlen, Netherlands), April 1979; "MBM La Garriga" in *Architectural Review* (London), August 1980; "Three interiors in Barcelona" in *Architectural Review* (London), October 1980; "New Housing Policy in Berlin" in *Quaderns* (Barcelona), March/April 1981; "Catalans in Berlin" in *L'Architecture d'Aujourd'hui* (Paris), October 1981; "Housing Development in Barcelona" in *Bauwelt* (Berlin), 30 April 1982; "MBM: la ultima modernidad y la primera memoria" by Josep Maria Montaner in *On* (Barcelona), April 1984.

Between—or beyound—an architecture meant to be drawn and an architecture meant to be built, there is built architecture that can be drawn (to be built, it had to be drawn beforehand). Between Piranesi and the practical manuals on house constructions are the essayists who, like Palladio, establish compositive bases upon either built examples or working drawings. So the drawing—the essential tool to control the composition and to check the design intentions—is, at the same time, a self-sufficient expression of an artistic proposal. It is this artistic proposal, understood as an intention to compose the building—"compose it" and "pose it" in its physical, psychological, or cultural setting—that is underlined in the various works we have carried out during 25 years of professional practice. Instead of attempting a systematic explanation, we can say that each building refers to elements and systems in a visual order composed and "posed." This approach to architecture can be classified in four distinct ways, though in reality they more often than not merge.

1) The conceptual thread leads through the relationship between the architectural project and the architectural and urban elements that have a constant tradition in the built environment. One aspect of this relationship is the minimalization of stylistic elements in an area where these elements are well defined. The relationship concerns not only the total form of the building itself but also the surface texture of the facade, which defines the "skin" of the environment. The persistent constructive play of artificial stone in and around the centre of Barcelona is an example.

2) Another aspect of this relationship is in the use of ordinary, anonymous elements that, even if they do not strictly correspond to the context, allow the architecture to be easily understood, because they are rooted in a solid but living tradition. Timber bay-windows, small scale traditional construction imposed upon a new urban building, and back galleries shifted round to the front facade are a few examples. These elements are often chosen for their deliberately fragile nature, which allows the new building to be absorbed into the neighbourhood as something provisional, not yet converted into a monumental object but, rather, a soft addition to a quietly changing neighbourhood whose character is maintained by a succession of these adaptable newcomers. Timber-slats, asbestos-cement, canvas blinds, and wooden shutters all suggest this reserved intention not to intrude with a rude, autocratic imposition: they are consistent with the user's desire for self-expression, within a composition of apparent disorder that supports this structure.

3) The relationship between architecture and the city can also be inverted, with part of the building reflecting the urban structure and texture as though it had allowed the city to carry on inside. This reference is visual rather than functional. The mistake of trying to impose on the left-over spaces the vitality of a city, by copying the social reality of the urban street, is avoided by restricting the image to a sequence of urban references within the architecture, even if the result is rhetorical or theatrical.

4) A more intensive architectural intervention is appropriate when the building or group of buildings act as an instrument of urban revival. When a street or neighbourhood has lost its initial vitality and decay has begun to set in, there is a need to create new centres of interest, rearrange a decadent disorder, reinterpret use, correct street perspectives, and relate urban incidents to the meaning of the places. The limits of this sort of intervention are always within the modest dimensional characteristics of architecture and its capacity to be read and understood in an easy code that is recognized by the man in the street; it must be close to that reality that is rooted in the historical process of the community and guarantees its coherent continuity.

These four "ways" are each an attempt to try to recover the proper role of architecture within the historical centres, its capacity to intervene in form and content without rejecting the familiar references of the social groups that both use and create within a process of continuing dialogue. The architect can work only like a beauty specialist or a cosmetic surgeon, whose task is always partial in that it cannot essentially change the human body or introduce a new interpretative code. Adjusting the contours of a nose or breast involves an agreement that, because of the mistakes of nature or the effects of wear and tear, there is a need for improvement; the make-up artist works according to the same kind of agreement. The make-up man and the cosmetic surgeon achieve, slowly, within the limits of the skills their professions have attained, a partial change in the human figure. The architect in relation to the city is in the same position: it is no exaggeration to say that in some respects the anatomy and biology of reality is the result of an archaeological superimposition of various make-ups and various partial adjustments, and it is that reality with which the architect must work.

To build in Europe almost always means to build in the historical city, especially if we understand by "historical" all that is both old and recent, the result of a dialectical process. Accordingly, the work of the architect in our cities should always be like that of the make-up artist or cosmetic surgeon. But the rapid growth of our cities, combined with the lack of limitation on private speculation, has destroyed the historical dialogue. The "new towns," "residential estates" and "slum clearances" involve attitudes and methods very different from those of the make-up artist and cosmetic surgeon. There is no previous structure upon which to work, so there can be no reflection of the old cities: the reality of their historical process cannot be imitated without the architect's committing the error of the ridiculous, be it the picturesque, monumental, folk, or revival. The challenge of virgin territory should be met with new constructions that are parallel to the large public works that have been refined and adjusted during the last 200 years and are now available to us charged with historical process, however unorthodox. The country is not the city, and to achieve an urban context rapidly new structures must be used—the ones we have already, the ones with a long visual history, the port, the railroad, the motorway, the dam, the quarry, and the airstrip.

—Martorell-Bohigas-Mackay

The partners in Martorell-Bohigas-Mackay are polemicists, and they have nicely portrayed some of the traps that recent Spanish architecture has fallen into—from the casualties of the revolution, those buildings that avoid reality in a make-believe world, to the particular pseudo-vernacularizing that amounts to a sick architecture, courting reality with formal irony and a certain amount of despair, to the faceless buildings that have come to be symbols of the hollow grey elite of the meritocracy. The architect rushing to stay in one place is the only constant in an inconstant milieu. The MBM answer, however, is not some sort of National Romanticism, with its dead-end in People's Democratic Architecture, nor a Technological Romanticism with its dead-end in a neutral, stillborn architecture, nor some utopian fantasy that never quite emerges from its pseudo-scientific test-tubes. MBM's credo is "poetic realism"—charging a building with imagination and suggesting the purpose of culture, the sort of architecture that always endeavours to be one step ahead of the printed word.

MBM condemns many of the vanities and anomalies of modern Spanish architecture. Neither the adolescent longing for a computer-based architecture with a comic-strip coding nor the overstessed axonometric cut-away mathematical vocabulary entirely escape their critical venom; neither is an "architecture-of-autobiography" nor a "blood-and-earth-architecture" safe. But, perhaps owing to their hypersensitivity to the limitations of most of the styles manifested by Spanish architecture today, they themselves seem unwilling to commit themselves to any style at all, and their "poetic realism" seems to mean no more than adopting a different genre for each design programme, hoping to find a better fit between the immediate conditions of the environment and the functional parameters than a more consistent "style" might allow. This method permits them to invent a succinct style from scratch, then bring it to realization and destruction within the span of a single building.

The rhythmic intermittence of the Meridiana Housing in Barcelona, an urban wall with occasional apertures, is a pertinent solution to the problems of a house-in-the-city, but it was abandoned as soon as it had been devised. MBM moved on to a kind of vernacular-run-amok at Santa Agueda, Benicassim: this labour-intensive-picturesque style, with its broken massing and throw-away feel, was indeed thrown away for the next major project, the housing for teaching staff at Pineda, which is much more compact and exacting. The Piher Factory at Granollers is an unashamed industrial shed. The apartments in Gerona are a Venturian elegy, the Thau School in Barcelona a gasketted dream of modernism. If this is "poetic realism," what is the difference between it and stripped classicism, or tourist architecture, or official monumentalism?

Still, a period of destruction, followed by one of what seems to the observer to be almost wilfully chaotic experimentation, is the classic progress of revolution—and revolutions are sometimes successful. Martorell-Bohigas-Mackay share an acute awareness of the problems and structure of urban life. It may be that the best is yet to come.

—Chris Fawcett

MASUDA, Tomoya.
Japanese. Born on Awaji Island, Hyogo Prefecture, 16 December 1914. Educated at the University of Kyoto, 1935-39, B.Arch. 1939. Lecturer, 1950-58, Assistant Professor, 1958-62, Professor, 1962-78,

and from 1978 Emeritus Professor, University of Kyoto (maintained atelier at the university). D.Arch., Univeristy of Kyoto, 1954; Visiting Professor, Sydney University, Australia, 1975. *Died* (in Kyoto) *in 1981.*

Works:

1957 Nantan-cho Town Hall, Hyogo Prefecture, Japan
   Institute for Radioactive Macromolecular Research, Neyagawa, Osaka Prefecture, Japan
   City Hall, Nagasaki (competition project)
1958 Rest House, Miyazu, Kyoto Prefecture, Japan
   Keage Purification Plant, Kyoto
   Onomichi City Hall, Hiroshima Prefecture, Japan
1959 Girls' High School, Suma, Kobe, Japan
   Toba Sewage Disposal Plant, Kyoto
   Engineering Faculty Buildings, Kyoto University
1961 Onomichi Assembly Hall, Hiroshima Prefecture, Japan
   Sumoto City Hall, Hyogo Prefecture, Japan
1962 Naruto City Hall, Tokushima Prefecture, Japan
   Kyoto University Atomic Pile Laboratory, Kumatori, Osaka Prefecture, Japan
   Kobayashi House, Kinugasayama, Kyoto
1963 Yamanouchi Purification Plant, Kyoto

   Suzuki Automotive Industries Main Building, Hamana-gun, Shizuoka Prefecture, Japan
   Higashiyama Hall, Kyoto
1964 Chishakuin Hall, Kyoto
   Memorial Assembly Hall, Kyoto University (project)
1965 Dormitory for the Tsuruya-Yoshinobu Company, Kyoto
   Master plan for *Expo '70*, Osaka (project)
1966 Shimizu Central Public Hall, Shizuoka Prefecture, Japan
1967 Heart Institute Laboratories, Tokyo
1968 Japan Furniture Centre, Harumi, Tokyo
1970 Toyooka Civic Centre, Hyogo Prefecture, Japan
   Monument to Typhoon Victims During A-Bomb Investigation, Hiroshima
1971 Engineering Faculty Main Office Building, Kyoto University
   Memorial Gymnasium, Kyoto University
   Okamoto House, Nantan-cho, Hyogo Prefecture, Japan
1972 Kitanada-Higashi Primary School and Kindergarten, Naruto, Tokushima Prefecture, Japan
1973 Hokke Club House, Kyoto
1973/
   82 Naruto Cultural Center, Tokushima Prefecture, Japan (project)
1975 Kuwajima Kindergarten, Naruto, Tokushima Prefecture, Japan
1976 Naruto Welfare Center for the Aged, Tokushima Prefecture, Japan

Publications:

By MASUDA: book—*Architecture Universelle Japon*, Geneva 1969; *Living Architecture: Japanese*, with photographs by Yukio Futagawa, London 1970; articles—"Struktur und Freiheit" in *Werk* (Zurich), October 1962; "A talk with Professor Masuda on fragments and fundamentals", interview, in *Architecture in Australia* (Sydney), October 1975.

On MASUDA: articles—"Town Hall, Minami-tan machi, Hyogo" in *The Japan Architect* (Tokyo), February 1958; "Onomichi City Hall" in *The Japan Architect* (Tokyo), September 1960; "Hohere Madschenschule in Suma, Kobe, Japan" in *Werk* (Zurich), no. 4, 1962; "A House in Kinugasayama" in *The Japan Architect* (Tokyo), August 1964; "Bauchronik: Eigenheim von Prof. Kobayashi, Kinugasayama, Kyoto" in *Werk* (Zurich), no. 5, 1964; "Siedlung mit Terrassenhausern bei Kobe, Japan" in *Werk* (Zurich), no. 10, 1964; "The Japan Furniture Center" in *The Japan Architect* (Tokyo), January/February 1968; "Laboratories for the Heart Institute" in *The Japan Architect* (Tokyo), December 1968; "The Chishaukuin Hall" in *The Japan Architect* (Tokyo), June 1969; "Naruto Civic Cultural Center" in *The Japan Architect* (Tokyo), May 1983.

"Nature" is apprehended in two ways in our traditional way of thought. One is: we do not act

Tomoya Masuda: Naruto Cultural Center, Japan, 1973-82.

upon it, we leave it intact; that is, nature is just "the given." The other is: we act freely upon "the given," naively following our own essential nature. These two visions are simultaneous and ambiguous. Just as "the given" is not merely naked physical nature, so is any artificial action not merely arbitrary or illogical. Both "nature" itself, that which the word "nature" signifies, and the attitude toward "nature," I assume to be "a-logical" or "non-logical." If the word "non-logical" does not mean illogical (id est, "not logical"), and if it conceivably implies the logical "non"—in other words, a logic of none—then it would be clear what and how the East, following its own nature, has constructed in "nature." It would then become evident how foresighted were the tea-house, flower arranging, gardening and its architecture, and, above all, the sense of time and space.
—Tomoya Masuda (1980)

Is Japanese architecture "form above all," as Peter Smithson has suggested—is it reducible to a "rectangular plane and a certain sort of curve"?

The large output of Tomoyo Masuda's atelier at Kyoto University has been consistently concerned with assessing the nature and formative roots of the Japanese architectural tradition vis-a-vis Western architectural biography. The fundamental distinction that Masuda draws between the two spatial enterprises rests on the "visible basis" of Western architecture and the "non-visible basis" of the Japanese. He cites the material aspects of classical and gothic forms as forming a visible basis in the European environment, in contrast to the way that columns alone signify Japanese space. Mannerism is the moment in Western history when "visibility" took over and wrapped itself independently around architectural superstructures: it would have continued to appear to us to be the only solution if modernism had not come along and cleared the air. Looking to the traditional Japanese house as an exemplar, the heroic architects chucked out visibility in favour of an architecture not determined by visual rules, proportions and geometries alone. But now visibility is beginning to creep in again through the back door—in the guise of post-modernism, post-metabolism, post-rationalism. The architecture of pure outlines of purpose just passed us by: there was nothing to remember it by, no mnemonic or associational network to make it adhere: it just drifted past as if it had never arrived in the first place. And that brings us back to square one. Visible rules hold sway again. "Difference" has again become a value, when only fifty years ago "difference" had been replaced with "similarity."

Masuda, in such works as the Kyoto University Gymnasium or the Higashiyama Hall, is intent on establishing a middle path, a neutral line between these polarities—not a clear-cut centre parting but an ambiguous zone of double meaning best described by the term *ryogi*. Not so objective and finite as "balance," it is more a matter of accommodating as many of the extremes on both sides as one can.

Another key consideration for Masuda is that we should see "others" as ourselves: we should design for ourselves, that is, for ourselves-as-others. What is the difference between designing for oneself and for oneself-as-others? An actor on the stage—he plays the part of a killer but must remain himself as well: the architect must become an actor.
—Chris Fawcett

MAY, Ernst.

German. Born in Frankfurt, 27 July 1886. Educated at University College, London, 1907-08; Technische Hochschule, Darmstadt, Germany, 1908-10; worked in the town planning office of Raymond Unwin, London, 1910-12; studied at the Technische Hochschule, Munich, under Friedrich von Thiersch and Theodor Fischer, 1912-13. Served in the German Imperial Army on the eastern and western fronts during World War I. Established private practice, Frankfurt, 1913; Technical Director, Regional Planning Authority, Breslau (now Wroclaw, Poland), 1919-21; Director, Public Housing Authority, Breslau, 1921-23; Director, Central Office for Refugee Welfare/Distressed People's Housing, Breslau, 1923-25; City Architect, Frankfurt, 1925-30; Director of the European Town Planning Team in the U.S.S.R., 1930-34; farmed in Tanganyika, 1934-37; in private practice, as architect and town planner, Nairobi, Kenya, 1937-54 (interned as an enemy alien, 1942-45); Head of the Planning Department, subsequently Adviser on City Planning and Housing Techniques, Neue Heimat Housing Development Organization, Hamburg, West Germany, 1954-60; in private practice, Hamburg, West Germany, 1960 until his death in 1970. Founder-Editor, *Das schlesische Heim*, Breslau, 1919–25, *Das neue Frankfurt*, 1925–30, and *Neue Heimat*, Hamburg, West Germany, 1954-60. Recipient: German Cross of Merit. Honorary D. Eng: Technische Hochschule, Hannover, West Germany; D. Phil.: University of Freiburg, West Germany; Honorary Professor, Technische Hochschule, Darmstadt, West Germany. Member, Akademie der Künste, Berlin. Honorary President, German Association of Housing, Town and Country Planning. Honorary Corresponding Member, British Town Planning Institute, and Royal Institute of British Architects. *Died* (in Hamburg, West Germany) *12 September 1970.*

Works:

1919 Cottages, Goldschmieden-Neukirche, Germany
1922 Plan for a housing development at Ohlau, Lower Silesia
1926 May House, Frankfurt
1926/
  27 Bruchfeldstrasse Housing Development, Frankfurt
    Ginnheim Housing Development, Frankfurt
    Praunheim Housing Development, Frankfurt
1928 Reform School, Bornheimer Hang, Frankfurt (with A. Locher)
    Niederrad Housing Development, Frankfurt (with H. Boehm)
    Westhausen Housing Development, Frankfurt
    Römerstadt Housing Development, Frankfurt
    Hohenblick Housing Development, Frankfurt
    Bornheimer Hang Housing Development, Frankfurt
    Riedhof-East Housing Development, Frankfurt
    Gartenstadt Goldstein Development, Frankfurt
    Tornow-Gelande Housing Development, Frankfurt
    Manundshainerstrasse Housing Development, Frankfurt
    Engelsruhe Development, Höchst, Frankfurt
    Miquelstrasse Housing Development, Frankfurt
    Plans for housing developments at Raimundstrasse, Riederwald, Rutschlehen, and Riedhof-West, Frankfurt
1928/
  30 Redevelopment plan for Frankfurt
1930/
  34 Town plans for Stseglovsk, Kusnetszk, Tirgan, Magnitogorsk, Stalinsk, Nishni-Tagil, and Leninakan, U.S.S.R.
    Regional plan for Moscow
1945/
  47 May House, Nairobi, Kenya
    Delamate Avenue Housing Development, Nairobi, Kenya
1947 City plan for Kampala, Uganda
    Community development plan for Naguru, Uganda
    Central Recreation Park, Kampala, Uganda
    Oceanic Hotel, Mombasa, Kenya
    Farmer's house, Limuru, Kenya
    Farmer's house, Molo, Kenya
    Aga Khan House, Oyster Bay, Dar-es-Salaam, Tanganyika
1950/
  51 Aga Khan School, Kisumu, Kenya
    Aga Khan Maternity Hospital, Kisumu, Kenya
    Cultural Center, with Shops, Offices and Hotel, Moshi, Tanganyika
1954/
  56 Hegholt Housing Development, Hamburg, West Germany (with Sprotte and Neve)
    Grunhofe Housing Development, Weissenstein, Bremerhaven, West Germany
    St. Lorenz Housing Development, Lübeck, West Germany
    Alte Vahr Housing Development, Bremen, West Germany
    Housing development, Aachen-West, West Germany
    Redevelopment plan for Neu-Altona, West Germany
    Apartment building, Lübeckerstrasse, Hamburg, West Germany
1956/
  70 May House, Hamburg, West Germany
    Rheinhausen Housing Development (competition project)
    Fennpfuhl Housing Development, Lichtenberg, East Berlin (competition project)
    Limes Housing Development, Frankfurt (competition project)
    Garath Housing Development, Düsseldorf, West Germany (project)
    Workers' Housing, Wulfen, West Germany (competition project)
    Neuen Vahr Housing Development, Bremen, West Germany
    Parkfeld Housing Development, Wiesbaden, West Germany (competition project)
    Klarenthal Housing Development, Wiesbaden, West Germany
    Dotzheim Housing Development, Wiesbaden, West Germany
    Rahlstedt Housing Development, Hamburg, West Germany
    Housing development, Stuttgart
    Eselsweg Housing Development, Mainz, West Germany
    Plan for the redevelopment of the centre of Bremerhaven, West Germany

Publications:

By MAY: articles—numerous contributions to *Das schlesische Heim* (Breslau), *Das neue Frankfurt*, and *Neue Heimat* (Hamburg).

On MAY: book—*Ernst May: Bauten und Planungen* by J. Buekschmitt, Stuttgart 1963; articles—"House in Kenya by Ernst May" in *Architects' Journal* (London), 20 July 1939; "Kampala Town Planning" in *Architects Yearbook*, London 1947; "Eigenheim des Architekten in Nairobi" in *Werk* (Zürich), June 1949; "House at Dar-es-Salaam" in *Architectural Review* (London), May 1953; "The One-Family House Versus Rebuilding the City" in *American Institute of Planners Journal* (Washington, D.C.), Fall 1956; "Ernst May" in *Der Aufbau* (Vienna), May 1957; "Ernst May: La sua abitazione ad Amburgo" in *Abitare* (Milan), May 1964; "Un architetto e una città: Ernst May a Francoforte" by Giorgio Grassi in *Controspazio* (Bari, Italy),

Ernst May: Romerstadt Housing Development, Frankfurt, 1928.

April/May 1970; "The New Frankfurt and Ernst May, 1925-1930" by Jean Castex, Jean-Charles Depaule and Philippe Panerai in *Cahiers de la recherche architecturale* (Roquevaire, France), December 1977; "Foreign Architects in the USSR" by Christian Borngraber in *Architectural Association Quarterly* (London), no.1, 1979.

From the time of his early studies in Munich and in England, Ernst May was much influenced by the ideas of Ebenezer Howard and the architecture of Raymond Unwin. He was an admirer of English domestic architecture championed by Muthesius and was a devotee of the Garden City movement. Yet his work for the new *Wohnkultur* was free from social and stylistic constrictions in a way that was not possible in England, for May's professional career coincided with a period of great social and political change in Germany.

As architect of Frankfurt in the 1920s, he designed the celebrated Römerstadt Housing Estate, which embodied some of the best English and Continental ideas of the time. Basically municipal low-income housing, Römerstadt was planned with small gardens and with something of the ideals of the Garden City movement, yet the architecture is avantgarde, owing much to the models of the Bauhaus circle. The peculiar economic difficulties within the Weimar Republic encouraged the use of experimental building techniques for cheapness, while standardized components and units were developed. May must therefore be seen as a major architect working within the tradition concerned to provide low-cost housing, which had developed from the nineteenth century.

He was invited to the Soviet Union to advise on town planning and led the teams responsible for the design of Tirgan and for the drafting of the Moscow Regional Plan. After only three years, however, he left Russia for East Africa, where he worked as a planning adviser.

His experience in the design of low-cost housing led to his appointment as consultant to the Heimat housing combine after the World War II. He specialized in the renewal of the shattered German towns and cities using techniques he had learned at Römerstadt. In his later years, he became concerned with the deteriorating quality of the environment and with the dehumanization of planning. Just as Soviet Russia did not live up to his expectations in the 1930s, so the postwar reconstruction in a new era also disappointed him. He became aware that the modern planner had the power to make an environment totally lacking in human qualities, and he saw that the wholesale rejection of the past for a chimerical technological paradise had brought new terrors to modern life.

May was primarily a creative architect who never lost sight of his early aims to create a decent environment for healthy human beings. At Römerstadt, he presided over an extraordinary marriage of ultra-modern simplicity in architectural design with the principles of the Garden City movement and thus broke away from the theories of Camillo Sitte and Muthesius that had influenced him in his early years. His 1919 designs for cottages at Goldschmieden-Neukirche reflect the influence of Unwin, his lifelong friend and mentor. These are still picturesque and traditional, in the enlightened eclecticism advocated by Muthesius, but Römerstadt, with its crisply cubic

buildings and bald, even stark, outlines, owes more to Professor Tessenow's housing schemes at Dresden or Bruno Taut's designs at Berlin-Falkenberg.

May has been represented as a left-wing idealist, an idea that has been fostered after his stay in the Soviet Union. In fact, he was nearest the Fabian Socialist position and remained sympathetic to this very British brand of idealism all his life, partly through his friendship with Unwin and partly through his adherence to the views of the Town and Country Planning Association. Despite internment in Kenya during the war as an enemy alien, he remained an enthusiastic admirer of liberal ideas from Britain until his death.

—James Stevens Curl

MAYBECK, Bernard Ralph.

American. Born in New York City, 7 February 1862. Apprentice cabinet-maker to the firm of Pottier and Stymus, New York, 1879-81; studied under Jules André, Ecole Nationale et Speciale des Beaux-Arts, Paris, 1882-86 (Silver Medal, 1885); at special courses of the University of California, Berkeley, 1894-96, 1898-1900; also attended the Ecole des Beaux-Arts, Arts et Metiers, Louvre and Sorbonne, in Paris, 1896-98. Married Annie White in 1890; children: Wallen and Kerna. Worked with architects John M. Carrere and Thomas Hastings, New York, 1886-88; Partner, Russell and Maybeck, Kansas

City, 1888; worked for Ernest Coxhead, San Francisco, 1889-90, and for A. Page Brown, San Francisco, 1891-94; in private practice, Berkeley, California, from 1894; Instructor in Drawing, University of California, Berkeley, 1894-97, and Director of Architectural Studies, Mark Hopkins Institute of Art, San Francisco, 1895-97; Manager of the Phoebe A. Hearst Competition for the architectural design of the University of California campus, 1896-1900 (travelled abroad extensively on competition business); Instructor in Architecture, University of California Berkeley, 1898-1903 (devised first complete curriulum in architecture); opened San Francisco office in 1902; retired from active practice, 1938. Supervising Architect, United States Shipping Board, 1917; Associate Architect, *Golden Gate International Exposition,* 1939. Member, Berkeley City Planning Commission; President, San Francisco Art Association. Founder, Council of Allied Arts, California. Exhibitions: *Domestic Architecture of the San Francisco Bay Region,* San Francisco Museum of Art, 1949; *Roots of Contemporary Architecture,* Los Angeles, 1956. Collection: College of Environmental Design, University of California, Berkeley. Recipient: Gold Medal, St.Louis Exposition, 1904; Gold Medal, San Francisco Exposition, 1915; Honor Award, 1950, Gold Medal, 1951, American Institute of Architects. M.A.: Mills College, Oakland, California, 1923; LL.D.: University of California, 1930. Honored Member, San Francisco Chapter, American Institute of Architects. Member, San Francisco Society of Architects; Société des Elèves de M. André, Paris. *Died* (in Berkeley) *3 October 1957.*

Works:

1886 Ponce de Leon Hotel, St. Petersburg, Florida (with Thomas Hastings)
1891 Crocker Building, San Francisco (as draftsman to A. Page Brown)
1892/
1902 Bernard Maybeck House, Grove and Berryman Street, Berkeley, California
1894 Swedenborgian Church, San Francisco (as draftsman to A. Page Brown)
1895 Keeler House, Highland Place, Berkeley, California
1896 Emma Kellogg House I, Palo Alto, California (destroyed, 1899)
     Hall House, Highland Place, Berkeley, California (destroyed 1956)
     Lawson House, Waring Street, Berkeley, California (destroyed)
1897 Davis House, Ridge Road, Berkeley, California (destroyed 1957)
1899 Town and Gown Club, Dwight Way, Berkeley, California (with later additions by other architects)
     Emma Kellogg House II ("Sunbonnet House"), Bryan Street, Palo Alto, California
     Reception Building, for Phoebe A. Hearst, Channing Way, Berkeley, California (moved to the University of California campus and converted to a gymnasium, Hearst Hall, 1901; destroyed, 1922)
     Reiger Huse, Highland Place, Berkeley, California (destroyed, 1958)
1900 Bridgeman House, La Loma Street, Berkeley, California
     McCrea House, Derby Street, Berkeley, California
1901 Flagg House, Shattuck Avenue, Berkeley, California
1902 Barn, University of California, Berkeley (project)
     Faculty Club, University of California, Berkeley (wth later additions by others)
     Whitney House, Hawthorne Terrace, Berkeley, California (destroyed by fire, 1923)

Hiram Kellogg House, Regent Street, Berkeley, California (relocated to Lyndon Street, Berkeley)
     Stockton House, LeRoy Avenue, Berkeley, California (destroyed by fire, 1923)
     Bunnell House addition, San Francisco
     Barnett House, San Francisco (project)
     Boke House, Panoramic Way, Berkeley, California
     Dresslar House, La Conte Avenue, Berkeley, California (destroyed by fire, 1923)
     Keeler Studio, Highland Place, Berkeley, California
1902/
03 Wyntoon (Phoebe Hearst country estate), McCloud River, Siskiyou County, California (destroyed)
1903 Cooley House, Haste Street, Berkeley, California (project)
     Clubhouse, Bohemian Club of San Francisco, Bohemian Grove, Russian River, California (two projects)
     Newall Brothers Store Building, San Jose, California (remodelled)
     Jones House, Berkeley, California (project)
     Thomas House additions, Berkeley, California (destroyed by fire, 1923)
     University of California Hospital, San Francisco (project)
1904 Gates House, South 13th Street, San Jose, California
     California Wine Association Exhibit, *St. Louis Exposition*
     Newall House remodelling, Pacific Street, San Francisco (with additional remodelling, 1906)
     Bettys House, Berkeley, California (project)
     Bunnell House movement to new site and remodelling, Broadway near Pierce Street, San Francisco
     Newall House remodelling, El Camino Real near Oakgrove, Burlingame, California (destroyed)
     Underhill House I, LeRoy Avenue, Berkeley, California (destroyed by fire, 1923)
     Outdoor Art Club Building, Blithedale Avenue, Mill Valley, California
     Ranson Beach House, Sunnyside Avenue, Oakland, California
1905 Farrington House, Arch Street, Berkeley, California (destroyed by fire, 1923)
     Diggles House, Lomita Park, San Mateo, California
     Tufts House I, Entrata Avenue, San Anselmo, California
1906 Hamilton Church, Belvedere and Waller, San Francisco (project)
     School, Morgan Hill, California
     Hillside Club Building, Cedar Street, Berkeley, California (with additions, 1922; destroyed by fire, 1923)
     Sanderson House, Lookout Place, Berkeley, California (destroyed by fire, 1923)
     Gregory House, Hilgard Street, Berkeley, California (project)
     Elston House, Aberdeen, Washington
     Unitarian Church, Cowper and Channing Street, Palo Alto, California (destroyed)
     Flagg Studio, Shattuck Avenue, Berkeley, California
     Miall House, Burlingame, California (project)
     Robinson House, El Camino Real, Burlingame, California (destroyed)
     Frey House, Berkeley, California (project)
     Stiles House, Piedmont, California (project)
     Tait House, East Oakland, California (project)
     Hopps House, Winding Way, Ross, California (with additions, 1925)
     Paul Elder Bookstore, Van Ness and Pine, San Francisco (destroyed)
     de Lemascheffsky House, Le Conte Avenue, Berkeley, California (project)

George Hansen Houses, Berkeley, California (projects)
     Evans House, Arch Street, Berkeley, California (project)
     Telegraph Hill Neighborhood House, Stockton Street, San Francisco
     Welch House, Larkin Street, San Francisco (project)
     Read House, Stockton, California (project)
     Rees House, La Loma and Virginia, Berkeley, California
1907 French House, Summer Street, Berkeley, California
     Senger House, Bay View Place, Berkeley, California
     Kern House, Dormidera Street, Piedmont, California
     Stebbins House remodelling, Berkeley, California
     Oscar Maurer Photographic Studio, LeRoy Avenue, Berkeley, California
     Gregory House, Greenwood Terrace, Berkeley, California
     Robinson House, Burlingame, California (project)
     Schneider House, Arch Street, Berkeley, California
     Lawson House, La Loma Avenue, Berkeley, California
     Saeltzer House, West Street, Redding, California
     Underhill House II, Tamalpais Road, Berkeley, California (destroyed by fire, 1923)
     Bath House for Hearst Hall, University of California, Berkeley (destroyed, 1922)
1908 Tufts House II, Culloden Street, San Rafael, California
     Roman House, Laurel Place, San Rafael, California
     Atkinson House, Durant Avenue, Berkeley, California
     Havens House, Wildwood Gardens, Piedmont, California (later remodelled)
     Library, for Briggs House, Los Gatos, California
     Social Hall, Unity Church, Bancroft and Dana Streets, Berkeley, California (destroyed)
1909 Goodman House, Berkeley, California (project)
     Flagg Summer House, Orr's Creek, Ukiah, California (destroyed, 1921)
     Roos House, 3500 Jackson Street, San Francisco (with additions: living room, 1913; garage, 1916; dressing room, 1919; study 1926)
     Randolph School, 2700 Belrose Avenue, Berkeley, California (now a residence)
     Goslinsky House, 3233 Pacific Avenue, San Francisco
     Rowell House, Mildreda and Forthcamp Street, Fresno, California (destroyed)
     Fry House, 32nd Avenue, San Francisco
     Thomas House, Eldridge Avenue, Mill Valley, California
     Bernard Maybeck House II, Buena Vista Way, Berkeley, California (destroyed by fire, 1923)
     Randolph School, Shattuck and Berryman, Berkeley, California (project)
1910 Thomas Studio, Greenwood Terrace, Berkeley, California (destroyed by fire, 1923)
     Dyer House, Los Gatos, California
     Decker House, Buena Vista Way, Berkeley, California (project)
     Apartment house, Lombard and Leavenworth Street, San Francisco (project)
     Power House, 1526 Masonic Avenue, San Francisco
     Shuman House, Sycamore Avenue, San Mateo, California
     San Francisco Settlement Association Club Building, 2520 Folsom Street, San Francisco (destroyed)

First Church of Christ Scientist, Dwight Way and Bowditch Street, Berkeley, California
1911 Young House, Green Street, San Francisco (project)
Boynton House, Buena Vista Way, Berkeley, California (temporary house; permanent house completed by A. R. Monro; destroyed by fire, 1923; subsequently rebuilt)
Jockers House, La Loma Avenue, Berkeley, California
Strawberry Canyon Bath House, University of California, Berkeley (project)
Towart House, Buena Vista Way and La Loma Avenue, Berkeley, California (destroyed by fire, 1923)
Design for Canberra, Australia (competition project)
Courthouse, Dayton, Nevada (competition project)
Schwartz House, Oakland, California (project)
1911/
13 Field houses for the de Fermery Playground, Mosswood Park Playground, and Bella Vista Playground, Oakland, California
1912 Flagg House II, Shattuck Avenue, Berkeley, California
Runyon House, Los Molinas, California (project)
Irving House, Sonora, California
Pacific Unitarian Church and School, Dana and Allston Way, Berkeley, California (project)
Steps and walk, for Underhill House, Rose Path and Euclid Avenue, Berkeley, California
San Francisco City Hall (competition project)
1913 Alameda County Infirmary, California (competition project)
Scott House, Vine and Scenic Avenue, Berkeley, California (destroyed by fire, 1923)
Young House, 51 Sotelo Avenue, Forest Hills, San Francisco
Parons Memorial Lodge, Sierra Club, Tuolumne Meadows, California
1913/
15 Town plan and hotel for Brookings Lumber Company, Brookings, Oregon (as projects: cottages, YMCA Club, and school)
1914 McFarlan House, Hawthorne Terrace, Berkeley, California (destroyed by fire, 1923)
Chick House, Chabot Road, Berkeley, California
Kennedy Studio, Euclid Avenue, Berkeley, California (destroyed by fire, 1923; rebuilt and annex added, 1923)
1915 Palace of Fine Arts, Livestock Pavilion, and "Housing of Hoo-Hoo" for the Pacific Lumbermen's Association, *International Exposition*, San Francisco
Hunt House, Spruce Street, Berkeley, California (relocated to Domingo Avenue, Berkeley)
Mathewson House, La Loma and Buena Vista Way, Berkeley, California
Whitney House, Keith Avenue, Berkeley, California
1916 Greene House, Chabot Road, Berkeley, California (destroyed)
Erlanger House, 270 Castenada, Forest Hills, San Francisco
Jackson House remodelling, Orchard Lane, Berkeley, California
Bingham House, San Ysidro Road, Montecito, California
Owens House, Ashmount Avenue, Oakland, California (with additions, 1920)
1917 Loeb House, 275 Pacheco Street, San Francisco (with additions, 1922)
Gay House, 196 Clarendon Avenue, San Francisco
1918 Hanna Houses, Crockett, California (project)
Temporary Red Cross Building, Civic Center Plaza, San Francisco

General plan for Mills College, Oakland, California
1918/
19 Town plan for Clyde, California
1919 Garage and service rooms for Rancho Lomo, Live Oak, Sutter County, California
Forest Hills Association Club Building, 381 Magellan Avenue, San Francisco (with E. C. Young)
Freeman Memorial Seat, Tucson, Arizona (with the sculptor Beniamino Bufano)
1920 Greeley House additions, 19th Avenue, Bakersfield, California
Stevenson House, Hollywood, California (project)
Oakland Memorial, California (project)
O'Keefe House, San Jose, California (project)
Morse Community House, Del Monte Properties, Pebble Beach, California (project; with Mark Daniels)
Fagan House, Portola Drive, Woodside, California
National Conservatory of Music, California Branch (project)
1921 Wright House, Etna Street, Berkeley, California
San Carlos de Borromeo Mission reconstruction, Carmel, California (project)
Floete House, Pebble Beach, California (project; with Mark Daniels)
Landsberger House, Carmel, California, (project)
Resort buildings, Glen Alpine Springs, El Dorado County, California
Outdoor Theatre for the Pilgrimage Play, Hollywood, California
Peers House, Old Truckee Road, Colfax, California
Calkins House, Rosemont Street, Oakland, California
Clark House, Hawthorne Terrace, Berkeley, California
1922 Ford House, Pebble Beach, California
Thomas House additions and remodelling, Pebble Beach, California
School, Pebble Beach, California (project)
Camp Curry kitchen additions, Yosemite Valley, California
School building on site of the 1915 fair, San Francisco (project)
Manning House, Pebble Beach, California (project)
Beckett House, Berkeley, California (project)
1923 Phoebe Hearst Memorial Building, University of California, Berkeley (project)
Joralemon House and Studio, Southampton Avenue, Berkeley, California
Loy House, Ellsworth Street, Berkeley, California
Sturm House, East Orange Grove Avenue, Glendale, California (project)
Kennedy House, Redding, California (project)
McMurray House, LeConte Avenue, Berkeley, California (destroyed by fire)
1923/
30 General plan for Principia College, East St. Louis, Illinois
1924 Giesler House, Buena Vista Way, Berkeley, California
Burnett House, Hilgard Avenue, Berkeley, California
"Sack House" (Bernard Maybeck House III), Buena Vista Way, Berkeley, California
1924/
29 Auditorium-Gymnasium-Museum, University of California, Berkeley (project)
1925 Hearst Memorial Gymnasium, University of California, Berkeley (with Julia Morgan)
Peers Office Building, Colfax, California (project)
Duncan House, Santa Rosa Avenue, Sausalito, California (project)
de Angulo House, 2815 Buena Vista Way,

Berkeley, California
Legge House, Panoramic Way, Berkeley, California (project)
Library and Recreation Hall, Chevy Chase School, Maryland (project)
Anthony House I, 3405 Waverly Place, Los Angeles
Staniford House, Ocean View Drive, Oakland, California
Smith House, San Francisco (project)
1926 Packard Automobile Showrooms, Van Ness Avenue, San Francisco (with Powers and Ahnden)
Hemet Hotel, Hemet, California (project; with M. E. Manning)
Hollis House, La Loma Avenue, Berkeley, California (project)
1927 Anthony House II, 3347 Waverly Drive, Los Angeles
Associated Charities Building, Gough and Eddy Street, San Francisco
Woolsey House, Sunset Drive, Kensington, California
1928 Harrison Memorial Library, Carmel, California
Packard Automobile Showroom, Los Angeles (with John Parkinson and Donald B. Parkinson)
Sunday School for First Church of Christ Scientist, Dwight Way, Berkeley, California (with Henry Gutterson)
Pillsbury House, Alvarado Road, Berkeley, California
Packard Automobile Showroom, Harrison Street, Oakland, California (with Powers and Ahnden; destroyed, 1974)
Anthony House III, with studio and gardens, 3435 Waverly Place, Los Angeles (with Mark Daniels)
1930/
38 Revised general plan for Principia College, Elsah, Illinois (with Julia Morgan)
1931 Chapel, Principia College, Elsah, Illinois (with Julia Morgan)
Maybeck Cabin, Twain Harte, California
Tufts House III, Buena Vista Way, Berkeley, California
1932 Paul Elder Book Store, Geary Street, San Francisco
1933 Wallen Maybeck House I, Buena Vista Way, Berkeley, California
Annie Maybeck House, Buena Vista Way, Berkeley, California
1935 House, 2786 Buena Vista Way, Berkeley, California
1935/
37 Ninth Church of Christ Scientist, San Francisco (project)
1936 Wells Cabin, Fuller Road, Twain Harte, California
Cole Chemical Company, St. Louis (project)
1937 Staniford House, Fresno, California (project)
Women of Berkeley Building, University Avenue, Berkeley, California
Wallen Maybeck House II, Purdue Avenue, Kensington, California
1938 Bernard Maybeck Studio, Maybeck Twin Drive, Berkeley, California
1939 Morris House, Edgecroft Road, Berkeley, California (with Mark White)
1940 Cemetery, South San Francisco (project; with Julia Morgan)
Aikin House, Buena Vista Way, Berkeley, California

Publications:

By MAYBECK: books—*Hillside Building* (booklet) Berkeley, California 1907; *Palace of Fine Arts and Lagoon*, San Francisco 1915; *The Principia College Plans*, St. Louis 1927; articles—"The Planning of a University" in *Blue and Gold* (University of Califor-

Bernard Maybeck: First Church of Christ Scientist, Berkeley, California, 1910.

nia Yearbook, Berkeley), 1900; "A Dream That Might Be Realized" in *Merchants Association Review* (San Francisco), November 1903; "House of Mrs. Phoebe A. Hearst in Siskiyou County, California" in *Architectural Review* (Boston), January 1904; "Palace of Fine Arts" in *Transactions of the Commonwealth Club of California* (San Francisco), August 1915; "Fine Arts Palace Will Outlast Present Generation" in *Architect and Engineer* (New York), November 1915; "Reflections on the Grauman Metropolitan Theatre, Los Angeles" in *Architect and Engineer* (New York), June 1923.

On MAYBECK: books—*Five California Architects* by Esther McCoy, New York 1960; *Bernard Maybeck: Artisan, Architect, Artist* by Kenneth H. Cardwell, Santa Barbara, California 1977; articles—"San Francisco Bay Portfolio" by William W. Wurster in *Magazine of Art* (New York), December 1944; "Bernard Ralph Maybeck, Architect, Comes Into His Own" by Jean Murray Bangs in *Architectural Record* (New York), January 1948; "Bernard R. Maybeck" by Jean Harris in *AIA Journal* (Washington, D.C.), May 1951; "A Visit with Bernard Maybeck" by F.D. Nichols in *Journal of the Society of Architectural Historians* (Philadelphia), October 1952; "Churches" in *Architectural Record* (New York), December 1956; "Maybeck: The Work of a Grass-Roots Visionary" in *Interiors* (New York), January 1960; "Bernard Maybeck, San Francisco Genius" in *AIA Bulletin* (San Francisco), April 1960; "How to Embalm a Building" in *Architectural Forum* (New York), November 1967; "The Dream Made Permanent" in *Progressive Architecture* (New York), February 1968; "Bernard Ralph Maybeck and the Principia: Architecture as Philosophical Expression" by Robert M. Craig in *Journal of the Society of Architectural Historians* (Philadelphia), October 1972; "Bernard Maybeck: factory products for a romantic architecture" in *AC: International Asbestos Cement Review* (Zurich), October 1979; "Two Houses with links to the past" by Charles K. Gandee in *Architectural Record* (New York), March 1980; "Bernard Maybeck's Wallen II House" by Thomas Gordon Smith in *Fine Homebuilding* (Newtown, Connecticut), April/May 1981; "Bernard Maybeck: experiments with cellular concrete" by Richard B. Rice in *L.A. Architect* (Los Angeles), May 1981.

Bernard Maybeck is one of the pivotal figures in the regionalist architecture of the San Fancisco Bay area. He was also an architect in the tradition of the artist—versatile, colorful, inventive, eclectic, full of the whimsy that makes art joyous and loved.

Maybeck was born in 1862 in New York, the son of a German immigrant wood carver in whose shop he apprenticed. He trained as an architect in Paris at the Beaux-Arts, learning that architecture had to be rationally thought out, that it had to utilize not only modern structural techniques but also traditional forms and values. He returned to New York, to work for his classmates Carrere and Hastings, then went to Kansas City and then San Francisco, which was still struggling to be "eastern" in its culture. The work of Maybeck and others pointed to a different, more relaxed, mode of life.

His many skills, ranging from disciplined but broad-handed designer to disciplined craftsman, and his wide eclectic tastes, afforded him an extremely wide palette. He was at home with almost any style, from Richardson to neo-classic, to Byzantine, to rural farm, to medieval, to romanesque-or whatever else he chose. Moreover, he could combine them, and often did.

Maybeck's work is characterized by an emphasis on vertical space dramatized by mixtures of scale in component structured assemblages. He saw architecture as a way of surrounding people with beauty. He used contemporary materials and techniques, direct structural expressions, innovative planning, and he was a master at handling the elements of architecture. He combined decorative crafts with historic images. Often he combined vernacular forms with "low art"—commonplace building materials and pieces, such as a factory-made window sash. His work also had a great deal of wit. He favored the humorous juxtaposition of materials whose scales were mixed and therefore surprising.

His best known building is the Palace of Fine Arts for the *International Exposition* of 1915 in San Francisco. It has, over the years, become so much of a landmark that, when it was faced with demolition, a successful effort was made to restore it. More innovative and expressive of the "Bay Area Culture" is the First Church of Christ Scientist in Berkeley, dating from 1910. Its massive wood structure is reminiscent of Japanese wood architecture, but the building is strictly "Bay area." The Oakland Packard Showroom, in Moorish style, is a grand space with rich applied decoration, unlike the First Church where the structure is its own visual embellishment.

Many of Maybeck's 150 buildings are houses. After the great fire in Berkeley he designed a number of houses for quick construction, utilizing a system of dipping burlap bags in wet plaster. Nailed in place, in several layers, they hardened into a strong and permanent wall.

Maybeck's work remains a favorite of the public and of the profession—to a large extent because it is not polemic but, rather, a rich feast for the senses, masterfully composed.

—Paul Spreiregen

MAYEKAWA, Kunio.

Japanese. Born in Niigata City, 14 May 1905. Educated at the University of Tokyo, Department of Architecture, graduated 1928; trained in Le Corbusier's, *q.v.*, office, Paris, 1928-30, and Antonin Raymond's, *q.v.*, office, Tokyo, 1930-35. Married Miyo Miura in 1945. In private practice, Tokyo, since 1935. President, Japan Architects Association, 1959-62; Vice-President, International Union of Architects, 1965-69. Recipient: Knight of the Royal Vasa Order, Sweden, 1959; Award, 1962, and Grand Prix, 1968, Architectural Institute of Japan; Asahi Newspaper Prize for Contemporary Architecture, 1962; Auguste Perret Prize, International Union of Architects, 1963; Suomen Leijonan Ritarikunnan Luokan Komentajamerkin, Finland, 1967; Japan Art Academy Award, 1974. Member of the Architectural Institute of Japan. Honorary Member, Mexican Institute of Architects, and Peruvian Institute of Architects; Corresponding Member, Royal Institute of British Architects; Honorary Fellow, American Institute of Architects. Address: Kunio Mayekawa and Associates, 8 Honshio-cho, Shinjuku-ku, Tokyo, Japan.

Works:

1935 Morinaga Candy Store, Ginza, Tokyo, and 15 other locations
1939 Employees' quarters for Kako Commercial Bank, Shingai, China
Arimine and Wadagawa Electric Power Station, Toyama, Japan
1940 Kishi Memorial Hall, Tokyo
Social Welfare Hall, Tokyo
1948 Keio University Hospital, Tokyo
1950/
62 Twenty-four Branch Offices, Nihon sogo Bank, Japan
1952 Head Office, Nihon sogo Bank, Tokyo
1953 National Museum of Modern Art, Tokyo
Apartment building, Hiroshima
1954 Kanagawa Concert Hall and Library, Yokohama

Nishihara Engineering Office, Tokyo
1955 International House of Japan, Tokyo (with Junzo Sakakura and Junzo Yoshimura)
1956 Educational Centre, Fukishima, Japan
1957 Prefectural Office, Okayama, Japan
Hanezawa Apartment Building, Tokyo
Shuzo Kaikan (Brewers' Club Cooperative Building), Kochi, Japan
Nippon Petrochemical Industry Office, Kawasaki, Japan
San-ei shoji Head Office, Nagoya, Japan
1958 Multi-story apartment building, Harumi, Tokyo
Japanese Pavilion, *World's Fair,* Brussels
City Hall, Hirosaki, Japan
1959 Setagaya Community Centre, Tokyo
1960 Kyoto Hall
Setagaya Ward Office, Tokyo
Gakushuin University, Tokyo
1961 Metropolitan Festival Hall, Tokyo
National Diet Library, Tokyo (with Makato Tanaka and Mido Associates)
1962 Kanagawa Prefectural Youth Centre, Yokohama
Cultural Centre, Okayama, Japan
1963 Library, Gakushuin University, Tokyo
Hotel Yaesu Ryumeikan, Tokyo
Okayama Museum, Okayama, Japan
1964 Kinokuniya Book Store Building, Tokyo
Community Centre, Hirosaki, Japan
Setagaya Museum, Tokyo
Japanese Pavilion, *World's Fair,* New York
1965 Janome Sewing Machine Company Head Office, Tokyo
1966 Community Centre, Saitama, Japan
1967 Building for the Monopoly Corporation of Japan, Tokyo
1969 Kinokuniya Book Store interior, San Francisco
Setagaya Ward Secondary Office, Tokyo
1970 Steel Automobile Pavilion, *Expo 170,* Osaka
Fuji Visitors' Centre, Yamanashi, Japan
1971 Speed Skating Stadium for the Winter Olympic Games, Sapporo, Japan
City Hospital, Hirosaki, Japan
Saitama Prefectural Museum, Omiya, Japan

1973 Resort Club House for the Kinokuniya Book Store in Awaji-shima, Hyogo, Japan
1974 Tokio Kaijo Building (Tokyo Marine and Fire Insurance Company), Tokyo
City Educational Centre, Yokohama
1975 Metropolitan Art Museum, Tokyo
1976 City Museum, Hirosaki, Japan
1977 Prefectural Museum, Kumamoto, Japan
Museum of East Asian Art, Cologne
1978 Prefectural Museum, Yamanashi, Japan
1979 City Museum, Fukuoka, Japan
1980 Prefectural Museum, Miyagi, Japan
1982 Prefectural Theater, Kumamoto, Japan
Gakusyûin University Library, Tokyo
1983 Kunitachi College Concert Hall, Kunitachi, Japan
Municipal Office of Naka-ward, Yokohama, Japan

Publications:

By MAYEKAWA: articles—"Thoughts on Civilization and Architecture" in *Bauen und Wohnen* (Zurich), 1965; "Formes et Fonctions" in *Architecture: Formes et Fonctions* (Lausanne), no. 13, 1967; "L'Humanisme et l'Architecture" in *Architecture: Formes et Fonctions* (Lausanne), no. 14, 1968; "La Décadence Psychologique des Architectes" in *Architecture: Formes et Fonctions* (Lausanne), no. 15, 1969; "Hommage à Sakakura" in *L'Architecture d'Aujourd'hui* (Paris), October/November 1969; "Vom Tod der Architektur" in *Kolner Stadt-Anzeiger* (Cologne), 5 December 1977.

On MAYEKAWA: book—*Three Japanese Architects: Mayekawa, Tange, Sakakura* by Alfred Altherr, Teufen, Switzerland 1968; articles—"Kulturzentrum in Tokio" in *Baukunst und Werkform* (Nuremberg), March 1962; "The Tokyo Metropolitan Festival Hall" in *Progressive Architecture* (New York), April 1965; "Art Museum in Japan" in *Arts and Architecture* (Los Angeles), September 1965; "The Saitama Prefectural Cultural Hall" in

Kunio Mayekawa: Metropolitan Festival Hall, Tokyo, 1961.

The Japan Architect (Tokyo), September 1966; "Saitama Prefectural Museum" in *L'Architecture d'Aujourd'hui* (Paris), September 1973; "Tokyo Marine and Fire Insurance Company" in *The Japan Architect* (Tokyo), September 1974; "Tokyo Metropolitan Museum of Art" in *Kenchiku Bunka* (Tokyo), January 1977; "Metropolitan Museum of Art, Tokyo" in *The Japan Architect* (Tokyo), May 1977; "Kumamoto Prefectural Art Museum" in *The Japan Architect* (Tokyo), April 1978; "Museum of East Asian Art, Cologne" in *Baumeister* (Munich), March 1979; "New Annex of the National Museum of Western Art", and "Fukuoka Art Museum" in *The Japan Architect* (Tokyo), May 1980; "The Museum of East Asian Art in Cologne" in *Deutsche Bauzeitschrift* (Gutersloh, West Germany), September 1980; "Miyagi Prefectural Art Museum" in *The Japan Architect* (Tokyo), August 1982.

Bibliography: *Kunio Mayekawa: Father of Modern Japanese Architecture* by James P. Noffsinger, Monticello, Illinois 1979.

More than half a century has passed since I went to Paris for the first time in my life, to learn about "modern architecture." I arrived at the Gare du Nord in Paris ten years after the armistice. France seemed to be enjoying her post-war prosperity but with some anxiety about the destiny of Western civilization. Oswald Spengler had published *Der Untergang des Abendlandes,* and I was shocked by the pessimistic opinions of Paul Valéry at the Société des Nations round table conference in Geneva in 1925.

In the 18th century, during the time of the Industrial Revolution in England, the Occidental countries began to have great confidence in the rationalist way of thinking, which has since been the basis of all science and technology; and it is quite obvious that all the brilliant fruits of modern civilization have encouraged Western people to believe in a rosy future for humanity.

But the optimism of the early 20th century has been destroyed completely by two world wars, and people have been struck dumb with confusion—just like the Babylonians whose ambitious Tower of Babel was torn down by the hands of God as punishment for their arrogance in wanting to equal God by building a tower. Today, it must be the task of the architect to assemble the broken pieces of brick and rebuild the human environment from no other motivation than real human need.

—Kunio Mayekawa

Kunio Mayekawa is undeniably the father of modern Japanese architecture. He has the unique distinction of having worked directly with Le Corbusier from 1928 to 1930 and with Frank Lloyd Wright's disciple Antonin Raymond from 1930 to 1935. During this period Mayekawa developed a keen understanding of the International Style. While in Le Corbusier's atelier, he worked on the Villa Savoye and the Pavillon Suisse, two of Corbu's most sophisticated and acclaimed projects. The experience left an indelible mark on his own work.

The Harumi Apartment Complex of 1958 is clearly indebted to the concepts developed for the Unité d'habitation at Marseilles by Le Corbusier. At Harumi, Mayekawa introduced to Japan the skip-floor apartment concept, while pioneering the use of reinforced concrete. Mayekawa first began using exposed concrete before the Second World War, and he continued to refine its use after the war in such outstanding projects as the Tokyo Metropolitan Festival Hall and the Gakushuin University buildings. In each case the articulation of architectural mass and the precision of detail reinforced the strength and clarity of the design.

Today, looking back over fifty years of architectural practice since his graduation from Tokyo University in 1928, Mayekawa draws a distinction between "pre-industrial architecture and post-industrial architecture," emphasizing the gradual shift from natural materials like stone and wood to man-made materials like steel, concrete and plastic. A pioneer of exposed concrete, Mayekawa has said of his own work, "I think the most outstanding example is the Tokyo Metropolitan Festival Hall."

A landmark building that integrated a cluster of theaters, performance and exhibition spaces into a unified architectural statement, the Tokyo Festival Hall, completed over two decades ago, remains one of the most influential and well conceived works of modern Japanese architecture. The heavy lintel which wraps around the interlocking theatrical spaces is reminiscent of Le Corbusier's bold entrance canopy to the Palace of the Assembly building in Chandigarh (also designed in the late 1950s). An unfortunate footnote to Japan's industrial growth is the destruction of the concrete at the Festival Hall due to the air pollution. Mayekawa laments, "We had to abandon this type of finish because of the air in Tokyo."

In the final analysis Kunio Mayekawa remains a creative artist and a master of his craft who has influenced nearly three generations of modern architects beginning with Kenzo Tange, who worked for Mayekawa from 1938 to 1942. Today Mayekawa continues to strive for architectural excellence: "I wish to create my architecture as the expression of my identity. I do not want to throw myself away as a merchandise in the market of the capitalist society!"

—Michael Franklin Ross

McCUE, Gerald Mallon.

American. Born in Woodland, California, 5 December 1928. Educated at the University of California, Berkeley, 1947-52, A.B. 1951, M.A. 1952. Married Barbara Walrond in 1951; children: Scott, Mark, and Kent. Partner, with Joseph P. Milano, in Milano and McCue, Berkeley, 1953-59; Principal, McCue and Associates, Berkeley, 1963-70; Principal, with David C. Boone and Frank Tomsick, McCue, Boone and Tomsick, San Francisco, 1970-76. Since 1976, Consulting Principal, MBT Associates, San Francisco. Member of the faculty, University of California, Berkeley, 1954-76: Professor of Architecture and Urban Design, 1966-76, and Chairman of the Department, 1966-71; Professor of Architecture and Urban Design since 1976, Associate Dean, 1976-80, and Dean since 1980, Harvard Graduate School of Design, Cambridge, Massachusetts. Exhibitions: *The Art of San Francisco,* San Francisco Museum of Art, 1962; *The Work of Gerald McCue and Associates,* University of California, Berkeley, 1966; *Architectural Work of McCue Boone Tomsick,* Redwood Association Gallery, San Francisco, 1972; *San Francisco Group Show,* California State Polytechnic University, Pomona, 1978, toured California. Recipient: Masonry Institute Award, 1963, 1964; National Design Merit Award, United States Department of Health, Education and Welfare, 1966; Governor's Honor Award, California, 1966; Prestressed Concrete Institute Award, 1968; National Council of Architectural Registration Boards Award, 1969; American Institute of Planners Award, Northern California Chapter, 1970; American Institute of Steel Construction Award, 1971; Edward C. Kemper Award, American Institute of Architects, 1971; United States General Services Administration Award, 1973; *Architectural Record* Award, 1973; Beautification Award, San Francisco Chamber of Commerce, 1976, 1977; *Print Magazine* Award, 1978. M.A.: Harvard University, 1977. Member, Lambda Alpha Honorary Land Economics Society, 1968. Fellow, American Institute of Architects, 1969. Address: Department of Architecture and Urban Design, Gund Hall, Harvard University, Cambridge, Massachusetts 02138, U.S.A.

Works:

1960 88-Inch Cyclotron, for the Lawrence Radiation Laboratory, University of California, Berkeley
1961 Stauffer Chemical Company Research Building, Richmond California
1963 Dow Chemical Company Research Center, Walnut Creek, California
1966 Fire House II, Berkeley, California
      Marina Master Plan and Harbormaster's Building, Berkeley Marina, California
1967 Chevron Research Laboratory, Richmond, California
1968 Gerald McCue House, Berkeley, California
      Milligan House, Galleon Ranch Road, Sea Ranch, California
      Ames Research Center, Moffett Field, California
1969 Life Sciences Building, Mills College, Oakland, California
1970 Djerassi House, Santa Cruz Mountains, California
      Alza Headquarters, Palo Alto, California
      12th and 19th Street/Broadway Subway Stations, Oakland, California, for the Bay Area Rapid Transit District
1972 Syntex Corporation Laboratories, Palo Alto, California
1975 Epstein House, Orinda, California
1976 IBM Santa Teresa Computer Programming Center, San Jose, California
1978 Oakes College, University of California at Santa Cruz

Publications:

By McCUE: books—*Creating the Human Environment,* with others, Urbana, Illinois 1970; *Interaction of Building Components During Earthquakes,* Cambridge, Massachusetts 1975; *Architectural Design of Building Components for Earthquakes,* Cambridge, Massachusetts 1978; *Building Response and Component Designs: An Enclosure Wall Study,* Cambridge, Massachusetts 1978; *IBM's Santa Teresa Laboratory,* Cambridge, Massachusetts 1978; articles—"Implications for ACSA of New Approach to Architectural Education" in *Journal of Architectural Education* (Washington, D.C.), August/December 1966; "The Role of the College of Environmental Design at Berkeley as a Training Ground for Architects" in *Architectural and Engineering News* (Philadelphia), June 1968; "Mendelsohn as a Teacher" in *Eric Mendelsohn,* Berkeley, California 1969; "Report of the AIA Committee on the Future of the Profession" in *Journal of Architectural Education* (Washington, D.C.), April 1970; "The Social Environment for Planning and Design" in *The Future Role of Professionals in the Built Environment,* Cambridge, Massachusetts 1974; "The Arch: An Appreciation" in *AIA Journal* (Washington, D.C.), November 1978.

On McCUE: book—*By Their Own Design,* edited by Abby Suckle, New York and St. Albans, Hertfordshire 1980; articles—"The Talent for the Sixties" and "Cyclotron in California" in *Architectural Forum* (New York), August 1961; "Roof of Red Cedar" in *Architectural Design* (London), March 1968; "McCue Boone Tomsick" in *Architectural Forum* (New York), April 1973; "Work by McCue Boone Tomsick" in *Architecture + Urbanism* (Tokyo), July 1977; "IBM's Santa Teresa Laboratory" in *Architectural Record* (New York), August 1977; "Oakes College, Santa Cruz" in *Baumeister* (Munich), November 1978; "U.C. Santa Cruz" in *AIA Journal* (Washington, D.C.), August 1979; "Silicon Style: IBM, Santa Teresa" in *Architectural Review* (London), May 1981.

Gerald McCue has combined an active career in

architectural practice with theoretical and practical work as a professor and researcher; he has, as well, maintained a high degree of involvement with professional organizations. His design theory and architectural practice are closely related. His primary aim is, and has been, to further the aims and the continued development of the modern movement in architecture. In McCue's theory and practice, this has involved a striving for a number of objectives. The prime objective is to utilize the most advanced technologies and methods of construction available. Ancillary objectives are the creation of forms that show user or observer the nature of the structure, the materials of construction, and the methods of assembly. These objectives are accomplished by the creation of prototypic designs that establish patterns of honest and direct expression.

McCue's career has progressed from following the classic prototypes of the modern movement to the production of new prototypes. In his view, new prototypes are necessary when neither Miesian exposed steel frames nor Corbusian concrete frames provide the best synthesis between activity enclosing space form and the materials and means of construction supporting it. His rocket testing station at Ames Research Center, Moffett Field, California, is an example of a contemporary and original expression of the Corbusian prototype. It follows what McCue calls a "homogeneous model," where structure and finish—whether wall, floor, columns, etc.—are as homogeneous as possible. This achieves, from the viewpoint of the modern movement, the fusion between modern building technology and honesty.

The IBM Santa Teresa Computer Programming Center near San Jose, California, serves as an example of a new prototype. It follows what McCue calls a "heterogeneous model" in that there is no consistency in structure and finish—whether walls, floor, columns, etc.—between the inside and the outside of the structure. Here honesty does not mean a mapping of inside unto outside, or vice versa; thus, the "honesty" of the modern movement undergoes some redefinition. To be honest now means that outside and inside both are contemporary and readable but that one is not readable from the other. This is a return to the concept of a façade that is separable from the interiorscape of a building complex.

The "heterogenous model" as new prototype reveals a number of converging forces on contemporary versions of the modern movement in architecture. Many people find the modern construction methods and materials displeasing and alienating, and for that, if for no other reason, desire a certain amount of artifice in the constructed environment. The distance between façade and interior may provide that degree of artifice. The current concern for security and defensibility of private space makes forms that demand high consistency between interior and exterior seem both psychologically and physically insecure. This often cited contemporary "narcissism" bespeaks a division between person and persona: interior and exterior. The realities of truly contemporary construction methods also make the "homogeneous model" a luxury few client can afford. Interior finishes can be made much more

cheaply from materials that are not suitable for exposure to the weather.

An architecture that is truly modern will forcefully symbolize a reading of the modern condition. McCue's recent work reflects an alienated, narcissistic, security conscious, and fragile postindustrial society of corporate and governmental gigantism. I wonder if different clients or a fundamentally nonmodern design philosophy might have given rise to a different reflection.

—Joseph B. Juhasz

McGRATH, Raymond.

British. Born in Sydney, New South Wales, Australia, 7 March 1903; emigrated to England, 1926, and to Ireland, 1940. Educated at Fort Street School, Sydney; University of Sydney (University Medal for English Verse, 1926), B.Arch. (first-class honours) 1926; awarded Wentworth Travel Fellowship, 1926; Research Student, Clare College, Cambridge, England, 1927-29. Served as an Official War Artist, England, 1939-40. Married Mary Catherine Crozier in 1930; children: Norman and Jennifer. In private practice, London, 1930-39; worked in the Office of Public Works, Dublin, 1940-68: Principal Architect, 1948-68; returned to private practice, Dublin, 1968 until his death in 1977. Consultant Architect, British

Gerald McCue: Epstein House, Orinda, California, 1975.

Raymond McGrath: Fischer's Restaurant, London, 1932.

Broadcasting Corporation, London, 1932. Professor, Royal Hibernian Academy, Dublin, 1968-77. Member of the 20th Century Group, and of the MARS (Modern Architecture Research) Group, London, in the 1930s. President: Royal Hibernian Academy, 1977. Fellow, Royal Institute of British Architects, Royal Institute of Architects of Ireland, and Society of Industrial Artists. *Died* (in Dublin) *2 December 1977.*

Works:

1928 Finella House remodelling and interiors, Queen's Road, Cambridge
1930 General Electric Company Stand, *Building Exhibition*, Olympia, London
1932 Fischer's Restaurant, New Bond Street, London
Studio, Broadcasting House, London
Rudderbar House (project)
1937 St. Anne's Hill (house), Chertsey, Surrey
Kingstone Store, Belgrave Gate, Leicester
1938 James Clark and Sons Stand, *Building Exhibition*, Olympia, London
1939 Chemical Factory, Buckinghamshire House, Hampstead, London
Airport Hotel (project)
Keene House, Carrygate, Leicestershire
1950 Cenotaph, Leinster Lawn, Dublin
Irish Embassy conversion, 17 Grosvenor Place, London

President of Ireland's House restoration, Dublin
1964 Kennedy Memorial Concert Hall, Dublin (project)
Dublin Castle restoration
1970 Matthew Gallagher Art Gallery, Royal Hibernian Academy, Dublin
1974 St. Anne's (house), Carrickmines, County Dublin
1979 New Headquarters for the Royal Hibernian Academy, Dublin

Publications:

By McGRATH: books—*Twentieth Century Houses.* London 1934; *Glass in Architecture and Decoration,* with Al Frost, London 1937, 1961; articles—"El Hospital de la Santa Cruz" in *Architectural Review* (London), May 1929; "Light Opera" in *Architectural Review* (London), January 1930; "Looking into Glass" in *Architectural Review* (London), January 1932; "Glass: An Integrally Decorative Material for the Architect and for the Industrial Designer" in *Country Life* (London), September 1941; "Australian Early Colonial" in *Architectural Review* (London), July 1948; numerous articles in *The Bell* (Dublin), 1940-54; "Rhapsody in Black Glass," interview, by Brian Hanson, in *Architectural Review* (London), July 1977.

On McGRATH: articles—"Finella: A House for Mansfield D. Forbes" by A.C. Frost in *Architectural Review* (London), December 1929; "Architects of Europe Today: Raymond McGrath, England" in *Pencil Points* (New York), June 1936; "A House in Surrey" in *RIBA Journal* (London), January 1938; "Chemical Factory, Buckinghamshire, England" in *Architectural Record* (New York), February 1940; "Keene House, Carrygate, Leicestershire" by Christopher Hussey in *Country Life* (London), August 1942; "Irish Embassy" in *Architectural Review* (London), May 1953; "Ireland's Modern Buildings" in *Architects' Journal* (London), September 1966; article in *Irish Builder and Engineer* (Dublin), 19 February 1972; "House at Carrickmines" in *Build Ireland* (Dublin), July 1975; "Raymond McGrath, 1903-1977" by David Saunders in *Architecture Australia* (Melbourne), April/May 1978; "'Simple Intime' in the work of Raymond McGrath" by Alan Powers in *Thirties Society Journal*, no. 3, 1982.

Raymond McGrath remains one of the great enigmas of architecture, in particular Irish architecture. Arriving in Ireland in 1940, at the age of thirty-seven, to take up a public appointment, he experienced not an architectural consciousness, as had been his good fortune in England, but a newly emerging literary consciousness born out of Ireland's declared policy of neutrality during World War II. John Betjeman, later Poet Laureate, was in Dublin then. So was Maurice Craig, the historian, who was later to become McGrath's great friend. The ambience of

Dublin suited him admirably, for he was a splendid writer as well as architect. He had published in England. His essay "The history of Architecture, the History of the Window," for his book *Glass in architecture and Decoration*, written with Al Frost in 1937, remains one of the finest expositions of architecture from 1800 to that year.

McGrath's writing talents were soon in evidence in Dublin. In the leading literary journal of the time, *The Bell*, published by Sean O Faolain and Peader O'Donnell, he wrote as well as illustrated many articles on architecture and the arts. He became intimately associated with the Royal Hibernian Academy, first as a Full Member, then as Professor of Architecture, and finally as Presiden—the first Architect/President since its founder, Francis Johnston.

McGrath had arrived, no less auspiciously, in England in 1926 and while undertaking post-graduate studies in Cambridge met his first client, Mansfield Forbes. The conversion of the Victorian house Finella for Forbes in 1928 has become legendary. Although a general awareness of the International Style was just being felt in England, it was clearly in evidence in Amyas Connell's High and Over house of 1929. Connell, from New Zealand, was later joined by his fellow countryman Basil Ward, and later still by Colin Lucas, to form a practice that is generally credited with the introduction of the International Style in England. Finella, however, was still an architecture of surfaces. But it did bring McGrath into contact with many other innovators, including the artists Henry Moore, Jacob Epstein, and Paul Nash and the architects Wells Coates and Serge Chermayeff.

The International Style, then well established in Germany, Holland, and France, became widely known in England through the 1932 essays of the *Architectural Review*. McGrath, fresh from Finella, was now working on Fischer's Restaurant, London, and, in conjunction with Coates and Chermayeff, on interiors for the BBC. These projects, together with a house, were illustrated in *Architectural Review*. His work began to have a significant effect on furniture and interior design, particularly his work in tubular steel and plywood. But it was his capacity to handly his projects as a series of planes using curved forms, neon lighting, and glass, the elements of Art Deco, that set McGrath apart at this time. And his collaboration with two conventional photographers, Dell and Wainwright, to illustrate his interiors, was a significant contribution to the development of architectural photography.

In 1934, after many years of preparation, he published *Twentieth Century Houses*. His best-known work, St. Anne's Hill, Chertsey, Surrey, a reinforced concrete house with landscaping by Christopher Tunnard, was completed in 1937. McGrath was now practicing in the company of many emigrés who were involved in firmly establishing the International Style in England. They included the Tecton and Mars groups, Gropius, Breuer, Moholy-Nagy, and Mendelsohn, as well as the native-born F.R.S. Yorke, Maxwell Fry, and Denys Lasdun. But, in 1940, rather than continue as a war artist, like many of his contemporaries, McGrath chose instead to accept an official appointment in Dublin as an architect with the Office of Public Works. Apart from the resulting cultural isolation, this appointment, by its nature, precluded private practice. He became Principal Architect in 1948, a post he held until 1968.

His works in Ireland include the unrealized projects for the Kennedy Memorial Concert Hall and a new headquarters for the Royal Hibernian Academy. His one piece of domestic architecture in Ireland, St. Anne's, Carrickmines, County Dublin, is very reminiscent of the earlier work, St. Anne's Hill, Chertsey.

McGrath's life was one of architectural and intellectual fulfillment, which, for its second half at least, seemed undeminished by the apparent indifference with which he was treated.

—Kevin Spencer

McHARG, Ian Lennox.

American. Born in Clydebank, Scotland, 20 November 1920; emigrated to the United States, 1954: naturalized, 1960. Educated at Harvard University, Cambridge, Massachusetts, 1946-50, B.Landscape Arch. 1949, M.Landscape Arch. 1950, M.City Planning 1951. Served as a Major in the British Army, commanding parachute troops, 1939-46. Married Pauline Crena de Iongh in 1947 (died, 1974); children: Alistair and Malcolm; married Carol Ann Smyser in 1977. Planner, Department of Health for Scotland, 1950-54. Since 1954, Professor of City Planning and Chairman of the Department of Landscape Architecture and Regional Planning, University of Pennsylvania, Philadelphia. Since 1963, Partner, with David A. Wallace, *q.v.*, William H. Roberts, and Thomas A. Todd, Wallace McHarg Roberts and Todd, Philadelphia; offices subsequently established in Los Angeles and Miami. Distinguished Science Lecturer, Brookhaven National Laboratory, Long Island, New York, 1968; Horace Albright Memorial Lecturer, University of California, Berkeley, 1969; Danz Lecturer, University of Washington, Seattle, 1971; Brown and Haley Lecturer, University of Puget Sound, Tacoma, Washington, 1972; Green Visiting Professor, University of British Columbia, Vancouver, 1974. Member, Committee on the Profession, American Society of Landscape Architects; Member of the Committee, White House Conference on Children and Youth; Member, United States Committee on Public Works. Recipient: Bradford Williams Medal, American Society of Landscape Architects, 1968, 1976; Morrison Medal, North American Wildlife Management Association, 1971; Creative Arts Award, Brandeis University, Waltham, Massachusetts, 1972; Allied Professions Medal, American Institute of Architects, 1972. D.H.L.: Amherst College, Massachusetts, 1970; D.H.: Lewis and Clarke College, Portland, Oregon, 1970; Bates College, Lewiston, Maine, 1978. Fellow, American Society of Landscape Architects, and Institute of Landscape Architects. Honorary Member, American Institute of Architects. Honorary Fellow, Royal Institute of British Architects. Address: Wallace, McHarg, Roberts and Todd, 1737 Chestnut Street, Philadelphia, Pennsylvania 19103, U.S.A.

Works:

1964 Plan for the valleys of Baltimore County
      Inner Harbor and Municipal Center, Baltimore
1966 Plan for Lower Manhattan (with others)
1967 Landscape plan for Washington, D.C.
1968 Richmond Parkway, Staten Island, New York (project)
1969 Ecological study for Minneapolis. Paul
1970 Metro Center, Baltimore (project)
      Skippack Ecological Study, Montgomery County, Pennsylvania
1972 Plan for the center of Los Angeles
1973 Plan for Northwest Baltimore (with I.M. Pei and Partners)
      Regional transportation plan for Denver
1974 Development plan for Amelia Island, Florida
1975 Pardisan Environmental Park, Tehran (project)
      I-95 Route Selection Study, Princeton, New Jersey
1976 Capitol Building, Washington, D.C. (project)

Publications:

By McHARG: book—*Design with Nature*, New York 1969; articles—"The Functions of Open Space Housing" in *The Architects Yearbook*, London 1955; "Can We Afford Open Space" in *The Architects' Journal* (London), 8-15 March 1956; "The Courthouse Concept" in *Architectural Record* (New York),

September 1957; "Ecology of the City" in *AIA Journal* (Washington, D.C.), December 1962; "Man and Environment" in *The Urban Condition*, edited by Leonard Duhl, New York 1963; "Ecological Determinism" in *The Future Environments of North America*, edited by Fraser Darling and John P. Milton, New York 1966; "Blight or a Noble City" in *Audubon Magazine* (New York), February/March 1966; "An Ecological Method of Landscape Architecture" in *Landscape Architecture* (Louisville, Kentucky), January 1967; "The Place of Nature in the City of Man" in *Challenge for Survival*, edited by Pierre Bansereau and V.A. Weadock, New York 1970; "Towards Comprehensive Ecological Planning" in *Plan* (Johannesburg), no.10, 1973.

On McHARG: articles—in *Life* (New York), 15 August 1969; in *Time* (New York), 10 October 1969; in *Fortune* (New York), February 1970; "A Sensible Plan for Future Development" in *Reader's Digest* (New York), August 1970; "Ian McHarg" by Dennis Fahrney in the *Wall Street Journal* (New York), 30 August 1971; article in the *Atlantic Monthly* (Boston), January 1974; "Planning for the Brave New World" by Roger Yee in *Progressive Architecture* (New York), June 1974; "Ian McHarg: Champion for Design with Nature" by Constance Holden in *Landscape Architecture* (Louisville, Kentucky), March 1977; "God and Man's Continuing Subjugation of Nature" in *Building Design* (London), 15 June 1979; "The Garden as a Metaphysical Symbol" in *RSA Journal* (London), February 1980.

*

With his book *Design with Nature*, Ian McHarg established himself as America's foremost landscape architect to stress the relationship of ecology to human land use. He believes that, prior to any development, the study of an area's ecological balances is imperative, if the impact of humanity on nature is to be better ascertained and minimized. In exhorting land use planners and developers to confront the totality of the landscape (and the implications of destruction of even a portion of that landscape), McHarg delights conservationists and greatly expands the province of traditional landscape architecture.

Viewing human actions as those of "a blind witless, low-brow, anthropocentric clod who inflicts lesions upon the earth," he asserts that people must act in harmony with nature rather than ignore it. Too much of our civilization has been constructed in spite of nature and has led to both human and natural catastrophe. Using such stunning examples as the flooding of the New Jersey shore, McHarg reveals the senseless waste that results from humanity's blindness to the needs of nature. He persuasively argues for an intensely ecological approach to development, one that would reconcile environmental and human needs.

McHarg has had the opportunity to implement his ideas on various projects. He employs a strict methodology that identifies flood plains, erosion-prone areas, frigid sites, soil drainage capacity, water table polluting areas, unstable bedrock, animal trails, flora patterns, outstanding scenery, historic structures, etc. on a series of overlapping maps. Through a process of elimination—as colored overlay is piled atop colored overlay—the area best suited for development emerges as the white portion of the map. From these pinpointed areas McHarg is able to make his final recommendations with regard to the proposed project.

Because it is such a pure, apparently deterministic approach, McHarg has been criticized for expounding mechanical solutions to difficult problems. Critics note his inability to deal with local political and business situations and point to the frequency with which political interests have compromised McHarg's theoretical solutions. His plan for northwest Baltimore certainly suffered this fate. A sprawling open valley, which McHarg had recommended remain intact while developments occurred on adjoining hills and plateaus, is now the victim of urban sprawl, the result of far too many "practical" decisions. That travesties of this sort occur comments more upon American political practice that upon McHarg's design procedures. To suggest that McHarg should encompass political considerations within his project plans is to completely misunderstand the man. He is a man with a purpose, a message to preach, and a plan to unfold. He expresses the need, and reveals a means, for people to develop in harmony with nature; the implementation of his schemes demands communal sanity. He is a teacher, who looks toward the long-term results of education rather than the short-term accomplishments of compromise.

—Don J. Hibbard

McINTYRE, (Robert) Peter.

Australian. Born in Melbourne, Victoria, 24 August 1927. Educated at Trinity Grammar School, Melbourne, matriculated 1944; University of Melbourne, 1944-50, B.Arch. 1950; Royal Melbourne Technical College, Dip.Arch. 1953; University of Melbourne, Dip.Town and Regional Planning 1955. Married the architect Dione Beatrice Cohen in 1954; children: Robert, Jane, Susan, and Anne. Worked in the office of his father, the architect Robert H. McIntyre, Melbourne, 1947, and for Stephenson and Turner, and Buchan Laird and Buchan, Melbourne, 1948; in private practice, Melbourne, 1950-53; Partner, with John and Phyllis Murphy and Kevin Borland, in Borland, Murphy and McIntyre, Melbourne, 1953-56; Partner, Peter and Dione McIntyre, Melbourne, 1956-61. Principal of McIntyre McIntyre and Partners Pty. Ltd., Melbourne (firm formed by consolidation of practices of Peter and Robert H. McIntyre), 1961-80, and McIntyre Partnership, Melbourne, since 1980. Director, International Planning Collaborative, Melbourne, since 1972 (partners: George Connor and Donald Wolbrink). Tutor, School of Architecture, University of Melbourne, 1951-53; Lecturer, Royal Melbourne Institute of Technology, 1957-60; Member of the Faculty of Architecture and Building, University of Melbourne, 1968-72. Founder and Director, *Architects' Revue,* University of Melbourne, 1948-54; Editor, with Robin Boyd, *Cross-Section,* Melbourne, 1951-53. Councillor, Royal Victorian Institute of Architects, 1963; President, Victorian Chapter, Royal Australian Institute of Architects, 1969-71; President, Royal Australian Institute of Architects, 1973-75. Exhibitions: *Olympic Pool Competition,* 1950; Academy of Science, Canberra, 1956; *High Court of Australia* travelling exhibition, 1972. Recipient: First Prize, Olympic Swimming Stadium Competition, Melbourne, 1953; Housing Service Award, 1954, Robin Boyd Environmental Award, 1975, Architectural Projects Award, 1975, Bronze Medal, 1977, 1978, New South Wales Chapter Award, 1980, and National Award, 1983, Royal Australian Institute of Architects; Sir James Barrett Memorial Medal, Town and Country Planning Institute, Melbourne, 1974; Special Recognition Award, American Society of Landscape Architects, Hawaii, 1968. Life Fellow, Royal Australian Institute of Architects, Royal Melbourne Institute of Technology, and Royal Australian Planning Institute. Associate, Royal Institute of British Architects. Officer, Order of Australia (A.O.), 1982. Address: McIntyre Partnership, 2 Hodgson Street, Kew, Victoria 3101, Australia.

Works:

1953 Beulah Hospital, Victoria

Peter McIntyre: McIntyre Sea House, Mornington, Victoria, 1979.

1954 Brunt House, The Belvedere, Kew, Victoria
    Snelleman House, 40 Kean Street, East Ivanhoe, Victoria
1954/
  56 Olympic Swimming Stadium, Melbourne (with Kevin Borland and John and Phyllis Murphy)
1955 Stephenson House, 42 Kean Street, East Ivanhoe, Victoria
    McIntyre House, 2 Hodgson Street, Kew, Victoria
1958 Shaw House, Eglington Street, Kew, Victoria
1959 Seymour Swimming Pool (project)
1961 McIntyre Ski Lodge, Mt. Buller, Victoria
    Peter Office Building, La Trobe Street, Melbourne
1962 Auski Ski Hire, Mt. Buller, Victoria
1963 Butt House, 16 View Road, Vermont, Victoria
    Molony's Ski Hire, Falls Creek, Victoria
1964 Ski Club of Victoria Apartments, Mt. Buller, Victoria
    Fairchild Factory, Croydon, Victoria
1965 Collingwood Football Club Grandstand, Victoria
    Loveridge Country Hardware Store, Berwick, Victoria
1966 Baldwin Country House, Birmingham Road, Mooroolbark, Victoria

1967 Ski Flats, Falls Creek, Victoria
1968 Morgan House, 9 Wheriside Avenue, Toorak, Victoria
1969 George Bass Motel, Lakes Entrance, Victoria
    Offices, 150 Lonsdale Street, Melbourne
    Motel, West Wyalong, New South Wales
1970 Offices, 180 William Street, Melbourne
1971 Ashley House, St. Kilda Road, Melbourne
    Offices, 450 St. Kilda Road, Melbourne
    Offices, 444 St. Kilda Road, Melbourne
1972 Bayside Shopping Centre, Frankston, Victoria
1973 A.M.P. Society Offices, Shepparton, Victoria
1973/
  74 Melbourne Strategy Plan
1974 Cadbury-Schweppes House, St. Kilda Junction, Melbourne
    Mt. Buller Planning Scheme, Victoria
    Hardies Offices, Braybrook, Victoria
1976 Apartments, Dryburgh Street, North Melbourne
1977 Knox City Shopping Centre, Stud Road, Knoxfield, Victoria
    Park Circle Shopping Centre, South Melbourne
1978 Australia Pacific House, 136 Exhibition Street, Melbourne
    Rob's Restaurant, Bulleen, Victoria

1979 The Jam Factory Shopping Centre, South
     Yarra, Melbourne
     National Bank, Bendigo, Victoria
     McIntyre Sea-House, Mornington, Victoria
     McIntyre Offices, Hawthorn, Victoria
1980 Windsor Hotel alterations, Melbourne
1981 Dinner Plain Alpine Village, Victoria
1982 Sunrise Beach Resort, Byron Bay, New South
     Wales
1984 Omski Ski Lodge, Mount Buller, Victoria

Publications:

On McINTYRE: book—*Old Continent— New Building: Contemporary Australian Architecture,* edited by Leon Paroissien and Michael Griggs, Darlinghurst, New South Wales 1983; articles—"R. P. McIntyre, 1973/74 Federal President, RAIA" in *Architecture in Australia* (Sydney), August 1973; "Knox City Shopping Centre" in *Architect* (Melbourne), February 1978; "Parliament House Competition" in *Transition* (St. Kilda, Victoria), November 1979; "Preserved for posterity" by Jane Hutchings in *Building Design* (London), 30 November 1979; "Jam Factory Shopping Centre" in *Architecture Australia* (Melbourne), January 1980; "Melbourne Olympics 1956" in *Architect* (Melbourne), June 1980; "Modern Australian Architecture," special issue of *Process:Architecture* (Tokyo), March 1981; "Houses in Australia," special issue of *Architecture Australia* (Melbourne), May 1983.

*

The objective of my work has been to find innovative solutions to architectural problems and at the same time to seek an appropriate emotional response from the user of the building and the community.

—Peter McIntyre

*

If Peter McIntyre were asked to summarize his design philosophy in one word, it would be "innovation." His practice has grown rapidly since he joined the family firm in the mid-1950s. The firm's output has been erratic in quality, reflecting a clientele with a wide range of attitudes to architecture.

When McIntyre was designing his first houses, Harry Seidler's book on architecture in Australia had just been published, and was having a profound influence on the thinking of young graduates. The same forces that influenced Seidler are, to some extent, reflected in McIntyre's own early work. There is the same interest in expressing structure and the same preoccupation with simple forms and direct geometry. The crowning achievement of this early period is the competition winning swimming complex for the Olympic Games held in Melbourne in 1956. The concept is remarkably simple. The major compression members are raked to accommodate seating on each side of the pool. They are tied together by roof trusses, the depth of which is reduced by the counterbalancing tension forces, and the whole is braced by delicate tension rods which are exposed on the exterior.

McIntyre had used the principle of tension structures before, in the Bush Nursing hospital at Beulah and in his own house at Kew. A number of his other houses of the same period are also noteworthy: like the works of many contemporary Australian architects (notably Robin Boyd and Roy Grounds, also from Melbourne) each house is an exercise emphasizing one aspect of architecture, such as shape, structure, volume, space, finish, or geometry.

During the 1960s the office of McIntyre and McIntyre turned its attention to commercial work, particularly low-cost, low-rental office buildings, pubs, and the development of winter sports facilities in the snow country just a few hours drive north of Melbourne. During the past decade or so, the firm has been engaged with Donald Wolbrink in the preparation of the City of Melbourne Strategy Plan—the first of its kind in Australia. The main feature of the plan is that it lays down the key strategies and goals for future growth without dictating the physical form it will take. The constraints of form are laid down in Action Plans that are developed for specific areas as and when required. It is unfortunate that rather than acting to prevent unrestrained development in the central business area, the strategy plan has merely stretched the ingenuity of commercial property developers who have brought every political, legal, and financial pressure on the city council to delay its adoption.

Most recently, Peter McIntyre has won acclaim for two buildings. Park Circle Shopping Centre is a small collection of single-storey shops built around a tiny public open space. The whole is tied together by a canopy of glass supported by a steel trussed folded plate. The construction is simple and finishes are cheap, indicating that this is a temporary use for a valuable development site. A delightful place to be in fine weather.

Knox City is a regional shopping centre and bus terminal located on the edge of metropolitan Melbourne. In external appearance and finish this building stands like a stronghold warding off the surrounding sea of cars and offering protection to the shopper. This image of a crusader castle is strengthened by the hollow concrete barbican guarding the covered way to the main entry. The interior is an enclosed pedestrian street two storeys high lined with small shops. At each end there is a department store. Attached to one side of the street is a tower containing rentable professional offices, a restaurant, and two small cinemas. Inside the protective walls the scale of the building is reduced to people-size as the street meanders and branches. At the junction, the floor is transformed into a small amphitheatre and the roof is pierced by pyramidal skylights. Here McIntyre has ignored the opportunity for exciting structural expression that was the hallmark of his earlier work. Instead of being directed upwards, the eye is invited to look at the shoppers below. This is an architecture in which people are the important ingredient.

—David Watson

McKINNELL, Noel Michael.

American. Born in Salford, Lancashire, 25 December 1935; moved to the United States, 1960: naturalized, 1983. Educated at the University of Manchester School of Architecture, 1953-58 (University of Manchester Travelling Scholarship, 1956), B.A. (honours) 1958; Columbia University School of Architecture, New York, 1959-60 (Fulbright Scholar, 1960), M.S.Arch. 1960; awarded Royal Manchester Institute Silver Medal, 1960. Married Jane D'Esopo in 1961; children: Caitlin and Phoebe. Associate Professor, Columbia University, 1960-62; Assistant Professor, 1963-66; Assistant Professor, 1963-66, Associate Professor, 1966-71, Professor of Architecture, 1971-83, and since 1983 Nelson Robinson Jr. Professor of Architecture, Harvard Graduate School of Design, Cambridge, Massachusetts. Since 1962, Partner, with Gerhard M. Kallmann, *q.v.,* and Henry Wood, Kallman, McKinnell and Wood, Architects, Inc., Boston. Professor of Architecture, University of Manchester (on leave from Harvard), 1972-74; Visiting Professor, Yale University, New Haven, Connecticut, 1976; Adjunct Professor, Columbia University, 1976-77. Exhibitions: Museum of Fine Arts, Boston, 1962; National Institute of Arts and Letters, New York, 1969; Metropolitan Museum of Art, New York, 1970; De Cordova Museum, Lincoln, Massachusetts, 1974. Recipient: Brunner Prize, National Institute of Arts and Letters, 1969; Honor Award, 1969 and 1982, Firm Award, 1984, American Institute of Architects; Precast Concrete Institute Award, 1969; Bartlett Award, 1969; Harleston Parker Medal, Boston Society of Architects, 1969, 1975 and 1983; Award of Merit, Concrete Industry Board, 1974; Bard Award, City Club of New York, 1977. M.A.: Harvard University, 1978. Address: Kellmann, McKinnell and Wood, Architects, Inc., 127 Tremont Street, Boston, Massachusetts 02108, U.S.A.

Publications:

By McKINNELL: books—*World Architecture,* contributing editor, London 1964–65; *Houses of Parliament Extension: A Competition Entry,* with Gerhard M. Kallmann, Cambridge, Massachusetts 1978; articles—interview in *Architects on Architecture,* edited by Paul Heyer, New York 1966, London 1967; "Movement Systems as Generators of Built Form," with Gerhard M. Kallmann, in *Architectural Record* (New York), November 1975.

*

See KALLMANN, Gerhard M.

MEIER, Richard Alan.

American. Born in Newark, New Jersey, 12 October 1934. Educated at Cornell University, Ithaca, New York, 1953-57, B.Arch. 1957. Worked with Frank Grad and Sons, New Jersey, 1957, Davis, *q.v.:* Lewis Davis, Brody, *q.v.:* Samuel Brody, and Wisniewski, New York, 1958-59, Skidmore, Owings and Merrill, *q.v.,* New York, 1959-60, and Marcel Breuer *q.v.,* and Associates, New York, 1960-63. Since 1963, Principal, Richard Meier and Associates, Architects, New York. Adjunct Instructor, 1963-66, Assistant Professor, 1966-69, and Adjunct Professor of Architecture, 1969-73, Cooper Union, New York; Visiting Lecturer/Critic, Princeton University, New Jersey, 1963, Syracuse University, Syracuse, New York, 1964, Pratt Institute, New York, 1965, and Yale University, New Haven, Connecticut, 1967; Resident Architect, American Academy in Rome, 1973; William Henry Bishop Professor of Architecture, Yale University, 1975, 1977; Visiting Professor, 1977, and Eliot Noyes Visiting Design Critic, 1980-81, Harvard University, Cambridge, Massachusetts. Chairman of the Awards Jury, American Institute of Architects, Philadelphia Chapter, 1972, American Academy in Rome, 1974, national AIA, 1975, and Pennsylvania Society of Architects, 1975. Exhibitions: AIA National Convention Exhibition, Washington, D.C., 1965, Portland, 1968, Boston, 1970, Detroit, 1971, and Washington, D.C., 1974; *40 under 40,* American Federation of the Arts, New York, 1966; Benjamin Franklin Parkway Fountain Competition, Architectural League, New York, 1966; *Vacation Houses,* AIA, New York, 1968; *Architecture U.S.A.,* United States Pavilion, *World's Fair,* Osaka, 1970; *Another Chance for Cities,* Whitney Museum, New York, 1970; National Housing Conference Exhibition, Washington, D.C., 1971; *Younger New York Architects,* Columbia University, New York, 1971; National Institute of Arts and Letters Exhibition, New York, 1971; *Low Rise High Density Housing,* Museum of Modern Art, New York, 1973; *Triennale,* Milan, 1973; *Due Architetti Americani,* United States Information Service, Milan, 1974; Columbia University, New York, 1974; Residential Design Exhibit, AIA, New York, 1974; University of California at Los Angeles, 1974; *Five Architects,* Princeton University School of Architecture, 1974; Cornell University, Ithaca, New York, 1974; *Architectural Studies and Projects,* Museum of Modern Art, New York, 1975; University of Houston School of Architecture, Texas, 1975; *The New York Five,* Art Net, London, 1975; *La Citta di Michelucci,* Basilica Alessandro, Fiesole, Italy, 1976; *Five Architects, New York,* at the *Mostra di*

Architettura, Naples, and toured Genoa, Zurich, Lausanne, Paris, Brussels and Helsinki, 1976; *Suburban Alternative,* at the *Biennale,* Venice, 1976; Cooper Union, New York, 1976; *Man Transforms,* Cooper-Hewitt Museum, New York, 1976; University of California at Los Angeles, 1976; *Idea as Model,* Institute for Architecture and Urban Studies, New York, 1976; Graham Foundation, Chicago, 1977; *200 Years of American Architectural Drawing,* Cooper-Hewitt Museum, New York, 1977; *New York: The State of Art,* Cultural Education Center, Albany, New York, 1977; *Design in Michigan,* Cranbrook Academy of Art Museum, Bloomfield Hills, Michigan, 1977; *Architecture,* Leo Castelli Gallery, New York, 1977; *Architecture: Seven Architects,* Institute of Contemporary Art, University of Pennsylvania, Philadelphia, 1977; *The Atheneum, Historic New Harmony, Indiana,* School of Architecture, Princeton University, New Jersey, 1978; *Architecture: Service/Craft/Art,* Rosa Esman Gallery, New York, and New Jersey State Museum, Trenton, 1978 *Richard Meier—Drawings and Collages,* Ballenford Architectural Books, Toronto, 1979; *Richard Meier: Collages and Architectural Drawings,* New Gallery of Contemporary Art, New Harmony, Indiana, 1979; *Collaboration: Artists and Architects,* Rosa Esman Gallery, New York, 1980; *Richard Meier: Matrix 58,* Wadsworth Atheneum, Hartford, Connecticut, 1980; *Richard Meier: Architectural Drawings, Models, Furniture Designs, Collages, Modernism Gallery, San Francisco, 1980; La Modernité—un projet inachevé,* at the *Festival d'automne,* Paris, 1982; *Richard Meier: Buildings and Projects 1965-1981,* Swiss Federal Institute of Technology, Zürich, 1982; *Richard Meier,* Max Protetch Gallery, New York, 1983; *ICSID Design '83,* Milan, 1983. Recipient: Excellence for House Design Award, 1964, 1968, 1969, and Award of Excellence for Design, 1977, *Architectural Record;* Homes for Better Living: Award of Merit, 1965, 1973, 1975, Homes for Better Living: First Honor Award, 1968, 1969, 1971, 1977; National Honor

Award, 1969, 1971, 1974, 1976, 1977, Award of Merit, 1970, Low and Moderate Income Housing National Award, 1970, and Bartlett Award, 1977, American Institute of Architects; House Competition Prize, 1965, and Award for Outstanding Residential Design, 1968, AIA, New York Chapter; Honor Award, AIA, New England Regional Council, 1968; Honor Award, United States Department of Housing and Urban Development, 1970; Brunner Prize, National Institute of Arts and Letters, 1972; Bard Award, City Club of New York, 1973, 1977; Award of Honor, New York Society of Architects, 1973; R. S. Reynolds Memorial Award, 1977; Design Award, New York State Association of Architects/AIA, 1978; Architectural Award of Excellence, American Institute of Steel Construction, 1978; Annual Award, *Progressive Architecture,* 1978; Pritzker Architecture Prize, Los Angeles, 1984. Fellow, American Institute of Architects, 1976. Address: Richard Meier and Partners, Architects, 136 East 57th Street, New York, New York 10022, U.S.A.

Works:

1962 Lambert Beach House, Fire Island, New York
1963 Design of *Recent American Synagogue Architecture* exhibition, Jewish Museum, New York
1964 Monumental Fountain, Benjamin Franklin Parkway, Philadelphia (competition project; with Frank Stella)
1965 Mr. and Mrs. Jerome Meier House, Essex Fells, New Jersey
      Frank Stella Studio and Apartment, New York (project)
1966 Dotson House, Ithaca, New York
      Renfield House, Chester, New Jersey
1967 Sona Shop, New York
      Smith House, Darien, Connecticut

Mental Health Facilities, West Orange, New Jersey (project)
Hoffman House, East Hampton, Long Island, New York
Rubin Loft renovation, New York (project)
1969 Saltzmann House, East Hampton, Long Island, New York
      Bronx Redevelopment Planning Study, New York
      House, Pound Ridge, New York
1970 Westbeth Artists' Housing, New York
      Health and Physical Education Building, State University College of New York at Fredonia (project)
      Charles Evans Industrial Buildings, at Fairfield and Piscataway, New Jersey (project)
1971 House, Old Westbury, New York
      Olivetti Branch Office Prototype, and Branch Office Prototype Modification
      Olivetti Training Center Dormitory, Tarrytown, New York (project)
      Olivetti Headquarters, Fairfax, Virginia (project)
1972 Twin Parks Northeast Housing, Bronx, New York
      Robert R. Young Housing, New York (project)
1972/
74 East Side Housing, New York (project)
1973 Douglas House, Harbor Springs, Michigan
      Paddington Station Housing, New York (project)
1974 Monroe Development Center, Rochester, New York (with Todd and Giroux)
      Shamberg House, Chappaqua, New York
      Museum of Modern Art, Villa Strozzi, Florence, Italy (project)
      Condominium House, Yonkers, New York (project)
      Undergraduate housing, Cornell University, Ithaca, New York (project)
1975 The Theatrum, New Harmony, Indiana

Richard Meier: High Museum of Art, Atlanta, Georgia, 1983.

Commercial building and hotel, Springfield, Massachusetts (project)

Wingfield Racquet Club, Greenwich, Connecticut (project)

1976   Bronx Developmental Center, New York

Maidman House, Sands Point, Long Island, New York

de Lone-Plukas House, Concord, Massachusetts (project)

Weber-Frankel Gallery, New York (project)

1978   Bronx Psychiatric Center Warehouse rehabilitation, New York

The Atheneum, and The Pottery Shed, New Harmony, Indiana

Aye Simon Reading Room, Guggenheim Museum, New York

Mr. and Mrs. Philip Suarez Apartment, New York

1979   House in Florida

Irwin Union Bank and Trust Company, Columbus, Indiana (project)

1980   Objects for Alessi Designs

1981   Hartford Seminary, Hartford, Connecticut

Renault Administrative Headquarters, Boulogne-Billancourt, France (project)

1982   Furniture for Knoll International

Elementary School, Columbus, Indiana

Housing Development, *Internationale Bauausstellung*, West Berlin (project)

1983   Giovanitti House, Pittsburgh, Pennsylvania

Siemens Office Building, Munich, West Germany (project)

Tableware for Swid Powell Designs

FIAT-Lingotto Factory Redevelopment, Turin, Italy (project)

High Museum of Art, Atlanta, Georgia

1984   Robert Helmick House, Des Moines, Iowa (project)

Joel Ehrenkranz House, North Salem, New York (project)

Des Moines Art Center, Iowa

Museum für Kunsthandwerk, Frankfurt, West Germany

Publications:

By MEIER: books—*Recent American Synagogue Architecture*, exhibition catalogue, New York 1963; *Richard Meier, Architect: Buildings and Projects 1966-1976*, New York 1976; *Richard Meier: Drawings of Four Objects, A Post Card Book 1976*, New York 1977; *On Architecture*, lecture paper, Cambridge, Massachusetts 1982; *Richard Meier, Architect: 1964/84*, with introduction by Joseph Rykwert, New York 1984; articles—"Planning for Jerusalem" in *Architectural Forum* (New York), April 1971; introduction to *Le Corbusier: Villa Savoye*, edited by Yukio Futagawa, Tokyo 1973; "Strategies: Eight Projects" in *Casabella* (Milan), May 1974; "Tre Recenti Progetti" in *Controspazio* (Bari, Italy), September 1975; "My Statement" in *Architecture + Urbanism* (Tokyo), April 1976; "Dialogue," with Arata Isozaki, in *Architecture + Urbanism* (Tokyo), August 1976; "General Remarks" in *The Japan Architect* (Tokyo), December 1976; "Olivetti Prototypes" in *L'Architecture d'Aujourd'hui* (Paris), December 1976; "A Word from Richard Meier" and "Dialogue: On Architecture," with Fumihiko Maki, in "White Existence—Richard Meier 1961-77," a special feature in *Space Design* (Tokyo), January 1978; "On the Spirit of Architecture" in *Architectural Digest* (Los Angeles), June 1981; "Remembering Breuer" in *Skyline* (New York), October 1981.

On MEIER: books—*The New York Times Book of Interior Design and Decoration*, New York 1966; *Art Today* by Ray Faulkner and Edwin Ziegfeld, New York 1969; *Young Designs in Living* by Barbara Plumb, New York 1969; *Architectural Record Book of Vacation Houses*, New York 1970; *History of*

Notable American Houses by Marshall Davidson, New York 1971; *Decorative Art in Modern Interiors* by Ella Moody, London 1971; *Architecture in a Revolutionary Era* by Julian Kulski, Nashville, Tennessee 1971; *Observations on American Architecture* by Ivan Chermayeff, New York 1972; *Five Architects: Eisenman/Graves/Gwathmey/Hejduk/Meier* by Kenneth Frampton and Colin Rowe, New York 1972; *Young Designs in Color* by Barbara Plumb, New York 1972; *Richard Meier: Smith House and House in Old Westbury* by Yukio Futagawa, Tokyo 1973; *Urban Design as Public Housing* by Jonathan Barnett, New York 1974; *Houses in the U.S.A.*, edited by Yukio Futagawa, Tokyo 1974; *Richard Meier: Douglas House, Michigan*, edited by Yukio Futagawa, Tokyo 1975; *Great Houses* by Walter Wagner, New York 1976; *Five Architects, New York* by Manfredo Tafuri, Rome 1976; *Wohnungsbau im Wandel von der Addition zur Integration* by David Mackay, Stuttgart 1977; *200 Years of American Architectural Drawing* by David Gebhard and Deborah Nevins, New York 1977; *Europa/America*, edited by Franco Raggi, Venice 1978; *Judith Turner Photographs Five Architects*, with introduction by John Hejduk, London and New York 1980; *American Architecture Now*, edited by Barbaralee Diamonstein, New York 1980; *Richard Meier: Matrix 58*, exhibition catalogue, Hartford, Connecticut 1980; *Richard Meier: The Art of Architecture*, exhibition catalogue, Atlanta, Georgia 1980; *GA 60: Richard Meier—The Atheneum, New Harmony, Indiana* by Paul Goldberger, edited by Yokio Futagawa, Tokyo 1981; *Collaboration: Artists and Architects* by Barbaralee Diamonstein, New York 1981; *New American Art Museums* by Helen Searing, New York and Los Angeles 1982; *Richard Meier: Buildings and Projects 1965-1981*, exhibition catalogue, Zurich 1982; articles—"The Very Personal Work of Richard Meier and Associates" by Joseph Rykwert in *Architectural Forum* (New York), March 1972; "Five on Five" in *Architectural Forum* (New York), May 1973; "Richard Meier: Public Space and Private Space" by Charles Hoyt in *Architectural Record* (New York), July 1973; "Architecture's Big Five Elevate Form" by Paul Goldberger in *The New York Times*, 26 November 1973; "Process Versus Style" by Wolf Von Eckardt in *The Washington Post*, 27 April 1974; "4 Projects by Richard Meier: Change and Consistency" by Charles Hoyt in *Architectural Record* (New York), March 1975; "Spatial Structure: Richard Meier," special issue of *Architecture + Urbanism* (Tokyo), April 1976; "The Gospel According to Giedion and Gropius Is Under Attack" by Ada Louise Huxtable in *The New York Times*, 27 June 1976; "Richard Meier: Architect" by Paul Goldberger in *The New York Times Book Review* (New York), 5 December 1976; "The Individual: Richard Meier" by Suzanne Stephens in *Progressive Architecture* (New York), May 1977; "Architectural Drawings as Art" by Ada Louise Huxtable in *The New York Times*, 12 June 1977; "Bronx Developmental Center," special issue of *Architecture + Urbanism* (Tokyo), November 1977; "White Existence—Richard Meier 1961-77," special feature in *Space Design* (Tokyo), January 1978; "Architecture: Richard Meier" by Paul Goldberger in *Architectural Digest* (Los Angeles), September 1978; "Five Frontiersmen" in *Newsweek* (New York), 6 November 1978; "Richard Meier: Master of Autonomous Architecture" in *AIT* (Stuttgart), no. 6, 1980; "Richard Meier: An American Architect" in *GA Document* (Tokyo), Summer 1980; "Richard Meier: Frankly Speaking" in *Interiors* (New York), October 1980; "Richard Meier: Two Projects in Context" in *Architectural Record* (New York), April 1981; "Richard Meier's New Furniture for Knoll" in *Architectural Record* (New York), November 1982; "Richard Meier Designs a New High for Atlanta" in *Interiors* (New York), October 1983; "Getty Museum Planned for L.A." in *Architects' Journal* (London), 18 January 1984; "Pritzker Prize for Meier" in *Building Design* (London), 27 April 1984; "Meier's Triumph" in *Building Design* (London), 3 May 1984; "Affirming

Modernism" in *Progressive Architecture* (New York), June 1984.

Bibliography: *Inorganic Architecture in the Work of Richard Meier: A Selected Bibliography*, Monticello, Illinois 1984.

*

The Paradox of the great cities is that in spite of the apparent denial of individual existence, there are human needs and hungers that the city answers. Large institutions are the city in microcosm. Their order is analogous to the articulation of public and private zones within a city. And within them exists wider possibilities of human intercourse within the continuity of urban existence.

Mine is an attempt to clarify and redefine a sense of order within society, to understand then a relationship between what has been and what can be.

But to gain any sense of my involvement, it is necessary to consult my work. Beyond theory, beyond historical reference, my meditations are on space, shape, light, and how to make them. My goal is presence, not illusion, and I pursue it with an unrelenting vigor.

—Richard Meier

*

To Richard Meier the process of building is an inorganic activity from the start; it is an intellectual pursuit to be thoughtfully considered from all angles. It is not surprising, then, that all aspects of his buildings are conceived in relation to their natural setting, even though to Meier the destruction of nature is implicit in man's creation of something new.

Perhaps this is why Meier articulates the material of his buildings with white paint: this brings out the surface and expresses the planar quality in relation to the more amorphous forms found in nature. He chooses white because it can creatively reflect the interchange between vertical space and natural light. The whiteness of his buildings is in purposeful contrast to natural surroundings.

In all of Richard Meier's houses, too, there is wood flooring which usually extends through the glass wall to an outside deck. He does not cover the floor in white tile because he wishes to express the difference between the horizontal floor plane and the vertical walls. (If the flooring were white, the spatial experience would be volumetric rather than planar.) The decking does not break with Meier's expression of contrast with nature, since, according to his philosophy, any material that has been shaped and reformed by man is already unnatural.

This is the era of the International Style, with the mass media making architectural information available throughout the world. Anyone's architectural style today is certainly influenced by this massive flow of information, and Richard Meier is no exception. The simplicity of Meier's work reflects some visual images of Le Corbusier and Alvar Aalto as well as some traits of the Japanese architectural style.

Comparing two of Meier's houses, the Smith House and the Douglas House, one can see that the latter is an improvement on the former; nevertheless, the intentions of the architect are clearly revealed in both cases. Both contain a clear separation of public and private spaces, with the circulation areas that connect these either articulated or not articulated. The interplay of the various spaces is well organized and designed according to his own, personal sense of aesthetics. From the exterior, one can always see a clear distinction between solid spaces and penetration of space derived from the building's relationship to the sun as well as from internal spatial arrangements.

The most distinctive aspect of Meier's design philosophy calls for the wrapping of spaces and their extension vertically, rather than horizontally—in contrast to, say, the Japanese house, which uses horizontal space to open the house towards the outside. Another important aspect of Meier's design is his sculptural effect. He creates this by adding and subtracting masses inside and outside the building, with the whiteness also contributing to the effect by unifying the surface and making volumetric deformations more pronounced.

It is wrong to assume, however, that Meier is devoted only to house design, for he has had such varied commissions as a modern museum in Florence, Italy and a hospital for the mentally retarded in the Bronx, New York. Both are superb designs and further evidence of his skilful articulation of circulation and precise composition of architectural elements.

—Ching-Yu Chang

MENDELSOHN, Eric.

American. Born Erich Mendelsohn in Allenstein, East Prussia, Germany, now Olsztyn, Poland, 21 March 1887; emigrated to England, 1933; naturalized, 1938; emigrated to the United States, 1941; naturalized, 1946. Studied economics at the University of Munich, 1907, and architecture at the Technische Hochschule of Berlin, 1908-10, and at the University of Munich, under Theodor Fischer, 1911-12. Served in the German Army, on the Russian and Western fronts, 1917-18. Married Luise Maas in 1915: daughter: Esther. Worked as a theatre designer and interior decorator in Munich, 1912-14; associated with the expressionist artists of the Blaue Reiter Group, Munich, 1914-15; practiced in Berlin, 1919-33; left Germany to escape persecution of the Jews, and lived alternately in London and Palestine, 1933-41; in partnership with Serge Chermayeff, *q.v.*, in London, 1933-39; settled in New York, 1941; practiced in San Francisco, 1945 until his death in 1953. Exhibitions: *Architecture in Concrete and Steel*, Galerie Paul Cassirer, Berlin, 1919; Gallery Contempora, New York, 1929; Architectural Association, London, 1931; *Triennale*, Milan, 1932; Museum of Modern Art, San Francisco, 1942; Art Institute of Chicago, 1942; City Art Museum, St. Louis, Missouri, 1944; Jewish Museum, New York, 1952; *Erich Mendelsohn: Ein Architekt skizziert*, Akademie der Künste, Berlin, 1960; Royal Institute of British Architects, London, 1962; *Eric Mendelsohn*, Akademie der Künste, Berlin, 1968; *The Drawings of Eric Mendelsohn*, University of California, Berkeley, 1969; *L'Opera di Eric Mendelsohn*, Istituto Nazionale di Architettura, Rome, 1972; *Funf Architekten aus funf Jahrhunderten*, Kunstbibliothek, Berlin, 1976 (travelled to Baden-Baden and Bonn, West Germany, and Zürich); *White City: International Style Architecture in Israel*, Jewish Museum, Tel Aviv, 1984-85. Recipient: First Prize, Cathedral Square Competition, Magdeburg, Germany, 1930; First Prize, Berlin Passenger Transport Company, Administration Building, 1931. *Died (in San Francisco) 15 September 1953.*

Works:

1911 Chapel, Hebrew Cemetery, Allenstein, Germany, now Olsztyn, Poland
1915 Becker House, Chemnitz, Germany, now Karl Marx Stadt, East Germany (project)
1920 Hausleben, Dorotheenstrasse, Berlin (destroyed)
1920/
24 Einstein Tower, Potsdam, Germany
1921 Office building, Kemperplatz, Berlin (project)
1921/
23 Herman and Company Hat Factory, Luckenwalde, Germany
Berliner Tageblatt Building, Jerusalemerstrasse, Berlin

1922 Two-family villa, Karolingerplatz, Charlottenburg, Berlin
1923 Weichmann Silk Store and Office, Gleiwitz, Germany, now Gliwice, Poland
Meyer-Kaufmann Textile Factory Power Station Building, Wuestegiersdorf, Germany
Sternfeld House, Heerstrasse, Berlin
Ruthenberg Central Electrical Works, Haifa, Palestine, now Israel (project)
Commercial Center, Haifa, Palestine, now Israel (competition project)
1924 Herpich Furriers Building, Leipzigerstrasse, Berlin
1925/
26 Temple of the Three Patriarchs, Tilsit, now Sovetsk, U.S.S.R.
1925/
27 Textile factory and industrial complex, Leningrad
1926 Schocken Department Store, Nuremberg
Cohen-Epstein Department Store extensions, Duisberg, Germany
1926/
28 Schocken Department Store, Stuttgart (destroyed)
1926/
29 Universum Cinema, Berlin

1927 Petersdorff Department Store, Breslau, Germany, now Poland
Deukon Dressmaking Building, Berlin
Power Station, Berliner Tageblatt Building, Jerusalemerstrasse, Berlin
Dr. Bejach House, New Babelsberg, Germany
Zoo Exhibition Hall, Berlin (project)
Yacht Club, Wannsee, Berlin (project)
Hebrew Cemetery, Königsberg, Germany (destroyed by Nazis)
Herpich Shop, Berlin
Trade Union Administration Building, Germany (project)
1927/
28 Woga Building Complex, Kurfürstendamm, Berlin
1928 Rudolf Mosse Pavilion, *Press Exhibition*, Cologne
Galerie Lafayette, Potsdamerplatz, Berlin (project)
1928/
29 Schocken Department Store, Chemnitz, Germany, now Karl-Marx-Stadt, East Germany
Metal Workers Union Building and Lindenstrasse redevelopment, Berlin (project)
1929 Chemical Syndicate Administrative Building, Berlin (project)
Palace of the Soviets, Moscow (competition project)
Mendelsohn House, Rupenhorn, Berlin
1930 Cathedral Square, Magdeburg, Germany (competition project)
Hebrew Youth Center, Essen, Germany
1930/
33 Bachner Department Store, Moravska-Ostrava, Czechoslovakia
1931 Columbus House, Potsdamerplatz, Berlin (destroyed)
Alexanderplatz redevelopment, Berlin (project)
Administration Building, Berlin Passenger Transport Co., Friedrichstrasse, Berlin (competition project)
Villa for the Duke of Alba, Madrid (project)
1932 Zinc Works, Magdeburg, Germany
1934/
36 Weizmann House, Rehovot, Palestine, now Israel
1935 Hotel, Southsea, Hampshire (project; with Serge Chermayeff)
de la Warr Pavilion, Bexhill-on-Sea, Sussex (with Serge Chermayeff)
Nimmo House, Chalfont St. Giles, Buckinghamshire (with Serge Chermayeff)

1935/
36 Master plan for Hebrew University, Mount Scopus, Jerusalem (project)
1936 Salman Schocken House, Jerusalem
Schocken Library, Jerusalem
House, Frinton Park, Essex (with Serge Chermayeff)
White City Housing Development, London (project: with Serge Chermayeff)
House, 64 Old Church Street, Chelsea, London (with Serge Chermayeff)
1937 Hotel, Garages and Shops Complex, Blackpool, Lancashire (project)
Commercial School, Jagur, Palestine, now Israel
1937/
38 Government Hospital, Haifa, Palestine, now Israel
1937/
39 Anglo-Palestine Bank, now National Bank of Israel, Jerusalem
Hadassah University Medical Centre, Mount Scopus, Jerusalem (renovated by Rechter-Zarhy-Rechter, 1976)
1939 Agricultural Institute, Rehovot, Palestine, now Israel
Daniel Wolf Research Laboratories, Rehovot, Palestine, now Israel
1942 Kaplan House renovation, Long Island, New York
1946/
50 Maimonides Health Center for the Chronic Sick, San Francisco (remodelled by others, 1953)
B'nai Amoona Temple and Community Center, St. Louis, Missouri
Temple and Community Center, Cleveland, Ohio
1947 Apartment building, Chestnut Street, San Francisco (project)
Walter Heller House, San Francisco (project)
Walter Haas House, San Francisco (project)
1948 Temple and Community Center, Washington, D.C. (project)
Beth El Temple and Community Center, Baltimore, Maryland (project)
1948/
52 Emanu-El Temple and Community Center, Grand Rapids, Michigan
1950/
51 Russell House, Pacific Heights, San Francisco
1950/
53 Varian Associates Electronic Research and Development Plant, Palo Alto, California
1950/
54 Mount Zion Temple and Community Center, St. Paul, Minnesota
1951 Emanu-El Temple and Community Center, Dallas, Texas (project)
Monument to the Jewish War Dead, New York (project)
1951/
53 Atomic Energy Commission Laboratories, Berkeley, California

Publications:

By MENDELSOHN: books—*Erich Mendelsohn: Structures and Sketches*, translated by H.G. Scheffauer, London 1924; *Amerika: Bilderbuch eines Architekten*, Berlin 1926; *Russland, Europa, Amerika: Ein Architektonische Querschnitt*, Berlin 1929; *Erich Mendelsohn: Das Gesamtschaffen des Architekten: Skizzen, Entwürfe, Bauten*, Berlin 1930; *Neues Haus—Neue Welt*, Berlin 1931; *Der Schöpferische Sinn der Krise*, Berlin 1932; *Three Lectures on Architecture*, Berkeley, California 1944; *Erich Mendelsohn: Letters of an Architect*, edited by Oskar Beyer, Munich 1961, New York and London 1967; articles—"Das Problem einer neuen Baukunst" in *Arbeitstrat für Kunst* (Berlin), 1919; "Architecture of Our Own Times" in *Architectural Association*

Erich Mendelsohn: Schocken Department Store, Stuttgart, 1928.

Journal (London), June 1930; "Background to Design" in *Architectural Forum* (New York), April 1953; "The 3-Dimensions of Architecture: Their Symbolic Significance" in *Symbols and Values*, New York 1954.

On MENDELSOHN: books—*Wright, Dudok, Mendelsohn* by Hermann Soergel, Munich 1926; *Moderner Zweckbau* by Adolf Behne, Munich 1926; *Eric Mendelsohn* by Arnold Whittick, London 1940, 3rd ed. 1965; *Il contributo di Mendelsohn alla evoluzione dell'architettura moderna*, Milan 1952; *Eric Mendelsohn* by Wolf Von Eckardt, New York and London 1960; *Theory and Design in the First Machine Age* by Reyner Banham, London 1960; *Modern Architecture: Expressionism* by Dennis Sharp, London 1966; *Eric Mendolsohn*, exhibition catalogue, Berlin 1968; *The Drawings of Eric Mendelsohn*, exhibition catalogue by Susan King, Berkeley, California 1969; *Eric Mendelsohn: Catalog of Sketches*, edited by Lotte Schiller, Mill Valley, California 1970; *Eric Mendelsohn: Opera Completa* by Bruno Zevi, with Louise Mendelsohn, Milan 1970; *Eric Mendelsohn*, exhibition catalogue, by Bruno Zevi, Rome 1972; *Die Architektur des Expressionismus* by Wolfgang Pehnt, Stuttgart 1973; *Funf Architekten aus funf Jahrhunderten*, exhibition catalogue, edited by Ekhart Berckenhagen, Berlin 1976; *Architekten Zeichnen*, edited by Claudius Coulin, Stuttgart 1980; *Visionary Architecture of the 20th Century* by Vittorio Magnago Lampugnani, Stuttgart and London 1982; articles—"Erich Men-

delsohn" by H. G. Scheffauer in *Architectural Review* (London), May 1923; "Puritanism in Art" by Aldous Huxley in *The Studio* (London), March 1930; "Erich Mendelsohn," special issue of *L'Architecture vivante* (Paris), Autumn/Winter 1932; "Mendelsohn" by Julius Posener in *L'Architecture d'aujourd'hui* (Paris), May 1932; "Undici Opera di Mendelsohn" by Edoardo Persico in *Casabella* (Milan), April 1934; "Current Architecture: Hospitals" in *Architectural Review* (London), February 1939; "Eric Mendelsohn" in *Architectural Forum* (New York), May 1947; "Eric Mendelsohn" in *Architectural Forum* (New York), April 1953; "Eric Mendelsohn" by Bruno Zevi in *Metron* (Rome), no. 49/50, 1954; "Mendelsohn" by Reyner Banham in *Architectural Review* (London), August 1954; "The Last Work of a Great Architect" by H. Schiller in *Architectural Forum* (New York), February 1955; "Eric Mendelsohn" by Irving D. Shapiro in *AIA Journal* (Washington, D.C.), June 1958; special issue of *L'Architettura* (Rome), September 1963; "Hadassah Hospital, Jerusalem" in *Baumeister* (Munich), September 1976; "Destruction of Eric Mendelsohn's Universum Cinema in Berlin" in *Architettura* (Rome), November 1979; "Theatre in a Building by Mendelsohn on Lehninger Platz" in *Bauwelt* (Berlin), 2 October 1981; "The Acting/Spatial concept of the Schaubühne" by Klaus Wever and Rudolf Biste in *Bühnentechnische Rundschau* (Velber, West Germany) April 1982; "The Universum Theatre" by Gae Aulenti in *Casabella* (Milan), April 1982; "Mendelsohn's Universum" by Bruno Zevi, Manfred Sack and Vittorio Magnago Lampugnani

in *Domus* (Milan), June 1982; "The First Sketch," special issue of *Daidalos* (Berlin), 15 September 1982; "Traces of Mendelsohn" by David Palterer in *Domus* (Milan), January 1984; "Tel Aviv, Showcase of Modernism, Is Looking Frayed" by Paul Goldberger in the the *New York Times*, 25 November 1984.

Many influences served to form Eric Mendelsohn's architecture; these he absorbed and combined into a strongly individual style. These influences could be enumerated as the spectacular and efficient engineering structures of the nineteenth century—he had a tremendous admiration for the Crystal Palace—the evolution of the modern machine, and modern art movements, especially art nouveau and expressionism. As well, he had a strong feeling for the structural potentialities of steel and reinforced concrete. All this is strongly reflected in the large number of sketch projects that he exhibited in 1919 at the outset of his career.

Among them were sketch projects for observatories which secured for him his first important commission: the observatory at Potsdam built for further researches into Einstein's theory of relativity. This now famous building is one of the best examples of Expressionist architecture. The exterior conforms to the interior structure of a square shaft with a square stairway, but the tower and base is a design of rhythms and curved shapes with deep, massive recesses derived partly from optical instruments. With the help of the light and shadow created by the design, it succeeds in giving the impression of mystery and symbolizes its purpose of scientific investigation into the nature of the universe. Mendelsohn's principal conscious aim in the design, however, was to achieve organic unity, a guiding principle in all his work. Einstein himself though of it as organic. A notable circumstance is that the finished building conforms in essential shapes to the original sketch. Mendelsohn always began an architectural project with a perspective sketch—a three dimensional concept—and the final in the series of such sketches was often like the finished building, as for example in the Schocken Store at Stuttgart. Mendelsohn used to say, "Look at the sketch, it's all there."

Most of Mendelsohn's subsequent buildings did not give quite the same scope for symbolic expression as the Einstein Tower. They are often distinguished by the careful relation of curved and rectangular forms, seen in his German work mainly in a series of departmental stores of which the most impressive are those at Stuttgart (now destroyed) and Chemnitz. In the former, the long horizontal lines of the main front are arrested by the spiral staircase glass tower, like a passage of music arrested by a vibrating chord. Mendelsohn used this motif frequently in a wide variety of building, in the de la Warr Pavilion, at Bexhill, in several buildings in Palestine, and perhaps most beautifully of all in the series of balcony-fronts in the Maimonides Health Center in San Francisco, where the straight horizontals are punctuated by a series of semi-circular projections. The relation of large, curved form to straight is used with good effect in the Chemnitz store with the long, convex, horizontal bands of golden travertine and glass in eight storeys arrested at both ends by staircase and lift grills. A similar dramatic treatment of curved forms is seen in the interior of the Universum Cinema, where the grand, unbroken sweep of the balcony front and seats is continued in the horizontal straight forms of the walls and echoed in the ceiling pattern.

One early influence on Mendelsohn was Greek art, as became apparent in a few designs such as the immense Columbus House in Berlin, in his own house in Berlin, in two houses in England, in the Hadassah University Medical Centre, Mount Scopus, Jerusalem, and in the Schocken House in Jerusalem. In these buildings, curved forms are used with great restraint; the main forms are large, plain, pale masses broken only by windows and a carefully calculated relation of verticals and horizontals to convey feelings of serenity and repose. This is seen particularly in hiw own house, which is very largely a design of square shapes, and it is significant that a partly enclosed exterior space against the house is designed for the performance of Greek plays.

To appreciate fully the de la Warr Pavilion, which Mendelsohn designed in collaboration with Serge Chermayeff, one must see a model of the whole design, for the building as it is now is only a part, and it has suffered from subsequent maltreatment. In the original, complete scheme, the building extends seawards with a circular swimming pool opposite the glass enclosure of the spiral staircase, with a lawn between, and a pier projecting from the swimming bath enclosure. The whole design is a fine combination of curved and rectangular forms.

Mendelsohn emigrated to the United States in 1941 and his principal works there were a series of temples and community centres for Jewish communities. They exhibit considerable variety of design. One of the most beautiful and characteristic is that at Cleveland, with its 100-foot dome. The site is slightly hilly and, in designing both the temple and the community centre, Mendelsohn carefully related the curved forms to the contours of the site. This is one of the best examples of his sense of organic unity, where a building is an integral part of its setting. In this guiding principle of Mendelsohn designs, each part shows by its character its relation to the whole. In addition, his work is characterised by decorative emphasis of purpose, which at times is symbolic.

The ideas such as dignity, aspiration, power, repose, solemnity, and gaiety suggested by the purpose and character of buildings imply symbolic shapes to which Mendelsohn gives dramatic emphasis, while taking these shapes as subjects for aesthetic effect.

—Arnold Whittick

MENDES da ROCHA, Paulo Archias.

Brazilian. Born in Vitoria, Espirito Santo, 25 October 1928. Educated at Mackenzie University, Faculty of Architecture and Town Planning, São Paulo, Dip.Arch. 1955. Served in the Brazilian Officers Reserve Corps (CPOR), São Paulo, 1949-51. Married Virginia Ferraz Navarro in 1955; children: Renata, Guilherme, Paulo, Pedro, and Joana. In private practice, São Paulo, since 1955. Professor, 1961-69, Director of Projects and University Councillor, 1965-67, and Coordinator of the Projects Department, 1969, University of São Paulo Faculty of Architecture and Town Planning. Member of the Council, 1958-61, Director of the Habitat Commission, 1971, and President, 1972-78, Brazilian Institute of Architects (IAB), São Paulo. Exhibitions: *Bienal*, São Paulo, 1961; *Beaubourg Competition Exhibition*, International Union of Architects, Paris, 1971; Museum of Contemporary Art, São Paulo, 1975. Recipient: First Prize, Legislative Palace Competition, Santa Catarina, Brazil, 1957; First Prize, Athletic Club Competition, São Paulo, 1958; President's Prize, *Bienal*, São Paulo, 1961; First Prize, Jockey Club Competition, Goias, Brazil, 1963. Address (office): Rua Bento Freitas 306, 5th Floor, Suite 51, 01220 São Paulo, Brazil.

Works:

1957 Legislative Palace, Florianopolis, Santa Catarina, Brazil (with Pedro Paulo de Melo Saraivo and Alfredo S. Paesani)
1958 Covered Gymnasium for the Paulistano Athletic Club, Rua Honduras, São Paulo
1960 Center for Child Care and Social Assistance, Cedral, São Paulo State
1962 Vila Maria School Complex, Sao Jose dos Campos, São Paulo State
    Taboao School Complex, Sao Bernardo do Campo, São Paulo State
    Forum Building, Avare, São Paulo State
    National Industrial Federation Headquarters, Brasilia
    Silveira Mello House, Piracicalia Garden City, São Paulo State (with Joao E. de Gennaro)
    Gaetano Miani House, Granja Julieta, São Paulo (with Joao E. de Gennaro)
1963 Jockey Club, Goiania, Goias, Brazil
    Malta Cardoso House, Jardim Guedala, São Paulo (with Joao E. de Gennaro)
1964 Cruz Secco House, Butanta, São Paulo (with Joao E. de Gennaro)
    Camargo Correia Building Company Office Building, São Paulo (competition project; with Joao E. de Gennaro)
    Apartment building, Haddock Lobo Street, São Paulo (with Joao E. de Gennaro)
    House, Mooca, São Paulo (with Joao E. de Gennaro)
    Paulo Mendes da Rocha House, São Paulo
1967 Vila Baeta School Complex, São Bernardo do Campo, São Paulo State
    COHAB Prefabricated Housing, São Paulo (project; with Joao E. de Gennaro)
    Cumbica Housing Estate, São Paulo (with J. B. Vilanova Artigas and Fabio Penteado)
1968 President Roosevelt State College, São Paulo

Housing complex, Guarulhos, São Paulo State
    SENAI Technical School, São Paulo
    SENAC Technical School, Campinas, São Paulo State
1970 Brazilian Pavilion, *Expo '70,* Osaka, Japan (with Flavio Motta, Julio Katinsky, and Ruy Ohtake)
    Fernando Millan House, São Paulo
    Mario Masetti House, São Paulo
1972 James Francis King House, São Paulo
    Children's Educational Centre, Jardim Calux, Sao Bernardo do Campo, São Paulo State
1973 Serra Dourada Municipal Stadium, Giania, Goias, Brazil
1974 Grota da Bela Vista Development, São Paulo (project)
1975 Municipal Insurance Headquarters, in the New Administrative Center, São Paulo
    Museum of Contemporary Art, University of São Paulo (with Jorge Wilhelm)
    Park Housing Development, Itatibam, São Paulo State (with Alfredo Paesani)
1976 Cultural and Convention Center, Campos do Jordao, São Paulo State
    National Agricultural Engineering Center, Fazenda Ipanema 7, Sorocaba, São Paulo State
    Antonio Junqueira de Azevedo House, São Paulo
1977 Monorail Station, Cuiaba, Mato Grosso, Brazil
    Comgas Company Administration and Technical Buildings, São Paulo
    University Center, Rondonopolis, Mato Grosso, Brazil
1978 Governor's Residence, Cuiaba, Mato Grosso, Brazil
    Calux Kindergarten, Sao Bernardo do Campo, São Paulo

Publications:

On MENDES da ROCHA: books—*Neue Möbel,* Stuttgart 1961; *Concours International pour la Realisation du Centre Beaubourg,* Paris 1971; *Grota da Bela Vista* (planning authority report), São Paulo 1974; articles—"Ginasio Coberto Clube Atletico Paulistano" in *Acropole* (São Paulo), November 1961; "Obra do Arquiteto Paulo A. Mendes da Rocha," edited by Flavio Motta, special issue of *Acropole* (São Paulo), August/September 1967; "Pavilhao Oficial do Brasil, Expo '70" in *Acropole* (São Paulo), March 1969; "Brazil's Pavilion" in *Kokusai Kentiku* (Tokyo), vol. 34, 1970; "Wohnhaus Paulo A. Mendes da Rocha" in *Architektur und Wohnen* (Hamburg), Summer 1973; "Dos Residencias en Brasil: Casa Millan e Casa Masetti" in *Summa* (Buenos Aires), February 1976; "Museu de Arte Contemporanea da Universidade de São Paulo" and "Grota da Bela Vista" in *Modulo* (Rio de Janeiro), no. 42, 1977; "Centro Nacional de Engenharia Agricola" in *Modulo* (Rio de Janeiro), no. 46, 1977; "Modern Brazilian Architecture," special issue of *Process: Architecture* (Tokyo), August 1980.

We try to achieve, in our own environment, a constant interaction between theoretical research and practical experiment, geared to the needs of a rapidly developing society. Our designs demonstrate not only our preference for an economy of language, but also the desire to use only those technical resources suitable for the revitalization of living and work areas, so as to improve the quality of life in the urban social environment.

—Paulo Mendes da Rocha

The modern architectural movement is not simply a movement to "modernize" architecture, to make it correspond to today's needs. It has as well, at times,

Paulo Mendes da Rocha: Covered Gymnasium for the Paulisto Athletic Club, Sao Paulo, 1958.

great deal of talk from architects and planners about man's "solidarity with nature." What this has usually meant in practice is a voracious and irreversible appropriation of the landscape to create works that dehumanize. The simplicity of approach, in both Mendes da Rocha and Niemeyer, also has to do with "solidarity," but it neither invades nor disturbs nature. Their architecture could be called fragile—not because they lacked the necessary financial resources and certainly not because they intended to demonstrate some dubious motive. It is a fragility that pays its respects to nature and rests on a firm belief in the solidarity of human beings and in the inevitability of change. It does not seek to impose a vision of society. Its true accomplishment is to keep nature intact, to remind man of his potential, and to allow for the advance of a new and more varied society.

—Flavio Motta

MERRILL, John Ogden.

American. Born in St. Paul, Minnesota, 10 August 1896. Educated at the University of Wisconsin, Madison, 1914-16; Massachusetts Institute of Technology, Cambridge, 1919-21, B.Arch. 1921. Served as a Captain in the Coast Artillery Corps, United States Army, 1917-19. Married Ross MacKenzie in 1918; children: Elizabeth Ross, John Jr. and Jean; married Viola Berg in 1946. Worked for Granger and Bollenbacher, Chicago; Chief Architect for the Mid-West States, United States Housing Administration, 1939. Joined Louis Skidmore, *q.v.*, and Nathaniel Owings, *q.v.*, already practising as Skidmore and Owings, Chicago (1936-39), to form Skidmore, Owings and Merrill, Chicago, New York, San Francisco, Portland, Oregon, Washington, D.C., etc., from 1939: retired from the firm in 1958. Director, Chicago Building Code Revision Commission, 1947-49. President, Chicago Chapter, American Institute of Architects. Exhibition: *Skidmore, Owings and Merrill*, Museum of Modern Art, New York, 1950; *Transformations in Modern Architecture*, Museum of Modern Art, New York, 1979. Recipient: Honor Award, American Institute of Architects, 1968. Fellow, American Institute of Architects. *Died* (in Colorado Springs, Colorado) *10 June 1975.*

been an attempt to regain an integrity for architecture, to create works that are significant in historical, artistic and human terms. Paulo Mendes da Rocha belongs to the generation whose connection with the modern movement is well established, and he may be characterized as an architect whose place in that movement has involved more than simply a response to the economic needs of people at a particular time and in a particular place.

To define Mendes da Rocha in terms of influences and antecedents, however, is to end up with a vast "family-tree" that, without extensive analysis and qualification, is more chaotic than illuminating. Although this is an over-simplification, it is more helpful to say that he is an architect of Brazil and that, in that context, he has been more interested in the confrontation between architecture and nature than in the confrontation between architecture and society. The architect to whom he can be most closely compared is Oscar Niemeyer.

Their works have much in common. Those who are tackling the problems of "crippling underdevelopment" may well be put off by such works—by the niceties of light, airy spaces, easy access, efficient circulation, and room for natural growth. For this world of elegance and charm is far removed from the world to which the great majority of

Brazilians belong. It is almost as if the architecture of Mendes da Rocha (and Niemeyer) were intended for a different species. It is an architecture that—like a sleek, aristocratic heron—lands gently in front of the inhabitant of central Brazil—a deformed, transformed man, nearer to geography than to history, a man more familiar with the trees of the Brazilian bush than the cultural references of a Niemeyer palace. From a certain perspective, it is easy to dismiss such work as stunning, even beautiful, but superfluous.

Yet such an analysis would miss the "accomplishment." The work of Mendes da Rocha creates a natural environment, reminding man of the earth's generosity, never condemning, in itself or by implication, what has gone before. It provides the setting in which we can examine the relationship of nature and architecture without recourse to knowledge of "technical," pseudo-scientific disciplines and their aggressive moralities. If this architecture seems remote from the man who looks at it, then it must be remembered that he looks at it with justified pleasure: because it is beautiful and because it suggests different perspectives, different kinds of reality. The architect has not thwarted his basic desire to communicate.

It is also well to remember that we have lived in a period in which there has been and continues to be a

See SKIDMORE, OWINGS AND MERRILL

MEYER, Hannes.

Swiss. Born in Basle, 18 November 1889. Educated at the Gewerbeschule, Basle, 1905-09; took evening courses in aesthetics at the Kunstgewerbeschule, Berlin, and in economics and land reform at the Landwirtschafts-Akademie, Berlin, under Professor Goecke, 1909-12; made study tour of England, 1912-13. Served in the Swiss Army, 1914-16. Married to Lena Bergner. Worked as a site superintendent, Stamm Brothers Building and Architectural Company, Basle, 1905-09; Assistant Architect, studio of Adolf Frohlich, Charlottenburg, Berlin, 1911-12; Assistant to Emit Schaudt, Berlin, 1912, and Georg Metzendorf, Munich, 1916-17; Architect, under Baurat Schmohl, Housing Welfare Section, Krupp Building Administration, Essen, 1917-18; in private practice, Basle, 1919-25; in partnership with Hans Wittwer, Basle, 1926-27; Master of Architecture, 1927-28, and Director (succeeded Gropius), 1928-30, Bauhaus School, Dessau, Germany: published

Bauhaus, 1928-29; Chief Architect of the Giprovtus Institutes of Technology and Higher Education, Consultant and Chief Architect to the Giprogor Town Planning Institute, and Chief Architect of the Standardgorproyect Town Planning Trust, all Moscow, 1930-31; Professor, VASI University of Architecture, Moscow, 1930-33; Professor, and Head of the Housing Advisory Council, Academy of Architecture, Moscow, 1934-35; in private practice, Geneva, 1936-39; Director, Institute of Urbanism and Planning, Mexico City, 1939-41; in private practice, Mexico City, 1941-49; Technical Director, Department of Workers' Housing, Ministry of Labor, Mexico City, 1942, and of La Estampa Mexicana Publishing House, Mexico City, 1947-49; returned to Switzerland, concentrating on theoretical studies for architectural publications, 1949 until his death in 1954. Member, German Land Reform Movement; Swiss Free Land Movement; Swiss Cooperative Movement; ABC Group, Switzerland; CIRPAC (Directing Committee of CIAM: Congrès Internationaux d'Architecture Moderne); Der Ring Architects Association, Berlin: VOPRA Architects' Association, Moscow; Managing Committee, Moscow Section, Association of Soviet Architects. Recipient: First Prize, German Trade Unions Federation School Competition, 1928. *Died* (in Crocifisso di Savosa, Switzerland) *19 July 1954.*

Works:

1916/
18 Kiel-gaarden Housing Development, near Essen (project; with Georg Metzendorf)
Margarethenhöhe Housing Development, near Essen (project; with Georg Metzendorf)
1918/
19 Pic-Pic Housing Development, Geneva (competition project)
1919/
21 Freidorf Co-operative Housing Estate, near Basle
Urbanization plan for Balsthal, Jura, Switzerland
1923 Central Cemetery, Basle (project)
1924 Co-op Show Window display, *International Co-operative Exhibition*, Ghent
1926 St. Peter's Primary School for Girls, Basle (competition project; with Hans Wittwer)
1926/
27 Palace of the League of Nations, Geneva (competition project; with Hans Wittwer)
1928/
30 Törten Housing Estate redevelopment, Dessau, Germany (with Bauhaus students; partially built)
German Trade Unions Federation School, Bernau, near Berlin
1929 Workers' Bank Building, Berlin (competition project)
1931/
32 Development and reconstruction plan for Greater Moscow (project; with Geimanson and Bücking)
1931/
36 Lenin School, Moscow (project; with Bauhaus student)
Housing development, Ishevsk, U.S.S.R. (project)
1932 Plan for the satellite town of Nishniy-Kurinsk, near Perm, U.S.S.R. (with the Standardgorproyect team; partially built)
Plan for the satellite town of Sozgorod Gorki, near Molotov, U.S.S.R. (with the Standardgorproyect team; partially built)
1933/
34 Plan for the capital city of Birobidjan, U.S.S.R. (with the Giprogor team, Gandurin and Salvin; partially built)
Redevelopment plan for Tschita, U.S.S.R. (project)

Redevelopment plan for Krassnojarsk, U.S.S.R. (project)
1934 Plan for the Perm Basin Industrial Zone, U.S.S.R. (project; with the Giprogor team, and Patapov)
Plan for the reconstruction of the town of Rybinsk, U.S.S.R. (project)
1938/
39 Jäggi Foundation Children's Home, Mümliswil, Solothurn, Switzerland
1941 Sports and Cultural Centre, Mexico City (competition project)
1942 Lomas de Becerra Housing Estate, Tacubaya, near Mexico City (project)
1946/
47 Agua Hedionda Spa Centre, Cauutla, Morelos, Mexico (project)
1947 Banco Nacional/Banco Internacional Headquarters, Mexico City (project)

Publications:

By MEYER: books—*The Freidorf Co-operative Housing Estate*, with J.F. Schar and H. Faucherre, Basle, 1921; *Hannes Meyer: Architettura o Rivoluzione: Scritti 1921-1942*, edited by Francesco Dal Co, Padua 1969; *Bauen und Gesellschaft: Schriften, Briefe, Projekte*, edited by Lena Meyer-Bergner, Dresden 1980; articles—numerous in specialist periodicals, including *Bauhaus* (Dessau, Germany), 1927-29.

On MEYER: book—*Hannes Meyer: Buildings, Projects and Writings* by Claude Schnaidt, Teufen, Switzerland and London 1965 (includes bibliography); articles—special issue of *Arquitectura y Decoracion* (Mexico City), October 1938; "Hannes Meyer" by Paul Artaria in *Werk* (Zurich), October, 1954; "Hannes Meyer" by Victor Bourgeois in *Ruimte* (Antwerp), May 1955; "The Work and Activities of the Architect and Town Planner Hannes Meyer 1889-1954" by Walter Münz in *Deutsche Bauzeitung* (Stuttgart), March 1961; "Hannes Meyer e la Scuola di Architettura" by Massimo Scolari in special Bauhaus issue of *Controspazio* (Bari, Italy), April/May 1970; "Hans Schmidt and Hannes Meyer in Moscow" by Christian Borngräber in *Archithese* (Niederteufen), November/December 1978; "Foreign Architects in the USSR" by Christian Borngräber in *Architectural Association Quarterly* (London), vol. 11, no. 1, 1979; "Hannes Meyer: architect, town planner, lecturer" by Klaus-Jurgen Winkler in *Architektur der DDR* (East Berlin), November 1979; "Hannes Meyer: Building" in *Architect* (Malta), July 1980; "Hannes Meyer and the early days of the GDR" by Klaus-Jurgen Winkler in *Architektur der DDR* (East Berlin), February 1982.

*

There are three good reasons for remembering and honouring Hannes Meyer. In the late 1920s he was the designer of a few highly progressive competition schemes. He was the second Director of the Bauhaus, after Gropius and before Mies van der Rohe, a post from which he was expelled on political grounds in 1930. And he believed that architecture was not art.

Traditionally his belief is explained as a manifestation of his Marxism, but, as with William Morris, the reverse might as easily be true. Meyer's design philosophy (though he was never plain in formulating his aesthetic principles) patently had the force of personal feeling commanding political philosophy. It probably began that way round—then it grew extreme. If Meyer believed only that design ideals should be subordinate to practical applications, it would have been an unexceptional, and unmemorable, position.

Meyer's pedagogically-forged extremism is durable precisely because it was so radical. His dialectical struggle with Moholy-Nagy (the Bauhaus's prime exponent of visual culture) forced

Meyer into exaggerated statements of the anti-visual. His advocacy of architecture as pure social science and sheer function became implacable. He held no brief for the accommodating pragmatism of formalist training, at least as far as his teaching theories were concerned: he opposed studio discussions about mere form. Ultimately, therefore, an aesthetic of anti-art was Meyer's contribution to architectural thought.

An anti-art aesthetic? What at the time was a seemingly blatant self-contradiction no longer holds after the lesson of an intervening fifty years of modernism and, more particularly, after the rise of semiology and its influence on modern aesthetic theory: Morris, Saussure and others have persuasively shown that nothing is without signification or aesthetic meaning. So Meyer with his contradictions has become a crucial figure to reassess. His conception of non-art architecture, or even anti-art architecture (if such a thing were possible, as it may be in the post-Saussure consciousness), would doubtless come across as a galvanic "statement" and hence a significant manifestation in the semiological books. His pure aesthetic neutrality, once achieved, would be loaded with values. Its very denials—unless invisible—would become emblematic.

Meyer's ironic failure to achieve these realizations of non-art in his own time, for example through the limited appreciation of such conceptual masterpieces as his competition drawings for the St. Peter's School, Basel (1926), has nevertheless not harmed his position with like-minded later fans, e.g. contemporary English neo-rationalists such as Cedric Price and Richard Rogers. In the end Hannes Meyer emerges both as a small historic figure, very much of his time—one especially sympathizes with his sad rootlessness, wandering from Russia to Mexico—and a far larger figure for the future.

—Nathan Silver

MEYER, Wilhelm Olaf.

South African. Born in Pretoria, 14 May 1935. Educated at the University of the Witwatersrand, Johannesburg, 1953-59 (Transvaal Institute of Architects First Prize, 1956, 1959; Gordon Leith Prize, 1959), B.Arch. 1959; University of Pennsylvania, Philadelphia, under Louis I. Kahn, *q.v.*, 1960-61 (Postgraduate Study Scholarship; Frank Miles Day Prize), M.Arch. 1961. Married Angela Winsome Murray in 1961; children: Arne and Alessandra. Partner, Watson, Peiser, Grobbelaar and Meyer, Pretoria, later also Johannesburg, 1961-66. Principal of Wilhelm O. Meyer and Partners Johannesburg, 1966-82, and Meyer Pienaar and Partners Inc., in Johannesburg and Durban, since 1982 (partners since 1971: Francois Pienaar; A. H. Olley; Jarmila Ondrackova; Floris Smith; Dexter Moren; Trevor Tennant). Guest Lecturer, University of Capetown, University of Natal, University of Pretoria, University of Potchefstroom, and University of the Witwatersrand, all South Africa, 1963-73. Founder-Member, Urban Action Group, Johannesburg, 1971, and Member of the Urban Action Teaching Group at the University of the Witwatersrand, 1973. Vice-President, 1976, and President, 1977, Transvaal Provincial Institute of Architects. Member of the Council of Architects, South Africa, since 1975; Chairman, South African Institute of Architects Housing Committee, 1977; Vice-President, 1979, President, 1983, South African Council of Architects; President-in-Chief, Inter-Bou, 1984. Exhibitions: Transvaal Academy Exhibition, Johannesburg, 1968; Pahlavi Library (Tehran) Exhibition in Tehran, Mexico City, Cape Town and Johannesburg, 1978. Recipient: First Prize, International Johannesburg Civic Centre Competition, 1962; Merit Award, South African Institute of Architects, 1964, 1966, 1972, 1975, 1977, 1981, 1983; First Prize,

Germiston Civic Centre Competition, 1973; Outstanding Young South African Award, 1973; Medal of Honour, Academy of Arts and Sciences of Architecture, 1980. Member, South African Institute of Architects, 1959; Associate, Royal Institute of British Architects, 1959. Address: Meyer Pienaar and Partners Inc., P.O. Box 52317, Saxonwold 2132, Johannesburg, South Africa.

Works:

1961/
62   Kenmauval Apartments, Pretoria (with the Watson Partnership)
1962/
63   Grupels Court Apartments, Pretoria (with the Watson Partnership)
     Botha Mansions Apartments, Pretoria (with the Watson Partnership)

Wilhelm O. Meyer: Verwoerdburg Urban Plan, South Africa, 1979.

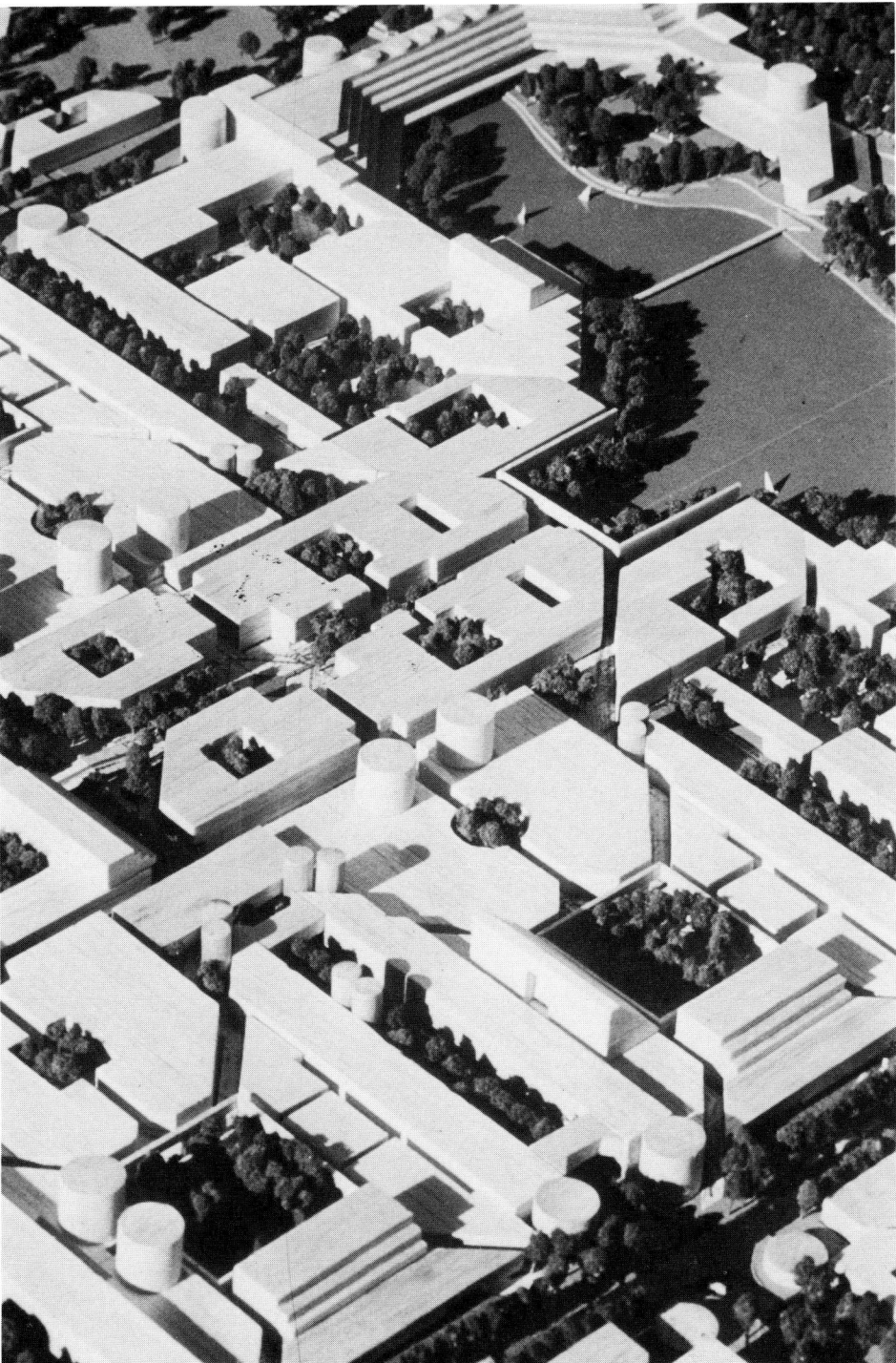

1963   Civic Centre, Johannesburg (with the Watson Partnership and Bryer and Partners)
1963/
64   Robinson House, Johannesburg (with Glen Gallagher)
1966/
67   Meyer House, Plettenberg Bay, South Africa
1968   Development plan for Rand Afrikaans University, Johannesburg (with Jan van Wijk and Partners)
1969   Development plan for Potchefstroom University, South Africa
       Architect's studio, Johannesburg
1969/
76   Student housing, Potchefstroom University, South Africa
1970/
75   Rand Afrikaans University, Johannesburg: Central Academic Facilities; Lecture Theatres; Laboratories and Library; Student Centre, Theatre and Sports Complex; Student Housing; Service Building and Central Plant (with Jan van Wijk and Partners)
1971/
75   Braamridge Head Office and Urban Centre, Johannesburg (with other firms)
1973   Civic Centre, Germiston, South Africa (competition project)
1973/
78   Potchefstroom University Biological Laboratories, stage I, and Education and Psychology Building, South Africa
1973/
79   Potchefstroom University Student Centre, Theatre and Sports Complex, South Africa (with Bannie Britz)
1975   Development plan for the University of Zululand, South Africa
       Urban plan for the Port Zimbali Resort Village, Natal North Coast, South Africa (with Revel Fox and Partners)
       Japan Architect Housing Competition, Tokyo (project)
1975/
76   McAdam House, Plettenberg Bay, South Africa
     Kruger House, Plettenberg Bay, South Africa
     Fihrer House, Plettenberg Bay, South Africa
     Sawmill and Factory, Plettenberg Bay, South Africa
     Sanctuary Vacation Village, Plettenberg Bay, South Africa (project)
1975/
77   Vaal Triangle College of Advanced Technology academic extension, Vanderbijlpark, South Africa
1976   University of Zululand Lecture Theatre Complex, South Africa
       Development plan for the University of the North, Transvaal, South Africa
       Development plan for Mabopane College of Advanced Technology, South Africa
       Rosebank Offices, Johannesburg
       Woodmead Town Houses, Johannesburg (project)
       Montgomery Park Town Houses, Johannesburg (project)
       Workers' Housing Village, Mabopane East, South Africa
1977   Development plan for the New Satellite Campus of Potchefstroom University, Vanderbijlpark, South Africa
       Development plan for University of Fort Hare, Cape Province, South Africa
       Student Housing, University of Fort Hare, Cape Province, South Africa
       Parliament Complex, High Courts, Presidential Suite and Ministries, Mmabatho, Bophuthatswana, Africa
1977/
78   Van der Wat House, Natures Valley, South Africa
     Perdikies House, Sandton, South Africa
     Pahlavi National Library, Tehran, Iran (competition project)
     New campus for Mabopane College of Advanced Technology, South Africa
1978   Hazyview Church, South Africa (competition project)
       Oppenheimer House, Witbank District, South Africa
       Meyer House, Parkview, South Africa
       Soweto Communal Centre, Soweto, South Africa
       Verwoerdburg New Town Plan, South Africa
       Fogel House, Johannesburg
       Spoormaker House, Johannesburg
1980   Jabulani Administration Centre, Soweto, South Africa
       Waddell House, Johannesburg
1981   Bloom House, Plettenberg Bay, South Africa
       Illman House, Johannesburg
       Ravensklip Old People's Homes for South African Railways, Johannesburg

Killarney Manor Apartments, Killarney, South Africa

Krugersdorp Civic Centre, Krugersdorp, South Africa

Everard Read Gallery, Rosebank, South Africa

Johannesburg Art Gallery extension, Johannesburg (to original Lutyens design)

Premier Group Headquarters, Killarney, South Africa

Fedmech Head Office, Vereeniging, South Africa (project)

Boumat Headquarters, Sandton, South Africa

Tai Long Wan urban plan, hotel and apartments, Lantau Island, Hong Kong (project)

Sturrock Park restaurant, pavilion and extensions for South African Railways, Johannesburg

1982 Endulini Office, Parktown, South Africa (project)

Eton Road Offices, Parktown, South Africa (project)

Alberton City Centre plan, pedestrianization and redevelopment, South Africa

Marine Parade Holiday Inn Hotel, Durban, South Africa

Collecott House, Sandton, South Africa

1983 Quartet development, Verwoerdburg, South Africa

Nasionale Pers Headquarters, Johannesburg

Rennies Executive Conference Centre, Wild Coast, Transkei

Beck Farm House, Cape Province, South Africa

1984 Roodepoort Country Club, Roodepoort, South Africa

Joshua Doore Shopping Centre, Nelspruit, South Africa

Ferndale Office Development, Randburg, South Africa

Publications:

By MEYER: articles—"The World of the House" in *South African Architectural Record* (Johannesburg), April 1965; "Values and the Making of Buildings" in *South African Architectural Record* (Johannesburg), November 1966; "Roofscapes" in *Habitat* (Johannesburg), no. 22, 1976; "The Architect's Responsibility for Better Building" in *Planning and Building* (Braamfontein), January 1976; "Beyond the Pigeonholes" and "Search and Exploration" in *South African Institute of Architects Golden Jubilee Congress Report*, Johannesburg 1977; "Homes Away from It All" in *Planning and Building* (Johannesburg), September 1977; "Pedro the Bull and Assorted Daisy Cows" in *Planning and Building Developments* (Braamfontein), April/May 1984.

On MEYER: book—*Meyer and Partners: Projects and Buildings 1967-1978*, Johannesburg 1978; articles—"Come Sara L'Architettura Africa" by J. Beinart in *Edilizia Moderna* (Milan), no. 89/90, 1963; "A Development Plan for Rand Afrikaans University" in *Architect and Builder* (Cape Town), May 1969; "Rand Afrikaans University" in *Bauen und Wohnen* (Zurich), November 1969; "Universities" by Julian Elliott in *Architectural Review* (London), April 1970; "Letter from Cape Town" by J. Morgan in *Architecture Plus* (New York), March 1974; "Johannesburg Revisited" by Theo Crosby in *RIBA Journal* (London), February 1976; "Pahlavi National Library" in *Domus* (Milan), August 1978; "Le Centre civique à Krugersdorp" in *Architecture d'aujourd'hui* (Paris), no. 219, 1981; "Tai Long Wan" in *Planning and Building Developments* (Braamfontein), March 1982; "Potchefstroom University" in *Architect and Builder* (Cape Town), July 1982; "In Progress: Museums" in *Progressive Architecture* (New York), August 1983; "Architecture as an

Object of Cultural Exchange" by Lindsay Bremner in *Architecture South Africa* (Cape Town), January 1984; "Killarney Manor" in *Planning and Building Developments* (Braamfontein), February 1984; "Allerton's Urban Renaissance" in *Planning and Building Developments* (Braamfontein), June 1984; "Meyer Pienaar and Partners" by Stephen Trombley in *RIBA Journal* (London), September 1984.

*

Any place succeeds even if it gives man only a glimpse of his highest aspirations. The great, the monumental, the awe-inspiring, the intimate, the socially responsible, the unassuming, the commonplace can all do this. Man's spirit can be touched by the unique and heroic as well as by the ordinary and humble in the complexity of human requirements and desires. Although these values can be circumstantially varied in their application, they cannot be invalidated or polarised into right or wrong. In man's history they are cyclical elements and not absolute. Order may thus include that which seems to be its opposite in the physical life condition of dualities and polarity. Even in doing so Ultimate Order is never escaped.

The golden thread of endeavour is perceived through anticipation and retrospection; prophecy and memory. Without considering two directions—backward and forward—the thread can have no continuity. Without considering both, in unison, there can be no thread. If something is loved deeply, it cannot be copied, but it can inspire a not dissimilar response. Reverence for the integrity of the original will only allow its essence to inform a later fragment of man's visual history.

In one's work the ramifications of various theories and images of the time are obviously present in suffused fashion behind what one does. But expression as such remains personal and belongs to the individual maker. This is part of his private world and fantasies for which he is not answerable to anyone. The art of the possible is no art without compelling visions in the impossible. But no matter the momentary and transitory foibles of expression one inadvertently journeys through from innovation through being cliché back to the same innovation in a new guise, the real interest one has in one's own work lies in how far it approaches the personal quest of interpretation of the timeless qualities and values in ever changing conditions and renewing circumstances.

For the architect, the work he does should always remain his way of expressing how he feels about and for his fellow man. It is as direct as that with no shorter cut and, constantly kept in mind, will act as the most reliable measure in all his concerns and sensibilities nurtured by deep inner awareness, whether these be social, aesthetic, practical or technical. Architecture means the thoughtful housing of the human spirit in the physical world. The architect becomes the enabling instrument only when he reaches in beyond himself. Ultimately, however, there is no shame or pity in architecture losing if life wins.

—Wilhelm O. Meyer

*

When Wilhelm O. Meyer studied at the University of the Witwatersrand during the late 1950s, the bloom had already gone off the influence there of the modern movement: that influence had been strongest in the 1930s and early 40s. There was a general searching about for a philosophical framework, for the architecture of the late 1950s was to a great extent dull and derivative, with few memorable works. Meyer was one of a group of young South Africans, which included Roelof Uytenbogaardt, Francois Pienaar, Danie Theron and Glen Gallagher who studied during the late 1950s and early 60s at the University of Pennsylvania under the then prevailing influence of Louis Kahn. On his return to South Africa, Meyer produced works that showed the influences of Kahn's formal approach: such apartment buildings as Grupels Court and Botha Man-

sions show a vigorous articulation of form, as does Robertson House (with Glen Gallagher).

Meyer participated with others in the winning scheme for the new Johannesburg Civic Centre, but both in detail and in overall form this scheme seems related to work in Johannesburg of the late 1950s: at that time the move away from the modern movement was characterized by detailed design, by some classical precedents, and, to an extent, by the influence of Fassler and the later work of Norman Hanson. The formal language of the Johannesburg Civic Centre was significantly different from the forms that Meyer chose for himself in his own work, particularly the design for the Rand Afrikaans University—his major work of the period: with its vigorous forms and its powerfully expressed enclosing shape, it was one of the most powerful images of a university of the 1960s. The style he achieved here expressed also the powerful drives within the Afrikaner community in South Africa. The form and the articulated shape, monumental scale, and, as Theo Crosby put it, "the Piranesian grandeur of the interiors" were entirely appropriate for the period.

There is in Meyer's work the development of two main themes: the search for a strong geometric form on a fairly monumental scale and the attempt to capture the "genius loci." He has been commissioned for several buildings of a similar kind—government, parliament and other institutional buildings—which he has done with considerable panache, and all have by their nature encouraged the formal and the monumental. The geometry of Germiston Civic Centre is somewhat freer than the others and shows a confident approach to the handling of relationships in a tighter urban context.

What distinguishes the subsequent work, such as the Pahlavi National Library competition entry and the parliament building projects, is the use of a simpler form for the building, with less articulation of the parts. This work is characterized by clarity of detailing and a great consistency of the parts to the whole. What one misses in these large-scale schemes is the gentler geometry and softer forms that only now and again have found their place in his work. Meyer's house for his parents in Plettenberg Bay, with its gentle shaping of the not too greatly articulated elements in plan, shows an appropriateness to site and relative smallness of scale that are welcome. Now that the period of heavy articulated forms in South African architecture has passed, Meyer moves into a period where possibly the commissions will be of a different nature and where this lighter touch and smaller scale may form part of his further development.

Meyer's work and that of his nearest collaborators and associates—Glen Gallagher, Bannie Britz and Francois Pienaar (a partner of long standing)—has been an important influence in South Africa, and there is for the period 1965-75 a discernible "school" in the Witwatersrand area that, though obviously revealing the influence of Louis Kahn, has steadily gained its own characteristic features. Influences have clearly been imported, but it is no longer a question of "alms from abroad," for there is in this work an exportable vision of its own.

—Hans Hallen

MICHELUCCI, Giovanni.

Italian. Born in Pistoia, 2 January 1891. Educated at the School of Architecture, Florence, 1908-11, Dip. Arch. 1911; Academy of Fine Arts, Florence, 1911-14. Served in the Italian Armyh, 1915-16. Married Aloisia Pacini in 1928. In private practice, Fiesole, since 1916. Teacher at the Institute of Art, Pisa, 1916-20, and Rome, 1920-28; Professor of Interior Design, School of Architecture, Florence, 1928-39; Professor, 1939-44, Chair in Urban Planning, 1944-45,

Giovanni Michelucci: Church of San Giovanni Battista, Campi Bisenzio, Florence, 1960-64.

Chair in Architectural design, 1944-45, and Dean of the School of Architecture, 1944-45, 1947-48, University of Florence; Chair in Architectural Composition, Faculty of Engineering, 1948-66, and since 1966 Emeritus Professor, University of Bologna. Director, *La Nuova Città*, 1945-56; Founder, Esperienza Artigiana, 1949; Director, *Panorami della Nuova Città*, 1950-52. Exhibitions: *Esposizione di Architettura Razionale*, Galleria di Palazzo Ferroni, Florence, 1932; *Ten Italian Architects*, Los Angeles, 1967; *La Città di Michelucci*, Palazzo del Comune, Fiesole, Italy, 1976; *Giovanni Michelucci*, Heinz Gallery, Royal Institute of British Architects, London 1978. Recipient: First Prize, *Italian Gardens Exhibition*, Florence, 1931; First Prize, with others, S. Maria Novella Station Competition, Florence, 1933; First Prize, with others, Master Plan of Pistoia Competition, 1936; First Prize, with others, Grazie Bridge Competition, Florence, 1954; Feltrinelli Prize, 1958; San Luca International Prize for Architecture, 1958. Address (office): Villa Il Roseto, Via Beato Angelico 15, 50014 Fiesole, Florence, Italy.

Works:

1916 Chapel, Caporetto, Italy
1920 House, Via Bellini, Pistoia, Italy
1921 War Memorial, Ancona, Italy (competition project)
1924 House, Via Rosselli, Montecatini, Italy
      Valdissena House, Pescia, Italy
1929 Balilla Headquarters, Piazza S. Francesco, Pistoia, Italy (with Raffaello Fagnoni)
1930 Valiani House, Via Mangili, Rome
      Dining Room Pavilion, *riennale*, Monza, Italy

1931 Valiani Villa, Via Prenestina, Rome
      Alfredo Casella Villa, Rome (project)
1932 Exhibition Halls, *Fiera Nazionale dell'-Artigianato*, Florence (with Pier Niccolo Bernardi, Gherardo Bosio, and Sarre Guarnieri)
1933 Master plan for University City, Rome (with others)
1935 S. Maria Novella Station, Florence (with others)
      Institute of General Physiology, Psychology and Anthropolgy, University City, Rome
      Institute of Mineralogy, Geology, and Paleontology, University City, Rome
      Covered Market, Piazza de Guidici, Florence (project)
1936 Master plan of Pistoia, Italy (competition project with A. Susini and L. Fuselli)
      Facade for *VI Mostra Mercato dell'-Artigianato*, Florence
1938 Government Building, Savona, Italy (competition project)
1939 Government Building, Arezzo, Italy
      Open-Air Theatre, E.42 District, Rome (project)
      Palace of Light and Water, E.42 District, Rome (project)
      Government Building, Savona, Italy (2nd project)
      Villa Contini-Bonacossi extensions, Viale Morin, Forte dei Marmi, Italy
      Tower conversion to house and gallery, Via Guicciardini, Florence (destroyed during World War II)
1946 Reconstruction of the area around the Ponte Vecchio, Florence
1947 Tower conversion, Vicolo dei Ramaglianti, Florence

1948 Funeral Chapel, S. Miniato al Monte, Italy
      House, Lido d'Albaro, Genoa
      Cassa di Risparmio Building, Viareggio, Italy
      Cassa di Risparmio Building, Volterra, Italy
1950 Stock Exchange, Pistoia, Italy
      Bathing Resort, Sori, Genoa (project)
      House, Via Montebello, Florence
      Baldassare House, Francavilla al Mare, Chieti, Italy (project)
      Skyscraper, Marsaglia Park, San Remo, Italy
1953 Caffe Donnini, Piazza della Repubblica, Florence
1954 Master plan for Ferrara, Italy (as consultant)
      Collina di Pentolungo Church, Pistoia, Italy
      Grazie Bridge, Florence (competition project); with E. Detti and D. Santi)
      Carrais Bridge, Florence (competition project; with E. Detti and D. Santi)
      Vespucci Bridge, Florence (competition project; with L. Cestelli-Guidi)
1956 Church of the Virgin, Via Bassa della Vergine, Pistoia, Italy
1957 Residential Zone and Church, Sasso Pisano, Italy
      Larderello Workers Village, Pisa
      Ventura House, Via Guicciardini 24, Florence
      INA Apartment Building, Via Guicciardini, Florence
      House, Via Monte Pania 1, Lido di Camaiore, Lucca, Italy
      Cassa di Risparmio Building, Via Bufalini, Florence
      Skyscraper, Livorno (project)
      Cabin, Torre S. Lorenzo, Italy (with L. Lugli)
      Società Larderello Building, Pisa
      Uffizi Gallery re-organization, Florence
1958 Master Plan for the Sorgane Quarter of Florence (as co-ordinator)

Citadel Gardens, Pisa
Galileo Center, Pisa (project)
1959 Institute of Geology, University of Bologna
Faculty of Letters and Philosophy, University of Bologna
Larderello Church, Pisa
Cemetery Church, Pistoia, Italy
Institute of Mathematics, University of Bologna
1961 Belvedere Church, Pistoia, Italy
Apartment buildings/shops, Lungarno del Tempio, Florence
1962 Giunti House, Viareggio, Italy
1963 Osteria del Gambero Rosso, Collodi, Pistoia, Italy
Memorial to the Victims of Kindu, Pisa Airport
Apartment/office building, Piazza Brunelleschi, Florence
1964 Church of St. John the Baptist, Autostrade del Sole at Campi Bisenzio, Florence
Concert Hall, Montecatini Terme, Italy (project)
Concert Hall and Art School, Ravenna (project)
Quadrio House, Milan (project)
Tomb of Dante (project)
1965 Rosetti House, Ravenna (project)
Monument to the Carabiniere, Fiesole, Florence
School and Village Garden, Arzignano, Vicenza, Italy
Institute of Chemistry, University of Florence (project)
1966 Skyscraper, Livorno
Borgo Maggiore Church, San Marino
1967 Arzignano Church, Vicenza, Italy
SIP Headquarters, Via Masaccio, Florence
Stock Exchange extension, Pistoia, Italy
Cassa di Risparmio Headquarters, Pistoia, Italy
Post office, Via Verdi, Florence
1969 Sampiva House, Arzignano, Vicenza, Italy
Bracco Chapel, Trespiano, Florence
1971 Master plan for Camaiore, Lucca, Italy
1972 Cangioli House, Pistoia, Italy
Scaglietti Chapel, Collodi Cemetary, Pistoia, Italy (project)
1973 Orangery reconstruction, Villa Strozzi, Florence (project)
1974 Tozzelli House, Pistoia, Italy
Plan for the center of Sesto Fiorentino, Italy
1975 Bastione Thyrion Secondary School, Pistoia, Italy
Post office, Viareggio, Lucca, Italy (with A. Pasquinucci)
Marble Experimental Center, Foce di Pianza, Carrarà, Italy (with B. Sacchi)
Monte dei Paschi di Siena Headquarters, Colle Val d'Elsa, Siena (project; with B. Sacchi)
Contrada del Palio Valdimontone Headquarters, Siena (project; with B. Sacchi)
Bini House, Pescia, Pistoia, Italy (with B. Sacchi)
Plan for the center of Arzignano, Vicenza, Italy (project; with B. Sacchi)
1976 Telecommunications Center, Pisa (with M. Innocenti)
Cassa di Risparmio Headquarters, Via Montalbano, Pistoia, Italy (with B. Sacchi)
Church, Livorno (project; with B. Sacchi)
Lacini House, Montemarcello, La Spezia, Italy (project; with B. Sacchi)
Friendship Monument, Church of St. John the Baptist, Autostrade del Sole at Campi Bisenzio, Florence
1978 San Bartolomeo Hospital, Sarzana, Italy (with M. Innocenti)
Novello Church, Cutigliano, Pistoia, Italy (project; with B. Sacchi)
Oratorio di San Leonardo conversion, Siena (project; with B. Sacchi)
1980/
83 Thermal Centre, Carrara, Italy (project; with B. Sacchi)
1980/
84 Sports Centre, Prato, Florence (project; with Mauro Innocenti)
1982 Monte dei Paschi di Siena Bank, Colle Val d'Elsa, Siena (with B. Sacchi)

Publications:

By MICHELUCCI: Books—*Filippo Brunelleschi*, Florence 1936; *Il Quartiere di Santa Croce nel Futuro di Firenze*, with A. Ardigo and F. Borsi, Rome 1968; *Brunelleschi Mago*, Florence 1972; *La Nuova Cittá*, edited by R. Risaliti, Pistoia, Italy 1975; *Non sono un Maestro*, Sarzana, Italy 1976; *Michelucci, il linguaggio dell'architettura*, with Franco Borsi, edited by Maria Cristina Buscioni, Rome 1979; *La felicita dell'architettura*, Pistoia 1981; articles—numerous in *Lo Stile* (Milan), 1942-43, *La Nuova Cittá* (Florence), 1946-56; "Ambienti Storici e Urbanistica Moderna" in *Domus* (Milan), no. 223/225, 1947; "La Ricostruzione in Toscana nell'Umbria e nelle Marche" in *Edilizia Moderna* (Milan), no. 40/42, 1948; "Felicita dell'Architetto" in *Domus* (Milan), no. 234, 1949; numerous in *Panorami della Nuova Cittá* (Florence), 1950-52, and *Urbanistica* (Turin), 1951-53; "Lettera per la Casa di Wright sul Canal Grande" in *Metron* (Rome), no. 51, 1954; "Come ho Progettato la Chiesa della Vergine" in *L'Architettura* (Rome), no. 16, 1957; "Sorgane: Quartiere Autosufficiente" in *Edilizia Popolare* (Rome), no. 16, 1957; "Punti Interrogativi" in *Quaderni della Nuova Cittá*, Florence 1957; "Rispondere ad una Esigenza Popolare con una Forma Culturalmente Efficace" in *L'Architettura* (Rome), no. 31, 1958; "Una Casa che non e un Villino, a Firenze" in *L'Architettura* (Rome), no. 35, 1958; "Chiesa di Larderello" in *L'Architettura* (Rome), no. 46, 1959; "La Scuola e La Cittá" in *Prospettive Storiche e Problemi Attuali dell'Educazione: Studi in Onore di E. Codignola*, Florence 1960; "La Concezione Architettonica della Chiesa" in *Civiltá delle Macchine* (Rome), no. 5, 1961; "Pensieri di Michelucci" in *L'Architettura* (Rome), no. 76, 1962; "De nombreuses chose d'abord obscures se sont éclairices et m'ont paru nouvelles" in *L'Architecture d'Aujourd'hui* (Paris), no. 113-114, 1964; "Sintonia" in *Domus* (Milan), no. 413, 1964; "Giustificazione di una Forma Architettonica" in *Autostrade* (Rome), no. 3, 1964; "L'Eglise de San Marino" in *L'Architecture d'Aujourd'hui* (Paris), no. 119, 1965; "Urbanistica: Problema Umano" in *Vita Sociale* (Pistoia, Italy), no. 2, 1966; "La Cittá del Dialogo" in *Testimonianze* (Florence), no. 85, 1966; "Il Cantiere" in *Vita Sociale* (Pistoia, Italy), no. 5/6, 1966; "La Genesi dell'Opera" in *Casabella* (Milan), no. 311, 1966; "Architettura e Societá Civile" in *Vita Sociale* (Pistoia, Italy), no. 3, 1967; "Lo Spazio e il Lugo dove l'Uomo construisce la sua Storia" in *Problemi della Cittá*, Padua 1967; "Considerazione di Urbanistica" in *A Proposito di una Polemica sul P. R. di Fiesole*, Pistoia, Italy 1969; "La Chiesa di Longarone" in *Civiltá delle Macchine* (Rome), no. 1, 1970; "La Cittá Antica nella Moderna" in *Firenze: Notizario del Commune* (Florence), no. 1, 1971; "Misura e Caratteri Umani della Cittá" in *Vita Sociale* (Pistoia, Italy), no. 146, 1971; "Giovanni Michelucci sulla Linguistica Architettonica" in *L'Architettura* (Rome), no. 227, 1974; "La Cittá e La Salute" in *La Riforma Sanitaria*, Pistoia, Italy 1974; "Una Chiesa che serva alla Cittá" in *Testimonianze* (Florence), April/May 1974; "Per una'altro Cittá" in *Parametro* (Bologna), May 1975; "Gilberto Rossini" in *Architettura* (Rome), May 1982; etc.

On MICHELUCCI: books—*Cassa di Risparmio di Firenze* by E. Berti and M. Gobbo, Florence 1958; *La Chiesa dell'Autostrada del Sole*, Rome 1964; *Giovanni Michelucci* edited by Franco Borsi, Florence 1966; *Giovanni Michelucci: Il Pensiero e le Opera* by F. Clemente and L. Lugli, Bologna 1966; *Michelucci* by M. Cerasi, Rome 1968; *Firenze Chiesa dell'Autostrada* by A. Ottani Cavina, Bologna 1968; *La Cittá di Michelucci*, exhibition catalogue, by Franco Borsi and others, Pistoia, Italy 1976; *Giovanni Michelucci* by Fabio Naldi, Florence 1978; *Giovanni Michelucci*, exhibition catalogue, Florence 1978; *La Chiesa di Longarone dell'architetto Giovanni Michelucci* by Franco Borsi and others, Florence 1978; *Giovanni Michelucci: la pazienza delle stagioni* by Ludovic Quaroni, Salvatore di Pasquale and Giovanni Landucci, Florence 1980; articles—"Giovanni Michelucci," special issue of *Space Design* (Tokyo), October 1979; "Interview with Giovanni Michelucci" by S. Cammilli in *Modo*, September 1980.

From the detachment and the impartiality of his S. Maria Novella Station in Florence, won in competition in 1933, to the saturnalia of the 1964 Church of St. John the Baptist near Florence, dedicated to the memory of the workers who lost their lives during the construction of the Autostrade del Sole, Giovanni Michelucci has never been afraid of practising abstinence one day, epicurism the next. One day he is a model of functionalist virtue, a paragon of philanthropic innocence, stainless and incorruptable, mobilising architecture for a good and righteous cause—and his buildings are principled and moral havens, harbours of ethical integrity and the cardinal virtues. Another day will find him egocentric, impatient to explore the voluptuousness in a detail here, the carnality in a material there, the earthiness of that section over there—on such a day, many diverse currents are ingeniously assimilated, resulting in intermittent architectonics irradiated with human involvement.

Obdurate members of both camps, the rationalists and the organicists, are usually outraged by Michelucci's blithe disregard for their carefully established and long maintained categories—but both camps might have something to learn from his contribution. Le Corbusier was constantly running into the same problem: architecture will always be bigger than the terms we invent to decribe it.

—Chris Fawcett

MIES van der ROHE, Ludwig.
American. Born Ludwig Mies in Aachen, Germany, 27 March 1886 (later adopted mother's name van der Rohe); emigrated to the United States, 1938: naturalized, 1944. Educated at the Domschule, Aachen, 1897-1900; Aachen Trade School, 1900-02. Served in the German Army, in the Engineer Corps, 1914-18. Married Ada Bruhn in 1914 (separated, 1925; died 1951); three daughters. Worked in his father's stonemason business, Aachen, 1900-02; draftsman in a stucco decorating business, Aachen, 1903-04; moved to Berlin and worked briefly in the office of an architect specializing in wood structures, 1905; apprenticed to the architect and furniture designer Bruno Paul, Berlin, 1905-07; in private architectural practice, Berlin, 1907-08; Assistant, with Walter Gropius, q.v., and Le Corbusier, q.v., in the office of Peter Behrens, q.v., Berlin, 1908-11; in private practice, Berlin, 1911-14 and 1919-37; in private architectural practice, Chicago, 1938 until his death in 1969 (firm continues as FCL Associates). Director of the Bauhaus at Dessau, 1930-32, and in Berlin, 1932 until it closed in 1933; Director of Architecture, Illinois Institute of Technology (formerly Armour Institute), Chicago, 1938-59. Co-Founder, *G* (Gestaltung) magazine Berlin, 1921; Director of Architectural Exhibits, Novembergruppe, Berlin, 1921-25; Founder, Zehner Ring, Berlin, 1925; First Vice-President, Deutscher Werkbund, Berlin, 1926-32, and Director of the Werkbund exhibition *Weissenhofsiedlung*, Stuttgart, 1927,

and of the Werkbund section, "The Dwelling," at the Berlin Building Exhibition, 1931; President, CIAM (Congrès Internationaux d'Architecture Moderne). Exhibitions (individual): Museum of Modern Art, New York, 1947; Art Institute of Chicago, 1968 (toured the United States, Canada and Europe); *A New City Square and Office Tower*, Royal Exchange, London, 1968; *Ludwig Mies van Rohe: Furniture and Furniture Drawings*, Museum of Modern Art, New York, 1977; *The Barcelona Pavilion—50 Years*, National Gallery of Art, Washington, D.C., 1979; *Mies van der Rohe: Interior Spaces*, Arts club of Chicago, 1982. Recipient: Royal Gold Medal, Royal Institute of British Architects, 1959; Gold Medal, American Institute of Architects, 1960; Gold Medal of Honor, with Philip Johnson, Architectural League of New York, 1960; Fine Arts Prize, City of Berlin, 1961; United States Presidential Medal of Freedom, 1963; Gold Medal, Bund Deutscher Architeken, Germany, 1966. D.F.A.: Carnegie Institute of Technology, Pittsburgh, Pennsylvania, 1960; Northwestern University, Evanston, Illinois, 1963; University of Illinois, Urbana-Champaign, 1964; D.Eng.: Institute of Technology, Karlsruhe, West Germany, 1950; Institute of Technology, Braunschweig, West Germany, 1955; LL.D.: University of North Carolina, Chapel Hill, 1956; D.H.: Wayne State University, Detroit, 1961. Member, National Institute of Arts and Letters, 1963. Member, Prussian Academy of Arts and Sciences, 1931; Commander (with cross), German Order of Merit, 1959. *Died* (in Chicago) *17 August 1969*.

Works:

1907 Riehl House, Neubabelsberg, Berlin
1911 Perls House (later Fuchs House), Zehlendorf, Berlin
1912 Kröller House, The Hague (project)
    Bismarck Memorial, Bingen am Rhein, Germany (competition project)
1913 House, Heerstrasse, Berlin
1914 Urbig House, Neubabelsberg, Berlin
    Mies van der Rohe House, Werder, Germany
1919 Glass Skyscraper, Friedrichstrasse, Berlin (competition project)
1920 Kempner House, Berlin (destroyed)
1921 Glass Skyscraper II, Berlin (project)
    Petermann House, Neubabelsberg, Berlin (project)
1922 Reinforced Concrete and Glass Office Building, Berlin (project)
1923 Brick Country House (project)
    Lessing House, Neubabelsberg, Berlin (project)
    Eliat House, Nedlitz bei Potsdam, near Berlin (project)
1924 Reinforced Concrete Villa (project)
    Traffic Tower, Berlin (project)
    Mosler House, Neubabelsberg, Berlin
1925 Municipal housing development, Afrikanischestrasse, Berlin
1926 Wolf House Guben, Germany
    Monument to Karl Liebknecht and Rosa Luxemburg, Berlin (demolished by the Nazis)
1927 Apartment Building (with furniture—e.g., the MR Chair—and interiors in collaboration with Lilly Reich) and General Plan, Werkbund exhibition *Weissenhofsiedlung*, Stuttgart
    Silk Exhibit, *Exposition de la mode*, Berlin (with Lilly Reich)
1928 Fuchs House (originally Perls House) additions, Zehlendorf, Berlin
    Remodelling of the Alexanderplatz, Berlin (competition project)
    Adam Building, Leipzigerstrasse, Berlin (competition project)

Ludwig Mies van der Rohe: IBM Building, Chicago, 1967.

Hermann Lange House, Krefeld, Germany (badly damaged in the war)

Esters House, Krefeld, Germany (badly damaged in the war)

1929 Office Building, Friedrichstrasse, Berlin (competition project)

German Pavilion (including furniture, e.g., the Barcelona Chair), International Exposition, Barcelona (demolished 1929; reconstructed 1983-84)

Electricity Pavilion, International Exposition, Barcelona (demolished)

Industrial Exhibits, International Exposition Barcelona (with Lilly Reich)

1930 Tugendhat House (with furniture and interiors), Brno, Czechoslovakia (badly damaged in the war; later converted to a gymnasium)

Country Club Building, Krefeld, Germany (competition project)

War Memorial, Berlin (competition project)

Gericke House, Wannsee, Berlin (competition project)

Philip Johnson Apartment interiors, New York

1931 House, and Apartment for a Bachelor, Building Exhibition, Berlin (demolished)

Court Houses (project)

1932 Lemcke House, Berlin

1933 Reichsbank, Berlin (competition project)

Factory Building and Power House for the Silk Industry, Vereinigte Seidenwerbereien AG., Krefeld, Germany

1934 Mining Exhibit, *German People—German Work* exhibition, Berlin

Mies van der Rohe House, Tyrol, Austria (project)

German Pavilion, International Exposition, Brussels (competition project)

Filling Station (competition project)

1935 Lange House, Krefeld, Germany (two projects)

Hubbe House, Magdeburg, Germany (project)

1937 Silk Industry Administration Building, Krefeld, Germany (project)

1938 Resor House, Jackson Hole, Wyoming (project)

1939 Preliminary master plan for the Illinois Institute of Technology, Chicago

1941 Revised master plan for the Illinois Institute of Technology, Chicago

1942 Museum for a Small City (project)

Concert Hall (project)

1943 Minerals and Metals Research Building, Illinois Institute of Technology, Chicago (with Holabird and Root)

1944 Library/Adminstration Building, Illinois Institute of Technology, Chicago (project)

1945 Alumni Memorial Hall, Illinois Institute of Technology, Chicago (with Holabird and Root)

Metallurgy and Chemical Engineering Building, Illinois Institute of Technology, Chicago (with Holabird and Root)

Chemistry Building, Illinois Institute of Technology, Chicago (with Friedman, Alschuler and Sincere)

Joe Cantor Drive-In Restaurant, Indianapolis (project)

1947 Cantor House, Indianapolis (project)

1948 Student Union Building, Illinois Institute of Technology, Chicago (project)

1949 Promontory Apartments, 5530 South Shore Drive, Chicago (with Pace Associates, and Holsman, Holsman, Klekamp and Taylor)

1950 Farnsworth House, on the Fox River, Plano, Illinois

Institute of Gas Technology, Illinois Institute of Technology, Chicago (with Friedman, Alschuler and Sincere)

Boiler Plant, Illinois Institute of Technology, Chicago (with Sargent and Lundy, and Frank Konnaker)

Central Research Laboratory, for the Association of American Railroads, Illinois Institute of Technology, Chicago (with Friedman, Alschuler and Sincere)

Cantor Commercial Center, Indianpolis (project)

Caine House, Winnetka, Illinois (project)

1951 McCormick House, Elmhurst, Illinois

Mechanical Research Building, for the Armour Research Foundation, Illinois Institute of Technology, Chicago (with Friedman, Alschuler and Sincere)

Steel-Frame Pre-fabricated Row House (project)

Pi Lambda Phi Fraternity House, University of Indiana, Bloomington (project)

Fifty by Fifty Foot-Square House (project)

860 and 880 Lake Shore Drive Apartments, Chicago (with Pace Associates, and Holsman, Holsman, Klekamp and Taylor)

Algonquin Apartments, Chicago (project; with Pace Associates)

1952 Chapel, Illinois Institute of Technology, Chicago

1953 Carman Hall: Faculty and Student Apartment Building, Illinois Institute of Technology, Chicago (with Pace Associates)

Mechanical Laboratory, for the Association of American Railroads, Illinois Institute of Technology, Chicago (with Friedman, Alschuler and Sincere)

Student Commons Building, Illinois Institute of Technology, Chicago (with Friedman, Alschuler and Sincere)

National Theatre, Mannheim, West Germany (project)

1954 Convention Hall, Chicago (project)

Master plan for the Museum of Fine Arts, Houston, Texas

1955 Bailey Hall, Illinois Institute of Technology, Chicago (with Pace Associates)

Cunningham Hall, Illinois Institute of Technology, Chicago (with Pace Associates)

1956 Physics-Electronics Research Building, Illinois Institute of Technology, Chicago (with C. F. Murphy Associates)

Crown Hall: School of Architecture and Design, Illinois Institute of Technology, Chicago (with C. F. Murphy and Associates)

Master plan for Lafayette Park, Detroit

Commonwealth Promenade Apartments, Chicago (with Friedman, Alschuler and Sincere)

900 Esplanade Apartments, Chicago (with Friedman, Alschuler and Sincere)

1957 Laboratory Building, for the Association of American Railroads, Illinois Institute of Technology, Chicago (with Friedman, Alschuler and Sincere)

Siegel Hall, Illinois Institute of Technology, Chicago (with Pace Associates)

United States Consulate, Sao Paulo, Brazil (project)

Quadrangle Apartments, Brooklyn, New York (project)

Bacardi Office Building, Santiago, Cuba (project)

1958 Metals Research Building, Illinois Institute of Technology, Chicago (with Holabird and Root)

Seagram Building, 375 Park Avenue, New York (with Philip Johnson, and Kahn and Jacobs)

Pavilion Apartments, Lafayette Park, Detroit

Joliet, La Salle and Nicolet Street Town Houses, Lafayette Park, Detroit

Battery Park Apartment Development, New York (project)

1959 Cullinan Hall, Museum of Fine Arts, Houston, Texas (with Staub, Rather and Howze)

Master plan for the Federal Center, Chicago

1960 Pavilion and Colonnade Apartments, Colonnade Park, Newark, New Jersey

1961 Bacardi Office Building, Mexico City (with Saenz, Cancio, Martin, Guttierez)

1962 Georg-Schafer-Museum, Schweinfurt, West Germany (project)

Home Federal Savings and Loan Association Building, Des Moines, Iowa (with Smith, Voorhees, Jensen)

1963 Lafayette Towers, Lafayette Park, Detroit

One Charles Center Office Building, Baltimore, Maryland

2400 Lakeview Apartments, Chicago (with Greenberg and Finfer)

Krupp Administration Building, Essen, West Germany (project)

1964 Meredith Memorial Hall, Drake University, Des Moines, Iowa

Mountain Place, Montreal (project)

Highfield House (apartment building), Baltimore, Maryland

1965 School of Social Service Administration, University of Chicago

1966 Church Street South School, New Haven, Connecticut (project)

Development plan for New Haven, Connecticut

Foster City Apartment Buildings, San Mateo, California (project)

1967 City Square and Office Tower, London (project; with William Holford and Partners)

IBM Building, Chicago (with C. F. Murphy Associates)

1968 Science Center, Duquesne University, Pittsburgh, Pennsylvania (with Paul Schweikher)

Nationalgalerie, West Berlin

Westmont Square, Montreal (with Greenspoon, Freedlander, Plachta and Kyrton)

Esso Service Station, Nun's Island, Montreal (with Paul LaPointe)

Commerzbank Office and Bank Building, Frankfurt (project)

1969 Toronto-Dominion Centre (as consultant; with John B. Parkin Associates and Bregman and Hamann)

Museum of Fine Arts additions, Houston, Texas

Blue Cross Building, Chicago (project)

High Rise Apartment Block I, Nun's Island, Montreal (with Philip Bobrow)

King Broadcasting Studios, Seattle (project)

High Rise Apartment Blocks II and III, Nun's Island, Montreal (with Edgar Tornay)

High Rise Apartment Block IV, Nun's Island, Montreal (completed by others)

Northwest Plaza, Chicago (project)

Dominion Square, Montreal (project)

American Life and Accident Insurance Company Building, Louisville, Kentucky (completed by others)

General plan for the Illinois Central Air Rights Development, Chicago

Two Illinois Center Building, Chicago (completed by others)

Loop College, Chicago (completed by others)

1970 111 East Wacker Drive Building, Chicago (completed by others)

Indiana Bell Telephone Company District Office, Columbus, Indiana (completed by others)

1973 Federal Center, Chicago (with A. E. Epstein and Sons, C. F. Murphy Associates, and Schmidt, Garden and Erikson: completed by associates)

Publications:

By MIES: books—*Bürohaus,* Berlin 1923, revised edition as *Der moderne Zweckbau,* Munich 1926; *Industrielles Bauen,* Berlin 1924; articles—"Hochhaus-projekt für Bahnhof Friedrichstrasse in Berlin" in *Frühlicht* (Berlin), January 1922; "Baukunst und Zeitwille" in *Querschnitt* (Berlin),

April 1924; "Briefe an die Form" in *Form* (Berlin), January 1926; "Rundschau: Zum Neuen Jahrgang" in *Form* (Berlin), February 1927; "Preface" and "Zu Meinen Block" in *Weissenhofsiedlung*, Deutscher Werkbund exhibition catalogue, Stuttgart 1927; "Werkbundaustellung: Die Wohnung Stuttgart" in *Form* (Berlin), September 1927; "Zum Thema: Austellung" in *Form* (Berlin), April 1928; "Uber Kunstkritik" in *Kunstblatt* (Berlin), June 1930; "Frank Lloyd Wright: An Appreciation" in *College Art Journal* (New York), Autumn 1946; "Das Schöne is der Glanz des Wahren" in *Neue Zeitung*, Berlin 1950; "Arbeitsthesen," "Uber die Form in der Architektur," "Die neue Zeit," and "Technik und Architektur" in *Programme und Manifeste zur Architektur des 20. Jahrhunderts*, Berlin, 1964.

On MIES: books—*Mies van der Rohe* by Philip Johnson, New York 1947, 3rd edition 1978; *Ludwig Mies van der Rohe* by Max Bill, Milan 1955; *Mies van der Rohe* by Ludwig Hilberseimer, Chicago 1956; *Architecture U.S.A.* by Ian McCallum, New York and London 1959; *The Master Builders* by Peter Blake, New York 1960; *Ludwig Mies van der Rohe* by Arthur Drexler, New York and London 1960; *Contemporary Architecture: Its Roots and Trends* by Ludwig Hilberseimer, Chicago 1964; *Mies van der Rohe: The Art of Structure* by Werner Blaser, New York, Stuttgart and London 1965; *Mies van der Rohe*, exhibition catalogue, by James Speyer and Frederick Koeper, Chicago 1968; *Mies van der Rohe* by Martin Pawley, Tokyo 1968, London 1970; *Ludwig Mies van der Rohe: Drawings in the Collection of the Museum of Modern Art* by Ludwig Glaeser, New York 1969; *Mies van der Rohe at Work* by Peter Carter, London and New York 1974; *Ludwig Mies van der Rohe* by Lorenzo Papi, Florence 1975; *Mies van der Rohe: Barcelona 1929* by J. P. Bonta, Barcelona 1975; *After Mies: Mies van der Rohe: Teaching and Principles* by Werner Blaser, New York, Basel and Stuttgart 1977; *Mies van der Rohe: die Villen und Landhausprojekte* by Wolf Tagethoff, Zürich 1980, Essen, West Germany 1981; *Mies van der Rohe: Interior Spaces*, exhibition catalogue by Franz Schulze, Chicago 1982; *Mies van der Rohe* by David Spaeth, with introduction by Kenneth Frampton, New York and London 1985; articles— "Farnsworth House" in *Architectural Forum* (New York), October 1951; "Seagram Building" by Arthur Drexler in *Architectural Record* (New York), July 1958; "Skyline: The Lesson of the Master" by Lewis Mumford in *New Yorker*, 13 September 1958; "Seagram Assessed" by William Jordy in *Architectural Review* (London), December 1958; "Ludwig Mies van der Rohe," edited by H. T. Cadbury Brown, special issue of *Architectural Association Journal* (London), July/August 1959; "Mies van der Rohe," edited by Peter Carter, special issue of *Architectural Design* (London), March 1961; "New Work of Mies van der Rohe" in *Architectural Forum* (New York), September 1963; "Mies van der Rohe" by Katherine Kuh in *Saturday Review* (New York), 23 January 1965; "Soaring Towers Gave Form to an Age" by Ada Louise Huxtable in *New York Times*, 19 August 1969; "Mies and the Closing of the Bauhaus" by Robert A. M. Stern in *Nation* (New York), 22 September 1969; "Ludwig Mies van der Rohe" in *Inland Architect* (Chicago), May 1977; "Confront-ation 1933—Mies van der Rohe and the Third Reich" by Elaine Hochman in *Oppositions* (New York), Fall 1979; "Mies' New National Gallery" by Peter Serenyi in *Harvard Architecture Review* (Cambridge, Massachusetts), Spring 1980; "Mies' Farnsworth House wins 25-year Award" in *AIA Journal* (Washington, D.C.), March 1981; "The Legacy of Museum Design of the 1960's" by Ada Louise Huxtable in the *New York Times*, 29 November 1981; "Mies Office Building Resurrected for the City" in *Building* (London), 15 January 1982; "City Rejects Mies" in *The Architects' Journal* (London), 29 September 1982; "Mies or Architecture in En-chained Liberty" by Paolo Melisi in *Domus* (Milan),

November 1982; film—*Mies van der Rohe* by Georgina van der Rohe, 1979.

Bibliographies—*Mies van der Rohe: A Bibliography*, thesis by Jessie F. F. Blackwell, University of London 1964; *Ludwig Mies van der Rohe: Master Architect (A Selected Bibliography)* by Robert B. Harmon, Monticello, Illinois, 1979; *Ludwig Mies van der Rohe: An Annotated Bibliography and Chro-nology* by David A. Spaeth, New York 1979.

As the world is a very large place, no sane person would hope to remake it; at most, an architect of great ambition might offer prototypes. That is what Ludwig Mies van der Rohe did. He liked to build not for the single client or site or brief but to solve, as he said, general "problems of building." He became celebrated as one of the several great masters of the modernist movement because as his work grew ever more basic, it attained exceptional sureness and clarity.

Mies—"van der Rohe" was his mother's surname—was a reformer deeply inspired by the past. Born in Aachen, Germany, he was taken as a child to worship each day in the chapel of Charlemagne. In later years, he recalled his admiration for the old and "clear" masonry buildings strong enough to have survived the centuries. His temperament was also formed by the nineteenth century: his sympathy for neo-classicism, his belief in the historical notion of the *Zeitgeist* or spirit of the time, and his idea that to express "the scientific and technological driving and sustaining foces of our time" was his moral duty. ("I work so hard," he said in 1963, "to find out what I have to do, not what I like to do.")

As a boy, Mies helped his father in the family stonecutting shop. He had no formal education in architecture; at fourteen, he went to work as a designer of traditional stucco ornaments. He moved on to Berlin in 1905 and soon apprenticed to Bruno Paul, an architect best known as a cartoonist and furniture designer. Mies very quickly immersed himself in the progressive movement. At twenty-one, he saw his first independent commission, the Riehl house, built near Berlin; it was not an innovative design, but a solidly crafted one, already suffused with his characteristic gravity. Mies's three years in the office of Peter Behrens, ending in 1911, confir-med this natural bent and also impressed him with the model of K. F. Schinkel's work, notably the Altes Museum (1823-1828) in Berlin, still in his mind when he designed the new National Gallery, built in Berlin at the end of life. Mies went to Holland in 1912 to work on a project for the Kröller country house, and there admired the "honesty" of H.P. Berlage's use of brick. From studying Berlage's Stock Exchange (1897-1903) in Amsterdam he decided that the goal of architecture should be "a clear construction."

After the years of his military service in 1914-1918, Mies's career suddenly matured. Three office-building projects of 1919-1921 revealed his intent of "driving to the essence of things." Two were towers of glass of steel framing; the last had walls of alternating bands of concrete and glass. Interior spaces were hardly indicated. Cantilever construc-tion was to lighten the mass while reducing each scheme to little more than repeated floors and supports. From his models, Mies discerned that "the play of reflections" on the glass would replace the traditional architectural values of sunlight raking across reveals to create shadows. Such prototypes forecast not only much of Mies's work during the 1950s and 1960s in North America but also an entire era of glass curtain-wall skyscrapers.

Having gone far toward an architecture he described as "almost nothing," Mies in a 1923 project for a brick country house revealed an aesthetic vocabulary drawn from de Stijl, the Dutch movement based on a Calvinist austerity very like his own. He had met Theo van Doesburg, its chief propagandist, in 1920. The walls of the brick house were planned as a dance of asymetrically balanced

meetings and crossings. De stijl also helped him generate the plans for the minimal yet elegant Barcelona Pavilion of 1929 (he spoke of his "shock" while designing it when he realized the aesthetic possibilities of the "free-standing wall"); for his courtyard house projects of the 1930s; and for the campus of the Illinois Institute of Technology, in Chicago, where he headed the department of architecture from 1938 to 1959.

Mies served as first vice-president of the Deutscher Werkbund, directed the great model housing expo-sition at Stuttgart in 1927, and directed the Bauhaus from 1930 to 1933. Most of his work in Europe remained unbuilt, and he entered his most fruitful period after World War II and in the United States. Meticulously proportioned buildings of glass sup-ported by slender steel members were to become his hallmark: the twin towers of flats at 860 North Lake Shore Drive in Chicago, the country house for Dr. Farnsworth near Plano, Illinois, and Crown Hall, the architecture building at I.I.T.—the last being one of a type in which he suspended the roof from trusses to leave the interior space all open and flexible. Among his other major buildings were the Seagram Building in New York and the Federal Center in Chicago.

Today, the discipline and Platonic purity of Mies's buildings cannot be challenged, but their high abstraction often looks grim and void. Relentless grid patterns and "universal" spaces too nearly express the anonymous and the bureaucratic, rather than any noble aspirations for individual or com-munal life. The prototypes appear too similar and unwilling to recognize the vast variety in human life and its daily functions. Their testament to science and technology is not so welcome, and their lack of colour, texture, warmth, and joy is noticeable. A new environmental awareness cannot accept their rel-ation to nature or their emphasis on thermally disastrous walls of glass along with sealed interiors. In reaching a naked clarity of structure Mies renounced too many human associations. Perfect in their own terms, his buildings hold forth little invitation to explore, to make one's self at home, or to deepen one's sense of place through time and intimacy.

—Donald Hoffmann

MINDLIN, Henrique Ephim.
Brazilian. Born in Sao Paulo, 1 February 1911. Educated at the Mackenzie School of Engineering, University of Sao Paulo, 1929-32, Dip.Arch.Ing. 1931. Married Helena Muniz de Souza; Vera Maria Bocaiuva Cunha; children: Katia and Tatiana. In private practice, Sao Paulo, 1933-41; in private practice, Rio de Janeiro, 1945-63, and also in partnership with Giancarlo Palanti, Sao Paulo, 1955-63; Partner (in the successor firm to the two partnerships), Henrique E. Mindlin, Giancarlo Palanti e Arquitetos Associados S.C. Ltda., Rio de Janeiro, from 1964 (name changed, on withdrawal of Palanti, to Henrique E. Mindlin e Arquitetos Associados S.C. Ltda., 1966, simplified to Henrique Mindlin Associados Ltda., 1969). Special Assistant to the Coordinator for Economic Mobilization, Construction Sector, Rio de Janeiro, 1942-44 (Re-presentative in the United States, 1943-44); Member, Subcommission for Housing, Council for Foreign Trade, Rio de Janeiro, 1944-45. Lethaby Professor of Architecture, Royal College of Art, London, 1961; Yonge Lecturer, Auburn University, Alabama, 1961; Professor, Federal University of Brazil, Rio de Janeiro, 1968-71. Member, Editorial Staff, *Acropole*, Sao Paulo, 1933-41; Editorial Consultant, *Ar-quitetura*, Rio de Janeiro, 1961. President, Instituto de Arquitetos do Brasil, 1970. Recipient: First Prize, Ministry of Foreign Affairs Annex Competition, Rio de Janeiro, 1942; Housing Prize, *Bienal*, Sao Paulo, 1951; First Prize, Israeli Paulista Congregation

Headquarters and Synagogue Competition, Sao Paulo, 1954; Honor Award, *Construcao Ingenieria Internacional*, 1958; First Prize, Bank of London and South America Competition, Sao Paulo, 1959; First Prize, Bank of London and South America Competition, Brasilia, 1960. Honorary Fellow, American Institute of Architects, 1960; Honorary Member, Society of Planning, Architecture and Visual Arts of Mexico, 1960, and National Society of Interior Designers, New York, 1960; Honorary Corresponding Member, Royal Institute of British Architects, 1963. Honorary Member, Brazilian Academy of Arts, 1968. *Died* (in Guanabara, Brazil) *6 July 1971.*

Works:

1938   Haberkamp House, Sao Paulo (project)
      Gross House, Sumare, Sao Paulo (project)
1939   Sousa Lima House, Sao Paulo (project)
      Carlos de Barros House, Sao Paulo (project)
      House, Rua Santa Adelaide, Sao Paulo (project)
1940   Santarem Building, Rua Barao de Campinas, Sao Paulo
      House, Placa Lucayas 146, Sao Paulo (project)
1942   Ministry of Foreign Affairs Annex, Rio de Janeiro (competition project)
      Hungria Machado House, Rio de Janeiro
1944   Palacio Itamarati alterations, Rio de Janeiro (project)
      Railway Employees Building modifications, Rio de Janeiro (project)
      Clinical Centre, Rua Conde de Lage, Rio de Janeiro
      Pan American Hotel, Rio de Janeiro (project)
      Hotel Rio Clara, Sao Paulo (project)
      Pan American Hotel, Belo Horizonte, Brazil (project)
      Two houses, Sao Paulo (project)
      Edgard de Almeida House interiors, Rio de Janeiro
1945   José Mindlin House, Sao Paulo (project)
      Condominium, Avenida Ipiranga, Sao Paulo
      Jacques Bloch House, Sao Paulo (project)
      Manoel Casoy House alterations, Sao Paulo (project)
      Tres Leoes Building, Sao Paulo (project)
      David Bank House interiors, Rio de Janeiro (project)
      Arthur Hehl Neiva House interiors, Rio de Janeiro (project)
      Samuel Klabin House interiors, Sao Paulo
      Palacio Tiradentes Conference Hall conversion, Rio de Janeiro (project)
      Sangirardi House, Niteroi, Rio de Janeiro
      Apartment building, Al. Barao do Rio Branco, Sao Paulo
      Pan American Hotel, Praia Vermelha, Rio de Janeiro (project)
1946   Office building, Rua Mario Ribeiro, Guaruja, Sao Paulo
      Apartment building, Rua Barata Ribeiro 432, Rio de Janeiro
      Apartment building, Guaruja, Sao Paulo
      Apartment building, Rua Belfort Roxo, Rio de Janeiro
      Apartment building, Rua Santo Amaro, Guaruja, Sao Paulo
      Hotel, Rua Couto Magalhaes 353, Sao Paulo
      Apartment building, Rua Araujo Gondim 46, Rio de Janeiro
      Jorge Zarur House, Rio de Janeiro
      Sao Geraldo Sanatorium, Rio de Janeiro
      Office building, Rua Ouvidor, Sao Paulo
      Ministry of the Exterior, Rio de Janeiro
1947   Domicini Shop, Rua Xavier de Toledo, Sao Paulo
      Claudio Medeiros Lima House, Estrada da Gavea 199, Rio de Janeiro
1948   José Carvalho House, Fazenda Nogueira, Bom Clima, Petropolis, Rio de Janeiro
      A Exposicao Copacabana Shop, Avenida N.

Senhora Copacabana 791, Rio de Janeiro
      Antenor Rezende House alterations, Rio de Janeiro
      A Exposicao Copacabana office interiors, Avenida 13 de Maio 23, Rio de Janeiro
      Hotel Ambassador modifications, Rua Senador Dantas 25-27, Rio de Janeiro
      José V. Carvalho House alterations, Rua Marques de Sao Vicente 205, Rio de Janeiro
      Inovacao Shop interiors and alterations, Rua Ouvidor, Rio de Janeiro
1949   Ducal Shop alterations, Sao Paulo
      Exposicao Tiradentes Shop interiors and alterations, Rio de Janeiro
      Hotel Comodoro interiors, Rua Duque de Caxias, Sao Paulo
1950   Dr. A. Bahia House interiors, Avenida Atlantica, Rio de Janeiro
      Capital Bank alterations and interiors, Avenida 13 de Maio, Rio de Janeiro
      Shop interiors, Avenida N. Senhora Copacabana 664, Rio de Janeiro
      Ceramus Building alterations, Avenida Atlantica 140, Rio de Janeiro
      Joao Alberto Dutra Leite Barbosa Inn, Avenida Presidente Dutra, Rio de Janeiro
      Ducal Shop interiors, Rua da Quitanda, Rio de Janeiro
      Augusto Lohnstein House, Rio de Janeiro
      Cogema Office interiors, Rua Mexico 31, Rio de Janeiro
      Housing development, Sao Paulo
      Ducal Shop interiors, Meier, Rio de Janeiro
      Palvino Montenegro Rocha Apartment interiors, Rio de Janeiro
      Office building, Rua Formosa 75-89, Sao Paulo
      Paulo Lynch House, Rio de Janeiro
      Office building, Rua Sao Bento, Sao Paulo
      A Exposicao Modas Building Complex, Exposicao Carioca, Rio de Janeiro
      Office building, Rua Barata Ribeiro 432, Rio de Janeiro
      Ducal Madureira Shop interiors, Rio de Janeiro
      Department store interiors, Copacabana, Rio de Janeiro
      Cogema Pavilion, Exposicao Rodoviaria, Rio de Janeiro
1951   Apartment building, Rua Bulhoes de Carvalho 181, Rio de Janeiro
      Mark Burke House, Rua Timoteo da Costa, Rio de Janeiro
      Apartment building, Rua Aristides Espinola, Rio de Janeiro
      Apartment building, Rua Taylor, Rio de Janeiro
      Banco do Brasil Headquarters, Rio de Janeiro (competition project)
      Banco de Credito Real Headquarters, Rua Sao Bento, Sao Paulo
      Harry Wentworth Hollmeyer House, Rua Timoteo da Costa, Rio de Janeiro
      José Carlos Moreira Salles House, Avenida Almirante Cochrane, Santos, Sao Paulo
      BOAC Office alterations, Avenida Rio Branco 251, Rio de Janeiro
      Library interiors, Rua Barao de Itapetininga, Sao Paulo
1952   Bus station, Placa 15 de Novembro, Rio de Janeiro
      Office building, Largo de Carioca, Rio de Janeiro
      Apartment building, Rua Raul Pompeia, Rio de Janeiro
      Natan Doiban House, Ilha do Governador, Rio de Janeiro
      Apartment building, Avenida Vieira Souto 336, Rio de Janeiro
      Hotel, Avenida Getulio Vargas, Rio de Janeiro
      Apartment building, Rua Padre Antonio Vieira, Rio de Janeiro
      Hotel, Avenida Ipiranga, Sao Paulo

Apartment building, Rua Consolacao, Sao Paulo
      Apartment building, Rua Timoteo da Costa, Rio de Janeiro
      Israeli Embassy alterations and new Consulate Building, Rua das Laranjeiras 361, Rio de Janeiro
      Urban and rural plan for Praia de Pernambuco, Sao Paulo
      Lauro de Carvalho Apartment alterations, Rio de Janeiro
1953   Vemag Shop interiors, Rua Piratini 1128, Rio de Janeiro
      Synagogue, Rua Capelao Alvares Silva 15, Copacabana, Rio de Janeiro
      Siderurgica Mannesmann, Belo Horizonte, Brazil (as consultant)
      Lauro de Souza Carvalho House, Petropolis, Rio de Janeiro
      A Exposicao Avenida reconstruction, Rio de Janeiro
      Israeli Cultural Headquarters, Rua Jose Higino 240, Rio de Janeiro
      Office building alterations and extensions, Rua Sorocaba 696, Botafogo, Rio de Janeiro
      Diana Danneman House, Rio de Janeiro
      Exposicao Madureira Shop, Rio de Janeiro
      Mannesmann City Housing Complex, Belo Horizonte, Brazil (project)
1954   Israeli Religious Association Headquarters, Community Centre and Temple, Rua General Severiano 166-177, Rio de Janeiro (project)
      George Hime House, Petropolis, Rio de Janeiro
      Israeli Paulista Congregation Headquarters and Synagogue, Rua Antonio Carlos, Sao Paulo (competition project)
      Horst Sekkel House, Rua Iposeira, Rio de Janeiro (project)
      Hebraica Headquarters, Rua das Laranjeira 346, Rio de Janeiro (project)
      Factory, Avenida Independencia, Sao Paulo (project)
      Federal Senate Headquarters, Avenida Rio Branco, Rio de Janeiro (competition project)
1955   Swissair Offices alterations, Rio de Janeiro (project)
      Auto Pecas Motorit Factory, Avenida Independencia, Sao Paulo
      Apartment building alterations, Ilha do Governador, Rio de Janeiro (project)
      KLM Airlines Offices alterations and interiors, Rio de Janeiro (project)
1956   Alzira Perestrello Apartment interiors, Rio de Janeiro (project)
      Copacabana Super Shopping Center, Rio de Janeiro (project)
      Avenida Central Building, Avenida Rio Branco 152-162, Rio de Janeiro
      Conjunto Vieira Souto Building, Rio de Janeiro (project)
1957   Apartment building, Rua Belizario Tavora, Rio de Janeiro (project)
      Pilot plan for Brasilia (competition project)
      Apartment building alterations, Rua Julio Otoni, Rio de Janeiro (project)
1958   Ultima Hora Building, Niteroi, Rio de Janeiro (project)
      Apartment building, Rua Visconde de Piraja 174-176, Rio de Janeiro
      Rudolf Mooshake House, Teresopolis, Rio de Janeiro (project)
      Feigenson/Telespark Office interiors, Rio de Janeiro (project; with Giancarlo Palanti)
      Olivetti Office/Shop interiors, Rio de Janeiro (project; with Giancarlo Palanti)
      Luiz Fernando Bocaiuva Cunha House alterations and extensions, Santa Tereza, Rio de Janeiro (project)
1959   Hotel Imperial, Petropolis, Rio de Janeiro (project)

Apartment building, Avenida Rui Barbosa, Rio de Janeiro (project)

Bank of London and South America, Rua 15 de Novembro, Sao Paulo (with Giancarlo Palanti)

Brazilian Pavilion, *Biennale*, Venice (project; with Giancarlo Palanti and Amerigo Nino Marchesin)

1960 Bank of London and South America, Setor Bancario Sul, Brasilia (competition project)

Hotel Rio Hilton, Rio de Janeiro (project)

Intercontinental Hotel, Brasilia (project)

Residential and commercial complex, Rua Jardim Botanico, Rio de Janeiro (project)

First National City Bank of New York, Setor Bancario Sul, Brasilia (project)

Hilton Hotel, Brasilia (project)

First National City Bank of New York, Avenida Rio Branca, Rio de Janeiro (project)

Metro Cinema alterations, Sao Paulo (with Giancarlo Palanti)

Hilton Hotel, Botafogo, Rio de Janeiro (project)

1961 First National City Bank Branch Office, Brasilia (project)

Globo Road and Television Building, Rua von Martrius, Rio de Janeiro (project)

Vera Simoes Bocaiuva Cunha House, Rua Joao Felipe 685, Santa Tereza, Rio de Janeiro

Apartment building, Rua Anibal de Mendonca 22, Rio de Janeiro

1962 José Smith Braz House, Brasilia (project)

First National City Bank of New York, Recife, Brazil

Australian Embassy, Brasilia (project)

State school, Rio Comprido, Rio de Janeiro (project)

State school, Meier, Rio de Janeiro (project)

British School extensions, Botafogo, Rio de Janeiro (project)

1963 Industrial complex, Sao Paulo (project; with Giancarlo Palanti)

Guanabara State Bank Headquarters, Avenida Nilo Pecanha, Rio de Janeiro

Instituto de Resseguros do Brasil Headquarters, Humaita, Rio de Janeiro (competition project)

Especifarma Laboratory, Sao Paulo (project; with Giancarlo Palanti)

Apartment building, Rua Marques de Sao Vicente, Rio de Janeiro (project)

José Mindlin House alterations, Sao Paulo (project; with Giancarlo Palanti)

Madureira de Pinho Building, Rio de Janeiro (project)

Bank of London and South America Headquarters alterations and extensions, Rio de Janeiro

Antonio Carlos de Almeida Braga House alterations, Rua Icatu 93, Gavea, Rio de Janeiro

Apartment building, Jardim Botanico, Rio de Janeiro (project)

Laranjeiras Residential/Commercial Complex, Rio de Janeiro (project)

Madureira National Shopping Center Commercial Complex, Estrada do Portelo 81-91, Madureira, Rio de Janeiro

1964 Bank of London and South America interior alterations, Recife, Brazil (project)

Netherlands Embassy, Brasilia

Town plan for the Troia Peninsula, Portugal

1965 Plan for the City Square, Guanabara, Brazil

1966 Lauro Simoes House alterations, Urca, Rio de Janeiro (project)

1967 *Jornal do Brasil* Headquarters and Industrial Plant, Avenida Brasil, Rio de Janeiro

Merchant Marine Center, Avenida Alfredo Agache, Rio de Janeiro (project)

Feasibility study for a hotel, Avenida Paulista, Sao Paulo

Ladeira do Leme Residential Complex, Rio de Janeiro (project)

1968 Electromar Factory extensions, Rio de Janeiro (project)

Banco de Lavoura Headquarters, Sao Paulo (competition project)

Sheraton Hotel, Avenida Niemeyer 121, Praia do Vidigal, Rio de Janeiro

Texaco do Brasil Building, Rio de Janeiro (project)

Office building, Rua Mayrink Veiga, Rio de Janeiro (project)

First National City Bank of New York, Belo Horizonte, Brazil (project)

Andarai Residential Complex, Guanabara, Brazil (project)

Divantex Factory, Sao Paulo (project)

IBM Building alterations, Avenida Presidente Vargas 1988, Rio de Janeiro

Banco da Lavoura Branch Office, Praca da Republica, Sao Paulo

Banco da Lavoura offices and computer rooms conversion, Rua Santo Andre 66, Sao Paulo

1969 First National City Bank of New York Branch Office, Avenida Nossa Senhora Copacabana 313, Rio de Janeiro

Elnorsa Factory, Pernambuco, Brazil (project)

IBM Factory and Offices, Sumare, Sao Paulo

First National City Bank of New York Headquarters alterations, Avenida Ipiranga, Sao Paulo

Banco da Lavoura Drive-in Branch Office, Sao Paulo (project)

Sheraton Hotel, Praia de Boa Viagem, Recife, Brazil (project)

Thomas de la Rue Works extensions, Rio de Janeiro (project)

First National City Bank of New York Headquarters alterations, Avenida Rio Branco 85, Rio de Janeiro

Banco Real de Investimentos Meeting Hall alterations, Sao Paulo (project)

Henrique de Botton House, Rua Aprazivel 85, Santa Tereza, Rio de Janeiro

1970 Intercontinental Hotel, Praia de Gavea, Guanabara, Rio de Janeiro

IBM Office Building interiors, Avenida Presidente Vargas, Rio de Janeiro (project)

First National City Bank of New York Branch Office alterations, Sao Paulo (project)

First National City Bank of New York Headquarters, Salvador, Brazil (project)

Credit-Card City Bank, Avenida Ipiranga 104, Sao Paulo

Maduriera do Pinho Office alterations, Rua 7 de Setembro 32, Rio de Janeiro

Publications:

By MINDLIN: books—*Modern Architecture in Brazil*, Rio de Janeiro 1956; *O Grande Hotel: Notas Sobre a Evolucao de un Programa* (professorial thesis), Rio de Janeiro 1962; *Prumadas de Circulacao em Edificios Altos* (professorial thesis), Rio de Janeiro 1962; *Tropico e lingua e literature, instituticao militar, energie solar, desporto, transportes, arquitetura, farmacopeia, musica, tropicalidade, como um conceito ecologico-geografico*, 2 vols., editor, with others, Recife 1974; articles—numerous in *Acropole* (Sao Paulo), 1933-41; "Walter Gropius" in *Jornal do Brasil* (Rio de Janeiro), July 1969.

On MINDLIN: books—*Henrique Ephim Mindlin: O Homen e o Arquiteto* by Celia Ballario Yoshida and others, Sao Paulo 1975; articles—"Apartment House, Guaruja, Santos" in *Pencil Points* (New York), April 1947; "Apartment Building, Sao Paulo," "Living in Brazil" and "Luxury Beach Hotel, Praia Vermelha" in *Architectural Forum* (New York), November 1947; "Brésil" in *L'Architecture d'Aujourd'hui* (Paris), January 1948; "Domestic Architecture in Brazil" in *L'Architecture d'Aujourd'hui* (Paris), August 1952; "Hotel Copan, Sao Paulo" in *Architectural Forum* (New York), October 1953; "Brazil: A New Oceanside Community" in *Architectural Record* (New York), June 1954; "Synagogue et Centre Culturel de la Communaute Israelite de Sao Paulo" in *L'Architecture d'Aujourd'hui* (Paris), June/July 1960; "Henrique E. Mindlin" in *Jornal do Brasil* (Rio de Janeiro), 18 February 1961; "Docencia Livre de Mindlin" by Jayme Mauricio in *Correio da Manha* (Rio de Janeiro), 31 August 1962; "Mindlin: Arquitetura" in *Correio da Manha* (Rio de Janeiro), 3 September 1970.

Henrique Mindlin started his career in Sao Paulo, in the years 1933-41, by erecting a few modernistic houses (following in the footsteps of Warchavchik) and the Santarem Building, a sober construction quite close in spirit to the work that Rino Levi was turning out at that time and to the modern Italian architecture of the years just prior to World War II.

In 1942 Mindlin moved to Rio de Janeiro, then still the capital of Brazil, and there came into contact with those architects who were engaged in the creation of a national architecture based on the theories of Le Corbusier. This influence had a profound effect on his subsequent work, and, with Lúcio Costa, Niemeyer, Reidy, Moreira and the Roberto Brothers, he began to actively contribute to the formation of the architectural idiom that was to give such a recognizable identity to the Brazilian version of the International Style. Some of Mindlin's major unbuilt projects belong to this period—the Foreign Affairs Ministry Annex, the Pan American Hotel at Praia Vermelha, and the Federal Senate Headquarters, all in Rio. But it is in his domestic architecture of the time that Mindlin most revealed his architectural creativity. The elements—butterfly roofs, chamfered walls in raw materials, glazed bays, sunscreens and wooden shutters—that characterize the houses for Lauro de Souza Carvalho and George Hime in Petropolis in 1953-54 are handled in a very personal manner, each plane visually detached from the adjoining one, disrupting the contention of the volumes and stressing a certain tension that exists in the composition of the mass.

In 1956 Mindlin started a new phase with the Avenida Central Building in Rio de Janeiro, the first steel-frame skyscraper erected in Brazil. His next works—for instance, the Bank of London in Sao Paulo and the First National City Bank of New York in Recife (a small, well-proportioned building pleasantly inserted into the existing urban scale)— are attempts to translate American curtain-wall office building principles into the local environment.

The Guanabara State Bank in Rio of 1963 marks another change in style, this time brought about by the use of exposed concrete and a brutalist vocabulary. Ribbon windows and concrete parapets alternate on the facade of the building, creating a strong horizontal pattern tied together by two powerful pylons. This "manner" would continue to be developed by Mindlin until the end of his life—either worked in a sobre vein, as in the project for the Merchant Marine Centre and in the *Jornal do Brasil* Building, both in Rio, or pushed towards more complicated articulations, as in the project for the First National City Bank of New York in Salvador.

The IBM Factory in Sao Paulo (1969) deserves special mention for its pioneering use of the spaceframe structure and for the exceptional attention paid to the technical problems inherent in an industrial building.

Henrique Mindlin's contribution to Brazilian architecture is not, however, restricted to his architectural production. As important as his technically innovative work—perhaps even more so—was the influence he exerted on his contemporaries both with the organization of his office and with his book *Modern Architecture in Brazil*, still virtually the only comprehensive source of information on the Brazilian movement.

His architectural firm, organized on a team-work system when the usual mode was still the individual practice, pointed the way to a work method that was suitable for coping with the ever-increasing complexities of projecting and designing architecture in a developing country. The firm is still in operation under the direction of Mindlin's partners, turning out such high quality works as the Souza Cruz Plant in Uberlandia (1975), and the *O Globo* Newspaper Industrial Building and a project for the head offices of C.V.R.D., both in Rio de Janeiro.

—Jorge Czajkowski

MITCHELL, Ehrman Burkman, Jr.

American. Born in Harrisburg, Pennyslvania, 25 January 1924. Educated at the Hill School, Pottstown, Pennyslvania, graduated 1941; University of Pennsylvania, Philadelphia, 1941-44, 1946-48 (Emerson Architectural Prize, 1948; Faculty Medal in Architecture, 1948), A.B. 1947, B.Arch. (summa cum laude) 1948. Served in the United States Navy, 1943-46. Married Hermine Strickler in 1948; children: Eric and Marianne. Associate Architect, Bellante and Clauss, London, 1951-58. Since 1958, Partner, with Romaldo Giurgola, *q.v.*, Mitchell/Giurgola Architects, Philadelphia; office established in New York, 1966. Vice-President, 1977, First Vice-President, 1978, and President, 1979, American Institute of Architects. Member of the Design Review Panel, United States Federal Reserve System; Board Member, American Australian Bicentennial Foundation. Exhibitions: University of Pennsylvania Museum, Philadelphia, 1965; Pennsylvania Academy of Fine Arts, Philadelphia, 1975; Columbia University, New York, 1977; *200 Years of American Architectural Drawing*, American Federation of Arts travelling exhibition, 1977-78; *Drawings Toward a More Modern Architecture*, The Drawing Center, New York, 1977, and Otis Art Institute Gallery, Los Angeles, 1978; *Roma Interrotta*, Rome, 1978. Recipient: First Award, 1961, Gold Medal, 1964, Honor Award, 1974, 1975, 1977, Architectural Firm Award, 1976, and Award of Merit, 1978, American Institute of Architects; Gold Medal, AIA, Philadelphia Chapter, 1961, 1964, 1972, 1974, 1977; Silver Medal, 1965, 1974, 1975, 1977, Distinguished Building Award, 1971, 1975, 1977, and First Honor Award, 1977, Pennsylvania Society of Architects; Gold Medal, Artists Guild of Philadelphia, 1966; First Prize, Wainwright State Office Complex Competition, St. Louis, 1974; Medal of Honor, AIA, New York City Chapter, 1975; Bard Award, City Club of New York, 1978; Design Award, *Urban Design*, 1978; Plaque of Honor, Federacion de Colegios de Arquitectos de la Republica Mexicana, 1984; Hazlett Award, Commonwealth of Pennsylvania, 1985. Fellow, American Institute of Architects, 1969; Honorary Fellow, Royal Canadian Institute of Architects, 1979; Fellow, Royal Australian Institute of Architects, 1980. Address: Mitchell/Giurgola Architects, 12 South 12th Street, Philadelphia, Pennsylvania 19107, U.S.A.

See GIURGOLA, Romaldo

MONEO Valles, José Rafael.

Spanish. Born in Tudela, Navarra, 9 May 1937. Educated at the Escuela de Arquitectura, Madrid, under Leopoldo Torres Balbás and Francisco Javier Saénz de Oíza *q.v.*, 1956-61. Served in the Spanish Army in Segovia, 1958 and 1959, and Pamplona, 1962. Married Belén Feduchi in 1963; children: Belén, Teresa, and Clara. Worked in the office of Jørn Utzon, *q.v.*, Hellebaek, Denmark, 1961-62; Assistant, Academia de Espana, Rome, 1963-65. Since 1965, in private practice, Madrid. Assistant Professor, Escuela de Arquitectura, Madrid, 1966-70; Professor of Architecture, Escuela de Arquitectura, Barcelona, 1971-85; Chairman, Department of Architecture, Graduate School of Design, Harvard University, Cambridge, Massachusetts, since 1985. Co-Founder/Editor, *Arquitecturas-Bis*, Barcelona, since 1974. Visiting Fellow, Institute for Architectural and Urban Studies, New York, 1976-77; Visiting Professor, Cooper Union, School fo Architecture, New York, 1976-77. Exhibitions: *10 Immagini per Venezia: mostra dei progetti per Cannaregio ovest*, Ala Napoleonica, Venice,1980; *La Modernité—un project inachevé*, Centre Georges Pompidou, Paris, 1982. Recipient: National Prize, Centre of Restoration Competition, Madrid, 1961; Premio de Roma, 1962; First Prize, Lucuna District Plan Competition, Vitoria, 1977. Address: José Rafael Moneo, Arquitecto, Oria 17, Madrid 2, Spain.

Works:

1961 Centre of Restoration, Madrid (competition project)
1962 Building on the Plaza del Obradairo, Santiago de Compostela, Spain (project)
1964 Madrid Opera House (competition project)
1965 Diestre Factory, Madrid Highway, Zaragoza, Spain
1966 Plaza de Toros extension, Pamplona, Spain
1967 Goméz-Acebo House, La Moraleja, Madrid
      City Hall, Amsterdam (competition project)
1970 Uremea Residential Building, San Sebastian, Spain (with Marquet, Zulaica and Unzurrunzaga)
      Primary school, Tudela, Spain
1971/
74 Housing Block with Picture Gallery, Paseo de la Habana, Madrid
1972 Eibar City Center, Spain (competition project)
1973 Stock Exchange, Madrid (competition project)
1975 Bankinter (bank office building), Paseo de la Castellana, Madrid (with Ramón Bescós)
      Fénix Mutuo Insurance Company Office building, Ramirez de Areliano 4, Madrid
1976 Town Hall, Huesca, Spain (competition project)
1976/
81 Town Hall, Offices, and City Centre Plan, Logroño, Spain
1977 Plan for the Lacuna District, Vitoria, Spain (competition project)
1978/
80 National Museum of Roman Art, Merida, Spain
1979/
81 Bank of Spain alterations and additions, Madrid

Publications:

By MONEO: articles—"Notas sobre la arquitectura griega" in *Hogar y arquitectura* (Madrid), July 1965; "Madrid: los ultimos veinticinco años" in *Informacion commercial española* (Madrid), no. 402, 1967; "La escuela de Barcelona" in *Arquitectura* (Madrid), January 1969; "El desarrollo urbano de Madrid en los 60" in *Cuadernos para el dialogo* (Madrid), April 1970; "Vitruvio y el buen salvaje" in *Arquitectura-Bis* (Barcelona), no.2,1974; "Gregotti and Rossi" in *Arquitecturas-Bis* (Barcelona), no.4, 1974; "Arquitecturas en las margenes" in *Arquitecturas-Bis* (Barcelona),no.12 1976; "Aldo Rossi: The Idea of Architecture" in *Oppositions* (New York), no. 5, 1978, and in *Space Design* (Tokyo), March 1978; "Architecture in the American University," with others, in *Lotus* (Venice), no. 27, 1980; plus numerous educational papers published by Escuela Tecnica Superior de Arquitectura, Barcelona, since 1971, and other articles in *Arquitecturas-Bis,* Barcelona, since 1974.

On MONEO: books—*Arquitectura española contemporanea* by Lluis Domènech, Barcelona 1967; *Contradictions in Living Environment* by David Mackay, London 1971; *La Modernite—un project inacheve,* exhibition catalogue, with texts by Jean-Philippe Chimot, Kenneth Frampton, Berthold Lubetkin and others, Paris 1982; articles—"José Rafael Moneo: Early Work," special issue of *Hogar y arquitectura* (Madrid); "Amsterdam City Hall Competition," special issue of *Arquitectura* (Madrid), April 1969; "José Rafael Moneo," special issue of *Nueva forma* (Madrid), January 1975; "Ten Architects in Venice" by Francesco Dal Co in *Architecture + Urbanism* (Tokyo), October 1980; "Enlargement of the Central Building of the National Bank in Madrid" in *Arquitectura* (Madrid), January/February 1981; "Housing on the Paseo de la Habana, Madrid" in *Arquitectura* (Madrid), March/April 1981; "The Work of Rafael Moneo" by Anton Capitel and others in *Arquitectura* (Madrid), May/June 1982.

*

Bankinter, which is my idea of true architecture, rises upon on a site in the Castellana, one of the streets with most character in Madrid, next to a small, eighteenth-century palace of delicate workmanship. Its restricted size shows the respect involved in its planning as an unobtrusive background against which the palace would assume greater importance and is indicative of a knowledge of the locality—of the implicit lines and of the limits imposed by law.

However, an interpretation of the frontage, which such planning appears to demand, becomes confused when one approaches the ordinary entrance, since the character of the independent features, which every building possesses, makes a great impression. Such independence is strongly emphasized by the horizontal line of the pavement. It must, then, be clear that the hazards and limitations—or, in short, the influence of the setting to which the work of architecture is subject—do not prevent the appearance of those disciplinary principles on which ultimately depend the formal structure of the object.

In Bankinter, some of these principles are well known and may even be called traditional: the emphasis placed on proportion, the interest shown in the definition of the various elements, the consideration for the construction, and the desire to give due value to the different materials. But adherence to such principles has not involved disregarding the value of the whole as a basis on which to found the planning operations; in Bankinter I have not, I hope, fallen into the temptation of concentrating on separate parts.

The desire for perfection, the eagerness to achieve correct proportions—an attribute of so-called classic architecture—has always been present throughout the execution of the work and this explains, perhaps, why both the work of the sculptor, Francisco López Hernández, the creator of the reliefs on the facade, and that of the painter, Pablo Palazuelo, to whom we are indebted for the plaster work in the entrance hall, has been incorporated without any need for special integration.

—José Rafael Moneo

*

José Rafael Moneo graduated in 1961 from the

Jose Rafael Moneo: Bankinter Building, Madrid, 1975.

Escuela de Arquitectura of Madrid where he had been a student of Leopoldo Torres Balbás, the famous historian and curator of the Alhambra, and of Francisco Javier Saénz de Oíza, the most brilliant architectural talent in Spain in the last twenty-five years. In his work, Moneo seems to have brought both of these influences together. He conceives of his professional life as teaching and criticism on one hand and as the practice of architecture on the other. His work—his own personality—is the result of that fortunate synthesis.

Moneo collaborated with Saénz de Oíza in the Torres Blancas projects of 1960-62. Then he went to Denmark to work with Utzon on the Sydney Opera House project. But after he had won the Premio de Roma in 1962 and a place in the Spanish Academy for two years, he began to show in his work that the final flowering of European utilitarian and expressionistic trends—evident in both Torres Blancas and the Sydney Opera House—would not determine his own future.

More careful than his teachers, Moneo produced a softened version of Nordic and Dutch traditions (current architecture in Madrid was sensitive to both); this trend is obvious in his competition projects for the Madrid Opera House and the Amsterdam Town Hall. To this conception he added, as it were, an evaluation of his own historic traditions and the possibility of rejecting what was thought of as modern—the International Style. This range of influences and aims is clear in his works of the 1960s—the splendid Urumea Building in San Sebastian, the Gomez-Acebo House in Madrid, the Primary School in Tudela, or the development in Pamplona.

In these early years, the 1960s, Moneo was one of the centers of interest and excitement in Madrid architecture. Now, in his maturity, he seems to have overcome the crises implicit in the 1960s with ease and with clarity. As an architect and as a teacher, Moneo has become one of the most important and dynamic figures in Spanish architecture.

Against crisis, Moneo defends the competence of architecture. From his commanding position as both professor and critic, he points out that discipline is the characteristic common to several architectures. Architecture, then, is a vast history in which the architect conscientiously looks for models and resources to convert or transform. (The courses Moneo taught at the Escuela de Madrid from 1966 to 1970 were "Projects" and "Analysis of Architectural Shapes.") This attitude is evident in the Bankinter in Madrid—even if its main interest has been in having achieved an apt urban solution for the Paseo de la Castellana, the main axis of the capital. In his competition projects for the Stock Exchange in Madrid and the Town Hall in Huesca, and in his Town Hall in Logroño, Moneo presents his reflections and answers to the way in which architecture can both merge into and build a city.

—Anton Capitel

MOORE, Arthur Cotton.

American. Born in Washington, D.C., 12 April 1935. Educated at St. Albans School, Washington, 1950-54; graduated 1954; Princeton University, New Jersey, 1954-60. A.B. (cum laude) 1958, M.F.A. 1960. Served as a Lieutenant in the United States Army, 1961. Married Patricia Stephan in 1966; son: Gregory. Worked in the office of Skidmore, Owings and Merrill, *q.v.*, New York, summers 1956-58; Ketchum and Sharp, New York, summer 1959. Satterlee and Smith, Washington, D.C., 1960-61, and Cloethiel Woodward Smith and Associates, Washington, D.C., 1961-65. Since 1965, Principal, Arthur Cotton Moore Associates, Washington, D.C. Contributing Editor on Urban Affairs, *The Washingtonian,* 1965-78. Professional Adviser, Committee Against the National Airport, 1966; Chairman, Committee on International Visitors, American Institute of Architects, Washington Chapter, 1969; Treasurer and Member of the Executive Committee, Georgetown Planning Council, Washington, D.C., 1970; Chairman of the Jury on the Presidential Reviewing Stand, 1972; Chairman, Subcommittee on Airports, Committee of 100 on the Federal City, 1973; United States Representative, State Department Trade Mission to Switzerland, The Netherlands, and Belgium, 1973; Member, Washington City Council Special Citizens Committee on Urban Renewal, 1973; Member of the Bicentennial Assembly of the District of Columbia, 1973; Member of the Board, Metropolitan Washington Planning and Housing Association, 1974; Member, Design Advisory Panel, City of Baltimore, 1975. Recipient: Excellence in Architecture Award, Metropolitan Washington Board of Trade, 1970; Honor Award, American Institute of Architects,

Potomac Valley Chapter, 1970; Citizens Association of Georgetown Award, 1971; Honor Award, AIA, Middle Atlantic Region, 1971; *Architectural Record* Award, 1972, 1977; *Progressive Architecture* Award, 1973; First Award, 1973, and Merit Award, 1976 (twice), Historic Preservation and Architectural Design, AIA, Washington, D.C. Chapter; American Association of School Administrators Award, 1976; *Design and Environment* Award, 1976; Owens-Corning Energy Award, 1976, 1977; First Honor Award, 1977 (twice), and Special Energy Citation, 1977, AIA, Northern Virginia Chapter; National Honor Award, AIA, 1977; Grand Award, National Association of Home Builders/*Better Homes and Gardens,* 1978 (twice). Address: Arthur Cotton Moore Associates, 1214 28th Street N.W., Washington, D.C. 20007, U.S.A.

Works:

1967 Rosslyn Air Terminal, Arlington, Virginia (project)
1969 Canal Square, Georgetown, Washington, D.C.
      House, 1600 Avon Place, Washington, D.C.
1970 Woodlawn Shopping Center, Woodlawn, Virginia
      Air rights proposal for downtown Washington, D.C.
      New Republic Office Building, Washington, D.C. (project)
1971 B and D Inland (mixed-use development), Washington, D.C. (project)
      Charleston Development, Charleston, South Carolina (project)
1972 Harris House, Arlington, Virginia
1973 Arthur Cotton Moore Associates Office Building, Washington, D.C.
1974 Remely Point Housing Development, South Carolina (project)
      Ohlandt Condominium, Charleston, South Carolina (project)
      Barney's Mixed-Use Development, Schenectady, New York (project)
1975 Chessie Georgetown Development, Washington, D.C. (project)
1976 The Foundry, Georgetown, Washington, D.C.
      The Cairo Apartments, Washington, D.C.
      Solar Energy Science Building, Madeira School, Greenway, Virginia
      Seven Old Buildings, Vanderbilt University, Nashville, Tennessee (project)
      Torpedo Plant (concept plan), Alexandria, Virginia
      Frederick Development (Black Horse Tavern and Kline Houses), Frederick, Maryland (project)
1977 Parking Facility, Vanderbilt University, Nasville, Tennessee
      Urban design for Columbia Pike, Arlington, Virginia (project)
      Times Square Adult Entertainment Center, New York (project)
      Shirlington Master Plan, Arlington, Virginia (project)
      Baltimore Fish Market (project)
      Redevelopment plan for Market Street, Baltimore (project)
      Plan for re-use of Lansburgh's Department Store, Washington, D.C. (project)
      Fairfax Cultural Center, Fairfax, Virginia (project)
1978 Lafayette Elementary School, Washington, D.C.
      Van Ness Apartments, Washington, D.C.
      Cooperative Finance Corporation Apartments, Washington, D.C.
      Cooperative Finance Corporation Office Complex, Washington, D.C.
      Bedford-Stuyvesant Commercial Complex (Restoration Plaza), Brocklyn, New York

Convention Center, Washington, D.C. (project)
      Tooks Way Housing Development, Columbia, Maryland
      Le Steak (restaurant), Washington, D.C.
      Cherry Hill (apartments), phase I and II, Washington, D.C.
      Bernstein House, Washington, D.C.
      Master plan for development for the Hechinger Company, Washington, D.C.
      Mixed-use development, 1312 30th Street, Washington, D.C.
      Guardian Federal Office Building, Washington, D.C.
      Greenberg Condominium, New Hampshire Avenue, Washington, D.C.
      Office building, 3030 M Street, Washington, D.C. (project)
      Redevelopment plan for Joseph Square Shopping Center, Columbia, Maryland
1979 Commercial Complex, Schenectady, New York
1980 The Old Post Office Development, Washington, D.C.
      Rockefeller Housing Development, Washington, D.C.
      Capital Hill Car Barn, Washington, D.C. (project)
      Dupont Circle Shopping Center, Washington, D.C. (project)
      Master plan for the Potomac School of Law, Washington, D.C.
1981 3600 M Street Building, Washington, D.C. (project)
      Hechinger Plaza Development, Washington, D.C. (project)
      Ellington School for the Performing Arts, Washington, D.C. (project)
      ACT/Proctor's Theatre, Schenectady, New York (project)
      5A Office Building, Baltimore

City Master Plans: Colmar Manor, Maryland, 1974; Downtown Nassau (and Bahamas Master Plan), 1975; York, Pennsylvania, 1976; Petersburg, Virginia, 1976; Columbus, Georgia, 1977; Norfolk, Virginia (waterfront), 1977; Nashville, Tennessee, 1977; Fort Wayne, Indiana, 1977; Baltimore, Maryland, 1978-; Schenectady, New York, 1979; Dearborn, Michigan, 1979; Rockville, Maryland, 1979.

Publications:

By MOORE: books—*New Town Legislation, Department of Housing and Urban Development,* Washington, D.C. 1969; foreword to *Historic Buildings of Washington,* Washington, D.C. 1973; articles—"Politics, Architecture and World Fairs" in *AIA Journal* (Washington, D.C.), April 1965; "The Pennsylvania Avenue Plan" in *St. Albans Bulletin* (Washington, D.C.), May 1965; "Adaptive Abuse" in *AIA Journal* (Washington, D.C.), August 1979; "The Retreat into Architectural Narcissism" in *AIA Journal* (Washington, D.C.), December 1980; numerous articles in *The Washingtonian,* 1965-78.

On MOORE: articles—"An Architecture of Issues" in *Progressive Architecture* (New York), July 1973; "A Study in Solar Energy Architecture" by Wolf Von Eckardt in the *Washington Post,* 16 February 1974; "Arthur Cotton Moore Associates of Washington: Practice Profile" by Mary E. Osman in *AIA Journal* (Washington, D.C.), May 1974; "Sunny Side Up" by Jim Murphy in *Progressive Architecture* (New York), February 1976; "Restoration of Confidence" by John Morris Dixon in *Progressive Architecture* (New York), November 1977; "Washington Architect Arthur Cotton Moore" by William Marlin in *Architectural Record* (New York), De-

Arthur Cotton Moore: Washington Harbor Project, 1982-88.

cember 1977; "Arthur Cotton Moore" by Wolf Von Eckardt in *New Republic* (Washington, D.C.), 25 February 1978; "Madeira School, Greenway" in *Informes de la construccion* (Madrid), March 1979; "Private House in Arlington, Virginia" in *Informes de la construccion* (Madrid), August/September 1979; "Low-Rise Housing in America," special issue of *Process:Architecture* (Tokyo), April 1980; "Private Residence, Washington, D.C." in *Architectural Record* (New York), May 1980; "Climate, Nature, and House," special issue of *Process:Architecture* (Tokyo), May 1982; "Learning from Bath" in *Progressive Architecture* (New York), August 1982.

ACM is concerned about the increasingly intramural and academic nature of even today's best architectural work. In order to counter architecture's growing separation from the mainstream of society, the firm acts not only as architects and planners but also at times as developers. By understanding and becoming involved in the political and economic basics of society, ACM has gained the freedom to influence the direction of many American cities and the real freedom to do and control the firms's design interests.

In planning, ACM has stressed an alternative-additive-incremental approach which entrepreneurs existing features and buildings with new construction into linkages to strategically reverse urban decline. In architecture, ACM has used adaptive reuse, incorporating of old fragments and historical allusions to build bridges or rapport with the general public. The preserved or evoked old images permit contrasting, free experimentation with new elements increasingly involving complete and curvilinear forms.

—Arthur Cotton Moore

Arthur Cotton Moore was an early critic of classic urban renewal and has continually sought means to influence the direction of his city, the nation's capital, and other cities, within and without traditional architectural practice. For more than ten years, Moore was architectural and urban critic for *The Washingtonian*, a glossy magazine in which he called attention to neglected problems and various proposed planning schemes with which he disagreed. Along with written criticisms of the status quo, he also published drawings and discussions of his suggestions for what should be done, involving himself in economic as well as architectural questions. He also frequently writes this sort of article for Washington's leading newspaper, *The Washington Post,* and serves on many official and ad hoc committees on urban planning. His conviction is that the gap between the profession and the public must be narrowed—partly by politicizing the population about architectural issues and partly by developing a rapport between people and the buildings themselves.

The project that first made Moore's name is Canal Square, in Washington's Georgetown neighborhood, one of the first major recycling projects in the country. A nineteenth century warehouse was joined to more than 75,000 square feet of new construction, sheathed in a similar dark brown brick. The complex contains offices, shops and a large restaurant laid out around a series of courtyards. Moore was one of the developers of Canal Square as well as the architect, and he frequently performs that role in other projects and even consults with interested community groups about how to develop such a project, including what retail mix pays and what political coalitions might be required to put the package together. He obviously does not agree that the architect is someone "who designs the building after all the decisions have been made."

Moore is not a preservationist as such but an urbanist with a taste for the variety and density that recycling can provide. His new construction often plays off the materials and details of the old, although until recently it was with a straightforward "clean-it-up-and-magnify-its-scale" modernist approach. The experience of incorporating different buildings into one complex has led him to a design position which values juxtaposition of dissimilar elements. His vocabulary has been quite fluid over the years—from the ribbon window bands and acute angles of his designs from ten years ago to the Buck Rogers moderne and neo-Palladian motifs of his current work. What has been consistent is a regard for the street and a propensity toward courtyard arrangements and traditional materials. Moore's practice is also distinguished by an interest in solar energy design, specifically the Madeira School Science Building, one of the first privately-financed, non-residential solar heated buildings in the country.

—Nory Miller

MOORE, Charles Willard.

American. Born in Benton Harbor, Michigan, 31 October 1925. Educated at the University of Michigan, Ann Arbor, under Roger Bailey, 1942-47, B.Arch. 1947: awarded University of Michigan George Booth Travelling Fellowship, 1949; Princeton University, New Jersey, under Jean Labatut, Enrico Peressutti and Louis I. Kahn, 1954-57 (Council of Humanities Fellowship, 1957), M.F.A., Ph.D. 1957. Served in the United States Army Corps of Engineers, in the United States and Korea, 1952-

54: Captain. Partner, Moore-Lyndon-Turnbull-Whitaker, Berkeley, California, 1962-64, and MLTW/Moore Turnbull, Berkeley, 1964-70; Principal, Charles W. Moore Associates, 1970-75. Since 1975, Partner, Moore Grover Harper, Essex, Connecticut; since 1976, Partner, Moore Ruble Yudel, Los Angeles. Assistant Professor, University of Utah, Salt Lake City, 1950-52, and Princeton University, New Jersey, 1957-59; Associate Professor, 1959-65, and Chairman of the Department of Architecture, 1962-65, University of California, Berkeley; Chairman of the Department of Architecture, 1965-69, Dean of the School of Architecture, 1969-71, and Professor of Architecture, 1969-75, Yale University, New Haven, Connecticut. Professor of Architecture since 1975, and Program Head in the School of Architecture since 1978, University of California at Los Angeles. Exhibitions: *40 under 40*, Architectural League of New York, 1965; University of Maryland, College Park, 1971; *Biennale*, Venice, 1976; University of Houston, 1976; Bologna, Italy, 1978; University of Michigan, 1978; Williams College, Williamstown, Massachusetts, 1978; *New American Art Museums*, Whitney Museum, New York, 1982. Recipient: Award, *Progressive Architecture*, 1962, 1963, 1964, 1965, 1966, 1967; Award, American Institute of Architects, 1965, 1966. Fellow, American Institute of Architects. Addresses (office): 1063 Gayley, Los Angeles, California 90024, U.S.A.; (home): 1725A Selby, Los Angeles, California 90024, U.S.A.

Works:

1957 House, 325 Via del Rey Road, Monterey, California
1959 House, 10 Chualar Place, Monterey, California
1961 Studio, 2508 Leavenworth Street, San Francisco
     Jobson House, Palo Colorado Canyon, California
1962 Jenkins House I, St. Helena, California (project)
     Bonham House I, Boulder Creek, California
     Moore House, Orinda, California
     West Plaza Condominium, Coronado, California (project)
     Seaside Professional Building, Seaside, California
     Master plan for the South Coast, Monterey, California (with Skidmore, Owings and Merrill)
     Master plan for Lone Hill Housing, San Jose, California
1963 Cortese House, Orinda, California (project)
     Legge House additions, Portola Valley, California
     Trueblood House additions, Palo Alto, California
     Turner House, Pebble Beach, California (project)
     Monte Vista Apartments, Monterey, California
1964 Athletic Club I, Sea Ranch, California
     Cudabach House renovation, Oakland, California (project)
     Gordon House renovation, Berkeley, California
     Jackson House, Santa Fe, New Mexico (project)
     Jenkins House II, St. Helena, California
     Jewell House, Orinda, California
     Morris-LaForge House, Boulder Creek, California (Project)
     Slater House, Stinson Beach, California
     Condominium I, Sea Ranch, California
     Goldsmith House renovation, Berkeley, California
1965 Bache House additions, Piedmont, California (project)

Charles Moore: **Kresge College, University of California, Santa Cruz, 1973.**

     Cornuelle House, Hillsborough, California (project)
     Halprin House I, Sea Ranch, California (project)
     Halprin House II, Sea Ranch, California (project)
     Johnson House, Sea Ranch, California
     Karas House, Monterey, California
     Kermeen House renovation, Orinda, California
     Krakauer House, Los Altos, California (project)
     Lawrence House additions, Palo Alto, California
     Martin House, Lake Tahoe, California
     Polk House renovation, Berkeley, California
     Talbert House, Oakland, California
     Condominium Hillside, Sea Ranch, California (project)
     Carmel Knolls Housing, Carmel Valley, California (project)
     Civic Center, Fremont, California (competition project)
     Plan for a Commercial Square, Novato, California
     Portland South Park, Lovejoy Plaza, Portland, Oregon (with Lawrence Halprin)
1966 Budge House, Healdsburg, California
     Halprin House III, Sea Ranch, California (project)
     Halprin House IV, Sea Ranch, California
     Harrison House, Santa Barbara, California (project)
     Johnson/Martin House, Lake Tahoe, California
     Knutsen House, Sonoma, California
     Lawrence House, Sea Ranch, California
     McClelland House, Sea Ranch, California (project)

     McNiven House renovation, Berkeley, California
     Otus House, Berkeley, California
     Saltzman House, Carmel, California
     Thomasian House, Orinda, California
     Truesdale House, Sea Ranch, California
     Turnbull Sr. House I, Carbondale, Colorado
     Vickery House, Sea Ranch, California (project)
     Arts Center, University of California, Berkeley (competition project)
     Urban renewal housing, Akron, Ohio (project)
     Cascade Project, Akron, Ohio (project)
1967 Boas House, Stinson Beach, California
     Moore House renovation, New Haven, Connecticut
     Morris House I, Sea Ranch, California (project)
     Pirofski House, Palo Alto, California (project)
     Spec I House, Sea Ranch, California (project)
     Stauffacher House, Mill Valley, California (project)
     Beckonridge Housing, Tacoma, Washington (project)
     College 6, University of California at Santa Cruz (project)
1968 Dahlen House, Santa Barbara, California (project)
     Hines House, Sea Ranch, California
     McElrath House, Santa Cruz, California
     Morris House II, Sea Ranch, California
     Ray House, Sea Ranch, California (project)
     Rigler House, Estes Park, Colorado
     Spec II House, Sea Ranch, California (prototype)
     Spec III House, Sea Ranch, California (prototype)

Weyerhauser Prototype House, Kansas City, Missouri

Bechtel Prototype Housing, Santa Catalina, California (project)

Conifer 4 Housing for the Elderly, Tacoma, Washington

Conifer 5 Housing, Tacoma, Washington

Church Street South Housing, New Haven, Connecticut

Gas Station Plaza Housing for the Elderly, New Haven, Connecticut

Los Angeles Psychiatric Building, Beverly Hills, California

Faculty Club, University of California at Santa Barbara

Housing, Hamden, Connecticut (project)

Athletic Club II, Sea Ranch, California

1968/
72 Peterson House I, Tacoma, Washington (project)

1969 Caygill House, Sea Ranch, California
Cornuelle House, New Hampshire (project)
Goodman House, Montauk, Long Island, New York (project)
Klotz House, Westerly, Rhode Island
La Boyteaux House, Orinda, California (project)
McComber House, Sea Ranch, California
Naff House, Pajaro Dunes, California
Reid House, Sea Ranch, California
Schub House, Long Island, New York (project)
Baker House, Sea Ranch, California
Bartell House, Sea Ranch, California
Binker House, Sea Ranch, California
Eastwood House, Sea Ranch, California
Edgerton House, Sea Ranch, California
Kohlmeister House, Sea Ranch, California
Kreps/Levine House, Sea Ranch, California
Larsen House, Sea Ranch, California
Matthews House, Sea Ranch, California
Whiteside House, Sea Ranch, California
Wickstead House, Sea Ranch, California
Wilson/Moore/King House, Sea Ranch, California
Tempchin House, Bethesda, Maryland (with Rurik Ekstrom)
Turnbull Sr. House II, Carbondale, Colorado
Low-income housing, Whitesburg, Kentucky (project)
Master plan for Russian Harbor, Jenner, California
Kansas City Mall

1970 Baer House addition, Monterey County, California (project)
Bransten House, Muir Beach, California (project)
Bransten House renovation, San Francisco
Gahagan House, Tamales Bay, California (project)
Koizim House, Westport, Connecticut
Moss House, Sea Ranch, California
Mentzer House, Sea Ranch, California
Rush House, Sea Ranch, California
Goodhart House, Sea Ranch, California
Deep River Housing, Essex, Connecticut (project)
Villa del Monte Housing for the Elderly, Seaside, California
Oak Street Turnkey Housing, Haight-Ashbury, San Francisco (project)
Huntington Station Urban Renewal Housing, Huntington, Long Island, New York
Tract A Townhouses, Vail, Colorado (project)
Boas Pontiac Building remodelling, San Francisco
Golden West Savings and Loan Association Office interiors, Capitola, California
Golden West Savings and Loan Association Office remodelling, Castro Valley, California
Golden West Savings and Loan Association Office interiors, Corte Madera, California
Golden West Savings and Loan Association

Office interiors, Eastridge, California (project)
Land use analysis: Nuclear Power Station, Davenport, California

1971 Church Street South Housing, New Haven, Connecticut
Robert T. Wolfe Apartments, New Haven, Connecticut
Triangle Pacific Development, Vermon, Connecticut
Housing for the elderly, Seaside, California

1972 Maplewood Terrace Housing, Middletown, Connecticut
Xanadune, St. Simon's Island, Georgia
Talmar Wood, Orono, Maine
Rudolph House, Captive Island, Florida
Goodman House, Long Island, New York (project)

1973 Essex Point, Condominiums, Deep River, Connecticut
Anderson Housing Development, Spriingfield, Massachusetts
Moore House, Essex, Connecticut
Halprin House, Sea Ranch, California
Kresge College, University of California at Santa Cruz
Murray House, Cambridge, Massachusetts

1974 Burns House, Santa Monica Canyon, California
Cold Spring Harbor Laboratories, Huntington, New York
Whitman Village Housing, Huntington, New York
Kingsmill on the James, Williamsburg, Virginia

1974/
75 Owen Brown Village, Columbia, Maryland

1975 Swan House, Southold, New York
Barber House, Guilford, Connecticut
Piazza d'Italia Fountain, New Orleans (project)
House, Madras, India
Moore House, Los Angeles

1976 House, near New York

1978 National Guard Armory, Norwich, Connecticut

1979 Riverfront Landing, Dayton, Ohio
Rodes House, Kenter Canyon, Los Angeles

1980 Sammis Hall, Cold Spring Harbor, Huntington, New York
St. Matthew's Parish Church, Pacific Palisades, California

1981 Dormitories, Quinnipiac College, Hamden, Connecticut
Kwee House, Singapore

1982 Williams College Museum of Art, Williamstown, Massachusetts
Tegel Harbour Development Master Plan, West Berlin (competition project)

Publications:

By MOORE: books—*The Place of Houses,* with G. Allen and D. Lyndon, New York 1974; *The Yale Mathematics Building Competition: Architecture for a Time of Questioning,* with N. Pyle, New Haven, Connecticut 1974; *Dimensions,* with G. Allen, New York 1976; *Body Memory and Architecture,* with K.C. Bloomer, New Haven, Connecticut 1977; articles—"New-Old Newport" in *Architectural Record* (New York), February 1959; "Hadrian's Villa" in *Perspecta* (New Haven), no. 6, 1960; "Sagamore" in *Journal of Architectural Education* (Washington, D.C.), Summer 1961; "You Have to Pay for the Public Life" in *Perspecta* (New Haven, Connecticut), no. 9/10, 1965 "Creating of Place" in *Image,* no. 4, 1966; "The Establishment Invites You to Join the Hushed and Sumptuous Appreciation of the Several Arts, Lincoln Center, Most Evenings; Arrival Optional but Difficult" in *Architectural Forum* (New York), September 1966; "Plug It In, Rameses, and See If It Lights Up, Because We Aren't

Going to Keep It Unless It Works" in *Perspecta* (New Haven, Connecticut), no. 11, 1967; "Church Street South Housing in New Haven," with G. Allen, in *Architect's Yearbook* (London), 1971; "Eleven Agonies and One Euphoria" in *Michigan Society of Architects Monthly Bulletin,* February 1971; "Charles W. Moore," interview, in *Kenchiku Bunka* (Tokyo), April 1971; "How Much Is a Monument Worth?" in *Journal of the Society of Architectural Historians* (Philadelphia), October 1972; "Schindler: Vulnerable and Powerful" in *Progressive Architecture* (New York), January 1973; "In Similar States of Undress" in *Architectural Forum* (New York), May 1973; "After a New Architecture: The Best Shape for a Chimera" in *Oppositions* (New York), May 1974; "Sea Ranch: A Second Look," with G. Allen and D. Lyndon, in *Architectural Record* (New York), November 1974; "Southerness" in *Perspecta* (New Haven), no. 15, 1975; "... Where Are We Now, Vincent Scully?" in *Progressive Architecture* (New York), April 1975; "Yale University Mathematics Building-Conclusion" in *Oppositions* (New York), no. 6, 1976; "Self-Portrait" in *L'Architecture d'Aujourd'hui* (Paris), March 1976; "Berlin: alt und neu," with others, in *Lotus International* (Venice), December 1976; "Magic, Nostalgia and a Hint of Greatness in the Workaday World of the Building Types Study," with R. Oliver, in *Architectural Record* (New York), April 1977; address in *North Carolina Architect* (Raleigh), November/December 1978; "A Personal View of Architecture" in *Arquitectura* (Madrid), July/August 1980; "Charles Moore", interview, in *Summa* (Buenos Aires), April 1981; "Interview One: Charles Moore" in *Transition* (St. Kilda, Victoria), June 1981; recording—*Designing with People's Desires,* tape cassette, London 1981.

On MOORE: books—*40 under 40,* exhibition catalog, by Robert Stern, New York 1965; *The Puzzle of Architecture* by Robin Boyd, Melbourne, London and New York 1965; *Selected Houses from Progressive Architecture,* New York 1966; *American Architecture and Urbanism* by Vincent Scully, New York 1969; *New Directions in American Architecture* by Robert Stern, New York 1969; *Nuove Ville* by Roberto Aloi, Milan 1970; *Global Architecture No. 3: MLTW/Moore Lyndon Turnbull Whitaker: The Sea Ranch* by Yukio Futagawa, Tokyo 1970; *Global Interiors No. 1: Houses in the U.S.A.* by Yukio Futagawa, Tokyo 1971; *Architecture 2000: Predictions and Methods* by Charles Jencks, New York 1971; *Observations in American Architecture* by Ivan Chermayeff, New York 1972; *Adhocism: The Case for Improvisation* by Charles Jencks and Nathan Silver, New York 1972; *A Visual History of Twentieth-Century Architecture* by Dennis Sharp, London and New York 1972; *Conversations with Architects* by J. W. Cook and H. Klotz, New York 1973; *A Guide to Architecture in San Francisco and Northern California* by David Gebhard and others, revised edition, Santa Barbara, California and Salt Lake City, Utah 1973; *Modern Movements in Architecture* by Charles Jencks, New York 1973; *Global Interiors No. 6: Houses in the U.S.A.* by Yukio Futagawa, Tokyo 1974; *Modern Architecture: The Architecture of Democracy* by Vincent Scully, New York 1974; *The Shingle Style Today* by Vincent Scully, New York 1974; *MLTW; Houses, 1959-75* by Yukio Futagawa, Tokyo 1975; *Europa/America,* edited by Franco Raggi, Venice 1978; *Houses for Sale,* edited by B. J. Archer, New York 1980; *American Architecture Now,* edited by Barbaralee Diamonstein, New York 1980; *Charles Moore* by Gerald Allen, New York 1980, St. Albans, Hertfordshire 1981; *New American Art Museums* by Helen Searing, New York 1982; articles—"Trends in Architecture: U.S.A.: Work by Charles W. Moore" in *Bauwelt* (Berlin), June 1963; "U.S.A.: Charles Moore, California" in *Architectural Design* (London), September 1963; "Charles Moore: Architecture and the New Vernacular" by David Gebhard in *Artforum* (New York), May 1965; "World Architects

2: Charles W. Moore and His Partners" in *The Japan Architect* (Tokyo), May and September 1965; "Charles W. Moore" in *Kenchiku Bunka* (Tokyo), April 1971; "Should Anyone Care About the 'New York Five'?" by P. Goldberger in *Architectural Record* (New York), February 1974; "White and Grey: Eleven Modern American Architects" in *Architecture + Urbanism* (Tokyo), April 1975; "Interior Architecture: Charles Moore—One Point of View" in *Progressive Architecture* (New York), April 1975; "Moore Is More: Cinq Portraits pour Chuck" in *L'Architecture d'Aujourd'hui* (Paris), March/April 1976; "America Now: Drawing Towards a More Modern Architecture" by R. Stern in *Architectural Design* (London), no. 6, 1977; "Charles W. Moore" by Yukio Futagawa in *Architecture + Urbanism* (Tokyo), 1978; "Art: Architectural Drawings: The Grace of Fine Delineation" in *Architectural Digest* (Los Angeles), March 1978; "Barrier-free Design" in *Progressive Architecture* (New York), April 1978; "The Work of Charles W. Moore", special issue of *Architecture + Urbanism* (Tokyo), May 1978; "Scourge of the International Style" in *Building Design* (London), 2 February 1979; "Charles Moore at Plymouth" in *RIBA Journal* (London), April 1979; "Morality and the Architecture of Charles Moore" in *Transition* (St. Kilda, Victoria), July 1979; "Charles Moore and Company", special issue of *GA Houses* (Tokyo), no. 7, 1980; "Charles Moore – Educator and Architect" in *New Zealand Architect* (Wellington), no. 2, 1981; "Charles W. Moore – The Gift of Urbanity" in *Architecture* (Paris), March 1981; "Charles Moore: Recent Projects" in *Architectural Review* (London), August 1981; "The Work of Charles Moore" in *Arkitekten* (Copenhagen), August 1983; "To Dare All" in *Connaissance des Arts* (Paris), September 1983; "Building Types Study 597: Religious Buildings" in *Architectural Record* (New York), February 1984.

Bibliography: *Charles Willard Moore: A Bibliography* by Marianne Dale, Monticello, Illinois 1979; *Charles W. Moore, North American Architect* by Florita Z. Louie de Malave, Monticello, Illinois 1985.

Charles Moore is a recognized and accomplished spokesman of a group who, together, constitute a dissident movement in American architecture. Born in 1925, he is a graduate of the University of Michigan and Princeton, from which he earned a PhD. His dissertation was on the role of water in architecture.

A characteristic of the "dissident" movement is that its practitioners possess a considerable background of scholarship, including an extensive and insightful knowledge of architectural history. They are also articulate and, since many of them hold teaching positions, they have a wide audience. Moore himself has been a teacher during much of his career, at the University of California at Berkeley, at Yale, and at the University of California at Los Angeles. As a practitioner much of his work has been authored under the firm identification "MLTW"—Moore, Lyndon, Turnbull, Whitaker.

Moore's dissidence is with a somewhat moralistic and socially directed position that modern architecture assumed. One can argue if that has been even partly fulfilled, or if indeed it is not business and institutional exigency that motivates and directs American architecture. Whatever it is, Moore takes exception to it.

As a counter offering, he poses a new set of objectives and possible accomplishments for architecture, and draws on an entirely different set of premises. Essentially his aim is that architecture be personalized, derived out of a condition of personal (client) predilection, out of metaphoric reference to site-setting and its historic and cultural connotation. Architecture should engage fancy, whim, historicism, myth, fantasy. It is less a medium for

moralizing an ideal; more an environment of symbols and connotations in the realm of sensed revelation, stimulated by psyche-arousing artifacts in space.

This direction came to wide professional attention with MLTW's design for the Sea Ranch, a coastal recreational community about 100 miles north of San Francisco. The buildings are of the most pragmatic, even ordinary construction. Their forms derive from their inner functions, site form, climate, and from recollections of summer-cottage architecture. It is a brilliant work, simple and elegant. It had great influence.

In the Faculty Club for the University of California at Santa Barbara, Moore has drawn on the personality of the place as a source of his design concept. That personality is one of theatrics, confounded but controlled. It is a reflection of "the California spirit" somewhat thwarted—as indeed that spirit is. The building has elements of "heraldry", befitting the traditional mood and even pretense of historic academic association.

In the design of the Kresge College at the University of California at Santa Cruz he has created a de Chirico-like stage set for the drama of student interchange. Again, it is composed of the most commonplace architectural elements, drawing even on the toy blocks of childhood.

Moore's faith is in the living out of each individual's personal destiny, not a social consciousness moralistically imposing itself through architecture, and certainly not some transposed stylistic architectural identification. His own consciousness is not easily dismissed.

—Paul Spreiregen

MORANDI, Riccardo.
Italian. Born in Rome, 1 September 1902. Educated at the School of Applied Engineering, Rome, Dip.Ing. 1927. Worked on earthquake-proof concrete churches in Calabria, 1928-31. In private practice, Rome, since 1931: concentrated on reinforced and pre-stressed concrete structures, from 1936. Visiting Lecturer at schools in Amsterdam, Zurich, London, Edinburgh, New York, Venice, Turin, Naples and Rome, from 1955; Adjunct Professor of Construction Technique, 1958, and Professor of Bridge Structure and Form, 1959, Faculty of Architecture, University of Florence; Professor of Bridge Construction, Faculty of Engineering, University of Rome, 1967; Research Teacher, Florida State University, Gainesville, 1970. Member, Superior Council of the Italian Ministry of Works; Member, Italian National Research Council. Exhibitions: *Architetture Italiane degli Anni i70*, Galleria Nazionale d'Arte Moderna, Rome, 1981; *Architecture for Arab Countries*, at the *Biennale*, Venice, 1981; *Cinema Exhibition*, Capitol Museum, Rome, 1983; *Modern Italian Architects*, Valle Giulia Museum, Rome, 1984. Recipient: Italian Association of Cement Manufacturers Prize, 1962; IN/ARCH Prize, Rome, 1966, and Liguria, 1969; Columbus Prize, International Institute of Communications, 1967; Freyssinet Prize, Fédération Internationale de la Précontrainte, 1970; XIII Samoter Prize, Verona, 1976; Honour Award, Technische Hochschule, Munich, 1979; Gold Medal, Institute of Structural Engineers, London, 1980; Architecture Prize, Accademia Nazionale dei Lincei, Rome, 1983; Plaque of Honour, Venezuelan Association of Engineers, 1983. Hon. D.Arch.: University of Reggio Calabria, 1983. Member, Accademia di San Luca, Rome, 1963; Honorary Fellow, Royal Society of Arts, London, 1963. Address (office): Viale G. Rossini 18, 00198 Rome, Italy.

Works:

1931 House, Viale Vaticano, Rome
1933 Piccini Car Park, Via Vittorio Emanuele, Rome
1934 Augustus Cinema, Rome
1935 Parish Church, Colleferro, near Rome
Giulio Cesare Cinema, Via Giulio Cesare, Rome
1939 House, S. Felice Circeo, Latina, Italy
1941 House, via Terme Deciane, Rome
1946 Astoria Cinema, Via Stoppani, Rome
1947 Alcyone Cinema, Via Lago di Lesina, Rome (with G. Gandolfi)
S. Nicolo Bridge, over the River Arno, Florence
1948 Bologna Cinema, Rome
Bridge over the River Fortore, near Serracapriola, Fiuggi, Italy
SRE Thermo-Electric Centre, S. Paolo, Rome
Valentino Bridge enlargement and restoration, River Calore (project)
1949 Calci e Cementi di Segni Cement Factory, Scafa S. Vantino, near Pescara, Italy
Grillo Bridge, over the River Tevere, near Rome
1950 House, Via Martelli, Rome
Espero Cinema, Via Nomentana, Rome
Bridge over the River Elsa, Tuscany, Italy
Match Factory, Zaule, Trieste
Auditorium, Academy of S. Cecilia, Rome
Floating Bridge, Paola Lake, near Sabaudia, Italy (project)
1951 Di Tommaso Barracks, Rome
SST Thermo-Electric Centre, Civitavecchia, Italy
Bridge over the River Arrestra, Genoa/Savona Motorway, Italy
Bridge over the River Tuy, Venezuela
1952 Eden Cinema, Rome
BPD Study Centre, Colleferro, near Rome
Bridge over the Lupara Stream, Genoa/Savona Motorway, at Arenzano, Italy
Aircraft Hangars, La Guaira, near Caracas, Venezuela (project)
1953 New Republic Bridge, Paguita, Caracas, Venezuela
Bridge over the River Storms, between Port Elizabeth and Cape Town, South Africa
Compere Bridge, over the River Liri, Sori, near Frosinone, Italy
Bridge over the River Adda, Lecco, Italy (project)
Verona Arena reinforcement
Bridges over the Agro and Fiumedinisi streams, Sicily
1954 Gornalunga Bridge, Enna, Sicily
Cerami Bridge, Galliano Castelferrato, Enna, Sicily
Lazzi Car Park, Florence
BPD Metallurgic Centre, Colleferro, Italy
Mooring Towers for electric cables across the Straits of Messina, Sicily
BPD Fibre Plant, Castellaccio, Anagni, Frosinone, Italy
1955 Bridge over the Tambura stream, Vagli di Sotto, near Lucca, Italy
Footbridge over the Lussia stream, Vagli di Sotto, near Lucca, Italy
Hydraulic Reservoir Aqueduct, Livorno (project)
Underground Reservoir, Caracas, Venezuela
SRE Thermo-Electric Centre, Fiumicino, Rome
1956 Maestoso Cinema, Via Appia, Rome
Genoa/Po Valley Motorway alterations, Bolzaneto, Genoa
Oreto Bridge, Palermo, Sicily (project)
Santa Barbara Thermo-Electric Centre, S. Giovanni Valdarno, near Florence
Amerigo Vespucci Bridge, over the River Arno, Florence

Riccardo Morandi: Central Rail Station, Baghdad, Iraq, 1980.

1957 Metronio Covered Market and Car Park, Via
Magna Grecia, Rome
Calci e Cementi di Segni Cement Factory,
Savignano, Italy
Bridge over the Sambro stream, Autostrada
del Sole, near Bologna
Bridge over Lake Maracaibo, Venezuela
Fiumicino International Airport Terminal,
Rome (competition project; with A.
Zavileeri, V. Monacco, and A. Luccichenti)
SENN Nuclear Establishment, Garigliano,
near Latina, Italy
1958 Bridge over the Tevere River, Magliana,
Rome
1959 ABCD Factory, Ragusa, Sicily
Underground Pavilion, Valentino Park, Turin
Palazzo del Lavoro, *Italia '61*, Turin (project)
Bridge over the River Tevere, Tor di Quinto,
Rome (project)
1960 Viaduct, Via Olimpica, Rome
Plan for raising of the Abu Simbel Temples,
Aswan, Egypt (project; with G. Colonetti
and P. Gazzola)
Bridge over the River Tartaro, Canda, Udine,
Italy (project)
SELT Thermo-Electric Centre, Valdarno,
Livorno
Bridge over the Columbia River, Canada
Overpass, CISA Motorway, Italy
1961 Olympic Stadium, Tehran (project)
Peugeot Building, Buenos Aires
Viaduct, Fiumarella Valley, near Catanzaro,
Italy
Bridge over the River Tevere, Autostrada del
Sole, near Attigliano, Viterbo, Italy
Monorail, *Italia '61*, Turin
1962 Aircraft Hangars, Alitalia Building, Fiumi-
cino International Airport, Rome
Bridge over the Port of Göteborg, Sweden
(project)
Bridge over the Vella stream, Sulmona, Italy
Piezometric Reservoir, EUR Zone, Rome
(project)
Bridge over the River Schelda, Antwerp
(project)

1963 Bridge over Lake Paola, Sabaudia, Latina,
Italy
1964 Sports Stadium, Munich (project)
Thermo-Electric Centre, Bastardo, Foligno,
Italy
Zeppieri Garage, Frosinone, Italy
1965 Bridge and Viaduct over the Polcevera Valley,
Genoa/Savona Motorway, Italy
Solferino Bridge, over the River Arno, Pisa
(project)
Bridge over the River Parana, Corrientes,
Argentina (project)
S. Nicola Bridge, Benevento, Italy
Bridge over the River Riachuelo, Buenos
Aires
Entella Viaduct, Genoa/Savona Motorway,
S. Luigi, Italy
Viaduct, Modica Valley, Ragusa, Italy
(project)
Calci e Cementi di Segni Cement Factory
additions, Colleferro, Italy
Bridge over the River Paranda, Zarate,
Argentina
Bridge over the Salerno/Reggio Calabria
Motorway, Sicily
Hotel/Restaurant, S. Felice Circeo, Latina,
Italy
1966 Viaduct, Latte Valley, near the Franco-Italian
border (project)
Wadi-Kuf Bridge, Libya
Overpass, Via Cristoforo Colombo, Casal
Palocco, Rome
Viaduct over the Favazzina stream,
Salerno/Reggio Calabria Motorway, Sicily
Bridge over the Rome/Fiumicino Airport
Motorway, Magliana, Rome
House, Salto di Fondi, Latina, Italy
1967 Bridge over the River Adige, Trento, Italy
Viaduct over the River Ontrano,
Salerno/Reggio Calabria Motorway, Sicily
1968 Bridge over the River Salso, Licata, Agrig-
ento, Sicily
1969 Bridge over the River Guyas, Guayaquil,
Ecuador
Sports Centre, Milan (with Ortensi, Mosco,
Musmesi and Stegher)

1970 Viaduct over the Tangential, Naples
Alitalia maintenance Centre for Boeing 747
Aircraft, Fiumicino International Airport,
Rome
Catania Airport, Sicily
Viadict over the Valley of Temples, Agrigento,
Sicily
Bridge over the River Magdalena, Barran-
quilla, Colombia
1971 ENEL Thermo-Electric Centre, Piombino,
Italy
Underground Car Park, Turin
ENEL Thermo-Electric Centre, Milazzo,
Italy
Underground Car Park, Brescia, Italy
Lecco Motorway, Italy
Bridge, Stmigliano, near Rome (project)
1972 Bridge, Barranquilla, Colombia
Naples Port and Motorway alterations
Bridge, Rande, Spain
1973 Focaro, Ruzzi and Arsella Viaducts, near
Chieti, Italy
Arvivo Viaduct, Italy
1974 Servia Bridge, Macedonia, Greece
Mededil Car Parks, Naples
Thermo-Electric Centre, Termini Imerese,
Italy
Bausan Wharf, Naples
1975 Pyramid Building, Abidjan, Ivory Coast
Carpinteto Viaduct, Potenza, Italy
Aircraft Hangars, at Fertilia, Alghero, Olbia,
and Elmas Cagliari, Sardinia
Air Force Barracks, Olbia, Sardinia
1976 Ergife Hotel, Via Aurelia, Rome
1977 Irminio Viaduct, Sicily
Cornice Bridge, Jeddah, Saudi Arabia
Apartment/office buildings, Jeddah, Saudi
Arabia
FATA Building, Turin (with Oscar Niemeyer)
Bridge, Jeddah, Saudi Arabia (project)
1978 Bridge, Abidjan, Ivory Coast
Bridge over the River Creek, Saudi Arabia
(project)
1980 Ohburn Bridge over the Jeddah-Medina
Road, Saudi Arabia
Luxury Hotel, Tripoli, Libya

Passenger Hall and Canopies for the new Central and East Rail Stations, Baghdad, Iraq (project)

1981 Two Tower Buildings for INAIL, Palermo, Sicily

Large Water Tanks in Italy and Nigeria (projects)

Air Terminal, Venice (project)

1982 Banca d'Italia Operational Centre, Frascati, Italy (project)

Posts and Telecommunications Building, Caltanissetta, Italy (project)

Al-Ain Airport, Persian Gulf (project)

1983 Cortes Bridge, near Madrid (competition project)

Footbridge, Algiers (project)

Sports Palace Building, Bari, Italy (project)

Railway Bridge, Attigliano, Italy

1984 Motorway Viaduct over the rio Colorio, near Stresa, Italy (project)

Motorway Viaduct over the River Fiumetta, near Stresa, Italy (project)

Motorway Viaduct over the River Scoccia, near Stresa, Italy (project)

Motorway Viaduct over the River Vallone, near Stresa, Italy (project)

Motorway Viaduct over the River Roddo, near Stresa, Italy (project)

Pre-stressing system employed in hundreds of structures (7 patents)

Publications:

By MORANDI: books—*Strutture di Calcestruzzo armato e di Calcestruzzo Precompresso*, Rome 1954; *Forma e Struttura dei Ponti*, Florence 1959; articles—"A bridge is a many splendoured thing", interview with Claudia Dona, in *Modo* (Milan), July/August 1982; "Contro la maledizione del cattivo rendimento", interview with E. Battisti, in *Casabella* (Milan), May 1983.

On MORANDI: books—*The Concrete Architecture of Riccardo Morandi* by Giorgio Boaga and Benito Boni, Milan 1962; *L'Architettura negli Impianti di Produzione e di Distribuzione di Energia Elettrica* by Mario Magistrelli, Rome 1963; *Scienzo delle Construzioni e Menzione Architettonica in Architettura Problemi*, Florence 1965; *Guida dell'Architettura Contemporanea in Roma*, Rome 1965; *New Italian Architecture* by Alberto Galardi, London and Stuttgart 1967; *Riccardo Morandi* by Lara-Vinca Masini, with introduction by Leonardo Ricci, Rome 1974; *Architetture Italiane degli Anni '70*, exhibition catalogue edited by Giovanna De Feo and Enrico Valeriani, Rome 1981; *Riccardo Morandi* by Giorgio Boaga, Milan 1984; articles—"The Story of a Visit to Northern Italy in October 1956" by R. Pedio in *Concrete Quarterly* (London), January/March 1957; "The Italian 'Morandi' System of Prestressing" by A. Carbone in *Indian Concrete Journal* (Bombay), vol. 31, no. 7, 1957; "An Underground Hall in Prestressed Concrete" in *Concrete Quarterly* (London), no. 47, 1960; "The Use of Prestressed Concrete in Architecture" by Henry J. Cowan in *Architectural Science Review* (Melbourne), March 1960; "Prestressed Concrete Crosses Lake Maracaibo" in *Engineering News Record* (New York), October 1961; "Riccardo Morandi" by Giorgio Boaga and Benito Born in *Architect and Building News* (London), 27 November 1963; "L'Oeuvre de Riccardo Morandi" by H. Hofacker in *Architecture Formes et Fonctions* (Lausanne), no. 11, 1964/65; "The Concrete Architecture of Riccardo Morandi" by Giorgio Boaga and Benito Boni in *Forum* (Hilversum, Netherlands), January/February 1966; "Roma senza Cuore" by Paoio Portoghesi in *Controspazio* (Bari, Italy), December 1969; "Les Ingenieurs et l'Architecture" by Serge

Ketoff in *L'Architecture d'Aujourd'hui* (Paris), no. 113/114, 1970; "Morandi's Bridges" in *Architectural Forum* (New York), October 1971; "L'Opera di Riccardo Morandi" by Lara-Vinca Masini in *Bolletino degli Ingegneri* (Florence), no. 6, 1972; "Our Lady of the Plateau" in *Architecture Plus* (New York), September/October 1974; "Tre Opere di Ricardo Morandi" in *Industria delle Costruzioni* (Rome), March 1976; "Nuova Sede della Fata" by Massimo Gennari in *Domus* (Milan), May 1977; "Fata European Group" in *Modulo* (Rio de Janeiro), November/December, 1979; "Flying Arches" in *Domus* (Milan), December 1980; "Commercial Centre in Abidjan" in *Industria delle Costruzioni* (Rome), no. 3, 1980; "Opere e progetti italiani del dopoguerra" in *Casabella* (Milan), May 1981.

All of Riccardo Morandi's work since the 1940s has aimed to redefine technological architecture in method and form, based on rationalist experimentation. He has restated and transformed the objects of the engineering tradition of the nineteenth century to conform to contemporary cultural and social needs. His bridges, viaducts and buildings are intended to be functional and their relationship with the landscape is, as with all man-made objects, one of seeking to qualify and redefine—but not in accordance with town-planning conception of "human scale"—the tradition of romantic idealism. Morandi's vision is quite different: he seeks a complete change of dimensional scale in which the architectural work becomes, as it were, a macro-support for a macro-functional operation. The relationship between architecture and space (and between architecture and nature) is identified in a sort of interchange, or interaction, aiming at a new environmental conception. By broadening his scale, he modifies and adapts the outlines of the landscape (as in the Valle del Latte Viaduct, the Wadi-Kuf Bridge, the Valley of the Temples Viaduct in Sicily, or the Columbia River Bridge in Canada), or tends to strain it to the breaking point (as in the Polcevera Viaduct over the "exploded" outskirts of Genoa, passing with a scornful disregard over the poor little buildings of run-down suburbs).

Despite their huge scale, Morandi's constructions are formally and plastically expressive. They relate to contemporary artistic movements, from "minimal art" to "land art." Often they achieve all the delicacy of an intricate gear system—as in the subtle frame of the Magliana Bridge or the Boeing 747 Aircraft Hangar at Fiumicino Airport in Rome. The outstanding feature of the hangar is the great sail roof, raised up and still seeming to rise, suspended like a halo, stretched from three large exterior pillars, transforming the hangar into a sort of shell whose outside form reflects the shape of the huge aircraft. It is this image that gives the work a symbolic character, so that it becomes a piece of token-architecture, one that functions as an ideal "key" for the coordination of site planning—a focus for the laying out of the site, step by step, in ideal proportions, at the culmination of which the channel of communications is transformed from the horizontal or suspended (as in bridges and viaducts) to the aerial, in a gigantic infrastructural supporting network.

Morandi's symbolism is just as apparent in his large industrial structures. For example, the Garigliano Nuclear Establishment involves a contemporary image, a "key" image, of a basilica. The image is not gratuitous. Morandi has both precisely read and commented upon a current transformation in architectural symbolism, in which the technological image for the illustration of productive power is being converted to one of a secular/sacral character. His image is encroaching, overwhelming, and apt.

Yet just as Morandi becomes comprehensible, in the sense that one tries to anticipate his visions, he seems to change. "Seems" because, again, it is only the observer who is slow to perceive. In the beautiful spiral steps of the Zeppieri Garage he transforms and interprets the spiral of Frank Lloyd Wright's

Guggenheim Museum in a quite deliberate personal manner—directly linking industrial and technological architecture with works of "culture" in contemporary architectural tradition.

—Lara-Vinca Masini

MOREIRA, Jorge Machado.

Brazilian. Born in Paris, of Brazilian parents, 23 February 1904. Educated at the National School of Fine Arts, University of Brazil, now the Federal University of Rio de Janeiro, 1927-32, Dip.Arch.Ing. 1932. Served as a Reservist in the Brazilian Army, Rio Grande do Sul, 1921. Married the architect Giusepina Pirro in 1957. Director of Architecture, Baerlein Construction Company, Rio de Janeiro, 1933-37. In private practice, Rio de Janeiro, since 1936. Works Coordinator, 1936-37, Member of the Commission, 1939-41, and Chief Architect, 1949-62, University City of the Federal University of Rio de Janeiro. Vice-President, 1953-55, 1959-61, 1961-63, 1963-65, and Member of the Superior Council, 1957-59, 1974-75, 1976-77, 1978-79, Institute of Brazilian Architects; Vice-President, 4th Congress of Brazilian Architects, Sao Paulo, 1954; President of the Jury, 2nd International Competition for Schools of Architecture, *Bienal*, Sao Paulo, 1955; Vice-President, National Congress of Engineers, Architects, and Agricultural Engineers, Rio de Janeiro, 1959; Member of the Federal Council of Engineering, Architecture and Agronomy, Rio de Janeiro, 1967-68; Member, Superior Council of Urban Planning, Rio de Janeiro, 1972-75; President, 1st Symposium on Development and Environment, Rio de Janeiro, 1973. President, Commission for Landscape Protection of Rio de Janeiro, since 1970. Exhibitions: 6th Pan American Congress of Architects Exhibition, Lima, Peru, 1947; *14th Beaux-Arts National Salon*, Rio de Janeiro, 1949; *Bienal*, Sao Paulo, 1953, 1957, 1961; *World's Fair*, Brussels, 1958. Recipient: First Prize, wih Affonso Eduardo Reidy, Rio Grande do Sul Railway Headquarters Competition, 1944; Honorary Prize, 6th Pan American Congress of Architects, Lima, 1947; Gold Medal, *14th Beaux-Arts National Salon*, Rio de Janeiro, 1949; First Prize, *Bienal*, Sao Paulo, 1953, 1957, 1961; Gold Medal, *World's Fair*, Brussels, 1958; Gold Medal, 1967, and Personality of the Year Award, 1978, Institute of Brazilian Architects; Brazilian Government Diploma for Public Service, 1972; State of Guanabara Medal, 1975. Address: Avenida Bartolomeu Mitre 380, CEP 22431, Rio de Janeiro, Brazil.

Works:

1933 2 Apartment buildings, Rua Prudente de Morais 982, Rio de Janeiro (later altered by others)

1934 George White House, Ladeira do Russell 37, Rio de Janeiro

Apartment building, Rua Republica do Peru 305, Rio de Janeiro (later altered by others)

Gaetano Vanutelli House, Rua Senador Correa 50, Rio de Janeiro (demolished)

Apartment building, Rua Senador Vergueiro 23, Rio de Janeiro

1936 Apartment building, Rio de Janeiro (project)

1937 Izabel Silva House, Rua General Rabelo 52, Rio de Janeiro

1937/

43 Ministry of Education and Health, Rio de Janeiro (with Le Corbusier, Oscar Niemeyer, Affonso Eduardo Reidy, Lúcio Costa; now the Palace of Culture)

1940 Administration Building, Rio Grande do Sul Railway System Pension Fund, Porto Alegre, Brazil (project)

1941 Capel Apartments, Rua Senador Vergueiro 66, Rio de Janeiro

S. Vicente de Paulo Home for the Elderly, Sao Borja, Brazil (later altered by others)

Administration Building, Public Service Pension Fund, Porto Alegre, Brazil (project)

1942 Medical Center, Federal University of Rio Grande do Sul, Porto Alegre, Brazil (project)

1943 Civic Center, Porto Alegre, Brazil (project)

1944 Headquarters for the Railway System of Rio Grande do Sul, Porto Alegre, Brazil (competition project; with Affonso Eduardo Reidy)

1945/
46 IPASE Tuberculosis Sanatoria, Correas and Rio de Janeiro (projects)

1946 Itatiaia Apartments, Rio de Janeiro (project; with Carlos Leão)

1947 Administration Building, Ferroviarios and Public Service Pension Fund, Porto Alegre, Brazil (project)

1947/
48 SNT Tuberculosis Sanatoria, Manaus, Salvador, and Belo Horizonte, Brazil (later altered by others)

1948 Antonio Ceppas Apartments, Rua Benjamin Batista 180, Rio de Janeiro

1949/
62 University City, of the Federal University of Rio de Janeiro: general plan; Institute of Child Care; Architecture and Urbanism School; Engineering School; Medical Cen-

ter; and Printing Works; also, projects for Pharmacy School; Nuclear Physics Institute; Microbiology Institute; Bio-physics Institute; Institute of Tuberculosis; University Stadium; and residential blocks

1950 IAPB Tuberculosis Sanatorium, Salvador, Brazil (project)

1952 Getulio Vargas Foundation Building, Rio de Janeiro (project)

Sergio Correa da Costa House, Rua Campo Belo 88, Rio de Janeiro

Antonio Ceppas House, Praca Atahualpa 86, Rio de Janeiro

Nike Apartments, Rio de Janeiro (project)

1953 IAPB Apartment Building, Rua Voluntarios da Patria 471, Rio de Janeiro (later altered by others)

1954 Floriano Farias House, Rua Eng. Alfredo Duarte 456, Rio de Janeiro

1955 Sergio Marques de Souza House, Rua Igarapava 14, Rio de Janeiro

1961/
65 Flamengo Park, Rio de Janeiro (with others)

1965 Restaurant for Flamengo Park, Rio de Janeiro (project)

IAPFESP Administration Building, Porto Alegre, Brazil (project)

1970 Alfredo Ornellas House, Nova Friburgo, Brazil (with Giuseppina Pirro de Moreira; later altered by others)

Benfica Park Estate (houses, apartments, and leisure area), Teresopolis, Brazil (project; with Giuseppina Pirro de Moreira)

Publications:

On MOREIRA: books—*Brazil Builds* by Philip Goodwin, New York 1943; *Dix Ans d'Architecture Contemporaine* by Sigfried Giedion, Zurich 1951; *Latin American Architecture since 1945* by Henry-Russell Hitchcock, New York 1955; *Modern Architecture in Brazil* by Henrique Mindlin, Rio de Janeiro 1956; *Brazil* by Elizabeth Bishop, in *Life World Library* series, New York 1962; *Arquitectura Actual de America*, Madrid 1966; *Quem é Quem nas Artes e nas Letras do Brasil*, Rio de Janeiro 1966.

I started my professional life in 1932, identified with the movement that strove to establish a new Architecture. In Brazil as well as in many other countries, this movement was an outcome of the world-wide campaign, from 1928, by CIAM (Congrès Internationaux d'Architecture Moderne). I had begun taking an active part in this struggle while still a student at the National School of Fine Arts in Rio de Janeiro. Lúcio Costa had been appointed Director of that School in 1931; he proceeded to change our education by "establishing a new manner of conceiving, projecting and building." Gregori Warchavchik—the pioneer of contemporary architecture in Brazil—was invited to teach us, and he made a very strong impression, arousing our enthusiasm for and understanding of Costa's initiative, and creating our consequent support of it. That same year, Frank Lloyd Wright's visit to Rio de Janeiro, and his activities here, were most important

Jorge Moreira: Architecture School, Federal University, Rio de Janeiro, 1957.

for the consolidation of the Modern Movement.

Having concluded my studies, I went to work for a construction company. All at once I felt how difficult it would be to practice architecture as I had come to feel it. I decided to make it a condition of my stay with the company that they allow me my freedom in designing. This condition having been accepted, I had no further problems during the period that I remained with them.

This basic requirement I still maintain. It is not that I want to impose my point of view; I always try to arrive, through a dialogue, at the most appropriate solutions to the client's needs, without, however, making any concessions that are contrary to the principles that I, as an architect, must fight for. This criterion has never made me walk out on a job. My opinions find justification in solid argumentation, and the client understands that I am trying to defend his own interests. I opened my private office in 1936.

I have enjoyed the privilege of knowing personally Frank Lloyd Wright, Richard Neutra, Walter Gropius, Alvar Aalto, Mies van der Rohe, Kenzo Tange, and Philip Johnson. Of greater significance, however, was the contact I had with Le Corbusier in 1937, when he came to Rio at the invitation of the Minister of Education and Health. The close relationship that we—the architects entrusted with the design of the new Ministry building—had with Le Corbusier during about three weeks, had a decisive influence on my professional development.

In the years that have elapsed since that time, Brazilian architecture has suffered the consequences of political, social, and economic changes, which have also affected the way we practice in our metier. And yet, my way of feeling architecture and its importance has remained unchanged. For me, to make architecture is still to conceive a work that endeavors to solve plastically the proposed problem, in accordance with the times, the materials, the technical and economic possibilities—by analyzing and considering any external factors that might influence the work; by giving heed to the impositions and habits of the milieu; by detailing and articulating all the architectural elements; and, finally, by always seeking the truth of purpose and function, in form as well as in materials. I always try to give my full assistance to the contractors on the building, so that the work is executed as it was conceived, fulfilling the needs of the client, and thus completing my task. I am also concerned with the environment of a proposed work, and of the work's significance within the environment. Once built, it becomes an element of the urban landscape, the harmony of which must always be preserved. For this reason, every architect must be urbanistically oriented.

In accordance with this principle, I have endeavored to collaborate rather actively in the establishing of urban regulations and norms that have in view the structuring of the city and the guidance of its future development, without loss to the natural landscape and to the material evidence of its history, the remains of which it is our duty to preserve.

I have had a constant interest in the institutional aspect of my profession, collaborating with and supporting our various associations—particularly the Institute of Brazilian Architects. This seems to me to be the only way to fulfill completely one's professional obligations.

I hope that the struggles and deceptions that are a part of our professional life will never discourage me or make me abandon the ideals that I have always held, ideals that are always being updated so that I may better serve architecture, whatever the occasion or the circumstances.

—Jorge Machado Moreira

The work of Jorge Machado Moreira is notable for its strict coherence and for its restrained use of form, which lend a classical simplicity to his buildings, making them the most representative examples of the rationalist tendency in Brazil.

Jorge Machado Moreira was a member of the team that created the design for the Ministry of Education and Health in Rio de Janeiro—with Le Corbusier, Lúcio Costa, Oscar Niemeyer, Affonso Eduardo Reidy, and others. His own first large-scale project was the Medical Center at Porto Alegre in 1942. It sets out architectural ideas that were to be developed in greater depth in the university buildings in Rio de Janeiro. In 1944 he collaborated with Affonso Eduardo Reidy in the national competition to design the new headquarters of the Rio Grande do Sul Railway, and their entry won first prize. The site for the new building was later changed and the project developed mainly by Reidy. In its exuberant use of shapes, the building has obvious links with the architectural movement of the 1940's and 1950's.

From 1949 until 1962 Jorge Machado Moreira directed the design office responsible for the new university at Rio de Janeiro. This enormous task included the urbanization of an area of approximately six square kilometres and the construction of buildings for a total of 40,000 people.

The project was only partially completed and is now being drastically altered. Of the twelve projects undertaken before 1962 (when the architect was indisposed as a result of a serious accident), only four major works were actually built: the Institute of Child Care; the Engineering School; the School of Architecture and Urbanism (which currently also houses the National School of Fine Arts and the University Administrative Center); and the Medical Center (now almost complete). Two of these buildings—the Institute of Child Care of 1953 and the School of Architecture and Urbanism of 1957—were awarded first prize in the 2nd and 4th Sao Paulo Bienal; the group of projects won a Gold Medal at the Brussels World's Fair in 1958.

The Institute of Child Care is a low building consisting of three parallel blocks (casualty, hospital and creche) linked by a transverse block and opening onto large gardens. The building is chiefly notable for its uncluttered detail and for its extensive internal and external surfaces, on which finishing materials are combined and juxtaposed with rare skill and taste.

The three larger buildings stand out like topological landmarks against the flat landscape of Fundão Island. A common identity is immediately established by the use of the same external material; by the clarity of line and the simplicity of the skyline; by the regularity of the windows, emphasized by their jutting sills and by the partitions that frame each gap; by the uniformity of design (two-storey buildings separated by landscaped patios and long narrow "blades" with blind lateral walls); and by the uniformity of scale and mood—that of monumental sobriety and simplicity. Yet the individuality of each building becomes apparent at closer range; then it is obvious that there are design features peculiar to each building, a response to specific functional needs. They demonstrate the wealth of possibilities that a limited vocabulary can offer when handled with dexterity.

This balance between individuality and identity—uniformity without monotony—is a rare and important contribution to contemporary town planning—all the more so in that it serves to point out the shortcomings of the more recent university buildings and of the great majority of projects of the same nature, where each building shrieks a strident individualism detrimental to the principles of harmony and restraint.

Two of Moreira's residential works are also outstanding. Despite the limitations imposed by the dimensions of the site and by zoning restrictions, the Ceppas Apartment Building is one of the best works of its kind in Rio de Janeiro. The Ceppas House, also in Rio, and subject to similar limitations, is an exceptional work—a large urban dwelling, extraordinarily spacious inside yet constructed on a site merely 430 metres square. The architect's proverbial perfectionism is obvious again in the fastidious attention to detail.

In his career Jorge Machado Moreira has also been constantly concerned with protecting architectural interests and with conservation. His active role in the profession—whether as a lecturer, competition judge, or member of special committees, particularly those having to do with revision of the laws relating to architecture—have won him innumerable important tributes, notably the Gold Medal and the Personality of the Year Award of the Institute of Brazilian Architects.

—Jorge Czajkowski

MORETTI, Luigi Walter.

Italian. Born in Rome, 2 January 1907. Studied humanities, Istituto Romano de De Merode, Rome; architecture, University of Rome, Dip.Arch. 1930. In private practice, Rome, from 1931. Founder, Istituto Nazionale di Ricerca Matematica e Operativa per l'Urbanistica (IRMOU), Rome, 1957. Founder-editor, *Spazio* magazine, Rome, 1956; also contributor to the magazines *Civilta delle Macchine* and *L'Architecture d'Aujourd'hui*. Exhibitions: *Triennale*, Milan, 1933, 1960; *Arte Sacra*, Rome, 1934; *Mostra delle Colonie Estive*, Circo Massimo, Rome, 1935; *International Exposition*, Rome, 1938; *Italian Youth Exhibition*, Rome, 1945; *Fiera di Milano*, Milan, 1946; *Expo '58*, Brussels, 1958; *Italia 61*, Turin, 1961; *La Casa Abitata*, Florence, 1965; *28/78 Architettura*, Palazzo delle Stelline, Milan, 1979; *Gli Annitrenta*, Palazzo Reale, Milan, 1982. Recipient: Valadier Prize, Rome, 1930; First Prize, Triennale Competition for Roman Studies, Rome, 1931; First Prize, Piazza and Nuovo Grande Teatro Competition, Rome, 1942; National Architecture Prize, Rome, 1957; Vallombrosa Prize, Rome, 1959; Gold Medal of the Professional Arts, Rome, 1960; Gold Medal, Ministry of Public Information, Rome, 1965; Architecture Prize, Accademia Nazionale dei Lincei, Rome, 1969. Honorary Fellow, American Institute of Architects, 1964; Academician, Accademia di San Luca, Rome, 1960. *Died* (in Isola di Capraia, Italy) *14 July 1973*.

Works:

1931 Palazzo Muccioli restoration, via Giulia, Rome (with Vallini)
Tower of the Militia site reorganization, Rome (with Corrado Ricci)
City Development Plan, Faenza, Ravenna, Italy (competition project; with Golfieri)

1932 Public Housing Complex, Lido di Ostia, Italy (with Vallini)
Villa Vallini, via Salaria/via Bruxelles, Rome (with Vallini)
Arch of Galliano restoration, Rome
Cola di Rienzo House restoration, Rome
Public Housing, Naples, Italy (competition project; with Poggi and Lizani)
Small Villa, Tivoli, Rome (project)
Sgombatti & Cerutti shop, corso Umberto, Rome
City Redevelopment Plan, Perugia, Italy (competition project; with Paniconi and Pediconi)
Post Office Headquarters, Naples, Italy (competition project)
Castel Fustao District Plan, Rome (project; with Montuori)
City Redevelopment Plan, Verona, Italy (competition project; with Fagioli, Paniconi, Pediconi and Tufaroli)
Palazzo De Vito alterations, via Panisperna, Rome
Building renovations, via Lisbona, Rome

1933 House for a Scholar, *V Triennale*, Milan (with Paniconi, Pediconi and Tufaroli)
Youth Centre, Piacenza, Italy

Youth Centre, Trastevere, Rome
Moretti House alterations, via Napoleone III, Rome
Small Palazzo, Aventino, Rome
Small Palazzo, Acilia, Rome
Small Blue Palazzo, corso Trieste, Rome
Mr. B. House, Caprarola, Viterbo, Italy
1934 Youth Centre, Trecate, Novara, Italy
Young Women's Centre, Piacenza, Italy
Arte Sacra exhibition layouts, Rome
Professor Curcio Studio interiors, via Vellestri, Rome
Palazzo del Littorio, *Mostra della Rivoluzione*, Rome (competition project)
1935 GIL General Command and Littorio Headquarters, additions, Foro Italico, Rome
Pavilion, *Mostra delle Colonie Estive*, Circo Massimo, Rome
1936 Film Academy, Foro Italico, Rome
Grand Hall, Foro Italico, Rome
Progettino Aureli, Rome
Main Auditorium of the Film Academy, Rome
Italian-German Friendship Building, Foro Italico, Rome
Esplanade, Foro Italico, Rome
Church of San Basilio I and II, Oreste Rosa, Rome
Church of San Basilio and San Nicola da Tolentino, Rome
Centocelle, Oreste Rosa, Rome
1937 Youth Centre, Urbino, Pesaro, Italy
Olympic Stadium, Rome (partly built)
Co-operative Building, Benzoni, Rome
Brennero Building, Rome
Berti Palazzo, Lido di Ostia, Rome
Balazzini Palazzo, Rome
Caio Duilio Baths, Lido di Ostia, Rome
Base for a sculpture by Scarpetta, Rome
Base for an unknown statue, Rome
Base for a statue of Balilla, Rome
Cesarea Domus, Rome
Risorgimento Co-operative Building I, Rome
Risorgimento Co-operative Building II, Rome
Il Nido Co-operative Building, Piazza Bologna, Rome
State Employees' Housing, Rome
Terraced Houses, Lido di Ostia, Rome
Villa Delle Penne, Fregene, Rome
Nicola di Crescenzio House, Rome
La Tirrena Co-operative Building, Lido di Ostia, Rome
Co-operative Building A, Rome
Co-operative Building B, Rome
Co-operative Buildings, Lido di Ostia, Rome
Il Nido Co-operative Building, via Garibaldi, Rome
Petrol Service Station, Rome
Newspaper Kiosk, Rome
Photo Kiosk, Rome
Cianocca, via Sistina, Rome
Little Church of San Crisognono restoration studies, Rome (project)
Old Sea-wall alterations, Cori, Latina, Italy
Heliotherapy Department alterations, in the Indoor Swimming Pool, Foro Italico, Rome
Youth Centre, Tivoli, Rome
Foro Italico Redevelopment Plan, Rome
Piazza Imperiale, at the *International Exposition*, Rome (competition project; with Fariello, Muratori and Quaroni)
Vallini Palazzo, viale Pineta, Lido di Ostia, Rome
Piazza dell'Impero and Entry Block, Rome
Open-Air Swimming Pool, Rome
Villa Falconi, Galloro, Rome
1938 Malgeri Chapel, Verano, Rome
Grand Theatre, *International Exposition*, Rome (not completed)
Aroma House, Ariccia, Rome
Sun House, Ariccia, Rome
Ministry of External Affairs Building, Rome (competition project)

1939 Amicucci Funeral Chapel, Tagliacozzo, L'Aquila, Italy
Foro Italico Redevelopment Plan 2, Rome
1940 Commemorative Cella, Foro Italico, Rome
Monument to Pius XI, San Pietro, Rome (competition project)
Tower renovations, Porta San Sebastiano, Rome
Tower renovation and restoration, Porta San Paolo, Rome
Hunting and Fishing Lodge, Brioni, Dalmatia, Yugoslavia
Cottage, Castel Fusano, Rome
Palazzo del Littorio, Mostra della Rivoluzione, Rome (competition project)
Youth Centre on the Foro Italico, Rome (sketch project)
San Alessio Higher Agrarian School, Rome
RR Military Police Headquarters and Zone Redevelopment Plan, Rome Moretti Tomb, Verano, Rome
Monumental Fountain, Foro Italico, Rome (project)
Sports Centre, Caserta, Italy
Sports and Youth Centre Exhibition layouts, Foro Italico, Rome
1941 College of Higher Classical Education, Foro Italico, Rome (project)
Provincial Economic Council Headquarters, Reggio Emilia, Italy
Piazzale San Pietro, Reggio Emilia, Italy
Sports and Youth Centre Exhibition layouts, Florence, Italy
Villa Camilli, Rome
Africa Italiana Plan, Rome (competition project)
Church, Gallo di Tagliacozzo, L'Aquila, Italy
House Type A, Tor Sapienza, Rome
House Type B, Tor Sapienza, Rome
Rural House, San Maria Nuova, Rome
Caffe Grande Italia coffee-bar, Rome
Grand Hotel, Dobbiaco, Bolzano, Italy
School of Horsemanship, the Forum, Rome
Pediment with Equestrian Statue, Foro Italico, Rome
Foresteria Nord Building, Foro Italico, Rome
Ferratella, Rome
Railway Services Redevelopment, Rome
Various Gardens, Foro Italico, Rome
Stadium Broadcasting Installation, Foro Italico, Rome
National Land Reclamation Centre, Latina, Italy
Youth Centre, Perugia, Italy
Trajan's Markets, Rome
Maria G. Garage, Rome
Youth Centre, Messina, Italy
Moretti House interiors, Rome
Testa House interiors, Rome
Sellani House interiors, Rome
Italian Youth exhibition layouts, at E42, Rome
Italian Youth exhibition layouts, Caprarola, Viterbo, Italy
Development Plan for Ostia Antica, Rome (project)
Adria Company Headquarters, Ostia Lido, Rome
Redevelopment Plan, Sanremo, Imperia, Italy
Theatre, Piacenza, Italy (project)
Autostrada Access Road, Puricelli, Rome
Pellicano Tomb, Verano, Rome
Piazzale Redevelopment, Ponente, Rome
Regina Margherita Development, Lido di Ostia, Rome
San Paolino alla Regola Church restoration, Rome
Via Guattani Development, Rome
Adua Bathing Company Installations, Lido di Ostia, Rome
Town Development, Signa, Florence, Italy (project)
Villa Von Matt, Monte Mario area, Camiluccia, Rome
Villa Blanc, EUR District, Rome

1946 Tubular Steel Pavilion, *Fiera di Milano*, Milan
1948 Boarding House, Via Corridoni, Milan
Hotel, Via Lazzaretto, Milan
Boarding House, Citta Universitaria, Milan
1949 *Nessuno sali a bordo* stage settings for Tatiana Pavlova, Rome
Astrea Co-operative Building, Moteverde Nuovo, Rome
1950 Il Girasole House, viale Bruno Buozzi
De Vito Estate Redevelopment Plan, Rome
1953 Office and Housing Complex (including Palmolive, Chlorodont, and Orestein e Kooper offices), corso Italia, Milan
Redevelopment Plan for Nuovo Terme, Viterbo, Italy (project)
Vidiri Apartment in Il Girasole House, Rome
1954 Villa La Saracena, Santa Marinella, Rome
Building Complex with five high-rise towers, Perego, Milan (project)
Marangoni Granetto House alterations and interiors, Milan
1955 National Academy of Dance (conversion of day-school buildings), Rome
1956 Borelli House, Santo Stefano, Grosseto, Italy
Village Redevelopment, Appia Antica, Rome
Workers Assistance Building alterations, Comacini, Varese, Italy
ENPAS Headquarters, via Bellini, Rome (project)
1957 National Architecture Prize Exhibition layouts, Rome and Milan
Archaeological Park, Rome
Inter-Municipal Plan, Rome
1958 Residential Development (from the old Eden Hotel), Nervi, Genoa, Italy (project)
Barene San Giuliano Urban Master Plan, Mestre, Venice, Italy (project)
Villa Sauli, via Corsica, Genoa, Italy
CEP Housing District, Livorno, Italy
Silenzi House alterations and interiors, Milan
Olympic Village, Rome (with Cafiero, Guidi, Libera, Luccichenti and Monaco)
Italian Pavilion, *Expo '58*, Brussels
New Residential Quarter Plan, Viareggio, Lucca, Italy
1959 Appia Antica Redevelopment Plan, La Caffarella, Rome
Alfano Residential Hotel, San Sebastiano District, Rome
Gerini Tolonia Apartment alterations, in the Villa Casale, Via Appia Antica, Rome
Bridge over the Tevere, Rome (competition project)
Royal Palace, Riyadh, Saudi Arabia (project)
Buildings, via San Giuseppe, Genoa, Italy
1960 San Francesco Saverio Missionary College, Val Canuta, Rome
Office and Residential Complex, Villa Di Sacalea, Palermo, Sicily
INCIS District Development, Strada di Decima (EUR), Rome
Castle alterations, Canossa, Reggio Emilia, Italy
IRMOU exhibit, XII Triennale, Milan
Office Complex Plan for the Instituto Massimo Area, Rome (project)
Health Exhibition layouts, at EUR, Rome
Architecture and Town Planning Exhibition layouts, Tunisia
Architecture and Town Planning Exhibition layouts, Algeria
Village restoration and alterations, Garganico, Rome
Assolombarda Headquarters, Milan (project)
Villa Modugno, Via Appia Antica, Rome (project)
1961 Terraced Houses by the sea (3), Santo Stefano, Grosseto, Italy
Lazio Pavilion, *Italia 61* Exhibition, Turin, Italy
Marangoni-Granetto House alterations and interiors, via dei Condotti, Rome
Watergate Residential Quarter, Washington, D.C.

Stock Exchange Tower Building, Place Victoria, Montreal, Quebec

1962 San Maurizio Apartment Building, Monte Mario, Rome

1963 Esso Oil Headquarters, Piazzale dell'Industria (EUR), Rome

Societa Generale Immobiliare Headquarters, EUR, Rome

Alcibiade Co-operative Apartment Building, Rome

Scarlino Regional Plan, Grosseto, Italy

Donoratico Regional Plan, Livorno, Italy

Villa Borghese Residential Centre Redevelopment Plan, Nettuno, Rome

Villa Generale Graziano, Genzano, Rome

Sicuri Building, via Micheli, Rome (project)

1964 Building restoration, Piazza San Lorenzo in Lucina, Rome

Piazza dei Cinquanento Redevelopment Plan, Rome (project)

New Urban Quarter Plan, Decima, Rome (project)

Istituto di Santo Spirito restoration, via Nazionale/via Venezia, Rome

Japanese Embassy restoration and interiors, via Venezia, Rome

ENPDEDP Headquarters Building, via Morgagni, Rome (project)

New Residential Centre Plan, Cinecitta, Torre Spaccata, Rome (project)

CIDA Auditorium, via Nazionale, Rome (project)

Faculty of Economics and Commerce, University of Rome (project)

1965 Fonti di Bonifacio VIII Thermal Complex alterations, Fiuggi, Frosinone, Italy

Casa Abitata Exhibition layouts, Florence, Italy

Torlonia Tomb, Trevi, Perugia, Italy

Valdoni Villas, Sperlonga, Latina, Italy

Capannelle District Urban Plan, De Filippi, Rome (project)

Termini-Risorgimento Central Trunk Line for the Metro, Rome

Metro Bridge over the Tevere, Rome

Manzolini Estate Urban Plan, via Cassia, Rome

1966 Sports Stadium and Olympic Complex, Teheran, Iran (project)

Royal Gardens, Teheran, Iran (project)

Mondragone Urban Development Plan, Caserta, Italy

Villa Borghese Underground Car Park, Rome

Samperi House interiors, Rome

SARA Building restoration, via Ripetta, Rome

Church at the Olympic Village, Rome (project)

1967 Sanctuary on Lake Tiberius, Tagbha, Israel (project)

Prince Borghese Estate Redevelopment Plan, Monte Argentario, Grosseto, Italy (project)

Cagno Estate Redevelopment Plan, Bari, Italy

Villa La Califfa, Santa Marinella, Rome

Building restoration and conversion, via del Valabro, Rome

Rural Development Studies, Incisa Bolgheri, Livorno, Italy

Santa Anastasia Church restoration, Circo Massimo, Rome

1968 Residential and Office Complex, San Berillo, Catania, Italy (project)

Engineers Club Headquarters, Kuwait (project)

El Aurassi Hotel, Algiers, Algeria

Villa Gabrielli, Affogalasino, Rome

Belli Zingone Estate Urban Redevelopment Plan, Casaletto District, Rome

Urban Residential Centre Plan, Libya

1969 Bedouin House, Kuwait

Apartments, Algiers, Algeria

School, Algiers, Algeria

1970 Club des Pins, Algiers, Algeria

Church of Maria Mater Eccleiae, Rome

Housing Development, via Marittima, Naples, Italy

Residential Complex at Olgiata, Rome

Algerian Embassy alterations and interiors, Rome

Villa Cascina Nuova, Santa Marinella, Rome

1971 Residential Complex on the Potomac, Alexandria, Virginia

Residential Complex, Roquencourt, Paris

High-rise Building, Montreal, Quebec (project)

Architectural Exhibition layouts, Madrid

1972 Villa Samaritani, Santa Severa, Rome

Villa De Angelis, Grottarossa, Rome

Villa Bucciante, Rome

OPHLM Commercial Centres, Algeria

Publications:

By MORETTI: book—*Apocalisse*, with P. Pascal, Rome 1964; article—"The value of profiles, and structures and sequences of spaces", in *Oppositions* (New York) October 1974.

On MORETTI: books—*Mostra dell'architettura italiana d'oggi*, exhibition catalogue by P. M. Bardi, Rome 1932; *Nuova architettura italiana* by A. Pica, Milan 1936; *Difficolta politiche dell'architettura in Italia, 1920-1940* by G. Veronesi, Milan 1953; *Schmiede und Schlosserarbeiten* by Hans Scheel, Stuttgart 1966; *Catalogo Bolaffi dell'architettura italiana 1963-66*, edited by P. C. Santini and G. L. Marini, Turin 1966; *50 immagini di architetture di Luigi Moretti*, with text by G. Ungaretti, Rome 1968; *Moretti*, edited by R. Bonelli, Rome 1975; *Il razionalismo e l'architettura in Italia durante il fascismo*, edited by S. Danesi and L. Patetta, Venice 1976; *28/78 architettura: cinquanta anni di architettura italiana dal 1928 al 1978*, exhibition catalogue edited by M. G. M. Bonadonna, Milan 1979; *Gli Annitrenta: arte e cultura in Italia*, exhibition catalogue by R. Barilli, C. De Seta, F. Irace and others, Milan 1982; articles—"The original Watergate scandal" by Wolf von Eckardt in *AIA Journal* (Washington, D.C.) April 1974; "Next to the Roman city walls: office building on the Piazzale Flaminio", in *Domus* (Milan) August 1975; "Underground car park in the Villa Borghese quarter, Rome", in *Architettura* (Rome) August/September 1978; "Mussolini's Bathroom" by Andrew Batey in *Archetype* (San Francisco), Summer 1979; "The Casa delle Armi in the Foro Italico, Rome, 1933-36" in *Modo* (Milan), November 1982.

Luigi Moretti studied architecture in his native Rome, obtaining his Laureato in Architecture in 1930. He was a very young, but leading member of Mussolini's Giovinezza Italiana, and through this contact and that of the ecclesiastical hierarchy, he attained a position of considerable importance with the power to advise his patrons on architectural appointments. Like many of his architectural contemporaries, he believed that the Mussolini regime could bring order and hope to the chaotic politics of Italy in the 1930s. He prepared a master plan for the Foro Mussolini in Rome and designed the personal Gymnasium and Baths for the Duce. The architectural character of his work at this time was a form of neoclassicism, using traditional and expensive materials, such as marble of great variety, and planning with lavish spaces on a grand scale. Much of his prewar work displayed this Roman monumental style, although his Fencing Academy (1935-6) at the Foro Mussolini showed the influence of the International Style. The hopes of those who believed in the Fascist promise of a rebirth of Italian culture were not fulfilled, and World War II produced a greater chaos than ever before in Italy. The reconstruction problem facing the Italian construction industry was enormous, and a major housing programme was promoted in which the architectural profession played an important part.

Moretti designed a number of housing projects in Rome and Milan, these including luxury apartments and houses for the Italian nobility, as well as low-cost apartment blocks such as the Casa Albergo in Milan which comprised several hundred dwelling units, extensive communal facilities, and administration offices. The architecture of these projects was typical of Moretti's approach to design; he did not accept the arguments of the European functionalists and in both his writings and his completed works he endeavoured to go beyond function and create buildings that were "both a physical reality and an ideal representation." This approach to architecture often led to a degree of uncertainty in Moretti's postwar work and his place in Italian architectural development is difficult to identify.

Moretti was always concerned with the way in which his buildings related to their surroundings, and as a dedicated urbanist he chose the shapes, materials and scale of his buildings with great care. One of his last buildings was a large office block in Piazzale Flaminio in Rome facing the ancient city wall and clearly visible from a long distance across the city. Here, the scale was reduced by building low, separated towers, but the roof features designed to hide ventilation and help the building to marry into the urban landscape, are unconvincing and cosmetic.

Moretti was an important Italian architectural critic and in the late 1940s and 1950s, he published and edited from his office in Rome the magazine *Spazio* in which he wrote a great many articles on the aesthetics of architecture, expressing his antipathy in general to the functionalist emphasis of the International Style and particularly to the fundamental principles of such international figures as Mies van der Rohe and Hannes Meyer.

In additions to his extensive work in Italy, Moretti executed commissions in Canada and the Watergate complex in Washington, D.C., better known for the famous scandal which led to the resignation of President Richard Nixon than for its architectural merits.

—Edward D. Mills

MORGAN, William.

American. Born in Jacksonville, Florida, 14 December 1930. Educated at the Harvard University Graduate School of Design, Cambridge, Massachusetts, under Josep Lluis Sert and Sigfried Giedion, 1955-58 (Holloway Scholarship; Lehman Fellow; Appleton Prize Fellow), M.Arch. 1958; Fulbright Grantee in Italy, 1958-59. Served as an officer in the United States Navy, in Korea and the Far East, 1952-55. Married Bernice E. Leimback in 1954; children: Newton and Dylan. Draftsman, for Paul Rudolph, Cambridge, part-time 1955-58, Smith, Hinchman and Grills, Detroit, summer 1957, and Reynolds, Smith and Hills, Jacksonville, Florida, 1959-60. Since 1961, Principal, William Morgan Architects, Jacksonville. Design Critic and Lecturer, Harvard Graduate School of Design, Cambridge, Massachusetts, 1981. Exhibitions: *A Decade of Architecture*, Jacksonville University Department of Fine Arts, 1971; *Transformations in Modern Architecture* Museum of Modern Art, New York, 1979. Recipient: Record Houses Award, *Architectural Record*, 1963, 1965, 1966, 1968, 1974, 1976, 1977, 1979, 1980; Wheelwright Fellowship, Harvard University, 1964; Design Award, American Institute of Architects, Florida Association, 1964, 1965, 1967, 1968, 1970, 1971, 1972, 1973, 1975, 1976, 1978, 1979, 1981, 1982, 1983, 1984; Homes for Better Living Award, American Institute of Architects, 1968, 1972, 1980; Graham Foundation grant, 1973; Honor Award, American Institute of Architects, 1974; Design Award, *Progressive Architecture*, 1975;

William Morgan: Federal Courthouse, Fort Lauderdale, Florida, 1978.

Design Award, United States General Services Administration, 1978; Mid-Career Fellowship, National Endowment for the Arts, 1979. Fellow, American Institute of Architects, 1975. Address: William Morgan Architects, 220 East Forsyth Street, Jacksonville, Florida 32202. U.S.A.

Works:

1961 William Morgan Apartments and Architectural Studio, Atlantic Beach, Florida
1962 James House, Atlantic Beach, Florida
     Williams House, Jacksonville Beach, Florida
1964 Gillespie Medical Clinic, Jacksonville Beach, Florida
     Rawls House, Jacksonville, Florida
     Williamson House, Ponte Vedra Beach, Florida
1966 Hatcher House, Jacksonville, Florida
     Place by the Sea Apartments, Atlantic Beach, Florida
     Ballentine House, Atlantic Beach, Florida
1968 Jacksonville Children's Museum, Florida
1969 Air Launched Weapons Training Facility, Mayport, Florida
     Stanley House, Gainesville, Florida
1970 Goodloe House, Ponte Vedra Beach, Florida
     Trainable Mentally Retarded School, Jacksonville, Florida
     Norfolk Sheraton Hotel, Virginia
1971 Savannah Elderly Housing, Georgia
     Florida State Museum, Gainesville
     Sheraton Inn, Hampton, Virginia
     Plaza Executive Centers, Miami

1972 Seascape at Hilton Head Apartments, Hilton Head Island, South Carolina
     Plummers Cove Apartments, Mandarin, Florida
1973 M. K. Dickinson House, Atlantic Beach, Florida
     220 East Forsyth Office Building (William Morgan offices), Jacksonville, Florida
     William Morgan House, Atlantic Beach, Florida
1974 Hilltop House, Central Florida
1975 Dunehouse Apartments, Atlantic Beach, Florida
     Oceanfront Condominium, Ocean City, Maryland
1976 Riverfront Esplanade, Norfolk, Virginia
     McCondichie House, Ponte Vedra Beach, Florida
1977 Police Memorial Building, Jacksonville, Florida
     Watkins House, Orange Park, Florida
1978 United States Post Office, Murray Hill, Jacksonville, Florida
     Regional Service Center for Duval County, Jacksonville, Florida
     Federal Building/United States Courthouse, Fort Lauderdale, Florida
     Community for Elderly Persons, Asheville, North Carolina
     J. C. Dickinson House, Gainesville, Florida
1979 Fish and Wildlife Interpretive Center, St. Marks, Florida
     Oceanfront Townhouses, Atlantic Beach, Florida
     United States Postal Facility, Arlington Station, Jacksonville, Florida

Tree House, Atlantic Beach, Florida
First District Court of Appeal, Tallahassee, Florida
1980 Jacksonville Electric Authority Enclosures, Jacksonville, Florida
1981 Prudential South Central Home Office Conceptual Design, Jacksonville, Florida
1982 Medical Clinic, Jacksonville, Florida
     Florida Conference Center, Tallahassee, Florida
     Neiman-Marcus Stores, Fort Lauderdale, Florida
1983 West Nassau Primary Care Center, Callahan, Florida
     Westinghouse Steam Turbine Generator Headquarters, Orlando, Florida
1984 Bloomingdale's Store, Miami
     Professional Office Building, Stuart, Florida
     Gilldorn Savings Association, Pawneee and Mount Zion, Illinois
     Mesa House, Austin, Texas
1985 Baptist Medical Pavilion, Jacksonville, Florida
     Professional Office Building, Jacksonville, Florida
     Submarine Base Headquarters Building, Kings Bay, Georgia

Publications:

By MORGAN; books—*Bucks County,* with photographs by Aaron Siskind, New York 1974; *Old Louisville: the Victorian Era,* with Samuel W. Thomas, Louisville, Kentucky 1975; *Louisville:*

architecture and the urban environment, Dublin 1979; *Prehistoric American Architecture*, Cambridge, Massachusetts 1980; articles—"Florida's Earth Architecture" in *The Florida Architect* (Miami), May/June 1975; "Strongboxes on Main Street" in *Landscape* (Berkeley, California), vol. 24, no. 2, 1980; "Louisville: city of paradoxes" in *Historic Preservation* (Washington, D.C.), May/June 1982; "Up to speed" in *Progressive Architecture* (New York), February 1983.

On MORGAN: books—*Decorative Arts and Modern Interiors,* annual, edited by Maria Schofield, London 1979; *Fifty Outstanding Architects of the World* by Ivica Mladenovic, Belgrade 1984; articles—"Teatro all Aperto" by Bruno Sevi in *L'Architettura* (Rome), January 1960; "Four Level House" by David Travers in *Arts and Architecture* (Los Angeles), June 1964; "Appartements-Jardins Atlantic Beach" by Renée Diamant-Berger in *L'Architecture d'Aujourd'hui* (Paris), April/May 1965; "William Morgan, Architect" by David Travers in *Arts and Architecture* (Los Angeles), May 1965; "Bright Young Men with Design on the Future" by Walter McQuade in *Fortune* (New York), July 1966; "The Earth" by C. Ray Smith in *Progressive Architecture* (New York), April 1967; "Interpod" by David Travers in *Arts and Architecture* (Los Angeles), April 1967; "From Flying Boxes to Stacked U's" by C. Ray Smith in *Progressive Architecture* (New York), June 1968; "Names: William Morgan" by Peggy Johnson in *Architectural and Engineering News* (Philadelphia), December 1969; "Museum Play In" by C. Ray Smith in *Progressive Architecture* (New York), November 1970; "Museum Architecture" by Michael Webb in *Museum News* (Washington, D.C.), March 1971; "Designing in, under, around and with the Earth" by Wolf Von Eckardt in the *Washington Post*, 8 April 1972; "Molding Our Man Made World" by Bess Balchen in *AIA Journal* (Washington, D.C.), February 1974; "Florida State Museum" by Gaitano Bologna in *Industria della Costruzioni* (Rome), November/December 1974; "Stepped Terrace as Breakwater" by C. Ray Smith in *Interiors* (New York), February 1975; "Earth Form House by William Morgan Echoes Florida's Pre-Colonial Past" by Barclay Gordon in *Architectural Record* (New York), May 1976; "Haus auf Vier Ebenen" by Jürgen Joedicke in *Bauen und Wohnen* (Zurich), September 1976; "Shaping Space" by Ed Fitzell in *Interior Design* (New York), January 1977; "McCondichie Residence, Hilltop Residence, Oceanfront Condominium" by Nakamura in *Architecture + Urbanism* (Tokyo), September 1977; "Breaking Down the Battlements" by Charles Hoyt in *Architectural Record* (New York), January 1978; "Underground Architecture" by Andrea O. Dean in *AIA Journal* (Washington, D.C.), April 1978; "Designs for Living" by Douglas Davis in *Newsweek* (New York), 6 November 1978; "Contemporary Houses of the World", special issue of *Architecture + Urbanism* (Tokyo), February 1979; "Celebration of Justice" in *Architectural Record* (New York), October 1979; "Architecture: William Morgan" by Frank Israel in *Architectural Digest* (Los Angeles), December 1979; "Private Residence, Gainesville, Florida" in *Architectural Record* (New York), mid-May 1980; "Forest House, Central Florida, 1979" in *Architecture + Urbanism* (Tokyo), July 1980; "Seminole Beach Housing in Florida" in *Industria delle Costruzioni* (Rome), September 1981; "Oceanfront Townhouses" and "Medical Clinic" in *Architecture + Urbanism* (Tokyo), April 1983; "First District Court of Appeal", "Jacksonville Electric Authority Enclosure", and "Florida Conference Center" in *Architecture + Urbanism* (Tokyo), August 1983; "Energy and earth sheltering revisited" in *AIA Journal* (Washington, D.C.), September 1983; "Architecture Souterraines" in *Decomag* (Montreal), February 1984; "Corte d'Appello Distrettuale a Tallahassee Florida" in *Industria delle Costruzioni* (Rome), June 1984.

*

A central concern of my work is the relationship of man to his environment. I seek to accommodate the needs of man by modifying his place on earth sensitively as possible. My interest in this direction had led me to search continually for the origins of architectural ideas in time and place on earth. My research explores the earliest beginnings of architecture with the view of assessing our present day activities and considering relevant directions for the future.

During the 1970s, I explored the evolution of architecture in the eastern United States for thousands of years before the arrival of Europeans. Presently I am inquiring into the prehistoric and traditional architecture of Micronesia; here stone cities, terraced mountains and distinctive buildings were created centuries ago by people on remote islands who worked with limited technologies. Their architecture successfully accommodated their needs in consonance with their environments.

It is my view that unique opportunities for meaningful architecture lie in our present day challenge of relating man and his institutions to his urban and rural environments. The elements of space, light, form, and movement take on new meaning through the perspective of history. Our continuing evolution constantly suggests new possibilities for architecture in the future.

—William Morgan

*

Since embarking upon an independent practice in the early 1960s, William Morgan has, in his architectural career, undergone a major metamorphosis. From spinning rather Miesian, functional cocoons of glass and other materials, he emerged from a ten-year study as one of the prime proponents of architecture as landscape. What at first appears to be an incredible transition in Morgan's approach reveals itself, upon closer inspection, to be a consistent maturation of ideas.

His early work adhered to strictly traditional, modern movement, neoclassical, functionalist forms, as exemplified by the Rawls and Williamson residences. These box-like dwellings present an austere facade to the public while employing extensive glass panels in the rear. Bold masonry "service towers," which house plumbing, utilities and baths, are a conspicuous design element, and a cantilevered roof provides structural support via hanger rods. A large, open, central living space, often two stories in height, dominates the interior. Snugly integrated within this "noble" space is an intimate fireplace area, and balconies overlook the space to afford myriad views. Morgan further explored the ramifications of this spatial disposition in an apartment complex, the Place by the Sea, and found it provided a "controlled variety within an agreeable order."

With later projects, such as the multi-level Ballentine and Hatcher residences, Morgan proved himself to be a masterful manipulator of interior spaces. These dwellings have as a focal point a central core that provides vertical circulation. Situated off either side of the core, at various levels, are living areas of different heights. The use of intimate fireplaces and balconies are reminiscent of his earlier designs, but the employment of a more complex spatial arrangement allows for a more varied and dynamic experience. The exteriors also display a more sophisticated handling, particularly in the Hatcher house. Numerous balconies penetrate its facade of naturally finished materials to create a dramatic pattern of light and shadow, which transcends the earlier unadorned curtain walls. While retaining a sense of functional utility and formal lines, these houses edge out into the twilight zone and explore the more humanistic aspects of classicism. However, a restrained formalism still dominates these designs, which is readily perceived in the buildings' relationship to their surroundings. The houses are built on and above the landscape and serve as platforms from which to observe nature. The environment is placed at a distance and regarded primarily as a source of scenic interest, to be considered architecturally only in the handling of the fenestration.

Morgan maintains this pronounced sense of classical control and order even in his more recently conceived "architecture as landscape" projects. His major public commissions of the past decade, the Florida State Museum in Gainesville and the Jacksonville Police Memorial Building, both belie the architect's strong commitment to rational order. Such elements as earth berm construction, a human scale, and expansive terraces, courtyards and promenades blend into an exceedingly formal, rigidly controlled pattern of interrelated spaces. These "earth form" designs do not so much disclose their proclaimed end, "buildings as landscape," as they do landscape as buildings. In these projects Morgan blurs the distinctions between building and landscape by employing natural elements as materials to be handled in a functional manner. A number of "earth form" residences, including the Hilltop House, well demonstrate this point. Featuring earth berm sides, the Hilltop House is a pyramid of monumental proportions that rises above the countryside. Although perpetuating the verdant sweep of the landscape, the residence is distinct from the surrounding terrain and functions in a manner similar to the Hatcher house, as an observatory.

A more successful attempt by Morgan to create a building as landscape is a duplex in Atlantic Beach, which is set into an existing sand dune. Situated on the ocean and following the rolling contours of the dune, the duplex intrudes as minimally as possible upon its natural setting. Only a curvilinear entry and a pair of oval porthole-like patios betray the presence of the dwelling in the earth. As such, this duplex points towards a feasible blending of landscape as architecture; however, the number of natural features that can be molded in such a manner appear to be rather limited.

The different stages of William Morgan's career all disclose him to be an extremely robust and innovative practitioner of functional formalism. He has consistently explored a wide range of possibilities which derive from the synthesis of the classical tradition and modern technology, and has developed various design solutions in an attempt to reconcile a functional approach with humanist needs.

—Don J. Hibbard

MORIYAMA, Raymond.

Canadian. Born in Vancouver, British Columbia, 11 October 1929. Educated at public and private schools in Vancouver, Hamilton, Ontario, and Tokyo; University of Toronto, 1949-54, B.Arch. 1954; McGill University, Montreal, 1954-57, M.Arch. 1957. Married Sachiko Miyauchi in 1954; children: Mark, Murina, Midori, Jason, and Ajon. In private practice, Toronto, since 1958: in partnership with Ted Teshima since 1969. Design Tutor, University of Toronto, 1961-63. Chairman of the Board, Ecological Research Ltd., Toronto, since 1969; President, Group One Ltd. (museum consultants), Toronto, since 1970. Chairman, Mid-Canada Conference Task Force on Environmental and Ecological Factors, 1969-70. Council Member, Ontario Art College, Toronto, 1972-73; Director, 1973-75, and Chairman of the Futures Committee, 1975, Canadian Guild of Crafts; Board Member, MTV Toronto, since 1979; Advisory Committee Member, MBA Arts Administration Programme, York University, Ontario, since 1982; Board Member, Canada Asia Pacific Foundation, since 1983. Exhibitions: National Gallery of Canada, Ottawa, 1977; Art Gallery of Ontario, Toronto, 1978; Winnipeg Art Gallery, Manitoba, 1982. Recipient: Massey Medal for Architecture, 1961; Award, *Canadian Architects Yearbook*, 1968; Pre-stressed

Raymond Moriyama: Metropolitan Toronto Library, 1977.

Concrete Institute Award, 1969; Citizen's Award, 1974; Massey Medal for Planning, 1976; Civic Award of Merit, Scarborough, Ontario, 1977; Japan Foundation Award, 1977; *Canadian Architect* Award of Excellence, 1979; OMRC Award of Excellence, 1979, 1981; Ontario Japanese Canadian Centennial Society Award, 1980; Stelco Design Award, 1980; City of Toronto Civic Award, 1980; Urban Design Award, 1982; Governor General's Medal for Architecture, 1982; Canadian Man of Distinction Award, DeBeers Foundation, 1983. LL.D.: Brock University, St. Catherines, Ontario, 1973; York University, Toronto, 1973; Trent University, Peterborough, Ontario, 1981; D.Ing.: Technical University of Nova Scotia, Halifax, 1980; Ryerson Fellowship, Ryerson Polytechnical Institute, Toronto, 1980. Fellow, Royal Architectural Institute of Canada, 1970; Member, Royal Canadian Academy of the Arts, 1973. Fellow, Royal Society of Arts, London, 1970. Address: Raymond Moriyama, Architects and Planners, 32 Davenport Road, Toronto, Ontario M5R 1H3, Canada.

Works:

1958   Private golf course, Toronto
1959   Gatehouse and Equipment Centre, for Crothers Caterpillar Ltd., Toronto
1960   Brady House, Scarborough, Ontario
        Comfort stations, Metropolitan Toronto Parks
1961   Civic Garden Centre, North York, Ontario
1962   Japanese-Canadian Cultural Centre, North York, Ontario
1964   Ernest Thompson Seton Park, North York, Ontario
        Master plan for the Ontario Science Centre, North York

1965   Raymond Moriyama, Architects and Planners Offices (renovation of service station), 32 Davenport Road, Toronto
1966   Convention Centre, Nassau, Bahamas (project)
        Master plan and site selections, Metropolitan Toronto Zoological Park, Scarborough, Ontario
        Minota Hagey Residence, University of Waterloo, Ontario
1967   John McCrae Senior Public School, Scarborough, Ontario
        Master plan of the Erindale Campus of the University of Toronto, Mississauga, Ontario
        Centennial Baptist Church, Markham, Ontario (project)
1967/
71   Waste Recycling Systems Research
1968   Jack Minor Public School, Scarborough, Ontario
        Human Kinetics Building, University of Guelph, Ontario
1968/
70   Cellular Building Systems Study
1969   Ontario Science Centre, North York
        Bell Telephone Hotel and Training Centre, Belleville, Ontario
1969/
70   Dynamic Structures Research (air curtain, wall and roof)
1970   Academic Staging Building, Brock University, St. Catherines, Ontario
        Fine Arts Building, phase II, York University, North York, Ontario
1971   Radio Station CKEY, Toronto
        Feasibility study of the Ministry of Urban Affairs, Ottawa, Ontario
1972   Centennial Arboretum Centre, University of Guelph, Ontario

L'Amoreaux Collegiate, Scarborough, Ontario
        Studios and Headquarters, Global Television Network, North York, Ontario
        Gazebo, King Township, Ontario
1973   Winnipeg Railway Study
        Scarborough Civic Centre, Ontario
1974   Minesing Swamp Study, Simcoe County, Ontario
        Northern Resources Exhibition Centre, Timmins, Ontario (project)
1975   Steam Attraction Centre, Muskoka, Ontario (project)
1976   Burnhamthorpe District Library, Mississauga, Ontario
        South Beach Urban Design, Miami Beach, Florida
        School for Outdoor Education Study, North York, Ontario
1977   Goh Ohn Bell Shelter, Toronto
        Metropolitan Toronto Library, Toronto
        National Gallery of Canada, Ottawa, Ontario (competition project)
        Energy Study, Toronto
1978   Malton Community Centre, Mississauga, Ontario
        Civic Centre Study, Barrie, Ontario
        Solar Heating Survey and Study, Toronto
1979   Stage One Experimental Theatre, Stratford, Ontario (project)
        Civic Centre Urban Design, Calgary, Alberta
        Performing Arts Centre, York University, North York, Ontario (project)
        Church of the Good Shepherd, Markham, Ontario
        Cedar Ridge Community Art Centre, Scarborough, Ontario
        Municipal Offices, Whitby, Ontario
        Multicultural Media Centre and Multilingual TV Headquarters, Toronto
        Meewasin Valley Conceptual Master Plan, Saskatoon, Saskatchewan
1980   Meewasin Valley Project Master Plan, Saskatoon, Saskatchewan
        Regional Art Gallery, London, Ontario
        Macdonald Stewart Community Art Centre, Guelph, Ontario
1981   Central Public Library, Peterborough, Ontario
1982   City Centre Plan, North York, Ontario (competition project)
1983   National Museum of Man, Ottawa, Ontario (competition project)
1984   Sudbury Science Centre, Sudbury, Ontario
        Canadian Music Centre, Toronto
        Science Complex, Brock University, St. Catharines, Ontario
        Government of Canada Building, Scarborough, Ontario
        Place St. Charles, New Orleans, Louisiana
        Office Building, 10 South La Salle, Chicago
        Civic Centre, Barrie, Ontario
        Transit and Pedestrian Mall, Main Street, Buffalo, New York
        Mono Cliffs Outdoor Education Centre, North York, Ontario
        National Music School of Canada, Toronto
        City Centre Central Library, North York, Ontario
        Maple Leaf Quay Waterfront Development, Toronto

Publications:

By MORIYAMA: articles—"Urban Renewal: Planning the Neighborhood" in *Royal Architectural Institute of Canada Journal* (Toronto), January 1958; "Trends in Motel Design" in *Royal Architectural Institute of Canada Journal* (Toronto), September 1960; "Thought Process and Intent: The Centennial Centre of Science and Technology, Toronto" in *Canadian Architect* (Toronto), September 1969;

"Design Process: Scarborough Civic Centre" in *Canadian Architect* (Toronto), November 1973; "New Metropolitan Library of Toronto" in *Architecture Concept* (Montreal), September/October 1977; "Metropolitan Library, Toronto" in *The Canadian Architect* (Toronto), January 1978.

On MORIYAMA: articles—"Three Projects by Moriyama and Watts, Toronto" in *Royal Architectural Institute of Canada Journal* (Toronto), June 1960; "Three-Hole Golf Course" in *Progressive Architecture* (New York), July 1962; "Workspace" in *Canadian Architect* (Toronto), February 1967; "Zoological Park, Metropolitan Toronto" in *Canadian Architect* (Toronto), November 1968; "Ontario's Participatory Museum" in *Architectural Record* (New York), August 1970; "A Civic Center for Scarborough, Ontario" in *Architectural Record* (New York), July 1974; "A Richness of Form, Space and Books" by Barry Downs in *Canadian Architect* (Toronto), January 1978; "Architecture, Meaning and Values: Raymond Moriyama and the New Metropolitan Toronto Library" by Joan M. Vastokas in *Artscanada* (Toronto), February/March 1978; "Meewasin Valley Project" in *The Canadian Architect* (Toronto), December 1979; "Peterborough Public Library, Ontario" in *The Canadian Architect* (Toronto), July 1981; "Japanese Bell House" in *The Canadian Architect* (Toronto), July 1982; "Architecture in Canada", special issue of *Bauwelt* (Berlin), 3 December 1982; "National Museum of Man" in *Section A* (Montreal), August 1984.

*

The consistency in the work of Raymond Moriyama is that of architectural personality applied to various building problems. In his designs, the richness of the psyche has remained free from the constraints of dogma. Each commission has brought interaction between the concerns of architect, client and user in the pursuit of an appropriate response. The range of possibilities he chooses to develop is unusual in the practice of modern architecture. Materials vary between buildings of similar use and form. There is a mix of angular and curved geometry. Motifs are sometimes invented or taken over from a generalized style or the work of other architects. The sophisticated viewer may object to the apparent lack of motivating rules or development of a personal style. In actuality, as one of Moriyama's buildings approaches a rule (e.g. a regulating geometry) or a specific style (e.g. a recognizable set of motifs), it unduly stresses that aspect of the design to the detriment of the whole.

There are various kinds of unity. Modern architecture favoured conceptual and formal unity; it rejected emotional and, by extension, spiritual unity if that can be considered descriptive of man's total existence. The architectural vocabulary employed by Moriyama fits within modern architectural practice. While ranging in source in contemporary time and place, it has the same simple, plain, undecorated look. As others do, he uses plants to soften the impact of the built environment. This architectural vocabulary is not one to which the general public is normally responsive, and its only imagistic allusions are to other architectural sources whose use might trouble connoisseurs. To most viewers, however, this issue is irrelevant in that all the forms are newly perceived and therefore equal within the context of the experience. Given the richness and diversity of contemporary existence, no specific form language will necessarily fit all occasions. As functional arangement, or structural system, or even energy consumption may generate different form solutions, so may less tangible but equal or more important concerns: uniqueness, personality. Or the form language itself might be subservient to other components of the total experience. The very nature of the intended building can establish its own significance which pre-exists the design. The form then becomes

supportive of the situation rather than presuming to create it.

Moriyama's success has been to match form with name and place to produce buildings that can be endowed with meanings associated with their purpose. The method of achieving this has been to establish psychological events within the overall fabric. Architects accustomed to conceptualizing the totality of a building design into a symbolic whole of metaphysical import may not see a relationship between the parts. The ordinary user will experience entry, shape, light, movement, colour, space as a series of events which cluster around the concept "library," or "civic centre," or "science centre." Such a set of sequential happenings allows some elements to have no other purpose than to enclose space or, at least, not to produce negative effects, while other forms create the desired experiences. Possibly because of the complexity of three-dimensional design, architects have learned to respond to simple orthogonal structures. By freeing the total building form from its symbolic function, Moriyama has been able to expend his creativity where it is most effective.

Current architectural dogma demands so many constraints as to severely limit design possibilities. By rejecting such stereotyped systems. Moriyama has freed himself to create effects where and how they are required, and at a scale and character that are appropriate. His buildings thereby include segments of creative brilliance where the non-rational amalgam of architectural elements comes together in a memorable experience. That it is the internal meaning of architectural experience evoked that is remembered, not the external medium of architecture employed, permits this diversity of means. The unifying theme is the inner sense of place where the architect's intent overrides and subjects his building vocabulary to the creation of a shaped event.

That Moriyama's buildings cannot be approached in the traditional formal terms of architectural theory sets them outside the mainstream of the architecture of the recent past. However, their popularity among the general public and the current broadening of architectural interests suggest that their consistent quality of result will lead to a critical reassessment of their value.

—Anthony Jackson

MORO, Peter.

British. Born in Heidelberg, Germany, 27 May 1911; emigrated to England, 1936: naturalized, 1947. Educated at the Technische Hochschule, Stuttgart, 1929-30, Berlin, 1930-34, and Zurich, 1934-36, Dip.Arch. 1936. Married Anne Vanneck in 1940; has three daughters. Practised with the Tecton Group, London, 1937-39; Lecturer, Regent Street Polytechnic, London, 1941-47; Associated Architect, Festival Hall, London County Council, 1948-51. Since 1952, Partner, with Michael Mellish, Michael Heard, Andrzej Blonski, Michael Merritt and Charles Peel, Peter Moro and Partners (now Peter Moro Partnership), London. Member of the Executive Committee, MARS (Modern Architectural Research) Group, London, 1938; founder-Member, 1961, and Vice President, 1978, Association of British Theatre Technicians; Member of the Council, Royal Institute of British Architects, 1967-73. Recipient: Bronze Medal, Royal Institute of British Architects, 1964; Civic Trust Awards, 1965, 1966, 1975; Plaisterer's Trophy, 1975; Peckham Society Award, 1976, 1980; Concrete Society Award, 1983. Fellow, Royal Institute of British Architects, 1948, and Society of Industrial Artists and Designers, 1957. C.B.E. (Commander, Order of the British Empire), 1977. Address: Peter Moro Partnership, 13 Rathbone Street, London W1P 1AF, England.

Works:

1939 House, Birdham, Sussex (with Richard Llewelyn Davies)
1948/
   51 Royal Festival Hall interiors, South Bank, London S.E.1
1954 House, Waldringfield, Suffolk
   Independent Television House and Studios, Kingsway, London
1957 Fairlawn Primary School, Lewisham, London
   Peter Moro House, Blackheath Park, London
1962 Hille of London Ltd. Offices and Showroom, Albermarle Street, London W.1
1963 Flats, for Audley Properties Ltd., Mayfair, London
1964 Playhouse Theatre, Nottingham
   Royal Opera House alterations, Convent Garden, London
1965 Secondary School and Youth Club, Cator Street, Peckham, London
   Primary School, Birstall, Leicestershire
   Hall of Residence, University of Leicester
1968 The Hansen House, Hertfordshire
1969 Gulbenkian Centre, Theatre and Television Studio, University of Hull, Yorkshire
1970 Associated Rediffusion Showrooms and Offices, London
   Greater London Council Housing, Comber Grove, Camberwell, London
1971 Theatre Royal alterations/remodelling, Bristol
1972/
   74 Greater London Council Housing, Barnado Gardens, Tower Hamlets, London
1973 Borough of Southwark Housing, Old Kent Road, London
1974 Borough of Southwark Housing, Montpelier Road, London
   Downside and Worth Boys Club with Swimming Pool, Southwark, London
   Greater London Council Housing, Fayland Estate, Wandsworth, London
   Greater London Council Housing, Clairview Road, Wandsworth, London
1975 Borough of Southwark Housing, Coxson Place, London
   Borough of Southwark Housing, East Street, London
   Riverside Theatre, New University of Ulster, Coleraine
1976 Borough of Southwark Housing, Earl Road, London
1977 Greater London Council Housing, Lebanon Gardens, Wandsworth, London
   Borough of Southwark Housing, Hamilton Square, London
1978 Borough of Southwark Housing, Queens Road/Pomeroy Street, London
   Greater London Council Housing, Hildenborough Gardens, Lewisham, London
   Piccadilly Theatre alterations, London
1979 Borough of Southwark Housing, Brimmington Central, London
   Borough of Southwark Housing, Pasley Road, London
1982 Theatre Royal, Plymouth, Devon
1983 BICC Headquarters refurbishment, London
1984 Taliesin Theatre and Arts Centre, University College, Swansea, Glamorgan

Publications:

By MORO: articles—"Queen Elizabeth Hall Appraisal" in *RIBA Journal* (London), June 1968; "Salle de Spectacles," special issue of *Architecture Francaise* (Paris), January/February 1969; "Theatres: A Design Guide" in *Architectural Design* (London), no. 3, 1973; "Fifteen Years of Theatre Design by Peter Moro," with S. Williams, in *RIBA Journal* (London), February 1979.

Peter Moro: Theatre Royal, Plymouth, Devon, 1982.

On MORO: books—*Architetture per lo Spectacolo* by Roberto Aloi, Milan 1958; *Modern Architecture in Britain* by Trevor Dannatt, London 1959; *Exhibition Design* by Misha Black, London 1959; *New Housing in Britain* by Brickman and Lewis, London 1960; *Ville nel Mondo* by Roberto Aloi, Milan 1961; *Schulbau* by Karl Otto, Stuttgart 1961; *Neue Einfamilienhauser* by Hoffman, Stuttgart 1962; *Architecture in Britain Today* by Michael Webb, London 1969; *The Politics of Architecture* by Anthony Jackson, London 1970; *The Modern Theatre* by Hannelore Schubert, London 1971; *Theatre Planning* by Roderick Ham, London 1972; articles—"Urban Housing Variations" by J.M. McKean in *Building Design* (London), 28 July 1978; "Housing in Pomeroy Street, Southwark, London" in *Baumeister* (Munich), August 1979; "Raising the roof" in *The Architects' Journal* (London), 12 May 1982; "Royal Progress" in *Building* (London), 14 May 1982; "Task force from the past" by Martin Pawley in *Building Design* (London), 25 June 1982; "Moving Performance" by Jonathan David in *Building Services* (London), September 1982; "Theatre Royal, Plymouth" by Derek Sugden and Gordon Nelson in *The Architects' Journal* (London), 13 October 1982; "Theatre Royal, Plymouth" in *Interior Design* (Morden, Surrey), January 1983.

I regard architecture as a service, not a vehicle for ego trips.

That is to say that a building must, as a matter of course, fulfill all functional requirements, both physical and emotional.

A building that works well but is aesthetically unsatisfactory is as bad as a beautiful building that fails to function properly on the physical plane.

The challenge, therefore, as I see it, is to combine in one's work aesthetic quality with practicability, not one at the expense of the other.

—Peter Moro

Peter Moro is an exemplar of Modern Movement architecture in England. His career began with Tecton before the Second World War, and he was on the executive of the MARS Group, but unlike that of many of his contemporaries his architectural practice in the 1980s retains its integrity; his buildings maintain a clarity and stylishness. There was no commercial sell-out in the '60s, nor loss of design nerve in the '70s; a recent major project, the important Plymouth Civic Theatre, completed in 1982, may be his finest building yet.

Typically, Moro would immediately qualify that word "his," also crediting Michael Mellish and Michael Heard, his partners for nearly 30 years. The practice has remained small and their output modest in quantity, but this is rather the result of the vagaries of patronage than of any ideological limit on size. Best known for a series of theatres, the partnership has designed a wide variety of buildings, and, in recent years, they have been offered a staple diet of local authority housing.

And their reputation need not rest on the larger buildings, for Moro has produced charming and sparkling little gems over a long period, works that clearly demonstrate his skill and intentions. His own house, for example, a cool white box floating over Blackheath greenery, is nevertheless undogmatic and friendly; in the Fairlawn Primary School in Lewisham, the precision of detail, materials and colour echoes the geometric Pasmore abstract which hangs in the hall, yet the school is humane and cheerful; the Hille Showroom and Offices in London's West End, a carefully scaled, modest, curtain-walled corner, hits the ground with a touch of virtuoso, with the precisely board-marked concrete, instead of being exposed to dirt, lichen and weather-staining, stands half a metre inside its crisp metal and glass cage. The counterpoint of textures, colours, planes and materials in these works is always deft, and the spaces therefore are pleasing both at a distance and in close contact.

Providing visual richness at all scales, but without a traditional decorative vocabulary, has engrossed Moro earlier when, at perhaps the most crucial point in his career, he found himself invited to join the design team for the Royal Festival Hall. It was Britain's first major non-utilitarian building for a decade, and, within Sir Leslie Martin's overall concept, Moro designed and detailed the interior of what is now recognized as one of the very few great buildings in modern Britain. It does not possess the "timelessness" that was the aim of the Modern Movement: not just the detail (the bent plywood, the flying boxes, the patterned carpet) but also the spaces and forms are clearly dated. The RFH is no longer admired as "new" but as "architecture," with its magnificent spaces, its quietly competent functioning, and, particularly, its consistency. Moro explored the decorative potential of the required lighting and the air handling and acoustic devices, well aware that the function of such a hall included an atmosphere of drama, of festivity and of anticipation.

These themes have been developed in the theatre projects that followed, from the very successful Nottingham Playhouse to the Plymouth Civic Theatre. Nottingham excites users and the public alike: its forms are clear and logical, inventively useful; its glittering detail is held within a simple geometry.

Moro is scathing about "false aesthetics," and never tries, for example, to hide a fly tower; rather, he would use it to compositional advantage. His antipathy to the Sydney Opera House is, he says, based on its being unable to perform its intended functions. As clearly, if unspoken, he feels an antipathy to forms that are generated from abstract imposed ideas rather than from the artistic exploitation of utilitarian necessities. The conviction is becoming rare in an era of little faith, but Peter Moro and Partners have shown that, with such convictions, they can produce architecture of consistently fine quality.

—J.M. McKean

MORTLOCK, (Harold) Bryce.

Australian. Born in Lithgow, New South Wales, 14 October 1921. Educated at the University of Sydney School of Architecture, under Leslie Wilkinson, and George Molnar, 1946-50 (George McCrae Prize for Construction, 1949), B.Arch. (honours and University Medal) 1950; worked in the office of Sydney Ancher, *q.v.*, Sydney, 1948-50; awarded Byera Hadley Travelling Scholarship, 1951; travelled in England and Europe, 1950-52. Served as Flying Officer and Instructor in the Royal Australian Air Force, in Australia and Canada, 1942-45. Married Peggy Evelyn Worley in 1948; children: Peter, Richard, and Philip. Worked in the Architect's Department of the London County Council, 1950-52; Partner, with Sydney Ancher and Stuart Murray, *q.v.*, Ancher, Mortlock and Murray, Sydney, 1953-64, and, with Ancher, Murray, and Ken Woolley, *q.v.*, Ancher, Mortlock, Murray and Woolley, Sydney, 1964-69; Director, Ancher, Mortlock, Murray and Woolley Pty. Ltd., Sydney, 1969-75; Director, 1975-82, and Consultant, since 1982, Ancher, Mortlock and Woolley Pty. Ltd., Sydney. Master Planner, University of Melbourne, since 1968; Director, Australian Building Industry Specifications Pty. Ltd., Sydney, since 1975; Editor-in-Chief, *Australian Building Specification* magazine, Sydney, since 1981. Visiting Professor, University of New South Wales, Sydney, 1981. Member of the Council since 1960, Honorary Treasurer, 1964-66, Vice-President, 1966-70, and President, 1970-72, Royal Australian Institute of Architects, New South Wales Chapter; Member, New South Wales Board of Architects, 1968-72; Member of the Advisory Committee to the New South Wales Ministry for Housing, 1968-75; Chairman of the Finance Committee, 1973, Member of the Council, 1973, Vice-President, 1973-75, and President, 1975-76, Royal Australian Institute of Architects. Exhibitions: Student Design Exhibition, London, 1951; *Ancher, Mortlock, Murray and Woolley, Sydney Architects 1946-76*, Art Gallery of New South Wales, Sydney, 1976 (toured Australia, 1977). Recipient: Alfred Bossom Medal, London, 1951; Sulman Prize, 1960, Merit Award, 1972, and Gold Medal, 1979, Royal Australian Institute of Architects, New South Wales Chapter; Queen's Jubilee Medal, 1977. Fellow, 1963, and Life Fellow, 1970, Royal Australian Institute of Architects. Member, Order of Australia (AM), 1982. Address: 5 Vernon Street, Cammeray, New South Wales 2062, Australia.

Works:

1954 House, Rayner Road, Whale Beach, New South Wales

1955 House, Ulm Street, Lane Cove, New South Wales

     House, Flaumont Avenue, Lane Cove, New South Wales

1956 House, Stonehaven Avendue, West Dubbo, New South Wales

1958 House, Herbert Avenue, Newport, New South Wales

1959 Badham House, Dolans Road, Cronulla, New South Wales

     House, Hendy Avenue, Collaroy, New South Wales

     House, Hull Road, Beecroft, New South Wales

1960 Materials and Structures Laboratory, University of Sydney

1961 House, Milray Avenue, Wollstonecraft, New South Wales

     Ski Lodge, Thredbo, New South Wales

     Civil Engineering Building, University of Sydney

1962 House, Cowdroy Avenue, Cammeray, New South Wales

1963 Chemical Engineering Building, University of Sydney

     House, Boronia Parade, Lugarno, New South Wales

     House, Karoo Avenue, East Lindfield, New South Wales

1964 Dental surgery, 40 Haldon Street, Lakemba, New South Wales

     House, Coppins Close, St. Ives, New South Wales

1965 Electrical Engineering Building, University of Sydney

     House, Mount Panorama, Bathurst, New South Wales

     House, Boronia Parade, Lugarno, New South Wales

     House, Castle Hill, Townsville, Queensland

1967 Peter Nicol Russell Engineering Faculty Building, University of Sydney

1968 Control Plan for Housing Development, Lyons, A.C.T.

1969 Town houses, 18 Shirley Road, Wollstonecraft, New South Wales

     Royal Australian Institute of Architects Headquarters, 2a Mugga Way, Red Hill, A.C.T.

     Student Union Building, Macquarie University, North Ryde, New South Wales (with Ken Woolley)

1970 Army Holiday Centre, Terrigal, New South Wales

     Master plan for the University of Melbourne

1971 Redevelopment area control plan for Turramurra, New South Wales

1972 City Office Building, 3 Spring Street, Sydney (with McConnel, Smith and Johnson)

     Town houses, 20 Almora Street, Mosman, New South Wales

     House, Fennell Bay, New South Wales

1974 Sports and Recreation Complex Control Plan, Mitchell College of Advanced Education, Bathurst, New South Wales

1975 Initial development work for the National Building Specification

     Durham Street Sports Centre Control Plan, Bathurst, New South Wales

     Markets Campus Plan, New South Wales Institute of Technology, Sydney

1977 University Square Precinct Plan, University of Melbourne

1980/
81 Corso Pedestrian Mall, Manly, New South Wales

1982/
84 Town Centre Development Control Plan, Tumut, New South Wales

Publications:

By MORTLOCK: books—*University of Melbourne Master Plan Report*, Melbourne 1970; *University of Melbourne Landscape Elements Report*, Melbourne 1974; *BIAC Report No. 5: The Use of the Master Specification*, Sydney 1974; *BIAC Report No. 16: A Building Classification System*, Sydney 1975; *University of Melbourne Master Plan*, report, Melbourne 1981; articles—"Model of the Design Process and the Problem of Values" in *Architecture in Australia* (Sydney), December 1965; "Towards a Reform of SfB" in *Architects' Journal* (London), April, May, and June 1966; "The Architect in the Community" in *Royal Australian Institute of Architects Journal* (Sydney), 1967; book review in *Australian Quarterly* (Sydney), no. 2, 1968; "Design of Union Buildings" in *University of Adelaide Union Newsletter*, August 1969; "President's Message" (editorials) in *Royal Australian Institute of Architects Bulletin* (Sydney), 1970-72; "Observations on McEwen's *Crisis in Architecture*" in *Architecture in Australia* (Sydney), June 1975; "Commonsense Conservation" in *Architecture in Australia* (Sydney), April/May 1977; "University of Melbourne—University Square Precinct Report" in *Architecture in Australia* (Sydney), July 1977; "Use and Misuse of Materials," with J. Roxburgh and G. Holland, in *Building Economist* (Sydney) September 1980; "The Structure of Building Communications," with V. F. Davies in *Building Economist* (Sydney), March 1981; "Sinful Pleasure" in *Architecture Australia* (Melbourne), September 1982; "Shock of the Old" in *Architecture Australia* (Melbourne), January 1983; "The Failure of Planning" in *Architecture Australia* (Melbourne), July 1983; "Architecture Outside Utopia" in *Architecture Australia* (Melbourne), November 1984.

On MORTLOCK: book—*Ancher, Mortlock, Murray and Woolley: Sydney Architects, 1946-76*, exhibition catalogue, by David Saunders and Catherine Bourke, Sydney 1976; *Old Continent—New Building: Contemporary Australian Architecture*, edited by Leon Paroissien and Michael Griggs, Darlinghurst, New South Wales 1983.

*

During the 1950s and 1960s, progressive architects believed that modern architecture's mission was to change the world. The pre-war prophecies of the European moderns—Corbusier, Gropius, Mies and others—were about to be fulfilled. New, pure building forms would be based on Cezanne's cube, cone, and cylinder. Modern technology would give us new, more efficient building methods and materials. Corb's Radiant City—immense slab blocks on pilotis separated by vast public open spaces—would make existing cities obsolete, to be swept away by comprehensive redevelopment and "sun, space, verdure." People's lives would be transformed. Henceforth they would be healthier, happier, richer, and eternally grateful for the benefits of modern art and architecture.

Well, of course, today it is only too obvious that it didn't work out like that. For one thing, environmental determinism—the effect of the environment on behaviour—had been grossly overestimated. The ethologists—Lorenz, Tinbergen, Morris, Ardrey, and many others—have shown that environments change species only through the mechanism of heredity over many generations and only when survival is involved. Man is no exception. The changes that modern architecture could make to man's environment had little effect on his survival as a species.

But they had a big effect on his capacity for being outraged, and it was the opposite of what modern architects intended. On the whole, people didn't like the new architecture. They acquired spokesmen like Malcolm MacEwen in *Crisis in Architecture* and Conrad Jamieson on BBC-TV. The mutterings swelled to a chorus and spread to the Sunday Papers. Baiting the professions is a popular sport, and the

Bryce Mortlock: Royal Australian Institute of Architects Headquarters, Redhill, A.C.T., 1969.

outrage has no doubt been exaggerated; after all, modern architecture has had its popular triumphs too. However, I think one point at least can be made, that insofar as architecture claimed to change the world, the world has given it the thumbs down. Comprehensive development is now a dirty word; it has destroyed potential conservation areas and scattered close-knit communities. The wind whistles through the undercrofts of the post-Corb skyscraper slums; at Pruitt-Igoe in the United States they even resorted to blowing up the buildings. The spaces between skyscrapers became no-man's land owned and loved by nobody. As to land-use efficiency, the residential densities were no higher than in the Georgian squares of London.

Utopia through architecture proved elusive, but unfortunately we didn't stop there. We laid claim to be guardians of the whole environment. I think it was Einstein who first said "the environment is everything that isn't me," and of course everybody is entitled to take an intelligent interest in what so closely concerns him. But we went further than that, and in so doing set ourselves up.

The environment became popular, and the heavies began to get into the act. Activist groups were formed to usurp the functions of government. Unions backed them. Builder's labourers took over planning. Everybody began minding everyone else's business.

In the middle of all this were the architects, with negligible political leverage, but in a most vulnerable position as potential scapegoats. Why? Because our work comes at the end of the decision-making chain. All the important decisions affecting the built environment—use, density, built form—are already made by politicians, aldermen, and planners by the time we come on the scene. The gross effects of bad planning decisions will not be mitigated by archi-

tectural treatment, no matter how sensitive. But the activist public ignores these decisions until they are embodied in our designs. Then it is we who are the villains, and we who are expected to bring the whole juggernaut to a halt by our sacrifice.

I think the time has come for us to give a lead in a new direction, towards minding one's own business. Voltaire's Candide, at the end of all his adventures, concluded that *il faut cultiver notre jardin*. Our architectural garden has always been designing buildings and getting them built. Let us get on with cultivating it, to the best of our ability. If everybody did that, we'd make a better world.

—Bryce Mortlock

Bryce Mortlock first became well known when his Badham House received the Sulman Prize for the best building of the year. The style comprised a true, detailed modular layout, simple materials sensitively but often unconventionally chosen, with an absence of applied finishes. The rational arrangement of economical materials and direct details anticipated what Robin Boyd later called the "Sydney School." It is in line with the Australian tradition of controlling sunlight to limit heat gain in summer, while making the best use of it in winter, and of using natural materials such as timber and brick.

In the 1960s, many architects in Sydney had the opportunity for large-scale work, and Mortlock's logical, pragmatic approach produced a series of functional and economic buildings, particularly for universities. He was involved not merely in the design of individual buildings but also in university precinct design and eventually in the planning of entire campuses, applying his principles to the logical use of land and the creation of spaces rather than building sites.

Mortlock was elected to the Council of the New South Wales Chapter of the Royal Australian Institute of Architects in 1960, became Chapter President in 1970, and Federal President in 1975. He was a highly articulate president. He was also active in devising a better method for specifications, which led to the development of a standard specification by a commercial computer specification service, whose copyright he donated to the Royal Australian Institute of Architects. In 1981 he became Editor-in-Chief of the *Australian Building Specification*, and in 1984, a member of the Building Standards Board of the Standards Association of Australia. More recently, he has also been teaching.

—Henry Cowan

MOSER, Werner Max.
Swiss. Born in Karlsruhe, Germany, 16 July 1896. Educated at E.T.H.: Eidgenössische Technische Hochschule, Zurich, under his father Karl Moser, 1915-19, Dip.Arch. 1919. Married Silva Schindler in 1923; children: Lorenz, Ruth, and Claudia. Worked in Rotterdam, 1921-22, with Frank Lloyd Wright, in Taliesin, Wisconsin, 1923-26, and in his father's architectural studio, Zurich, 1926. In private practice, Zurich, from 1928: in partnership with Max Haefeli and Rudolf Steiger from 1938. Visiting Lecturer, Harvard University, Cambridge, Massachusetts, 1955; Professor, E.T.H., Zurich, 1958-63. Exhibitions: *Der Neue Schulbau*, Kunstgewerbemuseum, Zurich, 1932; *Switzerland Planning and Building Exhibition*, Royal Institute of British

Architects, London, 1946; *Frank Lloyd Wright,* Zurich, 1950. Dr.Ing.: Technical University, Stuttgart, 1958. Member, Bund Schweizer Architekten, and Schweizerischer Werkbund. Honorary Fellow, Royal Institute of British Architects. Member, Akademie der Künste, Berlin. *Died* (in Zurich) *19 August 1970.*

Works:

1923 Office Building, Chicago (project)
1926 Terraced houses, Zürichbergstrasse, Zurich (project)
1929 Hagmann Boathouse, Erlenbach, Zurich (with Emil Roth)
1930 Semi-detached house, Hegibachstrasse, Zurich
  Budgeheim Old People's Home, Frankfurt (with Mart Stam)
  Eglisee Housing Development, Basle (with Emil Roth)
1931 Moser/Guggenbühl House, Eierbrechtstrasse, Zurich
1932 Neubühl Housing Development, Zurich (with Artaria and Schmidt, Max Haefeli, Rudolf Steiger and Emil Roth)
  Collegiate Building, Basle (competition project)
1933 Höngg School Complex, Zurich (competition project)
1934 Chiodera House, Küsnacht, Zurich
  Affoltern Church Hall, Zurich (competition project)
1935 Sury House, Riehen, Basle
1937 Studio Gubler, Unterengstringen, Switzerland
  Von Schulthess House, Zollikon, Zurich
1939 Congress Building and Concert Hall, Zurich (with Max Haefeli and Rufolf Steiger)
  Allenmoos Swimming Pool, Zurich (with Max Haefeli)
1941 Alstetten Reform Church, Zurich
1945 Prilly Housing Development, Lausanne (project)
1950 New Apostle Church, Geneva
  Church, Witikon, Switzerland (project)
1952 Cantonal Hospital, Zurich (with AKZ)
1953 Kienberger House, God Laret, St. Moritz, Switzerland
  Housing development, Hohenbühlstrasse, Zurich (with Max Haefeli)
1954 Fretz House, Zumikon, Zurich
  Eternit AG Office Building, Niederurnen Glarus, Switzerland (with Max Haefeli)
1957 Farbhof Housing Development, Alstetten, Zurich (with Max Haefeli and Rudolf Stieger)
1959 Jona School, Rapperswil, Switzerland (competition project)
1961 Dental Institute, University of Zurich
  E. F. Schmidt House, Rüschlikon, Switzerland
1962 Kornfeld Church, Riehen, Basle
1964 Palme Building, Zurich (with Max Haefeli, Rudolf Steiger, and André Studer)
1965 Aula University, Zurich (project)
1966 Neubühl Old People's Housing Development, Zurich (with Max Haefeli and Rudolf Steiger)
1967 ASM Administration Building, Zurich (with Max Haefeli and Rudolf Steiger)
1968 Bally Capitol, Bahnhofstrasse, Zurich
1973 Bungertwies School, Zurich (with Max Haefeli)

Publications:

By MOSER: books—*Das Kind und sein Schulhaus,* with Gonzenbach and Schohaus, Zurich 1933; *Frank Lloyd Wright: Sechzig Jahre Lebendige Architektur,* Winterthur, Switzerland 1952; *Wandlungen im Reformierten Kirchenbau in den Letzten Hundert Jahren,* Riehen, Switzerland 1965; *Gedanken über die Schweizer Architektur von 1916-1958,* Zurich 1969; articles—"Das Verhalten des Laien zur Heutigen Baukunst" in *Schweizerische Technische Zeitschrift* (Waben, Switzerland), no. 46, 1956; "Frank Lloyd Wright" in *Bouwkundig Weekblaad* (Antwerp), November 1959; "Die Bedeutung Frank Lloyd Wright für die Entwicklung der Gegenwartsarchitektur" in *Werk* (Zurich), December 1959; "Beiträge zur Schulbaureform" in *Schweizerische Bauzeitung* (Zurich), April 1965.

On MOSER: articles—"Double House near Zurich, Switzerland" in *Architectural Record* (New York), May 1934; "Tonhalle und Kongresshaus, Zurich" in *Werk* (Zurich), December 1939; "Bemerkungen zum Modernen Wohnhausbau" by Friedrich T. Gubler in *Werk* (Zurich), February 1941; "The Congress Building in Zurich" in *Architect and Building News* (London), March 1941; "House at Zollikon" in *Architectural Review* (London), March 1945; "Eglise à Zurich" in *L'Architecture d'Aujourd'hui* (Paris), December 1946; "Kerk te Zurich-Altstetten" in *Bouwkundig Weekblaad* (Antwerp), August 1948; "Werner Moser zum Siebzigsten Geburtstag" in *Werk* (Zurich), July 1966; "Swimming Baths and Sports Hall in School Complex, Zurich-Hottingen" in *Schweizerische Bauzeitung* (Zurich), November 1973; "Railway Architecture in Switzerland: Past Work and Three Contemporary Examples" by Bruno Oldermatt in *Schweizerische Bauzeitung* (Zurich), July 1974; "Haefeli, Moser, Steiger", special issue of *Archithese* (Zurich) March/April 1980.

Werner M. Moser belongs to the generation that established modern architecture in Switzerland. Like Max Haefeli, Rudolf Steiger, Hans Schmidt and Hans Wittwer, he studied at the E.T.H., Zurich, under his father Karl Moser. Yet, during the years 1915-19, when Karl Moser was totally committed to neo-clasicism, Werner Moser's early designs were marked by the influence of expressionism. There were other influences too. During his studies he spent some time with Paul Bonatz in Stuttgart; after graduation, like many other young architects of the time, he worked in Holland; and in 1923 he went to the United States where he worked with Frank Lloyd Wright. Wright's influence is evident in Moser's design for a multi-storey Chicago office building—at the same time the project reveals Moser's unequivocal adoption of "modernism."

After he returned to Switzerland, Moser's work revealed his adherence to the tenets of European New Building. Its peculiarly Swiss characteristics were a regard for topography, a breaking away from severe stereometry, and a preoccupation with design. During this period Moser was primarily concerned with school building. He took part in the school building exhibition in Zurich in 1932, published a book on the subject, *Das Kind und sein Schulhaus,* in 1933, and his designs and projects influenced school building in Switzerland for the next decade. Another important interest of his early work was the housing development: with collaborators, he built two Woba Union estates, the Eglisee Housing Development in Basle and the Neubühl Housing Development in Zurich. In these estates—in common with much of modern Swiss architecture—there is strong attention to detail, fine technical execution, and a particular attention to individual rooms. The components— standards of "classical modernism"—are slim, lightweight, and of high quality; there is a variety of materials, and the lighting effects are subtle.

Moser's joint practice with Haefeli and Steiger sprang from their friendship and similar interests. They received a number of major public commissions including the Congress Building and Concert Hall, the Allenmoos Swimming Pool, and the Cantonal Hospital—all in Zurich. These designs have in common their structure, emphasis of tactile qualities, open wall and ceiling elements, continuity of space sequence, transparent (planted) room dividers, and indirect lighting. They are also attempts to create a new festive and ceremonial monumentality in public buildings. They try, too, to relate well to their environments. The swimming pool, for instance, "fits" the totality of its park landscape: green areas are threaded in; the pavilions have a "provisional" quality.

Moser is now most remembered for his handling of space in his post-war plans for housing developments. He took into account the scale of the surroundings. High, medium and low-rise buildings were combined, and he treated the multi-storey building as a town planning element with diverse uses.

Moser was also interested in church building. He wrote on the subject, and he experimented in his own churches—putting the new in an old context (Altstetten Reform Church, Zurich), giving in to the influence of Wright (New Apostle Church, Geneva), or trying out the ideas of Aalto (Kornfield Church, Riehen).

His openness and his versatility—characteristics that made him a memorable architect—also marked his relationship with his students at the E.T.H.

—Ulrike Jehle-Schulte Strathaus

MOYA, (John) Hidalgo.
British. Born in Los Gatos, California, 5 May 1920. Educated at Oundle School; Royal West of England School of Art, Bristol, 1937-38; Architectural Association School, London, 1938-43, Dip.A.A. 1943. Married Jannifer Mary Innes Hall in 1947; children: Susan, Timothy, and Joanna. Since 1946, Partner, with Philip Powell, *q.v.,* Powell and Moya, and Powell, Moya and Partners, London (Michael Powell, Powell, and Moya, 1946-50; Powell and Moya, 1950-61; Powell, Moya, Robert Henley and Peter Skinner, 1961-73; Powell, Moya, and Skinner, 1973-76; Powell, Moya, Skinner, John Cantwell, and Bernard Throp, 1976-84; Powell, Moya, Skinner, Throp, Roger Burr, and John Haworth, since 1984). Exhibitions: Royal Institute of British Architects, London, 1974; Royal Academy, London, yearly since 1974. Recipient: First Prize, Pimlico Housing Competition, London, 1946; Bronze Medal, 1950, 1958, 1961, Architectural Award, 1967, and Royal Gold Medal, 1974, Royal Institute of British Architects; Festival of Britain Award, 1951; Civic Trust Award, 1961; Project Award, *Architectural Design,* 1965. Associate of the Royal Institute of British Architects, 1956. C.B.E. (Commander, Order of the British Empire), 1966. Address: Powell, Moya and Partners, 21 Upper Cheyne Row, London SW3 5JW, England.

See POWELL, Sir Philip

MOZUNA Kikoh, Monta.
Japanese. Born in Kushiro City, Hokkaido, 14 November 1941. Studied at the Department of Architecture, Kobe University, 1961-64. Principal, Monta Mozuna Mobile Molgue, Kobe, 1969-74. Since 1977, Principal of Monta Mozuna Kikoh Architects, Tokyo. Lecturer at Kobe University, 1965-77. Exhibitions: *The Contemporary Art Space,* City Museum, Yokohama, Japan, 1976; *Post-Metabolism,* Architectural Association, London, 1978; *A New Wave of Japanese Architecture,* Institute for Architecture and Urban Studies, New York, 1978 (toured the United States); *Biennale,* Venice,

Hidalgo Moya and Philip Powell: International Conference Centre, Westminster, London, 1984.

1980; *Terra 2*, Wroclaw, Poland, 1980; *Post Modernism*, Louisiana Museum, Humlebaek, Denmark, 1981; Ainu Ethnic Museum, Hokkaido, Japan, 1982; Stadtisches Museum, Dusseldorf, West Germany, 1983; Kushiro City Museum, Hokkaido, Japan, 1984; Kushiro Marshland Museum, Hokkaido, Japan, 1984. Address: Monta Mozuna Kikoh Architects, Sangubashi Silk-Haitsu, 5-52-6 Yoyogi, Shibuya-ku, Tokyo, Japan.

Works:

1972   Anti-Dwelling Box (M House), Kushiro City, Japan
1973   Labyrinth in the Labyrinth (project)
1975   Uchu-an (Cosmic Hermitage) I, II, III (project)
1976   Heaven Phase (T House), Wakayama, Japan
        Earth Phase, Koyasan, Japan
        Human Phase (T House), Kyoto
1977   Museum in Hokkaido, Kushiro, Japan
        Yin and Yang (S House), Kushiro, Japan
1979   Zen Temple (Eisho-ji), Tokyo
1980   Between Space (Y-House), Hiroshima, Japan

Publications:

By MOZUNA: book—*Kenchiku no Mugen*, Tokyo 1980; articles—"Anti-Construction" in *Kentiku* (Tokyo), September 1972; "Theory of Extension of Architecture" in *Kentiku* (Tokyo), March 1973; "Twin Architecture" in *Gendai Shisoh* (Tokyo), June 1973; "Esashioiwake" in *Kentiku* (Tokyo), April 1974; "Theory of Mobile Molgue" in *Space Design* (Tokyo), September 1974; "Manner of Mirrored Imagine House" in *Toshi-Jutaku* (Tokyo), October 1975; "Temple and Shrine", series, in *Shitsunai* (Tokyo), January 1977 to December 1978; "Manner of the Architecture of Earth, Water, Fire and Wind" in *Dento-To-Gendai* (Tokyo), vol. 50, 1978; "House with architecturalized yin-yang symbols" in *The Japan Architect* (Tokyo), June 1978.

On MOZUNA: book—*A New Wave of Japanese Architecture*, with introduction by Kenneth Frampton, New York 1978; articles—"An Anarchist's Guide to Modern Architecture" by Chris Fawcett in *Architectural Association Quarterly* (London), no. 3, 1975; "Monta Mozuna" by Makoto Ueda in *Japan Interior* (Tokyo), March 1978; "The Post Metabolists" in *Arquitectura* (Madrid), January/February 1979; 'AD Profile: Post-Modern Classicism" in *Architectural Design* (London), vol. 50, no. 5/6, 1980; "Hall of Mirrors" in *The Japan Architect* (Tokyo), November/December 1980; "Japan Through the Looking Glass", special issue of *Domus* (Milan), June 1981; 'Zen Temple, Eisho-ji, Tokyo" in *Architectural Review* (London), August 1981; "House, Tokyo" in *Architectural Review* (London), September 1981; "Japanese Designers", special issue of *Process: Architecture* (Tokyo), June 1983; "Residential Architecture", special issue of *GA Houses* (Tokyo), July 1983.

*

I, Monta Mozuna, the megalomaniac architect, following the examples of Vitruvius and Alberti, have compared architecture to the universe and developed an "architectural cosmos."

As the "cosmos" was created by a man, its endurance is very short and its scale is small. Its firmament can be easily touched by a hand, and its ground can be vibrated or sometimes even treaded through by a foot.

When it is overtaken by a storm, its firmament leaks and its ground is flooded. At a time like this, the "god" who takes charge of the cosmos must mend in a flurry the leaks in its firmament.

The architectural cosmos has the following three aspects: Celestial aspect, Terrestrial aspect and Human aspect. It is a trinitarian world derived from the universe that is symbolized by Zero. It is also a cosmological architecture that, as a universe model, represents the "planeto-terrestrial globe."

The architectural cosmos contains, as its spatial mythos, a reflected image of the beginning of the world or a dually reflected image of the cosmogony (Zohar, Kojiki, etc.).

Its system is based on the principles of Yin and Yang (Yi-King) and the binary system of Sephirot (Cabala). Its sacred structural principle is based on the ins and outs of the mechanism of universe.

The architectural cosmos, in addition, contains another context. The context consists of constructional theories, architectural idioms and structural techniques of modern architectures and architectural idioms and techniques of historical architectures. In other words, one can regard it as an architecture that combines modern techniques with symbolism.

The Celestial aspect is the "cast shadow" of a celestial figure (the Great Bear) that is projected on the earth's surface. The constellation projected on the earth has seven columns. The Celestial aspect was planned to eliminate the cartesian co-ordinates. It has, like a constellation, various imaginary lines (e.g., solid lines, broken lines, dotted lines, chain lines, etc.) that constitute a covering structure. It contains Yin-volumes and Yang-volumes.

The Terrestrial aspect has a "womb of Chimoshin" that is a symbolizing deity of the Mother Earth. It is a "stratigraphic-space-raising architecture". The Terrestrial aspect that has an inclination of 45 degrees is a plan and elevation at the same time. When it is projected vertically on the ground, it becomes a plan. When it is projected horizontally on human eyes, it becomes an elevation. It has two faces: positive and negative.

The Human aspect is a pace that reflects the physical and spiritual structures of a microcosm man. It uses "Sayado" that can be regarded as an architectural prototype of the Human aspect. The Sayado is a sort of covering "sheath structure" that has been used in a few Japanese religious buildings (e.g. Konjikido of Chusonji). It protects the shrine inside. The shape of the Human aspect is derived from the core of Le Corbusier's Garches. Its grilles are projected on the distorted covering structure.

The art of cosmological architecture is derived from those of the following building structures: Kanshinji, Koyasan with its lotus flower arrangement, Boro-Budar, Piazza del Campidoglio, etc.

The spatial system and composition of cosmological architecture are derived from the study of the following superbooks: *Kongokai mandara* (Vajradhatu-maha-mandala), *Taizokai mandara* (Mahakaruna-garbhodbhava-mandala), *Emerald Tablet, Zohar, Yi-King, Yuiitsu-Shinto-Myoboyoshu, Abid-harmakosa-sastra*, etc.

—Monta Mozuna

Michitaro Tada in his book *Shigusa no Nihon Bunka (The Japanese Culture of Gesture)*, presents a striking analysis of *monomare* (mimicry) as the definitive trait whereby Japanese culture is made known to the world at large and transmitted internally: "Briefly, we feel at the bottom of our hearts it's not a bad thing to copy. In fact, we don't consider it a negative phenomenon but rather something nostalgic we have known a long time." An essential element from which Japanese society is compounded is the rite of invitation into a group by means of identification—the stranger is immediately said to look like someone a member of the group knows—"As for our society, there is a kind of tacit premise among people who are alike that brings them together and into contact."

Where Monta Mozuna scores over Tada's analysis is in his understanding that "mimicry," "identity," "reflection," etc. are axiomatic in any culture, that identical twins are regarded with universal caution, that one's reflection in a mirror provokes speculation in every society, that symmetry is a global perception: his long elaborated "architecture-of-twins" has ruthlessly followed up these hunches. Uchu-an House features two identical forms at different scales facing each other; Human Phase (T House) has two identical forms of the same size linked by a bridge; Anti-Dwelling Box (M House) comprises a cube within a cube within a cube—this positing of a world within a world is one of the primal architectural episodes we are condemned to repeat ad nauseam.

More recently, Mozuna has begun to compliment his ironic mirrorings and knowing repetitions with a cosmological overlay—one house has its columns laid out according to a heavenly constellation, its stairs following a star-shaped course. This paranormal architecture-of-things-that-go-bump-in-the-night points to the supernatural forces conspiring to shape the laws of mimicry and reflection. He projects architecture as an astral body in which "the universe of mind intersects the physical universe at right angles and stretches into a different dimension." He wants to establish a building that corresponds to the centre of gravity to the soul—it involves the discovering and laying out of the working principles of the universe and the gathering of them together into one bag. Design must respect that each of us is not one person but a whole "ladder of selves" whose rungs can take each of us to separate

levels of pereception of the world's mysterious elements.

Mozuna has explored a further rung on his own ladder of selves and has changed his name to Kikoh Mozuna. So perhaps he ought to be given the double name Monta (Kikoh) Mozuna. And just why did he change it? A fortune-teller deemed it auspicious for him to change his name. When it came to publishing a book in 1980, *Kenchiku no Mugen* (The Architecture of Eternity) under his new name, Isozaki wrote an introduction mourning the death of the late Monta Mozuna in a mock obituary. But Mozuna, regardless of whether he styles himself Monta or Kikoh is alive and kicking, as his two monstrous *musea* for Hokkaido (1984) testify. They are his two largest and most ambitious projects yet realized, and it looks as though the change of name is proving lucky after all. It is a far from posthumous architecture suffering from *rigor mortis,* but a thing of fabulous realism, besotted visions and infectious arousals

To celebrate winning the Architectural Institute of Japan's award for his Kushiro City Museum, he went to the premier Shinto shrine at Ise to thank the *kami* (deity) for its help. He must also have thanked it for his new level on the ladder of selves.

—Chris Fawcett

MUCHOW, William Charles.

American. Born in Denver, Colorado, 28 July 1922. Educated at the University of Notre Dame, Indiana; University of Illinois, Urbana, B.Arch. 1947; Cranbrook Academy of Art, Bloomfield Hills, Michigan, under Eliel Saarinen, M.Arch. and Urban Planning 1948; awarded Rome Prize, 1948. Served in the United States Navy, 1942-46: Lieutenant junior grade; Captain of the U.S.S. Lovelace DE 198. Married Priscilla Williams in 1948; children: Mark, Marcelyn, Brian, Daryl and Kim. Since 1950, Principal of William C. Muchow Associates, Architects, Denver. Director, Key Savings and Loan Association, since 1972. Member, Colorado State Board of Architectural Examiners, 1967-77; President, National Council of Architectural Registration Boards, 1975-76; Member, Jury of Fellows, 1977-79, Chairman of the National Awards Committee, 1978, Chancellor of the College of Fellows, 1982-83, and Director of the Western Mountain Region, 1982-85, American Institute of Architects. Director, Downtown Denver Inc., since 1969, and the American Automobile Association, since 1970; Member, International Advisory Board, United States General Services Administration, since 1972; Member of the Design Review Board, McGraw Hill Edition, 1981-84, and University of Colorado, Boulder, 1982-85; Member of the Architectural Control Board, Denver Technological Centre, since 1983. Exhibitions: *Hardwood Industry Exhibition.* Museum of Science and Industry, Chicago, 1955 (furniture), 1959 (building); *Muchow Associates,* Colorado State University, Fort Collins, 1976; *American Association of School Administrators Exhibition,* Las Vegas, Nevada, 1977, and Atlanta, Georgia, 1978. Recipient: Award of Merit. 1954, and Honor Award, 1975, American Institute of Architects; Award of Merit, AIA/*Sunset Magazine*, 1957; Award of Excellence, *Architectural Record,* 1957; Award of Merit, 1957, 1958, 1967, 1969, 1974, 1976, Design Award, 1960, First Honor Award, 1964, and Honor Award, 1964, 1969 (twice), 1972, AIA, Western Mountain Region; First Honor Award, 1961, 1965, and Design Award, 1977, AIA, Colorado Chapter; Award of Excellence, American Institute of Steel Construction, 1961; Award of Honor, AIA/ Structural Clay Products Institute, 1963; Design Award, 1963, and First Design Award, 1971, *Progressive Architecture*; First Place, Denver Convention Center Competition, 1965; First Honor Award, AIA/United States Office of Education, 1966; Honor Award, AIA, Colorado

Chapter/Structural Clay Products Institute, 1969; Plaque Award, Downtown Denver Inc., 1974; Barlett Award, President's Committee on Employment of the Handicapped, 1975; Special Service Award Citation, Society of American Registered Architects, 1975; Special Citation, AIA/American Association of School Administrators, 1976; Honor Award, Construction Specifications Institute, 1977. Fellow, American Institute of Architects, 1968. Address: W.C. Muchow and Partners, 1725 Blake Street, Denver, Colorado 80202, U.S.A.

Works:

1951   Texas Company Office Building, Denver
1952   Merino High School, Merino, Colorado
1953   Two parking garages, Denver (with Fisher and Fisher)
1954   Muchow House, 618 South Monroe Way, Denver
        First Federal Savings and Load Building, Denver
1956   Brentwood Methodist Church additions, Denver
1958   Mullen High School, Fort Logan, Colorado
        Merino Elementary School, Merino, Colorado
        West Lakewood Elementary School, Lakewood, Colorado
        Washington Park Congregational Church, Denver
        Loveland Ski Lodge, Loveland Basin, Colorado
1960   First Federal Savings and Load Building additions, Denver
1961   Public Service Building, Denver (wth Berne, Baume and Polvnick)
        888 Logan Apartments, Denver (with Nat Sachter)
        Cherry Creek Medical Building, Denver
        Rockland Community Church, Lookout Mountain, Colorado
        Women's Club Building, Denver
        Silver State Savings and Load Building, Aurora, Colorado
1962   Prince of Peace Church remodelling, Denver
        First Federal Savings and Load Building, Englewood, Colorado
        Capitol Federal Savings and Load Building, Arvada, Colorado
1964   Methodist Church, Littleton, Colorado
        First National Bank, Loveland, Colorado
        Lincoln Towers Office Building, Denver (with Robert Hiester)
        Silver State Savings and Load Main Office Building, Denver
1965   Engineering Sciences Center, University of Colorado, Boulder (with Architectural Associates)
1966   First United Presbyterian Church, Denver
        Anchor Savings Association Building, Lawrence, Kansas
        Congdon House, 4150 East Quincy, Englewood, Colorado
1968   First Methodist Church, Laramie, Wyoming
        Federal Reserve Bank, Denver (with Ken R. White)
        Methodist Church, Cheyenne, Wyoming
        Dormitories, Hiram Scott College, Scottsbluff, Nebraska
        Bonfils-Stanton Regional Library, Lakewood, Colorado
1969   Logan Office Building, Denver
        Currigan Exhibition Hall, Denver (with Ream and Larson)
1970   Financial Programs Office Building, Denver
        Marina Center, Yellowstone National Park, Wyoming

Monta Mozuna: Anti-Dwelling Box, Kushiro City, Japan, 1972.

West Entrance Station, Yellowstone National Park, Wyoming

Savings and Load Building, Loveland, Colorado

Bergen Elementary School, Bergen Park, Colorado

Denver Center Office Building, Denver

Lions Head Gondola Terminals, Vail, Colorado

Farmers Union Office Building, Denver

1971 Albert L. Place Junior High School, Denver

Denver Technical Center Building II, Englewood, Colorado

Diners Club Office Building, Englewood, Colorado

1972 Jewish Community Center, Denver

Lincoln Center Office Building, Denver

Administration Building, Winter Park, Colorado (with Haller and Larson)

1973 Hellenic Orthodox Church, Denver (with Haller and Larson)

Park Central Office Building, Denver

Hamilton Life Insurance Building, Englewood, Colorado

1974 Fleming Law Building, University of Colorado, Boulder

Del Pueblo Elementary School, Denver

Greeley National Bank, Greeley, Colorado (with CNC/NHPQ)

Blue Cross/Blue Shield Office Building, Denver (with Ken R. White)

KKBNA Office Building, Lakewood, Colorado

Laredo Middle School, Englewood, Colorado (with Haller and Larson)

Office building, 18th and Central, Denver

1975 Henry Junior High School, Denver

Fine Arts Center, Colorado State University, Fort Collins

Cherry Creek Performing Arts Center, Englewood, Colorado

First Presbyterian Church additions, Boulder, Colorado

First National Bank, Westminster, Colorado

Auraria Higher Education Center Master Plan, Colorado (with A-5 Denver Inc.)

Auraria Higher Education Center Administration and Shops Buildings, Colorado (with A-5 Denver Inc.)

Smoky Hill High School, Englewood, Colorado (with Haller and Larson)

Metrobank Building, Denver

1976 Margaret Walters School for the Retarded, Arvada, Colorado

Robert Weiland School for the Retarded, Lakewood, Colorado

Heritage Elementary School, Englewood, Colorado (with Haller and Larson)

1978 Parking Garage, Denver Center for the Performing Arts

Governmental complex, Littleton, Colorado

Water Board Administration Building, Denver

Cherry Creek High School III, Englewood, Colorado (with Haller and Larson)

1979 Events and Conference Center, University of Colorado, Boulder (with Haller and Larson)

1980/
84 Guaranty National Insurance Offices, Denver, Colorado

Larken Office Building, Denver, Colorado

CGG Georex Properties Offices, Denver, Colorado

Rolm Telecommunications Corporation Offices, Denver, Colorado

Public Service Company Offices, 1480 Welton, Denver, Colorado

Berlinger House, Genesee Park, Golden, Colorado

Elementary and Middle Schools, Steamboat Springs, Colorado (with Robert Ralston Architects)

Columbia Middle School, Aurora, Colorado (with Haller and Larson)

Municipal Center, Lakewood, Colorado

Jefferson County Justic Center, Golden, Colorado

Eagle County Detention Facility, Eagle, Colorado

Central Energy Plant, University of Wyoming, Laramie

IBM Data Center, Boulder, Colorado

Ski Base Facilities, Winter Park, Colorado (with Haller and Larson)

Publications:

On MUCHOW: books—*Banken und Sparkassen*, Munich 1961; *Mid-Century Architecture in America*, Baltimore 1961; *Contemporary Houses Evaluated by Their Owners* by Thomas H. Creighton and Katherine M. Ford, New York 1961; *City Halls and Emergency Operating Centers*, Office of Civil Defense Brochure TR 32, Washington, D.C. 1966; *Existing Schools: Their Future*, Office of Civil Defense Brochure TR 53, Washington, D.C. 1968; *Housing: Adventures in Design*, New York 1973; *Architecture in America: Pictorial History*, vols. 1 and 2, by G.E. Kidder Smith, New York 1976; articles—"Denver Bank in mint condition" in *Interiors* (New York), September 1973; "Park Central" in *Architectural Record* (New York), April 1974; "Red striped blue cross" in *Architecture Plus* (New York), November/December 1974; "Centre for the Performing Arts, Denver" in *Baumeister* (Munich), May 1975; "Central Street, Colorado State University" in *Domus* (Milan), July 1976; "Currigan exhibition hall in Denver" in *Informes de la Construccion* (Madrid) April 1978; "Visual Arts Complex, Fort Collins" in *Architecture + Urbanism* (Tokyo), July 1978; "Evaluation: singular structure in Denver—Park Central" in *AIA Journal* (Washington, D.C.), February 1980; "Waterworks administrative offices, Denver" in *Baumeister* (Munich), September 1980.

William Muchow is a very successful practicing architect in Denver, Colorado, where nearly all of his architectural work is to be found. He has been able to combine a financially rewarding architectural career with a very high degree of design quality. Before the recent explosion of work by "outside" architects, Muchow's work kept the Denver area abreast of leading international trends in architecture,

William Muchow: Engineering Sciences Center, University of Colorado, Boulder, 1965.

although it has perhaps not been directly innovative of those trends. The look of the buildings is cosmopolitan; there is no particular striving to create a "Rocky Mountain Look."

Muchow's design philosophy stresses conscious awareness of technical and spatial problems, the solutions to which produce the envelope or facade of the building. Strictly speaking, there is no facade, as the technical/spatial approach produces "honest" buildings, the insides of which directly map unto the outside surface. The buildings have in effect been designed from the inside out. The "form making" then becomes an unconscious selection producing many alternatives which are successively eliminated, again for largely technical reasons. The language or expressive quality of a Muchow-designed building, then, tends to be an excellent representative of designed objects which communicate primarily the implicit value systems of a culture through explicit technological and technical excellence.

A case in point is the celebrated Blue Cross/Blue Shield building in Denver, which has become a local urban landmark. Building-height and zoning limitations produced an air-space or envelope which even when fully filled was hardly financially promising, given local land costs. The solution was to totally fill the air space and send cars to below the building so tha no precious land would be wasted on auto access or parking. The resulting building is a conventional skyscraper lying on its side, in the air, with autos sitting under it. The internal circulation plan is signalled on the outside by an outrageous red stripe going down the middle of the sleeping giant. The building, then, through strict attention to technical and spatial problems, is not only extremely interesting and visually striking, but also a witty if restrained comment on contemporary high-rise architecture. It celebrates this culture's preoccupation with efficiency and tool-like neatness, but in carrying that preoccupation to an extreme becomes an artistic expression of it—perhaps pushing people into a new and deepened awareness of themselves and their values.

The same approach to the Engineering Center at the University of Colorado, Boulder, produced right-side-up, high-rise classroom buildings that tower over the local low-rise, "hill-town" look and psychologically challenge the Rocky Mountain foothills to a face-off. The rigorous and unbending attention to space needs again turned the local scene topsy-turvy, mocking Boulder's "rural" pretensions.

What is missing in all this is an attention to people not as consumers or clients but as users of the insides of the buildings. One is tempted to paraphrase Amos Rapoport and say that, although strictly sociocultural solutions in architecture often produce technical excellence, sheer attention to technical excellence rarely is satisfactory from a socio-cultural stand-point. Indeed, one could hardly produce a more succinct statement of the unconscious values of our culture than that it values technology more than human beings.

—Joseph B. Juhasz

MULLER, Peter

Australian. Born in Adelaide, South Australia, 3 July 1927. Educated at St. Peter's School, Adelaide, 1944; University of Adelaide, 1944-48, B.E. 1948; South Australian School of Mines and Industries, Adelaide, 1945-48, F.S.A.S.M.I. 1948; University of Pennsylvania, Philadelphia, 1950-51 (South Australian Travelling Scholarship; Fulbright Scholarship; University Tuition Fellowship), M.Arch. 1951. Married Rosemary Winn Patrick in 1953 (divorced, 1964); children: Peter, Suzy, and James (died); married Carole Margaret Mason in 1964. Since 1953, independent architect, Sydney; since 1978, Principal, Regional Design and Research, Consultants, Marulan, New South Wales (associates: interior design—Alan Gilbert; research—Adrian Snodgrass; contracts—Christopher Carlisle). Visiting Tutor, University of New South Wales, Sydney, 1962; Director, National Capital Development Commission, Canberra, 1975-77. Address: Peter Muller, Architect, Bronte House, 470 Bronte Road, Bronte, New South Wales 2024, Australia.

Works:

1952 Audette House, Edinburgh Road, Castlecrag, Sydney
1954 Winns Department Store, Ware Street, Fairfield, Sydney
    Peter Muller House, 42 Bynya Road, Whale Beach, Sydney
1955 Walcott House, 40 Bynya Road, Whale Beach, Sydney
1956 Richardson House, 949 Barrenjoey Road, Palm Beach, Sydney
1957 McGrath House, 4 Dunara Gardens, Point Piper, Sydney
    Nicholson House, Angophora Crescent, Forestville, Sydney
1958 Walker House, 21 Arterial Road, St. Ives, Sydney
    Kindergarten, Barrenjoey Road, Palm Beach, Sydney
    Victa Administration Building, 318 Horsley Road, Milperra, Sydney
    Ward House, Foote Street, Templestowe, Melbourne
1959 Sculfer House, Livistonia Lane, Palm Beach, Sydney
    Richardson Ski Lodge, Thredbo Village, New South Wales
    Fogarty House, Dunalister Stud, Elmore, Victoria
1960 Southside Plaza Shopping Centre, Rockdale, Sydney
    McGrath Ski Lodge, Thredbo Village, New South Wales
    Gunning House, 369 Edinburgh Road, Castlecrag, Sydney
1960/
78 Eight Craftbuilt Prototype Houses, various locations around Sydney
1961 Patrick House, The Scarp, Castlecrag, Sydney
    Park House, Prince Alfred Parade, Newport, Sydney
1962 Creaser House, 1 Womerah Street, Turramurra, Sydney
    Hamilton House, 1 Pindari Place, Bayview, Sydney
    Purcell House, 14 Fisher Street, Balgowlah, Sydney
    Lance House, 1 Lindsay Avenue, Darling Point, Sydney
    Barling House, 4 Paradise Avenue, Clareville Beach, Sydney
1963 Barton House, Morella Place, Castlecove, Sydney
    Green House, 7 Wolseley Road, Point Piper, Sydney
    Walder House, Cabarita Road, Stokes Point, Sydney
1964 Lance House, Coolong Road, Vaucluse, Sydney
    Mitchell House, 20 Robe Terrace, Adelaide, South Australia
    I.P.E.C. Headquarters, 259 Glen Osmond Road, Frewville, Adelaide, South Australia
    Greenwood House, Mulgowrie Avenue, Balgowlah, Sydney
1965 Walder House, 61a Kambala Road, Bellevue Hill, Sydney
    I.P.E.C. Airfreight Terminal, Launceston, Tasmania
    Carroll House, Rockbath Road, Palm Beach, Sydney
    McArthur House, Tor Walk, Castlecrag, Sydney
1966 Dickson Hotel, Dickson, Canberra
    Hoyts Drive-in Theatre, Tamworth, New South Wales
1967 Hoyts Drive-in Threatre, Casula, Sydney
    Hoyts Cinema Centre, Bourke Street, Melbourne
1968 McGrath House, 8 Castra Place, Double Bay, Sydney
    Hoyts Drive-in Theatre, Bulleen Road, Bulleen, Melbourne
    Hoyts Drive-in Theatre, Mountain Highway, Wantirna, Melbourne
    Regent/Paris Theatres and Arcade, Rundle Street, Adelaide
    Schwarz House, Palmerston Street, Watson's Bay, Sydney
1969 Town houses, Trelawney Street, Woollahra, Sydney
    Turner House, 8 Sylvan Avenue, East Lindfield, Sydney
1970 Dulhunty Homestead: Nant Lodge, Glen Innes, New South Wales (with Albert Read)
    Steidler House, 9 Wentworth Street, Point Piper, Sydney (with Albert Road)
1971 Snider House, 12 Wolseley Crescent, Point Piper, Sydney (with Albert Read)
    Woolf House, 7 Gulliver Avenue, Vaucluse, Sydney (with Albert Read)
    Burrell Homestead: Rockdale, Armidale, New South Wales
1972 Peter Muller House II, Ubud, Bali, Indonesia
1973 Kayu Aya Hotel, Seminyak Kuta Beach, Bali, Indonesia
1978 Lian Cove Hotel, Batangus Luzon, Philippines
    Luxury Housing Settlement, Jubail Industrial Estate, Saudi Arabia
1979 Travelodge Condominium Apartments, Papeete, Tahiti
1980 Oberoi Kolva Beach Resort Hotel, Goa, India
1982 Karnak Oberoi Hotel, Luxor, Egypt
    Si-Rusa Resort Hotel, Point Dickson, Malaysia
1983 Townhouses(67), Sailfish Point, Gold Coast, Queensland

Publications:

By MULLER: monographs—*The Esoteric Nature of Griffin's Design for Canberra*, Canberra 1976; *The New and Permanent Parliament House*, with others, Canberra 1977; *Canberra and the New Parliament House*, with others, Dee Why West, New South Wales 1983.

On MULLER: books—*An Australian Identity* by Jennifer Taylor, Sydney 1972; *Fine Houses of Sydney* by Robert Irving, John Kinstler and Max Dupain, Sydney 1982; articles—"Molinari House" in *Architecture and Arts* (Melbourne), July 1954; "Audette House" in *Architecture in Australia* (Sydney), July/September 1955; special issue of *Architecture and Arts* (Melbourne), December 1955; "Peter Muller House" in *Architecture in Australia* (Sydney), January/March 1956; "Richardon House" in *Architecture and Arts* (Melbourne), August 1956; "House by Peter Muller" in *L'Architettura* (Rome), August 1958; "Craftbuilt Houses" in *Architecture in Australia* (Sydney), September 1961; article by David Saunders in *Art and Architecture* (Sydney), June 1971.

For the architect, it is not so much what he says as what he does. The depth of his understanding of function and significance in architecture is embodied in the structural forms of his work. Ideally, function and significance coincide in the form. However, due to the great Technological Seduction, function has preoccupied our present era to the almost total disregard of meaning.

There now emerge some architects concerned to find and express meaning as well as to fulfil functions in their work. The work becomes then a form receptive to the contemplative life of the spirit as well as a support to the active life of the body. There is much to recollect from the many traditional societies that recognize the unifying power of architectural forms whose origins reflect the proportions and harmonies of Nature.

—Peter Muller

Peter Muller was the earliest and most original of a circle of Sydney architects in the 1950s who were influenced by Frank Lloyd Wright. By nature an independent individual, he preferred to work alone, seeking new and innovative solutions to problems that arose from his particular response to a site or a client. His determination to use natural materials, to avoid synthetic finishes, and his feeling for the Australian landscape infected many of his Sydney contemporaries. But it was his creative attitude that set him apart, for much Australian architecture was derivative—and still is—borrowing, whenever necessary, stylistic terms from Europe and America. Muller avoided subservience to overseas styles by allowing himself to be influenced by cultures rather than by styles. He identified with the spiritual principles within a culture and so attained a deeper understanding of that culture's architecture. This attitude is peculiarly Australian: Muller conforms to a rural, essentially conservative architectural tra-

dition, issuing from the nineteenth century English Arts and Crafts movement and supported by the example of Walter Burley Griffin's buildings.

Wright had a direct influence on Muller, but there can be no doubt that Muller developed in an independent way, that his vision of architecture was sufficiently strong to be sufficiently his own, and that his distance from Wright enabled him to work in a freer manner than Wright's own students. This "distance" is crucial, because it enabled Muller to develop according to his own lights, and while there are similarities in their work, Muller has to be seen as an independent architect pursuing an organic ideal within the Australian context, rather than as a slavish neo-Wrightian.

Muller's architecture is characterized by a strong sense of geometry and axial composition; the repetition of simple geometrical elements imparts a pervasive unity to the forms, while the axial disposition of the parts responds to the romantic ideal of a building that is whole and simultaneously in a mystical union with nature. Muller has employed four different kinds of geometry—rectangular shapes organized about several opposed axes, usually three, of which one is dominant (Audette House; Muller House, Whale Beach); a related kind consisting of overlapping or connected squares along a diagonal growth axis (Nicholson House; Walcott House); a hexagonal geometry similar to Wright's; and circles (Richardson House).

Muller's private practice began almost as soon as he returned from overseas in 1952, when he was

asked to design Audette House. It is, to some extent, an immature work; it featured exposed timber trusses in much the same fashion as Taliesin West. The form of the building was defined by three axes; there was a longitudinal spine intersected by two transverse axes, one at ground level beside the entrance, the other on an upper level on the other side. Muller employed unprotected, exposed hardwood, and because he was unable to afford rustic masonry of the kind Wright had used in Falling Water, he imitated the appearance of masonry by inventing what came to be called "snotted brickwork."

His own house at Whale Beach, built some three years later, is a much more impressive work. It is based on a main spine intersected by a transverse axis of open galleries, with a third axis through the bedroom, and in his house Muller explored several themes. He carried the main living space out over and free of the precipitous sandstone outcrop on hardwood trusses that he supported on grey cement brick piers, to match the grey bark of the surrounding gum trees. He created maximum openness and identification with the landscape by using floor-to-ceiling plate glass and a long panel of glass in the roof over the entertainment area. He flooded the flat roofs so as to reflect the gums—a very beautiful, largely aesthetic notion of mirroring the landscape and so rendering the building invisible.

In the late 1950s, Muller built a number of modest, low-cost houses, such as Nicholson House, the Craftbuilt houses, and the Gunning House at Castlecrag. The Gunning House is a culmination of

Peter Muller: 1,000 Permanent Houses, Jubail, Saudi Arabia, 1977.

Muller's ideas on domestic architecture, and subsequent projects (Creaser House; Barton House) are elaborations on a larger scale of the earlier ideas. By the early 1960's, Muller was designing substantial commercial buildings for such companies as IPEC and Hoyts Theatres; of these, the Hoyts Cinema Centre, Melbourne, with its adaptation of the traditional Japanese system of bracket supports for supporting the edges of the floor slabs, is probably the most interesting.

It was not until the 1970s that new possibilities began to emerge in Muller's work, with the Kayu Aya Hotel on Kuta Beach, Bali. For some time, Muller had been interested in Asian culture, architecture, and crafts, but it was in Bali, for the first time, that he had an opportunity to further this interest. From the outset, Muller has avoided any idealization of industrialism in his architcture; if anything, his buildings have been a retort to the new International Style. In his Bali hotel, he was ideally placed to immerse himself in Balinese culture and to tap the rich decorative possibilities of Balinese crafts.

Muller's regionalist approach has considerably validity in Third World countries where it has been found that the whole imposition of International Style forms and techniques is not only expensive but also results in buildings that look alike all around the world. Muller employed Balinese craftsmen, using as much as possible their skills as both carvers and designers, mostly for the decoration of his buildings. But his concept went further, he used local materials and traditional methods of construction, even to the extent of following the ritual of cutting bamboo. The new hotel is a minor masterpiece of its kind.

Muller occupies an important place in postwar Australian architecture as the leading romantic architect of his time, one who has developed, as an alternative to the modern movement, an organic conception of architecture.

—Philip Drew

MURANO, Tohgo.

Japanese. Born in Karatsu, Saga Prefecture, 15 May 1891. Educated at the Waseda University School of Architecture, graduated 1918. Worked in Setsu Watanabe's architectural office, Osaka, 1918-29. Principal of Tohgo Murano Architects, Osaka (in partnership with Tiuchi Mori, as Murano and Mori Architectural Office, from 1949), 1929 until his death in 1984. Served as Chairman, Japan Architects' Organization; Member of the Central Council of Chartered Architects, Japan. Recipient: Red Cross Honorary Prize, Germany, 1935; Japan Art Acadeny Prize, 1953; Arts Council Prize, Osaka Prefecture, 1953; Annual Prize, 1954, 1956, and 1965, and Special Prize, 1972, Japan Architectural Society; Annual *Architects Yearbook* Prize, Tokyo, 1963; Prime Minister's Prize, Japan, 1974; Imperial Silver Goblet Award, 1974, and Imperial Silver Bowl, 1976. Honorary doctorate: Waseda University. Member, Japan Architects' Organization, and the Japan Art Academy; Honorary Member, Japan Architectural Society. Corresponding Member, Royal Institute of British Architects; Honorary Fellow, American Institute of Architects. Member, Order of the Blue Ribbon, Japan, 1958, and Order of Cultural Merit, Japan, 1967. Knight of St. Gregory Vatican, 1970. *Died* (in Takarazuka City) *26 November 1984.*

Works (all in Japan):

1931 Osaka Pension Apartment House, Osaka
     Minami Osaka Church, Osaka
1932 Morigo Company Branch Office, Takaracho, Tokyo
1935 German Cultural Research Institute, Higashi Ichijo, Kyoto Sogo Department Store, Kobe
     Argentina *Maru* and Brazil *Maru* ships' interiors
1936 Sogo Department Store, Osaka
1937 Watanabe Memorial and Public Hall, Ube
     Daimaru Department Store, Kobe
     Hieizan Hotel, Mount Hiei, near Kyoto
     Inspector's House, Daimaru Department Store, Kobe
1938 Town Office, Osho
     Village Office, Daisho, Hyogo Prefecture
1939 Nakayama House, near Ashiya, Osaka
1941 Nakabayashi House, Kyoto
     Ishihara Maritime Company Building, Tokyo
1942 Murano House, Ashiya, Osaka
1951 Shima Kanku Hotel, Shima Peninsula
     Tokyo Bank Club House, Takarazuka, Hyogo Prefecture
1952 Nakagawa House, Osaka
1953 Daishin Spinning Company Building, Nagoya
     Maruei Department Store and Hotel, Nagoya
     Sennichimae Grand Theatre, Osaka
1954 Takashimaya Department Store annex, Tokyo
     Kintetsu Hall, Osaka
1955 Kin-Ei, Kinki Cinema, Osaka
     Peace Memorial Cathedral, Hiroshima
     Fujikawa Gallery, Osaka
1956 Cafe Printemps coffee shop, Shinsaibashi, Osaka
     Press Hall, Kobe
     Dohton Restaurant, Osaka
1957 Tonda-ya Hotel, Minami-ku, Osaka
     Sogo Department Store and Yomiuri Auditorium, Tokyo
     Kintetsu Department Store, Tennoji, Osaka
     Rokko School Gymnasium and Lecture Hall, Mount Rokko, Kobe
1958 Murano House additions, Takarazuka, Hyogo Prefecture
     Public Hall, Yonago
     Yahata Central Community Centre, Hobashira Park, Kitakyushu City
     Fugetsu-do Building, Ginza, Tokyo
     Marubutsu Department Store and Ikeburu Station, Tokyo
     New Kabuki Theatre, Osaka
     Fugetsu Restaurant, Tokyo
1959 Kansai University Library, Osaka
     Yawata Public Hall, Kita-Kyushu, Fukuoka Prefecture
     Kitagawa (*sukiya* style) House, Tokyo
     Central Community Hall, Central Park, Kokura City
     Mikuyo Hotel Kasuien Annex, Kyoto
     Senshu Bank Head Office, Kishiwada, Osaka Prefecture
     Myoshinji Temple Hanazono Hall, Kyoto
1960 Indemitsu Kosan Company Tanimachi Petrol Station, Yorozu-machi, Osaka
     Textile Export Centre, Osaka
     Golf Club House, Takarazuka, Hyogo Prefecture
     City Hall, Yokohama
     Yoshimoto Building, Osaka
     Miyuko Hotel Pavilion Annex, Kyoto
1961 New Osaka Office Building (Shin-Osaka Building), Osaka
1962 Morita Building, Semba, Osaka
     Waseda University Literature Building (Bungakubu), Tokyo
1963 Miyako Hotel, Nagoya
     Nippon Life Insurance Company (Nihon Seimi) Building and Nissei Theatre, Hibiya, Tokyo
     Rest House on the Meishin Highway, near Lake Biwa
     Tonda-ya Restaurant (Saganoya), Kyoto
     Kansai University Special Lecture Theatre, Osaka
1965 Kansai University Specialist Library, Suita, Osaka
     Shgetsu-Tei House, Tokyo
1966 Chiyoda Life Insurance Company (Chiyoda-Seimi) Headquarters, Tokyo
     Forest Park Centre, Higashi-Kasugai District, Aichi Prefecture
     Naniwa-Gumi Office Building, Tokyo
1967 Catholic Church, Takarazuka, Hyogo Prefecture
1968 Osaka (Yaesu) Building, Tokyo
1969 Konan Women's College Lecture Hall, Kobe
     Japan Lutheran Theological Seminary, Tokyo
     Yushutsu Sen-i Kaikan, Osaka
     Trappist Monastery, Nishinomiya, Hyogo Prefecture
1970 Miyako Hotel Annex landscaping, Kyoto
     Bank of Tokyo Building, Osaka
     Hyogo Prefectural Modern Museum, Hyogo Prefecture
     Shima Tourist Hotel, Ise Shima National Park
1971 Hakone Botanical Gardens (Hakone Kumokuen) Rest Pavilion, Hakone
1973 Tea Ceremony Room in a department store, Tokyo
     Takashimaya Department Store, Okayama
1974 Akasaka Palace Guest House renovations, Tokyo
     Industrial Bank of Japan Building, Tokyo
1975 Nishiyama Memorial Hall, Kobe
     Keizo Koyama Art Museum, Komoro
1976 Hitachinomiya Family House, Tokyo
1977 Nadaman Tea House in the gardens of the New Otani Hotel, Tokyo
     Konan University Abe Memorial Library, Kobe
1978 Hakone Prince Hotel, Hakone
1979 Shojuso Guest House, Minato Ward, Tokyo
     Yatsugatake Art Museum, Suwa, Nagano Prefecture
1980 Bank of Tokyo Building, Kobe
     City Hall, Takarazuka, Hyogo Prefecture
1982 Takanawa Prince Hotel, Minato Ward, Tokyo

Publications:

By MURANO: articles—"Humanity and Architecture," with Teijiro Muramatsu, in *Japan Architect* (Tokyo), March 1974; "Hakone Prince Hotel" in *Japan Architect* (Tokyo), January 1979.

On MURANO: books—*The Architecture of Tohgo Murano 1931-1963,* Tokyo 1963; *Tohgo Murano,* Tokyo 1965; articles—"Tea Ceremony Rooms in a Department Store" in *Japan Architect* (Tokyo), October 1973; "Akasaka Palace Guest House" in *Japan Architect* (Tokyo), Seeptember 1974; "Industrial Bank of Japan, Tokyo" in *Japan Architect* (Tokyo), January 1975; "Keizo Koyama Art Museum" in *Japan Architect* (Tokyo), July 1976; "Abe Memorial Library, Konan University" in *Kenchiku Bunka* (Tokyo), January 1977; "Nadama Teahouse" in *Japan Architect* (Tokyo), April 1977; "Abe Memorial Library" in *Japan Architect* (Tokyo), May 1977; "Astounding: Togo Murano" by Kazuhiro Ishi'i in *Japan Architect* (Tokyo), June 1981; "Togo Murano: A Brilliant Past, a Brilliant Future" by Kazuhiro Ishi'i in *Japan Architect* (Tokyo), October 1982.

Bibliography—*The Architecture of Togo Murano, Dean of Japanese Architects* by James A. Noffsinger, Monticello, Illinois 1979.

Tohgo Murano's legacy of fifty years is a wealth of buildings that range in expression from direct functionalism to rich sensuousness to the restrained elegance of the *sukiya* style. Unlike several of his contemporaries, Murano did not study in Europe;

Tohgo Murano: New Kabuki Theatre, Osaka, 1958.

yet perhaps more than those of any other architect in Japan, his buildings show a subtle blending of past and present western architecture with the artistic heritage of Japan.

After graduation from Waseda University in 1918, Murano joined the Setsu Watanabe office in Osaka. In 1929 he established his own firm in that city and completed its first modern building, Sogho Department Store, in 1936. The success of this building lead to further commissions in commercial architecture, on which his early practice primarily was based.

Murano was among the pioneers who steered Japanese architecture through the reactionary years of the early postwar period. His buildings of that time show the spectrum of his diverse abilities that determined the characteristics of future work. Further commercial projects included the Takshimaya Department Store, Tokyo, (1952), which remains one of the most practical and pleasant of its kind anywhere in the world. At Hiroshima, the Chapel for World Peace (1953) displays his fascinating translation of western design. This strangely austere building appears to combine the concrete framing of Perret with Parisian Art Deco and a dash of Byzantine design. The massive, volumetric composition of the Yonago City Hall (1958) shows Murano in a rare, structurally expressive mood. Closely akin to this building is the Industrial Bank of Japan, Tokyo (1974). But for the Industrial Bank, the rough concrete, brick, and tile textures of Yonago have been replaced by the sleek precision of gleaming granite.

The most amazing of his buildings of the early 1960s is his building in Hibiya, Tokyo, which, behind its ordered and balanced Renaissance-inspired facade, houses Murano's most exuberant spaces—the foyers and auditorium of the Nissei Theatre. The rich materials and sinuous lines of the foyers are but preliminaries to the Gaudi-like colours and undulating curves of the continuous walls and ceiling of the auditorium, which gleam with glass mosaics and pearl oyster shells. Lighting from concealed sources adds to the mysterious quality of this truly fantastic space. A few years earlier, Murano had designed the new Kabuki Theatre in Osaka in a pseudo-traditional style.

Murano's imaginative expressionism shows most clearly in the Takarazuka Catholic Church (1967). The organically curved white walls of the structure are capped by a continuous copper roof that sweeps up from the spine with a fluidity that would be envied by Mendelsohn. Several of Murano's later buildings, including the Keizo Koyama Museum (1976), show a related earthy sensuality in their curved forms and white stuccoed walls that appear to grow organically out of the soil of their sites.

All that is best in Murano's architecture is evident in the Chiyoda Life Insurance Building in Tokyo (1965). The orderly structure that cleverly reduces the scale, the subtle blend of a delicate landscape with a large building accommodating 1,400 office workers, the gentle transition from site to building, the restraint yet mystical richness of the entry foyer, and the sensitivity of the Aikei teahouse in the *sukiya* style, make this one of the most accomplished buildings of its era.

Murano was a master of the modern *sukiya* style. The Kasuien Annex of the Miyako Hotel, Kyoto, 1959, the Shigetsu-Tei residence, Tokyo, 1965, and the Nadama Teahouse of the New Otani Hotel, Tokyo, 1977, amongst others, are harmonious and innovative compositions in this tradition.

Murano was a remarkable person, and through to the time of his death in 1984 at the age of ninety three, he remained a respected leader of the profession in Japan. In retrospect, his work now appears more relevant than perhaps it was even at the time of its construction. Murano's greatest attribute was that, despite the borrowing of compositional principles of the West, he always remained a traditional Japanese architect, introducing a fresh sensitivity into the discipline of modern technology. He provided a humanistic architecture rich with visual and tactile delights.

—Jennifer Taylor

MURCUTT, Glenn Marcus.

Australian. Born in Upper Norwood, London, England, of Australian parents, 25 July 1936; lived in New Guinea, 1936-41. Educated at Balgowlah Heights Public School, Sydney, 1943-44; Balgowlah Primary Public School, Sydney, 1945-49; Manly Boys' High School, Balgowlah, Sydney, 1950-55; part time architectural studies, under Noel Bazeley, University of New South Wales, Sydney, 1956-61, Dip.Arch. 1961. Served in the Royal Australian Air Force, Point Cook, 1956-57. Married Helen Kay in 1962 (divorced, 1979); sons: Nicholas and Daniel. Architectural Assistant in the office of Neville Gruzman, Sydney, 1956 and 1958-59; office of Levido & Baker, Sydney, 1956-57; office of John Allen and Russel Jack, Sydney, 1960-62; Architect, Keven J. Curtin and Partners, Sydney, 1962; Ian Fraser and Associates, London, 1962-64; Project Architect, Ancher Mortlock Murray and Woolley, Sydney, 1964-69. Since 1969, in private practice, Mosman, Sydney. Design Tutor, University of Sydney, 1970-78; Visiting Professor, University of New South Wales, Sydney, 1984. Recipient: Commonwealth Scholarship, 1957; Gray Mulroney Restoration/Renovation Award, 1972; Merit Award, 1975 (twice), 1976, 1977, 1978, 1979, 1981 (twice), 1982, and 1983 (twice), Wilkinson Award, 1976 and 1979, Blacket Award, 1977 and 1983, Robin Boyd Award, 1981, and Sir Zelman Cowen Award, 1983, Royal Australian Institute of Architects; Housing Industry Association Daily Mirror Design Design Award, 1980. Address: Glenn Murcutt, Architect, 12 Mandolong Road, Mosman, New South Wales 2088, Australia.

Works:

1960/
62 John T. Devitt House, Beacon Hill, Sydney
1968/
69 Glenn M. Murcutt House additions, Mosman, Sydney
1969/
72 Douglas L. Murcutt House, Belrose, Sydney
1970 B. Robertson House, East Killara, Sydney
1972 Justyn Armstrong House stage 1, Grenfell, Sydney
1972/
73 Laurie R. Short House, Terrey Hills, Sydney
1972/
74 Charles R. Cullen House, Peacock Point, Balmain, Sydney
1973 Dennis Wallis House alterations, Manly, Sydney
1974 Frank Hetherton House stage 1, Peacock Point, Balmain, Sydney
1974/
75 Marie I. Short Farmhouse, Crescent Head, New South Wales
1975 Barry J. O'Keefe House, Clifton Gardens, Sydney
1976/
77 House restoration, Poole Street, Longueville, Sydney
1977/
78 Karl Ockens House, Cromer, Sydney

1977/
79 Raymond Reynolds House, Woollahra, Sydney
1977/
80 Henric Nicholas Farmhouse, Mount Irvine, New South Wales
Justyn Armstrong House stage 2, Grenfell, Sydney
1978 Berowra Waters Inn conversion stage 1, Berowra Waters, New South Wales
1978/
80 Kenneth Carruthers rural workers' housing, Mount Irvine, New South Wales
1979/
80 N. Marsh and G. Freedman Offices, Woolloomoolloo, Sydney
1979/
82 Stuart Horney House, Warrawee, Sydney
1980 Engehurst (John Verge Villa) completion, Paddington, Sydney
1980/
82 John B. Carpenter House, Point Piper, Sydney
1980 Stephen Bonnitcha House alterations and additions, Drummoyne, Sydney
1980/
83 Zachary's Restaurant, Terrey Hills, Sydney
Sydney Ball and Lyn Eastaway House and Studio, Glenorie, Sydney
1981/
82 Frank Hetherton House stage 2, Peacock Point, Balmain, Sydney

Local History Museum and Tourist Information Centre, South Kempsey, New South Wales
Neville Fredericks Farmhouse, Jamberoo, New South Wales
1981/
83 New Catholic Presbytery and Community Hall, Mona Vale, Sydney
Hugh Munro Farmhouse, Bingara, New South Wales
Michael Rabbit House, Merewether, New South Wales
1982/
83 Michael Ramsden House alterations and additions, Blackheath, New South Wales
Berowra Waters Inn alterations, stage 2, Berowra Waters, New South Wales
1983/
84 Mervyn Finlay House, Hallidays Point, New South Wales
Tom Magney House, Binge Binge Point, New South Wales

Publications:

On MURCUTT: book—*Leaves of Iron: Glenn Murcutt, Pioneer of an Australian Architectural Form* by Philip Drew, Sydney, 1985; articles— "Glenn Murcutt's Houses" by Ian McDougall in *Transition* (St. Kilda, Victoria), November 1980;

Glenn Murcutt: Ball-Eastaway House, Glenorie, Sydney, 1980-83.

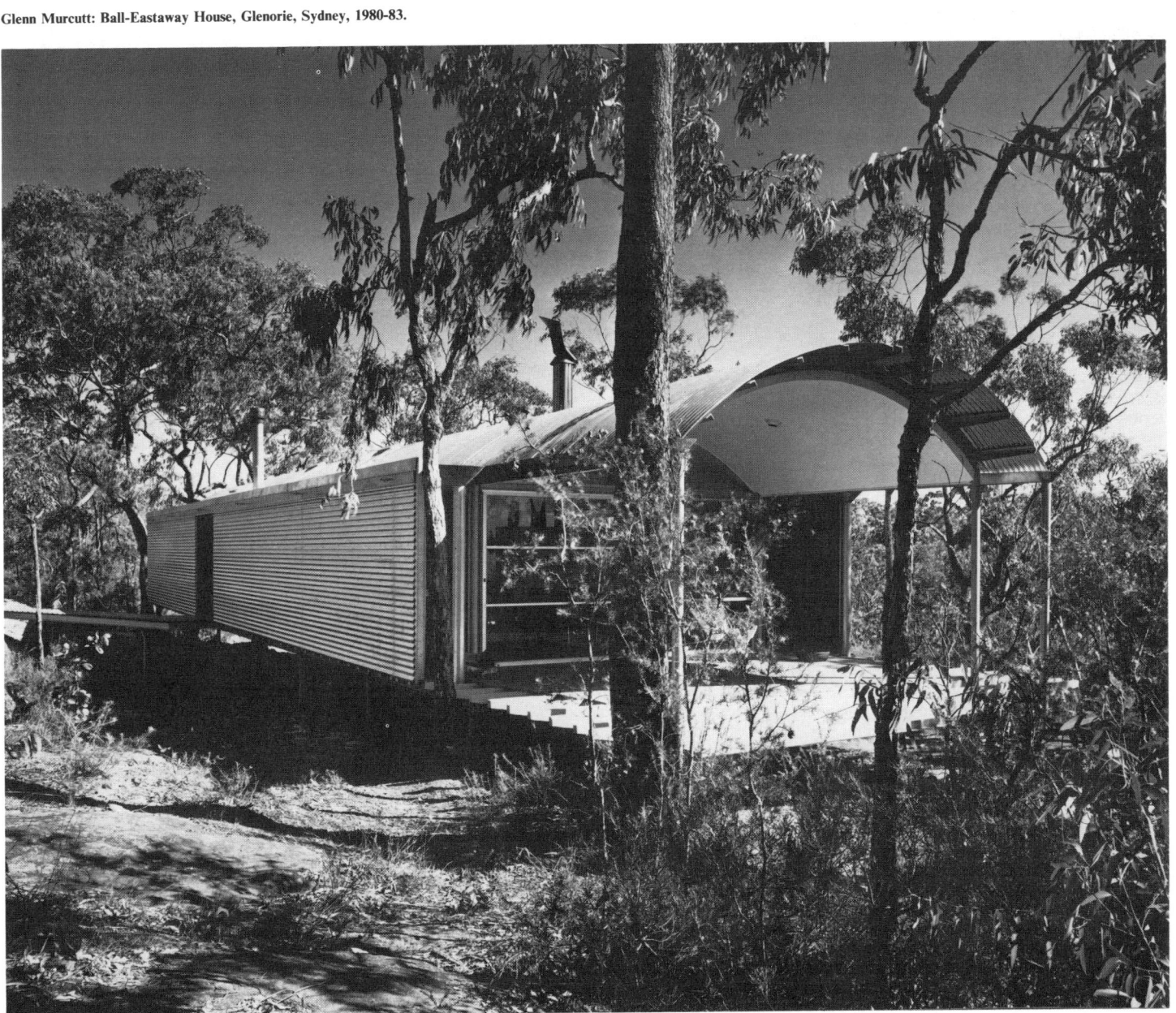

"Tin Roof Revival" by Johnny Grey in *Architectural Review* (London), June 1982; "Flashing Forms of Corrugated Steel for Weekend Farmers" by Andrew Metcalf in *AIA Journal* (Washington, D.C.), August 1982; "Revision of Corrugated Iron Tradition" by Jennifer Taylor in *Architecture + Urbanism* (Tokyo), November 1982; "Museum Boundaries" by Rory Spence in *Architectural Review* (London), February 1984; "Murcutt's Metal Vaults Shelter a Regional Museum" by Philip Drew in *AIA Journal* (Washington, D.C.), September 1984.

Because I am interested in people as individuals rather than as anonymous consumers of architecture, much of my architecture is domestic in character, with some of the work consisting of renovations. I have avoided major buildings by preference because in designing them, one is isolated from the users. Such large projects deprive one of both the stimulus and personal satisfaction of developing a building design from a close personal understanding of the client and his requirements.

The significant influences on my architecture have been the work of the Sydney architect S. E. Ancher; Mies van der Rohe's Farnsworth House; Pierre Chareau's Maison d'Alsace in Paris; the simple use of materials and forms, the movement of traffic, the modulation of daylight, and the spatial coherence of the folk architecture of the Greek islands; and, now, the Australian landscape.

I find myself strongly directed by climate when designing, allowing the penetration of the winter sunlight and excluding the sun in summer, thus modifying and affecting the micro-environment of my buildings. The use of gardens, pergolas, and simple sunlight and wind filters establishes a temperate gradient between the interior of my buildings and the surrounding environment. It should also be possible to be able to establish what the day is like outside whilst within one of my buildings. I am particularly interested in the language of a site, the question of appropriateness of building to landform, whether one designs merely a house on a farm or a farmhouse, for example.

The strong Australian sunlight, like that of Greece, requires, for me, simple forms, often white both outside and inside, allowing the structure of the native flora to be clearly silhouetted; the interest and variety develops from the play of light over the interior surfaces—a kind of natural decoration. In this sense, then, decoration should be inseparable from an outcome of materials, the light, and the site. Thus, decoration that consists entirely of applied textures and patterns has a life of perhaps one or two years before it has to be changed. But decoration that is the integration of objects, and the clarification of space and materials, has an enduring appeal.

I like simple, ordinary forms. The plans of many of my buildings are composed of pavilions on rectangular platforms which, while they are simple enough, represent a resolution of a complex series of demands. I see simplicity not so much as a disregard of complexity but as the clarification of the significant.

My interest in the ordinary expresses itself in my renovation work of typical Sydney suburban bungalows—of giving the ordinary something special—and in the use of galvanised corrugated iron not only for roofing but also for the external cladding of some of my houses. The proper recognition of corrugated iron as a handsome, versatile industrial building material was hampered by the prejudice derived from the wholesale misuse of this material in the nineteenth century, when it was inadequately insulated, and by the "tamed romantic Brutalism" which, until recently, has typified the Sydney School of architecture. I reject the affected rusticity, pretentious merging of building with the natural landscape, and feverish search for an "Australian style" of the Sydney School of architecture in favour of a more honest, straightforward kind of architecture.

I see the house as a comfortable refuge from the tensions and conflicts of the public world. Neverthe-

less, the house, particularly where it is located in an established street, should be sympathetic with the existing street patterns. In the future, architects will spend more time in renovating the existing building stock. This change is healthy, in my view, because it means that the architect will need to think much more carefully about how decisions affect both people and the existing architectural environment. I enjoy working with old buildings, or simply giving them a new life, in order to improve the wellbeing of the occupants—no matter how small the project.

—Glenn Murcutt

Australians have, in the main, been content fo faithfully follow the lead given by Britain and Europe, and, after World War II, by the United States, in architecture as in so many other matters. The emphasis on imitation in Australian architecture is a reflection of the prolongation of a colonial mentality long after the ending of actual colonial rule.

Attempts at developing an architecture belonging to the country and inspired by the local landscapes and conditions revealed themselves in numerous adaptations of Wright's prairie house style in the 1950s and in an identification with the work of Aalto, and, to a lesser degree, in a selective interest in traditional Japanese architecture. Glenn Murcutt, almost alone among his contemporaries, succeeded in the creation of an unmistakable Australian form that is imbued with the same hard/delicate quality as the landscape. Indeed, his Local History Museum and Tourist Information Centre at South Kempsey (1981-82) may, without exaggeration, be described as the first truly Australian building.

Murcutt succeeded in his quest for an endemic architectural form because he avoided, as much as possible, the imitation of overseas styles and models and sought instead to invent his own forms out of a consideration of local causes. To think of him exclusively as a Rationalist is to miss the point of his architecture entirely; his work is first and foremost a poetic statement in concrete building of his perception of the Australian landscape in and around Sydney. He is more accurately described as a Romantic-modern architect.

There are two main phases of development in the architecture—the first being an initial exploratory phase lasting from 1970 to 1973, during which Murcutt worked in a Miesian idiom and designed a series of accomplished glass pavilions, of which the Laurie Short house (1972-73) is the most impressive. In the second half of 1973, Murcutt undertook an architectural tour of the United States and Europe; this introduced him to the Pierre Chareau masterpiece, the Maison de Verre in Paris, and at the same time led to a more realistic appraisal of Mies's architecture at the Illinois Institute of Technology campus in Chicago. The trip, in its aftermath, opened the way for the subsequent second phase, which witnessed a fundamental realignment of his architecture with the region and is distinguished by an intensified involvement with Australian nature.

The tree, in particular, the *Angophora Costata*, thereafter served as the *leitmotiv* of his architecture, acting as a key which reveals the *genius* of the landscape. During this second phase, 1974-83, Murcutt wedded the minimalist Miesian pavilion to the vernacular, corrugated-iron hut of the countryside to produce a new type of long, thin house which somewhat resembles a detached verandah building. The Marie Short house, Crescent Head (1974-75), was the first of a series of houses that applied the new type. It was succeeded in 1980 by two remarkable farmhouses at Mount Irvine. The combination of refinement and primitiveness in the Neville Fredericks farmhouse, Jamberoo (1981-82), makes this one of Murcutt's most fascinating of the long, thin houses.

In 1983, Murcutt completed the Ball-Eastaway house at Glenorie, northwest of Sydney. Designed for two painters, his first all-corrugated-iron house, which he provided with an external sprinkler

arrangement to protect the house against bush fires, it represents the culmination of the architect's search for an architectural form in harmony with, and matching, the hard/delicate quality of the Australian bush.

Murcutt's combination of poetry and invention is unmatched among his contemporaries. This expression of a hard/delicate form has resulted in an open, independent architecture that turns its back on a subservient colonial past and draws near instead to the 40,000 year old traditions of the Australian Aborigines whose culture had grown into the land in a most remarkable way. His outlook is best illustrated by the West Australian Aboriginal admonition to "touch this earth lightly."

—Philip Drew

MURRAY, Stuart.

Australian. Born in Sydney, New South Wales, 27 October 1926. Educated at Fort Street Boys High School, Sydney, 1938-42; worked as a draughtsman with Wunderlich Ltd., Sydney, 1943-44; studied at the Sydney Technical College School of Architecture, under Henry Pynor, Sydney Ancher and Morton Herman, 1944-49, Dip.Arch. (civic design distinction) 1949; awarded New South Wales Board of Architects Research Bursary, 1950. Married Elizabeth Grime in 1952 (divorced, 1966); children: Anna, Andrew, Ruth and Daniel. Architectural Assistant with W. B. Griffin and Nicholls, Sydney, 1945-47, and with Sydney Ancher, Sydney, 1948-49; Architect with Denis Clarke Hall, London, 1949-51; Senior Architect, Intercon Ltd., London, 1952-53; Partner, with Sydney Ancher, *q.v.*, and Bryce Mortlock, *q.v.*, Ancher, Mortlock and Murray, Sydney, 1953-64; Partner/Director, with Ancher, Mortlock, and Ken Woolley, *q.v.*, Ancher, Mortlock, Murray and Woolley, Sydney, 1964-75; Founder-Director, North Sydney Planning Consultants, 1970-73. Since 1976, Principal, Stuart Murray Architect, North Sydney. Design Tutor, University of New South Wales Faculty of Architecture, Sydney, 1962, 1974-78; Member of the faculty, University of Sydney, 1965-75. Member of the Housing Committee, 1966-67, and Councillor and Chairman of the Environment Board, 1972-76, Royal Australian Institute of Architects, New South Wales Chapter. Exhibition: *Ancher, Mortlock, Murray and Woolley, Sydney Architects, 1946-76*, Art Gallery of New South Wales, 1976, and Australian tour, 1977. Recipient: First Prize, Waverley, New South Wales Town Hall Competition, 1957; First Prize, University of Newcastle Great Hall Competition, 1968. Fellow, Royal Australian Institute of Architects, 1966. Address: Stuart Murray Architect, 119 High Street, North Sydney, New South Wales 2060, Australia.

Works:

1949 House, Scotland Island, Sydney
1952 House, Amaroo Avenue, Turramurra, Sydney
      Hotel, Kingsford, Sydney
1959 House, Montah Avenue, Killara, Sydney
      House, Karoo Avenue, Lindfield, Sydney
1963 Housing, Northbourne Avenue, Canberra
      (with Sydney Ancher)
1964 Chemical Engineering School, University of Sydney
      Public Library, Gordon, Sydney

Stuart Murray: Apartments, Elizabeth Bay, Sydney, 1970.

1965 Offices, Milperra, Sydney
Architects' Studio, North Sydney
House, Careening Cove, Sydney
1966 House, Bilgola Heights, Sydney
Baby Health Centre, West Pymble, Sydney
Public Library, Turramurra, Sydney
1967 Carpark, Gordon, Sydney
Drive-In Restaurant, Bass Hill, Sydney
Town houses, Cremorne, Sydney
1968 Flats, Church Street, Woollongong, New
South Wales
Flats, Liverpool, Sydney
1970 Apartments, Elizabeth Bay, Sydney
Faculty Building, University of Sydney
1971 Nursing Hospital, Parramatta, Sydney
1972 Ski Lodge, North Perisher, Mount Kosciusko,
New South Wales
Great Hall, University of Newcastle, New
South Wales
1973 Offices, Ashfield, Sydney
1974 Aeronautics School, University of Sydney
Gymnasium and Library, Fort Street High
School, Petersham, Sydney
1976 Holiday Lodge, Robertson, New South Wales
Factory/Studio, North Sydney

Publications:

By MURRAY: papers—*Elements of Urban Environment*, Sydney 1972; *Contemporary Architecture and Environment*, Canberra 1976; article—"Sydney Ancher 1904-1979" in *Architecture Australia* (Melbourne), March 1980.

On MURRAY: books—*Australian Housing of the 70's* by Howard Tanner, Sydney 1976; *Ancher, Mortlock, Murray and Woolley, Sydney Architects, 1946-76*, exhibition catalogue, by David Saunders and Catherine Bourke, Sydney 1976; articles—"Community Housing, Canberra" in *Cross Section* (Melbourne), May 1963; "Apartments, Elizabeth Bay, Sydney" in *Cross Section* (Melbourne), July 1967; "Great Hall, University, Newcastle" in *L'Architecture d'Aujourd'hui* (Paris), no. 142, 1969; article by Diane Kell in *Constructional Review* (Sydney), May 1972; "Offices, Ashfield, Sydney" in *New South Wales Builder* (Sydney), June 1974; "Aeronautics School, University of Sydney" by Diane Kell in *Constructional Review* (Sydney), December 1974; "Australian Embassies" in *Arup Journal* (London), October 1976; "Innovative features of the Australian Embassy in Bangkok" in *Asian Building and Construction* (Hong Kong), May 1977; "RAIA Headquarters, A.C.T." in *Architecture Australia* (Melbourne), July 1978; "Modern Australian Architecture", special issue of *Process:Architecutre* (Tokyo), March 1981.

The early work attempted urbane, concise architecture, sparse and rectilinear; housing groups expressed privacy, and early sensitivity to environmental spaces (1959). Unity was sought in expression of quietly vivid Australian character under the influence of Sydney Ancher.

By the mid-1960's the use of more highly individual forms expressed the different influences of the programmes, producing sophisticated urban building (Apartments, Elizabeth Bay) of strongly sculpted construction, a blend of technical discipline with bold shaping (strong European influence).

Later a more complex organic technology produced handsomely rugged structures, strong and characterful. The Great Hall is scaled to total form rather than its component parts; it has large intention and a vivid series memorable in distant view, approach, entry and circulation (some Aalto influence).

In the early 70's a frankly industrial approach was adopted—the severing of building functions, building-block assemblies, overlapping profiles,

glass canopy roofs (Aeronatuics School, University of Sydney)—all the true components of the neo-functionalism of Stirling's work in the United Kingdom.

The buildings are lively in planning devices, internal spaces, external forms and siting, the latter two being used to integrate building and environment.

Inventiveness is used not merely to produce personal display, but as an imaginative and sensible response to the building programme, producing an intelligent solution to problems with a rich variety of architectural images.

—Stuart Murray

On the edge of a promontory overlooking Sydney Harbour stands a small jewel-like block of luxury apartments. Beaten copper gates open onto a travertine paved courtyard edged with regimented bay trees. But beyond this court one dare not go. Electronic sentinels guard this place as securely as did the eunuchs of Shahryar watch over his hareem. Inside the tower Shahrazad combs her hair and watches the boats sail past.

Stuart Murray looks upon his wayward and untypical building with some affection. He cheerfully acknowledges that his inspiration for the tight detailing and the opulent materials came from Italy via *Domus*. The baroque curves of the tower are reminiscent of Mendelsohn and Rudolph, whilst the urbane treatment of the ground floor entry shows the influence of Mangiarotti. The product of these diverse influences is one of the most sophisticated and elegant small buildings in Sydney.

Murray maintains that, in architecture as in the other arts, it is necessary to recognize influences and acknowledge sources. Two later buildings are typical of this approach and illustrate the way in which he is able to transform his inspirational sources into a personal style.

The Aeronautics School at the University of Sydney was completed while Murray was still a director of the firm Ancher, Mortlock, Murray and Woolley, and is one of a number of buildings in this precinct undertaken by them. This is a memorable building that can only be understood by spending some time in it. At first glance it is simply a long slab that spans a service road. The slab contains offices, service rooms, and access spaces. Tacked along the side of the slab, and articulated by a glazed slit at the junction, are the main workshops, laboratory and teaching spaces. This is an indeterminate plan: bits can be added or taken away from the central spine without destroying the basic form. But the simple plan is developed into a complicated and maze-like long section with branches and dead-ends in which it is easy to become lost. The interior of the spine is dominated by a glazed space which extends from ground level to the topmost storey. Finely detailed industrial glazing is supported by a three dimensional steel truss that hangs above stair and light wells. Finishes in this building are uncompromisingly industrial—concrete off-form without any special surface treatment, fairfaced brickwork infill panels inside and out, and heavy duty flooring. There is a certain maritime air about the place, and this quality is reinforced by the direct and simple details. Influences of Le Corbusier and James Stirling are recognizable but do not dominate that design. They do, however, endow this building with references that illuminate the way in which it is experienced.

The second building is a small office block located on a typical urban strip for a firm of building contractors. It is a simple, economic slab in bush-hammered concrete. Varying space requirements on each floor result in a stepped profile on the street facade. The lowest storey is set below ground level. The offices at this level look out onto a garden light-court and are protected from street noise by a landscaped embankment. Pedestrian access is via a bridge across the courtyard to a reception area on a gallery overlooking a public waiting space below. The introduction of the double-height space and the

conservatory style glazing on the external wall are reminiscent of the Aeronautics School. They transform an ordinary building into a delightful, urbane workplace.

The common thread that runs through Murray's work is a masterful understanding of scale. His buildings fit unfussily into the urban fabric, carefully maintaining the visual character of the street without in any way attempting to echo the architectural details of their neighbours. Those who come into contact with them find the experience essentially humanizing.

—David Watson

MYERS, Barton.

American. Born in Norfolk, Virginia, 6 November 1934; moved to Canada, 1968. Educated at the Norfolk Academy, Virginia, graduated 1932; United States Naval Academy, Annapolis, Maryland, 1952-56, B.S. 1956; University of Pennsylvania, Philadelphia, 1961-64, M.Arch. 1964; awarded University of Pennsylvania Chandler Travel Scholarship, 1965. Served as a Pilot in the United States Air Force, in the United States and England, 1956-61: Lieutenant. Married Victoria George in 1959; daughter: Suzanne. Worked with Louis Kahn, Philadelphia, 1964-66; Assistant Architect, Bower and Fradley, Philadelphia, 1966-68; Partner, with A.J. Diamond, *q.v.*, Diamond and Myers, Toronto, 1968-75. Since 1975, Principal, Barton Myers Associates, architects and planners, Toronto (associates: Donald Clinton; Bruce Kuwabara; Shirley Blumberg; Marianne McKenna; Thomas Payne); established second office in Los Angeles, 1980. Assistant Professor, University of Toronto Department of Architecture, 1968-70; Lecturer, Ontario College of Art, Toronto, 1970-71, and Division of Environmental Studies, University of Waterloo School of Architecture, Ontario, 1971-73; Visiting Professor of Architecture, Harvard University, Cambridge, Massachusetts, 1981, and University of Pennsylvania, Philadelphia, 1983; Thomas Jefferson Professor of Architecture, University of Virginia, Charlottesville, 1982; Professor of Architecture, University of California at Los Angeles, since 1983. Assistant Editor, Royal Architectural Institute of Canada Journal *Architecture Canada*, Toronto, 1968-69; Member, Advisory Committee for Design, National Capital Commission, Ottawa, 1968-74; Executive, Toronto Chapter, Ontario Association of Architects, 1972; Vice-Chairman, Toronto Chapter of Architects, 1973; Member, North Midtown Planning Group, Toronto, 1974-75; Founder and President, *Trace* magazine, Toronto, 1980-82. Exhibitions: *Harbour Front*, Toronto, 1975; *Urban Infill*, Science Centre, Toronto, 1975; Architectural Awareness Week Exhibition, Queens Park, Toronto, 1977; University of California, Los Angeles, 1979; *Barton Myers: Selected Works*, Old Dominion University, Norfolk, Virginia, 1980; Walker Art Center, Minneapolis, 1980; Canadian National Exhibition, Toronto, 1980; University of Toronto, 1980; Harbourfront, Toronto, 1981; Institute of Contemporary Arts, London, 1982; *Design Drawings*, Nova Gallery, Vancouver, 1982; *A Design Process, A Grand Avenue*, University of Virginia, Charlottesville, 1982; *Major Projects*, Akademie der Kunste, West Berlin, 1982; *Aesthetics for the Cold*, Buffalo, New York, 1983; Seagram Museum Exhibit, Waterloo University, Ontario, and University of Toronto, 1983; *Canadian Architects Abroad*, Harbourfront, Toronto, 1983; *The Urban Solution*, Toronto, 1983; University of California, Los Angeles, 1984; *Dreams of Development*, Toronto, 1984; *Monument*, Rijksuniversiteit Limburg, Netherlands, 1984. Recipient: Society of Graphic Designers of Canada Award, 1968 (twice); Annual Design Award, Ontario Association of

Architects, Toronto Chapter, 1969, 1971 (twice), 1976 (twice); Residential Design Award, Canadian Housing Design Council, 1971, 1975; Masonry Award, Canadian Design Council, 1972; Canada Council Grant, 1972; Design in Steel Award, 1973; Award of Merit, Toronto Historical Board, 1974; Landscape Ontario Award, 1977; House Award, *Architectural Record,* 1977; Design Award, City of Edmonton, 1978; Stelco Design Award, 1978; Habitation Space International Award, Switzerland, 1978; Design Award, *Progressive Architecture,* 1978, 1983; Award, *Urban Design,* 1978; NHRA Downtown Development Award, Norfolk, Virginia, 1981; Record Interiors Award, *Architectural Record,* 1981, 1982. Fellow, Royal Architectural Institute of Canada; Member, Society of Architectural historians, Tau Sigma Delta, Heritage Canada, American Institute of Architects, and the Royal Canadian Academy of Art. Address: Barton Myers Associates, 322 King Street West, Toronto, Ontario M5V 1J4, Canada.

Works:

1969 York Square (restaurant/shops complex), Yorkville, Toronto (with A. J. Diamond)
Housing Union Building, University of Alberta, Edmonton (with R. L. Wilkin)
Alcan Executive Headquarters interiors, Toronto (with A. J. Diamond)
Long range development plan for the University of Alberta, Edmonton (with A. J. Diamond)
Vidal Sassoon Salon interiors, Toronto (with A. J. Diamond)

1970 Ontario Medical Association Headquarters, Toronto (with A. J. Diamond)
Blade House, Virginia Beach, Virginia
Schwartz House, Virginia Beach, Virginia
Barton Myers House, Berryman Street, Toronto
Steel Equipment Building interiors, Toronto
1971 Canadian Television Housing Study, Toronto (with A. J. Diamond)
1972 Kew Beach Infill Housing and renovation, Toronto
Long range development plan for the University of Alberta, stage II, Edmonton (with A. J. Diamond)
1973 Apogee Infill Housing, Toronto
Union Facilities, University of Maryland, Baltimore
Town plan for Bronte, Ontario
1974 Wolf House, Roxborough Drive, Toronto
Rideau Street Mall, Ottawa
1975 Pickle Lake New Town and Housing, Ontario
Citadel Theare, Edmonton, Alberta (with R. L. Wilkin)
Barton Myers Associates Office interiors, Toronto
Dundas/Sherbourne Housing, Toronto (with A. J. Diamond)
1976 Lincoln Park Development Plan, Calgary, Alberta (with James McKellar)
York Row Infill Housing, Yorkville, Toronto (project)
Canadian National Railway Yards and Mainline Development Plan, Regina, Saskatchewan (project; with Stephen McLaughlin)
Canadian Pacific Railway Express Building, Toronto (project)

Canadian Pacific Railway Yards and Mainline Development Plan, Regina, Saskatchewan (competition project)
Canadian National Railway Station for Parkdale, Toronto (relocation)
Jones Avenue Branch Library renovation, Toronto
Spadina Commuter Parking Facility, Toronto (project)
Cinema Park Housing, Calgary, Alberta (project)
1977 Smith/Hamilton House, Newcastle, Ontario (project)
Townhouses, Ghent Square, Norfolk, Virginia
Urban Outdoors Inc. interiors, Toronto
Munn's United Church renovations, Oakville, Ontario
Monticello Arcade renovation, Norfolk, Virginia
Downtown plan review, Norfolk, Virginia
1978 Freemason Harbor Development Plan, Norfolk, Virginia
Alternatives to high-rise study, Edmonton, Alberta
Urban design study for the Urban Transportation Development Corporation
Downtown revitalization plan for Cambridge, Ontario
Yorkville Public Library alterations and additions, Toronto
Omnitown Housing Project, Toronto
Alcan interiors, Toronto
Downtown Athletic Club and Housing Project, Norfolk, Virginia
Griffin's Restaurant renovation, 110 York Street, Toronto

Barton Myers: Unionville Public Library, Ontario, 1983-84.

1979 Downtown Revitalization Study, Port Hope, Ontario

Grand Avenue Design, Bunker Hill, Los angeles (competition project)

Seagram Museum and Archives, Waterloo, Ontario

1980 Bellair Restaurant renovation, Toronto

Canadian Centre for Architecture, Montreal (project)

Embankment at Harbourfront, Spadina Quay, Toronto (competition project)

Central Library Feasibility Study, Los Angeles

1981 Royal Conservatory of Music Feasibility Study, Toronto

Wolf House renovations, Toronto

Telecommunications Museum Study, Brantford, Ontario

Dayton's Department Store, Minneapolis, Minnesota (project)

Multicultural Center/State Mall, Los Angeles

Office Building, 114-118 Hazelton Avenue, Toronto

Unionville Library, Markham, Ontario

1982 Office and Apartment Towers, Olympia and York, Toronto (project)

Center for the Performing Arts, Portland, Oregon

Buffalo and Allentown Revitalization Study, New York

National Gallery of Canada, Ottawa, Ontario (competition project)

City Hall, Mississauga, Ontario (competition project)

1983 Pasadena Center, Pasadena, California (project)

Shakespearean Festival Theatre alterations and addition, Stratford, Ontario

Don Watt and Associates Offices, Toronto

Royal Canadian Air Force Memorial, Ottawa, Ontario (competition project)

New Orleans Museum of Art, Louisiana (competition project)

petition project)

Carroll County Community College Master Plan, Baltimore, Maryland

1984 Hasbro Bradley Inc. Headquarters and Offices, Providence, Rhode Island

Hasbro Bradley Inc. Showrooms and Offices, New York

Avenue McGill College, Montreal (project)

Downer's Grove Development Plan, Chicago

Gottschalk and Ash Offices, Toronto

Howard Hughes Center Development Plan, Los Angeles

Wang Tower, Los Angeles

Canadian Broadcasting Corporation Development Plan, Toronto

IBM Westlake Park Master Plan, Dallas, Texas

Publications:

By MYERS: articles—"The Architecture of Accommodation" in *Habitat* (Ottawa), no. 3/4, 1977; "Weighting the Elements" in *Canadian Architect* (Toronto), November 1977; "Vacant Lottery" in *Design Quarterly* (Minneapolis), no. 108, 1978; "City Segments" in *Design Quarterly* (Minneapolis), no. 113/114, 1980; "A Grand Avenue: Design Process" in *Architecture + Urbanism* (Tokyo), August 1981; "Barton Myers and Associates" in *Spazio e Societa* (Milan), June 1984.

On MYERS: books—*On Streets*, edited by S. Anderson, Boston 1978; *Building with Words: Canadian Architects on Architecture*, with introduction by W. Bernstein and R. Cawker, Toronto 1981; *Modern Canadian Architecture* by Leon Whiteson, Toronto 1983; articles—"York Square" in *Canadian Architect* (Toronto), June 1969; "York Square" in *Progressive Architecture* (New York), September 1969; "York Square" in *Byggenkunst* (Oslo), September 1969; "York Square" in *Abitare* (Milan), October 1970; "Alcan Interiors" in *Canadian Architect* (Toronto), March 1971; "Ontario Medical Association" in *Canadian Architect* (Toronto), June 1971; "York Square" in *Architecture + Urbanism* (Tokyo), November 1971; "Work of Diamond and Myers" in *Architecture + Urbanism* (Tokyo), May 1972; "The Campus as a lesson in Urban Form—Students' Union Housing" in *Progressive Architecture* (New York), September 1972; "York Square in Toronto" in *Baumeister* (Munich), October 1972; "The Low Rise Alternative Urban Recycling" in *Time* (New York), 16 April 1973; "To Save a Fabric" in *Progressive Architecture* (New York), May 1973; "Student Street" in *Progressive Architecture* (New York), February 1974; "Students' Union Housing, University of Alberta" in *Architecture + Urbanism* (Tokyo), December 1974; "Diamond and Myers: Form and Reform" in *City Magazine* (Toronto), August/September 1975; "The Cutlery of Progress" by John Morris Dixon in *Progressive Architecture* (New York), February 1977; "Barton Myers" by C. Ray Smith in *Urban Design* (New York), Summer 1977; "A View of Contemporary World Architecture" in *The Japan Architect* (Tokyo), December 1977; "Canadian Citadel" in *Architectural Review* (London), July 1978; "A Perspective of Modern Canadian Architecture", special issue of *Architecture + Urbanism* (Tokyo), no. 5, 1978; "Wolf Residence" in *Architecture + Urbanism* (Tokyo), February 1979; "Tidewater Traditions" in *Progressive Architecture* (New York), October 1979; "Alcan Canada Products Ltd. Offices" in *Architectural Record* (New York), February 1981; "Housing, Norfolk, Virginia" in *Architectural Review* (London), March 1981; "The Battle of Bunker Hill" in *Trace* (Toronto), July/September 1981; "Bellair Cafe and Grill" in *Architectural Record* (New York), February 1982; "Innovative Architecture" in *Building Design* (London), 5 March 1982; "Redesigning Architecture" in *Financial Post Magazine* (Toronto), November 1982; "Barton Myers Proposes Warm, Lively Indoor Towns" in *Architectural Record* (New York), February 1983; "Barton Myers" in *Toshi-Jutaku* (Tokyo), August 1983; "Portland Center for the Performing Arts" in *Progressive Architecture* (New York), January 1984; "Barton Myers: Selected Projects" in *Architecture + Urbanism* (Tokyo), February 1984; "Solid Library in a Self-consciously Nostalgic Village" in *Architecture* (Washington, D.C.), September 1984; "National Gallery of Canada" in *Section A* (Montreal), Fall 1984.

*

Barton Myers Associates believes that architects and planners are most creative when confronting problems with difficult constraints, whether they be social, economic or physical. The ability to exploit circumstance and constraints is crucial to help bring about the accommodating aspects which make the work responsive to complex situations.

Members of the firm share personal interests in how things work and how things are made, and believe that the user as well as the builder appreciates these interests. The goal is to design buildings and details which are expressive of how they are put together. Buildings designed by the office of Barton Myers demonstrate how common off-the-shelf component parts, standard industrial systems, and composite structures can be selected, controlled, and modified to meet very particular building situations in the North American builders' market.

Each construction system and element is rigorously considered with respect to its functional, symbolic and cost appropriateness within the overall scheme. The assemblage and detail of the construction and the exposure of elemental system components create a sense of texture that is lacking in most contemporary buildings. Many of the projects make use of contemporary warehouse steel frame, metal decking and open-web steel joists, and the overlay of building sub-systems, when exposed and finely finished, contributes significantly to a quality of lightness and spaciousness.

The ultimate stress is on design excellence, and the resulting architecture is clear, composite, simply ordered in plan, while more complex spatially, and endowed with scale and ornamentation by means of elegant details, fittings and finishes. Stylistically, the work combines multiple references drawn from historical, vernacular and contemporary sources to increase the possible meanings. The projects of the office attempt to achieve a closely knit social and physical matrix where form and program are mutually supportive and the important issues of contemporary cities are addressed.

Barton Myers Associates has argued publicly for a strategy of consolidation of the inefficient physical fabric and building forms that continue to be developed in and around the typical uni-centred North American city with its high-density, high-rise downtown core and low-density suburban sprawl. The concept of urban consolidation demands a multi-centred city with a more balanced pattern of development densities and population distribution, with emphasis particularly on the middle-density range for lowd mid-rise residential design alternatives. Clearly, the major goals of a consolidation program are better utilization of land and municipal servicing, effective public transit networks, mixed land use development policies, and a wider range of housing choices with higher dwelling amenity.

The contextual aspects of our work are based on a respect for existing rights, urban fabric, and old/new combinations. An appreciation of tradition, historical models, popular culture, climate and building technology further influences the form and meaning of the architecture.

—Barton Myers

*

Barton Myers is a graduate of the University of Pennsylvania, influenced by Louis Kahn and the Philadelphia School. Since immigrating to Canada, Myers has been an active critic of the inefficiencies of the uni-centred North American city. He advocates an alternative strategy of *urban consolidation*, arguing for a multi-centred city of connected neighbourhoods, a more balanced distribution of development densities employing low-rise street-related forms, and efficient use of land, services and public transportation. Myers' architecture of consolidation must be understood within this polemic of urban reform, which reflects a pragmatic idealism working within the market place. His conception of the city is influenced by Jane Jacobs and Edmund Bacon.

Nearly all of the projects are either "infill" building types, which respect existing urban fabric, or connected, additive buildings as opposed to buildings as separate, isolated objects. Many of the projects retain existing buildings integrating "old" and "new" to maintain cultural continuity. Each project generally proposes a new social space in the form of the courtyard, the square and the galleria street.

Myers' work represents deliberate departures from the ideas and work of Louis Kahn. Designing for the Canadian climate, Myers has moved toward making simple, large building envelopes with unarticulated flat exterior surfaces and with articulated building elements within. Where Kahn believed that the "room" is the essential element of architectural composition, creating plans that represent a "society of rooms," Myers establishes the total building envelope as a single large "room" within which enclosures become "rooms within the room." Myers' idealization of the industrial warehouse as a generalized volume for living in is particularly evident in his steel construction essays which create twentieth century residential lofts. The incompleteness of the enclosures within the envelopes, the minimization of wall returns, dark corners and spaces, and the substitution of sliding walls for conventional doors disclose a heroic/claustrophobic spatial sensibility. Where Kahn generally maintained a rigorous distinction between "served" and "servant" spaces in his work, Myers integrates environmental support systems within habitable spaces. Service areas are rationally ordered in zones in plan.

The dominant configurative geometries are linear, orthogonal and planar, while the use of the circle, cylinder and curves is reserved to enclose and symbolize places of meeting or indicate special openings. Circumstantial inflections occur sparingly, with consistent use of the 45← angle to resolve corners, directional conditions and to indicate service elements.

The buildings are composite, made up of overlaid orders of exposed structural, mechanical and electrical systems. Connections between the discrete elements, fixtures and fittings are made visible, intentionally didactic.

In a design mode reminiscent of the work of Charles Eames, Myers selects and arranges common "off-the-shelf," "high-tech" and customized building components in out-of-context settings, juxtaposed with traditional, modern, and pop artefacts. The Myers schema, however, places greater weight on the construction elements than on vernacular and folk objects, to achieve a density of texture.

The facades of Myers' buildings fall into two groups. The first group could be called "infill frames," related primarily to the steel constructions in which the principal facades are rendered as minimal compositions of solid and large glazed panels set inside steel frames. The second group are the "faces," related to various concrete and frame structures, where brick is employed as a veneer deliberately expressed through its detailing to wrap the buildings in more complex and often gestural ways. Brick is consistently used as a reference to local vernacular traditions through type and colour selection. Openings are composed as simple geometric cut-outs in the frontal planes, emphasized by the concealment of window jambs and the use of large sheets of glass.

Myers brings together a number of diverse attitudes and tendencies rather than projecting a single "pure" style. The architecture is rational, clear and composite, reflecting the interaction of both a heroic morale and a reformative view of the urban implications of Modern Architecture.

—Bruce Kuwabara

N

NEFF, (Edwin) Wallace.

American, Born in La Mirada, California, 28 January 1895. Studied art in Munich, 1911-13, and in Geneva, 1913-14; attended the School of Architecture, Massachusetts Institute of Technology, under Ralph Adams Cram, 1915-17. Married Louise Up de Graff in 1925; children: Phyllis, Wallace and Arthur. Loft-Molder, American Shipbuilding Company, San Pedro, California, 1917-18; Delineator-Draftsman, office of the architect George Washington Smith, Santa Barbara, California, 1919; Partner, Neff and Edwards, Architects, Santa Barbara, 1919; Principal, Wallace Neff, Architect, Pasadena, California, 1922-33, and Hollywood, California, 1933 until he retired, 1975. Exhibitions: American Institute of Architects Exhibitions, Southern California Chapter, Los Angeles, 1924, 1930, 1938, 1950, 1958; *L.A. in the Thirties*, Art Galleries of the University of California at Santa Barbara, 1975. Collections: University of Southern California, Los Angeles; Huntington Library, San Marino, California. Recipient: Honor Award, American Institute of Architects, 1924 (twice), 1929, 1939, 1950, 1958; Egyptian Government Award for Housing, 1951. Fellow, 1956, and Fellow Emeritus, 1972, American Institute of Architects. *Died* (in Laguna Beach, California) *8 June 1982.*

Works:

1919 Edwin Neff House, Santa Barbara, California (with William Edwards)
1923 Walker House, San Pasqual Street, Pasadena, California
E. D. Libbey Stables, Ojai, California
Frances Marion Estate, Beverly Hills, California
1924 Ojai Valley Country Club, Ojai, California
Johnson House, Burleigh Drive, Pasadena, California
Delano House, Allen Avenue, Pasadena, California
1925 Wallace Neff House, Mendocino Street, Altadena, California
St. Elizabeth's Roman Catholic Church, Altadena, California
Hall House, Woodstock Road, San Marino, California
Motor Sales Building, Altadena, California
Bourne House, Lombardy Road, San Marino, California
Dumbolton House, Allen Avenue, Pasadena, California
Toms House, Lombardy Road, San Marino, California
Doane House, Shenandoah Road, San Marino, California
1926 Post House, Orlando Road, San Marino, California
Fairbanks House, Orlando Road, San Marino, California
Noble House, Burleigh Drive, Pasadena, California

Johnson House, Burleigh Drive, Pasadena, California
Bryant Ranch, Santa Ana Canyon, California
Visscher House, Prospect Lane, Pasadena, California
Lecky House, Armada Drive, Pasadena, California
Burr House, Carolwood Drive, Holmby Hills, California
1927 Barlow Estate, Sierra Madre, California
California Security Loan Building, Pasadena
Van Deinse Estate, Pasadena, California
Pickfair Estate additions, Beverly Hills, California
Forthman Hous, La Fayette Park Place, Los Angeles
1928 Gillette Ranch, Calabasas, California
Bush House, Lake Wells, Florida
Busch House, Hillcrest Avenue, Pasadena, California
Norman Chandler House, Nottingham Road, Los Angeles
Harry Culver Estate, Cheviot Hills, California
Collins House, Pasadena, California
Gartz House, Via Almar, Palos Verdes, California
King Vidor Estate, Tower Road, Beverly Hills, California
1929 Anderson House, Sunset Boulevard, Beverly Hills, California
Doheny Ranch, Santa Paula Canyon, California
Wallace Neff Office Building, Pasadena, California
Neff House, Orlando Road, San Marino, California
Edwin Neff House, South Orange Grove Boulevard, Pasadena, California
Turner House, Orlando Road, San Marino, California
Baer House, La Vereda Road, Santa Barbara, California
Thorne House, Los Altos Drive, Pasadena, California
1930 Richter House, Virginia Road, San Marino, California
Niblo Estate, Beverly Hills, California
Brigham Estate, Bel-Air, Los Angeles
Wurtzel Estate, Bel-Air, Los Angeles
1931 Millikan House, Normandy Drive, Pasadena, California
1932 William Goetz Hous (Louis B. Mayer House), St. Pierre Road, Bel-Air, Los Angeles
1933 Factory-built "Mobile Home," Los Angeles
1934 Doheny House alterations, Chester Place, Los Angeles
1936 Fredric March Estate, Beverly Hills, California
Garner House, Holliday Road, San Marino, California
1937 Miller Estate, Bel-Air, Los Angeles
1938 Joan Bennett House, Mapleton Drive, Hol-

mby Hills, California
King Vidor Estate II, Beverly Hills, California
1939 Doheny Memorial Library, Camarillo, California
1940 William Goetz House, Santa Monica, California
1941 "Air-form" concrete structures, Falls Church, Virginia
Doheny Memorial House of Studies, Washington, D.C.
1942 Thomas Ince Memorial Hospital, 29 Palms, California
1946 A. Neff "Air-form" House, Los Robles Avenue, Pasadena, California
1948 Bourne Estate, Palm Springs, California
1949 Hornstein Estate, Hidden Valley, California
1950 Duff Estate, Hollywood, California
1952 Browne Estate, Bel-Air, Los Angeles
1953 Groucho Marx Estate, Beverly Hills, California
Factor House, Beverly Hills, California
1955 Harpo Marx House, Palm Springs, California
1956 Gummo Marx House, Beverly Hills, California
George B. Miller House, Smoke Tree Ranch, Palm Springs, California
1957 Manressa Jesuit Retreat House Chapel, Azusa, California
Gymnasium, Pomona College, Claremont, California
1958 Edgar Richards Estate, Palm Springs, California
1960 Ralph Chandler House, Rossmore Street, Los Angeles
1963 Roy Eaton Estate, Hope Ranch, Santa Barbara, California
1964 Elizabeth Hay Bechtel Estate, Santa Barbara, California
1965 Singleton Estate, Holmby Hills, California
1969 Rovert K. Straus House, Hope Ranch, Santa Barbara, California
1975 Browne Estate II, Big Canyon, Newport Beach, California

Publications:

By NEFF: book—*Thin Shell Concrete Construction*, privately printed 1965.

On NEFF: books—*Architecture of Southern California: A Selection of Photographs, Plans and Scale Details from the Work of Wallace Neff*, Chicago 1964; articles—"An Artist in Adobe" by Harris Allen in *Pacific Coast Architect* (Los Angeles), August 1924; "Adventures in Architecture" by Harris Allen in *Pacific Coast Architect* (Los Angeles), September 1927; "Ranch House for E. L. Doheny, Santa Paula Canyon, California" in *Architectural Record* (New York), November 1930; "Residence of Joan Bennett, Holmby Hills, California" in *California Arts and Architecture* (Los Angeles), September 1938; "Wallace Neff, Architect: Some of His Recent Work" by Mark

Wallace Neff: Gillette Ranch, Calabasas, California, 1928.

Daniels in *Architect and Engineer* (Los Angeles), January 1941; "Ballyhooed Balloon" in *Architectural Forum* (New York), December 1941; "Bubble House" in *Architectural Record* (New York), December 1941; "Bubble House for Defense" in *Architect and Engineer* (Los Angeles), January 1942; "Grain Bins in Southwest Arizona" in *Architect and Building News* (London), 23 April 1943; "Airform House for a Desert Colony" in *Architectural Record* (New York), July 1944; "U.S.A." by André Bruyere in *L'Architecture d'Aujourd'hui* (Paris), July/August 1945; "Air-formed Concrete Domes" in *Progressive Architecture* (New York), June 1954; "Huntington/USC Archive Launched" in *LA Architect* (Los Angeles), December 1978.

My practice has been almost entirely confined to California, where problems of climate and site have to be contended with on every job. During the first years I applied the lessons I learned in five years study of the traditional architecture of Europe (1910-1914), when "modernism" was virtually unheard of.

I always admired the simpler architecture on the Continent. Clients in California were enthusiastic about having houses (my practice was domestic), which were reminiscent of the simpler architecture of Italy and France, and I was enthusiastic about giving them the "right" solution for their needs, using European precedents. However, I never had any illusion that my work was anything other than "Californian" in style, never "authentic" copies of something alien. I was always interested in structure (I learned the importance of structure from Ralph Adams Cram at MIT).

When the Depression of the 1930s wiped out my practice, I became interested in the problems of mass housing. The factory-built home I designed in 1934 sold for $800, but no one could afford even that.

My interest in "modern" was not stylistic. A thin shell concrete structure erected without forms seemed a rational answer to the problem of low-cost shelter at a time when low-cost shelter was needed. The "Airform" nethod of construction which I developed and patented proved more applicable in the underdeveloped countries than it did in the United States, where building was hemmed in by codes and special interests.

I was in practice for such a long time that my early work began to be admired in a nostalgic sort of way, and I got a lot of clients who were in love with the recent past. Once again, however, I was not under any illusion that my late work was "authentically" "1920s" or "1930s." It was done for people who lived in a different era, and I feel solves the problems of contemporary living.

—Wallace Neff (1980)

In 1921 Wallace Neff started a practice as an architect of large country and suburban houses. His involvement in the design and production of a factory-built "Mobile Home" in 1933, followed by his invention of the "Airform" concrete structure in 1941, seem a startling reversal of direction in midcareer. A close examination of his design approach reveals less inconsistency than might at first appear.

At the time that Neff started his practice, California was still receptive to almost any architectural influence. Frank Lloyd Wright and others had built "Mayan" buildings, and Schindler and Neutra were able to flourish as "moderns." Neff, who had spent years in Europe and received a "Beaux-Arts" education at M.I.T., turned out work which was closer in spirit to that of Bernard Maybeck. Each house was in a "style" appropriate to the client and the site, but the style was freely interpreted. The estate that Neff built in 1923 for Frances Marion, a hugely paid script writer, and her husband, a cowboy actor, was the architect's interpretation of "Hollywood." It included a Spanish bullring where the cowboy might perform, a Baroque gatehouse, an approach through Moorish arches, and a huge voissoired portal flanked by engaged columns which emerged above the roof as turrets topped by Oriental finials. The next year he built a very irregular planned "Normandy" mansion in a scale so small that the eaves almost touched the ground in many places. The reason for the adoption of this scale was to save as many as possible of the old oaks that covered the site.

Neff's work proved very popular in Southern California. As early as 1927 critics pointed out that it was widely imitated. Perhaps no single architect was more responsible than Neff for creating the eclectic "style" we associate with Southern California in the 1920s and 1930s.

In his country houses, where he did not have to contend with building codes, Neff perused his interest in structure. The Bryant Ranch (1926) and the Gillette Ranch (1928) employed a combination of adobe (mud) bricks, manufactured on the site, and reinforced concrete.

The Neff-designed "Mobile Home," christened the "Honeymoon Cottage" by its promoters, was assembled in the factory and trucked to the site.

In "Airform" construction a rubber-coated balloon is inflated and sprayed with concrete or plastic. The balloon is deflated and re-used as soon as the concrete or plastic is self-supporting. As far as is known, the twenty-one shells erected at Falls Church, Virginia, in 1941, were the first pneumatically formed structures where the entire structure was thin shell concrete. Neff went on to patent the process in 1942, and by the 1950s worthwhile social and general housing projects, including entire villages, had been built in South

Africa, French West Africa, Pakistan and Brazil.

Wallace Neff's services were constantly in demand because he approached each job in an uninhibited manner. His life left little time for polemics or introspection. Each client, whether a Hollywood millionaire or a native of an underdeveloped country, had a problem to be solved. This interest in problem solving gives philosophical consistency to Wallace Neff's prodigious career as an architect.

—Alson Clark

NELSON, George.
American. Born in Hartford, Connecticut, 29 May 1908. Educated at Yale University, New Haven, Connecticut, B.A. 1929, M.A. 1931; Catholic University of America, Washington, D.C., 1932; American Academy, Rome, 1932-34 (Rome Scholarship). In partnership with William Hamby, New York, 1936-41; Design Director, Herman Miller Furniture Company, Zealand, Michigan, 1946. Since 1947, Principal, George Nelson and Company, industrial designers, New York; since 1953, Partner, Nelson and Chadwick, architects, New York. Design Instructor, Yale University, 1931-32; Teacher of Design, Columbia University, New York, 1942-45; Visiting Critic in Architecture, Graduate School of Design, Harvard University, Cambridge, Massachusetts, 1972-73. Associate Editor, 1935-43, Co-Managing Editor, 1943-44, and Consultant, 1944-49, *Architectural Forum*, New York; Head, *Fortune/Forum* Experimental Department, Time Inc., New York, 1944-45; Editor, *Interiors*, New York, 1948-75. Member, New York State Council on Architecture, 1968-75. Program Chairman of the 15th Conference, 1965, and since 1965 Member of the Board of Directors, International Design Conference, Aspen, Colorado; Member, Board of Directors, Industrial Designers Society of America, 1967-69, and since 1972; Advisor, Visual Technology Center, Massachusetts College of Art, Boston, since 1982. Exhibition: *Nelson/Eames/Girard/Propst: The Design Center at Herman Miller,* Walker Art Center, Minneapolis, 1975-76. Recipient: Industrial Arts Medal, 1964, and New York Medal of Honor, 1979, American Institute of Architects; Distinguished Contribution Award, 1974, and Personal Recognition Award, 1981, Industrial Designers Society of America; Elsie de Wolfe Award, American Society of Interior Designers, 1975. D.F.A.: Parsons School of Design, New York, 1979; Minneapolis College of Art and Design, 1980. Fellow, American Institute of Architects, 1963; Industrial Designers Society of

America, 1968; Benjamin Franklin Fellow, 1960, and Honorary Royal Designer for Industry, 1973, Royal Society of Arts, London. Address: George Nelson Associates, 257 Park Avenue South, New York, New York 10010, U.S.A.

Works:

1940/
41 Fairchild House, 17 East 56th Street, New York (with William Hamby)
1944 Storagewall (with Henry Wright)
1946 Basic Storage Components
Gateleg Table
Slat Bench
1948 Herman Miller Showroom, Chicago
Executive Office Group
1950 Holiday house, Quoque, Long Island, New York (with Gordon Chadwick)
1952 Bubble Lamp, for the Howard Miller Clock Company
Rosewood Cases
1953 Herman Miller Showroom, New York
1954 Pedestal End Tables
Steelframe Group
1956 Information Center, Colonial Williamsburg, Virginia
Coconut Chair
Modular Seating
Omni System, for Structural Products Inc.
Thin Edge Cases
1957 Design of the *Education for Theatrical Design* exhibition, for the United States Information Agency, at the Sao Paulo *Bienal*
Day Bed
1958 Fire Alarm, for Acme Fire Alarm Company
Comprehensive Storage System
1958/
60 Design of the *Design Today in America and Europe* exhibition, for the Government of India; toured India
Design of the *Peaceful Uses of Atomic Energy* exhibition, for the Atomic Energy Commission, Cairo
Design of the *American National Exhibition*, for the United States Information Agency, in Moscow
1959 Loeb Student Center interiors, New York University, 566-576 La Guardia Place, New York
Catenary Group
1960 Tower Suite, Time-Life Building, 1271 Sixth Avenue, New York
1961 Design of the *Transportation USA* exhibition, for the United States Information Agency; toured Russia
Design of the Abbott Medical Exhibit, *World's Fair*, Seattle
Herman Miller Factory, Zeeland, Michigan
1963 Design of the *U.S.-Us Show*, for Herman Miller Company, toured the United States
Sling Sofa

1964 Herman Miller Showroom, Washington, D.C.
Action Office 1
Design of the Chrysler Exhibition, *World's Fair*, New York
Design of the United States Department of State exhibition, Hall of Presidents, *World's Fair*, New York
Design of the Irish Pavilion, *World's Fair*, New York
1966 Herman Miller Factory additions, Zeeland, Michigan
Herman Miller Showroom, New York
1967 Design of the *Industrial Design USA* exhibition, for the United States Information Agency; toured Russia
1968 Rosenthal Studio, New York
1970 Design of the *U.S. Treasury* exhibition, United States Department of the Treasury, Washington, D.C.
1970/
72 Design of the *Research and Development in the U.S.* exhibition, for the United States Information Agency; toured Eastern Europe
1971 Executive Office Group
1972 La Protagerie, 554 Fifth Avenue, New York
The Children's Place, West Hartford, Connecticut
The Children's Place, Willowbrook, New Jersey
The Children's Place, Echelon, New Jersey
1973 Aid Association for Lutherans Hospital, Appleton, Wisconsin
1974/
76 Design of the *USA '76: The First Two Hundred Years* exhibition, for the American Revolution Bicentennial Administration; toured 10 American cities
1976 Design of the *Latin American Exhibition*, Inter-American Cultural and Trade Center, Miami
1983 Design of the *Design Since 1945* exhibition, Philadelphia Museum of Art, Pennsylvania

Publications:

By NELSON: books—*Industrial Architecture of Albert Kahn Inc.,* New York 1939; *Tomorrow's House,* with Henry Wright, New York 1945; foreword to *Miller Furniture Company,* catalogue, Zeeland, Michigan 1952; *Living Spaces,* editor, New York 1952; *Chairs,* editor, New York 1953; *Display,* editor, New York 1953; *Storage,* editor, New York 1954; *Problems of Design,* New York 1957; *How to See: Visual Adventures in a World God Never Made,* Boston 1977; *George Nelson on Design,* New York 1979; articles—"Architects of Europe Today" in *Pencil Points* (New York), January/-March, May, July, September and November 1936, and January, March, June, August and October 1937; "Wright's

Houses" in *Fortune* (New York), August 1946; "There's a New Pattern in Furniture Behavior" in *House Beautiful* (New York), July 1947; "Styling Organization/Design" in *Arts and Architecture* (Los Angeles), August 1947; "Problems of Design: Ends and Means" in *Interiors* (New York), May 1948; "Blessed Are the Poor" in *Interiors* (New York), July 1948; "Problems of Design: The Dead-End Room" in *Interiors* (New York), November 1948; "Beware of Trends" in *Interiors* (New York), December 1948; "Mr Roark Goes to Hollywood: A Comment on Warner Brothers' Attempt to Intrepret Frank Lloyd Wright to the Masses" in *Interiors* (New York), April 1949; "Modern Furniture" in *Interiors* (New York), July 1949; "Business and the Industrial Designer" in *Fortune* (New York), July 1949; "Problems of Design: Modern Decoration [Notes on the Subscape, The Enlargement of Vision]" in *Interiors* (New York), November 1949, November 1950, and November 1951; "After the Modern House" in *Interiors* (New York), July 1952; "Good Design: What Is It For" in *Interiors* (New York), July 1954; "Handbook of European Architecture" in *Holiday* (New York), January 1960; "A Question for George Nelson and Paul Rudolph," with Paul Rudolph, in *Zodiac* (Milan), no. 8, 1961; "People-to-Product Relationship" in *Industrial Design* (New York), May 1962; "The French Like Glass" in *Architectural Forum* (New York), November 1962; "Switzerland" in *Architectural Forum* (New York), June 1963; "Prima dell'apertura, una visita alla Fiera di New York" in *Domus* (Milan), May 1964; "Design in America: The Last 25 Years: A Series of Interviews" in *Interiors* (New York), November 1965; "Obsolescence" in *Perspecta* (New Haven, Connecticut), no. 11, 1967; "Architecture for the New Itinerants" in *Saturday Review* (New York), 22 April 1967; "Design, Technology, and the Pursuit of Ugliness" in *Saturday Review* (New York), 2 October 1971; "The End of Architecture: Are Buildings About to Be Driven Underground or to Disappear" in *Architecture Plus* (New York), April 1973; "The Humane Designer" in *Industrial Design* (New York), June 1973; "The Designer as Social Catalyst" in *Canadian Architect* (Toronto), June 1973; "From Monuments to Bell Jars: George Nelson Predicts the End of Architecture" in *RIBA Journal* (London), October 1973; "The Hidden City: Making Our Cities Less Boring by Making Them Less Visible" in *Architecture Plus* (New York), November/ December 1974; "Design: The Business of Survival" in *Industrial Design* (New York), March 1975; "Do Small Companies Need Design?" in *Industrial Design* (New York), May/-June 1975; "Interiors: The Emerging Dominant Reality" in *Interiors* (New York), November 1975; "The Office Revolution" in *The Canadian Architect* (Toronto), June 1978; "Tents" in *Interiors* (New York), December 1978; "Why George Nelson is Seduced by Woven Architecture" in *Design* (London), April 1979; "Yes, the Designer is a Fool, but the Architect..." in *Modo* (Milan), May 1979; "Tribute to the Permissive Shell" in *AIA Journal* (Washington, D.C.), July 1981;

George Nelson: Comprehensive Storage System, 1958.

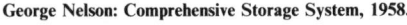

"Less Energy, More Work" in *The Architects' Journal* (London), 21 April 1982; "The Design Process" in *Interior Design* (New York), September 1983.

On NELSON: books—*Public Interiors* by Misha Black, London 1960; *The Art of Interior Design* by Victoria Kloss Ball, New York 1960; *Interior Design* by Arnold Friedmann, John F. Pile and Forrest Wilson, New York and Amsterdam 1970, 1976; *Industrial Design* by John Heskett, London 1980; *Environmental Interiors* by Mary Jo Weale, James W. Croake and W. Bruce Weale, New York and London 1982; articles—"The Storagewall" in *Architectural Forum* (New York), November 1944; "What Is Happening to Modern Architecture" in *Museum of Modern Art Bulletin* (New York), Spring 1948; "George Nelson Joins Interiors" in *Interiors* (New York), October 1948; "About the Job of Designing a Furniture Showroom" in *Interiors* (New York), May 1949; "The Projection of Industrial Design into Advertising" by Mildred Constantine in *Graphis* (Zurich), November 1953; "Examples of Work by George Nelson" and "The George Nelson Office: A Comprehensive Design Organization" in *Architectural Record* (New York), December 1957; "Designing the Moscow Exhibit" in *Architectural Record* (New York), November 1959; "The World of George Nelson" by Enzo Fratelli in *Zodiac* (Milan), no. 8, 1961; "Nelson's Way" in *Interiors* (New York), November 1963; "The Herman Miller Action Office" in *Interiors* (New York), December 1964; "Seven Significant Designers: An In-Depth Report" in *House Beautiful* (New York), October 1966; "Portfolio: Architecture" in *Perspecta* (New Haven, Connecticut), no. 11, 1967; "Conversation with George Nelson" in *Industrial Design* (New York), April 1969; "Designers in America: George Nelson and Company" in *Industrial Design* (New York), October 1973; "The Design Process at Herman Miller" in *Design Quarterly* (Minneapolis), no. 98/99, 1975; "Up to Earth" in *Progressive Architecture* (New York), April 1979; "Acorns to Oaks" in *Progressive Architecture* (New York), September 1980; "Visita el pail un disenador – se trata de George Nelson, Egresado de Yale" in *El Cronista* (Buenos Aires), April 1981; "Growth: The Magic Factors" in *Interiors* (New York), December 1982; "George Nelson" in *Architecture Intérieure Crée* (Paris), December 1983/February 1984.

Although he was trained as an architect, George Nelson's accomplishments extend to all phases of environmental design, and today he is known as one of the most talented industrial, graphic, and urban designers of the twentieth century. He has received international acclaim for his interiors, his unique designs for exhibition displays, his home and office furnishing inventions, and recently for proposing new concepts of urban growth.

After completing his undergraduate education at Yale University, Nelson began his career as a writer for several American architectural journals, and he was associate editor of *Architectural Forum* for almost a decade. During that time, he independently developed several new prefabricated architectural components. The most notable of these was a combination storage unit and room divider, known commercially as Storagewall (released in 1945). At roughly the same time, he invented, but did not develop, a complete, pre-formed one wall kitchen unit.

Storagewall brought Nelson to the attention of Herman Miller Inc., then still a small furniture manufacturer in Wisconsin. Even though Nelson had no experience in interior or industrial design besides his few, semi-architectural inventions, the president of that company still managed to eventually persuade him to join their staff. There, he continued to apply his keen mind towards creating radically new products for interior use, and soon

Nelson was a catalytic force in Herman Miller's growth.

He brought the now famous Charles Eames, a designer with similar multi-disciplinary inclinations, to the company, and Herman Miller soon became a mecca for the most talented industrial designers in the country. The company has always valued its design team as its chief commodity, and allowed them complete economic and temporal freedom to fully develop their new ideas. Herman Miller has remained dedicated to innovational design and high quality production, and has gained a reputation for European styling and craftsmanship. Today, largely as a result of Nelson's perseverance, it is America's most respected manufacturer of home and office furnishings.

Nelson's extraordinary ability to conceptualize environments in their totality, and erase distinguishing lines that have traditionally existed between interior, industrial, architectural and urban design, has been his chief asset throughout his career. With Herman Miller, and in independent practice, Nelson has developed countless schemes that are combinations of these disciplines, and are particularly effective because of this. Many of his designs for Herman Miller were complete living environments that were both furniture and architecture at once.

In the late 1950's, he applied this skill to a logical cause, the design of exhibitions. Soon he was clearly the leading American exhibition designer, and in 1959 he designed his acclaimed structure for the American national exhibition in Moscow. It used translucent fibreglass, molded into umbrella shapes, to create the roof and the display areas, while the columns regulated circulatory movement. Nelson has also designed many display cases, panel systems for vertical exhibitions, and numerous accompanying catalogues, including the brochure that accompanied the first exhibit of the Cooper Hewitt Museum, the Smithsonian Institution's National Museum of Design.

Throughout his professional career Nelson has remained a prolific writer, and his books and articles have had as much impact on contemporary design as have the ingenuity of his own creations. His 1977 release entitled *How to See* is his most personal. It is an extraordinary pictorial essay that displays design throughout our environment. There is some commentary, but the strongest statement is expressed by the careful selection of visual material.

Nelson is a quick thinker who has remained in the forefront of the design world for a third of a century, and continues to offer meaningful suggestions for future growth. Lately he has been concentrating more directly on issues of urban design, and he published numerous articles in the mid-seventies proclaiming the importance of revolutionizing our attitude towards architecture and the city as a whole. But whether the subject is architectural, industrial, or even completely hypothetical, Nelson has shown himself to be one of the sharpest problem solvers around, still happily kicking for design to bring more order and more beauty to our man-made environment.

—Mitchell B. Rouda

NELSON, Paul Daniel.

French. Born in Chicago, Illinois, 8 November 1895; emigrated to France, 1920; naturalized, 1973. Educated at Princeton University, New Jersey, 1913-17 (President, Princeton Triangle Club, 1916-17), Litt.B. 1917; Ecoles des Beaux-Arts, Paris, 1920-27 (Prix Guadet, 1927), D.P.L.G. 1927; influenced by the work of the Ecole de Paris: Braque, Léger, Miró, Giacometti, Arp, Derain, Hélion, Laurens, Calder, Bissière, Picasso, etc. Volunteered to join the Lafayette Escadrille, 1917, then served in the United States Air Force, in Italy and France, 1917-19: Lieutenant; Member, 1941, and President of the Washington, D.C. Chapter, 1942-43, American National Committee of "France Forever." Married Francine Lecoeur in 1920 (died, 1951); married the painter Maddalena Giannattasio in 1952; children: Ugo and Rory. In private practice, Paris, 1928-40; Architectural Consultant, 1941-42, and Job Captain, 1942-43, United States Housing Authority, Washington, D.C.; Consultant, Board of Economic Warfare and National Housing Agency, Washington, 1943-44; Chief of the Division of Urbanism and Building Industries, Supply Mission for France, Washington, 1944-45; returned to Paris and re-opened office there, 1945-67; Technical Assistant, French Ministry of Reconstruction, Paris, 1945-46; Professor and Director of the Franco-American Atelier of Architecture, Ecole Nationale Supérieure des Beaux-Arts, Paris, 1965-67; moved practice to Marseilles, and served as Professor and Director of the Franco-American International Atelier of Architecture, Ecole d'Art et d'Architecture de Marseille-Luminy, 1967-78. Special Consultant to the United States Public Heath Service, 1959, and to the Technical Department of the French Ministry of Public Health, 1961-62. Visiting Professor, School of Architecture, Pratt Institute, New York, 1957-58; Visiting Critic in charge of the Hopper Fellowship Competition, Yale University School of Architecture, New Haven, Connecticut, 1958-59; Visiting Professor, School of Architecture, Harvard University, Cambridge, Massachusetts, and School of Architecture, Massachusetts Institute of Technology, Cambridge, 1959-60, and Fellow of the Joint MIT/Harvard Center for Urban Studies, Cambridge, 1960. Exhibitions: Museum of Modern Art, New York, 1936; Palais de la Découverte, Paris, 1937. Collection: Museum of Modern Art, New York. Recipient: Graham Foundation Fellowship, 1957; Gold Medal, Société d'Encouragement à l'Art et à l'Industrie, 1968; Grand Medal of Honor, Académie d'Architecture, Paris, 1978. Honorary Member, Sociedad de Arquitectos Mexicanos, 1943; Member, American Institute of Architects, 1958. Chevalier, 1946, and Officer, 1956, Légion d'Honneur; Commandeur des Arts et Lettres, 1964. *Died* (in Trets, France) *30 August 1979.*

Works:

1928 Brooks House, 80 Boulevard Arago, Paris
1929 Art direction and sets for the United Artists' film *What a Widow!*, Hollywood, California
1930 Audio-visual theatre for the Joseph Kennedy House, Bronxville, New York (project)
1930/
32 Petite Maison de Santé, near Paris (project)
1932/
33 Health City of Lille, France (project)
1934 Surgical Pavilion of Ismailia, Egypt (project)
1936 National Center for the Columbia Broadcasting System, New York (project)
1936/
38 Suspended House, France (project)
1937/
38 Museum of Scientific Discovery, Paris (project; with Oscar Nitzchke and Frantz Jourdain)
1938 W.G.N. Broadcasting Theatre, Chicago (competition project; with Fernand Léger)
1941/
46 Research in urban planning for the United States Government
1946/
56 France-U.S.A. Memorial Hospital, Saint-Lô, France (with Roger Gilbert, Charles Sébillotte and Marcel Mersier)
1951/
52 Nurses' Home, Doctors' Home, and renovation of nursing units in the existing hospital, American Hospital of Neuilly, Paris

1954/
55 Badin Experimental House, rue Paul Couderc, Sceaux, France

1955/
56 Museum for Fernand Léger, Biot, France (project)

1957/
60 Research in America on hospital architecture

1961/
62 J. Walter Thompson Administrative Center, Paris (project)

1963/
68 Hospital, Dinan, France (with P. Devinoy and R. Lamourec)

1965/
74 Master plan and 500-bed hospital for the Arles Community Health Center, France (with P. Devinoy and Remondet)

1971 Plan for health care facilities in Tunisia (with P. Devinoy)

1975/
76 Paul Nelson House, Trets, France

Publications:

By NELSON: books—*Roof Framing*, with Thomas Rees, Milwaukee, Wisconsin 1927; *La Cité Hospitaliée de Lille*, Paris 1932; *Deux Etudes Hospitalières par Paul Nelson*, Paris 1936; *La Maison Suspendue*, Paris 1937; *Transformation de l'Architecture aux Etats-Unis*, Paris. 1946; articles—"La Maison de la rue Saint-Guillaume" in *L'Architecture d'Aujourd'hui* (Paris), November/December 1933; "L'Organisation Internationale des Cité Hospitalières" and L'air conditionné" in *La Revue des Hôpitaux* (Lyons), 1934; "Le Pavillon Chirurgical de Suez" in *Cahiers d'Art* (Paris), December 1935; "A Method of Architectural Procedure" in *Architectural Record* (New York), June 1937; "La Peinture Spatiale de Léger" in *Cahiers d'Art* (Paris), June 1937; "Le Palais de la Découverte" in *Cahiers d'Art* (Paris), no. 3/4, 1940; "American Architecture 1891-1941" in Architectural Record (New York), February 1941; "Researching for a New Standard of Living" in *Revere Copper and Brass Company Magazine* (New York), no. 2, 1942; "War Dormitories" in *Public Housing* (F.P.H.A.: Washington, D.C.), May 1942; "Design for Tomorrow" in *Perspecta* (New Haven, Connecticut), 1959; "An Integrated Approach to Design" in *Journal of the American Hospital Association* (Chicago), June 1959; "Mon ami Braque" in *Les Lettres Francaises* (Paris), 6 and 12 September 1962; "Le Théâtre et les Loisirs" in "Le Lieu Théâtral dans la Société Moderne" in *Revue du Centre National de la Recherche Scientifique* (Paris), 1963; "Collaboration Artistes-Architects" in *Melpomène* (Paris), 16 December 1964; "Corbu: C'etait un géant" in *Paris-Normandie* (Paris), 30 August 1965; "Un Brûleur d'Etapes" in *Les Lettres Francaises* (Paris), 2 and 7 September 1965; "Plomberie et Sanitaires Industrialisés in *Les Tables Rondes du Second Oeuvre* (Paris), October 1965; "L'homme, l'architecte, l'industrie du bâtiment" in *Techniques et Architecture* (Paris), 1966; "Vers le Centre de Santé" in *La Table Ronde* (Paris), March 1968; "Mutation ou Cessation" in *Le Carré Bleu* (Paris), no. 3/4, 1969.

On NELSON: books—*Hospitals: Integrated Design* by Isadore Rosenfield, 2nd edition, New York 1956; *Nouvelle Architecture Francaise* by Maurice Besset, Teufen, Switzerland 1967; *The New Architecture of Europe* by G. E. Kidder Smith, New York 1967; articles—"La Cité Hospitalière de Lille" by Christian Zervos in *Cahiers d'Art* (Paris), no. 8/10, 1932; preface by Christian Zervos to *La Cité Hospitalière de Lille* by Paul Nelson, Paris 1932; "The Surgical Pavilion of Suez" in *Architectural Record* (New York), June 1934; preface by Jean Hélion, "Termes de vie, Termes d'espace," to "Le Pavillon Chirurgical de Suez" by Paul Nelson in *Cahiers d'Art* (Paris),

December 1935; "Health City of Lille" in *Architectural Record* (New York), June 1938; "The Suspended House" in *Architectural Record* (New York), December 1938; "The Palace of Scientific Discovery" by John Burchard in *MIT Review* (Cambridge, Massachusetts), January/February 1939; "The Palace of Scientific Discovery" in *Architectural Record* (New York), February 1939; "Hôpital Hospice de Saint-Lô" in *L'Architecture d'Aujourd'hui* (Paris), November 1947; "Hôpital Hospice de Saint-Lô" in *L'Architecture d'Aujourd'hui* (Paris), January 1948; "Sun for Surgery at Saint-Lô" in *Life* (New York), July 1948; "L'Hôpital de Saint-Lô" in *L'Architecture d'Aujourd'hui* (Paris), no. 27, 1949; "Hospital at Saint-Lo, France" in *Architectural Review* (London), March 1949; "The Saint-Lo Hospital" in *Architectural Forum* (New York), September 1949; "Hôpital Memorial France-Etat-Unis, Saint-Lô, France" by Bridgeman in *L'Architecture d'Aujourd'hui* (Paris), no. 70, 1956; "Une Maison aux couleurs de Fernand Léger" in *Maison et Jardin* (Paris), July 1956; "Vers un Nouvel Humanisme," interview, by D. Valeix in *L'Architecture d'Aujourd'hui* (Paris), 1957; "Memorial Hospital" in *Progressive Architecture* (New York), October 1957; "Paul Nelson: La Maison Suspendue" by Aulis Blomstedt in *Le Carré Bleu* (Paris), no. 2, 1958; "For the Jersey Meadows: A Serpentine Band of Housing" in *Architectural Forum* (New York), April 1958; "Pratt Studies Jersey Meadows" in *Progressive Architecture* (New York), 1958; "La Forme Architecturale" by Aulis Blomstedt in *Le Carré Bleu* (Paris), no. 1, 1961; "Paul Nelson: Un Architecte Humaniste" by Michel-Louis Lacoste in *Informations et Documents* (U.S. Embassy, Paris), 1 November 1963; "Présentation Préliminaire de l'Hôpital de Dinan" in *L'Architecture d'Aujourd'hui* (Paris), no. 115, 1964; "Projet de l'Hôpital de Dinan" in *Techniques et Architecture* (Paris), no. 2, 1965; "Un Américain á Paris" by Ch. Galperine in *Notre République* (Paris), 3 February 1967; "Vers un Centre de Santé pour la Communauté: Arles" in *La Vie Collective* (Paris), October 1971; "Paul Nelson: An Interview" by Judith Applegate in *Perspecta* (New Haven, Connecticut) no. 13/14, 1971; "Plaido-yer pour le changement" by Anne Kandelman in *Le Carré Bleu* (Paris), no. 1, 1978; "About Paul Nelson (1895-1979)" by Anatole Kopp in *L'Architecture d'Aujourd'hui* (Paris), October 1979.

Bibliography: *Paul Nelson, The Humanist Architect* by Florita Z. Louie Malave, Monticello, Illinois 1984.

Ever since I began my studies of architecture in Paris I intended to be a creator, not a businessman (therefore I never maintained a big agency but chose the best associates, designers and engineers, as I went along, according to need). I was always interested in development. My interest in new methods and materials was combined with a constant interest in the development of "man"—this I learned from the artists of the Ecole de Paris, particularly from Braque. And I attempted to realize a synthesis between American technology and French humanism.

As my architecture was devoted to the development of man, I needed to learn how "man-in-progress" develops himself. And I discovered that he develops in two ways at the same time—as an individual and as a collective or social being. Parallel ways, but complementary: man goes from one to the other, and it is this alteration that enriches him—indirectly, while enriching his collectivity. From the moment that this process is admitted, then the conception of the house changes, because it becomes a closed form where it is possible for man and family to isolate themselves momentarily for their development needs (the Suspended House project). Conversely, collective architecture must be a free-standing form, opened on all sides. The "enriching" must

result necessarily from the contrast between the activities pertaining to these two forms (the goal is not form but man). In my opinion, therefore, the objective of architecture and of urban planning consists finally in responding to the needs of development of total man, from birth to death.

In my research in urban planning I discovered the fact that the most economical community units were also the most efficient—a discovery that was both economically staggering and qualitatively desirable. I came to believe that it is not a question of creating services—education, health, communications, etc—for a given population, but rather one of discovering the standards that determine the size of population necessary for the optimum efficiency of each service. And this led me to my theory about the organic structuration of the town as it should be.

To realize such a profound study of man's needs, and to reach an answer to these questions of needs by taking into account the future (with the hope of creating the least number of barriers to development). I was helped by a method of architectural procedure that I created in 1933-35 which I have used systematically ever since. This methodology is composed of three stages: the "non-architectural analysis," where the over-all aims are established by all concerned (specialists, engineers, arts and users); the "architectural analysis," devoted to the planning of ideal systems or forms of inter-relationships; and the "architectural synthesis," when design first crystallizes. This approach is dialectical in essence because it is based on continuous interchange (opposition and resolution) of the forces involved in the different fields. And, finally, it relies for beauty on the contrapuntal form of harmony that these melodies constitute as they enter into unison at certain points in the planning for over-all aims and principles.

These principles led me as an architect to develop a method of planning to facilitate to the maximum the provision of desirable development for man. Therefore, I have always started with "what should be done," which would permit me to lower my aim to "what can be done." This method eliminates immediately and continually any possibility of giving in to "what is usually done."

—Paul Nelson (1979)

"It has always been a principle of my architecture," Paul Nelson remarked in an interview, "to never limit the user to one way of doing things," and throughout his career he has been dedicated to the idea of "flexibility" as an architectural imperative.

Nelson was born in Chicago in 1895 and educated at Princeton University. A bomber pilot in France during World War I, he returned to Paris after the war to attend the Ecole des Beaux-Arts. In 1923, at the suggestion of his friend Le Corbusier, Nelson and several other young architects established an atelier under Auguste Perret, France's leading exponent in the use of reinforced concrete. By 1928 Nelson had his own office, and in 1930 he received a commission to design a small private clinic near Paris. In this project Nelson was to define several major themes that he would pursue for the remainder of his career. The psychological comfort of both patient and visitor, the architectural ramifications of modern medical technology, and the need for flexibility to accommodate changing environmental conditions were issues confronted in the clinic. They were greatly elaborated upon just two years later with a project for a teaching hospital and medical and nursing school complex in Lille. For this project Nelson invented and patented a "flexible curtain-wall" to allow for greater interior partition arrangements, though the wall was not put into use until construction of the France-U.S.A. Hospital at St Lô.

Throughout the 1930s, Nelson was involved in highly imaginative, often speculative architectural work, and in the invention of building or constructional systems. Specializing in hospital design, Nelson developed an egg-shaped operating room that allowed increased control over asepsis and lighting. It was also at this time that Nelson designed perhaps his best known project, the Suspended House (Maison Suspendue). Greatly influenced by Pierre Chareau's Maison de Verre, the Maison Suspendue consisted of prefabricated units for different functions suspended within a fixed steel cage. Touted as an "all-steel house," the Maison Suspendue was, for a short time, under consideration as the main theme construction for the 1939 New York *World's Fair*. Despite its wide publication, however, the house was never built, and the Trylon and Sphere were constructed at the Fair instead.

During World War II Nelson left France, though he was able to collaborate with Frantz Jourdain and Oskar Nitzchke on a research project for a Museum of Scientific Discovery (Palais de la Découverte). Drawings made for this unrealized building show a huge domed structure, strung with cables, and owing much to both Le Corbusier's design for the Palace of the Soviets and several of Melnikov's large exhibition projects.

Returning to France after the war, Nelson was named chief-architect for the France-U.S.A. Memorial hospital of St. Lô; it was completed in 1956 and is Nelson's finest medical building, incorporating many of his technological innovations. The architect's old friend Ferdinand Léger contributed a large mural to the entry of the hospital and, shortly before his death, collaborated with Nelson on a small residence near Paris (the Badin house at Sceaux), which boasted painted wall panels. After Léger's death, Nelson was asked to design a memorial museum for the painter. Situated over a hair-pin turn in the little winding town of Biot, the Léger museum, regrettably never built, is Nelson's most ingenious piece of site-planning, with the roof-terrace of the building creating a public plaza.

In 1957 Nelson received a Graham Foundation fellowship and his renewed contacts thereafter brought him back with increasing frequency. In 1959-1960 he taught at both Harvard and M.I.T., directing studies on a Progressive Patient Care Hospital in Cambridge.

Between 1960 and 1967 Nelson designed several large hospital complexes, including the 450 bed facility for the city of Dinan and a technologically sophisticated hospital and community mental health center in Arles. While working on the Arles center, Nelson moved to Marseilles where he helped set up the Franco-American Atelier of Architecture in the new School of Art and Architecture.

—Richard Lavenstein

NERVI, Pier Luigi.

Italian. Born in Sondrio, 21 June 1891. Educated at the University of Bologna, Italy, Dip.Ing. 1913. Officer in the Engineering Corps of the Italian Army, 1915-18. Married Irene Calosin in 1924; children: Antonio, Vittorio, and Mario. Engineer with the Società per Costruzioni Cementizie, Bologna, Italy, 1913-15 and 1918-23. In private practice, Rome, from 1923: Partner, Nervi and Nebbiosi, 1923-32; President, Ingg. Nervi and Bartolia, from 1932; Partner with sons Antonio, Mario, and Vittorio, Studio Nervi, 1960 until his death in 1979. Consultant Engineer, Unesco, Paris, 1952. Professor of the Technology and Technique of Construction, Faculty of Architecture, University of Rome, 1947-61. Exhibition: *Pier Luigi Nervi*, Centre d'Information du Bâtiment, Paris, 1962. Recipient: Certificate of Commendation, Institute of Structural Engineers, London, 1955; Brown Medal, Franklin Institute, Philadelphia, 1957; Exner Medal, Österreiche Gewerbevereines, Vienna, 1957; Gold Medal, American Institute of Architects, Philadelphia Chapter, 1958; Gold Medal, Confederazione Generale Italiana Professionisti-Artisti, Rome, 1958; Gold Medal, Royal Institute of British Architects, London, 1960; Alfred Lindau Award, American Concrete Institute,

1963; Award, Concrete Industry Board, New York, 1963; Emil Morsch Award, Deutsche Beton Verein, 1963; Gold Medal, American Institute of Architects, 1964; Gold Medal, Institute of Structural Engineers, London, 1968; Feltrinelli Award, Rome, 1968; Gold Medal, Académie d'Architecture, Paris, 1971. Honarary doctorates: University of Buenos Aires, 1950; University of Edinburgh 1960; Technische Hochschule, Munich, 1960; University of Warsaw, 1961; Harvard University, Cambridge, Massachusetts, 1962; Dartmouth College, Hanover, New Hampshire, 1963; Prague Polytechnic, 1966; University of London, 1969. Member, Accademia di San Luca, Rome, 1960. Honorary Member, American Institute of Architects, 1956; Honorary Member, National Institute of Arts and Letters, U.S.A., 1957; Foreign Member, Royal Academy of Fine Arts, Stockholm, 1957; Corresponding Member, Academia Nacional de Ciencias Exactas Fisicas y Naturales, Buenos Aires, 1959; Honorary Member, American Academy of Arts and Sciences, 1960; Corresponding Member, Bayerischen Akademie der Schönen Künste, Munich, 1960; Member, Royal Institute of Dutch Engineers, 1964; Member, Akademie der Künste, Berlin, 1964; Member, Institut des Beaux Arts, Paris, 1973; Foreign Member, Institut de France, Paris, 1973. *Died* (in Rome) *9 January 1979*.

Works (as structural engineer):

1927 August Cinema, Naples
1932 Municipal Stadium, Florence
       Circular Hangars in reinforced concrete and steel (project)
       Monumento della Bandiera, Monte Mario, Rome (project; with Rubens Magnani)
1934 Revolving house (project)
1935 Stadium, Rome (project: with Cesare Valle)
1936 Aircraft Hangars, for the Italian Air Force, Orvieto, Italy
       Biedano Valley Bridge, Viterbo, Italy (project)
1938 Silos for the Società Solvay, Rosignano, Italy (project)
1939 Viaduct (project)
1940 Pavilion of Italian Civilization, for the *Esposizione Universale* of 1942 (project; with P. M. Bardi)
       Palace of Water and Light, for the *Esposizione Universale* of 1942 (project)
1941 Aircraft hangars, for the Italian Air Force, at Orbetello, Torre del Lago, Italy (destroyed in 1944)
1942 Underground gasoline storage tanks, Italy
1943 984 foot span (project)
       660 foot span for railway station (project)
1945 Ferro-Cemento Warehouse, Rome
       Factory (project)
1946 Central Station, Palermo, Sicily (project)
       Pre-fabricated circular house (project)
1947 Swimming Baths, Naval Academy, Livorno, Italy
       Conte Trossi Wharf, San Michele di Pagano, Genoa (with Luigi Carlo Daneri)
1949 Air-insulated shed roof (project)
       Aircraft hangar, Buenos Aires (project)
1950 Restaurant Roof, Kursaal Beach Casino, Ostia, Italy (with Attilio La Padula)
       Exhibition Halls, Salone B and Salone C, Turin
1951 Salt Warehouse, Tortona, Italy
       Bridge over the River Reno, Sasso Marconi, Italy (project; with Carlo Castelli-Guidi)
1952 Tobacco factory, Bologna
       Roof of Hall, Chianciano Terme, Italy (with Mario Loreti and Mario Marchi)
1953 Gatti Wool Factory, Rome
       "System Nervi" pressure pipeline
       Lancia Factory, Turin (project)
       Sports Palace, Vienna (project; with Antonio Nervi)
1954 Main Railway Station, Naples (project; with Giuseppe Vaccaro and Mario Campanella)

Italian Cultural Institute, Stockholm (with Gio Ponti and Ture Wenerholm)
       Storehouses for Tobacco Factory, Bologna
       Tobacco Factory and Storehouses, Turin
       Tramcar Depot, Turin
1955 Fiat Factory, Turin
       Bridge over the River Tenza, Italy (project)
       Centre National des Industries, Paris (project; with Camelot, de Mailly and Bernard Zehrfuss)
1956 Exhibition Hall, Caracas, Venezuela (project)
1957 Unesco Headquarters, Paris (with Marcel Breuer and Bernard Zehrfuss)
       Palazzetto dello Sport, Rome (with Annibale Vitellozzi)
1958 Pirelli Building, Milan (with Gio Ponti, Alberto Rosselli, Antonio Fornaroli, Giuseppe Valtolina, Egidio dell'Orto and Arturo Danusso)
1959 Palazzo dello Sport, Rome (with Marcello Piacentini)
       Flaminio Stadium, Rome (with Antonio Nervi)
       Via Olimpica Overpass, Rome
       New Norcia Cathedral and Abbey, near Perth, Western Austalia (project; with Antonio Nervi and Carlo Vannoni)
       Railway Station, Savona, Italy (competion project)
1961 Palazzo del Lavoro, *Italia 61* exhibition, Turin
       George Washington Bridge Bus Station, New York
       Nathaniel Leverone Field House, Dartmouth College, Hanover, New Hampshire
1962 Burgo Paper Mill, Mantua, Italy
1963 Overpass, Genoa
1964 Covered Swimming Pool (project)
       Palazzetto dello Sport, Vicenza, Italy (project; with P. Maltauro)
1966 Portsmouth Cathedral extension, Hampshire (project; with Seeley and Paget)
       Cromodora Factory, Venoria Realie, Turin
       Stock Exchange Tower, Montreal (with Luigi Moretti)
       Office Building, Verona, Italy (project)
       Risorgimento Bridge, Verona, Italy
1967 MOTTA Autogrill, Padua, Italy (with M. Bega)
       Cultural Center, Tripoli, Libya (project)
1971 Church, San Remo, Italy (project; to be constructed)
       Papal Audience Hall, Vatican City
       St. Mary's Cathedral, San Francisco (with Pietro Belluschi, and McSweeney, Ryan and Lee)
       Cassa di Risparmio Headquarters, Venice (with A. Scattolin)
       Cultural and Convention Center, Norfolk, Virginia (with Williams and Tazewell)
1975 Ebute-Metta Station, Lagos, Nigeria (project)
       Stadium, Novara, Italy
       Ice Hockey Rink, Dartmouth College, Hanover, New Hampshre
       Um-Al Khanezeer Island Development, Baghdad, Iraq (project)
1978 International Labour Organization Office, Geneva (with Eugène Beaudouin)
       Pitt Rivers Museum, Oxford (project; with Powell and Moya)
1978 African Development Bank Headquarters, Abidjan, Ivory Coast (with E. Olympio)
       Italian Embassy, Brasilia
       Apartment/Office Building, Riyadh, Saudi Arabia (with ICE, Orsi and Koerne, Giudici and Stoppa, and Italprogetti)
       Austrian Embassy, Paris (as structural consultant; with Harry Seidler and Marcel Breuer)
       Railway Station, Cosenza, Italy (with Sara Rossi)
       Civic Library, Verona, Italy
       Church of S. Gaspare del Bufalo, Rome
       Good Hope Centre (exhibition hall), Cape Town

Publications:

By NERVI: books—*El lenguaje arquitectonico*, Buenos Aires 1950; *Art o scienza del costruire?*, Rome 1954; *Concrete and Structural Form*, London 1955; *Costruire correttamente*, Milan 1955, as *Structures*, New York 1956; *Nuove strutture*, Milan 1963, as *New Structures*, London and Stuttgart 1963; *Aesthetics and Technology in Building*, Cambridge, Massachusetts and London 1966; articles—"Arte e technica del costruire," in *Quadrante* (Milan), June 1931; "Pensieri sull'ingegneria" in *Quadrante* (Milan), October 1932; "Monumento alla bandiera" in *Quadrante* (Milan), December 1933; "Problemi della realizzazione architettonica" in *Casabella* (Milan), February 1934; "Un aviorimessa in cemento armato" in *Casabella* (Milan), April 1938; "Un arco monumentale in conglomerato no armato" in *Casabella* (Milan), August 1942; "Ancora sul senso dell' architettura" in *Domus* (Milan), March 1950; "Economica edilizia" in *La Casa* (Rome), April 1950; "Le proporzioni nella tecnica" in *Domus* (Milan), December 1951; "Possibilità costruttive ed architettonica della pre-fabbricazione strutturale" in *L'Architettura* (Rome), January 1952; "Precast Concrete Offers New Possibilities for Design of Shell Structures" in *American Concrete Institute Journal* (Detroit), February 1953; "L'Architecture du beton armé et le problème des coffrages" in *L'Architecture d'aujourd'hui* (Paris), July 1953; "Concrete and Structural Form" in *The Structural Engineer* (London), May 1956; "The Place of Structure in Architecture" in *Architectural Record* (New York), July 1956; "Reinforced Concrete Construction" in *Progressive Architecture* (New York), September 1957; "Critica delle strutture" in *Casabella* (Milan), January, February, March and April 1959; "Le strutture dell'Unesco" in *Casabella* (Milan), April 1959.

On NERVI: books—*Gli elementi dell'architettura funzionale* by Alberto Sartoris, Milan 1935; *Nuova architettura italiana* by Agnoldomenico Pica, Milan 1939; *Architettura moderna in Italia* by Agnoldomenico Pica, Milan 1941; *Italy Builds* by G E. Kidder-Smith, London and Milan 1955; *Pier Luigi Nervi* by G. C. Argan, Milan 1955; *The Works of Pier Luigi Nervi* by Jürgen Joedicke and Ernesto Rogers, Stuttgart and London 1957; *Pier Luigi Nervi* by Ada Louise Huxtable, New York 1960; *Structure in Architecture* by Mario Salvadori, Englewood Cliffs, New Jersey 1963; *Architettura moderna in Milano* by Agnoldomenico Pica, Milan 1964; *Architectural Engineering: New Structures* by Agnoldomenico Pica, New York 1964; *Pier Luigi Nervi* by Mate Major, Budapest 1966, Berlin 1970; *Nervi* by Jan Tomes, Prague 1967; *Pier Luigi Nervi* by Agnoldomenico Pica, Rome 1969; articles—"Homage to Pier Luigi Nervi" by Jean-Pol Hindre in *Espace* (Paris), no. 7, 1979; "Pier Luigi Nervi's Legacy" by Sergio Musmeci in *Architect* (Melbourne), August 1980; "Pier Luigi Nervi," special issue of *Process: Architecture* (Tokyo), April 1981; "The Historical Tradition of the Master Builder, 4: Pier Luigi Nervi" in *Small Scale Builder* (San Luis Obispo, California), no. 4, 1981.

Bibliography—*Work and Life of Pier Luigi Nervi, Architect* by Florita Z. Louie de Irizarry, Monticello, Illinois 1984.

As an architect in reinforced concrete, Pier Luigi Nervi was one of the most notable of this century. He evolved his own system of structural design, independently of others. It was mainly for large buildings of the hall type—exhibition pavilions, covered sports arenas, railway stations, aircraft hangars, warehouses and sports stadiums—and into the system he introduced variations in answer to needs and economy. The structures proved not only very efficient but also very attractive. In many buildings, he was both the structural engineer and the architect. In others, he collaborated with architects, but his special contribution to the design of the structure is usually strongly apparent. In the early years of his practice, he realized the limitations of in-situ concrete, especialy if speed and economy were to be secured, and he went on to design numerous pre-cast units that he used in conjunction with poured concrete in situ. One of these he termed *ferrocemento*. It consists of layers of fine steel mesh sprayed with cement mortar, and it can be used either for shell construction or for heavier units, with reinforcing rods inserted between the layers of mortar and mesh. With this basic system, he was able to introduce many variations as solutions to the different problems presented by each project.

Among his early spectacular works is the large Municipal Stadium at Florence for 35,000 people. (During the construction of the stadium, he realized the difficulties in creating such a structure of in-situ concrete.) The Stadium has several impressive features, among them the series of unusual spiral staircases projecting from the outer circumference of the building by means of curved, cantilevered members: they have the appearance of modern abstract sculpture. Impressive, too, is the shell canopy of the grandstand supported by a series of curved cantilevered beams.

The series of about a dozen large aircraft hangars for the Italian Air Force reveal Nervi's constant experimentation and evolution towards more efficient methods. For the earliest of these hangars, he employed in-situ concrete for the roof beams, and the method involved complicated shuttering. In the later hangars, he designed much lighter lattice pre-cast ribs for the roof, which were made in sections, assembled, jointed and held together at intervals by poured concrete ribs with forked ground supports. The arch is a low pointed Gothic, and the lattice beams make a diamond pattern, visually very attractive.

Among Nervi's finest achievements as an architect in reinforced concrete are the two immense exhibition halls in Turin, Salone B and Salon C, both very large structures erected in the incredibly short time of seven and six months. Salone B has a segmental roof span of 310 feet of corrugated section in which Nervi used his own method of pre-cast units of ferrocemento. These units have windows for roof lights, and are jointed and linked by ribs poured in situ, supported by four ribbed fans converging to the massive main supporting inclined concrete stanchions. At the end of the hall, is an apse for which he employed a different method. Here, the precast units, also made of ferro-cemento, form channels into which concrete is poured. In contrast to the perforated, corrugated main roof, the half-dome of the apse has a diamond pattern. The pattern of both roofs, although structurally determined, is highly decorative. In Salone C the diamond pattern is used, and light is admitted through a band between the triangular supports and the upper part of the roof.

Both of these methods were used in two well known later structures, the Palazzetto and the Palazzo dello Sport in Rome. Although he collaborated with two noted Italian architects—Vitellozzi in the Palazzetto and Piacentini in the Palazzo—it is clear that the essential design of the structures is Nervi's work. In the Palazzetto dello Sport, Nervi used the diamond pattern roof as in the Turin Salone C (with a similar, almost vertical band of fenestration at the lower edge of the roof), which, in this saucer dome, creates a very beautiful effect. It has been likened in effect to the fan vaulting of late Gothic. The external, sloping piers with triangular forked heads, which take the thrust of the roof ribs, provide a dramatic external effect. Here the sense of powerful structure and dramatic decorative effect are one.

In the Palazzo dello Sport, which is much larger, the corrugated form of roofing, as in the Turin Salone B, is adapted to the saucer dome with impressive effect, especially at the apex where the ribs converge to the cylindrical lantern. The thrust of the roof is taken by the mass of terraced seating, which in turn is supported by sloping piers. This construction is not, however, apparent in the general exterior view but is enclosed in a colonnade of slender members, which provides a covered passageway all around the building. Because of the colonnade, the exterior effect is not so impressive and structurally decorative as in the Palazzetto, Possibly, it was introduced by the collaborating architect.

The Unesco Headquarters in Paris is also a collaborative effort. Though different from his other work, it clearly shows Nervi's contribution in the structural design. The Y-shaped eight storey office block is supported on heavy, inclined concrete piers; adjoining it is the fan-shaped concrete conference hall of folded concrete slab construction. In this complex, Nervi permitted himself two very attractive decorative features: the generous sweep of a cantilevered shell canopy for the entrance and the external spiral stairway the whole height of the building, like a series of fans in concrete. Both have been mistaken, at first sight, for works of decorative abstract sculpture—which, of course, they are, while at the same time fulfilling a practical purpose.

Nervi belongs to that small group of structural engineers who have introduced methods that have created structures that are both spectacular and efficient. He was an engineer who was also an artist.

—Arnold Whittick

NETSCH, Walter Andrew Jr.

American. Born in Chicago, Illinois, 23 February 1920. Educated at the Massachusetts Institute of Technology, Cambridge, 1939-43, B.Arch. 1943. Served in the United States Army Corps of Engineers, 1943-46. Married Dawn Clark in 1963. Designer, for L. Morgan Yost, Kenilworth, Illinois, 1946-47. Joined Skidmore, Owings and Merrill, 1947: Designer, Chicago, 1947, Oak Ridge, Illinois, 1947-49, San Francisco, 1949-53, Tokyo, 1954, and Chicago, 1955; Partner, for Design, Chicago, 1955-72, Baltimore, 1972, and Chicago, 1972-79; retired, 1979. Has served as Member, Board of Directors, Metropolitan Housing and Planning Council of Chicago; Trustee, Museum of Contemporary Art, Chicago; Chairman, Planning Committee, American Institute of Architects, Chicago Chapter; Member, United States General Services Administration National Public Advisory Panel on Architectural Services; Chairman, Jury on Institute Honors, American Institute of Architects; and member, Advisory Council, Film Center, Art Institute of Chicago. Exhibitions: United States Air Force Academy, Colorado Springs, 1954; Miami University Art Museum, Oxford, Ohio, 1979; *Transformations in American Architecture*, Museum of Modern Art, New York, 1979; Zolla/Lieberman Gallery, Chicago, 1981. Recipient: R. S. Reynolds Award, 1964; Honor Award, and Bartlett Award, American Institute of Architects, 1978; Library Building Award, American Institute of Architects/American Library Association, 1978. D.F.A.: Lawrence University, Appleton, Wisconsin, 1968; Miami University, Oxford, Ohio, 1979. Fellow, American Institute of Architects, 1967. Address: 1700 North Hudson Street, Chicago, Illinois 60614, U.S.A.

Works:

1954   United States Naval Postgraduate School, Monterey, California

1962   Expansion plan for Northwestern University, Evanston, Illinois

1964   Chapel, United States Air Force Academy, Colorado Springs, Colorado

Publications:

By NETSCH: article—"Comprehensive Building Systems: Threat or Promise?" in *Building Research* (Washington, D.C.), September/October 1966.

On NETSCH: articles—"Northwestern University Expansion Plan" in *Progressive Architecture* (New York), August 1962; "Air Force Academy Chapel" in *Architectural Record* (New York), December 1962; "University of Illinois Campus Plan" in *Architectural Forum* (New York), May 1966; "University of Illinois" in *Architectural Forum* (New York), December 1968; "Field Theory: Forms as Process" in *Progressive Architecture* (New York), March 1969; "The Field Theory of Walter A. Netsch" in *Space Design* (Tokyo), June 1969; "The 'Visual Library' of Walter Netsch" in *Inland Architect* (Chicago), December 1970; "Field Theory" in *Bauen und Wohnen* (Zurich), October 1974; "Art Institute of Chicago" in *Architectural Review* (London), October 1977; "Netsch House" in *L'Architettura* (Rome), December 1977; "Building Types Study 537: Medical Facilities" in *Architectural Record* (New York), October 1979; "A New Museum by Walter Netsch of SOM Given Order By His Field Theory" in *Architectural Record* (New York), January 1980; "Miami University Art Museum, Oxford, Ohio" in *Deutsche Bauzeitung* (Stuttgart), August 1980; "Miami University Art Museum" in *Space Design* (Tokyo), August 1980.

With an M.I.T. background and a history of design experience, not only in the midwest but also in California and in Japan, Walter A. Netsch has made his name within the framework of Skidmore, Owings and Merrill, with whom he has been associated for more than thirty years.

Netsch is responsible for such works as the libraries of Northwestern University and the University of Chicago and the East Wing of the Art Institute of Chicago—dramatic, functional, beautiful by any standards. But perhaps the greatest interest has been in Netsch as the prime mover in "field theory." He has worked on the development of this theory since the 1960s, and in his own townhouse in Chicago he has created a kind of prototype, spaces with a variety of uses, main and subsidiary, from one basic unit. There are no corridors, and the open space dimension is carried out on the vertical as well as on the horizontal planes. The various levels spiral round a service core, engendering a diagonal more than a horizontal direction. Netsch is aware that the mode of living created by such surroundings will not suit the tastes and way of life of many people. It is not a style in which to grow old; superb agility is required to move around the different level accesses.

Netsch's aim has always been to apply the theory to larger constructions, to get away from the boredom of the square box. His first building to break away from the single rectangle was the United States Air Force Academy Chapel, and the first to actually employ the elements of field theory was the Community Social Center at Grinnell College, Iowa. But Netsch really drew attention to the theory with Chicago Circle.

Chicago Circle Campus of the University of Illinois took five years to plan and three years to build, and in 1965, with the completion of the first phase of building, the campus opened to 9,000 students. There are no residential buildings; Chicago Circle is essentially planned as an active commuter area, with a central open-air amphitheatre, relevantly an exposed gathering place, an allegory of the service core from which the life of a building generates. The Architecture and Arts Building shows strict adherence to field theory. Ground plans show the lattice work formed from the basic octagon, itself created from one rotating square placed upon another. These shapes lie beside each other, overlap, or extend, creating pinked edges instead of sharp angled corners.

Of the same period, Louis Jefferson Long Library at Wells College, Aurora, New York, is also constructed according to the principles of field theory. Space was required for a quarter million books, on open shelves, and seating for 328. Netsch's design comprises nine interlocking octagon "buds," forming an irregularly shaped perimeter, and there are magnificent wooded views from huge windows in all directions and at all angles. The odd-angled tent-like roof is supported by a series of eight interwoven beams sprouting from brick pillar bases, juxtaposing the trees, creating a link between nature and man. The two upper levels protrude at angles like giant theatre boxes, making the roof visible from all levels.

There has been considerable controversy on the advisability of the theory. The great point in its favour is, naturally, its flexibility; from the central core, "walls," in the form of library shelves, laboratory cabinets, or whatever corresponds to the function of the proposed building, create mobile boundaries. Allowances can be made for change and growth without great expense. On the other hand, perimeter walls are immense and costly.

Yet Netsch is not hardened in his principles. In the second phase at Chicago Circle he made every effort to solve the problems noted by students and faculty about the first phase. Netsch claims only that the "field theory is an ordering device, a way of looking at things." He most certainly compels us to look, and to think.

—Muriel Emanuel

Walter Netsch: Miami University Art Museum, Oxford, Ohio, 1978.

NEUTRA, Richard Josef.

American. Born in Vienna, Austria, 8 April 1892; emigrated to the United States, 1923: naturalized, 1929. Educated at the Second District Primary School, Vienna, 1898-1902; Sophiengymnasium, Vienna, 1902-10; studied architecture, under Rudolf Saliger, Karl Mayreder, and Max Fabiani, Technische Hochschule, Vienna, 1911-15 and 1917-18: Dip.Arch. 1918: influenced by Otto Wagner and Adolf Loos. Served as an Artillery Officer in the Imperial Austrian Army, in the Balkans, 1914-17. Married Dione Niedermann in 1922; children: Frank, Dion, and Raymond. Conducted seminar, with Karl Moser, at the Eidgenössische Technische Hochschule, Zürich, 1919; worked with the landscape architect Gustav Amann, Zürich, and in offices of Wernli and Staeger, Wadenswil, Switzerland, 1919-20, with Pinner and Neumann, and with Heinrich Stanner, in Berlin, 1921; City Architect, Luckenwalde, Germany, 1921; assistant architect, office of Eric Mendelsohn, *q.v.*, Berlin, 1921-23, and office of C. W. Short and Maurice Courland, New York, 1923; draughtsman, in the office of Holabird and Roche, Chicago, 1924 (met Louis Sullivan, Chicago, 1924); lived for three months with Frank Lloyd Wright, *q.v.*, Taliesin, Wisconsin, 1924; lived in the house of Rudolf Schindler, *q.v.*, Los Angeles, collaborating with him on various projects, including the League of Nations competition and the Group of Industry and Commerce projects, 1925-30; in private practice, Los Angeles, from 1925: in partnership with Robert E. Alexander, *q.v.*, Los Angeles, 1949-58, and with his son Dion in Richard and Dion Neutra and Associates, Los Angeles, 1965 until his death in 1970. Tutor, Academy of Modern Art, Los Angeles, 1928-29 (students: Harwell Harris *q.v.*, and Gregory Ain, *q.v.*). American Representative, Congrès Internationaux d'Architecture Moderne Conference, Brussels, 1929; Member, 1939-41, and Chairman, 1941-44, California State Planning Board; Member, California Board of Examiners, 1942-46; Member, Architectural Review and Advisory Panel, United States Navy, 1965; Consultant to the Austrian Government on the Building Research Organization, Vienna, 1969. Exhibitions (individual): Museo de Arte, São Paulo, 1950; University of California at Los Angeles, 1958; Kunstgewerbemuseum, Zürich, 1959; Museum of Modern Art, New York, 1982. Recipient: Honor Award, American Institute of Architects, Southern California Chapter, 1939, 1947, 1949, and 1963; Membership in Hall of Fame, World's Fair, New York, 1939; Bicentennial Silver Medallion, Columbia University, New York, 1954; *Wisdom Magazine* Award, 1957; Citation, United States Department of Commerce, 1957; Honor Prize for Architecture, City of Vienna, 1958; Gold Medal, Cuban Association of Architects, 1958; Order of Merit, Federal Republic of Germany, 1959; Wilhelm Exner Medal, Austrian Association of Crafts, 1959; Citation, United States Housing and Home Finance Agency, 1959; Arcadia Honor Award, 1959; Klimt Honor, Vereiningung Bildender Künstler, Vienna, 1961; Gold Medal, Ethiopia, 1967; Cross of the Republic of Germany, 1967; Gold Ring, City of Vienna, 1968; Gold Medal, American Institute of Architects (posthumous), 1977. Honorary doctorate: University of Graz, Austria, 1948; Technical University of Berlin, 1954; Adelphi University, Garden City, New York, 1963; University of Rome, 1965; and University of California at Los Angeles, 1969; Honorary Professor of Architecture, University of Madrid, 1969. Richard Neutra Room established at the Library of the University of California at Los Angeles, 1953. Fellow, American Institute of Architects, 1947; Member, National Institute of Arts and letters, 1964; Member, National Academy of Design, 1964. Honorary Member, American Institute of Landscape Architects, 1970. Corresponding Member, League of Philippine Architects, 1941; Honorary Member, La Sociedad de Arquitectos, Mexico, 1944; Honorary Member, Academy of Fine Arts, Brussels, 1952; Honorary Member, Royal Institute of British Architects, 1954;

Fellow, Royal Society for the Encouragement of Arts, Manufactures and Commerce, 1957; Honorary Member, Alberta Association of Architects, 1957; Corresponding Member, Accademia di San Luca, Rome, 1957; Honorary Member, Colombia Association of Architects, 1957; Honorary Member, Belgian Institute of Architects, 1958; Honorary Member, College of Academicians, Accademia di Belle Arti, Venice, 1958; Honorary Member, East African Institute of Architects, 1958; Corresponding Member, Académie d'Architecture, Paris, 1959; Honorary President, Tekhne: Office de Coopération et d'Assistance, Brussels, 1960; Honorary Member, Union of Hungarian Architects, 1963; Benjamin Franklin Fellow, Royal Society of Arts, London, 1965; Honorary Fellow, Sociedad Central de Arquitectos, Argentina, 1965; Honorary Member, Colegio de Arquitectos, Peru, 1965; Honorary President, Bund Deutscher Architekten, Germany, 1969; Honorary Member, Leonardo da Vinci Society, Italy, 1969. *Died* (in Wuppertal, West Germany), *16 April 1970.*

Works:

1915 Officers' temporary teahouse, Adriatic Coast, Serb' (now Yugoslavia)
1921 Public Housing Complex, Luckenwalde, Germany
1922 Commercial Centre, Haifa, Palestine (now Israel) (project; with Eric Mendelsohn)
1922/
  23 Housing Complex, Zehlendorf, Berlin (with Eric Mendelsohn)
1923 Library of Jewish Culture, Jerusalem (project)
1926/
  30 Rush City Reformed, Los Angeles (project)
1927 Jardinette Apartments, Los Angeles
    League of Nations Secretariat Plan (competition project; with Rudolph Schindler)
1929 Lovell House (Health House), Los Angeles
1933 Van Der Leeuw Research House (Neutra House), Silverlake, Los Angeles (destroyed by fire, 1963; rebuilt by Neutra, with his son Dion, 1964)
1935 Beard House, Altadena, California
    Corona Avenue School, Bell, Los Angeles
1936 Plywood Model House, Los Angeles
    Von Sternberg House (Ayn Rand House), San Fernando Valley, Los Angeles (demolished)
    Kraigher House, Downsville, Texas
    Catalina Ticket Office, Los Angeles
    Scholts Advertising Agency, Los Angeles
    California Military Academy, Los Angeles
1937 Beckstrand House, Palos Verdes, California
1938 Strathmore Apartments, Westwood, Los Angeles
    Emerson Junior High School, Westwood, Los Angeles
    Albert Lewin House, Santa Monica Beach, California
    William and Ilse Schiff Rowhouse, San Francisco
    John Nicholas Brown Vacation House, Fishers Island, New York (destroyed by Fire, 1975)
1939 National Youth Administration Centers, Sacramento and San Luis Obispo, California
    Amity Village, Compton, California
    McIntosh House, Los Angeles
    Davey House, Carmel, California
    Sciobereti House, Berkeley, California
    Eurich House, Los Altos Hills, California
1940 Kahn House, San Francisco
    Evans Plywood Company Building, Lebanon, Oregon
1941 Avion Village, Texas
    Maxwell House, Brentwood, Los Angeles
1942 Nesbitt House, Brentwood, Los Angeles
    Channel Heights, San Pedro, California
    Kelton Apartments, Westwood, Los Angeles

1944 Rural school buildings, Puerto Rico
    Health centers, Puerto Rico (projects)
1946 Kaufmann House (Desert House), Palm Springs, California
1947 Norwalk Service Station, Bakersfield, California
    Bailey Case Study House, Santa Monica Canyon, Los Angeles
1948 Tremaine House, Santa Barbara, California
    Aloe Medical Supply Building, Los Angeles
    Holiday house, Malibu, California
1950 Urban redevelopment plan for Sacramento, California (project; with Robert E. Alexander)
1950/
  53 Redevelopment plan for Elysian Heights, Los Angeles (project; with Robert E. Alexander)
    Eagle Rock Playground Club House, Los Angeles
1951 Hinds House, Los Angeles
    Northwestern Mutual Fire Insurance Building, Los Angeles
1952 Moore House, Ojai, California
1952/
  54 Territorial plan, Governor's Residence, and three schools, Guam (with Robert E. Alexander)
1953 Kester Avenue Elementary School, Los Angeles
    Community Hotel, San Pedro, California (with Robert E. Alexander)
1954 Child guidance clinic, Los Angeles (with Robert E. Alexander)
    Business Education Building, Orange Coast College, Costa Mesa, California (with Robert E. Alexander)
    Hacienda Motor Hotel, San Pedro, California
    Family Housing, Mountain Home, Idaho (with Robert E. Alexander)
1955 Medical Center, San Bernardino, California
    Mellon Science Building and Francis Scott Key Auditorium, St. John's College, Annapolis, Maryland (with Robert E. Alexander)
    Perkins House, Pasadena, California
1956 Gemological Institute of America Building, Brentwood, Los Angeles
    Amalgamated Clothing Workers Building, Los Angeles
    Chuey house, Los Angeles
    National Charity League Headquarters, Los Angeles (with Robert E. Alexander)
1957 Science Building, Arts and Music Auditorium, and Sports Facilities, Orange Coast College, Costa Mesa, California (with Robert E. Alexander)
    Miramar Chapel, La Jolla, California (with Robert E. Alexander)
    Alamitos Intermediate School, Garden Grove, California (with Robert E. Alexander)
    Nash House, Camarillo, California
    Ferro Chemical Company Office Building, Cleveland, Ohio (with Robert E. Alexander)
1958 Riviera Methodist Church, Redondo Beach, California (with Robert E. Alexander)
    Elementary Training School, University of California at Los Angeles (with Robert E. Alexander)
    Fine Arts Building, University of Nevada, Reno (with Robert E. Alexander)
    Palos Verdes High School, California (with Robert E. Alexander)
    Fine Arts Center, California State University, San Fernando (with Robert E. Alexander)
    Visitors' Center, Gettysburg, Pennsylvania (with Robert E. Alexander)
    Visitors' Center, Petrified Forest, Arizona (with Robert E. Alexander)
1959 Theatre, Düsseldorf (competition project)
    Museum of Natural History and Planetarium, Dayton, Ohio (with Robert E. Alexander)
1960 Singleton House, Los Angeles

Megastructure, Caracas, Venezuela (project; with Robert E. Alexander)

1962 Community Church, Garden Grove, California

1963 Swirlbul Library, Adelphi University, Garden City, Long Island, New York (with Robert E. Alexander)

United States Embassy, Karachi, Pakistan (with Robert E. Alexander)

Mariners' Medical Arts Center, Newport Beach, California

Lincoln Memorial Museum, Gettysburg, Pennsylvania (with Robert E. Alexander)

1964 Hall of Records, Los Angeles (with Robert E. Alexander)

Richard J. Neutra Elementary School, Lemoore, California (with Robert E. Alexander)

1965 Friedland House, Philadelphia

1966 Bucerius House, Navegna, Switzerland

Bewobau Housing Colony, Quickborn, near Hamburg, West Germany

Bewobau Housing Colony, Waldorf, near Frankfurt

Grelling House, Ascona, Switzerland

1967 Tower of Hope, Garden Grove Church, California (with Dion Neutra)

Rang House, Koenigstein, West Germany

Kemper House, Wuppertal, West Germany

Reutsch House, Wengen, Switzerland

1968 Pescher House, Wuppertal, West Germany

Delcourt House, Croix, France

1969 Orange County Courthouse, Santa Ana, California (with Ramberg and Lowrie)

Publications:

By NEUTRA: books—*Wie baut Amerika,* Stuttgart 1926, English edition, edited by Thomas Hines, Los Angeles 1979; *Amerika* (Neues Bauen in der Welt series), Vienna 1930, English edition, edited by Thomas Hines, Los Angeles 1979; *National Planning Methods of Mass Housing,* with the editors of the International Congress for New Building, London 1930; *House and Home,* with others, New York 1935; *Circle: Routes of Housing Advance,* with others, London 1938; *Preface to a Master Plan,* with others, Los Angeles 1942; *New Architecture and City Planning,* with Paul Zucker, New York 1945; *Architecture of Social Concern in Regions of Mild Climate,* São Paulo 1948; *Mysteries and Realities of the Site,* Scarsdale, New York 1951; *Survival Through Design,* New York and London 1954, Hamburg, Milan and Mexico City 1955; *Life and Human Habitat,* Stuttgart 1956; *Realismo biologico renacimiento humanistico en arquitectura,* Buenos Aires 1958, 1974; *Life and Shape* (autobiography), New York and Hamburg, West Germany 1962, Buenos Aires 1973; *World and Dwelling,* Stuttgart 1962, Barcelona 1963; *Building with Nature,* Stuttgart and Barcelona 1970, New York 1971; *Bauen und die Sinneswelt,* Dresden, East Germany 1977; articles—"Terminals-Transfers" in *Architectural Record* (New York), August 1930; "Gegenwärtige Bauarbeit in Japan" in *Die Form* (Berlin), January 1931; "Japanische Wohnung, Ableitung, Schwierigkeiten" in *Die Form* (Berlin), March 1931; "Umbildung chinesischer Städte" in *Die Form* (Berlin), January 1932; "Die industriell hergestellte Wohnung in USA Typungsschwierigkeiten" in *Die Form* (Berlin), March 1932; "New Elementary Schools for America" in *Architectural Forum* (New York), January 1935; "School in the Making" in *Nation's Schools* (Chicago), November 1937; Regionalism in Architecture" in *Architectural Forum* (New York), February 1939; "Research on Design of Dwelling-Units with Regard to Regional Differentiation" in *South African Architectural Record* (Johannesburg), February 1940; "Governmental Architecture in California" in *Arts and Architecture* (Los Angeles), August 1941; "Index of Liveability" in *Sunset* (Menlo Park, California), November 1943; "Class-rooms and Livingrooms" in *New Architecture and City Planning* by Paul Zucker, New York 1944; "Sea-land-transfer" in *Architectural Record* (New York), September 1946; "Human Setting in an Industrial Civilization" in *Zodiac* (Milan), no. 2, 1957; "Experience of the Theatre: Its Physiology" in *Arts and Architecture* (Los Angeles), May 1960.

On NEUTRA: books—*Organische Baukunst* by Hans Bernhard Reichow, Braunschweig, West Germany and Berlin 1949; *Richard Neutra,* exhibition catalogue, São Paulo, Brazil 1950; *Richard Neutra: Buildings and Projects,* edited by Willy Boesiger, vol. I, 1923-50, Zürich 1951, London 1965, vol. II, 1950-60, Zürich 1959, London 1965, vol. III, 1961-66, Zürich, London and New York 1966; *Richard Neutra* by Bruno Zevi, Milan 1954; *Richard Neutra: Is Planning Possible?* by Frederick Wright, Los Angeles 1958; *Richard Neutra* by Esther McCoy, New York 1960, London 1961; *Richard Neutra* (Contemporary Architects series), Tokyo 1969; *Richard Neutra* by Maté Pal, Budapest 1970; *Richard Neutra* by Rupert Spade, New York and London 1971; *Richard and Dion Neutra: Pflanzen, Wasser, Steine, Licht,* edited by H. Exner, D. Neutra, and H. Hamerbacher, Berlin and Hamburg, West Germany 1974; *Vienna to Los Angeles: 2 Journeys—Richard Neutra and Rudolph M. Schindler,* edited by Esther McCoy, Santa Monica, California 1979; *Richard Neutra and the Search for Modern Architecture* by Thomas Hines, New York and Oxford, England 1982; *The Architectue of Richard Neutra: From International Style to California Modern,* exhibition catalogue, by Arthur Drexler and Thomas S. Hines, New York 1982; articles—special issue of *L'Architecture d'aujourd'hui* (Paris), June 1948; cover story in *Time* (New York), 15 August 1949; special issue of *Baukunst und Werkform* (Darmstadt, West Germany), June 1955; special issue of *Espacio* (Havana), July 1955; special issue of *Canadian Architect* (Toronto), November/December 1957; special issue of *Vitrum* (Milan), May/June 1962; "Neutra est arrive" in *Réalites* (Paris), March 1965; special issue of *Arquitectura* (Madrid), September 1965; special issue of *DLW-Nachrichten* (Bietigheim/Wuertt, Germany), no. 75, 1967; special issue of *Kindai Kenchiku* (Tokyo), February 1968; special issue of *Home Magazine* (Los Angeles), February 1968; special obituary issue of *L'Architettura* (Rome), November 1970; "Designing for the Motor Age—Richard Neutra and the Automobile" by Thomas S. Hines in *Oppositions* (New York), Summer 1981; "Neutra Reappraised" by David Burney in *Architects' Journal* (London), 6 October 1982; film—*The Ideas of Richard Neutra,* Vienna 1968.

Bibliographies—*Richard J. Neutra and the Blending of House and Nature in American Architecture: A Selected Bibliography* by Robert B. Harmon, Monticello, Illinois 1980; *Richard Joseph Neutra: A Select Bibliography* by Lamia Doumato, Monticello, Illinois 1980.

*

Richard J. Neutra is a seminal figure in twentieth-century American architecture. His roots are wide and his influences strong. His work bears the unmistakable identity of its author, yet each project is uniquely appropriate.

He was born in the Vienna of the Hapsburgs in 1892, and the plan and imperious architecture of that city left a sense of opulence and elegance that was to emerge in his mature work, but in entirely new forms. His is a richness not normally found in the architecture of the first half of this century. That amplitude and complexity, never contrived, extended to his manipulation of space, internal and external.

The Vienna of his childhood and student days was a city rich in artistic and intellectual cross-currents. Among those architects whose work impressed him were Otto Wagner and Adolph Loos, whose dictum against ornament directed Neutra away from traditional forms. He graduated from the Vienna Technische Hochschule after serving in the Austrian Army in World War I. He left Austria in 1919 to work in Switzerland and them moved to Germany. In 1921 he joined Erich Mendelsohn to work on the Berliner Tageblatt building remodelling and the landmark Zehlendorf Housing Group. Believing that the future of modern architecture lay in America, he emigrated in 1923, worked in the east, and then in Chicago for the firm of Holabird and Roche. There, he met Louis Sullivan in that master's final days. At Sullivan's funeral in 1924, he met Frank Lloyd Wright and subsequently spent some time with Wright at Taliesen East. Most of Wright's work at that time was in Los Angeles, and Neutra decided to go there. Rudolph Schindler, a friend of student days, was also working in Los Angeles, and Neutra was to collaborate with Schindler on several projects.

In southern California, Neutra developed an especially appropriate regional architecture, adding a new dimension and direction to the several regional design systems in that area. His motifs, based on simple post-and-beam construction, were decidedly modern, and he avoided his predecessors' dependence on Mexican references. In residential architecture, with its range of design demands, his design philosophy came into its full range of effects and expressions. A particular hallmark of his work was the relationship between interior and exterior spaces; This he achieved with the use of large areas of glass and interpenetrations of interior and exterior space. He also employed rich landscaping to affirm his buildings' relationship to their climates and sites and to enrich his designs texturally.

Neutra was a great draftsman. His skill is seen in his rendering and plans, as also in his travel sketches, done in telling and rapid pastels. The originality of his creative mind is epitomized in the following episode: He was once given a psychological test. Asked where he would add an additional right arm to a perfectly formed human body, his reply startled his interrogators. "The human body is the result of millions of years of evolution. I would not do anything to change it. I reject the question!"

Neutra was a man of great physical stature. He was commanding in appearance and in word, and not a little arrogant. That may have accounted for the lack of major commissions which might otherwise have come to a man of such talent. But his work was popular—due, in part, to skilful architectural photography, namely that of Julius Shulman. That is not to demean the work but to recognize a then growing method of communicating architectural concepts and achievements.

Neutra's influence spawned a branch of southern California architecture—open, straightforward, assertive, unafraid of adjustment to site shape, and often possessing elements of formalistic flair, even bordering on playfulness. Among his more distinguished disciples are Robert E. Alexander, Gregory Ain, and Harwell Hamilton Harris, and the work of the large California firm Welton Beckett and Associates bears a considerable Neutra influence.

—Paul Spreiregen

NIEMEYER, Oscar.

Brazilian. Born in Rio de Janeiro, 15 December 1907. Educated at the Escola Nacional de Belas Artes, Rio de Janeiro, 1930-34, Dip. Arch. 1934. Married Annita Baldo in 1929; daugher: Anna Maria. Worked in the architectural studio of Lúcio Costa and Carlos Leão, Rio de Janeiro, 1935, and the studio of Le Corbusier, Paris, 1936; Architect, Departmento de Patrimonio Historico e Artistico Nacional, Rio de Janeiro, 1936-37; in private practice, Rio de Janeiro, 1937-56; Chief Architect,

NOVACAP (Government Building Authority), Brasilia, 1956-61 (architectural adviser since 1961); returned to private practice, Rio de Janeiro, 1961. Lecturer, School of Architecture, Federal University of Rio de Janeiro, since 1968. Founder Editor, *Modulo,* Rio de Janeiro, 1955. Exhibitions: *Oscar Niemeyer,* Musée des Arts Décoratifs, Paris, 1965; *Oscar Niemeyer,* Centre Georges Pompidou, Paris, 1979. Recipient: Honorary Citizen Award, New York, 1936; First Prize, National Athletic Center Competition, Rio de Janeiro, 1941; First Prize, Aeronautical Training Center Competition, Sao Jose dos Campos, Sao Paulo, 1947; Prix Joliot-Curie, Paris, 1956; Work Medal, Brazil, 1959; Lenin Award of the U.S.S.R., 1963; Benito Juarez Award, *Mexican Revolution Centennial,* Mexico City, 1964; Medal of the Polish Architectural Association, 1967; *L'Architecture d'Aujourd'hui* Award, 1968; Gold Medal, American Institute of Architects, 1970; Gold Medal, Académie d'Architecture, Paris, 1982. Honorary Member, American Academy of Arts and Sciences, 1949; Officer, Legion d'Honneur, France, 1980; Commander, Ordre des Arts et Lettres, France, 1982; Honorary Member, Academy of Arts of the U.S.S.R., 1983; Member, European Academy of Arts, Sciences and Humanities, 1983; Member, Comitato Internazionale dei Garanti, 1983. Address (office): Avenida Atlantica 3940, Cobertura, Copacabana, Rio de Janeiro, Brazil.

Works:

1936 Henrique Xavier House, Rio de Janeiro (project)
1937 Obra do Berco Nursery and Maternity Clinic, Rio de Janeiro
1937/
43 Ministry of Education and Health, Rio de Janeiro (with Le Corbusier, Lúcio Costa, Jorge Machado Moreira, and Affonso Eduardo Reidy; now the Palace of Culture)
1938 Oswald de Andrade House, Sao Paulo
Grande Hotel, Ouro Preto, Minas Gerais, Brazil
1939 Brazilian Pavilion, *World's Fair,* New York (with Le Corbusier)
1940 Design of the *Brazilian Industrial Exhibition,* Buenos Aires
1941 National Stadium, Rio de Janeiro
Water Tower, Rio de Janeiro
1942 Pampulha Development, with the Church of St. Francis of Assisi, Yacht Club, and Restaurant, Minas Gerais, Brazil
Oscar Niemeyer House, Gavea, Rio de Janeiro
1943 Kubitschek House, Pampulha, Minas Gerais, Brazil
Ofair House, Rio de Janeiro
1944 Prudente de Morais Neto House, Rio de Janeiro
Recreation Center, Rodrigos de Freitas Lagoon, Rio de Janeiro
1945 Yacht Club, Rio de Janeiro
1946 Boavista Bank, Rio de Janeiro
1947 Burton Tremaine House, Santa Barbara, California
1947/
52 United Nations Building, New York (with international team of architects, including Le Corbusier and Sven Markelius— Wallace K. Harrison, Chairman)
1948 Auditorium, Rio de Janeiro
1949 Mendes Country House, Rio de Janeiro
Gavea Hotel, Rio de Janeiro
House, Carvalho de Azevedo Street, Rio de Janeiro
O Cruzeiro Headquarters, Rio de Janeiro (project)
1950 Duchen Biscuit Factory, Sao Paulo
Libanais Club, Belo Horizonte, Brazil
Montreal Office Building, Sao Paulo
Quitandinha Hotel, Petropolis, Rio de Janeiro
House, Gavea, Rio de Janeiro

COPAN Office Building, Sao Paulo
Carlos de Britto Food Factory, Sao Paulo (project)
Julia Kubitschek Elementary School, Diamantina, Brazil
1951 Kubitschek Building Complex, Belo Horizonte, Brazil
Diamantina Hotel, Minas Gerais, Brazil
Ibirapuera Buildings, *IV Centennial Exhibition,* Sao Paulo (with Helio Uchoa, Zenon Lotufo, Eduardo Kneese de Mello, Gauss Estelita, and Carlos Lemos)
1952 Sul American Hospital, Rio de Janeiro
Miranda House, Gavea, Rio de Janeiro
1953 Aeronautical Training Center, Sao Jose dos Campos, Sao Paulo
Mineiro da Praducao Bank Headquarters, Belo Horizonte, Brazil
Oscar Niemeyer House, Canoas, Rio de Janeiro
1954 Apartment building, Belo Horizonte, Brazil
Cavanelas House, Pedro do Rio, Rio de Janeiro
1955 Museum of Modern Art, Caracas
Secondary school, Belo Horizonte, Brazil
Apartment building, Berlin
Public Library, Belo Horizonte, Brazil (project)
Getulio Vargas Foundation Headquarters, Rio de Janeiro
1957 Alvorada Palace (President's Residence), Brasilia
Brasilia Palace Hotel
1958 Supreme Court, Brasilia
Presidential Chapel, Brasilia
Planalto Palace (Presidential Offices), Brasilia
Three Powers Square, Brasilia
Congress Buildings, Brasilia
Brazilian Foundation Museum, Brasilia
Chapel of Our Lady of Fatima, Brasilia
National Theatre, Brasilia
1960 Main Square, University of Brasilia
Sciences Faculty, University of Brasilia
CEPLAN, University of Brasilia
National Steel Company Building, Brasilia
Dominican Theological Institute, Brasilia
1961 Stadium, Brasilia
1962 Arches Palace (Foreign Office), Brasilia
New Yacht Club, Pampulha, Minas Gerais, Brazil
Design of the *International Fair,* Tripoli
1963 Ministry of Justice, Brasilia
1964 Nordia Building Complex, Haifa, Israel (project)
Panorama Building Complex, Haifa, Israel (project)
University of Haifa, Israel
City in the Negev Desert, Israel (project)
1965 Rothschild House, Israel (project)
Redevelopment plan for the Algarve, Portugal
Brasilia Airport
Brazzaville Palace, Congo (project)
1966 Hotel, Madeira
French Communist Party Headquarters, Paris (with Jean de Roche and Chemetof)
Bloch Building, Rio de Janeiro
Redevelopment plan for Grasse, France (with Marc Emery)
1967 Dominican Convent, Saint Baume, France
1968 Mosque, Algiers
Redevelopment plan for Algiers
Civic Center, Algiers
Vertical Palace, Belo Horizonte, Brazil
Satetyles (Telecommunications Complex), Rio de Janeiro
Mondadori Building, Milan (with Luciano Pozzo)
Cuiaba University, Mato Grosso, Brazil
Ministry of Defense, Brasilia
1969 Constantine University, Algeria
Renault Office Building, Paris
1970 Hotel Nacional Rio, Rio de Janeiro
Brazilian Architects Institute, Brasilia
Stadium, Brasilia (project)

Cathedral, Brasilia
1971 Sciences and Technology Faculty, University of Algeria, Algiers
Human Sciences Faculty, University of Algeria, Algiers
1972 Moura Lacerda University, Ribeirao Preto, Sao Paulo
Denasa and Oscar Niemeyer Office Building, Brasilia
Frederico Gomes House, Rio de Janeiro
Bobigny Office Building, Paris
Cultural Center, Le Havre, France
Redevelopment plan for Dieppe, France (with Marc Emery)
Trade Center, Miami, Florida (project)
1973 Tour de la Défense (office building), Paris
Residence Hall, Oxford (project)
Music Center, Rio de Janeiro
Central Railway Station, Brasilia
1974 Foreign Office, Algiers
Safra Bank, Sao Paulo
Vice-President's Residence, Brasilia
Rio Towers, Rio de Janeiro
Telebras Office Building, Brasilia (with Carlos Magalhaes)
Josephine Jordan House, Rio de Janeiro
1975 Foreign Office Building II, Brasilia
1976 National Party Headquarters, Algiers
Mirza House, Rio de Janeiro
1977 Barra da Tijuca Redevelopment, Rio de Janeiro (with Marc Emery)
FATA Building, Turin (with Riccardo Morandi)
Bus Terminal, Londrina, Parana, Brazil
1978 Convention Center, Foz do Iguacu, Brazil
Theatre, Vicenza, Italy (with Frederico Motterle)
Anthropological Museum, Belo Horizonte, Brazil
Deputies Office Building, Brasilia
1979 Zoological Gardens, Algiers
Embratur Office Building, Brasilia
CESP Office Building, Sao Paulo
Business Quarter, Algiers
City Center Redevelopment, Barra, Rio de Janeiro
1980 Administrative Center, Pernambuco, Brazil (project)
Alcanorte Headquarters, Brazil (project)
1982 Convention Center, Abu Dhabi, United Arab Emirates (projects)
1983 Teotônio Vilela Memorial, Brazil
Samba Stadium, Brazil
1984 Cabanagem Monument, Brazil
Sixty Schools, State of Rio de Janeiro
Exhibition Center, Brazil (project)

Publications:

By NIEMEYER: books—*Mina Experiencia em Brasilia,* Rio de Janeiro 1961, Paris and Moscow 1963; *Textes et Dessins pour Brasilia,* Paris 1965; *Viagens: Quase Memorias,* Rio de Janeiro 1966; *Oscar Niemeyer,* Milan 1977; *A Forma na Arquitetura,* Rio de Janeiro and Milan 1978, Paris 1979; *Rio - de Província a Metrópole,* Rio de Janeiro 1980; articles—"Ce qui manque à notre Architecture" in *Le Corbusier: Oeuvres Completes,* edited by W. Boesiger, Zurich 1938; "Témoignages" in *L'Architecture d'Aujourd'hui* (Paris), October/November 1958; numerous articles in *Modulo* (Rio de Janeiro); recording—*Concrete Expression,* tape cassette and slides, London 1981.

On NIEMEYER: books—*The Work of Oscar Niemeyer* by Stamo Papadaki, New York and Tokyo 1950; *Modern Architecture in Brazil* by Henrique Mindlin, New York 1956; *Oscar Niemeyer: Works in Progress* by Stamo Papadaki, New York 1956; *Oscar Niemeyer* by Stamo Papadaki, New York and Ravensburg, Germany 1960; *Oscar Niemeyer* by

Oscar Niemeyer: Ministry of Defence, Brasilia, 1968.

Rupert Spade, London 1971; *Oscar Niemeyer* by Nelson Werncek Sodre, Rio de Janeiro 1978; *Architektur im Umbruch* by Jürgen Joedicke, Stuttgart 1979; *Oscar Niemeyer: Selbstdarstellung, Kritiken, Oeuvre,* edited by Alexander Fils, West Berlin 1982; articles—special issue of *Architectural Review* (London), March 1944; special issue of *Progressive Architecture* (New York), April 1947; special issue of *L'Architecture d'Aujourd'hui* (Paris), September 1947; special issue of *Architectural Forum* (New York), November 1947; special issue of *Architectural Review* (London), October 1950; "The Works of Oscar Niemeyer" in *L'Architecture d'Aujourd'hui* (Paris), August 1952; special issue of *L'Architecture d'Aujourd'hui* (Paris), October 1952; special issue of *Architectural Review* (London), October 1954; special issue of *L'Architecture d'Aujourd'hui* (Paris), October/November 1958; "Brasilia," special issue of *Acropole* (Sao Paulo), July/August 1970; special issue of *L'Architecture d'Aujourd'hui* (Paris), January/February 1974; "The Paradoxes of Oscar Niemeyer" by Bernard Huet in *L'Architecture d'Aujourd'hui* (Paris), March/April 1976; "Niemeyer in Turin" by Massimo Gennari in *Domus* (Milan), May 1977; "Niemeyer's One-Man Paris Show" by Odile Fillion in *Building Design* (London), 2 March 1979; "Introduction to Niemeyer" in *Summa* (Buenos Aires), October 1979; "Oscar Niemeyer", special issue of *Modulo* (Rio de Janeiro), 1980; "Department of Employment Offices in Bobigny" in *Construction Moderne* (Paris), Spring 1980; "Cultural Scientific Institute, Brasilia" in *AC: International Asbestos Cement Review* (Zurich), April 1980; "Completion of the Communist Party Headquarters in Paris" in *L'Architecture d'Aujourd'hui* (Paris), September 1980; "Flying Arches" in *Domus* (Milan), December 1980; "Oscar Niemeyer" in *Construction Moderne* (Paris), June 1982; "Maison de la Culture in Le Havre" in *L'Architecture d'Aujourd'hui* (Paris), September 1983; "Cultural Life in Le Havre" in *Construction Moderne* (Paris), December 1983; "Maison de la Culture du Havre" in *Mur Vivant* (Paris), no. 70, 1983.

When a form creates beauty it becomes functional and therefore fundamental in architecture.

The straight line, hard, inflexible, created by man, does not attract me. What does draw me is the free and sensual curve. The curve that I find in the mountains of my country, in the sinuousness of her rivers, in the clouds of the sky and the waves of the sea. The whole universe is made of the curve, the curved universe of Einstein.

—Oscar Niemeyer

Walter Gropius, discussing the work of Oscar Niemeyer with a group of his students at Harvard in the 1940s, referred to him as the *Paradiesvogel* (bird of paradise) of the architectural world. His work has always provoked very divergent responses—sometimes admiration, sometimes disparagement. Even today, it continues to be controversial.

The modern architecture of Europe, born in the depressed economy of the years following World War I, had necessarily a minimal standard morality or ethic as its basis. Exuberant, flamboyant images were never part of the modernist credo, and it took many years and divers influences before any visual richness began to be considered, much less explored. Even then, the suggestion was of forbidden fruit, an interest that needed constant justification. Although the influence of Le Corbusier has always been stressed in describing Niemeyer (and the description is apt, especially of the early work), the comparison is unnecessary for most of his buildings. Niemeyer's

creative genius is born of, and is a uniquely integral part of, the spirit and imagery of Brazil. One need only consider the almost unreal drama of those giant sugar loaf granite mountains right in the middle of Rio de Janeiro to recognize some of the profiles of Niemeyer's seemingly equally unreal building ideas.

Niemeyer has always accompanied the presentation of his designs with the most telling of thumbnail sketches. They contain the very essence of his design methodology. In a disarming way, they proceed along a logical path, outlining a process of elimination. First they suggest, then they are crossed out because of rational unsuitability, then they take a more logical direction—then take a leap and present an utterly disarming, simple, direct and yet visually poetic solution. To many architects who proceed in design with all kinds of hangups, who shackle their creative senses, these sketches often appear too simple, too easy—almost child-like and impossible—and they would be if it were not for the fact that on the next pages there invariably appears, quite miraculously and impeccably, the end result, an elegantly finished building, not deviating in the slightest from the essence contained in the seminal early sketches.

During some months in 1948 I briefly worked with Niemeyer and observed him at his work. In contrast to my experience of European/American procedure, he worked as I would imagine a painter or sculptor works. Sketches—intuitive gestures—ideas presented in a way to make the rationalist-oriented designer cringe. But my suspicions soon melted away when I subsequently realized how fundamentally unassailable were the inherent logic, the clarity, the structural and constructional plausibility of his work. This is not simply a personal perception; the results bear out the generalizations. Consider how many of his stunning concepts—Brasilia, huge universities in different parts of the world, museums, vast housing and office complexes—have in fact become reality. In our world, distrustful of artistic gestures, none of these projects would have been executed if they were not, however flamboyant the concepts, essentially of rationalist substance.

Niemeyer is an unassuming and humble man. While I worked for him he tried to discourage me from a long journey to Belo Horizonte just to see his buildings placed around a lake at Pampulha. "They are badly maintained, they are going to change the casino into a radio station... don't go." But I did—and seeing those structures under the brilliant tropical sky remains one of the memorable impressions of my career! They were certainly powerful enough to visually overcome disarranged interiors and dirty windows—more than one can say about most other modern architecture.

The deep humility and social consciousness of Niemeyer at first seem as unbelievable as his architectural visions. He accepted no fees for his first job, a nursery in Rio, and when the *brise-soleils* would not work, he paid for new ones out of his own pocket. For the design of his master work, Brasilia, he refused any fees other than his humble civil servant's salary. The evidence bears him out when he says, "I should be ashamed to be rich." When accepting the Lenin Prize at Brasilia, he spoke only of the need for government action to ease the miserable conditions of the workers who had built the city. He did not bask in the praise for his own work, but pointed out the social discrimination threatened by an imminent change to Lúcio Costa's plan for the city.

With all its looming social problems, there must indeed be hope for the future of Brazil—when the country has poets of the visual world with the humility of an Oscar Niemeyer.

—Harry Seidler

NOWICKI, Matthew.

Polish. Born Maciej Nowicki in Chita, Russia, of Polish parents, 26 June 1910; travelled extensively as a child and lived for some years in Chicago. Educated at the Art Institute of Chicago, 1921; School of Design, Gerson, Warsaw, 1925; Warsaw Polytechnic, 1929-36, M.Arch. 1936. Served as a Lieutenant in the Polish Army Artillery, 1939; participated in the Warsaw Insurrection, Home Army, 1944. Married Stanislawa Sandecka in 1935; had one son. In private practice, Warsaw, 1936-39; Assistant to Professor Swierczynski, Institute of Public Buildings, Warsaw, 1937-39; taught underground classes in architecture and town planning during the Nazi occupation, Warsaw 1939-45; Leader, Architectural Discussion Studio and Workshop, Warsaw, 1945; Design Chief, Capital Rebuilding Bureau (BOS), Warsaw, 1945-46; Cultural Attaché, Polish Consulate, Chicago, 1946; Polish Representative, United Nations Site and Building Committee, New York, 1946-47; Visiting Critic, Pratt Institute, Brooklyn, New York, 1947-48; Senior Professor of Architecture and Acting Head of the School of Design, North Carolina State College, Raleigh, 1948-51; employed by the architectural firm of Mayer and Whittlessey, New York, to begin firm's study for Chandigarh, the new capital city of the Punjab, India, 1949 until his death, 1951. Exhibition: Museum of Modern Art, New York, 1950. *Died* (in an airplane crash, in the Nile delta) *31 August 1951.*

Works:

1936/
37 National Bank Building, Warsaw (project)
   Ministry of Communications Building, Warsaw (project)
   Ministry of Work and Social Security Building, Warsaw (project)
   City redevelopment plan for Warsaw
1938 Local Government Building, Lodz, Poland
   Health Center, Druskienniki, Poland
   Tourist hotel, Augustow, Poland
   Sports and recreation center, ul. Podskarbinska, Warsaw
1939 Polish Pavilion, World's Fair, New York
1939/
45 Post-war city development plan for Warsaw
1943 Fregata Cafe interiors, Warsaw (with S. Sandecka)
   Latona Cafe interiors, Warsaw (with S. Sandecka)
1944/
45 Development plan for the city center of Warsaw
1944/
48 Chapel and Residence Hall, Center for the Blind, Laski, near Warsaw
1948/
53 Dorton Arena, *North Carolina State Fair*, Raleigh (project: with William Henry Dietrick)
1949 Buildings for Brandeis University, Waltham, Massachusetts (project; with Eero Saarinen)
1949/
51 State Library and Museum, Raleigh, North Carolina (project; with William Henry Dietrick)
   Preliminary studies for Chandigarh New Capital City, Punjab, India (for Mayer and Whittlessey)
1950 Circular Shopping Center, Columbus Circle, New York (project; with Clarence Stein)

Publications:

By NOWICKI: book—*The Writings and Sketches of Matthew Nowicki*, compiled by Bruce Harold Schafer, Charlottesville, Virginia 1973.

On NOWICKI: book—*Geschichte der Modernen Architektur* by Jürgen Joedicke, Stuttgart 1958; *Roots of Contemporary American Architecture*, edited by Lewis Mumford, New York 1959; *Polish Avant-Garde Architecture, 1918-1939* by Izabella Wislocka, Warsaw 1970; *Maciej Nowicki* by Tadeusz Barucki, Warsaw 1980; articles—"Matthew Nowicki" in *Architectural Forum* (New York), October 1950; "Matthew Nowicki," special issue of the *North Carolina State College School of Design Student Publication* (Raleigh), Winter 1951; "The Life, Teaching and the Architecture of Matthew Nowicki" by Lewis Mumford in *Architectural Record* (New York), June/August 1954; "Matthew Nowicki 1910-1951" by J. Hryniewiecki in *Projekt* (Warsaw), no. 1, 1957; "Matthew Nowicki" in *L'Architecture d'Aujourdhui* (Paris), September 1957; "The Writings and Sketches of Matthew Nowicki" by Bruce H. Schafer in *AIA Journal* (Washington, D.C.), July 1974; "A Radical settles down in Raleigh, North Carolina" by Ernest Wood in *AIA Journal* (Washington, D.C.), September 1980.

Matthew Nowicki was one of the most creative architects of his generation. But for his untimely death in 1951, he could well have found his place among the top few architects of the twentieth century. At the time of his death he was on the verge of realizing some of his most important projects, including a new city of Chandigarh in India, the planning of which was later completed by Le Corbusier. Although Le Corbusier's Chandigarh plans are well documented, there is little record of Nowicki's concept of super blocks and sketches for a whole range of civic and residential buildings. What sketches do exist, however, admirably show how Nowicki sympathetically and sensitively married the European design approach to local Indian materials, arts and building crafts. They show his love of drawing, which enabled him to express his ideas in three dimension rather than through plans in elevations.

Nowicki's early Polish training in engineering found a new scope in the United States where he was able to extend his mastery of somewhat repetitive post and beam construction to more daring and innovative structures. His sketches and projects, such as the Dorton Arena for the *North Carolina State Fair* and the State Library and Museum in Raleigh, are eloquent testimony to his creative abilities. His Arena is enclosed in two parabolic concrete arches that interest each other close to the ground and support the roof and frame the grandstands. His other designs include a circular shopping centre in Columbus Circle, New York, set above traffic at a busy intersection.

A less happy phase of Nowicki's work was his one time concern with the application of module to building, which he considered as a panacea for all architectural problems. This invariably produced monotony and occasionally forced solutions that were inappropriate to specific programmes.

As a teacher Nowicki is well remembered for his brief stint as a senior Professor of Architecture at North Carolina State College in Raleigh, where he was able to introduce important changes in a new curriculum. It united architecture, landscape architecture and city planning into a "single frame for the changing picture of the life of man," as he put it. His programme had four streams: design, structure, descriptive drawing and humanities. In many ways it was the forerunner of courses that schools of architecture later adopted during the 1960's and 70's. However, owing to the difficulties of implementation inherent in the bureaucratic environment of American tertiary institutions, many of his ideas were diluted.

Matthew Nowicki was far ahead of his time. he will be remembered for being one of the few architects who was able to get away from the then well accepted functional and somewhat stark approach of the modern movement and strive towards understanding and expression of a more humane architecture, softened by the local environment, tradition and culture, as his work in India so clearly indicates.

—B.S. Saini

NOYES, Eliot Fette.

American. Born in Boston, Massachusetts, 12 August 1910. Educated at Phillips Academy, Andover, Massachusetts, graduated 1928; Harvard College, Cambridge, Massachusetts, 1928-32, B.A. 1932; Harvard Graduate School of Architecture, Cambridge, 1932-35 and 1937-38 (Eugene Dodd Medal, 1935; Alpha Rho Chi Medal, 1938; American Institute of Architects Medal, 1938), M.Arch. 1938; awarded Wheelwright Travelling Fellowship, 1939. Served in the United States Air Force, 1942-45: Major. Married Mary Duncan Weed in 1938; children: Mary, Eliot Jr., Frederick, and Margaret. Worked as an architect on the Iranian Archaeological Expedition of the Oriental Institute of the University of Chicago, 1935-37; draftsman in the office of Coolidge, Sheply, Bulfinch and Abbot, Boston, 1938, and in the office of Walter Gropius, *q.v.*, and Marcel Breuer, *q.v.*, Cambridge, Massachusetts, 1939-40: Director of the Department of Industrial Design, Museum of Modern Art, New York, 1940-42 and 1945-46; Design Director for Norman Bell Geddes and Company, New York, 1946-47; in Private practice, as Eliot Noyes and Associates, New Canaan, Connecticut, 1947 until his death in 1977. Curator of Exhibitions, 1948-50, and Associate Professor and Critic of Architecture, 1948-

53, Yale University, New Haven, Connecticut. Consultant Director of Design, IBM Corporation, 1956-77, and Mobil Oil Corporation, 1964-77; Design Consultant to Westinghouse Electric Corporation, 1960-76, and to Pan American World Airways, 1969-72; Consultant on Design to the President of the Massachusetts Institute of Technology, Cambridge, 1972-77. President International Design Conference in Aspen, Colorado, 1965-70. Recipient: Design Award, *Progressive Architecture*, 1954; Award of Excellence for House Design, *Architectural Record*, 1956, 1957, 1959, 1971, and 1974; First Honor Award, and Centennial Medal, 1957, and Industrial Arts Medal, 1965, American Institute of Architects; Award of Merit, *House and Home*, 1957; Merit Award, United States Department of Housing and Urban Development, 1968; Merit Award, American Society of Landscape Architects, 1970; Design Medal, Society of Industrial Artists and Designers, London, 1971; Honor Award, Connecticut Society of Architects/AIA, 1975 (twice); Design Excellence Award, *Industrial Design*, 1975. D.F.A.: Carnegie-Mellon University, Pittsburgh, Pennsylvania, 1969. Fellow, American Institute of Architects, and Industrial Designers Society of America; Associate, National Academy of Design. Fellow, Royal Society of Arts, London. *Died* (in New Canaan, Connecticut) *18 July 1977.*

Works

1941 Jackson House, Dover Massachusetts
1950 Tallman House, New Canaan, Connecticut
      Bremer House, New Canaan, Connecticut
1951 Ault House New Canaan, Connecticut

Stackpole House, New Canaan, Connecticut
Hersey House, Southport, Connecticut
1952 Weeks House, New Canaan, Connecticut
1953 Briggs House, Redding, Connecticut
      Bubble Houses, Hobe Sound, Florida
1954 Bareiss House, Greenwich, Connecticut
      General Electric Corporation Wonder Home (exhibition project)
1955 Noyes House, New Canaan, Connecticut
1956 Bernhard House, Port Chester, New York
1958 IBM Corporation Office additions, Harrison, New York
1959 Simonsen Vacation House, Martha's Vineyard, Massachusetts
1960 Ohly Vacation House, Sherburne, Vermont
      First Federal Savings and Loan Association Building, Hagerstown, Maryland
1961 Noyes Ski House, Sherburne, Vermont
      IBM Branch Office Building, Arlington, Virginia
      IBM Branch Office Building, Los Angeles
1963 Rantoul Vacation House, Martha's Vineyard, Massachusetts
1964 IBM Aerospace Building Parking Garage, Los Angeles
      Timothy Dwight School, New Haven, Connecticut
      Time Capsule Pavilion, for Westinghouse Electric, World's Fair, New York
1965 IBM Areospace Building, Los Angeles
      Mobil Service Station Prototypes (55 built throughout the United States)
      Xerox Corporation Showroom interior, New York
      Westinghouse executive suite interior, Pittsburgh
1966 McKay Vacation House, Stratton, Vermont

Westinghouse Telecomputer Center and Office Building, Pittsburgh
      IBM Branch Office Building, Garden City, Long Island, New York
      General Fireproofing Company Showroom interior, New York
1967 General Fireproofing Company Sales Office and Showroom, Toronto
      Oliver Wolcott Library, Litchfield, Connecticut
      Salisbury Elementary School, Connecticut
      General Fireproofing Company Showroom interior, Toronto
      United Nations Pavilion, *Expo '67*, Montreal
1968 IBM Office Building additions, Harrison, New York
      Mobil Oil Company boardroom interior, New York
      IBM Pavilion, *Hemisfair*, San Antonio, Texas
1969 Preston House, Martha's Vineyard, Massachusetts
      Cummins Engine Company Sales and Service Buildings Prototypes
      IBM Computer Rooms Annex, Poughkeepsie, New York
      Meadow Street Fire Station, Norwalk, Connecticut
      Fire Drill Tower, Norwalk, Connecticut
      Study of elevated subway train stations, New York (project)
1970 Graham House, Greenwich, Connecticut
      Hodgson Vacation House, Snowmass, near Aspen, Colorado
      Mobil Oil Refinery Administration Building, Joliet, Illinois
      IBM Branch Office Building, Hamden, Connecticut

Eliot Noyes: Graham House, Greenwich, Connecticut, 1970.

Southside Junior High School, Columbus, Indiana

Mobil Site Feasibility Study, Farmers Branch Texas

1971 Mobil Stonybrook Center Customer Service Laboratory, Hopewell Township, New Jersey

Mobil Stonybrook Center Customer Service Laboratory, Hopewell Township, New Jersey

Mobil Oil Portuguese Headquarters Building, Lisbon

Master plan for Mobil Stonybrook Center, Hopewell Township, New Jersey

Pan American World Airways Passenger Terminal interiors, Kennedy Airport, New York

1972 Horton House, Stamford, Connecticut

Feasibility study: Wilton Library, Connecticut

Survey: Intercontinental Hotel, Cotonou Dahomey
omey

New Passenger Ship Terminal interiors, New York

IBM Headquarters lobby design, Armonk, New York

Mobil Oil Corporation Interior Design Standards (manual)

IBM Branch Office interiors, Baltimore

1975 Johnson House, Mystic, Connecticut

Wilton Library, Connecticut

1980 IBM Managment Development Center, Armonk, New York

Publications

By NOYES: book—*Organic Design and Home Furnishing*, New York 1941; *Symposium on the Esthetics of Automobile Design*, New York 1950; articles—regular column in *Consumer Reports* (Mount Vernon, New York), 1947-54; "Moods Are Not Accidents" in *Life* (New York), 15 February 1963; "25—Year of Appraisal," interview, in *Interiors* (New York), November 1965; "Continuing Study of the Window Wall" in *Architectural Record* (New York), 1967.

On NOYES: books—*Masters of Modern Architecture* by John Peter, New York 1958; *Architecture USA* by Ian McCallum, New York 1959; *Architecture Today and Tommorow* by Cranston Jones, New York 1961; *Vacation Houses* by William J. Hennessey, New York 1962; *Modern Houses of the World* by Sherban Cantacuzino, New York 1964; *Design and Planning*, Waterloo, Ontario 1965; *Design Coordination and Corporate Image* by F. H. K. Henrion and Alan Parkin, London and New York 1967; *Design in America* by Ralph Caplan, New York 1969; *The Corporate Search for Visual Identity* by Ben Rosen, New York 1970; *The Architectural Record Book of Vacation Houses*, New York 1970; *International Vacation Houses*, Stuttgart 1967; *International Shop Design*, Stuttgart 1967; *Great Houses*, edited by Walter F. Wagner, Jr., New York 1976; *Ferro-cement* by Stanley Abercrombie, New York 1977; *Contemporary Designers*, edited by Ann Lee Morgan, New York and London 1984; articles— "Concrete Bubble House" in *Architectural Record* (New York), May 1954; "IBM's New Corporate Face" in *Architectural Forum* (New York), February 1957; "Art at Home by Eliot Noyes" in *Art in America* (New York), Summer 1958; "A House for All Seasons" in *Life* (New York), 15 February 1963; "The Work of Eliot Noyes and Associates" in *Industrial Design* (New York), June 1966; "Eliot Noyes" in *Crée* (Paris), January/-February 1971; "Design for the Corporation" in *Progressive Architecture* (New York), October 1975; "Eliot F. Noyes, Architect and Designer of Office Equipment" in *RIBA Journal* (London), September 1977; "Eliot F. Noyes, 1911-1977" in *Progressive Architecture* (New York), September 1977; "Eliot Noyes, Architect and Designer" by Mark Brutton in *Design* (London), October 1977; "The First Among Us ... Eliot Noyes, 1910-1977" by Gilles de Bure and others in *Architecture intérieure Crée* (Paris), August/September 1978.

*

Eliot Noyes is as well known for his industrial design as he is for his architecture. He studied at Harvard Graduate School of Design in the early 1930s when the Beaux-Arts tradition was still the accepted curriculum. But, during his years at Harvard, he enlightened himself with the works of Le Corbusier who was drawing away from the traditionalism towards a revolutionary style of functional modernism. He interrupted his education at Harvard to participate as the delineator/recorder member of an archaeological expedition to Iran, as if to take a new perspective look at the Beaux-Arts curriculum with which he, too, was discontented.

He returned to Harvard to find that Gropius and Breuer had joined the faculty and were injecting into the curriculum this new spirit of modernism. His study of the Bauhaus, expounded by the new faculty, inspired his career-long reverence for the interrelationship of industrial design, architecture, painting, and sculpture. For Noyes, the complete architect was, like Le Corbusier, a painter, a sculptor, a furniture designer as well as a designer of building structure. Engineering, function, and art are the combined generators of design.

Noyes was, for a time, the Director of the Department of Industrial Design at the Museum of Modern Art, and there organized the furniture design competition out of which came the famous Eames chair. A wartime friendship with Thomas Watson, the future executive of IBM, developed into a designer-client association that changed the look of many IBM products. Noyes gave typewriters a sleek, smooth, modern design that showed that intricate, complicated machines can have an aesthetic beauty not inconsistent with their underlying expression of function. Noyes put aesthetics into Mobil gas stations, pumps, and accessories, giving that company a new corporate image through uniformity of design of its standardized parts with simple bold graphics. The function of the products was not compromised, just given an extra dimension with pleasing looks.

Noyes's houses convey his attempts to simplify the complicated. Usually they comprise simple rectilinear spaces, sometimes separated not by a material closure, but by the suggestion of closure through the use of furniture placement or wall screens. Almost a trademark of his is the common division of living space from dining space by a free-standing fireplace. There are definite separate activity-areas in his houses, but often one borrows extra expanse from an adjacent space.

Noyes predominantly used natural materials in simple configurations where each material often expresses more than itself. A stone fireplace in a house, for example, may extend to become a major structural element—a stone wall running the full length of the house perhaps terminating as a garden wall on the exterior. His own houses have a sparse, open, geometric plan and a straightforward, simply expressed structure that created an uncluttered background where his many art treasures and artifacts from extensive travels easily found places for display. He exhibited the Miesian celebration of the unadorned and straightforward use of materials to generate the bare, structural, essential space, refined or clad with a clean, tight skin.

—Stephen P. Hamilton

OBATA, Gyo.

American. Born in San Francisco, California, 28 February 1923. Educated at the University of California, Berkeley, 1941-42; Washington University, St. Louis, 1942-45, B.Arch. 1945; Cranbrook Academy of Art, Bloomfield Hills, Michigan, 1945-46, M.Arch. 1946. Married Majel Beth Chance in 1948 (divorced, 1971): children: Kiku, Nori, and Gen; married Nancy J. McGeehon in 1971 (divorced, 1984). Sr. Designer, Skidmore, Owings and Merrill, Chicago, 1947-50; Associate in charge of Design, Hellmuth, Yamasaki and Leinweber, St. Louis, 1951-55. Principal, with George Hellmuth, *q.v.,* and George Kassabaum, *q.v.,* 1955-78, Chairman of the Board, 1978-82, and Chairman and President since 1982, Hellmuth, Obata and Kassabaum, St. Louis. Affiliate Professor of Architecture, Washington University, St. Louis, since 1971. Recipient: Outstanding Alumni Citation, Washington University, 1964. Fellow, American Institute of Architects. Address: Hellmuth, Obata and Kassabaum Inc., Architects, 100 North Broadway, St. Louis, Missouri 63102, U.S.A.

Publications:

By OBATA: articles—"Some Suggestions for Urban Housing" in *Architectural Record* (New York), March 1961; "Dallas/Fort Worth Airport" in *L'Architecture d'Aujourd'hui* (Paris), March/April 1974.

*

I believe that architecture is the art of ordering space— whether it be a room, or a series of spaces creating a building, or a group of buildings creating a community. Working with an enormous palette of ideas, forms, materials and technology, the designer, with the client, has an opportunity to affect the essence of how people work, feel and live within these spaces. The volume an geometry of the buildings, the way natural light affects the space, the manner in which materials are applied and energy is used, and the relationship of the building to the site and environs are some of the many important considerations which define architectural space. By listening carefully to the client's needs, HOK is able to understand the variables of a project and to use the potential of those variables in arriving at the appropriate design solution.

—Gyo Obata

*

See HELLMUTH, OBATA AND KASSABAUM

OESTERLEN, Dieter.

German. Born in Heidenheim, Württemberg, 5 April 1911. Educated at the Goethe Gymnasium, Han-nover, Germany, graduated 1930; Technische Hoch-schule, Stuttgart, under Professor Schmitthenner, 1930-32; Technische Hochschule, Berlin, under Heinrich Tessenow, *q.v.,* and Hans Poelzig, 1932-36, Diploma 1936, M.Arch. 1939. Married Eva Freise in 1939; children: Friedrich, Mathis, and Bettina; married Eva Maria Stroedel in 1957. Since 1945, in private practice, Hannover, West Germany. Professor at the Technical University, Braunschweig, West Germany, 1952-76. Exhibitions: Art Circle, Hameln, West Germany, 1961; Kunstverein, Oldenburg, West Germany, 1971; Stadtisches Museum, Brauns-chweig, West Germany, 1972. Recipient: Schinkel-plakette, Berlin, 1938; First Prize, Cinema Compe-tition, West Germany, 1950; 3 Laves Prize, City of Hannover, West Germany, 1954; Krahe Prize, City of Braunschweig, West Germany, 1960; Award of Distinction, City of Bochum, West Germany, 1965; Bund Deutscher Architekten Prize, Bremen, West Germany, 1974; Recognition Prize, International Cembureau, Paris, 1975; three Prizes of the Bund Deutscher Architekten, Niedersachsen, West Ger-many, 1976; German Architecture Concrete Prize, 1977; Fritz-Schumacher-Prize, 1979; Niedersachsi-scher Culture Prize, West Germany, 1981. Member, Akademie der Künste, Berlin, since 1966. Address (office): Baumstrasse 11, 3000 Hannover 1, West Germany.

Works:

1946/
60 Market Church restoration, Hannover, West Germany
1951/
53 Filmstudio Cinema, Hannover, West Ger-many
1956/
58 Wilhelm-Busch School, Hannover, West Ger-many
1957/
59 Christ Church, Bochum, West Germany
1957/
62 Parliament Building for the Council of Nieder-sachsen, Hannover, West Germany
1959/
65 Church of Our Lady restoration, Bremen, West Germany
1960/
62 Andreanum School, Hildesheim, West Ger-many
1961/
67 German Soldiers Cemetery, Futa Pass, Flor-ence
1962/
63 Church of Jesus Christ, Sennestadt, near Bielefeld, West Germany
1962/
66 Conference and Concert Hall, Saarbrucken, West Germany
1963/
66 History Museum, Am Hohen Ufer, Han-nover, West Germany

1964/
67 Church of the Twelve Apostles, Hildesheim, West Germany
1967/
69 Administration Building, Volkswagen Works Foundation, Hannover, West Germany
   Administration Building, Chamber of Com-merce and Industry, Bielefeld, West Germany
   IBM Administration Building, Hannover, West Germany
1970/
71 Lamberti Church restoration, Oldenburg, West Germany
1971/
72 Institute for the Study of Materials and Soldering Techniques, Technical Univers-ity, Braunschweig, West Germany
1971/
73 Town Hall, Greven, West Germany
1972/
74 Administration Building, Concordia Insur-ance Company, Hannover, West Germany
1974/
75 Bischof Stahlin Geriatric Center, Oldenburg, West Germany
   City Art Gallery, Herford, West Germany
1976/
77 Theatre restoration and alterations, Mainz, West Germany
1977/
78 Die Arche Church Community Centre, Laat-zen, near Hannover, West Germany
78 Playhouse for the State Theatre, Braunsch-weig, West Germany (project)
1979/
85 Post Office Headquarters Administration Building, Bremen, West Germany
1980/
82 I.B.Z. Guesthouse, University of Göttingen, West Germany
1980/
83 German Embassy, Buenos Aires
1981/
83 Hilton Hotel, Mainz, West Germany (with G. Wagner)
1982/
84 Town Hall, Langenhagen, near Hannover, West Germany
1983/
85 Labour Office Administration Building, Gos-lar, West Germany
1984/
85 Opera House alterations for the State Theatre, Hannover, West Germany
   Dr. Meier AG Administration Building, Dollbergen, near Hannover, West Ger-many (project)
   City Hall, Rastatt, West Germany (project)

Publications:

By OESTERLEN: article—"Why Is There No Valid

Dieter Oesterlen: German Embassy, Buenos Aires, 1980-83.

Architectural Criticism?" in *Der Architekt* (Stuttgart), February 1979.

On OESTERLEN: book—*Dieter Oesterlen: Buildings and Projects 1946-63* by Alexander Koch, Stuttgart 1964; articles—"Old People's Centre in Oldenburg-Nadorst" in *Bauen und Wohnen* (Zürich), February 1974; "Concordia-Feuer Insurance Company Offices" in *Architektur und Wohnwelt* (Stuttgart), May 1975; "Art Gallery in Herford" in *Detail* (Munich), March/April 1976; "Art Gallery in Herford" in *Bauwelt* (Berlin), 21 May 1976; "A Good Integration with the Past" in *Construction moderne* (Paris), no. 13, 1978; "Herford Museum" in *Architecture + Urbanism* (Tokyo), October 1978; "Old People's Home in Oldenburg" in *Architektur und Wohnwelt* (Stuttgart), August 1979; "Hannover Is Quite Different from What You Thought It Was," special issue of *Der Architekt* (Stuttgart), January 1982.

*

I have been building for only a little more than twenty years, having began at about forty five years of age. After I received my diploma in Berlin in 1936, I was occupied with town planning in the prewar Nazi era, then there was the war until 1945, and then until 1955, there was a need to make up for the time lost as an architect in Germany cut off from architectural development.

I believe that a building arrangement grows from the actual town planning situation and that its characteristic plastic expression of shape (form-content) develops from the actual building problem. Since Mies van der Rohe and Scharoun, I regard the interlinking of exterior and interior spaces as an important specific of the new architecture. Everything—space as well as large and small forms—should be seized by this dynamic. Accordingly, I try to achieve a liveliness in my buildings with a tension in their spatial deployment and with pervasive, appropriate atmosphere, both goals to be achieved within controlled homogeneity of the interior and exterior appearance.

I have always considered the restoration of historic buildings (and the process of supplementing them with new buildings) as self-instructive, self-introspective, and self-measuring. A "feeling for" restoration seems essential to me. Nostalgia, which can be advantageous in momentary recollection, and its consequences—decorativeness, eclecticism—can only happen if the aims for the productive development of a new architecture are unclear or are intentionally abandoned.

—Dieter Oesterlen

*

I consider one of Dieter Oesterlen's buildings as particularly typical of his feeling for form, already apparent at the beginning of the still-disdained 1950s. It is his cinema in Hannover, with 600 seats in an underground area. There are two neon-lit words on the street facade: Film and Studio. The three straight lines of the "F" are continued down the outside wall, bend to the ceiling of the box office foyer, twist as a triple spiral around the central support of the main stairway, and glide freely with an asymmetric verve into the underground foyer. There, the projection room rises in a gentle arch in the ellipse of the auditorium. The side walls and ceiling are indirectly lit with strip lighting behind wood panels that become visible through the back lighting. For Oesterlen (as he says), a film lives from light. And so, architecturally, this cinema involves a play of light.

Oesterlen does without a curtain in front of the screen. Nothing in this Filmstudio is to remind us of the opera or the theatre, where the curtain still has a meaning: it covers the scenery, allows players surprise entries. In this cinema, and for the first time, Oesterlen designed a screen with two wings: they open at the beginning of the presentation like a book and close again at the end. Both wings have irregularly curved metal inserts which recall the highlights of an imaginary landscape.

The Hannover cinema is not typical of the whole of Oesterlen's work, of the crystalline body of his Christ Church in Bochum or of the cubist blocks of his housing and administration buildings. Yet this cinema is one of the best German examples of an architecture that, in its feeling for freedom of form, avoids the right angle and seeks a connection with organic growth.

—Christian Borngräber

O'GORMAN, Juan.

Mexican. Born in Coyoacán, Mexico City, 6 July 1905. Educated at Jesuit schools in Mexico City; National University of Mexico, School of Architecture, Mexico City, 1922-26, Dip.Arch. 1926; apprenticed to Carlos Obregón Santacilia, 1927; studied painting with Antonio Ruiz, Ramon Alba

Guedarrama, and Diego Rivera. Married Helen Fowler in 1941; daughter: Maria Elena. Worked in the architectural offices of José Villagrán García, Carlos Tarditi, and Carlos Contreros, Mexico City, 1927-29; Chief Draftsman, office of Carlos Obregón Santacilia, 1929-32; Head, Mexico City Department of Building Construction, 1932-34. In private practice, Mexico City, from 1934. Co-Founder, School of Architecture, 1932, and Professor of Architecture and Architectural Composition, 1932-48, National Polytechnic Institute, Mexico City. Founder, Workers' Housing Study Group, Mexico City, 1936. Exhibitions: *Anniversary of the Revolution*, Palace of Fine Arts, Mexico City, 1934; Museum of Modern Art, Palace of Fine Arts, Mexico City, 1948; Galerias del Bosque de Chapultepec, Mexico City, 1949; *Realismo y Fantasia en la Obra de Juan O'Gorman*, Palace of Fine Arts, Mexico City, 1950, and Morelia, Mexico, 1951; Institute of Mexican Art, Mexico City, 1961; *Salon de la Plastica Mexicana*, Mexico City, 1964; San Fernando Valley State College, California, 1964; *Art of Latin America since Independence*, Yale University, New Haven, Connecticut, 1966, and toured the United States; *Proyectos de Murales de Juan O'Gorman*, Palace of Fine Arts, Mexico City, 1968. Collections: Museum of Modern Art, New York; Palace of Fine Arts, Mexico City; Museum of Modern Art, Mexico City; Philadelphia Museum of Art, Pennsylvania. Recipient: First Prize, La Tolteca Painting Competition, Mexico City, 1930; First Prize for Mexico City, Excelsior Painting Competition, 1948; Diploma, City of Morelia, 1952; Diploma and Medal of Honor, School of Engineering and Architecture, National Polytechnic Institute, Mexico City, 1959; Diploma, National Institute of Mexican Youth, 1969; Diploma, Mexican College of Architects, 1970; Mexican National Art Prize, 1972. Member, National College of Architects of Mexico, 1956. Member, Bolivarian Society of Architects, Caracas, 1967. Member, Academy of Arts, Mexico City, 1971. *Died* (by suicide, in Mexico City) *January 1982*.

Works:

1924/
25 Frescoes for the Salon Bach (bar), Mexico City Numerous murals in Mexico City
1925/
28 Bank of Mexico reconstruction, Mexico City (with Carlos Obregón Santacilia)
    SSA (Secretaria de Salubridad y Asistencia Publica) Building, Mexico City (with Carlos Obregón Santacilia)
1927/
28 Lomas House, Chapultepec, Mexico City
    Mural, Pascual Ortiz Rubio House, Tizapán, Mexico
1929/
30 Diego Rivera House and Studio, San Angel Inn, Mexico City
    Juan O'Gorman House I, San Angel Inn, Mexico City
1931 Thomas O'Gorman House, Palmas, San Angel Inn, Mexico City
    Murals, Public Library, Azcapotzalco, Mexico (with Julio Castellaños)
1932/
34 Twenty-eight primary schools throughout Mexico, for the Ministry of Education, including schools at Tampico, Colonia Portales, Ilhuac Village, Xochimilco Village, Peravillo, and Coyoacán
    Technical School, Tresguerras Street, Mexico City
1934 Julio Castellaños House, Mexico City
    Manuel Toussaint House, Mexico City (project)
    Mexican Confederation of Labor Offices and Auditorium, Mexico City (project)
    Frances Toor House, Mexico City
1936 Sindicato de Electricistas Building, Calle

Orozco and Berra, Mexico City
1936/
37 Three murals, Mexico City Airport (2 now in the History Museum, Chapultepec Castle, Mexico City)
1939 Mural, Xochimilco Primary School, Mexico City
1940 Twelve murals, Cultural Association of Jewish Youth, Pittsburgh (project)
1941 Mural, Gertrude Bocanegra Public Library, San Agustin Church, Patzcuaro, Michoacán, Mexico
1941/
42 Mural, private house, San Angel Inn, Mexico City
1942/
43 Mural, Fred Davis House, San Jeronimo Lidice, Mexico (destroyed)
1944/
45 Museo Anahuacalli, Mexico (as consultant; with Diego Rivera)
1948 Mosaic murals, Conlon Nancarrow House, Las Aguilas, Mexico
1952/
53 National Library, State University of Mexico, University City, Mexico City (with Gustavo Saavedra and Juan Martinez de Velasco)
    Mosaic mural, Ministry of Communication and Public Works, Mexico City
1953/
56 Juan O'Gorman House II, Avenida San Jeronimo, San Angel Inn, Mexico City (destroyed, 1970)
1954/
56 Mosaic mural, Posada de la Mision Hotel, Taxco, Mexico
1960/
61 Mural, History Museum, Chapultepec Castle, Mexico City
1962/
65 Mural, Entrance Hall, Centro Interamericano del Seguro Social de la Unidad Independencia, San Jeronimo Lidice, Mexico (with Roberto Berdecio)
    Mural, Banco Internacional del Paseo de la Reforma, Mexico City
    Mosaic mural, San Cristobal Park, Santiago, Chile (as consultant/supervisor)
1966/
67 Mosaic mural, Convention Center Theatre, San Antonio, Texas
1968/
79 Murals, Room of the Revolution, History Museum, Chapultepec Castle, Mexico City

Publications:

By O'GORMAN: books—*El arte util y el arte artistico*, Mexico City 1932; *Autobiografia, antologia, juicios criticos y documentacion exhaustiva sobre su obra*, Mexico City 1973.

On O'GORMAN: book—*Builders in the Sun: Five Mexican Architects* by Clive Bamford Smith, New York 1967; articles—"Federal Schools of Mexico" in *Architectural Record* (New York), May 1934; "Contenido Politico de la Arquitectura" in *Edificacion* (Mexico City), September/October 1937; "Jardines del Pedregal da San Angel" in *Arts and Architecture* (Los Angeles), August 1951; "Biblioteca y Hemeroteca Nacional" in *Arquitectura* (Mexico City), September 1952; "Mexico City University: Its New Campus and Buildings" in *Northwest Architect* (Minneapolis), September/October 1952; "Mosaic Details from a House" in *Arts and Architecture* (Los Angeles), March 1955; "Mosaics" in *Arts and Architecture* (Los Angeles), February 1959; "Juan O'Gorman" by Mathias Goeritz in *Arquitectura* (Mexico City), December 1960; "Habitation à Mexico" in *L'Architecture d'Aujourd'hui* (Paris), June/July 1962; "O'Gorman

Cave House Disappears" in *Progressive Architecture* (New York), March 1970; "O'Gorman House" in *Architectural Design* (London), September 1970; "The Death of Juan O'Gorman by Esther McCoy in *Arts and Architecture* (Los Angeles) August 1982; "Modern Mexican Architecture", special issue of *Process: Architecture* (Tokyo) July 1983.

*

Juan O'Gorman was the eldest son of an Irish father and a Mexican mother, a genetic combination bound to produce a preponderance of imagination and fantasy over rational impulse, a condition favorable to creative work of fascinating iridescence as well as complex contradictions in theoretical pronouncements.

O'Gorman belonged to that generation of architects educated in the years when Le Corbusier's *Vers une Architecture* appeared and the architectural avant-garde hotly defended the favorite line, "La maison est une machine à demeurer," while conveniently forgetting such sentences as "L'architecture, c'est l'art par excellence" or "... est au delà des choses utilitaires" or "L'architecture est le jeu savant, correct et magnifique des volumes assemblées sous la lumière." After graduating from the Architecture School of the National University of Mexico and working for some years in the offices of various architects, O'Gorman built, between 1929 and 1932, a series of houses that are generally considered the first in Mexico to be designed according to the doctrines of Functionalism. Among these houses there was one for himself and two (a house and a studio) for Diego Rivera. At the time he was criticized for copying Le Corbusier's early houses in Paris. There is some truth in the charge—especially in the Diego studio, with its spiral stairs and sawtooth roof. But O'Gorman was only 24 years old at the time, and if he copied, he made the right choice.

During the following years O'Gorman designed and supervised the construction of twenty-eight schools for the Ministry of Education, strictly observing the rule of "maximum of utility for minimum of expense." And, while teaching design at the National Polytechnic Institute, O'Gorman instilled in his students the spirit of Functionalism: "Copying the monuments of antiquity, be they Aztec, Mayan, colonial or more recent works, means, as a pedagogical discipline, to engrave and to impress upon the mind of youth forms that were the product of other necessities and other construction methods and are therefore the farther away from our way of life the more mankind makes material progress."

Twenty years later, in a paper read at the Palace of Fine Arts, O'Gorman made this statement about his early architectural work (it sounds somehow like the confession of a penitent defector, accusing himself of having given in to bourgeois temptations): "What I want to have clearly established in writing is the fact that, for my own work, I took the architecture of Le Corbusier as a model and that makes me partly responsible for the implanting of Functionalism in our country; it is, at the same time, valid proof of my own lack of talent. This happened between 1926 and 1936, years during which I worked at actively applying the principles of Functionalism in Mexico. This mistake was especiallly grave, considering that within my reach was the knowledge of Frank Lloyd Wright's work, which was, at that time as it still is today, the contemporary expression of our own tradition. When I finally realized this error, I renounced architecture to dedicate myself to painting.... The Swiss puritanism of Le Corbusier's architecture is exactly the antithesis to the plastic arts of Mexico, from the antique Anáhuac down to the popular expressions of today."

If Frank Lloyd Wright's organic architecture was the supreme expression of the artistic tradition of Meso-America, Mexican architecture, too, should be, against all evidence, organic. On the other hand, Wright's Taliesin West is, according to O'Gorman, "the most magnificent modern house ... and one of

Juan O'Gorman: O'Gorman House II, San Angel Inn, Mexico City, 1956.

the most important works of art of all time. Its Mexican character is evident."

Today, all of these intertwined theories may seem both confusing and irrelevant, but the fortunate fact is that, about ten years after his flight from Functionalism (time that he spent painting a series of great alfresco murals and numerous excellent easel paintings in tempera), the architect O'Gorman suddenly emerged from his self-imposed exile, with the sword of Anti-Functionalism, the shield of Organic Architecture, and the battle cry Integration, ready to design, construct and complete in five years two buildings in Mexico City that made him famous through the world: the National Library at University City and his own house in the Avenida San Jeronimo.

Many murals had been painted in Mexico since the revolution, all of them on existing walls and mostly without any satisfactory relation to the architecture until, at mid-century, the idea of integrating sculpture and painting more closely into the building process became widely discussed. As with the great architectural monuments of the past from very different cultures—the Parthenon, Angkor Vat, Uxmal, or Chartres—the three arts should not be elaborated separately and later "put together," but should be worked out on the job, by the same people, in an act of simultaneous creation.

Conditions at the National Library were ideal for integration: O'Gorman was one of the three architects responsible for the project at the same time that he was the creator of the magnificent stone mosaics that surround the book stacks. The library was

widely admired and more photographed than any other modern building in the world, but it did not satisfy O'Gorman's desire for total integration: the murals that covered the rectangular box could not possibly hide it.

O'Gorman's own house, begun while he was finishing the library, is a work of ecologically integrated, pure organic architecture; it is the most significant creation of his life. He had bought a rather large plot at the edge of the vast lava bed south of Mexico City. Here he found a grotto hidden in the vegetation and used it to form two sides of the wonderful living room; part of the existing rock formation became the ceiling, and the remaining surfaces, mostly curved, he covered with coloured stone mosaics inside and outside. All kinds of minor technical difficulties beset him, but at last he realized his dream castle. He wrote in 1976: "This experiment in organic architecture was realized...for the principal purpose of being an outcry of protest in favor of humanism, perishing in the technological desert of our marvellous civilization."

After living in it for fifteen years, O'Gorman had to sell the house, and the subsequent owner destroyed it by pulling down a great part of the walls and covering the rest totally with a thick layer of cement—a crime that deprived the Mexican people of a singular monument that should have been protected by law. The loss almost broke O'Gorman's heart. He renounced architecture and dedicated himself to painting apocalyptic images haunting the deserts of technology.

—Max Cetto

OKADA, Shin'ichi.

Japanese. Born in Tokyo, 9 January 1928. Educated at the University of Tokyo School of Architecture and Graduate School of Architecture, B.Arch. 1955, M.A. 1957; Yale University Graduate School of Art and Architecture, under Paul Rudolph, *q.v.,* and Louis I. Kahn, *q.v.,* 1962-63, M.A. 1963. Married Hiroko Sakata in 1956; children: Makiko and Namihei. Architect for the Kajima Corporation, Tokyo, 1956-62; Designer, Skidmore, Owings and Merrill, *q.v.,* New York, 1964-65; Chief Architect, Kajima Corporation, Tokyo, 1965-69. Since 1969, President, Shin'ichi Okada, Architect, and Associates, Tokyo. Lecturer, Chiba University, 1966-69, and the University of Tokyo, 1971-73. Lecturer, Tokyo Metropolitan University, since 1974. Recipient: Kanagawa Prefecture Award, 1967; First Prize, Japanese Supreme Court Competition, 1969; Building Contractors Society Award, 1970, 1974; Architectural Institute Award, 1975. Address: Shin'ichi Okada Architect and Associates, No. 2—Kawa Building, 1-11-39 Akasaka, Minato-ku, Tokyo 107, Japan.

Works:

1966 Omura Children's Home, Nagasaki
1967 Idemitsu Kosan Clubhouse, Kanagawa, Japan
1968 Gymnasium, Nippon Dental College, Tokyo
       Hitachi Industries General Hospital, Hitachi, Japan

1970 Kajima Sendai Branch Office Building, Sendai, Japan
Kajima Kyushu Branch Office Building, Fukuoka, Japan
Kajima Head Office, Tokyo
1971 Gumma Cultural Center, Maebashi, Japan
Yanase Motors Branch Office, Fukuoka, Japan
1972 Hotel Ricci Sapporo, Sapporo, Japan
Idemitsu Kosan Research Center, Chiba, Japan
Niigata Campus, Nippon Dental College, Niigata, Japan
1973 City General Hospital, Kurashiki, Japan
Fukuoka Welfare Facility for the Elderly, Fukuoka, Japan
Okayama Young People's Lodge-in-Nature, Okayama, Japan
1974 The Japanese Supreme Court, Tokyo
Hotel Ricci Fukuoka, Fukuoka, Japan
Nissei Sangyo Hayama Clubhouse, Hayama, Japan
Research Laboratory, Japan Petroleum Exploration Company, Hamura, Japan
Japan Red Cross Blood Supply Center, Niigata, Japan
1975 SVAX Shinjuku Office Building, Tokyo
Okayama General Welfare Center, Okayama, Japan
Kurashiki Young People's Lodge-in-Nature, Kurashiki, Japan
1976 Tsukuba University, Tsukuba, Japan
1977 Anzen Motors Office Building, Tokyo
1978 Gumma Prefectural Library, Maebashi, Japan
Nissei Sangyo Yamanaka-Lake Clubhouse, Yamanashi, Japan
Niigata City Music Center, Niigata, Japan
Singapore Embassy, Tokyo
SVAX Nishishimmbashi Office Building, Tokyo
1979 Cultural Center, Tomakomai, Japan
Main Library, Tsukuba University, Tsukuba, Japan
Orient Museum, Okayama, Japan
Idemitsu Museum, Mitaka, Japan
Gyosei International High School, Chiba, Japan
Home for the Elderly, Yokohama, Japan
1980 Public Library, Tokorozawa, Japan
Metropolitan Police Headquarters, Tokyo
1981 City General Hospital, Ryozu, Japan
Urban Renewal of Mihara, Japan
Public Library, Koriyama, Japan
Public Library, Wakayama, Japan
1982 Community Village for Handicapped Persons, Hokkaido, Japan
1983 Cultural Gymnasium, Okayama, Japan
City Hall, Tomakomai, Japan
1984 City Music Center, Fukushima, Japan
Cultural Center, Ichinoseki, Japan
Public Library, Hachinohe, Japan
Kotaro Migishi Museum, Sapporo, Japan
Junior High School, Mitsu, Japan
National Welfare Center for Handicapped Persons, Tokyo
Japan Petroleum Exploration Company Branch Office, Nagaoka, Japan
Atomic Control Center, Hokkaido, Japan
1985 Okayama Public Museum, Okayama, Japan
City Museum, Hino, Japan
Fuji Women's College, Sapporo, Japan
Workers' Compensation Hospital, Toyama, Japan
Hospital of Tokyo University, Tokyo
Medical Association Hospital, Hakodate, Japan
Housing, Narita, Japan

Publications:

By OKADA: books—*Overseas Architecture*, nos. 1-
6 (Kajima, Tokyo), 1972-75; articles—"The Meaning of System in Design" in *Space Design* (Tokyo), May 1969; "Organization and Design: From Concept to Decision in Design" in *Kenchiku-Bunka* (Tokyo), March 1970; "The Process Toward the Physicalization of Architecture" in *Space Design* (Tokyo), January 1972; "The Meaning of System in Design" in *The Japan Architect* (Tokyo), January 1973; "The Inter-Relation Between Architecture and Human Life" in *Space Design* (Tokyo), December 1973; "Space and Symbol: The Development of the Architectural Concept in the Design of the Japanese Supreme Court" in *Space Design* (Tokyo), special issue 1974; "Niigata Municipal Music Center" in *The Japan Architect* (Tokyo), April 1978; "Walls and Tower" in *The Japan Architect* (Tokyo), January 1979; "Abstraction and Elaboration" in *Space Design* (Tokyo), September 1981.

On OKADA: books—*Beyond Metabolism: The New Japanese Architecture* by Michael Franklin Ross, New York 1978; articles—"Okada and Associates" in *Kenchiku-Goho* (Tokyo), December 1973; "The Path Shin'ich Okada Has Walked", special issue of *The Japan Architect* (Tokyo), January 1981; "Shin'ichi Okada", special issue of *Space Design* (Tokyo), September 1981.

Bibliography: *Shin'ichi Okada* by James P. Noffsinger, Monticello, Illinois 1982.

*

Several fundamental thoughts have occurred to me in the process of design:

The Wall: I find the wall a fundamental component that serves to create and determine space. By manipulating it by imposition, we succeed in generating and moving space as well as enclosing it. In the process it brings humankind into its fold. Furthermore, the wall becomes a step in the direction of developing the town.

The Heart Space: Of the spaces thus formed by the manipulation of the wall, we find generated the heart space. It is space that is able to adapt itself to the human situation—the place for a group to form, the place of communication, of human amelioration. A space fit to be called human, motherly space. The heart space might correspond to what Louis Kahn calls the "Room."

Catalytic Region: It is the region in which an object and another object lie contiguous to each other, confronting each other. Now the two objects exert force upon each other. It is a boundary region formed of two regions in touch with each other—such as the site and the road, the building and the earth, etc. These I find important and I believe that they deserve full attention when carrying out design. For we shall, in so developing the catalytic region, lead it into the realm of the urban.

Trunk Space: For complex architecture, and even for simple, independent structures, but more so for urban-size projects the generation of the trunk space is indispensable. In my design it becomes a key vocabulary. The street, the plaza and the mall are examples. But it is the region becoming more internalized, as is the spine, which deserves to be called the trunk space. The external/internal space of the main hall of the Japanese Supreme Court Building is one example that is very close to what I mean by trunk space.

Architectural Language: There is meaning in every architectural element. They form what we call the physical vocabulary. But against these there must be the vocabularization of each architectural concept, and the meaning of expression of each part of its content, that is, the conceptual vocabulary. By means of these two vocabularies (condensed into the architectural vocabulary), the complex structure may be brought into being, thereby evolving the architectural language. What is now the structuring architectural language device becomes the basis of a building structuring process. This we term the system of design.

—Shin'ichi Okada

*

Shin'ichi Okada is one of a select few Japanese architects who have had the technical skill, courage, and extraordinary design ability to leave the fold of one of Japan's Big Five design-build conglomerates. Okada succeeded in developing his own practice after being the chief designer for Kajima Corporation by winning the Japanese Supreme Court Building competition in 1969. His work for Kajima and his own work subsequently reveal the strong influence of his mentors at Yale University, Paul Rudolph and Louis I. Kahn.

Okada's buildings inevitably reflect the simple geometry and bold massing most often associated with Kahn. The head office of Kajima Corporation is composed of two massive towers shifted in plan to create a slot of space between them as an entrance, not unlike the shafts of brick at Richards Medical Building by Kahn. These large volumes shifted in plan appear again in Okada's "space walls" at the Supreme Court Building and, later, in a more refined statement at the Niigata Campus of the Nippon Dental College.

The overall impact of the Supreme Court Building itself is one of monumentality. It is massive, bold and imposing. Okada intended this impression, and in fact he believes in the need for monumentality in the overall urban design framework of our cities. He defines monumentality as possessing "scale that permits transmission into the future, continuity, long life, and the dream of durability in the face of change."

It is interesting to realize that "durability in the face of change" need not always be achieved through the heavy-handed use of bulky, capacious forms. It is true that the Egyptians employed a combination of massive size with simplicity of form to achieve longevity, but the delicate and serene Katsura Detached Palace has stood the test of time, albeit a shorter span, through the creative use of vernacular, natural materials and forms. This lesson was somehow never incorporated into Okada's design vocabulary.

A more sophisticated integration of forms and spaces with their environment was achieved by Okada at the Niigata Campus of the Nippon Dental College. Clusters of connected square blocks, with their projecting stair and service towers sheathed in clay tile, are arranged around a major campus outdoor quadrangle. The general esthetic is indebted to Kahn's Richards Medical Building, but the design attempts to develop Kahn's concept further and adapt it to this particular site. In this respect Okada is quite successful. The long, gray cold winters of this region produce powdery, white salt deposits from the ocean, which tend to collect on vertical panes of glass and erode exposed metal. Okada developed a system of clay-tiled vertical walls and steeply sloping glass skylights that protect the inhabitants from the bleak winters and shed the unsightly salt deposits, while allowing the warm sun to brighten the interior spaces.

All of Shin'ichi Okada's buildings tend to incorporate exterior space into the overall design concept, often with pleasing results. His structures, however, remain massive and geometrically purist. The success of the Niigata Campus and such other projects as the Gumma Cultural Center, the Omura Children's Home at Nagasaki, and the Kurashiki Young People's Lodge, indicates that we can expect a continuation of significant strong statements from the office of Shin'ich Okada.

—Michael Franklin Ross

OTAKA, Masato.

Japanese. Born in Fukushima prefecture in 1923. Educated at Tokyo University, Architecture Department, Dip.Arch. 1947, and Tokyo University Graduate School. Worked in the office of Kunio Mayekawa and Associates, Tokyo, 1949-61. In private practice, Tokyo, since 1961. Lecturer, Waseda University, Tokyo, and Tokyo University. Director, Japan Architects Association; Member of the Council, Architectural Institute of Japan; President, Agricultural Co-operation Architectural Study Stociety, Tokyo; Member, Board of Directors, Environmental Development Center, Tokyo. Founder Member, with Noboru Kawazoe, Kiyonori Kikutake, Fumihiko Maki, Kisho Noriaki Kurokawa, Kiyoshi Awazu, and Shinya Izumi, The Metabolist Group, Tokyo, 1960. Address: Masato Otaka and Associates, Odakyu Nishi Shinjuku Building, 1-47-1 Hatsudai, Shibuya-ku, Tokyo 151, Japan.

Works:

1954 Kanagawa Concert Hall and Library, Yokohama
1956 Education Center, Fukushima, Japan (with Kunio Mayekawa and Associates)
1958 Multi-storey Apartment Building, Harumi, Tokyo (with Kunio Mayekawa and Associates)
1961 Metropolitan Festival Hall, Tokyo (with Kunio Mayekawa and Associates)
1962 Kataoka Agricultural Union Co-operative Building, Japan
     Urban Platform Development, Sakaide City, Japan (project)

1964 Urban Platform Development, Otemachi, Japan (project)
     Japan Marine Workers' Union Hall, Tokyo
     Silk Center, Yokohama (competition project)
     Ueno Memorial Hall, Japan
1965 Hanaizumi Agricultural Union Co-operative Building, Japan
     City over Tokyo Bay (project)
1966 Tochigi Prefectural Health Insurance Building, Japan
1967 Yamanouchi Agricultural Union Cooperative Building, Japan
     Prefectural Center, Chiba, Japan
     Niihama Agricultural Union Co-operative Hall, Japan
1968 Nango-cho Agricultural Union Co-operative Building, Japan
     Makinohara Service Area and Rest House, Tokyo-Nagoya Expressway
     Central Library, Chiba, Japan
1970 Shizuoka Agricultural Co-operative Association Center, Japan
1972 Federation of Japan Automobile Workers' Union Education Center, Gotemba, Japan
     Housing Development, Chojuen, Japan
     Housing Development, Motomachi, Japan
1973 Apartment Building Development, Hiroshima, Japan
     Library, College of Industrial Technology, Nihon University, Tokyo
1976 Memorial Visitors' Center, Tsukuba, Japan
     Prefectural Art Museum, Chiba, Japan
1979 Prefectural Museum of History, Gunma, Japan
1980 Doho Park Gymnasium, Tsukuba, Japan
1982 Historical and Ethnic Archives, Miharu City, Japan
     Democratic Rights Memorial Hall, Fukushima, Japan

     Tama Center Master Plan, Tama, Japan
1984 Fukushima Museum of Art, Japan
     Museum of Modern Art annex addition, Kamakura, Japan
     Land Reclamation Development Plan, Yokohama, Japan
1985 Overseas Government Pavilion and Expo Theater, *Tsukuba '85* Exposition, Tsukuba, Japan

Publications:

By OTAKA: article—"Outline of the Tsukuba Expo '85", with others, in *The Japan Architect* (Tokyo), May 1984.

On OTAKA: articles—"Masato Otaka" in *Zodiac* (Milan), no. 3, 1958; "The Architects" in special issue on Japan of *Architectural Review* (London), September 1962; "New Architecture Assessed: Masato Otaka's Chiba Cultural Hall" in *Kokusai Kentiku* (Tokyo), May 1967; "Two Agricultural Co-operatives" in *The Japan Architect* (Tokyo), July 1967; "Experiments from Japan" in *Casabella* (Milan), March 1969; "New Developments in Japanese Architecture" in *Architectural Record* (New York), September 1970; "Education Center at Gotemba" in *The Japan Architect* (Tokyo), December 1972; "Apartments in Hiroshima" by Masaya Fujimoto in *The Japan Architect* (Tokyo), August 1973; "Mass Production in Housing" in *Bauen und Wohnen* (Zurich), March 1975; "Library, College of Industrial Technology, Nihon University" by Isao Takada in *The Japan Architect* (Tokyo), June 1974; "Chiba Prefectural Art Museum" by Noboru Kijima in *The Japan Architect* (Tokyo),

Masato Otaka: Fukushima Museum of Art, Japan, 1984.

February 1977; "Gunma Prefectural Museum of History" in *The Japan Architect* (Tokyo), March 1980; "History Museum in Takasaki" in *Detail* (Munich), May/June 1981; "Doho Park Gymnasium" in *The Japan Architect* (Tokyo), July 1981; "Gunma Prefectural Museum of History in Takasaki" in *Baumeister* (Munich), October 1981.

Bibliography: *Masato Otaka: Apprentice to Maekawa* by James P. Noffsinger, Monticello, Illinois 1980.

Having worked in Mayekawa's office for twelve years, during which time he was largely responsible for various works, including the Harumi Apartment Block on Tokyo Bay, Masato Otaka went on to become the oldest founder member of the Metabolist Group. Working particularly with Maki, he insisted on "Group Form" as the only valid urban instrument. To the dimensions of time and the three spatial dimensions, he added a fifth, the "dimension of the group." He hoped to generate fertile circumstances for the prismatic realization of city, and, in a series of projected urban accommodations and floating arcadia, he illustrated how "Group Form" could contribute to that ideal.

But those projects, when actually built, came to have a bitter realism about them. Otaka had learned (along with architects of Tange's generation) that despite the Metabolist plea for an untrammelled architecture, the result, when actually built, was inevitably a concrete and determinate object in the field of environmental relations. The resultant architecture has been a positing of lines and barriers in an ongoing filtering process whereby positive is separated from negative, yin from yang, wabi from sabi. The built element in Otaka's projects has come to assume a very deliberate and directing role: it does not try to be an entrepreneurial mechanism whereby urban transactions are effected; it manifests itself as the actual stuff (quiditas) of these exchanges.

Take his Chiba Prefectural Center of 1967: here the "thingness" is very evident: it is a place where civic justice is quite patently to be administered, a place where power is obviously manifest, a single object-crystal of self-evident truth to which all else must bow. There is no room to wonder whether this kind of justice is, in fact, as true as the whole enterprise is making out. Of course, answering such a question was not part of the architect's brief, and in a way he was right to gloss it over—yet one regrets that there isn't even the slightest crack or blemish in the building's logic of authority. His Gunma Prefectural Library (1978) also succumbs to the institutional – a civic bewilderness of rampant concretism, running away from the delights on offer at Mozuna's monumental architecture. To be civic doesn't necessarily mean one has to be grim or stern. But Otaka prefers to collaborate with those in power by giving them the kind of forbidding hideaways they so eagerly seek out. He leaves behind him a benumbed city, like a town under siege.

There is an interesting similarly between these projects and the main sanctuaries of some of the more prosperous of the new Japanese religions such as Soka Gakkai. The languages of civic and religious power overlap to an extent that might embarrass the Western observer, but to the Japanese they are reconcilable. I asked the architect responsible for the design of a temple in Kyoto for the new Buddhist sect, Konko-Kyo, why he had treated it in much the same vein as the coffee house he had designed elsewhere in Kyoto. With the headquarters of the sect carried out in Shinto style, the main sanctuary in Buddhist style, and the temple in Kyoto in a contemporary guise—under such conditions, he could make no sense of my question. The Japanese perceives and divides up his universe in a way quite distinct from ours, and we shouldn't be surprised by such apparent stylistic anomalies, any more than we should be surprised to find that in a recent poll of the religious practices of the Japanese, a great percentage of those polled professed to be believers in both Buddhism and Shinto.

—Chris Fawcett

OTANI, Sachio.

Japanese. Born in Tokyo, 20 February 1924. Educated at the University of Tokyo, Dip.Arch. 1946, D.Arch. 1951. Married Akiko Ochiai in 1952; daughter: Michiko. Worked as an architectural designer, office of Kenzo Tange, Tokyo, 1946-60. In private practice, Tokyo, since 1960. Lecturer, Department of Architecture, 1955-64, Assistant Professor of City Planning, 1964-71, and since 1971 Professor of City Planning, University of Tokyo. Exhibitions: *Contemporary Japanese Architecture*, toured Italy, 1968; *Sachio Otani: Pan-Pacific Prize Exhibition*, Honolulu, 1969. Recipient: First Prize, International Conference Hall Competition, Kyoto, 1963; Pan-Pacific Prize, American Institute of Architects, Hawaii Chapter, 1969. Member, Architectural Institute of Japan, and the City Planning Institute of Japan. Address: 3-22-15 Shoan, Suginami-ku, Tokyo 167, Japan.

Works:

1960/
61   Kojimachi District Redevelopment, Tokyo (project)

1960/
64   Tensho Kotai Jingu Religious Sect Headquarters, Yamaguchi Prefecture, Japan

1961/
63   Tokyo Children's Cultural Center

1963/
66   Kyoto International Conference Hall

1964/
69   The Wholesalers' Market Center, Toyama, Japan

1965/
66   Pavilion for Children, Children's Land, Kanagawa Prefecture, Japan (with sculptor Isamu Noguchi)
Japan Social Insurance Agency Office Building, Tokyo

1967/
68   Sagamihara Campus of Kitazato University, Kanagawa Prefecture, Japan

1967/
69   Kanazawa Institute of Technology, Ishikawa Prefecture, Japan

1967/
70   Sumitomo Fairytale Pavilion, *Expo '70*, Osaka
Tensho Kotai Jingu Religious Sect Headquarters extension, Yamaguchi Prefecture, Japan

1969/
70   Ohtsuka House, Tokyo
Kawaramachi High-rise Housing Estate, Kawasaki, Kanagawa Prefecture, Japan (project)

1969/
73   Kyoto International Conference Hall extension

1970/
71   Master plan for the west part of the Kawasaki Station Redevelopment, Kawasaki, Kanagawa Prefecture, Japan

1973/
75   Tensho Kotai Jingu Religious Sect Complex, Honolulu

1973/
77   Tensho Kotai Jingu Religious Sect Complex, Tokyo

1973/
80   National Institute of Environmental Study, Tsukuba Kenkyu Gakuen Toshi, Ibaragi Prefecture, Japan

1975/
76   Kanazawa Institute of Technology extensions, Ishikawa Prefecture, Japan

1978   Singapore Convention Center (project)
Ohtsuka Company Office Building, Tokyo

Publications:

By OTANI: books—*History of Urban Space Composition*, Tokyo 1972; *Regional Planning and Environment*, Tokyo 1972; *Life and the City*, Tokyo 1974; articles—"Urban Design and Architecture" in *Journal of Architecture and Building Science* (Tokyo), October 1965; "Urban Space and Community" in *Chiiki Kaihatsu* (Tokyo), May 1971; "Logic in Space Composition" in *Toshi Jutaku* (Tokyo), December 1971; "Matters Relating to Urban Renewal" in *Man and City*, Tokyo 1973; "Composition of Urban Space" in *Contemporary Policies in City Planning*, Tokyo 1973; "Historical Landscape Design and City Planning" in *Journal of Architecture and Building Science* (Tokyo), December 1973; "City Planning and Cultural Properties" in *Gekkan Bunkazai* (Tokyo), June 1975; "Contemporary Architecture and the Quality of Urban Space" in *Toshi Jutaku* (Tokyo), October 1975; "Low-rise Collective Housing" in *Toshi Jutaku* (Tokyo), May 1977; "The Role of City Planning in the Conservation of Historical Towns" in *Kankyo Bunka* (Tokyo), February 1978.

On OTANI: books—*New Japanese Architecture* by Egon Tempel, New York 1969; *The Complete Works of Contemporary Japanese Architects*, volume 18, edited by Isamu Kurita, Tokyo 1970; *Shinkenchiku-sha: A Guide to Japanese Architecture*, Tokyo 1971; *Beyond Metabolism: The New Japanese Architecture* by Michael Franklin Ross, New York 1978; articles—"The Tokyo Children's Culture Center" in *The Japan Architect* (Tokyo), September 1964; "The Headquarters of the Tensho Kotai Jingu Sect" in *The Japan Architect* (Tokyo), March 1966; "Kyoto International Conference Hall" in *Kokusai Kentiku* (Tokyo), July 1966; "Trapezoids Shape International Conference Center in Kyoto, Japan" in *Progressive Architecture* (New York), August 1966; "Palais des Conférences Internationales à Kyoto" and "Centre Religieux de la secte Tensho Kotai Jingu à Tabuse, District de Yamaguchi" in *L'Architecture d'Aujourd'hui* (Paris), September 1966; "The Architecture of Japan" in *Canadian Architect* (Toronto), January 1967; "Japanische Architecktur," special issue of *Baumeister* (Munich), August 1967; "Children's Land Juvenile Hall" in *The Japan Architect* (Tokyo), November 1967; "The Kitasate University, Sagamihara Campus" in *The Japan Architect* (Tokyo), October 1968; "Expo '70 Projects," special issue of *The Japan Architect* (Tokyo), April 1969; "Kanazawa Institute of Technology: Its Center and Its Civil Engineering Building" in *Kenchiku Bunka* (Tokyo), October 1969; "New Developments in Japanese Architecture" in *Architectural Record* (New York), September 1970; "New Trends in the Design of Public Operated Apartment Houses" in *Kenchiku Bunka* (Tokyo), December 1972; "Additions to the Kyoto International Conference Hall" in *The Japan Architect* (Tokyo), August 1973; "Kanazawa Institute of Technology" in *The Japan Architect* (Tokyo), April 1977; "Kanazawa Institue of Technology Library Center" in *The Japan Architect* (Tokyo) January 1983.

Bibliography: *Sachio Otani: Tange's Disciple* by James P. Noffsinger, Monticello, Illinois 1980.

Sachio Otani was one of Kenzo Tange's close

Sachio Otani: Kyoto International Conference Hall, Japan, 1966.

collaborators, working on some of the latter's earliest and best works such as the Hiroshima Peace Center. With the Tokyo Children's Cultural Center, he began his independent career, and since then his buildings, though few have been marked by a distinct style.

The Children's Center revealed his design approach, which has basically remained unchanged: an aggressive expression of the structure, a bold, sculptural handling of masses, and an intense articulation of functions. It also raised questions, which have persisted throughout his career, about his monumental sense of scale, here especially troubling in a building intended for children. More in keeping with its use is the Tensho Kotai Jingu Sect Headquarters, where the exposed concrete masses form an even more heroic ensemble.

The Kyoto International Conference Hall, which Otani designed on the basis of his winning entry in an open competition, is his representative building and shows both his strengths and weaknesses. One must applaud his effort to make a novel structural system of slanting columns and precast wall panels work. The system creates trapezoidal sections of different sizes and recalls a traditional method of wood consturction in Japan called *gassho zukuri:* thus the Hall may be considered Otani's contribution to the "Tradition Debate" that took place in the 1950's and 1960's. Otani has explored the architectural possibilities of this framework and has produced exciting visual effects, particularly on the outside, where (for example) interpreters' booths jut out of the conference hall. Yet the effort is all too visible inside, and the merit of having chosen this unorthodox system becomes debatable as the novelty wears off—when you have seen one room with a trapesoidal section, you have seen them all.

Otani is known as a theoretician and educator, and his Kojimachi Redevelopment Project is his essay in experimental urban design and housing. The dwelling units are self-contained and raised off the ground on stilts. The possibility of their fitting various ground contours is investigated, yet little else is shown to indicate that the project was meant for a specific site, much less one in central Tokyo.

The same slightly academic air prevails in Otani's more recent public housing project in Kawasaki, which was actually built. One can see his characteristic desire to explore new spatial organizations. In a typical building, the bottom half of the slab splays outward, creating inside what was intended to be a sheltered semi-public space. Unfortunately, nothing has been done with this space and it is dark and cavernous; one expects manacled prisoners to file past, not children and adults engaged in those spontaneous encounters the architect undoubtedly sought to promote.

In the end, it si not for his earnest investigations into new spatial organizations but for the indisputably dramatic sculptural expression of his forms that Otani's work will be remembered.

—Hiroshi Watanabe

OTTO, Frei.

German. Born in Siegmar, Saxony, 31 May 1925. Educated at the Schadow School, Zehlendorf, Berlin, as a trainee stonemason, 1931-43; Technische Hochschule, Charlottenburg, Berlin, 1932; Technical University of Berlin, under Freese, Bickenbach and Jobst, 1948-50 (on study trip to the United States, 1950-51), Dip.Ing. 1952, Dr.Ing. 1954. Did compulsory labour service, then served as a fighter pilot in the German Air Force, 1943-45; prisoner of war in France, 1945-47: Prison Camp Architect, Depot 501, Chartres, France, 1946-47. Married Ingrid Smolla in 1952; children: Angela, Bettina, Christine, Dietmar, and Erdmute. In private practice, Zehlendorf, Berlin, 1952-58; established architecture studio in Zehlendorf, Berlin, with Lohs, Bubner, Frank, Wehrhan, Medlin, et al, 1958-68. Since 1968, associated with Studio Warmbronn, with Bubner, Krier, Thorsteinn, Wright, Goedert, Goldsmith, Fritz, Doster, et al., Warmbronn, West Germany: since 1972 has worked only in collaboration with other architects, engineers, and surveyors. Adviser to the Large Tent Construction Division, L. Stromeyer and Company, Constance, West Germany, 1953-74; Adviser to Höchst AG on the use of technical fibers, 1973-75. Founder, Development Center for Lightweight Construction, Berlin, 1957. Since 1964 Professor and Director of the Institute for Lightweight Structures, and since 1976, Professor-in-Ordinary, University of Stuttgart. Visiting Professor of Design, Washington University, St Louis, 1958, Design Academy, Ulm, West Germany 1969, Yale University, New Haven, Connecticut, 1960, University of California, Berkeley, 1962, Massachusetts Institute of Technology/Harvard University, Cambridge, Massachusetts, 1962, University of Zulia, Maracaibo, Venezuela, 1962, National Institute of Design, Ahmedabad, India, 1966, and the International Summer Acedemy, Salzburg, Austria, 1971. Co-editor, *Arcus* magazine, Munich, since 1983. Exhibitions: *The Work of Frei Otto,* Museum of Modern Art, New York, 1971; *Leichtarchitektur: Frei Otto and His Teams 1955-1976,* travelling exhibition, North America, Europe, South Africa and the Middle East, 1975-78; *Natürliche Konstruktionen,* Institut für Auslandsbeziehungen, Stuttgart, 1981 (and world tour); *Leichtbau in Architektur und Natur,* Schussev Museum, Moscow, 1983. Recipient:

Paul Bonatz Prize, Stuttgart, 1971; City Architecture Prize, Cologne, 1971; Honorary Award for Use of Plastics, Club of Plastics Use, Munich, 1972; Thomas Jefferson Memorial Medal, University of Virginia, Charlottesville, 1974; Berlin Arts Prize, 1976; Auguste Perret Prize, with Rolf Gutbrod, International Union of Architects, 1976; Plaque, Bund Deutscher Architekten, 1978; Hugo Häring Prize, 1978; Deutscher Holzbaupreis, 1979; Aga Khan Award (with Rolf Gutbrod), 1980; Research and Technique Medal, Académie d'Architecture, Paris, 1982; Grand BDA Prize, Biberach, West Germany, 1982. Dr.Art/Arch: Washington University, St. Louis, 1973; D.Sc.: University of Bath, Avon, 1980; Honorary Professor, Technische Hochschule, Stuttgart, 1965, and University Federico Villareal, Lima, Peru, 1977. Honorary Fellow, American Institute of Architects, 1968; Royal Institute of British Architects, 1982. Member, Akademie der Künste, Berlin, 1970; Accademia di Archaeologica, Lettere et Belle Arti, Naples, 1983; Academie d'Architecture, Paris, 1983. Addresses: Berghalde 19, 7250 Leonberg-Warmbronn, West Germany; Institut für Leichte Flächentragwerke (IL), Universität Stuttgart, Pfaffenwaldring 14, 7000 Stuttgart 80 —Vaihingen, West Germany.

Works:

1953/
56 Social housing, Alexandrastiftung, Templehof, Berlin
1955 Tent Pavilions, *Bundesgartenschau,* Kassel, West Germany
1956 Tents, and Aircraft Hangars, *Gartenschau,* Saarbrucken, West Germany
Observation Pavilion, Oktoberfest, Munich
1957 Dance Floor Tent, Entrance Canopy, and Tent Shelters, *Bundesgartenschau,* Cologne
City of Tomorrow Pavilion, *Interbau,* Berlin
Small Exhibition Halls, Interbau, Berlin (with Gunschel and Carl Otto)
Cafe at Schloss Bellevue, Gropius Building, *Interbau,* Berlin (with Bubner and Lohs)
1958 Inselcafe Tent, *Saffa Exhibition,* Zürich
Tent Pavilion, *Gartenschau,* Saarbrucken, West Germany
1959 Frei Otto Studio, Türksteinweg 5, Berlin 37
1960 Tent for evangelist Billy Graham, Berlin
1961 Design of Evangelical Church Day celebrations, Olympic Stadium, Berlin
1962 Experimental structures, Deubau, West Germany
1963 Undulating Tent, Membrane Structure Hall, and Star Halls/Pavilions, Bundesgartenschau, Hamburg, West Germany
1964 Snow and Rocks Restaurant Pavilion, *Swiss National Exhibition,* Lausanne
1965 Retractable roof, Cannes, France (for Roger Taillibert)
Mobile theatre, for the Dutch Opera Foundation (project; with van den Broek and Bakema)
1967 German Pavilion, *Expo '67,* Montreal (with Rolf Gutbrod)
1968 Retractable roof for the Open-Air Theatre, Bad Hersfeld, West Germany (with Romberg and Bubner)
Institute of Light Surface Structures, Vaihingen, West Germany
1969 Arctic City (project; with Ove Arup and Kenzo Tange)
1970 Luisenburg Roof (project; with Romberg)
1971 Mobile large umbrella roof for the Music Pavilion, *Bundesgartenschau,* Cologne
1972 Roofs for the Olympic Stadium and Arenas, Munich (for Günter Behnisch; with Bubner, Aver, Büxel, and Fritz Leonhardt)
1973 Cultural Center, Abidjan, Ivory Coast (project; with Ove Arup and Rolf Gutbrod)
1974 Hotel and Conference Center, Mecca, Saudi Arabia (with Ove Arup and Rolf Gutbrod)

Mannheim Multi-Hall, West Germany
Spa and Recreation Centre, Baden-Baden, West Germany (competition project; with Rolf Gutbrod)
1976 Ministry of Industry and Electricity, Riyadh, Saudi Arabia (project; with Ove Arup and Rolf Gutbrod)
1978 Airfish High Performance Airship (project)
1978 Council of Ministers Building, Riyadh, Saudi Arabia (with Ove Arup and Rolf Gutbrod)
1980 Great Aviary, Hellabrunn, West Germany (with Happold)
"58 North" Climate-controlled Hall, Alberta, Canada (project; with Fullerton, Happold and Liddell)
1981 Sports Hall, King Abdul Aziz University, Jeddah, Saudi Arabia (with Gutbrod, Henning, Arup and Happold)
Mountain Tents for Pilgrims, Nuna, near Mecca, Saudi Arabia (prototypes; with Stone, Rasch and Angawi)
Diplomatic Club, Riyadh, Saudi Arabia (project; with Famous, Shibahi and Happold)
Foreign Office, Riyadh, Saudi Arabia (project; with Fritz, Kendel and Happold)
1982 Inflatable Barrage for the Rhein-Main-Donau Canal (project; with Giesecke, Happold and others)
Economical Housing on the Anhalter Platz, Berlin (IBA project; with Kendel, Happold and others)
1983 "Green" Housing Block, Sudrand Tiergarten, Berlin (IBA project; with Kendel, Gutbrod and others)

Publications:

By OTTO: books—*The Suspended Roof,* Berlin 1954; *Tensile Structures,* volume 1, with R. Trostel, Berlin 1962, and volume 2, with F.-K. Schlyer, Berlin 1966; *Natürliche Konstruktionen,* with others, Stuttgart 1982; *Schriften und Reden, 1951-1983,* edited by B. Burkhardt, Braunschweig, West Germany, and Stuttgart 1984; editor of *IL-Publications,* 25 volumes, Stuttgart, 1969-85; articles—"Vom Nest zur modernen Wohnstadt" in *Der Architekt* (Stuttgart), vol. 3, no. 12, 1954; "Vom ungeheizt schön warmen Haus und neuen Fenstern" in *Deutsche Bauzeitschrift* (Gutersloh, West Germany), no. 3, 1955; "Bauten für morgen?" in *Bauen und Wohnen* (Zurich), no. 3, 1955; "Die Stadt von morgen und das Einfamilienhaus" in *Baukunst und Werkform* (Nuremberg), no. 12, 1956; "Formes, techniques et constructions humaines" in *L'Architecture d'aujourd'hui* (Paris), no. 78, 1958; "Imagination et architecture" in *L'Architecture d'aujourd'hui* (Paris), no. 102, 1962; "Die Erdoberfläche" in *Bauen und Wohnen* (Zürich), no. 1, 1984; "Villes futures" in *L'Architecture d'aujourd'hui* (Paris), no. 115, 1964; "Ein Interbau und ein Spinnerzentrum" in *Deutsche Bauzeitung* (Stuttgart), September 1970; "Die neue Zeit der vielen Architekturen" in *Deutsche Bauzeitung* (Stuttgart), December 1972; "Die Europastadt" in *Deutsche Bauzeitung* (Stuttgart), December 1973; "Creation, Creativity and Architecture" in *Architectural Design* (London), no. 7, 1975; "Mit Leichtigkeit gegen Brutalistät" in *Deutsche Bauzeitung* (Stuttgart), January 1976; "Les formules qui menent l'architecture" in *L'Architecture* (Paris), no. 396, 1976; "Widernatürliche Architektur" in *Universitatsnachrichten* (Stuttgart), no. 50, 1977; "Wie weiter?" in *Schweizerische Bauzeitung* (Zürich), no. 16, 1977; "Naturliche Konstruktionen," with J. G. Helmcke and B. Burkhardt, in *Bauen + Wohnen* (Stuttgart) no. 4, 1978; "Der Pneu, Bauprinzip des Lebens" in *Bild der Wissenschaft* (Stuttgart), no. 15, 1978; "Biologie und Bauen" in *Durchblick* (Stuttgart), no. 6, 1980; "Das Aesthetische" in *Mitteilung des Instituts für leichte Flächentragwerke,* vol. 21, Stuttgart 1979; "Bauen in Natur und Technik" in *Forschung in der BRD,* Weinheim, West Germany 1983; recording—*Self-Designing Structures,* tape cassette and slides, London 1982.

On OTTO: books—*Documents of Modern Architecture: Shell Architecture,* edited by Jürgen Joedicke, Stuttgart and London 1963; *Tension Structures* by Conrad Roland, New York 1970; *The Work of Frei Otto,* exhibition catalogue, by Lüdwig Glaeser, New York 1971, revised as *Leichtarchitektur: Frei Otto and His Teams 1955-1976,* 1975, 1977; *Frei Otto: Form und Konstruktion* by Philip Drew, Stuttgart 1976; *Architektur in der Bundesrepublik* by Heinrich Klotz, Frankfurt 1977; *Architektur in Deutschland* by H. and M. Bofinger, J. Paul and H. Klotz, Stuttgart 1979; articles—"Frei Otto's Pneumatic Structures" in *Architectural Design* (London), July 1966; "Frei Otto Designs 1,865 Million Cubic Feet of Air" by R. L. Medlin in *Architectural Forum* (New York), April 1967; "Tents as Ideal Buildings" in *The Japan Architect* (Tokyo), July 1970; "Frei Otto at Work" in *Architectural Design* (London), March 1971; "Otto Biography" in *Industrial Design* (New York), June 1971; "Frei Otto: Biographical and Bibliographical Notes" in *Zodiac* (Milan), no. 21, 1972; "The Work of Frei Otto" in *Architecture Canada* (Toronto), 12 June 1972; "Garden Gridshell" by Tony Mitchell in *Building Design* (London), 25 April 1975; "When Is a Tent Not a Tent?" by Stephanie Williams in *Building Design* (London), 16 January 1976; "Swiss Cable Message" by Annette LeCuyer in *Building Design* (London), 8 June 1979; "Hotel and Conference Centre, La Mecca, Saudi Arabia" in *Domus* (Milan), June 1979; "Frei Otto Visit to Singapore" in *SIA Journal* (Sngapore), January/February 1980; "Frei Otto—Search for a Minimal Architecture" by Philip Drew in *Architect* (Melbourne), February 1980; "Otto's Desert Tent" in *Building Design* (London), 16 January 1981; "Frei Otto's New Work" in *MIMAR* (Singapore), April/June 1982; "Frei Otto" in *Architecture + Urbanism* (Tokyo), June 1982; "Natural Structure: Ideas and Plans of Frei Otto and his Team," special issue of *Deutsche Bauzeitung* (Stuttgart), July 1982; "Frei Otto—Recent Projects" in *L'Architecture d'aujourd'hui* (Paris), October 1982; "Aesthetic Truth" by E. Schunck in *Der Architekt* (Stuttgart), December 1982; "Frei Otto in Defence of Nature" by Walter Segal in *Architects' Journal* (London), 9 March 1983; "Looking for Wood in the Trees" by Lynda Relph-Knight in *Building Design* (London), 18 November 1983.

Bibliography—*Frei Otto's Tensile Structures: A Selected Bibliography* by Lamia Doumato, Monticello, Illinois 1979.

Frei Otto: Institute of Light Surface Structures, Vaihingen, West Germany, 1968.

Frei Otto is wholly responsible for the revival of the tent as a leading species of modern tensile architecture. The grid shell, of which the 1974 Mannheim Multi-Hall is the most recent example, may appear at first glance to be unrelated to pre-industrial tents, but in reality, it is a modern version of the traditional trellis tent of Central Asia. The tent and monumental architecture are not isolated phenomena; at various times in history, each has had an influence on the other. Otto's modest, early textile structures and his later, regular mesh, steel cablenet structures are open pavilions of the kind that has been such an important archetype of modern architecture and achieved its purest expression in the hands of Mies van der Rohe.

Modern tensile building was inspired, in the main, by the industrial suspension bridge; consequently, Otto's promotion of modest, prestressed, textile pavilions as an alternative prototype involved such a radically different conception of tensile form that he challenged current ideas on the nature and application of these structures. The much freer small-scale development of prestessed textile and cablenet pavilions in the 1960s is due, to a considerable extent, to Otto's pioneering efforts.

If, as Siegfried Giedion has asserted, construction is the subconscious of modern architecture, then Otto's role has been to enlarge and enrich its resources by the addition of an entirely new vocabulary of structural forms. His contribution is comparable to that of the other great twentieth-century shell builders and structural innovators, notably Candela, Torroja, Nervi, and Fuller.

Otto's architecture is a curious combination of Rationalism and Romanticism; it is, in the finest sense, an organic architecture that seeks to realize minimal-energy structures with shapes that correspond to the fundamental spatial laws of the universe. He belongs to the Rationalist strand of modern architecture in which architectural expression is achieved through the unhindered revelation of structure. Otto's emphasis on structural clarity, pure compression or tension stressed shapes, minimal surface, and material constructions all suggest a strong Rationalist bias and an extreme commitment to structural determinism of architectural form.

Otto's obvious Rationalism is allied to a thoroughly German kind of Romanticism, as shown in his reliance on such automatic processes as hanging chains, minimal soap films, and stretched fabrics and membranes to establish structural form, and in his consuming interest in biological structures. His emphasis on structural process as a primary design tool is innately Romantic because it respresents a rejection of culturally determined styles in architecture and a return to nature.

The highly curved shapes of Otto's pavilions are in striking harmony with landscape and biological forms; the artificial terrain of the large cablenet roofs counterpoints adjacent natural earth contours, and the Institute of Light Surface Structures at Vaihingen and the grid shell at Mannheim display disconcerting reptilian characteristics.

Otto's innovations have been of outstanding importance for the advancement of tensile architecture because he has combined research into the best forms for prestressed surface structures with the creation of the technical means to construct them. Traditional urban tents had predetermined, simple shapes, and twentieth-century engineers tended to follow this practice by adopting mathematically defined shapes for their structures. At a time when the analysis of cable structures was relatively undeveloped, Otto was able to explore a host of complex, indeterminate shapes and establish optimal geometries for his structures by using a range of model testing techniques. From the outset, Otto sought to discover the full range of anti-classically curved surfaces, the effect of various methods of supporting them, and the influence of various edge arrangements on the final shape.

The Snow and Rocks Restaurant pavilions at the *Swiss National Exhibition* at Lausanne in 1964 were Otto's first cablenets. Previously, all his roofs were made of cotton canvas with modest spans of from twenty to thirty metres. The Lausanne pavilions were transitional membrane-cablenet structures. The German Pavilion at *Expo '67* was Otto's first truly large-scale cablenet roof. With the completion of this pavilion, prestressed cablenet structures came of age, and, for the first time, the constructional means used matched the structural demands of large-scale prestressed structures having a freely sculptured surface topography. A new identity of form, structure, and construction was now feasible. The roofs of the main stadium and arenas of the 1972 Olympic Games at Munich added little to the Montreal achievement beyond the development of purely mathematical, computer-based procedures for determining cablenet patterns.

The small, early *Bundesgartenschau* textile pavilions are amongst Otto's most lyrical and successful works—the riverside shelter and dance pavilions at Cologne (1957) and the small, undulating star paviions at Hamburg (1963) were outstanding for their integration of aesthetics and construction. The close association of Otto and Peter Stromeyer, a leading tent manufacturer from Constance, undoubtedly contributed to the excellence of these early pevilions. The pre-1963 textile pavilions usually consisted of standard membrane elements arranged symmetrically in additive compositions. It was not until the mid-1960s, and his collaboration with the Stuttgart architect Rolf Gutbrod, that Otto began to explore picturesque, asymmetrical surfaces divided unevenly with interior low or high points. The Montreal Pavilion is the outstanding example of such a freely formed roofscape with its evocation of earthforms. The simply suspended auditorium roofs of the Hotel and Conference Centre at Mecca, (1974) are later fruits of Otto's collaboration with Gutbrod.

Otto exploited the inherent flexibility of textile structures by devising the convertible roof; its variable geometry allows the roof membrane to be retracted when not required. A great many such roofs have been constructed in Germany, France, and elsewhere, but none is so captivating as the roof for the Open-Air Theatrue at Bad Hersfeld (1968)

Since 1970, Otto has concentrated his attention on the analysis of biological material. Most of his genuine innovations were made prior to 1964, and his work sbusequently has involved an elaboration and detailed development of these early proposals. Otto's researches in the area of structure are remarkable for their diversity and inclusiveness. Today, he is no longer so active as a designer, and his influential role in Germany architecture is increasingly one of stimulating and guiding advanced architectural theory.

—Philip Drew

OUD, Jacobus Johannes Pieter.

Dutch. Born in Purmerend, 9 February 1890. Educated at the Quellinus Arts and Crafts School, Amsterdam; Rijksnormal School, Amsterdam; Technical University, Delft, Netherlands. Worked in the offices of Cuypers and Stuyt, Amsterdam, and of Theodor Fischer, Munich. In private practice, Purmerend, Netherlands, 1913-14; worked with W. M. Dudok, *q.v.*, in his studio, Leiden, Netherlands, 1915-16; in private practice, Leiden, Netherlands, 1916-18; City Architect, Rotterdam, 1918-33; in private practice, Rotterdam, 1933-54, and in Wassenaar, near The Hague, 1954 until his death in 1963. Founder-Member, with Theo van Doesburg and others, De Stijl group, Leiden, Netherlands, 1916-20; Founder, with Jan Wils and van Doesburg, De Sphinx Art Club, Leiden, Netherlands, 1917, and, with van Doesburg, *De Stijl* magazine, Leiden, Netherlands, 1917. Exhibitions: *Modern Architects*, Museum of Modern Art, New York, 1932; *J. J. P. Oud*, Rotterdam, 1951; *J. J. P. Oud: Bauten 1906-63*,

Neue Sammlung, Munich, 1965, and Akademie der Künste, Berlin, 1966; *The Architecture of J. J. P. Oud*, Florida State University, Tallahasee, 1978; *The Original Drawings of J. J. P. Oud*, Architectural Association, London, 1979; *Het nieuwe bouwen in Rotterdam, 1920-1960*, Museum Boymans-van Beuningen, Rotterdam, 1982. Honorary doctorate: Technical University, Delft, Netherlands, 1945. *Died* (in Wassenaar, Netherlands) *5 April 1963.*

Works:

1906 House, Purmerend, Netherlands
1911 Housing, for the Vooruit Company, Purmerend, Netherlands
1912 Cinema, Purmerend, Netherlands
      Country house, Aalsmeer, Netherlands
1915 Country house, Blaricum, Netherlands
      Public Baths, Purmerend, Netherlands (project)
      Military Convalescent Home, Den Helder, Netherlands (project)
1916 Leidendorp Housing Estate, Leiden, Netherlands (with W. M. Dudok)
      House, Broek, Waterland, Netherlands
      Housing, Velp, Netherlands (project)
1917 De Vonk Boarding School, Nordwijkerhout, Netherlands
      Allegonda House, Katwijk, Netherlands (with M. Kamerlingh Onnes; enlarged, 1927)
      School of Art and Trade, Den Helder, Netherlands (project)
      Terraced beach houses, Scheveningen, Netherlands (project)
1918 Terraced Housing (project)
      Reinforced Concrete Semi-Detached Housing (project)
1919 Spangen Housing Estate, Rotterdam (destroyed in World War II)
      Distillery/Shop, Purmerend, Netherlands (project)
      Factory/Offices, Purmerend, Netherlands (project)
1920 Tusschendijken Housing Estate, Rotterdam (damaged, 1943; reconstructed, 1950)
1922 Oud Mathenesse (semi-permanent) Housing Estate, Rotterdam
      House, Grunewald, Berlin (project)
1923 Temporary Administration Building, Oud Mathenesse Quarter, Rotterdam
1924 Workers' housing blocks (2), Hook of Holland
1925 De unie Cafe, Rotterdam (destroyed, 1940)
      Kiefhoek Workers' Village, Rotterdam
1926 Stianssi Hotel, Brno, Czechoslovakia (project)
      New Stock Exchange Building, Rotterdam (project)
1927 Basic Terraced Housing, Weissenhofsiedlung, Stuttgart
      Allegonda House extensions and remodelling, Katwijk, Netherlands
      People's University, Rotterdam (project)
1928 Church, Kiefhoek Workers' Village, Rotterdam
      Three-family house, Brno, Czechoslovakia (project)
1931 Blijdorp Workers' Housing Quarter, Rotterdam (project)
1934 Apartment Types (preliminary projects)
      Dinaux House, Rotterdam (project)
1935 House/Studio, Hillegersberg, Netherlands (project)
1936 Pfeffer Country House, Blaricum, Netherlands (project)
1938/
  42 Shell Company Corporate Headquarters, The Hague
1942/
  43 Plan for the centre of Rotterdam (project)
1943 Central Savings Bank, Rotterdam
1947 Workers' Terraced Housing Types (project)

1948 Dutch Steelworks Headquarters, Ijmuiden, Netherlands (project)
Dutch Soldiers' Monument, Grebbeberg Cemetery, Rhenen, Netherlands
1949 War Memorial, Dam Square, Amsterdam (with the sculptors John and Han Radecker)
1950 Esveha Company Offices, Rotterdam
Semi-detached house, Bloemendaal, Netherlands (project)
Plan for the San Lorenzo Complex, Rotterdam (project)
1951 Religious Centre, The Hague (project)
Workers' terraced housing, Arnhem, Netherlands (with N.P.A.M. van Hassel)
Water/Bell Tower, Emmeloord, Netherlands (project)
1952 South Holland Local Government Headquarters, The Hague
1952/
60 Bio Children's Convalescent Home, near Arnhem, Netherlands
School, The Hague
1954/
56 Utrecht Life Insurance Company Building, Rotterdam
1956/
63 Congress Hall Complex, The Hague
1958 De Hoge Veluwe Park-Keeper's House (project)
1960 House, Voorburg, Netherlands (project)
1962 Town Hall, Almelo, Netherlands (project)

Publications:

By OUD: books—*Het Hofplein-plan van Dr. Berlage,* Rotterdam 1922; *Holländische Architektur,* Munich 1926; *Nieuwe bouwkunst in Holland en Europe,* 's Graveland, Netherlands 1935; *Il Palazzo B.I.M. Shell,* The Hague 1951; *Zijn er nog architecten?,* The Hague 1959; *Mondriaan,* with L. J. F. Wijsenbeek, Zeist, Netherlands 1962; *Architecturalia voor bouwheren en architecten,* The Hague 1963; *Mein Weg in De Stijl,* Rotterdam 1962; articles—numerous in *De stijl* (Leiden, Netherlands), *De 8 en Opbouw* (Amsterdam), *i 10* (Amsterdam), and *De Groene Amsterdammer;* "Landhauser von Hermann Muthesius" in *Bouwkundig Weekblad* (The Hague), November 1913; "Over Cubisme, Futurisme, moderne bouwkunst" in *Bouwkundig Weekblad* (The Hague), September 1916; "Glas in lood van Theo van Doesburg" in *Bouwkundig Weekblad* (The Hague), August 1918; "Wohin fuhrt das neue Bauen: Kunst und Standard" in *Neue Zürcher Zeitung* (Zürich), September 1927; "Das flache Dachin Holland" in *Neue Frankfurt,* October/December 1927; "Architecture and the Future" in *The Studio* (London), December 1928; "The European Movement Towards a New Architecture" in *The Studio* (London), April 1933; "Mr. Oud Replies" in *Architectural Record* (New York), March 1947; "United Nations Headquarters" in *RIBA Journal* (London), October 1948; "Clarity in Town Planning" in *Housing and Town and Country Planning* (London), April 1949.

On OUD: books—*J. J. P. Oud* by Henry-Russell Hitchcock, Paris 1931; *Modern Architects,* exhibition catalogue, by Alfred Barr, Henry-Russell Hitchcock, and Lewis Mumford, New York, 1932; *J.J.P. Oud,* exhibition catalogue, by W. Jos de Gruyter, Rotterdam 1951; *J. J. P. Oud* by Giuliana Veronesi, Milan 1953; *J. J. P. Oud* by K. Wiekart, Amsterdam 1965; *J. J. P. Oud: Bauten 1906-63,* exhibition catalogue, by Wend Fischer, Munich 1965; *The Architecture of J.J.P. Oud, 1906-1963,* exhibition catalogue, by Gunther Stamm, Tallahasse, Florida 1978; *The Original Drawings of J.J.P. Oud, 1890-1963,* exhibition catalogue, London 1979; *Amsterdamse Bouwen, 1880-1980,* edited by Ids Haagsma and others, Utrecht, Netherlands and Antwerp, Belgium 1981; *Het Nieuwe Bouwen in Rotterdam, 1920-1960* by Wim Beeren, Rob Dettingmeijer, Frank Kauffman and others, Delft, Netherlands 1982; *J.J.P. Oud, Architect 1890-1963: Feiten en herinneringen gerangschikt* by Hans Oud, The Hague 1984; articles—special issue of *Sinkentiku* (Tokyo), 1924; "Entretiens sur l'Architecture Vivante: l'urbanisme en Hollande" by Jean Badovici in *Architecture vivante* (Paris), Summer 1925; "L'Evolution de l'architecture moderne en Hollande" by Theo van Doesburg in *Architecture vivante* (Paris), Autumn 1925; "The Architectural Work of J.J.P. Oud" by Henry-Russell Hitchcock in *Arts* (New York), February 1928; "J.J.P. Oud" by H.P.L. Wiessing in *Building* (London), July 1938; "Mr. Oud Embroiders a Theme" in *Architectural Record* (New York), December 1946; "Building at The Hague" in *Architectural Review* (London), April 1947; special issue of *Forum* (Amsterdam), no. 5/6, 1951; "Oud at 70" in *Bouwkundig weekblad* (The Hague), no. 23, 1960; "J.J.P. Oud" by Giuliana Veronesi in *Zodiac* (Milan), no. 12, 1963; "Notes on Oud" by Sergio Polano in *Lotus* (Venice), September 1977; "Functionalism Plus" in *Building Design* (London), 12 January 1979; "Along the Lines of Gradualness between Velp and Purmerend" by Gunther Stamm in *Bouw* (Rotterdam), 3 March 1979; "Cubism and De Stijl" by Gunther Stamm in *Bouw* (Rotterdam), 17 March 1979; "J.J.P. Oud's Blue Furniture" by Adina Riga in *Domus* (Milan), February 1980; "Student project: Fictitious Conversion of J.J.P. Oud's Terraced Housing in the Weissenhoffseidlung" in *AIT* (Stuttgart), no. 1, 1981; "Building or Make-Up—Oud's Preservation Work" by Ed Taverne in *Wonen TA/BK* (Heerlen, Netherlands), February 1983; "Architect Oud and Melody in architecture" by Hans Magdelijins in *Bouw* (Rotterdam), 15 and 29 October 1983.

*

Of all the leaders of the Modern Movement, it is the Dutchman J.J.P. Oud with his early method based on the mass-production and standardization of inexpensive working-class housing that has meant most to many of today's leading architects. A founder-member of the De Stijl group, Oud developed a style that is firmly that of the interrelationship of horizontal and vertical planes first understood by the Cubist painters and culminating in the severely geometric designs of the Neoplastic art of fellow De Stijl artist Piet Mondrian. The model for the proposed Purmerend factory, made in 1919, is a deliberate attempt to reproduce this severity with an obvious reliance on the simple relationships involving a series of interlocking forms and the inevitable cubic spaces left in between.

The influence of Frank Lloyd Wright is also crucial, arising partly from the exhibition of 1910 and partly from the fact that the spread of architectural magazines had resulted in Wright's ideas being both more widely known and certainly more accepted in Europe than in his native America.

This sympathetic amalgam of Wright and analytical Cubism led Oud to an essentially abstract concept of architecture and an intense distrust of the previous concern with hand-craft detailing and fussy ornamentation. This he saw as mere sentiment and even worse—"expressionistic"; he believed that materials, construction systems, and methods of production must be of the present and well-geared to the new machine age—fitted, in fact, to a life dependent on the machine. The standardization of the method of mass-production not only produced cheaper materials with which to build but also resulted in a uniformity that would inevitably lead to a social uniformity if used intelligently. Straight lines and clearcut forms were what was needed.

In 1917 Oud designed a row of seaside houses intended for an esplanade above the beach at Scheveningen, which are little more than a series of simple cubic masses, and it can be argued that in this unexecuted project of models and drawings, he is more concerned with the surface facade than with

controlled volume and that the link with Mondrian is clear.

The first built Rotterdam housing-estates at Spangen (1918-19) and Tusschendijken (1920), both of which were destroyed in World War II, were among the earliest schemes for low-cost, working-class housing and austerely built of brick. The later estates at Hook of Holland and Kiefhoek, also in Rotterdam, had a streamlined smoothness and sophisticated line that reflected an interest in something new. Oud's aim was to produce inexpensive building of a quality that would hint at real architecture.

The smallest, cheapest house could be mass-produced with enough variety in its design to provide a good, varied way of living for the workers who lived there. The style would be neutral and suggest a common anonymity; nowhere is the ideal better illustrated than in Oud's contribution to the Weissenhofsiedlung at Stuttgart in 1927. Here, he is seen at his inventive best amongst architects from five countries who offered their solutions to the growing housing problem and whose work has a remarkable consistency which led inevitably to what we now see as the International Style. Oud's terraced row was constructed of poured concrete—on-the-spot prefabrication—with typically vigorous projections and recessions and with the now almost obligatory flat roof. A well-thought-out arrangement of screens separated the houses that were stepped to conform to the slope of the ground. The interiors catered for accepted aspects of working-class life—"those without servants can well eat in the kitchen"—and the backyards offered ample opportunity for the necessary social contact. Modest in scale and in cost, they seemed the ideal solution.

In the early 1930s, however, Oud began to have doubts. He feared the danger of monotony and a sense of possible boredom and felt that his method limited him to little more than basic utilitarian problems. What he now envisaged was a happier balance between a strict objectivity of shape and an underlying gaiety which he hoped might bring an added richness through an increased variety of forms. He argued that the early fight for Modernism was over and that the battle had been won. A new evaluation was needed.

Oud's doubts have become our doubts, and an admiration for the early work, which is undoubtedly superior to anything he achieved later, leaves us thinking the same way. A new evaluation is needed and perhaps the revived interest in Oud, especially by the new re-thinking post-modernists, will help to provide the answer.

—John Furse

OWINGS, Nathaniel Alexander.
American. Born in Indianapolis, Indiana, 5 February 1903. Educated at the University of Illinois, Urbana, 1921-22; Cornell University, Ithaca, New York, 1927. Married Emily Otis in 1931 (divorced, 1953); children: Emily, Jennifer, Natalie, and Nathaniel Jr.; married Margaret Wentworth in 1954. Co-Founding Partner, with Louis Skidmore, *q.v.,* Skidmore and Owings, Chicago, 1936-39, and, with John Merrill, *q.v.,* Skidmore, Owings and Merrill, Chicago, New York, San Francisco, Portland, Oregon, Washington, D.C., etc., from 1939. Chairman, Chicago Plan Commission, 1948-51; Vice-Chairman, California Highway Scenic Roads Commission, 1964-67; Chairman, Temporary Commission on the Design of Pennsylvania Avenue, Washington, D.C., 1964-73, and Member of the Permanent Commission, 1973-82; Member, 1966-70, and Chairman, 1970-72, United States Secretary of the Interior's Advisory Board on the National Parks, Historic Sites, Building and Monuments,

Washington, D.C.; Chairman, Urban Design Concept Team for the United States Interstate Highway System, 1967-70. Trustee, American Academy in Rome. Exhibition: *Skidmore, Owings and Merrill*, Museum of Modern Art, New York, 1950. Recipient: Conservation Service Award, United States Department of the Interior, 1968; Gold Medal, American Institute of Architects, 1983. LL.D.: Ball State University, Muncie, Indiana, 1970; L.H.D.: Indiana University, Bloomington, 1973; Butler University, Indianapolis, 1976. Fellow, American Institute of Architects. *Died* (in Santa Fe, New Mexico) *13 June 1984.*

Publications:

By OWINGS: books—*The American Aesthetic*, New York 1969; *The Spaces in Between: An Architect's Journey*, Boston 1973; articles—"New Materials and Building Methods for the Chicago Exposition" in *Architectural Record* (New York), April 1932; "Economics of Department Store Planning" in *Architectural Record* (New York), February 1947; "What's New in Planning an Office Building?" in *Building* (London), December 1947; "Do We or Do We Not Orient the Bedroom?" in *Royal Architectural Institute of Canada Journal* (Toronto), September 1948; "Two Looks at Preservation" in *AIA Journal*(Washington, D.C.), February 1962.

Bibliography—*Nathaniel Owings of Skidmore, Owings, and Merril* by Lamia Doumato, Monticello, Illinois 1980

See SKIDMORE, OWINGS AND MERRILL

PANI, Mario.

Mexican. Born in Mexico City, 29 March 1911. Educated at elementary schools in Belgium and Italy; Lycée Janson de Sailly-Bachellor, Paris; Ecole Nationale Supérieure des Beaux-Arts, Paris, 1928-34, Dip.Arch. 1934; also awarded degree by the University of Mexico, Mexico City, 1934. Married Margarita Linaae in 1933; children: Margara, Mario, Jr., Ana, Eugenia, Enrique, Frederico, and Arturo. Since 1934, in private architectural practice, Mexico City. Chairman of the Board, Deplan S.A., international consultants, Mexico City, 1974-78. Professor of Architecture, University of Mexico, 1940-48. Founder and President, *Arquitectura Mexico* magazine, Mexico City, 1938-78. President of the Executive Board, Federal Public School Construction Program, Mexico City, 1944-48; Founder and Member of the Board, Colegio de Arquitectos de Mexico, 1946; Member of the Board, Committee for the Construction of Mexico City University, 1948-52; President, Regional Planning Commission of Acapulco, Mexico, 1951-53; Patron, San Carlos Museum of Art, 1954-78; Director, National Institute of Housing, Mexico City, 1955-64. Recipient: First Prize, Ciudad Victoria Stadium Competition, 1938; Bronze Medal, Marti Monument Competition, 1938; First Prize, House of Spain Competition, 1940; Gold Medal, VI Pan-American Congress, Lima, Peru, 1947; Gold Medal VII Pan-American Congress, Havana, Cuba, 1950. Honorary Fellow, Peruvian Institute of Urbanism, 1942, and American Institute of Architects, 1964. Address: (office) Paseo de la Reforma 369-1 Mezzanine, Mexico 5, D.F., Mexico.

Works:

1936 Reforma Hotel, Mexico City
1938 Thomas Bay Residence, Mexico City
1940 Hamburgo 293, 295, and 297, Mexico City
1941 Esplanada, Mexico City
1942 Perote Tuberculosis Hospital, Veracruz
Medical Center Master Plan, Mexico City (with José Villagrán García)
Alpes 1105, Mexico City
1943 Balsas 36, Mexico City
Rincon del Bosque, Mexico City
General Hospital, Saltillo, Mexico
Regional Hospital, Tulancingo, Mexico
1944 Alameda Hotel, Morelia, Mexico
Avenida Juarez 88, Mexico City
1945 Plaza Hotel, Mexico City
National School of Teachers, Mexico City
Reforma 334, Mexico City
1946 National Conservatory of Music, Mexico City
1947 Five elementary schools, Mexico City
Reforma-La Fragua, Mexico City (with Jesus Garcia Collantes)

1948 V. Carranza 70, Mexico City (with H. Galguera)
1949 Aleman 1080 Apartments, Mexico City (with Salvador Ortega)
1950 Secretariat of Water Resources Building, Paseo de la Reforma, Mexico City (with Enrique del Moral)
Costera 505, Acapulco (with Enrique del Moral)
1951 Regional plan for Yucatan, Mexico (with José Luis Cuevas and D. Garcia)
Regional plan for Merida, Mexico (with José Luis Cuevas and D. Garcia)
Dumas 130, Mexico City (with Enrique del Moral)
1952 Central Administration Building, University City, Mexico City (with Enrique del Moral and Salvador Ortega)
Juarez 950 Apartments, Mexico City (with Salvador Ortega)
Regional plan for Acapulco (with José Luis Cuevas)
Master plan for Guaymas, Sinaloa, Mexico (with José Luis Cuevas and D. Garcia)
Master plan for Culiacan, Sinaloa, Mexico (with José Luis Cuevas and D. Garcia)
Master plan for Mazatlan, Sinaloa, Mexico (with José Luis Cuevas and D. Garcia)
Mazaryk 170, Mexico City (with Enrique del Moral)
Lima House, Cuernavaca, Mexico
Master plan for University City, Mexico City (with Enrique del Moral)
1953 L. R. Montes House, Acapulco (with Enrique del Moral)
Pozo del Rey, Acapulco (with Enrique del Moral)
1954 Satellite City, Mexico City (with José Luis Cuevas and D. Garcia)
1955 Ixtlan, Mexico City
Ixtlan-Lomas Atlas, Mexico City
Acapulco Airport (with Enrique del Moral)
1956 Reforma 369 Condominium, Mexico City (with Salvador Ortega)
Santa Fe (2500 houses and apartments). Mexico City (with Luis Ramos)
1957 Los Cocos Condominium, Acapulco (with Salvador Ortega)
1958 Master plan for Matamoros, Mexico (with José Luis Cuevas and D. Garcia)
Tlanepantla 2000 Houses and Apartments, Mexico City (with Luis Ramos)
Reforma 368 Condominium, Mexico City (with Salvador Ortega)
Stadium, Ciudad Victoria, Mexico
1959 Banco Popular, Monterrey (with Salvador Ortega)
1960 Commercial Center, Satellite City, Mexico City (with Jesus Garcia Collantes)

1963 Immigration and Customs Building, Matamoros, Mexico (with H. Galguera)
Commercial Center, Cuernavaca, Mexico (with H. Gualguera)
Master plan for Juarez, Mexico
Master plan for Piedras Negras, Tamaulipas, Mexico
1964 Immigration and Customs Building, Nogales, Mexico (with H. Gualguera)
Nonoalco Tower, Mexico City (with Luis Ramos)
Commercial Center, Juarez, Mexico (with E. Molinar)
Exposition Center, Juarez, Mexico (with E. Molinar)
Commercial Center, Matamoros, Mexico (with H. Gualguera)
Tlatelolco City (12000 apartments), Mexico City (with Luis Ramos)
John F. Kennedy 5070 Apartments, Mexico City (with Luis Ramos)
General Studies for Mexican border cities, Baja California
Master plan for Nogales, Mexico
1965 Five tourism developments, Baja California
Vallejo 5600 Apartments, Mexico City (with H. Galguera)
Plateros 5510 Apartments, Mexico City (with Luis Ramos)
1970 Condesa del Mar Hotel, Acapulco
1974 Master plan for the reconstruction of Managua City, Nicaragua
1976 Master Plan for Xochimilco, Mexico
1980 Master Plan for the Paseo de la Reforma, Mexico City
1984 Urban Rehabilitation Plan, Tlatelolco, Mexico
"Urban Cellules" Apartment Blocks, Mexico City (projects)

Publications:

By PANI: books—*Eupalinos o el arquitecto,* translation of the work by Paul Valéry, Mexico City 1938; "*Los multifamiliares de pensiones,* Mexico City 1953; *La construcción de la Ciudad Universitaria,* with Enrique del Moral, Mexico City 1979; articles— "Presentation of the First Issue of Arquitectura" in *Arquitectura Mexico* (Mexico City), no. 1, 1938; "El Arquitecto Mario Pani escribe" in *Manana* (Mexico City), 3 December 1948; "The Housing Problem in Mexico City" in *Arquitectura Mexico* (Mexico City), no. 27, 1949; "Mario Pani lanza un reto a la critica" in *Mexico de Hoy* (Mexico City), 7 May 1949; "The Master Plan of the University City" in *Arquitectura Mexico* (Mexico City), no. 39, 1952; "Fundamental Ideas in the Planification of Acapulco" in *Ar-*

Mario Pani: Tlatelolco City Housing Development, Mexico City, 1964.

quitectura Mexico (Mexico City), no. 46, 1954; "First Housing Project for the Seguro Social Institute" in *Arquitectura Mexico* (Mexico City), no. 53, 1956; "Mexico: One Problem, One Solution" in *Arquitectura Mexico* (Mexico City), no. 60, 1957; "La Ciudad Satellite" in *Nivel* (Mexico City); May 1959; "Las Ciudades y sus planos reguladores" in *Novedades* (Mexico City), 23 August 1959; "Construction Control to Limit the Population Density in a Master Plan" in *Arquitectura Mexico* (Mexico City), no. 71, 1960; "Urban Renewal of Mexico City" in *Arquitectura Mexico* (Mexico City), no. 72, 1960; "La Ciudad Universitaria obra de equipo" in *Revista de America* (Mexico City), 20 January 1960; "Urban Renewal" in *Arquitectura Mexico* (Mexico City), no. 81, 1963; "25 Years Anniversary" in *Arquitectura Mexico* (Mexico City), no. 83, 1963; "Comentarios" in *Arquitectura Mexico* (Mexico City), no. 84, 1969; "Tlatelolco" and "The Economic Structure and Density of Tlatelolco City" in *Arquitectura Mexico* (Mexico City), no. 94/95, 1966; "Presentation" in *Arquitectura Mexico* (Mexico City), no. 96/97, 1967; "La Construccion de Tlatelolco" in *Siempre* (Mexico City), no. 877, 1970; "Eupalinos, the Architect" in *Arquitectura Mexico* (Mexico City), no. 106, 1972; "Urban Problems: The Street" in *Arquitectura Mexico* (Mexico City), no. 107, 1972; "Urban Problems" in *Arquitectura Mexico* (Mexico City), no. 109, 1974; "Richard J. Neutra" in *Arquitectura Mexico* (Mexico City), no. 110, 1974; "6th Centenial of Filippo Brunelleschi" in *Arquitectura Mexico* (Mexico City), no. 115, 1977.

On PANI: books—*Mexico's Modern Architecture* by I. E. Myers, New York 1952; *Art in Latin American Architecture* by Paul Damaz, New York 1963; *Builders in the Sun: Five Mexican Architects* by Clive Bamford Smith, New York 1967; *Diez arquitectos Mexicanos* by Alfonso de Neuvillete, Mexico City 1977; *Modern Architecture: Mexico,* edited by Shelly Kappe, Santa Monica, California 1981; *Mario Pani: biografia analitica* by Manuel Larrosa, Mexico City 1984; articles—"Mario Pani" in *Life* (New York), 17 March 1947; "Modern Mexico" by Ann Binkley Horn in *Architectural Record* (New York), July 1947; "Arte Moderne Mexicano" in *Arquitectura* (Havana), August/September 1948; "La Arquitectura Mexicana" in *Revista Nacional de Arquitectura* (Madrid), July 1949; "Arquitectura Actual" in *Arquitectura* (Lisbon), May 1950; "Urban Progress in Latin America" by Anatole A. Solow in *American City* (New York), November 1950; "The Overall Plan of Ciudad Universitaria" in *Arts and Architecture* (Los Angeles), August 1952; "Arquitectura Abstracta o Realista" in *Manana* (Mexico City), July 1953; "El Arquitecto Mario Pani" in *Arquitectura* (Havana), September 1953; "La Nueva Arquitectura Mexicana" in *Estudios americanos* (Seville), November 1953; "Mexiko Heute" in *Bauwelt* (Berlin), December 1953; "La Propieta orizontale arriva in Messico" in *Architettura* (Rome), January 1957; "Acapulco Airport, Mexico" in *Architectural Design* (London), February 1957; "Satellite City" in *Dimension* (Ann Arbor, Michigan), no. 1, 1958; "Pre-sidente Juarez Center" in *Architect and Building News* (London), January 1958; "The Towers of Satellite City" in *Arts and Architecture* (Los Angeles), May 1958; "Superblock in Mexico" in *Architectural Forum* (New York), May 1959; "Mario Pani" in *Construccion moderna* (Mexico City), September 1959; "Tlatelolco" in *Architecture d'aujourd'hui* (Paris), September 1960; "El Club de Yates de Acapulco y Mario Pani" in *Mundo hispanico* (Madrid), July 1968; "Hotel Condesa del Mar, Acapulco" in *Arquitectura Mexico* (Mexico City), January/February 1977; "The First Multi-family Estate is 30 Years Old" in *Arquitectura Mexico* (Mexico City), September/October 1978; "Hotel Condesa del Mar, Acapulco, Mexico" in *Nuestra Arquitectura* (Buenos Aires), no. 505, 1978; "Modern Mexican Architecture," special issue of *Process: Architecture* (Tokyo), July 1983.

Bibliography: *Mario Pani, Architect* by Florita Z. Louie de Irizarry, Monticello, Illinois 1983.

Educated in France, I obtained a degree in architecture at the Ecole des Beaux-Arts in Paris in 1934 and returned to my country with the intention of adapting my European learning to the social and cultural profiles of Mexico. It has been my continuous task to apply in Mexico the international principles of urbanism and architecture; for this reason, I have consistently promoted projects in which those principles could be applied without affecting the Mexican character and idiosyncracies.

The following projects are the one in which I achieved this goal, introducing in Mexico new concepts in urbanism and architecture:

1936: The first hotel to meet international standards
1947: Buildings high enough to allow population density appropriate to Mexico City's subsoil characteristics
1948: The first multi-habitational building with 1000 apartments
1950: The first super-block (University City)
1956: The first co-ownership building
1964: The first co-ownership city (Tlatelolco housing complex in Mexico City for 80,000 inhabitants)

The visual expression in vogue at the beginning of my studies in architecture was Art Deco of which there are excellent examples in Mexico; however, there is no trace of it in my work. My "architectural language" is that of the Bauhaus adapted to local climates and materials.

In Mexico, after Art Deco the Muralistic Movement came into being with formal expression in colonial as well as in contemporary buildings. My participation in that movement known in Mexico as "plastic integration" was with Jose Clemente Orozco, one of the greatest painters of all times. Together we experimented with what should rather be called "Interaction" than "Integration" between architecture and the visual arts in the campus of the National School of Teachers.

—Mario Pani

Mario Pani's Tlatelolco housing development, in the heart of Mexico City, typifies his concern with an affinity between the old and the new. This gigantic urban renewal project, covering 198 acres, was created to replace a squalid ghetto of 70,000 inhabitants. While excavating for this city within a city, the builders discovered many treasures from antiquity—among them a colonial chapel, Aztec pyramids, and a sixteenth-century cross—all of which were preserved in the Plaza of the Three Cultures.

Tlatelolco's 12,000 apartments are contained in 101 buildings ranging in height from four to twenty-two stories. Dominating the skyline is the tower of the administration and office building topped by a companile. The project has three medical and dental clinics, twelve creches, sports and social clubs, a cinema, multiple shopping areas, parking lots, and thirteen schools. The green spaces, which make up fifty percent of the total area, alleviate the harshness of the surrounding skyscrapers of concrete and steel.

Educated in Europe, Pani, on the return to his native Mexico, was appalled by the living conditions of the masses; subsequently, he became not only an architect but also a city planner. Because of his dedication and expertise, the Mexican Government has retained him to develop master plans for almost every city and region in Mexico—Acapulco, Mexico City, Yucatan, Guaymas, and even Baja California. He designed Mexico's first planned community—a satellite city for the capital. The color, forms, and scale of this city produce visual impact of impressive magnitude.

In 1947, Pani and Enrique del Moral were chosen to prepare the master plan for Mexico's University City. While directing this majestic project, they also found time to design the campus, the gardens, the sports stadium, and the Central Administration Building. This building, at the entrance to the University, exemplifies the beauty in Pani's work: the contrast of rough planes against smooth, the constant interplay of light and shadow, and the unique juxtaposition of muted serenity and blazing color. A three dimensional mural by David Alfaro Siqueiros adorns one wall, while adjacent to it, around the corner, is a wall of golden translucent onyx. The administrative offices are located in a twelve-storey tower connected to a three-story structure containing offices for student affairs. The tower, which rests on columns, is also adorned with a mural, and has a facade of glazed tiles, glass bricks, concrete, and carrera glass.

Pani's first commission, in 1936, was the design of Mexico City's Reforma hotel. The success of this luxury hotel led to other hotel commissions: the Plaza and the Alameda in Mexico City and the Condesa del Mar in Acapulco. Also, in Acapulco, he designed the International Airport with Enrique del Moral, the Yacht Club, and the Los Cocos Condominium.

In the late 1930s, he furthered his practice by entering every competition in which architects were invited to submit plans. His original, contemporary designs not only won awards but also attracted much attention. As a result, he was chosen to design Mexico City's first condominium of thirteen stories with a penthouse and, one of the first modern skyscrapers, the twenty-two story Secretariat of Hydraulic Resources Building, both on the Paseo de la Reforma.

In 1956, with architect Luis Ramos, he designed the Social es and Housing Unit of Santa Fe in Mexico City. This complete community for 14,000 inhabitants includes schools, creches, sports fields, social clubs, a medical clinic, a theatre, a shopping center, and public gardens.

"Mankind must build, in the next thirty-five years, more homes than it has built in the past five thousand years," says Pani, "to keep up with the growing population." Pani is one of the architects who, in combining beauty with efficiency, has shown the way.

—Peggy Cochrane

PARKIN, John Burnett.

Canadian. Born in Toronto, Ontario, 26 June 1911. Educated at the Adelaide Hoodless Public School, and the Delta College Institute, Hamilton, Ontario; studied architecture, at the University of Toronto, Dip.Arch. 1935. Married Jean Elizabeth Renshaw in 1943; children: John Burnett, Jr. and Ann. Worked for National Coal Board, London, and in office of architects Howard and Souster, London, 1935-37; in private practice, Toronto, 1937-47; Partner, with his brother Edmund T. Parkin and with John C. Parkin (no relation), q.v., John B. Parkin Associates, 1947-68, subsequently Parkin Architects Engineers and Planners, 1968-70; Partner, with Roy Marshall, Parkin Architects Engineers and Planners, Los Angeles, 1970 until his death in 1975. President, Association of Canadian Industrial Designers. Recipient: Premier Award of the Olympic Games, Helsinki, 1952; First Prize, Ontario Association of Architects Headquarters Competition, 1953; 14 Massey Foundation Medals, from 1954. Associate, University of Southern California, and California Institute of Technology; Fellow, Royal Architectural Institute of Canada; Royal Institute of British Architects; Honorary Fellow, American Institute of Architects. *Died (in Los Angeles) in August 1975.*

Works:

1946 Sunnylea School, Glenroy Avenue, Etobicoke, Ontario
1948 Christadelphian Church, Church Street, Toronto
1950 Central Collegiate Institute, Simcoe Street South, Oshawa, Ontario
     Hamden Memorial Hospital, Church Street, Weston, Ontario
1952 George Harvey Vocational School, Keele Street, York Township, Ontario
     Northwestern General Hospital, Keele Street, York Township, Ontario
1953 Yardley of London Plant and Offices, Curity Avenue, East York, Ontario
     Unity Church of Truth, Eglinton Avenue West, Toronto
1954 Robert Simpson Company Service Building, Lawrence Avenue West, North York, Ontario
     Ontario Association of Architects Headquarters, Park Road, Toronto
1955 Kenmore Industrial Development Plant, Warehouse and Power Plant, Etobicoke, Ontario
     Imperial Oil Office and Research Building, Sarnia, Ontario
     Ortho Pharmaceutical Office Building and Plant, North York, Ontario
1955/
57 Don Mills Shopping Centre, North York, Ontario
1956 Salvation Army National Headquarters and Temple Corps Building, Albert Street, Toronto
1958 Barber-Greene Plant and Offices, Barber-Greene Road, North York, Ontario
     Greater Niagara General Hospital, Niagara Falls, Ontario
     W. H. Collins Memorial Centre, Elliot Lake, Jamestown, Ontario
1959 Don Mills Collegiate Institute and Junior High School, The Donway East, North York, Ontario
     George Kennedy Public School, Weber Drive, Georgetown, Ontario
1960 Adams Brands Plant and Offices, Bertrand Avenue, Scarborough, Ontario
     Northern Electric Company Plant and Offices, London, Ontario
     Sun-Life Building, University Avenue, Toronto
     Hilldale Manor Home for the Aged, Oshawa, Ontario
     Primrose Club Building, Saint Clair Avenue West, Toronto
     Holy Blossom Temple additions, Bathurst Street, Toronto
     Imperial Oil Offices, North York, Ontario
1961 Elgin Centre Car Showrooms and Offices, Bay Street, Toronto
     Sidney Smith Building, University of Toronto
     St. Michael's College School additions and staff residences, Bathurst Street, Toronto
     Bawating Collegiate and Vocational School, Second Line East, Sault Sainte Marie, Ontario
     Knox Fellowship Centre and Chapel, Spadina Avenue, Toronto
     Dorothy Cameron Art Gallery, Yonge Street, Toronto
     Holy Rosary Parish Hall, Saint Clair Avenue West, Toronto
1963 Thomas J. Lipton Offices and Food Processing Plant, Bramalea, Ontario
     Sifto Salt Mill and Warehouse, Oxford Street, Goderich, Ontario
     Bell Telephone Company Equipment Building (No. 5 Crossbar Building), Markham, Ontario
     St. Mark's Presbyterian Church, Greenland Road, North York, Ontario
1963/
66 Toronto International Airport: Master Plan, Aeroquay, Control Tower, Administration Building, and Central Utilities Building
1964 Parking Garage, Germain Street, St. John, New Brunswick
     H. J. Heinz Company Factory extension, Leamington, Ontario
     Barber-Ellis Warehouse and Offices, Overlea Boulevard, Leaside, Ontario
     Simpson's Shop, Yorkdale Shopping Centre, North York, Ontario

Huntington University Residence, Larch Street, Sudbury, Ontario

Canadian Dental Association Office Building additions, St. George Street, Toronto

1965 McKinnon Industries Ltd. Building, St. Catharines, Ontario

Bata International Shoe Company Head Office, North York, Ontario

City Hall, Toronto (with Viljo Revell)

Oshawa Catholic High School, Stevenson Road North, Oshawa, Ontario

1965/
80 York University, Keele Street, North York, Ontario

1966 International Nickel Research Laboratory and Offices, Sheridan Park, Ontario

Warner-Lambert Research Institute, Sheridan Park, Ontario

Residential complex, University of Waterloo, Ontario

Thorvaldson Building, University of Saskatchewan, Saskatoon

Clarke Institute of Psychiatry, College Street, Toronto

Riverside Golf and Country Club, East Riverside, New Brunswick

1966/
75 Brock University, St. Catharines, Ontario

1967 I.B.M. Canada Head Office, North York, Ontario

Foundation Scottish Properties Office Building, Place du Canada, Montreal

Theatre, MacKay Pier, *Expo '67,* Montreal

Canadian National Pavilion, Ile Notre Dame, *Expo '67,* Montreal

1968 Simpson Tower Office Building, Toronto

1969 Union Railway Station, Ottawa

Toronto-Dominion Centre (consultant: Mies van der Rohe)

Publications:

By PARKIN: articles—"Post-War Planning of Schools" in *Royal Architectural Institute of Canada Journal* (Toronto), September 1942; "Tomorrow's Schools" in *Royal Architectural Institute of Canada Journal* (Toronto), July 1943.

On PARKIN: books—*Toronto International Airport,* Ottawa 1962; *John B. Parkin Associates,* Toronto 1966; articles—"Two Buildings by John B. Parkin Associates" in *Architectural Review* (London), November 1958; "Complete Professional Service for Diverse Industries" in *Architectural Record* (New York), December 1959; "John B. Parkin: Recent Work" in *Arquitectura* (Madrid), September 1966; "1500 Don Mills Road" by John C. Parkin in *Canadian Architect* (Toronto), May 1978; "Parkin" by John C. Parkin and Thomas Howarth in *Canadian Interiors* (Toronto), May 1978; "A Perspective of Modern Canadian Architecture," special issue of *Process: Architecture* (Tokyo), no. 5, 1978.

*

Together with his younger partner, John Cresswell Parkin (not related, despite the surname), John B. Parkin was a major figure in the establishment of modern architecture in Canada in the years following World War II. He helped to define architectural practice as a comprehensive corporate service. At the same time, he gained an international reputation for his firm, John B. Parkin Associates, as purveyors of a Canadian version of the austere and discplined design associated in the United States with Skidmore, Owings and Merrill and in the United Kingdom with Yorke, Rosenberg and Mardall. Parkin was himself a highly disciplined person of strong religious (Christadelphian) convictions who applied that rigor to his support of modern architecture in the late 1960s when Canadian architecture wavered uneasily between the familiar

and comfortable historical eclecticism of the well-established architects and the evangelical claims of younger protagonists of "modern."

Educated in the late Beaux Arts approach still taught at the University of Toronto in the 1930s, Parkin travelled in Europe after graduation and worked in England for the National Coal Board and Howard and Souster. He returned to Toronto to establish a small practice in 1937. Though his early work shows his personal interest and ability in design, his firm's design eminence became most closely associated with his younger partner, John Cresswell Parkin, who, in the firm's dominant years, carried responsibility for design. Nonetheless, John B. Parkin's interest and strongly expressed convictions about design provided a firm foundation for the work of his partner, as it did for the many talented architects who worked under their direction.

John B. Parkin's first houses, from the individual practice he established on his return from Europe, were examples of that attenuated historicism that is almost styleless but carries implicit references to either the mediaeval or classical tradition. There is certainly in Parkin's early work an emphasis on clarity, simplicity, and consistency that later emerged as the leading characteristic of the firm's design.

Parkin's later role was that of administrative leader rather than designer. He was known as a man of great integrity, direct and plainspoken, but also of great charm, who had the complete respect and trust of both colleagues and clients. He was able to reach important clients and attract and retain associates of outstanding ability to carry out their commissions. He shaped the firm to offer a service that was the corporate, industrial, equivalent of the Arts and Crafts model exemplified by Philip Webb and pioneered in the twentieth century by American practices such as Skidmore, Owings and Merrill. Total design by the unified group was the objective. To this end, the firm incorporated specialists in the design of structures, mechanical and electrical systems, interiors and furnishings, landscaping, and graphics. Furthermore, particular partners and associates developed specialized interests ranging from hospitals to airports. This objective was further expressed through a decided preference for prestigious and institutional clients who were prepared to allow the architect this complete control over programming, design, and construction.

The results are exemplified in the well-known buildings from the 1950s and 1960s, the Ontario Association of Architects Headquarters, Ortho Pharmaceutical, Toronto International Airport: Terminal One (the Aeroquay), Ottawa Union Station, Bata Shoes Head Office, and the IBM Head Office, all in or near Toronto. Terminal One is an outstanding example. Within John B. Parkin Associates, the key figure in its design was Lloyd Laity (later with John Carl Warnecke in San Francisco). The building united clarity of form and structure—central cubic parking garage in concrete elevated over arrival and departure levels, a ring structure in steel frame leading to departure gates—a masterly resolution of the interweaving movement of cars, buses, planes, passengers, friends, and spectators—with somewhat cold and formal interiors that displayed a remarkable wealth of specially commissioned Canadian art. The unanticipated advent of the jumbo-jet necessitated subsequent alteration and adaptation, but as originally conceived and executed within the Parkin airport plan, the building was a triumphant expression of the firm's virtues, themselves the result of John B. Parkin's vision.

—Michael McMordie

PARKIN, John Cresswell.

Canadian. Born in Sheffield, England, of Canadian

parents. 24 March 1922. Educated at the University of Manitoba, Winnipeg, 1940-44 (received University of Manitoba Travelling Fellowship; Thesis Prize, 1944), B.Arch. (honours) 1944; Harvard University, Cambridge, Massachusetts, under Walter Gropius, *q.v.,* 1944-47, M.Arch. (honours) 1947. Married Margaret Jeanne Warmith in 1948; children: John Jr., Geoffrey and Jennifer. Co-Founding Partner, with John B. Parkin, *q.v.,* and Edmund T. Parkin, and Partner in charge of Design, John B. Parkin Associates, Toronto, 1947-68; Senior and Managing Partner, Parkin Architects Engineers Planners, Toronto, 1968-70. Since 1971, Senior Partner, Parkin Architects Planners, Toronto (restyled as Parkin Partnership Architects Planners, 1976); current partners: Jack B. Mar, Peter H. Warren and Donald L. Wilson. President, Parkin Engineers Ltd., and Parkin-Arpac Ltd.; Director, Transo Corporation Ltd., Eastern Utilities Ltd. Lecturer, University of Toronto, 1947-48; Visiting Professor, McGill University, Montreal, 1966-67. President, 1955-58, and Chairman of the Committee of Past Presidents, 1958-60, Canadian Conference of the Arts; Chairman, National Industrial Design Council, 1959-61; Chairman, National Design Council, 1961-70; Governor, National Film Board of Canada, 1964-67; Chairman, Architectural Advisory Board, *Expo '67,* Montreal, 1965-67; Vice-Chairman, 1973, and Chairman, 1978, Board of Governors, Ryerson Polytechnical Institute, Toronto. Consultant, National Capital Commission, Ottawa, since 1962; Member of the International Council, Museum of Modern Art, New York, since 1966; President, Royal Canadian Academy of Arts, 1970-80. Recipient: Massey Medal in Architecture, 1950, 1955, 1958, 1964; Premier Canadian Architecture Award, Olympic Art Exhibition, Helsinki, 1952; Oscar Cahen Memorial Award, Art Directors of Toronto, 1960; Centennial Medal, Canada, 1967; Citation, Board of Directors, Canadian Corporation for the 1967 World Exhibition, 1968; Alumni Jubilee Award, University of Manitoba, 1968; Citation, Prime Minister of Canada, 1970; First Prize, National Gallery of Canada Competition, 1976; Queen's Silver Jubilee Medal, 1977. D.Eng.: Technical University of Nova Scotia, Halifax, 1977; D.Sc.: McGill University, Montreal, 1979. Fellow, Royal Architectural Institute of Canada, 1960. Fellow, Royal Institute of British Architects, 1954, Royal Society of Arts, London, 1962, and Society of Industrial Artists and Designers, London, 1967. Honorary Member, Japanese Canadian Cultural Centre, Toronto, 1966, Chambre de Commerce Francaise au Canada, 1967, and Association of Canadian Industrial Designers, 1972. C.C. (Companion, Order of Canada), 1972. Address: Parkin Partnership, 55 University Avenue, Toronto, Ontario M5J 2H7, Canada.

Works:

1953 John C. Parkin House, North York, Ontario

1954 Ontario Association of Architects Headquarters, Toronto

1955 Ortho Pharmaceutical Office Building and Plant, North York, Ontario

1962 Imperial Oil Offices, North York, Ontario

1963 Thomas J. Lipton Offices and Food Processing Plant, Bramalea, Ontario

1963/
66 Toronto International Airport: Master Plan, Aeroquay, Control Tower, Administration Building, and Central Utilities Building

1965 Bata International Shoe Company Head Office, North York, Ontario

McKinnon Industries Ltd. Building, St. Catharines, Ontario

1966 International Nickel Research Laboratory and Offices, Sheridan Park, Ontario

Etobicoke General Hospital, Ontario

1967 IBM Canada Head Office, North York, Ontario

John Cresswell Parkin: Marathon Realty Company Headquarters, Toronto, 1983.

1968 Simpson Tower Office Building, Toronto
1969 Union Railway Station, Ottawa
1971 Health Sciences Complex, Memorial University of Newfoundland, St. John's
1972 Safeco Insurance Company of America Offices, Mississauga, Ontario
1973 Eaton's of Canada Executive Offices interiors, Toronto
1976 National Gallery of Canada, Ottawa
1977 Computer Centre, Bank of Montreal, Scarborough, Ontario
1982 Health Sciences Complex, University of Ottawa
1983 Office Building, Bell Trinity Square, Toronto
        Marathon Realty Company Headquarters, Toronto
1985 Trade Centre and Arena, Hamilton, Ontario
        Provincial Offices for the College of Nurses of Ontario, Toronto

Publications:

By PARKIN: articles—"Relationships: Art and Architecture" in *The Structurist* (Saskatoon), October 1961; "Toronto 1980" in *The Globe and Mail* (Toronto), 4 November 1961; "Canadian Architecture since 1945" in the *Royal Architectural Institute of Canada Journal* (Toronto), January 1962; "Responsibility of the Architect to the Public and the Profession" in *AIA Journal* (Washington, D.C.), January 1964; "Architectural Disorder in Our Cities" in *AIA Journal* (Washington, D.C.), June 1965; two articles in the special issue on Canada of *Progressive Architecture* (New York), September 1972; "1500 Don Mills Road" in *Canadian Architect* (Toronto), May 1978; "Parkin," with Thomas Howarth, in *Canadian Interiors* (Toronto), May 1978.

On PARKIN: books—*John B. Parkin Associates,* Toronto 1966; *Building with Words: Canadian Architects on Architecture,* with introduction by W. Bernstein and R. Cawker, Toronto 1981; articles—"Canadian Cubes" in *The Architects' Journal* (London), December 1977; "The Canadian Wing" in *Architecture Concept* (Montreal), January/February 1978; "A Perspective of Modern Canadian Architecture", special issue of *Process: Architecture* (Tokyo), no. 5, 1978; "Parkin Partnership Offices, Toronto" in *Canadian Architect* (Toronto), September 1980; "Atrium Joins Towers" in *Canadian Architect* (Toronto), October 1983.

*

There are certain principles which I believe I have held fast for more than thirty years. My firms were never highly mobile ones in the sense that a one-man practice could be. We have never apologized for this, for we have always viewed this as a positive virtue necessitating, as it does, our avoidance of the ephemeral. We have never used the arbitrary, what is unreasonable, illogical or irrational. We have sought clarity of plan, clarity of structure, clarity in the use of materials and clarity of form.

The creation of beautiful plans and the creative pleasure attendant to the process has always been fundamental to architectural art. We have sought to place each and everything in its appropriate place.

The expression of our structures has usually been clearly evident in both elevation and plan; the bizarre structural forms which have been fashionable from time to tome have never been of our concern.

In the use of materials we have probably been doctrinaire in avoiding any arbitrary change of materials in the same wall plane, for example. We have always attempted to make materials do what is in their true nature. Our forms have been, I trust, a direct expression of plan and structure.

Our better buildings, the Ottawa Union Station and the Aeroquay (Terminal 1: Toronto Airport) for example, have always tended to accept the realities of convenience. In both these buildings the automobile was invited inside—surely a sensible notion in our climate. Both these buildings also demonstrate an idea which has always intrigued me, that is, the interaction of the two most important materials of our age—steel and concrete in juxtaposition. The circular ring building of the Aeroquay is steel, and its exterior clad in metal: the central rectangular solid is of concrete and of composite design directly expressed as such. The Union Station follows in the great railway tradition of a conspicuous metal roof poised against symmetric one-storey pavilions, wholly concrete in design. I was once told that the success of Union Station in Ottawa rested on the fact that it "looked like a station."

Architecture should enliven, ennoble and inspire, and not gratify or glorify the banal. The doctrine of innovation for its own sake, founded on creative obsolescence, is a practice we have always resisted. Our budgets and programs are sufficiently spartan and austere, although our forms need never reflect an austerity.

In attempting to set an even course in design policy over these more than thirty years, I have counselled my clients to avoid the momentary and the merely fashionable. No hyperbolic-paraboloids, and thin shells only where necessary: no fortresses in concrete and, I trust, only a rare judgmental error in the overwhelmingly pervasive use of concrete in the 1960s.

If I have a major regret, it would be related to a lack of opportunity to work to a greater extent in wood. This was owed, in the main, to the fact that most of our commissions have been of institutional or commercial nature and in urban settings with inhibiting codes. Otherwise, my partners and I have been privileged to undertake work in almost every building type—the regrettable exception being the highrise residential apartment building.

We have always tended to agree with the idea that every problem must be solved in an entirely radical way and believe, as others do, that the practice of architecture involves an accumulating sum of experience, the "software" of design method as well as the "hardware" of building technique.

—John C. Parkin

John C. Parkin has been completely identified first with the design work of John B. Parkin Associates and subsequently with the work of the firm he established following the end of the original firm in 1970, Parkin Architects Planners (now Parkin Partnership), winners of the 1976 competition for the new National Gallery of Canada.

With a large firm the work of the senior design administrator is inextricably bound up with the work of the colleagues whose work he supervises. One of the great achievements of John C. Parkin has been his ability to attract and collaborate with a succession of outstanding partners and associates, such as Douglas Rowland, now a partner in the successor firm to John B. Parkin Associates, Neish Owen Rowland and Roy, Toronto. Many others have passed through a period of apprenticeship with John C. Parkin and his colleagues to later eminence elsewhere.

Parkin is, nonetheless, directly identified with the design of the building that marked the first clear recognition of John B. Parkin Associates by Canadian colleagues, the Ontario Association of Architects Headquarters. The competition scheme had the same clear rectilinear frame and buff brick infill of the final structure, but in the course of development the design progressed from in situ reinforced concrete to the exposed steel frame that became a preferred feature of the Parkin style.

Other early projects of the firm show some variant tendencies that were to be resolved by the mid 1950s. An early butterfly-roofed rural school is one, the Toronto Salvation Army National Headquarters of 1956 is another. The latter, clad in buff brick, supported by round concrete columns, has sun shades extended over (south facing) windows, and perches a smaller flat as a separate block atop the main office building, which rises in turn from the ground level Auditorium block. The result seems close to Gropius's work of the same period, with perhaps a distant acknowledgement of Le Corbusier. The later work, of the 1950s and early 1960s, is more

comparable to the work carried out under Gordon Bunshaft by Skidmore Owings and Merrill and to that of Mies van der Rohe. Certainly the work of the firm's peak years was more in tune with contemporary American than European architecture. One exception was the Toronto City Hall of 1965, but even there execution of Revell's competition scheme through collaboration between the Finnish team and the Parkin staff led to a more closed, solid looking, earthbound building than the original drawings suggested.

John C. Parkin's influence within and without his practices has been pervasive both as a propagandist for good design and as a design critic. With John B. Parkin he became identified with the comprehensive "total" design best exemplified by buildings like Ortho Pharmaceutical, Terminal One (The Aeroquay at Toronto International Airport), the Bata Shoe Company and IBM Head Offices. These are buildings designed to stand apart as objects complete in themselves, set in landscapes varying from informal (Ortho Pharmaceutical) to the more formal (the Bata building on its platform). The buildings recall the eighteenth century play of Palladian formality against the "designed" landscape, none more so than John C. Parkin's own house.

The structures themselves were executed in black and white as far as possible with accent colours reserved for interiors and furnishings. For a while all lettering was (sans serif) Standard Medium, and Mies's Barcelona chairs were a popular adornment. The black painted recess at junctions (the "negative detail") was a ubiquitous device. The result was a considerable achievement in terms of consistency, clarity, quality of execution and, above all, in establishing a recognizable and memorable image for modern architecture.

In the mid-1960s, as the influence of Paul Rudolph and others became strong, the Simpson Tower and other buildings, in bush-hammered concrete and more plastic, irregular forms, reflected a loosening of the earlier discipline, as well as receptivity to the ideas of younger designers. Overall, however, the firm has continued the mid-century preference for unadorned, prismatic forms whose effect depends on scale and proportion supported by careful, reticent detail. The competition-winning (but abandoned) scheme for Canada's National Gallery was something of a departure, with its massively scaled, three-dimensional grid and diagonal screen facade, but more recent works such as the telephone company headquarters, Bell Trinity Square, re-emphasizes a tradition of austere geometry: evident "firmenesse" and "commoditie"; the grace and delicacy necessary for a "delite" more elusive, but characteristic of Parkin's best.

—Michael McMordie

PASANELLA, Giovanni.

American. Born in New York City, 13 January 1931. Educated at the Cooper Union, New York, 1949-53; Yale University, New Haven, Connecticut, 1954-58, M.Arch. 1958; awarded Yale Traveling Fellowship, 1958-59. Married Ann Kenigson in 1958; children: Marco and Nicolas. Designer with Edward Larrabee Barnes, q.v., New York, 1959-64; in private practice, as Giovanni Pasanella, Architect, New York, 1964-76. Since 1976, Partner, with Arvid Klein, Pasanella and Klein, Architects, New York. Architectural Consultant to the Chairman of the New York City Planning Commission, 1967, and to the Little Italy Restoration Association, New York, 1974-75. Critic in Architecture, Yale University, New Haven, Connecticut, 1963, and University of Kentucky, Lexington, 1964; Associate Professor of Architecture, 1965-68, and Project Director at the Institute of Urban Environment, 1965-66, Columbia University, New York; Critic in Architecture, and Visiting Fellow, Institute for Architectural and Urban Studies, New York, 1974. Exhibitions: Yale University Art Gallery, 1964; Columbia University School of Architecture, 1965; *40 under 40,* The Architectural League of New York, 1966; *The New City: Architectural and Urban Renewal,* Museum of Modern Art, New York, 1967; *Urban Design in New York,* New York City Planning Commission, 1969; *Architecture for the State University of New York College at Potsdam,* Katonah Gallery, Katonah, New York 1970; *Can Our Cities Survive?,* Whitney Museum, New York, 1970; *Architecture for the Arts,* Museum of Modern Art, New York, 1971; *Younger New York Architects,* Columbia University School of Architecture, 1972; *Architecture Lecture Series Exhibition,* Yale University School of Architecture, 1973; *Twin Parks,* Columbia University School of Architecture, 1973; *Giovanni Pasanella: Watercolors,* Galleria Il Ponte, Florence, Italy, 1983, 1984; *Pasanella + Klein: Recent Work,* Columbia University, New York, 1983. Recipient: *Architectural Record* Award, 1968, 1970, 1974; Residential Award, American Institute of Architects, New York Chapter, 1970. Address: Pasanella + Klein, 330 West 42nd Street, New York, New York 10036, U.S.A.

Works:

1965 Intensive Therapy Center for Infants, Staten Island, New York
　　　Richard Lemon House, Bedford, New York
　　　Godfrey Rockefeller House, Greenwich, Connecticut
　　　New campus master plan for Wykeham Rise School, Washington, Connecticut
1966 Giovanni Pasanella House, New York
1967 Science Building II, State University of New York College at Potsdam
　　　Twin Parks Urban Renewal Plan, Bronx, New York (with Jonathan Barnett, J. T. Robertson, Richard Weinstein, and M. Weintraub)
　　　Harlem Housing Study, New York (exhibition project)
　　　Alan Gray House, Wellfleet, Massachusetts
　　　Alex Rapaport House, Scarsdale, New York
1968 Negril Development Plan, Jamaica, West Indies (with Jonathan Barnett, Adelates Technical Services, J. T. Robertson, and Richard Weinstein)
　　　Chester Weinberg House, New York
　　　Charles Dunbar House, Winhall, Vermont
1969 Classrooms, Offices and Computer Center, State University of New York College at Potsdam
　　　Firehouse and Chief's Headquarters, New York
　　　Harry J. Brown House, Ringoes, New Jersey
　　　Robert L. B. Tobin House, New York
1969/
73 Twin Parks West, Bronx, New York
1970 Residential Complex B, State University of New York College at Purchase (project)
　　　Administration Building, State University of New York College at Potsdam
　　　Twin Parks Community Development, Bronx, New York (as consultant)
1970/
74 Twin Parks East, Bronx, New York
1971 Entrance Gates, Roads and Parking Area, State University of New York College at Potsdam
　　　William Clark House, Hilton Head Island, North Carolina (project)
　　　Albert Bernstein House, Roslyn Heights, New York
1972 Elementary School P205, New York
　　　Planning study for the Manhattan Landing Hotel Complex, New York
　　　Planning study for Hartz Mountain Industries, Hackensack Meadowlands, New Jersey

Giovanni Pasanella: Twin Parks West, Bronx, New York, 1973.

Joseph E. Seagram and Sons Office interiors, 800 Third Avenue, New York

Rehab Housing and Offices, Wallkill, New York

1973 Melrose Renewal Area Housing, Bronx, New York

Three Town Program Housing, Albany, New York

Ralph Peters House, Minerva, New York

Howard Bissell House, Jacksonville, Florida

Discount Corporation Trading Room and Offices, New York

1974 Harry Winston Office interiors, New York

Office Building, Des Plaines, Illinois

Owens Corning Fibreglass Computer Center, Granville, Ohio

1975 Little Italy Housing and Planning Study, New York

Elementary School P46, New York

Ronald Winston House, New York

Dr. Alan Grey House, Armonk, New York

Joseph E. Seagram and Sons Office interiors, Des Plaines, Illinois

1976 Columbia Grammar and Preparatory School, New York

Michael Schmitt House, Caftsbury, Vermont

Harry Winston Research Facility, New York

1977 Pueblo Nuevao Housing, New York

Fieldhouse and Hockey Rink, State University of New York, Fredonia

University Heights Housing, Bronx, New York

1978 Dr. Alan Grey House, Hartsdale, New York

Housing (Voluntary Residential Facilities), New York

Weber House, New Jersey

Joseph E. Seagram and Sons Office renovations and interiors, 375 Park Avenue, New York

1979 Little Italy Family Housing, New York

Joseph E. Seagram and Sons Office interiors, Lake Success, New York

Joseph E. Seagram and Sons Office interiors, Sherman Oaks, California

1981 Joseph E. Seagram and Sons Offices, Conference and Computer Centers, Laboratories and Aircraft Hangar, Rye, New York

Pasanella + Klein Offices, 330 West 42nd Street, New York

Mr. and Mrs. Charles Dunbar House, South Dartmouth, Massachusetts

1982 New York City Technical College renovations, City University of New York

Office interiors, Dallas, Texas

Office interiors, Mount Pleasant, New York

Joseph E. Seagram and Sons Executive Offices, 375 Park Avenue, New York

1983 Bernard Goldberg House, New York

Dining Hall renovation, College of Staten Island, New York

Beach Channel High School renovation, Queens, New York

Hangar 6 renovation, White Plains, New York

Publications:

On PASANELLA: books—*Architectural Record Houses of 1969* and *1970*, New York 1969, 1970; *The Shingle Style Today* by Vincent Scully, New York 1974; *Urban Design as Public Policy* by Jonathan Barnett, New York 1974, Tokyo 1978; *Housing* by John Macsai, New York 1976; *Pasanella + Klein, Architects: Public and Private Interventions in the Residential Field*, Rome 1982; *Giovanni Pasanella*, Florence, Italy 1983; *Pasanella + Klein, Architects: Recent Work*, Rome 1985; articles—"Lemon House" in *Art in America* (New York), May/June 1966; "The Work of Giovanni Pasanella" in *House Beautiful* (New York), July 1966; "Lemon House" in *Architecture d'aujourd'hui* (Paris), May 1967; "Lemon House" in the *New York Times,* 17 March 1968; "Residential Complex II" in *Architectural Forum* (New York), November 1970; "Twin Parks West" in the *New York Times*, 8 August 1971; "Twin Parks West" in *Building Design and Construction* (Chicago), April 1972; "Administration Building, Science II" in *Architectural Record* (New York), August 1972; "Grey House" *Architecture d'aujourd'hui* (Paris), September 1972; "Twin Parks West" in *Architectural Forum* (New York), June 1973; "Twin Parks West" in *Architectural Record* (New York), June 1973; "Twin Parks West" in *Apartment Construction News* (New York), August 1973; "Twin Parks West" in *Real Estate Forum* (New York), August 1973; "Joseph E. Seagram and Sons Inc." in *Progressive Architecture* (New York), September 1973; "Twin Parks West" in *Professional Builder* (Chicago), September 1973; "Bissell House" in *Architectural Forum* (New York), October 1973; "Twin Parks West" in the *New York Times,* December 1973; "Joseph E. Seagram and Sons Inc." in *Contract* (New York), March 1974; "Joseph E. Seagram and Sons Inc." in *Lighting Design and Application* (New York), July 1974; "Twin Parks West" in *Architecture + Urbanism* (Tokyo), July 1974; "The Work of Giovanni Pasanella" in *Architecture + Urbanism* (Tokyo), April 1975; "The Work of Giovanni Pasanella" in *L'Espresso* (Rome), 13 July 1975; "Joseph E. Seagram and Sons Inc." in *Interiors* (New York), September 1975; "Twin Parks West" in *Controspazio* (Bari, Italy), September 1975; "Twin Parks East" in *Architectural Record* (New York), August 1976; "Seagram Des Plaines" in *Architecture d'aujourd'hui* (Paris), August 1976; "Seagram Des Plaines" in *Architectural Record*

(New York), June 1977; "Twin Parks East" in *Controspazio* (Bari, Italy), June/July 1977; "Twin Parks East" in *Toshi Jutaku* (Tokyo), March 1978; "Giovanni Pasanella and the Architecture of the Possible" in *Parametro* (Bologna, Italy), May 1978; "Giovanni Pasanella, Klein— Recent Projects" in *Controspazio* (Bari, Italy), April/June 1981; "Recycling: Municipal Asphalt Plant" in *Architectural Record* (New York), November 1981; "Fredonia Fieldhouse, and Municipal Asphalt Plant" in *Architecture + Urbanism* (Tokyo), August 1982; "Mr. and Mrs. J. Arvid Klein Residence" in *Interni* (Milan), November 1982; "Little Italy Housing" in *Industria delle Costruzioni* (Rome), October 1984.

Giovanni Pasanella established his own practice in 1964 after working as a designer with Edward Larrabee Barnes, and since January 1976 he has been in partnership with Arvid Klein. He first attained prominence in 1967 as one of a group of young architects serving as consultants to the then chairman of the New York City Planning Commission. These advisers helped establish an urban design group within the Planning Commission which still functions today.

His firm does school and college buildings, medical and correctional facilities, urban planning and community development, commercial buildings and banks, multiple dwellings, houses, and interior design. But, to date, Pasanella is best known for his low-and middle-income housing projects constructed by the New York State Urban Development Corporation, the New York City Housing Authority, or various other public agencies, on so-called "vest pocket" sites. Such sites are irregular in shape and varied in topography, unlike the vast sites formerly cleared and leveled for urban renewal. These sites demanded a new kind of housing and massing design.

Three projects in the Bronx—Twin Parks Southwest, Twin Parks West and Twin Parks East—were a new departure when they were built in the late 1960s and early 1970s. The first two projects have floor-through, split-level apartments in which living and sleeping areas are separated by a half-level change in elevation. For what was believed to be the first time in any New York City highrise structure, public corridors and elevator stops do not serve every building level. Rather, one corridor and elevator stop serves 2 floors, saving 60 per cent of the public corridor space for redistribution into the apartments.

Twin Parks East is notable for the way in which it integrates 599 apartments at a density of 135 units per acre, an elementary school, parking facilities, community spaces, and a center for the aged.

Pasanella's multiple dwellings prove that highrise, high-density housing doesn't have to be bad. His work thus has served a major public purpose.

—Mildred F. Schmertz

PAYSSÉ-REYES, Mario.

Uruguayan. Born in Montevideo, 5 March 1913. Educated at the University of Montevideo Faculty of Architecture, under J. Vilamajo, 1932-37, Dip. Arch. 1937. Marrieed Emma Alvarez in 1940; children: Emma, Mario, Marcos, Monica, and Marcelo. Worked in the studio of J. Vilamajo, Montevideo, 1939-43. In private practice, Montevideo, since 1943. Professor of Architectural Projects, 1943-56, and since 1975 Director of the Faculty of Architecture, University of Montevideo. Secretary, First Assembly of the Institute of Architecture, Montevideo, 1945. Exhibitions (one-man shows): Faculty of Architecture, University of Montevideo, 1944, 1946, 1951, 1956, 1961, 1976; Center of Arts and Letters, Montevideo, 1963. Recipient: Medal of the Society of Uruguayan Architects, 1952, 1957, 1959, 1961,

1974. Member, College of Jurors, Society of Uruguayan Architects. Honorary Life Member, Central Society of Architects, Buenos Aires, 1969. Officer of the Academy of France, 1955; Academician, National Academy of Fine Arts, Buenos Aires, 1977. Address (office): General Santander 1725, Montevideo, Uruguay.

Works:

1936 House, Malvin, Uruguay
1937 Faculty of Architecture, University of Montevideo (competition project; with Julio Duhalde and G. Garcia Selgas)
1942 Low-cost housing, Uruguay (competition project)
1944 House, Carrasco, Uruguay (with Walter Chappe and Architectural Project School)
1945 Apartment building, Boulevard Artigas, Montevideo (with Julio Duhale and G. Garcia Selgas)
1945/
48 Zoological Gardens, Santiago Vasquez, Montevideo
1948 Apartment building, Pocitos, Montevideo
Hotel Waldorf Astoria, Punta del Este, Uruguay (competition project; with G. Garcia Selgas)
1950 House, Parque de los Aliados, Montevideo (project)
1951 House, Punta del Este, Uruguay
1955 Low-cost housing, Salinas, Uruguay
Payssé-Reyes House, Carrasco, Uruguay
Archdiocese of Montevideo Seminary (with Enrique Monestier and Walter Chappe)
1956 Transformable Building (project)
1957 Social Security Building, Calle Mercedes, Montevideo (competition project; with Walter Chappe, Fedor Tisch, and Mario Harispe)
1959 National Party Mutual Association Building, Montevideo (project; with N. Bascou, E. Faget, E. Ross, and C. Peluffo)
1961 Banco de La República Branch Office, Punta del Este, Uruguay (with Adolfo Poszi-Guelfi)
1964 Mount Olympus Building, Montevideo (competition project; with Perla Estable)
1965 Euro-Kursaal Building, Montevideo (competition project; with others)
1967 City Hall, Amsterdam (competition project; with Luis Patrone and Perla Estable)
1970 La Brava Housing Complex, Punta del Este, Uruguay (with Villegas-Berro, Mario Harispe, Gomez-Platero, Lopez-Rey, Perla Estable, and G. Lussich-Payssé)
La Pastora Housing Complex, Punta del Este, Uruguay (with Villegas-Berro, Mario Harispe, Gomez-Platero, Lopez-Ray, Perla Estable, and G. Lussich-Payssé)
1971 Belgrano University, Buenos Aires (with Villegas-Berro, Mario Harispe, Perla Estable, and G. Lussich-Payssé)
1972 Montecarlo Center, Montevideo (with Villegas-Berro, Mario Harispe, Perla Estable, and G. Guerra)
1973 Central Bus Station, Buenos Aires (with Villegas-Berro, U. Herran, Gomez-Platero, Perla Estable, Mario Harispe, A. Meijide, and G. Lussich-Payssé)
1974 Paraguayan Embassy, Brasilia (competition project; with Perla Estable, Nayla and Carlos Peluffo, G. Hughes, and M. Payssé-Alvarez)

Publications:

By PAYSSÉ-REYES: book—*Where Are We in Architecture?*, Montevideo 1967; articles—numerous, particularly in *Arquitectura* (Montevideo).

On PAYSSÉ-REYES: books—*Art in Latin American Architecture* by Paul F. Damaz, New York 1963; *New Directions in Latin American Architecture* by Francisco Bullrich, New York 1969; article—"Mario Payssé-Reyes," special issue of *Arquitectura* (Montevideo), December 1959.

The dwelling pictured was built in 1954-55 at the seaside resort of Carrasco, 17 kilometres from the city of Montevideo, and involved putting into practice theories that I had long been developing. It takes into account the climate, construction, economics, materials used, and the determinants of country and place.

Generally, my theories comprise these goals: that the architecture ought to be realized in such a way that the dwelling contributes to the happiness of the family; that it should allow for development, the possibility of change; and that the principles employed in a particular house should be the same in any house, no matter what the budget of the family, or the cost of the house, might be.

I am also concerned with these principles:

A house ought to have spaces that are both sheltered and open to the garden or exterior spaces. These intermediate spaces ought to be realized in such a way that they can be part of the exterior when the outside temperature allows and part of the inside when there is rain, wind, damp or too much sun and it is not pleasant or possible to be outdoors.

Good geometry is the guide to good architecture. Free spaces should be used only when there are determinants for those spaces: without autonomy of space there cannot be autonomy of shape or expression.

The proportion of openings to the outside should be adequate for light, temperature and comfort—for human sensibility. In Uruguay, the correct total area of outside openings is more or less 20%.

Materials should be used in their natural aspect and colour, to create an appearance of reality.

The plastic arts ought to be used in accordance with the principle laid down by Piet Mondrian 30 years ago: "By means of the unification of architecture, sculpture and painting, a new plastic reality will be created. Painting and sculpture should not be manifest apart from architecture, nor as mural art that destroys real architecture, nor as applied art. They should be part of the construction, to create an ambience not merely useful or rational but also pure and complete in its beauty."

The house at Carrasco conforms to Axel Munthe's description in his *Book of San Michele:* "The house was small, with few rooms, but it had courtyards and terraces from which to admire nature: the soul needs more space than the body."

—Mario Payssé-Reyes

One of the most outstanding figures in Uruguayan architecture in this century is Mario Payssé-Reyes. His importance derives from his work not only as an architect but also as a teacher: he is responsible for having dynamically revised the curriculum at the School of Architecture at the University of Uruguay, and he has been the unchallenged master of generations of Uruguayan architects. His solid theoretical grounding is obvious in his writings, yet he doesn't speak of architecture as only a play of forms but essentially sees it as being at the service of man. To him, architecture consists in working in accordance with determinants—the climate or the materials available for construction; in accordance with directives—function, building systems, economic imperatives, and so forth; and, lastly, in accordance with norms—plastic, aesthetic, or social. Architecture today is something more than simply the art of building; it is the art of transforming the entire habitat of man.

Some of Payssé-Reyes' works are already part of modern architectural tradition—for example, the Banco de La República in Punta del Este or his own private house in Carrasco: the latter has won praise

Mario Payssé-Reyes: Payssé-Reyes House, Carrasco, Uruguay, 1955.

from such internationally renowned figures as Richard Neutra and Bruno Zevi. For Payssé-Reyes, architectural emotion is achieved with the exaltation of the proposed program or subject, and his general principles may be summarized as: a simple and clear functional criterion; unification of interior spaces; relation of interior to exterior space, and full use made of the exterior; lighter, quicker, and cheaper building systems, such as steel or concrete; the employment of new materials and a greater use of transparent ones; a simplification of ornamentation; and a new integration of plastic arts. What architecture must be, according to Payssé-Reyes, is utilitarian in its objectives, and structurally rigorous, aesthetically demanding, and economically limited. The principal virtue of his architecture is simplicity, and functional and spatial values are his prime concerns. In this, he reveals the influence of the masters of the rationalist period, Le Corbusier, Gropius, and Mies van der Rohe, although the work of Frank Lloyd Wright has also left its mark.

Payssé-Reyes has always been concerned to improve the conditions of architecture in Uruguay. He carried out a series of studies of the climate of country, evaluating light, temperature, humidity, rains, winds, and so forth, from which he concluded that it was necessary to complement the enclosed and covered areas of buildings, particularly dwellings, with open and covered spaces; he also determined the proportion that must exist between built and empty spaces, taking into account, too, questions of economy, maintenance, security, and the sensibility of the local inhabitants. Payssé-Reyes also tends to make use of materials in the most expressive and simplest way; he respects their constructive possibilities and tries to preserve their unique textures and And his rigorous geometry confers on his work an unmistakable language, which is in turn reinforced by the manifest integration between architecture, sculpture and painting, in the plastic tradition of Joaquin Torres García.

—Jorge Glusberg

PEI, Ieoh Ming.

American. Born in Canton, China, 26 April 1917; emigrated to the United States, 1935: naturalized, 1948. Educated at St. John's Middle School, Shanghai; Massachusetts Institute of Technology, Cambridge, B.Arch. 1940; Harvard Graduate School of Design, Cambridge, Massachusetts, M.Arch. 1946. Served on the National Defense Research Committee, 1943-45. Married Eileen Loo in 1942; children: Ting, Chien, Li, and Liane. Instructor, then Assistant Professor, Harvard Graduate School of Design, 1945-48; Director of Architecture, Webb and Knapp Inc., New York, 1948-55. Since 1955. Partner, I. M. Pei and Partners, New York. Chancellor, American Academy and Institute of Arts and Letters, Washington, D.C., 1978-80. Member, National Council on the Humanities, Washington, D.C., 1966-70; Member, Urban Design Council of the City of New York, 1967-72; Member, National Urban Policy Task Force, American Institute of Architects, 1970-74; Member, Corporation of the Massachusetts Institute of Technology, Cambridge, 1972-77 and 1978-83; Member, Task Force on the West Front of the U.S. Capitol, American Institute of Architects, 1978-80. Recipient: Arnold Brunner Award, National Institute of Arts and Letters, 1961; Medal of Honor, American Institute of Architects, New York Chapter, 1963; Golden Door Award, International Institute of Boston, 1970; "For New York" Award, City Club of New York, 1973; Thomas Jefferson Memorial Medal, University of Virginia, Charlottesville, 1976; Elsie de Wolfe Award, American Society of Interior Designers, New York Chapter, 1978; Gold Medal, American Institute of Architects, 1979; Gold Medal of Honor, National Arts Club, 1981; Gold Medal, Alpha Rho Chi National Fraternity, 1981; Mayor's Award for Art and Culture, City of New York, 1981; Gold Medal, Academie d'Architecture, France, 1981; Pritzker Architecture Prize, 1983. D.F.A.: University of Pennsylvania, Philadelphia, 1970; Rensselaer Polytechnic Institute, Troy, New York, 1978; LL.D.: Chinese University of Hong Kong, 1970; Pace University, New York, 1972; President's Fellow, Rhode Island School of Design, Providence, 1979. Fellow, American Institute of Architects; Honorary Fellow, American Society of Interior Designers; Member, American Academy and Institute of Arts and Letters, American Academy of Arts and Sciences, the National Academy of Design, and American Philosophical Society. Honorary Fellow, Royal Institute of British Architects; Foreign Associate, Institut de France. Address: I. M. Pei and Partners, 600 Madison Avenue, New York, New York 10022, U.S.A.

Works:

1954/
59 Hyde Park Redevelopment, Chicago (with Harry Weese)
1955 Mile High Center, Denver
1958 Plan for Society Hill, Philadelphia (with Edmund N. Bacon)
1961 Plan for the Government Center, Boston
1962 Kips Bay Plaza, New York
   Slayton House, 3411 Ordway Street N.W., Washington, D.C.
   Town Center Plaza, stage I, 3rd/6th Streets N.W., Washington, D.C.
1963 Henry R. Luce Foundation Chapel, Taiwan
1964 Washington Square East/Society Hill, Philadelphia
   Green Center for the Earth Sciences, Massachusetts Institute of Technology, Cambridge
   Plan for the central business district of Oklahoma City
   School of Journalism: Newhouse Communications Center, Syracuse University, Syracuse, New York

1966/
67 Area Renewal plan for Bedford-Stuyvesant, Brooklyn, New York (with David A. Crane)
1967 University Plaza, New York University, New York
Hoffman Hall, University of Southern California, Los Angeles
National Center for Atmospheric Research, Boulder, Colorado
1967/
70 Air Traffic Control Tower, for the Federal Aviation Agency, at various airports in the United States
1968 Everson Museum of Art, Syracuse, New York
Des Moines Art Center addition, Iowa
Polaroid Corporation, Waltham, Massachusetts
1969 Bedford-Stuyvesant Superblock, Brooklyn, New York
1970 Master plan for Columbia University, New York
The Wilmington Tower, Delaware
Dreyfus Chemistry Building, Massachusetts Institute of Technology, Cambridge
National Airlines Terminal, Kennedy Airport, New York
1971 Cleo Rogers Memorial Library, Columbus, Indiana
1972 Mellon Art Center, The Choate School, Wallingford, Connecticut
Canadian Imperial Bank of Commerce Complex, Toronto
1973 Harbor Towers, Boston
Christian Science Church Center, Boston (with Arnaldo Cossutta)
88 Pine Street (office building), New York
Herbert F. Johnson Museum of Art, Cornell University, Ithaca, New York
1975 Chemical Engineering Facility: Ralph Landau Building, Massachusetts Institute of Technology, Cambridge
1976 Wilson Commons Building, University of Rochester, New York
Overseas-Chinese Banking Coporation Centre, Singapore
1977 Dallas City Hall, Texas
1978 East Building, National Gallery of Art, Washington, D.C.
1979 John Fitzgerald Kennedy Library Complex, Boston

Fragrant Hill Hotel, Beijing, China
Art Museum, University of Indiana, Bloomington
Convention and Exhibition Center, New York (project)
Industrial Credit Bank, Tehran
1980 West Wing, Museum of Fine Arts, Boston
Akzona Inc. Corporate Headquarters, Asheville, North Carolina
1981 Texas Commerce Tower, Texas Commerce Plaza, Houston
IBM Office Building, Purchase, New York
1982 Sunning Plaza, Hong Kong
1984 Arts and Media Center, Massachusetts Institute of Technology, Cambridge
1986 IBM Group Headquarters Building, Somers, New York
Gateway Complex, Singapore
New York Exposition and Convention Center, New York (with James Ingo Freed)
Raffles City, Singapore
1987 Le Grand Louvre museum extensions, phase I, Paris
Bank of China Tower, Hong Kong
Dallas Symphony Hall, Texas
1988 Mount Sinai Medical Center Complex, New York

Publications:

By PEI: articles—"The Nature of Urban Space" in *The People's Architects*, edited by Harry S. Ransom, Chicago 1964; "The Two Worlds of Architecture" in *AIA Journal* (Washington, D.C.), July 1979; "Buildings Are Not That Important... Social Fabric Is More Important", interview with Thomas Glynn, in *Challenge* (Washington, D.C.), December 1979; "I. M. Pei Talks on Chinese Architecture" in *Architectural Journal* (Beijing, China), no. 6, 1981; "I. M. Pei and Partners", with others, in *Space Design* (Tokyo), June 1982.

On PEI: books—*Global Architecture 41: National Center for Atmospheric Research, Boulder, Colorado/Christian Science Church Center, Boston Massachusetts*, edited by Yukio Futrgawa Tokyo 1976; *East Building, National Gallery of Art: A*

Profile, compiled by Richard McLanathan, Washington, D.C. 1978; *Drawings for the East Building, National Gallery of Art*, exhibition catalogue, Washington, D.C. 1978; *Inside New York's Art World* by Babaralee Diamonstein, New York 1979; *American Architecture Now*, edited by Babaralee Diamonstein, New York 1980; articles—"Pei in the Sky" by Astragal in *The Architects' Journal* (London), 28 August 1952; "How They Go About the Problem in Pei's Office" in *Architectural Record* (New York), September 1956; "The Builder's Architect" in *Architectural Forum* (New York), January 1959; "Paeans for Pei" in *Progressive Architecture* (New York), October 1963; "Good Luck, Mr. Pei!" in *Progressive Architecture* (New York), January 1965; "I. M. Pei and Partners" in *Architecture Plus* (New York), February 1973; "Humble Pei" in *Architectural Design* (London), July 1976; "Winning Ways of I. M. Pei" by Paul Goldberger in the *New York Times Magazine*, 20 May 1979; "I. M. Pei", special feature of *AIA Journal* (Washington, D.C.), June 1979; "I. M. Pei: Blueprint for Success" by Turner Lake in *TWA Ambassador* (St. Paul, Minnesota), October 1979; "I. M. Pei, Australia, and the Question of Time" in *International Architect* (London), no. 3, 1980; "I. M. Pei Speaking" in *Interiors* (New York), July 1980; "About I. M. Pei" in *Architecture* (Paris), August/September 1981; "The Third Way: The Architecture of I. M. Pei" in *Connaissance des Arts* (Paris), June 1982; "Discussions on Xiangshan Hotel" in *Architectural Journal* (Beijing, China), no. 3, 1983; "Pritzker Prize Won by I. M. Pei" in *Building Design* (London), 27 May 1983; "I. M. Pei Reflects On His Prize and His Architecture" by Eleanor Blau in *New York Times*, 2 June 1983; "I. M. Pei Goes Digging for Art in Paris" in *Building Design* (London), 2 September 1983; "Pei in the Sky" in *The Architects' Journal* (London), 15 February 1984; "Bank of China Calls In Pei for Hong Kong Headquarters" in *Building Design* (London), 13 April 1984; "The Stylish Artistry of I. M. Pei" by Peter Lemos in *Pan Am Clipper* (Los Angeles), November 1984.

Bibliographies: *The Buildings of I. M. Pei and His Firm* by James C. Starbuck, Monticello, Illinois 1978; *Pei's East Building of the National Gallery of Art* by James C. Starbuck, Monticello, Illinois 1979.

I. M. Pei: East Building, National Gallery of Art, Washington, D.C., 1978.

Ambiguity is everywhere in architecture, and most architects do a great deal of talking about it. I.M. Pei doesn't talk much, and his buildings don't represent manifestos of one architectural theory or another. Instead, he stands apart from the dispute and just builds the best way he knows how. There is still a cohesive philosophy evident in his work, but it is rational, not theoretical, and it is seldom stated verbally.

Pei has certainly been prolific: his firm has designed more than fifty major buildings, including several of the largest civic and corporate constructions of the decade. His work is strong, aggresively modern and highly successful. Nevertheless, Pei has hardly been an architectural hero. He doesn't spew the necessary epigrammatic pronouncements. Stripped of the hype that surrounds the work of many more "conceptual" architects, though, the work of I.M. Pei emerges clear, consistent, yet still innovative.

Design is very important to I.M. Pei, yet in many areas he has accepted the fact that a certain amount of standardization is necessary within the current uses of technology. He uses standardized parts frequently, but with restraint, for he is an exacting designer who refines details carefully, even at the occasional expense of maximum structural efficiency. His skilled use of technology both in terms of parts and modern structure is bold and expressive; nevertheless, he focuses on the interest of the client more than personal formal expressions.

Pei understands the importance of a philosophical approach, but he also knows the practical limitations that inevitably occur within design. He perfects the building functionally and emphasizes total, comprehensive planning, rather than the philosophical statement related to it. In the end, he embodies classical form with modern technology.

Pei's association with developer William Zeckendorf taught him a great deal: he understands architecture in a broad context, both environmentally and economically. His sense of reason and balance reflect this understanding, and the combination of rational restraint with a keen aesthetic sense and the unabashed use of structure and technical innovation is responsible for the vibrancy of his design.

Pei will not deny that he often compromises, but to him architecture is a profession of compromises relying on adept problem-solving relative to constraints. The process of design is a perfecting one, a pragmatic effort at successfully synthesizing a product from a total view of diverse and occasionally contradictory design issues. Pei remains aware and responsive to different contemporary architectural movements, but he continues to demonstrate a more acute concern for rational and structural architectural approaches.

—Ching-Yu Chang

PEICHL, Gustav.

Austrian. Born in Vienna, 18 March 1928. Educated at the Staatsgewerbeschule, Mödling, Vienna, 1943-44; Bundesgewerbeschule, Linz, Austria, 1946-48; Academy of Fine Arts, Vienna, under Clemens Holzmeister, *q.v.*, 1949-53, Dip.Arch. 1953. Married Elfriede Weinmayr in 1957; children: Markus, Katharina, and Sebastian. Since 1953, in private practice, Vienna. Professor at the Academy of Fine Arts, Vienna, since 1973. Political Cartoonist, as "Ironimus," in the *Süddeutsche Zeitung*, Munich, and *Die Presse*, Vienna, since 1955. Exhibitions: New York, 1965; Helsinki, 1968; *Biennale*, Venice, 1975; Palazzo Taverna, Rome, 1977; *Six Architects from the Schillerplatz*, Vienna, 1977; State Academy of Art, Dusseldorf, 1981; Norwegian Institute of Architects, Oslo, 1981; *Festival d'automne*, Paris,

1982. Recipient: City of Vienna Award for Architecture, 1969; Austrian State Award for Architecture, 1971; Reynolds Memorial Award, U.S.A., 1975. Member, Akademie der Künste, West Berlin, 1984. Address (office): Opernring 4, A-1010 Vienna, Austria.

Works:

1958 Urban plan for Gartenstadt Süd, Vienna (with Wilhelm Hubatsch and Franz Kiener)
1960 Public housing, Vienna
1960/
  62 Residential home, Grinzing, Vienna
1961 Elementary School, Krim, Vienna
  Interior design of the Caravelle Aircraft of Austrian Airlines
1962/
  64 Austrian Pavilion, World's Fair, New York
1963 Austrian Airlines Branch Office, Sofia
1963/
  65 Konvent der Dominikanerinnen: High School, Dormitories, Gymnasium and Cafeteria, Hacking, Vienna
1964 Austrian Pavilion, *Expo '67*, Montreal (project)
1965/
  67 RZ-Meidling Rehabilitation Center, Vienna
1964 Junior College with audio-visual display systems, Mistelbach, Austria (project)
  Contower Urban Housing (project)
1968 Austrian Pavilion, Helsinki Trade Fair
1969 ORF (Austrian Broadcasting Company) Branch Studio, Eisenstadt, Austria
1969/
  77 City of Vienna Public School, Diesterweggasse, Vienna
1970/
  72 ORF (Austrian Broadcasting Company) Stations at Linz, Salzburg, Innsbruck, and Dornbirn, Austria
1974 "Die Freyung zu Wien" Redevelopment Project, Vienna
1976 "Molino Stucky" Redevelopment Project, *Biennale*, Venice
1976/
  79 Earth Station for EFA (satellite communication company), Aflenz, Austria
1977 Vaduz Art Gallery, Liechtenstein (project)
1978 Wulle area urban plan, Stuttgart (project)
1978/
  81 ORF Broadcasting Station, Graz, Austria
  ORF Broadcasting Station, Eisenstadt, Austria
1979 Library, Karlsruhe, Germany (project)
  ORF Broadcasting Station additions, in Linz, Salzburg, Innsbruck and Dornbirn, Austria
  Water Detoxification plant, West Berlin
1980 Armeemuseum München urban plan, Munich (project)
1982 Technical Museum, Mannheim, West Germany (project)
  Radio Station, Argentinierstrasse, Vienna
1983 Design for the Papal Visit, Heldenplatz, Vienna
1984 IBA-Residence, Schlossstrasse, Vienna (project)

Publications:

By PEICHL: books—*Die veruntreute Landschaft*, Vienna 1978; *Architektur und Technik*, Vienna 1979; *Architektur aus Österreich*, with P. M. Bode, Salzburg, Austria 1980; *Gustav Peichl— Bauten, Projekte, Meisterschule*, Vienna 1981; as "Ironimus"—*Mein Österreich*, Munich 1974; *Der schwarze Riese: Helmut Kohl in der Karikatur*, editor, Vienna 1976; *Die siebziger Jahre*, Vienna 1979; *Grüne Helden— Graue Monster*, Munich 1983; article— "Architektur ist Sinnlich" in *Deutsche Bauzeitung* (Stuttgart), no. 5. 1978.

On PEICHL: articles—"ORF Studios" in *Architecture d'aujourd'hui* (Paris), December/January 1972/73; "ORF Radio Stations" in *Architectural Design* (London), January 1973; "Radio Four" by A. Best in *Design* (London), June 1973; "Relay Station, Alfenz" by Susan Doubilet in *Progressive Architecture* (New York), March 1984; "ORF Studio and Stage for Pope Johannes Paul II" by Shinichi Eto in *Architecture + Urbanism* (Tokyo), June 1984.

In the contemporary climate of specialization in the arts and sciences, there are a few strongholds where universality is preserved. Architecture is one of them.

Architecture exerts its influence over several generations. It is a prospect, an outlook, a vision of a new environment: that is the basis of its universality. It is equally clear that the claim to universality in no way implies a claim to totality. However, the interlinking of science, politics, research, and architecture is in full swing, and in recent years, the radical increase in man's conscious awareness of research activity is equal to the development in science itself.

But what makes planning and architecture so important are not only the economic and ethical but also the political and social consequences. In the typical State, politics makes use of architecture as a symbol. The better the architecture, the better the State.

We architects are the favorite scapegoats and whipping-boys in out society, but it is the client who is more guilty than the architect; architecture is, after all, conceivable without architects, but not without clients. Clients create the spirit of the age that architects have to portray.

The contemporary public client does not build, he consumes—building materials, money, the environment. For him, building is a meeting of requirements, an exhaustion of budget funds; building for the public client rarely has any aspect of "bringing up" or "bringing about." The large and powerful clients are the municipality, the town or city council, the company entrepreneur, and industry. The anonymity of the client leads to a loss of quality. Today's client is rarely one individual.

I should like architecture's aim to be understood as the process and structure of alterations in the spatial environment in which human society develops and changes. If we consider the invasion of the town and country by the same bleak curtain facades, then we realize the importance of the character of a locality and of individual personality to a lively picture of this world. It is worth recognizing the importance of the genius loci as a defence mechanism against the devastation of architecture.

Architectural criticism is also a question of aesthetics. I do not mean classical aesthetics, but a new aesthetic that is abstract or mathematical. It is not dependent, as is the classical aesthetic, on a philosophic concept, but—far removed—on a methodological one. It is not oriented towards subjective but largely towards objective measures. This aesthetic uses mathematical and empirical methods of procedure and makes use of abstract concepts. I love the classical aesthetic, but I am a willing slave to the technical aesthetic. There are technically perfect works that are aesthetically expressionless and unsatisfactory, but there is no architecture that is outstanding from an aesthetic viewpoint which is not also superb technically.

If the environment is not to become a routine copy, we must shape it not exclusively according to reason and purpose but also according to the senses. Architecture makes you feel serious or cheerful—according to its scale, volume or color. Architecture makes you sensuous!

—Gustav Peichl

From the same diploma year of 1953 at the Vienna Academy of Fine Arts as Gsteu and Holzbauer, and like them influenced by Clemens Holzmeister, Gustav Peichl is perhaps the leading representative

Gustav Peichl: ORF Broadcasting Station, Graz, Austria, 1979-81.

of the new generation of post-war Austrian architects.

His first works, of the early 1960s—for example, the Krim Elementary School and the Dominican Convent, both in Vienna—embody a feeling for pure form expressed in plain concrete and rendered surfaces. The explicit references to the International Style of the 1930s are emphasized by the strong horizontals that pervade the designs, and the buildings are superb examples of a finely perfected philosophy of internal planning.

Peichl's work developed in the later 1960s, becoming richer as the buildings shed their stylistically pure shells. The Meidling Rehabilitation Center in Vienna, though rational in planning terms, has a brutalist aesthetic of overhanging concrete terraces overlaid with symbolic gestures—three giant shiny metal spheres housing services on the roof—images that prefigure the mechanistic overtones of Peichl's series of near-identical radio stations for the ORF network throughout Austria.

Each radio station complex—organically planned with varying sized studios, control rooms and offices ranged around a central entrance hall—is given expression by a forest of gleaming aluminium ductwork that punches through a glazed roof—similar in feeling to the images of Bruno Taut. These ducts occasionally sprout out over the immaculately cast board-marked concrete exterior. The overall result is one of an unusually fine blend of whimsy and rationality, and the effect of architectural collage is heightened by the lattice-grids of walkways and antennae that seem to float above the ensemble. In these buildings Peichl never allows structure and services to impose their own rationale, regardless of the architectonic implications: elements are assembled for their picturesque effect, not their literal face value.

In his later work there is a growing concern for contextual design, in which buildings are considered relative to the surrounding built fabric. "Die Freyung zu Wien" is no run-of-the-mill rehabilitation scheme, but Peichl's earnest attempt at a symbiosis of nature and architecture—something also hinted at in his submission for the Venice *Biennale* of 1976. In the Vaduz Arts Center project the building is no longer treated as a free-standing sculptural object at all. Indeed, it is hard to discern a single "building" as such, so well integrated is the complex into the existing town morphology.

With these later works, Peichl's talents seem to have matured, so much so that he has become one of the leading modern movement architects who still finds he has a role in these post-modern times. In abandoning the monument, he has not forsaken architecture.

Yet, despite his eminence in the profession, Peichl's fame among the Austrian public at large comes from his alternative career as a political and social caricaturist. He remains best known as "Ironimus."

—Gerald Adler

PELLI, Cesar.
American. Born in Tucuman, Argentina, 12 October 1926; emigrated to the United States, 1952: naturalized, 1964. Educated at the University of Tucuman, 1944-49, Dip.Arch. 1949; University of Illinois, Urbana-Champaign, 1952-54, M.S.Arch. 1954; influenced by the teaching of J. Vivanco, E. Sacriste, E.

Rogers, and A. Richardson and by the work of Eero Saarinen, *q.v.*, Married Diana Balmori in 1950; children: Denis and Rafael. Director of Design, OFEMPE (government organization), Tucuman, Argentina, 1950-52; Associate Architect, Eero Saarinen and Associates, Bloomfield Hills, Michigan and Hamden, Connecticut, 1954-64; Director of Design, DMJM (Daniel, Mann, Johnson and Mendenhall), Los Angeles, 1964-68; Partner in charge of Design, Gruen Associates, *q.v.*: Victor Gruen, Los Angeles, 1968-77. Since 1977, Principal of Cesar Pelli and Associates, New Haven, Connecticut. Dean of the School of Architecture of Yale University, New Haven, 1977-84; Visiting Professor, University of Tucuman, Argentina, 1960; Visiting Professor of Architectural Design, University of Cordoba, Argentina, 1960; Charlotte Shepard Davenport Visiting Professor, 1972, and William Henry Bishop Visiting Professor of Architecture, 1974, Yale University School of Architecture; Visiting Professor, University of California at Los Angeles, 1975, 1976. Exhibitions: *Los Angeles 12*, Pacific Design Center, Los Angeles, 1976; *Biennale*, Venice, 1976; *A View of California Architecture: 1960-1976*, Museum of Modern Art, San Francisco, 1976-77; *Centennial— Art and Architecture*, New York, 1980; *New American Art Museums*, Whitney Museum, New York, 1982; *Trends in Contemporary Architecture*, National Gallery, Athens, 1982; *Fiat-Lingotto Project*, Turin, Italy, 1983. Recipient: Design Award, *Progressive Architecture*, 1966; Honor Award, American Institute of Architects, Southern California Chapter, 1968, 1969, 1975 (twice), 1976; First Prize, United Nations City Competition, Vienna, 1969; Arnold W. Brunner Prize, National Institute of Arts and Letters, 1978. Address: Cesar Pelli and Associates, 1056 Chapel Street, New Haven, Connecticut 06510, U.S.A.

Works:

1965 Sunset Mountain Park Urban Nucleus, Santa Monica, California (competition project)
1966 Century City Medical Plaza, Los Angeles
Teledyne Systems Laboratories, Northridge, California
Worldway Postal Center, Los Angeles
Federal Aviation Authority Office Building, Lawndale, California
1967 COMSAT Laboratories, Clarksburg, Maryland
Kukui Gardens Housing, Honolulu, Hawaii
Bunker Hill Third Street Tunnel extension, Los Angeles
1968 Pacific Center (offices and commercial complex), Vancouver, British Columbia
1969 Western Electric Office Building, Newark, New Jersey
United Nations City, Vienna (competition project)
City Hall, San Bernardino, California
1970 Commons and Courthouse Center, Columbus, Indiana
Security Pacific National Bank Building, San Bernardino, California
Ohrbach's Del Amo Department Store, Torrance, California
1971 Ohrbach's Cerritos Department Store, Cerritos, California
Pacific Design Center, Los Angeles
1972 Wells Fargo Office Building, Oakland, California
United States Embassy, Tokyo, Japan
1973 Clorox Office Building, Oakland, California
1974 Yale Music Center, New Haven, Connecticut (project)
Fox Hills Mall, Culver City, California
1975 Rainbow Center Mall and Winter Gardens, Niagara Falls, New York
1976 Daehan Kyoyuk Life Insurance Building, Seoul, Korea
1977/
84 Museum of Modern Art gallery expansion and residential tower, New York
1979/
81 Four-Leaf Towers, Houston, Texas
1979/
84 Office Building, 900 Third Avenue, New York
1979/
85 Four Stamford Forum, Stamford, Connecticut
1980/
83 Four Oaks Towers, Houston, Texas
1980/
85 Cleveland Master Plan and Clinic Building, Cleveland, Ohio
1981/
87 World Financial Center, Battery Park City, New York
1982/
84 Robert R. Herring Hall, Rice University, Houston, Texas
1983 ARCORP Town Center and Waterfront Master Plan, Weehawken, New Jersey
Fiat/Lingotto Redevelopment Plan, Turin, Italy (exhibition project)
1983/
85 University Apartments, University of Hartford, West Hartford, Connecticut
Century Executive Park, Hartford, Connecticut
1983/
87 Norwest Center, Minneapolis, Minnesota
1984 Mattatuck Museum, Waterbury, Connecticut (project)

Publications:

By PELLI: books—*Yale Seminars in Architecture*, editor, New Haven, Connecticut 1979-80; articles— "Open Line City" in *Progressive Architecture* (New York), June 1970; "Third Generation Architects" in *Architecture + Urbanism* (Tokyo), March 1971; "Four Days in May" in *Architecture + Urbanism* (Tokyo), September 1974; "Transparency: Physical and Perceptual" in *Architecture + Urbanism* (Tokyo), November 1976; "Conversation: Cesar Pelli on Architectural Technology" in *Architectural Record* (New York), August 1979; "My Favorite Building: The Crystal Palace" in *Architecture + Urbanism* (Tokyo), February 1980; "Skyscrapers" in *Perspecta* (New Haven, Connecticut), January 1982; "Architectural Form and the Tradition of Building" in *Via* (Philadelphia), November 1984; recording— *Skin and Bones*, tape cassette and slides, London 1980.

On PELLI: books—*12 Los Angeles Architects*, edited by N. Charles Slert and James R. Harter, Pomona, California 1978; *Europa/America*, edited by Franco Raggi, Venice 1978; *Houses for Sale*, edited by B. J. Archer, New York 1980; *Monographs on Contemporary Architecture: Cesar Pelli* by John Pastier, New York 1980; *By Their Own Design*, edited by Abby Suckle, New York and St. Albans, Hertfordshire 1980; *American Architecture Now*, edited by Barbaralee Diamonstein, New York 1980; *GA 59: Cesar Pelli/Gruen Associates* by Kenneth Frampton, edited by Yukio Futagawa, Tokyo 1981; *A Tower for Louisville*, edited by Peter Arnell and Ted Bickford, New York 1982; articles—"Cesar Pelli: Public Architect" by Sibyl Moholy-Nagy in *Architectural Forum* (New York), March 1970; "Cesar Pelli," special issue of *Architecture + Urbanism* (Tokyo), March 1971; "Cesar Pelli," special feature in *Architecture + Urbanism* (Tokyo), November 1976; "Cesar Pelli and the Use of Paper-thin Membrane Skins" in *Architect* (The Hague), May 1980; "Monuments of Nothingness?—The New Works of Cesar Pelli" in *Archithese* (Niederteufen, Switzerland), July/August 1980; "A New Phase of Cesar Pelli," special issue of *Space Design* (Tokyo), September 1980; "Pelli Unveils Battery Park City Plan" in *Building Design* (London), 5 June 1981; "The Sophisticated Skins of Cesar Pelli" by John Pastier in *AIA Journal* (Washington, D.C.), October 1981; "Pelli and Concrete Architecture" in *Architettura* (Rome), April 1983; "New Layers of Meaning: Works in Progress of Cesar Pelli" in *Architectural Record* (New York), July 1983; "Skyscrapers in the USA," special issue of *Bauwelt* (Berlin), 3 May 1984.

Bibliography: *Cesar Pelli's Designs* by Lamia Doumato, Monticello, Illinois 1979.

*

Architecture can claim to be the Mother of the Arts because of its deep roots in reality, a reality that nurtures it and establishes its limits. I need to work close to these roots. They are the primary source and feedback of my ideas. The circumstances in the these firm roots. Within them is the potential for the project. How source of opportunities in design. Design grows and expands from reality of each project are for me, when properly understood, the far it will be carried and in which direction depend on the quality of my judgement and my artistic skill. Seeking opportunities within a well-understood problem is the obverse of functionalism that sees in the same circumstances only a problem to be solved: a deterministic view that reduces options and allows no room for life. And much different from the formalist attitudes that will impose the same preconceived intentions on any circumstances. My commitment is to an architecture that celebrates life. For too long architecture has been absorbed with its death-defying qualities. An architecture that defies death has to accent the qualities of the non-living. It seeks above all massiveness and durability and it avoids the temporary or fragile. An architecture that enhances life accents perception, lightness, and change. The difference between a flower and a stone.

Architecture is not in the empty building but in the vital interchange between building and participant.

—Cesar Pelli

*

Cesar Pelli's intellectual approach to design was sharpened by his ten years in the office of Eero Saarinen, where there was ample time to study fully schemes for a variety of building types; this was a factor in his quick adjustment in Los Angeles to reduced time for design as well as smaller budgets. While he was head of design at DMJM and then Gruen Associates in Los Angeles from 1964 through 1977, he designed a cubic tower sheathed in glass from base to top with suppressed mullions and nondirectional flow of skin, and although his interest in the glass box was brief his preoccupation with transparency remains. He explored sculptural forms in glass, using recesses and projections and in some, a band of glass set at an angle to distort the images (San Bernadino City Hall), and in Pacific Design Center he turned the box on its side, crowed it with a glazed barrel vault, and introduced color, a blue ceramic glass. The non-monumental aspect of his buildings was emphasized by the extruded form, a form which allows the building to be cut off at many points (United States Embassy in Tokyo; Pacific Design Center).

During the 1960s, he designed two laboratories, both linear in plan, with a circulation spine along a high glazed wall through which additions can project (Teledyne Laboratories; COMSAT Laboratories). The circulation spine replaced stairwells, lobby, and lounges as places to meet. His most dramatic use of the circulation spine along a perimeter was in the award-winning design for United Nations Headquarters in Vienna, a multi-layered space stretching the entire length of the seven attached towers.

After leaving Los Angeles in 1977 to become Dean of the School of Architecture at Yale University, and opening his own office, he began to study forms which would reveal the lightness of the material and which were at home in their cityscapes. The tower for the Museum of Modern Art expansion is sheathed in eleven shades of brown and gray glass to blend into the brownstones of the street for an atmospheric perspective. In designing a tower with a curtain wall of stone, he was as intent on revealing it as a lightweight envelope (World Financial Center; Clinic Building for Cleveland Clinic Foundation). The World Financial Center Towers, faced in warm gray granite, relate to the World Trade Center Towers by the use of similarly dimensioned shafts and to other surrounding buildings by setbacks at the prevalent heights in the area. The towers are colonnaded at the base and crowned with copper-covered roof forms.

Herring Hall Graduate School of Business Administration at Rice University in Houston, Texas, respects Ralph Adams Cram's master plan and usage of materials, in this case brick, which Pelli used as a veneer, with stone and tile accents.

—Esther McCoy

PEÑA Ganchegui, Luis.
Spanish. Born in Oñate, Guipúzcoa, 29 March 1926. Educated at the National School, Oñate; College of Santa Maria, Vitoria, 1938-40; College of Santa Maria, San Sebastian, 1940-46; studied architecture and painting at the Mayor Nebrija College, Escuela Técnica Superior de Arquitectura, Madrid, 1946-58, Dr.Arch. 1958. Served in the University Militia, La Granja, Segovia. Married to Rosario Azpilicueta Aguilar; children; Maria, Rocio, Domingo, and Miguel. City Architect, San Sebastian, 1963-64. In private practice, San Sebastian, since 1964. Professor (in San Sebastian Department), Escuela Técnica Superior de Arquitectura, Barcelona. Exhibition: *La Modernité—un projet inachevé*, Centre Georges

Pompidou, Paris, 1982. Recipient: First Prize, Ulia National Competition, San Sebastian, 1962; Aizpurua Prize, 1964. Member, Conjunto Monumental de San Esteban, Murcia, Spain, 1977. Address (office): Reyes Católicos 14, 7th Floor, San Sebastian, Spain.

Works:

1959 Vista Alegre House, Zarauz, Guipuzcoa, Spain (with Juan M. Encio)
1963 Plaza de la Trinidad redevelopment, San Sebastian
Two houses, Olazabal, Motrico, Guipuzcoa, Spain
1964 Housing, Plaza Alcibar, Motrico, Guipuzcoa, Spain
Aizetzu House, Motrico, Guipuzcoa, Spain
Office building, Placencia de las Armas, Motrico, Guipuzcoa, Spain (project)
1965 Imanolena House, Paseo de San Nicolas, Motrico, Guipuzcoa, Spain
Entzus Housing, Motrico, Guipuzcoa, Spain
Mendixa Bar, Motrico, Guipuzcoa, Spain
Rosas Housing, Motrico, Guipuzcoa, Spain
Comanche Plant, Burgos, Spain
Arigain House, Oyarzun, Spain
Zubiando House, Oyarzun, Spain
1966 Yurrita I House, Oyarzun, Spain
Pharmaceutical Union Building alterations, San Sebastian
1967 Echezarreta House, Motrico, Guipuzcoa, Spain
Aritza House, Oyarzun, Spain
1968 San Francisco Church, Vitoria, Spain
Juan XXIII Co-operative Housing, San Sebastian
Donosti-Zarra Co-operative Housing, San Sebastian
Egoitza House, Oyarzun, Spain
1969 Arrasate House, Motrico, Guipuzcoa, Spain
Elu House, Motrico, Guipuzcoa, Spain
Fifty apartments, Ataun, Guipuzcoa, Spain
1970 Masach Apartments, Motrico, Guipuzcoa, Spain
El Puerto Housing, Motrico, Guipuzcoa, Spain
1971 Ganchegui House, Marquina, Spain (project)
Lizauer House, Onate, Spain (project)
Pharmaceutical Union Building, Eibar, Guipuzcoa, Spain
Pharmaceutical Union Building, Igara, Guipuzcoa, Spain
Belutene House, Oyarzun, Spain
Itarte Social Workshops, Irun, Guipuzcoa, Spain (project)
Ikastola Building, Ataun, Guipuzcoa, Spain (project)
Erriberane House, Oyarzun, Spain
1973 Maria y José School, Zumaya, Guipuzcoa, Spain
Iparraguirre Housing Complex, Motrico, Guipuzcoa, Spain
Twenty apartments, Ataun, Guipuzcoa, Spain
Erriberane Estate Plan, final phase, Oyarzun, Spain
1974 Pharmaceutical Union Building, San Sebastian
La Popa de Don Fausto Housing, Lequeitia, Vizacaya, Spain (project)
Silvester Perez Development Plan, Motrico, Guipuzcoa, Spain
1975 Housing block, Vitoria, Spain
Town Hall additions, Eibar, Guipuzcoa, Spain
Champagnot School, San Sebastian (project)
Yurrita II House, Oyarzun, Spain
1976 Gral Kursaal, San Sebastian (project)
Plaza de Tenis, San Sebastian (with sculptures by Eduardo Chillida)
Ikastola Building, Oyarzun, Spain
Plaza Monumento a los Fueros, Vitoria, Spain (with sculptures by Eduardo Chillida)

Luis Peña: Plaza de la Trinidad, San Sebastian, Spain, 1963.

1977 Euzkadi Monument, Oyarzun Cemetery, Guipuzcoa, Spain
Sagues Secondary School, San Sebastian (project)
Housing block, Bilbao, Spain (project)
Reina Maria Cristina Schools, San Sebastian (project)
Villa Adelka, San Sebastian
1981 Espana Industrial urban park, Barcelona (competition project)

Publications:

On PENA: books—*Arquitectura Espanola Contemporanea* by Luis Domenech Girbau, Barcelona 1968; *Luis Peña Ganchegui: conversaciones*, edited by Santiago Roqueta, Barcelona 1979; *La Modernité—un projet inacheve*, exhibition catalogue, with texts by Jean-Philippe Chimot, Kenneth Frampton, Berthold Lubetkin and others, Paris 1982; articles—"Luis Peña Ganchegui—empirismo, ironia, cultura" by Juan Daniel Fullaondo Errazu in *Forma Nueva* (Madrid), December 1970; "La tradicion viva en la obra de Luis Peña Ganchegui" by Miguel Angel Baldellou in *Hogar y Arquitectura* (Madrid), July/October 1974; "Peña Ganchegui, arquitecto euskera" by Luis Domenech in *Arquitecturas Bis* (Barcelona), September 1974; "Peña Ganchegui: de la arquitectura popular a la arquitectura de vanguardia" by Ramon Sanabria in *Hogares Modernos* (Madrid), October 1975; "Six Guipuzcoan Architects" in *Arquitectura* (Madrid), May/August 1977; "Small scale projects and works," special issue of *Lotus* (Venice), no. 22, 1979; "Villa Adelka" in *Quaderns* (Barcelona), November 1981; "The Terms of St. George's Dragon" in *Arquitectura* (Madrid), September/October 1982.

Since my time in Madrid came to an end, I have worked as an architect mainly in Motrico, a small village of some 5,000 inhabitants in Guipuzcoa, in the Basque Country. Because I work in a small Spanish village, the work I do is very far from using any kind of advanced technology.

In 1963 I was given the opportunity to take over the job of Municipal Architect of the beautiful city of San Sebastian, and I planned and directed the construction of the Plaza de la Trinidad in the Old Quarter, a square devoted to the Basque popular games. I gave up my post because I had strong feelings of incompatibility with the way in which the town was progressing and because I disagreed with the urban development plan that had been adopted.

I now carry on my profession in small communities of Guipuzcoa, such as Oyarzun (4,000 inhabitants). and Ataun (1,500 inhabitants) as well as in Motrico. Nevertheless, I do have continual contact with architects in Barcelona and Madrid through the "sesiones de critica" which take place each year in different cities of Spain.

Recently I have been involved in the planning of important urban spaces, such as the Plaza a la Mar in the Paseo del Tenis in San Sebastian, with sculptures by Eduardo Chillida, and the Plaza Monumento a los Fueros in Vitoria, also in collaboration with the same sculptor.

An interesting experience has been the construction of the Monumento a los Muertos for Euzkadi in the Cemetary of Oyarzun, built with a single mason, at the cost of 500,000 pesetas.

From the time that the Catalan architect, Oriol Bohigas, joined the Escuela de Barcelona, I have been attached to the school as a professor, working in its department in San Sebastian.

—Luis Peña

Over the past 25 years Luis Peña has produced work dedicated to a response to its surroundings. Without falling into the trap of local colour, he has contributed to the international movement in architecture with works suffused with local and national sentiment. As a result of this continuous search for the right ingredients, his work lacks the rigor of the avant-garde, but it has an uncanny feeling for place. His response to what the "feeling of place" means to people is so strong that his buildings seem to be a natural background to the everyday life of the Basques. His buildings, once built, seem always to have been there.

Mackintosh combined a national culture with an international movement; Luis Peña also looks for means to integration, but within the Basque Country. As far as architecture is concerned, the most significant feature of Basque culture is the closely-knit relationship of the community as expressed through the love of sport—that of the players and that of the spectators, who gamble on the outcome. Every corner, porch, street and square becomes a pitch for a favorite ball game; the characteristics and obstacles of each "pitch" influence the rules of each particular game, and the rules are agreed upon before play begins. This kind of full participation by neighbours in the use and management of their public spaces is inbred in all of Peña's architecture—so much so that he now seems to have deserted the architecture of buildings for the architecture of squares. His best are in San Sebastian—El Trinidad by the church and El Tenis by the sea, and in Vitoria—Plaza de los Fueros.

His housing developments consist of either large barn-like structures or an erratic string of street facades covered with a spider-like web of thin metal balconies. Both forms are characteristic of the Basque vernacular, translated by Peña into the language of modern architecture. His best housing is in Oyarzun and Motrico.

Peña's exploration of the relationship of the modern movement to place does not, however, merely consist of translating vernacular features; it also involves introducing a formal investigation of the movement itself into the local context. This intention is clear in the Mies-like precision of his Pharmaceutical Union Building in San Sebastian and his secondary school in Oyarzun. In the Pharmaceutical Union Building curved walls of glass brick and aluminium, mixed with concrete and rendered wall surfaces, do not, at first, look at all Basque. But it is a warehouse on a factory estate: it does not demand more, and Peña does not force the issue. The school, however, has been designed literally as a bridge between two neighbourhoods, and forms the background and wings of an open-air stage and playgound—a building acting an urban role.

Perhaps the most moving of Peña's designs is his small monument in Oyarzun Cemetery to those who died defending Basque liberties against Franco. It is like the old tombstones that lie up against the cemetery wall. Peña has rebuilt part of the rose-coloured wall with an open window that looks out onto the green farmlands beyond, marked with a black metal band like that which marks out the area on the wall and floor of a Basque ballgame. The window is "out of bounds"—symbolic of the injustice suffered by the martyrs. A flagpole is placed horizontally across the centre so that the Basque national flag can be hung either outside the cemetery or inside over the tomb. The flagpole leads the eye from the tomb to the fields, from the dead to the life they died for. Such symbolism would seem to suggest that Peña is a romantic, but, though he has a romantic streak, he is too much of an intellectual to fit any such easy generalization.

In his more recent work, Pena's command of the large public space has become more evident, be it the masterly loft of Onate town hall, or the large city park of Espana Industrial-Barcelona, with its artificial lake, giant dragon sculpture, and majestic and original light towers.

Apart from these and other major commissions outside the Basque Country, Pena devotes much of his time to teaching the younger generation in the small Basque school of architecture in San Sebastian.
—David Mackay

PENTEADO, Fabio Moura.
Brazilian. Born in Campinas, São Paulo State, 3 June 1929. Educated at the Ophelia Fonseca School, São Paulo, 1935-39; Instituto Mackenzie, São Paulo, 1940-48; Mackenzie University, Faculty of Architecture and Urbanism, São Paulo, under Eliziario Bahiana, 1948-53, Dip.Arch. 1953. Served in the Brazilian Air Force, 1948-49. Married Claude de Barros in 1958; children: Gabriel and Adriana. In private practice, São Paulo, since 1953. Member, Underground Transport Commission, São Paulo, 1959; Counsellor for Urbanism, National Planning Advisory Board, Brasilia, 1966. Instructor, School of Architecture and Urbanism, Mackenzie University, São Paulo, 1962-64. Architectural Editor, *Revista visão*, São Paulo, 1956-62; Organizer and Editor, *Brazilian Building Data Catalogue,* São Paulo, 1958; Director, *Arquitetos na TV*, Excelsior Television Network, Brazil, 1961-62. Director, *Arquiteto*, São Paulo, since 1974. Vice-President, Institute of Brazilian Architects, São Paulo Chapter, 1960-61; President, Executive Council, Brazilian Institute of Architects, 1966-68; Member, Executive Committee, International Union of Architects, Paris, 1969. Exhibitions: *Playa Girón Monument Competition Exhibition*, Havana, 1962; *International Theatre Exhibition*, Prague, 1967; *Bienal*, São Paulo, 1969; *Latin American Biennale*, Lima, 1970; *International Architecture Bienal*, São Paulo, 1973; *International Theatre Exhibition*, Prague, 1975. Recipient: First Prize, State Bank and Campineiro Club Competition, Campinas, Brazil, 1954; First Prize, Harmonia Club Competition, São Paulo, 1958; First Prize, and Gold Medal, *International Theatre Exhibition*, Prague, 1967; Gold Chain, Brazilian Institute of Architects, 1969; First Prize Jockey Club Social Building Competition, São Paulo 1974. Life Member of the Executive Committee, Brazilian Institute of Architects, 1968. Honorary Member, Colegio de Arquitectos de Mexico, 1969, Colegio de Arquitectos del Peru, 1969, and the American Institute of Architects, 1972. Address (office): Rua Bento Freitas 306, S1.801, 01220 São Paulo, Brazil.

Works:

1950 Domingos Solha House, Souzas, São Paulo
1954 Arnaldo Barbosa Apartment Building, São Paulo
     Sao Bernardo, Sao Caetano, and Santo Andre Water Treatment Stations, São Paulo State (with Ringo Kubota)
     State Bank and Campineiro Club, Campinas, São Paulo (competition project)
1956 Carlos Wathely Apartment Building, São Paulo
     Water Treatment Plant, Campinas, São Paulo (with Alfredo Paesani)
1958 Cabo Frio Hotel, Rio de Janeiro (project; with Ringo Kubota)
1960 Forum Building, Araras, São Paulo
     School, Campinas, São Paulo
     Sanitary Building, Barretos, São Paulo (project)
     Conselheiro Antonio Prado Technical School, Campinas, São Paulo
     Coffee Museum, Campinas, São Paulo (project)
     Carlos Monteiro Silva House, São Paulo
     Piracicaba Municipal Theatre, São Paulo (project; with Jose Ribeiro)
1961 School, Sao Caetano do Sul, São Paulo
     Electrotechnical Institute, São Paulo (project)
     Secondary school, Sao Bernardo do Campo, São Paulo (project)
1962 Apartment building, Dona Viridiana Street, São Paulo
     Noroeste Bank Branch Office, Guarulhos, São Paulo
     Bairro do Limao Housing Development, São Paulo (project)
     Playa Girón Monument, Museum, and Square, Cuba (competition project; with Ubirajara Gigliolli, José Ribeiro, Tito Livio Fraschino, and Vasco de Mello)
1963 Dock Workers' Housing Development, Santos, São Paulo (project)
1964 Harmonia Tennis Club Building, São Paulo (with Alfredo Paesani and Teru Tamaki)
     Founders' Monument, Goiania, Goias State, Brazil (project; with José Ribeiro)
1965 Water Treatment Plant, Pirassununga, São Paulo (project; with Alfredo Paesani and Teru Tamaki)
     Tourist Centre, San Sebastian, Spain (competition project; with Alfredo Paesani and Teru Tamaki)
1966 Water Treatment Plant II, Campinas, São Paulo (with Alfredo Paesani and Teru Tamaki)
     Opera House, Campinas, São Paulo (project; with Alfredo Paesani and Teru Tamaki)
     Sondeiker House, Jardim Marajoara, São Paulo (with Alfred Paesani and Teru Tamaki)
1967 Cumbica Housing Estate, São Paulo (with J. B. Vilanova Artigas and Paulo Mendes da Rocha)
1968 Cultural Centre, Campinas, São Paulo (with Alfredo Paesani and Teru Tamaki)
     Old People's Home, Campinas, São Paulo (project; with Teru Tamaki)
     Praca dos Azulejos Hotel, Campinas, São Paulo (project; with Alfred Paesani and Teru Tamaki)
     Julio de Mesquita Filho Hospital and School, Sao Paulo (with Teru Tamaki, Eduardo Almeida, and Giselda Visconti)
1969 Technical School, Vila Alpina, São Paulo (with J. P. Vilanova Artigas)
     Santa Casa da Misericordia Experimental Health Centre, São Paulo (with Teru Tamaki)
1970 Federal Technical School, Santos, São Paulo (project; with J. B. Vilanova Artigas and Paulo Mendes da Rocha)
     Alto Pinheiros Club Building, São Paulo (with Teru Tamaki)
     Fritz Strauss House, Campinas, São Paulo (with Teru Tamaki)
     Aziz Maluf House, Vinhedo, São Paulo (with Teru Tamaki)
1971 Tennis Club Building, Campinas, São Paulo (with Teru Tamaki)
     Twin Office Towers, São Paulo (project; with Teru Tamaki and Tito Livio Fraschino)
     Franklin Guidler House, Campinas, São Paulo (with Teru Tamaki)
1972 Office building, Alameda Santos, São Paulo (project; with Teru Tamaki)
     Pasargada Park Housing Estate, São Paulo (with Teru Tamaki; since altered)
     Ralton Purina Company Office Building, Volta Redonda, Rio de Janeiro (with Teru Tamaki)
     José Roberto Penteado House, Campinas, São Paulo (with Teru Tamaki)
1973 Cyrel Imobiliaria Housing Estate, São Paulo (project; with Teru Tamaki and Vasco de Mello)
     Chacara do Piqueri Housing Complex, with office tower and shops, São Paulo (project; with Decio Tozzi, Joao Walter Toscano, and Telesforo Christofani)
     State Administration Centre, São Paulo (project; with Teru Tamaki, Tito Livio Fraschino, and Hercules Merigo)
     Renewal plan for the historic town centre of Campinas, São Paulo (project; with Teru Tamaki and Tito Livio Fraschino)
     Ibiuna Land Development, São Paulo (with Teru Tamaki and Tito Livio Fraschino)
     Master plan for Fazenda Nossa Senhora do Carmo, Itaquera, São Paulo (with Teru Tamaki)
     Salto Housing Development, São Paulo (with Teru Tamaki)
     Ronald Levinsohn House, Rio de Janeiro (with Teru Tamaki and Tito Livio Fraschino)
1974 Jockey Club Social Building, São Paulo (competition project; with Teru Tamaki and Tito Livio Fraschino)
     Hermitage Hotel, Campinas, São Paulo (with Teru Tamaki)
     F.E.A.C. Urban Development, Campinas, São Paulo (project; with Teru Tamaki)

Fabio Penteado: Opera House, Campinas, Sao Paulo, 1966 (project).

Granja Sao Martinho Land Development, Campinas, São Paulo (project; with Teru Tamaki and Tito Livio Fraschino)

San Carlos Housing Development, São Paulo (project; with Teru Tamaki)

1975 Heleno Fragoso House, Rio de Janeiro (with Teru Tamaki)

1975/
77 Ten school buildings, São Paulo State (with Teru Tamaki and Hercules Merigo)

Eight branch offices for the São Paulo Savings Bank, São Paulo State (with Teru Tamaki, Hercules Merigo, and Nadia Cahen)

1977 São Paulo Light and Power Company Technical Installation Buildings, Sorocaba, Sao José dos Campos, São Paulo (with Teru Tamaki, Hercules Merigo, and Nadia Cahen)

Luiz Antonio Pires House, Campinas, São Paulo (with Teru Tamaki and Hercules Merigo)

1978 Cultural Centre: Theatre, Library and Art Gallery, Sao Bernardo do Campo, São Paulo (project; with Teru Tamaki)

Urban development plan for Sao Carlos do Pinaal, São Paulo (project; with Teru Tamaki and Jose Borelli)

Marcelino P. Barbosa House, Campinas, São Paulo (with Teru Tamaki and Jose Borelli)

José Steinberg House, Campinas, São Paulo (with Teru Tamaki, Hercules Merigo, and José Borelli)

Publications:

By PENTEADO: articles—monthly column on architecture in *Visao* (São Paulo), 1956-62.

On PENTEADO: articles—"Architectural Works Around Sao Paulo After Brasilia" in *Kokusai Kentiku* (Tokyo), June 1967; "Open Air Theatre Designed by Fabio Penteado" in *Binario* (Lisbon), January/February 1974; "Modern Brazilian Architecture," special issue of *Process: Architecture* (Tokyo), August 1980.

For a long time, São Paulo, in spite of its reputation as "the largest industrial centre in Latin America," remained a city whose cultural outlook was extremely conservative. Indeed, at Mackenzie University, where I studied architecture, any expression of modernism was generally considered bad taste, and architects such as Le Corbusier and even Oscar Niemeyer were sometimes quoted as being the dangerous proponents of Communist architecture.

After I received my diploma in 1953, combining my own efforts with those of a few of my more persistent colleagues, I began to use my first professional assignments as a means of teaching myself the necessary knowledge that I had not yet acquired. This self-teaching process was complemented by the experience that I gained as the architectural editor (1956-62) of an important Brazilian weekly, *Revista Visao*. As I was writing and learning, one of the aspects with which I was most concerned was the gap between the notions of human solidarity described in "Preliminary Thoughts" and what was actually achieved in the completed projects. Even when these projects incorporated the best design and the latest technology, they hardly ever seemed to me to fulfil the basic requirements of the original objectives.

After twenty-five years and several completed projects which, if nothing else, have kept my business alive, I believe that there have been a few occasions when I have been able to put into practice some of the ideas with which I was most concerned. These ideas can be seen in a few of the projects which try to live up to the ideal of total collective participation, although I do not know if the projects represent any real contribution: they were not specifically comissioned with this ideal in mind, nor was their value sufficiently appreciated. I like to regard them, however, as the preliminary plans for a party to which, when it takes place, I would very much like to be invited.

—Fabio Penteado

No study of Fabio Penteado's work should be restricted to questions of form, function and technique, although these aspects are sufficient evidence in themselves of the unquestionable quality of his buildings. The prime consideration is really one of response to purpose. Though function is partly determined by fixed parameters, a building is also influenced to a great extent by the architect's notions of the social role of architecture. The people/function relationship is carefully considered by Penteado in his projects, and the implicit possibilities are rethought and dealt with in a very dynamic way.

In practical terms: there is, in his work, a delicate balance between functional nuclei, the elements of which are precisely defined, and spatial complexes that are open to a variety of uses, that are designed to allow the user a wide range of interpretation. Further, his architectural aims are defined conceptually. A building may have a specific use, but it must never compartmentalize or exclude the changing world. A building should live *with* the world, inviting active participation from the user, assuming an almost didactic character by accepting and provoking a constant rediscovery of *rôle* and the consequent change to its social function.

Fabio Penteado's clients are the great Brazilian public: crushed, intimidated, discriminated against, and disoriented by the astonishing population explosion. His basic concern is with restoring dignity to their daily use of the man-made environment—a concern that is fundamental to his buildings. And, hence, his wider role, that of putting forward creative ideas and blueprints for mass architecture.

This task is of utmost importance: it is now forecast that the population of Brazil will double within the next twenty-five years. The capacity to implement such ideas as Penteado's will fall pitifully short of the expansion that is required. The deadlines for completion hardly allow time for prototypes to be tested or for monitoring the mistakes that multiply at an alarming rate in undertakings of this scale. There would be no point in proposing standardized models: they would be impracticable, not least because of the variety of cultural and geographical conditions. More relevant is any dialogue of ideas that can serve as a departure point in the formation of conceptual models. Penteado's work is concerned with just such ideas.

The Campinas Cultural Centre is one of a series of theatre projects that are the result of his research into architectural responses to leisure and culture. (His projects for the Piracicaba Municipal Theatre, the award winning Campinas Opera House, and the Sao Bernardo do Campo Cultural Centre are other examples.) The Campinas Cultural Centre is situated in the middle of a traditional Campinas square, but instead of "invading" the square, it replaces it: pedestrians pass over or through it in their search for the shortest way from A to B, and the building puts its various functions at the disposal of even the most casual user. Its four blocks are surmounted by an area that is entirely given over to the public, with tiered seating forming a large open-air theatre available for spontaneous events and public gatherings. Usable space is doubled. The volumes, laid out in the form of a mandala, are wonderfully dynamic: they vary in composition as the observer moves, standing out against each other with archaic monumentality, opening or closing the vistas. The tip of the large, leaning obelisk-tower does not emphasize its own base but marks the centre of the square and of the avenue that leads to it.

The Julio de Mesquita Filho Hospital and School, part of the Santa Casa de Misericordia Health Centre in São Paulo, is dedicated to the complex problem of providing medical care for a population of two million people in a state of abject poverty. This technical, dimensional and psychological impasse is resolved by a simple horizontal layout that can be grasped by the humblest of people. The hospital becomes a small town: the wards are the "suburbs" and the corridors are the "streets" where patients, doctors and visitors come and go, as do cleaning trolleys, food trolleys, and stretchers—as much as possible as if they were ordinary streets. In the centre of the building there is a large park with playing fields and places designed for the leisure needs of people of varying ages. It is all an attempt to incorporate the notion of healthiness within the community and to remove the tabu and disturbing connotations of sickness.

The "Santa Casa" is recognizable by its pediment of bare concrete, broken on each of the four sides by three arches seventy-one metres wide. This simple design suggests both the scale of the undertaking and the magnitude of its public function.

Penteado is also concerned to blend architecture with its surroundings—either through contrast or integration, depending on the individual circumstances. In the theatre projects, the space is developed architecturally to allow an expansion of activities centred around the buildings. This is also the case in the Aziz Maluf House in Vinhedo, the Fritz Strauss House in Campinas and, inversely—by landscaping the interior—in the Harmonia Tennis Club Building in São Paulo. Conversely, the "Santa Casa" and the Water Treatment Plant II in Campinas stand out in sharp definition against the surrounding landscape by virtue of the purity of their volumes.

Penteado has also expressed his ideas (and his idealism) in large urban plans. Of these, the Cumbica Housing Estate, already partially complete, has served for experiments in the establishment of work and planning systems hitherto not attempted on this scale; it has provided basic data for a study of the quality/quantity relationship and its economic implications in such a large-scale complex.

Penteado's profound involvement in activities specifically related to architecture is also characterized by a breadth of understanding born of his humanist viewpoint. As President of the Brazilian Institute of Architects during one of the most trying times in the political life of the country, he took great pains to grant his colleagues in need the support and solidarity of the Institute.

—Jorge Czajkowski

PENTTILÄ, Timo Jussi.

Finnish. Born in Tampere, 16 March 1931. Educated at the Institute of Technology, Helsinki, 1950-56, Dip.Arch. 1956. Served as an Ensign in the Finnish Infantry, 1956-57. Worked as a designer for Hytönen and Luukonen, Helsinki, 1953-54, Ström and Tuomisto, Helsinki, 1954-55, and for Aarne Ervi, q.v., Helsinki, 1957-59. Since 1959, in private practice, Helsinki; in partnership with Heikki Saarela, since 1972, and with Kari Lind, since 1974. Assistant Lecturer, University of Technology, Helsinki, 1959-60; Visiting Professor, University of California, Berkeley, 1968-69; Professor, Academy of Fine Arts, Vienna, since 1980. Vice-Chairman, SAFA: Association of Finnish Architects, 1968; Board Member, 1970-80, and President, 1976-80, Museum of Finnish Architecture, Helsinki. Exhibitions: *Bienal*, São Paulo, 1969; *Finland Builds*, Helsinki, 1970, 1976, and 1982; *Architettura fin-*

landese, Turin, 1973; *Finnish Architecture*, The Hague, 1975; *Timo Penttilä*, Academy of Fine Arts, Vienna, University of Stuttgart, and Technical University, Graz, Austria, 1979, SBG Galerie, Zürich, and Royal Institute of British Architects, London, 1980; *Architettura in Finlandia*, Ravenna, Italy, 1982; *Workshop of Arab Cities*, International Union of Architects World Congress, Cairo, 1985. Recipient: First Prize, City Theatre Competition, Helsinki, 1961; Architecture Award, State of Finland, 1976; Public Buildings Award, Finnish Institute of Cities, 1984. Knight of the Order of the Lion of Finland, 1971; Member of the Finnish Academy of Technical Sciences, 1978. Address: Timo Penttilä-Heikki Saarela-Kari Lind, Arkkitehdit Oy, Nervanderinkatu 5 D 44, 00100 Helsinki 10, Finland.

Works:

1958 Town Hall, Seinäjoki, Finland (competition project)
1959 Highway Construction Plan, Tampere, Finland
1960 Sports Hall, Turku, Finland (competition project)
1961 Exhibition and Sports Hall, Tampere, Finland (project)
City Hall, Helsinki (competition project)
Kaleva Church, Tampere, Finland (competition project)
1962 High School, Teisko, Finland
Salokunta Parish Hall, Karkku, Finland
Sampola Workers' Institute and Comprehensive School, Tampere, Finland
City Centre Plan, Oulu, Finland (competition project)
1963 Finnish Embassy, New Delhi (competition project)
Cultural Centre, Kemi, Finland (competition project)
1964 National Opera House, Madrid (competition project)
1965 Edvard Greig Hall, Bergen, Norway (competition project)
Master Plan for Vestamager, Denmark (competition project)
Commercial Institute, Tampere, Finland
1966 Pellonperäntie Row-Houses, Helsinki
Motel, Lappeenranta, Finland (project)
1967 City Theatre, Helsinki
Ratina Stadium, Tampere, Finland
Penttila Fishing Lodge, Inio, Finland
University of Oulu, Finland (competition project)
1969 Sauna Building, Sauna and Health Club, Humallahti, Helsinki (competition project)
1970 Nurses' School, Helsinki (project)
College of Music, Freiburg im Breisgau, West Germany (competition project)
1971 Congress Hotel, Yteri, Pori, Finland (competition project)
1974 Town Centre extension plan, Tapiola, Espoo, Finland
Imatran Voima Oy Head Offices, Vantaa, Finland
1975 City Institute, Espoo, Finland
Kansallis-Osake-Pankki Head Offices, Helsinki
Amusement Park Tower, Helsinki (competition project)
1976 National Opera House, Helsinki (competition project)
1977 National Cultural Centre, Manama, Bahrain (competition project)
Reima-Pukine Oy Textile Factory and Employees' Housing, Kankaanpää, Finland
Art Centre, Vaduz, Liechtenstein (competition project)
Forest Lodge, Inari, Lappland, Finland
Hanasaari Power Plant, Helsinki
1978 Pahlavi National Library, Teheran (competition project)

Gyllenberg Art Gallery, Helsinki (competition project)
1979 Suomen Sokeri Oy Head Offices, Tapiola, Espoo, Finland
Imatran Voima Oy Control Centre, Vantaa, Finland
Municipal Library, Vantaa, Finland (competition project)
1980 Domizil Head Offices, Brühl, West Germany
Hirviniemi Private Apartments, Helsinki
1981 Les Halles District redevelopment, Paris (competition project; with Roberto Menghi and Roberto Sambonet)
1982 City and Festival Hall, Ludwigsburg, West Germany (competition project)
Imatran Voima Oy Laboratory and Research Building, Vantaa, Finland
1983 Oy Nokia Ab Head Office, Espoo, Finland (competition project)
President's Official Residence, Helsinki (competition project)
Tête Défense development, Paris (competition project)
1983 Block of Flats, Gumpendorferstrasse, Vienna
1984 Anhalter Bahnhof, West Berlin (competition project)
Kansallis-Osake-Pankki Bank Headquarters restoration, Helsinki
Salmisaari Power Plant, Helsinki
1984 Perusyhtymä Oy Makrotalo Head Office, Tapiola, Espoo, Finland

Publications:

By PENTTILÄ: lecture papers—*The Limits of Rational Systems in Architecture*, Helsinki 1975; *Architecture and Realities of Construction*, Helsinki 1979; *Architecture as Part of Urban Culture*, Helsinki 1979; *Monuments of Democracy*, Helsinki 1982; articles—"Theory and Tradition" in *Arkkitehti* (Helsinki), no. 5/6, 1980; "Phänomene der Gegenwartsarchitektur" in *Deutsche Bauzeitung* (Stuttgart), no. 5, 1981; "The First Harvest of Environmental Thinking" in *Arkkitehti* (Helsinki), no. 2, 1982; "Architettura è un nome" in *Parametro* (Bologna), no. 106, 1982; "The Comprehensive View: Theory or Superstition?" in *Arkkitehti* (Helsinki), no. 7, 1982; "Debating Harmony: Criticism and Self-Criticism" in *Abitare* (Milan), no. 216, 1983.

On PENTTILÄ: books—*Nuove Ville—New Villas* by Robert Aloi, Milan 1970; *Timo Penttilä—Finnische Architektur*, exhibition catalogue, Vienna 1979; *Timo Penttilä*, exhibition catalogue, by Vittorio Magnago Lampugnani, Stuttgart 1979; *Timo Penttilä*, exhibition catalogue, by Vittorio Magnago Lampugnani, London 1980; *The Modern House* by David Mackay, Barcelona 1984; articles—"Salonkunta Parish Hall, Karkku" in *Arkkitehti* (Helsinki), no. 5, 1962; "City Theatre, Helsinki" in *RIBA Journal* (London), December 1967; "Ratina Stadium, Tampere" in *Deutsche Bauzeitschrift* (Gütersloh, West Germany), May 1969; "Hansaari Power Plant" in *Bauen und Wohnen* (Zürich), no. 11, 1975; "Thoughts about Architecture" in *Bauforum* (Vienna), no. 69/70, 1979; "Pahlavi National Library, Teheran" in *Arkkitehti* (Helsinki), no. 5/6, 1980; "Domizil Head Offices, Brühl" in *Architektur + Wettbewerbe* (Stuttgart), March 1981; "Suomen Sokeri Oy head offices, Tapiola" in *Architecture + Urbanism* (Tokyo) no. 5, 1982; "Private Apartments, Hirviniemi, Helsinki" in *Parametro* (Bologna), no. 106, 1982; "Bahrain National Cultural Centre, Manama" in *Form Function Finland* (Helsinki), no. 2, 1983.

Architecture is a vitally important means of intellectually and emotionally unlimited expression to man, and as such, is part of his cultural heritage. This is true even though architecture, also by its very

Timo Penttilä: Private Apartments, Hirviniemi, Helsinki, 1980.

nature, is intertwined with all the necessities of everyday life.

Architecture comes into existence only through the materialization of the ideas in unique situations, which is due to its heterogenous nature and the relative importance of many influencing factors. In an inexplicable way architecture also transcends the mere self-evident sum of these factors. Therefore I try to avoid preconceived ideas and the fallacies of dogmatism. My inspiration usually comes from the inside of the situation and differs case by case. The architecture of the Helsinki City Theatre, for example, reflects the unison of the natural topography of the site and the flow of people in the public spaces.

Modern technology and methodology are indispensable assets in the service of man, but they should not be the ultimate issues of architectural morality. The emphasis of my work has been and shall be on the satisfaction of human needs—practical as well as emotional.

—Timo Penttilä

Finland nowadays has only a few internationally known architects. Timo Penttilä is one of them. The number of his works is relatively small, but their quality is the better for that. It is significant that almost every one of his works has been published.

Penttilä's most important work is the City Theatre of Helsinki, which was built in 1964-67. Penttilä won the competition in 1961 when he was twenty nine years old with an entry that showed a sensitive adaptation to the site in a park district. This sensitivity remained constant throughout the entire building, right down to the smallest detail. The generous and finely harmonized succession of areas, beginning with the entrance up to the interior of the auditorium, is overwhelming. The materials are also finely harmonized, with bronze and ceramic tiles prevailing.

Certainly the Helsinki Theatre does not belong to the avant-garde—if that means untreated concrete and visible installations. But it would also be wrong to call the building "conservative"; its conception is quite too advanced for that. What, then, is it? And what sort of architect is Penttilä? In what "category" should he be placed?

Considering his previous buildings, one does find similarities to the designs of Alvar Aalto. His functional solutions and his generous conceptions of space suggest Aalto too. Nevertheless, he cannot really be called a student of Aalto, and he never worked with him. Contemplating again the equalized detail work of the Helsinki Theatre, one thinks of only one direct model—Aarne Ervi. The humanity of Ervi's architecture and his fine feeling for detail must surely have influenced Penttilä during the two years that he worked for him.

But, finally, Penttilä can't be classified. It would perhaps be more interesting to discover why his buildings are generally well accepted by their users and thought "beautiful" by other people. It is worth pointing out, because it becomes more and more obvious, how little recent experimental architecture has contributed to the beauty of our environment. This fact seems to be increasingly realized by the general public. This is not the place to discuss the so-called "lack of understanding" by the public and by builders of much modern architecture; I wish simply to pose the question, should not good architecture be something that is accepted by its users even when it involves innovations? Penttilä's architecture becomes more understandable in this context.

Penttilä does not follow vogueish trends, and he does not build for architectural critics. He is not a teacher who tries to educate his public; he refers to symbols and traditions that are accepted by his public, that is, by the users of his buildings. He is not seduced by the now-dominant Bauhaus purism; on the contrary, he is looking for values that functionalism is supposed to have thrown overboard. His interest is in the variety and continuity of forms and materials that belong to the tradition of our building culture, that are of significance and value. A comparison obtrudes with Eliel Saarinen, who, in spite of his generous conceptions, found the means to relate the forms and materials as well as the building tradition of Finland to the international movement (this is best seen in his earlier national romantic works, especially in the Helsinki Railway Station). Is Penttilä the successor of Eliel Saarinen?

—Antero Markelin

PEREIRA, William Leonard.

American. Born in Chicago, Illinois, 25 April 1909. Educated at the University of Illinois School of Architecture, Urbana, 1926-30, B.Arch. 1931. Served as an Assistant Regional Director, for California, United States Office of Civilian Defense, 1942-44. Married Margaret McConnell in 1934; children: William Jr. and Monica. Associated with Holabird and Root, Chicago, 1930-31; in private practice as William L. Pereira, Architect, Los Angeles, 1931-50; Partner, with Charles Luckman, Pereira and Luckman, Los Angeles, 1950-58. Principal and Chairman of William L. Pereira Associates, Los Angeles (other principals: G. L. Garvey; Jack Kassel; Neil W. Birnbrauer; Otto H. Kilian), 1958 until his death in 1985. Professor of Architecture, Design and Planning, University of Southern California, Los Angeles, 1949-59. Chairman, California Governor's Task Force on Transportation, 1967-68; Member, National Council of the Arts, 1967-68; Member, California Governor's Commission on Ocean Resources, 1967; Adviser, Aeronautics and Space Engineering Board, National Academy of Engineering, 1969-70; Member of the Science and Technology Council of the California Assembly, 1970; Architect-in-Residence, American Academy in Rome, 1971. Member of the Advisory Commitee, Crocker National Bank, California, 1963-85; Director, Urban America Inc., 1965-85; Director, American Film Institute, Washington, D.C., 1965-85. Recipient: Honor Award, American Institute of Architects, Southern California Chapter, 1963 (twice); Award of Merit, American Library Association 1963; Alumni Achievement Award, University of Illinois, 1973. Honorary doctorate: Otis Art Institute, Los Angeles, 1964; D.F.A.: Art Center College of Design, Los Angeles, 1971; D.L.: Pepperdine University, Malibu, California, 1974. Fellow, American Institute of Architects, 1958. Fellow, Academy of Motion Picture Arts and Sciences. Commander, Order of the Ivory Coast, West Africa. *Died* (in Los Angeles) *13 November 1985.*

Works

1939 Lake County Tuberculosis Sanitorium, Waukegan, Illinois
1950 Robinson's Department Store, 777 East Colorado, Pasadena, California
1952 CBS Television City, Beverly and Fairfax, Los Angeles
1953/
  58 University of California at Santa Barbara (as supervising architect)
1954 Marineland of the Pacific, Palos Verdes, California
1959/
  62 Master plan, new terminals and restaurant, Los Angeles International Airport
1960 Development plan for Irvine, California
1963 Public Library, Santa Fe Springs, California
  Olin Hall of Engineering, University of Southern California, Los Angeles
  West Fullerton Library, Fullerton, California
1964 Los Angeles County Museum of Art
  Avco Savings and Loan Association Building, 250 South Mills, Ventura, California
  Ahmanson Center, University of Southern California, Los Angeles
1965 Library, Crawford Hall, Steinhaus Hall, and Humanities-Social Sciences Building, University of California at Irvine (with Jones and Emmons, and Blurock and Ellerbrock)
  Dickenson Art Center, University of California at Los Angeles
  Booth Memorial Hall, University of Southern California, Los Angeles
1966 Norris Residence Hall, Occidental College, Eagle Rock, California
1969 Public Library, Buena Park, California

Master plan for the Houston Center, Texas
  Seaver Science Center, University of Southern California, Los Angeles
1970 Central Library, University of California at San Diego
  Braille Institute Library, Los Angeles
  Fine Arts Building, University of California at Irvine
1970/
  73 *Los Angeles Times* Building addition, Spring and 1st Streets, Los Angeles
1971 Cityview, Queens, New York
1971/
  73 Pepperdine University, Malibu, California
1972 Transamerica Corporation Building, San Francisco
  St. Francis Hotel tower addition, San Francisco
  Irvine Towers, Newport Center, Newport Beach, California
1973 Pacific Mutual Building, Newport Center, Newport Beach, California
  Great Western Savings Center, Beverly Hills, California
  Security Pacific Building, Flower and 6th Streets, Los Angeles
  Charles Lee Powell Hall, University of Southern California, Los Angeles
1974 Wells Fargo Bank Building, Newport Center, Newport Beach, California
1974/
  84 Qatar Planning Studies, Doha, Qatar
1976 Library/Multimedia Center, Golden West College, Huntington Beach, California
  Naval Hospital, Camp Pendleton, California
1977 Ameron Headquarters, Monterey Park, California
1977/
  80 SRI Buildings 22 and 23, Menlo Park, California
1978 Nissan Motors Engineering Center, Los Angeles
  Petroleum Research Institute, Caracas, Venezuela
  Three Broadway Stores, Southern California

1979 Naval Clinic, San Diego, California
  Herald Mail Newspaper Plant, Hagerstown, Maryland
  Los Angeles Times Satellite Plant expansion, Costa Mesa, California
  Aerojet General Headquarters, La Jolla, California
1980 Yanbu New Community, Saudi Arabia
  Two Transamerica Center, San Francisco
  Warmington Plaza, Santa Ana, California
1981 Yamaha Headquarters, Cypress, California
  Doha Sheraton Hotel, Doha, Qatar
  Hospital, University of California at Irvine
1982 American Airlines Corporation Headquarters, Dallas, Texas
  Avco Computer Center, Newport Beach, California
1983 Toyota National Headquarters, Torrance, California
  Avery International Headquarters, Pasadena, California
  Union Oil Research Center, Brea, California
1984 Sheraton Premiere Hotel, Universal City, California
  Tom Bradley International Terminal, Los Angeles Airport
  Nelson Research Center, Irvine, California
  Citicorp Building, San Francisco
  Los Angeles Times Satellite Printing Plant, Northridge, California

Publications:

By PEREIRA: articles—"The Architect and the Entrepreneur" in *AIA Journal* (Washington, D.C.), July 1962; "Campus Planning, University of California" in *Architectural Record* (New York), November 1964.

On PEREIRA: articles—"Two Current Works by William Pereira" in *Architectural Design* (London) September 1972; "Houston Center" by Charles

William Pereira: Sheraton Hotel and Conference Center, Doha, Qatar, 1981.

Delfante in *Urbanisme* (Paris), no. 137, 1973; "Great Western Savings Center" in *Domus* (Milan), September 1973; "Cityview Renewal Project, Borough of Queens, New York City" in *L'Architecture d'Aujourd'hui* (Paris), September/October 1973; "Pyramid from San Francisco" by F.E. Rontgen in *Polytechnische Tijdschrift* (The Hague), 21 December 1973; "Library of the University of California at San Diego" by L. Kahan in *Technique des Travaux* (Liege), January/February 1974; "Houston Center" by Edward K. Carpenter in *Urban Design* (New York), Autumn 1977; "Building Types Study 530: Heavy Duty Delights" in *Architectural Record* (New York), May 1979; "Building Types Study 546: Industrial Buildings" in *Architectural Record* (New York), July 1980; "Yanbu Neighborhood Takes Shape" in *Middle East Construction* (Sutton, Surrey), February 1982; "Doha Sheraton Hotel and Conference Center" in *Architecture + Urbanism* (Tokyo), October 1982.

Chicago-born William L. Pereira was a product of the Midwest. He studied at the University of Illinois, one of the great American schools of architecture, and worked in Chicago before settling in Los Angeles. But his work is a manifestation of an architectural and cultural energy that is clearly Californian.

Pereira's architectural work covers a broad range, including large-scale planning. His clients were large corporations and public companies as well as governmental agencies. His buildings are characterized not so much by a style as by stylistic wholeness and expression, for his goal seems always to have been to establish a fluent and immediately recognizable formal entity—a complete and spirited object as architecture.

Identifiability and symbol are always a principal emphasis of his work. In this respect his design reflects an urge identified with the Beaux-Arts approach to architecture, while the particular forms he employed are derived from those familiar in twentieth century Western art and sculpture. At the same time his designs are always extremely functional. One discerns in his finished work a disciplined search for functional appropriateness, a fluidity in the movement of people and processes. The combination of form and function is a clear-headed and optimistic California blend. If it is not profound, it is workable and affirmative, celebrating a moment and a time rather than attempting to probe depths. The work, like the man, is most congenial.

Among his accomplishments is the Marineland of the Pacific—a high achievement in the viewing of aquatic life and in handling large groups of people. Los Angeles International Airport, a far larger and more complex work, is a well-handled portal for the city. His Transamerica Corporation Building in San Francisco is a tall pyramidal tower standing with its own distinct identity amidst other tall buildings. Pereira also designed the striking tree-like library of the University of California at San Diego.

—Paul Spreiregen

PERESSUTTI, Enrico.

Italian. Born in Pinzano al Tagliamento (Udine), 28 August 1908. Educated at schools in Italy and Rumania, until 1927; studied architecture at the Milan Polytechnic School of Architecture, 1927-32, Dip.Arch. 1932. Served in the Italian Army, 1941-43. Married the architect Emma Pasquinelli in 1944; daughter: Marina. Founder Partner, with Gianluigi Banfi, *q.v.*, Ludovico Belgiojoso, *q.v.*, and Ernesto Nathan Rogers, *q.v.*, BBPR Architecural Studio, *q.v.*, Milan, 1932 until his death, 1973. Vice-Commissioner, CLNAI (Comitato di Liberazione Nazionale per l'Alta Italia), 1943; Member, Mun-

icpal Committee for the Master Plan for the city of Milan, 1946-47; Consultant Architect and Planner, CECA (Communauté Europeenne Charbon Acier), Luxembourg, from 1953; Consultant, Metropolitana Veneta, Venice, 1967-73. Co-director, Architetti del Movimento Moderno, Milan, from 1947; Member, CIAM (Congrès Internationaux d'Architecture Moderne), from 1935; Vice-President, ICSILD (International Council of Societies of Industrial Design), 1957-59. Editorial Board Member, *Quadrante* magazine, Milan, 1933-36, and *Metron* magazine, Rome, from 1946. Professor, Istituto Universitario di Architettura, Venice, 1957-59; Instructor in Industrial Design, Istituto Statale d'Arte, Venice, 1961-62; also Visiting Professor and Lecturer, Architectural Association School, London, 1950-51; Massachusetts Institute of Technology, Cambridge, 1952; Princeton University, New Jersey, 1953-59; Yale University, New Haven, Connecticut, 1957, 1962; and University of Illinois, Chicago, 1968. Member, Commissione per le Manifestazione d'Arte Moderna dell'Associazione tra i Cultori d'Architecttura 1935, and Maison des Artistes, Lausanne, 1939; Founder Member, Société Européene de Culture, 1950. Member of the Directive Committee, Associazione Disengo Industriale, Milan, 1957–59. *Died* (in Milan) *in 1975.*

Publications:

By PERESSUTTI: articles—"Sulla Funzione dei Materiali" in *Quadrante* (Milan), January 1934; "Urbanistica Corporativa: Piani Regolatori" in *Quadrante* (Milan), December 1934; "Incontri in Russia" in *Almanacco Letterario Bompiani*, Milan 1942; "Il Passaggio Ideale per la Casa" in *Domus* (Milan), August 1942; "Un Arredamento e una Dichiarazione" in *Domus* (Milan), October 1944; "Sul Convegno della Ricostruzione" in *Metron* (Rome), November/December 1945; "L'Uomo e gli Oggeti: Bere" in *Domus* (Milan), January 1946; "Sul Piano Regolatore: Funzioni e Caratteri della Città" in *La Voce di Milano*, February 1946; "L'Uomo e gli Oggeti: Dormire" in *Domus* (Milan), February 1946; "L'Uomo e gli Oggeti: Giocare" in *Domus* (Milan), March 1946; "L'Uomo e gli Oggeti: Mangiare" in *Domus* (Milan), April 1946; "La Lupa di Stagno non piace agli Architetti" in *Cronache di Bologna*, May 1947; "Sistemazione del Piazzale della Stazione di Bergamo" in *Metron*, (Rome), May/June 1948; "Parliamo di Gropius" in *Epoca* (Milan), September 1951; "Risolvere il Problema del Traffico" in *Milano-Sera*, 7 January 1954; "Moral Training for the Architect" in *Architecture and the University*, Princeton, New Jersey 1954; "La Sedia Thonet" in *Domus* (Milan), no. 290, 1954; "Case della CECA per gli Operai Siderurgici" in *Edilizia Popolare* (Rome), November 1955; "Un Convegno per la Protezione di Erice" in *Casabella* (Milan), no. 215, 1957; "Il Convegno dell'ASID a Beaford Springs" in *Stile Industria* (Milan), March 1959.

See BBPR ARCHITECTURAL STUDIO

PERKINS, Lawrence Bradford.

American. Born in Evanston, Illinois, 12 February 1907. Educated at the University of Wisconsin, Madison, 1924-25; Cornell University College of Architecture, Ithaca, New York, 1926-30, B.Arch. 1930. Married Margery Isabella Blair in 1932 (died, 1981); children: Dwight, Blair, L. Bradford, and Julia; married Joyce Ellen Sandler in 1982. Founding Partner, with Philip Will Jr., *q.v.*, and E. Todd Wheeler, Perkins, Wheeler and Will, Chicago, 1935-

46, subsequently Perkins and Will, 1946-64, and the Perkins and Will Partnership, 1964-70; Chairman of the Board, 1970-73, and since 1973 Director, Perkins and Will Architects Inc., Chicago; offices established in New York, 1951, and Washington, D.C., 1962. Adjunct Professor of Architectural Design, University of Illinois, Chicago, 1974-82; Visiting Professor, University of Illinois, Urbana-Champaign, since 1982. Member, 1945-65, and Chairman, 1948-54, 1963-65, Evanston Planning Commission, Illinois; Chairman, Advisory Board, Cook County (Chicago) Building Codes Commission, 1963-66; Director, Adlai Stevenson Institute of International Affairs, Chicago, 1965-75. Member of the Advisory Committee of the Cook County Forest Preserves, since 1963. Recipient: Chicagoan of the Year Award, 1960; 25 Year Award, American Institute of Architects, 1971; Distinguished Service Award, American Association of School Administrators, 1975; Dean of Architecture Award, American Society of Interior Designers, 1983. Fellow, American Institute of Architects, 1953. Address: Perkins and Will Architects, 2 North LaSalle Street, Chicago, Illinois 60602, U.S.A.

Works:

1940 Crow Island Elementary School, Winnetka, Illinois (with Eliel and Eero Saarinen)
1942 Rugen Elementary School, Glenview, Illinois
      Clyde Lyon Elementary School, Glenview, Illinois
1948 Greenbriar School, Northbrook, Illinois
      Blythe Park Elementary School, Riverside, Illinois
1949 Westwood Elementary School, Woodstock, Illinois
1952 Heathcote Elementary School, Scarsdale, New York
      Greenwood Elementary School, Woodstock, Illinois
      Glenbrook North High School, Glenview/-Northbrook, Illinois
      Hoover Elementary School, Neenah, Wisconsin
1953 Washington School, Evanston, Illinois
      Ralph Smith Elementary School, Hyde Park, Chicago
1954 Kellogg High School, Idaho (with Culler, Gale, Martell and Norie)
1955 Byron Junior High School, Shaker Heights, Ohio (with Michael Kane)
1956 Linton High School, Schenectady, New York
      Paige Elementary School, Schenectady, New York
1958 Richard E. Byrd School, Chicago
1960 Rockford College, Illinois
1963 United States Gypsum Building, Chicago
1964 Evanston Township High School, Illinois
      Charles Gates Dawes School, Evanston, Illinois
1965 Chute School, Evanston, Illinois
      Dalton Elementary School, Illinois
      Winnetka Public Library, Illinois
      First National Bank Building, Chicago (with C. F. Murphy Associates)
1976 Chapel, Ithaca College, Ithaca, New York (with A. Egner)

Publications:

By PERKINS: books—*Schools*, with Walter Cocking, New York 1949; *Workplace for Learning*, New York 1957; article—"Must We Live in Unlovely Cities" in *School Administrator* (Arlington, Virginia), Summer 1971.

On PERKINS: articles—"The Perkins and Will Partnership" in *Building Construction* (Chicago),

Lawrence Perkins: Heathcote Elementary School, Scarsdale, New York, 1952.

April 1969; "Return of the Megastructure" in *Architectural Forum* (New York), September 1973; "The Collective Campus" in *Interiors* (New York), November 1973; "First National Bank, Chicago" in *Informes de la Construccion* (Madrid), November 1973; "Medical Facilities" in *Architectural Record* (New York), September 1975; "Three Vocational Training Centers for the Petrochemical Industry in Saudi Arabia" in *Progressive Architecture* (New York), January 1978; "An Architectural Firm Helps Find New Markets for Outdated Schools" in *Architectural Record* (New York), August 1978; "Capital District Psychiatric Center at Albany" in *Interiors* (New York), December 1978; "Building Types Study 563: Health Care Facilities" in *Architectural Record* (New York), August 1981; "The New American Skyscrapers" in *L'Architecture d'Aujourd'hui* (Paris), April 1982; "Building Types Study 579: Schools" in *Architectural Record* (New York), August 1982.

Our architectural concern through the years has been service rather than architectural formulas. We have attempted to derive our architecture from the activities appropriate for the users, rather than impose some patent rectangle.

—Lawrence B. Perkins

Lawrence B. Perkins built the firm of Perkins and Will on two basic concepts. The first related to the nature of architecture, the second to the men and women who produce it. Perkins has always believed that a successful building project is the result of the combined contributions of many capable individuals. Furthermore, once the right team has been gathered, he believes that it should be allowed to operate freely so that the most creative ideas about design and technology can rise to the surface and be applied to the job at hand. Perkins and Will, founded in 1935, is now one of the largest firms in the United States, yet the team approach within a permissive atmosphere continues to prevail. And consequently,

their architecture remains varied in style and use of materials.

Rather than reflecting any preconceived stylistic or structural dogma, each project evolves from the compound circumstances of a particular building program, locale, client, and job team. Although projects may differ outwardly from one to another, there is nevertheless a common denominator that runs throughout the firm's work: buildings are appropriate to their situation and requirements.

The company's first major commission was the Crow Island School in Winnetka, Illinois, done in conjunction with Eliel and Eero Saarinen. Crow Island embodied a progressive design that turned away from traditional educational philosophy and form. Instead of a single anonymous rectangle, the school extends wings from a central block in order to distinguish age groups and activities through architectural massing. Each classroom opens onto a landscaped courtyard and has its own lavatory, sink and drinking fountain. Every aspect of the building is scaled to the children, right down to the furniture. Crow Island School had a tremendous influence on American academic design. It was a landmark in every sense, and it established the firm's sensitive expertise in educational architecture, a reputation that it still deservedly enjoys.

Although Perkins and Will has long specialized in institutional buildings, schools and hospitals particularly, the office has also expanded its interest and skill in commercial projects. Of all the commissions undertaken for the private sector, Perkins is perhaps most proud of and the firm most recognized for the soaring, plastic design of the sixty-storey First National Bank of Chicago.

Throughout his career, Perkins has assumed responsibility for some design and a great deal of management and client contact, and his leadership is indelibly stamped on every aspect of the firm's practice. He has always taken great interest in young people, and this is evidenced in both his commitment to teaching and in his willingness to create opportunities for the younger members of his organization.

—Linda Legner

PERRET, Auguste.

French. Born in Brussels, Belgium, of French parents, 12 February 1874. Educated at the Ecole des Beaux-Arts, Paris, under Julien Guadet, 1891-95 (Réconnaissance des Architectes Americains Prize, 1895). Married Jeanne Cordeau in 1902. Worked in his father's building construction firm, Paris, 1897-1905, and Partner, with brothers Gustave and Claude, in the successor company, Perret Frères, from 1905. Professor, Ecole des Beaux-Arts, Paris. Inspector-General of Public Works and National Palaces, France; Member, French National Committee for the Reconstruction; Chief Architect, Reconstruction of Le Havre; Member, Conseil Artistique des Musées Nationaux, Paris. President, Conseil Superieur de l'Ordre des Architectes, Cercle d'Etudes Architecturales, and Salon des Tuileries, all Paris. Recipient: Royal Gold Medal, Royal Institute of British Architects, and American Institute of Architects, 1948; Medal of Honor, Académie des Beaux-Arts, Denmark, 1949. Honorary doctorate: Helsinki Polytechnic, 1949. Officier, Légion d'Honneur, 1926. Officer, Order of the White Lion, Czechoslovakia, 1925, and of La Couronne du Chêne, Luxembourg, 1925. Member, L'Institut de France. *Died* (in Paris) *28 February 1954.*

Works:

1889 Temple Tower, *Exposition Universelle*. Paris
1890 House, Berneval, France
1896 4 six-storey houses, rue Sorbier, Paris
1898 Office building, 10 Faubourg Poissonière, Paris
1899 Municipal Casino, Saint Malo, France
1902 Apartment building, 119 Avenue de Wagram, Paris
1903 Cathedral, Oran, Algeria (project)
       Apartment building, 22 bis rue Franklin, Paris
1904 School, rue de la Tour, Paris
       Office building, Avenue Niel, Paris
1905 Garage, 51 rue de Ponthieu, Paris
       Villa, Montereau, France

1906 Office building, 48 rue Raynouard, Paris
1907 La Saulot Hunting Lodge, Salbris, France
1908 Docks at Saïda, Tiaret and Sidi-Bel-Abbès, Algeria (projects)
1911 French Legation, Istanbul
House extensions, Bièvre, France
1913 Théâtre des Champs Elysées, Paris (original project by van de Velde)
1914 Société Royale d'Harmonie Building, Antwerp (project)
1915 House, rue Claude-Lorrain, Paris
1916 Société Industrielle Docks [I], Casablanca
Chapel, Maurice Denis House, Saint Germain, Paris
1919 Société Industrielle Docks [II], Casablanca
Esders Clothing Workshops, 78 avenue Philippe-Auguste, Paris
1921 Madame Paul Jamot Monument, Montparnasse Cemetery, Paris
Marinoni Workshops, Wallut Foundry Buildings, and Grange Foundry Buildings, Montataire, Oise, France
Rozanes Jewellery Shop, rue de la Paix, Paris
FER Factory, Aulnois, France
Aircraft hangar, Villacomblay, France (project)
Terraced housing, Paris (project)
1922 Société MArseillaise de Crédit Building, 4 rue Auber, Paris
High-rise building (project)
Housing, Tours, France (project)
1923 Notre Dame Church, Le Raincy, near Paris
Durand Décors Workshops, rue Olivier-Metra, Paris
Grand-Quevilly House, near Rouen
Gaut House, rue Nansouty, Paris
Pont d'Argent (temporary aluminum structure), Théâtre des Champs Elysées, Paris
1924 Church Bell Tower, Saint Vaury, Creuse, France
Palais de Bois (temporary exhibition building), Porte Maillot, Paris
1925 Theatre, and Albert Levy Pavilion, *Exposition des Arts Décoratifs*, Paris
Crédit Hôtelier Building, rue de la Ville l'Evêque, Paris
Church of Saint Thérèse, Montmagny, Seine et Oise, France
Observation Tower, *Grenoble Exhibition*
House, Tours, France (project)
1926 Cassandre House, Versailles
Veret House, Noyon, France
Chana Orloff House, rue de la Tombe-Issoire, Paris
Aghia House, Alexandria, Egypt
Joan of Arc Basilica, Paris (project)
1927 Braque House, rue du Douanier, Paris
School, Parc Montsouris, Paris
Palace of the League of Nations, Geneva (competition project)
Dominican Convent, Cairo (project)
School for Young Girls, Constantine, Algeria (project)
1928 Bresy House, Villa Said, Algeria
Chapel, Arceuil, Seine, France
1929 Mela Muter House, Villa Seurat, Algeria
Church extensions, Juvisy-sur-Orge, France
Eiffel Monument, Paris
Chapel, Chalons, France
Colpach Monument, Luxembourg
Huré House, Boulogne-sur-Seine, Paris
Gordine House, Boulogne-sur-Seine, Paris
Galerie Katia Granoff Gallery extensions, Quai Conti, Paris
Ecole Normale de Musique, rue Cardinet, Paris
Oblates Convent, Saint Benoit, France
1930 Lange House, Avenue Ingrès, Paris
Musée Moderne (project)
Facade for the Galeries Lafayette, Paris (project)
1931 Capucine Monastery alterations, Saint Symphorien, France
Magnin Museum alterations, Dijon, France

Nubar Bey House, Garches, France
Society of Naval Works and Construction Building, Paris
Chapel, Vanves, France
Porte Maillot Redevelopment, Paris (project)
Palace of the Soviets, Moscow (competition project)
1932 Apartment building, 51-55 rue Raynouard, Paris
Marine National Building, Paris
State Printing Buildings, Paris (project)
Awad Bey House, Cairo
Chapel, Strasbourg (project)
Arsenal Building, Toulon (project)
Military Headquarters Complex, Algiers (project)
1933 Aghun House, Alexandria, Egypt
Government Buildings, Algiers (project)
Palace of Agriculture, Algiers (project)
Redevelopment plan for the Port of Metz, France, (project)
1934 Master plan, and Trocadéro, for the *World's Fair* of 1937, Paris (project)
Paul Lefèvre House, Sceaux, France
Mobilier National (National Guard) Building, Paris
1935 Pont de l'Arc, Paris
1936 Pershing Monument, Route de Versailles (project)
1937 Museum of Public Works, Paris
Palais de Chaillot, Paris (project)
1939 Iron and Aluminum Foundry, Issoire, France
Clock and Watch Factory, Besançon, France
Barbier Hugo Hospital, Algiers
Church, Carmaux, France (project)
Attaturk Monument, Turkey (project)

Auguste Perret: Mobilier National Building, Paris, 1934.

1940 Comedy Theatre, Istanbul, (project)
Thermal Baths, Paris (project)
Champs Elysées and Invalides Developments, Paris (projects)
Plaine de l'Arc Airport, Marseilles (project)
1945 Master plan for the reconstruction of Le Havre
1947 Place de la Gare reconstruction, Amiens
1948 Perret Tower, Amiens
Midy Laboratories, Neuilly, Paris
Olympic Stadium, Montessou, France (project)
1948/
53 Atomic Energy Commission Establishment, Saclay, France
1949 Airport, Marignane, France
Airport, Berre, France (project)
1950 New Town of Gif, France
1952 Church of St. Joseph, Le Havre
Town Hall, Le Harve
Aircraft hangars, Marignane, France
1953/
55 David Weill Building, Boulevard Berthier, Paris

Publications:

By PERRET: book—*Contribution à une Théorie de l'Architecture*, Paris 1952; articles—"Le Musée Moderne" in *Mouseion* (Paris), December 1929; "Architecture, Science et Poésie" in *La Construction Moderne* (Paris), October 1932; "Construire un Musée" in *Encyclopedie Francaise*, Paris 1938.

On PERRET: books—*A. et G. Perret et l'Architecture du Beton Armée* by P. Jamot, Paris and Brussels 1927; *Auguste Perret* by Ernesto N. Rogers, Milan 1955; *Auguste Perret* by Bernard Champigneulle, Paris 1959; *D'Une Doctrine d'Architecture: Auguste Perret* by Marcel Zahar, Paris 1959; *Concrete: The Vision of a New Architecture* by Peter Collins, London 1959; *A. and G. Perret: architectes francais, 1874-1954, 1876-1952*, C.N.A.M. publication, Paris 1976; *Auguste Perret* by Lamia Doumato, Monticello, Illinois 1982. articles—"A. et G. Perret" by Jean Badovici in *Architecture Vivante* (Paris), Summer 1925; "Auguste Perret and Brothers" in *The Architects' Journal* (London), December 1926; "Auguste Perret" by M. E. Cahen in *L'Architecture d'Aujourd'hui* (Paris), January 1930; special issue of *L'Architecture d'Aujourd'hui* (Paris), October 1932; "The Doctrine of Auguste Peret" by Peter Collins in *Architectural Review* (London), August 1953; "The Work of Auguste Perret" by Ernö Goldfinger in *Architectural Association Journal* (London), January 1955; "Classicism and Rationalism in Perret" by Jean Prouvé and Vittorio Gregotti in *Domus* (Milan), May 1974; "The Last of the Master Builders" by Ernö Goldfinger in *Building Design* (London), 7 March 1975; "Auguste Perret" by Francoise Very in *Architecture Movement Continuité* (Paris), November 1975; "A. et G. Perret" by J.B. Ache in *Construction Moderne* (Paris), May 1976; "Notre Dame of Le Raincy" in *Space Design* (Tokyo), September 1980.

Auguste Perret can justifiably be regarded as the creator of reinforced-concrete architecture, i.e. of an architecture in which all the elements of the reinforced-concrete structure remain visible externally and—as far as is practical—internally. Two fortuitous circumstances oriented him toward this research: the earliest systematic experiements in reinforced-concrete frame construction (patented in France by Hennebique in 1892) coincided with his own architectural training at the Ecole des Beaux-Arts; and his father, Claude Perret, was a building contractor who taught him to see architecture as literally "the art of building"—a methodical, carefully supervised process of assembling tectonic components.

Auguste Perret was also greatly influenced by Julien Guadet, who was not only his teacher at the Ecole des Beaux-Arts but also a personal friend. Guadet's theory of architecture was eventually published in book form, when it became the standard text on this topic for the next fifty years. Phrases such as "Truth is indispensable to architecture, and every architectural lie corrupts," and "Any project is bad if it is more difficult or more complicated to construct than necessary" indicate the doctrine he taught concerning the relationship between form and structure.

Auguste Perret's first opportunity to experiment systematically with the Hennebique system came in 1903 (i.e. when he was nearly thirty). His father wanted to construct an apartment building on a vacant lot in the fashionable residential district behind the Palais de Chaillot, but the area was too small for a profitable multi-story building in masonry. He initially opposed his son's proposal to build in reinforced-concrete (since Hennebique's patent precluded him from being the main contractor), but Auguste Perret eventually obtained his consent, and designed the building (22b rue Franklin) to take ingenious advantages of the topographical and legal constraints, and every advantage of the new structural system. The facade was covered with faience tiles, since concrete surfaces could not, at that time, be relied upon to resist the penetration of moisture. But the tiles were arranged in such as way as to express as clearly as possible the forms of the structural system employed.

After Claude Perret's death in 1905, Auguste and his brother Gustave changed the name of the firm to Perret Frères, and began specializing in reinforced-concrete construction. Initially they built only for other architects in accordance with the plans provided, but while so doing they experimented with the fundamental architectural problems that the new structural system presented. Of these, the most important (in Auguste Perret's opinion) was the problem of building reinforced-concrete *visibly*, as distinct from the then current assumption that the new material was only practicable as a concealed structural support.

Perret's first opportunity to demonstrate his solution to these problems occurred in 1922, when he was commissioned to design and build a large war-memorial church at Le Raincy, near Paris. Internally and externally, it was entirely of bare concrete. The roof was a thin shell; the slender vertical supports were carefully profiled monoliths; and the walls were a continuous grille of precast elements filled with stained glass. The beauty of the overall appearance effectively established the feasibility of using the new material to create a new architecture. As Henry-Russell Hitchcock asserts, it was at Notre Dame du Raincy that reinforced-concrete "came of age as a building material."

From then onward Auguste Perret's reputation as the pioneer of reinforced-concrete architecture was unchallengeable. But whereas the avant-garde theorists of the 1920's were mainly concerned with mass-produced housing and industrialization, Perret's research was directed towards technical refinements, whereby the system used at Le Raincy could be extended to every kind of monumental or multi-story building.

His main concern was to find methods of displaying the richness of the aggregate, to develop means of precasting all non-loadbearing elements, and to improve timber formwork in ways that would produce the most elegant profiles. The extent of his achievement can best be assessed by studying the apartment building that he designed and constructed at 51-55 rue Raynouard in 1932, and the Mobilier National (also in Paris) designed and built in 1934.

After World War II Auguste Perret was charged with the reconstruction of Le Harve, a large seaport completely flattened by aerial bombardment. His scheme was subject to some criticism at the time because it did not conform to the precepts of the CIAM "Athens Charter," but it effectively demonstrated his concept of architecture as a harmonious environment in sympathy with existing urban traditions.

—Peter Collins

PERRIAND, Charlotte.
French. Born in Paris, 24 October 1903. Educated in Bourgogne and Savoie, France, until 1919; studied design, under Maurice Dufrène, Ecole de l'Union Centrale des Arts Décoratifs, Paris, 1920-25; also attended the life-classes of Bernard Boutet de Monvel and André Lhôte, Académie de la Grande Chaumière, Paris, 1924-26. Married Jacques Martin in 1943; daughter: Pernette. In private practice, establishing her own studio in the Place Saint-Sulpice, Paris, 1927-30, and in the Boulevard du Montparnasse, Paris, 1930-37; assistant in charge of furniture and fittings, studio of Le Corbusier, *q.v.*, and Pierre Jeanneret, *q.v.*, Paris, 1927-37; in private practice as architect and designer, working with Jean Prouvé, *q.v.*, Pierre Jeanneret, and Georges Blanchon, Paris, 1937-40; established office for prefabricated building researches, in the rue Las-Cases, Paris, 1940; Industrial Design Consultant to the Japanese Ministry of Commerce and Industry, Tokyo, 1940-41; independent designer in Tokyo, 1941-42, and in Indochina, 1943-46. Since 1946, in private practice, Paris: worked frequently in Tokyo, 1953-56 and 1962-68, and in Rio de Janeiro and throughout Latin America, 1969-76. Member, Salon des Artistes Décorateurs, Paris, 1927; CIAM (Congrès Internationaux d'Architecture Moderne), 1928; Founder-Member, Union des Artistes Modernes, Paris, 1930; Member, Association des Etudiants et Artistes Révolutionnaires, Paris, 1931; Editorial Board Member, *Architecture d'aujourd'hui*, magazine, Paris, 1930-74; Consultant to the Ecole Régionale des Beaux-Arts et des Arts Appliqués, Besançon, France 1966-68; Jury President, International Office Furniture Competition, Paris, 1983-84. Exhibitions: *Exposition internationale des arts décoratifs*, Paris, 1925; *Salon des artistes décorateurs*, Paris, 1926, 1927, 1928; *Salon d'automne*, Paris, 1927, 1929; *Union des artistes modernes*, Musée des Arts Décoratifs, Paris, 1930; International Building Trades Exhibition, London, 1930; Trade Fair, Cologne, 1931; *Exposition Internationale*, Brussels, 1935; *Salon des arts ménagers*, Paris, 1936, 1952, 1957, 1958; *Exposition internationale*, Paris, 1937; *Tradition, selection, création*, Takashimaya Department Store, Tokyo and Osaka, 1941; *Exposition internationale de l'urbanisme et de l'habitation*, Paris, 1947; *Le Bazar*, Musée des Arts Décoratifs, Paris, 1949; *Synthesis of the Arts*, Takashimaya Department Store, Tokyo, 1955; Galerie Steph Simon, Paris, 1944-74; *La machine à s'asseoir: Le Corbusier, Charlotte Perriand, Pierre Jeanneret*, Palazzo dei Convegni, Rome, 1976; *Charlotte Perriand: un art de vivre*, Musée des Arts Décoratifs, Paris, 1985. Recipient: Ministry of Agriculture Award, Paris, 1938; Gold Medal, Académie d'Architecture, Paris, 1978. Officer, Ordre National du Mérite, France, 1978; Chevalier, Ordre des Arts et Lettres, France, 1981; Chevalier of the Légion d'Honneur, France, 1983. Address: 15 rue Las-Cases, 75007 Paris, France.

Works:

1927 Bar sous le toit, at *Salon d'automne*, Paris
1928 Furniture for the Villa Laroche, Paris
Dining-Room, *Salon des artistes decorateurs*, Paris
Furniture for the Villa Church, Ville-d'Avray, France
"Equipement d'habitation" furniture, *Salon d'automne*, Paris (with Le Corbusier and Pierre Jeanneret)
1929 "Maison Minimum" studies (project)
1930 Luterma display, International Building Trades Exhibition, London
Office furniture for the editor of *Semaine à Paris*, Paris
Music Room for the composer Jean Rivier, Paris
1930/
32 Swiss Building interiors, Cité Universitaire, Paris
1931 Chaise longue and cabinets, Trade Fair, Cologne, Germany
1932 Salvation Army Hostel interiors, Paris
House of Young Artists and Technicians, Paris (project)
1935 Bachelor Study, at the *Exposition internationale*, Brussels (with L. Sognot and R. Herbst)
1936 Lounge interiors, *Salon des arts ménagers*, Paris
Waiting-Room, Ministry of Agriculture, Paris
Studies for family and weekend houses and a mountain chalet (projects)
1937 Ministry of Agriculture displays, bathroom, mountain refuge and modular interiors, *Exposition internationale*, Paris
1937/
39 Experimental "refuge bivouac" high-altitude building, on Mount Joly, Haute-Savoie, France
1938 Curved Table in spruce from the Pavillon des Temps Nouveaux studies
Office interiors for Jean-Richard Block, Paris
1939 Hotel annexe, Vallée de Saint-Nicolas-de-Veroce, France

Mountain Hotel for the new winter sports complex at Méribel-les-Allues, Savoie, France

1941 *Tradition, sélection, création* exhibition layouts, Takashimaya Department Store, Tokyo and Osaka, Japan

1947 Maison Minimum interiors, *Exposition internationale de l'urbanisme et de l'Habitation,* Paris

1947 Franco-American Memorial Hospital interiors, Saint-Lô, France (with Paul Nelson and others)

1950 Kitchen Prototype I for the Unité d'Habitation, Marseille, France

Prefabricated interiors for the Marseille Unité d'Habitation, *Salon des arts ménagers,* Paris

1951 Furnishing prototypes for the Toulon development, *Salon des arts ménagers,* Paris

1952 Bathroom units, *Salon des arts Ménagers,* Paris

Student Quarters, Maison de Tunisie, Cité Universitaire, Paris

Bathroom fittings (with plumber J. Borot)

Air France Office interiors, Brazzaville, Congo (with J. Prouve)

1953 Student Apartment, Paris (with J. Prouvé, A. Salomon and Lagneau and Weill)

Hotel de France interiors, Conakry, West Africa (with J. Prouvé and Lagneau and Weill)

1955 *Synthesis of the Arts* exhibition layouts, Takashimaya Department Store, Tokyo

1957 *L'Art d'habiter au Japon* exhibit layouts, *Salon des arts ménagers,* Paris

Air France Office interiors, London (with P. Bradok)

1958 Housing for Petroleum Workers in the Sahara Desert, *Salon des arts ménagers,* Paris

1959 Communal Area interiors, Maison du Brésil, Cité Universitaire, Paris

Jean and Huguette Borot House renovations, Montmartre, Paris (with H. Prouvé)

Air France Office interiors, Tokyo (with J. Sakakura and R. Suzuki)

1959/
70 United Nations Conference Rooms and Assembly Hall renovations, Geneva (as consultant; with Beaudouin and Carlu)

1960 Mountain Chalet, Méribel-les-Allues, Sovoie, France

French Tourist Office interiors, London (with Ernö Goldfinger)

1962 Apartment interiors, Rio de Janeiro (with M. E. Costa)

Three sports stations, Vallée des Bellevilles, Savoie, France (competition project; with J. Prouvé and Candilis-Josic-Woods)

1965 Furniture and Display Stands, Musée National d'Art Moderne, Paris (with P. Faucheux)

1966 Japanese Ambassador's House interiors, Paris (with J. Sakakura and Riedberger)

1967/
82 Les Arcs Ski Stations 1600, 1800 and 2000, Savoie, France (with B. Taillefer, R. Godino and others)

1970 Apartment renovations, Paris

1975 Shiki Fabric House showroom interiors, Paris

1984/
85 *Un Art de vivre* exhibition layouts, Musée des Arts Décoratifs, Paris

Publications:

By PERRIAND: books—*Contact avec l'art japonais: selection, tradition, création,* editor, with Junzo Sakakura, Tokyo 1941; articles—"Wood or metal?" in *Studio* (London), April 1929; "L'Habitation familiale" in *Architecture d'aujourd'hui* (Paris), January 1935; "Equipement interieur" in *Techniques et architecture* (Paris) no. 7/8, 1948; "Le

Charlotte Perriand: Mountain Chalet, Méribel des Allues, France, 1946-52.

spectacle au Japon" in *Architecture d'aujourd'hui* (Paris), May 1949; "L'Art d'habiter," special issue of *Techniques et architecture* (Paris), June 1950; "Le Problème du rangement" in *Architecture d'aujourd'hui* (Paris), October 1954; "Une Tradition vivante," special issue of *Architecture d'aujourd'hui* (Paris), May 1956; "La Maison japonaise" in *Aujourd'hui* (Paris), April 1957; "Temoignage à Le Corbusier" in *Aujourd'hui* (Paris), no. 51, 1965; "Problèmes specifiques de trois vallées alpines" in *Architecture d'aujourd'hui* (Paris), June/July 1966; "Fifty Years since l'Esprit Nouveau," special issue of *Parametro* (Bologna, Italy), September/October 1976; "Jean Prouvé, 1901-1984," with others, in *Techniques et architecture* (Paris), April/May 1984; "Charlotte Perriand Looks Back (and Forward)," interview, with Charlotte Ellis and Martin Meade in *Architectural Review* (London), November 1984.

On PERRIAND: books—*New French Architecture* by Maurice Besset, Stuttgart and London 1967; *La Machine à s'asseoir: Le Corbusier, Charlotte Perriand, Pierre Jeanneret,* exhibition catalogue, by M. Di Puolo, M. Fagiolo and M. L. Madonna, Rome 1976; *Charlotte Perriand: un art de vivre,* exhibition catalogue, by Eugène Claudius-Petit, François Mathey and Yvonne Brunhammer, Paris 1985; articles—"Madame Perriand" in *Design* (Tokyo), November 1930; "La Fonction crée la ligne, un bureau de Charlotte Perriand" by Philippe Dôle in *Art et décoration* (Paris), no. 1, 1939; "Une Habitation au Japon" in *Techniques et architecture* (Paris), no. 7/8, 1946; "Mobilier étudié au japon par Charlotte Perriand" in *Architecture d'aujourd'hui* (Paris), March 1947; "Charlotte Perriand in Giappone" in *Domus* (Milan), May 1947; "Japanese Living Room" in *Architectural Review* (London), June 1947; "Elementi d'arredamento per la serie" in *Domus* (Milan), June 1953; "Mrs. Perriand's Fur-

niture and the Modulor" in *Kokusai-Kentiku* (Tokyo), December 1955; "Charlotte Perriand" by Jose Lluis Sert in *Aujourd'hui* (Paris), March 1956; "Les Grands Décorateurs—Charlotte Perriand" by Claude Salvy in *Les Nouvelles littéraires* (Paris), 31 June 1958; "Charlotte Perriand" in *Habitat* (Rio de Janeiro), January/February 1959; "Travel Agency" in *Architectural Review* (London), April 1963; "Charlotte Perriand" in *Architecture d'aujourd'hui* (Paris), April/May 1964; "Le Chalet de Charlotte Perriand en Savoie" in *Plaisir de France* (Paris), January 1966; "Furniture by Le Corbusier and Charlotte Perriand" in *Architectural Design* (London), July 1966; "Slouching toward Barcelona: Classic Chairs in form and Function" by Michael Lampert in *Progressive Architecture* (New York), February 1975; "Encounter with Charlotte Perriand" by Cella Manolin-Minart in *Modulo* (Rio de Janeiro), July/September 1977; "Un Architecte de l'anti-nostalgie" by Christine Clerc in *Elle* (Paris), 27 February 1978; "Apartment in Paris" by Yukio Futagawa in *Global Architecture* (Tokyo), no. 15, 1984; "French Government's Good Offices" in *Architectural Review* (London), March 1984; "Charlotte Perriand, architecte d'intérieur" by Genevieve Breerette in *Le Monde* (Paris), 7 February 1985; "Perriand in Perspective" by Charlotte Ellis in *Architects' Journal* (London), 13 February 1985; film—*Charlotte Perriand: créer l'habitat au XXe siècle,* French television film by Jacques Barsac, 1985; recording—*Charlotte Perriand, ou l'art d'habiter,* eight interviews by Paule Chavasse for *France Culture,* 1985.

I first met Charlotte Perriand in 1948 upon my arrival at *L'Architecture d'aujourd'hui* magazine, where she was already a member of the editorial committee. Editor André Bloc held her in deep affection, appreciating her candour, her attitude toward herself and others, and the strictness of her beliefs. She was by nature the faithful friend, the uncompromising rock, the even-stepped mountaineer who knows where she is going and who calmly solves each day's problems as they arise. The life of the committee at L'Architecture d'aujourd'hui was intense. Among the forty architects, André Bloc never made any decision without consulting Charlotte. He had full confidence in her judgement, whatever the topic under consideration.

Perriand spent her childhood in Paris and on a farm in Burgundy (previously in Savoie), at her paternal grandfather's. After training at the Union Central des Arts Décoratifs, at the Grande Chaumière, she took part in the 1923 Exposition des Arts Décoratifs and the 1927 Salon d'Automne. The books Vers une architecture and L'Art décoratif d'aujourd'hui opened her eyes and made her decide to meet Le Corbusier. That same year, 1927, she entered his atelier on the rue de Sèvres as a student in architecture and an associate for furniture.

Ten productive years followed. Besides furnishing the Laroche and Ville d'Avray villas, as well as the Swiss pavilion at the Cité Universitaire and the Salvation Army Refuge, she participated in home furnishing exhibitions. "We wanted to create a style of furniture accessible to all, and which, produced in an artisan manner, could be adapted to mass production," she explained.

In 1930, the Union des Artistes Modernes (UAM) united creative people from all disciplines. At the 1931 Cologne Fair, Le Corbusier, Pierre Jeanneret and Perriand presented a diorama of the "Plan Voisin" and furniture, including a metal-framed lounge chair, the culmination of long studies and a masterpiece universally acknowledged to this day.

The Le Corbusier atelier was an exciting climate precisely because it was staffed with young architects: Pierre Jeanneret, Alfred Roth, Junzo Sakakura, Josep Lluis Sert, Jean Bossu. Most of them belonged to CIAM and took part in its fourth meeting aboard the Patrix II, between Athens and Marseille. The convocation culminated in the drafting of ninety-five resolutions which later became the basis of the "Athens Charter", published in 1943 by Le Corbusier. The studio was a crucible where, in a climate of enthusiasm and friendship, all currents of research intersected as preliminary studies were made for the 1937 World's Fair. In addition, exhibitions succeeded one another, one of the most important being the Third Habitation Exhibition organized by L'Architecture d'aujourd'hui in 1936 at the Salon des Arts Ménagers, where Perriand presented a living room with furniture of her own creation.

In 1937, for the Paris World's Fair, the UAM obtained—not without a struggle—a spot for its pavilion. There, Le Corbusier, Pierre Jeanneret and Charlotte Perriand showed the prototype of a hotel sanitary unit manufactured by Jacob Delafon. As well, Perriand also presented several folding or combinable chairs, and—with Jeanneret and Andre Tournon as engineers—showed the "Bivouac Refuge" in co-operation with Aluminium Français in the High Mountain Equipment section.

At Porte Maillot, on a site reserved for Agriculture, Georges Monnet welcomed the new Le Corbusier/Pierre Jeanneret Pavillon des Temps Nouveaux, a large canvas tent which sheltered the Habitation and Leisure exhibit and the tenth meeting of CIAM. Nearby, with Fernand Léger, Perriand illustrated the Ministry of Agriculture's display of panels mounted on an open-air structure. "With Fernand Léger, work was transformed into recreation; every moment dazzled with colour and humour . . .," she recalls.

1937 also marked the end of the collaboration with Le Corbusier. "I left the atelier because of a desire for freedom, but that was not without heartbreak. Ten years spent with exceptional beings leave their mark," she noted.

The years 1938-39 saw research with wood, and a trend toward mountain projects, especially at Méribel-les-Allues, a new resort for winter sports. Then, in 1940, was initiated the Atelier at 15 rue Las Cases, with Jean Prouvé, Pierre Jeanneret and Georges Blanchon, to study temporary prefabricated buildings for the Aluminium Français plant at Issoires. But in February 1940, a strange invitation arrived for Perriand from the Ministry of Commerce and Industry of Japan, inviting her to become consultant in industrial arts—an invitation confirmed by Junzo Sakakura as testimony of the friendship that had developed in the Le Corbusier studio. So, in March 1941, Charlotte organized the exhibition Tradition, Selection, Creation in Tokyo.

But December brings Pearl Harbor. Blocked by war, Charlotte was able to leave Japan only for Indochina; from there, she was repatriated to France in 1946. But she had absorbed traditional Japanese culture: calm order, the philosophy of nothingness, refinement of detail, exterior-interior connection, notion of space in reduced areas, judicious use of a stone, of a small tree, of a sheet of water, or of a horizon line—symbols of the fact that man belongs to the universe.

In 1950, she designed the prototype kitchen for Le Corbusier's Unité de'Habitation in Marseille and then, with Jean Borot, a toilet-shower-tub-unit, presented in the Useful Forms section of the Salon des Arts Ménagers in 1952. That same year, she designed a student room in the Tunisia House of the Cité Universitaire, within the framework of the Space Group created by Andrè Bloc, where architects and plastic arts specialists worked together.

1955 saw the Synthesis of the Arts exhibit in Tokyo, with the collaboration of Sakakura and Martha Villages. Why Synthesis of the Arts? Because everything is integrated from the start in the design of a unit. She says, "I was creating harmonious units using tapestries of Le Corbusier, ceramic murals by Lèger, and furniture made up of standardized elements—risers and supports permitting the free assembly of bookcases, drawers of plastic materials, stackable seats and tables for entertaining, to be put away after use, freeing the space. The wood elements were to be manufactured in Japan, the metallic elements in the Jean Prouvé ateliers in Nancy." Later, those elements were produced by the Steph Simon Galerie in Saint Germain-des-Près. As a counterpart to her exhibition in Tokyo, Perriand organized, at the Salon des Arts Ménagers in Paris, an exhibit on the traditional Japanese art of living, with a selection of objects chosen by Sakakura and Yanagi, and a Japanese house designed by Ren Suzuki.

Overall, Perriand's work may be related to four themes she herself has defined: the art of the street, diversified creation, leisure in the mountains, and art for living. The art of the street, for Perriand, is an ephemeral art that obeys the laws of advertising and change. It is very important because it conditions the public to new forms. In that belief, she created the Steph Simon Galerie in Saint Germain-des-Prés (1955); the Air France offices in London (1957) and in Tokyo (1960), and the Shiki Fabric House showroom in Paris (1975). Of the Air France offices in Tokyo, which she had executed with Junzo Sakakura and Ren Suzuki, Perriand states, "Those premises were located on a street with movie houses displaying flashy advertising. I took the opposite position and built offices which were highly serene, made of white marble, and set against a background of an immense, luminous picture of the North Pole ice barrier seen from an airplane; it was suspended from cables and could be changed with each promotion campaign. That was assuming too much. The art of the street is an ephemeral architecture which becomes completely outdated approximately every ten years."

Another theme comes to life during that period: the idea that creation should be diversified, taking into account the places and programmes, the possibilities that derive from them, in order to achieve a greater richness of expression. For example, in the Maison du Sahara, presented at the Salon des Arts Ménagers in 1958, starting with standardized equipment, two modes of cabins were studied: one for sleeping, the other for living. Those cabins, air-conditioned during the day, opened their doors to the cool desert at night. A large tent sheltered them and provided a living space in the Bedouin manner.

In 1960, Perriand built her own chalet at Méribeles-Allues. "As long as I had to do a chalet traditional in techniques because of the specifications of the resort, I wanted to investigate the merits of the valley's indigenous housing: the perfect structural design of those peasant houses, the walls of flush stone topped with a separate frame which leaves openings that can be closed with pierced boards to air the stored hay. I kept the same structure, but closed the openings with fixed thermopanes or with sliding bay windows. Here I am, completely protected from draughts, from the cold, from the sun. I unite peasant traditions with the Japanese house. Who would believe this possible?"

Then, from 1967 to 1982, Perriand entered the world of concrete: planning and constructing the Station des Arcs in Savoie. Accommodations for 18,000 were spread among three resorts opened in 1982 at altitudes from 1,6000 to 2,000 metres.

"The leading idea of our first approach was to open wide interior spaces to the sun and nature, and to reduce closed circulation to a minimum. Arc 1600 was a laboratory of architecture. Arc 1800 and 2000 are resorts of a new type, based especially on an original concept of the hotel industry designed to attract an international clientele. We were faced with the need to innovate, densify, and to define the ideal balance between width and depth of a floor plan. It was necessary to standardize bathrooms, cooking areas, and storage areas, and to reduce installation time. We had to plan for everything—even teaspoons—and to build 500 livable studios between May 1 and November 30: a true challenge. In collaboration with a factory in Brittany which manufactured sanitary units for the French and foreign navies, and taking into account the planning, each morning we were able to deliver seven complete bathrooms, ready to be lifted by crane. That positive experience covered 3,000 units."

An art for living. That is the permanent goal that Perriand sets for herself; therefore, her task is far from complete. In the Atelier rue Las Cases, she works with her team. "The state of creativity is fragile," she says. "Creativity is spontaneous but, in order to preserve its freshness while achieving perfect execution, it needs to be nurtured, enriched by all members of the atelier. There is no competition, only synergy. The problem remains the same. On must express one's times. Changes occur which we cannot imagine. I take as my own motto that to walk is to move forward."

—Renée Diamant-Berger

PIACENTINI, Marcello.

Italian. Born in Rome, 8 December 1881; son of the architect Pio Piacentini. Educated at the Accademia di San Luca, Rome, 1901-04, Dip.Arch. 1904. Served in the Italian Army during World War I. In private practice, Rome, from 1906. Served as the Government Architect (principal architect to Mussolini). Professor, Scuola Superiore di Architettura, Rome. Editor, L'Architettura, Rome, 1922-43; President, National Committe on City Planning, and National Council of Architects. Recipient: First Prize, Civic Centre Competition, Bergamo, Italy, 1903; First Prize, Quirinal Traffic Tunnel Competition, Rome, 1908; First Prize, University of Bergamo Competition, Italy, 1910; Grand Prize for Architecture, World's Fair, Brussels, 1910; Grand Prize and Gold Medal, Esposizione di Roma, 1911; Special Grand Prize, Pan Pacific Exposition, San Francisco, 1915; First Prize, Memorial Arch Competition, Genoa,

1923; Gold Medal, City of Turin, 1935. Honorary doctorates: Accademia di Genoa, Urbino, Perugia, and Bologna. *Died* (in Rome) *in 1960.*

Works:

1903 Civic Centre, Bergamo, Italy (competition project)
1908 Quirinal Traffic Tunnel, Rome (competition project)
1910 Italian Pavilion, World's Fair, Brussels
      Master plan for the University of Bergamo, Italy
1911 Plan for the *Esposizione di Roma* (with A. Giustini and C. Bazzani)
      Palazzo delle Feste, Rome
      Pavilion, Piazza Colonna, Rome
      Villa Berlingier, Rome (with Pio Piacentini)
1915 Quirino Theatre restoration, Rome
      Villa Rusconi, Rome
      Vila Cavaglieri, Rome
      Villa Allegri, Rome
      Villa Page, Rome
      Villa Nobili, Rome
      Villa Gaspari, Rome
      Italian Pavilion, *Pan Pacific Exposition.* San Francisco
1917 Cinema, Rome (competition project)
      Villa, Via Settembrini, Rome
      Two villas, Viale della Regina, Rome
      Villa, Viale Liegi, Rome
      Terraced houses, Piazza del Viminale, Rome
      Restaurant, Rinascente Department Store, Rome
1918 Banca d'Italia Building, Piazza del Paramento, Rome
1919 Marmorata Bridge, Rome
1922 Cinema-Theatre Savoia, Florence
1925 Quirinetta Theatre, Rome
      Palazzo Pateras, Rome
      Villa Giovve, Rome
      Villa della Bitta, Roma
      Villa Peragallo, Rome
      Villa Testasecca, Rome
1926 Ambassador's Hotel, Rome
1927 Villa Glori Racecourse, Rome
      Master plan for the centre of Bergamo, Italy
      Argentina Theatre restoration, Rome
      Palace of the League of Nations, Geneva (competition project)
1927/
  32 Piazza della Vittoria, Brescia, Italy: Central Post Office, National Assurance Institute, and National Treasury of Social Assurance
1928 Casa Madre dei Mutilati, Rome
      War Memorial, Bolzano, Italy
      Law Courts, Messina, Sicily
1930 Cinema-Theatre Barberini, Rome
      Piazza Missori, Milan
      Cassa Nazionale delle Assicurazioni Sociali Building, Milan
1932 Memorial Arch, Genoa
      Via Regina Elena, Rome
      City Corporation Building, Rome (with G. Vaccaro)
      International Temple of Peace, Rome
      City Centre and Via della Conciliazione, Rome (with Attilio Spacciarelli)
      Luigi Cadorna Mausoleum, Pallanza, now Verbania, Italy
      Palazzo degli Studi, Foggia, Italy
      Wedekind Mausoleum, Acqui Ottolenghi, Italy
1933 University City, Rome (as chief architect; with Arnaldo Poschini, Pietro Aschieri, Giuseppe Capponi, Giuseppe Pagano, Giovanni Michelucci, Gaetano Rapisardi and Gio Ponti)
1934 Church of Christ the King, Rome
1936 Banca Nazionale del Lavoro Headquarters Rome
      Rectorate, University City, Rome

General Insurance Building, Jerusalem
1937 Italian Pavilion, *Exposition Internationale,* Paris
1937/
  40 *Esposizone Universale,* Rome (as supervising architect)
1938 Via Roma, Turin
1940 Law Courts, Milan
1941 Magna Grecia Museum Reggio Calabria, Italy
1942 Master plan for the E. 42 district, Rome (with others)
      Piazza della Vittoria, Genoa
      Master plan for University City, Rio de Janeiro (with V. Morpurgo)
1959 Palazzo dello Sport, Rome (with Pier Luigi Nervi)

Publications:

By PIACENTINI: books—*Architettura d'oggi,* Rome 1930; *Volto di Roma,* Rome 1945.

On PIACENTINI: books—*Architettura moderna in Italia* by A. Pica, Milan 1941; *L'Eclettismo a Roma 1870-1922* by Paolo Portoghesi, Rome 1969; *European Architecture of the Twentieth Century* by Arnold Whittick, London 1974; articles—"Marcello Piacentini mori nel 1925" by Bruno Zevi in *L'Architettura* (Rome), 1958; article by P. Marconi in *L'Architetto* (Rome), August 1960; "Marcello Piacentini—Fascist Architect Who Died 20 Years Ago" in *Architettura* (Rome), January 1981; "Radical Abstract and Cerebral" by Maristella Casciato in *Wonen-TA/BK* (Heerlen, Netherlands), July 1983.

*   *   *

To appreciate the work of Marcello Piacentini, it is essential to know its political and social background. Piacentini was Mussolini's principal architect throughout the major period of the Fascist regime. Mussolini dreamed of restoring the ancient glories of Imperial Rome and instigated numerous large reconstruction schemes for the centres of some of the principal cities. Piacentini carried out and made projects for several of these, principally at Brescia, Turin, and Rome. His best work in which his qualities as a planner and architect are most conspicuous, is the University City in Rome. Piacentini aimed in his design to combine the severe, Simple character of modern, concrete building wth classical monumentality—to combine in short the gradeur of Rome with the modern spirit, a goal inspired by his principal client.

His earliest large-scale, urban scheme, the Piazza della Vittoria at Brescia and the surrounding buildings, gives a clear indication of the character of his work. The buildings are constructed or reinforced concrete frames with brick infillings faced with marble, occasionally patterned, in the traditional Italian medieval and Renaissance manner. There is some mixture of traditional influences, Greek Roman, and Romanesque, but each is much simplified to flatness and bare outine. The immense Post Office building is a massive, square Greek portico; the Natonal Assurance Institute and Social Assurance Buildings have flat, simplified treatment with marble encrustation and Romanesque arcading.

A notable achievement in urban renewal is Piacentini's replanning and reconstruction of a central area of Rome to improve transport facilities as well as the setting of the fine buildings of ancient Rome and the Renaissance. The work was done in collaboration with Attilo Spacciarelli and involved the demolition of mean buildings and the introduction of a handsome avenue—the via della Concilizione—from the Tiber to the Piazza S. Pietro. It is a vast improvement in this central area, and it is difficult to resist the belief that the adverse criticism

that has been made is partly the result of its association with the Fascist regime.

Perhaps Piacentini's most conspicuous success is the University City in Rome, which invites comparison with the new building complex of London University. Both are classically inspired. In the former, there is a happier disposition of buildings, for the City is really a large garden in which monumental buildings are grouped and, for the most part, looking inward. Piacentini was the controlling architect, and he assembled a team of the best-known Italian architects to assist him. The general impression of the buildings is that overall, one mind controlled the essential character of the whole. The aims are explained by Piacentini himself. He is speaking of the Roman piazzi, which he says "are born of a symmetrical order, but the single buildings each take forms characteristic of their service. So it is with this University City. Born of an idea of a basilical and transept plan, it draws all its impressiveness from order and fundamental symmetry," and he speaks of the differences in the buildings. The undoubted unity of the whole could be criticized as possessing sameness, for the buildings follow in character Piacentini's own immense and dominating Rectorate building which also houses the Great Hall and Library. This sets the keynote of the whole. The lofty, square columns of the central portico; the patterning of windows on the plain, flanking blocks; the lettered frieze, and the large, sculptured reliefs give large-scale decorative notes to the walls, and the good proportion and monumental scale are impressive. This semblance of modernity given to the architecture of a classic Mediterranean clime is also a monumental expression of a political era.

—Arnold Whittick

PIANO, Renzo.
Italian. Born in Genoa, 14 September 1937. Educated at the Polytechnic, Milan, 1959-64, Dip.Arch. 1964. Married Magda Arduino in 1962; children: Carlo, Matteo, and Lia. Worked with architect-designer Franco Albini, *q.v.,* Milan, 1962-64, with his father E. Piano, Genoa, 1964-65, and with Z. S. Makowsky, London, 1965-70; since 1970, Partner, with Richard Rogers, *q.v.,* Piano and Rogers Architects, London, Paris, and Genoa; since 1977, Partner, with Peter Rice, Piano and Rice, engineers and architects, Genoa, Paris, and London; since 1980, Partner, with Richard Fitzgerald, Piano and Fitzgerald, Houston, Texas. Lecturer, Polytechnic of Milan, 1965-68; Visiting Lecturer, Columbia University, New York, 1967, University of Pennsylvania, Philadelphia, 1967, University of Bucharest, Rumania, 1968, and Polytechnic of Delft, Netherlands, 1969; Professor of Architecture, Architectural Association School, London, and Polytechnic of Central London, 1971; Visiting Lecturer, Unesco, Paris, 1973, and Oslo School of Architecture, 1976. Exhibitions: *Triennale,* Milan, 1967; Architectural Association, London, 1970; Musée des Arts Décoratifs, Paris, 1973. Recipient: First Prize, Place Beaubourg Competition, Paris, 1971; Auguste Perret Prize, International Union of Architects, 1978; Compasso d'Oro Award, Milan, 1981. Honorary Fellow, American Institute of Architects. Addresses: Atelier Piano, 14 Rue Sainte Croix de la Bretonnerie, 75004, Paris, France; Piano and Fitzgerald, 5075 Westheimer, suite 1260, Houston, Texas, U.S.A.; Studio Piano and Rice, Viale G. Modugno 22, 16156 Genoa, Italy.

Works:

1964/
  65 Reinforced polyester space-frames, Genoa

Renzo Piano: IBM travelling exhibition pavilion, 1982.

1965 Woodworking shop, Genoa
1966 Mobile sulphur-extraction building, Pomezia, Rome
Space-frame with inflatable units, Genoa
Pre-stressed steel and reinforced polyester structure, Genoa
1967 Shell-structure pavilion, *XIV Triennale,* Milan
Reinforced concrete construction system, Bologna
1968 Industrialized housing construction system, Genoa
Olivetti Factory Roof Components, Ivrea, Italy (with M. Zanuso)
1969 Residential district, Genoa
Olivetti-Underwood Factory Roof Components, Harrisburg, Virginia
1970 Shell/Esso Prefabircated Service Station System
Italian Industry Pavilion, *Expo '70,* Osaka, Japan
1970 Fitzroy Street Commercial Centre, Cambridge (with Richard Rogers and Fitzroy Robinson)
ARAM Inc. Medical Centre, Washington, D.C. (with Richard Rogers)
1971 B & B Italia Offices, Como, Italy (with Richard Rogers)
Clasp Italiana Ltd. Brockhouse Steel Structures (building system), Birmingham, England (with Richard Rogers)
1972 Universal Oil Products United Kingdom Head Office, and UOP Fragrances Ltd. Laboratory, Tadworth, Surrey (with Richard Rogers)
1973 Aston Martin Lagonda Ltd. Offices, Showroom, Restaurant, Squash Court and Housing, London (with Richard Rogers)
1975 PA Management Consultants (PATScentre) Research Laboratories, Workshops and Ancillary Administration Building, Cam-

bridge, England (with Richard Rogers)
Housing and recreation areas, for Globe Construction Ltd., at Basildon, Essex, England (with Richard Rogers)
1977 Institut de Récherche et de Coordination Acoustique, for Pierre Boulez, Paris (with Richard Rogers)
Centre Beaubourg, Paris (with Richard Rogers and Ove Arup and Partners)
Modular office system, Milan
1977/
80 Studio Piano workshop, Genoa
Lagny Factory housing and workshops, Marne-la-Vallee, France
1978 Kronenbourg factory building, Strasbourg, France
Emergency Housing wall-system
Housing estate, Cergy-Pontoise, France (competition project)
Mobile construction unit, Dakar, Senegal
Single-storey construction system with solar energy plant (competition project)
Industrialized construction system for evolving houses, Perugia, Italy
Transport vehicle for developing countries, Turin (project)
1978/
80 Fiat VSS experimental car, Turin
1978/
82 Quartiere Il Rigo housing estate, Corciano, Perugia, Italy
Holiday homes, Luca di Molare, Alessandria, Italy
1979 Design of *Open Site* television programme, for RIA Channel 2, Rome
Office factory for ANACT (project)
Neighborhood workshop, Otranto, Italy
1979/
81 Prototype emergency house, Macolim, Switzerland

1980 Multi-fuctional food centre, Genoa
Cultural centre (conversion of fifteenth century abbey), Passaggio di Bettona, Perugia, Italy
Exhibition complex, Milan (project)
Island of Burano restructuring plan, Venice
Shore and port development plan, Loano, Savona, Italy (project)
Civic centre and library, Loano, Savona, Italy (project)
1980/
81 Milanofiori Conference Centre structural system, Milan
Arvedi tubular structural system, Cremona, Italy
1980/
82 Neighborhood workshop, Bari, Italy
1981 Housing block renewal, Turin
Quartiere del Molo renewal plan, Genoa
Nationalgalerie extensions and housing, West Berlin (competition project)
1981/
83 De Menil Collection exhibition building, Houston, Texas
Banca Agricola Commerciale building, Reggio Emilia, Italy
1981/
84 Schlumberger Works conversion, Montrouge, Paris
1982 Organization of Arab Petroleum Exporting Countries (OPEC) building, Kuwait (competition project)
IBM travelling exhibition pavilions
Palazzo a Vela conversion for Alexander Calder exhibition, Turin
Centocelle/Torrespaccata Business Centre, Rome
Designs for the 1989 *World's Fair,* Paris (project)

Pietra area plan, Omegna, Novara, Italy (project)

Banca Agricola Commerciale branch building (conversion of printing-works), Modena, Italy (project)

1983 Metropolitan Railway stations (5), Genoa

1983/
84 Il Prometeo music research laboratory, Venice

1984 Water treatment plant integration plan, Genoa

Centre Georges Pompidou cinema extensions, Paris

Sesrieres ski resort master plan, Turin

Fiat Lingotto industrial complex conversion, Turin (as consultant)

Commercial Centre office buildings, Naples, Italy

Lowara Industries office extensions, Montecchio Maggiore, Vicenza, Italy

Keti: Kenya Energy Technology Institute, Nairobi

Leisure Centre, Cremona, Italy

Columbus Expedition 500th Anniversary designs, Genoa

Publications:

By PIANO: book—*The Building of Beaubourg*, with Richard Rogers and others, London 1978; *Antico e bello* with M. Arduino and M Fazio, Rome 1980; articles—"Architecture and Technology" in *Architectural Association Quarterly* (London), July 1970; "Il padiglione dell'industria italiana all 'Expo 70 di Osaka" in *Accaio* (Milan), November 1970; "Per un'edilizia industrializzata" in *Accaio* (Milan), February 1971; Piano and Rogers," with Richard Rogers, in *Architectural Design* (London), May 1975; "Mobilités des hypotheses alternatives de production" in *Werk-Archithese* (Zürich), November/December 1977; "Renzo Piano, Genova" in *Casabella* (Milan), November/December 1981.

On PIANO: books—*International Conference on Space Structures*, exhibition catalogue, London 1966; *IRCAM*, Paris 1977; *Costruire e ricostruire*, Udine 1978; *Das Centre Pompidou in Paris* by A. Fils, Munich 1980; *Renzo Piano/Pezzo per Pezzo*, exhibition catalogue, edited by G. Donin, Rome 1982; *La Modernité: un project inachevé*, exhibition catalogue, Paris 1982; *Storia di una Mostra Torino 1983*, Milan 1983; *Renzo Piano: progetti e architetture, 1964/1983* by Massimo Dini, Paris and Milan 1983, New York 1984; articles—"Structural Plastics in Europe" in *Arts and Architecture* (Los Angeles), August 1966; "Uno Studio Laboratorio" in *Domus* (Milan), October 1968; "Nuove techniche & nuove strutture per l'edilizia" in *Domus* (Milan), November 1968; "Industrial Roofing" in *Architectural Forum* (New York), March 1970; "Espo '70, Osaka" in *Accaio* (Milan), November 1970; "Industrialized Construction" in *Deutsche Bauzeitung* (Stuttgart), April 1971; "Concours Beaubourg" in *Architecture mouvement continuité* (Paris), November 1971; "Centre Beaubourg, Paris" in *Techniques et architecture* (Paris), February 1972; "L'Evoluzione del Progetto per il Centro Beaubourg" in *Domus* (Milan), June 1972; "Centre Beaubourg" in *Arkitekten* (Copenhagen), September 1972; "Piano + Rogers, Paris" in *Architecture d'aujourd'hui* (Paris), November/ December 1973; "B and B Italia Building" in *Architectural Design* (London), April 1974; "Centre Beaubourg" in *Acier-Stahl-Steel* (Brussels), September 1975; "Eiffel vs. Beaubourg" in *Werk-Archithese* (Niederteufen, Switzerland), September 1977; "Centro Beaubourg" in *Informes de la construccion* (Madrid), April 1978; "Colloquio con Renzo Piano" by Pierpeaolo Santini in *Ottagono* (Milan), June 1981; "Piano in Houston" in *Skyline* (New York), January 1982; "Renzo Piano," special issue of *Architecture d'aujourd'hui* (Paris), February 1982; "Renzo Piano" in *Architectural Review* (London), October 1982; "Renzo Piano, artisan du futur" in *Techniques et architecture* (Paris), no. 350, 1983; "Recent Werk van Renzo Piano" by Ronald Rogers in *Bouw* (Rotterdam), December 1983.

*

The relationship to natural environment in my work comes to fulfilment through three different experiences. First, a direct, physical relationship to nature, of which sometimes the building becomes a part. Second, viewing nature as language reference; recently some structural elements, such as casting pieces and lamellar-wood structures, conform to natural organic elements. Third, conceiving the space not only as a phenomenon realized through physical building elements—floors, walls, and ceilings—but also through those intangible elements of the space : light, air, colour, transparencies, and noise.

The Menil Collection Museum under construction in Houston, Texas, is in a natural environment in the centre of the city. A spacious exhibition hall is on the ground floor. The first floor we have entitled our "Treasure House," since it contains about 10,000 works in a variety of media kept in a state of ideal preservation. We decided to make the best use of available natural light to articular space. The building is a large platform, about 10,000 square metres erected five metres above the level of the park. Inside are a number of small gardens. The light enters through the transparent roof of the building and is refracted through a series of "leaves". These leaves of ferro-cement set up a double refraction between themselves as the light enters the building. The central part of the building is serviced by an internal promenade along its 120 metre length. The lighting continuously changes. Light is here the real protagonist of the space. We decided to construct the leaves in ferro-cement because it would permit us to create more organic shapes. The profile was derived from computer analysis and by experimenting with scale and full-size models. The ductile iron castings which collaborate structurally with the leaves were also developed through similar stages. The final result seems in many was inspired by nature itself.

The exhibition pavilion for IBM will travel to twenty European cities in the next two years. We used a polycarbonate structure with steel castins and lamellar woods. The building was conceived as a large greenhouse, its transparency allowing it to appear and disappear in the parks and gardens in which it will be erected.

The exhibition of 500 Calder sculptures in Turin during summer 1983 was in the sport centre: a building of 15,000 square metres with a thirty-metre high ceiling and no intermediate supports. The sunlight was completely obscured, and objects were directly illuminated by small halogen lamps. The light created a sort of magical space. We developed a system to generate breezes to move the Calder mobiles. The breezes, sounds coming from the sonorous Calders, and the light and the colour of the works themselves were all intangible elements that developed and manipulated the space.

In 1982 we began the restoration and redesigning of the new Schlumberger head office in Paris. We decided to replace the old courtyards which the buildings surround with an "urban park" 200 metres on each side. Nature is seen as a winner: it penetrates buildings, not stopping in front of the walls, but passing through them. Nature is the means for eliminating some of the sternness of this industrial complex and so create a pleasant work place.

With UNESCO in 1978 we worked on the restoration of Otranto in the south of Italy ad Burano, one of the small Venetian islands. These historical centres are the result of a stratification of ages and cultures, whose unity and articulation are well structured. In both locations, we constructed local workshops to aid artisans and inhabitants in the preservation and restoration of local building projects, using the most modern technology and instruments and sharing our knowledge with the people to activate their creative capacities.

The present crisis of the profession is due to an incompetence which hides the architect in a golden, pseudo-artistic world. This mystification leads the architect to take on a marginal role, abrogating the role of builder. There is, as well, often a total lack of sensibility on the part of the architect towards his client, with the architect seeing the creative experience as the fundamental objective of his work—rather than doing a service for the client. Understanding participation would be extremely useful.

All these examples have one thing in common: a refusal to separate the project from the construction. This is of great cultural importance. Unfortunately, in our society there is always the one who thinks and the one who performs, the one who plans and the one who constructs, but it is impossible to separate the two if we want to assure creative continuity in the architectural profession.

—Renzo Piano

*

Architecture can be analyzed according to how fully its maker expresses the building as an object, as a construct or as a container. By "an object" one means primarily an artifact to be appreciated: "construct" refers to the actual building methods and means; and "container" conveys how well the building's intended uses were fulfilled. Of course any successful architectural design has to take account of all three, but a polemical architect may preoccupy himself with one or perhaps two. Renzo Piano has been a constructor. While his buildings certainly encompass successfully all three objectives, structural developments are decidedly his conceptual points of departure.

Though national architecture means little today, there was something essentially Italian in his early pursuit of concrete factory frames and in his refining and perfecting of them. As with Nervi and other Italian masters. Piano's oppourtunities arose through the flexibility of the designer's professional role in Italy (engineers and architects can also be builders or developers, without ethical difficulty), together with the good luck of having industrialists in his own family who were able to commission some of his earlier work.

None of this would have come to international attention had Piano not met Richard Rogers in London and won the Centre Pompidou ("Beaubourg") competition with him and Ove Arup and Partners. Piano's contribution was equal to that of Rogers, but Piano was especially concerned with structure and overall design logic expressed in construction patterns. He functioned as an effective leader but even more as a smooth coordinator. As with Rogers, his social skills in the evolutionary process of that design have been underestimated, but they may be his most solid achievement to date, and even his greatest example to others.

—Nathan Silver

PIETILÄ, Reima.

Finnish. Born in Turku, 25 August 1923. Educated at the Institute of Technology, Helsinki, 1945-53, Dip.Arch. 1953. Served in the Finnish Army, 1942-44: Corporal. Married the architect Raili Paatelainen in 1961; daughter: Annukka. Architect in the City Master Planning Department, Helsinki, 1953-54; worked in the offices of architects Cedercreutz-Railo, and Viljo Revell, q.v., Helsinki, 1955-56; in private practice, since 1957, and with Raili Pietila, Helsinki, since 1960. Architect with the County Planning Department, State Building Administration Office, Helsinki, 1959-60. Professor of Architecture, 1973-79, and Dean of the Department of Architecture, 1978, University of Oulu, Finland; Visiting Professor and Lecturer, Washington University, St. Louis, 1966, Cornell University, Ithaca,

Raili and Reima Pietilä: Lutheran Church, Lieksa, Finland, 1982.

New York, 1972, Arlington University, Texas, 1977, Montana State University, Bozeman, 1984. Deputy Chairman, 1959-60, and Board Member, 1969-70, S.A.F.A.: Finnish Architects Association; Administrative Board Member, Industrial Design Association of Finland, since 1972, and Housing Association of Tapiola New Town, Finland, since 1977. Exhibitions: *Morphology-Urbanism*, Turku, Helsinki and Jyvaskyla, Finland, 1958; *Sketches*, Jyvaskyla, 1965, travelled to St. Louis, Columbus, New Haven, Mexico City and Venice, 1966-67; *Zone*, Helsinki, 1967, travelled to Lund, Sweden and Oulu, Finland, 1968-69; *Space Garden*, Museum of Finnish Architecture, Helsinki, 1971, and Kouvola Cultural Centre, Finland, 1972; *Notion-Image-Idea*, Aalto Museum, Jyvaskyla, and Museum of Finnish Architecture, Helsinki, 1974; *Contemporary Architecture in a Philosophic Experiment*, Porvoo, Finland, 1977; *Projects and Works*, North London Polytechnic, London, 1977; *Works, Sketches, Projects*, School of Architecture, Marseille, France, 1982; *Modern Islamic Architecture*, at the *Biennale*, Venice, 1982. Recipient: First Prize, Finnish Pavilion competition, for the 1958 World's Fair, Brussels, 1956; First Prize, Kaleva Church competition, Tampere, Finland, 1959; First Prize, Dipoli Congress and Student Centre competition, Otaniemi, Finland, 1961; First Prize, Suvikumpu Housing Development competition, Tapiola, Finland, 1962; First Prize, Finnish Embassy for New Delhi competition, 1963; First Prize, City Library competition, Tampere, Finland, 1978; First Prize, Lutheran Church competition, Lieksa, Finland, 1979; First Prize, President of Finland's Official Residence competition, Helsinki, 1984. Tapiola Medal, Finland, 1981; Prince Eugene Medal, Sweden, 1981. Honorary Foreign Member, Swedish Royal Academy of Liberal Arts, 1969; Honorary Member, S.A.F.A.: Finnish Architects Association, 1975; Honorary Life Member, American Institute of Architects, 1976; Honorary Member, Bund Deutscher Architekten, West Germany, 1983. Honorary Professor of Arts, Finland, 1971. Member, Academy of Technical Sciences, Finland, 1982. Honorary Doctorate: University of Oulu, Finland, 1983. Address: Raili and Reima Pietila

Architects, Livurinrinne 1 A 5, 00120 Helsinki 12, Finland.

Works

1953 Porin Sato Housing (competition project; with Viljo Revell and M. Jaatinen)
1958 Finnish Pavilion, World's Fair, Brussels

With Raili Pietilä:

1966 Kaleva Church, Tampere, Finland
Dipoli International Conference Centre, Institute of Technology, Otaniemi, Finland
1966/
69 Suvikumpu Housing Development, Tapiola New Town, Espoo, Finland
1967 Malmi Church, Helsinki (project)
1970 Central Government Offices Plan, Sief Palace Area, Kuwait City (project)
1972 Hvitträsk Sauna Bath Building, Eliel Saarinen Museum Centre, Kirkkonummi, Finland
Reidar Särestoniemi Swimming Pool, Sauna and Art Gallery, Kittilä, Lapland, Finland
1974 Dubai Corniche (project)
1975 Cultural Services Master Plan, Hervanta New Town, Tampere, Finland
1979 Congregational Centre, Leisure Centre, and Shopping Hall, Hervanta New Town, Tampere, Finland
1980 Kukkatalo house and garden centre, Suvikumpu, Tapiola, Finland
1981 His Highness The Emir's Office reception area extension, Sief Palace, Kuwait City
Council of Ministers Building, and Ministry of Foreign Affairs Building, Sief Palace Area, Kuwait City
1982 Lutheran Church, Lieksa, Finland
Suvituuli housing development, Suvikumpu, Tapiola, Finland
1983/
84 Cultural Axis Centre, stage 2, Hervanta New Town, Tampere, Finland
Old People's Home and Children's Nursery, Pori, Finland

Main Library, Tampere, Finland
Malminkartano experimental housing, Helsinki
1983/
85 Finnish Embassy, New Delhi, India
1984/
85 Official Residence of the President of Finland, Mantyniemi, Helsinki

Publications:

By PIETILÄ: books—*Centres and Noncentres*, Helsinki 1969; *Concept of Visual Entity in Environmental Design*, Wageningen, Holland 1971; *Architectures "Totales" et "Partielles" dans le contexte d'une image morphologique de l'environnement*, Arc-et-Senans, France 1973; *Notion, Image, Idea: Notes on Architectural Teaching*, Otaniemi, Finland 1974; *Leisure Time Architecture*, Helsinki 1977; articles— "La Morphologie de l'expression plastique" and "La Théorie de la composition" in *Le Carré bleu* (Paris), no. 1, 1958; "Hobby Dogs" in *Arkkitehti* (Helsinki), no. 6, 1967; "Local– Non–Local" in *Arkkitehti* (Helsinki), no. 7/8, 1967; "Dipoli: Literal Morphology" in *Arkkitehti* (Helsinki), no. 9, 1967; "The Zone" in *Arkkitehti* (Helsinki), no. 1, 1968; "Reima Pietila" in *Arkkitehti* (Helsinki), no. 7/8, 1976; "Essays on Architecture" in *Arkkitehti* (Helsinki), no. 5, 1977; Architecture That Directs Its Own Birth" in *Arkkitehti* (Helsinki), no. 6, 1977; "8 Ways to Break Free from Rabbit-Hutch Architecture" in *Arkkitehti* (Helsinki), no. 2, 1979; "The Architecture of Lieska Church," with Roger Connah, in *Arkkitehti* (Helsinki), no. 7, 1983.

On PIETILA: books—*Der Schluessel zur Architektur von heute* by Udo Kultermann, Düsseldorf and Vienna 1963; *Arquitectura finlandesa en Otaniemi* by Maria Lluisa Borras, Barcelona 1967; *New Finnish Architecture* by Egon Tempel, New York 1968; *Finland— Creation and Construction*, edited by H. Kallas and S. Nickels, New York 1968; *Modern Finnish Architecture* by Asko Salokorpi, New York 1970; *Multi-Family Housing* by David Mackay, Stuttgart 1974; *Meaning in Western Archi-*

tecture by Christian Norberg-Schulz, New York 1975; *800 Years of Finnish Architecture* by J. M. Richards, Newton Abbot, Devon 1978; *Il Labirinto dei Sabba: l'architettura di Reima Pietila* by Carmine Benincasa, Bari, Italy, 1979; *Genius Loci: Toward a Phenomenology of Architecture* by Christian Norberg-Schulz, London 1980; *A Dialectic of Architectural Systems and Poetry: Theory and Works of Reima Pietila*, thesis by Thomas John Burkle, University of Washington, 1983; *Kuwait: The Making of a City* by Stephen Gardiner, London 1983; *La Casa Unifamiliar: The Modern House* by David Mackay, Barcelona 1984; *Reima Pietila: Architecture, Context and Modernism* by Malcolm Quantrill, Helsinki 1984, New York 1985; articles—"Church at Tampere, Finland" in *Progressive Architecture* (New York), December 1961; "Dipoli and Kaleva Church" in *Domus* (Milan), December 1964; "Architettura finlandese: Reima Pietila" in *Comunita* (Milan), August 1965; "Pietila: Rebel in Finland" by Edward Mark Treib in *Architectural Forum* (New York), December 1967; "Reima Pietila" by Marika Hausen in *Paletten* (Stockholm), no. 4, 1967; "Pietila in the Seventies" by Akira Muto in *Architecture + Urbanism* (Tokyo), no. 9, 1974; "Reima Pietila and Raili Paatelainen" in *Jano arquitectura* (Madrid), no. 34, 1976; "Team 10 in Bonnieux: Reima and Raili Pietila" in *Deutsche Bauzeitung* (Stuttgart), November 1978; "Pietila's Step in a Different or New Direction" by William Miller in *Architecture + Urbanism* (Tokyo), no. 5, 1981; "Reima Pietila Observed" by Hiroshi Sasaki in *Process: Architecture* (Tokyo), no. 37, 1983.

My wife and I are figuratively married to architecture, as we live and work together as a married couple. Architecture is present also in our domestic life. Sitting over breakfast from six until eight in the mornings we talk of new ideas and solve practical detail problems: thus, the most creative and genuine experience of architecture comes to us undisturbed by the later busy work in the studio. Our weekends are completely dedicated to creative activity; thus architecture is our leisure, our hobby.

There are several working teams of married architects like ourselves still active in Finland, and we believe they will have an important role to play in improving the quality of architecture in the future.

We also believe that architecture, in its contemporary and inimitable form, is our basic cultural commodity and as such is original as art. And only as such can architecture help man to experience his environment profoundly and conceive the quality of his own culture. A genuine architecture helps man to be positively more acceptable and perceptive to himself. Design should not stop at the stage of a mere performance—form has also to convey emotion.

Architecture must be "local," expressing an appearance of the local nature. Finnish architecture should be organically one with its own evergreen Arctic forest, united with the "form-language" of the forest. Also, the rhythms of architectural structure and form should be national and characteristic, expressing the shape of space. Colours are to be closely related to nature, providing a strong tie to our cultural heritage. This architecture if freed from the international types of superficial generality and without fashionable names.

We strive for an architecture that by nature makes minds more sensitive to the built environment. We aim for this with all possible means, independent of any modern direction and moving freely amongst all the cultural periods of man. We try to do this without repeating ourselves.

We try to renew our basic grasp and vision in each new task. Thus we hope to bring forth a development and show that there are still areas in contemporary architecture open to exploration.

—Reima Pietilä

Reima Pietilä was born in Turku two years after Alvar Aalto received his architectural diploma in Helsinki at the age of 23. This places him in the generation of Finnish architects we might refer to as "post-Aalto", although Pietilä did not graduate until he was 30 and his first commission was not undertaken until 1957, when he was already 34. Thus hardly precocious, he is a late developer who has balanced relatively short spells of building with longer periods of thinking and working out his architectural philosophy. He is widely read in psychology, philosophy and cultural history; and, one of the most articulate of modern practiners, he expresses himself wittily in English.

He first attracted international attention with the design for the Finnish Pavilion at the Brussels World Fair, won in competition in 1956 and executed in 1958. References to Aalto, particularly to the sports hall at Otaniemi (1949-54), are clearly detectable in this pavilion. No further buildings came from Pietilä's studio until the mid-1960's. In the meantime, he married a fellow architect, Raili Paatelainen, in 1961, which has resulted in a continuity and harmony between home and office that is firmly within the Finnish tradition. The first products of this partnership were the "Dipoli" International Conference Centre for Otaniemi, and Kaleva Church in Tampere, both completed in 1966. Kaleva Church is one of the most successful religious interiors of this century, although the original concrete exterior was modified and clad in brick tiles at the request of the parish council, divorcing it entirely from the interior quality and expression it was intended to reflect.

With the successes of "Dipoli", Kaleva Church and the unrealized Finnish Embassy at New Delhi, Pietilä established himself as the master of an original architectural expression, a mastery he has retained in his recent successful competition entry for the new Tampere City Library. Also, by the time he undertook the design of the Suvikumpu housing area for Tapiola, Pietilä had emerged as the intellectual leader of his generation of Finnish architects, a situation deriving very much from his years of enforced contemplation, his model experiments and his contributions to *Le Carre Bleu*.

In recognition of his work he was awarded the national Professorship of Arts for 1971-72 and appointed to the Chair of Design in Oulu University in 1973. From 1973 until 1979 he divided his time between Oulu and an increasingly busy office in Helsinki. In 1972 he completed a small public sauna at the Hvittrask Cultural and Recreational Centre (formerly the studio home of Eliel Saarinen) and a sauna and art gallery for the Finnish painter Sarestoniemi at Kittila, Lapland. But his major works of the 70's centered on Tampere and Kuwait City. Just outside Tampere in the new town of Hervanta the Pietiläs designed a Lutheran parish centre and a leisure centre with shopping mall, the first stage of which was completed in 1979; while 1979 also brought first prize in the competition for the new Tampere City Library, with building due to be completed in 1986. The 70's were dominated, however, by work in Kuwait City on the Sief Palace District Buildings: this comprises an extension to the original Sief Palace to accommodate the Emir's Audience Hall, plus the Ministry of Foreign Affairs and the Council of Ministers Building. 1979 saw a limited competition for the replacement of Carl Ludwig Engel's Parish Church at Lieksa in Eastern Finland (1838) in which Pietilä took first prize, with the new church completed in 1982. In 1980 Pietilä's design for the Finnish Embassy at New Delhi (first prize in the original competition of 1963!) was revived and the project was completed in 1985. In 1983 he was elected to the Finnish Academy.

During the summer of 1984 Pietilä took the first prize in a national competition for the design of the official residence for the Finnish President, with the building scheduled for completion in 1986. 1985 saw the Pietiläs begin the design of their own country house at Tenhola on the south coast of Finland near Tammisaari, and construction of the smoke and normal saunas began in the summer of 1985.

—Malcolm Quantrill

PIKIONIS. Dimitris A.

Greek. Born in Piraeus in June 1887. Studied civil engineering at the Athens Polytechnic, 1904-08; painting and sculpture in Munich, 1908; architecture in Paris, 1909-12; drawing and ornamentation at the School of Fine Arts, Athens, 1923, Diploma 1923. Served in the Greek Army, 1912-21. Married Alexandra Anastasion in 1927; had two daughters and three sons. In private practice, Athens, 1923 until his death in 1968. Head, Architectural Team, Ministry of Rebuilding, Athens, 1946-47. Lecturer, 1921-23, Associate Professor, 1925-30, and Professor, 1930-57, National Technical University, Athens. Member, Greek Popular Art Association, 1937-40. Exhibitions: Academy of Fine Arts, Munich, 1961; *Dimitris Pikionis,* National Gallery, Athens, 1978; *Architecture of Pikionis,* Technische Hogeschool, Delft, Netherlands 1981. Member Academy of Athens, 1966. Member, Academy of Fine Arts, Munich, 1966. *Died* (in Athens) *27 August 1968.*

Works:

1921/
23 Moraitis House, Tzitzifies, Neo Faliro, Greece
1925 Karamanos House, Patissia, Irakliou Road, Athens
1926 School and Residence, Island of Egina, Greece (project; with E. Kriezis)
1927 Church of Agion Anargyron, Nea Ionia, Athens (project; with E. Kriezis)
    Papaloukas House, Chalepa Square, Athens
1928 Carayannis House, Mitsaki Road, Athens
1930 Papaioannou House, Markora Road, Patissia, Athens
1932 Summer Theatre, Marika-Kotopouli, Hayden Road, Athens
1933 School of Lycabetus, Athens
1933/
35 Garis House, Psychico, Athens
    Gionis House, Ellinico, Athens
    Caloyannis House, Ellinico, Athens
    Porfyras Tomb, Anastaseas Cemetery, Piraeus, Greece
    Paoli Family Tomb, Anastaseas Cemetery, Piraeus, Greece
    Gounaraki Family Tomb, First Cemetery, Athens
    Experimental School, University of Salonika, Greece
1936 Small building, Hayden Road, Athens (with N. Mitsakis)
1938 Craftsman's Pavilion, Neo Faliro, Greece (project)
1942 Mitsakis Gravestone design
1949 Efthymiadi-Menegaki Studio/House, Grypari Road, Patissia, Athens
1950/
57 Aixoni Housing Development, Glyfada, Greece (with others)
    Master plan for the surroundings of the Acropolis and the Hill of Philopappou, Athens
    Building complex, St. Dimitrios-Lombardiaris, Athens
1953 University of Salonika Forest Village, Pertouli-Trikalon, Greece
    Hotel Xenia, Delphi, Greece (with A. Papageorgiou)
    Garis House, Parnassos Road, Psychico, Athens
    Potamianos House, Ano Philothei, Athens
1960/
68 Children's playground, Philothei, Athens (with P. Pikionis and A. Coutsoyannis)
    Town Hall, Volos, Greece (project)
    Fortetzas Tourist Development, Rethymnon, Crete (project)
    Stamatopoulos House, Kypriadou, Athens
    Development surrounding the Velissarios Monument, Kymymi, Greece
    St. Paul's Church, Ethniki Estia, Greece

Publications:

By PIKIONIS: books—*Dodecanissos* (The Problem of Form), Athens 1950; *Antonis Sochos*, Athens 1961; *Fortetzas Tourist Development*, Athens 1966; *Autobiographical Notes*, Athens 1968; articles— "Our Popular Art and Us" in *Filiki Eteria* (Athens), April 1925; "The Painter Steris" in *Proia* (Athens), 23 April 1931; numerous articles in *Technica chronica* (Athens), 1933-58, *To trito mati* (Athens), 1935-37, *Aixoni* (Athens), 1950-54, and *Zygos* (Athens), 1956-66; "About Greek Tradition" in *Epoches* (Athens), January 1964.

On PIKIONIS: books—*Greek Art and Architecture 1945-1967* by Dimitris A. Fatouros, volume 8 of *Balkan Studies*, Salonika, Greece 1967; *The Architect Dimitris Pikionis* by Z. Lorentzatos, Athens 1969; *The Life and Work of Pikionis* by Ch. Tsilalis, Salonika, Greece 1969; *Dimitris Pikionis*, exhibition catalogue, Athens 1978; articles—"Entyposis ke crisis" by Fotis Politis in *Politia* (Athens), 26, 28 and 29 June and 4 July 1923; "House of Filotlei" in *Architectoniki* (Athens), no. 1, 1957; special issue of *Zygos* (Athens), January/February 1958; "A Quiet Creator Who Deeply Influenced Greek Architecture" by M. Kalligas in *To vima* (Athens), 20 May 1962; "Virtue and Form" by David Holden in *The Guardian* (London), 22 August 1963; "Architecture of the Road" by N. Kurokawa in *Ekistics* (Athens), November 1963; "The New Academician: Dimitris Pikionis" by A. Provelegios in *Nea estia* (Athens), 1 June 1966; "An Unknown Work of Pikionis" by N. Moutsopoulos in *Icones* (Athens), 26 August 1966; "L 'Architecture en Grèce" by Fr. Loyer in *SADG* (Paris), 2 July 1967; "Kinderspielplatze: Garten in Filothei bei Athen" by A. Papageorgiou in *Bauwelt* (Berlin), 1 July 1968; "Dimitris Pikionis: A Great Maitre" by K. Doxiades and "Pikionis: An Indelible Presence in the Neo-Hellenic World" by P. Psomopoulos in *To vima* (Athens), 1 September 1968; "The Life and Work of Pikionis" in *Architektoniki* (Athens), September/October 1970; "Dimitris Pikionis: His Work Lies Underfoot on Athens Hills" by Anthony C. Antoniades in *Landscape Architecture* (Louisville, Kentucky), March 1977; "Pikionis: Architecture as a Way of Life" by Dimitris A. Fatouros in *To vima* (Athens), 14 February 1979; "New Greek Architecture," special issue of *Wonen-TA/BK* (Heerlen, Netherlands), October 1981; "Dimitris Pikionis (1887-1968)" by Cees Zwinkels in *De Architect* (The Hague), January 1982; "Dimitris Pikionis (1887-1968)—Pioneer Greek Modernist" by Anastasia Dimitracopoulos in *Architectural Association Quarterly* (London), January-June 1982; "Pikionis Built a Way of Thinking" by Emile Chimintzas in *Forum* (Hilversum, Netherlands), June 1982.

*

Dimitris A. Pikionis played a singularly leading role in the formation of contemporary Greek architecture, and, even now, he continues to influence Greek architectural thinking. Pikionis also contributed to the development of Greek art, working with such artists as Kondoglou, Diamandolpoulos, Gkika, and Tsarouhis. He tried to coordinate architecture with artistic creation and to define their functions within the particular conditions of the Greek environment.

Pikionis used two basic organizing systems: one is the spatial relationship—geometric organization; the other is, as it were, life, the behavior that is evoked or even demanded by each space, the socio-cultural relationship.

The first system is one of relations between the under, over, and in-between limits (the "three limits" space definition); the continous and non-continuous; light and dark; the small and large in any spatio-situation; the interior and exterior of a building. He was concerned with neighborhood—the narrow pavement, moving between high walls, with a sudden opening where one lingers. That concern reveals itself in the volumes, small in size, in different variations, probably organized in "accumulative" order, with enclosures of large perpendicular planes—windows, doors, etc.

The second system involves human activities and behavior in each of these spaces—in the small atrium, enclosed all around by a high wall, next to, but removed from, the road; in the semi-covered space with the deep, sensual shadow; inside a cavity on a bright road; in the spaces of the many different occasions of private life, man alone, in small groups, or in public.

Relying on these two systems, Pikionis organized his space according to the demands (and possibilities) of his country and in the service of its people—so far as his time allowed and always with admirable virtuosity.

The works of Pikionis anticipate by twenty years the tendencies of today's architecture to aviod large, monolithic constructions—the high-rise and the over-size—and create small units structured in communications networks, closely related to the natural environment and to the psychological and physical scale of man.

All of his ideals are clearly revealed in his large and singularly significant reorganization of the area around the Acropolis with its carefully designed access routes, roads for car and pedestrians, and its pavilions and small squares. His abiding sociocultural philosophy is also expressed in the low-rise housing at Aixoni, near Athens, and in the play ground at Philothei, where the spaces for games reflect elements of mythology.

The inspiration of Pikionis's architecture is not, obviously, a superficial reading of what is called, conventionally, "popular architecture." His buildings are his own interpretation of a Greek and Mediterranean reality—an interpretation with a world-wide utility and a revoluntionary strength.

—Dimitris A. Fatouros

POLLINI, Gino.

Italian. Born in Rovereto, 13 January 1903. Educated in Rome, 1918-21; studied at the Faculty of Engineering, 1922-23, and the Faculty of Architecture, Milan Polytechnic, 1923-27, Dip.Arch. 1927. Served in the Italian Army, 1943. Married Renata Melotti in 1931; son: the pianist Maurizio Pollini. Founder Member, with Luigi Figini, *q.v.,* Guido Frette, Sebastiano Larco, Adalberto Libera, Carlo Enrico Rava and Giuseppe Terrapni, *q.v.,* Gruppo 7, Milan, 1927-29. In partnership with Luigi Figini, Milan, 1929-84. Since 1984, in private practice, Milan. Member, Municipal Committee for the Master Plan for the City of Milan, 1946. Professor, 1936-63, and Professor-in-Charge, 1963-68, Faculty of Architecture, Milan Polytechnic; Professor and Director of the School of Architecture, University of Palermo, Sicily, 1969-78. President, Lombardy Section, INU (Istituto Nazionale di Urbanistica), 1955-56. Member, CIAM (Congrès Internationaux d'Architecture Moderne), from 1929; Member, MIAR (Movimento Italiano per l'Architettura Razionale), 1930-32, and Quadrante, Milan, 1933-35. Exhibitions: Rationalist Architecture Exhibition, *Biennale*, Monza, Italy, 1927; *Triennale,* Monza, 1930; *Modern Architecture Exhibition,* Museum of Modern Art, New York, 1931; Union des Artistes Modernes, Paris, 1932; IV CIAM, Athens, 1933; CIAM Pavilion, *Triennale,* Milan, 1933; *Italian Aeronautical Exhibition,* Milan, 1934; VII CIAM, Bergamo, Italy 1949; *Italian Architecture,* London, 1952 (toured the United Kingdom); *The Modern Movement in Italy: Architecture and Design,* Museum of Modern Art, New York, 1953 (toured the United States); *Trien*

nale, Milan, 1954; *Mostra documentaria dell' architettura sacra italiana del dopoguerra,* Bologna, Italy, 1955; *Triennale,* Milan, 1960; *Milano 70-70,* Museo Poidi Pezzoli, Milan, 1971; *Domus: 45 anni dell' architettura,* Louvre, Paris, 1973; *Il razionalismo e l'architettura italiana durante il fascismo,* Venice, 1976; *Utopia e crisi dell'antinatura,* at the *Biennale,* Venice, 1978; *Design Process— Olivetti 1908-78,* University of California, Los Angeles, 1979; *28/78 Architettura,* Palazzo delle Stelline, Milan, 1979; *Figini e Pollini: architetti,* Milan, 1980; *F. Melotti/L. Figini e G. Pollini/R. Melotti,* Rovereto, Italy, 1984. Member, Accademia di San Luca, 1963. Address: Via Manin 3, 20121 Milan, Italy.

Works:

1927 Garage (project: wiht Gruppo 7)
Casa del Dopolavoro (project; with Gruppo 7)
1929 Regional Plan for Bolzano, Italy (competition project; with A. Libera)
1930 Electric House, *Triennale,* Monza, Italy (with Gruppo 7)
1931 De Angeli-Frua Offices, Milan (with Luigi Figini and Luciano Baldessari)
Bar Craja, Milan (with Luigi Figini and Luciano Boldessari)
1933 Artist's House and Studio, *Triennale,* Milan (with Luigi Figini)
1934 Sala dei Precursori, Italian Aeronautical Exhibition, Milan (with Luigi Figini)
Palazzo del Littorio, *Mostra della rivoluzione fascista,* Rome (competition project; with Luigi Figini, BBPR, and Luigi Danusso)
1934/
57 Olivetti Factory, Nursery School, Workers' Housing, and Social Services Centre, Ivrea, Italy (with Luigi Figini)
1935 Plan for the New Town of Ivrea, Italy (with Luigi Figini)
1936 Living Room and Roof Garden, *Triennale,* Milan (with Luigi Figini)
Brera Academy, Milan (with Luigi Figini, Pietro Lingeri, and Giuseppe Terragni)
Master plan for the Valle d'Aosta (with Luigi Figini, BBPR, Piero Bottoni, and others)
1939 Sala del Volo, Milan (exhibition project; with Luigi Figini)
1942 Villa Manusardi, Cartabbia, Italy (with Luigi Figini)
1946 Master plan for the centre of Milan (with Luigi Figini, BBPR, Piero Bottoni, Franco Albini, and others)
1948 Apartment and Office Building, Via Broletto, Milan (with Luigi Figini)
1951 INA-CASA Housing Estate, Via Harar, Milan (with Luigi Figini and Gio Ponti)
1952 Plan for the Borgo Porto Conte, Sardinia, Italy (with Luigi Figini)
1954 Church of the Madona of the Poor, Milan (with Luigi Figini)
1957 Apartment building, Via Circo, Milan (with Luigi Figini)
Hoepli Building, Milan (with Luigi Figini)
1963 Pozzi Ceramic Factory Industrial Complex, Sparanise, near Caserta, Italy (with Luigi Figini)
Church for the CEP Housing Scheme, near Bergamo, Italy (project; with Luigi Figini)
Hotel Largo Augusta, Milan (with Luigi Figini and C Blasi)
1968 Apartments, Milan
1972/
84 Department of Science Building, University of Palermo, Sicily (with V. Gregotti and G. Caronia)
1974 Student Study Centre, Conservatorio della SS. Nunziata, Palermo, Sicily (with P. Culotta, G. Laudicina, T. Marra, and F. Purini)
Villa Guida, Gunanzate, Italy (with Luigi Figini)

Gino Pollini: Church of Mater Ecclesiae, Rome, 1977 (project).

1976 IACP Housing Development, S. Giuliano Milanese, Italy (with Luigi Figini and G. Marini)

1977/
78 Church of Mater Ecclesiae, Rome (project; with Luigi Figini and G. Marini)

Publications:

By POLLINI: books—*Il piano regolatore della Valle d'Aosta,* with Luigi Figini, BBPR, Piero Bottoni and others, Ivrea, Italy 1943; *Elementi di architettura,* Milan 1966; *La residenza: esperienze di progettazione,* Palermo, Sicily 1973; articles—"Architettura," with Gruppo 7, in *Rassegna italiana* (Rome), December 1926; "Gli stranieri," with Gruppo 7, in *Rassegna italiana* (Rome), Rebruary 1927; "Impreparazione, incomprensione, pregiudizi" with Gruppo 7, in *Rassegna italiana* (Rome), March 1927; "Una nuova epoca arcaica," with Gruppo 7, in *Rassegna italiana* (Rome), May 1927; "Un Programma di architettura," with Luigi Figini and others, in *Quadrante* (Milan), May 1933; "La città funzionale" in *Urbanistica* (Turin), no. 3, 1934; "Relazione al progetto del Palazzo del Littorio," with Luigi Figini, BBPR and Luigi Danusso, in *Quadrante* (Milan), August/September 1934; "Origines de l'architecture moderne en Italie," with Luigi Figini, in *L'Architecture d'aujourd'hui* (Paris), June 1952; "Intervista con gli architetti Figini e Pollini" in *Edilizia popolare* (Milan), November/ December 1959; "Didattica e progettazione" in *Casabella* (Milan), no. 371, 1972; "Architettura e tecnica dall'Inghilterra" in *Parametro* (Bologna, Italy), February 1975; "CIAM de Bruxelles ad Atene: la città funzionale" in *Parametro* (Bologna, Italy), December 1976.

On POLLINI: books—*Figini e Pollini* by Eugenio Gentili, Milan 1959; *Figini e Pollini* by Cesare Blasi, Milan 1963 (includes bibliography); *Luigi Figini e Gino Pollini: architetti,* exhibition catalogue, edited by Vittorio Savi, Milan 1980; *La casa elettrica di Figini e Pollini* by Giacomo Polin, Rome 1982; *F. Melotti, L. Figini e G. Pollini, R. Melotti,* exhibition catalogue, by C. Melograni, Rovereto, Italy, 1984; articles—"Luigi Figini e Gino Pollini" in *Epoca* (Milan), December 1956; "Due opere di Luigi Figini e Gino Pollini" by Ludovico Quaroni in *Architettura* (Rome), no. 48, 1959; "Figini e Pollini" by S. Tintori

in *Casabella-Continuita* (Milan), October 1959; "Figini e Pollini" by Piercarlo Santini in *Comunita* (Milan), no. 76, 1960; "Figini e Pollini" in *Edilizia Moderna* (Milan), no. 82/83, 1963; "Figini e Pollini" by Joseph Rykwert in *Architectural Design* (London), August 1967; "Gino Pollini, architetto" in *Domus* (Milan), no. 501, 1970; "Bottoni, Figini, Pollini and BBPR and the Valle d'Aosta Plan, 1936" by Ezio Bonfanti in *Controspazio* (Bari, Italy), October 1973; "Palermo University" in *Domus* (Milan), October 1981.

See FIGINI, Luigi

POLSHEK, James Stewart.
American. Born in Akron, Ohio, 11 February 1930. Educated at Case Western Reserve University, Cleveland, Ohio, 1947-51, B.S. 1951; Yale University School of Architecture, New Haven, Connecticut, 1951-55, M.Arch. 1955; Royal Academy of Fine Arts, Copenhagen (Fulbright Fellow), 1956-57. Served as a meteorologist in the United States Navy Air Corps Reserve, 1953-60. Married Ellyn May Margolis in 1952; children: Peter and Jennifer. Worked with I. M. Pei, *q.v.,* and Associates, New York, 1955-56, with Ulrich Franzen, *q.v.* and Associates, New York, 1957-60, and with Westermann and Miller and Associates, New York, 1960-61. In private practice, as James Stewart Polshek and Associates, New York, 1962-80, and as James Stewart Polshek and Partners, New York, since 1980. Dean of the Faculty of the Graduate School of Architecture and Planning, Columbia University, New York, and Special Adviser to the President of Columbia for Planning and Development, since 1973. First Vice-President, American Institute of Architects, New York Chapter, 1970-71. Vice-President, Municipal Art Society, New York, 1974-80; Vice-President, Center of Building Conservation, New York; Vice-Chairman, Friends of Le Corbusier Inc.; Co-Chairman of the Executive Committee, Architects for Social Responsibility. Exhibitions: *40 under 40,* American Federation of Arts, New York, 1966; *Expo '70,* Osaka, Japan, 1970; *Another Chance for Cities,* Whitney Museum, New York, 1970; *Rise of an American Architecture,* Metropolitan Museum of Art, New York, 1970. Recipient: Building

Contractors Society Prize, Japan, 1965; Osaka Prefecture Architecture Prize, Japan, 1965; Gold Medal, Architectural League of New York, 1965; Project Award, 1969, Architectural Design Citation, 1981 (twice), 1983, 1984, *Progressive Architecture*; Hudson River Valley Commission Certificate, New York, 1969; Award of Excellence, American Institute of Steel Construction, 1971; Honor Award, American Institute of Architects, 1972; First Honor, Award, Connecticut Building Congress, 1974; Bard Award, City Club of New York, 1978. Fellow, American Institute of Architects, 1972. Address: James Stewart Polshek and Partners, 19 Union Square West, New York, New York 10003, U.S.A.

Works:

1959 Oster House, Stony Point, New York (with L. Schniewind)
1962 Oster Townhouse, New York
1964 Teijin Central Research Institute, Tokyo
1965 Teijin Textile Processing Research Institute, Osaka, Japan
1966 Big Brothers Inc. Residence, New York (with W. Toscanini)
1967 Stable Quadrangle rehabilitation, State University College of New York at Old Westbury (project)
Bedford-Stuyvesant Community Center, Brooklyn, New York (project)
Expo '70 Competition (project; with Arnold Saks)
1968 Donovan House, Port Washington, Long Island, New York (project)
Williams House, New York
Atlantic Terminal Urban Renewal Area Concept Plan, Brooklyn, New York
1969 Student Center, Wesleyan University, Middletown, Connecticut (project)
Recreation Structure, for Mr. and Mrs. Edgar Bronfman, Purchase, New York
1970 Clinton Youth and Family Center, YMCA of New York
Centennial Exhibit, Metropolitan Museum of Art, New York (with Arnold Saks)
George Jensen Store, Madison Avenue, New York (modified by others, 1974; destroyed, 1979)
Planning study for undergraduate dormitories at Wesleyan University, Middletown, Connecticut

1971 Dormitory and Academic Buildings, Rosemary Hall, Wallingford, Connecticut

New York State Bar Center, Albany

Service Group, State University of New York at Old Westbury

Atura Site 4B Housing (300 units), Atlanta Terminal Urban Renewal Area, Brooklyn, New York

Planning study for the Paterson, New Jersey Redevelopment Agency

Clinton Youth Center, West 54th Street, New York

Gellert House, Chappaqua, New York

Student Center, Wesleyan University, Middletown, Connecticut (project)

Central Plant, Wesleyan University, Middletown, Connecticut

1972 Materials Research Center, Allied Chemical Corporation, Morristown, New Jersey

Twin Parks East (housing), Bronx, New York

New student housing, Vassar College, Poughkeepsie, New York (project)

Comprehensive Consulting Center, Columbus, Indiana

Recycle Fuels Plant, Westinghouse Electric Corporation, Columbia, South Carolina

1973 Intermediate School 172, New York

Glen Ellen Ski and Recreation Center, Fayston, Vermont (project)

1974 Prototype manufacturing facility for the Westinghouse Company, Pittsburgh

1975 Helen Owen Carey Playhouse, Brooklyn Academy of Music, New York

Health and Physical Education Building, State University of New York at Old Westbury

1976 Brotherhood Synagogue restoration, New York

Health and Physical Education Building, Kingsborough Community College, Brooklyn, New York

Empire State Plaza (Albany Mall) Planning Study, Albany, New York

Allied Chemical Process Development, phase II (project)

Planning study for the Church of the Heavenly Rest and Day School

1977 Public Works Building, Englewood, New Jersey

Simon and Schuster Corporate Offices, New York

Student Residence, Skidmore College, Saratoga, New York (project)

1978 Trancas Associates Medical Center, Napa, California (with Peter Gluck)

Urban Issues Center, Villard House Restoration, New York

Norlin Corporation Offices, White Plains, New York

New York Society Library, New York

United States Customs House, New York

Consolidated Edison District 2 Business Office, New York

Consolidated Edison District 6 Business Office, New York

Harlem Shopping Mall, New York (project; with Bond and Ryder)

United States Consulate and Residence, Lyon, France (project)

1979 Consolidated Edison West Side Operations Center, New York

Hall of Fame restoration, Bronx, New York

Backer and Spielvogel Corporate Offices, New York

Delafield Estates, Riverdale, New York

Glenfield Middle School, Montclair, New Jersey

1980 Office Tower, 500 Park Avenue, New York

Rochester Cultural District Planning Study, Rochester, New York

Carnegie Hall restoration, New York

AMRO Bank Corporate Offices, New York

United States Embassy Chancery, Muscat, Oman

New York City Bar Association Building, New York

1982 Site J Development, Battery Park City, New York

North County Resource Recovery Facility, San Diego, California

1983 Stroh's River Place, Detroit, Michigan

Office Building, 44 Wall Street, New York

Harborside Corporation Office and Commercial Development, Jersey City, New Jersey

Theater of the Performing Arts, Miami Beach, Florida

IBM National Accounts Headquarters, White Plains, New York

1984 Seaport West Development, New York

Washington Place Apartments, New York

Dromenon Theater, New York

Publications:

By POLSHEK: article—"Architecture: The Synthesis of Art and Function" in *Connaissance des arts* (Paris), April 1981.

On POLSHEK: book—*American Architecture Now*, edited by Barbaralee Diamonstein, New York 1980; articles—"Functional Grid in Japan" in *Architectural Forum* (New York), August 1964; "An American Castle in Japan" in *Fortune* (New York), May 1965; "Laboratory 3: Research Placed on a Podium" in *Architectural Forum* (New York), May 1965; "A New York Studio di Architettura al Quaratasettesimo Piano" in *Domus* (Milan), February 1966; "The Young Innovators 1966" in *House Beautiful* (New York), July 1966; "Fluid Space" in *Interiors* (New York), September 1966; "Design Awards Program" in *Progressive Architecture* (New York), January 1969; "Teahouse by the Pool" in *Architectural Forum* (New York), May 1970; "Design for Merchandising" in *Architectural Record* (New York), February 1971; "Jugend und Familien-Treffpunkt in New York" in *Baumeister* (Munich), June 1971; "Clinton Youth and Family Center" in *Architectural Record* (New York), June 1971; "Work in Progress/James Polshek" in *Intellectual Digest* (New York), February 1972; "Tale of the Twin Park" in *Architectural Forum* (New York), June 1973; "Rosemary and Time" in *Architectural Forum* (New York), September 1973; "Allied Chemical's New Research Center" in *Architectural Record* (New York), August 1974; "James Polshek and Associates" in *Architecture + Urbanism* (Tokyo), April 1976; special issue of *Space Design* (Tokyo), July 1978; "Project for a Consulate, Lyon" in *Architecture d'aujourd'hui* (Paris), February 1980; "U.S. Consular Residence and Office, Lyon" in *Progressive Architecture* (New York), January 1981; "Health Care in Napa, California" in *Architectural Record* (New York), April 1981; "James Stewart Polshek and Partners: Offices for Backer and Spielvogel, Inc." in *Architectural Record* (New York), February 1982; "Repairs Renew Historic Colonnade" in *Engineering News Record* (New York), October 1982; "Rochester Convention Center" in *Progressive Architecture* (New York), January 1983; "500 Park Tower" in *Vogue* (Paris), April 1983; "Architecture: James Stewart Polshek" in *New York Magazine*, September 1983; "A Modernist Builds for the Future" in *Women's Wear Daily* (New York), July 1984; "Good Neighbor Policy" in *Architectural Record* (New York), July 1984.

*   *   *

For twenty-one years my work has been characterized by two patterns. One is a dependence on two and three-dimensional systems of geometric organization that are drawn from both classical and Japanese architectures. The other is an intellectual skepticism about the philosophical implications of applying those systems, a skepticism that has frequently caused me to disrupt or modify them. This use of the geometry inherent in natural morphologies (including bi-axial symmetries based on the human body) and an intuitive modification of them have characterized much of my work. One consequence of this has been that planar and sectional building organizations have often borne superficial resemblances to vernacular architecture, a melding of "primitive" and neoplatonic forms characterizing much of my work.

Other aspects of my work are so recurrent as to lead one to believe in a Freudian-defined role of the unconscious in physical design. Specifically, this refers to the above described dependence on bi-axial symmetry and also to a use of tripartite systems of plan and section organization. This latter manifests itself in the designs for the Teijin Central Research Institute (three service tower cores); the Service Group at the State University in Old Westbury (designed as three "L"-shaped buildings); the Bar Center in Albany, New York (tripartite graduated plan and section); a private Pool Pavilion (a plan of three interlocking squares); the Wesleyan Student Center (unbuilt; three-part scale breakdown of the High Street facade); and Intermediate School 172 (unbuilt; triple academic tower organization).

As a student, I looked for an architecture that was formally and historically consistent, since these qualities were more important to me than programmatic and urbanistic appropriateness. Ironically, since then, it is exactly the opposite that has signified most of my work. My interest is in commissions emphasizing contextualism, preservation of an historic patrimony, the addition of new building forms to old and the invention of formal vocabularies appropriate to each project. In each new project, I seek out form determinants that de-emphasize the massive ego investment and idiosyncrasy required in "virgin" design challenges. Topographically difficult sites, complex urban situations, the constraints of adaptive reuse, additions to occupied buildings, and historic preservation are several of the most common constraints. I have not been interested in the single house or the "one-off" boutique as an outlet for my art. For me, multiple housing and schools with a strong urbanistic focus, along with laboratories and industrial buildings with a strong technological basis, have been far more challenging and rewarding. Architecture that does not ultimately serve a larger social purpose I find inconsequential.

Current debates about the validity of modernism or the meaningfulness of postmodern architecture hold little interest for me. Midwestern pragmatism and a belief in the value of self-criticism have led me to conclude that the *act* of building must be of greater concern than the *theory* of building. I agree with Alexander Tzonis, who characterizes today's quasi-scientific, obscurantist theoreticians as "narcissistic—embracing elitism and hedonism while rejecting any interest in social responsibility and technological advancement." And, although my own work depends on vigorous applied architectonic systems, the interpretation and consequent expressions of specific client programs are what I have striven to perfect.

The first of three phases of practice, which began in 1963 with the design of the two industrial laboratories in Japan, ended with my appointment in 1973 as Dean of the Graduate School of Architecture and Planning at Columbia University. Both the dichotomy between ad hocism and order that characterizes my work and the social and political turmoil of the late 1960s ultimately led me to become interested in architectural education. This became a totally consuming passion between 1973 and 1978, during which period when I was charged with restoring the former stature of the school. Intense exposure to intellectually volatile architecture students and faculty, to their interest in theory as applied to the real world of building, and to their passion for history as paradigm has been intellectually stimulating for me and my staff and has increasingly had a significant impact on the quality of our work.

I was also appointed by President William McGill (and subsequently reappointed by President Michael I. Sovern) as Special Advisor to the President of the University for Planning and Design. This role allowed me to control the selection of architects for campus buildings, as well as to begin to restore the "urban design" integrity of McKim, Mead and White's plan for the campus. The "corrective medicine" became buildings and I used them to complete axes and mask nonconforming buildings constructed in the 1950s and 1960s. In this role, I have been instrumental in commissioning projects by Romaldo Giurgola, Gwathmey Siegel, John Stirling (unbuilt), Peter Gluck, Davis Brody, Prentice Chan and Olhausen, and Kliment and Halsband.

By 1978, with the school's stature reestablished and a national reputation reemerging, the stage was set for the third phase of practice. One of the "design problems" that had always been of interest, but whose solution proved elusive during my first "master builder" phase and my subsequent "educator" phase, was the rational and humane organization of a professional office. The challenge was to expand the diversity and scale of the office's commissions while simultaneously creating a design and management structure that would tap the talents of the exceptional young architects the office had always attracted but did not always know how to keep.

The first step was to take on two partners. Joseph Linden Fleischer is responsible for all management aspects of the office and Paul Spencer Byard, Jr. is responsible for all development. Both also run projects and are backed up by nine associates, five of whom, in addition to their project management responsibilities, have certain generic responsibilities: Timothy Hartung and Duncan Hazard handle all personnel and staffing questions, James Gainfort is responsible for building technology, Marla Appelbaum is responsible for interior design, and Sara Elizabeth Caples, for construction management. The four other associates, James Garrison, Tyler Donaldson, Richard Olcott, and Todd Schliemann, are the senior design associates and, with Neil Denari and me, form the Core Design Group of the office.

With this new office structure, my role has changed. While continuing to generate most partis, I have become a collaborator and teacher within the office. The members of the Core Design Group share a respect for the timeless tectonic principles of building and a belief in the need for an orderly, non-idiosyncratic approach to design. This collaborative approach has enriched the work of the office, allowing it to realize a more authentic expression of the conflicts and challenges of the time.

In the first six years (1978-1984) of the third phase, the office completed 500 Park Tower, the Rochester Convention Center, the Glenfield Middle School, and portions of the restoration of Carnegie Hall. Each of these major projects, in very different ways, embodies the shared visions and idealism of the partners, associates, and staff of James Stewart Polshek and Partners.

—James Stewart Polshek

James Stewart Polshek calls them his Cinderella commissions, but it must be one of the most extraordinary strokes of good fortune to befall any young architect. A Japanese visitor was so taken with Polshek's first independent commission, the Oster House, Stony Point, New York, that he invited Polshek to be the architect for a new central research institute for his company, Teijin Ltd., to be located outside Tokyo, a $32 million project. Polshek moved his family to Japan, established an office, and designed and supervised construction of a range of buildings, complex both organizationally and technically. The results show a calm strength and remarkable maturity. Much that is formative in

James Polshek: Office Tower, 500 Park Avenue, New York, 1980.

Polshek's subsequent work seems to result from this experience.

As a whole, his architecture has some unusual characteristics. There is distinct lack of stylistic continuity. Although the character of the work is strong, the strength comes not by idiosyncratic invention but from a programmatic and technical response to specific problems and specific contexts. He has undertaken a diverse range of projects—education buildings, institutional buildings, industrial buildings, labs, interiors, exhibitions—diverse, yet united in that they mostly pose unusual and demanding problems. The work has no dominant theme. It is in every case an intelligent response to the unique aspects of the program.

His architecture is at its best when there are strong constraints and a demand for ingenuity. In the accommodations for the New York State Bar Center, for example, the need to relate to a terrace of nineteenth-century townhouses enriched a work of sensitive contextualism. The new buildings are not simply respectful of the old, but in their mass and urban presence (apart from the curved stair), they seem almost vital new growth out of the old context. His work is least successful when neither context not problem offers any guidance. This is particularly true of the moderate-income housing project for the South Bronx, Twin Parks East. Here, the result is the antithesis of the previous example—raw, brutal, confused.

His work maintains a slow, even growth and in many ways, the most recent projects are his most distinguished. He has become known for sensitive, accommodating restorations in such significant New York buildings as the United States Customs House, Carnegie Hall, and the Vuillard House.

In many projects, large and small, he has demonstrated his strength as a constructor, a contextualist, and a synthesizer of the more extreme fashions of contemporary architecture. In the 500 Park Tower Amro Bank Building, his distinct abilities and strengths can best be seen. The problem was complex. It began with the acquisition of one of New York modernism's most elegant buildings, SOM's pavilion for the Pepsi Cola Company. The building on the corner of Park Avenue and East 59th Street had been empty for several years as developers struggled with the problem of producing a financially strong package out of an under-developed plot. Thus was only solved when the adjoining lot became available. Polshek's task was to develop the additional plot incorporating the SOM Building in a sympathetic way. The pivotal element of his solution is a vertical wall in grey granite, through which, at the base, a curtain wall emerges echoing the form of the existing work, suggesting a penetration and re-emergence of the older building into the mask of the new. The wall continues up carrying a transformation of the base curtain wall into stacks of brightly glazed apartment windows east and west. Though underplayed, there are pleasing references to past buildings: the association of granite mass to layered curtain wall seems to be indebted to the Howe and Lescaze Building for the Philadelphia Savings Funds Society of 1932 and to the Lumburg Holm entry design for the Tribune competition of 1924. There are small setbacks at the west edge of the granite wall as it moves higher, and in this Polshek is, perhaps, at his most mannerist, paying respects I presume to Rockefeller's Center. However, these charming, modest references are secondary to an arrangement of clustered towers which derive wholly from the elegant plans for the apartment. As competition between developers in Manhattan increases, there is a need not for the outrageous gesture but for the architecture of compromise in which continuity in the overall fabric is dominant. If all Manhattan were thus constrained, it could be a victory for good taste but emasculation of the city.

In many ways the nature of his architecture fits into the period after Gropius and before Kahn. Formal freedom is excused through contextualism; formal invention is excused through aspects of building technique or performance. He doesn't fit

easily with his contemporaries; compared with that of his New York colleagues, his work his conservative and makes few concessions to poetry. Yet, in his role as undemonstrative orchestrator of a building's parts, Polshek produces work of strength and honesty, and his inventiveness with technique and context raises it above the ordinary.

—Alan Balfour

PONTI, Gio(vanni).
Italian. Born in Milan, 18 DcNovember 1891. Educated at the Milan Polytechnic School of Architecture, 1918-21, Dip.Arch. 1921. Served in the Italian Army, 1916-18: awarded War Cross and Military Performance Medal. Married Giulia Vimercati in 1921; four children. Worked in the architectural studio of Mino Fiocchi and Emilio Lancia, Milan, 1921; Designer and Production Renovator, Richard Ginori Ceramics Factory, Milan and Florence, 1923-30; Partner, with Emilio Lancia, Studio Ponti e Lancia, Milan, 1927-33; Partner, with Antonio Fornaroli and Eugenio Soncini, Studio Ponti-Fornaroli-Soncini, Milan, 1933-45; Partner, with Fornaroli and Alberto Roselli, Studio Ponti-Fornaroli-Rosselli, Milan, 1952 until he retired, 1976. Professor, Faculty of Architecture, Milan Polytechnic, 1936-61. Director, *Stile*, Milan, 1941-47. Founder Editor, *Domus*, Milan, 1928-41, 1948-79. Director, Executive Board of the *Biennale*, Monza, subsequently the *Triennale*, Milan, 1933-79; General Supervisor, *Italia 61* exhibition, Turin, 1961, and the *Eurodomus* exhibition, Genoa and other Italian cities, 1966-69. President, Collegio Regionale Lombardo degli Architetti, Milan, 1957-60, and International Museum of Modern Architecture, Milan, 1961. Exhibitions: Florence, 1937; Galleria Gianferrari, Milan, 1939, 1951; Galleria dell' Obelisco, Rome, 1950; Institute of Contemporary Art, Boston, 1954, and toured the United States; Galleria La Bussola, Turin, 1955; AB Ferdinand Lundquist, Göteborg, Sweden, 1956; Galleria del Sole, Milan, 1956; Christofle, Paris, 1957; Liberty's, London, 1957; Galleria del Designo, Milan, 1959; *The Expression of Gio Ponti*, University of California at Los Angeles, 1966, and toured the United States; Galleria de Nieubourg, Milan, 1967; Galleria Toselli, Milan, 1978. Recipient: First Prize for Art, Accademia d'Italia, 1945; First Prize, University of Padua Faculty of English Competition, 1934; Compasso d'Oro for Industrial Design, 1956; Gold Medal, Académie d'Architecture, Paris, 1968. Honorary doctorate: Royal College of Art, London, 1968. Corresponding Member, Royal Institute of British Architects; Honorary Associate, American Institute of Architects. Member, Accademia di San Luca, Rome. *Died in September 1979.*

Works:

1921 Church, *Biennale*, Rome (exhibition project)
1925 House, via Randaccio, Milan (with Emilio Lancia)
      Richard Ginori Ceramics Factories conversions, Florence and Milan
1926 Bouilhet House, Paris
1927 Rinascente Department Store vestibule, Milan (with Emilio Lancia)
      Pavilion, *Fiera Campionaria*, Milan (with Emilio Lancia)
1928 Semanza House interiors, Levanto, Italy
      Memorial Monument, Milan (with G. Muzio, O. Cabiati, A. Alpago Novello and T. Buzzi)
1929 Hairdresser's salon, Malagoti, Milan
1930 Pavilion, *Biennale*, Monza, Italy (with Emilio Lancia)

Design of a flag for the Ospedale Maggiore, Milan
1931 Union Bank, Milan (with Emilio Lancia)
House, via Domenichino, Milan (with Emilio Lancia)
Borletti Tomb, Monumental Cemetery, Milan
1932 Borletti-House, via S. Vittore, Milan (with Emilio Lancia)
House, Bastioni di Porta Venezia, Milan (with Emilio Lancia)
1933 Littoria Tower (in steel), Parco di Milano, Milan (with Cesare Chiodi)
University City, Rome (with Giovanni Michelucci, Arnaldo Foschini, Pietro Aschieri, Giuseppe Capponi, Giuseppe Pagano, and Gaetano Rapisardi; Marcello Piacentini, chief architect)
House, corso Venezia, Milan
1934 Faculty of Mathematics Building, University City, Rome
House, via de Togni, Milan (with Emilio Lancia)
Palazzo de Littorio, Rome (competition project)
Faculty of English, University of Padua (competition project)
House, viale c. Zugna, Milan
1935 CIMA Building, Milan (with Luciano Baldissari)
Laporte House, Milan
Hotel, via Martello, Alto Adige, Italy (with Antonia Fornaroli and Eugenio Soncini)
House, via Ceradini, Milan
House, via Hajech, Milan
House, via Gustavo Modena, Milan
House, viale Regina Margherita, Milan (with Antonio Fornaroli and Eugenio Soncini)
House, corso Italia, Milan (with Antonio Fornaroli and Eugenio Soncini)
De Bartolemeis a Bratto Villas, Bresica, Italy
Entrance Hall, Ministero delle Corporazione, Rome
1936 Montecatini Building I, Milan (with Antonio Fornaroli and Eugenio Soncini)
Design of the *Catholic Press International Exhibition*, Vatican City
Italian Institute, Fürstenberg Palace, Vienna
Villa Marzotto, Valdagno, Italy (project; with Antonio Fornaroli, Eugenio Soncini, and Francesco Bonfanti)
Urban plan for Addis Ababa (with Giuseppe Vaccaro and Enrico del Dobbio)
1937 Liviano Building, School of Archeology, University of Padua (with the painter Massimo Campigli)
Domus Alba, via Goldoni, Milan (with Antonio Fornaroli and Eugenio Soncini)
Italian Pavilion (furnishings and ceramics), *World's Fair*, Paris
1938 Design of the *Vittoria Exhibition*, Padua
San Michele Hotel, Capri (project; with Bernardo Rudofsky)
Bungalows, Hotel Eden Roc, Cap d'Antibes, France (project)
RAI (Radio Associazione Italiana) Building, Milan (with Antonio Fornaroli, Eugenio Soncini and Nino Bertolata)
1939 Villa Donegani, Bordighera, Italy
Ferrania Office Building, corso Matteotti, Milan (with Antonio Fornaroli and Eugenio Soncini)
Building, San Babita, Milan (with Antonio Fornaroli and Eugenio Soncini)
Urban plan for Scalo Sempione, Milan (with de Finetti)
Costumes and scenery for *Il Pulcinella*, at the Teatro della Triennale, Milan
Great Hall and Basilica, Palazzo del Bo, University of Padua
Foreign Office, Rome (competition project; with Guglielmo Ulrich, R. Angeli, C. de Carli, and Eugenio Soncini)

Gio Ponti: Pirelli Tower, Milan, 1956.

Palazzo Marzotto, Milan (project; with Antonio Fornaroli, Eugenio Soncini, and Francesco Bonfanti)
1940 Villa Tataru, Cluj, Rumania (with Elsie Lazar)
Villa Marchesano, Bordighera, Italy
Staircase frescoes, University of Padua
Columbus Clinic for the Missionary Sisters of the Sacred Heart, Milan (with Antonio Fornaroli and Eugenio Soncini)
Ledoga Building, Milan (with Antonio Fornaroli and Eugenio Soncini)
Palazzina Salvatelli, Piazza Duse, Rome (with Antonio Fornaroli and Eugenio Soncini)
House, via Appiani, Milan (with Antonio Fornaroli and Eugenio Soncini)
INA-CASA Development, via Manin, Milan (project; with Antonio Fornaroli and Eugenio Soncini)
Giustiniani Apartment, Milan (project)
Fiat Building; Milan (with Antonio Fornaroli and Eugenio Soncini)
1943 Mondadori Building, Milan (project; with Antonio Fornaroli and Eugenio Soncini)
1944 Casa Barzanti, via Spiga, Milan
1945 North Railway Hotel and Office Building, Milan (project; with Antonio Fornaroli)
Ponti House I, Civate, Como, Italy
1946 Brustio Apartment, Milan
1948 Monumemt to the Victims of Ebensee Concentration Camp, Austria
House, via Lamarmora, Milan (with Antonio Fornaroli)
1949 Costumes and scenery for *Orfeo*, at La Scala, Milan
Villa Piodari, Rapallo, Italy (with Antonio Fornaroli)
Swimming Pool, Hotel Royal, San Remo, Italy
Self-illuminating furniture for the Casa Cremaschi, Milan
Mazzocchi Studio furnishings, via Monte di Pieta, Milan
Caffe espresso machinery, for La Pavoni, Milan
Sewing machines for La Visa, Voghera, Italy
1950 First Class Lobby, *Conte Grande* Liner (with Nino Zoncada)
Casino interiors, San Remo, Italy (with Antonio Fornaroli)
Villa Marchesano, San Remo, Italy
RAS Building, corseo Vittorio Emanuele, Milan (with Antonio Fornaroli)
Ceccato furnishings, Milan
Dulciora Shop, Milan
Vembi-Burroughs Offices, Genoa and Turin (with Antonio Fornaroli)
Villa Cremaschi interiors, Carate Urio, Como, Italy
1951 INA-CASA Housing Estate, via Harrar, Milan (with Luigi Figini and Gino Pollini)
Montecatini Building II, Milan
First Class interiors, on the liners *Giulio Cesare, Andrea Doria* and *Conte Bian camano* (with Nino Zoncada)
School complex, Chiavenna, Sondrio, Italy (with Antonio Fornaroli)
Model Hotel Room, *Triennale*, Milan
Steel cutlery for Argenteria Krupp, Milan, and Fraser, New York
Silver articles for Argenteria Krupp, Milan
Lamps for Greco, Milan
Leggera Chair, for Cassina, Milan
1952 Edison Electrical Centers, at Santa Giustina, Chiavenna, Cimego, Liri, Vinadio, Plantano d'Avio, and Stura Demonte, Italy (with Antonio Fornaroli and Alberto Rosselli)
Edison Building, Milan (with Antonio Fornaroli)
Villa Arata, Naples (with Antonio Fornaroli)
Oceania and *Africa* ships interiors
Technical School, Gonzaga Institute, Crescenzago, Milan (with Antonio Fornaroli)
Tables for the Singer Company, New York

1953 Faculty of Nuclear Physics, University of Sao Paulo (project)
Italian-Brazilian Center, Sao Paulo (project; with Liuz Contrucci)
Taglianotti House, Sao Paulo (project)
Swimming Pool, Hotel Royal, Naples
Distex Armchair, for Cassina, Milan
Furniture and Partition Walls, for Altamira, New York
Tap Fittings, for Gallieni, Vigano, and Marazza, Milan
Sanitary Fittings, for Ideal Standard, Milan
Lancia Building, Turin (with Antonio Fornaroli, Alberto Rosselli, and Nino Rosani)
Furniture, for Nordiska Kompaniet, Stockholm
Design of car bodywork, for Carrozzeria Touring, Milan
1954 Villa Planchart, Caracas
Italian Cultural Institute, Stockholm (with Pier Luigi Nervi and Ture Wenerholm)
Aldo Garzanti Center, Forli, Italy (with Antonio Fornaroli and Giulio Bosisio)
Industrialized House, *Triennale,* Milan (exhibition project)
1955 Arreaza House, Caracas
San Lucca Church, Milan (with Antonio Fornaroli and Alberto Rosselli
Villa Marmont, Zoagli, Genoa (with Antonio Fornaroli and Alberto Rosselli)
Ponti House II, Civate, Como, Italy
Superleggera Chair, for Cassina, Milan
Town Hall, Cesanatico, Pesaro, Italy (with Antonio Fonaroli and Alberto Rosselli)
Summer House, Arenzano, Genoa
Lamps, for La Luma, Milan
Alitalia Offices, New York
Cutlery, for Christofle, Paris
Supermarket, viale Zara, Milan (with Antonio Fornaroli and Alberto Rosselli)
Metal Desk, for Rima, Padua
Desk, for Chiesa, Milan
Cowhide carpet, for Colombi, Milan
1956 Pirelli Tower, Milan (with Pier Luigi, Nervi, Arturo Danusso, Antonio Fornaroli, Alberto Rosselli, Giuseppe Valtolina, and Egidio dell'Orto)
Handles, for Olivar, Borgomanero, Italy
Faculty of Architecture, Milan Polytechnic (with Giordano Forti)
Silver articles, for Christofle, Paris
Steel cutlery, for Argenteria Krupp, Milan
RAS House, via Nievo, Milan (with Antonio Fornaroli and Alberto Rosselli)
1957 House, via Dezza, Milan (with Antonio Fornaroli and Alberto Rosselli)
Melandri House, Milan (with Antonio Fornaroli and Alberto Rosselli)
FEAL Pre-Fabricated House, *Triennale,* Milan
Gorrondona House, Caracas (project)
Lamps, for Arredoluce, Milan
1958 Carmelite Convent, San Remo, Italy (with Antonio Fornaroli and Alberto Rosselli)
Government Office Building, Baghdad (with Antonio Fornaroli, Alberto Rosselli, Giuseppe Valtolina, and Egidio dell'Orto)
Assolombarda Building, Milan (with Antonio Fornaroli and Alberto Rosselli)
Villa Guzman-Bianco, Caracas (project)
Gallini Center, Voghera, Italy (with Antonio Fornaroli and Alberto Rosselli)
Cutlery, for Christofle, Paris
Eighth Floor Auditorium, Time and Life Building, New York
1960 Villa Nemazee, Tehran
Philips Building, Rome (with Antonio Fornaroli and Alberto Rosselli)
Alitalia Air Terminal interiors, Central Station, Milan
Hotel Parco dei Principi, Sorrento
1961 Montreal Tower (project)
Design of the *Italia '61* exhibition, Turin (with Pier Luigi Nervi)

1962 RAS Building, Milan (with Antonio Fornaroli, Alberto Rosselli, and Piero Portaluppi)
Montecatini Pavilion, *Milan Fair*
2 villas, Capo Stella, Elba (with Cesare Casati)
Hotel Storione, Padua (with Antonio Fornaroli and Alberto Rosselli)
Banca Antoniana, Padua (with Antonio Fornaroli and Alberto Rosselli)
Cassa di Risparmio di Padova e Rovigo, Padua (with Antonio Fornaroli and Alberto Rosselli)
House for the Mother Superior of Notre Dame de Sion, Rome (with Antonio Fornaroli and Alberto Rosselli)
Pakistan House Hotel, Islamabad (with Antonio Fornaroli and Alberto Rosselli)
1963 Shui Hing Stores, Hong Kong
Daniel Koo House, Hong Kong
Church of San Francesco, Milan
Bruckner Cultural Center, Linz, Austria (competition project; with Costanino Corsini and Giorgio Wiskeman)
Employees Residence, Varese Shoe Factory, Italy (with Antonio Fornaroli and Alberto Rosselli)
Cassa di Risparmio, Modena, Italy (with Antonio Fornaroli and Alberto Rosselli)
1964 Ministry Buildings, Islamabad, West Pakistan (with Antonio Fornaroli and Alberto Rosselli)
Anguissola House, Lido di Camaiore, Italy (project)
Hotel Parco dei Principi, Rome (with Antonio Fornaroli and Alberto Rosselli)
Chair, for Knoll, Milan
Banca dei Monte di Pieta Office and Apartment Building, Milan (with Antonio Fornaroli and Alberto Rosselli)
House Under Foil (project)
1965 Church, San Carlo Borromeo Hospital, Milan
Apartment/Office Building, Beirut (project; with Antonio Fornaroli and Alberto Rosselli)
1966 Law Courts, Verona (project; with Antonio Fornaroli and Alberto Rosselli)
1967 Bijenkorf Shopping Center, Eindhoven, Netherlands (with Theo Boosten, and the sculptors Mario Negri and Frans Gast)
Office building, via San Paulo, Milan (with Antonio Fornaroli and Alberto Rosselli)
1968 Plastic lamps, for Guzzini, Macerata, Italy
Furniture, for La Tecno, Milan
Piltello Housing Estate, Milan (with Antonio Fornaroli, Alberto Rosselli, A. Ferrari Angilella, and Giulio Ponti)
1969 Daniel Koo House, Marin County, California (project)
1970 Savoia Assicurazioni e Riassicurazioni Building, Milan (with Antonio Fornaroli and Alberto Rosselli)
Plan for the center of Munich (competition project; with Antonio Fornaroli and Alberto Rosselli)
1971 Taranto Cathedral, Italy
FEAL Building (project)
Center Beaubourg, Paris (competition project; with Alberto Ferrari)
Coordinating designs, for Zucchi, Milan
1972 Salzburg University (as consultant to Otto Prosinger and Martin Windisch)
Museum of Modern Art, Denver (with James Sudler and Joal Cronenwett)
1973 Decor, for D'Agostino Pottery, Salerno Italy
1976 Tiled flooring in Agostino ceramics, for Salzburger Nachrichten, Austria
1978 Painting on perspex, for the Shui Hing Stores, Singapore

Publications:

By PONTI: books—*La Casa all'Italiana,* Milan

1933; *Italiani,* with Leonardo Sinisgalli, Milan 1937; *Il Coro,* Milan 1944; *Cifre Parlanti,* Milan 1944; *Politica dell'Architettura,* Milan 1944; *Ideario,* Milan, 1945; *L'Architettura e un Cristallo,* Milan 1945; *Verso la Casa Esatta,* Milan 1945; *Ringrazio Iddio che le Cose non vanno a Mode Mio,* Milan 1946; *Paradiso Perduto,* Milan 1956; *Amate l'Architettura,* Genoa 1957, as *In Praise of Architecture,* New York 1960, Tokyo 1963; *Milano Oggi,* Milan 1957; *Nuvole sono Immagini,* Milan 1968; articles—numerous in *Domus* and *Stile,* Milan, and in other architectural and design periodicals throughout the world.

On PONTI: books—*Archiitettura d'Oggi* by Marcello Piacentini, Rome 1930; *Mobili Tipici Moderni* by G. C. Palanti, Milan 1933; *Tecnica dell'Abitazione* by G. Pagano, Milan 1936; *Architettura Moderna in Italia* by A. Pica, Milan 1941; *Difficolta Politiche dell'Architettura in Italia 1920-40* by Giulia Veronesi, Milan 1953; *Espressione di Giovanni Ponti* by James S. Plaut, Milan 1954; *Ponti Summing Up* by Mario Labo, Milan 1958; *Architettura Italiana Ultima/Recent Italian Architecture* by Agnoldomenico Pica, Milan 1959; *Modern Architecture* by Vincent Scully, New York 1965; *The Expression of Gio Ponti,* edited by Nathan H. Shapira, Minneapolis 1967; *28/78 Architettura,* exhibition catalogue, edited by Maria Grazia Mazzocchi Bonadonna, Milan 1979; articles—"Giovanni Ponti: dell Architettura al Disegno per l'Industria" by P. E. Gennarini in *Pirelli* (Milan), November/December 1951; "Pirelli Building, Milan" by Reyner Banham in *Architectural Review* (London), March 1961; "Scraping the Skies of Italy" by Edgar Kaufmann in *Art News* (New York), February 1966; "Ponti Is Dead" in *Building* (London), 21 September 1979; "Ponti—Loss to Design" in *Building Design* (London), 21 September 1979; "Obituary: Gio Ponti" in *Architects' Journal* (London), 26 September 1979; "Gio Ponti, 1891–1979" in *Domus* (Milan), October 1979; "Gio Ponti" in *Architectural Review* (London), December 1979; "Gio Ponti, 1891–1979" in *Architectural Design* (London) vol. 49, no. 12, 1979; "Obituary: Gio Ponti" in *Architect* (Malta) March 1980; "Gio Ponti, 1891–1979", special issue of *Space Design* (Tokyo), May 1981; "Gio Ponti—Three Opinions on the Man and a Look at His Latest Work" in *Modo* (Milan) October 1981.

Bibliography—*Gio Ponti* by Lamia Doumato, Monticello, Illinois 1981.

Modern man is born in a clinic and dies in a clinic. Is it therefore not surprising that he should spend the intermediate period between these two paramount events of his life in utterly soulless clinical environments? Architects, in moulding man's surroundings, have today unfortunately lost their magic touch. In the past, members of the profession were priests, astronomers or philosophers; in more ancient times they were conversant in the secret knowledge of celestial bodies and proficient in the understanding of essential terrestrial forms. This knowledge helped them to produce rarified works of art. Today, architecture is rarely able to transcend purely materialistic requirements. Architecture has become subservient solely to business interests ans speculation. What started as a path to enlightenment is now just a job!

Not so far for Gio Ponti. From the beginning of his career, Ponti's quest was a for a unique, individual creative ideology. Although a contemporary of members of the Italian Futurist movement, he was never in any way associated with their philosophy. Even in those early days he moved in a path isolated from surrounding thoughts and fashions. Gradually he developed an individualistic, sensitive approach in a multivalent and pluralistic expression of total design. His main influences came from close intimate friendships with Edoardo Persico, Bernard Ru-

dofsky and the painter Massimo Campigli: a reflection of his wide scope of vision. Following an initial academic and classical period of activity, he produced such significant pre-war projects as the Mathematics Building at Rome University (1934), the first Montecatini Building in Milan (1936) and the RAI offices in Milan (1938). The Montecatini design involved a remarkable evolution of standardization and architectural simplicity, in comparison to other works in Italy of that period. Contemporary to these works and also worthy of notice is his evocative hotel project for the Island of Capri, unfortunately never built, which manifested a deep ethnic understanding of the Mediterranean tradition. The particular relationship to site revealed in this project was to develop into a sensitive proficiency in grafting his work on to essential roots and in creating a progressive process of continuity, evolution and harmony in adapting his buildings to their particular environment.

Ponti's major contribution were, however, to come in later years in a remarkable integration of multi-disciplinary activities ranging from ceramics, painting, furniture and industrial design, theatre-sets and graphics, to architecture itself and town planning. In all of these activities (as well as in his long editorship of *Domus*), Ponti transcended purely materialistic requirements into a rare contemporary embodiment of truly poetic design concepts. The dogmatic imperatives of the early Modern movement, accompanied by declamatory revolutionary dialogue, resulted in a loss of spiritual values. In the mechanized soulless era of mass production that was to follow, Ponti's belief, plea and commitment was essentially for the individual, the particular and the unique. His total approach to architecture remained incontestably humanistic and essentially personal, respecting and glorifying both the onlookers and users of the buildings. In the best of Italian tradition (and what tradition it is!), Ponti's work evokes in its spectators a magical sense of ecstasy and fantasy. This is an expression of love and joy that transcends purely intellectual and technological values into the realm of the spirtual.

In all of his work there is constant evidence of his deep concern and inclination towards producing effects of lightness as opposed to heaviness and finite closed forms as opposite to infinite open ones; most of all, there is evidence of a deep understanding of what he referred to as the "poetry of precisions". This highly personalized approach produced a series of achitectural masterpieces that, despite their floating fantasy, are logically anchored to economic and rational criteria.

The Pirelli Tower in Milan (despite the changes from model to realization) must be considered as the jewel of modern skyscrapers: a diamond well cut and beautifully faceted. His Bijenkorf Shopping Center in Eindhoven brings a welcome air to the overcast sombre Nothern Skies of Holland: a space conceived for the glorification of the city. The Museum of Modern Art in Denver is as over-indulgent and Italiante as Caruso singing Neopolitan melodies, but equally infectious: a Baroque, mannerist expression as welcome and necessary as a golden touch of Mediterranean sun and as vital and rewarding as the best of Italian wines. The Cathedral in Taranto is perhaps his most successful religious building. A man of devout faith, Ponti manages to evolve the pure architectural spatial concept to a higher religious-spiritual one. "Religious architecture is not a matter of architecture but a matter of religion," Ponti tells us ...and so it is here. Its sun-scorched perforated lace-like facade evokes sculptured sounds against the timelessness of eternity. The rising fastigium recalls the elegant music of Tomasco Albinoni or Benedetto Marcello: crystallized sounds of romantic elegance. Ponti's concept of removing the stained glass evolves beyond that of the medieval cathedral and rings in clarion tones of conceptual clarity. Taranto's saffron-screen offers us a contact between spectator and infinity, between man and his Creator. The joy, belief and involvement of its maker is convincingly conveyed to the observer.

In the wide variety of his activities there is constant edivence that life, art and architecture were inseparable to Ponti. Her versatility was part of the grand tradition of the ancient masters of his land. In today's world, overwhelmed by the stolid facelessness of modern rationalism, we ask whether it is still possible for a contemporary building to be transformed into a poem. In perhaps the most difficult period of modern architecture Gio Ponti gave us a hopeful glimpse of a personal, positive, exuberant answer. For that accomplishment, his place in histroy is secure.

—Richard England

PORTMAN, John Calvin, Jr.

American. Born in Walhalla, South Carolina, 4 December 1924. Educated at the United States Naval Academy, Annapolis, Maryland, 1944; Georgia Institute of Technology, Atlanta, B.Arch. 1950. Served in the United States Naval Reserve, 1942-44. Married Joan Newton in 1944; children: Michael, John III, Jae, Jeffrey, Jana, and Jarel. Worked for Ketchum, Gina and Sharp, H. M. Heatley Associates, New York and Atlanta, 1945-49, and Stevens and Wilkinson, Atlanta, 1950-53; in private practice, Atlanta, 1953-56; Partner, Edwards and Portman, Atlanta, 1956-68. Since 1968, President of John Portman and Associates, Atlanta. President, Central Atlanta Progress, 1970-72. Principal, Portman Properties, Atlanta; Chairman of the Board, Portman Barry Investments Inc., Atlanta; Chairman of the Board, Atlanta Market Center; President, Peachtree Center Management Company, Atlanta; Chairman of the Board, Peachtree Purchasing, Atlanta; Chairman of the Board, Portman Hotel Company, Atlanta; Principal, Project Time and Cost, Atlanta; Director, Citizens and Southern Bank, Atlanta; Director, Commerce Club, Atlanta; Trustee, Atlanta Arts Alliance; Advisory Council Member, Agnes Scott College, Decatur, Georgia; Trustee, National Jewish Hospital and Research Center; Trustee, Scottish Rite Children's Hospital; Trustee, Georgia Tech Foundation. National Advisory Board Member, Georgia Institute of Technology, Atlanta, book1975-78; Director, Atlanta High Museum of Art, Georgia, 1982; Honorary Consul of Denmark in Atlanta. Recipient: National Citation, *Progressive Architecture,* 1956; Outstanding Young Man of the Year Award, Georgia Junior Chamber of Commerce, 1959; Distinguished Service Award, De-Kalb County Junior Chamber of Commerce, Georgia, 1960; Ivan Allen Award, American Institute of Architects, Northern Georgia Chapter, 1964; Outstanding Public Relations Award, Public Relations Society of America, Atlanta Chapter, 1967; Salesman of the Year Award, Sales and Marketing Executives of Atlanta Association, 1968; Golden Plate Award, American Academy of Achievement, 1968; Tau Sigma Delta Honorary Society Award, Georgia Institute of Technology, Atlanta, 1972; Atlanta Civic Design Commission Award, 1973; Architectural Excellence Award, American Institute of Steel Construction, 1973; Outstanding Humanitarian Award, National Jewish Hospital, 1973; Omicron Delta Kappa Award, Georgia State University, 1974; Design in Steel Award, American Iron and Steel Institute, 1975; Elsie de Wolfe Award, American Society of Interior Design, 1976; Georgian of the Year Award, Georgia Association of Broadcasters, 1976; City Association Award, Los Angeles, 1976; Brewer Award, Atlanta Convention Bureau, 1976; Merit Award, National Council for Community Services to International Visitors, 1976; Distinguished Service Medal, Georgia Business and Industry Association, 1977; Civic Leadership Award, Building Owners and Managers Association of Atlanta, 1977; Leadership and Accomplishment Award, Detroit University, Michigan, 1977; Medal for Innovation in Hotel Design, American Institute of

John Portman: Renaissance Center, Detroit, 1977.

Architects, 1978; Archdiocesan Medal for Architecture, Congress of the Greek Orthodox Church, 1980; Silver Medal, American Institute of Architects, Georgia Chapter, 1981; Distinguished Service Award, Empire Real Estate Board, Atlanta, 1984. LL.D.: Emory University, Atlanta, 1974. Fellow, American Institute of Architects. Member, Royal Order of the Knights of Dannenborg, Denmark, 1975; Officer, First Class, Royal Belgian Order of the Crown, 1983. Address: John Portman and Associates, 225 Peachtree Street, N. E., Suite 201, Atlanta, Georgia 30303, U.S.A.

Works:

1953 Fraternal Order of Eagles Building, Atlanta
1954 Henderson Office Building, Atlanta
1955 Lemer House, Atlanta
      Toubman House, Atlanta
1956 Midway Elementary School, DeKalb County, Georgia
1957 Southern Bell Executive Suite, Hurt Building, Atlanta
      Coggins Clinic and Drugstore, Atlanta
      Oglethorpe Demonstration School, Atlanta
1958 Jeff Davis Elementary School addition, Hazelhurst, Georgia
1959 YMCA Building, Southwest Side, Atlanta
      YMCA Building, West Side, Atlanta
      YMCA Building, Decatur, Georgia

1960 Carey Reynolds Elementary School, Doraville, Georgia (addition, 1966)
      Atlanta Merchandise Mart, Georgia (additions 1968 and 1985)
1961 Infirmary, Georgia Institute of Technology, Atlanta
      YMCA Building, Rome, Georgia
      Decorative Arts Center, Atlanta (additions 1970, 1979 and 1982)
1961 Peachtree Center, Atlanta
1962 Jamestown Shopping Center, College Park, Georgia
      Hawthorne Elementary School, Atlanta (additions, 1963, 1965)
      Fairburn High School addition, Fulton County, Georgia
1963 Pollack Paper Company Atlanta Plant addition
      Perry Homes addition, Atlanta
      Sequoyah High School, Doraville, Georgia (additions, 1964, 1965)
1964 John Portman House, Atlanta
      Trailways Bus Company Garage and Parking Deck, Atlanta
      Pollack Paper Company Plant addition, Birmingham, Alabama
1965 Greenbriar Shopping Center, Atlanta
      Service Center School, Atlanta
      Peachtree Center Building, Atlanta
      Antoine Graves House, Atlanta
      Dana Fine Arts Center, Agnes Scott College, Decatur, Georgia

      Herndon Elementary School, Atlanta
      Greenbriar Tire Center, Atlanta
      Greenbriar First National Bank, Atlanta
      Rich's Department Store, Greenbriar Shopping Center, Atlanta
      Greenbriar Theatre, Atlanta
      Trailways Bus Company Temporary Terminal, Atlanta
1966 Spalding Elementary School, Atlanta (addition, 1967)
      One Peachtree Street Building alterations and addition, Atlanta
      Midway Elementary School, Decatur, Georgia (addition, 1969)
      Pollack Paper Company Atlantic Plant addition
1967 Hyatt Regency Hotel, Peachtree Center, Atlanta (addition, 1971)
      C.W. Hill School, Atlanta
      Henderson High School, Chamblee, Georgia (additions, 1968, 1969)
1968 Atlanta Gas Light Tower, Peachtree Center, Atlanta
      Midnight Sun Restaurant, Peachtree Center, Atlanta
      Trailways Garage, Atlanta
1970 South Building, Peachtree Center, Atlanta
1971 J. F. Kennedy School and Community Center, Atlanta
      Hyatt Regency O'Hare Hotel, Chicago
      Blue Cross Office Building, Chattanooga, Tennessee

Alfred Blalock Elementary School, Atlanta
John Portman and Associates office interiors, Peachtree Center, Atlanta
Park Central Company Office Buildings (2), Dallas
Security Pacific National Bank, One Embarcadero Center, San Francisco
1974 Peachtree Cain Building, Peachtree Center, Atlanta
Hyatt Regency Hotel, Embarcadero Center, San Francisco
Levi Strauss Building, Two Embarcadero Center, San Francisco
Fort Worth National Bank (now Texas American Bank), Fort Worth, Texas
1975 Peachtree Center Shopping Gallery, Atlanta
World Trade Mart, Brussels
1976 Three Embarcadero Center, San Francisco
Peachtree Plaza Hotel, Peachtree Center, Atlanta
Peachtree Harris Tower, Peachtree Center, Atlanta
1977 Bonaventure Hotel, Los Angeles
Renaissance Center, phase I, Detroit
1979 Apparel Mart, Peachtree Center, Atlanta
1981 Four Embarcadero Center, San Francisco
Renaissance Center, phase II, Detroit
Ho Chung Marina, phase I, Sai Kung, Hong Kong
1982 Pavilion Inter-Continental Hotel, Singapore
1983 George Woodruff Physical Education Center, Emory University, Atlanta
1984 Rockefeller Center renovation, New York
1985 Marriott Marquis Hotel, Atlanta
Marriott Marquis Hotel, New York
Marquis One Office Tower, Peachtree Center, Atlanta
Courtland/Harris Parking Structure, Atlanta
Marina Square, Singapore
1986 Northpark Town Center, phase I, Atlanta
Post Mason Hotel, San Francisco
Landmark Plaza, Jakarta, Indonesia
Pertama Building, Kuala Lumpur, Malaysia
Inforum Building, Atlanta

Publications:

By PORTMAN: book—*The Architect as Developer*, with Jonathan Barrett, New York 1976; articles—"Atlanta Decorative Arts Center" in *Interiors* (New York), January 1961; "An Architecture for People and Not for Things" in *Architectural Record* (New York), January 1977; "Portman The Forerunner", interview, in *RIBA Journal* (London), October 1981; recording—*John Portman, Architect and Developer*, tape cassette, London 1977.

On PORTMAN: books—*GA 28: John Portman—Hyatt Regency Hotels* by Paul Goldberger, edited by Yukio Futagawa, Tokyo 1974; *American Architecture Now*, edited by Barbaralee Diamonstein, New York 1980; *GA 57: John Portman and Associates* by Paul Goldberger, edited by Yukio Futagawa, Tokyo 1981; articles—"John Portman: Atlanta's One-Man Urban Renewal Program" in *Architectural Record* (New York) January 1966; "Atlanta" in *Architectural Forum* (New York), April 1969; "The Architects Want a Voice in Redesigning America" by Gurney Breckenfield in *Fortune* (New York), November 1971; "John Portman: Architecture Is Not a Building" by Bernhard Leitner in *Arts in America* (New York), March/April 1973; "John Portman, Architect Plus" by Cathy Stanton in *AIA Journal* (Washington, D.C.), April 1975; "What to Do for an Encore" in *Architectural Record* (New York), June 1976; "John Portman, Architect-Developer" by Yukio Futagawa in *Approach* (Osaka), Autumn 1976; "Evaluation: San Francisco's Hyatt Regency Hotel as a Spatial Landmark" by John Pastier in *AIA Journal* (Washington, D.C.), October 1977; "Architect/Developer John Portman" in *RIBA Journal* (London), December 1977; "Hotels" and "In Progress: Portman Projects" in *Progressive Architecture* (New York), February 1978; "John Portman—Two Works" in *Architecture + Urbanism* (Tokyo), January 1979; "Atlanta—Capital of the New South" by Paul Gapp in *Chicago Tribune*, 26 March 1980; "Renaissance Center in Detroit" in *Casabella* (Milan), May 1980; "John Portman, An American Developer Architect" in *Der Architekt* (Stuttgart), May 1980; "Fat City" in *Interior Design* (New York), February 1981; "Times Square Hotel, New York" in *GA Document* (Tokyo), Winter 1981; "Circles in the Square" in *Interior Design* (New York), March 1982; "U.S. Giants 2: John Portman Speaks at the RIBA" in *Building* (London) 23 April 1982; "John Portman in London" in *The Architects' Journal* (London), 5 May 1982; "The Visible Lift" in *The Architects' Journal* (London), 15 June 1983; "Portman Place" in *Building Design* (London), 13 April 1984; "Portman: The Pavilion Inter-Continental, Singapore" in *Architect* (Melbourne), May 1984.

Bibliographies: *John Portman: An Introduction and Bibliography* by James C. Starbuck, Monticello, Illinois 1974; *John Portman of Atlanta* by Lamia Doumato, Monticello, Illinois 1981.

John Portman is Georgia-born and Georgia-educated as an architect and as a businessman. His work is the epitome of a successful blend of high finance and high-style architecture. That combination is as old in architecture as capitalism, but Portman has given it a new and fresh expression and dimension in American practice. At the same time as his work is financially successful, it is also enormously popular. People who would seldom go to see architecture visit Portman buildings and show them off to their visitors.

It is a tendency of American hotel architecture to be led in a particular direction at a particular time, usually by a particular architect. That architect is, currently, John Portman. His design motif is the urban hotel, self-contained in all its services and functions, and featuring an extremely large central atrium. His atriums are latter day urban forums. They are outfitted with shops, restuarants and lounges to assure a continuous vitality and animation, and they are spectacular in their verticval dimensions.

Portman's office provides all the design services required for executing one of his projects. He has also a commanding knowledge of the fiscal process of building development. Thus, his design skill is amply fortified by the normally controlling focus of financing. The two, combined, are powerful and unswerving. He commands resources of information that can withstand the severest forces of compromise.

As to the quality of his design, he is stylish without being superficial, and his lines, colors, materials and spaces are of great elegance. His buildings furnish a "sense of place" in many American cities that are otherwise lacking in such attributes of sociability.

Portman has practiced solely under his own name since 1968. Although most of his work is to be found in Georgia (particularly in Atlanta, and most notably in the Peachtree Center), his commissions include the Embarcadero Center in San Francisco, the Hyatt Regency O'Hare Hotel in Chicago, the World Trade Mart in Brussels, and—one of his most ambitious projects—the Renaissance Center in Detroit.

—Paul Spreiregen

PORTOGHESI, Paolo.

Italian. Born in Rome, 2 November 1931. Educated at the University of Rome, Dip.Arch. 1957. Since 1958, in private practice, Rome: in partnership with Vittorio Gigliotti, since 1964. Assistant Professor, 1958-61, and Professor, Faculty of Architecture and School for Monument Restoration, 1961-68, University of Rome. Since 1967, Professor of the History of Architecture, Milan Polytechnic (Dean of the Faculty of Architecture, 1968-75). Art Director, Officinia Edizioni, Rome, since 1964; Director/Editor, Controspazio, Bari, Italy, since 1969; Editor, *ITACA*, Rome, since 1977. Exhibitions: *Actual Alternatives*, L'Aquila, Italy, 1962; Galleria Il Bilico, Rome, 1966; Bauzentrum, Vienna, 1967; *Festival of Two Worlds*, Spoleto, Italy, 1967; *I Mostra triennale itinerante della architettura moderna italiana*, toured Italy, 1968; Hochschule für Bildende Künste und Bauzentrum, Hamburg, West Germany, 1969; Hochschule für Bildende Künste, Berlin, 1970; Kunst Haus, Göttingen, West Germany, 1970; Galleria Farnese, Rome, 1970; *Expo '70*, Osaka, Japan, 1970; Architects Association, Oslo, 1971; *Mostra triennale Iterinerante dell' architettura moderna italiani*, toured Italy, 1973; Galleria Il Milione, Milan, 1977; Galleria Pan, Rome, 1978; *Roma Interrotta*, Rome, 1978; Galleria Numerosette, Naples, 1978; *Transformations in Modern Architecture*, Museum of Modern Art, New York, 1979; *The Presence of the Past* at the *Biennale*, Venice, 1980. Recipient: National Award, Italian Institute of Architecture, 1963; Gold Medal, Ministry of Public Works, Rome, 1971. Member, Accademia di San Luca, Rome, 1966. Address (office): via XXIV Maggio 43, 00187 Rome, Italy.

Works:

1958 ENPAS Building, Pistoia, Italy
1959 Workers' housing, Castrovillari and Villa San Giovanni, Italy
Children's Hospital, Bari, Italy (project)
Baldi House, Rome
1960 Workers' housing, Modena, Italy
1961 Housing development (for 6,000 people), Reggio Calabria, Italy
INA-CASA Housing, in Cariati, San Marco Argentano, Carolei, and Mangone, Italy
1962 Housing development, Bagnara Calabria, Italy
1963 Old People's Home, Montecatini, Italy (project)
Office building, Rome
ENPAS Health Resort, Cesenatico, Italy
1964 Design of the *Michelangelo* Exhibition, Rome
1964/
67 Andreis House, Scandriglia, Italy
1965 600 houses, Naples (competition project)
Opera House, Cagliari, Italy
Canadian Pacific Tower, Montreal (project)
1966 SPECI Residential Development (for 1,000 people), Santa Marinella, Italy
1966/
71 Bevilacqua House, Gaeta, Naples
1967 Papanice Building, Rome
Master plan for the town of Colleferro, Italy
Italian Chamber of Deputies Office Building, Rome (competition project)
1968 Primary and secondary schools, Naples and Palermo
Church of the Holy Family, Salerno, Italy
Palace Hotel, Chianciano, Italy
Master plan for the town of Salerno, Italy (competition project)
1969 5,000 pre-fabricated houses, Kuwait
Social Services Center and Library, Avezzano, Vasto, Sulmona, Italy
Apartment building, Colle d'Arcaccio, Rome
Prefabricated schools, Asti and Rome
1969/
78 Technical college, L'Aquila, Italy
1970 Tersigni House, Ariccia, Italy

Paolo Portoghesi: Mosque and Islamic Centre, Rome, 1976 (project).

1972 Restoration of the old town of Salerno Italy
(as consultant)
Aparthotel Andalucia Mar, Marbella, Spain
Royal Jordanian Airlines and Royal Jordanian Army Housing (project)
Tourism development plan for Jordan
1973 International Airport, Khartoum, Sudan
Master plan for Khartoum, Sudan
1973/
74 Officers' Club, Khartoum, Sudan
1973/
78 Royal Court, Amman, Jordan
1976 Mosque and Islamic Center Rome

Publications:

By PORTOGHESI: books—*Guarino Guarini*, Milan 1956; *Borromini nella cultura Europea*, Rome 1964; *Michelangelo, architetto*, with others, Turin 1964; *Il Tempio Malatestiano*, Florence 1965; *Infanzia dell macchine*, Rome 1965; *Bernardo Vittone*, Rome 1966; *Roma barocca*, Rome 1966; *Borromini: architettura come linguaggio*, Rome 1967; *Dizionario di architettura e urbanistica*, editor, Rome 1968; *Roma: un'altra città*, Rome 1968; *L'Eclettismo a Roma 1870-1922*, Rome 1969; *Victor Horta*, Rome 1969, Tokyo 1976; *Roma del rinascimento*, Rome 1970, London 1972; *Le inibizioni dell'architettura*, Rome 1974; *La Seggiola di Vienna*, Rome 1975; *Album del liberta*, Rome 1975; *Album degli anni venti*, Rome 1976; *Album degli anni cinquanta*, Rome 1977; *Design e forme nuove nell'arredamento italiano*, with Marino Marini, Rome 1978; *Album degli Anni Trenta*, with Giovanna Massabrio, Rome 1978; *The Presence of the Past*, exhibition catalogue, with others, Milan and London 1980; *Dopo l'Architettura Moderna*, Bari, Italy 1981, New York 1982; *L'Angelo*

della storia, Rome 1982; articles—"Fear at Montecitorio: The New Building for the Chamber of Deputies: A Renunciation of Architecture" in *Controspazio* (Bari, Italy), September 1973; "Bottoni: 40 Years Fighting for Architecture," with others, in *Controspazio* (Bari, Italy), October 1973; "The Roman Palazzina" in *Casabella* (Milan), November 1975; "Le Inibizione dell'architettura moderna" in *Casabella* (Milan), December 1975; "The Research Continues" in *Controspazio* (Bari, Italy), December 1975; "Paolo Portoghesi and Virrorio Gigliotti," interview with Tatsuji Arono, in *Architecture + Urbanism* (Tokyo), May 1977; "Ideology and Original Sin" in *Controspazio* (Bari, Italy), June 1977; "National Competition for the New Administrative Centre of Florence" in *Controspazio* (Bari, Italy), December 1977; "The Architecture of Doubt" in *Controspazio* (Bari, Italy), January/February 1978; "Famous Houses" in *Summa* (Buenos Aires), July 1979; "Colour in Town/Colour in Turin" in *Domus* (Milan), January 1980; "Post-Modern Mosque," with Charles Jencks, in *Architectural Design* (London), no. 1/2, 1980; "Recent Projects," with G. Ercolani in *Controspazio* (Bari, Italy), January/March 1981; "Roma-Amor" in *Via* (Rome), vol. 5, 1982; "Interview," with A. Mendini and F. Irace, in *Domus* (Milan) July/August 1984.

On PORTOGHESI: books—*Alla ricerca dell'architettura perduta: le opere di Paolo Portoghesi e Vittorio Gigliotti* by Christian Norberg-Shulz, Rome 1975; *Paolo Portoghesi: progetti e disegni 1949-1979*, edited by Francesco Moschini, Florence and New York 1979; *Transformations in Modern Architecture*, exhibition catalogue, by Arthur Drexler, New York 1979; *Late-Modern Architecture* by Charles Jencks, London 1980; *Das Ende der Zuversicht* by

Wolfgang Pehnt, Berlin 1983; articles—"Fortresslike House on the Clifftop at Fontania, near Gaeta" in *Architecture Française* (Paris), October 1975; "Locus: Works by Paolo Portoghesi and Vittorio Gigliotti, 1971-1975" by Christian Norberg-Schulz in *Controspazio* (Bari, Italy), December 1975; "Project for the New State Palace in Amman" by Alfredo Passeri in *Industria delle costruzioni* (Rome), November 1977; "Portoghesi Picks Up the Pollen" by Martin Richardson in *Building Design* (London), 9 May 1980; "Portoghesi's Petals" in *Architectural Review* (London), August 1980; "Baroque modernism" in *Fifth Column* (Montreal), Summer 1981; "Embassy Revisited" in *Domus* (Milan), October 1982.

Bibliography—*Paolo Portoghesi: A Selected Bibliography of Books and Articles by and about Him* by Carole Cable, Monticello, Illinois 1983.

The works of Paolo Portoghesi, with Vittorio Gigliotti, transcend the rigidity and limitations of functional modern architecture by exploring more imaginative possibilities of form and meaning. Portoghesi has rediscovered the *Gestalt* qualities of Oriental architecture and Gothic, Baroque and Art Nouveau buildings. His concern with tradition is not limited to literal adaptation, but is an active transformation according to his own vision. He uses tradition in a new and creative way by absorbing the values of the past into forms of contemporary architecture. Portoghesi is also concerned with the environmental qualities of the site; he works to create harmony between a building and its users.

In the spirit of the revival of Baroque architecture (to which Portoghesi, one of our outstanding architectural historians, contributed immensely), his buildings rediscover space and movement as structural elements. In houses and large complexes, he uses a geometric vocabulary in a disciplined manner, relating the uniqueness of the topographical conditions to the specific aims of the client; examples are the Baldi, Andreis, Bevilacqua, and Tersigni houses, built between 1959 and 1971.

The rectangular geometry of the earlier phase of modern architecture is amplified and enriched by Portoghesi in these works in which he combines concave and convex spatial elements. In his more recent works, such as the Art Academy in L'Aquila and the public library in Avezzano, Portoghesi comes to a synthesis of his earlier achievements by integrating architectural form into the larger contexts of the environment. In his works carried out in the Middle East, as well as in his mosque in Rome, he has successfully integrated European and Islamic traditions into the formal vocabulary in a new synthesis.

Portoghesi is one of the outstanding scholars in the area of architectural history, concentrating as writer and teacher on Renaissance, Baroque, and late nineteenth century. He was also director of the architecture section at the *Biennale* in Venice and since 1984 has been in charge of all the various sections of the *Biennale*. Thus, Portoghesi has made a variety of important contributions to international architecture.

—Udo Kultermann

POWELL, (Arnold Joseph) Phillip.

British. Born in Bedford, 15 March 1921. Educated at Epsom College, Surrey, 1934-39; Architectural Association School, London, 1939-43 (SADG Medallist, 1943), Dip.A.A. (honours) 1943. Married Philippa June Eccles in 1953; children: Dido and Ben. Architectural Assistant to Frederick Gibberd, *q.v.*, London, 1943-45. Since 1946, Partner, with Hidalgo Moya, *q.v.*, Powell and Hoya, and Powell, Moya and Partners, London (Michael Powell, Powell, and Moya, 1946-50; Powell and Moya, 1950-61; Powell, Moya, Robert Henley, and Peter Skinner, 1961-73; Powell, Moya, and Skinner, 1973-76; Powell, Moya, Skinner, John Cantwell, and Bernard Throp, 1976-84; Powell, Moya, Skinner, Throp, Roger Burr, and John Haworth, since 1984). Member of the Royal Fine Art Commission since 1969. Exhibitions: Royal Institute of British Architects, London, 1974; Royal Academy, London, yearly since 1974. Recipient: First Prize, Pimlico Housing Competition, London, 1946; Bronze Medal, 1950, and Royal Gold Medal, 1974, Royal Institute of British Architects; Ministry of Housing and Local Government Award, 1953. Associate, 1944, and Fellow, 1956, Royal Institute of British Architects. Associate of the Royal Academy of Arts, 1972, and Royal Academician, 1977. O.B.E. (Officer, Order of the British Empire), 1957; Knighted, 1975; Companion of Honour, 1984. Address: Powell, Moya and Partners, 21 Upper Cheyne Row, London SW3 5JW, England.

Works (with Hidalgo Moya, and partners):

1946/
62 Churchill Gardens, Grosvenor Road, London
1949 Houses, Mount Lane, Chichester, Sussex
1951 Skylon, Festival of Britain, South Bank, London
1953 Houses and flats, Gospel Oak, London
Local authority housing, Inhurst, Baughurst, near Kingsclere, Hampshire (with Eric Chick)
1954 House, Toy's Hill, near Westerham, Kent
1955 Houses, Stokesheath Road, Oxshott, Surrey

1956 House, Leamington Spa, Warwickshire
Mayfield School, West Hill, Putney, London
1957 Admission Unit, Fairmile Hospital, near Wallingford, Berkshire
1961 Festival Theatre, Chichester, Sussex
1961/
72 Princess Margaret Hospital, Swindon, Wiltshire
1962 New building for Brasenose College, Oxford
1964 Admission Unit, Borocourt Hospital, near Henley, Oxfordshire
1966 Wexham Park Hospital, Slough, Buckinghamshire
1966/
75 Wycombe General Hospital, High Wycombe, Buckinghamshire
1967 Cripps Building, St. John's College, Cambridge
1967/
71 Wythenshawe Hospital, near Manchester
1968 Blue Boar Quad, Christ Church, Oxford
Swimming baths and assembly hall, Upper Richmond Road, Putney, London
Christ Church Picture Gallery, Oxford
1969 Magpie Lane Annex, Corpus Christi College, Oxford
1970 Dining Rooms, Bath Academy of Art, Beechfield House, Corsham, Wiltshire
British Pavilion, *Expo '70*, Osaka, Japan (with Takaki and Dodd)
1973 Plumstead Manor School, Plumstead Common, Woolwich, London
1974 Wolfson College, Oxford
Dining Rooms, Eton College, Buckinghamshire
1975 Houses and Flats, Lambeth, London
1976 Museum of London, London Wall, London
1976/
78 New buildings, Queens' College, Cambridge
1977/
78 Woolwich Military Hospital, London
1978 London and Manchester Assurance Company Headquarters, Winslade Park, Clyst St. Mary, Devon
1982 School for Advanced Urban Studies, Bristol University, Avon
National Westminster Bank, Shaftesbury Avenue, London
1983 Flats, Covent Garden, London
Maidstone Hospital, Kent
1985 International Conference Centre, Broad Sanctuary, Westminster, London

Publications:

On POWELL/MOYA: books—*The New Architecture in Great Britain* by Edward D. Mills, London 1953; *World's Contemporary Architecture*, volume 8, by Ino and Koike, Tokyo 1953; *Come si costruisce oggi nel mondo* by Carpanelli, Milan 1955; *Encyclopédie de l'architecture-Immeubles collectifs*, Paris 1956; *Die neue Schule* by Alfred Roth, Zürich 1957; *Encyclopédie de l'architecture nouvelle*, volume 2, by Alberto Sartoris, Milan 1957; *New Housing in Great Britain* by H. Bruckmann and D. L. Lewis, Stuttgart and London 1960; *Ebenerdig Wohnen* by Meyer-Bohe, Stuttgart 1963; *Encyclopaedia of Modern Architecture* by Gerd Hatje, London 1963; *Modern Buildings in London* by Ian Nairn, London 1964; *The New Museum* by Michael Brawne, London 1965; *Architecture in Britain Today* by Webb, London 1969; *Versammlungssttatten* by Ruhnau, Gütersloh, West Germany 1969; *Cambridge New Architecture* by Booth and Taylor, London 1970; *Student Housing* by Munnings and Allen, London 1971; *Neue englische Architektur* by Robert Maxwell, Stuttgart 1972; *Ospedali* by Aloi and Bassi, Milan 1972; articles—"Powell and Moya's Dash for Freedom" by Stephen Gardiner in *RIBA Journal* (London), March 1974; "P and M Strike Gold" in *The Architects' Journal* (London), 13 March 1974; "Royal Gold Medallists Powell and Moya" in *AA*

Notes (London), March/May 1974; "A Practice and Its Principles" in *Building* (London), 28 June 1974; "Powell and Moya Take Their Gold" in *RIBA Journal* (London), July 1974; "Powell and Moya: Architecture of Diffidence" in *Architettura* (Rome), November 1974; "Museum of London Opens" in *Building* (London), 3 December 1976; "Hospitals for Soldiers" in *Construction* (London), July 1979.

*

To define, even to myself, my approach to architecture, I find difficult. If I can detect principles, they are too often negative or humdrum—perhaps some are not principles at all: a mistrust of conscious struggling after originality (if originality grows out of the originalities of the problem, well and good); a mistrust, typically English perhaps, of the monumental approach, of making things big when they need not be; a mistrust of the attitude that treats any job as a "prestige job." A belief that each job—large or small, repetitive and standardized or nigglingly tailor-made—has an identity of its own and should not, in order to save its designer time and trouble, be allowed to become an arbitrary re-hash of one of its predecessors.

—Philip Powell

*

Philip Powell and Hildago Moya both trained at the Architectural Association School of Architecture during the war years when Frederick Gibberd was the principal, and Gibberd's individual approach to modern architecture is reflected in the work of Powell and Moya. They established their architectural practice in 1946 after winning the Pimlico Housing Architectural Competition. This development on the north bank of the River Thames was built in phases between 1946 and 1962 to replace some 33 acres of war-damaged property. Churchill Gardens, as it is now called, houses some 6,500 people in flats and maisonettes in a high-density layout devised to make the best use of this important riverside site. Every flat has a view of the river, and the general flat planning and site layout is strongly reminiscent of the early 1930s housing work of Walter Gropius in Berlin. Churchill Gardens, built with concrete frame and brick panels, is undoubtedly one of the most outstanding examples of postwar housing in Britain, and today, more than twenty years after completion, it is still well cared for and clearly appreciated by the residents. The human scale of this large complex and the excellent detail planning and design made Churchill Gardens a model that, unfortunately, too few have followed in recent years.

This attention to detail and understanding of human scale has become a Powell and Moya trademark, and although they have designed very little housing since Churchill Gardens, the standard of their work has been consistently high. Mayfield School, Putney (1956), has been rightly described as "subtle, elegant and humane." That description could be equally applied to all their subsequent work, which has included hospitals, swimming baths, and many college buildings at Oxford and Cambridge.

The Festival Theatre in Chichester (1961), a low-budget, hexagonal building, was one of the earliest examples of an arena stage in Britain. The design proved that good modern architecture is not necessarily dependent on expensive materials or a huge budget. In such works as the Cripps Building, St John's College, Cambridge (1967), Powell and Moya, with inherent sensitivity and understanding of materials applied to each new design problem, have produce architecture that is not original for the sake of originality but of a consistent high standard. They have earned many awards and the appreciation of those who use the buildings.

Powell and Moya received the Royal Gold medal of the Royal Institute of British Architects in 1974; this was the only occasion in more than 130 years that the award has been made to an architectural practice rather than an individual architect. One of the most recent buildings by this distinguished practice is the new London Museum, located on a difficult central

Philip Powell and Hidalgo Moya: London and Manchester Assurance Offices, Winslade Park Manor, Exeter, 1978.

city site: once again the resultant building is not only eminently practical; it also sets a high architectural standard, in striking contrast to much of the frankly commercial building that surrounds it.

In 1984, Powell was made a Companion of Honour, the first architect to receive this distinction; this was a very timely acknowledgement of the important role played by Powell and Moya in the development of postwar modern architecture in Britain.

—Edward D. Mills

PRATT, James Reece.

American. Born in Stamford, Texas, 25 March 1927. Educated at the University of Texas, Austin, 1944-50, B.Arch. 1950; Harvard University Graduate School of Design, Cambridge, Massachusetts, 1952-53, M.Arch. 1953. Served in the United States Navy, in the Pacific Theatre, 1945-46. Married Joanne Henderson in 1955; children: Sabrina, Alexandra, and Ilya. Field Administrator, Broad and Nelson, Dallas, 1951; Design Architect, A. L. Aydelott, Memphis, Tennessee, 1952, I. M. Pei, New York, 1953, Haefeli Moser Steiger, Zurich, 1954, and Broad and Nelson, Dallas, 1955-57; Partner, with Harold Box, Pratt and Box, Dallas, 1958-61; Partner, with Box and Philip Henderson, Pratt Box and Henderson, Dallas, 1961-84. Since 1984, Principal, James Pratt Architects, Dallas. Trustee, Dallas Museum of Fine Arts, 1964-68; Member, Professional Advisory Committee to the Dallas County Mental Health/Mental Retardation Board, 1967-71; Member, Board of Directors, The Greenhill School, Addison, Texas, 1967-73; Member, Task Force on Higher Education, Goals for Dallas, 1968-70; Member, Community Council of Greater Dallas Health Panel, 1971-75. Trustee, Dallas Health and Science Museum, since 1962; Trustee and Member of the Executive Committee, North Texas Educational Television Foundation, 1969-80; Trustee, Dallas Historical Society, 1978-80; Member, Dallas County Historical Commission, 1982-84. Co-Designer of the exhibitions, *A Study of Downtown Dallas,* 1957, and *The Better/Best Dallas,* 1958. Recipient: First Prize, Matico National Homes for Better Living Competition, 1959; Burlington Award for Interiors, 1975. Fellow, American Institute of Architects, 1973; Fellow, Dallas Institute of Humanities and Culture, 1982. Address: James Pratt Architects, 101 Trunk Avenue South, Post Office Box 19647, Dallas, Texas 75219, U.S.A.

Works:

1960 Children's Development Center (school for mentally handicapped children), Dallas
1961 Wilson House, 9035 Broken Arrow, Dallas
1962 St. Stephen Church, Mesquite, Texas
1963 The Great Hall, Apparel Mart, Dallas
1964 Hochstim House, 3725 Maplewood, Dallas
1965 College Inn, Eugene, Oregon
1966 Quadrangle Shopping Center, Dallas
1967 Master plan for the *State Fair of Texas,* Dallas
1968 Master plan for Griffin Square, Dallas
1969 Recognition Equipment Manufacturing Plant, Irving, Texas

1970 Waste Water Research Laboratory, Dallas
1971 Montgomery House, 3712 Beverly Drive, Highland Park, Texas
1972 Apparel Mart, phase III, Dallas
1973 Master plan for the Surrey Docks, London
1974 Greenhill Middle School and Laboratory Theatre, Addison, Texas
1975 Master plan for Brookhaven College; Farmers Branch, Texas
1976 Sloman House, 6009 St. Andrews Drive, University Park, Texas
1977 Patterson House addition, Crooked Lane at Strait Lane, Dallas
1978 Brookhaven College, phase I, Farmers Branch, Texas
1979 County Court House restoration, Dallas
1980 Dallas Museum of Art, Texas (as Managing Architect)
   Farrell-Wilson Farm Museum restoration, Plano, Texas
1982 Standard Casualty Home Offices, New Braunfels, Texas
1984 Sloman/Bower House, Dallas
   Exposition Plaza/Fair Park Link Urban Plan, Dallas

Publications:

By PRATT: books—*The Prairie's Yield: Forces Shaping Dallas Architecture from 1840-1962,* co-author, New York 1962; *COPE Guide to Environmental Education,* editor, Washington, D.C. 1970; *Urban Design in Dallas, Part I: Objectives,* Dallas 1970; *Environmental Encounter: Experiences in Decision Making for the Built and the Natural Environ-*

ment, co-author, Dallas 1979; *Farrell-Wilson Farm: Historic Report,* Plano, Texas 1980; articles—"A Matter of Choice" in *AIA Journal* (Washington, D.C.), May 1970; "How to Make Fair Park a Fair Park" in *D Magazine* (Dallas), March 1976; "An Archiect in Search of Dallas" in *Texas Architect* (Austin), November/December 1976; "Architectural Education for the 1980s" in *Texas Architect* (Austin), September 1980; "On Education for Practice: Three Questions" in *Tennessee Architect* (Nashville), September 1982; "Dallas: Remembered and Reimagined" in *Imagining Dallas,* edited by Gail Thomas, Dallas 1982; "Reflections on a Funeral" in *Texas Architect* (Austin), September 1982; "La Reunion: The Last Hurrah" in *Arts and Architecture* (Los Angeles), February 1984.

On PRATT: books—*Architectural Design Preview U.S.A.* by John Dixon, New York 1962; *Dallasights* by Lu, Weiming and others, Dallas 1978; articles—in *Architectural Forum* (New York), November 1959; in *Interiors* (New York), June 1974; "Dallas" by Donald Canty in *AIA Journal* (Washington, D.C.), March 1978.

I was trained just at the end of the era when Texas buildings still relied on a particular natural ventilation and were planned for the sun control needed in a hot, as well as a cold, locale. There was always a conflict between the logical form required by this sine qua non of comfort and the then-fashionable imported style. High styles had been derived in far more northern climes, and their forms only came to be possible in Texas when total climate control was available in the 1950's. We thought we could ignore nature. This was a critical point of architecture in the United States. From this time we would always have some form of climate control.

To an architect who grew up when one *had* to dine in the garden in the evening because it was the comfortable place, had to study in the shaded breezeway, and who slept on a deck in preference to a stifling bedroom, climate control was a great panacea for environmental ills, but it was not enough. The smells, the sounds, and the textures were missing. Before climate control we were trained to make buildings thin in one dimension to encourage the breeze. The fortunate side benefit was ever-changing daylight from at least two directions. There was bred in us an unconscious demand for a variety of sensory stimuli which the never-varying fluorescent bulb and the fixed tinted windows of big square plans ignore.

From a goal of satisfying immediate sensory demands in a single building one can expand to the wider purpose of answering more psychological needs in the design of environments. Clarifying and expressing those psychological purposes of art in architecture are what I want to be about as an architect. For their solutions are what make for excellence in building any environment.

The interrelation of forms in environment is one aspect of this attitude that is most often overlooked in building. The response of one creation to its existing neighbor helps make extra spaces for the one just added and gives more meaning to both. New possibilities for human contacts are revealed by these spaces between buildings when they are positively designed. In the city, buildings are pushed apart by the motor car into small pedestrian islands. I want to consciously knit them back together into a viable pedestrian fabric. It is the indoor or outdoor spaces which may faciliate community contact for the individual that interest me; I have gone about the world studying the components of such spaces for the past 30 years to better prepare myself to design them. They nearly always are multi-purposed in nature, and even though they have a formal working purpose, they as well have a recreational use. Creating the design solution to these complex functions is what challenges my ingenuity and imagination.

Another aspect of psychological purpose in architecture which interests me as a design problem is the creation of a more unique sense of place—but as part of its surrounding whole city. What are the constituent elements of a particular place? Physical and social? How can I employ them as architectural devices which both relate that place to its history and contribute to fresh buildings for today?

High art in the past came out od the vernaular of a particular locale—from down deep in its roots. Local

James Pratt: Brookhouse College, Farmers Branch, Texas, 1978.

materials, local cultural patterns, and local nature each contributed. Understanding and drawing from that vernacular are acts I want to better employ to help give substance to what I create. How can industrial artifacts and processes make as strong, as pungent, as special environments as those pre-industrial ones we admire? In what ways can a design be heightened with the particular light—both the quantity of light and its quality, its sharp direct hardness, or its soft diffuseness; its shadow and its color? What will enhance the particular topography, distill local nature to express the essence of that place? What should man's relation to the plant and animal world become in that locale?

I want to contribute pieces to a whole, be able to create a quiet background as well as a strong focal one. A work of architecture needs to be in harmony both with other buildings and with nature. I see a need to help man perceive better his relationship with his surroundings—both far and near—as he sits, stands, and moves at all kinds of speeds. How can I help men achieve grace in environments?

—James Pratt

James Pratt Architects is a Dallas office young in age but capable of wise decisions. In a diverse portfolio of work there is a strength of confident design. Like certain firms in the past (that of Eero Saarinen, for instance), Pratt and his partners make sure that each project is unique, as individual as the program requires—but totally designed.

No two projects have resembled one another; the linking thread is innovation and a progressive outlook. The European design of the Quadrangle Shopping Center, the witty and precise masonry construction of Brookhaven College, and the handling of scale within the Great Hall of the Apparel Mart, all in Dallas, are results of closely coordinated concepts, details, and materials.

In works for heavy public use, maintaining interest is a paramount consideration. Pratt has designed the Great Hall with seperate sub-spaces functioning within the massive exhibition space, providing for multiple usage and comfortable scale. At Brookhaven College the structural intrigue of floating brick beams add to the minute detailing. And Pratt is not afraid to test the new. His readiness to tamper with social habits is best seen in he Quadrangle, a little jewel of a shopping center. Off the beaten track but in a very swank area of Dallas, the Quadrangle is neither a mammoth, mindless shopping mall nor an endless American commercial strip à la Venturi. It invites the shopper to a quiet walk through many luxurious shops. Asking an American to abandon his automobile is a risky if not dangerous business, but the Quadrangle overcomes any withdrawal symptoms with intimate courtyards and spaces that invite exploration.

Pratt believes in "projects that can influence the form of the city." The volume of his firm is low but of high quality. Though an expansion to large scale projects is his goal, that goal is being achieved slowly, by careful choice. James Pratt Architects is a close-knit firm that believes in good design—often total design down to the doorknobs. Each of the partners doubles on duties, permitting closer contact to projects. It is a firm involvement, stressing teamwork and a flow of ideas throughout the staff.

Look to James Pratt and his partners to influence all areas of architecture. Their designs are confident and clear in vision. They are also interested in their community and the development of their profession: they helped in establishing a school of architecture at the University of Texas in Arlington. Their own lives involve the arts and urban affairs. Their varied capabilities and innovative approach puts them a cut above local and Texas-typical architecture, and will light the way to national and international fame.

—Logan Cravens

PRICE, Cedric.
British. Born in Stone, Staffordshire, 11 September 1934. Educated at the Cambridge University School of Architecture, 1952-55, M.A. 1955; Architectural Association School, London, 1955-57, Dip.A.A. 1957. Since 1960, Principal, Cedric Price Architects, London, Co-Founder, with Frank Newby, Light-weight Enclosures Unit, London, since 1969; Foun-der, Polyark: Architectural Schools Network, Lon-don, since 1971. Part-time Teacher, Architectural Association School, London, 1958-64. Chairman, Quality of Life Committee, Science Policy Found-ation Ltd., London, 1970-71. Exhibitions: *Cedric Price: The Evolving Image,* Heinz Gallery, Royal Institute of British Architects, London, 1975; *Forty London Architects,* Art Net, London, 1976; *Recent Works,* Architectural Association, London, 1979; *Houses for Sale,* Leo Castelli Gallery, New York, 1980 (travelled to James Corcoran Gallery, Los Angeles, and Texas Gallery, Houston, 1981); *In Memoriam Congress Hall Berlin,* Aedes Gallery, West Berlin, 1981; *Schemes,* Waddington Gallery, London, 1981; *The Home,* Architectural Associ-ation, London, 1982; *Cedric Price—25 Years,* Architectural Association, London, 1984. Associ-ate, Royal Institute of British Architects, 1959. Address: Cedric Price Architects, 38 Alfred Place, London WC1E 7DP, England.

Works:

1961 Aviary, London Zoo, Regent's Park, London (with Lord Snowdon and Frank Newby)
Fun Palace, for Joan Littlewood, Stratford East, London (project)
1964 Potteries Thinkbelt, Staffordshire (project)
1966 Oxford Corner House (public information hive), Central London (project)
1968 Development plan for the North Side of London Airport, Heathrow
Plan for adult education network and compo-nents, Greater Detroit and Oakland County, Michigan
1969 Computer Centre, British Transport Docks Board, London
Research on air structures, for the Ministry of Public Buildings and Works, London
1969 Design of short-life adaptive housing
1970 Temporary theatre, Amsterdam
Birmingham and Midland Institute Head-quarters, Birmingham
1971 Catering Complex, for J. Lyons and Com-pany, Blackpool Zoological Gardens, Lan-cashire
1972 Community Centre, for Inter-Action Trust, Kentish Town, London
Inflatable Roof Pedestrian Precinct, South-end, Essex

Cedric Price: The Cedric Price Aviary, Royal Veterinary College, London, 1981 (model).

Olympia Information Complex, Olympic Village, Munich

Development plan for the central area of Stuttgart (competition project; with Heini Wischer and Partners)

Two Tree Island Development, Southend, Essex (with Yorke, Rosenberg and Mardall)

1973 Variable, truckable conference facilities and specialized motor bus design (project)

Floating Breakwater and Marina, Abu Dhabi, United Arab Emirates (project)

Draft building code for single-skin air structures, Department of the Environment, London

1974 Student's Residential/Social Centre, Trondheim, Norway (competition project; with Archigram Architects)

1978 Generator, North Florida

1979 Westpen experimental cattle and sheep handling plant, Hampshire

Greenbird adjustable experimental aviary, Hampshire

1980 D.O.M. Offices, Cologne, West Germany (competition project)

Castel House, for an imaginary site in the United States (project)

1981 The Cedric Price Aviary, Royal Veterinary College, London

1982 Parc de la Villette development, Paris (competition project)

National Gallery extensions, London (competition project)

Airline Terminal, Luton Airport, Bedfordshire

1983 South Bank Development, London

Pavilions, Perth, Western Australia

1984 Mobile Gallery, Australia

Stowe Park Development, Stowe, Staffordshire

Publications:

By PRICE: books—*Learning: Developing Patterns of Urbanisation,* London 1970; *Air Structures,* London 1971; *Air Structures Bibliography,* 2 volumes, London 1972, 1973; *Predicament of Man,* London 1972; *Works II: Cedric Price,* London 1984; articles—guest editor of "What About Learning?," special issue of *Architectural Design* (London), May 1968; "Non-Plan: An Experiment in Freedom" in *New Society* (London), 21 March 1969; "Expediency" in *Architectural Design* (London), September 1969; "Safety Pins and Other Magnificent Designs" in *Pegasus* (New York), Spring 1972; "Public Spaces" in *London Architecture Club Magazine,* no. 2, 1978; "Beyond High Tech" in *L'Architecture d'aujourd'hui* (Paris), November, 1980; text, in *Tourism and the Environment,* London 1980; "Platforms, Pavilions, Pylons and Plants" in *Houses for Sale,* exhibition catalogue, New York 1980; "The Case Against Conservation" in *The Environmentalist* (London), no. 1, 1981; "A Summertime Breeze" in *AA Files* (London), January 1984. recording—*Technology is the answer, but what was the question?,* tape cassette and slides, London 1981.

On PRICE: book—*Planning for Diversity and Choice* by Stanford Anderson, Cambridge, Massachusetts 1968; *New Directions in British Architecture* by Royston Landau, London 1968; *The State of British Architecture* by Sutherland Lyall, London 1980; *Current Architecture* by C. Jencks and W. Chaitkin, London 1982; *How Architects Get Work,* London 1984; articles—"Life Conditioning" in *Architectural Design* (London), October 1966; "The Future Starts Now" in *Interior Design* (London), March 1968; "Rhetoric and Architecture" by Charles Jencks in *Architectural Association Quarterly* (London), Summer 1972; "Approaching an Architecture of Approximation" in *Architectural Design* (London), October 1972; "Price's Process" in *RIBA Journal* (London), January 1976; "Cedric Price—or Still Keeps Going When Everything Else Has Stopped" in *Architectural Design* (London), May 1976; "South Bank Saviour?" in *Building Design* (London), 3 February 1984.

*

Architecture and planning must, through its content, increase the range of imagination, invention, and ingenuity of its users. The reason for architecture is to encourage, rather than satisfy, people's appetite to behave, mentally and physically, in ways which they had previously thought impossible.

Architecture can best be judged by the untruths it establishes in other disciplines.

—Cedric Price

*

The ideological debate in British architecture during the last two decades has gained considerable strength and definition from Cedric Price, who represents one extreme point of view most articulately. Although his built work is by its very nature unlikely to appeal aesthetically to many of his fellow architects, he is nonetheless widely respected for his ideas and for his ability to defend them against considerable odds.

Price draws our attention to the negative and repressive side of architecure, to the way in which our actions are all too often restricted and conditioned by buildings originally constructed for other purposes and made incapable of change. He calls for flexibility and adaptability in architecture, believes in unpretentious and expedient buildings that can be used in a variety of foreseen and unforeseen ways, and believes, too, that buildings should have a predetermined life-span—in the case of most of his own built works, less than twenty years. In the interests of flexibility and easy demolition, he constructs most of his buildings of lightweight, dismountable materials. He is keen to exploit contemporary technology and disapproves of the widespread use of heavy, permanent construction, particularly in high buildings. He has pointed out how seldom architects seem to think, as they build, about how their work could be safely demolished.

Underlying Price's attitudes is a strong political commitment. He has long been a member of the Labour Party, and he dislikes architectural elitism and the production of monuments. Most of the profession, he says, is obsolete and incapable of responding to the needs of our time. Architecture should not be concerned with making statements or sending messages; that is surely the task of newsprint or television. Price's work can be consciously antiaesthetic in its pursuit of expediency. In his Inter-Action Centre, for example, he used temporary huts called Portakabins for part of the accomodation, generating the kind of ad hoc untidiness that most architects strive to avoid!

Price is also a pioneer of the non-building. An ingenious project for a university in Staffordshire, for example, involved the re-use of an abandoned railway with specially adapted carriages for lecture halls, which could move from town to town. Whereas most architects are only too keen to immortalize their thoughts in bricks and mortar. Price seems to strive to avoid doing so; if possible, he finds a solution to the problem that does not actually involve building, and he takes a perverse pride in seeing his works destroyed as they reach the ends of their allotted life-spans.

Price argues vigorously against the production of permanent, specific spaces for particular functions, always stressing the need for flexibility and the unpredictability of future use. He does not take very seriously the need for character and identity in buildings or the danger of disorientation in surroundings that change too frequently—issues that many other architects would put above flexibility and efficiency in use. It seems stangely inconsistent of Price that he acknowledges so fiercely the negative effects of architecture, yet remains so silent about the positive ones.

—Peter Blundell Jones

PROUVÉ, Jean.

French. Born in Paris, 8 April 1901; son of the painter Victor Prouvé. Educated in Nancy, France, until 1916; self-taught in architecture, but trained as a blacksmith and metalworker, under Émile Robert and Szabo, Paris, 1916-23. Served in the French Army, and worked with the Resistance in Nancy, 1940-44: Mayor of Nancy, after the Liberation, 1945. Married Madeleine Schott in 1924; children: Françoise, Claude, Simone, Hélène, and Catherine. Established own metal furniture and fittings workshop, Nancy, France, 1923-40, and in Nancy-Maxéville, 1944-54 (taken over as a pilot factory by the Pechiney Aluminium Company, 1947); Director of the Architectural Department, Compagnie Industrielle de Transport, Paris, 1954-66; in private practice as consultant engineer, in Paris and Nancy, France, 1966 until his death in 1984. Consultant engineer to CNIT and UNESCO, 1957-70. Instructor, Conservatoire National des Arts et Matières, Paris, 1957-71. Founder-member, Union des Artistes Modernes, Paris, 1930; President of the Jury, Centre Beaubourg Competition, Paris, 1971; President, Cercle d'Études Architecturales, Paris, 1971-77; National Commission Member, Foundation for Creative Works, Paris, 1982. Exhibitions: *Exposition des arts décoratifs,* Paris, 1925; World's Fair, Paris, 1937; *Exposition arts ménagers,* Paris, 1948, 1940, 1951, 1952, and 1958; *Exhibition of Applied Arts,* Hannover, West Germany 1951; *Triennale,* Milan, 1951; World's Fair, Brussels, 1958; Pavillon du Marsan, Musée des Arts Décoratifs, Paris, 1964 and 1966; Bern, 1965; Munich, 1965; *Salon des artistes décorateurs,* Paris, 1965; Copenhagen, 1966; *Villagexpo,* Saint-Michel sur Orge, France, 1966; Zürich, 1973; Karlsruhe, West Germany 1976; Geneva, 1977; Vienna, 1977; *Jean Prouvé, constructeur,* Museum Boymans-van Beuningen, Rotterdam, 1981; *Jean Prouvé: l'imagination constructive,* Institut Français d'Architecture, Paris, 1983. Recipient: Diploma of Honour, *Exposition des arts décoratifs,* Paris, 1925; Grand Prix, Cercle d'Étude Architectural, Paris, 1949; Reynolds Aluminium Prize, Le Havre, France, 1962; Prix Auguste Perret, Union Internationale des Architectes, 1963; First Prize, National Ministry of Education Competition, Paris, 1970; Prix Erasme, Paris, 1981; Grand Prix d'Architecture, City of Paris, 1982. Honorary Doctorates: École Polytechnique, Lausanne, Switzerland, 1969; University of Stuttgart, 1976. Member, Académie d'Architecture, France, 1975 (refused inscription, 1980); Honorary Fellow, Royal Institute of British Architects, 1982. Chevalier of the Order of Arts and Letters, France, 1965; Chevalier, 1950, and Officier, 1975, of the Légion d'Honneur, France; Chevalier of L'Étoile d'Anjouan, France, 1952, and of the Order of Leopold, Belgium, 1958. *Died* (in Nancy, France) *23 March 1984.*

Works (as engineer):

1923 Hôtel Thiers doorways, elevators, and ramps, Nancy, France (architect: Charbonnier)

1923/
25 numerous furnishings and interiors, Nancy, France

1925 Pavilion of Nancy doors, Reifenberg Pavilion doors and partitions, and Saint-Jean-de-Luz Casino elevator cages, at the *Exposition des arts décoratifs,* Paris

1929 Marbeuf Garage ramps and balustrades, rue Marbeuf, Paris (architect: Laprade)

1930 Stainless-steel interiors for the steamer Touko-ubia

1931 Musée des Arts Africains grills and railings, Paris (architect: Laprade)

Zoo grids and railings, Vincennes, France (architect: Laprade)

1932 General Government Buildings ironwork and metal fittings, Algiers (architect: Guiouchan)

Jean Prouvé: School Complex, St. Michel-sur-Orge, France, 1967.

1933 Gillet Lafond Building facade, Nancy, France
Cité Universitaire interiors and furniture, Nancy, France
Grange-Blanche Hospital operating theatres and sliding windows, Lyon, France (architects: Tony Garnier, Durand and Faure)
Tower Block metal fittings, Drancy, France (architects: Beaudouin and Lods)
1935 Compagnie Parisienne d'Électricité Offices steel facades and interiors, Paris (architect: Cassan)
Dupont Restaurant windows, doors, and ramps, Paris
Town Hall doors, partitions, and furniture, Boulogne-Billancourt, France (architect: Tony Garnier)
Rolland Garros Aéroclub, Buc, France (architects: Beaudouin and Lods)
1936 Peugeot Agency Building, Paris
Badet Shop frontage, Nancy, France
Railway Waiting-Room furniture, Strasbourg, France
Amos Brewery, Metz, France
1937 Ministry of Posts and Telecommunications folding doors, Paris (architect: Debat-Ponsan)

Portable toilet, World's Fair, Paris (for Le Corbusier and Jeanneret)
UAM Pavilion staircase, World's Fair, Paris (architects: Pingusson, A.J. Louis, and F.P. Jourdain)
Floating studio for fireworks, World's Fair, Paris
1938 Cinévox et Rex Cinema doors, verandahs, and cabins, Strasbourg, France (architect: Pingusson)
Maison du Peuple covered market, Clichy, Paris (architects: Beaudouin and Lods)
Housing Block ramps, staircases, and partitions, Drancy, France (architects: Beaudouin and Lods)
Maternity College bays, Meudon, France (architects: Beaudouin and Lods)
French Embassy metal furniture and fittings, Ottawa, Canada (architect: Beaudouin)
1939 Sédillot Hospital doors and ramps, Nancy, France
Workshop and Office staircases and portable partitions, Arnage, France (architect: Mallet-Stevens)
SCAL Office, Dormitory and Infirmary, Issoire, France (architect: Jeanneret)

Cinéma Marivaux, Luxembourg
French Embassy staircases, Moscow (architect: Beaudouin)
Exhibition screens, bays, partitions, and furniture, New York (architects: Borderel and Robert)
Combat Quarters Complex (800 units), for the 4th and 5th Armies, France
Gas tanks for trucks, France
1940 Carbonisation furnaces, France
"Pyrobal" furnace for low-combustion materials, France
Bicycle chassis, France
1941/
42 Monument railings, Place Stanislaus, Nancy, France
BCC Pavilions, Saint-Auban, France (architect: Jeanneret)
Experimental Centre swing doors and aircraft parts, Béziers, France (architects: Jeanneret and Escorsa)
1943 Meurthe et Moselle Prefecture doors, ramps, windows, and radiator housings, Nancy, France
Regional Police Headquarters, Nancy, France (architect: Bouyon)
Regional Urban Inspectorate, Nancy, France
1944 Lorraine District Housing (800 units) for the Ministry of Reconstruction and Town Planning, France
Fountains and railing repairs, Place Stanislaus, Nancy, France
BNCI Building furnishings, Nancy, France (architect: Michel André)
"Japy" windows, Nancy, France
"Lerebourg" partitions, doors, and metal fittings, Liverdun, France
Dr. Richard house, Vesoul, France
1945 Lorraine Maltworks doors and strongroom, Nancy, France
Cie Lorraine Electricity Works transformer doors and public lighting fitments, Nancy, France
Stofft Factory folding doors, Nancy, France
Daum Shop windows, Nancy, France
Éditions Braun folding doors and furniture, Mulhouse, France (architect: André)
Cie Grandval folding doors, Saint-Cloud, France
1946 Cité Universitaire student quarters, Nancy, France
GEC Company furnishings, Nancy, France
Place de la Carrière restoration, Nancy, France
Professor Capelle Office interiors, Nancy, France
Swiss Consultate interiors, registration desks, and tables, Nancy, France
Vilgrain Mill metal fittings, Nancy, France
Preventorium games room, Flavigny, France
Feburel Factory electrical installations, Jarménil, France
Dr. Bernard worktables, cupboards, and kitchen, Saint-Dié, France
College furnishings, Dieuze, France
Shop interiors, La Bresse, France (architect: Antoine)
La Lingerie de Soie shop interiors, Vittel, France
Colbert Swingbridge control cabin and fittings, Dieppe, France (architect: Teray)
"LMT3" tables, strongrooms, and fittings for the Marine Nationale, France
"Picard" metal garden gates, France
Pavilions, shower-rooms, windows, doors, and facades for the Sincotex Mining Company, France
Panels, doors, distributor-conveyor, and fittings, Dillingen, France
Post Office furniture, partitions, doors, counters, and strongrooms, Brussels
Lardit Factory monumental doors, France (architect: Bourgon)
1947 Saint-Gobain Exhibition Pavilion, Paris

Tobacco Factory interiors, Nancy, France

J.B. Thierry Hospital body-protectors, Nancy, France

Portico House and installations for the Prouve Workshops, Nancy-Maxéville, France

Glassworks Apprenticeship Centre and boarding facilities, Croismare, France (architect: H. Prouvé)

Millhouse grinding rooms, Bourbach le Haut, France (architect: Burcklé)

EDF portable barrage pavilions, Kembs, Ottmarsheim, France

Lesses Textiles pavilions, Vosges, France

Meuse Breweries dispensary pavilions, France

House, Carnac, France

School, Martigues, France (architects: Arati and Boyer)

Pavilion interiors and furniture, La Ferté, France

Pavilion, Dilligen, France

1948 Interiors, at the *Exposition arts ménagers*, Paris

Musée des Arts Décoratifs interiors, Paris

École Polytechnique interiors, Paris

"Ferembal" office interiors and fittings, Nancy, France

Laurent Bouillet Company office interiors, Nancy, France

OuHouse, Pont en Royan, France

Department of Civil Engineering Flight Trials Centre, Brétigny sur Orge, France

MRU demonstration houses, at Noisy le Sec, Château-Salins, Savoie, and Maxéville, France

1949 Château de la Muette portable partitions, for the Organisation Européenne de Coopération, Paris (architect: Démaret)

Vilgrain Mills elevators and metal fittings, Nancy, France (architect: Le Bourgeois)

Foundry and Steelworks Dormitories, Neuves-Maisons, France

Sablons School Complex, Saint-Pierre des Corps, France (architect: Dorian)

"Métropole" and "Coque" housing types for MRU, Meudon, France (architects: H. Prouvé and Sive)

Astronomical Research Institute metal framework, partitions, and strongrooms, Saint-Germain-en-Laye, France (architect: Counlon)

Building Federation facades and sliding windows, Paris (architects: Gravereaux and Lopez)

Unité d'Habitation suspended ceilings, Marseille, France (architect: Le Corbusier)

La Providence doors and sliding shutters, Marseille, France

"Métropole" type housing for the Electricity and Gas Company, Algiers

Exhibition Building interiors, Haiti (architect: Mirabaud)

Pavilion and furniture, Niamey, West Africa

1950 "Meudon" Pavilion type, *Exposition arts ménagers*, Paris

SFR roof laboratory, Paris (architect: Béri)

SFR laboratory doors and bays, Levallois-Perret, France

Cité Radieuse staircases, kitchens, and furnishings, Marseille, France (architect: Le Corbusier)

House for MRU of Rochelle, Royan, France

Mame Factory sheds, offices, and administration buildings, Tours, France (architects: Drieu-Larochelle and Zehrfuss)

School and Town Hall roofing, Saint-Pierre-des-Corps, France

Grand Jardin Lighthouse, Saint-Malo, France

Palais des Expositions and turnstiles, Lille, France (architects: Herbé and Gauthier)

Masurel Factory "TIM" prototype sheds, Tourcoing, France

IPD Office furniture and partitions, Douai, France (architect: Chomette)

Vaucousant Pavilion, Saint-Nicolas, France

School Complex interiors, Bouqueval, France

Haute-Provence Observatory cupolas, France (project; executed by Studal, 1957)

Alumaf ("Métropole") house and conservatory, Algiers

Three "Métropole" houses for E.G.A., Algiers

"Métropole" house for the Solétanche Company, Oran, Algeria

House, Abidjan, Ivory Coast

Two houses for Aluminium Francçais, Brazzaville, Congo

Sometima Pavilion, Brazzaville, Congo

Air France interiors and sundeck, Africa

Houses for ORSON and CFIA, France

1951 Shell-structure house, at the *Exposition arts ménagers*, Paris

OCE Building roofing, windows, and portable partitions, Paris

Franklin-Roosevelt Métro Station interiors, Paris

Salon of the Meridian, for the Obervatory of Paris (architect: Remondet)

Cegedur Building partitions, Avenue Marceau, Paris

Veterinary School partitions, Maison-Alfort, France (architect: Péchin)

Maisons Janicot shell-structure housing, Charenton, France (architect: H. Prouvé)

School, Aubervilliers, France (adapted by Studal)

Astronomical Research Institute folding doors, Saint-Germain-en-Laye, France

Dr. Dollander house facade, Nancy, France (architect: H. Prouvé)

UCMPI Rolling Mills ladies' room, libraries, and partitions, Hagondange, France (architect: Démaret)

House, Saint-Amé, France

Prometheus Monument, Amiens, France

Hospital doorways and operating-theatres, Saint-Lô, France (architect: Nelson)

Casino de la Grande Côte, Royan, France (architect: Ferret)

EDF Centre de Couesque hydroelectric dam doors, Toulouse, France

Dollander Family holiday home, Saint-Clair, France

Experimental School cantilevered bay, Montmorency, France (architect: Beaudouin)

Gas and Electricity Company sundeck, Rabat, Morocco (architect: Lenormand)

Société Générale roofing, sundeck, doors, facades, and public halls, Douala, Cameroon

Ultramarine Research Society house and sundeck, Abidjan, Ivory Coast

SAFIH Hotel facade, sundeck and frontage, Conakry, Guinea (architects: Lagneau and Weill)

National Bank bays and portable sundeck, Libreville, Gabon (architect: Chomette)

Niari Agricultural Society, Libreville, Gabon

EFFIAC doors and bays (for Africa), Paris

Shell-structure house, at the *Applied Arts Exhibition*, Hannover, West Germany

Staircases, doorways, window casements, and panels, at the *Triennale*, Milan

Eight Mobiloil Socony and Shell petrol stations, France

1952 School building, at the *Exposition arts ménagers*, Paris

Boulle College facades, Rue Pierre Bourdan, Paris (architect: Laprade)

Maternity College interiors, Nancy-Placieux, France

Shell petrol station, Épinal, France

School, Saint-Avold, France

Three school complex classrooms, La Chapelle-en-Servai, France

School, Orgeval, France

Department of Social Security facades, bays, and fittings, Le Mans, France (architect: Le

Couteur)

ASR School classrooms and cloister, Lorient, France

League of Teachers shell-structure vacation colony, Melun, France

Denis Pain Company school, Roubaix-Tourcoing, France

Faculty of Law folding partitions, Aix-en-Provence, France

CREPS Company staircase, desks, and amphitheatre seating, Aix-en-Provence, France (architect: Pouillon)

Merlan School facades and sundeck, Marseille, France

Préfecture partitions, Var, France

Gendarmerie Barracks panels, partitions, and doors, Lille, France

Standard Petrol Company shell-structure house, Lille, France

Hospital colony classrooms, desks, and stools, Saint-Brévine, France

Shell Company portable and folding panels, Abidjan, Ivory Coast

Administration Complex partitions and interior fittings, Dakar, Senegal

1953 Musée du Louvre folding doors and radiator housings, Paris

Building facades, Square Mozart, Paris (architect: Mirabaud)

Building facades and doorways, 29 rue Jean de Beauvais, Paris (architects: Herbé and Le Couteur)

Faculty of Medicine amphitheatre seating, Paris

Two school classrooms, Palaiseau, France

School, L'Hay-les-Roses, France

"Ferembal" panels and window casements, Nancy, France

Aéroclub reconstruction, Doncourt, France (architect: Le Corbusier)

Shell-structure school, Aubergenville, France

Festival Hall windows, doors, roofing, and framework, Lunery, France (architect: Sebillotte)

Five HLM houses, Lille, France

Fives-Lille Boys' Apprenticeship Centre roofing, Lille, France

CIL Park residence and two houses, Roubaix-Tourcoing, France (architect: Dubuisson)

Houilleries du Nord colliery library, France

Town Hall facade, Valenciennes, France

Five school classrooms and cloister, Bruxerolles, France

Mame Factory headquarters building, winter garden, and office for M. Mame, Tours, France (architect: Zehrfuss)

Postal Order Centre facade, Rennes, France

Préfecture facades, partitions, window panels, and doors, Nevers, France (architect: Robert)

SFR electronics factory, Saint-Egrève, France (architect: Gutton)

Mayoral School classrooms, cloister, and shell-roofing, Valence, France

Centre Dora facades, Marseille, France

Préfecture du Var panels and doors, Draguignan, France

City Administration Office facades and portable partitions, Bayonne, France

Lopez House interiors, Guerreville, France (architect: Lopez)

Merlin Gérin portable transformer prototype, Grenoble, France

Europe no. 1 Television Station facades and shell-structures, Monaco (architect: Notari)

School furniture and bays, at the Zürich Exposition, Switzerland

Austerlitz Railway Station platform shelter, Paris (project; executed by Studal, 1957)

1954 Centenary of Aluminium Pavilion, Paris (with Michel Hugonet)

Cité Universitaire interiors, Antony, France (architect: Beaudouin)

Seven school classrooms, Saint-Denis, France (architect: Lurçat)

Ten school classrooms, Mesnil-le-Roi, France (architect: Lopez)

School complex, Le Blanc-Mesnil, France (architect: Lurçat)

Jean Prouvé House, Nancy, France

School, Saint-Dié, France

Seven school classrooms, Custines, France

Four school classrooms, Genneville, France

H.L.M. woodland quarter, Lille, France

Housing Complex facades, Saint-Étienne, France (architect: Zehrfuss)

Housing Complex metal fittings, Saint-Jean-de-Maurienne, France (architect: Blanc)

Housing panels shutters and coverings, Froges, France (architect: Blanc)

Library, Marseille, France (architect: Pouillon)

Tobacco Factory sundeck, Marseille, France

Church fitments, Morsang sur Orge, France (architect: Fauraud)

Air France complex facades, Dakar, Senegal

1955 Institut des Pétroles, Rueil-Malmaison, France (as consultant)

1956 CNIT windows, Rond-Point de la Défense, Paris (architects: Camelot, Zehrfuss, and de Mailly)

Abbot Pierre house interiors, Pont Alexandre III, Paris

Source Cachat pump-room, Évian, France (architect: Novarina)

Avicole Buildings, Aix-en-Provence, France (executed by Goumy)

1957 Temporary Buildings, Villejuif, France

Renault Company reception hall, Flins, France (architect: Zehrfuss)

HLM housing development, Le Blanc-Mesnil, France (architect: Candilis)

Small portable churches, Forbach, France (executed by Goumy)

1958 "Sahara" housing, at the *Exposition arts ménagers*, Paris (with SETTAP and Charlotte Perriand)

Institut des Pétroles amphitheatre seating, Rueil-Malmaison, France

Roclaine Factory interiors, Saint-Étienne-du-Rouvray, France (architect: Gillet)

School, Bagnols-sur-Cèze, France (architects: Badani and Roux-Dorlut)

France and Luxembourg Pavilions, World's Fair, Brussels (with Gillet and Maillet)

1961 CNET Pavilion, Cachan, France (architect: Abraham)

Service Station, Bron-Parilly, France (architect: Gagès)

Berliet Experimental Centre, Saint-Priest, France (architect: Bornarel)

Library, Chemistry, Natural Science, and Nuclear Physics buildings, Faculty of Sciences, Lyon, France (architect: Perrin-Fayolle)

Sograph Offices, Grenoble, France (architect: Blanc)

Isotopic Separation Works, Pierrelatte, France

National School of Teacher Training, Le Havre, France (architect: Zehrfuss)

Rothschild covered swimming-pool, rue de l'Élysée, Paris (architect: de Galea)

Workers' housing prototypes, Pointe-Noire, France (architects: Lagneau and Weill)

Cantebonne Parish Centre, for the Micheville Steelworks, Villerupt, France

1962 Museum and Cultural Centre, Le Havre, France (architects: Lagneau and Weill)

Dr. Gauthier House, Saint-Dié, France

EDF Centre, Saint-George de Commiers, France (architect: Cholat)

Les Huiles Building for Berliet, Saint-Briest, France (architect: Bornarel)

Saint-Irénée Residence Building, University of Lyon, France (architect: Perrin-Fayolle)

La Madeleine Restaurant, University of Lyon, France (architect: Gagès)

Tennis Club, Lyon, France (architect: Perrin-Fayolle)

Merlin-Gérin Offices, Grenoble, France (architects: Pivot and Junillon)

La Dullage Cité Scolaire, Béziers, France (architects: Badani and Roux-Dorlut)

Mme. Seynave House, Beauvallon, France (architects: Hutchinson, Sauzet and Vilfour)

1963 Cité Universitaire Protestant Centre, Paris (architect: Le Caisne)

CIMT Social Welfare Building, Neuilly, France (architect: Deschler)

Church, L'Hay-les-Roses, France (architect: Picot)

Saint-Joseph Institute, Nancy, France (architects: Louis and André)

Haut-du-Lièvre Parish Centre, Nancy, France (architect: Louis)

Parish Centre, Cantebonne, France

Les Renardières Experimental Centre facades, Moret/Loing, France (architect: Le Couteur)

SNCF Railway Station, Orléans, France (architect: Hourlier)

Cité Universitaire residence and restaurant, Lyon, France (architects: Gagès and Villard)

Cité Scolaire Complex, Nevers, France (architects: Dufau and Robert)

Kronenbourg Brewery, Pointe-Noire, France

1964 Pavilion, Parc des Floralies, Orléans la Source, France

1965 Children's Nursery, Argenteuil, France (architects: Perottet and Deroche)

Two Pavilions, Parc des Floralies, Orléans la Source, France

CES Buildings, at Saint-Egrève, Grenoble, Le Vans, Bressuire, and Flavergnes, France (architects: Silvy, Belmont and Periller)

University Residences, Nanterre-la-Folie, France

Convent of the Clarisses, Poitiers, France (architect: Woods)

1966 Sports Centre facades, Saint-Maur-des-Fossés, France (architect: Madeline)

Paul Eluard School Complex, Argenteuil, France (architect: Dubrulle)

Two houses, "Tabouret" School, and Reception Hall, at *Villagexpo*, Saint-Michel-sur-Orge, France

Two houses at the Air France Centre, Arbonne, France

College, La Ferté-Bernard, France (architect: Barbé)

New Town Hall facades, Grenoble, France (architect: Novarina)

1967 Nobel Tower curtain-walls, Puteaux, France (architect: de Mailly Depusset)

Youth Club, Ermont, France

1968 Institute of Fisheries, Nantes, France

Palace of the Fair of Grenoble, France

College and Pavilion, Orléans la Source, France (architects: Andrault and Parat)

Autoroute petrol stations for Total France

New University, Berlin (architects: Candilis, Josic and Woods)

Institute of the Environment, Paris (architect: Joly)

Unesco Building V, Paris

Administration Offices, Le Vaudreuil new town, France

1970 Sandoz-France Laboratories, Rueil-Malmaison, France (architect: Zehrfuss)

Reimcourt Architectural School, Nancy, France (architect: Foliasson)

Mme. Jaoul House, Minguerin, France (architects: J.C. and C. Drouin)

Marne-La—Vallée Administration Buildings, Noisiel, France

Administration Offices, Melun-Sénart new town, France

1971 CAF Mountain Refuge, Les Evettes, France

(architects: Rey and Millet)

Faculty Buildings, Lyon-Bron, France (architect: Detcoud)

Faculty of Medicine, Rotterdam (architects: Choisy, Van Embden, Van Esinga, Roorda and Smelt)

1972 Polyester panels for the Matra company, France

University of Bron-Parilly, Lyon, France (architect: Dollander)

Secretariat-General for New Towns, Paris (architects: G. Autran and M. Macary)

1973 School, Trappes, France (architect: Merlin)

Alpes-Congres Building, Grenoble, France (architect: Claude Prouvé)

1974 Main Railway Station, Lyon-Perrache, France (architect: Gagès)

1976/
82 Works at the Forum des Halles, Paris

Works at the Vélodrome de Bercy, Paris

Works in the Quartier de l'Horloge, Paris

Lescot Buildings, Paris (architect: Willerval)

1981 Hertz Tower, Ouessant, France

Publications:

By PROUVÉ: articles—"L'Habitation de notre époque," edited by Colin Davidson, in *Architectural Association Journal*(London), December 1965; "Auguste Perret," with Vittorio Gregotti, in *Domus*(Milan), May 1974.

On PROUVÉ: *Industrial Architecture* by Benedikt Huber and Jean Claude Steineggar, Zürich and London 1971; *Jean Prouvé: Aspects of Innovation*, thesis by C. J. Mellor, University of Liverpool, 1978; *Jean Prouvé, constructeur*, exhibition catalogue, by W. A. L. Beeren, Jan van Geest, E. W. Kanthaus and others, Rotterdam and Delft, Netherlands, 1981; *Jean Prové: l'idée constructive* by Dominique Clayssen, Paris 1983; articles—"Jean Prouvé," special number of *Architecture* (Brussels), December 1954; "Jean Prouvé" in *Esthétique industrielle* (Paris), January/February 1957; "Jean Prouvé by Françoise Choay in *L'Oeil* (Paris), no. 46, 1958; "Jean Prouvé" by G. Gassiot-Talabot in *Cimaise* (Paris), no. 54, 1961; article in *Architectural Review* (London), August 1966; article in *Architectural Design* (London), February 1967; "The Future of Structures: Robert Le Ricolais, Jean Prouvé and René Sanger interviewed by Marie-Therese Mathieu" in *Recherches et architecture* (Paris), no. 10, 1973; "Foster, Prouvé and Loos in Paris" by Martin K. Meade in *Architects' Journal* (London) 9 March 1983; "The Great Tinsmith Jean Prouvé by François Chaslin in *Rassegna* (Milan), June 1983; "Jean Prouvé: Architect-Mechanic" by Michel Verres in *Architectural Review* (London), July 1983; "Prouvé Modern Movement Pioneer" by Nigel Newton in *Building Design* (London), 30 March 1984; "Obituary: M. Jean Prouvé" in *The Times* (London), 6 April 1984. films—*La Maison des jours meilleurs* by Jean Le Lardais, 1956; *Jean Prouvé, Constructeur* by Nadine Descendre and Guy Olivier, 1982.

Where have we got to with the industrialization of building (a subject on which we never stop talking)? Should we not, having stumbled about for nearly thirty years, take a new leap and finally find ourselves in front, this time, with the obstacles behind us? Really, the buildings of our time, small and large, industrial or commercial, are not on the whole as yet "of age." As for myself, I find only rarely that they harmonize with the other industrial productions of our time. They are too diffuse.

In fact, I do not know of any factory that is building, in large quantities, "conditioned" building elements which, benefiting from the industrial economic miracle of our time, could be used by all the specialists, architects, entrepreneurs, and eventually by the users.

I shall try to explain what I mean. I think we must take stock of the position—ask ourselves the question, "where are we?" Certainly, there is an architecture being built that we can call "modern"; let's say that it is contemporary. Most of us are agreed that it does not, on the whole, provoke the same architectural experience as that felt by people in front of the great ensembles of the past; that is undeniable. Would the reason not be a lack of courage in our use of the new materials that mechanization has put at our disposal? Is there not, too a deficiency of architectural inspiration in relation to these means?

It is important—and honest—to note that, amongst the mass productions of contemporary architecture, there are exceptions, exceptional, striking works—but, one must recognize, they are perhaps too particular. These works are deceptive in the extent to which they involve a spirit of industrialization, for they come from an execution that is only 'semi—industrial"; they involve the fabrication of a limited number of pieces. They are nothing more—for these unique works want to be personalized and signed.

Some think that this kind of peculiarity and diversity is desirable, but personally I think that it leads to disorder. We note that the old and admired architectural entities were often very uniform. That's a troubling thought. Industrialists are confused because, for the "personalities" of architecture, they are obliged to study and adapt continuously. The Master Builders, who are tempted to evolve, often make industrialists suffer by their personal demands, demands that are often inappropriate to the materials chosen. Such tasks are superhuman and cruel both to men and tools. Prices, too, are very high. And it happens that certain clever artisans, capable of improvisation, complete with the industrialists.

In fact, one has to be very competent to know, for example, what it is possible to obtain simply from a tipper press. It is only when one uses the press as a starting point that constructive inspiration can happen. To know how to take advantage of simplicity is, of course, not easy. But, in my opinion, everything stems from that. Any torment or any exploitation imposed on a basic material and in consequence on machines is economically indefensible.

Yet we must industrialize; we really have no choice. And, in my opinion, as an old practitioner, we must:

1) Bring architects closer to manufacturing. That will probably lead them to specialize, perhaps to integrate—but why not? Action at the heart of an innovative industry can be very exciting;

2) Imagine buildings as composed of elements, because the present way of manufacture is useless; it involves new materials being put to use in a traditional manner;

3) Use the elements as a starting point, from which all sorts of possible variations will come to mind— and those variations will in turn become new elements.

This process will lead to a worthwhile industrialization. The construction of motor cars—is that not the best example of what I mean? We owe the rationalization and the simplicity of the motor car to the recognition by the constructor of that which is technically possible. The same is now true for works of art, even for household items. Shall we remain incapable of perception in regard to that which is the framework of our lives—our accommodation? Is it not depressing that, in regard to that subject, a return to the past is now being advocated? what a failure that would be!

—Jean Prouvé (1980)

For sixty years, Jean Prouvé was the major figure in using industrial techniques in building. His especial love was for thin sheets of metal, formed and crimped

to give them strength. Prouvé usually worked closely and constructively with architects, but he was not an architect himself and was, in fact, critical of the profession of architecture, believing that the separation of designer and producer is one of the reasons for the low standard, both of design and construction, prevalent today.

During his long and diligent working life, Prouvé was an opportunist, taking the jobs that came, innovating and evolving where he could, often compromising and doing the ordinary where necessary for the continuity of his business. Two moments of this working life seem to be peaks when Prouvé was in the forefront of thought and development in architecture and building technology.

The first high spot in Prouvé's career was in the late 1930s when he built a series of buildings with the architects Beaudouin and Lods. Their Roland Garros Club for flying enthusiasts is a fair claimant to being the first totally indistrialized building— walls, roof, floors, ramp, and so forth were all pressed metal in this amazing building. The architects of the modern movement at that time were anxious to give their buildings a machine-made look, and machine-made elements, such as windows, were become normal, but no one else was going all the way and making the whole building an industrially designed and produced object. Destruction in the war probably prevented the Buc building from becoming a seminal twentieth-century building. A few years later, again with Beaudouin and Lods and this time also with Bodiansky, Prouvé built the Maison du Peuple in the Paris suburb of Clichy. It was a sizeable building with large moving parts—the 2,000 seat auditorium had floor, walls and roof that moved at the press of a button to change the space or to open it to the sky—and all was wrapped in an ingenious curtain wall of stressed skin panels held apart by coil springs. Forty years of weathering have not dealt kindly with the Maison du Peuple, for the weathering problems were not all solved, and the building has not had the sympathetic maintenance that it needed.

The second peak in Prouvé's career occurred in the 1960s with a series of single-storey, pressed-metal buildings. Workshops for the French atomic energy scientists at Pierrelatte, a holiday village for Air France at Fontainebleau, an exhibition village at St Michel-sur-Orge, and many other structures stand as evidence of a well-thought-out way of building in light, pressed metal. It is the way that these buildings are worked out with finess in every detail that impresses.

It may well be that Prouvé's prime importance was that he nagged at the consciences of architects everywhere. No one can say of industrialized building that it cannot be done, for Prouvé has done it. He has not adapted building to machine processes; he has worked it all out from scratch as if no one had ever built a building before. He has shown us all that there is a real alternative to the building construction that we have inherited from the middle ages. Through PROUVÉ, we can see that there is the alternative tradition of industrial design and industrial production. His single-minded, life-long dedication produced some tangible results, but the road is too hard for there to be many following the way that he was treading.

—John Winter

PRUS, Victor.
Canadian. Born in Poland, 24 April 1917; emigrated to England, 1940; emigrated to Canada, 1952; naturalized, 1957. Educated at the Technical University, Warsaw, 1935-39, Diploma 1939; University of Liverpool School of Architecture, 1945-47, Dip.Ing. Arch. 1947. Served as a Flying Officer in the Royal

Air Force, in the Middle East and Great Britain, 1940-45; Polish Cross of Valour (twice). Married the architect Maria Fisz in 1948. Assistant professor, Polish University College, London, 1947-50; Senior Executive Officer, *Festival of Britain,* London, 1949-51; Partner, with George Scolly, Prus and Scolly, Architects, London, 1950-52; Associate, V. Rother and Associates, Montreal, 1952-54; Assistant to Buckminster Fuller, Princeton University, New Jersey, 1953. Principal, Victor Prus, Architect, Montreal, 1954-70, and Victor Prus and Associates, Montreal, since 1970 (associates: Maria Prus; Jean Gareau). Visiting Professor, McGill University, Montreal, 1953, 1966, 1972; Professor, Ecole d'Architecture, Quebec, 1959; Visiting Professor, Graduate School of Architecture, Washington University, St. Louis, Missouri, 1978. Member, Canadian Housing Design Council, 1973-1974. Exhibitions: Victoria and Albert Museum, London, 1950; Montreal Museum of Fine Arts, 1958, 1960, 1963; Musée du Québec, 1964; Canadian Education Showplace, Totonto, 1968; Royal Canadian Academy, 1972; National Gallery of Canada, Ottawa, 1977; Place Desjardins, Montreal, 1978. Recipient: Massey Medal for Architecture, 1963; First Prize, Quebec Centennial Competition, 1964; First Prize, Royal Canadian Air Force Memorial Competition, 1969; First Prize, Montreal Congrès Centre Competition, 1978. Fellow, Royal Architectural Institute of Canada, 1968; Academician, Royal Canadian Academy, 1972; Member, Order of Architects of Quebec; Member, Town Planning Institute of Canada; Member, Corporation of Urbanists of Quebec. Honorary Fellow, American Institute of Architects, 1977. Address: Victor Prus and Associates, 1420 Sherbrooke Street West, Suite 301, Montreal, Quebec H3G 1K5 Canada.

Works:

1950   Public House, London (competition project; with Ernst Pollak)
1951   Display design, Physical World Exhibition, H.M.S. Campania, and Shipbuilding Section, Sea and Ships, Pavilion, *Festival of Britain,* London
1952   Office building, Jidda, Saudi Arabia (with G. Scolly)
1954   Webster House, Maitland, Ontario
1955   Public school, Lyn, Ontario
1956   Public school, Montague, Ontario
         Recreation centre, Kaplan, Louisiana (with N. Nehrbass)
1957   Experimental farm, Baton Rouge, Louisiana (with N. Nehrbass)
         Bowen House, Cornwall, Ontario
         Country club, Massena, New York (with Norval White)
1958   Lighter House Westmount, Montreal
1959   McLeod House, Brockville, Ontario
         Strub House, Beaurepaire, Quebec
1960   Rockland Shopping Centre, Mount Royal, Montreal (with I. Martin)
         Yacht Club, Senneville, Quebec
1961   Normandie Shopping Centre, Montreal (with I. Martin)
1962   Savoie Apartment Building, Westmount, Montreal
         Master Plan for Nuns' Island, Montreal (with Norbert Schoenauer)
         Polar Bear Zoo Enclosure, Granby, Quebec (with Buckminster Fuller)
1963   Hodgson House, Mount Tremblant, Quebec
1964   Centre Simard, Lac à l'Eau Claire, Quebec (project)
1966   Mount Royal Metro Station, Montreal
         Metro Bonaventure Terminus Complex, Mon-
1967   *Expo '67* Stadium Montreal
         Place Longueuil Civic and Shopping Centre, Longueuil, Quebec
1968   St. Augustin's Church, St. Bruno, Quebec
         James Lyng Polyvalent School, Montreal

Victor Prus: Metro Bonaventure Terminus Complex, Montreal, 1966.

1969 Royal Canadian Air Force Memorial Complex, Trenton, Ontario (competition project)
1970 Brudenell River Resort, Prince Edward Island
1971 Langelier Metro Station, Montreal
 Grand Théâtre de Québec City
1972 Conservatory of Music, Quebec City
1973 Molson House, Mount Tremblant, Quebec
1975 Centaur Theatres One and Two, Montreal
1977 Canada/France Astronomical Observatory, Mauna Kea, Hawaii
 National Gallery of Canada, Ottawa (competition project)
1978 Astronomical Observatory, Mount Megantic, Quebec
1979 Grantley Adams International Airport, Barbados, West Indies
1982 Place Longueuil, phase II, Montreal
1983 Palais de Congrès, Montreal

Publications:

By PRUS: papers—*Architecture et Terre des Hommes*, Montreal 1964; *Architecture and Human Ecology*, Montreal 1966; *The Role of the Arts in Contemporary Society*, Montreal 1967; *Two Theatres*, Urbana, Illinois 1970; *Architecture of Little Presence*, St. Louis 1975; *Theatre in North America*, Adelaide, South Australia 1975; *Architecture at the Service of the Community Theatre*, Adelaide, South Australia 1975; *Architecture of Condition: Heuristic Approach to Design*, St. Louis 1978; articles—"The Place of Shopping Centres in the City Today" in *Canadian Architect* (Toronto), February 1960; "On Subterranean Architecture" in *Canadian Architect* (Toronto), April 1963; "Metro Architecture" in *Architectural Design* (London), July 1967; "Expo Stadium in Retrospect" in *Architecture Canada* (Ottawa), April 1970; "Un Immeuble à la Mesure du Québec" in *Culture Vivante* (Quebec), May 1970; "Competitions for Canada" in *Review* (Toronto), Spring 1977.

On PRUS: books—*Three Centuries of Achitecture in Canada* by John Bland, Ottawa 1971; *Canadian Architecture 1960-1970* by Carol Moore Ede, Toronto 1971; *Pedestrian Revolution: Streets Without Cars* by Simon Breines, New York 1974; *Barbados Airport* by Mary Hall, Montreal 1978; *Montreal in Evolution* by Jean-Claude Marsan, Montreal 1981; *Contemporary Canadian Architecture* by W. Bernstein and R. Cawker, New York 1982; *Modern Canadian Architecture* by Leon Whiteson, Edmonton, Alberta 1983; *Twelve Proposals for the National Gallery of Canada and for the National Museum of Man*, edited by Odile Hénault, Montreal 1984; articles—"Public House Design" in *The Times* (London) 5 April 1950; "Pub Competition" in *Architectural Review* (London) April 1950; "Rockland Shopping Centre" in *Canadian Architect* (Toronto), February 1960; "Stadium for Expo '67" in *Architectural Design* (London), April 1967; "Two Subways" by Donald Canty in *Urban America* (Washington, D.C.), November 1967; "James Lyng School" in *Canadian Architect* (Toronto), January 1968; "Prus Wins RCAF Competition" in *Architecture Canada* (Ottawa), September 1969; "Le Grand Théâtre by Jacob Siskind in *The Gazette* (Montreal), 16 January 1971; "What's Up in Quebec's New Theatre" by Eric McLean in *The Montreal Star*, 23 January 1971; "Le Grand Théâtre de Québec" by André Blouin in *Vie des Arts* (Montreal), Summer 1971; "Brudenell Park" by J.A. Murray and others in *Canadian Architect* (Toronto), December 1971; "The House of the Five Pavilions" by Dan MacMasters in the *Los Angeles Times*, 28 April 1974; "Architects Praise Towns" by Patricia Lowe in the *Montreal Star*, 24 October 1974; "National Gallery Competition" in *Canadian Architect* (Toronto), April 1977; "Un Palais des Congrès sortant de l'ordinaire pour Montréal" by Marc Castro in *Bâtiment* (Montreal), October 1978; "Winning

Entry: Competition for Convention Centre, Montréal" in *Canadian Architect* (Toronto), February/March 1979; "Brudenell River Provincial Bank, Prince Edward Island" in *Canadian Architect* (Toronto), September 1979; "The 1976-77 Competition for the National Gallery of Canada" by Ruth Cawker in *Section A* (Montreal), June 1983; "Le Palais de Congrès de Montréal" by René Ferron in *Forces* (Montreal), no. 63, 1983; "The National Museum of Man" in *Section A* (Montreal), August 1984; "Palais de Congrès de Montréal" in *Canadian Architect* (Toronto), November 1984; films—*Dossier,* CBC television film, 1972; *A Modern Country* by T. Jaworski and L. Whiteson, 1984.

The reality of architecture lies not in the walls, the roof nor even in the spaces they enclose but rather in the ambience that results from the entire complex process. Such ambiences is subjectively perceived by the user and it must be our ultimate objective—as surely as making a home is the object of building a house. The form is merely a medium: it proceeds from a particular desire for a particular ambience.

Ambience is the abstract quality of condition, and I believe in architecture of condition rather than in architecture as a rhetorical statement or as an object of synthesis. Perhaps one can talk of the language of form, but it is preposterous to talk of the language of architecture. Our affectivity is pre-discursive: ambience affects us totally and at once. It is in such experience of architecture that its meaning resides.

But apprehension of meaning is often difficult in this post-modern frantic scramble for attention. The over-use of extravagant form places an impossible strain on the already over-taxed human sensibility. In this context the architecture of condition must be the architecture of moderate presence: neither stunning to the senses nor boggling to the mind but acceptive, inclusive and accountable.

—Victor Prus

Orthodox modern archiecture grew out of the teachings and practice of the Bauhaus in the 1920s. It was a revolutionary ideology based on a doctrine of moral integrity, rationalism, social relevance and puritanism. The movement came to flower during the post-war years, and like most pioneering movements, it overlooked, in its zeal, many of the important issues of architecture.

Victor Prus entered the architectural mainstream during the early 1950s, and except for a brief period of work in England, his professional life has centered in Ontario and Quebec.

Ideologically, his work often diverges from the accepted canons of modern architecture, insofar as he shifts the emphasis from traditional concerns of programme and construction techniques to expressional and humanitarian considerations. This does not mean that Prus's architecture is not contemporary. Quite the contrary, it attempts to fill a void by introducing extrinsic questions. Prus sees architecture as an intermediary process. He refers to his architecture as an "Architecture of Condition," one that finds its meaning in experience rather than expedience. Condition is the provision, or the prerequisite, for the occurence and the actualization of an *ambiance;* and *ambiance* is the abstract quality of condition which, for Prus, is the ultimate reality of architecture.

It is this pre-occupation that has created different attitudes and design expectations in his architecture. By rejecting the ultimate authority of programme, Prus accepts architecture as an act both subjective and objective, an interplay between intuition and reason. His architecture is one of accommodation, one that is willing to address itself to conflicting requirements without diffidence.

In the Grand Theatre de Quebec, two opposing objectives merge; the relationship of internal spacial considerations and contextual issues. Thus, the design strives to create an *ambiance* of illusion in which the spectator reacts to a continuum of experiences during the time-lapse of a journey through the theatre. At the same time, the design lets itself be governed by a powerful, if somewhat traditional, urbanistic consideration, namely, that the building becomes a visual focal point for the neighborhood. The result is a rich interior environment, dressed in a formal and very polite vestment. It is, what Venturi refers to, an "Architecture of Complexity and Contradiction."

In a similar manner, contradiction and opposition are acknowledged and used successfully in the design of the Montreal Congrès Centre. The building, an oblong, straddles a sunken exposed expressway in a longitudinal manner. The roadway separates two natural and very different zones of the city. Relating to each zone on its own terms, Prus produced a building with two totally different elevations, making his architectural integration a sympathetic graft in the urban tissue.

In the Royal Canadian Air Force Memorial Complex, Prus explores the possibility of superimposing varying *ambiances,* related to different spacial or movement conditions of the observer. The design recognizes three totally different, but equally important, levels of perception: from the air, from a motoring passer-by, and from a visitor on foot. Prus meets his objectives by making the building a landscape-form in which scale and form are perceived differently, depending upon the space-time relationship of the observer.

Whereas the French tradition of the Beaux Arts regarded the *plan* as the indispensable basis of architectural composition, Prus employs the *section* as his principal compositional tool. The Grand Theatre de Quebec, James Lyng Polyvalent School in Montreal, the Bonaventure Subway Station in Montreal, and the Grantley Adams International Airport in Barbados, all tell their story most clearly in their cross-sections, which disclose not only the formal substance of the design, but the hierarchical organization of space, the principal nodal points, the circulation lines and the structure.

It is difficult to sum up the work of Victor Prus. Unlike Rudolph or Mies, there is no neat chain of sequential events in which each part is developed or derived from the preceding one; there is no obvious chronology; there are no conspicuous common denominators. There is, however, a common concern and a consistency in attitude.

Prus's buildings are generally microcosmic statements of urbanism, in that they deal with interrelationships of scales, conflicts, and functions. They are structured around hierarchical principles of order and priorities. Prus is not a formalist. He is not a designer of beautiful objects, per se, nor is he a confirmed rationalist. He does not follow the credo that form is absolutely decided by its fulfilling function. Although he is a contemporary architect, he is not an avid camp-follower of the modern movement.

The architecture of Victor Prus is one of refinement, classical order, and is controlled by a sense of formal appropriateness. His architecture is a premeditative act striving for complete physical and psychological meaning.

—Adrian Sheppard

QUARONI, Ludovico.

Italian. Born in Rome, 28 March 1911. Educated at the University of Rome School of Architecture, 1928-34, Dip. Arch. 1934, and School of Town Planning, 1934-35. Served as a Lieutenant in the Italian Army, 1938-46: prisoner-of-war in India, 1941-46. Married Marcella Coromaldi in 1946; daughter: Sofia; married Gabriella Esposito in 1973; son: Massimiliano. Since 1935, in private practice, Rome. Assistant to Professor Del Dobbio, 1937, and to Marcello Piacentini, 1938, Faculty of Architecture, University of Rome; Professor of Town Planning, University of Rome and University of Naples, 1949-54; Professor of Planning, University of Florence, 1955-65. Professor of Architectural Composition, University of Rome School of Architecture, since 1964. Member, Advisory Board for Public Works, Rome; Member, Advisory Board, Academy of Fine Art, Rome; Vice-Chairman, Istituto Nazionale di Urbanistica. Exhibitions: *Italian Architecture of the Sixties,* toured Italy and Iran, 1972; *Utopia e crisi dell'antinatura* at the *Biennale,* Venice, 1978; *Architetture italiane degli anni '70,* Galleria Nazionale d'Arte Moderna, Rome, 1981. Recipient: Olivetti Prize for Planning, 1956; First Prize, with others, Turin Master Plan Competition, 1962; First Prize, with others, Government Office Building Competition, Rome, 1965. Member, Accademia Nazionale di San Luca, Rome, 1972. Address: Studio Quaroni, Via I. Nievo 61, 00153 Rome, Italy.

Works:

1934 Foreign Ministry Building, Rome (diploma project)
1935 Marine Colony, Riccione, Italy (competition project; with S. Donnini, B. Funaro, G. Roisecco, and F. Uras)
 Auditorium Building, Rome (competition project; with B. Fariello and S. Muratori)
 Heliotherapy Complex, Vercelli, Italy (competition project; with S. Donnini, B. Funaro, G. Roisecco, and F. Uras)
1936 Redevelopment Plan, Aprilia, Italy (competition project; with F. Fariello, S. Muratori, and E. Tedeschi)
 Group of small villas in the Gaeta region, Latina, Italy
 New Courthouse Complex, Rome (competition project; with S. Muratori)
 Regional Government Buildings, Livorno, Italy (competition project; with V. Colasanti, F. Fariello, and S. Muratori)
 Architettura attuale e la tradizione italiana exhibition layouts, Rome (with M. Piacentini)
 Doctor's Surgery, at the *Mostra dell'-Abitazione,* Rome (with G. Calza-Bini, V. Monaco, S. Muratori, F. Petrucci, and E. Tedeschi)
1937 Cassa Nazionale Malattie Headquarters, Rome (competition project; with E. Fuselli)

Palace of Art, Colle Oppio, Rome (project; with S. Muratori)
 Auditorium Development Plan, Villa Borghese, Rome (project; with F. Fariello and S. Muratori)
 Customs Buildings for the Alpine Passes (competition project; with F. Fariello, S. Muratori, and E. Tedeschi)
 Furniture Exhibition layouts, Fiera dell'Artigianato, Florence (project)
 Church and staging for an open-air mass, Foro Mussolini, Rome (project)
 Piazza della Nuova Stazione urban plan, Ostia Lido, Rome (with E. Fuselli)
 Monument to Don Jose Urquiza, Buenos Aires (competition project; with the sculptor F. Prati)
 Four room layouts, *Mostra Augustea della Romanita,* Rome (with V. Colasanti)
 Monument to Fallen Academicians, Foro Mussolini, Rome (project)
 Reception and Congress Building, EUR, Rome (competition project; with F. Fariello and S. Muratori)
1938 Piazza Imperiale, EUR, Rome (competition project; with F. Fariello and S. Muratori)
 Connecting Arterial Road from the Piazza Barberini to the Corso del Rinascimento, Rome (project; with G. Quaroni)
 Small Villa at Porto San Stefano, Grosseto, Italy
 Piazza Imperiale, Rome (executive project; with F. Fariello, S. Muratori, and L. Moretti)
 Palace of Ancient Art, and Palace of Modern Art, Rome (with F. Fariello and S. Muratori)
 Pavilion of Aluminium, *Mostra autarchica del minerale italiano,* Circo Massimo, Rome (with F. Fariello and S. Muratori)
 Sindacato Ingegneri exhibit layouts, *Mostra storica della bonifica meccanica,* Circo Massimo, Rome
 Sindacato Tecnici Agricoli, and Credito Agrario di Miglioramento exhibit layouts, *Mostra della bonifica integrale,* Circo Massimo, Rome
 Apartment Building, Piazza Istria, Rome
1939 Foresteria Building (conversion of exhibition pavilion), Circo Massimo, Rome
 City Redevelopment Plan, Galliate, Novara, Italy (competition project; with P. Airoldi)
 Luxury Villa, *Mostra dell'abitazione,* EUR, Rome
1940 City Redevelopment Plan, Biella, Italy (competition project; with A. Della Rocca and E. Lentini)
 Apartment extensions, Lungotevere degli Altivoti, Rome
 City Redevelopment Plan, Palermo, Sicily (competition project; with P. Airoldi, L. Racheli, G. Sterbini, and E. Lentini)
 Architecture exhibit layouts (3 sections), *VII Triennale,* Milan (with M. Piacentini)
 Ancient Peoples exhibit layouts, *Mostra della*

razza, Rome (with G. Marabotto)
1942 Small Villa, Cairate, Varese, Italy (project)
 Textile Factory, Brianza, Italy (project)
 Villa on the Ligurian Coast, Italy (project)
 Palazzo with Villas, Parioli, Rome (project)
1943 Votive Chapel, Cemetery of Clement-Town, India
 Shri Madhao Archway and Tower, Main Bazaar Square, Dewas, India
 New Industrial Centre and industrial zone plan, Dewas, India
 Access Road Development, Dewas, India
 Royal Residence Development, Dewas, India
1945 Villa on the Coast, Rapallo, Genoa, Italy (project)
1946 Railway Workers' Housing Development, Rome (with S. Garroni)
1947 Low-cost housing, San Rocco, Potenza, Italy (competition project; with S. Garroni)
 Low-cost housing, via Arecenza, Potenza, Italy (competition project; with S. Garroni)
 Railway Workshops, New Roma Termini Station, Rome (competition project; with M. Ridolfi, A. Cardelli, M. Fiorentino, A. Care, and G. Ceradini)
 New Parish Church, Prenestino, Italy (project; with G. Quaroni)
 Housing types for San Basilio, Rome (competition project; with M. Coromaldi and M. Fiorentino)
1948/
 58 Church of Santa Maria Maggiore (later San Franco), Francavilla a Mare, Italy
1949 Provisional Headquarters for the Council of Europe, Strasbourg, France
 Institute of Art, Rome (project; with M. Valori)
1950 Housing development, Tiburtino Quarter, Rome (with Carlo Aymonino)
1951 La Martella Housing Development, Matera, Italy (with M. Agati, F. Gorio, P. M. Lugli, and M. Valori)
 House, Via Innocenzo X, Rome (with Carlo Aymonino)
1952 La Martella Church, Matera, Italy
 Master plan for Ivrea, Italy (with A. Fiocchi, E. Ranieri, and N. Renacco)
1955 Master plan for the Canton Vesco, Ivrea, Italy
 School, Canton Vesco, Ivrea, Italy (with A. De Carlo)
1956 Master plan for Ravenna (with A. De Carlo, G. Salmoni, and P. L. Giordani)
 Church of the Holy Family, Genoa (with A. De Carlo, A. Mor, and A. Sibilla)
 "Pineta di Donoratico," Castagneto Carducci, Italy (project; with F. Gorio and A. De Carlo)
 Church of S. Gottardo, Genoa (project; with A. De Carlo, A. Mor, and A. Sibilla)
1957 INA-CASA Housing Development, S. Giusto, Prato, Italy (with M. Boschetti, A. De Carlo, and M. Giovannini)
 Two-level bridge, Dora River, Ivrea, Italy (project; with A. De Carlo, S. Musmeci, and B. Zevi)

1958 Master plan for Cortona, Italy (with A. De Carlo and M. Uccelli)

Italian Pavilion, World's Fair, Brussels (with others)

1959 Plan for Barene di S. Giuliano, Mestre, Venice (with M. Boschetti, A. De Carlo, G. Esposito, L. Giovannini, L. Menozzi, A. Polizzi, and T. Musho)

Master plans for the towns of Palmyra, Hasseke, Raqua, Kameshlie, and Sahra, Syria (with A. De Carlo, M. Boschetti, A. Livadiotti, and L. Giovannini)

1960 Master plan for the center of Tunis (with A. De Carlo, M. Amodei, and R. Consiglio)

1962 Punta Ala and Il Gualdo Developments, Castiglione della Pescaia, Italy (with R. Maestro, G. Esposito, S. Paoli, and A. Ponis)

Master plan for the center of Turin (competition project; with others)

1963 Lido di Classe Tourist Development, Ravenna (with N. D'Olivo, A. Manzone, and A. Quistelli)

1965 Government Office Building, Rome (competition project; with G. Esposito, M. Mibelli, and A. Quistelli)

Cassa di Risparmio Building, Ravenna, Italy (with E. Calanca, A. De Carlo, and C. Salmoni)

Marcellus Theatre restoration and additions, Orsini Palace, Rome (with L. Giovannini and G. Esposito)

Casilino Housing Development, Rome (with G. Esposito, R. Maestro, and L. Rubino)

1967 Master plan for Bari, Italy (with A. Quistelli, A. Renzulli, and R. Ferrari)

1969 Master plan for Reggio Calabria, Italy (with A. Quistelli and F. D'Orsi Villani)

Housing development, Lungomare Quarter, Bari, Italy (with A. Quistelli, A. Renzilli, and R. C. Ferrari)

Government Center, Kaskah, Tunis (project; with A. Amodei, R. Berardi, A. De Carlo, and B. Hagler)

1970 Lagoon Development, Tunis (with A. De Carlo)

Straits of Messina Bridge (competition project; with others)

New Gibellina Parish Church, Italy (with L. Anversa and G. D'Ardia)

Multi-purpose building, Grosseto, Italy (with E. Calanca)

1971 Banco di Roma, Filiale Romana, Rome (with E. Calanca)

1973 University of Calabria, Cosenza, Italy (competition project; with others)

University of Somalia Campus, Mogadishu (with S. Dierna)

Po River Industrial Area, Chioggia, Italy (project; with BBPR and others)

1975 University of Lecce, Italy (with R. C. Ferrari, S. Dierna, and A. Renzulli)

Plan for the "Asse Attrezzato," Rome (with M. Fiorentino, L. Passarelli, and B. Zevi)

1976 FIAT Housing Developments at several towns near Termoli and Cassino, Italy (with F. Karrer and L. Passarelli)

1977 Development plan for the S. Paolo and Collegno areas of Turin (with L. Passarelli and Livo Quaroni)

1980 Cultural Centre and Museographic Centre, Muscat, Oman (competition project; with L. Giovanini)

Historical Town Centre Development, Siena, Italy (with M. Neri)

Publications:

By QUARONI; book—*La Torre de Babele*, Padua, Italy 1967; *Immagine di Roma*, Bari, Italy 1969; introduction to *Die Stadtkrone* by Bruno Taut, Milan 1973; *Immagine di Roma*, Rome 1976;

Progettare un edificio, Milan 1977; *Franco Purini*, exhibition catalogue, Florence 1977; *Gaudi: immagine e architettura*, with Gabriele Morrione, Rome 1979; *Giovanni Michelucci*, with Salvatore di Pasquale and Giovanni Landucci, Florence 1980; *La citta fisica*, edited by Antonio Terranova, Rome 1981; articles—"La Communità Indiana" in *Metron* (Rome), 1947; "La situazione dell'architettura moderna in italia" in *Metron* (Rome), 1948; "Urbanistica e architettura" in *Urbanistica* (Milan), 1949; "L'Urbanistica per l'unita della cultura" in *Comunita* (Milan), 1952; "Indagine edilizia su Granasco," with L. Anversa and others, in *Inchiesta parlamentare sulla miseria*, Rome 1954; "La Città" in *Comunità* (Milan), 1954; "L'Architetto e l'urbanistica" in *Architettura d'oggi*, Florence 1954; "Volto della città" in *Comunità* (Milan), 1954; "Pianificazione senza urbanisti" in *Casabella* (Milan), 1954; "La chiesa, lo spazio interno" in *Casabella* (Milan), 1955; "Pianificazione urbanistica come mezzo di difesa dell'ambiente" in *Architettura* (Rome), 1956; "La difesa ed il rinnovamenta del paesaggio urbano e rurale" in *Architettura* (Rome), 1957; "Politica del quartiere" in *Urbanistica* (Turin), 1957; "Una città eterna: quattro lezioni da ventisette secoli" in *Urbanistica* (Turin), 1959; "Qualcosa si muove" in *Casabella* (Milan, May 1964; "School, Academy, Architecture" in *Controspazio* (Bari, Italy), November 1975; "Material for the Modern Movement" in *Parametro* (Bologna), March/April 1978; "Secret History of the Imagination," interview, with L.Menozzi in *Controspazio* (Bari, Italy), January/June 1983; "Domus Interview: Ludovico Quaroni" with Paolo Melis in *Domus* (Milan), July/August 1984.

Ludovico Quaroni: Barene di San Giuliano, Mestre, Venice, 1959 (model).

On QUARONI: book-*Ludovico Quaroni e lo sviluppo dell'Architettura moderna in Italia* by Manfredo Tafuri, Milan 1964; *Italian Architecture of the Sixties*, exhibition catalogue, with foreword by Giuseppe Tucci, Rome 1972; *Architetture italiane degli anni '70*, exhibition catalogue, edited by Giovanna De Feo and Enrico Valeriani, Rome 1981; *La monumentalità nell'architettura moderna* by Luciano Patetta, Milan 1982; articles—"Profilo di Ludovico Quaroni" by Riccardo Musatti in *Comunità* (Milan), no. 6, 1950; "Architetti italiani: Ludovico Quaroni" by Raffaella Crespi in *Comunità* (Milan), no. 54, 1957; "Progetti dello Studio Quaroni" by Antonio Quistelli in *Controspazio* (Bari, Italy), no. 2, 1973; "The Variety of Invariants" in *Architettura* (Rome), October 1977; "Multipurpose Development in Grosseto" by Giuseppe Nannerini in *Industria delle costruzioni* (Rome), February 1979; "Quaroni's project for the Teatro dell'Opera in Rome" in *Casabella* (Milan), March 1984; "Good and Bad Academy" by L. Benevolo in *Casabella* (Milan) June 1984.

I am both architect and planner. I can not conceive the division between the two. I am interested in the life within the buildings in the city, the people in the town, and the life of the town in its natural environment. Before 1960 I worked in support of town planning against architecture; since 1960 I have worked in support of architecture against planning. I have always been fond of town design and of an architecture integrated into the city. I believe that, even today, with new methods of analysis and design, architecture is a synthesis of function, technology, and form—but form has to arise from a correct use of the integration of functional and technological planning and design.

—Ludovico Quaroni

Among the generation of Italians who graduated in the early and mid-1930s, Ludovico Quaroni holds an important place not only as an architect but also as a planner and teacher. It is perhaps his influence as a didact and as a collaborator with younger architects in the postwar period for which he is best known in Italy. Outside Italy, however, his best known works are his churches, notably the Church of S. Franco at Francavilla al Mare, the church in his La Martella Housing Development at Matera, and the Church of the Holy Family in Genoa. None of these buildings is large, but they are startling. Not flamboyant, they have a great richness of conception and of detail. Their charm lies in clever and self-conscious manipulation of form, materials, and space, to tease the eye and propose visual paradox.

Quaroni's career has been interesting. Always a neo-classicist at heart, even in college, he slipped easily into the Fascist idiom in the late 1930s, and produced elegant compositions of great skill, the drawings for which are still admired. He served in the Italian Army during the war, was captured by the British in North Africa, and spent five years in a POW camp in India, where he worked on a few projects and taught architecture to his fellow prisoners. After the war, his work became softer. He became greatly involved with low-cost housing—at Tiburtino (an early conscious attempt to recreate a Roman urban vernacular), at La Martella, and at Prato. These schemes are characterized by modern planning ideas—buildings set back from streets, free geometry, and functional zoning—married to gracefully eclectic housing forms, and the result is surprisingly successful.

But since 1958, when he was one of the huge team responsible for the Italian Pavilion at the Brussels World's Fair, Quaroni has built comparatively little. He has, instead, concentrated on urban planning and on the teaching of that subject. It is a matter of regret that Quaroni's planning work reflects none of the charm and consideration of his buildings. His plans tend to be grandiose, to involve steadfastly illogical pattern-making—a far cry from the village of La Martella, which was admired throughout the world. Yet his reputation is assured: Quaroni can justly be accounted one of the great postwar Italian architects, if only for his housing projects and for his churches.

—Andrew Rabeneck

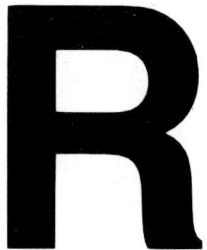

R

RAINER, Roland.
Austrian. Born in Klagenfurt, 1 May 1910. Educated at the Technische Hochschule, Vienna, 1928-33. Since 1947, in private practice, Vienna. Chief Planning Officer of Vienna, 1958-63. Professor of Housing and Town and Country Planning, Technische Hochschule, Hannover, West Germany, 1953-54; Professor of Building and Design, Technische Hochschule, Graz, Austria, 1955. Since 1956, Leader of the Architecture Master Class at the Akademie der bildenden Künste, Vienna. President, Austrian Kunstsenat, Vienna, 1980. Exhibitions: Akademie der bildenden Künste, Vienna, 1955 and 1978; Vienna, Essen, Hamburg, Cologne, and Karlsruhe, 1965; West Germany, Yugoslavia, and Turkey, 1980-82. Recipient: City of Vienna Architecture Prize, 1954; Austrian Cross of Honour in the Arts and Sciences, 1962; National Prize for Architecture, 1962; Austrian Arts and Sciences Award, 1979; Kardinal-Innitzer-Prize, Vienna, 1980. Honorary Fellow, American Institute of Architects, 1973; Honorary Member, Akademie der bildenden Künste, Vienna, 1980. Honorary Doctorate: Technische Universität, Vienna, 1982. Address: Fasholdgasse 3, 1130 Vienna, Austria.

Works:

1954 Prefabricated housing estate, Vienna (with Carl Auböck)
     Apprentices' Hall of Residence, Vienna
1956 Terraced housing, Ternitz, Lower Austria
1957 Artist's House, Kitzbühel, Austria
     "Town of the Future," *Interbau Exhibition*, Berlin
1958 Municipal Hall, Vienna
     Böhler Brothers Office Building, Elizabethstrasse 12, Vienna
1960 Steinbruch House, Burgenland, Austria
1961 New town for 100,000 people, near Bilbao, Spain (competition project; with others)
     Municipal Hall, Swimming Pool, and Housing Development, Ternitz, Lower Austria
1962 Mountain Holiday House (project)
1963 Lido, Ternitz, Lower Austria
     Housing development, Mauerberggasse, Vienna
     Evangelical church, Simmering, Vienna
1964 Housing development, Linz, Austria (project)
     Municipal Hall, Bremen, West Germany (with Säume and Hafemann)
1965 Stadium, Munich (competition project)
     Municipal Hall, Ludwigshafen, West Germany
1966 Austrian Pavilion, Plovdiv, Bulgaria
1967 Austrian Pavilion, *Expo '67*, Montreal competition project)
1969 Puchenau Garden City, phase I, Linz, Austria
1973 High School, Kagraner Anger, Vienna
     Television Centre, Kuniglberg, Vienna
     Covered swimming pool, adjacent to City Hall, Vienna
1976 Roman Catholic Pastoral Centre, Puchenau, Linz, Austria
1978 Puchenau Garden City, phase II, Linz, Austria
1980 Documenta Urbana housing group, Kassel, West Germany
     St. Michael's Roman Catholic Church, Leonding/Linz, Austria
     Attnang-Puchheim Garden City, Austria
1982/
83 Institute for Cable Communications, Ludwigshafen, West Germany
1983/
84 ORF Television Centre, stage III, Küniglberg, Vienna
1985 Housing Development, Leonfeldnerstrasse, Linz, Austria

Publications:

By RAINER: books—*Die Zweckmässigste hausform für erweiterung, neugründung und wiederaufbau von städten*, editor, Breslau 1944; *Die Behausungsfrage*, Zürich 1947; *Städtebauliche Prosa*, Tübingen, West Germany 1948; *Die Gegliederte und Aufgelockerte Stadt*, with Hubert Hoffmann and Johannes Göderitz, Tübingen, West Germany 1957; *Anonymes Bauen Nordburgenland*, Salzburg, Austria 1961; *Planungskonzept Wien*, Vienna 1963; Lebensgerechte Aussenräume, Zürich 1972; *Für eine Lebensgerechtere Stadt*, Vienna 1974; *Die Welt als Garten: China*, Graz, Austria 1976; *Anonymes Bauen im Iran*, Graz, Austria 1977; *Kriterien der wohnlichen Stadt*, Graz, Austria 1978; *Lebensgerechtes Bauen*, Graz, Austria 1978; *Bauen und Architektur*, Graz, Austria 1980; *Garten: Lebensraume, Sinnbilder, Kunstwerke*, Graz, Austria 1982.

On RAINER: books—*Roland Rainer: Bauten, Schriften und Projekte* by Peter Kamm, Tübingen, West Germany 1973; *Architektur aus Österreich seit 1960* by Peter M. Bode and Gustav Peichl, Salzburg, Austria 1980; articles—"Television Centre of Vienna" in *Werk* (Zürich), October 1973; "Municipal Swimming Baths, Vienna" in *Baumeister* (Munich), September 1976; "House of Dr. Bosch, Vienna" in *Bauen und Wohnen* (Zürich), December 1976; "Catholic Care Centre, Puchenau" in *Detail* (Munich), March/April 1978; "In the Centre of the Light" in *Bauwelt* (Berlin), 21 April 1978; "Puchenau Spiritual Welfare Centre" in *Architecture + Urbanism* (Tokyo), June 1978; "ORF Television Studios in Vienna" in *Deutsche Bauzeitschrift* (Gütersloh, West Germany), August 1978; "Living on the Ground" in *Deutsche Bauzeitung* (Stuttgart), January 1979; "Indoor Swimming Pool of Vienna Town Hall" in *Architecture + Urbanism* (Tokyo), August 1979; "St. Michael in Leonding" in *Kunst und Kirche* (Linz, Austria), February 1980; "Holy Buildings" in *Bauforum* (Vienna), July 1980; "Puchenau II" in *Bauwelt* (Berlin), 19 February 1982; "Documenta Urbana – Kassel 1982" in *Bauforum* (Vienna), March 1982.

*

After the disillusionment and disappointment over the result of postwar architecture and planning, our euphoria has changed to a world-wide scepticism about the triumph of production and the passion for technology and efficiency. We are now concerned with regaining personal, independent living areas—with space and volume in town planning—aims with which I have been concerned for thirty years in my speeches, my writings, and in my work for dwellings, housing estates, and garden cities.

We must still and continually defend this trend towards a more humane and more natural environment, a respect for ecology, against the latest inclinations of many architects to monumentatlity and "Architecture."

—Roland Rainer

Roland Rainer was Chief Planning Officer for the city of Vienna from 1958 to 1963—though it was only after a long struggle that he was able to carry out his general plan for rebuilding in the city. He first really made his mark there with the 1954 experimental estate of prefabricated, detached houses that he designed with Carl Auböck in deliberate contrast to the fortress-like blocks of flats built for workers in Vienna during the 1920s. His ideas on low buildings in cities were put forward in his book *Die Gegliederte und Aufgelockerte Stadt*. These ideas, both theoretically and practically, have had a great influence on younger Austrian architects, and postwar reconstruction in Austria has been largely inspired by Rainer and his school, with its emphasis on strict economy and rationality.

Rainer's own urban planning schemes outside Vienna include a municipal hall, swimming pool, and housing estate in Ternitz and Puchenau Garden City near Linz. He has been particularly in demand for his municipal halls with steel and reinforced concrete shells and suspension roofs; the first, Vienna Municipal Hall, for 16,000 people, was followed by municipal halls in the German cities of Bremen and Ludwigshafen. They are great multi-purpose buildings, the hall in Bremen being designed to cater for such varied events as cycle racing, ice shows, and political meetings, with grandstands placed along the two sides of a central arena that can be adapted as a track or an ice rink. The basic idea of the design consists in fusing the girders of the grandstands with the tensile members of the suspended roof into a single structure—in contrast to the Vienna hall, where the reinforced concrete grandstands support a steel trusswork.

After a visit to China in 1973, Rainer wrote the book *Die Welt als Garten: China*, which begins by asking the question, "Was könnte uns China sagen?" (What can China tell us?). Rainer's conclusion is that, above all, it can point the way to an improvement in urban living. Summing up some of the problems of modern cities, he argues: "At such a moment we must find interesting a world that for three or four thousand years has enabled many hundreds of millions of people in a relatively small area to live a cultivated existence—a world constructed not as a mechanism but grown like a garden."

—Konstantin Bazarov

Roland Rainer: ORF Television Centre, Kuniglberg, Vienna, 1983-84.

RAMIREZ VAZQUEZ, Pedro.

Mexican. Born in Mexico City, 16 April 1919. Studied with the architects José Luis Cuevas and Domingo Garcia Ramos, at the National School of Architecture, National University, Mexico City, 1941. Married Olga Campuzano in 1947; children: Pedro, Olga Maria, Javier and Gabriella. Since 1944, in private practice, Mexico City. Zone Chief for the State of Tabasco, Federal School Construction Program, Mexico, 1944-47; Head of the Department of Building Preservation, Mexican Ministry of Public Education, 1947-58; General Manager of the Administrative Committee, Federal School Construction Program, Mexico, 1958-64; Founder and Technical Director, Regional Center for School Construction, Mexico City, 1964-66. Secretary of Human Settlements and Public Works of the Mexican Government, since 1976. Professor of Architectural Design and Town Planning, National School of Architecture, Mexico City, 1942-58. Member of the Executive Committee, International Union of Architects, 1953-57; President, Society of Mexican Architects, and National Federation of Architects of Mexico, 1953-59; Founder and Director, Chapultepec Park Artistic and Cultural Unit, Mexico City, 1953-65; Member, ICOMOS (International Council of Monuments and Sites), 1965-76; President, XIX Olympic Games Organization Committee, Mexico City, 1966-70, and President of the Mexican Olympic Committee, 1972-74; Technical Adviser to the Institute of Political, Economic and Social Studies, 1969-70, and Secretary of Press and Propaganda, 1975, Institutional Revolutionary Party of Mexico; President, Industrial Design Seminar, Mexico City, 1970; Member of the International Council, Museum of Modern Art, New York, 1970; President, Metropolitan Autonomous University, Mexico City, 1974-75. Member of the International Olympic Committee, since 1972; Founder and Chairman of the Board of Directors of the Association of Friends of the National Museum of Anthropology, Mexico City, since 1974. Exhibitions: World's Fair, Brussels, 1958; World's Fair, New York, 1964; *Pedro Ramirez Vazquez, A Mexican Architect*, Grand Palais, Paris, 1982; School of Architecture, National University, Mexico City, 1985. Recipient: Golden Star, Belgium, 1958; Grand Prize, *Triennale*, Milan, 1960; Grand Prize and Gold Medal, *Bienal*, Sao Paulo, 1965; Gold Medal, Mexico City, 1969; Jean Tschumi Prize, International Union of Architects, 1969; Special Award, Industrial Designers Society of America, 1969; National Arts Prize, Mexico, 1973; Gold Medal, Académie d'Architecture, Paris, 1978; Gold Medal, 3rd Biennial of Architecture, Sofia, Bulgaria, 1983. Member, Society of Mexican Arcitects, 1953, and National Federation of Architects of Mexico, 1953; Acting Member, National Academy of History and Geography, Mexico, 1965; Founding Member, Academy of Arts of Mexico, 1968. Honorary Member, American Institute of Architects, 1953; Honorary Member, Industrial Designers Society of America, 1970; Member, Royal Society of Arts London, 1972; Emeritus Architect, National Academy of Architecture, Mexico, 1983. Knight of the Order of the Crown of King Leopold II, Belgium, 1958; Great Officer, Vasa Royal Order of Sweden, 1968; Great Chief, Ghana, 1968; Entrant, Golden Book of Israel, 1969; Great Officer, Order of the White Rose of Finland, 1969; Commander, Order of the Crown of Belgium, 1970. Address (office): Avenida de las Fuentes 170, Mexico 20, D.F., Mexico.

Works:

1944/
64 35,000 schools throughout Mexico (while working for the Mexican Ministry of Education)
1953 National School of Medicine, Mexico City (with Alvarez Espinosa, Hector Velazquez and Ramon Torres)
1954 Ministry of Labor and Social Welfare, Mexico City
1955/
57 Fifteen markets in Mexico City
1958 Mexican Pavilion, World's Fair, Brussels
1960 National Institute for the Protection of Infancy, Mexico City
Gallery of History, Chapultepec Park, Mexico City
1962 National Labor Conciliation Board, Mexico City
Mexican Pavilion, World's Fair, Seattle
Borderline Museum, Juarez, Mexico

1963/
64 Museum of the City of Mexico
    Museum of Modern Art, Chapultepec Park, Mexico City
    National Museum of Anthropology, Mexico City
    Mexican Pavilion, World's Fair, New York
1965 Ministry of Foreign Relations, Plaza of Three Cultures, Mexico City
    Aztec Soccer Stadium, Mexico City
1968 National Confederation of Chambers of Commerce, Mexico City
    Cauhtemoc Soccer Stadium, Puebla, Mexico
1970 Home of Girls and the Children's Hospital, Mexican Institution of Assistance to Children, Mexico City
1971 Market municipal plan for San Salvador, El Salvador (as technical adviser)
1972 Museum of African Art, Dakar, Senegal (project)
1974/
75 Pilsen High School, Chicago
1975 Siempre Magazine Building, Mexico City (project)
    Urban plan for a new capital city, Dodoma, Tanzania
1975/
76 Japanese Embassy, Mexico City (with Manuel Rosen and Kenzo Tange)
    Shrine of Guadalupe, Villa Gustavo A. Madero, Mexico City
1976 Master plan for Paseo Residencial, Monterrey, Mexico
    Fertilizantes de Centro America Building, San Jose, Costa Rica
    Mexican-Japanese School, Mexico City (with Manuel Rosen)
    Clinic and Social Sports Centre, Monterrey, Mexico
    Lomas Cemetery, Mexico City (project)
    Museum of Anthropology, Lima, Peru (project; as adviser)
1980 Congress Building, Mexico City
1981 International Olympic Committee Building, Lausanne, Switzerland
    DISA Company Building, Mexico City
1982 GMD (Grupo Mexicano de Desarrollo) Building, Mexico City
    Gruemint Office Building, Mexico City
    Cultural Centre, Tijuana, Mexico (with Manuel Rosen)
    Monument to Fray Anton de Montesinos, Santo Domingo, Dominican Republic
1982/
84 Ibero Americana University, Mexico City (advisor; with Rafael Mijares and Francisco Serrano)
    Musée du Louvre interior display, Paris (with others)
    Compania Mexicana de Aviacion Building, Mexico City (with Rafael Mijares and Andres Giovanini)

Publications:

By RAMIREZ VAZQUEZ: books—*4,000 Years of Mexican Architecture*, Mexico City 1956; introduction to *Mayan Architecture* by Henri Stierlin, Geneva 1964; *The National Museum of Anthropology*, Geneva 1968; *Codex of Time*, Mexico City 1976; *The History of Peoples and Cities: Codex of Human Settlements*, Mexico City 1982; *Mexican Popular Architecture*, Mexico City 1982; *The Space of Man*, Mexico City 1982; *Urban Development in Mexico*, 5 vols., Mexico City 1982; articles—"Interview with an Architect/Minister: Pedro Ramirez Vazquez" in *Architectes* (Paris), April 1979; "Restoration Programs in Mexico" in *Monumentum* (Guildford, Surrey), June 1983; "The Cathedral of Mexico and the Metropolitan Sacrarium" in *Monumentum* (Guildford, Surrey), December 1983.

On RAMIREZ VAZQUEZ: books—*Mexico's Modern Architecture* by I.E. Myers, New York 1952; *The Changing Shape of Latin American Architecture* by D. Bayon and P. Gasparini, Chichester, Sussex 1979; *11 Profils d'Architectes*, Paris 1982; articles—"National School of Medicine" in *L'Architecture d'Aujourd'hui* (Paris), April 1955; articles on prefabricated rural schools in *Der Architekt* (Stuttgart), August 1960, *Comunità* (Milan), September 1960, *L'Architecture d'Aujourd'hui* (Paris), September 1960, *L'Oeil* (Paris), September 1960, *Industrial Design* (New York), September 1960, *Architettura* (Rome), November 1960, *Architectural Review* (London), November 1960, and in *Domus* (Milan), December 1960; "National Museum of Anthropology" in *Architectural Record* (New York), June 1969; "Paseo Tollocan" in *Landscape Architecture* (Louisville, Kentucky), November 1976; "Tanzania Moves its National Capital Inland to Dodoma" in *Architectural Record* (New York), December 1979; "Museum of Black Culture in Dakar" in *Mur Vivant* (Paris), no. 56, 1980; "Modern Mexican Architecture", special issue of *Process: Architecture* (Tokyo), July 1983.

Bibliography: *Pedro Ramirez Vazques, The Architect* by Florita Z. Louie de Irizarry, Monticello, Illinois 1983.

In my opinion the mission of architecture is to give form to the spaces where man lives; it should be governed by the system of life and the technique of a given time, respecting at the same time the permanent and traditional esthetic values. In my work I have always endeavored to preserve these values, using contemporary solutions. Without imitating forms or repeating solutions I have tried, in the formal aspects, to preserve in the open spaces—in the patios, for instance—proportion and respect for the environment and the landscape, a generosity of dimensions, color, and the natural texture of materials, emphasizing the clarity and the sobriety of their use and harmony with their objective.

I also believe that architecture is a discipline meant to serve man; its mission consists not only in contributing forms and in planning works, but basically in representing an instrument of social politics. It is necessary to produce, simply and clearly, the architecture needed by our country, based on a deep knowledge of the peculiarities of our needs, both individual and collective, applying the

Pedro Ramirez Vazquez: Grupo Mexicano de Desarrollo Building, Mexico City, 1982.

technological progress of our time to the level of our economic possibilities in order to lead a better life at home, in the country and in the city. I have tried to reflect that concept in the rural school, in the house that grows, in the museums, in all sorts of buildings. Architecture is the material expression of its time, its objective being to serve man, not to achieve a form. Therefore, I have always been concerned with the importance of the work, giving it a human scale, not from a material point of view but bearing in mind the dignity of man and the social group to which he belongs.

Hence the scope of the museums I have built. These were conceived with the same idea: a museum, an objective and permanent educational building, must be easily understood by people of all cultural levels, must be a place where visitors will behold the objects it contains, will learn and be proud of their past and help them to be useful in the future.

The above ideas, which have inspired and guided my architectural work, reflect a desire to be useful to society and to act with intellectual honesty.

—Pedro Ramirez Vazquez

The architectural design of Pedro Ramirez Vazquez is stunningly original. Although he has designed many museums (and acted as an advisor to others), in Mexico, Africa, and Peru, his most famous is the National Museum of Anthropology in Mexico City. Housing one of the world's richest collection of archaeological treasures, this imposing edifice features an immense forecourt with bowers of trees shading benches and hand-hewn stone. The impressive entrance of smooth concrete and glass planes is flanked on either side with massive walls of rough, natural stone. Covering an eleven acre site, the complex contains an inner 600 foot long patio with an umbrella-like fountain fashioned from a sculptured bronze column topped with an aluminium overhang. The water, which cascades into black cantara paving, is re-circulated through small holes in the floor. Cut and fitted by hand, the cantara stone is evidence of Mexico's "mano de obra"—hand labor—reflecting pride of craftsmanship. Immense glass walls open the surrounding gardens and forests of the park into the interior of the museum, creating a blending of the indoors and outdoors, in conjunction with the past and the present, surpassing space and time.

His other work includes the School of Medicine for Mexico's University City: the buildings comprise three distinct units—the lecture halls, the laboratories, and a fan-shaped auditorium with 1,050 seats. From 1944 to 1964, 35,000 prefabricated schools were built from his plans in rural areas throughout Mexico. In 1976 he designed and built the Guadalupe Shrine for 10,000 persons inside and 30,000 more in the outside court. The architectural solution is a circular plan with a cover shaped like a tent to evoke Moses's pilgrimage with Decalogue, since it is a temple visited by numerous pilgrims. He also designed the National Parliament, including the House of Representatives and the Senate Chamber. The Mexican Government also commissioned him to design the Mexican pavilions for three World's Fairs—in New York, Seattle, and Brussels. Ramirez Vazquez's pavilion in Brussels was a small jewel set among the large pavilions of other countries. Comprising only 950 square yards, the structure was designed to represent Mexico as a progressive country rooted in an ancient culture.

Clean swept volumes and planes mark his Ministry of Labor and Social Security Building in Mexico City. Supported on round columns, the facade makes use of concrete, glass and light sandstone contrasting with dark lava. Ramirez Vazquez also designed many markets with thin-shell concrete roofs shaped like inverted umbrellas. These forms, derived from the awnings that cover the rural open markets, allow for natural light and cross-ventilation. His work is both distinguished and varied.

—Peggy Cochrane

RAPSON, Ralph.

American. Born in Alma, Michigan, 13 September 1914. Educated at Alma College, 1933-35; University of Michigan, Ann Arbor, 1935-38 (Phi Beta Kappa), B.Arch. 1938; graduate studies in urban and regional planning at Cranbrook Academy of Art, Bloomfield Hills, Michigan, 1938-40 (Cranbrook Scholarship). Married Mary Dolan in 1949; children: Richard and Thomas. In private practice, Chicago, 1942-46, and Cambridge, Massachusetts, 1946-54. Since 1954, in private practice, as Ralph Rapson and Associates Inc., Minneapolis. Head, Department of Architecture, Institute of Design, Chicago, 1942-46; Associate Professor, School of Architecture, Massachusetts Institute of Technology, Cambridge, 1946-54. Since 1954, Professor and Head, School of Architecture, University of Minnesota, Minneapolis. Thomas Jefferson Visiting Professor, University of Virginia, Charlottesville, 1967. Member of the Editorial Board, *Northwest Architect,* 1955-65; Commissioner, Minneapolis City Planning Commission, 1957-60; Member, Board of Directors, Walker Art Center, Minneapolis, 1959-63; Member, Architectural Advisory Board, United States General Services Administration, 1965-69; President, Minneapolis Chapter of the American Institute of Architects, 1967-68; Member, Board of Directors, Minnesota Society of Architects, 1967-70; Member, Low Income Housing Advisory Board, United States Metropolitan Planning Commission, 1969-72; Member, Transportation Task Force, Capitol Long Range Improvement Committee, Minneapolis, 1969-71. Architecture and Planning Consultant, University of Manitoba, Winnipeg, since 1957; Member, Minneapolis Committee on Urban Environment, since 1968 (past Vice-Chairman); Member, Architectural Advisory Board, University of Kansas, Lawrence, since 1970; Member, Community Development Task Force, Minneapolis, since 1971; Member, Architectural Advisory Board, United States Federal Reserve System, since 1977. Recipient: Parker Medal, State of Massachusetts, 1951; First Honor Award, 1954, 1975, Merit Award, 1955 (four times), and Bartlett Award, 1975, American Institute of Architects; Danish Government Medal, 1955; First Honor Award, 1958, 1959 (twice), 1963, 1964, 1972, 1973, Merit Award, 1960, 1961 (three times), 1965 (twice), 1972, 1974 (twice), and Honor Award, 1976, 1977, Minnesota Society of Architects; First Honor Award, Minneapolis Downtown Council, 1964; Award of Merit, Community Facilities Administration, 1964; First Design Award, *Progressive Architecture,* 1968, 1972; Honor Award, Pacific Region White Cement Architectural Awards Program, 1972; Honor Award, Minneapolis Committee on Urban Environment, 1972; Honor Award, United States Department of Housing and Urban Design, 1974 (twice); Barbara Flanagan Award, Minneapolis Committee for Urban Design, 1977; Honor Award, American Institute of Architects, Minnesota Chapter, 1977 and 1978; Minnesota Society of Architects First Gold Medal, 1979, and 25-year Award, 1983 and 1984; Richard Neutra Award, 1984. Fellow, American Institute of Architects. Address: Ralph Rapson and Associates Inc., 1503 Washington Avenue South, Minneapolis, Minnesota 55454, U.S.A.

Works:

1942 Willow Run Schools (3), Michigan (with Eero Saarinen)
1946 Gidwitz House, Chicago
1948 Gladstone Clinic and Apartments, McHenry, Illinois
1950 Eastgate Apartments, Cambridge, Massachusetts
1951/
53 United States Embassy Staff Apartments, Neuilly, Paris (with J. Vander Meuler)
1953 United States Embassy Office Building, Stockholm (with J. Vander Meuler)
United States Embassy Office Building, Copenhagen (with J. Vander Meuler)
United States Consulate and Apartments, Le Havre, France (with J. Vander Meuler)
United States Embassy, Athens (project; with J. Vander Meuler)
United States Embassy, The Hague (project; with J. Vander Meuler)
United States Embassy, Oslo (project; with J. Vander Meuler)
1954 united States Embassy Staff Apartments, Boulogne, Paris (with J. Vander Meuler)
1955 Gidwitz House II, Ravinia, Illinois
Hillside School and Dormitories, Northboro, Massachusetts
St. Peter's Lutheran Church, Edina, Minnesota
1958 Prince of Peace Lutheran Church for the Deaf, St. Paul, Minnesota
1959 Fargo City Hall and Memorial Auditorium, North Dakota
1960 St. Luke's Presbyterian Church, Minnetonka, Minnesota
1961 Mrs. Edward Brooks House, Long Lake, Minnesota
1963 Tyrone Guthrie Theatre, Minneapolis
State Capitol Credit Union Branch Office, Minneapolis
Wilder Residences for the Elderly, St. Paul, Minnesota
Pillsbury House, Wayzata, Minnesota
1964 Chateau Co-op Dining Club, Minneapolis
1969 St. Thomas Aquinas Church, St. Paul Park, Minnesota
1970 Hope Lutheran Church, Minneapolis
Butwin House, Mendota Heights, Minnesota
Cedar Riverside (housing and community complex), stage I, Minneapolis
1971 International Studies Building, University of Chicago (with Burnham and Hammond)
Performing Arts Center, University of California at Santa Cruz (with Henrick Bull)
1972 Rarig Building: Performing Arts Center, University of Minnesota, Minneapolis
1973 Humanities/Fine Arts Center, University of Minnesota at Morris
1974 Cedar Riverside (housing and community complex), stage II, Minneapolis
Cedar Square West (housing and community complex), stage I, Minneapolis
1975 Weyer House, Excelsior, Minnesota
1976 Recreation Facilities Building, Southern Illinois University, Carbondale
Classroom/Laboratory Building, St. Mary's Junior College, Minneapolis
The Glass Cube (Rapson House), Amery, Wisconsin
1977 First Federal Savings and Loan, Estherville, Iowa
1978 Tew House, Wayzata, Minnesota
Liu House, North Oaks, Minnesota
1978 Flesch/Davis House, Afton, Minnesota
Okoboji Condominiums, Estherville, Iowa

Publications:

By RAPSON: book—*Architects on Architecture,* edited by Paul Heyer, New York 1965; article—"The Ten Commandments of Architectural Design" in *Architecture Minnesota* (Minneapolis), November/December 1977.

On RAPSON: books—*Architecture U.S.A.* by Ian McCallum, New York 1959; *The Tyrone Guthrie Theatre,* Minneapolis 1963; *A New Theatre* by Tyrone Guthrie, New York 1964; *Contemporary Theatre Architecture* by Maxwell Silverman, New York 1965; *Theatre Design* by George Izenour, New York 1965; *Structure Systems* by Heinrich Engel,

Stuttgart 1967; *A Concise History of Western Architecture* by R. Furneaux Jordan, New York 1969; *New Town in America: The Design and Development Process,* edited by James Bailey, New York 1973; *Drawings by American Architects,* edited by Alfred M. Kemper, New York 1973; *Towards a Quality of Life,* edited by Lelah Bakhtiar, Tehran 1974; *Theatres and Auditoriums* by Harold Burris-Meyer and Edward Cole, Huntington, New York 1975; *The Architecture Book* by Norval White, New York 1976; *The New Downtowns* by Louis G. Redstone, New York 1976; *Architectural Present-ation Techniques* by William Wilson Atkins, New York 1976; *Architecture in the United States* by Ralph Hammett, New York 1976; articles— "Architecture for the Stage" in *Walker Design Quarterly* (Minneapolis), no. 58, 1963; "Tyrone Guthrie Theatre" in *Progressive Architecture* (New York), December 1963; "Theatres U.S.A.: Recent Designs by Ralph Rapson and John Johansen" in *Architectural Review* (London), April 1964; "Ralph Rapson: Artistic Virtuoso" by Mike Wilkinson in *Architecture Minnesota* (Minneapolis), May 1975; "Plane on Plain" in *Progressive Architecture* (New York), May 1980; "Architecture and Technology for a University Structure" in *Industria delle Costruzioni* (Rome), December 1980; "A Master of Modernism" by Frederick Koeper in *Architecture Minnesota* (Minneapolis), July/August 1984.

Architecture is not only a highly precise social and physical science but also a fine art—the processing of organizing and ordering space and relating it to society for our use, comfort, pleasure and spiritual satisfaction. In other words, it is the total act of converting and controlling, shaping and ordering the entire physical environment into an effective, ex-pressive and harmonious setting for human life. Quality and totality must be stressed; there is a dichotomy here: it is a conflict imposed by the effort to simultaneously satisfy both practical human needs and human aspirations. In a sense this dilemma is the conflict of technology versus cultural value.

In our search for significant environment the art of architecture must always control the science and technology of architecture, and the total must control the parts. The creative act must govern. Frank Lloyd Wright has given a clue in a beautifully stated passage:

In the arts, every problem carries within itself its own solution, and the only way yet discovered to reach it is a very painstaking way: to look sympathetically within the thing itself, to proceed to analyze and sift it, to extract its own consistent and essential beauty, which means its common sense truthfully idealized. There lies the heart of the poetry that lives in architecture.

Clearly this is the design process; however, the physical synthesis is quite another thing. Creativity is neither consistent nor predictable. The magic which the individual architect brings to each situation will vary, but it is nonetheless his grave responsibility to society.

An ancient Chinese Taoist philosopher—perhaps it was Confucius—wrote: "Lay more stress on the process through which perfection is sought than upon perfection itself." While I'm not certain that I agree completely with this—for no matter how excellent the process, the resultant design may still be poor—still, the process, the orderly systematic search, is vital and essential to a quality solution. Natural scientists have long perceived that form and process are indivisible aspects in organic growth.

As an educator, as well as a practicing architect and planner, I subscribe to the importance of the design process. This is particularly true in the education of designers, where it is far more import-ant to establish rational and creative thought process than simply a final design product.

Over the years I have organized ten check-points in my design search. These "ten commandments" are not listed here in any particular order; quite obviously one or another of these points will take precedence in any one specific situation. While laying little claim to their orginality, I do try to work with integrity and vigor within this general framework: 1) the need for economic/managerial responsibility; 2) need for historical continuity; 3) concern for the regional context and site conditions; 4) functional integrity in planning; 5) structural integrity; 6) integrity of technological advantage; 7) creative space; 8) the need for architectural expression; 9)the understanding and utilizing the potential of the period; and 10) totality of concept and totality of the creative act.

Igor Stravinsky has written: "The uninitiated imagine that one must await inspiration in order to create. That is a mistake." How true! Creative design is an agonizing and often lonely process. But it's an exhilarating, joyous and rewarding effort. And creativity is hard, loving work; while little is understood of creativity, near the heart of the creative process is the ability to maintain broad intuitive and emotional activity freely within the framework of endless hours of search and a vast amount of acquired knowledge along with endless experience.

Concerned and motivated as it is with the problems of humanity, there is seldom a black and white solution to any given environmental problem; rather, there is the great richness of the entire palette,

Ralph Rapson: Humanities/Fine Arts Center, Univerity of Minnesota at Morris, 1973.

limited only by the architect's inherent and developed qualities. Quite obviously, there is running through all of this the violent conflict of our highest hopes and aspirations with the daily press of reality—the dilemma of the dichotomy of the intellectual versus the emotional aspects of life. Technical means have always been and will continue to be the necessary means of achieving an enriched environment, but our great advantages will be of little value unless inspired by truly cultural values—values based on a genuine desire for harmonious and orderly environment, all stemming from an understanding and appreciation of the dignity of man and his aspirations. Fundamental to human survival is man's need to bring order to his environment. Unless he brings life's situations to an integrated whole, he cannot continue to grow and develop.

What I have been saying can perhaps best be summed up in this one short prescription found in Buddhism: "Develop an infallible technique, and then place yourself at the mercy of inspiration."

—Ralph Rapson

The architecture of Ralph Rapson emphasizes the straight line and its accompanying geometric shapes. Although his work displays many mechanistic and functionalist tendencies, this Minnesota architect has attempted to move beyond mere structural and material dictates to create spatially intriguing sculptural buildings. Grounded in a strong Miesian tradition, Rapson respects the need for structural integrity and functional planning; however, he does not limit himself by these approaches. He expands upon their theoretical foundations to create a more ornate, humanistic cube. For Rapson an architectural form is more than just a machine; it is a machine which may be enhanced via playful manipulation of space through the extension/accentuation of structural elements in a strictly decorative manner.

Control and order are the primary concerns of Rapson's architecture, and many restrained, formal designs have come out of his office. Such straightforward, unadorned structures as the United States embassies in Sweden and Denmark, St. Thomas Acquinas Catholic Church, the Prince of Peace Lutheran Church, and the State Capitol Credit Union indicate the main thrust of his work. However, a more dynamic plan, the Pillsbury House in Wayzata, Minnesota, more aptly reveals Rapson's ideals at their best.

One of the most ambitious domestic designs of the past fifteen years, the Pillsbury House consists of five separate, cube-shaped, brick pavilions which are linked by glass enclosed bridges. Skylights of various heights project above the flat roof and ostensibly serve as natural illumination sources. These functional elements provide a sculptural dimension and further enhance the airiness of the building which a cantilevered patio and raised concrete block foundation already establish. The fenestration, much of which is inset, further contributes to the sculptural nature of the dwelling through the creation of an undulating surface. The use of separate pavilions produces various courtyards, the spaces of which are determined by concrete block walls of varying heights. The structural approach applied to the exterior is vigorously perpetuated on the interior with a cubistic ceiling treatment resulting in multiple ceiling heights within each room. These interior and exterior elements combine to achieve a subtle, yet complex, spatial experience.

The Pillsbury House is an example of Rapson at his best. His handling of space mediates the formalistic geometric lines to create a provocative design. Such a playful use of space and forms fulfills Rapson's definition of architecture, the organization and ordering of an environment which relates to people's physical and spiritual use, comfort and pleasure. How well his more formal designs attain such an end depends upon how austere a definition is applied to the human condition and its needs.

—Don J. Hibbard

RAUCH, John.

American. Born in Philadelphia, Pennsylvania, 23 October 1930. Educated at Wesleyan University, Middletown, Connecticut, 1951; University of Pennsylvania, Philadelphia, 1953-57, B.Arch. 1957. Served in the United States Army, 1951-53, and in the reserves, 1953-55: Lieutenant. Partner, with Robert Venturi, *q.v.*, since 1964, and with Venturi and Denise Scott Brown, *q.v.*, since 1967, as Venturi and Rauch, 1964-80, and Venturi, Rauch and Scott Brown since 1980, Philadelphia (associates: Steven Izenour; David Vaughan). Lecturer, University of Pennsylvania, 1967-69. Chairman of the Awards Committee, 1968, and Chairman of the Official Practice Committee, 1969-70, American Institute of Architects. Exhibitions: *Gold Medal Awards,* Architectural League of New York, 1965; *The Work of Venturi and Rauch* toured the United States, 1965; *40 under 40*, Architectural League of New York, 1965; *The Work of Venturi and Rauch* Whitney Museum, New York, 1971; *The Invisible Artist*, Philadelphia Museum of Art, 1974; *The Work of Venturi and Rauch*, Pennsylvania Academy of Fine Arts, Philadelphia, 1975; *Suburban Alternatives: 11 American Projects*, Venice, 1976; *200 Years of American Architectural Drawing,* Cooper-Hewitt Musem, New York, 1977; *Drawings for a More Modern Architecture*, Drawing Center, New York, and Cooper-Hewitt Museum, New York, 1977; *Architecture 1: An Exhibition*, Leo Castelli Gallery, New York, and Institute of Contemporary Art, Philadelphia, 1977; *Roma Interotta*, Incontri Internazionali d'Arte, Rome, 1977-78; *Palaces for People*, Cooper-Hewitt Museum, New York, 1977; *Presence and Absence*, Galleria d'Arte Moderna, Bologna, Italy, 1977; *The Federal City in Transition*, Barbara Fiedler Gallery, Washington, D.C., 1979; *Venturi and Rauch: Architektur in Alltag Amerikas*, Kunstgewerbemuseum, Zurich, 1979 (toured Switzerland); *Venturi, Rauch and Scott Brown*, Galleria dell'Accademia, Florence, Italy, 1981; *Speaking a New Classicism*, Smith College, Northampton, Massachusetts, 1981 (toured the United States); *Architectural Fantasies*, American Institute of Architects Foundation, Washington, D.C., 1981; *Correspondences: Five Architects, Five Sculptors*, Palacio de las Alhajas, Madrid, 1982; *Buildings and Drawings by Venturi, Rauch and Scott Brown*, Max Protetch Gallery, New York, 1982; *Venturi, Rauch and Scott Brown: A Generation of Architecture*, Krannert Art Museum, University of Illinois, Urbana, 1984 (toured the United States); *250 Years of Drawings by Philadelphia's Architects*, Pennsylvania Academy of the Fine Arts, Philadelphia, 1985. Recipient: Graham Foundation Grant, 1963; Design Award, 1967, Honor Award, 1979, Urban Design and Planning Citations, 1980, 1981 and 1982, *Progressive Architecture*; First Prize, Yale University Mathematics Building Competition, 1970; Philadelphia Chapter Gold Medal, 1972, 1984; Adaptive Re-use Award, 1976, Honor Award, 1981, and Silver Award, 1984, National Honor Award, 1977, 1982, 1984, and Louis Sullivan Award, 1983, American Institute of Architects; Award of Merit, *House and Home*/American Institute of Architects 1973; *Print Magazine Casebook* Award, 1976 (three); *Urban Design* Case Studies Award, 1977; First Prize, Chinatown Redevelopment Competition, Philadelphia, 1979; Design Arts Recognition Award, National Endowment for the Arts, 1980; *Interiors* Award, 1980, 1983; Honor Award, Department of Housing and Urban Development, Washington, D.C., 1980; Award of Merit, *Administrative Management*, 1981; Certificate of Merit, Pennyslvania Historical and Museum Commission, 1983; East Pennsylvania Chapter Certificate of Merit, American Planning Association, 1983; Merit Award, Pennsylvania Society of Architects, 1983; Louis I. Kahn Citation, *American School and University,* 1984; Federal Design Achievement Award, 1984. Fellow, American Institute of Architects. Address: Venturi, Rauch and Scott Brown, 4236 Main Street, Philadelphia, Pennsylvania 19127, U.S.A.

See VENTURI, Robert

RAYMOND, Antonin.

American. Born Antonin Rajman in Kladno, Bohemia, now Czechoslovakia, 10 May 1888; emigrated to the United States, 1910; naturalized, 1914. Educated at the Realko, Kladno; Czech Higher Technical Institute, University of Prague, 1906-10; influenced by the work of Otto Wagner. Served in the United States Army Intelligence Corps, in France and Switzerland, 1917-19: 2nd Lieutenant. Married Noémi Pernessin in 1914; son: Claude. Worked in the office of Cass Gilbert, New York, 1910-12, and Frank Lloyd Wright *q.v.*, Chicago and Taliesin, Wisconsin, 1912-17, and for Wright in Tokyo, assisting on Wright's Imperial Hotel, 1919-20; established American Architect-Engineers, Tokyo, 1920-23; in private practice, Tokyo, 1923-37; returned to the United States via India, 1937: opened an office in New York, 1938, and a design studio in New Hope, Pennsylvania, 1939; in partnership with L. L. Rado, from 1946; returned to Japan and re-established practice there 1947. Honorary Consul of Czechoslovakia in Japan, 1925-27. Exhibitions: Rockefeller Center, New York, 1938; Takashimaya Department Store, Tokyo, 1952. Recipient: Medal of Honor, 1956, and Award of Merit and First Honor Award, 1957, American Institute of Architects. Fellow, American Institute of Architects, 1952. Honorary Life Member, Japanese Institute of Architects. Chevalier of the Légion d'Honneur, France; Officer of the Order of the White Lion, Czechoslovakia; Member, Order of the Corona d'Italia, Italy, and the Order of the Rising Sun, Japan. *Died* (in Langhorne, Pennsylvania) *21 November 1976.*

Works:

1917 de Vieux Columbier Theatre, New York
1920 Hoshi School, Tokyo
      Tanaka House, Tokyo
      Tokyo Lawn Tennis Club, Tokyo
1921 Women's Christian College, Tokyo
1922 Andrews Warehouse, Osaka
      Fukui House, Tokyo
1923 Goto House, Tokyo
      Raymond House, Reinanzaka, Tokyo (later re-erected at Morito Beach, Hayama, Japan)
1923/
33 St. Luke's International Hospital, Tokyo
1924 Convent and School of the Sisters of Notre Dame, Tokyo
      Dr. Read House, Reinanzaka, Tokyo
      Teten House, Tokyo
1925 Hagiwara House, Tokyo
      Siber-Hegner Warehouse, Yokohama, Japan
      Seaside Hotel, Kamakura, Japan (project)
1926 Convent and School for the Sisters of Notre Dame, Kobe, Japan
      Rising Sun Petroleum Company Offices, Yokohama
1927 Viscountess Hamao Summer House, Tokyo
      Socony Office Building, Yokohama, Japan
1928 Convent and School of the Sisters of the Sacred Heart, Okayama, Japan
      French Embassy alterations, Tokyo
      Italian Embassy Villa, Nikko, Japan
      Nagaoka House, Tokyo
      Oko House, Tokyo
1929 Manager's House, and Staff Housing, Rising Sun Petroleum Company, Yokohama
      Soviet Embassy, Tokyo (not supervised)
1930 Dunlop Rubber Company Factory, Kobe, Japan

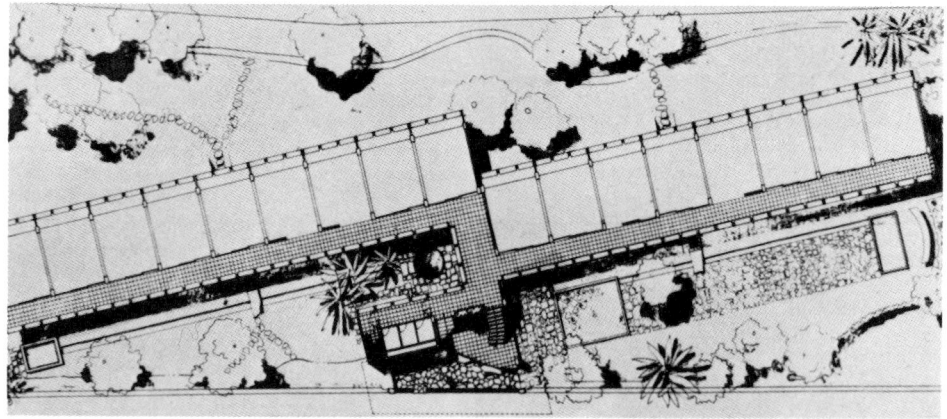

Antonin Raymond: Dormitories for an Ashram, Pondicherry, India, 1938.

Rising Sun Petroleum Company Service Stations in Tokyo, Yokohama, etc.
Tokyo Golf Club, Saitama
1931 Akaboshi Summer Cottage, Fujisawa, Japan
Troedsson Summer House, Nikko, Japan
Tokyo Steel Products Company Office Building, Kawasaki, Japan
1932 Akaboshi House, Tokyo
Otis Company Factory, Tokyo
Viscount S. House, Tokyo (project)
1933 Hatoyama House, Tokyo
Raymond Summer House, Karuizawa, Japan
1934 Brazil Coffee Shop, Tokyo
Chapel and Auditorium, Women's Christian College, Tokyo
Kawasaki House, Tokyo
James House, Shanghai
Ford Motor Company Assembly Plant and Office Building, Tsurumi, Japan (project)
Gymnasium, Sisters of Notre Dame School, Kobe, Japan
St. Paul's Church, Tokyo
Fukui Summer House, Atami, Japan
Kodera Summer House, Karuizawa, Japan
Oda Summer House, Karuizawa
1935 Blake House, Tokyo
Keller House, Tokyo
Walker House, Karuizawa, Japan
1936 National Cash Register Company Offices, Tokyo (project)
1938 Dormitories, Sri Aurobindo Ashram, Pondicherry, India
Piano designs for the Wurlitzer Company
1939 Pitt Petri Shop, Buffalo, New York
Raymond Farm, New Hope, Pennsylvania
1940 Defence Housing, Bethlehem, Pennsylvania
1941 Cambridge Glass Co. Wholesale Showroom, New York
Camp Upton (facilities for three Coast Artillery Regiments), Camp Upton, Long Island, New York
Docks for Panama (preliminary reports)
1942 Camp Kilmer Staging Area, Shelton, New Jersey
Camp Shanks Staging Area, Orangeburg, New York
Japanese Model Housing (for test purposes), Utah Proving Grounds
Prefabrication system for housing for Drycembly, Baltimore, Maryland
1943 Airport, housing and hospital facilities, Fort Dix, New Jersey
1944 New York City Department of Sanitation Garage, Brooklyn
U.S. Plywood Company Showroom, Boston
1945 Analysis and design proposals for Idlewild Airport, now Kennedy Airport, New York
Edward Keith Store, Kansas City, Missouri
Leister Housing, Bristol, Pennsylvania (project)
Long Island Railroad Station, Great River, New York

Prefabricated farm structures for the Stran Steel Company, Detroit
Regional Airport, Lexington, Kentucky (project)
Stores for Brown Fence and Wire Company, New Jersey
1946 Commercial Pacific Cable Company Offices, Guam (project; with L. L. Rado)
General Bronze Corporation Showroom, New York
Roadway Express Company Freight Terminal, Hoboken, New Jersey
1947 Master plan for the George School, Newton, Pennsylvania
Myrtle Beach Development, South Carolina (with L. L. Rado)
1948 Community Center, Summit, New Jersey (with the Allen Organization)
Community Center, Hickory, North Carolina (with the Allen Organization)
Electrolux Corporation Field House, Bronx, New York
Indian Government Office, New York
Master plan for the Levi Center Park, Omaha, Nebraska
Midtown Art Galleries, New York
St. Joseph's Catholic Church, Negros, Philippines
State Farm Insurance Company Recreation Center, Bloomington, Illinois
War Memorial Community Buildings, Housatonic, Massachusetts
Research and survey of glass use in farm buildings for the Libby Owens Ford Company
1949 Electrolux Corporation Recreation Center, Old Greenwich, Connecticut
Reader's Digest Building, Tokyo
Electrolux Corporation Industrial Building, Old Greenwich, Connecticut
1950 Two Standard Vacuum Oil Company Houses, Yokohama, Japan
1951 Master plan for the Anderson Air Base, Guam
Anderson Air Base Theatre, Guam
Neighborhood Recreation Center, Summit, New Jersey
Nippon Gakki Building and Yamaha Concert Hall, Tokyo
United States Army Engineers Base Maintenance Shop, Schenectady, New York
Harris House: United States Embassy Apartments, Tokyo
Perry House: United States Embassy Apartments, Tokyo
Jai Alai Arena, Tokyo (project)
Pan American World Airways Hotel, Tokyo (project)
1952 First National City Bank, Nagoya, Japan
Mikimoto Pearl Shop, Tokyo
Tokyo Film Building and Film Vault, Tokyo
United States Army Camp Drake and Camp Zama, Asaka, Japan

1953 Kitao Book Store (project)
Nippon Ita Garasu Office Building, Osaka (project)
Raymond Office and House, Azabu, Japan
Cunningham House, Tokyo
1954 St. Anselm's Church, Tokyo
Yasukawa Electric Company Office Building and Factory, Yawata, Japan
Yawata Steelworkers Union Memorial Hall, Yawata, Japan
1955 St. Alban's Church, Tokyo
St. Patrick's Church, Tokyo
Master plan for development of the shoreline, Long Beach, California
Yasukawa Gymnasium, Yawata, Japan
1957 Fuji Golf Club, Gotenba, Japan
Lutheran Church, Nobeoka, Miyazaki, Japan
Ito House, Matsuzakaya, Tokyo
1958/
60 Library, International Christian University, Mitaka, Tokyo
1958/
61 Gunma Music Center, Takasaki, Tokyo
1959 Golf Club, Moji, Japan
Rikkyo High School, Saitama, Japan
1959/
60 Iran Embassy, Azabu, Tokyo
1960/
66 Nanzan University, Nagoya, Japan
1961 Holy Cross Church, Tokyo
Chapel, Holy Ghost Hospital, Nagoya, Japan
Rikkyo High School, Shiki, Tokyo
St. Paul's Chapel, Rikkyo High School, Shiki, Tokyo
1961/
64 Matsuzakaya Department Store, Ginza, Tokyo
1963 Society Verbi Divini Monastery, Tokyo
Society Verbi Divini Seminary and Chapel, Nagoya, Japan
1965 San Carlos University, Cebu, Philippines
1966 Catholic Church, Shibata, Japan
International School, Nagoya, Japan
Society Verbi Divini Hostel, Maynooth, Ireland
Anglican Episcopal Church, Tokyo
1966/
69 Pan Pacific Forum, University of Hawaii, Honolulu
1968 Israeli Pavilion, *Expo '70*, Osaka (project)

Publications:

By RAYMOND: books—*Architectural Details,* with Noémi Raymond, Tokyo 1938, New York 1947; *Antonin Raymond: an Autobiography,* Rutland, Vermont 1973; articles—"On Japanese Residences," with Noémi Raymond, in *Antonin Raymond: His Work in Japan 1920-1935,* edited by K. Nakamura, Tokyo 1935; articles—"Concrete for New Designs" in *Architectural Record* (New York), January 1936; "Raymond Will Take Apprentices" in *Pencil Points* (New York), December 1939; "Working with USHA under the Lanham Act" in *Pencil Points* (New York), December 1941; "Toward True Modernism" in *Pencil Points* (New York), August 1942; "Buildings of 94X" in *Architectural Forum* (New York), May 1943; "A Hillside Built This House" in *Better Living* (New York), no. 18, 1943; "Housing: A Post-War Responsibility and Opportunity" in *AIA Journal* (Washington, D.C.), December 1945; "The Spirit of Japanese Architecture" in *AIA Journal* (Washington D.C.), December 1953; "The Doctrine of Auguste Perret" in *Architectural Record* (New York), January 1954; "Some Ideas Regarding an Organized Effort to Provide Public Housing in Japan" in *Hisaakira Kano* (Tokyo), 12 August 1955.

On RAYMOND: books—*Raymond's House,* Tokyo 1931; *Collection of Antonin Raymond's Work,*

Tokyo 1931; *Antonin Raymond: His Work in Japan 1920-1935,* edited by K. Nakamura, Tokyo 1935; *Modern Furnishings,* series 10, Tokyo 1937; *Organische Baukunst* by Hans Bernhard Reichow, Berlin and Braunschweig, West Germany 1949; articles— "Architect Comes Home from Japan" in *Architectural Forum* (New York), February 1939; "A Portfolio of Recent Works by Antonin Raymond" in *Architectural Forum* (New York), November 1941; "U.S. Architecture Abroad" in *Architectural Forum* (New York), March 1953; "U.S.A. Abroad" in *Architectural Forum* (New York), December 1957; "Antonin Raymond, Architect," edited by J. Killick, special edition of *Architectural Association Journal* (London), August 1962; "Urban School Design" in *Progressive Architecture* (London), March 1967; "A Conversation with Ladislav Rado" by William Marlin in *Architectural Record* (New York), May 1978.

It is difficult to summarize the architectural achievements of Antonin Raymond. His working life lasted for more than half a century, and his buildings are dotted all over the globe. However, during that long career he sometimes changed direction, and his widely scattered buildings are usually located far from the centres of architectural thought and development.

Like Richard Neutra and Rudolph Schindler, Raymond left Central Europe for the United States, where he gravitated to Frank Lloyd Wright. It was chance that made Wright send him to Japan to help with the hotel that he was building in Tokyo, but it was a chance that changed Raymond's life. Japan amazed the young Raymond and his designer wife Noémi. They felt that the architecture and the culture of Japan placed man more at ease with nature than was possible in the frenetic life of the cities of the west. The Raymond's life was rootless, but Japan gave them a home for much of their working lives.

At a time when the Japanese were full of admiration for all things Western, Raymond found great scope for his talents in Tokyo as numerous sizeable commissions came to him while he was still young. His earliest independent works were designed very much in the manner of Frank Lloyd Wright, and Raymond admitted that he found it difficult to throw off the style of his erstwhile employer. His own house, at Reinanzaka, Tokyo, completed in 1923, is the first break with the Wright manner and is Raymond's first mature design; with its plain surfaces and cubic forms, it must rate as a very early example of the International Style, as if Raymond were looking to Europe to free himself from Wright.

The decade following the completion of the Reinanzaka house saw the construction of a series of buildings of ever increasing quality. These buildings, in the cook International Style of the time, were often comparable with the German work of the same period. The 1928 alterations to the French Embassy in Tokyo were followed a couple of years later by the Tokyo Golf Club; this sequence of designs reached its apotheosis in two very beautiful houses, the Akaboshi House (1932) and the Kawasaki house (1934), for which Noémi designed the interiors.

Like Le Corbuiser, Raymond became dissatisfied with the limitations of the International Style, and by the early 1930's he was looking for richer forms and more tactile materials. His own summer house of 1933 at Karuizawa used sloping roofs and timber. It was based on the parti of the house Le Corbusier designed for a site in Chile, and Raymond suffered some cutting remarks from Le Corbusier for this shameless peice of cribbing, but the storm passed and Le Corbusier became an admirer of Raymond's work.

In 1937 the political climate made it difficult for an American to obtain work in Japan, and Raymond was asked to design some dormitories for an ashram in Pondicherry, India. Eighteen years previously, Raymond had imbibed the traditional spirit of Japan; now he did the same in India, living and working as a member of the ashram. The resulting buildings are perhaps Raymond's most distinguished design. Calm, elegant, climatically suitable with their vaulted roofs and louvred facades, they were his last buildings in Asia for a decade.

The approach of war brought Raymond back to the United States. At New Hope, Pennsylvania, he established his version of Wright's Taliesin. Here the family, assistants, and disciples would farm, build, and draw. The war years were spent as part of a large practice involved in wartime housing. After the war, in partnership with Ladislav Rado, he embarked on a second creative period. The postwar American work of Raymond and Rado as typified by the buildings for Electrolux at Old Greenwich, Connecticut, are pleasant, modest structures, but do not have the elan of his Japanese houses of the 1930's.

The commission by *Reader's Digest* magazine to build their new building in Tokyo brought Raymond back once again to his beloved Japan. The Reader's Digest Building, completed in 1949, was designed in Raymond and Rado's New York office; the first major postwar building in Japan, it immediately revived Raymond's Japanese practice. The Reader's Digest Building took the light, exposed, regular structure of the traditional Japanese building and added the louvres that he had learned to use at Pondicherry. A Japanese garden designed by Isamu Noguchi completed the scene of a revivified Japanese design.

In 1933 with his Karuizawa House, Raymond had turned away from the International Style to more folky, friendly forms. In 1953, making a similar turn, he built a house and office for himself at Azabu, with shoji screens and other features of traditional Japanese houses and framed the building in round logs.

Reinanzaka, Karuizawa, New Hope, Azabu—it is in the peaceful atmosphere of the houses that Raymond built for himself that we see him at his best. Raymond's buildings for others were sometimes good, often indifferent, but in his own home is an atmosphere of calm for the relaxation and restoration of the human spirit.

—John Winter

RECHTER, Yacov.
Israeli. Born in Tel Aviv, 14 June 1924; son of the architect Ze'ev Rechter. Educated at the Technion: Hebrew Technical Institute, Haifa, 1943-47, Dip. Arch. 1947. Served as a Lieutenant in the Israeli Army, 1947-49. Married Sarah Segal in 1947; Hannah Marron in 1957; children: Yonatan, Michael, Amnon, Ofra and Daphna. Assistant Architect to Ze'ev Rechter, Tel Aviv, 1946-50; Partner, with Ze'ev Rechter and Moshe Zarhy, in Rechter-Zarhy-Rechter, Tel Aviv, 1950-60, and, with Zarhy and Michael Peri, in Rechter, Zarhy—Architects, Peri—Engineer, Tel Aviv, 1960-75. Since 1975, in private practice as Yacov Rechter, Architect, Tel Aviv. Visiting Professor, Technion School of Architecture, Haifa, Israel, 1971-75. Chairman, America-Israel Cultural Foundation, Tel Aviv, 1976-80; Member of the Board of Governors, Technion University, Haifa, Israel, 1979-83; Member of the Council for Higher Education, Tel Aviv, since 1981; Board member, Tel Aviv Museum. Recipient: Rokach Prize for Architecture, 1964; Israel Prize for Architecture, 1973. Address (office): 150 Arlozorov Street, Tel Aviv, Israel.

Works (in Israel, unless noted):

1957 F.R. Mann Auditorium, Tel Aviv (with Z. Rechter and D. Karmi)
1958 Faculty of Archaeology, Jerusalem University, Giveat Ram Campus, Jerusalem
1960 Sprinzak Resort Hotel, Nazareth
1960/
  75 Out-Patients Clinics in Haifa, Ramat-Gan and Rehovoth
1961 Mivtachim Hotel, Nazareth
1965 Hilton Hotel, Tel Aviv
  Law Courts, Tel Aviv
  Two Apartment Buildings, Weitzman Institute, Rehovoth
1968 Mivtachim Hotel, Zikhron Yacov
1970 Conservatoire, Beer-Sheva
1970/
  80 Scientific Institute Master Plan, Kurdani
1974 Memorial and Cultural Building, Herzlia
  Hilton Hotel, Jerusalem
1975 Kaplan Hospital, Rehovoth
  Weitzman Institute Master Development Plan, Rehovoth
1975/
  84 Bank and Insurance Company Buildings, Tel Aviv area
1976/
  80 Giloh Housing Developments (2,700 apartments), near Jerusalem
1977 Astoria Hotel, Tel Aviv
1978 Carmel Hospital, Haifa
1979 Noga Hilton Hotel, Geneva, Switzerland (as Consulting Architect)
  Hadassa Hospital, Mount Scopus, Jerusalem
1980 Sheraton Hotel, Tel Aviv
1981 Central Library, Jerusalem University, Mount Scopus Campus, Jerusalem
1982 Sheraton Hotel, Jerusalem
  Laromme Hotel, Jerusalem
  Carlton Penta Hotel, Tel Aviv
1984 Waterfront Development, Tel Aviv
  L Quarter Housing (3,000 apartments) and Commercial Development, Tel Aviv
  Golda Cultural Center, Tel Aviv
  Marina City Commercial Development Master Plan, Tel Aviv
1985 School of Business Administration, Technion University, Haifa
  Merom Nave Civic and Residential Centrer, Ramat-Gan

Publications:

On RECHTER: articles—article in *Baumeister* (Munich), September 1975; "Three Buildings in Israel" in *L'Architettura* (Rome), November 1975; article in *Baumeister* (Munich), September 1976; "High on Giv'at Ram: The Jerusalem Hilton" by Betty Raymond in *Interiors* (New York), September 1976; "Recent Works of the Israeli architects Rechter Zarhy Peri" in *L'Architettura* (Rome), December 1976; article in *Baumeister* (Munich), May 1977; article in *Architectural Record* (New York), October 1977; "Memorial Building in Herzlia" in *Architecture in Israel* (Tel Aviv), 1978; "A New Five Star Hotel in Tel Aviv" in *Architektur und Wohnwelt* (Stuttgart), December 1979; "Carmel Hospital, Haifa" in *Architecture in Israel* (Tel Aviv), 1980; "Music Centre in Beersheba, Israel" in *Deutsche Bauzeitschrift* (Gutersloh, West Germany), October 1980; "Five Versions of Humane Rationalism in Israel" in *Architettura* (Rome), November 1983.

Immediately upon graduating from the Haifa Technion's faculty of architecture, Yacov Rechter joined with his father, the notable architect Ze'ev Rechter, to form in 1950 the firm Rechter-Zarhy-Rechter, which during the 1950s produced such major buildings as the Convention Halls (Binyanei Ha'oomah) in Jerusalem and the Mann Auditorium and Cultural Centre in Tel Aviv. After his father's death in 1960, the imprint of Yacov Rechter's design personality was felt even more strongly in the firm, and in the succeeding decades he has been largely responsible for several significant projects of high

Yacov Rechter: Giloh Housing Development, Talpiot, Jerusalem, 1976-80.

quality, for one of which—the Mivtakhim Resort Hotel in Zikhron-Ya'acov—he was awarded the prestigious Israel Prize in 1973.

At first glance, his work is stylistically diverse, but analysis reveals some persistent architectural themes. Of these perhaps the most important leit-motif is the device of the cellular facade, that is, the repetitive use of a basic element to create the overall form and pattern of the building. We see two significant variations of this theme. In many buildings—the Hilton Hotels in Tel Aviv and Jerusalem come to mind here—the individual elements are either highly-modelled or sharply facetted, uniting to create a rather simple overall form of great surface brilliance and intricacy of texture. In the Mivtakhim Resort Hotel, on the other hand, the individual cell is a rectilinear unit of pristine simplicity, but the manner of assembly is such as to generate an undulating facade form of great complexity. Thus the tension between simplicity and complexity, standardization and diversity, is always present in Rechter's work.

Rechter has an eye for a dramatic site, and the skylines of Jerusalem, Haifa and Zikhron Ya'acov are dominated by his designs. The Hilton tower is an elegant marker of one's approach to Jerusalem, if not an unquestionably appropriate symbol. The sinuous facade of the Zikhron-Ya'acov hotel, hugging the escarpment of the Carmel range, not only respects the landform but enhances it, in what must be one of Israel's most successful symbioses of landscape and the man-made object. The siting of Rechter's Carmel Hospital, recently completed in Haifa, is more controversial. Again, there is a sympathetic resonance between the spur of the mountain on which the building is located, and the magnificent, slope-wall, sculptured form of the hospital; but one may question whether the dominance of hill and flanking coastal plain by this massive, fortress-like structure is

the appropriate expression of a hospital in the urban hierarchy.

Another hospital recently completed by Rechter, of a less virtuoso kind, shows this talented architect at his very best. It is his reconstruction and radical expansion of Erich Mendelsohn's historic Hadassah Hospital on Mount Scopus, the war-torn hulk of which was recovered through the reunification of Jerusalem in 1967. Here Rechter, with great skill and understanding, combines the rigorous and complicated functional demands of a modern hospital with a loving care for the integrity of Mendelsohn's sadly-abused masterpiece. This respect for another's work shows restraint and sensitivity, qualities which, together with a precision in planning, a nicety of detail, and a response to context, combine to make Yacov Rechter one of the foremost of his generation in Israel's architecture.

—Gilbert Herbert

REIDY, Affonso Eduardo.
Brazilian. Born in Paris, France, 27 October 1909. Educated at the Escola Nacional de Belas Artes, Rio de Janeiro, 1927-30, Dip.Arch. 1930. Married Carmen Portinho in 1934. Worked in the Municipal Service Department, Rio de Janeiro, from 1934; Chief of the Division of Architecture, Municipal Works Department, Rio de Janeiro, 1934-47; Chief of the Planning Service, Housing Department, Rio de Janeiro, 1947; Director, Department of Urbanism, Municipal Works Department, Rio de Janeiro, 1948 and 1950-54. Assistant to Professor Warchavchik, 1930-31, Professor of Small Architectural Compositions, 1931, and Professor of City Planning,

1954, Faculty of Architecture and Urbanism, Federal University of Rio de Janeiro. Vice-President, 1944-45, and Life Member of the Advisory Board, Brazilian Institute of Architects. Exhibitions: *Bienal*, Sao Paulo, 1963; Lima, Peru, 1964; Tokyo, 1965. Recipient: Gold Medal, Escola National de Belas Artes, Rio de Janeiro, 1930; First Prize, with Gerson Pompeu Pinheiro, House of Good Will Competition, Rio de Janeiro, 1931; First Prize, *Bienal*, Sao Paulo, 1951. Livre Docente, Federal University of Rio de Janeiro, 1954. Honorary Fellow, American Institute of Architects, 1964. *Died* (in Rio de Janeiro) *10 August 1964*.

Works:

1931/
32 Home of Good Will (Hostel for Homeless Persons), Rio de Janeiro (with Gerson Pompeu Pinheiro)
1937/
43 Ministry of Education and Health, Rio de Janeiro (with Le Corbusier, Lucio Costa, Jorge Machado Moreira, and Oscar Niemeyer; now the Palace of Culture)
1938 Government Administration Building for the City Area, Rio de Janeiro (project)
1939 City Transport Service Offices and Workshops, Rio de Janeiro (project)
1944 Rio Grande do Sul Railway Administration Building, Porto Alegre, Brazil (project)
1947 Aviation Training Center, Sao Jose do Campos, Sao Paulo (project)
1947/
52 Pedregulho Housing Estate, Rio de Janeiro
1948 Redevelopment plan for the center of Rio de Janeiro (project)

Plan for Santo Antonio Hill Development, Rio de Janeiro

Pharmaceutical Factory, Rio de Janeiro (project)

1949 Pumping Station, Rio de Janeiro (project)

1951 Marechal Hermes Community Theatre, Rio de Janeiro

1952 Carmen Portinho House, Rio de Janeiro
Museum of Visual Arts, Sao Paul (project)
Gavea Housing Development, Rio de Janeiro

1954 Museum of Modern Art, Rio de Janeiro (destroyed by fire, 1978; now being reconstructed by Henrique Mindlin Associados)
Experimental school, Asuncion, Paraguay

1955 Dr. Couto e Silva House, Rio de Janeiro
Museum of Modern Art gardens, Rio de Janeiro (with Roberto Burle Marx)
Student Theatre, Rio de Janeiro (project)

1956 Master plan for Flamengo Park, Rio de Janeiro (with Roberto Burle Marx)

1957 City Employees Insurance Fund Headquarters, Rio de Janeiro

1959 World Health Organization Headquarters, Geneva (competition project)

1960 National Museum, Kuwait (competition project)
Bank of London and South America, Brasilia (compeetition project)
Paulo Bittencourt Footbridge, Rio de Janeiro

1960/
64 Open-Air Theatre, and Bandstand, Flamengo Park, Rio de Janeiro (projects)
Pavilions, Flamengo Park, Rio de Janeiro

Pavilion, Morro de Viuva Recreation Park, Rio de Janeiro (project)

1962 County house, Petroplis, Brazil
Forum, Pinacicaba, Sao Paulo (project)

Publications:

On REIDY: books—*Organische Baukunst* by Hans Bernard Reichow, Berlin and Braunschweig 1949; *The Works of Affonso Eduardo Reidy* by K. Franck, New York and London 1960; *L'Architettura Moderna in Brasile* by Sergio Bracco, Bologna 1967; *Latin America in its Architecture*, edited by Roberto Segre, New York and London 1981; articles—"Some New Architecture in Brazil" by S. Loweth in *The Architects' Journal* (London) 31 January 1946; "Pedregulho: ein wohnquartier in Rio de Janeiro" in *Werk* (Zurich), August 1953; "Brazil: Museum of Modern Art in Rio de Janeiro" in *L'Architecture d'Aujourd'hui* (Paris), January/February 1954; "Rio de Janeiro Museum of Modern Art" in *Architectural Review* (London), May 1954; "Conjunto Residencial Pedregulho" in *Informes de la Construccion* (Madrid), December 1956; "Versicherungsgebaude in Rio de Janeiro" in *Bauen und Wohnen* (Zurich), March 1960; "Affonso Eduardo Reidy" in *Zodiac* (Milan), no. 6, 1960; "Affonso Eduardo Reidy" in *Baukunst und Werkform* (Nuremberg) January 1962; "Affonso Eduardo Reidy" by Oscar Niemeyer in *L'Architecture d'Aujourd'hui* (Paris), September/November 1964.

Affonso Eduardo Reidy was, from the start of his career, involved with the introduction of functional modernism into Brazil. After absorbing various formative influences, he went on to build upon firmly, based principles of form and design and rapidly made his own distinctive contribution to the modern movement. When Lúcio Costa, the acknowledged father of modern architecture in Brazil, became director of the Escola Nacional de Belas Artes in 1931, he gathered round him a team of young architects, including Oscar Niemeyer and Reidy, and he appointed as head of his School of Architecture the Russian-born Gregori Warchavchik, who had been responsible for the very first modern-style architecture in Brazil. Reidy was made Warchavchik's assitant and thereafter combined practice with teaching. Another notable influence was Le Corbusier, who was invited to Rio in 1936 to design the now famous Ministry of Education and Health with a team which included Costa, Niemer and Reidy. Le Corbusier's forceful personality and powerful ideas naturally had a considerable effect, which can be seen in several characteristic features in Reidy's work as in Brazilian architecture in general, though they were modified and adapted to suit the particular climate conditions of Brazil

Reidy developed a subtly personal style that reached its full fruition in his Pedregulho Housing Estate, a loosely organized residental quarter for low-income public employees at subsidized rents; the estate included all the basic amenities such as a primary school, a health clinic, a laundry, a market, a gymnasium, a swimming pool and recreation areas. Traffic is not allowed in the area, and there are many

Affonso Eduardo Reidy: Pedregulho Housing Estate, Rio de Janeiro, 1952.

interesting geometrical contrasts and decorative features such as the murals of characteristic Latin *azulejos*, glazed tiles, of the school. The most striking feature is the great serpentine multistorey block of flats, 260 metres long, dominating the south side in great sweeping curves that follow the winding contours of the sloping hillside. The whole layout of the estate is indeed closely linked to the contours of the site, with the tall serpentine block of flats entered at middle-level from the hill slope, an idea suggested by earlier Le Corbusier projects in North Africa.

Many of Reidy's other projects are major urban planning schemes, such as his Gavea Housing Development in Rio, which extends the principles applied in the Pedregulho Estate. His superb plan for developing a new civic centre for Rio de Janeiro on Santo Antonio Hill was drawn up in 1948 and carried into execution in the following decades, though not without bureaucratic antagonism that prevented its full realization. The plan incorporates the ancient convent of Santo Antonio on the highest ground and other historic features such as the aqueduct, which becomes an enduring landmark of the city's traditional past, while a very considerable part of the land is given over to open spaces.

The Carmen Portinho house is on a steep hillside, with the garage and servants' quarters built directly on the ground, joined by the two sides of a sunken patio following the slope of the land to a main block which is raised on the characteristic pillars known as *Pilotis*, with a huge glass wall to the living room offering a view of the rich forest vegetation and a vast distant panorama.

With Carmen Portinho as construction engineer, the Museum of Modern Art in Rio de Janeiro is a further example of Reidy's designs in which two groups of buildings of different volumes are characterized by freely flowing wide spaces as well as by the novel ways in which natural daylight is combined with artificial lighting. The Museum clearly demonstrates the essentially spatial qualities of his architecture, with its geometrical contrasts almost sculptural in their impact, and his liking for an ingenious play of light and shade created by a combination of natural and artifical lighting. This is also true of his Museum of Visual Arts in Sao Paulo, again on a highly irregular site, but here given an expressive base structure with the Museum rising as a clear-cut triangular prism from it. His two theatres in Rio both have ingenious roofs. The earlier, the Marechal Hermes Community Theatre, in an industrial suburb of Rio, has a small auditorium seating only 300, and is also used for amateur performances as well as popular productions by professionals. The inverted double slope roof helps to integrate the external aspect with the internal layout, with the interpenetration of the two roof slopes, which corresponds to the auditorium section, serving a dual purpose: to the rear of the building it allows sufficient height for the stage with its scenery and cyclorama, while to the front it allows the lobby to be lit by a clerestory. Like all Reidy's projects, it shows him as a highly inventive architect who always arrived at technical and architectural solutions that are both personal and yet characteristically Brazilian.

—Konstantin Bazarov

REINIUS, Leif Axel

Swedish. Born in Stockholm, 24 May 1907. Educated at the Högre Realiäroverket, Stockholm, graduated 1925; Royal Technical University, Stockholm, 1925-29; Dip.Arch. 1929; student/assistant, in the office of Hakon Ahlberg, Stockholm, 1929-36; studied in Germany, Italy, and France, 1932. Married Ingrid Bergsten in 1936; children: Kristofer, Silja (died), Mikael, and Cornelia. Since 1936, in partnership with Sven Backström, *q.v.*, Stockholm. Editor, *Byggmästaren*, Stockholm, 1944-50. Recipient: Kasper Salin Award, Svenska Arkitekters Riksförbund, 1967; Prince Eugen Medal, 1970; Olle Engkvist Medal, 1973; Honorary Award, Stockholm Building Association, 1981. Member, Royal Academy for Free Arts, 1962. Knight Commander, Royal Order of Vasa, 1973. Address: Backström and Reinius, Storgatan 11, 114 44 Stockholm, Sweden.

see BACKSTRÖM, Sven

RENTON, Andrew.

British. Born in Dunfermline, Scotland, 22 May 1917. Educated at Dunfermline High School, 1929-34; Edinburgh College of Art School of Architecture, 1934-37, 1938-40 (Andrew Grant Travel Scholarship to the Cotswolds and Somerset, 1935, 1936; Royal Institute of British Architects Bronze Medallist, 1937; RIBA Scholarship to Italy, 1939), Dip.Arch. 1940 Served in the Royal Air Force in England, South Africa, India and Burma, 1940-46. Married Jessie Ballie Leith in 1940; Marjorie Julia Esdaile in 1977; sons: John and Andrew. Worked during college vacations for architect James Shearer, Dunfermline, 1932, 1933; worked in the office of Sir John Burnet Tait and Lorne, Edinburgh and London, 1937-38, in the office of Sir Robert Lorimer and Matthew, Edinburgh, 1946-48, and in the office of Basil Spence and Partners, London, 1948-49; Partner, Basil Spence and Partners, 1949-61; Principal, Andrew Renton and Associates, London, 1961-66; Partner, with Peter Howard and Humphrey Wood, Renton, Howard, Wood Associates, London, 1966-73, and Renton, Howard, Wood Partnership, London, 1973-74; Partner, Renton, Howard, Wood, Levin Partnership (with Gerald Levin), London 1974 until his death in 1982. Principal, Andrew Renton (Edinburgh), 1973-77. Member, Royal Institute of British Architects Publications Committee, 1961-65, Public Relations Committee, 1961-65, Council, 1968-74, London Regional Council, 1970-72, and London Environment Group, 1970-75; Member of the Council Architects' Benevolent Society, 1962-64, 1967-69; Member of the Council, Society of Industrial Artists and Designers, 1966-70, and Joint Honorary Treasurer, 1968-70; President, Cities of London and Westminster Society of Architects, 1970-72, and Founder and Chairman of the society's Conservation Group, 1970-74. Member of the Design Council Scottish Committee, 1974-82, and of the Design Index Selection Committee, 1975-82. Recipient: RIBA Architecture Award for London Region, 1967, and for Yorkshire Region, 1972; Civic Trust Award, 1967, 1972; Concours Cembureau Award, 1975. Associate of the Royal Institute of British Architects, 1940, and Fellow of RIBA, 1960. O.B.E (Officer, Order of the British Empire), 1972. *Died* (in London) *14 November 1982*.

Works:

1959 Thorn House Office Building, Upper St. Martin's Lane, London, W.C.2
1965 Saint Katherine Dock House (now the World Trade Centre), London E.1
1970 Edinburgh College of Domestic Science (now Queen Margaret College)
1971 Crucible Theatre, Sheffield
1972 Pure and Applied Sciences Buildings, University of Nottingham
 Department of Psychology, University of Sheffield
1974 River Clyde Study, Scotlan (competition project)
1977 Apartment restoration and conversion, Kensington Palace, London
1978 Saint Katharine by the Tower redevelopment, London, E.1

Publications:

By RENTON: articles—"Saint Katharine Dock House" in *East London Papers* (London), Summer 1969; "The Waterfront," with Charles McKean, in *Save the City: A Conservation Study of the City of London*, London 1977.

On RENTON: articles—"Rooms at the Tower" in *Building Design* (London), 28 September 1973; "Beyond the Tower" by Lance Wright in *Architectural Review* (London), December 1973; "Crucible Theatre, Sheffield" in *Arup Journal* (London), December 1973; "Crucible Theatre, Sheffield" in *Baumeister* (Munich), January 1974; "Edinburgh College of Domestic Science" in *The Architect* (London), May 1974; "Invergordon Aluminium Reduction Works" in *The Architect* (London), May 1974; "Tower Hotel, London" in *Deutsche Bauzeitschrift* (Gutersloh), September 1974; "Arts Centre, University of Warwick" in *Arkitekten* (Copenhagen), 23 March 1976; "Nottingham's Festival Hall" in *Architects' Journal* (London), 2 June 1976; "Crucible Theatre, Sheffield," in *Informes de la Construccion* (Madrid) April 1977; "Attractive, Maintenance-Free Structure in an Urban Setting" in *Concrete* (London), June 1980; "Tolmers Transformation" in *Architects' Journal* (London), 8 October 1980; "Concert Hall in Nottingham" in *RIBA Journal* (London), March 1981; "Mirror Buildings" in *London Architect* (London), July 1981; "Shaping the Theatre to Suit the Show" in *Design* (London), April 1982; "Obituary: Mr. Andrew Renton—Outstanding Modern Architect" in *The Times* (London), 23 November 1982; "Andrew Renton Dies Aged 65" in *Building* (London), 26 November 1982; "Renton of RHW Dies" in *Building Design* (London), 26 November 1982; "Andrew Renton (1917-1982)" by Humphrey Wood, in *Architects' Journal* (London), 1 December 1982; "Andrew Renton: Obituary" in *RIBA Journal* (London), January 1983.

My teaching always led me to believe that building (in the three-dimensional sense) made the university, the church, the house, or whatever the project happened to be.

Experience has however taught me that it is only people who can bring buildings alive. Nowadays it is only when the clients have a completely clear idea of what they wish to achieve and the politicians are in support of the project that the architect can get on with his job.

Architects now must get down to hard physical, social and economic facts and cannot as in the past create their own monuments with little regard for the users and their needs, buildings being treated as *objets d'art*. In my opinion, this present day challenge is all to the good.

—Andrew Renton (1980)

What is it that characterizes the varied output of Andrew Renton?—is it possible to find a common thread running through his various projects? The approach is clearly an inclusivist one, bent on establishing good urban manners and coming up with an appropriateness for each site in turn—for example, the way that even the sinuous rhythm of the distant Park Hill Housing Estate is embodied in the roof form of his Crucible Theatre, Sheffield. What is it that links this work with, say, the grand civic statement at St. Katharine Dock, London.

As far as one can see, it seems impossible to trace much of a connection between these projects (and our "auteur" theory might fail us), but in fact there is one idea enshrined and explored in most of Renton's work. The idea repeatedly tested and so far not discarded is, in fact, affirmation of interior at the expense of exterior: the latter is deliberately sacrified on behalf of the former.

This modus operandi is best demonstrated at the

Andrew Renton: Saint Katherine Dock House (now World Trade Centre), London, 1965.

Crucible Theatre. The interior lobby is an eloquent conclave of ramps, directions and stops, highlighted in dramatic colour coding: the experience is synaesthetic, whereby all of one's senses are fused together into one human receptor. But, outside, one is hard pushed to find even the slightest external corroboration of the internal event. The external super-structure enjoys a complicity of its parts one with another—there is clearly a vague, soft effort by each part to individualize itself, falling back and emptied of any correspondence with the logic of the interior. While the inside gives itself all at once, the exterior sits more like a delayed-action fuse, releasing itself by degrees. . . Whereas the interior is a fine denouement, the exterior can be only provisional.

To design from in to out is to restore the private at the cost of the public. Everything goes on "behind the door," and one needs a key to enter.

—Chris Fawcett

REVELL, Viljo (Gabriel).

Finnish. Born in Vaasa, 25 January 1910. Educated at the Technical University, Helsinki, 1928-36. Married Maire Hellin Myntti in 1941; children: Tuula, Sonja and Kati. Assistant in the office of Alvar Aalto, Helsinki, 1933-34; Partner, Kokko-Revell-Riihimaki, Helsinki, 1934-36; in private practice, Helsinki, 1936-64. Head of the Bureau of Reconstruction, Association of Finnish Architects, Helsinki, 1942-45. Recipient: First Prizes in the competitions: War Memorial Cenotaph, Helsinki,

1941; Teollisuuskeskus Building, Helsinki, 1949; Primary School, Meilahti, 1949; Primary School, Hyryla, 1953; Tampere Tasa Oy Company Building, Tampere, 1953; Primary School, Kauriala, 1955; Housing Development, Pori, 1955; Guards Barracks, Helsinki, 1957; City Hall, Toronto, 1958; KOP Building, Turku, 1960; KOP Building, Lahti, 1961. *Died* (in Helsinki) *8 November 1964.*

Works:

1935 "Glass Palace" Office Building, Helsinki (with N. Kokko and H. Riihimaki)
1937 Kesko Office Building, Vaasa, Finland
       Kuntsi House, Vaasa, Finland
1938 Halli Oy Office and Apartment Building, Vaasa, Finland
1945 Pihlajatie Apartment House, Helsinki
       Vänr, Stoolinkatu Apartment House, Helsinki
       Ollonqvist House, Espoo, Finland
1948 War Consumptives Rehabilitation Centre, Liperi, Finland
       Salo Villa, Karjalohja, Finland
       Henriksson Villa, Espoo, Finland
       Havula Villa, Tuusula, Finland
       Sato Oy Apartment Houses, Vaasa, Finland
       National Pensions Institute, Helsinki (competition project; with Keijo Petäjä and Torben Valeur)
1949 Helenius Villa, Vaasa, Finland
1950 Kelopuu Summer House, Sipoo, Finland
1951 Laajasalo Terrace House, Helsinki
1952 Teollisuuskeskus Industrial Centre, Office Building and Hotel, Helsinki (with Keijo Petäjä)
       Rantakatu Apartment House, Vaasa, Finland

       Maunula Apartment Houses, Helsinki (with Keijo Petäjä)
       Hakasalmi Oy Office Building, Helsinki (competition project)
1953 Meilahti Primary School, Helsinki (with Osmo Sipari)
       Children's Home, Tapiola, Finland
       Terrace House, Tapiola, Finland
       Tampereen Tasa Housing, Tampere, Finland (competition project: with E. Eerikainen)
       Housing Reform Plan (competition project; with E. Eerikäinen)
       Porin Sato Housing (competition project; with M. Jaatinen and Reima Pietilä)
1954 Sufika and Mäntyviita Housing, Tapiola, Finland
       Elementary school, Joensuu, Finland
1955 Hyvon-Kudeneule Knitwear Factory, Hanko, Finland
       Tallberg Villa, Helsinki
1956 Vaasanpuistikko Apartment Houses, Vaasa, Finland
       Malmönkatu Apartment House, Vaasa, Finland
1957 Didrichsen Villa, Helsinki
       Slev Factory, Kirkkonummi, Finland
1958 Tricol Factory, Inkoo, Finland
       Pyykönen House, Helsinki
       City Hall, Toronto, Canada (competition project; with Heikki Castren, Bengt Lundsten and Seppo Valjus)
1959 Hietalahdenkatu Apartment House, Vaasa, Finland
       Kaskenkaatajantie Apartment Houses, Tapiola, Finland
       Kaksoistornit Apartment House, Pori, Finland
1960 Tornitaso Apartment Houses, Tapiola, Finland

World Health Organization Office Building, Geneva, Switzerland (competition project; with Robert Ellenrieder, Bengt Lundsten and Seppo Valjus)
1961 Garrison Annex, Helsinki (with Heikki Castrén)
Didrichsen Art Gallery, Helsinki
Vatiala Funeral Chapel, Tampere, Finland
1962 Elementary school, Kauriala, Hämeenlinna, Finland
Commercial Centre, Vaasa, Finland
Nallentorni Apartment House, Tapiola, Finland
Peugeot Office Building, Buenos Aires, Argentina (competition project; with Heikki Castrén, Taivo Caspi and Kimmo Söderholm)
1963 KOP Bank Building, Turku, Finland
Munkkiniemenranta Apartment House, Helsinki
Koulukatu Apartment House, Vaasa, Finland
Kaunisto House, Helsinki
Kaskenhovi Terrace House, Tapiola, Finland
1964 City Hall, Toronto, Canada (with John B. Parkin Associates)
Oulunkylä Church, Helsinki (competition project; with Heikki Castrén)

Publications:

On REVELL: book—*Viljo Revell: Buildings and Projects*, edited by Kyösti Ålander, Helsinki 1966; articles—"Projet pour l'hôtel de ville de Toronto" in *L'Architecture d'Aujourd'hui* (Paris), vol. 33, no. 100, 1962; "Obituary: Viljo Revell" in *The Builder* (London), 13 November 1964; "Neues Rathaus in Toronto" in *Bauen und Wohnen* (Zurich), vol. 20, no. 8, 1968; "Civic Complex, Toronto, Canada" in *Architect and Builder* (Cape Town), November 1973; "Functionalist Monument: Helsinki's Glass Palace Get a Big Chance" by Cees Zwinkols in *De Architect* (The Hague), October 1979.

The young Viljo Revell's breakthrough in Finland came with the Lasipalatsi (Glass Palace) in 1935, which he designed in cooperation with Kokko and Riihimäki. This early functionalist building, originally intended to be only temporary, reflects influences of the 1930 Stockholm exhibition. From the beginning of his career, Revell acknowledged that he worked to promote international trends. As Alvar Aalto's assistant, together with Aarne Ervi, he worked, for instance, on the design of the Finnish Pavilion at the Paris *Worlds's Fair* in 1937. After World War II, Revell's own work showed that his approach diverged from the highly individual Aalto line, which was based on harmony and a conscious restraint with materials. Revell's works reflect the changes that were going on in post-war architecture internationally: he used the full potential of new materials, new concrete techniques and prefabricated elements to produce a non-ornamental mechanized urbanism that was completely new, particularly in Finland.

In 1948 Revell won a competition for a commercial building sponsored by various Finnish industrial organizations; it was to be the first large Finnish business building in the post-war period. Its strip windows and colonnade point to the International Style, and it also symbolized the emergence of the Finnish economy into a new era after the problems of the war and the post-war period of scarcity. The same new industrial modernism can be found in Revell's unit-built houses in the first phase of Tapiola (1954). He later turned to a more traditional technique in his designs for Tapiola, aiming at strong horizontal line. A large-scale town planning competition entry in 1953, for a suburb to the north of the city, never got beyond the competition stage. It featured two three-story lamellas of housing almost a kilometre long, following the ups and downs of the terrain, with an

Viljo Revell: Teollisuuskeskus Office Building, Helsinki, 1952.

internal service corridor. Revell and Osmo Sipari has experimented with this kind of twisting volume on a smaller scale in the Meilahti Primary School of 1953. In 1955 the Kudeneule Knitwear Factory was completed in Hanko, one of the Revell office's main projects before the design for Toronto City Hall. The factory integrated the rational qualities called for by industry into a basically rectangular, almost artificially modern, milieu.

The team involved in the Toronto City Hall competition of 1958—Heikki Castren, Bengt Lundsten and Seppo Valjus as well as Revell himself—created a powerful, symbolic-looking construction in which two concave towers shield a circular City Council Chamber. The final version (completed in 1964) made several compromises over the original plan in order to meet local demands. In a form that dominates the city centre, Toronto City Hall is a building that bears the hallmark of Revell's architecture, embodying the belief in technology of the '50s combined with the International Style's aspirations for the monumental. Here, as in several projects for city blocks (Helsinki, Vaasa), Revell reveals his powerful instinct towards the large entity, sometimes at the expense of detail. Yet, his small houses, such as the Villa Didrichsen in Helsinki, are also worked out down to the last detail, and the formalism that is sometimes perceptible in the larger works is not present.

The style of Revell's architecture has points of contact with Scandinavian functionalism, with the works of Le Corbusier, and with International Style and post-war industrial formalism. He was an architect of great character who made a major contribution to orienting Finnish architecture internationally and opening up its potential at home.

—Pekka Suhonen

RICCI, Leonardo.

Italian. Born in Florence, 8 June 1918. Educated at the University of Florence, under Giovanni Michelucci, 1938-41, Dip.Arch. 1941. In partnership with Leonardo Savioli, *q.v.*, and G. Gori, Florence, 1944-49. Since 1949, in private practice, Florence. Member of the Architecture Faculty, University of Florence, since 1945: Assistant Professor of Architecture, 1945-54; Professor of Architectural Composition and Design, 1954; Professor of Interior Design, 1954-55; Professor of Art and Architecture, 1954-60; Professor in charge of the Industrial Design Course, 1955-60; Professor in charge of the Second-Year Drafting Course, 1960-65; Professor of the

Elements of Architectural Composition and Design, 1964-65; Director, Town Planning Institute, since 1965; Professor of Town Planning, 1966-70; Head of the Faculty of Architecture, since 1971. Visiting Professor, Massachusetts Institute of Technology, Cambridge, 1960. Director, Town Planning Research Program, Italian National Committee for Research, 1964-66, 1966-67. Exhibitions: *La casa abitata*, Palazzo Strozzi, Florence, 1965; *Italian Architecture*, toured Italy 1965, 1973; *Utopia e crisi dell'antinatura*, at the *Biennale*, Venice, 1978. Recipient: Architecture Prize, *Bienal*, São Paulo, 1953; Naples Architecture Prize, 1955; Gold Medal, *Triennale*, Milan, 1958; Gold Florin Award, Florence, 1964; INARCH Prize, Florence, 1966. Member, Fine Arts Academy, Rome, 1962, San Luca Academy, Rome, 1963, and Teatina Academy for Sciences, Rome, 1964. Address (office): Via Bolognese Nuova, Monterinaldi, Florence, Italy.

Works:

1944/
45 Victory Bridge, Florence (competition project; with R. Gizdulich, G. Gori, G. Neumann, and Leonardo Savioli)
1945/
46 Plan for the reconstruction and redevelopment of Vicchio and Dicomano, Italy (with Leonardo Savioli)
Carraia Bridge, Florence (competition project; with G. Gori, G. Neumann, and Leonardo Savioli)
1946 Plan for the reconstruction and redevelopment of Empoli, Italy (competition project; with G. Gori and Leonardo Savioli)
Tourist and urban development plan for the Lido, Venice (competition project; with G. Gori and Leonardo Savioli)
Piazza d'Armi, Perugia, Italy (competition project; with G. Gori and Leonardo Savioli)
Grazie Bridge, Florence (competition project; with G. Gori and Leonardo Savioli)
1946/
47 Reconstruction plan for the Pontevecchio War-Damaged District, Florence (competition project; with G. Gori, E. Brizzi, and Leonardo Savioli)
Bridge over the Sieve River, Rufina, Italy (with G. Gori, G. Neumann, and Leonardo Savioli)
Bridge over the Arno River, Terranuova Braciolini, Italy (with G. Gori, E. Brizzi, and Leonardo Savioli)
Bridge over the Arno River, Figline Valdarno, Italy (with G. Gori, E. Brizzi, and Leonardo Savioli)
Group of four villas, for the directors of the Vetroflex Company, Florence (with G. Gori and Leonardo Savioli)
1947 San Romando District Redevelopment, Ferrara, Italy (competition project; with E. Gori, G. Gori, and Leonardo Savioli)
Bridge over the Arno River, Signa, Italy (competition project; with G. Gori, E. Brizzi, and Leonardo Savioli)
San Niccolo Bridge, Florence (competition project; with G. Gori, E. Brizzi, and Leonardo Savioli)
Bridge over the Serchio River, Calavorno, Italy (competition project; with G. Gori, E. Brizzi, and Leonardo Savioli)
Bridge over the Cecina River, Ponteginori, Italy (competition project; with G. Gori and Leonardo Savioli)
Mezzo Bridge, Pisa (competition project; with G. Gori and Leonardo Savioli)
Bridge over the Bisenzio River, Signa, Italy (with G. Gori and Leonardo Savioli)
Municipal Cemetery, Settignano, Italy (project; with E. Detti, R. Gizdulich, G. Gori, and Leonardo Savioli)

Saint-Gobain Workers' Garden City, Pisa (project; with G. Gori and Leonardo Savioli)
Design of the Artisans' Trade Fair, Florence (with E. Gori, G. Gori, and Leonardo Savioli)
1948 Bridge over the Sterza River, Bottaccina, Volterra, Italy (competition project; with G. Gori and Leonardo Savioli)
Design of the Artisans' Trade Fair, Florence (with E.Gori, G. Gori, and Leonardo Savioli)
Bridge over the Sterza River, Salitone, Volterra, Italy (with G. Gori and Leonardo Savioli)
Urban development building code for Lido di Camaiore, Italy (competition project; with G. Gori, E. Isotta, and Leonardo Savioli)
1948/
51 Flower and Fruit Market, Pescia, Italy (with E. Gori, G. Gori, E. Brizzi, and Leonardo Savioli)
1949 Design of the Artisans' Trade Fair, Florence (with E. Gori, G. Gori, and Leonardo Savioli)
1951/
63 Village of sixteen villas, Monterinaldi, Florence
1952 House, Beverly Hills, California
1953 Sets and costumes for the Boboli Garden Ballet, Florence
1953/
54 Village for 2,000 in the Sesto Hills, Florence (competition project; with G. Petrelli, Danilo Santi, and Leonardo Savioli)
1954 Quercianella Tourist Village, Livorno, Italy (project)
1954/
55 Plan for the San Frediano District, Florence (competition project; with G. Petrelli, Danilo Santi, and Leonardo Savioli)
1955 Leonardo Ricci Villa, Monterinaldi, Florence
Stage sets and scenery for Monteverdi's *Orfeo*, International Festival, Aix-les-Bains, France
Plan for Albisola Marina and for Albisola Superiore, Italy
1957 Borghese-Mann House, Forte dei Marmi, Italy
Housing Development Study for the CEP Workers' Housing Institution, Sorgane, Florence (project; with others)
1958 Balmain House, Island of Elba
Flower Market, San Remo, Italy (project)
1959 Goti Spinning Factory, Campi Bisenzio, Florence
1962 Plan for the Novoli Quarter, Florence (project; with others)
1962/
74 Montepiano Residential Village, Florence
1963 Cardon House, Castiglioncello, Livorno, Italy
Rossell House, Le Focette, Lucca, Italy
Experimental village, Riesi, Sicily
Workers Housing Development, Granaiolo, Genoa (project)
Residential Village, for GESCAL National Institute for Workers' Housing, Sorgane, Florence
1964 Giannini House, Rome
Design of the *Expressionism* exhibition, Palazzo Strozzi, Florence
1964/
68 Monte degli Uliva Village, Riesi, Caltanissetta, Italy
1965 Megalopolis (project; with Pennsylvania State University students)
Town plan for Pachino, Sicily
1967 Permanent Exhibition Centre, for the Artisans' Trade Fair, Florence (competiton project)
Municipal Cemetery Redevelopment, Montecatini, Lucca, Italy (project)
Layouts for the Italian Pavilion, *Expo '67*, Montreal

1972/
73 Master Plan for the University of Florence (competition project; with others)
1977/
78 Administrative Centre, Florence (competition project; with others)

Publications:

By RICCI: books—*Anonymous, XX Century*, New York 1962, as *Anonimo del XX secolo*, Milan 1965; *Leonardo Savioli*, with others, edited by Giovanni Fanelli, Florence 1966; articles—"Problemi per una nuova Maggioranza" in *Casabella* (Milan), May 1964; "The Architect: For Which Society?" in *Casabella* (Milan), December 1973; "Modern Art Gallery in Bologna" in *Architettura* (Rome), April 1976.

On RICCI: books—*Prima triennale itinerante d'architettura italiana contemporanea*, exhibition catalogue, edited by M. D. Bardeschi and L. V. Masini, Florence 1965; *Catalogo Bolaffi dell'architettura italiana 1963-66*, edited by P. C. Santini and L. Marini, Turin 1966; *New Directions in Italian Architecture* by Vittorio Gregotti, London and New York 1968; *Italian Architecture of the Sixties*, exhibition catalogue, with foreword by Giuseppe Tucci, Rome 1972; *Immaginazione megastrutturale dal futurismo a oggi*, edited by E. Crispolti, Venice 1979; articles—"A Monterinaldi, presso Firenze" in *Domus* (Milan), December 1957; "New Look on the Hills Near Florence" by Giulia Veronesi in *Zodiac* (Milan), no. 4, 1959; "The Involved Man: Leonardo Ricci" in *Progressive Architecture* (New York), August 1960; "La nascita di un villaggio per una nuova comunità, in Sicilia" in *Domus* (Milan), December 1963; "Birth of a Village in an Underdeveloped Area" in *Arts and Architecture* (Los Angeles), October 1966; "Città della terra: recherches d'urbanisme, Faculté de Florence" in *Architecture d'aujourd'hui* (Paris), October/November 1966; "Exploratory Research in Urban Form and the Future of Florence" in *Arts and Architecture* (Los Angeles), February 1967; "Abitazione à Firenze" in *Architecture: formes et fonctions* (Lausanne, Switzerland), No. 15, 1969; "Architettura a scala Urbana" in *Architettura* (Rome), May 1971; "The New Architecture of Florence" in *Architectural Record* (New York), February 1974.

*   *   *

After his studies under Giovanni Michelucci at the University of Florence, Leonardo Ricci soon purged his style of anything that suggested self-satisfaction or any notions of "subject before form." He thereafter devoted himself to international architectural questions—without reference to historic culture, conscious of the profound significance of contemporary conditions.

Ricci was one of the first Italian architects to change the treatment of materials in architecture, and he employs free, organic, natural forms full of powerful expressive content, putting forward the possibility of a new way of life related to today's needs in today's consumer society.

Ricci has anticipated some of the liberating alternative proposals of much of the current generation's radical architecture. In his research, he has combined the lessons of Frank Lloyd Wright with neo-expressionist demands, and this synthesis has led, in his work, to an individual version of International Brutalism.

More recently, Ricci has extended his architectural ideas to town planning. In his lectures, he has been offering theories on macrostructures and fluid communication facilities, proposing a whole series of investigations into great, organic "district cities" in which the natural components of the district are seen as parts of incessant, vital patterns of circulation.

—Lara-Vinca Masini

RICKARD, Bruce Arthur Lancelot.
Australian. Born in Sydney, New South Wales, 1
December 1929. Educated at Barker College, Sydney, 1937-46; studied architecture at Sydney Technical College, 1947-53, Dip.Arch. 1953; studied
landscape architecture at University College, London, 1954, and the University of Pennsylvania,
Philadelphia, 1956-57 (fellowship), M. Landscape
Arch. 1957; studied town planning at the University
of Sydney, 1958-59. Married Norma Mary Nivison
Charley in 1954; children: Peter (deceased) and Jane;
married Robin May Cooke in 1960; children:
Samuel, James, and Nicholas. Worked as a junior in
the offices of H. Ruskin Rowe, Sydney, 1947-49,
Sydney Ancher, *q.v.,* Sydney, 1949-53, and Fowell,
Mansfield and McLurcan, Sydney, 1952; Assistant,
Wallis Gilbert and Partners, London, 1954-55,
Garner and White, Philadelphia, 1956, George
Patton, Philadelphia, 1956, and Harberson, Hough,
Livingston and Larson, Philadelphia, 1957. Since
1959, Principal, Bruce Rickard and Associates,
Sydney. Temporary Lecturer, University of Sydney,
1958-59; Part-time Tutor, University of New South
Wales, Sydney, 1962-72 and 1974-76. Exhibitions:
Modern Sydney Domestic Architecture, Museum of
Modern Art, Melbourne, 1961; Farmer's Blaxland
Gallery, Sydney, 1961; Royal Agricultural Society
Easter Show, Sydney, 1964; Royal Australian
Institute of Architects Awards Exhibition, 1977
(toured Australia); *Old Continent—New Building,*
1983 (toured Australia). Recipient: Merit Award,
Royal Australian Institute of Architects, New South
Wales Chapter, 1972 and 1977. Address: Bruce
Rickard and Associates, 7 Ridge Street, North
Sydney, New South Wales 2060, Australia.

Works:

1953 Dickinson House, 26 Finlay Road, Turramurra, New South Wales
1954 Treloar House, The Avenue, Newport, New South Wales
1957 Clifton House, Prince Edward Parade, Hunters Hill, New South Wales
1958 Cohen House, 19 Rembrandt Drive, Middle Cove, New South Wales
1959 Malone House, Parni Place, Forestville, New South Wales
     Rickard House I, 51 Finlay Road, Warrawee, New South Wales
     Dibbs House, 39a Bardo Road, Newport, New South Wales
     Coventry House, Albert Parade, North Avalon, New South Wales
     Nairn House, Cronulla, New South Wales
1960 Reid House, 372 Old Northern Road, Castle Hill, New South Wales
     Marks House, 4 Deakin Place, Killara, New South Wales
1961 Midgeley House, Whale Beach Road, Whale Beach, New South Wales
     Smith House, Walker Place, McCarrs Creek, New South Wales
     Rickhard House II, 10 Kokoda Avenue, Wahroonga, New South Wales
     Courthouse, Narommine, New South Wales (with Ian McKay)
1962 Rolf House, 25a Finlay Road, Turramurra, New South Wales
     Armstrong House, 10 Cutler Road, Clontarf, New South Wales

Armit House, 22 Currugul Road, North Turramurra, New South Wales
     Cobb and Co. Drive-in Restaurant, Tempe, New South Wales
1963 Tennisen House, Burra Close, Mount Colah, New South Wales
     Fienberg House I, 27 Valerie Avenue, Chatswood, New South Wales
     Riddle House, 378 Deepwater Road, Castle Cove, New South Wales
     Shereline Homes Farmstead House, Showground, Sydney
1964 Lewis House, 37 Lynbrae Avenue, Beecroft, New South Wales
     Spring House, "Cloverdale," via Walcha, New South Wales
     Shereline Homes Executive House, Pennant Hills Road, Carlingford, New South Wales
1965 Marshall House, 61 Gordon Street, Clontarf, New South Wales
     Resanceff House, 14 Morella Place, Castle Cove, New South Wales
     Zador House, Boulevarde Street, Strathfield, New South Wales
     Mitchell House, 23 Rembrandt Drive, Middle Cove, New South Wales
     Sooster House, White Road, New Berrima, New South Wales
1966 Madden House, 27 Glenhaven Road, Glenhaven, New South Wales
     Davison House, The Esplanade, Kangaroo Point, New South Wales
     Hickey House, 2073 Pittwater Road, Bayview, New South Wales

Bruce Rickard: Richard House, Wahroonga, New South Wales, 1961.

1967 Armstrong House, 233 Cooyong Road, Terrey Hills, New South Wales
Curry House, 13 Sunnyridge Place, Bayview, New South Wales
Dell House, 169 Campbell Drive, Wahroonga, New South Wales
Heritage Homes Houses I, II, and III, Monterey Street, St. Ives, New South Wales
1968 Dolphin House, 3 Glenhaven Road, Glenhaven, New South Wales
1969 Connolly House, Colbran Road, Cheltenham, New South Wales
Mortuary chapel, Lady Davidson Hospital, St. Ives, New South Wales
1970 Allum House, 7 Berrilee Lane, Turramurra, New South Wales
Freeman House, 9 Kennedy Place, Church Point, New South Wales
McCreadie House, 72 Wandeen Road, Clareville, New South Wales
1971 Chapel, Lady Davidson Hospital, St. Ives, New South Wales
Car wash facilities, Mosman, Crows Nest, and Parramatta, New South Wales
1972 Car wash facilities, Canberra
1973 Whale Carwash, Gordon, New South Wales
1974 Car wash facilities, Bondi Junction, New South Wales
Fienberg House II, 19 Ocean Road, Palm Beach, New South Wales
Taylor House, Duke Street, Mittagong, New South Wales
1975 Townhouses, Ocean Shores, New South Wales (project)
Howard House, 3 Barclay Close, Pymble, New South Wales
Gee House, 2b North Parade, Hunters Hill, New South Wales
Lesslie House, Whitehall Road, Kenthurst, New South Wales
1977 Medium-density houses, Thurgoona, Albury-Wodonga, New South Wales (project)
1978 Medium-density houses, Bathurst, New South Wales (project)

Publications:

By RICKARD: article—"The Development of Canberra Landscaping" in *Architecture in Australia* (Sydney), December 1959.

On RICKARD: books—*Australian Housing in the Seventies* by Howard Tanner, Sydney 1967; *Living and Partly Living: Housing in Australia* by Ian McKay, Robin Boyd, Hugh Stretton and John Mant, Melbourne 1971; *An Australian Identity: Houses for Sydney 1953-1963* by Jennifer Taylor, Sydney 1972; *Old Continent—New Building: Contemporary Australian Architecture,* edited by Leon Paroissien and Michael Griggs, Darlinghurst, New South Wales 1983; articles—"The Growth of an Australian Architecture" by Milo Dunphy in *Hemisphere* (Canberra), August 1962; "Whale Carwash, Pacific Highway, Gordon, N.S.W." in *Architecture in Australia* (Sydney), August 1973; "House, Palm Beach" in *Architecture Australia* (Melbourne), January 1978; "Curry House" in *Architecture Australia* (Melbourne), November 1980; "Modern Australian Architecture," special issue of *Process: Architecture* (Tokyo), March 1981.

*

The bulk of my architectural work that has been built has been individual houses, the remainder being commercial work. Although I am very interested in housing on a larger scale and have designed some medium-density housing groups for government and developer/clients, none have, so far, been built.

I am not concerned merely with designing adequate buildings which shelter human activities from unpleasant sensations (such as wet, cold, heat) but buildings that allow and encourage people in their everyday life to enjoy and partake of the pleasant sensations emanating from climate and the natural and built environment, such as the well-being felt from sun in winter and shade in summer; the delight of seeing trees, plants, and the sky; the aesthetic pleasure of contemplating the play of space in a well-put-together built environment. The houses that I have built express this preoccupation; for example, my houses always, if possible, face north (similar to the south of the northern hemisphere), to catch the winter sun all day, and have northern terraces where it is as convenient for living activities to take place as it is indoors and often more pleasant. The outdoor areas also expand the usable living area of the house, allowing the family members greater choices for community or private activities. This aspect is of great importance to small units of medium- and high-density housing, where often families are condemned to living indoors only in crowded condition with little privacy and sometimes in units oriented in such a way as to never receive winter sun.

I care about the relationship of building to the site environment. My approach is to integrate the building with the site, for the building to reflect and emphasise in form, materials, and colour the dominant character of the site environment, whether it be on an undisturbed natural site with trees and rocks or a site in a man-made urban environment

Even though I consider the design of exterior appearance of my buildings and the spatial relationships that my buildings make with others, of greater moment to me is the interior spatial relationship and the play of major and minor spaces flowing together and sliding in sequence both horizontally and vertically as one moves about. While I try to obtain and be disciplined by a neat structural system, I try not to let the system dominate my design at the expense of spatial quality, but rather I try to exploit the unifying rythmic elements of the structural system.

In small buildings, I prefer to build with warm materials that require no further coating or decorating, such as brick, stone, timber, and glass. In buildings requiring large spans, I take up the challenge of building with steel and concrete and try to turn to account their innate qualities.

—Bruce Rickard

*

By the time Bruce Rickard returned to Australia in 1958, after four years overseas studying landscape design at the University of London and the University of Pennsylvania, the tide had turned and was beginning to run against the modern movement in Australia. Something of the conservatism of rural Australia had survived well into the 1950's in Sydney, and this factor, coupled with an undercurrent of romantic nationalism from the 1890s led to a wholesale rejection of the internationalism and machine aesthetics of modern architecture. Rickard arrived back in Australia at the crucial moment when the call for regionalism, climatic appropriateness, and an Australian identity in architecture was being voiced

Wright's Usonian houses were a revelation to Rickard, who recalls that on seeing Taliesin he was "impressed for the first time by a man-made environment." Rickard's free interpretation of Wright's 1930s language provided a focus for this somewhat romantic rejection of modern architecture, a movement that coalesced in a Wrightian school of domestic architecture in Sydney. Besides Rickard, the Sydney Wrightian School included Peter Muller, Neville Gruzman, Ian McKay, and several others and had a considerable impact on later postwar domestic architecture.

Rickard's style—he has built some sixty houses—unlike the romantic individualism of Peter Muller, is a rationalized version of late-1930s Wrightian motifs which have been stripped of their more idiosyncratic details. It would be trite to dismiss Rickard's Wrightian houses as mere copies and no more, for although Rickard has selected the best from Wright and adapted it to Australian circumstances, there are important, and fundamental, differences. For one thing, Wright's conception of the house as a protective cave-like refuge contrasts with the basic optimism of Rickard's houses which open onto the landscape and welcome light from the outside. Rickard avoids the cruciform plan and interpenetrating volumes intersecting at a central core of Wright's houses and prefers instead an elongated plan comprising a series of horizontally layered roof planes all facing north and, where the site permits, stepping back up the slope to admit daylight into the interior. The sun is a controlling factor in Rickard's houses. He strictly orients each house to the north and carefully calculates the roof overhangs to admit sunlight in winter and exclude it in summer. And instead of Wright's double pitched roofs, Rickard often uses a simple skillion roof superimposed above a lower horizontal one, to admit light deep within his houses. Rickard's houses are an intelligent interpretation of Wright; thus, there are similarities of style in the spatial form, horizontal expression, use of materials, and comfortable human scale. Rickard uses continuous strip windows, stained natural timber, rough sandstone walls, and progressive spatial sequences resulting in masterly Wrightian spatial compositions. The precise details throughout Rickard's houses demand a high standard of craft.

The Cohen house at Middle Cove (1958) is a long, low brick building with strong horizontal roof planes stepping backwards from the central living room. Rickard's house I at Warrawee (1959) and house II at Wahroonga (1961), particularly the latter, are consumate expressions of Rickard's artistry.

Rickard's reputation as an outstanding interpreter of the Wrighton domestic style is unfortunate in that it tends to obscure other quite different achievements. In the 1960s, Rickard designed a number of excellent carwash and service centres in Sydney with a precise engineering expression. Rickard's concern for extending quality design into the mass-housing market led to his involvement in a series of project houses for Shereline Homes and Heritage Homes; of these, the Executive Project House for Shereline is the most interesting. In his planning of individual house and town house types for the Ocean Shores Resort New Town, Brunswick Heads, Rickard was enabled to pursue his interest in the Usonian ideal.

Rickard's training as an architect and landscape designer allows him to see architecture as being of lesser importance than the design of the whole environment. In this respect, Rickard continues the tradition established in Australia by Walter Burley Griffin of land planning and environmental design.

—Philip Drew

*

RIDOLFI, Mario.

Italian. Born in Rome, 7 May 1904. Educated in Rome until 1918; worked for an engineering firm, and attended evening schools, Rome, 1918-24; studied at the School of Architecture, University of Rome, 1924-29, Dip.Arch. 1929, architectural travel scholarship, 1929; study-travels in Germany and Switzerland, 1933. Married (wife died, 1966). In partnership with the engineer Wolfgang Frankl, in Rome, 1934-39 and 1945-66, in Marmore, near Terni, Italy, 1966 until his death in 1984. Member of CIAM (Congrès Internationaux d'Architecture Moderne), and participant in MIAR (Movimento Italiano per l'Architettura Razionalista), from 1928. Co-director, *Metron* magazine, Rome, 1945. President, Accademia di San Luca, Rome, 1977-78. Exhibitions: *Mostra di Architettura Razionalista,* Rome, 1928 and 1931; *Le Architettura di Ridolfi e Frankl,* Palazzo Mazzancolli, Terni, Italy, 1979; *Architettura Italiane degli Anni' 70,* Galleria Nazionale d'Arte Moderna, Rome, 1981. Recipient: First Prize, Embassy Building Competition, Rome,

1930. Member, Academia di San Luca, Rome, 1960.
Died (by suicide, in Marmore, near Terni, Italy)
October 1984.

Works:

1925 Open-air Theatre by the sea (project)
Triumphal Arch in Memory of the War Dead (competition project)
1926 Elementary School, Rome (competition project; with A. Libera)
1927 Library in a Public Garden (project)
Regional Government Headquarters, Terni, Italy (competition project)
Elliptical Building (project)
1928 Low-cost furniture designs (competition project; with A. Libera)
Tower Restaurant, for the *Mostra di Architettura Razionalista*, Rome (project)
Hotel Building, for the *Mostra Architettura Razionalista*, Rome (project)
Tennis Spectator's Pavilion, for the *Mostra Architettura Razionalista*, Rome (project)
Flower Market, Piazza Monte d'Oro, Rome
Furniture for the Bucchi Fashion House, via Sistina, Rome
1929 Seaside Housing Colony, Castel Fusaro, Rome (project)
1930 Embassy Building in Latin America (competition project)
Theatre for the Opera Nazionale Dopolavoro (OND), via Capo d'Africa, Rome (competition project; with Fagiolo)
Caproni S79 aircraft interiors
Seaside Villa, for the *IV Triennale*, Monza, Italy (project)
1931 Children's Home, Isola del Giglio, Tuscany, Italy (project)
Commemorative Fountain, Piazzale della Stazione, Bologna, Italy (project)
Palazzata Buildings Complex, Messina, Italy (competition project; with Libera and Fagiolo)
Apartment Building, for the 2nd *Mostra Architettura Razionalista*, Rome (project)
Villas at Ostia Lido, Rome (competition project; with Fagiolo)
Urban Plan and Apartment Block, Ostia Lido, Rome (with Fagiolo)
House at Tor di Quinto, Rome (project; with A. Libera)
1932 Italian House, Tunisia (project)
Provincial Economic Council Headquarters, Pesaro, Italy (competition project)
Church for the Archdiocese of Messina, Italy (competition project)
Gymnasium for the Opera Nazionale Balilla (project)
1933 Balilla Building, Macerata, Italy (project)
Balilla Building, Potenza, Italy (project)
Post Office Building, Piazza Bologna, Rome
Fountain, Piazza Tacito, Terni, Italy
1934 Art Gallery, Piazza Colonna, Rome (with W. Frankl)
Technical Institute, Perugia, Italy (project; with W. Frankl)
PNF Headquarters, Via dei Trionfi, Rome (competition project; with Rossi, Cafiero and Rinaldi)
Rea Mansion, via di Villa Massimo, Rome (with W. Frankl)
1935 Public Swimming Pool, Villa Borghese, Rome
Testaccio Swimming Pool installations, Rome
1936 A. Bordoni Technical Institute, Pavia, Italy (with W. Frankl)
Leisure Centre, Tevere, Rome (with W. Frankl)
Colombo Mansion, via San Valentino, Rome (with W. Frankl)
1937 Caretti Inn, via Francespo Crispi, Rome (with Rossi)

Civilta Italiana Building, at EUR, Rome (competition project; with W. Frankl)
Armed Forces Building, at EUR, Rome (competition project; with W. Frankl)
1938/
39 Ministry for Italian Africa, Rome (competition project; with Rossi, Cafiero, Rinaldi, Legnani, Sabatini, and Frankl)
1939 Tuberculosis Prevention Centre, Pesaro, Italy (project; with W. Frankl)
1940 Fascist Professionals and Artists Confederation Building, Rome (project)
Prison prototype (project; with Rinaldi and Sabatini)
1940/
41 Agricultural Offices, Sant'Elia, Latina, Italy (project)
Palazzo del Littorio, Brindisi, Italy (project)
1942 Low-cost housing for the Castiglione Company
Via Baroni development, Rome
1945 Reconstruction Plan for Terni, Italy
1946 Bar-Kiosk, Piazza di Monte Savello, Rome
House for the Dependants of the Societa Terni, via Coletti, Terni, Italy
1947 Main Rail Station Carriage Works, Rome (competition project; with Quaroni, Cardelli, Firoentino, Care and Ceradini)
Penthouse construction, via Nicotera, Rome
1948 New Gallery at the Museo delle Terme, Rome
Palazzo del Drago restoration, Terni, Italy
Elettra Restaurant, Rome
House in the via Francesco Crispi, Naples, Italy (with W. Frankl)
1948/
49 INA-Casa Apartments, Italia Quarter, Terni, Italy (with W. Frankl)
Mansion Penthouse, via Paisiello, Rome (with Fiorentino and Frankl)
1949 Mansion in the via San Valentino, Rome (with W. Frankl)
Housing Type for UNRRA (project; with W. Frankl)
1949/
52 INCIS Apartments, via Ugo Bassi, Messina, Italy (with W. Frankl)
1949/
54 INA-Casa Housing Quarters, Via Tiburtina, Rome (with W. Frankl, L. Quaroni, C. Aymonino and others)
1950 UNRRA Apartments, Nopoli, Italy (with W. Frankl)
INA-Casa Apartments, Carignola, Italy (with W. Frankl)
Melchiorri Briganti House, Piazza del Mercato, Terni, Italy (with W. Frankl)
Cavalletti House, Piazza del Mercato, Terni, Italy (with W. Frankl)
Gallizia House, via Ardeatina, Rome (with W. Frankl)
1950/
51 Zaccardi Mansion, via G. B. De Rossi, Rome (with W. Frankl)
Chitarrini House, Largo Villa Glori, Terni, Italy (with W. Frankl)
1951 INA Apartments, Corso Vittorio Emanuele, Campobasso, Italy (with W. Frankl)
Luccioni Villa, via G. Carducci, Terni, Italy (with W. Frankl)
1951/
54 INA Apartments, viale Etiopia, Rome (with W. Frankl)
1952 Kussterman Mansion, via San Valentino, Rome (with W. Frankl)
Donatelli House, Largo Villa Glori, Terni, Italy (with W. Frankl)
INAIL Mansion, via Marco Polo, Rome (with W. Frankl)
1952/
53 Mancioli Mansion I, via Vulsci, Rome (with W. Frankl)
1952/
56 Secondary School, via Fratti, Terni, Italy (project; with W. Frankl)

1953/
55 Prison Building, Cosenza, Italy
Prison Building, Nuoro, Italy (with W. Frankl)
1954 Zaccardi Villas, via del Casaletto, Rome (with W. Frankl)
INA-Casa Apartments, via Donini, Livorno, Italy (competition project; with W. Frankl)
1954/
55 Astaldi Penthouse, via Porpora, Rome (with W. Frankl)
1955/
60 Olivetti Refuge, Canton Vesco, Ivrea, Italy (project; with W. Frankl)
1955/
61 Children's Home, Poggibonsi, Italy (with W. Frankl)
1956 INA-Casa Apartments, via Campegna, Naples, Italy (with W. Frankl)
INA-Casa Apartments, via Chiaiana, Naples, Italy (with W. Frankl)
1957/
58 CAP Apartments, Treviso, Italy (with Frankl, Gabbuti, Malagricci, Paladini, and Rinaldi)
1958 INA-Casa Apartments, Mareno, Italy (with W. Frankl)
1958/
60 INA-Casa Apartments, Conegliano, Italy (with W. Frankl)
INA-Casa Apartments, Belluno, Italy (with W. Frankl)
1959 Block of forty-four apartments, Terni, Italy (with W. Frankl)
1959/
60 Mancioli Mansion II, via Vulsci, Rome (with W. Frankl)
Franconi Houses, Corso del Popolo, Terni, Italy (with W. Frankl)
Staderini House, via Beccaria, Terni, Italy (with W. Frankl)
1959/
61 INA-Casa Apartments, via Villa Adriana, Tivoli, Italy (with W. Frankl)
1960 INA-Casa Apartments, Mestre, Italy (competition project; with W. Frankl)
1960/
61 Secondary School, via Fratti, Terni, Italy (2nd project; with W. Frankl)
1960/
63 Olivetti Refuge, Canton Vesco, Ivrea, Italy (2nd project; with W. Frankl)
1960/
64 FIAT Fratelli Fontana Complex, Terni, Italy (with W. Frankl)
1961 Industrial Technical Institute, Pietralta, Italy (competition project; with W. Frankl)
Nursery School, Trevisto, Italy (with W. Frankl)
1961/
63 Pallotta Houses, via Spada, Terni, Italy (with W. Frankl)
1962 Elementary School, Trevisto, Italy (with W. Frankl)
1962/
63 Shops and apartments for the Briganti Brothers, Terni, Italy (with W. Frankl)
IACP Housing Quarter, via Camaro, Messina, Italy
1964 Hospital, Campobasso, Italy (with Rossi and Frankl)
Clai Quarter Redevelopment Plan, Terni, Italy (with W. Frankl)
House, Marmore, near Terni, Italy
Bosco Development Plan, Piediluco, Italy (with W. Frankl)
ISES Apartments, Foggia, Italy (with Varetti, Bollati, Grassi and Frankl)
1965 Duomo Quarter Redevelopment Plan, Terni, Italy (with W. Frankl)
Solferino Quarter Redevelopment Plan, Terni, Italy
New Dock for the Lake of Piediluco, Italy (with W. Frankl)

1966 Prefabricated building components for the
Soprefin Company (with Malagricci and
Frankl)
Lina House, Marmore, near Terni, Italy
Politeana Building conversion, Terni, Italy
(project)
Nursery School, Spinaceto, Rome
1968 AGIP Motel, Settebagni, Rome (project)
1969 Motel, Belgrade, Yugoslavia (project)
1971/
75 Lana House, Cesi, Terni, Italy
1972/
73 De Bonis Houses, Porte delle Cavi, Terni,
Italy
1976 Stairway, Arrone, Terni, Italy
Angelici House completion, Cesi, Terni, Italy
1976/
77 Ottaviani House extensions, viale XX Settembre, Norcia, Terni, Italy
Lupatelli House, Vocabulo Piedimonte,
Terni, Italy
1977 Villa Luccioni extensions, via G. Carducci,
Terni, Italy
Francussi Penthouse, via della Remem-
branza, Arrone, Terni, Italy
1977/
78 Cresta House, Marmore, near Terni, Italy
(project)

Publications:

By RIDOLFI: book—*Manuale dell'architetto*,
editor, Rome 1946; articles—"Planning for an
Average-sized Town" in *Hinterland* (Milan), Jan-
uary/June 1980; "Nursery Schools" in *Domus*
(Milan), April 1980.

On RIDOLFI: books—*Architettura italiana oggi/
Italy's Architecture Today* by Carlo Pagani, Milan
1955; *Guide dell'architectura contemporanea in
Roma*, Rome 1965; *Il linguaggio grafico dell'architetto oggi* by L. Vanetti, Genoa 1965; *Catalogo
Bolaffi dell'architettura italiana 1963-1966*, edited
by Pier Carlo Santini and Giuseppe Luigi Marini,
Turin 1966; *New Directions in Italian Architecture*
by Vittorio Gregotti, London 1968; *Materiali per
l'analisi dell'architettura moderna: la prima
esposizione italiana di architettura razionale*, edited
by Michele Cannomo, Naples 1973; *Le architetture
di Ridolfi e Frankl*, exhibition catalogue, edited by
Francesco Cellini, Claudio D'Amato and Enrico
Valeriani, Rome 1979; *Architetture italiane degli
anni '70*, exhibition catalogue, edited by Giovanna
De Feo and Enrico Valeriani, Rome 1981; *50 Anni di
Professione*, edited by R. Bizzotto, L. Chiumenti
and A. Muntoni, Milan 1983; articles—"Palazzina
in viale di Villa Massimo a Roma" by P. Marconi in
Architettura (Rome), July 1937; "Stile di Ridolfi" by
Gio Ponti in *Stile* (Milan), January 1943; "Istituto
tecnico Antonio Bordoni a Pavia" in *Metron*
(Rome), January 1946; "Alcune opere recenti di
Mario Ridolfi" by Vittorio Gregotti in *Casabella*
(Milan), no. 210, 1956; "Unité de quartier à Rome"
in *L'Architecture d'aujourd'hui* (Paris), May 1956;
"Architetti italiani: Mario Ridolfi" by Guido Can-
ella and Aldo Rossi in *Comunità* (Milan), June/July
1956; "Mehrfamilienhauser in Rom" in *Baumeister*
(Munich), June 1959; "Opere recenti di Mario
Ridolfi" in *Casabella-Continuità* (Milan), March
1961; "Le carceri di Nuoro" in *Architettura* (Rome),
April 1964; "L'Ultimo lavoro di Mario Ridolfi" by
V. Vercelloni in *Controspazio* (Bari, Italy), June
1971; "Architecture of Mario Ridolfi", special issue
of *Controspazio* (Bari, Italy), November 1974; "A
Recent Project by Mario Ridolfi" in *Controspazio*
(Bari, Italy), September 1977; "The Opening Up
and Streetscape of the Corso del Porciuo in Terni"
in *Arquitecturas Bis* (Barcelona), March 1978;
"Architecture Arbitrarily Interrupted" in *Controspazio* (Bari, Italy), January/April 1979; "Overcoming
the Modern: Charles Moore, Mario Ridolfi and
Robert Venturi" by Luciano Rubino in *Ville Giardini* (Milan), July/August 1979; "An Exhibition and

Symposium on Ridolfi and Frankl" in *Controspazio*
(Bari, Italy), September/December 1979; "Why Is A
House Built?" by C. Morozzi in *Modo* (Milan),
October 1980; "AD Profile 32: From Futurism to
Rationalism" in *Architectural Design* (London),
no. 1/2, 1981; "Construction: Routes and Discour-
ses", special issue of *Lotus* (Venice), no. 37, 1983;
"Mario Ridolfi: Casa Luccioni in Terni 1977-79" in
Controspazio (Bari, Italy), January/June 1983; "A
Formidable Office: The Work of Mario Ridolfi" by
A. Soto in *Arquitectura* (Madrid), November/De-
cember 1983; "Ricordi di Mario Ridolfi" by L.
Benevolo in *Casabella* (Milan), December 1984.

*

Branded with the trademarks of Rationalist, Functionalist and Neorealist, the faces of architect Mario
Ridolfi are as complex as they are variable. He was
born in Rome in 1904, and thus belonged to a
generation of architects who defined themselves by
their adhesion to the canons of the Modern
Movement and its transformation into an Italian
functionalism with an international vocation. But
Ridolfi was a non-compliant, isolated case who
violated the architectural mandates of his contemporaries. Though his work espoused functionalism,
it transgressed predetermined compositions. He
decisively rejected architectural prototypes and
labels. Ignoring the renunciative Calvinist styles,
Ridolfi's designs found expression in the Italian
tradition by synchronizing vernacular forms and
materials with functional, modern styles. Belonging
to these styles were the lean-to roofs, balconies,
shutters, stones and bricks, railings, discontinuous
surfaces, irregular plans, sharp corners, and
ornamented facades. An architect who obstinately
followed his own ideas, Ridolfi produced structures
seen as discreet acts uncontaminated by ideology.

Although he was a member of MIAR
(Movimento Italiano Architetura Razionale), his
work often deviated from rationalist principles. In
fact, his early projects both adhered to the academic
tradition of the Roman School and explored German Expressionism. In 1924 he entered the Scuola
Superiore di Architettura in Rome, where he met
and collaborated with Adalberto Libera. Here
Ridolfi was inspired by Enrico del Debbio and
Pietro Aschieri, for his work at that time resembled
"rarefied classicism" and compositional techniques
linked to the Roman baroque. Simultaneously, the
Rationalist Movement invited him into architectural competition; designs for the school in Piazza
d'Arme in Rome (1926), the library in a garden
(1927), and the elliptical residence competition were
among his first achievements. His projects for the
restaurant tower and hotel (1928) and his thesis
project for a seaside colony at Castelfusano (1929)
also manifested Rationalist characteristics.

Ridolfi's visit to Germany and Switzerland in
1933 precipitated a change in his work; his contact
with the Expressionists enabled him both to overcome the antithesis between Rationalism and the
Roman School and to affiliate himself with the
former. Important works such as the Post Office in
Piazza Bologna (1933) and the competition for the
Palazzo di Littorio (1934) emerged as a result.
During the 1930s he developed a strong interest in
the "architecture of elements," stressing furnishings
and fixtures, and a fascination for the theme of the
house. The residences in Via de Villa Massimo
(1934), Via San Valentino (1936), designed with his
partner Wolfgang Frankl, and the model home at
E'42 (1940) testified to his didactic intrigue with this
theme.

Ridolfi's postwar activities were extensive, designing and reconstructing over eighty projects between 1945 and 1978 to add to his impressive
accomplishments since 1925. During an era of rapid
Western industrialization, his architecture sustained
a continuity between the distant past and the
functioning present. To establish this continuity
meant, however, divorcing himself from the Rationalist tradition and turning to a study of traditional
construction systems. When he designed vernacular

structures capable of fulfilling the demands of
modern urban society, his architecture bore yet
another label, Neorealism, one which Ridolfi himself contemptuously dismissed. His central concern,
rather, was to define an architectural language that
would be directly communicative for the poorer
classes who were viewed as the protagonist of
postwar reconstruction. The INA-Casa blocks of
the Tiburtino district in Rome represented to
Ridolfi and other young designers the chance to
experiment with a ground plan incorporating
American sociology and the populism of the Roman
baroque, characteristic of the new-Realist
Movement. In homage to the Italian culture, the
young architects used an ensemble of wrought iron,
Roman style brick vaults and details in the local
dialect, an attempt to rediscover the purity and
simplicity of rural Italian architecture. The *Manuale
dell'Architetto* of 1946, prepared by Ridolfi and G.
Calcaprina for the National Research Council, was
symptomatic of this period of reconstruction and
rediscovery. This book extolled traditional craftsmanship, thus promoting the building trade to the
vast unskilled labor force of underdeveloped country areas who were moving onto the cities. But the
book also furnished an essential contribution to the
projects involving subsidized housing projects.
Numerous important works derived from the brief
success of Neorealism, including Ridolfi's participation in the INA-Casa quarter project in Cerignola
(1950) and the houses in Viale Etiopia in Rome
(1951-1954).

Ridolfi's enthusiasm for the neo-realistic styles
was short-lived, however. After the failure of the
Tiburtino experiment in the 1950s, he concentrated
mainly on vernacular designs, and as a result
produced the Olivetti Nursery School in Ivrea
(1955-1963) and a series of inventions in the city of
Terni. In 1968 he was dealt yet another bitter
disappointment when his work with the Agip Tower
Hotel, a project which synthesized over forty years
of architectural experimentation, failed.

This misfortune represented the anti-climactic
end of an accomplished career, for he retired to
Marmore soon afterwards having contributed to a
mere nine housing projects throughout the next ten
years. In 1984 he committed suicide; apparently his
failure in 1968 presented an irreconcilible conflict to
his identity as an architect. But Mario Ridolfi did
not leave the world without distinction: he introduced German Expressionism to Italian architecture, and, through a revival of the vernacular,
encouraged postwar Rationalists to seek a language
which communicated expressly to the Italian culture.

—Carolyn Cole

RIETVELD, Gerrit Thomas.

Dutch. Born in Utrecht, 24 June 1888. Studied
drawing at the Municipal Evening School, Utrecht,
1906-08; architectural drawing with the architect P.
Houtzagers, Utrecht, 1908-11; architecture with P. J.
Klaarhamer, Utrecht, 1911-15. Worked in his
father's cabinet-making business, Utrecht, 1899-
1906; Draughtsman, C. J. Begeer's Jewellery Studio,
Utrecht, 1906-11; in private practice as a cabinet-
maker, Utrecht, 1911-19, and as an architect,
Utrecht, 1919-60: collaborated on architectural and
interior projects with Mrs. Truus Schroder-
Schrader, Utrecht, 1921-64; Partner, with J. van
Dillen and J. Van Tricht, Rietveld, van Dillen and
van Tricht, Utrecht, 1960 until his death in 1964.
Instructor in Industrial and Architectural Design,
Academie voor Beeldende Kunsten, Rotterdam and
The Hague, Academie van Beeldende Kunst en
Kunstnijverheids, Arnhem, Netherlands, and Acad-
emie voor Baukunst, Amsterdam, 1942-58. Member,

Gerrit Rietveld: Schroeder House, Utrecht, 1924.

with Van Doesburg, Huszar, Oud, and Wils, de Stijl Group, Leiden, Netherlands, and Utrecht, 1919-31; Founder-Member, CIAM (Congrès Internationaux d'Architecture Moderne), 1928; Dutch Delegate, CIAM, Frankfurt, 1929. Exhibitions: Modern Architecture Exhibition, Moscow, 1927; *Werkbund,* Vienna, 1932; *Biennale,* Venice, 1953; *Gerrit Rietveld,* Centraal Museum, Utrecht, 1958; *Rietveld, Architect,* Stedelijk Museum, Amsterdam, and Hayward Gallery, London, 1971-72; *Rietveld Schroder Huis 1925-1975,* Centraal Museum, Utrecht, 1975; *Architect Gerrit Rietveld in Limburg,* Bonnefantenmuseum, Maastricht, Netherlands, 1976; *Gerrit Rietveld,* De Zonnehof, Amersfoort, Netherlands, 1979. Honorary doctorate: Technical College, Delft, Netherlands, 1964. Honorary Member, Bond van Nederlandse Architecten, 1963. *Died* (in Utrecht) *25 June 1964.*

Works:

1920 Cornelis Begeer Shop, Utrecht
Dr. Hartog House interiors, Maarssen, Netherlands
1920/
22 Jeweller's shop, Amsterdam (destroyed)
1923/
24 Wessels Shop, Utrecht
1924 Van Huffel Chemist's Shop interiors, The Hague
Schroder House, Prins Hendriklaan, Utrecht (with Mrs. T. Schroder-Schrader)

1925 P. Ketting Study interiors, Utrecht
Dr. Muller Nursery, Utrecht
1926 Dr. Harrenstein Living Room, Amsterdam (with Mrs. T. Schroder-Schrader)
Weteringschans Bedroom, Amsterdam (with Mrs. T. Schroder-Schrader)
1927 Lommen House, Wassenaer, Netherlands (altered by other)
Birza Family House interiors, Utrecht (with Mrs. T. Schroder-Schrader; destroyed)
Normaal Housing (project; with Mrs. T. Schroeder-Schrader)
1928 Garage with Chauffeur's Living Quarters, Waldeck Pyrmontkade 10, Utrecht
1929/
58 Core Houses (projects)
1930/
31 Rowhouses, Erasmuslaan, Urecht (interiors with Mrs. T. Schroder-Schrader)
1930/
32 Rowhouses, for the Wiener Werkbund, Vienna
1931 Klep House, Montenspark 8, Breda, Netherlands
1931/
34 Studio houses, Blaricum and Laren, Netherlands (projects)
1932 Rowhouses, Robert Schumannstraat, Utrecht
House and Music School, Henriette van Lyndenlaan 6, Zeist, Netherlands
1933 Small Practical Houses (project)
Metz and Company Shop, Hoogstraat, The Hague (with W. Penaat)

1934 Row houses, Erasmuslaan, Utrecht (with Mrs. T. Schroder-Schrader)
Szekely House, Joh. Verhulstweg 70, Santpoort, Netherlands
1935 Hondius-Crone House interiors, Bloemendaal, Netherlands
Hillebrand House, Bloemlandscheweg 3, Blaricum, Netherlands
1936 Vreeburg Cinema, Utrecht (with Mrs. T. Schroder-Schrader)
Smedes House, van Weerden Poelmanlaan 1, Den Dolder, Netherlands
Mees House, Van Ouwenlaan 42, The Hague
1939 Hypothecair Crediet Bank, The Hague
Brandt-Corstius Summer House, Petten, Netherlands
1941 Verrijn Stuart Summer House, Breukelerveen, Netherlands
1942 Rietveld House (project)
1949 Smit House, Puntweg 8, Kinderdijk, Netherlands (project)
Van Ommeren House, Rijksstraatweg 158, Elst, Netherlands
1951 Stoop House, Beekhuizensweg 48a, Velp, Netherlands
Home for Spastic Children, Willemstad, Curacao
1952 Klaasen House, Taveernelaan 9, Den Dolder, Netherlands
1953 Bicycle Shed, Utrecht (destroyed)
1954 Van Ravensteijn-Hintzen house, Hoeflo 14, Laren, Netherlands
Driessen House, Hulkesteinscheweg 21, Arnhem, Netherlands

Dutch Pavilion, *Biennale,* Venice
Sculpture Pavilion, Sonsbeek Park, Arnheim, Netherlands (rebuilt at the Kröller-Müller Museum, Otterlo, Netherlands, 1965)
1954/
57 Housing, Hoograven, Utrecht (with van Grunsven and H. Schroder)
1955/
57 Housing, Utrecht (project; with J. Rietveld)
1956 Juliana Hall, and Entrance, Trade Fair, Utrecht (with others)
Visser House, Bergerdreed 6, Bergeyk, Netherlands (with H. Schroder)
De Ploeg Textile Works, Bergeyk, Netherlands (with G. Beltman, Engineers)
Institute for Applied Art, Wibautstraat, Amsterdam (project)
1956/
58 Scholten House, Kleiweg 32b, Baambrugge, Netherlands
1956/
68 Institute for Applied Art (Gerrit Rietveld Academy), Prinses Irenestraat 96, Amsterdam (completed by van Dillen and van Tricht)
1957 Blaha House, Villaparklaan 5, Best, Netherlands
Van Daalen House, Fasantlaan 14, Bergeyk, Netherlands
Press Room, Unesco, Paris
1957/
58 Schrale Beton Offices, Willemsvaart 21, Zwolle, Netherlands
1957/
59 Housing, Erasmusweg, Reeuwijk, Netherlands
1957/
63 Academy for Arts and Crafts, Onderlangs 9, Arnhem, Netherlands (completed by van Dillen)
1958 Parkhurst House, Oberlin, Ohio
1958/
59 De Zonnehof Exhibition Hall, Amersfoort, Netherlands
Van den Doel house, Monnikendammerzijweg 31, Ilpendam, Netherlands
1958/
61 Housing, Kanaleneiland, Utrecht
1958/
64 Primary school, Badhoevedorp, Netherlands
1958/
66 Auditorium, Hoofddorp Cemetery, Netherlands (completed by van Dillen)
1959 Ket Shop, Leeuwarden, Netherlands
Gemeentelijk Lyceum School, Doetinchem, Netherlands (with van Tricht)
1959/
60 Hamburger House, Korswater 9, Noordwijk, Netherlands
van Dantzig House, Harddraverslaan 60, Santpoort, Netherlands
Theissing House, Breitnerlaan 1, Utrecht
1960 Koot House, van Soutelandelaan, The Hague
1960/
65 Protestant Church, Zijdeveld, Uithoorn, Netherlands (with van Tricht)
1961/
62 Showroom, Design Centre, Amsterdam (partley destroyed, 1971)
1961/
63 Mado Shop, Oudegracht 119, Utrecht
1961/
64 Van Slobbe House, Zandweg 122, Heerlen, Netherlands
1961/
72 Centraal Museum extensions, Utrecht (with van Dillen)
1962 Poster Column, Eindhoven, Netherlands
1962/
63 Town Hall, Leerdam, Netherlands (project)
1962/
65 Savings Bank, Dedemsvaart, Netherlands
1963/
67 Steltman Jewellery Shop interiors, The Hague

Bosschaert House, Langewijnen 9, Laren, Netherlands (completed by T. Bakker)
1963/
72 Vincent van Gogh Museum, Amsterdam (with van Dillen and van Tricht)
1964 Miners' Barracks interiors, Eygelshoven, Limburg, Netherlands
Twente Technical High School Science Centre, Enschede, Netherlands (project)
1964/
67 Engelhard House, Straat van Mozambique 3, Amstelveen, Netherlands

Designs: Red-Blue Chair, 1918; Hanging Lamp, 1920; Berlin Chair, 1923; One-Piece Moulded Chair, 1927; Zig-Zag Chair, 1934; One-Piece Stamped Chair, 1942.

Publications:

By RIETVELD: books—*Over Kennis en Kunst, lezing-cyclus over stedebouw,* Amsterdam 1946; *Schroder Huis,* Amsterdam 1963; articles—numerous in *De 8 en Opbouw* (Amsterdam), 1932-1941; "Aanteekening bij Kinderstoel" in *De Stijl* (Leiden, Netherlands), no. 9, 1919; "Niet een landhuis maar een gewoon huis" in *Bouwkundig Weekblad* (The Hague), no. 44, 1926; "Interieur" in *International leergang voor vieuwe architectuur,* Delft, Netherlands 1930; "Nieuwe zakelijkheid in de Nederlandsche architectuur" in *De Vrijne Bladen,* Amsterdam 1932; "De nieuwe zkelijkheid in de architectuur" in *Leeuwarder Courant* (Leeuwarden, Netherlands), February 1933; "Vakverrotting" in *Bouwkundig Weekblad* (The Hague), no. 47, 1935; "Aangifte" in *Bond van Nederlandsche Architecten,* Amsterdam 1940; "De verhouding tusschen beeldhouwer en architect" in *Nieuwe Ultrechtsch Dagblad* (Utrecht), February 1947; "Het interieur" in *Bouwkundig Weekblad* (The Hague), no. 25, 1948; "Aspecten van het nieuwe bouwen" in *Forum* (Amsterdam), no. 2/3, 1949; "De bedoeling van de tentoonstelling" in *Schoonheid in huis en hof,* Amersfoort, Netherlands 1950; "Die Nachkriegsarchitektur in Holland" in *Werk* (Zürich), no. 11, 1951; "De Consequenties van het structuurplan van Utrecht voor de binnenstad" in *Bouwkundig Weekblad* (The Hague), no. 23/24, 1954; "Mondrian en het nieuwe bouwen" in *Bouwkundig Weekblad* (The Hague), no. 11, 1955; "Moord op Utrechts binnenstad: of levensvoorwaarde voor een stad" in *Elseviers Weekblad* (Amsterdam), October 1955; "De Jaarbeursgebouwen in 40 jaren" in *Forum* (Amsterdam), no. 3, 1956; "Ontwerper en materiaal" in *Visie* (Leiderdorp, Netherlands), no. 5, 1957.

On RIETVELD: books—*The Work of Gerrit Rietveld, Architect* by Theodore M. Brown, Cambridge and Utrecht 1958; *Rietveld tentoonstelling,* exhibition catalogue, Utrecht 1958; *Gerrit Rietveld: Bouwmeester van ein nieuwe tijd* by H. Schaafsma, Utrecht 1959; *Rietveld, 1924—Schroder Huis,* Hilversum, Netherlands 1963; *Gerrit Thomas Rietveld* by A. Buffinga, Amsterdam 1971; *Gerrit Rietveld, Architect,* exhibition catalogue, by I. L. Szenassy, Amsterdam 1971, London 1972; *Rietveld Schroder huis 1925-75,* exhibition catalogue by Gerrit Jan de Rook and Carel Blotkamp, Utrecht 1975; *Architect Gerrit Rietveld in Limburg,* exhibition catalogue edited by Istvan L. Szenassy, Maastricht, Netherlands 1976; *Instant Furniture* by Peter S. Stanberg, New York and London 1976; *Gerrit Thomas Rietveld: Furniture* by Daniele Baroni, Milan 1977, London 1978; *Gerrit Rietveld,* exhibition catalogue Amersfoort, Netherlands 1979; *Gerrit Rietveld, 1888-1964: een biografie* by Frits Bless, Amsterdam 1982; articles—"Proeve van kleurencompositie in interieur" by Theo van Doesburg in *De Stijl* (Leiden, Netherlands), no. 12, 1920; "Sculpture Pavilion, Arnhem, Holland" in *Architectural Design* (Lon-

don), no. 25, 1955; "Nieuw werk van G. Rietveld" in *De Groene Amsterdammer,* March 1956; special issue of *Forum* (Amsterdam), no. 3, 1958; "L'Oeuvre de Gerrit Rietveld" in *Architecture: formes et fonctions* (Lausanne, Switzerland), no. 6, 1959; "Gerrit Rietveld" in *Domus* (Milan), September 1965; "The Examples of Rational Buildings" by K. Drugowitsch in *Bauforum* (Vienna), January/February 1974; "Rietveld and His Museum Buildings" by E. Berg and H. Bak in *Arkitekten* (Copenhagen), 12 March 1974; "A Touch of De Stijl" by R. Yee in *Progressive Architecture* (New York), March 1975; "The Schroder House, 1924" by S. Nagao and Y. Tominaga in *Space Design* (Tokyo), March 1976; "Gerrit Rietveld" and "Mrs. Schroder and Her House" by Itzak Salomon in *Forum* (Hilversum, Netherlands), May 1980; "Rietveld: Myth and Reality" by Frits Bless in *Forum* (Hilversum, Netherlands), July 1981; "Photographic Report on Hoofdorp Cemetery Chapel" in *De Architect* (The Hague), January 1982.

Bibliography—*Gerrit Thomas Rietveld, 1888-1964* by Lamia Doumato, Monticello, Illinois 1983.

*

Gerrit Rietveld was an extraordinary architect. Almost all his work is provincial, even boring, yet there were brief moments when he was the most important architect and furniture designer in the world.

In 1918 Holland was an oasis of peace in a Europe at war, and it was in this Holland that Gerrit Rietveld produced his "red-blue" chair—a piece of furniture that was not too comfortable to sit on but was a delight to look at. It can be seen, in retrospect, as a demonstration of many of the concepts of the modern architecture that were to be invented during the course of the next decade. Rietveld was a cabinetmaker by training and made the chair himself; simple enough in construction, it was in its aesthetic that it was truly prophetic. Rietveld was a member of the de Stijl group and shared their love of bright colours and of rectangular planes sliding past one another. The red-blue chair was a de Stijl construction with bright colours and flat planes, but it also carried, in embryo, concepts such as the clear separation of supported planes and supporting framework and such as the reduction of designs to simple, unadorned rectangles that later architects were to develop in the design of buildings.

The chair was important, but the house that Rietveld designed for and with his friend Mrs. T. Schroder-Schrader was even more so. The house is small and stands on a tiny lot on Utrecht's Prins Hendriklaan, but it is clearly a manifesto building and the passing of more than half a century has not dimmed its impact. In 1924, when it was completed, Le Corbusier and Mies Van der Rohe were still fumbling through their early house designs, but the Schroder House is a mature work, a clear statement unequalled in Northern Europe this century.

De Stijl claimed to be liberators of space, and the Schroder House does not disappoint in that respect. In all the years since the Renaissance, space had been seen as confined, enclosed, ordered. Frank Lloyd Wright broke away from this limiting tradition and used space in a much freer way, and, due to the influence of Robert van't Hoff, Wright was admired and understood in Holland. But the Schroder House frees space far beyond that which Wright would sanction. The first floor is a flexible space—screens can be operated to make enclosed rooms or an open space. Big windows open the room to the outside; by placing side-hung casement windows opening away from the corner with no corner mullion, Rietveld removed the solidity and space-enclosing nature of the walls. For years, corners had been made solid; in the Schroder house the corner can be made nonexistent, and a new sensation of space, of limitless openness, has been gained.

The new sense of space achieved in the Schroder House would have been less meaningful were it not for the steel frame, used in a showy, wilful, but utterly consistent way. The architecture of open, flowing space is appropriate for steel-framed buildings, and here steel columns are enjoyed for their own sake and carried past the structure they support to emphasize the mood of continuity, of space extending beyond the confines of the house.

Ten years after the completion of the Schroder House, Rietveld built the everyday version, a row of houses, on an adjoining site in Utrecht's Erasmuslaan. Thoughtful, beautifully put together, and obviously very habitable, they are amongst the finest houses built in Europe at that time, but they lack the magic and the space games of the Schroder House, for by 1934 Rietveld had left the de Stijl movement, and he never again found a clear direction for his work. If the Erasmuslaan terrace is a come-down after the Schroder House, the later work of Rietveld can be said to continue the decline, for never again in thirty more years of practice did he design a building of world-scale influence and importance. He became a respectable but very local architect.

It was not only in Nazi Germany that modern architecture was frowned upon; for twenty years, Rietveld had little work and was considered demodé by the critics. Either because he had some sympathy with the reaction of the time or because he had to compromise to build at all, Rietveld's work in this period is often traditional, dull, and insipid. The nadir is reached in 1941 with the Verrijn Stuart Summer House at Breukelerveen, all thatch and waney-edge boarding, as if Hansel and Gretel had built a home by the lake.

The Schroder House made all the history books on modern architectur, while its architect seemed lost in a world of vernacular revival. In 1954 he staged a minor come-back. The Sculpture Pavilion in Arnheim's Sonsbeek Park stood for only a short while, but a decade later it was built again at Otterlo. This building has none of the smooth surfaces of the early buildings, but it does play de Stijl space-games, with walls extending outwards like the Barcelona pavilion. Then, in 1956, Rietveld turned to the curtain wall, which he handled very beautifully in the Institute for Applied Art, Amsterdam, with a totally high-tech image. The 1964 Van Slobbe House at Heerlen is probably the finest work from Rietveld's postwar period. A regular, almost Miesian frame is married with de Stijl planes—an irreconcilable conbination that somehow come off in this calm, masterly house. The Van Slobbe House is, however, the exception, and the general standard of the late work is not high. More typical is the brick de Stijl of the Dedemsvaart Savings Bank; structurally illogical, the design seems dated and dull.

—John Winter

ROBERTO ARCHITECTS.

Partnership; established, Rio de Janeiro, 1933, as M. M. Roberto, by Marcello Roberto (died, 1964) and Milton Roberto (died 1953); known as M. M. M. Roberto Architects, with Mauricio Roberto, 1942-64, and, under the direction of Mauricio Roberto, as M. Roberto Architects, since 1966. Exhibitions: Museum of Modern Art, Sao Paulo, 1958; *Brazilian Architecture,* Jedda, Saudi Arabia, and Lagos, Nigeria, 1976. Recipient: First Prize, Brazilian Press Association Headquarters Competition, Rio de Janeiro, 1936; Grand Golden Collar Award, Brazilian Institute of Architects, 1970; First Prize—Mint Building Competition, Rio de Janeiro, 1971; Alagados Urban Planning Competition, Salvador, Brazil, 1973; Taubate Administration Centre Competition, Sao Paulo, 1974; Usiminas Housing Competition, Ipatinga, Minas Gerais, Brazil, 1975; Convention Centre Competition, Salvador, Brazil, 1976; Tres Rios Urban Expansion Competition, 1976; Caji City Plan Competition, Salvador, Brazil, 1977; Buraquinho Tourist City Plan Competition,

Salvador, Brazil, 1978. Address: M. Roberto Arquitetos, Rua Siqueira Campos 43, Grupo 1006, Copacabana, Rio de Janeiro 22.031, Brazil.

Works:

1936 Brazilian Press Association Headquarters (ABI), Rio de Janeiro
1937 Airport Terminal Building and Hangars, Santos Dumont Airport, Rio de Janeiro
1941 Brazilian Insurance Institute Headquarters (IRB), Rio de Janeiro
1943 Industrial Institute Headquarters, Rio de Janeiro
Brazilian Insurance Institute Employees' Recreational Centre, Rio de Janeiro
1944 Pianco Apartment Building, Rio de Janeiro
Mamamguape Apartment Building, Rio de Janeiro
1944/
46 Sotreq Caterpillar Industrial Plant, Rio de Janeiro
1945 Roberto Building, Rio de Janeiro
1946 Mechanics' School, Rio de Janeiro
Faria Goes Summer Residence, Lake Araruama, Rio de Janeiro
1947 Institute of Pensions (IPASE) Employees' Apartment Building, Rio de Janeiro
1948 Faria Goes House, Rio de Janeiro
Naval Carpentry School, Niterói, Rio de Janeiro
1949 Carpentry and Weaving School, Vassouras, Rio de Janeiro
Brazilian Insurance Institute Office Building, Rio de Janeiro
1950 Weaving School, Petrópolis, Rio de Janeiro
Herbert Moses House, Gavea, Rio de Janeiro
1951 Ricardo de Albuquerque Workers' City, Rio de Janeiro
1952 Marques do Herval Offices and Shops, Rio de Janeiro
Arthur Monteiro Coimbra House, Jacarepagua, Rio de Janeiro
Apartment building, Cataguases, Brazil
1953 Samambaiba Apartment Building, Rio de Janeiro
1954 Shop and office, Samambaiba, Rio de Janeiro
School of Motor Engineering, Rio de Janeiro
Fátima e Finusia Apartment Building, Rio de Janeiro
Angel Ramirez Apartment Building, Rio de Janeiro
Guarabira Apartment Building, Rio de Janeiro
Tacito Prado House, Petrópolis, Rio de Janeiro
1955 Campello Apartment Building, Rio de Janeiro
Grumari Seaside Tourist Resort Development Plan, Rio de Janeiro
Tourist plan for the Cabo Frio Region of Rio de Janeiro
1956 School of Civil Construction, Rio de Janeiro
Polynuclear Metropolis: Urban Unit Cities Study (competition project)
Master plan of Imbituba City, Santa Catarina, Brazil
1957 Expansion plan for Tunis
1958 Souza Cruz Cigarette Company Headquarters, Rio de Janeiro
Banco da Amazonia, Brasilia
Guarapes Apartment Building, Rio de Janeiro
Bela Vista Apartment Building, Rio de Janeiro
Dalton Apartment Building, Rio de Janeiro
Barao de Sao Clemente Apartment Building, Rio de Janeiro
1960 Regina Yolanda Werneck House, Isle of Paqueta, Rio de Janeiro
1961 Cesar Thedim House, Cabo Frio, Rio de Janeiro
Apartment building, Laranjeiras, Rio de Janeiro

1962 Residential and hotel complex, Arenzano, Riviera del Poente, Italy
Getulio Vargas Hospital Annex and Ancillary Buildings, Rio de Janeiro
Ambulance, tuberculosis and public health buildings, Tijuco District, Rio de Janeiro
Moncorvo Filho Hospital, Rio de Janeiro
Club Building, Guinle Park, Rio de Janeiro
Apartment building I, Botafogo, Rio de Janeiro
1966 Apartment building II, Botafogo, Rio de Janeiro
1967 Development plan for Tres Rios, Rio de Janeiro
Building code for Araruama, Rio de Janeiro
Government Building, Sao Luiz, Brazil
1968 Bus Station, Tres Rios, Rio de Janeiro
Plan for Ribeirao Preto, Sao Paulo
Development plan for Betim, Minas Gerais, Brazil
1969 Apartment building, Ipanema, Rio de Janeiro
1969/
77 Bank of Brazil Administration and Data Processing Centre, Porto Alegre, Brazil
1969/
78 Bank of Brazil Administration and Data Processing Centre, Rio de Janeiro
1970 Development plan for Duque de Caxias, Rio de Janeiro
Development plan for Vitória, Espirito Santo, Brazil
Bank of Brazil Regional Headquarters, Sao Luiz, Brazil
1970/
77 Bank of Brazil Administration and Data Processing Centre, Sao Paulo
1971 Morro Nova Cintra Housing Development, Rio de Janeiro
1972 Priorities plan for Cabo Frio, Rio de Janeiro
Plan for the Niterói/Rio das Ostras Highway, Brazil
Urban master plan for Alagados, Salvador, Brazil (competition project)
BANESPA Banking Corporation Administration Centre, Sao Paulo
Nossa Senhora de Copacabana Parish Centre, Rio de Janeiro
Vera Simoes Summer Residence, Cabo Frio, Rio de Janeiro
1972/
77 Brazilian Academy of Letters, Rio de Janeiro
1973 Regional Bank of Brazil additions, Brasilia
Bank of Brazil Central Treasury, Rio de Janeiro
1974 Taubate Administration Centre, Sao Paulo
Marine Ministry interiors, Rio de Janeiro
Urban plan for Vila Oficinas, Curitiba, Brazil
Urban plans for Itapevi, Santo Andre, and Cotia, Sao Paulo
Santo Antonio do Catagua Urban Development, Taubate, Sao Paulo
1975 6th Naval District Headquarters, Sao Paulo
Youth Centre, Belo Horizonte, Minas Gerais, Brazil
Geovia Company Industrial Plant, Vitória, Espirito Santo, Brazil
Tourist development plan for Praia de Cacandoca, Ubatuba, Sao Paulo
1976 Santa Maria da Serra Tourist Centre, Barra Bonita, Sao Paulo
Bahia Convention Centre, Salvador, Brazil
Usiminas Housing, Ipatinga, Minas Gerais, Brazil
Bairro Ouro Verde Urban Development, Belo Horizonte, Minas Gerais, Brazil
Cidade Verde Urban Development, Betim, Minas Gerais, Brazil
Tourist plan for Barra Bonita, Sao Paulo
Plan for Caji, Salvador, Brazil

Roberto Architects: Brazilian Academy of Letters, Rio de Janeiro, 1972-77.

1977 International Insurance Company Headquarters, Rio de Janeiro

Urban expansion plan for Tres Rios, Rio de Janeiro

Acu da Torre Urban Development, Sao Joao da Mata, Bahia, Brazil

Urban development plan for Itapevi, Sao Paulo

1978 ERCO Company Factory, Santa Cruz, Rio de Janeiro

Urban development plan for Nova Lima, Minas Gerais, Brazil

Urban development plan for Santa Cruz, Rio de Janeiro

Tourism development plan for Buraquinho, Salvador, Brazil (competition project)

Tourism development plan for Morro de Guaratiba, Rio de Janeiro

1979 Data Processing Centre, Curitiba, Parana, Brazil

Data Processing Centre, Recife, Pernambuco, Brazil

1980 Urban development plan for Monte Alegre, Cabo Frio, Rio de Janeiro

Urban development plan for Sao Bernardo do Campo, Sao Paulo

Holiday Resort, Cabo Frio, Rio de Janeiro

Cultural and Recreational Center, Lagoa Rodrigo de Freitas, Rio de Janeiro

1981 Stock Exchange Headquarters, Rio de Janeiro

1982 Apartment Building, Cabo Frio, Rio de Janeiro

Apartment Building, Ipanema, Rio de Janeiro

Housing Development, Jacarepagua, Rio de Janeiro

1983 Hypermarket Disco, Rio de Janeiro (with others)

1984 Tourism development, Itacuruca Island, Rio de Janeiro

Tourism development, Jurujuba, Rio de Janeiro

Tourism development, Gamboa Beach, Itacuruca, Rio de Janeiro

Tourism development, Ilha das Cabras, Rio de Janeiro

1985 FUNENSEG Reassurance School, Rio de Janeiro

Summer Residence, Corumau, Bahia, Brazil

Publications:

On ROBERTO ARCHITECTS: articles—"Building for Business: New and Remodelled Office Buildings" in *Architectural Record* (New York), December 1940; "Brazilian Press Building" in *The Architects' Journal* (London), March 1941; "Cantilever Hangar, Santos Dumont Airport, Rio de Janeiro" in *Architectural Record* (New York), December 1942; "Cantilever Hangar" in *Architect and Building News* (London), March 1943; "Rio de Janeiro Airport" in *Architectural Review* (London), March 1947; "Flats in Rio de Janeiro" in *Architectural Review* (London), August 1947; "Building ABI, Rio de Janeiro" in *L'Architecture d'Aujourd'hui* (Paris), September 1947; "Education and Welfare in Brazil," "Living in Brazil," and "Office Buildings" in *Architectural Forum* (New York), November 1947; "Brésil" in *L'Architecture d'Aujourd'hui* (Paris), January 1948; "IRB Building at Rio de Janeiro" in *Architectural Review* (London), January 1948; "Arched Industrial Building Integrates Displat Repair and Office Space" in *Architectural Forum* (New York), November 1950; "Factory at Rio de Janeiro" in *Architectural Review* (London), January 1951; "The Work of Roberto, Roberto and Roberto, Architects" in *L'Architecture d'Aujourd'hui* (Paris), August 1952; "Buildings for Education" in *Progressive Architecture* (New York), February 1957; "Marcelo e Mauricio Roberto: Scioltezza e Liberta" by Giulia Veronesi in *Zodiac* (Milan), no. 6, 1960; "Data Processing Centre for the Sao Paulo Region Banco do Brasil" in *Modulo* (Rio de Janeiro),

December/January 1977-78; "Headquarters for the 6th Naval District in Sao Paulo" in *Modulo* (Rio de Janeiro), March/April 1979; "Data Processing Centre for the Banco do Brasil, Sao Paulo" in *Summa* (Buenos Aires), October 1979.

Bibliography: *The Robertos (Mauricio, Milton and Marcelo) Brazilian Family of Architects: A Bibliography* by Florita Z. Louie de Irizarry, Monticello, Illinois 1983.

A new technology is intended to be implanted in Brazil of nowadays. It is not easily done. Brazil is not easy at all. We need to be very realistic and very strict in regard to our dreams, our wishes, our needs.

The country grows at an average rate of 2.6 percent a year, and in the cities such percentile steps up to 4.4. Consequently, in ten years, that is in 1995, there will be eighty million new urbanized Brazilians, which represents, approximately, a need for 70 more cities like Brasilia or 140 cities like Niteroi.

In 1984, almost ten years before such will happen, we already owe 100 billion dollars to foreign countries and about one third of this amount inside our own country. 130 billion dollars on the whole: a most respectable sum. And let us not forget: our inflation has risen above 200 percent a year.

The most optimistic technicians in money claim as a solution a a six years' period of grace to settle this debt, followed by a long period at fixed interests to amortize the principal. I repeat, such is the optimists' claim, not that of the technicians of the present government. The period of grace is intended for investments in our industry in order to take up our development. Unfortunately, by the end of this time, in 1990, should the optimists' thesis be victorious, we shall be at five years from the above mentioned eighty million new urban inhabitants. Under these circumstances it is but evident that the expected population increase cannot and should not be given heed to by building new cities, neither Brasilias nor Niteróis.

It is the long-suffering, worn-out, well-known urban centers of our country that will have to support the heaviest part of the impact—cities like Rio the Janeiro and São Paulo, where almost every possible urban surgery has been undertaken: great avenues opened in the existing urban net, the sea pushed miles backwards, underground mass transport provided, and so on. And there is more. In these cities, the gradual increase of slum-inhabitants has been frightening, and it should not be forgotten that the Brazilian Financial System, just like the whole of Brazil, is undergoing a serious crisis.

No doubt, reality is dark and gloomy, but something has to be done. The population increase and consequent occupation of the great Brazilian urban centers are unalterable facts. We have got ten years ahead of us. Ten years, in urbanistic terms too short a period, and we have no money, in urbanistic terms a most tragic fact. On the other hand, however, we have highly qualified technicians: urbanists and architects who some years ago have shown the world that they are real experts.

A younger generation together with the older one will now have to face this tremendous challenge, and there is certainly no likeness whatsoever between what has to be done and what has already been done. Unfortunately, examples and our past experience will be of little avail.

The architects must have an enormous creativity and immense modesty. They are going to work in a poor and very complex country, in a most beautiful country with wonderful suffering people. New architectural and urbanistic parameters will have to be invented. They have to be simple and economical. They have to meet the need of everybody and not just that of a minority of rich people, which in numbers is growing more and more ridiculous.

New techniques have to be introduced. But they have to be very well-thought-over. We canot really fail to introduce them, but, and here I repeat, we have to choose those that meet the need of everybody and

not of a minority of the population. It is not the architects and urbanists who desire it; it is Brazil and its state of affairs that requires it.

—Mauricio Roberto

One of the teams most closely involved with the birth and development of modern architecture in Brazil was that of the Roberto brothers. The partnership was initially formed by the two elder brothers, Marcello and Milton, and was later expanded to include Mauricio, who eventualy took the office over on his own after the premature death of his brothers (in 1964 and 1953 respectively). Some years later he was joined by his two sons: Marcio Roberto, architect, in 1968, and Claudio Roberto, manager, in 1972. Up until the mid 1950s the Roberto brothers produced one of the most exuberant and personal strains of the Brazilian version of the "International Style," and contributed considerably to the freshness of its vocabulary.

The team's most notable building, the Brazilian Press Association Headquarters (ABI) in Rio in 1936, was one of the first modern designs to win an open architectural competition. This building is as important—historically and chronologically—as the famous Ministry of Education and Health Building built during the same period and in the same part of the city. The ABI Building brought together all the elements that were to become features of the Roberto brothers' subsequent work during this first phase of their practice: functionalist treatment of volume and facades, transparency of construction method, fluidity and ambiguity of interior/exterior limits, and spatial dynamism.

The ABI Building is also a pioneer in the use of *brises-soleil*—originally proposed by Le Corbusier, first used on this building, and subsequently almost the trademark of the Roberto brothers. These "sunbreaks" are made of fixed vertical "blades" that protect the office balconies from excessive sunlight: they seem to be carved out of the surface of the building and turned inwards, which gives the facade a somewhat compact and monolithic appearance. These superimposed sun-breaks were to appear in other projects in a more clearly stated form—for example, the concrete *grille* becomes a striking architectural feature in the case of the Santos Dumont Terminal, the Roberto Building, and the Fátima-Finusia Apartments. In other buildings—the Brazilian Insurance Institute Office Building or the Marques do Herval Building—the Roberto brothers employ another ingenious system—a lightweight structure with pivoted or swivelling aluminium parts.

The design of the headquarters of the Brazilian Insurance Institute (1941) is a more sophisticated and explicit expression of the principles of the ABI Building. The functional treatment of facades and volumes correspond more closely to the requirements of the interior. The symbolic functions—the director's office, for example—are expressed in an exceptionally free way. The colour scheme picks out the various elements of construction, emphasizing the rational construction approach while remaining discreet. This polychrome experiment was later to be developed and would become another hallmark of the Roberto brothers' work. It is evident in all its splendour in the facades of Santos Dumont Airport.

Also notable in this phase of the Roberto brothers' work is their treatment of the relationship between interior and exterior. In the case of the ABI Building and the Brazilian Insurance Institute, the entrance halls merge with the urban space: there is no separation of interior and pavement. The broad, open concourse of Santos Dumont Airport has a monumentality prescribed by its numerous columns—a technological requirement of its day. From the pavement outside, one can look through the concourse and enjoy and uninterrupted view of the airplanes. The concourse itself becomes an enormous symbolic portico: with its adjacent gallery, it puts passengers in the mood for the excitement of air travel. In the Brazilian Insurance Institute

Recreation Centre—a building of exceptional lightness and simplicity—the areas designated for living, leisure and games are interlinked and flow freely into one another.

In the Sotreq Caterpillar Industrial Plant, the Naval Carpentry School, and the School of Motor Engineering, the spatial dynamics are handled in a much more complex and unusual way. Several features—such as the stairways, mezzanines, walls or even secondary volumes—break with tradition and contribute to a closer link between interior and exterior. In the Sotreq building, three domes with different radii seem to shoot out at random, finally merging with the central body. In the schools, especially the latter, the architectural features are organized in an almost abstract way reminiscent of the constructivists. A similar treatment can be seen in certain of Rino Levi's projects and in Henrique Mindlin's houses, which attempt to dynamize the volume by separating it onto several planes. But with the Roberto brothers it is not the *volume* that is made dynamic but the *space* itself. This is perhaps their greatest contribution to Brazilian architecture. Sometimes the volume is maintained, but the surrounding space is opened up and its very "bareness" exploited. In other cases, shapes that create space are added or juxtaposed—the mouldings on the Fátima-Finusia and Marques do Herval buildings, for example. The treatment of these facades may at first sight appear gratuitous, but the rationale is precisely that of spatial dynamics.

It is strange that there is no expression of this language in the Roberto brothers' domestic architecture, which tends to be somewhat stilted or pretentious. Two rare exceptions are the Tacito Prado House in Petrópolis and the Sales Pavilion at Samambaiba (now completely transformed).

The designs of the first phase of the Roberto brothers' work, ending about the mid-1950s, involved an inventiveness and an intuitive, revolutionary treatment of architectural features that has only recently been studied and applied consistently. By contrast, their more recent buildings are chiefly concerned with mass and volume, to the detriment of spatial and symbolico-functional techniques.

The architectural output of this second phase can be divided into three different "styles." The most conventional of these styles comprises work such as the Banco da Amazonia in Brasilia and the Brazilian Adademy of Letters in Rio, variations of the theme of a monolithic volume supported by chamfered pillars. In the second "style" there is greater emphasis on the composition of the mass, as in the Nossa Senhora de Copacabana Parish Centre in Rio and the Bank of Brazil Administration and Data Processing Centres in Rio and in Sao Paulo. Of three cylindrical volumes of different heights and radii, the Saolo Paulo Centre is perhaps their most expressive design in this style. The third "style" is characterised by structures of tall pillars set out in proportion, supporting isolated volumes containing the functional components of the design. Theoretically it would be possible to place extra "boxes" in the spaces between the existing volumes without interfering with the normal running of the building. The visual effect of numerous columns crossing the remaining area is one of both chaos and fragility. Of the projects that were conceived along these lines, only one was built: the Bank of Brazil Administration and Data Processing Centre in Porto Alegre.

Town planning is now the most important part of Mauricio Roberto's work. The Robertos' first venture into this field was in 1955, with their design for a resort at Grumari Beach near Rio. This was soon followed by another plan of a similar nature for the Cabo Frio region. In 1956 Marcelo and Mauricio Roberto took part in the competition for a pilot plan for Brasilia. They were awarded third prize for their "Polynuclear Metropolis," which was to have consisted of seven urban units, each for 72,000 people. The units would have been urbanized and constructed in accordance with the requirements of the city's growth.

Of the more recent projects, the following are noteworthy: the plans for the integrated development of the towns of Duque de Caxias and Vitória and the designs for the area surrounding the Niterói/Rio das Ostras Highway and for the Barra Bonita Tourist Centre. The last two were designed to preserve and improve areas important to the ecologist and tourist alike. But of all the projects, the most interesting is a plan for the Alagados region of Salvador, which aims to regenerate a slum area of houses built on stilts without destroying the spontaneous urban structure and the community spirit that exists among the area's 90,000 inhabitants.

—Jorge Czajkowski

ROBERTSON, Howard Morley.

British. Born in Salt Lake City, Utah, U.S.A., of British parents, 18 August 1888. Educated at Eastfield House, Ditchling, Sussex; Malvern College, Worcestershire; Architectural Association School, London; Ecole des Beaux-Arts, Paris, Diploma 1913. Served in the British Army, in France, 1915-19: Military Cross, 1919. Married Doris Adeney Lewis in 1927. In partnership with the architect J. Murray Easton, London, 1919-31, and with Easton and E. Stanley Hall, London, 1932-40; Partner, Easton and Robertson, London, 1940-59, and Easton, Robertson, Cusdin, Preston and Smith, London, 1959 until his death in 1963. Technical Adviser, League of Nations Building, Geneva, 1927-29; Consultant Architect, National Services Hostels Corporation, London, 1939-45; Member of the Advisory Committee, United Nations Building, New York, 1947-48; Consultant, Unesco Building, Paris, 1951. Principal, and Director of Education, Architectural Association School, London, 1920-35. President, Royal Institute of British Architects, 1952-54. Recipient: Bronze Medal, 1928, 1936, Godwin Bursary, 1933, and Royal Gold Medal, 1949, Royal Institute of British Architects; Medal of the Essex, Cambridgeshire and Hertfordshire Allied Society of Architects, 1937. Fellow, Royal Institute of British Architects, 1925. Knighted, 1954. *Died* (in London) *5 May 1963*.

Works:

1925 British Pavilion, International Exposition, Paris (destroyed)
Royal Horticultural Hall, London (with J. Murray Easton)
1928 Private cinema, Imperial Institute, London
1929/
32 Liberty's Department Store, Regent Street, London W.1 (with J. Murray Easton)
1930 Office building, 52 Cornhill, London
House, South Kensington, London
Oxford University Press Warehouse, Neasden, London
1930/
39 Savoy Hotel modernization, London
1932 Royal Bank of Canada Building, 6 Lothbury, London
1932/
33 Nurses' Home, Children's Hospital, 37-46 Guildford Street, London
1933 Private cinema for Fox Films, London
House, Lake Zug, Switzerland
1935 British Pavilion, International Exposition, Brussels (destroyed)
1935/
39 Claridge's Hotel modernization, London
1936 British Pavilion, World's Fair, Johannesburg (destroyed)
1937 *The Practitioner* Office Building, 5 Bentinck Street, London

Private cinema for Publicity Films, London
Apartment block, Avenue Close, Regent's Park, London
Apartment block, St. Edmund's Terrace, Regent's Park, London
1938 Metropolitan Water Board Laboratories, New River Head, Rosebery Avenue, London (with J. Murray Easton)
1939 Electricity Company Showrooms, London (destroyed)
British Pavilion, World's Fair, New York
Sadler's Wells Theatre alterations and additions, London
1946 Sanatorium, Uppingham School, Rutland
1947/
52 Savoy Hotel modernization II, London
1949 Institute of Brewing Laboratories, Nutfield, Surrey
S.S. Rangitoto interiors, New Zealand Shipping Company (destroyed)
S.S. Rangitane interiors, New Zealand Shipping Company (now floating hotel, at Sullom Voe, Zetland)
1950 Cargo ship's interiors and living quarters, for Messrs. Watts, Watts and Company (destroyed)
Apartment block, Church Street, London
Apartment block, St. John's Wood Road, London
1951 Hatfield Technical College, Hertfordshire (now altered)
Hatfield Secondary Technical School, Hertfordshire (now altered)
S.S. Ruahine interiors, New Zealand Shipping Company (destroyed)
1952/
63 Master plan for the University of Reading, Berkshire (now altered)
1956 Bank of England Printing Works, Loughton, Essex
Faculty of Letters, University of Reading, Berkshire
1958 Bank of England Returned Note Building, Loughton, Essex
1961 Shell Centre Building, York Road, London
1961/
67 Lloyds Bank Regional Head Offices, Birmingham
1963 Bank of England Branch Offices, Bristol (now altered)

Publications:

By ROBERTSON: books—*The Principles of Architectural Composition*, London 1924; *Architecture Explained*, London and New York 1926; *Examples of Modern French Architecture*, with F.R.Yerbury, New York and Berlin 1928; *The Four Inns of Court*, New York 1930; *Modern Architectural Design*, London 1932, 1952; *The Post-War Home*, with others, London 1942; *Architecture Arising*, London 1944; *Reconstruction and the Home*, London and New York 1947; articles—"Modern Dutch Architecture" in *Architectural Review* (London), August 1922; "Modern Sweden" in *Architectural Review* (London), July 1924; "The Architecture of Finland" in *Architectural Review* (London), December 1924 and January 1925; "Architecture 1927—at the RIBA Galleries" in *Architectural Review* (London), June 1927; "Architecture 1928" in *Architectural Review* (London), June 1928; "A Pictorial Review of Modern Architecture in Europe," with F.R. Yerbury, in *Architecture* (London), November 1928/December 1930; "La Formation de l'Architecte en Angleterre" in *L'Architecture d'Aujourd'hui* (Paris), October/November 1933; "Architecture in Ankara" in *The Architect and Building News* (London), 8 April 1938; "The Domestic Scene: Contemporary Trends" in *Royal Architectural Institute of Canada Journal* (Toronto), November 1938; "The British Pavilion, New York World's Fair" in *The Builder* (London), 2 June 1939; "The New York World's Fair" in

Architectural Association Journal (London), July 1939; "Architecture 1919-1939" in *The Builder* (London), 2 February 1940; "B.I.N.C.: An Assessment" in *The Architect and Building News* (London), 28 November 1941; "Defence Housing in the U.S.A." in *The Architect and Building News* (London), 27 February 1942; "Como se evita el desordenado crecimento de las ciudades" in *Ingenieria y Arquitectura* (Bogota), November/December 1945; "Design of Interiors" in *Architectural Association Journal* (London), February/March 1947; "Quality in Architecture" in *The Architects' Journal* (London), 6 November 1947; "The American Scene" in *The Architect and Building News* (London), 19 March 1948; "The Seven Vamps of Architecture" in *The Builder* (London), 25 March 1949; "Inaugural Address" in *RIBA Journal* (London), November 1952; "The Architect's Dilemma" in *AIA Journal* (Washington, D.C.), February 1954.

On ROBERTSON: articles—"The Brussels Exhibition, 1935" in *Architectural Association Journal* (London), October 1934; "RIBA's New President, Mr. Howard Robertson" in *The Builder* (London), 20 June 1952; "Work by RIBA's New President" in *The Architects' Journal* (London), 26 June 1952; "Men of the Year—Howard Robertson" in *The Architects' Journal* (London), 15 January 1953; "Howard Robertson" by Reyner Banham in *Architectural Review* (London), September 1953; "A Traditional Architect" (obituary) in *The Times* (London), 6 May 1963; "Obituary" in *RIBA Journal* (London), June 1963.

*

Much of Sir Howard Robertson's work is in the late Renaissance manner, simplified by the deletion of classical ornament and the influence of the underlying steel and concrete construction, yet in a few buildings, such as those of the hall type, he was, with his partner, J. Murray Easton, in the forefront of modern developments. This emanated in part from his admiration, often expressed in hi writings, of some of the best modern continental architecture.

A notable development in Europe in the first quarter of the century for large buildings of the hall type was the parabolic rib construction, generally of reinforced concrete. An example of this in Robertson's work is the Royal Horticultural Hall, London, which he designed in collaboration with Easton. By a series of arches, approximately parabolic, a step structure is supported on either side, the vertical sections of which make four tiers of windows, while additional lighting is provided by an elliptical window in each bay. Ceiling heating, an early example, is provided by water-pipes embedded in the concrete soffit. This, for its time, very modern construction resulted in one of the most beautiful modern exhibition halls in Europe.

Robertson also designed many industrial buildings, offices and blocks of flats. Among the most typical of his designs, in the traditional simplified Renaissance manner, is the Nurses' Home of the Children's Hospital in Guildford Street, London, a steel-framed, brick-faced building with stone dressing on the two lower floors. It is a design of rectangular masses, well related, and there is an effective Greek reminiscence in the fluted columns of the two south portico entrances.

Robertson admired Mendelsohn's treatment of long horizontal facades arrested by circular vrtical features, and it was possibly this influence that prompted his design (in collaboration with Easton) of the Metropolitan Water Board Laboratories, London, in which a long curved two storey facade abuts a circular projecting entrance hall with vertical windows—but it lacks the cohesion of Mendelsohn's designs.

A spectacular later building, which must rank with the Horticultural hall as among Robertson's finest, is the Bank of England Printing Works, with its vast production hall, 800 feet long, with a clear span of 125 feet. (The structural engineer was Ove Arup.)

The roof consists of a series of asymmetrical arches which hold, on the north side, a stepped structure with windows forming the verticals. This is clearly an echo of the roof of the Horticultural Hall. Abutting it, on the south side, is the administration building, with a tall, six-storey vertically-emphasized entrance block and two long wings, one with continuous glazing forming a horizontal motif relating well with the verticals of the central blocks. Here are two contrasting structures determined by function, without stylistic integration—but the production hall is impressive.

Some of Robertson's later work in the simplified Renaissance manner, such as the immense and too obstrusive Shell Building on the South Bank, is apt to be rather dull, and it lacks the occasional originality of his best work. The demands of clients, however, can be inhibiting.

Sir Howard Robertson's work is of varied excellence: it includes some of the best modern buildings, but some is rather stereotyped. He was not immune to the influence of the wave of neo-classicism that spread over Europe during the 1930s.

—Arnold Whittick

ROBERTSON, Jaquelin Taylor.

American. Born in Richmond, Virginia, 20 March 1933. Educated at St. Mark's School, Southboro, Massachusetts, graduated 1951; Yale University, New Haven, Connecticut, 1951-55, B.A. 1955; Magdalen College, Oxford, England (Rhodes Scholar), M.A. 1957; Yale University (Koppers Student Architectural Design Scholarship), M.Arch. 1961; awarded Yale Travelling Fellowship, 1961. Married Marianna Neze in 1962. Worked as an architectural designer in the office of Sir Leslie Martin, *q.v.*, Cambridge, England, 1962-63, and Edward Larrabee Barnes, *q.v.*, New York, 1963-66; Principal Urban Designer, Urban Design Group, City Planning Commission, New York, 1968-69; Director, Office of Midtown Planning and Development, New York, 1969-72; City Planning Commissioner, New York, 1973; Vice-President, Arlen Realty and Development Corporation, New York, 1974-75; Director, Llewelyn-Davies and Partners, Tehran, 1975-77; Chairman, Llewelyn-Davies Associates, New York, 1977-78. Since 1978, Partner, J. T. Robertson Associates, New York. Lecturer, School of Architecture, Yale University, New Haven, Connecticut, 1964-65, and Columbia University School of Architecture, New York, 1965-67; Visiting Lecturer, Salzburg Seminar, Austria, 1973, and The New School, New York, 1973. Member, Board of Visitors, University of California at Los Angeles, 1971-72; Director, Parks Council, New York, 1971-75, International Design Conference at Aspen, Colorado, 1972-75, Architectural League of New York, 1972-75, Circle in the Square Theatre, New York, 1972-75, and Municipal Arts Society, New York, 1972-76. Exhibitions: *Forty under Forty*, Architectural League of New York, 1966; *The New City*, Museum of Modern Art, New York, 1967; *Urban Design*, New York, 1969; Institute of Architecture and Urban Studies, New York, 1977. Recipient: Albert S. Bard Award, City Club of New York, 1970; Parks Council Award, New York, 1971; Annual Design Award, *Progressive Architecture*, 1977. Address: 211 East 70th Street, New York, New York 10021, U.S.A.

Works:

1962 Louis Camu House, Alöst, Belgium (with Herman Lemaire)

1967 Isador Seltzer House, Sagaponick, New York
Madden House (project)
Master plan for Negril, Jamaica (with Sam Chang Associates)
1968 Twin Parks Urban Renewal Plan, Bronx, New York (with Jonathan Barnett, Giovanni Pasanella, and Richard Weinstein)
Lincoln Square Special Zoning District Plan, New York (with the Urban Design Group)
1969 Coney Island Urban Renewal Plan, Brooklyn, New York (with the Urban Design Group)
Plan for the Special Theatre District, New York (with the Urban Design Group)
Air Rights Transfer Legislation for New York City Landmarks (for Grand Central Terminal)
1969/
70 West Midtown Master Plan, New York (as Director, Office of Midtown Planning and Development)
1970 Jaquelin Robertson House renovation, 11 Punemere Lane, Easthampton, New York
Agronomics Office Building, Tehran (with Sam Chang Associates)
Clinton Urban Renewal Plan, New York (as Director, Office of Midtown Planning and Development)
1970/
72 Midtown Circulation Study and Plan, New York (as Director, Office of Midtown Planning and Development)
1971 Residential Multi-Use Zoning District Plan, New York (as Director, Office of Midtown Planning and Development)
1972 Fifth Avenue Special District Plan, New York (as Director, Office of Midtown Planning and Development)
Air Rights Transfer Legislation for Open Space, New York (as Director, Office of Midtown Planning and Development)
Times Square Special District Plan, New York (as Director, Office of Midtown Planning and Development)
1973 Queensboro Bridge Development Plan, New York (as Director, Office of Midtown Planning and Development)
Kaikaakko Development Plan, Honolulu (with Chester Rapkin)
1974 Hartford Square, Connecticut (with the Arlen Design Group)
Griffin Square, Dallas, Texas (with the Arlen Design Group)
1975/
78 Shahestan Pahlavi, Tehran (with Llewelyn-Davies and Partners, Tehran)
1977 Buford Scott House, 7612 Hill Drive, Richmond, Virginia (with Fred Cox)
1978 Lawrence Flinn House, Spaeth Lane, Easthampton, New York
Arco Chemical Corporation Research and Development Center, New Town Square, Philadelphia (with Davis Brody Associates)
1978 Museum of Modern Art Tower, New York (with Cesar Pelli)
1982 Koch-/Friedrich-Strasse Development, West Berlin (competition project; with Peter Eisenman)

Publications:

By ROBERTSON: articles—contributor, with Richard Weinstein, to *Urban Design as Public Policy* by Jonathan Barnett, New York 1973; "Machines in the Garden" in *Architectural Forum* (New York), April 1973; "Five on Five," with others, in *Architectural Forum* (New York), May 1973; "The Rediscovery of the Street" in *Architectural Forum* (New York), November 1973; "Shahestan Pahlavi" in *RIBA Journal* (London), February 1977; "Only Connect" in *Harvard Architecture Review* (Cambridge, Massachusetts), Spring 1980; "Gehry House in Santa Monica," with others, in *Arquitectura* (Madrid),

May/June 1980; "Three Vacation House Winners" in *Housing* (New York), September 1980; "Architecture as Urban Precinct" in *Architectural Record* (New York), October 1980; "Step Lightly On This Earth" in *Inland Architect* (Chicago), March/April 1983.

On ROBERTSON: articles—"Jaquelin Robertson: Ex New York City Planner Turned Developer's Architect" by Jane Holtz Kay in *Building Design* (London), 26 April 1974; "The Gamesman: Jaquelin Robertson" by Suzanne Stephens in *Progressive Architecture* (New York), May 1977; "A New City Center in Tehran" in *Progressive Architecture* (New York), January 1978; "American Architecture: After Modernism," special issue of *Architecture + Urbanism* (Tokyo), March 1981; "Building Types Study 560: Record Houses of 1981" in *Architectural Record* (New York), May 1981; "AD Profile: Architecture in Progress" in *Architectural Design* (London), no. 1/2, 1983; "Ohio Duo" in *Building Design* (London), 17 June 1983; "Urban Spacemen" in *Building Design* (London), 29 June 1984.

*

Architecture is a COMMUNAL art, both dependent upon and reactive to its surroundings. Unlike painting or sculpture, use and active social engagement is necessary to its appreciation. It is, very simply, man's most lasting and revealing artifact, as well as his most crucial and difficult aesthetic endeavor.

Architecture is not meant for museums—nor should it be judged by museum standards. It requires and serves LIVING—not VIEWING.

As an architect, I have been continually interested in the dialogue connecting seemingly opposite poles: ART and COMMERCE; OLD and NEW; LARGE and SMALL-SCALE DESIGN: PUBLIC and PRIVATE PRACTICE; OBJECT and CONTEXT; PLANNING and DESIGN; FLEXIBILITY and DETERMINACY; CITY and SUBURB; CAR and PEDESTRIAN. It is the comparison, juxtaposition, reconciliation, or delineation of these kinds of DIFFERENCES which leads to the creation of RELEVANT, LIVABLE, and SATISFYING ORDERS, which it is the architect's task to uncover.

My architectural concerns have largely focused on: a) *Historical Continuity:* Architecture is conservative and architectural changes are healthily INCREMENTAL not REVOLUTIONARY. Dictum: Mistrust POLEMICS; eschew UTOPIAS. b) *The Primacy of Context:* Buildings should observe the MANNERS OF THE PLACE. History, social/political and economic patterns, local conventions, the natural surroundings, taste and established language—these provide the architectural SETTING. Dictum: Ignore them at great risk. c) *Originality:* Not as important as it's cracked up to be. Dictum: Better to be good than original. d) *The Design of Cities:* Architects were intended to design cities. The order of the whole is more important than the order of the parts. Dictum: Designing cities is NOT like designing chairs. e) *Architecture/Planning/Development:* The three are inextricably interconnected. No architect who is ignorant of the *requirements* of the other two will be very useful as an urban designer, or even an aesthetically concerned citizen. Dictum: The architect should know how the world around him works. f) *Politics and Public Life:* All decisions, especially political ones, have design implications. If one wants to *positively* affect the quality of the built environment, one has to participate in government; they write the rules. Dectum: Pluralistic democracies depend on Citizen Bureaucrats: you get what you deserve. g) *Money:* It's important. Architects need it and need to understand how it works. Dictum: Only fools ignore money and power. h) *Variety:* Greatly over-rated. Most of the world's best architecture has been the *elaboration* of a few simple ideas, schemes, partis, details, etc. Dictum: There is greatness in consis-

tency; variety is most often a lack of focus—a handmaiden of triviality.

As a consequence of these concerns, my professional life has shifted between architectural design, urban design, planning, and development activity as well as between private practice and public sector involvement. I have worked for myself, for government, for a real estate firm, and for traditional architectural firms. I have taught and at the same time tried to understand and to participate in the market place. I have planned transit/pedestrian malls for large cities with the same enthusiasm as I have written zoning legislation and have designed cities in foreign cultures with the same attention to context as I have given small country houses in established regional settings. I have lived with compromise and accommodation. While I remain a "closet aesthete" and humanist whose motivating energies and tastes are essentially artistic, I am continually and fundamentally tainted by an undying addiction to the pulp world of politics and commerce, to art serving life.

—Jaquelin Robertson

*

Jaquelin Robertson, the architect, is an anomaly. An able designer whose reputation until recently has rested on three small house designs (one unbuilt), Robertson has for most of his career forsaken architecture for planning. He is an activist whose politics have led him away from building in the hope of serving architecture more broadly. His career provides interesting evidence of the degree to which participation in politics and development can allow a gifted architect to influence strongly the quality of the built environment.

Robertson's public career began when he joined with a group of friends to work with New York's mayor, John Lindsay, on problems of planning and development for the city. Robertson became Director of the Office of Midtown Planning and Development. His group had two modes of behavior. As architectural polemicists, they produced a number of elegantly detailed conceptual studies of areas in Midtown Manhattan in the cause of influencing subsequent development. These studies have had little tangible effect. As urban strategists, they devised incentive zoning plans in an attempt to advance certain qualities they considered valuable in the city. Developers were given concessions that could result in greater revenue from the development, in return for participating in improving the street level experience. Here there has been some success.

In 1974 Robertson moved from public to private participation in the process he had created. He became Vice-President of Planning and Design for Arlen Realty, who were engaged at that time with the Olympic Tower development. The building, designed by Skidmore, Owings and Merrill, descreetly incorporates an arcade, the product of Robertson's incentive zoning. When compared with Rockefeller Center across the street, however, the benefits to the pedestrian are hard to find.

His work with Llewelyn-Davies on Shahestan Pahlavi, a new town center for Tehran, as with the products of the Midtown Planning Office, has a markedly architectural character. In the careful drawings and sensitive diagrams, and in the superb model, there is marvellous invention, a curious hybrid of New York formalism and Iranian contextualism.

Until recently, Robertson's independent work as an architect comprised three little houses—one in Belgium, one in New York, and one never built. The two American designs—Seltzer House (built) and Madden House (projected)—are both remarkable and yet quite dissimilar. The Seltzer House is raw and bony; it shows all the inventive concerns of the early 1960s, but with a maturity, poise, and restraint that are remarkable for work so early in a career. The Madden House (from limited evidence) is an exceptional invention. Again, there are influences; a curious blend of Kahn and Rudolph, the compo-

sition has a dramatic and theatrical originality. It plays with illusional transparency in a way that belies its date. Perhaps, in all of Robertson's urban work, it has been the architect in him that has dominated. For example, one sees echoes of the Madden House in the buildings flanking the Nation Square of Shahestan Pahlavi.

Robertson's opportunism appears to involve a constant search for a setting that will allow the application of all his creative skills. The political game can encompass a vast range of intentions. In Robertsons's work, they seem above all to be a desire for architectural place-making, irrespective of the social or political context.

—Alan Balfour

ROCHE, (Eamonn) Kevin.
American. Born in Dublin, Ireland, 14 June 1922; emigrated to the United States, 1948: naturalized, 1964. Educated at the National University of Ireland, Dublin, 1940-45, B.Arch. 1945; did postgraduate work at the Illinois Institute of Technology, Chicago, 1948-49. Married Jane Tuohy in 1963; children: Eamon, Paud, Mary, Ann, and Alice. Designer, Michael Scott and Partners, Dublin, 1945-46, 1947-48; Architect with Maxwell Fry and Jane Drew, London, 1946, and with the United Nations Planning Office, New York, 1949; Associate, Eero Saarinen and Associates, Bloomfield Hills and Birmingham, Michigan, and Hamden, Connecticut, 1950-66 (Principal Associate in Design to Saarinen, 1954-61). Since 1966, Founder Partner, with John Dinkeloo, *q.v.*, Kevin Roche John Dinkeloo and Associates, Hamden, Connecticut. Member, Board of Trustees, American Academy in Rome, 1968-71, and Woodrow Wilson International Center for Scholars, Smithsonian Institution, Washington, D.C., 1969-71. Member of the Commission of Fine Arts, Washington, D.C., since 1969. Exhibitions: Museum of Modern Art, New York, 1968, 1971. Recipient: Arnold Brunner Award, American Institute of Arts and Letters, 1965; Creative Arts Award in Architecture, Brandeis University, Waltham, Massachusetts, 1967; Medal of Honor, American Institute of Architects, New York Chapter, 1968; Bard Award, City Club of New York, 1968, 1977, 1979; California Governor's Award for Excellence in Design, 1968; New York State Award, 1968; Bard Citation, Citizens' Union of New York, 1968; Total Design Award, American Society of Industrial Design, 1976; Grand Gold Medal, Academie d'Architecture, France, 1977; Pritzker Architecture Prize, 1982. D.Sc.: National University of Ireland, 1977. Academician, National Academy of Design; Member, National Institute of Arts and Letters; Honorary Fellow, Institute of the Architects of Ireland; Member, Royal Institute of British Architects; Member, Academie d'architecture, France; Member, Accademia Nazionale di San Luca, Italy. Address: Kevin Roche John Dinkeloo and Associates, 20 Davis Street, Hamden, Connecticut 06517, U.S.A.

Works (with John Dinkeloo):

1961/
68   Oakland Museum, California

1962/
64   IBM Pavilion, World's Fair, New York

1962/
67   Richard C. Lee High School, New Haven, Connecticut

1962/
69   Administration, Student Union, and Physical Education Buildings, Rochester Institute of Technology, New York

1963 Air Force Museum, Wright-Patterson Air
     Force Base, Ohio (project)
     Women's Resident Colleges, University of
     Pennsylvania, Philadelphia (project)
1963/
  65 Cummins Engine Company Components
     Plant, Darlington, England
1963/
  68 Ford Foundation Headquarters, New York
1964 National Center for Higher Education, Wash-
     ington, D.C. (project)
1964/
  74 Fine Arts Center, University of Massachus-
     etts, Amherst
1965/
  69 Knights of Columbus Headquarters, New
     Haven, Connecticut
     United States Post Office, Columbus, Indiana
1965/
  71 Power Center for the Performing Arts, Uni-
     versity of Michigan, Ann Arbor
1965/
  72 Veterans Memorial Coliseum, New Haven,
     Connecticut
1965/
  73 Creative Arts Center, Wesleyan University,
     Middletown, Connecticut
1966 Institute for the Study of Human Reproduc-
     tion, Columbia University, New York
     (project)
     National Fisheries Center and Aquarium,
     Washington, D.C. (project)
1966/
  72 Irwin Union Bank and Trust Company, Co-
     lumbus, Indiana
     Aetna Life and Casualty Computer Building,
     Hartford, Connecticut
1967/
  71 College Life Insurance Company of America
     Headquarters, Indianapolis
1967/
  78 Master plan for additions to the Metropolitan
     Museum of Art, New York (Temple of
     Dendur Pavilion; American Wing; Robert
     Lehman Pavilion; Michael C. Rockefeller
     Primitive Art Wing; European Art Wing;
     Sculpture Court)
1968 Small Orangerie, Columbus, Indiana (project)
1969 IBM Computer Technology Museum, Ar-
     monk, New York (project)
1969/
  75 Hotel and Office Building, stage I of the
     United Nations Development, New York
1969/
  77 Federal Reserve Bank of New York
1970/
  73 Cummins Engine Company Sub-Assembly
     Plant, Columbus, Indiana
1970/
  74 Richardson-Merrell Inc. Headquarters, Wil-
     ton, Connecticut
     Worcester County National Bank, Worcester,
     Massachusetts
1971 Design of the Bicentennial celebrations, Phila-
     delphia (project)
     Office complex, Toronto (project)
1972 Indiana and Michigan Power Company Com-
     plex/Headquarters, Fort Wayne, Indiana
     Cummins Engine Company Corporate Head-
     quarters, Columbus, Indiana
1973/
  76 Fiat World Headquarters, Turin
     Kentucky Power Company Headquarters,
     Ashland
1974 Center for the Performing Arts, Denver,
     Colorado (project)
1975/
  79 West Office Building, John Deere and Com-
     pany Headquarters, Moline, Illinois
1976 Visual and Communication Arts Building,
     Texas Christian University, Fort Worth
     Thomas J. Watson Research Center addition,
     72IBM Corporation, Yorktown Heights,
     New York

Kevin Roche and John Dinkeloo: Ford Foundation Headquarters, New York, 1963.

     Union Carbide Corporation World Head-
     quarters, Danbury, Connecticut
1977 Cummins Engine Company Corporate Head-
     quarters, phase II, Columbus, Indiana
     Bell Telephone Laboratories extensions, Hol-
     mdel, New Jersey
     General Foods Corporation Headquarters,
     Rye, New York
1978 Financial Services Headquarters, John Deere
     and Company, Moline, Illinois
1979 Conoco Inc. Petroleum Company Headquar-
     ters, Houston, Texas
     Office and Apartment/Hotel, stage II of the
     United Nations Development, New York
1980 Central Park Zoo, New York
     DeWitt Wallace Museum of Fine Arts,
     Colonial Williamsburg, Virginia
     E.F. Hutton Building, New York
1981 Thomas J. Watson Research Center additions
     II, IBM Corporation, Yorktown Heights,
     New York
     Block One Development, Denver, Colorado
     Ravinia Office Park, Atlanta, Georgia
1983 Bouygues World Headquarters, Paris
     Office Development, 60 Wall Street, New
     York

Publications:

By ROCHE: articles—"Architecture is a Language", interview, in *Architectes* (Paris), January
1979; "A Conversation with Kevin Roche" in
Perspecta (New Haven, Connecticut), no. 19, 1982;
recording—*An American Practice,* 2 tape cassettes,
London 1980.

On ROCHE/DINKELOO: books—*Modern Archi-
tecture* by Vincent Scully, New York 1961, 1974; *New
Architecture in New Haven* by Don Metz, Cambrid-
ge, Massachusetts 1966; *Architects on Architecture,*
edited by Paul Heyer, London 1967; *American
Architecture and Urbanism* by Vincent Scully, New
York 1969; *New Directions in American Architecture*
by Robert A.M. Stern, New York 1969, 1977; *Will
They Ever Finish Bruckner Boulevard* by Ada Louise
Huxtable, New York 1970; *GA 4: Kevin Roche John
Dinkeloo and Associates* by Hiroshi Hara, edited by
Yukio Futagawa, Tokyo 1971; *Observations on
American Architecture* by Ivan Chermayeff, New
York 1972; *Third Generation: The Changing Mean-
ing of Architecture* by Philip Drew, London 1972;
Conversations with Architects, edited by John W.

Cooke and Heinrich Klotz, London 1973; *Kevin Roche John Dinkeloo and Associates 1962-75* by Yukio Futagawa, Tokyo and Fribourg 1975; *GA Detail 4: Kevin Roche John Dinkeloo and Associates* by Nobuo Horumi, Tokyo 1977; *Kevin Roche, Architect: The Work of Kevin Roche John Dinkeloo and Associates,* edited by John O'Regan and Shane O'Toole, Dublin 1983; *GA 9: Kevin Roche John Dinkeloo and Associates,* edited by Yukio Futagawa, Tokyo 1984; articles—"Horizon" by Wolf Von Eckardt in *American Heritage* (New York), Summer 1971; "Kevin Roche and John Dinkeloo 1964-74," a special number of *Architectural Forum* (New York), March 1974; "Eero's Heir: The Work of Kevin Roche" in *Building Design* (London), 20 September 1974; "Two Splendid Fine Arts Centers by Roche Dinkeloo and Associates" in *Architectural Record* (New York), May 1975; "Three Buildings by Kevin Roche John Dinkeloo and Associates" in *Domus* (Milan), February 1976; "Two Business Buildings by Kevin Roche John Dinkeloo and Associates" in *Architectural Record* (New York), February 1976; "Tendencies in American Architecture: The Work of Kevin Roche John Dinkeloo and Associates" in *Parametro* (Bologna, Italy), July/August 1976; "Kevin Roche: Irish Architect in America" in *Introspect* (Dublin), December 1976; "Roche Diamond" in *Architectural Review* (London), April 1977; "Kevin Roche... Master of Architecture" in *Irish Builder and Engineer* (Dublin), April 1977; "A Change of Direction for Kevin Roche?" in *Architectural Record* (New York), August 1979; "Sheer and Shiny: Kevin Roche, Mega-Architect" in *Building Design* (London), 10 October 1980; "Roche at the RIBA" in *RIBA Journal* (London), December 1980; "Kevin Roche in Copenhagen" in *Arkitekten* (Copenhagen), 2 December 1980; "Roche: Pritzker Reaffirms the Mainstream" in *Progressive Architecture* (New York), June 1982; "The Architect Ought to Get Involved: Kevin Roche" in *Connaissance des Arts* (Paris), November 1982; "The Work of Kevin Roche" in *Architect and Builder* (Cape Town, South Africa), November 1982.

Bibliography: *Kevin Roche* by Lamia Doumato, Monticello, Illinois 1979.

Kevin Roche-John Dinkeloo and Associates is the most aesthetically daring Maurand innovative American firm of architects now working in the realm of governmental, educational, and corporate clients. As successors to the firm of Eero Saarinen and Associates, they appear to be also the successors, or at least strong contenders, to Skidmore Owings and Merrill in the area of large corporate facilities. The reasons are not difficult to see.

Their work in the past 18 years—some 35 major projects built and not built—demonstrates a kind of problem-solving for each specific situation that has produced, as it did for Eero Saarinen, works of distinct individuality and stylistic variety from project to project. We need only compare the Union Carbide headquarters in Connecticut, with the Fiat headquarters in Turin and the College Life Insurance headquarters in Indianapolis, to see the range of invention and variation applied to the design of suburban office complexes.

Their work has also continuously shown perceptive planning in relation to the environment—both urban and suburban. They were early innovators of urban public spaces—with the interior courts at the Ford Foundation Headquarters, the National Fisheries Center project, the National Center for Higher Education project, and the United Nations Development; with the park-covered Oakland Museum, which is the major monument of underground architecture; and with portico-arcades such as the one at the Columbus, Indiana Post Office. In terms of interior planning also they have been consistently innovative and refined in detailing inside and out, from the days when Warren Platner was the head of their interior design department to the more recent

office landscape scheme for Fiat headquarters. Their urban planning has been influential on other contemporary architects, especially the first schemes for the Worcester County National Bank and the Federal Reserve Bank of New York.

Their technical achievement, which is the province of John Dinkeloo, has made noteworthy advances in the use of slip-form concrete construction with inset steel members (Knights of Columbus Headquarters), of vast steel trusses (New Haven Coliseum) as well as in the use of materials such as raw poured concrete (Richard C. Lee High School; University of Massachusetts Fine Arts Center); weathering steel (Cummins Engine Plant, Darlington, England; Ford Foundation Headquarters); silo tiles (Knights of Columbus); and steel-and-glass curtain walls that are elegantly refined.

In their formal invention developed for individual planning requirements, there is always an element of surprise. Generally their solutions are so geometrically primal that they seem like the first project sketches or like first models blown up and built. Sometimes that surprise comes from an insight that appears unfailingly on target, reminding us of Dr. Johnson's definition of wit as that which makes us ask why we did not think of the idea ourselves. The work of Roche-Dinkeloo so often seems just right, obvious once revealed, almost inevitable—the idea of an urban interior park as at the Ford Foundation, the idea of elevating an urban tower high enough to let sunlight onto virtually all of a site, as at the Federal Reserve Bank of New York. Sometimes, on the other hand, their work appears to come from a flair for the arbitrary and the wilful, a kind of latter-day Boullée minimalism that makes us ask how the architects themselves ever got such an idea, as in the College Life Insurance complex.

At all times, however, the work of Roche-Dinkeloo is beautifully executed, daring and innovative, refined, and economically detailed. It is an architecture of contemporary size, of today's grandeur and richness. Yet it raises questions about out psychological responses. For all its currentness, the work of Roche-Dinkeloo is almost entirely abstract—in the mainstream of the Modern movement—and therefore virtually without reference to any recognizable traditional cultural symbolism. In this regard the architects come under censure from post-modern proponents of "Representational" architecture, which attempts, through associations with vernacular building or through analogies to classical or other forms and colors, to tell us about itself. The abstract geometries of Roche-Dinkeloo, their glassy, slick, smooth, impersonal surfaces, are, to a degree, alienated from mankind, almost other-wordly.

The principal cause of this alienation is the scale of their work. The Ford Foundation is only twelve storeys high but houses a garden that is one-third of an acre; the Air Force Museum project is designed to cover three and a half city blocks, the United Nations Development project is planned to cover two city blocks, and the National Fisheries Center project to have a greenhouse 600 feet long. But size alone is not the issue. Roche-Dinkeloo's projects are vast in appearance even when not in fact. The Knights of Columbus building, though only twenty-three storeys tall, presents an astonishing image when one is driving into New Haven. It looks as if the city built an electric plant as a gateway. "Please say 'Power Plant,'" Kevin Roche urged when I first made that observation. (Was it inevitable that he should design Power Center?)

Roche has long been enamored of the bigness and power of American industrial architecture—its factories and roadways—and the forms of that architecture are often reinterpreted, however abstractly, in his designs. The broad concrete bands (Richard C. Lee High School; Oakland Museum; Wesleyan University Arts Center) derive as much from highway bridges as from Frank Lloyd Wright's Falling Water; the weathering steel structures for factories (Cummins Engine Company projects) are idealized industrial architecture of the most direct

analogy and progression.

In the design of delicate and continuous steel-and-glass structures, however, the firm makes some of its highest marks. Those greenhouses are taut and uniform, pristine and elegant; they are at the same time abstract and generalized, even when they mirror and reflect the natural landscape, as at Power Center. With their awning-like structures (U.N. Plaza Hotel; Union Carbide Headquarters), they are only slightly more human. In their phantom awning development of steel without glass (Irwin Union Bank and Trust) they are dehumanized to an unearthly, dazzling degree.

These glistening greenhouse factories feed the aspirations of corporate magnates. The work of Roche-Dinkeloo realizes, it seems, the utopian dream of the industrial revolution, when, as now, corporations have progressed from manu-factories to management headquarters. The dream seems, in their work, realized, expanded to a superscale, ordered to a glittering tidiness, and suggesting the overbearing authority and the de-humanity of corporate existence. Roche-Dinkeloo designs appropriately and consummately for the princes of our day.

—C. Ray Smith

ROGERS, Archibald Coleman.
American. Born in Annapolis, Maryland, 29 September 1917. Educated at Lawrenceville School, New Jersey, 1932-35; Princeton University, New Jersey, 1935-39, B.A. 1939, M.F.A. 1942; United States Naval Postgraduate School, Annapolis, 1942-43, Dip.Naval Arch. 1943. Served in the United States Navy, 1942-46: Lieutenant. Married Lucia Bernadine Evans in 1947; children: Lucia and Coleman. Draftsman in the office of Cross and Cross, New York, 1939-40. Founder Partner, with Francis Taliaferro, George Kostritsky, and Charles Lamb, Rogers-Taliaferro-Kostritsky-Lamb, Baltimore, Maryland, 1946-69, and Chairman of the Board of the successor firm RTKL Associates, Baltimore, 1969-81. Zoning Commissioner, 1946-52, and Chairman of the Sanitary Commission, 1965, Anne Arundel County, Maryland. Lecturer, Virginia Theological Seminary, Alexandria, 1967-72. Member, Maryland Architectural Registration Board, 1958-67; Member, Architectural Review Board of Washington, D.C., 1963-66; Member, Maryland Arts Council, 1967-68; Chairman, Soviet-American Symposium on Urban Design, 1969, Israeli-American Symposium, 1969, and Indian Symposium, 1970; Trustee, Princeton University, 1972-76; President, American Institute of Architects, 1974. Address: RTKL Associates, 400 East Pratt Street, Baltimore, Maryland 21202, U.S.A.

Works:

1962 Charles Center, Baltimore
Urban redevelopment plan for Hartford, Connecticut
1966 Plan for downtown Cincinnati
Plan for downtown Eugene, Oregon
1968 Fountain Square, Cincinnati
1972 Plan for downtown Jacksonville, Florida

Publications

By ROGERS: novel—*The Monticello Fault,* Durham, North Carolina 1979; articles—"Towards a National Design Policy" in *Architectural Record* (New York), June 1967; "Russian Reconnaissance:

Stresses of Change" in *Progressive Architecture* (New York), August 1969; "The Ideas" in *Architecture: Formes et Fonctions* (Lausanne, Switzerland), 1971.

On ROGERS: articles—"Successful Cincinnati" by Ann Ferebee in *Design and Environment* (New York), Winter 1972; "Profile of the President of the AIA: Archibald C. Rogers" by Carol Rose in *AIA Journal* (Washington, D.C.), December 1973; "When an Architect Becomes a Novelist" by Andrea O. Dean in *AIA Journal* (Washington, D.C.), February 1979.

The following is an extract from my novel *The Monticello Fault* in which the hero and heroine argue about the nature of architecture. Joel, the architect, has become bogged down in the nuts-and-bolts of his design for a new museum building; the driving force of his original concept now eludes him. Lila, a painter, attempts to clarify, and perhaps help solve, his problem:

"Architecture no doubt lives by economics and stands by technology, but the architect is called to be an artist. It is an artist who stands at the heart of you, Joel Pellegrini, even if he is camouflaged in a business suit and is licensed to practise a profession. When you deny admittance to your intuition, you deny your calling. When you deny your calling, you risk atrophy. Intuition may be cruel, Joel, as cruel as living can be. But both are preferable to a walking death."

Joel could be stubborn, nearly as stubborn as Lila. He fought back.

"That's great! 'What is an architect?' The answer to this enigma appears below, inverted. So I stand on my head. 'An Architect is an artist wrapped in a professional inside a business man.' It sounds positively Churchillian, Lila."

Lila glared at him, her lips compressed, her eyes flashing a warning which Joel chose to ignore.

"I'll grant you this, Lila. Architecture *is* an art, but it's not architecture until it's built. To be built it has to be practical, its concept has to be realistic. Architecture isn't free like other arts, like music or poetry or painting. The architect is trammeled by reality. His art must be rational or it won't be built and won't be art. Where is there room for inspiration? Your paintings are inspired, Lila. I know that just as I know that a Mozart sonata or a Shakespearean sonnet is inspired. But what would happen if I admitted inspiration to my mind? How could a flash of insight, a pure and simple idea, survive translation into an economically sound and structurally safe building?"

Lila let him have it.

"*Never* say that to me. Never say that mine is the easier calling, that my art if freer than yours, that it is less rational, less real. *Never* again put me down, Joel Pelegrini."

She stormed at him, stamping her small, sandaled foot in fury. Joel was shaken. He sat down upon the drafting stool, regarding the new Lila.

Here was a Lila few had seen—imperious, passionate, flashing fire. Joel decided that he enjoyed this Lila, enjoyed too the contest that was building up between them. He started to interrupt. She ignored him and swept on, one question crowding upon the next.

"Is my palette more tractable than your economics or your stress-and-strains? Is my canvas less limiting than your site? Are not my visions compromised by my medium? My painting disciplined by my tools. Is my work unreal, irrational because it looks beyond time?" She again stamped her foot. "Is there no reality but this, this moment when one's foot treads the earth?"

Lila paused. Joel broke in. He meant to soothe her. He instead annoyed her.

Joel waffled.

"You are right, Lila. Of course you are right and I agree with you. Still, there is something different,

more difficult, about architecture, about the art of architecture."

Lila was scornful.

"There *isn't* any real difference, Joel. Architecture is an art like any other art, like music or poetry, and no more difficult. One art differs from another only in its raw material and in its medium for translating this material. Mozart's music flowed from his mind through his fingers to the keyboard. It flowed back to his mind through his ears. Was what came back identical with what flowed forth? How could it be? The poet wrestles with words to express his images, and words may well be the most intractable of all the media. My raw material is what I see about me and in my mind, translated imperfectly by my painting. Yours is the problem of sheltering society. Its solutions are translated, also imperfectly, by your buildings."

Lila smiled softly and to herself.

"We, you and I, Joel, are put here to be artists. We didn't ask for this assignment, but we cannot evade it. And what is our assignment?" Lila paused as if awaiting an answer. But she was no longer looking at Joel.

She answered.

"It is this. To listen. To accept within our emptiness the fertile radiance from eternity. To nurture the offspring it conceives within us. To let this then escape to life in the flesh with which we, and we alone, can clothe it so that it, my painting or your building, can then fulfill *its* assignment."

"But what is *its* assignment, Lila? My building

shelters a fragment of society. Your painting delights the eye and, from what I have seen, teases the mind. What more is there?"

"Those are the assignments of time, Joel. But art has another assignment from its parent beyond time. It is this. To speak its universal and wordless language to those it touches, to those who see my paintings and who indwell your buildings. To knit back together time and eternity during the brief moment of its speaking."

—Archibald C. Rogers

Archibald C. Rogers is the founder and former Chairman of the Board of RTKL Associates (established in 1946 as Rogers, Taliaferro, Kostritsky, Lamb), one of the leading practitioners of urban design in the United States and also a significant architectural firm. Rogers and his firm had an important role in the Charles Center redevelopment in downtown Baltimore, his home city, including the design of the public spaces. However, the firm's most important work is probably the plan for downtown Cincinnati, completed in 1966. This plan has become an exemplar of the way to include decision-makers necessary to the implementation of the plan in the process of creating the plan itself. Rogers set up a four-stage process: 1) reaching a consensus on the nature of the problems; 2) systematically reviewing available alternatives; 3) selecting the most desirable alternative; and 4) choosing the most effective way of attaining the selected objectives. Within each stage

Archibald Rogers: Fountain Square, Cincinnati, 1968.

Rogers was able to structure a series of decisions which were voted upon by a working committee of community leaders and then ratified by the Planning Commission and City Council. The plan, when completed, had also to be enacted in this way. Rogers had devised a planning process with its political support built in.

As a consequence of this process, the Cincinnati plan has been implemented much more successfully than most other planning documents. One of its most importat features is Fountain Square, also designed by RTKL. This Square has given downtown Cincinnati a new and important public space, which confers focus and identity on the new developments around it.

While RTKL has subsequently prepared downtown plans for many other cities, including Eugene, Oregon and Jacksonville, Florida, Rogers himself became interested in creating a national planning context. As president-elect and then president of the American Institute of Architects during 1973 and 1974, Rogers worked to create a National Growth Policy. It was adopted by the AIA. He then spent an additional year trying to create a coalition of other organizations that would support such a policy. The key to the National Growth Policy was the Growth Unit, which would produce a balanced plan and design for new development whether it took place as a new community or within an existing urban area. So far Roger's national planning efforts have met with little direct success, but they play an important part in creating the climate of opinion that may eventually lead to the adoption of such policies.

Rogers was more successful in influencing urban highway design. Through his efforts, an Urban Design Concept Team was established as part of the process of redesigning a controversial expressway project in Baltimore. Although the plans for this expressway have not gone forward, the concept of integrating land-use decisions and urban design with urban highway planning has been adopted in Federal highway legislation, and projects such as Westway in New York City would not have been possible without the work of Rogers and the Baltimore experience.

—Jonathan Barnett

ROGERS, Ernesto Nathan.

Italian. Born in Trieste, of an Italian mother and English father, 16 March 1909; acquired Italian citizenship, 1930. Educated at elementary school in Zurich, 1915-18; Gymnasium Tasso, Milan, 1918-21; Liceo Parini, Milan, 1921-27; Milan Polytechnic, 1927-32, Dip.Arch. 1932. Served in the Italian Army, 1933-35; during World War II interned in Vevey, Switzerland, 1943-45. Founder Partner, with Gianluigi Banfi, q.v., Ludovico Belgiojoso, q.v., and Enrico Peressutti, q.v., BBPR Architectural Studio, q.v., Milan, 1932 until his death, 1969. Lecturer, School of Architecture, 1962-65, Lecturer, Faculty of Art History, 1964-65, and Professor and Director of the Institute of Humanities, 1964-69, Milan Polytechnic. Editor, Le Arti Plastiche, Milan, 1931-33; Architectural Critic, La Fiera Letteraria, Milan, 1932-33; Editorial Adviser, Rassegne d'Architettura, Milan, 1932-34; Co-Editor, Quadrante, Milan, 1933-36; Editor, Atti del Sindicato Inter-provinciale Fascista degli Architetti, 1936; Joint Editor/Manager, Bulletin du Centre d'Etudes pour le Bâtiment, Lausanne, 1944-45; Editor/Publisher, Domus, Milan, 1946-47; Director, Architetti del Movimento Moderne, and Editor of their periodical Il Balcone, Milan, 1947; Editor, Casabella-Continuità, Milan, 1953-64. Member of CIAM (Congrès Internationaux d'Architecture Moderne), from 1935; Member of the Secretariat, Commissione per le Manifestazione d'Arte Moderna del'Associazione tra i Cultori d'Architettura, 1935, and Maison des Art-

istes, Lausanne, 1939; Member of the Committee, CNR (Consiglio Nazionale delle Ricerche), 1945; Founder Member, MSA (Movimento Studi Architettura), 1945, INU (Istituto Nazionale di Urbanistica), 1949, and Société Européenne de Culture, 1950; Member, Cercle d'Etudes Architecturales, Paris, 1950, Institut d'Esthetique Industrielle, Paris, 1951, Centro Studi Estetici, Milan, 1953, Zentralvereinignung der Architekten, Vienna, 1957, Association Internationale Critique d'Art, 1958, and Lega d'Igiene e di Profilassi Mentale, Rome, 1961. Honorary Member, American Institute of Architects, 1956, and Royal Institute of British Architects, 1963. Died (in Gardone, Italy) 7 November 1969.

Publications:

By ROGERS: books—Auguste Perret. Milan 1955; The Works of Pier Luigi Nervi, with Jürgen Joedicke, Stuttgart and London 1957; Esperienze dell'Architettura (collected essays), Turin 1958; Editoriali di Architettura (collected essays), Turin 1968.

On ROGERS article—"The Myth of Orpheus" by Benedetto Gravagnuolo and Alberto Zabban in Modo (Milan), May 1982.

Besides his activity as an architect, Ernesto Nathan Rogers was also a very prolific writer, the most influential writer among the Italians to reach a European public.

The son of a British insurance agent in Trieste and an Italian mother, Rogers was brought up in a literary household; his father was one of James Joyce's Trieste friends. Much of his secondary education was in Switzerland, and he was naturally cosmopolitan and polygot. An early flirtation with Futurism prompted his entry into the Fascist Party and into renouncing his British nationality. In 1927 he entered Milan Polytechnic with Banfi and Belgiojoso, whom he had met towards the end of his secondary schooling, and as a student he became editor of the general arts periodical Le Arti Plastiche to which he was already a contributor. With his associates he edited Quadrante, from 1933-36, which carried some of the most important polemics of the inter-war years. In 1935 all four associates joined CIAM. Rogers, as site architect of the Italian Merchant Navy Pavilion, on a barge moored in the Seine, travelled to Paris during the Exposition Internationale in 1937, but in 1938, when Italy adopted the German racial laws, he retired into anonymity, though he remained in Milan until forced to flee to Switzerland in 1943.

Rogers' disillusion with fascism was gradual, but by the beginning of the war it had passed into violent opposition. The internment camp at Vevey was regarded by such inmates as Rogers as a kind of college and contributed to the formation of the Partito d'Azione, which was to play an important part in immediate post-war Italian politics. Rogers was its agent at Vevey. He returned to practice with his surviving partners in 1945, and took over the editorship of Domus (to which, as well as Casabella, he had contributed before the war) from its politically compromised editors, making it the most exciting architectural magazine of the time; unfortunately, its high international reputation also led to its being abandoned by its usual lay home public, and Rogers was edged out. This, and other activities, lead to his becoming a permanent member of the Council of CIAM, with which he remained connected until its demise in 1959/60.

Rogers' most important influence was exercised through his editorship of Casabella-Continuità (1953-64) around which he gathered a group of young and important contributors (Giancarlo De Carlo, Vittorio Gregotti, Gae Aulenti, Marco, Zanusso, Aldo Rossi, etc.) and which he regarded as

an open seminar. Casabella became the most accurate recorder of the changes in Italian taste, which were taken up immediately by younger architects in Europe and the United States. Rogers consolidated this influence by his many lectures in Europe, America, Latin America, and China. His professorship in Milan was not to come until later, in 1964.

Although he never published a major book, Rogers' publications were frequent and prolific: some are collected in two volumes, Espierienza dell'Architettura in 1958 and Editoriali di Architettura in 1968. There is also a moving monograph on Auguste Perret. While, since the war, the Roman group of architects, with Bruno Zevi as their spokesman, wanted a concentration on local problems under the banner, oddly, of Frank Lloyd Wright, Rogers made Milan the centre of a cosmopolitan architectural activity by making the outside world familiar with Italian developments through the maximum exposure of the younger Italians to European and American cross-currents. His own philosophical developments are reflected more accurately in his writings than in the later work of BBPR, of which he continued to be an active partner. His particular concern with recent history as a foreshadow of current trends and his fascination with the Viennese brand of liberal rationalism and the architecture which it produced (Loos, Hoffmann, Behrens) has influenced the architecture of the 1970's more than it did that of his own lifetime, and it will probably continue to do so, through the group which he formed round Casabella.

—Joseph Rykwert

See BBPR ARCHITECTURAL STUDIO

ROGERS, Richard George.

British. Born in Florence, Italy, of British parents, 23 July 1933. Educated at the Architectural Association School, London, 1953-59 (First Year Prize), Dip.A.A. 1959; Yale University School of Architecture, New Haven, Connecticut, 1962-62 (Fulbright, Edward D. Stone and Yale Scholar), M.Arch. 1962. Served in the British Army, 1951-53. Married the architect Su Brumwell in 1960; Ruth Elias in 1973; children: Ben, Ab, Zad, and Roo. Partner, with Norman and Wendy Foster, q.v.: Norman Foster, and Su Rogers, Team 4, London, 1963-68, and Richard and Su Rogers, London, 1968-70. Since 1970, Partner, with Renzo Piano, q.v., London, Paris, and Genoa. Chairman of the Board, Tate Gallery, London; Member, United Nations Architects' Committee; Council Member, Royal Institute of British Architects, London; Vice-President, Aram USA Inc., Washington, D.C.. William Townsend Lecturer, University College, London, 1983; Eero Saarinen Professor of Architectural Design, Yale University, New Haven, Connecticut, 1984. Exhibitions: Biennale de Paris, 1963, 1967. Recipient: Architectural Design Awards, 1964, 1965, and 1968; Industrial Architecture Award, Financial Times, 1967, 1976, and 1983; House for Today Award, Ideal Home, 1968; Work of Outstanding Quality Award, 1969, Research Award, 1970, Regional Awards, 1975 and 1982, and Gold Medal, 1985, Royal Institute of British Architects; First Prize, Basildon Housing Competition, 1971; First Prize, Place Beaubourg Competition, Paris, 1971; Design Award, British Steel Corporation, 1975, 1982; Auguste Perret Prize, International Union of Architects, 1978; First Prize, Lloyd's Headquarters Competition, London, 1978; Premio Europeo Umberto Biancamano Award, 1979; Premier Award for Steel Structure, France, 1982; Eurostructpress Award, 1983. Royal Academician, 1979; Honorary Fellow of the American Institute of Architects and of the Royal

Academy of Art, The Hague; IBM Fellowship, 1981.
Address: Richard Rogers Partnership, 49 Princes
Place, Holland Park, London W11 4QA, England.

Works:

1967 Reliance Controls Ltd. Electrical Factory,
Swindon, Wiltshire
1970 Italian Industry Pavilion, *Expo ι70,* Osaka
(with Renzo Piano)
1970 Fitzroy Street Commercial Centre, Cambridge, England (with Renzo Piano and Fitzroy
Robinson)
ARAM Inc. Medical Centre, Washington,
D.C. (with Renzo Piano)
1971 B and B Italia Offices, Como, Italy (with
Renzo Piano)
Clasp Italia Ltd. Brockhouse Steel Structures
(building system), Birmingham, England
(with Renzo Piano)
International Distillers and Vintners Ware-
house/Office conversion, London
1972 Universal Oil Products United Kingdom
Head Office, and UOP Fragrances Ltd.
Laboratory, Tadworth, Surrey (with Renzo
Piano)
1973 Aston Martin Lagonda Ltd. Offices, Show-
room, Restaurant, Squash Court and Hous-
ing, London (with Renzo Piano)
1975 PA Management Consultants (PATScentre)
Research Laboratories, Workshops and
Ancillary Administration Building, Cam-
bridge, England (with Renzo Piano)
Housing and recreation areas, for Globe
Construction Ltd., Basildon, Essex (with
Renzo Piano)
1977 Institut de Recherche et de Coordination
Acoustique, for Pierre Boulez, Paris (with
Renzo Piano)
Centre Beaubourg, Paris (with Renzo Piano
and Sir Ove Arup and Partners)
1979 Lloyd's of London Headquarters

Publications:

By ROGERS: book—*The Building of Beaubourg,*
with Renzo Piano and others, London 1979;
recordings—*Piano and Rogers,* tape cassette, London 1976; *Genesis of the New Lloyd's underwriting
Room,* tape cassette and slides, London 1979.

On ROGERS: books—*By Their Own Design* by
Abby Suckle, London 1980; *Richard Rogers,* Lon-
don 1985; articles—"Piano and Rogers—
Beaubourg" in *Domus* (Milan), October 1971;
"Centre du plateau Beaubourg: concours d'idées,"
special issue of *Techniques et architecture* (Paris),
February 1972; "Piano and Rogers" in *Architects'
Journal* (London), 21 April 1972; "Piano and
Rogers: Centre Beaubourg" in *Architectural Design*
(London), July 1972; "Piano and Rogers" in
Architectural Design (London), no. 5, 1975; "Piano
and Rogers: Architectural Method" in *Architecture
+ Urbanism* (Tokyo), June 1976; "RIBA Discourse"
in *RIBA Journal* (London), January 1977; "Centre
Pompidou" in *Architectural Design* (London), no. 2,
1977; "Richard Rogers: Interview with Dennis
Sharp" in *Building* (London), 6 April 1979; "Rogers:
Ideal Site" in *Architects' Journal* (London), 30
January 1980; "Lloyd's Logic" in *Building* (Lon-
don), February 1980; "Rogers Revises Coin Street
Plans" in *Architects' Journal* (London), 14 January
1981; "Architects' Architecture" in *Archi-
tects' Journal* (London), 28 January 1981; "Billings-
gate Joins Office Space Pool" in *Building Design*
(London), 5 June 1981; "Six British Architects" in
Architectural Design (London), no. 12, 1981; "Napp
Laboratories, Cambridge" in *Architecture d'aujourd'hui* (Paris), June 1982; film—*Arena: Building
for Change,* BBC television film.

Ideology cannot be divided from architecture.
Change will clearly come from radical changes in
social and political structures. In the face of such
immediate crises as starvation, rising population,
homelessness, pollution, mis-use of non-renewable
resources and industrial and agricultural production, we simply anaesthetise our consciences. With
problems so numerous and so profound, with no
control except by starvation, disease, and war, we
respond with detachment. Today, at best, we can
hope to diminish the coming catastrophe by the
recognition of the existing human conditions and by
rational research and practice.

The importance of technology is in the application
of method to technique, whether one is talking of
sophisticated or primitive technology. The aim of
technology is to satisfy the needs of all levels of
society. Technology cannot be an end in itself but
must aim at solving long-term social and ecological
problems. This is impossible in a world where short-
term profit for the "haves" is seen as a goal, at the
expense of developing more efficient technology for
the "have nots." All forms of technology—from low
energy-intensive to high energy-intensive—must aim
at conserving natural resources while minimising
ecological, visual, and social damage to the environment, so that by using as little material as possible as
functionally as possible to answer new briefs, we
reach a self-sustaining situation where input equals
output.

A new distribution of ends and means is needed,
not based purely on a limited financial evolution of
human needs. In this context, it is as difficult to create
a truly socially oriented brief as it is to adapt and
translate it by the use of the correct technological
means.

—Richard Rogers

Richard Rogers: Lloyds Building, London, 1979-84 (model).

Richard Rogers is one of the few *emblematic* contemporary architects, concerned with advanced technology in architecture. This would put him deeply at risk of failure, or at least of design eccentricity, if he wasn't also a skilled manager, which he has proved to be without a doubt. Though many architects have aspired to produce highly technological works, Rogers has the ability to carry them out with repeated success. The formula seems to be that his clear design intentions are coupled with persuasiveness to clients, charisma to staff, and exhaustive research within a deceptively relaxed approach. These administrative and technical skills make his difficult design objectives attainable. If "design process" (to use that familiar if inert phrase) is a subject worth study, Rogers is a key person with whom to study it. High technology involves little risk of failure if ruthless practicality governs—and that seems to be Roger's way.

Winning the Beaubourg competition was a great achievement for Piano and Rogers, but not nearly so great as building it. Rogers was the most dynamic of the leaders. His team members later perceived their contributions as individually strong but also heightened by Rogers—a significant hint of how "effectiveness" was managed. A few slight (and diminishing) Archigram-style design resemblances therefore have little to do with Rogers's central qualities, the best of which prove a vital case for cultural progress and optimism (the weakest show an artiness that unfortunately gets well appreciated too).

Characteristic Rogers work are the PATScentre, the Centre Pompidou (Beaubourg), and Lloyd's of London. His works are developmentally consistent, so singling out a few is not to suggest the special but the more or less typical.

—Nathan Silver

ROSE, Peter.

Canadian. Born in Montreal, Quebec, 1 August 1943. Educated at Lower College, Montreal, 1955-61; Yale University, New Haven, Connecticut, 1961-70, B.A. 1966, M.Arch. 1970. Partner, with F. Andrus Burr and J.V. Righter, Rose/Burr/Righter Associates, Montreal, 1970-74; Designer, Arcop Associates, Montreal, 1972. Since 1970, President of Endless Construction Company, Montreal; since 1974, in private practice, as Peter Rose, Architect, Montreal. Visiting Critic in Architecture, Yale University, New Haven, Connecticut, 1974-78, Columbia University, New York, 1977, Carleton University, Ottawa, 1978, and Nova Scotia Technical College, Halifax, 1978. Exhibition: *Transformations in Modern Architecture*, Museum of Modern Art, New York, 1979. Recipient: Design Award, *Progressive Architecture*, 1978; Design Award, Ordre des Architectes du Quebec, 1978; Post Prize, McGill University School of Architecture, Montreal, 1978. Member, Ordre des Architectes du Quebec. Address (office): 1315 de Maisonneuve West, Montreal, Quebec, Canada.

Works:

1970 Peter Rose House, Magog, Quebec
1971 Graham House, Maisonville, Quebec (with F. Andrus Burr)
　　　Restaurant, Montreal (with F. Andrus Burr)
1972 Two prototype houses for native people, Bala, Ontario (with F. Andrus Burr)
　　　Vacation condominiums (300 units), St. Féreal, Quebec (project; with F. Andrus Burr)
　　　Prototype housing system for underdeveloped countries (project; with F. Andrus Burr)

1973 Plan for the ski area at St. Sauveur, Quebec (with F. Andrus Burr)
　　　Sinclair House, Jay Peak, Vermont (with F. Andrus Burr)
　　　Cummings House alterations, Knowlton, Quebec (with F. Andrus Burr)
　　　Cluster housing for doctors, Trudeau Institute, Saranac, New York (project; with F. Andrus Burr)
1974 Fortier House alterations, Magog, Quebec (with F. Andrus Burr)
　　　Winser House, Magog, Quebec (with F. Andrus Burr)
1975 Four block recycling scheme for Old Montreal (project; with F. Andrus Burr)
1976 Finlayson House, North Hatley, Quebec (with Mill Design and Research Center)
　　　Office Tower, Pointe Claire, Quebec (project; with Mill Design and Research Center)
　　　Elmwood School for Girls additions and alterations, Ottawa (project; with Mill Design and Research Center)
　　　Marosi House, North Hatley, Quebec
　　　Fortier House alterations, Magog, Quebec
1977 Bradley House, North Hatley, Quebec
　　　Johnson House, Ste. Agathe, Quebec
　　　Richer House, Ste. Agathe, Quebec
　　　C.I.C. Screen Printers Offices and Warehouse, Laval, Quebec
　　　Pavillon 70 (ski pavilion), St. Sauveur, Quebec (with Peter Lanken and J. V. Righter)
1978 Survey/evaluation of all Cree schools in Quebec
　　　Pavillon 70 alterations, and swimming pool, tennis courts, and landscaping at St. Sauveur, Quebec
1978 Housing for Crees (Nemeska Band), Champion Lake, Quebec

Peter Rose: **Bradley House, North Hatley, Quebec, 1977**

Cousineau House, Ayers Cliff, Quebec
Clubhouse, for Redbird Ski Club, Mont Tremblant, Quebec
Pinsonnault House alterations, Knowlton, Quebec
Shaughnessy House alterations, Montreal
1980 Montreal Skeet Clubhouse, Vaudreuil, Quebec
1983 House on Lake Memphremagog, Austin, Quebec (with M. Pimlott)

Publications:

On ROSE: books—*Supermannerism* by C. Ray Smith, New York 1977; *The Language of Post Modern Architecture* by Charles Jencks, New York 1978; *Transformations in Modern Architecture* by Arthur Drexler, New York, 1979; *Building with Words: Canadian Architects on Architecture*, with introduction by W. Bernstein and R. Cawker, Toronto 1981; articles—"Pavillon Soixante-Dix" in *Progressive Architecture* (New York), January 1978; "Private Residence at North Hatley" in *Architecture Concept* (Montreal), May/June 1978; "Nostalgie du Chateau" in *Progressive Architecture* (New York), March 1979; "Architecture in Canada," special issue of *Bauwelt* (Berlin), 3 December 1982; "A Proposal for the National Gallery of Canada" in *Architectural Design* (London), no. 5/6, 1983; "The Spirit and the Letter" in *Progressive Architecture* (New York), March 1983; "Ribkoff House, Austin, Quebec" in *Fifth Column* (Montreal), Summer 1983; "The Canadian Architect 1983 Awards of Excellence" in *The Canadian Architect* (Toronto), December 1983; "Building Types Study 600: Record Houses of 1984" in *Architectural Record* (New York), April 1984.

The influence of Charles Moore and Robert Venturi has, since the early 1960s, spread rapidly throughout the world, and most of the architecture designed under this influence is, at best, mediocre. This is largely due to the filtering down of architectural ideas and images—the second-hand, third-hand, and fourth-hand exposure (through books, journals, lectures, etc.) of most architects to the work of the Moore/Venturi High Architectural World. The level of understaning is shallow, and the resulting work is usually shallower. Accomplished people like Moore and Venturi must shudder at much of what gets built under their international wings.

But there are important exceptions to this general condition, such as the work of Peter Rose in Quebec. A native of Montreal, Rose completed his undergraduate and graduate degrees at Yale University. Robert Venturi and James Stirling were influential at Yale then; but of more significance is the fact that Rose was in the first class taught by Charles Moore in the Yale School of Architecture in 1966. The ideas and images came to Rose first-hand. And these ideas and images—particularly Moore's late-1960s rediscovery of vernacular architecture—were reinforced by Rose's travels between Montreal and New Haven through New England villages and farm country.

In addition to his use of false fronts and scale juxtapositions from Venturi and places of memories and big-time dreams from Moore, Rose's architecture has an additional layer of intelligently handled Quebec responses and references which save the works from being uncomfortable American transplants. In three buildings since 1975—two houses and a ski-lodge in Quebec—the huge chimneys are reminiscent of the chimney on the house Venturi designed for his mother in Chestnut Hill, Pennsylvania in 1962, and they recall Moore's 1969 Koizim House chimney in Westport, Connecticut; but Rose's chimneys are also like the prominent chimneys of seventeenth and eighteenth century Quebecois houses. His use of big, sweeping roofs recalls Venturi's 1962 Meis House Project for Princeton, New Jersey and Moore's California Sea Ranch roofs of 1966; but they are also functional snow-shedding

devices and relatives of the great Canadian railway hotel roofs. There is an overriding Northerness in Rose's compact plans (environmentally sensible), extensive use of wood, and most noticeably, Northerness in the proper, polite, serious composition of architectural elements.

Although there are teasers in his work (the very dramatic "sundeck as ski stage" in the Pavillon Soixante-Dix or the kitsch ceramic tile/fieldstone juxtaposition in the Marosi House fireplace), the work does not carry the sophisticated ironies and the complex readings available in Moore and Venturi's very American designs. Rose's work is not very ordinary, not very erotic, not very political, and not very controversial, all of which are possibilities taught by Moore and Venturi. But through learning from Quebec vernacular, Rose produces spirited architecture which has a friendly familiarity and a sense of belonging in the North.

—Larry Richards

ROSENBERG, Eugene.

British. Born in Topolčany, Czechoslovakia, 24 February 1907; emigrated to England, 1939: naturalized, 1947. Educated at primary and secondary schools in Nagy Tapolcsany, Hungary, 1912-18; secondary school in Topolčany, Czechoslovakia, 1918-20; State Industrial School for Building, Bratislava, Czechoslovakia, 1920-24; Technical University, Brno, Czechoslvakia, 1924-26; Technical University, Prague, 1926-28; Academy of Fine Arts School of Architecture, Prague, 1928, 1930-32, Dip.Arch. and Town Planning 1932; Atelier Le Corbusier, Paris, 1929; awarded Royal Institute of British Architects Diploma, London, 1946. Served in the Home Guard, 1943-45. Married Penelope Dorothy Wilkinson in 1946. Assistant to Havlíček and Honzik, Prague, 1932-33, Jan Gillar, Prague, 1933-34, and Josef Stepánek, Prague, 1934; in private practice, Prague, 1934-38; worked in the Department of Civic Design, University of Liverpool, under William Holford, *q.v.*, 1939-40; in internment camp, in Australia, 1940-42; Assistant to Rodney Thomas, London, 1942-43, and to F.R.S. Yorke, *q.v.*, London, 1943-44; Partner, F.R.S. Yorke and Eugene Rosenberg, London, 1944; Partner, with Yorke and Cyril Mardall, *q.v.*, Yorke, Rosenberg and Mardall, London, 1944-75. Recipient: Council of Industrial Design Award, 1959; Civic Trust Award, 1961, 1964, 1965, 1966, 1967, and 1969; Bronze Medal, Royal Institute of British Architects, 1961, 1966, 1967, and 1972; *Financial Times* Award, 1966 and 1969. Fellow, Royal Institute of British Architects, 1948. C.B.E. (Commander, Order of the British Empire), 1971. Address: 9 Chelwood House, Gloucester Square, London W2 2SY, England.

Works:

1929 Housing, Holesovice, Prague (project)
1931 Town plan for Trencin, Czechoslovakia (competition project; with J. Kucera)
 Airport, Ruzyne, Prague (competition project; with J. and K. Fiser, and J. Kinel)
1931/
 33 Red Cross Tuberculosis and Maternity Clinics, Topolčany, Czechoslovakia
1932 Workers Faculty Building, Prague (project)
1933 Town plan for Mukačevo, U.S.S.R. (competition project)
1934/
 35 Apartment block, Letrohradská, Prague
 Dr. Mokr House and Surgery, Topolčany, Czechoslovakia
1934/
 36 Apartment block, u. Pruhonu, Prague

 Two apartment blocks, u. Elektrárny, Prague
1935/
 37 Shops, offices and flats complex, Belkrediho Ul., Prague
 Low-cost apartment block, Schnirchova ul., Prague
1936 "Humanita" Workers' Cooperative Housing, Prague (project)
1936/
 38 Shopping arcades, offices and apartment blocks, Stepánska-Smečeky, Prague
1937 Grammar school, Topolčany, Czechoslovakia (project)
 Grammar school, Bratislava, Czechoslovakia (project)
 Primary schoool, Ludanice, Czechoslovakia (project)
 Stores, Nitra, Czechoslovakia (project)
 Stores, offices and flats complex, Prague (project)
1938 Department store, offices and flats complex, Prague (project)
 With Yorke, Rosenberg and Mardall:
1947 Luccombe House, Isle of Wight
 Cowley Peachey Housing, Middlesex
 Exhibition stands, Council of Industrial Design and Board of Trade, London
1948 Sigmund Pumps Factory, Gateshead, Durham
 Fort Corbletts House conversion, Alderney, Channel Islands
 Linden Doors Factory, Stowmarket, Suffolk (project)
 Temporary Outpatients Department, St. Thomas' Hospital, London
 Shebbear College Boarding School alterations, Devon
 Factories, Dagenham Docks, London (project)
1950 Barclay Secondary School, Stevenage, Hertfordshire
1951 John Lewis Department Store, Southsea, Hampshire (project)
 Dr. Cole House, Londonderry, Northern Ireland (with Corr and McCormick)
 Housing, King's Langley, Hertfordshire
 Susan Lawrence Primary School, London
 Elizabeth Lansbury Nursery School, London
 Housing, Brynmawr, Brecknock, Wales
 Hainault Forest Secondary School, Essex
1952 Sir William Nottidge School, Whitstable, Kent
 Sish Lane Housing, Stevenage, Hertfordshire
 College of Further Education, Merthyr Tydfil, Glamorgan, Wales
1953 Williams and Williams Exhibition Stand, Building Trades Exhibition, London
 The Mill House conversion, Wootton, Oxfordshire
 Warren Wood Secondary School, Rochester, Kent
 Upholland Grammar School, Wigan, Lancashire
 West Park Secondary School, Leeds
 Southalds Teachers' Training College Assembly Hall, Wimbledon, London
 Sheerwater Primary School, Woking, Surrey
 Causeway Green Primary School, Oldbury, Worcestershire
 North Mimms Boys' and Infants' School, Hertfordshire
1954 Steddall's Warehouse alterations, London
 Birchen Coppice Primary School, Kidderminster, Worcestershire
 Queensmead Secondary School, Ruislip, Middlesex
 London Transport Bus Garage and Depot, Loughton, Essex
 Hammerson Group Offices, Great New Street, London (project)
1955 Tudor House Home for the Infirm, Grayshott, Hertfordshire (project)
 Kerris Artists Studio conversion, Mousehole, Cornwall

Williams and Williams Offices, London (project)

Quarles Secondary Modern School, Romford, Essex

Master plan and stage I of the Leeds Polytechnic, West Yorkshire

Mark Hall Local Authority Housing, Harlow, Essex

Haileybury Boys Club, London

Bewdley Secondary School, Worcestershire

Kirkwall Place Housing, Bethnal Green, London

Kingswood School, Essex

1956 Boxgrove Housing prototypes

Wootton Rectory, Oxfordshire

Jack Straw's Lane House, Oxford, England

Tyrell and Green Store, Southampton, Hampshire

Dick Sheppard School, Tulse Hill, London

East Anglian Girls School, Bury St. Edmunds, Suffolk

Bradfield Secondary School, Yorkshire

Sigmund Pumps Factory extension, Gateshead, Durham (project)

North Mimms Boys' and Infants' School additions, Hertfordshire

College of Further Education extensions, Merthyr Tydfil, Glamorgan, Wales

Kingswood School extensions, Essex

1957 Southlands College Lecture block and Dining Room extensions, Wimbledon, London

Temple Moor Grammar School, Leeds, West Yorkshire

Stanley Outwood Secondary School, Yorkshire

Jewish Theological College, Montague Square, London

Oak Park Secondary School, Havant, Hampshire

Philip Harben House, 115 Great George Street, London

Dawley Secondary School, Shropshire

Interbau Housing, Berlin (project; with Werner Düttmann)

Master plan for the Bromsgrove Education Centre, Worcestershire

Timberlog Secondary School, Basildon, Essex

St. Paul's Secondary School, Addlestone, Surrey

Gatwick Airport, stage I, Sussex

Sir William Nottige school extensions, Whitstable, Kent

1958 Unilever House, Hamburg, West Germany (competition project)

Wokingham Infants School, Berkshire (competition project)

Jewish Board of Guardians Offices, London

Finnish Seamen's Mission, London

Chaucer Secondary School, Sheffield, South Yorkshire

Carmel College extensions, Wallingford, Berkshire

Brixton Synagogue Hall remodelling, London

Leeds Polytechnic, stage II, West Yorkshire

Tyrell and Green Store extension, Southampton, Hampshire

East Anglian Girls School alterations and additions, Bury St. Edmunds, Suffolk

1959 J. Spedan Lewis House, Longstock, Hampshire

Morsons Chemical Works, Enfield, Middlesex

Elephant and Castle Development, London (project)

World Health Organization Offices, Geneva (competition project)

Timber Development association Office Furniture, London (competition project)

Formation Furniture prototypes, for Bath Cabinet Makers Ltd.

Roman Road Housing, Bethnal Green, London

High Park School, Stourbridge, Worcestershire

St. Paul's School Hall alterations, Chertsey, Surrey

Brays Grove Secondary School, Harlow, Essex

College of Further Education, Bromsgrove, Worcestershire

Tennant Brothers Exhibition Stand, Club Trades Fair, London

Churchill College, Cambridge, England (competition project)

Upholland Grammar School extensions, Wigan, Lancashire

East Anglian Girls School alterations and additions, stage II, Bury St. Edmunds, Suffolk

1960 Watford Shopping Centre, Hertfordshire (project)

Rothwell Secondary School, stage II, Yorkshire

Warslow School, Staffordshire

United States Embassy, Grosvenor Square, London (with Eero Saarinen Associates)

Supasave Store, Southend, Essex

Staincliffe Hospital Geriatric Unit, Leeds, West Yorkshire

Altnagelvin Hospital, Londonderry, Northern Ireland

Passmores Comprehensive School, Harlow, Essex

D. Allford House, Persham, Surrey (project)

Brierly Hill Secondary School, Staffordshire

Rolls Royce Offices, Derby (project)

Telecommunications Engineering Building, Gatwick Airport, Sussex

Leeds Polytechnic, stage III, West Yorkshire

1961 N.J. Payne House, Shamley Green, Norfolk

Royal Masonic School, Ascot, Berkshire (project)

Bromsgrove High School, Worcestershire

Hob Green Primary School, Worcestershire

YRM and Norwich Union Insurance Societies Offices, Greystoke Place, London

Maternity and Outpatients Departments, Crawley Hospital, Sussex

Kew Bridge Development for British Rail, London (project)

Report on Creekside Refuse Disposal Depot, Deptford, London

Timber Development Association Wooden Furniture, London (competition project)

Kingswood School extensions, stage II, Essex

1962 Master plan for Kuwait Airport (with Sir Frederick Snow and Partners)

Elliott Brothers Welfare Building, Rochester, Kent (project)

Rotameter Factory, Croydon, Surrey (project)

Library, Cambridge University, England (project)

Southlands College: Queensmere Hostels, Lecture Block and Gymnasium, Wimbledon, London

Ark House, Rochford, Essex

Staff Residence, Crawley Hospital, Sussex

Barstable Comprehensive School, Basildon, Essex

College of Further Education extensions, stage II, Merthyr Tydfil, Glamorgan, Wales

North Mimms Boys' and Infants' School additions stage II, Hertfordshire

Haileybury Boys Club, stage II, London

Oak Park Secondary School extensions, Havant, Hampshire

Timberlog Secondary School extensions, Basildon, Essex

1963 Stamford House Swimming Pool, London

Rolleston Secondary School, Staffordshire

Rochdale College, Lancashire

Redevelopment scheme for the Dawley schools, Shropshire

John Lewis Warehouse, Stevenage, Hertfordshire (with Felix Candela)

Brewery redevelopment, Luton, Bedfordshire (project)

T.R. Evans House, Lacey Green, Buckinghamshire

A. Johnson and Company Factory and Offices, Wokingham, Berkshire

Harlow Training Centre, Essex

Cole Brothers Store, Sheffield

Shebbear College additions, Devon

East Anglian Girls School additions and alterations, stage III, Bury St. Edmunds, Suffolk

Bradford Secondary School extensions, Yorkshire

1964 Southlands College Staff Accommodation, Wimbledon, London

Development plan for the central area of Blackpool

Staff Residences, Altnagelvin Hospital, Londonderry, Northern Ireland

Kidd's Store, Leeds, West Yorkshire

Keddies Store, Southend, Essex

Temporary buildings for Crawley Hospital, Sussex

Development report on Luton Airport, Bedfordshire

Clements Store, Watford, Hertfordshire

Blythe Bridge Secondary School, Staffordshire

Belfast Synagogue

Mildmay Secondary School, Aveley, Essex

Adler Street Unit Workshope, London

Taylorian Institute Modern Languages Faculty, Oxford, England (project)

Dawley Secondary School extensions, Shropshire

Chaucer Secondary School extensions, Sheffield, South Yorkshire

College of Further Education extensions, Bromsgrove, Worcestershire

1965 Bakewell Secondary School, Derbyshire (project)

Gatwick Airport, stage II, Sussex

Simestow Comprehensive School, Tottenhall, Staffordshire

Romford Technical College, Essex

Chalvedon Comprehensive School, Basildon, Essex

Department of Electrical Engineering and Electronics, University of Liverpool

German Sailors' Home, London

Nurses Home and School, Crawley Hospital, Sussex

Gibbons Road Secondary School, West Willesden, London (project)

Control Building, Kuwait Airport

Rochdale College extensions, Lancashire

John Lewis Warehouse extensions, Stevenage, Hertfordshire

1966 Residential Buildings, Hamble College of Air Training, Hampshire (project)

Ada Street Unit Workshops, London

Local authority housing, Cadell Street, Tower Hamlets, London

Elliott Brothers Factory extensions, Borehamwood, Hertfordshire

Westwood hall and St. Edward's School, Leek, Staffordshire

Intermediate Terminal, Luton Airport, Bedfordshire

St. Thomas' Hospital, stage I, London (with W. Fowler Howitt)

Revision of the development plan, Library, Molecular and Engineering Sciences Building, stage I, and First Hall of Residence and Boilerhouse, University of Warwick, England

B. Henderson Guest Pavilion, Great Bedwin, Wiltshire

Elliott Brothers Factory, Rochester, Kent

College of Further Education extensions, stage III, Merthyr Tydfil, Glamorgan, Wales

Leeds Polytechnic, stage IV, West Yorkshire

St. Paul's Secondary School extensions, Addlestone, Surrey

Clements Store extensions, Watford, Hertfordshire
1967 Milkhouse Water House, Pewsey, Wiltshire
Operating theatres, Lambeth Hospital, London
Ancillary buildings, Redhill Hospital, Surrey
Avalon Furniture Offices and Showrooms, Yatton, Somerset
Bacton Street Housing, Tower Hamlets, London
Bath Cabinet Makers Furniture Factory
Royal Infirmary and Ancillary Buildings, Hull, Yorkshire
Ilford Training Centre, Essex
Sceptre Road Housing, Tower Hamlets, London
Stamford House Remand Home, Hammersmith, London
Terminal, Newcastle Airport, England
First Hall of Residence, stage II, University of Warwick, England
General Aviation Terminal, Gatwick Airport, Sussex
Queensmead Secondary School extensions, Ruislip, Middlesex
Leeds Polytechnic, stage V, West Yorkshire
Brays Grove Secondary School extensions, Harlow, Essex
1968 Boots Pure Drug Company Head Office, Nottingham, England (with Skidmore, Owings and Merrill)
Cottam Power Station, Nottinghamshire
Office Block, Gatwick Airport, Sussex
Cargo Area Canteen, Heathrow Airport, London
Cargo Area Airside Operations Building, Heathrow Airport, London
Second Hall of Residence, stage I, Physics Building, stage I, and Sports Pavilion and Playing Fields, University of Warwick, England
Fire Station, Luton Airport, Bedfordshire
Uxbridge Technical College, London
Willesden Secondary School, London
B. Henderson House conversion, Regent's Park, London
Old Street Concourse, London
Development plan for the University of Zambia, Lusaka
Timberlog Secondary School extensions, stage II, Basildon, Essex
St. Paul's Secondary School extensions, stage II, Addlestone, Surrey
Chaucer Secondary School extensions, stage II, Sheffield, South Yorkshire
John Lewis Warehouse extensions, stage II, Stevenage, Hertfordshire
1969 Computer Laboratory, University of Liverpool, Merseyside
Ealing Children's Home, London
Cargo Agents' Building, Heathrow Airport, London
Willis-Faber-Dumas Ltd. Computer Office interiors, Southend, Essex
Terminal, Stansted Airport, Essex
Kingshold Estate, King Edward's Road, Hackney, London
Second Hall of Residence, stage II, University of Warwick, England
Arts Centre and Chapel, University of Warwick, England (project)
Osprey Estate Housing, Bermondsey, London
Nash House Club Rooms interiors, The Mall, London
Associated Portland Cement Manufacturers Offices, Northfleet, Kent
Leeds Polytechnic, stage VI, West Yorkshire
Chalvedon Comprehensive School extensions, Basildon, Essex
1970 Crawley hospital, stage II, Sussex
Furness Withy and Company Apartment interior conversions, London
Sir William Gathwaite House interiors, London

Herman Miller Furniture Factory and Showrooms, Bath, Avon
Hangar, Luton Airport, Bedfordshire
Renal Dialysis Unit, St. Thomas's Hospital, London
Computer Centre, Lambeth Hospital, London
College of Further Education extension, stage II, Bromsgrove, Worcestershire
Rochdale College extensions, stage II, Lancashire
Sceptre Road Housing extensions, Tower Hamlets, London
1970/
72 Royal Infirmary and Ancillary Building extensions, Leeds, West Yorkshire
1971 Armstrong Cork Company office interiors, Uxbridge, Middlesex
Magistrates Court, Manchester, England
Keddies Store extensions, stage II, Southend, Essex
Arts Building, Computer Centre and Sports Centre, University of Warwick
Parsons Brown Office Building, Amoco Jetty, Milford Haven, Wales (project)
BEA (British European Airways) Office Building, Ruislip, Middlesex
BEA (British European Airways) Operational Offices, Heathrow Airport, London (project)
Chemistry Building, University of Zambia, Lusaka
Sizewell "B" Power Station, Suffolk (project)
Bromsgrove High School extensions, Worcestershire
Keddies Store extensions, Southend, Essex
1972 Tomo Estates Factory, Cowley Peachey, Middlesex
Furness House Office interiors, London
C and A Modes Computer Suite interiors, London
Battle Hospital, Reading, Berkshire
John Radcliffe Hospital, stage I, Oxford, England
Fieldhead Hospital, Wakefield, Yorkshire
Alcan Aluminium Smelter and Power Station, Lynemouth, Cumberland
Staff Residences, Churchill Hospital, Oxford
Schools of Education and Engineering, University of Zambia, Lusaka
South Western Hospital Departments, Lambeth, London
St. Thomas' Hospital Offices, Leadenhall Street, London
Keddie Commercial Centre, Southend, Essex (project)
Two Tree Island Marina, Essex (project; with Cedric Price)
New Arts Building, University of Liverpool, Merseyside
Feasibility study: Theodore Herzl Memorial Hospital, Israel
Northern Extension Terminal Building, Gatwick Airport, Sussex
Hindrey Place Housing, Hackney, London
John Radcliffe Hospital, stage II, Oxford, England
St. Thomas' Hospital, phase II, London
Wellington Hospital, St. John's Wood, London
W.D. and H.O. Wills Head and Western Division Offices and Factory, Bristol, Avon (with Skidmore, Owings and Merrill)
Central Electricity Generating Board Divisional Offices, Gloucester, England
Dashwood House Offices, Old Broad Street, London
St. Thomas' Hospital Office Development, Lambeth, London
Birchen Coppice Primary School extensions, Kidderminster, Worcestershire
High Park School extensions, Stourbridge, Worcestershire

Fire Station extensions, Luton Airport, Bedfordshire
1973/
75 Amersham General Hospital, Buckinghamshire
C and A Head Offices remodelling, London Offices, Eastcheap, London
Camden Health Centre, London
Development plan for Churchill/Warneford Hospitals, Oxford
Southern Extension and East Land Development, Gatwick Airport, Sussex
Slade Industrial Site, Oxford, England
National Westminster Bank Office Building, Southend, Essex
New Terminal, Luton Airport, Bedfordshire
John Radcliffe Hospital, stage III, Oxford, England
Feasibility study: Bio-Medical Centre, Lambeth, London (with Cusdin, Burden and Howitt)
Renslade Investments Ltd. Offices, The Hague
St. Thomas' Hospital, phase B, London
Guardian Properties Offices, The Hague
Ashmolean Art Gallery, Oxford, England
Organizational and building evaluation study: Commonwealth Development Finance Corporation Offices, London
Los Llanos Recreational Centre, Costa del Sol, Spain (project)
Library and Community Building, Albion Street, Southwark, London
Brixton Road Development, London
Territorial Army Centre, Camden, London
Tomo Estates Offices, Cowley Peachey, Middlesex
Royal Infirmary additions, Hull, Yorkshire
Keddies Store and Offices, stage III, Southend, Essex (project)
Psychiatric Day Unit, Battle Hospital, Reading, Berkshire
Crawley Hospital, stage IIa, Sussex
Yorke, Rosenberg, Mardall Offices, Turnmill Street, London

Publications:

On ROSENBERG: books—*The Modern Flat* by F. R. S. Yorke and Frederick Gibberd, London 1948; *The Architecture of Yorke Rozenberg Mardall*, introduction by Reyner Banham, London and New York 1972; articles—"Projekt zu einem Wohnblock in Holešovice" in *Stein Holz Eisen* (Stuttgart), no. 13, 1931; "Town Planning Competition: Horni-Sihot, Trencin" in *Stavitel* (Prague), no. 1, 1932; "Competition: Airport Prague-Ruzyne" in *Stavitel* (Prague), no. 4/5, 1932; "Workers Faculty" in *Stavitel* (Prague), no. 13, 1932; "Zwei Neuzeitliche Wohnbauten" by R. Hoffman in *Prager Tagblatt* (Prague), 28 January 1937; "Arcades in Stepanská, Prague" by Frantisek Zelenka in *Lidove Noviny* (Prague), 25 November 1938; "Immeubles de rapport à Prague" in *Architecture d'aujourd'hui* (Paris), October 1938; "Block of Flats, Prague" in *Architects' Journal* (London), 18 April 1940; "Arcades, Offices and Flats, Prague" in *Architects' Journal* (London), 11 July 1940; "Modern Architecture in Czechoslovakia" by F. R. S. Yorke in *Review* (London), no. 3, 1943; "The English Approach" by Hugh Casson in *Kvart* (Prague), no. 5, 1946; "Conversations with an Overseas Architect" by M. Kadlečiková in *Domov* (Prague), no. 3, 1964; "YRM's Shining Pot" in *Architects' Journal* (London), 8 May 1974; "Trouble at Two Tree Island" in *Building Design* (London), 19 July 1974; "Sickness and Wealth" in *Design* (London), September 1974; "Alcan Smelting Works in Lynemouth, Great Britain" in *Deutsche Bauzeitschritft* (Gütersloh, West Germany), October 1974; "Wills Factory and Headquarters, Hartcliff, Bristol" in *Architects' Journal* (London), 24 September

1975; "A Healthy New Building" by Vincent Smith in *Architecture Australia* (Melbourne), August/ September 1976; "British Art Gallery" in *Architecture d'aujourd'hui* (Paris), January/February 1977; "New Offices for Yorke Rosenberg Mardall in Briton Street" by Stevan Brown in *RIBA Journal* (London), March 1978; "A Place for Art" by Annette LeCuver in *Building Design* (London), 1 December 1978; "Taking Off at Gatwick" by Jack Christopher in *Building Design* (London), 2 March 1979.

Eugene Rosenberg was born in Slovakia and graduated in 1932 from the Academy of Fine Arts in Prague. Before qualifying, he had spent a year working intermittently in Paris for Le Corbusier, and when he left the Academy he worked for Havlíček and Honzik on the famous Pensions Institute in Prague, perhaps one of the first great monoliths in reinforced concrete and finished in white tiles. In 1939, two days before Hitler marched into Prague, Rosenberg arrived in London never to return permanently to Czechoslovakia. His reputation then rested on a series of modern buildings he had designed in Prague and elsewhere and his future upon an acquaintance in England with F.R.S. Yorke, Max Fry, and Frederick Gibberd.

To understand and appreciate Rosenberg's work and its origins, one should keep in mind that by 1934, when he was practising on his own account, Prague and Brno had become two acknowledged centres of the "international" modern movement and stood perhaps in the same relation to East Europe as Rotterdam to the West. The international movement—already being suppressed in Germany by Hitler—flourished in Prague and in Brno where Mies van de Rohe had built his celebrated Tugendhat House and where Bohuslav Fuchs also worked. It was a mainstream movement there, uncompromising and committed, with a strict geometrical discipline and much influenced by Le Corbusier and with close links with the Bauhaus. This was the architectural environment in which Rosenberg was brought up and in which he emerged to practice. His early work already outlined the course his architecture was to take in his maturity in England.

Most of these early buildings in Prague were blocks of flats and offices, and they already display a mastery of plan and section which was later to distinguish the work of the partnership Yorke, Rosenberg and Mardall, founded in London in 1944, with which Rosenberg was to spend most of his working life. these early buildings—offices and flats in the Stepánská-Smeeky and the Schnirchova ul.— also exhibit another characteristic, a clearly-stated structural geometry with a very sophisticated feeling for the plasticity of concrete. Rosenberg began his education as an engineer and subsequently switched to architecture, and throughout his career his planning has always related to a logical and consistent sense of structure.

The immediate impact of Rosenberg's work is one of ruthless logic, succeeded by a realization of the beauty that emerges from an intellectual discipline clearly expressed in the built form. It is Cartesian. It emerges in Prague and reaches through to the work in London years later. The major works of the partnership are, in the highest sense of the word, professional. There is nothing adventitious or casual but a classical, even Roman, simplicity of mass, a rigorous elimination of the irrelevant. Their buildings always make a clear, and often a grand, statement of intention and structure in the idiom of the international movement and demonstrate its increasing range and versatility—just as did Rosenberg's individual work in Prague.

In the early works, too, there is an elegance of detail, originating from simple elements. The structural discipline is echoed in the details such as shop fronts, balustrades, and railings formed from standard sections. Indeed, there seems to be a coherence in design, in structure, and in the use of materials between these buildings in Prague and some of those being built in England during the period—like Highpoint I. It was indeed an international movement, and Rosenberg has played no small part in it.

—Richard Sheppard (1980)

ROSSI, Aldo.

Italian. Born in Milan, 3 May 1931. Educated at the School of the Somaschi Fathers, Como, Italy, 1940-42; Collegio Alessandro Voltas, Lecco, Italy, 1943-46; studied under Ernesto N. Rogers, *q.v.*, and Giuseppe Samonà, *q.v.*, Polytechnic of Milan, 1949-59, Dip.Arch. 1959. Worked in the studios of Ignazio Gardella, *q.v.*, and Marco Zanuso, *q.v.*, Milan, 1956-57. Since 1959, in private practice, Milan: in collaboration with Gianni Braghiera, from 1971. Teaching Assistant to Ludovico Quaroni, *q.v.*, Scuola Urbanistica, Arezzo, 1963; Visiting Instructor from 1965, Professor of Architectural Composition, 1970-71, and Member of the Council from 1971, Polytechnic of Milan; Professor of Planning, Eidgenössische Technische Hochschule, Zürich, 1972-75; Professor of Architectural Composition, University of Venice, from 1975; Mellon Professor, Cornell University, Ithaca, New York, and Visiting Professor, Cooper Union, New York, 1976; Professor of Planning, Yale University, New Haven, Connecticut, 1980. Editor, *Casabella-Continuità*, Milan, 1955-64; contributor, *Societa*,

Eugene Rosenberg: St. Thomas' Hospital, London, 1975.

Milan, and Editorial Board Member, *Il Contemporaneo*, Milan, 1959. Director of the architectural section, *XV Triennale*, Milan, 1973, and of the *Biennale*, Venice, 1983; Director of the Interntional Seminar on Architecture, Santiago de Compostela, Spain, 1976. Exhibitions: *Triennale*, Milan, 1960; *Aldo Rossi*, Centro Arte Viva, Trieste, 1967; *Italian Architecture of the Sixties*, toured Italy and Iran, 1972-73; *Aldo Rossi: Bauten, Projekte*, Eidgenössische Technische Hochschule, Zürich, 1973; *Aldo Rossi/Louis Kahn/John Hejduk*, University of Stuttgart, 1974; *Aldo Rossi + 21 arquitectos españoles*, Palau de la Virrenia, Barcelona, 1975 (toured Spain); *Aldo Rossi*, Institute for Architecture and Urban Studies, New York, 1976; *Aldo Rossi*, Galleria Solferino, Milan, 1976; *Architecture I*, Leo Castelli Gallery, New York, 1977; *Abraham/Eisenman/Hejduk/Rossi*, Cooper Union, New York, 1977; *I nodi della rappresentazione*, Pinacoteca Comunale, Ravenna, Italy, 1978; *Aldo Rossi: progetti e disegni 1962-79*, Galleria Pan, Rome, 1979; *Aldo Rossi: alcuni mei progetti*, Galleria Antonia Jannone, Milan, 1979; *Aldo Rossi: disegni e progetti*, Galleria Cesare Manzo, Pescara, Italy, 1979; *Aldo Rossi in America*, Institute for Architecture and Urban Studies, New York, 1979; *Aldo Rossi: projects*, Max Protetch Gallery, New York, 1979; *The Architecture of Aldo Rossi*, Hayden Gallery, Massachusetts Institute of Technology, Cambridge, 1980; *Il Teatro del Mondo*, Galleria Antonia Jannone, Milan, 1980; *Un progetto per Firenze*, Cooperativa Libraria di Architettura, Naples, 1980; *City Segments*, Walker Art Center, Minneapolis, Minnesota, 1980 (travelled to Chicago, Fort Worth, Texas, Houston, Texas, and Purchase, New York, 1980-81); *Teatro e spazio scenico*, at the *Biennale*, Venice, 1980; *Aldo Rossi: modelli di architettura*, Galleria Antonia Jannone, Milan, 1981; *Architetture italiane degli anni '70*, Galleria Nazionale d'Arte Moderna, Rome 1981; *Aldo Rossi: architecture—Projects and Drawings*, Institute of Contemporary Arts, London, 1983; *Aldo Rossi*, Jamileh Weber Galerie, Zürich, 1983; *Aldo Rossi: Architecture—Drawings and Projects*, Blue Studio Architecture Gallery, Dublin, 1983; *Aldo Rossi: opere recenti*, Palazzina dei Giardini, Modena, Italy, and Rocca Paolina, Perugia, Italy, 1983; *The European Iceberg*, Art Gallery of Ontario, Toronto, 1985; *Aldo Rossi*, Galerie Tanit und Mollier, Munich, 1985. Recipient; First Prize, with Gianni Braghieri, Municipal Cemetery Competition, Modena, Italy, 1971. Address: Via Maddalena 1, 20122 Milan, Italy.

Works:

1960 Redevelopment plan for the Via Farina, Milan (project; with G. U. Polesello and F. Tentori)
  Ronchini Villa, Versilia, Italy (with L. Ferrari)
1961 Peugeot Building, Buenos Aires (competition project; with V. Magistretti and G. U. Polesello)
1962 Monument to the Resistance, Cuneo, Italy (competition project; with Luca Meda and G. U. Polesello)
  Monumental Fountain, City Hall, Milan (competition project; with Luca Meda)
  Country Club Building, Fagagna, Italy (project; with G. U. Polesello)
  School, Villa Reale Park, Monza, Italy (competition project; with V. Gavazzeni and G. Grassi)
  Museum of Contemporary History interiors, Milan (with M. Baffa, Luca Meda, and U. Rivolta)
  City Hall, Turin (competition project; with G. U. Polesello and Luca Meda)
1964 General plan and Steel Bridge, for the Triennale, Milan (with Luca Meda)
  Abbiategrasso Sports and Leisure Facilities, Ticino, Italy (project)
  Paganini Theatre and Piazza della Pilotta,

Parma, Italy (competition project)
1965 Residential redevelopment, Naples (competition project; with G. Grassi)
  Town Hall Square and Monumental Fountain, Segrate, Milan (partially realized)
  General building code and plan for Broni, Italy (project)
1966 Regional plan for Veneto, Italy (project; with G. Salmonà)
  Building code and plan for Certosa di Pavia, Italy (project)
  San Rocco Residential Complex, Monza, Italy (competition project; with G. Grassi)
1967 Building code and plan for the town centre of Sannazzaro de' Burgondi, Italy (competition project)
1968 City Hall, Scandicci, Italy (competition project; with M. Fortis and M. Scolari)
1969 School, Trieste (project; with R. Agosto, G. Grassi, and F. Tentori)
1970 Gallaratese 2 Apartment Complex, Milan
  De Amicis School restoration and additions, Broni, Italy
1971 General building code and plan for Abbiategrasso, Italy (project; with A. Balzani)
  Municipal Cemetery, Modena, Italy (competition project; with G. Braghieri)
1972 Town Hall, Muggio, Italy (competition project; with G. Braghieri)
1973 Municipal Cemetery, Modena, Italy (2nd competition project; with G. Braghieri)
  Single-family housing, Broni, Italy (with G. Braghieri)
  Layout of the International Architecture Section, *Triennale*, Milan
  Villa, Borgo Ticino, Italy (project; with G. Braghieri)
  General building code and plan for Fagnano Olona, Italy (project)
1974 Castle restoration and Bridge, Bellinzona, Italy (with G. Braghieri, B. Reichlin, and F. Reinhart)
  Single-family housing, Robbiate, Italy (with G. Braghieri)
  Local Government Office Building, Trieste (competition project; with G. Braghieri and M. Bosshard)
  Student Building, University of Trieste (competition project; with G. Braghieri, M. Bosshard, and A. Cantafora)
1976 Student Building, University of Chieti, Italy (competition project; with G. Braghieri and A. Cantafora)
  Municipal Cemetery, Modena, Italy (3rd project; with G. Braghieri)
1977 Houses at Mozzo, Italy (with A. Pizzigoni)
  "Roma Interotta" plan, Rome (project; with M. Bosshard, G. Braghieri, A. Cantafora, and P. Katzberger)
1978 City Centre Plan, Florence (competition project; with C. Aymonino and others)
  Elementary School, Fagnano Olona, Italy
  "Scientific Theatre" (project; with G. Braghieri and R. Freno)
1979 Houses at Zandobbio, Italy (with A. Pizzigoni)
  Secondary School, Broni, Italy
  Houses at Goito, Italy (with G. Braghieri and Coprat)
  Houses at Pegognaga, Italy (with G. Braghieri and Coprat)
  Floating Theatre (Teatro del Mondo), Venice (project)
  Symbolic Monument, Melbourne (competition project; with G. Braghieri and S. Getzel)
  District Library, Karlsruhe, West Germany (competition project; with G. Braghieri, C. Herdel, and C. Stead)
  Tower for the New Civic Centre, Pesaro, Italy (project)
1980 Canareggio West Development Plan, Venice (project; with G. Dubbini, A. de Poli, and M. Narpozzi)

Ghetto Area Plan, Pesaro, Italy (project; with G. Braghieri)
  Entrance Portal for the *Presenza del Passato* exhibition, Corderie, Venice
  Funeral Chapel (project; with C. Stead)
1981 Südliche Friedrichstadt housing development, Berlin (competition project; with G. Braghieri, C. Stead, and J. Johnson)
  Klosterli Area Plan, Bern, Switzerland (competition project; with G. Braghieri and C. Stead)
  House, Tiergarten, Berlin (project; with G. Braghieri and C. Stead)
  Villa in the Campagna Romana, Italy (project; with C. Stead)
1982 Kop van Zuid Area Plan, Rotterdam (project; with G. Braghieri and F. Reinhart)
  Carlo Felice Theatre reconstruction, Genoa, Italy (competition project; with I. Gardella, F. Reinhart, and A. Sibilla)
  Palladian 'Zitelle' redevelopment, Venice (project)
  New Palace of Congress, Milan (competition project; with M. Adjimia and G. Geronzi)
  Fontivegge Area Development Plan, Perugia, Italy (project; with G. Braghieri, V. Bega, G. Menghi, G. Geronzi, and M. Schleurer)
  "Fiera Catena" Area Plan, Mantua, Italy (competition project; with G. Braghieri and Coprat)
  Apartment Building with shops, Viadana, Italy (project; with G. Braghieri, C. Castagnoli, A. Gozzi and A. Medici)

Publications

By ROSSI: books—*Concorso per la ricostruzione del Teatro Paganini di Parma*, with Carlo Aymonino, Venice 1966; *L'Architettura della città*, Padua, Italy 1966; *Scritti scelti sull'architettura e la città*, edited by Rosaldo Bonicalzi, Milan 1975; *Ugo Carrega*, with Maria Teresa Balboni, Rome 1976; *Giovanni Bocaccio: II Decameron*, editor, Bologna 1977; *1977: un progetto per Firenze*, with Carlo Aymonino and others, Rome 1978; *Costruzioni del territorio e spazio urban nel Cantone Ticino*, with others, Lugano, Switzerland 1979; *Aldo Rossi*, exhibition catalogue, New York 1980; *A Scientific Autobiography*, Cambridge, Massachusetts and London 1981; *Teatro del Mondo*, with others, Venice 1982; *Il Libro Azzurro: i mei progetti 1981*, Zurich 1983; articles—"Un monumento ai partigiani" in *Casabella* (Milan), no.208, 1955; "L'Architetto e l'urbanistica" in *L'Urbanisme au service de l'homme*, edited by A. Gutton, Paris 1962; "Conversacion con Aldo Rossi" in *Construccion de la ciudad 2C* (Barcelona), 1972; "L'Habitation et la ville" in *L'Architecture d'aujourd'hui* (Paris), no. 174, 1974; "Architecture and Rationalism" in *Construccion de la ciudad 2C* (Barcelona), March 1977; "H. Schmidt and the Problem of Monotony" in *Werk/Archithese* (Niederteufen, Switzerland), May/June 1978; "I Live—Do I Decorate?", with D. Mazzoleni, in *Domus* (Milan) May 1982; film—*Ornamento e delitto*, 1973.

On ROSSI: books—*Aldo Rossi: Bauten, Projekte*, exhibition catalogue, Zürich 1973; *Aldo Rossi: Architektur des Rationalismus*, exhibition catalogue, Berlin 1974; *Aldo Rossi*, exhibition catalogue, New York 1976; *Aldo Rossi, Architetto*, exhibition catalogue, Milan 1976; *L'Architettura di Aldo Rossi* by Vittorio Savi, Milan 1977; *Aldo Rossi: Projects and Drawings 1962-1979*, edited by Francesco Moschini, Florence and London 1979; *Aldo Rossi in America, 1976 to 1979*. exhibition catalogue, with an introduction by Peter Eisenman, New York 1979; *City Segments*, exhibition catalogue, by Mildred S. Friedman, Minneapolis, Minnesota 1980; *Aldo Rossi* by Gianni Braghieri, Bologna, Italy 1981; *Il Gallaratese di Aymonino e Rossi* by C. Conforti, Rome 1981; *Aldo Rossi: opere recenti*, exhibition catalogue, edited by Vittorio Savi and Mario Lupani, Modena, Italy 1983; *Aldo Rossi: architecture— Projects and Drawings,* exhibition catalogue, with introduction by M. Bandini, London 1983; articles—"Elementi e costruzione: note sull' architettura di Aldo Rossi" by E. Bonfanti in *Controspazio* (Bari, Italy), no. 10, 1970; "Zu einer Ausstellung der Projekte von Aldo Rossi an der ETH—Zürich" by B. Reichlin in *Werk* (Zürich), no. 4, 1972; "La idea de arquitectura en Rossi y el cementiero de Modena" by José Rafael Moneo in *Elementi di composizione,* Barcelona 1973; "Aldo Rossi," special issue of *Construccion de la Ciudad 2C* (Barcelona), no. 2, 1975; "Rational Architecture" by Alan Colquhoun in *Architectural Design* (London), no. 6, 1975; "Aldo Rossi," special issue of *Architecture + Urbanism* (Tokyo), no. 65, 1976; "Aldo Rossi," special issue of *Construccion de la Ciudad 2C* (Barcelona), no. 5, 1976; "Aldo Rossi: una alternativa progresista para la arquitectura" by S. Frago and Malo de Molina in *Triunfo* (Madrid), no. 719, 1976; "Aldo Rossi: The Idea of Architecture" by José Rafael Moneo in *Oppositions* (New York), no. 5, 1978; "The Architecture of Dissent: Aldo Rossi and Ettore Sottsass" by Pier Carlo Santini in *Ottagono* (Milan), June 1978; "Elementary School at Fagnano Olona" in *Architecture + Urbanism* (Tokyo), June 1978; "The Works of Aldo Rossi" by C. K. Laine in *Crit* (Washington, D.C.), Spring 1979; "Aldo Rossi; Four Constructed Works", special issue of *2C Construccion de la ciudad* (Barcelona), December 1979; "Where 'ya comin' from, Aldo?" by Randy Cohen in *Fifth Column* (Montreal), Winter 1981; "Not Post-Modernism" by Dan Graham in *Artforum* (New York), December 1981; "Aldo Rossi and 21 Works", special issue of *Architecture + Urbanism* (Tokyo), 1982; "The Drawings of Aldo Rossi" in *Fifth Column* (Montreal), Autumn 1982; "Rossi and Radical Nostalgia" in *Plan* (Amsterdam), January 1983.

Bibliography—*Aldo Rossi* by Lamia Doumato, Monticello, Illinois 1982.

The work and theory of Aldo Rossi make up one of the most important statements in international contemporary architecture. Building practice needs reflection, theory needs practical experience, and Rossi's work benefits from his complex activities as teacher, editor of the magazine *Casabella,* and architectural historian. His studies in the typology and morphology of cities resulted in the book *L'Architettura della città,* a fundamental text in contemporary urbanism.

Building and city are united in Rossi's work; he deals with the urban fabric as an architect, not as a planner or designer. According to Rossi, the city is an agglomeration of objects of meaning and identity ("urban facts") relevant to the specific life of people in time and place. Cities are built over a long period of time; they include history; they are manifestations of political and social ideologies that shape the urban form. For Rossi the architect, history is not so much a sequence of events in time as objects recalled by memory and used as elements in the design process. The "urban fact" emerges from this process; it is the basis of the architect's work, that which reveals the identity of each given place. A strong emphasis on regional and local aspects of building and cities is also necessarily part of his work.

Rossi refers to his working method as 'rational', but he means more than a logical deduction from abstract facts. He means analogical thought—more complex than logical considerat ions. Rationalism deals with environment and people, meaning and history. In Rossi's own words, "The reducible specificity of architecture.SPT.SPT.SPT resides in the capacity to produce typical forms, which requires a particular knowledge of the past." Design thus becomes a process of selecting the appropriate type of 'plan' in a given context rather than a subjective statement.

Rationalism in architecture in Rossi's sense is a continuation of thinking patterns of the Enlightenment of the eighteenth century, as manifested in Boullée and Ledoux. Rossi's goal is the reconstitution of the architectural profession by these criteria, the creation of an autonomous architecture. His most important realizations—the housing scheme in Gallaratese in Milan (in collaboration with Carlo Aymonino), the elementary school in Fagnano Olona, the cemetery in Modena, and the Teatro del Mondo in Venice, as well as projects for Mozzo, Pegognaga, Goito, and Berlin—are paradigmatic and mysterious exemplifications of the theoretical basis from which Rossi operates. They are stimulating challenges for the situation of international architecture in the late twentieth century.

—Udo Kultermann

ROTH, Alfred.

Swiss. Born in Wangen, near Bern, 21 May 1903. Educated at primary and secondary schools in Wangen; Intermediate School, Solothurn, baccalaureate 1922; Federal Institute of Technology, Zürich, 1922-26. Worked with Le Corbusier, *q.v.,* and Pierre Jeanneret, *q.v.,* in Paris, 1927-28; in private practice, Göteborg, Sweden, 1928-30. Since 1931, in private practice Zürich. Design Critic, Washington University, St. Louis, Missouri, 1949-52, and Harvard University, Cambridge, Massachusetts, 1953; Professor of Architecture Federal Institute of Technology, Zürich, 1957-71. Editor, *Werk,* Winterthur, Switzerland, 1943-56. Exhibitions: *Switzerland Planning and Building Exhibition,* Royal Institute of British Architects, London, 1946; *Triennale,* Milan, 1957; *National Exhibition of Switzerland,* Lausanne, 1964; *Alfred Roth: Works,* Federal Institute of Technology, Zürich, 1983, and Technical University, Munich, 1984. Honorary doctorate: Technical University, Munich, 1977; University of Venice, 1984. Honorary Member: Royal Institute of British Architects, 1948; Royal Flemish Academy of Arts, Letters and Sciences, Brussels, 1948; Union of Modern Artists, Paris, 1949; Austrian Federation of Architects, 1955; Swedish Association of Arts and Crafts, 1956; Accademia di San Luca, Rome, 1980; Honorary Fellow, American Institute of Architects, 1966. Address: Bergstrasse 71, 8032 Zürich, Switzerland.

Works:

1928/
65   Industrial buildings in Wangen, Switzerland
1929/
30   200 low-cost apartments, Göteborg, Sweden
1930   Private house, near Göteborg, Sweden
1935/
36   Doldertal Apartment Blocks, Zürich (with Emil Roth and Marcel Breuer)
1936/
61   Houses in Zürich and Wangen, Switzerland
1937   Weekend House, Mammern, Lake Constance, Switzerland
1938/
46   Military buildings, Wangen, Switzerland
1939   Pavilion of Commerce, *National Exhibition of Switzerland,* Zürich (with Emil Roth)
1948   Kindergarten, Wangen, Switzerland
       Mechanical Laboratory extension, Federal Institute of Technology, Zürich
1948/
49   Swiss Tourist Office, Trafalgar Square, London
1950/
52   Primary school, Berkeley, near St. Louis, Missouri

1953/
55   *Contemporary Swiss Architecture* exhibition layouts, United States and Canada
1956   Secondary school, Wangen, Switzerland
1957   Swiss Pavilion, *Triennale,* Milan
1960   Roth House, Zürich
1961/
63   Primary school, Zürich
1962   Metal factory, Oerlikon/Zürich
1962/
72   Main Building and Natural Science Institute extensions, Federal Institute of Technology, Zürich
1965/
66   Shopping centre, Lucerne
1965/
69   Secondary school, Skopje, Yugoslavia
1966/
80   Schools, Kuwait
1968/
70   Commercial Centre Sabbag, Beirut, Lebanon
1972   Commercial building, Zürich
1977   Urban housing with shops and offices, Ajman, Persian Gulf (project)
       Bahrain National Oil Company, Bahrain (project)
1978/
82   Prefabricated schools, Kuwait
1978/
84   Abu Nuseir New Town, near Amman, Jordan (with Schindler and Schindler, Zürich, and Al Muhandis-Al Arabi, Amman)

Publications:

By ROTH: books—*Zwei Wohnhauser von Le Corbusier und Pierre Jeanneret,* Stuttgart 1927; *The New Architecture,* Zürich 1939, 6th edition 1976; *The New Schoolhouse,* Zürich 1950; *Begegnung mit Pionieren,* Zürich and Basel 1973, Tokyo 1975; articles—in *Werk* (Winterthur), 1943-56; "Some Critical Remarks on the Present State of Architecture" in *Architecture + Urbanism* (Tokyo), March 1980; "Rudolf Steiger 1900-1982" in *Werk, Bauen und Wohnen* (Zürich), November 1982.

On ROTH: books—*Gli elementi dell'architettura funzionale* by Alberto Sartoris, Milan 1931; *The Modern House* by F. R. S. Yorke, London 1934; *Switzerland Builds* by G. E. Kidder Smith, New York and Stockholm 1950; *A Decade of New Architecture* by Siefried Giedion, Zürich 1951; *Contemporary Architecture: Switzerland* by Yuichi Ino, Tokyo 1953; *Geschichte meines Lebens* by Henry van de Velde, Munich 1962; *Nationalisme et internationalisme dans l'architecture de la Suisse* by Jacques Gubler, Lausanne 1975; *Alfred Roth— Architect of Continuity,* with introduction by Stanislaus von Moos, Zürich 1984; articles—"Two Blocks of Flats in Doldertal, Zürich" in *AC: International Asbestos Cement Review* (Zürich), May 1982; "Modern House Blues— Absolutely Live" by Stefano Casciani in *Domus* (Milan), February 1983.

All my architectural endeavours and all my thinking are firmly based on the principles of the so-called functional architecture. But, for me, the complexity of the manifold functions does not permit me to reduce them to purely practical, technical, and economic ones—as is unfortunately true for the majority of present-day designs and buildings. The most important functions originate in man's psychological and human behaviour and in the demand for beauty, harmony, nobility, and inventiveness in general. This has been true for the architecture of all great historic periods. The differences between the essence and form of their art of building and ours can be found in the very different nature and maltitude of functions to be considered today and in our very

Alfred Roth: Bahrain National Oil Company, Persian Gulf, 1977 (project).

different creative possibilities to express them technically and artistically.

—Alfred Roth

The architectural ideas and creations of Alfred Roth are a logical continuation of the work of the pioneers of New Building in an honestly objective and constructive form of architecture. Roth believes in the undiminished validity of an architecture that answers its purpose. Functional appropriateness is a prime requirement of the user of the architecture and must be satisfied. From a conviction that our modern age is, at heart, creative and not imitative, as was the nineteenth century for example, Roth subordinates all conceivable questions of form to practical exigencies and holds the view that in this manner the psychological, spiritual, and aesthetic requirements in a building can be satisfied.

In particular, Roth has projected and built schools, both at home and abroad, which are a portrait of the logical consequence of an archi-

tectural creativity that finds its overwhelming expression in urbanistic, climatic, and logical functionality. Roth sees his works as timeless and resistant to the constant changes in architectural notions and views. He says: "Unfortunately today we see a progressive degeneration in established functional creative form. The most obvious causes are a spreading commercialization of architectural works and a frenzied striving for permanent novelty, chiefly for new forms which have no inner reason."

It is an interesting opinion of Roth's that a serious scientific criticism of architecture is lacking and that the extremely large range of possibilities in architectural form, broadcast through excessive commercial publication in architectural journals, has had a bad influence on the work of architects who, uncritically, pick up impulses from all sides and incorporate them in their own work without adequate reflection. In this respect one has to support him. It really is incomprehensible that we do not have an adequate critical examination of the suitability of today's architecture to its time, of an architecture

which is in fact a portrait of a disunited, spiritually and ethically divided, pluralistic society. I fully support Roth's view that we must prevent the architecture that shapes the face of our cities from becoming a plaything used for fashionable trends and cheap effects which nevertheless sell very well. We need a new draught of architectural ideas, feelings, and treatment, a revaluation of the ethical principles of our profession which, even if not scientific, must nevertheless be an honestly based expression of creative work. How compatible Roth's striving for a timelessness in architecture would be is another question. Architecture is always the portrait of a society and thus the expression of its culture. Even a society cannot escape its own shadow. Creative developments in the last decades have been particularly short-winded and short-lived. We see the frenzy of a modern age which less and less reflects upon itself in all spheres of life and must consequently stand the test of history.

—Justus Dahinden

ROUX-DORLUT Pierre.
French. Born in Puy, 10 October 1919. Educated at the Lycée de Puy, until 1937; studied architecture, Ecole Nationale Supérieure des Beaux-Arts, Paris, 1938, 1941-45, Dip.Arch, 1945. Served in the French Army, 1939-40. Married the architect Christine Gandziarek in 1957; children: Maya, Philippe, Michel. In private practice, with Daniel Badani, *q.v.*, in Paris, Abidjan, and Bône, since 1946. Architect-in-Chief for the Reconstruction, France, 1946-50; Consultant Architect to the Ministry of Construction for the districts of Gard, Pyrénées Orientales, and the Lozère, 1960-72, and of Calvados, since 1972. Currently, Architect-in-Chief of Civic Buildings and National Monuments; Architect-in Chief to the Ministry of Defence; Architect-in-Chief to the Ministry of Equipment; Consultant Architect to the Ministry of Culture; Member of the General Council for the Buildings of France, Schools and Colleges Department; Member of the Regional Commission on Architecture for the Basse-Normandie and Auvergne districts; Member of the Higher Studies Institute for the National Defence of Territory; and member of the Editorial Board, *L'Architecture d'Aujourd'hui* and *Architecture,* Paris. Professor of Architecture, Ecole des Beaux-Arts, Montpellier, 1946-55. Councillor, Syndicate of French Architects, and Order of Architects, Paris; Vice-President, Association of Engineers-Architects; First Commission Member, Office of Building, Seine District; Member, Group Espace, Paris. Exhibitions: Syndicate of Architecture, Paris, 1960; Congress of Architects, London, 1960, and Moscow, 1961; *Exposition Internationale des Formes Industrielles,* Paris, 1963; International Exposition, Stockholm, 1963; *Architecture Francaise de Recherches,* Paris, 1965; *Exposition Nationale de Beaux-Arts,* Paris, 1977; *Salon d'Automne,* Paris, 1977; *Decade d'Architecture,* Bâtimat, Paris, 1983. Recipient: Silver Medal, Académie d'Architecture, Paris, 1968; Gold Medal, Société d'Encouragement à l'Art et à l'Industrie, Paris, 1972; Silver Medal, City of Paris, 1977. Member, Académie d'Architecture; Chevalier de la Légion d'Honneur; Chevalier of the Order of Arts and Letters, France; Chevalier de l'Ordre de l'Etoile Noire du Benin. Member, Union Franco-Brittanique des Architects; Cercle d'Etudes Architecturales; Société des Architectes D.P.L.G. Address (office): 46 Avenue d'Iena, 75116 Paris, France.

See BADANI, Daniel

ROUX-SPITZ, Michel.
French. Born Michel Roux in Lyons, 13 June 1888; later adopted his mother's family name, Spitz. Educated at the Lycée Ampère, Lyons, 1899-1906; studied architecture under Tony Garnier, Ecole des Beaux-Arts, Lyons, 1908-11; student/apprentice, studio of Redon, Paris, 1912-13, 1919-20, and studio of Duquesne-Recoura, Paris, 1913-14; Prix de Rome Scholar, 1920-23. Served in the French Army, 1918-19. Married Suzanne Marcel in 1923; children: Jean and Francine. Worked for Édouard Herriot, Lyons, 1923-24; in private practice, Paris, 1924 until his death, 1957. Architect-in-Chief, Bibliothèque Nationale, Paris, 1932-55; also Architect-in-Chief to the National Refuge of Vincennes, the Ministry of Posts and Telecommunications, Ecole Superieure d'Application d'Agriculture Tropicale, Îlot 16 of the Prefecture de la Seine, the Lycée de Lyon, Saint-Maurice National Convalescent Home, and the General Treasury of Lyons. Member of the Council for Public Buildings, Paris, 1934-36. Professor of Architectural Theory, Ecole Nationale et Spéciale des Beaux-Arts, Paris, 1942-43. Editor-in-Chief, *L'Architecte* Magazine, Paris, 1925-33, and *Archi-* *tecture Francaise* magazine, Paris, 1943-44, 1945-50. Exhibition: *Exposition des Arts Décoratifs,* Paris, 1925. Recipient: Gold Medal, Casper-André Competition, 1909; First Prize, Clavel Stock Exchange Competition, 1910; First Prize, Archivist's Tomb Competition, 1913; First Prize, Hemerothèque Competition, 1920. Honorary Inspector-General of Public Buildings and National Palaces, France; Honorary Corresponding Member, Royal Institute of British Architects; Corresponding Member of the Royal Academy of Denmark; Associate Member, Royal Academy of Belgium. Commander of the Légion d'honneur, *Died* (in Dinard, France) *15 July 1957.*

Works:

1924/
29 Dental School and Dispensary, Lyons
Municipal Hall, La Croix Rousse, Lyons
1925 Monument to the Heroes of Dixmunde, Pierrefeu, France
Apartment building, Rue Guynemer, Paris
1925/
28 Monument to the Defense of the Suez Canal, Ismailia, Egypt
1928 Bathroom, *Salon des Artistes Décorateurs,* Paris
1928/
31 Apartment building, 89 Quai d'Orsay, Paris
1929/
31 Apartment building, Boulevard d'Inkermann, Neuilly, Paris
1930 Galeries Lafayette (department store), Boulevard Hausmann, Paris (competition project)
1930/
31 Apartment building, 3 rue de la Cité Universitaire, Paris
Apartment building, 115 Avenue Henri-Martin, Paris
Ford Building, Boulevard des Italiens, Paris
Apartment Building, Boulevard de Montparnasse, Paris
1930/
33 National School of Ceramics Sèvres, France
1931 Roux-Spitz Architectural Office, 33 rue Octave-Feuillet, Paris
Restaurant Milliet, Place Bellecour, Lyons
Main Railway Station, Perrache, Lyons (project)
Jewellery shop, Boulevard des Italiens, Paris
1931/
32 Apartment, rue de Franqueville, Paris
Apartment, rue Littolf, Paris
1931/
35 Central Post Office, 15th Arrondissement, Paris
1932 Apartment, Avenue Henri-Martin, Paris
Groupe Municipal d'Education Sociale Building, Vaise, Lyons
1932/
33 Annex, Bibliothèque Nationale, Versailles
National Convalescent Home, Saint Maurice, France
1935 Commissioners' Meeting Room, Paris
1935/
38 Postal, Telephone and Telegraph Regional Headquarters, Lyons
Hotel, Square Frères-Orban, Brussels
1935/
46 Bibliothèque Nationale redevelopment and renovation, Paris
1938/
39 Villa, Dinard, France
1939 Apartment, rue Littolf, Paris
1943 Hotel library, Neuilly, Paris
1943/
46 Housing developments in Paris (projects)
1946/
53 Department of Charts and Plans, Bibliothèque Nationale, Paris
1947/
49 Cité des Hauts Paves (housing development), Nantes, France
1948/
50 Postal, Telephone and Telegraph Regional Headquarters, Paris
1948/
51 Tropical Forestry Technical Centre, Nogent-sur-Marne, France
1953 Archives Annex, Bibliothèque Nationale, Paris
1955 Prints and Posters Central Building, Bibliothèque Nationale, Paris
Regional Hospital Centre, Dijon, France
1956 Town Hall, Saint Nazaire, France
1957 Regional Hospital Centre, Nantes, France
Faculty of Medicine and Pharmacy, Nantes, France (project)

Publications:

By ROUX-SPITZ: books—*Bâtiments et Jardins à l'Exposition des Arts Décoratifs,* Paris 1925; articles—"La création d'un ordre des architectes" in *l'Architecte* (Paris), 1929; "Opinions de M. Roux-Spitz" in *l'Architecture d'Aujourd'hui* (Paris), December 1930; "Contre le nouveau formalisme" in *l'Architecture d'Aujourd'hui* (Paris), April 1932; "Le domisme et l'urbanisme" in *Architecture Francaise* (Paris), no. 33, 1943; "L'Illusion des equipes d'architectes" in *Architecture Francaise* (Paris), no. 39/40, 1944; "D'un mois a l'autre," column, in *Architecture Francaise* (Paris), nos. 95-96, 1949.

On ROUX-SPITZ: books—*Michel Roux-Spitz: Réalisations,* 3 volumes, *1924-1932,* Paris 1936, *1932-1932,* Paris 1950, and *1943-1957,* Paris 1959; *L'Ecole de Paris: 10 architectes et leurs immeubles* by Jean-Claude Delorme, Paris 1981; *Michel Roux-Spitz: Architecte 1888-1957* by M. Raynaud, D. Laroque and S. Remy, Liège and Brussels 1983; articles—"Tendencies of the School of Modern French Architecture" in *Architectural Record* (New York), April 1929; "New Post Office, Lyons" in *The Architect and Building News* (London), 12 May 1939; "Cité des Hauts-Paves à Nantes" and "Quartier du Grand-Clos à Nantes" in *Architecture Francaise* (Paris), vol. 8, no. 73/74, 1947; "Le Centre Technique Forestier Tropical à Nogent-sur-Marne" in *Construction Moderne* (Paris), June 1954; "Postes et Telecommunications" in *Architecture Francaise* (Paris), November/December 1966; "Michel Roux-Spitz" by M. Raymond, P. Saddy and P. Celeste in *Architecture Mouvement Continuité* (Paris), no. 39, 1976.

Born in Lyons in 1888, Michel Roux-Spitz was a member of the generation that turned towards new underlying principals for architecture. He sought primarily the beauty of forms—and their logic, the kind of logic that Auguste Perret asserted in the economic, aesthetic and rational use of concrete.

Roux-Spitz reacted against the solemn mediocrities and rejected the decorative pastries that litter our towns. He drew up simple, logical and unadorned architectural plans that achieve the quality of expression appropriate to pure forms and appropriate, too, to the laws of architecture and construction. As well, he sought new solutions that would yet allow the user to "adapt;" at the same time he looked for new methods of building. He used techniques that allowed him to advance towards tomorrow's architecture.

In 1925 Roux-Spitz achieved a simple and significant kind of building. He erected in Paris, opposite the Luxembourg Gardens, a rental building of a hitherto unknown purity. He built in concrete clad with polished stones. The windows were treated in horizontal bands, one of the series being brought forward to break the monotony of the facade. This kind of housing provided agreeable and practical arrangements for the occupiers. Roux-Spitz conceived a number of this kind of building, always of impeccable quality, for he knew how to combine convenience with elegance.

Roux-Spitz was aware of all the currents in international architecture and with prgress in technology, but his knowledge and his much-envied organizational methods were always at the service of a sure sense of taste. He had a certain liking for pomp as well as for order, which reveals itself in his sumptuous villa in Dinard where stylish furniture seems to be at one with the architecture and where the garden is a succession of constructive elements. He believed in the permanence of certain laws of harmony.

When he was entrusted with the redevelopment and renovation of the National Library, he had to face very complicated, important and delicate problems. He solved them with a kind of lucid authority. On the one hand, he treated the Mansart gallery masterpiece and neighboring rooms with sober refinement. On the other hand, he dealt very surely with the depository at Versailles, giving it an aspect of totally serviceable functional modernism.

—Bernard Champigneulle

RUDOLPH, Paul Marvin,

American. Born in Elkton, Kentucky, 23 October 1918. Educated at the Alabama Polytechnic Institute, Auburn, 1935-40, B.Arch. 1940; Harvard Graduate School of Design, Cambridge, Massachusetts, under Walter Gropius, 1940-43, 1946-47, M.Arch. 1947; Wheelwright Scholar, in Europe, 1948. Served as a Lieutenant in the United States Navy, 1943-46. In partnership with Ralph Twitchell, Sarasota, Florida, 1948-52; in private practice, Sarasota, and New Haven, Connecticut, 1952-58; Chairman, School of Architecture, Yale University, New Haven, 1958-65. In private practice, New York, since 1965. Exhibitions: *Building Arts Exhibition*, Jewett Arts Center, Wellesley College, Massachusetts, 1960; *Work in Progress: Philip Johnson, Kevin Roche and Paul Rudolph*, Museum of Modern Art, New York, 1970. Recipient: First Prize, Rorimer Competition, American Institute of Decorators, 1940; Award of Merit, 1949, 1959, 1962, 1964, and First Honor Award, 1964, American Institute of Architects; Outstanding Young Architect Award, *Bienal*, Sao Paulo, 1954; First Design Award, *Progressive Architecture*, 1955; Arnold Brunner Prize, National Institute of Arts and Letters, 1958; National Gold Medal, *Building Arts Exhibition*, Wellesley College, Massachusetts, 1960; Architectural Award, Boston Arts Festival, 1961; Award of Excellence for House Design, *Architectural Record*, 1963; Honor Award, AIA, New York Chapter, 1969, and New England Regional Chapter, 1970; Award of Merit, Concrete Industry Board of New York, 1973; Honor Award, Federacion Panamericana de Asociaciones de Arquitectos, 1975; Elsie de Wolfe Award, American Society of Interior Designers, 1977. D.Arts: Colgate University, Hamilton, New York, 1966; D.F.A.: Florida State University, Tallahassee, 1970; Southeastern Massachusetts Technological Institute, North Dartmouth, 1970; H.H.D.: Auburn University, Montgomery, Alabama, 1972; Emory University, Atlanta, Georgia, 1981. Fellow, American Institute of Architects, 1970; Member, National Institute of Arts and Letters, 1971; Honorary Member, Instituto de Arquitectos de Puerto Rico, 1975; Fellow, American Society of Interior Designers, 1976; Honorary Professor, Universidad Federico Villareal, Lima, Peru, 1977. Address (office): 54 West 57th Street, New York, New York 10019, U.S.A.

Works:

1946 Denman House, Siesta Key, Sarasota, Florida (with Ralph Twitchell)
1947 Finney Guest House, Siesta Key, Sarasota, Florida (project)
   Miller House, Casey Key, Sarasota, Florida (with Ralph Twitchell)
1948 Revere Quality House, Siesta Key, Sarasota, Florida (with Ralph Twitchell)
   Healy Guest House ("Cocoon House"), Siesta Key, Sarasota, Florida (with Ralph Twitchell)
   Russell House, Sarasota, Florida (with Ralph Twitchell)
1949 Cheatham House, Lakeland, Florida (with Ralph Twitchell)
   Deeds house, Siesta Key, Sarasota, Florida (with Ralph Twitchell)
1951 Leavengood House, St. Petersburg, Florida (with Ralph Twitchell)
   Coward House, Siesta Key, Sarasota, Florida (with Ralph Twitchell)
   Burnette House, Sarasota, Florida (with Ralph Twitchell)
   Wheelan Cottage, Siesta Key, Sarasota, Florida (with Ralph Twitchell)
   Hook Cottage, Siesta Key, Sarasota, Florida
   Knott House, Yankeetown, Florida
1952 Design and layout of the *Good Design Exhibition*, Merchandise Mart, Chicago, and Museum of Modern Art, New York
   Walker Guest House, Sanibel Island, Florida
   Cohen House, Siesta Key, Sarasota, Florida
   Sanderling Beach Club, Siesta Key, Sarasota, Florida
1953 Siegrist House, Venice, Florida (with Ralph Twitchell)
   Biggs House, Delray Beach, Florida
   Hiss House ("Umbrella House"), Lido Shores, Florida
1954 United States Embassy, Amman, Jordan (project)
   Bostwick House, Palm Beach, Florida (project)
   Wilson House, Sarasota, Florida
   Taylor House, Venice, Florida
1955 Jewett Arts Center, Wellesley College, Massachusetts (with Anderson, Beckwith and Haible)
   Sarasota-Bradenton Airport, Florida (project)
   Burgess House, Burgess Island, Florida (Project)
   Plywood Association Experimental School (project)
1956 Four model houses for *Woman's Home Companion*
   Model house for the Homestyle Center, Grand Rapids, Michigan
   Applebee House, Auburn, Alabama
   Bramlett Equipment Company Office Building, Miami (project)
   Davidson House, Bradenton, Florida
   Inter-American Center, Miami (project: as architectural design consultant)
   Yanofsky House, Newton, Massachusetts
1957 Riverview High School, Sarasota, Florida
   Harkavy House, Lido Shores, Florida
   Blue Cross/Blue Shield Headquarters, Boston (with Anderson, Beckwith and Haible)
   Greeley Memorial Laboratory, Yale University Forestry School, New Haven, Connecticut
   Burkhardt House, Casey Key, Florida
1958 High School, Sarasota, Florida
   Art and Architecture Building, Yale University, New Haven, Connecticut
   Redevelopment plan for Church Street, New Haven, Connecticut (as consultant)
   McCandish House, Cambridge, Massachusetts
   Master plan for Tuskegee Institute, Alabama (project; with John S. Chase)

Deering House, Casey Key, Florida
1959 Parking garage, Temple Street, New Haven, Connecticut
   May Memorial Unitarian Church, Syracuse, New York
   Lake Region Yacht and Country Club, Winter Haven, Florida
   Liggett House, Tampa, Florida
1960 Married Student Housing, Yale University, New Haven, Connecticut
   Friedberg House, Baltimore
   Interdenominational Chapel, Tuskegee Institute, Alabama (with Fry and Welch)
   Vacation house, Greenwich, Connecticut, for *Woman's Day*
   Milam House, Jacksonville, Florida
   Daisley House, Inlet Cay, Florida
   Portland Cement Company Theme Center, *World's Fair*, New York (project)
   Cultural Center, Tuskegee Institute, Alabama (project; with Fry and Welch)
   RCA Advanced Designing and Styling Center (project)
   Pi Kappa Phi Fraternity House, University of Florida, Gainesville
1961 Ciba Pharmaceutical Company additions and cafeteria, Summit, New Jersey (project)
   Kappa Sigma Fraternity House, Auburn University, Alabama
   Manager's Office, Parking Authority, New Haven, Connecticut
   O'Brien Motor Inn, Waverly, New York (project)
   Silvas House, Greenwich, Connecticut
   Wallace House, Athens, Alabama
   Juvenile Detention Home additions, Bridgeport, Connecticut
1962 IBM Complex, East Fishkill, New York (with Walter Kidde)
   Ford Foundation Theatre (project)
   Free Library, Guilford, Connecticut
   Endo Laboratories Complex, Garden City, Long Island, New York (with Walter Kidde)
   Crawford Manor Housing for the Elderly, New Haven, Connecticut
   Master plan, dormitories, auditorium, and classroom building, Hotchkiss School, Lakeville, Connecticut
   Mental Health Building, Government Center, Boston (with Desmond and Lord, H.A. Dyer, and Pedersen and Tilney)
   Health, Welfare and Education Building, Government Center, Boston (with Desmond and Lord, H.A. Dyer, and Pedersen and Tilney)
   Christian Science Organization Building, University of Illinois, Urbana (with Smith, Seaton and Olach)
1963 Government Service Center, Boston (as coordinating architect)
   Orange County Government Center Office and Court House Building, Goshen, New York (with Peter Barbone)
   Southeastern Massachusetts Technological Institute, North Dartmouth (with Desmond and Lord)
   Creative Arts Center, Colgate University, Hamilton, New York
   Beneficient Church High-Rise Apartment Building, Weybosset Hill Housing Complex, Providence, Rhode Island
1964 City Hall, Syracuse, New York (project; with Ketcham-Miller-Arnold)
   John W. Chorley Elementary School, Middletown, New York (with Peter Barbone)
   Paul Rudolph Offices, West 57th Street, New York
1965 International Bazaar, Interama Project, Miami (project)
   Callahan House ("Southern House"), Birmingham, Alabama (project)
1966 Manoa Campus Visual Arts Center, University of Hawaii, Honolulu (project)

Master plan for the East Pakistan Agricultural University, Mymensingh (with William Grindereng)

Master plan for Stafford Harbor Resort Community, Virginia

Physical Sciences Building, Texas Christian University, Fort Worth (with Preston M. Geren)

Kinney House, Hamilton, New York (project)

Monteith College Center, Wayne State University, Detroit (project)

Hirsch House, New York

Brookhollow Corporation Office Building, Dallas (with Harwood K. Smith and Partners)

John Jay Park, New York (project)

Master plan for Northwest No. 1 Urban Renewal Area, Washington, D.C.

Caspi Penthouse, New York (project)

Beth El Synagogue additions, New London, Connecticut

1967 Graphic Arts Center and Apartments, New York (project)

Lower Manhattan Expressway Study, New York

Parcells House, Grosse Pointe, Michigan

Brown House, New York

Shore Dental Offices, New York

Three parks and playgrounds, New York (project)

Kaiser Apartment, New York

Endo Laboratories Office Building additions, Garden City, New York

Two apartment buildings, Bronx, New York

Master plan for Fox Hill, Staten Island, New York (with Jerraid L. Karlan)

Tracey Towers (apartment buildings and plaza), Bronx, New York (with Jerrald L. Karlan)

1968 Wilmot Road/Brookside Avenue Housing (mobile homes), New Haven, Connecticut

Married Student Housing (mobile homes), University of Virginia, Charlottesville (project)

Student Union, Southeastern Massachusetts Technological Institute, North Dartmouth

Stadium, Dammam, Saudi Arabia (project)

Magnolia Homes (mobile homes), Vicksburg, Mississippi (project)

Government Center (city hall, library, plaza, and police station), New Haven, Connecticut

Fort Lincoln Housing (mobile homes), Washington, D.C. (project)

Green House, Cherry Ridge, Pennsylvania

Additional buildings for First Church in Boston

1969 Raich House, Quoque, Long Island, New York (project)

Lewis House, Boston (project)

Burroughs Wellcome and Company Corporate Headquarters, Research Triangle park, Durham, North Carolina

Central City Library, Niagara Falls, New York

Waterfront Development (housing, school, commercial and community facilities), Buffalo, New York

Pistell House, Lyford Cay, Nassau, Bahamas (project)

Natural Science Building, State University of New York at Purchase

Gardner Cowles Apartment, New York

1970 Deare House, Great Neck, Long Island, New York

106th Street Housing and Neighborhood Development, New York (project)

Ten apartment towers, Kew Gardens, New York (project)

Rockford Center, Illinois

Industrial Park (office, industrial and commercial buildings), Hauppage, New York

House, Fort Worth, Texas

Shuey House, Bloomfield Hills, Michigan

Edersheim Apartment, New York

1971 Urban complex (apartments, commercial, recreational, and administration buildings), Beirut

Dweck House, Deal, New Jersey

Diaei Company Office Building, Nagoya, Japan

Davidson House additions, Bloomfield Hills, Michigan

1972 Community College, Staten Island, New York (project)

Entrecanales y Tavora Office Building, Madrid

1973 Apartment Complex, Miami (project)

Paul Rudolph Apartment, New York

Modular Housing (project)

East Northport Jewish Center Synagogue additions, East Northport, New York (project)

Dormitory, Davidson College, North Carolina (project)

1974 Pan-Lon Apartment Hotel, Jerusalem (project)

Os House, Atlanta

Pitts Theology Library addition, Emory University, Atlanta, Georgia

Niel C. Morgan House, Aspen, Colorado

Morgan Annex Housing Studies, New York

Marine and Skating Recreational Complex, Buffalo, New York

1975 Gary Strutin Apartment, New Rochelle, New York

Nancy Houston House, Westerly, Rhode Island

Chapel for Candler School of Theology, Emory University, Atlanta, Georgia

1976 Mr. and Mrs. Robert Bernhard House addition, Greenwich, Connecticut

Burroughs Wellcome Research Building additions, Research Triangle Park, North Carolina

1977 Mr. and Mrs. Ronald Fein House additions, Sands Point, New York

1978 Dr. Vallo Benjamin Apartment, New York

Mr. and Mrs. Richard Young House, Livingston Manor, New York

New Campus Entrance, Plaza and Gardens Plan, Tuskegee Institute, Alabama

Harrington Cancer Care Center, Amarillo, Texas

Mr. and Mrs. Rafael Carrillo Apartment, New York

Mr. and Mrs. Robert Heyada House, Deal, New Jersey

Zucker Company Apartment and Commercial Complex, New York

Zucker Company Loft Building conversion, New York

Burroughs Wellcome Toxicology/Experimental Pathology Building, Research Triangle Park, North Carolina

Mr. and Mrs. Dani Siegel House remodelling, Westhampton Beach, New York

Mr. and Mrs. Donald Zucker Townhouse remodelling, New York

1979 Marina Centre Developments, Singapore

Mr. and Mrs. Michael Glazer House, Los Angeles

Bass Brothers Office Buildings and Parking Garage, Fort Worth, Texas

Housing, Office and Shopping Complex with Plaza, Singapore

Apartment Building, Singapore

1980 Mr. and Mrs. Wylie Tuttle House, Maryland

Apartment Complex with Car Parking, Singapore

Ten Bungalows, Hong Kong

Mr. and Mrs. Henry Kwee House, Singapore

Electronic Data Systems Headquarters, Dallas, Texas (competition project)

Mr. and Mrs. Hugh Downs House, Connecticut

Stanley Marsh III Offices, Amarillo, Texas

Television Station for Stanley Marsh III,

Amarillo, Texas

1981 Coffee Memorial Blood Bank, Amarillo, Texas

Oxley Rise Condominium Housing, Singapore

Mr. and Mrs. Kenneth Sherman House addition and alterations, Wilton, Connecticut

Cambridge Research and Development Group Office alterations, Westport, Connecticut

1982 Pt. Yamano Utama Office Building, Jakarta Pusat, Indonesia

Burroughs Wellcome North Office Building, Research Triangle Park, North Carolina

Burroughs Wellcome Master Plan, Research Triangle Park, North Carolina

Mr. and Mrs. Mark Edersheim House alterations, Marmaroneck, New York

House for Beverly Park Estates, Beverly Hills, California

General Daniel "Chappie" James Center for Aerospace Science and Health Education, Tuskegee Institute, Alabama

1983 Michael Floersheim/Dr. Strauss Apartment remodelling, New York

John B. Rogers House/Office addition, Palm Beach, Florida

Bristol-Myers Research Laboratory, Connecticut (competition project)

Dr. and Mrs. Hillel Tobias House remodelling, Remsenburg, New York

1984 Mr. and Mrs. Eisner House remodelling, Westport, Connecticut

Science Building, Southeastern Massachusetts University, Boston

Mr. and Mrs. Michael Glazer House, Los Angeles

Mr. and Mrs. George Pavarini House, Greenwich, Connecticut

Mr. and Mrs. Wylie Tuttle House, Rock Hall, Maryland

Office Complex, Jakarta, Indonesia

Office and Commercial Building, Hong Kong

1985 Mr. and Mrs. Licht House addition, Hewlett Harbor, New York

Macy's Department Store, Danbury, Connecticut

Macy's Department Store, Riverchase, Birmingham, Alabama

Publications:

By RUDOLPH: books—*Architectural Education in the United States*, Washington, D.C. 1962; *Global Architecture 2: Frank Lloyd Wright—Fallingwater*, with Yukio Futagawa, Tokyo 1970; *Drawings*, edited by Yukio Futagawa, Tokyo 1972, Fribourg, Switzerland, 1974; *The Evolving City*, with Ulrich Franzen and Peter Wolf, New York 1974, 1976; articles—"The Spread of an Idea," editor, special issue of *L'Architecture d'Aujourd'hui* (Paris), 1950; "New Directions" in *Perspecta* (New Haven, Connecticut), Summer 1952; "Criticism of the United Nations Building" in *Architectural Forum* (New York), October 1952; "The Orientation of Modern Architecture" in *Sarasota Review* (Sarasota, Florida), 1953; "Notes on Row Housing" in *Pennsylvania Triangle* (Philadelphia), January 1953; "Regionalism and the South" in *AIA Journal* (Washington, D.C.), April 1953; "Evaluation of North Carolina Livestock Judging Pavilion" in *Architectural Forum* (New York), April 1954; "The Changing Philosophy of Architecture" in *Architectural Forum* (New York), July 1954; "On the New School Design Research Team" in *Archictectural Forum* (New York), September 1956; "The Six Determinants of Architectural Form" in *Architectural Record* (New York), October 1956; "Regionalism in Architecture" in *Perspecta* (New Haven, Connecticut), vol. 4, 1957; "A Personal Contribution to American Architecture" in *Architectural Review* (London), June 1957; "The Changing Face of

New York" in *AIA Journal* (Washington, D.C.), April 1959; "On Arts and Architecture" in *Arts and Architecture* (Los Angeles), August 1959; "The Creative Use of Architectural Material" in *Progressive Architecture* (New York), September 1959; "Architectural Education in the United States" and "A Question for George Nelson and Paul Rudolph," with George Nelson, in *Zodiac* (Milan), no. 8, 1961; "Paul Rudolph Cites Old Principles as a Basis for Analysis of Today's Work" in *Architectural Record* (New York), January 1962; "In Search of a Comprehensive Style" in *New Homes Guides*, New York 1963; "A View of Washington as a Capitol; or, What Is Civic Design" in *Architectural Forum* (New York), January 1963; "Architecture: The Patron and the Public" in *Response* (Princeton, New Jersey), April 1963; "Rudolph Calls Students to Task of Urban Design" in *Architectural Record* (New York), May 1964; "The essence of Architecture Is Space" in *House and Garden* (New York), November 1969; "Sibyl Moholy-Nagy" in *Architectural Forum* (New York), June 1971; "Alumni Day Speech: Yale School of Architecture, February 1958" in *Oppositions* (New York), October 1974; "A Conversation with Paul Rudolph" in *Architectural Record* (New York), March 1982.

On RUDOLPH books—*Architecture USA* by Ian McCallum, London 1959; *Theory and Design in the First Machine Age* by Reyner Banham, London 1960; *Architects on Architecture*, edited by Paul Heyer, New York and London 1967; *Paul Rudolph* by Yukio Futagawa, Tokyo 1968, English translation, by Rupert Spade, London 1971; *American Architecture and Urbanism* by Vincent Scully, New York and London 1969; *New Directions in American Architecture* by Robert A.M. Stern, New York and London 1969, 1977; *The Architecture of Paul Rudolph* by Sibyl Moholy-Nagy, New York and London 1970; *Global Architecture 20: Paul Rudolph—Interdenominational Chapel, Tuskegee Institute and Boston Government Service Center* by Yukio Futagawa and Carl Black Jr., Tokyo 1973; *Conversations with Architects*, edited by John W. Cooke and Heinrich Klotz, London 1973; *Follies: Architecture for the Late-Twentieth-Century Landscape* by B.J. Archer and A. Vidler, New York 1983; articles—"Yale's Paul Rudolph" by Russell Bourne in *Architectural Forum* (New York), April 1958; "Paul Rudolph: Away from Genealogy of the Celebrated Architects" by Hiroyasu Yamada in *Kokusai Kentiku* (Tokyo), June 1960; "Rudolph at the Cross-Roads" by Henry A. Millon in *Architectural Design* (London), December 1960; "Paul Rudolph" by Giulia Veronesi in *Zodiac* (Milan), no. 8, 1961; "Whither Paul Rudolph" by Peter Collins in *Progressive Architecture* (New York), August 1961; "Paul Rudolph: A Series of Articles," special issue of *Kokusai Kentiku* (Tokyo), April 1965; special issue of *The Japan Architect* (Tokyo), July 1970; special issue of *Architecture + Urbanism* (Tokyo), January 1975, July 1977; "Paul Rudolph's Manhattan Apartment" in *Architectural Record* (New York), January 1978; "New York Apartment" in *GA Houses* (Tokyo), no. 6, 1979; "Clustered Columns Play Hide-and-Seek" in *Architectural Record* (New York), July 1982; "William R. Candler Chapel, Emory University, Atlanta, Georgia" in *Architecture + Urbanism* (Tokyo), May 1983.

Bibliography: *the Work of Paul Rudolph* by Lamia Doumato, Monticello, Illinois 1979.

Paul Rudolph's volume of accomplishment is immense. He was fortunate that his talent and energy were led by the American building boom of the 1950s and 1960s. From the start of his own office in 1952 (after a four year partnership with Ralph Twitchell in Florida) to the present, Rudolph has worked upon approximately 160 commissions, built and unbuilt, fifty-eight of which were houses, apartment interiors, or additions and remodelings.

The remaining commissions comprise almost every conceivable building type or urban design problem of today: an embassy in Jordan, educational buildings, campus plans, master plans including buildings for major housing or civic projects, an airport, a parking garage, a motor inn, a theatre, a stadium for the kingdom of Saudi Arabia, a yacht and country club, office buildings, religious buildings including the superb Tuskegee Chapel, libraries, government or civic buildings, important exhibitions, various plans for parks and other recreational facilities, and uncounted miscellaneous projects. Some of this work was done during his seven-year stint as Chairman of the Department of Architecture at Yale University. All of it was done, and is being done, without a partner. Rudolph once said: "Let's face it, architects were never meant to design together.... Architecture is a personal effort, and the fewer people coming between you and your work the better.... If an architect cares enough and practices architecture as an art, then he must initiate design—he must create rather than make judgements."CEP Rudolph's initiations and creations have prefigured much of the design that has followed in the United States, Europe, and Japan. He continues to bring new concepts to the world of architecture which find their way into the work of nearly everyone else, becoming part of generalized building practice. His design is a synthesis of the ideas of Le Corbusier, Wright, and Kahn. It is heroic, humanistic, and sculpturally alive. His buildings are powerful interventions, creating new scale relationships in their surroundings. They are gateways, bridges, rallying points, creating great swirling outdoor environments and dynamic, intricately juxtaposed interior spaces. According to Ulrich Franzen: "He started the first real dialogue about architecture in the context of the city... this was a new approach to analyze problems of form and scale, space and function, as urban problems, rather than in the context of individual buildings." His two most spectacular exercises in urban form are the Boston Government Service Center and the Southeastern Massachusetts Technological Institute.

Rudolph continues to be interested in the concept of the industrialized, plug-in city and has devised several unbuilt schemes in which housing units similar to mobile homes and indeed manufactured by that industry would be hoisted into a steel or concrete framework and connected to the mechanical and electrical services. His unbuilt Graphic Arts Center project for New York City proposed, in his words, that "mobile homes be used as 20th century bricks" hung from cantilevered trusses.

In spite of his interest in industrialized processes, Rudolph long ago began to question the precepts of the Modern Movement. The generation of architects following him (led by Philip Johnson, who preceded him) do the same thing—declaring themselves to be postmodernists. Rudolph is one of the unacknowledged fathers of this new way of thinking. He was prescient as far back as the early 1960s when he said: "Action has outstripped theory. The last decade has thrown a glaring light on the omissions, thinness, paucity of ideas, naiveté with regard to symbols, lack of creativeness, and expressiveness of architectural philosophy as it developed during the 20's.... Many of our difficulties stem from the concept of functionalism as the only determinant of form. We cannot pretend to solve problems of space without precedent in form." Rudolph differs from the postmodernists, however, to the degree that his work is highly personal, competitive, and aggressive. The postmodernists claim to have more modest aims, but this may also reflect the fact that they have matured in a more modest economy. Like that of the postmodernists, Rudolph's work has, from the beginning, been tied to history, yet transformed in ways that are uncompromisingly his own.

—Mildred F. Schmertz

RUUSUVUORI, Aarno.
Finnish. Born in Kuopio, 14 January 1925. Educated at Tehtaanpuisto High School, Helsinki, graduated 1943; studied architecture at the Technical University, Helsinki, 1946-50, Dip. Arch. 1951; influenced by Aulis Blomstedt, *q.v.*, in whose office he worked while a student. Served as a Corporal in the Finnish Army, 1943-45. Married Anna Maria E. Jäämeri in 1970; children: Eva and Anu. In private practice, Helsinki, since 1952. Editor, 1952-55, and Editor-in-Chief, 1956-57, *Arkkitehtilehti* magazine, Helsinki; Assistant, 1952-59, Acting Professor of Architecture, 1959-63, and Professor of Architecture, 1963-66, Technical University, Helsinki; Director, Museum of Finnish Architecture, Helsinki, 1975-78. Chairman, Finnish National Committee of ICOMOS (International Council of Monuments and Sites), 1967-70, and of the Finnish Friends of Architecture, 1967-76; President, SAFA (Finnish Architects Association), 1982. Exhibitions: Jyväskylä, Finland (individual), 1969; Brno and Bratislava, Czechoslovakia (individual), 1969-70; *Contemporary Architecture in Finland*, toured the United States, 1955; World's Fair, Brussels, 1958; *Bienal*, São Paulo, 1961 and 1969; Royal Institute of British Architects, London, 1961; *Church Exhibition*, Milan, 1962; *Finland Builds*, Helsinki, 1971, 1972, and 1982; *Nature, Architecture, Design*, Helsinki, 1978. Recipient: Vainö Vähäkallio Scholarship, Helsinki, 1955; Lindahl-Thomé Scholarship, Helsinki, 1955; Kordelin Scholarship, Helsinki, 1957; Artist Scholarship, Helsinki, 1970 and 1973-75. Professor of Art, Finland, 1978-83. Member of SAFA (Finnish Architects' Association), 1952; Honorary Member, Architectguild, Helsinki, 1966; Member, Academy of Technical Sciences, Helsinki, 1979; Honorary Fellow, American Institute of Architects, 1982; Commander, Order of the Lion of Finland, 1983. Address: Architectural Office Aarno Ruusuvuori, Annankatu 15 B 10, 00120 Helsinki 12, Finland.

Works:

1961   Hyvinkää Church and Parish Center, Hyvinkää, Finland
        Pietinen Studio, Helsinki
1962   Apartment building, Merimienenk. 32, Helsinki
        City Real Estate Office renovation, Helsinki
1964   Huutoniemi Church and Parish Center, Vaasa, Finland
1965   Church and Parish Center, Tapiola, Espoo, Finland
1966   Weilin and Göös Printing Works, Tapiola, Espoo, Finland
        Orijärvi Mansion renovation, Orijärvi, Finland
        Prefabricated System House, Bökars, Finland
1967   Elementary school, Roihuvuori, Helsinki
        Marimekko Printing Works, Helsinki
1968   Police Headquarters, Mikkeli, Finland
        Kluuvi Office renovations, Helsinki
1969   Hellekis Mansion renovation, Hällekis, Sweden
1970   Helsinki City Hall renovation, stage I
1972   Rauhannummi Chapel and Cemetery, Hyvinkää, Finland
        Stunkel House, Grenolier, Switzerland
1973   Aberra House, Addis Ababa, Ethiopia
        Lilibeth House, Addis Ababa, Ethiopia
        Helsinki City Office Building renovation
        Paragon Office Building, Helsinki
1976   Real Estate Development Center, Addis Ababa, Ethiopia
        Klingspor Villa, Rossö, Sweden
1977   Halonen House, Kuusisaari, Helsinki
1979   Parate Printing Works, Helsinki
1980   Al Rashid Apartment Hotel, Riyadh, Saudi Arabia
1983   Klingspor Studio, Stockholm
1984   Restaurant Building for Holiday Resort, Kerimäki, Finland
        City Hall renovation, stage II, Helsinki

Aarno Ruusuvuori: Parate Printing Works, Helsinki, 1979.

Publications:

By RUUSUVUORI: books—*Business Architecture in Finland,* Helsinki 1959; *Single-Family Houses,* Helsinki 1960; *Alvar Aalto,* exhibition catalogue, Helsinki 1978; articles—text in *Finland Builds,* exhibition catalogue, Helsinki 1953; "Rauhannummi Funeral Chapel and Cemetery" in *Arkkitehti* (Helsinki), no. 7, 1973.

On RUUSUVUORI: books—*The New Churches of Europe* by G. E. Kidder Smith, London 1964; *World Architecture 2,* London 1965; *Asumme Lähellä Luontoa* by Anna-Liisa Ahmavaara, Helsinki 1966; *Uutta suomalaista arkkitehtuuria* by Pekka Suhonen, Helsinki 1967; *Neue finnische Architektur* by Egon Tempel, Stuggart 1968; *Architettura finlandese,* Turin 1973; *Finnish Architecture,* The Hague 1975; *Suočasná finská architektura* by Vladislav Dlesek, Prague 1975; *Mai finn építészet* by Elemér Nagy, Budapest 1976; articles—general survey of works in *Kokusai Kentiku* (Tokyo), April 1967; "Helsinki City Hall" in *Architecture + Urbanism* (Tokyo), no. 6, 1972; "Aarno Ruusuvori: Works" in *Kentiku* (Tokyo), no. 6, 1973; "Residence Halonen" in *Japan Interior Design* (Tokyo), no. 11, 1977; "Parate Printing Works" in *L'Architecture d'aujourd'hui* (Paris), no. 6, 1982; "Parate Printing Works" in *Techniques et architecture* (Paris), no. 6, 1982; "Aarno Ruusuvuori: Survey of Works" in *Le Carré Bleu* (Paris), no. 1, 1984; "Postwar Architecture in Nordic Countries" in *Architecture in Greece* (Athens), no. 18, 1984.

*

To me, architecture is a problem of space and light. The solution to this problem is backed by a rational structure.

In my work, I look for an appropriate frame for various human activities, a point of departure reduced to simple basic elements, rounded out and supplemented by developing activity.

—Aarno Ruusuvuori

*

Aarno Rusuvuori graduated as an architect in 1951, a memorable year in the history of modern Finnish architecture. For various reasons, World War II had interrupted the purity and simplicity of functionalism, which had made its breakthrough in the 1930s. During and after the war, in the 1940s, architects returned to traditional building forms, and their romanticism was affected not only in the overall structure but in the details as well. In 1951, however, some of the older generation of architects—Aulis Blomstedt, Yrjö Lindegren, Viljo Revell—rejected this romanticism in their work in favour of a return to international modernism.

Not enough attention has been paid to this period in architecture, but Ruusuvuori's thesis work—a project for the Finnish Embassy in Rome—is evidence that there was great admiration for the traditions of functionalism among students. Rationalism became Ruusuvuori's symbol. He prefers using cast fairface concrete, which he combines with other ascetic building materials. Nevertheless, it is the cool aestheticism and elegant detail that offer proof of his professional skill and give him his individuality.

Almost without exception, Ruusuvuori's buildings impress themselves on the mind: they have a certain pregnant form. One of the most expressive is the pyramid-shaped church in Hyvinkää, but generally, his individuality has been achieved with simpler overall forms.

In addition to the design of new buildings, Ruusuvuori has done a considerable amount of restoration—churches, town halls, building premises, and manor houses. In some cases, such as the renovation of the neoclassical Helsinki City Hall (from 1833), his methods have been extremely radical: only the outer walls and the most valuable rooms have been restored; everything else has become new, modern architecture. In work such as this, Ruusuvuori reveals his characteristic striving for simplicity and strong forms.

—Asko Salokorpi

S

SAARINEN, Eero.

American. Born in Kirkkonummi, Finland, 20 August 1910; son of the architect Eliel Saarinen, *q.v.*, and the sculptor and weaver Louise (Loja) Gesellius Saarinen; emigrated with his family to the United States, 1923: naturalized, 1940. Educated at primary and secondary schools in Michigan; studied sculpture at the Académie de la Grand Chaumière Paris, 1929-30;studied architecture at Yale University, New Haven, Connecticut, B.F.A. 1934; awarded Charles O Matcham Fellowship, for travel in Europe, 1934-36. Worked in the Office of Strategic Studies, Washington, D.C., 1942-45. married Lily Swann in 1939 (divorced, 1953); children: Eric and Susan; married Aline Bernstein Loucheim in 1954; son: Eames. Joined his father's architectural practice, Ann Arbor, Michigan, 1936: practiced with his father, 1937-41; Partner, with his father and J. Robert Swanson, Saarinen-Swanson-Saarinen, Ann Arbor, 1941-47, then, with his father, Saarinen, Saarinen and Associates, Ann Arbor, 1947 until his father's death in 1950; Principal of the successor firm, Eero Saarinen and Associates in Birmingham, Michigan, 1950 until his own death in 1961. Exhibition: *Design in America: The Cranbrook Vision 1925-1950,* toured the United States and Europe, 1983-84. Recipient: two First Prizes with Charles Eames, Furniture Design Competition, Museum of Modern Art, New York, 1940; First Prize, Jefferson National Expansion Memorial Competition, St Louis, 1948; Grand Architectural Award, Boston Arts Festival, 1953; First Honor Award, American Institute of Architects, 1955, 1956; First Prize, American Embassy Competition, London, 1965; Gold Medal, American Institute of Architects, 1962. M.A.: Yale University, 1949; LL.D.: Wayne State University, Detroit, 1961. Fellow, American Institute of Architects, and American Academy of Arts and Sciences. *Died* (in Ann Arbor) *1 September 1961.*

Works:

1937/
38 Community House, Fenton, Michigan (with Eliel Saarinen)
1938 Area plan for Goucher College, Baltimore (competition project; with Eliel Saarinen)
Berkshire Music Center, Tanglewood, Massachusetts (with Eliel Saarinen)
1938/
40 Kleinhans Music Hall, Buffalo, New York (with Eliel Saarinen)
1939 Smithsonian Institution Art Gallery, Washington, D.C. (project; with Eliel Saarinen and J. Robert Swanson)
1939/
40 Crow Island School, Winnetka, Illinois (with Eliel Saarinen, and Perkins, Wheeler and Will)
1940 Molded Plywood Chair (competition project; with Charles Eames)

1940/
42 Tabernacle Church of Christ, Columbus, Indiana (with Eliel Saarinen)
1941 Oberlin College, Ohio (project; with Eliel Saarinen and Richard Kimball)
Houses, school, and community hall, Center Line, Michigan (with Eliel Saarinen and J. Robert Swanson)
1941/
42 A.C. Wermuth HOuse, Fort Wayne, Indiana (with Eiel Saarinen)
Willow Run Housing Units, Michigan (with Eliel Saarinen and J. Robert Swanson)
1942 Schools, Willow Run, Michigan (with Eliel Saarinen and J. Robert Swanson)
Group plan and architectural scheme for Wayne State University, Detroit (competition project; with Eliel Saarinen and J. Robert Swanson)
Summer Opera House and Chamber Music Hall, Berkshire Music Center, Tanglewood, Massachusetts (with Eliel Saarinen)
1943 Lincoln Heights Housing Area, Washington, D.C. (with Eliel Saarinen and J. Robert Swanson)
1943/
44 Parliament Building, Quito, Ecuador (competition project; with Eliel Saarinen and J. Robert Swanson)
1944 Town plan for New Castle, Indiana (with Eliel Saarinen and J. Robert Swanson)
1944/
48 Edmundson Memorial Museum, Des Moines Art Center, Iowa (with Eliel Saarinen and J. Robert Swanson)
1945 Plan for Washtenaw County, Michigan (with Eliel Saarinen and J. Robert Swanson)
Development plan for Antioch College, Yellow Springs, Ohio (with Eliel Saarinen and J. Robert Swanson)
1945/
49 Women's Dormitory, Antioch College, Yellow Springs, Ohio (with Eliel Saarinen and J. Robert Swanson)
1946 H. H. Houston Community Development Plan, Outer Roxborough, Philadelphia (with Eliel Saarinen)
1946/
47 Campus development plan for Drake University, Des Moines, Iowa (with Eliel Saarinen and J. Robert Swanson)
Women's Dormitory, Drake University, Des Moines, Iowa (with Eliel Saarinen)
1946/
48 Christ Church, Cincinnati, Ohio (with Eliel Saarinen)
1946/
49 Science and Pharmacy Building, Drake University, Des Moines, Iowa (with Eliel Saarinen, J. Robert Swanson, and Brooks and Borg)
1947 Civic Center, Detroit (with Eliel Saarinen)
Campus development plan for Stephens Col-

lege, Columbia, Missouri (with Eliel Saarinen)
Chapel, Stephens College, Columbia, Missouri (with Eliel Saarinen)
Peoples Bank and Trust Company Building, Fort Wayne, Indiana (with Eliel Saarinen)
1948/
56 General Motors techinical Center, including interiors and furniture, Warren, Michigan (with Smith, Hinchman and Grylls)
1949 Buildings for Brandeis University, Waltham, Massachusetts (project; with Eliel Saarinen)
1951/
55 Dormitories/Dining Hall, Drake University, Des Moines, Iowa
1952/
55 Irwin Union Bank and Trust Company, Columbus, Indiana
1953/
55 Kresge Auditorium and Chapel, Massachusetts Institute of Technology, Cambridge
1953/
57 Milwaukee County War Memorial, Wisconsin
Miller House, Columbus, Indiana
1954 Master plan for the University of Michigan, Ann Arbor
1954/
58 Concordia College, Fort Wayne, Indiana
Dormitory, Vassar College, Poughkeepsie, New York
1955/
58 Women's Dormitory/Dining Hall, University of Chicago
1955/
59 United States Chancellery, Oslo
1955/
60 United States Embassy, Grosvenor Square, London (with Yorke, Rosenberg, Mardall)
1956/
59 IBM Building, Rochester, Minnesota
1956/
60 Law School, University of Chicago
1956/
62 Trans World Airlines Terminal, Idlewild Airport (now Kennedy Airport), New York
1957/
60 Law School, and Women's Dormitories, University of Pennyslvania, Philadelphia
1957/
61 Thomas J. Watson Research Center, IBM, Yorktown, New York
1957/
62 Bell Telephone Corporation Research Labotories, Holmdel, New Jersey
1957/
63 John Deere and Company Administration Center, Moline, Illinois
1958 David S. Ingalls Hockey Rink, Yale University, New Haven, Connecticut
1958/
62 Ezra Stiles College, and Morse College, Yale University, New Haven, Connecticut
1958/
63 Terminal Building, Dulles International Air-

Eero Saarinen: Trans World Airlines Terminal, Kennedy Airport, New York, 1962.

Publications:

By SAARINEN: book—*Eero Saarinen on His Work*, edited by Aline B. Saarinen, New Haven, Connecticut 1968; articles—"The Architecture of Defense Housing," edited by Edmond H. Hoben, in *National Association of Housing Officials Journal* (Chicago), no. 165, 1942; "Trends in Modern Architecture" in *Michigan Society of Architects Bulletin* (Detroit), May 1951; "Our Epoch of Architecture" in *AIA Journal* (Washington, D.C.), December 1952; "Six Broad currents of Modern Architecture" in *Architectural Forum* (New York), July 1953; "The Changing Philosophy of Architecture" in *Architectural Record* (New York), August 1954; "Function, Structure and Beauty" in *AIA Journal* (Washington, D.C.), July/August 1957; "Campus Planning: The Unique World of the University" in *Architectural Record* (New York), November 1960.

1958/
Dulles International Airport, Chantilly, Virginia, near Washington, D.C.

1958/
64 Repertory Theatre and Theatre Library/Museum, Lincoln Center, New York (with Skidmore, Owings and Merrill)

1959/
63 North Christian Church, Columbus, Indiana

1959/
64 Jefferson National Expansion Memorial (Gateway Arch), St. Louis

1960/
64 Columbia Broadcasting System Headquarters, New York

1964 School of Music, University of Michigan, Ann Arbor

International Airport, Athens

*

On SAARINEN: books—*Eero Saarinen* by Allan Temko, New York and London 1962; *Great Modern Architecture* by Sherban G. Cantacuzino, New York and London 1966; *Eero Saarinen* by E. J. Iglesia, Buenos Aires 1966; *Eero Saarinen* by Rupert Spade, New York and London 1971; *The Fourth Dimension in Architecture* by Edward and Mildred Hall, Santa Fe, New Mexico 1975; *St. Louis and the Arch* by Joel Meyerowitz, Boston 1980; *Design in America: The Cranbrook Vision 1925-1950*, exhibition catalogue, by Robert Judson Clark and others, New York 1983; *Contemporary Designers*, edited by Ann Lee Morgan, New York and London 1984; articles—"Now Saarinen the Son" by Aline B. Louchheim in the *New York Times Magazine*, 26 April 1953; special issue of the *Michigan Society of Architects Bulletin* (Detroit), July 1953; "Recent Works of Eero Saarinen" in *Zodiac* (Milan), no. 4, 1959; "The Diversity of Eero Saarinen" by Lawrence Lessing in *Architectural Forum* (New York), July 1960; "Eero Saarinen: Something Between Earth and Sky" by Allan Temko in *Horizon* (New York), July 1960; "Recent Work by Eero Saarinen" in *RIBA Journal* (London), November 1960; "Eero Saarinen 1910—1961" by Douglas Haskell in *Architectural Forum* (New York), October 1961; "Eero Saarinen 1910—1961" by Peter Carter in *Architectural Design* (London), December 1961; "Eero Saarinen: A Complete Architect" by Walter McQuade in *Architectural Forum* (New York), October 1962; "On Eero Saarinen" by Raymond Lichez in *Zodiac* (Milan), no. 17, 1967; "Pluralismo e prop-Architettura" by Bruno Zevi in *L'Architettura* (Rome), September 1967; "A View of Contemporary World Architecture," special issue of *The Japan Architect* (Tokyo), July 1970; "The Genesis of a Great Building and an Unusual Friendship" by William Hewitt in *AIA Journal* (Washington, D.C.), August 1977; "The World's Most Beautiful Airport?" by Allen Freeman in *AIA Journal* (Washington, D.C.), November 1980; "Eero Saarinen Spawn" by Nancy Lickerman Halik in *Inland Architect* (Chicago), May 1981; "Eero Saarinen in Perspective" by Andrea O. Dean in *AIA Journal* (Washington, D.C.), November 1981.

Bibliographies: *Eero Saarinen: His Life and Work* by Robert A. Kuhner, Monticello, Illinois 1975; *The Work of Eero Saarinen: A Selected Bibliography* by Lamia Doumato, Monticello, Illinois 1980.

*

To be born the child of a talented parent may be a blessing or a curse. Being the child of two such parents can only compound the situation. And for a child to follow in the profession of a talented parent may bring with it an even greater boon or risk.

For Eero Saarinen, being the son of the talented and famous architect, Eliel Saarinen, and the talented artist and artisan, Loja Gesellius Saarinen, was definitely a blessing. He lived in a home filled with creative activity and with creative people, visitors as well as his mother, father and sister. His early formal training was sporadic, at best, but he had ample opportunity for his own creative endeavours.

Having moved with his family to Bloomfield Hills, Michigan, when he was thirteen, Saarinen decided that, of all the arts, sculpture was his favorite and that he would become a sculptor. After a year in art school, he decided to become an architect rather than a sculptor, in spite of the fact that while a teenager his designs were mostly for sculpture and sculptural furniture. In later years, his love of sculpture was never lost. And eventually, when he became famous, as great an architect as his father had been—some think even greater—he also became the most sculptural architect of his era.

Eliel Saarinen was a notable architect before winning the second prize in the competition for the

Chicago Tribune Tower in 1922. The elder Saarinen's design, considered by many to be superior to the winner by Raymond Hood and John Mead Howells, brought with it worldwide publicity and recognition. Like his father before him, Eero Saarinen became a notable architect who later received world wide recognition for winning a competition—in 1948, for the design of the Jefferson National Expansion Memorial in St. Louis, later known as the Gateway Arch. He had achieved considerable stature before the competition in partnership with his father, and together they had designed a number of important buildings, including the Kleinhans Music Hall, Buffalo, New York; Crow Island School, Winnetka, Illinois, in association with Perkins, Wheeler and Will; and Tabernacle Church, Columbus, Indiana. He had won competitions before, the first for a design with matchsticks when he was twelve, and two first prizes, in 1940, for furniture designs made with Charles Eames for the Museum of Modern Art of New York City.

But the Gateway Arch established him firmly as one of the world's most important architects and established him as an individual architect, independently of his father. After his father's death in 1950, Eero Saarinen started his own practice, which grew quite rapidly. His buildings received wide publicity and won awards.

The buildings designed by the two Saarinens together gave little hint of the future development of Eero Saarinen as a designer. Most were excellent but unspectacular; they were relatively small and utilized natural materials. An exception was the large and complex General Motors Technical Center in Warren, Michigan, designed in association with Smith, Hinchman and Grylls, a multi-million dollar project completed in the 1950s after the elder Saarinen had died. The Technical Center style was what might be called classic modern of its time, with straight, clean lines, rectangular forms, in an almost Miesian manner. It, too, gave no indication of the future design directions of Eero Saarinen.

What followed was a tremendous outpouring of original work, each building different from the last and seemingly derived from some inner drive of Saarinen's toward inventive and sculptural forms. The Kresge Auditorium and Chapel, completed in 1955, at Massachusetts Institute of Technology, Cambridge, were perhaps, the first buildings to indicate the future directions of Saarinen's work. Both are daring in concept and sculptural in form. To follow were such notable buildings as those at Concordia College, Fort Wayne, Indiana; two buildings for IBM; the John Deere and Company Administration Center in Moline, Illinois; the Ingalls Hockey Rink at Yale; and the Trans World Airlines Terminal Building at John F. Kennedy Airport, New York City. In each succeeding design, Saarinen appeared to be trying to outdo the predecessors. And each brought him added fame and recognition. Along the way, he designed other buildings, some of which, such as the United States Embassy in London, were admired but not considered among his best.

During all the years of the 1950s, Saarinen continued to surprise and delight his admirers and to confound his critics. To both groups, he always seemed to be searching for the one design scheme that would be absolutely appropriate for each new building, searching for new horizons and seldom, if ever, looking back. While other noted architects seemed to be attempting to develop personal styles, in which each succeeding building derived from those they had designed before, Saarinen seemed to be developing an almost styleless philosophy in which each design sprang full-blown from his talent and toil almost as if he had never previously designed another building.

Needless to say, Saarinen's designs were, for the most part, fresh, intriguing, even mysterious. Saarinen himself came to be something of an enigma to the public and to his fellow architects. Some accused him of being primarily a showman, but others thought of him as possibly the most creative architect of his time. In the end, most had concluded that he really was a very creative architect, who was also a consummate showman.

In the late 1950s, Saarinen designed some of his greatest buildings. In 1961, successful, famous, and almost inevitably destined for even greater achievements, Saarinen died while undergoing brain surgery. He was only fifty-one, with what many thought would be the best of his architectural years ahead of him. A year later, he was awarded, posthumously, the highest honor of his fellow architects, the gold medal of the American Institute of Architects, an award his father had also won fifteen years before. In 1963, what many people consider his masterpiece, Dulles Airport, was completed.

Although he had not developed a style that others could follow and, perhaps, develop further, Eero Saarinen had left a creative legacy of originality in design that has influenced later architecture profoundly.

—William Dudley Hunt, Jr.

SAARINEN, (Gottlieb) Eliel.
American. Born in Rantasalmi, Finland, 20 August 1873; emigrated to the United States, 1923; naturalized, 1945. Educated at Klassillinenlyseo secondary school, Viborg, Finland, 1883-89; Realyceum secondary school, Tammerfors, Finland, 1889-93; simultaneously studied painting at the University of Helsinki and architecture at the Polytekniska Institutet, Helsinki, 1893-97; Dip.Arch. 1897. Married the sculptor and weaver Louise (Loja) Gesellius in 1904; children: Eva-Lisa (Pipsan) and the architect Eero Saarinen, q.v. Partner, with Herman Gesellius and Armas Lindgren, Gesellius-Lindgren-Saarinen, Helsinki, 1896-1905, and Gesellius-Saarinen, Helsinki, 1905-07; in private practice as Eliel Saarinen, architect, Helsinki, 1907-23; Evanston, Illinois, 1923-24, and Ann Arbor, Michigan, 1924-37; practised with son Eero in Ann Arbor, Michigan, 1937-41; Partner, with Eero and J. Robert Swanson, Saarinen-Swanson-Saarinen, Ann Arbor, Michigan, 1941-47; Partner, Saarinen, Saarinen and Associates, Ann Arbor, Michigan, 1947-50. Visiting Professor of Architecture, University of Michigan, Ann Arbor, 1924; Director, 1925-32, President, 1932-50, and Director of the Graduate Department of Architecture and City Planning, 1948-50, Cranbrook Academy of Art, Bloomfield Hills, Michigan. Chairman, City and Regional Planning Committee, American Institute of Architects, 1935. Exhibitions: Salon d'automne, Paris, 1907; Die grosse Kunstausstellung, Berlin, 1909; Internationale Baufach Ausstellung, Leipzig, Germany, 1913; Deutsche Werkbund Ausstellung, Cologne, 1914; Munksnas-Haga exhibition, Riddarhuset, Helsinki, 1915; Thumb Tack Club Annual Exhibition, Detroit Institute of Arts, 1924; Ausstellung Neuer Amerikanischer Baukunst, Berlin, 1926; International Architectural and Arts Exposition, New York, 1930; Loja and Eliel Saarinen, Architectural League of New York, 1931; Nordiska Byggnadsdag, Helsinki, 1932; Saarinen Family Exhibition, Detroit Institute of Arts, 1932; Saarinen Family Exhibition, Cranbrook Pavilion, Bloomfield Hills, Michigan, 1935; World's Fair, Paris, 1937; Loja and Eliel Saarinen, Norfolk Museum of Art and Science, Virginia, 1937; America Builds, Museum of Modern Art, New York, 1942 (toured the United States and Europe); Eliel and Loja Saarinen, Berea College, Kentucky, 1943; New Architecture of the United States, Cairo 1944; Design in America: the Cranbrook Vision 1925-1950, toured the United States and Europe, 1983-84; Saarinen in Finland, Helsinki, 1984; Furniture and Interior Architecture in the Work of Saarinen, Helsinki, 1984. Recipient: Bronze, Silver, and Gold medals, State of Finland, 1900; Gold Medal, Leipzig Exhibition, Germany, 1913; Gold Medal, Architectural League of New York, 1934; Academic Architects Society Medal, Copenhagen, 1939; Gold Medal, American Institute of Architects, 1947. Honorary Doctorates: Technische Hochschule, Karlsruhe, Germany, 1931; University of Helsinki, 1932; University of Michigan, Ann Arbor, 1933; Bethany College, Lindsburg, Kansas, 1936; Harvard University, Cambridge, Massachusetts, 1940; Drake University, Des Moines, Iowa, 1948. Honorary Professor, Finland. 1918; Fellow, American Institute of Architects, 1944; Academician, National Academy of Design, New York, 1946. Honorary Member: Imperial Academy of Art, St. Petersburg, 1906; Deutsche Werkbund; Zentrale Vereinigung der Architekten Österreichs, Vienna, 1913; Finnish Academy of Art, 1920; Society of Arts and Crafts, Budapest, 1921; Freie Deutsche Akademie des Stadtebaues, 1922; Royal Institute of British Architects, 1924; Michigan Chapter of the American Institute of Architects, 1925; Swedish Engineers Society, Detroit, 1926; Society of Finnish Architects, 1930; Architects' Society of Uruguay, 1931; Central Institute of Architects of Brazil, 1931; Council of Confidence, Art Academy of Finland, 1932; Michigan Society of Architects of Finland, 1936; Detroit Chapter of the American Institute of Architects, 1936. Commander First Class, Finnish Order of the White Rose, 1925; Grand Cross, Finnish Order of the Lion, 1946. Died (in Cranbrook Hills, Michigan) 1 July 1950.

Works:

1897 Tallberg Apartment Building, Helsinki (with Herman Gesellius and Armas Lindgren)
1898 Verdandi Insurance Company Building, Turku, Finland (competition project; with Herman Gesellius and Armas Lindgren)
Market Hall, Tampere, Finland (competition project; with Herman Gesellius and Armas Lindgren)
Henry van Gilse van der Pals Country House, Paloniemi, Lohja, Finland (with Herman Gesellius and Armas Lindgren)
Municipal Library, Turku, Finland (competition project; with Herman Gesellius and Armas Lindgren)
1899 Apartment block, Siltasaarentaku 12, Helsinki (with Herman Gesellius and Armas Lindgren)
Vuorio Villa, Helsinki (with Herman Gesellius and Armas Lindgren)
Pellervo Insurance Company Building, Helsinki (project; with Herman Gesellius and Armas Lindgren)
1899/1900 Finnish Pavilion, World's Fair, Paris (with Herman Gesellius and Armas Lindgren)
1901 Pohjola Insurance Company Building, Helsinki (with Herman Gesellius and Armas Lindgren)
1900 Tôrngren Villa, Espoo, Finland (with Herman Gesellius and Armas Lindgren)
1900/01 Pulkanranta Villa, Mäntyharju, Finland (with Herman Gesellius and Armas Lindgren)
Apartment block, Fabianinkatu 17, Helsinki (with Herman Gesellius and Armas Lindgren)
1900/03 Savings Bank, Tampere, Finland (with Herman Gesellius and Armas Lindgren)
1901 Sievers Villa, Helsinki (with Herman Gesellius and Armas Lindgren)
Church, Janakkala, Finland (project; with Herman Gesellius and Armas Lindgren)
1901/03 EOL Apartment Block, Helsinki (with Herman Gesellius and Armas Lindgren)
Olofsborg Apartment Block, Helsinki (with Herman Gesellius and Armas Lindgren)
1902 Hvitträsk (architects' houses and studio), Kirkkonummi, Finland (with Herman Gesellius and Armas Lindgren)

Westerlund Country House, Hvittorp, Kirk-
konummi, Finland (with Herman Gesellius
and Armas Lindgren)
Selin Villa, Miniato, Sökö, Espoo, Finland
(with Herman Gesellius and Armas Lin-
dgren)
Suur-Merijoki Country House, Viipuri, Fin-
land (with Herman Gesellius and Armas
Lindgren)
Paper mill, Voikkaa, Finland (with Herman
Gesellius and Armas Lindgren)
Vicarage, Jokioinen, Finland (with Herman
Gesellius and Armas Lindgren)
Municipal Library, Oulu, Finland (compe-
tition project: with Herman Gesellius and
Armas Lindgren)

1902/
06 Edelfelt EKA Villa, Kolo, Espoo, Finland
(with Herman Gesellius and Armas Lindgren)
1903 Church, Nilsiä, Finland (project; with Herman Gesellius and Armas Lindgren)
Bobrinsky Villa, Moscow (project; with Herman Gesellius and Armas Lindgren)
Castrén Villa, Espoo, Finland (with Herman
Gesellius and Armas Lindgren)
1904 Pirtti Artists' Club, Helsinki (with Herman
Gesellius and Armas Lindgren)
Luther Factory Club, Tallinn, Estonia (with
Herman Gesellius and Armas Lindgren)
Count Schouvaloff Memorial, Kursk, Russia
(with Herman Gesellius and Armas Lin-
dgren)
Bank building, Sortavala, Finland (with Her-
man Gesellius and Armas Lindgren)
Methodist church, Helsinki (with Herman
Gesellius and Armas Lindgren)
Nordic Bank Building, Helsinki (with Herman
Gesellius and Armas Lindgren)
Private house, Essen, Germany (competition
project; with Herman Gesellius and Armas
Lindgren)
Päivälehti Newspaper Building, Helsinki
(with Herman Gesellius and Armas Lind-
gren)

1904/
10 Finnish National Museum, Helsinki (with
Herman Gesellius and Armas Lindgren)
1905 Emmanuel Church, Helsinki (with Herman
Gesellius)
Palace of Peace, The Hague (competition
project; with Herman Gesellius)
Labour Union Building, Kotka, Finland (with
Herman Gresellius)

1905/
07 Molchow House, Remer Country Estate,
Mark Brandenburg, Germany (with Herman Gesellius)

1905/
14 Helsinki Railway Station
1906 Helsingin Sanomat Newspaper Building, Helsinki (with Herman Gesellius)
Oma Apartment Block, Helsinki (with Herman Gesellius)
Town Hall, Lappeenranta, Finland (project;
with Herman Gesellius)
1907 School building, Helsinki (project)
Keirkner Apartment interiors, Helsinki
1908 Parliament Building, Helsinki (competition
project)
School building, Turku, Finland (project)
Salamandra Insurance Company Building, St.
Petersburg, Russia (project)

1908/
13 Viipuri Railway Station, Finland (with Herman Gesellius)
1909 Winter Villa, Sortavala, Finland
Cederberg Mausoleum, Joensuu, Finland
(project)
1910 Tallberg Office Building II, Helsinki
Municipal Theatre, Tampere, Finland (competition project)
Industrial Exhibition Design, Helsinki (competition project)

Huber Office Building, Helsinki (competition
project)
1910/
15 Town plan for Munkkiniemi-Haaga, Finland
1911 Rigaer Gesellschaft Gegenseitigen Credits
Office and Apartment Building, Riga, Latvia (competition project)
Esto-Bank Building, Tallinn, Estonia (competition project)
1911/
12 Town Hall, Lahti, Finland
Esto-Bank Building, Tallinn, Estonia
1911/
13 Town plan for Tallinn, Estonia (competition
project)
1912 Town plan for Budapest
Suomi Insurance Company Building, Helsinki
(competition project)
Trade Union Building, Riga, Latvia (competition project)
School for Girls, Lahti, Finland
Town Hall, Tallinn, Estonia (project)
Town plan for Canberra (competition project)
1912/
13 Town Hall Joensuu, Finland
1913 Paulus Church, Tarto (Dorpat), Estonia

1914 Finnish Pavilion, San Francisco Fair (competition project)
Finnish Lutheran Congregational Hall, St.
Petersburg, Russia (project)
1915 Keirkner Villa, Helsinki
1916 Town plan for Munkkiniemi-Haaga, Finland
Keskuskatu Street layout, Helsinki
Swedish Theatre Annex and restoration,
Helsinki (project)
1916/
18 Pensionat Hotel, Munkkiniemi, Finland
1917 Trikkonen Office Building, Helsinki (project)
Trikkonen House, Helsinki (project)
1917/
18 City plan for Greater Helsinki
1919 Hospital Cairo (project)
Kalevala House, Munkkiniemi, Finland (project)
1922 Tribune Tower, Chicago (competition project)
1923 Plan for the lake front, Chicago (project)
1925 Christian Science Church, Minneapolis, Minnesota (project)
1926/
30 Cranbrook School for Boys, Bloomfield Hills,
Michigan

Eliel Saarinen: **Museum and Library, Cranbrook Academy of Art, Bloomfield Hills, Michigan, 1943.**

1926/
41 Cranbrook Academy of Art, Bloomfield Hills, Michigan
1927 Palace of the League of Nations, Geneva (competition project)
1928/
29 Saarinen House, Bloomfield Hills, Michigan
1929/
30 Kingswood School for Girls, Cranbrook, Bloomfield Hills, Michigan
Hudnut House, New York (with Ely Jacques Kahn)
1931 Stevens Institute of Technology, Hoboken, New Jersey
1931/
33 Institute of Science, Cranbrook, Bloomfield Hills, Michigan
1933 Alexander Hamilton Memorial, Chicago (project)
1935 Alko Factory and Office Building, Helsinki (competition project)
1937/
38 Community House, Fenton, Michigan (with Eero Saarinen)
1938 Area plan for Goucher College, Baltimore, Maryland (competition project; with Eero Saarinen)
Berkshire Music Center, Tanglewood, Massachusetts (with Eero Saarinen)
1938/
40 Kleinhans Music Hall, Buffalo, New York (with Eero Saarinen)
1939 Smithsonian Institution Art Gallery, Washington, D.C. (project; with Eero Saarinen and J. Robert Swanson)
1939/
40 Crow Island School, Winnetka, Illinois (with Eero Saarinen, and Perkins, Wheeler and Will)
1940/
42 Tabernacle Church of Christ, Columbus, Indiana (with Eero Saarinen)
1940/
43 Museum and Library, Cranbrook Academy of Art, Bloomfield Hills, Michigan
1941 Oberlin College, Ohio (project; with Eero Saarinen and Richard Kimball)
Houses, school, and community hall, Center Line, Michigan (with Eero Saarinen and J. Robert Swanson)
1941/
42 A.C. Wermuth House, Fort Wayne, Indiana (with Eero Saarinen)
Willow Run Housing Units, Michigan (with Eero Saarinen and J. Robert Swanson)
1942 Schools, Willow Run, Michigan (with Eero Saarinen and J. Robert Swanson)
Group plan and architectural scheme for Wayne State University, Detroit (competition project; with Eero Saarinen and J. Robert Swanson)
Summer Opera House and Chamber Music Hall, Berkshire Music Center, Tanglewood, Massachusetts (with Eero Saarinen)
1943 Lincoln Heights Housing Area, Washington, D.C. (with Eero Saarinen and J. Robert Swanson)
1943/
44 Parliament Building, Quito, Ecuador (competiton project; (with Eero Saarinen and J. Robert Swanson)
1944 Town plan for New Castle, Indiana (with Eero Saarinen and J. Robert Swanson)
1944/
48 Edmunton Memorial Museum, Des Moines Art Center, Iowa (with Eero Saarinen and J. Robert Swanson)
1945 Plan for Washtenaw County, Michigan (with Eero Saarinen and J. Robert Swanson)
Development plan for Antioch College, Yellow Springs, Ohio (with Eero Saarinen and J. Robert Swanson)
1945/
49 Women's Dormitory, Antioch College, Yel-

low Springs, Ohio (with Eero Saarinen and J. Robert Swanson)
1946 H. H. Houston Community Development Plan, Outer Roxborough, Philadelphia (with Eero Saarinen)
1946/
47 Campus development plan for Drake University, Des Moines, Iowa (with Eero Saarinen and J. Robert Swanson)
Women's Dormitory, Drake University, Des Moines, Iowa (with Eero Saarinen
1946/
48 Christ Church, Cincinnati, Ohio (with Eero Saarinen)
1946/
79 Science and Pharmacy Building, Drake University, Des Moines, Iowa (with Eero Saarinen, J. Robert Swanson, and Brooks and Borg)
1947 Civic Center, Detroit (with Eero Saarinen)
Campus Development plan for Stephens College, Columbia, Missouri (with Eero Saarinen)
Chapel, Stephens College, Columbia, Missouri (with Eero Saarinen)
Peoples Bank and Trust Company Building, Fort Wayne, Indiana (with Eero Saarinen)
1948/
50 General Motors Technical Center, Warren, Michigan (with Eero Saarinen and Smith, Hinchman and Grylls)
1949 Building for Brandeis University, Waltham, Massachusetts (project; with Eero Saarinen)

Publications:

By SAARINEN: books—*Munksnas-Haga,* with Gustaf Strengall, Helsinki 1915; *The Cranbrook Development,* Bloomfield Hills, Michigan 1931; *The City: Its Growth, Its Decay, It Future.* New York 1943; *Search for Form,* New York 1948; articles—"Stadtplanung für Reval" in *Der Stadtbau* (Cologne), no. 5/6, 1921; "Lausunto Eraista Helsingin Kaupungin Asemakaavaksmyksista" in *Helsingin Kaupungin Keskiosien Yleisasemakaavaehdotus,* Helsinki 1932; "Architecture in the Post-War World" in *Art Digest* (New York), August 1943; "Eliel Saarinen Receives the Gold Medal: The Citation and Mr. Saarinen's Response" in *AIA Journal* (Washington, D.C.), June 1947.

On SAARINEN: books—*L'Architecture à l'Exposition Universelle de 1900.* Paris 1900; *Konhistoria* by Carl G. Laurin, Stockholm 1901; *Kun Suuret Olivat Pienia* by Helmi Setala, Helsinki 1911; *Suomen Taiteen Historia* by Johannes Ohquist, Helsinki 1912; *Pro Helsingfors* by Bertel Jung, Helsinki 1918; *Ausstellung neuer amerikanisher Baukunst,* Berlin 1926; *The Story of Architecture in America* by Thomas E. Tallmadge, New York 1927; *Byggnaden som Konstverk* by Gustaf Strengell, Helsinki 1928; *Modern Architecture* by Henry-Russell Hitchcock, Jr., New York 1929; *History of the Skyscraper* by Francisco Mujica, Paris 1929; *Living Architecture* by Arthur Woltersdorf, Chicago 1930; *Byggnadskonst i Finland,* Helsinki 1932; *The New Architecture and the Bauhaus* by Walter Gropius, London 1935; *Modern Building* by Walter Curt Behrendt, New York 1937; *Architecture Through the Ages* by Talbot Hamlin, New York 1940; *Space, Time and Architecture,* by Siegfried Giedion, Cambridge, Massachusetts 1941; *The Architectonic City in Americas* by Hugo Leipziger, Austin, Texas 1944; *Toly kapitel om Munksnas* by Per Nystrom, Helsinki 1945; *Asemakaavaoppi* by Otto Meurman, Helsinki 1947; *Eliel Saarinen* by Albert Christ-Janer, Chicago, London and Toronto 1948; revised edition, Chicago 1979; *Eliel Saarinen ja'Suur-Tallinn'* by Igor Demkin, Tallinn, Estonia 1977; *Design in America: The Cranbrook Vision 1925-1950,*

exhibition catalogue, by Robert Judson Clark and others, New York 1983; articles—"Eliel Saarinen" by J. Robert Swanson in *Michigan Technic* (Ann Arbor), May 1924; "Eliel Saarinen" by Donnell Tilghman in *Architectural Record* (New York), May 1928; "L'Architecte Eliel Saarinen" by Gustaf Strengell in *L'Art vivant* (Paris), 15 October 1928; "Eliel Saarinen" by Bertel Jung in *Arkitekten* Copenhagen), no. 3, 1932; "Eliel Saarinen, Master of Design " by Kenneth Reid in *Pencil Points* (New York), September 1936; "Eliel Saarinen" by Aulis Blomstedt in *Arkkitehti* Helsinki), no. 11/12, 1943; "Eliel Saarinen: An Appreciation" by Kent Barker in *Journal of the Royal Architectural Institute of Canada* (Toronto), December 1944; "Gesellius-Lindgren-Saarinen" by Marika Hausen in *Arkkitehti* (Helsinki), no. 9, 1967; "The Helsinki Railway Station in Eliel Saarinen's First Versions, 1904" by Marika Hausen in *Studies in Art History 3,* Helsinki 1977; "Eliel Saarinen as the Interpreter of Urban Planning in His Own Time by Kirmo Mikkola in *Arkkitehti* (Helsinki), no. 4, 1981; "Eliel Saarinen Residence, Cranbrook Academy of Art" in *GA Houses* (Tokyo), July 1981; "The Finnish Horizon" by Kirmo Mikkola in *Byggekunst* (Oslo), no. 1, 1982; "Railway Station, Helsinki" by Akira Muto and Keibun Sano in *Space Design* (Tokyo), November 1982; "Eliel Saarinen," special issue of *Form Function Finland* (Helsinki), no. 2, 1984.

Bibliography—*Eliel Saarinen 1873-1950* by Lamia Doumato Monticello, Illinois 1980.

Eliel Saarinen is one of the few architects of modern times who has received less credit than he deserves. Many of his ideas are rooted in the pre-International Style days. During the height of the International Style vogue, they were virtually lost. However, they were ideas of such power that they have survived its demise and only now are they beginning to establish their place in the forefront.

In his drawing for the Chicago Tribune Tower competition, Saarinen, without resorting to stylistic eclecticism, established the concept of a tall building woven in all of its parts into a harmonious whole, a continuous flow from ground to sky. This is a stark contrast of the usuall high-rise of today, in which the typical floor is repeated mindlessly to the top, where the building is brutally cut off as a pair of scissors might cut a mechanically printed ribbon. Only now is the whole building beginning to return as the design unit.

Yet Saarinen's greatest message in that the object of architecture is not the building at all but rather the harmonious relationship of building and open space, and that this harmony does not stop at any arbitrary boundary or lot line but extends ever outward into the depths of the city. This led him to a major preocupation with city planning. In 1912 Saarinen enterd the competition for the design of the new capital of Australia, Canberra. Here, as in Chicago, his design was given second place, so his ideas remained on paper.

Saarinens opportunity actually to build the environment he had dreamed about came some ten years after his arrival in the United States from Finland, when George and Ellen Scripps Boothe founded the Cranbrook Academy of Art in Bloomfield Hills outside of Detroit and asked Saarinen to design it and the nearby boys' and girls' schools. Through his collaboration with Swedish sculptor Carl Milles and his work with his wife, the great weaver Loja, and others, he integrated art and crafts into architecture in a way that still is unmatched, and he created here one of the very few totally harmonious environments in the United States.

Saarinen did everything he could to turn the central flow of architectural energy away from preoccupation with the individual structure into concern for the larger organism of the city. The fact that his voice was ignored has exacted a tragic toll because of the inability of the design profession to

deal with the creative possibilities offered by the government program of urban renewal. Because so few had heeded his admonition, the profession as a whole was unprepared for the avalanche of responsibility that urban renewal placed on it, and made a terrible botch of a wonderful opportunity. In city after city in the United Staes, the basic urban fabric was torn apart for architectural non-entities, or, even worse, for vacant open wounds which still remain.

Saarinen saw clearly that his ideas would have their fullest expression in the distant future and set about to bridge the gap created by the misunderstanding and rejection which surrounded him. At Cranbrook, he established an Academy which, more than any other, resembled the Academy of classical times. Here, through personal contact, he was able to influence young minds with the vision he possessed in a way far more effective than he ever was able to achieve through his books. The students who worked with him there, including Charles Eames, Carl Feiss, Harry Weese, Harry Bertoia, Florence Knoll, and myself, are trying to bring these ideas alive today. Saarinen laid out for the architectural profession a design for its furture course which is may well decide to follow.

—Edmund N. Bacon

SAÉNZ DE OÍZA, Francisco Javier.

Spanish. Born in Madrid, 12 October 1918. Educated at the Escuela Tecnica Superior Arquitectura, Madrid; Colegio de Cataluna y Baleares, Barcelona, Dip-Arch. 1946. Since 1947, in private practice, Madrid. Professor from 1957, and Director, since 1981, Escuela Tecnica Superior Arquitectura, Madrid. Recipient: First Prize, with Laorga, Basilica of Aránzazu Competition 1949; First Prize, with Laorga, Basilica of La Merced Competition, 1949; Spanish National Architecture Prize, with Romaní y Oteiza, 1954; First Prize, Universidad Autonoma de Madrid Competition 1970; First Prize, Montecarlo Competition 1970; First Prize, University of Cordoba Competition, 1978. Address (office): Avenida de Portugal 55, Madrid, Spain.

Works:

1949 Basilica, Aránzazu, Spain (competition project; with Laorga)
       Basilica, La Merced, Spain (competition project; with Laorga)
1951 Entrevias Public Housing Development, Madrid
1954 Camino de Santiago Chapel, Spain (with Romani y Oteiza)
       Fuencarral Public Housing Development, Madrid
       Barrios de Puerta del Angel Public Housing Development, Madrid
1955 Batán Public Housing Development, Madrid
1960 House, Talavera de la Reina, Spain
1961 Ciudad Blanca Terraced Housing Development, Alcudia, Majorca
       Exhibition Hall, Huarte, Spain
1962 Torres Blancas Apartment Complex, Madrid
       Loyola Housing Development, Carabanchel, Spain (with J. L. Romany Aranda, E. Mangada Samain, and C. Ferran Alfaro)
1965 Horizonte Satellite Town, near Madrid (project; with J. L. Romany Aranda, E. Mangada Samain, and C. Ferran Alfaro)
1969/
70 Universidad Autónoma de Madrid y Bilbao, Madrid
1970 Montecarlo Development (competition project)
1971 Casa Huarte, Mallorca, Spain
1972/
76 Arturo Echevarria House, calle Lamiaco 27, La Florida, Madrid
1972/
80 Banco de Bilbao, Centro Azca, Madrid
1978 University of Cordoba, Spain (competition project)
1980 Islamic Centre, Madrid (competition project)

Publications

By SAÉNZ DE OÍZA: article—"El vidrio y la arquitectura" in *Revista nacional de arquitectura* (Madrid), September/October 1952.

On SAÉNZ DE OÍZA: book—*Architectura española contemporanea* by Luis Domenech Girbau, Barcelona 1968; articles—"Urbanizacion 'Ciudad Blanca,' Alcudia (Mallorca)" in *Cuadernos de arquitectura* (Barcelona), no. 58, 1964; "Grupo de Vivendas Loyola" in *Hogar y arquitectura* (Madrid), August 1965; "Einfamilienhauser" in *Baumeister* (Munich), December 1966; "Espagne—Madrid, Barcelone" in *L'Architecture d'aujourd'hui* (Paris), April/May 1970; "Competition in Cordoba" by Jeronimo Junquera in *Arquitectura* (Madrid), January/February 1978; "Seven Masters of Madrid and 7 + 7 Young Architects" by Alberto Campo Baeza in *Architecture + Urbanism* (Tokyo), March 1978; "The Banco de Bilbao Tower in the Azca Centre of Madrid" by Anton Capitel in *Arquitectura* (Madrid), January/February 1981; "Echevarria residence in La Florida, Madrid" in *Arquitectura* (Madrid), November/December 1981; "Olympic Projects for Barcelona" by O. Bohigas in *Casabella* (Milan), April 1984.

*

Francisco Saénz de Oíza is possibly the most complex and attractive personality in Spanish architecture of the last twenty-five years. His work is an exacting history of the progress of modern trends in this country.

His early career belongs to that period of historical reaction of the first years of Franco's regime, and his works of that time are a modernized version and revision of previously accepted conceptions. It was only during the 1950s that he began to break with these traditions. His original tendencies are still evident in the projects for basilicas in Aránzazu and La Merced, designed in collaboration with Laorga, both of which won their respective competitions to become accepted as "standards." But as the 1950s progressed, Saénz de Oíza's work began to show the growing influence of modernist ideals. In trying to make up for lost time, Saénz de Oíza (and other Spanish architects) moved quickly with an almost pre-ordained determination, towards the goal of "modernism", a goal that had been abandoned and lost among the tragedies and upheavals of the 1930s and 1940s.

Saénz de Oíza became one of the staunchest critics of official modern culture. He identified his ideal as that of the most orthodox modernism—a faith in architecture as a social response, encompassing what is functional and constructive. This ideal helps to explain his total dedication in the early 1950s to state-sponsored housing developments in Madrid—Barrios de Puerta del Angel, Fuencarral, Batán and Entrevías. All of these developments reveal his careful realism, his professionalism, and they became the basis of his influence.

In 1954 Saénz de Oíza and Romaní y Oteiza shared the National Architecture Prize for the Chapel on the Camino de Santiago. The influence of Mies is evident in the use of technology as an expressive tool. The Chapel testifies to the poetic force of such language; it seems to demonstrate that, no matter how diverse the subjects of works may be, technology is always of paramount importance.

In the late 1950s Saénz de Oíza seemed to change again, to be reacting to positions such as that of Bruno Zevi, who criticized the early ideas of the modern movement. The Ciudad Blanca in Alcudia expresses itself in terms of crude realism, and the House in Talavera de la Reina and the Exhibition Hall in Huarte reveal a Nordic influence—like much of the architecture of Madrid in the 1960s. Thereafter, his career, and his notions, progressed rapidly. In 1962, with the Torres Blancas Apartment Complex, his work transcended strictly national boundaries and, like the Sydney Opera House by Utzon, became the center of an international controversy. The explosion, to a great extent, was the destruction of early modernist ideals.

Yet, if this was a revolutionary moment in Spanish architecture, it was not pure revolution. The irony is that destruction of some of the primitive ideals of modernism coexist in Torres Blancas with a near perfect realization of other of those ideals. It may be that in Spain the very eagerness to import modern trends (trends that had developed more slowly in other countries) caused this kind of error; what is certain is that the work of Saénz de Oíza and that of many other architects of the time, is guilty of the error. Saénz de Oíza can be justly accused of searching for new ideals while in practice skilfully rescuing a concept of architecture that insists on rigorous functionalism and technological means.

Yet, since the late 1960s, there has been notable progress. Saénz de Oíza *has* gone on to produce works that more closely approximate his own ideas—the Universidad Autonoma de Madrid y Bilbao, the Montecarlo Development project, and the Casa Huarte in Majorca all show an increasing mastery. The Banco de Bilbao in Madrid confirms the trend; it is certainly one of the most sophisticated tower buildings in Europe. More recently, in the project for the University of Cordoba, Saénz de Oíza has created a strong work far removed from the mirage of modernism. His motto, "Utilitas, Firmitas, Venustas", suggests that he will persevere in his belief that the knowledge of architectural means is the way to make the old adage come true.

—Anton Capitel

SAFDIE, Moshe.

Canadian/Israeli. Born in Haifa, Israel, 14 July 1938; moved to Canada, 1955; acquired Canadian nationality (also retaining Israeli nationality), 1959. Educated at McGill University, Montreal, 1955-61, B.Arch. (honours) 1961. Reserve Soldier (Private) in the Israeli Army Corps of Education. Married Nina Nusynowicz in 1959; children: Taal and Oren. Architect with van Ginkel and Associates, Montreal, 1961-62, and with Louis I. Kahn, *q.v.*, Philadelphia, 1962-63; Section Head, Canadian Corporation for the 1967 World Exhibition, Montreal, 1963-64. In private practice, Montreal, since 1964, Jerusalem, since 1971, and Boston, since 1978. Visiting Professor, McGill University, 1970; Davenport Professor of Architecture, Yale University, New Haven, Connecticut, 1971. Since 1975, Professor of Architecture and Director of the Desert Architecture and Environment Department, Desert Research Institute, Ben Gurion University, Beersheva, Negev, Israel; since 1978, Professor of Architecture and Urban Design, Graduate School of Design, Harvard University, Cambridge, Massachusetts. Exhibitions: Baltimore Museum of Art, Maryland, 1973 (subsequently travelled to San Francisco, New York, Chicago, Ottawa, and Des Moines, Iowa); *Context,* toured the United States and Canada; *National Gallery of Canada,* Harvard Graduate School of Design, Cambridge, Massachusetts, and National Gallery of Canada, Ottawa. Recipient: Canadian Lieutenant-Governor's Gold Medal, 1961; Massey

Moshe Safdie: Habitat '67, Montreal, 1967.

Medal for Architecture, Canada, 1968; Gold Star Award, Philadelphia College of Art, 1970; Architect of the Year Award, American Institute of Registered Architects, 1971; Award of Excellence, *Canadian Architect*, 1972, 1973; Urban Design Concept Award, United States Department of Housing and Urban Development, 1980; New York Medal of Honor, American Institute of Architects, 1980; Rechter Prize, Association of Architects and Planners of Israel, 1982. Fellow, Royal Architectural Institute of Canada. Address: 100 Properzi Way, Somerville, Massachusetts 02143, U.S.A.

Works:

1967 Habitat '67, Montreal
1968 Habitat New York (project)
      Student Union, San Francisco State College (project)
      Fort Lincoln Urban Renewal Plan, Washington, D.C. (project)
1968/
72 Habitat Puerto Rico, San Juan
1970 Habitat for Tropaco, United States Virgin Islands (project)
      Habitat, Indian Carry, Saranac Lake, New York (project)
1971 Plan for Coldspring New Town, Baltimore, Maryland
1971/
79 Yeshivat Porat Joseph Rabbinical College, Jerusalem
1972 Master plan for Mamilah Central Business District, Jerusalem
1974 Desert Research Institute and Ben Gurion Archives, Sde Boqer, Negev, Israel
      Master plan for the Western Wall Precinct, Jerusalem

1976 Master plan for Keur Farah Pahlavi New Town, Senegal, West Africa
1977 Habitat Elahieh, Tehran
      Blood Transfusion Centres, Ivory Coast
1979 Landmark Square, Stamford, Connecticut
      Paley Youth Wing, Rockefeller Museum, Jerusalem
1980 Cambridge Center Master Plan, Cambridge, Massachusetts
1983 Maguer David School Complex, Hebrew College, Mexico City
      Robina Master Plan, Queensland, Australia
1984 Museum of Civilization, Quebec City
      Hebrew Union College, Jerusalem
      National Gallery of Canada, Ottawa

Publications:

By SAFDIE: books—*Beyond Habitat*, Cambridge, Massachusetts 1970; *For Everyone a Garden*, Cambridge, Massachusetts 1974; *Habitat Bill of Rights* (pamphlet), with Sert, Ardalan, Doshi, and Candilis, Tehran 1976; *Form and Purpose*, edited by John Kettle, Boston 1982; *Harvard Jerusalem Studio*, Cambridge, Massachusetts 1986; *Jerusalem: The Future of the Past*, Boston 1986; articles—"On from Habitat" in *Design* (London), October 1967; "Post Mortem on Habitat: Anatomy of a System" in *RIBA Journal* (London), November 1967; "The Changing Environment: Hell or Utopia?" in *Midway* (Chicago), Summer 1968; "Industrialized Buildings: Variety Within Repetition" in *Architecture Canada* (Toronto), November 1968; "Habitat '67" in *Beyond Left and Right*, edited by Richard Kostelanetz, New York 1968; "Presentation of Habitat, Puerto Rico and New York, Fort Lincoln and San Francisco" in *Architectural Design* (London), January 1969; "New Environmental Requirements for Urban Building"

in *Zodiac* (Milan), no. 19, 1969; "An Interview with Safdie" in *Ariel* (Jerusalem), 1973; "A View of Cities in 2024 A.D." in *Saturday Review/World* (New York), August 1974; "Collective Consciousness in Making Environment" in *The Frontiers of Knowledge*, New York 1975; "Entrevue avec l'architecte Moshe Safdie" in *Regards sur Israel* (Montreal), March/April 1975; "Private Jokes in Public Places" in *Inland Architect* (Chicago), November/December 1981; recordings—*Moshe Safdie*, tape cassette, London 1979; *Safdie in Jerusalem*, tape cassette and slides, London 1979.

On SAFDIE: books—*Habitat '67*, Ottawa 1967; *Third Generation* by Philip Drew, London 1972; articles—"Habitat '67" in *Engineering News Record* (New York), April 1965; "Habitat '67" in *Building Management* (Toronto), October 1965; "Correspondence Exchanged on Urban Problems" in *Business Quarterly* (London, Ontario), Summer 1966; "Habitat '67" in *Progressive Architecture* (New York), October 1966; "Habitat '67" by David Jacobs in *Horizon* (New York), Winter 1967; "Habitat '67" by Alexander Pyke in *Architectural Design* (London), March 1967; "Post Mortem on Habitat '67" by A.E. Komendant in *Progressive Architecture* (New York), March 1968; "Fort Lincoln Urban Renewal Project" in *Bauen und Wohnen* (Zürich), May 1969; "Moshe Safdie" by Israel Shenker in *Horizon* (New York), Winter 1973; "Building Systems and Growth: A Look into the Future" in *Designer* (New York), February 1974; "Seven Years after Habitat" in *Time* (Montreal), 15 July 1974; "Five Architects" in *Art and Architecture* (Tehran), April 1975; "Habitat Lives" in *Newsweek* (New York), 9 February 1976; "Safdie's Design for the Western Wall Precinct, Jerusalem" in *Baumeister* (Munich), August 1976; "New Mamilah Will Rise Outside Jerusalem's Walls" in *Architectural Record*

(New York), October 1977; "A New Setting for the Western Wall" by Mildred F. Schmertz in *Architectural Record* (New York), April 1978; "Rebuilding Jerusalem: The Work of Moshe Safdie's Practice" by Alan and Sylvia Blanc in *Building Design* (London), 10 November 1978; "Building a New Jerusalem" by Peter Davey in *Architects' Journal* (London), 29 November 1978; "Safdie Goes Back to Basics" by Annette LeCuyer in *Building Design* (London), 11 May 1979; "Jerusalem—Mamilla Central Business District Development" in *Urban Design International* (Purchase, New York), September/October 1980; "Exchange Between Moshe Safdie, James Rouse and Jane Jacobs" in *Urban Design International* (Purchase, New York), January/February 1981; "Musée National de la Civilization, Quebec City" in *Canadian Architect* (Toronto), December 1981; "Edifice E" in *Architecture Concept* (Montreal), January/February 1982; "Preservation and Renewal of Architecture and Urban Space," special issue of *Space Design* (Tokyo), October 1983; "Preview: National Gallery and Museum of Man" in *Canadian Architect* (Toronto), February 1984.

Rather than attempting to make a statement here on my work, I would prefer that readers refer to my writings listed above to learn of my theories and work as an architect.

—Moshe Safdie

*

Although nearly twenty years have passed since the revolutionary housing project Habitat was erected in Montreal in 1967, Israeli-born Moshe Safdie is still best known for this, the first major project of his career. Safdie studied at McGill University in Montreal, and then worked for two years in the office of Louis Kahn. He opened private practice in 1964, and he designed Habitat shortly thereafter. Nevertheless, his offices in Montreal and Jerusalem have been far from quiet since then, and much of his more recent work has demonstrated a continuing commitment to progressive experimentation, but with a more ripened sense of design and architectural finesse.

Habitat was a controversial project, criticized both because it looked unlike any piece of architecture that had ever been produced before that time, and because, like any prototype, it suffered from various miscalculations and mistakes that made the building terribly costly, partially inefficient, and occasionally unworkable. Still, as the first major prefabricated housing complex in the world, Habitat was indeed a breakthough. Safdie's unabashed design made no aesthetic compromises towards more conventional construction which it wasn't, and the use of the units as building blocks celebrated the independence and integrity of each component. An even more exciting gesture was Safdie's careful consideration of amenities such as private gardens, unobstructed views, and individual access, which proved that mass-produced housing need not be aimed only for the poor.

Far too few units (only 158) were built at Habitat to make the project and the prefabricating operation cost efficient, but Safdie repeated the project in Puerto Rico for a fraction of the cost. There, the bottom line per unit was low enough to qualify for government assisted programs designated for low middle-income housing.

In the late 1960s and early 1970s, Safdie's work became more diffuse, and his work included both small building projects, such as the San Francisco State College Student Union, and massive urban design schemes, including a much documented plan for a new town near Baltimore, Maryland, called Coldspring.

Transferring his attention to issues unlike those confronted in school and during his early career, when he focused his efforts almost exclusively on prefabricated housing, gave Safdie a chance to explore the potentials of prefabrication and his own

personal expression in completely different contexts. The experience proved to be a strengthening one, and when he began work on several projects in Jerusalem in the mid-1970s, he appeared more confident and capable than his earlier work had demonstrated. He designed a huge plaza for the large area now cleared in front of the Western Wall, the last remaining remnant of the retaining wall of the Second Temple and the holiest relic on earth for the Jewish people. It expertly uses level changes and geometrical ordering devices to create a space that allows ten people to pray in comfort, but could also accommodate a celebration of three thousand people, or a demonstration of fifty thousand. He also designed a twenty-acre business district for Mamilah, the former demilitarized zone that separated the old and new cities when the older portion was controlled by Jordan.

The most impressive of the Jerusalem projects, though, and the most significant in terms of Safdie's own personal expression, is his Yeshivat Porat Joseph Rabbinical College in the heart of the Jewish Quarter of the old city, overlooking the Western Wall Plaza. The school is an interesting mixture of bold structure, modern highlights (including repetitive, transparent glass domes that diffract colored light on their inner surfaces), and environmental sensitivity and response. Despite the frankness of the contemporary structure, the Yeshivat blends into the ancient city perfectly, and mimics traditional patterns of color, texture, shape and proportion.

All of the Jerusalem projects display the frenzied, but handsome sense of movement that has been a trademark of Safdie's work, but they also demonstrate an improved ability to deform that expression to remain sensitive to surroundings. Still, in plan, all of the projects continue to be organized largely based on geometrical maneuvers, not unlike those used at Habitat and the San Francisco Student Union. While the geometries that Safdie has favored throughout his career have certainly increased the rationality of his arrangements, they have also frequently been the biggest cause of economic difficulty, by jacking expense needlessly to retain theoretical design purity.

Regardless of the effectiveness of Safdie's geometry, his resolution of problems of high-density construction with completely three-dimensional solutions has been a great architectural contribution. Safdie is a theorist who should be admired for the boldness of his experimentation. If occasionally his work lacks the refinement of a more conservative practitioner, it is only because Safdie realizes that unless one dares to skirt failure, no advance can be made.

—Mitchell B. Rouda

SAKAKURA, Junzo.

Japanese. Born in Hashima City, Gifu Prefecture, 29 May 1901. Educated at the Tokyo University School of Art, 1923-27; studied architecture in Paris, 1929-30; apprentice/assistant in the office of Le Corbusier, Paris, 1931-36. Married Yuri Sakakura in 1939; children: Huruna, Miho, and Takenosuke. Worked as a community planner in Manchuria, 1939; in private practice, Tokyo, 1939-46; Principal, Junzo Sakakura and Associates, Tokyo, 1947 until his death 1969 (associates: Fumitaka Nishizawa, now President; Taisaku Cho; Seizo Sakata; Akira Yamaki; Shinichiro Takemura; Takenobu Ohta; and Toshitsugu Nunokawa); branch office established in Osaka, 1948. President, Japan Architects Association, 1964-68. Recipient: Grand Prize, *World's Fair*, Paris, 1937. *Died 1 September 1969.*

Works:

1937 Japanese Pavilion, *World's Fair*, Paris

1941 Iihashi House, Todoroki, Setagaya-ku, Tokyo
1941/
50 Pre-fabricated wooden houses, Tokyo
1944 Tatsumura House, Takarazuka Hyogo Prefecture, Japan
1948 Low-cost bamboo furniture
1950 Osaka Baseball Stadium
Takashimaya Department Store remodelling, Namba, Osaka
1951 Department of Higher Education, Franco-Japanese Institute, Tokyo
Kamakura Museum of Modern Art, Kamakura, Kanagawa Prefecture, Japan
Club Kanto, Chiyoda-ku, Tokyo
1952 Club Kansai, Osaka
1954 Taro Okamoto House, Minato-ku, Tokyo
Muroga House, Nikawa, Nishinomiya, Hyogo Prefecture, Japan
Suzuki House, Ashiya City, Hyogo Prefecture, Japan
Maruyama Hydro-Electric Power Plant, Gifu Prefecture, Japan
Tohkyu Kaikan Building, Shibuya, Tokyo
1955 International House of Japan, Minato-ku, Tokyo (with Kunio Mayeawa and Junzo Yoshimura)
Shiono House, Shukugawa, Nishinomiya, Hyogo Prefecture, Japan
1956 Tohkyu Bunka Kaikan Building, Shibuya, Tokyo
Diesel Memorial Gardens, Augsburg, West Germany
1957 Exhibition design at the *Triennale*, Milan
1958 Shirokiya Department Store remodelling, Tokyo
1959 Hajima City Hall, Gifu Prefecture, Japan
National Museum of Western Art, Taito-ku, Tokyo (with Le Corbusier, Kunio Mayeawa, Takamasa Yosizaka)
Silk Center, Yokohama
Hakuba Tokyu Hotel, Nagano Prefecture, Japan
Iga-Ueno City Public Hall, Mie Prefecture, Japan
Yamaha Company Employees' Seaside Recreation Center, Bentenjima, Hamamatsu, Shizuoka, Japan
1960 Exhibition design at the *Triennale*, Milan
Air France Office, in the Hibiya Mitsui Building, Tokyo (with Charlotte Perriand)
Hannan High School, Osaka
1961 Shionogi Pharmaceutical Company Central Laboratory, Osaka
1962 Kure City Hall and Cultural Center, Hiroshima Prefecture, Japan
Shionogi Pharamaceutical Company Warehouse and Office, Kuise, Hyogo Prefecture, Japan
Toray Company Basic Research Laboratory, Kanagawa Prefecture, Japan
1963 Saga Prefectural Gymnasium, Saga City, Japan
Highway Toll-Gate (prototype)
1964 Hiraoka City Hall, Osaka
Hotel Sanai (Park Hotel), Sapporo, Hokkaido, Japan
Iwate Broadcasting Company Building, Morioka City, Iwate Prefecture, Japan
Shipping Center, Takashimaya Department Store, Osaka
1965 Annex, Kamakura Museum of Modern Art, Kanagawa, Prefecture, Japan
Iga-Ueno City Hall, Mie Prefecture, Japan
Shin Akasaka Building, Minato-ku, Tokyo
Gymnasium, Ueno Municipal Nishi Primary School, Ueno City, Mie Prefecture, Japan
1966 Nagoya Termianl Station Building, Aichi Prefecture, Japan
Westside Concoures, Shinjiku Station and Underground Parking Garage, Shinjuku, Tokyo
Osaka Youth Outdoor Activities Center
1967 Gifu City Municipal Culture Center, Japan

Junzo Sakakura: Metropolitan Gymnasium Complex, Yumenoshima, Tokyo, 1976.

Yamaguchi Prefectural Museum, Yamaguichi City, Japan
Kohshiro Matsumoto House, Minato-ku, Tokyo
Odaskyu Department Store and Shinjuku Terminal Shinjuku, Tokyo
1968 Takashimaya Kohsakusho Furniture Factory, Minoh City, Osaka
Hajima City Municipal Cultural Center, Gifu Prefecture, Japan
Shionogi Pharmaceutical Company Factory, Settsu City, Osaka
1969 Hotel Blue Sky, Shirahama, Wakayama Prefecture, Japan
Kashikojima Country Club House, Mie Prefecture, Japan
Electric Power Pavilion, *Expo '70*, Osaka
25 Vocational schools, Thailand
Westside Annex Building, Shibuya Station, Tokyo

Publications:

By SAKAKURA: articles—"Temoinages pour Le Corbusier," with Nicholas Colley, in *L'Architecture d'Aujourd'hui* (Paris), February/March 1966.

On SAKAKURA: books—*Contemporary Architecture of Japan* by Shinje Koike, Tokyo 1954; *New Japanese Architecture* by Udo Kultermann, New York 1960; *New Directions in Japanese Architecture* · by Robin Boyd, New York 1962, 1968; *An Architectural Journey in Japan* by James M. Richards, London 1963; *Three Japanese Architects: Mayekawa Tange, Sakakura* by Alfred Alther, New York 1968; articles—"Three New Buildings in Osaka by Junzo Sakakura and Associates" in *Kokusai Kentiku* (Tokyo), May 1956; "Air France, Tokyo" in *The Japan Architect* (Tokyo), December 1960; "The Architects," in special issue on Japan of *Architectural Review* (London), September 1962; "Gusto di Junzo Sakakura" in *L'Architettura* (Rome), September 1965; "A Profile of Junzo Sakakura" by Ryuichi Hamaguchi in *The Japan Architect* (Tokyo), November 1966; "Hommage à Sakakura" by Mayekawa, Sato, Perriand, Prouvé and Takemura in *Architecture d'Aujourd'hui* (Paris), October/November 1969; "Blue Sky Hotel" in *Architectural Design* (London), March 1970; "Training Schools Operated by the Thailand Department of Vocational Education" in *The Japan Architect* (Tokyo) June 1971.

Bibliography—*Junzo Sakakura: Follower of Le Corbusier* by James Philip Noffsinger, Monticello Illinois 1980;

Architecture is presented to us by Junzo Sakakura as a compact entity that patiently awaits our coming in order to exist, then overflows our conception; it is there, in our midst, dense and impenetrable, like a stone or a tree; it endures; finally, it is what it is. These characteristics are perhaps a consequence of Sakakura's six-year meditation in the office of Le Corbusier.

At best, as in the courtyard houses in Osaka, Sakakura's work has a cave-like quality, featuring an interiority well directed and orchestrated by the thick concrete threshold he sometimes mounted around the site to present the architectural entity. At worst, the raw concrete imprisons, the entity interupts the flow of human occurrences, making of the architecture a ludicrously heavy mass. Sometimes the whole is relieved by a delicacy of curve, an organic incident, such as the pitched roofs on the Osaka Youth Outdoor Activities Centre, or an improbable angle or an unprecedented detail, such as the giant vantilation snorkels undermining the overzealous devotion to the developer's dream in the Shinjuku Station project.

Massive concrete work doesn't necessarily insist on absolute and nihilistic enclosure; there are ways of relieving it through modelling and perforation. Too often, however, Sakakura thought only of keeping out the forces of the Japanese city—for him, unknown terrors lurked in every corner, and his only thought was to keep them out of the private domain of his own project. But, of course, by so doing, he unwittingly added to the terrors of the public domain.

Some Japanese architects tend to design as if they were sitting an exam: each one works on his own, jealous of his own performance, selfish, ready to come up with a tenuous, barely consolidated result rather than own up that he might welcome a bit of help from his neighbour. In architecture, this attitude can produce an environment of urgent morphologies and sensational architectural monsters or one of notorious vanity and ostentatious consumption. Although much of Sakakura's work was strong and possibly enduring, it as often seemed to be guilty of one or the other flaws.

—Chris Fawcett

SALMONA, Rogelio.
Colombian. Born in Paris, France, 28 April 1929. Educated at the Universidad Nacional de Colombia, Bogota, 1947-48, 1957-62, Dip.Arch. 1962; student/ apprentice, studio of Le Corbusier, Paris, 1949-58; Ecole des Hautes Etudes Sociales, Sorbonne, Paris, under Pierre Francastel, 1948-57; Ecole d'Arts et Metiers, Paris, 1952-54. Married Michelle Clement in 1959; children: Pablo and Juan. In private practice, Bogota, since 1958. Exhibitions: Universidad Autonoma de Mexico City, 1977, 1979; Centre Georges Pompidou, Paris, 1980; Universidad Autonoma de Santo Domingo, Dominican Republic, 1981; Universidad de Panama, Republic of Panama, 1981; Sociedad Central de Arquitectos de Buenos Aires, 1982 (travelled to Cordoba, La Plata and Rosario, Argentina); Sociedad de Arquitectos del Uruguay, Montevideo, 1982; *Architecture and Cultural Identity,* Quebec University, Montreal, 1982; *Bienal: Patrimonio y Presente,* Colegio de Arquitectos de Chile, Santiago, 1983; *Arquitectura Latino Americana,* Instituto de Arquitectos, Porto Alegre, Brazil, 1983. Recipient: First Prize, Colombian Architects Association Headquarters Competition, Bogota, 1971; National Prize, Colombian Architects Association, 1977. Address: Residencias El Parque, Carrera 5, No. 26-39, Bogota, Colombia.

Works:

1959 El Polo (apartment building), Bogota (with Guillermo Bermudez)
High School, Bogota
1961 House, Santa Ana Sector, Bogota
1961/
63 Residencias los Cerros (low-income apartments), Bogota
1962 High School, Bogota
1963 Residencias San Cristobal (low-income apartments), Bogota
1965 Timiza (housing and urban development), Bogota (project)
House, Cabrera Sector, Bogota
House, Santa Margerita Sector, Bogota
1965/
70 Residencias El Parque (apartments), Bogota
1966 House, Los Rosales Sector, Bogota
Gutierrez House, Medellín, Colombia
1968 Amaral House, El Refugio Sector, Bogota
1969 Usatama (urban development), Bogota (project)
Low-rise, multi-family housing development, Pereira, Colombia (project)
1970 Calle 72 (apartment building), Bogota
El Museo (apartment building), Bogota
City Hall, Bogota
Independence Park renovation, Bogota
Alba House, El Chico Sector, Bogota
1971 El Rodadero (apartment building), Santa Marta, Colombia
El Retiro (apartment building), Bogota
Colombian Architects Association Headquarters, Bogota
Automobile and Touring Club Headquarters, Bogota (with Luis Esguerra)
Umaña House, Bosque el Retiro Sector, Bogota
1974 Rafael Nunez (housing and urban development), Bogota
1975 San Diego (office and housing complex), Bogota
Museum of Modern Art, Bogota
Puente House, Suba Sector, Bogota
1976 El Pinar (apartment building), Bogota
House, Bosque el Retiro Sector, Bogota
1977 Arango House, Bogota
Gómez House, Medellín, Colombia

Rogelio Salmona: Residencias El Parque, Bogota, Colombia, 1970.

1978 Alto de Los Pinos (apartment building), Bogota

Franco Country House, Tabio, Colombia

1978/
79 Housing and Urban Development, Cali, Colombia (project)

1979 Jorge Eliecer Gaitan Cultural Centre, Bogota

Boarding-House, Cartagena, Colombia

1984 Quimbaya Cultural Centre, Armenia, Colombia

Publications:

On SALMONA: books—*Multi-Storey Housing* by Karl Wilhelm Smith, Stuttgart 1966; *New Directions in Latin-American Architecture* by Francisco Bullrich, New York and London 1969; *Rogelio Salmona*, Buenos Aires 1975; *Crítica e Imagen* by Germán Tellez, Bogota, Colombia 1978; *Panorama de la Arquitectura Latino-Americana* by Damian Bayon and Paolo Gasparini, Barcelona 1978, as *The Changing Shape of Latin American Architecture*, Chichester, Sussex 1979; *Architectures Colombiennes* by Anne Berty, Paris 1981; articles—"In South America: After Corbu, What's Happening?" in *Progressive Architecture* (New York), September 1966; "Immeuble d'Habitation à Bogota" and "Habitat" in *Architecture d'Aujourd'hui* (Paris), February/March 1967; "Logements Economiques à Bogota" in *A.C. 49* (Zurich), 1968; "L'Architettura di Rogelio Salmona" in *Controspazio* (Bari, Italy), No. 8, 1972; "The Architecture of Rogelio Salmona" by J. A. Acebillo in *Arquitecturas Bis* (Barcelona), September 1975; "Amaral House, Bogota" in *Architecture d'Aujourd'hui* (Paris), no. 192, 1977; "The Recent Works of Rogelio Salmona", special issues of *Proa* (Bogota, Colombia), April and May 1983.

The works of Le Corbusier exerted a notable influence throughout the world, particularly in Latin America, where his ideas were adopted by a generation of architects who carried out the modernization of local architecture. Le Corbusier had also proposed urbanization plans for the South American cities of Buenos Aires and Rio de Janeiro, and in 1949 the Colombian government commissioned him to draw up a pilot plan for the capital, Bogota, a plan that was later developed by Josep Lluis Sert and Paul Lester Wiener. The plan is based on the principle of urban sectors; the land is divided into rectangular areas; there is an efficient rapid transit system. As in other Latin American countries, the influence of the International Style was already great in Colombia, and with the creation of the Bogota plan, Colombian architecture took a markedly rationalist road. It is within this context that the work of Rogelio Salmona should be analyzed.

Salmona worked for a number of years in Le Corbusier's studio in Paris, but on returning to Colombia he became, paradoxically, one of his former teacher's most outspoken critics. One of the reasons may well have been that the great man's precepts had begun to look more and more inappropriate in Colombia. During the 1950s a series of profound social changes had taken place. There was a displacement of masses of people to the cities, with an attendant deterioration of the environment; simultaneously, of course, there was wholesale real estate speculation, from which it followed that "rentability" became a prime criterion even for the architect. It is precisely in response to this new situation that Salmona developed his own ideas on architecture and urbanization—and these ideas have informed his work ever since.

His ideas are easily summarized. Architecture and city planning in Colombia are in a state of crisis created by the country's rapid urbanization and its attendant economic structure. This crisis is manifested in works that deny the most significant values of Colombian architectural culture, works that offer impoverished images and serve to decrease (rather than enhance) the variety of the urban morphology. Although there are excellent examples of modern architecture in Colombia, most modern works unfortunately support the generalization. By sacrificing the most important social, cultural, and topological values, architecture has given in to commercialism and conformity. The ideals of rationalist architecture do not provide the answer, for rationalist models are, almost by intention, foreign to the social and cultural values of their surroundings.

Salmona practices what he preaches. His vision is of an architecture that identifies with a particular and historical place and site, one that adds to by participating in its environment, and this vision is manifest in all his works, particularly the outstanding Residencias El Parque.

Salmona does not accept that the city must look like a chessboard—an image that has become almost an immutable fact of contemporary architecture. Because, with each project, he tries, as it were, to visualize the city afresh, his works are often greeted with controversy and an initial rejection that gradually dissipates as the virtues of his proposals become apparent. Further, he makes himself unpopular with a certain segment of his society by rejecting the goals of land speculation; in his work, he maintains occupation densities that are appropriate to people. And he often surprises by using his works to incorporate urban space into the environment—evidence of his belief that architecture is made for the whole man, that architecture is as much the property of the community as the sky.

Although this adroit handling of spatial volume is its most notable characteristic, his work is also interesting in other ways. For example, he is concerned with creating original, well-designed, low-cost housing for low-income groups. So are architects in many other parts of the world, but in Colombia there is a general attitude that fashionable architects create for fashionable clients; architecture involves a series of signs that denote prestige. As well, Salmona often uses brick, a material that is traditional to Colombia. The choice is not gratuitous. By using brick, he can relate his work to the existing urban landscape.

Yet perhaps, after all, Salmona's greatest accomplishment is that he has made his countrymen look at their cities. His main criticism of rationalist architecture and its seeming triumph is that now all cities, particularly Colombian ones, despite their historical, cultural, and regional differences, increasingly resemble one another. There is no sense of place; the constructions have no cultural or social meaning. He blames architect themselves for this decline—makes them responsible for contributing to urban chaos, for responding to extravagant rather than real needs, for giving in to economic power. He makes his countrymen regard the seemingly ubiquitous cement wall that destroys or blocks the Colombian landscape and reminds them that buildings occupy an urban space that belongs to the entire community.

Salmona has created an alternative. The Residencias El Parque are a good example. The building code allowed for one hundred percent land occupancy. Salmona used twenty percent of it for building and used the rest for open promenades and gardens for the use of the public. He proposed a series of volumes that would balance the needs of the program, economic rentability, and the characteristics of the site—and created buildings that present an outline appropriate to Bogota, encompass the green background of the city's mountains, and make use of the natural materials of the area. The never less than superb execution of his vision makes Salmona the most important figure in contemporary Colombian architecture.

—Jorge Glusberg

SAMONÀ, Giuseppe.

Italian. Born in Palermo, Sicily, 8 April 1898. Educated at the University of Palermo, Dip.Civ.Ing. 1922. Married Teresa Favara in 1923; children: Adele, Carmelo and Alberto. In private practice, Messina, 1922-58. Established office in Venice, 1936; Principal, with Giuseppina Marcialis Samonà and Alberto Samonà, Studio Samonà, Rome, 1958 until his death in 1983. Assistant Design Instructor, Faculty of Engineering, University of Messina, 1927-30; Instructor, Faculty of Architecture, University of Naples, 1931-36; Instructor, 1936-45, and Professor of Architectural Composition, and Director, 1945-71, Insitute of Architecture, Venice. Member, National Planning Legislation Committee, 1963-65; Senator of the Re-public of Italy, 1972. Exhibition: *Giuseppe Samonà*, Palazzo Grassi, Venice, 1975. Recipient: First Prize, Palazzata Resort Complex Competition, Messina, 1930; First Prize, Emergency Hospital Competition, Rome, 1947; Olivetti National Prize, 1958; First Prize, Regional Development Plan Competition, Messina, 1960; First Prize, City Centre Competition, Turin, 1962; Special Prize, New Sacca del Tronchetto Competition, Venice, 1964; IN-ARCH National Prize for Architecture, 1964. *Died* (in Rome) *in 1983*.

Works:

1922 Monument to the War Dead, Milan (project)

1923 Monument to the War Dead, Milan (2nd project)

1925 New Pulpit, Cathedral of Trento, Italy (competition project)

1928 parish churches, Calabria, Italy (projects)

Postal and Telecommunications Building, Naples (competition project)

Municipal Hall, Merano, Italy (competition project)

1929 Cathedral, La Spezia, Italy (competition project)

Palace of Justice, Campobasso, Italy (competition project)

1930 School of Science and Technical Institute, Syracuse, Italy (project; with Camillo Autore)

Villa Bellin restoration and alterations, Catania, Italy (with Camillo Autore)

New Seaside Resort Centre, Messina (competition project; with Camillo Autore)

Developement plan for Bolzano, Italy (competition project; with Enrico Calandra and Camillo Autore)

1931 Wool and Grain Market Building, Foggia, Italy (competition project)

1932 Giuffrida Funeral Chapel, Montevago, Agrigento, Italy

Giuffrida Country Villa, Montevago, Agrigento, Italy (project)

Church in Paradiso, Messina (competition project)

Church of Mary, Milazzo (competition project)

Church of San Filippo Neri, Messina (competition project)

Civil Service Building, Bari, Italy (competition project)

1933 Castellaneta Villa, San Severo, Foggia, Italy (project)

Passenger Terminal Building, Santa Maria Novena Station, Florence (competition project)

P.T.T. Services Building, Nomentano Quarter, Rome (competition project)

1933/
36 P.T.T. Services Building, Appio Quarter, Rome

1934 Exhibition Hall, *Exposition of the Fascist Revolution*, Rome (competition project)

1934/
35 Savings Bank Headquarters, Modena, Italy (competition project)

Apartment Building Development, Palermo (project)

Cinema lobby alterations, Ostia, Italy (project)

Auditorium, Rome (competition project)

1936 Police Magistrates Office Complex, Rome (competition project; with Mario de Renzi)

P.T.T. Employees' Apartment Building, via Taranto, Rome (project)

1936/
40 Government Officals House, Messina

1937 Casa Littoria, Rome (competition project)

1938/
40 Villa, Baia, Italy (project)

GIL Building, Messina (project)

INFAIL Headquaters, Messina (project)

San Paolo Bridge, Rome (project)

Apartment building, via Dalmazia, Rome (partially built)

Palace of Italian Civilization, E 42 Development, Rome (competition project; with Viola)

Palace of Agriculture and Land Reclamation, E 42 Development, Rome (project; with Marconi and Viola)

1939 INFPS Headquarters, Rome (competition project; with Viola)

Central Residential Development, Gaeta, Italy (project)

Development study of the Via Latina and Via Appia, Rome

1945 Crystal Palace Development, London (competition project)

Urban development plan for the Lavinaio Quarter, Naples

1946 Entrance Building, *Mediterranean Fair*, Palermo (project)

1947 INAIL Hospital, Rome (competition project)

1948 Apartment Building, Livorno (project)

Apartment Building, Turin (project)

1949 Office/Apartment Building, Sampierdarena, Genoa (project)

INA Office/Apartment Building, Treviso Italy

1950 Scimeni Villa, Mondello, Palermo

Apartment building, Rome

INAIL Revenue Building, Venice

1951 INA-CASA Housing Development, Palma Montechiaro, Italy (project)

INAIL Office Building, Livorno (project)

INAIL Hospital, Palermo (project)

1952 INAIL Office/Apartment Building, San Simeone, Venice (1st project; with E Trincanto)

INA-CASA Housing Development, Palma Montechiaro, Italy (project)

INA-CASA Housing Development, Sciacca, Italy

1953 INCIS Housing Development, Padua

INAIL Orthopaedic Hospital, Bari, Italy

Messina Seaside Resort Centre

SGES Headquaters, Palermo (1st project)

1954 INAIL Apartment Building, Livorno (project)

1955 Palazzo Camarata interior renovations, Palermo (project)

SGES Headquarters, Palermo (2nd project)

1956 Borgo Ulivia Experimental Housing Estate, Palermo (with Bonafede, Calandra, and Caracciolo)

INPS Headquarters, Messina Seaside Resort Centre

TIFEO Electrical Centre, Augusta, Italy

INAIL Office/Apartment Building, San Simeone, Venice

1957 Apartment Block, Block XI, Messina Seaside Resort Centre

Urban development plan for Brescia, Italy

1959 CEP Housing Development, Barene di San Giuliano Mestre, Venice (competition project; with Piccinato, Astengo, Calabi, and Majoli)

National Library, Rome (competition project; with Pizzetti and Quilici)

1960 Regional development plan for Messina (competition project)

Thermo Electric Stations (prototypes)

Apartment building, Syracuse, Italy

Villa in the Parco Flora, Albaro, Genoa (project)

Apartment/office building, Palermo

1961 ENEL Office Building, Milazzo, Italy (project)

SGES-ENEL Office Building, Palermo

TIFEO Thermo-Electric Station, Termini Imerese, Italy

ENEL Office Building, Syracuse, Italy

1962 Regional development plan for Milazzo, Italy (competition project)

Provincial development plan for Messina

Machinery/Servicing Buildings, Hydro-Electrical Centre, Sardinia (project)

Directional Centre for Turin (competition project; with Dardi, Mattioni, Pastor, Semerani, Tamaro, Trincanato, and Vianello Vos)

ENEL Thermo-Electric Centre, Trapani, Italy (project)

Provincial town plan for Trento, Italy

Regional development plan for Cavarzere, Venice (with Dardi, Trincanato and Bellemo)

Macchi House, Zitelle, Venice (project)

1963 National Providence and Credit Insitute Headquarters, Palermo (competition project)

Morroy-Persico Inn, via delle Regione, Palermo (project)

SCEIS commercial and development plan for Palermo

1964 Regional development plan for Villa San Giovanni, Italy

Office Building conversion, Mestre, Venice (project)

Territorial plan for the industrial belt of Milazzo, Messina (project; with Calandra and Bonafede)

New development plan for the Sacca del Tronchetto Venice (competition project; with Dardi, Mattioni, Pastor, Polesello, Tarmaro, Semarani, and Trincanato)

Regional development plan for Scilla, Italy

Comprehensive urban plan for Vajont, Italy

Group of villas, Falconarossa Baida, Palermo

1965 Regional development plan for Castiglione dello Stiviere, Garda, Italy (project; with Giovanazzi and Marconi)

Regional development plan for Cefalu, Sicily (project; with Doglio, Clandra, and Bonafede)

Regional development for Meda, Milan (project; with Cagna)

ANAS Divisional Headquarters, Palermo (project; with Cappellani and Di Cristina)

Mutual Insurance Company Building renovations, Largo Chigi, Rome (with Pizzetti)

1966 Mountain colony, near Ravenna

School complex, near Ravenna (project; as consultant architect)

Corso Clatafimi Residential Complex, Palermo (project)

Palazzo Francavilla restoration, Palermo (project; with Ziino)

Regional development plan for Palmi, Italy (with Doglio and Morabito)

1967 Chamber of Deputies Building, Rome (compition project)

Plan for the Veneta region, Italy (project; with others)

1968 Banco d'Italia Headquarters, Padua (with Pizzetti)

1969 Civic and Cultural Centre, Secondigliano, Naples (project; with Giannattasio)

Giuseppe Samonà: Banco d'Italia Headquarters, Padua, 1968.

Vulcanello Tourist Village, Vulcano Italy (project)

Permanent Road-Link Between Sicily and the Italian Mainland (competition project; with others)

1970 Civic, Cultural and Commercial Centre, Gibellina, Italy (project; with Gregotti and Pirrone)

1971 Portonovo Beach Development, Ancona, Italy (project)

Bank of Sicily Headquarters and Piazza Croci Redevelopment, Palermo (project)

New University of Cagliari, Italy (competition project; with others)

Territorial plan for the thermal zone of Sciacca, Sicily

1973 University of Calabria, Italy (competition project)

1974/
79 Theatre, Sciacca, Sicily

1975 Master plan for the centre of Florence (competition project; with others)

1976/
79 Plan for the old town centre of Montepulciano, Italy

1978 Apartment and office building, Fano, Italy

1980 Historic City Centre Plan, Palermo, Sicily (with G. De Carlo, B. DiCristina and A. M. Sciarra)

1981/
82 Town Centre Plan, Cadoneghe, Padua, Italy

Town Hall addition, Cadoneghe, Padua, Italy

1983 Tête-Defense Development, Paris (competition project)

Publications:

By SAMONÀ: books—*Elements Medioevali nell' architettura del secolo XVI in Provincia di Messina,* Naples 1935; *Monumenti Medioevali nel Retroterra di Cefalu,* Naples 1935; *Schemi Compositivi di Palazzi Napoletani del '500,* Naples 1935; *La Casa Popolare,* Naples 1935; *Il Duomo di Cefalu,* Rome 1940; *L'Urbanistica e l'Avvenire della Citta,* Bari, Italy 1959; *Venezia, Caduta e Salvezza,* Florence 1970; *L'Unita Architectura Urbanistica,* Milan 1975; *L'Urbanistica e l'Avvenire della Citta negli Stati Europei,* Rome 1975; *Il Dibattito architettonico in Italia, 1945-1975,* with C. Conforto and others, Rome 1977; articles—numerous in Italian periodicals since 1928, including *L'Architettura, Metron, Casabella, Urbanistica* and *Zodiac.*

On SAMONÀ: books—*Giuseppe Samaonà: La Casa Popolare degli Anni '30,* introduction by Mario Manieri-Elia, Padua 1973; *Giuseppe Samona: L'Unita Archiettura Urbanistica: Scritti e Progetti 1929-73* by Pasquale Lovero, Milan 1975; *Giuseppe Samona: Cinquant'Anni di Architettura,* exhibition catalogue, by Carlo Aymonino, Giorgio Cucci, Francesco dal Co, and Manfredo Tafuri, Rome 1975; articles—"Risveglio Architettonico in Sicilia" in *L'Architettura* (Rome), no. 11, 1932; "Recensione a Giuseppe Samona: La Casa Popolare" by Enrico Calandra in *L'Architettura* (Rome), no. 14, 1935; "Il Centro Traumatologico di Bari e Il Nucelo Residenziale in Padova dell'Architetto Giuseppe Samonà" by Giancarlo De Carlo in *Casabella* (Milan), no. 206, 1955; "Giuseppe Samonà" in *Cronache di Architettura* (Bari, Italy), no. 273, 1971; "Progetti dello Studio Giuseppe e Alberto Samona 1968-72" by Pasquale Lovero in *Controspazio* (Bari, Italy), no. 2, 1973; "Samona and Urban Architectural Unity" by Pasquale Lovero in *Parametro* (Bologna), September/October 1975; "Two Competitions" in *Casabella* (Milan), February 1980; "Giuseppe Samona" in *Arquitecturas Bis* (Barcelona), January/April 1980; "Giuseppe Samona, architetto," special issue of *Architetti Venezia* (Venice), November/December 1983; "Remembrances of Giuseppe Samona, 1898-1983" by Vittorio Gregotti

in *Casabella* (Milan), December 1983; "Giuseppe Samona, teacher and author, has died" in *Architettura* (Rome), January 1984.

Giuseppe Samonà summarized his own career as one devoted to architectural design, urban planning and political involvement. To this must be added a long and illustrious history as an educator.

In his architecture Samona leaned toward eclecticism and expressionism, the result of an interst in the differences rather than the commonalities in architectural-urban problems. General rules fail too often, he said, because they do not fit specific cases. His electicism ranged over a wide variety of forms and approaches in his architectural compositions, even allowing him the audacity to design a single building with quite dissimilar facades (the Banca d'Italia in Padua) in an attempt to harmonize with the particular character of each of the urban ambiences toward which the facades happened to face. His interest in expressionism in architecture helped to avoid standardization and to emphasize the uniqueness of each problem.

The unifying themes behind his work have been: the vision of nature with it complex interrelationships as an exemplar of cities and buildings; and a strong political bias toward socialism and a related emphasis on an architecture that can simultaneously respond to and fulfil political, social and economic goals together with those that are aesthetic and functional.

Several of his most dramatic architectural projects have been unrealized. These include the competition project for the Chamber of Deputies Building in Rome in 1967, which displays a vigorously thrusting composition of cantilevered volumes and planes partially supported by an irregualr arrangement of exaggeratedly slender "pilotis;" the Directional Centre for the city of Turin, 1962, similary composed of floating planes, but within an attenuated complex streching for nearly a kilometer from end to end; and the project for a villa in Baia, near Naples, of 1938-40, which, like the later works cited, seems to synthesize ideas derived from Wright, Le Corbusier and constructivism, but displays a compositional sophistication seldom realized by other architects until several decades later.

As much rewoned as an educator as a practicing architect, Samona, immediately after World War II, gathered together in the School of Architecture in Venice a variety of architects and artists who had been excluded from full participation in their professions by the Fascist regime, and in a manner reminiscent of Walter Groupius and the Bauhaus, forged a community spirit of progressivism which, for at least two decades, kept the Venice School in the forefront of modern architectural thought.

During the later half of his career a close collaborator was Egle Renata Tricanato, a reowned Venetian architect, scholar and teacher, whom he eventually married. He worked actively on urban and architectural projects almost until his death in Rome in his eighty-sixth year.

—Abraham Rogatnick

SANDROCK, Brian.

South African. Born in Bloemfontein, 10 November 1925. Educated at the Boys High School, Kimberley, matriculated 1942; University of Pretoria, Dip. Arch. 1952, M.Arch. 1959. Served as a pilot in the South African Air Force, seconded to the Royal Air Force, Italy, 1942-45: Lieutenant. Married Thelma Athene Wilson in 1951; son: Peter. Since 1953, in private practice, Pretoria. Lecturer in Design and the History of Architecture, University of Pretoria, 1954-59. Address: Halcyon Place, 426 King's Highway, Lynnwood, Pretoria 0081, South Africa.

Works:

1956/
84 Various buildings for the University of Pretoria

1960/
84 National Nuclear Research Centre, Pelindaba, near Pretoria

1962/
84 New campus for the University of South Africa, Pretoria

1975 Sandrock Studio and Penthouse, Lynnwood, Pretoria

1984 South African Medical and Dental Council National Headquarters, Pretoria

Publications:

By SANDROCK: article—"Pelindaba Today" in *Planning and Building Developments* (Braamfontein, South Africa), July/August 1979.

On SANDROCK: articles—"Human Sciences Building, Pretoria University" in *Planning and Building Developments* (Braamfontein, South Africa), May/June 1977; "Huis Magrietjie—New Women's Residence for the University of Pretoria" in *Architect and Builder* (Cape Town), South Africa, September 1982.

Brian Sandrock is probably the most distinguished and least publicized of the new generation of South African architects who emerged after World War II. His architectural training began during the poswar years of building austerity when the hoped-for architectural developments had not yet arrived and the profession was mainly occupied in overcoming the backlog of housing and in utilitarian building. The new wave of industry generated during the war was growing, however; a shift in political power, large-scale immigration from other parts of the world, and a loosening of ties with the United Kingdom brought new attitudes and values. One of the effects of these events on South African architecture was that the former English and American Beaux-Arts oriented influence on architectural practice and education (which had, in the 1930s, been breached by the influence of German and French thinking) faded.

Sandrock's teaching career at the new department of architecture at the University of Pretoria occurred during a period of radical change in architectural education; courses were no longer confined to design with particular emphasis on its artistic aspects but were reoriented towards an integrated and total concept of architecture and design was combined with the practical and technical sunjects of technical construction and the different faces of building sciences and services. In time, administration and economics came to be given more weight than before, and courses were broadened to include the humanities and the work of other design specialists.

The beginning of practice for Sandrock, and the accomplished associates he gathered round him after 1950, was in a climate of economic and population growth and expanding techndological and scientific developments in the field of electric power, the production of steel and other materials and building components—with architecture, subject to such imperatives, becoming less a personal art or the personal interpretation of individual needs. Sandrock's recognition of and use of science and technology in architecture has always gone hand in hand with his respect and concern for the needs of the human spirit, an approach which led him to the creation of fine architecture. In the main, this approach has been revealed within his exploration of the notably complex aspects of comprehensive planning for the long-term development of universities and nuclear research installations.

Brian Sandrock: University of Pretoria Stage I, South Africa, 1962-84.

The rationality of his planning, the enormous scale of projects, enriched by exotic and indigenous plants, creepers, shrubs, and trees, and, on occasion, their spectacular nature, reveals a talent that provides not olny vigour but also wit and elegance in buildings of an independent kind. He has also the ability, which is evident at Pelindaba, to make the Transvaal vernacular of brick and concrete merge into its setting or, with a splendid sense of structure and theatre, to command it: the delta-shaped administration bloack on the campus of the University of Pretoria, with its tall, swept back walls composed of complex, curving surfaces to shield the building against the western sun and traffic noise, provides a flat suburban setting with a point of focus. At the University of South Africa, the long, tiered administrative building, partly supported and cantilevered from a single, giant square column, dominates the capital city contained in the valley below.

—Doreen Greig

SARTORIS, Alberto.

Italian. Born in Turin, 2 February 1901. Educated at primary school and La Roseraie Professional School, Geneva, 1907-16; studied architecture, under Henri Gallay, Ecole des Beaux-Arts, and as a diploma-student in the office of architects Revillod and Turrettini, Geneva, 1916-17, Dip.Arch. 1923. Served in the Italian Army, Turin, 1921. Married Giovana Zoë Giovanna in 1922 (separated, 1929); Carla Prina in 1943. Collaborated with the architects Annibale Rigotti, Turin, and Raimondo D'Aronco, Udine, Italy, and the painter Felice Casorati, Turin, 1923-27; in private practice, Turin, 1923-39, and in Geneva, Rivaz, Lutry, and Cossonay, Switzerland, since 1930. Professor, Institut d'Architecture Atheneum, Lausanne, Switzerland, 1945-73; Professor of Architectural Composition and of the History of Art and Architecture, Académie Cantonale des Beaux-Arts, Sion, Switzerland, 1950-55; Professor of Art History, Université Populaire, Lausanne, Switzerland, 1951-53, and at the Faculty of Arts and Letters, Université de Lausanne, Switzerland, 1959-60; Professor of Urban Studies, Department of Architecture, Ecole Polytechnique Fédérale de Lausanne, Switzerland, since 1976. Associated with the Italian Futurist Movement, from 1920; co-founder, Movimento Italiano di Architettura Razionalista, 1928; founder-member, CIAM: Congrès Internationaux d'Architecture Moderne, and of Commissione Internazionale per la Realizazzione del Problema Architettonico Contemporanea, 1928; Artistic Counsellor, International Independent Cinema Cooperative, 1929; Member of Theo van Doesburg's De Stijl group, 1930; founder-member, Union des Artistes Moderne, and the Cercle et Carré artists' group, Paris, 1930; member, Abstraction-Création artists' group, Paris, 1931-36; founder-member, Abstract Artists Group of Como, Italy, 1935. Editor-in-Chief, *La città futurista*, Turin, 1929, *Présence*, Geneva, 1931, and *La città nuova*, Turin, 1932; Art and Architecture Critic, *Feuille d'avis officielle*, Geneva, 1931, and *Il popolo di Brescia*, 1939; Head of the Editorial Committee, *Architecture-Formes-Fonctions*, Lausanne, Switzerland, 1956. Secretary-General, Antonio Fontanesi Society for Fine Arts, Turin, 1923; Swiss Committee President, World Urbanism Day, 1935; President, School of Altamira, Spain, 1949; Vice-President, International Le Corbusier Association, 1974; President of the International Commission on Habitat, Art and Environment, East Berlin, 1975; International Association for the Development of African Architecture and Urbanism, 1975; International Association of Integrated Architecture and Urbanism, 1979; International Association for a Public Habitat, 1982; International Association of the 'Thirties, 1985. Exhibitions: Palazzo Reale, Monza, Italy, 1927; Musée Rath, Geneva, 1927; Museum of Modern Art, New York, 1927; *Biennale*, Venice, 1928, 1976; Galleria del Milione, Milan, 1932; Musée Jenisch, Vevey, Switzerland, 1932; Galleria d'Arte Moderna, Rome, 1933; Galleria Milano, Milan, 1934; Galleria Martano, Turin, 1972, 1983; Wroclaw, Poland, 1975; *Biennale*, Paris, 1977; Kunstmuseum, Münster, West Germany, 1978; Musée d'Art Moderne, Paris, 1978; Ecole Polytechnique Fédérale, Zürich, 1978; Musée des Beaux-Arts, La Chaux de Fonds, Switzerland, 1979; Galleria Nazionale d'Arte Moderna, Rome, 1979; Museo d'Arte Contemporanea, Milan, 1979; Calouste Gulbenkian Foundation, Lisbon, 1980; Academy of Fine Arts, Porto, Portugal, 1981; Royal Palace, Evora, Portugal, 1981; Galerie d'Art Moderne, Geneva, 1981; Museo Cortes, Naples, 1982; Centre d'Art Contemporain, Geneva, 1982; Le Nouveau Musée, Villeurbanne, France, 1982; Institute of Technology, Old Westbury, New York, 1982; Laboratorio Architettura Contemporanea, Rome, 1982; Manoir de la Ville, Martigny, Switzerland, 1983; University of Cincinnati, Ohio, 1983; Royal College of Art, London, 1983; Centre Georges Pompidou, Paris, 1984; Neue Nationalgalerie, West Berlin, 1984; Musée Cantonal des Beaux-Arts, Lausanne, Switzerland, 1984; Palazzo delle Belle Arti, Milan, 1985; Museu de Arte Contemporaneo, Sao Paulo, 1985; Centro de Arte y Comunicacion, Buenos Aires, 1985; *Triennale*, Milan, 1985. Recipient: Grand Prize for Architecture, Turin, 1927.

D.Sc.: Ecole Polytechnique Fédérale de Lausanne, Switzerland, 1976. Honorary Professor of Architecture, University of Buenos Aires, 1985. Honorary Member: Belgian Society of Modern Architects and Town Planners; Royal Institute of British Architects; Swiss Society of Engineers and Architects; Federation of Swiss Architects; Swiss Society of Painters and Sculptors; International Association of Art Critics; French Archaeological Society of the International Centre for Roman Studies; Institute of Studies of the Canary Islands; American Institute of Architects. Member, Société Française d'Architecture; Accademia Italiana Tiberina; Argentine Academy of Fine Arts; Royal Academy of Spain. Commander, Order of Merit, Italy. Addresses: (home) 8 rue des Etangs, 1304 Cossonay-Ville, Vaud, Switzerland; (office) 11 rue des Bons-Enfants, 1304 Cossonay-Ville, Vaud, Switzerland.

Works:

1920 Futurist Chapel (project)
Group of Editorial Buildings (project)
1921 Mediterranean Pergola in steel, glass, and concrete (projects)
1922 Housing, commercial, industrial, and urban building studies (project)
1922/
24 Aircraft and automobile chassis studies for Ceirano, Turin (projects)
Modern German architecture studies
1923 University Centre urban plan (project)
1923/
25 Suburban Building Complex, Turin (project)
1923/
26 Royal Buildings, Siam (with Annibale Rigotti)

Sanctuary Building, Gemona, Italy (with Raimondo D'Aronco)
Theatre Gualino, Turin (with Felice Casorati)
1924/
25 Santa Sindone and Baroque architecture studies, Turin
1925 Stadium quarter urban studies, Turin
Casa Minima ("the smallest house in the world": 6 × 6 m.), Turin
Professor Lionello Venturi Studio (project)
1926/
27 Rural multi-family housing for the Turin district (project)
1927 Workshop and industrial building complex, Geneva (project)
1927/
28 Comunità Autonome Artigiane Building and artisans' workshops, for the 1928 Exposition, Parco Valentino, Turin
1929 Theatre of the Avant-garde, Geneva (project)
Palace of Fine Arts, Milan (project)
1930 Villa-studio for the painter Jean Saladin van Berchem, Paris
House for the poet Henri Ferrare, Geneva
1931 Cité Cremaillère high-rise office building (project)
Notre Dame du Phare Cathedral, Fribourg, Switzerland (project)
1932 Catholic Church, Lourtier, Valls, Switzerland
Moret House, Martigny, Valls, Switzerland
Church, Sarreyer, Valls, Switzerland (project)
1932/
33 Société Immobilière Madeleine-Foncière Building, Vevey, Switzerland
Public Housing Block, Lausanne, Switzerland
1933 Villa Ghisletti, Geneva
1933/
35 Morand-Pasteur House, Saillon, Valls, Switzerland

Cercle de l'Ermitage Club interiors, Epesse, Vaud, Switzerland
1934 Institute of Music, Aigle, Switzerland
Selhofer Bookshop, Lausanne, Switzerland
Workers' Refectory at Frederic Fonjallaz House, Epesse, Vaud, Switzerland
Dr. Brum House, Lausanne, Switzerland
1936 Villa Selhofer, St.-Sulpice, Vaud, Switzerland (project)
House for a horticulturist, Geneva (project)
1937 Villa Gentinetta, Chexbres, Vaud, Switzerland
Campari restaurant conversions, Galleria Vittorio Emanuele, Milan (with Pietro Lingeri and Giuseppe Terragni)
Henri Ferrare House, Geneva
1938/
39 Houses and studios for the painters Italo and Vincenzo Grandi, at Vevey and Coseaux, Switzerland
Workers' Satellite City, Rebbio, Como, Italy (with Giuseppe Terragni)
1939/
40 Workers' Quarter, via Anzani, Como, Italy (with Giuseppe Terragni)
1940 Francis D. Berthoud et Cie Company Offices, Avanches, Vaud, Switzerland (projects)
1942 Sartoris House: Casa Ideale (project)
1950 Villa, Lutry, Vaud, Switzerland
1952 College, Lutry, Vaud, Switzerland
1952/
53 A. Farina House, Tenerife, Canary Islands (two projects)
1952/
55 Residential and Commercial Developments, Canary Islands (projects)
1953 Hotel Excelsior Turismo, Puerto de la Cruz, Tenerife, Canary Islands
Group of six garages, Renens, Switzerland
Villa, Prilly, Vaud, Switzerland

Alberto Sartoris: Lesieur Industrial Complex, Dunquerque, France, 1982-84.

1953/
54 Doctor Brunig Villa, Puerto de la Cruz, Tenerife, Canary Islands
1954/
55 Study Centre, Puerto de la Cruz, Tenerife, Canary Islands (project)
1955 Urban Plan for a Rural Town (project)
Rental Housing Complex, Crissier, Vaud, Switzerland
1955/
57 Church of Notre Dame du Bon Conseil, Louriter, Valls, Switzerland
1958/
59 Marinetti Tomb, Cimitero Monumentale, Milan (project)
1959 Residential quarter with hotel, gas station, and garages, Lutry, Switzerland
Charles Keller Commercial Building, Vienna (project)
Charles Keller Garage, Saint-Prex, Vaud, Switzerland
Post Office, Chatillens, Vaud, Switzerland
1960 World Centre for Health, Gingins, Vaud, Switzerland
Duplex Rental Apartment Building, Lutry, Switzerland
Huber House, St.-Sulpice, Vaud, Switzerland
1961/
62 Materco S.A. Factory, Mies, Geneva
1961/
64 Motel, Cully, Vaud, Switzerland (seven projects)
1962/
66 Housing Development, Lutry, Switzerland (seven projects)
1963/
65 Prefabricated Urban Complex, Varazze, Italy
1964 Chiolero House, Lutry, Switzerland
Housing and Office Block, Vassin, La-Tour-de-Peilz, Vaud, Switzerland
1964/
65 Old Town Quarter Redevelopment, Lutry, Switzerland
1965/
67 Mont-Fleuri Quarter Plan, Territet, Switzerland
1966 Villa Complex in a Park, Combe d'Aubagnac-Sete, Herault, France (project)
Guidetti Villa, Lutry, Switzerland
1967 Calabro-Sade Motels prefabricated expandable prototypes (projects)
Modular Urban Plan, Baugny-sur-Clarens, Vaud, Switzerland
Rental House, Montreux, Switzerland
1969 School Complex, Lutry, Switzerland (project)
1969/
71 Villa Complex, Canton of Vaud, Switzerland
1970 Dizerens Complex, Lutry, Switzerland
1971 Château des Planches, Montreux, Switzerland
1972 Petter Buildings Development, Lutry, Switzerland
1973 Sartoris House, Cossonay-Ville, Switzerland
1974 Private Clinic (project)
1974/
75 English Church restorations, Lausanne, Switzerland
Mastrangelo Villa, La Chésiaz-St. Légier, Switzerland
1976 Funerary Monument on the Bosphorus, Turkey (project)
1977 Museum of Art, Legnano, Italy (project)
1978 Spa Buildings, Stabio, Switzerland
1979 Monumental mosaics for the Museum of Legnano, Italy
1980 Town Plan for Mont-Fleuri, Switzerland (project)
1981 Hotel d'Angleterre, Cossonay-Ville, Switzerland (project)
1981/
82 Bona District Urban Plan, Carignano, Italy (project)
1982/
84 Lesieur Industrial Complex, Dunkerque,

France (with E. Cattani and P. Pastellas)
1985 Bobbià Family Chapel, Stabio, Switzerland
Guggenheim Museum, Venice, Italy (competition project; with L. Ferrario and D. Pastore)

Publications:

By SARTORIS: books—*Robert Mallet-Stevens, architecte*, Paris 1930; *Antonio Sant'Elia*, Milan 1930; *Baldo Guberti*, Milan 1932; *Gli elementi dell'architettura funzionale*, Milan 1932, 1935, 1941; *Vordemberge-Gildewart*, exhibition catalogue, Rome 1934; *Omaggio a Josef Albers*, exhibition catalogue, Milan 1934; *Willi Baumeister*, exhibition catalogue, Milan 1934; *Gli ambienti della nuova architettura*, Turin 1935; *A. A. Soldati*, exhibition catalogue, Rome 1936; *Interpretazioni di Mauro Reggiani*, exhibition catalogue, Milan 1936; *Mostra di pittura moderna italiana*, exhibition catalogue, Como, Italy 1936; *Montini visto da Sartoris*, exhibition catalogue, Milan 1937; *Det Moderna Hemmet*, Stockholm 1942; *Jozsef Molnar*, Budapest 1943; *Introduzione all'architettura moderna*, Milan 1943; *Sant'Elia e l'architettura moderna*, Milan 1944; *Mario Sitoni*, Milan 1946; *Encyclopédie de l'architecture nouvelle*, 3 vols., Milan 1948-57; *Leonard, architecte*, Paris 1952; *Piero della Francesca: The Arezzo Frescoes*, with Piero dei Francheschi, Paris and London 1957; *Catalogue de la Fédération Internationale au Film d'Art*, with Walter Gropius and Gerrit Rietveld, Brussels 1958-60; *Films sur l'art*, with André Chastel and others, Paris 1960; *Mauro Reggiani, monografia*, with G. M. Tabarelli, Milan 1960; *Jean Gorin*, exhibition catalogue, Milan 1962; *Gunter Fruhtrunk*, exhibition catalogue, Milan 1962; *Mostra Personale di Mauro Reggiani*, exhibition catalogue, Venice 1962; *Futurismo oggi*, with others, Rome 1967; *Luc Peire*, exhibition catalogue, Venice 1968; *Le mobilisme de Mary Vieira*, Milan 1968; *Jean Gorin: exposition retrospective*, exhibition catalogue, Paris 1969; *Luc Peire*, Bergamo, Italy 1970; *Gino Biasi*, exhibition catalogue, Udine, Italy 1970; *Mauro Reggiani*, exhibition catalogue, Turin 1971; *Bonfanti*, Paris 1971; *Metamorfosi delle arti*, Como, Italy 1971; *Vaquero*, Madrid 1972; *Sculptures en liberté*, Lausanne, Switzerland, 1973; *Jean Gorin*, Venice 1975; *Artur Jobin ou l'infiguration emblematique*, Cossonay, Switzerland 1975; *Lisbet Doyer*, Cossonay, Switzerland 1976; *F. T. Marinetti e l'architettura*, Rome 1977; *Significato del costruttivismo di Bertolio*, Milan 1978; *Portugal*, Lausanne 1979; *Die Kunst von Aldo Patocchi*, Schwetzingen, West Germany 1979; *Giorgio Nannei: oli sul tela 1975-1980*, exhibition catalogue, Milan 1980; *La lunga marcia dell'arte astratta in Italia*, Milan 1980; *Salvati e Tresoldi: architettura e design 1960-1980*, Milan 1980; *Les portraits d'architecture de Pietro Fontana*, Lausanne, Switzerland 1981; *Mario Botta, Transfigurer of Geometry*, Milan 1982; *L'Architecture de Luigi Ferrario*, Rome 1982; *Metaphysic of Architecture*, New York 1984; *Présence de l'architecture*, Milan 1985; *Temps de l'architecture—Temps de l'art*, Milan 1985.

On SARTORIS: books—*Alberto Sartoris, architecte* by Alexandre Mairet, Geneva 1927; *L'oeuvre critique et créatrice de l'architecte Alberto Sartoris* by Arnold Kohler, Geneva 1931; *Sartoris* by Michel Seuphor, Milan 1933; *Architetti di trent' anni: Alberto Sartoris* by P. M. Bardi, n.p. 1932; *Alberto Sartoris* by Paul Budry, Lausanne, Switzerland 1933; *L'architetto Alberto Sartoris*, exhibition catalogue, by Antonio Giulio Bragaglia, Rome 1933; *Architettura di Alberto Sartoris*, exhibition catalogue, by Bruno Moretti, Milan 1934; *Alberto Sartoris* by Rafaello Giolli, Milan 1935; *Alberto Sartoris* by René-Louis Piachaud, Lausanne, Switzerland 1939; *Alberto Sartoris* by Luis Felipe Vivanco, Santander, Spain 1951; *Alberto Sartoris: mezzo secolo di attivita*, exhibition catalogue, by A. Abriani, M. Fagiolo dell'Arco and others, Turin

1972; *Alberto Sartoris: l'architettura italiana fra tragedia e forma* by Alberto Cuomo, Rome 1978; *Alberto Sartoris*, exhibition catalogue, by Jacques Gubler, Zürich 1978; *Alberto Sartoris: un architetto razionalista*, exhibition catalogue, Rome 1979; *Alberto Sartoris*, exhibition catalogue, Lisbon 1980; *Au-delà du Taje: Rencontre avec Alberto Sartoris*, exhibition catalogue, by M. Alice Chico, Evora, Spain 1981; *Alberto Sartoris*, exhibition catalogue, Geneva 1981; *Incontro con Alberto Sartoris*, Stabio, Switzerland 1982; *Progetti e assonometrie di Alberto Sartoris*, exhibition catalogue by A. C. Quintavalle, A. Samona, P. Portoghesi and others, Rome 1982; *Alberto Sartoris et la Valais*, exhibition catalogue by Paul Auberson, Jacques Gubler, Michel Seuphor and others, Martigny, Switzerland 1983; *Alberto Sartoris/La Casa Morand- Pasteur*, Rome 1983; *Le Monde magique d'Alberto Sartoris* by Christian Leprette, with preface by Richard Meier, New York 1985; *Alberto Sartoris*, exhibition catalogue, São Paulo 1985; *Alberto Sartoris*, exhibition catalogue, Milan, 1985; articles—"Sartoris en Turin" by F. G. Mercadal in *Arquitectura* (Madrid) September 1928; "Alberto Sartoris" by Henri Ferrare in *21 Artistes du novecento italien*, Geneva 1930; "Alberto Sartoris" by Arnold Kohler in *Poligono* (Milan) March 1931; "Architettura di Alberto Sartoris" in *Il Resto di Carlino* (Bologna, Italy), 13 May 1933; "Alberto Sartoris" in *Architects' Journal* (London), 23 May 1935; "Avanti Savoia" by P. Morton Shand in *Architectural Review* (London), July 1935; "Alberto Sartoris, critico ed architetto razionalista" by L. Patetta in *Controspazio* (Bari, Italy) no. 6/7, 1970; "Sartoris e la matrice metafisica del razionalismo" by M. Fagiolo in *Ottagono* (Milan) December 1974; "Sartoris: The First Classicist of the Avant-Garde" by Oriol Bohigas in *Oppositions* (New York), Summer 1979; "Alberto Sartoris, Architekt" by T. Boga in *Werk* (Zürich) November 1982; "Sartorial Elegance" by Dennis Sharp in *Building* (London), 4 March 1983.

*

In praising the architecture of the 'twenties and 'thirties we are not latching wistfully on to a distant dream. If we speak today of the rationalist movement we are in no danger of losing our way among winding and neglected pathways, in the dead ends and sidings of a time long past. To peer into the currents of functional architecture is to have recourse to a living and still active history in order to penetrate spheres of creation that still retain all their potency today.

Indeed, I would repeat that the original rationalism (that of the true protagonists) has not yet completed its full, determining and international cycle. Although constantly under attack from all sides, it is currently in the midst of operations, positioned on the firing line, and engaged in open battle, as on the very first day: in open battle with academicism decked out in second-hand rags and sporting the grotesque mask of post-modernism, the poison of the century (even if we admit that negative experiences are sometimes useful and that, in this case too, there are exceptions).

After enduring the fiercest of attacks, the ideas and projects of functional architecture and town planning were virtually obliterated by the wave of accrhitects adhering to exclusively alimentary precepts, by insatiable promoters and the bastions of the régimes of money and mercantilism; and innovators and rational architects were thereby forced to act in secret and, during these sad times, temporarily to form a clandestine fellowship.

Fortunately, architects everywhere are now in the grip of a new creativity. And this creativity is apparent in every country where an ardent younger generation is enlisting in the ranks of neo-rationalism, while the surviving precursors of the new architecture impart to them their own knowledge, experience and vitality; in certain cases, indeed, precursor and continuator are working in collaboration with one another. A totally new rationalism is now coming to the fore, and is advancing and developing brilliantly by virtue of that irreversible law of intellectual constants which ensures the immortality of creative formulas and avant-garde ideas.

Rationalism still has total currency. It is still the playground of fantasy and social logic, of rational construction, of original conception and humanist invention.

—Alberto Sartoris

Alberto Sartoris is widely recognized as the first classicist of the architectural avant-garde. His career, begun in 1920, represents more than sixty-five years of critical revision of the Rationalist tradition. While his native Italy was governed in postwar years by anti-avant-garde attitudes, he demonstrated a pioneering will and determination to break the backwardness of Italian architecture and to integrate it with modern international ideals. He still remains critical of contemporaries who conform to elementary precepts, and of those insatiable developers who stifle innovative ideas in favour of mercantilism. His role as the bastion of neo-rationalist design included condemning the canons of post rationalism as "the poison of the century". Perhaps this militant predisposition prevented him from fully resolving his own architecture in built works, and from receiving proper recognition for his accomplishments.

During the 1930s, Sartoris was an active proponent of reason and tradition, and his mission—almost singular in the field of architecture—was to found an historical base for the Modern Movement. Functional architecture, as he saw it, must be interconnected with history, still living and active, in order to penetrate the spheres of creation that retain their potency today. He strove to consolidate this innovative line of thinking by emphasis on its social implications: "In renewing the art of construction, the civil spirit is renewed. In realizing the modern house, modern man is in a certain way defined."

In his fifty-three published books, it is clear that his iconographic summaries intend to establish stylistic consistencies applicable to the neo-rationalist tradition. The effort to produce a homogeneous group of general principles is visible in the absolutely autonomous treatment of the architectonic object. More than autonomous, Sartoris' work is virtually indifferent to the environment. Architecture is defined as a compositional consistency which finds its justification in history or in figurative suppositions, rather than in the situational response of the landscape or the city.

An important work from the early years of his career illustrates his role in the avant-garde: the pavilion for artisan communities in Turin (1927-29), which has been described as the first Italian rationalist building. The structure displays a codification of the classical style inside the Modern Movement; its pavilion features pilotis as a part of the continuity of a solid layer over a simply punctured pedestal; the shelves which shape the corners—ostensibly a functional support for exhibiting handicraft products—suggest the hard proportions of colonnades by Ledoux; the windows recompose the plan of the facade into a consistent and expressive skin, unlike the Corbusian window; and the asymmetrical top of the building contradicts the spontaneous fluidity and functional expressiveness of the terrace walls.

Frequently, the theme of prism and cylinder appear in Sartoris projects. In the house/studio designed in Paris in 1930, the central cylinder shape generated a whole system of cylindrical walls. Unlike the sensuous and sculpturally expressive curve so common to Le Corbusier, the wall is the result of a rigorous geometric formula.

Sartoris' own creative potential, however, seems to have been thwarted amid his repudiation of the Modern Movement's pioneers and his furious attacks on the post-rationalists. In those periods of which Zevi and Benevolo were the protagonists, he was forgotten as an architect and theoretician. The 1950s and 1960s saw him greeted with enthusiasm

by the Spanish and Latin Americans, while recent exhibitions have characterized him with labels as various as ingenious and professorial to heterodox and marginal. Such fluctuating recognition has doubtless contributed to his failure to create a body of outstanding built work. In spite of this handicap, his reputation as the uncompromising precursor of the avant-garde is secure.

—Carolyn Cole

SASAKI, Hideo.

American. Born in Reedley, California, 25 November 1919. Educated at Reedley Junior College, California, 1939; University of California, Berkeley, 1939-41; Central YMCA College, Chicago, 1943-44; University of Illinois, Urbana, 1944-46, B.F.A. in Landscape Arch. 1946; Harvard University, Cambridge, Massachusetts, 1946-48, M. Landscape Arch. 1948. Married Kisa Noguchi in 1951; children: Rin and Ann. Founder, Sasaki, Walker Associates, San Francisco, 1952-60; Principal, Sasaki, Strong and Associates, Toronto, 1960-66; Sasaki, Dawson, DeMay Associates, Watertown, Massachusetts, 1966-78. Since 1978, Principal (now Consultant), Sasaki Associates Inc., Watertown, Massachusetts. Instructor, Department of City Planning and Landscape Architecture, University of Illinois, Urbana, 1948-50, 1952-53; Instructor, 1950-52, 1953-70, and Chairman of the Department of Landscape Architecture, 1958-68, Harvard University. Member, United States Commission on the Fine Arts, 1962-71. Member of the Advisory Committee on Arts and Architecture, Kennedy Memorial Library, Boston, since 1970. Recipient: Collaborative Medal of Honor, with Eero Saarinen, Architectural League of New York, 1962; First Honor Award, United States Federal Housing Authority, 1963; First Honor Award, United States Bureau of Higher Education/American Institute of Architects, 1966; First Prize, Copley Square Competition, Boston, 1966; First Prize, St. Louis Gateway Mall Competition, 1967; American Society of Landscape Architects Medal, 1971; Allied Professions Medal, American Institute of Architects, 1973. DFA: University of Illinois, Urbana, 1982; DHL: University of Colorado, Boulder, 1984. Fellow, American Society of Landscape Architects, 1969. Address: Sasaki Associates Inc., 64 Pleasant Street, Watertown, Massachusetts 02172, U.S.A.

Works (landscape architecture):

1952 Jaycee Headquarters, Tulsa, Oklahoma
1959 Golden Gateway Development, San Francisco
1961 Stauffer Chemical Company Office Building, Richmond, California
1962 Foothill College, Los Altos Hills, California
1963 Pomeroy Green Industrial Center, Santa Clara Valley, California
1964 Alcoa Building, 1 Maritime Plaza, San Francisco
Dormitories, University of Rhode Island, Kingston
Engineering Complex, University of Colorado, Boulder
1965 Pomeroy West Industrial Center, Santa Clara Valley, California
Cabot, Cabot and Forbes Industrial Park, San Francisco
1966 Sasaki, Dawson, DeMay Associates Offices, Watertown, Massachusetts
Master plan for the University of Massachusetts at Amherst
Master plan for the University of Colorado, Boulder

Master plan for Kent State University, Ohio
1967 Gateway Mall, St. Louis (competition project)
Bell Telephone Laboratories, Holmdel, New Jersey
Civic Center, Los Gatos, California
Place Bonaventure Hotel, Montreal
1968 Sea Pines Plantation Master Plan, Hilton Head Island, South Carolina
1969 Alexandra Park, Toronto
Library Building, School of Architecture, University of Virginia, Charlottesville
Harbour Town Master Plan, Hilton Head Island, South Carolina
1970 Copley Square Development, Boston
Library, Providence College, Rhode Island
1971 Norfolk Airport, Virginia
State University of New York at Buffalo/Amherst
Wightman Tennis Center, Weston, Massachusetts
1972 MGIC Investment Corporation Headquarters, Milwaukee
Greenacre Park, New York
Weyerhaeuser Company Headquarters, Tacoma, Washington
1973 Constitution Plaza, Hartford, Connecticut
Plan for the Old Savannah historical district, Savannah, Georgia
1974 Master plan for the Columbia Point campus of the University of Massachusetts
Cedar Square West, Minneapolis
Promontory Point Housing, Newport Bay, California
Tobin Elementary School, Cambridge, Massachusetts
1976 Pennsylvania Avenue Development Corporation, Washington, D.C.
Pocantico Hills Estate, Tarrytown, New York
1977 Central Riverfront Master Plan, Minneapolis, Minnesota
1978 National Arboretum Master Plan, Washington, D.C.
1979 Minneapolis Great River Road Master Plan, Minneapolis, Minnesota
Hennepin Island Park, Minneapolis, Minnesota
US Capitol Plan Urban Design Concepts, Washington, D.C.
1980 Western Wyoming Community College, Rock Springs, Wyoming
1981 Yerba Buena Project Designs, San Francisco (as consultant)

Publications:

By SASAKI: book—*SA: Sasaki Associates Inc.—Planning, Architecture, Landscape Architecture, Civil Engineering, Environmental Services*, with Sasaki Associates, Watertown, Massachusetts 1975.

On SASAKI; articles—"Design of Exterior Space" by Jan C. Rowan in *Progressive Architecture* (New York), July 1960; "New England Portfolio" in *Landscape Architecture* (Louisville, Kentucky), April 1965; "Focusing University Development" in *Progressive Architecture* (New York), October 1966; "Castle in the Sky: Hotel Bonaventure" in *Interiors* (New York), October 1967; "Place Bonaventure" in *Architectural Design* (London), January 1968; "Most Popular Campus" in *Progressive Architecture* (New York), June 1973; "Place Bonaventure" in *Landscape Design* (London), February 1977; "Planting with Evergreens" in *Concrete Quarterly* (London), April/June 1977; "Winter Warm-Up on Summer Street" in *Contract Interiors* (New York), March 1978; "Building Types Study 525: Federal Architecture" in *Architectural Record* (New York), December 1978; "Kuwait Waterfront Project" in *Middle East Construction* (Sutton, Surrey), February 1979; "Three American Plazas" in *Landscape Design* (London), August 1979; "Is This the New England

Hideo Sasaki: Greenacre Park, New York, 1972.

Look?" in *Housing* (New York), December 1979; "A Complex Deal with Help from Uncle Sam" in *Housing* (New York), March 1980; "Banneker Plaza" in *Architectural Record* (New York), March 1982; "Building Types Study 591: Multifamily Housing" *Architectural Record* (New York), July 1983; "Reflections of Islam in the Cromwell Road" in *Landscape International* (Godalming, Surrey), January/February 1984.

Hideo Sasaki is one of the great professional success stories of our time. He was born and raised in California's hot south Central Valley and educated at Berkeley. With the onset of World War II he and his family were caught in the hysteria that resulted in the relocation of all west coast Japanese in various concentration camps. From there, as a result of a government policy that apparently considered Japanese in the east less dangerous than they would be in the west, he was able to go east to study and work in his field of landscape architecture. He taught at Illinois and Harvard (he had studied at both universities), and in 1958 became the Chairman of the Department of Landscape Architecture at Harvard. Here his extraordinary talents for communication, organization, and leadership began to blossom. Educational programs and his professional

practice grew together, each reinforcing and supporting the other. Students gained practical as well as theoretical knowledge, and Sasaki's office had a constant supply of eager workers. At no other school has there been such a consistent, thorough, and successful integration of teaching and practice.

So happily balanced a process could not maintain equilibrium forever. Eventually the office practice grew so demanding that Sasaki had to make a choice. He decided to give up teaching: the school was now well established, with a good faculty ready to take over. Thereafter the Sasaki office, in Watertown, Massachusetts, grew rapidly into a multidisciplinary firm that eventually employed 300 people, involved in architecture, engineering, and planning as well as landscape architecture.

That is the success story. What has been the qualitative level of the work turned out by this astonishing firm? Remarkably high. Sasaki went to Harvard in the wake of the modern design revolution that had occurred there in the late 1930s. He absorbed it, along with previous historical experience, and created a design/planning vocabulary that had both the freedom and the strength of that combination. Perhaps a little conservative from the free-swinging western point of view, his work, rich, strong and solid, struck the right notes at the right times and places, and earned him an enviable

clientele. Graduates from his classes and office have built what may well be called a Sasaki tradition throughout North America. Designer, planner, teacher, organizer, communicator, and salesman par excellence for the profession, Sasaki occupies a secure leading position in twentieth century landscape architecture. Now partially retired but still active, he is living in the east San Francisco Bay area.

—Garrett Eckbo

SAUER, Louis.
American. Born in Park Forest, Illinois, 15 June 1928. Studied medicine at DePauw University, Greencastle, Indiana, 1946-49, and architecture at Illinois Institute of Technology, Chicago, 1949-53, B.Arch. 1953; International School of City Planning, Venice, 1956; University of Pennsylvania, Philadelphia, 1957-59, M.Arch. 1959. Served in the United States Army, 1953-55. Married Elizabeth Mason in 1956; children: Christopher and Kathryn. Worked in the office of Jules Gregory, Lambertville, New Jersey, 1955-57, Milton Schwartz, Philadelphia,

1957-61, and Esbach, Pullinger, Stevens and Bruder, Philadelphia, 1959-61; Partner, with William Winchell, in Winchell and Sauer, Philadelphia, 1961-62; in private as Louis Sauer, Architect, Philadelphia, 1962-67; Partner, with Anthony Devito, Sauer and Devito, Philadelphia, 1967-69; Principal, Louis Sauer Associates, Philadelphia, 1969-79; President, Archiris Professional Corporation of Architects, Pittsburgh, Pennsylvania, 1982-85; Director, Lorenzi, Dodds and Gunnill, Pittsburgh, Pennsylvania, 1985-86. Since 1985, in private practice, as Louis Sauer Architect, Boulder, Colorado. Instructor, Drexel Institute of Technology, Philadelphia, 1960-65; Associate Professor, 1965-67 and 1974-77, and Adjunct Professor of Architecture, 1977-79, University of Pennsylvania, Philadelphia. Professor, 1979-85, Head of the Department of Architecture, 1979-81, and Director of the Institute of Building Science, 1981-82, Carnegie-Mellon University, Pittsburgh; Visiting Professor and Scholar, Massachusetts Institute of Technology, Cambridge, 1984-85; Professor, University of Colorado, Boulder, since 1985. Member, Housing Research Committee, and Design Committee, American Institute of Architects Commission on Environment and Design, 1973-74; Member, Design Advisory Panel, Department of Housing and Community Development, Baltimore, Maryland, 1973-74; Member, Research Advisory Panel, American Institute of Architects, 1974-75; Member, Advisory Committee on Behavior Science Research and Architectural Practice, AIA Research Corporation and National Endowment for the Arts, 1975-77. Member of the Editorial Board, 1974-77, Contributing Editor, 1973-77, *Journal of Architectural Research*, Philadelphia; Member, Community Development Committee, American Institute of Architects, since 1978; Research Advisor, National Science Foundation, since 1979; Board Member, Environmental Design and Research Association, 1982-84; Editorial Board Member, *Journal of Architectural and Planning Research*, Philadelphia, since 1983. Exhibitions: United States Pavilion, World's Fair, New York, 1964; Art Alliance of Philadelphia, 1975; University of Texas at Austin, 1974. Recipient: Honor Award, 1963, 1964, 1965, 1967, 1970, 1971, 1972, and 1978, and Silver Medal, 1967 and 1973, Pennsylvania Society of Architects; Award , 1963, 1965, 1968, 1969, 1970, 1971, 1972, and 1974, American Institute of Architects; Annual Award, Montgomery County Planning Commission, Pennsylvania, 1967; *Architectural Record* Award, New York, 1967; National Plywood Design Award, 1972; Biennial Award, United States Department of Housing and Urban Development, 1972 and 1976; Honor Award, Connecticut Society of Architects, 1974; Design Award, Greater Wilmington Development Council and Newcastle County Planning Board, Delaware, 1975; *Design and Environment* Award, 1975; Fellowship in Design, National Endowment for the Arts, 1978. Fellow, American Institute of Architects, 1973. Address: Louis Sauer Architect, 6367 Clearview Road, Boulder, Colorado 80303, U.S.A.

Works:

1961 Sachse Factory, Philadelphia (project)
Winchell House conversion, Philadelphia
1962 Urban renewal plan for the Morton area, Philadelphia
Louis Sauer House conversion, Lambertville, New Jersey
Cripps House, Lambertville, New Jersey
Hamilton House conversion, New Hope, Pennsylvania
Buten Duplex Townhouse conversion, Philadelphia
1963 Watson House conversion, Philadelphia
Waverly Court Housing, group I, Philadelphia (project)
1964 North Crossing Rental Housing, Willow Grove, Pennsylvania

Louis Sauer: Cincinnati Plaza, Ohio, 1977.

Pastorius Mews Housing Development, Philadelphia (project)
Cooper House, Margate, New Jersey (project)
Drake Mill House conversion, Chester County, Pennsylvania (project)
Addison Court Housing Development, Philadelphia (project)
Housing development, 7th and Lombard Streets, Philadelphia (project)
1965 Atrium Court Housing Development, Philadelphia (project)
Hornung House conversion, Philadelphia
Housing development, Willinboro, New Jersey (project)
Golf Course Island Housing Development, Reston, Virginia
McClennan House, Philadelphia
Park Purchase Condominium, Baltimore, Maryland (project)
St. Simeon's-by-the-Sea, Wildwood, New Jersey
1966 Waverly Court Housing, group II, Philadelphia
Housing conversions, tenth and Lombard Streets, Philadelphia
Rental apartments conversions, eleventh Street, Philadelphia
Viewmont Village (rental housing development), Scranton, Pennsylvania
Spring Pond (rental apartments and houses), Corning, New York
Housing development, fifth and Spruce Streets, Philadelphia (project)
1967 Lakeside Housing Development, Reston, Virginia (project)
Offutt Houses, Reston, Virginia
Penn's View Housing, Philadelphia (project)

Devito House conversion, Philadelphia
Harmony House Cooperative Housing Development, New Haven, Connecticut
Canterbury Gardens Cooperative Housing Development, New Haven, Connecticut
Grant and Morrison Houses, Philadelphia
Urban renewal plan for the Newhallville area, New Haven, Connecticut
Head House East Shops and Housing Development, Philadelphia (project)
Reed House, Great Barrington, Massachusetts
Leonard Frankel House, Margate, New Jersey
William Frankel House, Margate, New Jersey
Penn's Landing Square One Housing Development, Philadelphia (project)
Oakland Mills Village Centre, Columbia, Maryland
1968 Housing development, Locust Street, Philadelphia
Grundy Tower Housing Development, Bristol, Pennsylvania
Development plan for Fox Chase, Pennsylvania (project)
1969 Regency Square Housing Development, Cincinnati, Ohio
Second Street Housing Development, Philadelphia
Penn's Landing Square Two Housing Development, Society Hill, Philadelphia
Genesee Crossroads Housing Development, Rochester, New York (project)
Governor's Grove Housing Development, Middletown, Connecticut
North Crossing Rental Housing II, Philadelphia
Central Island Village, Islip, New York (project)

Sauer House conversion, Chestnut Hill, Philadelphia
1970 Condominium, Lombard Street, Philadelphia
Highrise low-cost rental apartment building, Warburton and Lamartine Streets, Yonkers, New York
Low-cost rental row-housing development, Warburton and Ashburton Streets, Yonkers, New York
1971 Oak Hill Terrace Housing Development, Penn Valley, Pennsylvania
Motel Complex, Penn's Landing Square, Philadelphia (project)
Strathallan Rental Housing for the Elderly, Rochester, New York (project)
Riverton Patio Housing Development, Rochester, New York (project)
Housing post-occupancy evaluation for the United States Department of Health, Education and Welfare
1972 Wilton Condominium, Wilmington, Delaware
Wilton Clubhouse, Wilmington, Delaware
Seascape Condominium, Avalon, New Jersey
1973 Plan for development of riverfront land, Cincinnati
Headmaster's House, Westtown School, Pennsylvania
Graver's Lane Rental Housing conversions, Philadelphia
1974 Development plan for Fell's Point, Baltimore
Land development plan for Boca Lago, Florida
Gypsy Hill Road Housing, Leighton, Pennsylvania
Crystal Gardens Housing Development, Corning, New York
Western Savings Bank at New Market, Society Hill, Philadelphia
Parcel 76 Housing Development, Washington D.C.
Orchard Mews Low-cost Housing Development, Baltimore
Crystal Gardens Housing Feasibility Study, Corning, New York (project)
Newmarket Commercial Complex, Philadelphia
1975
Hord House, Philadelphia
Broadway Market Rehabilitation, Fells Point, Baltimore, Maryland
1976
Inner Harbor West Housing Development Plan, Baltimore, Maryland
Marren House renovation, Harvey Cedars, New Jersey
1977 York Re-use Housing, York, Pennsylvania
Penn Housing, Philadelphia
Pine Street Houses, Philadelphia
Cincinnati Riverfront Plaza, Ohio
1978 One West Conway Rental Housing for the Elderly, Baltimore, Maryland
Harbor Walk Sales Housing, Baltimore, Maryland
Lower Town Development Strategy, St. Paul, Minnesota
1979
House rehabilitation, 1185 Fort Washington Avenue, Fort Washington, Pennsylvania
Washington Square West Low-Cost Housing rehabilitation, Philadelphia
Roberts House, Society Hill, Philadelphia
1980 House rehabilitation, 726 James Street, Pittsburgh
1981 Harbor Walk Condominium Housing, Baltimore, Maryland
1982 House rehabilitation, 605 Amberson Avenue, Pittsburgh Cards Plus shop, Pittsburgh
Westinghouse Cafeteria, South Boston, Virginia
Westinghouse Public Systems Company Strategic Facilities Plan, U.S.A.
Fred Rogers Tudor Manor, Latrobe, Pennsylvania

1983 East Liberty Commercial Revitalization Plan, Pittsburgh
DeCamp House, 622 St. James Street, Pittsburgh
Naval Air Training Center Housing, Lexington Park, Maryland
Western Center Development Plan, Canonberg, Pennsylvania
1984 The Rivercliff House, Point Pleasant, Pennsylvania
Newark Housing Strategies, Newark, New York
1985 Caine Hospital Redevelopment Strategies, Pittsburgh
Hamilton Estate Development Strategy, Lambertville, New Jersey
1986 Aries Property Development Strategies, Colorado Springs, Colorado
Low-Cost Single Parent Family Housing Strategies, Boulder, Colorado
Planning Research Corporation Architectural Strategies, San Diego, California
Jameson House rehabilitation, Boulder, Colorado

Publications

By SAUER: articles—"The Architect and User Needs" in *Behavior, Design and Policy Aspects of Human Habitats*, Madison, Wisconsin 1972; "How Six Families Use Space in Their Homes" in *Proceedings of the Third EDRA Conference*, Los Angeles 1973; "Some Thoughts on Design and Process in Housing" in *Modulus 10* (Charlottesville, Virginia), June 1974; "Differing Fates for Two Nearly Identical Housing Developments" in *AIA Journal* (Washington, D.C.), February 1977; "Man-Environment Knowledge and Design Criteria" and "A Framework for Considering Housing Costs" in *Proceedings of the Lebanon Housing Seminar*, Washington, D.C. 1977.

On SAUER: books—*The Housing Yearbook*, Washington, D.C. 1963; *The New York Times Book of Interior Design and Decoration*, edited by George O'Brien, New York 1965; *New Techniques of Architectural Rendering* by Helmut Jacoby, New York 1971; *Design for Human Affairs* by C. M. Deasy, New York 1974; *Apartments, Townhouses, and Condominiums*, edited by Elizabeth Kendall Thompson, New York 1975; *The Application of the Social and Behavioral Sciences to Environmental Design*, edited by Charles H. Kahn, Lawrence, Kansas 1976; *37 Design and Environment Projects*, edited by Ann Ferebee, Washington, D.C. 1976; *Entwurf und Planung: Stadthäuser*, edited by Paulhans Peters, Munich 1979; *Housing* by John Macooi, New York 1982; *Designing Your Client's House* by Alfredo De Vido, New York 1983; articles—"Louis Sauer's Works" in *Aujourd'hui* (Paris), January 1967; "Works and Methods of Louis Sauer" in *Toshi-Jutaku* (Tokyo), January 1969; "How to Work with Developers and Actually Enjoy It" in *Architectural Record* (New York), April 1973; "Penn's Landing Square" in *Progressive Architecture* (New York), March 1976; "Working Toward an Approach That Will Yield Lessons for Future Design" in *AIA Journal* (Washington, D.C.), August 1976; "Spring Pond Apartments" in *Wohnungsbau im Wandel* by David Mackay, Stuttgart 1977; "Building Types Study 523: Low-rise Housing" in *Architectural Record* (New York), October 1978; Cincinnatus Concourse and Forum" in *Architectural Record* (New York), June 1979; "Low-rise Housing in America," special issue of *Process: Architecture* (Tokyo), April 1980; "Evaluation—A Futuristic Gesture in Historic Society Hill" in *AIA Journal* (Washington, D.C.), June 1981.

I understand architecture to be a technological process and a product of society for heightening people's self-identity through solving specific man-

environment problems. As a process, it is intrinsically a cultural action for resource allocation involving complex issues and varied participants, to achieve political purposes. The major aspects concerning architecture are human needs, policies and programs allocating resources, community and neighborhood development, physical design, construction, distribution and occupancy, property maintenance and management. I have found that to the extent the interactions, separate goals, and disciplines of the individual participants in these aspects are understood, one can be effective in predicting and modifying the outcomes of the designed environment. Thus, architects, or others, may choose to intervene for greater influence upon the quality of the built environment.

—Louis Sauer

Louis Sauer is a no-nonsense, user-oriented architect from Philadelphia. His rather prolific firm has completed many fine buildings that have been conservative, but not conventional, and completely up-to-date, without being trendy. Sauer himself is a pragmatist, greatly aware of the importance of communication with the client, and sensitive to issues far broader than merely architectural design. Still, his buildings are neatly handsome and often slick. He has frequently proposed unique and surprisingly successful solutions to many difficult problems facing contemporary architects. He has readily accepted the challenges of some of the toughest building programs in America, and his portfolio includes an impressive number of successful public housing projects and in-fill urban designs.

In the Society Hill area of Philadelphia, Sauer has completed many six to ten-unit attached house complexes that have blended easily with the existing street patterns without compromising modernity or design freshness. By maintaining certain volumetric dimensions but distorting other, Sauer's houses are unusual and exciting in and of themselves, without damaging or significantly altering the local environmental character.

In the same neighborhood, but adjacent to the Delaware River, Sauer designed a new shopping center that clearly demonstrated his facile capability to produce a boldly imaginative solution reflecting the individual issues of a particular program. Residents had been long opposed to the development of a commercial center in the heart of this historic district, but Sauer finally developed a plan that did nothing to destroy the neighborhood's appearance. What is most surprising is that the new building he designed is a high-tech glass and stainless steel affair with exposed columns, beams, ducts, and pipes, all painted in bright, primary colors. This was accomplished by completely hiding the new center on all sides except the waterfront. Newmarket, as the complex is called, is masked on the other three sides by older residential units that were maintained and refurbished. The stores are located in the area that was once the yards for the surrounding homes, and it remains invisible until the pedestrian leaves the street zone, and enters a passage to penetrate within. An outdoor activity area designed for pedestrians surrounds the buildings of Newmarket, and extends to the backs of the houses. Towards the water the complex is allowed to reveal itself, where there is no concern with maintaining the quiet rhythms of the colonial streets.

Newmarket is also unusual because it explores a new method of merchandise display. There are no store windows, per se. Instead, the entire glass facade of the market reveals store interiors intended to serve as the displays themselves. The outdoor areas are certainly more exciting because of the interior motion visible through the glass walls.

Sauer has also completed a variety of public housing projects that are worthy of commendation. Two developers near New Haven, Connecticut, and several near Philadelphia, have proven Sauer to be capable of handling the hardest assignments. In all, he made snappy structures with easily identifiable individual units, and surprising variation for low-income developments. In Connecticut, he conducted interviews with future occupants to discover changes they would like to implement, and he revised the floor plan accordingly, without changing the size or overall cost of the housing.

Sauer is a strong, energetic, and forceful designer who is impressed by action, not words. He has made a commitment to keep architecture in close touch with the people it serves, and he has stayed a bit removed from the polemical debates of architecture, in order to be in the thick of its production.

—Mitchell B. Rouda

SAVIOLI, Leonardo.

Italian. Born in Florence, 30 March 1917. Educated at the Humanities Gymnasium, Florence, graduated 1935; University of Florence, under Giovanni Michelucci, 1935-40, Dip.Arch. 1941. Married Flora Wiechmann in 1950. In partnership with G. Gori and Leonardi Ricci, Florence, 1944-49. In partnership with Danilo Santi, Florence, 1950 until his death in 1982. Member of the Faculty of Architecture, University of Florence, from 1940: Professor of Town Planning and Landscape Architecture, 1951-82. Exhibitions: *Mostra della ricostruzione*, Rome, 1950; *Bienal*, São Paulo, 1953, 1957; *Disegni di Leonardo Savioli*, Galleria XXII Marzo, Venice, 1960; *Aspetti dell'arte contemporanea*, L'Aquila, Italy, 1963; *Disegni di Leonardo Savioli*, Galleria La Strozzina, Florence, 1963; *La casa abitata*, Florence, 1965; *Quadriennale*, Rome, 1966; *Mostra del marmo*, Carrara, Italy, 1966; *Italia 1965*, Tokyo, 1966; *Italian Architecture of the Sixties*, Tehran, 1972; *L'Art d'aujourd'hui*, Montauban and Nancy, France, 1972; *Young Italian Architecture*, toured Europe, 1972; *Biennale Internazionale della grafica*, Florence, 1972; *Mostra antologica*, Palazzo dei Diamanti, Ferrara, Italy, 1975; *Mostra antologica*, Sala San Ignacio, Arezzo, Italy, 1976; *Biennale*, Venice, 1978; *Mostra nazionale di grafica*, Capo d'Orlando, Italy, 1978; *Il disegno in Italia oggi*, Reggio Emilia, Italy, 1979; *Mostra di architettura*, Termoli, Italy, 1980; *Il materiale delle arti*, Milan, 1981; *Leonardo Savioli: grafico e architetto*, Palazzo del Podesta, Faenza, Italy, 1982, and Rome and Bologna, 1982. Recipient: Prize, *Bienal*, São Paulo, 1953; INARCH-DOMOSIC Prize, 1960; IN-ARCH Prize, 1963; Il Siglio d'Oro, 1965; Donatello Prize, 1965; First Prize, Flower Market Building Competition, Pescia, Italy, 1970; First Prize, Resort Development Competition, Cannes, France, 1973; INARCH-ANIACAP Prize, 1973. Member, Italian Art Academy, 1960. *Died* (in Florence) *11 May 1982.*

Works:

1942   District development plan for Livorno, Italy
1944/
45   Victory Bridge, Florence (competition project; with R. Gizdulich, G. Gori, Leonardo Ricci, and G. Neumann)
1945/
46   Plan for reconstruction and redevelopment of Vicchio and Dicomano, Italy (with Leonardo Ricci)
Carraia Bridge, Florence (competition project; with G. Gori, Leonardo Ricci, and G. Neumann)
1946   Plan for reconstruction and redevelopment of Empoli, Italy (competition project; with G. Gori and Leonardi Ricci)
Tourist and urban development plan for the Lido, Venice (competition project; with G. Gori and Leonardo Ricci)

Piazza d'Armi, Perugia, Italy (competition project; with G. Gori and Leonardo Ricci)
Grazie Bridge, Florence (competition project; with G. Gori and Leonardo Ricci)
1946/
47   Reconstruction plan for the Pontevecchio War-Damaged District, Florence (competition project; with G. Gori, Leonardo Ricci, and E. Brizzi)
Bridge over the River Sieve, Rufina, Italy (with G. Gori, Leonardo Ricci, and G. Neumann)
Bridge over the Arno River, Terranuova Braciolini, Italy (with G. Gori, Leonardo Ricci, and E. Brizzi)
Bridge over the Arno River, Figline Valdarno, Italy (with G. Gori, Leonardo Ricci, and E. Brizzi)
Group of four villas, for the Directors of the Vetroflex Company, Florence (with G. Gori and Leonardo Ricci)
1947   San Romando District Redevelopment, Ferrara, Italy (competition project; with E. Gori, G. Gori, and Leonardo Ricci)
Bridge over the Arno River, Signa, Italy (competition project; with G. Gori, Leonardo Ricci, and E. Brizzi)
San Niccolo Bridge, Florence (competition project; with G. Gori, Leonardo Ricci, and E. Brizzi)
Bridge over the Serchio River, Calavorno, Italy (competition project; with G. Gori, Leonardo Ricci, and E. Brizzi)
Bridge over the Cecina River, Ponteginori, Italy (competition project; with G. Gori and Leonardo Ricci)
Mezzo Bridge, Pisa, Italy (competition project; with G. Gori and Leonardo Ricci)
Bridge over the Bisenzio River, Signa, Italy (with G. Gori and Leonardo Ricci)
Municipal Cemetery, Settignano, Italy (project; with E. Detti, R. Gizdulich, G. Gori, and Leonardo Ricci)
Saint-Gobain Workers' Garden City, Pisa, Italy (project; with G. Gori and Leonardo Ricci)
Design of the Artisans' Trade Fair, Florence (with E. Gori, G. Gori, and Leonardo Ricci)
1948   Bridge over the Sterza River, Bottaccina, Volterra, Italy (competition project; with G. Gori and Leonardo Ricci)
Design of the Artisans' Trade Fair, Florence (with E. Gori, G. Gori, and Leonardo Ricci)
Bridge over the Sterza River, Salitone, Volterra, Italy (with G. Gori and Leonardo Ricci)
Urban development building code for Lido di Camaiore, Italy (competition project; with G. Gori, E. Isotta, and Leonardo Ricci)
1948/
49   Two prefabricated semi-detached villas (project; with E. Detti and Danilo Santi)
Villa, via del Larione, Ricoboli, Florence (with E. Detti and Danilo Santi)
Villa, San Domenico, Regresso, Florence (with E. Detti and Danilo Santi)
1948/
51   Flower and Fruit Market, Pescia, Italy (with E. Gori, G. Gori, Leonardo Ricci, and E. Brizzi)
1949   Design of the Artisans' Trade Fair, Florence (with E. Gori, G. Gori, and Leonardo Ricci)
Residential Zone, Savona, Italy (competition project; with E. Detti and Danilo Santi)
Pension, Forte dei Marmi, Italy (with E. Detti and Danilo Santi)
Design of the *Music Exhibition*, Palazzo Davanzati, Florence (with E. Detti and Danilo Santi)
1949/
51   Urban development building code for Florence (with L. Bartoli, E. Detti, S. Pastorini, G. Sagrestani, and the Florence City Technical Office)

1950/
51   Leonardo Savioli House, Certosa del Galluzzo, Florence
1951/
52   Piazzale Leonardo da Vinci, Mount Morello, Italy (project; with Danilo Santi)
1951/
58   Two semi-detached villas, San Francesco Village, Florence
Single-family house, San Francesco Village, Florence (with Danilo Santi)
1952/
53   Development plan for San Francesco Village, Florence (with Danilo Santi)
Eight semi-detached apartments, six apartments with shop, and complex of sixteen apartments, San Francesco Village, Florence (project; with Danilo Santi)
1953   Pinocchio Monument, Collodi, Pescia, Italy (competition project; with Danilo Santi and G. Gambone)
Fabrics shop, Prato, Italy (with Danilo Santi)
1953/
54   Village for 2,000 in the Sesto Hills, Florence (competition project; with Leonardo Ricci, Danilo Santi, and G. Petrelli)
Granary Barn conversion to Macchioro House, via delle Campora, Florence (with Danilo Santi)
1953/
64   Apartment building, San Francesco Village, Florence (with Danilo Santi)
1954/
55   Plan for the San Frediano District, Florence (competition project; with Leonardo Ricci, Danilo Santi, and G. Petrelli)
Two semi-detached villas, Poggio Gherardo, Florence (with Danilo Santi)
Torelli Villa, via Pana, Bellosguardo, Florence (with Danilo Santi)
1956/
57   Plan for Pomarance, Pisa, Italy
1956/
58   General plan for Prato, Italy (with T. Gatti and E. Rafanelli)
General plan for Montemurio, Italy (with Danilo Santi)
1957/
59   Building complex, Belvedere Quarter, Pistoia, Italy (with Danilo Santi and P. Melucci)
1958   Cinema, La Briglia, Florence (with Danilo Santi)
Villa Ventura, Regello, Italy (with Danilo Santi)
1958/
59   Urban development on the left bank of the Arno River, near Piazza G. Guerra, Empoli, Italy (competition project; with Danilo Santi)
1959   Church, Caprese Michelangelo, Italy (with Danilo Santi)
1959/
60   General plan for Volterra, Italy (competition project; with Danilo Santi)
1959/
61   Cooperative Housing Block, Pomarance, Italy (project; with Danilo Santi)
1960   Gebendinger Villa, Marignolle, Florence (with Danilo Santi)
Sacchelli Pension, Tonfano, Viareggio, Italy (with Danilo Santi)
Apartment building, via del Ponte alle Mosse, Florence (with Danilo Santi)
1960/
61   Covered market, Pomarance, Italy (with Danilo Santi)
Fischer Villa, Castello, Florence (with Danilo Santi)
1960/
65   Plan for Vaiano, Florence
1961   Melloni House, San Gaggio, Florence
1961/
62   Plan for the San Jacopino District, Florence (with Danilo Santi)

Leonardo Savioli: Project for an office building, 1976.

1961/
65 Building code and various buildins, via Tor-
cicoda, Isolotto, Florence (project; with
Danilo Santi)
1962 Low-cost holiday house, Tonfano, Italy (with
Danilo Santi)
Building on a Platform (projects; with M.
Dezzi Bardeschi, V. Giorgini, F. Gori, and
Danilo Santi)
Pension, Tonfano, Italy (project; with Danilo
Santi)
Design of *L'Oggetto moderno in Italia* exhi-
bition, Palazzo Strozzi, Florence (with
Danilo Santi and R. Vernuccio)
1962/
63 Plan for the Novoli District of Florence
1962/
64 Sandroni Villa, Arezzo, Italy (with Danilo
Santi)
1963 Design of *Le Corbusier* exhibition, Palazzo
Strozzi, Florence (with Danilo Santi and R.
Vernuccio)
Design of the *Jewellery Exhibition,* La Stroz-
zina Gallery, Florence
Inn with eighty Rooms, Tropea, Italy (project;
with Danilo Santi and S. Fabbri)
Wine Connoisseurs' Restaurant, San Casciano, Florence (project; with Danilo Santi)
Giandalia Villa, via Chiantigiana, Florence
(with Danilo Santi)

1963/
64 Development plan for the Green Belt, Castello, Florence (with Danilo Santi and S.
Fabbri)
1964 Torrini Building Plan, near via delle Campora,
Florence (with Danilo Santi)
Urban plan for Caprese Michelangelo, Italy
Jewellery Shop, Ponte Vecchio, Florence
(project; with Danilo Santi and S. Fabbri)
Glassware Shop, Venice (project)
1964/
65 Municipal Building Plan, Castiglio Fiorentino, Arezzo, Italy (with G. Fanelli and F.
Trivisonno)
Taddei Villa, San Domenico, Florence (with
Danilo Santi)
1964/
67 Apartment building, via Piagentina, Florence
(with Danilo Santi)
1965 Civic Center Plaza, San Francisco, California
(competition project; with G. Fanelli,
Danilo Santi, and F. Trivisonno)
Urban plan for the enactment of Statute 167,
Castiglioni Fiorentino, Arezzo, Italy (with
G. Fanelli, Danilo Santi, and F. Trivisonno)
1965/
73 Bayon Villa, San Gaggio, Florence
1966 Design of the *Florence at the Time of Dante*
exhibition, Certosa del Galluzzo, Florence
(with Danilo Santi)

Prefabricated room units, *La casa abitata*
exhibition, Plazzo Strozzi, Florence
1966/
68 Montecatini Cemetery extension, Italy (with
E. Brizzi and Danilo Santi)
1967/
71 Verrazzano Bridge, Florence (with C. Dame-
rini and V. Scalese)
1970/
71 New Flower Market, Pescia, Italy (competition project)
1971 City Planning Structure (project; with Danilo
Santi, G. Corradetti, and R. Buti)
1971/
72 Viaduct Bridge, over the River Indiano,
Florence (competition project)
Workers' Village, Volterrano, Italy (project;
with Danilo Santi, G. Corradetti, and S.
Giubbi)
1972 Catanzaro Airport, Italy (competition project)
1973 Genoa Airport (competition project)
Resort Development, Cannes, France (competition project)
1976 Office Building, Florence (project)
Subsidized Housing, Sermoneta Bassa, Italy
1976/
78 Administrative Centre, Florence (competition
project)
1979 University of Pisa, Italy (competition project)

1980/
81 Subsidized Building, Pistoia, Italy

Publications:

By SAVIOLI: books—*Il piano di ricostruzione di Dicomano*, Florence 1950; *Il verde nella città moderna*, Florence 1962; *I potessi di spazio*, Florence 1969; *Problemi di architettura contemporanea*, Florence 1973; articles—"Concorso per il Lido di Camaiore" in *Urbanistica* (Turin), no. 2, 1949; "Per un significato piu vero della pianificazione" and "La sistemazione urbanistica della piazza d'Armi a Perugia" in *Architetti* (Florence), no. 2, 1950; "Compiti attuali dell'urbanistica e dell'architettura" in *Architetti* (Florence), no. 6, "Gli sviluppi di Firenze dal 1900 fino ad oggi" and "Il Piano Regolatore di Firenze del 1951" in *Urbanistica* (Turin), no. 12, 1953; "Le case minime a Firenze" in *Urbanistica* (Turin), no. 14, 1954; "Il Piano Intercommunale del Territorio Fiorentino" in *Firenze*, Florence 1954; "I problemi del Piano di Ricostruzione di Firenze" in *La pianificazione intercomunale*, Turin 1957; "Urbanistica e architettura moderna nei centri storici monumentali" in *Quaderni della nuova citta*, Florence 1958; "Note su una villa a Populonia" in *Aujourd'hui* (Paris), no. 41, 1963; "Note su un negozio di calzature ad Arezzo" in *Architettura* (Rome), no. 120, 1965; "Il progetto di Paolo Jannone per un centro musicale a Firenze" in *Marcatre* (Milan), no. 23/25, 1966; "Spazio di coinolgimento" in *Casabella* (Milan), no. 326, 1968; "Trager und Einbaupakete" in *Bauen-Wohnen* (Munich), no. 2, 1975; "Il museo e la città" in *Casabella* (Milan), no. 443, 1979.

On SAVIOLI: books—*Disegni di Leonardo Savioli*, exhibition catalogue, by Giuseppe Marchiori, Venice 1960; *Disegni di Leonardo Savioli*, exhibition catalogue, by Umbro Apollonio, Florence 1963; *Leonardo Savioli*, edited by Giovanni Fanelli, Florence 1966; *Leonardo Savioli*, edited by Massimo Becatini, Florence 1974; *Leonardo Savioli: grafico e architetto*, exhibition catalogue, with introduction by Giulio Carlo Argan, Florence 1982; articles—"La mostra dell'oggetto moderne italiano" by Lara-Vinca Masini in *Abitare* (Milan), no. 14, 1963; "La casa abitata" by Lara-Vinca Masini and A. Pica in *Domus* (Milan), no. 426, 1965; "Leonardo Savioli" by M. Bottero in *World Architecture 3*, London 1966; "Art for the People: The Work of Leonardo Savioli" by Giuliano Chelazzi in *Deutsche Bauzeitung* (Stuttgart), January 1977; "The Cemetery of Montecatini" by Giovanni Klaus Koenig in *Architettura* (Rome), July 1978; "Project for Residential Structure in Sermoneta Bassa" in *Architettura* (Rome), August/September 1981; "Flora's Machine" by Adolfo Natalini in *Domus* (Milan), February 1982; "Flower Market in Pescia" in *Architecture d'aujourd'hui* (Paris), June 1982.

*
Leonardo Savioli always combined architectural research with a constant graphic and pictorial activity, in which he relied on the rhythmic repetition of a symbol to generate form; in turn, rhythm and symbol have become essential elements of his architecture. It is always by way of a symbol that Savioli relived and recreated the artistic experience of the past while proposing concepts for the future of the city—such as the stratification and concretization of plastic elements of different periods that, assembled in "technological" strata, project the present and future configuration of the city.

Starting from a spare, clear, architectural language, worked out in parallel slabs arranged in depth perspective (as in his own house at Certosa), Savioli moved on to the elaboration of rhythmically arranged volumetricunits, which became the foundation of his conception of self-contained composition, the creation of a landscape of forms not planned in advance but obtained from a series of additions. He moved from the plastic-technological object—detached, finite, and complete in itself (like the Via Piagentina block in Florence)—to a rejection of architecture that is self-contained and inward-looking for one that is global, directly connected with the course of life. This rejection followed a period of academic experiment and the university dispute of 1968. He called his new work the "architecture of behavior."

After a series of lectures—before and during the university dispute—like that of 1967 on "Poor Equipment for a Collective Structure" (during which some of the first proposals for "radical architecture" also emerged), Savioli shifted his theoretical research toward the elaboration of proposals for polyfunctional systems for contemporary art.

His later architecture reflects his theoretical position. He plans a modular structure in advance; it has a distinct technological-industrial reference, is roofed in and extensible, and provides a base containing all the technical necessities on which the user is able to erect a series of prefabricted concrete elements for his particular use. The structure is efficient, easy to build and manage, and creates residential units each different from the other—as in the two-apartment Bayon Villa at San Gaggio and in the project for a Workers' Village in the Volterrano.

—Lara-Vinca Masini

SCARPA, Carlo.
Italian. Born in Venice, 2 June 1906. Educated at the Technical School, Vicenza, 1917-19; studied architecture, Accademia di Belle Arti, Venice, 1920-25, Dip.Arch. 1926. Served in the Italian Army, 1926. Married Onorina Lazzari in 1934; son: Tobia. Assistant to the architect Vincenzo Rinaldi, Venice, 1922-24. In private practice as architect, designer and graphic artist, in Venice, 1927-62, in Asolo, 1962-72, and in Vicenza, 1972 until his death in 1978. Artistic Consultant to Murano Cappellin and Company Glassworks, Venice, 1927-30 and to Venini Glassworks, Venice, 1933-47; design consultant for the Venice *Biennale*, from 1941, and for Cassina and B & B furniture companies, Italy, 1969. Assistant Instructor, 1926-29, 1932-33, Professor 1933-76, Emeritus Professor, 1976-77, and Director, 1970-78, Istituto Universitario di Architettura, Venice; Head of Design Course, Istituto Artistico Industriale, Venice, 1945-47; Head of Visual Studies Course, Istituto Superiore di Disegno Industriale, Venice, 1960-61. Committee Member, International Glass Commission, Paris, 1962. Exhibition: *Nine Architects*, Venice, 1960; *Carlo Scarpa*, at the *Triennale*, Milan, 1960; *Architecture of the Museum*, Museum of Modern Art, New York, 1966; *Pursuit of New Structures*, at the *Biennale*, Venice, 1968; *Great Drawings from the Collection*, Royal Institute of British Architects, London, 1974; *Carlo Scarpa*, Accademia Olimpica, Vicenza, 1974; *Carlo Scarpa*, Institut de I'Environnement, Paris, 1975; *Carlo Scarpa*, Galeria I.D., Madrid, 1978; *Design & Design*, Palazzo delle Stelline, Milan, and Palazzo Grassi, Venice, 1979; *28/28 Architettura*, Palazzo delle Stelline, Milan, 1979; *Carlo Scarpa: disegni*, Accademia di San Luca, Rome, 1979; *Carlo Scarpa, 1906-1978*, Galleria dell'Accademia, Venice, 1984. Recipient: Diploma of Honour, *Triennale*, Milan, 1934; Olivetti National Award, Italy, 1956; Grand Prize of the Jury, *Triennale*, Milan, 1960; Gold Medal, Ministry of Public Information, Rome, 1962; IN-ARCH National Award, Italy, 1962; Regional Architecture Award, Verona, 1964; Architecture Prize of the President of the Republic, Italy, 1967; Accademia dei Lincei Prize, Italy, 1971. Honorary Member, British Institute of Design, 1970; Member, Accademia Olimpica, Vicenza, 1974; Honorary Member, Pierre Chareau Foundation, Paris, 1975; Academician, Accademia di San Luca, Rome, 1976. D.Arch.: Istituto Universitario di Architecttura, Venice, 1978. Member, Associazione per l'Architettura Organica, Venice. *Died* (in Sendai, Japan) *28 November 1978.*

Works:

1923/
24 Religious Buildings, Venice (as assistant to Vicenzo Rinaldo)
1924/
25 Villa Gioacchino Velluti annexe, Dolo, Venice
1925/
26 Palazzo Da Mula restoration and new industrial buildings for Cappellin and Company, Murano, Venice
Villa Angelo Velo restoration, Fintaniva, Padua, Italy (with Franco Pizzuto)
Velo Company dock-yards, Fontaniva, Padua, Italy (with Franco Pizzuto)
Industrial buildings and housing, Fontaniva, Padua, Italy (with Franco Pizzuto)
Villa Giovanni Campagnolo, Fontaniva, Padua, Italy (with Franco Pizzuto)
Villa Aldo Martinati, Padua, Italy (with Franco Pizzuto
1928 Glassware Shop interiors, Lungarno Guicciardini, Florence (demolished)
1931 Pastry Shop interiors, Frezzeria, Venice (demolished)
Ferruccio Asta House interiors and furnishings, Venice
1932 Academy Bridge, Venice (competition project)
1934 Plan for Mestre, Venice (competition project; with Mario de Luigi)
Lido Airport, Venice (project)
1935 Bassani Apartment, Cortina, near Belluno, Italy (project)
1936/
37 Ca Foscari (Faculty of Economics and Commerce) restoration, University of Venice
1937 Design of the *Venetian Jewels* exhibition, Venice
1940 Small apartments, San Gregorio, Venice (project)
1941 Design of the *Biennale*, Venice
Rizzo Tomb, Cemetery of San Michele, Venice
1942 Galleria Il Cavallino interiors, Riva degli Schiavoni, Venice
1946 Cinema, Valdobbiadene, Treviso, Italy (project)
1947 Giacomuzzi House, Udine, Italy (project)
Rental apartments and shops, Spalato Square, Padua (project)
Trans-Adriatic Society Offices, Venice (project)
1947/
49 Catholic Bank Headquarters, Tarvisio Udine (project)
1948 Design of the *Paul Klee* exhibition, *Biennale*, Venice
Catholic Bank Cervignano, Udine (competition project)
Bus Station, Piazza Mazzini, Padua (project)
Parish Church, Torre di Mosto, Venice (project)
1948/
49 Cinema, San Dona di Piave, Venice (project)
1949 Bauter Hotel, San Moise, Venice (Project)
Design of the *Giovanni Bellini* exhibition, Palazzo Ducale, Venice
Il Cavallino Gallery office interiors, Frezzeria, Venice
Apartment Building, Padua (project)
Guarnieri House, Lido, Venice (project)
4-storey rental apartment builing, Feltre, Belluno, Italy (project)
Danieli Hotel lobby, Venice (project)

Carlo Scarpa: Project for the Teatro Comunale, Vicenza, 1968-69.

1949/
50 Storeroom, and design of the *Publications Exhibition*, at the *Venice Film Festival*

1950 Ala Piavola de Franza Shop alterations, Venice (demolished)

Ferdinando Ongania Shop interiors, San Marco, Venice (demolished)

Telephone Company office alterations, San Marco, Venice (demolished)

Galleria Il Cavallino Art Publications Pavilion, *Biennale,* Venice

Bortolatto House, Cervignano, Udine (project)

1952 Design of the Italian Pavilion, and of the *Tiepolo* exhibition, *Biennale,* Venice

Design of the *Graphic Works by Toulouse Lautrec* exhibition, Palazzo Napoleonico, Venice

Historical Archives of Contemporary Art alterations, Ca'Giustinian, Venice (project)

Academy Gallery interiors and furnishings, Venice

1953 Design of *The 15th Century* exhibition, Town Hall, Messina

Correr Museum first floor gallery alterations, Venice

Villa Zoppas, Conegliano, Treviso, Italy (project)

National Gallery of Sicily restoration, Palazzo Abbatellis, Palermo

1954 Design of the *Art of Ancient China* exhibition, Palazzo Ducale, Venice

1954/
56 Academy Gallery interiors II, Venice

1955 Manlio Capitolo (public court) alterations, Rialto, Venice

Scatturin Lawyers' Office alterations, Venice

Museum Library and Cultural Centre, La Spezia, Italy (competition project; wtih G. d'Agaro, E. Detti, and V. Pastor)

1955/
57 Pedestal, for the Monument to a Partisan, Venice (demolished)

1955/
61 Veritti House, Udine

1956 Design of the *Piet Mondrian* exhibition, Gallery of Modern Art, Rome

Olivetti Mountain Colony, Brusson, Ivrea, Italy (competition project with G. d'Agaro, E. Detti, and V. Pastor)

Main Auditorium alterations, Ca'Foscari, Venice

Venezuelan Pavilion, *Biennale,* Venice

Six exhibition rooms remodelling. Uffizi Gallery, Florence (with Ignazio Gardella and Giovanni Michelucci)

1956/
57 Canova Museum alterations, Possagno Treviso, Italy

1957 Taddei House, Dorsoduro, Venice (project)

1957/
58 Olivetti Showrooms, San Marco, Venice

1958 Design of the *From Altichiero to Pisanello* exhibition, Castlevecchio Museum, Verona

Italian Pavilion interior, *Biennale,* Venice

Design of the *Murano Glassware* exhibition, Salviati and Company, San Gregorio, Venice

1959 Design of the *Vitality in Art* exhibition, Palazzo Grassi, Venice

Design of *A Century of Art in Murano Glass* exhibition, Verona

1960 Correr Museum second floor galleries alterations, Venice

Design of the *Frank Llyod Wright Memorial Exhibition*, Venice

Design of the *Erich Mendelsohn* exhibition, *Biennale,* Venice

1961 Design of the *Sense of Colour and the Mastery of Water* exhibition, *Italia '61,* Turin

Gavina Shop, Bologna (now the Simon Shop)

1961/
63 Querini Stampalia Library ground floor restoration and courtyard, Venice

1962 Design of the *Cima da Conegliano* exhibition, Treviso, Italy

1962/
63 Italian Pavilion alterations, *Biennale,* Venice (project)

1963 Cassina House, Ronco di Carimate Italy

(project)

Revoltella Museum alterations, Trieste (with Franco Vattolo)

Carlo Felice Theatre reconstruction, Genoa (project)

1964 Castelvecchio Museum restoration and alterations, Verona

Design of the *Giacomo Manzu* exhibition, Palazzo Napoleonico, Venice

1964/
65 Apartment Building, Grand Canal, Venice (project)

1964/
68 Zentner House alterations, Zurich

1965/
72 Benedetti House, Rome (project)

1966 Piazza del Duomo Development, Modena, Italy (project)

New Gallery reconstruction, Munich (competition project)

Design of the *Giorgio Morandi* exhibition, Italian Pavilion, *Biennale,* Venice

Entrance, Institute of Architecture, University of Venice (project)

1967 Design of *The Poem* exhibition, Italian Pavilion, *Expo '67,* Montreal

Design of the *Artuo Martini* exhibition, Treviso, Italy

1968 Design of the *Pursuit of New Structures* exhibition, *Biennale,* Venice

Design of *The Drawings of Erich Mendelsohn* exhibition, University of California, Berkeley

Design of the *Frescoes from Florence* exhibition, Hayward Gallery, London

Santini House, near Lucca, Italy (project)

Municipal Theatre, Vicenza, Italy (competition project)

1970 Design of the *Morandi* exhibition, Royal Academy, London

Masieri Memorial: Students Library and Housing, Grand Canal, Venice

1970/
72 Brion-Vega Tomb and Cemetery, San Vito, Treviso, Italy

1971/
72 Roth House, Asolo, Treviso, Italy (project)
1972 Lupi House, near Vicenza, Italy (project)
1972/
78 Carlo Felice Theatre, Genoa
1973 Fini Restaurant, Modena, Italy (project)
Library and Guest Rooms Annex, Querini
Stampalia Library, Venice (project)
Museum remodelling (final stage), Villa Strozzi, Florence (project)
1973/
75 People's Mutual Bank, Verona
1974 Design of the *Gino Rossi* exhibition, Treviso,
Italy
Design of the *Venezia-Byzantium* exhibition,
Palazzo Ducale, Venice
1974/
75 Villa Palazzetto exterior alterations, Monselice, Padua
Santa Caterina Convent conversation to
museum, Treviso, Italy (project)
Annex, Villa Matteazzi-Chiesa, Venice
1974/
78 National Museum, Messina
1975 Monument to the Victims of the '72 Terrorist
Outrage, Brescio, near Milan
1975/
76 Convent of San Sebastiano reconstruction
and estensions, Faculty of Literature and
Philosophy, University of Venice
1975/
77 Preservation plan for the ancient Roman
housing of Feltre, Italy
1976 Picasso Museum, Paris (project)
1977 Antoniana Bank Branch Office, Monselice,
near Padua (project)
Apartment interiors, Montecchio, Vicenza,
Italy
Design of the *Alberto Viani* exhibition, Venice
1977/
78 Week-end house for 3 families, Belluno, Italy
(with Hiroyuki Toyota)
1978 Zoppi House, Vicenza, Italy
Church of Torresino alter and paving, Padua,
Italy
Design of the *Carlo Scarpa* exhibition, Madrid
Design of the *Mario Cavaglieri* exhibition,
Rovigo, Italy

Designs: Glassware for Murano Cappelin and
Comapny, Venice, 1927-30, and for the Venini
Company, Murano, Venice, 1933-47; furniture,
particulary for the Gavina (now the Simon) Shop,
Bologna; and silverware.

Publications:

By SCARPA: book—*Memoriae Causa,* editor,
Verona 1977; article—"Interview with Carlo
Scarpa," with Barbara Radice, in *Modo* (Milan),
January/February 1979.

On SCARPA: books—*Carlo Scarpa—Architetto
Poeta* by Sergio Los, Venice, 1967; *Carlo Scarpa—
Architetto Poeta,* exhibition catalogue, by Sherban
Cantacuzino, London 1974; *Carlo Scarpa,* exhibition
catalogue, by Neri Pozza, Vicenza, Italy 1947; *Carlo
Scarpa,* exhibition catalogue, by Luciana Miotto-
Muret, Paris 1975; *Carlo Scarpa* by N. Pozza, Padua
1978; *Carlo Scarpa per Bernini,* edited by G. Scarpa,
Venice 1979; *Carlo Scarpa, Venezia 1906-Sendai
1978: I sette foglie giapponesi,* edited by G. Scarpa,
Venice 1979; *28/78 Architecura: Fifty Years of
Italian Architecture 1928 to 1978,* exhibition
catalogue, Milan 1979; *Carlo Scarpa a Castelvecchio,*
exhibition catalogue, edited by L. Magagnato, Milan
1982; *Carlo Scarpa* by P. Ceccarell and G. Mazzariol,
Venice 1984; *Carlo Scarpa* by M. A. Crippa, Milan
1984; *Carlo Scarpa, 1906-1978,* edited by Francesco
Dal Co and Giuseppe Mazzariol, Milan 1984; *Carlo*

Scarpa: il pensiero, il disegno, i progetti by Maria
Antonietta Crippa, Milan 1984; articles—"Opere
dell'Architetto Carlo Scarpa" by G. Mazzariol in
L'Architettura (Rome), no. 3, 1955; "I Premi Nazion-
ali di Architettura e Urbanistica a Carlo Scarpa e
Ludovico Quaroni" by Bruno Zevi in *L'Arch:tettura*
(Rome), no. 15, 1957; "Progetti di Carlo Scarpa" by F.
Tentori in *Casabella* (Milan), no. 222 1958; "Object on
View" by Michael Brawne in *Architectural Review*
(London), no. 753, 1959; "L'Architettura di Carlo
Scarpa" by S. Bettini in *Zodiac* (Milan), no. 6, 1960;
"Italia '61' Visual Poetry" by P. Gray in *The Observer*
(London), 14 May 1961; "Un 'Opera Distrutta di Carlo
Scarpa" by Pier Carlo Santini in *Zodiac* (Milan), no.
9, 1962; "Carlo Scarpa il Veneziano" by M. Bottero,
in *World Architecture 2,* London 1965; "Carlo
Scarpa—Architetto Veneziano" by M. Brusatin in
Controspazio (Bari, Italy), no. 3/4, 1972; "Scarpa:
L'Ornement est un Crime" by Pierre Joly in *L'Oeil*
(Lausanne), no. 223, 1973; "Carlo Scarpa" in
Architectural Review (London), December 1973;
"La 'Magie' de Carlo Scarpa" by Manfredo Tafuri
and "Locus Solus—Carlo Scarpa et le Cimetiere de
San Vito d'Altivole" by P. Duboy in *L'Architecture
d'Aujourd'hui* (Paris), no. 181, 1975; "Carlo Scarpa"
by Tadashi Yokoyama and Hiroyuki Toyota, special
issue of *Space Design* (Tokyo), June 1977; "Carlo
Scarpa: The Greatest Designer of Contemporary
Italian Architecture" in *L'Architettura* (Rome),
January 1979; "Obituary: Carlo Scarpa" in *Archi-
tectural Review* (London), February 1979; "Carlo
Scarpa in the 70s" special issue of *Architecture-
Mouvement-Continuité* (Paris), December 1979;
"Carlo Scarpa's 1st work" by Piercarlo Santini in
Ottagono (Milan), December 1980; "Carlo Scarpa:
last work—Banca Popolare di Verona" in *GA
Document* (Tokyo), no. 4, 1981; "Scarpa as
Educator" by Guido Pietropoli in *Progressive
Architecture* (New York), May 1981; "Farewell,
Caro Maestro" by Emilio Ambasz in *Progressive
Architecture* (New York), May 1981; "Carlo Scarpa:
Fragments 1926-1978" in special issue of *Rassegna*
(Milan), July 1981; "Carlo Scarpa, 1906-1978" by
Karljosef Schattner in *Baumeister* (Munich), Octo-
ber 1981; "Process and Theme in the Work of Carlo
Scarpa" by G. Zambonini in *Perspecta* (New Haven,
Connecticut), no. 20, 1984.

Post-war Italian architecture made a number of quite
specific and recognizable contributions; prominent
among them was the design of museum interiors.
Carlos Scarpa belonged to a small group of architects
who renovated a number of the great Italian
museums and who were occasionally also able to
demonstrate that their design skills did not depend
entirely on the juxatposition of new elements within
an old context. To thousands of visitors to the
Palazzo Abbatellis in Palermo, the Castelvecchio in
Verona, or the Correr Museum in Venice, it must
have come as perhaps both a surprise and a
revelation that a contemporary architect could treat
the art of the past—whether a painting or a
building—with such sympathy yet freshness. It was
not what they immediately associated with modern
architecture.
Scarpa's success may have been aided by two
strong interests that are closely related to each other:
decoration and the craft of building. What makes an
immediate impression in a building such as the
Venezuelan Pavilion in the grounds of the Venice
Biennale is not only the relation between the major
and minor volumes or the dissolution of the corner in
the way in which the glass in the roof joins the glass in
the wall, but also the detail of the screen hinge. A
simple device becomes a celebration that explains an
action, focuses the eye on an element of decreation,
and speaks of the care and skill with which the
building has been designed and put together.
These skills have also been put at the service of
showing objects of art in ways that have radically
altered our way of seeing and understanding them.
No setting can ever be non-existent or even neutral;
at its best it should be sympathetic. Scarpa has been

able to devise such settings through an understanding of the unique attributes of the object. At the
Palazzo Abbatellis, for instance. Francesco
Luarana's bust of Eleanor of Aragon, seen at the end
of a vista through two doorways, is raised slightly
above its metal support so that none of its form will
be visually interrupted; behind it the background of
green painted panels emphasizes the outline of the
white marble and at the same time provides within a
tall room an environment in scale with the size of the
sculpture and the delicacy of its carving.
Scarpa's work is deeply rooted in the Venetian
tradition; at the same time he has been enormously
influenced by Frank Lloyd Wright. Not only do his
drawings resemble those of Wright, but he has taken
up Wright's preoccupation with architecture as a
plastic, intensely three-dimensional art. From
Wright and Charles Rennie Mackintosh he has also
inherited a belief in a kind of visual density that
derives from both form and materials and the way in
which they are detailed—what Kahn writing about
Scarpa described as "the sense of the wholeness of
inseparable elements."
Scarpa's work began to make an impact in the
middle 1950's, long before notions of conservation,
respect for the past, or the recognition of the
possibilities of decoration were seriously mooted.
The contribution that he and a number of his Italian
contemporaries made was thus to awaken among
architects both an altenative view of the past and a
new way of relating it to the present—of perhaps
understanding the value of a continuity in tradition.

—Michael Brawne

SCHAROUN, Hans.

German. Born in Bremen, 20 September 1893.
Educated at the Technische Hochschule, Charlot-
tenburg, Berlin, 1912-15. Married Anna Marie
Hoffmeyer in 1920; Margit von Plato in 1960.
Worked in the office of Paul Kruchen, Berlin, 1913-
15, and served as site architect to Kruchen on the
East Prussia Rebuilding Programme, 1915-18; in
private practice, Insterburg, Germany, 1919-25; in
partnership with Adolf Rading, Berlin, 1926-28; in
private practice, Berlin, 1932 until his death in 1972.
City Planning Officer, Berlin, 1945-47; Founder,
Planungskollektiv, Berlin, 1946. Professor of Archi-
tecture, Academy of Arts, Breslau, (now Wrocaw,
Poland), 1925-32; Senior Professor of Town Plann-
ing, Technical University, Berlin, 1946-58; Head,
Institute of Building Studies, Berlin, 1947-51. Mem-
ber, Glaserne Kette (Glass Chain), Berlin, 1919;
Member, Works Council for the Arts, Berlin, 1919;
Member of Der Ring, Berlin, 1926. President,
Akademie der Künste, Berlin, 1955-68. Exhibitions:
Weissenhofsiedlung, Stuttgart, 1927; *German Garden
and Industry Exhibition,* Leignitz, 1927-28; *Deut-
scher Werkbund Exhibition,* Breslau, (now Wrocaw,
Poland), 1929; *Building Exhibition.* Berlin, 1931;
Hans Scharoun, Akademie der Künste, Berlin, 1967
and 1969; *Hans Scharoun,* Institute of Contempor-
ary Arts, London, 1974; *Museumsbauten—Entwurfe
und Projekte,* Museum am Ostwall, Dortmund, West
Germany, 1979. Recipient: First Prize, Cathedral
Square Competition, Prenzlau, Germany, 1919;
First Prize, Market Place Competition, Insterburg,
Germany, 1921; First Prize, Leiderhalle Competition, Stuttgart, 1949; First Prize, Theatre Compe-
tition, Kassel, West Germany, 1952; First Prize, Old
People's Home Competition, Berlin, 1952; Fritz
Schumacher Prize, Hamburg, West Germany, 1954;
Berliner Kunst Prize, 1954; First Prize, Town
Planning Competition, Bremen, West Germany,
1956; First Prize, Berlin Philharmonie Competition,
1956; Federal Grand Cross of Merit, 1959; Medallion, Free Arts Academy, Hamburg, West Germany,
1959; First Prize, Mehringplatz Development Competition, Berlin, 1963; Bund Deutscher Architekten
Prize, 1964; First Prize, Library of Prussian Culture

Hans Scharoun: State Library, Berlin, 1967-68.

Competition, Berlin, 1964; Auguste Perret Prize, International Union of Architects, 1965; First Prize, Wolfsburg Theatre Competition, West Germany, 1965; Honorary Citizenship, Berlin, 1969. Honorary doctorates: Technische Hochschule, Stuttgart, 1954; University of Rome, 1965. Senator of the Technical University of Berlin, 1962. *Died* (in Berlin) 25 *November 1972.*

Works:

1911 Church, Bremerhaven, Germany (competition project)
1913 Plan for the Kaiser-Wilhelm-Platz, Geestemunde, Germany (competition project)
Kruchen House, Buch, near Berlin (with Paul Kruchen)
Freymuth Sanatorium, Babelsberg, near Berlin (with Paul Kruchen)
Grunewald Sanatorium, near Berlin (project; with Paul Kruchen)
1914 Hospital, Mariendorf, near Berlin (with Paul Kruchen)
Community Hall, Angerburg, Germany (competition project)
1915 Town plan for Gumbinnen, East Prussia (project)
1916 Riding School/Temporary Church conversion, Walterkehmen, East Prussia
Inn, Goldaper Lake, East Prussia (project)
1917 Community Hall, Kattenau, East Prussia
1917/
18 Farmhouse, Thierfeld, near Gumbinnen, East Prussia
1918 Semi-detached houses, with stables, near Insterburg, East Prussia
1919 State Housing Development, Insterburg, East Prussia (project)
Tivoli Theatre conversion, Insterburg, East Prussia (project)
Cemetery, Dortmund, Germany (competition project)
Cathedral Square, Prenzlau, Germany (competition project)
Town Hall, Emmerich, Germany (competition project)
Swimming Baths, Prenzlau, Germany (competition project)

1920 Two houses, Pregelstrasse, Insterburg, East Prussia
Gutzheit House conversion, near Gumbinnen, East Prussia
Kamswyken Housing Development, near Insterburg, East Prussia
Cultural Centre, Gelsenkirchen, Germany (competition project)
Matheus Muller Works extensions, Eltville, Rheinhessen, Germany (competition project)
Town Hall and Church Square, Lyck, East Prussia (competition project)
Museum of Medicine, Dresden, Germany (competition project)
1920/
21 Town planning scheme for Insterburg, East Prussia (competition project)
1921 Railway Station Post Office, Bremen, Germany (competition project)
Market Place, Insterburg, East Prussia (competition project)
1921/
22 Farmhouse conversion, Sahtilten, East Prussia
1922 Farmyard with forge and riding stables, Kuinen, East Prussia
Stock Exchange Building, Königsberg, East Prussia (competition project)
Chicago Tribune Building (competition project)
Multi-Storey Office Building, Friedrichstrasse, Berlin (competition project)
Granary Building, Wertheim, East Prussia
Town Hall, Wesel, Germany (competition project)
Single-family houses, Insterburg, East Prussia
Gobert House, Sodehnen, East Prussia
Kant Monument, Königsberg, East Prussia (competition project)
1923 Office and apartment building conversion, Insterburg, East Prussia
1923/
24 Apartment blocks, Parkring, Insterburg, East Prussia
1924 Prince Albrecht Gardens Buildings, Berlin (competition project)
1924/
25 Munsterplatz, Ulm, Germany (competition project)

Public Buildings, Bad Mergentheim Spa, Württemberg, Germany
Business Premises, Frankfurt (competition project)
1925 Professor Siegel House, Insterburg, East Prussia (project)
Tannenberg Monument, Germany (competition project)
Town Hall, Bochum, Germany (competition project)
Konitzer Shop, Marienburg, East Prussia (project)
Water Tower (three competition projects)
Bridgehead Building, Cologne (competition project)
1926 Station Square, Duisburg, Germany (competition project)
Variable Apartment Block Dwellings (project)
Popelwitz Housing Development, Breslau (now Wrocaw, Poland) (competition project)
1927 Exhibition Site and Fairground, Berlin (competition project)
Town Hall, Insterburg, East Prussia (competition project)
Exhibition Hall, Breslau (now Wrocaw, Poland) (two projects)
Transportable Wooden House, *German Garden and Industry Exhibition,* Liegnitz
Single-family house, *Weissenhofsiedlung,* Stuttgart
Redevelopment plan for Ministry Gardens, Berlin (project; with Peter Behrens, Adolf Rading, Heinrich Tessenow, and Martin Wagner)
Offices and fire station, Breslau (now Wroctow, Poland) (competition project)
Reichstag Building extensions, Berlin (two competition projects)
Swimming Baths, near the Zoo, Berlin (project)
Apartment block, Dahlem, Berlin (project)
1928 Evangelical Church, Zimpel, Breslau (now Wroclaw, Poland) (competition project)
School, Zimpel, Breslau (now Wroclaw, Poland) (competition project)
Civic Hall and Exhibition Hall, Bremen, Germany (competition project)
School buildings, Schlichtallee, Lichtenberg, Berlin (competition project)
Single-Family House (competition project)
Hotel, Wesermunde, Germany (project)
Richard Wagner Monument, Leipzig Germany (competition project)
1928/
29 Apartment block, Kaiserdamm, Charlottenburg, Berlin
1929 Single People's Apartment Block, *Deutscher Werkbund Exhibition,* Breslau (now Wroctaw, Poland)
Housing, Kaiserstrasse, Bremerhaven, Germany
Apartment block, Heidelberger Platz, Wilmersdorf, Berlin (project)
Apartment block, Paulsbornerstrasse, Wilmersdorf, Berlin (project)
German Iron and Steel Company Exhibition Pavilion, Desta, Germany (project)
1929/
30 Apartment block, Hohenzollerndamm 35-36. Wilmersdorf, Berlin
1930 Law Courts, Invalidenstrasse, Tiergarten, Berlin (competition project)
Housing development, Siemenstadt, Berlin
Apartment block, Lindner, Berlin (project)
Schlachtensee-type Terraced Housing (project)
Halensee-type Terraced Housing (project)
Apartment block, Flinsberger Platz, Wilmersdorf, Berlin (destroyed, 1944; rebuilt by others, 1963)
Civic Hall, Rostock, Germany (competition project)

1931 Leiser Company Shop Sign, Berlin (project)
War Memorial, Thuringer Wald, Germany (competition project)
Steinhausen House conversion, Falkenhain, near Berlin (project)
Bauwelt Contemporary House, Berlin (competition project)
Housing, Kottbusser Tor, Kreuzberg, Berlin (project)
Housing, Treseburger Ufer, Neukolln, Berlin (project)
Housing, Hauptstrasse, Schönerberg, Berlin (project)
Housing, Kaiserdamm, Charlottenburg, Berlin (project)
"Worolet" Housing Types (project)
Three Moller Single-Family Houses, Potsdam, near Berlin (project)
Apartment Block with Access Galleries, Berlin (project)
Lobau-type Single-Family House (project)
Two semi-detached houses (project)
Suburban-Housing Scheme, Berlin (project; with Edwin Gutkind)
Housing and Cinema, Spandauer Damm, Charlottenburg, Berlin (project)
Two-storey apartment blocks, Berlin (project)
Four-storey apartment blocks, Berlin (project)
Housing, Wannsee, Berlin (project)
Apartment block, Reichstrasse, Charlottenburg, Berlin (project)
Plan for Central Corridor Block Apartments, Berlin (project)
Apartment block, Hindenburgplatz, Bremerhaven, Germany (project)
1932 Single-Family House (three projects)
Square Building Apartment, Berlin (project)
The Growing House, Berlin (exhibition project)
Apartment block, Landsberger Allee, Lichtenberg, Berlin (project)
Cinema, Bremerhaven, Germany (project)
Panke Park, near Berlin (project)
Transportable House (project)
Apartment block, Hohenzollernring, Spandau, Berlin
Wenzeck House, Frohnau, Berlin
Schuldenfrey House, Garystrasse 26, Dahlem, Berlin
Apartment block with variable flats (project)
Apartment block, Berlin (project)
Single-family house with arcade (project)
1933 Apartment block, Zweibruckerstrasse 38-46, Spandau, Berlin
Variable Dwelling (project)
Schminke House, Löbau, Saxony, Germany
Strauss House, Huninger Strasse, Dahlem, Berlin
Town plan for Stockholm (competition project)
Apartment block, Alexanderplatz, Berlin (project)
Mattern House, Bornim, Potsdam, near Berlin
Housing development, Kladow-Hottengrund, Berlin
1934 Loeser and Richter Works conversion and extensions, Lobau, Saxony, Germany
Single-family housing group, Burgerpark, Westermunde, Germany (project)
Hotel holiday houses, Vietznau, Switzerland (project)
Muller-Oerlinhausen Mosaic Works Shop, Charlottenburg, Berlin
Professor Gocht House, Berlin (project)
1935 Baensch House, Hohenweg 9, Spandau, Berlin
Hoffmeyer House, Friesenstrasse 6, Bremerhaven, Germany
Pflaum House, Falkensee, near Berlin
1936 Housing, Kaiserstrasse 224, Bremerhaven, Germany
House, Heiligensee, Berlin

Moll House, Grunewald, Berlin (destroyed), 1944)
1937 Housing, Elbestrasse, Bremerhaven, Germany
Moller House, Zermutzelsee, near Altruppin, Brandenburg, Germany
1937/
38 Noack House, Potsdam, near Berlin
1938 Biskupski House, Zermutzelsee, near Altruppin, Brandenburg, Germany
Housing, Blessmannstrasse, Bremerhaven, Germany
Kruger House conversion, Rehwiese 4, Nikolasse, Berlin
Bonk House, Bornim, Potsdam, near Berlin
Housing, Humboldtstrasse, Reinickendorf, Berlin (project)
Just House, Schlachtensee, Berlin (project)
Apartment Block conversion, Yorkstrasse, Bremerhaven, Germany (project)
1939 Weidhaas House, Leipzig Germany (two projects)
Silbermann Family Garden Bath-House, Havel, Brandenburg, Germany
Scharf House, Miquelstrasse 39a/b, Schmargendorf, Berlin
Mohrmann House, Falkensteinstrasse 10, Lichtenrade, Berlin
1940 Housing, Kaiserstrasse 240-54, Bremerhaven, Germany
Endell House, Kleinen Wannsee 30b, Wannsee, Berlin
Studio conversion, Kantstrasse 12, Charlottenburg, Berlin
1941/
43 Central Laundry, Berlin (project)
1942 Weigand House, Borgsdorf, near Berlin
1943 Muller-Oerlinghausen House conversion, Kressbroon/Bodensee, Germany
Moller House extension, Zermutzelsee, near Altruppin, Brandenburg, Germany
1946 Berlin City Plan (project; with Planungskollektiv Group)
Deutschland Plastic House (project; with Karl Bottcher)
Exhibition Gallery, Friedrichstrasse Station, Berlin (project)
1948 Wilhelm House, Kladow, Berlin (project)
America House conversion, Bremerhaven, West Germany
Gerd Rosen Exhibition Gallery (project)
1949 Opera House, Leipzig, East Germany (competition project)
Cellulose Factory, Rothensee, Magdeburg, East Germany (project)
Neighborhood Unit Housing, Friedichshain, Berlin (project)
Leiderhalle, Stuttgart (competition project)
Institute of Building conversion, German Academy of Sciences, Berlin
1950 Schminke House extensions, Löbau, Saxony, Germany (project)
Shops and apartments, Kurfurstendamm 182, Charlottenburg, Berlin (project)
1951 Primary school, Darmstadt, West Germany (project)
American Memorial Library, Blucherplatz, Kreuzberg, Berlin (competition project)
1952 Heinrich-Mendelsohn Building, Kaiserdamm, Charlottenburg, Berlin (competition project)
Siemenstadt Centre, Jungfernheideweg, Berlin (project)
City Theatre, Kassel, West Germany (competition project)
Old People's Home, Tiergarten, Berlin (competition project)
Plan for the development of Helgoland, West Germany (competition project)
1953 National Theatre, Mannheim West Germany (competition project)
1954 Theatre, Gelsenkirchen, West Germany (competition project)

1954/
59 "Romeo and Juliet" Flats, Zuffenhausen, Stuttgart
1955 Private school, Bergneustadt, West Germany (competition project)
Office building, Hannover, West Germany (competition project)
New Market, Hamburg, West Germany (competition project)
City Plan for Marl, Westphalia, West Germany (as project consultant)
Restaurant, Hansaviertel, Berlin (project)
Wella Company Administration Buildings, Darmstadt (two competition projects)
Stoeher House, Darmstadt
Apartment block extensions, Goebelstrasse 1-9, Siemenstadt, Berlin (original building by Bartning)
1956 Town plan for Bremen, West Germany (competition project)
Orphanage, Botnang, Stuttgart (project)
Krupp Convent, Essen, West Germany (competition project)
Development plan for the Hansaviertel, Tiergarten, Berlin (project)
Single-family houses, Hansaviertel, Tiergarten, Berlin (project)
1956/
61 Housing, North Charlottenburg, Berlin
1956/
62 Geschwister Secondary School, Lunen, Westphalia, West Germany
1957 School, Holterhofchen, Hilden, Westphalia, West Germany (competition project)
Civic Hall, Bremen, West Germany (competition project)
Shopping centre, Goebelplatz, North Charlottenburg, Berlin (project)
1958 Concert Hall, Saarbrucken, West Germany (competition project)
Plan for Spandau Old Town, Berlin (project)
Rothenburg House conversion, Dahlem, Berlin (project)
State Savings Bank, Stuttgart (project)
Town Hall, Marl, Westphalia, West Germany (competition project)
1959 Berlin as Capital City (competition project)
Plan for Reeperbahn-Millerntor, Hamburg, West Germany (project)
1960 Studio flat, Berlin (project)
1961 School for Social Studies, Linz, Austria (competition project)
1961/
63 "Salute" High-Rise Block, Stuttgart
1961/
68 School, Marl, Westphalia, West Germany
1962 Foreign Students Hostel (project)
Leere Vasen Housing Development, Boblingen, near Stuttgart
Dumont Schauberg Publishers Offices, Cologne (project)
1963 Dom-Romerberg-Bereich, Frankfurt (competition project)
Berlin Philharmonie, Kemperplatz, Tiergargen, Berlin
Redevelopment plan for Mehringplatz, Kreuzberg, Berlin (competition project)
1963/
71 German Embassy, Brasilia
1964 Neven-DuMont House, Cologne (project)
Concert Hall, Pforzheim, West Germany (competition project)
Theatre, Zürich (competition project)
SP Offices, Hamburg, West Germany (competition project)
Library of Prussian Culture, Tiergarten, Berlin (competition project)
1965 Housing, Rauhe Kapf, Boblingen, near Stuttgart
1966 Tormann House, Bad Homburg van der Hohe, West Germany
Faculty of Architecture Building, Technical University of Berlin

Chapel of St. John, Glockengarten, Bochum, West Germany

Church of the Transfiguration of Christ, Viktoria-Luise-Platz, Schöneberg, Berlin (project)

Art Centre and Hostel, Matthaikirchplatz, Tiergarten, Berlin (project)

1967/
78 State Library, Berlin
1968 "Red Garage," Zuffenhausen, Stuttgart
Kopke House, Im Dol 10, Dahlem, Berlin
1969 Housing, Hasenbergsteige, Stuttgart (project)
1970 Church and Parish Centre, Rabenberg, Wolfsburg, West Germany
Kindergarten, Detmerode, Wolfsburg, West Germany
High-rise apartment block, Zabel-Kruger-Damm, Reinickendorf, Berlin
AOK Headquarters Building, Mehringplatz, Kreuzberg, Berlin
German Maritime Museum, Bremerhaven, West Germany
1971 "Orplid" High-Rise Apartment Block, Boblingen, near Stuttgart
1973 City Theatre, Wolfsburg, West Germany
1978 Philharmonie Chamber Music Hall, Tiergarten, Berlin (completed by others)
State Institute for Musical Research and Museum of Musical Instruments, Tiergarten, Berlin (completed by others)

Publications:

By SCHAROUN: articles—"Struktur in Raum und Zeit" in *Handbuch moderner Architektur*. Berlin 1957; "Raum und Milieu der Schule" in *Bauen und Wohnen* (Zürich), April 1961; preface to *Baroque: Italie et Europe Centrale* by Pierre Charpentrat, Fribourg, Switzerland 1964.

On SCHAROUN: books—*Hans Scharoun*, exhibition catalogues, by Heinrich Lauterbach, Berlin 1967, 1969; *Global Architecture: The Berlin Philharmonic Concert Hall* by Yukio Futagawa and Hiroshi Sasaki, Tokyo 1973; *Expressionist Architecture* by Wolfgang Pehnt, London 1973; *Fantastic Architecture* by Ulrich Conrads and Hans G. Sperlich, London 1973; *Hans Scharoun: Bauten, Entwürfe: Texte*, edited by Peter Pfankuch, Berlin 1974; *Hans Scharoun* by Peter Blundell Jones, London 1978; *Het Nieuwe Bouwen International; CIAM—Housing, Town Planning*, exhibition catalogue, by R. D. Oxenaar and A. van der Woud, Delft, Netherlands 1983; *Architekture-Raume: Idee und Gestalt bei Hans Scharoun* by Eckehard Janofske, Braunschweig and Wiesbaden, West Germany 1984; articles—"Hans Scharoun: oeuvres récentes" in *L'Architecture d'aujourd'hui* (Paris), September/November 1960; "Hans Scharoun: Ein Beitrag zum organischen Bauen" by Margit Staber in *Zodiac* (Milan), no. 10, 1962; "L'Opera di Hans Scharoun e la sua influenza a Lunen" in *L'Architettura* (Rome), October 1963; "Hans Scharoun," special issue of *Bouwkundig Weekblad* (Amsterdam), October 1963; "The Work of Hans Scharoun" by Udo Kultermann in *Binario* (Lisbon), January/February 1974; "Hans Scharoun: An Exhibition of His Work" by Peter Blundell Jones in *Building Design* (London), 8 November 1974; "Hans Scharoun: A Short Discussion of His Work" in *The Architect* (London), December 1974; "Late Work of Scharoun" by Peter Blundell Jones in *Architectural Review* (London), March 1975; "Hans Scharoun: An Introduction" by Peter Blundell Jones in *Architectural Design* (London), July 1978; "Hans Scharoun" by Peter Blundell Jones in *RIBA Journal* (London), November 1978; "Light on Scharoun" by Colin St. John Wilson in *Architectural Review* (London), April 1979; "Required Reading: Berlin State Library" by Dennis Sharp in *Building* (London), 4 January 1980; "Hans Scharoun: State Library, Berlin" by Manfred Speidel in *Architecture + Urbanism* (Tokyo), May 1980; "Meaning from Contrast: Scharoun's Philharmonic in Berlin" by Eckehard Janofske in *Daidalos* (Berlin), 14 March 1982; "Hans Scharoun—Dead Ten Years Ago" by Max Onsell in *Bauwelt* (Berlin), 26 November 1982; "Scharoun Houses" by Peter Blundell Jones, in *Architectural Review* (London), December 1983; recording—*Hans Scharoun*, tape cassette and slides by Peter Blundell Jones, London 1979.

*

Hans Scharoun's early work was a mixture of international modernism and expressionism. His flats at the *Deutscher Werkbund Exhibition* in 1929, though strictly functional in conception, have some expressionist features and are full of curves and pierced splayed walls. He was responsible for the general layout of the housing at Siemenstadt, Berlin, in 1930, and his own contribution to the scheme also shows traces of expressionism.

Although Scharoun's work falls into two distinct parts, before and after World War II, the buildings he designed during the war are of considerable interest. Scharoun was not a popular architect before the war, but he built a number of remarkable houses, among which the Schminke House, Löbau, is outstanding. Arranged at first-floor level, it has a free, open plan divided only by light-weight moveable partitions. The house has generous balconies which curve and sweep around it.

His houses were always very skilfully sited, making the maximum use of ground and cross-country views. He did not hesitate to plan a living room facing north if the best outlook was in that direction, but he always compensated for the lack of sunlight by providing smaller winders in the same room looking southward. His greatest skill was in the creation of interior space incorporating outlook, comfort, and surprise, the last often obtained by the use of converging and then widening walls in the form of a venturi. The direction of the best views was always marked on his sketch plans; houses were clearly seen to be created round these aces. Apart from this determination to make the best use of the site, there is nothing geometrical about his plans; they flow freely and logically and without constraint. He never seems to have been much concerned with external appearances, usually leaving them to take care of themselves, sometimes with not very happy results

During World War II, his designs were officially unpopular, but he still continued to design private houses, clothing his expressionist plans in skilfully designed traditional exteriors which either deceived or satisfied the authorities.

It was not until after the war that Scharoun came into his own as the Expressionist of the age. Outstanding among his postwar designs was the City Theatre for Kassel, which was never built because the client doubted whether the design could be constructed. It was the design for the Romeo and Juliet Flats in Stuttgart-Zuffenhausen, in 1954-59, that firmly established him. Here the plan, almost devoid of right angles, points in nine different directions, while odd-shaped curved and pointed balconies add to the startling and dramatic silhouette. In spite of their curious and even frightening appearance, the flats are extremely popular and are snapped up the moment they come onto the market.

Scharoun's best-known work, the Berlin Philharmonie, is one of the world's great concert hall interiors clad in a drab and collapsed-looking exterior. The hall, reached from a dramatic polygonal foyer where staircases shoot off Piranesi-like at all angles, is built up of parcels of seating round the orchestra. Each parcel contains about the same number of seats as there are players in the orchestra, and the effect is to reduce the overall scale of the interior without lessening the total sense of space. For once, the siting of the building is far from ideal. It deserves an enclosed site; instead, it looks overexposed, like jelly on a flat dish.

Scharoun's German Embassy in Brasilia shows his use of floor space at its most prodigal, with frequent changes of level and many oddly-shaped rooms. Externally, boldly expressionist use is made of sun screens.

Scharoun also built several schools notable for their immense spread and their logical planning within what at first appears to be an incomprehensible jumble. Elevations—or, more properly, exteriors—were allowed to develop themselves, and detailing is heavy but simple and modest.

The Maritime Museum in Bremen contrasts with most of Scharoun's other buildings in that it is comparatively simple in conception. But the plan and general conception of the City Theatre in Wolfsburg astounds by the extravagance of its spread, above all in its foyer and cloakrooms. It has much in common with the Berlin Philharmonie. The Berlin City Library, sited opposite Mies van der Rohe's National Gallery, is Scharoun's last and largest building. At first sight its plan seems very wasteful, although the various functions are skilfully integrated. No doubt, as in all Scharoun's buildings, it will be found to have some fine interiors.

—Gontran Goulden

SCHINDLER, Rudolph Michael.

American. Born in Vienna, 5 September 1887; emigrated to the United States, 1914. Educated at the Imperial Technical Institute of Vienna, 1906-11; Vienna Academy of Arts, under Otto Wagner, 1909-14. Married Sophie Pauline Gibling in 1919 (separated in the 1930s); son: Mark. Worked as a draftsman for Mayr and Mayer, Vienna, 1911, and for Ottenheimer, Stern and Reichert, Chicago, 1914; joined the office of Frank Lloyd Wright, q.v., Chicago, as an unsalaried employee, 1916: became a paid employee, 1918; sent by Wright to oversee work on the Barnsdall Houses, in Los Angeles, 1920-21; in private practice, Los Angeles, 1921 until his death in 1953: in collaboration with Richard Neutra and Carol Aronovici, 1925-31. Lecturer, Chicago School of Applied Art, 1917. Exhibitions: Scripps College, Claremont, California, 1950; University of California at Santa Barbara, 1967; Stedelijk Museum, Amsterdam, 1969; Royal Institute of British Architects, London, 1969; Museum Villa Stuck, Munich, 1985. Schindler Archive and Study Center established, Los Angeles, 1980. *Died* (in Los Angeles) *22 August 1953*.

Works:

1912 Hotel Rong, Vienna (project)
Hunting Lodge, Vienna (project)
Actor's Clubhouse, 6 Dorotheergasse, Vienna (for Mayr and Mayer)
1912/
13 Crematorium and Chapel, Vienna (project)
1914 Summer House, near Vienna (project)
Neighborhood Center, Chicago (competition project)
1915 Hotel, Chicago (project)
Bar, Chicago (project)
Martin House, Taos, New Mexico (project)
1915/
16 Homer Emunim Temple and School, Chicago (project)
1916 Store Front, Chicago (project)
Central Administration Building, Chicago (project)
Women's Club, Chicago (project)
Lee House remodelling, Maywood, Illinois
Hampden Club, Chicago
1916/
17 Log House (project)
1917 House, Oak Park, Illinois (project)
1917/
18 Buena Shore Club, Chicago

Rudolph Schindler: Lovell Beach House, Newport Beach, California, 1926.

1918 Children's Corner, Art Institute of Chicago (project)
1919 One-room apartment, Chicago (project)
     Memorial Community Center, Wenatchee, Washington
     Staley House, Waukegan, Illinois
     Shampay House, Chicago
     Workmen's Colony (Monolith Homes), Chicago (project)
1920 Temporary House for J.B. Irving, Wilmette, Illinois (project)
     Theatre, Shops, and apartments, Olive Hill, Los Angeles (project; with Frank Lloyd Wright)
     Barnsdall Houses A and B, Olive Hill, Los Angeles (with Frank Lloyd Wright)
     Bergen Free Public Library, Jersey City, New Jersey (Competition project)
     Industrial Housing, Los Angeles (project)
     House, 7 Greenwood Common, Berkeley, California
1921 Walt Whitman School, Los Angeles (project)
     Korsen Bungalow Court, Los Angeles (project)
     Playmart Skyscraper, Los Angeles (project)
1921/
   22 Schindler/Clyde Chase Double House, 833 North Kings Road, Hollywood, California

1922 Helena Rubinstein Beauty Salon, Los Angeles
     Binder and Gross Apartment Building, Soto Street, Los Angeles
     Burrell Duplex, Hollywood, California
     Henderson Double House, Los Angeles
     Caplan Apartment Building remodelling, Los Angeles
     Lacey Duplex, 830-832 Laguna Avenue, Los Angeles
     Kent House, Los Angeles (project)
     Mix House, Los Angeles (project)
     Campbell House, Los Angeles (project)
     Duncan House, Los Angeles (project)
     Lindquist House, Hollywood, California (project)
     Baker Photographic Studio, Los Angeles
     Temple Apartment Building, Hollywood, California (project)
     Popinoff Cabin, Coachella, California
     Burrell House, Los Angeles (project)
1922/
   24 Davies House, Los Angeles (project)
1922/
   25 Floren Duplexes and Apartments, Harper and Romaine and La Jolla and Romaine, Hollywood, California
1923 Friedman/Kopley Apartment Building, 115 North Soto Street, Los Angeles

Paine Duplex, 1024 Havenhurst Avenue, Los Angeles
Lovell House, Hollywood, California (project)
Lowe House, Eagle Rock, California (with Frank Lloyd Wright)
Hotel Wind and Sea alterations, La Jolla, California (project)
Warne House, Hollywood, California (project)
Art Room, Hollywood Public Library, California (project; with Douglas Donaldson)
Physical Education Club Lodge, Topanga Ranch, Topanga Canyon, Los Angeles County (project)
Neville Store and Hotel, Hollywood, California (project)
Helena Rubinstein House alterations and remodelling, Greenwich, Connecticut
Leswin/Leepa Beach Studio and Store, Castel La Mar, California
Pueblo Ribera Community, 230 Gravilla Street, La Jolla, California
Baker House, Hollywood, California (project)
Kruetzer Apartment Building, 1620-1626 North Gower Street, Los Angeles
Four-flat Building, 4327 Harold Way, Los Angeles
1924 Popinoff Desert House, Coachella, California (project)
     Lovel Vacation House, Wrightwood, California
     Braun Apartment Building remodelling, 6092 Selma Avenue, Los Angeles
     Packard House, 931 North Gainsborough Drive, South Pasedena, California
     Peoples Bank, Los Angeles (project)
     Plotkin House, Los Angeles (project)
     Barnsdall Houses garden wall and landscaping, Olive Hill, Los Angeles
     Gibling House, Los Angeles
     Nurembega Heights Hotel, Burbank, California (project)
1924/
   33 Levin House, 2376 Dundee Place, Los Angeles
1925 Barnsdall Houses remodelling, Olive Hill, Los Angeles
     Popinoff Hotel and Bungalow Community, Coachella, California (project)
     Howe House, 2422 Silver Ridge Avenue, Los Angeles
     Hotel Elsinore, Elsinore, California (project; with A.R. Brandner and Richard Neutra)
     Wading Pool and Pergola, for Barnsdall Houses, Olive Hill, Los Angeles
     Photographic Studio, Ambassador Hotel, Los Angeles (project)
     Lovell Ranch House, Fallbrook, California
     Furniture for Lovell House children's workshop, Los Angeles
     Sullivan/Kent Tea Room, Los Angeles
     Brudin House, El Monte, California (project)
     Breacher Apartment Building, Los Angeles
     Park Ranch House, Fallbrook, California
1925/
   26 Lovell Beach House, 1242 Ocean Avenue, Newport Beach, California
     Weiner House remodelling, 1120 Court Street, Los Angeles
     Briggs House, Newport Beach, California (project)
     Sorg House, 600 South Putney Avenue, San Gabriel, California
     Exhibition Room, Berkeley, California (project)
     Morgenthau Studio, Palm Springs, California (project)
     Leah-Ruth Shop, Long Beach, California
     Haines Health Food Store, Los Angeles
     League of National Building (competition project; with Richard Neutra)
     Brown Apartments, Hollywood, California (project)

Hain House, Los Angeles

Hennessey Brothers, Apartment Building, Los Angeles (project)

Levy Apartment Building, Los Angeles (project)

1926/
28 Martec House, Los Angeles (project)

Price House, Los Angeles (project)

1926/
40 Manola Court Apartment Building, 1811-1813 Edgecliff Drive, Los Angeles

1927 Freeman House furniture, 1965 Glencoe Way, Hollywood, California

Hotel Elsinore, Elsinore, California (2nd project; with A.R. Brandner)

Miller Apartment Building, Los Angeles (project)

Four-flat building, Pasadena, California

Aesop's Store, Los Angeles

Temporary Outdoor exhibition pavilion, Barnsdall Houses, Olive Hill, Los Angeles

Garden Apartments, Los Angeles (project)

Miller Apartment Building, Los Angeles (project)

Napolitano Oil Mill, 676 Clover Street, Los Angeles

Richardson House remodelling, 8272 Marmont Way, Los Angeles

Zaczek House, Los Angeles (project)

Translucent House (Barnsdall House), Palos Verdes, California (project)

Amusement Center, Los Angeles (project)

1927/
28 Falcon Flyers Country Club, Near Wasco, Kern County, California (project)

1928 Twin Harbour Community, Cataline Island, California (project)

Slemons House, Los Angeles (project)

Art Gallery, Lake Merritt, Oakland, California (project)

Braxton House, Venice, California (project)

Barnsdall House remodelling, Olive Hill, Los Angeles

Golden Pyramid, Los Angeles (project)

Wolfe Summer House, Avalon, Cataline Island, California

Sets for *Soul of Raphael*, Trinity Auditorium, Los Angeles

Braxton Gallery, Hollywood, California

Grokowsky House, 816 Bonita Drive, South Pasadena, California

1929 Hotel, Hollywood, California (project)

Diffin House remodelling, Avalon, Catalina Island, California (project)

Coffee Shop for Tucson Holding Company, Arizona (project)

Wolfe School of Costume Designing, Los Angeles

Satyr Bookshop, Los Angeles

Lavana Studio Building, Los Angeles (project)

Automobile Show Room, Lincoln Garage Building, Beverly Hills, California (with H. Sachs)

Lingerbrink Cabin, Calabasas, California

J.J. Newberry Storefront, Los Angeles (project; with H. Sachs)

Paradise Resort, Ontario, California (project)

Cabin No. 1, Park Moderne, Blackbird Way, Woodlands Hills, California

Effie Dean Cafe, Los Angeles (project)

Frankel Apartment Building, Los Angeles (project)

Vorkapic House remodelling, 2100 Benedict Canyon, Beverly Hills, California

Easter Puppet Show, Los Angeles

1930 Shore House, Venice, California (project)

Cohan Market, Los Angeles (project)

Exposition Buildings and Park, Los Angeles (project)

Bennati House remodelling, Los Angeles (partially executed)

Elliot House, 4237 Newdale Drive, Los Angeles

Wing Hotel and Subdivision, Banning, California (project)

Nobby Knit Store, Los Angeles (project)

Kopenlanoff Desert House, Palm Springs, California (project)

Kopenlanoff Subdivison, Palm Springs, California (project)

Auditorium and Civic Center, Richmond, California (competition project)

1930/
31 George/Freedman Store, Los Angeles (project)

1931 Cherry Apartment House, 3910 South Walton Street, Los Angeles

Marx House remodelling, 1557 North Courtney Avenue, Los Angeles

Stojano House garage, 8501 Dahlia Street, Los Angeles

Highway Bungalow Hotel (project)

Von Koerber House, 408 Monte d'Oro, Hollywood Riviera, Torrance, California

The Embassy Restaurant and Arcade, Los Angeles

1933 House, Park Moderne, Blackbird Way, Woodland Hills, California

Hanna House, Los Angeles (project)

Lierd/Todd House, Los Angeles (project)

Standard Oil Service Station (prototype)

Donnell's Desert Hotel, Twenty-Nine Palms, California (project)

Brown, Smith and Moore Automobile Store, Los Angeles (project)

Max Company Show Windows, Los Angeles (project; with A.R. Bradner and B.P. Paradise)

1932/
33 Bread Pit Stores, Los Angeles

1932/
34 Sardi's Restaurant, Hollywood, California

Lindy's Restaurant, Hollywood, California

1932/
36 Veissi House, Hollywood, California

1933 Schindler Shelters (prototypes)

Farr Dance Hall, Denver (project)

Oliver House, 2236 Micheltorena Street, Los Angeles

Union Oil Service Station (prototype)

Lock House, Los Angeles (two projects)

Perstein House, remodelling and furniture, 111 Tamalpais Road, Berkeley, California

The Oven (retail bakery), Los Angeles

Grauman Restaurant, Los Angeles (project)

Panel Post Constructions (prototypes)

1934 Buck House, Eighth and Genessee Streets, Los Angeles

Dondo House, remodelling, 583 Tamalpais Road, Berkeley, California (project)

King House remodelling and furniture, 10354 La Grange, Westwood, California

Kipp House remodelling, 1773 Griffith Park Boulevard, Los Angeles

Pavaroff House, remodelling and furniture, 1641 North Crescent Heights Boulevard, Los Angeles

Ransom House, Palm Springs, California (project)

Rheingold House remodelling, 8730 Sunset Boulevard, Los Angeles

House, Leimert Park, Los Angeles (project)

Nerenbaum Service Station (project)

1934/
35 Van Patten House, 2324 Moreno Drive, Los Angeles

Haines House, 5112 Alishia Drive, Dana Point, California

1934/
37 Bennati Mountain Cabin, Lake Arrowhead, California

1935 Stander House remodelling, 2006 La Brea Terrace, Hollywood, California

Stander Apartments, Los Angeles (project)

O'Reilly Mountain Cabins (project)

Heraty House, Los Angeles (project)

Delahoyde House, Los Angeles (project)

First Baptist Church of Hollywood, California (project)

DeKeyser Double House, 1911 Highland Avenue, Hollywood, California

Shep House, Los Angeles (two projects)

Standor House remodelling, Los Angeles

1935/
36 Geggie House, Pasadena, California (two projects)

Walker House, 2100 Kenilworth Avenue, Los Angeles

1936 Fitzpatrick House, 8078 Woodrow Wilson Drive, Hollywood Hills, California

Sunset Medical Building, 6642 Sunset Boulevard, Hollywood, California

Jacobs House, Beverly Glen, California (two projects)

Mack House, Hollywood, California (project)

Kaun Beach House, 112 Western Drive, Richmond, California

Schuettner House, Los Angeles (project)

Seligson House remodelling, 1671 Orange Grove Drive, Los Angeles

Seff House remodelling and furniture, Los Angeles

Miller House, Los Angeles (project)

Warshaw House, Los Angeles

Kipp Craft Workshop, Los Angeles

Pavaroff House, Beverley Hills, California (project)

Mack House, Los Angeles (project)

Two McAlmon Houses, 2721 Waverly Drive, Los Angeles

Panel Post Constructions (second prototypes)

1936/
37 Berkoff House, Los Angeles (project)

1936/
38 Zaczek Beach House, 114 Elen Avenue, Playa Del Rey, California

Modern Creators Store, Holloway Drive and Palm Avenue, Hollywood, California

1937 Lingenbrink Store, 8750 Holloway Drive, Hollywood, California

Lowe House II, Eagle Rock, California

Rodakiewicz House, 9121 Alto Cedro Drive, Los Angeles

Rose Beach Colony (project)

Warren House remodelling and furniture, 1115 North Beverly Drive, Hollywood Hills, California

Ryan Beach House (project)

Renisoff House, Los Angeles (project)

Kipp House remodelling, 1773 Griffith Park Boulevard, Los Angeles

1938 Yates House remodelling, 1735 Micheltorena Street, Los Angeles

Bubeshko Apartment Building, 2036 Griffith Park Boulevard, Los Angeles

Rosenthal Apartment Building, Los Angeles (project)

Sharples Studio House, Los Angeles (project)

Southall Studio House, 1855 Park Avenue, Los Angeles

Timme House, Los Angeles (project)

Westby House, 1805 Maltman Avenue, Los Angeles

Wilson House, 2090 Redcliff Street, Los Angeles

Wolff House, 4008 Sunnyslope Avenue, Studio City, California

Francis House, Hollywood Hills, California (project)

Hanna House, Los Angeles (project)

Morgan Photographic Shop, Hollywood, California (project)

Shep House, Los Angeles (project)

Burke House/Apartment, Newport Beach, California (project)

Djey/Aldrich House, Los Angeles (project)

Lockheed 27 Airplane interiors (two projects; with H. Sachs)

Panel Post Constructions (third prototypes)

1939 Falk Apartment Building, 3631 Carnation Avenue, Los Angeles

Goodman House remodelling, 2149 Casitas Avenue, Altandena, California
Lingenbrink Store, 12560 Ventura Boulevard, Studio City, California
Bissiri House, Los Angeles (project)
Balkany House, North Hollywood, California (project)
Hub Office Building Los Angeles (project)
Mackey Apartment Building, 1137 South Cochran Avenue, Los Angeles
Wong House remodelling, Santa Monica, California
Kaun Beach House, Richmond, California

1940 Lingenbrink Store, Studio City, California
Droste House, 2035 Kenilworth Avenue, Los Angeles
Goodwin House, 3807 Reklaw Drive, Studio City, California
Hodel House remodelling and furniture, 1800 Huntington Drive, San Marino, California
Rodriguez House, Glendale, California (project)
Lapotka Apartments, Los Angeles (project)
Houses, 423, 429 and 433 Ellis Avenue, Inglewood, California (with E. Richard Lind)
Van Dekker House, 5230 Penfield Avenue, Canoga Park, California
Sax House, Los Angeles (project)
Strader House, North Hollywood, California (project)
Taylor House, South Pasadena, California (project)

1941 Rodriguez House, 1845 Niodrara Drive, Glendale, California
Carre House, Los Angeles (project)
Hartigan House, Hollywood Park, California (project)
Hiler Studio House, Hollywood, California
Bubeshko Apartment Building addition, 2036 Griffith Park Boulevard, Los Angeles
Byers House, Van Nuys, California (project)
Gibling House, Los Angeles (project)
Druckman House, 2764 Outpost Drive, Los Angeles
Periere House, Los Angeles (project)
Karz Apartments, Los Angeles (project)

1942 Albers House remodelling, 2781 Outpost Drive, Los Angeles
Harris House, Los Angeles
Pennington House remodelling, Thousand Oaks, Camarillo, California
Falk Apartment Building, Los Angeles (three projects)
Officers' Club, Palm Springs, California (project)

1943 Howenstein House remodelling, South Pasadena, California
Fisher House, Los Angeles (project)
Langley House remodelling, 841 Stone Canyon, Brentwood, California
Marker House remodelling, Los Angeles (project)

1944 Bethlehem Baptist Church, 4900 South Compton Avenue, Los Angeles
Litt House remodelling, 3050 Menlo, Glendake, California
Nickerson House remodelling, 681 Norton Street, Los Angles
Hollywood Women's Club remodelling, Los Angeles (project)
Rosco Duplex remodelling, 6000-6002 La Prada Park, Los Angeles
Thomasset Apartment remodelling, Los Angeles (project)
Starkey House remodelling, 2330 Merrywood, Los Angeles
Sabsay House studio addition, Los Angeles

1945 Roth House, 3624 Buena Park Drive, North Hollywood, California
Schick House, North Hollywood, California (project)
Braden House, North Hollywood, California (project)

Compinsky House, Burbank, California (project)
Gold House, 3758 Reklaw Drive, Los Angeles
Medical Arts Building, 12307 Ventura Boulevard, Studio City, California
Presburger House, 4255 Agnes Avenue, Studio City, California

1946 Daugherty House, 4635 Louise Avenue, Encino, California
Kermin Medical Building, Los Angeles (project)
Toole Desert House, Palm Village, California
Kallis House, 3580 Multiview Drive, Studio City, California
Harvey House remodelling, Los Angeles
Howatt House, Laguna Beach, California (project)
Lord Leigh Showroom and Offices, 847 South Santee, Los Angeles
Redesdale Avenue Apartments, Los Angeles (project)
Spangler House, Los Angeles (project)
Lingenbrink Store additions, 8750 Holloway Drive, Hollywood, California
West Pottery Works, Los Angeles
Gallagher Apartments, Los Angeles (project)

1946/
49 Tietz Medical Offices, Los Angeles
Armon House, 470 West Avenue 43, Los Angeles

1947 Mangaldas House, Los Angeles (project)
Courcio House remodelling, Los Angeles (project)
Schick and Associates Rest Home, Los Angeles (project)
Virginia Duplex, Los Angeles (project)
Trumbo House, Los Angeles (project)
Borisof House, Los Angeles (project)

1948 Lechner House, 11606 Amanda Drive, Studio City, California
Schick and Associates Motel, Los Angeles (project)
Gibling House, Los Angeles (project)
Ott Apartment Building, Beverly Hills, California (project)
Laurelwood Apartments, 11833 Laurelwood Drive, Studio City, California
Sax House, Los Angeles (project)
Drive-In Theatre, Los Angeles

1949 Washington Palace Motel, Los Angeles (project)
Janson House, 8704 Skyline Drive, Hollywood Hills, California
Penthouse, Beverly Hills, California (project)
Blembel House, Hollywood, California (project)
Meyers House remodelling, 2040 Oakstone Way, Hollywood, California

1949/
50 Tischler House, 175 Greenfield Avenue, Bel Air, Los Angeles
Inaya House, Beverly Hills, California (project)

1950 Tucker House, 8010 Farholm Drive, Hollywood, California
Gordon House, remodelling, 6853 Pacific View Drive, Hollywood Hills, California
Kaynor Manufacturing Company, 811 East 17th Street, Los Angeles
Zacek Beach House additions, Playa Del Rey, California

1950/
51 Ries House, 1404 Miller Drive, Los Angeles
Erlik House, 1757 Curson Avenue, Hollywood, California

1950/
52 Skolnik House, 2567 Glendower Avenue, Los Angeles

1952 Apartment, Los Angeles (project)
Elmer House, Hollywood, California (project)
Esther McCoy House into duplex conversion, 2434 Beverly Boulevard, Santa Monica,

California (not completed)
Schlesinger House, 1901 Myra Avenue, Los Angeles

1953 Marks House remodelling, 1052 Manzanita Street, Los Angeles

Publications:

By SCHINDLER: book—*Collected Papers,* Los Angeles 1948; articles—"A Cooperative Building" in *T-Square* (Philadelphia), February 1932; "Space-architecture" in *California Arts and Architecture* (Los Angeles), January 1935; "Furniture and the Modern House" in *Architect and Engineer* (San Francisco), December 1935 and March 1936; "Architect—Post War—Post Everybody" in *Pencil Points* (New York), October 1944 and November 1944; "Reference Frames in Space" in *Architect and Engineer* (San Francisco), April 1946.

On SCHINDLER: books—*International neue Baukunst* by Ludwig Hilberseimer, Stuttgart 1928; *New World Architecture* by Sheldon Cheney, New York 1930; *The Book of Modern Houses* by Patrick Abercrombie, London 1936; *Southern California Country* by Carey McWilliams, New York 1946; *Architecture, Ambition and Americans* by Wayne Andrews, New York 1955; *Five California Architects* by Esther McCoy, New York 1960; *R. M. Schindler,* exhibition catalogue, Santa Barbara, California 1967; *The Architecture of the Well-Tempered Environment* by Reyner Banham, London 1969; *Schindler* by David Gebhard, New York 1972; *Vienna to Los Angeles: 2 journeys—Richard Neutra and Rudolph M. Schindler,* edited by Esther McCoy, Santa Monica, California 1979; articles—"An Eastern Critic Looks at Western Architecture" by Henry Russell Hitchcok in *California Arts and Architecture* (Los Angeles), December 1940; "West Coast Architecture: A Romantic Movement Ends" by Esther McCoy in *Pacific Spectator* (Stanford, California), Winter 1953; "Four Schindler Houses of the 1920's" by Esther McCoy in *Arts and Architecture* (Los Angeles), September 1953; "Roots and Contemporary Architecture" by Esther McCoy in *Arts and Architecture* (Los Angeles), October 1956; "Rudolph Schindler" by Hans Hollein in *Der Aufbau* (Vienna), no. 3, 1961; "Letter of Louis H. Sullivan to R. M. Schindler" by Esther McCoy in *Journal of the Society of Architectural Historians* (Philadelphia), December 1961; "Rudolph Schindler" by Hans Hollein in *Bau* (Vienna), no. 4, 1966; "Dedicato a Schindler" by Herman Hertzberger in *Domus* (Milan), September 1967; "The Renewed Interest in Popularity of Schindler's Architecture" by Esther McCoy in the *Los Angeles Times,* 23 October 1967; "Rudolph Schindler: A Pioneer Without Tears" by Reyner Banham in *Architectural Design* (London), December 1967; "Ambiguity in the work of R. M. Schindler" by David Gebhard in *Lotus* (Milan), no. 5, 1968; "R. M. Schindler" by Esther McCoy in *Lotus* (Milan), no. 5, 1968; "The Least Appreciated: Rudolph Schindler" by Walter Segal in *Architects' Journal* (London), 19 February 1969; "The High and Low Art of Rudolph Schindler" by Dan O'Neill in *Architectural Review* (London), April 1973; "Notes on the Work of Rudolph M. Schindler," special issue of *Architecture + Urbanism* (Tokyo), November 1975; "Aspects of the house—3 projects by Schindler" by David Sisan in *Canadian Architect* (Don Mills, Ontario), February 1981; "Rudolph M. Schindler 1887-1952" by Daniel Treiber in *Architecture—mouvement—continuité* (Paris), June– September 1981; "Rudolph M. Schindler's King's Road House" by Murray Silverstein in *Fine Homebuilding* (Newtown, Connecticut), August/ September 1981; recording—*Schindler in California,* tape cassette and slides by Esther McCoy, London 1980.

Bibliography—*A Viennese in California—the Architecture of Rudolph M. Schindler: An Introductory Bibliography*, Monticello, Illinois 1983.

The importance of Rudolph Schindler as a highly original architect of the modern movement is a recently accepted fact, and much of this reassessment depends on the tardy recognition that his Beach House, designed in 1922 and built during 1925-26 for the naturist author Dr. Phillip Lovell, compares most favourably with what Le Corbusier, particularly in his innovative Maison Citrohan, was doing at the same time, Schindler, it is now realized, is not merely an "interesting outsider"—outside the limits of the International Style, that is—but a builder of immense subtlety of meaning, well able to handle the most diverse architectural and symbolic problems.

Trained in Vienna by Otto Wagner and influenced by the designs of Charles Rennie Mackintosh and the thinking of Adolf Loos—his essay on "Ornament and Crime" had a lasting effect—Schindler is very much the artist-architect, and indeed his tentatively erotic figure drawings are close in manner to those of Gustave Klimt and Egon Schiele. In a manifesto published in 1912 he stated, "The cave was the original dwelling. A hollow abode pile was the first permanent house. To build menaqt to gather and mass material, allowing it to form empty cells for human shelter." And this sculptuarl method is the basis of much of what he built. The manifesto is an important document, for everything that Schindler achieved is in some way related directly to its youthful ideals.

In America, first in Chicago and then in Los Angeles, he proved a most prolific designer, both when working alone and later with Frank Lloyd Wright, a man he much admired. Eventually, he found Wright a little too overpowering and began to work in collaboration with his close friend, the engineer Clyde Chase. In 1921, with Chase, he built their two-family house on Kings road to the west of Hollywood, at a time when the newly emerging motion picture industry was all the rage. From this time on, Schindler and Los Angeles are pretty well inseparable.

The house is of prime importance to a full understanding of his basic architectural philosophy. It is one of the most original concepts of the 1920s, being conceived solely in terms of living needs and not as an essay in spatial form or formal virtuosity! The mood is very much one of modesty and restraint. For the first time, the garden is seen as an integral part of the house, and the accepted traditional distinction between the outside and inside is taken to be false. This is, of course, an important legacy of his association with Wright. The house is designed as a series of private rooms and cooperative areas—"zones"—and conceived primarily as a single, enclosed environment intended to "combine the solidity of the cave with the light-weight characteristics of a tent." Here again there are hints of Wright and the thinking of the manifesto. Schindler was obviously happy with the house and lived and worked in it until his death in 1953.

The Lovell Beach House is one of the most important early modern houses. It is almost Constructivist in feeling. The open, box-like inner area consists of two tray-like planes supported on the outside by a concrete frame which enables the two planes to connect easily with each other. The outisde-inside counter-balance is well controlled and typically restrained.

Schindler kept in touch with developments in Europe, and a detailed file of cuttings from the leading architectural magazines was ever at hand. He was very aware of the Dutch De Stijl group—especially the work of the architect-designer Gerrit Riteveld—and there is certainly something of Rietveld in the Beach House. Its form is a knowing amalgam of the positive expression of structure as advocated by the Constructivits and the sculptural interplay of the planes and volumes of De Stijl. Dr. Lovell was an ideal client, and the two men worked in

complete harmony to achieve a synthesis of health and modernity based on privacy and informal, communal living in the open air.

In recent years, interest in the philosophy behind the building of the Beach House has served to point out the fact that at a time when Le Corbusier was making his no doubt well-deserved reputation as the le;ading architect of the new style and publishing *Towards a New Architecture*, Schindler had, in two houses, built a logical extension to the thinking of his own equally pertinent manifesto—yet was virtually unknown. it is now clear that his partial distaste for the International Style—the style for the twentieth century—is the reason for Schindler's past neglect, but now that a new evaluation of the concept of internationalism is called for, there can be little doubt that Schindler will rightly be seen to have been one of the most original architects of the Modern Movement.

—John Furse

SCHLESINGER, Frank.

American. Born in New York City, 17 September 1925. Educated at Middlebury College, Vermont, 1946-48; University of Illinois, Urbana, 1948-50, B.S. 1950; Harvard University Graduate School of Design, Cambridge, Massachusetts, 1950-54, M.Arch. 1954. Served in the United States Navy, 1943-46. Married Draga Ann Christy in 1971; children: Christy, Katherine, Danny, Nike, Jeff, and (stepson) Francis. Designer, for Hugh Stubbins, *q.v.*, Cambridge, Massachusetts, 1953-55, for Marcel Breuer, *q.v.*, New York, 1955-56, and (part-time) for Louis I. Kahn, *q.v.*, Philadelphia, 1957-58. Principal, Frank Schlesinger, Architect, Philadelphia since 1956 and Washington, D.C. since 1972. Instructor, University of Pennsylvania, Philadelphia, 1957-58; Visiting Critic, Columbia University, New York, 1962-63, and University of Pennsylvania, 1965. Since 1971, Professor of Architecture, University of Maryland, College Park. President, Harvard Graduate School of Design Alumni Association, 1971-73. Exhibitions: *National Gold Medal Exhibit*, Architectural League of New York, 1965; *40 under 40*, Architectural League of New York, 1965; *Frank Schlesinger, Architect*, Philadelphia Art Alliance, 1968. Recipient: Honor Award, American Institute of Architects, Philadelphia Chapter, 1960-65, 1968, and 1969; Honor Award, 1960, 1961, and 1963-65, Bronze Medal, 1965 and 1969, and Silver Medal, 1973, Pennsylvania Society of Architects; Design Award, *Architectural Record* 1960 and 1974; Arthur Wheelright Fellowship in Architecture, Harvard University, 1963; Design Award, *Progressive Architecture*, 1966, 1967, 1969, 1972 and 1974; Honor Award, American Institute of Architects, Northern Chapter, 1975 (twice); Distinguished Designer Sabbatical Fellowship, National Endowment for the Arts, Washington, D.C., 1984. Fellow, American Institute of Architects, 1970. Address (office); 732 17th Street NW, Washington, D.C. 20006, U.S.A.

Works:

1953 Schlesinger House, Lexington, Massachusetts
1958 Bernstein House, Princeton, New Jersey
1960 Schlesinger House, Doylestown, Pennsylvania
1960/
70 Girl Scout Camp Structures, Quakertown, Pennsylvania
1962 Oberman House, Princeton, New Jersey (project)
     Katz House, Norristown, Pennsylvania (project)

Rittenhouse Swim Club, Philadelphia (with T.R. Vreeland)
Research Laboratory, University of Pennsylvania, Philadelphia (with T. R. Vreeland)
1963 Beachcomber Swim Club, Philadelphia (with T. R. Vreeland)
1964 Blumenthal House, Princeton, New Jersey
     Zisman House, New York (project)
     Lemmon House, Gladwyne, Pennsylvania
1965 Medical Offices/Apartments, Bristol, Pennsylvania (project)
     Plan for the urban renewal of the Mercer-Jackson area, Trenton, New Jersey
1965/
66 Plan for the urban renewal of the Genesee Crossroads area, Rochester, New York
1967 Service station, Buffalo, New York
     Oritsky House, Reading, Pennsylvania
     Fisher House, Doylestown, Pennsylvania (project)
1967/
69 Plan for the urban renewal of the Waterfront area, Buffalo, New York
1968 Fairmount Park Nature Center, Philadelphia
     Malkiel House, Princeton, New Jersey (project)
1969 Office Building, South Coventry, Connecticut (project)
1970 Genesee Crossroads Plaza, Rochester, New York
     St. Mary's at the Cathedral, Philadelphia
     Girl Scout Dining Hall, Quakertown, Pennsylvania
     Dining Hall, Cheyney, Pennsylvania (project)
1971 Dino's Restaurant, Columbia, Maryland
1972 Housing for the Elderly, Bristol, Pennsylvania
1973 Wisconsin Avenue Condominiums, Washington, D.C. (project)
     Low and Middle-Income Housing, Rochester, New York (with Gindel and Johnson)
     Christy Village Ski Condominiums, Beech Mountain, North Carolina
     Marina and Village Center, Syracuse, New York
1974 Waterfront Condominiums, Annapolis, Maryland
1975 Senate Auto Service Center/Garage, Washington, D.C.
     Westover Apartments, Washington, D.C. (with Kerr-Reno)
     Boathouse, Syracuse, New York (project)
1976 1301 Pennsylvania Avenue Office Building, Washington D.C.
1978 National Plaza Hotel/Office Building, Washington, D.C. (with Mitchell/Giurgola)
1981 Presidential Office Building extension, Washington D.C.
     Marine Guards Headquarters, Port-au-Prince, Haiti
1983 Holy Name Friary, Silver Spring, Maryland

Publications:

On SCHLESINGER: articles—"Megastructures" in *Progressive Architecture* (New York), July 1968; "Genesee Crossroads Plaza" in *Architecture d'aujourd'hui* (Paris), September 1968; "Fairmount Park Nature Center" in *Progressive Architecture* (New York), January 1969; "Oritsky Residence" in *Progressive Architecture* (New York), April 1970; "Girl Scout Dining Hall" in *Architectural Forum* (New York), October 1971; "Tubular Steel Residence" in *Progressive Architecture* (New York), January 1972; "Genesee Crossroads Plaza" in *Progressive Architecture* (New York), March 1972; "St. Mary's at the Cathedral" in *Progressive Architecture* (New York), January 1974; "Christie Village Condominiums" in *Architectural Record* (New York), May 1974; "Grundy Tower, Bristol, Pennsylvania" in *Architectural Record* (New York), May 1977; "1301 Pennsylvania Avenue" in *Architectural Record* (New York), May 1978 and May

Frank Schlesinger: 1301 Pennsylvania Avenue Office Building, Washington, D.C., 1976.

1982; "Schlesinger Residence" in *Toshi-Jutaku* (Tokyo), August 1983.

Since 1972, Frank Schlesinger has successfully combined in architectural practice based in downtown Washington, D.C., with a teaching position at the suburban University of Maryland on its College Park campus. His firm, which he established in 1956 in Philadelphia, has won more than thirty design awards at national, state, and local levels. In 1977, he became architect for the Quadrangle Development Corporation for the rejuvenation taking place along Pennsylvania Avenue on its western end near the White House.

The structure known as 1301 Pennsylvania Avenue is the first office building to be completed in the area being restored by the Pennsylvania Avenue Development Corporation (PADC), an agency of the United States Government. Three years later, in 1984, construction was completed on National Place, a major mixed-use project developed by Quadrangle and the Marriott Corporation. Schlesinger, in association with Mitchell/Giurgola, won the PADC-sponsored competition. The winning design, selected from three national competitors, was the only solution which proposed to preserve the historic National Theatre.

Schlesinger currently has three projects in various stages of completion—a Franciscan Monastery in Montgomery County, Maryland; an addition to the Presidential Office Building in Washington; and the Marine Guard Quarters in Port-Au-Prince, Haiti. Over the years, the firm has engaged in work ranging from private homes to housing and institutional projects in the multimillion-dollar category. In addition, it has brought a high level of design to a number of projects with which aesthetics are seldom associated, such as an underground garage/pedestrian bridge and a prototype service station, to mention just two. For the small architectural firm to survive, Schlesinger knows that principals such as himself must provide extensive experience in the coordination and direction of interdisciplinary teams of planners, landscape architects, and engineers.

As a professor of architecture, Schlesinger is deeply concerned about today's architectural students and about the world they observe and will soon join as practitioners. Modern architecture, as he sees it, is not dead; instead, it allows for a range of approaches from Wright to Mies to a variety of present-day innovators. Students somehow tend to look at all of this in terms of "fashion," he says, adding, "What it amounts to is a misreading of architectural history." Regarding his own practice, Schlesinger expresses the hope that his work does not respond to a fad or a particular time.

—Robert E. Koehler

SCHNEBLI, Dolf.

Swiss. Born in Baden, Aargau, 27 December 1928. Studied architecture, ETH: Eidgenössische Technische Hochschule, Zurich, 1948-51; Graduate School of Design, Harvard University, Cambridge, Massachusetts, under Josep Lluis Sert, *q.v.*, M.Arch. 1954 (Wheelwright Fellowship, 1956). Married; children: Tobias, Raffaella, and Alessandra. Worked as assistant in the office of Daniel Girardet, Mulhouse, Switzerland, 1951-53, with The Architects Collaborative (TAC), *q.v.*, Cambridge, Massachusetts, and in the studio of Josep Lluis Sert, *q.v.*, New York, 1954-56. In private practice, Agno, Ticino, Switzerland, 1958-71. Since 1972, Principal, Dolf Schnebli and Associates (now Dolf Schnebli + Tobias Ammann Architekten + Partner), Agno and Zurich (Associates: Tobias Ammann, Isidor Ryser, Ernst Engeler, Bernhard Meier, and Alfio Indemini). Assistant Instructor, Harvard Graduate School of Design, Cambridge, Massachusetts, 1959-60; Visiting Professor, Washington University, St. Louis, Missouri, Harvard Graduate School of Design, Cambridge, Massachusetts, and the University of California, Berkeley, 1964; Professor, ETH: Eidgenössische Technische Hochschule, Zurich, since 1971. Exhibitions: *Swiss Architecture Today*, toured the U.S.S.R., Poland, Hungary, Rumania, Czechoslovakia, and the German Democratic Republic, 1968-73; *Tendenzen Neuere Architektur im Tessin*, ETH: Eidgenössische Technische Hochschule, Zurich, 1975 (toured Europe); *Architecture 70/80 in Switzerland*, Kunsthalle, Basel, Switzerland, 1981 (travelled to Vienna, Rome, Padua, Montreal and Turin); *Dolf Schnebli, Architect*, ETH: Eidgenössische Technische Hochschule, Zurich, 1984 (toured the United States). Recipient: Award of Merit, United States Higher Education Facilities Design Awards, 1966. Member, Federation of Swiss Architects; Federation of Swiss Planners; Association of Swiss Engineers and Architects. Addresses: ETH: Eidgenössische Technische Hochschule, HIL Gebäude, ETH-Honggerberg, 8093 Zurich, Switzerland; Dolf Schnebli + Tobias Ammann Architekten + Partner, Brunnenhofweg 30, 8057 Zurich, Switzerland; Dolf Schnebli + Tobias Ammann Architetti + Associati, Via Oro, 6982 Agno, Switzerland.

Works

1950 Hunting Lodge, Bernau, Schwarzwald, West Germany
1953 Cultural Center, Basel, Switzerland (competition project)
1954 School, Baden, Switzerland (competition project)
 Crematorium, Baden, Switzerland (competition project)
1958 Schnebli House, Agno, Switzerland
1959 Congress Building, Geneva (competition project; with Jean Messerli)
 Palace of Congress, Ascona, Switzerland (competition project)
 Costioli House, Campione, Italy (with Isidor Ryser)
 Mattioli House, Campione, Italy (project; with Isidor Ryser)
 Interform Houses, Origlio, Switzerland (with E. Theiler)
1960 School Centre, Trevano, Switzerland (competition project)
 Barracks Complex, Aarau, Switzerland (competition project)
 Church, Ennetbaden, Switzerland (competition project)
 School, Chiasso, Switzerland (competition project)
 Fountain, Agno, Switzerland (with Sam Magee)
 Casette 3S Housing, Breganzona, Switzerland (project; with Robert Matter)

Secondary School, Locarno, Switzerland (with Isidor Ryser, Ernst Engeler, Bernhard Meier and Klaus Vogt)

1961 Station Quarter Development, Baden, Switzerland (competition project)

Technical College, Windisch, Switzerland (competition project; with Robert Matter and Isidor Ryser)

Church, Sarnen, Switzerland (competition project)

Hall Complex, Muttenz, Switzerland (competition project; with Robert Matter and Isidor Ryser)

1962 Town Design Plan, Sins, Switzerland (competition project)

Congress Hall, Locarno, Switzerland (competition project)

Commercial School, Bellinzona, Switzerland (competition project)

Maillet Studio, Verscio, Switzerland (with Klaus Vogt)

School, Pregassona, Switzerland (competition project)

Theatre, Neuchâtel, Switzerland (competition project; with Robert Matter)

1963 Hall Complex, Burgdorf, Switzerland (competition project)

Leu House, Novaggio, Switzerland

Sulzer House, Astano, Switzerland (project)

Lichtenhahn House, Carabbia, Switzerland (with Klaus Vogt and Sam Magee)

1964 Jesuit Retreat, Schönbrunn, Switzerland (competition project)

Ledergerber House, Seedorf, Switzerland (with Bernhard Meier)

Hoteliers Centre, *Expo*, Lausanne, Switzerland (with Hans Howald and R. Haussmann)

Leisure Exhibit, *Expo*, Lausanne, Switzerland

Palace of Congress, Lugano, Switzerland (competition project)

Swimming Pool, Bellinzona, Switzerland (competition project)

St. Anna Institute, Lugano, Switzerland (project; with Robert Matter)

Church, Buchs, Aarau, Switzerland

1965 Community Housing, Lugano, Switzerland (with Isidor Ryser)

Swimming Pool, Wohlen, Switzerland (with Robert Matter)

School, Wohlen, Switzerland (with Robert Matter and Klaus Vogt)

Hospital, Lugano, Switzerland (competition project)

1966 Haussmann House extensions, Vernate, Switzerland (with Robert Matter)

Swiss School, Naples, Italy (with Robert Matter, Isidor Ryser, Ernst Engeler and Bernhard Meier)

District Hospital, Baden, Switzerland (competition project)

1967 Plaza and Lakeshore Development, Caslano, Switzerland

Steinmann House alterations, Aranno, Switzerland (with Ernst Engeler)

Town Plan, Dättwil, Switzerland (competition project)

Town Design Plan, Littau, Switzerland (with Robert Matter)

1968 Housing Complex, Lichtenstein (competition project)

Children's Home, Bissone, Switzerland (with Isidor Ryser, Ernst Engeler and Bernhard Meier)

Streiff House, Minusio, Switzerland (with Isidor Ryser and Bernhard Meier)

Karrer House, St. Abbondio, Switzerland (with Bernhard Meier)

1969 Town Design Plan, Zofingen, Switzerland (competition project)

Old People's Home, Biasca, Switzerland (competition project)

Rolla House alterations, Poiana, Switzerland (with R. Roduner)

1970 Catholic Church, Oberentfelden, Switzerland (with Isidor Ryser and Fred Schaepe)

Pozzi House, Agno, Switzerland (with Ernst Engeler)

G. Savarese Holiday Village, Vico Equense, Italy (project)

Saxer House, Bissone, Switzerland (project; with Robert Matter and Isidor Ryser)

Municipal Centre, Littau, Switzerland (project; with Robert Matter)

Schoolhouse, Muri, Switzerland (competition project)

Slaughterhouse Complex, Basel, Switzerland (competition project; with D. Oertel)

Post Office, Bellinzona, Switzerland (competition project)

Children's Home, Sachseln, Switzerland (competition project; with Robert Matter and Isidor Ryser)

1971 Schoolhouse, Baden, Switzerland (competition project; with Robert Matter)

Law School, Washington University, St. Louis, Missouri (with Anselevicius and Montgomery, Robert Matter and William Rupe)

1972 Children's Home, Altdorf, Switzerland (competition project)

Broom County Cultural Center, New York (competition project; with Robert Matter and William Rupe)

Altbühl Housing Redevelopment, Furttal, Switzerland (competition project; with Bruno Pfister)

Diem House extension, St. Abbondio, Switzerland (with Tobias Ammann)

Elementary School, Breganzona, Switzerland (project; with Ernst Engeler)

Jung House, Intragna, Switzerland (with Tobias Ammann)

Chiodoni House, Agno, Switzerland (with Isidor Ryser)

1973 Drinking Fountain, Zurich (competition project; with P. Selmoni, M. Dolinski and Phil Rolla)

Housing Redevelopment in Haberacher, Baden, Switzerland (competition project; with Bruno Pfister)

Gotthard Bank remodelling, Lugano, Switzerland (with R. and T. Haussmann, Bernhard Meier and Alfio Indemini)

1974 Primary School, Ruopigen-Littau, Switzerland (with Klaus Dolder and Dommann/Pluss)

Church, Davos, Switzerland (competition project; with Werner Wegmann)

Nursery School, Locarno, Switzerland (with Bernhard Meier and Tobias Ammann)

School Centre, Ponte Tresa/Croglio, Switzerland (competition project; with Tobias Ammann)

Housing Redevelopment, Rancate, Switzerland (competition project; with Isidor Ryser, M. Dolinski and Tobias Ammann)

1975 Gotthard Bank Headquarters, Lugano, Switzerland (project; with Bernhard Meier)

Lindenfeld Town Design Plan, Lucerne, Switzerland (with Werner Wegmann)

Municipal Offices, Berne, Switzerland (competition project; with Isidor Ryser)

SBB Training Centre, Löwenberg, Switzerland (competition project; with Tobias Ammann)

Housing Redevelopment, Winterthur, Switzerland (competition project; with Bruno Pfister, T. Indermühle and M. Dolinski)

SBB Drinking Fountain (competition project; with Philip Rolla and M. Dolinski)

Cemetery, Neuenhof, Switzerland (competition project; with Werner Wegmann)

Meier-Bucher House remodelling, Cimo, Switzerland (with Bernhard Meier)

Redevelopment Plan, Locarno, Switzerland

(with Bruno Brocchi and G. Bisagni)

Botti House remodelling, Torricella, Switzerland (with Alfio Indemini)

1976 Retziki Psychiatric Centre extensions, Thessaloniki, Greece (project; with Fredi Gubler and U. Rötemund)

Swimming Pool, Witikon, Switzerland (competition project; with Peter Quarella)

Reutenen Redevelopment, Frauenfeld, Switzerland (with Tobias Ammann and Werner Wegmann)

Town Design Plan, Niedermatt, Lucerne, Switzerland (project)

1977 Gilly House remodelling, Aranno, Switzerland (with Bernhard Meier)

Wolk House, Magliaso, Switzerland (with Isidor Ryser and Bernhard Meier)

Old People's Home, Agra, Switzerland (competition project; with Isidor Ryser)

Sports Centre, Tenero, Switzerland (competition project; with Isidor Ryser)

Pastificio Vecchio Bakery remodelling, Cavigliano, Switzerland (with Tobias Ammann, Bernhard Meier and Alfio Indemini)

B. Frei/R. Siegrist House remodelling, Origlio, Switzerland (with Bernhard Meier and Alfio Indemini)

1978 Kolb House, Gorduno, Switzerland (with Tobias Ammann and Bernhard Meier)

Town Planning Study, Dübendorf, Switzerland (competition project; with Ernst Gisel)

Lorenzetti House remodelling, Losone, Switzerland (with Tobias Ammann, Alfio Indemini and Silvano Lanzi)

Dimitri Theatre, Verscio, Switzerland (with Tobias Ammann, Bernhard Meier, Ernst Engeler and Alfio Indemini)

Dimitri School, Verscio, Switzerland (with Tobias Ammann, Bernhard Meier and Alfio Indemini)

St. Angelo College, Loverciano, Switzerland (with Bernhard Meier)

School, Montagnola, Switzerland (competition project; with Isidor Ryser)

Pfister Condominiums, Locarno-Monti, Switzerland (with Tobias Ammann and Isidor Ryser)

1979 Rieger House remodelling, Pian Rancate, Switzerland (with Tobias Ammann, Ernst Engeler and Alfio Indemini)

Prison, Regensdorf, Switzerland (competition project; with Axel Fickert)

Gerwig House, Brissago, Switzerland (with Tobias Ammann and Silvano Lanzi)

1980 Condominium Building, Ponte Tresa, Switzerland (with Isidor Ryser)

Jecklin House, Costa Borgnone, Switzerland (with Tobias Ammann, Bernhard Meier and Alfio Indemini)

Old People's Housing, Novaggio, Switzerland (competition project; with Isidor Ryser)

Friedrichstadt Housing Development, West Berlin (competition project; with Axel Fickert)

Münzlishausen Residential Redevelopment, Baden, Switzerland (project; with Bernhard Meier and F. Gellera)

Baur House remodelling, Gordevio, Switzerland (with Tobias Ammann and Alfio Indemini)

Diener House remodelling, Costa, Switzerland (with Tobias Ammann and Alfio Indemini)

1981 Piazza del Sole development, Bellinzona, Switzerland (competition project; with F. Gellera)

Housing Development on the River Limmat, Zurich (competition project; with Axel Fickert)

Elementary School, Bissone, Switzerland (with Ernst Engeler)

Spichiger House remodelling, Sassalto/Intragna, Switzerland (with Tobias Ammann, Isidor Ryser and Alfio Indemini)

Weber House, Zumikon, Switzerland (with F. Gellera)

Mühlegasse Housing Development, Baar, Switzerland (with Werner Egli, Hans Rohr and Frank Vogel)

Albergo della Posta boarding-house, Astano, Switzerland (with Tobias Ammann, Ernst Engeler and Bernhard Meier)

School, Egg, Switzerland (competition project; with F. Gellera)

Straumann House remodelling, Cugnasco, Switzerland (with Tobias Ammann and Isidor Ryser)

De Angelis Workshops, Agno, Switzerland (competition project; with Tobias Ammann, Alfio Indemini and Silvano Lanzi)

School, Hedingen, Switzerland (competition project; with Tobias Ammann and F. Gellera)

Jauslin House renovations, Someo, Switzerland (with Tobias Ammann, Alfio Indemini and Silvano Lanzi)

Stock Exchange Building, Zurich (competition project; with F. Gellera)

PCW low-cost housing development, Unter den Halde, Wurenlingen, Switzerland (project; with Paolo Kolliker)

PCW low-cost housing phase I, Wurenlingen, Switzerland (with Paolo Kolliker)

1982 Town Hall and Sports Installation, Origlio, Switzerland (competition project)

Moneta Commercial Building, Baden, Switzerland (competition project; with Paolo Kölliker)

Tiefebrunnen Tram Depot rebuilding, Zurich (competition project)

Parish Centre, School and Bus Terminus, Leukerbad, Switzerland (project; with Isidor Ryser and Patrik Huber)

Biering House, Banco, Switzerland (project; with Tobias Ammann and Bernhard Meier)

Etang-Long Development, Crans, Switzerland (competition project; with Patrik Huber and Steven Fong)

Low-cost Housing, Santomenna, Italy (project; with Tobias Ammann and Ernst Engeler)

Leiser House, Vaux-sur-Morges, Switzerland (project)

1983 Old People's Home, Hallau, Switzerland (competition project; with Patrik Huber)

Muhleareal Development, Thun, Switzerland (competition project; with Ueli Schweizer and Tobias Ammann)

Lazzarini Del Grosso/Nicoloso Houses, Moghegno, Switzerland (with Tobias Ammann, Bernhard Meier and Silvano Lanzi)

Südstrasse Housing Development, Zurich (project)

Humbel House, Zurich (project)

Brentano House, Brugg, Switzerland (project)

Kaufmann House, Winterthur, Switzerland (project)

Villa Giulia, Naples, Italy (project)

Neuweiler House remodelling, Gandria, Switzerland (with Tobias Ammann and Alfio Indemini)

Feller Building Entrance Hall, Horgen, Switzerland (project; with Paolo Kölliker and Kenneth Kao)

Rosa House, Caslano, Switzerland (with Tobias Ammann, Bernhard Meier and Alfio Indemini)

Opera de la Bastille, Paris (competition project; with Miroslav Sik and Sara Spiro)

Zentrum Littau Building, Littau, Switzerland

(project; with Isidor Ryser, Patrik Huber and Marcel Meili)

1984 Monotti House, Cavigliano, Switzerland (with Tobias Ammann, Bernhard Meier and Silvano Lanzi)

S.A.M.E. Marina, Vico Equense, Italy (project; with R. Tropeano and C. Pfister)

School, Dättwil, Switzerland (competition project; with Bea Ammann, Markus Wassmer and Regula Kloti)

1985 Zentrum Littau Housing, Littau, Lucerne, Switzerland

Publications:

By SCHNEBLI: articles—guest editor, *Deutsche Bauzeitung* (Stuttgart), no. 8, 1969; "Eretria", with Paul Hofer, in *Werk/Archithese* (Zurich), September 1977; "Seldwyla" in *Werk/Archithese* (Zurich), September/October 1978; "Ruepigen in Littau" in *Archithese* (Niederteufen, Switzerland), May/June 1980; "Public Competitions in Architecture" in *Werk, Bauen und Wohnen* (Zurich), March 1981; "Energy and Architecture" in *Archithese* (Niederteufen, Switzerland), July/August 1981.

On SCHNEBLI: books—*Das Neue Schulhaus* by Alfred Roth, Zurich 1966; *World Architecture 3*, edited by John Donat, London 1966; *Pianificazione e disegno delle università*, edited by Giancarlo De Carlo, Rome 1968; *Arts of the Environment*, edited by Gyorgy Kepes, New York 1972; *Architecture 70/80 in Switzerland* by Werner Blaser, Basel and Stuttgart 1982; *Dolf Schnebli*, exhibition catalogue, Zurich 1984; articles—"House at Campione d'Italia" in *Architectural Design* (London), September 1962; "Casa privata a Carabbia, Ticino" in *Architecture Formes et Fonctions* (Lausanne, Switzerland), no. 12, 1965; "Swiss High School" in *Architectural Forum* (New York), January/February 1966; "Habitation a Carabbia, Suisse" in *L'Architecture d'Aujourd'hui* (Paris), February/March 1966; "Schulhauser—Kindergarten" in *Werk* (Zurich), August 1966; "Schools" in *Baumeister* (Munich), January 1967; "Mehrfamilienhauser, Hausergruppe" in *Werk* (Zurich), May 1967; "Recent Swiss Architecture and Architects", special issue of *Casabella* (Milan), "Soziale Wohnbauten in der Via Trevano/Torricelli, Lugano" in *Bauwelt* (West Berlin), 5 February 1968; "La Scuola Svizzera di Napoli" in *Architettura* (Rome), March 1968; "Swimming Pools" in *Werk* (Zurich), September 1968; "Dolf Schnebli and His Work" in *Deutsche Architecktur* (East Berlin), September 1968; "Down a Hillside in Naples" in *Architectural Forum* (New York), March 1969; "Kindergarten in Bissone, Ticino" in *Werk* (Zurich), January 1974; "Limited Experiments in Housing Construction" in *Bauen und Wohnen* (Zurich), June 1974; "Church in Oberenfelden, Switzerland" in *Architettura* (Rome), February 1978; "Kindergarten in Locarno" in *Deutsche Bauzeitschrift* (Gutersloh, West Germany), November 1978; "Contemporary Architects 11: Dolf Schnebli" by Fumihiko Maki in *Architecture + Urbanism* (Tokyo), November 1978; "Zurich Riverfront Competition" by Mario Botta in *Lotus International* (Milan), no. 25, 1979.

*

Architecture is something rational—rational in the sense of the French rationalists. It is built upon premises, and the result can be judged against those premises. The difficulty lies in the premises. Parts of them are measurable—soil condition, orientation towards the sun, climate, strength of materials, etc. Others are not so easily quantifiable—such as social conditions, history, the client, and not least the architect himself. The architect, like any human being, inherits some qualities from his birth, but much more he learns through experience. I therefore think that the biography of the architect is an important part of these premises. I therefore often tell my students, rather than to study the publica-

tions of the current architectural scene, they would do better to look into their own biography for inspiration.

My work has the imprint of my biography. My first encounter with architecture happened when I was eighteen years old. In an architect's office in Geneva, I found books by Le Corbusier. His work as an artist and architect were and still are a source of inspiration. My studies in Zurich, work in France, Summer school in Venice (1952), work in the United States with Sert, Chermayeff and Gropius, the studies at Harvard, the year I spent on the landway from Greece to India (1956), and the opening of my own office in Ticino in 1958 are still part of work I do today. I believe that urbanism, architecture, and design are the same disciplines. Since 1954, when I worked as an instructor in Harvard Graduate School of Design, I have always tried to teach and work in private practice at the same time. I see my work as a continuous struggle based on my thinking about daily life and the continuity of architecture as a discipline.

—Dolf Schnebli

*

Dolf Schnebli creates architecture for its own sake. He does not pretend to be a sociologist who attempts to interpret or depict life through symbolism or geometric allusion. On the contrary, he sees life emanating from the details of his constructions, in the way a column meets a slab, or a stair lands in a hall. Because of this rational attitude, his buildings are strikingly commodious and functional. His close attention to these elements and his pragmatic insistence on spatial organization divorce him from many colleagues in the Modern Movement who express themselves through abstraction and reductionism.

Schnebli's architectural vision can be attributed largely to his international experience. His home and first practice originate in German-speaking Zurich, though a professional migration to Agno—a city only three hours away, but culturally separated by its location on the Italian borders of Switzerland—enabled him to be in constant touch with his intellectual allies. Prior to this move, he had worked in France and studied at Harvard University in the United States. At Harvard, he came in contact with the distinguished architects Josep Lluis Sert and Serge Chermayeff—but was equally influenced in ensuing years by the work of Mies, Aalto, Frank Lloyd Wright and Siegfried Giedion. In addition, his visits to the U.S.S.R., Poland, Hungary, Rumania, Czechoslovakia, and the German Democratic Republic have certainly influenced his present thinking. Yet, Schnebli has been careful not to confuse their diverse architectural languages, and instead translates them into his own vocabulary. His syntax, moreover, adheres ever faithfully to the canons of Le Corbusier, whose work as an artist and architect remains the prime source of his inspiration.

His work as it applies to the humanist tradition has earned him international renown. These designs apparently deviate from his rationalist discipline, as his architecture frequently has social, political and economic implications. The humanism in his work is particularly visible in the intersection between construction and spatial organization. Schnebli may also be characterized as a people's architect; his buildings are an integral part of the culture they serve, for they depend on the skills and traditional craftsmanship still practised by Swiss and Italian masons, carpenters and stone-workers. The conflict between humanism and rationalism is thereby resolved: the buildings function not only for the people, but people equally serve the buildings. Architecture, as he understands it, is the expression of thought, converted into work, which is ultimately rational construction. If it is only destined to represent and define human use or behaviour, it is

Dolf Schnebli: Zentrum Littau Housing, Lucerne, Switzerland, 1985.

robbed of the logic derived from memory, and thereby of its intrinsic rationality.

Schnebli's careful attention to the detail of his materials is owed to Le Corbusier, who argued that certain elements, including pilotis, roof terraces, free plan and open facade, were essential to his new architecture. He then transforms Corbusier's poetics into architecture as manifested function, a number of his housing developments and other complexes featuring terraced layouts as a free agglomeration of cellular units, instead of presenting a pictorial unity. One example is his house at Campione d'Italia. Schnebli's chief goal was to make the house blend with the strong landscape of its surroundings. He favoured brick and concrete for the exterior, and used natural wood for the windows and doors. The floors were made of clay tiles, whilst the interior walls and ceiling were finished in white stucco. Although in the entire house there is no span longer than nine-and-a-half feet, change of floor levels give the structure a rich, spacious feeling. This house, typical of his work, reinforced his commitment to the spatial unit.

The same no-nonsense pragmatic attitude is demonstrated throughout his thirty-five year career. His work consistently speaks for itself, free from abstraction or metaphysical allusion. Nothing is implied beyond what the immediate surface shows. A rationalist in the purest sense, Schnebli has learned to fuse humanism into his work, enabling it to be more practicable and comfortable.

—Carolyn Cole

SCHWARZ, Rudolf.

German. Born in Strasbourg, 15 May 1897. Educated at the Technical University of Berlin, 1915-19; State Academy of Arts, Berlin, under Hans Poelzig, 1919-23. Worked as a government architect in Cologne, 1923-25; taught at the Bau-und Kunstgewerbeschule, Offenbach, 1925-27; Director, Kunstgewerbeschule, Aachen, 1927-34; in private practice, Aachen, 1934-40; Chief of Reconstruction and Planning Lothringen, 1941-44; prisoner-of-war, 1944-46; Chief City Planner, Cologne, 1946-52; in private architectural practice, in Frankfurt and Cologne, 1953 until his death, 1961. Professor of Town Planning, Staatliche Kunstakademie, Dusseldorf, 1953-61. Member, Deutscher Werkbund; Bund Deutscher Architekten; Görres-Gesellschaft. Exhibitions: Akademie der Künste, Berlin, 1963; Akademie der Architektenkammer Nordrhein-Westfalen, Dusseldorf, 1981. Recipient: First Prize, Frauenfriedenskirche Competition, Frankfurt, 1927 (with Dominkius Böhm); German Service Cross, 1951; Fritz Schumacher Prize, Hamburg, 1952; Art Prize, Nordrhein-Westfalen, 1958; First Prize, Reichstag Reconstruction Competition, Berlin, 1960. Member, Akademie der Künste, Berlin; Akademie für Städtebau und Landesplanung, Germany. *Died* (in Cologne) *3 April 1961.*

Works:

1928 Castle, Festival Hall and Chapel reconstruction, Rothenfels-am-Main, Germany

1929 Youth Hall, Aachen (with Hans Schwippert and Johannes Krahn)

Waldfriedhof Cemetery, Aachen (with Johannes Krahn)

1930 Corpus Christi Church, Aachen (with Hans Schwippert and Johannes Krahn)

1931 College of Sociology, Aachen (with Hans Schwippert and Johannes Krahn)

1932 Liebfrauen Church interiors, Leipzig

Parish Church, Ilsenburg/Harz, Germany (project)

Parish Church, Milwaukee, Wisconsin (project)

1933 St. Abert Chapel, Leversbach, near Düren, Germany

Semi-detached house, Lovenich, near Cologne

Schrage House, Bruck, Cologne

Parish Church, Grosssteinheim-am-Main, Germany (project)

2 houses, Landhaus, Essen

Doctor's house, Duisburg, Germany

1936 Parish Church with Hall, Lichtefelde, Berlin (project; with Emil Steffan)

Parish Church, Aschaffenburg-Damm, Germany (project)

Dr. Fruhauf Surgery, Offenbach/Main, Germany

1937 Church, Gross Zschocher, Leipzig (project)

Church and Parish Hall, Windorf, Leipzig (project)

Gothic Parish Church extensions, Burgstadt/Main, Germany

Baroque Parish Church interiors, Wasserlosin-Untefranken, Germany

Parish Church interiors, Ketzin, Brandenburg, Germany

Fluhe House, Duisburg, Germany

1938 Gymnasium/Church of Christ the King conversion, Fulda, Germany

Schwarz House, Frankfurt

Church and Parish Hall, Gropelingen, Bremen (project)

1940 Pilgrimage Church interiors, Mariental, Westerwald, Germany

1941 Cathedral interiors, Trier, Germany (as consultant architect)

1941/
44 Regional and reconstruction plans for Lothringen, Germany

1942 Parish Church, Hanau, Germany (project)

New Gothic Church interiors, Bockenheim, Frankfurt

1943 Church of Mary Queen of Peace, Oberrodinghausen, Germany (with Johannes Krahn)

1944 St. Catherine's Church extensions, Krickenau, Germany

1946/
52 Reconstruction plans for the city of Cologne

1947 Saint Heribert Church reconstruction, Deutz, Cologne (with Josef Bernard)

Church, Durwiss, near Aachen (project)

Temporary church, Gey, near Düren, Germany (project)

Church, Bilderstockehen, Cologne (project; with Emil Steffan)

Church, Kirchen/Sieg, Germany (project)

1948 St. Paul's Church/Political Discussion Hall conversions, Frankfurt (with Eugen Blank, Johannes Krahn, and Gottlob Schaupp)

Liebfrauen Church choir fittings, Frankfurt

Marien Hospital Chapel interiors, Frankfurt

1949 Borromeo Chapel reconstruction, Munster (competition project)

1950 Pilgrimage Church reconstruction, Kalk, Cologne

St. Catherine's Church reconstruction, Niehl, Cologne (with Hermann Pfeiffer)

1952 Roman Church reconstruction, Johannisberg, Rheingau, Germany (with Rudolf Steinbach)

Maria Himmelfahrt Church, Wesel, Germany

Girls' Upper School, Darmstadt (project)

All Saints' Anglican Church, Marienburg, Cologne (with Josef Bernard)

Cathedral interiors, Munster (competition project)

1953 Liebfrauen Church interiors, Trier, Germany

St. Anna's Church, Parish Hall and Kindergarten, Duisburg, Germany

State Theatre, Manheim (project with Josef Bernard and Wilhelm Kiphahn)

Industrial development plans for Kopsack, Germany (with Josef Bernard)

1954 St. Albert's Church, Andernach, Germany

St. Michael's Church and Oratory, Frankfurt

St. Joseph's Church, Braunsfeld, Cologne (with Josef Bernard)

1955 Plan for the Rhein Braun Colliery, Germany

Mechtern Church reconstruction, Ehrenfeld, Cologne

Liebfrauen Church reconstruction, Mulheim, Cologne

1956 St. Anna's Church, Düren, Germany

Parish Church with Rectory and Meeting Hall, Graveneck/Lahn, Germany

Altar, for the Assembly of German Catholics, Cologne

Schwarz House, Mungersdorf, Cologne

Festival Hall reconstruction, with Chapel, Gurzenich, near Cologne (with Karl Band)

Pedagogical Academy, Munster (competition project; with Josef Bernard)

1957 Cathedral Precinct, Cologne (competition project; with Karl Band)

Wallraf-Richartz Museum reconstruction, Cologne (with Josef Bernard)

St. Mary's Church interiors, Oberhausen, Germany (with Josef Bernard)

Church of the Holy Cross, Bottrop, Germany (with Josef Bernard)

St. Francis Church, Bedingrade, Essen

Parish Hall and Youth Centre, Niehl, Cologne

St. Andrew's Parish Church, Ruttensheid, Essen

St. Joseph's Church, Merzig, Saarland, Germany (competition project)

1958 Parish Church of the Holy Family, Oberhausen, Germany (with Josef Bernard)

Collegiate Church Spire, Bocholt, Germany (with Josef Bernard)

St. Mauritius Church, Wiesbaden (competition project)

Town Hall, Marl, Germany (competition project)

Memorial Church to the Victims of National Socialism, Plotzensee, Berlin (as consultant architect)

1959 Vetus-Latina Institute, Archbishopric of Kloster Beuron, Germany

St. Antonius' Church Frohnhausen, Essen

Church of Mary the Queen, Saarbrucken

St. Boniface's Church, Forst, Aachen

St. Pius' Church with Recotry and Parish Hall, Barmen, Wuppertal, Germany

1960 St. Christophorus Church and Social Centre, Niehl, Cologne

St. Gertrude's Church and Social Centre, Schweinheim, Aschaffenburg, Germany

Primary school, Nippes, Cologne

St. Boniface's Church and Social Centre, Wetzlar, Germany

St. Raphael's Church, Gatow, Berlin

St. Vitalis Church interiors, Mungersdorf, Cologne

St. Ludger's Church, Vohwinkel, Wuppertal, Germany

St. Florian's Church and Social Centre, Vienna

St. Teresa's Church and Social Centre, Donau, Linz, Austria

Church with Rectory and Kindergarten, Hausen, near Offenbach, Germany

Theatre, Dusseldorf (competition project)

Catholic Church, Soest, Westphalia, Germany (competition project)

Reichstag, Berlin (competition project)

Town Hall, Cologne (competition project)

Chamber of Commerce, Bremen (competition project)

Plan for a Town Square, Wolfsburg, Germany (competition project; with S. Szekessy)

Publications:

By SCHWARZ: books—*Vom Bau der Kirche*, Aachen 1938, as *The Church Incarnate*, Chicago and

Rudolf Schwarz: St. Joseph's Church, Braunsfeld, Cologne, 1954.

London 1958; *Von der bebauung der Erde, Heidelberg 1949; Kirchenbau,* Heidelberg 1960; *A Pugin Bibliography,* Charlottesville, Virginia, 1963; *Wegweisung der Technik und andere Schriften zum Neuen Bauen,* edited by Maria Schwarz and Ulrich Conrads, Braunschweig 1979; articles—"Dominikus Böhm und sein Werk" in *Moderne Bauformen* (Stuttgart), vol. 26, 1927; "Das Zukunfttige Köln" in *Bauen und Wohnen* (Zurich), vol. 4, 1949; "Der Neue Kirchenbau" in *Werk* (Zurich), April 1949; "Dominikus Böhm" in *Baukunst und Werkform* (Nuremberg), February 1955; "Einige Bemerkungen zu St. Michael in Frankfurt" in *Das Münster* (Munich), July/August 1955; "Architektur als heiliges Bild" in *Baukunst und Werkform* (Nuremberg), vol. 10, no. 3, 1957; "Die Kirche zum Heiligen Kreuz in Bottrop" in *Das Münster* (Munich), May/June 1958.

On SCHWARZ: books—*Rudolf Schwarz,* exhibition catalogue, edited by Maria Schwarz, O.M. Ungers and others, Heidelberg 1963; *Rudolf Schwarz,* exhibition catalogue, edited by Manfred Sundermann, Claudia Lang and Maria Schwarz, Bonn 1981; articles—"The Architecture of Rudolf Schwarz" by H. A. Reinhold in *Architectural Forum* (New York), January 1939; "Neuen Kirchenbauten von Rudolf Schwarz" in *Bauen und Wohnen* (Zurich), no. 12, 1949; "Europe's Great New Churches" in *Architectural Forum* (New York), December 1957; "Das Erste Museum der Nachkriegszeit" in *Baukunst und Werkform* (Nuremberg), no. 1, 1958; "The 'Seven Archetypes' of Rudolf Schwarz" in *Architectural Record* (New York), June 1958; "New Church Architecture in Germany" by G. E. Kidder Smith in *Architectural Record* (New York), June 1962; "Das Erbe von Rudolf Schwarz" in *Das Münster* (Munich), January/February 1967; "In

Memoriam Rudolf Schwarz" by Rudolf Bernard in *Das Münster* (Munich), January/February 1972.

*   *   *

Rudolf Schwarz is best known for his Catholic churches, though he was not so exclusively a church architect as his older contemporary Dominikus Böhn—he designed such important secular buildings as the College of Sociology in Aachen and the Wallraf-Richartz Museum in Cologne, and he worked in city planning and post-war reconstruction. But he has been described (by G.E. Kidder Smith) as "probably the most profound church architect of our time," because for him religious architecture was not limited to mere building, but reflected the basic philosophical thinking that is strongly evident in his book *Vom Bau der Kirche.* Schwarz's work has been called an "architecture parlante" because the buildings are meant to suggest and embody metaphysical ideas, to be "high inhabitable pictures like life-size parables."

This does not mean that Schwarz was not a modern functionalist architect, for it was in accordance with that basic doctrine "form follows function" that he became a pioneer of the one-room open-plan type of church interior. His work was part of the Liturgical Revival, a movement to return to the most ancient concept of Christianity in which priest and laity were intimately one within the mystical body of the Church, and the prototypes of his early church buildings ere the great basilicas of pagan Rome, which were open halls of justice. A highly significant example, which prompted much controversy when it was first built in 1930, is the Corpus Christi Church at Aachen, a very plain simple rectangular hall without aisles, a severe enclosed space, with the altar mounted on a platform so that it is clearly visible from any point, the outside, with its

belfry tower having an equally stark simplicity, the whole full of a concentrated austere religious purpose.

Schwarz felt that a religious building should be a "mighty refuge," and in many of his post-war designs he sought to provide a spiritual "fortress" of enduring solidity and strength against the outside world. The solid towering walls of St. Michael's Church in Frankfurt rise unbroken by windows, for this church is lit only by a continuous window band just below the roof. The plan is an ellipse with trefoil chapels, so that the main body is a great oval room surrounded by a gently curving wall which gives much less feeling of confinement than would a similar rectangular space, producing a serenely calm interior lit only from high above. The idea came on a journey through the Aare Gorge, when Schwarz found himself "hemmed in by staring rocks lit only high up through a small gap to the open sky. I saw this gorge as a common human experience: a menacing world towering all around with but a glimpse of the open sky whose silver light shimmers down from the highest region. This experience found its architectural expression in St. Michael's."

Another highly original shape, which is equally a thoughtful interpretation of the new liturgical concepts, is St. Anna's Church in Düren (a town almost totally destroyed by bombing), built with stone retrieved from rubble to make a large massive L-shaped church with sheer exterior walls. The highly unusual plan of the Church of the Holy Cross, Bottrop, a brick parabola with the open end sheathed only in glass, is a direct realization of an idea put forward in the form of a parable years earlier in Schwarz's book. Similarly, the Church of Mary the Queen in Saarbrucken expresses the idea of Mary as Queen directly in its plan of four horizontal conjoined parabolas which give the appearance of a crown, lit by glazed half parabolas at the meeting point, so that light is focused as a dazzling architectural spotlight at the crossing.

These highly original constructions are never mere gimmicks, but always attempts to make the buildings more directly functional and open in accordance with the requirements of the modern liturgical movement. And they have made Schwarz generally acknowledged, along with Dominikus Böhm, as one of the great innovators of modern church design.

—Konstantin Bazarov

SCHWEIKHER, (Robert) Paul.

American. Born in Denver, Colorado, 28 July 1903. Educated at the University of Colorado, Boulder, 1921-22; Art Institute of Chicago, 1922-23; Illinois Institute of Technology, Chicago, also the Chicago Atelier, nights 1924-26; Yale University School of Architecture, New Haven, Connecticut, under Otto Faelton and Sheppard Stevens, 1927-29, B.F.A. 1929; travelled and studied in Europe (Matcham Fellowship), 1929-30. Served in the United States Naval Reserve, in Virginia, Illinois and California, 1942-45: Lieutenant junior grade to Lieutenant Commander. Married Dorothy Miller in 1923; son: Paul. Worked as a draftsman with Granger and Bollenbacher, Chicago, 1923-25, and with David Adler, Chicago, 1925-27; assistant designer with Russell Wolcott, Chicago, 1927, 1928; free-lance architect, 1930-31; Chief Designer with Philip B. Mather, Chicago, 1931-33; Designer and Site Planner, General Houses Inc., Chicago, 1933-34; Principal and Senior Partner, with Theodore Warren Lamb and Winston Elting, Schweikher, Lamb and Elting, Architects, Chicago, 1934-42, and Schweikher and Elting, Chicago, 1946-52; Professor of Architecture and Chairman of the School of Architecture, Yale University, also in private practice as Paul Schweikher Associates, New Haven, Connecticut, 1953-57; Professor of Architecture and Head of the Department of Architecture, Carnegie-Mellon University, Pittsburgh, also in private practice as Paul Schweikher Associates, Pittsburgh, 1957-69. In private practice, Sedona, Arizona, since 1970. Director, American Institute of Architects Chicago Chapter School, 1939-40; Member, Board of Directors, Arts Club of Chicago, 1939-56; Member, Civic Design Committee of Chicago, 1941-42; Member, City Planning Commission of Pittsburgh, 1961-63; Member of the Advisory Council, Princeton University School of Architecture, New Jersey, 1961-69. Visiting Critic/Lecturer: School of Fine Arts, Art Institute of Chicago, 1939; University of Illinois, Urbana, 1947, 1952; Yale University, 1947, 1950, 1951; Washington University, St. Louis, 1949; Arizona State University, Tempe, 1949, 1975; Tulane University, New Orleans, 1950; University of Kansas, Lawrence, 1950; University of Minnesota, Minneapolis, 1952; Western Reserve University, Cleveland, 1957; Syracuse University, New York, 1959; Princeton University, 1960. Exhibitions: one-man—Art Institute of Chicago, 1941; Yale University, 1947, 1969; Akron Art Institute, Ohio, 1948; University of Chicago, 1949; University of Illinois, 1949-50; Tulane University, 1949-50; University of Texas at Austin, 1951; University of Kansas, 1951; University of Minnesota, 1951; Carnegie Institute of Technology, Pittsburgh, 1957; Princeton University, 1960, 1963; Catholic University, Washington, D.C., 1960; Carnegie Institute Museum, Pittsburgh, 1962, 1965; Arts and Crafts Center, Pittsburgh, 1967; Harvard University, Cambridge, Massachusetts, 1968; Arizona State University, Tempe, 1974; Graham Foundation Gallery, Chicago, 1984 (with William Ferguson Deknatel); group—Museum of Modern Art, New York, 1933, 1951; Sokolniki Park, Moscow, 1959; Architectural League of New York, 1960; American Institute of Architects Center,

Washington, D.C., 1960; American Federation of Arts, toured U.S.A. and South America, 1962-64; *Chicago Architects*, toured U.S.A. 1976-77. Collections: Schweikher Collection, Northern Arizona University Library, Flagstaff; Architectural Department, Art Institute of Chicago. Recipient: Grand Prize, General Electric Homes Competition, 1935; First Award, Church Architectural Guild of America, 1955; Design Award, *Progressive Architecture*, 1956, 1957, 1960; Distinguished Citizen Award, Denver, 1958; Honor Award, 1959, and Merit Citation, 1962, American Institute of Architects, Chicago Chapter; Ford Foundation Research Grant, 1962; Architect of the Year Award, Junior Chamber of Commerce, Pittsburgh, 1966; Artist of the Year Award, Arts and Crafts Center, Pittsburgh, 1967. Honorary M.A.: Yale University, 1953. Address: R.R. No.3, High Tor, Sedona, Arizona 86336, U.S.A.

Works:

1932 Charles W. Eliason House, Chicago (project)
1936 Berg House I, Glen Ellyn, Illinois
Third Unitarian Church, Chicago
Dushkin House, Winnetka, Illinois
Johnson House, Chicago
Lowenstein House, Highland Park, Illinois
1937/
41 Upton House I, Scottsdale, Arizona
Berg House II, Glen Ellyn, Illinois
1938 Rinaldo House, Downers Grove, Illinois
Schweikher House, Roselle, Illinois
1939 Emerson Settlement House, Chicago
Housing project, Rockford, Illinois
Barry House, Glenview, Illinois
Cooperative Community, Glenview, Illinois
Foster House, Hinsdale, Illinois
Guenther House, LaPorte, Indiana
L.D. Kern House, Roselle, Illinois
M.A. Kern House, Roselle, Illinois
Williams House, Glen Ellyn, Illinois
Voevodsky House, Libertyville, Illinois
1940 Flatley House, Western Springs, Illinois
Stone House, Topeka, Kansas
1941 McVey House, Glen Ellyn, Illinois
Archie M. Schrom House, Highland Park, Illinois
1942 Officers Quarters, United States Naval Training Station, Great Lakes, Illinois
William Fleming House, Highland Park, Illinois (project)
1946 Goebel House, Barrington, Illinois
House for *Life* magazine, New York
Usonia Cooperative II, White Plains, New York
Wooster House, Skokie, Illinois
1947 Burda House, Mount Prospect, Illinois
Kessel House, Glenview, Illinois
Landis House, Flora, Indiana
Stary House, Lisle, Illinois
1948 Lew House, White Plains, New York
Upton House addition, St. Joseph, Michigan
Upton House II, Scottsdale, Arizona
Tom Darlington House, Paradise Valley, Arizona (project)
1949 Fine Arts Center, Maryville College, Tennessee
Beatty House, Lake Forest, Illinois
1950 Burhans House, Peoria, Illinois
Finch House, Paradise Valley, Arizona
Horton House, Valparaiso, Indiana
Rockwell House, Flossmoor, Illinois
Eli Brown Office Building, Louisville, Kentucky (project)
Porter Office Building, Chicago (project)
1951 First Methodist Church, Plainfield, Iowa
Faith United Protestant Church School, Park Forest, Illinois
Carpenter House, Libertyville, Illinois
Elting House, Libertyville, Illinois
Harring House, Highland Park, Illinois

Keller House, South Bend, Indiana
Otis House, Libertyville, Illinois
Orphan asylum, Chicago (project)
Decker House, Peoria, Illinois (project)
1952 Cazenovia Elementary School, New York
Residence for the Mentally Ill, Chicago Medical Center
Beaugureau House, Barrington, Illinois
Bennett House, Tyron, North Carolina
Harvey Studio, Libertyville, Illinois
Shiller House, Glen Ellyn, Illinois
Yacht Club, St. Joseph, Michigan (project)
1953 Elementary school, Roselle, Illinois
Samuel Tyndale Wilson Chapel/Theatre, Maryville College, Tennessee
Elementary school, Schaumburg, Illinois
Faith United Protestant Church, Park Forest, Illinois
Gray House, St. Joseph, Michigan
Lloyd-Smith House, Huron Mountain, Michigan
Parker House, Palatine, Illinois
Ross House, St. Joseph, Michigan
1954 Frazel House, Wayne, Illinois
Law School, University of Chicago (project)
Grace Lutheran School and Church, Teaneck, New Jersey (project)
1955 First Universalist Church, Chicago
Josiah Willard Gibbs Research Laboratory, Yale University, New Haven, Connecticut (with Douglas Orr)
Long-range plan for Yale University, New Haven, Connecticut (project)
1956 Reactor Building, University of Buffalo, New York (project)
Seymour Knox Wing, Museum of Fine Arts, Buffalo, New York (project)
Hotel Machu Picchu, Lima, Peru (project)
1957 Fine Arts Center and Music Unit, University of Buffalo, New York
Women's Dormitory, New Haven State Teachers College, Connecticut (with Earl Carlin)
1958 Unitarian Church, Evanston, Illinois
Studio Theatre, Carnegie Institute of Technology, Pittsburgh
Carnegie Institute Museum alterations, Pittsburgh
Public library, Watertown, Connecticut
Campus Activities Building, Carnegie Institute of Technology, Pittsburgh
1959 Women's Dormitory, Maryville College, Tennessee
Chicago Hall Language Center, Vassar College, Poughkeepsie, New York
1960 Trinity United Presbyterian Church, East Liverpool, Ohio (with James Porter)
Somerville Hospital, Massachusetts (project; with William Metcalf)
1961 Exhibition cases for the Carnegie Institute Museum, Pittsburgh
1962 The Ideal Theatre, Pittsburgh (project; with George Izenour)
1965 Knoxville Branch, Carnegie Library, Pittsburgh
1966 Cooperative apartments, Kittanning, Pennsylvania (project)
1967 Student Union Building, Duquesne University, Pittsburgh
Medical Office Building, Steubenville, Ohio (with James Porter)
Wright House, Fox Chapel, Pennsylvania
Municipal Fine Arts Center, Concert House and Theatre, Erie, Pennsylvania (project; with George Izenour)
1968 Thompson House, Seal Harbor, Maine
Apartment building for the elderly, Pittsburgh (project)
Scattered hillside housing, Pittsburgh (project)
Keller House, St. Joseph, Michigan (project)
1969 Science Center, Duquesne University, Pittsburgh (with Mies van der Rohe as supervising associate)

Paul Schweikher: Chicago Hall Language Center, Vassar College, Poughkeepsie, New York, 1959.

1970 WQED-WQEX Educational Television Station, Pittsburgh
      YMCA Building, Pittsburgh (project)
1974 Schweikher House II, Sedona, Arizona
1978 Schweikher studio, workshop and house complex, Sedona, Arizona

Publications:

By SCHWEIKHER: articles—"A Chicago Housing Project", with George Fred Keck, in *Architectural Record* (New York), March 1933; "Chicago Must Plan to Save Its Life" in *Real Estate Magazine* (Chicago), July 1939; "Decay and Revival of American Cities" in *Illinois Society of Architects Bulletin* (Chicago), September 1939; "Architectural Bandwagon" in *The New Humanist* (Chicago), March 1955; "The Architectural Virtues" in *Pittsburgh Post-Gazette,* July 1961; "The Architecture of Usefulness" in *Yale Literary Review* (New Haven, Connecticut), September 1966.

On SCHWEIKHER: books—*Neuzeitlicher Verkehrsbau* by K. Wittman, Potsdam 1931; *Work of Young Architects in the Middle West* by Henry-Russell Hitchcock and Philip Johnson, New York 1933; *Tomorrow's Houses* by Nelson and Wright, New York 1945; *American Interior Design* by Meyric R. Rogers, New York 1947; *A Decade of New Architecture* by Sigfried Giedion, Zurich 1951; *Built*

in USA: Postwar Architecture, edited by Henry-Russell Hitchcock and Arthur Drexler, New York 1952; *What is Modern Interior Design?* by Edgar Kaufmann Jr., New York 1953; *Churches and Temples* by Paul Thiry, Richard M. Bennett and Henry L. Kamphoefner, New York 1954; *Architecture USA* by Ian McCallum, New York 1959; *The Architecture of America* by Burchard and Bush-Brown, Boston 1961; *Chicago's Famous Buildings,* edited by Arthur Siegel, Chicago 1966; *Chicago Architects* by Stuart E. Cohen, Chicago 1976; *Architecture in Context: The Avant-Garde in Chicago's Suburbs — Paul Schweikher and William Ferguson Deknatel* exhibition catalogue by J. Zukovsky and B. Blum, Chicago 1984; articles—buildings and projects published in articles in *Architectural Forum* (New York), November 1939, October 1940, August 1942, January 1946, May 1947, October 1947, November and December 1952, April 1956, May 1959, December 1961, January 1962, March 1966, and July/August 1967; *Architectural Record* (New York), December 1936, November 1941, March 1943, December 1946, July 1947, November 1947, December 1951, April 1955, June 1955, June 1956, August 1957, April 1959, September 1959, and February 1966; *Architecture + Urbanism* (Tokyo), July 1971; *House and Garden* (New York), December 1950; *House and Home* (New York), October 1957; *Architecture d'Aujourd'hui* (Paris), April/May 1957; *Life* (New York), April 1947; *Nuestra Arquitectura* (Buenos Aires), April 1947, August 1952, October 1952, November/December 1956; *Pencil Points* (New York), February 1940, December 1946;

Progressive Architecture (New York), November 1950, January 1957, November 1957, January 1960, December 1961, February 1962, December 1965, and September 1967; *Vogue* (New York), July 1957; "Austerity in Concrete" in *Architectural Forum* (New York), December 1961; "Four Theaters for the Ford Foundation" in *Progressive Architecture* (New York), February 1962; "Homage to Paul Schweikher" in *Charette* (Philadelphia), January 1963; "Power for Culture" in *Progressive Architecture* (New York), December 1965; "Pittsburgh Library—Class Amid the Clutter" in *Architectural Forum* (New York), March 1966; "Architecture on Campus" in *Architectural Forum* (New York), July/August 1967; "Three Houses, Three Generations" in *Progressive Architecture* (New York), November 1967; "At the Top of the Mountain" in *Fine Homebuilding* (Newtown, Connecticut), August/September 1983.

*

The April 1939 issue of *Architectural Forum* presented some of the work done up to that time by my associate Theodore Warren Lamb and me. The editor had asked that we write a short introduction. We wrote in part the following:

Our working philosophy is made up of growing and changing ideas and we hesitate to crystallize it into irrevocable statements.
We try to solve the vital problems of satisfying the requirements, creating simple, workable structure,

orienting the structure to sunlight, to prevailing winds and to the physical character of the site.

Ted Lamb was killed in an airplane accident in 1943 while on his way to London. I have had a number of partners and associates since, but the above tenet serves still as a direction-finder.

Otto Faelton and Sheppard Stevens influenced me as a student at Yale. Longer lasting influences were those of: David Adler—my employer for two years; from him I learned to see scale, proportion, and detail. Mies van der Rohe—a close friend; we had many long talks about architecture, other architects, and his collection of Schwitters. Buckminster Fuller—I was one of a small group that worked (nights) with Fuller on the first "Dymaxion" house in 1933. George Howe—my predecessor (as Chairman of the School of Architecture) at Yale, a dear friend, a cherished companion: he was a sharp critic. Louis Kahn—it was my privilege to teach with him (and to be taught by him) at Yale; he was an occasional guest at Carnegie-Mellon in the '60s.

—Paul Schweikher

Paul Schweikher's forte is sensitive selection and honest expression of materials. He uses materials with enduring qualities and indigenous textures: brick, stone, tile, wood, copper, lead, steel and concrete. Rarely does he resort to traditional finish materials; when he does, it is usually for functional reasons. As he has said:

It is better as a whole to be satisfied with a closer acquaintance with a few basic materials and to concentrate on those with the same sincerity and honesty given to present day plan—that an integration of plan and material and ultimately building may become a truly representative architecture.

Schweikher makes little distinction between exterior and interior materials, as at the Knoxville Branch Library in Pittsburgh: concrete block walls, exposed concrete structural frame, and granite paving carry the material theme throughout the building, unifying the design. He conceives of walls as complete three-dimensional units without front and back, finished or unfinished side. The interior face of an exterior wall, by definition, is of the same material.

The design of Trinity United Presbyterian Church, East Liverpool, Ohio, demonstrates Schweikher's thorough knowledge of precast concrete. At the intersection of columns and beams, exposed lead beam caps and lead plugs skillfully express the inner function of post-tensioning strands. Slit windows separate the concrete block exterior walls from the columns, clearly defining structural and non-structural elements. Concrete blocks, carefully proportioned and left exposed reveal the indigenous aggregates.

At the Unitarian Church in Evanston, Illinois, Schweikher turned to reinforced concrete and glass to make a brutal statement in material. The exterior has two end walls entirely of glass, captured between massive concrete sidewalls and roof structure. Huge fins project out from the sidewalls and merge with the main concrete roof beams to form a rigid frame. Very narrow glass slits punctuate the otherwise unrelenting severity of the smoothly-finished, inward-sloping sidewalls.

Schweikher's quest for explicit honesty in exposing natural finishes and structural elements required careful integration of architectural, mechanical and electrical systems. A narrow mechanical bay bisecting the Knoxville Branch Library supplies air through the sidewalls of the high-ceilinged, sky-lit reading rooms. Strip fluorescent down lights, mounted on the shelving units, provide lighting in the stack areas and keep the exposed concrete, double-tee ceiling uncluttered. At the Fine Arts Center at Maryville College, Tennessee, Schweikher made no attempt to conceal the mechanical and electrical systems; he deliberately exposed pipes, conduits,

light fixtures and heating units in front of finished materials. At the Stone House in Topeka, Kansas, a symbiotic relationship exists between material expression and mechanical function. Here, an under-floor radiant heating system freed the living space of mechanical equipment and necessitated the use of brick pavers as a floor material and heat sink.

With the proliferation of today's dropped-ceiling, extruded-aluminium, gypsum board buildings, Paul Schweikher's work stands pointing in another direction: honest expression of basic materials resulting in a more representative architecture.

—Geoffrey Lee Farnsworth

SCOTT, Michael John.

Irish. Born in Drogheda, 24 June 1905. Educated at Belvedere College, Dublin, 1917-23; School of Art, Dublin, and School of Acting, Abbey Theatre, Dublin, 1923-26; articled to Jones and Kelly, architects, Dublin, 1923-26. Married Patricia Nixon in 1932; children: Anthony, Michael, Brian, Niall, and Ciarin. Architectural Assistant, Charles J. Dunlop, Architect, Dublin, 1926, and Office of Public Works, Dublin, 1927; acted with the Abbey Players, Dublin, on tour in the United States, winter 1927-28. In private practice, Dublin, from 1928, as Principal, Michael Scott, Architect, 1928-58, and Michael Scott and Associates, 1958-66, and Senior Partner, Michael Scott and Partners, 1966-74, and (with Ronald Tallon, Robin Walker, and Niall Scott) Scott Tallon Walker/Architects, Dublin and London, 1974 until he retired in 1977; consultant to Scott Tallon Walker, since 1977. Co-Founder and Chairman, Building Centre of Ireland, 1958-77. Founder and Executive Committee Chairman, Rosc international art exhibitions, Dublin, 1967-80; Chairman of the Council, Dublin Theatre Festival, 1968-82; Chairman, Gate Theatre, Dublin, since 1982. Exhibitions: (landscape drawings), Dawson Gallery, Dublin, 1967, 1975, and 1978; (architecture), Bank of Ireland Exhibition Hall, Dublin, 1975. Recipient: Silver Medal, City of New York, 1939; Triennial Gold Medal, Royal Institute of the Architects of Ireland, 1953-55; Royal Gold Medal, Royal Institute of British Architects, 1975; Distinguished Service Cross, Federal Republic of Germany, 1977. Hon.Dip.Arch.: College of Technology, Bolton Street, Dublin, 1967; Hon.Dr.: Royal College of Art, London, 1969; Litt.D.: Dublin University, 1970; D.Sc.: Queen's University of Belfast, 1977. Fellow, Royal Institute of the Architects of Ireland, 1948. Honorary Member, Royal Society of Ulster Architects, 1967; Honorary Fellow, American Institute of Architects, 1972; Honorary Fellow, Institute of Structural Engineers, London, 1976. Member, Icelandic Order of the Falcon, 1974. Address (office); 19 Merrion Square, Dublin 2, Ireland.

Works:

1929 North Wing, St. Ultan's Children's Hospital, Dublin
1930 Gate Theatre conversion, Dublin
1936 Laois County Hospital, Portlaoise, Ireland
1937 Offaly County Hospital, Tullamore, Ireland
1938 "Geragh" (Scott House), Sandycove Point, Dun Laoghaire, County Dublin.
1939 Pavilion of Ireland, World's Fair, New York
1949 Irish Transport Board Bus Chassis Factory, Dublin (now Central Engineering Workshops of the Office of Public Works)
1951 Irish Transport Board Bus Garage, Donnybrook, Dublin
1953 Irish Transport Board Bus Station/Department of Social Welfare Office Building, Store Street, Dublin

1954 McCairns Motors Ltd. Car Assembly and Service Garage, Santry, Dublin
1956 Stewarts and Lloyds of Ireland Ltd. Warehouse and Office Building, Port of Dublin Ballroom, Shelbourne Hotel, Dublin
1959 Brown and Polson Ltd. Factory, Inchicore, Dublin
1966 Abbey Theatre, Dublin (with Ronald Tallon)

Publications:

By SCOTT: articles—"Inaugural Address" in *Green Book: Journal of the Architectural Association of Ireland* (Dublin), 1937-38; "The Abbey as I Remember It" in *The New Abbey Theatre*, supplement to *Irish Times* (Dublin), 18 July 1966; "An Aspect of Man and His Environment" in *Green Book: Journal of the Architectural Association in Ireland* (Dublin), 1968; "Michael Scott on Dublin," interview, with Consuelo O'Connor in *An Taisce: Ireland's Conservation Journal* (Dublin), September/October 1978; "Art and Architecture" in *Art about Ireland*, Dublin 1979.

On SCOTT: articles—"Comhaimsirigh Michael Scott" in *Indui* (Dublin), 10 August 1951; "Men of the Year" in *Architects' Journal* (London), 20 January 1955; "Michael Scott" in *Irish Times* (Dublin), 17 September 1955; "Michael Scott" in *Irish Architect and Contractor* (Dublin), October 1956; "Michael Scott and Partners" by Alan Colquhoun in *Architectural Design* (London), February 1968; editorial comment by Martin Reynolds in *Irish Builder and Engineer* (Dublin), 7 September 1968; "Michael Scott: Father Figure of Irish Architecture" in *Building and Contract Journal* (Dublin), 12 June 1969; "The Royal Scott" by Lance Wright in *Architects' Journal* (London), 22 January 1975; "Irish Gold" by Neil Steedman in *Building Design* (London), 24 January 1975; "Michael Scott, Man and Architect" in *Build* (Dublin), February 1975; "Scott/Tallon/Walker" by Neil Steedman in *Yearbook of the Royal Institute of the Architects of Ireland* (Dublin), 1975-76; "The Shamrock Building" by Nicholas Sheaff in *Irish Arts Review* (Carrick-on-Suir, Ireland), Spring 1984.

As a pupil of Jones and Kelly, I recall playing my part in the detailing of Ireland's last classical civic building, Cork City Hall. I was, of course, also expected to "switch to Gothic" when it was thought that the occasion demanded this. On first encountering modern architecture, initially in its Swedish (and Dutch) forms, through the eyes of Frank Yerbury, those of us who were weaned to it from this training background tended to see the modern movement as something which we were "for," in opposition to others who were "against," without analyzing too clearly the various strands which made it up, or our own positions in it. Those who were "against" were forced into some species of eclectism (full-dress classical or gothic had by that time priced itself out of all but the ecclesiastical market) or Art Deco, a style in which I also served my brief time (but distinctions among different segments of the opposition were considered irrelevant once a commitment to modern architecture had been declared).

I would consider my glass-walled Irish Pavilion in the 1939 New York World's Fair, along with my own house at Sandycove Point, to be my first recognizably modern-movemnet buildings, although my county hospitals at Portlaoise and Tullamore were both significant steps—albeit in somewhat different directions—along my chosen path: Portlaoise, a very frank expression of both the hospital brief and its crude, or at least low-tech, mass concrete structure, painted in the stunning white of the period, and Tullamore, with its juxtaposition of stone arches and Dudok-type stair towers.

My Irish Pavilion was to be, however, my last exercise in its genre. Although Ireland was neutral in the 1939-45 war, shortages of supply put building on any scale out of the question, and my practice was hard put to survive on small alteration works, offering little scope for creativity of any kind. As with a great many architects of my generation, who took their first faltering steps in modern architecture within the shadow of war clouds ahead, a magic moment had passed beyond recall by the time the major commissions from Coras Iompair Eireann (nationalized transport) reached me in the immediate postwar years. Although the bus terminal and offices at Store Street, Dublin, must be reckoned the principal work of my architectural career, this building bears many signs of the loss of architectural foothold, perhaps loss of innocence, which those who reached their maturity just as war broke out suffered from the interruption of their creative flow.

The Store Street building was completed in 1953. From then to the end of the decade was a lean time in Ireland, during which emigration reached its peak. Although bitterly disappointed that the immediate postwar boom had proved yet another false start to my chances of creating a real corpus of good modern buildings in Ireland, I did at least have the opportunity, with this enforced freedom from major commissions, to look at the several directions in which modern architecture was seen to be dividing. The still well which I first drew inspiration had become a whirlpool in which I was now trying to define my position.

What I began to see as the true gospel of modern architecture was clarified for me most eloquently, many years later, by Peter Carter, at one time a member of Mies van der Rohe's staff and author of *Mies van der Rohe at Work*, in a lecture delivered in University College, Dublin, in December 1975. As this lecture was delivered in my honour—as one of a series of events organized by my colleagues in Ireland to celebrate my Royal Gold Medal year—I take leave

to quote from it, in lieu of any profession of my own faith:

...because today's technology provides architects with a wide range of choice, the freedoms it brings may only too easily be interpreted as *license* for *irrational* individualism of a most egregious kind.

By concentrating upon a STRUCTURALLY oriented architecture, our work as a whole would acquire REASON as its basis, and GENERALITY in its application. For, in a MORPHOLOGICAL interpretation of STRUCTURE may be found a sound GENERAL PRINCIPLE upon which the architecture of *our time* might develop, as it indeed did in the past.

While this PRINCIPLE OF STRUCTURE remains secure, the MAINSTREAM of architectural development will not be easily side-tracked.

And, furthermore, we shall be properly prepared for the time when our present *needs* and *means* give way to others and so initiate a new cycle in the development of architecture.

The *philosophy of architecture* could be interpreted as having both CONSERVATIVE and RADICAL strains, without implying contradictory aims.

CONSERVATIVE: Because in its basic ingredients are to be found the *traditional* principles of structural order, spatial relation and proportion.

RADICAL: Because it accepts as prime determinants the significant driving and sustaining forces of our time—those of science, technology, industrialism and economy.

Furthermore, in its realization as *architecture*, this philosophy often becomes *sociologically* radical, in that we may sense in the very HUMILITY of the spaces many of its buildings offer, the acquisition of civilizing freedoms from wilful architectural manipulation and anachronistic custom.

At the beginning of this lecture I noted that the one characteristic shared by all the great architectural

epochs of the past was that their BUILDERS restricted themselves to very clear PRINCIPLES, yet this did not inhibit the range or the variety of their work. And, upon due reflection, I think that many will agree that *that* is, perhaps, the only way we too may make an architecture of *some* SIGNIFICANCE.

When, in 1958, at the onset of a new period of great expansion in Ireland, I decided to make my chief assistants at that time, Robin Walker and Ronald Tallon, associates in a reconstituted practice, to become partners later, I was happy to feel that this doctrine of architecture would be safe in their hands and, subsequently, in the hands of my son Niall. The third member of my 1958 crew, Patrick Scott, also joined in the creation of the new firm but left shortly afterwards to devote his full time to painting and freelance designing.

—Michael Scott

There were three important aspects concerning the formative years of Michael Scott. He chose an articled training, a decision precipitated no doubt by the rather erratic nature of academic facilities at that time in Ireland. He went into private practice very early in his life, which, somhow, gave him the opportunity to travel and pursue briefly and ultimately dismiss other careers in acting, in ballet no less, and as a painter. Then there was the relative isolation of Ireland. Little effective dialogue with European mainland influences was possible during this period. It is doubtful that Corbusier's *Towards a New Architecture* of 1927 would have reached Ireland, or Pevsner's *Pioneers of Modern Design* of 1936, not to mention the *Architectural Review* and, in particular, its famous essays of 1932 by Morton Shand and Wells Coates. Certainly there was the Christ the King Church in Cork (1936) by Barry

Michael Scott: Irish Transport Board Bus Station, Store Street, Dublin, 1953.

Byrne, a Chicago architect; there was, too, the whole literary revival in Ireland; then in full ferment; finally, there was the Irish Stained Glass movement, which had reached its high point in the work of artists such as Michael Healy, Harry Clarke and Evie Hone. All this occurring in a country just finding its nationalistic feet, putting together only in 1937 a constitutional basis for its future.

Nevertheless, Scott was learning the language of contemporary expression in architecture. An early office block by Jones and Kelly, his employers, provided him with an introduction. On establishing his own practice in 1928, there were many projects such as his own house, hospitals, and theatre conversions to allow him to extend his syntax. But it was the Irish Pavilion for the New York World's Fair in 1939 that demonstrated his command. In this stylish, curvilinear work, with its glazed curtain wall cladding, flat roof slab, and two-storey volume may be seen an excellent manifestation of Scott's fluency. There are echoes of the Mies Barcelona Pavilion of 1929. There is the same comprehension of space, one rectilinear, one curvilinear, but three-dimensional for all that: the canvas of architecture had, for Scott, been filled in. Sculpture by Herkner, paintings by McGonigal and Keating, and lettering by Gill were included as integral elements of his deign.

Back in Dublin, coincidentally, this very architecture was finding another expression in a new terminal for the airport (1939) by Professor Desmond Fitzgerald—a Bauhaus-inspired design. With these two buildings, then, though separated by several thousand miles, Ireland was shaking off the last remnants of the revival period.

In the mid-1940s, there came the commission for the Bus Station in Dublin and, with it, official recognition at home as well as abroad. Opened in 1953, after many vicissitudes, including a change of client, it still retains its original qualities—the planning of the awkward island site; the use again of architectural volumes, particularly the great curving concourse enhanced and unified by its column disposition and diagonal floor finish; the complex planning so evident at each floor level; the superb detailing throughout.

Of course there have been criticisms; it has been condemned as eclectic. But then, as Peter Collins says in his book *Changing Ideals in Modern Architecture*, this is no bad thing. In the Dublin Bus Station Scott eschews all formalism in detail planning in favour of a freer interpretation of the design brief. His capacity to do this is demonstrated in the way that spaces are put together, the way each reflects its function, the way that their complex hierarchy is evolved. Their disparate environmental needs are provided for; the rationale of structure in architecture is well articulated. Scott has—albeit with notable assistance from Ove Arup and Jorgan Varming—become fully literate. Naturally, it is tempting to look for overseas influences. Le Corbusier's Cite de Refuge, a Salvation Army hostel opened in Paris in 1933, has an obvious elevational similarity but it would be impertinent to labour it.

The introduction of associates into his practice in 1959 and partners some years later brought to an end Scott's accredited architectural work. Yet, for Scott, an evangelical role, with a very special concern for the visual arts, continued: he has participated, and continues to participate, in virtually every national institution having to do with the arts. Most of his citations highlight his pioneering role in architecture, indeed in all the arts in Ireland, and his inclusion in this publication is further endorsement of his achievements.

—Kevin Spencer

SCOTT BROWN, Denise.

American. Born Denise Lakofski in Nkana, Zambia, 3 October 1931; emigrated to the United States, 1958: naturalized, 1967. Educated at Kingsmead College, Johannesburg, South Africa, 1938-47; University of the Witwatersrand, Johannesburg, 1948-51; Architectural Association School, London, under Arthur Korn, *q.v.*, 1952-55, A.A. Diploma and Certificate in Tropical Architecture 1956; University of Pennsylvania, Philadelphia, under H. Gans, Louis I. Kahn, *q.v.*, D. A. Crane, R. B. Mitchell, W. L. C. Wheaton, W. Isard, C. Rapkin, P. Davidoff and B. Harris, 1958-60, M.City Planning 1960; M.Arch. 1965. Married the architect Robert Scott Brown in 1955 (died, 1959); married the architect Robert Venturi, *q.v.*, in 1967; son: James. Worked as a student architect with various firms in Johannesburg and London, 1946-52; Architectural Assistant to Ernö Goldfinger, *q.v.*, and Dennis Clarke Hall, London, 1955-56, to Giuseppe Vaccaro, Rome, 1956-57, and to Cowin, DeBruyn and Cook, Johannesburg, 1957-58; Assistant Professor, School of Fine Arts, University of Pennsylvania, Philadelphia, 1960-65; Visiting Professor, School of Environmental Design, University of California, Berkeley, 1965; Associate Professor, School of Architecture and Urban Planning, University of California at Los Angeles, 1965-68 (initiated Urban Design Program). Since 1967, Architect and Planner, and later Partner, with Robert Venturi and John Rauch, *q.v.* (associates: Steven Izenour; David Vaughan), Venturi and Rauch, and since 1980, Venturi, Rauch and Scott Brown, Philadelphia: Partner-in-Charge of Urban Planning. Visiting Professor in Urban Design, Yale University School of Architecture, New Haven, Connecticut, 1967-70 (Fellow of Morse College since 1970); Visiting Critic, Rice University, Houston, Texas, 1969; Regents Lecturer, University of California at Santa Barbara, 1972; Chairwoman, Evaluation Committee for the Industrial Design Program, Philadelphia College of Art, 1972; Member of the Visiting Committee, School of Architecture and Urban Planning, Massachusetts Institute of Technology, Cambridge, 1973-83; Baldwin Lecturer, Oberlin College, Ohio, 1975; Visiting Professor, University of Pennsylvania School of Fine Arts, Philadelphia, 1982, 1983. Advisory Committee Member, Temple University Department of Architecture, Philadelphia, since 1980; Curriculum Committee Member, Philadelphia Jewish Children's Folkshul, since 1980; Advisor, United States National Trust for Historic Preservation, since 1981; Policy Panel Member, National Endowment for the Arts Design Arts Program, 1981-83; Board Member, Society of Architectural Historians, 1981-84; Capitol Preservation Comittee Member, Commonwealth of Pennsylvania, since 1983. Exhibitions: *The Work of Venturi and Rauch*, Whitney Museum, New York 1971; *The Invisible Artist*, Philadelphia Museum of Art, 1974; *The Work of Venturi and Rauch*, Pennsylvania Academy of Fine Arts, Philadelphia, 1975; *Suburban Alternatives: 11 American Projects*, Venice, 1976; *Women in American Architecture*, Brooklyn Museum, New York, 1977; *Architecture: Seven Architects*, Institute of Contemporary Art, Philadelphia, 1977; *Venturi and Rauch: Architektur in Alltag Amerikas*, Kunstgewerbemuseum, Zurich, 1979 (toured Switzerland); *Venturi, Rauch and Scott Brown*, Galleria dell' Accademia, Florence, Italy, 1981; *Architecture of the State University of New York at Purchase*, Neuberger Museum, Purchase, New York, 1981; *Correspondences: 5 Architects, 5 Sculptors*, Palacio de las Alhajas, Madrid, 1982; *Buildings and Drawings by Venturi, Rauch and Scott Brown*, Max Protetch Gallery, New York, 1982; *Venturi, Rauch and Scott Brown: A Generation of Architecture*, Krannert Art Museum, University of Illinois, Urbana, 1984 (toured the United States); *House/Work*, First Women's Bank, New York, 1984; *250 Years of Drawings by Philadelphia's Architects*, Pennsylvania Academy of the Fine Arts, Philadelphia, 1985. Recipient: First Prize, Yale University Mathematics Building Competition, 1970; Gold Medal, 1972, and Adaptive Re-use Award, 1976, American Institute of Architects, Philadelphia Chapter; Casebook Award, *Print Magazine*, 1976 (twice); *Urban Design* Case Studies Award, 1977; National Association of Schools of Art Award, 1979; Recognition Award (three) and Honor Award, Department of Housing and Urban Design, 1980; *Progressive Architecture* Award, 1980, 1981, 1982; Historic Preservation Award, 1980, and Certificate of Merit, 1983, Pennsylvania Historical and Museum Commission; Hazlett Memorial Award, Commonwealth of Pennsylvania, 1983; Certificate of Merit, American Planning Association, Eastern Pennsylvania Chapter, 1983. DFA: Oberlin College, Ohio, 1977; DHL: New Jersey Institute of Technology, Newark, 1984. Member, Architectural Association, London, American Planning Association, and Alliance of Women in Architecture; Associate of the Royal Institute of British Architects. Address: Venturi, Rauch and Scott Brown, 4236 Main Street, Philadelphia, Pennsylvania 19127, U.S.A.

Works:

1963 Study of the Neighbourhood Garden Association of Philadelphia
      Plan for the new tri-state New York Metropolitan Region, for the Office of Regional Development of the State of New York (with Marc Emery)

1967/
70   "Mass Communication on the People Freeway" (project: subway stop design; with Robert Venturi and B. Adams)
      "Learning from Las Vegas" (research project on symbolism in commercial architecture; with Robert Venturi and Steven Izenour)
      "Remedial Housing for Architects; or, Learning from Levittown" (research project on residential symbolism and popular taste; with Robert Venturi and P. Schmitt)

With Venturi and Rauch:
1968 Walker and Dunlop Office Building, Transportation Square, Washington, D.C. (project; with Caudill Rowlett Scott)

1968/
70   Rehabilitation plan for South Street, Philadelphia

1970 Mathematics Building, Yale University, New Haven, Connecticut
      Survey and analysis of subway station facilities, Philadelphia
      Humanities Classroom Building, State University of New York at Purchase
      Master plan and urban design of California City, California

1971 Lawton Plaza redevelopment plan, New Rochelle, New York
      Great Western Cities Inc. Office Building, California City, California (project)

1972 Master plan for the Bicentennial International Exposition Site at Eastwick, Philadelphia (with other firms)

1973 Windsor Hotel conversion plan, Cape May, New Jersey
      Preliminary design for prototypical neighborhood and community shopping centers for Saga Harbor, new community south of Miami, Florida
      Housing, Washington Square West Urban Renewal Area, Philadelphia (project)
      Renewal plan for the Seneca-Susquehanna area, Harrisburg, Pennsylvania
      Design of the Bicentennial celebration on and around Benjamin Franklin Parkway, Philadelphia
      South Central Philadelphia Neighborhood Development Program

1973/
75   Fairmount Manor and the Poplar Community (planning study for lawsuit, Shannon v. H.U.D.)

1974 Natural Science Museum, Roanoke, Virginia (project)

City Edges: design study for the improvement of road and water entrances to Philadelphia (with Murphy Levy Wurman)

Feasibility study for a residential community near Phoenix, Arizona

1975 Revitalization study of the Strand, Galveston, Texas

1976 Franklin Court, Independence National Historical Park, Philadelphia

Allen Memorial Art Museum renovation and additions, Oberlin College, Ohio

Faculty Club, Pennsylvania State University, University Park

Signs of Life: Symbols in the American City exhibition plan, Smithsonian Institution, Washington, D.C.

1977 Proposal for the rejuvenation of Main Street and The Hollow, Boonton, Jew Jersey

Urban design study for Heritage Plaza West, Salem, Massachusetts

Planning study for St. Christopher's Hospital for Children, Philadelphia

Expert testimony on environmental impact for Harvey Cedars, New Jersey

Planning study for Old City, Philadelphia

1978 Planning study for Washington Avenue, Miami Beach

Planning study for Jim Thorpe, Pennsylvania

Urban design for Western Plaza, Pennsylvania Avenue, Washington, D.C.

Arisbe Museum (Charles S. Peirce House), exhibition and graphic designs, Milford, Pennsylvania

1979 Best Products facade design, Oxford Valley, Pennsylvania

1980 Museum fur Kunsthandwerk, Frankfurt, West Germany (competition project)

Borough of Princeton development plan and urban design study, New Jersey

Borough of Jenkintown development planning study, Pennsylvania

1981 Hennepin Avenue transportation and development plan, Minneapolis, Minnesota (with Bather, Ringrose, Wolsfeld, Jarvis, Gardner, Inc.)

1984 Republic Square district plan, Austin, Texas

1985 Downtown Center City Plan, Memphis, Tennessee

Westway Riverfront Park, New York (with Clarke and Rapuano)

Laguna Gloria Art Museum, Austin, Texas

New Building, Seattle Art Museum, Washington

Denise Scott Brown's industrial designs include furniture, fabrics and homewares for: Fabric Workshop (Philadelphia), 1983; Alessi International (Milan), 1983, 1985; Formica Corporation (New York), 1983; Swid Powell, (New York), 1984, 1985; Knoll International (New York), 1984; Elective Affinities (Milan), 1985; Arc International (Milan), 1985.

Publications;

By SCOTT BROWN: books—*The Highway*, exhibition catalog, with Robert Venturi, Philadelphia 1970; *Aprendiendo de Todas Las Cosas*, with Robert Venturi, Barcelona 1971; *Learning from Las Vegas*, with Robert Venturi and Steven Izenour, Cambridge, Massachusetts 1972, 1977; *Signs of Life: Symbols in the American City*, exhibition catalog, with Steven Izenour, New York 1976; articles—"Natal Plans" in *Journal of the American Institute of Planners* (Washington, D.C.), May 1964; "The Meaningful City" in *Journal of the American Institute of Planners* (Washington, D.C.), January 1965; "Development Proposal for Dodge House Park" in *Arts and Architecture* (Los Angeles), April 1966; "Will Salvation Spoil the Dodge House?" in *Architectural Forum* (New York), October 1966; "Team 10, Perspecta 10, and the Present State of Architectural Theory" in *Journal of the American Institute of Planners* (Washington, D.C.), January 1967; "The Function of a Table" in *Architectural Design* (London), April 1967; "Planning the Powder Room" in *AIA Journal* (Washington, D.C.), April 1967; "Housing 1863" in *Journal of the American Institute of Planners* (Washington, D.C.), May 1967; "Teaching Architectural History" in *Arts and Architecture* (Los Angeles), May 1967; "Planning the Expo" in *Journal of the American Institute of Planners* (Washington, D.C.), July 1967; "The Bicentennial's Fantasy Stage" in *Philadelphia Evening Bulletin*, 8 March 1968; "A Significance for A & P Parking Lots; or Learning from Las Vegas," with Robert Venturi, in *Architectural Forum* (New York), March 1968; "Mapping the City: Symbols and Systems" in *Landscape* (Santa Fe, New Mexico), Spring 1968; "Little Magazines in Architecture and Urbanism" in *Journal of the American Institute of Planners* (Washington, D.C.), July 1968; "Urbino" in *Journal of the American Institute of Planners* (Washington, D.C.), September 1968; "On Ducks and Decoration," with Robert Venturi, in *Architecture Canada* (Toronto), October 1968; "Venturi versus Gowan," with Robert Venturi, in *Archi-*

tectural Design (London), January 1969; "On Pop Art Permissiveness and Planning" in *Journal of the American Institute of Planners* (Washington, D.C.), May 1969; "Learning from Lutyens," with Robert Venturi, in *RIBA Journal* (London), August 1969; "The Bicentennial Commemoration 1976," with Robert Venturi, in *Architectural Forum* (New York), October 1969; "Mass Communication on the People Freeway; or, Piranesi Is Too Easy," with Robert Venturi, in *Perspecta* (New Haven, Connecticut), no. 12, 1969; "Co-op City: Learning to Like It," with Robert Venturi, in *Progressive Architecture* (New York), February 1970; "Reply to Pawley—'Leading from the Rear',"with Robert Venturi, in *Architectural Design* (London), July 1970; "Education in the 1970's—Teaching for an Altered Reality" in *Architectural Record* (New York), October 1970; "Learning from Pop" and "Reply to Frampton" in *Casabella* (Milan), May/June 1971; "Some Houses of Ill-Repute: A Discourse with Apologia on Recent Houses of Venturi and Rauch," with Robert Venturi, in *Perspecta* (New Haven, Connecticut), no. 13/14, 1971; "Ugly and Ordinary Architecture; or, The Decorated Shed," with Robert Venturi, in *Architectural Forum* (New York), part I, November 1971, and part II, December 1971; "Bicentenaire de l'Independence Americaine," with Robert Venturi,

Denise Scott Brown: Cover of the Republic Square District Plan, Austin, Texas, 1984.

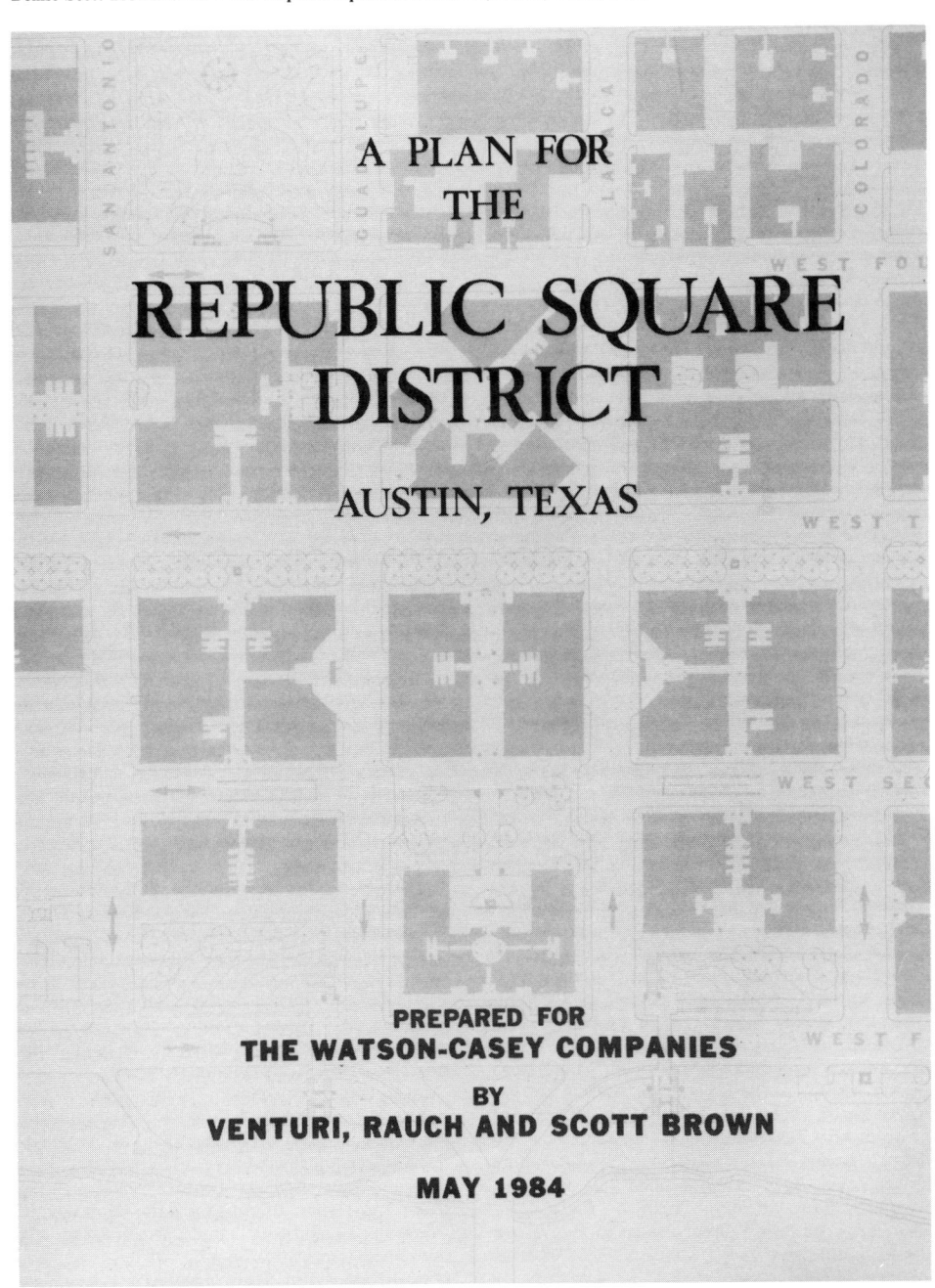

A PLAN FOR THE

REPUBLIC SQUARE DISTRICT

AUSTIN, TEXAS

PREPARED FOR
THE WATSON-CASEY COMPANIES
BY
VENTURI, RAUCH AND SCOTT BROWN

MAY 1984

in *L'Architecture d'Aujourd'hui* (Paris), November 1973; "Evaluation of the Humanities Building at Purchase," with Elizabeth and Steven Izenour, in *Architectural Record* (New York), October 1974; "Functionalism Yes, But ...," with Robert Venturi, in *Architecture + Urbanism* (Tokyo), November 1974; "House Language," with others, in *American Home* (New York), August 1976; "On Architectural Formalism and Social Concern: A Discourse for Social Planners and Radical Chic Architects" in *Oppositions 5* (New York), Summer 1976; "Suburban Space, Scale and Symbol," with others, in *Via* (Philadelphia), 1976; "Zeichen des Lebens, Signes de Vie" in *Archithese* (Zurich), no. 19, 1976; "Elusive Outcome" in *Progressive Architecture* (New York), May 1977; "On Formal Analysis as Design Research" in *Journal of Architectural Education* (Washington, D.C.), May 1979; "Die Stadt als Zeichensystem" in *Werk-Archithese* (Zurich), September/October 1979; "Revitalizing Miami" in *Urban Design International* (Purchase, New York), January/February 1980; "Architectural Taste in a Pluralistic Society" in *Harvard Architecture Review* (Cambridge, Massachusetts), Spring 1980; "Denise Scott Brown", interview, in *Particular Passions*, edited by Lynn Gilbert and Gaylen Moore, New York 1981; "With People in Mind" in *Journal of Architectural Education* (Washington, D.C.), Fall 1981; "An Urban Design Plan" in *Design Quarterly* (Minneapolis), no. 117, 1982; "Drawing for the Deco District" in *Archithese* (Niederteufen, Switzerland), 4 March 1982; "Denise Scott Brown", interview, in *Penn in Ink* (Philadelphia), Spring 1983; "A Worm's View of Recent Architectural History" in *Architectural Record* (New York), February 1984.

On SCOTT BROWN: books—*American Architecture and Urbanism* by Vincent Scully, New York 1969; *New Directions in American Architecture* by Robert A.M. Stern, New York 1969; *Will They Ever Finish Bruckner Boulevard?* by Ada Louise Huxtable, New York 1970; *After the Planners* by Robert Goodman, New York 1971; *Wasteland: Building the American Dream* by Stephen A. Kurtz, New York 1973; *Conversations with Architects* by John W. Cook and Heinrich Klotz, New York and London 1973; *Architettura Radicale* by Paolo Navone and Bruno Orlando, Milan 1974; *Supermannerism: New Attitudes in Post Modern Architecture* by C. Ray Smith, New York 1977; *Women in American Architecture: A Historic and Contemporary Perspective*, by Susana Torre, New York 1977; *Le Spose del Vento* by Luciano Rubino, Verona, Italy 1979; *Venturi and Rauch: Architektur im Alltag Amerikas*, exhibition catalogue by Stanislaus von Moos, Zurich 1979; *Venturi, Rauch and Scott Brown*, edited by Gianni Pettena and Maurizio Vogliazzo, Milan 1981; *Venturi, Rauch and Scott Brown: A Generation of Architecture*, exhibition catalogue by Rosemarie Haag Bletter, Urbana, Illinois 1984; articles—"Are the Venturis Putting Us on" by Ursula Cliff in *Design and Environment* (New York), Summer 1971; special issue of *Architecture + Urbanism* (Tokyo), October 1971; "Ms. Scott Brown Keeps Her Own Taste to Herself" by Patsy McLaughlin in *Pennsylvania Gazette* (Philadelphia), December 1971; "Interview: Denise Scott Brown" by Linda Groat in *Networks* (Los Angeles), no. 1, 1972; "Venturi and Venturi, Architectural Anti-Heroes" by Barbara Flanagan in *34th Street Magazine* (New York), 13 April 1972; "The Venturis—American Selection" by Deborah Waroff in *Building Design* (London), 4 August 1972; "Women in Professions: Architecture" by Vivien Raynor in *Viva* (London), May 1974; "Venturi and Rauch 1970-74," special issue of *Architecture + Urbanism* (Tokyo), November 1974; "Thirty-Six Women with Real Power Who Can Help You" by Donnal Israel and David C. Berliner in *Cosmopolitan* (New York), April 1975; "Architect for Pop Culture" by Maralyn Lois Polak in *Philadelphia Inquirer*, 8 June 1975; special issue of *Progressive Architecture* (New York), October 1977; "Recent Works by Venturi and Rauch", special issue of

Architecture + Urbanism (Tokyo), January 1978; "The Social Thought of Denise Scott Brown and Robert Venturi" and "Venturi and Rauch as Planners" by Jean-Louis Sarbib in *L'Architecture d'Aujourd'hui* (Paris), June 1978; "Miami Beach" by David Morton in *Progressive Architecture* (New York), August 1980; "Rude Graphics, or Learning from Las Vegas" by Teresa Reese in *Print* (New York), September/October 1980; "Venturi, Rauch and Scott Brown", special issue of *Architecture + Urbanism* (Tokyo), December 1981; "Women in Architecture" by Andrea O. Dean in *AIA Journal* (Washington, D.C.), January 1982; "Learning from Denise: The Role in Architecture of DSB" by Mildred F. Schmertz in *Architectural Record* (New York), July 1982; "Contradiction and Complexity Create a Home" by John Duka in *New York Times*, 28 October 1982, "Venturi, Rauch and Scott Brown" in *Progressive Architecture* (New York), January 1983; "At Home: Venturi/Scott Brown House" by Charles K. Gandee in *Architectural Record* (New York), September 1983; "Personal Patterns" by Martin Filler in *House and Garden* (New York), January 1984; "Portrait: Robert Venturi and Denise Scott Brown" by Jonathan Z. Larsen in *Life* (New York), November 1984.

Bibliographies: *Denise Scott Brown* by Lamia Doumato, Monticello, Illinois 1982; *Venturi, Rauch and Scott Brown*, Monticello, Illinois 1982.

*   *   *

In the mid-1950s, in London, I saw an article on a surprising and beautiful American building, It was a Brutalist building. Given our view of America, we had not expected to see such a sympathetic architecture there and we had never heard of the architect, although he appeared to be quite old, 56. (We were, of course, in our early 20s.) The architect was Louis I Kahn and the building was the Trenton Bath House ...

The Philadelphia School that I knew in the late 1950s and early 1960s as a student and professor at Penn was different from the one that has been described in publications by architects and journalists. Its genesis in city reform gave it a broader scope than has been recognized by most architectural historians, linking it to the New Deal and social thought of the Old Left at the one end, and to the initiation of the Civil Rights Movement and the New Left at the other. In the late 1940s, Mayor Joseph Clark invited G. Holmes Perkins, an architect and professor at Harvard, to head the School of Fine Arts at the University of Pennsylvania. The new dean brought with him and built around him an interdisciplinary team of architects, planners, and landscape architects. His new school resembled the Harvard school upon which it was based. However, the seeds of dissolution of such schools were within it, even as it was first founded, and the further addition of faculty members from different backgrounds eventually exploded the Harvard model. In that explosion originated some of the most important trends of thought in architecture and planning in the 1960s and 1970s ...

Paul Davidoff, a law student and graduate from the planning department, directed planning thought at Penn toward social action. This was 1958-59 and, in an otherwise quiescent campus, something unusual was buzzing around the planning department. I think it was the New Left. Here, long before it was visible in other places, was the elation that comes with the discovery and definition of a problem: poverty. The social planning movement engulfed Penn's planning department. It spread to the civic design program, but was held at bay by the architects who went about their business as usual. At faculty meetings, planners accused architects of being arrogant, but even the most churlish social planners didn't know where to put Lou Kahn. Although he called a pox on all their houses, he seemed to have everyone's respect. In the midst of this argument, computers moved in, bewitching the planners but not

yet the architects. The battle shifted from one between architects and humanists to one betweeen humanists and technocrats, with architects in both camps. I sat in the middle between architects and planners, pulled and buffeted. Each side seemed so right except when it was all wrong. How could the protagonists be so one-sided? My New Brutalist background tied in equally well with Kahn and Gans. The esthetic impulse that the social planners went to lengths to negate did not seem inadmissible, or indeed deniable, to me, nor was it necessarily elitist and undemocratic. On the other hand, how could the faculty in the architecture department turn their backs on what the planners were saying? If for no other reason than to keep their esthetic eyes fresh, the architects needed their systems broken by the social reality the planners represented. But despite a brief and faddish fling in the 1960s with radical chic, few architects and fewer historians heard the message of the social planners. We did.

The work of our firm will be misunderstood and wrongly placed until it is seen in a broader intellectual context than is usual in architectural discussion today. This context spans architectural philosophies on both sides of the Atlantic, including but also antedating those of the Modern Movement, and it encompasses areas of history and social thought that lie beyond the purview of most architectural critics. Critics who ignore the social and cultural dimension in our thought see only historical sources in our symbolism. However, the ideas that led to the decorated shed were derived from a wider panoply of events than those that generated Radical Eclecticism. Failure to depict the full scope of our context leads to misinterpretation of our content. Our work should be seen whole. Our research should be matched to our design. Our planning and urban design should be compared with our architecture. The social comment in *Learning from Las Vegas* should be related to the architectural prescriptions. Such an overview would suggest a reinterpretation of our architecture and would support our claim that we are not Postmodernists, except perhaps in the theological sense.

—Denise Scott Brown

*   *   *

As a principal in the firm of Venturi, Rauch and Scott Brown, Denise Scott Brown has pursued a career in both the practice and teaching of architecture, planning and urban design. Educated at the University of Witwatersrand, Johannesburg, the Architectural Association School, London, and at the University of Pennsylvania, Scott Brown has made a significant theoretical contribution to the firm's production, notably in the development of large planning projects and exhibitions. She has written extensively, particularly on issues of social conditions and their relation to architecture and planning.

Since the publication of Robert Venturi's Complexity and Contradiction in Architecture in 1966, the firm has publicly established a polemical attitude that utilizes history as a model for architectural problem solving. In numerous articles and a later book, *Learning from Las Vegas*, Denise Scott Brown has, as co-author, put considerable emphasis on the inherent value of the commercial vernacular of America's recent past and continuing present. She has consistently theorized that the current cultural environment is not one that calls for heroic communication through pure architecture. She advocates, instead a richness in architectural meaning through the use and adaption of conventional forms.

Consistently, the firm's projects seem to be designed around a parti that is unassertive and familiar. The development of the partis, however, most often yields details that can best be thought of as discordant fragments. The complexity and confusion introduced by these transfigured elements is intended to provoke a re-evaluation of conceptual content of the work. This architecture may be ordinary or "familiar" in two basic modes: in how it is constructed and in how it is seen. Artistically, the use of conventional elements in Venturi's work involves careful adaptations of symbolic imagery. This approach, while remaining functionally conventional, promotes an architecture of meaning rather than expression.

Denise Scott Brown's interests, however, extend beyond the realm of architecture's traditional limits. Her particular education and consequent exposure to the social planning theories of writers such as Paul Davidoff and Herbert Gans have instilled a deeply-rooted concern for the philosophical gap between architects and sociologists. Her research, in both theory and practice, has focused on ways in which architects can better utilize social insight and express social concern. Approaching this investigation as both an architect and a planner, Scott Brown more readily distinguishes formal components as being defined by both perceptual and symbolic qualities. She is concerned not only with what we see in form, but also with what we understand from what we see. Her aim has been to show that the architect's concern with form and its aesthetics can be reconciled with social concern and social idealism.

In defense of the firm's investigative work with Las Vegas and Levittown, Scott Brown repeatedly differentiates between the concepts of "learning" and "enjoying." She promotes the separation of one variable, such as the formal vernacular of Levittown or Las Vegas, as part of a process of analysis and design. This investigation of form is intended as a means of producing innovations in architectural theory and form-making that are more receptive to the needs and life-styles of different types of people. The appeal is to architects not to be overly self-righteous—Ato allow the lower middle class its own version of the suburban environment. In defense against the charges of social irresponsibility, Scott Brown responds that the origin of these charges lies not in the avowed realms of capitalist social evils or in isolated formal doctrine, but in the fact that the lower middle class symbolism of the forms of Las Vegas and Levittown is offensive to the upper middle class tastes of many architects.

Although this view might be construed as being non-dialectical in nature, it does raise the issues of social concern in architecture to a highly consequential level. We have here an almost polemical stance that calls for a comprehensive understanding of the social concerns and immediate problems confronting architecture today. This is not a philosophy that replaces idealism with realism but rather one that concentrates visionary and idealistic energies on immediate concerns within the confines of existing means.

—S. Fiske Crowell, Jr.

SCUTT, Der.

American. Born in Reading, Pennsylvania, 17 October 1934. Studied at Wyomissing Polytechnic Institute, Pennsylvania, 1952-55; Pennsylvania State University, University Park, 1957-59, B.Arch. 1959; Yale University, New Haven, Connecticut, 1959-61, M.Arch. 1961 (Winchester Wirt Travelling Fellowship, 1961). Married Leena Liukkonen in 1967; children: Hagen and Kirsti Karina. Architectural apprentice, Eastern Engineering Company, Reading, Pennsylvania, 1952-55; Assistant Architect in the offices of Jochen Weinert, Hagen, West Germany, 1955-56, Philip Johnson, q.v., New York, 1957, Vincent G. Kling, Philadelphia, 1958, Edward Durell Stone, q.v., New York, 1961-62, and Paul Rudolph, q.v., New York, 1962-65; Architect, 1965-67, Associate, 1967-75, with Ely Jacques Kahn, q.v., and Robert Allan Jacobs, Kahn and Jacobs Architects, New York; Associate, 1975-76, Partner, 1976-79, Poor Swanke, Hayden and Connell Architects, New York; Partner, Swanke,

Hayden, Connell and Partners Architects, New York, 1979-81. Since 1981, in private practice, New York. Lecturer in Architecture, Barlow School, Amenia, New York, 1964-65; Guest Critic in Architecture, 1967, and Visiting Critic in Architectural Design, 1982, 1983, Yale University, New Haven, Connecticut. Director, United States Institute of Theatre Technicians, 1970-72; Secretary, New York Chapter of the American Institute of Architects, 1970-72; Chairman of the Scholarship Awards Committee, 1970-72, Executive Committee Member from 1970, Vice-President for Architecture, 1972-73, and Chairman of the Brunner Scholarships Committee, 1976-77, Architectural League of New York; New York Board member, 1971-72 and 1974-75, National Planning Board Member, 1971-72 and 1972-73, New York Vice-President, 1972-73, New York President, 1973-74, and Chairman of the Publications Committee, 1979-80, Illuminating Engineering Society; Chairman, Commission Internationale de L'Eclairage, 1978. Contributing Editor, *Lighting Design and Application* magazine, New York, since 1972. Exhibitions: *Forty Under Forty*, Architectural League of New York, 1966; *Trump Tower*, Continental Center at Urban Center, New York, 1981. Recipient: Rotary International Travel Fellowship to West Germany, 1955-56; First Prize, Marble Institute of America Competition, 1957; First Prize, Glen Gery Shale Brick Corporation Competition, 1958; First Prize, Summitville Tile Company Competition, 1958; Professional Contribution Award, American Institute of Architects, 1961; *Architectural Record* Award of Excellence, 1970, 1974, 1975; First Award, Better Rochester Building Program, 1970; Lumen Lighting Award, 1970 (twice), 1972, 1973, 1975, 1977, 1981, 1982, E. F. Guth Award, 1970, Applied Lighting Competition Award, 1970 (twice), Award of Merit, 1974, 1982, and Distinguised Service Award, 1976, Illuminating Engineering Society; New Jersey Business Good Neighbor Award, 1973; Work in the Public Interest Award, Manhattan Community Board, 1981; Annual Award, New York Concrete Industry Board, 1982; Fifth Avenue Association Award, New York, 1983; Award of Excellence, Building Owners and Managers Association, 1984; Bard Award, City Club of New York, 1985. Fellow, Illuminating Engineering Society, 1979. Member, American Institute of Architects; Architectural League of New York; Municipal Art Society of New York. Address: Der Scutt Architect, 244 Fifth Avenue, New York, New York 10001, U.S.A.

Works:

1965 Francis C. St. John Library, Amenia, New York

1966 Boston Safe Deposit and Trust Company Building, Boston (project)

1967 Barlow School Master Plan, Amenia, New York (project)

1967/
68 Hotel, Theatre and Commercial Development, Pennsylvania Avenue, Washington, D.C.

1969 Eastern Airlines Terminal alterations and concourses, John F. Kennedy Airport, New York (project)
Dining Hall and Student Center, Barlow School, Amenia, New York (project)
Crossroads Office Building, Rochester, New York

1971 Office Building and Minskoff Theatre, One Astor Plaza, New York

1971/
74 Westchester Day School Master Plan, Marmaroneck, New York (project)

1973 Western Union Headquarters, Upper Saddle River, New Jersey
W. A. Di Giacomo Associates Office interiors, 1133 Avenue of the Americas, New York

Lower Manhattan Cultural Center, New York (project)
Roure Bertrand Dupont Perfumery Center, Administration and Production Plant, Teaneck, New Jersey
Hercules Inc. Master Plan and Computer Building, Wilmington, Delaware

1974 Equitable Life Assurance Computer Center, Easton, Pennsylvania

1976 Grand Central Station Terminal resoration and lighting, New York

1977 New York City Convention Center Study, New York

1978 American Security Bank restoration, Washington, D.C.

1978/
84 Trump Tower Luxury Condominium and Commercial Building, New York

1979 Barnes Group Corporate Headquarters, Bristol, Connectitcut

1980 Bowery Savings Bank restoration, New York
Public Service Gas and Electric Headquarters, Newark, New Jersey
Northwestern Mutual Life Insurance Headquarters, Milwaukee, Wisconsin (with Sasaki Associates)
Grand Hyatt Hotel, New York (as Design Consultant)

1981 Guardian National Bank Headquarters, Hempstead, New York (project)
Trump Barbizon Plaza Condominium Tower, Central Park South, New York (project)

1981/
84 Store and Building Entrance Design, 650 Fifth Avenue, New York (project)

1981/
86 Condominium Tower, 100 United Nations Plaza, New York

1982 Bowery Savings Bank Data Processing Facility, New York (project)
Health Club and Retail renovations, Bally's Park Place Casino, Atlantic City, New Jersey (project)
Roure Bertrand Dupont U.S. Headquarters addition and renovation, Teaneck, New Jersey

1982/
85 Hong Kong and Shanghai Bank Corporate Office Building, New York

1983 Drom International U.S. Headquarters, Montvale, New Jersey (project)
Codex Corporation Headquarters, Manchester, Massachusetts (competition project)

1983/
85 Office Building renovation, 100 Fairfield Avenue, Bridgeport, Connecticut

1984 Hand Surgery Clinic, St. Luke's Roosevelt Hospital Center, New York
Pfizer Inc. Corporate Headquarters expansion, zoning and concept plan, New York
Office Building, 520 Madison Avenue, New York

1984/
86 West Houston Street Hotel, New York
LoGuidice/Chatwal Condominiums, West 23rd Street, New York
Office Building renovation, 505 Park Avenue, New York

1985 Continental Center Corporate Headquarters, New York
Police Headquarters, 73rd Precinct, Brooklyn, New York

1985/
86 East Side Airline Terminal Commercial and Condominium Development, New York

Publications:

By SCUTT: articles—"Architecture of the 70s" in *The Office of the 70s*, Elmhurst, Illinois 1970; "A Quest for Original Thinking in Interior Office Design" in *The Office* (Stamford, Connecticut),

June 1970; "Esthetics in Ceiling Systems Lighting" in *International Lighting Review* (Amsterdam), vol. 24, no. 2, 1973; "Merging the Disciplines" in *Progressive Architecture* (New York), September 1973; "The Minskoff Theatre—One Astor Plaza" in *Theatre Design and Technology* (New York), October 1973; "Lighting the Innerspaces" in *Interior Design* (New York), May 1974; "The Many Faces of Light" in *Designers West* (Los Angeles), October 1975; "Gracing the Skyline—Not Disgracing It" in the *New York Times*, 22 September; "Midtown Zoning: Leave It Alone" in the *New York Times*, 10 May 1981; and numerous articles in *Lighting Design and Application* (New York), 1971-86.

On SCUTT: books— *Community and Privacy* by Serge Chermayeff and Christopher Alexander, New York 1963; *Cities Fit To Live In* by Walter McQuade, New York 1971; *Adhocism* by Charles Jencks and Nathan Silver, London and New York 1972; *Urban Design as Public Policy* by Jonathan Barnett, New York 1974; *Supermannerism* by C. Ray Smith, New York 1977; *The Skyscraper* by Paul Goldberger, New York 1981; *An Introduction to Urban Design* by Jonathan Barnett, New York 1982; *Trump Tower* by Sy Rubin and Jonathan Mandell, Winston-Salem, North Carolina 1984; articles— "Construction Starts on Astor Plaza" in the *New York Times*, 11 October 1968; "Record Interiors of 1970: Offices for W. A. DiGiacomo and Associates" in *Architectural Record* (New York), January 1970; "Architect's Apartment, New York City" in *Architectural Record* (New York), August 1970; "Young Architects in Firms" in *Architectural Record* (New York), December 1972; "The Minskoff Theater" in *Theatre Crafts* (Emmaus, Pennsylvania), September 1974; "Light as Art" in *Interior Design* (New York), August 1975; "New Lighting in Grand Central" in *Interior Design* (New York), September 1976; "A New York Blockbuster of Superior Design" by Ada Louise Huxtable in the *New York Times*, 1 July 1979; "Trump: The Development of a Manhattan Developer" by Howard Blum in the *New York Times*, 26 August 1980; "Architect Der Scutt—He's A One-Man Glitzkrieg, This Fair-Haired Boy of Architecture" by Lindsy Van Gelder in the *Daily News* (New York), 29 September 1980; "Der Scutt Breaks Away" by Sharon Churcher in *New York Magazine*, 3 August 1981; "The Sky's the Limit" by Douglas Davis in *Newsweek* (New York), 8 November 1982; "Der Scutt Plans 80 Room Hotel Near Soho" in *New York Construction News*, 14 May 1984; "Trumping the Competition" in *Interiors* (New York), June 1984; "Der Scutt Architect" in *Architecture + Urbanism* (Tokyo), July 1984; "Der Scutt: A Profile" in *The Designer* (New York), August 1984.

I am not inclined to favor frivolous architectonic and cosmetic appliqué. I despise the extreme of decoration; too much "brutalism" is too raw for me. I believe that too much improvisation in commercial architecture at times can be irresponsible. I am profoundly concerned with motivating the occupant. To that end, I am intrigued with bold forms and spaces which are relevant to the function and commensurate with the scale of the project. I like variety and complexity as long as the solution is logical. I have great concern for both electric and natural light and its manipulation with respect to the interior environment. The entrance and procession embodying surprise, comfort, delight and variation, and logical organization are important planning parameters. I believe a building becomes architecture when the orderly inclusion of the above

Der Scutt: Trump Tower, New York, 1983.

motivates the occupant with a positive sensory stimulation. The degree of architectural magnificence depends on the measure of the skillful manipulation of form, space, light, material, and detail.

The history of architecture can teach us a great deal.

—Der Scutt

Der Scutt has always thought big and high. He dropped out of his undergraduate course at Pennsylvania State University which he considered lacking in imagination, and made good use of a year's fellowship in Germany, where he mastered the language, worked on construction sites and became an impeccable draughtsman. With this experience behind him, plus a masters degree from Yale, he wanted only to involve himself in large-scale projects. By the time he went into private practive he was almost fifty, but his formative period—almost twenty years—working with the architectural "kings" of the 1960s and 1970s, Philip Johnson, Vincent Kling, Edward Durell Stone, Paul Rudolph and Ely Jaques Kahn, had given him the opportunity to express his theories within the context of the most prestigious building trends of those years.

Scutt is still fascinated by the form of the skyscraper and its ability to capture natural, unencumbered light. Lighting has always been an especial interest, and not merely an aesthetic one; he feels strongly about the effect of certain types of illumination on the eye, is constantly in touch with the latest research in lighting needs, and expanding his knowledge about eye fatigue and the requirements of the eye in work environments. he notes that too often architect and lighting engineer do not work together: "Light values must be set, then designed for—lighting sources should be integrated with architectural form."

In 1974, Scutt met property developer Donald Trump. Trump was impressed with Scutt's design of One Astor Plaza, which broke away from the mould of glass boxes with sawn-off tops by its more sculptural approach. The meeting resulted in a number of projects for this developer with the Midas touch, culminating in Scutt's most famed building—the Trump Tower, completed in 1984. The 58-storey block on New York's Fifth Avenue demonstrated Scutt's feeling that, "too much Brutalism is too raw". Contrasting with the huge and solid concrete block of former years, Trump Tower positively ripples, and inside is revealed a glorious mix of textures—glass, marble, brass, even a waterfall—all seen at their best in airy spaces suffused with filtered light.

Scutt's passion for light, and for particular lighting requirements, tends to influence his choice of textures that reflect natural or interior illumination in such a way as to extend or exaggerate its path. This can be seen to remarkable effect in the angular brass construction of the enormous 33,000 square foot gallery of Continental Center in downtown New York. Here, air and light are clearly considered right from the moment of conception up to the end of the project.

Relationship with clients are exceptional. Scutt is a designer who answers to them rather than to architectural critics. Client needs are a prime concern, and despite his repputation for being a strong-willed and imperious perfectionist, Scutt is sought after for his ability to dynamically create and deliver environments that recognize the function of the structure and the behaviour of its occupants.

Currently, the main body of Scutt's work is to be seen only in the Eastern States of America, but projects on the drawing board and in development stages look set to inspire more than casual interest from Europe and further afield and to bring Scutt to the brink of intenational renown.

—Muriel Emanuel

SEGAL, Walter.
British. Born in Ascona, Switzerland, 15 May 1907; emigrated to England, 1936: naturalized, 1939. Educated at the Technische Hoogeschule, Delft, Netherlands, 1927; under Hans Poelzig, Technische Hochschule, Berlin, 1929; Eidgenössische Technische Hochschule, Zürich, 1931-32, Dip.Arch. 1932. Married Eva Bradt in 1938 (died, 1950); married Mary Moran Scott in 1962; has six children. In private practice, Ascona, near Locarno, Switzerland, 1932-33, Porza sopra Lugano, Switzerland, 1933-34, and Palma, Majorca, 1934-35; Excavation Architect, Cairo Museum, 1935. In private practice, London, 1936 until his death in 1985. Studio Master, Architectural Association School, London, 1944-48; Bannister Fletcher Professor, Bartlett School, University College London, 1973; Assistant Lecturer, Thames Polytechnic, London, 1976; Visiting Professor, University of Pennsylvania, Philadelphia, 1978. *Died* (in London) *27 October 1985.*

Works:

1931 Small House, Berlin (competition project)
1932 Casa Piccolo, Ascona, Switzerland
1933 House, Terreno, Palma, Majorca
       House, Calle Dos de Mayo, Palma, Majorca
       Restaurant, Cuidad Marina, Ibiza
1937 School for the *News Chronicle*, London (competition project)
       Factory, Holly street, London
1938 Furniture designs
1940 U.K. Ministry of Supply Hostels in Blackpole, Gloucestershire; Steeton, Gloucestershire; and Kirby, Liverpool (2).
1945 Block of flats, Leigham Court Road, Streatham, London
1950 Housing estate, St Anne's Close, Highgate, London
       Housing estate, West Heath Gardens, Hampstead, London
1951/
   61 House, Crooked Usage, Finchley, London
       House, Neeld Crescent, Hendon, London
       House, Dennis Lane, Stanmore, Middlesex
       House, Brent, London
       House, The Boltons, Kensington, London
       House, Church Road, Bushill Park, London
1961 House, Rugby Road, Twickenham, Middlesex
1963 House, West Heath Road, Hampstead, London
       House, Fideris, Grisons, Switzerland
       Tretol Office Building, Edgware Road, Colindale, London
       Block of flats, Chesham Street, Chelsea, London
       Factory and office building, Ramsgate Street, Dalston, London
1964 Block of flats, Rutland Gate, London
       Block fo flats, Ovington Square, London
1965 Maisonettes, Compayne Gardens, Hampstead, London
       Terraced housing, Tasker Road, Hampstead, London
       Temporary "rationalized timber" house, Highgate, London
1966 Block of flats, Cat Hill, East Barnet, London
       Block of flats, Salmon Way, Wembley, Middlesex
1967 Block of flats, Bedford Road, Feltham, Middlesex
       Walter Segal House, Highgate, London
1968 Timber House, Ballygarrett, Ireland
1969 Timber house, Chapel Street, Halstead, Essex
1970 Timber house, Main Street, Yelling, Huntingdonshire
       Timber house, North Chailey, Lewes, Sussex
       House addition, 40 Old Church Lane, Wembley, London
1971 House, Ballycummisk, County Cork, Ireland
       House, North Common, Chailey, Sussex

House, Woodbridge, Suffolk
1974 House extension, Woodbridge, Suffolk
1976 Social Centre, University of Sussex, Brighton (project)
1977 Two-storey house, Mill Hill, London
1977/
80 Lewisham Self-Build Housing Association, London
1978 Housing schemes for the Solon Housing Association, London (project)

Publications

By SEGAL: books—*Planning and Transport*, London 1945; *Home and Environment*, London 1948, 1953; *Housing: A Survey of the Post-War Housing Work of the London County Council 1945-49*, London 1949; *Housing for People*, London 1979; articles—"Building a House in Majorca" in *Architect and Building News* (London), June 1942; "Patio House: Variations on a Theme" in *Architect and Building News* (London), February 1943; "The Small House in Urban Areas" in *Architect and Building News* (London), June 1943; "Site Layout and Technique" in *Journal of the Royal Architectural Institute of Canada* (Toronto), January 1945; "Small Houses in America" in *Architect and Building News* (London), July 1948; "Changing Trends in Site Layout" in *Arena* (London), March 1966; "A Man on His Own" in *Architect and Building News* (London), October 1968; "Architecture: The Assertive and the Unobtrusive" in *Architect and Building News* (London), September 1969; "Readier for Compromise" in *Architects' Journal* (London), April 1970; "Mart Stam" in *Architects' Journal* (London), June 1970; "Ernst May 1886-1970" in *Architects' Journal* (London), September 1970; "Art in Revolution" in *Architects' Journal* (London), February 1971; "Aalto Up-to-Date" in *Architects' Journal* (London), January 1972; "The Neo-Purist School of Architecture" in *Architectural Design* (London), June 1972; "Scharoun" in *Architectural Review* (London), February 1973; "Home—Sweet Home?" in *RIBA Journal* (London), October 1973; "Into the Twenties" in *Architectural Review* (London), January 1974; "Meeting Gropius Again" in *Architects' Journal* (London), 13 February 1974; "Wood in Architecture" in *The International Book of Timber*, London 1975; "An Architect's Approach to Architecture" in *RIBA Journal* (London), July 1977; "View from a Lifetime" in *RIBA Transactions* (London), no. 1, 1982; "Post-Modern Recession" in *Architects' Journal* (London), 17 February 1982; "Segal on Segal" in *Architects' Journal* (London), 10 March 1982; "The Other Schinkel..." in *Architects' Journal* (London), 15 December 1982; recording—*Walter Segal*, 2 tape cassettes with comments by John Wells-Thorpe and Colin Boyne, London 1977.

On SEGAL: books *The Life, Writings and Work of Walter Segal*, thesis by H. C. Smyth, University of Newcastle, England 1973; *Walter Segal* by John Maule McKean, Stuttgart and Zürich 1980; articles—"Hostel for Factory Workers" in *Architect and Building News* (London), May 1942; "Proposed House at Mill Hill" in *Architect and Building News* (London), November 1947; "The ABSE House" in *Architect and Building News* (London), April 1949; "Factory and Warehouse" in *Architects' Journal* (London), October 1958; "House at Highgate" in *Architects' Journal* (London), March 1966; "A Certain Satisfaction in Building a Shelter for Oneself" by John Maule McKean in *Architects' Journal* (London), 3 September 1975; "Das Segal Konzept: Hauser aus der Baustoffhandlung" in *Baumeister* (Munich), November 1975; "Walter Segal: Pioneer" by John Maule McKean in *Building Design* (London), 20 and 27 February 1976; "Liberation Through Technology" in *Building Design* (London), 27 February 1976; "The Segal System" by

John Maule McKean in *Architectural Design* (London), no. 5, 1976; "Walter Segal: The Compleat Architect" in *Architects' Journal* (London), 13 April 1977; "Segal's Other Buildings" in *Architects' Journal* (London), 20 April 1977; "Segal Self-Build Hits Bureacratic Chaos" in *Architects' Journal* (London), 16 August 1978; "Segal's Self-Build Starts in Lewisham at last" in *Architects' Journal* (London), 11 October 1978; "Students Build a Timber House" by Manfred Goss in *Deutsche Bauzeitung* (Stuttgart), January 1979; "The Green House" in *Architects' Journal* (London), 27 August 1980; "Do-It-Yourself Vernacular" by Charlotte Ellis in *Architects' Journal* (London), 17 December 1980; "Architects' Architecture" in *Architects' Journal* (London), 28 January 1981; "Self-Build Housing in Lewisham, London" in *AC* (Zürich), April 1981; "Segal's First Half Century in Practice" by Charlotte Ellis in *Architects' Journal* (London), 7 April 1982; "Being the Builder Builds Own Being" by Jan Westra in *Openhouse* (Eindhoven, Netherlands), no. 3, 1982.

*

It is extremely interesting to see the way that Walter Segal's reputation has grown on the basis of a relatively small number of buildings. In particular, he has attracted the attention of a generation of younger architects who have grown dissatisfied with the increasingly detached and managerial role of the architect. There is no doubt that professionalism has had some of the effects that its original critics, including Lethaby, feared; architects have become detached from the building process to such an extent that many problems such as building faults, high costs, uninventive construction and failure to realize the potential of either traditional crafts or new techniques can be attributed to it.

Segal, perhaps without really intending it, began to point a way back to a better synthesis with building, when he had to design himself a temporary and extremely low-cost house in his garden in the mid-1960s. Using standard and uniform timber members, board sizes, rationalized framing, and a radically different attitude to foundations, he produced a prototype that became a model for a series of other designs in which he has gone on refining and developing his method. It was an approach that lent itself as well to owner-builders as to clients who wanted low-cost buildings put up by builders. He developed a system of drawings that greatly simplified communication with the few tradesmen that were needed to construct his designs, and he personally supervised and took on many of the tasks of a general contractor for his clients, thus being able to control costs, details, and quality in a way few architects who operate in conventional practice are able to do.

In the course of this development, Segal has naturally encountered those authorities who administer regulations and control development, and Segal's reputation among many architects has been enhanced by his having become quite militant in the fight against petty bureaucrats who cannot tolerate the refreshing iconoclasm of his general approach to design.

—Cedric Green

SEIDLER, Harry.

Australian. Born in Vienna, Austria, 25 June 1923; emigrated to Australia in 1948: naturalized, 1958. Educated at the Wasagymnasium, Vienna, 1932-38; University of Manitoba, Winnipeg, 1941-44, B.Arch. 1944; Harvard University, Cambridge, Massachusetts, under Walter Gropius, *q.v.*, and Marcel Breuer, *q.v.*, 1945-46, M.Arch 1946; also studied design, under Josef Albers, Black Mountain College, Beria, North Carolina, 1946. Married Penelope A. M. Evatt in 1958; children: Timothy and

Pauline. Chief Assistant to Marcel Breuer, New York, 1946-48; worked with Oscar Niemeyer, *q.v.*, Rio de Janeiro, 1948. Since 1948, Principal of Harry Seidler and Associates, Sydney. Visiting Professor, Harvard University Graduate School of Design, 1976-77, and University of British Columbia, Vancouver, 1977-78; Thomas Jefferson Professor of Architecture, University of Virginia, Charlottesville, 1978; Visiting Professor, University of New South Wales, Sydney, 1980, and University of Sydney, 1984. Trustee, Art Gallery of New South Wales, Sydney, 1976-80; Councillor, University of New South Wales, Sydney, 1976-80. Collections: Museum of Modern Art, New York; Harvard University, Cambridge, Massachusetts. Recipient: Sir John Sulman Medal, Royal Australian Institute of Architects, 1951, 1967, 1981, and 1983; Wilkinson Award, Royal Australian Institute of Architects, 1965, 1966, and 1967; Pan Pacific Citation, American Institute of Architects, 1968; Gold Medal, Royal Australian Institute of Architects, 1976. Life Fellow, Royal Australian Institute of Architects, 1970; Fellow, Australian Academy of Technological Sciences, 1979. Honorary Fellow, American Institute of Architects, 1966; Honorary Member, Académie d'Architecture, Paris, 1982. O.B.E. (Officer, Order of the British Empire), 1972. Address: Harry Seidler and Associates, 2 Glen Street, Milsons Point, New South Wales 2061, Australia.

Works

1949/
54 Houses, Sydney
1957 Master Plan for McMahons Point high density housing, Sydney
1960 Apartment block, Ithaca Gardens, Elizabeth Bay, Sydney
Ciba Chemical Company Administration and Warehouse Building, Orion Road, Lane Cove, Sydney
1960/
67 Australia Square redevelopment, Sydney (with Pier Luigi Nervi)
1961 Blues Point Tower apartment block, McMahons Point, Sydney
Office and Warehouse Building, Harris Street, Ultimo, Sydney
1962 The Rocks redevelopment project, Sydney Cove
Apartment block, 40 Victoria Street, Potts Point, Sydney
1963 Apartment block, Stephen' Street, Paddington, Sydney
Apartment block, Kimberley Street, Diamond Bay, Sydney
1963/
65 Apartment block, 58 Roslyn Gardens, Rushcutters Bay, Sydney
1964 Town houses and apartment housing, Canberra
1965 Apartment block, 85 Elizabeth Bay Road, Elizabeth Bay, Sydney
1965/
66 Apartment block, 29 Ocean Avenue, Double Bay, Sydney
1965/
68 Space Frame Building, Bourke Road, Alexandria, Sydney
1966/
67 Apartment blocks, Edgecliff Road, Edgecliff, Sydney
Seidler House, Killara, Sydney
1967 Apartment blocks, Maloney Street, Rosebery, Sydney
1967/
68 Housing project for fellows and research scholars Australian National University, Canberra

Harry Seidler: M. L. C. Centre Office Tower, Sydney, 1971-77.

1968 Urban redevelopment scheme, Sydney Apartment block, 100 Elizabeth Bay Road, Elizabeth Bay, Sydney

1970 Condominium apartments, Acapulco, Mexico

Memorial to Martyrs, Rookwood, Sydney

1970/
75 Commonwealth Government Trade Group Offices, Kings Avenue, Barton, Canberra

1971 Mid-City Centre, George and Pitt Streets, Sydney

1971/
72 Office building 41 McLaren Street, North Sydney

1971/
73 Seidler and Associates Office and Administration Building, Milsons Point, Sydney

1971/
77 M.L.C. Centre Office Tower and Theatre Royal, Martin Place, Sydney

1972 Conzinc Riotinto of Australia Headquarters, office tower and commercial redevelopment, Collins Street, Melbourne

1973 Apartment housing project, Bushey Park, Singapore

Commonwealth Government Offices, Tuggeranong, Canberra

1973/
77 Australian Embassy, Quai Branly, Paris

1974/
76 Fairfield Central Library, Cabramatta, Sydney

Torin Factory, Penrith, Sydney (with Marcel Breuer and Associates)

1975/
77 Municipal Offices, North Sydney

1976 LaTrobe University Library, Victoria

Baraduda Town Centre, Albury-Wadonga, New South Wales

1978/
79 Home Unit Apartments (72), Broadbeach, Queensland

1978/
80 Theatre and Funtion Complex, Ringwood Civic Centre, Melbourne

1979 Parliament House, Canberra (competition project)

1979/
80 Hillside Housing, Kooralbyn, Queensland
8 Townhouses, Belconnen, A.T.C.

1980 Office and Apartment Building, Jalan Ampang, Kuala Lumpur, Malaysia

1980 Weapons Workskhop, Department of Defence, Garden Island, Sydney

1980/
84 Hong Kong Club and Office Building redevelopment, Hong Kong

1981 New World urban development, Singapore

1982 Office Building, Grosvenor Place, Rocks Area, Sydney

1982/
84 Civic Centre and Municipal Offices development, Waverley, Victoria
Eleven townhouses, Yarralumla, A.C.T.

1983 Offices, Retail and Apartment development, Riverside, Brisbane, Queenland
Hilton Hotel, Brisbane, Queensland
Theatre and Cultural Centre, Frankston, Victoria

Publications:

By SEIDLER: articles—in *Arts and Architecture* (Los Angeles), January 1948, January, February, and June 1949, January, May, and September 1950, November 1951, November 1953, May 1954, May, November and December 1955, August and December 1956, January and September 1957, February, April and July 1958, January, October and December 1959, January, March, July and November 1960, January, May, June, August and December 1961, May June, August and November 1962, February and October 1963, June and July 1964, October and November 1965; *Architectural Review* (London), September, October and November 1951, November 1952, May 1954, August 1956, October 1959, May 1961, July and August 1963, November 1964, July 1966, November 1967, June 1968, March 1969, October 1970, April, May and September 1972, March 1976, March 1977, and October 1978; *Bauen und Wohnen* (Zürich), October 1952, April 1955, March and July 1956, September 1957, March 1958, December 1959, March 1960, July 1961, October 1962, November 1963, June 1964, January, May and June 1966, January and Feburary 1969, September 1975, September 1976, November 1978; *M.D.* (Stuttgart), April 1958, July 1961, June 1962, August and October 1963 May, June, October and December 1964, March, April and November 1965, April 1968, July 1969, June 1971, May 1972, February 1973; *L'Architecture d'aujourd'hui* (Paris), no. 20, 1952, September 1954, no. 73, 1957, no. 86, 1959, no. 103, 1962, nos. 113-114, 1964, no. 120, 1965, no. 130, 1967, no. 150, 1970; *Domus* (Milan), February 1952, September 1953, July 1963, April 1964, August 1968, May 1972, July 1975, September 1977, November 1978; *Architectural Design* (London), April 1959, April 1960, December 1961, November 1962, May 1963, September, October and November 1964, September 1965, October 1966, June 1967, March 1972; *Architectural Forum* (New York), September 1960, January 1962, August 1963, March 1968, April 1969, November 1970; *Deutsche Bauzeitschrift* (Gütersloh, West Germany) June 1961, May and October 1962, October 1963, July 1964, February 1965, September and November 1966, May, August and September 1967, January, February, July and August 1969, April 1970, July 1972; *Architecture Plus* (New York), February 1973; *Architecture Australia* (Melbourne), October 1949, December 1951, April and July 1954, January 1955, December 1958, May and June 1961, May 1962, June 1965, July 1966, February, June, August and December 1967, April, August and November 1968, June 1969, February and August 1970, April 1971, April and June 1972, November 1973, August and December 1974, December 1975, June/July 1976, March and July 1977, November 1978, January 1979, May and September 1982, January and November 1983, March and June 1984; *Architecture + Urbanism* (Tokyo), May and October 1976, January 1979, October 1980; *Toshi-Jutaku* (Tokyo), June, August and September 1983.

On SEIDLER: books—*Living Spaces* by G. Nelson, New York 1952; *Houses, Interiors and Projects 1949-54*, Sydney 1954, 1959; *The Modern Factory* by Edward D. Mills, London 1959; *The Australian Ugliness* by Robin Boyd, Melbourne 1960; *Best Australian Houses* by N. Clerehan, Melbourne 1961; *New Buildings in the Commonwealth* by J.M. Richards, London 1962; *Encylopaedia of Modern Architecture* by G. Hatje, London 1963; *Harry Seidler 1955-63*, Sydney, Paris and Stuttgart, 1963; *High Density Living* by R. Jensen, London 1966; *Apartments* by S. Paul, New York 1967; *Architecture in Australia: A History* by J.M. Freeland, Melbourne 1968; *Australia Square*, Sydney 1969; *Australian Style* by B. Hayes, London 1970; *Office Buildings* by R. Hohl, London 1968; *Living and Partly Living* by McKay, Boyd, Stretton and Mant, Melbourne 1972; *Architecture for the New World: The Work of Harry Seidler* by Peter Blake, Sydney, New York and Stuttgart, 1973; *Houses Architects Design for Themselves*, edited by Walter F. Wagner, Jr., New York 1974; *Houses Architects Live In*, New York 1977; *Planning and Building Down Under: New Settlement Strategy and Current Architectural Practice in Australia*, Vancouver, British Columbia 1978; *Harry Seidler: Australian Embassy/Ambassade d'Australie, Paris* by Peter Blake, Sydney, New York and Stuttgart 1979; *Two Towers, Harry Seidler: Australia Square MLC Centre* by Philip Drew, Sydney and Stuttgart 1980; *By Their Own Design* by Abby Suckle, New York 1980; *Australian Architecture 1901-51: Sources of Modernism* by Donald Leslie, Sydney 1980; *Medium Density Housing in Australia*, edited by Bruce Judd and John Dean, Canberra 1983.

*

The underlying credo of morlity in modern architecture has largely been lost or forgotten, or has undergone such mutation as to become unrecongnizable. The demand that there be a consequential three way simultaneous design process at the basis of architectural design decisions, which brings into a happy marriage considerations of social use, aethestics, and technology, is ignored in the wilful capriciousness which characterizes so much of the new man-made world that has come into existence.

To regain some direction which could restore a discernible cultural aim to take the place of the prevalent "free for all"—and the commercially motivated "something new every Monday morning"—desperate efforts of the unskilled—it may be well to recall the high principles and clear consequentiality expressed by some of the pioneers; their demand was for basic integrity and an intrinsic honesty of approach. Let us think simply and realistically of the tasks. It is the cardinal brief for the designer to find solutions which, in addition to all "architectural" considerations, will be objects that can be produced naturally and appropriately in a given socio-economic climate. To extract from an existing environment the essential character that is its very own and develop an inevitably complimentary solution, is as important as finding answers simultaneously to technological questions. One can not exist at the exclusion of the other.

Practically such solutions will:

Strive toward the exquisite understatement inherent in consequential systems to take the place of today's fashionable devotion to ostentatious complexity.

Contrive systematic solutions and their components such as will "invite" variation. The more parts of a system are assembled, the more interesting and visually enticing the totality will become, rather than duller and more soul-destroying, as is the present-day norm.

Devise and maximize systems of mechanization appropriate and "in tune" with the particular task. These must not only stop at considerations of structure and cladding (as is so often the limit of prevalent thought), but will also encompass simulaneously intergral solutions to the problems posed by all services (without the usual nightmarish afterthought complications of most "modern" buildings).

Pursue with purity and directness the problems of connections and detail which will recur wherever identical situations generate them (in contrast to adhoc traditional detailing which contributes so much to the high cost of buildings).

In the shaping of elements, give free reign to the expression of the laws of nature—not what is "imagined" to be so by many struturally naive architects—but the unassailable physical truth of statics. Great richness of expression can result from such a search which will have that irreplaceable quality of longevity—of remaining valid—being born of the immutable and irrevocable truth of nature.

Aesthetically such solutions will:

Exploit a visual vocabulary their stems from the conviction that architecture is and always was above all an ART form, and that an interrelation and interdependence between all the visual arts

Be aware that consistent visual pheonema have emerged in our time which have given rise to recognizable basic design criteria forming a common denominator to most visual endeavours; amongst these are:

The subtle orchestration of the intricacies of space. Twentieth century man's eyes and senses crave space in a new way as only our technology can muster (as against the great spatial work of, for instance, the Baroque). The sense of the infinite and simultaneously intimate—the sense of the beyond.

The channelling of a space and surfaces in opposition or tension; the "pulling apart" of confining areas and their disposition in contradiction (the curve against countercurve—the juxtaposition and sequencing of compressive low to the surprise of high).

Visual tension, the balance of unequals, generated in surfaces as in the juxtaposition of material (synthetic smooth against natural rough—warm colour against cold).

The use of counterpoint; once a strong visual element is chosen, it must find its re-use or echo throughout the work (as against the arbitrary assembly of unrelated forms).

A single, strong idea of form coupled with a solution to planning which must be disarmingly simple—a "Gordian Knot" kind of solution, with the character of the inevitable and of a reproducible prototype.

—Harry Seidler

Harry Seidler's early houses from 1949 to 1954 established an authentic version of modern architecture in conformity with Bauhaus principles in Australia. The consistency and unfailing high quality of design and execution of Seidler's subsequent work set a standard for modern architecture in Australia. Seidler's design orientation presents a number of contrasts with the mainstream of postwar architecture in Australia; his buildings are uncompromisingly international in a country where conservative regionalism is the rule. And whereas the creative wave of Australian architecture has tended towards a kind of romanticism inspired by Wright and Scandinavian ideas, Seidler's architecture is an example of academic rationalism in so far as it emphasizes standardization and concentration, the perfection of a limited number of established themes, the clear articulation of architectonic form, and the expression of architecture as structural form on motifs taken from contemporary painting or sculpture which he uses to generate a range of compositions from which he selects the most suitable form.

The Australia Square Office Tower marks the beginning of a change in Seidler's architecture away from tensional composition derived from Josef Albers and a De Stijl type of elementarist composition towards a more static classical compostition inspired by Norman Carlberg's sculpture and the paintings of Frank Stella. The use of circular and quadrant geometries in Seidler's architecture in the 1970s betrays a significant shift away from functionalism and towards classicism. The Trade Group Offices, Canberra are the clearest expression of the new classicism in Seidler's work. Seidler's rationalism is manifested in the meticulous consideration of details and their standardisation and in a preoccupation with the mastery of technology. In his recent public buildings, Seidler has transformed structure and services into decorative sculpture. Seidler was assisted in the sculptural expression of his structures (notably the variable-profile concrete "T" beams) by Peter Miller, a Sydney structural engineer, and Pier Luigi Nervi.

The main influences on Seidler were Albers and Marcel Bruer; from Albers, Seidler learned to think in visual terms, while Breur showed him how to assemble and articulate his building elements. Breur's influence can also be detected in Seidler's choice of materials, especially Breuer's juxtaposition of smooth, artificial materials and natural, rough materials and the fluid treatment of space.

Of the early houses, it was the Rose Seidler (1949-50) and the Rose houses built at Turramurra that made the greatest impact on Seidler's Australian contemporaries. While working in Breur's New York office form September 1946 to March 1948, Seidler was involved in the Robinson House, Williamstown (1946-47), and the Breuer House I in New Canaan, Connecticut (1947). Some features, mainly relating to the planning, were carried over from these American houses and reapplied in

Seidler's new Australian houses. The R. Seidler House, for example, has a bi-nuclear plan (developed by Breuer in 1943) similar to the Robinson House, and the Rose House was closely related in its plan to the Breuer House. These early Seidler houses should not be thought of as mere copies, since they reveal an independance of thought, professional competence, and care for the quality of construction that compares more than favorably with Breuer's own houses.

Seidler was busy throughout the 1950s designing houses for private clients; then, in the early 1960s he received commissions for apartment and office buildings. In nearly all his apartment buildings, from the earliest ones close to the centre of Sydney at Camperdown, Elizabeth Bay, Rushcutter's Bay, and Edgecliff, to the apartments for Australian embassy staff in Paris, Seidler consitently applied a split-level arrangement with access on alternate floors. The Blues Point Tower Apartments, North Sydney, with its staccato rhythm of staggered glass enlivening the exposed facades, is probably the most interesting of Seidler's apartment buildings. In 1961 Seidler designed Lend Lease House Offices, Sydney, which with its prominent use of adjustable aluminium louvres for sun control, was the first of a series of important projects, of which the M.L.C. Centre, Sydney, is a later example. The most famous, and deservedly so, is the Australia Square project, Sydney, which was a major town planning triumph in overcoming the problems of piecemeal development in the central business district and a formidable statement of Seidler's uncompromising rationalism. Pier Luigi Nervi made an important contribution in the design of the floor system for the first two floors of the tower.

In 1964-68, Seidler was also involved in Canberra group housing schemes, which were remarkably successful. Seidler's own house at Killara (1966-67), located in a bush setting reminiscent of Wright's Falling Water, is an essential statement of the architect's values. Seidler is still very much a European, never having lost the Viennese sense of decorum from which his buildings take their formal quality and dignity. The major themes of structural clarity, material economy in the construction, spatial interplay of related levels, and disciplined selection of materials are all there.

The early 1970s were an expansive period for Seidler, he built offices for his firm at Milson's Point, Sydney, and completed three major projects: the Trade Group Offices, Canberra, the Australian Embassy in Paris, and M.L.C. Centre, Sydney. The offices at Milsons Point and the Embassy are major works typlifying the shift in Seidler's style towards classicism.

Following the stagnation of the post-Whitlam era, the 1980s witnessed a resurgence of design activity and building for Seidler, who found himself engaged on a wide range of housing, cultural, and commercial redevelopment projects at a very large scale. Of these, the most significant were the Ringwood Theatre and Funtion Complex (1978-80), the Hong Kong Club and Office Building (1980-84), and the Grosvenor Place (begun 1982), and Riverside (begun 1983), towers in Sydney and Brisbane respectively. The Grosvenor Place complex is an urban colossus that promises to be Seidler's most comprehensive work to date, involving as it does an enlightened experiment in the rational use of energy that goes some way to answering the critics of such costly and extravagent real estate monuments.

In these more recent large complexes for city centres, there is little that is demostrably new formally; the preoccupation with the earlier quadrant and opposed circular geometries is extended, and, in the most extreme instance, the Hong Kong Club, this results in a modern Baroque fantasy in insitu concrete. But all of this is far less important than Seidler's evident commitment to draw together the fragmented and disparate functions of the city heart into a civilized setting for urban life that is at once coherent and ordered.

Seidler has played an important role in the

establishment of modern architecture in Australia. His stature as an architect can be assessed in two ways: first, in relation to his Australian contemporaries, and second, as a student of Gropius, Albers, and Breuer. His architecture is therefore an extension rather than a reflection, as most Australian architecture is, of the international modern movement. Seidler's architecture is unquestionably important both in a local sense and internationally, although recognition has tended to come more readily from outside Autralia.

—Philip Drew

SEIFERT, Ivan.

French. Born in Zagreb, Yugoslavia, 23 December 1926; emigrated to France, 1955: naturalized, 1969. Educated at the University of Zagreb, Department of Architecture, under Vladimir Turina, 1945-51 (Student Prize, 1950), Dip.Arch.Ing. 1951. Married Miryana Vujicic in 1955; children: Sanda, Marc, Patrick, and Anne. Town Planner, Town Planning Institute, Zagreb, 1951; Architect, Office Haberle, Zagreb, 1952-55, office of Pierre Vago, *q.v.*, Paris, 1955-57, Stafford, Moor and Farington, Sydney, 1957-58, and Atelier L.W.D., Paris, 1958-61. Since 1961, Partner, A.T.E.A. (Atelier d'Etudes Architecturales), Neuilly, Meudon, France (partners: Guy Lagneau, Michel Weill, Jean Dimitrijevic, Paul Cordoliani, Henri Coulomb, and Renzo Moro). Technical Adviser, S.E.T.A.P. (Société pour l'Etude Technique d'Aménagements Planifies), Neuilly, Meudon, since 1961. Address: A.T.E.A., 3 rue Marcel Allegot, 92190 Meudon, France.

Works:

1952 Cinema, restaurant, and bowling club complex, Bregana, Yugoslavia
Electrical Centre, Institute for Shipbuilding Research, Zagreb
1954 Hydroelectric Power Station, Jablanica, Yugoslavia
1956 Apartment building, rue Erlanger, Paris
1957 McMahons Point Residential Development, Sydney (project with others)
Laboratories, University of Sydney
Office building, Sydney
Villas, University of Sydney
Factory, Sydney
1958 Qantas Airlines Airport Hanger, Sydney
Slaughterhouse, University of Veterinary Studies, Sydney
Central Bank for the West African States, Lome, Togo
1959 Citroen Exhibition Hall, Abidjan, Ivory Coast
1960 Hotel Transatlantique, Ouargla, Algeria
Chargeurs Réunis Apartment Buildings, Libreville and Port Gentille, Gabon
1961 Low-cost housing, Ouargla, Algeria
1962 Apartment buildings, Gif-sur-Yvette, France
Apartment buildings, Brest, France
1963 High School and College of Education, Bamako, Mali (with Tekhne)
1964 Faculty of Literature Building, University of Nice, France
Library, University of Nice, France
1966 National Bank of Madagascar, Antananarivo
1967 Bank of France, Cannes, France
Apartment building, Landivisiau, France
1968 Apartment buildings and houses, Cergy-Pontoise, France
1969 E.S.S.E.C.: Institute for Advanced Studies in Economics and Commerce, Cergy-Pontoise, France
1970 Highway Bridge Restaurant, Lancon, France

1971   Airport, Bamaklo, Mali (with Tekhne)
       Highway Hotel, Macon, France
1972   Apartment building, Cergy-Pontoise, France
1973   Bank of France, Clermont-Ferrand, France
1974   Bank of France, Créteil, France
1975   Popular Bank Group Training Centre, Cergy-
       Pontoise, France
1976   Teaching and Research Centre for Advanced
       Studies in Commerce and Management,
       Sophia-Antipolis, France
1977   Two Schools, Cergy New Town, France
       Housing (77 units), l'Isle d'Abeau, France
1978   Commercial Centre, l'Isle d'Abeau, France
       Information Centre, Evry, France (project)
1979   Cultural Centre, Poissy, France (project)
       Solar Central Heating for a winter sports
       resort (project)
1980   Housing (180 units) and shops, Poissy, France
       Housing (400 units), Châtillon-sous-Bagneux,
       France (project)
       Municipal Library, Poissy, France (project)
1981   Housing renovations (1,500 units), Paris
       region
1983   New Town Centre, Cergy-Pontoise, France
       Town Centre, Tremblay-les-Gonesse, France
       (project)
1984   Information Centre, Marne la Vallée, France
       (project)
       Cite Universitaire development, Cergy, Fra-
       nce (project)

Publications:

On SEIFERT: book—*Guide de l'architecture dans les villes nouvelles*, Paris 1979; articles—"Sport Parc Rijeka-Susak" in *L'Architecture d'aujourd'hui* (Paris), December 1949; "Institute for Shipbuilding Research" in *Arhitektura* (Zagreb), no. 1, 1954; "Skyscraper or Eight-Story Building?" in *Vjesnik* (Zagreb), 21 December 1954; "A Redevelopment Project for McMahons Point" in *Arts and Architecture* (Los Angeles), February 1958; "Central Bank for West African States" in *Progressive Architecture* (New York), December 1962; "University of Nice—Faculty of Literature" in *Technique et architecture* (Paris), December 1964; "Creators of the Institute" in *Le Courier* (Antananarivo, Madagascar), 9 March 1968; "High School and College of Education, Bamako, Mali" in *L'Architecture d'aujourd'hui* (Paris), November 1968; "University of Nice Faculty of Literature and University Library" in *Technique et architecture* (Paris), October 1969; "Hopes and Possibilities—Ivan Seifert, Architect" in *Telegram* (Zagreb), 21 December 1971; "E.S.S.E.C.: Institute for Advanced Studies in Economics and Commerce" in *Architecture intérieure* (Paris), November 1973; "E.S.S.E.C." in *Reflets* (Paris), January 1974; "E.S.S.E.C.: Institute for Advanced Studies in Economics and Commerce" in *Planen und Bauen* (Zürich), June 1974; "Training Centre for the Popular Bank Group, Cergy-Pontoise" in *Le Bâtiment-Bâtir* (Paris), May 1977; "Centre de formation des Banques Populaires" in *Construction moderne* (Paris), October 1977; "Deux projets à Cergy-Pontoise" in *Construction moderne* (Paris), March 1982; "Centre d'enseignement et de recherche" and "Centre de formation à Cergy" in *Mur vivant* (Paris), January 1983; "C.E.R.A.M." in *Images* (Paris), February 1984; "Centre de la ville nouvelle de Cergy" in *Moniteur* (Paris), September 1984.

*

Architecture and architects have not been spared by the crisis which has shaken our economy for some years; I think, however, that the problems of our profession arose much earlier. The profession of architect, once regarded as one of the most eminent, has lost its prestige and its respectability.

We are told daily that we have not learnt to adapt ourselves to new situations, to new techniques, to a society in continuous evolution. Perhaps some architects have known how to adapt to new situations only too well, and perhaps this is precisely the reason for a certain deterioration in the profession. The sudden increase in demand for dwellings and installations after the war provoked a tidal wave in construction. The demand was such that speed was often more important than quality; to have a roof over one's head was of greater consequence than the proportions of a facade! Suddenly architects faced a promising future, and a large number of young people were attracted to the profession; unfortunately, vocation and talent were not always deciding factors in their choice. With high stakes and few references, the problem was how to make one's name, how to *sell* one's architecture. Instead of becoming a creator, the architect became a salesman.

For the less gifted, to be effective was enough. They claimed that they could solve any problem by using curtain walls to replace facades and by using system building which allowed everyone to produce everything (except good projects). By eliminating practically all research and by always repeating ready-made solutions from other projects, they became ubiquitous "specialists" in dwellings, educational establishments, and so forth, monopolizing entire building sectors. They became essential assistants, because legislation required than an architect be called in for certain kinds of buildings. We have this kind of architect to thank for a large number of housing estates, for school buildings that recall barracks, and for the contempt of the public at large for "contemporary architecture."

More gifted architects had to take the opposite path. In order to sell their architecture, they had to be different. They had to invent a new architecture every day; architecture became a consumer item, following fashion, changing with ever-increasing rhythm.

It is not surprising that the public, disgusted with the mediocrity of some architects and confused by the search for ever more unusual forms of other architects (forms often accentuated by aggressive colour), sought refuge in the so-called "inspired" values of the past (witness the current infatuation for the individual house "in the French manner" and certain very formal projects for the center of Paris). One wonders whether architecture will arrive at the year 2000 in reverse gear. To get out of this absurd situation, we must rethink the art of building. Before you can find a remedy you must establish a diagnosis.

In the old towns, every building was different. Nevertheless, the whole gave an impression of unity and harmony by the use of identical or similar materials, by the same building techniques, by the human scale; and form clearly expressed function. Architecture in the past was easily understood by the public; it provided a sense of security. Our towns today are no longer reassuring. We flee from them at every opportunity. The best proof: the congestion on the motorways every weekend. The perfection of completely rationalized plans that do not take into account the human being's deepest desires has produced neither towns nor habitat but groups of

Ivan Seifert: C.E.R.A.M. Teaching and Research Centre, Sophia-Antipolis, France, 1976.

zones of specific activity and machines for living, working, or shopping. In our towns, disorder and a lack of unity are the consequences of the desire of many architects to do their work without bothering to adapt their project to what already exists.

The global result is generally disappointing, despite the sometimes undeniable quality of the components. It is not surprising that, with such results, the public doubts the competence of our profession. It is up to us to give proof to the contrary.

—Ivan Seifert

From Yugoslavia, where he was born, trained as an architect, and worked for a time, Ivan Seifert came to France to broaden his experience, then settled permanently. He first worked with me, collaborating notably on the Interbau Hansaviertel Apartment Building and in the competition for the Library of the University of Bonn.

After working in Australia, Seifert returned to France, and for many years now has been a member of the A.T.E.A. architectural team within which he has conceived and executed numerous works, in Africa as well as France, that are always interesting and often of great quality—for example, E.S.S.E.C. (Institute for Advanced Studies in Economics and Commerce) in the new town of Cergy-Pontoise, near Paris. Seifert's work is characterized by a thorough research into form and volume—not by arbitrary plastic compositions but by a dynamic expression of functions and a studied use of materials.

—Pierre Vago

SEIFERT, Robin (Richard Seifert).

British. Born of Swiss parents, in Switzerland, 25 November 1910. Educated at the Central Foundation School, London, 1920-28; University College, University of London, 1928-33, Dip.Arch. 1934. Served in the Corps of Royal Engineers, 1940-44, and in the Indian Army, 1944-46; Certificate for Meritorious Services, Home Forces, 1943; Honorary Lieutenant Colonel, 1946. Married Josephine Jeanette Harding in 1939; children: Brian, John, and Anne. Since 1934, Principal of R. Seifert and Partners, London (current partners: H.G. Marsh, A.G. Henderson, J.M. Seifert, R.F. Morris, R.J. Jenkins, S. Alexander, H.E. Morgan, and J. Clowes); office established in Glasgow, 1970. Member of the Road Safety Council, 1970-73; Member, British Waterways Board, 1971-74; Member of the Council, Royal Institute of British Architects, 1971-74. Exhibition: *Seifert Architecture*, Royal Institute of British Architects Heinz Gallery, London, 1984. Recipient: Civic Design Award, 1970; E.E.C. Constructional Steelwork Award, 1978; Architect Award, Royal Institute of British Architects, 1983. Fellow, University College London, 1971. Fellow, Royal Institute of British Architects, 1945, and Royal Society of Arts, 1976. Address: R. Seifert and Partners, 164 Shaftesbury Avenue, London WC2H 8HZ, England.

1955   Woolworth House, Marylebone Road, London
1960   Kellogg House, Baker Street, London
1962   Dunlop House, King Street, St. James's, London
1965   Nat. West House, Stratford Place, Piccadilly, London
1966   Centre Point (office building), St. Giles Circus, London
       Royal Garden Hotel, Kensington, London
       I.C.T. Headquarters Building, Putney, London
1967   Drapers Gardens (bank headquarters), London

Gateway House, Piccadilly, Manchester
1968   Tolworth Towers (local council offices), Surbiton, Surrey
       Guinness Mahon Bank, Gracechurch Street, London
1969   Britannia Hotel, Grosvenor Square, London
1970   I.C.I. Research Laboratories, Blackley, Manchester
1971   A.T.V. Centre, Birmingham
       Lloyds Bank, City of London
1971/
72   Shopping Centre and Council Housing, Erith, Kent
1972   Whittington House, Alfred Place, London
       Anderson Cross (shopping mall, offices, residential buildings, and bus station), Glasgow
1973   Park Tower Hotel, Knightsbridge, London
       Sobell Sports Centre, Islington, London
       International Press Centre, Shoe Lane, London
       Holiday Inn, George Street, London
       Surrey Lane Housing, Wandsworth, London
       London Metropole Hotel, Edgware Road, London
1974   *Times* Newspaper Building, Printing House Square, London
       London Penta Hotel, Cromwell Road, London
       St. John's Ambulance Headquarters, Windsor, Berkshire
1975   National Exhibition Centre and Metropole Hotel, Birmingham
       British Steel Corporation Research Laboratories, Middlesbrough, Yorkshire
       IPC Offices, Kings Reach, Southwark, London
       Melia Hotel and Residential Complex, South Bank, London
1976   London Heathrow Airport Hotel
       Maples Furniture Store, Tottenham Court Road, London
       Wembley Conference Centre, London
       Tower Warehouse, London Docks
       Princess Grace Hospital, Nottingham Place, London
       Houses and offices, King Street, Hammersmith, London
1978   Minet Insurance Company Headquarters, Leman Street, London
       Metropolitan Police Headquarters, Putney, London
       B.A.T. Building, Victoria Street, London
       New Blackfriar's Station and Guinness Peat's Headquarters, London
1979   Shopping mall, King Street, Hammersmith, London
       Gamages redevelopment, Holborn, London
       National Westminster Bank Tower, Bishopsgate, London
       Euston Square (new station and office development), Euston, London

Publications:

By SEIFERT: article—"London's Buildings: Technical Advances Point to an Exciting Future" in *Chartered Surveyor* (London), September 1972.

On SEIFERT: books—*Londoners* by Richard Bourne, London 1981; *A Broken Wave: The Rebuilding of England 1949-1980* by Lionel Esher, London 1981; articles—"The Man Who Did All This and Became an Architect by Accident" by Judy Hillman in the *Evening Standard* (London), 22 June 1965; "Architects and Their Offices: R. Seifert and Partners" by Mary Haddock in *Building* (London), 10 February 1967; "Centre Point: Symbol of the Sixties" in *Building* (London), 24 May 1968; "Drapers Gardens" in *Building* (London), 6 August 1968; "Seifert-on-the-Hill" in *Architects' Journal*

(London), 7 October 1969; "Tomorrow's Hotels" in *Architect and Building News* (London), 5 November 1970; "Seifert on Our Skyline" in the *Sunday Times Magazine* (London), 13 February 1972; "The Post House Hotel, London Airport" in *Architectural Review* (London), September 1972; "R. Seifert" in *Building Design* (London), October 1972; "Two Sides of a Street" in *Architects' Journal* (London), 22 August 1973; "Hospital Remedy: Princess Grace Hospital, London" by Martin Spring in *Building* (London), 21 July 1978; "The Highest Building in Europe: The National Westminster Bank Tower" in *Building* (London), 4 August 1978; "Seifert's Wrenaissance" by David Atwell in *Architects Journal* (London), 21 February 1979; "London's Latest Tower" in *Chartered Quantity Surveyor* (London), August 1980; "NatWest Tower—A Review" in *Building* (London), 23 January 1981; "Seifert Goes Mediaeval for London Bridge" in *Building* (London), 20 February 1981; "Seifert's Camden Scheme to Go Ahead" in *Architects' Journal* (London), 4 March 1981; "Space for Mermaid" in *Building Design* (London), 10 July 1981; "Seifert for Limehouse" in *Architects' Journal* (London), 10 February 1982; "Water Based Formula" in *Building* (London), 12 February 1982; "Seifert Speaks" in *Architects' Journal* (London), 21 April 1982; "Colonel Seifert's Coat of Many Colours" in *Building Design* (London), 23 April 1982; "Wonderland" in *Architects' Journal* (London), 26 May 1982; "Richard Seifert: The Man Who Changed London" in *Bauforum* (Vienna), no. 98, 1983; "Seifert Design for Surrey Docks Site" in *Building Design* (London), 24 February 1984; "The Adelphi" in *Building* (London), 9 March 1984; "Alternative Medicines" in *Building* (London), 20 July 1984; "Brickbats and Mortar" by Charles Knevitt in *The Times* (London), 21 November 1984.

*

Postwar architecture has long been the subject of debate, clouded by strong criticism against all that has been done. There is no defence against bad architecture, but I would prefer to treat all the mistakes and successes as part of an experimental era leading to the unique in design and technology. All architecture communicates—many try to evade this fact whilst under the spell of modernistic dogma.

It is right that everyone is now taking an interest in the design of our buildings. If there had been the same kind of interest in the early 1950s, the building boom might have started off on the right foot. Most people live and work in buildings that are far removed from their architectural ideal. Many of us have a preference for Nash terraces and there has been much talk about a "human scale" in building, but one must try to balance the preservation of historic and architectural places with the vital need of a community to rebuild. Whilst Nash terraces have their remarkable attraction (and it must be remembered that they were "speculative" housing developments), it would be monotonous and uninteresting if urban cities were full of Nash terraces without a variation of style. Comprehensive developments that respect their neighbours, the skyline, conservation areas, and views from the parks and bridges, should not be architecturally frustrated, unless we wish to see our great cities submerged into a skyline that can only be viewed from the street and not from panoramic points of vantage.

The architect has always been a creator, but today, among other things, he has to be a technologist, a lawyer, a cost controller, conservationist, sociologist, and administrator. When he has been all these things to his client and to society—only then perhaps can he dwell on the hope for the future. He must grapple with the problems of energy saving, pollution, economics, road sprawl—the combination of these problems must, in the future, necessarily tax the mind of every architect, who, with the encouragement of governments and the people, must look to an architectural era when technology, together with the elements of nature, will create a new architectural definition to our way of working and living.

I hope that we are now moving into a new post modern period. We have learnt a great deal about spatial organization, clarity, and refinement of details, which have characterized most of the world's greatest epochs of architecture. They stand for the rational, the abstract, and the universal in their internal competition with the subjective, the evocative, and the particular.

—Robin Seifert

Robin (also known as Richard) Seifert formed his architectural practice when he qualified in 1934. His first works were on private housing estates. After World War II, his office won a number of commissions for industrial estates, including large complexes at Woolwich and at Brighton. His interest in new techniques in building, and his desire to reject the traditional methods of cladding and construction, led him to develop an expertise in concrete as a structural and expressed material at a time when brick and stone were difficult to obtain in Britian. He embraced technologies and models developed in America and in Europe, involving the maximum use of concrete in sculptured forms for the buildings themselves, and exploiting the homegeneous possibilities of concrete as the skin and bones of architecture.

His architecture is, in his own estimation, greatly influenced by Gropius, and Seifert sees Gropius as the seminal force on modern architecture, mid-way between the philosophies of Lloyd Wright on the one hand and those of Le Corbusier on the other. Seifert has certainly created buildings that startle. The complicated castings needed for Centre Point, for example, are indicative of his commitment to concrete as a cladding and structural material, and have made possible a tall building with a distinctively modelled character. The Royal Garden Hotel in Kensington is a more conventional slab with antecedents firmly in both the Gropius and Corbusier camps, while the London Penta Hotel combines both sculptured shapes and the simpler rectangular slabs. Yet the apparent clarity of the main forms of these buildings is perhaps dimmed by the handling of their bases. The slender tower of Centre Point, for example, becomes confused with the lower building at its foot, while the simple slab-like form of the Royal Garden Hotel has several structures at the *piloti*-like base that detract from the simple geometry of the building as a whole.

Although Seifert moved away from concrete as a cladding material after 1971 and now favours a return to traditional claddings such as brick and granite for their appearance and durability, his latest great tower-block for the National Westminster Bank in the City of London is perhaps the apotheosis of his belief in advanced building technology. It has been described as one of the most elegant of all the towers in the City, and it is technically among the most sophisticated. The concrete core is surrounded by light, curtain-walled offices and supports the tallest office-block in England.

Seifert has succeeded in building up one of the largest and most successful practices in the United Kingdom. His firm has carried out a great number of large schemes that are startling, dynamic, and spectacular, but the true sophistication of Seifert's work lies in his exploitation of technology to achieve his effects, of which perhaps the National Westminster tower is the greatest expression, although once again the base of the building is uncertainly handled.

—James Stevens Curl

Robin Seifert: Centre Point Office Building, London, 1966.

SELIGMANN, Werner.

American. Born in Osnäbruck, Germany, 30 March 1930; emigrated to the United States, 1949: naturalized, 1955. Educated at Cornell University, Ithaca, New York, under Romaldo Giurgola, Thomas Canfield, Abraham Geller, and Buckminster Fuller, 1950-54, B.Arch. 1954; Technische Hochschule, Braunschweig, Germany, under F. W. Kraemer, 1958-59. Married Jean Lois Liberman in 1954; children: Raphael and Sabina. Principal, Werner Seligmann and Associates, Cortland, New York, since 1961. Instructor, University of Texas at Austin, 1956-58; Research Assistant, Technische Hochschule, Braunschweig, 1958-59; Instructor, E.T.H.: Eidgenössische Technische Hochschule, Zurich, 1959-61; Assistant Professor, 1961-65, and Associate Professor, 1965-74, Cornell University; Professor, Harvard University, Cambridge, Massachusetts, 1974-76. Since 1976, Dean of the School of Architecture, Syracuse University, New York. Exhibitions: *American Synagogue Architecture,* Jewish Museum of New York, 1963; *40 under 40,* Architectural League of New York, 1965; *American Architecture,* Musée d'Art Moderne, Paris, 1966; *Another Chance for Cities,* Whitney Museum, New York 1971; *Works of Werner Seligmann and Associates,* Andrew Dickson White Museum, Cornell University, 1971; *Another Chance for Housing,* Museum of Modern Art, New York, 1973; *White and Grey,* University of California at Los Angeles, and Museum of Modern Art, Pasadena, California, 1971; Istituto Nazionale di Architettura, Rome, 1974; *Two Hundred Years of American Synagogue Architecture,* Rose Art Museum, Brandeis University, Waltham, Massachusetts, 1976; *Werner Seligmann: Recent Competition Projects,* Syracuse University, New York, 1983 (travelled to Florence, Italy, 1984); *Prinz Albrecht Palais Competition,* Martin Gropius Building, West Berlin, 1984; *Nouvelle Direction de L'Architecture Moderne,* Institut Francais d'Architecture, Paris, 1985. Address: Werner Seligmann and Associates, 9 Homer Avenue, Cortland, New York 13045, U.S.A.

Works:

1963 Beth David Synagogue, Binghamton, New York
Waterfront Study, Lake George Village, New York
1965 Waterfront Urban Design Study, Buffalo, New York

1966 Plan for Urban Renewal Area I, Binghamton, New York
1967 Science Building II, State University of New York at Cortland
1967/
69 Heritage Park, Elmira, New York (project)
1968/
70 Community renewal plan for Utica, New York
Plan for the Model Cities Area, Binghamton, New York
Plan for the Woodburn Court Area, Binghamton, New York
1970 Urban Renewal/NDP Area 1 Design, Utica, New York
1971 Administration Building, Willard State Hospital, Willard, New York
1972 Rehabilitation Center, Willard State Hospital, Willard, New York (with F.P. Wiedersum)
Dormitory, Huntington Camp, Raquette Lake, New York
1973 New York State Urban Development Corporation Low- and Middle-Income Housing, Elm Street, Ithaca, New York
New York State Urban Development Corporation Low- and Middle-Income Housing, Maple Avenue, Ithaca, New York
Rehabilitation study of the Court Street Area, Binghamton, New York
1974 New York State Urban Development Corporation Low- and Middle-Income Housing, Menands, New York
1975 New York State Urban Development Corporation Housing for the Elderly, Olean, New York
Impact study for the Capri Theatre, Binghamton, New York
1979 Central Fire Station, Olean, New York
Community Building, North Barry Street, Olean, New York
1981 Center Ithaca Housing, Office and Commercial Complex, Ithaca, New York
1982 Civic Center, Monroeville, Pennsylvania (competition project)
1983 Opera de la Bastille, Paris, France (competition project)
Riverfront Development, Fort Lauderdale, Florida (competition project)
1984 Cultural Arts Pavilion, Newport News, Virginia (competition project)
Prinz Albrecht Palais Development, West Berlin (competition project)

Publications:

By SELIGMANN: articles—"Assessing Broadway East" in *Progressive Architecture* (New York), October 1974; "Runcorn: Historical Precedent and the Rational Design Process" in *Oppositions 7* (New York), Winter 1976-77; "The Mountains and the Machine", with Pilar Viladas, in *Progressive Architecture* (New York), July 1982.

On SELIGMANN: book—*Low-rise Housing* by John Macsai, New York 1976; articles—"Rehabilitation Center, Willard State Hospital" in Architectural Forum (New York), December 1970; feature article in *Progressive Architecture* (New York), May 1973; "U.D.C. Housing, Ithaca, New York" by Charles Moore in *Oppositions 3* (New York), May 1974; "Willard Administration Building" by Michael Dennis in *Progressive Architecture* (New York), May 1976; special issue of *Architecture + Urbanism* (Tokyo), December 1976; "A Fitting Image? Olean Central Fire Station" in *Progressive Architecture* (New York), July 1980; "Filling the Void: Center Ithaca" in *Progressive Architecture* (New York), July 1982; "Dismayed: Scurf from Iron: Unforgivable" in *Bauwelt* (West Berlin), 1 June 1984; "Berlin: Prinz Albrecht Palais Competition" in *Lotus International* (Milan), no. 42, 1985.

*   *   *

In an age of widespread architectural fads, rapidly changing stylistic trends and an often arcane language of explanation, Werner Seligmann's work remains rooted in the mode of classical modernism. Born in Germany, but educated in the United States (at Cornell University), Seligmann has developed an architectural vocabulary the sources of which can be traced to Frank Lloyd Wright and, principally, Le Corbusier.

Seligmann's early work, particularly his Beth David Synagogue in Binghamton, New York, is ambitious, even in its obvious enthusiasm and debt to Frank Lloyd Wright. In its overall appearance and general massing (and in the revealing symmetrical cross-section), Beth David Synagogue shares significant resemblances to Wright's Unity Temple. The plan is an amalgam, however, exhibiting a Wrightian symmetry but inflected with modern mannerist tendencies, as in the skewed geometry of the stairs that run from the lower level to the sanctuary. The special, sculptural spaces (the small chapel, for instance) recall a more distinctly Corbusian aesthe-

Werner Seligmann: Olean Central Fire Station, New York, 1979.

tic. Constructed of concrete block, the building is both oddly rugged and elegant, a sensitive composition in the delineation of and contrast between exposed block bearing walls and non-bearing plastered screen walls.

Seligmann's subsequent work shows the influence of Wright supplanted by the ghostly presence of Le Corbusier. The Willard State Hospital Administration Building, Willard, New York, is, in boldest terms, a Corbusian white box set in the landscape. A study in clarity, the double loaded corridor plan is rigorously simple, as is the overall organization of the building. Architectural interest and complexity comes through a series of contrasting polar opposites: the thinness of the structure and cladding system (a simple steel frame and metal enclosure) versus the spatial depth of the plan. A centralized service wall runs the length of the corridor; functional interruptions along the wall punctuate the space, providing pocket entries for offices and special rooms. The lobby exhibits its own particular dispositions of a free plan, where oversized stairs and landing float within a space which is, in turn, enclosed by a free glass facade.

Built during a time of considerably revived interest in the architecture of Le Corbusier, Seligmann's Willard Administration Building is an interpretive excursus into an historical approach to building, not unlike those historic, distinctly Corbusian referential buildings by Richard Meier (and in some cases, Michael Graves) which date from the same period.

Seligmann's best known project to date is his Urban Development Corporation housing, which comprises 235 units of publicly assisted low-cost housing in the college town of Ithaca, New York. Here it is the spirit rather than the actual example of Le Corbusier that pervades the complex, while the real inspiration for the design comes from the brilliant Halen Housing Estate by Switzerland's Atelier 5 in 1961.

Like the Halen scheme, Seligmann's UDC housing is situated on a sloped site and comprises a variety of individual unit types. Instead of including the landscaped roof terraces that distinguish Halen, which Seligmann could not use due to UDC budget restrictions, most units enclose an atrium. Within a rigorous, tightly-controlled framework Seligmann manages to develop both the intensely repetitive basis of the scheme and a sense of each unit's individuality, aided by a series of internal pedestrian streets. An earlier site plan, more lavishly landscaped with a green fissure running through it, is more attractive, though, like other amenities, unhappily cut for lack of funds.

Currently dean of the Architecture School at Syracuse University, Seligmann formerly taught architecture at Harvard, Texas, Cornell and the ETH in Zurich. Committed to the principles and, seemingly, the aesthetic of the modern movement, Seligmann has managed to stamp his architecture with a spirit of rational clarity, tempered with sensitivity and elegance.

—Richard Lavenstein

SERT, Josep Lluis.
American. Born in Barcelona, Spain, 1 July 1902; emigrated to the United States 1939: naturalized, 1951. Educated at the Escuela Superior de Arquitectura, Barcelona, M.Arch. 1929. Married Ramona Longás in 1938; daughter: Maria. Assistant to Le Corbusier *q.v.*, and Pierre Jeanneret, *q.v.*, Paris, 1929-31; in private practice, Barcelona, 1929-37 (organized GATCPAC group of architects affiliated with CIAM (Congrès Internationaux d'Architecture Moderne); lived in Paris, 1937-39; Co-Founder and Partner, with Paul Lester Wiener and Paul Schulz, Town Planning Associates, New York, 1939-57; in private practice Cambridge Massachusetts, 1957-58.

Partner, with Huson Jackson and Ronald Gourley, Sert, Jackson and Gourley, Cambridge, Massachusetts, 1958-63, and Sert, Jackson and Associates Cambridge, Massachusetts, 1963 until his death in 1983. Professor of City Planning, Yale University, New Haven, Connecticut, 1944-45; Professor of Architecture and Dean of the Graduate School of Design, Harvard University, Cambridge, Massachusetts, 1953-69, also Consultant to the Harvard Planning Office, 1956-69, Emeritus Professor, 1969-83; Thomas Jefferson Memorial Foundation Professor of Architecture, University of Virginia, Charlottesville, 1970-71. Member, Board of Directors and Planning Committee, Citizens Housing Council of New York, 1945; President, CIAM, 1947-56; Chairman, Planning Board of Cambridge, Massachusetts, 1957; Chairman, American Institute of Architects Committee on the National Capital, 1964; Member of the Advisory Council, Princeton University School of Architecture and Urban Planning, 1972-74, Exhibitions: *J.L. Sert,* Spanish Museum of Contemporary Art, Madrid, 1978; *Museumsbauten,* Museum am Ostwall, Dortmund, West Germany, 1979; *CIAM,* Rijksmuseum Kröller-Müller, Otterlo, Netherlands, 1983 (toured the Netherlands). Recipient: Thomas Jefferson Medal, University of Virginia, 1970; FAD (Fomento de las Artes Decorativas) Award, Barcelona, 1974; Gold Medal, Académie d'Architecture, Paris, 1975; Architectural First Award, 1977, and Gold Medal, 1981, American Institute of Architects; Gold Medal, Colleges of Architecture of Spain, 1981; Gold Medal, State Government of Catalunya, Spain, 1981; Gold Medal, Ministry of Culture, Madrid 1982. Honorary M.A.: Harvard University, Cambridge, Massachusetts, 1953; Lit.D.: Boston University, 1963; Art.D.: Boston University, 1968; D.Arch.: Universitat Politecnica, Barcelona, 1981. Fellow, American Institute of Architects; Member, National Institute of Arts and Letters and American Academy of Arts and Sciences. Honorary Member: Royal Architectural Institute, Canada; Royal Society of Arts, London; Royal Institute of British Architects; Academie Royale, Belgium; Akademie der Künste, Berlin; Royal Academy of Arts, London; Society of Architects, Mexico; Institute of Urbanism, Peru; Académie d'Architecture, France; Sociedad de Arquitectos, Colombia. *Died* (in Barcelona) *15 March 1983.*

Works:

1929 New resort community for the Costa Brava, Spain (exhibition project)
1931 Apartment house, Calle Muntaner 342-348, Barcelona
1933/
    35 Master plan for the City of Barcelona (with GATCPAC, Le Corbusier, and Pierre Jeanneret)
1934 Leisure City, Castelldefels, near Barcelona (project; with GATCPAC)
1934/
    36 Casa Bloc (low-rent apartments), Paseo Torras y Bages 105, Barcelona (with GATCPAC)
1935 Weekend houses, Gerraf, Spain
    Central Anti-Tubercular Dispensary, Calle Torres Amat, Barcelona (with J. Torres and J. Subirana)
1937 Spanish Pavilion, World's Fair, Paris (with Luis Lacasa)
1945 Motor City, Brazil (project)
1948 New City of Chimbota, Peru (project)
1949 Sert House, Locust Valley, Long Island, New York
1949/
    51 Master plan for Medellin, Colombia
1950/
    52 Master plan for Tumaco, Colombia
    Master plan for Cali, Colombia
1951 Church, Puerto Ordaz, Venezuela (project)

1951/
    53 Master plan for Bogotá, Colombia (with Le Corbusier)
1954/
    55 Pilot plan for the resort of Varadero, Cuba
1955/
    56 Studio for Joan Miró, Palma, Mallorca
1955/
    57 Presidential Palace, Havana (project)
1955/
    58 Master plan for Havana
1955/
    60 United States Embassy, Baghdad
1958 Sert House, Cambridge, Massachusetts
1958/
    59 Center for the Study of World Religions, Harvard University, Cambridge, Massachusetts
1958/
    60 New England Gas and Electric Association Headquarters, Boston
1958/
    65 Holyoke Center, Harvard University, Cambridge, Massachusetts
1959/
    64 Museum of Contemporary Art, for the Maeght Foundation, Saint-Paul-de-Vence, France (with Bellini, Lizero and Gozzi)
1960 House for Georges Braque, Saint-Paul-de-Vence, France (project)
    East Hills Housing (Action Housing), Pittsburgh (demonstration Planned Unit Development project; with Walter Gropius, Carl Koch, John Ormsbee Simonds, and B. Kenneth Johnstone)
1960/
    67 Charles River Campus of Boston University (with Hoyle, Doran and Berry and Edward T. Steffian and Associates)
1961 House, Ibiza, Spain
1963 Carpenter Center for the Visual Arts, Harvard University, Cambridge, Massachusetts (with Le Corbusier; as supervisory architect)
1963/
    65 Peabody Terrace Married Students Housing, Harvard University, Cambridge, Massachusetts
1964/
    66 Dormitory, Library, Dining and Activity Center, Guelph University, Ontario (with Project Planning Associates)
1965/
    70 Six houses, Punta Martinet, Ibiza, Spain
1966/
    72 Martin Luther King Elementary School, Cambridge, Massachusetts
1967/
    68 Urban renewal plan for the central business district of Worcester, Massachusetts
1969 Carmelite Convent, Carme de la Paix, Mazille (Cluny), France
    Master plan for a resort community on the Frioul Islands, Marseille, France
1970/
    73 Undergraduate Science Center, Harvard University, Cambridge, Massachusetts
1971/
    75 Eastwood Housing, Roosevelt Island, New York
    Riverview Housing, Yonkers, New York
1972/
    75 Fundación Joan Miró Center for the Study of Contemporary Art, Montjuich Park, Barcelona (with Anglada, Gelabert and Ribas)
1974 Les Escales Park Housing, Barcelona (with Anglada, Gelabert and Ribas)
1977 Caixa d'Estalvis de Catalunya (offices and cultural center), Barcelona
1978/
    81 Autopistas (road service buildings, hotel, shops, and restaurants), La Junquera, Spain
1981 National Centre for Science and Technology Master Plan, Riyadh, Saudi Arabia

West Campus Housing, Massachusetts Institute of Technology, Cambridge
1982 Porta Catalana Road Service Building Complex, French/Catalan border, Spain

Publications:

By SERT: books—*Can Our Cities Survive?*, Cambridge, Massachusetts and London 1942; *The Heart of the City*, edited with E. N. Rogers and J. Tyrwhitt, New York and London 1952; *Antoni Gaudí*, with James Johnson Sweeney, Stuttgart, London and New York 1960; *The Shape of Our Cities*, with J. Tyrwhitt, Tokyo 1961; *Ibiza: fuerta y luminosa*, Barcelona 1967; *Cripta de la Colonia Güell de Antoni Gaudí*, Barcelona 1969; articles—"The Human Scale in City Planning" in *New Architecture and City Planning*, edited by Paul Zucker, New York 1944; "Urbanism en Amerique du Sud," with Paul Lester Wiener, in *L'Architecture d'aujourd'hui* (Paris), December 1950/January 1951; "The Changing Philosophy of Architecture" in *Architectural Record*

(New York), August 1954; "Architecture and the Visual Arts" in *Harvard Foundation for Advanced Study and Research Newsletter* (Cambridge, Massachusetts), 31 December 1954; "The Architect and the City" in *The City in Mid-Century*, edited by H. Warren Dunham, Detroit 1957; "What Became of CIAM?," with Walter Gropius, Le Corbusier, and Siegfried Giedion, in *Architectural Review* (London), March 1961; "Remembering Le Corbusier" in *AIA Journal* (Washington, D.C.), November 1965; "Below the Alhambra" with Frank Woods, in *Architectural Review* (London), March 1980; "The Lucid Vanguard," interview, in *Quaderna* (Barcelona), May/June 1982.

On SERT: books—*José Luis Sert* by Knud Bastlund, Zürich and London 1967; *Sert: Mediterranean Architecture*, edited by Maria Lluisa Borrás, Barcelona and Paris 1974, Boston 1975; *Sert's Architecture in the Miró Foundation* by Bruno Zevi, Barcelona 1976; *J. L. Sert* by Jaume Freixa, Barcelona 1979, Zürich and Munich 1980; *J. L. Sert*, exhibition catalogue, Madrid 1978; *L'Architecture*

fonctionelle: le projet de J. L. Sert pour l'Ecole des Beaux-Arts de Besançon pose la question by Marie-Josee Lement, Paris 1982; articles—"Sert's Concept of Living" by S. Anderson in *Architectural Design* (London), August 1965; "Sert: works and Projects 1929-1973," special edition of *Cuardenos le arquitectura* (Barcelona), November/December 1972; "Ten Years Past at Peabody Terrace" by Jonathan Hale in *Progressive Architecture* (New York), October 1974; "A Portfolio of Design for Display" by Gerald Allen in *Architectural Record* (New York), October 1974; "The Last Works of J.L. Sert in Barcelona" by David Ferrer in *Arquitectura* (Madrid), March 1975; "A Certain Feeling: Interview with J. L. Sert" by Peter Murray in *Building Design* (London), 23 May 1975; "Miro and Sert in Barcelona" by Pierre Joly in *L'Oeil* (Paris), September 1975; "Towards a Housing Manifesto" by Marie Dulac in *Architecte* (Paris), June 1976; "A Study Center for Contemporary Art" by Roland Penrose and "Sert for Miro" by David Mackay in *Architectural Review* (London), July 1976; "Hommage to Catalonia—Fundación Joan Miró" by Mildred F. Schmertz in *Architectural Record* (New York), March 1977; "The Urbane and

Josep Lluis Sert: Centre Joan Miro, Barcelona, 1975.

Varied Buildings of Sert, Jackson and Associates" by Andrea O. Dean in *AIA Journal* (Washington, D.C.), May 1977; "AIA Presents 1981 Gold Medal to Josep Lluis Sert" in *Architectural Record* (New York), January 1981; "Homage to a Catalonian" by Robert Campbell in *AIA Journal* (Washington, D.C.), February 1981; "Jose Lluis Sert: His Work and Ways," special issue of *Process: Architecture* (Tokyo), December 1982; "In memoriam: Jose Lluis Sert's House at Harvard" by Emilio Donato in *Arquitectura* (Madrid), March/April 1983; "Jose Lluis Sert: Noted Architect and Harvard Dean" by Robert Campbell in *Harvard Graduate School of Design News* (Cambridge, Massachusetts), March/April 1983; "Jose Lluis Sert, 1.7.1902—15.3.1983," special issue of *Q* (Barcelona), April 1983; "Jose Lluis Sert 1902-1983" by Willo von Moltke in *Progressive Architecture* (New York), June 1983; "Jose Lluis Sert— Persevere and Criticise" by Oriol Bonigas in *Casabella* (Milan), July/August 1983.

Josep Lluis Sert, as a disciple of Le Corbusier and former President of CIAM, played an important role in the development of the early planning theories of the Modern Movement and through his design projects and writings, contributed significantly to their acceptance. For example, he helped prepare the Modern Movement's seminal planning manifesto, the Athens Charter of 1933, which formalized and codified the new concepts.

With the exception of Le Corbusier, Sert had more influence upon the built world of housing and planning than any other CIAM member and as much as any architect of his generation. In his long career, he collaborated in the preparation of approximately twelve master plans at the scale of the city or town, at least three within the scope of a neighborhood or district, six for large-scale housing developments, and two for entire campuses.

Sert's high-rise, high-density housing projects disprove the currently fashionable criticism that such housing is inhumane, the cause of feelings of isolation and helplessness and contributory to delinquency, vandalism, and the collapse of the family. Sert's housing—most notably the Peabody Terrace Married Student's Housing at Harvard University, Eastwood on Roosevelt Island in New York City, and Riverview in Yonkers—is very humane indeed. Sert was a leading spokesman for, and designer of, balanced, compact housing designed with an equal emphasis upon community and privacy within a range of densities. In his housing, Sert managed to achieve a workable balance between the number of dwelling units and the supporting services provided, such as schools, day-care centers, recreational facilities, shopping and other amenities. He strives to obtain a proper balance between people and automobiles, buildings and open space, people and trees, as well as passive and active recreation.

His housing offers a variety of dwelling sizes and plan layouts to provide a range of choices to families and individuals of different needs and lifestyles. In his schemes, most units have cross-ventilation, good views in two directions, natural light, and sunlight. In massing and fenestration Sert followed the Modulor dimensioning of Le Corbusier, paying great attention to scale, color, and texture.

Sert's campus work at Harvard and for the Charles River Campus of Boston University also exhibits his interest in high-density urban design. He has written, "An urban campus is a cultural center within a city, and should set an example of good planning and good design for the city. It is, in a way, a micro-city, and its urbanity is the expression of a better, more civilized way of life."

Sert also did distinguished work at the scale of the single building. For example, he showed great skill in the design of museums. The Foundation Maeght in St. Paul-de-Vence and his most recent museum in Barcelona are both composed of carefully proportioned spaces, shaped in a variety of ways, with many different ceiling heights, sources of light, and degrees of openness. For museums and other buildings which

need to make maximum use of natural light, Sert developed prominent semi-circular light scoops, which he used so often they become a trademark. The Barcelona museum houses the paintings and sculpture of Sert's friend, Joan Miro. The work of the latter—spontaneous, joyful, rooted in the subconscious—is at the opposite end of the spectrum from Sert's eminently rational, scientific, conscious design.

—Mildred F. Schmertz

SHARON, Arieh.

Israeli. Born in Yaroslaw, Poland, 28 May 1902; emigrated to Palestine in 1920, and worked and lived on the Kubbutz Gan Shmuel, 1920-26; acquired Israeli nationality, 1948. Educated at the Staatliche Bauhaus, Dessau, Germany, under Walter Gropius, *q.v.*, Hannes Meyer, *q.v.*, Josef Albers, Paul Klee, and Wassily Kandinsky, 1926-29, graduated 1929. Married Gunta Stoelzl in 1928; Haya Sankowsky in 1932; children: Yael, Eldar, *q.v.*: Eldar Sharon, and Uri. In charge of the architectural office of Hannes Meyer in Berlin, and supervised building of the Educational Centre of the Trade Unions in Bernau, Berlin, 1929-31; in private architectural practice, Tel Aviv, 1932-39; townplanner and civic designer, Tel Aviv, 1940-48; Director and Chief Architect of the National Planning Agency of Israel, 1948-53; Partner, in an architectural practice, with Benjamin Idelson, Tel Aviv, 1954-64, and with his son Eldar Sharon, Tel Aviv, 1964 until his death in 1984. Member of the Executive Committee, International Union of Architects, Paris, 1963-67; Chairman, National Council for National Parks and Nature Reserves, Israel, 1964; Chairman, Standards Institution of Israel, 1965-69; President, Association of Engineers and Architects in Israel, 1965-71. Exhibitions: *Kibbutz und Bauhaus*, Bauhaus Archive, Berlin (toured Germany, Switzerland, Mexico, and The United States), 1977-79. Recipient: Israel Prize for Architecture, 1962; Gold Medal, Mexican Institute of Architecture, 1964; Rokach Award, Tel Aviv, 1963, 1971. Honorary Member, Royal Institute of British Architects, 1962, Akademie der Künste, Berlin, 1965, and the Bund Deutscher Architekten, 1967; Honorary Fellow of the American Institute of Architects, 1970. *Died* (in Paris) *24 July 1984*.

Works:

1924/
  26 Buildings for the Kibbutz Gan Shmuel, Palestine
1929 Vocational school in Zlin, Czechoslovakia (competition project; with Anton Urban)
1932 Histadrut Pavilions, Levant Fair, Tel Aviv
1933/
  34 Cooperative housing, Tel Aviv
1934/
  35 Brenner House, Histadrut Centre, Tel Aviv
1935/
  37 Beilinson Hospital, Petah Tikva, Palestine
1936 Institute for Physical Culture, Haifa
      Agricultural Cooperative Centre, Tel Aviv
1937/
  38 Hamashbir Cooperative Centre, Jaffa
1937/
  39 Apartment houses, Tel Aviv
      Apartment houses, Ramat Gan, Palestine
      Apartment houses, Haifa
1938 Kibbutz layout, Ein Hashofet, Palestine
1938/
  40 Cooperative housing, Tel Aviv
1939 Kibbutz Dining Hall, Gan Shmuel, Palestine
      Kibbutz Dining Hall, Sarid, Palestine
      Kibbutz layout, Dalia, Palestine
1940 Kibbutz layout, Kfar Glikson, Palestine

1940/
  42 Ohel Theatre Building, Tel Aviv
1941 Kibbutz layout, Mishmar Hayam, Palestine
1942 Kibbutz layout, Alumot, Palestine
1944 Vocational school, Tel Mond, Palestine
1945 Kibbutz Kindergarten, Gan Shmuel, Palestine
      Kibbutz school community, Beit Alpha, Palestine
1945/
  48 Chen Movie Theatre and Offices, Tel Aviv
1946 Kibbutz school community, Ma'abarot, Palestine
      Histadrut Trade Union School, Tel Aviv
1947 Wingate Institute for Physical Education, Nethanya, Palestine
1948 Lessin House of Culture, Tel Aviv
1948/
  52 Solel Boneh Headquarters, Tel Aviv (with Dov Karmi)
1949 School building, Kiryat Yam, Israel
1949/
  53 Urban and new town plans for Israel (with National Planning Agency)
1950/
  70 Beilinson General Hospital, Peta Tikvah, Israel (with Ora Fradis and Benjamin Idelson)
1954 Forum, Technion, Haifa (with Benjamin Idelson)
1954/
  60 Municipal Hospital, Ichilov, Tel Aviv (with Ora Fradis, M. Rafaeli, and Benjamin Idelson)
1955/
  57 Neighbourhood housing, Nazareth (with Benjamin Idelson)
1955/
  62 Regional Hospital, Beersheba, Israel (with Benjamin Idelson)
1956/
  58 Churchill Auditorium, Technion, Haifa (with Y. Bregman, A. Kinsbrunner, and Benjamin Idelson)
1958 Israel Pavilion, World's Fair, Brussels (with Arieh Elhanani and Benjamin Idelson)
1958/
  60 Library and Senate Building, Technion, Haifa (with Moshe Kletter and Benjamin Idelson)
1959/
  60 Workers Bank Headquarters, Tel Aviv (with Neomi Paz and Benjamin Idelson)
1959/
  61 Yakhin Pectin Factory, Petah Tikva, Israel (with Ziona Leshem and Benjamin Idelson)
1959/
  64 Yad Vashem Memorial, Jerusalem (with Arieh Elhanani and Benjamin Idelson)
1960 Dormitories, Hebrew University, Jerusalem (with Benjamin Idelson)
1960/
  65 Housing, Kiryat Yam, Israel (with Y. Rosenberg and Benjamin Idelson)
1961 Faculty of Chemistry, Hebrew University, Jerusalem (with Benjamin Idelson)
      Ezrat Nashim Mental Hospital, Jerusalem (with Benjamin Idelson)
1961/
  63 Gratz Elementary School, Tel Aviv (with Benjamin Idelson)
1961/
  65 Jewish Agency Headquarters, Tel Aviv (with Benjamin Idelson)
1962 Beit Yakhin Office Building, Tel Aviv (with Shmuel Schwartz and Benjamin Idelson)
1963 Master plan for Ife University, Nigeria (with Benjamin Idelson)
1963/
  65 Labour Sick Fund Headquarters, Tel Aviv (with Ziona Leshem and Benjamin Idelson)
      Regional Clinic, Rehovot, Israel (with Micha Amitai and Benjamin Idelson)
      Humanities Building, Ife University, Nigeria (with AMY Limited and Benjamin Idelson)

Arieh Sharon: Convalescent Home, Tiberias, Israel, 1971.

1964 Halls of Residence, Ife University, Nigeria (with AMY Limited and Benjamin Idelson)

Hasneh Building, Beersheba, Israel (with Benjamin Idelson)

Radio and Television Building, Jerusalem (with Elling Bureau, Eldar Sharon, and Moshe Kletter)

1964/
66 Electric power station, Ashdod, Israel (with Moshe Kletter and Benjamin Idelson)

1964/
68 Regional Hospital, Eilat, Israel (with A. Yaski, A. Alexandroni, and Benjamin Idelson)

1964/
70 Hamaschbir Office Building, Tel Aviv (with Shmuel Schwartz and Benjamin Idelson)

1965/
68 Agricultural Cooperative Headquarters, Tel Aviv (with A. Kaplan, E. Mashiah, and Eldar Sharon)

1965/
71 Convalescent home, Tiberias, Israel (with Harold Rubin and Eldar Sharon)

1965/
72 Rambam Government Hospital, Haifa, (with E. Kanner, Ora Fradis, and Eldar Sharon)

1965/
76 Tel Giborim General Hospital, Tel Aviv (with Moshe Kletter, Zalman Shohat, and Eldar Sharon)

1966 Medical Centre, Tel Aviv (with Moshe Kletter, Ora Fradis, Yuval Geni, and Eldar Sharon)

Regional Hospital, Ashdod, Israel (project; with Y. Rosenberg, Ziona Leshem, and Eldar Sharon)

1966/
68 Kibbutz Memorial Museum, Yad Mordechai, Israel (with Yoram Diamant, M. Dubravsky, and Eldar Sharon)

1966/
70 Geha Mental Hospital, Petah Tikva, Israel (with Yoram Diamant and Eldar Sharon)

1966/
74 Tel Giborim Nurses' School, Tel Aviv (with Moshe Kletter, Zalman Shohat, and Eldar Sharon)

1967 Pavilion Hospital for Developing Countries (project; with others)

Israel Pavilion, *Expo '67,* Montreal (with David Resnik and Eldar Sharon)

Beeri Apartment Houses, Tel Aviv (with Dov Karmi, E. Mashiah, and Eldar Sharon)

1967/
68 Housing, Beersheba, Israel (with Shmuel Schwartz and Eldar Sharon)

1967/
69 Housing estate, Nazareth (with Avi Kaplan and Eldar Sharon)

1967/
70 Library, Ife University, Nigeria (with AMY Limited, Harold Rubin, and Eldar Sharon)

1967/
72 University Medical School, Tel Aviv (with Eldar Sharon)

1968 Health Sciences Centre, Bangkok (with Benjamin Idelson, G. Zippor, AMY Limited, and Eldar Sharon)

Vice-Chancellor's Residence, Ife University, Nigeria (with AMY Limited, Harold Rubin, and Eldar Sharon)

1968/
69 Town Hall, Kiryat Yam, Israel (with E. Kanner and Eldar Sharon)

1968/
70 Master plan for the Old City and environs, Jerusalem (with David A. Brutzkus and Eldar Sharon)

1968/
72 Institute of Education, and Secretariat, Ife University, Nigeria (with AMY Limited, Harold Rubin, and Eldar Sharon)

1969 Tiergarten Museum, Berlin (competition project; with Eldar Sharon)

Civic Centre, Sdeh Boker, Israel (with Eldar Sharon)

1969/
74 Bank of Israel Headquarters, Jerusalem (with Y. Rosenberg and Eldar Sharon)

1970 Military hospital, San Salvador (with AMY Limited and Eldar Sharon)

Adam Hacohen Apartment Houses, Tel Aviv (with Shmuel Schwartz and Eldar Sharon)

1970/
73 Israel America House, Tel Aviv (with M. Tintner, George Perel, and Eldar Sharon)

1971 City Hall, Amsterdam (competition project; with Eldar Sharon)

1972 Oncology Pavilion, Rambam Hospital, Haifa (with D. Rubinstein and Eldar Sharon)

Neighbourhood housing, Eilat, Israel (with Eldar Sharon)

UNIDO and IAEA Conference Centre, Vienna (competition project; with Eldar Sharon)

Prefabricated bungalows, Ghana (with Eldar Sharon)

1972/
73 Fast Hotel, Jerusalem (with George Perel and Eldar Sharon)

1972/
75 Radar Memorial, near Jerusalem (with George Perel and Eldar Sharon)

1972/
76 Hotel, Sharem-el-Sheikh, Israel (with Yoram Diamant and Eldar Sharon)

Municipal Centre, Rehovot, Israel (with George Perel and Eldar Sharon)

Assembly Hall, Ife University, Nigeria (with AMY Limited, Harold Rubin, and Eldar Sharon)

Soroka Health Centre, Beersheba, Israel (with Micha Amitai, Ora Fradis, and Eldar Sharon)

1972/
82 Medical Centre, Tel Aviv (with Moshe Kletter, Yuval Geni, and Eldar Sharon)

1973 Container housing for OHW, New York (project; with Harold Rubin and Eldar Sharon)

Misawa Home Housing Scheme, Japan (project; with Harold Rubin and Eldar Sharon)

1973/
75 Field School, Kfar Etzion, Israel (with Charles Dorell and Eldar Sharon)

1973/
76 Gilo Neighbourhood, Jerusalem (with Y. Rosenberg and Eldar Sharon)

Maccabi Sports Centre, Tel Aviv (with George Perel and Eldar Sharon)

1974 Negev Museum, Sdeh Boker, Israel (with Eldar Sharon)

1974/
78 Asaf Harofe Hospital, Zerifin, Israel (with Eldar Sharon)

1977 Apical Hospital and College for Health Sciences, Ife, Nigeria (with Eldar Sharon, Egboramy Company, and Yeheskel Rosenberg)

1978 Isaka Island Vacation Village, Nigeria (project; with Eldar Sharon, Egboramy Company and Yuval Geni)

Publications:

By SHARON: books—*Physical Planning in Israel*, Tel Aviv 1955; *Hospitals in Developing Countries*, Tel Aviv 1967; *Hospitals in Israel and Developing Countries*, Tel Aviv 1968; *Planning Jerusalem: The Old City and Its Environs*, Jerusalem 1973; *Kibbutz + Bauhaus*, Stuttgart and Massada 1976; articles—"Planning and Israel" in *Israel and Middle East* (Tel Aviv), March 1952, and in *Town Planning Review* (Liverpool), April 1952; "Collective Settlements in Israel" in *Town Planning Review* (Liverpool) January 1955; "Hospitals in Israel" in *World Hospitals* (London), vol. 1, 1964; "Medical Centres and Hospitals in Developing Countries" in *Dialogue in Development* (Proceedings of the 2nd World Congress of Engineers and Architects in Israel), Tel Aviv 1970; "Planning Jerusalem" in *Ekistics* (Athens), November 1974.

On SHARON: books—*Ospedali* by Roberto Aloi and Carlo Bassi, Milan 1973; *Wohnen in Eigenen Haus* by Gerhard Schwab, Stuttgart 1976; *New Israeli Architecture* by Amiram Harlan, London and East Brunswick, New Jersey 1982; articles—"Cast in History, Not in Concrete" by Wolf Von Eckardt in the *Washington Post* (Washington, D.C.), 26 August 1972; "Haifa Transporation Centre", in International Lighting Review (Amsterdam) no. 3, 1976; "Transport in Haifa" in *Deutsche Bauzeitschrift* (Gütersloh, West Germany), September 1976; "Obituary: Mr. Arieh Sharon" in *The Times* (London), 3 August 1984.

The long and productive career of Arieh Sharon, extending over half a century, embraced many phases: the farmer and practical builder on the kibbutz; the pioneer modern architect; the public servant, directing the urban and regional planning programmes of the new state of Israel; and the successful architect in private practice, not only helping to shape Israel's architecture, but also significantly contributing to the development of the Third World. Threaded through this long saga of achievement there are three continuous strands, three components of his attitude to architecture and to life. It is only when these strands are woven together that the pattern is complete; and it is when the components are brought into congruence that Sharon's architecture is at its most powerful.

The first component is idealism, the capacity to be moved by an idea, the capacity for devotion and service to a cause, be it the Zionist-socialism of his youth or the ideal of the new architecture that he imbibed at the Bauhaus—both, in their ways, dreams of building a shining new world. It was this idealism which led Sharon to devote many creative years to the design of kibbutzim; which almost tempted him to follow Hannes Meyer to a career in the Soviet Union; and which, after the founding of the State of Israel in 1948, induced him to accept the new government's invitation to create and direct a National Planning Agency, through which he advocated that policy of decentralization which underlay Israel's new towns programme, which initiated the proper planning of the major urban concentrations, and which sought—through propaganda and exhibition—to make the general public planning-conscious.

After idealism—or perhaps linked to it—is Sharon's eternal avant-gardism, his pioneering spirit, his eagerness to be in the vanguard of new development, in the forefront of new movements—not only in responding to new challenges, but also in creating new symbols. The spirit of the *chalutz*, or pioneer, brought Sharon to Eretz Israel in 1920; during the 1930s he played a central role in the making of a modern architecture in Israel, a natural revolutionary stance for an architect who had sought out the Bauhaus for his education; and in the decade prior to his death in 1984, as advanced architectural posture moved into its post-modern phase, he joined forces with his son Eldar and other young Israeli architects of that generation that he delighted to call "the sabra avant-garde," seeking once again to put a new face on Israel's architecture and perhaps to attempt to give it new meaning.

It must be said that the drive to be in the avant-garde is both a strength and a weakness: at best the pioneering spirit is a creative force, discarding the shackles of the past, generating new and valid solutions to present and future problems; but there is always an inherent danger, when new architectural forms are sought, that it is not for their relevancy, but for mere novelty's sake. The control mechanism that prevents this trivialization of the creative spirit is found in the third component of Sharon's architectural attitude: his essential pragmatism, his concern with reality as well as dream, practice as well as theory, action as well as idea. It is Sharon the pragmatist who first learned architecture through direct building experience, in his kibbutz days; who was more strongly attracted by the Bauhaus's credo of learning by doing than by its polemical debates on abstract issues; and who found his architectural inspiration in the guidance of Hannes Meyer, the apostle of the functionalist approach and the *neue sachlichkeit*. Pragmatism is the very essence of Sharon's early architectural work: the honest and direct use of materials, the austere simplicity of architectural form, the functional efficiency of his planning, the growing awareness of climatic constraints. It is in evidence not only in his more modest projects, such as his many apartment blocks or in his kibbutz and housing area developments (where economic factors are a powerful lever for pragmatism), but also in the larger, more complex, and functionally more demanding institutional buildings—especially the university complexes and hospitals—that he designed. This pragmatism is particularly evident in the fecund period when he worked in association with Benjamin Idelson, when, in my view, his creative talent was at its peak—mature, disciplined, yet powerfully inventive.

The motivating power of Sharon's work is his idealism, expressed both in architectural and social terms; the freshness and excitement lies in his natural thrust towards the vanguard, the new and the untried. It is when these traits are coupled with the iron discipline of the pragmatist, who harnesses his dream to the real world, and derives his vision from the constraints of reality, that good architecture can be made. It is to Sharon's credit, and greatly to architecture's benefit, that he so often succeeded in achieving this elusive synthesis of the real and the ideal.

—Gilbert Herbert

SHARON, Eldar.

Israeli. Born in Tel Aviv, Palestine, now Israel, 27 November 1933; son of the architect Arieh Sharon, *q.v.* Studied under Alfred Neumann, Faculty of Architecture, Technion, Haifa, Dip.Arch, 1956. Served in the Engineering Corps of the Israeli Defence Forces, 1956-58: Captain. Married Ruth Sharon in 1953; Ilana Sharon in 1971; children: Arad, Smadar, and Eran. Worked in the office of Arieh Sharon and Benjamin Idelson, Tel Aviv, 1958; partner in architectural practice with Alfred Neumann and Zvi Hecker, *q.v.*, Tel Aviv, 1958-64; partner, with Arieh Sharon, Sharon and Sharon Architects, Tel Aviv, 1964-84. Since 1984, in private practice, Tel Aviv. Recipient: First Prize, Bat Yam Municipality Building Competition (with Zvi Hecker), 1958. Address: Hayarkon Street 70, Tel Aviv, Israel.

Works:

1960 Bat Yam Town Hall, near Tel Aviv (with Zvi Hecker and Alfred Neumann)

1962 Dubiner Apartment House, Ramat Gan, near Tel Aviv (with Zvi Hecker and Alfred Neumann)

Club Méditerranée Holiday Camp, Achsiv, Israel (with Zvi Hecker and Alfred Neumann)

1964 Officers' Academy, near Mitzpe Ramon, Israel (with Zvi Hecker and Alfred Neumann)

Radio and Television Building, Jerusalem (with Elling Bureau, Arieh Sharon, and Moshe Kletter)

1965/
68 Agricultural Cooperative Headquarters, Tel Aviv (with A. Kaplan, E. Mashiah, and Arieh Sharon)

1965/
71 Convalescent Home, Israel (with Harold Rubin and Arieh Sharon)

1965/
72 Rambam Government Hospital, Haifa, Israel (with E. Kanner, Ora Fradis, and Arieh Sharon)

1965/
76 Tel Giborim General Hospital, Tel Aviv (with Moshe Kletter, Zalman Shohat, and Arieh Sharon)

1966 Medical Centre, Tel Aviv (with Moshe Kletter, Ora Fradis, Yuval Geni, and Arieh Sharon)

Regional Hospital, Ashdod, Israel (project; with Y. Rosenberg, Ziona Leshem, and Arieh Sharon)

1966/
68 Kibbutz Memorial Museum, Yad Morde- chai, Israel (with Yoram Diamant, M. Dubravsky, and Arieh Sharon)

1966/
70 Geha Mental Hospital, Petah Tikva, Israel (with Yoram Diamant and Arieh Sharon)

1966/
74 Tel Giborim Nurses' School, Tel Aviv (with Moshe Kletter, Zalman Shohat, and Arieh Sharon)

1967 Pavilion Hospital for Developing Countries (with Benjamin Idelson, J. Hertz, G. Zip- por, A. Leitersdorf, I. Belsitzman, and Arieh Sharon)
Israel Pavilion, *Expo '67*, Montreal (with David Resnik and Arieh Sharon)
Beeri Apartment Houses, Tel Aviv (with Dov Karmi, E. Mashiah, and Arieh Sharon)

1967/
68 Housing, Beersheba, Israel (with Shmuel Sch- wartz and Arieh Sharon)

1967/
69 Housing Estate, Nazareth, Israel (with Avi Kaplan and Arieh Sharon)

1967/
70 Ife University Library, Nigeria (with AMY Limited, Harold Rubin, and Arieh Sharon)

1967/
72 University Medical School, Tel Aviv (with Arieh Sharon)

1968 Health Sciences Centre, Bangkok, Thailand (with Benjamin Idelson, G. Zippor, AMY Limited, and Arieh Sharon)
Vice-Chancellor's Residence, Ife University, Nigeria (with AMY Limited, Harold Rubin, and Arieh Sharon)

1968/
69 Town Hall, Kiryat Yam, Israel (with E. Kanner and Arieh Sharon)

1968/
70 Old City and environs master plan, Jerusalem (with David A. Brutzkus and Arieh Sharon)

1968/
72 Institute of Higher Education, Ife University, Nigeria (with AMY Limited, Harold Rubin, and Arieh Sharon)
Ife University Secretariat, Nigeria (with AMY Limited, Harold Rubin, and Arieh Sharon)

1969 Tiergarten Museum, West Berlin (with Arieh Sharon)
Civic Centre, Sdeh Boker, Israel (with Arieh Sharon)

1969/
74 Bank of Israel Headquarters, Jerusalem (with Y. Rosenberg and Arieh Sharon)

1970 Military Hospital, San Salvador, El Salvador (with AMY Limited and Arieh Sharon)
Adam Hacohen Apartments Houses, Tel Aviv (with Shmuel Schwartz and Arieh Sharon)

1970/
70 Israel America House, Tel Aviv (with M. Tintner, George Perel, and Arieh Sharon)

1971 City Hall, Amsterdam (competition project; with Arieh Sharon)

1972 Oncology Pavilion, Rambam Hospital, Haifa, Israel (with D. Rubinstein and Arieh Sharon)
Neighborhood Housing, Eilat, Israel (with Arieh Sharon)
UNIDO and IAEA Conference Centre, Vienna (competition project; with Arieh Sharon)
Prefabricated Bungalows, Ghana (with Arieh Sharon)

1972/
73 Fast Hotel, Jerusalem (with George Perel and Arieh Sharon)

1972/
75 Radar Memorial, near Jerusalem (with George Perel and Arieh Sharon)
Hotel, Sharem-el-Sheikh, Israel (with Yoram Diamant and Arieh Sharon)
Municipal Centre, Rehovot, Israel (with George Perel and Arieh Sharon)
Assembly Hall, Ife University, Nigeria (with AMY Limited, Harold Rubin, and Arieh Sharon)
Soroka Health Centre, Beersheba, Israel (with Micha Amitai, Ora Fradis, and Arieh Sharon)

1972/
82 Medical Centre, Tel Aviv (with Moshe Klet- ter, Yuval Geni, and Arieh Sharon)

1973 OHW Container Housing, New York (project; with Harold Rubin and Arieh Sharon) Misawa Home Housing Scheme, Japan (project; with Harold Rubin and Arieh Sharon)

1973/
75 Field School, Kfar Etzion, Israel (with Cha- rles Dorell and Arieh Sharon)

1973/
76 Giloh Neighborhood, Jerusalem (with Y. Rosenberg and Arieh Sharon)
Maccabi Sports Centre, Tel Aviv (with George Perel and Arieh Sharon)

1974 Negev Museum, Sdeh Boker, Israel (with Arieh Sharon)

1974/
78 Asaf Harofe Hospital, Zerifin, Israel (with Arieh Sharon)

1977 Apical Hospital, and College for Health Sciences, Ife, Nigeria (with Egboramy Company, Y. Rosenberg, and Arieh Sharon)

1978 Isaka Island Vacation Village, Nigeria (project; with Egboramy Company, Yuval Geni, and Arieh Sharon)

1980/
82 Nurses' Residential Building, Asaf Harofe Hospital, Zerifin, Israel

Publications:

On SHARON: books—*World Architecture One*, edited by John Donat, London 1964; *Modern Architecture in Colour* by Udo Kultermann, London 1965; *Twentieth Century Architecture* by John Jacobus, London 1969; *A Visual History of Twen- tieth Century Architecture* by Dennis Sharp, Lon- don 1972; *Town Halls and Community Centres*, Munich 1973; *New Israeli Architecture* by Amiram Harlap, East Brunswick, New Jersey, and London 1982; articles—"Due opere dello studio Arieh ed Eldar Sharon ed Associati" in *Architettura* (Rome), June/July 1973; "Universitè d'Ife" in *Techniques et Architecture* (Paris), November 1973; "Geha Men- tal Hospital" in *Baumeister* (Munich), March 1974; "Due impianti medici in Israele" in *Architettura* (Rome), July 1975; "Les modèles exportés" in *Architecture Francaise* (Paris), December 1976; "Honeycomb on a hillside in Israel" in *Ideal Home* (London), April 1977; "Apartment Block, Ramat Gan" and "Municipal Buildings of Bat Yam" in *Summarios* (Buenos Aires), April 1979; "Back to Bauhaus with Chutzpah—Nurses' Hostel in Haifa" in *Building Design* (London), May 1981.

One can, and one perhaps ought to, compare the design of a good house with the design of a good university campus and the design of a good city. They all provide for a place to live, work, sleep and engage in cultural, creative and recreative activities, and they all have to accommodate sufficient services to make the complex work. The difference is only in quantity and in scale, and it is scale which seems to be one of the key factors that has been neglected in twentieth century architecture.

The gargantuan development of new towns, un- iversity campuses, neighbourhoods and cities of today seems to be almost totally centered around the car, the road system and the interests of the speculative real estate dealer/developer. This has led with rare exceptions to the complete neglect of human scale in design and city planning. The old traditional key factor in all good design—namely sensitive regard to reasonable walking distances— has been completely forgotten in the process.

The principles of what has traditionally been considered as a good home or house seem to apply cross-culturally to most Mediterranean societies. A good Greek house, a Pompeian house, a traditional Jewish (Talmudic) house or an Arab house—all have an entrance court leading to an interior court around which the various living and sleeping quar- ters are organized. Similarly, many of the traditional colleges follow closely the same pattern. A Persian madrasa, a Greek academia or Oxford and Cam- bridge colleges were built around a central court. Students' and teachers' quarters, class rooms, din- ing halls, recreation rooms and libraries were desig- ned around this central court, thus rendering all college facilities accessible within comfortable walk- ing distance. The traditional college was almost without exception an integral part of the historical city, and located within immediate walking distance from the city centre.

This pattern repeats itself in all historical small cities. For the inhabitants of these cities, work- place, church, government house, market-place, etc., were all within convenient walking distance. The Old City of Jerusalem, as a living example, has a parameter of 800 on 900 meters. It is subdivided by two main axes: south-north and east-west, has a large open space of the Holy Mount on its eastern section, and within its walled space live more than 25,000 people. The city provides for the religious and commmercial needs of a large hinterland population, as well as for international pilgrimage and trade, contains a disproportionately large num- ber of temples, markets, schools, and government offices, and yet it is still one of the best and most beautiful cities to live in.

May we deduce solutions from all these examples on an urban scale for a modern town with tens of thousands of people living together, a town which none the less preserves its human scale? The answer, I think, is positive. The shape of a town that can be grasped by the human eye, easy walking distances for pedestrians, removal of the car from the com- plex. Can we use modern technology in such a way as to make life in the city more attractive for people to live and dwell in, instead of escaping from it? In short, the revival of an old dream: creating a place to be in.

—Eldar Sharon

Eldar Sharon is the son of the distinguished Israeli architect Arieh Sharon, with whom he had practised for a number of years. There are now several projects entirely under Eldar Sharon's name, and therefore an assessment of his independent work is becoming possible.

Particularly interesting is the nurses' residence at the Asaf Harofeh medical center. Although on the surface this project is highly reminiscent of the collaborative work with his father, a closer examina- tion reveals some quite interesting differences. Arieh Sharon, educated at the Bauhaus, was instrumental in inserting an interpretation of Bauhaus ideas and ideals into the Israeli context. As this was worked out with his son Eldar, the overall expression was spartan: minimalist, angular, redundant, ins- titutional, severe—it spoke of willing submission of the individual to state and community—of a re- expression of traditional and modern European (Ashkenazi) values into a context of shared, precious, scarce material resources.

In the nurses' residence at Asaf Harofeh, this lean language is shot through with purely decorative, re- created industrial-age artifacts. If one knows some- thing of the history of the building, then one knows that through a series of mischances and tough architectural decisions, craft has come to be presented under the guise of prefabrication. The building, irrespective of its history shows prefabrication as the illusion and craftsmanship as the reality. The project for all its seeming institutional severity is a part-whimsical statement about the pseudo-functionalism of the original Israeli-Bauhaus-settler aesthetics and ethic. It says in effect that that original spartan ethic was (at least in part) a facade and an ornamental device—a surface denial of deep-seated aesthetic commitments to pure European-oriented ornament.

Yet, these nurses' rooms are still ultra-small, ultra-minimal, hard and unyielding in their structure. This is the Israeli reality—but a reality that has by now become part-ornamental, part-facade—like Fidel Castro's beard and military fatigues—or the fatigues of an Israeli general. The ornamental touches are not used to soften or to hide the scarcity of room, of resources, of luxuries. Rather, they are there as a reminder of the separateness of expression from necessity—of the minimalism of self expression when faced with the demands of the community.

In this "neo-Bauhaus" vocabulary, the younger Sharon reveals deeper contradictions within Israeli values than in any of the previous collaborative work with his father. In going solo, the place of individual expression, of decorative surface lamination, of the decorativeness of spartan "uniforms," of the relation between individual and community values, is no longer taken for granted—no longer assumed to be simply, naively, and straightforwardly given. Rather, the spartan reality is partly mocked and thus contrasted to Athenian possibility.

—Joseph B. Juhasz

SHEPPARD, ROBSON AND PARTNERS.

Partnership; established by Richard Sheppard (1910-82), Jean Shufflebotham (died, 1974), and Geoffrey Robson (born 1918), in London, 1947. Partners: William Mullins, Gordon Taylor, John Heywood, A.C.F. Morris, Anthony Furlong, and Richard Young; with Geoffrey Robson as consultant to the practice since 1979. Associated firm: Sheppard, Robson and Partners (overseas), established in Jersey, Channel Islands, 1976. Recipient: Royal Institute of British Architects Awards, 1953, 1961, 1962, 1967, 1968(twice), 1974, 1975, and 1979; Civic Trust Awards, 1963, 1966, 1968, 1969(twice), 1971, 1972, and 1975; Office of the Year Award, 1975; First Prize in the competitions—Churchill College, Cambridge, England, 1959; Telford New Town, Shropshire, 1978; Design Centre, London, 1979; Al-Omma Mosque, Tripoli, Libya 1980; Office/Industrial Development, Teddington, Middlesex, 1981; Arabian Gulf University Master Plan, Bahrain, 1981; Merck, Sharpe & Dohme Research Laboratories, Essex, 1981; Shopping Development, Bracknell, Berkshire, 1982; Prime Minister's Offices, Bahrain, 1982. Address: 77 Parkway, Camden Town, London NW1 7PU, England.

Works:

1952 Harrowfield Secondary Boys School, Harold Hill, Essex
1953 Offices for Swan Hunter and Wigham Richardson, Wallsend on Tyne
1954/
66 Royston School, Hertfordshire
1954/
67 Churchfields School, West Bromwich, Staffordshire

1954/
70 Burton-on-Trent Technical College, Staffordshire
1955 Oswestry Secondary Modern School, Shropshire
1956 Tollington school, Creighton Avenue, London
Hurlingham Girls School, Peterborough Road, Fulham, London
1956/
61 Riley Comprehensive School, Bloxwich, Walsall, Staffordshire
1959/
66 School of Navigation, Newton Road, Warsash, Southampton
1959/
68 Chatham Walderslade Secondary School, Kent
1960/
71 Worcester Technical College
1960/
76 William Edwards School, Stifford Clays Road, Grays, Essex
1961/
66 Loughborough University, Leicestershire
1961/
73 Redditch College of Further Education, Worcestershire
1963 Digby Hall, University of Leicester, England
1964/
68 Imperial College of Science and Technology, South Kensington, London
1964/
72 West Midlands College of Education, Gorway, Walsall, Staffordshire
1964/
73 Merz Court, Science/Arts Buildings, and Hatton Gallery, University of Newcastle upon Tyne
1965/
73 Brunel University, Uxbridge, Middlesex
Churchill College, Cambridge, England
1967 Wallasey Grammar School, Cheshire
1968 St. Albans School, Hertfordshire
1968/
77 South Bromsgrove School, Charford Road, Bromsgrove, Worcestershire
1969 Administration Building, University of Southampton, Hampshire
1969/
75 Central redevelopment of Waltham Cross, Hertfordshire
1969/
76 The City University, St. John Street, London
1974 Collingwood College, University of Durham, England
Social Amenity Centre and Library, Campus West, Welwyn Garden City, Hertfordshire
Welwyn/Hatfield Sports Centre, Welwyn Garden City, Hertfordshire
Richard Sheppard, Robson and Partners Offices, Parkway, London
1974/
75 Offices and shops at 12/13 and 34/36 Lime Street, London
1976 Conference Centre and Library for King Edward's Hospital Fund for London, Albert Street, London
Offices at 150/152 Fenchurch Street, London
1976/
80 Wood Green Shopping City, London
1977/
78 Manchester Polytechnic
1978 Offices at 105/109 Cannon Street, London
Conference centre, Fairmile Court, Cobham, Surrey
Housing, Lymington Road, Camden, London
Rayleigh Laboratory extensions, Southampton University, Hampshire
British Airports Authority Offices, Gatwick Airport, Sussex (competition project)
Police College, Tripoli, Libya (project)
Exhibition Centre, Ibadan, Nigeria (project)

Naval Hospitals, in Bandat Abbas, Tehran, and Bandar Pahlavi, Iran (project)
1978/
80 Brookfield House office refurbishment, London
1978/
81 Inveresk House office refurbishment, Aldwych, London
1979 Office refurbishment, 58-60 Moorgate, London
Supermarket and flats, Blackheath, London (project)
Office Building redevelopment, 10 Dover Street, London (project)
Design Centre, The Haymarket, London (competition project)
Shopping Centre, Chineham, Basingstoke, Hampshire (competition project)
Orthopaedic and Accident Hospital, Shagamu, Nigeria (project)
Survey Department Offices, Tripoli, Libya (project)
Traffic Control Centre, Tripoli, Libya (project)
Police Records Department, Tripoli, Libya (project)
Ministry of Foreign Affairs Headquarters, Riyadh, Saudi Arabia (competition project)
Arab Centre for Vocational Training, Sebratha, Libya (project)
Golf Club Professionals' Shop refurbishment, Seer Green, Buckinghamshire
1979/
81 Housing rehabilitation, Lithos Road, Hampstead, London
1980 St. Peter's Primary School, Greenwich, London
Bishop Challoner Roman Catholic School, Basingstoke, Hampshire
Pierrepoint School additions, Frensham, Surrey
Shopping Centre, Rainham, Kent
Office refurbishment, 39 Dover Street, London
Office refurbishment, 48 Copthall Avenue, London
Office refurbishment, 10 Old Bond Street, London
New Housing, Aylesham, Kent (project)
Electrical Research Association development plan, Leatherhead, Surrey (project)
Great St. Thomas Apostle Development, City of London (project)
Flats, Putney, London (project)
Residential buildings, Christ Church College, Oxford, England (competition project)
Office Building feasibility study, 8 Moorgate, London (project)
Malayan Bank Headquarters Complex, Kuala Lumpur, Malaysia (competition project)
Mansoura Paediatric Hospital, Egypt (project)
Advanced Studies Complex, Kuwait (project)
Diplomatic Club, Riyadh, Saudi Arabia (competition project)
The Al-Omma Mosque, Tripoli, Libya (competition project)
1981 St. Alphege Church repairs, Greenwich, London
Civic Centre, Chelmsford, Essex
Moor House alterations and refurbishment, Moorfields, London
Charnwood Shopping Centre alterations, Loughborough, Leicestershire
St. Peter's Church of England School additions, Redditch, Worcestershire
Office refurbishment, 47/48 New Bond Street, London
Office and Residential Development, 73-77 East Street, Epsom, Surrey
Office refurbishment, 13 Regent Street, London
Residential Wing, Mansfield College, Oxford, England (competition project)

Sheppard, Robson and Partners: The City University, St. John Street, London, 1976.

Hersham Central Redevelopment, Surrey (competition project)

Vilamoura Housing Complex, Algarve, Portugal (competition project)

National Centre for Constructional Laboratories, Baghdad, Iraq (competition project)

Arabian Gulf University master plan, Bahrain (project)

Housing Scheme, Manila, Philippines (project)

1983 Royal London House refurbishment, Finsbury Square, London

Office, shops and residential building, 106-110 Brompton Road, London

Office refurbishment, 8-10 Great George Street, London

Imperial Cancer Research Centre, South Mimms, Hertfordshire

Office Headquarters Building, Westbrook Mills, Godalming, Surrey

Office refurbishment, Albermarle House, Piccadilly, London

Office Building, 9-10 Philpot Lane, London

Office Development, 10/13 Ludgate Broadway, London

Office refurbishment, Albemarle Street, London

Merck Sharpe & Dohme Pharmaceutical Research Laboratories, Harlow, Essex

Post Office Letter-Sorting Office, Maidstone, Kent

Commissary Warehouse, R.A.F. Lakenheath, Suffolk

Central Area Shopping Development, Bracknell, Berkshire

Civic Centre stage 2, Chelmsford, Essex

Lewisham Hospital phases 1A and B, London

1983/
84 Shelley House Office Building, Noble Street, London (project)

Biological Research Laboratories, South Mimms, Hertfordshire (project)

Factory Development, Teddington, Surrey (project)

Office Building, 1-4 Bury Street, London (project)

Composite Recreation Facility, R.A.F. Fairford, Gloucestershire (project)

Culver Shopping Precinct, Colchester, Essex (project)

Shopping Centre refurbishment, Eastgate, Colchester, Essex (project)

Housing Development, Tortola, British Virgin Islands, West Indies (project)

Khulafa Street Redevelopment, Baghdad, Iraq (project)

Naaish Khana, Khadiyama Redevelopment, Baghdad, Iraq (project)

Al-Gaylani Education Centre, Baghdad, Iraq (project)

National Centre for Constructional Laboratories, Baghdad, Iraq (2nd project)

Prime Minister's Offices, Bahrain (project)

Villa Harthiya Guest Palace, Baghdad, Iraq (project)

Personnel Housing, R.A.F. Alconbury, Cambridgeshire (project)

Publications:

By SHEPPARD/ROBSON: book—*The Planning of Science Laboratories in Schools*, London 1956.

On SHEPPARD/ROBSON: books—*A Broken Wave: the rebuilding of England, 1940-1980* by Lionel Esher, London 1981; *Sheppard Robson: Architects* by Alastair Best, Charles McKean, Peter Murray and others, London 1983; articles—"The Work of Richard Sheppard, Robson and Partners" in *Architectural Design* (London), July 1957; "Churchill College, Cambridge: An Essay in Form and Quality" by H.N. Brockman in *The Financial Times* (London), 5 June 1964; "The Oxbridge Double" by Michael Manser in *The Observer* (London), 26 July 1964; "Brunel University" by Diana Rowntree in *The Guardian* (London), 25 February 1965; "Massive Simplicity Beside the Cam" by Michael Webb in *Country Life* (London), 25 November 1965; article in *Kentiku* (Tokyo), March 1968; "The City University" by H. N. Brockman in *The Financial Times* (London), 8 October 1970; "Sheppard's Path" in *Architects' Journal* (London), 14 March 1973; "Friendly Face of Culture" by Stephen Gardiner in *The Observer* (London), 21 April 1974; "Architects Have the Best Office" by Roy Levine in *The Financial Times* (London), 20 October 1975; articles in *Art and Architecture* (Tehran), December 1975, March 1976; "Higher Education at Lower Cost" by Tony Aldous in *Country Life* (London), 12 February 1976; "Finding the Perfect Partnership" by Stephen Gardiner in *The Observer* (London), 24 September 1978; "Building Rehab" in *Building* (London), 16 February 1979; "City Polish—Two Office Buildings" in *Architects' Journal* (London), 28 March 1979; "Shopping in Style" in *Building Design* (London), 13 April 1979; "Large scale Campus" in *Building Design* (London), 11 May 1979; "All Saints Building, Manchester Polytechnic" in *RIBA Journal* (London), August 1979; "Mews Memory" in *Architects' Journal* (London), 30 January 1980; "Offices in Cannon Street, London" in *Industria delle costruzioni* (Rome), June 1980; "Working to Rule" in *Interior Design* (Morden, Surrey), March 1981; "Shop City Nears Completion" in *Building Design* (London), 20 March 1981; "Revealing Designs" in *Architects' Journal* (London), 1 July 1981; "Architectural Practice in London" in *Industria delle costruzioni* (Rome), December 1981.

"Modern" architecture seeks to derive its formal content from the exploration of a problem rather than its adaption to a preconceived form. As a practice, we believe that "modern" architecture is vigorous and vital and that its full growth and development is to come. We do not think that it has become an historical digression and that a return to past forms is likely or desirable—although certainly possible. We think there is a place for the vernacular in in-fillig but that generally only a design discipline based upon the scale and technological resources of our society can meet present conditions

Our approach is thus pragmatic and we hope that every one of our buildings creates its own identity. There is no identity kit, and if there is a resemblance between one and another we are glad, but this is not our aim. We do not theorise about forms, techniques, and user needs but endeavour to find an answer which most nearly fits our information about these requirements and think that the design should meet them in an economic, practical, and significant way. We do not seek, indeed have never produced, personal, individual, quirky expressions, nor distorted the problem in any respect in order to do so. We believe that form, proportion, rhythm, texture, and, consequently, style are functions which vary in terms of the problem and are never constant. We are extremely conscious of the dichotomy inherent in the architect's role. We are engaged as the owner's agent to design for a (usually) unknown and anonymous tenant. Society has created a chasm between the user, a tenant, and the owner and his architect. The interests of the two seldom coincide and we all, in our various ways, try to bridge the gap. But in this relationship lies the impersonality of modern building and the modern state. Both may be benevolent by intention but are distant in the result. We believe that the purpose, form, and organisation of a building should be immediately comprehensible externally and internally by the disposition of volumes and their expression. Scale and mass must also be manipulated in relation to site and intention. It is important that buildings should create a sense of relation and responsibility with the user. The vandal insults authority but if we can produce something which people are proud of and pleased to occupy, then environmental conditions are enriched and dignified.

—Sheppard, Robson and Partners

Sheppard, Robson and Partners originated at the Architectural Association School of Architecture during its wartime evacuation to Hadley Wood, near Barnet. As a member of the teaching staff, Dick Sheppard recognized the qualities in one of the leading students, Geoffrey Robson, and after office experience, a partnership was formed that has both personally and professionally been an outstanding success. Both partners are designers first and businessmen afterwards, and so consistent is the firm's work, which is always of a high standard, that it is difficult to tell who was individually responsible. No building is more revealing than their own offices in Camden Town, London—an imaginative re-use of poor space at the rear of shops.

Sheppard and Robson's chief claim to fame, however, will undoubtedly rest with Churchill College, Cambridge, resulting from a competition which they won in 1959. Although visually the architectural idiom is modern, the plan shows Sheppard's particular sensitivity to history and appreciation of the values of the form of the traditional Oxford and Cambridge colleges. These were based on the square quadrangle, a shape both practical and contemplative that grew from the medieval cloister. At Churchill College, the squares are planned to follow one another in informal sequence, recomposed from history to be free and liberal in their grouping (not unlike academics in converse). The elevation of this unusual plan reflects the advanced way of thought at the time and, like all the firm's detailing, is strong, sometimes to the point of abruptness. Truth to material suggested that the

concrete which forms the building material should express its timber shuttering, and sometimes (as with the Greek conversion of timber form into stone) timber form has been transposed into concrete.

It was in a similar vein of boldness, imagination and appreciation of arts other than architecture that this distinguished firm organized the removal of a famous modern fresco that was deteriorating in a barn in Cumbria to a new position in their university buildings at Newcastle.

—Geoffrey Jellicoe

SHINOHARA, Kazuo.

Japanese. Born in Shizuoka, 2 April 1925. Educated at the Institute of Technology, Tokyo, B.Eng. 1953, D.Eng. 1967. Served in the Japanese Army, in Japan and Korea, 1945. Married Kumiko Sasaki in 1951; children: Miwako, Rieko and Hikaru. Since 1954, in private practice, Tokyo: established studio at Tokyo Institute of Technology, 1962. Instructor, 1953-61, Associate Professor, 1962-69, and Professor of Architecture since 1970, Tokyo Institute of Technology; Visiting Professor of Architecture, Yale University, New Haven, Connecticut, 1984. Exhibitions: *Two Houses in a Department Store,* Odakyu Department Store, Shinjuku, Tokyo, 1964; *Kazuo Shinohara: 30 Maisons Contemporaines,* Société Francaise des Architectes, Paris, 1979 (travelled to Aachen, West Germany, 1980; Lausanne, Switzerland, 1981; Zurich, 1981; Palma, Spain, 1981); *Kazuo Shinohara,* Institute for Architecture and Urban Studies, New York, 1981 (travelled to New Haven, Connecticut, 1982; Montreal, Quebec, 1983; Winnipeg, Manitoba, 1983; Cambridge, Massachusetts, 1983); *The Works of Kazuo Shinohara,* Architectural Institute of Japan, Tokyo, 1984. Recipient: Architectural Institute of Japan Prize, 1972. Address: Tokyo Institute of Technology, O-Okayama 2-12-1, Meguro-ku, Tokyo, Japan.

Works:

1954 House in Kugayama, Tokyo
1958 House in Kugayama II, Tokyo
  Tanikawa Residence, Tokyo
1960 House in Komae, Tokyo
1961 House in Chigasaki, Japan
1962 Umbrella House, Tokyo
1963 House with a Big Roof, Tokyo
  House with an Earthen Floor, Karuizawa, Japan
1965 North House in Hanayama, Kobe, Japan
1966 Asakura Residence, Tokyo
  House in White, Tokyo
  House of Earth, Tokyo
1968 South House in Hanayama, Kobe, Japan
  Yamashiro Residence, Yokohama
  Suzusho Residence, Hayama, Japan
1970 Shino Residence, Tokyo
  The Uncompleted House, Tokyo
1971 Cubic Forest (private house), Kawasaki, Japan
  Repeating Crevice (private house), Tokyo
  Sea Stairway (private house), Tokyo
  Sky Rectangle (private house), Tokyo
  Prism House, Yamanaka-ko, Japan
1972 House in Kugahara, Tokyo
1973 House in Higashi-Tamagawa, Tokyo
  House in Seijo, Tokyo
1974 Tanikawa Residence, Karuizawa, Japan
1975 House and Art Gallery, Karuizawa, Japan
1976 House in Uehara, Tokyo
  House in Itoshima, Fukuoka Prefecture, Japan
1978 House in Ashitaka, Numazu, Japan
  House in Hanayama no. 3, Kobe, Japan

  House on a Curved Road, Tokyo
1980 House in Hanayama no. 4, Kobe, Japan
1981 House Under High-Voltage Lines, Tokyo
1982 Ukiyo-e Museum, Matsumoto, Japan
  Higashi-Tamagawa Complex, Tokyo

Publications:

By SHINOHARA: books—*Residential Architecture,* Tokyo 1964; *Theories on Residences,* Tokyo 1970; *Kazuo Shinohara: 16 Houses and Architectural Theory,* Tokyo 1971; *Theories on Residences II,* Tokyo 1975; *Kazuo Shinohara II: 11 Houses and Architectural Theory,* Tokyo 1976; *Kazuo Shinohara,* with Yasumitsu Matsunaga, New York 1982; articles—"Houses Are Art" in *Shinkenchiku* (Tokyo), May 1962; "The Three Primary Spaces" in *The Japan Architect* (Tokyo), August 1964; "A Theory of Residential Architecture" in *The Japan Architect* (Tokyo), October 1967; "Beyond Symbol Spaces" in *The Japan Architect* (Tokyo), April 1971; "Abstractions from the East" in *The Japan Architect* (Tokyo), May 1974; "Irrational City and Space Machine" in *Skinkenchiku* (Tokyo), March 1975; "When Naked Space is Traversed" in *The Japan Architect* (Tokyo), February 1976; "The Third Style" in *Shinkenchiku* (Tokyo), January 1977; "The Savage Machine As An Exercise" in *The Japan Architect* (Tokyo), March 1979; "Towards Architecture" in *The Japan Architect* (Tokyo), September 1981; "Interview: Kazuo Shinohara" in *Transition* (St. Kilda, Victoria), February 1982; "After Modernism", with Kenzo Tange, in *The Japan Architect* (Tokyo), November/December 1983.

On SHINOHARA: books—*New Directions in Japanese Architecture* by Robin Boyd, New York and London 1968; *Kazuo Shinohara: Architecte Japonais – 30 Maisons Contemporaines,* Paris 1980; articles—"Kazuo Shinohara's Architectural Theory" by Hiroki Onobayashi in *The Japan Architect* (Tokyo), February 1967; "Heretical Spaces" by Koji Taki in *Shinkenchiku* (Tokyo), July 1968; "Kazuo Shinohara und die japanische Wohnarchitektur" by Irmtraud Schaarschmidt in *Die Kunst* (Munich), March 1971; "Significant Spaces" by Koji Taki in *The Japan Architect* (Tokyo), April 1971; "Kazuo Shinohara and Residences" by Akira Ohashi in *To the Age of Interior,* Tokyo 1971; "With a Sensation of Freedom: Houses Designed by Kazuo Shinohara" by Irmtraud Schaarschmidt in *Bauwelt* (Berlin), February 1976; "Kazuo Shinohara" by Toyoo Itow in *History of Residences in Showa Era,* Tokyo 1976; "Jap Savagery" in *Architectural Review* (London), August 1977; "Kazuo Shinohara: Una Filosofia de la Vivienda," special issue of *Summarios* (Buenos Aires), October 1977; "Absence of Architecture" by Yasumitsu Matsunaga in *Kenchiku Bunka* (Tokyo), October 1978; "Kazuo Shinohara", special issue of *Space Design* (Tokyo), January 1979; "A House/Room" in *Bauwelt* (West Berlin), 2 February 1979; "Kazuo Shinohara: Architectural Space Explorations", special issue of *The Japan Architect* (Tokyo), March 1979; "Primary Spaces: Houses by Kazuo Shinohara" in *Progressive Architecture* (New York), May 1980; "La geometrie emotionelle de Shinohara" by Gilbert Luigi in *Neuf* (Brussels), 6 July 1980; "Japan Through the Looking Glass", special issue of *Domus* (Milan), June 1981; "House, Tokyo" in *Architectural Review* (London), September 1981; "Two Shinohara Houses" in *The Japan Architect* (Tokyo), September 1981; "Oppositions: The Intrinsic Structure of Kazuo Shinohara's Work" in *Perspecta* (New Haven, Connecticut), no. 20, 1983; "Thirty Controversial Houses", special issue of *L'Architecture d'Aujourd'hui* (Paris), April 1983; "New Museum for Japa-

Kazuo Shinohara: House under High-Voltage Lines, Tokyo, 1981.

nese Ukiyo-e Woodblock Prints" in *Progressive Architecture* (New York), May 1983; "Japanese Architecture 1: Shinohara's Machine" in *De Architect* (The Hague), February 1984; "Ein Philosoph der Architektur" in *Frankfurter Allgemeine Zeitung* (Frankfurt), April 1984; "High-Wire Act" in *House and Garden* (New York), August 1984; "Kazuo Shinohara's Savage Machine and the Place of Tradition in the Modern Japanese Residence" in *Journal of the Society of Architectural Historians* (Washington, D.C.), May 1984.

Bibliography: *Kazuo Shinohara: Japan's Leader in Residential Architecture* by James P. Noffsinger, Monticello, Illinois 1982.

I was very struck by a photograph of the elevation of a fighter plane labeled as one of the most important craft of its kind in the United States Naval Air Force. To enable this craft to perform its special combat functions, all possible technical expertise and skill had been lavished on production. But, seen from the elevation, the plane lacked the smooth and stream-lined form one generally associates with aircraft. The square jet intakes, the adjustable wings, and the fuselage seemed to have been clumsily connected together so that each could perform its functions with maximum efficiency. This startlingly powerful machine is capable of producing the image of an intrepid bird in flight. In contrast, the standard streamlined aircraft recalls an ornamental water fowl afloat on a pond.

My reference to this dangerous aircraft-weapon is similar to the quotational use architects of the early Modern Movement made of biplanes in visual analogies to exemplify the relationship between form and function.

Another example of the same kind of clumsiness is the spacecraft that first took man to the surface of the moon. The aluminium-covered plastic installed on the craft to protect it from solar heat and minute meteorites during its passage through space free of air resistance impressed me as being even more roughly assembled than the elevation of the fighter. Totally lacking in elegance, from an architectural standpoint, the mooncraft was extremely refreshing for me to behold and made me wonder if a similar architecture did not exist.

An architecture of this kind would not be one of associating forms with other definite points of reference but would instead cut the form free of all extraneous background. It would be a design based on the response relation between form and function that was a classical theme of modern architecture once.

Though it has lost its absolute nature, the dual association of function and form is by no means without effect today. However, half a century of technological development has altered the conditions for this fundamental architectural theme. From the two photographs I mentioned, I discovered a solution to the problem of function and form. But the machine objects in my analogy are no the mechanical bodies themselves but only parts of them.

Of course, the mooncraft could be called a complete machine, but in effect it was only the nose of a much larger mechanical assemblage. The analogy between form and function and the machine is derived not from the whole, but from the parts.

The particular fighter represented is capable of dealing with twenty-four distant enemy targets, six of which can be struck simultaneously with missiles. The essential nature of the latest weaponry is to be found in invisible mechanisms making this kind of action possible. It is not a characteristic manifested in solid, physical matter.

New products resulting from novel technology have a freshness of shape that nourishes the theme of function and form. As I have said, whereas the architects of the 1920s used the machine as a whole in their analogies, I prefer to employ only a part and even then do not always make visual analogies.

In today's newspaper (July 13, 1981), I saw an advertisement claiming that the world's largest electronic brain was contained within a package no more then fifty cubic centimeters and could operate one basic circuit calculation in 350/1,000,000,000,000 of a second.

Human beings often employ spatial modifiers to express the semantic contents of words—"high" performance of "close" relations are examples. The classical idea of the relation between form and function was predicated on this customary way of thinking. Today, "big" does not mean powerful. Elevating the performance level of calculators depends first of all on technology for the minimization of heat generation in circuitry. When this obstacle was overcome, calculators steadily diminished in size. In other words, the simple rectilinear relation between form and function was invalidated.

The participants in the Modern Movement of the 1920s made form and function a central issue and, working with it, developed a series of revolutionary solutions. However, it was this same theme that caused some people to declare, a few decades later, that the Modern Movement had died. It seemed then that all beautiful, fresh answers to the issue had been exhausted. Technology was altered to render the rectilinear, straightforward operations of Modern Architecture inefficacious. It is, however, mistaken to assume from this that the very issue of form and function has lost its validity.

Boarding a plane in Accra, the capital of Ghana, in the morning, I arrived in Geneva while it was still light. The orderly streets of this city, one of the cleanest and loveliest in Europe, had a slightly stifling effect on me as I walked them. In contrast, the capitals of the several West African nations I had been visiting had seemed lively and bustling. Along their streets stand buildings copied from their suzerain states, painted in bright African colors and placed beside small, cheaply built structures. The total impression can scarcely be called beautiful from the Modern architecture standpoint. But the out-rageousness of the scene charms, along with the brightly clad, gracefully moving people who live there.

By no means a beautiful city, Tokyo has a quality of its own, a mood that is totally unlike those of spacious modern European cities with their great weight and mass of tradition. Even from the standpoint of Modernist urban theory, the main streets of small West African capitals are more orderly than what is to be found in Tokyo. No city in the world demonstrates the variety of building types or the disorder of decorative surface colors and forms that Tokyo offers. Chaos is the only word to describe the total effect. Still, I cannot uncondition-ally reject the chaos of this city. Chaos precedes destruction. But from place to place, in the vast village that is Tokyo, vitality and activity charge the streets to make this one of the most exciting cities in the world.

In the past, Tokyo was a sprawling aggregate of wooden domestic and other architecture practically never more than two stories. A hundred years ago, when the nation underwent a reversal of political direction and launched a program of modernization and Westernization, the low wooden building were gradually replaced with copies or imitations of European-style architecture. The main parts of the city burned in World War II but have since been rebuilt on a scales larger than before. The miraculous development into an industrialized society that made this possible filled the city with all kinds of industrial products and the planless distribution of which was tolerated by an apathetic Japanese society.

One aspect of this tolerance—or absorption power—is the way Japanese people use forms and even words borrowed from their parent cultures in purely decorative ways. If the words look nice, their true meaning is a matter of no importance. Foreign words often appear as shop and product names in situations that are not actually suited to true semantic contents and in colorful mixture with Chinese characters and the characters of the Japanese-syllabary systems. Foreign words and their Japanese-syllabary transcriptions appear side by side in colors for which there seems to be no system of orderly selection. At night, the scene becomes more dazzling with the inclusion of a high-industrial society's amusement technology. though it is possible to condemn all this as chaos, a "culture" that has advanced to such a stage still deserves a fair evaluation.

At one time I participated in a judging panel for the *Consultation Internationale pour l'Amenagement du Quartier des Halles,* in Paris. I was slightly surprised to hear the ease with which French architects talk about urban axes and urban symbolism. A Japanese architect who lives in Paris explained to me that this was not unordinary, but I could not help reflecting that the application of such terms to town planning in Japan would require cautious consideration. The axis in Europe stirs up associations with planning during imperialism of fascism. But symbolism for Japanese is automatically associated with emperor worship.

For me, the city must be considered with Tokyo as a starting point. Pursuing the European city image is an illusion, as were the megalomaniac, technologically ordered city projects fashionable twenty years ago. This is more than a matter of taste; I can see no other valid starting point than the chaos that is Tokyo.

Small wooden houses are still a part of Tokyo anarchy. Their strictly ordered interiors suggest the persistence, even in fragmentary form, of the culture that produced the tea ceremony, *Ikebana* floral arranging, and the *No* drama. But the effective limits of these old customs extend only to the small, immediate spaces of daily life and not as far as local neighborhoods, let alone the city. Still the same system of order transcends the city space to find application in politics and society, where it provides an old-fashioned vertical hierarchy for the symbolic emperor system and for the organization of big business.

The European system, in which personal freedom is established in the small space of the home and leads to the planning of republican freedom in the larger city space, is an inversion on all levels of the Japanese one.

In the design of a single building, the method whereby anarchy is expressed as a major subject can lead to the establishment of an architectural logic. This is not to say, however, that the problem of anarchy is solved on a miniature scale. Any building that sets out to be no more than a part of anarchy is unable to deal with anarchy. I have no use for miniatures that adulate anarchy.

Anarchy cannot logically be a method; simplification and abstraction are opposed to it. Expectations can be placed on anarchy, not from a planning standpoint, but only from the standpoint of probabilities. The greatest probability for anarchy to produce vitality and liveliness occurs when buildings designed and produced on the basis of the most advanced technology of the age and replete with totally decorous beauty are submerged in the planlessness of the street.

If this too is unsatisfactory, the architect could try to plan specified, orderly regions using ideas raised by brilliant skill to a religious level, not unlike the *ville radieuse.* But, no matter how much brilliance used to design them, even radiant cities are likely to be buried in drastic chaos by their surrounding regions. The illogical gap between this and orderly spaces nourishes the vitality of chaos.

To ensure its continued vitality, progressive anarchy must constantly alter its structure. Vitality is in a sense synonymous with urban freedom. A city that is ceaselessly generating such vitality is mankind's greatest, unintentionally created machine.

The masters of Modern architecture pursued the combination of form and function in some works with religious self-control. Architects eager to produce works that were opposed to the spirit of Modernism boldly disregarded the classical rule between form and function. In other words, they capriciously combined forms that were thought to have no need to conform to functional demands.

Architects felt free from functional restraints and directed their attentions towards operations upon forms. They placed operation on top of operation and pursued this simplistic one-way street to still further operations. Modernist thought had strongly stressed experiments in conforming to new materials and structures, new techniques, and changes in domestic and social life. The opponents of Modernist thought, however, consider all this meaningless. Though they have acquired maximum freedom in the creation of forms, their architecture is nevertheless destined to follow a one-way street. Modern Architecture can be compared to a long first act of a play. The audience had become bored towards the end and now welcomes a brief, light, comical interlude full of irony and parody on the action that has already taken place. But the audience accepts this only as an interlude that does not need to be taken seriously. "Everyone laughs at a good joke on first hearing. Repeated hearings of the same anecdote rarely provoke mirth," as Bruno Zevi has noted.

Attempts of this kind represent differentiations and reinterpretations of history divorced from their significant context, and reassembled in comical parodies. It is a fashion. It is logically correct for anti-Modernist architecture to reintroduce the old styles that Modern architecture rejected, as long as reintroduction incorporates the operations of differentiation and reinterpretation.

The orthodox interpretation of traditionalism is one in which the present culture is seen through the past. The time gap between the time at which the so-called traditional element was created and the time when it is used, involves unintentional differentiation and reinterpretation that are difficult to avoid. Architecture in which this process is intentional and in which method is central is of an entirely different kind.

Corresponding to a disillusionment with technology, some Japanese architects abandoned their pursuit of Western thought and attempted to find new architectural knowledge in old Japanese traditions. In cultural fields, it is not uncommon, especially in Japan, for artists to return after a period of vigorous exploration to an evaluation of traditional values in their old age. This approach presupposes encounters with mythical spaces that transcend all historical fact. Though characterized by a different circuit, this too is a kind of traditionalism. Tradition is wide; therefore, at the necessary time, it will allow free interpretation. But tradition is mighty and so will always invalidate any mistaken interpretations.

I have always regarded the Japanese architectural tradition seriously and through my association with it evolved a number of definitions concerning the character of Japanese space. The Japanese architectural tradition has provided me with both concepts and methods fundamental to my architecture at the present. It paved the way for my abstract architecture.

Today, tradition no longer occupies my thoughts. I regard present reversions to tradition and history as being nothing more than interludes, and I suspect that soon the second act of Modern architecture will begin, and it will begin with a redifinition of function.

Orderly, geometric identical steel-and-glass highrise buildings arranged along a spine vanishing to a point such as those in *la ville radieuse* crystallized the method and thought of architecture of the 1920s. But history left its dreams unfulfilled with *la ville radieuse* being only an ephemeral, bright apparition in architectural history.

From the early stage of my career, my concept of the city connoted chaos. Nonetheless, I still have great respect for *la ville radieuse* as a summation of the spirit of the 1920s. Its blueprints are fiction, but not illusion.

A rigorously ordered, transparent building of steel and glass was once planned and such revolutionary answers to the issue of the combination of form and function demonstrated the essential nature of the Modern architecture of the 1920s. This outstanding architect of the time created an almost religious regularity between form and function. He strove to produce maximum meaning through minimum vocabulary and syntax. Although one system and one form unifies their entire spaces, this was not his final goal. He sought unbounded freedom above all. My initial goal was to evoke definite expressions in a single space by using one theme and a minimum number of operations. While responding to Japanese architectural tradition, I had the greatest admiration for the masters who produced splendid solutions to the question of function and form operating within a different environment but a common context.

I no longer attempt to unify all spatial elements for the sake of one major theme, even at this new stage in my career, I sense a freedom in using minimal elements and syntax. For this reason, I revere the architect who produced primary spaces in steel and glass for the sake of ordering everything to a single intention.

It is unlikely that the Modern architecture of the 1920s would, if resuscitated, have any meaning. In the early part of my career, I tried not to follow the way of Western Modern architecture via its Japanese counterpart. An emotional encounter with the Japanese architectural heritage encouraged me to give up my former speciality for architecture and helped me choose my architectural starting point. This led me to freeze temporarily the admiration I had then for the architecture of the 1920s. Then, following its own particular contextual course, my own architecture gradually approached the machine, that crystallization of the spirit of the 1920s. I even now employ the same word. My passage through the spirit of the 1920s was essential.

Since I do not believe in the existence of total meaninglessness, I am convinced that something relative can result even from elements that have lost meaning and have reduced to the zero degree. A major theme of my work, the search for zero degree established a context in which meaning was eliminated from symbolic space. I do not plan to return along the path I have trod but turn to start again in a new direction. My new destination is a primary space, a functional space. Since what I call my second style, I have used various adjectives to describe the points I have passed: neutral, inorganic, naked, and so on. Tangents drawn through these points all meet in the domain of the machine. Since the late 1970s, the machine has been my major theme.

I selected the machine, one of the elements that is thought to have made Modern architecture barren, as a means of visualizing my own ideas about architecture. Though this may look an anachronism, it is, in fact something that has autonomously developed along the path my architecture has followed.

If symbolic meanings remain, they are stripped away. Parallel with this, a check operation is performed to halt all movement in the direction of conceptual assembly. I call a machine a physical system in which objects are simply joined together in a *sachlich* manner.

Unquestioning faith in technology resulted in *la ville radieuse* and the glass skyscraper. The machine as an architectural analogy connoted sleekness, clarity, and unity. The outstanding architects of the 1920s had a vision of the near future of society and the city. Their brilliant projects were happy synchronizations of the fact and functions in a period of social revolution.

The machine I am attempting to put together is a set of parts with zero meaning. Even I am not certain what rules I shall find most suitable for the joining of such parts. Anarchy and clumsiness are parts of both the city and technology that arrest my attention at the present. My zero-degree machine will be assembled under the same conditions as the machine used as an architectural analogy in the 1920s, since it will have *function* as its keyword. But my machine will not be international. It will have a name and nationality clearly indicated.

—Kazuo Shinohara

Japanese tradition was of profound import to Shinohara while a student, and his personal comprehension of it was incorporated in his first residential work e Kugayama House, Tokyo (1954). "I selected the elevated floor system, since it is historically one of the two prototypical forms of Japanese houses... the (interior) finishes expressed my longing for things Japanese." In what he describes as his first phase, he employed the lightweight timber construction, the beaten earth floor (such as House with an Earthen Floor, Karuizawa, 1963), and the irrational, non-functioning 'wasteful spaces' of Japan's primordial tradition.

His second phase was intimated in the Uncompleted House, Tokyo (1970) involved the use of the cube as the exterior shell of the house and a 'fissure space' for the centre of the interior. It was not until the Cubic Forest House, Kawasaki (1971) that the second phase came to fruition in the raw neutrality of spaces and cruel and characterless exteriors. His disaffection with vernacular solutions reared its head more and more... "tradition is always powerful and will always find ways of invalidating any mistaken interpretation."

His work continued to increase in 'savagery', with heavy concrete slanting roofs and more extreme design solutions. The House in Karuizawa (1975), was fractured into two curved segments, while the House in Itoshima (1976) had been butchered into two halves. Shinohara was now entering what he calls his third phase, which was officially reached in the House of Uehara, Tokyo (1976). Shinohara's intent to completely divest things of sentimental content is manifest in this phase. The House in Uehara is seminal 'savage forest', a kaleidoscopic disorientation effected by the awkward concrete columns and braces reaching out at contentious 45-degree angles. He is now trying to construct a 'zero-degree machine', which will be assembled under the same conditions as the machine that was was used in the architectural analogy in the 1920s, since it will have function as its keyword. But his machine will not be international, for its name and nationality will be clearly indicated.

Like Isozaki's, his work has proceeded through three phases or 'manners', and their two architectural lives read like a tale of two metamorphoses. Whereas Isozaki's work has advanced from the pugnacious, drunken modern forms of his adolescence and assumed a more dignified mien befitting his conception of design-maturity, Shinohara's projects have moved from a tentative, virginal and introspective tradition to the more pitiless and atrocious modernities of his own maturity. His preferred theory of history is the retrogressive one, which insists that, for all our efforts, we will never reach civilization, and must follow our pre-ordained route to perfidy.

—Chris Fawcett

SHIRAI, Seiichi.
Japanese. Born in Kyoto, 5 February 1905. Studied philosophy and architectural history at the Karl Reprecht University, Heidelberg, Germany, and the Friedrich Humboldt University, Berlin, under Karl Jaspers and Max Desoir, 1928-31. Married Teruko Kawamura in 1938; children: Hyōsuke and Ikuma. Director, Shirai Architectural Institute, Tokyo, 1935, until his death in 1983. Recipient: Kotaro Takamura Award, 1960; *Architectural Annal* Prize, 1969; Architectural Institute of Japan Award, 1969; Mainichi Art Award, 1970. *Died* (in Kyoto) *22 November 1983.*

Works:

1936 Kawamura House, Tokyo

1937   Kanki-sō (house), Shizueka Prefecture, Japan
1942   Shimanaka Mountain Lodge, Nagano Prefecture, Japan
1950/
51   Akinomiya Village Office, Akita Prefecture, Japan
1954/
55   Atomic Bomb Memorial Building (project)
1955   Hansobo Buddhist Temple (project)
1955/
56   Matsuida Town Office, Gunma Prefecture, Japan
1956   Ogachi Town Office, Akita Prefecture, Japan
1958   Hondō of the Zenshoji (main part of a Buddhist temple), Tokyo
1962/
63   Ohato Branch of the Shinwa Bank, Nagasaki Prefecture, Japan
1963   Tokyo Branch of the Shinwa Bank
1963/
65   Shicho-sha (private house), Kureha, Toyama, Japan
1966/
75   Shinwa Bank Head Office, Sasebo, Nagasaki Prefecture, Japan
1967/
70   Kohaku-an (Shirai House), Ebara-cho, Nakano-ku, Tokyo
1968/
71   Sakuestsu-ken (private house), Negishi-cho, Yokote, Akita Prefecture, Japan
1971/
72   Shiribetsusan-ryo (villa residence for a pharmaceutical company), Hokkaido, Japan
     St. Sebastian House (classroom), Ibaraki Christian Junior College, Ibaraki Prefecture, Japan
1972/
74   NOA Building, Tokyo

1974   Sanat Chiara Chapel, Ibaraki Christian Junior College, Ibaraki Prefecture, Japan
1980   Shoto Museum, Shibuya Ward, Tokyo
1981   Sekisuikan-Shizuoka Municipal Art Museum, Shizuoka Prefecture, Japan

Publications:

By SHIRAI: Book—*Buddhism and Architecture,* volume 12 of the *Complete Works of World Architecture,* Tokyo 1960; *Koshikyo-shocho* [The World of my challigraphy], 3 volumes, Tokyo 1970, 1976, 1978; articles—"Tendan" in *Shinkenchiku* (Tokyo), September 1955; "Stone Buddhist Images of China" in *Shinkenchiku* (Tokyo), October 1955; "Something Jomon-like" in *Shinkenchiku* (Tokyo), August 1956; "Tofu" in *Living Design* (Tokyo), October 1956; "Meshi" in *Living Design* (Tokyo), November 1956; "Taian no nijo" in *Shinkenchiku* (Tokyo), August 1957; "On Carlo Scarpa" in *Space Design* (Tokyo), June 1977; "Bruno Taut: Memorandum" in *Space Design* (Tokyo), December 1978.

On SHIRAI: books—*Seiichi Shirai,* volume 9 of *The Complete Works of Contemporary Japanese Architects* by Isamu Kurita, Tokyo 1970; *The Architecture of Seiichi Shirai* by Takashi Hasegawa and others, Tokyo 1974; *Seiichi Shirai,* edited by Aiko Hasegawa, Tokyo 1976; *The Architecture of Seiichi Shirai and His World,* edited by Noboru Kawazoe, Tokyo 1978; *Study of the Works of Seiichi Shirai,* Tokyo 1978; articles—"Zenshoji Temple" in *Kenchiku Bunka* (Tokyo), June 1963; "Residence on Kureha Hill" in *Kenchiku Bunka* (Tokyo), January 1966; "Debut Works of Architects" in *Kokusai Kentiku* (Tokyo), October 1966; "The Noah Building" in

Japan Architect (Tokyo), February 1975; "Sei'ichi Shirai," special issue of *Space Design* (Tokyo), January 1976; "Shibuya Ward Shoto Museum of Art" in *Approach* (Tokyo), Winter 1980; "Shoto Museum" in *Japan Architect* (Tokyo), May 1981; "Sekisuikan-Shizuoka Municipal Serizawa Keisuke Art Museum" in *Kenchiku Bunka* (Tokyo), October 1981.

Bibliography—*Sei'ichi Shirai: Japanese Architect of the Alternative* by James P. Noffsinger, Monticello, Illinois 1982.

As the noted writer Junichiro Tanizaki observed, Japanese architecture begins with the spreading of a roof over the land to create a domain of shadows, which is then paritioned as necessary. One might say, on the other hand, that Western architecture begins with the creation of the wall in vertical contradistinction to the land. Despite the century of modernization and the apparent adaptation to Western building methods, the Japanese, lacking a tradition of masonry construction, have yet to exploit fully the architecture qualities of walls.

Educated in Europe (where he studied German philosophy) but sensitive to traditional Japanese culture, Seiichi Shirai was very conscious of this. Perhaps no other Japanese architect is so aware of what one might call the existential meaning of the wall and of the expressive potential of wall surfaces.

The Kaisho-kan and the NOA Building are two exercises in the startling juxtaposition (in the former, lateral; in the latter, vertical) of roughly dressed stone and slick metal panels. The facade of his famous Shinwa Bank Head Office in Sasebo consists of two seemingly unconnected masses: one a dark, bronze mass on a white, stone base and the other, a white,

Seiichi Shirai: Hono of the Zenshoji, Tokyo, 1958.

travertine mass cantilevered from a dark core. Unlike, say, Louis Kahn, his concern for walls is not structuralist. Through the interplay of different tactile and visual values, Shirai compels us to confront the wall as surface.

His buildings repel the causal visitor. In the Kaisho-kan, the oddly shaped windows, deliberately unaligned, seem to encode some recondite wisdom or the enigmatic language of a secret fraternal society. In the Shinwa Bank, the building's base literally curls away from the sidewalk like a fastidious man who finds himself in low company.

Entry (i.e., the penetration of the wall), as one might expect, is never a simple matter in a Shirai building. This is true even in his earliest work. In the residence called Kanki-so, built in the 1930s, an exterior stairway takes one to the second floor terrace from which entrance is effected. Inside, one finds oneself on a theatrically raised stage with carved balustrade, from which one steps down into a whitewashed room with dark, exposed timber members and a fireplace at the other end. There is the same (sometimes exaggerated) sense of drama in his other works. In the Kaisho-kam, which is, of all things, a computer center, the prevailing image is distinctly sexual: one enters via a thin slit in the sandstone-faced front of the building. The same overtly womb-like image is used for the entrance to the NOA Building. It is, however, his unbuilt project for the Atomic Bomb Building, designed to house drawings of the catastrophe, which most graphically expresses the theme of rebirth or resurrection. The actual exhibition area is a white volume cantilevered from a dark core, standing aloof and protected by a moat of water. One enters from a separate building, via a tunnel from which one rises by a stairway inside the core, which is lit from above.

His interiors are often sealed, artifically lit spaces. Shirai has remarked that philosophy is born only where there is enclosure and that the only truly enclosed space in traditional Japanese architecture is the tea-ceremony room. In the sense that his spaces turn the visitor back onto himself and are essentially contemplative, Shirai's work is in great contrast to much of postwar Japanese architecture, which was long preoccupied with technological utopia and the rapidly growing economy.

His Japanese-style buildings, too, are striking, but it is his so-called Western buildings that are the most remarkable for their somewhat eccentric individuality and for the commentary that they make on modern society by the aloofness of their external forms and the reflective quality of their inner spaces.

—Hiroshi Watanabe

SIMONDS, John Ormsbee

American. Born in Jamestown, North Dakota, 11 March 1913. Educated at Michigan State University, East Lansing, 1930-35 (Arnold Scheele Award), B.S. in Landscape Architecture 1935; Graduate School of Design, Harvard University, Cambridge, Massachusetts, under Joseph Hudnut, Bremer Pond, Walter Chambers, Marcel Breuer and Walter Gropius, 1963-39 (Topiarian Cup, 1938; Samuel Hershey Prize, 1938; Eugene Dodd Medal, 1939), M. Landscape Arch. 1939. Served as a site planner for war housing and military construction during World War II. Married Marjorie C. Todd in 1943; children: Taye, Todd, Polly and Leslie. Park Planner and Construction Supervisor, Michigan State Department of Parks, in the Upper Peninsula, 1935-36; Partner, Simonds and Simonds, landscape architects, Pittsburgh, 1939-70, and Collins, Simonds and Simonds, landscape architects-planners, Washington, D.C. and Pittsburgh, 1952-70. Since 1970, Senior Partner (Emeritus since 1983), EPD: The Environmental Planning and Design Partnership, Pittsburgh and Miami Lakes, Florida (partners:

Philip Douglas Simonds; Paul Dorr Wolfe; C. Richard Hays; Geoffrey L. Rausch; Jack R. Scholl). Instructor in Site, Community, Urban and Regional Planning, Department of Architecture, Carnegie Institute of Technology, Pittsburgh, 1955-67. Chairman of the Committee on Education, 1952-53, Vice-President, 1959-63, Member of the Executive Committee, 1959-67, President, 1963-65, and Chairman of the Committee on the Profession, 1961-63, American Society of Landscape Architects, and President of the ASLA Foundation, 1965-67; United States Consultant on Community Planning, Inter-American Center for Housing and Planning, Bogota, Colombia, 1960, 1961; Member of the Executive Council, Harvard Graduate School of Design Alumni Association, 1960-63; Founding Member, Interprofessional Commission on Environmental Design, 1963; Member, Joint Committee on the National Capitol, 1964-65; Chairman, Urban Parks and Open Spaces Panel, White House Conference, 1965; Member of the Board of Urban Advisers, Federal Highway Administration, 1966-68; Chairman, Design Awards Jury, Landscape Architecture and Conservation, United States Army Corps of Engineers, 1968; Member, President's Task Force on Resources and the Environment, 1968-70; Chairman, Panel on Environmental Impact Statements, Interprofessional Commission on Environmental Design, Airlie Conference, 1972; Board Member, Hubbard Educational Trust, 1974; Member of the Governor's Resource Management Task Force, Florida, 1979-80. Exhibitions: American Society of Landscape Architects exhibitions, 1945-75. Recipient: Honor Awards in the categories of community planning, housing, civic design, parks and recreation, school and campus planning, transportation, and environmental design, from the American Society of Landscape Architects; Honorary Citation, ASLA, Pennsylvania Chapter, 1968, ASLA Medal, 1973; Top Men of the Year Citation, *Engineering News-Record*, 1973; Charles L. Hutchinson Medal, Chicago Horticultural Society, 1979; Sigma Lambda Alpha Award, Council of Educators in Landscape Architecture, 1979. D.Sc.: Michigan State University, 1968. Fellow, American Society of Landscape Architects, 1965; Associate, National Academy of Design, 1969; Honorary Associate, American Institute of Architects, Pennsylvania Chapter. Fellow, Royal Academy of Design, London, 1970; Honorary Corresponding Member, Royal Town Planning Institute, London, 1973. Address: The Loft, 17 Penhurst Road, Pittsburgh, Pennsylvania 15202, U.S.A.

Works (landscape architecture/planning):

1936 Marquette State Park, Michigan
1939/
   55 Site and landscape planning for more than 200 private residences and estates in Pennsylvania, Ohio, Indiana and Michigan
1947/
   49 Ten prototype parklets, The City of Pittsburgh
1952 North Allegheny High School and Campus, Allegheny County, Pennsylvania (with Mitchell and Ritchey)
   Aviary/Conservatory, Pittsburgh (with Button and McLean)
   Broadhead Manor (public housing community), Pittsburgh (with Mitchell and Retchey)
   Beechwood Park and Swimming Pool, Pittsburgh (with B. Kenneth Johnstone and Associates)
   Greater Pittsburgh Airport (with Joseph Hoover)
   John Kane Hospital, Allegheny County, Pennsylvania (with Mitchell and Ritchey)
   General Medical Hospital, Pittsburgh (with Mitchell and Ritchey)
   North View Heights (public housing community), Summer Hill, Pittsburgh (with Mitchell and Ritchey)

1953 Mellon Square, Pittsburgh (with Mitchell and Ritchey)
   St. Clair Hospital, Allegheny County, Pennsylvania (with Kuhn, Newcomer and Valentour)
   Lower Hill Redevelopment, Pittsburgh (with Mitchell and Ritchey)
1954 North Allegheny Elementary School, Allegheny County, Pennsylvania (with Mitchell and Ritchey)
   Fraternities, Carnegie Tech, Pittsburgh (with Lawrence and Anthony Wolfe)
   Civic Auditorium, Pittsburgh (with Mitchell and Ritchey)
   Sewickley Academy, Pennsylvania (with B. Kenneth Johnstone)
1955 Cannon-McMillan High School, Cannonsburg, Pennsylvania (with Kuhn, Newcomer and Valentour)
   Improvement program for the Pittsburgh City Reservoirs
   Seton Hill College Campus, Pennsylvania (with Celli-Flynn)
   United States Army Nike Housing (5 sites), Allegheny County, Pennsylvania
1956 Redevelopment plan for Rankin, Pennsylvania
   North Triangle Redevelopment, Philadelphia (with Lester A. Collins)
   Clara Barton School, Allegheny County, Pennsylvania (with Button and McLean)
   Improvements to Fort Meade, Maryland (with Lester A. Collins)
1957 Grandview Park, Pittsburgh
   Equitable Plaza, Pittsburgh (with Schell and Deeter)
   Mt. Lebanon High School Campus and Fields, Mt. Lebanon, Pennsylvania (with Kuhn, Newcomber and Valentour)
   Lockhaven Hospital, Lockhaven, Pennsylvania (with B. Kenneth Johnstone)
   Physically Handicapped Children's School, Allegheny County, Pennsylvania (with B. Kenneth Johnstone)
1958 Sewickley Heights Estates, Pennsylvania
   Development plan for Allegheny College Campus, Meadville, Pennsylvania
   Allegheny Center Redevelopment, Pittsburgh (with Mitchell and Ritchey)
   Santee Fill, Annapolis Campus, Maryland (with Lester A. Collins)
   Children's Hospital, Pittsburgh (with B. Kenneth Johnstone)
1959 Chautauqua Institution Campus, Chautauqua, New York (with Lester A. Collins)
   Allegheny County Regional Park System, Pennsylvania (with Griswold, Winters and Swain, and Ezra Stiles)
1960 Physical Education Complex, University of Pittsburgh (with Mitchell and Ritchey)
   Underground Zoo, Pittsburgh (with Lawrence and Anthony Wolfe)
   East Hills Housing (Action Housing), Pittsburgh (demonstration Planned Unit Development project; with Walter Gropius, Josep Lluis Sert, Carl Koch, and B. Kenneth Johnstone)
   St. Thomas of the Fields, Allegheny County, Pennsylvania (with John Pekruhn)
1960 Miami Lakes New Town, Miami Lakes, Florida (with Lester A. Collins)
1961 Recreation study for the Kinzua Reservoir, Warren County, Pennsylvania
   Comprehensive plan for Clairton, Pennsylvania
   Pittsburgh Stadium and Riverfront Park (with Deeter, Ritchey and Sippel)
   Westinghouse Research Center, Pittsburgh (with Deeter, Ritchey and Sippel)
1962 Conceptual plans for Wacker Drive, Chicago (with Barton-Aschman)
   Mount Union Public Housing Community, Pennsylvania (with Curry, Martin and Taylor)

John Ormsbee Simonds: Pelican Bay Coastal Community, Collier County, Florida, 1984.

1963 Recreation plan for Twelve Mile Island, Allegheny County, Pennsylvania (project)
1964 Shopping Mall, East Liberty, Pennsylvania
1964 Master Plan for Chicago Botanic Garden, Chicago
1965 Allegheny Commons (revised master development plan), Pittsburgh
Virginia Outdoor Recreation Study
1966 Comprehensive parks and recreation plan for Baltimore
Downtown urban renewal plan for Parkersburg, West Virginia
Founder's Square, Louisville, Kentucky (with Lawrence Melillo)
1967 Redevelopment plan for the central area of McLean, Virginia
Master plan for the proposed community of Tatoosh, Washington (project)
Washington Road Shopping Mall, Mt. Lebanon Township, Pennsylvania
1968 Environmental action plan for Chattanooga and Hamilton County, Tennessee
1968 Landscape architecture for the Metropolitan Area Transit Authority, Washington, D.C.
Jacaranda (planned community of 9 square miles), Broward County, Florida
Model Cities Rehabilitation Plan for the Mott-Haven District, New York
1969 Center City Redevelopment, Cumberland, Maryland
Multiple use opportunities plan, East-West Freeway, Milwaukee

1970 Downtown urban renewal plan for Huntington, West Virginia
Riverfront, Louisville, Kentucky (with Lawrence Melillo, and Doxiades and Associates)
Transit Expressway Revenue Line, Allegheny County, Pennsylvania (project; as planning consultant)
Fermont New Town Feasibility Study and Plan, Quebec
1971 Master plan for Ohiopyle State Park, Pennsylvania
Development plans for the new community of Saga Bay, Dade County, Florida
Highway illumination concept plan, Virginia Department of Highways (with Hayes, Seay, Mattern and Mattern)
The Springs (new community), Orlando, Florida (with Nils Sweitzer)
1972 Master plan for Fisher Island, Dade County, Florida (project)
Opportunity Park and Redevelopment, Akron, Ohio
Cary Arboretum, Duchess County, New York
Revised master plan for the Missouri Botanic Garden, St. Louis
Corridor location, design and multiple use opportunities plan, Interstate Highway 110, Pensacola, Florida (with Beiswenger, Hoch and Associates)
Location alternatives, Leesburg, Virginia Bypass

1973 Space utilization study, Interstate Highways 64 and 77, Charleston, West Virginia
Development plan for the waterfront, Toledo, Ohio
Multimodal transportation study for Pennsylvania state park and recreation areas (project)
Shoreline protection and development program, Lake Ontario, Finger Lakes Region, New York
Environmental improvement study of Highway VA I-66, Fairfax and Arlington Counties, Virginia
1974 Riverbend Plaza, South Bend, Indiana (with Clyde E. Williams and Associates)
1974/
82 Regional Center Development and Master Plan, Weston, Florida
1975 Transportation alternatives study, I-66 Corridor, Fairfax and Arlington Counties, Virginia (with Howard, Needles, Tammen and Bergendoff)
1976 Revised master plan and site development, Holden Arboretum, Mentor, Ohio
Comprehensive plan for St. George Island, Franklin County, Florida
Development plan for West Palm Beach, Florida
Master plan for the new community of Pelican Bay, Florida
ITT Community Development Corporation 100 square mile land replanning, Florida

Plan for Key Island, Naples, Florida
1977 Campus planning, Pennsylvania State University, University Park
Pennsylvania National Cemetery, Indiantown Gap (with Burt, Hill and Associates)
Neville Island Regional Park, Allegheny County, Pennsylvania
Beachfront, Hollywood, Florida (project)
Corridor study, Grant Street, Pittsburgh (project)
1978 Toledo International Park, Ohio (project)
Dade County Marina, Florida (project)
Plan for the Carnegie Mellon University Campus, Pittsburgh (project)
1979/
80 Riverfront Study, Saginaw, Michigan
1980/
81 Waterfront Recreation Study, Lee County, Florida
1981 Blue Ridge Parkway Feeder Link Alternatives, North Carolina
1982 Office and Industrial Park Master Plan, Broward County, Florida
1982/
83 Riverfront Study, Fort Lauderdale, Florida
1984 Las Olas Streetscape and Trafficway improvements, Fort Lauderdale, Florida
Development Plans for six new community parks, Collier County, Florida

Publications:

By SIMONDS: books—*Landscape Architecture: The Shaping of Man's Natural Environment*, New York 1961, revised as *Landscape Architecture: A Manual of Site Planning and Design*, New York 1983; *A Report on the Profession of Landscape Architecture*, editor, Washington, D.C. 1963; *Virginia's Commonwealth*, editor, Richmond 1965; introduction to *Landscape Gardening* by Andrew Jackson Downing, New York 1967; *The Freeway in the City*, editor, Washington, D.C. 1968; *Outdoor Recreation Facilities Manual*, U.S. Army Corps of Engineers, Washington, D.C. 1973; contributions to *Encyclopaedia of Urban Planning*, edited by Arnold Whittick, New York 1974; *Earthscape: A Manual of Environmental Planning*, New York 1978; articles—"Miami Lakes New Town" in *Parks and Recreation* (Washington, D.C.), October 1970; "The Mobile Society: A Look to the Future" in *Consulting Engineer* (New York), March/April 1974; "Self-Destruction of an Island Paradise" in *Landscape Architecture* (Louisville, Kentucky), January 1976; "From Scrabble and Ooze" in *Landscape Architecture* (Louisville, Kentucky), March 1978.

On SIMONDS: articles—"Figures in a Landscape" in *Landscape Architecture* (Louisville, Kentucky), January 1964; article in *The Engineering News Record* (New York), 9 March 1972; article in *AIA Journal* (Washington, D.C.), October 1978.

The work of the landscape architect, or "architect of the landscape," is the design of functional and expressive out of door spaces and places. These are created within the context of the natural and manbuilt environment, and range in scope and complexity from a child's playlot to a recreational park, university campus, or the conceptual planning of a community or new town.

On larger commissions the landscape architect often serves as a member of a closely coordinated professional team, which includes architects, engineers, planners, and scientist-advisers. A generalist, the landscape architect brings to the planning-design process specialized training in the physical sciences—such as physiography, geology, hydrology, biology, and ecology—and a feeling for the land, human relationships and design.

The past several decades have witnessed a remarkable evolution in the practice of landscape architecture. Within this brief span of time the emphasis has shifted from the design of large estates and sumptuous resorts for the wealthy to subdivisions, public works projects, public housing, urban renewal, military installations, freeway improvements, national, state and urban parks—and more recently to river basin studies and comprehensive resource planning. It has been the privilege of the members of our firm to have had an active role in this dynamic transformation.

—John Ormsbee Simonds

John Ormsbee Simonds is a founding partner of Environmental Planning and Design, a firm that consists of more than thirty professionals who are experienced in all phases of landscape architecture and planning. It has engaged in more than 500 projects since the founding of the original partnership in 1939. The firm is national in scope, and its work includes programs in regional development, urban renewal, and municipal comprehensive planning and zoning. The office engages in the design of waterfront and water-related projects, pedestrian malls, downtown urban plazas and botanical gardens. It plans industrial sites, highway and transit facilities, and park and recreational space and serves a large variety of institutions including hospitals, schools, and churches.

Since such work demands highly complex forms of collaboration, it is difficult to assess Simonds as an individual designer. Because of the immense success of his firm in both its volume and quality of work, Simonds must by considered first as an immensely skillful specialist, a person who knows how to respond to the expressed needs of many segments of society, how to formulate problems and agree upon alternatives. His books, most notably *Landscape Architecture: The Shaping of Man's Natural Environment*, reveal a philosophy of planning rooted in a knowledge of historical forms enriched by extensive travel as a young man in Japan, Korea, China, Burma, Bali, India, and Tibet. By his own account, his travels taught him that "one plans not places or spaces or things—one plans experiences.... Form must take its shape from the planned experience, rather than the experience from the preconceived form.... The living, pulsing, vital experience, if conceived as a diagram of harmonious relationships, will develop its own expressive forms. And the forms evolved will be as organic as the shell of the nautilus; and perhaps, if the plan is successful, they may be as beautiful."

—Mildred F. Schmertz

SIREN, Heikki.
Finnish. Born in Helsinki, 5 October 1918. Educated at Suomalainen Yhteiskoulu, Helsinki, matriculated 1939; Technical University, Helsinki, under J. S. Siren, Dip.Arch. 1946. Served in the Finnish Army, 1939-45: Lieutenant. Married the architect Kaija Tuominen (i.e., Kaija Siren, *q.v.*), in 1944; children: Kirsi, Sara, Jukka and Hannu. Worked in the office of Professor J. S. Sirén, Helsinki, 1944-48. Since 1949, Partner, with Kaija Siren, Arkkitehtitoimisto Kaija ja Heikki Siren, Helsinki; branch office established in Linz, Austria, 1962-74, Kotka Finland, 1969-75, and Zurich, Switzerland, 1979-83. Special teacher of architecture, Helsinki University of Technology, 1957-58; Guest Lecturer, University of Technology, Trondheim, Norway, 1960; Director, Architectural Seminar, University of Technology, Vienna, 1966. Exhibitions: *Bienal,* Sao Paulo, 1957, 1961; *Exposition d'Art Contemporain* (own stand), Paris, 1963. Recipient: Väino Vähäkallio Fellowship, 1948; First Prize, Housing Reform Competition, Helsinki, 1953; Gold Medal, *Bienal,* Sao Paulo, 1957, 1961; First Prize, Brucknerhaus Concert Hall Competition, Linz, 1962; Auguste Perret Award, Union Internationale des Architectes, 1965; First Prize, Reichsbrucke Competition, Vienna, 1977; Silver Plaque, SAFA Finnish Architects Association, 1978; First Prize, Conference Palace Competition, Baghdad, 1978; Camillo Sitte Prize, Vienna, 1979; Architectural Prize, State of Finland, 1980; Medal of the Academy of Sciences, Finland, 1980; Grande Medaille d'Or, Academie d'Architecture, Paris, 1980; Medal of the University of Technology, Helsinki, 1984; Finnish Cultural Foundation Prize, 1984. Honorary Professor, Helsinki, 1970; Member, Finnish Academy of Technical Sciences, 1971; Honorary Doctor of Technology, University of Technology, Tampere, 1982; Foreign Member, Academie d'Architecture, Paris, 1983. Address: Arkkitehtitoimisto Kaija ja Heikki Siren, Lounaisväylä 8A, 00200 Helsinki 20, Finland.

Works (with Kaija Siren):

1948 Scenery for the play *Miriam,* Kansanteatteri, Helsinki
1949 Tomb of the Fallen, Tarvasjoki, Finland
1950 Apartment building, Kalevankatu 46, Helsinki
Apartment building, Savonkulma, Kuopio, Finland
1950/
73 Tech Town, Otaniemi, Finland
1951 Kankainen Manor House restoration, Kalvola, Finland
Tech Town Sauna, Otaniemi, Finland
1951/
60 Siren House, Lauttasaari, Helsinki
1952 Servin Mökki Restaurant, Otaniemi, Finland
Apartment building, Hatsalanpuisto, Kuopio, Finland
1953 Tuura Vacation House, Suomusjärvi, Finland
Soiniemi Villa, Vihtr, Finland
Tikkakoski Home for Children, Tiokkakoski, Finland
Apartment building, Otakallio 1, Otaniemi, Finland
1954 Small Stage, Finnish National Theatre, Helsinki
Kimmeltie Rowhouse Development, Tapiola, Finland
Scenery for the play *Wanderer,* Finnish National Theatre, Helsinki
Concert Hall, Lahti, Finland
Kontiontie Rowhouse Development, Tapiola, Finland
1955 Ylitalo Vacation House, Sjökulla, Finland
Leppäniemi Manor restoration, Loppi, Finland
Apartment building, Kivalterintie 18-20, Helsinki
Otsolahden Lämpö Garage, Tapiola, Finland
1956 Suomen Koneliike Office Building, Helsinki
Helkama Villa, Vihti, Finland
Otalaakso Apartment Building, Otaniemi, Finland
Apartment building, Kivalterintie 17-19, Helsinki
Apartment buildings, Ritokalliontie 1 and 3, Helsinki
Bockholm Sauna, Barösund, Finland
1956/
72 Shell Service Stations, Finland
1957 Otaharju Apartment House, Otaniemi, Finland
Aarnivalkea School, Tapiola, Finland
Aarnivalkea School Teachers' Apartments, Tapiola, Finland
Rowhouses, Näätätie 19, Helsinki
Chapel, Otaniemi, Finland
1958 Eskola Vacation House, Sjökulla, Finland
School, Kauklahti, Espoo, Finland
Housekeeper Institute, Kauniainen, Finland

1959 Otanotko Apartment Building, Otaniemi, Finland
       Otsonpesä Linked Houses, Tapiola, Finland
       House interior, Välskärinkatu 7, Helsinki
       Finlayson Industrial Building elevation, Tampere, Finland
1960 Maria Sauna, Iniö, Finland
       Olkahinen Elementary School, Aitolahti, Finland
       Rowhouses, Kanneltie, Helsinki
       Kehrääjä Apartment Building, Tapiola, Finland
       OSA I Apartment Building, Otaniemi, Finland
       Peurasaari School, Kemi, Finland
1961 Interior for the yacht *Kuohhuneiti*, Helsinki
       Water Tower, Loviisa, Finland
       Church, Orivesi, Finland
       J. S. Sirén Tombstone, Helsinki
       Alppilan Tehdastalo Building for small industries, Helsinki
       Finnish Workers' Savings Bank, Kotka, Finland
       Tapiolan Lämpö Central Garage, Tapiola, Finland
       Kauklahti Children's Complex, Espoo, Finland
1962 Interior for Valtimo KOP, Porvoo, Finland
       Karhuranta Apartment Building, Tapiola, Finland
       Sauna at Kankainen Manor, Kalvola, Finland
       Otsonlinna Apartment Building, Tapiola, Finland
       OAS II Apartment Building, Otaniemi, Finland
       Otakallio II Apartment Building, Otaniemi, Finland

       Iltarusko Rowhouses, Tapiola, Finland
       Finnish National Theatre restoration, Helsinki
       Pappilansalmi School, Hamina, Finland
       Complex for the Aged, Kauklahti, Espoo, Finland
       Apartment building, Kauklahti, Espoo, Finland
1963 New chapel and cemetery, Espoo, Finland
       Ympyräkeskus Office Building, Hamina, Finland
       Rowhouses development, Hagen, West Germany
       Helsinki Cathedral restoration, Helsinki (plan by J. S. Sirén)
       Oulu Oy Office Building, Oulu, Finland
       Pihlajamäki Shopping Centre, Helsinki
       Apartment buildings, Oravankatu 3-5, Karhula, Finland
       Apartment building development, North Tapiola, Finland
       Apartment building, Kauklahti, Espoo, Finland
       Siren stand, *Exposition d'Art Contemporain*, Paris
1964 Apartment building, Lounaisväylä 8, Helsinki
       Pusenius House, Kotka, Finland
       Rauma-Repola Kitchen Furniture (project)
       Apartment building, Pikalähetintie 14-18, Helsinki
       Nurmes Administration Building, Nurmes, Finland (plan by J. S. Sirén)
       Konela Automobile Repair Shop, Helsinki
1964/
  65 Bird House and Ostrich Hall, Korkeasaari Zoo, Helsinki
1965 Kallio Municipal Offices, Helsinki
       Finnish Workers' Savings Bank, Tampere, Finland

       Bank of Finland restoration, Vaasa, Finland
       Log cabins, Rantasalmi Oy, Finland
       Björkbodan Tehdas Oy Fittings, Finland
       Tapionsolu Linked Houses, Tapiola, Finland
1966 Shopping centre, North Tapiola, Finland
       Atrium House Development, Louhentie 1, Tapiola, Finland
       5 private houses, Tapiola, Finland
       Apartment building development, Kalliola, Kotka, Finland
       Residential development, Krefeld, West Germany
       Pieksämäki Savings Bank, Finland
1966/
  69 Lingonso Vacation Island, Barösund, Finland
1966/
  70 Polar houses and row houses, Finland
1967 Sisko Aho Tombstone, Helsinki
       Spiral staircase, Högfors, Finland
       Town Hall, Kankaanpää, Finland
       Tornionlaakso Savings Bank, Tornio, Finland
       Punjo Villa, Espoo, Finland
       Apartment building, Kääpäkatu 8, Karhula, Finland
1967/
  74 Vacation village, Lacanau, France
1968 Scenery for the play *Rosencrantz and Guildenstern Are Dead*, Finnish National Theatre, Helsinki
       Linked houses development, Polar Village, Vantaa, Finland
       KOP Circular Building, Helsinki
       Tapion Auto Office Building, Tapiola, Finland
       Tampereen Keskus Office Building, Tampere, Finland
       Oy Lohja Ab Directors' Residence, Lohja, Finland

Heikki and Kaija Siren: Chapel, Otaniemi, Finland, 1957.

Asko Kitchen Furniture (project)
1968/
71 Apartment house development, Ristinkallio, Karhula, Finland
1968/
74 Pirkkola Sports Park, Helsinki
1968/
76 Apartment building development, Karhuvuori, Kotka, Finland
1969 Kontula Parish Hall, Helsinki
Myllypuro Parish Hall, Helsinki
Espoonlahti Apartment Building, Espoo, Finland
House interior, Hollantilaisentie 1, Helsinki
Espoo Mixed Secondary School, Kauklahti, Espoo, Finland
Roinela Sauna, Järvenpää, Finland
1970 Apartment building, Jukolantie 11, Kouvola, Finland
"La Pierrefitte" attached houses development, Paris
Lauttasaari Co-Educational School, Helsinki
Apartment building, Kauklahti, Espoo, Finland
Parish Centre, Kankaanpää, Finland
1971 Oiva Soini Tombstone, Helsinki
Apartment building, Kääpäkatu 12, Karhula, Finland
Jussi Vacation House, Barösund, Finland
Co-operative Bank, Kotka, Finland
1971/
75 Sports Center, Kankaanpää, Finland
1972 Apartment building, Kymenlaaksonkatu 14, Kotka, Finland
Finnish Co-Educational School of Helsinki
"Johanna" Trawler
Björkholm Vacation House, Snappertuna, Finland
1973 Kaikka Vacation House, Barösund, Finland
Hakkarainen Vacation House, Bromary, Finland
Muurahainen Vacation House, Kangasala, Finland
Suulisniemi Apartment Building Development, Karhula, Finland
1974 Brucknerhaus Concert Hall, Linz, Austria
Apartment buildings, Kalliola, Kotka, Finland
Vitamaki Apartment Building, Kouvola, Finland
Town plan for Lentävänniemi, Tampere, Finland
Rank Xerox Head Office, Espoo, Finland
Utsjoki Golf Club and Restaurant, Karuizawa, Japan
Sapokan Vuokratalot Apartment Buildings, Kotka, Finland
1974/
75 Kolmio Apartment House Development, Kotka, Finland
1975 Viitapuisto Apartment Building, Kouvola, Finland
Log Buildings, Huvila Seppälä, Finland (project)
Raatimikko Business Building, Mikkeli, Finland
1976 Alatornio Parish Hall, Tornio, Finland
Golf Club, Onuma, Hokkaido, Japan
Vacation Centre, Hakone, Japan
1977 Juvatalo Office Building, Tapiola, Finland
Reichsbrücke, Vienna
1978 Opetustalo School of Economy, Helsinki
Conference Palace, Baghdad
1979 Lutheran Parishes Office Building, Helsinki
1981 Reichsbrucke, Vienna (as members of team)
1982 Conference Palace, Baghdad
1984 KOP Kamppi Offices, Helsinki
Dormitory and apartment buildings, Tech Town, Otaniemi, Finland
Housing development, Tapiola, Finland
1984 Scenery for the Finnish National Theatre, Helsinki
Finnish Embassy, Riyadh, Saudi Arabia

Publications:

On the SIRENS: books—*Arquitectura Finlandesa: Alvar Aalto, Heikki Siren, Reima Pietila*, Barcelona 1971; *Kaija and Heikki Siren, Architects,* edited by Erik Bruun and Sara Popivits, Helsinki 1977, Dusseldorf 1978; *Heikki and Kaija Siren: Finnish Design Team* by Lamia Doumato, Monticello, Illinois 1980; articles—"Kaija and Heikki Siren, Architects" in *Architettura* (Rome), no. 29, 1958; "Work of Heikki Siren" in *Kindaikenchiku* (Tokyo), no. 19, 1965; "The Northern Architects Kaija and Heikki Siren" in *Space Design* (Tokyo), no. 10, 1975.

The Finnish log-built village, old grey buildings with their fences, gates and courtyards; white plastered houses on the Mediterranean; restrained and disciplined wooden architecture that blends into the Japanese landscape—indigenous architecture has still some amazing power; it can move one with its simplicity and genuineness.

It is obvious that the lasting significance of these buildings stems from the strength of creation behind them. They do not only meet the given need, but also often rise beyond it to the non-rational quality of architecture. Instinct, intuition and imagination are integral to creative work of permanent value.

An architect's working methods arise from his own characteristic quality, his experience and his training. The stress laid on different aspects of planning varies, depending on the requirements and conditions of age. The special character of each project is the primary premise for planning, which may have a visionary, technological, aesthetic or purely morphological basis.

Still, a clear plan is absolutely vital, as it is a synthesis based on all aspects of the problem.

Max Reinhardt, an "architect" of the stage, said that even in his most fantastic productions he was operating in a sphere "only a hand's breadth" above reality.

Architecture creates the "stage" for human life, which has in itself all the elements for illusion. The unrestrained imagination of the designer can easily break the delicate balance that should exist between nature and the built environment.

The architect has to define the desired atmosphere, the relationship between the building and its surroundings, and then to find the appropriate means to create this intangible quality of the work.

—Kaija and Heikki Siren

The work of Kaija and Heikki Siren began in the 1950s and reached its first peak towards the end of the decade, when the University of Technology area in Otaniemi was built.

At that juncture Brutalism was beginning to spread throughout the world; a few years later Metabolism appeared in public for the first time, with utopic proposals for bearing constructions of great span and interchangeable secondary units, which later materialized in a simplified form. Then, under the influence of the demand for variability and flexibility, came what is called container architecture, the architecture of neutral cells in which it was often only possible to find one's bearings by means of various information systems—when it appeared both unnecessary and unavoidable to introduce industrialized building. The youth revolt in the U.S.A. led the way to dome and shelter architecture and the houseboats in Sausalito. On the other hand, the single family house facing a garden appeared to be a hopeless anachronism, while densely populated areas and high-rise buildings were thought to be a necessity.

Those who consciously experienced these tendencies and currents finally have had to accept with resignation that many of the waves have disappeared, leaving no trace in the sand. When the waters claimed there were a few rocks left on the beach,

recently covered but now once more a visible witness to their own abiding quality. If I am not mistaken, some of Kaija and Heikki Siren's buildings can be counted among these survivors.

Here we confront an architectural problem of long standing and one that will persist into the future. It concerns the relationship between form and space, the creation of a frame that does not limit human activity but facilitates it, the relationship between redundancy and information, the relationship between the known and the new. Undoubtedly it is sound architecture, not that of exaggeration and the grandiose gesture, which finds expression in the work of these architects—an architecture characterized by clarity and restraint.

The chapel of Otaniemi was one of the buildings which at that time made an abiding impression and exercised an influence on us younger architects on the Continent: two walls which enclose the forecourt and church area, a sloping roof, light coming in from the rear and a view over the altar area out into a natural setting—a simple house of brick and wood. Seldom has more been created by such simple means! This building, apparently so simple, contains, however, a set of problems which are worth thinking over. Much in modern architecture appears simple, but is in fact not simple, merely monotonous. True simplicity lies in that which has, so to speak, regained simplicity; it does not constitute the first step but the last step in a lengthy and laborious process. Simplicity is so rare today because we lack the patience and time to allow the form to mature. Thus some buildings strive to make an impression at any price, because some people—and rightly—revolt against monotony, but on the other hand do not have sufficient time or patience to make their way from the stage of great and unbridled gestures back to simplicity. For those actually participating in an epoch it is often difficult to realize when this stage of simplicity has been reached. One often has to be content with assumptions. Presumably the only criteria are stability in time and durability over a longer, if also limited, period of time.

Reflections on architecture are linked, beyond the rational, with values that are not based on reason. Heikki Siren once expressed this more simply. According to him, anything that cannot be grasped comes from the heart.

Anonymous indigenous architecture is one of the sources of inspiration for both these architects. What they find fascinating in it is not just its simplicity and originality, but the creative power, the unerring instinct.

Heikki Siren, who has himself designed stage-settings, labels architecture a stage for human life. If this formula is taken in earnest, we find that behind it lies hidden the idea that playfulness is a legitimate and necessary means in architecture. This element of playfulness is indeed found in their work. It does not force itself upon one; it appears instead with restraint; it is no guiding principle, merely a hint—for example, the white fencing outside the row houses on Kontiontie in Tapiola.

In any discussion of Finnish architecture the landscape typical of the country is often mentioned. In the Western world God and nature are typically conceived to be at different poles. For the Japanese, on the other hand, the divine reveals itself in nature, and nature is itself divine. Something of this latter concept is perceptible in the work of the Sirens, for otherwise it is difficult to understand why, for example, the natural setting seen through the glass altar wall in the Otaniemi chapel is permitted to be a part of the church area and why the cross does not stand inside the church, but in front of it, in the forest.

I have attempted here a few notes that may contribute to an understanding of the Sirens. Of course I hardly dare hope that I have succeeded in explaining very much, but I might add that, with Kaija and Heikki Siren, life and architecture complement one another: the simplicity, originality and sincerity of their own lives is reflected in their architecture.

—Jürgen Joedicke

SIREN, Kaija

Finnish. Born Katri Anna-Maija Helena Tuominen in Kotka, 23 October 1920. Educated at Kotkan Tyttölyseo, Kotka, matriculated 1939; Technical University, Helsinki, under J. S. Sirén, Dip. Arch. 1948. Married the architect Heikki Siren *q.v.*, in 1944; children: Kirsi, Sara, Jukka and Hannu. Since 1949, Partner, with Heikki Siren, Arkkitehtitoimisto Kaija ja Heikki Siren, Helsinki; branch office established in Linz, Austria, 1962-74, Kotka, Finland, 1969-75, and Zurich, Switzerland, 1979-83. Exhibitions: *Bienal,* Sao Paulo, 1957, 1961; Exposition d'Art Contemporain (own stand), Paris, 1963. Recipient: Gold Medal, *Bienal,* Sao Paulo, 1957, 1961; Auguste Perret Award, Union Internationale des Architectes, 1965; Architectural Prize, State of Finland, 1980; Grande Medaille d'Or, Academie d'Architecture, Paris, 1980; Finnish Cultural Foundation Prize, 1984. Foreign Member, Academie d'Architecture, Paris, 1983. Address: Arkkitehitoimisto Kaija ja Heikki Siren, Lounaisväylä 8A, 00200 Helsinki 20, Finland.

See SIREN, Heikki

SIZA Vieira, Alvaro Joaquim de Melo.

Portuguese. Born in Matosinhos, 25 June 1933. Educated at the University of Oporto School of Architecture, Portugal, under Fernando Tavora, 1949-55, Dip.Arch. 1955. Married Maria Antonia Marinho Leite in 1962 (died, 1973); children: Alvaro and Joan. Since 1954, in private practice, Porto, Portugal: worked with Fernando Tavora, 1955-58. Professor of Architecture, University of Oporto, Portugal, since 1965. Exhibitions: *Siza Arkitekt i Porto*, Copenhagen, 1975, and Aarhus, Denmark, 1976; *Alvaro Siza, arquitecto*, Barcelona, 1976; *Europa/America*, at the *Biennale*, Venice, 1978; *Alvaro Siza, architetto 1954-79*, Milan, 1979; *La Modernite—un projet inacheve*, Centre Georges Pompidou, Paris, 1982; *10 New Buildings*, Institute of Contemporary Arts, London, 1983. Correspondent, Academie d'Architecture, Paris, 1971. Address (office): Rua da Alegria 399, Porto 4000, Portugal.

Works:

1954/
57 Four houses, Afonso Henriques Avenue 394, Matosinhos, Portugal
1956/
59 Parish Center, Matosinhos, Portugal (partially built)
1957/
59 Carneiro de Melo House, Boavista Avenue, Porto
1958/
63 Boanova Restaurant, Avenue Marginal, Leca da Palmeira, Matosinhos, Portugal (with Alberto Neves, Antonio Meneres, Botelho Dias, and Joaquim Sampaio)
1958/
65 Quinta da Conceicad Swimming Pool, Matosinhos, Portugal
1959 Caulkers Monument, Porto (project: with Alcino Soutinho, Augusto Amaral, and the sculptor Lagoa)
1960 Factory canteen, Matosinhos, Portugal (demolished)
1960/
62 Rocha Ribeiro House, Duarte Pacheco 502, Maia, Portugal
1960/
63 Lordelo Cooperative Building, Prof. Augusto Nobre 193, Porto, Portugal

1961/
66 Leca Swimming Pool, Avenue Marginal, Leca da Palmeira, Matosinhos, Portugal (partially built)
1962/
65 Ferreiro da Costa House, Azenha Decima Street 258, Matosinhos, Portugal
1964/
68 Alves Costa House, Praia de Moledo, Meledo do Minho, Portugal
1965/
69 Alves Santos House, Padre Afonso Soares Street, Povoa do Varzim, Portugal
1966 Cotton warehouse, Sousa Aroso Street, Matosinhos, Portugal
1967 Motel, Coimbra, Portugal (project)
1967/
70 Manuel Magalhaes House, Combatentes Avenue 1954, Porto, Portugal
1968 Office Building, Porto, Portugal (project)
1969 Borges Bank, Vila do Conde, Portugal (project)
1970 Domus Cooperative Supermarket, Boavista Avenue 3324, Porto, portugal
1970/
72 Caxinas Housing Estate, Praia de Caxinas, Vila do Conde, Portugal (partially built)
1971 Alcino Cardoso House, Lugar da Gateira, Moledo do Minho, Portugal
1971/
74 Sottomayor Bank, Dr. Antonio José de Almeida, Oliveira de Azemeis, Portugal

1972 Mobil Housing Estate, Matosinhos, Portugal (project)
Marques Pinto House, Porto, Portugal (project)
Domus Cooperative Supermarket, Alvaro Gomes 112, Porto, Portugal
Housing estate, Ovar, Portugal (project)
1972/
73 Sottomayor Bank, Visconde Guedes Teixeira Avenue, Lamego, Portugal
1973 Housing estate, Ovar, Portugal (second project)
Gallery, Campo Alegre 1192, Porto, Portugal (partially built)
Azeitad House, Azeitad, Portugal (project)
1973/
76 Beires House, Alberto Pimentel Street, Povoa do Varzim, Portugal
1973/
77 Bonca Residents Association Housing, Boavista Avenue, Porto, Portugal
1974/
77 S. Victor Residents Association Housing, Senhora das Dores, Porto, Portugal
1975 Restaurant Pico do Areeiro, Madeira (project)
1976 Barredo Renewal, Fontetaurina 191-192, Porto, Portugal
Largo da Lada Barredo Renewal, Porto, Portugal (project)
1976/
77 Antonio Carlos House, S. Joao de Deus Street, Santo Tirso, Portugal

Alvaro Siza: Caxinas Housing Estate, Vila do Conde, Portugal, 1972.

1977 Francelos House, V. Nova de Gaia, Portugal (project)

1977/
79 Cooperative housing, Bairro da Malagueira, Evora, Portugal

1979 Görlitzer Bad Swimming Pool, Berlin (competition project)

1980/
82 Housing Group, Charlottenburg, Berlin (project)

Caixa General de Despositos Offices, Matosinhos, Portugal (project)

1980/
84 Banca Borges & Irmao Building, Vila do Conde, Portugal

Publications:

By SIZA: articles—in *Lotus 13* (Milan), December 1976; in *Proceedings of the Seminario Internacional de Arquitectura*, Santiago de Compostela, Spain 1977; in *Europa/America*, exhibition catalogue of the *Biennale*, Venice 1978; in *Arquitectura* (Lisbon), March 1979.

On SIZA: books—*Architektur 1940-1980* by Adolf Max Vogt, Berlin, Frankfurt and Vienna 1980; *La Modernite—un projet inachevé*, exhibition catalogue, by Jean-Philippe Chimot, Kenneth Frampton, Berthold Lubetkin and others, Paris 1982; *Ten New Buildings*, exhibition catalogue, by Martin Lazenby and Robert Maxwell, London 1983; articles—"Tres obras de Alvaro Siza" by Nuno Portas in *Arquitectura* (Lisbon), July 1960; "Un analisis de la obra de Alvaro Siza" by Pedro Vieira de Almeida in *Hogar y arquitectura* (Madrid), January 1967; "Archittettura recenti di Alvaro Siza" by Vittorio Gregotti and "Note sul significato dell'architettura di Alvaro Siza nell'Ambiente Portoghese" by Nuno Portas in *Controspazio* (Bari, Italy), September 1972; "Arquitecturas en Las Margenes" by José Rafael Moneo and "Alvaro Siza" by Oriol Bohigas in *Arquitecturas bis* (Barcelona), March 1976; "Alvaro Siza, architetto" by Bernard Huet and "Il metodo di Siza" by Pierluigi Nicolin in *Alvaro Siza, architetto 1954-79*, exhibition catalogue, Milan 1979; "Alvaro Siza Vieira—Projects and Achievements, 1970-1980," special issue of *Architecture d'aujourd'hui* (Paris), October 1980; "Alvaro Siza," special issue of *Architecture + Urbanism* (Tokyo), December 1980; "Name to Reckon With" in *Building Design* (London), 13 February 1981; "Alvaro Siza Vieira's Guggenheim Transformation" in *International Architect* (London), no. 4, 1981; "Echoes of the Portuguese Tradition" in *Arkkitehti* (Helsinki), no. 8, 1983; "Architecture as Modification," special issue of *Casabella* (Milan), January/February 1984; "Berlin Game" in *Building Design* (London), 17 February 1984; "Siza i Vieira: Banca a Vila do Conde" in *Domus* (Milan), November 1984.

*

Most of my works were never fulfilled; some of the things I did were carried out only in part, others were profoundly changed or destroyed.

That's only to be expected.

An architectonic proposition, whose aim it is to go deep into the existing transforming trends, into the clashes and strains that make up reality, a proposition that intends to be more than a passive materialization, refusing to reduce that same reality, analysing each of its aspects, one by one—that proposition can't find support on a fixed image, can't follow a linear evolution.

Nevertheless, and for the same reason, that proposition can't be ambiguous, neither can it restrain itself to a disciplinary discourse, however sure it seems to be.

Each design is bound to catch, with the utmost rigour, a precise moment of a flittering image in all its shades. The better you can recognize that flittering

quality of reality, the clearer must your design arise. It is the more vulnerable as it is true.

That may be the reason why only marginal works (a quiet dwelling, a holiday-house miles away) have been kept as they were originally designed.

This is the outcome of participation in a process of cultural transformation, of construction/destruction. But something remains. Pieces are kept here and there, inside ourselves, perhaps gathered by someone, leaving marks on space and on people, melting in a process of total transformation.

We are now putting them together, to make the spaces between them become images and give them a meaning and to make each of them have a meaning when faced with the others *sous la lumière*.

In that space there can be found the last little stone and the last little conflict.

We change space as we change ourselves—by pieces, confronted with "the other" collectively and individually.

Nature, the abode of man, and man, the creator of Nature, both absorb everything, embodying or rejecting it in a transitory way, as everything leaves its mark on them.

Departing from isolated pieces, we search the space that bears the pieces.

—Alvaro Siza

*

Possibly the most important characteristic of Alvaro Siza's work—that to which the new Portuguese architecture owes so much—is his ability to break down the stylistic elements of "Racionalismo" and recompose them so that they come to be part of "Manierismo." The Modernist tradition of Form expresses itself with originality in Siza's work in three different ways: in the autonomy of space; in relation to surroundings; and in method of positioning.

Siza's works are always based on unity of space and volume, and it is this that makes them stand out as autonomous objects. They are all comprehensible as artefacts in which, thanks to the handling of components, there is an absolute coherence of function and form, varied though they may all be in content and arrangement. Thus, in the case of the Magalhaes House, the walls, screens and pillars all play their part in implying the dialectic of continuous fluidity within finite and limited space; in contrast, the Sottomayor Bank in Oliveira de Azemis uses these same elements to give the impression of spatial fluidity, broken up, as it were, into an unlimited succession of independent sectors. The fundamental reasoning behind the finished work lies in the way in which space can be held under tension, always achieved through the use of familiar means in an ambiguous setting within the actual composition.

Architecture is fundamentally intended, then, as an independent unity of concept and form; but despite this independence, it always manages, without sacrificing its radicality, to accommodate well to its surroundings. All Siza's work can also be understood, therefore, as a response to the rural or urban context to which it belongs, despite the fact that this accommodation is never achieved through imitation, and certainly not in terms of those "environmental pre-existences" of which the Italians were so fond in the 1950s and 1960s. Siza is able to respond to the environment without detracting from the functional and stylistic identity of his architecture, and, moreover, he establishes an effective dialectical tension within it. In his plans for the Via Alfonso Henriques, Porto, he manages to make the new buildings stand out even though they are adapting to the existing curve of the street; they are integrated into the existing architecture in a now almost legendry manner. The way in which the surroundings are reflected in the mirror surface of the facade is characteristic of the way in which he visually re-integrates the urban landscape, without, however, affecting the independent value of his own contribution. Another example is the way in which the swimming pool at Leca hides between the structure of the roadway and the first rocks of the

beach, but nevertheless yields nothing of its own identity to its surroundings and does not disappear as though camouflaged. In the case of the residential complex in the Bonca district of Porto, Siza even seems to introduce a fundamental change of form and typology in the surroundings themselves, suggesting that architecture has within it the means of transformation—the view of the Modernists in their most optimistic moments; but he also makes a sufficient response to the basic topographical, as well as sociological and symbolic, elements of the residential area of which it forms a part.

The differences between (on the one hand) the Bonca development and (on the other) the incomplete Caxinas Housing Estate indicate that, when faced with the same conflicting objectives of autonomy versus appropriateness, Siza evolves very different solutions, depending on the individual situation, the physical, economic, productive and environmental needs. In this sense one might say that his designs are always based on situation—or that they are more appropriately defined according to the "contextual whole" than to any dogma of a priori assumptions—more of a conditioned response than an abstract ideology. Siza would without doubt have the approval of John Dewey, who defined research as "the controlled transformation of an indeterminate situation into one so determined in its constituent relations that it converts the separate elements of the original situation into a unified whole." In Siza's work the disruption and recomposition of Rationalist language has shown itself to be a fitting instrument for adaptation to the expressive force of situation.

—Oriol Bohigas

SKIDMORE, Louis.

American. Born in Lawrenceburg, Indiana, 8 April 1897. Educated at the Bradley Polytechnic Institute, now Bradley University, Peoria, Illinois, graduated 1917; Massachusetts Institute of Technology, Cambridge, 1921-24 (Rotch Special Student Prize, 1924), B.Arch. 1924; awarded Rotch Travelling Fellowship, 1926-29: Visiting Scholar, American Academy in Rome, 1927. Served in the United States Army, in England, 1918-19. Married Eloise Owings in 1930; children: Louis Jr. and Phillip. Worked for Maginnius and Walsh, 1924-26; Chief of Design, and Assistant to the General Manager, *Century of Progress Exposition,* Chicago, 1929-35. Co-Founding Partner with Nathaniel Owings, *q.v.,* Skidmore and Owings, Chicago, 1936-39 (established New York branch, 1937), and, with John Merrill, *q.v.,* Skidmore, Owings and Merrill, Chicago, New York, San Francisco, Portland, Oregon, Washington, D.C., etc., from 1939; retired from the firm in 1955. Served as President, New York Building Congress; Chairman, Advisory Council of the School of Architecture Princeton University, New Jersey; Consultant Architect to the United Nations, New York, and to the University of Michigan, Ann Arbor. Exhibitions: *Built in U.S.A. 1932-1944,* Museum of Modern Art, New York, 1944; *Skidmore, Owings and Merrill.* Museum of Modern Art, New York, 1950. Recipient: Medal of Honor, 1948, and Gold Medal, 1957, American Institute of Architects; Distinguished Alumni Award, Bradley University, 1952. LL.D.: Bradley University, 1952. Fellow, American Institute of Architects. *Died (in Winter Haven, Florida) 27 September 1962.*

Publications:

By SKIDMORE: book—illustrations for *Tudor in Architecture* by Richard Chamberlain, New York

1929; article—"New York Proposes a World Capital for the United Nations" in *Architectural Forum* (New York), November 1946.

See SKIDMORE, OWINGS AND MERRILL

SKIDMORE, OWINGS AND MERRILL.

Partnership; established in Chicago by Louis Skidmore, *q.v.*, and Nathaniel Owings, *q.v.*, as Skidmore and Owings, 1936, and with John Merrill, *q.v.*, as Skidmore, Owings and Merrill, 1939; branch offices established in New York, 1937, subsequently in San Francisco, Portland, Oregon, Washington, D.C., Boston, Los Angeles, Houston, Texas, and Denver, Colorado. Current Partners include: Bruce J. Graham, *q.v.*, Raul de Armas, Robert H. Armsby, David M. Childs, Walter H. Costa, James R. DeStefano, Robert Diamant, Lawrence S. Doane, William M. Drake, Jr., Thomas J. Eyerman, Richard C. Foster, Richard A. Giegenack, Marc E. Goldstein, Parambir S. Gujral, Robert A. Halvorson, Alan D. Hinklin, Robert P. Holmes, Robert A. Hutchins, Srinivasa Iyengar, Richard C. Keating, John L. Kriken, Diane Legge Lohan, Michael A. McCarthy, John O. Merrill, Jr., Leon Moed, Maris Peika, David A. Pugh, Adrian D. Smith, Kenneth A. Soldan, Douglas F. Stoker, Robert L. Wesley, Gordon L. Wildermuth, John H. Winkler and Carolina Y.C. Woo. Exhibition: *Skidmore, Owings and Merrill*, Museum of Modern Art, New York, 1950. Addresses: 33 West Monroe Street, Chicago, Illinois 60603; 220 East 42nd Street, New York, New York 10017; One Maritime Plaza, San Francisco, California 94111; 900 S.W. Fifth Avenue, Portland, Oregon 97204; 1201 Pennsylvania Avenue N.W., Washington, D.C. 20004; 334 Boylston Street, Boston, Massachusetts 02116; 70 Universal City Plaza, Universal City, California 91608; 400 One Shell Plaza, Houston, Texas 77002-4906; 1775 Sherman Street, Suite 1100, Denver, Colorado 80203, U.S.A.

Principal Works:

1942/
46 Atom City, Oak Ridge, Tennessee
Recreation and Welfare Buildings, Great Lakes Training Center, Illinois
1949/
50 Lake Meadows (housing development), Chicago
Terrace Plaza Hotel, Cincinnati
Brooklyn Hospital, New York
1952 Lever House, Park Avenue, New York
H.J. Heinz Company Vinegar Plant, Pittsburgh
1954 Manufacturers Hanover Trust, Fifth Avenue Branch, New York
United States Consulate, Dusseldorf
1955 Hilton Hotel, Istanbul
1957 Connecticut General Life Insurance Company, Bloomfield, Connecticut
United States Navy Service School, Great Lakes, Illinois
Karl Taylor Compton Laboratories, Massachusetts Institute of Technology, Cambridge
1958 Reynolds Metals Company Building, Richmond, Virginia
Inland Steel Company Headquarters, Dearborn and Monroe Streets, Chicago
1959 John Hancock Mutual Life Insurance Company Building, San Francisco
Crown Zellerbach Corporate Headquarters, San Francisco

1960 PepsiCo Inc. World Headquarters, Park Avenue, New York
United Airlines Hangars and Flight Kitchen Complex, San Francisco
Union Carbide Building, Park Avenue, New York
Parke Davis and Company Offices and Research Laboratories, Kalamazoo, Michigan
1961 Chase Manhatten Bank, New York
Upjohn Pharmaceuticals Company, Kalamazoo, Michigan
First National City Bank, Houston
1962 United States Air Force Academy, Colorado Springs
United Airlines Headquarters, Chicago
Solar Telescope, Kitt Peak, Arizona
1963 Emhart Manufacturing Company Offices, Bloomfield, Connecticut
Beinecke Rare Book and Manuscript Library, Yale University, New Haven, Connecticut
1964 Tennessee Gas Corporation Headquarters, Houston
1965 American Republic Insurance Company Building, Des Moines, Iowa
Civic Center, Chicago
Brunswick Building, Chicago
Library/Museum and Vivian Beaumont Theatre, Lincoln Center, New York
Mauna Kea Beach Hotel, Hawaii
University of Illinois at Chicago Circle
Banque Lambert Office and Bank Building, Brussels
H.J. Heinz Company Ltd. Headquarters, Hayes Park, Middlesex, England
1966 Life Sciences Building, Illinois Institute of Technology, Chicago
1967 Marine Midland Building, 140 Broadway, New York
Hartford Fire Insurance Company Building, San Francisco
1968 Oakland-Alameda County Coliseum, Oakland, California
Alcoa Building, Golden Gate Center, San Francisco
Bank of America Headquarters, San Francisco
Boots Pure Drug Company Ltd. Headquarters, Nottingham, England
1970 John Hancock Center, Chicago
International Bank for Reconstruction and Development, Washington, D.C.
1971 One Shell Plaza Office Building, Houston
Lyndon Baines Johnson Library and Sid W. Richardson Hall, University of Texas at Austin
Trans World Airlines Office Building, Kansas City
1973 W.R. Grace Building, 1114 Avenue of the Americas, New York
1974 First Wisconsin Center (bank/office building), Milwaukee
Royal Gazette Newspaper Plant, Hamilton, Bermuda
Sears Tower, Chicago (World's tallest building)
Hirshhorn Museum and Sculpture Garden, Washington, D.C.
W. D. and H. O. Wills Headquarters and Tobacco Processing Facility, Bristol, England
Philip Morris Cigarette Manufacturing Plant, Richmond, Virginia
1975 Harris Trust and Savings Bank, Chicago
Baxter Travenol Laboratories Headquarters, Deerfield, Illinois
Tour Fiat high-rise building, Paris
1976 Ohio National Bank, Columbus, Ohio
Sha Tin Reclamation Project New Town, Hong Kong
Washington Mall Plan and Constitution Garden, Washington, D.C.
1977 Apparel Mart and Holiday Inn, Wolf Point, Chicago

Art Institute of Chicago addition and School of Art, Chicago
Yanbu New Town Master Plan, Saudi Arabia
IBM Office interiors, Armonk, New York
California First Bank, San Francisco
1978 Hyatt International Hotel, Surabaya, Indonesia
Europoint IV Office Building, Rotterdam
Portland Transit Mall, Portland, Oregon
Texaco Headquarters, Harrison, New York
Banco do Occidente, Guatemala City, Guatemala
Miami University Art Museum, Oxford, Ohio
Mayo Clinic Community Medicine Facility, Rochester, New York
1979 Town Master Plan, Irvine, California
United States Customs House renovation, Portland, Oregon
Georgetown Plaza Hotel Complex, Washington, D.C.
1980 King Abdul Aziz International Airport, Jeddah, Saudi Arabia
Arthur Andersen and Company Office interiors, Chicago
First Federal Savings and Loan of Little Rock, Arkansas
Louise M. Davies Symphony Hall, San Francisco
1981 City Hall, Columbus, Indiana
Vista International Hotel, New York
University Kebangsaan Master Plan, Kota Kinabalu, East Malaysia
Three First National Plaza Building, Chicago
1982 Menninger Foundation Building, Topeka, Kansas
Georgia-Pacific Center, Atlanta, Georgia
West Hotel Guest Quarters, Houston, Texas
Clinic for Massachusetts General Hospital, Boston
Tenneco Employee Center, Houston, Texas
1983 ENERPLEX (Prudential) Office Building, Princeton, New Jersey
Irving Trust Operations Center, New York
Allied Bank Plaza, Houston, Texas
Central Area Plan, Chicago
Gulf Mineral Resources Corporation Building, Denver, Colorado
1984 Royal Dutch Shell Headquarters addition, The Hague, Netherlands
National Commercial Bank, Jeddah, Saudi Arabia
University Place/University Green Multi-Use Complex, Cambridge, Massachusetts
Northwest Frontier Province Agricultural University Master Plan, Peshawar, Pakistan
Southeast Financial Center, Miami, Florida
1985 LTV Center, Dallas, Texas
Hughes Aircraft Company Building, Los Angeles
Harvard Square Subway Station, Cambridge, Massachusetts
Citicorp Plaza, Los Angeles
First Canadian Centre, Calgary, Alberta
State Office Building, San Francisco
1986 United States Embassy, Moscow
Shearson American Express interiors, New York
Lucky-Goldstar Headquarters, Seoul, Korea
Rowes Wharf Multi-Use Complex, Boston

Publications:

On SKIDMORE/OWINGS/MERRILL: books— *Skidmore, Owings and Merrill* by Mario José Buschiazzo, Buenos Aires 1958; *Skidmore, Owings and Merrill: Architects,* New York 1960; *The Architecture of Skidmore, Owings and Merrill 1950-*

Skidmore, Owings and Merrill: Lever House, New York, 1952.

1962 by Henry-Russell Hitchcock and Ernst Danz, New York and Stuttgart 1962, London 1963; *Skidmore, Owings and Merrill* by Christopher Woodward and Yukio Futagawa, Tokyo 1968, New York and London 1970; *The Architecture of Skidmore, Owings and Merrill 1963-73* by Arthur Drexler and A. Menges, Stuttgart and New York 1974; *Skidmore, Owings and Merrill, 1936-80* New York 1981; *Skidmore, Owings and Merrill: Architecture and Urbanism, 1973-1983* by Albert Bush-Brown, Stuttgart and New York 1984; articles—"Skidmore, Owings and Merrill", special issue of *Architecture + Urbanism* (Tokyo), January 1974; "Recent Works of Skidmore, Owings and Merrill", special issue of *Space Design* (Tokyo), May 1979; "SOM's Computer Approach" in *Architectural Record* (New York), August 1980; "Corporate Architecture: A Profile of Skidmore, Owings and Merrill" in *Crit* (Washington, D.C.), Fall 1980; "SOM at Midlife" in *Progressive Architecture* (New York), May 1981; "A Stage in the Work of Skidmore, Owings and Merrill" in *De Architect* (The Hague), June 1981; "The Architecture of Skidmore, Owings and Merrill" by Bruce Graham in *RIBA Transactions* (London), no. 4, 1983; "Skidmore, Owings and Merrill" in *Architecture + Urbanism* (Tokyo), March 1983.

Bibliography: *Skidmore, Owings and Merrill, 1936-1983* by Frances C. Gretes, Monticello, Illinois 1984.

When Louis Skidmore and Nathaniel Owings worked together on the Chicago *Century of Progress Exposition* in 1933, it became clear that they were a good team. They formed their partnership in Chicago in 1936, and Skidmore opened their New York office a year later. As they were aiming at large-scale commissions to be tackled by a group approach, it was inevitable that the office would become multi-disciplinary, so, within a few years, John Merrill, an engineer, was made a partner. Whilst all the partners performed primarily organizational and client contact roles, Skidmore was the most sensitive designer, Merrill, the practical engineer, and Owings, the organizer.

During its first decade, the practice was more renowned for competent large-scale work than for individual architectural achievement. In such an environment it is not easy to sort out where the individual talents lay, but the fact remains that the first design breakthrough for Skidmore, Owings and Merrill came from the New York office whilst it was in Skidmore's care.

The founding partners of SOM did not claim to be great architects, but they did claim to be able to "produce the people who produce the architecture." After World War II, the New York office produced Gordon Bunshaft, and his Lever House of 1952 and Manufacturers Hanover Trust Company of 1954 put SOM at the forefront of the world architectural scene. Bunshaft is rightly credited with the design of these spare, shiny buildings. Skidmore retired just at the moment when his office was producing architecture of fame and quality. Bunshaft became famous, but it was Skidmore who made it all possible.

Merrill was involved with the laying of the foundations for the mighty architectural practice that SOM was to become. His retirement in the 1950s meant that he did not stay long to share the period of worldwide fame that the firm enjoyed in the decades following the completion of Lever House. Yet the legacy of the engineer amongst the founding partners is clear to see, for SOM has since numbered amongst its partners engineers of the stature of Fazlur Khan and Myron Goldsmith, and much of the firm's work concerns the relationship between architecture and structure.

Because he was younger than his two partners and because they retired early, Owings was the only one of the three founding partners to have been involved with the firm in its two halcyon decades following the completion of Lever House. He made no claim to be a first-rate designer; he was the organizer, the impre-

sario who recognized and supported talent, who got others to give their best. The system at SOM was for each project to have a partner in charge to deal with the client, a project manager to deal with the business side, and a designer to be cossetted and supported and encouraged to design the best possible building with the minimum of interference. Owings had observed how other firms had designers at a fairly low level in the hierarchy and how these designers got frustrated as their seniors chopped and changed their work, so he saw to it that at SOM talented designers were backed up and supported by others in the firm.

It was its organizational ability, not its design ability, that first brought fame to Skidmore, Owings and Merrill, and it is precisely in getting a large team of architects to work well together that Owings excelled. During World War II, when most American practices were severely reduced in size, SOM was commissioned to design and build Oak Ridge, Tennessee, the city for the workers on the first A-bomb. SOM required an office some 450 strong for this project, and this gave Owings the chance to exercise his talents and the firm the experience to tackle the big jobs, the organization clients, and the bureaucracy of the postwar decades.

Chicago played a big part in the origins of SOM, and Chicago had, at the turn of the century, a considerable skill at urban organization. SOM revived this tradition and its own organizational talents into action with vast urban redevelopment schemes such as Lake Meadows on Chicago's South Side, which started construction in 1950. Such developments, where the land is cleared and a series of towers erected, have since gone out of favour, but Lake Meadows remains one of the best in the genre.

Gordon Bunshaft put the firm on the architectural, as opposed to the organizational, map with Lever House in 1952. The shiny, glamorous skin and the open space around this tower made it an instant success, and businessmen the world over wanted similar buildings to give them the image of sophistication and efficiency. The powerful combination of organizational and design skills put SOM in a class of its own, and a long series of corporate headquarters of magnificence gave the firm a well-deserved place as world pacesetter of this building type. As time went by, other talented designers within SOM took its designs in different directions, and Bunshaft himself shifted his ground, so that by the mid-1960s, SOM buildings ceased to be clearly recognizable from the products of other offices. But the concern for quality, for detail, and for intelligent building remained.

—John Winter

SLAATTO, Nils.

Norwegian. Born in Lillehammer, 22 June 1923. Educated at the Norges Tekniske Høyskole, Trondheim, Dip.Arch. 1947. Married Margit Bleken in 1949; children: Helge, Egill Eindride, Martin, and Brynhild. Division Architect, Vadsø-Tana, during the rebuilding of Finmark, 1948-50; worked in the Farmers Building Office, Oslo, 1950-58. In partnership with Kjell Lund, *q.v.*, Oslo, since 1958. Vice President, Federation of Norwegian Architects, 1969-71. Exhibitions: *Works of Lund and Slaatto*, Det Kongelige Dankse Kunstakademie, Copenhagen, and Det Finske Arkitekturmuseum, Helsinki, 1975, toured universities and architecture schools in Europe and England, 1975-78; *Lund and Slaatto*, Architects' Association, Bergen, Norway, 1981; *Lund og slaatto—Arkitekter i 25 Ar*, Norwegian Architecture Museum, Oslo, 1953; *Lund og Slaatto—Skapande Ordning*, Academy of Free Arts, Stockholm, 1984. Recipient: First Prize, Akerhaus County Agricultural School Competition, Arnes, Norway, 1958; The Concrete Award, Federation of Norwegian Architects/Norwegian Concrete Associ-

ation, 1964, 1977; The Wood Prize, Norwegian Concrete Association/Council for Tree Information, 1966; Stundt's Award, 1972, and Houen's Award, 1976, Federation of Norwegian Architects; First Prize, Norwegian Civil Engineers Main Office Building Competition, Oslo, 1970; First Prize, Eidsvåg Church Competition, Bergen, 1970; First Prize, National Gallery Extension Competition, Oslo, 1972; First Prize, National Theatre Extension Competition, Oslo, 1973; First Prize, Bank of Norway Competition, Oslo, 1973; First Prize, Cultural Centre Competition, Stavanger, 1980; Prize of Honour, Society of Useful Arts, Oslo, 1981. Address: Kjell Lund og Nils Slaatto, Arkitekter, Bygdøy Alle 13, Oslo 2, Norway.

See LUND, Kjell

SMITH, Ivor Stanley.

British. Born in Leigh-on-Sea, Essex, 27 January 1926. Educated at the School of Art, Southend-on-Sea, Essex, 1941-42; Bartlett School of Architecture, University College, University of London, 1943-45; Cambridge University School of Architecture, 1948-50, M.A. 1950; Architectural Association School, London, 1950-52, Dip.A.A. 1952. Married Audrey Laurence in 1947; has four children. Senior Architect, City Architect's Department, Sheffield, Yorkshire, 1952-61. Partner, Lupton and Smith, Oxford, 1962-66, subsequently Ivor Smith and Cailey Hutton, Oxford and Bristol, since 1966. Visiting Teacher, Cambridge University School of Architecture, 1963-69; Professor of Architecture, and Director, University College School of Architecture, Dublin, 1969-73; Professor of Architecture, and Head, University of Bristol School of Architecture, 1975-82; Visiting Professor, National University of Singapore, 1983-84, and Heriot-Watt University, Edinburgh, 1983-85. Recipient: Bronze Medal, Royal Institute of British Architects, 1961; Civic Trust Award, 1967, 1969; Ministry of Housing and Local Government Medal, 1969; Department of the Environment Award, 1970, 1983, and Design Medal, 1975; First Prize, Bristol Docks Competition, 1981. LL.D.: National University of Ireland, Dublin, 1974. Associate, Royal Institute of British Architects. Address: Ivor Smith and Cailey Hutton Architects, 19 Charlotte Street, Bristol 1, England; and Pond House, Northend, Henley, Oxfordshire RG9 6LG, England.

Works:

1961 Park Hill Neighbourhood Development, Sheffield
1966 Housing, Heston Grange, Middlesex
1967 Two houses and studio, Ewelme, Oxford, England
1969 Old people's and family housing, Dibleys, Blewbury, Berkshire
1970 Suburban housing, Rushey Mead, Leicester
1971 King Street redevelopment, stage I, Cambridge, England
1974 Magdalen College School master plan, stage I, Oxford, England
     Magdalen College feasibility studies for student residences, Oxford, England
1977 King Street redevelopment, stage II, Cambridge, England
     Greenleys Activity Centre, Milton Keynes, Buckinghamshire
     SSM Priory, Willen, Buckinghamshire
     Somerville College alterations and additions, Oxford, England
1979 Old people's housing, St. Peter's Vicarage, Poole, Dorset

Ivor Smith: King Street Development, Cambridge, 1977-79.

1981   Housing (500 dwellings), Exwick Farm, Exeter, Devon
1982   Old People's Housing, Wallingford, Oxford, England
1983   Leisure Park, near Newbury, Berkshire

Publications:

By SMITH: articles—"Louisiana, Museum of Modern Art" in *RIBA Journal* (London), April 1965; "Architect's Approach to Architecture" in *RIBA Journal* (London), July 1967; "Architecture—A Celebration" in *New Universities Quarterly* (Bristol), Autumn 1976; "Reflection in Action" in *New Universities Quarterly* (Bristol, England), Spring 1984.

On SMITH: articles—"Second Interests" in *Building* (London), February 1974; article in *Architects' Journal* (London), December 1974; "Dialogue Indoors" in *Architectural Review* (London), November 1975; article by Robert Langton in *Architects' Journal* (London), October 1976; article in *Baumeister* (Munich), December 1977; "Two Community Centres" by Penny McGuire in *Building Design* (London), 23 June 1978; "On the Waterfront" in *Architects' Journal* (London), 2 January 1980; "Council Housing Bristol Fashion" in *Building* (London), 4 January 1980; "Rural Retreat" in *Architects' Journal* (London), 17 June 1981; "Domestic Feel" by Anthony Williams in *Building* (London), 25 September 1981; "Home for the Aged in Poole" in *Baumeister* (Munich), March 1982.

*   *   *

The practice of Ivor Smith and Cailey Hutton has always had a particular interest in the way cities, towns, and villages develop. This had had an influence on the sort of work taken on, which has tended to be especially concerned with the way buildings relate to and modify their context. The office has tried to develop a better understanding of housing, community building and urban design as well as the implications of making buildings in certain ways.

To many people, both laymen and professionals, the present situation in architecture appears confused. Yet there is a growing amount of work being done which has as its basis a rational approach, an endeavour to see whole issues, and an understanding of the way things relate. At the same time, this recognizes the need for acknowledging in a very human way the complexities of living. It includes an awakened interest into what gives architecture meaning—the way everything is affected by and yet modifies its context, whether at the scale of a building within the urban fabric or at the scale of detail within a building.

Some aspects of our work can be easily defined and measured, but many aspects are indeterminate. Even though these involve value judgements, they can nevertheless be studied in as rigorous a way as the more easily measurable issues. From this can be built up a body of understanding which can be called "theory," substantial enough to support decisions and quite apart from matters of taste.

—Ivor Smith

*   *   *

Underlying Ivor Smith's work is a reasoned approach to architecture, seen as a complex series of inter-relationships between people and their surroundings. He regards as too simple the tendency to concentrate on particular aspects as conveyed by such puritanical slogans as "Form follows Function" or "Honesty of Structure" or the notion that architecture is an expression of the architect's personality. For Ivor Smith the architect's role is to provide a background to human activity. Human living is what matters, and the architect's job is to provide a background full of meaning and significance in relation to its context.

Ivor Smith's developing architectural theory has emerged as a synthesis of his accumulated experience. The underlying assumption is that there are a number of universal principles or standards related to problems generated by our times that can be identified and understood. They exist as a complex series of inter-relationships that always occur, at every scale, whatever technology is used. They are generating factors in design work, supplying reason and motivation to support the decisions and choices made; everything else is of less importance. When all these relationships and interactions are considered in a rational way, the number of options left that must be determined by personal opinion, preference or taste is drastically reduced and no longer a cause of conflict; instead, they can serve to give the necessary richness and diversity or character to places.

Among the basic generators of design, Ivor Smith distinguishes the following relationships: the work to *context* (landscape, urban fabric, land use); to *routes* (external, internal); to *environment* (climate, heat, light, sound); to *groupings* (individuals, groups, crowds); and to *interface* (outside/inside, public/private). These relationships are brought together in a complex "fit."

By concentrating on these primary relationships, the designer is more likely to get the large elements right. The finer details relating to the functional activity are then more likely to be right and to occupy their proper role. Smith refers often to historical analogy or precedent, which for him provides a way of transferring ideas from similar situations, relates to common experience that can be shared, communicated and discussed, evokes broader issues, and opens up opportunities. This concern is "not with the images of the past but with the underlying order; not with appearances but with the innate structure and the relationships from which it has sprung."

One aspect of *context* that he sees as important is a respect for the "grain" of the map—the pattern and intensity of black on white. The "grain" is caused by a variety of factors—routes, uses, life styles—that have established themselves in balance over the years. If architects ignore the grain, they are likely to upset this balance and damage the city system and cause it to lose its coherence.

The relationship of built form to *routes* is a generative factor determining the pattern of settlements as well as buildings. Routes provide a "coding" system, a comprehensive large-scale frame within which small scale diversity can occur without chaos. "They can provide the public order that allows for private freedom, informal social contacts or public celebrations." Relationship to *environment* means the way in which buildings are used to moderate climate, light, heat and sound. They should be planned to require the minimum correction to their integral environment and minimum artificial heating, lighting and ventilation—and to consume the minimum amount of energy.

By *groupings,* the vast numbers of people involved in almost any activity, Smith conveys his concern with ways of breaking down these numbers "in order to make the world a more humane and hospitable place." However, he criticizes the concept of dividing settlements into neighbourhood units, clustered around a primary school and other communal facilities, arguing that that kind of imposition does not allow people the necessary freedom to choose contacts and patterns of living. But he also criticizes the concept of open plan offices, without corridors and with maximum contact between great numbers of workers, for imposing too much freedom, which may have a paralysing effect. "The problem of large numbers applies elsewhere. It is not just that 'small is beautiful'—which has the ring of putting the clocks back—but that small when it is identifiable in relation to the large is meaningful."

Such architectural factors as the need to mark the entrance, or the different treatment of outside and inside, are referred to by Smith as *interface* relationships. Interface is about edges, where the internal demands of the street are simultaneously ordered. This implies reconciliation, and it is in this reconciliation that the architect exploits his skill.

The inter-relationship between all these factors is very complex: they do not always fit. But Ivor Smith does not look for an exact fit, for something that is neat and tidy. He argues that the people for whom he designs do not operate precisely, they change their minds and do unpredictable things; he is, therefore, looking for something looser, not too specific, even ambiguous, that will allow for a range of opportunities and choices, so that people can live in the way they want.

—Teresa Czaplinska-Archer

SMITH, Whitney Rowland.

American. Born in Pasadena, California, 16 January 1911. Educated at the University of Southern California, Los Angeles, 1929-34, B.Arch. 1934. Married Virginia Hill in 1936; children: Annabel and Gregory. Worked in various architects' offices, and in private practice, Pasadena, 1941-46; Partner, with Wayne R. Williams, Smith and Williams, Pasadena, 1946-73. In private practice, Pasadena, since 1973. Instructor in Advanced Planning and Architecture, University of Southern California, Los Angeles, 1941; Instructor in Architecture and Planning, Scripps College, Pomona, California, 1945-52. Member, Planning Commission of South Pasadena, 1953, and Community Redevelopment Agency of South Pasadena, 1954-62. Recipient: Honor Award, 1946 (twice), 1951 (three times), 1954, 1957 (twice), and Merit Award, 1957 (twice), American Institute of Architects, Southern California Chapter; Honor Award, 1950, 1957, Merit Award, 1957, 1959, and Award of Excellence, 1959, AIA, Pasadena Chapter; Merit Award, national AIA, 1952, 1954 (twice), 1958; First Award, Community Arts Association, Santa Barbara, California, 1954; Merit Award, *House and Home/Sunset Magazine/AIA,* 1956 (twice); Merit Award, *House and Home,* 1956; Merit Award, National Association of Home Builders, 1957; First Award, *American Home,* 1957; Merit Award, 1957, 1961, and Honor Award, 1961, *Sunset Magazine/AIA;* Los Angeles Beautiful Award, 1958; Merit Award, Church Architectural Guild, 1959; Merit Award, AIA: Homes for Better Living, 1962. Fellow, American Institute of Architects, 1957. Address (office): 1517 Fair Oaks Avenue, South Pasadena, California 91030, U.S.A.

Works:

1937 Milton R. Jones House and Office, Claremont, California
1938 George L. Coates House, 232 N. Oliveras, Altadena, California
1942 Bradley House, Pasadena, California
     MacLean House, Pasadena, California
1943 Linda Vista Shopping Center, San Diego
1947/
50 Mutual Housing Association Community Development, Hanley Avenue at Rochedale, Los Angeles (with A. Quincy Jones and Edgardo Contini)
1948 Williams House, 4211 Glenwood, Mount Washington, Los Angeles
     Johnson Motors Showroom and Shops, Pasadena, California
1949 Whitney R. Smith House, Pasadena, California
     Griffith Park Girls' Camp, Griffith Park Boulevard, East Hollywood, Los Angeles (with A. Quincy Jones and Edgardo Contini)
     Sale House, 1455 Oriole Drive, Beverly Hills, California
1950 Clarke House, 1557 Oriole Lane, Beverly Hills, California
1951 Dean's Residence, Occidental College, Los Angeles
     Nursery School, All Saints Episcopal Church, Pasadena, California
1952 Blaisdell Medical Building, 547 East Union, Pasadena, California
     Crowell House, 949 South San Rafael, Pasadena, California
1953 Fisher-Hauch Clinic, Pomona, California
1954 Blue Ribbon Tract Housing, Northridge, California
     Manning Medical Building, Pasadena, California
     Children's Chapel, Neighborhood Church, Pasadena, California
1956 Thorpe Insulation Plant, Los Angeles
     Grandview Construction Company Office Building, Gardena, California
     Millikan Religious Education Building, Neighborhood Church, Pasadena, California
1957 Smith and Williams Architectural Office, Pasadena, California
     Mobil Service Station, Anaheim, California
     Mobil Service Station, La Mirada, California
     Royce Children's Clinic, Pasadena, California
     College Car Wash, Pasadena, California
1958 Van Vechten Laundry, Pasadena, California
     Office building, 1414 Fair Oaks, South Pasadena, California
1959 Swimming Facilities, Scripps College, Pomona, California
     International Chemical Workers Local 146, Lompoc, California
     Seabyrd Restaurant, Newport Beach, California
     Oscar's Restaurant Chain, Southern California
     Civic Center, Buena Park, California
     Westcott Building, Los Angeles
     Port Holiday Recreation Community, Lake Meade, Nevada
1960 Community development, California City
1961 Mission Bay Water Recreation Development, San Diego (as consultant)
     McCarthy Office Building, Pasadena, California
     St. Paul's Lutheran Church, Monrovia, California
1964 Recreation Center, University of California at Los Angeles
1965 W. H. Friend Offices and Warehouse, 100 West Green at DeLacey, Pasadena, California
1967 Residence Halls, California Polytechnic State University, Pomona
     Central Power Plant, California Institute of Technology, Pasadena
1972 Neighborhood Church, 1 Westmoreland Place, Pasadena, California
     Ikebana House Flower Arranging Studio, San Marino, California
1973 Vedanta Society Convent, Hollywood, California
1977 Science and Art Buildings, Westridge School for Girls, Pasadena, California
1979 Gymnasium, Westridge School for Girls, Pasadena, California
     Henry E. Huntington Memorial Library addition, San Marino, California
1980 J. T. Thorpe Office Building, Monterey Park, California
1981 Tenneco West Development Plans, Bakersfield, California (as consultant)
1982 Development Plans for Pico Rivera and Downey, California (as consultant)

Publications:

By SMITH: books—*The Architect Looks at Housing the Aging,* editor, Los Angeles 1958; *Planning of Homes for the Aged,* with others, Chicago 1959.

On SMITH: books—*Standards for Regional Recreation* by Wayne R. Williams and others, Washington D.C. 1958; *Architecture U.S.A.,* edited by Ian McCallum, London 1959; articles—"Planning for Specialists" in *Los Angeles County Medical Bulletin,* October 1956; "Buildings by Smith and Williams" in *Architectural Review* (London), May 1957.

Southern California from 1941 to the present has been a good place for an architect to work. First, there have been interesting clients in a wide variety of fields, and, second, there have been many vital and qualified consultants and collaborators with whom to work.

I have had the good fortune to practice as an architectural partner with Wayne R. Williams over a period of 27 years. Together we designed nearly every classification of architectural work from a garden tea house to a complete city. We expanded our architectural team as required: corporate members included Robert P. Meyerhof, Philip C. Patterson, R. Stuart Denker and others. A Permanent Col-

Whitney R. Smith: Neighborhood Church, Pasadena, California, 1972.

laboration was formed with Simon Eisner (city planner) and Garrett Eckbo (the landscape architect), and was called Community Facilities Planners (C.F.P.). C.F.P. developed plans for more than 40 major projects.

Other ad hoc team members have included Victor Gruen and Associates; Kariotis and Kesler; Selje, Bond and Stewart; Edgardo Contini; A Quincy Jones; Joseph Amestoy; and many others.

I have acted as developer for four office buildings. I believe that all architects can improve their understanding and experience by developing some projects for themselves.

I have taught "architectural appreciation" courses, and I strongly believe that any major improvement in architectural design will come from emphasizing the education of the general public rather than the practicing architect.

For the past ten years or so, I have been in private practice as an individual. I contract for all supporting design and engineering services and retain on an ad hoc basis some forty consultants for this purpose. These consultants are highly qualified persons, many of whom I have worked with for many years, and they make possible what I consider to be a highly efficient and creative team.

—Whitney R. Smith

Whitney R. Smith worked for a short time in the office of Harwell Hamilton Harris, and he considers Harris to have been a great influence on his work; he also acknowledges his debt to Kem Weber and Charles and Henry Greene.

During World War II Smith designed the Linda Vista Shopping Center at San Diego, notable because it was one of the first such projects to be built around a central green ("Grass Grows on Main Street"), with parking on the perimeter behind the buildings. After the war, during a short partnership with Quincy Jones and Edgardo Contini, he was instrumental in designing two important projects in the Los Angeles area—the "goodsie-woodsie" Mutual Housing Association Community in upper Brentwood and the Griffith Park Girl's Camp, a wood, post-and-beam structure which is more of an open shelter than a building.

During his long partnership with Wayne R. Williams, he had many commissions for commercial buildings, schools, churches, etc., but his greatest contribution was in domestic architecture, much of it in Pasadena. His partner liked verticals, Smith—reflecting perhaps his debt to the Greene Brothers—worked with horizontals. He customarily used panel-post construction with four-by-eight-foot infills, usually of plywood and glass. Smith coped with Pasadena's hot summer climate by using materials such as adobe brick and by opening interior spaces to the prevailing breezes through sliding glass doors. Often the entrance to his houses was through a lath greenhouse with planting by Garrett Eckbo visible from all parts of the living space. This lath house treatment was also a characteristic of some of his larger designs, such as the office building at 1414 Fair

Oaks in South Pasadena.

Since most of his houses were built on subdivisions of old estates, they were from the first usually surrounded by large trees which formed a theatrical setting for the precise modular buildings.

In the 1970s Smith has usually designed in what might be called a neo-Shingle style, the new buildings at Westridge School in Pasadena being cases in point. His project in 1979 for a major addition to the Henry E. Huntington Memorial Library in San Marino is appropriately Beaux Arts in inspiration.

—Robert Winter

SMITHSON, Alison.

British. Born Alison Margaret Gill in Sheffield, 22 June 1928. Educated at Sunderland Church High School, County Durham, 1934-39; George Watson's Ladies College, Edinburgh, 1939-43; South Shields High School for Girls, County Durham, 1943-44; School of Architecture, University of Durham, 1944-49; influenced by the work of Le Corbusier, *q.v.* Married Peter Smithson, *q.v.*, in 1949; children: Simon, Samantha, and Soraya. Temporary Technical Assistant, London County Council Architects Department, London 1949-50. Since 1950, in partnership with Peter Smithson, London. Associated with the Independent Group and with Team 10. Exhibitions: *Parallel of Life and Art*, Institute of Contemporary Arts, London, 1953; *Architecture and Technology*, London, 1961; *Painting and Sculpture of a Decade 1954-64*, Tate Gallery, London, 1964; *Triennale*, Milan, 1968; *Line of Trees...A Steel Frame*, Art Net, London, 1975, and Fruit Market Gallery, Edinburgh, 1976; *Sticks and Stones*, at the *Biennale*, Venice, 1976; *Sperrymoor and Kingsbury*, Serpentine Gallery, London, 1977; *House of the Future*, at *The Way We Live Now*, Victoria and Albert Museum, London, 1978; *Sheffield University, Churchill College*, Clear Gallery, Rome, 1979, *24 Doors to Christmas*, Kettle's Yard, Cambridge, England, 1979; *Christmas pax Hogmanay*, Fruit Market Gallery, Edinburgh, 1980/81. Collections: Victoria and Albert Museum, London; Royal Institute of British Architects Drawings Collection, London. Address: Alison and Peter Smithson, Architects, Cato Lodge, 24 Gilston Road, London SW10 9SR, England.

Works (with Peter Smithson):

1954   Hunstanton Secondary Modern School, Norfolk
1956   Sanders Garage, Bark Place, London
    House of the Future, *Ideal Home Exhibition*, Olympia, London
    Patio and Pavilion, *This Is Tomorrow* exhibition, Whitechapel Gallery, London
1957   Watford House, Devereux Drive, Watford, Hertfordshire

1960   Caro House, Frognal, Hampstead, London
    Wayland Young Pavilion, 100 Bayswater Road, London
1961   Iraqi House, Piccadilly, London
1962   Fonthill Folly, Upper Lawn, West Tisbury, Wiltshire
1963   Occupational Health Unit, Park Royal Hospital, London
1964   The Economist Building, St. James's Street, London
1970   Road, etc., in Street, Somerset
    Garden Building, St. Hilda's College, Oxford, England
1972   Robin Hood Gardens (housing), Robin Hood Lane, London
    Ansty Plum Studio, Garage and Store, Wiltshire
1978   Amenity stage 1, University of Bath, Avon
1981   Second Arts Building, University of Bath, Avon
1983   Entrance hall, University of Bath, Avon
1984   Amenity stage 2, University of Bath, Avon

Publications:

By Alison SMITHSON: books—*Uppercase*, with Peter Smithson, London 1960, revised edition as *Urban Structuring*, London and New York 1967; *Team 10 Primer*, editor, London 1965, Cambridge, Massachusetts 1968; *Portrait of the Female Mind as a Young Girl*, novel, London 1966; *The Euston Arch*, with Peter Smithson, 1968; contribution to *The Evacuees*, edited by B. S. Johnson, London 1968;

Ordinariness and Light: Urban Theories '52-'60 and Their Application in a Building Project '63-'70, with Peter Smithson, London 1970; *Without Rhetoric: An Architectural Aesthetic 1955-1972*, with Peter Smithson, London and Cambridge, Massachusetts 1973; *Feedback*, London 1973; *The Tram Rats: A Story for Adults and Children*, with Peter Smithson, London 1976; *Places Worth Inheriting*, London 1978; *Anthology of Christmas*, Bath, Avon 1979; *24 Doors to Christmas*, Cambridge, England 1979; *Anthology of Scottish Christmas pax Hogmanay*, Edinburgh 1980; *The Heroic Period of Modern Architecture*, with Peter Smithson, Milan and London 1981; *Team 10 out of CIAM*, editor, London 1982; *The Shift in our Aesthetic, 1950-78*, with Peter Smithson, London 1982; *AS in DS*, Delft, Netherlands 1983; articles— "Florence: Arno Approach," in *Architectural Design* (London), September 1972; "Ruminations on Founders Court" in *Architectural Design* (London), August 1973; "Collage of Photographs" in *Architectural Design* (London), November 1973; "Travel Notes" in *Feedback* (London), December 1973; "Collective Design: The Violent Consumer; or, Waiting for the Goodies" in *Architectural Design* (London), May 1974; "Collective Design: Reappraisal of Concepts in Urbanism" in *Architectural Design* (London), July 1974; "How to Read and Recognize Mat-Building" in *Architectural Design* (London), September 1974; "Collective Design: Collective Quality" in *Architectural Design* (London), November 1974; "Collective Design: The Good-Tempered Gas Man" in *Architectural Design* (London), March 1975; "Team 10 at Royaumont, 1962" in *Architectural Design* (London), November 1975; "The Tram Rats: A Story for Adults and Children"

Alison and Peter Smithson: Second Arts Building, University of Bath, 1981.

in *Art Net* (London), July 1976; statement on The Tram Rats, with Peter Smithson, in *Net 3* (London), July 1976; "Alvar Aalto," with Peter Smithson, in *Ark: Arkkitehti* (Helsinki), August 1976; "In Pursuit of Lyrical Appropriateness" in *Spazio e società* (Florence), Autumn 1976; "Kreutzburg Study: Berlin 1975" in *Lotus* (Venice), December 1976; "Four Visits: Arme de Salut: 1948, '54, '59, '76," with Peter Smithson, in *Bauwelt* (Berlin), January 1977; "Adamsez Sanitary Fittings" in *Design Magazine* (London), June 1977; "The City Centre Full of Holes" in *Architectural Association Quarterly* (London), no. 9, 1977; "Quality of Place" in *Spazio e società* (Milan), January 1978; "On Amancio d'Apoim Guedes" in *Architecture + Urbanism* (Tokyo), June 1978; "The Smithsons . . . Gone Swimming" in *Art Net Rally* (London), July 1978; "Where the Dream Has Landed" in *Spazio e società* (Milan), December 1979; "Hole in the City, Damascus Gate, Jerusalem" in *Mac Nine* (Glasgow), April 1981; "Layers and Layering" in *Spazio e società* (Milan), June 1981; "Louis Kahn: Invitation to Otterlo" in *Arquitecturas* (Barcelona), June 1982; "The Legacy of the Modern Movement" in *Spazio e società* (Milan), December 1982; "A Quarter of a Century Working in Berlin" in *Architectural Design* (London), May 1983; "AS in DS: A Sensibility Primer" in *B-Nieuws* (Delft, Netherlands), July 1983; "Response to Australia" in *Architecture Forum* (Brisbane, Queensland), January 1984; "The Grown and the Built: The Landscape That Can Survive and the Lewerentz Connection" in *Spazio e società* (Milan), March 1984.

On the SMITHSONS: articles—"Beyond Garden Lane" by Anthony Pangaro in *Architecture Plus* (New York), June 1973; "Robin Hood Gardens" in *Architecture + Urbanism* (Tokyo), February 1974; "Alison and Peter Smithson: Gentle Cultural Accommodation" in *L'Architecture d'aujourd'hui* (Paris), January/February 1975; "The Smithsons: A Profile" by John Maule McKean in *Building Design* (London), May 1977.

Bibliographies: *Bibliography of the Works of Alison and Peter Smithson* by the Smithsons, London 1975-84 (regularly updated); *Alison Smithson* by Lamia Doumato, Monticello, Illinois 1982.

*

My current concern is with the quality of place. Related to the built environment, quality is not only visual; it concerns a satisfactory life in various kinds of place . . . supportive places that give out energy . . . the revitalization of existing groups of buildings by new buildings . . . the pleasure of use of the environment transmitted through the other four senses: touch, smell, feel, sound. The term *quality of place* can be further rounded out to include such aspects of experience as the sense of reassurance which certain densities convey . . . the time-ordering of a city by the ebb and flow of under or over-use of such a place as the market . . . the quality of placement of new buildings so that they renew each town's own identity . . . that reconnective quality that dovetails each building into place . . . the rightness of choice of site for the patterns of movement a development will attract . . . the voice in terms of the bulk of a new building and whether this speaks truly of the contribution the activity in the building will make to the quality of life in the town . . . whether the rightness of placement reflects a sense of social order.

In this rounded-out definition, quality of place seems to have two natures: the tangible, or built form; and the intangible, or social form. The tangible qualities are man-made; ordered, articulate, classifiable, physical, often very obvious forms. The intangible qualities are those of human connection, attitude, and accepted (therefore difficult to observe) patterns of use. The tangible quality of place has to do with the acts of form-giving. Intangible quality of

place has to do with those acts by which the community clothes the built fabric with further levels of meaning . . . the stuff and decoration of the urban scene . . . the feeling of knowing how to use spaces responsibly. My act of form-giving has to invite the occupiers to add their intangible quality of use.

—Alison Smithson

*

Alison Smithson's contribution to the highly-successful partnership with her husband Peter is less noticeable than one might expect as the Smithsons admit to no division of labour and consequently speak with one voice. This has been the accepted pattern since their marriage in 1949 when they began work on the Hunstanton School. Credit and comment are equally shared, and the solidarity against criticism is total. When asked to contribute personally to the "Women in Architecture" edition of *Architectural Design* in August 1975, Alison smithson began her statement with the usual "We."

Like her husband, she finds the constant need to express herself in words, and it is perhaps here, in the many contributions to the influential architectural press, that we see her at her most personal. A short piece in *The Evacuees* tells of the early years, and in her novel *Portrait of the Female Mind as a Young Girl*, there are clear insights into the sources of much of her architectural philosophy. Her commitment to Team 10 is well illustrated by the care and consideration she took in editing the *Team 10 Primer*—a vital document for those concerned with the evolution of the Modern Movement.

In the early days of the meetings of the Independence Group, her concern with the difficulties of everyday living and intuitive understanding of the social implications of working-class street "culture" played an important part in the thinking around the 1952 Gold Lane Project and consequently in the ideas behind the recent scheme for Robin Hood Gardens.

The affection she retains for the days at the Institute of Contemporary Arts and the real influence they had on English Pop Art is genuine, and her many broadsides fired at Banham offer some of the more stimulating comments on what she sees as the inadequacies of the architectural establishment. Often aggressive in her tone of voice, she is ever concerned with the idea of identity and meaning of the most mundane day-to-day existence, and her contribution to the most important husband and wife team of recent times cannot be doubted.

—John Furse

SMITHSON, Peter Denham.

British. Born in Stockton-on-Tees, County Durham, 18 September 1923. Educated at Stockton-on-Tees Grammar School 1934-39; studied at the University of Durham School of Architecture, 1939-42 and 1945-47, and in the Department of Town Planning, 1946-48; Royal Academy Schools, London, 1948-49; influenced by the work of Le Corbusier, *q.v.*, and Mies van der Roche, *q.v.* Served as a Lieutenant in the British Army, Queen Victoria's Own Madras Sappers and Miners, in India and Burma, 1942-45. Married Alison Margaret Gill (*q.v.:* Alison Smithson) in 1949; children: Simon, Samantha, and Soraya. Temporary Technical Assistant, London County Council Architects Department, 1949-50. Since 1950, in partnership with Alison Smithson, London. Associated with the Independent Group and with Team 10. Exhibitions: *Parallel of Life and Art*. Institute of Contemporary Arts, London, 1953; *Architecture and Technology*, London, 1961; *Triennale*, Milan, 1968; *Line of Trees . . . A Steel Frame*, Art Net, London, 1975, and Fruit Market Gallery, Edinburgh, 1976; *Sticks and Stones, Biennale*, Venice

1976; *Art into Landscape*, Art Gallery, Middlesborough, County Durham, 1977; *A Pahlavi Selection*, Art Net, London, 1978; *La Modernité, un projet inachévé*, Centre Georges Pompidou, Paris, 1982; *Architettura nei paesi islamici*, at the *Biennale*, Venice, 1983. Collections: Victoria and Albert Museum, London; Royal Institute of British Architects Drawings Collection, London. Address: Alison and Peter Smithson, Architects, Cato Lodge, 24 Gilston Road, London SW10 9SR, England.

Publications

By Peter SMITHSON: books—*Uppercase*, with Alison Smithson, London 1960, revised edition as *Urban Structuring* London and New York 1967; *The Euston Arch*, with Alison Smithson, London 1968; *Ordinaries and Light: Urban Theories '52-'60 and Their Application in a Building Project '63-'70*, with Alison Smithson, London 1970; *Bath: Walks Within the Walls*, London 1971, Bath, Avon 1980; *Without Rhetoric: An Architectural Aesthetic 1955-1972*, with Alison Smithson, London and Cambridge, Massachusetts 1973; *The Heroic Period of Modern Architecture*, with Alison Smithson, Milan and London 1981; *The Shift in our Aesthetic*, 1950-1978, with Alison Smithson, London 1982; articles—"Simple Thoughts on Repetition" in *Architectural Design* (London), August 1971; "Toulouse-le-Mirail: Reactions" in *Architectural Design* (London), October 1971; "Signs of Occupancy" in *Architectural Design* (London), February 1972; "Vehicles, Mechanisms, Services: Another Ordering" in *Architectural Design* (London), June 1972; "Florence: Arno Approach," with Alison Smithson, in *Architectural Design* (London), September 1972; "Collective Design: Initiators and Successors" in *Architectural Design* (London), October 1973; "Shadrach Woods" in *Architectural Design* (London), November 1973; "Interactions and Transformations: Urban Structure and Urban Form" in *Architectural Design* (London), January 1974; "To Embrace the Machine" in *Architectural Design* (London), April 1974; "The Free University and the Language of Modern Architecture" in *Domus* (Milan), May 1974; "Collective Design: Lightness of Touch" in *Architectural Design* (London), June 1974; "Thorpe Thewles Viaduct" in *Architectural Design* (London), July 1974; "Collective Design: Making the Connections" in *Architectural Design* (London), May 1975; "Affirmation: Church at The Hauge, Aldo van Eyck architect" in *Architectural Design* (London), June 1975; "Thinking of Louis Kahn" in *Architecture + Urbanism* (Tokyo), September 1975; "The Space Between" in *Oppositions* (New York), October 1975; "Louis Kahn's Centre for British Art, Yale" in *RIBA Journal* (London), April 1976; "Ronald Jenkins: Oration" in *Arup Journal* (London), April 1976; "Oxford and Cambridge Walks" in *Architectural Design* (London), June 1976; statement on The Tram Rats, with Alison Smithson, in *Net 3* (London), July 1976; "Alvar Aalto," with Alison Smithson, in *Ark: Arkkitehti* (Helsinki), August 1976; "Four Visits: Arme de Salut: 1948, '54, '59, '76" with Alison Smithson in *Bauwelt* (Berlin), January 1977; "Apropos Terni + Words on Centre Pomidou" in *L'Architecture d'aujourd'hui* (Paris), Febraury 1977; "Making Another Connection" in *Arkitekten* (Copenhagen), June 1977; "Risking More to the Future" in *ILAUD Annual Report* (Urbino, Italy), 1977; "Beaux Arts" in *Oppositions* (New York), Spring 1978; "Charles Eames" in *RIBA Journal* (London), October 1978; "Once a Jolly Swagman" in *Architectural Design* (London), December 1978; "Some Further Layers" in *ILAUD Annual Report* (Urbino, Italy), 1978; "A baton rompus" in *Actualité de la Charte d'Athenes* (Strasbourg, France), February 1979; "Chains of Remembrance" in *IDZ Werkstadt* (Berlin), September 1979; "Working within an Inherited Language" in *AIA Journal* (Washington, D.C.) January 1980; "In Praise of Cupboard Doors" in *ILAUD Annual Report*

(Urbino, Italy), 1979: "Fruit from the Tree of Inquiry" in *Spazio e societa* (Milan), September 1980; "Three Generations" in *ILAUD Annual Report* (Urbino, Italy), 1980; "Bakema" in *Forum* (Amsterdam), Summer 1981; "The Masque and the Exhibition" in *ILAUD Annual Report* (Urbino, Italy), 1981; "For Jean Prouvé" in *Institut d'Architecture* (Paris), February 1983; "Passing It On" in *Architectural Review* (London), May 1984.

As I find I can read the theoretical writings only of those architects whose work I have already fallen in love with, this has led my life into the channel cut in this century by Le Corbusier, Mies van der Rohe, and Walter Gropius. Action first, writing later. With a strong sense of obligation to the continuity of architecture itself. Of English theoretical writing, only Uvedale Price remains in my mind, ill-rememberedly important. And Ruskin, in snatches. But always the thing itself catches me first...the English landscape garden, Florence, and Venice. It was Palladio who took me to Wittkower.

It is architecture on the ground, buildings being built, that I enjoy; like Maigret, I feel suffocated by theory without the intention of action and not arising from it. My own work and theoretical writing is somehow always the same...deeper into the same things. But it is for others to talk about that.

—Peter Smithson

In equal partnership with his wife Alison, Peter Smithson is responsible for three of the most important buildings built in England since World War II. The legendary secondary school at Hunstanton, Norfolk, designed in 1949, started in 1952, and finished in 1954, is the true foundation of the Smithsons' youthful international reputation. The Economist Building in St. James's Street, London, completed in 1964, is one of the most sophisticted complexes in twentieth century architecture, and the more recent housing at Robin Hood Gardens, also in London and completed in 1972, is a concrete attempt at solving the ever-present problem of mass-housing.

Labelled "New Brutalist" by Banham, the work shows influences clearly. "Mies is great but Corb communicates" is the familiar admission, and this subtle combination of formal articulate styling tempered by an essentially human understanding of the day-to-day working pattern of ordinary people is the basis of the method.

The Hunstanton School is essentially Miesian in concept; wherever you stand you see exactly how the building is made and with what materials. There is no ambiguity. The Economist Building is conceived as an articulate series of functional movements involving not only those who work there and those who play in the select confines of the adjacent Boodles, but also the man in the street, the pedestrian who cuts through the piazza to avoid the traffic chaos in nearby Picadilly.

Robin Hood Gardens, in London's East End, is an attempt to put into built fact the ideas on mass housing—working-class housing, that is—first suggested in the Golden Lane Project of 1952 with its Le Corbusier-inspired "street-decks" and the thinking based on the fascination for "street culture" that so obsessed those connected with the *This Is Tommorrow* exhibition held at the Whitechapel Gallery in 1956. Much of Peter Smithson's early ideas can be seen in relation to the Independent Group meetings held at the Insitiute of Comtemporary Arts, London, in the mid 1950s and his reaction to the sudden influx of imagery from across the Atlantic. His later visits to America and to Japan are of prime importance.

Unquestionably the most articulate of recent architectural polemicists, he has made an important contribution to the academic side of the profession; words have been as important to him as the buildings. The Smithsons have, in fact, written much and built comparatively little. The continually provocative writing—especially in the early days of *Architectural Design*—has had a telling effect on those to whom the Smithsons embody the continuation of the progressive ideas of the Modern Movement. This reputation has been enhanced by their regular involvement with other leading young architects in the highly influential and truly international Team 10. The importance of this "loose association of friends" to the Modern Movement, since its formation at Dubrovnik in 1956, is well illustrated in the *Team 10 Primer*—edited by Alison Smithson.

Recently, in a short piece written for the Jubilee Edition of the *Architectural Review,* Peter Smithson has drawn attention to the change that has taken place in the neighbourhoods that he has come to know well over the last twenty-five years and states that a new "form" is needed to ensure that the reality of these neighbourhoods is retained. It is true to say that, twenty-five years after Hunstanton, those concerned with what must be done are waiting to hear what "form" he has in mind—a hint of which can be seen in the recent and current building at the University of Bath.

—John Furse

See SMITHSON, Alison

SOLERI, Paolo.

American. Born in Turin, Italy, 21 June 1919; emigrated to the United States, 1955. Educated at the Turin Polytechnic, 1941-46, D.Arch. (honors) 1946; Fellow, Frank Lloyd Wright Foundation, Taliesin West, Scottsdale, Arizona, 1947-48. Married Carolyn Woods in 1949; children: Kristine and Daniela. In private practice, Turin, and Southern Italy, 1950-55. Since 1956, President, the Cosanti Foundation, Scottsdale. Distinguished Visiting Lecturer, Arizona State University, Tempe. Exhibitions: *Visionary Architecture*, Museum of Modern Art, New York, 1961; *Two Urbanists: The Architecture of Buckminster Fuller and Paolo Soleri*, Brandeis University, Waltham, Massachusetts, 1964; *The Architectural Vision of Paolo Soleri*, Corcoran Gallery, Washington, D.C., 1970, toured New York, Chicago, Ottawa, Berkeley, California, and Phoenix, Arizona; *2 Suns Arcology: The City Energized by the Sun*, Xerox Center, Rochester, New York, 1976; *Envision Cities of the 21st Century*, Miami-Dade Community College, Florida, 1980; *Utopian Visions in Modern Art*, Hirshhorn Museum, Washington, D.C., 1983; *Yesterday's Tomorrows*, National Museum of American History, Washington, D.C., 1984; *Space for Peace: Architektur Vision*, Graz, Austria, 1984. Collection: Soleri Archives, Howe Architecture Library, Arizona State University, Tempe. Recipient: Graham Foundation, Fellowship, 1962; Guggenheim grant, 1964, 1967; Design Award, *Progressive Architecture*, New York, 1979; Gold Medal, World Biennale of Architecture, Sofia, Bulgaria, 1981; Silver Medal, Academie d'Architecture, Paris, 1984. Honorary doctorates: Dickinson College, Carlisle, Pennsylvania; Moore College of Art, Philadelphia; Arizona State University. Address: The Cosanti Foundation, 6433 Doubletree Road, Scottsdale, Arizona 85253, U.S.A.

Works

1948 Bridge (project)
1949 The Dome House, Cave Creek, Arizona (with Mark Mills)
1953 Artistica Ceramica Solimene Ceramics Factory, Vietri-sul-Mare, near Palermo, Sicily
1956 Earth House, Scottsdale, Arizona
1956/
76 The Cosanti Foundation, Scottsdale, Arizona
1958/
67 Mesa City (project)
1966 Outdoor Theatre, Institute of American Indian Arts, Santa Fe, New Mexico
1970 Arcosanti (community for 5,000 people), near Cordes Junction, Arizona
1970/
85 Arcosanti: South and North Vaults; East and West Housing; Foundry Apse; Ceramics Apse; Crafts III; Laboratory Building; Soleri Unit; Greenhouse Housing
1981 Deconcini House, Phoenix, Arizona

Publications:

By SOLERI: books—*Arcology: The City in the Image of Man*, Cambridge, Massachusetts 1970; *The Sketchbooks of Paolo Soleri*, Cambridge, Massachusetts 1971; *The Bridge Between Matter and Spirit Is Matter Becoming Spirit*, New York 1973; *Fragments: A Selection from the Sketchbooks of Paolo Soleri*, London 1981; *The Omega Seed*, New York 1981; *Food Chain and Metamorphosis*, Scottsdale, Arizona 1983; *Arcosanti: An Urban Laboratory*, San Diego, California 1983; *Space for Peace*, Scottsdale, Arizona 1984; *Paolo Soleri's Earthcasting*, Layton, Utah 1984; *Technology and Cosmogenesis*, Montgomery, Alabama 1985; articles—"Two Suns Arcology" in *Architectural Association Quarterly* (London), no. 2, 1976; "In the Beginning Was the City", interview, in *Architectes* (Paris), September/October 1977; "Arcosanti, Valletta Theatre Complex", with Richard Schwadel, in *Architecture + Urbanism* (Tokyo), March 1979; "Vernacular Architecture", interview, in *Architectes* (Paris), May 1979.

On SOLERI: books—*The Architecture of Bridges*, New York 1948; *Architects on Architecture*, edited by Paul Heyer, London 1967; *Visionary Cities: The Arcology of Paolo Soleri* by Donald Wall, New York and London 1970, 1971; *The Arcology of Paolo Soleri*, thesis by P. Studdert, University of Newcastle-on-Tyne 1973; articles—"Paolo Soleri" by Jeffrey Cook in *Architectural Association Quarterly* (London), April 1969; "Quella che Soleri Chiama Arcologia" in *Domus* (Milan), May 1969; "Prophet in the Desert" by Ada Louise Huxtable in the *New York Times*, 15 March 1970; "Arcology of Paolo Soleri" by Sybil Moholy-Nagy in *Architectural Forum* (New York), May 1970; "Paolo Soleri Thinks Very Big" by Sherwood Davidson Kohn in the *New York Times Magazine*, 27 July 1970; "The Architectural Vision of Paolo Soleri" in *L'Architecture d'Aujourd'hui* (Paris), October 1970; "Paolo Soleri: The Philosophy of Urban Life" by Henryk Skolimowski in *Architectural Association Quarterly* (London), Winter 1971; "Soleri: 'Plumber with a Mind of St. Augustin'" by E. Hibgee in *AIA Journal* (Washington, D.C.), February 1971; "Soleri's Arcology: A New Design for the City" by S. Kostof in *Art in America* (New York), March 1971; "The Individual as Institution" by W.I. Thompson in *Harper's* (New York), September 1972; "Job Site for Utopia" by J.M. Dixon in *Progressive Architecture* (New York), April 1973; "Arcosanti: Pueblo and Acropolis" by Chuck Simmons in *Mountain Gazette* (Denver), October 1973; "Paolo Soleri: A Flight from Flatness" by John Elkington in *Architectural Association Quarterly* (London), vol. 6, no. 1, 1974; "Arcosanti: Dream City" by Douglas Davis in *Newsweek* (New York), 16 August 1976; "Arcosanti: A Utopia in Construction" in *Domus* (Milan), April 1977; "Review: Paolo Solari" in *Crit* (Washington, D.C.), Spring 1978; "Soleri and the Arcosanti Experience" in *Building* (London), 15 December 1978; "Paolo Soleri at the RIBA" in *RIBA Journal* (London), March 1979; "Soleri: Architect/Philosopher" in *Architecture* (Paris), February 1980; "Soleri's Arcosanti" in *Bouw* (Rotterdam), 5 February 1983.

Paolo Soleri: Arcosanti, near Cordes Junction, Arizona, begun in 1970.

Bibliographies: *AA Library Bibliography No. 4: Paolo Soleri*, London 1972; *Paolo Soleri: A Bibliography* by Mary Vance, Monticello, Illinois 1980.

The Cosanti Foundation is a not-for-profit organization pursuing the research and development of an alternative urban environment. Given that the ecological, logistic, economic, cultural and energy problems of present cities are closely interwoven, it is the Foundation's understanding that long-term solutions must be sought within a comprehensive perspective. For the past twenty years the Cosanti Foundation has been experimenting with an urban reorganization of highly integrated three-dimensional complexes called Arcologies (from architecture-ecology), urban concepts reinforcing the interdependence between population, resources and diverse urban functions. Arcology is seen also as a societal framework that can give a higher quality to humankind's physical, psychological and aesthetic well-being.

Present related research investigates the use of solar energy within arcologies. The focus is on the use of peripheral, extensive greenhouses employed for both food production and as solar collectors from which heat energy is directed to the town complex to meet heating and cooling needs on a community scale.

The gathering and structuring of cities into three-dimensional space maximizes the urban benefits of interaction and accessibility while minimizing the costs of energy, raw materials, and land. Logistically, the self-contained design of the arcology would result in: conservation of energy and resources; preservation of land for agriculture and recreation; elimination of the diffused sprawl of commercial services and community facilities; elimination of the need within the urban landscape for the automobile, a prime cause of pollution and waste; and highly integrated and ecomomically efficient heating, cooling, lighting, delivery systems and waste disposal

mechanisms. In addition, arcology can be an instrument for cultural intensification and social integration while meeting the private needs of the individual. Every resident would have immediate and unlimited access to the lively urban center as well as to a vast natural landscape. Arcology is an environment that offers a satisfying synthesis of city and country dwelling.

The construction of Arcosanti began in 1970 in the mesa country of central Arizona, seventy miles north of Phoenix. When completed the town of 4,500-5,000 people will rise twenty-five stories, cover thirteen acres of an 860 acre land preserve, and serve as a study center for the social, economic, and ecological implications of its architectural framework. To date, more than 2,500 students and professionals of all ages, races and backgrounds have participated in experiental workshops and seminars, teaching and learning from one another through the building of Arcosanti.

—Paolo Soleri

Paolo Soleri received his training at Turin Polytechnic, graduating with a doctorate in architecture in 1946. Awarded a scholarship, he went to the United States where he took up an apprenticeship with Frank Lloyd Wright in Arizona from January 1947-September 1948. Somewhat disillusioned with Taliesin West and accompanied by his equally disenchanted friend Mark Mills, Soleri set up—hermit-like—in the desert. In 1949, having just married his best client's daughter, Soleri together with Mills built a remarkable masonry and dome house for his mother-in-law at Cave Creek, Arizona. The next year Soleri returned to Turin with his wife; they designed craft objects and built a *Leoncino* (a camper converted from a lorry large enough to house three people), which incorporated a solar device. In it they moved to Southern Italy in 1951 and began specializing in ceramics. At Vietri-sul-mare, near Palermo, Soleri designed his first major building, a

ceramics studio and workshop large enough for a one-family business. The Ceramica Artistica Solimene, completed in 1953, faces the Mediterranean and consists of an expansive top-lit workshop built from reinforced concrete and faced externally with glazed pots. It was an early experiment in the strict use of locally available materials, handcraft and engineering, all of which were to become important features of Soleri's later work in Arizona.

Soleri and his wife returned to the American desert in 1955 and settled into the, then, relative peace of Scottsdale in Paradise Valley, Arizona, close to Phoenix and Taliesin and near to mother-in-law. On a flat arid five-acre site Soleri began to build his Cosanti Foundation and sketch out his blueprints for alternative urban environments. Cosanti was the original workshop base out of which came the ideas for *Arcologies* (a name given to the alternative urban habitats compounded of *Architecture* and *ecology*) and eventually "Arcosanti," the prototype settlement now under construction at Cordes Junction eighty miles further north from Scottsdale. At Cosanti the first experiments in new building techniques and forms commenced, firstly with the so-called "earth house" (concrete forms cut from the ground) and in 1978 the concrete exhibition gallery. Here Paolo Soleri started making ceramic wind bells and eventually established a foundry and workshop on site for casting metal bells. This activity, still the main income-making source for Cosanti, now also operates at Arcosanti.

A recurring design theme in Soleri's work has been on bridges and "bridge-cities." He first achieved recognition in this engineering field through the publication of some of his designs in the book *The Architecture of Bridges* issued by the Museum of Modern Art, New York, in 1948. Soler's work came to the wider attention of the American public through a large scale exhibition of his arcology and bridge projects held at the Corcoran Gallery, Washington, in 1970. There he presented his ideas in model form, establishing his priorities for an alternative urban future based on a concentration or "a miniaturization" (after Teilhard de Chardin) of city elements into single large urban structures. His concept was in direct opposition to the ideas of planners such as Doxiades and their notion of spread-out cities (Ecumenopolis) which, in Soleri's view, lacked both ecological balance and architectural significance.

The same year Soleri set out to build one of these arcologies, the one for an "Arcosanti," on the 860-acre site at Cordes Junction, a point on the Arizona map that gives access to the main highways. Situated on a mesa which has similar characteristics to a hypothetical scheme he drew up some years before, Arcosanti will eventually provide accommodation for 4500-5000 people. It will rise twenty-five stories, will be pedestrian oriented and will cover only thirteen acres of the incredibly beautiful site. It is unique and, according to Soleri, will serve as a prototype for further schemes. The design aspects of the project are interesting and innovative. What was learnt at Cosanti about concrete casting has been developed to a high degree at Arcosanti, and experiments have been carried out in the decoration of surfaces and moulding. Two large vaults have been constructed as well as "solar" apses and a more conventional workshop block. The whole scheme is being built largely by volunteers, summer student apprentices and work-people who share Soleri's personal vision. It has gone through numerous modifications but is at last emerging as a viable alternative proposition for the future.

Soleri has developed his original design to take into account the new urgent needs for energy conservation in building; in conjunction with experts from the University of Arizona, he has designed more advanced solar systems. He explains this development at some length in his article "Two Suns Arcology" (*AA Quarterly*, vol. 7, no. 2, 1976).

His involvement with the project has been time consuming, and the need to raise the necessary capital to complete the project (possibly 15-20 years from now) has taken Soleri from Los Angeles to Delhi as well as most of the European capitals over the past decade on lectures, broadcasts and promotional tours. Arcosanti yearly Arts and Music Festivals have been arranged to bring large numbers to the site (10,000 people in one day in 1978), not simply to share in the delights of Arizona's special musical event but also to experience at first hand the new environmental concept. The second stage of the project includes theatre and workshop centres to house such events.

Through all this activity Paolo Soleri himself remains a calm, introspective, frugally minded individual possessed by the desire to continue and complete the vision of a new order for "urban man." His own writings and pronouncements on the wider implications of his philosophy (enshrined in his completely unfathomable book *The Bridge Between Matter and Spirit*) are now displaying a much more intense interest in metaphysics, theology and what he calls "eschatology." He defines man's (and by that he means also woman's) present situation as untenable and the modern city—with its inherent destructive characteristics—as unacceptable. Thus he seeks to find restitution in the "new man" who has a vision strong enough to take him forward into new areas of spirituality and find new hope in a close knit urban way of life

—Dennis Sharp

SORIANO, Raphael Simon.
American. Born in Rhodes, Greece, 1 August 1907; emigrated to the United States, 1924: naturalized, 1930. Educated at Rhodes College, St. Jean, 1919-22; University of Southern California, Los Angeles,

B.Arch. 1934. Worked with Richard Neutra, *q.v.*, Los Angeles, 1932-35, and with the Los Angeles City Planning Commission, 1935-36. In private practice, Los Angeles, 1936-53, and Tiburon, California, since 1953. Visiting Professor, Tulane University, New Orleans, 1956, University of Arizona, Tucson, 1959, McGill University, Montreal, 1959, Yale University, New Haven, Connecticut, 1959-60, Cornell University, Ithaca, New York, 1961-62, and Washington University, St. Louis, 1962-63. Exhibitions: World's Fair, Paris, 1937; Pan-American Congress, Havana, 1951, and Mexico City, 1952; Museum of Modern Art, New York, 1952; Fine Arts Museum, Houston, 1952; *Bienal*, São Paulo, 1953; International Industrial Exhibition, Moscow, 1958; Yale University, New Haven, Connecticut, 1960; City Art Museum, St. Louis, 1962; *The Twentieth Century House*, Museum of Modern Art, New York, 1962; *Historical Housing 1930-1940*, University of California at Santa Barbara, 1975. Recipient: *Progressive Architecture* Award, 1947; American Institute of Architects Award, 1949, 1951, 1956, 1957, 1958, 1959, 1960, 1962; Pan American Congress Award, 1951, 1954; *Architectural Record* Award, 1956; *House and Home* Award, 1960. Fellow, American Institute of Architects. Honorary Member, Society of Mexican Architects. Address (office): 21 Main Street, Belvedere, Tiburon, California 94920, U.S.A.

Works:

1935   Lipetz House, 1843 Dillon, Los Angeles
1936   Kimpson-Nixon House, 380 Orlena, Los Angeles

Raphael Soriano: World Peace Center, Alcatraz Island, San Francisco Bay, 1969 (project).

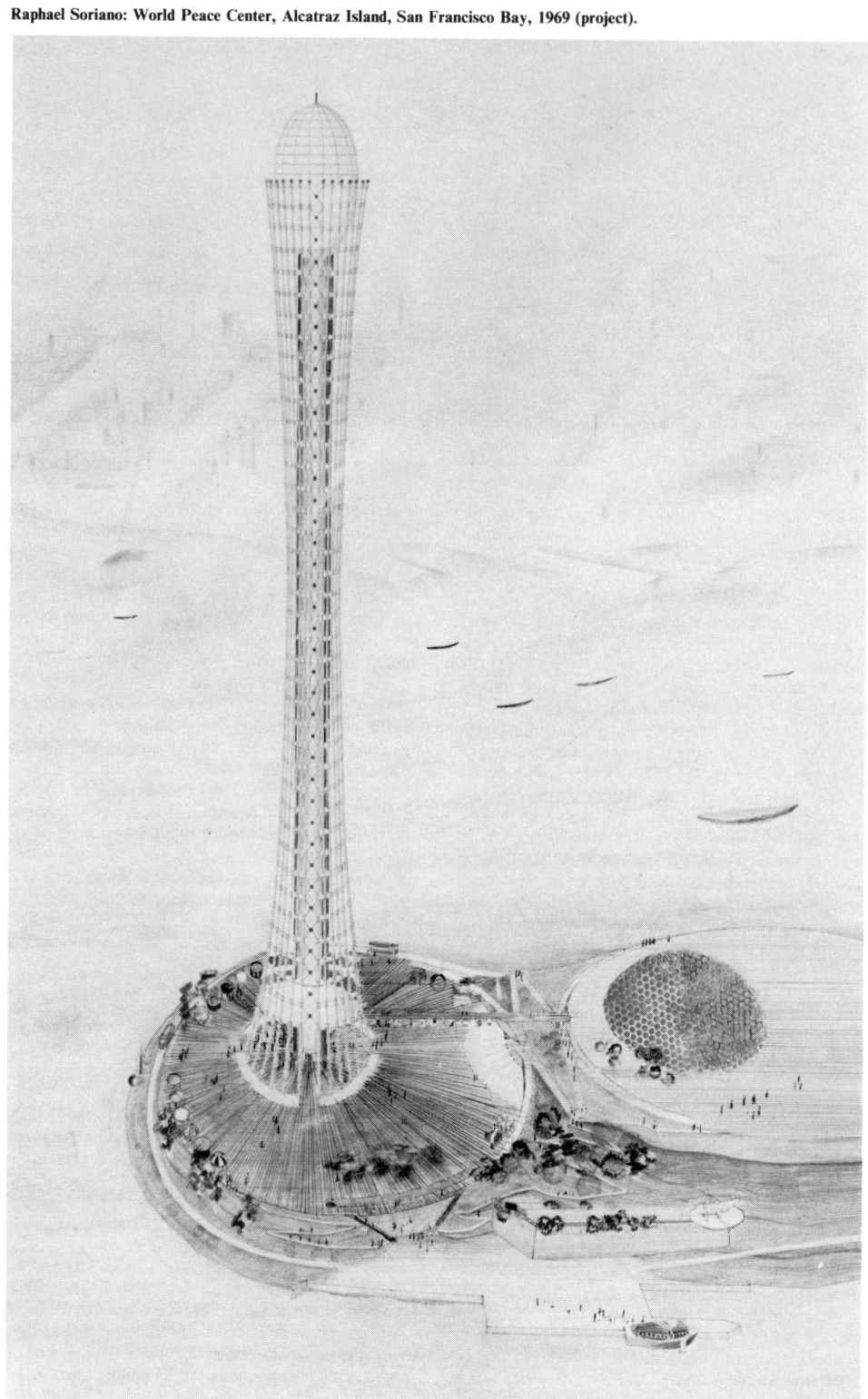

1937 Los Angeles Jewish community Center, 2317 East Michigan, Los Angeles
1938 Ross House, 2123 Valentine, Los Angeles
1939 Polito House, 1650 Queens Road, Hollywood, Los Angeles
    Gogol House, 2190 Talmadge, Los Angeles
1940 Lukens House, 3425 West 27th Street, Los Angeles
    Koosis House, 1941 Glencoe, Los Angeles
    Strauss-Lewis House, 3131 Queensbury, Los Angeles
1941 House, Avenue 37, Mt. Washington, Los Angeles
1948 Horticultural Center, for the Hallawell Seed Company, San Francisco (demolished, 1965)
    Ciro of Bond Street Shop, San Francisco (with Serge Chermayeff)
    Case Study House, for *Arts and Architecture*, Pacific Palisades, California
1950 Colby Apartments, 1312 Beverly Green Drive, Los Angeles
    Noyes House, 111 Stone Canyon, Los Angeles
    Julius Shulman House and Studio, 7875 Woodrow Wilson, Los Angeles
    Touriel Medical Building, 2608 West Santa Barbara, Los Angeles
1951 Schrage-Hallauer House, 2648 Commonwealth, Los Angeles
1959 Houses, 20 and 24 Longfellow Road, Mill Valley, California
1969 World Peace Center, Alcatraz Island, San Francisco Bay (project)

Publications:

By SORIANO: article—"Interview: Raphael Soriano" in *Archetype* (San Francisco), Spring 1979.

On SORIANO: books—*Architecture U.S.A.*, edited by Ian McCallum, London 1959; *Architects on Architecture*, edited by Paul Heyer, London 1967; *The Second Generation* by Esther McCoy, Salt Lake City, Utah 1984; articles—"Dos Casas en California: Raphael S. Soriano, Arquitecto" in *Arquitectura* (Mexico City), July 1941; "House by Raphael Soriano" in *Arts and Architecture* (Los Angeles), October 1945; "Un Architetto in una società Industrializzata" by Geoffrey Holroyd in *Edilizia Moderna* (Milan), April 1955; "Steel Frame House by Raphael S. Soriano" in *Arts and Architecture* (Los Angeles), January 1956; "Genetrix: Personal Contributions to American Architecture" in *Architectural Review* (London), May 1957; "A Hillside House by Raphael S. Soriano" in *Arts and Architecture* (Los Angeles), August 1960; "Raphael S. Soriano, FAIA" in *Architectural and Engineering News* (Philadelphia), February 1963; "Recent Domestic Architecture" in *Bauen und Wohnen* (Zürich), June 1967; "Scholars Back Soriano Proposal" in *San Francisco Examiner*, 13 October 1969; "On the Mies Edge" in *Domus* (Milan), February 1981.

The modern movement in California, at a certain moment in time, owed much to European emigrés— Richard Neutra, Rudolph Schindler and Raphael Soriano. Soriano emerged out of Neutra's office and his architecture owed much to Neutra, but his work was more ordered, more regular, more classic. An amalgam, one is tempted to think, of the California of his adoption and his native Aegean.

There is a fundamental difference between his prewar and his postwar work. Before the war, he was a mainstream, modern architect, designing white cubes in the Bauhaus tradition, but after the Case Study House of the late 1940s, he changed to structures of steel and to a less formal way of building.

It was his houses of the late 1930s that first brought him fame. Influenced by Neutra's designs for the Kahn house and the Brown house, they marry the rectangular white aesthetic of the European modern movement with the ubiquitous American balloon frame and try to express the balloon frame by exposing the studs as vertical elements through the long strips of glazing. Without going all the way with Neutra and his "Biorealism," Soriano nevertheless shared Neutra's underlying care for climate and environment, and the sharp forms of the early houses are softened in the later structures by broad overhangs to protect the windows from the powerful Los Angeles sun.

In the late 1940s, the West Coast magazine *Arts and Architecture* commissioned a series of Case Study Houses by Los Angeles architects, and these houses tended to be steel framed, with a hard-edged structure enclosing relaxed indoor/outdoor living spaces so appropriate to the local climate and life style. These houses launched Charles Eames, Pierre Koenig, and others on their architectural careers, but Soriano was already a mature house designer. His case study house, with a steel frame of round columns, and a heavy fascia combined with lush semi-tropical planting and light infill panels, made the steel frame seem at home in Southern California and led to a series of commissions for steel houses which must be regarded as his most beautiful works. Of particular delight is the house for the architectural photographer Julius Shulman, where the steel frame extends out over the terrace to enclose it with planting. A particular Soriano skill was the filtering of the strong California sun through diffuse membranes to make habitable outdoor spaces; the filter could be plants as at the Shulman house, corrugated plastic sheet in the Griffiths Park Apartments, wood slats for a nursery garden in San Francisco.

The 1953 move from Los Angeles to a waterside office in Marin County gave him a delightful place in which to work, but little local success. The woodsy Bay Region Style was too strong in the San Francisco area for Soriano to be appreciated and understood, and he remained an outsider.

—John Winter

SOSTRES Maluquer, Josep Maria.

Spanish. Born in La Seu d'Urgell, Lerida, 15 May 1915. Educated at the Escuela Superior de Arquitectura, Barcelona, Dip.Arch. 1946. In private practice, Barcelona, since 1947. Adjunct Professor of Art and Architectural History, 1957, Head of the First Year Course, 1958-59, Antoni Gaudí Professor of Architecture, 1960-61, and since 1962 Professor of Architectural History, Escuela Tecnica Superior Arquitectura, Barcelona. Founder Member, Group R, Barcelona, 1952; Member of the Founding Committee, Amigos de Gaudí Foundation, Barcelona, 1953. Exhibitions: Galerias Layetanas, Barcelona, 1952, 1958; *Bienal*, Sao Paulo, 1957. Recipient: First Prize, Low-Cost Housing Competition, Barcelona, 1949. Corresponding Member, Union Professionelle des Architectes, Saint Luc, Brussels. *Died* (in Barcelona) 8 February 1984.

Works:

1948 Elias Family House alterations and extension, Bellver de Cerdanya. Lerida, Spain
1948/
  50 6 houses, Tallo District, Bellver de Cerdanya, Lerida, Spain
    Hotel, Montseny, Spain (project; completed by Fogars de Montclus)
1949 Low-Cost Housing, Barcelona (competition project; with others)
1951 Elias Family Vault, Tallo Cemetery, Bellver de Cerdanya, Lerida, Spain

1952 Cusi House, La Seu d'Urgell, Lerida, Spain
    Tabau House, Bellver de Cerdanya, Lerida, Spain
1953 Brau House, Muntaner and Reus Streets, Barcelona (project)
1953/
  55 Farras House, Andorra
    Agustí House, Sitges, Spain
1955 Design of the *Third Exhibition of Group R*, Barcelona (with F. Basso)
    Hostel Valira, Andorra (project)
    Alonso House, Ciudad Diagonal, Barcelona (completed by others)
    Four apartments, Torredembarra, Tarragona, Spain
1955/
  58 M.M.I. House, Ciudad Diagonal, Barcelona
1956 Design of the *Gaudí Exhibition*, Salon del Tinell, Barcelona
1956/
  57 Hotel Maria Victoria, Puigcerdà, Gerona, Spain
1957 Iranzo House, Ciudad Diagonal, Barcelona
1960/
  61 Cloister Garden landscaping, Cathedral of La Seu d'Urgell, Lerida, Spain
1963/
  65 *El Noticiero Universal* (newspaper) Building, Barcelona
1968 Hernandez Pijuan Studio interiors, Barcelona
1971/
  73 Xampeny House, Ventola, Gerona, Spain
    Campana House, Ventola, Gerona, Spain

Publications:

By SOSTRES: book—*Josep Maria Sostres: Writings*, edited by Pep Quetlas and José Maria Torres Nadal, Murcia, Spain 1983; articles—"Sentiment and Symbolism of Space" in *Projects and Materials* (New York), September/October 1949; "El Funcionalismo y la Nueva Plastica" in *Boletin de Informacion de la Direccion General de Arquitectura* (Madrid), July 1950; "La Arquitectura Monumental" in *Revista Nacional de Arquitectura* (Madrid), May 1951; "Nikolaus Pevsner: Primer Historiador de la Arquitectura Moderna" in *Destino* (Barcelona), May 1952; "Situacion de la obra de Gaudí en relacion con su epoca y trascendencia actual en Arquitectura" in *Revista Nacional de Arquitectura* (Madrid), July 1953; "Luis Domènech y Montaner: Arquitecto del Orfeo Catala" in *La Vanguardia* (Barcelona), 13 February 1958; "Henry van de Velde" in *Cuadernos de Arquitectura* (Barcelona), no. 13, 1958; "Frank Lloyd Wright" in *Cuadernos de Arquitectura* (Barcelona), no. 37, 1959; "Un Esquema de la Arquitectura actual en Finlandia" in *Cuadernos de Arquitectura* (Barcelona), no. 39, 1960; "Paisaje y diseno" in *Cuadernos de Arquitectura* (Barcelona), no. 64, 1966.

On SOSTRES: books—*La Arquitectura Moderna* by Gillo Dorfles, Oriol Bohigas, and José Martorell, Barcelona 1956; *Arquitectura Espanola Contemporanea* by Luis Domènech, Barcelona 1968; *Polemica d'Arquitectura Catalana* by Oriol Bohigas, Barcelona 1970; articles—"Bellver de Cerdaña (Lerida)" in *Revista Nacional de Arquitectura* (Madrid), June 1953; "Josep Maria Sostres" by Luis Domènech in *Arquitecturas Bis* (Barcelona), May 1974; "Dos Obras Recientes de Josep Maria Sostres" in *2C Construccion de la Ciudad* (Barcelona), June 1975; "Josep Maria Sostres," special issue of *2C Construccion de la Ciudad* (Barcelona), August 1975; "In Memoriam: Josep Maria Sostres" in *Arquitectura* (Madrid), January/February 1984.

Because of the Civil War, and because he had been ill as a child, Josep Maria Sostres did not qualify as architect until he was 30 years old. It was during these

Josep Maria Sostres: *El Noticero Universal* **Building, Barcelona, 1965.**

long formative years that he acquired a wider culture than is usual in the study of architecture. He not only read about architecture, he also read poetry; in addition, painting became more than just a pastime to him. He could count among his friends both artists and poets. After qualifying in 1946 he visited Italy and was impressed by Terragni's buildings. This background led him into direct opposition to the general cultureless atmosphere that gripped Spain, in particular the universities. Under Franco's dictatorship the Modern Movement was associated with the Republican Government and was actively discouraged. Within this context a small group of architects gathered together in Barcelona under the open-ended name of "Grupo R" in 1952: the main objective of the group was to establish connections back to the rationalist architects of the 1930's, to recover a lost culture and to bring it back into Spanish society. Sostres, who had already published four fundamental articles on the subject, became the natural theoretical leader of the group. At the same time his keen interest in Antoni Gaudí led him to become one of the founder-members of the "Amigos de Gaudí," and it was as a result of his hard work that Gaudí was finally recognized internationally.

Yet Sostres is more than just an influential theoretician and polemicist. Although he has constructed only about a dozen architectural works, four of these works constitute corner-stones of modern architecture in Catalonia: Hotel Maria Victoria in Puigcerdà; Casa Agustí in Sitges; M.M.I. House in Ciudad Diagonal; and the *El Noticiero Universal* Building in Barcelona.

Hotel Maria Victoria, in the Pyrenees border town of Puigcerdà, is within the mainstream of functional architecture with its clearly expressed structure and use, but at the same time it incorporates an Aaltolike organic appreciation of place, each of its three facades responding to the little square and narrow side street, with commanding views over the cliffs of this hillside town. The facades have been designed to fit into the urban context rather than to serve as a functional expression of internal use.

The Casa Agustí, on the Mediterranean, responds to the climate by breaking down the essentially simple cubic concept to create a series of sheltered outside rooms. A double facade protects the bedrooms from the heat, and the cube is excavated away under the staircase to allow light and breezes across the ground floor living area. The single-storey library and study are separated from the main house by a pergola, and the walls of the house extend, Mies-like, into the garden, to create an enclosure.

The M.M.I. House reveals an extraordinary synthesis of early modern architecture, including nearly all of the classical Mondrian-like compositional elements—flat roof terrace, alternative walls of glass and solid rendered surfaces—and a plan that revolves around a glass-walled patio. In this very carefully detailed building, Sostres made the rich vocabulary of the 1930's available for the 1950's.

Sostres was a firm believer in the Modern Movement. He was capable of absorbing the lessons of history and place without rejecting the Movement's early rational tradition. His *El Noticiero Universal* Building, with its severe regular window pattern, glazed on the same plane as the stone facing, is a superb example of civic manners in providing a background architecture to complement Cerda's Barcelona street plan and to fit in beside its neighbours.

In 1962 Sostres was awarded the chair of history at the Barcelona School of Architecture. Since then, however, he led a somewhat retired life both academically and professionally. He died in 1984.

—David Mackay

SOTTSASS, Ettore, Jr.
Italian. Born in Innsbruck, Austria, of Italian parents, 14 September 1917. Educated in Turin, 1928-34; studied architecture at the Polytechnic, Turin, 1935-39, Dip.Arch. 1939. Served in the Italian Army, in Montenegro and Sargiaccato, 1942-45. Married Fernanda Pivano in 1949; lived with Eulalia Grau, 1970-75, and with Barbara Radice since 1976. Associated with the designer Luigi Spazzapan, Turin, 1937-40. Since 1946, in private practice as architect, and since 1958 as an industrial designer, Milan: Principal, Sottsass Associati, Milan, since 1980. Designer Consultant to the Olivetti Company since 1958: established additional design office for Olivetti, at Ivrea, near Turin, 1960. Foundermember, Global Tools group, Milan, 1975; worked with Studio Alchymia designers' group, Milan, from 1979; founder, Memphis design group, Milan, 1981. Exhibitions: *Triennale*, Milan, 1954, 1957, 1960; *Miljö for en ny planet*, National Museum, Stockholm, 1969; *Italy: The New Domestic Landscape*, Museum of Modern Art, New York, 1972; *Ettore Sottsass Jr.*, International Design Centre, Berlin, 1976, toured Europe, Israel and Australia; Cooper-Hewitt Museum, New York, 1976; *28/78 Architettura*, Palazzo delle Stelline, Milan, and Palazzo Grassi, Venice, 1979; *Design Process Olivetti 1908-1978*, University of California at Los Angeles, 1979; *Italian Re-Evolution*, La Jolla Museum of Art, California, 1982; *Memphis*, Victoria and Albert Museum, London, 1982; *Design since 1945*, Philadelphia Museum of Art, 1983. Recipient: Premio Compasso d'Oro, Milan, 1959. Honorary doctorate: Royal College of Art, London, 1968. Address (office): Via Manzoni 14, 20121 Milan, Italy.

Works:

1934 Apartment Building, Turin (project)
1947 Church, QT8 Quarter, Milan (competition project)
     Design of the Oggetti per la Casa exhibition, *Triennale*, Milan
     Chair design in "legno panforte"
     Salon Réalités Nouvelles, Paris
1948 Grassotti Display Stand, *Food Fair*, Turin
     Cogne Display Stand, *Automobile Show*, Turin
1949 Villas (projects)
1950 INA-CASA Housing Development, Savona, Italy (competition project)
1951 INA-CASA Housing Development, Novara, Italy (competition project)
1952 School, Siliqua, Sardinia (project; with Ettore Sottsass Sr.)
     Golf Club, Lerici, Italy
     Four two-storey houses, Romentino, Novara, Italy (project)
     INA-CASA Apartment Building, Arborea, Sardinia (project)
1952/
54 INA-CASA Housing Development, Carmagnola, near Turin
     INA-CASA Housing Development, Meina, Lake Maggiore, Italy
1956 Galleria del Naviglio, Milan
     Galleria del Cavallino, Venice
1957 Cineaste's Apartment interiors, Milan
     Design of the Italian Glass Exhibition, Triennale, Milan
1958 Dentist's House interiors, Genoa

1960 Atrium Entrance Hall, *Triennale,* Milan
1961 Design of the Prime Materials Exhibition, *Italia '61,* Turin
      Design of the *Italian Painting Exhibition,* Bolles Gallery, San Francisco
      Villa by the Sea (project)
1963 Design of *I Biennale d'Arte,* Bari, Italy
1964 Galleria Il Quadrante, Florence
1965 Galleria Sperone, Turin
      Fetrinelli Photographic Library, Turin
      Living Room, *La Casa Abitata,* Florence
1968 Olivetti Display Stand, *La Macchina della Informazione,* Turin
      Pomodoro Apartment interiors, via Vigevano 3, Milan
1969 Tantra Ceramics
1969/
73   Synthesis 45 Office Equipment and Furniture for the Olivetti Company
1970 Yantra Ceramics
      Cometa Lamp and Furniture for the Poltronova Company
1970/
72   Glassware for the Vistosi Company
1972 Mickey Mouse Table for the Bonacina Company
1973 Lighting for the Erco Company
      Pornographic Architecture (projects)
1977 Nonsense Architecture (projects)
1978 Customized Car for Fiorucci (project)
1979/
80   Bauhaus I and II Furniture Series, for Studio Alchymia
1981 Furniture for the Memphis group
1982/
83   Fiat Lingotto Redevelopment, Turin (competition project)

Publications:

By SOTTSASS: books—*Europa e America,* exhibition catalogue, Turin 1946; *Arte Astratta e Concreta,* Rome 1948; *Ceramiche del Tenebre,* exhibition catalogue, Milan 1963; *Miljö for en ny Planet,* exhibition catalogue, Stockholm, 1969; articles—"Coerenza di Neutra" in *Domus* (Milan), November 1946; "Le Case Camminano" and "E inutile che cerchiate sezioni auree nelle case di Wright" in *Avanti* (Milan), April 1947; "Case false e vere" and "Standard" in *Avanti* (Milan), May 1947; "La Triennale" in *Avanti* (Milan), June 1947; "L'Architettura no fu Nuova" in *Avanti* (Milan), August 1947; "La Carta degli Architetti e degli Operai" in *Avanti* (Milan), December 1947; "Significato dello Standard" in *Comunita* (Rome), March/April 1949; "Architettura Popolare in Sardegna" in *Comunita* (Rome), June 1951; "Antoine Pevsner" in *Domus* (Milan), April 1953; "Alberghi e Tende" in *Domus* (Milan), October 1953; "Gusto per il Rustico" in *Domus* (Milan), January 1954; "Le Corbusier e il Mediterraneo: Due Mostre di Le Corbusier" in *Domus* (Milan), February 1954; "Liberty: La Bibbia di Mezzo Secolo" in *Domus* (Milan), March 1954; "Struttura e Colore" in *Domus* (Milan), October 1954; "Katsura: Villa Imperiale a Sud-Ouest di Kyoto" in *Domus* (Milan), November 1954; "Lussuoso e finito" in *Domus* (Milan), December 1954; "Piccola Storia del Cartellone Pubblicitario" in *Stile Industria* (Milan), January 1955; "Graffica Popolare" in *Stile Industria* (Milan), April 1955; "Disegno Magico" in *Stile Industria* (Milan), October 1956; "Disegno e Produzione del Mobile" in *Atti del Collegio Regionale Lombardo degli Architetti,* Milan 1957; "Chiariti i Misteri della Pittura Astratta" in *Avanti* (Milan), February 1958; "Adriano Olivetti" in *Stile Industria* (Milan), May 1960; "Design" in *Domus* (Milan), January 1962; "Automatizzazione e Design" in *Stile Industria* (Milan), April 1962; "Viaggio a Oriente: Birmania" in *Domus* (Milan), June 1962; "Viaggio a Oriento: Japur e il Palazzo" in *Domus* (Milan), August 1962; "Viaggio a Oriente: Templi in India" in *Domus*

(Milan), November 1962; "Dada, New Dada, New Realists" in *Domus* (Milan), February 1963; "Civiltà del Danubio nelle Riviste" in *Domus* (Milan), May 1963; "Man Ray: Il Dada è morto: Viva Il Dada" and "Viagga a Oriente: Agra e le Pitture Sulle Case" in *Domus* (Milan), January 1964; "Pop e non Pop (a proposito di Michelangelo Pistoletto)" in *Domus* (Milan), May 1964; "Offerta a Siva" in *Domus* (Milan), January 1965; "Viaggio a Occidente: Che cosa fanno il dentro?" and "Viaggio a Oriente: Nepal" in *Domus* (Milan), March 1966; "Breve Sondaggio in Germania" in *Domus* (Milan), April 1966; "Memoires di Panna Montata" in *Domus* (Milan), December 1966, January 1967, December 1967, March 1969, and March 1970; "Gli Archizoom" in *Domus* (Milan), October 1967; "Un Posto in Citta" in *Domus* (Milan), July 1968; "A Philosophy of Light" in *Space Design* (Tokyo), February 1970; "Una Lettera in Ritardo" in *Domus* (Milan), February 1971; "Graffi d'Amore sulla pelle del Pianeta" in *L'Uomo Vogue* (Milan), April 1971; "Environment per il Lavoro d'Ufficio" in *Rassegna Modi di Abitare Oggi* (Milan), November/December 1971; "Objects as Memories" in *Casabella* (Milan), February 1974; "Ettore Sottsass 1955-75" in *Binario* (Lisbon), August/September 1976; "A Day in the Life of a Designer" in *Crée* (Paris), September 1977; "Memphis: Interview with Ettore Sottsass", with S. Lane, in *Arts and Architecture* (Los Angeles), no. 1, 1983; "Conversation with Ettore Sottsass", with Alessandro Mendini, in *Domus* (Milan), October 1983.

On SOTTSASS: books—*Forme Nuove in Italia* by Agnoldomenico Pica, Milan and Rome 1957; *Architettura italiana ultima/Recent Italian Architecture* by Agnoldomenico Pica, Milan 1959; *Interior Design* by Arnold Friedmann, John F. Pile and Forrest Wilson, New York and Amsterdam 1970, 1976; *Architettura Radicale* by Paola Navone and Bruno Orlandoni, Milan 1974; *Sottsass's Scrap Book: Drawings and Notes by Ettore Sottsass Jr.,* edited by Federica Di Castro, Milan 1976; *Ettore Sottsass Jr.: de l'objet fini à la fin de l'objet,* exhibition catalogue, Paris 1976; *Ettore Sottsass Jr.,* exhibition catalogue, Jerusalem 1978; *28/78 Architettura,* exhibition catalogue by Maria Grazia Mazzocchi Bonadonna, Milan 1979; *Memphis: The New International Style* by Barbara Radice, Milan 1981; *Ettore Sottsass Jr.,* by Penny Sparke, London 1982; articles—"Introduzione ad Ettore Sottsass Jr." by Pier Carlo Santini in *Zodiac* (Milan), no. 11, 1963; "Ettore Sottsass Jr.: Mobili 1965" in *Domus* (Milan), December 1965; "Cahier di Ettore Sottsass Jr., 1966" in *Lotus* (Venice), no. 3, 1966-67; "Six Design Offices in Europe: Ettore Sottsass Jr." by Gilles de Bure and Gerard Negreanu in *Crée* (Paris), May 1974; "Ettore Sottsass" by Solange Thierry, Monelle Hayot, and Odette-Helene Gasnier in *L'Oeil* (Lausanne), January/February 1977; "Architecture of Dissent: Aldo Rossi and Ettore Sottsass" by Pier Carlo Santini in *Ottagono* (Milan), June 1978; "Ettore Sottsass Jr., his latest projects" by Barbara Radice in *Space Design* (Tokyo), December 1979; "Disco in Lebanon" by Marco Zanini in *Modo* (Milan), May 1981; "Competition for the Fiat-Lingotto Plant", special issue of *Architettura* (Rome), May 1984; "The Turin Collection" by I. Latham in *Building Design* (London), 18 May 1984.

*   *   *

What Ettore Sottsass Jr. exhibited at *Italy: The New Domestic Landscape* at the Museum of Modern Art in 1972 were super-sensual postulates for a ritualized interior, counter-design, building as commentary.

His works "represent a series of ideas, and not a series of objects to be put on the market this evening or tomorrow morning.... The aim is not to achieve a product but to...provide ideas." Sottsass is not in the least concerned with making furniture, or in creating an elegant, "cute," sweet or amusing environment, and still less is he concerned with designing "silent" objects that will allow the spec-

tator to remain calm and happy within his psychic and cultural status quo. His aim is to break "the interminable chain of psycho-erotic self-indulgences about 'possession'... of objects." And one can only reflect that that kind of goal will certainly impose a responsibility on whomever ventures to use the objects. "Eliminating the protective layer of alibis we build around ourselves always necessitates great commitment."

Sottsass wants design to come to terms with that catalogue of needs that our industrial-productive society has drawn up, and he insists that this can happen only if the designed objects have a detached, disinterested, uninvolved quality—so that they gradually fade away, disappearing into the general texture of domestic life, acting as a frame for the rites of cooking, sleeping, entertaining. He envisages "house" not as a barricaded fortress, containing the tombs of the occupants' memories, but rather as a sort of living plasma of demountable elements that can at any moment provide the most suitable setting—sinuous or rigid, transparent or closed—for the drama that is about to take place. "The pieces of furniture move like beasts of the sea; they diminish or increase, they go to right or left, up or down; they coalesce into colonies, dissolve into dust, solidify into rocks or soften into plankton." By being so amorphous and chameleon-like, and by means of its neutrality and mobility and its ability to clothe any ceremony without becoming involved in it, "house" may promote a greater consciousness of environment and of the creative role that we can play. Surely, if we can accept "house" in the way that Sottsass describes, then this would be an auspicious beginning to the demystification of that solemn morbidness with which the environment is normally regarded.

Sottsass's furniture and design, whether of his earlier technological inquiry or his later design-self, delving into primitivisms, archaisms, and cunning eccentricisms with the Memphis Group, suggest totems of domesticity: around them flow the rites of the bed, the oven, the hearth, the front door, the stairs. His house is a shrine-like chamber in which the acts of greeting, discussion, eating, cleaning, breathing, get separated from their human vessels and lay on the floor like debris. This is no orgy of consumption, no diversion, no camp operetta, but a perspective onto an expanded inventory of urban qualities.

—Chris Fawcett

SPENCE, Basil Urwin.
British. Born in Bombay, India, of British parents, 13 August 1907. Educated at George Watson's College, Edinburgh, 1920-25; Heriot-Watt University Architectural School, Edinburgh, 1925-29; Bartlett School of Architecture, University College London, 1929-30. Served in the British Army, 1939-45; Major. Married Mary Joan Ferris in 1934; children: Milton and Gillian. Worked as an assistant in the office of Edwin Lutyens, London, 1929-30; architect, working with William Kininmonth, in the office of Rowand Anderson and Paul, Edinburgh, 1931-33; Partner, Rowand Anderson and Paul, Edinburgh, 1934-37; in private practice, Edinburgh, 1937-39, as Basil Spence and Partners, Edinburgh, 1946-63; partnership divided into Sir Basil Spence, London, 1964-76, Spence Glover and Furguson, Edinburgh, 1964-74, and Spence Bonnington and Collins, London, 1964-70; Sir Basil Spence International (now The Sir Basil Spence Partnership), London established 1974. Adviser to the Board of Trade for the British Industries Fair, London, 1947, 1948, and 1949; served as Planning Consultant to universities of Edinburgh, Southampton, and Nottingham, and to Basildon New Town. First Hoffman Wood Professor of Architecture, University of Leeds, 1955-56; Professor of Architecture, Royal Academy,

London, 1961-68. Member of the Council, 1952, Vice-President, 1954-55. Honorary Secretary, 1956, and President, 1958-60, Royal Institute of British Architects; Member, Fine Arts Commission, London, 1956-70; Treasurer, Royal Academy, London, 1962-64. Recipient: Festival of Britain Award, 1951; First Prize, Coventry Cathedral Competition, 1951; Saltire Society Award, 1952; Bronze Medal, Royal Institute of British Architects, 1962; Award of Merit, City of Coventry, Warwickshire, 1970; Grand Médaille d'Or, Académie d'Architecture, Paris, 1974. Honorary Fellow, Royal College of Art, London, 1962; D.Litt.: University of Leicester, England, 1963, University of Southampton, Hampshire, 1965; LL.D: University of Manitoba, Winnipeg, 1963. Fellow, Royal Institute of British Architects, 1947; Associate of the Royal Scottish Academy, 1952; Associate of the Royal Academy, 1953, and Royal Academician, 1960; Royal Designer for Industry, 1960. Honorary Fellow, American Institute of Architects, 1963; Honorary Member, Accademia di San Luca, Rome, 1973. Knighted, 1960; O.M. (Order of Merit), 1962. *Died* (in Eye, Suffolk), *19 November 1976*.

Works:

1935 House for Miss Reid, Murryfield, Edinburgh
1937/
    39 Broughton Place (Dr. Elliot House), Lothian, Scotland
        Quothquhan Lodge (Sir Erskine-Hill House), Lothian, Scotland
1938 House for Mrs. Spence (his mother), Edinburgh
1939 Griblock (Lord Colville House), Stirlingshire, Scotland
1946 *Britain Can Make It* exhibition, London (as Chief Architect)
1947 *Enterprise Scotland* exhibition, Edinburgh (as Chief Architect)
1949 *Scottish Industries Exhibition*, Glasgow (as Chief Architect)
1950 Housing, Dunbar, East Lothian, Scotland
        Housing, Selkirk, Scotland
1951 *Heavy Industries Exhibition*, at the Festival of Britain London (as Chief Architect)
        Sea and Ships Pavilion, Festival of Britain, London
        Housing, Shepperton, Middlesex
1952 Saltire Award Flats, Newhaven, Edinburgh
        Duncanrigg Secondary School, East Kilbride, Scotland
1954 Ecclesfield Secondary Modern School, Yorkshire
        School, Sydenham, London
        St. Ninian and St. Martin's Church, Whilthorn, Scotland
1955 Parsons Cross Secondary School, Sheffield, England
        Church, Clermiston, Scotland
1956 Trinity College Chapel, Glenmorgan, Scotland
1957 St. Martin's School, Shropshire
        St. Chad's Church, Bell Green, Coventry, Warwickshire
        St. Oswald's Church, Tile Hill, Coventry, Warwickshire
        Church of St. John the Divine, Willenhall, Coventry, Warwickshire
1958 St. Paul's Church, Ecclesfield, Yorkshire
        Housing, Basildon New Town, Essex
        House, Oxlease Estate, Hatfield, Hertfordshire
        Wray House, Wimbledon, London
1959 St. Catherine's Church, Sheffield, England
        St. Aidan's Church, Leicester, England
        Thorn House (office building), St. Martin's Lane, London
        Research and Teaching Building, University of Liverpool

1960 Undergraduate Residence, Queen's College, Cambridge, England
        Physics Building, University of Liverpool
        Aeronautics and Mechanical Engineering Building, University of Southampton, Hampshire
        Glen Eyre Residences, and Economics Building, University of Southampton, Hampshire
1961 St. Francis' Church, Newall Green, Wythershawe, Lancashire
        Spence House, Beaulieu, Hampshire
1962 Cathedral of St. Michael, Coventry, Warwickshire
        Scottish Widows Life Assurance Building, Edinburgh
        Power Station, Trawsfynydd, Wales (original design and as consultant)
        Housing II, Basildon New Town, Essex
        High-rise housing, Gorbals, Glasgow
        Senior Common Room, University of Southampton, Hampshire
        Falmer House, University of Sussex, Brighton
1963 Music Rooms, Trinity College, Glenmorgan, Scotland
        Arts Building, and Chemistry Building, University of Southampton, Hampshire
1964 Hampstead Civi Centre, Library and Swimming Baths, London
        Two Houses, Banalbufar, Majorca
        Research Building, University of Edinburgh
        Nuffield Theatre, and Civil and Electrical Engineering Building, University of Southampton, Hampshire
        Library, phase I, University of Sussex, Brighton
1965 Princess Street Housing, Edinburgh
        Animal Research Building, University of Edinburgh
        Chemistry Building, University of Exeter, Devon
        Chemistry Building, University of Sussex, Brighton
        St. Aidan's College, University of Durham, England
1966 Crematorium, Mortonhall, Edinburgh
        Terminal, Glasgow Airport
        Meeting House, University of Sussex, Brighton
        Students Union Building, Physics Building, Lecture Theatre, University of Exeter, Devon
1967 Library, Staff Club and Canteen, University of Edinburgh
        Physics Building, University of Exeter, Devon
        Geology/Botany Building, University of Southampton, Hampshire
        Physics Building, University of Sussex, Brighton
        St. Matthew's Church, Reading, Berkshire
1969 Municipal Library, Newcastle upon Tyne, England
        Tizard Building extension, University of Southampton, Hampshire
        Recreation Building, and Biology Building University of Sussex, Brighton
1970 Household Cavalry Barracks, Knightsbridge, London
        Town Hall and Civic Centre, Sunderland, County Durham
        House, Fawwara, Malta
        Boathouse, Carmel College, Wallingford, Berkshire
        Institute of Development Studies, University of Sussex, Brighton
1971 Chancery, British Embassy, Rome
        Rivierstaete Building, Amsterdam (original design and as consultant)
        Library, phase II, University of Sussex, Brighton
1972 Administration Building, University of Sussex, Brighton
1973 Zoology Building, University of Southampton, Hampshire

1974 Parliament Building extension, Wellington, New Zealand (original design and as consultant)
        Palais des Nations extension Geneva (as consultant)
1975 Bank of Piraeus, Athens
        Northampton Lodge, Canonbury, London
        Arts Building, University of Sussex, Brighton
        Geology and Mining Building, University of Newcastle, England
1976 Queen Anne's Mansions Office Development, London (original design and as consultant)
1977 Kensington and Chelsea Civic Centre, London
        Mariposa Luxury Apartments, Cannes, France
        Ionian Popular bank, Piraeus, Greece

Publications:

By SPENCE: books—*Exhibition Design*, with others, edited by Misha Black London 1950; *The Cathedral of St. Michael, Coventry*, London 1962; *Phoenix at Coventry: The Building of a Cathedral*, London 1962, 1964; *Out of the Ashes: A Progress Through Coventry Cathedral*, with Henk Snoek, London 1963; *The Idea of a New University: An Experiment in Sussex*, with others, edited by David Daiches, London 1964; *New Buildings in Old Cities*, Southampton, Hampshire 1973; articles—"The Modern Church" in *RIBA Journal* (London), July 1956; "Sir Basil Spence on His Work," interview, with John Donat in *The Listener* (London), 18 February 1965.

On SPENCE: books—*Profils d'architectes—architectures originales du XXe siecle*, edited by C. Massin and the Académie d'Architecture, Paris 1981; *A Broken Wave: The Rebuilding of England, 1940-1980* by Lionel Esher, London 1981; articles—"Basil Spence" in *The Observer* (London), 14 June 1959; "Sir Basil Spence" by Lewis Mumford in *New Yorker* (New York), 10 March 1962; "The Very Model of a Monumental O.M." by Peter Lewis in *Queen* (London), 4 December 1962; "Pillar of Architecture" by David Pryce-Jones in *Telegraph Magazine* (London), 28 September 1973; "Obituary; Sir Basil Spence' by James Richards in *The Times* (London), 20 November 1976; "The Day Sir Basil Fainted" by Hugh Casson in *The Observer* (London), 21 November 1976; "Obituary" by Richard Sheppard in *RIBA Journal* (London), January 1977; "Obituary" by Sir Frederick Gibberd in *Architectural Review* (London), April 1977; "Sir Basil Spence: An Architect's Appreciation" by Colin Campbell in *Scottish Review* (Edinburgh), Spring 1977; "Old Guard, Avant-Garde" by Lawrence Wodehouse in *Building Design* (London), 23 February 1979; Films for Television—*Using Our Eyes: Exploring Space*, BBC Television, 1958; *About Religion: Coventry Cathedral*, ATV, 1960; *Tempo Architecture*, Iris Production Television, 1962; *Out of Burning: Coventry Cathedral*, ATV, 1962; *Checkpoint: Sir Basil Spence's House*, BBC Television, 1963; *Living Architects*, Thames Television, 1971.

Sir Basil Spence was raised and received part of his architectural training in Edinburgh. He came to London to work in the office of Sir Edwin Lutyens on the designs of the government buildings for New Delhi in India. His association with Lutyens influenced the whole of his architectural career, for Spence's work carried the Lutyens stamp of monumentality, complete with a deep appreciation of building form and composition. iIn a truly individual way, Spence developed a form of modern architecture that carried on the Lutyens tradition in contemporary terms,

Basil Spence: Chancery Building, British Embassy, Rome, 1971.

using both modern and traditional forms and materials.

His work immediately following World War II was largely concerned with exhibitions and designed part of the 1951 Festival of Britain South Bank Exhibition, the Sea and Ships Pavilion. In 1950 he entered and subsequently won the architectural competition for the rebuilding of Coventry Anglican Cathedral; this event was to have a profound effect on his life's work. The assesors report described the design as "one which shows the author has qualities of spirit and imagination of the highest order." The design, for which Spence prepared all the drawings personally, retained the ruins of the war-damaged Cathedral Church as a memorial shrine and entrance to the new Cathedral, which was planned at right angles to the ruined shell.

The New Coventry Cathedal, which can seat 2,000 people, was consecrated on 25 May 1962; it has been hailed by many critics as one of the outstanding religious buildings of our time. Some, less enthusiatsic, pointed out that the elongated plan is not in keeping with recent liturgical thinking, which favours a plan form that encourages the congregation to gather round the altar, rather than view it from a distance. This criticism takes no account of the difficulties of the site and ignores the fact that it was Spence's wish to bring the altar forward, in front of the choir, to reduce the apparent distance between the focal point of the Cathedral and the congregation. This revision to the design was not approved by the Reconstruction Committee, and the original plan was therefore retained. Time alone will decide the place of Coventry Cathedral in the history of British architecture. There is no doubt that the ordinary visitor finds much that is satisfying and inspiring. Each year thousands of people visit the Cathedral; it is estimated that more than one million visitors have passed through its doors since the day of consecration.

Spence's intention was that the Cathedral should represent all that is best in our day and age, to the glory of God, and the work of many artists has been included: the tapestry by Graham Sutherland, stained glass by John Piper and Lawrence lee, sculpture by Jacob Epstein and many others, all designed to compliment rather than compete with the building. Of all the buildings Spence designed, Coventry Cathedral stands out as his personal work, for he involved himself in arduous lecture and money-raising tours on behalf of the Reconstruction Committee and concerned himself with every detail of the design and execution of the work.

To many laymen, Coventry Cathedral represents the best of contemporary architecture, and apart from Wren, Spence is the only architect that they can name. This one building will rightly ensure that Spence's name is never forgotten.

The controversy that developed over the design of Coventry Cathedral was often repeated with other buildings designed by Spence, for although, initally, the Cathedral dominated his life and work, his services were in constant demand and he received many other commissions. Among the more important were Thorn House, the University of Sussex, the British Embassy in Rome, the Knightsbridge Barracks, and the Hampstead and Kenington Civic Centres. Each of these works has received its share of praise and condemnation. In particular, the Knightsbridge Barracks was considered by some critics as too massive a structure for a site on the edge of Hyde Park, but when the smaller, mediocre towers that fringe the Royal Parks are considered in relation to Spence's tower, they become insignificant, petty intrusions, whereas the knightsbridge tower has a monumental character, boldly modelled and challenging. Spence was a rare architectural genius, able to develop a genuine monumentality through the medium of contemporary design.

This particular skill is clearly shown in his Rome Embassy design. In a city of great monuments, Spence fitted in naturally and produced a building of great personal character that nevertheless acknowledged the scale and character of its neighbours.

Towards the end of his career, Spence seemed to feel, not without justification, that the professional critics were often unfair in their comments about his buildings. For example, the building that replaced Queen Anne's Mansions by St James's Park, for which he was consultant, was severely castigated by the architectural press when the design were first published. This very large office building faced with Portland stone occupies a very important site in London. Now that it is complete, it is clear that once again the critics misjudged Spence's skill, for the new building is exactly right in its setting—primarily because of the scale, sculptural form, and massing developed by its architect.

Spence received many honours at home and overseas, including a knighthood and the Order of Merit. He was always able to pass his enthusiasm on to others—students, friends, or audience; he was totally committed to architecture, and his boundless enthusiasm and total sincerity won clients and even critics over to his side in the end. History will without doubt regard Spence as perhaps the last great architectural figure of the twentieth century, who perhaps would have been more at home in earlier times, but who nevertheless left a permanent record of personal achievement, in times when anonymity seems to be regarded as a desirable characteristic.

—Edward D. Mills

STAM, Martinus Adrianus.

Dutch. Born in Purmerend, 5 August 1899. Studied drawing at the Rijksnormaalschool voor Tekenonderwijs, Amsterdam, 1917-19. Married the architect Lotte Beese in 1934. Student/Draughtsman, office of J. M. van der Mey, Amsterdam, 1917-19; Draughtsman, office of Granpré Molière, Verhagen and Kok, Rotterdam, 1919-22; worked in the offices of Hans Poelzig and Max Taut, *q.v.*, Berlin, 1922, Werner Moser, *q.v.*, Zurich, 1923-24, A.Itten, Thun, Switzerland, 1924-25, and J. A. Brinkman, *q.v.*, and L. C. van der Vlugt, Rotterdam, 1925-28; Guest Lecturer in City Planning, Bauhaus School, Dessau, Germany, 1928-29; worked with Ernst May, *q.v.*, on city planning in the U.S.S.R., 1930-34; in private practice, with Lotte Beese and W. van Tijen, Amsterdam, 1935-39; Director, Institute for Industrial Arts Education, Amsterdam, 1937-48, Academy of Fine Arts, Dresden, 1948-50, and of the Kunsthochschule für Bildende und Angewandte Künste, East Berlin, 1950-52; worked in collaboration with B. Merkelbach and P. Elling, Amsterdam, 1953-56; established own practice, Amsterdam, 1956: closed studio in 1966 and moved to Switzerland. Editor, with Hans Schmidt, Hannes Meyer, *q.v.*, El Lissitzky, and Emil Roth, *ABC*, Zurich, 1924-28; President, Opbouw Group, Rotterdam, 1926-28; Founder Member, CIAM (Congrès Internationaux d'Architecture Moderne), 1928; Co-Founder, GKF (Association of Practitioners of Applied Arts), Amsterdam, 1945; Editor, with Brusse, Jaffé, Kloos, Rietveld and Sandberg, *Open Oog*, Amsterdam, 1946; Co-Organizer, with Mesquita, Sandberg, and van den Broek, Goed Wonen (Good Living) Foundation, Amsterdam, 1947. Exhibitions: *Mart Stam*, Gemeentemuseum, The Hague, 1969; *Building 20-40*, van Abbemuseum, Eindhoven, Netherlands, 1971.

Works:

1920 City plan for The Hague (competition project)
1920/
   30 Budge Foundation Old People's Home, Frankfurt (with Werner Moser)
1922 German Bookprinters Association Building, Dudenstrasse, Berlin (with Max Taut)

Am Knie Office Building (project)
Reinforced Concrete and Glass Office Building, Königsberg, Germany (competition project; with W. von Walthausen)
1924 Wolkenbügel Office Building, Moscow (project; with El Lissitzky)
City plan for Trautenau, Czechoslovakia (competition project)
St. Wendel School, Germany (project)
1925 School, Thun, Switzerland (project)
Shopping Centre with Cafe-Restaurant, Laan van Meerdervoort, The Hague (competition project)
Railway Station, Cornavin, Geneva (project)
1926 Plan for Rokin Square, Amsterdam (competition project)
1926/
   27 Housing Block with Three Apartment Types, Amsterdam (project)
1926/
   30 van Nelle Factory, Rotterdam (with Brinkman and van der Vlugt)
1927 Bus Station (project)
Terraced housing, Weissenhof Estate, Stuttgart
Water Tower, Amsterdam (project)
1927/
   28 Plan for the Hofplein, Rotterdam (project; with the Opbouw Group)
1928 N. V. Van Berkel's Patent Office, Keileweg, Rotterdam (project)
Baba House, Prague (project; built in 1933 to revised plans)
1929/
   31 Hellerhof Housing Development, Frankfurt
1930/
   31 City plan for Magnitogorsk, U.S.S.R.
1931/
   32 Open-Air Theatre, Urals, U.S.S.R. (project)
1932/
   33 City redevelopment and reconstruction plan for Makejevka, U.S.S.R.
1933/
   34 City Plan for Orsk, U.S.S.R.
1936 Apartment building, Anthonie van Dijckstraat, Amsterdam (with W. van Tijen and Lotte Beese)
1937 Town Hall, Amsterdam (competition project; with W. van Tijen, Lotte Beese and H.A. Maaskant)
1938 Plan for the Bos and Lommer District, Amsterdam
1938/
   39 Layout for *de Trein* (Dutch Railways Centenary Exhibition), Amsterdam
1939 Fokker Factory Exhibition Stand (project)
Dutch Pavilion, *World's Fair*, New York
1940 Dutch Pavilion, *Trade Fair*, Cologne (project)
1942 Crematorium with Columbarium, The Hague (competition project)
City expansion plan for Rotterdam (with the De 8 Group)
1949 Reconstruction plan for the Old City, Dresden, Germany
1954 City plan for Nagele, Nordoostpolder, Netherlands
1956/
   59 Housing Complex, for the Het Osten Catholic Building Commission, Dr. H. Colijnstraat, Amsterdam (with Merkelbach and Elling)
1957 Plan for the Hansaviertel District, Berlin
1957/
   59 N. V. De Geillustreerde Pers Office Building, Stadhouderskade, Amsterdam (with Merkelbach and Elling)
1958 Beatric Apartment Building, Dopperkade/Beethovenstraat, Amsterdam
1959/
   61 Princesse Apartment Building/Office/Garage Complex, Beethovenstraat, Amsterdam
1962 Apartment building with self-service shop, Linnaeusstraat/Polderweg, Amsterdam
1963 Mahuko High-Rise Office Building, De Tijd-Maasbode, Amsterdam

1964 Sports Center, De Boelelaan, Amsterdam
1965 Country house, Hierden, near Harderwijk, Netherlands

Publications:

By STAM: articles—"Kollektive Gestaltung" in *ABC* (Zurich), no. 1, 1924-25; "Die Reklame," with El Lissitzky, and "Modernes Bauen 1" in *ABC* (Zurich), no. 2, 1924-25; "Modernes Bauen 2" and "Modernes Bauen 3" in *ABC* (Zurich), no. 3/4, 1924-25; "Der Raum die Fläche, das Volumen, der Volumenkomplex," with H. Schmidt, in *ABC* (Zurich), no. 5, 1924-25; "Der Zusammenbruch der Monumentalität in Rotterdam 1922, 1926, 1928" in *ABC 2* (Zurich), no. 4, 1927-28; "Das Mass—Das richtige Mass—Das Minimum-Mass" in *Das Neue Frankfurt*, no. 3, 1929; numerous articles in *De 8 en Opbouw* (Amsterdam), 1935-42; "Die Architektur-Konzeption El Lissitzkys" in *El Lissitzky*, exhibition catalogue, Basle and Hanover 1965, 1966; "Armoede of Welstand" in *Open Oog* (Amsterdam), no. 1, 1946; "Behoudzucht" in *Open Oog* (Amsterdam), no. 2, 1946.

On STAM: books—*Holländische Architektur* by J. J. P. Oud, Munich 1926, 1927; *Grosstadt Architektur* by Ludwig Hilberseimer, Stuttgart 1927; *Modern Dutch Builders* by F. R. Yerbury, London 1931; *De Stijl 1917-1931: The Dutch Contribution to Modern Art* by H. L. C. Jaffé, Amsterdam 1956; *Theory and Design in the First Machine Age* by Reyner Banham, London 1960; *Die Weissenhofsiedlung* by Jürgen Joedicke and Christian Plath, Stuttgart 1968; *Mart Stam: Documentation of His Work 1920-1965*, with introduction by G. Oorthuys, London 1970; *Building 20-40*, exhibition catalogue, Eindhoven, Netherlands 1971; *CIAM: Dokumente 1928-1939*, edited by Martin Steinmann, Basle and Stuttgart 1979; *Amsterdamse Bouwen 1880-1980*, edited by Ids Haagsma and others, Utrecht and Antwerp 1981; *Visionary Architecture of the 20th Century* by Vittorio Magnago Lampugnani, Stuttgart and London 1982; *Modern Architecture Since 1900* by William J. R. Curtis, London 1982; *Architectuur en Planning: Nederland 1940-1980*, edited by S. Umberto Barbieri, Rotterdam and Amsterdam 1983; *Guide all'architettura moderna: De Stijl* by Giovanni Fanelli, Rome 1983; articles—special issue of *Bouwkundig Weekblad* (The Hague), 23 December 1969; "Mart Stam" by Walter Segal in *The Architects' Journal* (London), 3 June 1970; "Weissenhof, 50 Years Later" by Norbert W. Daldrop in *Moebel Interior Design* (Leinfelden), February 1977; "The Development of the Weissenhof Estate in Stuttgart" by Babo Rasch in *Deutsche Bauzeitung* (Stuttgart), November 1977; "Mart Stam— 80 years old" by Adalbert Behr in *Architektur der DDR* (East Berlin), August 1979; "Mart Stam and the Arts and Crafts Movement" by Caroline Boot in *Wonen-TA/BK* (Heerlen, Netherlands), June 1982; "Traces of Stam" in *Forum* (Hilversum, Netherlands), April 1983; "The Van Nelle Factory in Rotterdam" by S. Umberto Barbieri in *Casabella* (Milan), September 1983; "Conservation of the Modern" by F. Irace in *Domus* (Milan), April 1984; "Stuttgart Tribute" in *Building Design* (London), 1 June 1984.

Mart Stam belongs to that group of functionalist architects who, in the late 1920s, had an appreciable influence on the development of international architecture and, in particular, its ideology. Among the members of this group were the collaborators on the social critical review *ABC* (1924-28): Stam, Hans Schmidt, Hannes Meyer, and El Lissitzky. Their influence was such that in 1928 Meyer became Director of the Bauhaus in Dessau and Mart Stam, guest lecturer. And it was Stam, Meyer, and Schmidt who, in 1928, created the famous concluding declaration at the first CIAM (Congrès Internationaux d'Architecture Moderne), thereby thwarting Le Corbusier's intention of putting forward his own conceptions. Even during the preparations for the Weissenhof Estate in Stuttgart in 1927, Stam, with his socialist ideas, was an opponent of Le Corbusier, the independent artist. In Holland, from 1926-28, after Oud's resignation, Stam took over as the active president of the architects' association Opbouw.

This group of architects, which was known as the radical left wing of the avant-garde, had strong social commitments. Van Loghem, a colleague of Stam's has expressed their attitude as follows: "The whole of our creative thinking was directed to ideas of social revolution." Because the West did not offer these architects an opportunity to realize the goal of a renewal of society, they hoped to achieve it in Communist Russia within the framework of the Five Year Plan. From 1930 onwards, Stam, Schmidt, and Meyer, together with Ernst May, André Lurcat, and others, went to the U.S.S.R. as specialists, involved mainly in the building of the new Russian industrial towns. Between 1932 and 1934, however, a change occurred in Communist dogma: the "Ideology of Labor" was transformed into the "Ideology of Socialist Man." The foreign specialists were reproached with building inhuman towns, and, as a result, they had to leave Russa. There was something ironically comic in their situation: in Russia they were dismissed as decadent bourgeois architects; in the West they were received as cultural bolshevists.

And, yet, the group was completely serious. Influenced by Marxist theory, the *ABC* architects wanted to fulfil the essential spiritual and material needs of all mankind. In order to achieve this goal, they took the path of pure science and technique; they consistently turned away from the traditional formal demands of architecture. They believed in the technical neutrality of architecture, seeing it as a problem of organization. Hannes Meyer said: "The devaluation of all works of art is indisputable, and without doubt their replacement by an exact science is only a question of time." These basic ideas permeate the 1928 CIAM Declaration: "Town planning is the organization of all the functions of collective life in the town and in the country. Town planning can never be determined by aesthetic considerations but exclusively by functional deductions. The most important factor in town planning is the systematic arrangement of functions—a) housing; b) work; and c) recreation (sport, pleasure). Means to the fulfilment of these functions are a) land division; b) traffic regulation; and c) legislation." The Athens Charter of 1933—with its well-known four functions division and its scientific, analytic method of Functionalism—also owes much to the work of the *ABC* architects group.

The understanding of architecture as science (analysis) as opposed to architecture as art (intuition) brought about tensions in the CIAM. In 1938 Giedion described the two opposing tendencies as productive of architectural discussion, but after World War II, a shift took place within the CIAM and more emphasis was thereafter placed on architecture as art (Team 10).

Stam's work can be divided into two periods, 1920-34 and 1934-65; the transition coincides roughly with his return from Russia in 1934. It is the first period that is of most importance.

Stam is a representative of the Dutch "Whites" of the 1920s, along with Rietveld, Oud, Duiker, and van der Vlugt. During this period, he played a very special role, which can be perhaps be compared with that of Theo van Doesburg; they were spokesmen for new tendencies, and both made a creative contribution to conceptions of architecture. While van Doesburg propagated the De Stijl aesthetic with his cubes and squares composition, Stam took a new road. Influenced by Russian Constructivism and Futurism, he became one of the leading spokesmen of Functionalism.

Architectonically, Stam's Constructivist contribution is of particular importance. With brilliantly drawn constructivist perspective-projects, he created a sensation in international specialist offices—with the Königsberg Office Building, the Wolkenbügel variations, the Geneva-Cornavin Railway Station, the Rokin in Amsterdam, and so on. It was in a similar spirit that these well-known Constructivist-inspired buildings were exected in Holland at the end of the 1920s—Duiker's Sanatorium in Hilversum and the Open-Air School in Amsterdam, and van der Vlugt's Rotterdam Stadium and, to a certain extent, the van Nelle Factory. (Compare, too, the Constructivist project by Le Corbusier for the Soviet Palace in 1931.)

Of Stam's dozen or so executed buildings, his contribution to the Weissenhof Estate is architecturally the most valuable. He created this work, terraced housing, during the period when he collaborated, between 1925-28, in the architectural practice of Brinkman and van der Vlugt (when he also took part in various works for which van der Vlugt was responsible, for example, the van Nelle Factory). Stimulated by Marcel Breuer's chair experiments, Stam also designed for the Weissenhof Estate a two-legged, sprung tubular steel chair—as did Mies van der Rohe; it was presumably in preliminary discussions about the exhibition that Mies adopted Stam's basic idea. Further, Stam's functionalist town planning schemes for Russia (1930-34) are remarkable, as is his project for an open-air theatre in the Urals.

Thanks to the currently available monographs on the Dutch "Whites" of the 1920s, and because of the research that was necessary to produce these studies, this group can now be assigned their appropriate place in architectural history. Besides his contribution to Stuttgart, Stam is important principally for his Constructivist and town planning projects and for his inspirational role as spokesman for Functionalism. In a critical examination of his completed works, one should be guided not only by his own ideologies but also by this directive from his adversary Le Corbusier who, at the beginning of the 1920s, said: "The development of form is the architect's touchstone."

—Arnulf Lüchinger

STEIDLE, Otto.

German. Born in Munich, 1943. Educated at the Volksschule, Milbertshofen, Munich, 1949-56; Wirtschaftsaufbauschule, Munich, 1956-59; apprentice in an architectural studio, Munich, 1960-62; studied engineering, Staatsbauschule, Munich, 1962-65, Dip.Ing. 1965; Kunstakademie, Munich, 1965 and 1969. Partner, Muhr and Steidle Architectural Office, Munich, 1966-69. Since 1969, Principal, Steidle und Partner, Munich (partners: Patrick Deby and Roland Sommerer); second office established in West Berlin, 1981. Co-founder, SEP City Planning Group, Munich, 1974, and the Planungsgruppe fur den Elementar- und Primar-bereich, Munich, 1976. Professor of Design and Functional Planning, University of Kassel, West Germany, since 1979; Professor of Design and Construction, Technical University, West Berlin, since 1981. Recipient: Deubau Prize, Essen, West Germany, 1981. Address: Steidle und Partner, Gentnerstrasse 13, 8000 Munich 40, West Germany.

Works:

1971 Seven terraced houses, Gentnerstrasse, Munich (with D. Thut and J. Freiberg)
1971/
73 Community Centre for four parishes, Munich
1974 Housing Development, Nuremberg/Langwasser, West Germany (with P. Deby, G. Niese and R. Sommerer)

1974/
76 BMW Workers' Housing Complex, Dingolfing, West Germany (with P. Deby and G. Niese)

1975 House, Luxemburgstrasse, Munich (with J. Freiberg, G. Niese and R. Sommerer)
Housing Group, Peter-Paul-Althaus-Strasse, Munich

1976 Vocational School Centre, Kempen, West Germany (project; with Rico Armbruster)
Kindergarten, Erdweg, West Germany
Housing Group, Osterwaldstrasse, Munich (with R. Sommerer and J. Freiberg)

1977/
79 St. Michael's Church, Rosenheim, West Germany

1978 Apartment and Commercial Building, Leopoldstrasse/Ainmillerstrasse, Munich

1980 Infill Housing, Karl-Theodor-Strasse, Munich (with R. Sommerer)
Psychotherapy Home, Kassel, West Germany (project; with M. Bunge and J. Freiberg)

1982 International Conference Centre, Rüdesheimer Platz, Wilmersdorf, West Berlin (with S. Geiger and A. Lux)

1984 Gruner und Jahr Publishing Offices, Hamburg, West Germany (with Uwe Kiessler)
Group of four "green" houses, West Berlin

1985 Energy-efficient houses, Federal Garden Exhibition, West Berlin

Publications:

By STEIDLE: articles—"Elementa '72 . . . No Experiment" in *Der Architekt* (Stuttgart), January 1977; "Town Houses from Industrial Parts, Munich" in *Deutsche Bauzeitung* (Stuttgart), January 1980; "A Newspaper City at Hamburg Harbor", with Uwe Kiessler, in *Bauwelt* (West Berlin), 2 March 1984; "Das 'Prinzip Hoffnung' in der Erneuerung der Stadt" in *Archithese* (Niederteufen, Switzerland), November/December 1984.

On STEIDLE: books—*Architecture in Deutschland* by H. and M. Bofinger, H. Klotz and J. Paul, Berlin, Mainz and Stuttgart 1979; *Architektur in Deutschland '83*, edited by Jürgen Joedicke, Stuttgart 1984; articles—"System-built Community Centres" in *Baumeister* (Munich), April 1974; "Vocational School Centre in Kempten" in *Baumeister* (Munich), March 1976; "Prefabricated Housing in Nuremberg-Kangwasser" in *Domus* (Milan), September 1977; "Adapatable Housing—Three Examples in Munich" in *Baumeister* (Munich), December 1977; "Grouped Homes, Munich" in *L'Architecture d'aujourd'hui* (Paris), April 1978; "Kindergarten in Erdweg" in *AC: International Fibrecement Review* (Zurich), January 1979; "Flats and Office Building in Munich" in *Baumeister* (Munich), April 1980; "Home for Psychotherapy in Kassel" in *L'Architecture d'aujourd'hui* (Paris), April 1981; "Church in Rosenheim" in *Deutsche Bauzeitung* (Stuttgart), June 1982; "Closing a Gap in Munich" in *Baumeister* (Munich), November 1982; "Centre for Scientist from Abroad" in *AC: International Fibrecement Review* (Zurich), April 1984.

*

User-participation, communication, and—in later work—particular attention to the environment are the four components that define the work of Otto Steidle. He encountered little difficulty in involving the user in his best-known early work, a row of terraced houses in Munich-Schwabing (1971); he himself lived in one of the seven houses, while his sister and friends moved into the others. This group of dwellings, which were built with prefabricated parts of an industrialized building system, left all internal arrangements to the occupier. When Steidle constructed low-cost housing, he knew it was not possible to predict the needs of an unknown future tenant, so the practical planning with the occupier had to be replaced by a rich assortment of homes

suitable for conversion and extension.

Stairways and walkways are a continuing great interest for Steidle. More than a practical link to the shortest route, they define semi-public areas in their own right. Steidle furnishes them with niches and seating arrangements, and places them so that they encourage informal encounters. At the International Conference Centre in Berlin (1982), which, on town-planning grounds, is divided into individual building units, a long diagonal stairway runs along the courtyard side, butts onto the rear wings, sprouts bridges to the access galleries, and connects areas in common use, such as conservatory, hall, library, theatre and exhibition area. With its eaves and gables, the building relates well to older neighboring civic structures. The Gruner und Jahr publishing offices in Hamburg (1984, in collaboration with Uwe Kiessler) was conceived by Steidle not as a large administration block but as a small town with public squares, streets, lanes and courtyards, since it seemed to him that a building to house 2,500 workers would not otherwise have fitted into the small-town nature of the location.

Working with renowned experts on energy conservation, Steidle put their advice to architectonic use. On the Berlin conferences centre he set a steep roof and glazed the south face to create a conservatory. Warm air is fed into the heating plant circulation. Glazed loggias and vestibules act as energy-saving buffer zones. At the 1985 Berlin Federal Garden Exhibition, energy-efficient houses featured glazed tower-like roof structures to gain heat from the sun.

Steidle's intensive preoccupation with functional requirements has led to the development of an unmistakable style. His buildings display a basic and provisional structure, which lends them a superb adaptability—even if not fully exploited by clients. Stairways and balconies form a spacious filigree around the inner areas. Materials are not exotic or extravagant, but are richly employed: wooden laths, wire trellises, metal or concrete sections direct from the building catalogue. Frequently, his buildings radiate an improvised cheerfulness, a quality which is rare in German architecture.

—Wolfgang Pehnt

STEPHEN, Douglas Cruden.

British. Born in Fraserburgh, Scotland, 4 May 1923. Educated at the American School, Shanghai, China, 1923-33; China Inland Mission School for Boys, Chefoo, now Yentai, Shantung, China, 1934-37; Royal High School, Edinburgh, 1938-39; St. Asaph County Grammar School, North Wales, 1940-42; University of Liverpool School of Architecture, 1942-43; Architectural Association School, London, under Arthur Korn, *q.v.*, and H.T. Cadbury-Brown, 1945-48, 1952-53. Married the architect Margaret Olivia Dent in 1947 (divorced, 1965); children: John and Jan. Assistant Designer with John Lansdell, London, 1948-49; Architectural Assistant to Ernö Goldfinger, *q.v.*, London, 1949-50; Part-time Architectural Assistant to H.T. Cadbury-Brown, London, 1950. Since 1954, Founder Partner, with Margaret Dent, Douglas Stephen and Partners, London (current partners: Stephen; Dent; Barnaby Milburn; Robert Maxwell). Governor for Events, and Council Member, 1983, Policy Committee Member, 1983-85, and Vice-President for Public Affairs, 1984, Royal Institute of British Architects, London. Exhibitions: Royal Academy, London, 1974; Museum of Modern Art, New York, 1978; *British Buildings*, Royal Institute of British Architects, London, 1984; *Contemporary British Architecture*, British Council touring exhibition, 1984. Recipient: Ministry of Housing and Local Government Award, 1964; South West Region Award, Royal Institute of

British Architects, 1977; Constrato-Steel Award, 1978; *Architectural Design* Project Award, London, 1984. Address: Douglas Stephen and Partners, 42-44 Beak Street, London W1R 3DA, England.

Works:

1949/
54 Manor house modernization, North Houghton, Hampshire (with Margaret Dent)
House conversions, London (with Margaret Dent)
Exhibitions and shops, London and Glasgow (with Margaret Dent)
House, East Horsley, Surrey

1951 Civil Engineering and Irrigation sections, *Festival of Britain*, Kelvin Hall, Glasgow (with Margaret Dent)

1954 Pottery showroom and offices, Baker Street, London (now demolished)

1955 Showroom and maisonettes, Crawford Street, London W.1 (project)

1956 Haslerigge Road Primary School extension, South London
Apartment block, Lansdowne Road, London W.11 (project)
Apartment block, 103-105 Harley Street, London W.1
Apartment block, 62-64 Wimpole Street, London W.1

1959/
63 Office building, Deansgate and St. Mary's Gate, Manchester

1959/
64 Centre Heights (shops, offices and flats development), Swiss Cottage, London (with Panos Koulermos)

1961/
64 The Mount (apartment block), Bedford Gardens, London W.1
Pre- and post-natal clinic, Acton, London (with Alan Forrest)

1962/
65 Crossover maisonettes, Craven Hill Gardens, Paddington, London (with Kenneth Frampton)

1963/
67 Hereward Centre (shopping centre), Peterborough (with Elia Zenghelis and David Bradley)

1964 Evelyn's Secondary School, Yewsley, Middlesex (project; with Alan Forrest)
Southwood Park Apartments, Highgate, London (with Robert Maxwell)
UAM House (office building), Watford, Hertfordshire (with David Wild and Ed Jones)

1965 Evelyn's Secondary School, Yewsley, Middlesex (with Alan Forrest and Claire Watson)

1965/
66 Housing, Dover, Kent (with Margaret Dent)
Old people's housing, Cosser Street, London (project; with David Bradley)
Low-rise high-density housing, Cramer Street, London (project; with David Bradley)

1965/
69 Rodwell Tower, Piccadilly, Manchester

1966 Housing, Joel Street, Middlesex (project)
Royal College of Art conversion, London (with Elia Zenghelis)
Office building, Waltham Cross, Hertfordshire (project; with Robin Spence)
Brunel Centre, stage 1 and master plan, Swindon, Wiltshire (with Robert Maxwell)
Shops, offices and flats development, Swiss Cottage, London (project)
Housing, Breakspear Road, Hillingdon, London (project)
Kitchen range for Boulton and Paul (project; with Robin Spence and David Bradley)
Greater London Council low-rise high-density housing, Drummond Street, Camden, London (with Robert Maxwell)

French Embassy high-security penthouse extension, London (with Robert Maxwell and Barnaby Milburn)

1967 Greater London Council Housing, Middleton Street, Bethnal Green, London (with Robin Spence and David Bradley)

Branch Library, South Ruislip, Middlesex (with Robin Spence)

1968 Brunel Centre, stage 11, Swindon, Wiltshire (with Adrian Gale, Gerard Gilgallon and Barnaby Milburn)

1969 St. Paul de l'Etoile Satellite Town, La Gude, Var, France (project; with Martin Richardson and Margaret Dent)

Mechanical garage, Boston (project; with Anton Furst)

1971 Office building, Manchester (project; with Barnaby Milburn)

Hotel, Earl's Court, London (project)

Low-income housing, Nassau, Bahamas (with David Bradley)

Hotel, Bahamas (project; with Kenneth Frampton)

Historic building rehabilitation, London (project; with Margaret Dent)

Housing rehabilitation, Southwark, London (project; with Margaret Dent)

1972 Two social services buildings, Luton, Bedfordshire (project; with Robert Maxwell)

Housing Advice Centre, Hillingdon, London (with Charles Sands)

1973 Brunel Centre, stage III, Swindon, Wiltshire (with Barnaby Milburn and BDP)

Hotel complex, M4 Motorway, Wiltshire (project; with Barnaby Milburn)

Two libraries and three social services buildings, Hillingdon, London (with Charles Sands)

Apartment block, Fitzjohn's Avenue, London N.W.3 (project)

Office building, London Road, East Grinstead, Sussex (project; with Barnaby Milburn and Stephen Gage)

Flats, Hove, Sussex (project; with Charles Sands)

Housing, Ascot Road, Haringay, London

(with Robert Maxwell, Andrew Preece, David Lyall and Margaret Dent)

Health Centre, Bounds Green, London (with Stephen Gage)

Neo-classical house, Hampstead, London

1974 Gallagher Tobacco Showroom, Bond Street, London W.1 (project; with Achille Castiglione)

1975 St. James's Churchyard Shopping Centre conversion, Piccadilly, London W.1 (project)

1976 Historic house rehabilitation, Chelsea, London (project)

1977 National Magazine Company Headquarters, London (project)

Three permanent exhibition buildings for Concorde' prototypes (project I: with Robert Maxwell; project II: with Barnaby Milburn, Stephen Gage and Stephen Buck; project III: with Carl Laubin and Robert Hughes)

Four hotels for shrine sites for pilgrims, Iraq (project; with Barnaby Milburn, Robert Hughes, Stephen Buck and Carl Laubin)

1977/ 78 Urban renewal plan for Kendall Square, Cambridge, Massachusetts (project; with Barnaby Milburn, Stephen Buck, Robert Hughes, Robert Maxwell and Carl Laubin)

1978 Brunel Centre, stage IV, Swindon, Wiltshire (with Barnaby Milburn, Robert Hughes, Stephen Buck and Carl Laubin)

Victorian office building rehabilitation, Poland Street, Soho, London (with Stephen Gage)

Victorian warehouse rehabilitation, Folgate Street, London E.1 (project)

1979 Above Bar Church, Southampton (project; with Stephen Buck)

1980 Telford New Town, Shropshire (project; with Robert Maxwell and Banaby Milburn)

1980/ 81 Holyhead Terminal Building and Rail Station, Wales

1981 Offices, housing and leisure centre, Swiss Cottage, London (project; with Barnaby Milburn and Carl Laubin)

British Rail/Sealink Terminal Building, Holyhead, Wales (project; with Barnaby Milburn, Robert Hughes and Carl Laubin)

1982 Apartments and offices, Park Road, London (project; with Stephen Gage)

1983 Timberhill Area Urban Renewal Plan, Norwich, Norfolk (project; with Barnaby Milburn and Robert Hughes)

1984 C19 Warehouse refurbishment, Warwick Street, London (with Geraldine Walder)

Apartment Housing, Drayton Gardens, London (with Stephen Gage and Simon Colebrook)

Health Centre, Highgate, London (with Stephen Gage)

Commercial Centre and Urban Renewal, Newmarket, Suffolk (with Barnaby Milburn and Michael Emptage)

Site 4 Development, London Docklands (project; with Delaney, McVeigh and Pike)

Canary Wharf Development, London Docklands (with Delaney, McVeigh and Pike)

Town Centre Development, Port Harcourt, Nigeria

Close Housing, Hampstead, London (project; with Geraldine Walder)

Front Entrance Steps, Royal Institute of British Architects, London

Crown Yard, Newmarket, Suffolk

Central Area Development, Norwich, Norfolk

1985 Hotel, Canary Wharf, London Docklands (project)

Central Area Shopping Centre, Ipswich, Suffolk

Douglas Stephen: Brunel Centre, Swindon, Wiltshire, 1966-78.

Publications:

By STEPHEN: book—*British Buildings 1960-64,* with Kenneth Frampton and Michael Carapetian, London 1965; articles—"Institute of Technology at Otaniemi, Finland" in *Architectural Design* (London), February 1968; "25 Years of British Architecture 1952-1977: Commercial Buildings" in *RIBA Journal* (London), May 1977; "Less Than Utopian Geometry" in *London Architect* (London), July 1981.

On STEPHEN: articles—"Douglas Stephen and Partners" by Robert Maxwell in *Architectural Design* (London), September/October 1977; "Healthy Restraint: Bounds Green Health Centre, London" by Anthony Williams in *Building* (London), 13 July 1979; "Douglas Stephen Takes Issue With the Architectural Press" in *London Architect* (London), June 1981; "RIBA to Boost Work and Cut Bureaucracy" by Ian Martin in *Building Design* (London), 28 August 1981; "Tuesdays at the RIBA" in *RIBA Journal* (London), October 1981; recording—*True Grit,* tape cassette by Robert Maxwell, London 1980.

*

Having entered architectural practice at the beginning of the fifties, I belong to an immediate post-war generation which felt very closely in touch with the sources of the modern movement on the Continent, and indeed saw modern architecture as a cause to fight for in Britain.

The enjoyment of functional empiricism in the post-war period was partly an appreciation of its flexibility in relation to the varying demands of different jobs, but also a desire to exploit its own potential for structuring this diversity with a visual order. There were crucial differences in the modern style as practised in Le Corbusier and Terragni, say, or in Gropius or Breuer, and I belonged to a circle whose discrimination between such stylistic nuances had been sharpened by the teaching of Colin Rowe. It was this unequivocal influence also which enabled one to see modern architecture as being as much due to stylistic invention as to empirical necessity.

The willingness to accept an arbitrary or preconceived mental element in works of architecture enables them to be treated as vehicles of expression for ideas. This approach is probably the main explanation for the marked classicism and narrow eclecticism which has characterized my own work of our practice today.

I have never ceased to regard architecture as a practical art, which uses technology of necessity but never becomes subservient to it. Between demands of the programme, the resources of technology, I always look to a means of making the buildings communicate. In that way I hope to be equal to the task of responding to the social implications in a programme, and enlarging the depths of meaning that mere buildings may have for most people.

—Douglas Stephen

*

As a student, Dougals Stephen was remarkable amongst his contemporaries for his enthusiasm and drive. While still a student he undertook many small commissions for exhibition stands, and this led to his being responsible for an extensive area of the exhibition mounted in Glasgow in 1951 as part of the *Festival of Britain* celebrations, under the aegis of the late Sir Basil Spence. This experience of actually getting things built was an important factor in his early success as a practitioner.

The buildings of this early period are in one sense works of immaturity, but they also display a thorough professionalism and certainly reflect the confidence which during the postwar period most architects placed in the benefits of redevelopment. However, two aspects of the work of this early period were remarkable: the apartments at Harley Street and Wimpole Street stand out, not for their

functionalist aesthetic, but for their classicism; while the flats at Bedford Gardens are ultra-modern in a distinctly European, not an English, way. The difference of approach suggests the opening up of a polemic within Stephen's understanding of architecture, and betrays an interest in style and the theory of style which is quite other than the single-mindedness of a practitioner who wants only to get things built.

Stephen's awareness of these stylistic choices indicates an inner intellectuality at variance with his surface qualities of empiricism and entrepreneurial initiative. The potential was present from the beginning for the discovery of an approach to architecture which could reconcile the demands of the programme with a conscious refusal of a purely programmatic inspiration. This also perhaps explains how his practice developed into a gentle patronage in which others could join in this quest. The recital of those who worked there as associates and later distinguished themselves in their own right as radical designers or theorists is testimony to the generous spirit in which he worked: Panos Koulermis, Kenneth Frampton, Elia Zenghelis, Robin Spence, Adrian Gale, Edward Jones, and Peter Jamieson all contributed to the work of the office and helped to produce a varied output which never took the facile imprint of a "house style."

In the early 1970s, this period of eclectic search was succeeded by a more concentrated period of consolidation. The practice was enlarged by the addition of Robert Maxwell and Barnaby Milburn, and gave itself the task of attempting to reconcile the diversity of approaches in a more consistent theoretical method. From this middle period have come the various buildings constructed at Swindon for the Borough of Thamesdown. These buildings make positive spaces between each other and with the adjoining parts of the town. Each building is distinctive, so that a single character is not imposed on a large slice of the town, but rather between them they sketch out a way of dealing with the comprehensive redevelopment without the usual penalties of uniformity and visual impoverishment. Technological possibilities are explored in the interests of making an up-to-date facility, but they do not take over as the predominant content of the architecture, imposing a uniformity of appearance. The various glazed canopies are made out of modern materials with modern technology, yet they are also reminiscent of nineteenth-century arcades and railway architecture, appropriate to a railway town. These buildings represent the maturing of Stephen's original perception that style and function have to be attended to separately, and reconciled, along with a more general reconciliation between classical and modern, between the claims of development and those of environment and history.

—Robert Maxwell

STERN, Robert A. M.

American. Born in New York City, 23 May 1939. Educated at Columbia University, New York, B.A. 1960; Yale University, New Haven, Connecticut, M.Arch. 1965. Married Lynn Solinger in 1966 (divorced, 1978); son: Nicholas. Worked for the Perkins and Will Partnership, Washington, D.C., summer 1964; Program Director, The Architectural League of New York, 1965-66; Designer, Office of Richard Meier, New York, 1966; Consultant to Philip Johnson for *Eye on New York* television documentary, CBS-TV, and Member, Mayor Lindsay's Task Force on Urban Design, 1966-67; Consultant, Small Parks Program, New York, 1966-70; Urban Designer and Assistant for Design Policy to Assistant Administrator Samuel Ratensky, Housing and Development Administration, New York, 1967-70; Partner, Robert A. M. Stern and John S. Hagmann, architects, New York, 1969-77. Since

1977, Principal, Robert A. M. Stern Architects, New York. Lecturer, 1970-72, Assistant Professor, 1973-77, Associate Professor, 1977-82, Professor since 1982, and Director of the Temple Hoyne Buell Center for the Study of American Architecture since 1984, Columbia University, New York (Chairman, Committee on Lectures and Exhibits, since 1971, and College Departmental Representative, since 1973). William Henry Bishop Visiting Professor, Yale University, 1978. Member, Board of Directors, Yale Arts Association, 1968-72; Vice-President, Cunningham Dance Foundation, 1969-73; Member, Architecture Committee, Whitney Museum, New York, 1970-76; President, 1973-77, and Executive Committee Member since 1977, Architectural League of New York; Visiting Fellow, 1974-76, Architectural Education Program Advisor, 1974-77, and Trustee since 1983, Institute for Architecture and Urban Studies, New York; Director, New York Chapter, American Institute of Architects, 1976-78. Trustee, American Federation of the Arts, since 1967; Member, Mayor's Panel of Architects, New York, since 1975; Board Member, Society of Architectural Historians, New York, 1975-78; Editorial Consultant, Architectural History Foundation, New York, 1979-83; Board Member, Preservation League of New York, since 1984. Exhibitions: group shows—*The Roosevelt Island Competition,* Architectural League of New York, 1975; *Biennale,* Venice, 1976; *Palaces for the People,* Cooper-Hewitt Museum, New York, 1977; *Drawing Toward a More Modern Architecture,* Drawing Center and Cooper-Hewitt Museum, New York, 1977; *Art and Contemporary Architecture,* David Findlay Galleries, New York, Fall 1977; *Celebration of Water,* Cooper-Hewitt Museum, New York, 1978; *Transformations in Modern Architecture,* Museum of Modern Art, New York, 1979; *City Segments,* Walker Art Center, Minneapolis, 1980; *Speaking a New Classicism,* Smith College, Northampton, Massachusetts, 1981; *Collaboration: Artists and Architects,* Architectural League of New York, 1981; *Post-Modernism Comes to England,* Architectural Design Gallery, London, 1981; *Ornamentalism,* Hudson River Museum, Yonkers, New York, 1983 (travelled to the Fendrick Gallery, Washington, D.C., and University of Texas, Austin); *A Tribute to Contemporary Architecture,* University Place Gallery, Cambridge, Massachusetts, 1984; *Ideas/Ideal/Deal/Real,* University of Maryland, College Park, 1985; one-man shows—North Carolina School of Design, Raleigh, 1976; Art Net, London, 1977; Architectural Club, Miami, 1978; Young Hoffman Gallery, Chicago, 1981; Neuberger Museum, State University of New York at Purchase, 1982. Organized: continuing series of exhibits for the Architectural League of New York, 1965-66; *40 under 40,* American Federation of the Arts travelling exhibition, 1966; *Another Chance for Cities,* Whitney Museum, New York, and tour, 1970-71; *Some Younger New York Architects,* Columbia University and Boston Architectural Center, 1971-72; *Ornament in the 20th Century,* Cooper-Hewitt Museum, New York, Fall 1978; *Trends in Contemporary Architecture* New Gallery of Contemporary Art, Cleveland, 1978. Collection: Tehran Museum of Contemporary Art. Recipient: Award of Honor, New York Society of Architects, 1974; First Prize, Roosevelt Island Housing Competition, New York, 1975; Certificate of Honor, New York State Association of Architects, 1975; Certificate of Merit, New York State Association of Architects/American Institute of Architects, 1976; Award of Merit, *House and Home/AIA,* 1977; Residential Design Award, AIA, New York Chapter, 1977; First Honor Award, Homes for Better Living, *Housing,* 1978; Lumen Award, New York Section, Illuminating Engineering Society/International Association of Lighting Designers, 1978, 1982, 1983; National Honor Award, American Institute of Architects, 1980, 1985; Distinguished Architecture Award, 1982, 1984 (twice), 1985, and Medal of Honor, 1984, American Institute of Architects, New York Chapter; *Interiors* Award, New York, 1982, 1985; *Builder Magazine* Award, New York, 1984; First Honor Award,

Robert Stern: Point West Place Office Building, Framingham, Massachusetts, 1983-84.

American Institute of Architects, Westchester/Mid-Hudson Chapter, 1984; Award of Excellence, *Architectural Record*, New York, 1984. Fellow, American Institute of Architects, 1984. Address: Robert A. M. Stern Architects, 211 West 61st Street, New York, New York 10023 U.S.A.

Works

1968 Wiseman House, Montauk, Long Island, New York
1969 Tiffeau-Busch Ltd. Showroom and Offices, New York
1970 Showrooms for Helen Harper Inc., New York
1971 William White Jr. Apartment, New York
        Poolhouse and related facilities, Danziger House, Purchase, New York
1972 Beebe House and outbuildings, Montauk, Long Island, New York
        Kretchmer Apartment, New York
        Danziger Apartment, New York
1973 Eisner Apartment, New York
        Source Securities Corporation office alterations, New York (additional alterations, 1975, 1976)
1974 Poolhouse, for Bourke House, Greenwich, Connecticut
        Ferris Booth Hall additions and alterations, Columbia University, New York (project)
        Lang House, Washington, Connecticut
        Library, Museum, and Civic Plaza, Biloxi, Mississippi (project)
        University Hotel, John Jay Hall, Columbia University, New York (project)
1975 Dooney and Bourke Factory, Norwalk, Connecticut (project)
        Tennis Club, for King/Hitzig Productions, New York (project)

Squash Courts and Club Facility, for Bourke Enterprises, Newton, Massachusetts (project)
        Development plan for the city of Regina, Saskatchewan (competition project)
        Cullman House additions and alterations, Stamford, Connecticut
        Ehrman House and outbuildings, Armonk, New York
        Leonard Stern Townhouse, New York
        Hope Solinger Apartment, New York
        Solinger and Gordon Law Offices, New York
        Roosevelt Island Housing, New York (competition project)
1976 Danziger House additions and alterations, Purchase, New York
        Ferrin House, East Hampton, Long Island, New York
        Ski Lodge, Killington, Vermont (competition project)
        Development plan for Singer Island, City of Riviera Beach, Florida (competition project)
        St. Joseph's Village for Senior Citizens (competition project)
        Student Television Studio, Ferris Booth Hall, Columbia University, New York (project)
        State Capitol Annex Building, St. Paul, Minnesota (competition project)
        Subway Suburb, *Biennale*, Venice
197   Jerome Greene Building, School of Law, Columbia University, New York
        Bourke House, Seal Harbor, Maine
1978 Rodman Rockefeller Apartment, New York
        Millstein Townhouse, New York
1979 Erbun Fabrics Inc. Showroom, New York
        First Avenue Squash Club, New York
        Catlin House, Dublin, New Hampshire
        Maynard House, East Hampton, Long Island, New York

Cohen Apartment, New York
        Silvera House, Deal, New Jersey
        Hitzig Apartment, New York
        International House renovation, New York
        Smetana Medical Suite, New York
        Prototypical facade for Best Inc.
1980 Cohn House, Llewellyn Park, New Jersey
        Cohn House, Chilmark, Martha's Vineyard, Massachusetts
        Lawson House, East Quoque, Long Island, New York
        House, King's Point, New York
        Modern Architecture After Modernism Pavilion, at *Forum Design*, Linz, Austria
        Chicago Tibune Tower, Chicago (exhibition project)
        Strada Novissima exhibit, at the *Biennale*, Venice, Italy
        Carpasso Apartment, Fifth Avenue, New York
        City Hall annex, Cincinnati, Ohio
        House, Farm Neck, Oak Bluffs, Massachusetts
        DOM Headquarters, Bruhl, West Germany (competition project)
        Garibaldi Meucci Museum, Staten Island, New York
        House, Glen Cove, Long Island, New York
        San Juan Capistrano Library, California (competition project)
        Saper House additions, Woodstock, New York
        Catlin and Cos Offices, New York
1981 Ram Island House, Shelter Island, New York

Publications:

By STERN: books—*40 Under 40: Young Talent in*

Architecture, exhibition catalogue, New York 1966; *New Directions in American Architecture*, New York 1969, 1977; *George Howe: Toward a Modern American Architecture*, New Haven, Connecticut 1975; introduction to *The PSFS Building* (booklet), Philadelphia 1976; foreword, with Wilder Green, to *200 Years of American Architectural Drawings* by David Gebhard and Deborah Nevins, New York 1977; *Europa/America: Architetture Urbane Alternative Suburbane*, with others, *Biennale* exhibition catalogue, Venice 1978; commentary to *Philip Johnson: Collected Writings*, New York 1979; *The Artist's Eye: American Architectural Drawings, 1779-1979*, with Deborah Nevins, New York 1979; *The Anglo-American Suburb*, editor, with John Montague Massengale, London 1981; *Raymond Hood*, with Thomas P. Catalano, New York 1982; *East Hampton's Heritage*, with Clay Lancaster and Robert Hefner, New York 1982; *New York 1900* with Gregory Gilmartin and John M. Massengale, New York 1983; articles—"PSFS: Beaux Arts Theory and Rational Expressionism" in *Journal of the Society of Architectural Historians* (Philadelphia), May 1962; "Relevance of the Decade 1929-1939" in *Journal of the Society of Architectural Historians* (Philadelphia), March 1965; "Paul Rudolph: The First Twenty-Five Years" in *Kokusai Kenchiku* (Tokyo), May 1965; editor of *Perspecta* (New Haven, Connecticut), no. 9/10, 1965; "Constitution Plaza One Year After" in *Progressive Architecture* (New York), December 1965; "A Static Gallery" in *Progressive Architecture* (New York), April 1966; "Random Shots at USA 65" in *Progressive Architecture* (New York), May 1966; "Stompin' at the Savoye" in *Architectural Forum* (New York), May 1973; "Tape Recorder Chats" in *Architectural Record* (New York), May 1973; "Raymond Hood" in *Progressive Architecture* (New York), July 1974; "Yale 1950-1965" in *Oppositions* (New York), October 1974; "Toward an Architecture of Symbolic Assemblage" in *Progressive Architecture* (New York), April 1975; editor of "White and Gray," special issue of *Architecture + Urbanism* (Tokyo), April 1975; "A Serious Discussion of an Apparently Whimsical House" in *Architectural Record* (New York), July 1975; "Park Avenue Is Almost All Right (Maybe)" in *Architectural Record* (New York), February 1976; "Letter to the Editor" in *Oppositions* (New York), Winter 1976; "Robert Stern on Jim Stirling" in *Design Quarterly 100* (Minneapolis), Spring 1976; "Gray Architecture: Quelques Variations Post-Modernistes Autour de l'Orthodoxie" in *L'Architecture d'Aujourd'hui* (Paris), August/September 1976; guest editor of "40 Under 40 + 10," special issue of *Architecture + Urbanism* (Tokyo), January 1977; "At the Edge of Modernism" in *Architectural Design* (London), April 1977; "Forum: The Beaux-Arts Exhibition" in *Oppositions* (New York), Spring 1977; "Letter to the Editor" in *Contract Interiors* (New York), July 1977; "Further Thoughts on Millbank," with George Baird and Charles Jencks, in *Architectural Design* (London), July/August 1977; "Report: New York Notebook" in *Architecture + Urbanism* (Tokyo), August 1977; "The Evolution of Philip Johnson's Glass House, 1947-48" in *Oppositions* (New York), Fall 1977; "Something Borrowed, Something New" in *Horizon* (New York), December 1977; "After the Modern Movement" in *The Japan Architect* (Tokyo), December 1977; "Venturi and Rauch: Learning to Love Them" in *Architectural Monographs* (London), vol. 1, 1978; "New Directions in Modern American Architecture: Postscript" in *Architectural Association Quarterly* (London), nos. 2/3, 1978; "The Suburban Alternative: Coping with the Middle City" in *Architectural Record* (New York), August 1978; "How to Redesign New York" in *Art News* (New York), November 1978; "Models for Reality: Some Observations" in *Great Models* (Student Publication: North Carolina State University School of Design, Raleigh), no. 27, 1978; "Drawing from Models," with Frances Halsband, R. M. Kliment, and Richard B. Oliver, in *Journal of Architectural Education* (Washington, D.C.), September 1978; "Doubles of Post-Modern" in *Harvard Architecture Review* (Cambridge, Massachusetts), vol. 1, 1979; "With Rhetoric: The New York Apartment House" in *Via* (Philadelphia), vol. 4, 1980; "Interview: Robert A. M. Stern", with Jay Murphy, in *Dimensions* (Lincoln, Nebraska), vol. 2, no. 1, 1981; "Behind the Facades", interview with Charles Gandee, in *Architectural Record* (New York), March 1981; "An Interview with Robert A.M. Stern" in *Crit* (Washington, D.C.), Spring 1981; "Robert Stern on Modern Architecture" in *Architect and Builder* (Cape Town, South Africa), April 1982; "Duplications of Post-Modernism" in *Arquitectura* (Madrid), September/October 1982; "The Temple of Love and Other Musings", interview, in *Historic Preservation* (Washington, D.C.), September/October 1982; "Robert Stern and Michael Graves", interview with Katherine Dolgy, in *Fifth Column* (Montreal), Fall 1983; recording—*The Presence of the Past*, tape cassette and slides, London 1980.

On STERN: books—*The Roosevelt Island Competition*, exhibition catalogue, edited by Barbara Goldstein, New York 1975; *Wohnen im Eigenen Haus* by Gerhard Schwab, Stuttgart 1976; *The Form of Housing*, edited by Sam Davis, New York 1977; *The Language of Post-Modern Architecture* by Charles Jencks, London 1977; *Decorative Art and Modern Interiors 1978*, volume 67, edited by Maria Schofield, New York 1978; *Post-Modern Classicism* by Charles Jencks, London 1980; *American Architecture Now*, edited by Barbaralee Diamonstein, New York 1980; *Robert A. M. Stern: Buildings and Projects 1965-1980*, edited by Peter Arnell and Ted Bickford, New York 1981; *Robert Stern*, edited by David Dunster, with introduction by Vincent Scully, London 1981; *After Modern Architecture* by Paolo Portoghesi, New York 1982; *The Charlottesville Tapes*, edited by Jaquelin Robertson, New York 1985; articles—"Lang Residence: Where Are We Now, Vincent Scully?" by Charles Moore in *Progressive Architecture* (New York), April 1975; "Residence for an Academical Couple, Washington, Connecticut, 1973-74" in *Architecture + Urbanism* (Tokyo), April 1975; "The Work of Robert A. M. Stern and John S. Hagmann," special feature in *Architecture + Urbanism* (Tokyo), October 1975; "Stern Dimensions" in *Progressive Architecture* (New York), June 1976; "Les Cendres de Jefferson" by Manfredo Tafuri, and "Robert Stern/John Hagmann" in *L'Architecture d'Aujourd'hui* (Paris), August/September 1976; "Architecture: Letting Go with Color" in *House and Garden* (New York), September 1976; "Stern Star Estrella: La Obra de Robert A.M. Stern" in *Arquitecturas Bis* (Barcelona), September 1976; "40 under 40: Robert A.M. Stern" in *Architecture + Urbanism* (Tokyo), January 1977; "Grand Allusions" by Suzanne Stephens in *Progressive Architecture* (New York), February 1977; "The Stern View" by Jane Holtz Kay in *Building Design* (London), 11 February 1977; "Robert Stern," interview, by Bob Maltz in *Building Design* (London), 10 June 1977; "Robert A. M. Stern's Two Houses" by Paul Goldberger in *Architecture + Urbanism* (Tokyo), September 1977; "The Re-emergance of Color as a Design Tool" by Nory Miller in *AIA Journal* (Washington, D.C.), October 1978; "Designs for Living" by Douglas Davis in *Newsweek* (New York), 6 November 1978; "U.S. Architects: Doing Their Own Thing" by Robert Hughes in *Time* (New York), 8 January 1979; "The Doubles of Post-Modern" in *Harvard Architecture Review* (Cambridge, Massachusetts), Spring 1980; "Robert A. M. Stern projects" in *Controspazio* (Bari, Italy), April/June 1981; "Five Projects of Robert A. M. Stern" in *Architecture + Urbanism* (Tokyo), June 1981; "Robert A. M. Stern—From Perspecta to Post-Modern" in *Architectural Design* (London), vol. 51, no. 12, 1981; "The Maturing of Robert Stern" by Paul Goldberger in the *New York Times*, 4 April 1982; "Robert A. M. Stern" in *Architecture South Africa* (Cape Town), May/June 1982; "Three Interiors by Robert Stern" in *Architectural Review* (London), July 1982; "The Residential Works of Robert A. M. Stern", special issue of *Architecture + Urbanism* (Tokyo), July 1982; "Decoration is Not a Crime" in *Connaissance des Arts* (Paris), May 1983; "Architecture: Robert A. M. Stern" by Vincent Scully in *Architectural Digest* (Los Angeles), June 1984; "The Trend-Setting Traditionalism of Architect Robert A. M. Stern" by Carol Vogel in the *New York Times Sunday Magazine*, 13 January 1985.

Many of the cherished orthodoxies of the Modern Movement are now being supplanted by new concerns and beliefs. While these may not yet define a theory of architecture, a few beliefs that now guide my work may have wider implications for understanding the architectural climate of our time: 1) applied ornament is no crime; 2) buildings that refer to other buildings in the history of architecture are more meaningful than those which do not (this used to be called "eclecticism"); 3) buildings that refer and defer to the buildings around them gain strength over those that do not (this might be called "contextual integration"); 4) buildings that associate with ideas about specific events which caused them to be made are more meaningful than those which do not; the pursuit of specific images to convey ideas about buildings is relevant to design; 5) architecture is a story-telling or communicative art. Facades are not diaphanous veils; nor are they the affirmation of deep structural secrets. They are mediators between buildings as "real" constructs and those illusions, allusions and perceptions necessary to put buildings in closer contact with their social, cultural, historical and physical milieu.

Language and Meaning: In issues of form, as opposed to issues of technology or functional accommodation, orthodox modern architecture has been unwilling to accept known paradigms; over and over, the leading architects of the past generation have struggled to invent new forms that would replace those from the past which had become widely accepted as symbols. Rather than searching for ways of saying new things in traditional languages, our most inventive Modern architects have attempted with very modest success to invent a new, exclusive, absolute, universal architectural language. Nonetheless, at this point in time, the new language of modernism cannot be ignored no matter how limited it may appear to be in relationship to the great architectural languages of the past. In certain situations the modernist language is very potent: as in the designs of factories and other industrial buildings and especially in the components of buildings including the furniture which was the specialty of the Bauhaus. But, for most situations, especially those affecting the private realm of habitation and the public realm of institutional and urban design, the language of modernism—especially its dialect known as the International Style—has often proven incapable of subtle expression. The modernist styles are abstract rather than associative, conceptual rather than perceptual, technologically rather than culturally based. Modernism has become a narcissistic exercise about the making of buildings. As such, it has cut itself off not only from its role as a cultural act but also from its own formal traditions.

I believe that architectural form is related to symbolic intention and not technological expression; that architectural design is based on a known integration of lessons learned from those buildings that one admires and clients value—whether the client be individuals or the public and its institutions; and that forms from the past must be manipulated in relationship to particular and environmental situations. I believe that such a process of integration and manipulation—which used to be called eclecticism—can enrich our work and thereby make it more familiar and, possibly, more meaningful not only to the people who use buildings directly but also to those who merely see them in passing. The idea of eclecticism in architecture ought not to be embarrassing; after all, virtually every architect chose his or her art and profession out of admiration for buildings which were already in existence.

In the same way that many architects talk about functional programs which cause work to emerge in a particular way, and about the constraints of site, budget, and so on, which also serve to shape it, architects should be willing to talk about the forms of earlier architecture which have spoken directly to them. And it seems perfectly logical to me that details and sometimes whole images from admired work of the past find their way into current work just as portions of the literature of the past find their way into much of the poetry and prose of our time and just as our spoken language has within it certain phrases adopted whole from foreign languages.

Ornamentalism is the handmaiden of eclecticism. It is a paradox that when the Modern Movement threw out applied ornament it took over the characteristics of ornamentation—natural imagery, plasticity and continuity—even, on occasion, representationalism—and used them to establish not only a new language but also a new grammar of building form. This had the effect of turning whole buildings into utilitarian ornaments. Contrast Howell and Hood's *Chicago Tribune* building with Adolf Loos's project: one an image of a gothic tower, the other literally a doric column. At present, it seems that the use of familiar ornamental devices from the past is one way of making architecture more accessible. The articulation of new and old elements is deliberately blurred in my work: my feet are firmly placed on both sides of the line of historical imperative. I am both Modern and contemporary, anxious to reinforce tradition without losing sight of the fact that though I can choose to speak an old language, I will need to coin new phrases and, of course, to say new things.

I believe that design is, in part, a process of cultural assimilation. Though design includes problem-solving, the functional and technological paradigms called for in the vast majority of situations with which we deal have been established over the past 200 years: hence we can discuss building typology. Our task is to question the formal prejudices—or are they paradigms?—which dog us at what I regard as the end of modernism. And such questioning cannot come only from within the well-spring of an individual architect's "talent": it must also emerge from a knowledge of history, a concern for the state of the architectural art at a given moment, and a serious respect for the aspirations of clients. It must be continuously reaffirmed that individual buildings, no matter how remotely situated from other works of architecture, form part of a cultural and physical context. As a culture, as architects, we know so very much. What must be done is to face this knowledge squarely—and in so doing face the world around us, taking it for what it is, incrementally adapting the objects and ideas in it to our needs, while we in turn adapt to its demands. My attitude toward form, based on a *love for and knowledge of history*, is not concerned with accurate replication. It is eclectic and uses collage and juxtaposition as techniques to give new meaning to familiar forms and, in so doing, to cover different though not necessarily new ground. Mine is a confidence in the power of memory (history) combined with the action of people (function) to infuse design with richness and meaning. If architecture is to succeed in its efforts to participate creatively in the present, it must go beyond the iconoclasm of the Modern Movement of the last fifty years as well as the personal and often self-indulgent formalism of so much recent work and, strengthened by the fullest possible reading of its own past, recapture for itself a basis in culture.

—Robert A. M. Stern

An architect whose didactic gifts need to be assessed in his historical essays, lectures, and critical writing, as well as in his buildings, Robert A. M. Stern was a notable author and teacher of design before he began his own practice. This particular position as critic-*cum*-architect may look a bit like that of Robert Venturi, and it does somewhat derive from him, but

Stern is more than somewhat stylistically at variance with Venturi. Taking off from Venturi's preoccupations with American vernacular design and the sense of history (Venturi always seems more concerned with the sensation than the history), Stern has developed a stronger historicism, its sensations dogmatically controlled into sensibilities.

In Stern's own presentation of his work, he has seen himself as an "inclusivist," for his mix of references and themes, as opposed to the "exclusivists," the modern movement masters and, lately (according to Stern) their partly neo-Corbusian acolytes like Meier and Hejduk. For observers outside the salons and schools of New York, New Haven, and Philadelphia, with their esoteric architectural preoccupations, the inclusivists and exclusivists might look the same, since Stern and the rest use like vocabularies of stucco, contrasting solids and voids, flat planes, thin surfaces, deliberately skimpy details, tepid shapes, and (in Stern and several, but not all, practitioners) seductive curves, decorator-y colours, and no interest in expressing structure. Occasional infighting between such as the "New York Five" and their critics, the "Five on Five" (the latter including Stern), seems remote and precious in places like England, where Piano and Rogers and Norman Foster show their remorseless technological bent, or in Japan, France and Belgium, where really hairy ad-hocists offer a more relaxed, more vulgar, less contrived manifestation of what could be read as the linguistic analogy in aesthetics.

But, not even 50 until 1989, Stern continues to mature and strengthen. Admirers can find his best recent work at La Jolla, California, and in houses at Martha's Vineyard, Massachusetts.

—Nathan Silver

STILLMAN AND EASTWICK-FIELD.

Partnership: established, London, 1949, by John Stillman (born 1920), Elizabeth Eastwick-Field (born 1919), and John Eastwick-Field (born 1919). Current Associates: Humphrey Lukyn Williams, John Howe, David Stephens, and David Chisholm. Partners have acted as Assessors for awards of the Civic Trust, Department of the Enviroment, Central Council for the Disabled, and the Country Landowners Association, and as External Examiners at the Universities of Wales, Manchester, Newcastle, and London, as well as acting on councils and committees for the Royal Institute of British Architects, British Standards Institute, and Architectural Association. Exhibition: *150th Anniversary Retrospective Exhibition,* University College, London, 1978. Recipient: Bronze Medal, 1962 and 1977, and Housing Design Award, 1981, Ministry of Housing and Local Government/Department of the Environment; Civic Trust Awards, 1966, 1967, 1968, 1970, 1973, 1978, 1979, and 1981; South West Region Award, 1966, London Region Award, 1983, Royal Institute of British Architects; Donaldson Medal (John Eastwick-Field), University College, London, 1978. Address: 18 Highbury Place, London N5 1QT, England.

Works:

1946 Cecil Sharp House/English Folk Dance and Song Headquarters rebuilding, London (pre-partnership: J. and E. Eastwick-Field with Hugh Pite)
1953 Crocker Farm Builders, Minety, Wltshire
1955 Blackwell School Hall and Gymnasia, Harrow, Middlesex
1956 Krabbe House, Calcot, Reading, Berkshire
       Camden School for Girls redevelopment, London

Goldup House, Whitchurch, Berkshire
1958 New Wing for the Children's Hospital, Marlborough, Wiltshire
1959 Concrete Ltd. Exhibition Stand, *Building Exhibition,* London
1960 Post Office, Putney, London
       Fulbourne Housing Estate, Bethnal Green, London
       Halls of Residence and Staff Housing, College of Aeronautics, Cranfield, Bedfordshire
       Rayners School for the Deaf, Penn, Buckinghamshire
1961 Municipal Depot, Welwyn Garden City, Hertfordshire
1962 Hide Tower Housing Scheme, Westminster, London
       Housing, Oxlease, Hatfield, Hertfordshire
1963 Students Union Building, University of Keele, Staffordshire
1964 Mackintosh Hall Cultural Centre and Girls School, Gibraltar
1965 Hampstead School, London
1966 Housing, community centre, and shopping development, West Ham, London
       Residential School for the partially sighted, Exeter, Devon
       Residential and commercial development, Dufours Place/Marshall Street, Soho, London
       Advanced Science Wing, Camden School for Girls, London
       New Assembly Hall, Market Harborough Grammar School, Leicestershire
       Primary school, Market Harborough, Leicestershire
       Engineering Complex Brunel University, Uxbridge, Middlesex
       Training centre for the handicapped, Hackney, London
1968 Sports Hall, Totnes School, Devon
       Trevelyan College for Women, University of Durham, England
1970 Allington Park Primary School, Allington, Kent
       Grove Lane Housing Scheme, Camberwell, London
       Brixham Primary School, Devon
       Plympton Grammar School Development, Devon
       Ilfracombe Comprehensive School, Devon
1971 Physics, Polymer Science, and Nuclear Science Buildings, Brunel University, Uxbridge, Middlesex
       Edward VI School, Totnes, Deveon
       Clissold Park Comprehensive School, Stoke Newington, London
       Housing, Brecknock Road, Holloway, London
1972 Princess Marina Psychiatric Hospital, Northamptonshire
1973 Sir James Knott Hall, Trevelyan College, University of Durham, England
1975 New VIth Form House, Roedean School, Brighton, Sussex
       Weedon Bec Primary School, Northamptonshire
       Blackheath Bluecoat School Development, London
       Malpas County High School Development, Cheshire
       Frodsham County Secondary School, Cheshire
       Drama Workshop and Science Extensions, Hampstead School, London
1976 Housing and day nursery, Gresham Road, Brixton, London
       Housing, Wheelwright Street, Islington, London
       Welldon Park First School, Harrow, Middlesex
       University College development plan and stage I, Buckingham
       Chace Wing, Enfield District Hospital, Middlesex

Stillman and Eastwick-Field: Westside School for Girls, Gibraltar, 1976-82.

Nantwich School Development, Cheshire
Newton Abbot Schools Development, Devon
Housing, nursery and community buildings, Walterton Road, Paddington, London
School sports hall, Axminster, Devon

1976/
82 Westside School, Montagu Basin, Gibraltar
1977 Corby Community Hospital and Health Centre development, phase I, Northamptonshire
Housing, Nelson Gardens, Bethnal Green, London
School for Delicate Children, Kennington, London
Sheltered housing for old people, Myatts Fields, Brixton, London
Housing, phase II, Wheelwright Street, Islington, London
Palmers Estate housing rehabilitation, Turnell Park, London
Working girls hostel and adult training centre, Highbury, London
Irthlingborough School Development, Northamptonshire
1978 Old people's housing, Prentis Road, Streatham, London
Old people's housing, Stockwell Road, Clapham, London
Flats rehabilitation, Nevern Place, Earls Court, London
Gymnasium Camden School for Girls, London

Housing, Palmers Estate, Tufnell Park, London
Mayflower Family Centre, London
1979 Day Centre for the Physically Handicapped, Highbury, London
Boiler House, St. Anne's Hospital, Tottenham, London
Infectious Diseases Unit, St. Anne's Hospital, Tottenenham, London
1980 Chemistry Building, University College, London
Student Residences rehabilitation, Brunel University, Uxbridge, Middlesex
1981 Single-Person Housing, Wandsworth, London
Egyptology Department and Museum, University College, London
Housing rehabilitation, Walthamstow, London
1982 Academic Offices, Brunel University, Uxbridge, Middlesex
Research Laboratries, University College, London
Design Technology and Mult-Media Workshops conversion, Brunel University, Uxbridge, Middlesex
1983 Community Hospital, Clacton, Essex
Mortuary Building, Chase Farm Hospital, Enfield, Middlesex
Raine's Foundation School, Tower Hamlets, London
1984 Kitchens and Staff Dining-Room, Chase

Farm Hospital, Enfield, Middlesex
Sheltered Housing, Highbury, London
Ambulance Station and Nurse Education Centre, Stoke Mandeville Hospital, Buckinghamshire
Single-Person Housing II, Wandsworth, London
Pharmaceutical Research Institute, Camden, London
Doctor's Group Practice Offices, Hackney, London
Sixth Form Centre, Camden School for Girls, London
1985 Victoria Park Development Feasibility Study, Hackney, London

Publicatins:

By STILLMAN AND EASTWICK-FIELD: books—*Building in Cob Pise and Stabilized Earth* by John Eastwick-Field and Elizabeth Eastwick-Field, London 1947; *Design and Practice of Joinery* by John Eastwick-Field and John Stillman, London 1958, 1961, 1966, 1973.

On STILLMAN AND EASTWICK-FIELD: books—*Scheibe, Punki und Hugel* by Gustav Hassenpflug and Paulhans Peters, Munich 1966; *Planning for Play,* edited by Lady Allen of Hurtwood,

London 1968; *New British Architecture* by Robert Maxwell, London, 1972; *A Guide to Modern Buildings in London,* edited by Charles McKean and Tom Jestico, London 1976; articles—"Hexagon College for Durham" in *Times Educational Supplement* (London), 15 March 1958; "Young Architects" by James Stirling in *Architectural Design* (London), June 1958; "The Brains Behind the Builders" in *The Times* (London), September 1958; "Hide Tower, London" in *Bauen und Wohnen* (Zürich), September 1962; "Building Brunel" by Diana Rowntree in *The Guardian* (London), 25 February 1965; "The Visionary Village" by Diana Rowntree in *The Guardian* (London), 22 March 1966; "Architects Top Ten" by George Mansell in the *Sunday Telegraph* (London), 1 July 1966; "A Lesson from the Rock" by Robert Bond in *The Surveyor* (London, 17 July 1980; "Individual Lives" in *Architects' Journal* (London), 17 December 1980; "Refloating the Mayflower" by Anthony Williams in *Building* (London), 27 November 1981; "Pilgrim's Progress" by Danica Ognjenovic in *Interior Design* (New York), April 1982; "Mayflower Family Centre, Newham, London" in *Baumeister* (Munich), July 1982; "Youth Club at the Mayflower Family Centre Development" in *RIBA Journal* (London), August 1982.

We do not bring to projects preconceived ideas of planning, design, or construction. We believe that a closer study of clients' needs and of the site and its surroundings is the key to successful design. Each project will make its own demands for the type of construction and materials—as witness the many beautiful and unselfconsious indigenous buildings throughout the world

We believe that building must ultimately become far more sophisticated, but until economic and other circumstances permit a more rapid development to technology, we realize there are risks in setting aside tradition and using methods and materials.

We believe that architects have an obligation both to build soundly and to use their trained sensibilities to stretch visual imagination.

—John Stillman
—John Eastwick-Field
—Elizabeth Eastwick-Field

Years ago, critic Ian Nairn wrote that Stillman and Eastwick-Field "have always been honest and sometimes dull also. Not the dulleness of someone with nothing to say, but the honesty which if presented with an unexciting programme refuses to dramatise it artificially." There are no great set-pieces in the portfolio of Stillman and Eastwick-Field. Rather, theirs is a record of sound and honest architecture, architecture that desires first and foremost to satisfy the people who use it while remaining true to the materials and methods of construction it has employed.

The practice started life in 1949, full of the zeal of building a better Britain out of the wreckage of the war. By that time John Eastwick-Field had put in a period working for the Building Research Station and teaching at the Architectural Association. With his wife, Elizabeth, also an architect, he carried out several commissions, including the rebuilding of Cecil Sharp House, the headquarters of the English Folk Dance and Song Society. John Stillman brought to the practice special interests in school building and in standards and specification that have proved to be lifelong.

The three combined an admiration for the work of Mies, Aalto and Le Corbusier with a healthy scepticism for the strict mores of Modern Movement. Like so many other practices founded just before the postwar building boom got under way in earnest, for more than twenty years Stillman and Eastwick-Field enjoyed a wide range of major commissions for schools, hospitals, university colleges, workshops, and housing. While their buildings were never far from the forefront of the current fashion, the partners were preoccupied with combining style with technical excellence. An early example is the 226 foot high Hide Tower, Westminster, a succesful example of prefabrication in a tall residential building (incidentally, for elderly people) which remains popular with its tenants today.

In the early 1960s, a new strain appeared in their work: a concern to make their buildings smaller in scale and readily comprehensible to their users. This was particularly true of their schools, often designed for the handicapped or for very young children. The West of England School for Partially Sighted Children, in Exeter, completed in 1966, was conceived in traditional manner as an intimate group of brick-clad buildings designed to encourage the children to venture out of doors. In 1971, at their Edward VI School at Totnes, traditional materials were skillfully handled to produce a sensitive alternative to the conventional postwar school. The 1982 Westside School, a girls' comprehensive in Gibraltar, bears the fruit of these exercises in an excellent design for a warm climate: groups of classrooms, in buildings of white forticrete blocks with pitched, tiled roofs, set around planted courtyards.

With the cutbacks in large, public sector commissions for new buildings in the late 1970s, the work of the practice has turned more to feasibility studies, research into energy conservation for the Building Research Station, and rehabilitation and conversion of existing buildings—for example, David Stephens' chemistry laboratories for students and pharmaceutical laboratories for Sandoz at University College, London, and David Chisholm's sensitive extension of a Norman Shaw school for the Raine's Foundation in Bethnal Green. In new building, the practice has opted for a crisply detailed style, normally in red brick, with pitched roofs tiled with traditional slates or clay pantiles, timbered window frames and staircase rails, and bright, primary-coloured paints for other points of detail, as can be seen in John Stillman's Community Hospital at Clacton in Essex, Elizabeth Eastwick-Field's recent boilerhouse for St Leonard's Hospital, David Chisholm's Nurse Education Centre at Stoke Mandeville Hospital, and Humphrey Lukyn Wiliams' Acadamic Offices at Brunel University.

—Stephanie Williams

STIRLING, James Frazer.
British. Born in Glagow, Scotland, 22 April 1926. Educated at the Quarry Bank High School, Liverpool, until 1941; Liverpool School of Art, 1942; University of Liverpool School of Architecture, 1945-50 (exchange student in New York, 1949), Dip.Arch. 1950; School of Town Planning and Regional Research, London, 1950-52. Served as a Lietenant in the Paratroops, 1942-45; in D-Day Landing with 6th Airborne Division, 1944. Married Mary Shand in 1966; children: Benjamin, Kate and Sophie. Worked as Senior Assistant, Lyons, Israel and Ellis, *q.v.*, Lyons, Israel, Ellis and Gray, London, 1953-56; in partnership with James Gowan, *q.v.*, London, 1956-63; in private practice, London, 1964-70. Since 1971, Partner with Michael Wilford, James Stirling and Partner (now James Stirling, Michael Wilford and Associates), London. Visiting Teacher, Architectural Association, London, 1955. Regent Street Polytechnic, London, 1956-57, and Cambridge University School of Architecture, 1958; Royal Institute of British Architects Lecturer, 1965. Davenport Professor, Yale University, New Haven, Connecticut, since 1967; Visiting Professor, Akademie der Künste, Düsseldorf, since 1977; Banister Fletcher Professor, London University, 1977; Architect-in-Residence, American Academy, Rome, 1982. Exhibitions: *James Stirling: Three Buildings,* Museum of Modern Art, New York, 1969; Heinz Gallery, Royal Institute of British Architects, London, 1974; *Biennale,* Venice, 1976; Walker Art Center, Minneapolis, Minnesota, 1977; Leo Castelli Gallery, New York, 1977; *Roma Interotta,* Rome, 1978; *Museum Projects,* Dortmund University, West Germany, 1979; *Manhattan Townhouses,* New York, 1980; *Three German Projects,* Royal Institute of British Architects, London, 1980; *Fogg Museum New Extension: Drawings,* Fogg Museum, Cambridge, Massachusetts, 1981; *Ten New Buildings,* Institute of Contemporary Arts, London, 1983; *Model Futures,* Institute of Contemporary Arts, London, 1983. Recipient: Brunner Award, National Institute of Arts and Letters, U.S.A., 1976; Alvar Aalto Medal, Finland, 1978; Gold Medal, Royal Institute of British Architects, 1980; Pritzker Prize, 1981. Honorary Doctorate: Royal College of Art, London, 1979. Honorary Member, Akademie der Künste, Berlin, 1969; Accademia delle Arti, Florence, 1979; Accademia Nazionale di San Luca, Rome, 1979; Bund Deutscher Architekten, West Germany, 1983; Honorary Fellow, American Institute of Architects, 1976; Fellow, Royal Society of Arts, London, 1979. Associate of the Royal Institute of British Architects, 1950. Address: James Stirling, Michael Wilford and Associates, 75 Gloucester Place, London W1H 3PF, England.

Works:

1956 House, Isle of Wight
1957 Expandable House (project)
         Low-rise flats, Ham Common, Richmond, London
         Private house conversion, London
         Churchill College, Cambridge, England (project)
1957/
    59 Low-rise houses and flats, Preston, Lancashire
1958/
    61 Dining Hall, Brunswick Park Primary School, London
1959 Selwyn College, Cambridge, England (project)
1959/
    63 Engineering Department, University of Leicester, England
1960/
    64 Old people's home, Blackheath, London
         Children's home, Frogmore, Wandsworth, London
1964/
    67 History Building, Cambridge University, England
1964/
    68 Flats, Camden Town, London
         Andrew Melville Hall, University of St. Andrews, Scotland
1965 Dorman Long Headquarters Building, Middlesbrough, Yorkshire
1966/
    71 Florey Building, Queen's College, Oxford, England
1967/
    76 Housing, Runcorn New Town, Cheshire
1968 Redevelopment study, New York (with A. Baker)
1969 Siemens AG Building, Munich (project)
1969/
    72 Olivetti Training School, Haslemere, Surrey
1969/
    76 Low-cost housing, Lima, Peru
1970 Derby Town Centre (project)
1971 Olivetti Headquarters, Milton Keynes, Buckinghamshire (project)
         Arts Centre, University of St. Andrews, Scotland (project)
1975 Wallraf-Richartz Museum, Cologne (project)
         Museum for Northrhine/Westphalia, Düsseldorf (project)

1976 Government Centre, Doha, Qatar (project)
Regional Centre for Tuscany, Florence (with Castore, Malanima, Rizzi)
1977 Revision to the Nolli Plan for Rome (project)
1977 Administration Centre, Wilaya de Skikda, Algeria
Museum of Science and Technology, Tehran
Dresdner Bank, Marburg, West Germany
1977/
  84 Art Gallery addition, National Museum, Stuttgart
1979 Design and Feasibility Study for Tate Gallery extensions, Millbank, London
1979/
  81 Architecture School extensions, Rice University, Houston, Texas
1979/
  84 Fogg Museum new building, Harvard University, Cambridge, Massachusetts
1980/
  85 Tate Gallery extension (Turner Museum), Millbank, London

Publications:

By STIRLING: book—*James Stirling,* with Robert Maxwell, New York 1983.

On STIRLING: books—*The New Brutalism* by Reyner Banham, London 1966; *Architecture in Britain Today* by Michael Webb, London 1969; *The Politics of Architecture* by Anthony Jackson, London 1969; *Dizionario encyclopaedia d'architettura e urbanistica* by Paolo Portoghesi, Rome 1969; *Architecture 2000* by Charles Jencks, London 1971; *The Third Generation* by Philip Drew, Stuttgart, 1972; *New British Architecture* by Robert Maxwell, Stuttgart 1972; *Modern Movements in Architecture* by Charles Jencks, London 1973; *Design in Architecture* by G. Broadbent, London 1973; *Saper vedere L'architettura moderne* by Bruno Zevi, Turin 1973; *James Stirling,* exhibition catalogue, with introduction by Reyner Banham, London 1974; *James Stirling: Buildings and Projects 1950-74,* London, New, York, Stuttgart, Milan and Tokyo, 1975; *Dortmunder Architekturhefte 15: Museumbauten— Entwurfe und Projekte seit 1945,* exhibition catalogue, edited by Josef Paul Kleihues, Dortmund, West Germany 1979; *James Stirling: Buildings and Projects 1950-1980,* edited by Peter Arnell and Ted Bickford, with an essay by Colin Rowe, New York 1984; articles—"The Work of Stirling and Gowan" by Arthur Korn in *Architecture and Building News* (London), January 1959; "Two Works by James Stirling: A Portrait" by Hiroshi Hara and Yukio Futagawa in *Kokusai Kentiku* (Tokyo), January 1965; "The Anti-Pioneers" by Nikolaus Pevsner in *The Listener* (London), 5 January 1967; "L'Opera di James Stirling" by L. Biscogli in *Casabella* (Milan), June 1967; "Observations on New British Architecture" by T. Stevens in *Bauen und Wohnen* (Zürich), December 1967; "Pop non Pop" by Charles Jencks in *Architectural Association Journal* (London), Winter 1968; "James Stirling: Buildings and Projects 1950-1967" in *Kentiku Architecture* (Tokyo), January 1968; "Lucky Jim" in *Building Design* (London), 25 May 1973; "James Stirling: Five Projects" in *Genghia Architecture* (Taiwan), June 1973; "An Extra Dimension" by N. Jones in *RIBA Journal* (London), April 1974; "A Modern Neo-Classicist" by M. Girouard in *Country Life* (London), May 1974; "A Detonation in Glass and Brick" by Charles Jencks in *Times Literary Supplement* (London), 21 June 1974; "Transformations in Style" by Kenneth Frampton in *Architecture + Urbanism* (Tokyo), February 1975; "Jim the Great" by G. K. Koening in *Casabella* (Milan), March 1975; "James Stirling at the IUA Congress, Spain" in *Building Design* (London), May 1975; "The Language of Architecture" by Charles Jencks in *Sunday Times Magazine* (London), 10 August 1975; "Anglo-Scottish Architect with Anglo-International Reputation" in *House and Garden* (London), October 1975; "Inside James Stirling" in *Design Quarterly* (Minneapolis, Minnesota), April 1976; "Stirling Gets Aalto Medal" in *Architects' Journal* (London), 14 December 1977; "Stuttgart National Gallery Extension and Workshop Theatre" in *Architectural Design* (London), no. 8/9, 1979; "Back with a Bang" by J. M. McKean in *Building Design* (London), 7 September 1979; "Stirling Quality" by J. M. McKean in *Building Design* (London), 14 September 1979; "Stirling Gets the Gold" in *Building Design* (London), 29 February 1980; "Stirling Gold" by A. Best in *Architects' Journal* (London), 5 March 1980; "Stirling on the Gold Standard" by G. Stamp in *The Spectator* (London), 29 March 1980; "James Stirling: Royal Gold Medal for Architecture" in *RIBA Journal*

James Stirling: New State Art Gallery and Workshop Theatre, Stuttgart, 1977-84.

(London), March 1980; "The British Architect Who Works Abroad" in *House and Garden* (London), June 1980; "Stirling Receives Pritzker Prize" in *Progressive Architecture* (New York), June 1981; "James Stirling: Dynamic Dissonant" in *Connaissance des arts* (Paris), November 1981; "James Stirling—Work in Progress" in *Casabella* (Milan), April 1982; "The Man behind the Tate's New Work of Art" by Deyan Sudjic in *The Times* (London), 19 April 1983; "Stirling Revalued" by Deyan Sudjic in *Sunday Times Magazine* (London), 22 January 1984; "New Museums Harmonize with Art" by Paul Goldbergen in the *New York Times*, 14 April 1985. film—*James Stirling's Architecture*, BBC/Arts Council, London 1973.

Bibliography—*The Architecture of Inconsistency in the Work of James Frazer Stirling: A Selected Bibliography* by Robert B. Harmon, Monticello, Illinois 1981.

I ceased to believe in Frank Lloyd Wright's philosophy of "truth to materials" when I saw for the first time a building by Palladio—where the peeling columns were in fact made of bricks—and not of marble or stone, as I had naively assumed from the books.

I believe that the shapes of a building should indicate—perhaps display—the usage the way of life of its occupants, and it is therefore likely to be rich and varied in appearance, and its expression is unlikely to be simple. The collection (in a building) of forms and shapes which the everyday public can *associate* with and be *familiar* with—and *identify* with—seems to me essential. These forms may derive from staircases, windows, corridors, rooms, entrances, and so forth, and the total building could be though of as an assemblage of everyday elements recognizable to a normal man and not only an architect. For instance, in a building we did at Oxford University some years ago, it was intended that you could recognize the historic elements of courtyard, entrance gate towers, cloisters, as well as a central object replacing the traditional fountain or statue of the college founder. In this way, we hoped that students and public would not be *disassociated* from their cultural past. The particular way in which functional-symbolic elements are put together may be the "art" in the architecture.

I am wary of what seems to me banal and arrogant solutions of tents, space frames, domes, and bubbles covering everything—these technocratic solutions may be valid for single-usage spectator activities, but if carried into normal everyday building can only *subvert* the richness and variety of life.

If the expression of functional-symbolic forms and familiar elements is foremost, the expression of structure will be secondary, and if structure shows, it is not in my opinion the engineering which counts but the way in which the building is put together that is important. It is desirable not to eliminate the traces of the human hand in carpentry or bricklaying, and by the same token it is necessary to express the assemblage process of most prefabricated systems; similarly with the use of colour pigmentation in plastics to delineate the separate parts.

We are not much concerned with the imagery of space flight or super-advanced technology, as I think an architect usually has to make to with the technology which is normal and is cost-wise available to him. According to what is appropriate for a particular building problem, the building could, I think, be made of any materials—old or new, traditional or technological—and the whole spectrum of the past, from earth works to plastics, is usable according to the differing economic/climate conditions prevailing in different countries.

—James Stirling

In terms of architectural ingenuity, the work of James Stirling can be seen as the most powerful expression of the contemporary international situation. His development over more than two decades has rightly been described as the mirror of architectural development in general: "It has fallen to James Stirling to express the revolutionary intentions of a new generation in the medium of hard building and all this has provided a tradition which makes questioning not only to be expected but du jour, which is in its own way moving architecture forward on an international front" (Alvin Boyarsky in *Architectural Design*, November 1968). In comparison with his fellow architects of the "Third Generation," Stirling, who has always been more articulate than most of them, has become a prototype for postwar international architectural development.

Stirling's early work reflects his critical dialogue with the late work of Le Corbusier and architectural history and at the same time is a statement of independence. In 1957 he wrote: "Today, Stonehenge is more significant than the architecture of Sir Christopher Wren." His housing in Ham Common and Preston and his old people's home in Blackheath document the concern for communal vitality and neighborliness in terms of a direct articulation of space and circulation which is in direct opposition to prevalent stylistic and aesthetic concerns. Since 1962 Stirling has argued against the obsession with decorating the skin of buildings. He does not accept the traditional functionalist attitude but prefers instead an integration of form and function using imagery as the connecting link. Architecture is, in his own words, "not a question of style of appearance; it is how you organize spaces and movement for a place and activity." For him, from and space are to be experienced in relation to an inherent meaning given to the building by the architect.

A second phase in Stirling's development is strongly articulated in a sculptural and ambivalent use of materials and a dialectical approach toward meaning. This is documented in his buildings for the engineering faculty of the University of Leicester, the history department at Cambridge, the dormitories for the University of St. Andrews, and in the Runcorn New Town housing—each a powerful articulation of the required solution. Stirling integrates the industrial potential appropriately into the architectural form. Metaphorically he uses the image of the greenhouse, the battle ship, constructivist architecture in Russia, and skyscraper design in America, as well as engineering structures such as the launching ramps at Cape Kennedy and housing of the eighteenth century in England. The integration of pre-existing imagery into the built form gives complex meaning to his work and creates a greater harmony between environment and tradition.

Since 1970 Stirling has intensified historical imagery and urban concern, the project for the Town Centre at Derby being the most radical example. In other projects, such as the museum in Düsseldorf, he has included parts of the existing urban fabric which surrounds the new building. The project for the Wallraf-Richartz/Museum in Cologne goes even further in an attempt to correct the existing urban site. By means of the new museum he harmoniously unifies the three isolated units—the Cathedral, the railway station, and the Hohenzollern Bridge. Major works of the 1980s, such as the Staatsgalerie in Stuttgart and the project for the Science Center in Berlin, as well as additions to existing structures in Cambridge, Massachusetts and Houston, Texas, give a summary of Stirling's design philosophy and at the same time open up perspectives for new creative development.

Stirling's concept of contemporary architecture is concerned with the humanization of the environment. Humanistic considerations dominate all technological, economic, and aesthetic preconceived ideas and ideologies. Architecture has to reestablish its own criteria for evaluation; for Stirling this obviously means creating in harmony with common sense, tradition, the existing environment, and a concern for people.

—Udo Kultermann

STONE, Edward Durell.

American. Born in Fayetteville, Arkansas, 9 March 1902. Educated at the University of Arkansas, Fayetteville, 1920-23; as apprentice to Henry R. Shepley, Boston, 1923-25; Harvard University, 1925-26; Massachusetts Institute of Technology School of Architecture, 1925-26; Rotch Travelling Scholar, in Europe, 1927-29. Served as a Major in the United States Air Force, 1942-45. Married Orlean Vandiver in 1931 (divorced, 1950); children: Edward Jr. and Robert; married Maria Eleana Torchio in 1954 (divorced); children: Benjamin and Maria; married Violet Campbell Moffat in 1972; daughter: Fiona. Worked with the consortium of architects designing Rockefellar Center, New York, 1929-35; in private practice, New York, 1935 until his death, 1978: President, Edward Durell Stone and Associates, New York; offices established in Palo Alto, California, Los Angeles, and Chicago. Instructor in Advanced Design, New York University, 1935-40; Associate Professor of Architecture, Yale University, New Haven, Connecticut, 1946-52; Visiting Critic, Princeton University, New Jersey, 1953, and University of Arkansas, Fayetteville, 1955, 1957-59. Trustee, American Federation of the Arts; Director, American National Theatre and Academy; Director, Whitney Museum, New York. Recipient: Architectural League of New York Medal, 1937, 1950, 1953; Grand Prize, Pittsburgh Glass Competition, 1938; First Prize, *House and Garden*, 1939; Gold Medal, 1955, and Honor Award, 1958, 1967, American Institute of Architects; Architectural Achievement Award, Copper and Brass Reserve Association, 1963; Architectural Excellence Award, Metropolitan Washington Board of Trade, 1965; John F. Kennedy Award, Institute of North American Studies, Barcelona, 1966; Building Award, *Business Magazine*, 1966; First Prize, American Society of Landscape Architects Competition, 1973. D.F.A.: University of Arkansas, Fayetteville, 1951; Colby College, Waterville, Maine, 1959; Hamilton College, Clinton, New York, 1962; M.F.A.: Otis Art Institute, Los Angeles, 1961; L.H.D.: University of South Carolina, Columbia, 1964. Fellow, American Institute of Architects; Member, National Academy of Design. Member, National Institute of Arts and Letters, and Fellow, American Academy of Arts and Sciences, 1960. Fellow, Royal Society of Arts, London, 1960. *Died* (in New York) *6 August 1978.*

Works:

1933   Mandel House, Mt. Kisco, New York
1937   House, 4 Buckingham Street, Cambridge, Massachusetts (with Carl Koch)
1939   Goodyear House, Old Westbury, Long Island, New York
       Museum of Modern Art, West 53rd Street, New York (with Phillip Goodwin)
1946   El Panama Hotel, Panama City
1951   Fine Arts Center, University of Arkansas, Fayetteville
1954   United States Embassy, New Delhi
1957   Government Hospital, Lima, Peru
       Stanford University Medical School and Hospital, Palo Alto, California
       Graf House, Dallas
1958   United States Pavilion, *World's Fair*, Brussels
       Stuart Pharmaceutica Company, Pasadena, California
1959   Edward Durell Stone House (conversion of brownstone), 130 East 64th Street, New York
       Gulf Service Station, Kennedy International Airport, New York
       Central Library, 1213 Newell Avenue, Palo Alto, California
       Mitchell Park Branch Library, 3700 Middlefield Road, Palo Alto, California
1960   American Federation of the Arts Building interior conversion, 41 East 65th Street, New York

1961 Harvey Mudd College, Claremont, California
    Institute of Nuclear Science and Technology, Islamabad, Pakistan

1962 Perpetual Savings Bank, Wilshire Boulevard and Malcolm, Los Angeles
    Perpetual Savings Bank, Wilshire Boulevard and McCarty, Los Angeles
    Foster and Wells Fargo Buildings, 1015 East Hillside Boulevard, Foster City, California
    Commodore Apartments, Foster City Boulevard, Foster City, California

1963 State University of New York at Albany
    Beckman Auditorium, California Institute of Technology, Pasadena
    General Community Hospital of the Monterey Peninsula, Carmel Highway, Monterey, California
    Theatre, Loyola University, 7101 West 80th Street, Los Angeles
    Center for Continuing Education, University of Chicago
    Public School 199, 270 West 70th Street, New York

1964 National Geographic Society, 17th and M Streest N.W., Washington, D.C.

1965 Huntington Hartford Gallery of Modern Art, Columbus Circle, New York (now the New York City Department of Cultural Affairs)
    City Hall, Paducah, Kentucky

1966 Museum of Art, Ponce, Puerto Rico
    Bush Memorial Stadium, St. Louis

1968 General Motors Building and Plaza, 58th/59th Streets at Fifth Avenue, New York (with Emerby Roth and Sons)
    Phillips Hall of Education, University of Southern California, Los Angeles
    Social Science Building, University of Southern California, Los Angeles

1969 *Buffalo Evening News* Building, Buffalo, New York
    Fine Arts Center, Amarillo, Texas
    Master plan for the Florida State Capitol Complex, Tallahassee (with Smith and Hills)
    Civic Center, Seaside, California

1970 Ahmanson Center, 3731 Wilshire Boulevard, Los Angeles
    NASA Building, Cambridge, Massachusetts (now the Federal Department of Transportation)
    School of Law, University of Alabama, University
    Eisenhower Hospital, Palm Desert, California
    City Hall, Palo Alto, California

1971 John F. Kennedy Center for the Performing Arts, Washington, D.C.

1972 Gerontology Center, University of Southern California, Los Angeles
    Law Center, Georgetown University, Washington, D.C.

1973 PepsiCo World Headquarters, Purchase, New York.

1974 Standard Oil Building and Plaza, East Randolph Street, Chicago (with Perkins and Will)

1975 Bankamericard Center, Green and Arroyo Parkway, Pasadena, California
    Davidson Conference Center, University of Southern California, Los Angeles

Publications:

By STONE: books—*The Evolution of an Architect,* New York 1962; *Recent and Future Architecture,* New York 1967; article—"Kitchens: Efficiency Is Not Enough" in *Architectural Record* (New York), May 1962.

Edward Durell Stone: Standard Oil Building, Chicago, 1974.

On STONE: articles—"Recent Work by Edward Durell Stone" in *Architectural Forum* (New York), July 1941; "Meet Edward Stone" in *House Beautiful* (New York), September 1945; "Genetrix: Personal Contributions to American Architecture" in *Architectural Review* (London), May 1957; "Educaitonal Work of Edward D. Stone" in *Architectural Record* (New York), February 1958; "The Work of Edward D. Stone" in *Architectural Record* (New York), March 1959; "Minoru Yamasaki and Edward Durell Stone" in *Zodiac* (Milan), no. 8, 1961; "New York Is the Office of Ed Stone" in *Architectural Forum* (New York), October 1961; "New Work, Serene and Classic, by Edward Durell Stone" in *Architectural Record* (New York), October 1962; "Recent Work of Edward Durell Stone" in *Architectural Record* (New York), October 1964; "Theatres" in *Progressive Architecture* (New York), October 1965; "Public Buildings" in *Architectural Forum* (New York), November 1971; "Two California Hospitals by Edward Durell Stone" in *Architectural Record* (New York) September 1972; "Sculpture in a Broad Landscape" by Lanning Roper in *Country Life* (London), 21 April 1977; "Edward Durell Stone, 1902-1978" in *Arts and Architecture* (Los Angeles), April/July 1979; "Cultural Colossi—Kennedy Centre at 10" by A. O. Dean in *AIA Journal* (Washington, D.C.) August 1981.

Bibliographies—*Architectural Versatility and the Work of Edward D. Stone: a selected bibliography* by Robert B. Harmon, Monticello, Illinois 1980; *Edward Durell Stone: A Bibliography* by James R. Christopher, Monticello, Illinois 1984.

*

At the least, Edward Durell Stone was representative of the essentially fragmentary nature of the history of modern architecture. In the course of a career which emerged from the infancy of the International Style and ended in the unsettled eclecticism of the late 1970's, Stone's work was periodically, and often temporarily, emblematic of that congruence of forces that generate "newness" in architecture. The significance of the work is as discontinuous and erratic as the vagaries of popular taste. Stone himself disparaged mass culture: "It is impossible for me to associate these mass-assembled, catch-penny structures with permanent architecture. They bear more resemblance to the latest automobile, dependent upon shining, metallic finish and doomed to obsolescence." Yet much of his own legacy is similarly fleeting, dependent upon surface manipulations and the repeated application of "stock parts."

In his later, most productive years (the Monumental Period), the deterioriation of intended permanence into transience became increasingly pronounced as Stone settled into a more restricted vocabulary, rooted in the classicisim of the New Delhi Embassy and reapplied endlessly from Paducah to the Potomac. Supported by the popular press and a certain cultural appropriateness (to both India and the United States), New Delhi quickly became a symbol of a "new architecture," its lacy grillwork and sensuous courtyard juxtaposed with a classic symmetry and proportion, the elephantine Great Seal above the entry. As a result, the building was accepted and praised by both the giver and receiver, and, indeed, some twenty years later, John Kenneth Galbraith (then the Ambassador) was to pronounce it "perhaps the most beautiful building ever accomplished by the government of the United States." Frank Lloyd Wright, according to Stone, called it "one of the finest buildings of the past hundred years." In the context of Stone's work, the Embassy was a rare example of a building that synthesized both potent cause and dramatic effect.

The subsequent output of building designs—both built and unbuilt—eroded the pedestal which supported the Embassy's reputation by displaying in endless redundancy not only the formalism of the composition, but its elements as well. The fragile

determinism of New Delhi disappeared in a search for "universality."

The distillation of the vocabulariy was accompanied by the increasingly messianical perception of the architect's role (no doubt infused by the aura of Frank Lloyd Wright). The result is disastrous. Where there can be tolerance for such romantic banality in lesser structures—gas stations and resort hotels—the magnitude of intention in such buildings as the Kennedy Center in Washington, D.C., the General Motors Building New York and the Florida State Capital turns the object to portentuous kitsch. Like other artifacts of mass-culture—the automobile, the mobile home—they attempt to signify status by the manipulation of styles. At Best, they are objects for unconsidered or uneducated enjoyment; at worst, they are pompous and dull. They are merely buildings of effect.

Just as Stone's later buildings pander to man's instincts for beauty in a way that annihilates meaning, his ventures into complex and large scale design reveal a similar vacuousness. The consummation of the Stone-Rockerfeller Connection—the campus of the State University of New York at Albany—is the academic companion of Wallace Harrison's South Mall and reflects Stone's "quest for order" and formal simplicity. The result is exemplary of the academic facism of the 1960's. The architect, overly consumed with occupying the podium of good taste, became the conveyor of banality.

Stone's contribution must be judged in terms of the considerable popular impact of his later work. However, the episodic nature of his career contains strata—each somewhat separate from the other—that contain some elements of lasting worth. For example, his early flirtation with the International Style followed an important contribution to the design of the interior of Radio City Music Hall, and resulted in the elegant Panama Hotel and residences that helped introduce the modern style to the Northeastern United States. The signal building of this period—and, perhaps, of Stone's career—was the Musum of Modern Art in New York City (with Philip Goodwin). Even with later additions, the exterior of the museum has sustained virtues of high modernism that are absent in his later, more monumental work. At the same time, the careful manipulation of the interior space of the rectangle is vastly superior to Stone's other cultural palaces—the Kennedy Center or the Huntington Hartford Gallery of Modern Art in New York.

Stone urged that each architect should "try to find his own handwriting... his own expression" yet, save for the early work, there is little that is personal and private in his work.

—Robert Segrest

STONOROV, Oscar.

American. Born in Frankfurt am Main, Germany, 2 December 1905; emigrated to the United States, 1929: naturalized, 1937. Apprenticed to a stonecutter in Florence, and studied anatomy and mathematics at the University of Florence, 1924-25; studied at E.T.H.: Swiss Federal Institute of Technology, Zurich, under Karl Moser, 1925-28; worked for the architectural firm of André Lurcat, and studied sculpture with Aristide Maillol, Paris, 1928-29. Married Elizabeth Foster in 1938; children: Katrina, Andrea, Barbara, and Derek. In private practice, Philadelphia, 1932 until his death, 1970: in partnership with Alfred Kastner, 1932-36, George Howe, *q.v.,* 1942-43 and Louis I. Kahn, *q.v.,* 1942-48. Organized the exhibition *Sixty Years of Living Architecture: The Work of Frank Lloyd Wright,* Palazzo Strozzi, Florence, 1951, European tour, 1951-53, and North American tour, 1953-54. Served as Director of the Philadelphia Housing Association,

and of the Philadelphia Citizens Council on City Planning. Exhibitions: *Built in U.S.A. 1932-1944,* Museum of Modern Art, New York, 1944; *Better Philadelphia Exhibition,* Philadelphia, 1947. Recipient: Fairmont Art Association Award, Philadelphia, 1965. Fellow, American Institute of Architects. Member, Pennsylvania Association of Architects; City Policy Commission, Philadelphia; New Jersey Society of Architects; American Institute of Planners. *Died* (in a plane crash, with union leader Walter Reuther) *9 May 1970.*

Works:

1928/
29 Karlsruhe Municipal Hospital, Germany (project; with Edwin Blos)
1929 2 Houses, Zurich (with Willy Boesiger)
      Private clinic, Karlsruhe (project)
1930 State Theatre of the Ukraine, U.S.S.R. (competition project; with Willy Boesiger)
      Rural Hospital for the Southern States, for the Julius Rosenwald Foundation (project)
      Forrest House, Java Farm, Edgewater, Maryland (project)
1931 Weyman Biological Laboratory, North Carolina
      Clark Foreman Apartment interiors, New York
      Palace of the Soviets, Moscow (competition project; with Alfred Kastner)
1932 Carl Mackley Houses (housing development), for the Federation of Full-Fashioned Hosiery Workers, Philadelphia (with W. P. Barney)
1933 Mrs. Frank Foster House interiors, Haverford, Pennsylvania
      Mrs. John Wintersteen House interiors, Chestnut Hill, Pennsylvania
      M. B. Montgomery Studio, Philadelphia
      Howard City (housing development), Washington, D.C. (project; with Hilyard Robinson)
1934 Public housing development, Meadville, Pennsylvania (project)
      Pre-fabricated houses, for the Republic Steel Corporation, various locations including Huntington Terrace, Bethesda, Maryland
      Recreation Center, Bangor, Pennsylvania
      Minard Hamilton Penthouse interiors, New York
      Federation of Hosiery Workers Union Hall, Philadelphia
1935 Public housing (Public Works Administration No. 6002), Camden, New Jersey
      Academy of Music interiors, Philadelphia
      Freedman Store, Philadelphia
      Housing renovation, Waverly Street, Philadelphia
1936 Westfield Acres (public housing development), Camden, New Jersey (with Joseph Hettel)
      Collier House, Arlington, Virginia (project)
      Frank B. Foster House remodelling and additions, Phoenixville, Pennsylvania
      Mouth Hygiene Clinic, Philadelphia
      Patchell Estate Housing Development, Philadelphia (project)
      Rosenfeld Apartments, Camden, New Jersey
      Spooner House, Philadelphia (project)
      Public housing development, Paterson, New Jersey (project)
1938 School, Charlestown Playhouse, Pennsylvania
      Oscar Stonorov House, Avon Lea, Phoenixville, Pennsylvania
      Louis Dublin Week-end House, Westport, Connecticut (project)
      Cavanaugh House, Falls Church, Virginia (project)
      Davis House alterations, Chestnut Hill, Pennsylvania

Clement T. Branch Village (public housing development), Camden, New Jersey (with Hettel Associates)

Public housing development, New Britain, Connecticut (project; with Ludorf and Bishop)

1939 Youth Center, East Springfield, Pennsylvania (project)

Children's World Exhibition, *New York World's Fair* (with Goerge Howe, Herbert Spiegel and Cornelius Bogert)

Public housing development, Aliquippa, Pennsylvania

Public housing development, Ambridge, Pennsylvania

Public housing development, Beaver Falls, Pennsylvania (2 projects)

1940 Resident workshop, National Youth Administration, Philadelphia

Public housing development, Audubon Village, New Jersey (with Hettel Associates)

Tonnies House, Bryn Mawr, Pennsylvania

1941 Sidney Biddle House, Philadelphia

Walter Phillips House, Torresdale, Pennsylvania (with Edmund N. Bacon)

Design of the *Organic Design* Exhibition, Museum of Modern Art, New York

Design of a furniture exhibition at Bloomingdale's Department Store, New York

Design of a furniture/defense house exhibition at Gimbel's Department Store, Philadelphia

Eunice Richardson Apartment interiors, New York

Public housing development, Middletown, Pennsylvania

1941/
43 Carver Court Housing, Coatesville, Pennsylvania (with George Howe and Louis I. Kahn)

1942 Pennypack Housing, Philadelphia (project; with George Howe and Louis I. Kahn)

Phoenixville Hospital alterations and additions, Pennsylvania (project)

Broudo House, Philadelphia

Display house for the *Ladies Home Journal*

Frey House remodelling, Radnor, Pennsylvania

1943 Lincoln Road Housing, Coatesville, Pennsylvania (project; with George Howe and Louis I. Kahn)

Lily Ponds Housing, Washington, D.C. (project; with George Howe and Louis I. Kahn)

Willow Run Housing, Detroit (project; with Louis I. Kahn)

Thermostore, Gimbel's, Phoenixville, Pennsylvania

194X Hotel, Philadelphia (competition project; with Louis I. Kahn)

International Ladies Garment Workers Union Offices interior alterations, Philadelphia

International Upholsterers Union Offices interior alterations, Philadelphia

International Union of Master Ship Workers Offices, Camden, New Jersey

1944 Motion Picture Operators Union Building, Philadelphia

Pennypack Buildings, Philadelphia (with Louis I. Kahn)

Borough Hall alterations and additions, Phoenixville, Pennsylvania

Lucius Crowell House additions, Charlestown, Pennsylvania

Cosmetics Department and Shoe Salon, Gimbel's Department Store, Philadelphia

1945 Health Clinic extension and alterations, 22nd and Locust Streets, Philadelphia (with Louis I. Kahn)

Paul Darrow House alterations and additions, Philadelphia

Pre-fabricated steel house, for the Harman Corporation

Moskalik House, 2018 Spruce Street, Philadelphia

Plan for the North Triangle, Philadelphia

Philadelphia Psychiatric Hospital extension (project)

Radbill House, Merion, Pennsylvania

Coward Shoe Company alterations, Philadelphia

1946 Charlestown Playhouse additions, Pennsylvania

Unity House (International Ladies Garment Workers Union Building), Pike County, Pennsylvania (project)

Thom McCann Shoe Store alterations and additions, 69th Street, Philadelphia

Solar House (project)

House, 2036 Rittenhouse Square, Philadelphia

Memorial Playground, Philadelphia

Evans House, Philadelphia (project)

Psychiatric Hospital, Monument Avenue, Philadelphia (project; with Louis I. Kahn)

1947 Offices and Cafeteria, Container Corporation of America, Philadelphia (project; with Louis I. Kahn)

DuPont Theatre (project)

Plan for the expansion of the Drexel Institute, Philadelphia

Franklin Institute additions, Philadelphia

Plan for the redevelopment of the "Triangle," University of Pennsylvania, Philadelphia

Design of the *Better Philadelphia Exhibition*, Philadelphia (with Edmund N. Bacon)

Garage, Filbert Street, Philadelphia (project)

1948 Captain Beczewski House, Philadelphia

Lucius Crowell House alterations and additions, Charlestown, Pennsylvania

Design of the *Yardville Exhibition* for *McCall's Magazine* and Gimbel's Department Store, Philadelphia

Plan for the redevelopment of North 8th Street, Philadelphia

1949 Coward Glass Front Shoe Store, Philadelphia (with Louis I. Kahn)

Brégy House alterations and additions, Philadelphia

Redevelopment plans for the Harman Corporation

Cherokee Village (housing development), Philadelphia

Kelly's Oyster House (restaurant), Philadelphia

Housing development, Valley Forge, Pennsylvania (project)

Leonni's Restaurant, Philadelphia

Plan for the Southwest Temple Redevelopment Area, Philadelphia

Plan for the 32nd and Walnut Streets Area, Philadelphia

Plan for the 22nd and College Avenue Area, Philadelphia

Solidarity House (United Auto Workers Office Building), Detroit

Design of the *Washington Sesquicentennial Exhibition*, Corcoran Gallery, Washington, D.C.

Penn Drexel Corporation Building, Philadelphia

Holmes House alterations and additions, Charlestown, Pennsylvania

1950 Flower Service Corporation Offices, Philadelphia

Exhibition house for *Life* magazine

Exhibition house for Peasewood Woodwork Company, Cincinnati

Fleer Corporation Offices, Philadelphia

1951 Clark House, Philadelphia

Louis Martin House, Cheltenham, Pennsylvania

Y.M.C.A. Building remodelling, Philadelphia

1952 Alexander Frey House, Pocano Hills, Pennsylvania

1953 Display House, *Philadelphia Home Show*

Louis Forman House, Wyncotte, Pennsylvania

East Falls Elementary School, Pennsylvania

1954 Playground, 8th and Brown Streets, Philadelphia

Hetzell Playground, Philadelphia

Penrose Playground, Philadelphia

1955 Solidarity House additions, Detroit

Plan for the redevelopment of the Gratiot-Lafayette Area, Detroit

Hasselquist House, Charlestown, Pennsylvania

1956 Northeast Municipal Building, Bustleton Avenue, Philadelphia

Cow/Sheep Barn, Pennsylvania State University, University Park

1958 Plan for the redevelopment of the Washington Square East Area, Philadelphia

1959 Plan for the redevelopment of Newark Plaza, New Jersey

1961 Hillman Brass and Copper Company Offices and Warehouse, Willow Grove, Pennsylvania

Plan for Hartford, Connecticut

Plan for the central business district of Sharon, Pennsylvania

1962 Unitarian Fellowship Hall, Cherry Hill, New Jersey

Hopkinson House (apartments), Philadelphia

Oakland Park Apartments, Philadelphia (project)

Schuykill Falls (public housing development), Philadelphia

1963 Forestry Center, Pennsylvania State University, University Park

Schenk Memorial Building (Lutheran Church), Philadelphia

Plan for the central business district of Lansdale, Pennsylvania

1964 Georgia Pacific Corporation Offices and Warehouse, King of Prussia, Pennsylvania

Hotel, Bombay (project)

Government of India, Pavilion, *World's Fair*, New York

Lincoln National Bank alterations, Philadelphia

Charlestown Elementary School, Pennsylvania

Housing development, for the Andean Development Corporation, Bogota, Colombia (project)

Lutheran Memorial Church, Blackwood, New Jersey

1965 *India Caravan Exhibition* (project)

Stonorov Architectural Offices, Chestnut Street, Philadelphia

Northeast Medical Center, Philadelphia

Computer Facilities Center, Pennsylvania State University, University Park

Plaza Apartments, Philadelphia

Valley Forge Medical Center and Hospital alterations, Pennsylvania

1966 Rural Teaching Hospital Prototype, for Dr. Lalla Iverson, India

Best of Life Park Housing for the Elderly, Atlantic City, New Jersey

Casa Fermi Housing for the Elderly, Philadelphia

Pump Valve Company additions, Philadelphia

Plan for the central business district of Burlington, New Jersey

Plan for Merchantville, Pennsylvania

1967 Public housing development, South Coatesville, Pennsylvania

Stephen Smith Towers Housing for the Elderly, Philadelphia

Master plan for the Smith, Kline and French Corporation, Applebrock Farm, Pennsylvania

1968 James Sutton House additions, Bryn Mawr, Pennsylvania

John F. Hartranft School and Community Services Center, Philadelphia

St. Paul's Church School, Annapolis, Maryland

Animal Health Research Complex, East Goshen Township, Pennsylvania

Welsh Road Branch Library, Philadelphia

Community plan for the East Park, Philadelphia

1969 318-320 South 4th Street additions and alterations, Philadelphia

Community Health Care Center, Temple University, Philadelphia

Lutheran Home for the Elderly, Germantown, Philadelphia

Teaching Hospital, Temple University, Philadelphia

1970 Henry Most House alterations, Charlestown, Pennsylvania

United Auto Workers Family Education Center, Onoway, Michigan (renamed Walter and Mary Reuther Memorial Family Education Center)

Urban renewal plan for the Downtown East Area, Reading, Pennsylvania

Study of mental retardation facilities, for the Pennsylvania State Office of Mental Retardation

Veterans Stadium, Philadelphia

St. Christopher's Hospital for Children, Philadelphia

Library, Cheney State College, Chester County, Pennsylvania

Plan for the township of East Windsor, New Jersey

Master plan for the *Michigan State Fair*

Youth Study Center, Philadelphia

Smith, Kline and French Laboratories, Chester County, Pennsylvania

Casa Vivarelli, Pistoia, Italy

Publications:

By STONOROV: books—*Le Corbusier: His Work 1909-1929*, with Willy Boesiger, Zurich 1929; *Why City Planning Is Your Responsibility*, with Louis I. Kahn, New York 1942; *You and Your Neighborhood*, with Louis I. Kahn, New York 1944; article—"Theatres" in *New Architecture and City Planning*, edited by Paul Zucker, New York 1944.

On STONOROV: book—*Built in U.S.A. 1932-1944*, exhibition catalogue edited by Elizabeth Mock, New York 1944; articles—"Philadelphia Exhibition" in *Architectural Forum* (New York), December 1947; "Yardville" in *McCall's* (New York), February 1949; "Three Shoe Stores" in *Architectural Forum* (New York), December 1949; "Good Land Use + Good Architecture + Long Earning Life" in *House and Home* (New York), February 1956; "Die Stadt in Automobilizertalter" in *Bauen und Wohnen* (Zurich), September 1957; "The Importance of Being Oscar" in *Greater Philadelphia*, November 1962; "Philadelphia Landmark: Hopkinson House" in *Architectural Forum* (New York), April 1963; "Housing—Still Man's Primary Building Need" by Arthur Ziegler Jr. in *Charette* (Philadelphia), July/August 1967; "Profile" in *The New Yorker*, 5 August 1967; "L'idea di Oscar Stonorov" by Bruno Zevi in *L'Architettura* (Rome), July 1970; "Oscar Stonorov: Public Housing Pioneer" by Ursula Cliff in *Design and Environment* (New York), Fall 1971; special issue of *L'Architettura* (Rome), June 1972; "An Architecture for Labor in Post-Industrial America" in *AIA Journal* (Washington, D.C.), October 1972.

Although Oscar Stonorov was a strongly individual figure, his work is almost a diagram of the development of the social concerns of architecture over the forty years in which he practiced.

One of his first prize-winning designs, in 1931, was the Moscow Palace of the Soviets (with Alfred Kastner), a monument to what seemed to be the new era in art and architecture. As the world-wide depression deepened, and as monumental opportunities for architects diminished, he turned his attention increasingly to the problem of providing decent, pleasant housing for the urban working class. Stonorov always had an unusual facility for seeing where the intellectual action was, and during the 1930's he joined an extraordinary group of young architects and planners in Philadelphia who made that city the pioneer in contemporary American city planning.

Stonorov's first important Philadelphia work, Carl Mackley Houses, housing for the hosiery workers' union, reflects his conviction that "housing . . . is no longer so much a question of naked shelter only. It is the demand for the reorganization of rotten communities into stable, sane, and healthy societies." In addition to the bright, airy apartments, Stonorov's design incorporates the ideals of mutual aid that were then part of the intellectual climate: a cooperative nursery school (which flourished for years) and a cooperative grocery. Stonorov was not only co-designer of the project, but, as an adroit political manipulator, was also largely responsible for having funding for it and other low-cost housing included in the National Industrial Recovery Act of 1933.

After the war, when he and Edmund N. Bacon designed the enormously influential *Better Philadelphia Exhibition*, his planning had become more ambitious, and the wide boulevards, rehabilitated neighborhoods, and multi-level shopping malls set a pattern that Philadelphia is still following. In neighborhood rehabilitation, Stonorov used methods thirty years ago that comtemporary planners keep rediscovering. He went into the neighborhoods himself and talked to residents on street corners and candy stores, finding out from them what they wanted in their future environment. He devised a system in which the future owners themselves worked out their down-payments by participating in the construction.

Stonorov had begun his career as a sculptor, studying under Maillol in Paris, and he remained a practicing sculptor all his life, in later years maintaining a studio outside Florence. His last major work, the United Auto Workers Family Education Center, represents a fusion at last of his architecture and sculpture: from the austerity of his earliest housing for the hosiery workers he had moved to buildings where the richness of sculptural form is as important as the structural elements.

—Ursula Cliff

STUBBINS, Hugh Asher, Jr.

American. Born in Birmingham, Alabama, 11 January 1912. Educated at the Georgia Institute of Technology, Atlanta, 1929-33, B.S. in Architecture 1933; Harvard University Graduate School of Design, Cambridge, Massachusetts, 1933-35 (Appleton Scholarship, 1933-34; Boston Society of Architects Prize, 1934; Warren Prize, 1934, 1935), M.Arch. 1935. Served in the United States Naval Reserve, 1933-39. Married Diana Hamilton Moore in 1938 (divorced, 1960); children: Michael and Hugh Asher III; married Colette Fadeuihle in 1961. Worked as a designer draftsman with R. B. Wills, Boston, 1935-37; Principal, with Marc Peter, in Peter and Stubbins, Boston, 1937-39; Chief Designer, Miller, Martin and Lewis, Birmingham, Alabama, 1939-40; in private practice, Boston, 1940-41; Vice-President, The Stereographic Company, Cambridge, 1941-42; Draftsman, Radio Research Laboratory, Cambridge, 1942-43; Assistant to the President, Polaroid Corporation, Cambridge, 1943-45. Since 1949, President of Hugh Stubbins and Associates, Cambridge, Massachusetts; since 1969, Principal, Hugh Stubbins/Rex Allen Partnership, Cambridge, Massachusetts, and San Francisco. Instructor and Assistant to Walter Gropius, Graduate School of Design, 1940, Assistant Professor, 1945, Associate Professor, 1946-52, Chairman of the Department of Architecture, 1953, Member of the Visiting Committee, Graduate School of Design, 1958-72, and since 1978 Member of the Alumni Council of the Graduate School of Design, Harvard University; Visiting Critic-in-Residence, Yale University, New Haven, Connecticut, 1948-49, and University of Oregon, Eugene, 1950; Thomas Jefferson Professor of Architecture, University of Virginia, Charlottesville, 1979; Guest Lecturer, Lawrence Institute of Technology School of Architecture, Southfield, Michigan, 1981, and Notre Dame University School of Architecture, Indiana, 1982. Member, Arts and Architecture Committee, Kennedy Memorial Library, 1964; Vice-President, American Institute of Architects, 1964-65; Director, Benjamin Franklin Foundation, Berlin, 1964-69; Chairman, Design Advisory Committee, Boston Redevelopment Authority, 1964-76; Chairman, Selection Committee, Thomas Jefferson Memorial Chair, University of Virginia, Charlottesville, 1965-70; Vice-President, 1968-69, and President, 1969-70, Boston Society of Architects; Chairman, South Atlantic Regional Conference Awards Committee, 1974; Member, Jury of Fellows, American Institute of Architects, 1974-75. Member, Design Review Panel, Worcester, Massachusetts Redevelopment Authority, since 1966; Secretary, Rotch Traveling Scholarship Committee, since 1971; Member, Mayor's Panel of Architects, New York City, since 1972; Member, AIA Housing Committee, since 1978; Member, National Advisory Board, Georgia Institute of Technology, since 1978; Member of the Foreign Business Council of Massachusetts, since 1978; Advisory Commission Member on Foreign Buildings Operations, United States Department of State, 1980-83; Chairman, American Institute of Architects Honor Awards Commission, 1980. Exhibitions: Museum of Modern Art, New York, 1946; *Triennale*, Milan, 1947. Recipient: First Prize, American Gas Association National Competition, 1938; First Prize, *Progressive Architecture* National Competition, 1946; Award of Merit, American Institute of Architects, 1950, 1961, 1966, 1970; First Design Award, *Progressive Architecture*, 1954; Harleston Parker Gold Medal, 1955, 1981; Top Award, *The School Executive*, 1956; Silver Medal, Architectural League of New York, 1958; Award of Excellence, *Architectural Record*, 1959, 1967; Boston Arts Festival Award, 1961, 1963; Design Award, *Progressive Architecture*, 1961; Award of Merit, American Library Association, 1966; Design Award, AIA, New England Regional Council, 1966, 1979, 1980; Award of Merit, United States Office of Education, 1966; Award of Excellence, 1966, 1970, and Special Citation, 1983, American Institute of Steel Construction; Architectural Firm Award, AIA, 1967; Award of Excellence for Design, *Architectural Record*, 1971; Award of the Year, Prestressed Concrete Institute, 1971; Collaborative Achievement in Architecture Medal, AIA, 1972; Award of Merit, Institute of Southern Affairs and the Southern Academy of Letters, Arts and Sciences, 1973; Gold Medal for Excellence in Design, Tau Sigma Delta, 1975; Award for Excellence, *Design and Environment*, 1975; Award of Merit, AIA/American Library Association, 1976; Merit Award for Excellence in Design, Guild for Religious Architecture, 1976; Special Energy Award, AIA/American Association of School Administrators, 1978; Bard Award, City Club of New York, 1978; AIA New York Chapter Award, 1978; Boston Society of Architects Award, 1978; Boston Exports Honor Award, 1978; Award of Excellence, Building Owners and Managers Association of New York, 1978; Award of Excellence, *Urban Design*, 1978; National Honor Award, American Institute of Architects, 1979; Thomas Jefferson Medal, 1979; R. S. Reynolds Memorial Award, 1981. Fellow of the American Academy of Arts and Sciences, 1957, and of the American Institute of Architects, 1960; Academician, National Academy of Design, 1974. Honorary Fellow, Mexican Society of Architects, 1974. Address: Hugh Stubbins and Associates Inc., 1033 Massachusetts Avenue, Cambridge, Massachusetts 02138, U.S.A.

Works:

1950 Adams Residence, Concord, Massachusetts
1954 Veterans housing, Wellesley, Massachusetts
      Back Bay Center, Boston (project)
      The Country School, Weston, Massachusetts
1955 United States Legation, Tangier, Morocco
      Better Homes and Gardens House, Chicago
      Dracut Junior/Senior High School, Dracut, Massachusetts
      Piney Point Beach Club, Marion, Massachusetts
1956 Animal Rescue League, Boston
      Sharpe House, Poujac, Rhode Island
      330 Beacon Street Apartment House, Boston
      Shaughnessy Elementary School, Lowell, Massachusetts
1957 Congress Hall, Berlin
1959 Woodland Elementary School, Weston, Massachusetts
      Continental Terrace Apartment House, Cambridge, Massachusetts
      Scientific Engineering Institute, Waltham, Massachusetts
1960 Loeb Drama Center, Harvard University, Cambridge, Massachusetts
      Unitarian Church, Concord, New Hampshire
      Gulf Coast Community College, Panama City, Florida
      Charlesbank Apartment House, Boston
1961 Brookline Farm, Massachusetts (project)
1962 Beverly School for the Deaf, Massachusetts
      Graduate student housing, Massachusetts Institute of Technology, Cambridge
1962/
  69 Various buildings, including hi-rise dormitories, dining commons, etc., University of Massachusetts, Amherst
1962/
  75 Various buildings, including dormitories, theatre complex, etc., Mount Holyoke College, South Hadley, Massachusetts
1965 Physics Building and Dormitory, Princeton University, New Jersey
      Maimonides School, Brookline, Massachusetts
      Falmouth Intermediate School, Falmouth, Massachusetts
      Countway Library of Medicine, Harvard University Medical School, Boston
      Gymnasium, Bowdoin College, Brunswick, Maine
1966 North East Primate Center, Harvard University, Southboro, Massachusetts
      Senior Center, Bowdoin College, Brunswick, Maine
1967 Dana Hall School, Wellesley, Massachusetts
      Fine Arts Building, Rochester Institute of Technology, New York
      Administration Center, Brandeis University, Waltham, Massachusetts
1968 Union Mutual Life Insurance Company Office Building, Portland, Maine
      Gymnasium, Oberlin College, Ohio
      National Technical Institute for the Deaf, Rochester Institute of Technology, Rochester, New York
      Decorative Arts Wing, Boston Museum of Fine Arts
      Student Union, Brandeis University, Waltham, Massachusetts
1969 1033 Massachusetts Avenue Office Building, Cambridge, Massachusetts
1971 Veterans Stadium, Philadelphia
1972 Academic complex and hockey rink, Tabor Academy, Marion, Massachusetts
      Technical School, Shiraz Technical Institute, Iran

      Master Plan, Hampshire College, Amherst, Massachusetts
1973 Library, Alfred University, Alfred, New York
1974 The Bank, Manchester, New Hampshire
      Southeastern Massachusetts University, North Dartmouth
1976 Master Plan, Law School and Graduate School of Business Administration, University of Virginia, Charlottesville
      Public Library, Newburg, New York
      Pusey Library, Harvard University, Cambridge, Massachusetts
1977 Hewlett-Packard Company, Waltham, Massachusetts
      Y.M.C.A., Worcester, Massachusetts
1978 Citicorp Center, New York (with Emery Roth and Sons)
      St. Peter's Church, New York
      Federal Reserve Bank of Boston
1981 Scottish and York Headquarters, Princeton, New Jersey
1983 Commonwealth Pier Project, Boston
      Pittsburgh/Jenkins Empire Building, Pittsburgh, Pennsylvania
      Prudential Company Development Plan
1984 Republic Bank Preliminary Master Plan, Southland, Texas
      Carnegie Center Development Plan, Pittsburgh, Pennsylvania
      Kuwait Bank, Kuwait City, United Arab Emirates
      Cousteau Ocean Center, Norfolk, Virginia
      Crerar Library, University of Chicago
      General Services Administration Federal Office Building, Boston
      Marriott Hotel, Copley Place, Boston
      Pacwest Center, Portland, Oregon

Publications:

By STUBBINS: book—*The Design Experience*, New York and London 1976; articles—"College Dormitories: What Do Colleges Really Want?" in *Architectural Record* (New York), April 1946; "Und die Antwort des Architekten" in *Baukunst und Werkform* (Nuremberg), no. 1, 1958.

On STUBBINS: books—*Architecture U.S.A.*, edited by Ian McCallum, London 1959; *Architects on Architecture*, edited by Paul Heyer, New York 1966, London 1967; articles—in *Architectural Forum* (New York), April 1945; *Architecture d'Aujourd'hui* (Paris), July 1947; *Architectural Forum* (New York), September 1949; *Progressive Architecture* (New York), November 1953; "U.S. Center Slated for Berlin" by Thomas H. Creighton in *Progressive Architecture* (New York), September 1955; "Machine Made America" by Ian McCallum in *Architectural Review* (London), May 1957; "Berlin Congress Hall" in *Architectural Record* (New York), December 1957; *Progressive Architecture* (New York), January 1958; *Architectural Forum* (New York), June 1959; *Architectural Record* (New York), March 1963; *Architectural Record* (New York), August 1975; *Baumeister* (Munich), June 1976; "Seventh Heaven: Citicorp" in *Building Design* (London), September 1977; "At the Core of the Apple" in *Progressive Architecture* (New York), December 1978; "Hugh Stubbins: Architecture in the Spirit of the Times", special issue of *Process: Architecture* (Tokyo), no. 10, 1979; "Newcomers Out West" in *Interiors* (New York), December 1980; "Skyscrapers in New York" in *Bouw* (Rotterdam), 28 May 1983.

*

Buildings are built, after all, to fulfill specific needs and to adapt to specific environments. Their ability to do this should form a part of any critical study we make or any building we design. "Today we live in a civilization, which in contemporary terms may be

measured by the state of its architecture. The primary art of any civilization is that which most immediately dominates and motivates the life styles of people of that civilization. Everywhere, consciously or subconsciously, we are motivated—and often dominated—by the shapes we see and their proportions in relation to us. Contemporary society is reflected to an enormous extent in its shapes and proportions, and indeed it can be said that architecture in the modern world is essentially the cultural bridge between Art and Science, since the modern architect is both an artist and a scientist. While it remains an inspiring pleasure to read the genius of a poet, or to listen to the genius of a musician, or to see the genius of a painter or a photographer, it is for the contemporary mind often a greater inspiration to be able to *feel* the beauty of a structure, which one can touch and exist within...."

I have a deep respect for *function*. The planning problems *must* be solved. The building must not only work for the user, but also be flexible for the future. Structure is of great importance. It should be forthright, logical and honest. It should have integrity, which does not mean it necessarily has to be expressed. A building in some way should express its purpose as well as have a unity in itself. It must be a whole thing, rather than a lot of elements strung together. Integration within its environment is important, for if we are to avoid physical chaos—with which we are now surrounded—we must respect the existing fabric, be it natural or manmade. In the long view, to be new or exciting may not be as important as to be courteous and restrained. I hasten to say that I do not mean that, within these parameters, we should not exploit fully all the ideas and philosophy plus the technology, methods and materials at our command.

Perhaps most of all it is important to realize that at any time we are just a link between the past and the future—and we must see ourselves as evolving from one and leading to the other, despite the ever-present temptation to deny our forebears. Since, in the last analysis, architecture reflects society's priorities and purposes, our architectural heritage is a unique expression of history and the progress of *man*.

What monuments we leave behind us in the form of buildings reveal more clearly than *anything* else, the value we place on the *quality* of life.

Architecure finally speaks of the nobility of man's existence and the desire to make life happier while we live on this earth.

—Hugh A. Stubbins, Jr.

*

If many young architects had their first choice, or older ones a second, the kind of architect that Hugh Stubbins is might well be the kind they would want to become.

Stubbins is a designer, a very good one, but his concept of design, unlike that of some of his contemporaries, is concerned not only with aspects of space, form and esthetics, but also with rigorous solving of the problems of building sites, circulation, materials, environmental systems and structures, as well as the needs and purposes of clients. And Stubbins is deeply concerned with the needs, problems and aspirations of the people who will occupy and use his buildings. Undoubtedly Stubbins would agree that good design is the essential, central ingredient of all good architecture, but it certainly is not the only one. Enlightened programming and excellence in planning, function and technology are also integral ingredients.

Attention to all of these elements has shaped the kind of architect Hugh Stubbins has become, very close to the ideal of the complete architect, adept at obtaining commissions for his firm, a good business man, a successful designer, a good manager. As a result, he has developed a successful firm that consistently produces buildings that many believe to be beautiful. At the same time, his buildings work,

Hugh Stubbins: Citicorp Center, New York, 1978.

and they are completed on schedule and within their budgets. And, for the most part, his clients are delighted with the results.

Perhaps even more delighted are the people who occupy and use these buildings. This state of affairs has existed for a long time, through the long series of smaller and medium-sized buildings, schools, houses, college buildings and the like that Stubbins has designed over the years. However, it is not uncommon for good architects to produce humane, livable, interesting and comfortable environments in such buildings. Recently, Stubbins has produced such amenities in some very large buildings, a rare occurrence indeed.

In a large office building, Citicorp Center, completed in 1978 in New York City, Stubbins has produced an environment composed of great plazas, shops, restaurants, a church and other elements that capture the imagination, and usually the fancy, of all who experience it. In this building Stubbins gave new life to an urban area that formerly was occupied during the day only by those who were there on business and was completely deserted at night. Perhaps the most telling fact is that the great public spaces of this building are constantly filled with people in action or in repose, all enjoying themselves and experiencing fine architecture, from early morning until late every night, every day including weekends. In the Federal Reserve Plaza, completed in Boston later in 1978, Stubbins has created another such environment. Buildings like these not only provide humane environments for people, but also go a long way toward revitalizing the decaying centers of the cities in which they are built.

Hugh Stubbins admits to having been influenced by Walter Gropius, Marcel Breuer and Alvar Aalto. Their influences have deeply affected his philosophy, his intellect and his ideals, but have affected his style very little. In fact, it might be said that each of his buildings has its own style, derived from its own program, needs and problems. In each, the attempt has been made to discover the exact solution for the individual problems. Accordingly, Stubbins has not produced any radical, new overall style and no high-sounding theories. All he produces is consistently excellent architecture that people admire and enjoy.

—William Dudley Hunt, Jr.

STUDIO PER.

Partnership; established, Barcelona, 1965. Partners: Pep Bonet, *q.v.;* Cristian Cirici, *q.v.;* Lluis Clotet, *q.v.;* and Oscar Tusquets, *q.v.* Address: Caspe 151, Barcelona 13, Spain.

SYRKUS, Helena.

Polish. Born Helena Niemirowska in Warsaw, 14 May 1900. Studied architecture at the Institute of Technology, Warsaw, 1918-23; humanities and philosophy at the University of Warsaw, 1923-25. Married Szymon Syrkus, *q.v.,* in 1926. Practiced with Szymon Syrkus, Warsaw, 1926 until his death, 1964; in private practice, Warsaw, 1964 until her death in 1982. Vice-Chairman, 1939-42, and Chairman, 1942-45, PAU (Underground Architecture and Town Planning Studio), of WSM (Warsaw Housing Co-operative); Secretary, Economic and Social Planning Unit, KRN (Underground Polish Government), 1943-45; Chairman, Propaganda Department, and Vice-Chairman of the Spatial Planning Committee, BOS (Capital Rebuilding Bureau), Warsaw, 1945-46; Secretary-General, NROW (Supreme Council for the Reconstruction of Warsaw),

1946. Lecturer, Institute of Architecture and Town Planning, Warsaw, 1949-51. Adjunct, 1949-52, Assistant Professor, 1952-55, Adjunct Professor, 1955-66, Professor, 1966-70, and Emeritus Professor, 1970-82, Technical University, Warsaw. Member of the Executive Committee, Union International des Architects, 1948-58. Member, Committee of Architecture and Town Planning, Polish Academy of Sciences, 1960-82. Secretary, Praesens group, Warsaw, 1926-39, Editor of the *Praesens* journal, 1926, 1930, and Member of the Praesens Design Team, 1930-39; Member, 1929-57, and Secretary, 1933-39, Polish Branch of CIAM (Congrès Internationaux d'Architecture Moderne): Vice-President, International Council of CIAM, 1947. Exhibitions: *Warsaw of the Future,* Warsaw, 1936; *Warsaw Lives Again,* toured the United States and the United Kingdom, 1946; Tenth Anniversary Exhibition, Warsaw, 1955; International Union of Architects Exhibition, The Hague, 1955; Warsaw National Institute of Technology for National Economy, 1960; *Constructivism in Poland 1923-1936: Blok/Praesens,* Lodz, Poland, Essen, West Germany, and Otterlo, Netherlands, 1973; *Tendenzen der Zwanziger Jahre,* Berlin, 1977, London, 1978; *Het Nieuwe Bouwen Internationaal: CIAM,* Rijksmuseum Kroller-Muller, Otterlo, toured Netherlands, 1983. Collections: Museum of Modern Art, Lodz, Poland; Museum of Architecture, Wroclaw, Poland. Recipient: First Prize, with Szymon Syrkus, Old People's Home Competition, Kutno, Poland, 1928; First Prize, with Szymon Syrkus, Teachers Sanatorium Competition, Srodborow, Poland, 1932; Polish Medal of Freedom, 1945; Golden Cross of Warsaw Reconstruction, 1947; Polish Anniversary Medal, 1955; Merit Prize, Polish Ministry of Education, 1954, 1966; Honorary Award, International Congress of Intellectuals for Peace, Wroclaw, Poland, 1958; World Peace Committee Award, 1959; Golden Cross of Merit, Warsaw, 1960; Honorary Golden Badge, Central Committee of Housing Co-operatives, Warsaw, 1964; First Prize, Czuby Housing Development Competition, Lublin, 1973; Polish Thirtieth Anniversary Medal, 1974; Polityka Book Prize, Warsaw, 1977; Honorary Award, Polish Historians Association, 1977; Honorary Award, Warsaw City Council Culture Department, 1977; Celebration Medal, Warsaw Institute of Technology, 1977. Commander, Order of Polonia Restituta, 1956. *Died* (in Warsaw) *19 November 1982.*

Works: With Szymon Syrkus:

1927 Simultaneous Theatre, Warsaw (with A. Pronaszko and Z. Leski)
1929 Old People's Home, Kutno, Poland
1930 Housing Units with Steel Structures (project; with St. Hempel)
1931 Polish Teachers Association Building, Warsaw
       House, King's Hill, Skolimow, Poland (with St. Hempel)
1932 Teachers' Sanatorium, Srodborow, Poland (competition project; with St. Hempel)
1934 Experimental Theatre, for Irena Solska, Zoliborz, Warsaw
1935 Association of Workers Housing Co-operative, Grudziadz, Poland
1936 Rakowiec Housing Development, stage I, Warsaw (with the Praesens Team)
       House, Warsaw (with St. Hempel)
1937 House, Saska Kepa, Warsaw (with St. Hempel)
       Houses in Grzybowska, Zlota, and Jaworzynska Streets, Warsaw (with St. Hempel)
1939 Rakowiec Housing Development, stages II and III, Warsaw
       Sanatorium, Konstancin, Poland (with St. Hempel)
       Dairy (competition project; with St. Hempel)

1945 Housing developments for Rakowiec and Kolo, Warsaw (projects; with PAU)
       General plan for a "Socialist Warsaw" (project; with PAU)
1949 Meeting Hall, Rakowiec Housing Development, Warsaw (with WSM)
       Kolo Housing Development, stage I, Warsaw
       City Gasworks reconstruction, Kredytowa Street, Warsaw
       Belgian Consulate reconstruction, Warsaw
       Yugoslav Embassy reconstruction, Piekna Street, Warsaw
       Atheneum Theatre conversion, Warsaw
1951 School, Filtrowa Street, Warsaw
       Narodowy Bank Polski, Warsaw (competition project)
       School, Krolikarnia, Warsaw
       OK Saska Plan, Warsaw
       Theatre, Lodz, Poland (competition project)
1954 Praga Housing Development, phase I, Warsaw
1960 Pre-fabricated Slab Systems for Housing Units (project)
       Tatary Housing Development, Lublin, Poland
       Pre-fabricated Reinforced Units (project; with others)
       Praga Housing Development, phase II, Warsaw (project; with others)
       Kolo Housing Development, phase IV, Warsaw (with others)

Helena Syrkus only:

1973 Czuby Housing Development, Lublin, Poland (competition project)
1974 Tarchomin Housing Development, Warsaw (competition project)
1978 Housing Development, Warsaw (competition project)

Publications:

By H. SYRKUS: books—*Nowoczesne Osiedle Robotnicze* (Modern Workers Housing), with Szymon Syrkus, Katowice, Poland 1931; *Le Mur Exterieur,* with Szymon Syrkus (CIAM Paper), Athens 1933; *La Genealogie de l'Architecture Functionnelle,* with Szymon Syrkus (CIAM Paper), Zurich 1938; *Ob sluga Spoleczna Jako Czynnik Ksztaltujacy Osiedle* (Communal Services: An Aid to Create a Sense of Community in Housing Estates), with Szymon Syrkus (PAU Paper), Warsaw 1940; *Osiedle Spoleczne na tle Dzielnicy, Miasta, Regionu* (The Social Housing Unit in Relation to District, Town and Region), Warsaw 1941; *Organizacja Wykonawstwa Odbudowy Warszawy* (How to Reconstruct Demolished Warsaw), with Roman Piotrowski, Cracow 1944; *Tezy Urbanistyczne Odbudowy Warszawy* (Town Planning Aspects of Rebuilding Warsaw), with Roman Piotrowski, Warsaw 1945; *Udzial Spoldzielczosci Mieszkaniowej w Realizacji Pierwszego Trzyletniego Planu Godpodarczego dla Warszawy* (Part Played by Housing Co-operatives in the Realization of the First Three Year Economic Plan for Warsaw), with Szymon Syrkus, Warsaw 1946; *Les Cite Souvrieres à Varsovie,* Zurich 1949; *Hommage à Cor van Eesteren,* with others, Amsterdam 1967; *Hommage à Giedion,* with others, Basle 1971; *Hommage à Walter Gropius,* Berlin 1974; *Ku Idei Osiedla Spolecznego* (Towards the Idea of a Social Housing Estate), Warsaw 1976; *Kazimierz Malewicz* (in French), Warsaw 1978; articles—numerous in Polish architectural journals, and "Production des Logements en Masse," with Szymon Syrkus, in *L'Architecture d'Aujourd'hui* (Paris), no. 1, 1932; "De l'Architecture et de la Production des Logements," with Szymon Syrkus, in *L'Equerre* (Liege), nos. 7/8, 1935; "Industrialisation du Bâtiment en Pologne," with Szymon Syrkus, in *Les Chantiers dans Le Monde* (Paris), no. 3/4, 1948, reprinted in *L'Architecture devant ses Taches Nouvelles,* Lausanne 1948; "Planning and Housing in Warsaw," with Szymon Syrkus, in *The Architects Yearbook,* Lon-

Helena and Szymon Syrkus: Apartment Building, Saska Kepa, Warsaw, 1937.

don 1949; "La Rationalisation des Projects et de la Construction des Habitation" in *Livre du IVme Congrès UIA*. Rotterdam 1955; "La Recontre d'Architectes et d'Elus Municipaux à Varsovie" in *Revue UIA* (Paris), no. 5, 1954; "Sozialer Wohnungsbau und Baurationalisierung in Warschau: Wohnquartier Kolo," with Szymon Syrkus, in *Das Werk* (Zurich), January 1959.

On H. and S. SYRKUS: books—*Gli Elementi dell'Architettura Funzionale* by Alberto Sartoris, Milan 1932; *Circle: International Survey of Constructive Art,* edited by J. L. Martin, Ben Nicholson and Naum Gabo, London 1937; *The Culture of Cities* by Lewis Mumford, New York and London 1938; *Introduzione all'Architettura Moderna* by Alberto Sartoris, Milan 1944; *Constructivism in Poland 1923-1936: Blok/Praesens,* exhibition catalogue, Lodz 1973; *Nowa Architektura Polska, diariusz lat 1971-1975* by T. Przemyslaw Szafer, Warsaw 1979; *CIAM: Dokumente 1928-1939,* edited by Martin Steinmann, Basle and Stuttgart 1979; *Het Nieuwe Bouwen Internationaal: CIAM – Housing, Town Planning,* exhibition catalogue by R. D. Oxenaar and A. van der Woud, Delft 1983; articles—"Kolo Housing Development" in *Revue UIA* (Paris), nos. 4 and 5, 1954; "Habitation 1945-55" in *Livre du Ivme Congrès UIA,* Rotterdam 1955; "Simultaneous Theatre and Irena Solska Theatre Projects," summary of a thesis by Bozena Frankowska in *Pamietnik Teatralny* (Warsaw), no. 2, 1962; "Syzmon Syrkus und die Gruppe Praesens" in *Bauwelt* (Berlin), January 1965; Polish Architecture: the contribution of Helena and Szymon Syrkus" by Teresa Czaplinska-Archer in *Architectural Association Quarterly* (London), October 1981: "In Memory of Helena Syrkus" by G. Greslieri in *Parametro* (Bologna), December 1982; "Helena Syrkus 1900-1982" by A. Roth in *Werk, Bauen und Wohnen* (Zurich), May 1983.

The life and work of Helena and Szymon Syrkus are inseparably linked with the history not only of Polish but also of international avant-garde architectural thought. The fundamental principle of their long partnership is that social co-operation is more rewarding than competition and rivalry.

In 1926, through the initiative of Szymon Syrkus, the avant-garde group of Modernists, *Praesens,* was formed, and their journal published their theories of a new architecture. Working within the framework of CIAM, with such internationally eminent architects as Le Corbusier, Gropius, Giedion and Moser, Helena and Szymon Syrkus were co-authors of the Athens Charter, and the Polish Branch, which they represented through the thirty years of its existence, was one of the most radical wings of the organization. They were given moral support in Poland by Toeplitz and Tolwinski, leading organizers of social housing projects. These men entrusted the architects of *Praesens* with the design of the Rakowiec Housing Development for the Warsaw Housing Co-operative, and the *Praesens* architectural/town planning studio was set up to realize this commission.

The Rakowiec project, which was presented to the Third Congress of CIAM in Brussels in 1930, was an illustration of Le Corbusier's dictum, "Il n'y a pas d'Architecture sans Urbanisme." By considering the indelible natural characteristics, such as the geographical location of the city within central Europe, the climate, morphology, and the main lines of communication of the country itself, the Syrkus's were able to define the major factors influencing the function of the city and to formulate a rational framework for its development. As a result of this work, they were able to create a theory of social housing for the district, town or region. This theory, first formulated in the Underground Architecture and Town Planning Studio (PAU) during the Nazi occupation of Poland, was later documented by Helena Syrkus in her book *Ku Idei Osiedla Spolecznego.*

The characteristic traits of most of their subsequent work were an emphasis on uniting architecture with social demands, an integration of theoretical architecture and town planning research with the practical design and realization of the social housing estate, and a constant attempt to apply modern building techniques to the construction of cheap, small, and generally accessible apartments, by using standard pre-fabricated units.

There are four consecutive stages in their work. First, between 1917 and 1926, their study and work involved a search for concepts to unify the widely divergent creative aims of the avant-garde—

postulates for a new architecture. It was a period of contact with the avant-garde milieu of the 1920s in Moscow, Cracow, Berlin and Paris, and the futurist group Katarynka and later the Blok Group in Warsaw, experiences that helped to form Szymon Syrkus's ideas and their development in *Praesens*.

The formation of *Praesens* is the beginning of the second phase in their career, which was characterized by a crystallization of their ideas about approach and the character and tasks of the new functionalist architecture. They stated their ideology in the first issue of the *Praesens* journal: "By way of experiment, architecture provides new apportunities, not only plastic as it might seem, but also social. For architecture changes the social pattern, as the social pattern changes architecture." According to Syrkus, the only solution measuring up to twentieth century expectations was to combine architecture with industry, to adjust it to the technical possibilities offered by industrial production. He assumed that a proper understanding of progress would prompt a flexible architecture, one that could easily be adapted to the rapid changes occurring in everyday life. He believed that architecture had to adapt with these changes—which it could do: new solutions were being continually introduced in the building industry as a result of human inventiveness, the noblest feature of man. New building—making use of all the technical opportunities offered by modern industry, and fulfilling the needs of people—ought as well to integrate dwellings with their surrounding environment.

Their involvement with CIAM greatly influenced their further work and their third period of creativity, which spans the 1930s and the Second World War. It begins with the opening of the *Praesen* Architectural Studio in 1931 and their work on Rakowiec. In designing Rakowiec, they applied an arrangement of columns in the skeleton support structure which created the most advantageous conditions for planning flats. By applying and refining this modular system, they managed to formulate certain principles according to which the whole development could be designed, and these principles were later used in planning new housing developments and even new towns. As early as 1931, by introducing a modular system that would allow for mass pre-fabrication, the Syrkus's tried to solve the problem of building houses on huge developments.

The design of Rakowiec and its partial realization in the pre-war period, combined with their theoretical work with CIAM and CIRPAC, culminated in a full realization of their social housing theory and its illustration in projects created underground during the war years for further housing developements and for a general plan for a future Warsaw. This period is characterized by a continual broadening of interest, a movement towards large-scale spatial and regional planning, and a consciousness of the real social, organizational and political factors responsible for the development of the environment.

The liberation of Poland in 1945 brought a political system that allowed the full realization of the ideas that the Syrkus's had struggled for all of their lives—the fourth and conclusive phase in their work. They saw their theories put into practice, and, at Warsaw Technical University, were able to pass on these theories to others. A high point of this period is the realization of the Kolo Housing Development between 1947-49, which so accurately reflects their ideas that in 1978 it was placed under a preservation order and classified as a historical monument.

During the period 1954-60 Helena and Szymon Srykus carried out research into the standardization of the construction of houses and prepared a prototype project of pre-fabricated elements. They elaborated their research in further projects, and, in their own view, achieved the "clearest" expression of their theories in the Tatary Development in Lublin of 1960.

Szymon's theoretical work, only partially realized in his lifetime, was continued by his widow Helena, until her death in 1982.

—Teresa Czaplinska-Archer

SYRKUS, Szymon.

Polish. Born in Warsaw, 24 April 1893. Educated at the Technische Hochschule, Vienna, 1911-12, Graz, 1912-14, Riga, Moscow, and Warsaw, 1915-22; studied painting and architecture at the Academy of Fine Art, Cracow, 1918-20, and sculpture at the Ecole des Beaux-Arts, and drawing at the Académie Colarossi, Paris, 1923-24. Served as a technical engineer in the Polish Army, 1915-17; interned in Auschwitz Concentration Camp, 1942-45. Married Helena Niemirowska (i.e., Helena Syrkus, *q.v.*) in 1926. Worked in various architectural practices, on building sites and as a designer in film studios, Berlin, 1922-23; assistant in the architectural studios of Leon Chifflot and and Gustave Umdenstock of the Académie des Beaux-Arts, Paris, 1923-24, and in the practice of H. Gay, Warsaw, 1925-26; practised with Helena Syrkus, Warsaw, 1926 until his death, 1964. Chairman, PAU (Underground Architecture and Town Planning Studio) of WSM (Warsaw Housing Co-operative), 1939-42; Vice-Chairman and Director, Town Planning Section, BOS (Capital Rebuilding Bureau), Warsaw, 1945. Chairman, Architecture Department, Unit of Sociology in Architecture, Institute of Architecture and Town Planning, Warsaw, 1949-51; Professor of Design, Technical University, Warsaw, 1949-64. Vice-President, SARP (Polish Architects Association), 1934-37, 1944-46; Chairman of the Research Centre, Polish Association of Housing Reform, 1947-49; Chairman, Section of Technology Progress in the Building Industry, Polish Committee on State Prizes, 1949-64; First Secretary, Institute of Technology Branch, Communist Party of Warsaw, 1950. Member, Katarynka futurist group, Cracow, 1918-20, and Blok group, Warsaw, 1925; Founder Member, Praesens Group, Warsaw, 1926-39, Member of the Editorial Board of the *Praesens* journal, 1926-39, and Member of the Praesens Design Team, 1929-39; Member, Executive Committee, CIRPAC (Comité Internationale pour la Résolution des Problèmes de l'Architecture Contemporaine), 1927-57; Member, Polish Branch of CIAM (Congrès Internationaux d'Architecture Moderne), 1929-57. Exhibitions: Modern Architecture Exhibition, Warsaw, 1926; *Machine Age*, New York, 1927; *International Theatre Exhibition*, New York, 1927; *Functional Warsaw*, London, 1934; *Warsaw of the Future*, Warsaw, 1936; *Warsaw Lives Again*, toured the United States and the United Kingdom, 1946; Tenth Anniversary Exhibition, Warsaw, 1955; International Union of Architects Exhibition, The Hague, 1955; Warsaw National Institute of Technology for National Economy, 1960; *Constructivism in Poland 1923-1936: Blok/Praesens*, Lodz Poland, Essen, and Otterlo, Netherlands, 1973; *Tendenzen der Zwanziger Jahre*, Berlin, 1977, London, 1978; *Het Nieuwe Bouwen Internationaal: CIAM*, Rijksmuseum Kroller-Muller, Otterlo, toured Netherlands, 1983. Collections: Museum of Modern Art, Lodz, Poland; Museum of Architecture, Wroclaw, Poland. Recipient: First Prize, Old People's Home Competition, Brzesc, Poland, 1928; First Prize, with Helena Syrkus, Old People's Home Competition, Kutno, Poland, 1928; First Prize, *Home Trade Fair*, Poznan, 1929; First Prize, with Helena Syrkus, Teachers Sanatorium Competition, Srodborow, Poland, 1932; Polish Medal of Freedom, 1945; Golden Cross of Warsaw Reconstruction, 1947; Diploma, Royal Institute of British Architects, 1954; Polish Anniversary Medal, 1955; Merit Prize, Polish Ministry of Education, 1955; First Class Award, Committee of Town Planning and Architecture, Warsaw, 1956; Golden Cross of Merit, Warsaw, 1960. Honorary doctorate: Technische Hochschule, Graz, Austria, 1963. Honorary Member, Royal Institute of British Architects, 1937. Commander, Order of Polonia Restituta, 1956. *Died* (in Warsaw) *in 1964.*

Works:

1926 Housing Development (project; with T. Zarnower and M. Szczuka)
Bialystok Church (competition project; with H. Oderfeld)

1927 Simultaneous Theatre, Warsaw (with A. Pronaszko, Z. Leski, and Helena Syrkus)
Palace of the League of Nations, Geneva (competition project; with H. Oderfeld)

1928 Old People's Home, Warsaw (with H. Oderfeld and E. Seydenbeutel)
Artificial Silk Factory, Tomaszow Mazowiecki, Poland (with H. Oderfeld)
Old People's Home, Brzesc, Poland

1929 Fertilizer Pavilion, *Home Trade Fair*, Poznan

With Helena Syrkus:

1929 Old People's Home, Kutno, Poland

1930 Housing Units with Steel Structures (project; with St. Hempel)

1931 Polish Teachers Association Building, Warsaw
House, King's Hill, Skolimow, Poland (with St. Hempel)

1932 Teachers' Sanatorium, Srodborrow, Poland (competition project; with St. Hempel)

1934 Experimental Theatre, for Irena Solska, Zoliborz, Warsaw

1935 Association of Workers Housing Co-operative, Lodz
Association of Workers Housing Co-operative, Grudziadz, Poland

1936 Rakowiec Housing Development, stage I, Warsaw (with the Praesens Team)
House, Warsaw (with St. Hempel)

1937 House, Saska Kepa, Warsaw (with St. Hempel)
House in Grzybowska, Zlota, and Jaworzynska Streets, Warsaw (with St. Hempel)

1939 Rakowiec Housing Development, stages II and III, Warsaw
Sanatorium, Konstancin, Poland (with St. Hempel)
Dairy (competition project; with St. Hempel)

1945 Housing developments for Rakowiec and Kolo, Warsaw (projects; with PAU)
General plan for a "Socialist Warsaw" (project; with PAU)

1949 Meeting Hall, Rakowiec Housing Development, Warsaw (with WSM)
Kolo Housing Development, stage I, Warsaw
City Gasworks reconstruction, Kredytowa Street, Warsaw
Belgian Consulate reconstruction, Warsaw
Yugoslav Embassy reconstruction, Piekna Street, Warsaw
Atheneum Theatre conversion, Warsaw

1951 School, Filtrowa Street, Warsaw
Narodowy Bank Polski, Warsaw (competition project)
School, Krolikarnia, Warsaw
OK Saska Plan, Warsaw
Theatre, Lodz (competition project)

1954 Praga Housing Development, phase I, Warsaw

1960 Pre-fabricated Slab Systems for Housing Units (project)
Tatary Housing Development, Lublin, Poland
Pre-fabricated Reinforced Units (project; with others)
Praga Housing Development, phase II, Warsaw (project; with others)
Kolo Housing Development, phase IV, Warsaw (with others)

Publications:

By S. SYRKUS: books—*Osiedle w Celle i w Kassel* (Housing in Celle and Kassel), Katowice, Poland 1931; *Nowoczesne Osiedle Robotnicze* (Modern Workers' Housing), with Helena Syrkus, Katowice, Poland 1931; *Le Mur Extérieur*, with Helena Syrkus (CIAM Paper), Athens 1933; *Warschau: Funktionele Stadt*, with Jan Chmielewski (CIAM Paper), Zurich 1934; *Warszawa Funkcjonalna* (Functional Warsaw), with Jan Chmielewski, Warsaw 1935; *La Généalogie de l'Architecture Functionnelle*, with

Helena Syrkus (CIAM Paper), Zurich 1938; *Obsluga Spoleczna Jako Czynnik Ksztaltujacy Osiedle* (Communal Services: An Aid to Create a Sense of Community in Housing Estates), with Helena Syrkus (PAU Paper), Warsaw 1940; *Udzial Spoldzielczosci Mieszkaniowej w Realizacji Pierwszego Trzyletniego Planu Godpodarczego dla Warszawy* (Part Played by Housing Co-operatives in the Realization of the First Three Year Economic Plan for Warsaw), with Helena Syrkus, Warsaw 1946; *Referat o Akademii Architectury* (About the Academy of Architecture), Warsaw 1951; articles—numerous in Polish architectural journals, and

"Architecture Opens the Volume" in *Machine Age,* exhibition catalogue, New York 1927; "Debate on the Modern Theatre" in *International Theatre Exhibition,* exhibition catalogue, New York, 1927; "Production des Logements en Masse," with Helena Syrkus, in *L'Architecture d'Aujourd'hui* (Paris), no. 1, 1932; "Nuova Teorie di Teatro" in *Quadrante* (Milan), no. 11, 1934; "De l'Architecture et de la Production des Logements," with Helena Syrkus, in *L'Equerre* (Liege), nos. 7/8, 1935; "Logis et Loisirs: Cas d'Application: Villes et Campagnes" in *Le Livre du Vme Congrès CIAM,* Paris 1938; "Industrialisation du Bâtiment en Pologne," with Helena Syrkus,

in *Les Chantiers dans le Monde* (Paris), no. 3/4, 1948, reprinted in *L'Architecture devant ses Tâches Nouvelles,* Lausanne 1948; "Planning and Housing in Warsaw," with Helena Syrkus, in *The Architects Yearbook,* London 1949; "A Critical Appraisal of Habitat at Present" in *Le Livre du Xme Congrès CIAM,* Dubrovnik 1956; "Sozialer Wohnungsbau und Baurationalisierung in Warschau: Wohnquartier Kolo," with Helena Syrkus, in *Das Werk* (Zurich), January 1959.

See SYRKUS, Helena

TAILLIBERT, Roger.

French. Born in Châtres-sur-Cher, 21 January 1926. Studied at the École du Louvre, Paris, 1949-50; École Nationale Supérieure des Beaux-Arts, Paris, 1950-55, Dip.Arch. (honours) 1955; Prix de Rome Scholar, 1957-59; Laureate of the Institut de France, for research, 1959. Served in the French Army, 1952. Married Béatrice Pfister in 1965; daughter: Sophie. Since 1960, in private practice, Paris. Member, Commission on Public Buildings, France, 1968-71; Member of the Architectural Commission of Lille and Toulouse, France, 1972-75; Member, Architectural Commission of Paris, 1974-77. Researcher in Sports Building Structures, for the French Ministry of Sports, since 1966; Consultant Architect to the City of Montreal, since 1972; Member of the French National Architectural Commission, since 1976; Chief Architect and Conservator, Grand Palais des Champs-Elysées, Paris, 1977-83, and Palais de Chaillot, Paris, since 1983. Exhibitions: *Architecture and Sports*, Mexico City, 1968; *CIAM Exhibition*, Montreal, 1976; *2 Prix Européens*, Cembureau, France, 1978. Recipient: Gold Medal, Académie d'Architecture, 1971; Grand National Prize in Arts and Letters, for Architecture, 1976. Architect-in-Chief of Civic Buildings and National Palaces; Member, Académie d'Architecture, 1972. Chevalier of the Légion d'Honneur; Commander of the National Order of Merit, 1972. Honorary Fellow, Royal Society of Arts, London, 1975; Member, Institut de France, 1983. Address (office): 163 rue de la Pompe, 75116 Paris, France.

Works:

1962 D.A.F. Factory, Survilliers, France
1965 Covered swimming pool, Deauville, France
1967 Olympics Training School, Font-Romeu, Pyrenées, France
 Carnot Swimming Pool (with movable roof), Paris
1968 Research laboratory, Castres, Tarn, France
1970 Pharmaceutical products factory, Castres, Tarn, France
 Parc des Princes Stadium, Paris
1970/
74 Plateau de Bel Air (new town), near St.-Germain-en-Laye. France
1972 Stadium Nord, Lille, France
1972/
74 Sports and Cultural Center, Chamonix, France
1974/
76 Olympic Complex, Montreal: Stadium Sports Center, Swimming Pools Complex, and Plazas
1974/
78 Sports Center and School, Castres, Tarn, France
1975 National Ski and Alpine School, Chamonix, France
 Baltimore Stadium, Maryland

1976 Hotel Intercontinental, Montfleury, Cannes, France
 Municipal Library, Castres, Tarn, France
 Lycée Nord, Toulouse, France
1977 Nuclear power plant, Tournus, France (project)
 Prefecture of Tarn and Garonne Building, Montauban, France
1978 Faculty of Pharmacy, University of Toulouse, France
 National Engineering School, Gabès, Tunisia
 European Parliament, Luxembourg
 Jolimont School Complex, Toulouse, France
1978/
80 Olympic Water Sports Centre, Kirchberg, Luxembourg
1978/
84 National Geographic Centre, Amman, Jordan
1979 Telephone Exchange Buildings in Cannes, Marseille, and Aix-en-Provence, France
1980 INSEP National Institute of Sports, Paris
1981 Golf and Country Club, Yamoussoukro, Ivory Coast
1982 Military Sports Complex, Baghdad, Iraq (competition project)
1982/
84 Gold Club and Sports Centre, Abidjan, Ivory Coast
1983 Scientific High School, Sèvres, France
 Ice Skating Rink, Abu Dhabi, United Arab Emirates (competition project)
1983/
84 INSEP Judo and Boxing Centre, Paris
 Nuclear Plants at Penly-Civaux, France
1984 Officers Residential and Sports Club, Abu Dhabi, United Arab Emirates (competition project)
 Police Centre, Cergy-Pontoise, France
1984/
85 Guyancourt Apartment Buildings, St. Quentin en Yvelines, France
 Gros Boulaincilliers Commercial and Community Development, Paris
1985 Apartment Buildings, Enghien, France
 Coca-Cola Plant and Warehouses, Grigny, France
 Country Club and Sports Centre, Portmarly, France
 Les Tourelles Swimming Pool refurbishment, Paris

Publications:

By TAILLIBERT: books—*Construire l'avenir*, Paris 1977; *Annales de l'Institut du Bâtiment*, editor, Paris 1977; article—"Industrialized Telephone Exchange" in *Mur vivant* (Paris) no. 58, 1980.

On TAILLIBERT: books—*Histoire mondiale de l'architecture* by Michel Ragon, Paris 1971; *Guide d'architecture contemporaine de France*, Paris 1972;

Montreal Olympique by Marc Emery, Montreal 1976; *Roger Taillibert* by René Huyghe, Paris 1977; articles—"The New European Parliament Building" in *Building Design* (London), 10 February 1978; "The Prefecture for the Tarn-et-Garonne" in *Mur vivant* (Paris) no. 58, 1980; "Three Works by Roger Taillibert" in *Informes de la construccion* (Madrid), September 1980; "Olympic Swimming Pool in Luxembourg" in *L'Architecture d'aujourd'hui* (Paris), December 1982.

*

For a quarter of a century, architecture has been for me a means to give better expression to man's needs and to give him a better way of life. Each building, each work of art, is an essential element in scientific, technological development, and often a delight to the new users. Although materials have varied little, man exploits their performance with an ever more precise vision. Architecture, thanks to the spirit of research and application, becomes a medium that all developed nations would like to see applied, with the necessary talent, to all their needs.

In all my works, my most sought-after goal is the "well-being of man," but there is always also the possibility that one may find an unknown space within one's own culture. There should be no superfluity, no aggression, and also one tries to stay as far as possible from the negative aspects of form, forms without the conviction of stability or of functional structure; one tries to explore new paths without obstacles or servility to past notions.

To have recourse to the purest geometric form, to adapt it, to carve it in space, to make it audacious and pleasing—that is an achievement that must everywhere bring to man the balance that he seeks in the "chasms of contemporary towns." Matter shapes space; it does not rend or brutalize it. In the harmony of its volumes describing the outward appearances of places, the architecture of a growing world shapes a better way of life in an environment that is always in search of better solutions. Permanently inventive conceptions cause technique to blossom, and that is a form of success that only the erosion of time will ennoble or destroy.

—Roger Taillibert

*

The ideal that Roger Taillibert pursues is to produce a structure as if it has sprung from the earth, at the same time making it appropriate to a given program and revealing very clearly the resources of contemporary construction. He uses the most modern means at his disposal to achieve the quintessence of each project, taking his design to the very limit of defiance. It is not surprising that he has this attitude of mind. A great sportsman since his early youth, Taillibert seems driven to push back the limits of the possible.

If he considers architecture as involving a harmonization of space, then he does not attempt to achieve that harmonization according to any dominant aesthetic. It is, rather, an organic and rational harmonization, that which can result from a precise use of materials and techniques selected for their

Roger Taillibert: Covered Swimming Pool, Deauville, France, 1965.

potential. For Taillibert, architecture is an exact and logical organization of matter and space.

This is not to imply that he rejects the aesthetic or social implications, as such, of construction. They exist for him—but they can only be consequences, not aims. Plastic beauty, functionalism, scale, or symbolic implication are the elements that, in the intuitive process of creation, result from the harmonious combination of other elements—the ingenuity and precision of technical calculations, experimentation, the choice and marriage of materials, adaptation to the economic conditions of the program, and the integration of the project to the site.

These ideas inform recent works, the Olympic installations at Montreal, the Olympic Water Sports Center at Kirchberg, Luxembourg, and the nuclear power plant in Tournus—works accomplished with means it would not have been possible to use in earlier works, the Parc des Princes Stadium in Paris, the Sports and Cultural Center in Chamonix, the D.A.F. Factory in Survilliers, or the Olympics Training School at Font-Romeu in the Pyrénées.

—Renée Diamant-Berger

TAKEYAMA, Minoru.

Japanese. Born in Sapporo, 15 March 1934. Educated at Waseda University, Tokyo, 1952-58, B.Arch. 1956, M.Arch. 1958; Harvard University, Cambridge, Massachusetts, 1959-60 (Fulbright Scholar), M.Arch. 1960. Worked for TAC, Josep Lluis Sert, and Hideo Sasaki, Cambridge, 1960-61, for Paul Lester Wiener, Isamu Noguchi, and Harrison and Abramovitz, New York, 1961-62, and for Jørn Utzon, Arne Jacobsen, Finn Juhl and Henning Larsen, in Copenhagen, 1962-64. Since 1965, President of Minoru Takeyama and the United Actions, Tokyo; office established in Sapporo, 1975. Lecturer, School of Architecture, Royal Danish Academy of Fine Arts, 1963-64. Assistant Professor, 1965-76, and since 1976 Professor, Musashino Art University, Tokyo. Visiting Critic, Waseda University, 1965, Hokkaido University, 1966, Kyushuh Institute of Technology, 1972, and Nagoya Institute of Technology, 1972; Visiting Professor, University of California, Berkeley, Spring 1976 and 1977, University of Hong Kong, 1982, and National University of Singapore, 1983. Member of the Board, Japan Architects Association, since 1975; Architects Selection Committee Member, City of Tokyo, 1982-84; Contributor, *Shinkenchiku* magazine, Tokyo, from 1983. Member, ArchiteXt, with Takefumi Aida, Takamitsu Azuma, Mayumi Miyawaki, and Makoto Suzuki, since 1971. Exhibitions: *Bienal,* Sao Paulo, 1957; *Body Furniture,* Tokyo, 1970; *Body Lighting,* Tokyo, 1974; *Terra-1,* Poland, 1975; *A New Wave of Japanese Architecture,* toured 10 American cities, 1978; *Graphic Architecture,* Tokyo, 1978; *Minoru Takeyama,* Hekiso-kan, Tokyo, 1980; *Homage to Palladio,* Italian Cultural Center, Tokyo, 1980; *Minoru Takeyama, 1970-1980,* University of Hong Kong, 1981; *The House as Model,* Good Design Corner, Tokyo, 1981; *The House as an Image,* Louisiana Museum, Humlebaek, Denmark, 1981; *Post-Modernism in Japan,* Galleri Falsted, Copenhagen, 1982; *The State Mosque of Iraq,* Baghdad, 1983; *Japan Air: Seven Architects,* Rotterdam, 1984. Recipient: Grand Prize, *Bienal,* Sao Paulo, 1957; Shogyo Design Association Award, 1971, 1974; Wheelwright Fellowship, Harvard University, 1971; Fulbright Research Fellowship, 1975; Silver Medal, Japan Display Design Association, 1975; Honorable Mention, Islamic Cultural Center Competition, Madrid, 1980; Special Prize, World Biennale of Architecture, Sofia, Bulgaria, 1981. Address: Minoru Takeyama and the United Actions, 5-1-10-501 Minami-Aoyama, Minato-ku, Tokyo, Japan.

Works:

1958 House, Tokyo (ROH)
1959 Recreational facilities for the Mastic Tile Company (COM; competition project)
1960 City Hall, Boston (COB-o; competition project)
1961 Urban design for the Mastic Tile Company (COM; competition project)
1963 National Theatre of Japan (COT; competition project)
1965 Savarian Restaurant interiors, Tokyo (IOG)
Pandora Restaurant interiors, Tokyo (IOP)
Design for bath units (DON)
House, Børnholm, Denmark (ROB; project)
1966 House, Sapporo, Japan (ROT-1)
Housing units (COB; competition project)
Mammina Fashion Store interiors, Tokyo (IOM-1)
Transparent House (ROGg; project)
1967 City Center, Espoo, Finland (COE; competition project)
Yamagiwa Electric Hardware Store interiors, Tokyo (IOY-1)
Yamagiwa Parlor interiors, Tokyo (IOY-2)
Municipal Cemetery, Mito, Japan (POM)
1968 Young Men's Lodge, Nagano, Japan (BON)
Shingle House, Tokyo (ROK)
City Hall, Amsterdam (COA; competition project)

"Situationer" (NOS-1; conceptual model)
United Nations Conference Center, Vienna (COW; competition project)
Mammina Fashion Store interiors, Kobe, Japan (IOM-2)
Yamagiwa Showroom interiors, Tokyo (IOY-3)
Memorial Tower for War Victims, Hokkaido, Japan (MOO)
"Shu Pub" Shoe Store, Tokyo (IOO-1)
Utonai Leisure Center, Hokkaido, Japan (BOU)
Tops Coffee Shop interiors, Tokyo (IOT)
Kinichikan Department Store, Sapporo, Japan (BOK; project)

1970 Ichi Ban Kahn Omni-Rental Stores, Tokyo (BOS-1)
Fuji Heavy Industry Labor Union Hall, Saitama, Japan (BOF)
Ni Ban Kahn Omni-Rental Stores, Tokyo (BOS-2)
New experimental college, Thy, Denmark (BONec; project)
"Living Room" (MOS-2; conceptual model)
Multi-family house, Tokyo (ROI)
Relocatable Kindergarten Units, Copenhagen (DOK; project)
"Body Furniture" (XOF)

1971 Compound houses, Tokyo (ROSh/B)
Iwakura Office Building, Hokkaido, Japan (BOI-1)
Place Beaubourg, Paris (COP; competition project)
Shell Gas Station exterior, Tokyo (EOsh)
House, Sapporo, Japan (ROSg)
Yamatake exterior, Sapporo, Japan (EOT)

1972 Pepsi Cola Canning Plant, Mikasa, Hokkaido, Japan (BOP-1)
Kurashiki Factory conversion (POK; project)
Tack Restaurant, Hokkaido, Japan (BOI-3)
Tom Store exterior, Hokkaido, Japan (EOI)
Redevelopment plan for the Ugawara Coast Line, Japan (POU)
"Yamaha Sound Woods," Shizuoka, Japan (POY; project)
House, Lahore, Pakistan (ROPk; project)
Sambi Restaurant, Los Angeles (BOSn; project)
"Body Lighting" (lighting fixture; XOE)

1973 Hotel Beverley Tom, Tomakomai, Hokkaido, Japan (BOI-4)
Island of Chirin, Kyushu, Japan (POT; project)
Nichiro Saloon interiors, Tokyo (ION)
Combined house, Hakone, Japan (ROT/M; project)
City of Tomakomai Shopping Arcade, Hokkaido, Japan (EOTm; project)
Design of store facade for National Electric Shops (EON)
Onuma Lakeshore Development, Hakodate, Japan (POH; project)

1974 House, Asahikawa, Hokkaido, Japan (ROA)
House, Tomakomai, Hokkaido, Japan (ROW-1)
High-density, low-rise housing, Tomakomai, Hokkaido, Japan (ROW-2; project)
Design of the Environment of the Northern Region exhibition, Sapporo, Japan (XOH)
Misawa Homes Showroom interiors, Tokyo (ION)
Yamagiwa Record Shop interiors, Tokyo (IOY-5)
Yamagiwa Parlor interiors, Chiba, Japan (IOY-6)
House, Sapporo, Japan (ROIw)
Stage design for the musical Himiko, Tokyo (DOH)

1975 Porto Santos Island Development (COS; competition project)
"Earthtecture" (XOT; exhibition project)
House, Tokyo (ROU)
House, Sapporo, Japan (ROY)
Rehabilitation Center, Sapporo, Japan (PON)

"Shu Pub" Shoe Store, Tokyo (IOO-6)
Shell Garden Super Market, Tokyo (BOSh; project)
Self-help community, Manila (COM; competition project)

1976 Sapporo Art Park, Hokkaido, Japan (POS; project)
Bankei Rehabilitation Center, Sapporo, Japan (PON; project)
Atelier Indigo (own studio), Sapporo, Japan (ROO)
Summer House, Hokkaido, Japan (RON)
Summer House, Hokkaido, Japan (ROOg)
Prefabricated house, Sapporo, Japan (ROIw)
"Shu Pub" Shoe Store, Tokyo (IOO-7)
House, Sapporo, Japan (ROKu)
House, Tokyo (ROSz)

1977 House, Sapporo, Japan (ROOg)
House, Fukushima, Japan (ROH)
Unique Bazaar Store, Tokyo (IOM)
Medical Center, Sapporo, Japan (BOK; project)
Agricultural Fair Exhibition layouts, Sapporo, Japan (XOF)

1978 Department Store "109", Shibuya, Tokyo (BOT)
Pops Restaurant, Kasukabe, Tokyo (BOYm)
Uny Shopping Center, Nagoya, Japan (BOUn)
House, Sapporo, Japan (ROKm)
House, Tokyo (ROSz)

1979 Nakamura Memorial Hospital, Sapporo, Japan (BON)
House, Sapporo, Japan (ROIb)
House, Tokyo (RONm)
Hungry Horse Restaurant, Tokyo (IOH)
Islamic Cultural Center, Madrid (COI; competition project)

1980 Shell Garden Store, Tokyo (Bosh)
Apartment House, Tokyo (BOF/F)
House, Tokyo (ROKn)
Studio Building, Musashino Art University, Tokyo (BOM-1)
Building no. 10, Musashino Art University, Tokyo (BOM-2)
House, Sapporo, Japan (ROSk)
Flore Coffee Shop, Yokohama, Japan (IOY-1)
Tricolor Coffee Shop, Yokohama, Japan (IOY-2)

1981 Abu Nuwaz Development and Conservation Project, Baghdad, Iraq (COAb; competition project)
Abu Dhabi International Conference Halls, United Arab Emirates (COAd; competition project)
Tikrit and Samara Redevelopment Plan, Iraq (POT/S; with PCI)
Merchandise House, Sapporo, Japan (RON1)
Office Building, Osaka, Japan (BOMk; project)

1982 House, Kawasaki, Japan (ROKm)
Photo Studio Building, Tokyo (BOHt)
State Mosque of Iraq, Baghdad (COMs; competition project)
The Peak Development, Hong Kong (COHk; competition project)
Hotel Hamaya, Sapporo, Japan (BOHm; project)
Hotel Princess, Mexico City (BoMx; project)

1983 Opera House, Paris (COPo; competition project)
Housing Complex, Peking and Shanghai (RONl; project)
Candy Factory, Nara, Japan (BOMk)
High-Rise Office Building, Tokyo (BOPk; project)
History Museum, Cairo, Egypt (COEg; competition project)
Tokyo Mosque, Shibuya, Tokyo (BOMs; project)

1984 Multi-Use Building, Kyoto, Japan (BOKy)

Publications:

By TAKEYAMA: books—Jørn Utzon and His Intentions, Tokyo 1966; Music and Architecture, Tokyo 1966; Space Perception, Tokyo 1966; Scandinavian Design, Tokyo 1967; How to Design Shops and Stores, Tokyo 1972; Blue Nirvana-Language vs. Architecture, Tokyo 1973; Autobiography of an Architect, Tokyo 1973; Food and Environment, Tokyo 1974; Meaning of Street, Tokyo 1977; translation of The Language of Post-Modern Architecture by Charles Jencks, Tokyo 1978; Language in Architecture, Tokyo 1983; articles—"Notes on Housing Space" in Kindaikenchiku (Tokyo), June 1959; "On Arne Jacobsen" in Space Design (Tokyo), March 1965; "The Common Trends in Northern Culture" in Design (Tokyo), April 1966; "Urban Design and Architecture in Northern Europe" in Shinkenchiku (Tokyo), January and February 1967; "Tivoli as an Urban Textile" in Design (Tokyo), January 1967; "Situationism in Architecture" in Kindaikenchiku (Tokyo), May 1968; "Space Relationships" in Kenchiku (Tokyo), September 1968; "Henning Larsen and His Works" in Kindaikenchiku (Tokyo), November 1968; "Space Situationing" in Toshijutaku (Tokyo), March 1969; "Revolving Interior" in Kindaikenchiku (Tokyo), March 1969; "Forbidden Space" in Japan Interior (Tokyo), November 1969; "New Experiments in Space Design" in Japan Interior (Tokyo), April 1970; "The Surface Reflects Contents" in Kenchiku (Tokyo), July 1970; "Reinstatement of Surface Structure" in The Japan Architect (Tokyo), August 1970; "On Territory" in Space Design (Tokyo), August 1970; "Expo '70" in Arkitekten (Copenhagen), no. 6, 1970; "Street-Scaping" in Japan Interior (Tokyo), April 1971; "The Living Room" in The Japan Architect (Tokyo), July 1971; "Use-ology" in Japan Interior (Tokyo), October 1971; "Civil Design" in Japan Interior (Tokyo), November 1971; "IEG (Imago-Encephalo-Graph)" in Space Design (Tokyo), March 1972; "Phenomena-Analysis of Urbanity" in Shotenkenchiku (Tokyo), April 1972; "Fashion and Architecture" in Kenchikuzasshi (Tokyo), July 1972; "Urban Interior" in Japan Interior (Tokyo), August 1972; "Language in Architecture" in Space Design (Tokyo), January 1973; "Unfinished Harmony in Space" in Kenchiku (Tokyo), January 1973; "The Greening Environment" in Kankyobunka (Tokyo), March 1973; "Revising Architectural Internationalism" in Architecture + Urbanism (Tokyo), May 1973; "Counter Architecture I" in Kenchikubunka (Tokyo), August 1973; "Interior Landscape" in Japan Interior (Tokyo), August 1973; "Pedagogical Architecture" in Architecture + Urbanism (Tokyo), October 1973; "Counter Architecture II" in Kenchikubunka (Tokyo), January 1974; "IEG of Minoru Takeyama" in Space Design (Tokyo), January 1974; "Distorted Form" in Japan Interior (Tokyo), April 1974; "Anthrophobia" in Kenchikubunka (Tokyo), June 1974; "Human Grouping and House Collecting" in Kenchikubunka (Tokyo), August 1974; "Space Dynamics" in Japan Interior (Tokyo), October 1974; "New Dimension of Architects' Education" in Kenchikuzasshi (Tokyo), October 1974; "Regionalism in Hokkaido: Design and Community" in Japan Interior (Tokyo), January 1975; "Community" in Japan Interior (Tokyo), January 1975; "Street Semiology" in Kenchikubunka (Tokyo), February 1975; "Urban Environment of San Francisco" in Japan Interior (Tokyo), November and December 1975; "Japanese Interior Design as Paradox" in Japan Interior (Tokyo), December 1975; "On Japanese Heterogeneity" in Japan Interior (Tokyo), February 1976; "Image Synthesizing" in Kindaikenchiku (Tokyo), May 1976; "Heterology in Architecture" in The Japan Architect (Tokyo), June 1976; "Offensive Space/Defensive Space" in Japan Interior (Tokyo), September 1976; "Arts and Urban Environment" in Mainichi News (Tokyo), 24 and 31 October 1976; "Outside-in and Inside-out" in Space

Minoru Takeyama: Nakamura Memorial Hospital, Sapporo, Japan, 1979-80.

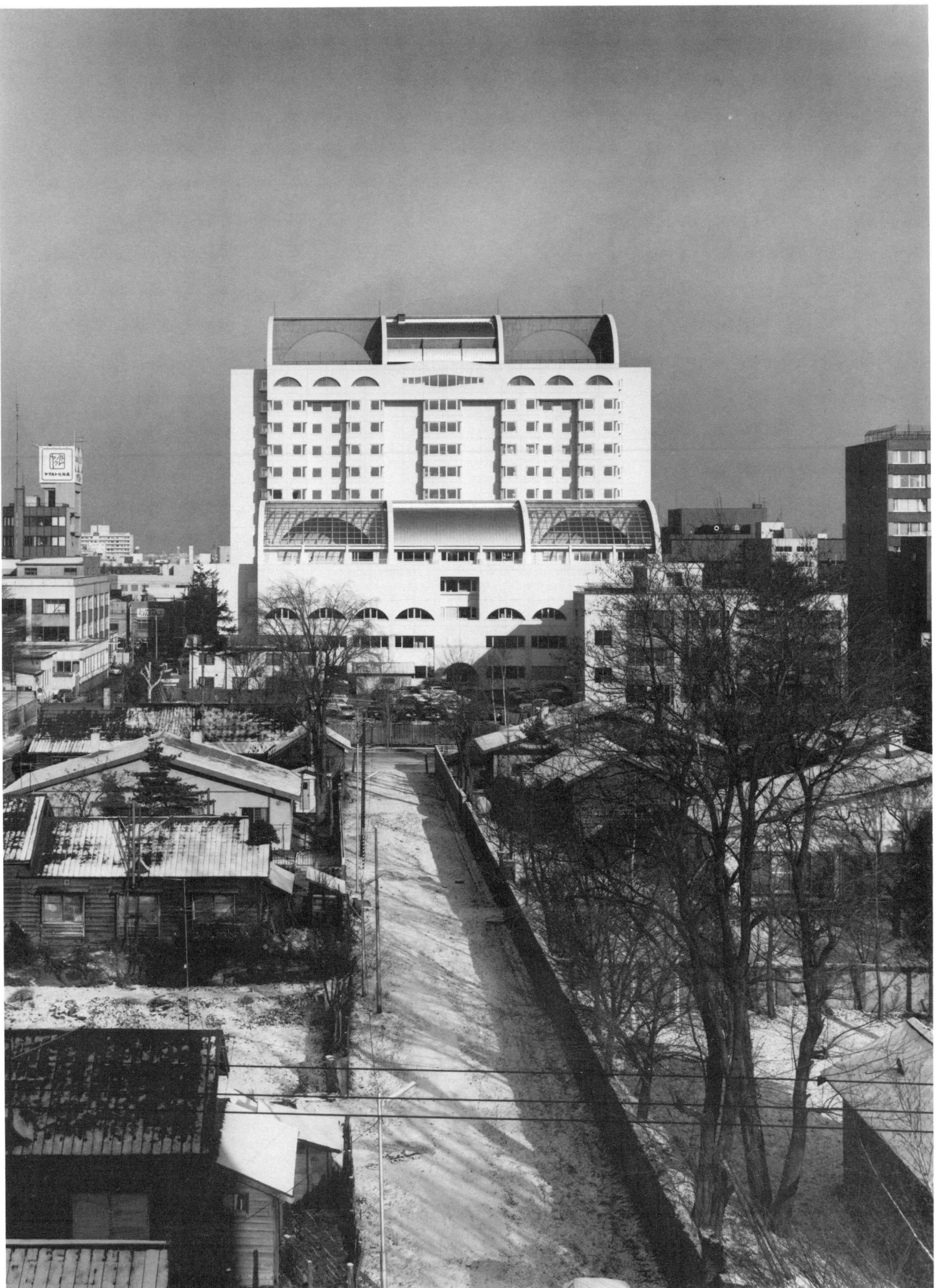

Design (Tokyo), November 1976; "Soft Technology in Architecture" in *Kenchikuka* (Tokyo), November 1976; "White Landscape" in *Japan Interior* (Tokyo), March 1977; "Architecture and Non-Architecture" in *Japan Interior* (Tokyo), August 1977; "Form and Image" in *Shinkenchiku* (Tokyo), September 1977; "Counter Architecture III" in *Kenchikubunka* (Tokyo), September 1977; "Extremely Private Space" in *Japan Interior* (Tokyo), September 1977; "Expressive Urbanism" in *Kenchikubunka* (Tokyo), September 1977; "Atelier Indigo" in *The Japan Architect* (Tokyo), January 1978; "Panoramic Views" in *Intellect and Sensitivity* (Tokyo), February 1978; "Sad Space and Happy Space" in *Japan Interior* (Tokyo), March 1979; "Background to Post-Modernism" in *Architecture + Urbanism* (Tokyo), October 1979; "The Vigeland Sculpture Gardens, Oslo", with others, in *Space Design* (Tokyo), March 1980; "The Architect's Role and Social Demands" in *Shinkenchiku* (Tokyo), August 1980; "Form versus Function" in *Shinkenchiku* (Tokyo), July 1981; "Louisiana Museum, Humlebaek", with Nobuo Sekine, in *Space Design* (Tokyo), October 1981; "Time Out, Time In" in *Space Design* (Tokyo), February 1982; "Nakamura Memorial Hospital" in *The Japan Architect* (Tokyo), March 1982; "Architecture and Communication" in *Japan Interior* (Tokyo), August 1982; "On Memphis" in *Space Design* (Tokyo), March 1983; "About Diversity" in *The Japan Architect* (Tokyo), October 1983.

On TAKEYAMA: books—*Modern Movements in Architecture* by Charles Jencks, London 1973; *The Language of Post Modern Architecture* by Charles Jencks, London 1977, 1978; *Beyond Metabolism: The New Japanese Architecture* by Michael Franklin Ross, New York 1978; *A New Wave of Japanese Architecture*, with introduction by Kenneth Frampton, New York 1978; *The New Japanese House* by Chris Fawcett, London 1980; *Color Outside* by Tom Porter, London 1982; *Fifty Outstanding Architects of the World* by Ivica Mladjenovic, Belgrade 1984; articles—"ArchiteXt and the Problem of Symbolism" by Charles Jencks in *The Japan Architect* (Tokyo), June 1976; "ArchiteXt" in *The Japan Architect* (Tokyo), June 1976; "Post Metabolism" in *The Japan Architect* (Tokyo), October/November 1977; "An Anarchist's Guide to Modern Architecture" by Chris Fawcett in *Architectural Association Quarterly* (London), no. 3, 1978; "The Black Boxes of Minoru Takeyama" in *Los Angeles Times*, 26 February 1978; "An Overview of Japanese Architecture" by Paul Goldberger in the *New York Times*, 22 December 1978; "The Post Metabolists" in *Arquitectura* (Madrid), January/February 1979; "Takeyama's Hospital as a Landmark" in *The Yomiuri* (Tokyo), 11 August 1981; "Takeyama's Works Abroad" in *Shinkenchiku* (Tokyo), October 1981; "Building Ten, Musashino Art University" in *The Japan Architect* (Tokyo), August 1982; "Symbolic Association" by David Morton in *Progressive Architecture* (New York), December 1982; "Architecture and Eros" by Chris Fawcett in *Vision* (Hong Kong), no. 12, 1983.

Bibliography: *Minoru Takeyama: Japanese Architect of Heterogeneity* by James P. Noffsinger, Monticello, Illinois 1982.

*

Architecture is the "relator" which governs the inter-relation between expression and content in its signification. For architectural phenomena, Japan can be compared to a huge kaleidoscope of signs which presents extremely heterogeneous visions. This heterogeneity in visual effects shares a homogeneous content which is socio-culturally characterized by its racial, religious and linguistic univalence. In other words, in this cultural climate, the architect's creativity is the "relator" of heterogeneous expression and homogeneous content.

"Homo" or "hetero"—we can define this "like-ness" or "unlikeness" relationship as a basic continuity between two entities, which is one of the fundamental gestalt factors from which a man confirms his orientation and existence. Hypothetically, I have been using a scale to measure a sense of continuity by inserting three degrees, *analogy, homology* and *heterology,* between the extremes of "likeness" and "unlikeness." Simply speaking, analogy involves associating similar contents in spite of differences of form and structure; e.g., a bird's wing and an insect's wing, *Homology,* on the other hand, lets us find a similarity of form but not content (such as function); e.g., a bird's wing and a dog's leg. In both cases the continuity can be investigated through similarity or "likeness."

Heterology involves establishing a relationship between two entities in terms of metaphysical meaning. The continuity can still be measured in dissimilar or "unlike" elements. For example, try to relate a turtle's head to a mushroom. They have nothing in common biologically. Their forms and contents are different. However, in Japan, these two are both phallic symbols! They are related not in their intrinsic meaning but in their symbolic meaning, which is a product of the deeply-rooted historical sub-culture of particular human minds.

Through *heterology* we can trace continuous relationships between factors linked neither in structure nor in content in terms of their extrinsic meaning within a particular culture. It is a conceptual tool to cope with the increasing multivalence and dissimilarity of our environmental phenomena. *Heterology* can even be seen to be oriented towards the future if we look back at the evolution of urbanism and architecture. For as the built environment has evolved from the rural to the urban through successive stages of agriculture and industry, and as architectural space has evolved in its primary context from the pragmatic to the semantic through various degrees of functionalism, so too have the concepts dealing with the continuity of such stages changed from the stage of *analogy* to that of *heterology* through that of *homology.* As our perception evolved from one stage to the next, the original meaning of architecture has lost its intrinsic motivation in favor of an increasingly arbitrary intent.

As an architect coping with the sub-culture of a kaleidoscope of multiple architectural signs, I find that one of the basic intentions of my work is to confirm the relation between heterogeneous expression and homogeneous content. Evaluating the phenomena of architectural language, I have changed my aim from time to time—such as reacting against the homegeneity of the content at some times or escalating the heterogeneity of the visual experience at other times. No matter which quality predominated, the architectural meaning has, however, remained with the relationship itself between the two sides, content and expression.

The "discontinuous continuity" of my past challenges in architectural creativity could be classified into the following stages (as far as the chronology of rhetoric is concerned):

During the first period of my architectural practice, after my return to Japan after being abroad for a few years, my intuitive views led me to maintain an arbitrary conception of the surrounding urbanism as a *unicellular* organism. Most architects think analogically; my ideas were analogically oriented too; I emphasized the similarity of contents. In unicellular organisms a single cell is encapsulated by a membrane which functions as a sort of communication link between the internal life and the external stimuli. To me the membrane was more meaningful than the core inside. I expected the surface of material things to have a similar mediating function between the hidden dimensions within buildings and the exposed happenings of the external environment. By and by, however, the surface became, for me, self-contained, independent in its own expression, and even gave up its primary function as a mediator. The first stage of my heterological rhetoric was to disconnect the inter-relation between the inside and the outside, as expressed in those works designated

BOS-1, BOS-2, BOF, EOT, EOSh, Earth-texture, etc.

The basic content of the heterogeneous environmental structure of Japan, which is based on a homogeneous socio-culture, seemed to me like the structure of "brotherhood" which is different from that of "neighborhood." Originally various neighbors try to depend upon a certain contract to create a uniform neighborhood of homogeneous quality, while brothers, who have common kinship, often behave in different ways from one another. One brother participating in the same brotherhood does not depend on formal agreement to join the native company. I would compare the difference between "brother" and "neighbor" with the difference between "paradigm" and "syntagm" respectively in linguistics. The syntagmatic context, in my interpretation, is based on a chain of *metonymy* (neighbor to neighborhood) and is, therefore, a contrasting relation, while the paradigmatic context is an oppositional relation, collecting unconscious metaphors (brothers to brotherhood).

(In fact, metaphor in architectural language is very arbitrary and unstable. It is absent from man's consciousness and topologically brings up man's memories and associations. Metaphors are the offspring of the *meso-* and *paleo-cortex* of the human brain. While searching for a meta-language of architectural signification, I borrowed immaturely from the knowledge of "brain architects.")

As a result, my surrounding environment was no longer a *unicellular* organism but began to dwell in my own brain, and architecture which seemed to be a relator between expression and content functioned as a *neurone,* the basic element of communication. IEG (Imago-encephalo-graph) is a product of this stage of my architectural conceptions, together with BOP, BOI, SIT-1, SIT-2, and Body Furniture.

Neither a brother nor a neighbor can resist mortality: life and death are the common destiny. It is within a sequence of time, and on that score, that man describes the proof of his existence. According to brain physiologists, time perception is one of the basic human privileges (as well the privilege of perceiving signs). We share the power of perceiving space with other animals; in fact, a nesting animal can do a better job of creating space ecologically than we can. In notating the syntagmatic context, in terms of time sequence, we need a linear score to show contrasting relations. In the paradigmatic context, the score will become more complicated to include various fragments of metaphor. In order to describe the multivalence of Japanese cultural phenomena, I feel that we need a very particular score that can clarify topologically superimposed signs.

My effort is to conceive space as "time-teller," to tell "what time space is" at constantly changing sequences. As far as heterology is a methodology to stipulate "discontinuous continuity" in architecture, this is one of the most promising developments at present. With this conviction, I have done such works as IOO, ROW-1, ROW-2, DOX, COP, ROO, and my challenge is still, patiently, to go on.

—Minoru Takeyama

*

Minoru Takeyama is one of the wonderful enigmas on Japan's contemporary architectural scene. He is often puzzling and contradictory, yet always creative, inventive and witty. As Robert Venturi pointed out in his classic indictment of modern architecture, complexity and contradiction can be very positive attributes. Venturi claimed that he liked elements "which are hybrid rather than 'pure,' compromising rather than 'clean,' distorted rather than 'straightforward,' ambiguous rather than 'articulated.'" These contradictory qualities of inclusion are an apt place to begin to describe the complex work of Minoru Takeyama.

·Like abstract paintings Takeyama named his two attention grabbing pleasure palaces of 1970, Ichiban-khan and Ni-ban-khan, which translate simply into Number-one-building and Number-two-building. Ichi-ban-khan is a black metal and glass space ship with a layering of horizontal stripes to ward off low flying aircraft. Ni-ban-khan, the symbol of post-modern architecture, is a collage of op-art and catalogue components combined into a powerful image in the visually rich Shinjuku entertainment section of Tokyo. Recently Takeyama had Ni-ban-khan repainted into a single piece of op-art sculpture, reinforcing the concept that buildings should be adaptable to change and impermanency.

Like Arata Isozaki, Takeyama represents Japan's new Mannerism in which wit and metaphor are part of the architectural package. In his Pepsi-Cola Canning Plant in Mikasa, Hokkaido, and in the Hotel Beverley Tom in Tomakomai, Takeyama employs visual puns and double entendre to satirize the building functions. The truncated cylindrical form of the Pepsi Canning Plant has a sloped roof which allows melted snow to collect and vaporize at the central boiler plant of the building. As the foggy mist rises on the cold Hokkaido landscape it appears that one of America's most popular soft drinks is being manufactured from melting Japanese snow. At the Hotel Beverley Tom, which is located in a bleak industrial section of Tomakomai, Takeyama has wrapped this large-scale phallic symbol in an industrial black metal skin which parodies the huge oil tankers and silos that accent the landscape.

Takeyama is a master at employing catalogue components and modern technology as visual playthings with which to make larger-than-life toys for people. When his parents asked him to update their somewhat time-tested seventy-year old traditional wooden house, Takeyama wrapped the exterior in diagonal metal siding, giving it a most contemporary look and an energy-efficient insulated enclosure simultaneously; however, he left the interior exactly as it had always been. From the outside it is a sleek, chic modern house, but inside it is a simple traditional Japanese house in which his parents feel most comfortable.

To test the concept of impermanence and flexibility in architecture, Takeyama designed his own house as a series of eight cubes which can theoretically be rearranged in 45,656 configurations. I wonder if anyone is keeping score? Thus far it seems that Minoru Takeyama's richly coded symbolism and mannerist heterogeneity have brought us an architecture that gives the viewer both a sense of joy and wonder.

—Michael Franklin Ross

TANGE, Kenzo.

Japanese. Born in Osaka, 4 September 1913. Educated at the University of Tokyo, Department of Architecture, 1935-38, and Graduate School, 1942-45, D.Eng. 1959. Married Toshiko Kato in 1949; Takako Iwata in 1971; children: Michiko and Noritaka. Principal, Kenzo Tange & Urtec, urbanists and architects, Tokyo, since 1961. Professor of Architecture, 1946-74, and since 1974 Professor Emeritus, University of Tokyo. Visiting Professor, Massachusetts Institute of Technology, Cambridge, 1959-60, and Harvard University, Cambridge, Massachusetts, 1972. Recipient: First Prize, Memorial to the Creation of Greater East Asia Competition, 1942; First Prize, Japanese Cultural Center Competition, Bangkok, 1943; First Prize, Hiroshima Peace Center Competition, 1949; First Prize, Tokyo Metropolitan Government Office Competition, 1952; Annual Prize, Architectural Institute of Japan, 1954, 1955, 1958; Pan Pacific Citation, American Institute of Architects, Hawaii Chapter, 1958; International Prize for Art and Architecture, *L'Architecture d'Aujourd'hui*, 1959; Building Contractors of Japan Society Prize, 1960, 1965, 1966, 1969, 1970; Diploma of Merit, International Olympic Committee, 1964; Gold Medal, Royal Institute of British Architects, 1965; Asahi Newspapers Prize, Japan, 1965; Special Prize, Archi-

tectural Institute of Japan, 1965, 1970; President's Medal, Architectural League of New York, 1966; Gold Medal, American Institute of Architects, 1966; Gold Medal, Société d'Encouragement au Progrès, France, 1967; Order of the Yugoslav Star, 1968; Medal of Honor, Royal Academy of Arts, Denmark, 1968; Thomas Jefferson Memorial Foundation Medal, U.S.A., 1970; Gold Medal of the President of Italy, 1970; Prime Minister's Award, Japan, 1971; Gold Medal, Académie d'Architecture, France, 1973; SARP Medal, Institute of Polish Architects, 1973. D.F.A.: State University of New York at Buffalo, 1962; D.Eng.: Technische Hochschule, Stuttgart, 1962; D.Arch.: Polytechnic, Milan, 1964; D.Sc.: University of Hong Kong, 1970; D.Litt.: University of Sheffield, England, 1970; D.Art.: Harvard University, 1971; University of Buenos Aires, 1978; Honorary Professor, Universidad Nacional Federico Villareal, Peru, 1977. Honorary Fellow, American Institute of Architects; Honorary Member, American Academy of Arts and Letters, and Akademie der Künste, Germany; Sociedad Bolivariana de Arquitectos, Venezuela, 1978; Venezuelan Architects Association, 1978; Corresponding Member, Academie d'Architecture, France, 1979; Associate, Institut de France Academie des Beaux-Arts, Paris, 1983. Member, Order of St. Gregory the Great, Vatican, 1970, and Order of Merit of Science and Arts, West Germany, 1976; Commander, National Order of Merit, France, 1977; Commander, Order of Merit, Republic of Italy, 1979; Gran Oficial de la Orden El Sol del Peru, 1983. Address: Kenzo Tange & Urtec, 7-2-21 Akasaka, Minato-ku, Tokyo, Japan.

Works:

1942 Memorial to the Creation of Greater East Asia Co-Prosperity Shere, at Mt. Fuji, Japan (competition project)
1943 Japanese Cultural Center, Bangkok (competition project)
1946/
47 Master Plan for Hiroshima
1949/
55 Hiroshima Peace Center
1952/
57 Tokyo Metropolitan Government Offices
1953 Kenzo Tange House, Tokyo
1955/
58 Prefectural Government Office, Kagawa, Japan
1957/
58 Imabari City Hall, Ehime, Japan
1958/
60 Kurashiki City Hall, Okayama, Japan
1959/
60 Tokyo Restructuring Plan (project)
1959/
64 Ichinomiya Housing Project, Kagawa, Japan
1960/
61 Totsuka Country Club House, Kanagawa, Japan
1960/
62 Nichinan Cultural Center, Miyazaki, Japan
1960/
64 Tsukiji Redevelopment Plan, Tokyo
1961/
64 National Gymnasia for the Tokyo Olympics St. Mary's Cathedral, Tokyo
1961/
67 Press and Broadcasting Center, Yamanashi, Japan
1962/
64 Prefectural Gymnasium, Kagawa, Japan
1965/
66 Resorts Master Plan, Bandai Inawashiro City, Fukushima, Japan (project)
City Center Reconstruction Project, Skopje, Yugoslavia
1965/
67 Dentsu Office Building, Tokyo

University of the Sacred Heart, Taipei, Taiwan
1966/
67 Yukari Nursery School, Tokyo
Shizuoka Press and Broadcasting Center, Tokyo
1966/
68 Takasaki and Maebashi City Regional Plans, Gunma, Japan (project)
International School of the Sacred Heart, Tokyo
City Axis Master Plan, Kyoto (project)
1966/
70 Kuwait Embassy and Chancery, Tokyo
Master plan, trunk facilities, and Festival Plaza, *Expo '70*, Osaka (as head of group of architects)
1967/
68 Master Plan for Flushing Meadow Sports Park, New York City (project; with Marcel Breuer and Lawrence Halprin)
1967/
69 Master Plan for Yerba Buena Center, San Francisco (project; with McCue, Boone and Tomsick, and Lawrence Halprin and Associates)
1967/
70 Shizuoka and Shimizu City Regional Plans, Shizuoka, Japan (project)
Olivetti Technical Center, Kanagawa, Japan
Master plan for Morioka City, Iwate, Japan
New Northern Development, Bologna, Italy (project)
1968/
70 Press and Broadcasting Center, Shizuoka, Japan
1968/
71 Japan in the 21st Century Plan, Tokyo (project; as head of a physical and socio-economic team)
1969 New Central Station, Skopje, Yugoslavia
International Air Terminal Building, Kuwait
1970/
71 City Regional Plan, Trieste, Italy (project)
1970/
74 Minneapolis Arts Complex (with Parker Klein Associates)
1971 Sports Arena, Yerba Buena Center, San Francisco (project; with McCue, Boone and Tomsick, and Lawrence Halprin and Associates
University, hospital, and dormitory, Oran, Algeria
Librino New Town, Catania, Italy (project)
1971/
74 Master Plan for Fiera District Center, Bologna, Italy (project)
1972 Akasaka Prince Hotel, Tokyo
Inner Harbor Residential Development, Baltimore (with Cochran, Stephenson and Donkervoet, and Parker Klein Associates)
Palace for King Faisal, Jeddah, Saudi Arabia (project)
1972/
74 Bulgarian Embassy and Chancery, Tokyo
1973 Hokusetsu New Town Center, Hyogo, Japan
Andalouses Tourist Complex, Oran, Algeria
Apartment Towers, Tehran (project)
Pilgrims Accommodation Master Plan, Muna, Saudi Arabia (project; with GK Industrial Design Associates)
1973/
77 Turkish Embassy and Chancery, Tokyo
Headquarters Building, University of Tokyo
1974 Farah Park Hotel, Tehran (with Mir-Djalali and Detail Consulting Company)
Sacred Garden of the Buddha's Birthplace, Lumbini, Nepal
Abbasabad New City Centre, Tehran (project; with Louis Kahn)
1974/
75 Matsue City Master Plan, Shimane, Japan (project)

1974/
77 Sogetsu Hall and Offices, Tokyo
1975 Imperial Iranian Embassy, Tokyo
New Presidential Palace, Damascus, Syria (with Mohammad Nofal)
Public Garden, Damascus, Syria (with Mohammad Nofal)
Sports City, Damascus, Syria (with Mohammad Nofal)
Fiera District Center Architectural Design, Bologna, Italy (project; with Pierluigi Giordani, Ferdinando Forlay, Ettore Masi, and Gianpaolo Mazzucato)
1975/
76 Japanese Embassy, Mexico City (with Pedro Ramirez Vazquez and Manuel Rosen)
1976 King Faisal Foundation Headquarters Complex, Saudi Arabia
Institute of Architecture and Urbanism, Oran, Algeria
Bab-Ezzouar III University City, Algeria
Yarmouk University, Amman, Jordan (with Jafar Tukan and Partners)
1976/
78 Hanae Mori Building, Tokyo
1977 Government Center Master Plan, Doha, Qatar (project)
New City Hall, Shahstan Pahlevi, Tehran (project)
Amir's Palace, Doha, Qatar
1977/
82 King's Palace and Crown Prince's Palace, Jeddah, Saudi Arabia
1978 Government Capitol Complex Master Plan, Rabat, Morocco
1979 King Faisal Foundation phase II, Riyadh, Saudi Arabia
Federal Capital Central Area Development, Abuja, Nigeria
Main Buildings, Abuja, Nigeria
1980 Overseas Union Bank Centre, Singapore
City Telecommunications Centre, Singapore
City Administration Centre, Naples, Italy
Koseinenkin Culture and Service Centre, Hiroshima, Japan
Ichinomiya Housing Project, Takamatsu City, Japan
1981 National Assembly Building, Abuja, Nigeria
Presidential Complex, Abuja, Nigeria
Supreme Court Building, Abuja, Nigeria
Ministry of National Planning, Abuja, Nigeria
G. B. Building, Singapore
Nanyang Technological Institute, University of Singapore
Brickfield Hill Development, Sydney, Australia
Hyogo Prefectural Museum of Art, Hyogo, Japan
1982 International Petroleum Centre, Singapore
Toin School, Kanagawa, Japan
Saudi Arabian Chancellery, Riyadh, Saudi Arabia
Ehime Culture Centre, Ehime, Japan
Arabian Gulf University, Manama, Bahrain
King's Centre, Singapore
Shaha Alam Town Centre, Shah Alam, Malaysia

Publications:

By TANGE: books—*Katsura: Traditional and Creation in Japanese Architecture,* Tokyo and New Haven, Connecticut, 1960, 1972; *A Plan for Tokyo,* with the Kenzo Tange Team, 1960; *Ise: Origin of Japanese Architecture,* with Noboru Kawazoe, Tokyo 1962, Cambridge, Massachusetts 1968; *Japan in the Future,* Tokyo 1966; *Japan in the 21st Century,* with the Kenzo Tange Team, Tokyo 1971; *Architecture and Urban Design,* Tokyo 1975; articles—"Creation in Present-Day Architecture and the Japanese Architectural Tradition" in *The Japan Architect* (Tokyo), June 1956; "Architecture and Urbanism" in *The Japan Architect* (Tokyo), October 1960; "Prophecies from Kenzo Tange" in *Arquitecto Peruano* (Lima), March/June 1977; "Architecture and Socio-cultural Development" in *Arkitekten* (Copenhagen), March/April 1979; "Interview with Kenzo Tange" in *Architectes* (Paris), November 1981; "Kenzo Tange: Architectonic Autobiography", with Manfredo Tafuri and others, in *Plan* (Amsterdam), February 1982; "After Modernism", with Kazuo Shinohara, in *The Japan Architect* (Tokyo), November/December 1983.

On TANGE: books—*Kenzo Tange* by Robin Boyd, New York and London 1962; *Kenzo Tange 1946-58: Reality and Creation,* Tokyo 1966; *Kenzo Tange 1955-1964: Technology and Humanity,* Tokyo 1966; *Three Japanese Architects: Mayekawa, Tange, Sakakura* by Alfred Altherr, Teufen 1968; *Kenzo Tange* by Paolo Riani, Florence and London 1969; *Kenzo Tange* by Isamu Kurita, Tokyo 1970; *Philosophy of Contemporary Architects: Kenzo Tange* by M. Naka, Tokyo 1970; *Kenzo Tange 1946-1969: Architecture and Urban Design* by Udo Kultermann, Zurich and London 1970; *Kenzo Tange* by Noboru Kawazoe, Tokyo 1976; *Kenzo Tange* by A. V. Ikonnnikov, Moscow 1976; *Kenzo Tange,* by H. R. von der Muhll, Zurich 1978; articles—"Kenzo Tange" by Udo Kultermann in *Das Kunstwerk* (Stuttgart), November/December 1960; "Reflection on Kenzo Tange's Tokyo Bay Plan" by Peter Smithson in *Architectural Design* (London), October 1964; "Junzo Sakakura, Kunio Maekawa and Kenzo Tange" by N. Hozumi and J. Dodd in *Architectural Design* (London), May 1965; "New Arts Complex in Minneapolis" in *Domus* (Milan), September 1973; special number of *The Japan Architect* (Tokyo), August/September 1976; "Tehran Town Hall" in *Mur Vivant* (Paris), no. 47, 1978; "A Day with the Architect Kenzo Tange" in *Arquitectura Mexico* (Mexico City), November/December 1978; "Kenzo Tange and URTEC", special issue of *The Japan Architect* (Tokyo), July/August 1979; "Kenzo Tange and URTEC", special issue of *Space Design* (Tokyo), January 1980; "Kuwait Airport" in *Middle East Construction* (Sutton, Surrey), November 1980; "Abuja, Nigeria's New Capital City" in *RIBA Journal* (London), July 1982; "Kenzo Tange in Bologna" in *Architettura* (Rome), February 1983; "Kenzo Tange and URTEC", special issue of *Space Design* (Tokyo), September 1983; "Friend of Kings" in *Asian Building and Construction* (Hong Kong), March 1984.

Bibliography: *Kenzo Tange: Modern Japan's Genius Architect* by James P. Noffsinger, Monticello, Illinois 1980.

Kenzo Tange's work reflects and cyrstallizes the changing political and economic climate of Japan in a quarter century, from the nationalism of World War II, through defeat and reconstruction, to the renewed search for national identity and growth in confidence. Despite finer distinctions to be made in his changing concerns, it is possible to divide his career into two parts, whose major interests are the synthesis of Japanese traditions and modern architecture and the realization of a Metabolist vision of the city.

Western architecture arrived in Japan with the Meiji Restoration more than a century ago. Since then Japanese architectural history for the most part has faithfully mirrored the trends and preoccupations of Europe and America. But recurring throughout those years of adaptation was the idea of a return to native values and forms. (Chuta Ito and Sutemi Horiguchi in their respective ways attempted to broaden the architectural vocabulary to include Japanese and Oriental sources, and they both promoted a reappraisal of traditional works.) World War II and the heightened nationalist sentiment provided the context for Tange's debut, a successful entry in the competition for a Memorial to the Creation of Greater East Asia Co-Prosperity Sphere, followed by another first place in the competition for a Japanese Cultural Center in Bangkok. The former was inspired by Shinto shrines, while the latter made references to palaces. The wartime pressure to employ such references was powerful and even the modernist, Mayekawa, succumbed to it; but with Tange the revivalism seems to have come more naturally, as a personal reaction against conventional modern architecture. After the war, the Occupation naturally dampened such enthusiasms, but even when Tange produced buildings in a modern, specifically Corbusian manner, such as the Hiroshima Peace Center, there were indirect Japanese references.

In the 1950s tradition again became an active issue, and Tange was a leading participant in the so called "Tradition Debate." The blending of Japanese and modern forms in his buildings of the time is more skillful than in his wartime designs. His own house, with its pilotis and core, manages to be modern while recalling ancient "raised floor dwellings" of Japan. The Kagawa Prefectural Government Office, with its application of traditional wood details in concrete on the facade, was much admired and copied. The debate slackened by the 1960s, yet the definitive traditionalist building was finished in 1964. Tange capped the first phase of his career with the National Gymnasia for the Tokyo Olympics. This pair of suspension structures with their sweeping curved roofs is reminiscent of Japanese traditional architecture without indulging in direct references. The masterful asymmetric arrangement of the roofs and the dynamic balance in the siting of the pair show how well Tange had assimilated traditional techniques. Here at last Tange accomplished what his predecessors had not, demonstrating that modern architecture need not necessarily be Western. Ironically, however, this proved to be an end and not a beginning, for Tange was by then engaged in a different problem.

The 1960s in Japan saw the increasing activity of the Metabolists, many of whom had been associated with Tange. The second phase of Tange's career must be seen against that background; even though he himself was not a Metabolist, his work was sympathetic to theirs. In fact they owed a great deal to Tange's proposal to structure the chaotic growth of Tokyo—his Tokyo Plan, 1960—a startling suggestion to extend the city over the bay. It called for a linear trunk of motorways, from which branched giant housing units. This early megastructure approach provided a starting point for the Metabolists. Their attempt to analyze the modern city as an organic unit subject to growth, decay and renewal recalls traditional Japanese ideas of cycles and change and thus may be said to continue indirectly the 1950s preoccupation with cultural identity.

The movement produced a number of buildings by Kurokawa, Kikutake and others, but none was quite as explicit as or on a scale comparable to that of Tange's Yamanashi Press and Broadcasting Center. Service and stair towers double as structural columns and floors span them freely according to different functional requirements. Gaps were left to indicate the possibility of future growth. It is without question a striking building. But like a great deal of Metabolist work, the polemics far outdistanced the realized architecture. The random quality of the space layout was more apparent than real—once fixed, the layout was no more flexible than in a conventional structure—and the mechanical services which are housed in the ostensibly more permanent infrastructure may be subject to the most rapid obsolescence.

Yamanashi inaugurated the second phase of Tange's career, one which paralleled Metabolist activity. The Corbusian references disappeared, as did the traditionalist. Gone too was the contained, integrated character of his earlier work. Yukari Nursery School, Sacred Heart University, the original project for Dentsu in Tokyo, and the Kuwait

Embassy all suggest in their different ways an incompleteness and the possibility of growth and change. Yet the paradox is that this possibility is forfeited at the same time by the artfulness of the carefully asymmetric designs—one feels that any addition or subtraction would be an unwelcomed disturbance. In his first phase, Tange subordinated parts to the whole, so that structure, mass and space became tightly integrated unity. In office buildings or single-purpose structures, this mattered less, but there was strain when the program was at all complex. What could not be accommodated conventionally in the whole had to be left out; hence the little boxes that clutter the base of St. Mary's Catherdral. In his second phase, an entire building was fragmented and reassembled into a system. The result, at first glance, may seem more complex, yet the buildings remain expressions of spontaneity and are in reality static and closed.

The 1970 Osaka Exposition, for which he provided the master plan and the theme pavilion, a giant space frame, epitomized the Metabolist movement with its celebration of technology. At last a true megastructure had been built. But like the National Gymnasia, this proved to be the climax of a period and not the start. The era of rapid economic growth came to an end, and with it the more ambitious Metabolist dreams.

Since then Tange's work has been increasingly outside Japan, and he has expressed a loss of interest in the old tradition issue. Yet his successful buildings have all been rooted in the Japanese past directly or indirectly, and it is his National Gymnasia, which best resolved the problem of tradition, that remains his best work and the peak of twentieth century Japanese architecture.

—Hiroshi Watanabe

TANIGUCHI, Yoshiro.

Japanese. Born in Kanazawa, Ishikawa Prefecture, 24 June 1904. Studied at the Imperial University of Tokyo (now Tokyo University), in the Architecture Department of the School of Engineering, 1925-28, Dip.Arch. 1928; made a study tour of Europe, 1928-29. Married Kinu Mitsui in 1931; 3 children. In private practice, Tokyo, from 1930: Partner, with Shinsake Takamiya, in Taniguchi, Takamiya and Associates. Assistant Professor, Tokyo University, 1931; Professor, 1943-65, and Emeritus Professor, 1965-79, Tokyo Institute of Technology. Director, Museum Meiji-mura, Inuyama, Japan, from 1965. Member of the Cultural Properties Specialist Council of Japan, from 1952. Recipient: Arts and Sciences Prize, 1942, and Works Prize, 1949, Japan Institute of Architects; Japan Academy of Arts Award, 1961. Member, Japan Academy of Arts, 1962. *Died* (in Tokyo) *in 1979.*

Works:

1932 Hydraulics Laboratory, Institute of Technology, Tokyo
1937 Mr. K. House, Tokyo
      Keio-Gidyuku Primary School, Tokyo
1947 Toson Kinendo Memorial Hall, Kamuro, Japan
1951 Medical Department Building, Keio University, Tokyo
1952 Lecture Hall, Institute of Technology, Tokyo
1955 Weekend Houses (10), Karuizawa, Nagano Prefecture, Japan
1956 Chichibu Cement Company Factory no. 2, Chichibu, Saitama Prefecture, Japan
      Golf Clubhouse, Sagamihara, Kanagawa Prefecture, Japan
      Swimming Pool, Tokyo
1957 Saeki Weekend House, Koji-machi, Tokyo

1958 Oto-Tachibana-Hime Memorial, Sagamihara Golf Course, Kanagawa Prefecture, Japan
      Centennial Monument, Keio University, Tokyo
      Kei Hara Memorial Hall, Morioka City, Japan
1959 Chidorigafuchi Cemetery for the War Dead, Chiyoda-ku, Tokyo
      City Hall, Aomori, Japan
      City Hall, Takasaki, Japan
      Torikyo Hotel, Atami, Shizuoka Prefecture, Japan
      Auditorium Building, Institute of Technology, Ookayama, Tokyo
1960 Togu Palace for Crown Prince Akihito, Akasaka, Tokyo
1962 Slhiseido Cosmetics Company Building (Shiseido Kaikan), Chuo-ku, Ginza, Tokyo
      Okura Hotel, Tokyo
1963 Funi Zen Study Temple, Yoyogi, Tokyo
      Auditorium for the Keio Private School and Kindergarten, Shibuya, Tokyo
      Mori Ogai Memorial Library, Komagome, Tokyo
      Yacht Harbour for the Olympic Games, Enoshima Island, Kanagawa Prefecture, Japan
1965 Furukawa Library, Nagoya University, Aichi Prefecture, Japan
      Yamatane Art Museum, Nihombashi, Chuo Ward, Tokyo
1965/
  66 Josen-ji Temple, Shibuya, Tokyo
1965/
  68 Gallery of Eastern Antiquities, National Museum, Ueno Park, Tokyo
1966 New Imperial Theatre (Teigeki Kaikan), Marunouchi, Tokyo
1967/
  69 National Museum of Modern Art, Kita-no-maru Park, Chiyoda Ward, Tokyo
1967/
  71 Josen-ji Temple Cemetery Grounds and Buildings, Shibuya, Tokyo
1968/
  71 Okura Hotel, 46 Joseph Israel Straat, Amsterdam (with Y. Shibata, B. Bijvoet and G. H. M. Holt)
1969 Ishikawa Public Museum, Kanazawa, Japan
1972 Tokyo Kaikan Office Building, Chiyoda Ward, Tokyo
1972/
  74 Akasaka (Togu) Palace Guest House addition, Minato Ward, Tokyo
1973 Kawabun Restaurant Annex (Hall of the Water Mirror), Nagoya, Japan
1974/
  75 Japan Academy, Tokyo
      House at Yukigawa, Ota Ward, Tokyo
1975/
  76 Eiji Yoshikawa Memorial Building, Ome, Tokyo
      Fukui Sogo Bank Branch Office, Seiwa, Miyuki-ko, Japan
1976/
  78 Municipal Library, Kanazawa, Ishikawa Prefecture, Japan
1977/
  78 Shieido Art Museum, Kakegawa, Shizuoka Prefecture, Japan
1979 Town Offices, Kitashiobara, Japan (project)
      Mr. B. Guest House (project)

Publications:

By TANIGUCHI: books—*Kiyoraka na Isho* [Architectural design and aesthetics], Tokyo 1948; *Isho Nikki* [Addresses, essays and lectures], Tokyo 1954; *Gendai no me* [Today's Focus], Tokyo, 1955; *Shigakuin Rikyu* [The Shigakuin Imperial Villa], Tokyo 1956; *Kenchiku*, Tokyo 1960; articles— "Gallery of Eastern Antiquities" in *The Japan*

Architect (Tokyo), December 1968; "Tokyo Kaikan" in *The Japan Architect* (Tokyo), April 1972.

On TANIGUCHI: books—*New Japanese Architecture* by Udo Kultermann, New York 1960; *An Architectural Journey in Japan* by James M. Richards, London 1963; *New Japanese Architecture* by Egon Tempel, New York 1969; *A Guide to Japanese Architecture*, Tokyo 1971; articles—"The Personality and Works of Taniguchi" by Ryuichi Hamaguchi in *Shinkenchiku* (Tokyo), January 1956; "Memorials by Yoshiro Taniguchi" in *Shinkenchiku* (Tokyo), October 1958; "Architects of the Month" in *The Japan Architect* (Tokyo), January/February 1959; "Palace for the Crown Prince, Akasaka, Tokyo" in *The Japan Architect* (Tokyo), July 1960; "The Architects," in special issue on Japan of *Architectural Review* (London), September 1962; "The Shiseido Building" in *The Japan Architect* (Tokyo), March 1963; "Yoshiro Taniguchi and His Work" in *The Japan Architect* (Tokyo), May 1966; "Vision de Paix" by Frederic D. Debuyt in *Art d'Eglise* (Ottignies, Belgium), no. 139, 1967; "Hotel Okura, Amsterdam" in *The Japan Architect* (Tokyo), March 1972; "Seiwa Branch of the Fukui Sogo Bank" in *The Japan Architect* (Tokyo), November 1976; "Toward a Revitalization of Form" in *Architecture + Urbanism* (Tokyo), February 1977; "Eiji Yoshikawa Memorial at Ome" in *The Japan Architect* (Tokyo), May 1977; "Kanazawa Municipal Library" in *The Japan Architect* (Tokyo), January 1980.

Bibliography—*Yoshiro Taniguchi: Artist-Architect of Japan* by James Philip Noffsinger, Monticello, Illinois 1981.

*

We are apt to perceive Yoshiro Taniguchi as an arch-conservative and reactionary because of the Establishment status that he achieved. It is true that in his public buildings (e.g., Togu Palace, Hotel Okura, and the Eastern Antiquities Gallery of the National Museum), he took the path of traditionalism that modernism had rejected and that he developed a decorative style that had great popular appeal. But he also left behind a body of work, particularly in his youth, which is attractive to the modernist, namely the handsome neo-classical schools (Keio University), the stern and poetic literary monuments and memorial halls (Toson Kinendo), and a factory of a classicist beauty unrivalled in modern Japan (Chichibu Cement); he is indeed one of the masters of modern Japanese architecture.

His work was always in conscious contrast to that of modernists such as Mayekawa and Tange, and he continually broadened the possible range of modern architectural vocabulary in Japan. He had a wide following that included the general public, intellectuals and the ruling elite, yet his architecture was by no means "populist;" it was in fact, very difficult to understand. Why, then, is its appeal wider and deeper perhaps than that of the work of Tange or Mayekawa?

That appeal is due not simply to the traditionalism of his late work, but also to his classicist rigor and "class," his deep involvement in his design, his attitude toward architecture as philosophy and toward architectural expression as poetry, as well as to the characteristic decorative spaces of traditionalist motifs in his later years. He managed to reconcile the apparently conflicting worlds of classicism and ornament, insofar as he could maintain the ideals of *Zweckmassichkeit* and *Sachlichkeit*, to create a non-eclectic, non-derivative style. This reconciliation is clear in his Hotel Okura, the Imperial Theatre, and the Tokyo Kogyo University Memorial Hall. These works appealed to the general public, although they were disregarded by many modernists. They constituted his unspoken criticism of the structuralist and heroic yet (for lack of ornament) slightly anaemic forms of modern architecture.

Taniguchi was from the start also a man of letters, and in his writings he expressed the deep impression made on him by the neo-classicism of Schinkel and the traditionalism of Tessenow. What is interesting is that from early on he showered criticism on what he saw as inorganic rationalism and arbitrary formal manipulation. He did not go so far as to espouse decoration, yet he did not reject it either. It was therefore quite natural for him to turn toward traditional decorative patterns via a re-evaluation of traditional culture. Whereas Tessenow created a world of stark, absolute order, taking an anti-international, regionalist stance, Taniguchi, while also anti-international, developed finally a world of ornamental beauty.

His is not a light, simple world of patterns, however, but is unexpectedly dark and heavy. There is, beyond his planar, compositional world, a profound incomprehensibility. There is neither formality nor clarity of concept. His world is created from what most modern architects threw away along with ornament: craftsmanship, studied proportions and treatment of details. It is an expression of corporeality, the aftermath of a struggle between self-restraint and a will to express. Proportions are deliberately distorted in a way contrary to traditional Japanese architectural order *(kiwari)*. The cumulative effect of such details contrasts with the conceptuality of modern architecture and results in an illegible totality, yet his work, whether we like it or not, is almost awesomely overpowering and replete in evidence of a will. This corporeality, that is, the vestige of the designer's struggle and thought, requires the maximum self-restraint and formal control. Taniguchi clearly possessed both this restraint and the will to express; that is what gives the effect of darkness and weight to his designs. Yet this quality or "aura" is impossible to capture on photographs, and it is a pity that Taniguchi's architecture may be thus misunderstood. Yet amid the current post-modern reconsideration of what architecture really is, his work is valuable for the alternative approach that it suggests.

—Katsuyoshi Arai

TAUT, Bruno.

German. Born in Königsberg, 4 May 1880. Trained in the studio of architect Bruno Mohring, Berlin, 1900-03; educated at the Technische Hochschule, Stuttgart, under Theodor Fischer, 1903-05. Married to Hedwig Wollgast; son: Heinrich. Practised in Berlin, 1908-21; City Architect, Magdeburg, Germany, 1921-23; in partnership with his brother Max Taut, *q.v.,* and Franz Hoffmann, Berlin, 1923-31; practised in Moscow, 1932-33, Tokyo, 1933-34, and Ankara and Istanbul, Turkey, 1935 until his death, 1938. Chief Architect, GEHAG Housing Program, Berlin, 1924-32. Chairman, Arbeitsrat für Kunst, Berlin, 1918; Editor/Publisher, *Die Gläserne Kette* chain letter, Berlin, 1919-23, and *Frühlicht* magazine, Magdeburg, 1921-22. Exhibitions: *Arbeitsrat Exhibition of Unknown Architects,* Berlin, 1919; *Paris-Berlin,* Centre Pompidou, Paris, 1978; *Bruno Taut zum 100. Getburtstag,* Akademie der Künste, West Berlin, 1980. *Died* (in Istanbul, Turkey) *24 December 1938.*

Works

1902 Crematorium (project)
1903 Monument (project)
1904 Fountain (project)
    School, Schramberg, Germany (competition project)
    Gravestones (projects)
    School, Rottweil, Germany (competition project)

    Building Facade Types, Bautzen, Germany (project)
1905 Main Railway Station, Karlsruhe (competiton project; with Max Taut)
    Country Houses, Tilsit, now Sovetsk, Russia (competition project)
    Circular Church (project)
    Church, Lichtenthal, Germany (competition project)
    Orphanage, Strasbourg, Germany (competition project)
    Workers' Housing Development (project)
    Kursaal additions, Cannstadt, Germany (project)
    Kindergartens (projects)
1906 Village Church interiors, Unterriexingen, Germany
    Department Store (competition project)
    Grammer School, Diedenhofen, Germany (competition project)
1907 Main Railway Station, Leipzig, (competition project)
    Church interiors (competition project)
    Housing Development, Hamburg (competition project)
1908 Main Railway Station, Darmstadt (competition project; with Karl Bonatz and Georg Martin)
    Harkotschen Iron Mills Turbine-House, Wetter/Ruhr, Germany
1909 Apartment building facade, Bismarckstrasse 10, Charlottenburg, Berlin (with Heinz Lassen; demolished)
1910 "Ettershaus" (management recreation facilities), for Siemens-Halske Company, Bad Harzburg, Germany
    Wertheim Department Store extensions, Leipzigerstrasse, Berlin
    High School, Zehlendorf, Berlin (competition project)
    Trade Distribution Company Pavilion, *Clay, Cement and Lime Industries Exhibition,* Baumschulenweg, Berlin
1911 Apartment/office buildings, Bismarckstrasse 1 and 20, Charlottenburg, Berlin (demolished)
    Apartment/office buildings, Kottbusser Damm 2-3, Neuköln, Berlin (demolished) Apartment/office building, Kottsbusser Damm 90, Neuköln, Berlin
    Reibedanz House, Dahlem, Berlin
    Plan for housing at Johannisthal, Berlin
    Apartment buildings, Hardenbergstrasse 1 and 2, Charlottenburg, Berlin (demolished)
    Village Church interior restoration, Nieden, Kreis Prenzlau, Germany
    Office building facade, Linkstrasse 12, Mitte, Berlin (demolished)
1912 Apartment building, Hardenbergstrasse 3a, Charlottenburg, Berlin (demolished)
    Apartment building, Tiegertenstrasse 34a, Tiergarten, Berlin (demolished)
    Landscaping of the Rudesheimer Platz, Zehlendorf, Berlin (competition project)
    Redevelopment plan for Neuköln, Berlin (competition project; with Max Taut)
1913 "Monument to Steel" Pavilion, *International Building Trades Exhibition,* Leipzig (with Franz Hoffmann)
1914 Master plan for Am Falkenberg (garden suburb), Grunau, Berlin (partly built)
    Reform (garden suburb), stage I, Magdeburg, Germany
    Heinrich Mittag Department Store alterations, Breiter Weg 155, Magdeburg, Germany (demolished)
    Reibedanz Steam Laundry, Teilestrasse 23, Tempelhof, Berlin
    Third Secession Building facade, Kurfürstendamm 232, Charlottenburg, Berlin (with Max Taut; demolished)
    Luxfer Prism Syndicate "Glashaus" Pavilion, *Werkbund Exhibition,* Cologne (with Franz Hoffmann)

    Redevelopment plan for Kladow, Berlin (competition project)
1915 Oheim Mineworkers' Housing Development, Katowice, Poland (partly built)
1916 House of Friendship Building, Istanbul (competition project)
1920 Lindenhof (single-people's housing development), Schöneberg, Berlin (demolished)
    Hermann Essig Tombsone (project)
    Miners' Housing Development, Ruhland, Senffenberg, Germany (project)
    Folkwang School, Hagen, Germany (project)
1921 Reform (garden suburb), stage II, Magdeburg Germany
    Master Plan for the development of the Elbe riverbank, Magdeburg, Germany (1st project)
    Skyscraper Office Building, Kaiser-Wilhelm-Platz, Magdeburg, Germany (project)
    4 exhibition halls, *Middle-German Exhibition,* Rotenhornpark, Magdeburg, Germany
    Open-Air Cinema and Park-Keeper's House, *Middle-German Exhibition,* Rotenhornpark, Magdeburg, Germany (projects)
    Heinrich Mittag Department Store reconstruction, Magdeburg, Germany (project)
1922 Site utilization plan, Magdeburg, Germany (1st project)
    War Memorial, Domplatz, Magdeburg, Germany (project)
    Hotel, Kemperlatz, Charlottenburg, Berlin (competition project)
    Stadt Köln Hotel/Office Building, Magdeburg, Germany (project)
    Chicago Tribune Tower (competition project)
    Stadt und Land Agricultural Exhibition Hall, Wilhelm-Kobelt-Strasse, Magdeburg, Germany (now Hermann-Gieseler Sports Hall)
    Master plan for the development of the Elbe riverbank, Magdeburg, Germany (2nd project)
    Cemetery, Magdeburg, Germany (project)
1923 Site utilization plan, Magdeburg, Germany (2nd project)
    Eichwalde Housing Development, stage I, Waldstrasse, near Berlin
    Completion plan for Am Falkenberg (garden suburb), with Festival Hall, Grunau, Berlin (project)
1925 Schillerpark Housing Development, stage I, Wedding, Berlin
    Plan for the *Hein und Scholle* exhibition, Braunschweig, Germany
    Eichwalde Housing Development, stage II, Waldstrasse, near Berlin
    Primary school, Senffenberg, Germany (project)
1927 Hufeisensiedlung Housing Estate, stage I, Britz, Berlin
    Housing development, Paul-König-Strasse, Hohenschönhausen, Berlin
    Bruno Taut House, Wiesenstrasse, Zossen, Dahlewitz, Germany
    Single-family housing development, Waldschulstrasse and Lanchenweg, Eichkamp, Berlin
    Apartment building, Weigandufer, Neuköln, Berlin
    Apartment building, Leinestrasse, Neuköln, Berlin
    Apartment buildings, Fuldastrasse 22-23, Neuköln, Berlin
    Terraced houses, Weststrasse, Johannisthal, Berlin
    Workers' apartments, Weissenhof Estate, Stuttgart (demolished)
    Berthold House, Offenbachstrasse 10, Markkleeberg-West, Germany
    Dammweg Community School, Neuköln, Berlin (partly built)
1928 Schillerpark Housing Development, stage II, Wedding, Berlin
    Housing development, Grellstrasse, Prenzlauerberg, Berlin

Apartment building, Schönlanker Strasse, Prenzlauerberg, Berlin

Apartment building, Olivaer Strasse 1-11, Prenzlauerberg, Berlin

Attilahohe Housing Development, Attilastrasse, Berlin

Apartment building, Ossastrasse 9-16a, Neuköln, Berlin

Apartment building, Normannenstrasse 13-18, Lichtenberg, Berlin

Apartment building, Trierer Strasse 8-18, Weissensee, Berlin

1929 Beach resort facilities for Zossen, Rangsdorf, Germany (project)

Friedrich Ebert School, Luckenwalde, Germany (project)

1930 Apartment building, Gartenstrasse 22-25, Weissensee, Berlin

Housing development, Carmen-Sylvastrasse, now Erich-Weinert-Strasse, Prenzlauerberg, Berlin

Friedrich Ebert Housing Development, Togostrasse, Wedding, Berlin

Pedagogical Academy, Essen (competition project)

Law Courts, Invalidenstrasse, Berlin (competition project)

Housing development, Buschallee 24-107, Weissensee, Berlin

Paradies Housing Development, Hundsfelderstrasse, Bohnsdorf, Berlin

Ideal Housing Development, Franz-Konrer-Strasse, Britz, Berlin

1931 Forest Housing Development, stage I, near Onkel Toms Hütte, Zehlendorf, Berlin (with Hugo and O. R. Salvisberg)

Housing development extension, Parchimer Allee, Britz, Berlin

1932 Intourist Hotel, Sverdlor Square, Moscow (competition project)

Housing development, near Kursk Station, Moscow (project)

Trade Union Hall, Moscow (project)

New road plan for the area Gorky Street to Red Square, Moscow (project)

Cultural Centre, Moscow (project)

1934 Ikoma Mountain Development Plan, near Osaka, Japan (project)

Turkish Embassy, Tokyo (project)

1936 Okura House, Tokyo (now altered)

Hingo House interiors, Atami, Japan

1937 Technical University, Ankara, Turkey (project)

Chemical Institute, Ankara, Turkey (project)

Theatre, Ankara, Turkey (project)

1938 Languages and History Faculty Buildings, University of Ankara, Turkey

Bruno Taut House, Ortakoy, Turkey

Ataturk Lyceum, Anakara, Turkey (with Asim Komurcuoglu)

Ministry of Culture Exhibition Buildings, *International Exposition*, Izmir, Turkey

Professor Nissen House, Ortakoy, Turkey (project)

Parliament Building, Ankara, Turkey (project)

Institute for Girls, Izmir, Turkey (partly built)

Boys' Boarding School, Trabzon, Turkey (completed by Franz Hillinger)

Middle School, Cebeci, Turkey (completed by Franz Hillinger)

Kemal Ataturk Catafalque, Ankara, Turkey

Publications:

By TAUT: books—*Monument der Eisens*, Leipzig 1913; *Glashaus: Werkbundausstellung Köln*, Cologne 1914; *Ein Architekturprogramm*, Berlin 1918, reprinted in *Programme und Manifeste zur Architektur des 20. Jahrhunderts*, edited by Ulrich Conrads, Berlin 1964; *Die Stadtkrone*, with Paul Scheerbart and others, Jena, Germany 1919; *Alpine Architektur*,

Hagen, Germany 1919; *Der Weltbaumeister*, Hagen, Germany 1920; *Organisation des Bauwesens*, Berlin 1920; *Die Auflösung der Städte, oder die Erde eine gute Wohnung*, Hagen, Germany 1920; *Die Neue Wohnung*, Leipzig 1924, 4th edition 1926; *Bauen: Der neue Wohnbau*, edited by Der Ring group, Leipzig 1927; *Ein Wohnhaus*, Stuttgart 1927; *Modern Architecture*, London 1929; *Die neue Baukunst in Europa und Amerika*, Berlin 1929; *Nippon mit europaischen Augen gesehen*, Tokyo 1934; *Die Architektur des Westens mit ihrer Bedeutung für Japan*, Tokyo 1934; *Grundlinien der Architektur Japans*, Tokyo 1936; *Bildende und angewandt Kunst*, Tokyo 1936; *Homes and People of Japan*, Tokyo 1937; *Architekturlehre: Grundlagen, Theorie und Kritik*, Tokyo 1936, Istanbul 1938; *Wiederentdeckung der Schönheit, Japans*, Tokyo 1939, 1962, 1965; *Frühlicht: Eine Folge für die Verwirklichung des neun Baugedankens*, Berlin 1963; articles—numerous in architectural journals, 1913-32, including "Für die neue Baukunst" in *Das Kunstblatt* (Berlin), no. 1, 1919; "The Nature and Aims of Architecture" in *The Studio* (London), March 1929; "My Siedlungen" in *Lotus* (Venice), September 1977; "The Earth—A Good Home" in *Oppositions* (New York), Fall 1978.

On TAUT: books—*Die Gläserne Kette* by Udo Kultermann, Leverkusen, Germany 1963; *Bruno Taut 1880-1938* by Kurt Junghanns, East Berlin 1970; *Bruno Taut – Baumeister einer neuer Welt* by Iain Boyd Whyte, Stuttgart 1981, as *Bruno Taut and the Architecture of Activism*, Cambridge 1982; articles—"Bruno Taut: A Visionary in Practice" by H. G. Scheffauer in *Architectural Review* (London), December 1922; "Obituary: Prof. Bruno Taut" by Walter Segal in *RIBA Journal* (London), 23 January 1939; "Bruno Taut e la rivista 'Frühlicht'" by Ulrich Conrads in *Edilizia Moderna* (Milan), no. 86, 1965; "Prophet of the Future Environment" by H. H. Waechter in *AIA Jounral* (Washington, D.C.), September 1973; "The Glass Dream" by Dennis Sharp in *Architecture + Urbanism* (Tokyo), September 1973; "A Taut Facade and Building Control" in *Bauwelt* (Berlin), 12 August 1977; "Development of the Weissenhof Estate in Stuttgart" by Bodo Rasch in *Deutsche Bauzeitung* (Stuttgart), November 1977; "Bruno Taut", special issue of *Forum* (Hilversum), vol. 26, no. 6, 1978; "Bruno Taut Once Again", special issue of *Space Design* (Tokyo), December 1978; "Bruno Taut, 1880-1938" by Franziska Bollerey and Kritiana Hartmann in *Bauwelt* (Berlin), 15 December 1978; "Bruno Taut" by A. Lancelle in *AIT* (Stuttgart), vol. 88, no. 5, 1980; "Bruno Taut" by G. Kosel, K. Junghanns and H. Taut, in *Architekur der DDR* (East Berlin), April 1980; "Bruno Taut" by Julius Posener in *Bauwelt* (Berlin), 18 July 1980; "Bruno Taut (1880-1938): Utopia and Hope" by Francesco Dal Co in *Casabella* (Milan), July/August 1980; "Bruno Taut and the Temple of Industry" in *Archithese* (Zurich), July/August 1980; "Bruno Taut—Realist and Visionary" by Gerhard Ullmann in *MD: Moebel Interior Design* (Stuttgart), September 1980; "Bruno Taut—Shaper of Solid Forms" by Hans Jorg Rieger in *Aktuelles Bauen* (Zurich), March 1981; "Bruno Taut" by Lekha Sarkar in *Aktuelles Bauen* (Zurich), July 1982.

*   *   *

More than an architect, more than a writer, Bruno Taut was a Utopian, a dreamer. His disillusion with the conservatism, elitism and traditionalism of German society at the start of the new century, which turned to despair as he witnessed the outbreak and the course of the First World War, provoked him to direct his own attentions towards the future. Inspired partly by the new collectivism of the U.S.S.R., and partly by the open democracy of Britain and Holland, he envisaged a new society born of cooperation, constructing for itself an almost magical environment of sparkling alpine cities, with pillars, vaults, arcades and bridges of coloured glass, all radiating as much love as they did light. Taut believed that the stronger the conviction of the

society and the more harmonius its spirit, the more extraordinary and the more poetic would be its architecture. His sketches, therefore, should not be read as architectural fantasies but as social fantasies.

But while Taut thought of architecture principally as an expression or a symbol of the quality of the society who created it, he also recognized within it the potential for provoking change. He saw that the new architecture, with its new technologies and its new materials, might anticipate, and thus encourage, as new social order. Taut regarded the phenomemon of industrialization as significant because it generated these new technologies and new materials, but he rejected its image as the basis for any new architectural aesthetic, any new style. Indeed, his own designs diverged considerably from those of the Bauhaus and his fellow pioneers. Angular, geometric, crystalline structures and motifs recur throughout his work, suggesting the influence of Gothic, oriental and Islamic architecture, each of which, significantly, expressed the aspirations and achievements of their society and culture rather than the genius of a single individual.

The building which most clearly illustrated Taut's architectural vision was the Glass Pavilion at the *Werkbund Exhibition* in Cologne in 1914. A glass dome and glass walls enclosed a gallery with a glass inlaid floor, from which a glass staircase led to a subterranean waterfall—a strangely mystical celebration of a new indutrial product. Taut dedicated the Pavilion to Paul Scheerbart, the visionary poet whose lyrical exposition of the potential of a glass architecture had largely inspired the design. Taut's period as planner and architectural advisor to the city of Magdeburg produced little of any architectural significance but did fulfill his commitment to building for a new society. His greater contribution to the new architecture, and to the German Expressionist movement in particular, came not from his buildings but from his writings and his correspondence. It was he who coordinated and broadcast the ideas of the group, first in the Utopian chain letter, *Die Gläserne Kette* (The Glass Chain), which included among its correspondents Hans Scharoun, Walter Gropius, Hermann Finsterlin and Hans and Wassili Luckhardt, and subsequently in his magazine *Frühlicht* (Daybreak), a title fully expressive of Taut's anticipation of the dawning of a new age.

—Bob Allies

TAUT, Max.

German. Born in Königsberg, 15 May 1884. Educated at the Königsberg Gymnasium; apprentice in carpentry and building trades, Königsberg; studied at a building trade school, 1903-05. Served in the German Army, 1914-18. Married Margarete Wollgast in 1914. Worked in the office of Mies van der Rohe, *q.v.*, Berlin, 1905, and in the studio of Hermann Billing, Karlsruhe, Germany, 1906-11; in private practice, Berlin, from 1911: in partnership with Franz Hoffmann, 1918-50 (with Hoffmann and his brother Bruno Taut, *q.v.*, 1923-31); barred from any public commission by the Nazis, 1933-45. Founder-Director, Architectural Department, Fine Arts Academy, Berlin, 1945-53. Founder-Member, Berlin Arbeitsrat für Kunst, 1918, Novembergruppe, Berlin, 1919, Der Ring architects' union, Berlin, 1920, Deutscher Werbund, 1946, and the Bund Deutscher Architekten, 1948. Exhibitions: *German Arts and Crafts Exhibition*, Dresden, Germany 1906; *Werkbund Exhibition*, Cologne, 1914; *The Growing House*, Berlin, 1928; *Max Taut*, Akademie der Künste, Berlin, 1964; *Max Taut 1884-1967; Zeichnungen, Bauten*, Akademie der Künste, Berlin, 1984. Recipient: Gold Medal, Arts and Crafts Exhibition; Dresden, Germany 1906; Gold Medal, *Building Exhibition*, Leipzig, Germany 1913; German Cross of Merit, 1957. D.Eng.: Technische Hochschule, Karlsruhe, Germany 1958. Member, Akademie der Künste, Berlin, 1955. *Died* (in Berlin) *26 February 1967.*

Works:

1905 Main Railway Station, Karlsruhe (competition project); with Bruno Taut)
1911/
  12 School, Finsterwalde, Germany
1912 Water Tower, Nauen, Germany (competition project)
  Redevelopment plan for Neuköln, Berlin (competition project; with Bruno Taut)
1913 Koswig Textile Factory; Finsterwalde, Germany
  Werdandi-Bundes Hall, *Building Exhibition,* Leipzig, Germany (with F. Seesselberg)
1913/
  15 Realgymnasium, Nauen, Germany
1914 Third Secession Building facade, Kurfüstendamm 232, Charlottenburg, Berlin (with Bruno Taut; demolished)
1919 Church (project)
1920 Wissinger Family Vault, Stahnsdorf, Berlin
  Heinrichshofen Exhibition Hall, Magdeburg, Germany (with F. Mutzenbecker)
1921 Revolving House (project)
1922 *Chicago Tribune* Tower (competition project)
1922/
  23 Federation of German Trade Unions Building, Wallstrasse, Berlin
1922/
  25 German Printers Building, Dudenstrasse, Berlin (with Mart Stam)
1923 S.K.F. Norman Factory, Berlin (competition project)
1926 Federation of German Trade Unions Hall, *Gesolei Exhibition,* Düsseldorf
1927 House, Hiddensee, Germany
  Apartment building development, Reinickendorf, Berlin
  Werkbund Housing, Weissenhof Estate, Stuttgart
1928 Housing estate, Eichkamp, Berlin
1928/
  29 Dorotheen-Lyceum School, Kopenick, Berlin
  School complex, Lichtemberg, Berlin
1929/
  30 State Administration Building, Breitenbachplatz, Dahlem, Berlin
1929/
  31 Federation of German Trade Unions Building, Frankfurt
1930/
  32 Cooperative Wholesale Bakery, Spandau, Berlin
1931/
  32 Cooperative Department Store, Oranienplatz, Berlin
1949 Radio Station, Hannover, West Germany (project)
1949/
  52 Reuter Housing Estate, Bonn
1952/
  53 Ludwig-Georg-Gymnasium, Darmstadt, West Germany
1954/
  55 Apartment building, Methfesselstrasse, Berlin
1955/
  64 August-Thyssen Housing Development, Vietlinden, Duisburg, West Germany
1957 Apartment building development, Bismarckstrasse, Stieglitz, Berlin
1964 Central Children's Home, Berlin

Publications:

By TAUT: book—*Bauten und Plane,* with introduc-

tion by Adolf Behne, Berlin 1927; article—"My Siedlungen" in *Lotus* (Venice), September 1977.

On TAUT: book—*Max Taut,* exhibition catalogue, by Julius Posener, Berlin 1964; *Max Taut 1884-1967: Zeichnungen, Bauten,* exhibition catalogue, Berlin 1984; articles—"Aufgaben für den Siedlungsarchitekten zur Eichkamp-siedlung von Max Taut" by Fritz Hellwag in *Das Schöne Heim* (Berlin), April 1930; "Max Tauts Gewerkschaftshaus in Frankfurt" in *Wasmuths Monatshefte für Baukunst* (Berlin), vol. 15, 1931; "Un Grand Edifice de Max Taut" by Christian Zervos in *Cahiers d'art* (Paris), no. 3, 1928; "Die Lichtenberger Schulen" in *Wasmuths Monatshefte für Baukunst* (Berlin), vol. 16, 1932; "Entwurf für ein Funkhaus in Hannover" and "Neue Siedlung für Bonn am Rhein" in *Architektur und Wohnform* (Stuttgart), no. 6, 1949; "Max Taut funfundsechzig Jahre" by Joachim Steinecke in *Neue Bauwelt* (Hamburg, West Germany), no. 19, 1949; "Neue Bauten von Max Taut" in *Bauwelt* (Berlin), 10 May 1954; "Max Taut zum Gedenken" by Kurt Junghanns in *Deutsche Architektur* (East Berlin), February 1968; *Max Taut: Brother and Contemporary of Bruno Taut* by Hans-Joachim Kadatz in *Architecktur der DDR* (East Berlin), April 1980.

Max Taut differed from his brother Bruno in his greater awareness of reality. After an apprenticeship as a carpenter, Taut attended a building trades school and later worked in Hermann Billing's studio. From 1911, he was active as an architect in private practice, and from 1918 he worked in partnership with Franz Hoffmann. Together with Walter Gropius and Bruno Taut he was a founder of the Berlin Arbeitsrat für Kunst and was later a member of Der Ring, an association to which all the leading avant-garde architects belonged in the middle 1920s.

From the period immediately after World War I, several interesting projects, such as the Revolving House of 1921 as well as structures such as the expressionistic Wissinger Monument in Berlin-Stahnsdorf of 1920. Taut completed the building for the Federation of German Trade Unions in Berlin in 1923, employing the ferroconcrete framework as a visible element; the interior details reveal an expressionist influence. The Federation of German Trade Unions Building in Frankfurt of 1931 demonstrates in classical form the use of a ferroconcrete framework as an architectural tool.

Taut was invited to build two residential buildings for the Weissenhof Estate in Stuttgart in 1927, evidence of the extraordinary regard in which his work was held by his contemporaries. During this same period, as well as doing residential buildings, housing estates (e.g., the Eichkamp Estate, Berlin, 1928), and adminstrative and office buildings, he also designed a series of school buildings, including the Berlin-Lichtenberg School Complex of 1928-29.

As architect for the trade unions, and as a wellknown champion of modern architecture, Taut was excluded after 1933, from any public commissions. He was able to complete only a few residential buildings.

After the war, he was once again able to pursue his career to its full extent, and he went on to create variants of his outstanding structures of the 1920s—for example, the Ludwig-Georg-Gymnasium in Darmstadt. His Reuter Estate in Bonn is one of the outstanding achievements of German postwar building.

—Jürgen Joedicke

TEAM ZOO.
Cooperative formed in Tokyo, Japan, 1971. Members include: Atelier Zo, founded by Koichi Otake

(born in Sendai, Japan, 1938), Reiko Tomita (born in Tokyo, 1938), and Hiroyasu Higuchi (born in Shizuoka, Japan, 1939), in 1971; Atelier Mobile, founded by Kinya Maruyama (born in Tokyo, 1939), in 1970; Atelier Iruka, founded by Tsutomi Shigemusa (born in Yokohama, Japan, 1946); Atelier Gaii; Atelier Garuda; Atelier Hoenkan; and other studios. Exhibition: *A New Wave of Japanese Architecture,* Institute for Architecture and Urban Studies, New York, 1978 (toured the United States). Recipient: Artistic Encouragement Award, Ministry of Education, Tokyo, 1978 (Atelier Zo); Architectural Institute of Japan Prize, 1981 (Atelier Mobile). Address: Team Zoo/Atelier Mobile, Kikui-cho 61, Shinjuku-ku, Tokyo, Japan.

Works:

1972 Children's Museum, Okinawa, Japan (Atelier Zo)
  Nursery School, Kazenoko, Japan (Atelier Mobile)
1974 Youth Friendship Center, Suzuka, Japan (Atelier Zo)
  Domo Arabeska (house), Japan (Atelier Zo)
  Domo Celankato (house), Japan (Atelier Zo)
1975 Kazura Clinic, Kazura, Chiba Prefecture, Japan (Atelier Mobile)
  Village Community Center, Nakijin, Okinawa Prefecture, Japan (Atelier Zo and Atelier Mobile)
1976 Youth Friendship Center, Hiki, Saitama Prefecture, Japan (Atelier Zo)
  Tsukuba Golf Club, Higashi, Ibaragi Prefecture, Japan (Atelier Mobile)
  Nursery School, Honjo, Japan (Atelier Mobile)
1977 Municipal Library, Komaki, Aichi Prefecture, Japan (Atelier Zo and others)
  Coucou House, Japan (Atelier Mobile)
1979 Domo Balena (house), Yokohama, Kanagawa Prefecture, Japan (Atelier Iruka)
  Workers' Hostel, Nishikicho, Japan (Atelier Zo)
  House in Ameku, Japan
  Domo Romba (house), Japan (Atelier Iruka)
1980 Fujima Housing Complex, Kudan, Tokyo (Atelier Mobile)
  Municipal Community Center (Shinkushan), Miyashiro, Saitama Prefecture, Japan (Atelier Zo)
1981 Kasahara Primary School, Miyashiro, Saitama Prefecture, Japan (Atelier Zo)
  City hall, Naga, Okinawa Prefecture, Japan (Atelier Mobile and Atelier Zo)
  Domo Bikky (house), Japan (Atelier Zo)
1982 Domo Verda and Domo Kunkurba (houses), Japan (Atelier Iruka)
  Wakaba Nursery School, Hanamaki, Iwate Prefecture, Japan (Atelier Mobile)
1983 Tokiwa Nursery School, Mizusawa, Iwate Prefecture, Japan (Atelier Mobile)

Publications:

On TEAM ZOO: book—*A New Wave of Japanese Architecture,* with introduction by Kenneth Frampton, New York 1978; articles—"Saitama Prefectural Youth Friendship Center" in *Japan Architect* (Tokyo), April 1977; "Nakijin Village Center" in *Japan Architect* (Tokyo), February 1978; "Komaki Municipal Library" in *Japan Architect* (Tokyo), August 1978; "The Post Metabolists" in *Arquitectura* (Madrid), January/February 1979; "Domo Baleno" in *Japan Architect* (Tokyo), November/December 1980; "Primary School in the Tobudabutsukoen Area of Tokyo" in *Architecture d'Aujourd'hui* (Paris), June 1982; "Miyashiro Municipal Community Center" and "Naga City Hall" in *Japan Architect* (Tokyo), July 1982; "Team Zoo and Their Work" by P. Goulet in *Architecture d'Aujourd'hui* (Paris), September 1982; "Atelier Mobile and

Their Contribution to Team Zoo" in *Architecture d'Aujourd'hui* (Paris), December 1982; "Thirty Controversial Houses" by Marc Emery in *Architecture d'Aujourd'hui* (Paris), April 1983; "Kasahara Primary School in Miyashiro" in *Japan Architect* (Tokyo), November/December 1983; "Wakaba Nursery School" and "Tokiwa Nursery School" in *Japan Architect* (Tokyo), April 1984.

A "zoo" can mean a collection of caged beasts, or more colloquially the scene of raunchy, uninhibited behaviour often associated with college students. Both meanings are implied to a certain extent by the "zoo" in Team Zoo. A collection of architectural ateliers, some with animal names such as *zo* (elephant) and *iruka* (dolphin), Team Zoo was started by former Waseda University graduates, and in the sense that the team is a group of equals, it remains collegial if no longer collegiate in spirit. If "funky" in the context of a zoological garden refers primarily to the prevailing odor, in the context of Team Zoo the adjective is used most often to describe the earthy quality of its architecture, which more decorous designers find, and are presumably intended to find, offensive.

Like their late mentor, Takamasa Yosizaka, the members of Team Zoo have a deep interest in indigenous architecture in the Third World, and this is apparent in their work in Okinawa, the most southern and least developed of Japanese prefectures. Cheap available materials and low technology—concrete blocks employed as the left-in-place formwork for reinforced concrete—are used in highly inventive ways in the Nakijin Community Center and the Nago City Hall. Ample shaded areas are created to deal with the heat of the subtropical climate, and effective use is made of natural ventilation, particularly in the city hall. Bold colors and the incorporation of local craftwork (*shiisa* or clay lions) enliven the city hall, which must be counted among the most imaginative examples of public architecture in postwar Japan.

"Contextual" is an overworked term and is, moreover, inapplicable in their instance since it is used most frequently to describe work that is designed to fit into an urban environment and their best buildings are in suburban or rural environments. Yet their close attention to the particulars of local culture creates a close if not entirely seamless connection between buildings and their contexts. Vines of local plants (e.g., wood rose and bougainvillea in Okinawa; a local variety of grape in Miyashiro) are frequently extended over the roof and literally bind a building to the land.

Organic imagery is often found in their work (e.g., Domo Arabeska), but the team members are catholic in their tastes and draw their inspiration from many sources. The Miyashiro Community Center suggests a classical amphitheater on the outside and has wood detailing inside revealing the influence of the Arts and Crafts movement. Domo Celakanto (named after the coelacanth) has an exterior that calls to mind the Expressionist work of Hugo Haring as well as the proboscis of a Concorde. What the team members seem to abhor most of all is consistency, at least consistency of a stylistic kind. Their works are exuberant, sometimes to the point of being boisterous, and unconventional, sometimes to the point of being grotesque. However, at all times their buildings exude a tremendous energy, or animal spirits, and that seems entirely appropriate in works created by the denizens of a zoo.

—Hiroshi Watanabe

TENGBOM, Ivar Justus.
Swedish. Born in Vireda, near Jönköping, Sweden, 7 April 1878. Educated at the School of Building, Chalmers Technical College, Göteborg, Sweden, 1894-98; Royal Academy of Arts School of Architecture, Stockholm, 1898-1901 (Royal Gold Medal, 1901), Dip.Arch. 1901. Married Hjördis Nordin in 1905; children: Anders, Ann Mari, Yvonne, and Ulf; married Madeleine Douglas in 1931. Worked in the office of Erik Lallerstedt, Stockholm, 1901-03; in partnership with Ernst Torulf, Göteborg, Sweden, 1903-12: in charge of the Stockholm office of the partnership, 1906-12; in private practice, Stockholm, 1912-62. Architect to the Stockholm Royal Palace, 1922-59, and to the Drottningholm Royal Palace, 1922-62; Director-General, National Board of Building and Planning, Stockholm, 1924-36. Instructor at the Free Academy of Architecture, private school founded by ex-students of the Royal Academy of Arts, including Osvald Almqvist, *q.v.*, and Sigurd Lewerentz, *q.v.*, Stockholm, 1910-11; Professor, Royal Academy of Arts School of Architecture, Stockholm, 1916-20. Editor, *Arkitektur* magazine, Stockholm, 1908-11. Exhibitions: *Nordic Classicism 1910-1930*, Museum of Finnish Architecture, Helsinki, 1982; *Ivar Tengbom 1878-1968*, Architectural Association, London, 1982. Recipient: First Prize, with Ernst Torulf, Borås Town Hall Competition, Sweden, 1907; First Prize, Högalid Church Competition, Stockholm, 1912; First Prize, Stockholms Enskilda Bank Competition, 1912; First Prize (shared), Stockholm Concert Hall Competition, 1920; First Prize, with Anders Tengbom, Bonnier Publishing House Competition, Stockholm, 1938; Royal Gold Medal, Royal Institute of British Architects, 1938. Fellow, Royal Academy of Arts, London, 1947; Member, Accademia di San Luca, Rome, 1947. *Died* (in Stockholm) *6 August 1968.*

Works:

1904/
05 City Hall, Stockholm (competition project; with Ernst Torulf)
1906 A. Brunius Villa, Stockholm
1907/
10 Town Hall, Borås, Sweden (with Ernst Torulf)
1911 Church, Arvika, Sweden
1911/
23 Högalid Church, Stockholm
1912/
15 Stockholms Enskilda Bank Building, Stockholm
1913 Scandinavian Bank Building, Stockholm (competition project)
1913/
19 Housing Development, Diplomatstaden, Stockholm
1919/
20 Johnson Office Building reconstruction, Stockholm
1920/
26 Stockholm Concert Hall
1926 University of Commerce, Stockholm
1926/
28 Swedish Match Company Head Office, Stockholm
1928/
34 Esselte Office Building, Stockholm
1931/
32 "City Palace" Office Building, Stockholm
1935 Savings Bank, Örebro, Sweden
1937/
48 Bonnier Publishing House, Stockholm (with Anders Tengbom)
1938/
40 Swedish Institute, Rome
1938/
41 Church restoration, Halmstad, Sweden
1942/
44 Åtvidaberg Office Building, Stockholm
1943/
44 Savings Bank, Enköping, Sweden
1946/
50 Cathedral restoration, Uppsala (competition project)
1947/
49 Cathedral restoration, Skara, Sweden
1948/
51 Foreign Office rebuilding and restoration, Stockholm
1954/
62 Drottningholm Palace Park restoration, Sweden (with Walter Bauer and Nils G. Wollin)
1956/
58 Royal Palace Museum restoration, Stockholm

Publications:

By TENGBOM: article—"How Yesterday Made Possible Today's Swedish Architecture," interview, with Eugene Clute, in *American Architect* (New York), August 1931.

On TENGBOM: books—*100 Blad Svensk Byggnadskonst*, with introduction by Harald Boklund, Malmö, Sweden 1923; *Trettiotalets Byggnadskonst i Sverige*, edited by Hans Brunnberg, Hans-Fredrik Neumuller and Inga Mari Lonnroth, Stockholm 1943; *Nordisk Arkitektur 1946-1949*, edited by Gustaf Lettstrom and others, Stockholm 1950; *Sweden Builds* by G. E. Kidder Smith, New York and Stockholm 1956; *Nordic Classicism 1910-1930*, exhibition catalogue, edited by Simo Paavilainen, Helsinki 1982; articles—"Ivar Tengbom" by George Nelson in *Pencil Points* (New York), November 1935; "Royal Gold Medal Presentation to Professor Ivar Tengbom" in *RIBA Journal* (London), 11 April 1938; "L'Istituto svedese in Roma" by Francesco Fariello in *L'Architettura* (Rome), September 1942; "Bonnierhuset" and "Fagersta Lasarett" in *Byggmästaren* (Stockholm), 7 June 1951; "Un Immeuble industriel à Stockholm" by Martin Raberg in *La Construction moderne* (Paris), March 1956; "Obituary: Ivar Tengbom" in *Building* (London), 16 August 1968; "Ivar Tengbom 1878-1968" by Björn Linn in *Arkitektur* (Stockholm), October 1968; "Swedish Neo-Classicism of the 1920s," special issue of *Arkitektur* (Stockholm), no. 2, 1982; "Swedish Grace: Modern Classicism in Stockholm," special issue of *International Architect* (London), no. 8, 1982; "Ivar Tengbom 1878-1968" by Stuart Knight in *Architectural Association Events List* (London), November 1982; "The Swedish Influence: Ivar Tengbom" by Alan Powers in *Architectural Association Files* (London), July 1983.

In 1910 a conflict developed at the Academy of Arts in Stockholm between Professor Grundstrom and some of the students of architecture. Six students, including Osvald Almqvist, Gunnar Asplund, Sigurd Lewerentz, and Melchior Wernstedt, left to found a private school of architecture with Carl Bergsten, Ragnar Östberg, Ivar Tengbom, and Carl Westman as tutors. The ideals on which the school was founded were in opposition to the neoclassicism prevalent at the Academy and can be best described as those of "national realism," in which traditional Swedish vernacular and structural elements were mixed with a straightforward approach to design that attempted to return to first principles.

If Östberg had been an exponent of a picturesque use of eclectic elements, Tengbom was perhaps nearer the neoclassical thought of his time than were his colleagues. He began to move away from national realism, even though he had been one of the movement's leading theorists. He commenced a search for geometrical precision and for a crisp, light, rational architecture. His work became gradually restrained and simplified, and his development was marked by his insistence that the earlier neoclassical movement was only a step on the journey in search of purity of form, something that had already been discovered by Boullée, Ledoux, Kreis, Tessenow, and Soane. However, instead of the immense build-up of massive forms so characteristic of the French neoclassicists of the Academy in Rome, Tengbom moved steadily towards modernism, although his conversion was scarcely spectacular.

The importance of Tengbom in the context of Scandinavian architecture lies in his influence as a teacher and as a theorist as well as in his example as a leader in the drive towards a new architecture. His oeuvre spans neoclassicism, rational realism, and early modernism.

—James Stevens Curl

TERRAGNI, Giuseppe.

Italian. Born in Meda, Milan, 18 April 1904. Educated at the Technical School, Como, 1917-21; Milan Polytechnic, School of Architecture, 1921-26, Dip.Arch. 1926. Served in the Italian Army, on the Greek and Russian fronts, 1939: repatriated to Italy; died of after-effects of exhaustion. In private practice, with his brother Attilo, Como, 1927-39. Founder Member, with Frette, Larco, Libera, Figini, Pollini, and Rava, Gruppo 7, and MIAR (Movimento Italiano per l'Architettura Razionale), 1926. Founder-Editor, with Ciliberti, Lingeri and others, *Valori Primordiali* magazine, Como, 1937. Exhibitions: *III Mostra delle Arti Decorattive*, Monza, 1927; *Werkbundausstellung*, Stuttgart, 1927; *Esposizione di Architettura Razionale*, Rome, 1928; *Giuseppe Terragni*, Como, 1949. *Momenti di Giuseppe Terragni*, Galleria Pantha Arte, Como, 1981; *Terragni: poesia della razionalita*, Istituto Mides, Rome 1983. Recipient: First Prize, Como Master Plan Competition, 1934; First Prize, Busto Arisizio Secondary School Competition, 1934. *Died* (in Como) *19 July 1943*.

Works:

1926 Villa Saibene (project)
     Swiss Metropole Hotel restoration, Como
1927 Gas Works, Rome (project)
1928 Novocomun Apartment Building, Como
1929 Hospital, Milan (competition project)
     Tennis Chalet (project)
1930 Vitrum Store, Como
     Strecchini Tomb, Como
     Ladies' hairdressers shop, Como
1932 Sala del '22, *Mostra della Rivoluzione Fascista* Rome
     War Memorial, Erba Incino, Italy
     Ortelli Tomb, Cernobbio, Italy
     Tailor's shop, Monza, Italy
     Aeroclub, Como (project)
     Cathedral (project)
     Lake or Seaside House (project)
     Land Reclamation Monument (project)
1933 Ghiringheli House, Milan (with Pietro Lingeri)
     Toninello House, Milan (with Pietro Lingeri)
     Artist's Lakeside House, *Triennale*, Milan (with Gruppo di Commo)
     Covered Market, Como
     War Memorial, Lake Como (with Enrico Pampolini; from a design by Sant'Elia)
     School, Malpensata Quarter, Lecco, Italy
1934 Master plan of Como (competition project; with P. Bottoni, Pietro Lingeri, and others)
     Busto Arsizio Secondary School (competition project; with L. Mosca)
     Palazzo Littorio Rome (projects A and B; with Carminati, Lingeri, Vietti, Saliva, and the artists Nizzoli and Sironi)

1935 Rustici House, Milan (with Pietro Lingeri)
     Lavezzari House, Milan (with Pietro Lingeri)
     Post Hotel, Piazza Volta, Como
     Scarfatti Monument, Col d'Echele, Italy
     Pedraglio House, Como
1935/
36 Brera Acadamy School, Milan (two projects; with Pietro Lingeri, Luigi Figini, and Gino Pollini)
     Casa del Fascio, Como (now the Casa del Popolo)
     Pirovano Tomb, Como
1936 Lakeside Villa (project)
1937 Bianca House, Siveso, Italy
     Casa del Floricoltore, Rebbio, Italy
     Canton Library, Lugano, Switzerland (competition project)
     Nuovo Campari Restaurant, Milan (with Pietro Lingeri and Alberto Sartoris)
     Palazzo dei Congressi, E 42 District, Rome (competition project; with Pietro Lingeri and C. Cattaneo)
     Asilo Sant'Elia (kingergarten), Como
     Palazo Littorio, stage II, Rome (project)
     Danteum, Via dell'Impero, Rome (with Pietro Lingeri)
     Satellite quarter, Rebbio, Italy (with Alberto Sartoris)
1938 Tool Factory enlargement, Missagia, Como
     Fiera Campionaria, Milan (competition project; with Bottoni, Lingeri, Mucchi, and Pucci)
1939 Palazzo dei Congressi, E 42 District, Rome (2nd project)
     Casa del Fascio, Lissone, Italy (with A. Carminati)
     Giuliani-Frigerio House, Como
     Housing development, Via Anzani, Como

Publications:

By TERRAGNI: articles—"Architettura," with Gruppo 7, in *Rassegna Italiana* (Milan), December 1926; "Gli Stranieri," with Gruppo 7, in *Rassegna Italiana* (Milan), February 1927; "Impreparazione, Incomprensione, Pregiudizi," with Gruppo 7, in *Rassegna Italiana* (Milan), March 1927; "Una Nuova Epoca Arcaica," with Gruppo 7, in *Rassegna Italiano* (Milan), May 1927; "Architettura di Stato?" and "Lettera sull'Architettura" in *L'Ambrosiano* (Milan), February 1931; "Discorso ai Comaschi" in *L'Ambrosiano* (Milan), March 1940; "A relazione sul Danteum" in *Oppositions* (New York), Summer 1977.

On TERRAGNI: books—*Giuseppe Terragni* by M. Labo, Milan 1947; *Ritratto di Giuseppe Terragni* by M. Radice, Como 1949; *Difficolta Politiche dell'Architettura in Italia 1920-40* by Giulia Veronesi, Milan 1953; *Eredeta di Terragni e lo Sviluppo dell'Architettura Italiana 1943-68* (Congress papers), Como 1968; *Omaggio a Terragni* by Bruno Zevi, Milan 1968; *Giuseppe Terragni e la citta di razionalismo Italiano* by E. Mantero, Bari, Italy 1969; *Giuseppe Terragni* by Bruno Zevi, Bologna 1980; *Il Danteum di Terragni, 1938* by L. Schumacher, Rome 1980; *Momenti di Giuseppe Terragni*, exhibition catalogue, Como 1981; *Quindici anni divita e di lavoro con l'amico e maestro Giuseppe Terragni* by L. Zuccoli, Como 1981; *Giuseppe Terragni, 1904-1943*, edited by M. Fosso and E. Mantero, Como 1982; *Giuseppe Terragni: La Casa del Fascio*, edited by L. Ferrari and D. Pastore, Rome 1982; *Terragni: poesia della razionalita*, exhibition catalogue, edited by Fabio Mariani, Rome 1983; articles—"The Casa del Fascio at Como, Architect Giuseppe Terragni" in *The Architect and Building News* (London), July 1937; "Giuseppe Terragni" by P. M. Bardi in *Il Vetro* (Milan), July/August 1943; "Giuseppe Terragni" by Pietro Lingeri in *Quaderni della Facolta di Architecttura* (Milan), 1945; "Omaggio a Terragni" by A.

Podesta in *Emporium* (Bergamo), April 1948; "Terragni, Lingeri and Italian Rationalism" by Panos Koulermos in *Architctural Design* (London), March 1963; special edition of *L'Architettura* (Rome), July 1968; "Terragni" by A.D.P. in *Domus* (Milan), October 1968; From Object to Relationship II: Giuseppe Terragni" by Peter D. Eisenman in *Perspecta* (New Haven, Connecticut), no. 13/14, 1971; "Levels of Meaning in Terragni: The Danteum Project" by Thomas Schumacher in *Parametro* (Bologna), May 1976; "Giuseppe Terragni" by Claudio Maneri in *Architecture + Urbanism* (Tokyo), September 1976; "Giusepe Terragni: Subject and Mask" by Manfredo Tafuri in *Oppositions* (New York), Winter 1977; "The Subject and the Mask" in *Lotus* (Venice), no. 20, 1978; "Palladio or Terragni?" by Maurice Cooper in *Building Design* (London), 22 February 1980; "Figurative Paintings and Drawings by Giuseppe Terragni" in *Modulus* (Charlottesville, Virginia), 1980/81; "Terragni and Italian Rationalism" by Gerda ten Cate in *Bouw* (Rotterdam), 29 May 1982; "Giuseppe Terragni," special issue of *Rassegna* (Milan), September 1982; "Terragni," special issue of *2C Contruccion de la Ciudad* (Barcelona), November 1982.

Giuseppe Terragni was one of the pioneer architects of the modern movement in Italy, and produced some of its most significant buildings in a brief career that lasted only 13 years between his graduation in Milan in 1926 and his call-up into Mussolini's army in 1939. Not only was his achievement cut short by his death as a result of his experiences fighting on the Russian front, but also he had less work than he otherwise might have done because he was one of the very few architects who, in the bitter debate that raged round architecture in Italy during the fascist period, held out for a completely new approach.

Wrenching architecture away from neo-classical and neo-baroque revivalism and eclecticism was particularly difficult in Italy: no other country was so heavily overshadowed by its artistic past. The Futurists reacted to this by demanding a violent break with the past, but the principal Futurist architect, Antonio Sant'Elia, was unable to realize any of his utopian visions, leaving only sketches of unbuilt projects behind him when he was killed in the First World War. His example and his legend were the inspiration of the Italian movement for rationalist architecture of the 1920s and 1930s. Some of his drawings for other projects were used by Terragni and Prampolini in the design of their War Memorial, a stark symmetrical composition of abstract forms on the shores of Lake Como.

When, in 1926, Terragni and other progressive members of Gruppo 7 issued the manifesto that made them the leaders in the fight against revivalism, they adopted only a moderately advant-garde position, much less aggressive than that of the Futurists, calling for clarity and honesty in the use of materials but emphasizing that "we do not intend to break with tradition: transforms itself and takes on new aspects beneath which only a few can recognize it. The new architecture, the true architecture, should be the result of a close association between logic and rationality."

The fight for modern architecture was carried on not only in lively polemics in magazines but also, practically, in exhibitions such as the Monza *Biennale* and Milan *Triennale*, which gave the rationalist architects, who otherwise had to rely on private commissions, rare opportunities for experimentation. Terragni exhibited many fascinating models and protects, and in 1932 he designed a hall for the *Mostra della Rivoluzione Fascista* in Rome.

Those of his designs actually executed form a small but remarkable group; nearly all of them are in Como where he practiced and which was then the centre of modern Italian architectural experiment. These works form the nucleus of the language of Italian rationalist of modernistic architecture, the first of them being the Novocomum Apartment Building, a block of flats behind the stadium in

Giuseppe Terragni: Casa del Popolo, Como, Italy, 1932-36.

Como, harsh and deliberately modernistic, clearly derived from earlier German and Russian experiments. Terragni's architecture achieved both maturity and a more distinctively Mediterranean character in the Casa del Fascio (now known as the Casa del Popolo), which has come to be regarded as one of the most brilliant formal excercises of the 1930s: in it, Terragni translated into a distinctively southern language the possibilities latent in designing with a reinforced concrete skeleton. Floors of offices are simply arranged round an intenal court, so that the building is a hollow cube, with the front, which is seen across the piazza outside the cathedral, opening up an exposed structural frame whose wall does not fill the space between piers and beams but is set back. There is no ornament, simply a beautifully proportioned arrangement of solids and voids whose violent contrasts of light and shade create a dramatically punctuated architectural dialogue. The proportions are those of classical architecture, and it was this complete and cunning fusion of modernism and tradition which once made this building so controversial, leading Giuseppe Pagano to denounce it as an example of "17th century affectation applied to Functionalism." This unique blend has been excellently summed up by Reyner Banham: "For those who believe that modern architecture is still subject to the grand old rule, it is proof that the rules are still valid. For those who believe that modern architecture has to do with social progress, it is the machine aesthetic at its most heartlessly elegant."

Terragni next designed a striking kindergarten, the Asilo Sant'Elia, again using courtyards and open frames to produce airy spaces for children to work and play in. Otherwise, Terragni built a number of houses and apartments, mostly simple unadorned structures that make elegant use of such features as balcony frames and sun screens. At his early death he left behind a large number of architectural and town-planning schemes and a collection of controversial writings on architecture. In many ways his career resemble that of Sant'Elia, except that Terragni did actually manage to realize some of his buildings, buildings that have played an important role in the development of modern Italian architecture.

—Konstantin Bazarov

TESSENOW, Heinrich.

German. Born in Rostock, 7 April 1876. Educated at the College of Education, Rostock, 1892-93; apprentice carpenter in his father's workshop, Rostock, 1894-96; College of Building, Neustadt, Mecklenburg, Germany, 1896; College of Building, Leipzig, 1897; (assistant railway designer, Danzig, 1898-1900); Technische Hochschule, Munich, under Karl Hocheder and Friedrich von Thiersch, 1900-01. Married Elly Mathilde Charlotte Schülke in 1903. Worked with the architect Martin Dülfer, Munich, 1901-02; Instructor, Municipal College of Building, Sternberg, Germany, 1902, and Municipal College of Building, Lüchow, Germany, 1903; worked at Paul Schultze-Naumburg's Saalecker Workshops, 1904; Instructor, Arts and Crafts School, Upper Trier, Germany, 1905-09; Assistant to Professor Martin Dülfer, Technische Hochschule, Dresden, 1909-10; in private practice, in Hellerau, Germany, 1910-13, Vienna, 1913-19, Hellerau, 1919-20, Dresden, 1920-26, and Berlin, 1926 until his death, 1950. Professor, School of Arts and Crafts, Vienna, 1913-19; Professor, Academy of Arts, Dresden, 1920-26;

Head of Master Studio, Academy of Fine Arts, Berlin, 1926-34; Professor, 1926-41, Emeritus Professor, 1941-50, and Lecturer, 1945-50, Technische Hochschule, Charlottenburg, Berlin; Teacher, 1934, and Part-time Director of the Master Studio, 1936, United Schools for Liberal and Applied Arts, Berlin. Founder, Deutscher Werkbund, 1910; Founder, Crafts Center/Community, Hellerau, Germany, 1919; Member, Novembergruppe, Berlin, 1921; Founder Member, Der Ring architects group, Berlin, 1926; Chairman, Deutscher Werkbund, Berlin, 1949. Exhibitions: *Heinrich Tessenow*, Berlin, 1961; *Heinrich Tessenow*, Architectural Association, London, 1977. Honorary doctorates: University of Rostock, 1919; Technische Hochschule, Stuttgart, 1929. Honorary Life Member, Bund Deutscher Architekten, 1950. Honorary Corresponding Member, Royal Institute of British Architects, 1937. Member, Prussian Academy of Fine Arts, Berlin, 1920, and Academy of Arts, Berlin, 1950. *Died* (in Berlin) *1 November 1950.*

Works:

1902 Vicarage (project)
Tessenow Seaside House, Sternberg, Germany (project)
Vorstadt Two-Family House (project)
Garden Pavilion (project)

1902/
03 Schön Boarding House, Sternberg, Germany

1903 Semi-Detached Housed (project)
Four-Family Houses (project)
7 Terraced One-Family Workers House (project)
Corner Houses with 2 Shops (project)

Am Buchenwald Villa (project)
Facade for a Two-Family House (project)
Small Town House (project)
Country House by the Sea (project)
Porter's House (project)
Single-Family House (project)
Bismarck Tower (project)
Country Lodging House (project)
Funeral Monument (project)
Parish Church (project)
Small Town Hall (project)
Entrance Gate (project)
1904 Country House (project)
Haus auf der Höhe (single-family house)
(project)
Two-Family House (projects)
Burial Vault (project)
Garden Pavilion (project)
Three-Family House (project)
1905 Single-family houses, Neu-Dölau Housing
Estate, near Halle/Saale, Germany
4 Terraced Single-Family Houses (project)
Single-family house, near Mülheim/Ruhr,
Germany
Single-Family House (project)
Einsiedelei Two-Family House (project)
4 terraced single-family houses, Weiden Hous-
ing Estate, near Cologne
Country House, Saratoff, Russia (project)
Workers' House (project)
Six-Family House (competition project)
Two-Family Country House (project)
2 Semi-Detached Workers' Houses (project)
Forest Cemetery (project)
1906 Country House on the Ruhr (project)
Single-family house, Mintard, near Mül-
heim/Ruhr, Germany
12 Semi-Detached Houses (project)
Single-family terraced houses, Bad Brösen,
near Danzig
Single-Family Terraced Housing (project)
Single-Family House, Eifel Plateau, Germany
(project)
2 Single-Family Semi-Detached Houses (project)
Three-Family House (project)
2 Semi-Detached Two Family Houses (project)
Fountain for Small Town Market Square
(project)
Corner House, Bad Brösen, near Danzig
(project)
1906/
07 State Electricity Company Workers' Housing,
Trier, Germany
1907 Vicarage (2 projects)
Holiday House, Vorpommern, Germany (competition project)
Single-Family Terraced Housing, Ohren-
strasse, Trier, Germany (project)
Rural Single-Family House (project)
Holiday House on the Ruhr (2 projects)
Village School with Teachers' Housing (project)
1908 Single-Family Terraced Housing (project)
2 Semi-Detached Single-Family Houses (project)
Single-Family House (project)
Single-Family Terraced House (project)
2-Storey Terraced Housing (project)
2 semi-detached houses for Civil servants,
Mettlach an der Saar, Germany
Public Baths (project)
1909 Single-Family House in the Ruhr Valley
(project)
1910 Haus zum Wolf (Schmidt House), Hopfen-
garten, near Magdeburg, Germany
8 single-family houses, Am Schänkenberg,
Hellerau, Germany
Metzges House, Remagen/Rhein, Germany
Israeli Young Farmers' Educational Institute, Steinhorst, near Celle, Germany
Dalcroze Institute for Physical Education,
Hellerau, Germany

Single-Family Terraced Housing (project)
1910/
11 12 single-family terraced houses, Am Schänkenberg, Hellerau, Germany
2 single-family houses, Heideweg 24-26, Hellerau, Germany
Single-family house, Tännichtweg 2, Hellerau,
Germany
Single-family terraced house, Hohensalza,
Germany
Single-family house, Auf dem Sand 12, Hellerau, Germany
Single-family house, Heideweg 22, Hellerau,
Germany
Gehlig House, Tännichtweg 1, Hellerau, Germany
2 semi-detached single-family houses, Am
Schänkenberg 17-19, Hellerau, Germany
2 semi-detached single-family houses, Tännichtweg 6-8, Hellerau, Germany
Single-family house, Karl-Liebknechtstrasse,
Hellerau, Germany
4 five-family houses, Dresdenerstrasse, Hellerau, Germany (project)
1911/
13 8 single-family houses, Am Schänkenberg and
Am Pfarrlehn, Hellerau, Germany
1912 Nau-Rosser Single-Family House and Studio,
Lostau, near Magdeburg, Germany
4 semi-detached single-family houses for
factory workers and officials, Wald-
kirchen/Erzgebirge, Germany
1912/
13 5 single-family terraced houses, Am Pfarrlehn
4-12, Hellerau, Germany
1913 Single-family house, Falkenberg Garden City,
Berlin
Single-family house, Tännichtweg 14, Hellerau, Germany
Elementary/High School, Hellerau, Germany
(project)
Six-Family Terraced Housing, Groba-Riesa
Housing Estate, Hamburg (project)
1914 4 single-family terraced houses, Am Schänkenberg 38-40, Hellerau, Germany
Viennese Kunstgewerbeschule Rooms, Werkbund Exhibition, Cologne
1916 Cemetery monument, Vienna
1916/
17 Böhler House, Oberalpina/St. Moritz, Switzerland
1917 Single-family terraced houses, Rähnitz, Dresden (project)
Municipal Monument to the Dead of World
War I (competition project)
1919 Post-War Housing Development, Rähnitz,
Dresden (project)
Rural Housing Settlement, Rähnitz, Dresden
(project)
1919/
20 Graf Doret Mansion, Czomahaya, Hungary
20 22 single-family houses and 2 multi-family
houses, Public Housing Estate, Possneck,
Thuringia, Germany
Schnitterkaserne Terraced Housing (project)
Free-Standing Single-Family House (project)
Workers' Housing, Schleswig-Holstein, Ger-
many (project)
Mansion for State Secretary Busch, Bussow,
Mecklenburg, Germany
Single-Family Terraced House (project)
Four-Family House for a Small Town (pro-
ject)
1921 Kleinstes Dauerhaus (single-family house),
Rähnitz, Dresden (project)
Semi-detached single-family state housing,
Rannersdorf Estate, Schwechat, Vienna
1922 11 connected single-family houses, Edwin-
Hoernle-Strasse 19-39, Hellerau, Germany
1924 Mansion, Bavaria (project)
Bridge over the River Elbe, Meissen, Germany
Krauss Family House, Schwarzenberg, Ger-
many (project)
1925 Regional School, Klotzsche, near Dresden

Oberbayern Restaurant, and Cupola with 2
Side Halls for Main Exhibitions, Quadre-
nnial Exhibition, Dresden
Dresdener Anzeigers Office Building, Dresden
(competition project)
Berliner Sezession Exhibition Building, Berlin
(competition project)
1926 Gallery interiors, and Inner Courtyard, Inter-
national Art Exhibition, Dresden
Am Rosenhof Restaurant, *Garden Exhibition*,
Dresden
1927 Single-Family house, Mineworkers' Estate,
Finkenherd, Frankfurt an der Oder, Germany
Freudenberg House, Heidelberg (project)
City Swimming Hall, Gartenstrasse, Berlin
Rengen Family Tomb, Kamnist, Germany
Trade School, Charlottenburg, Berlin (com-
petition project)
Redevelopment plan for the Ministry Gar-
dens, Berlin (project; with Peter Behrens,
Adolf Rading, Hans Scharoun, and Martin
Wagner)
1927/
30 Heinrich-Schütz School, Kassel
1928 3 four-family houses, Am Fischtal 58-60,
Zehlendorf, Berlin
6 single-family terraced houses, Am Fischtal
62-66, Zehlendorf, Berlin
2 single-family houses, Am Fischtal 2 and 2A,
Zehlendorf, Berlin
Castle Hotel conversion, Kassel (destroyed)
Crown Prince's Palace/Museum of Modern
Painting conversion, Berlin (destroyed)
Country House on the Ruhr (project)
1928/
29 Single-Family houses conversion, Neutor-
strasse 26, Neubrandenburg, Germany
1929 Music High School, Charlottenburg, Berlin
(project)
Aschrott Foundation Old People's Home,
Kassel (competition project)
Church, Karlshafen, Germany (project)
1930 Tessenow House, Sophie-Charlotte-Strasse 7,
Zehlendorf, Berlin
Busch Family Tomb, Büssow/Neumark, Germany
1930/
31 Memorial to the War Dead, Berlin (reno-
vation/conversion of Schinkel's Neue
Wache)
1931 Goethe House enlargement, Am Frauenplan,
Weimar
Church, Karlshafen, Germany (project)
Elisabeth-Heim Institute for Cripples, Rostock (project)
Students' Lodging House, Berlin (project)
Regimental Hall of Honor, Magdeburg Cathedral, Germany (project)
1932 Cassinone Family Tomb, Vienna
1933 Reichshauptbank Building extensions, Berlin
(competition project)
1934 House, Aue/Erzgebirge, Germany (project)
1935 Crafts School, Königsberg, Germany (project)
Hubbe und Fahrenholtz Administration Building, Magdburg, Germany
1936 Single-Family House and Three-Family House, Rügen, Germany (competition project)
Hindenburg Memorial and Barracks, Magdeburg, Germany
Hall layouts, *Olympic Art Exhibition*, Berlin
Plan for the Trommelplatz, Königsberg, Germany (competition project)
1937 12 single-family houses, Iserhorstweg, Neu-
strelitz-Kiefernheide, Germany
Monument to the War Dead of the Stargard
Region, Neubrandenburg, Germany
1938 Barracks, Helmstedt, Germany (project)
Dohrn Family Cemetery, Gut Hökersdorf,
near Stettin, Germany
Bridge over the River Weichsel (project)
1941 Administration Building, Braunschweig, Ger-

many (competition project)

Junker Works Housing Estate, Magdeburg, Germany (project)

1942 Plan for the Diedrichshagen Satellite Town, Warnemünde, near Rostock

Barlach Tomb, Ratzeburg, Germany (project)

1942 Mosigkau Community Housing Development, near Dessau, Germany (project)

Plan for the Drewitz Satellite Town, Potsdam, Berlin

1943 Cottage/Tessenow House conversion, Güstrow, Siemitz, Germany

1946 Town reconstructrion plans for the German towns of Pasewalk, Friedland, Woldegk, Neubrandenburg, Rostock, and Demmin

1947 Small Farmhouse, Single-Family House with Workshop, and Rural Single-Family House, for the Mecklenburg Region, Germany (project)

Plan for the reconstruction of the old city of Lübeck

Plan for the reconstruction of the old town of Mecklenburg

1948 Café Niederegger, Lübeck (project)

Publications:

By TESSENOW: books—*Zimmermannsarbeiten*, Freiburg 1907, Munich 1921; *Der Wohnhausbau*, Munich 1909, 3rd edition 1927; *Hausbau und dergleichen*, Berlin 1916, 3rd edition 1928; *Handwerk und Kleinstadt*, Berlin 1919; *Das Land in der Mitte*, Hellerau, Germany 1921; *Die kleine und die grosse Stadt. Aus dem Nachlass*, edited by Hans Hasche, Munich 1961; *Kleine Schriften von Heinrich Tessenow: Enthält die Aufsätze "Handwerkerarbeit und Fabrikarbeit" und "Die Farbe im Stadtbild,"* Hamburg 1967; *Die Zeichnungen von Heinrich Tessenow*, Berlin 1981.

On TESSENOW: books—*Heinrich Tessenow*, exhibition catalogue, Berlin 1961; *Heinrich Tessenow 1876-1950* by Gerda Wangerin and Gerhard Weiss, Essen 1976; articles—"Arbeiten von Heinrich Tessenow und seinen Schulern" by Werner Hegemann in *Wasmuths Monatshefte für Baukunst* (Berlin), vol. 9, no. 9, 1925, and vol. 10, no. 2, 1926; "Paul Wolff und Heinrich Tessenow" in *Wasmuths Monatshefte für Baukunst* (Berlin), vol. 11, no. 4, 1927; "Heinrich Tessenow" by Oskar Gehrig in *Mecklenburgische Monatshefte* (Mecklenburg, Germany), no. 11, 1927; "Heinrich Tessenow" by Peter Meyer in *Werk* (Zurich), no. 8, 1934; "Heinrich Tessenow zum 60. Geburtstag" in *Frankfurter Zeitung* (Frankfurt), 5 April 1936; "Heinrich Tessenow" by Bruno Reichlin in *Casabella* (Milan), no. 7, 1970; "Heinrich Tessenow" by Steen Eiler Rasmussen in *Bauwelt* (Berlin), April 1976; "Two Masters: Hans Poelzig and Heinrich Tessenow" by Julius Posener in *Lotus* (Venice), September 1977; "The Last 100 Years: The Masters" by Luciano Rubino in *Ville Giardini* (Milan), June 1979.

Heinrich Tessenow, with his strongly puritanical "reductive-classicism," does not fit easily into any 20th century movements. Although his work is unequivocally associated with the time span of New Building, Tessenow was much more interested in the human and social aspects of a new building than in the creation of a new style.

After completing an apprenticeship as a carpenter in his father's business in Rostock, Tessenow studied building and then studied architecture at the Technische Hochschule, Munich, under Karl Hocheder and Friedrich von Thiersch. He then worked with Martin Dülfer, who became a strong influence, and from 1902-03 he taught at the building colleges in Sternberg (Mecklenburg) and in Lüchow (Hanover). Still in search of solid experience, he joined Paul Schultze-Naumburg's Saalecker Workshop in 1904.

This educational history is indicative of Tessenow's goals: like Mebes and Ostendorf, he believed that a fundamental renewal of architecture could be guaranteed only by a return to solid traditions. Because of his disagreement with Schultze-Naumburg's theories, he left the workshop in 1905 and went on to teach in the Arts and Crafts School in Upper Trier. Then, from 1909-1910 he worked as an assistant to Martin Dülfer at the Technische Hochschule in Dresden.

From 1910, Tessenow was able to begin translating into reality his vision of an appropriate, objective architecture, depending less on spectacular artistic ideas than on functional craft traditions. He completed his best known works in 1910-13, the Dalcroze Institute for Physical Education in Hellerau and housing for the Hellerau Garden City. Tessenow's strength lay in the re-use of strong, classical elements in a completely different form. His reduction of the architectonic medium of expression went so far that, to many of his contemporaries, even his houses seemed over-purist. Tessenow considered the objectivity of these buildings not as a style but rather as a necessary result of his function-related work methods. And, in fact, it was especially in his houses that Tessenow best conveyed his extraordinary feeling for spatial atmosphere and the human dimension.

During 1913-19 Tessenow taught at the School of Arts and Crafts in Vienna. World War I and the European revolution made a deep impression on him. Unlike Taut, Mendelsohn or Scharoun, who foresaw the coming of a new age of creativity, Tessenow felt very deeply the burden of the war and the chaos it left behind. He rejected the city. He came to believe that he could achieve a new social cohesion for people only in "organic" and "in themselves viable" small towns. Man again became the center of his attention and his work; his ideals became not dissimilar to those of William Morris, and in 1919 he founded a Crafts Center/Community in Hellerau.

During 1920-26 he taught at the Academy of Arts in Dresden, and in 1926 he was appointed Professor at the Technische Hochschule, Charlottenburg; thereafter he worked and practiced in Berlin. His teaching in Berlin was extraordinarily important to him. He used his position as a forum to criticize all formalism and to propound his belief that "A minimum of display is the decisive factor," During this period, until World War II, Tessenow began to follow new paths, particularly in school architecture. He turned away from symmetry as a principle of order, and in these large buildings rediscovered an objective, purist expression of form. By careful staggering of the structure, he included nature within the ground plan and kept building details within the crafts tradition. It was precisely in this reliance and refinement of a particular tradition that Tessenow differed from Gropius or Mies van der Rohe who wanted to break with tradition, even in building detail. In these years Tessenow naturally belonged with representatives of "New Objectivity" without necessarily adhering to all of their philosophy. Buildings like the Heinrich-Schutz School in Kassel (1927-30) or the City Swimming Hall in Berlin (1927) clearly demonstrate this attitude. In 1928 the estate "Am Fischtalgrund" in Zehlendorf was completed: his work there documents Tessenow's continuing preference for economical, lovingly arranged single-family houses even on high-density estates. In 1930/31 Tessenow was commissioned to transform Schinkel's Neue Wache in Berlin into a memorial to the dead of World War I—a task he handled with extraordinary sensitivity and refinement.

Tessenow soon experienced difficulties after the seizure of power by the National Socialists. In 1934 he was forced to give up his teaching post at the Academy of Fine Arts in Berlin. Under pressure from his former pupil, Albert Speer, he did try to make compromises, but his designs were more and more frequently rejected by the Nazis. Like Paul Bonatz, Tessenow was totally helpless against the continual excessive demands on him, and he was, in effect, forced to retire from teaching and his practice in

1941. But in 1945 he was able to resume teaching at Charlottenburg. His principal post-war activity was in planning the reconstruction of the old town centers, which he regarded as an opportunity to realize the small town ideal he had been propagating since 1918. He worked, on and off, on plans for various towns, most notably Mecklenburg and Lübeck, until his death in 1950.

In the last few decades there has been a continual increase in the estimation of Tessenow's work—despite the fact that he always adopted a middle stance and cannot therefore really be said to belong either to the reactionary "Heimatstil" movement or the radical "New Objectivity." More important than any classification of his style has been the recognition that Tessenow, like Hugo Häring, is one of the very few important 20th century architects who have fostered an individual primarily modest and human architecture. Few architects have dealt as seriously and as profoundly as Heinrich Tessenow with the problems of high-density housing and of housing for those of modest means.

—Frank Werner

TESTA, Clorindo.

Argentinian. Born in Buenos Aires in 1923. Studied at the Faculty of Architecture and Urbanism, Buenos Aires University. In private practice, Buenos Aires. Member, Buenos Aires Regulating Plan Team, 1948. Member, Group of Thirteen, Buenos Aires. Exhibition: *Clorindo Testa: La Peste en Ceppaloni*, Galeria Florida 948, Buenos Aires, 1978. Recipient: First Prize, Civic Center Competition, La Pampa, Argentina, 1956; First Prize, Provincial Government House Competition, La Pampa, Argentina, 1956; Gold Medal, World's Fair, Brussels, 1958; First Prize, Bank of London and South America Headquarters Competition, Buenos Aires, 1960; National Painting Prize, Instituto Torcuato Di Tella, Buenos Aires, 1961; First Prize, National Library Competition, Buenos Aires, 1962; Arte de America Prize, 1965; Grand Prize, *Bienal*, Sao Paulo, 1977. Member, National Fine Arts Academy, Buenos Aires, 1977. Address (office): Sante Fe 1821-6P, 1123 Buenos Aires, Argentina.

Works:

1951 Argentine Construction Chamber Building, Buenos Aires (with Dabinovic, Gaido and Rossi)

1956/
61 Bus Terminal, Santa Roas, La Pampa, Argentina (with Rossi, Gaido and Dabinovic)

1956/
63 Provincial Government House, Santa Rosa, La Pampa, Argentina (with Dabinovic, Gaido and Rossi)

1959/
66 Bank of London and South America Headquarters, Buenos Aires (with SEPRA)

1962 National Library, Buenos Aires (project; with A. Cazzaniga de Bullrich and F. Bullrich)

1970 Central Naval Hospital, Buenos Aires (with Lascara and Genoud)

1975 Aerolineas Argentinas Building, Catalinas Norte, Buenos Aires (with Lascara and Rossi)

1976 Presidente Plaza Hospital, La Rioja, Argentina

1979 Government Hospital, Ivory Coast, Africa Cultural Center (18th century building conversion), Buenos Aires (with Bedel and Benedit)

1982 Paseo de la Recoleta Development, Buenos Aires (with Demaria and Genoud)

Publications:

By TESTA: paper—*Hacia una Arquitectura Topologica*, with Jorge Glusberg, Lima 1977; articles—"A Professional Without Anguish", interview, in *Arquitecturas Bis* (Barcelona), January/March 1981; "Interview with Clorindo Testa" in *Summa* (Buenos Aires), July 1981.

On TESTA: books—*Clorindo Testa* by Julio Llimas, Buenos Aires 1962; *New Directions in Latin American Architecture* by Francisco Bullrich, New York 1969; *Clorindo Testa: La Peste en Ceppaloni*, exhibition catalogue, Buenos Aires 1978; *The Changing Shape of Latin American Architecture* by D. Bayon and P. Gasparini, Chichester, Sussex 1979; *Architekten der Dritten Welt* by Udo Kultermann, Cologne 1980; articles—"Clorindo Testa" in *Revista de Arquitectura* (Buenos Aires), no. 38, 1953; "Hospital Presidente Plaza, La Rioja" in *Nuestra Arquitectura* (Buenos Aires), no. 498, 1976; "Apartment Buildings in Buenos Aires", special issue of *Summa* (Buenos Aires), December 1978; "The United Holland Bank Headquarters, Buenos Aires" in *Summa* (Buenos Aires), March 1979; "National Library" in *Conescal* (Mexico City), October/December 1979; "House in Tortuguitas, Province of Buenos Aires" in *Summa* (Buenos Aires), August 1980; "Housing Block at Castex 3335, Buenos Aires" in *Summa* (Buenos Aires), April 1981; "Houses in Argentina, Chile and Uruguay" in *Summa* (Buenos Aires), October 1981; "New Cultural Centre for Buenos Aires" in *Summa* (Buenos Aires), September 1982; "Clorindo Testa: The Work of an Artist", special issue of *Summa* (Buenos Aires), January/February 1983; "Cultural Centre in Buenos Aires" in *Summa* (Buenos Aires), April 1983; "Interior Architecture", special issue of *Summa* (Buenos Aires), December 1983.

*   *   *

The most significant figure to have appeared on the Argentine architectural scene in the last two decades or so is undoubtedly Clorindo Testa. He began his work in 1948 as part of the team for the Buenos Aires Regulating Plan. After spending two years in Italy, where he began painting, he returned to Buenos Aires and developed his activities as an architect, frequently associating with divers colleagues for each project. Since then, it has been as difficult to classify him according to a particular style as it is to comprehend his work according to any explicit (or implicit) theoretical posture. Possessing a bold talent, a powerful creative imagination, and an exquisite sensibility, Testa likes to allow his buildings to speak for themselves. As he himself points out, "What I wanted to say is what is said by the buildings I made."

Some clues, however, do exist. In a paper presented jointly with the author, before the Frederico Villarreal University in Lima in 1977, entitled *Towards a Topological Architecture*, Testa outlines his attitude about the habitat. Criticizing the urbanization proposals of the Athens Charter, he points out that the assumptions about the quality of life that might be obtained through the division of the city into "functional" areas have been undermined in less than forty years: "Functionalism forgot social reality, and I believe that one cannot speak of an urbanistic change if there exists a division between political, social and human factors." The creation of spaces for particular functions is meaningless, if these spaces don't primarily address the problem of the elimination of the solitude of the individual who lives in the midst of the crowd. This vision, of an architecture of synthesis, is verifiable in his own works.

The Bank of London and South America is considered by many people to be the most important building erected in Buenos Aires in the last half century because of its significant values. it was done in collaboration with the SEPRA team, which has a wealth of experience in Argentina, and has been

Clorindo Testa: National Library, Buenos Aires, 1962-84.

praised by critics of international renown such as Nikolaus Pevsner; it has, as well, awakened an unusual interest in the average inhabitant of Buenos Aires. The inside is conceived as one great unitary space which encompasses five levels; these levels jut out or appear as hanging trays, generating series of spaces which are surbordinated or integrated to a central one; the structural solution is of a "brutalist" image. The rupture of an image of box-wrapping is manifest in the resolution of the inside-outside link, in the creation of a transition area, coinciding with the entrance, which allows for the perception of the whole at pedestrian level. Testa was equally concerned with the "linkage" with neighboring buildings and respect for the urban environment, and he has rescued the street as a vital experience. The maturity of the design and the profound technical resolution produce an enormous impact.

Yet despite the formal beauty and ingenuity of the building, function has not been sacrificed to form; on the contrary, a deft integration exists between form and function—as it does in the administrative blocks of La Pampa, which were, additionally, subjected to particular weather conditions. But perhaps the best indication of Testa's ability to combine dazzling

form with superb functionalism is his hospital in Africa, his most ambitious work.

The design of the hospital reveals Testa responding to, and solving the problems, of a number of particular conditions: 1) institutional conditions (the client, Health Ministry, Government of the Ivory Coast); 2) social conditions (geographical venue; possible population of the hospital; types of services; assistance activities; teaching centers; research centers); 3) technical conditions (350 beds; 28,000 square metres with a central volume in the shape of a hollowed-out prism pierced by ramps); 4) natural conditions (strong winds, heavy rainfall, red earth, vegetation made sparse by clearing work; horizontal land; constant temperature of 30←C); 5) geopolitical conditions (highway crossing in the center of the country; nearby city of 35,000 people); 6) institutional and social conditions of consumption (non-existence of hospital centers in neighboring countries; predominant endemic diseases, etc.); 7) aesthetic conditions (production of an architectural event). The space-time succession, that is to say the constitution of a serial system to which the spectator gains access, is nothing more (or less) than the clear and gradual manifestation of the process of the design, leading to an understanding of the final architectural discourse.

The designs of Clorindo Testa do not project a reality—they constitute it. The act of projection and the act of building are not independent stages, but one single proposal within a total structure.

—Jorge Glusberg

THE ARCHITECTS COLLABORATIVE (TAC).

Partnership; established, Cambridge, Massachusetts, 1945, by Walter Gropius, *q.v.*, Norman Fletcher, Jean Fletcher, John Harkness, Sarah Pillsbury Harkness, Robert MacMillan, Louis McMillen, and Benjamin Thompson, *q.v.*; TAC International established in 1960; TAC Incorporated, 1964. Current Principals: Norman Fletcher, John Harkness, Sarah Pillsbury Harkness, Louis McMillen, and Alex Cvijanovic, Roland Kluver, John F. Hayes, Peter W. Morton, Leonard Notkin, Richard Brooker, James E. Burlage, Howard F. Elkus, H. Morse Payne, Perry K. Neubauer, Walter Rosenfeld, Jr., Richard A. Sabin, John P. Sheehy, David G. Sheffield, and H. Malcolm Ticknor. Recipient: Boston Arts Festival Award, 1954, 1956, 1959, 1960, 1963, 1964; Parker Medal, Boston Society of Architects, 1961, 1973, 1978; American Institute of Architects Award, 1964, 1966, 1967, 1970, 1971, 1972, 1974, 1976, 1977, 1978, 1979; Prestressed Concrete Institute Award, 1966, 1983; American Society of Landscape Architects Award, 1967; United States Department of Housing and Urban Development Award, 1968; American Concrete Institute Award, 1972, 1984; United States General Services Administration Award, 1973; First Prize, Johns Manville Building Competition, Colorado, 1973; Connecticut Society of Architects Award, 1974; First Prize, Arab Investment Company Building Competition, 1976; First Prize, Abu Dhabi Library Competition, 1976; American Institute of Steel Construction Award, 1979; Energy Conservation Award, Owens-Corning Fiberglas Corporation, 1982; Passive Solar Design Award, 1982; White House Citation, United States Department of Consumer Affairs, 1983; Concrete Industry Board of New York Prize, 1984. Addresses: 46 Brattle Street, Cambridge, Massachusetts 02138; 639 Front Street, San Francisco, California 94111, U.S.A.

Works:

1946 Ryan House, Cambridge, Massachusetts
Poppleton House, Dayton, Ohio
Lexington Nursery School, Massachusetts (project)
Skiing hut, Franconia, New Hampshire (project)
Library, Willimantic, Connecticut (project)
Kaplan House, Newton, Massachusetts
Usiskin House, Long Island, New York (project)
1947 Brockelman House, Worcester, Massachusetts
Neil House, Andover, Massachusetts
Wolfers House, Maine
Peter House, Cape Cod, Massachusetts
Catheron House, Foxboro, Massachusetts
Heywood House reconstruction, Maine
Town plan for Michael Reese Hospital, Chicago
1948 Hua Tung University, Shanghai, China (project)
Peter Thacher Junior High School, Attleboro, Massachusetts
Lawrence House, Lexington, Massachusetts
McMahon House, Lexington, Massachusetts
House, Providence, Rhode Island

England House, Pittsfield, Massachusetts
Howlett House, Belmont, Massachusetts
Elementary school, Sherborn, Massachusetts (project)
1949 Pillsbury House, Rumford, Rhode Island
Field House, Cape Cod, Massachusett
Graduate Center, Harvard University, Cambridge, Massachusetts (with Brown, Lawford and Forbes)
1950 Park buildings, Lexington, Massachusetts
Apthorp House, Concord, Massachusetts
Hechinger House, Washington, D.C.
England House, Washington, D.C.
Napoli House, Concord, Massachusetts
Theatre, New Rochelle, New York (project)
Medical center, Mt. Kisco, New York (project)
Barnes House reconstruction, Belmont, Massachusetts (project)
1950/
65 Dormitory (Boylston, Emerson, Fay) alterations, Harvard University, Cambridge, Massachusetts
1951 Business school, Attleboro, Massachusetts
Burncoat Secondary and Senior Schools, Worcester, Massachusetts (with A. Johnson)
Pillsbury House, Milton, Massachusetts
Vischer House furniture, Indiana
Vannah House, Foxboro, Massachusetts
Stichweh House, Hanover, Massachusetts
Elementary and secondary schools, Amesbury, Massachusetts (project)
Donelly Bureau reconstruction, Boston (project)
Bradley House (project)
Housing and Home Finance Agency Headquarters, San Jose, Costa Rica (project)
Wasco Flashing Corporation, Cambridge, Massachusetts (project)
Five Fields Housing Complex, Lexington, Massachusetts
Houses, Lake Barcroft, Falls Church, Virginia
American University Office Building, Washington, D.C. (project)
Mulcahey Elementary School, Taunton, Massachusetts
Pilgrim Park Elementary School, Warwick, Rhode Island
Elementary school, Providence, Rhode Island
Senior school, Concord, New Hampshire
American Association for the Advancement of Science Office Building, Washington, D.C.
Shops, for the Hechinger Company, Falls Church and Alexandria, Virginia
Designs/models for school and college furniture for the Thonet Factory
Cole House, Cambridge, Massachusetts
Baruch House, Newton, Massachusetts
Lang house, Newton, Massachusetts
Elementary school, Cambridge, Massachusetts
Elementary school, North Adams, Massachusetts
Caulfield House reconstruction, Washington, D.C.
1953 McCormick and Company Office Building, Chicago
Wherry District Housing, for the United States Navy, Quonset, Rhode Island
Back Bay Center, Boston (with Pietro Belluschi, Carl Koch, Hugh Stubbins, and Walter Bogner)
National Education Association Building (project)
Burke House, Center Harbour, New York
1954 Flagg Street Elementary School, Worcester, Massachusetts (with A. Roy)
Shopping center, Saugus, Massachusetts (with Ketchum, Gind and Sharp)
Overholt Thoracic Clinic, Boston
1955 Elementary school, Waltham, Massachusetts
Secondary school, Attleboro, Massachusetts

1956 Elementary school, West Bridgewater, Massachusetts
Housing at Otis Air Force Base, Falmouth, Massachusetts
United States Embassy, Athens
1957 Oheb Shalom Temple, Baltimore
Littleton Junior-Senior High School, Massachusetts
Pioneer Valley Regional High School, Northfield, Massachusetts
1958 William F. Pollard Junior High School, Needham, Massachusetts
Elementary school, Stoughton, Massachusetts
Dormitories, for Phillips Academy, Andover, Massachusetts
Reyim Synagogue, Newton, Massachusetts
Boylston Hall, Harvard University, Cambridge, Massachusetts
Murchison House, Provincetown, Massachusetts
Pan American Building, New York (as consultant architects; with Pietro Belluschi, on plan of Emery Roth and Sons)
Jewish Community Center, Hartford, Connecticut
1959 Elementary school, Acton, Massachusetts
Britz-Buckow-Rudow Settlement, West Berlin (project)
Apartment block, Hansa District, Berlin
Hollis Hall, Harvard University, Cambridge, Massachusetts
Shiffman Humanities Center and Olin-Sang American Civilization Center, Harvard University, Cambridge, Massachusetts
Putterham Branch Library, Brookline, Massachusetts
Academic Quadrangle, Brandeis University, Waltham, Massachusetts
1960 L.G. Hanscom Field Elementary School, Lincoln, Massachusetts
Elementary school additions, Kingston, Massachusetts
Dormitories, Brandeis University, Waltham, Massachusetts
Northeast Elementary School, Waltham, Massachusetts
East Hills, Pittsburgh (with Carl Koch and Sert, Jackson)
Gould Hospital, Presque Isle, Maine
Parkside Elementary School, Columbus, Indiana
Hoffman Laboratory of Experimental Geology, Harvard University, Cambridge, Massachusetts
Chase Manhatten Bank, Great Neck, Long Island, New York
Hemoglobin Laboratory alterations, Children's Hospital Medical Center, Boston
1961 Levi Warren High School additions, Newton, Massachusetts
Peter Bent Brigham Hospital, Boston
School of Law, Economics and Business Administration, University of Tunis
1961/
73 Wayland High School, Massachusetts
1962 Mount Kisco Elementary School, New York
McCann Regional Vocational High School, North Adams, Massachusetts
Thomas M. Evans Science Building, Arts and Communications Center, George Washington Hall alterations, Sylvia Pratt Kemper Memorial Chapel, and Copley addition to the Oliver Wendell Homes Library, Phillips Academy, Andover, Massachusetts
Julia L. McCarthy Elementary School additions, Acton, Massachusetts
New Trier Township High School, Winnetka, Illinois
IBM Federal Systems Division, Gaithersburg, Maryland
1963 Higher Teacher Training College, Bamako, Mali
Mount Kisco Middle School, New York

Development plan for the Moses Brown School, Providence, Rhode Island

Air-Supported Athletics Facilities, Forman School, Litchfield, Connecticut

St. George's School, Newport, Rhode Island

Pound Ridge Elementary School additions, New York

1964 Britz-Buckow-Rudow Center, West Berlin (project)

Schofield Elementary School, Wellesley, Massachusetts

Lexington High School, Massachusetts

Dormitory and Commons Building Quadrangle, Clark University, Worcester, Massachusetts

Bennington Regional High School, Vermont

North Bennington Fire House, Vermont

Master plan for Redwood Shores, Redwood City, California

Development plan for four state parks in West Virginia

1965 Rosenthal China Factory, Selb, Germany

Master plan for a university at Mosul, Iraq

Clinical Research Center alterations, Children's Hospital Medical Center, Boston

Redwood Shores Community Development, Redwood City, California

Development plan and additional buildings, Eaglebrook School, Deerfield, Massachusetts

Plan for Abbott Academy, Andover, Massachusetts

Chelmsford Junior High School, Massachusetts

YMCA Building, Warren Street and Washington Park Boulevard, Boston

1965/
72 Development plan for the Virginia Polytechnic Institute, Blacksburg

1966 Concord Junior High School, Massachusetts

Faculty Tower, University of Baghdad

Higher Teacher Training College, Kano, Nigeria

Greylock Residential Houses, Williams College, Williamstown, Massachusetts

Jewish Community Center, Worcester, Massachusetts

YMCA Building, Roxbury, Massachusetts

Beveridge Hall additions, Mount Hermon School, Massachusetts

Gymnasium and Swimming Pool, Northfield School, Massachusetts (project)

Multi-Purpose Dormitory Building, Rensselaer Polytechnic Institute, Troy, New York

New Trier West High School, Winnetka, Illinois (with Perkins and Will)

Fox Lane Middle School, Bedford, New York

McFarland Elementary School additions, Chelmsford, Massachusetts

Plum Cove Elementary School, Gloucester, Massachusetts

TAC Office Building, Cambridge, Massachusetts

1966/
76 Blue Hills Regional Vocational High School, Canton, Massachusetts

1967 Experimental buildings for a primary and secondary school at Britz-Buckow-Rudow, West Berlin

Huntington Art Gallery addition, West Virginia

Tower East Office and Commercial Building, Shaker Heights, Ohio

Rosenthal Glassworks, Amberg, West Germany

Town plan for Selb, Germany

East Greenwich High School, Rhode Island

Camp Hill Auditorium alterations, Mount Hermon School, Massachusetts

1968 Kennedy Federal Building, Civic Center, Boston

Development plan for Butler University, Indianapolis

Boys Club of Boston, Warren and Cliff Streets, Roxbury, Massachusetts

Freshmen Dormitory, Rensselar Polytechnic Institute, Troy, New York

Weston High School, Massachusetts

School and Child Day Care Center, Gropiusstadt, West Berlin

Westborough Senior High School, Massachusetts

Children's Inn, Children's Hospital Medical Center, Boston

1969 Hillside Elementary School, Needham, Massachusetts

TAC Office Building additions, Cambridge, Massachusetts

Maple Road Elementary School, Chelmsford, Massachusetts

Biology, Geology and Education Building, Virginia Polytechnic Institute, Blacksburg

IBM Space Systems Center, Gaithersburg, Maryland

Chott Maria Agricultural School, Sousse, Tunisia

Optics and Space Guidance Laboratories,

The Architects Collaborative: Johns-Manville Company World Headquarters, Jefferson County, Colorado, 1976.

NASA Electronics Center, Cambridge, Massachusetts

Composite Medical Facility, Otis Air Force Base, Falmouth, Massachusetts (project)

1970 Chelmsford High School, Massachusetts

Marshfield High School additions, Massachusetts

Peabody School, Concord, Massachusetts

Emerson School additions, Edgartown, Massachusetts

James L. Hanley Education Center, Providence, Rhode Island

Vocational School additions, Providence, Rhode Island

Teaneck Educational Complex, New Jersey (project)

Macgregor House (dormitory), Massachusetts Institute of Technology, Cambridge

Faculty and Classroom Buildings, University of Tunis

Research Buildings, National Institute of Child Health, Bethesda, Maryland (project)

Development plan for Dickinson College, Carlisle, Pennsylvania

Graduate School of Dentistry, Boston University Medical Center

Office and Computer Building, Massachusetts Hospital Association Headquarters, Burlington

1970/
74 Teaching and Research Buildings alterations, Harvard Medical School, Boston

1971 Parking Garage, New England Deaconess Hospital, Boston

Nauset Regional High School, Eastham, Massachusetts

Norwalk Senior High School, Connecticut

Expansion plan for Worcester Academy, Massachusetts

Anita Tuvin Schlechter Auditorium and Arts Center, Dickinson College, Carlisle, Pennsylvania

Jewish Community Center, Wilmington, Delaware

Central Veterinary Laboratory, Sotuba, Mali

Roxse Housing Development, Roxbury, Massachusetts

Khamis Mushayt Hospital, Saudi Arabia

Tabuk Hospital, Saudi Arabia

Basic Paediatric Research Laboratory, Children's Hospital Medical Center, Boston

Park Plaza, Boston (project)

Waterfront Parcel A-6 Commercial Development, Boston (project)

1972 Church Park Apartments, Boston

Museum of Comparative Zoology, Harvard University, Cambridge, Massachusetts

Powder House Community Elementary School, Somerville, Massachusetts

Tufts/New England Medical Center, Boston

Electrical and Industrial Engineering Building, Virginia Polytechnic Institute, Blacksburg

Second House (dormitory), Massachusetts Institute of Technology, Cambridge (project)

Development plan for Southern Illinois University, Edwardsville

research Laboratories and Animal Quarters Building, Harvard Medical School, Boston

Nursing and Allied Health Sciences Building, University of Vermont Medical School, Burlington

1973 Weston Middle School, Connecticut

Women's Dormitory, Virginia Polytechnic Institute, Blacksburg

IBM Components Building, East Fishkill, New York

Development plan for the United States Military Academy, West Point, New York

Plan for development of tourism in Jaz Valley, Budva, Yugoslavia

Walden Square Housing Development, Cambridge, Massachusetts

Fenway Housing for the Elderly, Boston

Amathus Hotel, Limassol, Cyprus

El Tropicana Hotel, Panama City (project)

Proger Health Services Buildings, and Dental Health Sciences Buildings, Tufts/New England Medical Center, Boston

American Institute of Architects Headquarters, 1735 Pennsylvania Avenue N.W., Washington, D.C.

Ely Park Housing, Binghamton, New York

Health Services Complex, University of Minnesota, Minneapolis

Crown Center, Kansas City, Missouri

1974 Norwell High School, Massachusetts

No. 6 Dormitory alterations, Groton School, Massachusetts

South Station conversion to an Arena, Boston (project)

Maine Medical Center, Portland

Maineway Plaza, Portland (project)

Temple Israel, Boston

Sterling and Francince Clark Art Institute, Williamstown, Masachusetts (with Pietro Belluschi)

Coram Library, Bates College, Lewiston, Maine

1974/
79 Development plan for the Capitol Center, Tallahasse, Florida

1975 Angelo Patri School (Bronx Intermediate School 137), 2225 Webster Avenue, Bronx, New York

Pre-fabricated school, Kuwait City

Wolcott House voncersion, Milton Academy, Massachusetts

Audubon New Community Development, phase 1, Amherst, New York

Echelon Office Building, New Jersey

Tourism development study for the Republic of the Philippines

Classroom and Office Buildings, Southern Illinois University, Edwardsville

Health and Physical Education Building, Virginia Polytechnic Institute, Blacksburg

Radiology and Surgery Department extensions, Children's Hospital Medical Center, Boston

Clinical Laboratory, New England Deaconess Hospital, Boston

Shawmut Bank Headquarters, 67 Milk Street, Boston

1976 Foster Gallery of Contemporary Art, Boston

Quincy Elementary School, Boston

Lincoln Park Community School, Somerville, Massachusetts

School of Nursing, New England Deaconess Hospital, Boston

Union Hospital, Lynn, Massachusetts

Johns-Manville World Headquarters, Jefferson County, Colorado

Charleston Savings Bank, Boston

Maine State Office Building, Augusta

Hotel Bernardin Resort Complex, Piran, Yugoslavia

Radiation Therapy Building, New England Deaconess Hospital, Boston

Nos. 1-4 Dormitory Units alterations, Groton School, Massachusetts

Forbes House conversion to Student Residences, Milton Academy, Massachusetts

1977 Seeley Mudd and Biochemical Research Buildings, Harvard Medical School, Boston

St. Mary's Hospital entensions and alterations, Kansas City, Missouri

Fiduciary Trust Building, Boston

Athletics Facilities extensions, Harvard University, Cambridge, Massachusetts

Visual Arts Instructional Facility, State University College of New York at Purchase

Building and Grounds Center, and Goodwin House, Milton Academy, Massachusetts

1978 Friends Community, North Easton, Massachusetts

Porto Carras Tourist Resort, Sithonia, Greece

Sheraton Hotel additions, Kuwait City

Holyoke Revitalization Plan (Heritage State Park), Masachusetts (project)

Environmental impact study of Route 44, Plymouth, Massachusetts

Plan for Smith College, Northampton, Massachusetts

Kuwait Fund Office Building, Kuwait City

Arab Investment Company Headquarters, Riyadh, Saudi Arabia (competition project)

Academic Center, Boston University (project)

Tourist development study of Contadora Island, Panama

Pine Cay Resort Development, Turks and Caicos Islands, West Indies

Tennessee Valley Authority Headquarters, Chattanooga (project)

Sheraton Hotel, Baghdad

Jewish/Hillside Medical Center, New Hyde Park, New York

Amoskeag Bank, Manchester, New Hampshire

Institute of Public Administration, Riyadh, Saudi Arabia

Performing Arts Building, Virginia Commonwealth University, Richmond

Ainsworth Gymnasium, Smith College, Northampton, Massachusetts

Physical Education Building, Bates College, Lewiston, Maine (project)

Athletics Facilities, United States Military Academy, West Point, New York (project)

Auditorium, University of Baghdad

Primary Care Center, University of Virginia, Charlottesville

Sheraton Hotel, Basra, Iraq

1979 Tourist development study for the Republic of Ireland

Hotel Inter-Continental, Sharjah, United Arab Emirates

Petra Historical Site Development, Jordan

Jerash Historical Site Development, Jordan

Intensive Care Unit, Children's Hospital Medical Center, Boston

New York State Veterans Home, Oxford, New York

Corning YMCA Building conversion, New York

Government Ministerial Office Building, Bahrain

South Station Transportation Center, Boston

1980 IBM Building, Sterling Forest, New York

Meredith Corporation Headquarters, Des Moines, Iowa

Abu Dhabi National Library and Cultural Center

Two Thousand Housing Units, Baghdad, Iraq

Blue Cross/Blue Shield Headquarters, New Haven, Connecticut

Kuwait Foundation for the Advancement of Science, Kuwait City, United Arab Emirates

LIJ Hillside Medical Center and Parking Structure, New Hyde Park, New York

Yanbu Housing Community, Saudi Arabia

Fine Arts Department Project, Bates College, Lewiston, Maine

Copley Place Central Area, Boston

Westin Hotel, Copley Place, Boston

Friends Community, phase III, North Easton, Massachusetts

Indonesian Embassy, Washington, D.C.

Johnson Wax Office Building and Parking Facility, Racine, Wisconsin

Kuwait News Agency, Kuwait City, United Arab Emirates

Maine National Bank renovations, Portland, Maine

Medical Office Building, St. Joseph's Hospital, Tampa, Florida

Parking Garage, St. Joseph's Hospital, Tampa, Florida

Faculty Housing, University of Baghdad, Iraq

Veterans Administration Medical Center,

West Roxbury, Massachusetts
Yanbu Community Facilities, Saudi Arabia
1981 National Institute of Electricity and Electronics, Tlemcen, Algeria
School of Natural Resources, University of Vermont Medical School, Burlington
Theatre, Hotel, and Parking Development, Copley Place, Boston
St. Francis/St. George Hospital, Cincinnati, Ohio
Western Pennsylvania Hospital, Pittsburgh
Mosul Five-Star Hotel, Mosul, Iraq
Hospital and Parking Garage, Temple University, Philadelphia
University of Baghdad extension, Iraq
Bell Laboratories Telecommunications Facility, Freehold, New Jersey
Khulafa Street Redevelopment, Baghdad, Iraq
Maidan Square Transportation Center, Baghdad, Iraq
Department of Education Building, Tallahassee, Florida
10.P Clinic, Veterans Administration Medical Center, Boston
Reader's Library, University of Virginia, Charlottesville
Wang Laboratory, Dublin, Ireland
Bering Office Tower, Houston, Texas
1982 Central National Museum, Riyadh, Suadi Arabia
Composite Medical Facility, Loring Air Force Base, Limestone, Maine
National Union Hotel, Limassol, Cyprus
United States Post Office General Mail Facility, Springfield, Massachusetts
University of Southern Florida Library, Sarasota
Beechwood Ohio Office Complex, Cleveland, Ohio
Cabot Corporation Conference Center, Billerica, Massachusetts
North Shore Community College, Beverly, Massachusetts
Community Cancer Center, St. Joseph's Hospital, Tampa, Florida
1983 Bapst Library renovations, Boston College, Chestnut Hill, Massachusetts
Bahrain Exhibition and Conference Center, Bahrain
Athletic Facility, Cornell University, Ithaca, New York
Twenty-First Century Laboratory, Oklahoma State University, Stillwater
Mixed-Use Offices, Union Square, San Francisco
Washington College Master Plan, Chesterfield, Maryland
New England Telephone Headquarters, Burlington, Vermont
Sharp American Corporation United States Headquarters, Mahway, New Jersey
South Bluffs Development, Memphis, Tennessee
1984 Aberthaw-Hudson Office Building, Hudson, Massachusetts
Arlington-Hadassah Mixed-Use Complex, Boston
Fine Arts Center, Bates College, Lewiston, Maine
Student Union, Florida State University, Tallahassee
Metropolitan Executive Conference Center, Marlborough, Massachusetts
Ministry of Public Works Headquarters, Kuwait City, United Arab Emirates
Shattuck Office Park, Andover, Massachusetts
Sweetbrook Nursing Home expansion, Williamstown, Massachusetts
Combs Cancer Research Building, University of Kentucky, Lexington
Business School, Virginia Polytechnic Institute, Blacksburg

Town Center Multi-Use Complex, Walnut Creek, California
Ingalls Associates Headquarters, Boston

Publications:

By TAC: books—*Town Plan for the Development of Selb* by Walter Gropius and TAC, Cambridge, Massachusetts 1970; *A Design Manual for Parking Garages* by Sergio Brizzi and TAC Graphics, Cambridge, Massachusetts 1975; *Streets: A Program to Develop Awareness of the Street Environment*, Boston 1976; *Building Without Barriers for the Disabled* by Sarah P. Harkness and James N. Groom Jr., New York 1976.

On TAC: books—*The Architects Collaborative 1945-1965*, edited by Walter Gropius and others, Teufel, Switzerland, 1966; *The Architects Collaborative Inc: TAC 1945-1972*, Barcelona 1972; Articles—"The Architects Collaborative" in *Arts and Architecture* (Los Angeles), August 1946; "The Architects Collaborative" in *Baukunst und Werkform* (Nuremberg), vol. 10, 1957; "Genetrix: Personal Contributions to American Architecture" in *Architectural Review* (London), May 1957; "The Architects Collaborative" in *Architectural Record* (New York), April 1959; "Gropius e TAC: Lavori Recenti" by Clifford H. Morse and Mario Brunati in *Casabella* (Milan), September 1967; "Unity Within Diversity" by Jane Holtz Kay in *Building Design* (London), 18 October 1974; "The Architects Collaborative: Recent Works" in *Architecture + Urbanism* (Tokyo), July 1978; "Bold Discretions: The Work of TAC Interiors" by David Morton in *Progressive Architecture* (New York), September 1978; "Factory in Which Light and Air Were Formgivers" in *AIA Journal* (Washington, D.C.), September 1979; "More Than Just Energy" in *Progressive Architecture* (New York), April 1980; "Berlin 1980: Bauhaus-Archive" in *Ottagono* (Milan), June 1980; "Community School Design" in *The Architects' Journal* (London), 13 August 1980; "Ainsworth Gymnasium at Smith College" in *Architectural Record* (New York), September 1980; "TAC: The Heritage of Walter Gropius", special issue of *Process: Architecture* (Tokyo), October 1980; "In the Centre of Downtown Boston" in *Architectural Record* (New York), July 1981; "Evaluation—Relic of Sixties Strategies" in *AIA Journal* (Washington, D.C.), May 1982; "The DC Compound" in *Progressive Architecture* (New York), October 1983; "Lighting Strategies: Case Study—TAC's CIGNA Office Building, Bloomfield, Connecticut" in *Architecture* (Washington, D.C.), October 1984.

Bibliography: *The Architects Collaborative (TAC): A Bibliography of Books and Articles, 1945-83* by Edward Teague, Monticello, Illinois 1984.

"By synchronizing all individual efforts, the team can raise its integrated work to higher potentials than is represented by the sum of the work of just so many individuals." (Walter Gropius, 1945).

With this statement as a guiding principle, the eight founding partners of TAC recognized at the outset in 1945 that the complex problems facing the profession made the collaborative process essential. Not merely an assemblance of a team of specialist, collaboration is an attitude about how people should work together and toward what ends. The process goes on within an organizational structure that evolved and continues to evolve in response to new needs

Essential to the structure is a weekly meeting of TAC's Board of Directors to decide business policy and to review work in progress. Policy decisions rely heavily upon recommendations from consultive and research committees, and the decisions that emerge

from the weekly meetings are complemented through the office of the President.

Equally essential to TAC's approach is the firm's division into teams varying in number and composition—each working on a specific project. The intimate character of these semi-autonomous groups, headed by senior members of the firm, avoids the anonymity of persons and designs often associated with larger scale.

All projects receive review through the weekly meetings of principals and associates. In order to preserve the artistic integrity of the team, criticisms with respect to design are not binding, but the responsible give and take within these sessions clarifies and broadens the vision of the team members. Collaboration extends as well into work with other firms such as engineers and specialists in the fields of education, health, acoustics and transportation.

It was from a sense of urgency to solve problems on a larger scale that TAC grew from a firm of eight partners to an office of over two hundred. Had the group remained small, it would have been barred from participation in today's major problems of health, education, and urban design whose solutions require the creative resources of many people. Moreover, the system of teams makes it possible to continue giving problems of smaller scale the same degree of personal attention and involvement

A mutual respect for each other's interests over the years has led to a wide variety of work, both in this country and abroad. This same breadth of interests will characterize TAC's future work as well. Through all changes, it is intended that the spirit that guides this practice be continuous and reflect itself in a physical environment which advances the quality of human life.

—The Architects Collaborative

The original nucleus of The Architects Collaborative was Walter Gropius, then Chairman of the Department of Architecture at Harvard University, who believed in the beneficial and even mandatory nature of team effort in the architectural profession. The theoretical tone inherent in this advocacy of collaborative effort finds a direct correspondence in the polemics of Gestalt philosophy, which was pervasive in Western Europe during the 1920s and 1930s; it also relates directly to the teaching methods that were established at the Bauhaus, where Gropius was director from 1919 to 1928. Gropius's participation in the initial development of TAC was integral to the creation of its general and continuing aesthetic philosophy, that the totality of a design is greater than the simple sum of its individual parts or creators.

TAC has grown from the original eight partners to a company of more than two hundred people. That growth was a response to the complexity, and size, of many modern design commissions. In turn, the company is now able to draw on the resources of what is now, in effect, a large, multi-disciplinary design organization. At the same time, and unlike some other firms, TAC has retained the original small team concept, making it possible for them to continue to give smaller scale works a high degree of responsible design input.

The idealism of this concept must, of course, become slightly modified in practice, for the economic demands in the operation of a large firm necessitate a very careful evaluation of smaller, less profitable ventures. And, as with all viable business structures in a capitalist society, TAC must make an effort to conduct a successful business venture and must often find it difficult to justify innovative theoretical directives at the risk of corporate profitability. The sheer size of the Collaborative, which gives the firm such a strong core of resources, may also tend to modify and compromise the conceptual and idealistic energy that is possible in more individual solutions.

There are, however, many positive gains. Within TAC, collaboration has aspired to be more than just an assemblance of a team of specialists; it involves an attitude about "group work" that is essentially creative, in that it continues to adapt itself, its methods and solutions, in response to new problems within a dynamic society. The team concept, too, involves both practicality and idealism: TAC teams are each different because each team is a response to a particular job, but each team is a reflection of TAC's attempt to preserve the individuality of persons and their work.

The concept of collaboration extends beyond the confines of the office to directly encompass all professions involved in a particular project. Certainly, the inclusion of engineers and construction-related groups is not unique to the architectural design process of this firm alone, but there is at TAC a professional ambition to be responsible to all peripheral and constituent design issues and to enhance the sensitivity, and skill, of designers by provoking constructive criticism from their associates.

The influence of Walter Gropius is obvious in TAC's approach to architecture as a search to appreciate the specific as it relates to the larger context and the individual as part of the collective, in a modern cultural environment the complexities of which necessitate collaboration and common method. Because of this philosophy and the success of their methods, and because they have denied an esoteric approach in their work in order to achieve a more general exposure, TAC has well designed a wide variety of buildings and dealt with a considerable range of problems. In particular, their interest in the social determinants of architecture has attracted many clients for housing, educational and social projects, not only in the Northeastern United States, but also, increasingly, throughout the world.

—S. Fiske Crowell, Jr.

THIRY, Paul.

American. Born in Nome, Alaska, 11 September 1904. Educated at the University of Washington, Seattle, under Carl Gould and Arthur Herrman, 1923-28 (Bobb and Gould Prize, 1926; Gladding McBean Prize, 1926; American Institute of Architects Medal, 1928), B.Arch. 1928; Ecole des Beaux-Arts, Fontainebleau, France, under Jacques Carlu and Victor Laloux, 1927, Dip.Arch. 1927. Married Mary Thomas in 1940; children: Paul Jr. and Pierre. In private architectural practice, Seattle, since 1929: Partner, Thirty and Shay, 1935-39; Partner, Jones, Bouillon, Thiry and Syliaasen, involved in war work in Seattle, Renton, Port Orchard, Tacoma and Hanford, Washington, and in Alaska, 1940-45; returned to private practice, 1945-71; since 1971, President of Thiry Architects Inc. Member, 1952-61, and Chairman, 1953-54, City of Seattle Planning Commission; Member of the Executive Board, Puget Sound Regional Planning Council, 1954-57; Member, 1956-61, and Vice-Chairman, 1958-61, United States Department of the Interior Historic American Buildings Survey Board; Member, President's Council on Pennsylvania Avenue, Washington, D.C., 1962-64; Member, 1963-75, and Vice-Chairman, 1972-75, National Capital Planning Commission; Member, John F. Kennedy Memorial Library Committee, Cambridge, Massachusetts, 1964; Member, United States Postmaster-General's Council for Research and Engineering, 1968-70; Architect-in-Residence, American Academy in Rome, 1969; Advisory Council Member, United States Peace Corps, 1982-84. Exhibitions: *World's Fair*, Brussels, 1958; *World's Fair*, New York, 1964; *Salon d'Art Sacré*, Musée d'Art Moderne, Paris, 1954; *National Gold Medal Exhibition*, Architectural League of New York, 1956; *Arquitectura Actual de America*, Madrid, 1965; Annual Exhibition, National Academy of Design, New York, 1968; *New American Architecture*, New Delhi, 1973. Recipient: Paul Bunyon Award, Seattle Chamber of Commerce, 1949; Distinguished Citizen in the Arts Award, Seattle City Council, 1962; Citation for Community Design, American Institute of Architects, 1965; American Iron and Steel Institute Award, 1965; American Institute of Steel Construction Award, 1965; Herbert Adams Medal, 1974, and Henry Hering Medal, 1976, National Sculpture Society; Certificate of Appreciation, United States Army Corps of Engineers, 1977; Outstanding Architecture and Engineering Award, Society of American Military Engineers, 1977; Outstanding Contribution Award, American Planning Association, Washington State Chapter, 1982; Seattle Chapter Medal, American Institute of Architects, 1984. Honorary Diploma, Colegio de Arquitectos, Santiago, Chile, 1965; D.F.A.: St. Martin's College, Olympia, Washington, 1970; D.F.A.: Lewis and Clark College, Portland, Oregon, 1979. Fellow, American Institute of Architects, 1951, and Chancellor of the College of Fellows, 1962-64; Member, Society of Architectural Historians (Director, 1967-70); Academician, National Academy of Design, 1967. Honorary Member, American Institute of Interior Designers, 1962, National Sculpture Society, 1963, and American Institute of Planners, 1975. Officier d'Académie, France, 1950. Address: Thiry Architects Inc., 800 Columbia Street, Seattle, Washington 98104, U.S.A.

Works

1930 Saint Edward Catholic Church, Shelton, Washington
1938 Catholic Archbishop's Chancery, Seattle
1940 A. S. Kerry House, Beaconfield, Washington
1940/
  44 Federal Public Housing Authority Projects, including 6,000 dwellings and appurtenant community facilities, shopping centers, schools, etc., Port Orchard, Washington (with Jones, Bouillon and Sylliaasen)
1940/
  48 Our Lady of the Lake Catholic Church and School, Seattle
1943/
  44 United States Navy Advance Base Depot, Tacoma, Washington (with Jones, Bouillon and Sylliaasen)
1944 Du Pont de Nemours Town Plan, Hanford, Washington (with Jones, Bouillon and Sylliaasen)
1945 Ceramics Kiln Building, University of Washington, Seattle
     Stimson Building, Salt Lake City, Utah
1947 I. F. Laucks House, Orcas Island, Washington
1947/
  67 Electrical Engineering Building, University of Washington, Seattle
1948 Botany Experimental Greenhouses, University of Washington, Seattle
1948/
  50 Christ the King Catholic Church and School, Seattle
1949 Dairy Plant Plan, Washington State University, Pullman
1950 Museum of History and Industry, Seattle
1950/
  58 Regents Hill Women's Residence, Washington State University, Pullman
1952 Charles and Emma Frye Museum, Seattle
1953 St. George Catholic Church and Friary, Seattle
1954 North East Branch Public Library, Seattle
     Powerhouse and Visitors Center, Chief Joseph Dam, Bridgeport, Washington
     United States Army Corps of Engineers Administration Building, Auburn General Depot, Washington
1955 Northgate Public Elementary School, Seattle

1956 St. Pius X Convent, Parish Hall and School, Mountlake Terrace, Washington
     Operational Training Building, McCord Air Force Base, Tacoma, Washington
1957 Washington State Library, Olympia
1957/
  62 *Century 21 Exposition*, Seattle (principal architect)
1958 Francis H. Brownell Jr. House, Seattle
     Cedar Park Public Elementary School, Seattle
     Haggard Hall of Science, West Washington University, Bellingham
     Naval and Marine Corps Reserve Training Center, Seattle, Washington
1959 State Capitol Campus Plan, Olympia, Washington
1960 Viking Center-Student Union Building, West Washington University, Bellingham
     First National Bank Pavilion, *Century 21 Exposition*, Seattle
     Corregidor/Bataan Plan, Philippines (competition project)
1961 Presbyterian Church and Center, Mercer Island, Washington
     State of Washington Theme Building, International Exhibit Building, and Entertainment Center Buildings, *Century 21 Exposition*, Seattle
     United States Embassy, Santiago, Chile
1962 Kalman Brauner House, Seattle
     Higginson Hall of Residence for Women, West Washington University, Bellingham
     Nalley Theater and Exhibition Building, and Ford Motor Company Pavilion, *Century 21 Exposition*, Seattle
     Seattle Center
     Libby Dam-Lake Koocanusa Project Comprehensive Plan, Libby, Montana
     Libby Dam, Powerhouse, Visitors Center and Facilities, Libby, Montana
1963 West Washington University Campus Plan, Bellingham
     Seattle Center Comprehensive Plan
1964 Seattle Center Coliseum
     Extension of the West Front of the United States Capitol, Washington, D.C. (as consultant)
1965 Vedanta Center Ramakrishna, Seattle
     Seattle Center Contemporary Arts Museum
     World War II Memorial, Utah Beach, France (as consultant)
1966 St. Demetrios Greek Orthodox Church and Center, Seattle
     Delta Upsilon Fraternity, University of Washington, Seattle
1966/
  68 National Capital Transit Agency, Washington, D.C. (as consultant)
1966/
  70 United States Department of Agriculture Building extension, Washington, D.C. (as consultant)
1967 St. Martin's College Campus Plan, Olympia, Washington
     Border Patrol Station, Spokane, Washington
     Border Patrol Station, Blaine, Washington
1967/
  72 Riverfront development, Spokane, Washington (as consultant)
1968 Aubrey Watzek Campus Library, Lewis and Clark College, Portland, Oregon
1968/
  74 Lewis and Clark College Campus Plan, Portland, Oregon
1969 Jewish Community Center, Mercer Island, Washington
     Agnes Flanagan College Chapel, Lewis and Clark College, Portland, Oregon
     4th Infantry Division Monument, Sainte Marie du Mont, France
     Burton Hall Men's Residence, St. Martin's College, Olympia, Washington
1970 Christ Episcopal Church, Tacoma, Washington

Paul Thiry: Seattle Center Coliseum, Washington, 1964.

1971 Hartsfeld Residence Buildings, and North-western School of Law, Lewis and Clark College, Portland, Oregon
Washington Mutual Savings Bank Headquarters, Seattle
1973 Biology-Psychology Center, Lewis and Clark College, Portland, Oregon
1975 Enlisted Men's Club, Naval Air Station, Whidbey Island, Washington
1978/
84 Libby Dam Reregulation Project, Libby, Montana (as consultant)
1979 Seattle First National Bank Seaboard/-Downtown Branch, Seattle, Washington
1982 Saint Demetrios Greek Orthodox Church Community Center, Seattle, Washington

Publications:

By THIRY: books—*Churches and Temples*, with R. Bennett and H. Kamphoefner, New York 1953; *Eskimo Artifacts*, with Mary Thiry, Seattle 1978; articles—"Architecture Today: A Symposium" in *Liturgical Arts* (New York), November 1950; "Call to Arms" in *AIA Journal* (Washington, D.C.), December 1954; "Contemporary Church Architecture" in *AIA Journal* (Washington, D.C.), October, 1955; "Esthetics and Architecture" in *AIA Journal* (Washington, D.C.), June 1956; "Progress Dilemma" in *AIA Journal* (Washington, D.C.), October 1956, and in *Pacific Architect and Builder* (Seattle), April 1957; "Total Design" in *AIA Journal* (Washington, D.C.), December 1959; "On Design" in *Pacific Architect and Builder* (Seattle), February 1961; "Unmemorial or in Memoriam" in *AIA Journal* (Washington, D.C.), March 1962; "Basic Needs of Cities" in *Tacoma News Tribune* (Tacoma, Washington), March 1962; "Washington in Transition" in *AIA Journal* (Washington, D.C.), January 1963; "There Are Many Ways to Create a Desert" in

Architectural Record (New York), May 1965; "Northwest Today" in *Seattle Post Intelligencer*, December 1965; "Our Cities Today: Chaos or Challenge?" in *AIA Journal* (Washington, D.C.), January 1966; "Water and the Environment" and "Architectural Treatment of Dams" in *Arts and Architecture* (Los Angeles), July 1967; "Libby Dam: An Engineer Talks Esthetics" in *AIA Journal* (Washington, D.C.), November 1968; "Planning of Washington as a Capital" in *AIA Journal* (Washington, D.C.), April 1974; Washington, D.C., The Capital" in the *Washington Post*, May 1974.

On THIRY: books—*Tomorrow's House* by Nelson and Wright, New York 1945; *Contemporary Church Art* by Anton Heinze, New York 1956; *Modern Church Architecture* by Christ-Janer and Foley, New York 1962; *Architecture in America* by G.E. Kidder Smith, New York 1976; articles—"The Work of Paul Thiry" in *Nuestra Arquitectura* (Buenos Aires), July 1949; articles in *Sinkentiku* (Tokyo), April 1956 and May 1956; "Profile III: Paul Thiry" by Robert E. Koehler in *Pacific Architect and Builder* (Seattle), February 1961; "Names: Paul Thiry FAIA" in *Architecture and Engineering News* (New York), November 1961; article in *Vitrum* (Milan), November 1963; "West Coast Architects IV: Paul Thiry" by Esther McCoy in *Arts and Architecture* (Los Angeles), January 1965; "Paul Thiry, Architect" by Robert Wilmsen in *Symposia* (Portland, Oregon), January 1965; "Una Capanna Sol Fiume" in *Abitare* (Milan), October 1965; "Seattle Center Coliseum" in *Vitrum* (Milan), October 1967; "Libby Dam to Wed Concrete and Esthetics" in *Engineering News Record* (New York), 14 August 1969; "Libby Dam Project" by Andrea O. Dean in *AIA Journal* (Washington, D.C.), April 1977; "Elements of Northwest Style" in *Pacific Northwest Magazine* (Seattle, Washington), March 1983; "Paul Thiry and the Emergence of Modernism in the Northwest" by Meredith Clausen in *Pacific Northwest Quarterly* (Tacoma, Washington), July 1984.

For the first time in the history of man we appear to be faced with an overwhelming urge to build everyplace and anywhere. This urge carries us far beyond the recognition of existing values or the correctness of what we do. We are overrun by those obsessed with the doctrine of progress, who find no place or thing immune from their immature judgement and unrestrained activities. Therefore, in a more practical and realistic way, it behoves us to study carefully the requirements of our day. We should do this with reference to the past and with consideration for the future. We must know one place is not the same as another. We need to know the difference between the wilderness, the rural, and the urban.

ARCHITECTURE
If there is to be physical and mental betterment on earth it most assuredly rests with the world of architecture to give direction and to take steps to lead the way. The world of architecture is a world of building and of planning. It is the privilege of the architect to provide man with environment. It is singularly his duty to look at situations objectively... because architecture is the direct result of man's occupation of space. It would seem significant that architecture is of prime importance to the life of man and that it is his inseparable companion, for surely without it, he reverts to the primitive state. We are faced with a new pace in architecture, one which does not reconcile itself with the past. It follows no historic pattern nor does it find compatibility in form or appearance with structures of our traditional inheritance. Inter-mixtures must be viewed with concern.

Architecture can no longer be merely plan and facade. It is necessary to go beyond, into the wide ranges of cause and effect of action and reaction, and into the reasons for force... more particularly, into counter-force. Today we need an architecture that is in itself counter-force, that extends on a vast scale to a comprehension of environment, both natural and man-made. As the pace quickens, the environmental equations change and methods of realization change with them. This change cannot be regarded as a salvation for old patterns. Opposed philosophies must be reconciled. Where the differences involve structure, a choice must be made.·

ARCHITECTURE: A CONTINUING PROCESS

Our greatness will be measured in how we meet the progress dilemma—the problem of preservation and exploitation—and how we cope with the apathetic and irresistible forces of destruction, which, strangely enough, move through construction. Others may toy with interplanetary travel and satellite substations in the stratosphere, but for the present let us make this a world of beauty and of order. Where we detract from nature let us add back twofold with human quality. Before us is the world as it is and before us is the world as it should be. Ours is the choice. To labor the day or to envision the morrow.

—Paul Thiry

The name of Paul Thiry is synonymous with Pacific Northwest architecture, although his influence in the field of design is far more than a regional matter. This "influence," for the most part, has never really received the recognition it deserves from his peers.

Since he began his practice in Seattle, fifty years ago, Thiry has matched his contributions to design with those to his profession, to his community and to his country. The latter are particularly noteworthy, for he was a Presidential appointee to the National Capital Planning Commission for a number of years, always doing his homework, flying from coast to coast for just about every meeting. A scholar and an historian, he has assembled what is probably one of the best private collections on the history of the nation's capital. He also was a Presidential appointee to the Peace Corps Advisory Board, serving from 1982 to 1984.

Often a champion of unpopular—and generally controversial—causes, Thiry has refused to remain silent on affairs of state that affected the environment, man-made or otherwise, whether they be on the home front in Seattle, where he has lived and practiced all his adult life, or on the West Front of the U.S. Capitol itself. More than one delegate to the national convention of the American Institute of Architects in 1966 remembers when he came to loggerheads with the establishment in what was virtually a one-man show, convincing the members on the floor to table a motion regarding the restoration of the West Front wall.

Thiry, to be sure, has mellowed over the years, but the truth of the matter is that while he often appeared to be a voice crying in the wilderness, he was found later to be speaking about the most feasible solution to the issue at hand.

Charles Dunshire, in a *Seattle Post-Intelligencer* editorial of December 14, 1984, referring to Thiry's appearance on a panel at the local AIA Chapter's Senior Council banquet, wrote: "He has been quiet in recent years, but he found his voice again one evening last week, and it was as assertive as ever." Dunshire went on: "Council President Fred Bassetti, in introducing his profession's local elder statesman, noted that Thiry in 1961 had advocated covering the downtown section of the freeway with a landscaped tier to bind up the municipal wound created by the superhighway, at what now seems the incredibly low cost of $2 million. Bassetti also credited Thiry with having advanced a plan for saving King County's Green River before, as Bassetti put it, 'it became covered with asphalt.'" Thiry then told his audience, "in no uncertain terms," that two current proposals were bothering him: the downtown convention center and the Metro bus tunnel beneath Third Avenue.

Thiry is as equally adroit as a writer as he is a speaker—and his interests are legion.

As for his architecture in general, Thiry has always maintained this basic concern: "buildings should be good neighbors." And so his have been—and still are. His Library for the Washington State Capitol in Olympia, while respecting the traditional forms already there, was expressed in a contemporary medium. An architectural innovator in a number of areas, he pioneered the use of prefabrication of parts, among them wood lamination, tilt-up concrete, and precast and prestressed concrete walls and trusses. His Christ the King Church in Seattle, 1948, was one of the first to place the congregation around the altar in a semicircle.

As principal architect for the *Century 21 Exposition* in Seattle in 1962, Thiry employed the same common sense approach that has been the trademark of his design career. What he wrote before the fair opened in 1962 was indeed to come true: "Century 21 is designed not only for the excitement of the moment, but many of its structures and facilities are planned as a permanent adjunct to a projected Seattle Center of lasting significance. . . . Seattle World's Fair will be a phoenix among fairs." Anyone who has visited the site—to attend an opera, a ballet, or a sporting event in Thiry's own Coliseum, which he designed as the theme structure—will attest that once again the architect was a prophet.

An evaluation of Thiry's work would be incomplete without a reference to Libby Dam in Montana, which one critic called "a powerful, respected work of architecture." For any Army Corps of Engineers project to have an architect involved from start to finish is almost inconceivable, and few but Thiry would have seen it through. But in visiting dams through the U.S.A., he found that the construction of most of them had disfigured natural surroundings and that many contained visually discordant and disconcerting architectural elements.

All of this echoes Thiry's philosophy when he wrote: "A building's form and relationship to its neighbors not only affects the visual aspects of the whole, but the ensemble reflects on the quality of the individual unit. Too often a nonconformance not only detracts from itself but also disfigures the total scene."

For his lifelong contributions, Thiry received the first American Institute of Architects Medal to be presented by the Seattle Chapter in 1985.

—Robert E. Koehler

THOM, Ronald James.

Canadian. Born in Penticton, British Columbia, 15 May 1923. Educated at the Vancouver School of Art, 1941-43, 1944-47, Dip.Art 1947. Served as a navigator in the Canadian Air Force, 1943-44. Married Molly Golby in 1963; children: Emma, Adam, and, from previous marriage, Robin, Sidney, Aaron and Bronwen. Joined Thompson, Berwick, Pratt and Partners, Vancouver, as an apprentice, 1947: Partner, 1958-63. Since 1963, Principal, Thom Partnership, Toronto. Director, Toronto Cultural Advisory Corporation, since 1974. Exhibitions: Royal Canadian Academy of Arts Travelling Exhibition, 1971; National Gallery of Canada, Ottawa, 1973; Institute for Theatre Technology Exhibition, Anaheim, California, 1975; Toronto City Hall, 1976; *Spectrum Canada,* Royal Canadian Academy of Arts Travelling Exhibition, 1976; University of Toronto School of Architecture, 1979; *Transformations in Modern Architecture,* Museum of Modern Art, New York, 1979. Collection: University of Calgary Archives, Alberta. Recipient: First Prize, Massey College Competition, Toronto, 1963; Massey Medal, 1963; Citations of Excellence (4), International College and University Conference and Exposition, Atlantic City, New Jersey, 791970; Design Award, Canadian Institute of Architects, Toronto Chapter, 1970; Merit Award, Canadian National Design Council, 1971; Canadian Housing Design Council Award, 1971; First Prize, for North America, Aluminium Building Products Design Competition, 1973; Award of Excellence, *Canadian Architect Yearbook,* 1974; Award of Merit, Ontario Masons' Relations Council Architectural Awards Programme, 1975; Award of Merit, Low Energy Building Design Awards, Public Works office of Canada, 1979; Design Award, Architectural Institute of British Columbia, 1982; Restoration Award of Excellence, *Canadian Architect Yearbook,* 1974; Award of Merit, Ontario Masons' Relations Council Architectural Awards Nova Scotia Technical College, Halifax, 1973. Associate, 1971, and Member, 1973, Royal Canadian Academy of Arts; Fellow, Royal Architectural Institute of Canada, 1973. Officer, Order of Canada, 1981. Address: The Thom Partnership, 47 Colborne Street, Suite 401, Toronto, Ontario M5E 1E3, Canada.

Works:

1963 Massey College, University of Toronto
1963/
71 Trent University, Peterborough, Ontario (temporary buildings: Catherine Parr College and Rubidge Hall, 1963-64; Master Plan, 1964; Champlain College, Lady Eaton College, Thomas J. Bata Library, Chemistry Building, and Reginald Faryon Bridge, 1964-71)
1967 Sir Sandford Fleming College, master plan and phase I, Peterborough and Lindsay Campuses, Ontario
Polymer Pavilion, *Expo '67,* Montreal
Pottow House, Toronto
Narod House, Vancouver
Sandwell House, Caledon, Ontario
Stewart House, Caledon, Ontario
1968 College Education Centre, North Bay, Ontario
Social Science Building, Queen's University, Kingston, Ontario
Master plan for the Civic Square, Hamilton, Ontario
1970 Shaw Festival Theatre, Niagara-on-the-Lake, Ontario
Sir Sandford Fleming College, phase II, Peterborough, Ontario
Frum House, Oxbow Avenue, Toronto
1971 Fraser House, Toronto
1972 Price Hotel, Don Mills, Ontario
Metropolitan Toronto Zoo, Scarborough, Ontario (with Clifford and Lawrie, and Crang and Boake)
1973 Home for the Aged, Picton, Ontario
The Thom Partnership Offices, 47 Colborne Street, Toronto
Ridpath's Store, Toronto
Goh House, King City, Ontario
Horne House, Caledon, Ontario
1974 Oakville Theatre, Oakville, Ontario
Sir Sandford Fleming College, phase II, Lindsay, Ontario
1976 Marathon Office Campus, Toronto
Mark Erin Homes, Mississauga, Ontario
Bayview-Finch Townhouses, Toronto
Market Square, Toronto
Bonnycastle House, Calgary, Alberta
1977 Confederation Square, Toronto (project)
Lester Pearson College of the Pacific, Pedder Bay, Vancouver (with Barry Downs)
Dodek Cottage, Roberts Creek, British Columbia
Crematorium, Montreal
Silverspring Apartments, Toronto
Summit Golf Club, Aurora, Ontario
Women's Cultural Centre, Toronto
Troumassee Hotel, St. Lucia, West Indies
1978 Transport Canada Training Institute, Cornwall, Ontario

Ryerson Architecture Building, Toronto
Sir Sandford Fleming College, phase III, Peterborough, Ontario
Convention Centre, Kitchener, Ontario
Creditview Housing, Mississauga, Ontario
1979 Chateau Laurier Hotel renovations, Ottawa
Burlington Hotel and Condominiums, Ontario
Deerfoot Business Centre, Calgary, Alberta
Prince Hotel, Toronto
Atria North Complex, Toronto
1980 Sir Stanford Fleming College, Frost Campus, Lindsay, Ontario
1981 St. Lawrence Non-Profit Housing, Toronto
1982 Office Building, 2 Confederation Square, Toronto
1983 St. Lawrence Centre for the Performing Arts, Toronto

Publications:

By THOM: book—*Exploring Toronto,* with others, Toronto 1972, 1973, 1974; articles—"Art Centre: A Critical Analysis" in *Canadian Architect* (Toronto), July 1963; "Toronto City Hall: A Critique" in *Canadian Architect* (Toronto), October 1965; "The Many-Headed Client" in *Canadian Architect* (Toronto), September 1966; "Voice" in *Canadian Architect* (Toronto), July 1970; "Comment: Freedom at a Price" in *Canadian Architect* (Toronto), August 1973; "Critique: George Brown College of Applied Arts and Technology, Toronto" in *Canadian Architect* (Toronto), March 1974; "Toward Design" in *Canadian Architect* (Toronto), September 1977.

On THOM: articles—"Architect Ron Thom Shapes a Mantle of Privacy for a Vigorous House" in *House Beautiful* (New York), September 1969; "Thomas J. Bata Library, Trent University" in *Canadian Architect* (Toronto), August 1971; "Progress Report: Metro Zoo, Toronto" in *Canadian Architect* (Toronto), October 1974; "New Theatres on the Niagara River" by Tony Coutade in *Theatre Design and Technology* (New York), Fall 1975; "Stahl" in *Baumeister* (Munich), April 1977; article in *Process: Architecture* (Tokyo/Pittsburgh), May 1978; "The Thom Partnership" in *Canadian Interiors* (Toronto), June 1979; "Metropolitan Toronto Zoo" in *Architecture + Urbanism* (Tokyo), September 1979; "Lester B. Pearson College" in *Summarios* (Buenos Aires), September/October 1979; "Atria North Office Complex, Toronto" in *Canadian Architect* (Toronto), February 1980; "Pauline McGibbon Cultural Centre, Toronto" in *Canadian Architect* (Toronto), April 1980; "The Atrium" in *Canadian Architect* (Toronto), July 1982; "Atrium Office Building in Toronto" in *Baumeister* (Munich), September 1982; "Roy Thomson Hall, Toronto" in *Canadian Architect* (Toronto), October 1982; "Reopened for Business: Toronto's Confederation Life Building" in *Canadian Heritage* (Toronto), October/November 1982; "Putting the Clock Back" in *Cue* (Faringdon, Oxfordshire), May/June 1983; "Remodelled Theatre" in *Canadian Architect* (Toronto), October 1983.

*

I see architecture as expression inevitably reflecting time, place, cultural mores and attitudes. This implies both conscious and unconscious expression, and it applies to good and bad architecture alike.

Consequently it has always been fairly easy to place very accurate dates on buildings and to be reasonably accurate about their roots.

This suggests that architects should consider architecture as a vehicle of expression that should reflect its raison d'etre.

In order to achieve this, the architect must be as aware as possible of any and all needs that the specific building is to serve. He must be prepared to listen. He must not "create" in his own vain vacuum and expect life to respond by adapting, even though life is forever showing itself capable of doing this. In most cases there need not be unresolvable conflicts between the priorities of the architect and those of users.

As cities increase in size and complexity there becomes a much greater overlapping of the various functions of living, and with that develops a growing interdependence of all the parts. Architects therefore must become increasingly aware of this fact of life, and become more willing than they have been in the past to be affected by conditions surrounding and beyond their immediate work.

Less and less does architecture exist in splendid isolation. Architecture must now recognize the need to assist the cohesiveness of the social fabric, and not be a contributor to mass chaos. To achieve this goal, a greater involvement with other disciplines and the willingness to accept their widsoms will be required of architects in the future than has been expected of them in the past. And this of course demands a change of attitude on the part of architectural educators.

There will also have to be changes in the area of public education as society more and more feels the effects of interdependence and as it becomes more and more a participatory society.

Ron Thom: Champlain College, Trent University, Peterborough, Ontario, 1964-71.

The media in all its forms must become much less oblivious to such a basic and all pervasive topic of life. Even though as a society we are largely visually illiterate, we are not immune to the effects of our created environment.

For all this, it must be said that architecture at its best still has the inherent power to celebrate the human functions it accommodates and that there is nothing to suggest that the new constraints that may come should impede the ability of architecture to extend and enrich life in our society.

—Ron Thom

Integrity is what characterises Ron Thom's work, not simply integrity of overall design but integrity to site and to extant buildings. Even such large projects as Trent University reflect a care for siting and topography on the one hand that is manifested on the other by a meticulous care for all the details of design work down to the cutlery and ashtrays. It is conventional to compare his work to that of Frank Lloyd Wright, but his care for detail has more in common with the work of Arne Jacobsen—as in Jacobsen's St. Catherine's in Oxford. Thom is less dogmatic than Wright; he has more respect for local materials and the quality of the life to be lived within his buildings. Massey College is not only (rightly) turned inward from a noisy intersection around a quiet and deceptively arranged quadrangle, but it is also broken up into many "houses," both to preserve intimacy and to reduce noise. Not all of the details of its construction are ideal; residents complain about the inflexibility of the fixtures, but fifteen years after its construction it shows the evidence of contented life—in its public rooms especially—that would be the envy of many other academic architects.

The use of brick with broken, pierced or recessed walls at Massey is characteristic of Thom's conviction that the architect is both activist and observer. He must, Thom believes, "be willing to make adjustments in his design until the architecture becomes a full expression of the life of which it is a part." Plainly, academic work, such as Massey, Trent, the Sir Sandford Fleming Colleges and the Lester Pearson College, is congenial to these aims. Its success is attested to by a student at Trent: "One is never conscious of its being architecture. The place works and is comfortable."

Thom's continuing affection for brick and cedar in such varied projects as the Fraser House, the Toronto Zoo, and the Shaw Festival Theatre is evidence of his West Coast roots, but it is of a piece with his concern for detail and site. And in the midst of the blank horror of much that is being built in Ontario, it is a welcome alternative. At Trent it is often overlooked that Thom not only incorporated local stone into the faceted walls of his building but also adapted old houses in the town with a genius and respect that is almost unheard of amongst contemporary renovators. And it is the same genius that he has brought to one of his recent projects, the development of Confederation Square in Toronto, where a Victorian office building is not only preserved but also restored and a new building attached to it, picking up its lines and reticulation.

—D.D.C. Chambers

THOMPSON, Benjamin.

American. Born in St. Paul, Minnesota, 3 July 1918. Educated at Yale University, New Haven, Connecticut, 1937-41, B.F.A. 1941. Served as a Lieutenant in the United States Navy, 1942-45. Married Mary Okes in 1942 (divorced, 1967); children: Deborah, Anthony, Marina, Nicholas and Benjamin Jr.; married Jane Fiske McCullough in 1969. Founder-Partner, TAC: The Architects Collaborative, Cambridge, Massachusetts, 1946-65; Founder and Chair-

man of the Board, Design Research International Inc., Cambridge, 1953-70. Since 1966, President, Benjamin Thompson and Associates, Cambridge. Chairman, Department of Architecture, Harvard University, Cambridge, 1963-68. Exhibition: *Three Architects at Williams College,* Williams College, Williamstown, Massachusetts 1976. Recipient: Honor Award, 1966, 1970, 1972, and First Honor Award, 1974, American Institute of Architects, New England; State Arts Award, Maine, 1967; Centennial Award, Wayne State University, Detroit, 1967; Library Buildings Award, AIA/American Library Association, 1968, 1974; Honor Award, national AIA, 1968, 1971, 1978; Harleston Parker Award, 1971, 1973, 1977, Neighborhood Housing Award, 1974, and Honor Award, 1977, Boston Society of Architects; President's Medal of Honor, Kirkland College, Clinton, New York, 1972; Award of Excellence, AIA, Western Massachusetts, 1974; Case Studies Award, *Urban Design,* 1977; Bartlett Award, AIA/President's Committee on Employment of the Handicapped, 1978; International Design Award, American Society of Interior Designers, 1978; Special Award, American Society of Landscape Architects, 1978. Address: Benjamin Thompson and Associates, One Story Steet, Cambridge, Massachusetts 02138, U.S.A.

Works:

With TAC—
1953 Burke House, Center Harbour, New York
1958 Boylston Hall, Harvard University, Cambridge, Massachusetts
1959 Hollis Hall, Harvard University, Cambridge, Massachusetts
 Academic Quadrangle, Brandeis University, Waltham, Massachusetts
1959/
 62 Sylvia Pratt Kemper Chapel, Science Building, Arts and Communications Center, and Oliver Wendell Holmes Library, Phillips Academy, Andover, Massachusetts
1960 Chase Manhattan Bank, Great Neck, Long Island, New York
 Dormitories, Brandeis University, Waltham, Massachusetts
1964 North Bennington Fire House, Vermont
1965 Abbott Academy, Andover, Massachusetts (planning only)
1966 Greylock Residential Houses, Williams College, Williamstown, Massachusetts

With Benjamin Thompson and Associates—
1966 Nathan Hale Dormitory, Phillips Academy, Andover, Massachusetts
 Master plan for the new campus of Kirkland College, Clinton, New York
 Heller Buildings, Brandeis University, Waltham, Massachusetts
1967 Rabb Graduate Center and Lown Building, Brandeis University, Waltham, Massachusetts
 Dormitories and Fraternity Building, Colby College, Waterville, Maine
 Mount Anthony Union High School, Bennington, Vermont
1968 Bronfman Science Center, Williams College, Williamstown, Massachusetts
 Music Building and Buckley Recital Hall, Amherst College, Massachusetts
1969 Design Research Headquarters, Cambridge, Massachusetts
1970 Faculty Office Building and Classroom/Administration Building, Harvard Law School, Cambridge, Massachusetts
 Coolidge Bank and Trust Building, Watertown, Massachusetts
1971 New Co-Educational Facility (school conversion), St. Paul Academy, Minnesota
 Plumley Village East Housing Community, Worcester, Massachusetts

1972 J.P. Holland School, Dorcester, Massachusetts
 Berkshire Community College, Pittsfield, Massachusetts
 Gutman Library and Research Center, Harvard University, Cambridge, Massachusetts
 Campus Plan, Academic facilities and Dormitories, Kirkland College, Clinton, New York
1973 Housing program for the elderly, Cambridge, Massachusetts
1975 Cape Cod Bank and Trust Building, Hyannis, Massachusetts
1976 Soldiers Field Road Housing, Harvard University, Boston
1976/
 78 Faneuil Hall Market Place, Boston
1977 Alaska State Capital Competition Plan, Willow, Alaska (with Jonathan Barnett and M. Paul Friedberg)
1977/
 78 St. Anthony Main (restoration of riverfront district), Minneapolis
 Intercontinental Hotel Complex, Abu Dhabi, United Arab Emirates
 Law School, New York University, Washington Square, New York
1977/
 82 IBM Offices, Burlington, Vermont
1979 Intercontinental Hotel, Al Ain, United Arab Emirates
 St. Paul Academy and Summit School, St. Paul, Minnesota
 Department of Redevelopment and Alumni Affairs, Dartmouth College, Hanover, New Hampshire
1980 Harborplace Development, Baltimore, Maryland
1981 St. Anthony Main Mixed-use Development, Minneapolis
 Matep-Medical Area Total Energy Plant, Boston
 Service Center for the Medical Area Service Corporation, Boston
 National Fire Protection Association Building, Quincy, Massachusetts
 Opus 2 Office Center and Rauenhorst Corporate Headquarters, Minnetonka, Minnesota
1982 Strawbridge and Clothier Food Hall, Philadelphia
1983 Pavilion in the Old Post Office, Washington, D.C.
1983/
 84 South Street Seaport Museum, New Fulton Market, New York
1984 Hotel Semiramis Intercontinental, Cairo, Egypt
1985 Ordway Music Theater, St. Paul, Minnesota

Publications:

By THOMPSON: articles—in *The New Yorker,* 28 December 1963; "The Spirit of Sanity" in *Connection: Visual Arts at Harvard* (Cambridge, Massachusetts), February 1964; in *Interiors* (New York), June 1964; "Proposal for a Case Method System in Architectural Education" in *Indian Builder Annual* (New Delhi), 1965; "Questions Posed in the Harvard Yard" in *AIA Journal* (Washington, D.C.), April 1965; in *Interiors* (New York), July 1965; "An Interview with Benjamin Thompson" in *Interiors* (New York), November 1965; "An Architect Views His Environment" in *Architectural Record* (New York), January 1966; "Modern Not Monotonous—Let's Build a New Boston for the People" in the *Boston Globe,* 8 May 1966; "Design Research Story" in *Mobilia* (Cambridge, Massachusetts), September 1966; "Boston Is a Growing Thing" in the *Boston Globe,* 26 March 1967; "The World Around Us—Towards an Architecture of Joy and Human

Benjamin Thompson: New Fulton Market, New York, 1983-84.

Sensibility" in *Architectural Record* (New York), September 1967; "Visual Squalor and Social Disorder—A New Vision of the City of Man" in *Architectural Record* (New York), April 1969.

On THOMPSON: books—*Architects on Architecture,* edited by Paul Heyer, London 1967; *Three Architects at Williams College,* exhibition catalogue by John Stamper, Williamstown, Massachusetts 1976; articles—"Two College Libraries" in *Architectural Record* (New York), August 1974; "Harvest Restaurant, Cambridge" in *Contract Interiors* (New York), July 1977; "Building Types Study 510: The Case for Design Quality" in *Architectural Record* (New York), December 1977; "An Old Market Place Given New Life in Boston" in *AIA Journal* (Washington, D.C.), May 1978; "Building Types Study 527: Retail Malls" in *Architectural Record* (New York), February 1979; "Building Types Study 547: Four Resort Hotels" in *Architectural Record* (New York), July 1980; "The Pull of Pageantry" in *Interiors* (New York), September 1980; "Harborplace, Baltimore" in *Urban Design International* (Purchase, New York), November/December 1980; "Baltimore's Lively Downtown Lagoon" in *AIA Journal* (Washington, D.C.), June 1981; "Tod Inlet, Vancouver Island" in *Urban Design International* (Purchase, New York), July/August 1982.

*

When we come down from the clouds a meaningful architecture will be created in our time. When we come to grips with our present, there is a chance we will influence the future. Isolation is a terrible state, and architecture of the mountain top has no relevance. Buildings communicate when they connect to the meaningful flow of our own age. Architecture should reflect man's hope and faith, interpret life and transmit joy. The very act of building is a symbolic act of confidence.

We have only begun to recognize architecture's real importance and function in modern life. The space between buildings and the space within buildings may be more important than the photographable facades that preoccupy designers and critics alike. While many professionals continue to design for the static vision of the camera, others are beginning to realize that the dynamics of life and people, the nature of the whole human habitat, is our task. After all, we spend our lives in and around buildings, and, more than we know, our lives are shaped by their qualities—for better or worse.

—Benjamin Thompson

*

In part, it must come from the association with Gropius, but mostly the moral tone conveyed by Benjamin Thompson's architecture is a reflection of the character of the man. A cultural conservative, Thompson has strong faith in the power of architecture. In his writings, he bemoans the collapse of standards and the continual worsening of the American environment.

He was one of the TAC partners in charge of the Harvard Graduate Center built in Cambridge, Massachusetts in 1949, still the most convincing of all the Gropius work in America. What in the 1940s and 1950s was the most advanced of post-war Modernism in America later developed in the 1960s and 1970s with such calm and evolutionary consistency that its remarkable quality became lost in its unremarkable form. Thompson separated from the Collaborative in 1966, but his work remained faithful to its cause. Until the mid 1970s only two problems caused him to stretch his architecture principles into creating works of remarkable quality. The first was a literal showcase for a product design and marketing enterprise, "Design Research," founded by Thompson in 1953, reflecting a concern, as Gropius and Behrens had before him, not only with producing well designed buildings for working in but also with offering well designed products to serve them. (Thompson remained a Chairman of the company until 1970.) The second was the brilliant and theatrical redevelopment of the Faneuil Hall Marketplace, Boston, which revealed a too long hidden sensual and indulgent side to Thompson's nature.

The inventive contextualism of Faneuil Hall has been followed by similar events in Baltimore Harborplace, and in New York at the South Street Seaport. Harbor Place consists of pavilions whose form is ahistorical, but in terms of stage management, repeats the character of Quincy Market. In New York's South Steet, however, the Fulton Market and Pier 17 are wholly new objects whose nature derives from an extension of historical models. They are not selfconscious replications of past styles, rather they are sensitive reconstructions whose morphology in both language and materials distills the essence of past types. Fulton Market is a brick shed, a cheap 1920s brick shed, which gains great vitality from a generous undulating metal canopy suspended over the sidewalk on metal cables, rising on the corners with swaying swaggering grace. By such basic means, Thompson, echoes the mood and the public presence of nineteenth-century market buildings.

Similar qualities have been applied to the project for a market waterfront in Burlington, Vermont, in which, judged by the drawings, a convincing nineteenth-century narrative character will be established. In commercial work the results are undistinguishable from the mainstream of American practice, however, it is in his most recent public project that the measure of his significance can be gauged; the Ordway Music Theatre for St. Paul, Minnesota. A building which incorporates the most complex advances in theatre technology yet whose physical presence reveals the strengths and weaknesses of Thompson's perspective. It is undemonstrably modern. There is no concession to past style. It asymmetrically presents to the public square the faceted windows of the grand foyers. By day it is a rather anonymous, ungainly hulk, reminiscent of similar civic theaters in Germany and Scandinavia; in the evening the brightly lit interior reaches into the public place and presents the audience as public theater. Though historical in its public presence, the interior is an exquisitely constructed abstraction of a nineteenth-century proscenium horseshoe auditorium and stage. The walls are acoustically treated in wooden straps cut into infinitely varied shapes and this extends to other elements which in the nineteenth-century theater may have been merely decorative; here they serve to improve the sound quality. What meaning can one find in this contradiction, between a modern, unsigned, expressive exterior and a historically based perpectival interior? Is performance constrained by the antimodern proscenium frame? Does this theatre exist only to serve the past? How much more intriguing would have been the inversion in which public order was ironically implied on the outside and spacial ambiguity given freedom on the inside. In this play between autocratic order and the provocative of new order, Thompson has all the skills: but, seems uncertain of where he stands. He may be modern on the outside but in substance he is a conservative reactionary and as such is exactly appropriate to the times. His concern with historical continuity, human scale, with the craft of building and with the re-establishment of evolutionary forms in restoring the fabric of cities so much more wholesome and trustworthy than much of the idiosyncratic speculation that has followed the proclamation of post-modernism.

—Alan Balfour

TIGERMAN, Stanley.

American. Born in Chicago, Illinois, 20 September 1930. Educated at Senn High School, Chicago, 1944-48; Massachusetts Institute of Technology, Cambridge, 1948-49; Institute of Design, Chicago, 1949-50; Yale University School of Architecture, New Haven, Connecticut, 1959-61 (Alpha Rho Chi Medal, 1961), B.Arch. 1960, M.Arch. 1961. Served as a Petty Officer Second Class in the United States Navy, 1950-54. Married Judith Richards in 1956; JoAnn Kinzelberg in 1968; Margaret McCurry in 1979; children: Judson and Tracy. Architectural Draftsman with George Fred Keck, Chicago, 1949-50, T. David Fitz-Gibbon, Norfolk, Virginia, 1952-54, A.J. Del Bianco, Chicago, 1954-56, and with Milton M. Schwartz, Chicago, 1956-57; Designer, Skidmore, Owings and Merrill, Chicago, 1957-59; Architectural Draftsman with Paul M. Rudolph, New Haven, Connecticut, 1959-61; Chief of Design,

with Harry M. Weese, Chicago, 1962-62; Partner, with Norman Koglin, Tigerman and Koglin, Chicago, 1962-64; Principal, Stanley Tigerman and Associates Ltd., Chicago, 1964-82. Since 1982, Principal of Tigerman, Fugman, McCurry, Architects, Chicago. Professor of Architecture, 1965-71, and Adjunct Professor, 1980, University of Illinois at Chicago Circle; Architect-in-Residence, American Academy, Rome, 1980. Visiting Professor/Critic/Lecturer: Washington University, St. Louis, 1962-64; University of Houston, Texas, 1962-64, 1976, 1977; Northwestern University, Evanston, Illinois, 1962-64; Cornell University, Ithaca, New York, 1964, 1977; Cardiff College of Art, Wales, 1965; Cooper Union, New York, 1966-71; University of Notre Dame, Indiana, 1966-71; University of California, Berkeley, 1966, 1977; Institute for Architecture and Urban Studies, New York, 1975; Smithsonian Institution, Washington, D.C., 1975, 1976; Columbia University, New York, 1976; Virginia Polytechnic Institute, Blacksburg, 1976; Harvard University, Cambridge, Massachusetts, 1976; University of Detroit, 1976; Roosevelt University, Chicago, 1976; University of Kansas, Lawrence, 1976; University of Utah, Salt Lake City, 1977; University of Maryland, Baltimore, 1977; Miami University, Oxford, Ohio, 1977; Rhode Island School of Design, Providence, 1977; University of Illinois, Urbana, 1977; University of Arkansas, Fayetteville, 1977; Society of Fine Arts, Quincy, Illinois, 1977; Ball State University, Muncie, Indiana, 1978; Harvard University, Cambridge, Massachusetts, 1978, 1982; University of North Carolina, Charlotte, 1978, 1982; Miami University, Oxford, Ohio, 1979; University of Cincinnati, Ohio, 1980; University of Houston, Texas, 1981; Tulane University, New Orleans, Louisiana, 1981; University of Nebraska, Lincoln, 1981; Cranbrook Academy, Bloomfield Hills, Michigan, 1983. Chairman, American Institute of Architects Institute Honors Jury, 1977. American Correspondent of *L'Architecture d'Aujourd'hui*, Paris, since 1966. Member, Chicago Seven. Exhibitions: Norfolk Art Museum, Virginia, 1954; Art Institute of Chicago, 1954, 1964, 1965, 1973, 1977; Washington University, St. Louis, 1962; B.C. Holland Gallery, Chicago, 1962; Walker Art Center, Minneapolis, 1965; Art Center, Midland, Michigan, 1965; Northwestern University, 1966; Northern Illinois University, DeKalb, 1966; Roosevelt University, 1966; Evanston Art Center, 1969; Kansas City Art Research Center, 1969; Arts Association, Springfield, Illinois, 1970; University of Chicago, 1975; Cooper Union, New York, 1976; *Seven Chicago Architects*, Richard Gray Gallery, Chicago, 1976; Harvard University, 1976; Museum of Contemporary Art, Chicago, 1976; *Biennale*, Venice, 1976, 1978; University of Houston, 1976, 1977; University of California, Berkeley, 1976, 1977; *Bienal*, Sao Paulo, 1976; Drawing Center, New York, 1977; University of California at Los Angeles, 1977; *City Segments*, Walker Art Center, Minneapolis, 1979; *Collaboration: Artists and Architects*, Architectural League of New York, 1981. Also a painter and sculptor: exhibitions at various museums and universities. Recipient: Award of Excellence for Design, *Architectural Record*, New York, 1970, 1978, 1979, 1980; Award of Merit, American Institute of Architects, 1970; Distinguished Building Award, AIA, Chicago Chapter, 1971, 1973 (twice), 1975 (twice), 1977 (twice), 1978, 1979 (six times), 1981, 1982, 1983; Gold Medal Award for Excellence in Masonry, Metropolitan Chicago Masonry Council, 1974; Award of Merit, AIA/*House and Home* and American Home, 1974; Annual Award, for continued excellence of design, Illinois AIA, 1976; Award of Merit, Chicago Lighting Institute, 1976; Distinction Award, 1977, and Honor Award, 1978, Illinois Council of the American Institute of Architects; *Chicago* Magazine Art Award, 1978; *Progressive Architecture* Award, New York, 1980 (twice); National Honor Award, American Institute of Architects, 1982; Masonry Institute Award, 1982; Architecture Award, Gypsum Drywall Contractors

of Northern Illinois, 1983. Address: Tigerman, Fugman, McCurry, Architects, 444 North Wells Street, 2C, Chicago, Illinois 60610, U.S.A.

Works:

1962/
64 Pickwick Village Townhouses, Chicago
   Habenicht House, Elgin, Illinois
1963 O'Grady House, Park Ridge, Illinois (project)
1963/
64 Chaplan House, Park Forest, Illinois
1963/
69 Woodlawn Gardens Low-Rise Housing, Chicago
1966 Kaplan House remodelling, Chicago
   Barovsky and Ehrlich Offices, Chicago
   Loyola Housing Project, Chicago
1966/
68 Bower's House, Wilmette, Illinois
1966/
69 Nun's Island Low-Rise Housing, Montreal
1966/
76 Five polytechnics in Bangladesh
1968 Chicago Dwelling Association Housing
   Inner city apartment remodelling, Chicago
1969 Texas prototype gas station (project)
1969/
74 St. Benedict's Abbey Church and Print Shop remodelling, Benet Lake, Wisconsin
1970 Atlantis Resort Complex, Grand Bahamas (project)
   Housing for indigents, Chicago (project)
   Park Place Apartments, Chicago
1970/
71 Brodley House, Chicago
1970/
73 Vollen Barn, Burlington, Wisconsin
1972 Instant Football (megastructure project)
   Board of Education feasibility study, State of Illinois (project)
   Art Museum, Northern Illinois University, DeKalb (project)
1972/
73 Kelmer Arlington Industrial Building, Arlington Heights, Illinois
   Hot Dog House, Harvard, Illinois
   Frog Hollow, Berrien Springs, Michigan
1973 Metal and Glass House, Glencoe, Illinois
1973/
74 Townhouse, Tucson, Arizona (project)
1974 Richard Gray Gallery, Chicago
   Bottega Glascia, Chicago
   House and Garden prototype kitchen
   Loop College, Chicago (project)
   Marks House, Hollywood, California (project)
1974/
78 Piper's Alley Commercial Mall, Old Town, Chicago
   Prairie Brook Apartments, Palatine, Illinois
   Illinois Regional Library for the Blind and Physically Handicapped, Chicago
1975/
77 Arby's Restaurant, Chicago
   Daisy House, Porter, Indiana
1976 Stone-Levin Apartment, Chicago
   St. John's Catholic Cathedral, Champaign-Urbana, Illinois (project)
   Tackbary House, Barrington, Illinois (project)
   Zipper Townhouses (project)
1976/
77 Walner Law Office, Chicago
1976/
78 "Animal Crackers" (Blender House), Highland Park, Illinois
   Ukrainian Institute of Modern Art, Chicago
1976/
80 National Archives Center of the Baha'i's of the United States, Wilmette, Illinois
   Labadie House, Oakbrook, Illinois (project)

1977/
79 "Tigerman Takes a Bite out of Keck": Walner House addition, Highland Park, Illinois
Kastel House, Chicago
Anti-Cruelty Society Building, Chicago
1977/
80 Sam's Cut-Rate Liquors Building, Chicago
1978 "A Kosher Kitchen (for a Suburban Jewish American Princess)": Desser House addition, Wilmette, Illinois (project)
"Dante's Bathroom" (project)
1978/
79 Private House, Lisle, Illinois
Cavey's Restaurant, Manchester, Connecticut
Private Condominium House, Chicago
Private House, Ogden Dunes, Indiana
1978/
80 Stokman Chamber Music Festival designs, Door County, Wisconsin
PSM Condominiums, Cook County, Illinois
1978/
81 Pensacola Place Development, Chicago
1979 Best and Company Building, Chicago (exhibition project)
City Segment, Minneapolis, Minnesota (exhibition project)
1979/
80 Private House, Highland Park, Illinois
Private House II, Highland Park, Illinois
Arthur Frank Law Offices, Chicago
Chair designs for Knoll International (project)
Fisherman's Cove Housing, Palatine, Illinois
Georgian London in the Crystal Palace (project)
1980 Private Apartment remodelling, Chicago
Private House, King's Point, Long Island, New York
Metalstand Showroom at the Merchandise Mart, Chicago (with Richard Saul Wurman)
Walner Law Office II, Chicago
Private House, Crete, Illinois (project)
Architectural League of New York Project (exhibition project; with Richard Haas)
Sam's Cut-Rate Liquors II, Chicago
Private House, Barrington Hills, Illinois
Private House addition, Highland Park, Illinois
Chicago and State High-Rise Apartments, Chicago (project)
1981 Private House remodelling and addition, Winnetka, Illinois
Davis Furniture prototypes, for *Interiors* magazine, New York
Thonet Showroom Exhibition design, Chicago
Sam's Wine Warehouse, Chicago
Private House remodelling, Chicago
1982 Private House, Highland Park, Illinois
Knoll International Corporate Park and Showroom, Houston, Texas
"Storehouse" Building, Chicago
Urban Villa, West Berlin
Central Area Plan, Chicago
Decorative Screen prototype, for Rizzoli International
Furniture prototypes, for Formica Corporation
Country House, Washington, Connecticut
Private House remodelling, Lakeside, Michigan
1983 Decorative Objects, for Swid Powell Designs
Weekend House, Lakeside, Michigan
Helmsley Spear Office Building renovation, Chicago

Publications:

By TIGERMAN: book—*Versus: An American Architect's Alternatives*, with Ross Miller and Dor-

othy Metzger Habel, New York 1982; articles—introduction to *Chicago Architects* by Stuart Cohen, Chicago 1976; "Chicago Architectural Heritage" in *Arquitectura* (Madrid), March/April 1979; "Daisy House, Porter, Indiana" in *GA Houses* (Tokyo), no. 6, 1979; "George Fred Keck, 1895-1980", with Stuart Cohen, in *Chicago Architectural Journal,* vol. 1, 1981; "The Chicago Architectural Club, 1895-1940", with John Zubowsky, in *Chicago Architectural Journal*, vol. 2, 1982; "The Residential Works of Robert A.M. Stern", with others, in *Architecture + Urbanism* (Tokyo), July 1982.

On TIGERMAN: books—*Chicago on Foot* by Ira J. Bach, Chicago 1969, 3rd edition 1977; *New Directions in American Architecture* by Robert A.M. Stern, New York 1969; *Urban Structures for the Future* by Justus Dahinden, New York 1972; *Chicago 1930-1970* by Carl Condit, Chicago 1974; *Art: Search and Self-Discovery* by James A. Schinneller, Worcester, Massachusetts 1975; *Housing* by John Macsai and others, New York 1976; *Unbuilt America* by Alison Sky and Michelle Stone, New York 1976; *Megastructure* by Reyner Banham, New York 1976; *Seven Chicago Architects,* catalog of the exhibition at the Richard Gray Gallery, Chicago 1976; *Europa/America*, edited by Franco Raggi, Venice 1978; *Collaboration: Artists and Architects* by Barbaralee Diamonstein, New York 1981; *Gehry, Site, Tigerman: trois portraits de l'artiste en architecte* by Olivier Poissiere, Paris 1981; articles—"The Nation's Largest Low-Rise Project" in *Architectural Forum* (New York), May 1971; "Aeroport," special issue of *L'Architecture d'Aujourd'hui* (Paris), June/July 1971; "Young Architects in the United States" by Esther McCoy in *Zodiac* (Milan), no. 13, 1973; "Stanley Tigerman in Bangladesh" by M.W. Newman in *Inland Architect* (Chicago), February 1973; "Upgrading Barns to Be Inhabited by People" in *Architectural Record* (New York), June 1974; "Grandes Orgues et Petites Industries" in *L'Architecture d'Aujourd'hui* (Paris), July/August 1974; "Chicago Revisited," special issue of *Interior Design* (New York), December 1974; "Interior Architecture: Fashion with Style" in *Progressive Architecture* (New York), December 1974; "Weese versus Mies" in *Architectural Record* (New York), April 1975; "A House That Thinks for Itself" in *House and Garden* (New York), July 1976; "Tigerman Shapes a Fresh New Library for the Blind" by Nory Miller in *Inland Architect* (Chicago), September 1976; "Seven Chicago Architects" in *Architecture + Urbanism* (Tokyo), May 1977; "The Diversity in Design Among Chicago Architects Today" in *Architettura* (Rome), December 1977; "On the Town with the Lively Chicago Seven" in *Inland Architect*

(Chicago), February 1978; "Chicago Seven" in *Architecture + Urbanism* (Tokyo), June 1978; "Works of Stanley Tigerman" in *Space Design* (Tokyo), October 1978; "Stanley Tigerman vs. Frank O. Gehry" in *GA Houses* (Tokyo), no. 6, 1979; "Tigerman Sees the Light in Architecture" in *Building Design* (London), 23 March 1979; "Stanley Tigerman Pure American" in *De Architect* (The Hague), May 1979; "Stanley Tigerman: Recent Projects" in *Architecture + Urbanism* (Tokyo), November 1979; "The Ghost of Mies v. The Chicago Seven" in *Plan* (Dublin), January 1980; "Tigerman Embraces Mother Nature" in *Interiors* (New York), April 1980; "Arby's, Chicago" in *Industria delle Costruzioni* (Rome), October 1980; "The Split Infinitive of Stanley Tigerman" in *International Architect* (London), no. 6, 1981; "Stanley Tigerman House Projects" in *Controspazio* (Bari, Italy), April/June 1981; "Stanley Tigerman: An Anti-Platonic Stance" in *Transition* (St. Kilda, Victoria), September/December 1981; "House with a Pompadour, Lake Michigan" in *Architecture + Urbanism* (Tokyo), November 1982; "Houses", special issue of *GA Houses* (Tokyo), March 1983; "A Piece of the American Quilt" in *Progressive Architecture* (New York), April 1984.

Bibliography: *Chicago Seven* by Lamia Doumato, Monticello, Illinois 1982.

One of the reasons that American architecture has always been essentially apolitical is due to the sparsity of a country that even now has one of the lowest population densities in the world. Political posturing, in some ways, grows out of the need to react to excessive/obsessive laws which, in turn, come into existence to order density. Europe is d has been for some time now nse. Its architecture is a representation of reactions to density. Rules concerning the needs of a collective stem, in part, from the tension created by unordered proximities. Thus Europe babel of the many languages concentrated there nds to be represented by an architecture required to order intrinsic chaos.

America, unencumbered by excessive density, was founded and continues to operate on the principle of the individual. America's architecture has always represented the pluralist possibilities evolving from individualism tempered by common cause. American architecture, traditionally an amalgam of European antecedent forms adapted to individual concerns, is a unique synthesis of classical traditions made expedient through capitalism.

The American architect has always struggled with the unresolved dialetic of a dualism born of morality

Stanley Tigerman: Illinois Regional Library for the Blind and Physically Handicapped, Chicago, 1978.

tempered by expediency. Nearing the end of the twentieth century the heels of the heroic phase of modern architecture victorious representation itself of America's heroic World War II aspirations, American architects now face the challenge of coming to grips with the less-than-heroic represent-ation of unwanted involvement first in Vietnam and now in Central America. Only in America could an architecture of doubt, conditioned by skepticism force its way to the surface of a vessel designed normally to contain an optimistic content.

So...how does one become an American archi-tect today?

1. By remaining vulnerable

2. By socratic reflection tempering a normally optimistic architectural disposition

3. By treading "the narrow ridge" Martin Buber once described as separating rampant individualism from dogmatic collectivism.

4. By faith tempered by reason

...America for me is all of this, and an American architect has the dual obligation of reflecting his beliefs and doubts simultaneously, since that is what his pluralist culture contends with each day.

—Stanley Tigerman

Stanley Tigerman has tackled with style and imagin-ation many of the architectural issues that have evolved during his career. He has approached middle income and public housing with early and comme-ndable interpretations of vernacular modes. He added his own efforts to the 1960s utopian fascin-ation with high-technology megastructures. And he has worked in the very real forum of third world developing countries in Bangladesh. He has built high-rise and below ground; for speculative devel-opers and the Cuisinart set; in brick, concrete, wood and metal.

Throughout he has been a kind of architectural scavenger, years before (or after) that kind of eclecticism gained acceptance. For the first decade, the strongest influences were his former employers, Walter Netsch and Harry Weese, his teacher Paul Rudolph, and latter-day Chicagoan Mies van der Rohe. Later, the list expanded in all directions to include John Hejduk, Charles Moore, Art Moderne, de Stijl and many more.

In recent years, his previously stylistically diverse practice has begun to come together into a progress-ive development of designs—some built, some not—that are increasingly sensual and theatrical. As early as the Glass commissions (apartment and boutique), Tigerman's deftness with soft curves and three-dimensional staging became apparent. Subsequent designs have continued to expand the vocabulary which increasingly includes biomorphic shapes, bright color, topiary, and imagery which both in detail (e.g. his repeated use of Magritte cloud-filled skies) and as *objet trouvé* makes allusions to other things.

The names of the buildings have become an element of play as well as explanation: to wit, Hot Dog House, Animal Crackers, Zipper Townhouses, Dante's Bathroom, Kosher Kitchen for a Suburban Jewish-American Princess, Tigerman Takes a Bite out of Keck (a rippled effluvia of an addition to a modernist George Fred Keck house).

The metaphors are sometimes related to the project—for instance, the Daisy House, in the shape of male genitalia, is built for a man who owns strip joints—and sometimes, although not ideologically, surreal. Frequently they are intended to amuse—like a two-car garage shaped and painted like the cars themselves—and just as frequently to shock—church confessionals whose plans come from the sections of standard lavatory fixtures.

Almost invariably the work is marked by formal inventiveness, sculptural and compositional finesse and attentiveness to detail. The pop and por-nography, historicism and literary reference are like formal building blocks. That architecture should be jaunty, appealing and an "experience" is really the message.

As well as a prolific architect, Tigerman has been a central influence on the architectural community of Chicago in the 1970s through the group Chicago Seven, conferences, exhibits and competitions. The activities focused not only on creating a community of discussion among Chicago designers and en-couraging talented beginners to participate, but also in putting architectural issues before the archi-tectural, art and general public.

—Nory Miller

TOMBAZIS, Alexandros Nicholas.

Greek. Born in Karachi, Pakistan, 10 April 1939. Educated at elementary and secondary schools in London and Athens, 1945-57; Athens Technical University, 1957-62, Dip.Arch.Eng. 1962. Served as an Officer in the Building Department of the Greek Navy, 1962-64. Married Alexandra Cozzika in 1964; children: Despina and Nicholas. Assistant, Athens Technical University School of Architecture, 1962-65; Scientific Assistant, Doxiades Associates, At-hens, 1964-65. Founder and Principal, Alexandros N. Tombazis and Associates, Athens, since 1963, and Abu Dhabi, 1974-76, and Dubai, United Arab Emirates, since 1974. Exhibition: Centro Edile, Milan, 1984. Recipient: First Prize—National School Buildings Organization Competition, At-hens, 1963; Civil Servants' Pension Fund Office Building Competition, Athens, 1968; Demokritos Nuclear Research Centre Headquarters Compe-tition, Athens, 1969; Public Electricity Company Headquarters Competition, Athens, 1971; General Cement Company Headquarters Competition, At-hens, 1971; National Bank for Industrial Develop-ment Headquarters Competition, Athens, 1972; Chronic Disease Hospital Competition, Korydallos, Piraeus, Greece, 1972; Athens University Faculty of Law Competition, 1977; Town Hall Competition Kifisia, 1977; Bank of Greece Solar Kindergarten Competition, Athens, 1981; Klafthmonos Square Monument Competition, Athens, 1981; and five prizes, Ministry of Planning, Housing and Environ-ment, Athens, 1983. Address: Meletitiki Company Ltd., Alexandros N. Tombazis and Associates, 1 Aristodemou Street, Athens 106 76, Greece.

Works:

1963 Greek National School Buildings Organiz-ation Prototypes (competition project)

1964 Greek State Railways Headquarters, Athens (competition project)

1965 Chios Archaeological Museum, Greece (com-petition project)

1966 Greek Pavilion, for *Expo '67*, Montreal (competition project)

Athens Technical University Boarding House (competition project)

University of Athens Hospital (competition project; with Biris and Sartzetaki)

Urban housing for the Shikenshiku-Sha Com-pany, Tokyo (competition project)

1967 Athens Historical War Museum (competition project)

Espoo City Centre, Finland (competition project)

Epiros Poultry Cooperative Plant, Ioannina, Greece (with Th. Sartzetaki)

1968 Civil Servants' Pension Fund Office Building, Athens (competition project)

Telephone booth prototype (competition project)

Hellenica Beauty and Toiletry Laboratory, Maroussi, Athens

A. Svolos House, Kinetta, Greece

V. Katsambas House, Kifisia, Greece

Akti Mytina Tourist Village, Lemnos, Greece

1969 Grava School Complex, Athens (competition project)

Athens Central Market and Commercial Centre (competition project)

E. Diakos Apartment Building, P. Psychico, Athens

Psimaras House, Glyfada, Athens

Nea Smyrni Elementary School Complex, Athens

Van der Graaf Accelerator Building, De-mokritos Nuclear Research Centre, Aghia Paraskevi, Athens

Gold Exhibits Section, National Archaeolog-ical Museum, Athens

Demokritos Nuclear Research Centre Head-quarters, Aghia Paraskevi, Athens

Olympos Cement Depot, Volos, Greece

VESO Kernal-Oil Plant, Corinth, Greece

1970 Piraeus Port Authority Office Building Greece (competition project):

Technikos Cosmos Company Apartment Complex, Kastri, Athens (competition pro-ject)

St. Paul Accident Hospital extension, Kifisia, Greece (project)

1971 Perugia City Centre, Italy (competition pro-ject)

Public Electricity Company Headquarters, N. Falero, Athens (competition project)

General Cement Company Headquarters, Kifisia, Greece

Demokritos Nuclear Research Centre Radi-ation Laboratory, Aghia Paaskevi, Athens

Difros Apartment Complex, Ag. Varvara, Athens

1972 National Electricity Organization Training Centre, Drosia, Athens (competition pro-ject)

Prodomi High-rise Residential Complex, Kis-ifia, Greece

High Tension Laboratory, Athens Poly-technic

King Paul National Foundation Boarding House, Molai, Lakonia, Greece

Athens College, Bodosakeio Elementary Sch-ool, Kantza, Attica, Greece (with Perkins and Will)

National Bank for Industrial Development Headquarters, Athens

Yacht Marina for the Greek Tourist Organiz-ation, Salonica, Greece

1973 School for Tourist Professions, for the Greek Tourist Organization, Anavissos, Attica, Greece

1974 Technical School, Lamia, Greece

Fix Day Care Centre, P. Falero, Athens

Pediatric Clinic and Spastics Unit, Athens Pediatric Centre, Maroussi, Athens

Catholic Church Office Building, Athens

First-class hotel, Abu Dhabi, United Arab Emirates

A. Chandris Company Cable Plant, Volos, Greece

1975 Abu Dhabi Conference City, United Arab Emirates (competition project)

Apartment complex, Al Saman, Sharjah, United Arab Emirates

Kouloura Fund Health Centre, Hydra, Greece

1976 A. Frangoyiannis House, Ekali, Athens

Al Futtaim House, Dubai, United Arab Emirates

1977 Town Hall, Kifisia, Greece

Town Hall, Psychico, Greece (competition project)

Technical Chamber Office Building, Larissa, Greece (competition project)

Secondary school complex, Piraeus, Greece (competition project)

Technical Schools complex, Chalkida, Greece (competition project)

National Bank of Greece Pensions Home (competition project)

Secondary schools complex, Chania, Crete (competition project)
Acropolis Archaeological Museum, Athens (competition project)
Chronic Disease Hospital, Korydallos, Piraeus, Greece.

1978 A. Mavrakakis House, Ano Voula, Athens
Agricultural University Library, Athens
Faculty of Law Building, University of Athens
Two National School Organization school complexes, Ano Liossia, Athens
Heios I Solar House, Trapeza Aigialeias, Greece
Deithnis Techniki Office Building, Sina and Akadimias Streets, Athens
Bank for the Industrial Employees Fund offices, Athens (project)

1979 Solar Village 3, Lykovyrissi, Athens
C. Sofianos passive solar house, Ekali, Athens
A. Romanos house, Kifisia, Greece
Aluminium de Grèce headquarters interiors, Athens
Mitropoleos Square landscaping, Athens

1980 National Mortgage Bank housing complex, Komotini, Greece
National Mortgage Bank housing complex, Xanthi, Greece
G. Tolis house, Kambos Despoti, Trikala, Greece

Shopping Centre, Kifisia, Greece

1981 Ch. Metaxopoulos apartment building, Glyfada, Athens
A. Mavarakakis passive solar house, Perdica Egina, Greece
Bank of Greece solar kindergarten, Holargos, Athens
TEB office building, Athens (with A. Athanasoulï-Triha)
Luxury Tourist Village, Rhodes, Greece (project; with F. Kydoniates)
100 and 500kw Photovoltaic Plants, Kythnos and Agia Roumeli, Greece

1982 Mosque for Mr. Majid Al Futtaim, Dubai, United Arab Emirates (project)
Library building, Benaki Botanical Institute, Kifisia, Greece (project)
Faculty of Medicine, Ionnanina University, Greece (project)
Chania Technical University, Crete (project)

Publications:

By TOMBAZIS: articles—"The Spacestructure System" in *Architecture in Greece* (Athens), vol. 2, 1968; "Greek Vernacular Architecture" in *Architecture in Greece* (Athens), vol. 3, 1969.

On TOMBAZIS: book—*Guide to Postwar Architecture in Greece, 1945-1983* by O. B. Doumanis, Athens 1984; articles—in *Architektoniki* (Athens), 1963, 1968; *Arkkitehtuuri Kimpailuja* (Helsinki), no. 8, 1967; *Architektur Wettbewerbe* (Stuttgart), vol. 52, 1967; *L'Architecture d'aujourd'hui* (Paris), no. 134, 1967; *The Japan Architect* (Tokyo), no. 127, 1967, no. 322, 1984; *Architecture in Greece* (Athens), vol. 2, 1968, vol. 3, 1969, vol. 4, 1970, vol. 5, 1971, vol. 6, 1972, vol. 8, 1974, vol. 10, 1976, vol. 11, 1977, vol. 18, 1984; *Bauen und Wohnen* (Zürich), no. 8, 1971; *E + P* (Frankfurt), 1971, 1972, 1974; *Design in Greece* (Athens), vol. 3, 1972, vol. 4, 1973, vol. 8, 1977, vol. 11, 1980; *L'Architettura* (Rome), August 1972; *Architectural Review* (London), no. 908, 1972; *Technodomica* (Athens), no. 2, 1976, no. 19, 1978; *DBZ* (Gütersloh, West Germany), no. 22, 1977.

A considerable number of the projects that we have had the opportunity to work on have been awarded to us as the result of architectural competitions called for either by the State or by private individuals. There is a law, in fact, in Greece which requires that most public work be awarded in such a manner; this in my opinion, is a very favourable situation from many points of view. The problems, however, that exist are many—for example, a number of these projects do not get built; the designer does not supervise

Alexandros Tombazis: Difros Apartment Complex, Athens, 1971.

construction, so he has no say in the alterations that are made to his design!; the whole system for awarding public contracts for construction is not based on any consideration of quality but only upon the lowest price offered; and any large project—of which there are quite a number—,is a ten-year love affair with at least as many ups and downs!

—Alexandros N. Tombazis

The projects of Alexandros N. Tombazis represent exemplary exceptions to the usual offhand solutions that the low state of building technology in Greece. He has never been preoccupied with arguments on regionalism or the "Greekness" of his projects, as has been the case with many other Greek architects. He can be regarded as the Greek architect par excellence who is constantly alert to advancements of building technology and the state of architecture abroad and who introduces these innovations to his native land. He does so after questioning their adaptability to Greece, through exhaustive and in-depth studies, with the help of the most gifted technologists of the country. His office, small by western standards, has produced a great number of diverse building types including residential, educational, industrial, administrative, health and tourist facilities.

Tombazis's work reflects a variety of formal influences. Some of his early projects were heavily influenced by Le Corbusier's form-making language. A number of subsequent projects followed the conceptual and stylistic vocabulary of the Metabolists. The house in Kinetta, one of Tombazis masterpieces, is perhaps the best Metabolic residence ever constructed anywhere on earth. Some of his latest projects—an entry for the first panhellenic competition for the new Museum of Acropolis and another entry for the town hall in Psychico—arouse memories of the work of James Stirling, especially his History Faculty Building at Cambridge. There have been a few instances—in which when he has dealt with traditional expressions. An historic zoning ordinance or the unique nature of the project demanded it—in spite of the multiplicity of Tombazis's formal expressions, one thing is certain: he is a brilliant interpreter of the form vocabulary he sets about to exploit. In every case, his projects are integrated design packages, with most appealing craftmanship and appealing elevations.

Tombazis's office is still young by western professional standards, but it has participated in and won a great number of Greek architectural competitions and has also been distinguished by major awards in international competitions. There is no doubt that this firm also enjoys the trust of its Greek, as well as its Middle Eastern, clientele. If the firm exploits its authority and the trust gained during the first decade of its practice and if it goes beyond the conventionalities of generally accepted "good architecture," it will most certainly produce "unique" architecture, distinguished by its own personality, unburdened by the formal memories of other nations, and expressive of twentieth-century Greece. The unfortunate early death in the summer of 1977 of Takis Zenetos, pioneer in the search for a technologically correct Greek architecture, puts an additional burden on Tombazis's shoulders. In recent years, he has been preoccupied with bio-climatic and solar design, sensitive to microclimates and energy conservation, and has produced quite a few exemplary projects of this type. His firm has the ability—and he is the only current Greek practitioner who has the background—to produce a viable, all-inclusive, technologically correct Greek architecture.

—Anthony C. Antoniades

TORROJA y MIRET, Eduardo.

Spanish. Born in Madrid, 27 August 1899. Studied constructional engineering, Dip.Eng. 1923; awarded honorary qualification as architect (posthumously), School of Architecture, Madrid, 1967. Practiced in Madrid from 1923: Partner, with Manuel Sanchez Arcas, 1934-35. Founder-Director, Instituto Técnico de la Construcción del Cemento, Costillares, Madrid (now, Instituto Eduardo Torroja). Visiting Professor, Harvard University, Cambridge, Massachusetts; Princeton University, New Jersey; Raleigh Architectural College, North Carolina; Massachusetts Institute of Technology, Cambridge; University of Buenos Aires. President, International Federation of Pre-stressing; President, Association of Shell Structures. Collection: Instituto Eduardo Torroja, Côstillares, Madrid. Recipient: First Prize, Zarazuela Racecourse Competition, 1936. *Died* (in Madrid) *15 June 1961.*

Works:

1925 Tempul Aqueduct, Guadalete River, Jerez de la Frontera, Spain
1926 Sancti-Petri Bridge, Spain
1933 Market Hall, Algeciras, Spain (with Manuel Sánchez Arcas)
      Aire Aqueduct, University City, Madrid
      Quince Ojos Aqueduct, University City, Madrid (with M. L. Otero and A. Aguirre)
      Stadium Tramcar Station, University City, Madrid (not completed)
      Cantarranas Retaining Wall, Madrid
1934 Operating theatre, and Sun balconies, University City Hospital, Madrid
1935 Zarazuela Racecourse, Madrid (with Carlos Arniches and Martin Dominguez)
      Frontón Recoletos (Pelota Game Hall), Madrid (with Secundino Zuazo; destroyed during the Spanish Civil War)
      Church, Villaverde, Spain
1936 Reinforced Concrete Water Tower, Zarazuela Racecourse, Madrid (project)
1938 Factory Building, Seville (project)
1939 Brick Water Tower, Zarazuela Racecourse, Madrid
      Alloz Aqueduct, Alloz, Spain
      Martin Gil Viaduct, Esla River, near Leon, Spain
      Tordera Bridge, near Barcelona
1939/
   47 La Muga Bridge, over the Muga River, Spain
1942/
   45 Torrejon Aircraft Hangar, Madrid
      Aircraft Hangar, Barajas, Spain
1943 Las Corts Football Stadium, Barcelona (with J. M. Sagnier)
1948/
   51 Instituto Técnico de la Construcción y del Cemento, Costillares, Madrid
1949 Aircraft Hangar, Cuatro Vientos, Spain
1950 Railway Station Roof, Orense, Spain (project)
1952 Church, Pont de Sert, Lerida, Spain (with J. R. Mijares)
      Chapel of the Ascension, Xerrallo, Spain (with J. R. Mijares)
1953 Pre-stressed Concrete Shrine/Shelter, Sancti Spirit, Spain
1956 Half-Mile Aqueduct (project)
      Cañelles Dam, near Lerida, Spain
      Water Tank, Fedala, Morocco
      Cylindrical Shell Chapel (project)
      Timber Church (project)
1957 Shell-Roof, for the Táchira Club, Caracas, Venezuela (with F. Vivas)
      Skew Slab Bridge (project)

Publications:

By TORROJA: books—*Variantes Modernas en las Estructuras de Puentes,* Madrid 1944; *Fundamentos para el calculo de estructuras lineales planas,* Madrid 1949; *Bridges and Aqueducts,* Raleigh, North Carolina 1957; *Razon y ser de los tipos estructurales,* Madrid 1956, as *The Philosophy of Structures,* Berkeley, California 1958; *The Structures of Eduardo Torroja* (autobiography), New York 1958; *Logik der Form,* Munich 1961: articles—"Problems and Possibilities of Concrete Shells" in *The Builder* (London), 18 April 1958; "The Influence of Structural Form in Architecture" in *Architectural Association Journal* (London), February 1961; "Raison et être des types structurax" in *Architecture de Lumière* (Paris), no. 12, 1965; and numerous technical publications for the Consejo Superior de Investigaciones Cientificas, Madrid, 1942-61.

On TORROJA: Bibliography—*Eduardo Torroja y Miret, Architect-Engineer (Madrid, Spain): A General Bibliography* by Florita Z. Louie de Irizarry, Monticello, Illinois 1983; articles—"Eduardo Torroja" by G. Wastlund in *Byggmastaren* (Copenhagen), 1 February 1950; "Torroja's Sculptural Concrete" in *Architectural Forum* (New York), February 1955; "Vocazione Iberica per la Forma" in *Domus* (Milan), April 1956; "Bridges and Aqueducts" in *North Carolina School of Design Journal* (Raleigh), vol. 7, no. 2, 1957; "Un Maestro delle Strutture: Eduardo Torroja" by G. Pizzetti in *Casabella* (Milan), no. 217, 1957; "Les Structures Spatiales d'Eduardo Torroja" by Alberto Sartoris in *Architecture: Formes et Fonctions* (Lausanne), no. 6, 1959; "Eduardo Torroja" by Jürgen Joedicke in *Bauen und Wohnen* (Zurich), no. 11, 1960; "Eduardo Torroja 1899-1961" by M. Dezzi-Bardeschi in *Casabella* (Milan), August 1961; "Eduardo Torroja" by F. Cassinella in *Cuadernos de Arquitectura* (Barcelona), no. 46, 1961; "Un copertura smontabile a struttura metallica" in *Architettura* (Rome), June 1962.

Eduardo Torroja y Miret was one of the great architect-engineers of this century, rivalled only by the Italian Pier Luigi Nervi. As a result of Torroja's genius and pioneering efforts, Spanish architecture achieved legendary qualities, particularly in the enclosure of space, structural concepts, and the daring use of material, especially concrete, raising it from prosaic to poetic levels.

Three works, striking for their conceptual simplicity and underlying logic, demonstrate Torroja's incredible structural skill. Moreover, they emphasize the importance of teamwork and collaboration between architect and engineer, which the exploitation of traditional and new materials, and changing ideals, demanded.

In the Market Hall at Algeciras, Torroja, with Manuel Sánchez Arcas, created a superb 156' diameter low profile spherical dome of shell concrete pierced with a zenithal skylight at the centre. In Madrid, Torroja collaborated with Secundino Zuazo to realize the Frontón Recoletos. Designed for the game of pelota, the building was imaginatively roofed with two cylindrical vaults, intersecting at right angles and spanning 107' over a length of 180'. It was built in 80 days. Light was admitted to the interior by ingeniously conceived skylights, integral with the structural shells. The Fronton Recoletos was destroyed during the Spanish Civil War, but Torroja was convinced that its continuous construction would have permitted restoration, especially if it had been shored after damaged.

Elsewhere in Madrid, Torroja realized his masterpiece, the Zarazuela Racecourse, designed in association with the architects Carlos Arniche and Martin Dominquez. Determined by the strict functional necessities of racegoers for unrestricted views, shade, and freedom of movement, Torroja's revolutionary roof structure has been described as a "veritable ballet of eggshell concrete butterflies." The roof is composed of a series of shell concrete cantilevered hyperbolic sectors 42' long, counterbalanced by a series of similar shells 23' long, stabilized by anchor ties. The miraculously thin shells vary from 2' to 5·5'. It withstood severe bombardment during the Civil

War, and its graceful appearance was somewhat marred, but it remains structurally sound.

Without Torroja's engineering skill it is doubtful whether these works would have been realized with such panache. Certainly architecture elsewhere at that time suggests that there was an enormous creative gulf between Torroja and his contemporaries.

Later works by Torroja display his growing confidence; they are all expressions of his dazzling genius. Bridges, aqueducts, dams, water towers, factories, stadia, and even a coal bunker, were raised from a strictly utilitarian level to structural and aesthetic sublimity. Examples are the Alloz Aqueduct, 1,340' in length; Las Corts Football Stadium, Barcelona, where the steel roof cantilevers 83' over the spectators; the water tank at Fedala, with a 925,000 gallon capacity; and the Instituto Técnico de la Construcción y del Cemento in Madrid (founded by Torroja), where a 26' high dodecahedron makes a superb coal bunker and where the circular dining hall and pergola over a peripheral pathway are spectacular.

Torroja's inspiration is also evident in such churches as that at Pont de Sert, Lerida, where the structure of the composite shell vaults is spiritual. His project for the Táchira Club in Caracas, Venezuela, with stepped concrete shell, is masterly and moving as it elegantly adjusts its form to various levels.

Such was the quality of Torroja's work that Frank Lloyd Wright was moved to say, "he has expressed the principles of organic construction better than any engineer I know." His works, moreover, can be understood as a reflection of Spain's precarious economic state: Torroja was prevented from using expensive constructional methods and materials, a limitation that he converted to inspiration.

In his autobiography, *The Structures of Eduardo Torroja*, he makes the following statement: "I have tried to understand as completely as possible all the factors involved and apply my ingenuity to achieve a satisfactory solution both structurally and economically. My final aim has always been for the functional, structural and aesthetic aspects of a project to present an integrated whole both in essence and in appearance."

That is undoubtedly what Eduardo Torroja achieved: he raised structural engineering to unprecedented heights and created some of the world's most beautiful structures.

—Harold Booton

Works:

1936 "Berisville" (block of 7 flats), Symonds Street, Auckland (with E. R. Morton)
1945 House, Selwyn Road, Auckland
1954 Memorial Pavilion, Mt. Albert Grammar School, Auckland
1957 All Saints Church, Ponsonby, Auckland
1958 St. Oswald's Church, Auckland
1961 Christ Church, Papakura, Auckland (with Frank Jones)
1963 St. Matthew's Church, Helensville, Auckland (with Frank Jones)
1964 St. John's Church, Te Awamutu, New Zealand (with Frank Jones)
1970 Private swimming pool and loggia, Mojácar, Spain
1978 Cathedral of the Holy Trinity nave, tower and site development, Auckland (with Gillespie, Newman, Pearce)
1982 St. Mary's Church relocation to the Holy Trinity Cathedral Cluster, Parnell, Auckland
1984 King's School Chapel additions, Auckland (with D. Schofield and M. Brown)

Publications:

By TOY: articles—"The University" in *New Zealand Herald* (Auckland), 20 December 1948; "The Adventure of Architecture," parts I and II, in *New Zealand Institute of Architects Journal* (Wellington), May and June 1953; "Architecture 30 Years A.F." in *Home and Building* (Auckland), April 1962; "Design and Its Wholeness" in *New Zealand Institute of Architects Journal* (Wellington), May 1964; "Design Decisions in Architectural Practice" in *New Zealand Institute of Architects Journal* (Wellington), August 1967 and February 1968; "Guest Speaker—Prof. Ole Dybbroe" in *Home and Building* (Auckland), May 1971; "Shapes of Urban Growth in *University of Auckland News*, August 1971; "Auckland: Water City of the South Pacific" in *Auckland at Full Stretch*, edited by Graham Bush and Claudia Scott, Auckland 1977.

On TOY: articles—"Toy Interview," with Ed Haysom, in *Auckland Architectural Association Bulletin*, October 1976; "A Man in His Place" by Boyce Richardson in *New Zealand Listener* (Wellington), 18 June 1977; "The Toy Plan for the University" in *A History of the University of Auckland 1883 to 1983* by Keith Sinclar, Auckland 1984.

Correspondences and contradictions between the potentialities of natural and architectural forms can then be grasped through a common imagery of closure and openness and movement. Design becomes an orchestration of building and natural structures at all or any levels, from town to room to lamp-post.

If the theory is to be practically effective some way must be found of making it available not just occasionally but generally at the inception of building projects. As a model for this purpose we established at the Auckland School of Architecture a design theatre. This gathered together, round a discussion space, examples of natural and architectural structures graphcally interpreted in accordance with the theory, and with particular refeence, since this is an Auckland school, to the natural structure of the Auckland region as its base. The theatre was intended to be a tool to help reveal to all those involved the environmental implications of their building design decisions. Such a focus for building work, with appropriate reference to local conditions, could clearly be repeated in other regions and at different levels within the region.

My own practice interest tends to zoom in on the bay form with which, in an infinite variety of nature's proportions, inland as well as by the sea. Auckland and indeed most of New Zealand is bountifully blessed. Three dimensional, and transitional by virtue of its qualities both of connectedness and separateness (connecting by water or land, separated by its land rim), the bay has great potential for resolving many of the apparent conflicts of present day community—the demands, for instance, of outer relatedness on the one hand but of identity on the other. The outstanding example of the bay in its (mainly) built form is to be found in the self-renewing and beautifully modulated piazza and piazzetta of San Marco at Venice.

At the level of smaller gatherings and buildings, the bay form as forecourt, porch, and canopied interior is interesting. This is the "open hand" really, open vertically to the sky still, but as well opening in front over the land—because to receive, to give are transcendent acts certainly, but also warm and earthy things to do. All Saints Church, Ponsonby, is of this type.

Again, the bay is the form of the maori marae, a traditional place for gathering and greetings and farewells. So, whether we are of Polynesian or European descent, this is for us an important form in common. Through it we can, if we wish, build the means for that mutual cultural intercourse and understanding which is one of the happier dreams of people in this land.

—R. H. B. Toy

TOY, Richard Horton Beauclerc.

New Zealander. Born in Ignace, Ontario, Canada, 9 May 1911; emigrated to New Zealand, 1923. Educated at Mt. Albert Grammar School, Auckland, 1927-29; Auckland University College, 1930-36, B.Arch. 1936; St. John's College, Auckland, 1932-34; University of New Zealand Travelling Scholar in Architecture, 1937; Trinity College, Dublin, 1949-50, Ph.D. 1950. Served as a Major in the New Zealand Army, 1939-43. Married Cushla Gwyn Hammond in 1938 (divorced, 1969); married Sally Elizabeth Collier in 1969; children: Michael, Alison, And Brian. Architectural Assistant, offices of E. R. Morton, Auckland, 1936, M. K. Draffin, Auckland, 1936, and S. Heaps, London, 1937-38. In private practice, Auckland, snce 1939. Lecturer, 1939-50, Senior Lecturer, 1950-57, Professor of Architectural Design, 1957-77, and since 1977 Professor Emeritus, School of Architecture, University of Auckland. Fellow, St. John's College, Auckland, since 1964. Recipient: Bronze Medal, 1949, and Building of the Year in Auckland Award, 1957, New Zealand Institute of Architects. O.B.E. (Officer, Order of the British Empire), 1982. Address (office): 23 Seccombes Road, Epsom, Auckland 3, New Zealand.

In the past, building generally has responded in a whole sort of way, purposefully and often imaginatively, to the shapes and structure of its elemental heritage, its earth-sky-water-light context, wherever that may be. Most modern work makes a minimum reponse—practice, so-called—the overall and individual effects of which are deadening and especially noticeable in a place like New Zealand where the great bulk of the building in its beautiful landscape is of recent origin. My academic and practical interests have centred round ideas of enchancing what should be in any builiding project this very vital relationship.

Until recently such ideas received little support, but now it seems to me that the climate is becoming favourable to their growth; there is a more "anima" and less "animus" like way of relating to the environment, a motivation shown in spreading conservation movements. The pursuit of these ideas involves, on the academic side, developing a theory of nature's structure which can display, in terms corresponding to those of arcitectural theory, the potentialities of the land, practical and cultural, for human dwelling (and, of course, for letting it be). The potentialities we are concerned with here are those for accommodating and asserting the inward and outward manifestations of life and its transitons.

R. H. B. Toy creates an architecture concerned with the marriage of earth and sky. The words are always on his lips; his hand is always drawing them; his architecture is made with them, an architecture resonant with themes of the immanent and transcendental in human experience. Living and working in the heart of Auckland, he demonstrates in his daily life as in his architecture the intimate connection, for young and old, with the earth's loveliness and the freedom of the open sky. In his architecture—earthbound masonry with light, open timber enclosures above—he continues to work with timber when it has been abandoned by others. His buildings are amongst the loveliest in the country.

Toy has devoted his life to helping others as a teacher; he is loved by students in a society in which it is difficult to admit and express this feeling, and he is recognized by everyone as excelling in the understanding of form in the natural landscape and perceiving the relation of that landscape to built architecture. His buildings are small, but their architectural reference is broad.

Toy is guided by hs belief in the public art of architecture, at home in its natural setting, as a celebration of the society he loves. With this conviction he has quietly embellished a city and

Richard Toy: Saint Mary's Church relocation, Parnell, Auckland, 1982.

region with urban and rural parish churches, culminating in a cathedral. This hierarchy of levels of community is a theme in his work, senstively grafted to a context of other buildings, characterized by a respect for the old, encouraging gradual shaping of space with time a tempering of 20th century spatial rehtoric and technical confidence with sensitivity to places and people.

He is concerned with the careful opening of traditional forms without destroying them; floating roof canopies; partial dissolution of massive form into spatial ambiguities and linearities; opened forecourts complemented by the welcoming covering of space in the manner of the Polynesian marae.

All of his themes of space, material and form are embodied in his cathedral design—the tremulous canopy, the enclosure of space, the opened forecourt, the upthrust vertical, the place, the society, aware of itself in its setting. Toy shares with Patrick Geddes a belief in this awareness as a means of growth.

He is prompted in his work by compelling personal experience of three-dimensional space in relation to the human being, an awareness that the space of architecture in integral to the space of nature. Thus his works, often unassuming in purpose, evince a powerful aesthetic and lead through connection to the deepest purposes in life; it is an architecture quietly assertive of the dignity of man, concerned with universal themes, both encompassed by and encompassing land and society.

It is an architecture that will persist.

—John D. Dickson

TURNBULL, William, Jr.

American. Born in New York City, 1 April 1935. Educated at St. Mark's School, Southboro, Massa-chusetts, 1948-52; Princeton University, New Jersey, under William Shellman and Heath Licklider, 1952-56, B.A. 1956; Ecole des Beaux-Arts, Fontainebleau, 1956; Princeton University, under Jean Labatut, Enrico Perussutti, and Louis I. Kahn, 1956-59, M.F.A. 1959. Served in the United States Army Corps of Engineers, 1959-60. Married Wendy Woods in 1967 (divorced); children: Ramsey and Connor; married Mary E. Griffin in 1985. Designer, Skidmore, Owings and Merrill, San Francisco, 1960-63; Designer, President Kennedy's Pennsylvania Avenue Commission, Washington, D.C., 1963; Partner, Moore, Lyndon, Turnbull and Whitaker, Berkeley, California, 1963-65, and MLTW/Moore Turnbull, Berkeley, 1965-70; Principal, MLTW/Turnbull Associates, San Francisco, 1970-84. Since 1984, Director, William Turnbull Associates, San Francisco. Lecturer, College of Environmental Design, University of California, Berkeley, 1965-69; Visiting Professor, University of Oregon, Eugene, 1966-68; Lecturer in Architecture, Stanford University, Palo Alto, California, 1974-77; Visiting Critic, Massachusetts Institute of Technology, Cambridge, 1975, Yale University, New Haven, Connecticut, 1977, 1981 and 1986, and University of California, Berkeley, since 1978. Member, Citizens' Technical Advisory Committee to the California Legislative Joint Committee on Open Space Lands, 1968-71; Member, Design Review Board, Sausalito, California, 1976-78; Chairman, National Honor Awards Jury, American Institute of Architects, 1977. Design Consultant, World Savings and Loan, since 1976; Member of the Council on the Arts, Massachusetts Institute of Technology, 1976-80; Design Consultant to The Formica Corporation, 1977-85. Exhibitions: *40 under 40*, The Architectural League of New York, 1966; *MLTW*, The Architectural League of New York, 1966; *MLTW*, University of Oregon, 1967; *Centennial Exhibition*, University of California at Santa Barbara, 1968; *The California House*, Oakland Museum of Art, California, 1972, 1975; *Surroundings*, Walnut Creek Civic Arts Gallery, California, 1974; *Two Hundred Years of Santa Clara Valley Architecture*, Triton Museum of Art, Santa Clara, California, 1976; *Princeton Beaux Arts and Its New Academicism*, Institute for Architecture and Urban Studies, New York, 1977; A *View of California Architecture 1960-1976*, Museum of Modern Art, San Francisco, 1977; *50 Years of Princeton Architecture from Labatut to Geddes*, Princeton University, 1977; *200 Years of American Architectural Drawing*, Cooper-Hewitt Museum, New York, 1978; *Drawings for a More Modern Architecture*, Drawing Center, New York, and Otis Art Institute, Los Angeles, 1978; Architecture Exhibition, Ball State University, Muncie, Indiana, 1978; *William Turnbull*, Bonnafont Gallery, San Francisco, 1981; *The California Condition*, La Jolla Museum of Art, California, 1982; Louisiana World Exposition, New Orleans, 1984. Recipient: House of the Year Award, *Architectural Record*, 1962, 1967, 1969, 1970, 1972, 1973, 1983; Merit Award, 1962, 1968, 1975 (twice), Special Award, 1964, 1968, and Honor Award, 1964, 1972 (twice), American Institute of Architects/*Sunset Magazine*; Award of Merit, 1963, 1967, 1978, Honor Award, 1978, and Centennial Design Award, 1982 (twice), AIA, Bay Region; First Honor Award, 1963, 1976, and Merit Award, 1966, 1970, AIA/*House and Home*; California Governor's Award for Planned Communities, 1966; National Honor Award, AIA, 1967, 1968, 1973; Community Design Award, 1970, and Honor Award, 1982 (three), AIA, California; First Honor Award, 1970, Honor Award, 1974, and Design Award, 1981, *Progressive Architecture*; Award, AIA/United States Department of Housing and Urban Development, 1972; Honor Award, AIA, Connecticut, 1977; Award of Merit, AIA/American Library Association, 1978; Award of Honor, San Francisco Art Commission, 1982; Award of Honor, AIA, East Bay, 1983; Award of Merit, Pacific Coast Builders, 1983; Design Award, American Wood Concil, 1984. Fellow, Kresge College, University of California at

Santa Cruz, 1973. Fellow, American Institute of Architects, 1976. Address: William Turnbull Associates, Pier 1½, The Embarcadero, San Francisco, California 94111, U.S.A.

Works:

1959 Ellis Island Plan, New York (master's thesis project)
1960 Civic Center Fountain, Seattle (competition project)
  Governor's Mansion, Sacramento, California (competition project)
  Matterson House, Monterey, California
1961 City Hall, Boston (competition project)
1962 Jenkins House I, St. Helena, California (project)
  Moore House, Orinda, California
  West Plaza Condominium, Coronado, California (project)
  Seaside Professional Building, Seaside, California
  Master plan for the South Coast, Monterey, California (with Skidmore, Owings and Merrill)
  Master plan for Lone Hill Housing, San Jose, California
1963 Cortese House, Orinda, California (project)
  Legge House additions, Portola Valley, California
  Trueblood House additions, Palo Alto, California
  Turner House, Pebble Beach, California (project)

Monte Vista Apartments, Monterey, California
Plan for Pennsylvania Avenue, Washington, D.C. (project; as staff designer)
1964 Athletic Club I, Sea Ranch, California
  Cudabach House renovation, Oakland, California (project)
  Jewell House, Orinda, California
  Morris-LaForge House, Boulder Creek, California (project)
  Slater House, Stinson Beach, California
  Condominium I, Sea Ranch, California
1965 Cornuelle House, Hillsborough, California (project)
  Halprin House I, Sea Ranch, California (project)
  Halprin House II, Sea Ranch, California (project)
  Johnson House, Sea Ranch, California
  Karas House, Monterey, California
  Krakauer House, Los Alto, California (project)
  Lawrence House additions, Palo Alto, California
  Martin House, Lake Tahoe, California
  Polk House renovation, Berkeley, California
  Talbert House, Oakland, California
  Condominium Hillside, Sea Ranch, California (project)
  Carmel Knolls Housing, Carmel Valley, California (project)
  Civic Center, Fremont, California (competition project)
  Plan for a Commercial Square, Novato, California

Portland South Park, Lovejoy Plaza, Portland, Oregon (with Lawrence Halprin)
1966 Budge House, Healdsburg, California
  Halprin House III, Sea Ranch, California (project)
  Halprin House IV, Sea Ranch, California
  Harrison House, Santa Barbara, California (project)
  Knutsen House, Sonoma, California
  Lawrence House, Sea Ranch, California
  McClelland House, Sea Ranch, California (project)
  Otus House, Berkeley, California
  Saltzman House, Carmel, California
  Thomasian House, Orinda, California
  Truesdale House, Sea Ranch, California
  Turnbull Sr. House I, Carbondale, Colorado
  Vickery House, Sea Ranch, California (project)
  Arts Center, University of California, Berkeley (competition project)
  Urban renewal housing, Akron, Ohio (project)
  Cascade Project, Akron, Ohio (project)
1967 Boas House, Stinson Beach, California
  Morris House I, Sea Ranch, California (project)
  Pirofski House, Palo Alto, California (project)
  Spec I House, Sea Ranch, California (project)
  Stauffacher House, Mill Valley, California (project)
  Beckonridge Housing, Tacoma, Washington (project)

William Turnbull: The American Club, Victoria Island, Hong Kong, 1985 (model).

College 6, University of California at Santa Cruz (project)

1968 Dahlen House, Santa Barbara, California (project)

Hines House, Sea Ranch, California

McElrath House, Santa Cruz, California

Morris House II, Sea Ranch, California

Ray House, Sea Ranch, California (project)

Spec II House, Sea Ranch, California (prototype)

Spec III House, Sea Ranch, California (prototype)

Weyerhauser Prototype House, Kansas City, Missouri

Bechtel Prototype Housing, Santa Catalina, California (project)

Conifer 4 Housing for the Elderly, Tacoma, Washington

Conifer 5 Housing, Tacoma, Washington

Faculty Club, University of California at Santa Barbara

Housing, Hamden, Connecticut (project)

Athletic Club II, Sea Ranch, California

1968/
72 Peterson House I, Tacoma, Washington (project)

1969 Caygill House, Sea Ranch, California

Klotz House, Westerly, Rhode Island

La Boyteaux House, Orinda, California (project)

McComber House, Sea Ranch, California

Naff House, Pajaro Dunes, California

Reid House, Sea Ranch, California

Baker House, Sea Ranch, California

Bartell House, Sea Ranch, California

Binker House, Sea Ranch, California

Eastwood House, Sea Ranch, California

Edgerton House, Sea Ranch, California

Kohlmeister House, Sea Ranch, California

Kreps/Levine House, Sea Ranch, California

Larsen House, Sea Ranch, California

Matthews House, Sea Ranch, California

Whiteside House, Sea Ranch, California

Wickstead House, Sea Ranch, California

Wilson/Morre/King House, Sea Ranch, California

Tempchin House, Bethesda, Maryland (with Rurik Ekstrom)

Turnbull Sr. House II, Carbondale, Colorado

Master plan for Russian Harbor, Jenner, California

Kansas City Mall

1970 Baer House addition, Monterey County, California (project)

Bransten House, Muir Beach, California (project)

Bransten House renovation, San Francisco (project)

Gahagan House, Tamales Bay, California (project)

Mentzer House, Sea Ranch, California

Rush House, Sea Ranch, California

Goodhart House, Sea Ranch, California

Villa del Monte Housing for the Elderly, Seaside, California

Oak Street Turnkey Housing, Haight-Ashbury, San Francisco (project)

Tract A Townhouses, Vail, Colorado (project)

Boas Pontiac Building remodelling, San Francisco

Golden West Savings and Loan Association Office interiors, Capitola, California

Golden West Savings and Loan Association Office remodelling, Castro Valley, California

Golden West Savings and Loan Association Office remodelling, Corte Madera, California

Golden West Savings and Loan Association Office interiors, Eastridge, California (project)

Pembroke Dormitories, Brown University, Providence, Rhode Island

Land use analysis: Nuclear Power Station, Davenport, California

1971 King House renovation, La Selva Beach, California

Schaefer House, Sonoma County, California (project)

Schink House, Woodside, California (project)

Edgerton House additions, Sea Ranch, California

York House, Oakland, California

Bay Ranch Condominium, Point Reyes, California (project)

Arcata National Building remodelling, San Francisco

Gentry Office Building, Dublin, California (project)

Golden West Savings and Loan Association Building, Albany, California (project)

Golden West Savings and Loan Association Building, Santa Cruz, California (project)

Feasibility plan for low-income housing and housing for the elderly, Pittsburg, California

1972 Boise Cascade System Houses, Lake Country, California (project)

Haas House renovation, San Francisco

Hayes House, Comptche, California (project)

Hepler House, Palo Alto, California

Pirofski House additions, Palo Alto, California

O'Connor House, Sea Ranch, California

Dunlavey House, Sea Ranch, California (project)

Starbird House, Santa Clara County, California

MLTW/Turnbull Associates Office remodelling, San Francisco

Beta Theta Pi Fraternity Building remodelling, Stanford University, Palo Alto, California (project)

Hill Plan, Nashville, Tennessee (project)

Vail-Boothcreek Plan, Vail, Colorado (project)

1973 Dillingham House renovation, San Francisco

Foster House renovation, San Francisco

Halprin House additions, Sea Ranch, California

Jacobs House, Sausalito, California (project)

Johnson House additions, Sea Ranch, California

Perini House additions, San Rafael, California

Rosenberg House, Sea Ranch, California (project)

Shanley House, Morris County, New Jersey

Christensen House, Sea Ranch, California

Stone House, California (project)

Sunset Magazine Prototype House, Menlo Park, California (project)

Sylvia House, Santa Rosa, California

Turnbull Jr. House renovation, Sausalito, California

Kresge College, University of California at Santa Cruz

Owen Brown Village Housing, Columbia, Maryland (project)

Oceanic Properties Cluster Housing, Sea Ranch, California (demonstration unit only)

Richardson Highlands Housing, Marin City, California (project)

Franklin Square, Franklin, Tennessee (project)

Design Research Building remodelling, San Francisco

Sherman Clay Building, Portland, Oregon (project)

Sylvia Corporation Yard, Sea Ranch, California

World Savings and Loan Association Office renovation and interiors, San Francisco

Arts Facility, Kresge College, University of California at Santa Cruz

Old Farm Plan, West Haven, New Jersey (project)

Plan for Owen Brown Village, Columbia, Maryland

1973/
75 Turnbull Sr. House III, Far Hills, New Jersey (project)

1974 Bowles House additions, San Francisco

Devendorf House, Sea Ranch, California

Fall River Cabins, Glenburn, California

Newton Townhouse, San Francisco (project)

Coon House, Sea Ranch, California (project)

Kanner House, Sea Ranch, California

Marshall House, Sea Ranch, California

Potter House, Sea Ranch, California

Wong House, Sea Ranch, California (project)

Ziegler Townhouses, Franklin, Tennessee (project)

Sedway-Cooke Planning Offices, San Francisco

Newman Office interiors, San Francisco

Sterling Vineyards Tasting Room additions and remodelling, Calistoga, California

C.L.O.T.H. Building remodelling and interiors, San Francisco

1975 Bertram House renovation, Sea Ranch, California (project)

Hayes House renovation, San Francisco

Peterson House II, Columbia, Maryland

Sloan House, Franklin, Tennessee

Zimmermann House, Fairfax County, Virginia

La Fuente Restaurant remodelling, San Francisco

1976 House, Lafayette, California

Sagan House, Tahoe, California (project)

Kauai Condominium, Lolea, Kauai, Hawaii (project)

Prince Kuhio Building renovation, Kauai, Hawaii (project)

Wine and Cheese Shop remodelling, San Francisco (project)

Minnesota Capitol addition, St. Paul (competition project)

1977 Lilienthal House additions, Napa, California

Moss House, Sea Ranch, California

Trestle Beach Housing, Santa Cruz County, California

World Savings and Loan Association Building, Santa Maria, California

World Savings and Loan Association Building remodelling, La Jolla, California

World Savings and Loan Association Building, Seal Beach, California

Library and Cultural Center, Biloxi, Mississippi

Master plan and landscaping for Garin Park, Fremont, California (project; with Garrett Eckbo)

A. G. Monastery Plan, Carmel Highlands, California (project)

1978 American Wood Council House Beautiful I, Las Vegas, Nevada (project)

American Wood Council House Beautiful II, Las Vegas, Nevada

Allewelt House, Modesto, California

Brown House, Locke, California

Caygill House addition, Sea Ranch, California

DiGiorgio House, Napa, California

Foster House addition, Healdsburg, California

Hart/Pryor House remodelling, Chevy Chase, Maryland

Hines House, Aspen, Colorado (project)

Keenan House, Napa County, Californian (project)

Leaper House additions, San Francisco

Lee House, San Francisco

Lindzey House, Sea Ranch, California

Markham Winery additions, Napa County, California

McElrath House additions, Santa Cruz, California

Pirofski House additions, Palo Alto, California

Scarlett House, Woodside, California (project)

Sedway House additions, San Rafael, California

Baxter House, Sea Ranch, California

Steltzner House remodelling, St. Helena, California

Trefethen House additions, Napa County, California

Yoerg House remodelling, Atherton, California

Sausalito Point Housing, Marin County, California (project)

Hart/White Property Housing, West Virginia (project)

Jewels by Jacques Building interiors, Richmond, California

World Savings and Loan Association Offices, Stanford Shopping Center, California

Mark Fenwick Offices interiors, San Francisco (project)

Santos and Haircutter interiors, San Francisco (project)

California Harvest Shops interiors, San Francisco (project)

Schoen-Snedeker/Anchorage interiors, San Francisco

Toys in the Tower interiors, San Francisco

Beadazzled interiors, San Francisco

Almaden Shopping Plaza interiors, San Jose, California

Serramonte Shopping Center remodelling, San Francisco (project)

Sterling Vineyards Private Reserve Building Calistoga, California (project)

Johnson/Turnbull Vinyards remodelling and planning, Napa County, California

Public Library remodelling, Sausalito, California

Nature Conservatory Interpretive Center, Big Creek, California

Nature Conservatory Interpretive Center, Santa Cruz Island, California

State Coastal Conservancy Plans for Casper, Cambria and Whiskey Shoals, California

Hudson Planning, Big Sur, California

Briggs Property Plan, Carmel Highlands, California

Ocean Meadows Plan, Mendocino, California

A. G. Monastery Union Shell Plan, Monterey, California

1979 Site 5 Office Building, Sacramento, California

Library, Sausalito, California

1980 Brown House, Locke, California

Carroll House, San Francisco

Head Royce School, Oakland, California

Herst House, Ross, California

Mayfield Mall and Mini Mall, Mount View, California

Embarcadero Promenade, San Francisco

Cakebread Cellars, Rutherford, California

1981 Twichell Plan, San Francisco

Lee House, San Francisco

Phelan House, Evanston, Illinois

Fisher Vineyard, Santa Rosa, California

Rabkin House, Sausalito, California

De Bruyn House addition, Sausalito, California

1982 Davidow House, Kauai, Hawaii

Embarcadero Center Theater, San Francisco

Edwards House, Chappaquiddick, Martha's Vineyard Island, Massachusetts

North San Matero County Center for the Arts, California

Trestle Beach Condominiums, Soquel, California

Courtyard House, Aspen, Colorado

Parcel 10 Development, Woodrun Place, Snowmass, Colorado

Church Divinity School of the Pacific Rehabilitation, Berkeley, California

1983 The Coach Store, San Francisco

Sherman Clay Building, Sutter Street, San Francisco

Manager's Residence, Chateau Montelena, Calistoga, California

California Fish Growers' Facilities, Bodega Bay, California

Johnson/Turnbull Vineyard, Oakville, California

Helmholz House, Healdsburg, California

St. Anne's Church and Rectory, Fremont, California

Centennial Condominiums, Vail, Colorado

Sweetwater Country Club, Houston, Texas

Hyatt Regency Hotel interiors, 5 Embarcadero Center, San Francisco

1984 Boalt Hall Physical Plant improvements, University of California, Berkeley

Motlow House remodelling, Berkeley, California

Cakebread Cellars Master Plan, Rutherford, California

Reingold House, Wrightwood, California

Milligan House, Sea Ranch, California

Doubleday House remodelling, Green Street, San Francisco

Doubleday Offices remodelling, Lombard Street, San Francisco

Robbins House interiors, St. Helena, California

Pettit and Martin Law Offices interiors, San Francisco

Theel Condominiums, Dana Point, California

Smith/Kennon House, Santa Monica, California

Wonderwall, Centennial and Bayou Lagoons, at the Louisiana World Exposition, New Orleans

Woodrun I Condominiums, Snowmass Village, Colorado

LeBoeuf Lamb Leiby MacRae Law Offices interiors, San Francisco

Stepanian House addition, San Francisco

Newton Winery Offices, St. Helena, California

Snowmass Base Village Condominiums, Colorado

Corte Madera Plan, Corte Madera, California

1985 Naegele House, Santa Monica, California

Heil House, Sea Ranch, California

Brown House, San Rafael, California

Montgomery House, Waveland, Mississippi

Witherspoon House, Inverness, California

Escher House, Rutherford, California

Evers House, Healdsburg, California

Pease House, Sonoma, California

Spencer House, Oakville, California

Chesapeake Genetics, Chesapeake City, Maryland

Drucker House, Ross, California

Ahearn House, Charleston, South Carolina

Yoerg House, Atherton, California

American Club, Victoria Island, Hong Kong

Publications:

By TURNBULL: books—*Global Architecture: MLTW/The Sea Ranch*, edited by Yukio Futagawa, Tokyo 1971; illustrations for *The Place of Houses* by Moore, Lyndon and Allen, New York 1974; *Global Architecture: Sea Ranch Details*, Tokyo 1976; articles—"Zimmermann House, Fairfax County, Virginia" in *GA Houses* (Tokyo), no. 1, 1976; "An Interview with William Turnbull, Jr." in *Transition* (St. Kilda, Victoria), March 1980; "William Turnbull, Jr.", interview, in *Architecture* (Washington, D.C.), March 1985; "William Turnbull: interview", with Bill Hersey, in *San Francisco Bay Architects' Review*, Spring 1985.

On TURNBULL: books—*The Architecture of Monuments* by Thomas Creighton, New York 1962; *World Architecture 2, 3* and *4: U.S.A.* by John Donat, London and New York 1965, 1966, 1967; *American Architecture and Urbanism* by Vincent Scully, New York 1969; *New Directions in American Architecture* by Robert A. M. Stern, New York 1969, 1977; *Nuove Ville* by Roberto Aloi, Milan 1970; *Observations in American Architecture* by Ivan Chermayeff, New York 1972; *Drawings by American Architects*, New York 1973; *Global Interiors: Houses in the U.S.A. 6*, edited by Yukio Futagawa, Tokyo 1974; *Houses by MLTW, 1959-1975* by Yukio Futagawa, Tokyo 1975; *Unbuilt America* by Alison Sky and Michelle Stone, New York 1976; *Bay Area Houses*, edited by Sally Woodbridge, New York 1976; *Drawings for a More Modern Architecture*, exhibition catalog, Los Angeles 1978; articles—*Geijutsi Seikatsu* (Tokyo), November, 1968; *Kenchiku Bunka* (Tokyo), April 1971; *Architecture + Urbanism* (Tokyo), November 1972; "Barn House at Sea Ranch, California" in *Architecture + Urbanism* (Tokyo), October 1974; "Outside In" in *Progressive Architecture* (New York), February 1976; "House in a Box" in *Architectural Review* (London), June 1976; "Two One-Family Houses" in *Arkitekten* (Copenhagen), March 1977; "House in Great Falls, Virginia" in *Baumeister* (Munich), July 1977; "University of California at Santa Cruz" in *AIA Journal* (Washington, D.C.), August 1979; "Mellow Yellow" in *Progressive Architecture* (New York), August 1979; "William Turnbull Jr.—Bonnafont Gallery" in *San Francisco Chronicle*, 17 May 1981; "The California Condition" in *LA Architect* (Los Angeles), December 1982; "Mixed Metaphors: The New Orleans Fair" in *Progressive Architecture* (New York), May 1984; "On the Banks of the Mississippi" in *Building Design* (London), 8 June 1984.

The work of MLTW has evolved in many ways over the last ten year period. Primarily we believe in "place making," that architectural quality derived from site and insight that allows the participant to feel a heightened consciousness of being alive and enjoying the awareness of it. We try to identify and celebrate the individual with all his hopes and aspirations in an increasingly complex and mechanized world.

Within the realm of the automobile, "strip" development, and plastic subdivisions, we in California still look back to the land itself for basic insights—sun, topography and microclimate. We feel that our buildings must be well-rooted in their environments, drawing from the landscape's inherent resources while at the same time commenting on owner's idosyncrasies, desires and budgets.

It seems to us that a building, to provide more than mere shelter, must have a conceptual idea, one that speaks to an insight of the client's needs, both tangible and intangible, and thereby to excellence in architecture. To be successful, a building must be compelling for the mind—as well as keeping out the rain.

The Sea Ranch Condominium (1965) provided a solution for multi-family vacation housing by preserving open land and clustering units. It combined simple repetitive pieces under large roofs that followed the ground contours and resembled "big houses" in the grand seashore tradition (albeit in our case Western and rural). Interiors of vacation homes, we felt, need not be stiff and formal, as proper faces put on for neighborhood consumption in the everyday world. Our condominiums had kitchens and baths stacked like furniture (and painted that way), while bedrooms were two-story derivations of an old four-poster bed. Construction as a heavy timber cage pragmatically solved the structural forces of wind and earthquake, while poetically reminding the inhabitant that the northern coast of California is still a rough, wild, frontier environment.

Ten years later the Zimmermann House, outside

Washington, D.C., is a maturation of our concerns with "place" and conceptual image. In this project the owners were at odds with one another about what constituted a house. Mr. Zimmermann felt that a house should be a place of light-filled spaces, while Mrs. Zimmermann wished to have one of many porches recalling her childhood in the old summer houses of Maine. The house wanted to be, in essence, a "grand porch" enclosing an inner house whose roofs themselves became useful decks within this grand superannuated gazebo. The porch has a translucent fiberglass roof to let in overall light, a device we first used on the Swimming/Tennis Facility at Sea Ranch. the exterior of the porch is covered in 1 × 4 lattice work to filter the sunshine, frame views, and establish a boundary between the inside and outside worlds. Simple plywood walls and aluminum windows of the inside house continue our respectful involvement with common builder materials and the simplicity of detail. The structure of the porch cage is made up of groupings of small pieces of wood, from 2 × 12's to 2 × 6's, with fewer pieces as the structure grows above the ground, Like the Condominium, these carrying and bracing members are all exposed for the eye and the mind two perceive. The deceptively simple structure sits quietly on a rise of ground overlookin farmland and the Potomac River. A paradox pleasantly resolved.

Architecture without space and light is devoid of interest. In its making, architecture should delight the mind, respect the purse, and consume the intellect.

—William Turnbull, Jr.

William Turnbull Jr. is a narrative architect. His buildings are carefully crafted fables about shelter, program, site, climate, tradition, and movement through space. His Zimmermann house near Washington D.C. makes a virtue of a contradictory program. The husband wanted lots of light and the wife wanted lots of porch, to recall summers on the verandah of a house in Maine. But a conventional porch would have cut off much of the light. So Turnbull made it unconventional. He abstracted a traditional porch relative—the gazebo—and cast it over the entire house. He produced a dramatic compromise: a sunshade which is also a light filter. The net-like pattern of lathwork even recalls the porch screens of McKim, Meade and White's Newport Casino and the general porch look of late nineteenth century New England summer houses. The moral here is that history is always new.

Another house, on a ranch near Modesto in the hot sun Joaquin Valley of California, required greater protection from the sun as well as privacy for each member of a large family, which nevertheless liked to live out of doors. The house appears to be a large, simple, rectangular, hip roofed pavilion surrounded by verandahs rhythmically marked off in bays. The image combines the sheltering quality of General Mariano Vallego's Verandah-grit Petaluma Adobe—the classic California ranch house—with an almost Palladian manipulation of symmetry and proportion. It looks new but familiar at the same time, in the manner of the best Bay Region work of William Wurster. But the interior reveals a surprise O. Henry ending to this tale of life on the ranch. For the single enclosing roof form hides two quite separate houses—one for the parents and one for the children. The two structures are connected by a courtyard which is protected but not covered by a section of the roof which has been cut away leaving only the supporting timbers. Here, too, the light is filtered, now through a timber screen, and the court becomes a down-home oasis for recuperation after the round-up.

It is fitting that a storytelling architect should design a house for books. Turnbull's Biloxi Library and Cultural Center in Mississippi provides the backdrop for the imaginary journey which every reader makes. A library is a place for people to sit while their minds wander away. But before they sit down they can be put in the proper reflective mood.

The story here is about entrance and departure, about the way a series of thresholds can accentuate the sensation of arrival. The building resembles an abstracted lobster: the two pincers or wings define a central entrance courtyard, past a flagpole and the original tiny wood frame library which has been preserved. The door is framed in a flat gable capped with a rectangular cut-out or empty belfry at the top. The simple abstract image brings to mind the front stoops of small town churches, schools, and meeting houses of once upon a time. A short passage leads to the high, wide main reading room. To the left is the two story circular circulation (!) "temple," a central desk surrounded by interpenetrating framing devices. Beyond and through the circulation desk, which is also a circulation space, lies the exhibition hall. Entrance here consists of a passage dividing a dramatic double stairway leading up to the light. Another major entrance, or exit, leads outside through the corner of the building. The walk from either side of the building to the circulation desk at the center is a theatrically controlled journey. After all, borrowing a book is a very special event and should be commemorated.

Turnbull's architecture is important because it fashions memorable and modern settings out of ordinary and historical elements. He transforms buildings into places and makes them fun to read.

—Daniel Gregory

TUSQUETS Guillen, Oscar.

Spanish. Born in Barcelona, 14 June 1941. Educated at the Deutsche Schule, Barcelona, 1950-54; Escuela de Artes y Oficois Artísticos, Llotja, Barcelona, 1954-58; Escuela Tecnica Superior de Arquitectura, Barcelona, 1958-65. Served in the Spanish Army, in Tarragona and Lérida, 1961, 1962, 1965: 2nd Lieutenant. Married Beatriz de Moura in 1964. Worked in the architectural studio of Federico Correa and Alfonsa Mila, Barcelona, 1961-64; formed the partnership Studio PER, with Christian Cirici, *q.v.*, Lluis Clotet, *q.v.*, and Pep Bonet, *q.v.*, Barcelona, 1965. Professor in charge of Projects, Escuela Tecnica Superior de Arquitectura, Barcelona, 1975-76, 1979-80. Director of Culture, Colego Arquitectos Cataluña y Baleares, Barcelona, 1966-67, 1976-78. Exhibitions: *Arquitectura del Studio PER*, Lérida, 1971; *Triennale,* Milan, 1973; *Arquitectura y Lágrimas,* Sala Vincon, Barcelona, 1975; *Centenario de la Escuela Tecnica Superior de Arquitectura de Barcelona,* Palacio Nacional, Barcelona, 1977; *Festival of Films about Architecture,* Centre Georges Pompidou, Paris, 1978; *Transformations in Modern Architecture*, Museum of Modern Art, New York, 1979; *Biennale,* Venice, 1980; *The House as Image*, Louisiana Museum, Humlebaek, Denmark, 1981; *The Presence of the Past*, Paris, 1981, San Francisco, 1982; *Ten New Buildings*, Institute of Contemporary Arts, London, 1983; *Tea and Coffee Piazza*, Milan and New York, 1983; *Tusquets and Clotet Watercolours*, San Francisco and Los Angeles, 1984; *Idee Prozess Ergebnis*, IBA, Berlin, 1984; *Biennale,* Paris, 1985. Collections: Museum of Modern Art, New York; Centre Georges Pompidou, Paris; Architektur Museum, Frankfurt; World Gallery, New York; Bonnafont Gallery, San Francisco. Recipient: Premio F.A.D., Barcelona, 1965, 1972, 1979, 1980, 1983; Gold Delta Award for industrial design, Barcelona, 1974, 1979, 1980; First Prize, Rambla de la Bisbal competition, Gerona, 1975; National Restoration Award, Madrid, 1980; First Prize, Faculty of Medicine Extension competition, Barcelona, 1980; Critics' Design Prize, Barcelona, 1984. Address: Studio PER, Caspe 151, Barcelona 13, Spain.

Works:

1963 Colegio Mayor San Raimundo de Peñafort, Barcelona (with Lluis Clotet)
1965 Editorial Lumen Offices, Barcelona (with Lluis Clotet)
   Emilio Blay House interiors, Barcelona (with Lluis Clotet)
   Apartment Block I, Cadaqués, Gerona, Spain (with Lluis Clotet and Xavier Carulla)
   Sonor Hi-Fi shop and studio, Barcelona (with Lluis Clotet and Xavier Carulla)
1968 Gremio Vidrieros Building, Barcelona (with Lluis Clotet and Xavier Carulla)
   Maspons-Ubina Studio, Barcelona (with Lluis Clotet and Xavier Carulla)
   Fonda Sala Restaurant, Olost de Llusanes, Barcelona (with Lluis Clotet and Xavier Carulla)
   Ibars Offices, Barcelona (with Lluis Clotet and Xavier Carulla)
   Casa Fullá apartment building, Barcelona (with Lluis Clotet and Santiago Loperena)
   Single-family housing, La Atmella del Vallés, Barcelona (with Lluis Clotet and Xavier Carulla)
   Solitari Apartments, Cadaqués, Gerona, Spain (with Lluis Clotet and Xavier Carulla)
   El Colomer Apartment Complex, Cadaqués, Gerona, Spain (with Lluis Clotet, Santiago Loperna, and Anna Bohigas)
   Casa Penina (house), Cardedeu, Barcelona (with Lluis Clotet, Santiago Loperena, and Anna Bohigas)
   Ancla Roja Apartments, Salou, Tarragona, Spain (with Lluis Clotet and Anna Bohigas)
   Miro Otro exhibition plan, Barcelona (with Lluis Clotet, Pep Bonet, and Cristian Cirici)
1970 Gil Sala residential additions, Barcelona (with Lluis Clotet, Santiago Loperena, and Anna Bohigas)
1971 Casa Regas (house), Llofriu, Gerona, Spain (with Lluis Clotet, Santiago Loperena, and Anna Bohigas)
   Puig and Cadafalch Housing Block, Mataró, Barcelona (with Lluis Clotet, Santiago Loperena, and Anna Bohigas)
   Union Lloyd Travel Agency Building, Barcelona (with Lluis Clotet, Santiago Loperena, and Anna Bohigas)
1972 Aerojet Travel Offices, Barcelona (with Lluis Clotet, Santiago Loperena, and Anna Bohigas)
   Belvedere Georgina (house), Llofriu, Gerona, Spain (with Lluis Clotet, Santiago Loperena, and Anna Bohigas)
1973 Mozart-Fortuny Apartments, Sant Cugat del Valles, Barcelona (with Lluis Clotet, Santiago Loperena, and Anna Bohigas)
   Aerojet Travel Offices, Palma, Majorca (with Lluis Clotet and Santiago Loperena)
   Alpes Building, Hospitalet, Barcelona (with Lluis Clotet, Santiago Loperena, and Anna Bohigas)
1974 Tusquets Family Apartment alterations, Barcelona (with Lluis Clotet, Santiago Loperena, and Anna Bohigas)
   Casa Vittoria (house), Pantelleria, Italy (with Lluis Clotet)
   Stephanie Apartment, Barcelona (with Lluis Clotet, Santiago Loperena, and Anna Bohigas)
   Sahutuje Studio, Barcelona (with Lluis Clotet, Santiago Loperena, and Anna Bohigas)
1975 Jacob Levy Apartment, Barcelona (with Luis Clotet, Santiago Loperena, and Anna Bohigas)
   Feria Textiles Exhibition Stand, Valencia (with Lluis Clotet)
1976 Housing group, Sardanola, Barcelona (with Lluis Clotet, Santiago Loperena, and Anna Bohigas)
   New Building for the Colegio de Arquitectos

Oscar Tusquets: **Museum of Modern Art, Frankfurt, 1983 (project).**

de Catalunya, Barcelona (competition project)

1976/
79 Apartment building, Calle Circunvalcion Alta, Cerdanyola, Barcelona (with Lluis Clotet)

1978 Santa Maria de Gallecs Planning Study, Mollet de Valles, Barcelona (with Lluis Clotet and Xavier Sust)

Housing Complex, Gran Via, Barcelona (with Pep Bonet, Christian Cirici and Lluis Clotet)

Pomes Gardens planting, Font Clara, Gerona, Spain

1978/
79 Casa en el Golf single-family house, Golf de Santa Cristina de Aro, Gerona, Spain (with Anna Bohigas)

La Balsa Restaurant and Apartment, Calle Infanta Isabel, Barcelona (with Lluis Clotet and Anna Bohigas)

1979/
80 Fortuny Swimming Pool, Calle Fortuny, Sant Cugat del Valles, Barcelona (with Lluis Clotet)

Casa Thomas restoration, Calle Mallorca, Barcelona (with Christian Cirici, Pep Bonet and Lluis Clotet)

1979/
82 Faculty of Medicine extensions, University of Barcelona (with Lluis Clotet, Fransesc Basso and Carles Diaz)

1980/
81 Del Liceo al Seminario district redevelopment, Raval quarter, Barcelona (with Lluis Clotet)

1981 Casa Calico single-family house, Bagur, Gerona, Spain (project)

1981/
83 Banco de Espana branch office, Gerona, Spain (project; with Lluis Clotet and Ignacio Paricio)

1981/
84 Palau de la Musica and Sant Fransesc Church remodelling, Calle Amadeo Vives, Barcelona (with Lluis Clotet, Carles Diaz and Ignacio Paricio)

1982 Sastreria Groc tailor's shop facade renovation, Rambla de Catalunya, Barcelona (with Anna Bohigas)

1983 Convent dels Angels development, El Raval, Barcelona (with Lluis Clotet, Carles Diaz and Ignacio Paricio)

Museum of Modern Art, Frankfurt-am-Main, Germany (competition project; with Lluis Clotet, Claudia Mann, Carles Vinardell and Ignacio Paricio)

Azulete Restaurant glass dining-room, Via Augusta, Barcelona (with Pepe Cortes, Ignacio Paricio and Enric Torrent)

1983/
84 Casa en el Maresme single-family house, Premia de Dalt, Barcelona (project; with Ignacio Paricio and Carles Vinardell)

Mas Abello housing complex, Reus, Tarragona, Spain (with Carles Diaz, Carles Vinardell an Carles Basso)

1984 Azulete Bar interiors in a Modernist house, Via Augusta, Barcelona (with Are Oliver)

La Puntilla Cultural Centre auditorium, Las Palmas, Canary Islands (with Agustin Juarez, Maribel Correa, Diego Estevez and Ignacio Paricio)

Publications:

By TUSQUETS: books—*Neutral Corner*, Barcelona 1965; *Arquitectura Modernista,* with Lluis Clotet, Barcelona 1968; *Arquitectura Gótica Catalana,* with Lluis Clotet, Barcelona 1968; *Arquitectura y Lágrimas,* with Lluis Clotet, Barcelona, 1975; also designed the series of books *Cuadernos Infimos, Cauderno Marginales, La Sonrisa Vertical, Acracia,* and *Los 5 Sentidos,* Barcelona 1969-80; articles—"Elogio de los espacios tontos" in *Nuevo Ambiente* (Barcelona), no. 16, 1969; "Porque Cruyff si y Alvar Aalto no?" in *Arquitecturas Bis* (Barcelona), May 1974; "B.D. Ediciones de Diseno y su local en Madrid" in *Arquitectura* (Madrid), nos. 204-205, 1977; articles, with Lluis Clotet—"Acondicionamento sala estar y comedor" in *Cuadernos Arquitectura* (Barcelona), no. 4, 1965; "Viviendas en Hospitalet de Llobregat" in *Hogar y Arquitectura* (Madrid), October 1968; "Casa Regas" in *Cauderno Arquitectura* (Barcelona), July/August 1972; "El chalet masia" in *Mobelart* (Barcelona), October 1972; "Belvedere Georgina casita unifamiliar" in *Cuadernos Arquitectura* (Barcelona), September/October 1973; "Mi Terraza, Studio PER en el Industrial Design de la Triennales de Milan" in *Hogares Modernos* (Barcelona), November 1973; "Biblioscala de un piso en Barcelona" in *Nuevo Ambiente* (Barcelona), March/April 1974; "Manzana Puig i Cadafalch" in *Cuadernos de Arquitectura Anuario* (Barcelona), no. 109, 1975; "Viviendas en Sant Cugat" in *Cuadernos de Arquitectura Anuario* (Barcelona), no. 110, 1975; "Vivir en la Ciudad" in *Habitat,* Barcelona 1975; "Learning from Venturi" in *Quaderns d'Arquitectura* (Barcelona), 1984.

On TUSQUETS: books—*Arquitectura Espanola Contemporanea* by Lluis Domenech, Barcelona 1968; *Casa Vittoria, Pantelleria* by the Habitat editors, Barcelona 1976; *El Studio PER o los confines de la Arquitectura actual* by J. Muntañola, Barcelona 1976; *Arquitecturas Catalanas* by Helio Piñon, Barcelona, 1977; *The Language of Post-Modern Architecture* by Charles Jencks, London 1977; *Topogenesis uno* by Joseph Muntanyola, Barcelona 1979; *Eclectisismo y Vanguardia* by Ignaci Sola Morales, Barcelona 1982; *Clotet-Tusquets* by Claudia Mann, Barcelona 1983; *The Modern House* by David Mackay, Barcelona 1984; *Spanish Contemporary Architecture* by E. Bru and J. L. Mateo, Barcelona 1984; articles—"Los Premios FAD" by Oriol Bohigas in *Serra d'Or* (Barcelona), January 1967; "Canaletas Neighbourhood" by David Mackay in *World Architecture,* London 1968; "Uma Ionja em Barcelona" in *Architectura* (Lisbon), January 1968; "Chalet en una ciudad jard." in *Nuevo Ambiente* (Barcelona), no. 15, 1969; "Exposición Miró Otro" in *Summa* (Buenos Aires), 20 November 1969; "Vivre dehors: Autour de patios-terrasses" in *Maison Francaise* (Paris), June 1971; "Obras de Clotet-Tusquets," special issue of *Hogar y Arquitectura* (Madrid), July 1971; "Los Premios de interiorismo FAD 1971" in *Hogares Modernos* (Barcelona), January 1972; "Allestimento a Barcelona" in *Domus* (Milan), October 1972; "Nuevas Tendencias de la Arquitectura española" in *Arquitectura* (Madrid), May 1972; "Belvedere Georgina" in *Nuevo Ambiente* (Barcelona), September 1973; "Casa Regas Llofriu" in *Nuevo Ambiente* (Barcelona), November 1973; "Casa Georgina" in *Toshi Yutaku* (Tokyo), November 1973; "Introducir una vivienda functional en un Belvedere Palladiano" in *Domus* (Milan), no. 522, 1973; "Opiniones sobre el Belvedere" by Correa, Sust, and Fiores in *Jano Arquitectura* (Barcelona), December 1973; "Agencia Viajes Aerojet" in *Nuevo Ambiente* (Barcelona), March 1974; "Gil Sala Building" in *Toshi Yutaku* (Tokyo), no. 8, 1975; "El plano en el espacio" by X. Sust in *Jano Arquitectura* (Barcelona), December 1975; "Casa Vittoria en la isla de Pantelleria" in *Arquitecturas Bis* (Barcelona), May/June 1976; "Anarchist's Guide" by Chris Fawcett in *Architectural Association Quarterly* (London), vol. 7, no. 3, 1976; "C'e un designer sul trapezio" by Bruno Zevi in *Espresso* (Milan), 23 July 1977; "Studio PER," special issue of *Architecture + Urbanism* (Tokyo), April 1977; "Per, uno per uno, tutti per tutti" by Alessandro Mendini in *Modo Milano* (Milan), November 1977; "Iberia," special issue of *Archithese* (Niederteufen), November/December 1979; "Come Palladio, oltre Palladio" by Barbara Radice in *Casa Vogue* (Milan), November 1980; "Studio PER" in *Domus* (Milan), January 1981; "Nuova vita per il Palazzo della Musica" by Franco Apra in *Casa Vogue* (Milan), September 1982; "Studio PER" in *El Croquis* (Madrid), August/October 1983; "La casa omerica" by Donatella Smetana in *Casa Vogue* (Milan), July/August 1984.

There it comes, the Great Circus of the Culture of Architecture with artists from all over the world. The foolhardy Archigrams, the Tendenzas, rigorous lion-tamers, the Radicals, famous contortionists, the Five Architects, reincarnation of the clown in the thirties . . . and a lot more.

The happy strolling band runs untiring around the world, sets up its tent in any Congress or University and develops the show, always new, always repeated. Ideal towns, universal panaceas, paternalist warnings . . . there isn't any relation with what one really builds, but the circus is like that: a healthy evasion.

It is very difficult to be able to perform in this show, yet from time to time some death or the dictation of fashions causes some vacancies. The new artists are recruited in the most sophisticated universities, where one doesn't waste time in practical training, as its pupils are not going to build that much. It isn't easy for Spanish provincials like us to obtain a role in this troupe.

Nevertheless, as every day the possibility to realize a work becomes more remote, a work that would allow us to really intervene in our surroundings—that is, an architectonical work—we exercise ourselves in pirouettes and jumps, hoping that one day the great circus will notice us.

—Oscar Tusquets

See CLOTET Ballus, Lluis.

Studio PER is four architects in related practices in one office. Apart from administrative convenience, what really binds them together is that they share the same approach to architecture in valuing positively its cultural objectives. Their architecture is essentially intellectual. They are eager to discuss, argue, and defend their work against all criticism in order to explore all the rich possibilities available to their avant-garde position. This makes their buildings, and their explanations, often contradictory—but that is the price of an open mind—adventure and doubt. But this attitude, which is almost literary rather than visual, would be of little interest if it were not backed up by secure professional ability, compositional control, and a sensitive feeling for proportions.

Lluis Clotet and Oscar Tusquets have, until recently, been one practice. From the beginning they were immersed in the neo-realist, historically-based, so-called Barcelona School of Architecture that achieved a coherent local style during the 1960's and 70's. It was based on program analysis, environmental integration, economic use of materials, and constructional detailing as a basis for decoration. Their apartment building Casa Fullà in Barcelona and the private house Casa Penina are the most representative of this period.

The small week-end house, "Belvedere Georgina," in Llofriu, is so ironic in poking fun at the modern movement and so dexterous in its use of historical vocabulary that at first it seems to be just a brilliant example of pop art in architecture. The house in conceived as a garden pavilion in the form of a temple in homage to the motor-car, which makes the week-end house possible. The car is parked under a classical pergola, and one enters the house down through the pit. Part of the pavilion is cut away to form a sheltered court, and the missing section is painted on the walls. The window shutters are designed and placed according to the proportions and rules of classical composition, allowing the real windows to be placed haphazardly behind, according to the dictates of the interior function. Though the image of the house is an irrelevant exercise in pop history, it has given the authors the freedom to extend the frontiers of architectural composition in its own right to give a cultured solution to the building so that it reads well in the landscape and allows the exterior and interior design to overlap independently.

It is through this "second reading" of their architecture that one finds the common denominator that runs through their buildings—be it the outside rooms defined by concrete columns in the Vittoria house on the Island of Pantelleria or the split-level row housing in Sant Cugat.

The recent work of Tusquets shows a disenchantment of the Modern Movement and an increasing fascination for eclectic classical models as shown in his proposals for alterations to the Palau de la Musica in Barcelona, a private house in Premia del Dalt (Barcelona), and social housing in Reus.

The common freshness and professional skill of Clotet and Tusquets, and that of their associates in Studio PER, together with their sensitive alertness to current architectural fashion, enable them to translate new concepts quickly into the local Catalan cultural context. It is a task that is needed if the modern movement is to take root geographically.

—David Mackay

U

UNGERS, Oswald Mathias.

German. Born in Kaiseresch/Eifel, 7 December 1926. Educated at elementary and high schools in Mayen, Germany, 1932-47; Technische Hochschule, Karlsruhe, under Egon Eiermann, 1947-50, Dip. Arch. 1950. Served in the Germany Army, 1945-46. Married Liselotte Gabler in 1956; children: Simon, Sophia and Sibylle. In private practice, Cologne, since 1950, Berlin, since 1964, and Ithaca, New York, since 1970. Professor and Ordinarius (Chair in Urban Design), Technical University, Berlin, since 1963 (Dean of the Faculty of Architecture, and Senator, 1965-67; Vice-Dean of the Faculty of Architecture, 1967-68); Visiting Critic, 1965, 1967, Chairman of the Department of Architecture, 1969-75, and since 1975 Professor of Architecture, Cornell University, Ithaca, New York. Visiting Professor, Harvard University, Cambridge, Massachusetts, 1973; Professor of Architecture, University of California at Los Angeles, 1974-75; Visiting Professor, Technical University, Vienna, 1979. Co-Director, *Interbau* international building exhibition, Berlin, 1984. Exhibitions: *Bienal*, Sao Paulo, Brazil, 1957; *20 German Architects*, Warsaw and Chicago, 1960; *Cologne Architects' Buildings*, Cologne, 1963; *James Stirling and O. M. Ungers*, Zurich, 1965; *German Architecture*, Moscow, 1967; *Rational Architecture*, London, 1975; *Nine International Architects*, Dortmund, 1976; *Biennale*, Venice, 1976; *MantransForms*, Cooper-Hewitt Museum, New York, 1976; *The Sparkling Metropolis*, Guggenheim Museum, New York, 1978; *Museum Buildings since 1945*, Museum am Ostwall, Dortmund, 1979. Recipient: First Prize, Frankfurt Kommende Competition, 1960; First Prize, Berlin 4. Ring Competition, 1975; Special Award, University of Bremen, 1976; First Prize, Hotel Berlin Competition, 1977; First Prize, Kammergericht Competition, Berlin, 1978; First Prize, Badische Landesbibliothek Competition, Karlsruhe, 1980; First Prize, Melkerei Solar House Competition, Landstuhl, 1979; First Prize, Exhibition Centre Competition, Frankfurt, 1980. Address (office): 60 Belvederstrasse, 5000 Cologne 41, Germany.

Works:

1951 Single-family house, Oderweg, Dünnwald, Cologne
Clothing Factory and residential building, Aachenerstrasse, Braunsfeld, Cologne
Multi-family housing, Hültzstrasse, Braunsfeld, Cologne
1953/
58 Institute for Science Studies, Oberhausen, Germany
1956 Student housing, Lindenthal, Cologne
1957 Housing complex, Nippes, Cologne
Apartment block, Dellbrück, Cologne
Two-family house, Cologne
1958 Apartment block, Hansaring, Cologne
1959 Ungers House, Müngersdorf, Cologne
Apartment block, Wuppertal, Germany

1959/
62 Housing complex, Poll, Cologne
"Deutsche Order" (renovation, Frankfurt Kommende), Frankfurt
1960 Art Gallery, Dusseldorf (competition project)
Single-family house, Bensberg, Germany (project)
1960/
61 Single-family house, Odenthal-Erberich, near Cologne (with Max Bill and Olivio Ferrari)
Bold House, Odenthal-Erberich, near Cologne (with Max Bill and Olivio Ferrari)
1961 Single-family house, Bad Homburg, Germany
Single-family house, Overath, Germany
Roman-German Museum, Cologne (competition project)
Preparatory School, Beuel, Germany (competition project)
1961/
63 Garden City Development, Zollstock, Cologne (competition project)
1962 Single-family house, Henneg/Sieg, Germany
1962/
65 Master plan for a housing complex and apartment block for the elderly, Cologne New City, Seeberg, Cologne (competition project)
1964 Student housing, Enschede, Netherlands (competition project; with J. Sawade and G. Geist)
1964/
66 Märkisches Viertel Housing Estate, West Berlin
1965 Museum Complex, Tiergarten, West Berlin (competition project)
German Embassy, Rome (competition project; with J. Sawade)
Preparatory School, Mayen, Germany (competition project; with U. Fleming)
1966 Housing Estate, Ruhwald, Berlin (competition project)
1967/
68 Housing II, Ruhwald, Berlin (project; with Josef Paul Kleihues, H. H. Moldenschardt, and others)
1972 Blauer See Development, Rüsselheim, Germany (competition project)
Federal Ministries, Bonn (competition project)
1973 Plan for the district redevelopment of Düren, Germany (competition project; with R. Koolhaas, K. L. Dietzsch and A. Krieger)
Systematization master plan for the Tiergarten, Berlin (competition project; with R. Koolhaas, P. Allison and D. Allison)
1975 4th Ring Reconstruction, Lichterfelde, Berlin (competition project; with R. Koolhaas and K. Dietzsch)
Aller-Möhe New Town, Hamburg (competition project; with B. Haffner and K. Mekeez)
Housing, Roosevelt Island, New York (competition project)
Housing estate, Widdesdorf, Cologne (project)

Wallraf-Richartz Museum, Cologne (competition project)
1976 University Complex, Bremen (competition project)
Castle Park, Braunschweig, Germany (project)
Morsbroich Castle addition, Leverkusen, Germany (project)
Housing, Marburg, Germany (project)
1977 Hotel Berlin, West Berlin (competition project)
Südliche Friedrichstadt Plan, Berlin (project)
1978 Hotel Budapesterstrasse, Berlin (competition project)
Severins Quarter Development, Altstadt, Cologne (competition project)
1978/
79 Courts of Justice, Berlin (competition project)
Multi-family housing, Schillerstrasse, Charlottenburg, Berlin
Woolworth Store facade design, Wedding, Berlin
1979 Technical Centre, West Berlin Savings Bank, Berlin (competition project)
Melkerei Solar House, Landstuhl, Germany (competition project)
Ackerhof City Development Plan, Braunschweig, Germany (competition project)
1979/
80 Technical High School, Bremerhaven, Germany (competition project)
Alfred-Wegener-Institute for Polar Research, Alten Hafen, Bremerhaven, Germany
1979/
83 Housing development, Lützowplatz, Berlin
1979/
84 German Architecture Museum, Schaumainkai, Frankfurt
1980 Marktplatz Development, Hildesheim, Germany (competition project)
1980/
82 Multi-family housing, Miquelstrasse, Berlin
1980/
83 Galleria and Exhibition Hall 9, Frankfurt
1980/
84 Badische Regional Library, Karlsruhe, Germany
1981 Karstadt Department Store, Tempelhof, Berlin (competition project)
Barmer Exchange Bank, Wuppertal-Barmen, Germany (competition project)
Westkunst temporary museum in the Exhibition Hall, Deutz, Cologne
Friedrichstadt Town Plan, Berlin
1981/
83 Konstantinplatz Redevelopment, Trier, Germany
1982 German Library, Frankfurt (competition project)
German Embassy Residence, Washington, D.C. (competition project)
Federal Postal Museum, Frankfurt (competition project)
1983 Museum of Modern Art, Frankfurt (competition project)
Paulsplatz Redevelopment Plan, Frankfurt

Gruner + Jahr Publishing Office, Hamburg (competition project)

1983/
84   Gleisdreieck Fair and Exhibitions Building extensions, Frankfurt

Publications:

BY UNGERS: books—*Die gläserne Kette: Visionare Architekturen aus dem Kreis un Bruno Taut 1919-1920,* exhibition catalog, with Udo Kultermann, Leverkusen, Germany 1963; *Rudolf Schwarz,* 1963; *Die Erscheinungs Formen des Expressionismus der Architektur,* Cologne 1964; *Veroffentlichungen zur Architektur,* 27 volumes, general editor, Berlin 1965-69; *Optimale Wohngebietsplanung,* with Horst Albach, Wiesbaden 1969; *Kommunen in der Neuen Welt 1740-1971,* with Liselotte Ungers, Cologne 1972, Barcelona 1978; *Dortmunder Architekturhefte 11: Planungsbeispiel Siedlung Hochlarmark Recklinghausen,* with G. Borchers, Dortmund 1978; *Kommentar zum Wettbewerb Kammergericht Berlin,* Cologne 1979; *The Urban Garden—Student Projects for the Sudliche Friedrichstadt Berlin,* editor, with Hans F. Kollhoff and Arthur A. Ovaska, Cologne 1979; articles—"Für eine Lebendige Baukunst" in *Bauwelt* (Berlin), August 1961; "Aus einem vortrag vor dem Akademischen Architektenverein in Hannover" in *Baukunst und Werkform* (Nuremberg), August 1961; "Zum 'Weltplanungsprogramm' von Buckminster Fuller" in *Bauwelt* (Berlin), no. 45, 1961; "Insegnamento sviluppo e ricerca" in *Casabella* (Milan), no. 300, 1965; "Planning and Accident" and "Structure-Quality-Dimension" in *Bau* (Zurich), June 1967; "Grossform" in *Aujourd'hui: Arts et Architecture* (Paris), October 1967; "Form in der Grosstadt" in *Werk* (Zurich), November 1967; "Big Forms in Habitation" in *L'Architecture d'Aujourd'hui* (Paris), May 1969; "Utopische Kommune in Amerika" in *Werk* (Zurich), June 1970, July 1970, August 1970, March 1971, and August 1971;

"Northwest-Zentrum: Adhoc Heart of a City?", with Liselotte Ungers, in *Architectural Forum* (New York), October 1970; "City Problems in a Pluralistic Mass Society" in *Transparent* (Vienna), May 1971; "Towards a New Architecture," with Reinhard Gieselmann in *Programs and Manifestoes in 20th Century Architecture* by Ulrich Conrads, Cambridge, Massachusetts 1972; "Early Communes in the U.S.A.," with Liselotte Ungers, in *Architectural Design* (London), August 1972; "Berlin Free University: Nine Evaluations," with others, in *Architecture Plus* (New York), January/February 1974; "Le Comuni del Nuovo Mondo," with Liselotte Ungers, in *Lotus* (Venice), no. 8, 1974; "Oswald Mathias Ungers: Theories, Ideas and Proposals," with Vittorio Gregotti, in *Lotus* (Venice), no. 11, 1976; "A Vocabulary: Oswald Mathias Ungers' Plans for Rebuilding the Town of Marburg" in *Lotus* (Venice), June 1977; "Suggestions and Proposals for Five Workers' Housing Estates," with Josef Paul Kleihues, in *Bauwelt* (Berlin), April 1978; "The Architecture of Collective Memory" in *Lotus* (Venice), no. 24, 1979; "Humanistische Architektur" in *Deutsches Architektenblatt* (Stuttgart), 1 September 1979; "Una teoria trasformazione morfologiche," interview with Marcello Panzarella, in *Architettura* (Rome), January/February 1980.

On UNGERS: books—*Neue Deutsche Architektur* by Ulrich Conrads and Werner Marschall, Stuttgart 1962, as *Contemporary Architecture in Germany,* New York 1962 as *Modern Architecture in Germany,* London 1962; *Architettura tedesca del secondo dopoguerra* by Giovanni Klaus Koenig, Bologna 1965; *Wohnen in neuen Siedlungen,* Stuttgart 1965; *Neue Wohnhauser* by Olinde and Walter Meyer-Bohe, Stuttgart 1966; *The New Brutalism* by Reyner Banham, New York 1966; *Twentieth Century Architecture: The Middle Years 1940-65* by John Jacobus, New York 1966; *Mehrgeschossiger Wohnungsbau* by Karl Wilhelm Schmitt, Stuttgart 1966, as *Multi-story Housing,* New York 1966; *Neue Stadt Köln-*

Chorweiler by Harald Ludmann and Joachim Reidel, Stuttgart 1967; *New Directions in German Architecture* by Gunther Feuerstein, New York and London 1968; *Reisefuhrer zur modernen Architektur—Deutschland* by Grete Hoffman, Stuttgart 1968; *German Architecture 1960-1970* by Wolfgang Pehnt, New York 1970; *Architettura Razionale* by Enzio Bonfanti and others, Milan 1973; *Wohnungsbau—The Dwelling—L'Habitat* by Harald Deilmann and others, Stuttgart 1973; *Entwurfe und Planung 21: Studentheime* by Hans Schmalscheidt, Munich 1973; *Megastructures—Urban Futures of the Recent Past* by Reyner Banham, New York 1976; *Architektur in der Bundesrepublik—Gesprache mit Gunter Behnisch, Wolfgang Boring, Helmut Hentrich, Hans Kammerer, Frei Otto, Oswald Mathias Ungers* by Heinrich Klotz, Marburg, Germany 1977; *Gestaltung einer neuen Welt—Kritische Essays zur Architektur der Gegenwart* by Heinrich Klotz, Lucerne 1978; *Rational Architecture 1978—The Reconstruction of the European City,* Brussels 1978; *Dortmunder Architekturhefte 15: Museumsbauten,* edited by Joseph Paul Kleihues, Dortmund 1979; *Architektur in Deutschland,* edited by H. and M. Bofinger, H. Klotz and J. Pahe, Stuttgart 1979; *Architektur 1940-1980* by Adolf Max Vogt, Frankfurt 1980; articles—"Bauten and Projekte von O. Mathias Ungers" in *Bauwelt* (Berlin), 22 February 1960; "Focus VI: O. M. Ungers" by Ulrich Conrads in *Zodiac* (Milan), no. 9, 1962; "I protagonisti dell'architettura contemporanea: O. M. Ungers" in *Rassegna dell'Istituto di Architettura e Urbanistica* (Rome), December 1965; "Germania di Oggi: O. M. Ungers" by L. Bisogli in *Casabella* (Milan), May 1966; "Betrachtungen über das Schaffen der Architekten O. M. Ungers" by Jürgen Paul and "Oswald Mathias Ungers: Ein Beitrag zur Architektur" in *Deutsche Bauzeitung* (Stuttgart), July 1966; "O. M. Ungers—Sozialer Wohnungsbau 1953-1966" in *Baumeister* (Munich), May 1967; "The Contribution of Oswald Mathias Ungers to Architecture" by Carlo Aymonino in *Controspazio* (Bari, Italy), November 1975; "O. Mathias Ungers" by Vittorio Gregotti in *Lotus* (Venice), January 1976; "Oswald Mathias Ungers" in *Dortmunder Architekturausstellung,* edited by Josef Paul Kleihues, Dortmund 1976; "Ungers at Columbia" by Steven Holl in *Skyline* (New York), October 1979; "Un messaggio a Mathias Ungers da un altro mondo" by Aldo Van Eyck in *Spazio e Società* (Milan), December 1979; "The Case of O. M. Ungers" by Eric Watson in *Skyline* (New York), February 1980.

Bibliography: *The Architecture of Oswald Mathias Ungers: A Bibliography* by Gerardo Brown-Manrique, Council of Planning Librarians, Monticello, Illinois 1977, rev. ed. 1980.

The New Abstraction: the formal language of such an architecture is a rational and intellectual one, not based on accidents or sudden fanciful inspiration. Emotion is controlled by rational thinking, and this is stimulated through intuition. The dialectical process between the two polarities is almost essential in a creative process aimed towards a gradual improvement of ideas, concepts, spaces, elements and forms. It involves the process of abstraction until the object in it fundamental structure, the concept in its clearest geometry and the theme in its most impressive image appear.

To accomplish this level of clarity, the architectural concepts have to be carried through history and seen not as isolated events, as spontaneous inspirations, as clever tricks or as a 'menu of specialities', but as something which does not change at all, which is permanent, and which only proceeds through continuous stages of transformation. The New Abstraction means exactly that: the transformation of ideas and concepts in the course of history. A more precise New Abstraction in architecture will revive basic concepts of space which have occurred in all historical periods: for instance, the four column

O. M. Ungers: Galleria Exhibition Hall, Frankfurt, 1980-83.

space, the concept of walls, the courtyard block, the gate, the cruciform building, the square, the circle, the cylinder, the pyramid, and the perfect cube – regular geometric and volumetric forms which as universal orders of abstraction represent a quality of permanence. It is not the differentiation of colour and form, of material and style, that will be of importance and significance, not the abundance of shapes, volumes and spaces, but the restriction and economy of means. The New Abstraction should be the representation of the essential.

—O. M. Ungers

On a fine Spring day in Vienna I met with O. M. Ungers to talk about architecture.

We discovered that there are three trends that lead us both to expect the worst for the development of architecture: first, the trend towards imitative historicism in which the new is merely a banal quotation from the past, and design exhausts itself in copying and signifies nothing; secondly, the trend to romanticism through kitsch, which discerns the lofty pretension of architecture as artistic concern and considers itself original in the sense of "something for everyone;" and thirdly, the trend of the "downpath path," that is, the architect's flight from his own responsibility into the political hide-and-seek of so-called "participation" in which (in a democratic interpretation of architecture) the will of the people decides how a house or a street or a square in the town shall look. Ungers believes that the architect alone must take full responsibility for the shaping of the environment, that this responsibility is also political and above all undivided and entire. Architects must find the courage to represent their understanding of form.

Ungers wants to advance to autonomy of form by means of asceticism and discipline in planning, so that with simple forms, on the one hand, geometric systems will break down complexity, but, on the other hand, chance as a creative dimension will be impossible. An intellectualized aesthetic with a certain monumental pretension will result.

Ungers says, "Architecture means an analytical discussion with the environment which is developed and stamped by time." Form is the outcome of a dialectical process between the complex given facts of a situation and a particular period of time as well as the defined ideal images that result. So that architecture may remain humanistic and not become hostile to the user, Ungers proposes Contextualism, the integration of actual circumstances without imitating those circumstances. Contextualism is not pragmatic or solely utilitarian, nor should it prevent innovation in architecture.

Ungers regards architectural creations as individual solo performances for which the architect is responsible and must assume the associated challenges. He feels that the collective or civil initiative has not yet furnished any convincing evidence that it is a discoverer or producer of cultural performances. In the history of the West these performances have always been produced by individuals. Twenty years ago, in a manifesto, Ungers said: "Freedom lives only in the constant discussion of individuals with reality and in the perception of inner personal responsibility towards place, time and man."

I asked Ungers what he meant, then, by social architecture, and what significance he attached to his archetypal forms.

He said: "Social architecture is a degree of quality (not quantity) in the design of public places—that is, halls, foyers, galleries, streets, squares. The public place, experienced and lived in by the community, is the most important basis of identity for people in the town."

And he regards the archetypes not simply as fixed forms that allow for continual use and which everyone understands, but also as the conceptual in architecture, its maintenance of value, its timeless expression of excellence. By means of analogies which the architect works at and recomposes, architecture as expression, despite its pretensions to

"autonomous form," will become abundant and full of fantasy.

—Justus Dahinden

URABE, Shizutaro.

Japanese. Born in Kurashiki, Japan, 1909. Studied architecture, Imperial University, Kyoto, Dip.Arch. 1934. Worked as chief maintenance engineer for Soichiro Ohara on the redevelopment plan for Kurashiki Rayon Company (now Kuraray) and the Kurashiki town district, from 1935: Founder, Kurashiki Architectural Research Institute, Kurashiki, 1962 (re-named Kurashiki Architectural Office, 1965). Founder-Partner, with Masakazu Morimoto, Urabe and Morimoto architectural firm (now S. Urabe and Associate Architects), Osaka, 1962. Part-time Lecturer, Osaka University, 1954-55, and Kyoto University, 1962-66. Recipient: Mainichi Newspapers Shuddan Bunka Sho Prize, Tokyo, 1961; Annual of Architecture Prize, Tokyo, 1963; Architectural Institute of Japan Prize, Tokyo, 1964. Address: S. Urabe and Associate Architects, Shin-Hankyu Building, 12-39 Umeda-1 chome, Osaka 530, Japan.

Works:

1950 Archaeological Museum, Kurashiki, Japan
1953 Inn with a Pub (project)
1956 Kurashiki Inn, Kurashiki, Japan
1959 El Greco Coffee Shop, Kurashiki, Japan
1960 Japanese Arts and Crafts Museum (Manakata Museum), Osaka
1961 Ohara Art Museum Annex, Kurashiki, Japan
1962 Aizenbashi Children's Day Nursery, Osaka
1965 Kuraray Kokufudai Apartment House, Kurashiki, Japan
Takizawa Ironworks Company Factory, Okayama, Japan
Kokusai (International) Hotel, Kurashiki, Japan
1964 Takeuchi House, Kurashiki, Japan
Kuraray Takatsuki Apartment House and Dormitory, Kurashiki, Japan
1964 Aizenbashi Hospital, Osaka
Yasuda Fire and Marine Insurance Company Apartment House, Kurashiki, Japan
Youth Hostel, Kurashiki, Japan
1966 Hamako Building, Kochi City, Japan
Tokyo Zokei Daigaku (University of Art and Design), Hachioji, Tokyo
Rest Home in Hattori Green, Japan
Asahi Broadcasting Offices, Tokyo
Funai Credit Union Head Office, Tokyo
Ryobi Bus Company Terminal, Saidaiji, Japan
1967 Ryobi Bus Company Terminal, Tanashima, Japan
Youth Hostel, Konoike Park, Nara, Japan
Municipal Museum of Folklore, Saijo, Japan
Rokko Hankyu Building, near Osaka
Research Building phase 1, Women's Christian University, Tokyo
Noguchi House, Kurashiki, Japan
Hotel (project)
1968 Yasuda Fire and Marine Insurance Company Apartment House, Jiyugaoka, Japan
Kuraray Central Research Institute, Kurashiki, Japan
1969 Nishitetsu Grand Hotel, Fukuoka, Japan
Yasuda Fire and Marine Insurance Apartment House, Fugigaoka, Japan
Horibe House, Kurashiki, Japan
Okayama Garden Restaurant, Kamido, Okayama, Japan
Kominkan Cultural Centre, Kurashiki, Japan

Kurabo Memorial Hall, Kurashiki, Japan
1970 Senri Hankyu Hotel, Toyonaka, near Osaka
Hotel Plaza, Oyo Ward, Tokyo
Sapporo Beer Company Computer Centre, Sweiwa Kyobashi, Chuo
1971 Coffeekan Coffee House, Kurashiki, Japan
Kawasaki Steel Company, Apartment House no. 10, Mizushima, near Kurashiki, Japan
Nippon Synthetic Chemical Company Research Institute, Tokyo
Chamber of Commerce and Industry, Kurashiki, Japan
NHK Broadcasting Hall, Kobe, Japan
Meiji Milk Products Factory, Okayama, Japan
Matsushita Memorial Archives Building, Kii Scenic Hills Park, Wakayama, Japan
Water Authority Offices, Kurashiki, Japan
Dentist Association Hall, Okayama, Japan
Suehiro Main Shop, Suehiro, Japan
Kurashikikan Tourist Offices, Kurashiki, Japan
1972 Municipal Culture Centre, Tamano, Japan
Guest house, Kanebo, Japan
Civic Hall, Kurashiki, Japan
Momoyamadai Grand Mansion, Kurashiki, Japan
1973 Castle Park East Office, Osaka, Japan
Apartment House H-1, Semboku New Town, Japan
Police Headquarters, Sonezaki, Osaka
Yasuda Kasai Apartment House no. 2, Osaka
Municipal Dowa Kaiho Hall, Nishinari, Japan
Civic Hospital, Tamano, Japan
1974 Fukuoka Bank Narayamachi Branch Office, Fukuoka, Japan
RSK Rose Garden Restaurant, Kurashiki, Japan
Ivy Square Development, Kurashiki, Japan
Yuhigaoka Prefectural Library, Osaka
Kurosumikyo Shintozan Great Hall, Kuroi, Japan
1975 Women's Hospital Dormitory, Kanebo, Japan
Cancer Research Institue, Kanebo, Japan
Kawasaki Steel Training Centre, Mizushima, near Kurashiki, Japan
1975/
81 Central Hospital extensions and renovations, Kurashiki, Japan
1976 Forestry Youth Training Centre, Miyazaki Prefecture, Japan
Senri Hankyu Hotel phase 2, near Osaka
Tatsumi House, Kurashiki, Japan
1977 Civic Centre and Fire Station, Hirano, Japan
Nikka Whisky Company Houses, Nishinomiya, Japan
Fukuoka Bank Minami-gaoka Branch Office, Fukuoka, Japan
1978 Nikko Hotel, Narita, Japan
Jiro Osaragi Memorial, Hall, Yokohama, Japan
Fukuoka Bank Tsukikuma Branch Office, Fukuoka, Japan
Hamako Confectionery Building, Kurashiki, Japan
1979 Ryobi Store, Tsureshima, Japan
Hospital, Mure, Japan
House of the Founder of Kurosumikyo
Fukuoka Bank Ogori Branch Office, Fukuoka, Japan
1980 Yasuda Fire and Marine Insurance Company Building, Ichinomiya, Japan
Yasuda Fire and Marine Insurance Company Building, Yukuhashi, Japan
Kurashiki City Hall, Kurashiki, Japan
Protected Buildings renovations by the Kurashiki River, Kurashiki, Japan
Sanshu Asuke Yashiki Buildings Complex
Rokko Memorial Hall
Yasuda Fire and Marine Insurance Company Apartment House, Suizenji, Japan
Port Island Line Station, Kurashiki, Japan

Station forecourt and buildings, Kurashiki, Japan
1981 Port Island Building, Kurashiki, Japan
Historical Archives Building, Yokohama, Japan
Raku Building/Seisensha Building, Kurashiki, Japan
Fukuoka Bank Munakata Branch Office, Fukuoka, Japan
Music Circle Office, Osaka
Red Cross Hospital, Musashino, Japan
Yasuda Fire and Marine Insurance Company Building, Tsuyama, Japan
1982 Medical Society Hospital, Innoshima, Japan
Orthopaedic Rehabilitation Hospital, Osaka
Youth Hostel, Nara, Japan
Recreation Centre, Tamano, Japan
Biwako Research Institute, Lake Biwa Ko, Japan
Agricultural Park, Kobe, Japan
1984 Kanagawa Prefectural Archives of Modern Literature, Yokohama, Japan

Publications:

By URABE: articles—"A Personal View of Frank Lloyd Wright" in *Kokusai Kentiku* (Tokyo), March 1965; "Nature and Humanity" in *The Japan Architect* (Tokyo), October 1972; "Osaragi Jiro Commemorative Hall" in *Kenchiku Bunka* (Tokyo), June 1978.

On URABE: books—*An Architectural Journey in Japan* by J. M. Richards, London 1963; *A Guide to Japanese Architecture,* Tokyo 1971; articles—"Japan Craft Museum, Osaka" in *The Japan Architect* (Tokyo), January 1961; "Kurashiki International Hotel" in *The Japan Architect* (Tokyo), May 1964; "Tokyo University of Art and Design" in *Kenchiku Bunka* (Tokyo), June 1966; "The Kurashiki Central Research Center" in *The Japan Architect* (Tokyo), November 1968; "The Nishitetsu Grand Hotel, Fukuoka" in *The Japan Architect* (Tokyo), October 1969; "The Hotel Plaza, Oyodo, Osaka" in *The Japan Architect* (Tokyo), February 1970; "Kurashiki Civic Center" in *The Japan Architect* (Tokyo), October 1972; "Tamano Civic Hospital" in *The Japan Architect* (Tokyo), April 1974; "Kurashiki Ivy Sqaure" by Maskazu Morimoto in *The Japan Architect* (Tokyo), October 1974; "Transformation of a Spinning Factory into a Hotel and Exhibition Areas" in *Recherche et Architecture* (Paris), no. 29, 1977; "Japanese City and Architecture: Kurashiki," special issue of *Process:Architecture* (Tokyo), July 1982; "Kurashiki Central Hospital" in *The Japan Architect* (Tokyo), August 1982; "Japanese Signs," special issue of *Process:Architecture* (Tokyo), December 1983.

Bibliography—*Shizutaro Urabe: Modular Architect of Japan* by James Philip Noffsinger, Monticello, Illinois 1979.

*   *   *

Kurashiki is a small town in west Japan where Urabe has done most of his work. The town's vernacular idiom is unique – it has heavy walls of beaten earth like those used for traditional storehouses (*Kura*). The walls divide house from house, house from city, and Kurashiki from other towns.

Kurashiki at 6:30 in the morning; a place reveals itself before one's eyes into the gradual build-up of a picture. The light fashions a sense of direction: one is conscious, with every step, of facing this way or that. Kurashiki, where day meets night exactly half way, was a good setting for morning. No one was there. I was free to look at just what I pleased. The river. A bridge spans it in a low arc that recognizes the fundamental properties of matter. The sublime reflection of the thick green water. The place is well

made, solid and void in the right mix. Walking through it is a matter of following the walls. There are times when everyone likes to withdraw from the world of immediate pressures: this is a good place for that. One's thought, like one's feet, follows the walls—a series of right and left turns into scenes differentiated in volume and colour. Again and again, one's path crosses where one has been before, but always the approach is from a fresh angle, eye and foot taking it in, surveying it all. It could be a channel made from stone walls some two or three metres high, the path itself a metre broad. From time to time the channel bends, so that although the path is heading straight it leads, in fact, through a series of gentle curves. Imprisoned by the walls, one gets along as best one can, subject to the will of the walls at all times. Nonetheless, I walk.

Shizutaro Urabe. His is a vernacular rescued from the museums and resuscitated. A revivalist fervour is tempered by a sober analysis of actuality. 1001 nights in Japanese architecture. His method—the plastic reorganization of the *kura* (storehouse), which, along with the castle, constitutes the heavy, massive stream of Japanese history. (For Urabe, Japan is a rampart). The Ohara Museum is a fortified city wall: he ennobles the concrete by craft techniques, suggesting an alternative to concrete brut, leading towards a kind of archivist's architecture.

Though tendentious, what he says is never without substance. Inside the Kokusai Hotel, there is an explicit medievalizing tendency—heavy wood and cast-iron bannisters, copper light fittings, bulky, textured elements—a fortress against modernity. The inteior of the Ohara Museum comprises violent juxtapositions of opposing histories in space: one walks through Bannister Fletcher, its pages reorganized randomly, with the Japanese section more or less at the beginning. Even Tange, in his nearby City Hall, takes a temporary break from his exclusivism. Wood details are transposed into concrete, but his tentative move out to Kurashiki is cancelled by the universal interior, where piles of civic documents lay inaccessible and gathering dust in the liquid and undefined space. There's no mark man can make on it. Urabe goes in the opposite direction, making all the marks himself and, consequently, little room for man as well. But that's to exaggerate. It's perhaps best to describe it as a didactic quality, like a basic primer in architectural history, and the graphic quality there is part of it. Problems? One might mistake the inside of the theatre for a play, the interior of the museum for the exhibits—but it's hard to consider them as real problems.

Urabe maintains that man dosen't make history, but history makes man. He swims against the current of architecture. His brief-case is full of books on world history. He speaks of Greece, Rome and Kurashiki in the same breath. He is also subtly changing gear from his former and almost exclusively local referents to take on board a jazzed-up cartoon Classicism too – see his City Hall (1980), or his Hospital (1981). (To a packed hall, he writes on the board "shapes are shadows.") He has his arms outstretched and slowly brings them together in front of him, compressing more and more history into a single crystal form, which acts as the paradigm for all his designs.

—Chris Fawcett

UTZON, Jørn.

Danish. Born in Copenhagen, 9 April 1918. Educated at the Ålborg Katedralskole, Copenhagen, until 1937; studied architecture, under Steen Ejler Rasmussen and Kay Fisker, *q.v.*, Royal Academy of Arts, Copenhagen, 1937-42, Dip.Arch. 1942. Married Lis Fenger in 1942. Assistant architect in the offices of Paul Hedquist and Gunnar Asplund, *q.v.*, Stockholm, 1942-45, and in the office

of Alvar Aalto, *q.v.*, Helsinki, 1946; made study-tours of Europe and North Africa, 1947-48, and the United States (including Taliesin), and Mexico, 1949. In private practice, in Copenhagen, 1950-62, in Sydney, Australia, 1962-66, and in the United States, Switzerland and Denmark, since 1966. Visiting Professor, University of Hawaii, Honolulu, 1971-75. Exhibition: *Transformations in Modern Architecture,* Museum of Modern Art, New York, 1979. Recipient: First Prizes in the competitions— Skaanske low-cost housing, Denmark, 1953; High-rise housing, school and community centre, Elineberg, Sweden, 1954; Sydney Opera House, Australia, 1957; Danish Labour Party Education Centre, Copenhagen, 1958; Town Plan of Frederiksberg, Denmark, 1959; State Theatre complex, Zurich, 1964; Parliament and Congress Centre, Kuwait, 1972. Gold Medal, Royal Academy of Arts, Copenhagen, 1945; Eckersberg Medal, 1957; Honour Plaque, Bund Deutscher Architekten, 1966; Mobel Prize, 1970; Gold Medal, Royal Australian Institute of Architects, 1973; Gold Medal, Royal Institute of British Architects, 1978; Lakerol Prize, 1979; Architecture Prize, Danske Arkitekters Landsforbund, 1981; Alvar Aalto Medal, 1982. Honorary Fellow, Royal Australian Institute of Architects, 1965; American Institute of Architects, 1970. Address: Bossemagergade 77, 3150 Hellebaek, Denmark.

Works:

1945 Crystal Palace Development, London (competition project, with Tobias Faber)
Crematorium (project)
1946 Water Tower, Bornholm, Denmark
1947 Housing Development, Morocco (project)
Central Railway Station, Oslo (project; with Arne Korsmo)
Paper Factory, Morocco (project)
1948 School of Commerce, Göteborg, Sweden (project; with Arne Korsmo)
Development plan for the Vestre Vika area, Oslo (project; with Arne Korsmo)
1952 Jørn Utzon House, Hellebaek, Copenhagen
Development plan for the Skøyen-Oppsal area, Oslo (project; with Arne Korsmo)
1952/
53 House, Holte, Denmark
House, near Lake Furesö, Denmark
1954/
60 Elineberg Housing Estate, Denmark (with E. and H. Andersson)
1956/
66 Opera House, Sydney (completed by others, 1973)
1957/
60 Kingohusene Housing Estate, near Elsinore, Denmark
1958 Workers' High School, Hojstrup, Denmark
High School, Hellebaek, Copenhagen (project)
1959 Melli Bank, Tehran
Pavilions Complex, World's Fair, Copenhagen (competition project)
1960 National Museum, Copenhagen (competition project)
Town development plan for Elviria, Denmark (competition project)
1962/
63 Danish Co-operative Building Company Housing Development, Fredensborg, Denmark
1963 Art Museum, Silkeborg, Denmark (project)
1964 Municipal Theatre, Zurich (competition project)
1967 Sports Stadium, Jeddah, Saudi Arabia (project)
1968 Utsep Mobler Flexible Furniture (project)
1969 School Centre, with Technical College, Herning, Denmark (project)
Espansiva Byg A/S Timber Component House System (project)

1971/
73 Utzon House, Porto Petro, Mallorca, Spain
1972- National Assembly Complex, Kuwait
1976 Bagsväerd Church, Copenhagen
1978/
80 Public Swimming Pool and Recreation Centre, Copenhagen (project)
1979/
81 Heart Society Health and Recreation Center/ Village, Vendsyssel, Denmark (project)

Publications:

By UTZON: books—*Sydney Opera House*, Sydney 1962; *Sydney Opera House*, booklet with slides, Venice, California 1975; *GA 61: Church at Bagsvaerd*, Tokyo 1981; articles—"Eget bus ved Hellebaek, Denmark" in *Byggekunst* (Oslo), no. 34, 1952; "Platforms and plateaux" in *Zodiac* (Milan), no. 10, 1962; "Elements in the way of life", interview with Markku Komonen, in *Arkkitehti* (Helsinki), no. 2, 1983.

On UTZON: books—*Third Generation: The Changing Meaning of Architecture* by Philip Drew, London and Stuttgart 1972; *Transformations in Modern Architecture*, exhibition catalogue by Arthur Drexler, New York 1979; *Australian Art and Architecture*, edited by Anthony Bradley and Terry Smith, Melbourne 1980; *Visionary Architecture of the 20th Century* by Vittorio Magnago Lampugnani, Stuttgart and London 1982; articles—"Jørn Utzon: A New Personality" in *Zodiac* (Milan), no. 5, 1959; "The Sydney Opera House" in *Architecture in Australia* (Sydney), September 1960; "Platforms and Plateaux: Ideas of a Danish Architect" in *Zodiac* (Milan), no. 10, 1962; "Terrasserne, Fredensborg" in *Arkitektur* (Copenhagen), August 1964; "The Work of Jørn Utzon" in *Kokusai Kentiku* (Tokyo), November 1965; "The Sydney Opera House" by Peter Keys and Colin Brewer in *Architecture in Australia* (Sydney), December 1965; "Utzon: The End" by Robin Boyd in *Architectural Forum* (New York), June 1966; "The Utzon Story" in *Architectural Review* (London), June 1966; "Jørn Utzon" in *Bauen und Wohnen* (Zurich), September 1966; "The Work of Jørn Utzon," special issue of *Arkitektur* (Copenhagen), no. 1, 1970; "Pedagogical Architect" in *Architecture + Urbanism* (Tokyo), October 1973; "Magnum Opus" by Kerry Stephenson in *Building Design* (London), 12 October 1973; "Utzon's Medal for Life Saving" in *The Architects' Journal* (London), 28 June 1978; "Utzon's Latest: Church in Bagsväerd" by Philip McLean in *Building Design* (London), 27 October 1978; "Bagsväerd Church" in *Arkitektur DK* (Copenhagen), May 1982; "Jorn Utzon's House, Porto Petro, Mallorca" in *Cuaderns* (Barcelona), September 1982; "Elegant in the Desert" by Stephen Gardiner in *Building Design* (London), 1 October 1982; "Nordic Architects", special issue of *Quaderns* (Barcelona), April/June 1983; "Echoes of the Far East in a House in the Far North" in *House and Garden* (London), March 1984.

Bibliography—*Jørn Utzon* by Lamia Doumato, Monticello, Illinois 1984.

Jørn Utzon became well-known with one extraordinary piece of architecture, the Sydney Opera House, which is probably the most outstanding building designed in modern times. Yet all of his work, from an early competition for the Crystal Palace in London to the Bagsväerd Church in Copenhagen, shows a powerful imagination and a sensitive skill that goes far beyond Danish "impeccability" and makes him one of the most important contemporary architects. In the aftermath of many recent intellectual debates, young architects today frequently look at his work in search of what is "real" in architecture in its most basic sense.

Utzon graduated from the architectural school of the Royal Academy of Fine Arts in 1942, having as his teachers the enormously influential and respected Kay Fisker and Ejler Rasmussen. Initially he worked in the office of Gunnar Asplund and Alvar Aalto; later he spent a period of study at Frank Lloyd Wright's Taliesin East. Eventually the work of the three masters shaped the convictions and the character of Utzon's architecture: he was able to incorporate into his own work the balanced, disciplined juxtaposition of Asplund, the imaginative gestures of Aalto, and the organic structures of Wright. Yet his own work matured in an absolutely singular way, with poetical statement strengthened by a professional skill and a spontaneous dedication to those infinite manifestations of human life that make architecture.

Utzon's architecture is founded and developed upon four main principles: the influence of the work of his masters, a laboriously-achieved adherence to a tradition, the understanding that architecture is to be lived in, and an attention to structure and constructive processes. The result is an architecture from which one inevitably learns, since rather than declaring a prior intellectual intent, it contains that intent not only within the strength of a personality but also as the synthesis of the aspirations of all those who will live within its spaces. An early indication of Utzon's preference for an impeccable construction sequence is the two houses built in 1952-53, one for himself in Hellebaek, the other near Lake Fureso, where a distinctive relation between supporting and supported elements is realized.

Utson experimented extensively with the idea of raised terraces, platforms, and imaginary roofs that make gestures toward the sky like foliage of tall trees tossed by the wind. A number of his terrace sketches are evocative of the ground platforms of Monte Alban in Mexico. In fact, the design that gave him fame, the Sydney Opera House, is conceived as a structure of grand dimensions rising above a system of terraces, so ingeniously proportioned in its parts as to appear much smaller in drawings. The two series of carefully-shaped reinforced concrete shells covering the halls, described as elliptic paraboloids, rise more than two hundred feet above the ground level. They were engineered by Ove Arup, and by virtue of their shape, their mass is placed where it is most advantageous structurally. Thus the design is the result of a successful integration of the work of an architect and an engineer who together produced an unforgettable architectural image. The overall scale achieved in the complex is not only adequate to Sydney Harbor, but it also develops a focus which collects into one vision the otherwise scattered elements built on its periphery. Unfortunately, Utzon was forced to abandon the supervision of the work in the midst of construction, and the interior work of the building clearly reflects his departure.

After the Sydney Opera House, Utzon received a number of commissions and prizes not necessarily followed by construction, such as the project for the Zurich Theatre in 1964. In 1976 construction was completed of the Bagsväerd Church, a subtle and beautiful building. It rises like a simple cluster of farm buildings in a suburban area of Copenhagen, its masses of light grey walls complemented by the glittering reflection of glass roofs. The plan consists of a sequence of meeting rooms, courts, and halls which gradually increase in dimension, culminating in the church assembly hall. This changing of vertical dimension is reflected outside, while in plan all rooms are continued within the limit of two skylighted corridors, which eventually become part of the assembly hall itself. To this alternate sequence of dimensions corresponds a particular choice of materials that includes an undulating reinforced concrete ceiling, terminating in a larger wave and capturing the penetration of daylight into the central hall. The free profile of the shell is framed by the rhythmical sequence of the 2.2 meter module of the supporting elements, and is complemented by transparent wood partitions. An harmonious intimacy is achieved within the building in contrast to the subtle ambiguity of the outside, thus reflecting the public and private nature of the architecture. This building expresses an aspiration for spirituality which is complex, intimate and yet common to people; it does so with simple protective signs, leaving the actual making of symbols to the user. The architecture here does not declare a malaise or the inner contradiction of a society, for the architect knows that architecture can be generated only by aspirations for a better world built from life experience—a hopeful aspect of man's endeavors, not the mirror of his confusion.

Utzon's work always proceeds from an accurate consideration of site conditions into the articulation of a program within a precise building discipline. Such a discipline comes from the observance of natural laws and from structural integrity, but Utzon's architecture transcends the mere art of building: it evolves its forms into a poetic invention that has a strength and harmony not unlike the forms of Nature herself.

Recent years have seen the near completion of another monumental work which may be another landmark for Utzon's life work and for architecture in general: the new Parliament for Kuwait. The complex of offices and chambers is modularly built around an internal street leading to a large assembly space, as a loggia of greater proportion supported by hollow columns and roofed with precast concrete catenary-shaped trusses. This canopy opens to the sea laterally as a solemn gesture of uncompromising beauty.

—Romaldo Giurgola

UYTENBOGAARDT, Roelof Sarel.

South African. Born in Cape Town, 23 June 1933. Educated at the Voortrekker High School, Cape Town, 1947-50; University of Cape Town, under L. W. Thornton-White, 1950-56, B.Arch. 1956; British Academy in Rome, 1957-59 (Royal Institute of British Architects Rome Scholarship); University of Pennsylvania, Philadelphia, under Louis I. Kahn and David A. Crane, 1959-61 (University of Pennsylvania Scholarship; Kahn Scholarship; American Institute of Planners Student Award, 1961), M.Arch. and M.C.P. 1961. Married Mariane Meyer in 1957; children: Ritva, Renera, Mariane. Assistant to the architect Koppel Brown, Kitwe, Zambia, 1955-57; City Planning Designer, Boston Redevelopment Authority, 1961-63; Partner, with Peter J. Pelser, Uytenbogaardt and Pelser, Cape Town, 1963-66; Principal, Roelof S. Uytenbogaardt, Architect, Cape Town, 1966-71; Principal, with Ian Macaskill and Peter Schneider, Uytenbogaardt, Macaskill and Schneider, Cape Town, 1971-77; Principal, Uytenbogaardt and Macaskill, Cape Town, 1977-80. Since 1981, Principal of Roelof S. Uytenbogaardt and Norbert Rozendal, Cape Town. Senior Lecturer in Architecture, 1966-70, since 1971 Professor and Head of the Department of Urban and Regional Planning, and since 1977 Dean of the Faculty of Fine Art and Architecture, University of Cape Town. Visiting Critic, University of Pennsylvania, 1966, and Columbia University, New York, 1967. Member of the Committee, Cape Provincial Institute of Architects, 1966-71. Recipient: Bronze Medal, Cape Provincial Institute of Architects, 1965, 1967. Address: Uytenbogaardt and Rozendal, 7 Ellerslie Road, Wynberg, Cape Town 7735, South Africa.

Works:

1955 McKerrel House, Kitwe, Zambia
DRC Church Manse, Kitwe, Zambia
Small block of flats, Kitwe, Zambia

Roelof Uytenbogaardt: Sports Centre, University of Cape Town, 1977.

1956 African Market, Kitwe, Zambia
Hepworth House, Kitwe, Zambia
1963 Van Zyl Shop, Paarl, South Africa
Primary school, Cape Town (project)
Old Age Home, Cape Town (project)
School, for the Cape Provincial Administration, Parow, Cape, South Africa
1964 Dutch Reformed Church, Welkom, Orange Free State, South Africa
Dutch Reformed Seminary, Cape Town (project)
1966 Development plan for Goodwood, Cape Town (with Barac, Hirst and Field)
Small Hotel, Worcester, Cape, South Africa (project)
House, Seaforth, Cape Town (project)
1967 Bonwit Clothing Factory, Cape Town
Mellini House, Cape Town (project)
Suter House garden and pool, Cape Town (projects)
1968 Crown Mines Property Development (for 40,000 people), Ormonde, Johannesburg (project; with Urban Design Consultants)
1969 Shell International Offices, Bethlehem, Orange Free State, South Africa (project)
Shell International Depot, Ceres, Cape, South Africa (project)
1970 Gunners Circle Shopping Centre, Epping, Cape Town
1972 Plan for the development of the beach front at Jeffreys Bay, South Africa (project)
1973 Werdmuller Centre, Claremont, Cape Town
1974 Dido Valley Group Housing, Simonstown, South Africa (project)
Runciman Drive Housing, Simonstown, South Africa (project)
1975 De Wet House, Caledon, Cape, South Africa
Garden of Remembrance, Simonstown, South Africa
1976 Belhar Housing, Cape Town
Dorman Housing Development, Hout Bay, Cape Town
1977 Sports Centre, University of Cape Town
Mitchell Plain Housing (2,500 units), Cape Town

1978 Belhar Low-Cost Housing (5,500 units), Cape Town
Steinkopf Community Centre, Steinkopf, Cape, South Africa

Publications:

By UYTENBOGAARDT: book—*Housing: A Comparative Analysis of Urbanism in Cape Town*, with others, Cape Town 1977; article—"The New Urban Environment" in *South African Architectural Record* (Johannesburg), 1966.

On UYTENBOGAARDT: books—*World Architecture 2* by John Donat, London 1965; *A Guide to Architecture in South Africa* by Doreen Greig, Cape Town 1971; articles—"The Symbolic City" by David A. Crane in *American Institute of Planners Journal* (Washington, D.C.), November 1960; "N. G. Kerk, Welkom-Wes" by Neville Krige in *Huisgenoot* (Cape Town), February 1967; "Werdmuller Centre" in *Planning and Building Developments* (Braamfontein, South Africa), September/October 1975; "Werdmuller Centre" in *Architect and Builder* (Cape Town), May 1976; "Belhar Group Housing" in *Planning and Building Developments* (Braamfontein, South Africa), March/April 1977; "UCT Sports Centre" in *Architect and Builder* (Cape Town), January 1978; "Steinkopf" in *Architect and Builder* (Cape Town), June 1978; "Garden of Remembrance, Simonstown" in *Architecture South Africa* (Cape Town), September 1979; "Steinkopf Community Centre" in *Architecture South Africa* (Cape Town), Spring 1980.

*   *   *

The real concerns of architecture belong to the realm of the timeless. Architecture transcends generations and is for all people. Its continued development is sought in the works of individuals responding to the specifics of place. Regional, local and particular context, as the constraints set up by the given reality and purpose of the building program, is of continued assistance to the design process. In

architecture is also the beginning of urbanism, and urbanism again acts as a powerful informant to architecture. In this process there is no sense of the frantic, as one is involved in a continuum in which all of architecture plays a part. Originality is not a goal but a wonderful result of the bringing together of all factors of creativity, and at all times it will be steeped in the experience of that which came before, has been assimilated and given new meaning by the understanding of the present.

—Roelof S. Uytenbogaardt

As a result of his brilliant student career at the University of Cape Town School of Architecture, Roelof S. Uytenbogaardt was awarded the Rome Scholarship in 1957 and spent his first post-graduate years at the British School in Rome. This contact with the historical architecture of Rome and Italy was of particular importance in his formative years, which culminated in a period in the United States where, like so many other graduate students at the time, he came under the powerful influences of Kahn, Crane and the post-Carpenter Center Corbusier.

After two years of study and work in architecture, urban design and planning in Philadelphia and Boston, Uytenbogaardt returned to work in Cape Town: he started with a small church, went on to a shop, some industrial work, a large commercial complex, and an indoor sports centre. At the same time he has been involved in individual and group housing developments.

To some extent this period has been a process of working through an eclectic rag-bag of the dominant influences of the formative period—the Kahnian influence in the Welkom Church of 1964 and the Bonwit Clothing Factory of 1967, the "style Corbu" in parts of the Werdmuller Centre in 1973 and, to a lesser extent, in the University of Cape Town Sports Centre of 1977. An emphasis on influences would, however, create a superficial view about a number of specific and highly-original architectonic assemblages, only the elements of which indicate a genealogy of remembered images and styles. The Werdmuller Centre is a serious attempt to gain new understandings of how to make a naturally conditioned and adaptive shopping complex that is actually habitable. The Sports Centre, again, is a contribution to a clearer understanding of how to put together a complex variety of university space types. His planning work has ranged from a project for a large new sub-urban development for 40,000 persons at Ormonde, Johannesburg, to a review of the Cape Town Foreshore Scheme, to several other urban design exercises including important research and development in urban low-cost housing of various types.

All the work, whether architecture or urban design, reflects a view that the visible world is shaped by deep structures, underlying causes and human motivations that it is the role of the architect to explore, understand, and make manifest. It also reflects the view of a "true believer" of the 1960s, a believer in absolute values: it is the role of the architect not only to translate these underlying forces into architectonic form but also to interpret human motivations in the name of man in the abstract.

Roelof Uytenbogaardt is one of the major architectural talents on the African sub-continent, and it is sad to reflect that, perhaps because of malign neglect, his work is not better known internationally. His architectronic virtuosity is at least equal to that of the Australian architect John Andrews, but Uytenbogaardt brings to his work additional levels of perception and involvement. It is worth noting that Uytenbogaardt is an experienced light aircraft pilot: perhaps it is this perspective that enables him to X-ray hidden environmental structures and settlement patterns from above. It is also noteworthy that he has recently also become an avid cyclist. We could speculate that his future work may reflect both the lofty contemplation of aerial absolutes and also a stocktaking of the imperfect hopes and aspirations of ordinary people and enterprises.

—Julian Elliott

VADÁSZ, György.

Hungarian. Born in Budapest, 18 February 1933; son of the architect Mihály Vadász. Educated at the Technical University, Budapest, under Károly Weichinger, Pál Csonka, Frigyes Pogány and Máté Major, 1952-57, Dip.Arch. 1957; Master School of the Union of Hungarian Architects, 1958-60, M.Arch. 1960. Served in the Hungarian Army, 1954, 1955. Married Katalin Pusztai in 1954 (divorced, 1964); married Vera Pöhl in 1964; children: György, Katalin, Bence, and Eszter. Architect-Planner with the Office of Urban Studies, Budapest, 1957; Head Planner, Office of Industrial Buildings, Budapest, 1958-64. Since 1964, Head of the Department of Architecture, Office of Urban Studies, Budapest. Chief architect of Baja City, Hungary, from 1983. Lecturer, Faculty of Architecture, Technical University, Budapest, 1963-75. Director, Master School of the Union of Hungarian Architects, 1978-82. Member of the Directorate, City Improvement Society of Budapest, since 1984. Exhibitions: *Travelling Theatre,* Royal Festival Hall, London, 1961; Masters School of the Union of Hungarian Architects Exhibition, Budapest, 1961; *International Agricultural Fair,* Budapest, 1962, 1967, 1970; *György Vadász and Tibor Vilt,* Museum of Art, Budapest, 1970; Dwellings Exhibition, Architects Union of the U.S.S.R., Moscow, 1972; *Works of György Vadász,* Sofia, 1973, Varna, 1974, Mongolia, 1975, and Zurich, 1978; Union of Hungarian Architects Exhibition, Budapest, 1977; *Hungarian Architecture 1945-75,* Stuttgart, 1978; *György Vadász,* Szombathely, Budapest and Baja, 1979; *Works of György Vadász,* Kiskunhlas, 1980; Architecture Exhibition, Moscow, 1980; *Györgyt Vadász,* Sopron, 1981; Architecture Exhibition, Berlin, Warsaw and Copenhagen, 1981; *György Vadász,* Baja, 1982; *György Vadász,* Debrecen 1983; *György Vadász/Imre Varga,* at the *41st Biennale,* Venice, 1984. Recipient: Ybl Prize, Ministry of Construction, Budapest, 1972; Art Prize for the György Dózsa Monument, Budapest, 1974; Excellent Worker of the Building Industry Award, Budapest, 1975; Gold Medal, Ministry of Instruction, Budapest, 1976; Pro Urbe Prize, Zalaegerszeg, Hungary, 1979; National Architecture Prize, Hungary, 1979, 1980; Architecture Prize, *Biennale of Architecture,* Sofia, 1984; Pro Arte Prize, Budapest, 1984; and prizes in numerous architectural competitions since 1961. Address (office); Herman Otto utca 2/b, 1022 Budapest, Hungary.

Works:

1958 House, Szeged, Hungary (with György Tokar)
1961 ZIM Works, Kecskemét, Hungary
1962 Week-end houses, *International Agricultural Fair.* Budapest (exhibition project)
1963 VTR Office Buildings, Szekesfehérvár, Hungary
　　　Zugió Knitwear Factory Social Center, Budapest
1967 MHSZ: Hungarian Association of Defence Headquarters, Budapest
　　　ABC Department Store, Budapest
　　　Week-end houses, *International Agricultural Fair,* Budapest (exhibition project)
1968/
　70 Füred Square Shopping Center, Budapest
1971/
　78 Hospital Pavilions, Téténya Street, Budapest (with Péter Katona)
1972 Residence for Diplomats, Budakeszi Street, Budapest (with Anna Perczel)
1975/
　81 Gellért Mountain water-basin, walls and landscaping, Budapest
1976 National Cemetary of Mohács, Hungary (with Gusztáv Szlezak)
1978 City Centre, Zalaegerszeg, Hungary
　　　MEDOSZ: Agricultural Workers Trade Union Headquarters, Budapest (with András Mézáros)
　　　Thermal Bath interiors, Gellert Mountain, Budapest (with Márta Fohl)
1982 Ceremonial Square, Zalaegerszeg, Hungary
　　　Krisztina Telephone Exchange Building, Budapest
1983 Double Villa, Fonyód, Hungary
1984 City Centre Development with flats and shops, Baja, Hungary
　　　Calvinist Church, Pécs, Siklós, Hungary
　　　Postal Headquarters and Telephone Exchange, Baja, Hungary
　　　Main Square Development Plan, Baja, Hungary
　　　City Centre Development, Karcag, Hungary
　　　MONIMPEX Housing Complex, Budapest
　　　Hungarian Exhibition, *Biennale,* Venice (with sculptor Imre Varga)

Publications:

By VADÁSZ: articles—"Take a Signal" in *Association of Hungarian Architects Bulletin* (Budapest), no. 4, 1968; "Ideas about the Artistic Order" in *Jelkep* (Budapest), no. 4, 1980; "Shaping the Environment in the Second Half of the 20th Century; or, Misconstrued Functionalism" in *Interpress Grafik* (Budapest), no. 1, 1983; and numerous articles in Hungarian newspapers since 1960.

On VADÁSZ: books—*Nogyar épitészettörténet* by Rados Jeno, Budapest 1971; *Hungarian Architecture 1945-75,* exhibition catalogue, Stuttgart 1978; *Modern épitészettörténeti* by Kubinszky, Budapest 1978; *Neue Architektur in Ungarn* by Jenö Szendröi, Budapest 1978; *XLI Biennale di Venezia 1984: Ungheria,* exhibition catalogue, with an introduction by Geza Csorba, Budapest 1984; articles—"Mohács" in *Baranyai Muvelodes* (Budapest), no. 4, 1976; "Wohnhaus in Budapest" in *Bauwelt* (Berlin), no. 3, 1978; "György Vadász" in *Architektur der DDR* (Berlin), August 1979; "Die historische Gedenkstadte von Mohacs" in *Der Aufbau* (Vienna), no. 10, 1980; films—*National Cemetery of Mohács,* ÉTK film, Budapest 1978; *Four Excellent Hungarian City Centres,* ÉTK film, Budapest 1982; *Zalaegerszeg,* Hungarian television film, Budapest 1983; *Articles and Works of György Vadász,* ÉTK video, Budapest 1984.

*

It was my father who taught me what was good and beautiful – not with words, but with his life. "Whatever you do, reflect your true self— even with the minutest of your gestures." I have been trying to keep to this ever since. But I am different, not like him. My one and only virtue is what I do and, perhaps, the way I do it. I really believe in my work as an intellectual and emotional challenge to be overcome.

More and more am I fascinated by landscape, plants and nature: I am more fascinated nowadays by a nice tree than by a nice building. If only we could bend our carnivorous technology to the service of humanity once more, to save our landscape on the outside and man on the inside. Even a house can radiate love, just as fear and coldness emanate from the inhuman architecture of inhuman periods in history. This intrinsic, radiating love heals us, and it is this remedy we must now employ.

—Gyorgy Vadász

*

In the new society formed after the Second World War, in which there has been a total upheaval within those professions concerned with faith and the intellect, the architect has had to assume, along with his initial role as a constructor, the increasingly important roles of educator and priest. In Hungary György Vadász has not been afraid to assume this new vocation and responsibility and to leave behind the dead end of ordinary production. He seeks to foresse, to master in advance, the ways in which his architecture will be perceived.

This attitude leads him to work in several directions with different objectives—commercial buildings (large shops, commerical centres), housing (bocks of flats and individual houses), offices and socio-cultural buildings (hospitals, an opera house, a library, etc.); he has even created commerative furniture and monuments.

In his work Vadász leaves nothing to chance. With the meticulous attention to detail of a goldsmith he has composed such works as the town centre of Zaalegerszeg, where he went beyond the functional and material and made well-orchestrated elements spring into space—the modelling of facades (balcony rails, cornices, copings, the proportions fof solids and voids), urban furniture (lighting), urban focal points (fountains), etc. In this spatial sequence much is imparted by the play of materials and the richness of the colours in the prefabricated panels which make up the exterior of the buildings.

Vadász uses a vocabulary of warm materials in coloured plasters, glazed surfaces and metallic tracery, and joins them with an animated placing of volumes to create in space an atmosphere which is both dynamic and static. Vadász fascinates with his ability to say so much with so little.

—Zdravko Natchev

VAGO, Pierre.

French. Born in Budapest, Hungary, 30 August 1910; emigrated to France, 1928: naturalized, 1933. Educated at the Ecole Spéciale d'Architecture, Paris, under Auguste Perret, 1928-32, Diploma (first class) 1932. Served in the Marine Nationale, 1934, 1939-44: Medaille de la Resistance, 1945. Married Monique Lesourd in 1934 (died, 1949); children: Jean-Pierre, Florence, Michel and Catherine; married Nicole Cormier in 1968. In private practice, Paris, since 1934. Director of Architectural Studies, Ecole Supérieure d'Architecture, Tournai, Belgium, 1956-66. Professor of Architecture and Urban Design, Sommerakademie für Bildende Kunst, Salzburg, 1971-75. Chief Editor, 1931-49, and Chairman of the Editorial Board, 1950-75, *L'Architecture d'Aujourd'hui*, Paris. Founder, Réunions Internationales d'Architectes, 1932; Secretary-General, 1948-68, and since 1968 Honorary President, Union Internationale des Architectes, Paris; Secretary-General, 1957-59, and President, 1963-65, ICSID (International Council of Societies of Industrial Design), Brussels. Has served on the jury of numerous international competitions including: Berlin Centre; WHO Headquarters, Geneva; Tunis Centre; Tel Aviv Centre; Madrid Opera House, UNIDO Headquarters, Vienna. Recipient: Grand Prix d'Architecture, Paris, 1959. Honorary doctorate: University of Stuttgart, 1972, and University of Budapest. Honorary Member of the Royal Institute of British Architects, of the American Institute of Architects, and of the Bund Deutscher Architekten. Chevalier of the Légion d'Honneur, 1958. Commander of the Order of Gregoire le Grand, 1959, of the Cross of the South, Brazil, 1961, and of the Order of Alfonso El Savio, Spain, 1975; Officier, Ordre des Arts et des Lettres, France, 1984. Member, Akademie der Künste, Berlin; Académie d'Architecture, Paris. Address: Le Valparon, 77123 Noisy sur École, France.

Pierre Vago: University of Lille, France, 1975.

Works:

1928 Memorial to Joan of Arc (competition project)
1934 Pre-fabricated Steel House, *Exposition de l'Habitation*, Paris
1934/
35 Various houses, apartments and shops, Paris
1936 French Section, *Triennale*, Milan
1937 Architects Club House, *World's Fair*, Paris (with Jean Démaret)
1945/
47 Master plan for the historic cities of Arles, Beaucaire and Tarascon, France
1947/
48 Master plan for Le Mans, France
1948/
54 Reconstruction of the Bouches-du-Rhône area, France (chief architect)
1948/
59 Buildings for the Bank of Algeria in Algiers, Batna, Biskra, etc.
1950 School, Tarascon, France
Church of St. Pierre, Arles, France
190 housing units, Martigues, France
1951 School, Arles, France
Mineral water factory, Arles, France
Dominican Convent, Monteils, Aveyron, France
United States Army Depot, Landes-de-Bussac, France
1952 School, Montrouge, Paris
1953 Central Bank of Tunisia, Tunis
Housing units, St. Cloud, Paris
Church, Carry-le-Rouet, France
Dominican Chapel, Etrépagney, France

Gyorgy Vadász: City Centre Housing Development, Zalaegerszeg, Hungary, 1976-78.

1954 St. Therese Church, Le Mans, France
Villas, Hydra, Algeria
Housing estates in the South of France
1955 Technical College, Marseilles
1955/
57 Housing (2,000 apartments), Le Mans, France
1956 Le Bon Marché, Algiers
1957 Apartment building, Hansaviertel, West Berlin
Church, St. Cyr, Versailles
1958 Basilica of St. Pius, Lourdes (with Eugene Freyssinet)
St. Michel Clinic, Toulouse
1959 Technical University, Le Mans, France
1960 Residence du Parc, Le Mans, France
1961 Technical School, Beaucaire, France
1962/
76 Sablons Quarter, Le Mans, France
1965 Centre of the new town of Ashdod, Israel (competition project)
1968 Library, University of Bonn (with Fritz Bornemann)
1970 Monastery at Nazareth
Master plan for Luxembourg
1971 Monastery Church, Prouille, France
1973 French Cultural Centre, Jerusalem
1975 University of Lille
1977 Museum and Hostel, Lourdes
1978 Church for 5,000 worshippers, Lourdes (project)
1980/
82 Pilot Project for Coatzacoalos, Mexico (with Carl Auböck)

Publications:

By VAGO: book—*Robert Mallet-Stevens*, Bari, Italy 1980; articles—"Architecture in France and the Contemporary Problem of Style" in *The Studio* (London), October 1939; "Architettura e Carattere Urbano" in *Domus* (Milan), December 1955; "France, 1969" in *L'Architecture d'Aujourd'hui* (Paris), July/August 1969; "The Architectural Profession in France" in *Der Architekt* (Stuttgart), June 1974.

On VAGO: books—*Peter Vago* by Máté Major, Budapest 1982; *Pierre Vago* by F. Carbajal de la Cruz, Mexico City 1984; articles—"Basilica of St. Pius, Lourdes, France" in *Architectural Design* (London), June 1959; "Bibliothèque de Bonn, Allemagne" in *L'Architecture d'Aujourd'hui* (Paris), February/March 1962; "Siège de Calberson à Paris" in *L'Architecture d'Aujourd'hui* (Paris), December 1963/January 1964; "Literature and Law Buildings for Lille" in *Recherche et Architecture* (Paris), no. 42, 1980; "An Efficient Articulation for a More Liberal Management: University of Lille" in *Architettura* (Rome), December 1981.

Pierre Vago was born in Budapest in 1910; his mother was the famous singer Ghita Lenart; his father, Joseph Vago, was a well known architect of the modern movement before 1914, associated with the German Werkbund. When Pierre was eight years old, the family moved to Italy, and Italian became his second language; he also speaks German fluently, and since 1928, when he moved to Paris, French has been his language. His life in different countries prepared him for the international rôle he was to play in architecture.

As a poor student of architecture in Paris, Vago supplemented his meagre allowance by writing. Hard working and astonishingly precocious, he gained his first honours in architecture at the age of eighteen in an international competition for a "memorial to Joan of Arc." He studied under Auguste Perret at the Ecole Spéciale d'Architecture. Perret introduced reinforced concrete into architecture, and the influence on Vago of Perret's doctrine of the paramount imortance of construction in arcitecture has been very strong.

Vago belongs to that generation of young architects who rejected both the traditional architecture still prevalent in France as well as the lack of solid craftmanship of the avant-garde. From the beginning his aim has been to provide the new architecture with a firm theoretical and practical base, to bring about a concentration of its dispersed efforts and an exchange among proponents of its different tendencies. The periodical *L'Architecture d'Aujourd'hui,* founded in 1930, of which Vago was the editorial secretary and soon the editor, was originally to be named *Construire:* the name implies a programme. *L'Architecture d'Aujourd'hui* was international in outlook. It made known in France the achievements and trends of the new architecture throughout the world. Vago's international background and Perretist outlook enabled him to make the review very quickly the most important publication in architecture in Europe.

In 1932 he founded the Reunions Internationales des Architects (R.I.A.), which was to develop after the Second World War into the Union Internationale des Architectes (U.I.A., founded in 1948), of which Vago was the Secretary-General, that is to say, the organizer. The organization is less one-sided than the CIAM (of which he was also a member); it is also truly international. From the beginning the socialist countries were represented, and U.I.A. is one of the few associations in which professional people from both parts of the world can engage in a free exchange of opinions. This accomplishment is due to Pierre Vago's wide outlook, his ability to act as a moderator, and his comprehensive and balanced outlook. The first congresses—Moscow, 1932; Milan, 1933; and Prague, 1935—were even then events of outstanding importance. Vago gave a forum and centre to architects in all countries struggling to break away from traditionalism.

It might be said that Vago's organizing activity is the most conspicuous part of his work; however, he has not neglected his professional work as an architect and town planner. In fact, he considers creative work to be the most important part of his life. He has practised architecture since 1934. In that year he showed a prefabricated steel house at the *Exposition de l'Habitation* in Paris; in 1937 he built—with Jean Demaret—the Architects Club House at the *World's Fair* in Paris. Towards the end of the war he supervised the regional planning of the Côte des Maures, the area of the Côte d'Azur between Cannes and Toulon, and in 1947 he was appointed Chief Architect for the reconstruction and development of the ancient towns of Arles, Avignon, and Beaucaire. As architect for the Bank of Algeria he built a number of office buildings in Algeria and Tunisia. As a result of an international competition, he built, with Fritz Bornemann, the great library at Bonn; and in 1957 he was one of the foreign architects who built blocks of flats in the "Hansaviertel" in Berlin. Pierre Vago's best known building is the underground chapel at Lourdes for 25,000 pilgrims, a great work of architecture—and of construction.

—Julius Posener

VALLE, Gino.

Italian. Born in Udine, 7 December 1923; son of the architect Provino Valle, and brother of the architect Nani Valle. Educated at the Marinelli High School, Udine, 1938-41, graduated 1941; Istituto Universitario di Architettura, Venice, 1942, 1945-48, Dip.Arch. 1948; at Harvard Graduate School of Design, Cambridge, Massachusetts (Fulbright Scholar), 1951-52. Served in the Italian Navy, 1943-45: trained at the Brioni Naval Academy, later prisoner-of-war in Germany. Married Piera Ricci Menichetti in 1961; children: Piero and Carla. Partner, with father Provino, 1948-55, and since 1955 Principal, Studio Architetti Valle, Udine. Associate Professor, 1954-55, 1972-77, and since 1977 Professor of Architecture, Istituto Universitario di Architettura, Venice. Chairman, Industrial Design Course, Venice School of Art, 1962-63; Lecturer, Royal Institute of British Architects, London, 1965; Visiting Professor, University of Natal, Durban, South Africa, winter 1967; Visiting Critic, Harvard Graduate School of Design, 1970-71. Vice-President, ICSID (International Council of Societies of Industrial Design), Brussels, 1967-71. Exhibitions: *4th Bienal,* Sao Paulo, Brazil, 1957; Galleria Nazionale d'Arte Moderna, Rome, 1959; *Italian Industrial Design,* Illinois Institute of Technology, Chicago, 1959; *First International Exhibition,* Musee des Arts Decoratifs, Paris, 1963; *Gino Valle,* Royal College of Art, London, 1964; *Utopia e crisi dell'antinatura,* at the Biennale, Venice, 1978; *Architetture italiane degli anni '70,* Galleria Nazionale d'Arte Moderna, Rome, 1981; *The European Iceberg,* Art Gallery of Ontario, Toronto, 1985. Recipient: Gold Medal, 1954, Silver Medal, 1957, *Triennale,* Milan; Gold Compasses Award, Rinascente, Milan, 1956, 1962; First Prize, National Competition for the Monument to the Resistance in Udine, 1959; IN/ARCH Prize, Rome, 1960; AITEC National Prize, Rome, 1962; Luxaflex International Prize, 1963. Member, Accademia di San Luca, Rome, 1975. Address: Studio Architetti Valle, 13 piazza primo Maggio, 33100 Udine, Italy.

Works:

1951 Ghetti House, Codroipo, Italy (with Nani Valle)
1954 Migotto House (now Pozzi House), Pasian di Prato, Italy (with Provino and Nani Valle)
    Quaglia House, Sutrio, Italy (with Provino and Nani Valle)
    Cassa di Risparmio Bank, Udine (with Provino and Nani Valle)
1955 Cassa di Risparmio Bank, Latisana, Italy (with Provino and Nani Valle)
    Bellini House, Udine (with Nani Valle)
    Hospital, Portogruaro, Italy (with Nani Valle)
1957 Flats and offices, Trieste (with Provino and Nani Valle)
1958 Town Hall, Treppo Carnico, Italy (with Nani Valle)
1959 Chiesa Graphic Works, Udine
1960 Apartment building, Via Marinari, Udine (with Firmino Toso)
1961 Zanussi Factory Offices, Pordenone, Italy
    Nicoletti House, Udine
    Scala Ceramics Factories in Orcenigo and Roccasecca, Italy
1963 Sipre Pre-Fab Factory, Udine
    Zanussi Warehouses, Milan and Rome
    Therapeutic Institute, Lignano, Italy
    Town Centre Plan, Nevegal, Italy
    Municipal Theatre, Udine
1964 Thermal Baths Complex, Arta, Udine
1965 Office building, Udine
1966 Twin House (Red House), Udine
1967 Vine Factory, Risano, Italy
1968 Messaggero Veneto Printing Works, Udine
1969 Zanussi Service Spine, Pordenone, Italy
    Monument to the Resistance, Udine (with Federico Marconi and Dino Balsadella)
1971 Apartments and offices, Udine (with P. Ricci Menichetti)
1973 Zanussi DP Centre, Pordenone, Italy
1974 Town Hall, Casarza, Italy (with P. Ricci Menichetti)
    Geatti Warehouse and Showrooms, Terenzano, Italy
    Factory, Portogruaro, Italy

1976 Zoppas Factory Canteen, Susegana, Italy
1977 Tomb of Pier Paolo Pasolini, Casarsadella Delizia, Pordenone, Italy
1978 Fantoni Factory, Offices and Service Buildings, Osoppo, Italy
    Valdadige Pre-Fabricated Schools, Udine and Venice
    Office Building, Agrate, Milan (project; with M. Broggia and M. Burkardt)
    Office Building, Pomezia, Rome (project)
1979 IACP Public Housing, Udine
    Residential Development, Buia, Italy (with P. Ricci Menichetti)
1982 Galvani Office Building, Pordenone, Italy (with A. Carnelutti, A. De Gillia and N. Zizzutto)
1983 IBM Centre, Basiano, Milan (with Fiat Engineering)
    Banca Commerciale Italiana, New York

Publications:

By VALLE: articles—"La Scuola Internazionale estiva del CIAM 1952 a Venezia" in *La Rivista Pirelli* (Milan), December 1952; "Applicazioni della struttura spaziale continua ad ottaedri" in *Rassegna Tecnica della Regione Friuli Venezia Giulia* (Venice), January 1955; "Friuli Venezia Giulia: Aspetti della regione a statuto speciale e problemi del piano di sviluppo" in *Urbanistica* (Turin), no. 40, 1963; "Discourse: Gino Valle" in *RIBA Journal* (London), May 1965; "La Funzione dell'industrial Designer" in *Congresso Accaio,* Luxembourg 1965; "Otto Riposte sui Problemi del Design: La Educazione dell'Industrial Designer" in *Edilizia Moderna* (Milan), no. 85, 1965; "Intervista Registrata nella Primavera del 1970" in *Zodiac* (Milan), December 1970; "Architecture as planning practice", with Vittorio Gregotti, in *Casabella* (Milan), September 1979; "Interview with Gino Valle", in *Architettura* (Rome), April 1982.

On VALLE: books—*Ville in Italia* by Roberto Aloi, Milan 1960; *Una Svolta nelle Costruzioni* by Konrad Wachsmann, Milan 1960; *10 Profili di Artisti della Regione Friuli Venezia Giulia* by Dino Dardi, Venice 1965; *Catalogo Bolaffi dell'Architettura Italiana 1963-66,* edited by P. C. Santini and G. L. Marini, Turin 1966; *Immaginazione Megastrutturale dal Futurismo a Oggi,* edited by E. Crispolti, Venice 1979; *Architetture italiane degli anni '70,* exhibition catalogue edited by G. De Feo and E. Valeriani, Rome 1981; *The European Iceberg,* exhibition catalogue edited by G. Celant, Milan 1985; articles—"Architettura di Giovani" by Giuseppe Samonà in *Casabella* (Milan), May 1955; "Tre Banche dello Studio Valle" by Francesco Tentori in *Casabella* (Milan), December 1956; "Una Costruzione a Trieste" by Luciano Semarani in *Casabella* (Milan), April 1958; "The Work of Studio Valle" by Joseph Rykwert in *Architecture and Building* (London), April 1958; "Condominium in Trieste" by Reyner Banham in *Architectural Review* (London), November 1958; "La Distruzione Pianificata" by Francesco Tentori in *Casabella* (Milan), February 1959; "Tre Opere ed un Progetto" by Francesco Tentori in *Casabella* (Milan), April 1959; "Il Monumento alla Resistenza" by Bruno Zevi in *L'Espresso* (Rome), May 1959, and in *L'Architettura* (Rome), August 1959; "10 Anni di Attivita Valle" by Francesco Tentori in *Casabella* (Milan), December 1960; "15 Anni di Architettura Italiana" by Francesco Tentori in *Casabella* (Milan), May 1961; "World Studio Valle" by Reyner Banham in *Architectural Review* (London), June 1961; "World" by Reyner Banham in *Architectural Review* (London), January 1962; "Presente e Futuro della Architettura Industriale in Italia" by Roberto Giuducci in *Zodiac* (Milan), January 1962; "The Look of Industry" in *Architectural Forum* (New York), April 1962; "Gino Valle" by Giuseppe Mazzariol in *Zodiac* (Milan), October 1963; "The Work of Gino Valle" by Joseph Rykwert in

Gino Valle: Zanussi Factory Offices, Pordenone, Italy, 1961.

Architectural Design (London), March 1964; "Things Seen" by Edward Lucie-Smith in *The Times* (London), 21 April 1964; "Edificio Termale" by Maria Bottero in *Zodiac* (Milan), April 1965; "Architetture di Gino Valle" by Joseph Rykwert in *Domus* (Milan), May 1965; "Alle Porte di Milano" by Joseph Rykwert in *Domus* (Milan), May 1970; "Gino Valle: Edifici Industriali" by Joseph Rykwert in *Domus* (Milan), November 1970; "Italian Suavity," editorial in *Architectural Forum* (New York), April 1971; "Gino Valle" by F. Dal Co and M. Manieri in *L'Architecture d'Aujourd'hui* (Paris), September/October 1975; "La Necessita dell'Architettura" by F. Dal Co in *Lotus International* (Milan), no. 11, 1976; "Incontri con i Protagonisti" by P. Carlo Santini in *Ottagono* (Milan), March 1976; "New type layouts for elementary and secondary schools", in *Industria delle Costruzione* (Rome) no. 5, 1979; "Factory, Udine, Italy" by J. Glancey in *Architectural Review* (London), October 1979; "Fabbrica Fantoni", in *Progressive Architecture* (New York), September 1980; "Green-Red Houses", in *Domus* (Milan), September 1980; "Colour—part of architecture", in *Abitare* (Milan), May 1981; "Residential area in Udine", in *l'Architecture d'Aujourd'hui* (Paris), September 1981; "New Housing Project in Venice" by G. Polin in *Casabella* (Milan), March 1982; "Fantoni Factory", in *l'Architecture d'Aujourd'hui* (Paris), June 1982; "Coloring Blocks" by D. Morton in *Progressive Architecture* (New York), October 1982; "The Architecture of Gino Valle" by P. Fumagalli in *Werk, Bauen und Wohnen* (Zurich), July/August 1983; "IBM Distribution Centre in Pordenone" by P. A. Croset and G. Polin in *Casabella* (Milan), March 1984.

Italian architecture of the last thirty years serves as a dramatic mirror of contradictory tendencies that reflect and epitomize the general condition of Western culture. The ideas and buildings produced have been called the work of an uncertain generation, a generation that has witnessed a progressive alienation from the reality of the process of urban development and construction. With typical generosity, Italian architects have labored under the burden of a great number of attitudes, unfortunately not always bringing them to mature consequences. Any attempt to understand the situation is made even more difficult by the fact that the work of critics and analysts is greatly affected by their political convictions, allegiances that frequently intertwine and react with the political attitudes of the architects themselves. Nevertheless, in spite of a variety of "ruptures" and "alternatives," architec-

tural culture in Italy retains a fundamental continuity. It seems that in Italy transformations are only possible in terms of a deep-rooted philosophy of settlement and its idealization into form. This pressing drive for idealization causes, more than is warranted, a search for the exceptional, at times proposed brilliantly, yet often contrasting sharply with the common sense with which life makes its signs. Gino Valle belongs to that roster of architects who express this common sense in their work; and this may well be the reason for the durable quality of Valle's buildings, both technologically and visually.

The city of Udine, where he works, is a town of respectable and often beautiful buildings, already characterized by the activity of G. D'Aronco, one of the most gifted architects of the Italian "liberty." The tradition of building properly and accurately is deep-seated there, and Valle's office is definitely part of that tradition. It is a family office, a strong qualification in itself, which began with Provino Valle, a designer of several important buildings in the city, and followed by the partnership of his two children, Gino and Nani. Gino Valle was educated both in Italy and at Harvard, where he graduated in 1952. Since that time he has completed a large number of projects, most of them built in the region where he lives. Their design is based on the translation of the tenets of the modern movement into a professional experience pointing toward "significance" in architecture. This significance rests in a methodology of design more than in a vocabulary of forms. Valle focuses upon the realization of a "catalog" of elements, a catalog that includes modules of human activities as well as modules of form. These compositional elements are laboriously investigated, scrutinized, and related to the framework of the urban environment.

The results of this continuous and thoughtful professional activity are buildings the forms of which are generated from the design of a program before the actual "reaching-out" for images. It is appropriate that much of Valle's work deals with industrial buildings. The need for a strict adherence to programmatic demands in such buildings is in keeping with the adoption of a methodology of composition of elements, which ends by having a profound influence on the formal vocabulary. The solutions for the Zanussi Factory Offices of 1961 and the computer center for the same company in 1973 are far apart in time but very close conceptually and in terms of their formal references. It is precisely this sense of continuity, both logical and linguistic, that constitutes the "significance" of Valle's work. The same significance is to be found in the architecture of farmhouses, residences, and other "ordinary" structures in the Friuli region.

Few of his works are relatively independent of programmatic limits. One is the somber monument to the Resistance in Udine (1969), while another is the Town Hall of Casarza (1974), where the separate structures of a meeting hall and offices are involved in highly formalistic exercises.

Yet even in these instances Valle's work is in a distinctive position with respect to post-war Italian architecture. Within the process of radical transformation that Italian society is undergoing, Valle's work maintains (and in many ways expands) the responsibilities of professionalism in a free society. His investigations of the process of programming and methods of approach to design consciously place the architect at the center of the process of production. For even if the parameters of the architecture of the present may be different from those of the past, the needs are the same: to relate those humanistic functions to architecture without which is has little reason to exist.

—Romaldo Giurgola

VAN DEN BROEK, Johannes Hendrik.
Dutch. Born in Rotterdam, 4 October 1898. Educated at the Rijswerkschool, Nijmegen, Netherlands, 1913-17; Technical University, Delft, 1919-24, Dip.Arch. 1924. In private practice, Rotterdam, 1927-37; in partnership with Johannes Brinkman, *q.v.*, Rotterdam, 1937-48; Principal, with Jacob Bakema, *q.v.*, Architectengemeenschap van den Broek en Bakema, Rotterdam, 1948 until his death, 1978. Professor of Town planning, Technical University, Delft, 1947-64; Supervisor, Academy of Architecture, Amsterdam, 1966-76. President, Good Living Foundation, Rotterdam, and Efficient Housing Foundation, Rotterdam, 1948-67; Member, Executive and Professional Committees, International Union of Architects, 1948-67; Member of the Council, Bouwcentrum, Rotterdam, 1948-67. Member, CIAM (Congrès Internationaux d'Architecture Moderne), from 1947, and Team 10, from 1963. Exhibitions: *Bouwen voor een open samenleving*, Boymans Museum, Rotterdam, 1963, toured The Netherlands, Germany, Austria and Italy; *Pampus*, Stedelijk Museum, Amsterdam, 1965, toured The Netherlands, Austria and the United States; *Samen Bouwen*, Town Hall, Schoonhoven, Netherlands, 1972, toured Australia and Germany; *Progetti e Opere*, Castello Nuovo, Naples, 1974, toured Italy. Recipient: Dutch Critics Prize, International Associ-

ation of Art Critics, 1972. Honorary Member, American Institute of Architects, Royal Institute of British Architects, Zentral Vereingung Architekten Oesterreichs (Austria), and Bund Deutscher Architekten (Germany). Officer, Orange-Nassau Order, Netherlands, 1950; Knight, Order of Nederlandse Neeuw, 1966. Chevalier, Légion d'Honneur, France, 1939; Member, of Order of La Couronne, Belgium, 1958. *Died* (in The Hague) *6 September 1978.*

Works:

1927/
29 Housing, with shops and restaurant, Mathenesserplein, Rotterdam
1930/
32 Office and apartment building, Mathenesserlaan-Binnenweg, Rotterdam
1931/
33 High-rise apartment block, Schiekade, Rotterdam
1931/
34 Housing estate, Vroesenlaan, Rotterdam
1934 Low-cost housing, Rotterdam (competition project)
1935/
36 Public housing, Mathensserdijk, Rotterdam
1936 Doctor's house, Keizersgracht, Amsterdam (competition project)
1936/
37 Public housing, Schepenstraat, Rotterdam
1936/
38 Public housing, Stadhoudersweg, Rotterdam

1937 Dutch Pavilion, *World's Fair,* Paris
Hospital, Terneuzen, Netherlands (projects)
Plate Holiday House, Rockanje, Netherlands (project)
1937/
38 Public housing, Statenweg, Rotterdam
Holland-America Lines Departure Hall, Wilhelminakade, Rotterdam
Ten Horst-Vorgel House, Vierhouten, Netherlands
Niehuis-van den Berg Office extensions, Pastoriestraat, Rotterdam
1937/
39 Snoek House, C.N.A. Looslaan, Hillergersberg, Rotterdam
1937/
40 Van Ommeren N.V. Office Building, Antwerp
1938 House of Art and Science, Rotterdam (project)
Nygh House, Rotterdam (project)
1938/
39 Public Housing, Vroesenlaan, Rotterdam (with Wilhelmus Theodorus Hyacinthus ten Bosch and Albert Otten)
Gestel House, Bentincklaan, Rotterdam
de Arend Central Club House, Rotterdam
Public housing, Bentincklaan, Rotterdam
1938/
40 Low-cost housing, Tarwebuurt, Rotterdam-South

1939 Mass Exhibition Hall of 1941, Rotterdam (project)
Public housing, Statensingel, Rotterdam (project)

1940/
41 Workers' housing, Rotterdam
Temporary shops, Mathenesserlaan, Rotterdam
1941 Garden Housing Estate, Wilgenplas, Rotterdam (project)
Blaak Development Plan, Rotterdam (competition project)
1941/
43 Tollens and Company Dye and Lacquer Factory, Overschiesweg, Overschie, Netherlands
Public housing, Rotterdam-South
1941/
45 Gispen N.V. Factory and Office Building extensions, Stationsweg, Culemborg, Netherlands
1941/
48 Strijp I Terrace Housing, Strijp, Eindhoven, Netherlands
1942 Development plan for the Hofplein, Rotterdam (competition project)
Engels N.V. Slaughterhouse, Garage and Canteen, Landsmeer, Netherlands (project)
1942/
43 Van Nelle Company Warehouse extensions, van Nelleweg, Rotterdam
1943 Reconstruction plan for Schiedamsesingel-Binnenweg, Rotterdam (project)
Post-war public housing, Rotterdam (project; with the Woning-Architectuur Group)
Maritime Centre, Vasteland, Rotterdam (project)
1944 Slaughterhouse and cattle-market, Rotte, Rotterdam (project)

J. H. van den Broek and Jacob Bakema: Lijnbaan Shopping Centre, Rotterdam, 1953.

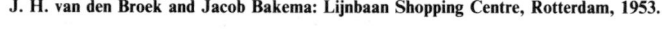

1945 Wevers Circus, Blijdorp, Rotterdam (project)
      Parish Centre, Rotterdam-South (project)
1945/
  49 Ardath Tobacco Company extensions, Spui-
      weg, Dordrecht, Netherlands
1946 Reform Church, Kralingen, Rotterdam (pro-
      ject)
1946/
  47 Nederlandse Agrarische Industrie Factory
      rebuilding, Poeldijk, Netherlands
1946/
  48 Aircraft Hangar reconstruction, Ypenburg,
      Netherlands
1946/
  49 Holland-America Lines Warehouse and Off-
      ice Building, Wilhelminahaven, Rotterdam
      Thomsen's Havenbedrif Harbour Building,
      Lekhaven, Rotterdam
1947 Main Hall, Volksuniversiteit, Diergaardesin-
      gel, Rotterdam (project)
      Single-family housing (project)
      Terraced housing, Hook of Holland (project)
1947/
  50 Strjp II Terrace Housing, Strijp, Eindhoven,
      Netherlands
      Holland America Lines Harbour Building,
      Rijnhaven, Rotterdam
1947/
  51 Lamers and Indemans N.V. Factory, Parallel-
      weg, Hertogenbosch, Netherlands
1948 Church Community Centre, Charlois, Rotter-
      dam (project)
1948/
  50 Two semi-detached houses, Hornlaan, Bev-
      erwijk, Netherlands
      Nederlandse Kroonkurk Mij. N.V. Factory
      and Office Building, Sluisjesdijk, Rott-
      erdam
1948/
  51 Termeulen-Wassen-van Vorst Shopping Baz-
      aar, Binnenweg, Rotterdam
1948/
  53 City Transport and Motor Services Building,
      Schiekanaal, Rotterdam
1949 Pendrecht Housing Estate, Rotterdam (pro-
      ject)
      Artists Centre (project)
1949/
  50 Layout and buildings for the *Rotterdam Ahoy*
      exhibition, Stadtpark, Rotterdam
      Zuid Shipping Union Medical Services Build-
      ing, St. Jobsweg, Rotterdam
1949/
  51 Van Houten and Zn. Metalworks Shop and
      Office Building, Bierstraat, Rotterdam
      Mill and bakery extensions, Binnenhaven,
      Wageningen, Netherlands
      Anthony Veder N.V. Shipping Bureau exten-
      sions, Westplein 11, Rotterdam
1949/
  52 Van der Meer House remodelling, Prins Bern-
      hardkade, Rotterdam
1949/
  53 Lijnbaan Shopping Centre, Rotterdam
      Ypenhof (van den Broek House), Kraling-
      seweg 179, Rotterdam
      Secondary school with gymnasium, Coppel-
      stockstraat, Brielle, Netherlands
1950 Cinema, Hengelo, Netherlands (project)
      Public housing, Drente, Netherlands (project)
      van den Broek/Bakema Office extensions,
      Westerkade, Rotterdam
      Van Leer Company Administration Building,
      Stadionplein, Amsterdam (competition
      project)
      Auction Building, Marconistraat, Rotterdam
      (project)
      Bataafse Petroleum Company Administr-
      ation Building, The Hague (competition
      project)
      Uttman House, Bennekom, Netherlands (pro-
      ject)
1950/
  51 Aircraft hangar, Ypenburg, Netherlands

Terrace housing, Heeswijkstraat, Voorburg,
      The Hague
1950/
  53 Holland-America Lines Works Building, Wil-
      helminakade, Rotterdam
1951 Hoving House, Drachten, Netherlands (pro-
      ject)
      Pendrecht Housing Estate, Rotterdam (pro-
      ject; with Opbouw Group)
      Sanders House, Vught, Netherlands (project)
1951/
  52 Hispano Suiza N.V. Factory, Terheyden-
      seweg, Breda, Netherlands
      Esso Service Station, Ungerplein, Rotterdam
1951/
  53 Zuid Shipping Union Station, Bananenstraat,
      Rotterdam
      Veder N.V. Warehouse and Office Building,
      Ijsselhaven, Rotterdam
      Public housing, Blankenburgersingel, Over-
      schie, Rotterdam
1951/
  54 Terrace shops and houses, Lange Nieu-
      wstraat, Velsen, Netherlands
1951/
  61 Metallurgy Laboratory, Technical Univers-
      ity, Delft
1952 Veder House, Kralingseweg, Rotterdam (pro-
      ject)
1952/
  53 Niehuis-van den Bergh Works Building with
      Housing Havenstraat, Rotterdam
1952/
  54 de Klerk Furniture Shop, Nieuwe Binnenweg,
      Rotterdam
      Public housing, Molenleystrat, Breda, Neth-
      erlands
      Huf Shoe Store, Hoogstraat, Rotterdam
      Horticultural School, Burgmeester H. van
      Sleenstraat, Brielle, Netherlands
      Public housing, with shops, Burgmeester Bau-
      mannlaan, Rotterdam
      Ten Cate and Company Administration Buil-
      ding, Spoorstraat, Almelo, Netherlands
1952/
  55 Public housing, with shops and restaurant,
      Pleinweg, Zuidplein, Rotterdam
      Boilerhouse and Laboratory of Heating Tech-
      niques, Technical University, Delft
1952/
  56 Terraced and public housing, Maarten Har-
      pertszoon Tromstraat, Brielle, Netherlands
1953 Alexanderpolder Housing Estate, Rotterdam
      (project; with Opbouw Group)
      Van Giessen and Zn. Wharf, Office and Shops
      enlargement, Krimpen an der Ijssel, Neth-
      erlands
      Veder N.V. Office remodelling, Westerkade,
      Rotterdam (project)
      Hotel, Rotterdam (project)
      Van Ommeren N.V. Office Building, Wester-
      laan, Rotterdam (project)
1953/
  54 Housing, Breedveldsingel, Rotterdam
      Layout and buildings for the *E 55* exhibition,
      Rotterdam
1953/
  55 Nurses Home, Westersingel, Rotterdam
      Housing development, Geuzenveld, Amst-
      erdam
      Navy Sports Centre, Schulpweg, Rotterdam
1953/
  56 Rotterdamsche Kolen Centrale Office and
      Warehouse Building, Waalhaven, Rotter-
      dam
1954 Sonneveld House Redevlopment, Schiedam-
      sevest, Rotterdam
1954/
  56 Public housing, with shops, Mariniersweg,
      Rotterdam
1954/
  57 Galeries Modernes Department Store, Hoog-
      straat, Rotterdam
      Town Hall remodelling, Marktplein, Brielle,

Netherlands (with Philippus Bolt and C.
      Baert de la Faille)
1954/
  58 Reformed Church, Burgemeester Honnerlage
      Gretelaan, Schiedam, Netherlands
      T.N.O. Metallurgy Laboratories, Rotterdam-
      seweg, Delft
1955 Visser House, Papendrecht, Netherlands (pro-
      ject)
      Zwolsman N.V. Head Office, Utrecht (pro-
      ject)
      Sanders House, Juliaanlaan, Rotterdam
      Sports Park, Madestein, The Hague (project)
      Congress Hall, The Hague (project)
1955/
  57 Shopping Centre, Zuiderwinkels, Nagele, Ne-
      therlands
      School for the Retarded, Burgmeester H. van
      Sleenstraat, Brielle, Netherlands
      Prefabricated public housing, Rijswijk, Neth-
      erlands
1955/
  59 Terraced and public housing, Vrederust Oost,
      The Hague
1955/
  60 Montessori School, Schimmelpenninckstraat
      20, Rotterdam
1956 Hotel, Zeestraat-Javastraat, The Hague (pro-
      ject)
      Alexanderpolder Housing Estate, Rotterdam
      (project; with Opbouw Group)
      Single-family housing, Karpendonk, Eind-
      hoven, Netherlands (project)
      Diepen House, Wassenaar, Netherlands (pro-
      ject)
      Youth Hostel, Oostvoorne, Netherlands (pro-
      ject)
      Theatre, Zwartenweg, The Hague (project)
      Nievelt-Goudriaan and Company Office
      Building, Veerkade, Rotterdam (project)
      Frik House extensions, Heerenveen, Neth-
      erlands (project)
      Centre Building, Emmen, Netherlands (pro-
      ject)
1956/
  57 Public housing, Hengelolaan, The Hague
      Van Giessen an Zn. Offices remodelling,
      Krimpen an der Ijssel, Netherlands
      Wieringa House, Hobbemastraat 2, Middel-
      harnis, Netherlands
1956/
  58 Klein Driene Development, Hengelo, Neth-
      erlands
      Ierland-van Zanten Shop, Lijnbaan, Rot-
      terdam
1956/
  61 World Broadcasting Building, Witte Kruis-
      laan 55, Hilversum, Netherlands
1957 Viewing Tower, Stadtpark, Rotterdam (pro-
      ject)
      Shopping Centre, Vlaardingen, Netherlands
      (project)
      Maritime Centre, Scheveningen, The Hague
      (project)
1957/
  58 'T Heechterp District Development, Leeu-
      warden Ost, Netherlands
1957/
  59 Nord-Kennermerland Regional Plan, North
      Holland
1957/
  60 Apartment tower block, Hansaviertel, Berlin
      Diaconessenhuis Clinic extensions, Wester-
      singel, Rotterdam
      Medical Cenre, de Cordesstraat, Hook of
      Holland
      Aerod Hydro-dynamics Laboratories, Techn-
      ical University Delft
      Het Parool Newspaper Building, Amsterdam

1958 Netherlands Pavilion, *World's Fair,* Brussels
      (with Gerrit Rietveld and Joost Willem
      Cornelis Boks)
      Lummus Nederland N.V. Office Building,

Plaspoelpolder, Rijswijk, Netherlands (project)

Landbouwhuis (Agricultural Centre), Paternosterstraat, Alkmaar, Netherlands (project)

Capital Centre, Berlin (competition project)

Ter Meulen House, Oude Zeeweg, Noordwijk, Netherlands (project)

Vlaardingen Nord Buildings, Vlaardingen, Netherlands (project)

Margarine AG/Unilever Office Building, Valentinskamp, Hamburg (competition project)

Shopping Centre, Culemborg, Netherlands (project)

1958/
59 Van Welzenes N.V. Factory, Spijkenisse, Netherlands

1958/
60 *Floriade* horticultural exhibition layouts, Stadpark, Rotterdam
Reformed Church, Ring, Nagele, Netherlands
van Roosbroeck House, Barendrechtseweg, Barendrecht, Netherlands (demolished)

1958/
61 Dura N.V. Office Building, Raadhuisplein, Rotterdam
Analytical Chemistry Laboratories, Technical University, Delft

1958/
62 Town Hall, Marl, Germany

1958/
63 Central Post Office Building, Prinses Beatrixlaan, The Hague

1959 De Nederlanden 1845 Insurance Building, Adelheidstraat, The Hague (competition poject)
Shopping Centre, Laan van Meerdervoort, The Hague (project)

1959/
61 Meerwaldt House, Baarsweg, Hoogvliet, Netherlands
Lamers and Indemans N.V. Factory extensions, Parallelweg, Hertogenbosch, Netherlands
Shopping centre, with maisonettes, Bergen, Netherlands
Terraced houses with shops, Prins Hendrikstraat, Hook of Holland

1959/
62 Grain Testing Laboratories, Technical University, Delft
Leeuwarden Noord Housing Estate, Leeuwarden, Netherlands
Shopping Centre, with houses, Binnenhof, Amstelveen, Netherlands

1959/
63 Road Construction Laboratories, Technical University, Delft

1959/
64 School of Engineering Lecture Building, and School of Architecture Lecture Building, Technical University, Delft

1960 World Health Organization Building, Geneva (competition project)
Radio and television station, Kuwait (project)
Cultural Centre, Leverkusen, Germany (competition project)

1960/
61 Van Buchem House, Offenbachlaan 5, Hillegersberg, Rotterdam
Van Wijk House, Distelstraat 4, Hook of Holland
De Klerk House, Tsjaikofskilaan 7, Hillegersberg, Rotterdam

1960/
62 Post Office, Binnenhof 64, Amstelveen, Netherlands
Junior School and Kindergarten, Smeetslandsedijk, Rotterdam
Raiffeisenbank Building, Prins Hendrikstraat, Hook of Holland
Van Giessen and Zn. Canteen and Drawing Office, Krimpen an der Ijssel, Netherlands

Office building with shops, TuftmarktKalvermarkt, The Hague

1960/
63 High-rise apartment block, Mariahoeve, The Hague (project)
Office building, Oostingstraat, Emmen, Netherlands
Elementary School, Emmercompascum, Emmen, Netherlands

1960/
68 Town Hall, Terneuzen, Netherlands

1961 Elementary School, Erica, Emmen, Netherlands (project)
Fortgens House, Straatweg, Rotterdam (project)
Timp Hose extensions, Grindbank, Laren, Netherlands (project)
Steilshoop Housing Estate, Hamburg (competition project)
Frik House, Heerenveen, Netherlands (project)
Shopping Centre, Heemskerk, Netherlands (project)
High School for the Social Sciences, Linz, Austria (competition project)
Plan for Wulfen New Town, Westphalia, Germany (competition project)
Shopping Centre, Jagershoef, Eindhoven, Netherlands (project)
High-rise apartment block, Rozenburg, Netherlands (project)

1961/
62 Auditorium, Technical University, Delft
Central Post Office, Velperweg, Arnhem, Netherlands
Wierda House, Burgemeester Falkenlaan, Heerenveen, Netherlands

1961/
63 Philips N.V. Works Housing, Strijpsestraat, Eindhoven, Netherlands
Van Wilgen House, Mahlersingel, Rotterdam

1962 Development plan for the Woensel District, Eindhoven, Netherlands
Town Hall, Offenbach am Main, Germany (competition project)
Nordwestadt Centre, Frankfurt (competition project)
Centre Building, Spoorstraat, Nimwegen, Netherlands (project)
Van de Sande Wijbrand House, Straatweg, Rotterdam (project)
Ljnbaan Shopping Centre extension, Lijnbaan, Rotterdam
University of the Ruhr, Bochum, Germany (competition project)
Philips N.V. Works Housing, Geldorp, Netherlands

1962/
63 Expansion plans for Hengelo North, Netherlands

1964 Protestant Student Community Centre, Mainz, Germany (competition project)
Town Hall, Jerusalem (competition project)
Town plan for Skopje, Yugoslavia (competition project)
Sociedad Immobiliaria y del Gran Kurssal Maritimo S.A., San Sebastian, Spain (competition project)

1964/
68 Drachten Elementary School, Netherlands

1964/
69 Hermes Student Club, Rotterdam

1965 Zwijndrecht Secondary School, Netherlands
Leo van Ireland House, Rotterdam
Mobile Theatre, for the Dutch Opera Foundation (project; with Frei Otto)

1965/
70 M.B.O. Covered Shopping Centre, Leeuwarden, Netherlands

1965/
71 Drachten Elementary School for Handicapped Children, Netherlands

1965/
76 Town Hall, Ede, Netherlands

1966/
68 Corpac Office Building, Tilburg, Netherlands

1966/
69 Apartment building, Tilburg, Netherlands

1966/
73 Nurses' Dormitory, Leidschendam, Netherlands

1966/
74 I.C.Z. Hospital, Apeldoorn, Netherlands

1967 Sanders House reconstruction, Schiedam, Netherlands

1968 Medical School, Accra, Ghana
Urban distric development plan for Diemen, Netherlands
Exotarium (tropical garden), The Hague
Town Hall, Amsterdam (competition project)

1968/
73 Cultural and Community Centre, Winschoten, Netherlands

1968/
76 D.S.H.B. Old People's Housing, Delft, Netherlands

1969 Shell Company Administration Building, Hamburg (competition project)
Lommerrijk Sports Centre Residential Buildings, Rotterdam
Town Hall and Apartments, Weert, Netherlands
University of Brussels (competition project)
Mummelmannsberg Comprehensive School, Hamburg (competition project)
Student Dormitories, Delft, Netherlands

1970 Netherlands Pavilion, *World's Fair*, Osaka, Japan (with Carel Weeber)

1971 University Economics Faculty Building extension, Rotterdam (project)

1971/
73 de Grave Home for the Retarded, Gorinchem, Netherlands

1971/
76 Erasmus College Secondary School, Zoetermeer, Netherlands

1973 Zeckendorf House, The Bahamas
Sunter Town Plan, Djakarta, Indonesia (project)
Kurhaus District redevelopment, Scheveningen, Netherlands (as supervising architect)
Barre Molen Windmill restoration, Zoeterwoude, Netherlands

1974 City centre plan for Eindhoven (project; with Herman Hertzberger)
World Trade Centre, Rotterdam (competition project)
Traffic plan for Kloekamp and Main Railway Station, The Hague
Kaatstraat renovation, Utrecht

1975 Renovation of the Weerdjes District, including apartment buildings, Arnhem, Netherlands

Publications:

By van den BROEK: books—*Habitation*, volumes 1-3, Rotterdam 1945-65; *Creatieve Krachten in de Architectonische Conceptie*, Delft 1948; *Woonmogelijkheden in het nieuwe Rotterdam*, with Willem van Tijen, Johannes Brinkman and Huig A. Maaskant, Rotterdam 1941; *Beginselen van Kerkbouw*, The Hague 1954; *Gids voor Nederlandse Architectuur* with Meischke and Boot, Rotterdam 1955; *Scholen*, Rotterdam 1956; articles—"Wie wil goed wonen?" in *Goed Wonen* (Amsterdam), January 1948; "1898-1948: Viftig jaar Nederlandse Architectuur" in *Bouw* (Rotterdam), September 1948; "Open Brief aan J.J.P. Oud," with Jacob Bakema, in *De Groene Amsterdammer* (Amsterdam), 6 December 1952; "Bedrifsgebouwen" in *Forum* (Amsterdam), April/May 1953; "Bouwkunst in dienst van de kerk" in *Wending 8* (Amsterdam), no. 10/11, 1953/54; "Moderne Architektur in moderner Stadtplanung" in *Aachener Zeitung* (Aachen), 25 January 1955; "Efficiente Woningbouw, Standaardplattegronden," with others, in *Bouw* (Rotterdam), 18 July 1955; "Cultuur, Architectuur, Techniek" in *Bouw* (Rotterdam), 23 July 1955; "Efficiente Woningbouw: Hernieuwde activeit van de Studiegroep," with others, in *Bouw* (Rotterdam), 24 January 1959; "Stadt und Wohnung im heutigen Licht" and "Konstruktion und Gestaltung im industriellen Wohnungsbau" in *Der Architekt* (Stuttgart), April 1959; "Stad en jeugd—jeugd en stad" in *Bouw* (Rotterdam), 16 July 1960; "Uit Inleiding" and "Doelmatigheid en creativeteit in de woningbouw" in *Delftse School* (Delft), November 1961; "Velen hebben vaal aan hem te danken: In Memoriam B. Merkelbach" in *Bouw* (Rotterdam), no. 44, 1962; "Bewoners moeten mogelijkheid tot variatie hebben" in *Algemeen Dagblaad* (Rotterdam), 3 November 1962.

On van den BROEK: books—*CIAM 1959 in Otterlo,* Stuttgart 1959; *Architektur und Stadtebau: Das Werk van den Broek und Bakema,* edited by Jürgen Joedicke, Stuttgart 1963; *Bouwen voor een open samenleving,* exhibition catalogue, Rotterdam 1963; *van den Broek/Bakema,* edited by Camillo Gubitosi and Alberto Izzo, Rome 1976; *Architecture-Urbanism: Architecten-gemeenschap van den Broek en Bakema,* edited by Jürgen Joedicke, Stuttgart 1976; articles—"Het Bureau van den Broek en Bakema" by Willem van Tijen in *Forum* (Amsterdam), June 1957; "Costruzioni degli Architetti Jacob Bakama e Johannes van den Broek" by G. Perugini in *L'Architettura* (Rome), September 1959; "van den Broek und Bakema," special issue of *Bauen und Wohnen* (Zurich), October 1959; "Brinkman, Brinkman, van der Vlugt, van den Broek, Bakema" by B. Housden, special issue of *Architectural Association Journal* (London), December 1960; "The Architecture of Van den Broek" by Jord den Hollander in *De Architect* (The Hague), January 1979; "Exhibition 'The appropriate architecture of Van den Broek'" by Wim J. Van Heuvel in *Polytechnisch Tijdschrift* (The Hague), April 1981; "Housing in the Hague" in *Bouw* (Rotterdam), 30 April 1983.

J. H. van den Broek (he was always known by his initials), was born in 1898 at Rotterdam in the Netherlands, where he also studied architecture. Between 1924 and 1937 he was in practice on his own account; from 1937 to 1948 he was in partnership with Brinkman, and in 1948 he joined Jacob Bakema.

van den Broek was of the same generation as architects like Ernö Goldfinger, born at the right time to witness the remarkable architectural developments in Europe of the 1920s and 1930s, but not then experienced or practised enough to influence them. In the work and career of van den Broek, as of Goldfinger, we can see the realization and extension of the Modernist ideals made relevant to a more realistic and politically secure Europe than the one before the war.

Although van den Broek's Dutch Pavilion at the Paris exhibition of 1937 secured his reputation as a practitioner of an elevated version of the International Style, his most familiar contributions to European architecture has been with Team 10, a post-war off-shoot of CIAM. Team 10 encouraged a view of architecture which reflected the utopianism of the 1960s. Of the members of Team 10 (Candilis, Josic, Woods, the Smithsons, Ralph Erskine and Stefan Wewerka), van den Broek's contribution is perhaps the most anonymous and the one which can be least appropriately applied to the group's credo of "building towards society's realisation of itself."

Stylistically, van den Broek refined the Modernism of the 1930s into a thin, tight and neat glacial mode, well suited to the corporate needs of the 1950s. Precision and lightness are twin dominating characteristics of his style.

—Stephen Bayley

van EESTEREN, Cornelis.

Dutch. Born in Kinderdijk, Alblasserdam, 4 July 1897. Educated at schools in Alblasserdam and Dordrecht, until 1912; apprenticed as a carpenter and builder, Dordrecht, 1912-14; studied architecture, Academie van bleeldenden Kunsten en technischen Wissenschaft, Rotterdam, 1915-17, Dip.Arch. 1917; higher building studies, Academie voor Bouwkunst, Amsterdam, 1919-22, Rome Prize, 1922; city planning studies, Institut d'Urbanisme of the Sorbonne, and Ecole des Beaux-Arts, Paris, 1923-24; also apprentice draughtsman in the studios of architects W. Kromhout, Rotterdam, 1915, W. Verschoor, The Hague, and G. J. Rutgers, Amsterdam, 1919-21. Worked with the architect Pineau, Paris, 1924; studio-chief, office of architect Jan Wils, Voorburg, 1924-27; in private practice, Rotterdam and Amsterdam, from 1927. Member of the Commission for Fine Buildings, Rotterdam, 1925-28; Chief Architect, City Planner, then Head of the Town Planning Department, City of Amsterdam, 1929-59; Member of the Study-Group for Landscape and Planning of the Ijsselpolder, Kontak Commission, Amsterdam, from 1942; Member of the Advisory Council on Urban Design for the Amsterdam District, from 1957; Advisor, 1959, and Chairman of the Urban Design Advisory Committee, 1960-64, Amsterdam Building Office; Member of the Advisory Committee on District Planning, Amsterdam, from 1965. Guest Professor of Urban Building Studies, Staatliche Bauhochschule, Weimar, Germany, 1927-30; Professor of Urban Planning, Academie voor Bouwkunst, Amsterdam, 1932-36; Professor of Urban Design, Technische Hogeschool, Delft, 1947-67. Member, with the artist Theo van Doesburg, De Stijl movement, in Paris and Amsterdam, 1923-31; Founder-Member, De Opbouw architects group, Amsterdam, from 1925; Co-founder, The Hague branch of the Filmliga Institute for Pioneer Art Films, 1927-29; Member, De 8 architects group, Amsterdam, from 1929; Chairman, CIAM (Congres Internationaux d'Architecture Moderne), 1930-47; Member of the Postwar Housing Study Group, Amsterdam, 1943; Chairman, Union of Dutch City Planners (BNS), 1946-51; Member of the Permanent Urban Design Commission, Union International des Architectes, from 1948. Exhibitions: De Stijl, Galerie de l'Effort Moderne, Paris, 1923; *Salon d'Automne,* Paris, 1923; *Der neue Schulbau,* Switzerland, 1932; *De rationele woonwijk,* Amsterdam, 1932; *De Stijl,* Camden Arts Centre, London, 1968; *De Stijl—Visions of Utopia,* Walker Art Center, Minneapolis, toured U.S.A. and Netherlands, 1981-82. Recipient: First Prize, Bouwkunst en Vriendschap Competition, Rotterdam, 1917; First Prize, Unter den Linden Competition, Berlin, 1925; David Roell Prize, Prince Bernhard Foundation, Amsterdam, 1968. Honorary Member, Union of Dutch Urban Planners, 1967; Honorary Corresponding Member, Royal Institute of British Architects, 1937; University of Santiago School of Architecture, Chile, 1958; Academie d'Architecture, Paris, 1960; German Academy of Urban Design and Planning, 1960. Knight of the Order of the Dutch Lion, 1960; Member, Akademie der Kunste, Berlin, 1964. Address. Weldam 11, 1081 HN Amsterdam, Netherlands.

Works:

1918 Urban Building Studies for the Alblasserdam region, Netherlands (projects)

1921/
23 Amsterdam University Hall (project; with additions by Theo van Doesburg)
Private Town-house (project; with Theo van Doesburg)

1922 Private House (project; with Theo van Doesburg)

1923 Leonce Rosenberg House (project; with Theo van Doesburg)
Studio-house for an artist (project; with Theo van Doesburg)

Royal Dutch Academy of Sciences Building, Amsterdam (project)
House, Alblasserdam, Netherlands
House by a river, Alblasserdam, Netherlands (project)

1924 House in Zorgvliet Park, The Hague, Netherlands (project)
Traffic Studies, Paris
Rokin Development, Amsterdam (competition project)
City Plan with viaduct roads (project; with Theo van Doesburg)

1925 Shopping Precinct with Cafe-Restaurant, Laan van Meerdevoort, The Hague
Unter den Linden Redevelopment Plan, Berlin (competition project)

1927 Water Tower, Dunen, near Wassenaar, Netherlands (competition project; with M. S. Jongkind)

1928 Main Auditorium of the Agricultural High School, Wageningen, Netherlands (competition project)
Regional Music School, Frankfurt-on-Oder, Germany (as consultant)

1928/
40 Schools, Housing and Urban Development of the Carl Reinierszkade, Eerensplein, and other districts, The Hague (with Merkelbach and Karsten)

1929/
31 Theo van Doesburg House and Studio, Meudon-val-Fleury, France (with Theo van Doesburg)

1933/
52 Frankendaal Housing and Urban Development, Amsterdam

1939/
51 Slotermeer Development, Amsterdam

1941 Hofplein and Blaak Redevelopment, Rotterdam (project; with De 8 architects)

1944 Reconstruction Plan for Rotterdam

1949 Dorf Nagele Plan, Nordostpolder, Netherlands (with Merkelbach and De 8 architects)

1958 City Plan for Osorno, Valdivia Province, Chile

1959/
64 City Plan for Lelystad, Netherlands

1975 City Reconstruction Plan, Nijmegen, Netherlands

Publications:

By van EESTEREN: books—*CIAM: Rationelle Babauungsweisen,* Frankfurt 1930; *Het Algemeen Uitbreidingsplan,* Amsterdam 1934; *De conceptie van onze hedendaagse nederzettingen en cultuurlandschappen,* Amsterdam 1948; *Het plan, zijn functie en estetische aspecten,* n.p. 1958; *Stedebouwkundig plan voor Lelystad,* The Hague 1965; *Zweedse autografie,* n.p. 1967; *De congres van U.I.A. te Moskou 1958: Bouw en herbouw van steden 1945-1957,* Delft 1966; articles—"Het Waardhuis te Elshout" in *Bouwkundig Weekblad* (Amsterdam), 13 April 1918; "Vers une construction collective", with Theo van Doesburg, in *De Stijl* (Leiden), no. 6/7, 1924; "Moderne Stedebouwbeg in selen de praktijk" in *De Stijl* (Leiden), no. 10/11, 1924/25; "Naar aanleiding van de prijsvraag voor een watertoren te Wassenaar" in *i 10* (Amsterdam), nos. 1 and 3, 1927; "10 jaar De Stijl" in *De Stijl* (Leiden), no. 7, 1927; "Haus am Fluss" in *Der Cicerone* (Leipzig), no. 19, 1927; "Woonhuis te Nunspeet" in *i 10* (Amsterdam), no. 2, 1928/29; "In memoriam Theo van Doesburg" in *De Stijl* (Leiden), final issue, 1932; "De functioneele stad" in *De 8 en Opbouw* (Amsterdam), 25 May 1935.

On van EESTEREN: books—*'s-Gravenhage als woonstad,* The Hague 1927; *Bouwen-Bauen-Batir: Holland* by J. B. van Loghem, Amsterdam 1932; *Poetica dell'architettura neo-plastica* by Bruno Zevi, Milan 1953; *De Stijl: 1917-1931* by H. L. C. Jaffe,

Amsterdam 1956; *Architettura Moderna in Olanda* by Giovanni Fanelli, Florence 1968 *Cor van Eesteren* by Reinder Blijstra, Amsterdam 1971; *De Stijl 1917-1931: Visions of Utopia* by H. L. C. Jaffe, Oxford 1982; *Guide all'architettura moderna: De Stijl* by Giovanni Fanelli, Rome 1983; *Anfange einer neuen Architektur* by Manfred Bock, The Hague and Wiesbaden 1983; articles—"Cornelis van Eesteren, mestro de la arquitevtura contemporanea, cumple 70 anos" in *AUCA* (Santiago), no. 9, 1967; "Prof. C. van Eesteren 4 Juli 70 jaar" by H. L. C. Jaffe in *Bouwkundig Weekblad* (Amsterdam), no. 85, 1967; "Cornelis van Eesteren" by H. L. C. Jaffe in *Architectural Design* (London), December 1967; "Colloquium on architecture and town planning in Hamburg" by Hilde de Haan in *De Architect* (The Hague), June 1981.

Cornelis (Cor) van Eesteren was born at Kinderdijk (a town noted for the quality of its shipbuilding and machine-making skills), Netherlands, in 1897. His family had long been connected with the building industry, and the young Cor trained as a draughtsman and carpenter. Having decided to become an Architect, he joined the office of the Expressionist Willem Kromhout in 1915 and graduated with Honours from the Rotterdam Academy of Fine Arts and Technical Sciences in 1917. From that time, his chief interests developed in the field of town planning, and in 1918 he worked as a planner at Alblasserdam, near his birthplace, and also collaborated with architects in The Hague and in Amsterdam on various schemes. Like many Netherlands architects of the time, van Eesteren was influenced by the work of Frank Lloyd Wright, partly as a legacy of Berlage's enthusiasms, and this is evident in the building he designed for the Royal Netherlands Academy of Sciences.

The award of a major prize in 1922 led to travels in Germany to study traditional brick architecture, but the visit led to Weimar and meetings with the personalities associated with the Bauhaus, including Theo van Doesburg (1883-1931). From that time, the German and Dutch experimenters had a profound effect on van Eesteren, and 1923 saw a collaboration with van Doesburg, who designed the interiors for two houses by van Eesteren and who introduced the latter to Mondrian. The older van Doesburg excercised a considerable influence on van Eesteren, who rapidly absorbed the notions of the De Stijl movement: the two men produced a manifesto entitled *Vers une construction collective*, also signed by Rietveld, and participated in the famous De Stijl exhibition held in Rosenberg's Galerie de l'Effort Moderne in 1923. Designs for houses by van Eesteren dating from this period demonstrate an increasing concern with the interrelationship of internal and external spaces, and indeed with the qualities of inhabited volumes themselves, although the effects were often harsh and stark in the extreme.

In 1924 van Eesteren took over management of the office of Jan Wils, who was working on the Amsterdam Stadium in preparation for the Olympic Games of 1928. The following year, van Eesteren won first prize in a competition for the remodelling of the Unter den Linden in Berlin, and he produced plans for major changes in central Paris and in Amsterdam; these were characterised by high-rise blocks and huge traffic arteries cut through the urban fabric.

Such fashionable successes led to van Eesteren's appointment in 1929 as Chief Architect of the Town Planning Department of the City of Amsterdam, although his duties did not preclude plenty of private work and part-time jobs. He supervised the planning of Amsterdam for nearly half a century, and the General Extension Plan of 1936 is regarded as his most important work.

From 1930 to 1947 he was president of the Congrès Internationaux d'Architecture Moderne (CIAM), in which organisation he had led the Dutch National Working Group entrusted with the search for a language of appropriate symbols for town planning, a pretentious exercise that proved interminable and, ultimately, sterile. In 1947, van Eesteren was appointed Professor of Town Planning at the Technical University of Delft where he contributed to the decline of the influence of Granpré Molière in favour of the doctrine of empiricism. He retired from this post in 1967.

Van Eesteren based much in his theories on demographic studies and on an analysis of the different needs of various groups in society. His plans were dependent on the concept of population density, a subject on which (like others), he was dogmatic. During the 1920s and 1930s, he attempted to apply the design principles of the De Stijl movement to town planning. Opinion about his work is divided: some see van Eesteren as a great exponent of the fresh and "revolutionary" ideas of the 1920s, while others see in his oeuvre the seeds of the destructive tendencies in postwar European town planning, including the promotion of highrise blocks and excessive traffic penetration and pollution in urban centres. Van Eesteren's concerns with standardisation, "rationalisation," and the rejection of the unmeasurable in his plans have been paralleled in many countries, with less than happy results.

—James Stevens Curl

VAN EYCK, Aldo.

Dutch. Born in Driebergen, Netherlands, 16 March 1918. Educated at King Alfred School, Hampstead, London, 1924-32; Sidcot School, Winscombe, Somerset, 1932-35; Building School, The Hague, 1938; E.T.H.: Eidgenössische Technische Hochschule, Zurich, 1939-43. Married Hannie van Roojen in 1943; children: Tess and Quinten. Worked as an architect in the Public Works Department, Amsterdam, 1946-50. In private practice, The Hague and Amsterdam, since 1952; in partnership with Theo Bosch, 1971-82, and with Hannie van Eyck-van Roojen, since 1982. Editor, *Forum* magazine, Amsterdam, 1959-63, 1967. Lecturer in Art History, Enschede Art School, Netherlands, 1951-55; Tutor in an art school, Amsterdam, 1951-66; tutor at the Academy of Architecture, Amsterdam, 1956-61; Visiting Critic/Lecturer, University of Pennsylvania, Philadelphia, Washington University, St Louis, Harvard University, Cambridge, Massachusetts, Tulane University, New Orleans, the School of Architecture, Singapore, and the University of Trondheim, Norway, 1961-68; Professor, Institute of Technology, Delft, since 1968; Guest Professor, E.T.H., Zurich, 1977-78; Paul Philippe Cret Professor of Architecture, University of Pennsylvania, Philadelphia, 1978-83. Member, De 8 en Opbouw, Amsterdam, from 1946; Dutch Delegate to CIAM (Congrès Internationaux d'Architecture Moderne), from 1947; Member, COBRA, Copenhagen, Brussels, and Amsterdam, 1948-51. Member, Team 10, since 1953. Exhibitions: *Greater Number*, at the Triennale, Milan, 1968; *Europa-America: 25 Contemporary Architects*, at the *Biennale*, Venice, 1967; *Nine Architects*, toured Germany and Switzerland, 1976-77; *Aldo van Eyck: Buildings, Ideas, Photographs*, National Gallery of Greece, Athens, 1983; International Union of Architects Exhibition, Cairo, 1985. Recipient: City of Amsterdam Architecture Prize, 1964; First Prize, Protestant Church Competition, Driebergen, Netherlands, 1965; First Prize, Town Hall Competition, Deventer, Netherlands, 1967; First Prize, with Theo Bosch, Nieuw Markt Master Plan Competition, Amsterdam, 1970; First Prize, with Hannie van Eyck, Historical Museum Competition, Zwolle, Netherlands, 1971; Rotterdam-Maaskant Prize, 1982; Wihuri International Prize, Helsinki, 1982. Honorary Doctorates: New Jersey Institute of Technology, 1979; Tulane University, New Orleans, 1979. Honorary Member, Staat-liche Kunstakademie, Dusseldorf, 1979; Member of the Royal Academy of Arts and Sciences, Belgium, 1981; Honorary Fellow, American Institute of Architects, 1981; Honorary Member, Bund Deutscher Architekten, Germany, 1983. Address (office): Dorpstraat 44, Loenen a.d. Vecht, Netherlands.

Works

1946 Tower Room conversion, Zurich
1947/
74 Approximately 700 children's playgrounds, Amsterdam (with the Public Works Department)
1948 Heldring en Pierson Bank conversion, The Hague
1949 van Eyck Apartment conversion, Amsterdam
1950 "Ahoy" Entrance Sign, *National Maritime Exhibition,* Rotterdam
1952 Blue-Violet Room, Stedelijk Museum, Amsterdam
1954 64 houses for the elderly, Amsterdam (with Jan Rietveld)
1955 House, Herman Gorterstraat, Amsterdam (with Jan Rietveld)
1955/
56 3 schools, Nagele, N.E. polder, Netherlands (with H. P. D. van Ginkel)
1957/
60 Children's Home Amsterdam
1965 Protestant Church, Driebergen, Netherlands (competition project)
1966 Sculpture Pavilion, Arnhem, Netherlands
1967 Town Hall, Deventer, Netherlands (competition project)
1968 Design of the Greater Number Pavilion, *Triennale,* Milan
 Camping sanitary facilities, Loenen a.d. Vecht, Netherlands
1968/
70 Low-income housing, Lima, Peru (with Sean Wellesley Miller)
 Roman Catholic Church, The Hague
1969 Visser House extensions, Bergeik, Netherlands (original house by Gerrit Rietveld)
 Schmela Art Building, Dusseldorf
1970 Verberk House, Venlo, Netherlands
 Master plan for the Nieuw Markt area, Amsterdam (competition project; with Theo Bosch)
1971 Historical Museum, Zwolle, Netherlands (competition project; with Hannie van Eyck)
1974/
76 G. J. Visser House, Retie, Belgium
1975/
77 Housing, Zwolle, Netherlands (with Theo Bosch)
1975/
79 Hubertus Home (for single parents and their children), Amsterdam (with Hannie van Eyck)
1980/
83 Huize Padua psychiatric clinic, Boekel, Netherlands (with Hannie van Eyck)
1982/
83 Clinic for Drug Addicts, Helmond, Netherlands (with Hannie van Eyck)
 Siemens AG new buildings, Nuremberg, Germany (with Hannie van Eyck)
1984 Protestant Church for the Moluccan Community, Deventer, Netherlands (with Hannie van Eyck)
 ESTEC/ESA New Conference Centre and Restaurant, Noordwyk, Netherlands (with Hannie van Eyck)

Publications:

By van EYCK: articles—"CIAM 6, Bridgewater:

Aldo Van Eyck: Home for Single-Parent Families, Amsterdam, 1975-79.

Statement Against Rationalism, 1947" in *A Decade of Modern Architecture* by Sigfried Giedion, Zurich 1954 and *CIAM Otterlo* by Oscar Newman, Stuttgart and London 1961; numerous articles in *Dutch Forum* (Amsterdam), including "Wij Ontdekken Stijl" (We Discover Style), no. 2/3, 1949; "De Bal Kaatst Terug" (The Ball Bounces Back), no. 3, 1958; "Het Verhaal van een Andere Gedachte" (The Story of Another Idea), no. 7, 1959; "There is a Garden in Her Face," no. 3, 1960/61; "The Medicine of Reciprocity, Tentatively Illustrated," no. 6/7, 1962; "Steps Toward a Configurative Discipline," "The Pueblos of New Mexico," and "The False Client and the Great Word NO," no. 4, 1962; "Anna Was, Livia Is, Plurabelle's To Be," July 1967; and "Dogen," July 1967, reprinted as "The Interior of Time: A Miracle of Moderation" in *The Meaning of Architecture,* edited by Charles Jencks and George Baird, London 1969, and, with "The Kaleidoscope of the Mind," in *Via* (Philadelphia), no. 1, 1968; "Giancarlo De Carlo and Urbino" in *Zodiac* (Milan), no. 16, 1966; "The Enigma of Multiplicity (Mourn Also for All Butterflies)" in *Harvard Educational Review* (Cambridge, Massachusetts), vol. 39, no. 4, 1969; "What Is and Isn't Architecture" in *Lotus* (Venice), no. 28, 1980; "Lumière, Couleurs et Transparence" in *L'Architecture d'Aujourd'hui* (Paris), October 1981; "Aldo van Eyck: Annual RIBA Dicourse" in *RIBA Journal* (London), April 1981; "R.R.P. (Rats, Posts and other Pests)" in *Architectural Design* (London), no. 7, 1981; "Ex turigo semper aliquid novum" in *Archithese* (Zurich), no. 5, 1981; "By Definition" in *Forum* (Amsterdam), June 1982.

On van EYCK: books—*Netherlands Architecture since 1900* by R. Blijstra, Amsterdam 1960; *Modern Movements in Architecture* by Charles Jencks, London 1973; *Once Arquitectos* by Oriol Bohigas, Barcelona 1976, Cambridge, Massachusetts 1977; *Aldo van Eyck, Projekten 1948-1961,* Groningen, Netherlands 1981; *Aldo van Eyck: Hubertus House,* with texts by Herman Hertzberger, Francis Strauven and others, Amsterdam 1982; *Aldo van Eyck, Projekten 1962-1976,* Groningen, Netherlands 1983; *Aldo van Eyck Ax Bax* by Jan van Geest, Georges Candilis, Giancarlo De Carlo, and Suzana and Dimitris Antonakakis, Athens 1983; *The Modern House* by David Mackay, Barcelona 1984; *Architecture in an Age of Scepticism* by Denys Lasdun, London 1984; *Aldo van Eyck,* edited by Francis Strauven, Antwerp 1985; articles—"Polder and Playground" by John Voelcker in *The Architects Yearbook,* London 1955; "Children's Home in Amsterdam" by Bruno Zevi in *L'Architettura* (Rome), no. 6, 1961; "The Vicissitudes of Ideology" by Kenneth Frampton in *L'Architecture d'Aujourd'hui* (Paris), no. 177, 1975; "Church at The Hague" by Peter Smithson in *Architectural Design* (London), June 1975; "The Web and the Labyrinth" by Pierluigi Nicolin in *Lotus* (Milan), no. 11, 1976; "Street Urchin, Mother's House, Amsterdam" by Peter Buchanan in *Architectural Review* (London), March 1982; "Weaving Chaos into Order: Home for Single-Parent Families, Amsterdam" by Susan Doubilet in *Progressive Architecture* (New York), March 1982.

Blight has crept over our field in recent years. I shall, therefore, draw on the *Team 10 Primer* and say what I have said before. I wish—still wish—to identify a building with that same building entered—hence, with those it shelters; and define space—each space built—simply as the appreciation of it. This "circular" definition, whilst excluding all academic abracadabra, includes what should never be excluded: those entering that space, appreciating it. Architecture can do no more, nor should it ever do less, than accommodate people well, assit their homecoming. The "rest"—a sign here or a symbol there—will either take care of itself or does not matter.

If making a building has become too difficult, the dilemma is complete. But is it really all the difficult? Does it really require a genius to avoid the meagre or a sage to bypass silliness? It is painfully true of architecture that it is not just good quality that counts, but a significant quantity of that quality. A nice school built here is of no use to a child elsewhere. So why not start with this: persuade those narrow border lines—the hard and harsh ones—to loop generously and gracefully into articulated in-between places and, having done so, give each space the right "inner horizon" for the gratifying sense of reference it provides. That buildings could help mitigate stress is no longer a desirable objective! On the contrary: fostering conflict—even provoking it wilfully—has become a trend, like those other flirtations with adbsurdity, irony, banality, inconsistency and "Rome," of course. Affecting mannerism by misquoting from true mannerism, which, though reflecting inner conflict, also resolved it by coaxing troublesome paradoxes into significant form, is particularly selfish. Essential meaning is thus abused and wasted. Eclectics everywhere are producing little more than a single standard mono-mix with the opposite in mind no doubt. But never mind the Minnesota Six and their like! What is needed is better functionalism. For there is no such thing as a solid teapot that also pours tea. Such an object might be a penetrating statement about something, but is simply is not a teapot. Neither is there, nor shall it come to pass that there ever will be, such a thing as a building intentionally contradictory, absurd, banal, trivial or disconcerting that is still a building—or architecture. Marcel Duchamp invented many puzzling things, but they were significantly *not* buildings. Anyway, history—that great gathering body of experience—is there in the mind's interior—to be used and not spilt (I am referring to what I wish to call the R.R.P. – Rats, Posts and other Pests).

—Aldo van Eyck

Aldo van Eyck's reputation as a leading architect of the post war European avant-garde is based on his simple concern that a building must not only provide real practical space but also offer the opportunity for possible alternative activities for those who come to use it. It must be structurally and formally adaptable; consequently, the language of its construction can have more than one meaning.

Van Eyck is a man of considerable personal charm and modesty, and there is a fundamental humanity about his whole approach to architecture that is clearly reflected in everything he has done. From the early, and much admired, Amsterdam Children's Home to the recent Home for Single Parents and their children also in Amsterdam, there is a continuity of common sense that underlines his very real concern for the identity of the individual and a realization that the architect must build for each man and all men, as quite obviously they no longer feel the necessity to build for themselves. Worrying about the increasingly formless nature of society, coupled with an avowed distaste for the "boredom of hygiene," van Eyck has increasingly looked outside the accepted Western European tradition for his solutions. The Pueblos and the Dogon and later his work in the shanty-town "Barriados" of Peru have led him away from his original formal mathematical method into an area that always involves some element of surprise. He likes us to come upon his buildings without quite knowing what to expect and without fully understanding the reason for them until we recognize it instinctively. There is a real horror of what he has called the "organized nowhere." His comment the architecture need do no more than "assist man's homecoming" underlines a concern for controlled alternatives, *not* the mere irrational ambiguities that characterise the "ad hoc" thinking of the Post Modernists, whom he utterly despises.

The much quoted act of sympathetic recognition—"Bump!—Sorry. What's this? Oh hello!"— is typical of his fondness for what he sees as a poetic approach to architecture; it hints at a lingering admiration for Le Corbusier and also accounts for his commitment to Team 10—the "loose association of friends" whose admitted responsibility for the recent evolution of mainstream Modern Movement thinking has proved so fruitful for the continuation of the European tradition.

Though undeniably part of this tradition, van Eyck refuses to be a part of mere history, and that is his appeal to those concerned with the vital problem of training a formal identity, both socially and architecturally, in the face of intense commercial pressure. The concern for the individual is genuine, and the need for a form that offers more than one solution essential. Van Eyck is not concerned with "Utopia" but with the day-to-day existence of the individual in what he sees as a formless society.

—John Furse

van WIJK, Jan.

South African. Born in Roberts Heights, 2 May 1926. Educated at Oranje Meisieskool, Bloemfon-

tein, 1933; Robert Heights Primary School, 1934; Beach Primary School, East London, 1935-36; Roberts Heights Primary School, 1937; Grey College, Bloemfontein, 1938; Langenhoven Primary School, Pretoria, 1939; General Brink Primary School, Roberts Heights, 1939; Afrikaans Boys High School, Pretoria, 1940-43; University of Pretoria School of Architecture, 1944-49, B.Arch. 1949. Married Erna Marais in 1960. Student Assistant in the offices of Verhoef, Smit and Viljoen, Pretoria, 1946, and office of Norman Eaton, Pretoria, 1948; Assistant Architect, Meiring and Naude, Pretoria, 1949-50, Cape Town, 1951-56, Brian Colquhoun and Partners, London, 1956, Kahn and Jacobs, New York, 1957, and Smit and Viljoen, Pretoria, 1958; Partner, Daan Kesting and Jan van Wijk, Pretoria, 1959-62; in private practice, Pretoria, 1962-67; Senior Partner, Jan van Wijk and Partners, Pretoria and Johannesburg, 1968-75. Since 1975, Chairman of Vennootskap Jan van Wijk Incorporated, with co-directors Cas Nel, Albert Lintvelt, Hans Wilreker and Leon van Schaik, Johannesburg; branch office at George, Cape Province. Also director, Tendenda Investment Company, and Linea Documentation Company, Johannesburg, since 1975. Chairman of the Architectural Education Committee, South African Council for Architects, Pretoria, 1983; External Examiner, University of Pretoria, 1983, 1984. Exhibitions: Museum of Gideon Malherbe, Paarl South Africa, 1975; *Architects' Thinking*, Institute of South African Architects, Pretoria, 1982; *Soweto Hospital Computer Drawings*, Institute of South African Architects, Johannesburg, 1983. Recipient: Institute of South African Architects, Award, 1973, 1978; Medal of Honour, South African Akademie vir Wetenskap en Kuns, 1983. Address: Vennootskap Jan van Wijk Incorporated, 5th floor, Metal Box Centre, 25 Owl Street, Auckland Park 2092, Johannesburg, South Africa.

Works:

1950/
56 South African Broadcasting Corporation Studios and Offices, Cape Town (with Meiring and Naude)
1957 Hotel, Jamaica, West Indies (project)
Motel, Long Island, New York (project)
American Airlines Terminal, Kennedy Airport, New York (as assistant)
Seagrams Building, New York (as assistant)
1959 Tennis Clubhouse, Pretoria
Shops, offices and flats complex, Lydenburg, South Africa
Church Hall, Parkhurst, Johannesburg
Church, Moregloed, Pretoria
1960 Church, Universiteitsoord, Pretoria
Streicher House, Lydenburg, South Africa
Dr. van der Merwe House, Machadodorp, South Africa
1962 Chemist's shop, offices, and bank complex, Thabazimbi, South Africa
1963 De Leeuw House, Pretoria
Dr. Aucamp Cave House, Pretoria
Jan van Wijk House, Pretoria
Motel, Thabazimbi, South Africa (project)
1964 Rembrandt Tobacco Corporation Art Pavilion, Johannesburg
Motel, Nelspruit, South Africa (project)
1965 Post Office, Kleinbos, Stormsriver, South Africa
Luckhoff Beach House, Kleinmond, South Africa
Bonuskor Offices and Shops, Nelspruit, South Africa
1966 Church, Sasolburg, South Africa
1967 Resort Town, Natal Northcoast, South Africa (project; with D. Theron)
Bonuskor Company House, Komatipoort, South Africa

Municipal Electric Company Substation, Offices and Workshops, Paarl, South Africa
Ster Theatres Cinemas, Shops and Ice Rink Complex, Pretoria
Fire Brigade Station and Housing, Verwoerdburg, South Africa
Arconpark Church, Vereniging, South Africa
Rand Afrikaans University, Johannesburg (with Wilhelm O. Meyer)
1968 Dr. Wessels Bushveld House, Hoedspruit, South Africa
1969 De Necker Bushveld Camp, Klaserie, South Africa
Indian Reformed Church, Laudium, Pretoria
Telephone Exchange Secretariat/Laboratories, Pretoria (with O. Verhoef, W. Mare and F. Viljoen)
1971 De Necker Holiday Bungalow, Knysna, South Africa
1973 Municipal Electricity Company Offices and Workshops, Kempton Park, South Africa
Rembrandt Tobacco Corporation Cigarette Factory, Heidelberg, Transvaal, South Africa
Rembrandt Tobacco Corporation Store, Paarl, South Africa
Fruit Stall, Sabie Park, South Africa
Housing development, Sabie Park, South Africa
Rembrandt Tobacco Corporation Workers' Housing Scheme, Paarl, South Africa
Dr. Wessels Bushveld House, Sabie-Sand Game Reserve, South Africa
Recreation Centre, Sabie Park, South Africa
Dr. Rupert Bushveld House, Transvaal Lowveld, South Africa
1974 Church Hall, Aucklandpark, Johannesburg
Church complex, Brackenhurst, South Africa
Irish Brigade/Anglo-Boer War Monument, Johannesburg
Students Housing, phase II, Rand Afrikaans University, Johannesburg
Wilderness House, Wilderness, South Africa
Sub-Economic Housing Scheme, Kleinkrantz, South Africa (project)
1975 Afrikaans Language Symbol, Paarl, South Africa
Condeda Development Company Office Building, Pretoria
Belvidere Holiday Resort, Knysna, South Africa (project)
Church complex, College Park, Vereninging, South Africa
Sub-economic houses and town development, Breidbach, King Williamstown, South Africa
Gazankulu Government Buildings, Giyani, Transvaal, South Africa
Kruger House, Johannesburg
Kloof-en-Dal Church Complex, Johannesburg
1976 Students Housing, phase III, Rand Afrikaans University, Johannesburg
Experimental holiday houses, Sabie Park, South Africa
Town Square Development, Paarl, South Africa
1977 Tourist camp, Pacaltsdorp, South Africa
Oudemeester Workers' Housing, Stellenbosch, South Africa
Van der Merwe Beach House, Still Bay, South Africa
Housing scheme, Tembisa, Transvaal, South Africa
Economic housing, Breidbach, King Williamstown, South Africa
Jan van Wijk Beach House, Wilderness, South Africa
1978 I. C. Breweries Beer Distribution Depot, Johannesburg
Gazankulu Ministers' Houses, Giyani, Transvaal, South Africa
Holiday resort, Oyster Bay, South Africa

Jan Van Wijk: Gazankulu Government Buildings, Giyani, Transvaal, 1975.

Historic houses restoration, Stellenbosch, South Africa
Army Mess and Single Men's Headquarters, Middleburg, Transvaal, South Africa
Oudemeester's Workers' Housing Scheme, Stellenbosch, South Africa
1979 Army Quartermaster's Complex, George, South Africa
Industrial Development Corporation Head Office, Sandton, South Africa
Industrial School for Girls, George, South Africa
Old People's Home, George, South Africa
2,000-bed Hospital, Soweto, Johannesburg
Iscor Housing, Pretoria
1980 Post Office Workers' Housing, Soweto, Johannesburg
Rembrandt Tobacco Corporation Cigarette Factory, phase 2, Heidelberg, Transvaal, South Africa
Urban Foundation Housing Scheme, Pimville, Soweto, Johannesburg
1981 Rand Life Assurance Office Building, Parktown, Johannesburg
Jan van Wijk House, Randburg, South Africa
Urban Foundation Multi-purpose Centre, Soweto, Johannesburg
Police Station, Kliptown, South Africa
Factory Flats, Kathlehong, Germiston, South Africa
1982 South African Broadcasting Corporation Flats, Randburg, South Africa
Josh Heyman House, Johannesburg
Manpower Technical Centre, Mmabatho, Bophuthatswana
Hotel Marina alterations, Margate, Natal, South Africa
1983 Mission Opera de Bastille, Paris (competition project)

BMW Head Office, Midrand, South Africa (competition project)
Housing, Netherlands (competition project)
Sanlam Factory Flats, Wadeville, South Africa
Engelbrecht Holiday Camp, Sabiepark, South Africa
1984 Classrooms, Sports Complex and Engineering Faculty, Rand Afrikaans University, Johannesburg
Manpower Centre, Mabopane, Bophuthatswana
Meintjies House, Johannesburg
Rand Aksepbank Lowveld Guest House, Malelane, South Africa

Publications:

On van WIJK: articles—"Afrikaans Language Monument, Paarl" in *Architect and Builder* (Cape Town), March 1975; "Rand Afrikaans University" in *Planning and Building Developments* (Braamfontein), May/June 1976; "Conenda, Pretoria: new branch office for architects" in *Architect and Builder* (Cape Town), February 1979; "Rand Afrikaans University student housing phase 2" in *Architect and Builder* (Cape Town), May 1979; "Satellite Park, Stellenbosch" in *Architecture South Africa* (Cape Town), June 1979; "Up in time for the big thirst" in *Architect and Builder* (Cape Town), February 1981.

*   *   *

Being of Africa, this continent, especially South Africa where I was born and bred, had a marked influence on my development as an architect. Its wide ranges, its plains and semi deserts, its mountains, rocks, trees, its bush and semi-tropical regions brought me close to nature. Africa's indigenous architecture—reed huts, adobe huts, thatched roofed settlements near the waterhole, the organically-shaped enclaves with meandering walls, encircling baobab trees, the earthy whole encompassing the social structure, the patterns of plains and dry riverbeds, the patchland agriculture, the greys, the yellows, the reds, oranges and browns, and bright blue skies, tremendous thunderstorms and droughts—all these made me believe that architecture is a clayey thing, a moulded sculpture, flowing as part of the soil.

A rock, a tree, a hillock, a dry riverbed, would ask for a building—no, would ask for someone to outline the building that is already there, has been there since long past, to define what it wants to be given shape to in its midst. Difficult requests, set by nature, because what do you do to a commercial building in a city where nature in a sense is excluded? And yet, the building is "seen," defined in the mind's eye, then sketched and modelled, given shape, and then drawn by means of instruments, in order to have it built. At times even the computer questions the validity of the resulting curves. And those materials that come straight, are bent, cut, moulded so that they do not form a box but enclose spaces of various shapes and experience, as if the soil or site itself gave birth. And those that cannot be bent and shaped are so arranged that the whole seems plastic, organic. Granted, only one of the many avenues of architecture but one that constantly asserts itself and wants to be explored. In the city proper, with its constraints and harsh building regulations, the battle is really on, with some success. In the suburban scene, where nature is present, more success. With housing schemes and smaller buildings, churches, clinics, club houses, theatres, etc., having fun becomes possible.

The chosen example of my work is a culmination

of the above, being a dynamic symbol in reinforced hammered concrete made and moulded from and rooted in the soil of Africa and depicting the origin and growth potential of a dynamic language, Afrikaans, my mother tongue, which is a modern Western language of Africa. Height: 57m.; two years building time; completed 1975.

But this is only part of the big game of architecture, from Vitruvius to moon landings, art and technology, intuition and reason, feeling and logic. From preconceived visions, to be drawn, to be built, or from the other end, a logical sequence of structured thinking through the vision to the product—all trying to seek the golden thread of man's never-ending quest of enclosing a space. In this quest many have joined and have contributed and still contribute to the final products being more than the sum of the constituent parts. This search for unity in cross-fertilizing diversity goes on.

—Jan van Wijk

The symbiotic relationship of architectural education at the University of Pretoria with the work of the city's most prominent architects lead to a most productive architecture in Pretoria during the late 1940s and early 1950s. The leaders of that movement included Norman Eaton, Helmut Stauch, Professor Meiring and Gordon Mackintosh. The influences upon them and upon the young architects ranged from the spluttering end of the modern movement of the 1930s that had revolved around Martienssen in Johannesburg to the strong influence of Le Corbusier, as seen in the Brazilian work of the time and published in *Brazil Builds*. Jan van Wijk worked on the South African Broadcasting Building in Cape Town, by Meiring and Naude, and there the Brazilian influence is most clearly seen.

The influences of this period seem the strongest in van Wijk's houses and other projects of the early 1960s. The organic forms that Eaton at times sought and (possibly because of his strong roots in the classical) could not reach except in the paving and site works of some of his buildings, and which draw upon the free forms of African themes, such as those represented by the Zimbabwe ruins, van Wijk was to develop and take further. His design for the Monument at Paarl is an excellent example of these qualities in his work.

Van Wijk's collaboration with Meyer on the Rand Afrikaans University lead to a design that, with its tightly expressed and articulated shapes, is much more characteristic of Meyer and his colleague Pienaar. This influence clearly had an effect on van Wijk's subsequent work, for that work shows much greater geometric formalism than previously—as in the New Telephone Exchange in Pretoria.

The importance of van Wijk's work lies in its roots in one of the most vigorous architectural periods in South Africa and in its continuation of the themes that grew out of that time: a direct sensitivity to climate, excellence in siting, and an inventive freedom in the choice of an appropriate form. Some of these influences have been suppressed in South Africa in the last decade or so, as articulated forms and geometric rigidity have become the dominant themes, supported as they are by a strong and imported philosophic influence. Van Wijk may well return to the earlier themes in his work.

—Hans Hallen

VECSEI, Eva.

Canadian. Born Eva Hollo in Vienna, Austria, of Hungarian nationality, 21 August 1930; emigrated to Canada, 1957: naturalized, 1962. Educated at the School of Architecture, University of Technical Sciences, Budapest, 1948-52, B.A. 1952. Married the architect Andrew Vecsei in 1952; children: Andrea and Paul. Assistant Professor, School of Architecture, University of Technical Sciences, Budapest, 1952-53; Architect, Architectural Institute of Residential Design (Lakoterv), Budapest, 1953-56; Design Developer, 1958-64, and Associate, 1964-70, Affleck, Desbarats, Dimakopoulos, Lebensold, Size, architects, Montreal; Associate, Dimitri Dimakopoulos, Architect, Montreal, 1970-73; Principal, Eva H. Vecsei, Architect, Montreal, 1973-76; Partner, Eva Vecsei—Dan Hanganu, Montreal, 1977; Principal, Eva H. Vecsei, Architect, Montreal, 1978-84. Since 1984, Principal of Vecsei Architects, with Andrew Vecsei, Montreal. Design Advisory Committee Member, National Capital Commission of Canada, 1981. Exhibition: *Les Femmes Exposent*, Centre Georges Pompidou, Paris, 1978. Recipient: 5 Massey Architecture Awards, 1960-70; Award of Excellence, *The Canadian Architect*, Toronto, 1983. Address: Vecsei Architects, 1405 Bishop Street, Montreal, Quebec H3G 2E4, Canada.

Works:

1954 Housing for Miners, Tatabanya, Hungary
1955/
56 Housing Project and School, Lagymano, Budapest
1960/
70 Place Bonaventure, Montreal (with Affleck, Desbarats, Dimakopoulos, Lebensold, Size)
   Life Science Building, Dalhousie University, Halifax, Nova Scotia (with Affleck, Desbarats, Dimakopoulos, Lebensold, Size)
   Laval Civic Centre, Quebec (with Affleck, Desbarats, Dimakopoulos, Lebensold, Size)
   Student Centre, McGill University, Montreal (with Affleck, Desbarats, Dimakopoulos, Lebensold, Size)
   St. Gérard Majella Church, St. Jean, Quebec (with Affleck, Desbarats, Dimakopoulos, Lebensold, Size)
   St. Thomas D'Aquin Church, Quebec
   Pavilion George Frederick, Drummondville, Quebec (with Affleck, Desbarats, Dimakopoulos, Lebensold, Size)
1973/
76 La Cité, Montreal: 3 residential buildings; office building; hotel; recreational club; 3 cinemas; shopping centre; parking, gardens and terraces (with Dobush, Stewart, Longpré, Marchand and Goudreau)
1976 City Centre Master Plan, Karachi, Pakistan (with Yasmen Lari and John Schrieber)
   Five Restaurant interiors, Montreal
1977 Studio Two renovations, National Film Board, Montreal (with Dan Hanganu)
1978 Concept and Feasibility Study for East Block, 1910 Wing, Parliament Hill, Ottawa, Ontario
1982 Office Building, 1500 Boulevard Maisonneuve, Montreal (with M. Panzini)
   Sternthal House, Westmount, Montreal (with M. Panzini)
   Office Building, 445 Boulevard St. Lawrence, Old Montreal (with M. Panzini)
   Sunar Showroom, Montreal (with M. Panzini)
1984 National Aviation Museum Concept Designs, Rockliffe, Ontario (with A. Lillakas)
   Hull Core Area Ideal Building Height Control Study, Quebec
   Collège Marie de France extension and new school, Montreal

Publications:

By VECSEI: article—La Cité de la métropole" in *Architectural Concept* (Montreal), May/June 1977.

On VECSEI: books—*History of Modern American Architects* by Zoltan Kosa, Budapest 1973; *History of Modern Architecture* by Zoltan Kosa, Budapest 1975; articles—"Human Settlements: World News: L'Architecte de La Cité—Eva Vecsei" by Claude R. Lussier in *Décormag* (Montreal), January 1977; article by Mildred F. Schmertz in *Architectural Record* (New York), January 1978; "Moving Through Time" in *Interiors* (New York), June 1983; "The Canadian Architect 1983 Awards of Excellence" in *The Canadian Architect* (Toronto), December 1983.

*

My definition of Architecture: building of shelters which satisfy the psycho-sociological needs of our society.

The prehistoric shelter-building or even the creation of present day working space is not architecture per se; it becomes architecture when it goes beyond its mere function, i.e., when it appeals to us at the *intellectual level* and at the *level of sensory perception* as well.

The modern movement is almost blameless on the intellectual level. It taught us to look for harmony between the structural system and the plan, materials and details. We learned the beauty of simplicity and economy of repetitiveness. It taught us to respect function—or, at least, the physical aspect of it. But repetition, simplicity and predictability alone are not yet virtues; they often mean the absence of creativity and inventiveness. Simplicity is often boring, and it is well known that a boring environment often provokes neurotic behavior.

If we acknowledge the necessity of a perceptually more stimulating architecture, especially in urban environments, we should also recognize all the parties to whom it should be addressed. The effect on the so-called "other users" is equally important: those who live nearby or, by seeing our structures every day, are affected by their presence, i.e., those whose environment is altered by our architectural activity.

I feel that present day architectural design should put more accent on the sensory level. Instead of the uniform surface, anonymous massing, parts of the building should be identifiable by and with the user. (Apartments, working spaces, etc. should be recognized from the exterior.) The "episode of decoration" should have a comeback, together with the more adventurous surface treatment, the greater variation of void and solid on the facade.

The dual role of roofscape should be fully exploited again; i.e., as the fifth elevation of the building (this cannot be ignored in urban situations, where it is often within view) and as a new source of semi-public space. The surface of our buildings should have the tactile appeal which makes the architecture of the great epochs so visually exciting.

These are some of the aspects I tried to incorporate in the recent La Cité mixed-use project. The three residential buildings—1350 units—are strongly sculptured by the variety of different expressions of some eighty apartment types. These towers are adjacent to pools, recreational terraces, and a plaza—all built over the commercial infrastructure utilizing the landscaped roof slabs as public and semi-public spaces.

To sum up: the aesthetic quality of our urban environment must be improved. Architecture should become a perceptually more stimulating experience than it is presently. It should become, again, *the* source of visual pleasure and civic pride.

—Eva Vecsei (Montreal, 1980)

*

Hungarian-born Eva Vecsei spent her first twelve years as an architect in Montreal working first as a design developer then as an associate of Affleck, Desbarats, Dimakopoulos, Lebensold and Size. While there, she was in charge of the design of

Eva Vecsei: La Cité, Montreal, 1977 (model).

several large projects, and, still in her thirties, she became head project designer with partner-in-charge R. T. Affleck for one of the largest buildings in the world—Place Bonaventure in Montreal. Constructed on a six-acre site with one million square feet of retail mart space, 100 thousand square feet of office space, and a 400-room roof top hotel, Place Bonaventure was built just in time for the opening of *Expo '67* and cost $80 million in 1967 dollars.

Her second mammoth project is La Cité, Montreal's first large-scale mixed-use comprehensive downtown development. This project, completed in 1977, is the first job designed by Vecsei as head of her own office, which she opened in 1973. The project, constructed on a seven-acre site, consists of a 26-story office building, a 500-room hotel, three 30-story residential towers, and a two-level, 220 thousand-square-foot retail area that provides all weather connection between all parts of the project. The total cost of La Cité was $120 million in 1976 dollars.

These facts and figures are significant because no woman architect has ever before had such broad responsibility for the design and construction of projects of this magnitude and excellence. Vecsei has had the opportunity to display a nearly full range of design abilities—her own geometric and spatial skills, her knowledge of architectural form and theory, and the power to coordinate, integrate and synthesize the knowledge of others.

It is unlikely that projects of the size of Place Bonaventure and La Cité will be built again in Canada in the near future. Vecsei is now engaged in smaller work that makes a lesser demand upon her organizational talents and a larger one upon her expressive skills. The results will deserve attention.

—Mildred F. Schmertz

VENTURI, Robert Charles.

American. Born in Philadelphia, Pennsylvania, 25 June 1925. Educated at the Episcopal Academy, Philadelphia, graduated 1943; Princeton University, New Jersey, under Donald Drew Egbert and Jean Labatut, 1943-50, B.A. 1947 (Phi Beta Kappa), M.F.A. 1950; American Academy, Rome (Rome Prize Fellowship), 1954-56. Married the architect Denise Scott Brown, *q.v.*, in 1967; son: James. Worked as a designer for the firms of Oscar Stonorov, Philadelphia, Eero Saarinen, Bloomfield Hills, Michigan, and Louis I. Kahn, Philadelphia, 1950-58; Partner, with Paul Cope and H. Mather Lippincott, Venturi, Cope and Lippincott, Philadelphia, 1958-61, and, with William Short, Venturi and Short, Philadelphia, 1961-64. Partner, with John Rauch, *q.v.*, since 1964, and with Rauch and Denise Scott Brown since 1967, Venturi and Rauch, and since 1980, Venturi, Rauch and Scott Brown, Philadelphia (senior associates: Steven Izenour, David Vaughan). Assistant Professor, then Associate Professor of Architecture, University of Pennsylvania, Philadelphia, 1957-65; State Department Lecturer in the U.S.S.R., 1965; Architect-in-Residence, American Academy in Rome, 1966; Charlotte Shepherd Davenport Professor of Architecture, Yale University, New Haven, Connecticut, 1966-70; Visiting Critic, Rice University, Houston, Texas, 1969; Walter Gropius Lecturer, Graduate School of Design, Harvard University, Cambridge, Massachusetts, 1982. Member, Panel of Visitors, School of Architecture and Urban Planning, University of California at Los Angeles, 1966-67; Trustee, American Academy in Rome, 1969-74; Member, Board of Advisers, Department of Art and Archaeology, Princeton University, New Jersey, 1969-72, and since 1977. Member, Board of Advisors, School of Architecture and Urban Design,

Princeton University, New Jersey, since 1977, and of the Ossabaw Island Project, Savannah, Georgia, since 1977. Exhibitions: *Gold Medal Awards*, Architectural League of New York, 1965; *The Work of Venturi and Rauch*, toured the United States, 1965; *40 under 40*, Architectural League of New York, 1966; *The Work of Venturi and Rauch*, Whitney Museum, New York, 1971; *The Invisible Artist*, Philadelphia Museum of Art, 1974; *The Work of Venturi and Rauch*, Pennsylvania Academy of Fine Arts, Philadelphia, 1975; *Suburban Alternatives: 11 American Projects*, at the *Biennale*, Venice, 1976; *200 Years of American Architectural Drawing*, Cooper-Hewitt Museum, New York, 1977; *Drawings for a More Modern Architecture*, Drawing Center, New York, and Cooper-Hewitt Museum, New York, 1977; *Architecture 1: An Exhibition*, Leo Castelli Gallery, New York, and Institute of Contemporary Art, Philadelphia, 1977; *Roma Interotta*, Incontri Internazionali d'Arte, Rome, 1977-78; *Palaces for People*, Cooper-Hewitt Museum, New York, 1977; *Presence and Absence*, Galleria d'Arte Moderna, Bologna, Italy, 1977; *The Federal City in Transition*, Barbara Fiedler Gallery, Washington, D.C., 1979; *Venturi and Rauch: Architektur im Alltag Amerikas*, Kunstgewerbemuseum, Zurich, 1979 (toured Switzerland); *Venturi, Rauch and Scott Brown*, Galleria dell'Accademia, Florence, Italy, 1981; *Speaking a New Classicism*, Smith College, Northampton, Massachusetts, 1981 (toured the United States); *Architectural Fantasies*, American Institute of Architects Foundation, Washington, D.C., 1981; *Correspondences: 5 Architects, 5 Sculptors*, Palacio de las Alhajas, Madrid, 1982; *Buildings by Venturi, Rauch and Scott Brown*, Max Protetch Gallery, New York, 1982; *Ornamentalism*, Hudson River Museum, New York, 1983 (travelled to the University of Texas, Austin, and the Fendrick Gallery, Washington, D.C.); *Venturi, Rauch and Scott Brown: A Generation of Architecture*, University of Illinois, Urbana, 1984 (toured the United States); *Robert Venturi: Architect's Furniture*, Synderman Gallery, Philadelphia, 1985; *250 Years of Drawings by Philadelphia's Architects*, Pennsylvania Academy of the Fine Arts, Philadelphia, 1985. Recipient: Graham Foundation Grant, 1963; Design Award, *Progressive Architecture*, 1967; First Prize, Yale University Mathematics Building Competition, 1970; Gold Medal, 1972, and Adaptive Re-use Award, 1976, American Institute of Architects, Philadelphia Chapter; Award of Merit, *House and Home*/AIA, 1973; Arnold W. Brunner Memorial Prize in Architecture, National Institute of Arts and Letters, 1973; Creative Arts Award, Brandeis University, Waltham, Massachusetts, 1976; Casebook Award, *Print Magazine*, 1976 (three times); Honor Award, 1977, and Medal, 1978, AIA; Case Studies Award, *Urban Design*, 1977; Medal of Achievement, Philadelphia Art Alliance, 1978; Citation, National Association of Schools of Art, 1980; Hazlett Memorial Award, Commonwealth of Pennsylvania, 1983; Thomas Jefferson Memorial Foundation Medal, University of Virginia, Charlottesville, 1983; Louis Sullivan Award, International Union of Bricklayers and Allied Craftsmen, 1983. D.F.A: Oberlin College, Ohio, 1977; Yale University, New Haven, Connecticut, 1979; University of Pennsylvania, Philadelphia, 1980; Princeton University, New Jersey, 1983; D.H.L.: New Jersey Institute of Technology, Newark, 1984. Fellow, American Institute of Architects; American Academy in Rome; Accademia Nazionale di San Luca, Rome. Address: Venturi, Rauch and Scott Brown, 4236 Main Street, Philadelphia, Pennsylvania 19127, U.S.A.

Works:

1960   Dudley L. Miller House, East Hampton, Long Island, New York
1963   Alan Zinzer House, Woodbury, Connecticut
      Vanna Venturi House, Philadelphia

1964   H. Justice Williams House restoration, stage I, Philadelphia
1965   Guild House: Elderly People's Housing, Philadelphia
      Footlighters Theatre, Paoli, Pennsylvania (project)
1965/
  69   Philadelphia General Hospital renovation and additions
1965-   F. Otto Haas House additions, Ambler, Pennsylvania
1966   Entrance Building, Mausoleum and Memorial Tower, Princeton Memorial Park, New Jersey (project; with Richard Cripps)
1967   Community Center: Y.M.C.A., City Hall and Library addition, Philadelphia (project)
      Renewal plan for Hennepin Avenue, Mineapolis
1968   Renewal feasibility study of Hot Springs, Arkansas
      H. Justice Williams House restoration, stage II, Philadelphia
      Nathaniel Lieb House, Long Beach Island, New Jersey
      Two-Bay Fire Station, Columbus, Indiana
      Walker and Dunlop Office Building, Transportation Square, Washington, D.C. (project; with Caudill Rowlett Scott)
      Drs. George Varga and Frank Brigio Medical Office Building, Bridgeton, New Jersey
1968/
  70   Rehabilitation plan for South Street, Philadelphia
1969   St. Francis de Sales Church renovation, Philadelphia
1970   Feasibility study of office, commercial and theatre complex for Times Square, New York
      Survey and analysis of subway station facilities, Philadelphia
      Master plan and urban design of California City
1971   Lawton Plaza redevelopment plan, New Rochelle, New York
      Great Western Cities Inc. Office Building, California City (project)
1972   Bato Paper Company Warehouse, Greenwich, Connecticut
      Convention Center conversion plan, Niagara Falls, Ontario
      Master plan for the Bicentennial International Exposition Site at Eastwick, Philadelphia (with other firms)
1973   West Mount Airy Clustered Housing Plan, Philadelphia
      Preliminary design for prototypical neighborhood and community shopping centres for Saga Harbor, new community south of Miami, Florida
      Horace Bushnell Memorial Hall alterations, Hartford, Connecticut (with George Izenour)
      Humanities Classroom Building, State University of New York at Purchase
      Feasibility study for the re-use of the Philadelphia College of Art
      Neighborhood health center for the Southeast Philadelphia Community Corporation (project; with William Mann Sr.)
      Housing, Washington Square West Urban Renewal Area, Philadelphia (project)
      David Trubek House, Nantucket Island, Massachusetts
      George Wislocki House, Nantucket Island, Massachusetts
      Renewal plan for the Seneca-Susquehanna area, Harrisburg, Pennsylvania
      Prototype designs for lighting, street furniture and signs, University of Pennsylvania (competition project)
      Design of the Bicentennial celebration on and around Benjamin Franklin Parkway, Philadelphia

Robert Venturi: Wu Hall, Butler College, Princeton University, New Jersey, 1983.

South Central Philadelphia Neighborhood Development Program (as consulting architect and planner)

1974 Four-Bay Fire Station, New Haven, Connecticut

Natural Science Museum, Roanoke, Virginia (project)

Public park and recreational facility, East River, New York (project; with Coffey Levine and Blumberg)

Kevin Cusak House, Sea Isle City, New Jersey

Peter Brant House, Greenwich, Connecticut

Design study for the improvement of road and water entrances to Philadelphia (with Murphy Levy Wurman)

Feasibility study for a residential community, phase I, near Phoenix, Arizona

1975 Revitalization study of The Strand, Galveston, Texas

Carll Tucker II House, Mount Kisco, New York

Community Center Building, Philadelphia Naval Base

1976 Franklin Court, Independence National Historical Park, Philadelphia

Allen Memorial Art Museum renovation and additions, Oberlin College, Ohio

Faculty Club, Pennsylvania State University, University Park

Educational Facility for Morris Arboretum, Philadelphia (project)

Peter Brant House, Vail, Colorado

200 Years of American Sculpture installation design, Whitney Museum, New York

American Painting Bicentennial exhibition design, Pennsylvania Academy of Fine Arts, Philadelphia

Philadelphia: Three Centuries of American Art exhibition design, Philadelphia Museum of Art

1977 Catalog-Showroom for Basco Inc., Concord, Delaware

Marlborough-Blenheim Hotel renovation and additions, Atlantic City, New Jersey (project)

Palley's Jewellers renovation, Atlantic City, New Jersey

INA Capital Management Corporation office interiors, Philadelphia

Peter Brant House, Bermuda

Proposal for the rejuvenation of Main Street and The Hollow, Boonton, New Jersey

Urban design study of Heritage Plaza West, Salem, Massachusetts

Planning study for St. Christopher's Hospital for Children, phase I, Philadelphia

Signs for the central business district of Salem, Massachusetts

1978 Arisbe Museum (Charles S. Peirce House), exhibition and graphic designs, Milford, Pennsylvania

Man, Land and the Environment exhibition design, Hartwell Regional Visitors Center,

South Carolina (competition project)

Old City development and planning study, Philadelphia

Marcia B. Tucker Estate development plan, Mount Kisco, New York

Social Sciences Buildings, State University of New York at Purchase

Conservation Laboratory, Philadelphia Museum of Art, Pennsylvania

1979 United States Pavilion and exhibition design for the 1982 International Exposition on Energy, Nashville, Tennessee (competition project)

Australian Parliament House, Canberra (competition project)

Best Products exterior facade, Oxford Valley, Pennsylvania

Institute for Scientific Information Headquarters, University City Science Center, Philadelphia

Knoll International Showroom and Conference Room, New York

Preservation study for Jim Thorpe, Pennsylvania

Washington Avenue Corridor plan, Miami Beach, Florida

Buildings re-use study, Lackawanna Avenue, Scranton, Pennslyvania

William Penn exhibition design and urban study, Philadelphia

Computer exhibition design, University of Pennsylvania, Philadelphia

1980 Borough of Jenkintown development planning study, Pennsylvania

Borough of Princeton development plan and urban study, New Jersey

Western Sector Plaza design, Pennsylvania Avenue, Washington, D.C. (with George F. Patton)

Venturi, Rauch and Scott Brown Offices, Philadelphia

Museum fur Kunsthandwerk, Frankfurt, West Germany (competition project)

Frankfurter Messe Exhibition Complex, Frankfurt, West Germany (competition project)

1981 Benedict Yedlin Inc. Office Building, Montgomery Township, New Jersey (project)

Wheelabrator-Frye Headquarters expansion, Hampton, New Hampshire (project)

Settlement Music School addition and renovation, Philadelphia

Carroll Newman Library addition and renovation, Virginia Polytechnic Institute and State University, Roanoke (with Vosbeck, Vosbeck, Kendrick and Redinger)

Chinatown Single and Duplex Townhouses, Philadelphia

Houston Hall Student Center interiors, University of Pennsylvania, Philadelphia

Residential Development, Princeton, New Jersey (project)

Hennepin Avenue transportation and development plan, Minneapolis, Minnesota (with Bather, Ringrose, Wolsfeld, Jarvis, Gardner, Inc.)

Philadelphia Museum of Art expansion master plan, Pennsylvania

Contemporary American Realism Since 1960 exhibition design, Pennsylvania Academy of the Fine Arts, Philadelphia

1982 Park Regency Condominiums, Houston, Texas

1983 Metropolitan Apartment Block (conversion of YMCA building), Philadelphia

Little Hall Dormitory addition, Princeton University, New Jersey

Gordon Wu Hall new dining and social facilities, Butler College, and Wilcox Hall alterations, Princeton University, New Jersey

Commons Residential Colleges addition, Princeton University, New Jersey

Welcome Park, Philadelphia

Rockefeller and Mathey Colleges exterior renovations, Princeton University, New Jersey

1984 Natural History exhibit design, Philadelphia Zoological Gardens, Pennsylvania

Nassau Street Entrance relocation, Princeton University, New Jersey

College Walk improvements, Princeton University, New Jersey

1985 Southwest Quadrant master plan, Central Business District, Austin, Texas

Downtown Center City plan, Memphis, Tennessee

Westway Riverfront Park, New York (with Clarke and Rapuano)

Graduate School of Management and Organized Research, University of California, Irvine (project)

Commercial and Residential Building, Baghdad, Iraq (project)

Princeton Inn social/dining facility alterations, Forbes College, Princeton University, New Jersey

Natural Habitat Primate Center, Philadelphia Zoological Gardens, Pennsylvania

Laguna Gloria Art Museum, Austin, Texas

Tarble Student Center (Clothier Hall conversion), Philadelphia

Molecular Biology Building plan, Princeton University, New Jersey

New building, Seattle Art Museum, Washington

Industrial designs include furniture, fabrics and homewares for: Fabric Workshop (Philadelphia), 1983; Alessi International (Milan), 1983, 1985; Formica Corporation (New York), 1983; Swid Powell (New York), 1984, 1985; Knoll International (New York), 1984; Elective Affinities (Milan), 1985; Arc International (Milan), 1985.

Publications:

By VENTURI: books—*Complexity and Contradiction in Architecture*, New York 1966, Tokyo 1969, Paris 1971, Barcelona 1972; *The Highway*, exhibition catalogue, with Denise Scott Brown, Philadelphia 1970; *Aprendiendo de Todas Las Cosas*, with Denise Scott Brown, Barcelona 1971; *Learning from Las Vegas*, with Denise Scott Brown and Steven Izenour, Cambridge, Massachusetts 1972, 1977; articles—"The Campidoglio: A Case Study" in *Architectural Review* (London), May 1953; "Project for a Beach House" in *Architectural Design* (London), November 1960; "Weekend House" in *Progressive Architecture* (New York), April 1961; "A Justification for a Pop Architecture" in *Arts and Architecture* (Los Angeles), April 1965; "Three Projects: Architecture and Landscape, Architecture and Sculpture, Architecture and City Planning" in *Perspecta* (New Haven, Connecticut), no. 11, 1967; "Trois bâtiments pour une ville de l'Ohio" in *L'Architecture d'Aujourd'hui* (Paris), December 1967/January 1968; "A Significance for A & P Parking Lots; or, Learning from Las Vegas," with Denise Scott Brown, in *Architectural Forum* (New York), March 1968; "A Bill-Ding Board Involving Movies, Relics and Space" in *Architectural Forum* (New York), April 1968; "On Architecture" in *L'Architecture d'Aujourd'hui* (Paris), September 1968; "On Ducks and Decoration," with Denise Scott Brown, in *Architecture Canada* (Toronto), October 1968; "Venturi versus Gowan," with Denise Scott Brown, in *Architectural Design* (London), January 1969; "Learning from Lutyens," with Denise Scott Brown, in *RIBA Journal* (London), August 1969; "The Bicentennial Commemoration 1976," with Denise Scott Brown, in *Architectural Forum* (New York), October 1969; "Mass Communications on the People Freeway; or, Piranesi Is Too Easy," with Denise Scott Brown, in *Perspecta* (New Haven, Connecticut), no. 12, 1969; "Co-op City: Learning to Like It," with Denise Scott Brown, in *Progressive Architecture* (New York), February 1970; "Reply to Pawley—'Leading from the Rear'," with Denise Scott Brown, in *Architectural Design* (London), July 1970; "Some Houses of Ill Repute: A Discourse with Apologia on Recent Houses of Venturi and Rauch," with Denise Scott Brown, in *Perspecta* (New Haven, Connecticut), no. 13/14, 1971; "Ugly and Ordinary Architecture; or, The Decorated Shed," with Denise Scott Brown, in *Architectural Forum* (New York), part I, November 1971, part II, December 1971; "Bicentenaire de l'Indépendance Américaine," with Denise Scott Brown, in *L'Architecture d'Aujourd'hui* (Paris), November 1973; "Functionalism Yes, But . . . ," with Denise Scott Brown, in *Architecture + Urbanism* (Tokyo), November 1974; "Plain and Fancy Architecture by Cass Gilbert at Oberlin" in *Apollo* (London), February 1976, in an expanded version in *Allen Memorial Art Museum Bulletin* (Oberlin, Ohio), no. 2, 1976-77; "A Reaction to Complexity and Contradiction in the Work of Furness" in *Pennsylvania Academy of the Fine Arts Newsletter* (Philadelphia), Spring 1976; "Learning from Aalto" in *Progressive Architecture* (New York), April 1977; "A Definition of Architecture as Shelter with Decoration on it" in *Architecture + Urbanism* (Tokyo), January 1978; "Learning the Right Lessons from the Beaux Arts" in *Architectural Design* (London), January 1979; "Allen Memorial Art Museum, Oberlin" in *Werk/Archithese* (Zurich), January/February 1979; "Interview: Robert Venturi and Denise Scott Brown" in *Harvard Architec-*

ture Review (Cambridge, Massachusetts), Spring 1980; "Interview with Robert Venturi" in *Modo* (Milan), November 1981; "Il Proprio Vocabolario" in *Gran Bazaar* (Milan), 1982; "RIBA Discourse" in *RIBA Journal* (London), May 1982; "Diversity, Relevance and Representation in Architecture" in *Architectural Record* (New York), June 1982; "On Aalto", with others, in *Quaderns* (Barcelona), April/June 1983; "Proposal for the Iraq State Mosque, Baghdad" in *L'Architecture d'Aujourd'hui* (Paris), September 1983.

On VENTURI/RAUCH/SCOTT BROWN: books—*American Architecture and Urbanism* by Vincent Scully, New York 1969; *New Directions in American Architecture* by Robert A. M. Stern, New York 1969; *Will They Ever Finish Bruckner Boulevard?* by Ada Louise Huxtable, New York 1970; *Architecture for the Arts: The State University of New York College at Purchase*, New York 1971; *The Work of Venturi and Rauch*, exhibition catalogue, by Vincent Scully, New York 1971; *After the Planners* by Robert Goodman, New York 1971; *Third Generation: The Changing Meaning of Architecture* by Philip Drew, New York 1972; *Wasteland: Building the American Dream* by Stephen A. Kurtz, New York 1973; *Conversations with Architects* by John W. Cook and Heinrich Klotz, New York and London 1973; *Architettura Radicale* by Paolo Navone and Bruno Orlando, Milan 1974; *The Shingle Style Today* by Vincent Scully, New York 1974; *Global Architecture 39: Venturi and Rauch* by Paul Goldberger and Yukio Futagawa, Tokyo 1976; *Supermannerism: New Attitudes in Post Modern Architecture* by C. Ray Smith, New York 1977; *New Directions in American Architecture* by Robert Stern, New York 1977; *Architectural Monographs 1: Venturi and Rauch*, edited by David Dunster, London 1978; *Transformations in Modern Architecture* by Arthur Drexler, New York 1979; *Venturi and Rauch: Architektur im Alltag Amerikas*, exhibition catalogue by Stanislaus von Moos, Zurich 1979; *Origini ed eclisse del movimento moderno* by Cesare De Seta, Bari, Italy 1980; *Venturi, Rauch and Scott Brown*, edited by Gianni Pettena and Maurizio Vogliazzo, Milan 1981; *Poetica y Arquitectura* by Josep Muntanola, Barcelona 1981; *Immagini del Post-Moderno*, edited by Claudio Aldegheri and Maurizio Sabini, Venice 1983; *Venturi, Rauch and Scott Brown: A Generation of Architecture*, exhibition catalogue by Rosemarie Haag Bletter, Urbana, Illinois 1984; articles—"Are the Venturis Putting Us On" by Ursula Cliff in *Design and Environment* (New York), Summer 1971; "Robert Venturi," special issue of *Architecture + Urbanism* (Tokyo), October 1971; "Venturi and Rauch" in *L'Architecture d'Aujourd'hui* (Paris), December 1971/January 1972; "Architecture in '71: Lively Confusion" by Ada Louise Huxtable in the *New York Times*, 4 January 1972; "Venturi and Venturi, Architectural Anti-Heroes" by Barbara Flanagan in *34th Street Magazine* (New York), 13 April 1972; "The Venturis—American Selection" by Deborah Waroff in *Building Design* (London), 4 August 1972; "In Love with Times Square" by Ada Louise Huxtable in the *New York Review of Books*, 18 October 1973; "Venturi and Rauch 1970-74," special issue of *Architecture + Urbanism* (Tokyo), November 1974; "Franklin Court" in *Progressive Architecture* (New York), April 1976; "The Rise and Fall of Main Street" by Ada Louise Huxtable in the *New York Times Magazine*, 30 May 1976; "The Venturi 'Anti-Style' of Architecture" by Ada Louise Huxtable in the *New York Times*, 30 January 1977; special issue of *Progressive Architecture* (New York), October 1977; "The Recent Nine Works of Venturi and Rauch" by Shinichiro Kikuchi in *Architecture + Urbanism* (Tokyo), January 1978; "Venturi and Rauch," special issue of *L'Architecture Aujourd'hui* (Paris), June 1978; "Doing Their Own Thing" by Robert Hughes in *Time* (New York), 8 January 1979; "Venturi, Rauch and Scott Brown", special issue of *Summarios* (Buenos Aires),

May 1979; "Study of Architectural Works 5: On Venturi" in *Architecture + Urbanism* (Tokyo), May 1979; "On Venturi 2" in *Architecture + Urbanism* (Tokyo), July 1979; "Philadelphia: Venturi City" by Thomas Hine in *Today* (Philadelphia), 23 September 1979; "Repetition and Differentiation in the Architecture of Robert Venturi" in *Parametro* (Bologna, Italy), January/February 1980; "Interiors: Knoll Center by Robert Venturi" in *Architectural Record* (New York), March 1980; "Venturi and the Classic Modern Tradition" by Andrew MacNair in *Skyline* (New York), March 1980; "Learning from Venturi" by Martin Filler in *Art in America* (New York), April 1980; "Architecture: Robert Venturi" by Carol Vogel in *Architectural Digest* (Los Angeles), October 1980; "Life After Mies" by Pilar Viladas in *Interiors* (New York), January 1981; "Venturi, Rauch and Scott Brown", special issue of *Architecture + Urbanism* (Tokyo), December 1981; "Venturi and Rauch: House in Delaware" in *International Architect* (London), no. 9, 1982; "Venturi, Rauch and Scott Brown" by Charles Jencks in *Architectural Design* (London), January/February 1982; "Robert Venturi—In Love with the Art of Building" by Paul Goldberger in the *New York Times*, 19 September 1982; "Venturi's Master Class" by Robert Gutman in *The Architects' Journal* (London), 7 September 1983; "Venturi in Princeton" by Mark Swenarton in *Building Design* (London), 2 December 1983; "Mr. Post-Modern" by Douglas Davis in *Newsweek* (New York), 9 July 1984; "Venturi's Unashamed Eclecticism" in *Design* (London), October 1984; "Portrait; Robert Venturi and Denise Scott Brown" by Jonathan Z. Larsen in *Life* (New York), November 1984.

Bibliographies: *Robert Charles Venturi: A Bibliography* by Lamia Doumato, Monticello, Illinois 1978; *Venturi, Rauch and Scott Brown*, Monticello, Illinois 1982.

In the progression of our ideas about appliqué, first as spatial layering, then signboard, and then ornament, we came to appliqué as representation in architecture. Representation in this context involves the *depiction* as opposed to the *construction* of symbol and ornament. Manifestations of this approach to symbolism in architecture are essentially two-dimensional and pictorial.

—Robert Venturi (1985)

Robert Venturi is presently one of the most original talents in contemporary architecture in the United States; his projects and writings provide a critical, underlying strength for the alternatives to the American functionalism that developed in the late 1950s. He has also been instrumental in devising an architectural language that has its counterpart in the Pop movement in the figurative arts.

A knowledge of Venturi's preparation as an architect is important for an understanding of his attitudes and his work. He graduated from the Princeton University School of Architecture, which was directed at that time by the revered Professor Labatut, one of the last representatives of the Beaux Arts system in education. Venturi first became associated with the office of Eero Saarinen, where, among other projects, he worked on the design of the Milwaukee County War Memorial Center. The building design retains the characteristics of Saarinen's work; nevertheless, the dynamic contrast between the cantilevered elements and the rigid setting of the plan reveals Venturi's characteristic search for an ambiguous balance within the structure as a whole. After spending a term as a Fellow of the American Academy in Rome, he designed a house in Chestnut Hill, Philadelphia, where an intense concern for the quality of daylight is revealed in his emphasis upon the large roof-top light chambers; it is a concern that, during his time in Italy, Venturi

must have seen similarly embodied in the architecture of the late Roman Baroque and the late eighteenth century in Naples. In 1957 Venturi became a member of the faculty of the University of Pennsylvania School of Architecture, where he taught a course on architectural criticism; this course eventually provided the basis for his book *Complexity and Contradiction in Architecture*. The book made his ideas well-known among architects, students, and critics; for Vincent Scully, for example, it is the most important writing on the making of architecture since Le Corbusier's *Vers une architecture*. The book elaborates the articles of a gentle manifesto in which Venturi makes a clear break with the multitude of "-isms" presented as alternatives to the shallow surface of Functionalism; it re-introduced architecture in the multitude of its spontaneous manifestations, including that of the often-condemned current building industry. It is an imaginative manifesto, inspired in part by the "will to be" of the great Louis Kahn, who nevertheless was unable to comprehend Venturi's appreciation of the circumstantial and the ordinary. During his tenure at the University of Pennsylvania, Venturi stated his case as an architect with the design submitted for the F. D. Roosevelt Memorial in Washington, D.C. It is a work of unquestionable quality, one that exists simultaneously as a large billboard perceptible at great distance, a place for cars to pass by and park, and an area of small gardens for art objects to be perceived at close range.

During the same period Venturi designed a number of small houses, including a house for his mother in Chestnut Hill, built in 1963. At this point the conceptual attitude and the formal vocabulary of Venturi's work are clearly pronounced and decisively developed on two levels: the large-scale element of distant view (billboard, chimney, roof shapes), responding in part to the Kevin Lynch precepts in urban design, and the texture of surfaces in close view, the current products of the American building industry and home developers (aluminum sash, varieties of textured bricks, colored tiles, etc.). The Brutalist tendency in architecture had already conditioned the current American taste for such choices. However, the implication of Venturi's reinforcement of these choices was far-reaching, as it involved a substantial criticism of the modern movement, particularly of Mies van der Rohe's aesthetics ("Less is more"), a criticism that Brutalism never shared. Venturi's reply, "More is more," became programmatic; the "true" honest things for which to search became the objects of everyday use, particularly those that were used as symbols of activities: the products of the advertising and distribution industry, used furniture, light signs, and graphic announcements.

However, Venturi's work still remains firmly bound to the basic tenets of the modern movement. His building plans always observe the requirements of function, program, and activities, and his architecture never becomes lost in the stimulus of historicism. In reacting to post-modernist claims heavily dependent upon historical recollections, Venturi recently declared that for him the "modern movement was almost right." His architecture above all gives importance to the making of a place; the juxtaposition of textures and materials is used to establish a condition quite different from the one obtained when the main preoccupation is the abstract depiction of space. Instead, his architecture is inherently scaled to human use, comfort, entertainment, and memories.

The theoretical preoccupations that often make Venturi a vigorous polemicist also frequently affect his architecture, which at times cannot overcome the limitation of being demonstrative. However, Venturi shows an uncommon artistic sensitivity in projects such as the Transportation Building in Washington D.C. (rejected by the Art Commission), the Humanities Classroom Building for the State University of New York at Purchase, the competition project for the Yale Mathematics Building, a

series of houses built on Nantucket Island, which represent a sophisticated view of contextual architecture, and finally in Franklin Court in Philadelphia, where he becomes totally free from polemic positions. The work done in close collaboration with Denise Scott Brown is of great significance in defining conceptual approaches, as well as in developing a consciousness for social conditions. This partnership made possible the extensive exploration into the nature of the suburbs that culminated in the book *Learning from Las Vegas*, in which Venturi's familiar theory of the "ordinary" was further illustrated.

In recent years the office of Robert Venturi has been active in a variety of projects which extend from the new Westway in Manhattan, New York, to the dining hall addition at Princeton University. The latter is a building of considerable importance as it emphasizes in particular the attitude of the architect towards the built environment. The building takes into consideration the surrounding structures with the result of truly enhancing the entire environment in the area through an attentive use of materials and ornamental elements, and yet maintains the offscale impact of some of its elements such as the stone cladding above the entryway. This touch is one of the continuing aspects in the Venturi design of sudden change of dimensions which effectively produces a startling sense of engagement in each one of his buildings.

If a single statement could express Robert Venturi's contribution to architecture, it would have to be that, with his work and his writings, Venturi has opened a window on the contradictory and yet extraordinary landscape of built America. In doing so he caused the improvised, the casual, and the contingent to become part of our real environment, not bypassed or ignored; new structures both inspire and become part of such a reality. This view has rightly captivated the imagination of many young architects, and will continue to have a lasting effect on their work.

—Romaldo Giurgola

VILLAGRÁN GARCÍA, José.

Mexican. Born in Mexico City, 22 September 1901. Educated at the Colegio del Sagrado Corazon, Mexico City, 1908-13, 1914-15; Colegio Frances, Mexico City, 1916-17; School of Architecture of the Academia de San Carlos, now the National School of Architecture of the Universidad Nacional Autonoma de Mexico, Mexico City, 1918-22, Dip.Arch. 1923. Married Concepcion de la Mora in 1935; son: Enrique. Worked as an architect for the Department of Public Health, Mexico City, 1924-35. In private practice, Mexico City, since 1935. Consultant Architect, National Committee of the Campaign Against Tuberculosis, 1939-47; Consultant Architect for Hospital Construction, Secretariat of Public Health and Welfare, Mexico City, 1943-45; Consultant Architect for Hospitals in the Western Hemisphere, World Health Organization, Washington, D.C., 1951. Professor of Architectural Composition, 1924-35, Professor of Architectural Theory, 1926-35, 1936-57, and Director, 1933-35, National School of Architecture, Mexico City. Member, Board of Governors, Universidad Nacional Autonoma de Mexico, 1953-70. Exhibition: *Bienal*, Sao Paulo, 1955. Recipient: Architecture Prize, *Bienal*, Sao Paulo, 1955; National Art Prize, Mexico, 1968. Member, Colegio Nacional de Arquitectos de Mexico. Address (office): Dublin 7, Mexico 6, D.F., Mexico.

Works:

1922 Hotel, Lake Patzcuaro, Mexico (project)
1925 Institute of Hygiene, Popotla, Mexico City

1929 Tuberculosis Sanatorium, Huipulco, Tlalpam, Mexico City
Children's Health Dispensary Building, Mexico City
Milk Production Building, Popotla, Mexico City
1934 Children's Day School No. 5, Mexico City
1935 José Villagrán García House, Dublin 7, Mexico City
Palma Office Building, Mexico City
1937 National Cardiological Institute, Mexico City
1941 Apartment building, Avenida Insurgentes 444, Mexico City
Surgical Block, Huipulco Sanatorium, Tlalpam, Mexico City
Children's Hospital, Mexico City
1942 Chronic Tuberculosis Patient's Block, and Manuel Gea Gonzalez Hospital, Huipulco Sanatorium, Tlalpam, Mexico City
Medical Center Master Plan, Mexico City (with Mario Pani)
Tuberculosis Sanatorium, Zoquipan, Jalisco, Mexico
1943 Mundet Sports Park, Mexico City
Hospital de Jesus Office Building, Mexico City
1943/
46 Hospitals plan for the Republic of Mexico
1944 Mexico University College, Mexico City
1945/
46 Regional schools plan for Mexico
Costa Rica Primary School, Mexico City
1946/
50 Condesa Office Building, Mexico City
1948 Gante Parking Garage, Mexico City
1951 National School of Architecture Complex, Universidad Nacional de Mexico, Mexico City
1952 Las Americas Cinema and Office Building, Mexico City

1953 Cumbres Primary and Secondary School, Mexico City
Lafragua Office Building, Mexico City
National Mission Seminary, Tlalpam, Mexico City
1954 Centro Inmobiliario America Complex, Mexico City
Rastro y Frigorificos Works/Office Complex, Mexico City
San Cosme Market Building, Mexico City
San Lucas Market Building, Mexico City
1963 Hotel Maria Isabel, Mexico City
Hotel Alameda, Mexico City
Ford Motor Company Office Building, Mexico City
Tacubaya, La Viga, and Coyoacan Preparatory Schools, Universidad Nacional de Mexico, Mexico City
1965 Mixcoac and Insurgentes Preparatory Schools, Universidad Nacional de Mexico, Mexico City
1966 National School of Architecture additions, Universidad Nacional de Mexico, Mexico City
1967 University Centre additions, Universidad Nacional de Mexico, Mexico City
1970 ICA Constructora Company Offices, Mexico City
1976 Complex of 20 buildings for the National Cardiological Institute, Mexico City (Hospital, Outpatients Clinic, Scientific Research Block, Nursing School, Cardiologists' School, Residential Block)

Publications:

By VILAGRÁN GARCÍA: books—*Panorama de 50 Anos de Arquitectura Mexicana Contemporanea*, Mexico City 1950; *Problemas en la Formacion del Arquitecto*, Mexico City 1964; *Arquitectura y Restauracion de Monumentos*, Mexico City 1967; introduction to *Builders in the Sun* by Clive Bamford Smith, New York 1967; *Estructura Teorica del Programa Arquitectonico*, Mexico City 1972; *Esencia de lo Arquitectonico*, Mexico City 1972; *El Mayor Problema de la Arquitectura Actual*, Mexico City 1974; *La Forma en Arquitectura*, Mexico City 1975. articles—"Apuntes para un estudio" in *Arquitectura* (Mexico City), nos. 3-12, 1939-43; "La Iglesia Catolica ante la Arquitectura de la Epoca" in *Arquitectura* (Mexico City), no. 14, 1943; "Poco para Mucho y Mucho para Poco" in *Arquitectura y lo Demas* (Mexico City), vol. 1, no. 4, 1945; "Ideas Regentes en la Arquitectura Actual" in *Arquitectura* (Mexico City), no. 48, 1954; "La Ensenanza de la Arquitectura" in *Revista ENA* (Mexico City), no. 1, 1959; "Notas acerca de la carrera de arquitecto" in *Revista ENA* (Mexico City), no. 3, 1960; "Meditaciones sobre una crisis formal de la arquitectura" in *Cuadernos de Arquitectura* (Mexico City), no. 4, 1962; "6 Temas sobre la Proporcion en Arquitectura" in *Cuadernos de Bellas Artes* (Mexico City), nos. 7, 8 and 10, 1962; "Teoria de la Arquitectura" in *Cuadernos de Arquitectura* (Mexico City), 1964.

On VILLAGRÁN GARCÍA: book—*Parkhauser Tiefgaragen* by Dietrich-Klose, Stuttgart 1965; articles—"School/Home for Small Children" in *Architectural Record* (New York), June 1936; "Arquitectura en Mexico" in *Arquitectura* (Mexico City), April 1939; "Children's Hospital, Mexico City" in *Architectural Record* (New York), October 1944; "Edificios para estacionamento de automoviles" and "Edificios para despachos" in *Arquitectura* (Mexico City), June 1951; "Museo de Arte y Escuelo de Arquitectura" in *Arquitectura* (Mexico City), September 1952; "José Villagrán García," special issue of *Arquitectura* (Mexico

Jose Vilagrán García: National Cardiological Institute, Mexico City, 1976.

City), September 1956; "Hotel Maria Isabel, Mexico, D.F." in *Arquitectura* (Mexico City), June 1962; "Fabrique de Ventilateurs près de Mexico" and "Hotel Alameda a Mexico" in *L'Architecture d'Aujourd'hui* (Paris), September 1963; "Hotel Maria Isabel, Mexico City" in *Architectural Design* (London), September 1963; "National Cardiology Institute" in *Arquitectura Mexico* (Mexico City), November/December 1978.

The work which I have developed during the 56 years of service to my country as an architect can be divided into two categories. The first is of a didactic nature; the second is professional architecture itself.

The Didactic: The idea that is basic to my teaching of the Theory of Architecture is that architecture is *the art of constructing habitable space for the human being;* or, to put it into its four demensions—the physical, the biological, the psycho-instinctive, and that pertaining to the spirit. Or, as summed up in the classical definition of Seneca: the animal, the rational, and the free.

Professional Architecture: I have tried, for 56 years, to realize and apply in my works the ideas explained in my architectural teaching, invariably pursuing these aims, the works should have axiological and concurrent worth as objects with economic/constructive usefulness; that they should be factological—in other words, that their form should accord with complex totality; that they should be aesthetically positive and expressive in themselves; and, finally, that they should have social value in the service of the community in which they find themselves.

—José Villagrán García

After the turn of the century revolution, Mexican artists tried to find a link with pre-Hispanic times through the subjects developed in their murals, the battle of the Indian race against the conquistador—Diego Rivera is an example. And a similar phenomenon, an approach to a past destroyed by violence, happened in architecture during the first decades of this century as the result of a search for authentic expressions. It is in this context that the work of José Villagrán García, known as the father of modern rationalism in Mexico, really achieves its importance.

Villagrán's influence stems not so much from works actually built (although some of them, such as the National School of Architecture in Mexico's University City, are an example in themselves), but from his constant preaching in classrooms and lectures, based on a profound analysis of the European theoreticians. Villagrán was always solidly against the imitation of historic styles, even if Mexican: "What originally was a spontaneous identification with Colonial and pre-Cortez forms has become more and more critically inconsistent and has led our people down pathways to the worst expression of taste in this century."

According to Villagrán, a work of architecture acquires status as such only if utilitarianism, technology, and social, functional and formal factors have been integrated in the design. This makes it easy to understand his opposition to "dressing" architecture with fashionable silks. In 1925 he suggested that "Mexican contemporary architecture is the fruit of the historical development of our art in search of theoretical doctrinal orientation and of expressions which are part of our culture."

Villagrán's ideas were initially influenced by Le Corbusier, particularly *Vers une Architecture* and Le Corbusier's "living machine" concept, and by Gropius, to whom he specifically refers. Discussing criticism of the new Mexican architecture that he proposed, he said: "Those who have referred to the new Mexican architecture as functionalist, meaning by that to imply that it has ignored the aesthetic in order to satisfy utility and society, are unaware of the doctrine put forward by our School of Architecture, and probably also unaware of what has been

pointed out in a similar vein, although in a different way, by European functionalists like Gropius."

Villagrán repeatedly urged young Mexican architects to identify with their time and place. He warned against a divorce between doctrine and practice and against expressions of a decorativist, atechtonic and extemporaneous formalism. One of Villagran's principles is truth in architecture, accompanied by logical thought (the object is created through objective reasoning, not subjective emotion). Truth and logic, in a milieu tending towards exalting rediscovered native pre-Columbian values, will ensure that modern architecture's message is heard, with all the risks implicit in a movement that precisely has an objective the abolishing of all ornamentalism (as in Loos) and all vestiges of "picturesque-ism." This is why Villagrán's architecture, for example, did not involve (as did the work of some of his disciples and followers) the integration of the wall with its surfaces—a mode that, nevertheless, to a considerable extent, identifies some of the best-known works of modern Mexico.

The opposition between a culture that possessed traditional and popular artistic elements, a culture that welcomed any stance that stressed national values, and the principles of a different attitude in architecture, one that appealed to design guidelines unassociated with whatever is not "functionalist," and therefore tending to impress forms not identifiable with specific sectors and places—this opposition was not exclusive to Mexico after the second decade of this century. But it was intense in Mexico, and the effort to popularize the ideas of modern architecture had to overcome difficulties not present in other places. The importance of José Villagrán García and his lessons is that, by sheer effort, he was able to introduce the contemporary world to Mexican architecture.

—Jorge Glusberg

VILLANUEVA, Carlos Raúl.

Venezuelan. Born in Croydon, Surrey, England, of Venezuelan parents, 30 May 1900. Educated at the Lycée Condorcet, Paris; Ecole des Beaux-Arts, Paris, under Gabriel Heraud, Dip.Arch. 1928. Married Margot Arismendi in 1933; children: Francisco Raul, Jose Carlos, Pavlona and Carlos Raul. In private practice, Caracas, Venezuela, 1929 until his death, 1975. Architect to the Ministry of Public Works, Caracas, 1929-39; Consultant Architect, Banco Obrero (Workers' Bank), Caracas, 1940-60. Founding Professor of Architecture, University of Venezuela, Caracas, from 1944. Founder President, Venezuelan Association of Architects; President, Venezuelan National Board of Historic and Artistic Protection and Conservation; Founder Director, National Planning Commission. Exhibition: *Carlos Raúl Villanueva*, Museo de Caracas, 1976. Recipient: Architecture Prize, *Exposition Internationale*, Paris, 1937; Diploma of Merit, Pan American Congress of Architecture, Lima, Peru, 1947; Citation of Merit, *Bienal*, Sao Paulo, 1957; National Architecture Prize, Venezuela, 1963. Dr.Arch.: University of Venezuela, Caracas, 1961. Honorary President, College of Architects of Venezuela; Officer, Orden del Libertador, Venezuela, 1945. Chevalier, Légion d'Honneur, France, 1939; Honorary Corresponding Member, French Society of Urbanism, 1948; Honorary Member, American Institute of Architects, 1952, and Royal Institute of British Architects, 1959; Honorary Associate, Institute of Urbanism of Peru. *Died* (in Caracas) *16 August 1975.*

Works:

1929/
    30 Church of San Francisco de Yare, Caracas

          Bolivar House restoration, Caracas
1931 Bullring, Maracay, Venezuela
1935 Museo de los Caobos, Caracas
1937 Venezuelan Pavilion, *World's Fair*, Paris
1939 Gran Colombia School, Caracas
1941 Redevelopment of the El Silencio Quarter, Avenida Bolivar, Caracas
1943/
    44 General Rafael Urdaneta Housing Development, Maracaibo, Venezuela
1943/
    45 Dos de Diciembre Housing Development, Caracas (with José Manuel Mijares, José Hoffman and Carlos Branco)
1944/
    47 Master plan for University City, University of Venezuela, Caracas
1945 Medical Center, University City, Caracas
1947 Technical/Industrial School, Caracas
1948 Francisco de Mirando Housing Development, Caracas
1950 Ciudad Tablitas (housing development), Caracas
1950/
    52 Olympic Stadium, University City, Caracas
1951 Villanueva House, La Florida, Caracas
1952 Aula Magna (main auditorium), Library, Plaza Cubierta and Walks, and the Botanical Institute, University City, Caracas
1953 Small Concert Hall, University City, Caracas
1954 El Paraiso Housing Development, Caracas (with Carlos Celis and José Manuel Mijares)
          Humanities, Science, and Physics buildings, University City, Caracas
          Cerro Piloto Housing Development, Caracas
1955 School of Dentistry, University City, Caracas
1955/
    57 23 de Enero High-Rise Housing Development, Caracas (with C.C. Cepero and José Manuel Mijares)
1956 Institute of Petroleum Engineering, University of Zulia, Maracaibo, Venezuela
1957 School of Architecture and Urbanism, School of Pharmacy, and Olympic Swimming Stadium, University City, Caracas
          Ascension Chapel, 23 de Enero Development, Caracas
1958 Villanueva House, Caraballeda, Venezuela
1961/
    64 Fundación La Salle Office Building, Caracas
1967 Venezuelan Pavilion, *Expo '67,* Montreal (with E. Trujillo)
1968 Museo de Bellas Artes, Caracas (project)

Publications:

By VILLANUEVA: books—*Caracas of Yesterday and Today*, Caracas 1943, 1950; *Caracas en tres tiempos*, Caracas 1966; articles—"La Ciudad y su Historia" in *Boletin de Universidad Central* (Caracas), January 1964; "Lettre de Colombia" in *Architecture: Formes et Fonctions* (Lausanne), vol. 12, 1965/66; "Fonction-Formation-Position" in *Architecture: Formes et Fonctions* (Lausanne), vol. 15, 1969.

On VILLANUEVA: books—*Latin American Architecture since 1945* by Henry-Russell Hitchcock, New York 1955; *Masters of Modern Architecture* by John Peter, New York 1958; *Baukunst der Gegenwart* by Udo Kultermann, Tübingen 1958; *Art in Latin American Architecture* by Paul F. Damaz, New York 1961; *Carlos Raúl Villanueva and the Architecture of Venezuela* by Sibyl Moholy-Nagy, Stuttgart and London 1964; *Panoramica de la Arquitectura Latinoamericana* by Damián Bayón and Paolo Gasparini, Barcelona 1977, as *The Changing Shape of Latin American Architecture: Conversations with Ten Leading Architects*, New York and Chichester, Sussex 1979; *Architektur 1940-1980* by Adolf Max

Vogt, Berlin, Frankfurt and Vienna 1980; *Latin America and Its Architecture*, edited by Roberto Segre, New York and London 1981; articles—"Caracas University City" in *Arts and Architecture* (Los Angeles), November 1954; "La Casa di Villanueva" and "Nuovi Quartieri a Caracas" in *Domus* (Milan), April 1956; "Housing Projects in Caracas," "La Maison de l'architecte Carlos Raúl Villanueva" and "Unité d' Habitation à Caracas" in *L'Architecture d'Aujourd'hui* (Paris), October 1956; "Three Cubes" in *Architectural Forum* (New York), September 1967; "Obituary" in *AIA Journal* (Washington, D.C.), December 1975; "Homage from Venezuela to Carlos Raúl Villanueva" in *Arquitecturas Bis* (Barcelona), November 1976.

Carlos Raúl Villanueva's real importance lies not merely in his built works, but also in his underlying attitude to architectural design, for much of his work has become a prototype for subsequent works by architects throughout Latin America. An initiator of new methods and new standards, Villanueva was also a creator of the first rank.

At first the bullring at Maracay, his earliest major work, does not seem particularly "modern." Bullfighting is a rigidly traditional sport, a fact that Villanueva acknowledges in his design: the structure is a compromise of new materials, the demands of expanded space, and historical continuity. Thus, the massive arena is surmounted all around by the lace-like lightness of its top arcade, and Moorish-style horse-shoe arches span its entrance. But, with this work, Villanueva introduced to South America a skeleton structure actually *expressed* through its concrete stress-members, as Perret had done in Europe some 50 years previously.

In his redevelopment of the El Silencio Quarter in Caracas, Villanueva revealed his concern for the quality of the human environment, and in his development of the University City of the University of Venezuela, Caracas, this feeling is most triumphantly expressed. His accomplishment is particularly evident in his conception of the covered plazas and walks: more than a mile of covered walkway undulates around the hillside on which the university is situated, its wave-like progression, varying in height, providing a cool shelter as its pre-stressed, pre-poured concrete units on cantilevered supports curve around planted islands. Low shelters give way to lofty halls, which in turn give onto terrazzo-floored plazas that provide shaded gathering places throughout the university complex. At almost every focal point in this vast structure Villanueva collaborated with artists who created sculptural and mural "accents" integrated into the work as a complete architectural entity—a notable success being Alexander Calder's multi-coloured "clouds" hanging from the ceiling of the main auditorium (the Aula Magna), not only acting as sound baffles for musical concerts, but also transforming the massive interior into a light and airy space.

Villanueva's Olympic Stadium at University City illustrates how severely practical his designs could be, while at the same time achieving an aesthetic magnificence. Seating 30,000 people, the stadium is supported on almost invisible concrete columns; the grandstand, with locker-rooms and other facilities ingeniously tucked below, is covered by a breathtaking cantilevered free span of pre-stressed concrete beams. Clean ramps, also in concrete, sweep up to the terraces of seating to complete a totally harmonious blend of stressed forms.

University City is magnificent, the work of a master. Villanueva may, however, have his most lasting influence in housing.

Just prior to commencing work on University City, he was commissioned to design a low-cost housing development for low-income families in Maracaibo. Previously such developments had been sponsored by industrial concerns whose only interest was to locate workers in rows of conveniently drab and monotonous barracks for as little expense as possible. Villanueva rose to the occasion by creating

a new standard of housing at an equally low cost, arranging the 1,000 one-family houses and several three-storey multiple dwellings concentrically around urban centres of community facilities—schools, shops, churches, and gathering-places—Short but broad streets opened out at the fronts of the houses, and individual yards and pedestrian walkways at the rear were designed to enhance the character of the neighborhood. Villanueva had built up to a standard, rather than down to a cost.

While he was Consultant Architect to the Workers' Bank, Villanueva further developed the lessons of Maracaibo in two residential estates in Caracas—23 de Enero and El Paraiso—perhaps the finest low-to middle-income housing complexes in Venezuela. Instead of spreading single-storey "ranchos" all over what was (and still is, thanks to his scheme) an environmentally beautiful hillside, he built a blend of low-rise and high-rise blocks in a coherent pattern that stresses horizontal movement rather than a vertical stabbing at the sky. The peasants who live in these blocks enjoy cool breezes from the hillside, rather than the expensive ground-level mugginess reserved for the fashionable rich.

It is difficult to believe that these developments were greeted with harsh and bitter criticism when they were first built, for today they have become a synonym—as has all of Villanueva's work—for qualitative rather than quantitative design.

—Colin Naylor

von BRANCA, Alexander Freiherr.

German. Born in Munich, 11 January 1919. Educated at the Landeschulheim, Neubeuern, Germany, 1931-37; University of Munich, 1946-48; E.T.H.: Eidgenössischen Technischen Hochschule, Zurich, 1948-50. Served in the German Army, 1938-40. Married Theresa Freifau zu Guttenberg in 1952 (died, 1953); married Carolina Bernasconi in 1955; children: Franziskus, Emanuela, Alexandrea, Matthias, and Benedicta. In private practice, Munich, since 1950. Architect, Heimat Building Department, City of Munich, since 1972. Recipient: Cultural Prize, City of Munich, 1957; Honour Award, City of Burghausen, 1978; Ludwig-Thoma-Medal, Munich, 1980; Monument Conservation Medal, Munich, 1980; Europa-Nostra-Prize, Würzburg, 1981; Architecture Prize, City of Munich, 1983; Merit Cross and Star, Principality of Liechtenstein, 1984; München Leuchtet Prize, City of Munich, 1984. Member, Bavarian Order of Merit, and Akademie der Künste, Munich. Member, Papal Order of Sylvester, and Accademia dei Virtuosi al Phanteon, Rome. Member, Order of the Royal Knight of Malta. Address (office): Gauss-strasse 1, 8000 Munich 80, West Germany.

Works:

1954 Volksbank, Weiden, Germany
      Church, Herzogspitalstrasse, Munich
1955 Buttermelcher Church, Munich
      Flats for diplomats, Thiemestrasse, Munich
1957 Klenze Grammar School, Munich
1957/
  58 Old people's home, Pullach, Munich
1957/
  60 Monastery for the Styler Missionaries, Munich Church, Greifenberg, Germany
1959/
  61 Church, Rohrbach, Germany
1960 Haniel House, Haimhausen, Germany
1962 Church, Weissenburg, Germany
1962/
  64 Stanischeff House, Munich
1962/
  65 St. Matthias Church, Füstenried, Germany

1963/
  66 German Embassy, Madrid
1963/
  67 Savings Bank, Wasserburg, Germany
1963/
  71 Family holiday house, Naumburg, Germany
1964 von Branca House, Oberfohringerstrasse, Munich
      Church, Langwasser, Germany
1964/
  68 Raiffieisen Insurance Building, Munich
1964/
  69 Church, Beuel, Bonn
1965/
  67 Church, Jettingen, Germany
1965/
  68 Catholic Monastery and Church, Schönstatt, Germany
1966/
  69 Castle Church, Hirschberg, Germany
1966/
  71 Treatment Center, Bad Füssing, Germany
1967/
  69 Class House, Harsewinkel, Germany
1969 Dante Grammar School, Munich
1970/
  71 Underground (Subway) Station, Marienplatz, Munich
1970/
  74 St. Thomas More Church, Neusäss, Augsburg
      Central Library, University of Regensburg
1971 Flats for old people, Heidelberg
1971/
  72 Village school, Neubeuern, Germany
      Press City, Olympic Village, Munich
1971/
  75 Postal Administration Building, Freiburg
      St. Ulrich's Catholic Academy, Augsburg
1972/
  74 Regional Insurance Building (LVA), Perlach, Munich
1972/
  78 Student Union, University of Würzburg
1973/
  75 4 underground (subway) stations, Bonn
1973/
  77 Chapel and School, Catholic Monastery, Schönstatte, Germany
1973/
  81 Neue Pinakothek Art Gallery, Munich
1977/
  79 Church Centre, Diesenbach/Regenstauf, Germany
      Hertie Department Store, Würzburg, Germany
1977/
  80 Guest House, Bad Füssing, Germany
      Savings Bank Headquarters, Aschaffenburg, Germany
1977/
  82 Woodland Cemetery, Leutkirch, Germany
1978- Museum, Vaduz, Liechtenstein (competition project)
1978/
  81 Raiffeisen-Zentralbank Administration Building, Munich
      Local Government Administration Builiding, Aschaffenburg, Germany
1978/
  83 Nonntal Housing Development, Berchtesgaden, Germany
1979/
  82 St. Salvator Parish Church, Nördlingen, Germany
      Sanatorium, Griesbach, Germany (with Hummel and Hofmeister)
1979/
  84 German Embassy, Vatican City, Rome
      Raiffeisen-Zentralbank Building, Augsburg, Germany

Alexander von Branca: Bayerische Raiffeisen-Zentral Bank, Munich, 1978-81.

1980/
82 Guesthouse, Catholic Monastery, Schönstatt, Germany
Funeral Chapel, Catholic Monastery, Schönstatt, Germany
Böhrer family house, Aschaffenburg, Germany

1980/
83 WVG Office and Commercial Building, Munich

1980- Mortgage Offices layout and extensions,
Wiesbaden, Germany

1981/
84 Underground (subway) Station, Theresien-
wiese, Munich (with A. and B. Martens)

1981- Old City restoration, Regensburg, Germany
Bayernwerk Administration Building, Munich

1982/
83 Sanatorium Plazas, Griesbach, Germany

1982- Priests' Seminary, Augsburg, Germany
Father Joseph Kentneich Reception Hall,
Catholic Monastery, Schönstatt, Germany
Schönstatt Marienschwestern Provincial
Buildings, Kosching, Germany

1983- Government Centre, Esslingen, Germany

Publications:

By von BRANCA: articles—"Aufsatz über das
Wohnen" in *Süddeutsche Zeitung* (Munich), July
1972; "Aufsatz über Architektur und Denkmalss-
chutz" in *Augsburger Allgemeine*, July 1974; "Denk-
mal und Stadtbilpflege in Bamberg" in *Schönere
Heimat* (Munich), March 1975; "Das Zeit-
gemässe—oder der Mut zum Unzeitgemässen" in
Der Architekt (Stuttgart), 1976; "Die Chance des
Regionalismus in der Architektur" in *Der Architekt*
(Stuttgart), 1976; "Brücken zwischen moderner
Architektur und Denkmalspflege" in *Deutsches
Architektenblatt* (Stuttgart), May 1976; "Verfall der
Gestaltsaussage" in *Civitas/Rund um den Bau*
(Zurich), 1977; "I Feel an Obligation to Form" in
Der Architekt (Stuttgart), January 1979; "The Pin-
akothek in Munich" in *Bauwelt* (Berlin), 22 May
1981.

On von BRANCA: articles—"L'Architecte Alex-
andre von Branca" in *Art d'Eglise* (Ottignies, Bel-
gium), no. 114, 1961; "Klenze-Oberrealschule,
München" in *Baumeister* (Munich), March 1964;
"Architect-Parents Plan Their Own Highly Modern
House in Munich" in *House Beautiful* (New York),
January 1966; "Meeting Place for Church and the
World: St. Ulrich, Augsburg" in *Architektur und
Wohnform* (Stuttgart), July 1975; "Administration
Building in Munich-Perlach for Landesversicherun-
gsanstalt Oberbayern" in *Baumeister* (Munich),
October 1975; "Regensburg University" in *Baumei-
ster* (Munich), May 1976; "Oberpostdirektion
Freiburg" in *Bauwelt* (Berlin), January 1977; "Cult
and Church Architecture" by Werner Finke in
Münster (Munster, Germany), vol. 33, no. 1, 1980;
"International Competition for the Kunsthaus in
Vaduz" in *Baumeister* (Munich), August 1980;
"Urban Renewal in East Munich—Market for
Haidhausen" in *Baumeister* (Munich), October
1980; "Hertie Department Store in Würzburg" in
Deutsche Bauzeitung (Stuttgart), December 1980;
"The New Pinakothek in Munich" by Michel Huth
in *Connaissance des Arts* (Paris), March 1981;
"Three Buildings in Munich" by Peter Davey in
Architectural Review (London), June 1981; "Bank
Building and Offices" in *Detail* (Munich), July/
August 1982; "County Building in Aschaffenburg"
in *Baumeister* (Munich), September 1982.

Art is inextricably linked with the definition of Man
and with his self-image. Image and representation in
the process of change is also a considered act. In
disconnected and distorted pictures we exhibit a
caricature of ourselves, not our real human potential; in one-dimensionality we exhibit the limitations
of a vision which no longer recognizes the complexity of the world. Art, and also architecture, thereby
takes on a new dimension—the dimension of salvation—since we are dealing here with the being or
non-being of Man in all his complexity.

It is Man's task to retrieve this dimension of art
and architecture—in a plural society most especially. The task consists in re-establishing an image of
Man that is not simply the image of a moment, an
endlessly abbreviated definition of humanity, but an
image rooted in the human continuum, in all its
valencies and dimensions, over aeons of time. From
this, the correct relationship to the whole must
necessarily follow, with no reference to any modernism or superficiality.

—Alexander von Branca

The abundant work of Alexander von Branca
suggests community and a profound basis, that
which, over the ages, can be transposed and reflected with strength in architecture. I therefore put to
him the question of art in architecture—art as a
message from man to man about his place in the
world, his seeing and non-seeing, his perception and
non-perception.

Von Branca believes that in a work of art both
primitive and contemporary human experience are
similarly visible; the work of art, therefore, has an
irrefutably informatory content. The true value of a
creative work is not merely its quality within its
particular aesthetic category; the value is also in its
message to the next one, to the other, who, as a
human being, lives with the same horizon of experience, even when hundreds of years intervene.
Von Branca confirms the absolute necessity of
continuity through tradition and the symbolic value
of architecture as expression over ages and generations. There is a "supertemporal truth" in architecture. In other words, we can not extract modern
architecture from its historical context, its associations with history, and regard "modern" as a quality
per se.

Or, rather, we should not be able to do so. If the
architecture of our century is regarded within a
historical context, there is more conformism than
courage—uniformity, lovelessness, a technical ingenuity with a failure of design. Von Branca thinks
that our work has become spiritually poorer; that is,
it has failed to "connect" with the life of man. Most
of our works involve a giving in to the ethos of small
effort for high return; all want to rule but none will
serve. Von Branca, conversely, sees art as involving
a high seriousness—listening to, looking at, serving
and giving to the purpose of the work, so that man,
the observer, can understand and explain why it
exists.

Everything that is created lives. Even the
apparently dead lives, and in many ways the historic
is more alive than the contemporary. There can be
no such thing as historicism! Von Branca sees
architecture's present task as primarily that of
revealing to mankind the life in things. We must be
concerned with discovery and with revelation; we
must create works that prove themselves by per-
suading us to look at the environment not only with
the outer eye but also with the inner eye. Von Branca
believes that architecture must be associative, must
inform, must contribute to the world of the imagination without which we, as creative beings, cannot
live. Architecture must construct horizons of expectation, and it must have an aura like that of people
themselves, who meet each other, who respond, who
are attracted or repulsed. Von Branca told me of his
first visit to the Pantheon in Rome, when, on
entering, he stopped, moved back, because the
"inner radiance" of the building was so powerful.

Our materialistic architecture cannot express
such radiance. It can no longe seize hold of life. Von
Branca deplores the one-sidedness, the functionalism of our works: they are comfortable, well-made,
and often they have quality, but they do not live, and
their lifelessness makes people sad and drives them
to escape into the past, where liveliness is easier to
find. Von Branca wants to bring it back to our time,
as a "message upwards and downwards," and he
defines the message as that of love. For von Branca
sees the absence of life as the absence of love, and he
fears that lovelessness is the fate of our time.

It is a serious and earnest vision, and it pervades
all of his work.

Yet there are problems. Von Branca wants to
eliminate isolated individualism as the inheritance
of a misunderstood notion of "artistic freedom."
One could argue that, even if it appears to be a
medium of expression for everyone, art is always
isolated and individual in its development: the great
works of architectural history are always unique,
the product of the individual ego. And an architecture that is humble yet resolute in its autonomy is
often the one that sets free the creative potential that
separates the real work of art from the indifferent
average. Also, von Branca thinks that the future
development of architecture depends on whether
people can escape from the slavery of materialism.
But materialism is increasingly the only aim of our
lives, and if the possible renaissance of architecture
depends not so much on constructed details as on
attitude to life—well, that is a tall order.

I asked von Branca about the relationship of
theory to practice, between his philosophy and
reality. His answer was unequivocal: theory and
practice are one! That is a lofty claim, and with von
Branca it is entirely sincere. Yet, I wonder. Even
with the greatest care for, and love in, our work, we
architects have to accept a good measure of im-
potence in our achievements, and I think we seek to
compensate for this impotency with theory. But this
is not to offer a darker vision, or to contradict von
Branca. "Theory corrects practice, practice corrects
theory," and in the reciprocal fertilization of correction there can be a creative beginning.

—Justus Dahinden

VON GERKAN, Meinhard.

German. Born in Riga, Lithuania, 3 January 1935;
Lived in Posen (Poznan), Poland, 1939-45; moved to
West Germany in 1945. Studied physics and law,
University of Hamburg, West Germany, 1954-55;
architecture, Technical University of Berlin, 1956-
60; architecture, Technical University of Bruansch-
weig, West Germany 1960-64, Dip.Arch.Eng. 1964.
Married Gerda Kuhn in 1959; children: Florence and
Franziska. Since 1965, Partner, with Volkwin Marg,
von Gerkan-Marg + Partner, Hamburg, West
Germany; branch offices in Berlin and Munich
(additional partners since 1972; Rolf Niedballa,
Karston Brauer, Andreas Sack and Klaus Staratz-
ke). Taught at the Freie Akademkie der Künste,
Hamburg, West Germany 1972-74; Professor of
Architectural Design, Technical University of
Braunschweig, West Germany, since 1974. Member
of the Board, Chamber of Architects, Hamburg,
West Germany since 1969. Recipient: First Prize,
Pahlavi National Library Competition, Tehran,
1978; Concrete Architecture Prize, 1979; Bund
Deutscher Architekten Prize, 1979, 1980, and 1981.
Member Bund Deutscher Architekten; Free
Academy of Arts, Hamburg, West Germany.
Address; von Gerkan-Marg + Partner, St Benedict-
strasse 8, 2 Hamburg 13, West Germany.

Works:

1966 Kohenmann House, Hamburg, West Germany
1966/
68 Storman Public Hall, Oldesloe, Germany
(with Schedje)

Meinhard von Gerkan: Sports Centre, University of Kiel, West Germany, 1974.

1966/
69 Max Planck Institute, Lindau, Germany (with Störmer)

1967/
70 Sports Complex, Diekirch, Luxembourg (with Störmer)

1968/
70 Poppenbuttel Apartment House, Hamburg, West Germany

1968/
74 Terminal, Roads, bridges and other facilities at Tegel Airport, Berlin (with Nickels)

1969/
71 Alsterufer Apartment House, Hamburg, West Germany

1970/
74 Control tower, Power Station and Operations Building, Tegel Airport, Berlin (with Nickels)

1972/
74 Shell Company Head Offices, Hamburg, West Germany (with Wieche)
   Sports Centre, University of Kiel, West Germany (with Nickels)

1973/
74 Sound-deadening bunkers, Tegel Airport, Berlin

1973/
75 Aral Company Head Office, Bochum, West Germany
   Munich Airport II
   Bilwerder-Allermohe New Town, Hamburg, West Germany (with Erler, Wolske, Nickels and Ohrt)

1974/
75 Tax Office, Oledburgh, West Germany (with Patschan)

1947/
77 Psychiatric Institute, Rickling, West Germany

1974/
80 Hansaviertel Development, Hamburg, West Germany

1975/
76 Kolhofen Residential Area, Hamburg, West Germany

1975/
77 Technical College, Bad Oldesloe, West Germany (with Wieche)
   European Patent Office, Munich

1976 Der El Beida Airport, Algeria

1976/
78 Gross Bleichen modernization, Hamburg, West Germany
   Bergedorf Polytechnic, Hamburg, West Germany

1976/
84 Passenger and Freight Terminal, Algiers Airport, Algeria

1977 Hyatt Hotel, Abu Dhabi, United Arab Emirates
   Moscow Airport (project)

1977/
78 Town houses, Hamburg, West Germany
   MAK Company Head Office Building, Kiel, West Germany (with Borockstedt and Discher
   Ministry of the Interior, Kiel, West Germany
   Pahlavi National Library, Teheran, Iran (competition project)
   Police Headquarters Office, Panckstrasse, Berlin (competition project)
   Taxi Bay Roofing, Tegel Airport, Berlin

1977/
79 "Fabrik" Building reconstruction, Hamburg, West Gemay

1977/
80 Taima and Sulayyil residential development, Saudi Arabia

1977/
81 House "G," Blankenese, Hamburg, West Germany

1977/
82 Otto-Versand Headquarters extensions, Hamburg, West Germany
   Community Centre, Ritterstrasse, Stade, West Germany

1978 City Hall, Mannheim, West Germany (competition project)
   Kammergericht City Plan, Berlin (competition project)

Federal Ministry of Trade, Bonn (competition project)

1978/
80 Biochemical Institut, University of Braunschweig, West Germany

1978/
83 Park-House, Poststrasse, Hamburg, West Germany

1979 Central Library, Auditorium and Sprts Hall, University of Oldenburg, West Germany (project)
   Town Housing, Tiergarten, Berlin

1979/
80 City Swimming Pools, Spandau, Berlin (competition project)

1979/
82 Rickling Psychiatric Clinic Buildings, Falkenhorst, West Germany

1979/
83 Rickling Psychiatric Clinic Buildings, Thetmarshof, West Germany
   Custodial Housing Block, Südring, Hamburg, West Germany

1980/
81 Renaissance Hotel, for Ramada, Hamburg, West Germany

1980/
83 Sports Institute, Bad Schwartau, West Germany
   Lufthansa Airline Headquaters, Hamburg, West Germany
   Office Building, Hohe Bleichen, Hamburg, West Germany

1981 Kiel Castle renovations, Kiel, West Germany

1981/
82 Energy-saving house, *International Bauausstellung* Berlin

1981/
83 ZOB Office and Residential Building, Bad Schwartau, West Germany
   Plaza Hotel, Hillmannpaltz, Bremen, West Germany
   "Black Box" electronics sales building, Berlin
   Office Centre, Mainz, West Germany

Publications:

By von GERKAN: books—*Architektur 1966-1978: von Gerkan Marg und Partner*, with others, Stuttgart 1978; *Architektur 1978-1983: von Gerkan, Marg und Partner*, with others, Stuttgart 1983; articles—"Neubau des Flughafen Berlin Tagel" in *Berliner Bauwirtschaft*, no.598, 1972; "Quo Vadi? Zum Wettbewerbswesen" in *Deustsches Architektenblatt* (Stuttgart), no. 13. 1974; "Viefalt in der Einheit: neuplanung für den Flughafen Berlin-Tegal" in *Duetsches Architektenblatt* (Stuttgart) no. 21, 1974; "Architekten sind nicht an allem schuld" in *Die Zeit* (Hamburg, West Germany) 21 February 1975; "Gedanken zum Berufbild und zur Berufspraxis de Architeken heute" in *Detail* (Munich), no. 3, 1975; "Schnorkel gegen Raster" in *Die Zeit* (Hamburg, West Germany) 29 August 1975; "Gestalting unsere Unwelt" in *Verband Wohnugsunternehmen* (Munich), no 11, 1975; "Architektur kritisch—Ein Bau widerlegt seine Ideologie: FU-Berlin—Die Rostlaube" in *Der Architekt* (Stuttgart), no 11 1975; "Elemente der Flughafenplanung: Hamburg-Kaltenkirchen, Flughafen München II, Flughafen Berlin-Tegel" in *Bauen und Wohnen* (Zurich). March 1976; "Verkehrsbauten als zentrale Aufgabe der Umweltgestaltung" in *Der Architeckt* (Stuttgart), no. 11, 1976; "Der Computer als Ersatz für den hohlen Bauch" in *Bauwelt* (Berlin), no. 34, 1976; "The Conditions for Architecture" in *Der Architekt* (Stuttgart), February 1979; "The Work of von Gerkan, Marg und Partner" in *Space Design* (Tokyo), April 1979; "The Urban Residence" in *Bauen und Wohnen* (Zurich), July/August 1979; "Specialize of Generalize?" in *Bauwelt* (Berlin), 12 October 1979.

On von GERKAN: books—*Bauen in Deutschland* by Alfred Simon, Essen West Germany 1969; *Deutsche Kunst seit 1960. Vol. 4 Architecture* by Paclo Nestler and peter M. Bode, Munich 1976; *Architektur in Deutschland* by H. and M. Bofinger, J. Paul and H. Klotz, Stuttgart 1979; *Bauen der 70er Jahre in Berlin* by Rolf Rave, Hans-Joachim Rave and Jan Rave 1980; *Architektur in Deutschland '83*, edited by Jürgen Joedicke, Stuttgart 1984; articles—"Ein Burg aus Glas" in *Stern*, (Hamburg, West Germany), no. 30, 1970; article on the Shell Headquarters in *Baumeister* (Munich), no.5, 1970; "Architektenportrat Meinhard von Gerkan und Volkwin Marg" in *Deutsche Bauzeitung* (Stuttgart), no. 5, 1972; article on the European Patent Office in *Baumeister* (Munich), no 11, 1972; article on Berlin Airport in *Bauwelt* (Berlin), no. 45, 1974; "Weiche nach Wehen—Flughafen Berlin-Tegel" in *Der Spiegel* (Berlin), 14 October 1974; "Ein Hallelujah Für Zwei Architekten" in *Die Zeit* (Hamburg, Werst Germany, 25 October 1974; "Die glorreichen Sieben der duetschen Architekur" in *Welt am Sonntag* (Bonn), 7 November 1976; article on the Sports Centre at the University of Kiel in *Domus* Decmber 1977; article on the Pahlavi National Library in *Stern* (Hamburg, West Germany), 18 May 1978; "Tegel Airport Services Building" in *Architecture + Urbanism* (Tokyo), July 1979; "Vocationbal School Centre in Hamburg-Bergedorf" in *Baumeister* (Munich), January 1980.

*   *   *

Primary in importance in our design efforts is the attempt to render "personality"and "identity" to each building. The diversity of our construction task—from the one-family dwelling to the airport—and their respective situations with regard to environment and ecology—extending from Schleswig Holstein to the Persian Gulf—entails a mulitude of differences in identity. We have never attemped to conceal such differences by means of standardizing. We much prefer to discover the substance-oriented peculiarity of a project, or its particular reference to environment, to ultimately find for the traits of identity we have thus discovered the best and most suitable means of design.

The means by which we try to establish correspondene of form to the respective content are various—constructional, spatial, plastic three-dimensional, decorative-aesthetic, topographical—but they are in no way merely of a formal nature—in the usual meaning of the team in the architectural vocabulary. We do not use any preconceived formal solution which we can fit to every problem, but we try to find a specific answer to every specific question.

More than by any other factor our design work is determined by the regularity of goemetry. When it has not seemed feasible to derive form the specific requirements posed by the building site or from the urban environment components to shape the architectural character, we have drawn the structuring framework of our designs from geometry. With geometry the law of natural sciences becomes the guide for artistic form-finding and creation. That may seem to imply a lack of creative power or of formal imagination, but it is the means of discover selfdiscipline, to seek out valid and timeless forms of architecture. We have almost never freely invented an architectural form; each form is either bound to the requirements imposed by the building site and/or to the specific function, but mostly it is bound to both of these and also to goemetric laws.

As variously as we may try to solve each architectural assignment—without an dogmatic prejudices—we do also claim to understand our role as architects in society. We conder ourselves experts in the design and maintenance of order in our environment. That role demands, on the one hand, taking into account the needs of society and, on the other hand, resolutely and purposefully influencing, with the authority of competent experts, permanent changes in the environment. Idoelogical contempt or a know-it-all attitude, in these concerns is surely just an inappropriate as is an uncritical striving for fulfillment at any price.

—Meinhard von Gerkan

*   *   *

Although as students they were already successful in architecture competitions (anonymously, in the service of other architects), Meinhard von Gerkan and his partner Volkwin Marg won seven first prizes, some of them in international competitions, in the first year of their joint practice. The exceptional and meteoric rise of two beginners, unknown and without means, to the rank of international stars was made possible by the modern practice, particularly prevalent in Germany, of inding architects through competion for practically all public and most large private building projects.

The principal reasons for von Gerkan and Marg's success are that they conscientiously fulfill the quantitive programme; pragmatically develop their architecture from an analysis of function, local environment, and topography; and rarely seek suuport from geometric forms. Their designs do not obey a univers repertoire of form or direction but are an "interpretation related to the content and situation of the actual project." Their buildings are not stylistically characterized by an unmistakable personal handwriting; they can, and do, include all the architectural feature of our time.

All of Von Gerkan and Marg's buildings are brilliantly conceived and executed. Some are Exemplary—for example, the Sports Centre at the University of Kiel. Others, like the airport building at Berlin-Tegel, are international stature.

—Manfred Sack

WACHSMANN, Konrad Ludwig.
American. Born in Frankfurt-on-Oder, Germany, 16 May 1901; emigrated to the United States, 1941: naturalized, 1947. Educated at elementary and junior high school, Frankfurt-on-Oder, 1907-15; apprentice carpenter and cabinet-maker, Frankfurt-on-Oder, 1915-20; studied at the School of Applied Arts, Berlin, 1920; Academy of Art, Dresden, under Heinrich Tessenow, 1920-22; Academy of Art, Berlin, under Hans Poelzig, 1923-24. Married Judith Wachsmann; daughter: Ray. Worked as an unpaid assistant, studio of Le Corbusier, Paris, 1924-25; draughtsman-designer, then Chief Architect, Christoph and Unmack prefabricated building company, Niesky, Silesia, 1925-28; in private practice, Berlin, 1928-32; Assistant City Planner, Granada, Spain, 1933-34; in private practice, Rome, 1935-38; interned, then served in the French Army, in Grenoble and Aix-en-Provence, 1939-41; collaborated with Walter Gropius on the General Panel prefabrication system, New York, 1941-49: Technical Director and Executive Vice-President, 1942-45, President, 1945-48, and Chairman, 1948-49, General Panel Corporation, New York, and Burbank, California; in private practice as designer of structural systems, in Chicago, 1949-60, in Genoa, Italy, 1960-63, and in Los Angeles, 1964 until his death, 1980. Publisher and Editor, three issues of *Eidon* photographic magazine, Rome, 1934-35. Professor and Director of the Institute of Advanced Building Research, Institute of Design, Illinois Institute of Technology, Chicago, 1949-56; Professor of Architecture and Director of the Building Institute, 1964-72, and Professor Emeritus, 1972-80, University of California, Los Angeles; also Visiting Lecturer at the University of Karlsruhe, Unversity of Tokyo, Haifa Technion University, Ulm Hochschule fur Gestaltung, Salzburg International Summer Academy, Lausanne Ecole Polytechnique, New York State University at Buffalo, Yale University and the University of Texas at Austin, from 1955. Member of the Board of Governors, Bauhaus Archive, Berlin, 1969. Exhibitions: *General Panel System*, American Institute of Architects, New York, 1943; *Mobilar Structure*, Museum of Modern Art, New York, 1946; *Toward Industrialization of Building*, Illinois Institute of Technology, Chicago, 1950; *Konrad Wachsmann: retrospective*, Illinois Institute of Technology, Chicago, 1954; *Konrad Wachsmann*, toured Germany, 1956-57; *Building in our time*, Galerie Wuerthle, Vienna, travelled to Munich and Zurich, 1958; *Corbusier and Wachsmann*, Galleria Nazionale d'Arte Moderna, Rome, travelled to Amsterdam, Delft and Essen, 1959; *Konrad Wachsmann—50 Years of Life and Work*, University of California, Los Angeles, toured the United States and Canada, 1971-74. Collection: Wachsmann Archive, Huntington Library, San Marino, California. Recipient: Rome Prize, Prussian Ministry of Culture, Berlin, 1932; Medal of Honour (with Walter Gropius), Pan-American Congress of Architecture, 1951; Gold Medal, First Biennial of Design Methodology, Rome, 1970. Honorary D.Ing.: University of Stuttgart, 1973; University of Southern California, 1977.

Extraordinary Member, Academy of Arts, Berlin, 1973; Honorary Associate Member, American Institute of Architects, Southern California Chapter, 1976. *Died* (in West Los Angeles) *25 November 1980.*

Works:

1925/
28 Block-built house for Mr. V., Niesky, Poland
Earth Sciences Institute, Ratibor, Poland
Prefabricated Hotel Complex with School and Hospital, for Curacao, West Indies
Children's Convalescent Hospital, Spremberg, Germany
Prefabricated Tennis Club-house, Berlin
Weekend House, Frankfurt-on-Oder, Germany (project)
Youth Hostel in the Mountains (competition project)
Steel Bridge over the Rance River, France (project)
1928/
29 Albert Einstein Country House, Caputh, near Potsdam, Germany
1928/
32 Doctor's House and Office, Jueterbock, near Berlin
1930 Single-family house and row-houses, for *Bauwelt* magazine, Berlin (competition projects)
1931 Torkret advertising tower, at the *Internationale Bauausstellung*, Berlin
1932/
33 Timber Building types (5), for the Deutscher Werkbund Exhibition, Stuttgart (project)
1935/
38 Reinforced concrete apartment building, Rome
Reinforced concrete market hall, Rome
Office building with underground cinema and garage, Rome (project)
Country houses, near Rome
Country house, Capri, Italy
1938/
39 Tubular steel construction system, Grenoble, France (project)
Universal plywood panel construction system, Grenoble, France
1941 Leisure Center, Key West, Florida (project; with Walter Gropius)
1941/
42 General Panel prefabrication system, New York (with Walter Gropius)
1942 Convalescent Home, Key West, Florida (project; with Walter Gropius)
1943/
46 Mobilar Construction System, New York
1946 General Panel Corporation factory, Burbank, California
Studio interiors, New York (with Serge Chermayeff)
1947/
49 The Marshall Plan duplex house, 6643 Lindenhurst, Los Angeles

1949 General Panel House, 2861 Nichols Canyon, Los Angeles
1950/
53 Aircraft Hanger tubular steel structural system for the U.S. Air Force
1950/
56 Armco stainless steel curtain wall system (with Woody Garber and others)
1954 Convention Center, Chicago (project; with Mies van der Rohe)
1955 School pavilion space frame system, Tokyo
1956 Siegfried Giedion mountain chalet, Switzerland
Concert Hall cantilevered timber roof structure, Salzburg
1957 Instant-change aluminium and plastic structure system (project)
1958 Mechanical Museum modular plywood panel system (project)
1959 Floating Exhibition Complex aluminium components, Lake Leman, Lausanne, Switzerland (project)
1961/
72 Italsider Steel Company high-rise headquarters, Genoa, Italy
Harbour Area installations and urban plan, Genoa, Italy
1966 Adaptable component system for high-rise buildings (project)
1966/
70 Civic Center, California City
1967 Convention Center of 2,000-feet square, on four supports (project)

Publications:

By WACHSMANN: books—*Holzhausbau: Technik und Gestaltung*, Berlin 1931; *Holz im Bau*, Stuttgart 1957; *Neuzeitliches Bauen mit Holz*, exhibition catalogue, Stuttgart 1959; *Wendepunkt im Bauen*, Wiesbaden 1959, as *The Turning Point in Building: structure and design*, New York 1961; *Aspekte* (photographs), Wiesbaden 1961; *Prefabbricazione*, Bari, Italy 1962; *Industrializzazione dell'Edilizia*, Bari, Italy 1965; *Selbstdarstellung*, Dusseldorf 1973; articles—"Holzbau" in *Wasmuths Lexicon der Baukunst*, Berlin 1931; "Mobilar Structures" in *Pencil Points* (New York), March 1946; "Construction—a revolutionary structural system" in *Arts and Architecture* (Los Angeles), April 1946; "Ein Konstruktionssystem fur Hallenbauten" in *Baukunst und Werkform* (Nuremberg), no. 9, 1954; "Building in our time" in *Architectural Association Journal* (London), April 1957; "L'Utensile del nostro tempo" in *Civilta delle Macchine* (Rome), May/June 1957; "Das Studium in Team" in *Bauen und Wohnen* (Zurich), October 1960; "Concetti di Architettura" in *Casabella* (Milan), October 1960; "Research: the mother of invention" in *Arts and Architecture* (Los Angeles), April 1967; "Viewpoint" in *Designers West* (Los Angeles), May 1970; "Industrialization of Housing in the USSR" in *California Savings and Loan Journal* (Pasadena), June 1971; "Towards the Year 2,000" interview with Walter Menzies, in *Building Design* (London), 6 August 1976.

On WACHSMANN: books—*Corbusier and Wachsmann*, exhibition catalogue with introduction by Giulio Carlo Argan, Rome 1959; *Konrad Wachsmann—50 Years of Life and Work Toward Industrialization of Building*, exhibition catalogue with introduction by John Hubbard, Los Angeles 1971; *The Packaged House—Dream and Reality* by Gilbert Herbert, Haifa 1981; *The Dream of the Factory-Made House: Walter Gropius and Konrad Wachsmann* by Gilbert Herbert, Cambridge, Massachusetts 1984; articles—"Kleine und grosse Bauten in neuer Holzbautechnik" in *Bauwelt* (Berlin) 10 December 1931; "Recreational Center for Key West, Florida" in *Architectural Forum* (New York), August 1942; "Prefabrication System for Architects" in *Pencil Points* (New York), April 1943; "Expansible Prefab House for Postwar" in *Architectural Record* (New York), December 1944; "La Prefabrication aux Etats-Unis" in *L'Architecture d'Aujourd'hui* (Paris), January 1946; "General Panel Corporation System" in *Techniques et Architecture* (Paris), November/December 1946; "Architect's Studio of Konrad Wachsmann" in *Interiors* (New York), February 1947; "The House in Industry" in *Arts and Architecture* (Los Angeles), November 1947; "Ein Beispiel dreidimensionaler Struktur" by Hans Curjel in *Werk* (Zurich), October 1954; "Wachsmann's Magic" in *Shinkenchiku* (Tokyo), July 1955; "Profile: Konrad Wachsmann" in *Der Aufbau* (Vienna), February 1959; "Konrad Wachsmann" by Paul Ipsen in *Arkitektur* (Copenhagen), March 1960; "La Sintassi Spaziale di Konrad Wachsmann" by Giulio Carlo Argan in *Casabella* (Milan), October 1960; "The Work of Konrad Wachsmann" in *Arts and Architecture* (Los Angeles), May 1967; "Great Builders of the 1960s", special issue of *The Japan Architect* (Tokyo), July 1970; "Konrad Wachsmann: toward industrialization of building" by Ward Robertson Jr. in *AIA Journal* (Washington, D.C.), March 1972; "Whole Earth Men: Fuller and Wachsmann" in *Inland Architect* (Chicago), July 1973; "Konrad Wachsmann" in *Building Design* (London), 31 August 1973; "Konrad Wachsmann Dead" in *Building Design* (London), 12 December 1980; "Death of Konrad Wachsmann" in *AIA Journal* (Washington, D.C.), January 1981; "Konrad Wachsmann: May 12, 1901—November 25, 1980" by Esther McCoy in *L.A. Architect* (Los Angeles), January 1981; "Konrad Wachsmann, 1901-1980" in *UIA: International Architect* (London), no. 5, 1981; "Einstein's Summer House, in Caputh, Potsdam" by Martin Muschter in *Architektur der DDR* (Berlin), May 1981; "Remembering Konrad Wachsmann" by Kurt Liebknecht in *Architektur der DDR* (Berlin), July 1981; "Konrad Wachsmann 1901-1980" by Barbara Goldstein in *Architectural Design* (London), no. 3/4, 1982.

For more than fifty years, Konrad Wachsmann devoted his life's energy toward the industrialization of building, and his effect on the development of the architectural profession has been staggering. As inventor, architect, and engineer, Wachsmann is a truly monumental figure. Although few of his schemes have ever been executed or mass produced to the extent that he envisioned, his innovative ideas continue to dominate technical advancement in architecture; he remains the giant of his field.

Already prolific in Germany before World War II, Wachsmann matured substantially after emigrating to America in 1941. In 1942, in collaboration with Walter Gropius, Wachsmann developed the building system for General Panel Corporation, which was the first time true flexibility was achieved using standardized building parts. Then, in 1946, his Mobilar Stuctures offered similar universal variability in a primarily structural component system. His philosophy in both inventions was to standardize basic units, rather than complete walls,

windows, columns or beams. Further, his joints were directionless, and the components could be used in horizontal or vertical positions; they were fully interchangable. This enabled infinite combinations to be made with a very limited number of prefabricated elements. The desirable economic advantages of standardization and mass production were finally achieved without compromising the possibility of original architectural expression.

Wachsmann continued to explore the potentials of industrialized building in the thirty-four years until his death in 1980, centering his activities first at the Illinois Institute of Technology, and then at the University of Southern California's Graduate Program on Industrialization, which he founded in 1965. In all that time his message has remained clear. All of his designs allow great freedom in construction and connection, and never impose monotony. For all his interest in mass production, he never stood apart from the world of architecture and its spirit.

His book *The Turning Point*, released in English in 1961, revealed his love for the precision of modern technology, but ended with a powerful statement insisting that technology and art did not stand apart. The same year he published *Aspekte*, a collection of his own photos. It demonstrated his own sense of precision, but still bore testament to his acute sensitivity to detail and impulse.

Wachsmann consistently propounded this dual message of precision and sensitivity throughout his life. His devotion to technology was unfaltering, but it was tamed by an extraordinary understanding of art and the value of beauty.

—Mitchell B. Rouda

WALKER, Derek.

British. Born in Ribchester, Lancashire, 15 June 1931. Educated at the Leeds School of Architecture and Town Planning, and at the University of Pennsylvania, Philadelphia, 1951-57. Married Jill Messenger in 1958; children: Matthew and Icarus. Principal, Derek Walker and Partners, architects and planners, Leeds, London and Liverpool, 1958-60, and Walker, Wright, Schofield, interiors and graphics, London, 1965-70; Chief Architect and Planner, with overall responsibility for architectural design and planning, Milton Keynes Development Corporation, Buckinghamshire, 1970-76. Since 1976, Principal, Derek Walker Associates, architects, planners, and landscape architects, Milton Keynes, London and Los Angeles, and Walker, Wright, Day, interiors, graphics, and lightweight structures, London. Vice-Chairman, Consortium of Consultants to the Società Generale Immobiliare, Italy, 1978-82. Third Year Master, University College, Dublin, 1968-70; Visiting Professor, University of Pennsylvania, Philadelphia, 1976-77, and University of Southern California, Los Angeles, since 1977. Governor, Chelsea College of Art, London, since 1968; Consultant, since 1977, and Chairman of the Design Awards Panel, since 1980, *Architectural Design* magazine, London. Exhibitions: *Derek Walker: Furniture and Sculpture*, Woollands, London, 1960; *Milton Keynes*, Salone Internazionale dell'Industrializzazione Edilizia, Bologna, Italy, 1976; *Derek Walker: Projects*, University of Southern California, Los Angeles, 1976; *Art into Landscape*, Serpentine Gallery, London, 1977-78; *Derek Walker: Recent Projects*, Architects Gallery, Rome, 1978; *Transformations in Modern Architecture*, Museum of Modern Art, New York, 1979; *Tre Oci*, Venice, 1980. Recipient: Civic Trust Award, 1965 (twice), 1967, and 1968; *Architectural Design* Award, 1966, 1967, and 1968, and Grand Project Award, 1966; Industrial Architecture Award, *Financial Times*, 1969; Constrado Steel

Award, 1972; Housing Award, Department of the Environment, 1973 and 1977; Office of the Year Award, 1974; First Prize, Silver Jubilee Architectural Competition, London, 1976; Royal Institute of British Architects Awards (2), 1979; European Architectural Heritage Award, 1981. Addresses: Derek Walker Associates, The Old Rectory, Great Linford, Milton Keynes, Buckinghamshire MK14 5AX, England; 20 Golden Square, London W1R 3PA, England; Granada Building, Suite 30, South Lafayette Park, Los Angeles, California, U.S.A.

Works:

1964 Johnson House, North Rigton, Yorkshire
1965 Churnin House, Collingham, Yorkshire
  Holiday village, Scarborough, Yorkshire
  Templenewsam Urban Planning Development, Leeds, West Yorkshire
  Cayton Bay Holiday Village, Yorkshire
1966 Gould House, Leeds, West Yorkshire
  Village plan for Sherburn in Elmet, Yorkshire
  Housing Association, Park Place, Harrogate, Yorkshire
  Housing, Cheadle, Manchester
1967 Hollies Old People's Home, Leeds, West Yorkshire
  St. Benedict's Church, Garforth, near Leeds, West Yorkshire
  Serenson House, Liverpool
  Sacred Heart Church, Leeds, West Yorkshire
  Heckmondwike School, Yorkshire
1968 Ingledew Housing Association, Leeds, West Yorkshire
  VW Showroom System, United Kingdom
  Shaw Lane Housing, Leeds, West Yorkshire
  Pontefract Church, Yorkshire
  Doyle Dane Bernbach Advertising Agency, London
1969 Housing, Runcorn New Town, Cheshire
  Mental Villas, Royal Earlswood Hospital, Surrey
  WASS Car Showrooms and Maintenance Depot, Leeds, West Yorkshire
1970/
76 Milton Keynes, Buckinghamshire (as Chief Architect and Planner)—Central Area development; Central Area housing for 30,000 people; developments in existing towns, Cofferidge Close in Stony Stratford and Brunel Centre in Bletchley; village plans for Great Linford, Woughton, Woolstones, Broughton, Shenley Church End, Shenley Brook End, Loughton, Willen, Milton Keynes Village, Simpson, and Old Bradwell; infrastructure system; housing, Coffee Hall, Neath Hill, Fullers Slade, Bradville, Linford, Fishermead, Springfield, and Tinkers Bridge; industrial developments, Kiln Farm, Stacey Bushes, Bleak Hall, and Manor Farm; City Club, Central Milton Keynes; SBI System for Industry; Lanhall Private Housing; Canalside Private Housing; Scicon Computer Centre; Parks System; Grid Road Landscape Strategy
1977 City Club Mark III, Sculpture Park, Oldbrook Housing Structure Plan, and E1.2 Housing, Milton Keynes, Buckinghamshire
1978 Heelands 9 Housing, Milton Keynes, Buckinghamshire
  Housing and schools, Jubail, Saudi Arabia
  Plan for MIZDA Village Development, Libya
  Building system for Habitat, Milan
  VW Distribution Depot, Grimsby, Lincolnshire
  Whitney Museum Development, New York (with Foster Associates)
  Islamic Cultural Centre, Riyadh, Saudi Arabia

1979/
  81 Main Business Centre, Jubail, Saudi Arabia
1980/
  82 Residential Zone for 50,000 People, Jubail, Saudi Arabia
     Entertainment Module, Venice, Italy (project)
1981- Wonderworld Theme Park and related industries development, Corby, Northamptonshire
     Mosque, Jubail, Saudi Arabia
1982 District Planning Impact Study, Corby, Northamptonshire
     L'Oreal Headquarters, London
     Everards Brewery, Corby, Northamptonshire
     "Kop van Zuid," Rotterdam (project)
     Bus Station, Jubail, Saudi Arabia
     Shopping Centre, Jubail, Saudi Arabia
1982/
  83 Urban Planning Update, Jubail New City, Saudi Arabia
1983 Garden Centre, Corby, Northamptonshire
     D.R.S. Computer Centre, Milton Keynes, Buckinghamshire
     Leisure Development, Stockton Racecourse, County Durham (project)
     Leisure Development, Aintree Racecourse, Lancashire (project)
1984 Hotel, Milton Keynes, Buckinghamshire
     Stadium, Wonderworld Theme Park, Corby, Northamptonshire
     Entrance and Retail Complex, Wonderworld Theme Park, Corby, Northamptonshire
     Energy Building, Wonderworld Theme Park, Corby, Northamptonshire

Publications:

By WALKER: book—*Architecture and Planning of Milton Keynes*, London 1979; *Los Angeles—Architecture and Culture*, London and New York 1982; *British Architecture*, London 1983; articles—"System Building for Industry" in *Architectural Design* (London), October 1972; "Milton Keynes" in *Domus* (Milan), April 1973; "The Design Policy of Milton Keynes," special issue of *Architectural Design* (London), June 1973; "Central Area and Central Area Housing, Milton Keynes," special issue of *Architectural Design* (London), August 1974; "The Housing Dilemma" in *Architectural Association Quarterly* (London), no. 3, 1974; "The Social Planning of Milton Keynes" in *Architectural Association Quarterly* (London), no. 4, 1974; "Central Area of Milton Keynes" in *Domus* (Milan), December 1974; "The Emerging City," special issue of *Architectural Design* (London), December 1975; "Landscaping: Clipped and Unclipped" in *Architectural Design* (London), September 1976; "Aluminium in Building" in *RIBA Journal* (London), May 1977; "The Management and Politics of City Building" in *Industrialization Forum* (Montreal), October 1977; "Shopping Building, Milton Keynes" in *RIBA Journal* (London), May 1979; "Prince's Palace, Riyadh" in *Architectural Design* (London), April 1981; "Los Angeles" in two special issues of *Architectural Design* (London), nos. 11/12, 1981, and 3/4, 1982; "British Architecture," special issue of *Architectural Design* (London), no. 3/4, 1981; "Profile: Derek Walker" in *Architectural Design* (London), June 1982; "Animated Architecture" and "Wonderworld", in *Architectural Design* (London),

September 1982; "Modern Olympiad" in *Building Design* (London), 20 and 27 July 1984; "Los Angeles Olympics 1984" in *Architectural Review* (London), August 1984.

On WALKER: book—*Architecture in Britain* by Michael Webb, London 1968; articles—"A City of Villages" by David Rock in *The Built Environment* (London), October 1973; "A Celebration of Systems" in *Progressive Architecture* (New York), November 1973; "System Building for Industry" in *Techniques et Architecture* (Paris), February 1974; "Milton Keynes: The Beautiful City" by Robert Maxwell in *Architectural Association Quarterly* (London), vol. 6, 1974; "GRP Housing" in *Bauen und Wohnen* (Zürich), June 1975; "GRP—Those in Favour" by Alastair Best in *Design* (London), June 1975; "The Price of Street Appeal" by Alastair Best in *Design* (London), August 1975; "Milton Keynes: New Town in England" by Rene Elvin in *Architektur der DDR* (Berlin), December 1975; "Milton Keynes Factories" by John Winter in *Architects' Journal* (London), 22 and 27 December 1976; "Cofferidge Close, Stony Stratford" by Terence Farrell in *Architects' Journal* (London), 1 November 1978; "Whitney Museum of Art" in *Architectural Record* (New York), August 1979; "Whitney Museum, New York" in *Domus* (Milan), November 1979; "Whitney Art Museum" and "Mizda Village, Libya" in *Architectural Review* (London), January 1980; "Case Study—Milton Keynes" in *RIBA Journal* (London), June 1981; "Bradwell Abbey" in *Architecture d'Aujourd'hui* (Paris), June 1982; "Vier Ontwerpen voor Rotterdam-Zuid" in *Wonen-TA/BK* (Heerlen, Netherlands), December 1982;

Derek Walker: Wonderworld, Corby, Northamptonshire, 1981 (model).

"L'Oreal Headquarters, Kensington" in *Architectural Review* (London), February 1983; "Landscape Project, Park Futures" in *Architects' Journal* (London), December 1983.

An interest in design in all scales, furniture and component design to city and urban structuring, the inter-relationship of people and places, the manipulation of interior and exterior space.

A fascination for many years with leisure development has culminated in the Wonderworld project which combines entertainment and leisure facilities with a great deal of participatory and educational presentations on a thousand-acre site. The crucial interest for the practice has been its assimilation of new complementary skills, special effects, filmmaking, graphics, and leisure engineering.

More and more I see architecture as a response to personal initative and public demand. It is useless to sell outworn stylistic philosophies in the name of historic succession. Large-scale opportunity has freed me from the need to compromise within "house style" formality. My practice will always seek to express itself within a tradition of experiment and widening experience, with a particular emphasis on variety of approach, as each project develops its momentum by analysis of needs, site location, local tradition, client response, and personal curiosity.

I hope to remain internationally oriented with the realization that the shared experience in education, filmmaking, graphics, writing, and landscape can combine with one's major experience in architecture and planning to offer, particularly in schools of architecture and the confines of a "teaching" office, the kind of background in which the young architect and designer can flourish and develop.

—Derek Walker

Derek Walker is principally known as the chief architect and planner of Milton Keynes, Britain's newest, and possibly last, "New City," where, from 1970 to 1976, he directed the architectural and planning team assembled for the project.

Appointed chief architect at the age of thirty-eight, Walker was responsible for knitting the new city of 250,000 people into the existing rural structure of 22,000 acres of North Buckinghamshire. It was a challenge to which Walker responded with characteristic and infectious enthusiasm, assembling around him some of the brightest available people; indeed, for several years, his team became somthing of a Mecca for the most talented British graduate designers.

The work of the Milton Keynes group also became a prime focus of interest for those involved in architecture in its widest meaning. There was a vast array of projects, including housing for 10,000 newcomers a year, eleven village plans, the largest central area scheme in Europe, a parkland system of 5,000 acres, a new system for industrial building, a blueprint for infrastructure standards, as well as experimental, mass-produced, glass-reinforced plastic housing units, lightweight structure enclosures, a pop art City Club with electric-toy play-gardens, and romantic treelined walks through a central park with observation cone, water carpet, and water organ to be "played" by the inhabitants of the new-style City. The scheme encapsulated many of the lifestyle aspirations of the 1960s, but they were designed as serious contributions to a richer urban experience.

Walker, however, eventually found himself unable to involve himself fully in projects beyond the design stage, being simultaneously active as administrator, "salesman," and dismantler of bureaucracies. So, in 1976, he resigned from the Milton Keynes Development Board to re-establish his former practice, where he had previously achieved considerable success and a full mantle-shelf of architectural awards, with work ranging from large-scale planning solutions, housing, churches, community and commercial buildings, to major interiors and furniture design, all illustrating his obvious enjoyment of technique and the art of "putting the bits together." He has reformed the practice in the direction of his ideal vision—a design group that might be characterized as an amalgam of the practices of Eero Saarinen and Charles Eames (an "amalgam" because Saarinen never did enough graphics and Eames never did enough architecture); it is their inherent flexibility that Walker so much admires, and he is building a small team of twelve to fourteen designers drawn from many disciplines and able to work together effectively at many different levels.

In late 1978 a consortium was formed to act as consultants to the Italian multi-national group, Società Generale Immobiliare. Besides Walker, the group includes such internationally known figures as James Stirling, Richard Rogers, Frei Otto, Norman Foster, Renzo Piano, and Ove Arup and Partners. Walker's position as Consultant Representative and Vice-Chairman gives some indication of the importance he has achieved internationally and the respect that these associates have for them. Walker recognizes the Utopian optimism in the aspirations of the group, but he argues forcibly that, even if the group is unsupported by major commissions, it will at least achieve a regular dialogue between idea-makers that can only be helpful to the individuals and to their work.

Unlike most of his collaborators in the consortium—Foster, Stirling, Rogers *et al.*—Walker's personal stylistic enthusiasms are difficult to characterize. He insists that his only criteria is appropriateness and that he therefore refuses to adopt or even search for a "house style." In his commercial and industrial work he can be said to be nearest to his close friend Foster—with an interest in flexibility, clean detailing, and prototype solutions. But his domestic work achieves a character born out of a fascination, developed from his experiences at Milton Keynes, with the breakdown in scales necessary in the field of large-scale public housing.

Walker is a designer of liberal interests. Cautious of gratuitous architectural gestures in his own work, he refuses to post-intellectualize his buildings after the design process. He feels a pragmatic realism about the architect's responsibility to the user, an overwhelming optimism for the future, and a belief in the designer's ability to work effectively towards it.

—Tom Heneghan

WALLACE, David A.

American. Born in Chicago, Illinois, 30 August 1917. Educated at the University of Pennsylvania, Philadephia (Chandler Fellow; Paris Prize in Architecture, 1939), B.Arch. 1941, M.Arch. 1950; Harvard University Graduate School of Design, Cambridge, Massachusetts, M.City Planning 1950, Ph.D. in Planning 1953. Served in the United States Army Corps of Engineers, in the United States, England, France, Belgium, and Germany, 1941-46: Major. Married Joan Heatly Dulles in 1954; stepson: Robert. Supervising Planner, Chicago Housing Authority, 1950-51; Partner, Wallace and Schoenbrod, Chicago, 1950-53; Assistant Director, Marshall Field Foundation Study of Housing of Low-Income Groups, Chicago, 1951-53; Director of Planning and Development, Redevelopment Authority of the City of Philadelphia, 1953-57; Director, Planning Council of the Greater Baltimore Committee, 1957-61; Partner, with Ian L. McHarg, *q.v.*, William H. Roberts, and Thomas A. Todd, Wallace McHarg Roberts and Todd, Philadelphia, 1963-79. Since 1979, Partner, with Roberts, Todd, David C. Hamme, Richard W. Huffman, and Charles B. Tomlinson, Jr., Wallace Roberts and Todd, Philadelphia. Assistant Professor of Planning, University of Chicago, 1953. Professor of Planning, 1961-72, and since 1972 Adjunct Professor of Planning, University of Pennsylvania. Member, Board of Governors, American Institute of Planners. Recipient: Design Award, *Progressive Architecture*, 1973. Fellow, American Institute of Architects. Address: Wallace Roberts and Todd, 1737 Chestnut Street, Philadelphia, Pennsylvania 19103, U.S.A.

Works:

1959   Charles Center Master Plan, Baltimore
1964   Plan for the valleys of Baltimore County
1964- Inner Harbor and Municipal Center, Baltimore
1966   Plan for Lower Manhattan (with others)
1967   Landscape plan for Washington, D.C.
1968   Richmond Parkway, Staten Island, New York (project)
1969   Ecological study for Minneapolis-St. Paul
1970   Metro Center, Baltimore (project)
       Skippack Ecological Study, Montgomery County, Pennsylvania
1972   Plan for the center of Los Angeles
1973   Plan for Northwest Baltimore (with I. M. Pei and Partners)
       Regional transportation plan for Denver
1981   Downtown strategy plan, Norfolk, Virginia
1983   Master Plan for the United States Capitol, Washington, D.C.
1984   Liberty State Park Master Plan, Jersey City, New Jersey
       Mission Bay Master Plan, San Francisco

Publications:

By WALLACE: books—*The Future of Metro Center/Baltimore*, Baltimore 1969; *Metropolitan Open Space and Natural Process*, editor and co-author, Philadelphia 1970; articles—"The Relationship of Official and Citizen Planning Programs" in *Planning 1958* (American Society of Planning Officials), Chicago 1958; "Renaissance in Baltimore" in *Traffic Quarterly* (Westport, Connecticut), January 1960; "Renaissancemanship" in *Journal of the American Institute of Planners* (Washington, D.C.), August 1960; "Planning the City's Center," senior editor, in *Journal of the American Institute of Planners* (Washington, D.C.), February 1961; "Conceptualizing Urban Renewal" in *University of Toronto Law Journal*, vol. XVIII, no. 3, 1968; "Diary of a Plan," with William C. McDonnell, in *Journal of the American Institute of Planners* (Washington, D.C.), January 1971; "Urban Design as Science" in *Urban Design International* (Purchase, New York), November/December 1979; "Downtown Norfolk Redevelopment" in *Urban Design International* (Purchase, New York), January/February 1981.

On WALLACE: articles—"Health Care" in *Progressive Architecture*, (New York), February 1969; "Amelia Island, Florida" in *L'Architecture d'Aujourd'hui*, (Paris), October/November 1972; "Baltimore: An Abandoned Harbor . . ." in *Design and Environment*, (New York), Summer 1973; "Amelia Island" in *Architectural Design*, (London), January 1974; "All is Here at the Microcosmic Zoo-Park for Tehran" in *Landscape Architecture*, (Louisville, Kentucky), January 1974; "Planning for the Brave New World—Profile: Wallace, McHarg, Roberts and Todd" in *Progressive Architecture*, (New York), June 1974; "Tehran, Iran—Pardisan, an Environmental Park" in *Design and Urban Environment*, (New York), Winter 1975; "Master Plan for the Capitol Assigned" in *AIA Journal*, (Washington D.C.), July 1975; "Nigeria Plans its New Capital" in *Urban Design International*, (Purchase, New York), January/February 1980; "Mission Bay" in *Progressive Architecture* (New York), January 1984.

David Wallace: Baltimore Inner Harbor, 1964.

David A. Wallace is a founder and senior partner of WMRT (Wallace, McHarg, Roberts and Todd) and the successor firm Wallace, Roberts and Todd, a leading urban design and planning firm located in Philadelphia.

Wallace's most important early experience was as Supervising Planner for the Chicago Housing Authority, Director of Planning for the Philadelphia Redevelopment Authority, and then Staff Director of the Planning Council of the Greater Baltimore Committee, the latter a not-for-profit group that had a quasi-governmental character. These experiences gave him a thorough knowledge of the nature and workings of American city government and became the foundation of his work as a consultant urban designer and planner. In 1961, Wallace became Professor of Planning at the University of Pennsylvania, and he has been closely identified with that university ever since.

The early work of the firm followed naturally from Wallace's Baltimore experience: the Inner Harbor Plan for Baltimore and the Plan for the Valleys of Baltimore County. The Inner Harbor Plan has continued to occupy the firm up to the present time, and many of its proposals have now been realized. An outmoded pier area has been replaced by a public park, surrounded by office towers and housing Wallace, Roberts and Todd (WRT) has now done plans for cities all over the United States and some work overseas, specializing in downtown redevelopment and environmental analysis. The firm's work is characterized by its application of the planning philosophy identified with the University of Pennsylvania.

That philosophy involves "comprehensive planning," a theory devised to combat the short-sightedness found in many specific plans which focus too closely on an immediate problem. WRT likes to begin with an environmental analysis and, often,

with extensive social and demographic analyses, such as those used in their planning for the Denver Rapid Transit District. "Scientific rigor" is another principle long-pursued at the University of Pennsylvania, and, within the limits of the budgets for planning studies, at WRT, the difficulty is, of course, that planning requires predictions about human behaviour, and predicting human behaviour is not an area which scientific progress has been very marked.

Pursuit of comprehensiveness and science has not diminished the WRT's commitment to practical answers for immediate problems, and they continue to demonstrate a clear-headed awareness of both the usefulness and the limitations of city planning.

—Jonathan Barnett

WARCHAVCHIK, Gregori.

Brazilian. Born in Odessa, Russia, 2 April 1896; emigrated to Brazil, 1923: naturalized, 1930. Studied architecture at the University of Odessa; Reale Istituto Superiore di Belle Arti, Rome, Dip.Arch. 1920. Married Mina Klabin in 1927; children: Ilia Mauricio and Sonia. Worked in the office of Marcello Piacentini, Rome, 1920-23; in private practice, Sao Paulo, 1923-31, Rio de Janeiro (collaborating with Lúcio Costa), 1931-33, and Sao Paulo from 1934. Professor of Small Architectural Compositions, National School of Fine Arts, Rio de Janeiro, 1931. Member, CIAM (Congrès Internationaux d'Architecture Moderne), 1929-42. Exhibitions: Housing Congress Exhibition, Sao Paulo, 1931; Beaux-Arts Exhibition, Rio de Janeiro, 1931;

Salon of Tropical Architecture, Rio de Janeiro, 1933; Modern Art Exhibition of the Sociedade Pro-Arte Moderna, Sao Paulo, 1933; *Brazil Builds*, Museum of Modern Art, New York, 1943; *Bienal*, Sao Paulo, 1951, 1953, 1959, 1963; *Brazilian Architecture*, London, Copenhagen and Aarhus, 1957; *Warchavchik e la Introducao da Nova Arquitecture no Brasil*, Museo de Arte, Sao Paulo, 1965-66; *Gregori Warchavchik; Retrospective*, Museo de Arte, Sao Paulo, 1975. Recipient: Architecture Prize, *Correio da Manha*, Rio de Janeiro, 1965. *Died* (in Sao Paulo) *27 July 1972.*

Works:

1927/
28 Gregori Warchavchik House, Santa Cruz Street, Sao Paulo (altered, 1935)
1928/
29 Max Graf House, Mello Alves Street, Sao Paulo (destroyed)
1929 House, Avanhandava Street, Sao Paulo (destroyed)
    Joao Souza Lima House, Sao Paulo
    Candido da Silva House, Sao Paulo
    Public housing estate, Barao de Jaguara Street, Sao Paulo
    Studio for Two Artists (project)
1930 Middle-class housing estate, Dona Berta and Alfonso Celso Streets, Sao Paulo
    "Modernistic House," Itapolis Street, Sao Paulo
    Luiz da Silva Prado House, Bahia Street, Sao Paulo
    Studio for an Artist (project)
1931 Antonio da Silva Prado House, Estados Unidos Street, Sao Paulo (destroyed)

Medical Association Building interiors, Sao Paulo

Nordschild House, Toneleros Street, Rio de Janeiro (destroyed)

Harmonia Tennis Club House, Sao Paulo (project)

Guimaraes da Fonseca House, Sao Paulo (project)

Lincoln Nodari Apartment Building, Rio de Janeiro (project)

Bar and Restaurant, Copacabana, Rio de Janeiro (project)

1932 Manoel Dias Penthouse Apartment interiors, Rio de Janeiro

Rolim Goncalves House, Sao Paulo (project)

Alfredo Schwartz House, Rio de Janeiro (with Lúio Costa; destroyed)

Two houses for Mrs. Gallo, Rio de Janeiro

1933 Duarte Coelho House, Rio de Janeiro (destroyed)

Workers' housing estate, Gamboa, Rio de Janeiro

1938 Cia. de Melhoramentos Gopouva House, Sao Paulo (destroyed)

1939 Apartment building, Barao de Limeira Street, Sao Paulo

Praca de Republica Redevelopment, Sao Paulo (competition project)

Three rental houses, Avenida Europea, Sao Paulo

1940 Liuba Klabin House, Sao Paulo (since altered)

Town Hall, Sao Paulo (competition project; with Villanova Artigas)

1943 Rau Crespi House, Guaruja, Sao Paulo

1946 Mrs. Jorge Prado Beach Pavilion, Guaruja, Sao Paulo (since altered)

1949 Warchavchik Beach House, Guaruja, Sao Paulo

1950 Raquel Simonsen House, Alemanha Street, Sao Paulo

Crespi Farm House, Sao Paulo State (project)

1952 Renzo Palhari House, Alemnha Street, Sao Paulo

Paulistano Club Building, Sao Paulo

1953 Pinheiros Club Ballroom, Sao Paulo

1954 Cicero Prado Office Building, Avenida Rio Branco, Sao Paulo

Regatas Tiete Club Building, Sao Paulo

Publications:

By WARCHAVCHIK: articles—"Acerca de Arquitectura Moderna" [The 1925 Manifesto] in *Correio da Manha* (Rio de Janeiro), 1 November 1925, reprinted in *Tribuna da Imprensa* (Rio de Janeiro), 27/28 August 1960; "Architecture: Report on the 3rd CIAM Congress in Brussels 1930" in *Cahiers d'Art* (Paris), no. 2, 1931; "Arquitectura Viva" in *O Jornal* (Rio de Janeiro), 1 December 1931; introduction to *Architecture of Social Concern in Regions of Mild Climate* by Richard Neutra, Sao Paulo 1948; plus numerous other writings in the daily newspapers of Rio de Janeiro and Sao Paulo, 1925-61.

On WARCHAVCHIK: books—*Gli Elementi dell' Architettura Funzionale* by Alberto Sartoris, Milan 1931; *Brazil Builds* by Philip L. Goodwin, New York 1943; *Modern Architecture in Brazil* by Henrique Mindlin, Rio de Janeiro and Amsterdam, 1956; *The New Art in Brazil* by Pietro Maria Bardi, Milan 1956; *Arquitectura Contemporanea* by Udo Kultermann, Barcelona 1958; *Warchavchik e la Introducao da Nova Arquitectura no Brasil* by Gilberto Ferraz, Sao Paulo 1965 (includes complete list of Warchavchik's newspaper articles); *Gregori Warchavchik: Retrospective,* exhibition catalogue, Sao Paulo 1975; *Latin America in Its Architecture,* edited by Roberto Segre, New York and London 1981; articles— "L'Architecture Moderne au Brésil" by Pierre Louis Flouquet in *Chantiers* (Brussels), October 1947; "Habitations Individuelles au Brésil" in *L'Architecture d'Aujourd'hui* (Paris), June 1948; "Les Origines de l'Architecture Nouvelle à l'Amerique Latine" by Alberto Sartoris in *Architecture: Formes et Fonctions* (Lausanne), 1958; "La Nueva arquitectura Brasilena" by Alberto Sartoris in *Informes de la Construccion* (Madrid), no. 105, 1958.

*

Gregori Warchavchik was the great pioneer of modern architecture in Brazil. Born in Russia and trained in Italy, he arrived in Brazil in 1923 and settled in Sao Paulo where he became closely associated with a group of avant-garde intellectuals who had taken part in the "Modern Art Week" in 1922. Architecture had had no important representation at that seminal event, and it was only in 1925, with the publication of Warchavchik's manifesto "About Modern Architecture," that the issue of creating a new architecture suitable to the times was raised.

The first modernistic work built in Brazil was Warchavchik's own house in 1927/28. Seen today, it strikes one as a sober building of classicizing tendencies solved in a simplified Art-Deco vocabulary, with matching interiors. At the time, however, it provoked a turmoil, because the prevailing taste militated against so straightforward an architecture. One of the most interesting features of the house is the large covered veranda onto which the main rooms open at the rear. Although ill matched to the rest of the house (it is rather picturesque in appearance), it shows the architect's concern with the local climate.

During the 1930s, one-family houses predominanted in Warchavchik's professional practice. The "Modernistic House" of 1930 and the houses for Luiz da Silva Prado of 1930 and Antonio da Silva Prado of 1932 deserve being singled out for the mature handling of their cubistic volumes, enhanced by the use of very few architectural elements.

The "Modernistic House" has a unique place in the history of the development of modern Brazilian architecture. It was exhibited for a whole month, fully furnished and decorated, and during that time was visited by 30,000 people, and this fact, and the polemics the house provoked, helped to bring about a gradual change in public opinion. In Rio de Janeiro the same role was performed by Warchavchik's Nordschild House of 1931 and the Manoel Dias penthouse apartment, displayed in 1932.

The Antonio da Silva Prado house was, however, unquestionably the best project of the period. Outstanding for the daring cantilever of the roof over the front terrace and for the enormous hide-away sliding glass doors which connect the living room directly to the outside, it was much ahead of its time stylistically.

In 1940 Warchavchik took the second prize at a competition for the Sao Paulo Town Hall. It was one of the few large scale projects in his career, and its main interest was in the flexibility of the internal partitioning and in the careful reorganization of the urban space in which it was to be placed.

During the 1940s, Warchavchik's vocabulary, until then decidedly puristic, took a new look, fostered by its use of natural, raw materials. The Crespi House (1943), where the small site inspired the ingenious solution of lifting the bedroom wing on stilts and fitting the other rooms and a veranda underneath, and Mrs. Prado's thatched beach house (1946), both built in the sea-side resort of Guaruja, exemplify quite clearly this new tendency.

But at about this time, Brazilian architecture would take a course that was not foreseen in Warchavchik's work. In Rio de Janeiro a direct contact with Le Corbusier, coupled with a growing awareness of the country's cultural heritage, spurred by the recent creation of the Historical and Artistic Patrimony Protection Service, would result in a highly original indigenous movement, which flourished in the work of Lúcio Costa, Niemeyer, Reidy, Moreira, and the Roberto brothers, a movement that would become internationally renowned in the next twenty years. The main difference between this movement and Warchavchik's work is in the markedly national feeling of the movement and its creativeness, brought about by a freedom in the handling of the orthodox modern vocabulary.

Nevertheless, Warchavchik remains an important figure, as much for the articles he published to defend his principles as for his architectural work. And his brief stay as a teacher at the Architectural Department of the Beaux Arts School in Rio de Janeiro (1931), together with the work he was then erecting in Rio, had a profound influence on the first generation of modern Brazilian architects.

—Jorge Czajkowski

WARNECKE, John Carl.

American. Born in Oakland, California, 24 February 1919. Educated at Oakland High School, graduated 1937; Stanford University, California, 1937-41, B.Arch. (cum laude) 1941; Graduate School of Design, Harvard University, Cambridge, Massachusetts, under Walter Gropius, 1941-42, M.Arch. 1942. Children: John Carl Jr., Rodger, Margaret, and Frederick. Worked for Miller and Warnecke (father's firm), Oakland, California, 1945; Principal, John Carl Warnecke and Associates, San Francisco, 1946-58, and Warnecke and Warnecke, San Francisco, 1951-58. Since 1958, Chairman and Chief Executive Officer, John Carl Warnecke and Associates, San Francisco, New York, Washington, D.C., and Los Angeles. Member, National Commission on the Fine Arts, Washington, D.C., 1963-67. Recipient: Arnold Brunner Prize, National Institute of Arts and Letters, 1957. Associate, National Academy of Design, 1958; Fellow, American Institute of Architects, 1962. Address: John Carl Warnecke and Associates, 417 Montgomery Street, San Francisco, California 94104, U.S.A.

Works:

1956 American Embassy, Bangkok, Thailand (project)

1960/
68 Asilomar Hotel and Conference Grounds, Pacific Grove, California

1960/
69 Stanford University, California: University Bookstore and Post Office; J. Henry Meyer Undergraduate Library; Nathan Cummings Art Building; Roscoe Maples Athletic Pavilion; Student Residences

1962 Mabel McDowell Elementary School, Columbus, Indiana

1963 Nob Hill Condominium, San Francisco

1964/
69 Student residences, University of California, Berkeley

1965 Del Monte Regional Shopping Center, Monterey, California

1966 College of the Desert, Palm Desert, California
John F. Kennedy Memorial, Arlington Cemetery, Virginia

1967 Lafayette Square, Washington, D.C.: New Executive Office Building; United States Court of Claims Building; Townhouse renovation and Park

1969 Master plan for the California State Capitol, Sacramento
Hawaii State Capitol, Honolulu (with Belt, Lemmon and Lo)
Renwick Gallery restoration, Washington, D.C.

1970 Moffitt Library, University of California, Berkeley

Lauinger Library, Georgetown University, Washington, D.C.

Kaiser Center for Technology, Pleasanton, California

Residence Halls, University of Massachusetts, Amherst

Regency at Kahala Hotel, Honolulu

1971 Chinese Cultural Center/Holiday Inn Hotel, San Francisco

Hilton Hotel Tower, San Francisco

1972 Marco Polo Apartments, Honolulu

Pacific Telephone and Telegraph Equipment Building, stage I and II, Oakland, California

1972/
78 Neiman-Marcus Stores in Beverly Hills, California; Fort Worth, Texas; Newport Beach, California; Northbrook, Illinois; and St. Louis

1974 Bergdorf Goodman Store, White Plains, New York

New York Telephone Equipment Building, New York

The Pasadena Center, Pasadena, California

Rhode Island Hospital Trust National Bank Headquarters, Providence

United States Naval Academy, Annapolis, Maryland: Master Plan; Mickelson and Chauvenet Halls; Nimitz Library; and Rickover Engineering Building (with George M. Ewing Co.)

1976 Hewlett-Packard Microelectronics Plant, Santa Rosa, California

Student Residences, Georgetown University, Washington, D.C.

1977 American Telephone and Telegraph Co. Lines Headquarters, Bedminster, New Jersey

South Terminal, Logan International Airport, Boston

Breakers Row Apartments, Palm Beach, Florida

Aid Association for Lutherans Headquarters, Appleton, Wisconsin

Hennepin County Government Center, Minneapolis

Sun Co. Headquarters, Radnor, Pennsylvania

Trident Training Facility, Bangor, Washington (with Tracey-Brunstrom and George M. Ewing Co.)

Science Center, University of Richmond, Virginia

Neiman-Marcus Galleria, Washington, D.C.

State Compensation Insurance Fund Home Office Building, San Francisco

1978 Ventura County Government Center, Ventura, California (with Daniel L. Dworsky)

1979 George Washington University, Washington, D.C.

Ontario Civic Center, California

Federal National Mortgage Association Headquarters renovation, Washington, D.C.

1980 Brea Civic Cultural Center, California

1981 Village A Student Housing, Georgetown University, Washington, D.C.

1982 Large Animal Hospital, Tufts University, Boston, Massachusetts

Opera Plaza Condominiums, San Francisco

1983 San Jacinto Office Tower, Dallas, Texas

1984 Sports Arena, University of Nevada, Las Vegas

Trusthouse Forte/Westbury Hotel, New York

Trusthouse Forte/Alrae Hotel, New York

Publications:

By WARNECKE: article—"Another View of the History of a Campus", with Robert J. Evans, in *AIA Journal* (Washington, D.C.), February 1980.

On WARNECKE: book—*Architects on Architecture*, edited by Paul Heyer, London 1967; articles—"The Recent Work of John Carl Warnecke" in *Architectural Record* (New York), March 1960; "The Humanist Architecture of John Carl Warnecke" in *Architectural Forum* (New York), December 1960; "Those New Buildings on Lafayette Square" in *Architectural Record* (New York), April 1968; "Hawaii State Capitol: New Forms for the

John Carl Warnecke: United States Court of Claims Building, Washington, D.C., 1967.

Newest State" in *Architectural Record* (New York), May 1969; "The 1974 AIA Honor Awards: Seven New Buildings, Two Not So New" in *AIA Journal* (Washington, D.C.), May 1974; "John Carl Warnecke, Architect" in *Amerika Magazine* (Moscow), 1975; "Neiman-Marcus: Northbook" in *Interior Design* (New York), November 1976; "Impressive New Government Center Around a Grand Atrium" in *Architectural Record* (New York), March 1977; "Logan Airport: The New South Terminal" in *Architectural Record* (New York), September 1977; "The Aid Association for Lutherans" in *Architectural Record* (New York), February 1978; "Los Angeles Harbor Department Administrative Office Facility" in *Architectural Record* (New York), mid-August 1978; "Sun Company Inc." in *Interiors* (New York), February 1979; "Building Types Study 528: Three Office Buildings" in *Architectural Record* (New York), March 1979; "Trident Training Facility" in *Architectural Record* (New York), June 1979; "AT&T Long Lines Headquarters" in *Interior Design* (New York), November 1979; "The Fairfax Hotel" in *Architectural Digest* (Los Angeles), April 1980; "Small Is Beautiful" in *Interiors* (New York), July 1980; "Market Street, San Francisco" in *AIA Journal* (Washington, D.C.), August 1980; "Henle Students Village, Georgetown University" in *Baumeister* (Munich), November 1980; "Capitol Hill's New Colossus" in *Time* (New York), 17 January 1983; "The Kennedys at Lafayette Square" in *Progressive Architecture* (New York), January 1984.

The key to the firm's approach to each problem is its belief that the right solution will grow out of a sensitive, comprehensive understanding of each client. Every project is approached with a searching examination of the client's traditions, needs, and aspirations. The firm believes that each institutional or individual client has a spirit and style uniquely his own, and it is this spirit and style that the firm seeks to discover and express. The precisely right solutions vary greatly in physical form and appearance, depending as they do upon the unique combination of the client, his program, his budget, his site, and its environment.

The site and environment have a powerful influence on the design of each project. Every new project, whatever its size, is a part of a larger community. The project's total physical, social, and historical setting is the subject of careful study that precedes design.

The firm has been asked to work in some of the world's most beautiful natural environments where nature provides inspiration for design: the hills of San Francisco; California's Redwood Forests; the tropical beauty of Hawaii and Tahiti; the Great Plains of the Midwest; the deserts of Palm Springs and Saudi Arabia; the dramatic Navajo lands; the rich color of Cali, Colombia adjacent to the lush tropical Andes; and the canals and klongs of Bangkok. In these places the approach is to blend the buildings harmoniously into the surroundings—so it might be said that the structures are shaped in such a way that the setting is more beautiful than it was before.

The firm has been asked to design in places—equally beautiful—which were built by man over generations: the environs of the White House; historic Annapolis; the campuses of the University of California and Stanford University; old Monterey; the Royal Palace grounds of Honolulu; fashionable Nob Hill; a site adjacent to the Imperial Palace in Tokyo; and the historic residential area of Neuilly in Paris. In historic places such as these, the needs of the present must show respect for the past. Here, basic plans, new forms, masses, materials, colors, and textures are designed in sympathy with the place and its history. At the same time each element is planned to solve the problems of the present and to express the continuity that provides a link to the future as well as the past.

In other environments, such as busy commercial districts or the featureless patterns of unplanned suburbs, the setting has less influence on the designs. Here a structure is treated as an entity in itself. In the design of a big city hospital, an airport, an industrial plant, a suburban research center or a downtown office building, new types of buildings and twentieth-century architecture emerge to meet today's needs. Contemporary forms, structural systems and new functions make the strong statements needed to express the purpose, vigor, and significance of each client.

In other places we have created whole new environments—new communities, parks, college campuses, capitol complexes. Here, in projects of broad scope and scale, new ideas and images must be developed. In these places creative solutions to design give new character to the surrounding and evoke new moods, and establish new ways of life.

Another aspect of the firm's approach to design is best expressed by its diversity of experience. By working on all types of projects in the mainstream of contemporary life, the firm maintains the breadth and vitality essential to creative design. This diversity also provides an enlarged knowledge within the firm which can be used to deal with new problems or channeled into the specialized development and refinement of any particular project or building type. Although each design grows out of its unique program, site, and place in history, strong threads of continuity run through all the firm's work.

Finally, experience has proved that a complete integration of planning, architecture, engineering, landscape architecture, and interior design is necessary for excellence in design. The firm believes that there is basically one unified design profession rising above the separate design disciplines.

—John Carl Warnecke

John Carl Warnecke belongs to that generation of unstructured dissidents who in the late 1950s and 1960s searched for ways out of the minimalism to which modern architectural thought seemed to lead. Like others of that period, among them Harry Weese, Edward Durell Stone, Philip Johnson, and Paul Rudolph, Warnecke turned to traditional materials, the forms of exotic as well as classical architecture, and urban design configurations from Mediterranean cultures. Educated under Gropius at Harvard but also schooled in the firm of his Beaux-Arts-trained architect father, Warnecke talks in terms of buildings being good neighbors, both culturally and physically.

His design for the American Embassy in Thailand, the project that made his reputation but was never built, is an attempt to approximate traditional Thai architecture. It was to be raised on stilts over a manmade pool, colonnaded, flanked by a decorative screen balustrade, and topped by a floating pagodalike roof.

That design led to the Hawaian State Capitol commission, with its volcano-like silhouette, open to the sky in homage to a culture that has once worshipped the forces of weather and edged in emphatic ribbed patterns in recollection of the traditional wood construction.

Within his own culture, Warnecke's taste for non-Western sensibilities sometimes outstripped his good neighborliness. His elementary school in Columbus, Indiana, which he describes as reflecting "the character of South Indiana with its flat terrain accentuated by tall Victorian houses, barns and silos" strikes most visitors as bearing far more noticeable resemblance to a Japanese teahouse than to a mid-western farm.

Warnecke's penchant for decoration as well as place has led to a co-mingling of stylistic motifs on most projects. The famous Lafayette Square design, which found a way to save a row of nineteenth century houses and a historic park and still provide needed government offices, combines mansard roofs, bay windows, colonial brick (abeit in high-rise form), tracery and Saracen arches. Throughout his career Warnecke has shown preference for lower

tech materials (except for the most recent buildings such as the Aid to Lutherans Association Headquarters), inflected massing to minimize scale, and articulation of public space. Like others of his generation, he turned to Italy and Greece for direction. Fountains, arcades, colonnades, atriums, courtyards, paved piazzas and balconies are used in various interpretations in most of the important projects.

Although Warnecke's work can be criticized for less than fastidious proportions and historical details that can be as coy as convincing, his career has thrown the issues of context and non-monumentality into the public eye as effectively as anyone's. And especially during the early 1960s, when his friendship with President John F. Kennedy made him particularly visible, Warnecke gave an impetus to the preservation movement that has never been fully acknowledged.

As Warnecke's reputation grew, so did the firm, now numbering around two hundred people with permanent offices in four major American cities. The design approach has undergone a concomitant expansion but continues to emphasize blending new architecture with old, mitigating the impact of modern size and materials, and providing public gathering spaces.

—Nory Miller

WARREN, (Frederick) Miles.

New Zealander. Born in Christchurch, 10 May 1929. Educated at Christ's College, Christchurch (Soames Scholarship); University of Auckland School of Architecture, 1949-50 (Auckland University College Prize for Excellence in Architecture), Dip. Arch. 1951. Worked for the architects Cecil Wood, Christchurch, 1946-47, R. C. Munro, Christchurch, 1948, and W. H. Trengrove, Christchurch, 1951-52, and for the London County Council, England, 1953-54. In private practice, Christchurch, since 1955: in partnership with G. T. Lucas, 1956-57, and, with M. E. Mahoney, as Warren and Mahoney, since 1958. Member of the Council, New Zealand Institute of Architects, 1967-68. Chairman, New Zealand Architects Education and Registration Board, since 1976. Exhibition: New Zealand Institute of Architects Exhibition, C.S.A. Gallery, Christchurch, 1973. Recipient: Gold Medal, 1960, 1964, 1969, and Silver Medal, 1969, 1973, 1979, New Zealand Institute of Architects; Pan Pacific Architectural Citation, 1966. Fellow, New Zealand Institute of Architects, 1965. C.B.E. (Commander, Order of the British Empire), 1974; K.B.E. (Knight, Order of the British Empire), 1985. Address: Warren and Mahoney, Post Office Box 1527, Christchurch, New Zealand.

Works:

1958 Flats, Dorset Street, Christchurch
     South Island Dental Nurses Training School, Christchurch
     Karitane Hospital, Christchurch
1959 J. Ballantyne and Company Department Store, Christchurch
     Haywrights Riccarton Department Store, Christchurch
1960 Hall of Residence, Christchurch College Laboratories, Christ's College, Christchurch
1961 Wool Exchange, Christchurch
     Christchurch Memorial Garden Crematorium
1962 Student Union and Ngaio Marsh Theatre, Canterbury University, Christchurch
1963 Student Union, Auckland University
1964 Student Union, Massey University, New Zealand

Miles Warren: Saint Patrick's Church, Napier, New Zealand, 1983-84.

British Secondary Boarding School, Port Vila, New Hebrides
Wool Exchange, Dunedin, New Zealand
Warren and Mahoney Office and House, Christchurch
1965 Christchurch Town Hall and Civic Centre
Government House, Honiara, Solomon Islands
Condominium Government Office, Port Vila, New Hebrides
British Primary School, Port Vila, New Hebrides
Lenakel Hospital, Tanna, New Hebrides
Mendana Hotel, Honiara, Solomon Islands
1966 Burns Philp Ltd. Department Store, New Hebrides
S.I.M.U. Office Building, Christchurch
Haywrights Department Store, Ashburton, New Zealand
1967 Canterbury Frozen Meat Company Offices, Christchurch
International Importing Company Offices, Christchurch
1968 Thorngate (office building), Christchurch
Northlands Shopping Centre, Christchurch

1969 North Canterbury Catchment Board Offices, Christchurch
Guardian Royal Exchange Building, Christchurch
British Service Base Hospital, Vila, New Hebrides
Maidment Theatre, Auckland
Medbury Preparatory School, Christchurch
1970 Library, Christ's College, Christchurch
Travelodge Hotel, Queenstown, New Zealand
Haywrights Department Store, Christchurch
Frankton Arms Hotel, Queenstown, New Zealand
Wendover Maternity Hospital, Christchurch
1972 A.E.Q. Office Building, Christchurch
Williams City Centre, Wellington
Maheno Tavern, Oamaru, New Zealand
Brydone Hotel, Oamaru, New Zealand
S.I.M.U. Office Building, Timaru, New Zealand
Avon Broadcasting Company Office Building, Christchurch
Woolshed Restaurant, Wellington
Terrace House (office building), Christchurch
1973 City Library, Timaru, New Zealand

Dominion Mutual Securities Building, Christchurch
Colonial Mutual Life Insurance Building, Christchurch
Burma Motor Lodge, Wellington
Assembly Hall, Medbury Boys School, Christchurch
Gloucester Street Shopping Arcade, Christchurch
ICI Office Building, Christchurch
1974 Sports Hall, Christ's College, Christchurch
Gymnasium and Laboratories, Rangi Ruru Girls School, Christchurch
St. Peter and Paul Primary School, Lower Hutt, New Zealand
Atkinson and Forbes Car Park and Shops, Christchurch
Haywrights Sydenham Supermarket, Christchurch
S. R. Halliwell Office Building, Christchurch
Leisure Lodge Motor Inn, Nelson, New Zealand
Transport House Offices, Christchurch
1974/
79 Chancery, New Zealand Embassy, Washington, D.C.
1975 S.I.M.U. Office Building, Dunedin, New Zealand
Leisure Lodge Motor Inn, Dunedin, New Zealand
Roman Catholic Cathedral restoration, Christchurch
1976 Radio New Zealand Office Building, Christchurch
Latimer View House (office building), Christchurch
Feltex House (office building), Auckland
1977 Haywrights Ltd. Shopping Mall, Christchurch
1978 Shopping Arcade, Greenwood Estate, Christchurch
New Zealand Army Memorial Museum, Waiouru, New Zealand
New Zealand Refrigeration Nominees Office Building, Christchurch
Allied Properties Office Building, Auckland
House restoration, Governors Bay, New Zealand
1979 National Mutual Life Association Office Building, Christchurch
Canterbury Library, Christchurch
1980 Ashton House, Wellington
Boarding House refurbishment, Christ's College, Christchurch
Fletcher Challenge Head Office, Lambton Quay, Wellington
Regent Theatre, Christchurch
AL349own Hall, Wellington
1981 Canterbury Centre, Christchurch
College House Teaching Block, Christchurch
Oaks Shopping Centre, Wellington
New Printing Hall, Christchurch Press Company, Christchurch
Southern Cross Hotel refurbishment, Dunedin, New Zealand
Community and Arts Centre, Tauranga, New Zealand
Triangle Centre, Christchurch
City Administration Building, Waitemata, New Zealand
Wellington Show Association Building, Wellington
Wesley Trust Retail Development, Wellington
1982 A. A. Mutual Building, Wellington
Northern United Building, Wellington
Radford Retail Complex, Wellington
Civic Administration Building, Rotorua, New Zealand
Union House, Auckland
Collegiate Auditorium, Wanganui, New Zealand
1983 Academy Hotel refurbishment, Wellington
Coster House, Canterbury, New Zealand

Easterbrook Apartments, Christchurch
Levin Theatre, Levin, New Zealand
Marlborough Theatre, Blenheim, New Zealand
Millwood House, Wellington, New Zealand
N.Z.I.G. New Building, Wellington
St. Patricks's Church, Napier, New Zealand
Kaiwaka Point Housing, Taupo, New Zealand
1984 A.E.Q. Flats, Christchurch
Burdon House, Nelson, New Zealand
Charles House, Canterbury, New Zealand
Art Department, Christ's College, Christchurch
Wigram Park Housing Development, Christchurch
National Insurance House, Wellington
Davis House, Christchurch
D.I.C. Development, Wellington
Ferguson House, Bay of Islands, New Zealand
Gunn House, Nelson, New Zealand
Holy Trinity Church alterations, Nelson, New Zealand
A. Jensen Factory, Christchurch
Cathedral re-ordering, Nelson, New Zealand
New Ward, Nurse Maud Hospital, Christchurch
St. Bernadette's New Church Building, Christchurch
Chapel, St. Margaret's College, Christchurch
Drama Room, St. Margaret's College, Christchurch

Publications:

By WARREN: articles—"Style in New Zealand Architecture" in *New Zealand Architect* (Wellington), no. 3, 1979; " . . . . in decent obscurity" in *Home and Building* (Auckland), no. 5, 1979.

On WARREN: articles—in *Architectural Review* (London), October 1959; "Three Christchurch Office Buildings by Warren and Mahoney" in *New Zealand Institute of Architects Journal* (Wellington), September 1972; "Ownership Flats for Williams Development Holdings Ltd." in *New Zealand Institute of Architects Journal* (Wellington), April 1975; "Coringa Country Club" in *New Zealand Architect* (Wellington), February 1978; "Feltex Centre, Symonds Street, Auckland" in *Home and Building* (Auckland), vol. 40, no. 5, 1978; "The Waioury Memorial Army Museum Appraisal" by Ross Brown in *New Zealand Architect* (Wellington), no. 3, 1979; "New Zealand Chancellery" in *Home and Building* (Auckland), no. 5, 1979; "The Well-Mannered Embassy" by Wolfgang Eckhardt in *New Zealand Architect* (Wellington), no. 5, 1979; "New Zealand Embassy Carries on Washington's Diplomatic Building Boom" in *Architectural Record* (New York), January 1980; "A Mini Palace—65 Cambridge Terrace" in *Home and Building* (Auckland), no. 5, 1980; "Warren Flat" in *New Zealand Architect* (Wellington), no. 5, 1980.

*

Miles Warren is a distinguished, compulsive designer who really enjoys his profession. His buildings, from a highly productive office, are dotted all around his home city of Christchurch and appear up and down New Zealand, even extending as far as the Pacific Islands and Washington, D.C.

His work includes government, university and office buildings; hospitals, theatres and auditoriums; commercial, retail and sports buildings; banks, hotels and restaurants; religious buildings, restorations, flats and "one off" houses for special clients. In all this variety and development, Miles Warren has produced two outstanding works: the Christchurch Town Hall and Civic Centre, and his own office-town house. Both are designed from a clear rational basis, with spaces sensitively and scientifically organized, and are a vivid indictment of all those who think that modern architecture is dead. The Christchurch Town Hall and Civic Centre was a triumph for Warren and Mahoney, as it was also for Dr. Harold Marshall who pioneered the control of lateral reflections of sound in the auditorium. Scientifically, it was a first in the world, and a major breakthrough in the history of architecture in New Zealand. To savour a symphony concert in this Christchurch auditorium – in all its richness of colour, reverberance and symbolic reference – is to enjoy the finest musical auditorium in the country. The space has a strong, silent classical discipline, but surprisingly a rich overlay of Romanticism as well. And it is the creative combination of romantic place-making and the scientific creation of a machine for making enveloping music in that gives this auditorium its reverberant realism and its exciting fantasy. With all its nuances of suggestion and symbol, the Christchurch auditorium cannot be understood by reason alone. In this design, Warren stood alone – and he wore New Zealand's classically modern crown with good reason. It was perhaps his one true moment of international glory.

Architecture for Miles Warren is the delight and pleasure of making things well. It is the craft of good workmanship—a minor science and technique. At the same time he is hard-headed enough to realize that though architecture occasionally becomes high art, such work has to be subsidized by more standard and repetitive projects.

Historically Miles Warren is the product of the last stages of the art and crafts free school tradition in New Zealand. Trained by Cecil Wood, Miles Warren experienced early in his career the craft of the architect at work. The great merit of this system was the value it placed upon the all-embracing approach to design: everything was seen to matter. Even draughtmanship was worthy of attention. This love of drawing is still there in Miles Warren, and he has the confidence and skill to draw in front of his clients. In this way he seeks out their needs and inspires their confidence.

Warren supplemented the last stages of his arts and crafts training with full-time study at the Auckland School of Architecture when it was under the influence of the "Group" architects. His post-graduate years were spent working on Roehampton and travelling in Europe, where he came under the influence of Le Corbusier's *beton brut* and the Italian formalists. Returning to New Zealand in the mid-1950s, he worked these Brutalist influences out in concrete at Christchurch College, which won him a gold medal.

More recently his work has developed in response to the ever-increasing opportunities available to New Zealand's top architect. Despite added pressure, he still creates work that seems remarkably fresh and invigorating, at a time when the architectural profession throughout the world has been in general losing confidence. Perhaps Miles Warren's secret lies in his ability to gain creative revitalization from constantly building a new house for himself and living in his own architecture. Currently his romanticism is served by restoring a colonial country retreat in the foothills of the Banks Peninsula, where he indulges his two passions – art and gardening.

Miles Warren is totally committed to his profession and to the pursuit of excellence. He believes that order is better than chaos, creation better than destruction, gracefulness and forgiveness better than violence and vendetta.

—Russell Walden

WATANABE, Youji.

Japanese. Born in Naoetsu City, 14 June 1923. Educated at the High School of Arts and Crafts, Takada, 1936-41; Assistant to Professor Takamasa Yosizaka at the Architectural Institute of Waseda University, Tokyo, 1955-58; qualified as an architect, 1957; special postgraduate student of city planning at Waseda University, 1969-73. Served in the Japanese Marine Corps, 1944-45: 2nd Lieutenant. Worked for the Nippon Stainless Steel Manufacturing Company, Tokyo and Naoetsu, 1941-47, and in Dr. Kume's Architectural Office, Tokyo, 1947-55. In private practice, Tokyo, 1958 until his death in 1983. Lecturer in Architecture, Waseda University, since 1964; Visiting Lecturer, Montana State University, Bozeman, and the University of Auckland, New Zealand, 1983. Exhibitions: *VIII Salone Internazionale della Industializzazione Edilizia*, Bologna, 1972; Centre Georges Pompidou, Paris, 1976; *CAYC Travelling Exhibition*, Argentina, 1977; Centro Edile Library, Milan, 1977; Museum of Modern Art, New York, 1978. *Died* (in Tokyo) *2 November 1983.*

Works:

1949 Reinforced concrete apartment houses (competition project)
1950 Fujisawa City Hall, Japan
Grave of the Unknown Soldier (competition project)
Restaurant, Yokohama/Kaikan Building Yokohama (with Dr. Kume's Office)
1952 Hamamatsu City Hall, Japan (with Dr. Kume's Office)
Tenrikyo Hall, Tokyo (competition project)
1953 Shimbashi Branch of the Daiwa Bank, Tokyo (with Dr. Kume's Office)
Makino House, Tokyo (with Dr. Kume's Office)
1954 Shibuya Toei Theatre, Tokyo (with Dr. Kume's Office)
Cultural Center for Aichi Prefecture (competition project)
Cultural Center for Shizuoka Prefecture (competition project)
National Diet Library (competition project)
1955 Asai House, Tokyo (with Dr. Kume's Office)
Town Hall, Takaoka, Japan (with Dr. Kume's Office)
1956 Ryumon Book Warehouse, Nara, Japan
Monument of the 2000th Anniversary of the Birth of Buddha, India (competition project)
City Hall, Nagasaki (competition project)
1958 Osawa Fishing House, Chichibu-Tama National Park, Japan
Niigata Hospital of Labor Office, Naoetsu, Japan
House with store (competition project)
1959 Kagoshima Office and House, Niigata, Japan
Hatonosu Youth Hostel, Chichibu-Tama National Park, Japan
Konishi Building, Tokyo
1960 Otaba Fishing House, Chichibu-Tama National Park, Japan
1961 Miyama Heights (rest house), Chichibu-Tama National Park, Japan
Youji Watanabe Office Building, Tokyo
Zendoji (temple), Itoigawa, Japan
1962 Miyakozushi Restaurant, Tokyo
Yamazaki House ("Tategarami"), Tokyo
1963 Japanese National Theatre (competition project)
International Conference Hall, Kyoto (competition project)
1964 Monden Villa, Fuji, Japan
Minoda House ("Igeta"), Tokyo
Allegheny Public Square, Pittsburgh, Pennsylvania (competition project)
Master plan for Naniwa University of the Arts, Japan (competition project)
Single-family houses (3), Hollywood, California (competition project)

Youji Watanabe; Sky Building no. 3, Tokyo, 1970.

Shijo Ohashi Bridge Kyoto (competition project)
1965 Plan for the development of tourism in Nippon-Land (competition project)
Exhibition Hall, Japan Architecture Center, Tokyo (competition project)
Fune Teahouse, Tokyo
1966 Takagi House, Isogo, Japan
Miyata House, Tokyo
Shinozaki House, Matsudo, Japan
Yotsuya Station, Japan National Railways (competition project)
The Farmhouse (competition project)
1967 Head Office Building, *Expo '70*, Osaka (competition project)
High-rise Apartment Buildings in Steel (competition project)
Hokkaido Memorial Tower, Japan (competition project)
Sanwa Building, Tokyo
Iwakata House, Naoetsu, Japan
1968 Nishida House, Tokyo
Sky Building No. 2, Tokyo
Ishida House, Tokyo
Dr. Minezaki House ("Dragon Fort"), Ito, Japan
Pavilion, *Expo '70*, Osaka (competition project)
1969 Japanese Supreme Court (competition project)
1970 Sky Building No. 3, Tokyo
Meiwa Building, Tokyo
International Tourism Center, Hakone, Japan (competition project)
1971 Habitat '70 (project)
Sky Building No. 5, Tokyo
W-H Concrete Prefab (project)
Opera House, Belgrade, Yugoslavia (competition project)
Centre Beaubourg, Paris (competition project)
National Headquarters for TANU, Tanzania (competition project)
1972 Community Plaza (competition project)
Kamoshida Building, Tokyo
Yamazaki House ("Site in Air"), Tokyo
1973 Kuramae Tower Building, Tokyo
Daisho Building, Tokyo
Housing, Komyoike-Senboku New Town, Japan (competition project)
1974 Public Housing, Damascus, Syria (competition project)
1975 Tanaka House, Naoetsu, Japan
Polto Santo Island (competition project)
Urban Environment of Developing Countries, centering on Manila (competition project)
1976 U.A.E. Development Bank International Hotel (competition project)
Dr. Minezaki Clinic, Tokyo
1977/
78 Pahlavi National Library, Tehran (competition project)
Center and Shops for Little New Town, Shizuoka, Japan
1978 Nago City Hall, Okinawa (competition project)
1979 Islamic Cultural Centre, Madrid (competition project)
1980 New Architectural Institute of Japan Building, Tokyo (competition project)
Hi-No-Maru Building, Tokyo (project)
1981 Tokyo Building (project)
1982 Mito City Housing, Japan (competition project)
The Peak Development, Hong Kong (competition project)
1983 Opera de a Bastille Development, Paris (competition project)

Publications:

By WATANABE: books—*Approach to Architecture*, Tokyo 1974; articles—"An Argument on Architectural Offices" in *Kenchiku-bunka* (Tokyo), May 1956; "Religious Architecture and Glass" in *Glass* (Tokyo), August 1962; "The Interior Without Upholstery"in *Kenchiku-chishiki* (Tokyo), November 1964; "Zendoji Temple of Shunanzan" in *Kenchiku-chishiki* (Tokyo), December 1964; "Miscellaneous Thoughts on the Architecture of South America" in *Kenchiku-techo* (Tokyo), March 1969; "The Architectural Competition for the Supreme Court" in *Shinkenchiku* (Tokyo), April 1969; "An Account of a Trip to Iceland" in *Kenchiku-kai* (Tokyo), June 1969; "Opinion to the Supreme Court" in *Kentiku* (Tokyo), June 1969; "History and Race in Architecture Impressions of Latin America" in *Densetsu Guide* (Tokyo), no. 41, 1970; "Sky Building No. 3/HABITAT '70" in *The Japan Architect* (Tokyo), October 1970, "Industrialization of the Japanese House" in *Technical Japan* (Tokyo), no. 2, 1971; "Residence Tategarami" in *Kentiku* (Tokyo), November 1971; "My Heretical Architecture" in *Shitsuanai* (Tokyo), November 1971; "W-H Concrete Prefab" in *Kenchiku-kai* (Tokyo), January 1972; "Campus Layout" in *Waseda University News* (Tokyo), June 1972; "Housing of Tomorrow—More Pilotis" in *Kanna* (Tokyo), no. 56, 1972; "At the Invitation of SAIE '72" in *Journal of Architecture* (Tokyo), January 1973; "'See,' 'Know,' 'Comprehend:' Architecture of Europe" in *Kenchiku-kai* (Tokyo), January 1973; "My View of Architecture" in *Contemporary Architects of Japan*, volume 23, Tokyo 1974; "My Education in Architecture" in *Journal of Architecture* (Tokyo), April 1976.

On WATANABE: books—*Modern Movements in Architecture* by Charles Jencks, New York 1973, Tokyo 1976; *Contemporary Architects of Japan*, volume 23, Tokyo 1974; *Contemporary Architecture of the World*, Tokyo 1982; *Fifty Outstanding Architects of the World* by Ivica Mladjenovic, Belgrade, Yugoslavia 1983; articles—"Some Thoughts on the Dragon Fort" by Takamasa Yosizaka in *Shinkenchiku* (Tokyo), April 1969, and in *The Japan Architect* (Tokyo), June 1969; "Architechnics" in *Architecture Plus* (New York), May/June 1974; "Heretical Architecture of Y. Watanabe" in *The Asahi* (Tokyo), 11 September 1974; "It's a Building" in *International Herald Tribune* (Paris), 25 September 1974; "Paradoxical Solid of Isozaki" by Charles Jencks in *Shinkenchiku* (Tokyo), January 1975.

Commentary on my project HABITAT PLAN
1. Argument against the existing conception of "facing south," the "East-West Axis (Latitude)" in architecture. It is a "South-North Axis (Longitude)" project. (Connection with the universe, the earth, plants and human beings is the starting point of this idea.)
2. Desire to produce and industrialize architecture and experiment with iron architecture.
3. Announcement of the argument against the contemporary world which is mainly occupied by researchers, like civil engineers who do not understand the arts, the city planners.
4. An experiment which is a transcendental condition and "art" without allowing variations to human beings, the city and life by industrialization.

Basis of the HABITAT PLAN
A. 1) Sun. 2) View. 3) Equality for all, and infinity in privacy.
B. 1) Whether or not to include streets and transportation in the city. 2) If the city is altered, the existing method of redeveloping a city will not be used. First of all, streets will be constructed for transportation; after that, buildings around the street will be taken away to create public plazas and schools—it's an opposite view that streets and house lots should be changed to buildings and plazas.

Advantages and defects of my plan, in the event of the alteration of Tokyo
1) In that case, a window or a balcony with a width of two metres, facing south, will be installed per person: the same number of people will be accommodated in only one-half to one-third of existing residential quarters.
2) Surplus residential quarters will be changed to park and public establishments: the area of each establishment will be definite, accordingly the city will be operated smoothly and will be habitable.
3) Transportation will be by pilotis methods; accordingly, there will be no difficulty in commuting and traffic jams will be dissolved.
It is, however, still doubtful whether the conditions mentioned above will be essential or possible, and the HABITAT PLAN may be an experiment in irrationality: the result may be realizations as in Sky Building No. 3.

—Youji Watanabe (1980)

Youji Watanabe (not to be confused with Toyokazu Watanabe, that other architectural controversialist in Osaka) had the tendency, once having established the metaphor by which a particular building is to be known, to court that metaphor to the very end. Having got hold of some legitimate analogy by which to approach a project, he followed it right through and out the other side—beginning on one side in the cool lucid dawn of rationalism, he ended up in the steamy dusk of the irrational and the spooky.

In all our thinking we are guided by models and archetypes, metaphors that allow our individual concepts to come together—"The Tree of Life," "The Pyramid of Power," "The Scales of Justice." Through exaggeration and caricature he mocked these deep-seated correspondences. The image of a house-as-a-bus that haunted the prefabrication boffins for a long while he appropriated for his Sky Building No. 3, and the metaphor is somehow left dangling before us while all else has vanished. The image of architecture as lithe and supple, as a bird, as in Saarinen's TWA Terminal in New York—Watanabe pricked its pretensions by making an apartment block in the semblence of a penguin. He took on similar imagery in the Dragon Fort in Ito, a house and clinic for a pediatrician, Dr. Minezaki: initially the house was to resemble the bridge of a battleship, but the plan was later modified to suggest the coiled body of a great dragon. "Children usually dislike doctors, but this house has become a playground for them because of the rising vehicular approach, the rotating turntable in the entrance and the limitless appeal of the spiralling shape."

Architecture need not necessarily be a cage, a lost tract, a suicide machine, a monster of brilliant and erudite torture let loose on man. It need not ride roughshod over man, that abstract and negligible entity. Architecture need not be that thing that architects have recourse to in the same way that alcoholics have recourse to drink. It need not be a cast-off fancy dress, a box of obsolete gadgets, a clockwork toy with the key missing. Watanabe has shown us that in some buildings we can feel our perceptions heightened, as though we had just sprouted antennae. He demonstrated that the "instant of the world" that the architect builds need not necessarily threaten, that it can equally calm and soothe to such an extent that a building can even come out to us, flowing, throbbing, beating up against us both from without and within. The voice we hear in architecture need not necessarily be that of the architect's but can be the unification of all aspirations.

—Chris Fawcett

WEARDEN, Clifford.

British. Born in Preston, Lancashire, 15 August 1920. Educated at Preston Grammar School, 1932-37; University of Liverpool, School of Architecture, 1938-40, 1946-48, B.Arch. (honours) 1948, and Department of Civic Design, 1948-49, Dip. Civic Design 1949. Served as a Pilot in the Fleet Air Arm of the Royal Navy, 1940-46; Lieutenant, Royal Naval Volunteer Reserve. Married Elsie Sherman in 1953; Pauline Noel Tinsley in 1969; children: Amanda, Sarah and Charlotte. Assistant Architect, Lipson and Kaad, Sydney, 1945, York and Sawyer, New York, 1946-47, and George Grenfell Baines Group, Preston, 1947; Architect/Planner, Architekt Wilhelm, Zug, Switzerland, 1948; Project Architect, Sir Basil Spence and Partners, London, 1949-54, and Trehearne and Norman Preston and Partners, London, 1954-55. Principal, Clifford Wearden and Associates, architects/town planning consultants/designers, London, 1955 until he retired, 1981. Member of the Council of the Architects Registration Council, since 1966. Exhibitions: *Summer Exhibition,* Royal Academy, London, 1963, 1971; *National Federation of Housing Societies Exhibition,* Royal Institute of British Architects, London 1971; *Jubilee Exhibition,* Architectural Association, London, 1977; *Transformations in Modern Architecture,* Museum of Modern Art, New York, 1979. Member, Society of Industrial Artists and Designers, 1969. Address: 29 Kingsley Place, London N6 5EA, England.

Works:

1950 Ecclesfield Colley Secondary Modern School, Sheffield (with Sir Basil Spence and Partners)
1952 Coventry Cathedral ruins preservation (with Sir Basil Spence and Partners)
1953 Noonamena House, Onslow Road, Burwood Park, Weybridge, Surrey
1958 Service House, Inchmery, Exbury Estate, Hampshire
1960 Banqueting Hall, Carpenters Hall, London Wall, London E.C.2 (with H. Austen Hall)
1961 Interiors of directors' offices, Watney House, Palace Street, London S.W.1
1963 Pepler House (apartment block), Wornington Road, London W.10 (with Peter Deakins)
1964 Ferndene (cluster housing complex), 123 Slough Lane, Kingsbury, London N.W.9 (with Peter Deakins)
1965 Office interiors, 17 Lansdowne Road, Croydon, Surrey (with Malcolm Wildsmith)
1967 National Westminster Bank, 43 Kingsway, London W.C.2
1968 Lancaster West Urban Village Master Plan, London W.11 (with Malcolm Wildsmith, Peter Simpson and Derek Latham)
1970 Lancaster West Urban Village, stage I, London W.11 (with Ken Price and Nigel Whitbread)
1972 *Readers Digest* Service Department, Ply-mouth, Devon (project; with Ken Price and John Chatwin)
1974 Director's Office, Royal Botanic Gardens, Kew, London (project; with Simon Bensasson)
1977 Public Cleansing and Social Services Departments Sub-Depot, Kensington and Chelsea Borough Council, Barandon Road, London W.11 (with Siu Wing Kwok)
1978 Office extension, 24 Lisson Grove, London N.W.1.

Publications:

On WEARDEN: books—*Architecture in Britain Today* by Michael Webb, London 1969; *Dwelling Houses* by Giampiero Aloi, Milan 1970; *Guide to Modern Buildings in London* by Charles McKean and Tom Jestico, London 1976; articles—"Comprehensive Redevelopment, Kensington" in *Architectural Review* (London), January 1966; "Housing, Kensington, London" in *Architect and Building News* (London), 7 September 1966; "Housing, Kingsbury, London" in *Architectural Review* (London), November 1966; "Housing" in *Architects' Journal* (London), 16 November 1966; "Group d'Immeubles à Kingsbury, Londres" in *L'Architecture d'Aujourd'hui* (Paris), February/March 1967; "Double-Decked Village" in *Architectural Forum*

Clifford Wearden: Ferndene Housing Development, Kingsbury, London, 1964.

(New York), April 1967; "Hausgruppe in Kingsbury, London" in *Baumeister* (Munich), May 1967; "Hausgruppe in Kingsbury, London" in *Bauwelt* (Berlin), 24 July 1967; "Statt Stadtteilnurteilsanierung" in *Baumeister* (Munich), December 1970; "Models of Integration 1: Housing Group in Slough Lane, Kingsbury" by Horst Klement and Peter Rumpf in *Bauwelt* (Berlin), 6 May 1974.

For as long as I can remember, I have had a compelling desire to be totally involved with the design and construction of buildings, their interiors and the space between. This force has directed my life's pursuit, but although I have practised architecture and its allied disciplines now for more than thirty years, I am as much at a loss as ever to comprehend why it dominates my life, although I am aware that many others share this compulsion in varying degrees and directions.

I believe it is the existence of this force that makes it difficult for most creative people to explain their aims, and I have found the process of self-analysis involved in preparing this statement a very valuable experience.

During the total creative process I try to involve my clients as much as possible to ensure that their needs and values are fully appreciated and put into effect. The process usually starts with a series of informal discussions, and in this build-up of the brief I encourage thinking in terms of actual needs rather than preconceived images of solutions.

I consider it dangerous to resort to realistic shapes and forms too early in the design process, and I prefer to make only diagrammatic studies until I am satisfied that the brief has been properly formulated, the broad-based research completed, and a hierarchy of values evolved.

Through the years I have employed increasingly more sophisticated methods of working as new techniques—such as network analysis and cost planning—have been devised.

I make use of scale models to assist in the design process and, wherever necessary, full-size mockups of complex structural details and full-size samples to agree such things as texture and colour.

I regard every stage as having a design content, whether it be the formulation of the brief, writing a specification, making a working drawing, or instructing the builder during construction. I believe it is this constant concern for detail in the general pursuit of excellence that leads me to have successive love affairs with my buildings.

This must be the most difficult period to date in which to practise and survive for any sensitive architect. As a profession we have been mercilessly and I believe unfairly criticised for our recent works, and this has coincided with an economic recession within an age of rapid technological, social and cultural change. In this country there has, at the same time, been a rapid increase in the amount of complicated, restricting and often senseless building and planning legislation published and constantly amended.

It is therefore more than ever vital to remain as flexible as possible within this constantly changing situation and to endeavour to satisfy every need presented by the brief from the most commonplace to delight.

There is, of course, no perfect solution, and the most that one can hope to achieve is the most appropriate balance of the needs presented by the brief within the framework of the existing situation.

—Clifford Wearden

Clifford Wearden's most successful project must be "Ferndene" at Kingsbury, London, a group of thirty-seven dwellings for the Hastoe Housing Society. A plan with a restrained thrust to it in three directions (the fourth being the approach way), the building suddenly assumes in section and elevation a multitude of variegations, facets, and apertures picked out in concrete or brick; the houses break out

into a multiplanar mass whose juggling and high-wire antics suggest a clowning all-the-fun-of-the-fair vernacular of the best kind, without having to actually resort to pitched roofs or pantiles to make its case. Out of the slow, well-considered and easy rotation of the plan, the actual architecture of it all pops out as a more mobile and witty affair—where the plan drags its heels, the building as a whole is eager and on the alert, looking for anything that might come its way. The complexity of reference, the sustained orchestration, the little nodes of interest here and there—all such elements point to different readings of the plan-as-text: it is as though, in this instance, the section was not just a resolution of the plan but an urban commentary on it, a caricature no less.

An "island of urbanity in Metroland," it compresses bits of village, town and suburb together in the making of a little sample of city. In the eyes of the Local Authority it makes sense in costguide and Parker Morris terms, yet in more earth-related terms it also makes sense. Of course, its organic constitution could have been played up more, but the complex's suggestions are nonetheless sufficient to lift us out of Metroland into some more substantial place.

—Chris Fawcett

WEEKS, John.

British. Born in London, 5 March 1921. Educated at Dulwich College, London, 1933-38; Architectural Association School, London, 1938-42, 1946-47, A.A. Diploma 1947. Served as a Sergeant in the Education Corps of the British Army, 1942-45. Married Barbara Lilian Munn in 1955; children: Julia and Timothy. Assistant Architect, Research Division, London Midland and Scottish Railways, London, 1947-48; Architect, Hills West Bromwich Ltd., West Bromwich, Staffordshire, 1949; Assistant Architect, involved in an investigation into function and design of hospitals, London, 1950-56; Deputy Director, Division of Architectural Studies, Nuffield Foundation, London, 1956-60; Studio Master, Architectural Association School, London, 1960. In partnership with Richard Llewelyn-Davies, *q.v.*, London, 1960-81: currently, Chairman, Llewelyn-Davies Weeks, Architects, Planners and Health Services Consultants. Part-time Senior Lecturer, Bartlett School of Architecture and Planning, University College, University of London, 1961-72. Member of the Council, Center on Environment for the Handicapped, 1975-77; Council Member, 1975-83, and Vice-President, 1976-77, Architectural Association, London; Chairman of the British Health Care Export Council, 1982-84. Exhibitions: *This is Tomorrow*, Whitechapel Gallery, London, 1956; *Artist Versus the Machine*, Building Centre, London, 1963; *Cybernetic Serendipity*, Institute of Contemporary Arts, London, 1968; *Jubilee Exhibition*, Architectural Association, London, 1977. Recipient: Bronze Medal, Royal Institute of British Architects, 1957; West Suffolk Award to Architects, 1957. Fellow, Royal Institute of British Architects, 1964. Address: Llewelyn-Davies Weeks, Brook House, Torrington Place, London WC1E 7HN, England.

Works (with Richard Llewelyn-Davies, 1950-81):

1952 Nuffield House, Musgrave Park Hospital, Belfast
1954 Diagnostic Centre, Corby, Northamptonshire
1955 House, Mayford, Surrey
1957 Mignot Memorial Hospital, Alderney, Channel Islands
       Rushbrooke Village Housing, Bury St. Edmunds, Suffolk

1958 *The Times* Newspaper Office Building, London (with Ellis, Clarke and Galleraugh)
1960 Students Residence and Dining Room, Imperial College of Tropical Agriculture, Trinidad, West Indies (with Colin Laird Associates)
       Meeting halls and laboratories, Zoological Society, London
       Nuffield Institute of Comparative Medicine, London
1961 The Stock Exchange redevelopment, London (with Fitzroy Robinson)
       Sun Alliance Insurance Building, London (with Fitzroy Robinson)
       Northwick Park Hospital and Clinical Research Centre, Harrow, Middlesex
1963 Tate Gallery extension, London
       Town Centre Development, phase I, and Sports Centre, Basingstoke, Hampshire (with Ian Fraser Associates)
1966 Barmston Village Housing Project, Washington New Town, County Durham
1968 Experimental Pathology Research Building, St. Mary's Hospital, Paddington, London
       Stantonbury Housing Scheme, Milton Keynes, Buckinghamshire
1968/
74   University Teaching Hospitals, in Ottawa, Ontario; St. John's, Newfoundland; and Saskatoon, Saskatchewan
1970 Youth Treatment Centre, Birmingham
       University Children's Hospital, Leuven, Belgium (with Felix Tanghe and Delarue)
       Medical Centre, Flinders University, Adelaide, South Australia (with the South Australia Department of Public Works)
1971 York District Hospital, England
       Sciences laboratories, National Hospital for Nervous Diseases, London
       Salmaniya Medical Centre, Bahrain
1972 Metal Box Company Headquarters Building, Reading, Berkshire
       Singapore General Hospital, Outram Road, Singapore (with INDECO)
       General Hospital, Doha, State of Qatar
1973 Normanby College Education Centre, King's College Hospital, London
1974 Health Sciences Centre, University of Khon Kaen, Thailand (with Kingston Reynolds Thom and Allardice)
1975 Cancer Research Foundation, Sutton, Surrey
       Rayne Institute Research Laboratories, University College Hospital, London
1976 Voluntary Research Trust Research Laboratory Building, King's College Hospital, London
1977 Mount Hope Medical Centre development plan, Trinidad, West Indies
1978 St. Mary's Hospital and Medical School redevelopment, Paddington, London
1983 Hammersmith Hospital and Royal Postgraduate Medical School redevelopment, London

Publications:

By WEEKS: articles—"The Hertfordshire Achievement," with Richard Llewelyn-Davies, in *Architectural Review* (London), June 1952; "Progress in Planning Hospitals" in *RIBA Journal* (London), January 1959; "New Developments in Hospital Design and Construction" in *The Hospital* (London), July 1959; "Sterilizing Practice in Hospital—Architectural Problems" in *The Hospital* (London), October 1959; "Current Trends in Hospital Planning" in *The Hospital* (London), October 1959; "Planning for Growth and Change" in *The Architects' Journal* (London), July 1960; "The Children's House, Amsterdam" in *Architectural Design* (London), July 1960; "Mechanization and Hospital Design" in *Architectural Design* (London), January

John Weeks: Northwick Park Hospital, Harrow, Middlesex, 1961.

1961; "Cost Control—Hospital Building" in *Architectural Design* (London), January 1961; "Review of General Hospitals—Functional Studies of the Main Departments (Bouwcentrum, Rotterdam)" in *The Architects' Journal* (London), April 1962; "Indeterminate Architecture" in *Transactions of the Bartlett Society* (London), May 1964; "Hospitals for the 1970's" in *Hospital Management Planning and Equipment* (London), November 1964, and in *RIBA Journal* (London), December 1964; editor, special issue on hospital architecture of *Architectural Review* (London), June 1965; "Indeterminate Hospital Design on Urban Sites" in *Hospital Management* (London), June 1966; "Indeterminacy in Architecture" in *The Listener* (London), June 1967; "Hospital Design for Growth and Change" in *World Hospitals* (London), January 1969; "Studies in Hospital Design During the Next Twenty-One Years," with Peter Cowan and in *Hospital Management Planning, Equipment* (London), May 1969; "Hospital Design (Architecture in Israel)" in *Journal of the Association of Engineers and Architects in Israel* (Haifa), June 1969; "Multi-Strategy Buildings" in *Architectural Design* (London), October 1969; "Designing for Patient Care, Education and Research" in *World Hospitals* (London), November 1969; "Indeterminate Dimensions in Architecture" in *Baumeister* (Munich), November 1969; "Planning the Gasthuisberg Project," with Gavin Maxwell, in *World Hospitals* (London), April 1970; "Northwick Park Hospital" in *L'Architecture d'Aujourd'hui* (Paris), July 1970; "Design Strategy for Flexible Health Sciences Facilities," with Gordon Best, in *Health Services Research* (Chicago), Autumn 1970; "Designing for Indeterminacy" in *Architectural Review* (London), November 1971; "Hospital Design" in *Architectural Design* (London), July 1973; "Alvar Aalto" in *The Listener* (London), Summer 1976; 'Distribution of Room Sizes in Hospitals," with Gordon Best, James Cheyne and Ellen Leopold, in *Health Services Research* (London), Autumn 1976; "The Wellington Hospital, St. John's Wood" in *The Architects' Journal* (London), Spring 1977; "Hospital Building" in *RIBA Journal* (London), Jubilee Issue, May 1977; Designing and Living in a Hospital: An Enormous House" in *RSA Journal* (London), July 1979; "Richard Llewelyn-Davies in *The Architects' Journal* (London), 11 November 1981; "Hospitals 3: Buildings to Visit" with Mike Nightingale, in *RIBA Journal* (London), August 1982; "Approachable Hospitals" in *Hospital Management* (London), April 1984; "Design Trends—Implications on Building and Converting Laboratories" in *Design, Construction and Refurbishment of Laboratories*, Chichester, Sussex 1984.

On WEEKS: books—*Meaning in Architecture* by Charles Jencks, London 1969; *Parameters and Images* by L. Brett, London 1970; *A Broken Wave* by L. Esher, London 1981; articles—review in *The Architects' Journal* (London), 2 February 1972; "Hospitals in a Village Context" by Bob Allies in *Building Design* (London), 16 March 1979.

*

For the greater part of my professional life I have specialized in hospital design. Hospitals as a building type have a number of curious properties (aside from the expected ones of complicated function, and often, great size) which marks them off from typical architect's commissions. All hospitals require to grow and change as they adjust to the changes in their catchment area population and as medical and nursing techniques alter. Since they may take many years to design and construct, it is not unusual for the architect's original brief to be out of date in many places as soon as they are opened.

The architect's brief is only one incident in the life of a hospital which will continue to change during the whole of its existence. Thus the architect is deprived of the traditional basis for his design—a full and accurate description of the functions his building will have to accommodate.

It follows that the architect is not able to determine the final form of the building and that he must design an "indeterminate" hospital, on the assumption that his brief is incomplete and probaby wrong.

In successive projects I have been searching for a method of design which takes as its starting point provision for irregular and unforeseeable growth and change—an indeterinate architecture—to replace the conventional ideal of finite formal composition.

Architectural design has as its objective a building which can be continuously modified by its occupants without losing its integrity. Buildings must be lived in to stay alive, and their inhabitants' modifications to the fabric are visible evidence of the life process.

A tree has a shape which is the result of all external environmental factors acting on its own internal mechanisms. At every stage of its life a tree has a shape and size which perfectly balances these. Few observers are critical.

Good design, for a living building, will allow it to age as does a tree.

—John Weeks

*

In 1960, John Weeks, now Chairman of Llewelyn-Davies Weeks Architects, was already advocating an approach to planning that would allow for growth of unforeseeable volumes, while still maintaining some kind of comprehensible form—he was reacting against the typical urban growth patterns, best illustrated by hospitals, whereby expedient additions and fillings-in created the characteristic formlessness which the city was assuming. By the principle of space continuity, he managed to establish a way of relinquishing our concept of planning as an exercise in finite geometry in favour of a concept based on an extendible communication sytem. In other words, to use his analogy, a duffle coat in place of a tailor-made suit. But he added a rider to his manifesto right from the start: the danger exists that flexibility, if uncritically adopted, costs too much and tempts those concerned not to think out their problems in advance—"it is not to be used simply to justify indecisive planning."

By the 1970s, with the completion of his Northwick Park Hospital and of the Medical Centre, Flinders University, Adelaide, his fledgling "responsiveness' had matured into a full-scale multistrategy architecture of indeterminacy. This I-Ching arcchitecture of lattice systems and independent subsystems demotes determinism to second place behind that of the life of the building; it entails the letting go of the Platonic side to design and understanding architecture as a kind of time-frame. Japanese Metabolist projects failed, for they ony had the appearance of indeterminacy—their real guts were nostalgic and heroic. Cedric Price's Interaction Centre, Weeks feels, is much better resolved, for it carries more vividly evidence of its users' lives.

An indeterminate architecture doesn't get in the way; at a fundamental level it recognizes and appreciates the reality of people's opinions and gives them the right to exercise them. At Northwick Park, Weeks was trying to deal with the problem of sheltering an organization which has a rate of growth and change so great that it makes its buildings obsolete before they decay naturally. Looking at such precedents as the nineteenth century railway station and exhibition shed, where engineers, uninhibted by the contemporary architectural morality that expects a close fit between form and function, he noted that they fabricated easily extendible linear spaces which at the same time did not condition the arrangement of internal affairs. His only criticism of these nineteenth century buildings was that they nonetheless still looked finite and complete. At Northwick Park he deployed the elements of nineteenth century flexibility—separate buildings tied together by an independent internal street—but he didn't insist on achieving a unity of constant relationships; instead he came up with a geometric aformalism that wrapped around the close-knit communications clusters. This demonstration of an

architecture of kinetic densities and intervals, however, has been matched by some of hardly recent work of the partnership, and one is inclined to wonder if that doesn't make the theory of an architecture-of-chance sound rather hollow today?

—Chris Fawcett

WEESE, Harry Mohr.

American. Born in Evanston, Illinois, 30 June 1915. Educated at Massachusetts Institute of Technology, Cambridge, 1934-38 (Roche Prize, American Institute of Architects, 1938), B.Arch. 1938; Yale University, New Haven, Connecticut, 1936-37; Cranbrook Academy of Art, Bloomfield Hills, Michigan, 1938-39 (Fellow in City Planning); Research Assistant, Bemis Housing Foundation, M.I.T., 1939-40. Served as an Engineering Officer in the United States Navy, 1942-46. Married Kate Baldwin in 1945; children: Shirley, Kate and Marcia. Designer, Skidmore, Owings and Merrill, Chicago, 1940-41, 1946-47; Partner, with Benjamin Baldwin, Baldwin and Weese, Kenilworth, Illinois, 1941-42. Since 1947, Chairman of the Board of Harry Weese and Associates, Chicago; office established in Washington, D.C., 1966, Miami, Florida, 1977, Los Angeles, 1981, and Singapore, 1983. Chairman, Building Committee, Council for the Restoration of the Alder-Sullivan Auditorium Theatre, Chicago, 1964-67; Member of the Mayor's Committee for the Preservation of Chicago's Historic Architecture, 1972; Member of the Task Force on Federal Architecture, National Endowment of the Arts, 1973; Chairman of the Task Force on Rebuilding the City, 1973, and President of the Chicago Chapter, 1975, American Institute of Architects; Architectural Consultant, United States Department of State Foreign Buildings Program, 1973-76. Chairman of the Urban Form Committee since 1968, and Member of the Lakefront Committee since 1968 and of the Transportation Committee since 1970, Metropolitan Housing and Planning Council of Chicago; Member, American Institute of Architects Capital Architects Advisory Committee, since 1972; Member, National Council on the Arts, 1974-80; Member, Architectural Review Panel of the Board of Governers of the United States Federal Reserve System, since 1974; Member, Design Arts Committee, National Council on the Arts, since 1980. Publisher, *Inland Architect* magazine, Chicago. Recipient: Distinguished Building Award, 1959, 1967, 1969, 1970 (twice), 1971, 1974, 1975, 1978, Honor Award, 1968, 1970, and Distinguished Interior Architecture Award, 1980, American Institute of Architects, Chicago Chapter; Honor Award, 1960, and Restoration and Rehabilitation Award, 1963, American Institute of Architects/ Chicago Association of Commerce and Industry; First Prize, Masonry Institute, 1962; Brunner Prize, National Institute of Arts and Letters, 1964; Merit Award for Design Excellence, United States Department of Housing and Urban Development, 1965 (twice); National Honor Award, 1969, 1970, 1973, 1977, 1983, and Firm of the Year Award, 1978, American Institute of Architects; Chicago Beautiful Award, 1969, 1976, 1979; Award of Excellence for House Design, *Architectural Record*, 1970; Architectural Award of Excellence, American Institute of Steel Construction, 1970; Award of Excellence, Chicago Tile Institute, 1971; Honor Award, United States General Services Administration, 1972; Honor Award, *House and Home*, 1973; Award of Excellence, Development Council Foundation, Champaign County, Illinois, 1973; City Beautiful Award, Dayton, Ohio, 1973; Prestressed Concrete Institute Award, 1974, 1975; Illinois Association of School Boards Award, 1974; Award for Excellence, *Environmental Design*, 1975; Design

Harry Weese: United States Embassy Housing, Tokyo, 1983.

Award, Greater Wilmington, Delaware Development Council, 1975; National Design for Transportation Award, 1981 (twice); Grand Award, National Association of Home Builders, 1981; Merit Award, American Society of Landscape Architects, Florida Chapter, 1981; Preservation Alliance Award, Louisville, Kentucky, 1982; First Prize, Second Biennial Highway Design Competition, Federal Highway Administration, 1982; Union of Polish Architects Award, Second World Biennale of Architecture, 1983; Illinois Indiana Masonry Council Award, 1983; Award of Excellence, Post-Tensioning Institute, Washington, D.C., 1983; Merit Award, American Institute of Architects, D.C. Chapter, 1983. Fellow, American Institute of Architects, 1961; Academician, National Academy of Design. Address: Harry Weese and Associates, 10 West Hubbard Street, Chicago, Illinois 60610, U.S.A.

Works:

1951 Master plan for the Cummins Engine Company, Columbus, Indiana
1953 Master plan for Drake University, Des Moines, Iowa
1956 United States Consulate Staff Apartments, Accra, Ghana
     Apartment building, 277 East Walton Street, Chicago
     Residence Hall, University of Chicago
1958 United States Embassy and Staff Apartments, Accra, Ghana
1959 Professor Gale Johnson House, Chicago
     Hyde Park Redevelopment, Chicago (with I. M. Pei and Loewenberg and Loewenberg)
1960 KLM Airlines Offices, Chicago

Old Town Apartment Building, 235 West Eugenie Street, Chicago
     Master plan for Cornell College, Mount Vernon, Iowa
1962 Arena Stage Theatre I, Washington, D.C.
1963 Illinois Center for the Visually Handicapped, Chicago
     Northern Baptist Theological Seminary, Hinsdale, Illinois
1964 Newberry Library renovation, Chicago
     Otter Creek Country Club, Columbus, Indiana
1965 Jens Jensen School, Chicago
     IBM Office Building, Milwaukee
     First Baptist Church, Columbus, Indiana
     Kenwood Gardens, Chicago
1966 Cummins Engine Company Manufacturing Plant, Columbus, Indiana
     Outdoor Garden, Art Institute of Chicago
     Science Complex, University of Colorado, Boulder
     Chicago Teachers' Union Apartment Building
1966- Metro Subway System, Washington, D.C.
1967 Alder-Sullivan Auditorium Theatre restoration, Chicago
     Orchestra Hall renovation, Chicago
     Master plan for the Lincoln Park Zoo, Chicago
     Master plan for the Field Museum of Natural History, Chicago
1968 Air India Staff Housing, Bombay
     Building 64, Cummins Engine Company, Columbus, Indiana
     Library and Auditorium, Rochester Institute of Technology, New York
     South Lower Campus Project, University of Wisconsin, Madison

Science Building, Beloit College, Wisconsin
Time & Life Building, East Ohio Street, Chicago
Fort Lincoln Housing for the Elderly, Washington, D.C.
Master plan for Reed College, Portland, Oregon
1969 Seventeenth Church of Christ Scientist, Chicago
     Latin School, Chicago
     Center for the Performing Arts, Milwaukee
     St. Louis Junior College
1970 Bank Street College of Education, New York
     Interama: Caribbean Pavilion, Miami, Florida (project)
     Atlas Crankshaft Manufacturing Facility, Fostoria, Ohio
     District of Columbia Interstate Highway Study
     Southwest Washington (D.C.) Urban Renewal
1971 Greenwood Park Apartments, Chicago
     Science Building, Cornell College, Mount Vernon, Iowa
     Shadowcliff (house), Door County, Wisconsin
     Office Building and Art Center, Cincinnati
     Education and Communications Building, and Physical Education Building, University of Illinois at Chicago Circle
     Master plan for Lake Michigan College, Benton Harbor, Michigan
     Master plan for Park Forest South, Illinois
     Master plan for St. Louis Junior College
     Master plan for the new town of Lake Lure, Waukegan, Illinois
     Master plan for the Avery Coonley School, Downers Grove, Illinois

1972 Arena Stage Theatre II, Washington, D.C.
Actors Theatre, Louisville, Kentucky
Given Institute of Pathobiology, Aspen, Colorado
IBM Laboratory and Office Building, Endicott, New York
Master plan for the West Campus of Massachusets Intstitute of Technology, Cambridge
Master plan for the Theatre of Western Springs, Illinois
Master plan for Ghent District Housing, Norfolk, Virginia

1973 Crown Center Hotel, Kansas City
Research Building, Chicago Botanical Gardens
Credit Card Center, American Oil Company, Raleigh, North Carolina
IBM Central Utilities Plant, Endicott, New York
Levis Faculty Center, University of Illinois, Urbana
Center for Advanced Study, University of Illinois, Urbana
LaSalle Plaza Office Building, LaSalle and Lake Streets, Chicago
First National Bank, Dayton, Ohio

1974 Lake Village East, Chicago
Credit Card Center, American Oil Company, Des Moines, Iowa
Northwest Medical Arts Building, Arlington Heights, Illinois
Theatre remodelling, Boston University
Fine Arts Building, Carleton College, Northfield, Minnesota
345 West Fullerton Apartment Building, Chicago
Hyde Park Townhouses, Chicago
Village Hall, Oak Park, Illinois
Social Sciences Campus, State University of New York, Buffalo-Amherst Branch
Plan for the restoration and expansion of the State Capitol, Montgomery, Alabama
Master plan for Pershing Square, Kansas City

1975 Federal Correctional Center, Chicago
Fine Arts Building and Student Center, Drake University, Des Moines, Iowa
51st and King Drive Building rehabilitation, Chicago
Grand Central Station redevelopment, New York (project)
Solar House, University of Delaware, Wilmington
Library, University of Massachusetts, Boston
United States Courthouse Annex, Chicago
John Knox Home Apatment Building, Norfolk, Virginia
Grace Street Housing for the Elderly, Chicago
West Willow Townhouses, Chicago
Master plan for the Downtown Core of Baltimore
Master plan for the 3A Interstate Highway System, Baltimore

1976 Mercantile Bank, Kansas City
Library, Williams College, Williamstown, Massachusetts
First National Bank, Albuquerque, New Mexico
Gymnasium, New Trier High School, Winnetka, Illinois
Northwest Industries office interiors, Chicago
Science Building, Cornell College, Mt. Vernon, Iowa
School of Medicine, Southern Illinois University, Carbondale
Plan for the development of the riverbank, Chicago
Trans Union Corporation Office Building, Lincolnshire, Illinois

1977 Wheaton National Bank, Wheaton, Illinois
Civic Center, Middletown, Ohio
Terman Engineering Center, Stanford University, California
Keck, Cushman, Mahin and Cate office interiors, Chicago

1978 Marriott Hotel, North Michigan Avenue, Chicago
Euclid Place, Oak Park, Illinois
Rosenberg Townhouses, Chicago
Study for the National Park Service, Chicago
Floating marina, Navy Pier, Chicago (project)
Plan for the renovation of the Loop Elevated Railway, Chicago

1978 Dade County, Florida Transportation System (as architectural consultant)
Plan for the Northeast Corridor (Boston to Washington, D.C.), for the United States Federal Railroad Administration
Riyadh Airport Community, Saudi Arabia
Field Museum of Natural History renovation, Chicago
Convention/Entertainment Center, Grand Rapids, Michigan
Newberry Library renovation and expansion, Chicago
Multi-Purpose Building, Stateville Prison, Joliet, Illinois
1100 Lake Shore Drive (apartments), Chicago
Harwick Administration Building, Mayo Clinic, Rochester, Minnesota
Theatre, University of Chicago
Pesch House, Lake Forest, Illinois
Plan for the Niagara Frontier Transportation Authority
Minnesota State Prison, Stillwater
Steelcase Showroom, Chicago
200 South Wacker Drive Office Building, Chicago
Rivermouth Complex, Chicago (project)
Neiman Marcus retail store, Oak Brook, Illinois
Union Underwear Corporate Headquarters, Bowling Green, Kentucky
Intercontinental Hotel, Chicago (project)

1978- Printers Row Housing, South Dearborn Street, Chicago

1979 Brown Forman Warehouse renovation, Louisville, Kentucky
Radisson Hotel Entrance and Storefront, Chicago
Northwest Industries interiors, Sears Tower, Chicago
United States Embassy Housing, Tokyo
Design Development for People's Gas Vocational School, Chicago

1980 American Medical Association Project X, Chicago (project)
Sun-Times Offices, Chicago (project)
City Hall, Crown Point, Indiana (project)
Music Hall renovation, Kansas City, Missouri
McLean Gardens Housing, Chicago (project)

1980- South Cove Marina, New Buffalo, Michigan
Brown Colman and Dement Office Building, Kalamazoo, Michigan

1981 Anchorage Library, Alaska (project)
United States Embassy Housing, Accra, Ghana (project)
Interfaith Chapel, Snowmass, Colorado (project)
Carbondale Library, Illinois

1981- Buildings for South California Rapid Transit District, Los Angeles
Adams/Wabash Station renovation, Chicago Transit Authority, Chicago
Multi-Modal Transportation Center, Gary, Indiana

1982 Alter House, Indiana Dunes, Indiana
Lobby renovation, 75 East Wacker Drive, Chicago
Criswell Housing, Austin, Texas (project)
MAT Associates Hotel, New Orleans, Louisiana (project)
Bankers Trust interiors, Chicago

Post Office and Customs House renovations, St. Louis, Missouri

1982- Campeau/Criswell Master Plan, Dallas, Texas

1983 Singapore Mass Rapid Transit Development, Singapore (as Consultant)
Downtown Redevelopment Master Plan, Hanover Park, Illinois
Zaiser House, Naples, Florida (project)
Office Building renovation, 545 North Michigan Avenue, Chicago
First National Bank of Maryland interiors, Chicago
United States Embassy Housing, Tokyo

1983- High-rise Office Building, 411 East Wisconsin, Milwaukee, Wisconsin
Atlas Crankshaft Factory Building, Chicago

1984 Cutler House, Aspen, Colorado (project)

1984- IBM Office interiors, Milwaukee, Wisconsin
Dormitory renovation, McCormick Theological Seminary, Chicago
Heritage Bank interiors, Milwaukee, Wisconsin
Kenosha Marina Master Plan, Kenosha, Wisconsin
Heritage Landings Master Plan and Housing, Mineapolis, Minnesota
Chicago and Northwest Railroad Trainshed renovation, Chicago

Publications:

By WEESE: articles—"Chicago and Urban Designs" in *American Institute of Planners Reporter and Review* (Washington, D.C.), December 1958; "Random Thoughts on Architectural Controls and Their Effect on Cities" in *AIA Journal* (Washington, D.C.), March 1961; "Opinion: Tax Reform and Land Reform" in *Inland Architect* (Chicago), July 1972; "The Issue Is Tall Buildings" in *AIA Journal* (Washington, D.C.), January 1973; "Arbor Day Thoughts" in *Morton Arboretum Quarterly* (Lisle, Illinois), Spring 1974; "What's Next for Chicago" in *Commerce Magazine* (Chicago), October 1974; "Tribute to Alvar Aalto" in *Arkkitehti* (Helsinki), August 1976; "Perspective III: Preservation" in *Journal of Architectural Education* (Washington, D.C.), November 1976; "What Next, Chicago?" in the *Chicago Daily News*, 7 May 1977; "Chicago and its River" in *Chicago Magazine*, August 1979; "The Chicago Plan Commission" in *Inland Architect* (Chicago), April 1980; "The World Is But A Passing Stage" in *Inland Architect* (Chicago), July/August 1981; "New Rehab Code Vital—How About a Vote?" in the *Sun-Times* (Chicago), 3 March 1982; "Back Come the Trolleys" in *Inland Architect* (Chicago), May/June 1982; "Date with a Decade—The Import of the 1992 World's Fair", with others, in *Inland Architect* (Chicago), July/August 1982; "Housing for the U.S. Embassy in Tokyo", with Toshihiko Kimura, in *The Japan Architect* (Tokyo), September 1983; "Troubled Allies at O'Hare" in *Inland Architect* (Chicago), November/December 1983; "Expo 1992" in *Inland Architect* (Chicago), May/June 1984.

On WEESE: books—*Architecture U.S.A.*, edited by Ian McCallum, London 1959; *Three Architects at Williams College*, exhibition catalogue by John Stamper, Williamstown, Massachusetts 1976; *Chicago Architects* by Stuart Cohen, Chicago 1976; *Der Offene Kamin-Folge 3* by Fritz Barran, Stuttgart 1976; articles—"Wide-Open Bank" in *Architectural Forum* (New York), August 1952; "Suburban Menace" in *AIA Bulletin* (Chicago), November 1954; "Starting a Tradition" in *Time* (New York), 4 March 1957; "The Office of Harry Weese Associates, Chicago" in *Inland Architect* (Chicago), September 1957; "Eyeful in Africa" in *Architectural Forum* (New York), September 1959; "Arena Stage" in *Architectural Review* (London), June 1960; "Washington Builds a True Theatre-in-the-Round" in *The Times* (London), 27 December 1961;

"Il Teatro Arena Stage a Washington" in *Edilizia Moderna* (Milan), March 1963; "Architect Counts City's Blessings" in *Milwaukee Journal*, 10 March 1964; "A Baptist Church by Weese" in *Architectural Record* (New York), December 1965; "First Baptist Church" in *L'Architecture d'Aujourd'hui* (Paris), April/May 1966; "How to Keep Your Landmarks and Have Them, Too" in *Progressive Architecture* (New York), October 1966; "Subways Don't Have to Be Miserable" in *Fortune* (New York), April 1967; "Harry Weese Should Have His Way with Chicago" in *Esquire* (New York), June 1968; "Monumental Weese" in *Architectural Review* (London), December 1968; "Summer House in Muskola Lake District" in *DBZ/Deutsche Bauzeitschrift* (Gutersloh), May 1969; "New Weese Buildings Create a Downtown Complex" in *Progressive Architecture* (New York), June 1969; "Harry Weese, FAIA" in *Interiors* (New York), November 1970; "Vacanze a picco sul lago Michigan" in *Domus* (Milan), October 1971; "Apartments in Chicago" in *Architecture + Urbanism* (Tokyo), October 1971; "Good Weese" in *Architectural Review* (London), February 1972; "Harry Weese" in *Revue Moderne des Arts et de la Vie* (Paris), January 1973; "Harry Weese and Associates of Chicago" in *Space Design* (Tokyo), February 1976; "Metro's Designer" in *Washington Post*, 24 June 1977; "Goodbye Art Deco" in *Progressive Architecture* (New York), August 1977; "Washington Metro" by Colin Amery in *Architectural Review* (London), February 1978; "Harry Weese of Chicago" in *AIA Journal* (Washington, D.C.), May 1978; "Mercantile Bank Building, Kansas City" in *Informes de la Construccion* (Madrid), March 1979; "First National Bank in Albuquerque" in *Informes de la Construccion* May 1979; "Rest Assured—Harry Weese is Keeping Chicago" in *Chicago Tribune Magazine*, 20 May 1979; "Harry Weese: Humanism and Tradition", special issue of *Process: Architecture* (Tokyo), no. 11, 1979; "Architecture in the 80s" in *Inland Architect* (Chicago), January/February 1980; "Urban Repair in Washington, D.C." in *Baumeister* (Munich), April 1980; "Building Types Study 553: Embassies and Consulates" in *Architectural Record* (New York), December 1980; "Given Medicine" in *Architectural Review* (London), April 1981; Weese Offices in Chicago" in *Baumeister* (Munich), January 1982; "Chicago Architects" in *Chicago Tribune*, 17 October 1982; "Divide and Restore" in *Progressive Architecture* (New York), November 1983; "Harry Weese: Two and Three Dimensional Sober Calligraphy" in *Architettura* (Rome), January 1984.
Bibliography: *Harry Mohr Weese* by Lamia Doumato, Monticello, Illinois 1981.

Architecture's main duty is to innovate. It is not pander to trivia. It is not to destroy or supercede randomly. Its mission presently would seem to be one of regeneration. Consolidate and cultivate the garden of the future.

As populations in industrial nations level off, it would seem wise to study the history of European cities, matured over a thousand years. It would be tragic if the U.S.A, the offspring of Europe, and the most wasteful of nations, found itself with architecture as a fragile and embarassed residue among the ruins of once promising cities. This need not happen. Meanwhile, people are taking matters into their own hands.

Their regenerated city will be denser, greener, more permanent, and more responsive to human needs and individual creativity. People will live in town and go to work on the fringes. Its center will be its brain, its heart, and throbbing with the ongathering of institutions, culture, circus, and commerce for the enjoyment and creativity of all. It will be what a Paris is now and what a Chicago could become, root and branch, the better of a number of worlds, the city where the good life, in Aristotle's words, can be led. Upon this we seem to agree. But it will not be easy, neither in a socialist nor in a capitalist context.

Archaic land tenure, monopolies, anarchy, and corruption thrive in both worlds.

An architects will have more difficulty fulfilling their true mission as form givers, as the complexities of conflicting demands, constituencies, lobbies, and specialists could lock us in the ivory tower. The social contract of architecture needs to be rediscovered and restated. It must neither be elitist nor utopian but in terrestrian terms.

—Harry Weese

Harry Weese is a native of Chicago, where he has based his practice, begun in 1947. He recieved his architectural training at the Massachusetts Institute of Technology in the 1930s, time when the curriculum revolved around both the Beaux-Arts and Bauhaus influences. He subsequently studied urban planning at the Cranbrook Academy near Detroit, under Eliel Saarinen. There, Eero Saarinen, though his junior, became a mentor.

Unlike the work of many noted contemporary architects, Weese's does not bear a recognizable stamp. It is characterized, rather, by a painstaking attention to the specific design problem at hand. It is from a deep understanding of each problem—its setting, its historical relations, and particularly its unique functional requirements—that his design solutions arise. The nature of his projects and the requirements of American practice compel him to operate a large office, but he has always been in full control of it. Every design project is done under his guidance.

His work includes a wide range of building types—theatres, office buildings, houses, churches, public housing, schools, and so forth. He has also maintained a position of spokesman for causes and issues in planning and architecture whch he feels compelled to address, mainly in Chicago.

Weese was among the first major designer architects to work in the area of historic restoration. The specific work was the great Chicago Auditorium Theatre, designed in the nineteenth century by Louis Sullivan and Dankmar Adler.

He was also selected to be the design architect for the stations and public facilities of the rail rapid transit system of Washington, D.C. His approach to this project reveals his general approach to all problems. He saw that the problem of the station designs was recognizability by passengers—a familiar sequence of arrival or departure experiences. The varying constraints and conditions of each station needed a familiar consistency of theme rather than "variety." Indeed, there would be more than enough forces trying to pull the stations apart, creating confusion. His solution was to design a system of component parts, a "system of systems," for individual designers to utilize in the many stations. It has worked admirably and is among the outstanding works of public architecture in America.

Weese's other projects include the First Baptist Church, Columbus, Indiana; the renovation of the Field Museum of Natural History and Orchestra Hall in Chicago; the Time-Life Building in Chicago; Arena Stage in Washington, D.C.; the Latin School, Chicago; the Federal Correctional Center, Chicago; and the Terman Engineering Center at Stanford University, California.

—Paul Spreiregen

WEINSTEIN, Richard S.
American. Born in New York City, 30 November 1932. Educated at Brown University, Providence, Rhode Island, B.A. 1956; Columbia University, New York, M.A. in clinical psychology; Harvard University, Cambridge, Massachusetts; University of Pennsylvania, Philadelphia, under Louis I. Kahn,

q.v., Romaldo Giurgola, q.v., Robert Venturi, q.v., and Robert Le Ricolais (Arthur Spade Brook Gold Medal for Design, 1961), M.Arch. 1961; Prix de Rome Scholar, American Academy in Rome, 1963. Served in the United States Army, 1956-58. Married to Sandra Cohen; children: Alexander and Nicolas. Worked for I. M. Pei, q.v., Edward Larrabee Barnes, q.v., and Skidmore, Owings and Merrill, q.v. New York; Director, Manhattan Planning Office, Department of City Planning, New York, 1966-68, and Mayor's Office of Lower Manhattan Development, New York, 1968-74. Since 1974, in private practice, as Richard S. Weinstein Associates Inc., New York. Project Director, Museum of Modern Art Expansion Projects, 1975-77. Project Director, 42nd Street Redevelopment Projects, New York, since 1978; President, New Sources of Funding Inc., New York, since 1978. Member, Board of Directors, The Theatre Development Fund, New York, New York Landmarks Conservancy, and the Architectural League of New York; Member, Visiting Committee, Harvard Graduate School of Design. Exhibition: Museum of Modern Art, New York, 1966. Address: Richard S. Weinstein Associates Inc., 200 Park Avenue, Suite 3024, New York, New York 10017, U.S.A.

Works:

1966/
67 Twin Parks Urban Renewal Plan, Bronx, New York (with Giovanni Pasanella, Jonathan Barnett, Jaquelin Robertson, and M. Weintraub)

1966/
74 Numerous zoning ordinances, embodying complex urban design criteria, for the Lower Manhattan Waterfront, Lincoln Square, Greenwich Street, Theatre District, etc., for the New York City Government

1969 Negril Development Plan, Jamaica, West Indies (with Giovanni Pasanella, Jonathan Barnett, Adelates Technical Services, and Jaquelin Robertson)

1971 House, Montreal

1974/
75 Master plan/design guidelines for Park Central (mixed commercial development), near Dallas

1975/
77 Apartment Tower, for the Museum of Modern Art, New York (project)

76/
77 Development plan for Floyd Bennett Field, Gateway National Recreation Area, New York
Museum of Pueblo and Navajo Art, Santa Fe, New Mexico (project)

Publications:

By WEINSTEIN: article—"Demeter and the Snow Queen" in *Architectural Forum* (New York), October 1973.

On WEINSTEIN: book—*American Architecture Now*, edited by Barbaralee Diamonstein, New York 1980; article—"White and Gray: Twelve Modern American Architects" in *Architecture + Urbanism* (Tokyo), April 1975.

Architecture is about institutions. Architects should understand and be able to use to their advantage the legal, financial, and political methodoligies of the market place, which underline the institutional structure of contemporary society. This should enable them to find metaphors which express directly the character of our experience of institutional structure, our experience of membership, and our search for a system of values from which to make choices. Mastery of these methodologies also places the architect in a position of advantage with the political and financial establishments which have always controlled the construction of buildings and cities.

—Richard S. Weinstein

Richard S. Weinstein is a leading exponent of the practice of urban design using innovative forms of public-private partnerships and what he calls "venture philanthropy."

One of a group of young architects who joined the administration of New York City Mayor John Lindsay in 1967, Weinstein became the head of the Mayor's Office of Lower Manhattan Development. His most notable achievements were the creation of special zoning districts, in which land-use regulations—previously proscriptive in nature—were used to achieve positive architectural results. These districts, including the Theatre District, the Lincoln Square District, the Greenwich Street District, and the Lower Manhattan Waterfront, became increasingly complex and sophisticated. For the first time they created a means of achieving coordinated development of portions of a city incrementally through the medium of land-use regulation. Whether these innovations will prove completely successful still remains to be seen. They are dependent on the vagaries of the private real estate market, and it will be years before any one district will be developed completely.

After leaving the New York City government in 1974 to start his own practice, Weinstein wrote design guidelines for the 300-acre Park Central project near Dallas. These guidelines amount to a voluntary special zoning district that coordinates and gives form to a development proceeding incrementally over a long period of time. It is to be used by the developer in drawing up lease and sale agreements for individual parcels within the project.

Weinstein also put together the controversial proposal in which the Museum of Modern Art in New York City sought to develop an apartment house using the "air-rights" (additional floor area permitted by zoning) of the Museum and Garden, transferring these development rights to property adjacent to the Museum. Weinstein is now taking this principle farther by establishing a not-for-profit corporation, New Sources of Funding, which specializes in helping non profit institutions realize the potential of similar "sleeping assets."

Before entering city government, Weinstein worked for a number of architectural firms, including I. M. Pei and Partners and the Office of Edward Larrabee Barnes, and received the Prix de Rome of the American Academy in 1963. He continues to keep his hand in as an architectural designer. His best-known building is a large private house iun Canada, which shows the influence of his teacher, Louis I. Kahn, but also evokes recollections of French chateaus and the work of H. H. Richardson.

—Jonathan Barnett

WEJCHERT, Hanna.

Polish. Born Hanna Adamczewska in Radom, 29 July 1920. Educated at the Warsaw Technical University, 1939-46, Dip.Arch. 1946, Ph.D. 1959. Interned in Ravensbruck concentration camp, 1944-45. Married Kazimierz Wejchert, *q.v.*, in 1962; daughter: Dorota. In partnership with Kazimierz Wejchert since 1947. Member of the faculty of the Warsaw School of Architecture since 1946: Assistant Lecturer in Town Planning, 1946-59; Lecturer, 1959-62; Assistant Professor, 1962-70; Associate Professor, 1970-75; Professor, since 1975. Vice-Chairman of the Council, TUP (Towarzystwo Urbanistow Polskich), Warsaw, 1968–72; Member

of the Town Council of Tychy, Poland, 1969-73; Member, Committee of Architecture and Town Planning, Polish Academy of Science, 1978. Vice-Chairman, SARP (Architectural Association of Poland), since 1974. Exhibitions: *Terra 1*, Wroclaw, Poland, 1975; Exhibition of County Regional Plans, Warsaw, 1978; Association of Polish Architects Exhibition, in Warsaw, Rzeszów and Katowice, Poland, 1984. Recipient: Golden Cross of Merit, 1951; Ministry of Town Planning and Architecture Award, 1955 and 1957; Golden Badge of Merit, Katowice, Poland, 1959; Polish State Prize, 1964; Ministry of the Environment Prize, 1974; Ministry of Higher Education Prize, 1977; Badge of Merit, Tychy New Town, 1978; Ministry of Construction Prize, Warsaw, 1978; Honour Prize, Association of Polish Architects, 1983. Address (office): ul. Orezna 45, Warsaw, Poland.

Works (all with Kazimierz Wejchert):

1951 Master plan for Tychy New Town, Poland
1952 Master plan for the North District of Tychy, Poland
1958 Recreation Centre, Paprocany, Poland (project; with Z. Lojewski)
Memorial Monument, Tychy, Poland (project)
Town Centre Plan, Warsaw (competition project; with team)
Wiosna Ludów Square, Poznán, Poland (competition project; with A. and M. Czyzewski)
1960 North Park, Tychy, Poland (with H. Okolowicz-Krzes)
1962 Master plan for the South District of Tychy, Poland
Tychy Central Railway Station Area Development, Poland (with M. Niklewicz)
Town Hall and District Community Party Headquarters, Tychy, Poland (with W. Jaciow and E. Piasecki)
1965 MNO Apartment Buildings, Tychy, Poland (with A. and M. Czyzewski)
Eartecznik Holiday Centre, Wisla Reservoir, Poland (with W. Jaciow and E. Piasecki)
1966 Krzyki District Development, Wroclaw, Poland (competition project; with A. and M. Czyzewski)
1967 Victoria Square, Warsaw (competition projects; with G. Chodkowski)
Atrium Housing Development, Tychy, Poland (with M. and A. Czyzewski)
Paderewski Housing Devlopment, Katowice, Poland (competition project; with A. and M. Czyzewski)
One-family houses, North District, Tychy, Poland (project)
1969 Monument, Tychy, Poland (with J. Jarnuszkiewicz)
1970 Plan for the centre of Sieradz, Poland (competition project; with J. Chmielewski, G. Chodkowski, and Z. Dembowska)
1971 Town Centre, Jena, East Germany (with G. Chodkowski)
Recreation Centre, Dzierzno Lake, near Gliwice, Poland (competition project; with A. Gawlikowski and S. Gzell)
1972 Polanczyk Recreation Centre, Solina Reservoir, Poland (with A. Gawlikowski and S. Gzell)
Sports Stadium, Tychy, Poland (with Z. Lojewski)
Development plan for the town of Ostroleka, Poland (competition project; with J. Chmielewski and G. Chodkowski)
Plan for the centre of Wloclawek, Poland (competition project; with M. Dziekoński)
1973 Shopping and Community Centre, Tychy, Poland (competition project; with M. Dziekonski)
1974 Atrium Housing Development, ul. Orezna, Warsaw (with D. Putkowski)

1975 Plans for the urban centre and for housing, South District of Tychy, Poland
1976 Master plan for the expansion of Podkowa Lesna, near Warsaw (with K. Domaradzki and R. Dziekoński)
Plan for the centre of Lomza, Poland (project; with J. Chmielewski, A. Gawlikowski, and E. Haduch)
1977 Master plan for the satellite town of Jaroszowice, Tychy, Poland (with T. Kazimierski)
City Centre, Kiel, West Germany (competition project; with M. Dziekonski)
1978 Master plan for the Stella district of Tychy, Poland (with A. Czyzewski)
1979 Les Halles Redevelopment Plan, Paris (competition project; with D. Wejchert and T. Plebański)
Old Town Master Plan, Radom, Poland (with E. Kola Kowski and T. Kazimierski)
Zuzanna District Master Plan, Tychy, Poland (with B. Wlodarczyk)
Ursula District Master Plan, Tychy, Poland (with Z. Lojewski)
1980 Karolina District Master Plan, Tychy, Poland (with M. Czyzewski)
1981 Honorata District Master Plan, Tychy, Poland (with M. Czyzewski and J. Wlodarczyk)

Publications:

By H. WEJCHERT: books—*Wplyw Realizacji na Przemian Miasta* (The influence of Realization on the Changing Image of a Town), Warsaw 1964; *Przestrzenne Uksztaltowanie Osiedli Mieszkaniowych Wznoszonych Metoda Uprzemyslowiona w Swietle ich Realizacji w Polsce* (monograph), Warsaw 1964; *Mieszkanie, Zespol Mieszkaniowy i Miasto na tle Budowy N. Tychow: Sprawy Mieszkaniowe* (Flats, Housing Estates and Town: The New Town of Tychy), Warsaw 1964; *Z Problemow Urbanistyki Miast Poludniowej Szwecji* (monograph), Warsaw 1967; *Miasto Przyszlosci* (Town of the Future), with Kazimierz Wejchert, Warsaw 1973; *Domy Atrialne* (Atrium Housing), Warsaw 1974, 1978; *Small Towns*, with Kazimierz Wejchert, Warsaw 1984; *Ksztaltowanie Zespolow Mieszkaniowych*, Warsaw 1984; articles—"O Realizacji Planu Zagospodarowania m. Garwolin" in *Dom: Osiedle: Mieszkanie* (Warsaw), January 1947; "Studia Zakladu Urbanistyki w Malych Miastach" in *Biuletyn Historii Kultury* (Warsaw), April 1949; "Szesc Ratuszy," with Kazimierz Wejchert, in *Architektura* (Warsaw), April 1950; "Prace Planist. przy Odbudowie Starego Miasta w Olsztynie" in *Miasto* (Warsaw), May 1951; "Problemy Malego Regionu" in *Architektura* (Warsaw), May 1962; "Problemy Miast Szybko Rozwijajacych sie w Polsce," with Kazimierz Wejchert, in *Miasto* (Warsaw), September 1964; "Uzbrojenie Podziemne Miasta a Przemiany Struktury Przestrzennej Osadnictwa," with Kazimierz Wejchert, in *Miasto* (Warsaw), April 1965; "Hidden Remains of Old Buildings as a Problem of Modern Local Planning" in *City* (London), no. 3/4, 1970; "Indywidualne Budownictwo Miszkaniowe w Planowaniu Miast i Stref Zurbanizowanych" in *Sprawy Mieszkaniowe* (Warsaw), February 1971; "Presentation: Tychy New Town," with Kazimierz Wejchert, in *Architektura* (Warsaw), February 1972; "Historia Nadal Optymistyczna" in *Architektura* (Warsaw), February 1972; "Uwagi o Mieszkaniu Przyszlosci," with Kazimierz Wejchert, in *Sprawy Mieszkaniowe* (Warsaw), February 1973; "Nowe Tendecje w Ksztaltowaniu Zespolow Mieszkalnych w Miastach" in *Architektura* (Warsaw), September/October 1974; "Spatial Structure of Small and Middle Size Towns," with Kazimierz Wejchert, in *Geographia Polonica* (Warsaw), no. 32, 1975; "New Towns in Poland," with Kazimierz Wejchert, in *New Towns*, University Park, Pennsylvania 1976.

On H. and K. WEJCHERT: books—*Vom Städtebau der Welt* by F. Jaspert, Berlin 1961; *Les Villes Nouvelles* by Merlin Pierre, Paris 1969; *L'Urbanisme contemporaine* by W. Ostrowski, Paris 1970; *The Architecture of Poland* by Brian Knox, London 1971; *Städtebau der Socialistischer Lander* by E. Goldzamt, Berlin 1975; articles—"Neue Städte in Polen" by J. Heuer in *Neue Heimat* (Hamburg, West Germany), no. 8, 1958; "Der Nachbar in Osten" by G. Kuhne in *Bauwelt* (Berlin), no. 19, 1962; "L'Urbanisme Pologne" by H. Skibniewska in *Architecture d'aujourd'hui* (Paris), no. 118, 1964-65; "La Ville nouvelle: Nowe Tychy" by J. Fourquier in *Planification et urbanisme en Pologne*, Paris 1970; "We Present Attitudes: The Wejcherts on the City," editorial in *Architektura* (Warsaw), April 1977.

Contemporary architecture should grow from the roots of local conditions and traditions and from national culture.

The architect's task—resulting from the needs of rapid population growth—has changed from the scale of one building to the scale of the building complex. One should, therefore, not speak merely about the architecture of buildings; rather, one has to compose and create the architecture of space. Its form, proportions, and tensions generate the framework of people's lives to a much greater extent than do particular buildings.

The large-scale character of the building industry, the size of the areas that are being urbanized, and the industrial production of building elements increase the danger of uniformity and lack of character in urban patterns. The way to counteract this possibility lies in the conscious design of space, backed up by an acquaintance with the theory of appearances, seeing, the analysis of perception, and psychological factors.

On an urban scale, the creation of new values has become necessary. It should happen through the introduction of new urban patterns, which would become plan-generating elements and would provide the basis for further rational developments of urban form.

The unplanned development of the great towns creates the danger that conditions of life may deteriorate. This can be prevented if planning authorities attempt to create settlements of medium-sized towns (100,000-150,000 inhabitants); such units encourage conditions that are suited to people and closer to nature.

The space in an urban environment should divide itself—should be so formed that it divides—into intimate housing space, one's everyday surroundings, and into communal space, accessible to everyone.

Housing environments should ensure contact between the dwellings and the local terrain and landscape, a goal that can be obtained by creating buildings "not exceeding the height of trees," i.e. not more than four stories.

In order that each generation need only contribute a small stage to the historical process of building, we should respect the acheivements of previous ages and the recources accumulated by the current generation. A skillful reference to existing buildings is the most appropriate cultural continuation.

In the field of education, we consider it most important that the teachers transmit to their students not only knowledge but also creative and social attitudes.

We consider the role of the architect to be that of servant to society. Architectural work is not owned by the designer but by the consumer. In making plans for the future, the designer still has the right and the obligation to rely not only on reason, knowledge, and skill, but also, to an equal degree, on intuition. This combination is nearly always decisive in the development of architectural thought.

—Hanna and Kazimierz Wejchert

The most important aspect of the careers of Hanna and Kazimierz Wejchert has been their design work, which involves both architecture and town planning. They have also been involved in forming a "team, " for most of the tasks in which they have been engaged exceed the capabilities of two people. Equally important has been their theoretical work, which they treat as a synthesis of their accumulated experience. They are regarded as the founders of a "new school of architectural thinking, combining the European cultural heritage with new social ideas to guide future development."

Their basic principles include the acceptance of the social role of the architect/town planner (they regard their profession as providing a social service) and the belief that architectural and town planning problems are inseparable. The designer should not think to himself, "I built my town" or "My town includes . . . ," but should instead regard the town as belonging to the people who live there, for whom he designs only a certain framework that they can assimilate, accept, and develop.

Another crucial principle is their treatment of space as architecture; they refer to the space between buildings, and to streets, squares and green areas as being capable of creating feelings of belonging and social identification. The Wejcherts have also developed techniques for producing and motivating design decisions—techniques that do not always precisely conform with accepted regulations and conventions. And, finally, this too might be listed as a principle, that the Wejcherts believe in communication—with the public, with their team, with the client/investor, and with the contractor and other specialists in the design process—a communication informed by an understanding of users' needs and the specialists' tasks.

The Wejcherts produced the master plan for the new town of Tychy in 1951, and construction of the town, for 100,000 inhabitants, has been proceeding under their supervision for the past twenty-five years. It has proved to be for them an experimental testing ground, where the architectural and town planning concepts propagated and taught by them at the Warsaw School of Architecture have been tried and corrected over a long period.

Their basic assumption in the planning was that as Tychy would be a new town with no existing roots, it has to have a clear pattern that could be easily comprehended. From a social point of view, it had to be a Socialist city in which there could be no "good" or "bad" districts. As well, they tried to create a certain framework of commonly used space differentiated from the space of the individual—space within a dwelling and its immediate surroundings.

Their work on the Tychy plan give rise to a new theory about crystallizing plan elements. In the first stage of the project, the Wejcherts approached the planning, as they themselves admit, in an intuitive way. But as they worked, certain elements—crystalizing elements—suggested themselves, elements that, comprehensible to each user, help in the orientation and readibility of urban space. In medieval towns, the marketplace usually provided one such element; it explicity defined a particular space, the shape and character of which depended entirely on the wealth of the inhabitants and on local cultural traditions. In the plan for Tychy, the basic planning element was provided by two intersecting axes: a railway line running east-west and a green belt running north-south, with a explicitly articulated central point—the station. The main streets, just over one-half mile long, were built on the grid and defined the area of the centre. On each of the corners, they planned a complex of squares

Hanna and Kazimierz Wejchert: Ursula District of Tychy New Town, Poland, 1979.

with district services for the four housing districts, each with 25,000 inhabitants.

The Wejcherts attempted to preserve the hierarchical structure of the city, from the neighbourhood unit through the estate and community, up to the district. They regarded this hierarchy as one that should not be tampered with. "Our task has been to build a town, not a group of housing estates separated from each other and not creating an urban formation. The town is not an agglomeration of housing estates with a shopping centre. The town is an organic creature." The Wejcherts believe that the "natural" development of the town often creates spatially unattractive patterns. In their opinion, the most interesting towns are those of the Middle Ages that had one market, towns that later, in the seventeenth century, grew into new towns seeded with new elements that crystallized their plans and ordered the areas of development—new clusters of service and trading units, town halls, churches, squares, and so forth. The Wejcherts believe that many contemporary plans (including those in Poland), the creation of which has involved great difficulties, have suffered just precisely because of the absence of such crystallizing elements.

Another major subject of their research has been in devising a theory of urban composition: man's perception of space, the creation of specific images, the planner's ability to use a variety of elements for spatial composition.

Parallel with their work at Tychy, the Wejcherts are conducting research on the inner spatial structure of small and medium-sized towns. This work will provide the basis in the future for evolving strategic development plans for Tychy. Another practical result will be development plans for a number of small towns conceived of as plans for buildings rather than simply plans for general spatial development—for, as the Wejcherts often stress, "in small towns each building plays a role."

The Wejcherts live in two towns—Warsaw, where they teach, and Tychy, where they build. They are, as they say, fascinated by reality and by the need to realize their projects, a stong characteristic of the War generation, who have a dominating sense of duty to their country.

—Teresa Czaplinska-Archer

WEJCHERT, Kazimierz.
Polish. Born in Smolensk, Russia, 14 May 1912. Educated at the Warsaw Technical University, 1929-35, Dip.Arch. 1935, Ph.D. 1944. Served in the Polish Army, 1935-36, 1939; prisoner-of-war in Bergen-Belsen, 1944-45. Married Janina Pawluc in 1934 (divorced); children: Kazimierz, Ewa, and Dorota; married Hanna Adamczewska (i.e., Hanna Wejchert, *q.v.*) in 1962. Inspector, Warsaw Surveying Office, 1936-37; in private practice, Warsaw, 1937-39; Member, Polish Country Planning Team, 1946-47. In partnership with Hanna Wejchert since 1947. Chief Designer of Tychy New Town, Poland, since 1951. Member of the faculty of the Warsaw school of Architecture since 1946: Assistant Lecturer on Town Planning, 1946-51; Deputy Professor, 1951-55; Associate Professor, 1955-65; Professor, since 1965, and Director of the Spatial Planning Institute, 1971-78. Visiting Professor, Wroclaw University, Poland, 1948, Technical University of Berlin, 1962, Technische Hochschule, Hamburg, West Germany, 1962, and Essen, West Germany, 1963, Technical University of Helsinki, 1969, Technische Hochschule, Dresden, 1972, and Darmstadt,

West Germany, 1973, Institute of Regional Planning, Barcelona, 1974, Technical University of Vilnius, Lithuanian S.S.R., 1974, Institute of Architecture, Moscow, 1975, and Technische Hochschule, Dresden, 1976. Member of the Council, SARP (Architectural Association of Poland), 1949-55, 1960-70, 1974, and Chairman of the SARP Section at Tychy, Poland, 1955-70; Chairman, Society of Polish Town Planners, 1955-57; Chairman, Town Planning Section, Committee of Architecure and Town Planning, Polish Academy of Science, 1960-75. Exhibitions: *Terra 1*, Wroclaw, Poland, 1975; Exhibition of County Regional Plans, Warsaw, 1978; Association of Polish Architects Exhibition, in Warsaw, Rzeszów, and Katowice, 1984. Collection: Architectural Museum, Wroclaw, Poland. Recipient: Polish 10th Anniversary Medal, 1955; Ministry of Town Planning and Architecture Award, 1955, and 1957; Polish Golden Cross of Merit, 1956; Polonia Restituta Cross, 1956; Golden Badge of Merit, Katowice, Poland, 1959; Polish State Prize, 1964 and 1984; Ministry of Higher Education Prize, 1974; Ministry of the Environment Prize, 1974; 30th Anniversary Medal, 1974; Polish Medal of Merit, 1975; Gottfried von Herder Prize, Vienna, 1976; Honour Prize, Polish Association of Architects, 1983. Member, Order of the Banner of Labour, 1970. Corresponding Member, Deutsche Akademie für Städtebau, 1977, and Polish Academy of Science, 1978. Address (office): ul. Orezna 45, Warsaw, Poland.

Publications:

By K. WEJCHERT: books—*The Polish Small Town as a Town Planning Problem*, Warsaw 1947; *Tychy New Town*, Warsaw 1960; *Miasto na warsztacie* (Town in the Making), Warsaw 1969, Warsaw and Washington, D.C. 1974; *Sociological Studies as an Element of Town Planning* (monograph), Warsaw 1970; *Miasto Przyszlosci* (Town of the Future), with Hanna Wejchert, Warsaw 1973; *Elementy kompozycji urbanistycznej* (Elements of Town Planning Composition), Warsaw 1974, 1984, in German: Warsaw 1978; *Problemy identyfikacji przestrzeni we wspolczesnych zespolach mieszkaniowych* (Space Identification in Contemporary Mass Housing Development), Warsaw 1975; *Rola elementow krystalizujacych w planach zabudowania* (Role Played by the Crystalizing Elements in Development Plans), Warsaw 1977; *Small Towns*, with Hanna Wejchert, Warsaw 1984; articles—"Prace Zakl. Urb. PW. na Ziemiach Odzyskanych" in *Architektura* (Warsaw), September 1948; "Szesc Ratszy," with Hanna Wejchert, in *Architektura* (Warsaw), April 1950; "Pieknomiasta in *Miasto* (Warsaw), August 1952; "Indywidualnosc miasta a prefabrykacja" in *Miasto* (Warsaw), April 1956; "Tychy New Town" in *Town and Country Planning* (London), April 1956; "Nowe Tychy" in *Architektura* (Warsaw), June 1957; "Städtebau in Polen" in *Städtebau in Ausland*, Berlin 1963; "Problemy Miast Szybko Rozwijajacych sie w Polsce," with Hanna Wejchert, in *Miasto* (Warsaw), September 1964; "Uzbrojenie Podziemne Miasta a Przemiany Struktury Przestrzennej Osadnictwa," with Hanna Wejchert, in *Miasto* (Warsaw), April 1965; "Tereny i urzadzenia sportowe w planowaniu przestrzennym" in *Urzadzenia sportowe*, Warsaw 1966; "Designing and Executing Sports Facilities in Tychy" in *Biuletyn IUA* (Warsaw), no. 30, 1972; "Presentation: Tychy New Town," with Hanna Wejchert, in *Architektura* (Warsaw), February 1972; "Uwagi o Mieszkaniu Przyszlosci," with Hanna Wejchert, in *Sprawy Mieszkaniowe* (Warsaw), February 1973; "Spatial Structure of Small and Middle Size Towns," with Hanna Wejchert, in *Geographia Polonica* (Warsaw), no. 32, 1975; "New Towns in Poland," with Hanna Wejchert, in *New Towns*, University Park, Pennsylvania 1976.

See WEJCHERT, Hanna

WIENS, Clifford Donald.
Canadian. Born in Glen Kerr, Saskatchewan, 27 April 1926. Educated at Banff School of Fine Arts, Alberta, 1945; University of Saskatchewan, Saskatoon, 1946; Moose Jaw Technical School, Saskatchewan, 1948; Rhode Island School of Design, Providence, 1949-54, B.Arch. 1954. Married Patricia Elizabeth Leigh in 1955; children: Mieka, Robin, Inga, Susan, Nathan, and Lisa. Designer, Stock and Ramsey, architects, Regina, Saskatchewan, 1954-55, and Joseph Pettick, architect, Regina, 1955-57; President, Wiens and Associates, Regina, Saskatchewan, 1957-81. Since 1981, President, Wiens Johnstone Architects Ltd., Regina, Saskatchewan. Visiting Lecturer, University of Saskatchewan Faculty of Sociology and Faculty of Art, 1966-67; Visiting Professor, University of Manitoba, Winnipeg, 1968; Visiting Lecturer, North Dakota State University, Grand Forks, 1970; Visiting Professor, University of Calgary, 1977. President, Saskatchewan Association of Architects, 1970; Member of the Canadian Advisory Committee on Art for Public Buildings, Ottawa, 1974-76. Exhibitions: Canadian Federation of Artists Exhibition, 1964, 1969, 1970; *The Architecture of Clifford Wiens*, Art Gallery of Ontario, Toronto, 1967. Recipient: Merit Award, and Award of Excellence, National Design Council of Canada, 1967; Precast Concrete Institute Award, United States and Canada, 1967; Massey Medal, 1967, 1970; First Award, American Institute of Architects, 1975. Fellow, Royal Architectural Institute of Canada; Associate, Royal Canadian Academy of Arts. Address (office): 2139 Albert Street, Regina, Saskatchewan S4P 2V1, Canada.

Works:

1959 St. Joseph's Church, Whitewood, Saskatchewan
     Pense Elementary School, Pense, Saskatchewan
1960 Pilot Butte School, Pilot Butte, Saskatchewan
     Bell City Motel, Regina
     Kern Motel, Regina
     Kenley Apartments, Regina
     Interprovincial Steel Company Building, Regina
     Balgonie School, Balgonie, Saskatchewan
     Lumsden Eight-Room School, Lumsden, Saskatchewan
1961 St. Mark's Candle Schop, Lumsden, Saskatchewan
     Spivak Apartments, Regina
     Cindercrete Plant, Regina
     4 auditoriums for the Regina Public School Board
1962 Mennonite Brethren Church, Hill Avenue, Regina
     Morse High School, Morse, Saskatchewan
     Kramer House, Mission Lake, Saskatchewan
1963 Lashburn Ten-Room School, Lashburn, Saskatchewan
     Morton House, Regina
     Lough House, Regina
1964 Lebret School, Lebret, Saskatchewan
     Herbert School additions, Herbert, Saskatchewan
1965 McCannell School, Regina
     Darke Hall additions, University of Saskatchewan, Regina
     Weyburn Service Centre, Weyburn, Saskatchewan
     Poultry Science and Horticultural Building, University of Saskatchewan, Saskatoon (project)
1966 North Battleford Service Centre, North Battleford, Saskatchewan
     Lumsden School, Lumsden, Saskatchewan
     Maple Creek Camp and Picnic Grounds Administration Building, Trans-Canada Highway, Maple Creek, Saskatchewan

Clifford Wiens: Heating and Cooling Plant, University of Saskatchewan, Regina, 1967.

Ward Johnston Warehouse, Saskatoon, Saskatchewan

Lloydminster Creamery Plant, Lloydminster, Saskatchewan

1967 Minto Christian Education Centre, Moose Jaw, Saskatchewan

Church of Our Lady, Moose Jaw, Saskatchewan

Central Heating and Cooling Plant, University of Saskatchewan, Regina

Percival Mercury Motor Sales Building, Regina

Melfort, Co-op Creamery Plant, Melfort, Saskatchewan

1968 4-H Campsite, Birsay, Saskatchewan

Hodgeville-Central Butte School additions, Saskatchewan

1969 Crestview Chrysler Showroom, Regina

Silton Chapel, Silton, Saskatchewan

1970 Simpson School additions, Yorkton, Saskatchewan

Holy Rosary Cathedral interior renovations, Regina

Bertmar Investments Store, Moose Jaw, Saskatchewan

1971 Blakeney House, Regina

1972 St. Joseph School additions, Regina

Maintenance Building, University of Saskatchewan, Regina

Unity Separate School additions, Unity, Saskatchewan

Legislative Building renovations, Regina

Engineering and Physics Building, Unversity of Saskatchewan, Regina (project; with others)

1973 Motor Services Shop, Regina

Traders' Building renovations, Regina

Mount Royal School, Regina

Yorkton Creamery Plant, Yorkton, Saskatchewan

1974 Toronto/Dominion Head Office Building, Regina

Public Library and Art Gallery, Swift Current, Saskatchewan

Spa Building, Nakusp Hot Springs, British Columbia

1975 Native Auto Shredder Plant, Regina

East Central School, Prince Albert, Saskatchewan

Saskatchewan Association of Rural Municipalities Office Building, Regina

1976 Dr. Martin LeBoldus High School, Regina

Joseph Burr Tyrell High School, Fort Smith, North West Territories

Native Metal Industries Office Building, Regina

1977 Elementary School, Regina

Senior Citizens Recreations Centre, Prince Albert, Saskatchewan

Senior Citizens Apartment Complex, Weyburn, Saskatchewan

Canadian Imperial Bank of Commerce Data Service Centre, Regina

Holy Rosary Cathedral restoration (after fire), Regina

1978 Royal Bank of Canada Office Building, Regina

Fire Station No. 6, Regina

Hillsdale Baptist Church, Regina

Royal Canadian Mounted Police Swimming Pool, Regina (project)

Study of the Moose Jaw River Valley, Saskatchewan

National Gallery of Canada, Ottawa (competition project)

1979 Northwest Water Storage Reservoir, Regina, Saskatchewan

1980 Kindergarten Schools, at Nut Lake, John Smith and White Bear Reserves, Saskatchewan

1981 Diary Producers Co-operatives Creamery, Regina, Saskatchewan Pedestrian Overpass Bridge, Regina, Saskatchewan

Creamery, Regina, Saskatchewan

Golden Mile Shopping alterations and renovations, Regina, Saskatchewan

Cote Reserve Indian School, Cote, Saskatchewan

1982 Balcarres School addition and renovation, Saskatchewan

Parkway Office Building, Regina, Saskatchewan

1983 Canadian Broadcasting Corporation Centre, Regina, Saskatchewan

Camrose Lutheran College Classroom Building, Camrose, Alberta

Wihak, Karasin and Thomas Dental Offices, Regina, Saskatchewan

Golden Mile Office and Mall alterations, Regina, Saskatchewan

Founders Hall relocation and restoration, Camrose Lutheran College, Camrose, Alberta

1984 Tkach Law Office, Regina, Saskatchewan

Elevator installation, Holy Rosay Cathedral, Regina, Saskatchewan

Outdoor Theatre, Moose Jaw, Saskatchewan

New City Hall, Prince Albert, Saskatchewan

11th Floor Offices and interiors, Bank of Montreal, Regina, Saskatchewan

Cathedral Area Senior Citizens Apartments, Regina, Saskatchewan
Cathedral Neighborhood Centre, Regina, Saskatchewan
New Albert School, Regina, Saskatchewan
Dairy Producers Co-operatives Ltd. Creamery, Prince Albert, Saskatchewan
Visitor Information Centre, Fleming, Saskatchewan

Publications:

By WIENS: book—*Silton Chapel*, Vancouver 1970; articles—"The Design Canada Structural Steel Awards Program" in *Design Canada* (Ottawa), 1966; "The Design Canada Concrete Institute Awards Program" in *Design Canada* (Ottawa), 1967; "Weather Shelter" in *Canadian Architect* (Toronto), October 1972; "Spiral Tee Pee" in *Wood World* (Vancouver), Summer 1972; "The 1974 Canadian Architects Yearbook Award of Excellence" in *The Canadian Architects Yearbook 1974*, Toronto 1974; "Industrial Design—Why Better Products?" in *Saskatchewan Business Forum* (Regina), March 1975; "Regionalism and Reality" in *The Canadian Architect* (Toronto), October 1979; "Data Graphics—Division of Wiens Johnstone Architects Ltd." in *Regina Today*, June 1983; "From Mies to Metaphors" in *The Canadian Architect* (Toronto), May 1983.

On WIENS: books—*The Architecture of Clifford Wiens*, exhibition catalogue, Toronto 1967; *Canadian Architecture 1960/70*, Toronto 1971; *Holzbau Atlas*, Munich 1979; *Building with Words: Canadian Architects on Architecture*, with introduction by W. Bernstein and R. Cawker, Toronto 1981; *Modern Canadian Architecture* by Leon Whiteson, Toronto 1983; *Fifty Outstanding Architects of the World* by Ivica Mladenovic, Belgrade 1984; articles—"St. Joseph's, Whitewood, Saskatchewan" in *Canadian Architect* (Toronto), February 1961; "Interprovincial Steel Office Building" and "St. Mark's Shop" in *Canadian Architect* (Toronto), March 1962; "Hill Avenue Mennonite Brethren Church, Regina" in *Royal Architectural Institute of Canada Journal* (Toronto), December 1963; "Architecture of the Prairies" by Hans Elte in *Royal Architectural Institute of Canada Journal* (Toronto), June 1965; "Administration Building" in *Canadian Architect* (Toronto), November 1966; "Significant Architects '67" in the *Canadian Architects Yearbook*, Toronto 1967; "Out on the Plains" in *Progressive Architecture* (New York), September 1970; "That Magnificent Mud-Reinforced Concrete" by Walter McQuade in *Fortune* (New York), December 1970; "National Gallery Competition Results" in *Canadian Architect* (Toronto), April 1977; "Superstars of the Skyscrapers" in *En Route* (Toronto), March 1978; "Clifford Wiens—A New Profile" in *News Wave* (Regina, Saskatchewan), April 1980; "Regina Office of Wiens Johnston Architects Ltd." in *Architects' Forum* (Vancouver), July/August 1981; "Computers in Architecture", special issue of *Architects' Forum* (Vancouver), vol. 4, no. 2, 1984.

The process of design for an architectural commission has become extremely complex. It is a complexity that needs to be understood and identified. A kind of equation must be struck that gives weight to the order of priorities that will guide the design process. Central to this equation is the reality of the client. With each commission the fullest respect and attention should be given to the client's needs and resources. To do otherwise is to lose credibility and consequently the opportunity to serve again, for without the client the privilege of shaping space does not exist. That the client may experience a new design awareness in the design process should be anticipated and understood by the architect. Frequently the limits set by the client at the beginning of a project are not the same limits set at the end of the project. The architect must therefore develop the ability to communicate the evolutionary design possibilities to the client at the formative stages.

The focus of architecture exists in the expression of both the essential and the unique. It is my conviction that there is a quality of uniqueness inherent in each design problem. To remove the element of uniqueness from architecture, as is occurring in the somewhat mindless mass production of buildings today, represents a kind of technical cloning for which we can, at best, only congratulate ourselves at having mastered technique. To clearly articulate the essential and unique activities of human use, the essential and unique aspects of the site and the essential and unique characteristics of available materials and construction systems represents, for me, and excitement of the design process.

The design process can begin very slowly towards synthesis or spring full blown, depending on the understanding that is brought to the design problem. Where it must slowly, the process is one of developing a working relationship of all elements, however mediocre the articulation of that relationship may be at first. As these relationships develop, I begin to identify what is essential and what is unique and concurrently begin to search for the kind of spatial configurations that will enclose and separate human activity with the greatest clarity. From the understanding of spatial needs, a structural framework begins to suggest itself. It is extremely important, at this point, that the fullest implications of all technical and environmental concerns are fully realized. Each element of the design should fulfill itself in terms of its own discipline while contributing to the whole. The design process, therefore, involves many cycles of critical analysis, each cycle spawning its own mutations. It is often these mutative developments that offer the greatest opportunity for unique and expressive qualities in the design. When a design is most fitting to its use and to the spirit of its own making, it can be considered to be complete, to be fully synthesized, to be unique.

—Clifford Wiens

Clifford Wiens has the ability to distill a building to its essence and to express the distillation in simple floor plans and eye-catching forms. Most of his buildings are modest in size and limited in function, so his approach to design has yet to pass the test of a complex programme. This does not, however, detract from the effectiveness of what he has already done.

His Administration Building for Maple Creek Camp, and Silton Chapel, and Mennonite Brethren Church in Regina, the Interprovincial Steel Company Building and his Heating Plant for the University of Saskatchewan all have symmetrical plans. The Silton Chapel and the heating plant are perfect squares. His weather shelter design is a helix; the St. Mark's Shop is a circle, with circular porthole windows. Wien's preoccupation, then, with rigid and simple geometry is evident.

Although his plans are formal and static, it is in three dimensional form that Wiens lightens his seriousness and achieves some of the memorable effects that have enhanced his reputation. It must by remembered that he is designing for the Canadian prairie, and he seems to want to do two things: to express in built form the horizontality visually in order to make his building stand out as an "event." One of his standard techniques is to isolate the roof structure from the main base of the building; in effect, this allows a horizontal plane to pass visually through the elevation. The floating roof structure is then free to be exploited as a "flag" and is frequently enhanced by sinking the base of the building into the ground (as in the Silton Chapel and the St. Mark's Shop). By these means he achieves both purposes—expressing the horizontal site yet interrupting it. Lowering the building also gives a sense of shelter (though, ironically, his weather shelter is not lowered). This is one of the few concessions Wiens makes to the harshness of his environment; he is more consistently concerned with a visual response than a physical one. Nevertheless, his buildings are not inappropriate, and visually they make a strong and sensible contribution to the built environment of his region.

—Kent Hurley

WILL, Philip, Jr.

American. Born in Rochester, New York, 15 February 1906. Educated in Rochester public schools, 1912-22; Phillips Academy, Exeter, New Hampshire, 1922-24; Cornell University College of Architecture, Ithaca, New York, 1924-30 (Clifton Beck with Brown Medal; Charles Goodwin Sands Medal; Thesis Medal, 1930), B.Arch. 1930. Married Caroline Elizabeth Sinclair in 1933; children: Elizabeth and Philip. Worked as an architectural draftsman, Gordon and Kaelber Architects, Rochester, 1928-29, and Shreve, Lamb and Harmon, New York, 1930-33; Associate Architect, General Houses Inc., Chicago, 1933-34, and South Park Gardens, 1934. Founding Partner, with Lawrence Perkins, q.v., and E. Todd Wheeler, Perkins, Wheeler and Will, Chicago, 1935-46, subsequently Perkins and Will, 1946-64, and the Perkins and Will Partnership, 1964-70; Senior Vice-President, 1970-71, and Vice-Chairman, 1970-73, Director, 1973-83, and Chairman, 1975-83, Perkins and Will Architects Inc., Chicago; offices established in New York, 1951, and Washington, D.C., 1962. Director, Illinois Council, American Institute of Architects, 1947-49; Director, 1947-51, Second Vice-President, 1951-52, and President, 1952-54, Chicago Chapter of the AIA; Chairman, Citizens of Greater Chicago, 1954; President of the Alumni Council of the College of Architecture, 1954-56, Trustee, 1963-73, and Chairman of the Trustee Committee on Buildings and Grounds, 1966-73, Cornell University; Second Vice-President, 1956-58, First Vice-President, 1958-60, and President, 1960-62, National AIA; Member, 1959-64, and Chairman, 1965, City of Evanston (Illinois) Planning Commission; Chairman, Committee on the Performance Concept, Building Research Advisory Board, Washington, D.C., 1965. Recipient: Cruceiro Sul do Brasil, 1961; Special Citation of Merit, AIA, 1968; 25 Year Award, AIA, 1971; The Cornell Medal, 1973; Outstanding Service Award, AIA, 1982. Fellow, American Institute of Architects, 1951. Honorary Fellow, Royal Architectural Institute of Canada, and the Philippine Institute of Architects; Honorary Member, Le Sociedad de Arquitectos Mexicanos, and La Sociedad de Arquitectos del Peru. *Died* (in Venice, Florida) *22 October 1985.*

Works:

1933 Logan House, Northfield, Illinois (as associate archiect to Howard Fisher)
1934 Steel House, *Century of Progress Exposition*, Chicago (for General Houses Inc.)
1937 Philip Will Jr. Residence, Evanston, Illinois
1939/
40 Crow Island School, Winnetka, Illinois (with Eliel and Eero Saarinen)
1952 Heathcote School, Scarsdale, New York
1954 Rockford Memorial Hospital, Illinois
1957 Willage (Philip Will Jr. Summer Cottage), Higgins Lake, Michigan
1958 Cornell University Engineering Campus, Ithaca, New York
International Minerals and Chemical Corporation Building, Skokie, Illinois

1960 Pure Oil Company Office Building, Palatine,
      Illinois
      Stamford Hospital, Connecticut
1963 U.S. Gypsum Building, Chicago
1964 National College of Agriculture, Chapingo,
      Mexico
1965 Scott Foresman Office Building, Glenview,
      Illinois
      Lutheran School of Theology, Chicago
1966 First National Bank, Chicago (with C. F.
      Murphy Associates)
      Salsbury Laboratories, Charles City, Iowa
1967 Orchard Ridge Campus, Oakland Commun-
      ity College, Farmington, Michigan
1969 Abbott Laboratories, Lake County, Illinois

Publications:

By WILL: articles—"The Future of the Architec-
tural Profession" in *Louisiana Architect* (New
Orleans), December 1961; "Ahead Lies a New
Frontier" in *Florida Architect* (Miami), January
1962; "The Architect Serves His Community" in
AIA Journal (Washington, D.C.), May 1962

On WILL: articles—"The Perkins and Will Partnership" in *Building Construction* (Chicago), April

1969; "Return of the Megastructure" by Suzanne
Stephens in *Architectural Forum* (New York), Sep-
tember 1973; "First National Bank, Chicago" in
Informes de la Construccion (Madrid), November
1973; "Medical Facilities" in *Architectural Record*
(New York), September 1975.

As humane architecture, a building must relate to
people. It must provide an environment that delights beholder and occupant, which inspires respect, productivity, and ultimate sense of rightness.
                                    —Philip Will Jr. (1980)

Philip Will Jr. was co-founder (with Lawrence
Perkins) of Perkins and Will of Chicago, one of
America's largest and most active architectural
firms. After working for Gordon and Kaelber in his
home town of Rochester, New York, and Shreve,
Lamb and Harmon in New York City, Will moved
to Chicago and a position with General House Inc.,
a firm headed by architect Howard Fisher. General
Houses did early work in prefabricated houses
designs, mostly in the modernist manner. Will, in
fact, was responsible for the prefabricated steel
house that General Houses showed in the 1934
Century of Progress Exposition in Chicago. Three

years later he built his own house in Evanston,
Illinois, an elegant frame structure whose originality
rested in a graceful mixture of the ground-hugging
profiles of Frank Lloyd Wright's earlier Prairie
Style, with volumetric elements related to the International Style.

The firm of Perkins, Wheeler and Will was
established in 1935. Following the lean Depression
years, which were marked by only occasional
modest residential work, Will and his colleagues
undertook their first major commission (with Eliel
and Eero Saarinen), the Crow Island School in
Winnetka, Illinois. This was a radical design which
featured the articulation of individual classrooms
and study areas, and Will played a far greater role in
the overall planning of Crow Island than he has
been given credit for. The project launched Perkins
and Will (Wheeler left the firm in 1946) in the design
of academic institutions, a field in which they have
continued to distinguish themselves.

Perkins and Will's later work was wide-ranging in
function and often in scale. Will himself was chiefly
involved in the design of the headquarters for Scott
Foresome in Glenview, Illinois and the U.S. Gypsum Building, one of the most discussed works of
the post-World War II phase of Chicago commercial building.
                                    —Franz Schulze

Philip Will: Heathcote School, Scarsdale, New York, 1952.

WILLERVAL, Jean

French. Born in Tourcoing, 28 September 1924. Educated at the Ecole Nationale Supérieur des Beaux-Arts, Paris; studied painting, 1943-44, and architecture, 1945-51. Married the achitect Anna Mazurkiewicz in 1951; children: Carine, Isabelle and Bruno. In private practice, Paris since 1959; established office in Lille, France, 1962 (associates: Pierre Rignols and Andrè Lagarde). Consultant Architect to the French Ministry of Equipment, since 1964; Consultant Architect for the Paris Master Plan, since 1975; Member of the Commission on Architecture and Urbanism of the City of Paris, since 1976. Professor, Department of Architecture, Ecole Nationale Supérieure des Beaux-Arts, Paris, since 1958; Professor and Chairman, l'Ecole Supérierieure d'Architecture de San Luc, Tournai, Belgium, since 1964. Exhibition: Centre Georges Pompidou, Paris, 1976. Recipient: First Prize, Pre-Fabricated School Competition, 1960; First Prize, Town Hall Plaza Competition, Lille, France, 1961; First Prize, Palace of Justice Competition, Lille, France, 1962; First Prize, National Agronomic Research Center Competition, Theix, France, 1962; First Prize, Lille Roubaix-Tourcoing Center Competition, 1970; First Prize, Doubs District Administration Buildings Competition, France, 1972; Grand Silver Medal, Académie d'Architecture, 1972; First Prize, Lille-Est New Town Commercial Center Competition, France, 1973; First Prize, National Family House Competition, 1974; Grand National Prize in Architecture, 1975, 1976; First Prize, General Tax Collec-tion Centre Competition, Martinique, 1981; First Prize, City Centre Reconstruction Competition, Beirut, 1983. Member, Académie d'Architecture; Chevalier, Order of Arts and Letters, 1976; Chevalier, Légion d'Honneur, 1976. Address (office): 52 rue Pernety, 75014 Paris, France.

Works:

1962/
73   12,000 flats in French new towns
1963/
75   National Institute of Agronomic Research, Theix, France
1968   Hall of Justice, Lille, France
1973   Fire Brigade Barracks (Caserne Messéna), Boulevard Masséna, Paris
1974   Pernod Factory and Headquarters, Créteil, France
1975   Town Hall, Bordeaux
1976   Banque Populaire du Nord Headquarters, Lille, France
      Lock Lookout Station, Lille, France
      "Le Forum" Business and Shopping Center, Lille, France
1977   Nuclear power plants in Flamanville, Belleville, and St. Alban/St. Maurice, France
      Town Hall, Fort-de-France, Marinique
      "Le Mercure" Business Center, Roubaix, France

      Hypermarket, Lille, France
1978   Polish Consulate, Lille, France
1980   Control Data Headquarters and Laboratories, Marne-la-Vallée France
      Hewlett Packard Headquarters and Laboratories, Evry, France
1981/
82   Les Halles Development, Paris
1982/
84   Two tower blocks, La Defense district, Paris
1983   Contemporary Art Museum, Dunkerque, France

Publications;

By WILLERVAL: article in *Galerie des Arts*(Paris), July 1983.

On WILLERVAL; articles—"Fire station on the Boulevard Masséna" in *Architectural Française* (Paris), July/August 1973; "Nuclear Centres" in *Crée* (Paris), February 1976; "Centre Mercure, Roubaix" in *Architecture d'Aujourd'hui* (Paris), February 1979; "Paris' Second Longest Planning Wrangle Comes to an End" in *Building Design* (London), 13 February 1981; "The Leaning Tower of Pernod" in *Deutsche Bauzeitung* (Stuttgart), October 1981; "The Toll-Booths of Saint Avold" in *Construction Moderne* (Paris), October 1981; "Per-

Jean Willerval: **Museum of Contemporary Art, Dunquerque, France, 1983.**

nod Solar Complex at Lyon" in *Recherche et Architecture* (Paris), no. 45, 1981; "Headquarters and Laboratories of Control Data" in *Mur Vivant* (Paris), July 1983; "Contemporary Arts Museum at Dunkirk" in *Arbitare* (Milan), October 1983; "Building Lescot— Les Halles" in *Mur Vivant* (Paris), October 1983; "Nuclear Power Plant in St. Alban" in *Contemporary Architecture* (Lausanne Switzerland), no. 5, 1983/84; "Preservatrice Insurance Headquarters—La Defense", in *Techniques et Architecture* (Paris), August/September 1984.

My ideas on architecture are simple. When I have to construct a building, whatever it is, I always start with the principle that I have to create a master work—in the medieval sense of the word—that is to say, a perfect work, complete in all its details. This work is meant for the men who will live or work there. Of course, it must meet all the functional criteria that our age requires, but I am less and less of a purist in this respect. Contrary to what one might think, dry and precise functionalism is not an exact science and can be adapted to an unusual fantasy born from structural requirements or the nature of the site.

The problem with architecture is mastery of the contructed space; interior and exterior are but one, and one must pass from one to the other without a break. There is no facade street, no facade garden; all facets of the work must be treated nobly. Man inhabits this place, and he has to find himself as ease both inside and out, and there is no detail that can be neglected in the arrangement of the place where he lives and works.

When I am asked to construct large buildings that are to take their place in a city's profile, I still believe that we must construct buildings that, by their quality, their proportions, their beauty, will polarize the diffuse feelings of citizens who like to refer to "places" that attract them and of which they are proud. A town hall is not a magma of cells more or less well put together; it is a public "place." It is built once every 100 or 200 years and is above passion and party. It must be exemplary; it must provoke the pride of citizens by its serene beauty. I do not construct a building thinking that it may be destroyed in ten years. I have a horror of provisional architecture. I take my profession seriously.

As for the architectural signature that I seek, it is to be found in three complimentary goals: 1) unity within and without—emphasis on the built sector without artifice and without deceit but without depriving oneself of the pleasure of the design of forms, and a search for transparencies, for the path of light throught the building, giving it life, as with time passing; 2) creation according to the scale of vision of the passerby who doesn't life his head, a varied and familiar world that both attracts and distracts him; and 3) appropriateness—the consideration, finally, that a large building takes its place in the city and that its own beauty can be an end in itself. One reaches for another scale of values. This architecture is seen; it belongs to everyone; it should be a source of joy for those who contemplate it every day.

—Jean Willerval

Jean Willerval occupies a not insignificant position among French architects of the postwar generation. He is a conscientious worker who wants to do architecture rather than business and to recognize his responsibilities rather than to escape them in woolly theorizing, absurd non-architecture, scandalous utopias, or the fashion for the past. His work is distinguished not by any apparent consistency but by a continual search, more or less successful and always sincere. He does not yet seem to have found the way to express his personality, but it is likely that maturity will help him to develop a more distinctive line.

Worthy of particular mention among his principal executions are the Hall of Justice, Lille, still bearing the traces of his academic training as an architect but already showing his desire to be of his time; the

excellent fire station on on the Boulevard Massena in Paris; but especially his building for the apertif firm of Pernod in the new town of Créteil, near Paris, where Willerval gives proof of a great mastery of form and of a controlled freedom in the conception of the whole as well as in the details. In recent years, Willerval's professional activity has expanded considerably. But he has been able to resist the temptations of fashion, of so-called "Post-Modernism". Apart from the brief digression of the Les Halles commission, Willerval has moved in his own direction: the functional solution of posed problems, with intelligent use of today's technology; investigation of pure forms, avoiding the tedious without making any concession to the superficial, aftificial, anecdotal, ordecorative.

—Pierre Vago

WILLIAMS, Amancio.

Argentinian. Born in Buenos Aires, 19 February 1913. Educated at the University of Buenos Aires, Faculty of Engineering, 1931-34, and Faculty of Architecture, 1938-41, Dip.Arch. 1941. Served as a Reserve Officer in the Argentine Air Force, 1934-38. Married; children: Veronica, Florencia, Teresa, Ines, Gloria, Claudio, Cristobal, and Pablo. In private practice, as architect, designer and city planner, Buenos Aires, since 1941. Exhibitions: International Exhibition of Architecture, Paris, 1947; Harvard University, Cambridge, Massachusetts, 1951, 1955 (one-man); *Architecture of Latin America*, Museum of Modern Art, New York, 1955-56; University of Buenos Aires, 1955 (one-man); *World's Fair*, Brussels, 1958; International Exposition, Moscow, 1958; *Bienal*, Sao Paulo, 1961; *Art of Latin America Since Independence*, Yale University, New Haven, Connecticut, 1966; Museum of Modern Art, New York, 1968; Universidad de la Republica, Montevideo, 1975; *Visionary Drawing of Architecture and Planning*, Drawing Center, New York, 1979. Recipient: Gold Medal, *World's Fair*, Brussels, 1958; Laurel de Plata Award, Ateneo Roariano, Buenos Aires, 1971; Biennial Honor Award, Sociedad Central de Arquitectos, Argentina, 1972. Member, National Academy of Fine Arts, Buenos Aires, 1959. Honorary Fellow, American Institute of Architects, 1962; Honorary Member, Institute of Hispanic Culture, 1965; Honorary Member, College of Architects of Peru, 1965; Honorary Architect, University of Montevideo, 1970; Honorary Professor, Universidad Nacional Federico Villareal, Lima, Peru, 1977. Address (office): Virrey Loreto 1940, Buenos Aires 1426, Argentina.

Works:

1939 Self-supporting Roof Structure (project)
1942 Dwellings in Space, Buenos Aires (project; with Delfina Galvez de Williams and Jorge Vivanco)
Jorge Black House, Bariloche, Argentina
1942/
43 Casa Amarilla O.V.R.A. Housing Development, Buenos Aires (project)
Extendible Partition Wall (project)
1942/
53 Concert Hall (Hall for Plastic Spectacle and Sound), Buenos Aires
1943 Complex of Apartment Blocks, Buenos Aires (project)
House in the Parque Pereyra Iraola, Mar del Plata, Argentina
House in Martinez, Albardon, Buenos Aires Province

House, Buenos Aires (project)
Triangular Housing Block, Mar del Plata, Argentina (project)
Regional plan for Patagonia, Argentina
1943/
45 "House over the Brook", Mar del Plata River Valley, Argentina
1944 House, Escobar, Buenos Aires Province
Transport and communications study, Buenos Aires
1945 Country house, General Pueyrredon District, near Mar del Plata, Argentina (with Jorge Butler)
International Airport, Buenos Aires (project; with Cesar Janello, Colette Boccara and Jorge Butler)
Plan for the City of Buenos Aires
1946 Armchair in Leather and Wood
Office and commercial complex, Buenos Aires (with Cesar Janello, Colette Broccara and Jorge Butler)
1947 National master plan for the Ministry of Public Health, Argentina
1947/
58 Regional plan for the Parana Delta and Buenos Aires Region
1948 Central City Redevelopment, Cordoba, Argentina (project; with Gomes Molina)
City and regional plan for Corrientes, Argentina
Missionary-Boat for Disease Prevention in the Parana Delta, Argentina (project)
Office Building Suspended by Cables, Buenos Aires (project)
1948/
53 Curuzu-Cuatia Hospital, Corrientes, Argentina
Esquina Hospital, Corrientes, Argentina
Mburucuya Hospital, Corrientes, Argentina
1949 Design of the *Architecture and Urbanism of Our Times* exhibition, Galeria Kraft, Calle Florida, Buenos Aires
Doctor's house and surgery, Palermo, Buenos Aires
1949/
50 Various objects in steel and plastic
1951 House for a horticulturist, El Tigre, Argentina
1951/
52 Reinforced Concrete Vaulted Roof (prototype; with Julio Pizetti)
1952 House with ground-floor shop, Munro, Argentina
1953 House in the Forest, Parana Delta, Argentina (project)
1954 Various pre-fabricated structures
1954/
55 Reinforced Concrete Shell Service Station, Avellaneda, Argentina (project)
1955 Health Center, Mar del Plata, Argentina (project)
1955/
57 Apartment building, Buenos Aires (project)
1956/
57 Bedroom and library furniture
Francisco de Ridder Apartment interiors, Avenida Alvear 1491, Buenos Aires
1957/
58 Regional and city plan for El Tigre, Argentina
1958 Ignacio Pirovano Penthouse conversion, Buenos Aires
1959 Universidad Catolica Argentina alterations and renovations, Buenos Aires
1960 Huinca-Loo Mansion extensions and alterations, Province of Buenos Aires
Industrial School with Shell Roof, Olvarria, Argentina (project)
Textiles Supermarket and Showrooms, Bernal, Argentina
Monument for the Marist International Congress, Buenos Aires
1961 Di Tella Family Summer House and Art Gallery, Punta del Este, Argentina (project)

Amancio Williams: House Over the Brook, Mar del Plata, Argentina, 1943-45.

Olivetti Company Housing Estate (competition project)

1962 Furniture shop (conversion of existing apartment building), Buenos Aires

20-storey building, Avenida Libertador, Buenos Aires (project)

Iggam Company Factory and Office Building, Cordoba, Argentina (project)

Monument to the Composer Alberto Williams, Buenos Aires

1963 Apartment alterations, Gelly Obes and Guido Streets, Buenos Aires

Alterations to 2 floors of an apartment building, Hippolito Irigoyen 1782, Buenos Aires

1964 Library, Students Residence, Zavalia 2048, Buenos Aires

Pastoral Care Center, Berlin (project)

1965 Biochemical Laboratory, Juncal 1720, Buenos Aires (project)

1966 Olivetti Shop and Showrooms alterations, Buenos Aires (project)

Olivetti Exhibition Pavilions (project)

Bunge y Born Pavilion, Sociedad Rural Building, Buenos Aires

1967/
68 Church of Our Lady of Fatima, Pilar, Argentina

1967/
70 Bonomo House, Buenos Aires

1968 West German Embassy, Plaza Alemania, Buenos Aires (project; with Walter Gropius)

Argentine Industrial Union Building, Buenos Aires (competition project; with Luis Santos, Alejandro Bonomo and Eduardo Rojkind)

Hugh-Rise Building, Buenos Aires (project)

1968/
69 Tilda Thamar House, Vte. Lopez District, Buenos Aires (project)

1968/
71 Sirio Libanes Country Club, Pergamino, Argentina (with Ricardo Mackinlay and Delfina Galvez de Williams)

1969 San Vicente de Paul Hospital, Oran-Salta, Argentina (competition project; with Luis Santos)

Canumar-Empresa Naviera Office Building, Calle 25 de Mayo, Buenos Aires (project; with Luis Santos)

Juan Carlos Ongania House, Las Lomas de San Isidro, Argentina (project; with Luis Santos)

Raul Desmaras House, Las Lomas de San Isidro, Argentina (project; with Luis Santos)

Bernardo Mandelbaum House, San Isidro Boating Club, Argentina (project; with Eduardo Leston)

1969/
70 Cultural Center, Cume-Co Estate, Pirovano, Buenos Aires Province (project)

1970 L. U. 9 Radio Station, Mar del Plata, Argentina

1971/
72 City and neighborhood planning study of Corrientes, Argentina

1972 Monument with Laser Beams, near the Colón Theatre, Buenos Aires (project)

1974/
75 The City That Humanity Needs (urban study project)

1977 Pierano Apartment alteration, Buenos Aires

Ignacio Pirovano Apartment alterations, Parera 3, Buenos Aires

S.A.C.A.F.I. Offices, Sargentos 435, Buenos Aires

1978 Office building, Belgrano, Buenos Aires (project)

General San Martin Monument, Pirovano, Buenos Aires

1978/
80 Cross in the River Plate, Buenos Aires (project)

1982 Parc de la Villette Develpment, Paris (competition project)

Publications:

By WILLIAMS: articles—"La Ciudad que Necesita la Humanidad" in *Clarin* (Buenos Aires), 25 November 1977; "Orientar al País para Abordar una Nueva Época" in *La Nación* (Buenos Aires), 12 October 1978; "Descubrimiento arqueologico en la Quebrada del Toro" in *La Nacion* (Buenos Aires),

23 January 1983; film—*Altar Monumantal: Primer Congreso Mariano Interamericano*, with Horacio Coppola, Buenos Aires 1960.

On WILLIAMS: books—*L'Architecture Nouvelle* by Alberto Sartoris, Milan 1954; *Amancio Williams* by Raul Gonzalez Capdevila, Buenos Aires 1955; *New Directions in Latin American Architecture* by Francisco Bullrich, New York 1969; articles— "Amancio Williams: House Over the Brook", special issue of *Nuestra Arquitectura* (Buenos Aires), no. 8, 1947; "Systeme d'habitations collectives en gradins" in *L'Architecture d'Aujourd'hui* (Paris), no. 16, 1947; "Una nueva unidad estructural" in *Nueva Vision* (Buenos Aires), no. 5, 1954; "Tres hospitales en la Provincia de Corrientes" in *Nueva Vision* (Buenos Aires), no. 9, 1957; "Proyecto para una fabrica Iggam S.A." in *Summa* (Buenos Aires), no. 5, 1966; "La concepciones del diseno en la trascendente obra de Amancio Williams" in *Conviccion* (Buenos Aires), 26 May 1979; "De la ciudad inhabitable a la ciudad espacial" in *La Nacion* (Buenos Aires), 11 October, 1981; films—*Amancio Williams* by Manuel Antin, Buenos Aires 1967; *Amancio Williams*, produced by Sucesos Argentinos, Buenos Aires 1968; *Departamento de Ignacio Pirovano* by David Lamelas, Buenos Aires 1971.

The realization of my work has been very difficult here in Argentina, but I consider that its importance is in the value of its ideas.

In the last few years I have been very active studying and promoting a theme that is, I think, at this moment, the great need of mankind. It has to do with human habitat. Until now I have used as a title (and also as a slogan) "The City That Humanity Needs." The press in Argentina and Uruguay have given me a great deal of support. All of the newspapers and the best magazines have published articles, and I have lectured on the radio and televsion, at the National Academy of Fine Arts, and at the University of Uruguay. Considering that the Argentina newspapers have a circulation of something like 500,000 copies I suppose that until now, in different issues, more than 10 million copies have been circulated on this theme. Now, critics in the States have begun paying attention to this work, and I have been asked to lecture there.

—Amancio Williams

As a foreword to a magazine presentation of the works of Amancio Williams, in 1947, Le Corbusier wrote: "The three Americas, which up to fifty years ago were still the land of colonists and colonization, are still countries which aspire to steep themselves in the latest branches of knowledge. Life races ahead there: these countries beckon life, and life bursts in them. It manifests itself through a form of building which develops beyond all our customs, all our conceptions. Here we have Buenos Aires, which, through succeeding jolts, through contrast and reaction, and through the action of limited but intensely cultivated groups, an avant-garde society, reaches the level of the most captivating reality in architecture. Here we find, for instance, as a first post-war contact, the fresh appearance of creations in the fields of city planning and architecture, filled with the breadth of oceans and of the pampus, a great breadth, liberated from meaniness. Here, then, are the works of Amancio Williams and of his team in Buenos Aires."

The quotation is apt, for Amancio Williams, who was then thirty-four years old, had already carried out the Dwellings in Space project, a project for an airport for Buenos Aires, and, in particular, had designed and oversaw the construction of the famous House Over the Brook in Mar del Plata, considered "the most audacious and independent creation of that generation of Argentine architects." That decade, the 1940s, saw the greatest output from Williams, who was to have a notable influence on a professional environment that was still strongly tied to more or less orthodox "styles" and (with a few isolated exceptions) hadn't seemed to notice the existence of a new architecture emerging as a consequence of European and American movements at least thirty years earlier.

Unfortunately, William's studies and projects are much more numerous than his actual buildings, perhaps because, as he himself observes, the necessary finance to realize such projects is always missing. Nevertheless, those studies have profoundly affected not only Argentine architecs but also all those who have seem them at exhibitions throughout the world and in the architectural press. He has been, and remains, a master of contemporary Argentine architecture.

His principles, in his own words, are: "working with every freedom in space; handling the three dimensions freely; searching within technology for true expression; working with a sense of unity; reaching a synthesis; working with a sense of the permanent." And, it is necessary to "employ all of our creative forces, the forces of culture, and to apply science to our development." The two constants in all his work are the application of science and the manipulation of, and attention to, space.

A fundamental concern of his work has been to free the ground of the city, to respect or create green spaces—he admires Le Corbusier's "building in space" concept. This interest in spatiality applies to individual buildings as well as to cities as a whole: besides the works mentioned above, his projects for an office building in downtown Buenos Aires and his Hall for Plastic Spectacle and Sound also demonstrate his consistent and continuous interest in space—as do his more recent studies in the field of planning.

Three works remain seminal.

The House Over the Brook, completed in 1945, was an attempt to achieve a three-dimensional structure which would leave the ground level free, that is, an intergrated and complex system that would do away with pillar supports. His solution was to achieve support via a curved foil with a parabolic section, which works in conjunction with the concrete floor of the main level of the dwelling and with the beams that surround it, in such a way that the tensions of the whole determined the final shape.

In an urban environment, there is his project for an office building. It was conceived as having an outer structure of four huge concrete columns with beams and upper arcades, also made of concrete, from which were hung the horizontal planes of each floor, through the employment of steel struts acting exclusively through traction—thus eliminating columns from the standard storey. The complex was of four blocks separated from one another and from the ground by airy open spaces which, in the case of the access level tier, reached a height of almost twenty metres.

Presenting his project for Dwellings in Space in 1942—set up on an urban lot measuring 14.50 by 43 metres, between party walls—Williams stated that "the plastic solution is obtained on the basis of technology, the only road to avoid falling into capriciousness," and its cost "turned out to be, when the calculation was made, considerably less than that of an ordinary apartment house of the same category and capacity, which was studied at the same time and the cost of which estimated for comparison purposes." As well, the Dwellings in Space had the notable advantages of open yard ventilation, natural lighting, exposure to sunlight, natural insulation, and views.

This kind of dwelling, expanded on an urban scale, showed itselt to be ideal for creating different types of housing for social groups of differing economic levels. Marcel Breuer noted that the ground surface was made use of in three different ways: for shops, general circulation, etc.; for dwellings; and for gardens. And, as Williams himself pointed out after creating the project, the ground plan of the dwellings presented fundamental analogies with the typical native country house, through the relationship between the three basic elements: house, verandah, and green space.

—Jorge Glusberg

WILLIAMS, (Evan) Owen.

British. Born in Tottenham, London, in 1890. Educated at Tottenham Grammar School, London; University of London, B.Sc. 1911; student/ apprentice, Electric Tramways Company, London, 1905-11. Married Gladys Tustian in 1915 (died, 1947); children: one son and one daughter; married Doreen Baker in 1947; children: one son and one daughter. Architect/Engineer, Trussed Concrete Company, later Truscon, London, 1912-13; Chief Aeroplane Designer, Wells Aviation Ltd., London, 1913; in private practice as civil engineer and architect, London, 1919-39; in partnership with T. S. Vandy, London, 1939 until his death, 1969. Consulting Civil Engineer, *British Empire Exhibition*, London, 1922-24; Consulting Engineer for Motorway Construction to the Ministry of Transport, London, 1945-69. Exhibition: *Owen Williams, 1890-1968*, Architectural Association, London, 1976. Recipient: Silver Medal, City and Guilds Institute, London, 1911; Telford Gold Medal, Institute of Civil Engineers, London, 1927, 1961. Member, Institution of Civil Engineers; Associate Fellow, Royal Aeronautical Society. K.B.E. (Knight Commander, Order of the British Empire), 1924. *Died 23 May 1969.*

Works:

1912 Shipyard in reinforced concrete, Poole, Dorset (with Reinforced Concrete Engineers)
      Gramophone company factory, Hayes, Middlesex (with Truscon; now the E.M.I. Building)
1913 Prototype aeroplanes, for Wells Aviation Ltd.
1914/
18 Concrete ships
1919 Walls Factory, Acton, London
1920 Tannery, Runcorn, Cheshire
1921 Ice-making plant, Hull, Yorkshire
1922/
24 Stadium and layouts for the *British Empire Exhibition*, Wembley, London (with J. Simpson and M. Ayrton)
1923 Palace of Industry, *British Empire Exhibition*, Wembley, London
1925 Parc des Attractions, *International Exposition*, Paris
1925/
30 Wansford Bridge, Huntingdon
      Findhorn Bridge, Scotland
      River Spey Bridge, Scotland
      Montrose Bridge, Scotland
      Lea Valley Viaduct, North Circular Road, London
1926 Cotton seed crushing mill, Adana, Turkey
1930 Cumberland Garage, near Marble Arch, London
      Dorchester Hotel, Park Lane, London (consulting engineer in early stages; completed by others)
1932 Boots Factory, Beeston, Nottingham
      Daily Express Building, London (as consulting engineer; in association with Ellis and Clarke)
      Road/Rail Bridge, Charing Cross, London (project)
      Waterloo Bridge, London (project)
1933 Cement factory, Thurrock, Essex
      Hunt Partners Factory extension, London
1934 Empire Swimming Pool and Sports Arena, Wembley, London

Pioneer Health Centre, St. Mary's Road, Peckham, London

Sainsbury's Warehouse, Rennie Street, Southwark, London

1935 Lilley and Skinner Warehouse, Pentonville Road, London

1936 Housing, Stanmore, Middlesex

1937 Odhams Printing Works, Watford, Hertfordshire

Provincial Newspapers Offices, Salisbury Square, London

Daily Express Building, Glasgow (as consulting engineer)

Boots Factory, Beeston, Nottingham

Removable restaurant, Wembley Stadium, London

Synagogue, Dollis Hill, London

1939 *Daily Express* Building, Manchester (as consulting engineer; in association with Ellis and Clarke)

1939/
45 Concrete ships

1945 Motorway design for the U.K. Ministry of Transport (as consulting engineer)

1948 Olympic Games installations, Wembley Stadium, London

1950/
54 British Overseas Airways Corporation Maintenance Headquarters and Hangars, London Airport, Heathrow

1959 *Daily Mirror* Building, London (as consulting engineer; in association with Anderson, Forster and Wilcox)

M1 Motorway, stage I: London to Birmingham

1966 Viaduct, Port Talbot, Wales

1967 M1 Motorway, stage II: Birmingham to Doncaster, Yorkshire

River Usk Bridge, Newport, Monmouthshire

1,000-foot twin tunnel, Crindau Ridge, Newport, Monmouthshire

1968 Midland Link Motorways

1969 Box-Girder Bridge over the Channel, England to France (project)

Publications:

By WILLIAMS: books—*The Philosophy of Masonry Arches,* London 1927; *The Design and Construction of the M1,* with O. T. Williams, London 1961.

On WILLIAMS: book—*The Law of Least Action: Sir Owen Williams' Career, 1922-1939,* thesis by D. Cottam, Liverpool University 1980; articles—"Pioneer Health Centre, Peckham, London" in *Architectural Record* (New York), June 1935; "Neue Bauten von Sir Owen Williams" in *Moderne Bauformen* (Stuttgart), November 1935; "Warehouse for Messrs. Lilley and Skinner" in *Architectural Review* (London), September 1936; "Synagogue at Dollis Hill" in *The Architect and Building News* (London), 25 March 1938; "Sir Owen Williams" by Alfred Roth in *Werk* (Zurich), April 1947; "BOAC Headquarters at London Airport" in *The Builder* (London), 4 November 1955; "The New Mirror Building" in *The Architect and Building News* (London), 8 March 1961; "Sir Owen Williams" by Michael Gold in *Zodiac* (Milan), no. 18, 1968; "Sir Owen Williams" by Stephen Rosenberg, Warren Chalk and Stephen Mullin in *Architectural Design* (London), July 1969; "Green Lines" by J. M. Richards in *The Architects' Journal* (London), 1 February 1976; "Keeping in Style" by Stephen Games in *The Architects' Journal* (London), 8 July 1981.

*   *   *

After practice in civil engineering Sir Owen Williams became structural engineer and architect of several notable buildings during the 1930s. These were

designed when the "new architecture," that is functional building with synthetic materials—steel, concrete, glass, laminated timber, plastics and numerous others, in which precise mathematical calculations are possible—was gradually spreading mainly from Germany and Central Europe to England. Owen Williams was among the first in England to use the constructional methods that had been developed, and he used them with considerable success. Such methods often made possible a more efficient fulfilment of the building's purpose.

Among the more spectacular of these buildings is the Boots Factory at Beeston, Nottingham. In this structure he used, for the first time in England I think, concrete mushroom columns supporting large concrete floor slabs, a method invented by the Swiss engineer, Maillart, several years earlier. The edges of the concrete floors form strong courses of the otherwise unbroken glass screens that form the walls of this large factory. By this method the utmost natural light could be introduced into large areas of the interior, and it was, when erected, one of the most progressive industrial buildings in Europe.

Owen Williams used the mushroom column and floor slab construction in many subsequent buildings, such as the cement factory at Thurrock in Essex and the Peckham Health Centre, London.

In Maillart's first use of this method the mushroom heads were circular; in Williams' use of them in the Boots Factory they were large square reversed pyramids. In the Peckham Health Centre cantilevered crossheads surmount cruciform columns, an elegant variation of the structure. Architecturally this building represents Williams' finest achievement. It is a rectangular three-storey structure of reinforced concrete with concrete slab floors, and glass screens for external walls similar to the Boots Factory. The various parts of the building are grouped round a central swimming bath. Particularly effective is the centre part of the south-west facade which has a series of six circular box windows on the two upper storeys above the arcade columns of the children's recessed play space.

The Empire Swimming Pool, at Wembley, is also a notable structural design. It is one of the largest covered spaces in England, 341 feet long with a roof span of 236 feet. Its building was based on a horizontal grid which permitted the use of standardized units contributing to a speedy erection in about six months. The ingenious pitched roof is constructed of a series of three hinged arches in reinforced concrete buttressed by vertical concrete shafts linked to the concrete gallery and to the roof members by concrete fins, a very conspicuous, rather heavy external feature.

Although essentially a structural engineer, specializing in reinforced concrete, Owen Williams was, at the same time, architect of some of the most notable buildings erected in England in the 1930s. Like many structural engineers he was inclined to consider that if the structure is right and fulfilled its purpose well, then good appearance would come of itself—yet some of his designs, especially that of the Peckham Health Centre—show an undoubted sensitivity to aesthetic effect.

—Arnold Whittick

WILLIAMS-ELLIS, (Bertram) Clough.

British. Born in Northampton, 28 May 1883. Educated at Oundle School; Trinity College, Cambridge; Architectural Association School, London. Served as a Major in the Welsh Guards and the Royal Tank Corps, British Army, in France, 1914-18: Military Cross; mentioned in despatches. Married Amabel Strachey in 1915; children: Susan, Charlotte, and Christopher (died). In private practice, London and Merioneth, Wales, 1905-14, 1919 until his death, 1978. Served as First Chairman, Stevenage New Town Development Corporation, Hertfordsh-

ire; President, Institute of Landscape Architects; President, Design and Industry Association; Vice President, Council for the Preservation of Rural Wales; Chairman, Glass Industry Working Party; Member, Grand Council, British Travel Association National Parks Committee; National Trust Committee for Wales; Government Committee on Art and Industry; Art Committee, University of Wales; Advisory Council for Welsh Reconstruction; Trunk Roads Advisory Committee. LL.D.: University of Wales, 1971. Fellow, Royal Institute of British Architects. C.B.E. (Commander, Order of the British Empire), 1958; Knighted, 1972. *Died* (in Penrhyndeudraeth, North Wales) *8 April 1978.*

Works:

1905/
14 Small institution building, Oxford

Five houses, Oxford

House alterations and additions (2), Oxford

Sports Pavilion, University College, Oxford

Aberuchaf Cottage, Abersoch, Caernarvonshire

Farmhouse, Glasfryn Estate, Caernarvonshire

Steam Laundry reconstruction, Cambridge

Village Hall, Stone, near Aylesbury, Buckinghamshire

Park cottages, Cricket St. Thomas, near Chard, Somerset

Farmstead buildings, Byfleet, Surrey

House restoration and alterations, Moynes Park, Essex

House alterations, Normandy Park, Surrey

House alteratons, additions and new lodge, Burton Court, Hertfordshire

Princess Christian's Farm Colony, Kent

Rectory, near Pentraeth, Anglesey

Rectory and Church, Prentrefelin, Caernarvonshire

Llangoed Castle rebuilding, Breconshire

Church restoration, Crickadarn, Breconshire

Village Square, Cushendun, County Antrim, Ireland

Hunting box and stables, Brechfa, Carmarthenshire

Sham ruins, on islet near Holyhead, Anglesey

Old people's housing, Swavesey, Cambridgeshire

School reconstruction, farmhouse, monument and gates, Wroxall Abbey, Warwickshire

House restoration, Plas Hen, Dolgellau, Merioneth

Cottages, Guys Cliff, Warwickshire

House, near Woking, Surrey

Cottages, Compton, Surrey

Battersea Dog's Home master plan and rebuilding, London

House, Stanmore, Middlesex

Hunting box and stable alterations, near Finmere, Buckinghamshire

Waddington Manor restoration and alterations, Oxfordshire

Llechwyddgarth Hall restoration and alterations, Llangynog, Montgomeryshire

Small industrial hamlet, near Leamington, Warwickshire

House alterations, Stoke Bruern Park, Northamptonshire

Dower House alterations, Easton Neston, Northamptonshire

Entrance gates, Gayton House, Northamptonshire

Cleve Court alterations, Kent

Wolverton Court reconstruction and additions, Warwickshire

Country Life House, Gidea Park, Essex (competition project)

Ridgeway House, near Wellington College, Berkshire

House alteratons, Strawberry Hill, Kent

Plas Brondanw orangery, gardens and new lodge, Merioneth

Spectator Cottage, Marrow Downs, Surrey (competition project)

1918/
39 War Memorial Tower, Garreg, Merioneth

Palace of Industry, pavilions and displays, *British Empire Exhibition* (1925), Wembley, London (as co-ordinating architect)

House alterations, Gilwell Park, Essex

Glenmona House rebuilding, Cushendun, County Antrim, Ireland

Maud Cottages, Cushendun, County Antrim, Ireland

Cushendun Village additions, County Antrim, Ireland

Lord McNaughton Memorial Hall and School, Giant's Causeway, County Antrim, Ireland

Bushmill Central School, County Antrim, Ireland

Youth Hostel, Loggerheads, Flintshire

Government House alterations, Guernsey, Channel Islands

Memorial Hospital alterations, Portmadoc, Caernarvonshire

Ex-servicemen's housing scheme, Ashtead, Surrey

Hospital, Blaenau Ffestiniog, Merionethshire

St. Cross Mill alterations, Winchester, Hampshire

House restoration, near Ticehurst, Sussex

House restoration and additions, Carregfelin, Caernarvonshire

House with studio and garden, Swiss Cottage, London

Three houses, Hampstead, London

Savoy Court restoration and additions, Denham, Buckinghamshire

House/public school conversion and additions, Stowe, Buckinghamshire

House/Bonar Law College conversions and additions, Ashridge Park, Berkshire

New hamlet, Ashridge Park, Berkshire

Cumnor House, Oxfordshire

Gardens and temples, Eaglehurst, Hampshire

Farm buildings, Avon Tyrel, Hampshire

Summit Station, Mount Snowdon, Caernarvonshire

Church of Christ Scientist, Belfast

House, Belfast

School, Belfast

House, near Romsey, Hampshire

Bolesworth Castle reconstruction and gardens, Cheshire

Hotel conversion, and Angel and Neptune Houses, Portmeirion, Merioneth

Kilve Court restoration and alterations, Somerset

Country house, near Andover, Hampshire

House, Littlestone, Kent

Deudraeth Castle-Hotel conversion, Merioneth

House, near Ashburton, Devon

House, Stapledown, Surrey

House, near Walton Heath, Surrey

House alterations and additions, Royston, Hertfordshire

Doctor's house and surgery, Penrhyndeudraeth, Merioneth

White Cottage, near Portmeirion, Merioneth

Girls' boarding school, near Guildford, Surrey

Great Hundridge Manor alterations and additions, Buckinghamshire

Milton Court restoration, Surrey

House alterations, near Burnham, Somerset

House/Hotel conversion and extensions, Newlands' Corner, Surrey

Country house and cottage, Harrowhill Copse, Surrey

Co-operative Society Store, Pwllheli, Caernarvonshire

House, Pencaenewydd, Caernarvonshire

Cross Hill House alterations, Adderbury, Oxfordshire

House alterations, Attingham Park, Shropshire

Aitcham House alterations, Shropshire

Layton Hall alterations, Shropshire

New Ladies' Carlton Club and Swimming Pool, London

Grosvenor Crescent, London (demolished)

English Speaking Union, Charles Street, Mayfair, London

Oxford and Cambridge Club Ladies' Annex, Pall Mall, London

Bladen Lodge reconstruction, The Boltons, Kensington, London (demolished)

House reconstruction, Hill Street, Mayfair, London

Marcel Boulestin Restaurant, Leicester Square, London

Sloane House alterations, London

Romney House reconstruction, Hampstead, London

Coed Coch House reconstruction and alterations, Denbighshire

Palatial Official/Commercial Residence, Shanghai, China

Two small houses, Tientsin, China

Leigh Coppings Farm alterations and extensions, Kent

Clough Williams-Ellis: Maud Cottages, Cushendun, Northern Ireland, 1925.

Laugharne Castle alterations, Carmarthenshire

Brondanw Tower, Merioneth

Hubbards Hall reconstruction and additions, Essex

Two houses, Chichester harbour, Sussex

Funtington Lodge alterations, Bosham, Hampshire

Little Cassiobury House alterations and additions, Hertfordshire

House and gardens, Caversham Place, near Reading, Berkshire

Laughton House extensions, Lincolnshire

Methodist Chapel, Llanstumddwy, Caernarvonshire

Farmhouse, Pentrefelin, Caernarvonshire

Bridge, Carmarthen Town

Caversham Heights House additions, Berkshire

New Hall and Chapel, Bishop's Stortford College, Essex

House, Plover's Field, Newland's Corner, Surrey

House restoration, Maids-of-Honour Row, Richmond, Surrey

Cornwall Manor reconstruction, Oxfordshire

Hartsbourne Grange reconstruction, Hertfordshire

Restaurant, Laughing Water, Cobham, Kent

Plan for the town, and three houses, Llanbedrog, Caernarvonshire

Doctor's house/surgery conversion, Pwllheli, Caernavonshire

House, near Brickenden, Hertfordshire

House, Rhos-on-Sea, Denbighshire

House, Deganway, Caernarvonshire

1945/
71 Portmeirion and Brandanw Estates renovation, Merioneth

Plan for the town of Bewdley, Worcestershire

Plan for the town of Weston-super-Mare, Somerset

Doctor' house, Somerset (with Lionel Brett)

Plan for the town of Reddith, Worcestershire (with Patrick Abercrombie and Lionel Brett)

House restoration Gegin Fawr, Aberdaron, Caernarvonshire

House restoration, Plas-yn-Rhiw, Caernarvonshire

House, near Llanfaelrhys, Caernarvonshire

Home Farm House, Aston Tirrold Manor, Berkshire

Beudy Newydd reconstruction, Merioneth

Glanddyfi Castle alterations, Montgomeryshire

New mansion building, Rhiwlas, Merioneth

New mansion and pavilion, Voelas, Denbighshire

National Forest Park Hall, Caernarvonshire

Warden's house, Beddgelert, Caernarvonshire

Beach cafe/restaurant, Criccieth, Caernarvonshire

Restaurant, Conway Falls, Denbighshire

Old Bridge House alterations, Pembroke Town

New Lodge, Ty Newydd Llanstumddwy, Caernarvonshire

House rebuilding, Plas Brondanw, Merioneth

The Drum House, Croesor, Merioneth

Lloyd George Grave, Memorial and Museum, Caernarvonshire

House restoration and additions, Tyn-y-rhos, Brynkir, Caernarvonshire

Nantclwyd Hall reconstruction with farmhouse and inn additions, Denbighshire

House reconstruction and extensions, Nant-y-Glyn, Caernarvonshire

Giant's Causeway renovations, County Antrim, Ireland

Entrance gates and monument, Bodrhyddan Park, Flintshire

Crown house and gardens, Barford St. John, Oxfordshire

Prescote Manor Gardens, Oxfordshire

House, Porth-y-Castell, Merioneth

Park layout and extensions, Dunwood House, Yorkshire (partially realized)

House alterations and extensions, Cwm Bychan Gerddi Blwog, Merioneth

New buildings and Plas Canol extensions, Portmeirion, Merioneth

New buildings, Dalton Hall, Westmorland

Temple in the Park, Hatton Grange, Shropshire

Lloyd George Memorial, Westminster Abbey, London

Caroline Thorpe Monument, near Cobbaton, Devon

Publications:

By WILLIAMS-ELLIS: books—*Cottage Building in Cob, Pisé, Chalk and Clay*, London and New York 1919, revised edition, with John and Elizabeth Eastwick-Field, as *Cottage Building in Cob, Pisé, and Stabilised Earth*, London 1947; *The Pleasures of Architecture*, with Amabel Williams-Ellis, London 1924, 3rd edition 1954; *England and the Octopus*, London 1928, Portmeirion, Wales 1975; foreword to *The DIA Cautionary Guide to St. Albans*, London 1929; *The Architect*, London 1929; *Land of My Fathers*, with others, London 1930; *Lawrence Weaver*, London 1933; *Architecture Here and Now*, with John Summerson, London 1934; *Britain and the Beast*, editor, London 1937; *Snowdonia*, Portmeirion, Wales 1939; *Plan for Living*, London 1941, 1944; *The Adventure of Building*, London 1946; *On Trust for the Nation*, London 1947; *Royal Festival Hall, London*, London 1951; *Town and Country Planning*, London 1951; *Portmeirion Still Further Explained*, Birmingham 1956; *Portmeirion: The Place and Its Meaning*, London 1963, Portmeirion, Wales 1973; *Roads in the Landscape*, London 1967; *Architect Errant*, London 1971; *Around the World in Ninety Years*, London 1979.

On WILLIAMS-ELLIS: articles—"Plas Brondanw, Merioneth" by Christopher Hussey in *Country Life* (London), 5 and 12 September 1957; "From Portmeirion" in *The Architect and Building News* (London), 3 August 1966; "Clough's Magnificent Folly" by James Morris in the *Observer Colour Magazine* (London), 7 September 1969; "Antrim's Discreet Holiday Resort" by James Stevens Curl in *Country Life* (London), 6 May 1976; "The Fanciful Genius of Portmeirion Who Built to Delight" by Martin Wainwright and Michael Morris in *The Guardian* (London), 10 April 1978; "Sir Clough Williams-Ellis: Sensibility, Skill and Intuition" by Frederick Gibberd in *Building Design* (London), 14 April 1978; "Sir Clough Williams-Ellis 1883-1978" by E. Maxwell Fry in *RIBA Journal* (London), June 1978; "Wales's Universal Architect" by Richard Haslam in *Country Life* (London), 21 July 1983; "The Town of Sir Clough: Portmeirion" in *Abitare* (Milan), May 1983; "Folly of Portmeirion Neglect" by Alison Barker in *Building Design* (London), 4 August 1983.

The contribution to architecture and to the quality of the environment of Sir Clough Williams-Ellis has been considerable, although critics excessively sympathetic to modernism have tended to ignore his achievements.

From the beginnings of his career, Williams-Ellis showed a concern for the environment and for picturesque and pleasing compositions that was anathema to fashionable 'progressives.' His most famous work, the village of Portmeirion in north Wales, embraces his most characteristic strengths: a respect for the natural site and a love of eclectic motifs to achieve agreeable compositions. Elements derived from Italy and Spain combine with more indigenous domestic vernacular forms to create a modern village that delights the eye. On a smaller scale, but full of visual pleasures, is his work for Ronald and Maud McNeill at Cushendun, County Antrim, Northern Ireland, comprising The Square, Glenmona House, and Maud Cottages.

Both Portmeirion and Cushendun demonstrate the genius of Williams-Ellis as a composer of picturesque architectural groupings. Less well-known today are his work for the Wembley Exhibition of 1925, the Bishop's Stortford College Chapel, the conversion of Ashridge Park in Hertfordshire, and the various churches and schools in England, Wales, and Ireland. His designs for memorials and monuments possess a serenity that owes much to the classical language of architecture, notably the Lloyd George mausoleum and the Westminster Abbey memorial, and the recent monument to the first wife of Jeremy Thorpe. He wrote a fine appreciation of the life and work of Sir Laurence Weaver, the historian of monuments and memorials.

As a writer himself, Williams-Ellis was entertaining, witty, and civilized. His *Cottage Building, England and the Octopus, The Pleasures of Architecture*, and *Architect Errant* are eloquent testimonies of his great love of beauty, his hatred of ugliness and of philistinism, and his immense worries about waste, destruction, and stupidity. As editor of *Britain and the Beast* (1937) he argued for coherent, wise, and civilized planning policies to protect the countryside and the national heritage from greed, from pusillanimous attitudes, and from destruction. His choice as first Chairman of the first New Town Development Corporation (Stevenage) might have given us a great new town incorporating the wonderful environmental aspects of Portmeirion and Cushendun on a much larger scale, but unfortunately his brand of cultivated sensibility was out of tune with the realities of post-war Britain as well as with the aims of his colleagues, and so a prosaic utilitarianism with no delight and certainly no 'useless' picturesqueness was to prevail.

Williams-Ellis died in 1978. The world, and especially the beleaguered world of traditional architecture and three-dimensional creativity in town planning, is the poorer for his passing.

—James Stevens Curl

WILSON, Colin St. John.

British. Born in Cheltenham, Gloucesterhire, 14 March 1922. Educated at Felstead School, Essex, 1935-40; Corpus Christi College, Cambridge, 1940-42, M.A. 1942; Bartlett School of Architecture, University College London, 1946-49, Dip.Arch. 1949. Served as a Lieutenant in the Royal Naval Volunteer Reserve, 1942-46. Married Muriel Lavender in 1955 (divorced); married Mary Jane Long in 1972; children: Sarah-Jane and Harry. Architectural Assistant, Verner O. Rees and Partners, London, 1949-50, and in Housing Division, London County Council Architects Department, 1950-55; Principal Architect, Property Development Company, London, 1955-56; in private practice, and in association with Professor Sir Leslie Martin, Cambridge and London, 1956-70. Since 1971, Senior Partner, and Director since 1981, Colin St. John Wilson and Partners, London (other directors: John Collier, M. J. Long, and John Honer). Lecturer, Department of Architecture, Cambridge University, 1956-59; Fellow of Churchill College, Cambridge, 1960-72; Visiting Critic, Yale University School of Architecture, New Haven, Connecticut, 1960, 1964, 1983 and 1985; Bemis Visiting Professor of Architecture, Massachusetts Institute of Technology, Cambridge, 1970-71. Professor of Architecture, Cambridge University, since 1975; Fellow of Pembroke College, Cambridge, since 1977. Trustee, Tate Gallery, London, 1974-80, and the National Gallery, London,

1977-80. Exhibitions: Architectural Association, London, 1951, 1954; *This Is Tomorrow*, Whitechapel Gallery, London, 1956 (designed exhibition); *Contemporary Artists and Architects in the U.K.* (film), at *Expo '67*, Montreal; *Solutions to Energy Conservation in Buildings*, Royal Institute of British Architects, London, 1976; *British Architecture*, Architectural Design Gallery, London, 1982; Royal Academy of Arts, London, 1984; *Architects For Social Responsibility*, Max Protetch Gallery, New York, 1985. Fellow, Royal Institute of British Architects. Address: Colin St. John Wilson and Partners, Highbury Crescent Rooms, 70 Ronalds Road, London N5 1XW, England.

Works:

1951 Coventry Cathedral, Warwickshire (conpetition project; with Peter Carter)
1952 Narrow-Frontage Maisonette Prototype
      Shell Company Service Station (competition project; with Peter Carter)
1954 Housing estate, Bentham Road, Hackney, London
      University of Sheffield, Yorkshire (competition project; with Peter Carter)
1955 High-Level Helicopter Station (project; with Peter Carter)
1955/
   57 Residential building, Hereford Square, London (with Arthur Baker)
1956 Design of the *This Is Tomorrow* exhibition, Whitechapel Gallery, London
      Science Faculty Layout and Physics Buildings, University of Leicester (with Sir Leslie Martin)

King's College Hostel, Cambridge (project; with Sir Leslie Martin)
1957/
   58 Factory and laboratory, Welwyn Garden City, Hertfordshire (with Sir Leslie Martin and Sir Ove Arup)
1957/
   59 Architecture Department extension, Scroope Terrace, Cambridge University (with Alex Hardy)
1957/
   62 Harvey Court Residential Building, Gonville and Caius College, West Road, Cambridge (with Sir Leslie Martin)
1958 Housing project, Borough of St. Pancras, London (with Sir Leslie Martin)
1959/
   64 3 libraries, Manor Road, Oxford University (with Sir Leslie Martin)
1960 Royal Holloway College Campus Layout, University of London (with Sir Leslie Martin)
1960/
   64 William Stone Residential Building, Peterhouse, Trumpington Road, Cambridge (with Sir Leslie Martin)
1961/
   64 2 houses, Grantchester Road, Cambridge
1962/
   64 British Museum Library, London (project; with Sir Leslie Martin)
1965 Grandstand, Newmarket Racecourse, Suffolk (project)
      Residential building, St. John's College, Queens Road, Cambridge (project)
      Keiller House, Virginia Water, Surrey (project)

1965/
   69 Cornford House, Conduit Head, Madingley Road, Cambridge
1965/
   70 Civic and Social Centre, St. Johns Gardens, Liverpool (project)
1965/
   71 Agricultural Research Council Biochemistry Laboratory, Babraham, Cambridge (with Michael Brawne)
1969 British Museum Development Plan, London (project)
1970 British Library Building, Bloomsbury, London (project)
1970/
   79 British Museum West Wing Extension, London
1973 Lucas Industries Corporation Headquarters, Shirley, Birmingham (competition project)
      New County Hall, Northampton (project)
1974/
   77 Housing, Borough of Haringey, London
1975- British Library Building, St. Pancras, London
1982 Abbey National Headquarters Building, Milton Keynes, Buckinghamshire (competition project)
1983 City Polytechnic, Hong Kong (competition project)
      Dolls House (competition project)
1984 New Library Building, Queen Mary College, University of London
1985 Bishop Wilson School Memorial Library, Springfield, Chelmsford, Essex
      Catering and Commercial Development, Queen Mary College, University of London

Colin St. John Wilson: British Library Building, Euston Road, London, 1975 (project).

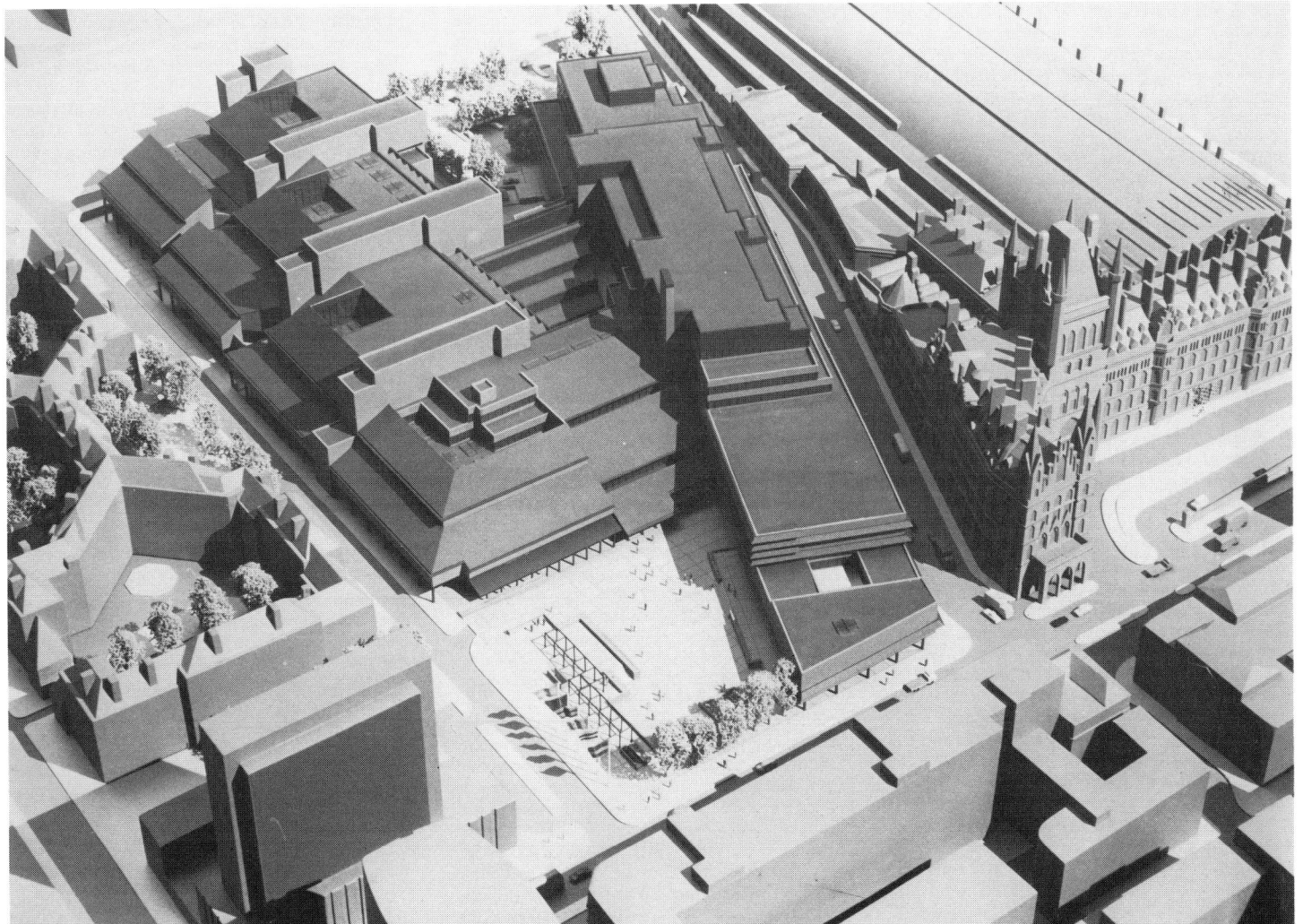

Publications:

By WILSON: articles—"Architect and Patron" in *The Observer* (London), 4 June 1950; "Towards a New Cathedral" in *The Observer* (London), 7 January 1951; "The Vertical City" in *The Observer* (London), 17 February 1952; "Eduardo Paolozzi and Nigel Henderson" in *Cambridge Review* (Cambridge), 1957; "The Collegiate Court," with J. L. Martin, in *Architectural Review* (London), July 1959; "Open and Closed" in *Perspecta* (New Haven, Connecticut), no. 7, 1961; "Letter to an American Student" in *Program* (New York), no. 3, 1964; "Gerrit Rietveld: 1888-1964" in *Architectural Review* (London), December 1964; "Modus Operandi" in *Cuadernos de Arquitectura* (Barcelona), no. 72, 1969; "Alvar Aalto and the State of Modernism" in *International Architect* (London), no. 2, 1979; "Architecture—Public Good and Private Necessity" in *RIBA Journal* (London), March 1979; "Light on Scharoun" in *Architectural Review* (London), April 1979; "The Modern Tradition" in *Arkkitehti* (Helsinki), no. 3, 1983; "Speer and the Fear of Freedom" in *Architectural Review* (London), June 1983; "Large Public Spaces" in *Tiili* (Helsinki), no. 4, 1984; "The Historical Sense" in *Architectural Review* (London), October 1984; "Waterhouse's Law Courts Project" in *The Architects' Journal* (London), 26 June 1985; "Sacred Games" in *Architectural Review* (London), July, 1985.

On WILSON: book—*Architektur 1940-1980* by Adolf Max Vogt, Berlin, Frankfurt and Vienna 1980; articles—"Arbeider 1958-67" by Christian Norberg-Schulz in *Byggekunst* (Oslo), no. 3, 1967; "Colin St. John Wilson" by Kasumasa Yamashita in *The Japan Architect* (Tokyo), April 1968; "Colin St. John Wilson o la Seriedad en el Proceso Arquitectonico" by Marcial Echenique in *Cuadernos de Arquitectura* (Barcelona), no. 72, 1969; plus articles on major buildings in *Architectural Design* (London), October 1959, July 1960, November 1962, November 1965, June 1967, *Architectural Review* (London), September 1965, November 1971, *Domus* (Milan), August 1968, and *RIBA Journal* (London), April 1976; "Portrait of the Artist: Colin St. John Wilson" in *The Architects' Journal* (London), 11 October 1978; "New Building for the British Library" in *Architectural Review* (London), December 1978; "Museum Expands" in *Building Design* (London), 26 January 1979; "British Museum Extension, Bloomsbury, London" in *Architectural Review* (London), January 1981; "The City Polytechnic, Hong Kong" in *Architectural Design* (London), 3 April 1984; "Wilson's Drum" in *Architectural Review* (London), October 1984.

*

I believe that architecture serves a more fundamental need, than we normally suppose. For, harassed by continual change, we need somehow to be made at home in the world and to that end we must be served not only at the level of utility and visual pleasure but also at a deeper psychological level where both the reality and the image of wholeness and of structure in the environment restore us to a measure of balance amid all our contradictions. If this were not so, then the present discontent with the state of our cities would be less impassioned, for I do not believe that questions of convenience or of aesthetics alone would lead to such distress.

From this it follows that our first aim is to understand the nature of the real needs for building in our time, and here the architect's contribution divides into two. In the first instance he must assist in drawing up a "programme" of those needs which can be defined in terms of operational order, economic priority and technical feasibility: and it is clear that this task he cannot perform on his own. I have for nearly thirty years engaged with this problem in many different ways—working both within a local government office and within private practice, designing buildings for private individuals, for developers, for industry, for universities, for local and for national government agencies; I have built for myself both home and place of work; and I have been both competitor and assessor in various competitions. On every occasion it has been a question of starting from scratch! Furthermore, the "client" in the form of a committee is often a will-of-the-wisp, forever changing personnel, priorities and programme and, in any case, acting as the sponsor rather than the user of the proposed building. If we then add to this tenuous relationship the further strain of continual technological innovation, it becomes clear that we are confronted with a whole pattern of operations which is cut off from any of the gentle give-and-take by which traditional procedures have evolved in a balanced way.

As a teacher (since 1956) I have been able to study this issue not only in terms of professional practice but also from a theoretical point of view; and this view has occasionally been amplified by development of certain aspects to a level of formal rigour by research students. Out of all this I have built up an unshakeable conviction that the only course to be pursued today is in the first instance the patient elaboration of whatever technique is suitable to ensure a proper dialogue between Architect and user of the building. This can be laborious in a large building (for the British Library we had to computerise 8,000 bits of information), but it is the essential foundation. Secondly, upon that foundation the architect can then not only invent a design but also submit it to controlled criticism and revision: and here it is important to realise that, for criticism to be creative, it must be firmly controlled in this way. Finally, at the end of the day, the architect must invent a design which will not only stand up to the test of use but will also answer to those deep and less rational needs to which I have alluded above. If it can fulfill them to, then it will raise the whole issue to that moment of architectural realization in which a frame for the actions of men suddenly focuses into a place where those actions are not merely made possible but are made manifest, are made, perhaps for the first time, vivid and recognisable to themselves, and their identity preserved against erosion. When this happens mere building has become architecture.

That, unlike the drawing up of a statement of needs, is an act of imagination, and it can be performed only by an architect.

—Colin St. John Wilson

*

A building is a string of events belonging together, progressing from basement to roof and back again. This line is derived from the very factual cycle of living that we can all observe. Colin St. John Wilson, tired of architects' overblown polemics and sterile products has refined his ambitions to following the chain of existence at its most elementary; he has elected to elevate the basic living configurations into a sensitive architecture-of-place. His recent, judiciously measured, vernacularizing projects also exemplify this caution; he has no truck with the enforced fairy-tale of post modernism.

One ploy he resorts to, in order to avoid the indecent propositions of formalism, is the plan: the planimetric interplay of hanging gardens in the Library Group, Oxford (1959-64) is an early paean to the plan, which in this case is made to stand up in a three-dimensional way. In the pin-wheel massing of the aborted Liverpool Civic Centre, we can see quite clearly that the main push is from the plan. Similarly, in the Northampton County Hall project's Aalto-like sweeping armature, it's the plan that is leading.

In the splintered, punctured, stretched brick and timber-skin of Cornford House, Cambridge, there is a remarkable break out from the plan, and the perforated, disjointed vernacular wraps around the broken massing in a masterly dwelling spiral. It's only when Wilson comes to employ this same technique in the more recent large-scale projects that there is a sense of mismatching; nonetheless, the vernacular idiom still allows him a little moderation in the face of the escalating immoderation that the urban architect feels is expected of him. In his British Library, at last being realized along London's Euston Road, you have a better match between city and vernacular; nonetheless, it could well be seen as a shaken and tormented urban *topos* recalling a collision. It might be called a collision between its two major wings, a collision between its village-like out-world and Aalto-like in-world, a collision between the architectural mind and body, here and there, now and then, Nobody is seriously injured, save the architectural critic, whose job in dealing with such paradoxes if far from easy.

Wilson's work is formed by the "twin texts" of "out-there" (actuality) and "in-here" (in the mind); he sees the need to re-establish a Cézanne-like *rapprochement* between these polarities as the foundation for an architecture that can make sense of what ever may confront it. Only an architecture that can both embrace and yet distance at the same time has the possibility of ringing true.

—Chris Fawcett

*

WILSON, (Leslie) Hugh.
British. Born in London, 1 May 1913. Educated at Haberdasher Ake's School, London, 1923-29; studied at the Regent Street Polytechnic School of Architecture, London, 1929-32. Married Monica Chrysavye Nomico in 1938 (died 1966); children: Rosemary, Pamela and Andrew. Assistant Architect, office of Herbert Shepherd and Louis Blanc, London, 1933-39; Chief Architectural Assistant, then War Damage Officer, City Surveyor's Office, Canterbury, Kent, 1939-45; City Architect, 1945-56, and Planning Officer, 1949-56, Canterbury, Kent; Chief Architect and Planning Officer, Cumbernauld New Town, Dumbarton, Scotland, 1956-62; in private practice, London, 1962 until his death in 1985: in partnership with John Lewis Womersely, as Hugh Wilson and Lewis Womersely Architects and Town Planners, 1964-85. Technical Advisor on Urban Development, Ministry of Housing and Local Government, London, 1965-67; Director, Property Services Agency, Department of the Environment, London, 1973-74. Chairman, London Docklands Joint Committee, 1977-81, and Board member, London Docklands Development Corporation, 1981-84. Vice-President, 1960-61 and 1962-64, Senior Vice-President, 1966-67, and President, 1967-69, Royal Institute of British Architects. Member of the Traffic Signs Committee, 1961-62, and Advisory Council Member on Road Research, 1967-68, Ministry of Transport, London; Member of the National Council for Building and Civil Engineering Industries, Ministry of Public Building and Works, London, 1969-71; Member of the Royal Fine Art Commission, London, 1971-85; Member of the Central Housing Advisory Committee, Department of the Environment, London, 1972-74. Recipient: Royal Institute of British Architects Town Planning Award, 1956; Saltire Housing Award, 1961, 1964 and 1965. D.Sc.: University of Aston, Birmingham, England 1969. Distinction in Town Planning, London, 1956; Honorary Fellow, Royal Architectural Institute of Canada; Fellow, Royal Town Planning Institute, London; Honorary Fellow, American Institute of Architects; Honorary Fellow, Institution of Structural Engineers, London; Fellow, Chartered Institute of Building, London; Honorary Member, Akademie der Künste, West Berlin. Officer, Order of the British Empire (OBE), 1952; Knighted, 1967. *Died* (in London) 20 July 1985.

Hugh Wilson: Housing at Ravenswood 10, Cumbernauld New Town, Scotland, 1965.

Works:

1945/
56 Simon Langton Girl's School, Canterbury, Kent
Reed Avenue School, Canterbury, Kent
St. Stephen Primary School, Canterbury, Kent
Frank Hooker School, Canterbury, Kent
Church of England Secondary School, Canterbury, Kent
Simon Langton Boys' School, Canterbury, Kent
1957 Cumbernauld New Town Plan, Dunbarton, Scotland
1962 Skelmersdale New Town Plan, Lancashire
1963 Education Precinct, Manchester, Lancashire
1964 Redditch New Town Plan, Worcestershire
Irvine New Town Plan, Aye, Scotland
1965 Northampton Expansion Plan, Northamptonshire
Teesside Sub-Regional Plan, Durham
Exeter Central Area Plan, Devon
Glasgow University, Scotland
Housing at Ravenswood 10, Cumbernauld New Town, Dunbarton, Scotland
1966 Oxford Central Area Plan, Oxfordshire
Brighton Central Area Plan, Sussex
1967 Cardiff Central Area Plan, Wales
1968 Torbay Central Area Plan, Devon
Lewes Central Area Plan, Sussex
1969 Housing at Winyates, Redditch New Town, Worcestershire
1975 Housing at South Malling, Lewes, Sussex
1976 National Westminster Bank, Exeter, Devon

1978 Sheltered Housing for the Elderly, Croydon, Surrey
Whitgift Almhouses conversion and alterations, Croydon, Surrey
Sports Hall, Whitgift School, Croydon, Surrey
1982 Housing for the Elderly, Croydon, Surrey
1984 Whitgift School extension, Croydon, Surrey

Publications:

By WILSON: books—*Cumbernauld: Report on the Central Area*, Cumbernauld, Scotland 1960; *Building: A Joint Venture*, lecture paper, Boreham Wood, Hertfordshire 1972; articles—"Britains Failure to Make Use of its Architects" in *The Times* (London), 29 November 1968; "A Single Voice," interview, in *Building* (London), 9 July 1976; "The Building Debate" in *Building* (London), 25 February 1977.

On WILSON: articles—"Girls' Secondary School at Canterbury" in *The Architects' Journal* (London), 15 March 1951; "The Architect in Canterbury" in *The Architects' Journal* (London), 4 June 1953; "Men of the Year" in *The Architects' Journal* (London), 17 January 1957; "Cumbernauld New Town, Mark II" in *The Architects' Journal* (London), 1 October 1959; "The Planning and Development of Cumbernauld" in *The Builder* (London), 9 September 1960; "Flatted Factory, Cumbernauld" in *The Architect and Building News* (London), 17 April 1963; "Housing and Cumbernauld New Town" in *Architectural Review* (London), February 1964; "New Town Design—Cumbernauld and

After" in *RIBA Journal* (London), May 1964; "Town Planning in Great Britain" in *L'Architecture d'Aujourd'hui* (Paris), June/July 1967; "The Plan for Irvine" in *Town and Country Planning* (London), October 1967; "The Architect's Contribution" in *AIA Journal* (Washington, D.C.), December 1969; "Housing at Colshaw Farm" in *The Architects' Journal* (London), 8 May 1974; "Cumbernauld New Town" in *Landscape Design* (London), February 1976; "Into the 1980s" in *Building Design* (London), 11 June 1976; "Manchester Education Precinct" in *The Architects' Journal* (London), 29 September 1976; "Central Services Building, Huddersfield Polytechnic" in *Yorkshire Architect* (Sunderland), January/February 1978; "Playing to the Gods" in *Building Design* (London), 20 February 1981; "Obituary: Sir Hugh Wilson—Planning New Towns and Redeveloping Old" in *The Times* (London), 24 July 1985.

*

It was mainly in the sphere of planning new towns that Sir Hugh Wilson did his most original and memorable work. The first and most distinctive of these was Cumbernauld, and hill town in Scotland. A notable feature of this is the separation of pedestrian and vehicular traffic possibly more complete than in any former new town. But the most spectacular and original concept in this plan in that of the town centre which Wilson designed in collaboration with Geoffrey Copcutt. It is a vast megastructure, one of the largest in the world, where all the central facilities of the town are concentrated in one enormous building of eight levels. The lowest, for vehicular traffic, includes the central spine road which passes underneath the immense super structure. At this lowest level are loading docks for the shops above and parking areas. The other levels comprise a series of pedestrian ways, with the floors linked by escalators, lifts, stairs, and ramps. The various levels contain complete shopping facilitites, offices, recreational and cultural facilities, banks, a hotel, a public house, a health clinic, a library, a church, a community centre, restaurants, and cafes, while at the top level is a row of penthouses. The complex is all ingeniously worked out. The design may have been partly prompted by the cold, wet, and windy weather of this hill top in Scotland. Anyhow, it is a notable solution of a difficult problem. It deservedly was among the first of the American R.S. Reynolds Memorial Awards for Community Architecture.

This imaginative conception made Wilson famous, with the result that he was much in demand to plan more new towns and the urban renewal of several existing town centres. Of the new towns, he prepared plans for Skelmersdale in Lancashire, Redditch near Birmingham, Irvine in Scotland, and Northampton, which is really a considerable extension of a fairly large existing town.

In the plan for Skelmersdale, the segragation of pedestrian and vehicular traffic is adopted. The walkways cross the roads by means of underpass and elevated ways. The town centre is again a concentraton of facilities—shops, offices, entertainment—and includes an ecumenical centre for several religious, the whole provided in two large buildings. The shopping area is on the first floor, with malls linking squares, while the ground floor is devoted to servicing.

In the plan for Redditch, again there is segregation of pedestrian and vehicular traffic; with a ring road round the centre, much of which is for public transport only. The centre, partly a development of the existing one, thus integrates the old and new. The new part includes a covered, air-conditioned shopping precinct on the first floor while a multi-storey car park is adjacent, the two being connected by a bridge.

In collaboration with his partner Lewis Womersley, Wilson prepared two plans for the new town of Irvine in Scotland. In the first plan, the town centre was in the geographical centre, but in the revised plan, the centre was near the coast, as it was thought that this would be more attractive to tourists. Both plans show the centres as mainly pedestrian at several levels.

Some of the residential areas are notable for ingenious layout. In one, there is a series of squares, each with internal courts to which terrace houses face. The courts have lawns, trees, and children's play spaces with boulders and log fencing, and there is a network of footpaths through the whole area. Each court also has a service road access (but no through road) for vehicles. Garages and parking are at one corner of each square near the service entrance. The terrace houses surrounding each square are very attractive with facades that have a dramatic black-and-white finish. This is some of the most aesthetically distinctive low-cost housing in a new town.

Northampton offers a further example in Weston Favel of a shopping centre provided in a large building with roofed and spacious pedestrian ways.

Wilson was on the pioneer architects in providing the closed-in, multi-level town centre, of which Cumbernauld is the first and most impressing example. For the first time, the whole town centre, with the provision of all facilities for a population of 60,000, was concentrated in one immense, storeyed building.

—Arnold Whittick

James Wines:Indeterminate Facade: Best Products Showroom, Houston, Texas, 1975.

WINES, James.

American. Born in Oak Park, Illinois, 27 June 1932. Educated at Syracuse University, New York, 1950-55, B.A. 1955. Married Gul Seden in 1956 (divorced, 1967); daughter: Suzan. Worked as a sculptor, New York, exhibiting internationally and completing several large public commissions, 1955-67. Since 1969, Founder and Principal of SITE Inc., New York: in partnership with Emilio Sousa, Alison Sky and Michelle Stone, since 1973. Professor of Art, New School for Social Research, New York, 1960, 1961, The School of the Visual Arts, New York, 1965, 1971, and New York University, 1965, 1977; Artist-in-Residence, Cornell University, Ithaca, New York, 1969, and the State University of New York at Buffalo, 1970; Mellon Professor of Architecture, Cooper Union, New York, 1977; Architect-in-Residence, Dartmouth College, Hanover, New Hampshire, 1977. Since 1975, Professor of Architecture at the New Jersey School of Architecture, Newark. Exhibitions: Whitney Museum, New York, 1973; Museum of Modern Art, New York, 1975; *Biennale*, Venice, 1975; Centre Pompidou, Paris, 1975; Australian Museum Travelling Exhibitions, 1976-77; *Buildings for Best Products, U.S.A.*, Museum of Modern Art, New York, 1979; *SITE: Buildings and Spaces*, Virginia Museum of Art, Richmond, 1980. Recipient: Rome Prize, American Academy in Rome, 1956; Guggenheim Fellowship, 1962; Ford Foundation Grant, 1964; National Endowment for the Arts Grant, 1973; Graham Foundation Grant, 1974. Address: SITE Inc., 60 Greene Street, New York, New York 10012, U.S.A.

Works:

1969 Education Place, University of Northern Iowa, Cedar Falls (project; with Cynthia Eardley and Dana Draper)
 Everson Museum Plaza, Syracuse, New York (project)
1971 Physics/Astronomy Plaza, University of Wisconsin at Milwaukee (project; with Dana Draper)
1972 Peeling Facade, Best Products Store, Richmond, Virginia (with Cynthia Eardley)
 Crossroads Apartments, Peekskill, New York (project)

With Alison Sky:
1973 Intermediate School 25 Courtyard, New York (project)

 Rainbow Center Plaza, Buffalo, New York (competition project)
1974 Four Arts Society Plaza, Palm Beach, Florida (project)
1975 Indeterminate Facade, Best Products Showroom, Houston, Texas
 Interstate 80 Roadway, Nebraska (project)
 Molino Stucky Grain Mill Plaza, Venice (project)
 Parking Lot Building, Best Products Showroom, Southern California (project)
1977 Notch Building, Best Products Showroom, Sacramento, California
1978 Ghost Parking Lot, Hamden Plaza, Hamden, Connecticut
 Tilt Showroom, Best Products Showroom, Towson, Maryland
 Best Anti-Sign, Best Products Distribution Center, Ashland, Virginia
 Building Renovation, 341 Madison Avenue, New York (project)
 Terrarium Showroom, Best Products Showroom (project)
1979 Hialeah Water Showroom, Best Products Showroom, Miami, Florida
 Cutler Ridge Showroom, Best Products Showroom, Miami, Florida
1980 Forest Building, Best Products Showroom, Richmond, Virginia
 Perpetual Savings and Loan Association prototype bank, Rapid City, South Dakota
1980/
81 Twist Building, Best Products Showroom, Quaker Ridge, New Jersey
1981 Famolare Shoes interiors, New York
 Walt Disney Animation exhibition design, Whitney Museum, New York
 Highrise of Homes theoretical housing (project)
1982 Williwear Fashion Showroom, New York
1983 Space Statiopn Video Games Center, New York
 Bedford House (Mr. and Mrs. Ralph Evans house), Bedford, New York
 McDonald's Restaurant, Berwyn, Illinois
1984 Williwear Men's Showroom, New York
 Inside/Outside Showroom, Best Products Showroom, Milwaukee, Wisconsin

Publications:

By WINES: books—*Highrise of Homes/SITE*, with Patricia Phillips, New York 1982; articles—"Public

Art, Private Gallery" in *Art in America* (New York), January 1970; "The Case for Site Oriented Art" in *Landscape Architecture* (Louisville, Kentucky), July 1971; "Straatkunst," with Nancy Goldring in *Tijdschrift voor Architectuur en Beeldende Kunsten* (Heerlen), January 1972; "Peekshill Melt," with Nancy Goldring, in *The Art Gallery* (Ivorytown, Connecticut), March 1972; "The Case for the Big Duck" in *Architectural Forum* (New York), April 1972; "La Point de Vue de l'Automobiliste" in *L'Architecture d'Aujourd'hui* (Paris), November 1972; "Notes from a Passing Car" in *Architectural Forum* (New York), September 1973; "Urban Art—Assisting the Assisted Readymade" in *Casabella* (Milan), May 1974; "Dearchitecturization" in *Architecture + Urbanism* (Tokyo), part I, June 1974, part II, July 1975; "Ent-Architekturierung" in *Kunstforum International* (Mainz), October 1974; "The Iconography of Disaster" in *Architectural Design* (London), June 1975; "De-architecture" in *L'Architettura* (Rome), June 1975; "De-architecturization" in *Arts in Society* (Madison, Wisconsin), Fall/Winter 1975; "Il Linguaggio Eretico della Disarchitettura" in *Modo* (Milan), November 1977; "The Architecture of Risk" in *Architecture Intérieure/Crée* (Paris), March and May 1978; "Architecture and the Crisis of Communication" in *Via* (Philadelphia), vol. 4, 1980; "Best: SITE and the psychological effects" in *Architecture Intérieure Crée* (Paris), March/April 1980; "Walls Have Meaning", interview, in *Building Design* (London), 24 October 1980; "Wines on SITE" in *RIBA Journal* (London), December 1980; "La Facade Indeterminate, Magasin Best" in *L'Architecture d'Aujourd'hui* (Paris), February 1981; "1989—What Universal Exhibition?" in *Connaissance des Arts* (Paris), July/August 1983; "Public Space Design" in *Domus* (Milan), July/August 1984; recordings—*The Further Adventures of 'De-architecture'*, tape cassette, London 1979; *SITE: Architecture as Art*, 2 tape cassettes, with Alison Sky, London 1980.

On WINES: books—*Buildings for Best Products, U.S.A.*, exhibition catalogue, New York 1979; *SITE: Architecture as Art*, with texts by Pierre Restany and Bruno Zevi, London and New York 1980; *SITE: Buildings and Spaces*, exhibition catalogue, Richmond, Virginia 1980; *Gehry, Site, Tigerman: trois portraits de l'artiste en architecte* by Olivier Boissiere, Paris 1981; *Jahrbuch für Architektur—Neues Bauen, 1980, 1981*, Frankfurt 1981; articles—"Site" in *Art and Artists* (London), October 1971; "New Concepts for Public Space Combine Art and Architecture" by Janet Bloom in *Architectural Record* (New York), February 1972; "L'intorno Scolpito" by Bruno Zevi in *L'Architettura* (Rome), May 1973; "James Wines" by Toshio Nakamura in *Architecture + Urbanism* (Tokyo), Summer 1974; Indeterminate Facade" by Toshio Nakamura in *Architecture + Urbanism* (Tokyo), July 1975; "Pre-disastro nel Texas" by Lisa Ponti in *Domus* (Milan), October 1975; "SITE-ations" by Judith Goldman in *Art News* (New York), October 1975; "Houston Falling" by Douglas Davis in *Newsweek* (New York), 22 December 1975; "SITE: Indeterminate Facade" by Franco Raggi in *Casabella* (Milan), March 1976; "Surrealism Comes to Shop Center" by C. Ray Smith in *The Village Voice* (New York), 15 March 1976; "Crumbling Facades" by Peter Marsh in *Building Design* (London), 6 August 1976; "Halfway Between Building Design and Modern Art" by William Marlin in the *Christian Science Monitor* (Boston), 11 March 1977; "Safe as Houses?" by Dennis Sharp in *The Guardian* (London), 8 June 1977; "Architect's Unstable Designs Relieve Monotony" by Paul Goldberger in the *New York Times*, 27 June 1977; "Monumento al Cossumatore" by Bruno Zevi in *L'Espresso* (Rome), 31 July 1977; "Fragmentation in California" by Lisa Ponti in *Domus* (Milan), August 1977; "The Drums Go Bang and the Symbols Clang" by Sydney Baggs in *Architecture Australia* (Sydney), November 1977; "Business among the Ruins" by Wolf Von Eckardt in the *Washington Post*, 14 January 1978;

"Through the Looking Glass" by Lance Wright in *Architectural Review* (London), March 1978; "La De-Architecture dei SITE" by Giovanni Ralli in *Casa Vogue* (Milan), November 1979; "Buildings for Best Products" in *Skyline* (New York), February 1980; "Insights on SITE" by Pilar Viladas in *Interiors* (New York), August 1980; "Vintage Wines" in *The Architects' Journal* (London), 29 October 1980; "Notes on the Philosophy of SITE", special issue of *Summarios* (Buenos Aires), December 1980; "SITE: Architecture and Environmental Architecture", special issue of *Space Design* (Tokyo), August 1981; "SITE—New York" in *Ufficiostile* (Milan), September/October 1981; "Gruppo SITE" by Manuela Cerri Goren in *Vogue* (Milan), March 1982; "Arbeiten von SITE" in *Werk, Bauen und Wohnen* (Zurich), May 1982; "Designing the Unthinkable" in *Newsweek* (New York), 8 November 1982; SITE—Architekturpositionen Abseits von Architektur" in *Umriss* (Vienna), January 1983; "The Bricks Come Tumbling Down" by Wolf Von Eckardt in *Time* (New York), 28 November 1983; "Between Utopia and Apocalypse: Five Projects by SITE" in *Architectural Record* (New York), March 1984; "Metamorphoses", special issue of *L'Architecture d'Aujourd'hui* (Paris), June 1984; "A New Site for SITE" by Herb Smith in *Architectural Record* (New York), October 1984.

My work is a fusion of art and architecture. It is a form of hybridism, combining aspects of both disciplines which I have called "de-architecture". This term refers to a theoretical perspective for examining the conventional definitions separating art and architecture, expanding their meanings, and using buildings to change public response to the sociological and psychological significance of the commonplace environment. De-architecture is an inversion for critical effect, a context for gaining new perspectives, and a disassembly of those presumptive, etched-in-granite, notions of what *is* and *isn't* architecture in the interests of finding more flexible interpretations of this essential public art.

In contrast to this century's architecture traditions, I believe that the ideas a building communicates as an extension of its own functions, or relation to historical traditions, are neither as interesting, nor as relevant, as those it absorbs from its immediate social/cultural context. Stated another way, rather than develop architecture from the inside out, my buildings evolve from the outside in.

I support architecture as art, versus architecture as design. To me, art represents the liberty to explore a rich variety of sources for visual content. Design, on the other hand, implies a priority of some practical nature which is then resolved by the superficial application of aesthetic principles to a specific problem. Art responds primarily to the subconscious rituals and impulses of society. Design is nothing more than a compromise of art in deference to the expedient.

Architecture (with a capital "A") is not my final objective; but, instead is treated as a "subject matter" or raw material for art. Architecture, in effect, is the throwaway, the found object, the redundant piece of information to be acted upon and transformed into something more interesting. My buildings are not intended to be viewed as exercises in the manipulation of form, space, and structure for their own sake (or, as some kind of sculptural extension of function). They are, rather, structures which use the familiar definitions of architecture as a means of inversion and the exploration of ideas which may, or may not, have anything to do with the conventional significance of shelter.

It is my view that architecture, because it represents the universal need for shelter, is the only physical presence which can rightfully be used as a means of creating true public art. All other art forms—painting, sculpture, crafts, etc. are only

incidentally, or by self-conscious choice, a part of the public domain. Contrary to using art as a decorative or applied accessory to buildings, my work is an endeavor to eliminate the distinctions which have always separated art and architecture. I feel my work is valid public art because it cannot exist in any other context without a total loss of meaning.

There is a general view, (inherited from Modernist Architecture tradition) that works of "private art"—created from an objectified, gallery-oriented, perspective—can simply be plunked down in, on, or adjacent to buildings and become "public" by this mere act of installation. The aesthetic and conceptual content of this kind of integration of the arts is based on nothing more than the decision of placement itself—which is to say, there is no content. As an alternative, my work has introduced the idea of public art as a psychological dialogue, creating a provocative mental connection between buildings and their contexts. The definition of "integration" in this case does not refer to the function of public art as a collection of homogenized formal consistencies in its relation to architecture. Instead, it refers to public art as a means of commentary on architecture. The physical components of what might traditionally be described as "as art" (as differentiated from the building) are related by mental associations—for example, art as the inversion of architecture, art as the analysis of architecture, art as the condition of becoming or reducing architecture.

—James Wines

Visions of bricks cascading from a false front, incomplete corners, and peeling walls spring to mind with the mention of the name of James Wines. Noted for such deviant design concepts, SITE (originally Sculpture in the Environment), the firm Wines heads, injects a whimsical element into the ponderous architectural scene of post-1960s America. However, more than mere playfulness is at work in these endeavors; the definition of the role of art and architecture, architect and artist, is intensely scrutinized and challenged.

Assuming an antagonist role, Wines has proven himself to be a delightfully literate and refreshingly engaging critic of the sterile, totalitarian aspects of function-oriented architecture and the application of gallery precepts to art in public places. His humorous, almost facetious, essays such as "The Case for the Big Duck," "Notes from a Passing Car," "De-Architecturization" and "The Iconography of Disaster" deplore the "Techosplat" sensibility that pervades so much of modern urban design and reject the concept of art as applied decoration or exhibitable object. Labeling modern public space art as "charm bracelet sculpture," and introducing such sublime ideas as D.D.T. (Duck Design Theory) with its "form follows fantasy" postulate, Wines raucously re-examines the state of the arts in America.

Finding them totally out of touch with reality, he suggests a rejection of the Bauhaus and avant-garde traditions and espouses the redefinition of the role of architecture to a position more responsive to public needs. He recognizes that engineering and design solutions are not the ends of architecture, but merely two of the means. Rather than being the thrust of architectural endeavors, engineering and design are tools to be used by architects, who should strive to make artistic statements within a sociocultural context.

Transcending the written word, Wines has attempted to apply his ideas to the too often impenetrable realm of implementation. The state Street Park in Binghamton, New York, with its series of massive, undulating, dock-like structures rolling the length of a full city block, well reflects his attempt to eliminate the focus on public art and architecture as separate entities. While a monumental sculpture in its own right, appreciated by both automobilists and pedestrians, it is more than just a sculpture as it invites and anticipates physical interaction. Functionally reminiscent of Lawrence Halprin's Lovejoy Fountain in Portland, Oregon, it adorns the landscape as a flexible pedestrian-recreation-leisure space.

Wines's more radical, and controversial, Best Products showrooms literally decimate the facade of the traditional functional box. These showrooms break down the conventional expectations of architectural design and attack the Bauhaus sensibility with a vivarious vengeance. Again sculpture and architecture are integrated to transform a static "art object" into an event which encourages people to interact with their surroundings. The juxtaposition of a minimally designed commercial box with a seemingly decomposing facade, provokes at least a second look or a gleeful exclamation of confrontation, if not a questioning of what is happening. As the antithesis of "Technosplat" design, these structures supplant the intransigent answers of functionalism with a more humanistic situation of action-reaction, question-ponder.

The Best showrooms, while a delight to behold, present a rather limited solution to the problem of discovering a new humanistic architecture. Primarily functioning as statements against institutionalized, totalitarian architecture, they are ephemeral forms that assume the existence of a staid establishment for their impact.

Recent project proposals by SITE indicate Wines has moved away from such reactive architecture and has entered a phase that explores situationally appropriate architectural solutions. Rather than merely decryin established norms, the proposed prototype for the Perpetual Savings & Loan based in Rapid City, South Dakota, makes an architectural statement on the Savings and Loan's position within the community. Designed to stand alone on the prairie, this thirty seven foot cube is split diagonally through the use of contrasting materials. The front presents a brick Greek revival entry, a traditional icon of fiscal stability; the rear is composed of regional stone, and represents the institution's innovative responsiveness to local conditions.

Similarly, SITE's "Highrise of Homes" proposal, which debuted at Chicago's Young/Hoffman Gallery in September 1981, attempts to intergrate the public's "spontaneous and idiosyncratic preference in popular styles of dwelling" with the development of highrise apartments. This schematic presents a highrise frame infilled on each floor with a variety of single family houses, complete with lawns and shrubbery. Although the proposal received broad coverage in the architectural press, to date it has been implemented only in the pages of the future-oriented comic book, *Sabre*, where Heironymous Skull lives in one of the Lynchburg, Virginia units. Such depictions, rising out of a mire of functionalism, leads one to hope that Wine's commissions and proposals may eventually lay a persuasive foundation on which a future of tantalizing forms will be erected.

—Don J. Hibbard

WOMERSLEY, (Charles) Peter.

British. Born in Newark, Nottinghamshire, 24 June 1923. Educated at the Architectural Association School, London, under Arthur Korn, 1947-52, Dip.A.A. (honours) 1952. Served in the British Army 1942-46. In private practice, Scotland, 1953-78; founded practice in Hong Kong, 1962: architectural consultancy in Hong Kong, 1979, until he retired, 1984. Recipient: Grand Project Award, Architectural Design, 1964; Civic Trust Award, 1965 (twice), 1968; Edinburgh Architectural Association Medal, 1965, 1973; Bayer International Award, 1977; Scotland Award, Royal Institute of British Architects, 1975. Associate of the Royal Scottish Academy, 1966. Lives in Hong Kong and Italy. Addresses: Apartment A-2, Repulse Bay Apartments, Repulse Bay, Hong Kong; Eremitaggio 36, Torri del Benaco, Lago di Garda, Italy.

Works:

1954 Farnley Hey (house), Huddersfield, Yorkshire
1957 High Sunderland (house), Galashiels, Selkirk, Scotland
The Rig (architect's house), Gattonside, Melrose, Scotland
1960 Church Square Council Houses, Galashiels, Selkirk, Scotland
1962 House, Camberley, Surrey

Peter Womersley: Klein Studio, Galashiels, Scotland, 1972.

1963 Peninsula Hotel modernization, Hong Kong
1963 Port Murray (house), Maidens, Culzean, Scotland
1964 Fairy Dean Football Stand, Galashiels, Selkirk, Scotland
1965 Psychiatric Admission Unit, Haddington, Lothian, Scotland
Sports Centre, University of Hull, Yorkshire
1967 Doctors Group Practice Building, Kelso, Scotland
Roxburgh County Buildings, Newton St. Boswells, Roxburgh, Scotland
1968 House, Bath, Somerset
Transplantation Surgery Unit, Western General Hospital, Edinburgh
1969 St. George's Office Building, Hong Kong
1970 Midland Bank Headquarters, Huddersfield, Yorkshire
1972 Bernat Klein Studio, Galashiels, Selkirk, Scotland
1978 Boilerhouse, Melrose Hospital, Scotland
Sports Centre, Coatbridge, Strathclyde, Scotland

Publications:

By WOMERSLEY: article—"Architect's Approach to Architecture" in *RIBA Journal* (London), May 1969.

On WOMERSLEY: book—*Scotstyle: 150 Years of Scottish Architecture* by Fiona Sinclair, Edinburgh 1984; articles—"Focus on a Valley View" by S. F. Lewis in *Ideal Home* (London), October 1972; "The Architect's office, Gattanside" in *Baumeister* (Munich), November 1972; "Bernat Klein Studio" in *Architecture + Urbanism* (Tokyo), July 1974; "Transforming a Drawing Office into a Living-Room" in *House and Garden* (London), November 1978.

*

Peter Womersley, although he is English, has spent most of his professional life in Scotland. For much of this time he worked alone, never employing more than three or four assistants, partly because of his belief that he must be personally involved in all his projects. His work consists of small, one-off schemes, in each of which (in his own words) he has striven "to experiment aesthetically, producing at the same time a building which stands up to both gravity and weather, and satisfies the client in use and as an investment." Peter Womersley regards each problem as an individual one, an "affair of the heart," as he puts it, and believes that each architectural solution should be a "fresh re-building of experience gained on other buildings."

That said, one notes that his designs evolve their own constructional and aesthetic systems. Increasingly—due in part to his travels and to his work in Hong Kong—Womersley has become fascinated by the application of basic geometry to architecture. He has always acknowledge his debt to Mies van der Rohe, and expressed it most clearly in his use of a rectangular grid and of simple open volumes broken down into smaller related spaces. However, Womersley recognizes that the Miesian doctrine can easily lead to sterility, and thus we find him turning more to Wright for inspiration in the imaginative expression of materials. In his detailing, as in his planning, he aims to refine "to the apparent simplicity which alone is satisfying."

In the early years of his practice, his preferred material was timber; later, when he turned to reinforced concrete, he used timber as shuttering, and thus suggested a continuing line of development. Such changes were simultaneously an expression of his desire to experiment with more sculptural forms and of his wish to explore the technical poentialities of concrete. With both materials he realizes the importance of structural honesty, but feels that a building should display a "convincing whole" rather than be a "structural demonstration."

The essence of Peter Womersley's architecure is most strikingly demonstrated in the Bernat Klein Studio, near Galashiels, with its beautiful siting and eloquent use of glass, concrete, and blue-black brick. It is arguably the outstanding Scottish building of the 1970s.

—Peter Willis

WONG, Jackson Chack Sang.

Hong Kong Citizen. Born in Hong Kong, 16 June 1930. Educated at St. Joseph's College, Hong Kong, 1945-50; Hong Kong University School of Architecture, under R. Gordon Brown, 1950-55 (Lee Hysan Gold Medal, 1953), B.Arch. (first class honours) 1955. Married Annie Leung Kit Wah in 1962; children: Eugenia, Felix and Raymond. Assistant Architect to Professor R. Gordon Brown, Hong Kong, 1955-57; Founder-Partner, Wong and Ng and Associates, Hong Kong, 1957-64, and Wong, Ng, Ouyang and Associates, Hong Kong, 1964-72; Principal Partner, Wong and Ouyang and Associates, Hong Kong, 1972-83 (other partners: Leslie Ouyang, Thomas Y. K. Kwok, and Lam Wo Hei). Since 1981, Principal Partner, WOA Architects, Singapore. Director, Wong and Ouyang (Singapore), Pte. Ltd. design consultants, since 1981; Director, Wong and Ouyang (HK) Ltd., Hong Kong, since 1983; Director, Wong and Ouyang (China Projects) Ltd., since 1984. President, Hong Kong Institute of Architects, 1973-74. Recipient: Wah Yuen Chuen Residential Development Prize, Hong Kong, 1977; Merit Prize, Singapore Island Country Club Competition, 1983. Addresses: Wong and Ouyang (HK) Ltd., Alliance Building, 130-136 Connaught Road Central, Hong Kong; Wong and Ouyang (Singapore) Pte. Ltd., 302 Orchard Road, 03-03 Tong Building, Singapore 0923.

Works:

1955 House, 8 Purves Road, Hong Kong
House, 12 Cooper Road, Hong Kong
1958 House, Anderson Road, Hong Kong
1959 Jardin's Lookout Residents Association Clubhouse, Hong Kong
Valley Villa, Blue Pool Road, Hong Kong
1960 the Box House, Fei Ngo Shan Road, Hong Kong
1961 House, 21 Cooper Road, Hong Kong
1963 House, Clearwater Bay Road, Hong Kong
Clearwater Bay Apartments, Hong Kong
1964 Kwun Tong District Government Offices, Kowloon, Hong Kong
Kwun Tong Royal Jockey Club Health Centre and Maternity Home, Kowloon, Hong Kong
Hyatt Hotel, Nathan Road, Kowloon, Hong Kong
Skyscraper Apartment Building, Tin Hau Temple Road, Hong Kong
Silver Strand Garden Townhouse, Nam Tau Sha, Hang Hau, Hong Kong
1965 Link's Estate Townhouse, Hong Kong
Kwun Tong Mansion, Yuet Wah Street, Hong Kong
1966 Chinese Y.M.C.A. Building, Waterloo Road, Kowloon, Hong Kong
Villa Monte Roza Apartments, Stubbs Road, Hong Kong
Cape Mansion Apartments, Mount Davis Road, Hong Kong
De La Salle Secondary School, Kam Tsing Village, Fan Ling, New Territories, Hong Kong

Chiap Hua Clocks and Watches Factory, Kwun Tong Road, Hong Kong
Jackson Wong Residence, 80 Chung Hom Kok Road, Hong Kong
1967 Dragon Court Apartments, Waterloo Road, Hong Kong
1968 Man Cheong Office Building Des Voeux Road West, Hong Kong
Magazine Heights Apartments, 17 Magazine Gap Road, Hong Kong
Tai On Cinema and Apartment Building, Shaukiwan Road, Hong Kong
Harilela House, Cambridged Road, Hong Kong
St. Joseph's Primary School, Morrison Hill, Hong Kong
Belvedere Court Townhouses, Shouson Hill Road, Hong Kong
Concordia Lutheran Anglo-Chinese School, Cloud View Road, Hong Kong
Chan Sui Ki College, Homatin, Hong Kong
1971 Unicorn Gardens Apartments, Shouson Hill Road, Hong Kong
Hong Kong Adventist Hospital, Stubbs Road, Hong Kong
Turtle Cove Villas, Red Hill, Hong Kong
Twin Bay Villa Townhouse, Clearwater Bay Road, Hong Kong
1972 Chong Gene Chong College, Chaiwan, Hong Kong
Pearl City Commericial and Residential Complex, Hong Kong
Dah Chong Hong Motor Services Centre, Cheung Sha Wan, Hong Kong
Din Wai Factory, Hoi Yuen Road, Hong Kong
1973 Residence, 20 D.E.F. Broadwood Road, Kowloon, Hong Kong
1974 Monte Verde Apartments, 41 Repulse Bay Road, Hong Kong
Stephen Mansion Apartments, Belfran Road, Hong Kong
Hutchinson House Office Building, Harcourt Road, Hong Kong
1975 Westlands Gardens Housing, Quarry Bay, North Point, Hong Kong
Oblates Fathers Primary School, Yuk Yat Street, Hong Kong
Holiday Inn, Nathan Road/Mody Road, Kowloon, Hong Kong
1976 Hand Shing Office Building, Hong Kong
Eastern Commercial Centre Office Building, Hong Kong
Causeway Bay Commerical Building, Sugar Street, Hong Kong
Outboard Marine Industrial Building, Tsing Yi Island, Hong Kong
Yan Garden Housing, Waterloo Road, Hong Kong
Hiranand House Office Building, Mody Road, Kowloon, Hong Kong
Holiday Inn, Manila, Philippines
Dah Chong Hong Motors Service Building, Quarry Bay, Hong Kong
1977 CMA Pre-vocational School, Nam Cheong Street, Hong Kong
Car Park and Car Repair Building, Wing Fong Street, Kwai Chung, Hong Kong
Champion Office Building, Nathan Road, Hong Kong
Mrs. Jenny Wong House, Hang Hau, Hong Kong
Yue Hwa Chinese Products Emporium Department Store interiors, Hong Kong
Nan Fung Sun Chuen Housing, Tai Koo Valley, Hong Kong
Hyde Towers Apartments, Kwun Tong, Hong Kong
Honest Motors Car Showroom and Office Building Leighton Road, Hong Kong
Braemar Hill Mansion Housing, Hong Kong
China Building, Peddar Street/Queen's Road Central, Hong Kong
1978 Honest Motors Showroom and Office Build-

Jackson C. S. Wong: Holiday Inn Harbor View, Hong Kong, 1981.

ing, Causeway Bay, Hong Kong
Braemar Hill Mansion Residential Development, North Point, Hong Kong
Leung Shek Chee College Secondary School, Sau Mau Oing, Hong Kong
Golden Villas Townhouses, Silverstrand, Hong Kong
1979 La Salle College Secondary School, Kowloon, Hong Kong
Sino Centre Office and Commercial Building, Mongkok, Hong Kong
Tai Po Government Disrict Office Building, Tai Po Market, Hong Kong
Holiday Inn, Islamabad, Pakistan
Holiday Inn, Penang, Malaysia
1980 Admiralty Centre Office and Commercial Building, Queensway, Hong Kong
Hang Seng School of Commerce, Shatin, Hong Kong
Shatin City One Residential and Commmercial Complex, Shatin, Hong Kong
Worldwide House Office Building, Central, Hong Kong
Cape Villa Terraced Houses, Chung Hom Kok, Hong Kong
Flamingo Garden Terraced Houses, Fei Ngo Shan, Hong Kong
Shangri-La Hotel, Tsimshatsui East, Hong Kong
Beverly Villa Apartments, Boundry Street, Hong Kong

Tsimshatsui Centre Office and Commercial Building, Tsimshatsui East, Hong Kong
1981 Holiday Inn Harbour View, Tsimshatsui East, Hong Kong
Kwai Chung Godown (warehouse), Kwai Chung, Hong Kong
Chi Lok Fa Yuen High-rise Housing, Tuen Mun, Hong Kong
Wah Yuen Chuen High-rise Housing, Ha Kwai Chung, Hong Kong
Jat Min Chuen High-rise Housing, Shatin, Hong Kong
1982 Carrian Centre Office Building, Wanchai, Hong Kong
Crocodile House Office Building, Central, Hong Kong
Sino Square Office and Commercial Building, Tsimshatsui East, Hong Kong
Euro Trade Centre Office and Commercial Building, Central, Hong Kong
Sunny Villa High-rise Apartments, Tsuen Wan, Hong Kong
Whampoa Terminal Building, Hunghom, Hong Kong
Holiday Inn Hotel, Karachi, Pakistan
Fung House Office Building, Queensway, Hong Kong
Nelson Square Office and Residential Complex, Vancouver, British Columbia (with Romses Kwan and Associates)
Holiday Inn Hotel, Johore Bahru, Malaysia

Sun Hing Industrial Building, Tuen Mun, Hong Kong
City Garden High-rise Residential Complex, North Point, Hong Kong
1983 Peak Villas Bungalows, The Peak, Hong Kong
Citicorp Centre Office Building, Causeway Bay, Hong Kong
Estoril Court High-rise Apartments, Mid-Level, Hong Kong
Elm Tree Towers High-rise Housing, Jardine's Lookout, Hong Kong
1984 Monterey Court High-rise Housing, Jardine's Lookout, Hong Kong
Hollywood Plaza Office and Commercial Development, Mongkok, Hong Kong
Cornwall House Factory, Quarry Bay, Hong Kong
Whellock House Office Building, Central, Hong Kong
Dah Chong Hong Motor Service Centre, Kowloon Bay Reclamation, Hong Kong
South Sea Industrial Building, Tuen Mun, Hong Kong

Publications:

On WONG: articles—"An Architect's House" in *Far East Architect and Builder* (Hong Kong), September 1966; "Holiday Inn: Linking Up" in *Asian*

Architect and Builder (Hong Kong), August 1974; "Latest Holiday Inn Has 650 Rooms" in *Asian Building and Construction* (Hong Kong), June 1975; "Cross Design Comes out Tops" in *South China Morning Post* (Hong Kong), 27 July 1977; "Wong and Ouyang and Associates, Hong Kong" in *Asian Building and Construction* (Hong Kong), November 1979; "Tao Ho Blocks" in *Architectural Review* (London), December 1979; "Twin Tower Complex Above Hong Kong Metro Station" in *Asian Building and Construction* (Hong Kong), September 1980.

Hong Kong as an economic society has been very active, highly efficient, and really realistic, with no exception for the building industry. Land cost in Hong Kong is probably the most expensive among its neighbouring countries, if not the highest in the world. Therefore, to survive in the highly competitive building industry, a developer or his consultants has a unique order of priorities, that is, to achieve: 1) the maximum total floor area in any development; 2) the most economical structure, as most buildings are high-rise; 3) an architectural scheme that requires the least time either for design and/or for construction; and 4) the best form and elevational treatment that does not adversely affect the other priorities, at no significant extra cost to the development.

These priorities are reflected in the works with which I have been involved. As a result they appear simple and straight-forward. I have found that simplicity in form, with explicit structural expression in exterior design, and "clean cut" planning solutions meet less resistance from all concerned.

Coverage of the roof area of a building still plays a crucial part in the development potential of a building site in Hong Kong, which also prevents any architectural articulation or architectural projection or indentation that sacrifices floor area or reduces the commercial viability of a project.

I believe in proportion and consistency. I find that refinement of proportion is one of the few areas with which a client is not concerned; and consistency in architectural detailing enables a building to stand out better in a crowded built environment. Recently my experience has shown that the reflective surface of a building does not necessarily have an adverse visual impact on its surroundings so long as it reflects images.

I believe that the interior of a building should reflect the structural system of the building and, if possible, the architectural form of a building exterior. Occupants in a building—with a few exceptions—should preferably be aware of the exterior surroundings at all times. A building interior to me is a controlled environment, designed for activities within a space. Lighting is an important means of creating an interior atmosphere, even more so than colour. People react to colour differently, and the colour of a surface is subject to changes according to light sources.

The architectural statement of a building should be simple and forceful to maintain its identity harmoniously in busy and over-crowded surroundings.

—Jackson C. S. Wong

Jackson C. S. Wong came from a Swatow background. Among Chinese, the inhabitants of Swatow are known for their defined code of ethics and for their rather Sicilian approach to issues and solutions: Jackson Wong is no exception.

He is a product of the University of Hong Kong under Gordon Brown, the former principal of the Architectural Association. His architecture is direct and controlled. He is committed to the grand scheme of things. He understands thoroughly the spatial determinants used by the private sector to define architecture. He accepts these as his base because they allow him to create the kind of architecture that large development groups and the government can relate to if not understand. He is

uncompromising on details, carefully matching these to the scale of his projects.

It is not unreasonable to say that the grand and the formal are still important and essential components necessary to hold urban architecture together. It is unavoidable that such an architecture often suffers from a sense of individual scale but Wong, like Pei and Portman, is committed to the urban collective scale and its purpose. His architecture can be described as sophisticated urban containers for collective activities. Wong's intention in architecture is fundamentally Palladian but his moves and actions leading to this realization must be described as Von Clausewitzian.

—K. C. Lye

WOODS, Shadrach.

American. Born in Yonkers, New York, 30 June 1923. Studied engineering at New York University, 1940-42, and literature at Dublin University, 1945-48. Served in the United States Naval Reserve, 1941-45. Married Clarissa Labaugh in 1946. Worked with Georges Candilis, *q.v.,* in the office of Le Corbusier, Paris, 1948-51; associated with Candilis in ATBAT-Afrique, Casablanca, 1951-55; Partner, with Candilis and Alexis Josic, *q.v.,* Candilis-Josic-Woods, Paris, 1955-63; worked with Candilis in Paris, 1963-67; in private practice, New York, 1970-73: Principal, Woods, Weintraub Associates. Lecturer, Yale University, New Haven, Connecticut, 1967; Professor of Architecture, Harvard Graduate School of Design, Cambridge, Massachusetts, 1968-73; appointed William Henry Bishop Visiting Professor of Architecture, Yale University, 1973 (declined because of ill health). Member, Team 10, from 1962. Recipient: First Prize, Marseilles Housing Competition, 1959; First Prize, Toulouse-le-Mirail New Town Competition, 1960; First Prize, Free University of Berlin Competition, 1963. *Died* (in New York) *31 July 1973.*

Works:

1951/
55   Musulman Collective Housing Development, Casablanca (with Vladimir Bodiansky and Georges Candilis)
1952/
54   Master plan for the city of Casablanca (with Vladimir Bodiansky and Georges Candilis)
1954/
55   Opération Million: 3,600 housing units, France, particularly the Paris suburbs (with Georges Candilis and Alexis Josic)
1956/
61   Plan and housing for the new town of Bagnols-sur-Cèze, France (with Georges Candilis and Alexis Josic)
1959   Housing (4,000 units), Marseilles (with Georges Candilis and Alexis Josic)
1960   Urban prefabricated houses, Algeria (competition project; with Georges Candilis and Alexis Josic)
Master plan for the new town of Toulouse-le-Mirail, France (with Georges Candilis and Alexis Josic)
1961   New town of 30,000 inhabitants, Caen, France (competition project; with Georges Candilis and Alexis Josic)
New town of 10,000 inhabitants, Hamburg, West Germany (competition project; with Georges Candilis and Alexis Josic)
1962   University for 2,000 students, Bochum, West Germany (competition project; with Georges Candilis and Alexis Josic)

1963   Plan for the center of Frankfurt (project; with Georges Candilis and Alexis Josic)
Master plan for Fort Lamy, Chad, Africa (with Georges Candilis and Alexis Josic)
Master plan of the Free University of Berlin (with Georges Candilis and Alexis Josic)
1964/
65   Cité Artisanale (Workshop Center for Artisans), Sèvres, France (with Georges Candilis and Alexis Josic)
Ski Resort, Vallée de Belleville, France (with Georges Candilis and Jean Prouvé)
Val d'Asua Residential Development, near Bilbao, Spain
1966   Steilshoop Regional Center, Hamburg, West Germany (with Georges Candilis)
1967   Redevelopment plan for the Bonne Nouvelle, Paris
1969   Redevelopment plan for the SoHo District, New York
1970   Redevelopment plan for Karlsruhe, West Germany
Douglas Circle, Central Park, New York (project)

Publications:

By WOODS: books—*Urbanism Is Everybody's Business,* with J. Pfeufer, Stuttgart 1968, 1970; *What U Can Do,* Houston, Texas 1970; *The Man in the Street: A Polemic on Urbanism,* London 1975; *Toulouse le Mirail: Birth of a New Town,* with Georges Candilis and Alexis Josic, Stuttgart 1975; articles—"Why Revisit Le Pavillon Suisse" in *Architectural Forum* (New York), June 1965; "Conversation on Urbanism," with Roger Vailland, in *Perspecta* (New Haven, Connecticut), vol. 11, 1967; "Strive for Uniformity?" in *Architecture Canada* (Toronto), April 1967; "Waiting for Printout" in *Perspecta* (New Haven, Connecticut), vol. 12, 1969.

On WOODS: books—*New French Architecture* by Maurice Besset, London and Stuttgart 1967; *Candilis, Josic, Woods* by Jürgen Joedicke, Stuttgart 1968; articles—"Candilis, Josic, Woods" in *Cimaise* (Paris), January/February 1961; "Atelier Candilis, Josic, Woods" in *Architectural Design* (London), January 1965; "Shadrach Woods 1923-1973" by Peter Smithson in *Architectural Design* (London), November 1973; "Shadrach Woods: A Personal Remembrance" by P. C. Papademetriou in *Architecture in Greece* (Athens), vol. 8, 1974; "Team 10 at Royaumont" by Alison Smithson in *Architectural Design* (London), November 1975.

Although Shadrach Woods was trained as an architect and began his career in Le Corbuiser's office, his most notable accomplishements were in the field of urban design. As early as the mid 1950s, Woods focused his attention on the increasingly apparent failures of modern urban life, and designed several new town plans, low-income housing projects, and public health facilities for communities throughout the world.

When the radicalism of the 1960s swept the Western world, Woods took a forefront position as champion of the urban inhabitant. During his association with Candilis and Josic in Paris (1955-1967), Woods produced many significant urban schemes as well as several individual buildings. Together, the group developed a policy of "urbanism" that Woods retained after the partnership was dissolved. In the last years of his life, Woods devoted himself even more selflessly towards the implementation of these ideas.

Urbanism, according to Woods and his associates, is the methodical process by which we organize our cities. It is not a purely physical expression, because it refers not only to the organization of our buildings, but also to the structuring of our service, transportation, and energy networks, as well as to the development of our economic systems. All of these elements determine urban form.

Woods was frustrated by the apparent stagnation of the metabolism of the overall urban form, despite the radical and accelerating changes of the individual systems. For instance, Woods condemned, with others, the singularity of pedestrian and vehicular traffic zones. Such zones had become acutely antiquated, he insisted, because technology had produced new vehicles that now travelled too fast to retain any relationship to human beings on foot.

When he planned, Woods attempted to reform more than just the physical composition of the city, even though he certainly pushed for much physical reformation. "It is clear that no formal composition can provide an answer to these problems," he wrote in 1961, "because the answers of all formal compositions are static, precise, and fixed. Today's buildings are obsolete in five years. Our object is not to make the building flexible, but to make the urban complex flexible enough to foster short life buildings as well as long ones."

Woods felt there was a great urgency to the development of urbanistic solutions, because he sensed that every mistake now being perpetrated would compound itself as we were forced to live in an inadequate environment. In a pamphlet published by Rice University in 1970, Woods pleaded to students to rebel against the status-quo. Despite our limited power as pawns of "the state, the institutions, and the corporations that are the most pernicious forces in society," he told them, we must use whatever skill or power we do wield to alter the current suicidal directions of society. This alteration, he insisted, involved not merely the prevention of negative changes in our cities through the use of organized community resistance, but also the presentation of alternative solutions to real economic problems.

In his final projects in New York, Germany, and France, Woods showed what kind of alternative solutions he meant. His innovative ideas have now become axiomatic: reasonable, anti-opportunistic growth can be accomplished only through sensitive, small scale renewal and renovation, not through the senseless destruction and complete rebuilding of large tracts of still viable communities.

—Mitchell B. Rouda

WOOLLEY, Kenneth Frank.
Australian. Born in Sydney, New South Wales, 29 May 1933. Educated at Sydney Boys' High School, 1946-49; trainee in the Government Architect's Branch, New South Wales Department of Public Works, Sydney, 1950-54, and studied at the University of Sydney, 1950-54, B.Arch (honours) 1954 (University Medal; Sulman Medal; Stephenson Turner Medal); awarded Byera Hadley Travelling Scholarship, 1955. Married Cythia Anne Stuart in 1957 (divorced, 1979); children: Howard, Anna, and Simon; married Virginia Braden in 1980. Design Architect, Government Architect's Branch, Sydney, 1955-56 and 1957-63; Assistant Architect, Chamberlin, Powell and Bon, *q.v.*, London, 1956-57; Partner, with Sydney Ancher, *q.v.*, Bruce Mortlock, *q.v.* and Stuart Murray, *q.v.*, Ancher, Mortlock, Murray and Woolley, Sydney, 1964-69; Director, Ancher, Mortlock, Murray and Woolley Pty. Ltd., Sydney, 1969-75. Since 1975, Director, Ancher, Mortlock and Woolley Pty. Ltd., Sydney: now Senior Director. Visiting Tutor and Critic, University of Sydney, and New South Wales Institute of Technology, Sydney; Visiting Professor, University of New South Wales, Sydney, 1983-84. Member, New South Wales Board of Architects, 1960-72, New South Wales Board of Architectural Education, 1969-72, and Royal Aus-

tralian Institute of Architects Aboriginal Housing Panel, 1972-76. Member, New South Wales Building Regulations Advisory Committee, 1960-74; Member of the Quality Review Committee, Darling Harbour Redevelopment Authority, Sydney, 1985. Exhibitions: *Sulman Award Exhibition,* Royal Australian Institute of Architects, Sydney, 1963; *RAIA Member Exhibition,* Sydney, 1964; *Australian Exhibition,* at Expo '67, Montreal, 1967, and *Expo '70,* Osaka, Japan, 1970; RAIA Awards Exhibitions, Sydney, 1968-84; *Ancher, Morlock, Murray and Woolley, Sydney Architects, 1946-76,* Art Gallery of New South Wales, Sydney, 1976 (toured Australia, 1977); *Pleasures of Architecture,* Sydney, 1980; *Competition for the Quay,* Sydney, 1983; *Old Continent— New Building,* toured Australia, 1983-85; *Triennale of World Architecture,* Belgrade, Yugoslavia, 1985. Recipient: Taubman House Competition Prize (with Michael Dysart), 1958; Sulman Medal, 1962, Bronze Medal, 1962, and Wilkinson Award, 1962 and 1968, 1983, Blacket Award, 1964, 1969, and Civic Design Award, 1983, Royal Australian Institute of Architects; St. Regis-ACI Sisalkraft Travelling Scholarship, 1968; Merit Award, Royal Australian Institute of Architects, New South Wales Chapter, 1972, 1976, 1978, 1979, 1980 (twice), 1981, 1982, and 1984; First Prize, Department of Criminology Competition, Canberra, 1979; First Prize, Lend Lease Homes Competition, Lane Cove, Sydney, 1980; First Prize, National Archive Competition, Canberra, 1983; First Prize, Gateway Site Competition, Sydney, 1983; C. S. Daley Medal, Canberra, 1984. Fellow, 1965, and Life Fellow, 1976, Royal Australian Institute of Architects. Address: Ancher, Mortlock and Woolley Pty. Ltd., 40 Collins Street, Surry Mills, New South Wales 2010, Australia.

Works:

1955/
57 Chapel and Sisters Home, St. Margaret's Hospital, Sydney
Chemistry School, University of Sydney (with H. Rembert and P. Webber)
1958 Low-Cost Exhibition House, Cherybrooke, Pennant Hills, New South Wales (with Michael Dysart)
1958/
62 Fisher Library, University of Sydney (with T. O'Mahony)
1959 Descon Factory, Brookvale, New South Wales (now demolished)
1960 Mona Vale Hospital, New South Wales (with C. Weatherburn)
1960/
62 Recreation Hall and Chapel, Lidcombe State Hospital, New South Wales
1960/
64 New South Wales State Government Offices, Sydney
1961 Three exhibition houses, Kingsdene, New South Wales (with Michael Dysart)
Windsor Courthouse restoration, New South Wales
1961/
78 3,000 project houses, Sydney and throughout Australia
1962 Macquarie Field House restoration, Liverpool, New South Wales
Woolley House, Mosman, New South Wales
1963 Spiral Fountain, State Office Block, Bent Street, Sydney
Baudish House, Middle Cove, New South Wales
1964 Culhane House, Hunters Hill, New South Wales
Rothery House, Strathfield, New South Wales
Theatrette and Premier's Suite interiors, State Office Block, Sydney
Student Union, University of Newcastle, stage 1, New South Wales

1964/
66 St. George Technical College, stage III, New South Wales
F. C. Pye Field Environment Laboratory, Canberra
1965 Myers House, Mosman, New South Wales
1965/
68 The Penthouses, Darling Point, New South Wales
1965/
69 Student Union Building, Macquarie University, North Ryde, New South Wales (with Bryce Mortlock)
1966 Ullr Ski Lodge, Perisher Valley, New South Wales
Six townhouses, Milson Road, Cremorne Point, New South Wales
1967 Macquarie Town Housing, Ryde, New South Wales (project)
1967/
68 Six townhouses, Gillies Street, Wollstonecraft, New South Wales
Three-storey apartments, Shirley Road, Wollstonecraft, New South Wales
Staff House, University of Newcastle, New South Wales
1967/
71 Seventh Day Adventist Church, Canberra
1968 Student Union Building, University of Newcastle, stage II, New South Wales
Kindergarten, La Perouse, New South Wales
Six-storey apartments, Fairfax Road, Bellevue Hill, New South Wales
Kinneil Hotel and Apartments (project)
1968/
71 Wentworth Student Union Building, University of Sydney
1969 Steel House for the Future (research project)
Small office building, Greenmansions Street, St. Leonards, New South Wales
Twelve-storey flats, Reynolds Street, Cremorne, New South Wales
1970/
77 Town Hall House, Sydney Square and Arcade, and Town Hall alterations and restoration, Sydney
1970/
78 Government Detached and Atrium Houses (600), Canberra
St. Andrew's Cathedral restoration, Sydney
1971 Woden Churches Centre, Canberra
Woden School for Retarded Children, Canberra
1972 500 apartments, Victoria Point, Sydney (project)
1972/
77 Woden Health Centre and Woden Library, Canberra
1973 108 group houses, Liverpool, New South Wales
Kippax Health Centre, Canberra
100 holiday houses, Fiji
1973/
75 Master plan for the Commonwealth Scientific and Industrial Research Organization (C.S.I.R.O.) Black Mountain Campus, Canberra
1973/
78 Australian Embassy, Bangkok, Thailand
1974 High density housing, Rhodes, Sydney (project)
Wolloomooloo Action Plan Urban Design Study
Soi Attakarn Prasit Embassy Housing, Bangkok, Thailand (project)
Woden Child Care Centre, Canberra
1974/
78 Kippax Townhouses, Canberra
100 townhouses, village centre, and new town pilot project, Holsworth, New South Wales
1975 Precast Concrete House (project)
Master plan and site development for the Academy of Science, Canberra

1975/
78 Infill housing and Victorian period house restoration, Glebe, New South Wales
1976 Pettit House, Canberra
1976/
79 Rare Book Library, University of Sydney (project)
1,000 apartments and urban development, Darlinghurst Hill, Sydney (project)
1977/
79 Radio station, Vila, New Hebrides
1978 West Amenities and Project Control Facility, Garden Island Naval Dockyard, Sydney
Radio station, Honiara, Solomon Islands
Pettit House, Dee Why, New South Wales
Bathurst Housing, New South Wales (competition project)
1978/
80 Australian Institute of Criminology, Canberra (project)
Housing (56 units), Woolloomooloo, New South Wales
1979 Central Lighting Master Plan Study, Canberra
1980 Woolley House, Paddington, Sydney
1980/
83 Guided Missile Launch System Repair Facility, Garden Island Naval Dockyard, Sydney
Church of Jesus Christ of the Latter Day Saints Chapel, Leura, Blue Mountains, New South Wales
1980 Housing (220 units), Best Street, Linley Cove, New South Wales
1981/
83 Yarralumla Townhouses, Canberra
1982 Cadets' Mess, at the Australian Defence Force Academy, Canberra (with Department of Housing and Construction)
Goodman House, Pymble, New South Wales (project)
House at Fingal Bay, Tweed Heads, Queensland
Residential, Office, and Shops Development, Manly, New South Wales
1982/
83 Queenscliff Surf Pavilion, Manly, New South Wales
1982/
84 Denning Offices, Gordon, New South Wales
The Anchorage housing (350 units), Tweed Heads, Queensland
Australian Federal Police Headquarters Plan, Canberra
1983 Gateway Plan, Circular Quay, Sydney (competition project)
Parliamentary Triangle Study, Canberra (with National Capital Development Commission)
Fleet Wharf Design and Coordination, Garden Island, Sydney
Beauchamp House renovation and restoration, Canberra
1983 National Archives, Canberra
Hill House, Mosman, New South Wales
1984 Office Building, George Street, Paramatta, New South Wales
Office Building, Parkes Street, Paramatta, New South Wales
Woolley Weekend House, Palm Beach, New South Wales
Overlapping Housing, Rushcutters Bay, Sydney
Portal Building Studies, Garden Island, Sydney
Commonwealth Law Courts, Paramatta, New South Wales
1984 National Archives Design Development, Canberra
1985 B. Pettit Weekend House, Scotlander Island, New South Wales
Glass Houses Exhibition layouts, Royal Botanic Gardens, Sydney

Publications:

By WOOLLEY: book—*Ken Woolley— Drawings*, edited by Virginia Woolley, Sydney 1983; articles—"Air Conditioning" in *Australian Building Science and Technology* (Sydney), October 1964; "How Australians Should Be Housed" in *Economic Society of Australia Journal* (Sydney), March 1967; statement in *Towards an Australian Architecture* by Harry Sowden, Sydney 1968; "Concrete" in *Building Science Forum* (Sydney), June 1970; "Project Housing" in *Sunday Review* (Sydney), 1971; "Australia's Terrace Houses" in *Architectural Forum* (New York), May 1971; "Australian Domestic Architecture" in *Art and Australia* (Sydney), June 1971; "Tertiary Education Buildings" and "Travel Sketches" in *Architecture in Australia* (Sydney), August/September 1976; "Heritage Legislation in New South Wales" in *Architecture in Australia* (Sydney), May 1978.

On WOOLLEY: books—*Australia's Home* by Robin Boyd, revised edition, Melbourne 1952; *The Puzzle of Architecture* by Robin Boyd, Melbourne 1965; *Towards an Australian Architecture* by Harry Sowden, Sydney 1968; *In the Making* by Craig McGregor, Harry Williamson and David Moore, Melbourne 1969; *Australian Style* by Babette Hayes and April Hersey, Sydney 1970; *Living and Party Living* by McKay, Stretton and Mant, Melbourne 1971; *444 Sydney Buildings* by Richard Apperly and Peter Lind, Sydney 1971; *An Australian Identity* by Jennifer Taylor, Sydney 1972; *Housing in the Seventies* by Howard Tanner, Sydney 1976; *Ancher, Mortlock, Murray and Woolley, Sydney Architects, 1946-76* by David Saunders and Catherine Bourke, Sydney 1976; *Fine Houses of Sydney* by Robert Irving, John Kinstler and Max Dupain, Sydney 1982; *Medium Density Housing in Australia* by Bruce Judd and John Dean, Canberra 1983; *Old Continent—New Building: Contemporary Australian*

Ken Woolley: Australian Embassy, Bangkok, 1973-78.

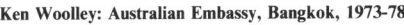

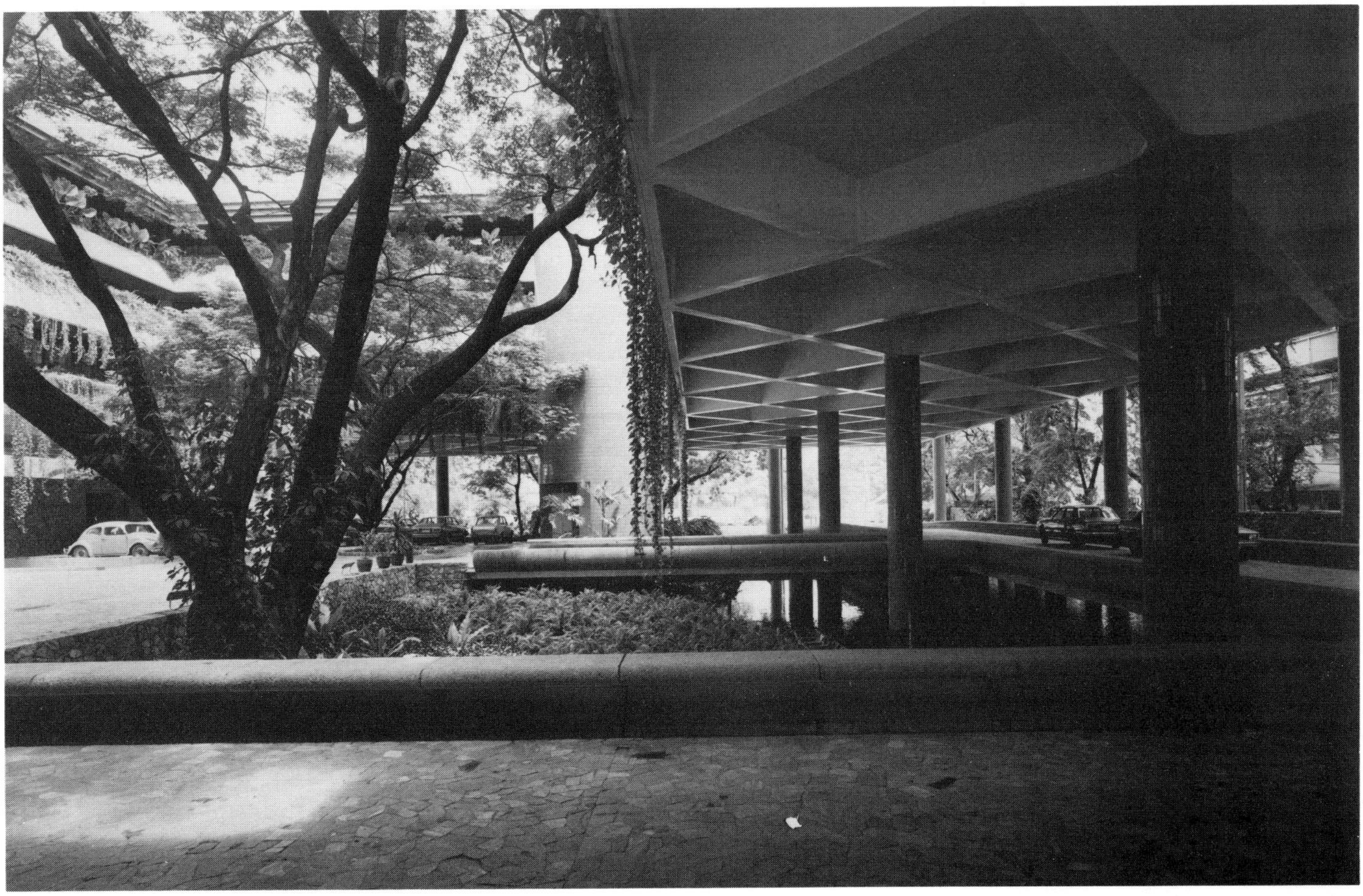

Architecture, edited by Leon Paroissien and Michael Griggs, Darlinghurst, New South Wales 1983; *Details in Australian Architecture* by Roger Pegrum, Canberra 1984; *Fifty Outstanding Architects of the World* by Ivica Mladjenovic, Belgrade, Yugoslavia 1984; articles—"Gateway to More" by Col James in *Architecture Bulletin* (Sydney), no. 1/2, 1982; "Woolley House" in *Architecture Australia* (Melbourne), July 1984; "Detailing, National Identity and a Sense of Place in Australian Architecture" in *UIA International Architect* (London) no. 4, 1984.

Early on, it seemed to me that the dogma of the conventional modern movement had not come to terms with humanist values. Its functional and visual shortcomings were apparent in the failure to resolve elements incompatible with an overall concept. Thus, my early work, in the 1950s, tended to pay respect to Aalto for his informal and accidental effects and to Mies for the rigour of his detailing.

There followed a conviction that directness of detail and a reassessment of traditional values were needed, and, when applied to domestic and related work, these produced a style that Robin Boyd called "a tamed romantic kind of Brutalism." With other participants as well, this approach became known as the Sydney School. Perhaps because ti was expressed in rather warm and traditional materials—brick, tile, and timber—there evolved a preconception of the style which often left it unrecognised in other types of buildings, because of its tendency to approach each problem afresh.

I believe, like Venturi, that some buildings are naturally ordinary and demand general, rather traditional responses, whereas others are special and generate particular solutions. I seem to have had many opportunities in both areas and regard the ordinary buildings, for example for low-cost housing, to be just as important as particular, special buildings. It is possible to misinterpret the special responses as intentional moves towards a new style or simply as lack of a consistent style.

All of my work, it seems to me now, has been based on finding a framework (not necessarily frame construction) which is capable of acting as a reference for all the functional and aesthetic requirements of the programme. That is, a system or discipline which encompasses the geometry, construction technique, and planning arrangements and sets up the potential for variations and complexities which can enhance the design, serving a myriad of minor functional and humanistic subtleties. Ideally, the elements have an inherent capability of permutation by chance and by functional determinants. The achievement of this framework is an effort of synthesis based on analysis and understanding.

The recently completed Town Hall development in Sydney covers a broader range of activites than before. From a basic requirement for ordinary offices on a standard budget, the building becomes the source of a major civic design exercise. The historic Town Hall is restored, its acoustics improved, facilities for audiences extend into the new building, and a new complex of civic spaces forms a Town Square. Direct access is gained to a major underground station, and pedestrian movement on the whole city block is transformed. The restoration work, which also involved St. Andrew's Cathedral for the National Trust is another interest for which I would like to have more time.

Further new directions are seen in the Australian Embassy in Bangkok, which revives the traditional pavilion standing in water and is clad in golden yellow temple tiles. The most recent project at the Sydney Naval Dockyard is designed with a stressed skin steel plate structure, like the superstructure of the ships it services.

A major, central, urban, high-density housing scheme will start soon. It creates new urban streets from a predominantly low-rise solution, utilising them for open space, circulation, visual interest, and security. Variation and complexity are developed around a standard, low-cost construction technique employing all its geometric possibilities together with added variable components—balconies, doorways, bays and terraces, shop fronts, and the like.

Like most architects, I have been plagued in recent years by unbuilt projects, innovative but ill-fated. Many of these are due to the failures of the planning profession, which also deserves criticism for prescribing real building solutions into regulations, stifling creative development.

I am still very involved with drawing, both as a record, as in travel sketches, and as a means of communication. Drawing is also the medium in which to work out the development of basic ideas.

As for the future, I hope to see architects concentrating on a truly sensitive language and insisting on the responsibility for the environment's being placed where it belongs, with political planning. (1978)

Looking from the vantage point of 1985, my earlier statement seems to mark the end of a period. I think that is probably true of many architects in the first edition. A number of projects listed then were in fact completed, notably the Australian Embassy in Bangkok, the design of which dates from 1973. The large urban housing project at Darlinghurst, for which I had such hopes, was abandoned. The key designs from the late 1970s were the Institute of Criminology and my new house at Paddington. The former was the result of a competition and proceeded to full contract documentation before being suspended and later abandoned. The house was built and received the same award as my 1962 house at Mosman. My most significant current project is the National Archives in Canberra, the result of a limited competition. Earlier, I stressed my interest in an architectural discipline, which ordered the necessary chaos and complexity of individual expression while not suppressing them. I have now come to understand the tension between order and chaos as the essential ingredient of architectural quality and to better recognise the need for the classical and the romantic, representing order and chaos, to appear with different emphasis appropriate to the place and the programme of any building. I have become increasingly aware of the importance of comprehension of a building and thus the signification of meaning by building elements. So the development of architecture as expression through something broadly analogous to language has concerned me deeply and appears, perhaps with varying degrees of exploratory success, in all the recent work.

—Ken Woolley

Since the age of 23 years Ken Woolley has been making notable contributions to Australian architecture. He has maintained a front line position through the high quality of his architecture and its relevance to the circumstances and mood of the time of its creation. The buildings produced over this period exhibit a consistency in fundamental ideals but a wide diversity in formal compositions. Always evident in his work are an understanding of and a delight in building materials be they rough and rustic or refined and precise, the exploration of spatial variety, the exploitation of the properties of light, and a united relationship between building, site and setting. Ever changing are the characteristics and forms of the individual buildings which provide unique answers in terms of programme and location and Woolley's current position in his restless search for appropriate expression.

Woolley's initial opportunities to design prominent buildings arose from his position as Assistant Architect in the Government Architect's Branch of the Public Works Department of New South Wales. Of the early buildings Fisher Library (with T O'Mahony), 1958-62, the main resource centre of the University of Sydney, and the composite steel and concrete framed State Government Offices, Sydney, 1960-64, show a remarkable ability and confidence in their compositions and in the use of new technologies.

In 1964 Woolley joined the highly respected Sydney firm of Ancher Mortlock and Murray. Before leaving the Government Architect's Office he had become involved in project housing design and, with his own house at Mosman, had established a reputation as a leading figure in the regional romantic "Sydney School" movement. His brick and tile "Sydney School" buildings of the sixties, which included the Student Union at the University of Newcastle, were inspired by the terrain, colours and textures of the Australian bushland sites. Off-saw timber and rough clinker bricks, carefully chosen to blend with surroundings, were put together with great care and craftsmanship. These buildings, often of several levels, followed the contours and reflected the slopes in the raking roof planes. The resulting interior spaces were rich in their earthy colours and heavy textures and dramatically lit through high openings in the walls and roofs. These buildings were influential towards establishing an ethic in Australian architecture that was widely shared for over a decade.

Perhaps Woolley's greatest contribution to the environment has come in the field of housing, for, with over 4,000 individual houses built to his designs, he has played a major part in raising the standard of the average suburban dwelling. His single houses and multiple housing schemes share roots in the vernacular. Traditional materials are used and in large developments the units are so arranged on stepped levels or in groups so as to provide privacy, a sense of intimacy and a domestic scale.

Woolley is equally at home in the city as in the suburbs or the country and his subsequent multistoried city buildings retain the Brutalist aesthetic of the 'Sydney School' but are constructed primarily of concrete. These are more expressionistic works that exploit the sculpturaal and structural possibilities of the material. These qualitites are present in Town Hall House, 1970-77, which was designed for the historic precinct of the Sydney Town Hall and the Cathedral of St Andrew. It is but one element of a highly successful extensive civic design project for the street levels and underground system of a central city block. The most structurally lucid and expressive of Woolley's buildings is the Australian Embassy in Bangkok, 1973-78, where the lush water-logged garden and sheathing golden toned tiles bring a traditional local flavour to a fine example of rational modern architecture.

The second Woolley House, built in the inner city suburb of Paddington, 1980, introduced fresh concerns that were to influence the future direction of his architecture. Here the precipitous terrain and the surrounding mixed housing types determined the nature of the house that rears up from the site below as a white sculptural tower clinging to the cliff. Woolley's experience in housing shows in the quite ingenious plan which places the rooms on three levels in close relationship to a central stairwell. New in his work are the strong street edging properties of the flat plane of the facade and the explicit references to the language of the older adjacent architecture.

The Church of Jesus Christ of the Latter Day Saints (Mormon) at Leura and the Surf Pavilion of Queenscliff further extend the use of the flat plane to define the building envelope and the use of typological forms. Both buildings also indicate Woolley's new interest in buildings as toy-like objects. In addition they also exhibit an increasing level of spatial complexity. Slicing axes through the plans control the organisation of spaces that are highly varied in three dimensions. The sensitive play of such moulded form with subtly introduced light makes the Mormon Chapel one of the most delightful of Woolley's interior spaces. The Surf Pavilion is a fun building with a story-book lookout tower and an outer shell of colonnaded walls coloured beige like the sand and an inner core painted the russet of the cliffs and the brick buildings of the townscape behind. The roof of the hall curves in wave-like forms suggestive of the movement of the ocean. In its mood, visual accord and performance, the Queenscliff Surf Pavilion provides a clear example of what Woolley means by 'appropriate' architecture. The contrast these buildings provide with those designed at the same time for the naval dockyard of Garden Island in Sydney demonstrates how the individuality of Woolley's architecture is largely determined by context. The West Amenities and Project Control Facility and the Guided Missile Launching System Repair Unit are strongly technological in their imagery and they sit as blue-grey mechanical objects amongst the ships and cranes of the dockyards.

While Woolley insists he remains a functionalist at heart his recent buildings are becoming less pragmatic and draw more on the imagination. There is increasing emphasis on the cultural, rather than the physical, basis for design and the buildings themselves show a new elegance and richness. The design for the Australian Archives for a lakeside site in the Parliamentary Triangle in Canberra is a resolved composition of layered spaces ordered by a graduated spatial progression that reaches its climax under the central dome. The language of the Archives building derives from Walter Burley Griffin's 1912 drawings in his submission for the design of the capital, the architectural elements of Canberra's landmarks of the earlier decades and the new Parliament House by Mitchell Giurgola Thorp. Woolley's building seeks to stand, in the Canberra tradition, as an independent object and at the same time to establish compositional affinity with the Griffin plan and the existing objects within it. It is the most ambitious example of Woolley's constant concern from the overall context of his architecture. This is notably a classical building that brings a new grand dimension to Woolley's creative abilities with space and light.

Ken Woolley is an informed and aware architect who is constantly looking ahead for better solutions. His latest projects suggest that he is moving towards a new level of creativity and that his most compelling works are yet to be built.

—Jennifer Taylor

WRIGHT, Frank, Lloyd

American. Born in Richland Center, Wisconsin, 8 June 1867; moved with his family to Weymouth, Massachusetts, 1874; settled in Madison, Wisconsin, 1877. Educated at Second Ward School, Madison, 1879-83; University of Wisconsin School of Engineering, Madison, 1885-87. Married Catherine Lee Tobin in 1889 (separated, 1909; subsequently divorced); children: the architect Lloyd Wright, *q.v.,* John, Catherine, Frances, David and Llewellyn; left family to live with Mrs. Mamah Bortwick Cheney, 1909 until her death in the Taliesin fire, 1914; married Miriam Noel in 1915 (separated, 1924; died, 1927; married Olgivanna Lazovich in 1925; children: Iovanna and (by wife's previous marriage) Svetlana. Worked as a Junior Draftsman for Allen D. Conover, Madison, 1885-87, and for Lyman Silsbee, Chicago, 1887; Assistant Architect, 1888-89, and Head of the Planning and Design Department, 1889-93, Adler and Sullivan, Chicago; in partnership with Cecil Corwin, Chicago, 1893-96; in private practice in the Chicago suburb of Oak Park, 1896-97, and in Chicago, 1897-1909; travelled with Mrs. Cheney to Europe, and stayed in Fiesole, near Florence, 1909-11; built first Taliesin house and studio, and resumed practice, Spring Green, Wisconsin, 1911; re-opened Chicago office, 1912; Taliesin partially destroyed by fire and rebuilt as Taliesin II, 1914; established office in Tokyo in conjunction with work on the Imperial Hotel, 1915-20: while in Japan compiled Spaulding Collection of Japanese Prints, now in the Museum of Fine Arts, Boston; worked on first concrete "texture block" houses, California, 1921-24; Taliesin II partially destroyed by fire and rebuilt as Taliesin III, 1925; Worked in La Jolla, California, 1928; established southwestern headquarters, Ocatillo, at

Chandler, Arizona, 1928-29; established Wright Foundation Fellowship at Taliesin, 1932 (with annual winter transfer of Fellowship activities from Spring Green to Chandler, Arizona, 1933-38, and to Scottsdale, Arizona, from 1938); worked on major theoretical studies for Broadacre City from 1933; built Taliesin West, Paradise Valley, near Scottsdale, Arizona, 1938; continued to practice in Wisconsin and Arizona until his death, 1959; students formed Taliesin Associated Architects on his death to complete various works. Exhibitions: Chicago Architectural Club, 1894, 1898, 1899, 1900, 1901, 1902, 1907; Museum of Modern Art, New York, 1931, toured the United States and Europe; *Broadacre City,* Pittsburgh, 1935; Museum of Modern Art, New York, 1940; *Sixty Years of Living Architecture: The Work of Frank Lloyd Wright,* Palazzo Strozzi, Florence, 1951, European tour, 1951-53, and North American tour, 1953-54; *Mile High Building,* Sherman Hotel, Chicago, 1956; *An Architect and His Client: Frank Lloyd Wright and Francis W. Little,* Metropolitan Museum of Art, New York, 1973; *The Decorative Designs of Frank Lloyd Wright,* Renwick Museum, Smithsonian Institution, Washington, D.C., 1978; *Frank Lloyd Wright and the Prairie School,* Musée de la Seita, Paris, 1983. Collections: Frank Lloyd Wright Foundation, Taliesin, Spring Green, Wisconsin and Taliesin West, Paradise Valley, near Scottsdale, Arizona; Frank Lloyd Wright Collection, Avery Library, Columbia University, New York; Northwestern University, Evanston, Illinois. Recipient: Kenchiko Ho Citation, Royal Household of Japan, 1919; Royal Gold Medal, Royal Institute of British Architects, 1941; Gold Medal, American Institute of Architects, 1949; Gold Medal, AIA, Philadelphia Chapter, 1949; Peter Cooper Award, 1949; Centennial Award, *Popular Mechanics,* 1950; Star of Solidarity, City of Venice, 1951; Medici Medal, City of Florence, 1951; Gold Medal, National Institute of Arts and Letters, 1953; Brown Medal, Franklin Institute, Philadelphia, 1954; Freedom of the City, Chicago, 1956. M.A.: Wesleyan University, Middletown, Connecticut, 1939; D.F.A.: Princeton University, New Jersey, 1947; Yale University, New Haven, Connecticut, 1954; University of Wisconsin, Madison, 1955; LL.D: Florida Southern College, Lakeland, 1950; D.Phil.: University of Wales, Bangor, 1956. Member, National Institute of Arts and Letters, 1949. Honorary Member: Academie Royale des Beaux Arts, Brussels, 1927; Akademie Royal der Künste, Berlin, 1929; National Academy of Brazil, 1932; Royal Institute of British Architects, 1941; National Academy of Architects, Uruguay, 1942; National Academy of Architects, Mexico, 1943; National Academy of Finland, 1946; Royal Academy of Fine Arts, Stockholm, 1953. *Died* (in Phoenix, Arizona), *9 April 1959.*

Works:

1885 University Avenue Power House, Madison, Wisconsin (project)
1887 Hillside Home School Building I, for the Misses Lloyd Jones, Spring Green, Wisconsin (converted to Taliesin Fellowship Complex, 1933)
 Misses Lloyd Jones House, Spring Green, Wisconsin (project)
 Unitarian Chapel, Sioux City, Iowa (project)
1889 Frank Lloyd Wright House, Oak Park, Illinois
1890 Charnley House, Ocean Springs, Mississippi
 MacHarg House, Chicago
 Louis Sullivan House, Ocean Springs, Mississippi
 Cooper House, La Grange, Illinois (project)
1892 Charnley House, 1365 North Astor Street, Chicago
 Blossom House, Chicago
 Clark House, La Grange, Illinois
 Emmond House, La Grange, Illinois
 Mrs. Thomas Gale House, Oak Park, Illinois

 Harlan House, Chicago
 McArthur House, Chicago
 Parker House, Oak Park, Illinois
 Albert Sullivan House, Chicago
 Victoria Hotel remodelling, Chicago Heights
1893 Lake Mendota Boathouse, Madison, Wisconsin
 Walter Gale House, Oak Park, Illinois
 Lamp Cottage, Lake Mendota, Madison, Wisconsin
 Frank Lloyd Wright House playroom addition, Oak Park, Illinois
 Lake Morona Boathouse, Madison, Wisconsin (project)
 Library and Museum, Milwaukee (competition project)
1894 Winslow House, River Forest, Illinois
 Bagley House, Hinsdale, Illinois
 Bassett House remodelling, Oak Park, Illinois
 Peter Goan House, La Grange, Illinois
 Roloson Apartments, Chicago
 Wooley House, Chicago
 Concrete Monolithic Bank (project)
 Orris Goan House, La Grange, Illinois (project)
 McAfee House, Chicago (project)
1895 Francis Apartments, 4304 South Forrestville, Chicago
 Francisco Terrace Apartments, 253 North Francisco, Chicago
 Moore House, Oak Park, Illinois
 Waller Apartments, Chicago
 Williams House, River Forest, Illinois
 Young House alterations, Oak Park, Illinois
 Amusements Park, Wolf Lake, Illinois (project)
 Baldwin House, Oak Park, Illinois (project)
 Lexington Terrace Apartment Building, Chicago (project)
 Luxfer Prism Company Skyscraper, Chicago (project)
1896 Format for *House Beautiful* magazine
 Goodrich House, Oak Park, Illinois
 Roberts House remodelling and Stable, Oak Park, Illinois
 Romeo and Juliet Windmill Tower, Hillside Home School, Spring Green, Wisconsin
 Devin House, Chicago (project)
 Perkins Apartment, Chicago (project)
 Roberts Houses (4), Ridgeland, Illinois (project)
1897 Heller House, 5132 South Woodlawn, Chicago
 Frank Lloyd Wright Studio (addition to house), Oak Park, Illinois
 George Furbeck House, Oak Park, Illinois
 Wallis Boathouse, Lake Delavan, Wisconsin
 All Souls Building, Lincoln Center, Chicago (project)
 Chicago Screw Company Factory Building, Chicago (project)
1898 Rollin Furbeck House, Oak Park, Illinois
 River Forest Golf Club, Illinois
 Smith House, Oak Park, Illinois
 Mozart Gardens Restaurant remodelling, Chicago (project)
 Waller House, River Forest, Illinois
1899 Husser House, Chicago
 Waller House remodelling, River Forest, Illinois
 Cheltenham Beach Resort, near Chicago (project)
 Eckhart House, River Forest, Illinois (project)
 House (project published in *Architectural Review,* London)
1900 Jesse Adams House, Longwood, Illinois
 William Adams House, Chicago
 Bradley House, Kankakee, Illinois
 Dana House, Springfield, Illinois
 Foster House, Chicago
 Goldsmith House, Lake Delavan, Wisconsin
 Hickox House, Kankakee, Illinois
 Pitkin Lodge, Desbarats, Ontario, Canada
 Wallis House, Lake Delavan, Wisconsin

Frank Lloyd Wright: Robie House, Chicago, 1909.

Abraham Lincoln Center, Chicago (project)
Home in a Prairie Town (project Published in *Ladies Home Journal,* New York)
Francis W. Little House I, Peoria, Illinois (project)
Motion Picture Theatre, Los Angeles (project)
School, Crosbyton, Texas (project)
A Small House with Lots of Room in It (project published in *Ladies Home Journal,* New York)
1901 Davenport House, River Forest, Illinois
Universal Portland Cement Company Exhibition Pavilion, Buffalo, New York
Henderson House, Elmhurst, Illinois
Hills House remodelling, Oak Park, Illinois
Jones House, Boathouse and Gate Lodge, Lake Delavan, Wisconsin
River Forest Golf Club additions, Illinois
Thomas House, Oak Park, Illinois
Gatehouse and Gardener's Cottage, for Waller House, River Forest, Illinois
Gate Lodge remodelling, for Wallis House, Lake Delavan, Wisconsin
Stables, Wilder House, Elmhurst, Illinois
1902 Willits House, Highland Park, Illinois
Fricke House, Oak Park, Illinois
George Gerts Double House, Whitehall, Michigan
Walter Gerts House, Whitehall, Michigan
Heurtley House remodelling, Marquette Island, Michigan
Heurtley House, Oak Park, Michigan
Hillside Home School Building II, for the Misses Lloyd Jones, Spring Green, Wisconsin (now part of Taliesin)
Francis Little House II, Peoria, Illinois
Ross House, Lake Delavan, Wisconsin
Spencer House, Lake Delavan, Wisconsin
Lake Delavan Yacht Club, Wisconsin (project)
Metzger House, Ontario, Canada (project)
Mosher House (project)
House, Oak Park, Illinois (project)
Waller House I, Charlevoix, Michigan (project)
Yahara Boat Club, Madison, Wisconsin (project)
1903 Barton House, Buffalo, New York
Freeman House, Hinsdale, Illinois
Martin House, Oak Park, Illinois

Scoville Park Fountain, Oak Park, Illinois
Walser House, Chicago
Chicago and Northwestern Railway Stations for the Chicago suburbs (project)
Lamp House I, Madison, Wisconsin (project)
Roberts Quadruple Block Plan (24 houses), Oak Park, Illinois (project)
Waller House II, Charlevoix, Michigan (project)
Frank Lloyd Wright Studio-House, Oak Park, Illinois (project)
1904 Larkin Building, Buffalo, New York
Cheney House, Oak Park, Illinois
Lamp House II, Madison, Wisconsin
Martin House and Conservatory, Buffalo, New York
Baldwin House I, Kenilworth, Illinois (project)
Bank Building I, Dwight, Illinois (project)
Clarke House, Peoria, Illinois (project)
House, Highland Park, Illinois (project)
Scudder House, Desbarats, Ontario, Canada (project)
Ullman House, Oak Park, Illinois (project)
Larkin Company Workmens' Rowhouses, Buffalo, New York (project)
1905 Adams House, Highland Park, Illinois
Baldwin House II, Kenilworth, Illinois
Bank Building II, Dwight, Illinois
Brown House, Evanston, Illinois
E-Z Polish Factory, 3005 West Carroll, Chicago
Gilpin House, Oak Park, Illinois
Glasner House, Glencoe, Illinois
Hardy House, Racine, Wisconsin
Heath House, Buffalo, New York
Johnson House, Lake Delavan, Wisconsin
Lawrence Memorial Library interior, Springfield, Illinois
Rookery Building entrance, lobbies and balcony-court remodelling, LaSalle Street, Chicago
Barnes House, McCook, Nebraska (project)
House on a Lake (project)
Varnish Factory (project)
Concrete Apartment Building, Chicago (project)
Pergola and Pavilion for Moore House, Oak Park, Illinois (project)
1906 Unity Temple, Oak Park, Illinois

Beachy House, Oak Park, Illinois
De Rhodes House, South Bend, Indiana
Fuller House, Glencoe, Illinois
Gridley House, Batavia, Illinois
Hoyt House, Geneva, Illinois
Millard House, Highland Park, Illinois
Nicholas House, Flossmoor, Illinois
Petit Mortuary Chapel, Belvedere, Illinois
River Forest Tennis Club, Illinois
Shaw House remodelling, Montreal
Bock Studio-House, Maywood, Illinois (project)
Devin House, Eliot, Maine (project)
Fireproof House for $5,000 (project published in *Ladies Home Journal,* New York)
Gerts House, Glencoe, Illinois (project)
Ludington House, Dwight, Illinois (project)
Shaw House, Montreal (project)
Stone House, Glencoe, Illinois (project)
1907 Garage, for Blossom House, Chicago
Cummings Real Estate Office, River Forest Illinois
Fabyan House remodelling, Geneva, illinois
Fox River Country Club remodelling, Geneva, Illinois
Hunt House, La Grange, Illinois
Larkin Company Pavilion, *Jamestown Exposition,* Virginia
Fricke House alterations, Oak Park, Illinois
Pebbles and Balch Shop, Oak Park, Illinois
"Tan-y-deri" (Porter House), Spring Green, Wisconsin
Sutton House, McCook, Nebraska
Tomek House, Riverside, Illinois
Westcott House, Springfield, Ohio
McCormick House, Lake Forest, Illinois (project)
Municipal Art Gallery, Chicago (project)
Porter House II, Spring Green, Wisconsin (project)
1908 Coonley House ("Zoned" Prairie House), Riverside, Illinois
Browne's Bookstore, Chicago
Davidson House, Buffalo, New York
Evans House, Chicago
Gilmore House, Madison, Wisconsin
Horner House, Chicago
Francis Little House, Wayzata, Minnesota
May House, Grand Rapids, Michigan
Roberts House, River Forest, Illinois

Stockman House, Mason City, Iowa
Baker House I, Wilmette, Illinois (project)
Stables, for Brigham House (project)
Guthrie House, Sewanee, Tennessee (project)
Horseshoe Inn, Estes Park, Colorado (project)
Melson House, Mason City, Iowa (project)

1909 Robie House, 5757 South Woodlawn, Chicago
Arcade Building, Chicago
Gale House, Oak Park, Illinois
Baker House II, Wilmette, Illinois
City National Bank and Hotel, Mason City, Iowa
Francis Little House additions, Peoria, Illinois
Copeland House alterations, Oak Park, Illinois
Ingalls House, River Forest, Illinois
Steffens House, Chicago
Stewart House, Montecito, California
Thurber Art Gallery, Chicago
Ziegler House, Frankfort, Kentucky
Brown House, Geneva, Illinois (project)
City Dwelling with Glass Front (project)
Larwell House, Muskegon, Michigan (project)
Lexington Terrace, Chicago (2nd project)
Parker Studio remodelling (project)
Roberts House, River Forest, Illinois (project)
Town Hall, Glencoe, Illinois (project)
Town of Bitter Root, Darby, Montana (project)
Bathing Pavilion, for Waller House, Charlevoix, Michigan (project)
Waller Rental Houses (3), River Forest, Illinois (project)

1910 Amberg House, Grand Rapids, Michigan
Blythe and Markley Law Office remodelling, Chicago
Como Orchard Summer Colony, Darby, Montana (partly executed)
Irving House, Decatur, Illinois
Universal Portland Cement Company Exhibit, Madison Square Garden, New York
Frank Lloyd Wright House-Studio, Viale Verdi, Fiesole, Italy (project)

1911 American System Ready-Cut Houses, for Richards Company, Milwaukee (prototypes)
Angster House, Lake Bluff, Illinois
Balch House, Oak Park, Illinois
Pavilion, Banff National Park, Alberta, Canada
Booth House, Glencoe, Illinois
Gardener's Cottage, for Coonley House, Riverside, Illinois
Lake Geneva Inn, Wisconsin
Taliesin, Spring Green, Wisconsin (living quaters destroyed by fire, 1914)
Adams House I, Oak Park, Illinois (project)
Booth Summer Cottage (project)
Christian Catholic Church, Zion, Illinois (project)
Greenhouse, for Coonley House, Riverside Illinois (project)
Coonley Kindergarten, Riverside, Illinois (project)
Cutten House, Downer's Grove, Illinois (project)
Esbenshade House, Milwaukee (project)
Walter Gerts House alterations, River Forest, Illinois (project)
Garage and Stables, for Health House, Buffalo, New York (project)
Madison Hotel, Wisconsin (project)
North Shore Electric Train Waiting Stations for the Chicago suburbs (project)
Porter House III, Spring Green, Wisconsin (project)
Schroeder House, Milwaukee (project)
Frank Lloyd Wright House, Chicago (project)

1912 Coonley Playhouse, Riverside, Illinois
Greene House, Aurora, Illinois
Park Ridge Country Club additions and alterations, Illinois
Dress Shop, Oak Park, Illinois (project)
Florida House, Palm Beach (project)
Kehl Dance Academy House and Shops, Madison, Wisconsin (project)
San Francisco Call Press Building (project)
Schoolhouse, La Grange, Illinois (project)
Small Townhouse (project)
Taliesin Cottages (2), Spring Green, Wisconsin (project)

1913 Adams House II, Oak Park, Illinois
Francis Little House II, Wayzata, Minnesota
Midway Gardens (including interiors), Chicago (destroyed)
Block of city row houses, Chicago (project)
Carnegie Library, Ottawa, Ontario, Canada (project)
Hilly House, Brookfield, Illinois (project)
Kellogg House, Milwaukee (project)
Mendelsohn House, Albany, New York (project)

1914 Mori Oriental Art Studio, Chicago
Taliesin II, Spring Green, Wisconsin (living quarters; original studios and workshops remained intact; rebuilt living quarters again destroyed by fire, 1925)
Concert Gardens, Chicago (project)
Jackson Houses (3) (project)
State Bank, Spring Green, Wisconsin (project)
United States Embassy, Tokyo (project)
Vogelsang Dinner Gardens, Chicago (project)

1915 Bach House, Chicago
Brigham House, Glencoe, Illinois
German Warehouse, Richland Center, Wisconsin
Ravine Bluffs Housing Development and Bridge, Glencoe, Illinois
Chinese Hospital (project)
Chinese restaurant, Milwaukee (project)
Lake Shore House (project)
Model Quarter-Section Development, Chicago (project)
Wood House, Decatur, Illinois (project)

1916 Bagley House, Grand Beach, Michigan
Hollyhock House (Barnsdall House), Los Angeles
Bock House, Milwaukee
Carr House, Grand Beach, Michigan
Duplex apartments, for Minkwitz Ready-Cut Systems, Milwaukee
Vosburgh House, Grand Beach, Michigan
Behn House, Grand Beach, Michigan (project)
Converse House, Palisades Park, Michigan (project)
William Allen White House remodelling, Emporia, Kansas (project)

1917 Allen House, Whichita, Kansas
Hunt House, Oshkosh, Wisconsin
Hayashi House, Tokyo
Odawara Hotel, Nagoya, Japan (project)
Powell House, Wichita, Kansas (project)

1918 Fukuhara House, Hakone, Japan
Yamamura House, Ashiya, Japan
Count Immu House, Tokyo (project)
Viscount Inouge House, Tokyo (project)
Motion picture theatre, Tokyo (project)

1919 Gallery for Japanese Prints, for the Spaulding Collection Boston (project)
Monolith Homes, Racine, Wisconsin (project)

1920 Barnsdall Houses A and B, Los Angeles
Cantilevered Skyscraper (project)
Theatre, shops and apartments, Olive Hill, Los Angeles (project)

1921 Mrs. Thomas Gale House, Whitehall, Michigan
Giuy Gakuen School of the Free Spirit, Tokyo
La Miniatura (Millard House), Pasadena, California
Doheny Ranch development, near Los Angeles (projects)
Glass and Copper Skyscraper (project)
Baron Goto House, Tokyo (project)

Block House, Los Angeles (project)

1922 Imperial Hotel, Tokyo
Little Dipper (Barnsdall Kindergarten), Los Angeles
Freeman House, Los Angeles
Lowe House, Eagle Rock, California
Storer House, Los Angeles
Johnson Desert Compound and Shrine, Death Valley, California (project)
Merchandising Building, Los Angeles (project)
Desert Springs (house), Mojave Desert, California (project)
Tahoe Summer Colony (cottages and barges), Lake Tahoe, California (project)

1923 Ennis House, Los Angeles
Moore House, Oak Park, Illinois (rebuilding after fire)
Martin House, Buffalo, New York (project)

1924 Indian Figure Sculptures, Madison, Wisconsin (in conjunction with the Nakoma Project)
Gladney House, Fort Worth, Texas (project)
Nakoma Country Club, Madison, Wisconsin (project)
National Life Insurance Company Skyscraper, Chicago (project)
Planetarium, Sugar Loaf Mountain, Maryland (project)

1925 Taliesin III, Spring Green, Wisconsin (living quarters only; original studios and workshops, 1911, remained intact)
Millard Gallery, Pasadena, California (project)
Phi Gamma Delta Fraternity House, University of Wisconsin, Madison (project)
Steel Cathedral, New York (project)

1926 Covers for Liberty magazine
Kinder Symphony Playhouse, Oak Park, Illinois (project)
Skyscraper Regulation, Chicago (project)
Standardized Concrete and Copper Gas Station (project)

1927 Arizona Biltmore Hotel, Phoenix (with Albert McArthur)
Martin House, Derby, New York

1928 Ocatillo (Wright's Soutwestern headquarters), Chandler, Arizona
Beach Cottages Ras-El-Bar Island, Damiette, Egypt (project)
Blue Sky Burial Terraces, Buffalo, New York (project)
Cudney House, Chandler, Arizona (project)
Jones House I, Tulsa, Oklahoma (project)
Low-cost concrete block houses, Chandler, Arizona (project)
San-Marcos-in-the-Desert Resort Hotel, Chandler, Arizona (project)
San Marcos Hotel alterations, Chandler, Arizona (project)
San Marcos Water Gardens, Chandler, Arizona (project)
School for negro children, La Jolla, California (project)
Simple block house, Chandler, Arizona (project)
Young House, Chandler, Arizona (project)

1929 Jones House II, Tulsa, Oklahoma
St. Mark's Tower, New York (project)

1930 Vases and glassware for Leerdam Glass, Netherlands
Automobile with Cantilevered Top (project)
Cabins for desert or woods, Chicago YMCA (project)
Grouped apartment towers, Chicago (project)
Noble Apartment House, Los Angeles (project)

1931 Capital Journal Building, Salem, Oregon (project)
House on the Mesa, Denver (project)
Three schemes for A Century of Progress, 1933 World's Fair, Chicago (project)

1932 Autombile and airplane filling and service stations (project)

Cinema and shops, Michigan City, Indiana (project)
Conventional House (project)
Prefabricted sheet steel farm units (projects)
Highway overpass (project)
Life House (project)
New Theatre (project)
Norm of the Prefabricated House (project)
Overhead Filling Station (project)
Prefabricated sheet steel and glass roadside markets (project)
Willey House I, Minneapolis (project)
1933 Taliesin Fellowship Complex, Spring Green, Wisconsin (addition to existing Hillside Home School; partly executed, theatre destroyed by fire, 1952)
1934 Broadacre City model and exhibition plans
Willey House II, Minneapolis
Helicopter (project)
Road Machine (project)
Train (project)
Zoned House No. 1 (project)
1935 Falling Water (Kaufmann House), Bear Run, Pennsylvania
Hoult House (1st Usonian House), Wichita, Kansas (project)
Lusk House, Huron, South Dakota (project)
Marcus House, Dallas (project)
Zoned City House (project)
Zoned Country House (project)
Zoned Suburban House (project)
1936 Hanna House, Palo Alto, California
Jacobs House, Westmoreland, Wisconsin
S. C. Johnson Administration Building, Racine, Wisconsin
Roberts House, Marquette, Michigan
Chandler Hotel remodelling, Chandler, Arizona (project)
Little San Marcos-in-the-Desert Resort Inn, Chandler, Arizona (project)
1937 Wingspread (Johnson House; "The Last Prairie House"), Racine, Wisconsin
Edgar J. Kaufmann Sr. Offices, Pittsburgh
All-steel houses (100), Los Angeles (project)
Borglum Studio, Black Hills, South Dakota (project)
Bramson Dress Shop, Oak Park, Illinois (project)
Memorial to the Soil (chapel), Southern Wisconsin (project)
Notz House, Pittsburgh (project)
Garage, for Parker House, Janesville, Wisconsin (project)
1938 Guest House, for Falling Water (Kaufmann House), Bear Run, Pennsylvania
Midway Farm Buildings, Taliesin, Spring Green, Wisconsin
Rebhohn House, Great Neck, Long Island, New York
Taliesin West (Wright's Winter headquarters), Scottsdale, Arizona
House for a Family of $5,000-$6000 Income (project for Life, New York)
Jester All-Plywood House, Palos Verdes, California (project)
Johnson Gatehouse and Farm Group, Wind Point, Wisconsin (project)
Jurgensen House, Evanston, Illinois (project)
McCallum House, Northampton, Massachusetts (project)
Monona Terrace, Civic Center, Wisconsin (project)
Pinetree House (Smith House), Piedmont Pines, California (project)
1939 Armstrong House, near Gary, Indiana
Goetsch-Winkler House I, Okemos, Michigan
Rosenbaum House, Florence, Alabama
Schwartz House, Two Rivers, Wisconsin
Sturges House, Brentwood Heights, California
Suntop Homes (quadruple house), Ardmore, Pennsylvania
Bell House, Los Angeles (project)
Carlson House, Superior, Wisconsin (project)

Crystal Heights Hotel, Shops and Theatres, Washington, D.C. (project)
Front gates, Taliesin, Spring Green, Wisconsin (project)
Lowenstein House, Mason City, Iowa (project)
Mauer House, Los Angeles (project)
Spivey House, Fort Lauderdale, Florida (project)
Usonian House Development (7 buildings), Okemos, Michigan (project)
1940 Baird House, Amherst, Massachusetts
Bazett House, Hillsborough, California
Christie House, Bernardsville, New Jersey
Community Church, Kansas City, Missouri
Euchtman House, Baltimore
Lewis House, Libertyville, Illinois
Manson House, Wausau, Wisconsin
Pauson House, Phoenix, Arizona
Pew House, Madison, Wisconsin
Pope House, Falls Church, Virginia
Sondern House, Kansas City, Missouri
Auldrass Plantation, near Yemassee, South Carolina
Model House, Museum of Modern Art, New York (exhibition project)
Nesbitt House, Carmel Bay, California (project)
Eaglefeather (Oboler House), Los Angeles (project)
Pence House, Hilo, Hawaii (project)
Rentz House, Madision, Wisconsin (project)
Watkins Studio, Barnegate City, New Jersey (project)
Methodist Church, Spring Green, Wisconsin (project)
1940/
59 Florida Southern College, Lakeland
1941 Affleck House, Bloomfield Hills, Michigan
Griggs House, Tacoma, Washington
Oboler Gatehouse and Retreat, Los Angeles
Richardson House, Glenridge, New Jersey
Snowflake (Wall House), Plymouth, Michigan
Barton House, Pine Bluff, Wisconsin (project)
Dayer Music Studio, Detroit (project)
Ellinwood House, Deerfield, Illinois (project)
Field House, Peru, Illinois (project)
Mountain Lakes (Guenther House), East Caldwell, New Jersey (project)
Petersen House, West Racine, Wisconsin (project)
Schevill House, Tucson, Arizona (project)
Sigma Chi Fraternity House, Hanover, Indiana (project)
Sundt House, Madison, Wisconsin (project)
Waterstreet Studio, near Spring Green, Wisconsin (project)
1942 Solar Hemicycle (Jacobs House), Middleton, Wisconsin
Burlingtham House, El Paso, Texas (project)
Circle Pines Center, Cloverdale, Michigan (project)
Cloverleaf Quadruple Housing, Pittsfield, Massachusetts (project)
Cooperative Homestead (housing for Detroit Auto Workers; project)
Foreman House, Washington, D.C. (project)
1943 Hein House, Chippewa Falls, Wisconsin (project)
McDonald House, Washington, D.C. (project)
Richardson Restaurant and Service Station, Spring Green, Wisconsin (project)
1944 S.C. Johnson Research Tower, Racine, Wisconsin
Pergola House (Loeb House), Redding, Connecticut (project)
Harlan House, Omaha, Nebraska (project)
Wells House, Minneapolis (project)
1945 Friedman House, Pecos, New Mexico
Grant House, Cedar Rapids, Iowa
Taliesin Dams, Spring Green, Wisconsin
Adelman Laundry, Milwaukee (project)

Berdan House, Ludington, Michigan (project)
Elizabeth Arden Desert Spa, Phoenix, Arizona (project)
Glass House (project for Ladies Home Journal, New York)
The Wave (Haldorn House), Carmel, California (project)
Slater House, Rhode Island (project)
Stamm House, Lake Delavan, Wisconsin (project)
1946 Brauner House ("Usonia II"), Okemos, Michigan
Walter House and River Pavilion, Quasqueton, Iowa
President's House, Olivet College, Michigan (project)
Dayer House and Music Pavilion, Bloomfield Hills, Michigan (project)
Garrison House ("Usonia I"), Lansing, Michigan (project)
Hause House, Lansing, Michigan (project)
Housing for the State Teachers College, Lansing, Michigan (project)
Morris House I, San Francisco (project)
Munroe House, Knox County, Ohio (project)
Newman House ("Usonia I"), Lansing, Michigan (project)
Oboler Studio, Los Angeles (project)
Panshin House, State Teachers College, Lansing, Michigan (project)
Pinderton House, Cambridge, Massachusetts (project)
Pinkerton House, Fairfax County, Virginia (project)
Rogers Lacy Hotel, Dallas (project)
Sarabhi Administration Building and Store, Ahmedabad, India (project)
Van Dusen House ("Usonia I"), Lansing, Michigan (project)
1947 Alpauch House, Northport, Michigan
Bullbullian House, Rochester, Minnesota
Master plan for Galesburg Village Dwellings, Kalamazoo, Michigan
Guest House alterations, Falling Water (Kaufmann House), Bear Run, Pennsylvania
Keys House, Rochester, Minnesota
Lamberson House, Oskaloosa, Iowa
First Unitarian Society Meeting House, Madison, Wisconsin
Master plan for Parkwyn Village Dwellings, Kalamazoo, Michigan
Master plan for Usonia Homes, Pleasantville, New York
Wetmore Auto Display Room and Workshop, Detroit (project)
Bell House, East St. Louis, Illinois (project)
Black House, Rochester, Minnesota (project)
Boomer House, Phoenix, Arizona (project)
Butterfly Bridge, over the Wisconsin River, Spring Green, Wisconsin (project)
Cottage Group Resort Hotel, Hollywood, California (project)
San Antonio Transit Company Depot, Texas (project)
Daphne Funeral Chapels, San Francisco (project)
Grieco House, Andover, Massachusetts (project)
Hamilton House, Brookline, Vermont (project)
Hartford House, Hollywood, California (project)
Houston House, Schuyler County, Illinois (project)
Keith House, Oakland County, Michigan (project)
Marting House, Northampton, Ohio (project)
Palmer House, Phoenix, Arizona (project)
Pike House, Los Angeles (project)
Pittsburgh Point Park (project)
Ayn Rand House, near Redding, Connecticut (project)
Sports Club, Hollywood, California (project)

Wheeler House, Hinsdale, Illinois (project)
Wilkie House, Hennepin County, Minnesota (project)
Valley National Bank, Tucson, Arizona (project)

1948 Adelman House, Fox Point, Wisconsin
Alsop House, Oskaloosa, Iowa
Anthony House, Benton Harbor, Michigan
Buehler House, Orinda, California
Eppstein House, Galesburg Village, Kalamazoo, Michigan
Greiner House, Parkwyn Village, Kalamazoo, Michigan
Fountainhead (Hughes House), Jackon, Mississippi
Laurent House, Rockford, Illinois
Levin House, Parkwyn Village, Kalamazoo, Michigan
Mossberg House, South Bend, Indiana
Pratt House, Galesburg Village, Kalamazoo, Michigan
Rosenbaum House addition, Florence, Alabama
Smith House, Bloomfield Hills, Michigan
V. C. Morris Shop, San Francisco
Walker House, Carmel, California
Welziemer House, Oberlin, Ohio
Adelman House, Fox Point, Wisconsin (project)
Barney Cottage, Spring Green, Wisconsin (project)
Bergman House, St Petersburg, Florida (project)
Bimson Penthouse, Phoenix, Arizona (project)
Crater Resort, Meteor Crater, Arizona (project)
Daphne House, San Francisco (project)
Ellison House, Bridgewater Township, New Jersey (project)
Feenberg House, Fox Point, Wisconsin (project)
Hageman House, Peoria, Illinois (project)
Margolis House, Kalamazoo, Michigan (project)
McCord House, North Arlington, New Jersey (project)
Miller House, Pleasantville, New York (project)
Muehlberger House, East Lansing, Michigan (project)
Pittsburgh Point Park (2nd Project)
Prout House, Columbus, Indiana (project)
Scully House, Woodbridge, Connecticut (project)
Smith House, Ann Arbor, Michigan (project)
Valley National Bank and Shopping Center, Sunnyslope, Arizona (project)

1949 Sondern House additions, Kansas City, Missouri
Cabaret-Theatre, Taliesin West, Scottsdale, Arizona
Edwards House, Okemos, Michigan
Friedman House, Usonia Homes, Pleasantville, New York
McCartney House, Parkwyn Village, Kalamazoo, Michigan
Serlin House, Usonia Homes, Pleasantville, New York
Weisblatt House, Galesburg Village, Kalamazoo, Michigan
Bloomfield House, Tucson, Arizona (project)
Dabney House, Chicago (project)
Drummond House, Santa Fe, New Mexico (project)
Goetsch-Winkler House II, Okemos, Michigan (project)
Griswold House, Greenwich, Connecticut (project)
John House, Oconomowoc, Wisconsin (project)
Lea House, Ashville, North Carolina (project)
Publicker House, Haverford, Pennsylvania (project)

Southern Crossing, San Francisco Bay Bridge (project)
Kaufmann Self-Service Garage, Pittsburgh (project)
Theatre, for the New Theatre Corporation, Hartford, Connecticut (project)
Windforhr House, Fort Worth, Texas (project)
YMCA Building, Racine, Wisconsin (project)

1950 Anderton Court Center, Beverly Hills, California
Berger House, San Anselmo, California
Brown House, Parkwyn Village, Kalamazoo, Michigan
Carlson House, Phoenix, Arizona
Carr House, Glenview, Illinois
David House, Marion, Indiana
Gillin House, Dallas
Harper House, St. Joseph, Michigan
Matthews House, Atherton, California
Meyer House, Galesburg Village, Kalamazoo, Michigan
Miller House, Charles City, Iowa
Muirhead House, Plato Center, Illinois
Neils House, Minneapolis
O'Donnell House, East Lansing, Michigan
Palmer House, Ann Arbor, Michigan
Schaberg House, Okemos, Michigan
Shavin House, Chattanooga, Tennessee
Smith House, Jefferson, Wisconsin
Sweeton House, Merchantville, New Jersey
Winn House, Parkwyn Village, Kalamazoo, Michigan
Wright House, Phoenix, Arizona
Zimmerman House, Manchester, New Hampshire
Achuff House, Wauwatosa, Wisconsin (project)
Auberbach House, Pleasantville, New York (project)
Bush House, Arkansas (project)
Carroll House, Wauwatosa, Wisconsin (project)
Chahroudi House I, Lake Mahopac, New York (project)
Conklin House, New Ulm, Minnesota (project)
Grover House, Syracuse, New York (project)
Hargrove House, Berkeley, California (project)
Jackson House, Madison, Wisconsin (project)
Jacobson House, Montreal (project)
Montooth House, Rushville, Illinois (project)
Sabin House, Battle Creek, Michigan (project)
Leon Small House, West Orange, New Jersey (project)
Southwestern Christian Seminary, Phoenix, Arizona (project)
Stevens House, Park Ridge, Illinois (project)
Strong House, Kalamazoo, Michigan (project)
Wassel House, Philadelphia (project)

1951 "Usonian Automatic" (Adelman House), Phoenix, Arizona
Austin House, Greenville, South Carolina
Chaddroudi House II, Lake Mahopac, New York
Elam House, Austin, Minnesota
Fuller House, Pass Christian, Mississippi
S. C. Johnson Office alterations, Racine, Wisconsin
Kinney House, Lancaster, Wisconsin
Kraus House, Kirkwood, Missouri
Pearce House, California
Reisley House, Usonia Homes, Pleasantville, New York,
Rubin House, Canton, Ohio
Staley House, Madison, Ohio
Clarke Cottage, Carmel, California (project)
Hall House, Ann Arbor, Michigan (project)
Haynes House, Fort Wayne, Indiana (project)
Boulder House (Kaufmann House), Palm Springs, California (project)
Schevill Studio, Tucson, Arizona (project)

1952 Blair House, Cody, Wyoming
Brandes House, Bellevue, Washington
Goddard House, Plymouth, Michigan
Hillside Playhouse redesign and rebuilding, Spring Green, Wisconsin
Hillside Theatre Curtain, Spring Green, Wisconsin
Lewis House, Tallahassee, Florida
Lindholm House, Cloquet, Minnesota
Marden House, McLean, Virginia
Pieper House, Paradise Valley, Arizona
Teater House, Bliss, Idaho
Affleck House II, Bloomfield Hills, Michigan (project)
Bailleres House, Acapulco, Mexico (project)
Clifton House, Oakland, New Jersey (project)
Cooke House, Virginia Beach, Virginia (project)
Leesburg Floating Gardens, Florida (project)
Paradise on Wheels (trailer park), Paradise Valley, Arizona (project)
Sturtevant House, Oakland, California (project)
Swann House, near Detroit (project)
Wainer House, Valdosta, Georgia (project)
Zeta Beta Tau Fraternity House, University of Florida, Gainesvile (project)

1953 Boomer Cottage, Phoenix, Arizona
Dobkins House, Canton, Ohio
Penfield House I, Willoughby, Ohio
Riverview Terrace (restaurant), Spring Green, Wisconsin
Sander House, Stamford, Connecticut
Usonian Exhibition House (pavilion), New York
Robert Llewellyn Wright House, Silver Springs, Maryland
Brewer House, East Fishkill, New York (project)
Lee House, Midland, Michigan (project)
Masieri Memorial Building, Grand Canal, Venice (project)
Seacliff (Morris House II), San Francisco (project)
Pieper and Montooth Office Building, Scottsdale, Arizona (project)
Point View Residences (apartment towers), Pittsburgh (project)
FM Radio Station, Jefferson, Wisconsin (project)
Rhododendron Chapel, Bear Run, Pennsylvania (project)
Restaurant, Yosemite National Park, California (project)

1954 Bachman-Wilson House, Millstone, New Jersey
Boulter House, Cincinnati
Christian House, Lafayette, Indiana
Clark-Arnold House, Columbus, Wisconsin
Hollyhock House remodelling, Olive Hill, Los Angeles (exhibition project)
Fawcett House, Los Banos, California
Feiman House, Canton, Ohio
Frederick House, Barrington, Illinois
Greenberg House, Dousman, Wisconsin
Hagan House, Uniontown, Pennsylvania
Keland House, Racine, Wisconsin
Price House, Bartleville, Oklahoma
Price House, Phoenix, Arizona
Thaxton House, Houston
Barnsdall Park Municipal Gallery, Los Angeles (project)
Christian Science Reading Room, Riverside, Illinois (project)
Tipshus Clinic, Stockton, California (project)
Cornwell House, West Goshen, Pennsylvania (project)
Freund Department Store, San Salvador, El Salvador (project)
Rebhuhn House, Fort Meyers, Florida (project)
Schwenn House, Verona, Wisconsin (project)

1955 Dallas Theatre Centre
Decorative fabrics and wallpapers for Sch-

umacher and Company

Hoffman House III, Manursign Island, Rye, New York

Kalil House, Manchester, New Hampshire

Lovness House, Stillwater, Minnesota

Pappas House, St. Louis County, Mississippi

Rayward House, New Canaan, Connecticut

Sunday House, Marshalltown, Iowa

Tonkens House, Cincinnati

Tracy House, Seattle

Turkel House, Detroit

Adelman House, Whitefish Bay, Wisconsin (project)

Barton House, Downers Grove, Illinois (project)

Blumberg House, Des Moines, Iowa (project)

Boswell House I, Cincinnati (project)

Christian Science Church, Bolinas, California (project)

Coats House, Hillsborough, California (project)

Cooke House (Usonian Block Scheme II), Virginia Beach, (project)

Dlesk House, Manistee, Michigan (project)

Gillin House, Hollywood, California (project)

Jankowski House I, Oakland County, Michigan (project)

Korrick's Department Store alterations, Phoenix, Arizona (project)

Lenkurt Electric Company Administration/Manufacturing Building, San Mateo, California (project)

Miller House, Milford, Michigan (project)

Morris Guest House, San Franciso (project)

Neuroseum (hospital and clinic), Madison, Wisconsin (project)

Oboler House II, Los Angeles (project)

"One Room House," Phoenix, Arizona (project)

Pieper House, Phoenix, Arizona (project)

Sussman House, Rye, New York (project)

Wieland Motel, Hagerstown, Maryland (project)

1956 Price Tower (office and apartment building), Bartlesville, Oklahoma

Annunciation Greek Orthodox Church, Milwaukee

Hoffman Auto Showroom, New York

Bott House, Kansas City, Missouri

Kundert Clinic, San Luis Obispo, California

Meyer Clinic, Dayton, Ohio

Friedman House, Deerfield, Illinois

Music Pavilion, Taliesin West, Scottsdale, Arizona

Nooker House (Lloyd Wright Studio) restoration, Oak Park, Illinois

Pre-Fab I, for Marshall Erdman Associates, Madison, Wisconsin

Scott House (Roberts House) alterations, Riverside, Illinois

Smith House, Kane county, Illinois

Spencer House, Brandywine Head, Delaware

Stromquist House, Bountiful, Utah

Walton House, Modesto, California

Boebel House, Boscobel, Wisconsin (project)

Bramlett Hotel, Memphis, Tennessee (project)

Usonian Automatic House Designs (projects; with Taliesin students)

Golden Beacon (skyscraper), Chicago (project)

Gross House, Hackensack, New Jersey (project)

Hunt House, Scottsdale, Arizona (project)

Tonkens Loan Office, Cincinnati (project)

Mile High Skyscraper, Chicago (project)

Mills House I, Princeton, New Jersey (project)

Quietwater (Morris House), Stinson Beach, California (project)

New Sports Pavilion, Belmont, Long Island, New York (project)

O'Keefe House, Santa Barbara, California (project)

Roberts House, Seattle (project)

Schuck House, South Hadley, Massachusetts (project)

Stillman House, Cornwall on Hudson, New York (project)

Vallarino Houses, Panama City (project)

1957 Boswell House II, Cincinnati

Fasbender Clinic, Hastings, Minnesota

Gordon House, Aurora, Oregon

Juvenile Cultural Study Center, Building A, University of Wichita, Kansas

Kinney House, Amarillo, Texas

Pre-Fab II, for Marshall Erdman Associates, Madison, Wisconsin

Schultz House, St. Joseph, Michigan

Lindholm Service Station, Cloquet, Minnesota

Trier House, Des Moines, Iowa

Duey Wright House, Wausau, Wisconsin

Wyoming Valley School, Wisconsin

Adams House, St. Paul, Minnesota (project)

Nezam Ameri Palace, Tehran (project)

Arizona State Capitol, Papago Park, Phoenix (project)

Baghdad Cultural Center, Iraq (project)

University of Baghdad, Iraq (project)

Bimson "Usonian Automatic" House, Phoenix, Arizona (project)

Brooks House, Middletown, Wisconsin (project)

Hartman House, Lansing, Michigan (project)

Hennesy House, Smoke Rise, New Jersey (2 projects)

Herberger House, Maricopa County, Arizona (project)

Highway Motel, Madison, Wisconsin (project)

Fisher Housing Project, Whiteville, North Carolina (project)

Hoyer House, Maricopa County, Arizona (project)

Juvenile Cultural Study Center, Building B, University of Wichita, Kansas (project)

Gate Lodge, Falling Water (Kaufmann House), Bear Run, Pennsylvania (project)

McKinney House, Cloquet, Minnesota (project)

Miller House, Near Roxbury, Connecticut (project)

Mills House II, Princeton, New Jersey (project)

U. S. Rubber Company Model Exhibition Houses, New York (exhibition project)

Moreland House, Austin, Texas (project)

Postal Telegraph Building, Baghdad, Iraq (project)

Post Office, Spring Green, Wisconsin (project)

Schanbacher Store, Springfield, Illinois (project)

Shelton House, Long Island, New York (project)

Sottil House, Cuernavaca, Mexico (project)

Stracke House, Appleton, Wisconsin (project)

Wedding Chapel, Claremont Hotel, Berkeley, California (project)

Wilson House, Morgantown, North Carolina (project)

Zieger House, Grosse Island, Michigan (project)

1957/
66 Marin County Government Center, San Rafael, California

1958 Albin House, Bakersfield, California

Lockbridge, McIntyre and Whalen Clinic, Whitefish, Montana

Olfelt House, St. Louis Park, Minnesota

Petersen Cottage, Lake Delton, Wisconsin

Pilgrim Congregational Church, Redding, California (partly executed)

Leuchauer Clinic, Fresno, California (project)

Colgrove House, Hamilton, Ohio (project)

Crosby-Lambert House, Colbert County, Alabama (project)

Franklin House, Louisville, Kentucky (project)

Guttierez House, Albuquerque, New Mexico (project)

Hanley Airplane Hangar, Benton Harbor, Michigan (project)

Jones Chapel (Trinity Chapel), University of Oklahoma, Norman (project)

Lagomarsino House, San Jose, California (project)

Libbey House, Grand Rapids, Michigan (project)

Lovness Cottages, Stillwater, Minnesota (project)

Mike Todd Universal Theatre, Los Angeles (project)

Pre-Fab III, for Marshall Erdman Associates, Madison, Wisconsin

Pre-Fab IV, for Marshall Erdman Associates, Madison, Wisconsin

Spring Green Auditorium, Wisconsin (project)

Unity Chapel, Taliesin Valley, Spring Green, Wisconsin (project)

1959 Grady Gammage Memorial Hospital Auditorium, Arizona State University, Tempe

Beth Sholom Synagogue, Elkins Park, Pennsylvannia

Guggenheim Museum, New York

Art Gallery, Arizona State University Tempe (project)

Donahoe House, Phoenix, Arizona (project)

Furgatch House, San Diego, Califonia (project)

Mann House, Putnam County, New York (project)

Penfield House II, Willoughby, Ohio (project)

Daniel Wieland House, Hagerstown, Maryland (project)

Gilbert Wieland House, Hagerstown, Maryland (project)

1960 Enclosed Garden, for Mrs. Frank Lloyd Wright, Taliesin, Spring Green, Wisconsin

Publications

By WRIGHT: books—*Ausgeführte Bauten und Entwürfe von Frank Lloyd Wright* (the Wasmuth Portfolio), Berlin 1910, as *Frank Lloyd Wright: The Early Work*, New York 1968; *The Japanese Print: An Interpretation*, Chicago 1912; *Experimenting with Human Lives*, Los Angeles 1923; *The Life Work of the American Architect Frank Lloyd Wright*, edited by H. Th. Wijdeveld, Sandport, Netherlands 1925, New York 1965; *Modern Architecture*, Princeton, New Jersey 1931; *Two Lectures on Architecture*, Chicago 1931; *An Autobiography*, New York and London 1932, revised edition New York 1943, London 1945; *The Disappearing City*, New York 1932, revised edition as *When Democracy Builds*, Chicago 1945, revised edition as *The Living City*, New York 1958; *Architecture and Modern Life*, with Baker Brownell, New York and London 1937; *An Organic Architecture*, London 1939; *Frank Lloyd Wright on Architecture: Selected Writings 1894-1940*, edited by Frederick Gutheim, New York 1941; *Genius and the Mobocracy*, New York 1949, 1954, London 1972; *The Future of Architecture*, New York 1953, London 1955; *The Natural House*, New York 1954; *An American Architecture*, edited by Edgar Kaufmann, New York 1955; *The Story of the Tower*, New York 1956; *A Testament*, New York 1957; *Drawings for a Living Architecture*, New York 1959; *Frank Lloyd Wright: Writings and Buildings*, edited by Edgar Kaufmann and Ben Raeburn, New York 1960; *The Drawings of Frank Lloyd Wright*, edited by Arthur Drexler, New York 1962; *Architecture: Man in Possession of His Earth*, edited by Iovanna Lloyd Wright and Patricia Coyle Nicholson, New York 1962, London 1963; *Buildings, Plans and Designs*, New York 1963; *Architectural Essays from the Chicago School*, with others, Chicago 1967; *Studies and Executed Buildings*, Chicago 1975; *In the Cause of Architecture: Essays by Frank Lloyd Wright for the*

Architectural Review 1908-1952, edited by Frederick Gutheim, New York 1975; *Letters to Apprentices*, with commentary by Bruce Brooks Pfeiffer, Fresno, California 1982; *Letters to Architects*, Los Angeles 1984.

On WRIGHT: books—*Frank Lloyd Wright* by H. de Vries, Berlin 1926; *In the Nature of Materials 1887-1941: The Buildings of Frank Lloyd Wright* by Henry-Russell Hitchcock, New York 1942; *Frank Lloyd Wright* by Bruno Zevi, Milan 1947; *Taliesin Days: Recent Architecture of Frank Lloyd Wright* by Edgar Kaufmann, New York 1952; *Frank Lloyd Wright* by Enrico Tedeschi, Buenos Aires 1955; *Frank Lloyd Wright to 1910: The First Golden Age* by Grant C. Manson, New York 1958, 1979; *Frank Lloyd Wright: Rebel in Concrete* by Alysea Foresee, Philadelphia 1959; *Frank Lloyd Wright* by Vincent Scully Jr., New York and London 1960; *Frank Lloyd Wright* by Peter Blake, New York 1960, London 1963; *Frank Lloyd Wright: A Biography* by Finis Farr, New York 1961; *Frank Lloyd Wright: Living Architecture* by Doris Ransohoff, Chicago 1962; *Frank Lloyd Wright: America's Greatest Architect* by Herbert Jacobs, New York 1965; *Frank Lloyd Wright: A Study in Architectural Content* by Norris Kelly, Englewood Cliffs, New Jersey 1966; *Frank Lloyd Wright: His Life, His Work, His Words*, edited by Olgivanna Lloyd Wright and others, New York 1966; *Frank Lloyd Wright: Public Buildings* by Martin Pawley, Tokyo 1967, London 1970; *Two Great Architects and Their Clients: Frank Lloyd Wright and Howard Van Doren Shaw* by Leonard K. Eaton, Cambridge, Massachusetts 1969; *Frank Lloyd Wright* by Marco Bardeschi, Florence 1970, London and New York 1972; *Frank Lloyd Wright* by Charlotte Willard, New York 1972; *Frank Lloyd Wright: An Interpretive Biography* by Robert Twombly, New York 1973; *The Prairie School: Frank Lloyd Wright and His Midwest Contemporaries* by H. Allen Brooks, Toronto 1972; *Prairie School Town Planning 1900-1915: Wright, Griffin, Drummond* by Courtney Graham Donnell, New York 1974; *The Architecture of Frank Lloyd Wright: A Complete Catalog*, compiled by William Allin Storrer, Cambridge, Massachusetts 1974, 1978; *Houses by Frank Lloyd Wright*, edited by Yukio Futagawa, Tokyo 1975; *Frank Lloyd Wright's Usonian Houses: The Case for Organic Architecture* by John Sergeant, New York 1976; *The Decorative Designs of Frank Lloyd Wright* by David A. Hanks, Washington, D.C. 1977; *Frank Lloyd Wright: Three Quarters of a Century of Drawings* by Alberto Izzo and Camillo Gubitosi, London and Florence 1977, London 1979; *Apprentice to a Genius* by Edgar Tafel, London and New York 1979; *Frank Lloyd Wright, His Life and Architecture* by Robert C. Twombly, New York and Chichester, Hampshire 1979; *Measured Drawing: Frank Lloyd Wright in Japan* by Masami Tanigawa, Tokyo 1980; *Frank Lloyd Wright's Hanna House*, New York, London, and Cambridge, Massachusetts 1981; *Writings on Wright*, edited by H. Allen Brooks, London, and Cambridge, Massachusetts 1981; *Frank Lloyd Wright* by Thomas A. Heinz, New York, London and Barcelona 1982; *Guide to Frank Lloyd Wright and Prairie School Architecture in Oak Park* by Paul E. Sprague, Chicago 1983; *Frank Lloyd Wright: A Research Guide to Archival Sources* by Patrick J. Meehan, New York and London 1983; *Kings of Infinite Space: Frank Lloyd Wright and Michael Graves* by Charles Jencks, London and New York 1983; *Man About Town: Frank Lloyd Wright in New York City* by Herbert Muschamp, Cambridge, Massachusetts and London 1983; *Frank Lloyd Wright's Robie House* by Donald Hoffman, New York 1984; *The Robie House of Frank Lloyd Wright* by Joseph Connors, Chicago 1984.

Bibliographies: *Frank Lloyd Wright: A Selective Bibliography* by Ruth L. Gough, Worcester, Massachusetts 1941; *What Men Have Written About Frank Lloyd Wright: A Bibliography* by Bernard Karpel, New York 1955; *Frank Lloyd Wright: A Biblio-graphy*, compiled by Oak Park Public Library, Illinois 1969; *Frank Lloyd Wright in Print 1959-1970* by James Muggenberg, Charlottesville, Virginia 1972; *Frank Lloyd Wright: A Bibliography* by Kenneth and Jane Starosciak, New Brighton, Minnesota 1973; *Frank Lloyd Wright: An Annotated Bibliography* by Robert L. Sweeney, Los Angeles 1978; *Frank Lloyd Wright's Fallingwater: The House and Its History* by Donald Hoffman, New York 1978; *Frank Lloyd Wright on Urban Design and Planning* by Patrick J. Meehan, Monticello, Illinois 1978; *Frank Lloyd Wright: Organic Architect and Planner* by Cortus T. Koehler, Monticello, Illinois 1978; *Frank Lloyd Wright: A Study in Architectural Content* by Norris Kelly Smith, Watkins Glen, New York 1979; *The Frank Lloyd Wright Book Reviews* by Patrick J. Meehan, Monticello, Illinois 1980; *Frank Lloyd Wright's Imperial Hotel, Tokyo: Preservation Attempts* by James P. Noffsinger, Monticello, Illinois 1980; *Chicago School of Architecture: A Selected Bibliography* by Robert B. Harmon, Monticello, Illonois 1982; *An Update on Frank Lloyd Wright (1867-1959) and Some Sources for Review*, Monticello, Illinois 1983. Filmography: *The Frank Lloyd Wright Motion Picture Guide* by Patrick J. Meehan, Monticello, Illinois 1983.

Frank Lloyd Wright is of the American tradition of Emerson, Thoreau, and Whitman; his strength and inspiration were drawn from the soil, the products of natural growth, and the lessons which they taught. His materials were taken from the land—wood (unplaned and stained rather than painted), stone, and clay brick—and though he honoured the machine because of its ability to process, standard-ize, and simplify, he had passed beyond that stage of feeling obliged, as did his European counterparts, to express symbolically a machine aesthetic in his architecture. A brilliant psychologist, he understood human needs and administered to them through his work. Above all he sought "repose," a restful environment free of tension which catered to the mental health and happiness of the indweller.

To help achieve this, Wright evolved a new concept of interior space: this is his matchless contribution to the future of architecture. Rooms of a house, prior to his time, were box-like although occasionally aligned with large openings in between them. Each room had a single function. Wright changed all that. His "rooms" overlap and interpenetrate—often at the corners. Use areas are defined by screening devices and subtle changes in ceiling heights. A single space serves a variety of functions depending upon (and this is the essential point) the position of the observer. That is to say, spaces are defined rather than enclosed, and use is relative (to the individual) rather than absolute (one room having one use).

Wright also generated a new vocabulary of architectural forms. In the 1920s he began experimenting with shapes other than the right angle. 30, 45, 60, and 120 degree angles began to enter his work, both in plan and in elevation; also the circle, arc, and spiral. Although ridiculed when they first appeared, these forms, in the latter third of our century, have now been generally accepted by the architectural profession.

Wright was born in Richland Center, Wisconsin, in 1867. Two youthful experiences (in addition to his mother's determination that he be an architect) particularly influenced him as a designer. The first was his training with Froebel kindergarten "gifts," which instilled in him a sense of order, proportion, and an appreciation for the relation between basic geometric shapes. Because of his training he based his plans, and later his elevations as well, on a unit (his word) system which governed all elements in the design. The second most significant experience was working summers on his uncle's farm; it was there that he gained his appreciation and respect for the land, nature, and the materials that nature produced.

After a brief, inconclusive stint at the University of Wisconsin where he took some mechanical drawing and basic mathematics courses, Wright departed (1887) for Chicago where he spent some months in J. L. Silsbee's office (an architect devoted to residential designs which for over a decade had an impact on Wright's work) before seeking employment with Adler and Sullivan where he remained until 1893. These were the years of the Auditorium, the Wainwright Building, and the Chicago World's Fair. Once on his own, Wright designed the Winslow house (1894), a strong, monumental work which summed up the ideals of classicism without recourse to Classical forms. This was not, however, what he felt architecture to be, and throughtout the decade he sought an expression more suitable to the natural setting and the materials of the region. A variety of experiments characterized these years that con-cluded in 1900 with what has become known as the prairie house. Long, low, hovering planes that extend laterally as porches and porte-cocheres, these buildings were L, T, or cruciform in shape with overlapping, interpenetrating spaces. The plans adhered to a basic unit system of design. The materials were either brick or unplaned (stained) wood and plaster.

Until the outbreak of the 1914 war he continually evolved the prairie house toward greater abstraction. Roofs and balconies gradually became flat, hovering slabs, and a geometric interplay between verticals and horizontals replaced an emphasis upon wall. Compare, for example, the Willits house (1902), Robie house (1909), and Coonley playhouse (1912) in this regard. Wright's non-residential work certain-ly played a role in this development: the Larkin Administration Building (1904) and especially Unity Temple (1906) reiterated the geometric shapes of the Froebel toys and demonstrated the uselessness of a visible roof. When Wright's drawings were published in Europe by Ernst Wasmuth as 100 large litho-graphs, it is these designs which were included and which irrevocably altered the course of European architecture from that moment onward.

Wright spent more than a year in Europe (he had visited Japan in 1905) preparing the Wasmuth publication, and upon his return began building Taliesin in Wisconsin—on lands he had helped farm in his youth. There, while he was in Chicago finishing the Midway Gardens buildings (the most abstract of his designs to date), a deranged servant murdered seven members of Wright's household and burned Taliesin to the ground. The shock left its impact. In terms of architecture it seemed to direct him toward more solid, protective forms, as if to create a shelter against the outside world. The more formal, massive California houses (Barnsdall, Millard, Ennis, etc) are typical. The 1920s, slighted by Wright's biographers because of his limited number of executed works, were, I believe, incredibly rich in an inventive sense and established the direction of his work for 30 years to come. Domestic tranquility returned to him by the late 1920s, and in 1932 he published his *An Autobiography* and founded the Taliesin Fellowship, a group (eventually about 60) of apprentices who built buildings and did domestic chores, as well as working at the drafting boards. He had reached 65, had no commissions, and spent his time giving a few public lectures and designing Broadacre City, which was not really a city at all but rather a car oriented segment of semi-rural America.

In 1936 his luck changed. He designed and built both Fallingwater and the Johnson Administration Building. These thrust Wright into the limelight; the Museum of Modern Art in New York exhibited his work, and the January 17th, 1938 issue of *Time* featured him on its cover—against the backdrop of Fallingwater. Commissions, particularly for lower middle income housing, began to come in. Wright's response was the Usonian (United States-ian) house, a logical development from the earlier prairie house. The Jacobs House was the first of these homes wherein Wright achieved a remarkable degree of variety and openness in buildings of truly restricted size. Built upon a concrete slab into which the radiant heating was incorporated, the house was limited in construction almost entirely to wood, bricks, and glass, these materials having the same natural finish both inside and out.

During this last quarter century of his remarkably long life, Wright produced work the range and variety of which seemingly knew no bounds. Aside from his Usonian and other houses he built the Guggenheim Museum, Price Tower, Beth Sholom Synagogue, Annunciation Greek Orthodox Church, and Marin County Buildings, most of which evolved from his earlier experiments in unorthodox shapes and forms. Near Phoenix, Arizona, he built Taliesin West as a winter retreat and it is there that he died on April 9th, 1959, in his 92nd year, leaving behind a legacy which will nourish architecture for generations to come.

—H. Allen Brooks

WRIGHT, (Frank) Lloyd.

American. Born in Oak Park, Illinois, 31 March 1890; eldest son of the architect Frank Lloyd Wright, *q.v.* Educated at public school in Oak Park, 1895-97; Hillside Home School, near Spring Green, Wisconsin, 1898-1907; University of Wisconsin, Madison, 1907-09. Married Elaine Hyman in 1917 (divorced, 1925); married Helen Taggart in 1926; son: Eric. Assisted his father in the preparation of drawings for the Wasmuth Portfolio, in Florence, and travelled in Europe, 1909; worked at the Harvard Herbarium, Cambridge, Massachusetts, and as a landscape draftsman in the office of Olmsted and Olmsted, Boston, 1910-11; worked in the Olmsted and Olmsted Nursery, and as a landscape architect for the firm of Frederick Law Jr., San Diego, California, 1911; architectural draftsman/delineator, office of Irving J. Gill, San Diego and Los Angeles, 1912-15; in partnership with Paul G. Thiene, as landscape architects, Los Angeles, 1915; established independent office as architect and landscape architect, Los Angeles, and became Head of the Design and Drafting Department of Paramount Studios, Los Angeles, 1916-17; worked for Standard Aircraft Company, Elizabeth, New Jersey, and Curtis Airport Company, Long Island, New York, 1918; Draftsman, Rouse and Goldstone, New York, 1919; worked with his father on the landscaping of Barnsdall Houses and Olive Hill, Los Angeles, 1919-20; worked as a landscape architect for William J. Dodd, Los Angeles, 1920-21; in private practice as a landscape architect, Los Angeles, working closely with his father, 1922-26; in private practice as an architect, Los Angeles, 1924-72. Chairman, Los Angeles Delegation, International Housing Congress, Mexico City, 1939. Exhibitions: *Lloyd Wright,* University of Oklahoma School of Architecture, Norman, 1964; *Four Decades of Living Architecture: Lloyd Wright, Architect,* The Building Center, Los Angeles, 1966; *Lloyd Wright, Architect: 20th Century Architecture in an Organic Exhibition,* University of California at Santa Barbara, 1971. *Died* (in Santa Monica, California) *31 May 1978.*

Works:

1910 "A Prairie House," Oak Park, Illinois (project)
1914/
15 Landscaping of the new industrial city of Torrance, California (with Olmsted and Olmsted)
1915/
16 Site plan and landscaping for Playa Del Rey, California (project)
Severence Estate Landscaping, Pasadena, California (with Paul G. Thiene)
Meyer Estate landscaping, Beverly Hills, California (with Paul G. Thiene)

1917/
18 Various sets for Paramount Studios, Hollywood, California
1919/
20 Barnsdall Houses/Olive Hill landscaping, Los Angeles
1920 Country Club landscaping, Phoenix, Arizona (project)
Dodd Estate landscaping, Beverly Hills, California
1921 Preuss Estate landscaping, Hollywood, California
Weber House, 3923 West 9th Street, Los Angeles
1921/
22 Santa Monica High School landscaping, California (project)
1922 Henry Bollman House, 1530 Ogden Avenue, Hollywood, California
Otto Bollman House, 2200 Braidview Terrace, Hollywood, California
Lyman Commercial Center, Sierra Madre, California (project)
Taggart House, 5423 Black Oak Drive, Los Angeles
University Club landscaping, Los Angeles
1923 Stage set for *Julius Caesar* (Gordon Craig production), Hollywood Bowl, Hollywood, California
Doheny Ranch landscaping, Beverly Hills, California
Oasis Hotel, 125 Palm Springs Canyon Drive, Palm Springs, California
Sierra Madre City Park, California (project)
Storer House landscaping, Hollywood, California (supervised construction for Frank Lloyd Wright)
1924 Ennis House landscaping, Los Angeles (supervised construction for Frank Lloyd Wright)
Freeman House landscaping, Los Angeles (supervised construction for Frank Lloyd Wright)
Ellen True Rookery Tent-Houses, Palm Springs, California (one built)
Mausoleum (project)
1924/
25 Shell for the Hollywood Bowl, Hollywood, Caifornia (project)
1925 Carr House, with landscaping, Lowry and Rowena Streets, Los Angeles
Gilkerson House landscaping, Chevy Chase, Glendale, California
Howe House, Beverly Hills, California
City of the Future, Los Angeles (project)
Civic Center, Los Angeles (project)
Stahl House, Beverly Hills, California (project)
Landscaping plan for Oshkosh, Wisconsin (project)
1925/
26 House, Palm Springs, California (project)
1926 Five-Room House, Los Angeles (project)
Studio House, Los Angeles (project)
Desert Hacienda, Palm Springs, California (project)
Concrete Block House, Chevy Chase, Glendale, California (project)
Four-Room House, Chevy Chase, Glendale, California (project)
Calori House, Chevy Chase Drive, Glendale, California
Derby House, 2535 Chevy Chase Drive, Glendale, California
Eliot House, Chevy Chase, Glendale, California (project)
Fairfax Theatre, Los Angeles (project)
Farrell House, 3209 Lowry Road, Los Angeles
Johnson House, Chevy Chase, Glendale, California (project)
Lewis House, 2947 Graceland Way, Chevy Chase, Gendale, California
Millard House studio addition, 645 Prospect Crescent Way, Pasadena, California
Nelson House, Los Angeles (project)

Oliver House, Chevy Chase, Glendale, California (project)
Sowden House, 5121 Franklin Avenue, Los Angeles
1926/
28 Navarro Houe, 5609 Valley Oak Drive, Hollywood, California
1927 Counselman House, 4905 Lockhaven Street, Eagle Rock, California
Martin House, Palm Springs, California (project)
Wilkes Theatre and Shops, Hollywood, California
Lloyd Wright Studio/House, 858 North Doheny Drive, Los Angeles
Dune House, near Palm Springs, California (project)
Connell Hillside House, Los Angeles
1927/
28 Lake Arrowhead Hotel and Bungalows, California
1928 Behn House, Chevy Chase, Glendale, California (project)
Yucca-Vine Market, for Raymond Griffith, Hollywood, California
McDowell House, Chevy Chase, Glendale, California (project)
Metzler House, Camarillo, California (project)
Upman House garden, Altadena, California
Shell for the Hollywood Bowl, Hollywood, California
1929 Backman Store, Tarzana, California
Bassett House landscaping, Los Angeles
Furniture, for Carrol Jones, Los Angeles
Albert Marple Stores facade remodelling, Los Angeles (project)
1930 Plan for Boeing Aiport, Burbank, California (project)
Day House remodelling, Los Angeles
Apollo Baths, Henderson Gymnasium, Los Angeles (project)
Group of Stores, for L. D. Owens, Hollywood, California (project)
Professional Office Building, Hollywood, California (project)
City of Los Angeles Art Department sculpture and garden (project; with Harold Swartz)
Harold Swartz House, Los Angeles (project)
Tibbett House remodelling, Beverly Hills, California
Jake Zeitlin Book Shop, Los Angeles
Plan for Los Angeles Airport (project)
Design of exhibition space for pre-Columbian art, Stendahl Gallery, Los Angeles
1931 Children's Outdoor Theatre, Olive Hill, Los Angeles (project)
Roman Catholic Cathedral, Los Angeles (project)
Kellogg Ranch, Banning, California (project)
Drive-In Open Air Market and Restaurant, Monrovia, California
1932 Furthman House remodelling, Bel Air, Los Angeles
Halfhill Apartments, Los Angeles (project)
Richardson House, Eagle Rock, California (project)
Apartment Building, Hollywood, California (project)
1933 Apollo Baths, Henderson Gymnasium, Los Angeles (2nd project)
Behn House, Westwood, California (project)
Hanna House, Chevy Chase, Glendale, California (project)
Tule Mat Houses, Imperial Valley, California (project)
1933/
34 Howland House, 502 Crescent Drive, Beverly Hills, California
Cascades Club, Palm Springs, California (project)
1934 Connell House remodelling and furniture, Los Angeles
Newman House remodelling, 627 North Can-

Lloyd Wright: Wayfarer's Chapel, Palos Verdes, Califonia, 1951.

on Drive, Beverly Hills, California
Tony Price/Gladys Barbieri Book Shop and Bindery remodelling, Hollywood, California
Samuel House, 570 North Bundy Drive, Beverly Hills, California

1934/
37 Avery House, 365 Rockingham Avenue, Los Angeles
1935 Claudette Colbert House, 615 North Faring Road, Los Angeles
Kaufman House remodelling, Los Angeles
Niles House, Los Angeles (project)
Sauer House, St. Louis (project)
Smith House, Chevy Chase, Glendale, California (project)
Westlake Medical Building, 676 Westlake Avenue, Los Angeles
1936 Griffith Ranch House, 4965 Rigoletto Street, Canoga Park, California
Theta Chi Fraternity House, University of California at Los Angeles (project)
Jake Zeitlin Book Store, Los Angeles

1936/
41 Day House remodelling, Los Angeles
Evans House, 554 North Bundy Drive, Los Angeles
1937 Butterworth House, Los Angeles (project)
Brower House, Pacific Palisades, California (project)
Edens House remodelling, Los Angeles
Gracy House, Austin, Texas (project)
Haight House, Los Angeles (project)
Jones House, Burbank, California (project)
Lazarus House, Los Angeles (project)
Motel, Los Angeles (project)
Ruby House, Beverly Hills, California (project)
1938 Blalock House, Los Angeles (project)
Christian Science Church, Monrovia, California (project; with William Gray Purcell)
Henricks Press Building, Litchfield, Illinois (project)
Benthuysen House remodelling, Los Angeles
Vidor House, Los Angeles (project)
1939 Four-Square Housing, Los Angeles (project)

Haight House remodelling, Beverly Hills, California
Smith House, Los Angeles (project)
Tibbet Ranch House, near Bakersfield, California (project)

1939/
40 Ramona Gardens Public Housing Project, Los Angeles (with George J. Adams, Ralph C. Flewelling, Eugene Weston Jr., and Lewis Eugene Wilson)
1940 Degener House, Los Angeles
Greer House, 9200 Haskell Avenue, Los Angeles
Lubsen House, 1262 Rubio Avenue, Altadena, California
Othman House, 2200 Broadview Terrace, Los Angeles
Swann House, Hope Ranch, Santa Barbara, California (project)
Tibbet House remodelling, Encino, California (project)
1941 Nelson Eddy Studio, Los Angeles (project)
Kaufman House remodelling, Los Angeles
Kaye House I, Los Angeles (project)
Kellogg Perchino Breeding Farm, Pahrump Valley, Nevada (project)
Lewis House remodelling, Los Angeles
Rouben Mamoulian House, Los Angeles (project)
Robertson House II, Los Angeles (project)
Earl Stendahl Studio-House, Los Angeles
1941/
42 Aliso Village Public Housing Project, First Street and Mission Road, Los Angeles (with George J. Adams, Walter S. Davis, Ralph C. Flewelling, Eugene Weston Jr., and Lewis Eugene Wilson)
1942 Degener House, Los Angeles (project)
1944 Warren Smith House, Los Angeles (project)
Fairmont Hotel remodelling and tower, San Francisco (project)
Schuyler House, Los Angeles (project)
Tourtellotte House, Palos Verdes, California (project)
1945 Benjamin House, Los Angeles
Brewer House, Pacific Palisades, California
Cardenas House, Oracle, Arizona (project)
Crosby House, North Hollywood, California (project)
Greer Dressmaking Plant, Los Angeles
Kaye House II, Westwood, Los Angeles (project)
Mel Smith House, Los Angeles (project)

1946 Loew House, Los Angeles (project)
Antaky Textile Manufacturing Plant, New York (project)
Anne Baxter House remodelling, Los Angeles (project)
Gainsburg House, 1210 Journey's End Drive, La Canada, California
Huntington Hartford Outpost Club, Hollywood, California (project)
Huntington Hartford Reunion Tract, Los Angeles (project)
Kuttler House remodelling, Los Angeles
Caravansary and Administration Buildings, Institute of Mental Physics, Yucca Valley, California
Redlich House, 602 North Arden, Beverly Hills, California
Stendal Candy Factory, Burbank, California (project)
Frank Wyle Residential Development, Los Angeles
1946/
47 Reitz House, Los Angeles
1946/
48 Jascha Heifetz House remodelling and studio, Beverly Hills, California
1946/
51 Swedenborg Memorial Chapel ("The Wayfarer's Chapel"), Portuguese Bend, Palos Verdes, California

1947 Kenneth Baxter House, San Mateo, California (project)
Beatrice Wood House, Ojai, California
1948 Charles House landscaping, 1210 Benedict Canyon Drive, Beverly Hills, California
Christian Science Reading Room, Fontana, California (project)
Powell House, Los Angeles (project)
1949 Blalock Apartments, Alhambra, California (project)
De Jonghe House, 9020 Crescent Drive, Los Angeles
Dorland House, 1370 Morada, Altadena, California
Healy House, 565 Perugia Way, Los Angeles
Jester House, 32 Narcissa Drive, Portuguese Bend, Palos Verdes, California
Nabel House, 2323 La Mesa Drive, Santa Monica, California
Newman House, 14148 Sunset Boulevard, Pacific Palisades, California
Platt House, Los Angeles (project)
Huntington Hartford Pool Pavilion, Pacific Palisades, California
1949/
50 Huntington Hartford Theatre Square, Hollywood, California (project)
1949/
65 Hill and Dale Nursery and Kindergarten, 16706 Marquez Avenue, Pacific Palisades, California
1950 Alfred Erickson House, 5408 Stauder Circle, Minneapolis
Arthur Erickson House, 5501 Londonderry Road, Edina, Minnesota
Frank Jones House, Covina, California
Shulman House and Carport, Los Angeles
1951 Slater HOuse, La Habra, California (project)
Snow Chapel, Ile Begras, Montreal (project)
1951/
54 Huntington Hartford Vine Street Theatre, Hollywood, California (project)
1951/
59 Jascha Heifetz House additions, 1520 Gilcrest Drive, Beverly Hills, California
1952 Set for the touring production of *John Brown's Body* (Charles Laughton production)
Charles Laughton House pool and dressing room, Los Angeles
1952/
56 Kropp House and Carport, near Grayslake, Illinois
1953 Babcock House, San Diego (project)
Brown House, Los Angeles (project)
Dell House, Los Angeles
Huntington Hartford Fine Arts Galleries, Outdoor Theatre, and Sculpture Gardens, Hollywood, California (project)
Wagner House, Palos Verdes, California (project)
1953/
54 Honeycutt House, 14674 Los Altos Park, Los Angeles
1954 Cafeteria and Cottages, Institute of Mental Physics, Yucca Valley, California
1955 Pent-O-Rama House, Santa Barbara, California (project)
Swedenborg Memorial Chapel, El Cerrito, California (project)
Joshua Tree Land Development, California (project)
1956 Roberts Children's House, Institute of Mental Physics, Yucca Valley, California
Moore House, 504 Paseo del Mar, San Pedro, California
1957 Polster House, Beverly Hills, California
Howard House remodelling and landscaping, Encino, California
Bartfield House, Thousand Oaks, California (project)
Good Shepherd Community Church, Des Plaines, Illinois
1958 Dunham House, Palos Verdes, California
Levand House, Beverly Hills, California

Mace House, 8292 Hollywood Boulevard, Los Angeles
St. Luke's Presbyterian Church, Rolling Hills, California (project)
1959 Lumbleau House, 22158 Pacific Coast Highway, Malibu, California
Stein House and Garage, Granada Hills, California (project)
1960 Charles Laughton House remodelling, furniture, and garden, Los Angeles
Robert Wright House landscaping, Bethesda, Maryland
Pihl House, Edina, Minnesota (project)
Karasik House and Carport, 436 Spaulding Drive, Beverly Hills, California
1961 Pilgrimage Playhouse remodelling, Los Angeles (project)
Mount Olivet Lutheran Church addition, Minneapolis (project)
Piatigorsky/Steiner Chess Club remodelling, Los Angeles
1961/
65 Pico-Robertson Shopping Mall, Los Angeles (project)
1962 Hare House remodelling, Bel Air, Los Angeles
Huntington Hartford Portal Project, Sunset Bay, California (project)
Piatigorsky House entrace gates, Beverly Hills, California
Regional urban plan for Los Angeles County (project)
1963 Bowler House, Palos Verdes, California
Harris House, Orange County, California (project)
Todd Theatre, Los Angeles (project)
Johnson House, 7017 Senalda Road, Hollywood, California
Pfeiffer/Hulet House, Coral Gables, Miami (project)
1964 Terrance Park Apartment, Orange County, California (project)
World Folk Park, Burbank, California (project)
Holiday Bargain Fair and Service Station, Minneapolis (project)
1965 Erickson Family Memorial Garden, Lakewood Memorial Park, Minneapolis (project)
Lombardi House, 804 Los Gatos Road, Palos Verdes, California
Daniel Wright House additions, Phoenix, Arizona
Daniel House landscaping, Los Angeles
Church of the New Jerusalem, Los Angeles (project)
Piatigorsky House guest house remodelling, Los Angeles
1965/
72 First Christian Church, Avenue de los Floras and Kusts Avenue, Thousand Oaks, California
1967 Moorehead House pavilion and loggia additions, Rolling Hills, California
1968 La Rue House, Los Angeles (project)
Alexander House, Thousand Oaks, California (project)
1968/
69 Westfair Shopping Center, Springdale Street and Warner Aenue, Huntington Beach, California (project)
1969 Triangle Park Shopping Center, Long Beach, California (project)
1970 Nabel House landscaping and swimming pool, Santa Monica, California
1970/
71 Urban Recreation Center, Dallas (project)
1971 Bellenson House, Simi Valley, California (project)

Publications

By WRIGHT: articles—"A New Art" in the *Los*

Angeles Times, mid-winter number, 1929; "Woven and Designed by Maria Steinhof" in *California Arts and Architecture* (Los Angeles), November 1940; "Aliso Village Group Housing Project Result of Coordinated Planning" in *Southwest Builders and Contractors* (Los Angeles), May 1943.

On WRIGHT: books—*The Ferro-Concrete Style* by Francis S. Onderdonk, New York, 1928; *The New World Architecture* by Sheldon Cheney, New York 1930; *Modern American Design* by R. I. Leonard and C. A. Glassgold, New York, 1930; *California Gardens* by Winifred S. Dobyns, New York 1931; *Residential Architecture in Southern California* by Paul R. Hunter and Walter L. Reichardt, Los Angeles 1939; *Built in U.S.A.* by Henry-Russell Hitchcock and Arthur Drexler, New York 1952; *Lloyd Wright,* exhibition catalogue, Norman, Oklahoma 1964; *Four Decades of Living Architecture: Lloyd Wright, Architect,* exhibition catalogue, Los Angeles 1966; *Lloyd Wright, Architect: 20th Century Architecture in an Organic Exhibition,* exhibition catalogue, by David Gebhard and Harriette von Breton, Santa Barbara, California 1971; articles—"Portrait of Lloyd Wright" by Carter Ludlow in the *Los Angeles Examiner,* 3 November 1961; "So Wright Turns" by Arthur Miller in the *Los Angeles Herald Examiner,* 4 September 1966; "Lloyd Wright" by Esther McCoy in *Arts and Architecture* (Los Angeles), October 1966; "Lloyd Wright on Design" by Judy Cool in the *Los Angeles Herald Examiner,* 21 May 1967; "Lloyd Wright" by Esther McCoy in *Progressive Architecture* (New York), July 1978.

Bibliography—*Lloyd Wright: A Prairie School Architect* by Patrick J. Meehan, Monticello, Illinois 1978.

Lloyd Wright's talents were scattered over several fields in his formative years, and the unifying thread was his landscape design, which he used to modify or enhenace a structure. His early training in landscaping was as a draftsman in the Boston office of Olmsted and Olmsted, a position he took after his return from Europe where he had assisted his father, Frank Lloyd Wright, in preparation of drawings for the Wasmuth Portfolio.

His first job in an architectural office was in San Diego as a draftsman at age 23 for Irving Gill, and his admiration for Gill's unadorned cubic forms of concrete affected his own work. His houses of the twenties and thirties blended his father's decorative style of the teens and twenties with the planar surfaces of Gill; the cubic forms were always clear, and ornament tended to be concentrated in small areas, usually around openings, as in the Churrigueresque style.

Wright's aesthetic was based on the wall, but theatrical features such as overscaled openings, two story fireplaces and complex ornament gave his buildings a closer relationship to German Expressionism than to the work of his father or Gill; but Wright's interest in music and theatre, and his employment for a year in the design department of a film studio (from which industry a number of his clients came), is a more likely source. The houses of the twenties and thirties are often scaleless—or are scaled to the easel rather than the street—which gives them special interest in a post-Miesian age.

Wright had a more temperate side, as seen in designs for less venturesome clients, based on his father's Prairie Style adapted to the California climate. There was also an inventive side—the use of a slipform technique for the concrete walls of his 1923 Oasis Hotel, Palm Springs; schemes for city plans that proposed elevated roads made of compacted waste from city dumps.

With the completion of his Wayfarers' Chapel at Palos Verdes, Wright's work became more widely known. The glass-walled structure, framed with heavy wood bents and light steel members, is open to a grove of redwoods. The arch form of the bents, and the roof, built up of triangular-shaped solid and transparent materials, give a Gothic character to the open chapel. Wright, as was typical, considered the planting before the design, a sequence that today makes most of his building an integral part of the site.

—Esther McCoy

WURSTER, William Wilson.

American. Born in Stockton, California, 20 October 1895. Educated in Stockton elementary schools; Stockton High School, graduated 1913; University of California, Berkeley, 1912-13; worked for a surveyor, 1913-14; returned to the University of California, and studied naval architecture and marine engineering, 1914-16; shipped to sea, in the Pacific, as an engineer, 1916-18; returned to the University of California, 1919-20, B.Arch. (honors) 1920. Married Catherine Bauer in 1940 (died 1964); daughter: Sarah. Assistant, office of architect E. B. Brown, Stockton, 1910; worked for the architectural firm of John Reid, Jr., San Francisco, 1920; worked in the office of the Filtration Division, City of Sacramento, California, under the architect Charles Dean, 1921-22; travelled in Europe, 1922-23; worked for the firm of Delano and Aldrich, New York, 1923-24; returned to California to design a filtration plant for the East Bay Water Company, 1924-25; in private practice, San Francisco, 1926-43; Partner, with Theodore Bernardi and Donn Emmons, Wurster, Bernardi and Emmons, San Francisco, 1945 until his death, 1973. Fellow, Graduate School of Design, Harvard University, Cambridge, Massachusetts, 1943-44; Dean of the School of Architecture and Planning, Massachusetts Institute of Technology, Cambridge, 1944-50; Dean of the College of Architecture, 1950-59, Dean of the College of Environmental Design, 1959-63, and Dean Emeritus, 1963-73, University of California, Berkeley. Chairman, Architects Advisory Committee, U.S. National Housing Agency, 1942; Chairman 1949-50, and California State Member, 1959-67, National Capitol Park and Planning Commission; Member of the Architectural Advisory Panel, Office for Foreign Buildings, U.S. State Department, 1958-63. Exhibition: *Built in U.S.A. 1932-1944,* Museum of Modern Art, New York, 1944. Recipient: First Prize, Golden Gateway Redevelopment Project Competition, San Francisco, 1959; Gold Medal, American Institute of Architects, 1969. LLD: University of California, Berkeley, 1964. Fellow, American Institute of Architects; American Academy of Arts and Sciences; Royal Academy of Fine Arts, Copenhagen; Member, Akademie der Künste, Berlin; Honorary Corresponding Member, Royal Institute of British Architects; Affiliate, American Institute of Planners. *Died* (in Berkeley, California) *19 September 1973.*

Works:

1927 Smith House, Russell Street, Berkeley, California
Gregory Farmhouse, Canham Road, Scotts Valley, Santa Cruz, California
1931 Yerba Buena Club, *San Francisco Fair*
1932 Henderson House, Bromfield Road, Hillsborough, California
1933 Converse House, Santa Rita Street, Carmel, California
Eiskamp House, Brewington Avenue, Watsonville, California
1934 Sanderson House, Bristol Avenue, Stockton, California
1936 Pope House, Bromfield Road, Hillsborough, California
House, 215 Western Drive, Richmond, California

Jensen House, La Vereda Street, Berkeley, California
1937 Terraced houses, 757-763 Bay Street, San Francisco
House, 737 Bay Street, San Francisco
Henning House, Chiltern Road, Hillsborough, California
Mendenhall House, Emerson Street, Palo Alto, California
1938 Van Deusen House, Hawthorne Terrace, Berkeley, California
1939 House, 2633 Green Street, San Francisco
House, 30 Cragmont Avenue, San Francisco
House, 2560 Divisadero Street, San Francisco
Corbus House, Felton Drive, Menlo Park, California
Raas House, Cowper Street, Palo Alto, California
Strauss House, Stonewall Road, Berkeley, California
1940 House, 1641 Green Street, San Francisco
Dinkelspeil House, Ascot Road, Hillsborough, California
Farley House, Stonewall Road, Berkeley, California
1941 Carquinez Heights (housing), Vallejo, California
Parker Houses, Sacramento, California
Field House, Bristol Avenue, Stockton, California
Timby House, Knoll Drive, San Carlos, California
1942 Stern Hall, University of California, Berkeley
Lamberson House, Alvarado Road, Berkeley, California
House, 3655 Clay Street, San Francisco
Lyman House, Selby Lane, Atherton, California
Schuckl Canning Company Office Building, Fair Oaks Avenue, Sunnyvale, California (now California Growers and Canners Building)
1943 Valencia Gardens (housing), 15th Street, San Francisco (with Harry Thomsen)
1945 House, 250 Locust Street, San Francisco
1948 House, San Carlos Avenue, Sausalito, California
1949 Shuman House, Mountain Home Road, Portola, California
1951 House, 25 Raycliff Terrace, San Francisco
House, 2745 Larkin Avenue, San Francisco
1952 House, 2795 Vallejo Street, San Francisco
House remodelling, Chiltern Road, Hillsborough, California
1954 House, 301 Locust Street, San Francisco
Center for Advanced Studies in the Behavioral Sciences, Stanford University, Palo Alto, California
1955 Two cottages, Greenwood Terrace, Berkeley, California
1958 House, 850 El Camino del Mar, San Francisco
1958/
65 Capitol Tower Apartments, Sacramento, California (with Edward Larrabee Barnes and DeMars and Reay)
1959 Medical Plaza, Stanford University, Palo Alto, California
Married Student Housing, Stanford University, Palo Alto, California
Stern Hall additions, University of California, Berkeley
Strawberry Canyon Recreation Center, University of California, Berkeley
1960 New building for the Woodside Community Church, Woodside, California
1961 First Unitarian Church, Lawson Road, El Cerrito, California
1961/
63 Golden Gateway Redevelopment Project (master plan, garages, point towers and town houses along Jackson Street), San Francisco (with DeMars and Reay)
1962/
67 Ghirardelli Square renovation and remodel-

ling, San Francisco
1964 Civic Auditorium remodelling, San Francisco (with Skidmore, Owings and Merrill)
1965 Sarah Dix Hamlin School, 2129 Vallejo Street, San Francisco
Woodlake Residential Community, San Mateo, California
Cowell College, University of California at Santa Cruz
1967 Northpoint, 2211 Stockton Street, San Francisco
1970 The Ice Houses I and II (conversion of warehouses to interior design showrooms), 1265 Battery and 151 Union Streets, San Francisco
1970/
71 Bank of America World Headquarters, San Francisco (with Skidmore, Owings and Merrill; design consultant Pietro Belluschi)

Publications:

By WURSTER: articles—"From Log Cabin to Modern House" in the *New York Times Magazine,* 20 January 1946; "Building Now: How You Can Meet the 50 Per Cent Rise in Building Costs" in *House and Garden* (New York), May 1946; letter in *Architectural Forum* (New York), March 1947; "When Is a Small House Large" in *House and Garden* (New York), August 1947; "Architectural Education" in *AIA Journal* (Washington, D.C.), January 1948; "Architecture Broadens Its Base" in *AIA Journal* (Washington, D.C.), July 1948; "The Unity of Architecture and Landscape Architecture" in *Landscape Design,* exhibition catalogue, San Francisco 1948; "The Outdoors in Residential Design" in *Architectural Forum* (New York), September 1949; "The Architectural Life" in *Architectural Record* (New York), January 1951; "The Great Arch of the Jefferson National Expansion Memorial in St. Louis, Missouri" in the *St. Louis Post-Dispatch,* September 1956; "Row House Vernacular and High Style Monument" in *Architectural Record* (New York), August 1958; "Indian Vernacular Architecture: Wai and Cochin," with Catherine Bauer, in *Perspecta 5* (New Haven, Connecticut), January 1959; "The University and the Environmental Design Professions" in *College of Environmental Design Exhibition,* exhibition catalogue, Berkeley, California 1959; "College Planning" in *Architectural Record* (New York), September 1959.

On WURSTER: book—*Built in U.S.A. 1932-1944,* exhibition catalogue, edited by Elizabeth Mock, New York 1944; articles—"Building Types: Homes $7,500 and Under" in *Architectural Record* (New York) March 1938; "Case Study House 3" in *Arts and Architecture* (Los Angeles), June 1945; "Meet William Wurster" in *House Beautiful* (New York), June 1945; "William Wilson Wurster" in *Architectural Forum* (New York), July 1943; "A New Structural Method Builds a New Campus" in *Architectural Forum* (New York), June 1950; "Profilo di un Architetto Americano: William Wilson Wurster" in *Architettura* (Rome), May 1957; "Genetrix: Personal Contributions to American Architecture" in *Architectural Review* (London), May 1957; "L'Architetto William Wilson Wurster" by Richard C. Peters in *Casabella* (Milan), April 1960; "Recent Works of William Wurster" in *Architectural Record* (New York), January 1963; "The Western House" in *AIA Journal* (Washington D.C.), June 1968; "Three Houses Built for Summer" in *House and Garden* (New York), June 1970; "W. W. Wurster, Architect, Dies" by C. Anspacher in *San Francisco Chronicle* (San Francisco) 20 September 1973; "U.C. Santa Cruz" by D. Gregory and others in *AIA Journal* (Washington, D.C.) August 1979; "William Wilson Wurster" by Richard C. Peters in *Journal of Architectural Education* (Washington, D.C.), November 1979; "William Wilson Wurster—A Northern Californian Modernist Architect" by William P. Coburn in *Archetype* (San Francisco), Autumn 1980.

William Wurster: Cowell College, University of California, Santa Cruz, 1965.

William Wilson Wurster has been called "the great American regionalist—an architect who was both a pioneer and a prophet." Alvar Aalto, the internationally known Finnish architect, said of Wurster, "He is a man who loves people, loves to build for people, and never loses sight of this happiness." As architect, planner and educator, Wurster's achievements were extraordinary. From his famous Gregory Farmhouse, Santa Cruz, in 1927, to the award winning Ghirardelli Square, San Francisco, in 1967, the quality of his work always remained true to his unyielding belief that architecture should be a forthright response to local and regional needs and conditions. His buildings are simple, direct and honest, qualities which, for those who knew him, precisely reflect his philosophy of being—a philosophy of simplicity, directness and honesty of expression. As a person, Wurster was a great humanitarian. As an architect he was internationally known for his leadership in the development of a regional expression. As an educator, Dean Wurster's vision, leadership and determination expanded the scope of professional architectural education to include concern for the total environment.

Wurster's work has a unique place in American architecture. During the late 1920s and in the 1930s he developed an architecture which suited the region, most notably in the Bay Area of Northern Califor-nia. His understanding of the social and economic conditions, climatic variances, materials, methods of building and the architectural heritage of the area stimulated the expression "Bay Region Style." If style is a conscious language of form, then Wurster's work does not fit this catalog term. His architecture was a rational answer to given conditions rather than the concretization of any predetermined visual image. It was a straightforward expression based on a good deal of knowledge and common sense. Derived from regional sources as a response to local human needs, it transcended the fashionable and exemplified a simple, direct design approach that suited the place, the climate, and the way of life of the people.

Wurster believed architecture, as a complicated social art, had to acknowledge the total environment. This implied that the importance of architecture was not the isolated building itself, but its relation to the people, the community and all other buildings. He knew that human environments created by architects cannot help but influence the ultimate users and thus felt that "the importance of all architectural things must be measured by its meaning for people" and must be concerned with the everyday things that shape their physical and psychological needs and aspirations.

After World War II Wurster joined forces with long-time friends and employees Theodore Bernardi and later Donn Emmons and formed the now famous firm Wurster, Bernardi, and Emmons in 1946.

Because of Wurster's belief that good architecture should be available to people in all walks of life, no work was too big or small for the firm, and they did everything from kitchen remodelings to company headquarters. Even though the scale of the projects dramatically enlarged in later years to include government buildings, college campuses, churches, large housing complexes and bank headquarters, the firm continued in the Wurster tradition, building many wonderful houses. That unfailing sense of simplicity and directness of a decade before is still evident in all the work, and the intentional modesty, informality and lack of strain remained the keynote in their approach.

The significance of Wurster's architecture was perhaps best stated by the noted American landscape architect, Thomas D. Church. When Wurster received the American Institute of Architecture's highest honor, The Gold Medal, in 1969, Church wrote: "Wurster's buildings of 40 years ago sit confidently in the world of today. His buildings of today will seem inevitable 40 years from now."

—Richard C. Peters

Y

YAMASAKI, Minoru.

American. Born in Seattle, Washington, 1 December 1912. Educated at the University of Washington, Seattle, 1930-34, B.Arch. 1934; New York University, 1934-35. Married Teruko Hirashiki in 1941; children: Carol, Taro, and Kim. Designer, Githens and Keally, New York, 1935-37; Designer, Draftsman and Job Captain, Shreve, Lamb and Harmon, New York, 1937-43; Designer, Harrison and Fouilhoux, New York, 1943-44; Designer, Raymond Loewy Associates, New York, 1944-45; Chief Architectural Designer, Smith, Hinchman and Grylls, Detroit, 1945-49. Since 1949, Principal, Minoru Yamasaki and Associates, Troy, Michigan: in partnership, with Joseph Leinweber, Yamasaki, Leinweber and Associates, Detroit, 1949-55; and, with Leinweber and George Hellmuth, *q.v.*, Leinweber, Yamasaki and Hellmuth, St. Louis, 1949-55. Instructor of Water Color, New York University, 1935-36; Instructor of Architectural Design, Columbia University, New York, 1943-45. Exhibitions: *Buildings for Business and Government*, Museum of Modern Art, New York, 1957; *International Building Exposition*, Berlin, 1957; *Living Today*, Corcoran Gallery, Washington, D.C., 1958; World's Fair, Brussels, 1958; *American National Exhibition*, Moscow, 1959; University of Chicago, 1959; University of Michigan, Ann Arbor, 1959; Architectural League of New York, 1959 (retrospective); John Herron Art Institute, Indianapolis, 1959 (retrospective); Michigan Society of Architects, Detroit, 1960; Honolulu Academy of Arts, 1960 (retrospective); Michigan State University, East Lansing, 1960; Oberlin College, Ohio, 1960; De Young Museum, San Francisco, 1960 (retrospective); University of Washington, Seattle, 1960; *National Gold Medal Exhibition*, toured the United States 1960-61; *New Directions in Architecture*, American Institute of Architects, Wisconsin Chapter, Milwaukee, 1960; *AIA Convention Exhibition*, Philadelphia, 1961; *Century 21* (World's Fair), Seattle, 1962; *AIA Convention Exhibition*, Miami Beach, 1963; *Arquitectura Actual de America*, Instituto de Cultura Hispanica, Madrid, 1965; *Synagogue Architecture and Sculpture*, Jewish Community Center of Cleveland, 1966; *Minoru Yamasaki: The Architect and His Use of Sculpture as an Integral Part of Design*, Staempfli Gallery, New York, 1967; *Spaces for Sport and Culture*, Olympic Games, Mexico City, 1968; Meadow Brook Art Gallery, Oakland University, Rochester, Michigan, 1974 (retrospective). Recipient: Design Award, *Progressive Architecture*, 1956; Architectural Institute of Japan Award, 1957; Gold Medal, American Institute of Architect, Detroit Chapter, 1959; Alumnus Summa Laude Dignatus Award, University of Washington, Seattle, 1960. D. H.: Wayne State University, Detroit, 1960; D.Arch.: University of Michigan, Ann Abor, 1961; D.F.A.: Rensselaer Polytechnic Institute, Troy, New York, 1961; Bates College, Lewiston, Maine, 1964; Franklin and Marshall College, Lancaster, Pennsylvania, 1976; D.H.L.: Carleton College, Northfield, Minnesota, 1967; LL.D.: University of Saskatchewan, Regina, 1967; D.Arch. Design: Eastern Michigan University,

Ypsilanti, 1979. Fellow, American Institute of Architects, 1960; Fellow, American Academy of Arts and Sciences, 1960. Address: Minoru Yamasaki and Associates, 350 West Big Beaver Road, Troy, Michigan 48084, U.S.A.

Works:

1950 Louis Baker House, Greenwich, Connecticut
     Daniel W. Goodenough House, 234 Lothrop, Grosse Pointe Farms, Michigan
1955 S. Brooks Barron House, 19631 Argyle Crescent, Detroit
1956 Terminal Building, Lambert Airport, St. Louis
1957 United States Consulate-General Office Building and Staff Headquarters, Kobe, Japan
1958 McGregor Memorial Community Conference Center, Wayne State University, Detroit
     American Concrete Institute, Seven Mile Road, Detroit
1959 Reynolds Metals Regional Sales Office Building, Northland Drive, Southfield, Michigan
     United States Pavilion, *Agriculture and Trade Fair*, New Delhi
1961 Civil Air Terminal, Dhahran, Saudi Arabia (architectural design and detailing only)
1962 *Century 21* (World's Fair) Buildings, Seattle (architectural design and detailing only)
1963 Michigan Consolidated Gas Company Office Building, Woodward Avenue, Detroit (architectural design and detailing only)
1964 North Shore Congregation Israel Temple, Sheridan Road, Glencoe, Illinois
     Queen Emma Gardens Apartment Buildings, Honolulu
     Northwestern National Life Insurance Company Office Building, Minneapolis
     IBM Office Building and Garage, Seattle (architectural design and detailing only)
     Prentis Building, Wayne State University, Detroit
1965 William James Hall, Harvard University, Cambridge, Massachusetts
     Woodrow Wilson School of Public and International Affairs, Princeton University, New Jersey
     Classroom and Laboratory Buildings, University of Saskatchewan, Regina
1966 Century Plaza Hotel, Century City, Los Angeles
1967 Manufacturers and Traders Trust Company Office and Bank Building, Buffalo, New York
     Library, University of Saskatchewan, Regina
1968 Ala Moana Apartments, Honolulu
     Japanese Cultural and Trade Center, San Francisco (with Van Bourg/Nakamura and Associates)
1969 Eastern Air Lines Terminal, Logan International Airport, Boston (architectural design and detailing only)

1972 Styling and Product Planning Building, Chrysler Corporation, Highland Park, Michigan
1973 Horace Mann Educators Office Building, Springfield, Illinois
     Basic and Clinical Science Facility, Medical College of Ohio at Toledo
1974 World Trade Center, New York (with Emery Roth and Sons)
     Congregation Beth El Temple, Bloomfield Township, Michigan
     Colorado National Bank Office Building, Denver
1975 Montgomery Ward and Company Headquarters Office Building, Chicago
     Century Plaza Towers and Garage, Century City, Los Angeles (architectural design and detailing only)
1976 College Center, Franklin and Marshall College, Lancaster, Pennsylvania
     Performing Arts Center, Tulsa, Oklahoma
1977 Bank of Oklahoma Office Building, Williams Center, Tulsa, Oklahoma
     Rainier Square Bank Tower, Seattle (architectural design and detailing only)
1978 Federal Reserve Bank, Richmond, Virginia
     Office Building Complex, for the Arabian Monetary Agency, Riyadh, Saudi Arabia
1979 Miyako Hotel, Tokyo
1980 Royal Reception Pavilion, International Airport, Jeddah, Saudi Arabia
1982 100 Washington Square, Northwestern National Life Insurance Company Office Building, Minneapolis
1983 Government Center Office Building, Toledo, Ohio
     Shiga Sacred Garden Temple, Shinji Shumei-kai, Shiga Prefecture, Japan
     Head Office Building, Saudi Arabian Monetary Agency, Riyadh, Saudi Arabia
1986 HAW'A Islamic Women's Center (shopping, cultural, educational and recreational facility), Jeddah, Saudi Arabia
1988 Eastern Province International Airport (Western Main Terminal, Royal Reception Terminal, Mosque and Parking Structure, Control Tower), Saudi Arabia
     World Trade Center (retail complex, office tower, hotel, parking structure), Bangkok

Publications:

By YAMASAKI: books—*Minoru Yamasaki: the architect and his use of sculpture as an integral part of design*, exhibition catalogue, Berne 1967; *A Life in Architecture*, Tokyo and New York 1979; articles—"Notes in Passing" in *Arts and Architecture* (Los Angeles), July 1959; "The Present State of Architecture" in *Dicta* (St. Louis), January 1963; "Humanist Architecture for America and Its Relation to the Traditional Architecture of Japan" in *RIBA Journal* (London), January 1961; "A Philosophy" in *Design* (Bombay), January 1972; "Architecture East and West" in *Architect and Builder* (Cape Town),

February 1976; "Shinji Shumei-kai Temple" in *The Japan Architect* (Tokyo), September 1983.

On YAMASAKI: articles—"The Morality of Modern Architecture" in *Architectural Forum* (New York), May 1956; "Profilo di un Architetto Americano: Minoru Yamasaki" in *L'Architettura* (Rome), November 1956; "The Architecture of Minoru Yamasaki" in *Architectural Record* (New York), May 1957; "Minoru Yamasaki" in *L'Architecture d'Aujourd'hui* (Paris), April 1958; "American Architect, Yamasaki" by Russell Bourne in *Architectural Forum* (New York), August 1958; "A Conversation with Yamasaki" in *Architectural Forum* (New York), July 1959; "Minoru Yamasaki's Works of Late" in *Kokusai Kentiku* (Tokyo), February 1960; "Minoru Yamasaki: Projets et Réalisations Récents" in *L'Architecture d'Aujourd'hui* (Paris), April/May 1960; "Soaring Ribbed Vaults to Dominate Yamasaki's Design for Seattle Fair" and "Yamasaki's New Expression of 'Aspiring Verticality'" in *Architectural Record* (New York), August 1960; "Six New Projects by Yamasaki" in *Architectural Record* (New York), July 1961; "Minoru Yamasaki's Recent Buildings" by Ada Louise Huxtable in *Art in America* (New York), Winter 1962; "Yamasaki's Dhahran Airport" in *Architectural Record* (New York), March 1963; "Yamasaki's First Tower" in *Architectural Forum* (New York), May 1963; "Structure Plays Leading Role in Latest Yamasaki Designs" in *Architectural Record* (New York), December 1963; "Minoru Yamasaki" in *Architectural Record* (New York), September 1964; "Bearing Wall Expressed in a Skyscraper" and "Natural, Appropriate Use of Concrete Shells" in *Architectural Record* (New York), February 1965; "Structure and Design" in *Fortune* (New York), June 1965; "Recent Work of Minoru Yamasaki" in *Casabella* (Milan), January 1966; "The Century Plaza: A Resort in Mid-City" in *Architectural Record* (New York), August 1966; "Minoru Yamasaki Designs His Own Office" in *Architectural Record* (New York), September 1968; "The Greatest Skyscraper of Them All" in *Reader's Digest* (New York), July 1969; "Airports" in *Architectural Record* (New York), August 1970; "Works of Minoru Yamasaki" in *Informes de la Construccion* (Madrid), October 1974; "The Architect Was Told 'World Trade,' So He Planned Big" in *Smithsonian Magazine* (Washington, D.C.), January 1978; "Tradition Rekindled" in *Architectural Record* (New York), June 1983.
Bibliography: *Serenity and Delight in the New Architecture as Exemplified in the Work of Minoru Yamasaki: A Selected Bibliography* by Robert B. Harmon, Monticello, Illinois 1981.

For me as an architect, my life has been a constant search for the best combination of aesthetics and function in the buildings I design. For several years, as a result of the influences I received during my trips around the world, I tended to overdesign and overdecorate some of our buildings. But about the time of the India Fair, I began to think of the functional needs of people in an urban environment, and this led me to correct these excesses when designing our buildings. For the last twenty years, I have adhered to the idea of using the least possible amounts of materials to attain the desired strength and stability without compromising either aesthetics or function.

When I read the following Emerson quotation in his essay entitled "Beauty," it only served to strengthen my resolve:

beauty rests on necessities: the line of beauty is the result of perfect economy. The cell of the beehive is built at that angle which gives the most strength with the least wax. The bone or the quill of the

Minoru Yamasaki: Northwestern National Life Insurance Building, Minneapolis, 1964.

bird gives the most alar strength with the least weight

There is not a particle to spare in natural structures. There is a compelling reason in the uses of the plant for every novelty of color or form; and our art saves material by more skillful arrangement; and reaches beauty by taking every superfluous ounce that can be spared from a wall and keeping its strength in the poetry of columns.

I feel very strongly that man is much happier when his environment consists of delicate elements, beautifully proportioned, whether they are of wood or stone, concrete or steel. I thoroughly dislike being in interiors of buildings which are made of cold, rough and massive brick, concrete or stone. I much prefer the softness of wood and plaster and floors of carpet or, in Japan, *tatami*, because of the comfort they provide and the humane feeling that these materials impart. Obviously, there have been successful spaces built in beautifully polished marbles and other stones but, basically, for the interior, where one must spend most of his time, I prefer the softer materials. I have used polished marbles in both residential and office interiors, relatively sparsely, and in more monumental areas such as public lobbies, where polished or honed marble seems more appropriate to me. The rougher materials mentioned earlier seem much more suitable in gardens and on exterior walls, not in interior spaces where they are uncomfortable and abrasive when people come into contact with them. I enjoy materials delicately designed and pleasing to the touch as well as to the eye.

Whenever I am in Japan, I try to make time to visit some classic expression of their architectural tradition. Wandering through the structures or sitting in the gardens, I find myself renewed, once again determined to make these the standards by which I will develop my work. Modern man spends too much time thinking of ways to improvise and supposedly improve upon designs, usually to the detriment of true aesthetics. Objects and buildings become too overdone, too trendy, giving them no lasting meaning. It is this we must contemplate on and try to avoid.

A general assessment of what I have learned in my practice is that architecture is to create shelter, usable and livable areas for man so that he may go about living his life productively and happily in all the variety of activities in which he needs and wishes to be involved. We must provide protection from the normal elements of climate—wind, sun, rain, snow, cold and heat—as well as from the more violent aspects of nature, such as fire, earthquakes, hurricanes, etc.

Beyond these basics, the architecture we build should give man an aesthetic emotional fulfillment so that whether he goes from home to work or to other activities in which he may be involved, he can anticipate the pleasure of his destination.

—Minoru Yamasaki

Minoru Yamasaki has attempted to provide American architcture with a new tradition of democratic humanism enhanced by his special understanding of the problems of scale and of serenity as derived from Japanese models. This attempt at synthesis of individualistic and democratic Western ideals with Japanese models based on contrary principles takes place in a Miesian concern for purity of understatement. The results have often proven to be contradictory rather than harmonious—an outcome not out of keeping with the ironic and contradictory mode of the times from which the buildings spring.

His Federal Science Pavilion for the *Century 21* World's Fair (Seattle, 1962) was widely heralded as setting such a humanist theme for architecture. With a mood and massing highly reminiscent of St. Mark's Square, this structure constantly combines in its formal aspect the vertical parallels dominant in

American highrise architecture with the arches and spires of monastic Europe. The scale and serenity derive from the formal arrangement of masses, especially the central sculptural spires.

This theme, especially the formal arrangement of vertically and its resolution in Gothic arches, is, however, stretched to absurdity in the World Trade Center in New York, Yamasaki's most significant and important commission. This design is absurd in much the same way as Theatre of the Absurd or Surrealist Art: in maximization of self-referential incongruity. Extended into the sky, the narrow parallels defining the windows (and the exterior, load-bearing lattice structure) close in on themselves and create sky-spires of negative space. The very towers themselves meet in the infinity of their verticalness, yet forming another Gothic mega-arch infinitely higher than their Seattle predecessors. This theme is set at the base with the "human scale" set of lattices. These lattices actually form physical arches as opposed to the implicit arches of the towers. The final resolution of the human scale, then, as elaborated by this building, occurs in the sky, in the infinity of space; this is an ironic pie-in-the-sky humanism, offering salvation in the not-here and not-now.

From the walkway of the Brooklyn Bridge or the New Jersey Palisades, WTC shimmers. This is architecture as art; Op Art to be exact. The eye cannot discern whether it is looking at a series of crisscrossing lines or a series of verticals—here the American-European-Japanese synthesis is clearly unresolvable on the retinal level, and the building is a challenge to the academicism of the New York skyline rather than a solution of its contradictory elements.

In reality, WTC, and for that matter Seattle Science Pavilion, is about as humanistic, democratic, or serene as a 1964 Lincoln Continental. They are physical objects that are humanistic, democratic, and serene for those few who can afford them, politically, economically, ecologically. That the WTC uses as much electricity as a Swedish city of 200,000 is neither an accomplishment of sociotechnical progress nor a joke. As an office building, WTC provides little in the way of amenity for anyone but the top executives working in it; economically, it is a drain on city and region; politically, it serves a commerical-governmental elite physically and socially isolated from the people whom, by democratic principles, it is supposed to serve.

Rather than creating a humanist tradition or a foretaste of the twenty first century, the architecture of Yamasaki emerges as an ideal realization, an end-of-the-line for a set of technical, social, and aesthetic standards. These standards of accomplishment are expressed by two implicit doctrines brought to final fruition in WTC: 1) architecture is site-free and prototypic—building design is a sub-category of industrial product design; and 2) architecture is the creation of monumental sculpture—purity of form synthesis is a criterion that overrides and is separate and separable from social, political, and environmental responsibility. Judged by these standards, Yamasaki's creations are indeed masterpieces.

—Joseph B. Juhasz

YORKE, Francis Reginald Stevens.
British. Born in Stratford upon Avon, Warwickshire, 3 December 1906. Educated at Chipping Camden School, Gloucestershire; University of Birmingham School of Architecture and Town Planning. Married Thelma Austin Jones in 1930; had two daughters. In private practice, London, 1930-35; in partnership with Marcel Breuer, London, 1935-37; worked under William Holford on government war work, 1939-44; Partner, with Eugene Rosenberg, *q.v.*, and Cyril Mardall, *q.v.*, Yorke, Rosenberg

and Mardall, London, 1944 until his death, 1962. Founder Member, MARS Group, London, 1932; Assistant Editor, *The Architects' Journal,* London, 1933; Editor, *Specifications* (annual), London, 1935-62. Recipient: Council of Industrial Design Award, 1959; Civic Trust Award, 1961; Bronze Medal, Royal Institute of British Architects, 1961. Fellow, Royal Institute of British Architects. C.B.E. (Commander, Order of the British Empire), 1962. *Died* (in London) *10 June 1962.*

Works:

1933 Reinforced Concrete Houses (2), Gidea Park, Essex (with William Holford, A. Stephenson and A. Adams)
1935 Reinforced Concrete House, Nast Hyde, Hatfield, Hertfordshire
1936 Civic Centre of the Future (project; with Marcel Breuer)
1937 Sea Lane House, East Preston, Sussex (with Marcel Breuer)
1939 Seven Cottages, Stratford upon Avon, Warwickshire (with F.W.B. Yorke)
1939/
44 Government depots, camps and factories, England (with William Holford)
1940 Flats, Camberwell, London (with Arthur Korn)
 With Yorke, Rosenberg, Mardall:
1947 Luccombe House, Isle of Wight
 Cowley Peachey Housing, Middlesex
 Exhibition stands, Council of Industrial Design and Board of Trade, London
1948 Sigmund Pumps Factory, Gateshead, Durham
 Fort Corbletts House conversion, Alderney, Channel Islands
 Linden Doors Factory, Stowmarket, Suffolk (project)
1949 Temporary Outpatients Department, St. Thomas' Hospital, London
 Shebbear College Boarding School alterations, Devon
 Factories, Dagenham Docks, London (project)
1950 Barclay Secondary School, Stevenage, Hertfordshire
1951 John Lewis Department Store, Southsea, Hampshire (project)
 Dr. Cole House, Londonderry, Northern Ireland (with Corr and McCormick)
 Housing, King's Langley, Hertfordshire
 Susan Lawrence Primary School, London
 Elizabeth Lansbury Nursery School, London
 Housing, Brynmawr, Brecknock, Wales
 Hainault Forest Secondary School, Essex
1952 Sir William Nottidge School, Whitstable, Kent
 Sish Lane Housing, Stevenage, Hertfordshire
 College of Further Education, Merthyr Tydfil, Glamorgan, Wales
1953 Williams and Williams Exhibition Stand, *Building Trades Exhibition,* London
 The Mill House conversion, Wootton, Oxfordshire
 Warren Wood Secondary School, Rochester, Kent
 Upholland Grammar School, Wigan, Lancashire
 West Park Secondary School, Leeds
 Southlands Teachers' Training College Assembly Hall, Wimbledon, London
 Sheerwater Primary School, Woking, Surrey
 Causeway Green Primary School, Oldbury, Worcestershire
 North Mimms Boys and Infants School, Hertfordshire
1954 Steddall's Warehouse alterations, London
 Birchen Coppice Primary School, Kidderminster, Worcestershire
 Queensmead Secondary School, Ruislip, Middlesex

 London Transport Bus Garage and Depot, Loughton, Essex
 Hammerson Group Offices, Great New Street, London (project)
1955 Tudor House Home for the Infirm, Grayshott, Hertfordshire (project)
 Kerris Artists Studio conversion, Mousehole, Cornwall
 Williams and Williams Offices, London (project)
 Quarles Secondary Modern School, Romford, Essex
 Master plan and stage I of the Leeds Polytechnic
 Mark Hall Local Authority Houising, Harlow, Essex
 Haileybury Boys Club, London
 Bewdley Secondary School, Worcestershire
 Kirkwall Place Housing, Bethnal Green, London
 Kingswood School, Essex
1956 Boxgrove Housing prototypes
 Wootton Rectory, Oxfordshire
 Jack Straw's Lane House, Oxford
 Tyrell and Green Store, Southampton
 Dick Sheppard School, Tulse Hill, London
 East Anglian Girls School, Bury St. Edmunds, Suffolk
 Bradfield Secondary School, Yorkshire
 Sigmund Pumps Factory extension, Gateshead, Durham (project)
 North Mimms Boys and Infants School additions, Hertfordshire
 College of Further Education extensions, Merthyr Tydfil, Glamorgan, Wales
 Kingswood School extensions, Essex
1957 Southlands College Lecture Block and Dining Room extensions, Wimbledon, London
 Temple Moor Grammar School, Leeds
 Stanley Outwood Secondary School, Yorkshire
 Jewish Theological College, Montagu Square, London
 Oak Park Secondary School, Havant, Hampshire
 Philip Harben House, 115 Great George Street, London
 Dawley Secondary School, Shropshire
 Interbau Housing, Berlin (project; with Werner Düttmann)
 Master plan for the Bromsgrove Education Centre, Worcestershire
 Timberlog Secondary School, Basildon, Essex
 St. Paul's Secondary School, Addlestone, Surrey
 Gatwick Airport, stage I, Sussex
 Sir William Nottidge School extensions, Whitstable, Kent
1958 Unilever House, Hamburg (competition project)
 Wokingham Infants School, Berkshire (competition project)
 Jewish Board of Guardians Offices, London
 Finnish Seamen's Mission, London
 Chaucer Secondary School, Sheffield
 Carmel College extensions, Wallingford, Berkshire
 Brixton Synagogue Hall remodelling, London
 Leeds Polytechnic, Stage II
 Tyrell and Green Store extensions, Southampton
 East Anglian Girls School alterations and additions, Bury St. Edmunds, Suffolk
1959 J. Spedan Lewis House, Longstock, Hampshire
 Morsons Chemical Works, Enfield, Middlesex
 Elephant and Castle Development, London (project)
 World Health Organization Offices, Geneva (competition project)
 Timber Development Association Office Furniture, London (competition project)
 Formation Furniture prototypes, for Bath

 Cabinet Makers Ltd
 Roman Road Housing, Bethnal Green, London
 High Park School, Stourbridge, Worcestershire
 St. Paul's School Hall alterations, Chertsey, Surrey
 Brays Grove Secondary School, Harlow, Essex
 College of Further Education, Bromsgrove, Worcestershire
 Tennant Brothers Exhibition Stand, *Club Trades Fair,* London
 Churchill College, Cambridge (competition project)
 Upholland Grammar School extensions, Wigan, Lancashire
 East Anglican Girls School alterations and additions, stage II, Bury St. Edmunds, Suffolk
1960 Watford Shopping Centre, Hertfordshire (project)
 Rothwell Secondary School, stage II, Yorkshire
 Warslow School, Staffordshire
 United States Embassy, Grosvenor Square, London (with Eero Saarinen Associates)
 Supasave Store, Southend, Essex
 Staincliffe Hospital Geriatric Unit, Leeds
 Altnagelvin Hospital, Londonderry, Northern Ireland
 Passmores Comprehensive School, Harlow, Essex
 D. Allford House, Persham, Surrey (project)
 Brierly Hill Secondary School, Staffordshire
 Rolls Royce Offices, Derby (project)
 Telecommunications Engineering Building, Gatwick Airport, Sussex
 Leeds Polytechnic, stage III
1961 N.J. Payne House, Shamley Green, Norfolk
 Royal Masonic School, Ascot, Berkshire (project)
 Bromsgrove High School, Worcestershire
 Hob Green Primary School, Worcestershire
 YRM and Norwich Union Insurances Societies Offices, Greystoke Place, London
 Maternity and Outpatients Departments, Crawley Hospital Sussex
 Kew Bridge Development for British Rail, London (project)
 Report on Creekside Refuse Disposal Depot, Deptford, London
 Timber Development Association Wooden Furniture, London (competition project)
 Kingswood School extensions, stage II, Essex
1962 Master plan for Kuwait Airport (with Sir Frederick Snow and Partners)
 Elliott Brothers Welfare Building, Rochester, Kent (project)
 Rotameter Factory, Croydon, Surrey (project)
 Library, Cambridge University (project)
 Southlands College: Queensmere Hostels, Lecture Block and Gymnasium, Wimbledon, London
 Ark House, Rochford, Essex
 Staff Residence, Crawley Hospital, Sussex
 Barstable Comprehensive School, Basildon, Essex
 College of Further Education extensions, stage II, Merthyr Tydfil, Glamorgan, Wales
 North Mimms Boys and Infants School additions, stage II, Hertfordshire
 Haileybury Boys Club, stage II, London
 Oak Park Secondary School extensions, Havant, Hampshire
 Timberlog Secondary School extensions, Basildon, Essex

Publications:

By YORKE: books—*The Modern House,* London

1934; *The Modern House in England,* London 1937; *The Modern Flat,* with Frederick Gibberd, London 1937, 1950; *A Key to Modern Architecture,* with Colin Penn, London 1939; *Flooring Materials,* with C. Roy Fowkes, London 1948; *The New Small House,* with Penelope Whiting, London 1954; article—"Modern Architecture in Czechoslovakia" in *Review* (London), no. 3, 1943.

On YORKE: book—*The Architecture of Yorke Rosenberg Mardall,* introduction by Reyner Banham, London and New York 1972; articles— "Taking off at Gatwick ... 25 Years Later" by Jack Christopher in *Building Design* (London), 2 March 1979; "Airport Building", in *RIBA Journal* (London), March 1981; "Modern Masters: Yorke, Rosenberg, Mardall" by Colin Davies in *Building* (London), 20 March 1981; "Terminal Grounded" in *Building Design* (London), 20 November 1981; "No More Heroes" by Deyan Sudjic in *Building Design* (London), 8 January 1982.

*

F.R.S. Yorke was one of the small group of architects who introduced modern architecture into Britain during the 1930s. While England after the First World War remained true to the tradition of neo-Georgian, the continent has long been seething with twentieth century ideas. The most influential revolutionary was Le Corbusier, followed closely by Walter Gropius of the Bauhaus. In the 1920s the ideas percolated into English schools of architecture, but it was not until later that the new concept of internationalism in architecture began to acquire the force of reality. After the Second World War, however, the new style flowered as the expression of a new society, and Yorke was able to practice his art unrestricted by academic tradition.

Although Yorke was undoubtedly inspired by Le Corbusier, he was himself an artist of the highest calibre, not given to imitation. His work at its best was almost classical in its purity of form. Of all his immediate post-war works, perhaps it is for his schools that he will be best remembered. Among these was one specially built for the 1951 *Festival of Britain* exhibition of architecture in the Lansbury neighbourhood in Poplar. The exploitation of glass and reinforced concrete was dramatic. The external space design seemed to flow into the building; from outside, it was possible to see the interior with its rich and colorful ceramics. The so-called International Style was soon to run into difficulties with less experienced and sensitive designers, but during his period Yorke pioneered, illuminated and gave distinction to architecture that will always be part of architectural history.

Yorke was not one to suffer fools gladly, but his personal charm and business acumen enabled him to build up a business with two equally distinguished partners, a firm that has continued after Yorke's death, as Yorke, Rosenberg and Mardall, in his own tradition of the impersonal and international, acknowledging their continuing debt to Le Corbusier and Mies van der Rohe.

—Geoffrey Jellicoe

YOSHIDA, Isoya.
Japanese. Born in Tokyo, 19 December 1894. Educated at the Kaisei Middle School, Tokyo, 1909-13; Department of Architecture, Tokyo Art School, now Tokyo University of Fine Arts, 1915-23, Dip. Arch. 1923; travelled in Europe, 1925. Married

Hatsué Yoshida in 1939. In private practice, concentrating on "Sukiya" style (traditional Japanese modular design), Tokyo, 1925 until his death, 1974. Lecturer, 1941-46, Professor of Architecture, 1946-61, and Professor Emeritus, 1962-74, Tokyo University of Fine Arts. Exhibitions: *Furniture Designs of Isoya Yoshida,* Takashimaya, Tokyo, 1952; *Expo '70,* Osaka, Japan, 1970. Recipient: Japan Arts Academy Award, 1952; Japan Cultural Medal, 1964. Member, Japan Arts Academy, Japan Architects Association, and Japan Institute of Architects. Honorary Member, Architects Association of Mexico, and American Institute of Architects. *Died* (in Tokyo) *24 March 1974.*

Works:

1931 Sekiya House, Tokyo
1934 Kokei Kobayashi House/Studio, Tokyo
1935 Gimpu-so House, Tokyo
1936 Shuho Yamakawa Studio, Tokyo
     Kineya Villa, Atami, Japan
     Nobuko Yoshiya House, Tokyo
1939 New Park Hotel, Matsushima, Japan
1940 Hoshun Yamaguchi House, Tokyo
     Oshima House, Tokyo
     Iwanami Villa, Atami, Japan
     Aoki House, Tokyo
1940/
  62 Shinkiraku Japanese-style Restaurant, Tokyo
1942 Fugetsu Teahouse, Shizuoka, Japan
1944 Isoya Yoshida House, Kanagawa Prefecture, Japan
1949 Kato House, Kamakura, Japan
1951 Kabukiza Theatre, Tokyo
1951/
  58 Ryuzaburo Umehara House/Studio, Tokyo
1953 Tsurutoku Japanese-style Restaurant, Tokyo
1954 Koyoen Tsuruya Japanese-style Restaurant, Hyogo Prefecture, Japan
     Hoshun Yamaguchi Studio, Kanagawa Prefecture, Japan
1955 Bunrakuza Theatre, Osaka
     Kosaburo Yoshizumi House, Tokyo
1956 Botan Japanese-style Restaurant, Osaka
     Yamagata House, Tokyo
1957 Kanzaburo Nakamura House, Tokyo
     Suzuki House, Tokyo
1958 Meijiza Theatre, Tokyo
     Japan Academy of Arts Center, Tokyo
1959 Tsuruya Japanese-style Restaurant, Osaka
1960 Sasaki House, Tokyo
     Yaeko Mizutani House, Tokyo
     Goto Art Museum, Tokyo
     Yamato Bunka Hall, Nara, Japan
1961 Gyokudo Art Museum, Tokyo
1962 Nobuko Yoshiya House, Kanagawa Prefecture, Japan
     Kitazawa Center, Nagano Prefecture, Japan
     Japan Cultural Center, Rome
1963 Kitamura House, Kyoto
1964 Okazaki Tsuruya Hall, Kyoto
     Shigeru Yoshida House, Kanagawa Prefecture, Japan
1965 Matsuoka House, Kyoto
1965/
  73 Royal Hotel, Osaka
1966 Murakami Kaishin Hall, Tokyo
1967 Inomata House, Tokyo
1968 Narita-san Shinsho-ji Temple, Chiba Prefecture, Japan
     Chugu-ji Temple, Nara, Japan
1969 Sinsuke Kishi House, Shizuoka Prefecture, Japan
     Mangan-ji Temple, Tokyo
1970 Kitagawa Shop, Tokyo
     Matsushita Pavilion, *Expo '70,* Osaka
1971 Mikiya House, Tokyo
     Iikura Hall, Ministry of Foreign Affairs, Tokyo
1972 Prince Chichibu House, Tokyo
     Mitsukoshi Silver House, Tokyo

Publications:

On YOSHIDA: books—*Architect Isoya Yoshida's Work,* edited by Yoshida, Tokyo 1949; *Isoya Yoshida* (Modern Japanese Architects Series), edited by Kurita, Tokyo 1974; *Works of Isoya Yoshida* by Gakuji Yamamoto, Tokyo 1976; articles— "Bunrakuza Theatre" in *Kenchiku Bunka* (Tokyo), April 1956; "Restaurant à Osaka" in *L'Architecture d'Aujourd'hui* (Paris), May 1956; "Classic Modern Hall for the Academy of Arts" in *Shinkenchiku* (Tokyo), July 1958; "Académie d'Art Japonais, Tokio" in *L'Architecture d'Aujourd'hui* (Paris), April/May 1960; "A Profile of Isoya Yoshida" in *The Japan Architect* (Tokyo), January/February 1969; "A Tribute to the Memory of Isoya Yoshida" by Teijo Ito in *Architecture + Urbanism* (Tokyo), May 1974; "Renovation of the Bamboo Hall of the Restaurant Shinkiraku" by Motoyoshi Itagaki in *The Japan Architect* (Tokyo), January 1982; "Mikiya Residence" in *The Japan Architect* (Tokyo), October 1982.

Bibliography—*Isoya Yoshida: Modern/Traditional Architect of Japan* by James Philip Noffsinger, Monticello, Illinois 1980.

*

The reconciliation of tradition and modernity was a major theme for modern Japanese architecture. Isoya Yoshida, along with Tange and Kikutake, was one of the few architects to have succeeded in this task, and when one considers that he achieved it in the genre of wood structures, creating the so-called modern *sukiya* style and establishing it as a popular art, his achievement must be ranked at least the equal of Tange's.

Yoshida's work may be divided into that of three periods. The first period saw the pursuit, primarily in private houses and Japanese style restaurants, of a modernization of the *sukiya* and of the establishment of the modern *sukiya* style; the second (post-war) phase saw in public buildings, theaters and art museums the pursuit of a Japanese design in concrete; and the third phase (from the mid-1960s on) saw the formal search for a truly Japanese terminology purged of Chinese influences in religious architecture, a field that had been dominated by very strict stylistic rules.

These phases are distinctions that Yoshida himself once made with regard to his career, but common to these three periods is a search for Japanese spaces and Japanese architecture, and in this search he completely upset the traditional paradigm and its customary order and rules. His approach may be termed *contraventionalism,* and when furthermore one reflects on his love of technical invention, his progressivism and his confident self-advocacy, one may well consider him more akin to Le Corbusier than Le Corbusier's desciple, Mayekawa.

There are many reasons that account for the unique modernity of Yoshida's *sukiya* spaces, but the most striking is his overthrow of the modular systems of traditional wood architectural design. Yoshida introduced the okabe system, a method that hides structural columns inside the wall, into the *sukiya* style, and (disregarding the .9 m. × 1.8 m. module) placed wood pilasters "where [he] wanted to." He also tried such inventive techniques as removing the corner columns from wood structures to create corner windows and reversing the traditional chiaroscuro of Japanese spaces, making the ceiling, wall and floor in that order become darker by the use of artificial lighting. These, together with electrically operated partitions and *shoji* that slide completely into walls, might well have been inspired by the stage mechanisms and lighting effects of the traditional plays that he loved and was familiar with from youth.

In his second phase too he was a traditionalist who constantly rebelled against tradition, often using walls and pilasters and creating a style of flat roof with extremely thin edge. In his religious architecture, he developed a simple roof-supporting system that did away with the Chinese order *(tokyo)*. This spirit of rebellion—the rejection of models and in their stead the espousal of free creation and invention—is indeed true to the original spirit of *sukiya*, which was created in the middle of the sixteenth century as a style for the emergent bourgeois class, and it is because of this attitude that Yoshida's *sukiya* is truly modern, light and urbane, in contrast to the work of other modern practitioners of traditional wood architecture such as Horiguchi, Murano, Taniguchi and Tange. Yoshida alone spent his entire life removed from the fashion of European modernism or the International Style: his independence can be attributed to his birth and upbringing as a proud, Tokyo bourgeois, his deep confidence in and love of traditional bourgeois culture, and his urbane view of architecture as a background for this culture. This anti-modern modernism that Yoshida embraced lives on and contains within it an unlimited potential for the future.

—Katsuyoshi Arai

YOSIZAKA, Takamasa.

Japanese. Born in Tokyo, 13 February 1917. Educated at the Maison des Petits, Geneva, 1921-23; Ecole de l'Etoil du Matin, Tokyo, 1924-29; Ecole Internationale, Geneva, 1929-33; Waseda University, Tokyo, graduated 1941. Served in the Imperial Japanese Army, 1942-45. Married Hukuko Kono in 1945; children: Masakuni, Masamitu, and Feliza. In private practice, Tokyo, 1945 until his death in 1980; President, Atelier U, Tokyo, 1965-80. Worked in the studio of Le Corbusier, *q.v.*, Paris, 1950-52; Manager, Equatorial Africa Expedition, 1957-58; Leader, Mount McKinley Expedition, Alaska, 1960. Head of the Department of Architecture, Waseda University, Tokyo, 1964-66, and Sangyo Gizyutu Sensyu Gakko, Tokyo, 1964-69; Dean, School of Science and Engineering, Waseda University, 1969-72. President, Architectural Institute of Japan, 1973-74. Director, Metropolitan Planning Institute, Tokyo, 1974 until his death in 1980; President, Japan-China Architectural Technique Friendship Association, 1974-80, Institute of Living Studies, Tokyo, and Quantity Surveyors Institute, Tokyo, Exhibition: *Panoramiru*, Odakyu Hall, Tokyo, 1975. Recipient: First Prize, Ginza Leisure District Project, Tokyo, 1946; First Prize, Sibuya Leisure District Project, Tokyo, 1946; First Prize, *Bienal*, São Paulo, 1954, 1955, and 1957; Ministry of Education Prize, *Biennale*, Venice, 1957; Leopoldville Cultural Center Prize, Belgian Congo, 1959; Architectural Institute of Japan Award, 1963; Planning Institute of Japan Award, 1974. Member of the Légion d'Honneur, France. *Died (in Tokyo) 17 December 1980.*

Works:

1946 Ginza Shopping and Leisure District, Tokyo (project)
Sibuya Shopping and Leisure District, Tokyo (project)
1947 Waseda Educational/Cultural District, Tokyo (project)
1950 Imamura House, Tokyo
1953 Oikawa House, Tokyo
1955 Yosizaka House, Tokyo
Tiba Nissan Service Station, Iba, Japan
1956 Ura House, Tokyo
Japanese Pavilion, *Biennale*, Venice
1957 Masuda House, Tokyo
Sogo House, Tokyo
Kondo House, Tokyo
Maruyama House, Tokyo
1958 Meisei High School, Osaka

Kaisei High School, Nagasaki
1959 Karasawa Mountain Lodge, Kamikoti, Japan
Maison Franco-Japonaise, Tokyo
Nationa Museum of Western Art, Taito-ku, Tokyo (with Le Corbusier, Kunio Mayekawa, and Junzo Sakakura)
1960/
63 Kureha Middle School, Toyama, Japan
1961 Kurosawaike Mountain Lodge, Myoko, Japan
Oosaka Keiza Daigaku Ski Hut, Sirouma, Japan
City Hall, Gozu, Japan
1964 Takeda House, Tokyo
Tateyamaso Mountain Lodge, Midagahara, Japan
1965 Akabosi House, Kugenuma, Japan
Arukokai Ski Hut, Tadesina, Japan
Tenryu River Monument, Hamamatu, Japan
1965/
67 Redevelopment plan for Tokadanobaba, Japan
Daigaku Seminar Housing, Hatiozi, Tokyo
1966 Kurosawaike Mountain Lodge, II, Myoko, Japan
Takayama Rest House, Takayama, Japan
1966/
67 Oosima Pilot Plan, Motomati, Japan
1967 Higuti House, Tokyo
Matudo Minami Primary School, Tiba-ken, Japan
Oosima Daisan Middle School, Oosima, Tokyo
Oosima Daiiti Middle School, Oosima, Tokyo
Oosima Sasikizi Primary School, Oosima, Tokyo
Town Hall and Library, Oosima, Tokyo
Meika Building, Tokyo
1968 Nozawa Spa Lodge, Nozawa, Japan
Husaziiso Mountain Lodge, Tateyama, Japan
Karasawa Mountain Lodge II, Kamikoti, Japan
Space Museum, Ikomayama, Osaka
Development plan for Nagaone, Titibu, Japan
1969 Oono House, Tokyo
Gokurakuzaka Ski Hut, Bizyodaira, Japan
Seikatu Center, Seikatu, Japan
Development plan for Sagamiko, Japan
Redevelopment plan for the shopping quarter, Yamaga and Misumi, Japan
1970 Sin'ei Distribution Center, Tokyo
Printers and Food Manufacturers Collective Estate Development, Kagosima, Japan
1971 Izawa House, Tokyo
Yamada Bokuzyo Mountain Lodge, Naganoken, Japan
Kurobedaira Daikanho Mountain Lodge, Toyama-ken, Japan
Working Youth Athletic Center, Asikaka, Japan
Rural housing development, Hirayaga, Japan
Rural housing development, Kamo, Japan
1972 Iizuka House, Takata, Japan
Ootu House, Kasiwa, Japan
Kobayasi House, Matumoto, Japan
Working Women's House, Morioka, Japan
1973 Nisiyama House, Azumi, Japan
Youth Center Covered Pool, Morioka, Japan
Environment renewal plan for Ootamati, Japan
1974 Misawa House, Hayama, Japan
Environment renewal plan for Hiragatyo, Japan
1975 Sakurai High School Gate, Sakurai, Japan
Environment renewal plan for Hatinohe and Sannohe, Japan
1976 Kosizuka House, Tokyo
Horikawa House, Tokyo
Environment renewal plans for Inagawa and for Ninohe, Japan

1977 Metoki Rural Children's Park, Sannohe, Japan
Environment renewal plans for Daitotyo, Kanasago, and Dezima, Japan

Publications:

By YOSIZAKA: books—*Introduction to the Study of Dwellings*, Tokyo 1950; *Le Corbusier*, Tokyo 1953; *Environment and Form*, Tokyo 1955; *A House, A School*, Tokyo 1960; *From Primitive to Civilized*, Tokyo 1961; *Study of Dwelling*, Tokyo 1965; *GA 18: Le Corbusier—Chapelle Notre Dame du Haut*, edited by Yukio Futagawa, Tokyo 1971; *Directives*, Tokyo 1972; *Century 21 Japan*, with others, Tokyo 1972; *GA 18: Le Corbusier—L'Unité d'Habitation, Marseille*, edited by Yukio Futagawa, Tokyo 1972; *Moi, j'aime pas la mer*, Tokyo 1973; *the Sendai Plan*, with others, Tokyo 1973; *GA 30: Corbusier—Chandigarh*, edited by Yukio Futagawa, Tokyo 1974; *World Architecture*, Tokyo 1976; *Proposition for a Re-Arrangement of Quarters*, with others, Tokyo 1976; *Korean Rural Agglomerations*, with others, Tokyo 1976; *Korean Rural Agglomerations*, with others Tokyo, 1976; translations into Japanese—*Le Modulor* by Le Corbusier, Tokyo 1952; *Le Modulor II* by Le Corbusier, Tokyo 1959; *Silent Cities* by Norman Carver, Tokyo 1966; *Vers une architecture* by Le Corbusier, Tokyo 1976; *Le Corbusier: oeuvres completes*, 8 volumes, Tokyo 1971-78; *Erreurs monumentales* by Michel Ragon, Tokyo 1972; *Le Charte d'Athene* by Le Corbusier, Tokyo 1976; *Le Modulor I and II* by Le Corbusier, revised edition, Tokyo 1976.

On YOSIZAKA: book—*Contemporary Japanese Architects: Takamasa Yosizaka*, Tokyo 1971; articles—in *Kentiku* (Tokyo), May 1961, January 1966, January 1971; *Tosi Zyutaku* (Tokyo), August 1975.

*

What is an architect? It seems that I have been reckoned as an architect, so what I have been doing must be what an architect does. But as for art, a painter or a sculptor will do better; as for enterprise, a business will do better, a politician will do better; as for technique, an engineer will do better; as for workmanship, a craftsman will do better; and as for life, a housewife will do better. Nevertheless, an architect dreams— to build a beautiful house, to build a lively city, a build a prosperous nation, yes, and to build world peace, wielding only the power dictated by the value of his own conscience, believing that it may be the omnipotent key to solve any problem.

People's concern can be classified into five grades: first, the world within and the one immediately in touch with his body; then the world encircling him and useful to him; and the wider world supporting the favorable conditions to realize the above items; further out, there must be a world swarming with disturbing forces which infiltrate everywhere—do we have to conquer this world too? And there is an even bigger world included in the universe which we can only imagine intellectually. Greedily, an architect acts, dealing with this greatest world, wishing to relate it to the first-mentioned world.

Result: the task seems to be beyond his power, but he struggles brandishing a theory named "Discontinuous Unity," and inventing a tool named "Method Through Discovery," trying to bring all the five worlds into a consistent whole and to express them coherently.

"Discontinuous Unity," because the contemporary world drives towards individual respect on one hand and at the same time towards the promotion of group consciousness, the former tending towards diversity and chaos, the latter searching for a discipline of unity yielding to coercion. This contradiction must be solved in plan, section, and

Takamasa Yosizaka: Maison Franco-Japonaise, Tokyo, 1959.

form. Even floors, walls, ceilings, windows, doors, and other elements—as well as building materials and building equipment produced in industry with precision—became independent and need to be gathered together to form one house. It is through finding a construction method that design can be enhanced to its philosophic and aesthetic value. The clue to the solution can only be reached by "discovering" the fundamental problem through the conditions in each case, on each occasion. Capable of becoming the finding of solutions for other's problems, it is a fascinating play worth risking one's life.

—Takamasa Yosizaka (1980)

Takamasa Yosizaka, one of the pioneers of modern architecture in Japan, spent many years in Europe, both as a student and as an employee of Le Corbusier's atelier. Like his compatriots Junzo Sakakura and Kunio Mayekawa, Yosizaka emerged from the experience of working with Le Corbusier deeply colored; his earliest work in Japan greatly recalled the material, formal, and compositional sense of Corbu in the mid-1950s.

Yosizaka's own house (1955), for example, used a visible structural system of concrete posts and slabs, infilled with block much like at Maisons Jaoul. His container and platform system is much like that of the famous Domino House scheme, and, physically,

the Yosizaka residence resembles Corbusier's early, purist, Citrohan house. The Japan Pavilion at the Venice *Biennale*, designed by Yosizaka in 1956, employs a similar structural frame, but the encasing envelope is less disrupted, and the result is much akin to the Tokyo Museum of Western Art, designed by Corbusier's office with project supervision by Yosizaka, Sakakura, and Mayekawa.

In time, though, Yosizaka's designs moved away from heavy *beton brut* and other formal explorations that resembled Corbusier. The Gozu City Hall of 1961 must be considered a key work in this regard. Although still constructivist, the building celebrates technology whimsically. A huge office block is thrown into the air, supported by concrete trellises that look like the structural support for a huge bridge, which is, in fact, what the building has become.

The Maison Franco-Francaise, of the same period, demonstrates Yosizaka's growing consciousness of context. It is a very sculptural building finished in a rich, deep red. The front has been masked by a screen studded with Roman letters, however, to confirm the bland massing of many of the simpler buildings in urban Japan.

As his concern for adequate contextual response grew, Yosizaka recieved several planning commissions. In the mid-1960s, in his redevelopment plans for Oosima, Motomati, and Tokadanobaba, he explored three-deimensional public spaces and natural, flexible planning within a structured

approach. His Daigaku Seminary Housing at Hatiozi, Tokyo, displays the same ideas, but at a more refined level and a smaller scale. The housing units are simple, repeated elements that descend down the slope of the site, but the total plan is dominated by several singular elements. The Headquarters and Main Seminar House tower above the residence blocks like Arabesque minarets or medieval campaniles. They unify the design by offering common, identifiable monuments that have come to characterize the complex.

The combination of many units arranged randomly, with a strong, unifying formal element, reflects Yosizaka's important notion of "Discontinuous Unity." There are many different values of philosophy that must all be expressed in architecture, he claims. While his buildings often suggest this diversity, he also tries to create a "natural understanding that may contribute to peace." He accomplishes this by unification and clarification, by joining complexity with simplicity.

Yosizaka was a higly intelligent designer with a strong background in both Western and Japanese design approach. He melded these by incorporating in design his understanding of contextual and human concerns, as well as abstract form. His career was one of transformation, but was consistently characterized by the inclusion of many different ideas, without compromised integrity.

—Ching-Yu Chang

ZABLOCKI, Wojciech.

Polish. Born in Warsaw, 6 December 1930. Educated at the School of Architecture, Cracow, 1949-54, M.A. 1954; Warsaw School of Architecture, Ph.D. 1968. Married Alina Janowska in 1963; children: Marcin, Michal, and Katarzyna. Since 1955, in private practice, Warsaw; has also worked in the State Design Office, Cracow, since 1955. Co-Editor, *Architektura*, Warsaw, 1967-71. Former fencing champion: four times World Fencing Champion, and five times Polish Champion; Member of the Polish Olympic Team in sabre fencing, 1949-65: twice placed second in Olympic Fencing Events. Member, Polish Olympic Committee, 1965-72; Vice-President, Polish Fencing Association, 1968-72. Vice-President, Polish Branch, Sport and Recreation Section, International Union of Architects, since 1970. Exhibitions: *Constructions*, Warsaw, 1969; *Buildings*, Projects and Ideas, Vienna, and Warsaw, 1982; *Old Aleppo and Countryside*, Aleppo and Damascus, Syria, and Warsaw, 1983; *Architecture and Landscape of the Syrian Coast*, Aleppo, Syria, 1984. Collection: Museum of Architecture, Wroclaw. Recipient: Polonia Restituta Honorary State Award, 1960; Ministry of Building Award, 1964, 1972, and 1975; Ministry of Culture Award, 1968; Polish Olympic Committee Award, 1981. Address (office): ul. Kaniowska 21B, 01-529 Warsaw, Poland.

Works:

1958 Cement Works, Chelm, Poland
1959 Gypsum Factory, Dolina Nidy, Poland
1962 Olympic Training Centre, Warsaw
1964 Covered Ice Rink, Gdansk, Poland (competition project; with M. Wróbel, W. Szymán-ski, and Zórawski)
1965 Westerplatte Monument, Gdansk, Poland (competition project; with the sculptor G. Zemla)
     Poznan Museum (competition project)
1966 Monument to the Silesian Uprising, Katowice, Poland (with the sculptor G. Zemla)
1970 Municipal Hall, Lublin, Poland (project; with S. Kuś)
     Sports Centre, Nowa Ruda, Poland (project; with W. Humiecki)
1972 Sports Centre, Konin, Poland (with L. Sz-wedowski)
     Catholic Church, Konin, Poland (project; with S. Kuś)
1973 Sports Hall, Bydgoszcz, Poland (competition project; with W. Humiecki)
     Sports Centre, Glasgów, Poland (project; with S. Kuś)
     Covered Ice Rink, Glogów, Poland (project; with S. Kuś)

Covered Ice Rink, Toruń, Poland (project; with W. Humiecki)
     Cepelia Tower House, Warsaw (project; with W. Humiecki)
1974 Sports Centre, Pulawy, Poland (with S. Kuś)
     Sports Hall, Tarnobrzeg, Poland (project; with J. Bodasiński)
     Sports Centre, Kielce, Poland (competition project; with J. Bodansiński)
     Training Centre, Bydgoszcz, Poland (project; with W. Humiecki)
     Sports Centre, Warsaw (with S. Kuś and R. Wilczynski)
1975 Sports Centre, Tomaszów Maz., Poland (project; with W. Humiecki)
     War Memorial, Tomaszów Maz., Poland (project)
     Twin Atrium House, Warsaw
     Sports Hall, Grudziadz, Poland (with J. Bod-asiński)
     Sports Hall, Warsaw (competition project; with J. Bodasiński and S. Kus)
1975- Sports Centre, Zgorzelec, Poland (with S. Kuś)
     Sports and Recreation Park, Tarnobrzeg, Poland
1976 War Memorial, near Kolobrzeg, Poland (project; with the sculptor Pastwa)
     Olympic Sports Centre, Poznan (competition project; with J. Bodasiński)
     Sports Hall, Kielce, Poland (project; with M. Dziurla)
     Elana Sports Hall, Toruń, Poland (project; with T. Spanili)
1976- Sports Park, Kielce, Poland (with J. Bodasin-ski ánd M. Dziurl)
1977 Sports Centre, Leszno, Poland (project; with J. Golebiowski)
     Swimming Pool, Ciechanów, Poland (project; with S. Kuś)
     Small Sports Hall (project; with S. Kuś)
1977- Sports hall, Leszno, Poland (with NOWAK and R. Czyzak)
1978 Slowacki Monument, Warsaw (project; with the sculptor E. Wittig)
1978- Covered Ice Rink, Siedlce, Poland (with W. Humiecki)
     Terrace House, Warsaw (project)
     Tower House "Polam," Warsaw (project; with A. Derentowicz)
1979 Polam Lamp Factory, Warsaw (project; with A. Szulc)
1980 Tennis Hall, Warsaw
     Sports Hall, Gorlice, Poland (with A. Szulc)
1981 Residential Building Warsaw (with D. Rz-ewuska)
     Polonez Sports Hall, Warsaw (project; with A. Szulc)
1982 Sports Centre, Aleppo, Syria (with Fauzi

Khalifa, and Milihouse + Polservice Team)
1983 Centre for the Mediterranean Games of 1987, Latakia, Syria (with Milihouse + Polservice Team)
     Khan Assad Paša Building reconstruction, Damascus, Syria (project)
1984 Tent Villa, Damascus, Syria
     Shell Villa, Damascus, Syria
     Sports Hall, Glogow, Poland (project)
     Sport City Hotel, Latakia, Syria (project)

Publications:

By ZABLOCKI: books—*Z Workiem Szermierc-zym po Swiecie* (with Fencing Bag Around the World), Warsaw 1962; *Podroze z Szabla* (Travelling with Sabre), Warsaw 1965; *Czynny Wypoczynek w Zakladzie Pracy* (Recreation in Factories), Warsaw 1966; *Architecture for Active Recreation in Towns*, Warsaw 1978; *Szabla i piórkiem* (with Sabre and Pencil), Warsaw 1982; *Ciecia prawdziwa szabla* (Cuts with War Sabre), Warsaw 1984; articles—"Architektura i Konstrukcja Hali Sportowej Yo Yogi: Kenzo Tange" in *Inzynieria i Budownictwo* (Warsaw), no. 10, 1965; "Architektura Olimpijska" in *Dyst Olimpijski*, Warsaw 1966; "Architektura Obiektów Sportowych" in *Dysk Olimpijski*, Warsaw 1967; "Sport Centrum in Warschau" in *Bauen und Wohnen* (Zürich), no. 7, 1967; "Monument des Insurges Silesiens" in *Architecture d'aujourd'hui* (Paris), no. 9, 1967; "Tworczośćczy Produkcja?" in *Architektura* (Warsaw), no. 133, 1967; "Wladyslaw Hasior: Nowe Relacje" in *Architektura* (Warsaw), no. 410, 1967; "Stalowe Konstrukcje Jerzego Jar-nuszkiewicza" in *Architektura* (Warsaw), no. 498, 1967; "Sport we Wspolczesnym Spoleczenstwie" in *Architektura* (Warsaw), no. 213, 1968; "Ogrody Japońskie" in *Architektura* (Warsaw), no. 9, 1969; "Magiczne Kolo Polskiej Architektury" in *Architektura* (Warsaw), no. 2/3, 1969; "Denkmal der Schlesischen Aufstande" in *Deutsche Architektur* (East Berlin), no. 6, 1970; "Sportzentrum Konin" in *Sport und Baderbauten* (Düsseldorf), no.;1, 1972: "Sport Approaches Nature" in *Poland* (Warsaw), no. 3, 1972; "O Architekturze lgrzysk Olimpijskich w Monachium" in *Architektura* (Warsaw), no. 5/6, 1972; "Sala Gier w Warszawie" in *Architektura* (Warsaw), no. 12, 1972; "Salle sportive polyvalante à Bydgoszcz" in *Architecture d'aujourd'hui* (Paris), no. 11/12, 1973; "Hallen Sportzentrum in Pulawy" in *Sportstattenbau und Bäderanlogen* (Cologne), no. 4, 1975; "Centre Sportif, Konin, Pologne" in *Architecture Contemporaine* (Lausanne, Switzerland), 1979-80; "Tennis Hall, Warsaw, Poland", in *Architecture contemporaine* (Lausanne, Switzerland), 1981-82.

On ZABLOCKI: books—*Elspresja Sil w Architek-*

Wojciech Zablocki: Sports Centre, Warsaw, 1974.

turze Wspolczesnej (Expression of Forces in Contemporary Architecture) by J. Slawinska, Warsaw 1970: *New Polish Architecture* by P. Szafer, Warsaw 1973; *Atlas of Warsaw Architecture* by J. Chroscicki and A. Rottermund, Warsaw 1977; *Nowa architektura polska, diariusz lat 1971-75* (New Polish Architecture, 1971-75) by T. P. Szafer, Warsaw 1977; *Nowa architektura polska, diariusz lat 1975-80* (New Polish Architecture, 1975-80) by T. P. Szafer, Warsaw 1981; article—"New Sports Architecture of W. Zablocki" by A. Glinski and Bruszewski in *Architektura* (Warsaw), no. 12, 1975.

My personal attitude to architecture is the result of my identification with the user, especially as far as the "perception" of the architectural form created by myself is concerned. That means I try to design such architecture which will please me—an imagined user—instead of trying to affect any specific user.

My lack of interest in getting into the client's favours results in a particular psycho-sociological marketing to find the client's taste being substituted by the principle *cognosce te ipsum*, and more or less precise indentification with the imagined users. Such an attitude permits a very personal relation with any contemporary fashion or architectural style and enables me to act according to the principle "end justifies means." I suspect many architects share my point of view but not all of them will admit it, out of authentic or excessive modesty.

I must confess that my ideas do not come to me out of themselves. Thrown on my own resources, I arduously and consciously search for them in different categories of reality: in the organic world of animals, shells, crystals, sculpture, and in the historic architecture of various nations, particularly my beloved Polish timber architecture. I often attempt consciously to design my architectural forms to look similar to those which impressed me strongly in the past. These reminiscences are sometimes close, sometimes remote, and at times traceable only to myself.

In spite of several changes in my architectural "style," some elements have remained constant. I simply cannot get away from them. My inclination towards monumentalism is one of these conditionings. This disposition prevents me from designing small, scattered forms related to the terrain. The other is the tendency towards constructivism—the use of static characteristics of a building and treating the construction details sculpturally.

Working in a uniformity of convention tires me and makes me fear the repetition of my own concepts. Therefore, from time to time, I try to change the way of designing the forms or choose different materials and construction methods—even if the first attempts in this "new style" are not so satisfying as the fully-elaborated and tested methods. This is one of the reasons for my change of cultural scene three years ago. My latest designs and realizations are being created in Syria. The necessity of adjusting to a different climate and a rich tradition of architectural forms—nomads' tents, Byzantine and Crusader architecture, and magnificent Islamic buildings—allowed me to start the search for new forms which influence my designs in Poland.

—Wojciech Zablocki

How the architect's mentality and personality are expressed and how his individual mark is made on the designed object are concerns in the work and design approach of Wojciech Zablocki. He belongs to the postwar generation of Polish architects, and for the past twenty-five years his work has been very specific, individual, and controversial. Zablocki attempts to integrate the dynamics of structural form with an architecture that aims at the expressive synthesis of new technical possibilities.

He was an active sportsman for many years and an Olympic champion. He is interested in the psychology of sports and recreation and, indeed, has been responsible for most of the new sports halls and centres in Poland. His personal experience has influenced his views on how space for sports and recreation should be organized. Any sport requires concentration. Also, the technical infrastructure is important, as is easy access to other related sporting activities.

Starting with these assumptions, Zablocki concentrates his interest on the most rational plan for a multi-functional interior. He treats the exterior as a shell requiring large-scale roof profiles; he believes that the exterior must take into account both practical and symbolic functions. A crucial role is played by the form of the architectural-structural solution adopted.

Zablocki is often accused of creating buildings that have "formalistic tendencies" and criticized for not paying sufficient attention to context, the landscape, or neighbouring buildings. He accepts these criticisms but remarks at the same time that "the search for future and new architectural, structural and urbanistic solutions is no longer popular today, the reason lying in the crisis of mostly stereotyped and monotonous modern architecture, which has caused people to become interested in the past." He empohasizes that all the visions of romantic utopias, whatever their appeal, were not able to stop the process of civilization, demographic growth, and the development of new technologies.

Zablock's ideology is close to that of Frei Otto and to the expressionist tendencies of the work of Kenzo Tange and Saarinen. He admits, too, that he often surrenders to an inspiration emerging from a fascination with organic structures.

In 1962, for the Olympic Training Centre in Warsaw, Zablocki conceived of a form of several small pavilions with roof structures hanging on cables, reminiscent of hammocks, sails, or tents stretched between trees. This impression is further intensified by the separation of the suspended form of the roof structure from the horizontal brick podium wall by a band of glazing. After a period of applying suspended roof structures of cable or mixed arch-cable design to many buildings and projects, until repetition of the same structural principle had resulted in its perfection, Zablocki moved away from this concept and explored the possibilities of new forms of expression in frame structures and space-frames. His most recent works are an amalgam of previous experience—hanging structures complented by frame structures.

A preoccupation with the problems of roof structures for large, multi-function sports halls and a search for the expression of logic and beauty in their construction are the dominant traits of Zablocki's work. Accusations that this kind of architecture does not fit many situations and perhaps creates universal but unrelated buildings does not worry him. The descriptions that he uses— hammocks, sails, Concorde, bird, butterfly—convey taking off, hovering, flying, and these metaphors suggest perfectly the dynamic character of his architecture. He is unusually consistent in his design approach, does not stand for any compromise solutions, stakes everything on the "natural" beauty of structure and the dynamics of shape, and creates his buildings not for the grey, universal mass but for individuals of a strong and dynamic temperament— very much like his own.

—Teresa Czaplinska-Archer

ZABLUDOVSKY, Abraham.

Mexican. Born in Bialostock, Poland, 14 July 1924; emigrated to Mexico, 1927: naturalized, 1941. Educated at the Universidad Nacional Autonoma, Mexico City, in the National Preparatory School, 1941-42, and the National School of Architecture, 1943-49, Dip.Arch. 1949. Married Alinka Kuper in 1953; children: Gina, Jaime, and Moisés. In private practice, Mexico City, since 1949: in partnership with Teodoro González de León, q.v., since 1968. Director, INURBA S.A., Mexico City, since 1973; Advisor to the Director, CODEUR, Mexico City, since 1978. Teacher of Composition, 1965-67, and currently Lecturer and Advisor, Universidad Nacional Autonoma, Mexico City. Currently, Lecturer and Advisor to the Museum of Modern Art, Mexico City. Exhibitions: *XX Centuries of Mexican Architecture*, El Colegio de México, Mexico City, 1965, and toured Mexico; Colegio Nacional de Arquitectos, Mexico City, 1969; *Arquitectura Contemporánea Mexicana*, Galeria Misrachi, Mexico City, 1969; *The Photography of Architecture and Design*, Los Angeles, 1977; *Mexican Architecture*, Mexico City, 1978; *Transformations in Modern Architecture*, Museum of Modern Art, New York, 1979; *Modern Architecture: Mexico*, SCI-ARC Architecture Gallery, Los Angeles, 1981; *Latinamerica 82*, West Berlin, 1982; *Contemporary Third World Architecture*, Pratt Manhattan Center

Gallery, New York, 1983 (toured the United States). Recipient: First Prize, with Teodoro González de León, El Colegio de México Competition, Mexican City, 1973; Premio Nacional de Ciencia y Arts (with Teodoro Gonzalez de Leon), Mexico City, 1982. Honorary Fellow, American Institute of Architects, 1982. Address: Avenida Mexico 99 B, 06100 Mexico, D.F., Mexico.

Works:

1958 House Paseo de las Palmas 1210, Mexico City
     House, Paseo de las Palmas 635, Mexico City
1962 Housing development, Satélite, Mexico
1965 Apartment building, Schiller Street, Mexico City
     Apartment building, Av. Cumbres de Acultzingo 12 and 20, Mexico City
1966 House, Moraván 180, Mexico City
1967 House, Sierra de la Breña 84, Mexico City
1971 House, Palacio de Versalles 235, Mexico City
1979 Condominium Apartments Building, Edgar Allan Poe Street 28, Mexico City
     City Theatre, Tuxtla Gutierrez, Chiapas, Mexico
1980 Tourist Centre, La Costa Can Cun, Mexico (project)
     Multibanco Mercantil de Mexico Headquarters, Montes Uralas 620, Mexico City
     Condominium Apartment Buildings, Cumbres de Acutzingo Street 26, Mexico City
1984 San Pedro Plaza Shopping Center, San Antonio, Texas (project)
     City Theatre, Aguascalientes, Mexico (project)

With Teodoro González de León:
1963/
  77 Eight planning surveys for various Mexican cities
1968 José Luis Cuevas House, Galeana 109, Mexico City
1969/
  70 Office building, Nuevo León and Campeche, Mexico City
     Office building, Campos Eliseos 169, Mexico City
     Office building, Presidente Masarik 191, Mexico City
1969/
  71 Mixcoac Towers, Mixcoac-Lomas de Plateros, Mexico City
1970/
  73 Vallejo-La Patera (1418 apartments), Avenida Vallejo/Torres/de los Cien Metros/ Margarita M. de Juárez, Mexico City (with Armando Franco)
1971 Two Apartment buildings, Avenida de las Fuentes and Fuente de la Templanza, Tecamachalco, Mexico City
1972 Two Apartment buildings, Victoria 34, Echegarary, Mexico
     Sports and Civic Center (public square movie theatre; library; club; gymnasium; swimming pool; etc.), Sor Juan Inés de la Cruz 45, Tlalnepantla, Mexico
1972/
  73 Cuahtémoc District Municipal Building, Mexico City (with Luis Antonio Zapiain and Jaime Ortiz Monasterio)
     Two Apartment buildings, Fuente de las Pirámides 20 and 22, Tecamachalco, Mexico City (with Rosemberg)
1973 Conasupo Branch Stores, throughout Mexico
     INFONAVIT Building (administrative offices for workers' housing development), Mexico City
1973/
  75 Mexican Embassy, Brasilia (with J. Francisco Serrano)

1974/
  75 El Colegio de México (library; seminar rooms; computer center; offices; auditorium; cafeteria; parking), Mexico City
     Twenty-Five-story apartment building, Tecamachalco, Mexico City
     Rufino Tamayo Museum, Oaxaca, Mexico (project)
1979 National Pedagogical University, Mexico City
1981 Tamayo Museum Complex, Chapultepec Park, Mexico City
1982 Office Tower Block, Avenida Palmas, Mexico City
1984 Cultural and Services Building, Chichen-Itza, Yucatan, Mexico

Publications:

By ZABLUDOVSKY: published lectures—*Las ciudades, el hombre, el artista*, Mexico City 1974; *La Arquitectura y las Artes Visuales*, Mexico City 1975; *Arquitectura Contemporánea Israelí*, Mexico City 1976; *Importancia y Significado de la Bauhaus*, Mexico City 1976; *Kibbutz-Bauhaus*, Mexico City 1979.

On ZABLUDOVSKY/GONZÁLEZ DE LEÓN: books—*Arquitectura Contemporánea Mexicana*, exhibition catalogue, Mexico City 1969; *Ocho Conjuntos de Habitacion*, Mexico City 1976; *Ten Mexican Architects* by Alfonso de Neuvillate, Mexico City 1977; *The Photography of Architecture and Design* by Julius Shulman, New York 1977; *Mexican Architecture: The Work of Abraham Zabludovsky and Teodoro González de León* by Paul Heyer, New York 1978; articles—"Immeuble d'habitation à Mexico" in *L'Architecture d'Aujourd'hui* (Paris), September 1963; "Mexico City Office Building" in *American Concrete Institute Journal* (Detroit), May 1976; "Contrapuntal Buildings" by Felix Sanchez in *Arquitectura* (Mexico City), November/December 1976; "An Arresting View to the South" in *Architectural Record* (New York), October 1977; "Mexican Embassy, Brasilia" by G. Cataldi in *Industria delle Costruzioni* (Rome), April 1978; "Colegio de México" by G. Cataldi in *Industria delle Costruzioni* (Rome), May 1978; "College for Post-Graduate Research" in *Architettura* (Rome), January 1979; "Works of the Architects González de León and Zabludovsky" in *Summarios* (Buenos Aires), January 1980; "The Colegio de Mexico" in *Casabella* (Milan), July/August 1980; "The Tamayo Museum" in *Arquitectura Mexico* (Mexico City), July/ August 1981; "Colegio de Mexico in Mexico City" in *Baumeister* (Munich), August 1981; "The Tamayo Museum" in *Architectural Record* (New York), September 1981; "Contemporary Art Museum in Mexico City" in *Techniques et Architecture* (Paris), April/May 1982; "The Rufino Tamayo Museum in Mexico City" in *Industria delle Costruzioni* (Rome), June 1982; "Modern Mexican Architecture", special issue of *Process: Architecture* (Tokyo), July 1983.

Architecture is an activity devoted to confining a space that man uses for some purpose. In fulfilling this function, it is materialized into an object that is, by its nature, plastic volume.

Such a volume is an invention that, like all inventions, is based on influences, on existing forms; it springs from its predecessors, from needs.

Sullivan used to say that in the problem lies the solution. The architect's method is the precise conjoining of unknowns to organize space. The first stage in the functional scheme is to delve into the problem, the site, the micro-climate, the psychological and economic context. This is the program. Taking the program as his starting-point, the architect determines the number and size of the spaces, their dimensions and their reciprocal relationships. This, rather than any other point, is where the contemporary architect begins. But the method of creation ends up by being a unitary creative process in which each step arises from the one which precedes it and, at the same time, receives feedback from the one which follows. Everything has its explanation and its own justification. And yet no method automatically leads to a solution. The architect's task is a creative one, and though the form of the object is determined by reference to probable concrete data and to its function, the design process means that different types of influence operate on different individuals.

While it may be true that the solution lies within the problem, it would be simplistic to apply the norm that form follows function. The aim of research into the conditioning factors of a project is not to find the greatest number of relationships between them, but rather the basic ones, the marrow of the problem, and through these to imagine the synthetic spatial relationship. That is, the synthesis of the problem and its basic space must be found first, and into these what is secondary—the vast majority of marginal elements—is easily adapted: the synthesis of the problem lies in the form adopted.

—Abraham Zabludovsky

The work of Abraham Zabludovsky and Teodoro González de León has been one of maturity in linear evolution. Their work is a direct confrontation with the facts of architecture, towards conclusions that are increasingly sophisticated and more sensitized as design responses within the specificity of a building's context, both environmental and cultural. Pedro Ramirez Vazquez, Minister of Human Settlements and Public Works in the José Lopez Portillo government, identified González de León and Zabludovsky as Mexico's new generation of architects. He sees their work as truly contemporary because it ignores none of the technical innovations of our time and because it utilizes the available construction systems and materials to the maximum of their potential.

Both men were strongly influenced by Le-Corbusier, and González de León spent two years in his atelier. In their work in Mexico, however, perfomed both singularly and in association, Zabludovsky and González de León have included many more diverse sources, and their response has grown and changed considerably. Their work is plastic, express structure coherently and constantly, and has often used color in a boldly imaginative way. Their work is not an isolated effort, and it explores many conclusions germane to the seminal ideas of the Modern Movement, but in general theirs is an architecture that is more than the sum of European and United States influences. It is not conditioned by any rationalist or singular idea, bt rather it develops from experience. One senses that they see modern architecture as the manifestation of a new and progressive social order rather than of any disciplining ideology.

Zabludovsky and González de León make pragmatic use of simple, available means and their work looks beyond the functionalist premise for a synthesis that includes a form-idea relative to all the functions, the general urban and local conditions, materials and their maintenance, and all pertinent economic factors. They, like many counterparts around the world, find architecture anything but the easy "form follows function" notion; they are more dependent for their inspiration on the main idea that comes from a broader synthesis. This is seen in several of their public projects of recent years, as well as in the consistent development and refinement of their ideas.

Their Colegio de México (1975) is one of their strongest designs, and evokes recollections of convents and monasteries of sixteenth century Mexico as well as the theme idea of building related to patio. The building is accomplished in an unequivocally twentieth century expression. It is not the conscious incorporation or copying of elements and forms from the past but the spirit of the past—the durable values—that the designers seek to respect and capture in a language relevant to their time. The Colegio does not dwell in a wishful land of nostalgia. It deals with reason confirmed by substance and moved by passion.

Abraham Zabludovsky and Teodoro González de León: El Colegio de Mexico, Mexico City, 1975.

From the early days of usually solid and wellmannered responses to building problems, Zabludovsky and González de León have emerged to a new, invigorated awareness of the design challenge. "There are no twelve year old geniuses in architecture," remarked Le Corbusier. Architecture is a field for irrepressible optimism and it demands a tenacious staying power. González de León and Zabludovsky, as individuals and a collaboration, are filled with both. For them, the Colegio appears as both an end and a beginning, the conclusion of the first half of their careers and the promise of a future that lies ahead. The seeds are sown, and if the fruits are equal to the promise, the architecture of the Americas can only be richer.

—Paul Heyer

ZANUSO, Marco.

Italian. Born in Milan, 14 May 1916. Studied at the Faculty of Architecture, Polytechnic of Milan, 1935-39, Dip.Arch. 1939. Served in the Italian Navy, 1940-45: Lieutenant; Military Cross of Valour. Married Marialisa Pedroni in 1944; daughters: Federica, Lorenza and Susanna. Since 1945, in private practice as architect and industrial designer, Milan. Director, *Domus* magazine, Milan,1947-49; Editor, *Casabella* magazine, Milan, 1952-54. Professor Extraordinary of Industrial Design, 1965-76, Professor of the Development of Materials, 1966-68, Professor of Industrial Design from 1976, Member of the Athens Commission, 1980-82, President of the Department of Planning and Production from 1981, and President of the Council of Address from 1982, Faculty of Architecture, Polytechnic of Milan. City Councillor, 1956-60, Member of the Building Commission, 1961-63, 1967-69, and Member of the City Planning Commission, 1961, Milan; Member of CIAM: Congres Internationaux d'Architecture Moderne, from 1956; President, Associazione Disegno Industriale (ADI), Milan, 1957-58, 1958-59, 1966-74; Administration Council Member, *Triennale*, Milan from 1977; Regional Councillor, IN/ARCH Architectural Commission, Milan, from 1977. Exhibitions: *Marco Zanuso*, at the Festival of Two Worlds, Spoleto, Italy, 1967; *Le Design Francais*, Centre de Creation Industrielle, Paris, 1971; *Italy: The New Domestic Landscape*, Museum of Modern Art, New York, 1972; *Design and design*, Palazzo delle Stelline, Milan, and Palazzo Grassi, Venice, 1979; *Design Since 1945*, Philadelphia Museum of Art, 1983; *Marco Zanuso*, Galeria B. D. Ediciones de Diseno, Barcelona and Madrid, 1983; *Deus ex Machina*, Parma, Italy, 1984. Collections: Museum of Modern Art, New York; Philadelphia Museum of Art. Recipient: Grand Prize and Gold Medal, 1948, 1951, 1954, 1964, Gold Medal, 1957, and Silver Medal, 1960, *Triennale*, Milan; Compasso d'Oro award, Milan, 1956, 1962, 1964, 1967, 1979; Silver Medal, Villa Olmo exhibition, Como, Italy, 1957; Gold Seal, *La Casa Abitata* exhibition, Florence, Italy, 1965; Interplas Award, London, 1965; Two Gold Medals and Honour Award, Biennale of Industrial Design, Liubliana, Yugoslavia, 1966; Gold Medal, Colloquio Internazionale d'Estetica Sperimentale, Rimini, Italy, 1966; Gold Medal, International Design Congress, Yverdon, Switzerland, 1969; SAIE Prize, Associazione Italiana per Edilizia Industrializzata, 1971; Bolaffi Prize, Turin, 1972; Medal of the Comune of Milan, 1984; President of the Republic's Medal, Italy, 1984. Address: Via Laveno 6, 20148 Milan, Italy.

Works:

1952 Filiale Linoleum Shop, Milan

Two-Family House at QT8, Milan (with R. Menghi)
1953 Office Building, Milan (with R. Menghi)
1954/
55 Nursery and Maternity Home, Lorenteggio, Milan
City Villa, Via Monterosa/Via Settiniano, Milan
1955/
57 Olivetti Headquarters, Buenos Aires, Argentina
Olivetti Headquarters, Sao Paulo, Brazil
1956 Ceramics Factory and Staff Housing, Palermo, Sicily
1957 Bachelor Apartment, Milan
1958 Necchi Offices, Pavia, Italy
Hotel Punta San Marino, Arenzano, Genoa, Italy (with I. Gardella and G. Venezioani)
1959 Kindergarten, Gubbio, Italy
Case Rosse houses, Capo San Martino, Arenzano Pineta, Italy
1960/
63 FEAL Housing, Milan
1962 Hotel, Porto Conte, Sardinia (project; with F. Clerici and A. Simon)
Vacation House I, Arzachena, Sardinia
1963/
64 Vacation House II, Arzachena, Sardinia
1965 Housing Block in the Via Laveno, Milan
1967 Brinnell Factory, Casella d'Asolo, Treviso, Italy
1968/
70 Olivetti Headquarters, Crema Scarmagno, Italy
Olivetti Headquarters, Marcianise, Italy
1970/
72 Edgars Ltd. Headquarters, Johannesburg, South Africa
1972 Grado Conference Centre, Venezia Giulia, Venice
1974 Longarone Cemetery, Belluno, Veneto, Italy (with G. Avon and F. Tentori)
1974/
77 IBM Italia Factory, Segrate, Milan
1977 Vacation House, Lake Como, Italy
1978 Press House, Lydenburg, South Africa
1979 Teatro Fossati renovations, Milan
1979/
82 IBM Italia Factory, Palomba, Rome
1979- New Building for the Piccolo Teatro, Milan
1980 Albergo Continental bank, shop and residential conversion, Milan (project)
1981 Palazzo delle Notarie Buildings renovations, Reggio Emilia, Italy (project)

Zanuso's industrial designs include furniture for: Moretti e Bianchi, 1949, Arflex, 1951-78, Cedit, 1955, 1968, Gavina, 1959, Palini, 1960, Bonacina, 1961, Techniform, 1962-64, Kartell, 1963-64, 1972, C & B, 1967, Brionvega, 1969-70, Lumenform, 1969, Elam, 1969-70, Zanotta, 1969-71, 1978, Mim Mobili, 1970, Anic, 1972, Lanerossi, 1972, Fiat, 1972, Boffi, 1972, Steiner, 1973, Poggi, 1975-79, and Poltrona Frau, 1982; products for: Borletti, 1956, Homelight, 1956-59, Girmi/Subalpina, 1958, Brionvega, 1961-77, Auso/Siemens, 1964-66, Necchi, 1964, 1972, Terraillon, 1969-70, Aurora, 1970, Parma Shop, 1970, Vortice, 1972-74, Saffa, 1975, Sorin Biomedica, 1981, Fusital, 1982, Villeroy e Boch, 1982, FEAL, 1983, and Solani Ebs, 1984.

Publications:

By ZANUSO: books—*La macchina per cucire*, exhibition catalogue, Milan 1962; *Elementi di techologia dei materiali come introduzione allo studio del design*, Milan 1967; *La progettazione e l'organizzazione degli ambienti di lavoro*, with Pierluigi Nicolin, Milan 1974; articles—"Non dimentichiamo la cucina" in *Domus* (Milan), no. 197, 1944; "Dibattito sull'insegnamento dell'Industrial Design" in *Stile Industria* (Milan), no. 21, 1959; "L'Industrial Design non e un metodo na un

mestiere" in *Rivista Ideal Standard* (Milan), December 1961; "La scelta del design" in *Stile Industria* (Milan), February 1962; "Dibattito sulla scuola di Industrial Design" in *Abitare* (Milan), no. 10, 1962; "Mezzo secolo di experienze in una citta pilota della progettazione industriale" in *La Repubblica* (Milan), vol.4, no. 18, 1979; "The Drawings of Heinz Franck", with others, in *Modo* (Milan), September 1980; "Planning: conversation with Marco Zanuso", interview, in *Architettura* (Rome), March 1982.

On ZANUSO: books—*Forme nuove in Italia* by Agnoldomenico Pica, Milan 1957; *Architettura per lo spettacolo* by Robert Aloi, Milan 1958; *Architettura italiana ultima/Recent Italian Architecture* by Agnoldomenico Pica, Milan 1959; *Alberghi, motels, ristoranti* by Robert Aloi, Milan 1961; *Architettura industriali conterporanee* by Robert Aloi, Milan 1965; *Catalogo Bolaffi dell'architettura italiana 1963-66*, edited by P. C. Santini and G. L. Marini, Turin 1966; *Idee per la casa*, edited by Franco Magnani, Milan 1969, as *Modern Interiors*, London 1969; *Le Design Francais*, exhibition catalogue with introduction by Francois Mathey, Paris 1971; *Zanuso*, edited by Trevor Wilson, Melbourne 1971; *Marco Zanuso: Designer* by Gillo Dorfles, Rome 1971; *Italy: The New Domestic Landscape*, exhibition catalogue edited by Emilio Ambasz, New York and Florence 1972; *Il design in Italia 1945-1972*, by Paolo Fossati, Turin 1972; *In Good Shape—Style in Industrial Products 1900-1960* by Stephen Bayley, London 1979; *Design and design*, exhibition catalogue with texts by Angelo Cortesi, Carla Venosta, Arthur Pulos and others, Florence 1979; *Industrial Design* by John Heskett, London 1980; *Environmental Interiors* by Mary Jo Weale, James W. Croake and W. Bruce Weale, New York and London 1982; *Design Since 1945*, exhibition catalogue edited by Kathryn B. Hiesinger and George H. Marcus, Philadelphia 1983; articles— "Marco Zanuso Experiments with Air" in *Interiors* (New York), April 1953; "Marco Zanuso: un architetto della seconda generazione" by Vittorio Gregotti in *Casabella* (Milan), no. 216, 1957; "Asilo-nido di Lorenteggio a Milano" in *Casabella* (Milan), no. 218, 1957; "A Milano per uno scapolo" in *Domus* (Milan), September 1958; "Un asilo a Gubbio" in *Domus* (Milan), January 1960; "Ad Arenzano Pineta, le case rosse" in *Domus* (Milan), August 1960; "Architettura italiana 1963", special issue of *Edilizia Moderna* (Rome), no. 82/83, 1964; "Case in granito ad Arzachena, Olbia" in *Architettura* (Rome), January 1965; "Vacation Fortress on Sardinia" in *Architectural Forum* (New York), June 1967; "Bauten fur die Industrie" in *Werk* (Zurich), February 1969; "Know a Place—Make a Home" in *Abitare* (Milan), August/September 1973; "Longarone Cemetery, Belluno" by R. Pedio in *Architettura* (Rome), February 1975; "IBM Main Offices at Segrate" in *Casabella* (Milan), April 1977; "An Intricate Beehive" in *Planning and Building Developments* (Braamfontein, South Africa), July/August 1978; "House on Lake Como" in *Architectural Review* (London), October 1979; "Conference Centre in Grado" in *Architettura* (Rome), January 1980; "Lydenburg, South Africa" in *Abitare* (Milan), January/February 1981; "Five Houses by Marco Zanuso", special issue of *Ville Giardini* (Milan), December 1981; "IBM a Segrate, Milano" in *Architettura* (Rome), December 1982; "IBM a San Palomba, Roma" in *Industria delle Costruzioni* (Rome), no. 145, 1983; "Ristrutturazione Teatro Fossati" in *Casabella* (Milan), no. 508, 1984; "Palazzo dei Congressi a Grado" in *Parametro* (Bologna, Italy), no. 135/136, 1985.

Marco Zanuso's reputation as a leader in postwar Italian design was first established with his work on household appliances and furnishings. His important designs in this area include the 1951 Lady chair, which was an early combination of metal and upholstered foam rubber; the 1962 enammelled, sheet-metal Lambda chair and the 1971 Mancuso coffee table. All of these designs are notable for an elegance which arises directly out of their function, highlighting Zanuso's impeccable sense of form. It is this sense, allied to a comparable feeling for structure, which has distinguished Zanuso's buildings.

From the beginning it was clear that he was determined to bring a clean, technological approach to his architecture. This accorded naturally with the postwar housing programmes which were very receptive to a more functional modern style. The two-family house that Zanuso designed with Roberto Menghi at QT8, Milan (1952) demonstrates this concept of function-related elegance with its division into three different bodies. The central body is of minimum dimensions, in which are the kitchen, pantry, bathroom and staircase; the other two blocks contain living-rooms and bedrooms facing south. On the mezzanine floor a porch-shaped terrace leads intop the orchard garden. Built in brick, with the internal portion roofed in waterproofed concrete, it is a combination of two intersected volumes, connected by a minor block. The two lateral bodies have spacious windows and vaulted roofs. Attention to symmetry is emphasized gy the identical dimension of window and porch openings in these two lateral bodies.

One of the most important characteristics of Zanuso's work is his special concern for natural landscape. While working on the Olivetti HQ at Sao Paolo, Brazil (1955/57) he insisted that the first publication of the work should open with a photgraph of clouds, because he felt that these were an inevitable background to any Brazilian landscape. Nevertheless, the resulting building, with its vault-covered central body, each vault embedded in and supporting the others, has been described as "proudly technoligical".

This sensitivity to a natural environment is further apparent in his design of a Vacation House at Arzachena, Sardinia (1963-64). Here he made use of the red, yellow and white granite which is a traditional building material for the area, and he employed native building methods. As a result, the granite which occurs naturally on the site continues from the walls of the house down the slope to the sea. Outside, the houses have a blocked-up, defensive look; from the inside they open out onto splendid views. This "rustic" approach is here applied with considerable finesse.

It was this Sardinain project that Zanuso recalled when designing the Press House at Lydenburg, South Africa (1978). Once again, Zanuso's special respect for the landscape is in evidence as the architecture blends with the natural setting, the stone walls of the building running out across the land becoming part of it. With its careful mixture of cultural references from various sources, the Press House manages to be both ancient and modern at the same time. It has been described as a huge chameleon which changes colour and skin as the seasons shift. But this is not to say that the building has been absorbed into the landscape, rather it is a prime example of balancing a strong and well-marked natural environment with a comparably defined human presence. The final effect is that of a building which belongs in its surroundings, as though it has been there for ages.

It is not surprising that a man with Zanuso's background in industrial design should be drawn to work on industrial complexes. Indeed, he has said that his favourite subject is the factory in which he finds the heart of modern society. The Edgardale complex which Zanuso designed as the headquarters of Edgars Stores in Johannesburg (1970-72) demonstrates his approach to the problem of building a single structure to accomodate activities that previously took place in several (in this case, seventeen) different buildings. It also illustrates Zanuso's ability to take into account the demands of a man-made landscape. Aware that the building was within sight of a complex highway intersection which afforded changing views depending on the traffic flow, Zanuso chose to conceive a volumetric

development that would offer fragments of the facade oriented in different directions, and connected to each other by means of strongly articulated visual hinges. The result is not a routine building, but an "environmental structure"—a dynamic framework capable of responding to the transformations of relationship between function and spatial organisation. Within this framework a pleasant working environment becomes, in effect, an intricate beehive.

Zanuso has always been keen to serve his native city of Milan in his capacities as City Councillor, member of the City's Planning and Building Commissions, as well as through his teaching post at the Milan Politecnico. He has also been active in editorial positions, particularly at the Milan—based "Casabella" magazine. There are several examples of Zanuso's work in the City, but perhaps the most interesting is the most recent, the renovation of the Teatro Fossati and the subsequent construction of the new Piccolo Teatro.

In the case of the Teatro Fossati, Zanuso was faced with the task of revitalising a building which had suffered a long decline, ending with its total abandonment after the war. Now it was to be restored to house an experimental theatre and a drama school, and to act as an adjunct to the new Piccolo Teatro. The building is made up of two closely linked but separate blocks: the elliptically planned theatre of brick walls and wooden roof, and the drama school next door, a reinforced concrete structure. Of the old theatre the original brick facade onto the Via Rivoli (the street dividing it from the new Piccolo Teatro) has been conserved, plus the stage with two pairs of columns and the roof over the stage supported on wooden trusses. The architectural lay-out reflects the idea of the pre-existing theatre with its outer load-bearing elliptical walls which start at the ground floor and determine the entire volume of the theatre. It is hard to define Zanuso's work on this project. It is not simply a job of restoration, as too much new adaptation has been done, nor is it a new building as there were too many regulating constraints of conservation. However, the most significant design idea to be employed is that of a total space in which the spatial distinction between stage and public is left undefined by means of an organisational flexibility of both scenic equipment and seating layout, to the point of apparently changing the traditional concept of theatre "all'italiana". This is achieved through the possibility of using the same spatial elements by both public and actors alike. This reflects a conception of flexibility of the theatrical lay-out within the fixity of architectural space. One can only imagine the important role that the new Piccolo Teatro will have within this complex siting and functional choice, both in terms of its scale (1200 seats) and its monumental character as an isolated object which will act as a watershed between different and continuous urban systems.

The most recent example of Zanuso's factory design is the IBM Italia Factory at Palomba, Rome (1979-82). Situated in a typical example of Latium lowlands, the factory required a careful study of the site's configurations with its changing, delicate orography. As a result this understandably bulky development was built along the levels suggested and imposed by the landscape. Rejecting the idea of a camourflage concealment as being inconsistent with the quantity and function expressed by the new installation, Zanuso as opted instead for a gradual visual inclusion in the folds of the land. The ground plan is based upon the repetition of approx. 3,500 square metres, through which the production facilities are articulated. The whole development has a main body of seven square blocks arranged in an "L"-shape. Four big towers, corresponding to each pair of modules, contain the systems and services in a solution which, by decentralizing the production area from the offices and warehouses, helps to keep work noise low and also saves a considerable amount of energy.

Zanuso has said that it is important for an

architect never to "resist" a landscape, and the work of this exceptional designer with his commitment of form and function clearly demonstrates his extraordinary sensitivity to an existing enironment and his ability to effect change in that environment so that it seems the most natural of developments.

—Paul Ryan

ZEHRFUSS, Bernard Louis.

French. Born in Angers, 20 October 1911. Educated at Stanislas College, Ecole Nationale des Beaux-Arts, Paris, 1928-39 (Premier Grand Prix de Rome, 1939), Dip.Arch. 1939. Volunteer in the Free French Army, 1942; Lieutenant in the Reserves. Married Simone Fanny Samana in 1950; daughter: Dominique. Chief Government Architect and Adjunct Commissioner of City Planning, Housing and Tourism, Tunisia, 1943-48. Since 1948, in private practice, Paris. Architect to the Council of Construction, Algeria, 1950-54, and Paris Region, 1955-62. Chief Architect of Civic Building and National Monuments, France, since 1955 (Inspector-General of Civic Building and National Monuments, 1965-68). Recipient: Gold Medal, Society for the Encouragement of Art and Industry, France, 1960. Honorary Member, American Institute of Architects, and Royal Society of Arts, London. Officer of the Légion d'Honneur; Officer of the Order of Merit; Member of the Institut de France, 1983. Chevalier of the order of Danebrog, Denmark; Officer of the Republic of Tunisia. Address (office): 9 rue Arsène Houssaye, 75008 Paris, France.

Works:

1943/
48 Public buildings, schools, housing, hospital, and hippodrome, Tunisia
1947 Gammartti National Cemetery, Tunisia
1950 Mame Printing Works, Tours, France
1952 Renault Factory, Flins, France
1955 National Centre for Industry and Technology (CNIT), La Défense, Paris (with Camelot and de Mailly)
1958 Unesco Buildings I, II, and III, Paris (with Marcel Breuer and Pier Luigi Nervi)
1958/
78 Housing complexes, Paris region, Nancy and St. Etienne, France
1960 University of Tunis
Summer Palace for the Shah of Iran, Tehran (project)
1963 Unesco Building IV, Paris
Cultural Centre, Frankfurt (project)
1965 Faculty of Sciences, University of Tunis
French Embassy, Rabat, Morocco (project)
Hotel du Mont d'Arboir, Megève, France
1966 Design of the exhibition *Hommage à Le Corbusier,* Louvre, Paris
1968 Danish Embassy, Paris
1969 Unesco Building V, Paris
1970 French Embassy, Warsaw
1971 Ministry of Finance interiors, Paris
1972 Siemens Company Headquarters, Saint-Denis, near Paris (with Burckhardt)
Sandoz Company headquarters, Paris
1973 Jeumont Schneider Company Headquarters, Paris
1974 Spie Batignolles Headquarters, Paris
1975 Gallo-Roman Underground Museum, Lyon, France
1976 Design of the exhibition *Hommage à André Malraux,* Louvre, Paris

Bernard Zehrfuss: Unesco Building VI, Paris, 1977.

1977 Unesco Building VI, Paris
1978 French National Railways (SNCF) Head-quarters, Paris (project)
1979 New Housing Quarter Plan, Tunis
1980 Unesco Buildings extensions and new layouts, Paris (with Breuer Associates)
Bercy International Sports Centre, Paris (competition project)
1981 Housing Development, 15th Arrondissement, Paris
1982 Unesco Office Development, Paris

Publications:

By ZEHRFUSS: articles—"Architecture: évolution ou révolution" in *L'Architecture d'aujourd'hui* (Paris), February 1965; "L'homme dans la ville" in *La NEF* (Paris), July 1965; "Hommage à Le Corbusier" in *Lettres francaises* (Paris), August 1965; article on Paris in *Figaro* (Paris), February 1968; "Fernand Léger and Architecture" in *Europe* (Paris), 1971; article on Paris in *Le Monde* (Paris), August 1972; "Le cadre du bonheur 'La Ville'" in *Cultures* (Paris, no. 4, 1976; "L'homme et sa ville" in *La NEF* (Paris), June 1977.

On ZEHRFUSS: books—*Tunisie vivant*, Paris 1946; *World's Contemporary Architecture*, Tokyo 1953; *Architecture du 20ème siècle*, Paris, 1964; *Architecture of the West*, Moscow 1972; *Les Défis de l'an 2000*, Paris 1977; *Des architectures pour mieux vivre*, Paris 1980; articles—"Tunisia" in *L'Architecture d'aujourd'hui* (Paris), October 1948; "Fifth Building for Unesco" in *Architecture Francaise* (Paris), July/August 1973; "Siemens Headquarters in Saint-Denis" in *Baumeister* (Munich), November 1973; "Archaeological Museum in Lyons" in *Architecture Francaise* (Paris), April 1975; "Lyon" by Pierre Kjellberg in *Connaissance des Arts* (Paris), February 1976; "Archaeological Museum in Lyons Which Is Almost Entirely Buried Underground" in *Concrete Quarterly* (London), April/June 1977; "Archaeology Museum in Lyons" in *Casabella* (Milan), January 1979.

In all of the works that I have built, I have always searched for different solutions and different ex-pressions. Architecture has been, for me, a perpetual beginning again; it is conditioned, in effect, by one's interpretation of the given program and by the function of the chosen site. The choice of archi-tectural means, the disposition of the plan, the relationship of volumes, the harmony of parts—everything depends on this idea. Some examples from my works will illustrate this search:

The placement of the Renault Factory in Flins in the countryside on the banks of the Seine or the Mame Printing Works in Tours alongside the Loire.

The grand arch of the Centre National des Industries et des Techniques at La Défense which stands at the east-west axis of Paris.

The insertion of the building complex of Unesco into an historic environment of Paris; the sunken patios which complete the composition without making it dull.

The swimming pool of the Hotel du Mont d'Arboir in Megeve from which one sees a panorama of the French Alps.

The new University of Tunis modelled on the nearby hills of the town.

The Gallo-Roman Museum in Lyon which, sunken into the slope of a hill, does not change the site of the Roman theatre of Fourvières.

—Bernard Zehrfuss

After the armistice in 1940 Bernard Zehrfuss settled down with a small group of friends in an abandoned village of Provence; ecologists before the fact and in advance of fashion by a quarter of a century, they tried to breathe new life into picturesque Oppède. Then he was called to Tunisia where, with his faithful companions—among them the wise but lazy Paul Herbé, Le Couteur, Auproux, Marmey, Patout, all architects of enthusiasm and merit—he was respo-nsible for the planning and rebuilding of that beautiful country. The "team of twenty" that he inspired did an excellent job, the benefits of which Tunisia keeps to this day.

The successes achieved by Zehrfuss as the head of the Tunisian department entrusted with develop-ment and reconstruction, his human qualities and his organizational capabilities naturally destined him for high responsibilities in liberated France. Import-ant projects were entrusted to him—the Renault complex at Flins, a remarkable industrial achieve-ment; embassies, university buildings, and so forth. Bit it was his participation with Breuer and Nervi in the building of Unesco Headquarters in the heart of Paris that brought him to the forefront of current architecture. One recognizes the hand of Nervi in the structure of the great hall and that of Breuer in the conception of the administrative sector—but Zeh-rfuss, too, was unquestionably important: it was he who was later solely responsible for the numerous enlargement, extensions and new building for the world organization, and he has known how to maintain, in spite of very difficult conditions at times, a high quality. Brought into the limelight by his spectacular achievement, Zehrfuss was given com-missions for many private sector administrative buildings for important multi-national companies—Sandoz, Siemens, Schneider, and others. Also in collaboration, there is his well-known National Centre for Industry and Technology at La Defense, justifiably criticized for its siting (a criticism acknow-ledged by Zehruss) of which the principal point of interest lies in the great vault by the engineer Esquillan.

Zehrfuss courageously refused to put his name to the alterations required of his project for the development of the Bercy warehouse area in Paris; in his initial prize-winning scheme one finds again all the qualities of this architect. The same is true of a more recent but so far little-known work of great quality, the Gallo-Roman Museum in Lyon.

—Pierre Vago

ZEIDLER, Eberhard H.

Canadian. Born in Braunsdorf, Germany, 11 Jauary 1926; emigrated to Canada, 1951: naturalized, 1956. Educated at the Bauhaus, Weimar, Germany, 1945-48; Technische Hochschule, Karlsruhe, 1948-49, Dip.Ing. 1949. Married Jane Abbott in 1957; chil-dren: Margaret, Robert, Katy and Christina. Desig-ner, office of Eiermann and Lindner, Karlsruhe and Osnabruck, 1949-51; Associate in charge of Design, Blackwell and Craig, Toronto, 1951. Partner, Blackwell, Craig and Zeidler, Toronto, 1954, and successor firms Craig and Zeidler, 1955-63, Craig, Zeidler and Strong, 1963-75, and Zeidler Partner-ship/Architects, 1975-80. Since 1980, Principal Part-ner, with Alfred C. Roberts, Zeidler Roberts Part-nership/Architects, Toronto. Lecturer in Architec-tural Design, 1953-55, Visiting Professor, 1983-84, and Adjunct Professor since 1984, University of Toronto. Recipient: National Design Award, 1962, 1967, 1972; Design Award, Masonry Council, 1964, 1965, 1966, 1968, 1970, 1971, 1974; Award of Excellence, *Canadian Architecture*, 1969, 1970, 1971, 1974; Precast Concrete Institute Award, 1970; Eedee Award, 1971; Design Award, *Progressive Architecture*, 1972; American Iron and Steel Ins-titute Award, 1973; Ordre des Architectes du Québec Award, 1978; Urban Design Award, 1978, 1980, 1981; Honor Award, American Institute of Architects, Detroit Chapter, 1979; University of California at Los Angeles School of Architecture Urban Planning Award, 1980; National Honor Award, American Institute of Architects, 1980; Design Canadian Award, 1981; Governor General's Medal for Architecture, Canada, 1982; Ontario Renews Award, 1983; Urban Land Institute Award, 1983; Canadian Housing Design Council Award, 1983; Interior Designers of Ontario Award, 1983; Ontario Masons' Relations Council Award, 1983; Design and Planning Award, Builder's Choice, 1984; Concrete Building Award, Builder's Choice, 1984; Concrete Building Award, 1984. Address: Zeidler Roberts Partnership/Architects, 315 Queen Street West, Toronto, Ontario M5V 2X2, Canada.

Works:

1953 Grace Church, Peterborough, Ontario
1954 St. Giles Church, Peterborough, Ontario
1955 Memorial Centre, Peterborough, Ontario
Hamilton House, Peterborough, Ontario
1957 West Ellesmere Church, Toronto
1963 Parkwood United Church, Toronto
Beth Israel Synagogue, Peterborough, On-tario
1964 General Hospital, Whitby, Ontario
Ajax and Pickering Hospital, Ajax, Ontario
1965 Forester House, Toronto
Burnview Apartments, Toronto
1966 Grant Sine Public School, Cobourg, Ontario
1967 Health Sciences Centre, McMaster Univer-sity, Hamilton, Ontario
Physical Sciences Building University of Guelph, Ontario
Ross Memorial Hospital, Lindsay, Ontario
Centennial Recreation Centre, Scarborough, Ontario
Municipal Building, Ajax, Ontario
Municipal Building, Pickering, Ontario
1968 T.A. Stewart Vocational School, Peterbor-ough, Ontario
1969 Ontario Place, Toronto
Fanshawe School of Applied Arts and Tech-nology, London, Ontario
Korah Collegiate and Vocational School, Sault Sainte Marie, Ontario
1970 Dr. Joseph O. Ruddy Hospital, Whitby, On-tario
Osler School of Nursing, Toronto
1971 Harbour City, Toronto
Regional hospitals, New Brunswick
Willow Park Public School, Scarborough, Ontario
1972 General Hospital, Detroit (with Kessler Associates and Giffels Associates)
Wayne State University Clinic, Detroit (with Kessler Associates and Giffels Associates)
Civic Hospital, Peterborough, Ontario
Sussex Hospital, New Brunswick
Dumont Hospital, New Brunswick
Central Laundry, Hamilton, Ontario
1973 Eaton Centre, Toronto (with Bregman and Hamann)
1975 Health Sciences Centre, Edmonton, Alberta
Mont Sainte Marie Condominiums and Con-ference Centre, Gatineau, Quebec
Canadian Imperial Bank of Commerce Build-ing, Calgary, Alberta
Regional Hospital, St. Johns, New Brunswick
1976 Century Place, Belleville, Ontario
1977 Chalmers Hospital, Fredericton, New Bruns-wick
1978 Trinity Square Development, Toronto
Mississauga Hospital, Ontario
Young People's Theatre, Toronto
Kensington Housing Development, Toronto
1978/
84 Glen Cedar Public School, Newmarket, On-tario
1979 Queen's Quary Terminal, Toronto
Agnes McPhail Public School, Scarborough, Ontario
1980 Yerba Buena Gardens, San Francisco

Eberhard Zeidler: Ontario Place, Toronto, 1969.

1981 Gallery At Harborplace, Baltimore, Maryland
College of Physicians and Surgeons of Ontario, Toronto
1982 Canada Place, Vancouver, British Columbia
Ontario Pavilion, *Expo '86*, Vancouver, British Columbia
Metroplex Plaza, Kuala Lumpur, Malaysia
1983 Canadian Red Cross Society, Ottawa, Ontario
Sick Children's Hospital, Toronto
1984 Sunnybrook Hospital, Toronto

Publications:

By ZEIDLER: books—*Healing the Hospital*, Toronto 1974; *Multifunktionale Architektur im stadtischen Kontext/Multi-Use Architecture in the Urban Context*, Stuttgart and Paris 1983, New York 1984; articles—"Notes on Church Architecture" in *Royal Architectural Institute of Canada Journal* (Toronto), December 1956; "Expo '67 in Montreal" in *Deutsche Bauzeitung* (Stuttgart), August 1967; "Designing for the Unknown Future" in *The Business Quarterly* (London, Ontario), April 1973; "McMaster and Beyond" in *National Hospital and Health Care* (Sydney), November 1975; "Planning for Flexibility" in *National Hospital and Health Care* (Sydney), December 1975; "Montreal Olympics" in *Bauen und Wohnen* (Zurich), November 1976; "Architects, Developers Have a Moral Duty to Lead the Way to a Better Environment" in *Real Estate Development Annual* (Toronto), August 1977; "Build Hospitals for Future Change" in *Hospital Administration in Canada* (Toronto), February 1978; "The Lost Dimension" in *Bauen und Wohnen* (Zurich), July/August 1978; "Multi-use Buildings" in *Bauen und Wohnen* (Zurich), October 1979; "Architecture: The Fine Art of Survival" in

Canadian Architect (Toronto), February 1980; "Urban Counterpoints" in *RIBA Transactions* (London), vol. 1, no. 1, 1982; "Edmonton Hospital" in *Canadian Architect* (Toronto), May 1983; "Hospital Architecture" in *Architecture Minnesota* (Minneapolis), May/June 1983; "Humanized High-Tech—At What Cost?", with Peter Hemingway, in *Canadian Architect* (Toronto), February 1984.

On ZEIDLER: book—*Building with Words: Canadian Architects on Architecture*, with introduction by W. Bernstein and R. Cawker, Toronto 1981; articles—"Peterborough Memorial Community Centre" in *Canadian Architect* (Toronto), November 1957; "Ajax Municipal Building" in *Canadian Architect Yearbook* (Toronto), 1967; "Madawaska Valley District High School" in *Deutsche Bauzeitung* (Stuttgart), June 1968; "Thomas A. Stewart and Auburn Vocational Schools" in *Domus* (Milan), December 1968; "Ajax-Pickering Hospital" in *Deutsche Bauzeitung* (Stuttgart), September 1969; "McMaster University Health Sciences Centre" in *Architectural Review* (London), April 1970; "McMaster University" in *L'Architecture d'Aujourd'hui* (Paris), June 1970; "McMaster University Health Sciences Centre" in *The Lancet* (London), October 1970; "Harbour City" in *Baumeister* (Munich), October 1970; "Ontario Place" in *Deutsche Bauzeitung* (Stuttgart), April 1971; "McMaster University" in *Architectural Forum* (New York), June 1971; "Dr. Joseph O. Ruddy General Hospital" in *Architectural Record* (New York), September 1971; "Ontario Place, Toronto" in *Canadian Architect* (Toronto), October 1971; "Harbour City" in *Progressive Architecture* (New York), January 1972; "University of Guelph/Fanshawe College" in *Baumeister* (Munich), January 1972; "McMaster University" in *Bauwelt* (Berlin), June 1973; "McMaster University" in *Architectural Design* (London), July 1973; "McMaster University" in

Architecture Francaise (Paris), November/December 1973; "Ontario Place Children's Village" in *Architectural Review* (London), February 1974; "McMaster University" in *Architektur und Wohwelt* (Stuttgart), October 1974; "Zeidler Residence" in *House Beautiful* (New York), January 1975; "Toronto Eaton Centre" in *Bauen und Wohnen* (Zurich), December 1975; "Toronto Eaton Centre" in *Domus* (Milan), March 1976; "Toronto Eaton Centre" in *Progressive Architecture* (New York), June 1977; "Toronto Eaton Centre" in *Nikkei Architecture* (Tokyo), August 1978; "A Perspective of Modern Canadian Architecture", special issue of *Process: Architecture* (Tokyo), no. 5, 1978; "Toronto Eaton Centre" in *Progressive Architecture* (New York), December 1978; "Young People's Theatre" in *Baumeister* (Munich), April 1979; "Detroit Receiving Hospital" in *Architectural Record* (New York), April 1980; "Profile on Eberhard Zeidler" in *Saturday Night Magazine* (Toronto), December 1980; "Architects on Architecture" in *Building* (London), 23 October 1981; "The Dilemma of Design" in *Deutsche Bauzeitung* Stuttgart), January 1983; "Eaton Centre, Toronto" in *Architettura* (Rome), April 1983; "From Mies to Metaphors" in *Canadian Architect* (Toronto), May 1983; "Eberhard H. Zeidler—Projects" in *City and Country Home* (Toronto), Spring 1983; "Arcades", special issue of *Aktuelles Bauen* (Zurich), June 1983; "Waterfront Renovation" in *Canadian Architect* (Toronto), October 1983; "Detroit Receiving Hospital and Wayne State Clinic Building" in *Architecture + Urbanism* (Tokyo), October 1983; "The Canadian Architect 1983 Awards of Excellence" in *Canadian Architect* (Toronto), December 1983; "Queen's Quay Terminal, Toronto" in *Deutsche Bauzeitung* (Stuttgart), May 1984; "Alberta Atrium" in *Architectural Review* (London), July 1984; "Twelve Proposals for the National Gallery of Canada and for the National Museum of Man", special issue of *Section A* (Montreal), August 1984; "Queen's Quay Terminal" in *Builder Magazine* (Washington, D.C.), October 1984.

My architectural training began in one of the sandboxes of a small Silesian town that took most of its architectural heritage from Viennese precedents.

Maybe I should take this into consideration if I want to understand my emotions towards architecture. My amateur architectural status ceased when I started to study in the newly re-opened Bauhaus at Weimar after the War.

In 1951 I came to Canada I got some small commissions (churches, houses) and taught at the University of Toronto. I was engulfed in a turmoil of frantic activity, the growth period of Canada after the Second World War. I hoped in doing so that I would not only find myself but also build in a better way. I felt that the international style of Bauhaus lacked the emotional quality that I was searching for. Yet the blinds we all were wearing due to the doctrines of Modern Architecture were difficult to discover.

We cannot underestimate the power of architectural theories, especially if they are converted through misuse into dogmas, becoming blinds to the designer, preventing him from seeing the total horizon.

Architecture means something slightly different to all of us; to some it may represent the necessity of building, to others excess of opulence—the Taj Mahal; it may mean the isolated individual building to some, to others the vitality of all man-made environment.

Yet architecture is all of these things. It is necessity and it is folly—if song is folly. It is the detail of the small individual building and it is the totality of our man-made world.

It is only when we equate all of our man-made environment with architecture that we can attempt to understand how it influences our life. Architecture is the shell of our life and therefore our past, our present and our future.

Modern architecture saw beauty in form only as the aftermath of funcion and construction, but not as an independent emotional force that could equally influence form.

We are looking today with astonishment at Victorian architecture and re-discovering its philosophy, finding many things that are amazingly useable. The irritating thought nags at us, that progress might be a circle rather than a straight line.

Architecture must be seen, walked through, it must be touched and experienced. Architecture must be lived in. Magazines, photographs and theories have become substitutes for the real thing, obscuring the world before us.

And yet here is their power: theories can either widen or narrow our views of this world. They can help us to understand it better and grasp the meaning of its complexity or they can limit and restrict our creative abilities. We are just awakening from such experience.

Architecture is our life, and like life it is the struggle for survival. It is the job of being alive and is the search for life's meaning.

Architecture will always transcend words and be perceived on a level that cannot be reached by logic. We have realized the dangerous power of a theory to limit our ability to conceive the totality of architecture.

Modern architecture has left us with as rich a heritage as the forgotten masters of Victorian times, now that we have escaped its dogma and are again able to see beyond its borders.

Ultimately, the Pleasure of Form and Space, which is architecture, transcends words and becomes the poetry of our subconscious.

—Eberhard Zeidler

Tied as it supposedly is to the broad abstracted characteristics of its time—social, economic, political—architecture is usually treated as a very serious art form. Modern architecture particulary has, in the mainstream, taken the mundane forms of ordinary real estate construction as the basis of its style—simple, rectangular, straightforward, with subsequently just a touch of embellishment—forms that derived from warehouses and factories. Collaterally, modern form givers have also been very serious men. The principled Gropius, the enigmatic Mies, the paranoid Corbu were all types well-known in the annals of art where tragedy is felt to be intrinsically superior to comedy.

This situation requires the architectural viewer to ponder the buildings around him soberly. The exception has been the exposition where the general public has expected to be dazzled and architects have allowed themselves (if somewhat self-consciously) to let down their hair and stretch their imaginations. More recently, in our ever more sophisticated consumer society, it has been recognised that while buildings probably do not much affect our behaviour, they can attract or repel; and while certain building types such as schools have captive users, others like fast food outlets need our custom and are their own advertisements. The visual attractions of Main Street have thereby entered the architect's vocabulary. From another direction, the scientific interest in the psycho-sociology of users' needs is recognizing that a joy of living is just as natural as a fascination with suffering and death. Architects representing the spirit of the times can therefore now legitimately include the ligher aspects

of human existence: excitement, humour, entertainment, pleasure.

Two large building complexes by Eberhard Zeidler are excellent examples of what might be termed Expo Art. Ontario Place is described as a fun centre and is close in spirit to a permanent exhibition ground. Eaton Centre features a multi-story shopping arcade and offices and is fun architecture made out of a standard building problem. The architectural language employed is generically the same in both and shows that imagination can be extended to buildings that are not functionally designated as amusing. The cable structures, tent forms and dome, over-water walkways and hung stairways at Ontario Place, which sits offshore in Lake Ontario and includes a moored warship, are oddly limited to a more marine aesthetic in Eaton Centre. The connection is not simply that ship-like motifs have been used but that the multi-level space arrangement with its connecting escalators and bridges, and the use of metal and glass with exposed industrial-type components for lighting and air-handling, provide the character of the machine aesthetic which the early moderns equated with a dynamic technologically exciting world. The relationship is furthered by a geometry of angles and curves, and even the streetside advertisements are hung in a manner reminiscent of lifeboats. The quality of design, however, is enlivened and accentuated in subtly amusing details that raise the comparison above a mere copy. The metaphor is elaborated by ad hoc events in layout, shape and connections that enrich the texture of the design and add to the riot of light, movement, sound and colour. Allied to the abundance of planting in the controlled environment under the glass roof, the centre provides a successful contrast to the major street it runs alongside.

The popularity of both Ontario Place and Eaton Centre in a city where a growing number of modern buildings have found favour in the public imaginations, indicates the potentialities of the modern style beyond its until recently self-imposed limitations. That this direction needs further broadening is evidenced by another large building designed by Zeidler, the Health Sciences Centre for McMaster University, Hamilton, in which a related form idiom seems less appropriate to the situation. When modern architecture offered a closed style as its response to what was perceived as a definable historical era, it rejected the previous century's concern for the classical principle of propriety. Nonetheless a contemporary architecture has to support the many different qualities of activities that have given rise to various building types. Such a spectrum of needs, each with its own different perceptual requirements, suggests a variety of means to achieve the desired ends. Zeidler's work explores such possibilities.

—Anthony Jackson

NOTES ON ADVISERS AND CONTRIBUTORS

ABERCROMBIE, Stanley. Contributor. Architect in private practice, New York.. Editor, *Interior Design*, New York. Former Editor of *Interiors*, New York, Architecture Editor of *AIA Journal*, Washington, D.C., and Senior Editor of *Architecture Plus*, New York. Contributor to the *Wall Street Journal, Progressive Architecture, Artforum, Journal of the Society of Architectural Historians, Design, Architecture + Urbanism*, and other periodicals. **Essays:** Alvar Aalto; Ulrich Franzen.

ACHLEITNER, Friedrich. Contributor. Professor of the History of Building Construction, Akademie der Bildenden Künste, Vienna. Architectural Critic, *Die Presse*, Vienna, 1962–72. Author of *Hosn Rosn Baa* (with H. C. Artmann and Gerhard Rühm), 1959; *Lois Welzenbacher* (with Ottokar Uhl), 1968; *Prosa, Konstellationen, Montagen, Dialektgedichte, Studien*, 1970; *Quadratroman*, 1973; *Die Ware Landschaft* (editor), 1977; *Der Werkbund*, 1978; *Österreich-Architekturführer*, 3 volumes, 1980–83. **Essays:** Hans Hollein; Wilhelm Holzbauer; Clemens Holzmeister.

ACKERMANN, Kurt. Contributor and entrant: see his own entry. **Essays:** Fritz Leonhardt.

ADLER, Gerald. Contributor. Author of a thesis on William Holden, 1978. **Essays:** Gustav Peichl.

ALINGTON, W. H. Contributor and entrant: see his own entry. **Essay:** Ian Athfield.

ALLIES, Bob. Contributor. Architect in private practice, London. Lecturer at Cambridge University. Contributor to *Architectural Review* and *Designers Journal*, London. **Essays:** Ahrends Burton and Koralek; Edward Cullinan; Bruno Taut.

ANTONIADES, Anthony C. Contributor. Architect in private practice, Greece, New Mexico, and Texas. Professor, University of Texas at Arlington. Author of *Introduction to Environmental Design*, 1973; *Contemporary Greek Architecture*, 1979; *Architecture and Allied Design*, 1980; *Poetics of Architecture*, 1985. **Essays:** Kazuhiro Ishii, Ricardo Legorreta; Alexandros N. Tombazis.

ARAI, Katsuyoshi. Contributor. Lecturer at the Bunka-Gakuin School of Architecture, Tokyo. Author of *A Study of an English New Town: Runcorn*, 1969; *A Study of Modern Architecture: Le Corbusier* (in preparation). Contributor to *Architecture + Urbanism* and *Kenchiku Bunka*. **Essays:** Yoshiro Taniguchi; Isoya Yoshida.

ARNOLD, Christopher. Contributor. President, Building Systems Development Inc., San Francisco. Lecturer in the Department of Architecture, University of California, Berkeley, 1975–79. Joint Author of *Building Configuration and Seismic Design*, 1982. **Essays:** Mario J. Ciampi; Ernest J. Kump.

BACON, Edmund N. Contributor and entrant: see his own entry. **Essay:** Eliel Saarinen.

BAIRD, George. Contributor and entrant; see his own entry. **Essays:** Melvin Charney; Jerome Markson.

BALFOUR, Alan. Contributor. Professor and Director of Programs in Architecture, Georgia Institute of Technology, Atlanta. Formerly, Research Associate, Massachusetts Institute of Technology, 1970; *Rehab: Strategies and Techniques*, 1973; *Rockefeller Center: Architecture as Theatre*, 1978. **Essays:** John Hejduk; Donlyn Lyndon; James Stewart Polshek; Jaquelin Robertson; Benjamin Thompson.

BARNETT, Jonathan. Contributor and entrant: see his own entry. **Essays:** David A. Crane; David Lewis; Archibald C. Rogers; David A. Wallace; Richard S. Weinstein.

BATTLE, T. Q. Contributor. Chairman of Towco Ltd. (U.K.). Author of *The Chimney Book*, 1977. Regular contributor to *The Architects' Journal*. **Essay:** Chamberlin Powell and Bon.

BAYLEY, Stephen. Contributor. Director of the Conran Foundation, London. Formerly, Lecturer at The Open University (U.K.), and University of Kent, Canterbury. Author of *In Good Shape: Design in Industrial Products 1900–1960*. 1979; *The Albert Memorial*, 1981; *Harley Earl and the Dream Machine*, 1983. **Essays:** Theo Crosby; Howell, Killick, Partridge and Amis; C.S. Mardall; J. H. van den Broek.

BAZAROV, Konstantin. Contributor. Freelance writer and researcher, London. Author of *Landscape Painting*, 1980. **Essays:** Franco Albini; Charles Herbert Aslin; Dominikus Böhm; Rifat Chadirji; Ignazio Gardella; Wassili Luckhardt; Roland Rainer; Affonso Eduardo Reidy; Rudolf Schwarz; Giuseppe Terragni.

BEEBY, Thomas Hall. Adviser and entrant; see his own entry.

BIERMANN, B.E. Contributor. Professor of Architecture, University of Natal, Durban. Author of *Boukuns in Suid-Afrika*, 1954; *Red Wine in South Africa*, 1971. **Essay:** Hans Hallen.

BLUNDELL JONES, Peter. Contributor. Visiting Lecturer in Architecture, Cambridge University. Author of *Hans Scharoun: A Monograph*, 1978. **Essays:** James Gowan; Ron Herron; Cedric Price.

BOHIGAS, Oriol. Contributor and entrant: see his own entry. **Essay:** Alvaro Siza.

BOOTON, Harold (died, 1983). Contributor. Formerly, architect and planner in private practice, Leeds, Yorkshire, and Principal Lecturer in Architecture, Leeds School of Architecture. Author of *Architecture of Spain*, 1966; *Great Traditions of Western Architecture* (with Bruce Allsopp and Ursula Clark), 1967; *Renaissance Architecture and Ornament in Spain*, 1970. **Essay:** Eduardo Torroja y Miret.

BORNGRÄBER, Christian. Contributor. Architectural historian, Berlin, and organizer of exhibitions of German and Russian culture of the 1920's. Author of *Kunst in die Produktion!—Sowjetische Kunst während der Phase der Kollektivierung und Industrialisierung 1927–1933* (with others), 1977; *Stilnovo: Design in den 50'er Jahren—Phantasie und Phantastik*, 1979. **Essays:** Paul Baumgarten; Helmut Hentrich; Dieter Oesterlen.

BRAWNE, Michael. Contributor and entrant: see his own entry. **Essay:** Carlo Scarpa.

BROCKMAN, H. A. N. (died, 1980). Contributor. Architectural Correspondent, 1961–1979, and Architectural Consultant, *The Financial Times*, London. Senior Architect, Ministry of Local Government, 1946–61. Author of *The Caliph of Fonthill: An Architectural Biography of William Beckford*, 1956; *The Architect in Industry*, 1965. **Essay:** Trevor Dannatt.

BROOKS, H. Allen. Contributor. Professor of Fine Art, University of Toronto. Past President, Society of Architectural Historians (U.S.A.). Author of *The Prairie School: Frank Lloyd Wright and His Midwest Contemporaries*, 1972, 1975, and *Frank Lloyd Wright and the Prairie School*, 1984, and editor of *Writings on Wright: Selected Comment on Frank Lloyd Wright*, 1981. **Essay:** Frank Lloyd Wright.

CANDILIS, Georges. Contributor and entrant: see his own entry. **Essay:** Vladimir Bodiansky.

CAPITEL, Anton. Contributor. Architect in private practice, Madrid. Professor of Architectural Design, Escuela Tecnica Superior de Arquitectura, Madrid. Author of *José Antonio Coderch 1945–1976*, 1978, and *La Arquitectura de Luis Moya Blanco*, 1981. Editor of *Arquitectura*, Madrid. Contributor to *Arquitecturas Bis, Jano Arquitectura, Contróspazio* and *Boden*. **Essays:** Alejandro De La Sota; José Rafael Moneo; Francisco Saénz de Oíza.

CETTO, Max (died, 1980). Contributor and entrant: see his own entry. **Essay:** Juan O'Gorman.

CHAMBERS, D. D. C. Contributor. Associate Professor of English, University of Toronto. Author of *Lost Cities*. Essays: A. J. Diamond; Ron Thom.

CHAMPIGNEULLE, Bernard. Contributor. Architectural critic, Paris. Author of *Auguste Perret*, 1959. Essay: Michel Roux-Spitz.

CHANG, Ching-Yu. Contributor. Architect in private practice (Architectural Space Network), Tokyo. Lecturer in the Graduate Program, School of Engineering, Nihon University, Tokyo. Formerly, Assistant Professor, Carnegie-Mellon University, Pittsburgh, Pennsylvania, and Associate Professor, School of Architecture, Technical University of Nova Scotia, Halifax. Contributor to *Space Design, Architecture + Urbanism, The Japan Architect*, and *Architecture Plus*. Essays: Edward Larrabee Barnes; Jonathan Barnett; Romaldo Giurgola; Victor A. Lundy; Fumihiko Maki; Richard Meier; I. M. Pei; Takamasa Yosizaka.

CHELAZZI, Giuliano. Contributor. Architect in private practice, Florence, Italy. Contributor to *Pan Arte, Deutsche Bauzeitung, L'Architettura*. Essays: Helge Bofinger; Justus Dahinden; Egon Eiermann; Rolf Gutbrod.

CLARK, Alson. Contributor. Director of the Architecture and Fine Art Libraries, University of Southern California, Los Angeles. President of the Southern California Chapter of the Society of Architectural Historians, 1976–78. Essays: Robert E. Alexander; Wallace Neff.

CLIFF, Ursula. Contributor. Associate Editor, *Industrial Design*, New York. Essay: Oscar Stonorov.

COCHRANE, Peggy. Contributor. Architect in private practice, California. Past President, Association of Women in Architecture. Member of the Editorial Board, *L.A. Architect*. Author of *Yucatan* (musical), 1977; *I Gave at the Office* (play), 1978; *The Witchdoctor's Cookbook*, 1979; *The Witchdoctor's Manual*, 1979; *How to Reject Rejection*, 1979. Essays: Edward A. Killingsworth; Pierre Koenig; Mario Pani; Pedro Ramirez Vazquez.

CODRINGTON FORSYTH, James. Contributor. Partner, ArkiNova Architects and Planners, Gavle, Sweden. Technical Officer, Building Standards Institution, Sweden. Formerly, Regional Planner, Järfälla kommun, Sweden; Part-time Instructor in Architecture, Royal Technical College, Stockholm. Joint Editor of *Kök med standard*, 1979. Contributor to *Architectural Review* and *Building Design*. Essay: Sven Backström.

COLE, Carolyn. Contributor. Freelance writer, London. Essays: Kamran Diba; Joan E. Goody; Allan Greenberg; Mario Ridolfi; Alberto Sartoris; Dolf Schnebli.

COLLINS, Peter (died, 1981). Contributor. Formerly, Professor of Architecture, McGill University, Montreal. Author of *Concrete: The Vision of a New Architecture*, 1959; *Changing Ideals in Modern Architecture*, 1969; *Architectural Judgement*, 1971. Essay: Auguste Perret.

COLLYMORE, Peter. Contributor. Architect in private practice, London. Author of *House Conversion and Renewal*, 1975; *Ralph Erskine*, 1982. Essay: Ralph Erskine.

COLVIN, Brenda. Contributor and entrant: see her own entry. Essay: Sir Geoffrey Jellicoe.

COOK, Jeffrey. Contributor. Professor of Architecture, Arizona State University, Tempe. Author of *Architectural Anthology*, 1966, 1969, 1972; *The Architecture of Bruce Goff*, 1978; *Passive Solar '78*, 1979. Essay: Bruce Goff.

COWAN, Henry J. Contributor. Professor Emeritus of Architectural Science, University of Sydney (formerly Dean of Architecture). Editor, *Architectural Science Review*. Past President, Building Science Forum of Australia. Author of *The Master Builders; Architectural Structures; Dictionary of Architectural Science;* and numerous other books. Essays: David Jackson; R. N. Johnson; Bryce Mortlock.

CRAVENS, Logan. Contributor. Freelance designer. Essays: O'Neil Ford; James Pratt.

CROWELL, S. Fiske, Jr. Contributor. Senior Designer, Perry, Dean, Stahl and Rogers, Boston. Instructor, Boston Architectural Center. Essays: Serge Chermayeff; Denise Scott Brown; The Architects Collaborative.

CURL, James Stevens. Contributor. Architect and town planning consultant (U.K.). Author of *European Cities and Society*, 1970; *The Victorian Celebration of Death*, 1972; *City of London Pubs* (with Timothy M. Richards), 1973; *Victorian Architecture: Its Practical Aspects*, 1973; *The Cemeteries and Burial Grounds of Glasgow*, 1975; *The Erosion of Oxford*, 1977; *English Architecture: An Illustrated Glossary*, 1977; *Mausolea in Ulster*, 1978; *The Architecture, Planning, and History of the Estates of the Drapers' Company in Ulster*, 1979; *A Celebration of Death*, 1980; *Classical Churches in Ulster*, 1980; *The History, Architecture, and Planning of the Estates of the Fishmongers' Company in Ulster*, 1981; *The Egyptian Revival*, 1982; *The Life and Work of Henry Roberts (1803–76), Architect*, 1983; *The Londonderry Plantation 1609–1914*, 1985. Essays: Osvald Almqvist; Jacob Bakema; Eugène Beaudouin; Victor Bourgeois; Johannes Brinkman; Lúcio Costa; Harald Deilmann; Giorgio Grassi; Pierre Jeanneret; Sigurd Lewerentz; Ernst May; Robin Seifert; Albert Speer; Ivar Tengbom; Cornelis van Eesteren; Clough Williams-Ellis.

CURTIS, William J. R. Contributor. Author and Lecturer. Author of *Le Corbusier/English Architecture of the 1930's*, 1975; *A Language and a Theme: The Architecture of Denys Lasdun and Partners*, 1977; *Le Corbusier at Work: The Genesis of the Carpenter Center for the Visual Arts* (with Eduard Sekler), 1978; *Modern Architecture Since 1900*, 1982. Essays: Wells Coates; Sir Denys Lasdun; Berthold Lubetkin.

CZAJKOWSKI, Jorge. Adviser and contributor. Professor of Architecture, Federal University of Rio de Janeiro. Brazilian Correspondent, *Architecture*, Paris, 1975–77. Author of *Since Brasilia: Modern Brazilian Architecture* (in preparation); *Retrato do Brasil* (with others; in preparation). Essays: Sergio Bernardes; João Filguéiras; Joaquim Guedes; Rino Levi; Henrique Mindlin; Jorge Machado Moreira; Fabio Penteado; Roberto Architects; Gregori Warchavchik.

CZAPLINSKA-ARCHER, Teresa. Contributor. Architect in private practice, Sydney, Australia. Author of *James Stirling: Theory and Practice* (thesis: Wroclaw Technical University, Poland), 1978. Contributor to *Architectural Association Quarterly*, London, and to *Sztuka* and *Architektura*, Warsaw. Essays: Buszko and Franta; Oskar Hansen; Bohdan Lachert; Ivor Smith; Helena Syrkus; Hanna Wejchert; Wojciech Zablocki.

DAHINDEN, Justus. Contributor and entrant: see his own entry. Essays: Günter Behnisch; Alfred Roth; O. M. Ungers; Alexander von Branca.

de MARÉ, Eric. Contributor. Freelance writer and architectural photographer, London. Formerly, Editor of *The Architects' Journal*, London. Author of *The Canals of England*, 1950; *Scandinavia*, 1952; *New Ways of Building* (editor), 1952; *Time on the Thames*, 1952, 1975; *New Ways of Servicing Buildings*, 1954; *The Bridges of Britain*, 1954, 1975; *Gunnar Asplund*, 1955; *London's Riverside*, 1958; *Photography and Architecture*, 1961; *London's River: The Story of a City*, 1964; *Swedish Cross-Cut: The Story of the Göta Canal*, 1965; *London 1851: The Year of the Great Exhibition*, 1972; *The London Doré Saw*, 1973; *Wren's London*, 1975; *The Victorian Wood-Block Illustrators*, 1979; *A Matter of Life or Debt*, 1983, 1984. Essay: Gunnar Asplund.

DEVINE, Mary Elizabeth. Contributor. Professor of English, Salem State College, Massachusetts. Author of *Restoration and 18th Century Theatre Research: A Bibliography of Criticism 1900–68* (with Carl J. Stratman and David G. Spencer), 1971; *Appearances*, 1980. Essay: Charles William Brubaker.

DIAMANT-BERGER, Renée. Contributor. Writer and architectural historian, Paris. Editor, *L'Architecture d'Aujourd'hui*, Paris, 1948–72. Secretary of the Group Espace, 1950–66. Author of *Group Espace*, 1950; *Arne Jacobsen*, and the monographs *Jean Balladur; Gaston Jaubert; Bernard de la Tour d'Auvergne; Jean Le Couteur; Auguste Arsac; Legrand et Rabinel*; and *Daniel Badani/Pierre Roux-Dorlut*. Essays: Edouard Albert; Daniel Badani; Bernard de la Tour d'Auvergne: Alexis Josic; Charlotte Perriand; Roger Taillibert.

DICKSON, John D. Contributor. Senior Lecturer in Architecture, University of Auckland, New Zealand. Essay: R. H. B. Toy.

DREW, Philip. Contributor. Architect in private practice, Sydney, Australia. Australian Correspondent, *Architecture + Urbanism*, Tokyo. Technical Editor, Architectural Press, London, 1970–71, Visiting Assistant Professor, University of Idaho, 1972–73, Senior Lecturer, University of Newcastle, 1974–83, and Visiting Associate Professor, Washington University, St. Louis, 1982–83. Author of *Third Generation: The Changing Meaning of Architecture*, 1973; *Frei Otto: Form and Structure;* 1976; *Tensile Architecture*, 1979; *Two Towers*, 1980; *The Architecture of Arata Isozaki*, 1982; *Leaves of Iron: Glenn Murcutt, Pioneer of an Australian Architectural Form*, 1985. Essays: John Andrews: Robin Boyd; Peter Corrigan: Richard Le Plastrier: Peter Muller: Glenn Murcutt; Frei Otto; Bruce Rickard; Harry Seidler.

DÜTTMANN, Martina. Contributor. Editor with the Archibook Publishing Company, Berlin. Formerly, Editor, *Bauwelt*, Berlin. Editor of *Information uber Gestalt*, 1974; *Reihe Skizzenbucher*, 1975; and *Reihe Werkstadtbucher*, 1976. Essay: Werner Düttmann.

ECKBO, Garrett. Contributor and entrant: see his own entry. Essay: Hideo Sasaki.

EDER, Rita. Contributor. Researcher, Instituto de Investigaciones Estéticos, National University of Mexico. Author of *Dada Documentos* (with Ida Rodriguez), 1977; *Imagen Historica de la Fotografia en Mexico* (with Nestor García Canelini), 1978; *Alberto Gironella*. Essay: Mathias Goeritz.

ELLIOTT, Julian. Contributor and entrant: see his own entry. Essays: Ron Kirby; Roelof S. Uytenbogaardt.

EMANUEL, Muriel. Contributor. Freelance researcher, editor and writer, London. Editor of *Israel: A Survey and Bibliography*, 1971; *Contemporary Architects*, 1980. Essays: Max Abramovitz; Yona Friedman; Walter A. Netsch; Der Scutt.

ENGLAND, Richard. Contributor and entrant: see his own entry. Essay: Gio Ponti.

FABER, Tobias. Contributor. Professor and Rector, School of Architecture, The Royal Academy of Fine Arts, Copenhagen. Author of *Rum, Form og Funktion*, 1962; *Dansk Arkitektur*, 1963, 1976; *Arne Jacobsen*, 1964; *Alberobello*, 1967; *Neue Dänische Architektur*, 1968; *En Kinarejse*, 1979. Essay: Jørgen Bo.

FARNSWORTH, Geoffrey Lee. Contributor.

Architect and Associate with Schmidt, Garden and Erikson, Chicago. **Essay:** Paul Schweikher.

FATOUROS, Dimitris A. Contributor. Rector and Professor of Architecture, and Director of the Laboratory of Design and Industrial Aesthetics, University of Thessaloniki, Greece. Formerly, Member of the Editorial Boards of the annual reviews *Architecture in Greece* and *Design in Greece*, and currently of *Urban Ecology*. Regular contributor to *To Vima*, Athens. Author of *The Consciousness of Architectural Work*, 1952; *Courses of a Systematic Theory of Architecture*, 2 volumes, 1971–73; *Change and Reality in the University*, 1975; *The Scientist and the Authority*, 1979; *The Syntax of Space and Geometry of the Architectural Work*, 1979; and editor (with others) of *Problems of Production and Organization of Space*, 1979; *Architectural Organization and Expression*, 1981. **Essays:** Dimitris Antonakakis; Aris Konstantinidis; Dimitris A. Pikionis.

FAWCETT, Chris. Contributor. Research Fellow, Kyoto University, and Instructor at Kyoto Art College, Japan. Author of *The New Japanese House*, 1980; *Against History* (forthcoming). Contributor to the *Architectural Association Quarterly*, *Architectural Design*, *Tulane Architectural Review*, *Toshi Jutaku* and *Shinkenchiku*. **Essays:** Takefumi Aida; Yoshinobu Ashihara; Gae Aulenti; Colquhoun and Miller; Hiromi Fujii; Patrick Gwynne; Hiroshi Hara; John M. Johansen; Martorell-Bohigas-Mackay; Tomoya Masuda; Giovanni Michelucci; Monta Mozuna; Masato Otaka; Andrew Renton; Junzo Sakakura; Kazuo Shinohara; Ettore Sottsass, Jr.; Shizutaro Urabe; Youji Watanabe; Clifford Wearden; John Weeks; Colin St. John Wilson.

FISCHER, Volker. Contributor. Deputy Director of the German Architecture Museum, Frankfurt. Formerly, Councillor for Cultural Affairs, Marburg, West Germany. Author of *Nostalgie, Geschichte und Kultur als Trodelmarkt*, 1980; *Die Revision der Moderne, Postmoderne Architektur 1960–80*, with Hans-Peter Schwarz and Andrea Gleiniger-Neumann, 1984; *Bauen heute — Architektur der Gegenwart in der Bundesrepublik Deutschland*, with others, 1985; editor, with Gunther Rotermund, *Jahrbuch fur Architektur*, 1984. **Essays:** Raimund Abraham; Rem Koolhaas.

FURSE, John. Contributor. Lecturer in Visual Communication, Plymouth Polytechnic, Devon. Author of *Michelangelo*, 1975. **Essays:** Giancarlo De Carlo; J. J. P. Oud; Rudolph Schindler; Alison Smithson; Peter Smithson; Aldo van Eyck.

GILMONT, Darius. Contributor. Freelance writer, designer, and student architect, Manchester, England. **Essay:** Mario Botta.

GIURGOLA, Romaldo. Contributor and entrant: see his own entry. **Essays:** Jørn Utzon; Gino Valle; Robert Venturi.

GLUSBERG, Jorge. Contributor. Director, Center of Art and Communication, Buenos Aires. President, Argentine Section of the International Association of Art Critics. Associate Professor, New York University. Delegate Counsellor, International Union of Architects. Corresponding Editor, *Leonardo*, U.S.A., and *D'Ars*, Milan. Editor, Bulletin of the International Union of Architects, and Co-director, *Revista de Estetica*. Author of *Towards a Topological Architecture* (with Clorindo Testa), 1977; *Rhetoric of Latin American Art*, 1978; *Socio-Semiotic of Architecture*, 1978; *Myths and Magic of Fire, Gold and Art*, 1978; *From Incan Habitat to the Lima of the Future*, 1979; *Theory and Criticism of Architecture*, 1979; *Clorindo Testa, Painter and Architect*, 1983; *School of Architecture: Drawings from Architects*, 1983; *Six Mexican Architects*, 1984. **Essays:** Mario Roberto Alvarez; Antonini Schon Zemborain; Baudizzone-Erbin-Lestard-Varas; Eladio Dieste; Manteola, Sánchez Gómez, Santos, Solsona, Architects;

Mario Payssé-Reyes; Rogelio Salmona; Clorindo Testa; José Villagrán García; Amancio Williams.

GOULDEN, Gontran (died in 1985). Contributor. Director, The Building Centre, London, 1962–74, and Deputy Chairman, The Building Centre Group, 1974–77. President, The Architectural Association, 1956–57; Treasurer, International Union of Architects, 1965–75. Author of *Bathrooms*, 1966. **Essays:** Otto Bartning; Hugh Casson; Willem Dudok; Kay Fisker; Arne Jacobsen; Hans Scharoun.

GOWAN, James. Contributor and entrant: see his own entry. **Essay:** Peter Cook.

GRAF, Urs. Contributor. Architect, editor and publisher, Berne. Art Critic, *Werk*, Zurich, 1969–75. Author of *Berner Szene* (with Rös Graf), 1973; *Beispiele aus dem Grenzbereich Kunst: Architektur* (exhibition catalogue; with Rös Graf), 1975. **Essay:** Atelier 5.

GREEN, Cedric. Contributor. Senior Lecturer in Architecture, University of Sheffield, Yorkshire. **Essays:** Richard England; Walter Segal.

GREGORY, Daniel. Instructor in Architectural History, Carnegie-Mellon University, Pittsburgh. **Essay:** William Turnbull, Jr.

GREGOTTI, Vittorio. Adviser and entrant; see his own entry.

GREIG, Doreen. Contributor. Architect and writer, Johannesburg. President of the Convocation of the University of the Witwatersrand, Johannesburg. President, Transvaal Institute of Architects, 1959, 1965, South African Institute of Architects, 1972–74, and South African Council for Architects, 1973–75. Author of *Herbert Baker in South Africa*, 1970; *A Guide to Architecture in South Africa*, 1971; *The Diffusion of Dutch Culture Abroad in the Seventeenth and Eighteenth Centuries*, 1985. **Essays:** Steffan Ahrends; Brian Sandrock.

HALLEN, Hans. Contributor and entrant: see his own entry. **Essays:** Julian Elliott; Wilhelm O. Meyer; Jan van Wijk.

HAMILTON, Stephen P. Contributor. Architect in private practice, Massachusetts. Instructor, Boston Architectural Center. Architectural Book Reviewer for *Library Journal*, New York. **Essays:** Peter Blake; Eduardo Catalano; Dan Kiley; Carl Koch; Eliot Noyes.

HARROP-ALLIN, Clinton. Contributor. Associate Professor, Department of the History of Art, University of South Africa, Pretoria. Author of *Norman Eaton: Architect*, 1975. **Essay:** Norman Eaton.

HAWKINS, Lucinda. Contributor. Formerly, Deputy Editor, *Studio International*, London. **Essays:** Pietro Belluschi; Charles Warren Callister; Ezra Ehrenkrantz; John Lautner.

HAYES, Mary. Contributor. Freelance writer and lecturer on the visual arts, London. **Essay:** Lyons, Israel, Ellis and Gray.

HEINONEN, Raija-Liisa (died, 1978). Contributor. Curator of Archives, Museum of Finnish Architecture, Helsinki, 1975–78. Author of *The Breakthrough of Functionalism in Finland*, 1979. **Essay:** Erik Bryggman.

HENEGHAN, Tom. Contributor. Unit Master at the Architectural Association School, London. Freelance writer on architecture for *Building Design*, London. **Essay:** Derek Walker.

HERBERT, Gilbert. Contributor. Mary Hill Swope Professor of Architecture, Technion: Israel Institute of Technology, Haifa. Lecturer in Architecture, University of the Witwatersrand, Johannesburg, 1947–61; Reader in Architecture and Town Planning University of Adelaide, South Australia, 1961–

1968. Associate Editor, *South African Architectural Record*, Johannesburg, 1949–60. Author of *The Synthetic Vision of Walter Gropius*, 1959; *Martienssen and the International Style: The Development of Modern Architecture in South Africa*, 1975; *Pioneers of Prefabrication: The British Contribution in the Nineteenth Century*, 1978; *The Dream of the Factory-Made House: Walter Gropius and Konrad Wachsmann*, 1984. **Essays:** Norman Hanson; Dov Karmi; Ram Karmi; Al Mansfeld; Yacov Rechter; Arieh Sharon.

HEYER, Paul. Contributor. Architect in private practice, New York. Professor of Architecture, and Co-Chairman of the Graduate Department of Architecture, Pratt Institute, Brooklyn, New York. Editor of *Architects on Architecture: New Directions in America*, 1966; and author of *Mexican Architecture: The Work of Abraham Zabludovsky and Teodoro González de León*, 1978. **Essay:** Abraham Zabludovsky.

HIBBARD, Don J. Contributor. Architectural Historian, State of Hawaii. Architectural Historian, State of Idaho, 1975–78. Author of *Normal Hill*, 1978; *Weiser: A Look at Idaho Architecture*, 1978; *The View from Diamond Head*, 1985. **Essays:** Vernon DeMars; Joseph Esherick; Ian McHarg; William Morgan; Ralph Rapson; James Wines.

HOFFMANN, Donald. Contributor. Art and Architecture Critic, *The Kansas City Star*. Editor of *The Meanings of Architecture: Buildings and Writings by John Wellborn Root*, 1967; and author of *The Architecture of John Wellborn Root*, 1973; *Frank Lloyd Wright's Fallingwater*, 1978; *Frank Lloyd Wright's Robie House*, 1984. **Essay:** Ludwig Mies van der Rohe.

HUNT, William Dudley, Jr. Contributor. Consulting Editor, John Wiley and Sons Inc., New York and Chichester. Senior Editor, *Architectural Record*, New York, 1958–63; Publisher, *AIA Journal*, Washington, D.C., 1964–72 (Publishing Director of the AIA, 1970–72). Editor of, and contributor to, *Comprehensive Architectural Services*, 1965; *Creative Control of Building Costs*, 1967; *Architectural Graphics*, 1981; *Architects' Data*, 1980; author of *Contemporary Curtain Wall*, 1958; *Total Design*, 1972; *Encyclopedia of American Architecture*, 1979; *American Architecture: A Field Guide to the Most Important Examples*, 1984. **Essays:** Welton Becket; Wallace K. Harrison; Richard Llewelyn-Davies; Eero Saarinen; Hugh A. Stubbins, Jr.

HURLEY, Kent. Contributor. Assistant Dean, and Director of the Sandwich (Co-op) Program, Faculty of Architecture, Technical University of Nova Scotia, Halifax. **Essays:** Gustavo da Roza; Clifford Wiens.

JACKSON, Anthony. Adviser and contributor. Professor of Architecture, Nova Scotia Technical College, Halifax. Author of *The Politics of Architecture*, 1970; *A Place Called Home*, 1976; *The Democratization of Canadian Architecture*, 1978; *The Future of Canadian Architecture*, 1979; *Space in Canadian Architecture*, 1981. **Essays:** Ray Affleck; George Baird; Barry Downs; Macy DuBois; Raymond Moriyama; Eberhard Zeidler.

JELLICOE, Geoffrey. Contributor and entrant: see his own entry. **Essays:** Holger Blom; Roberto Burle Marx; Brenda Colvin; Dame Sylvia Crowe; Philip Dowson; Eric Lyons; Sheppard, Robson and Partners; F. R. S. Yorke.

JOEDICKE, Jürgen. Contributor. Professor, and Director of the Institut Grundlagen der modernen Architektur und Entwerfen, University of Stuttgart, since 1967; in architectural practice with Walter Mayer, Stuttgart and Nuremberg, since 1973. Editor of the series *Documents of Modern Architecture*. Author of *A History of Modern Architecture*, 1958; *Office Building*, 1959; *Shell Architecture*, 1963; *Hugo Häring: Schriften, Entwürfe, Bauten*, 1965;

Architecture since 1945: Sources and Directions, 1969; *Angewandte Entwurfsmethodik für Architekten*, 1976; *Architektur im Umbruch: Geschichte, Entwicklung, Ausblick*, 1979; *Space and Form in Architecture*, 1984. **Essays:** Kurt Ackermann; Richard Döcker; Friedrich Wilhelm Kraemer; Horst Linde; Heikki Siren; Max Taut.

JORDY, William H. Adviser. Henry Ledyard Goddard Professor of Art, Brown University, Providence, Rhode Island. Editor (with Ralph Coe) of *"American Architecture" and Other Writings* by Montgomery Schuyler, 1961; and author of *American Buildings and Their Architects*, 2 volumes, 1976.

JUHASZ, Joseph B. Contributor. Associate Professor of Environmental Design, and Director of the Environmental Design Division, College of Design and Planning, University of Colorado, Boulder. Author of *Environments: Notes and Selections on Objects, Spaces and Behavior* (with Steven Friedman), 1974. **Essays:** Alden Dow; Garrett Eckbo; Herb Greene; Morris Lapidus; Gerald McCue; William C. Muchow; Eldar Sharon; Minoru Yamasaki.

KELL, Diane. Contributor. Editor of the *Constructional Review*, Sydney. **Essay:** Keith E. Cottier.

KINGDON, Jonathan. Contributor. Lecturer in Fine Art, Ruskin School of Drawing, Oxford University. Author of *East African Mammals: An Atlas of Evolution in Africa*. **Essay:** Richard Hughes.

KOEHLER, Robert E. Contributor. Freelance editor and writer, Washington, D.C. Editor, *AIA Journal*, Washington, D.C., 1965–73. Co-editor of *Current Techniques in Architectural Practice*, 1976; editor of *Personnel Practices Handbook*, 1978. **Essays:** Charles Blessing; Frank Schlesinger; Paul Thiry.

KOENIGSBERGER, Otto. Contributor. Emeritus Professor of Development Planning, University College of the University of London. Editor, *Habitat International*, since 1977. Author of *Construction of Ancient Egyptian Doors*, 1936; *Housing in Ghana* (with Charles Abrams and Vladimir Bodiansky), 1956; *Housing in Pakistan* (with Charles Abrams), 1957; *Housing in the Philippine Islands* (with Charles Abrams), 1958; *Metropolitan Lagos* (with others), 1962; *Development and Urban Renewal in Singapore* (with Charles Abrams and Susumu Kobe), 1963; *Roofs in the Warm Humid Tropics* (with Robert Lynn), 1966; *Climate and House Design* (with Carl Mahoney and Martin Evans), 1970; *Manual of Tropical Housing* (with others), 1972; *Planning Legislation*, 1975; *The Implementation of Urban Plans*, 1977; *Planning Education in Poor Countries*, 1977; etc. **Essay:** James Cubitt.

KULTERMANN, Udo. Adviser and contributor. Professor of Architecture, Washington University, St. Louis. Formerly, Director, City Art Museum, Leverkusen, West Germany. Author of *Architecture of Today*, 1958; *Hans und Wassili Luckhardt*, 1958; *Dynamische Architektur*, 1959; *New Japanese Architecture*, 1960; *Junge deutsche Bildhauer*, 1963; *New Architecture in Africa*, 1963; *Der Schluessel zur Architektur von heute*, 1963; *New Architecture in the World*, 1965; *History of Art History*, 1966; *Architektur der Gegenwart*, 1967; *The New Sculpture*, 1967; *Gabriel Grupello*, 1968; *The New Painting*, 1969; *New Directions in African Architecture*, 1969; *Kenzo Tange*, 1970; *Art and Life*, 1970; *New Realism*, 1972; *Die Architektur im 20. Jahrhundert*, 1977; *Ernest Trova*, 1978; *Scultura contemporanea*, 1979; *Architecture of the Seventies*, 1980; *Architects of the Third World*, 1980; *The Basilica of Maxentius*, 1985; *Contemporary Architecture in Eastern Europe*, 1985. **Essays:** Arata Isozaki; Uttam C. Jain; Leon Krier; Rob Krier; Paolo Portoghesi; Aldo Rossi; James Stirling.

KUWABARA, Bruce. Associate, Barton Myers Associates, Toronto. Visiting Critic of Architecture, Technical University of Nova Scotia, Halifax, and University of Waterloo, Ontario; Tutor, University of Toronto. **Essay:** Barton Myers.

LAURIE, Michael. Contributor. Professor of Landscape Architecture, University of California, Berkeley. Author of *An Introduction to Landscape Architecture*. 1975. Co-editor, *Gardens Are For People* by Thomas D. Church, 1963. **Essay:** Thomas D. Church.

LAVENSTEIN, Richard. Contributor. Architect with Rivkin-Weisman Architects, New York. Formerly, Instructor, School of Architecture, Washington University, St. Louis. **Essays:** George Howe; Paul Nelson; Werner Seligmann.

LEGNER, Linda. Contributor. Free-lance writer on architecture, Chicago. **Essays:** Hellmuth, Obata, and Kassabaum; Lawrence B. Perkins.

LEWCOCK, Ronald. Contributor. Aga Khan Professor of Architecture and Design for Islamic Cultures, Massachusetts Institute of Technology, and Lecturer, Architectural Association School, London. Formerly, Senior Lecturer, School of Architecture, University of Natal, South Africa and Fellow of Clare Hall, Cambridge, England. Editor of the architectural entries for the *Encyclopaedia of Southern Africa* and *Everyman's Encyclopaedia*. Author of *Early 19th Century Architecture in South Africa*, 1963; *Sana, An Arabian Islamic City*, 1984. **Essay:** Revel Fox.

LLOYD, Michael. Contributor. Consultant in private practice, Oslo. Formerly: Dean of the Faculty of Architecture, Kumasi, Ghana; Principal, Architectural Association School of Architecture, London; Consultant Head, Hull School of Architecture. Author of *Teknisk Tegning og Skissering*, 1960; *Environmental Impact of Development Activities*, 1975. **Essays:** Sverre Fehn; Knut Knutsen; Arne Korsmo.

LÜCHINGER, Arnulf. Contributor. Architect and writer, The Hague. Director of Arch-Edition Den Haag. Author of *Structuralism in Architecture and Urban Planning*, 1980; *Herman Hertzberger, Buildings and Projects 1964–1984*, 1985; *Alltagliche Architektur*, with N. John Habraken, 1985. Contributor to *Bauen und Wohnen* and *Architecture + Urbanism*. **Essays:** Piet Blom; N. John Habraken; Herman Hertzberger; Mart Stam.

LYE, K. C. Contributor. Professor and Dean of Architecture, University of Hong Kong. Formerly, Professor and Head, Department of Architecture, University of Manitoba. Author of *The Architecture of Self-Help Communities*, 1978. **Essays:** Tao Ho; Sumet Jumsai; Jackson C. S. Wong.

MACKAY, David. Adviser, contributor and entrant: see his own entry. **Essays:** Ricardo Bofill; Pep Bonet; Lluis Clotet; José A. Coderch; Josep María Jujol; Luis Peña; Josep Maria Sostres.

MAKINSON, Randell L. Contributor. Curator, The Gamble House: Greene and Greene Library, School of Architecture, University of Southern California, Los Angeles. Author of *A Guide to the Work of Greene and Greene*, 1974; *Greene and Greene*, 2 volumes, 1977–78. **Essay:** Henry Mather Greene.

MARKELIN, Antero. Contributor. Professor of Urban Design, University of Stuttgart. Editor of *Mensch und Stadtgestalt*, 1974; author of *Stadtbild in der Planungspraxis* (with M. Trieb), 1976. **Essay:** Timo Penttilä.

MARTIN, Linda. Contributor. Architect working in the Bristol Housing Association. Formerly in private practice, Oslo. **Essay:** Kjell Lund.

MASINI, Lara-Vinca. Contributor. Art critic and

editor, Florence. Author of *Le Tombe dei Re a Saint Denis*, 1966; *La Cattedrale di Wells*, 1967; *Savioli*, 1967; *Gaudi*, 1969; *Riccardo Morandi*, 1973; *Progetto Struttura, Metodologia del Design*, 1975; *Simbolismo*, 1979. Regular contributor to *Domus*, *Quadrum*, *NAC*, *L'Architettura*, *Art and Artists*, etc. **Essays:** Carlo Aymonino; Angelo Mangiarotti; Riccardo Morandi; Leonardo Ricci; Leonardo Savioli.

MAXWELL, Robert. Contributor. Partner of Douglas Stephen and Partners, London. Dean of Architecture, Princeton University. Formerly, Professor of Architecture, University College of the University of London. Author of *New British Architecture*, 1972; *Venturi and Rauch*, 1978. **Essay:** Douglas Stephen.

McCOY, Esther. Adviser and contributor. Architectural writer and historian, Los Angeles. Contributing Editor, *Arts and Architecture*, Santa Monica, and *Progressive Architecture*, New York. Author of *Five California Architects*, 1960, 1975; *Neutra*, 1960; *Modern California Houses*, 1962, 1978; *Craig Ellwood*, 1968; *Vienna to Los Angeles: Two Journeys*, 1979; *The Second Generation*, 1984. **Essays:** Gregory Ain; J. R. Davidson; Harwell Hamilton Harris; A. Quincy Jones; Cesar Pelli; Lloyd Wright.

McKEAN, J. M. Contributor. Freelance architect and critic, London. Tutor, Architectural Association School, London; Director of the First Year Course, North East London Polytechnic School of Architecture. Former Technical, then News Editor of *The Architects' Journal*, London. Author of *Architecture of the Western World* (with others), 1979; *Masterpieces of Architectural Draughtsmanship*, 1980. **Essays:** Michael Brawne; Peter Moro.

McMORDIE, Michael. Contributor. Professor of Architecture, Faculty of Environmental Design, University of Calgary. President, Society for the Study of Architecture in Canada. **Essays:** Arthur Erickson; John B. Parkin; John C. Parkin.

MILLER, Nory. Contributor. Assistant Editor, *AIA Journal*, Washington, D.C. Formerly, Managing Editor, *Inland Architect*, Chicago, and Architecture Critic of the *Chicago Daily News*. **Essays:** Warren J. Cox; Bertrand Goldberg; Hugh Newell Jacobsen; Arthur Cotton Moore; Stanley Tigerman; John Carl Warnecke.

MILLS, Edward D. Contributor. Senior Partner, Edward D. Mills and Partners, Architects, London. Author of *Architecture as a Career*, 1945; *The Modern Factory*, 1951; *The Modern Church*, 1956; *The New Architecture in Great Britain*, 1953; *Factory Building in Great Britain*, 1967; *The Changing Workplace*, 1972; *The National Exhibition Centre*, 1976; *Building Centre Guide to Building Maintenance*, 1984; *Churchbuilding* (in preparation). **Essays:** Architects Co-Partnership; E. Maxwell Fry; William Graham Holford; Ely Jacques Kahn; Luigi Moretti; Philip Powell; Basil Spence.

MIOTTO-MURET, Luciana. Contributor. Professor of Modern Architectural History, Université de Paris VIII-Vincennes. Author of *Carlo Scarpa*. 1975. Contributor to *L'Architecture d'Aujourd'hui*, *Revue de l'Art*, *L'Architecture* and *Spazio e Società*. **Essays:** Pierre Chareau.

MOTTA, Flavio. Contributor. Professor of the History of Art and Architecture, Faculty of Architecture and Urbanism, University of Sao Paulo. Regular contributor to *Acropole*, Sao Paulo. **Essay:** Paulo Mendes da Rocha.

MURPHY, Elizabeth. Contributor. Architect. Author of *Eileen Gray* (thesis: North London Polytechnic), 1976; *The Eileen Gray House at Castellar, near Meudon*, 1977. **Essay:** Eileen Gray.

NAIRN, Janet. Contributor. Freelance writer, Los Angeles. **Essay:** Frank O. Gehry.

NATCHEV, Zdravko. Contributor. Architect in private practice, Nanterre, France. Contributor to *Neuf, L'Architecture d'Aujourd'hui, Crée,* etc. **Essays:** Imre Makovecz, György Vadász.

NAYLOR, Colin. Associate editor and contributor. Freelance researcher, editor and writer, London. Formerly, Editor, *Art and Artists,* London. Editor of *Contemporary Artists,* 1977; *Contemporary Photographers,* 1987. **Essays:** William W. Caudill; Enrique del Moral; Barnett Gruzen; Helmut Jahn; Edward F. Knowles; Lucien Kroll; Carlos Raúl Villanueva.

NEVEL, Robert B. Contributor. Teaching Assistant, School of Architecture, Washington University, St. Louis. **Essay:** Zvi Hecker.

OSBALDESTON, Roger. Contributor. Associate Professor of Landscape Architecture, California Polytechnic State University, San Luis Obispo. **Essay:** Lawrence Halprin.

OSTLER, Timothy. Contributor. Architect in private practice. London. Author of *Pancho Guedes: The Collective Unconscious of Architecture* (thesis: University of Sheffield), 1978; *Amancio Guedes* (forthcoming). **Essay:** Amancio Guedes.

PATTERSON, Gordon. Contributor. Senior Partner, Gordon Patterson and Partners, landscape architects, Stevenage, Hertfordshire. Co-Author of *Gardens of Mughal India,* 1960. **Essay:** Hans Luz.

PEGRUM, Roger. Contributor. Architect and Planner in private practice, Sydney. Associate Professor in Architecture, University of Sydney. Author of *The Bush Capital; Australian Architects: Philip Cox; Details in Australian Architecture.* **Essay:** Daryl Jackson.

PEHNT, Wolfgang. Adviser and contributor. Editor for Arts and Architecture, Deutschlandfunk, Cologne. Editor of *Encyclopedia of Modern Architecture,* 1964; *Die Stadt in der Bundesrepublik,* 1974; and author of *New German Architecture 1960–1970,* 1970; *Expressionist Architecture,* 1973; *Der Anfang der Bescheidenheit,* 1983; *Das Ende der Zuversicht,* 1983. **Essays:** Ferdinand Kramer; Otto Steidle.

PETERS, Richard C. Contributor. Professor and Chairman of the Department of Architecture, College of Environmental Design, University of California, Berkeley. President, Association of Collegiate Schools of Architecture, 1979–82. Author of *William Wilson Wurster: An Architect of Houses.* **Essay:** William Wilson Wurster.

POSENER, Julius. Contributor. Emeritus Professor, Hochschule der Künste, Berlin. Author of *Anfänge des Funktionalismus,* 1964; *Garden Cities of Tomorrow,* 1968; *Hans Poelzig,* 1970; *From Schinkel to the Bauhaus,* 1974; *Berlin on the Road Towards a New Architecture,* 1979; *Collected Writings from Half a Century,* 1979. **Essay:** Pierre Vago.

QUANTRILL, Malcolm. Contributor. Professor of Architecture, Texas A and M University. Deputy Editor, *Art International,* Zurich. Director, Architectural Association, London, 1967–69, Dean of the School of Environmental Design, Polytechnic of North London, 1973–80, and Professor of Architecture and Urban Design, University of Jordan, 1980–83. Author of *Ritual and Response in Architecture,* 1974; *Monuments of Another Age* (with Esther Quantrill), 1975; *Alvar Aalto: A Critical Study,* 1983; *Reima Pietila, Architecture, Context and Modernism,* 1984; *Aalto and After* (in preparation); and *The Environmental Memory* (in preparation). **Essay:** Reima Pietilä.

RABENECK, Andrew. Contributor. Managing Director, Building Systems Development (U.K.) Ltd., London. Consultant Editor, *Architectural Design,* London 1970–78. Author of *Planning Office Space* (with others), 1976; *Encyclopaedia of Architecture and Technical Innovation* (with others), 1979. **Essays:** Christopher Alexander; BBPR; Ludovico Quaroni.

RICHARDS, Larry. Contributor. Assistant Professor, Faculty of Architecture, and Campus Design Coordinator, Technical University of Nova Scotia, Halifax; Vice-President, Networks Ltd., Halifax. Atlantic Regional Editor, *Decormag,* Montreal. **Essay:** Peter Rose.

RODRIGUEZ, Ida. Contributor. Researcher, Instituto de Investigaciones Estéticos, and Professor, Faculty of Philosophy, National University of Mexico. Author of *La critica de arte en México,* 1964; *El arte contemporáneo,* 1964; *El surrealismo y el arte fantástico de México,* 1969; *Pedro Friedeberg,* 1972; *Una década de critica de Arte,* 1974; *Herbert Bayer: Un Concepto Total,* 1975; *Dada Documentos* (with Rita Eder), 1977. **Essay:** Max Cetto.

ROGATNICK, Abraham. Contributor. Professor of Architecture, University of British Columbia, Vancouver. Contributor to *Architectural Review, Architectural Design, Artforum, Artscanada* and *The Canadian Architect.* **Essays:** Douglas Cardinal; Giuseppe Samonà.

ROSENBERG, Eugene. Contributor and entrant: see his own entry. **Essays:** Bohuslav Fuchs; Josef Havlíček.

ROSS, Michael Franklin. Contributor. Director of Architectural Programs, Daniel, Mann, Johnson and Mendenhall, Los Angeles. Visiting Professor of Architecture, University of California at Los Angeles. West Coast Correspondent, *Progressive Architecture,* New York; Member of the Editorial Board, *L.A. Architect.* Author of *Beyond Metabolism: The New Japanese Architecture,* 1978. **Essays:** Takamitsu Azuma; Kisho Kurokawa; Anthony Lumsden; Kunio Mayekawa; Shin'ichi Okada; Minoru Takeyama.

ROUDA, Mitchell B. Contributor. Freelance architectural writer. Formerly, Assistant Editor, *Stylos Architecture* (formerly *Process: Architecture,* Pittsburgh and Tokyo). Author of *Emerging Architecture in the Emerging World,* 1979. **Essays:** Nader Ardalan; Lewis Davis; Louis I. Kahn; Leandro V. Locsin; George Nelson; Moshe Safdie; Louis Sauer; Konrad Wachsmann; Shadrach Woods.

ROWNTREE, Diana. Contributor. Architect in private practice, Hexham, Northumberland. Architecture Correspondent of *The Guardian,* London, 1955–66. Author of the *Penguin Handbook of Interior Design,* 1964. **Essay:** Ove Arup.

RYAN, Paul. Contributor. Freelance writer, London. **Essays:** Guido Canella; Marco Zanuso.

RYKWERT, Joseph. Contributor. Professor of Art, University of Essex, Colchester, and Slade Professor of Fine Arts, Cambridge University. Author of *The Golden House,* 1947; *Church Building,* 1966; *On Adam's House in Paradise,* 1972; *The Idea of a Town,* 1976; *The First Moderns,* 1980; *The Necessity of Artifice,* 1983; *Robert Adam,* 1984; *Richard Meier,* 1984, and editor of *The Ten Books of Architecture* by Alberti, 1955. **Essays:** Luigi Figini; Vittorio Gregotti; Ernesto Nathan Rogers.

SACK, Manfred. Contributor. Editor of *Die Zeit,* Hamburg. Author of *Architektur in der Zeit,* 1979; *Das deutsche Wohnzimmer,* 1980; *Lebensraum: Strasse,* 1982; *Einfache Paradiese,* 1985. **Essays:** Gottfried Böhm, Hermann Fehling, Josef Paul Kleihues; Meinhard von Gerkan.

SAINI, B. S. Contributor. Professor and Head of the Department of Architecture, University of Queensland, Brisbane. Author of *Architecture in Tropical Australia,* 1970; *Building Environment: An Illustrated Analysis of Problems in Hot Dry Lands,* 1973. **Essays:** Charles M. Correa; John Dalton; Robin Gibson; Matthew Nowicki.

SALOKORPI, Asko. Contributor. Head of the Research Department, Museum of Finnish Architecture, Helsinki. Author of *Modern Finnish Architecture,* 1970; *Guide to Finnish Architecture,* 1979. **Essay:** Aarno Ruusuvuori.

SCHMERTZ, Mildred F. Adviser and contributor. Senior Editor, *Architectural Record,* New York, Visiting Lecturer, Yale University School of Architecture, New Haven, Connecticut. Editor of, and contributor to, *Campus Architecture,* 1972; *Open Space for People,* 1974; *Office Building Design,* 1975. **Essays:** Edmund N. Bacon; Gunnar Birkerts; Cambridge Seven; B. V. Doshi; M. Paul Friedberg; Robert Geddes; Gerhard M. Kallmann; Tasso Katselas; Giovanni Pasanella; Paul Rudolph; Josep Lluis Sert; John Ormsbee Simonds; Eva Vecsei.

SCHOENAUER, Norbert. Contributor. Professor of Architecture (former Director of the School of Architecture), McGill University, Montreal. Formerly, Senior Adviser for Planning and Design, Canadian Ministry of State for Urban Design. Author of *The Court-Garden House* (with S. Seeman), 1962; *University Housing in Canada* (with J. Bland), 1966; *Architecture Montreal,* 1967; *Introduction to Contemporary Indigenous Housing,* 1973; **Essay:** Irving Grossman.

SCHULZE, Franz. Contributor. Hollender Professor of Art, Lake Forest College, Lake Forest, Illinois. Art Critic of the *Chicago Sun-Times.* Contributing Editor, *Art News,* New York, and *Inland Architect,* Chicago. Author of *Fantastic Images: Chicago Art since 1945,* 1972; *100 Years of Architecture in Chicago* (with Oswald W. Grube and Peter C. Pran), 1976. **Essays:** Thomas Hall Beeby; Irving J. Gill; Bruce J. Graham; Ludwig K. Hilberseimer; George Fred Keck; Fazlur Khan; William Lescaze; Philip Will, Jr.

SEGREST, Robert. Contributor. Associate Professor of Architecture, Georgia Institute of Technology, Atlanta. **Essay:** Edward Durell Stone.

SEIDLER, Harry. Adviser, contributor, and entrant: see his own entry. **Essays:** Marcel Breuer; Oscar Niemeyer.

SEKLER, Eduard F. Contributor. Osgood Hooker Professor of Visual Arts and Professor of Architecture, Harvard University, Cambridge, Massachusetts (formerly, Director of the Carpenter Center for the Visual Arts at Harvard). Author of *Wren and His Place in European Architecture,* 1956; *Proportion: A Measure of Order,* 1965; *Le Corbusier at Work: The Genesis of the Carpenter Center for the Visual Arts* (with William J. R. Curtis), 1978; *Josef Hoffmann, das architektonische Werk,* 1982; and editor of *Historic Urban Spaces I–IV,* 1962–71; *Master Plan for the Conservation of the Cultural Heritage in the Kathmandu Valley,* 1977. **Essay:** Josef Hoffmann.

SEOW, E. J. Contributor. Professor of Architecture (formerly Head of the School of Architecture), University of Singapore. **Essays:** William S. W. Lim; Datuk Lim Chong Keat.

SHARP, Dennis. Contributor. In private practice as an architect, London. Formerly, Senior Lecturer, Architectural Association School, London, and Founder Editor of the *Architectural Association Quarterly,* Architectural Consultant to *Building,* London, and Board Member, International Committee of Architectural Critics. Author of *Area Rejuvenation: Rochdale,* 1965; *Modern Architecture and Expressionism,* 1966; *Sources of Modern Architecture,* 1967; *The Picture Palace and Other Buildings for the Movies,* 1969; *The Bauhaus* (with film strips), 1970; *A Visual History of Twentieth Century Architecture,* 1974; editor of *Planning and Architecture,* 1968; *Glass in Modern Architecture,* 1968; *Glass Architecture by P. Scheerbart,* 1972; *Manchester,* 1969; *Henry van de Velde: Theatres 1904–14,* 1974; *The Rationalists,* 1978; *The English

House by H. Muthesius, 1979; *Alfred Bossom's American Architecture 1903–26*, 1984. **Essay:** Paolo Soleri.

SHARON, Arieh (died, 1984). Adviser and entrant: see his own entry.

SHEPPARD, Adrian. Contributor. Architect in Montreal. Associate Professor of Architecture, McGill University, Montreal. Former partner in the firm of Desnoyers, Mercure, Gagnon, Sheppard, architects, Montreal. **Essay:** Victor Prus.

SHEPPARD, Richard (died, 1982). Contributor and entrant: see Sheppard, Robson and Partners. **Essay:** Eugene Rosenberg.

SILVER, Nathan. Contributor. Architect in private practice, London. Head of the School of Architecture, North East London Polytechnic. Formerly, Architecture Critic of the *New Statesman*, London. Author of *Lost New York*, 1967; *Adhocism: The Case for Improvisation* (with Charles Jencks), 1972; *The Centre Pompidou* (forthcoming). **Essays:** Bernard Feilden; Hannes Meyer; Renzo Piano; Richard Rogers; Robert A. M. Stern.

SMITH, C. Ray. Contributor. Writer, editor, design critic, and architecture historian. Formerly, Editor, *Interiors, Residential Interiors*, and *Theatre Crafts*, and Feature Editor, *Progressive Architecture—New York*. Author of *The American Endless Weekend*, 1973; *Supermannerism: New Attitudes in Post-Modern Architecture*, 1977; and editor of *The Shapes of Our Theatre* by Jo Mielziner, 1970; *The Theatre Crafts Book of Costume*, 1973; *The Theatre Crafts Book of Make-Up, Masks, and Wigs*, 1974. **Essays:** Luis Barragán; Peter D. Eisenman; Michael Graves; Charles Gwathmey; Hugh Hardy; Frederick Kiesler; Kevin Roche.

SPENCER, Kevin. Contributor. Architect, Dublin; Research officer with a state-sponsored organization. **Essays:** Raymond McGrath; Michael Scott.

SPEIREGEN, Paul. Contributor. Architect and planner, Washington, D.C. Broadcaster on National Public Radio (U.S.A.). **Essays:** Gordon Bunshaft; Hassan Fathy; Buckminster Fuller; Bernard Maybeck; Charles W. Moore; Richard J. Neutra; William L. Pereira; John Portman; Harry Weese.

STRATHAUS, Ulrike Jehle-Schulte. Contributor. Member of the staff of the Institute of Architectural History and Theory, Eidgenössische Technische Hochschule, Zurich. Author of *Bauten im 20. Jahrhundert*, 1977; *Kunst der Gegenwart* (with others), 1978. **Essay:** Werner M. Moser.

SUHONEN, Pekka. Contributor. Writer and art critic, Helsinki. Author of *New Finnish Architecture*, 1967; *Finland Creates* (with J. Fields and David Moore), 1976. **Essays:** Aulis Blomstedt; Viljo Revell.

TANNER, Howard. Contributor. Architect in private practice, Sydney. Lecturer in Architectural and Landscape History and Conservation, University of Sydney. Author of *Restoring Old Australian Houses and Buildings*, 1975; *The Great Gardens of Australia*, 1976; *Australian Housing in the Seventies*, 1976; *Architects of Australia*, 1980. **Essay:** Philip Cox.

TAYLOR, Jennifer. Contributor. Associate Professor in Architecture, University of Sydney. Author of *An Australian Identity*, 1972; *John Andrews: Architecture and Performing Art* (with John Andrews), 1979. **Essays:** Sydney Ancher; Col Madigan; Tohgo Murano; Ken Woolley.

UHLIG, Günther. Contributor. Professor of Housing and Town Planning, University Fridericiana, Karlsruhe, West Germany. Co-editor, *Arch* magazine, Stuttgart. Author of *Kulturelle Modelle der Bau- und Wohnreformbewegungen: Das Zentralküchenhaus im Kontext von Architektur- und Stadtplanungsstrategien bis 1933*, 1980. **Essay:** Ludwig Leo.

VAGO, Pierre. Adviser, contributor and entrant: see his own entry. **Essays:** Georges Candilis; Michel Ecochard; Eugène Freyssinet; Jean Ginsberg; Albert Laprade; Marcel Lods; André Lurcat; Ivan Seifert; Jean Willerval; Bernard Zehrfuss.

WALDEN, Russell. Contributor. Reader in the History of Contemporary Architecture, Victoria University of Wellington, New Zealand. Senior Lecturer, Birmingham School of Architecture, England, 1972–78. Editor of *The Open Hand: Essays on Le Corbusier*, 1977; *Le Corbusier: Ideals and Realities* (Ph.D. dissertation, University of Birmingham, England), 1978; *Voices of Silence: The Chapel of Futuna*, 1986. **Essays:** W. H. Alington; Le Corbusier; Miles Warren.

WATANABE, Hiroshi. Adviser and contributor. Writer and architect, Tokyo. Contributor to *Architecture, Progressive Architecture*, and other periodicals. Translator, *Space in Japanese Architecture* by Mitsuo Inoue, 1985. **Essays:** Tadao Ando; Sutemi Horiguchi; Kiyonori Kikutake; Sachio Otani; Seiichi Shirai; Kenzo Tange; Team Zoo.

WATSON, David. Contributor. Senior Lecturer in Architecture, University of Melbourne. **Essays:** Don Hendry Fulton; Peter McIntyre; Stuart Murray.

WERNER, Frank. Contributor. Assistant Professor of Architecture, University of Stuttgart. Architecture Critic, *Stuttgarter Zeitung*. Author of *Old Town with New Life*, 1975; *Paul Bonatz 1877–1956*, 1977. **Essays:** Paul Bonatz; Hugo Häring; Heinrich Tessenow.

WHITTICK, Arnold. Adviser and contributor. Architectural historian and writer, London. Formerly, Chief Editor, *Building Materials* and *Encyclopaedia of Urban Planning*, London. Author of *History of Cemetery Sculpture from Ancient Times to the Norman Conquest*, 1938; *Erich Mendelsohn: A Biography*, 1940, 1955; *War Memorials*, 1946; *The Small House Today and Tomorrow*, 1947; *European Architecture in the Twentieth Century*, 3 volumes, 1950–74; *Symbols and Design*, 1960; *The New Towns: Their Origins, Achievements and Progress* (with Sir Frederic Osborn), 1963; *Ruskin's Venice*, 1976. **Essays:** Peter Behrens; Constantinos Doxiades; Jane B. Drew; Aarne Ervi; Sir Frederick Gibberd; Ernst Gisel; Walter Gropius; Sir Charles Holden; Sven Markelius; Eric Mendelsohn; Pier Luigi Nervi; Marcello Piacentini; Hans Poelzig; Sir Howard Robertson; Sir Owen Williams; Hugh Wilson.

WILLIAMS, Sheldon. Contributor. Art critic and journalist, London. Artistic Adviser to Rona Ltd., London. Author of *Situation Humaine*, 1968; *Verlon*, 1969; *A Background to Sfumato*, 1970; *Voodoo and the Art of Haiti*, 1972; *20th Century British Naives and Primitives* (with others), 1978; *The World Encyclopaedia of Naive Art* (with others), 1979; and editor of *The Rona Guide to the World of Naive Art*, 1979. **Essay:** Max Bill.

WILLIAMS, Stephanie. Contributor. Architectural critic and historian. Formerly, Editor of *Architects' News*, and Features Editor of *Building Design*, London. Contributor, *Sunday Times, Christian Science Monitor, South China Morning Post*, and *Asian Wall Street Journal*. **Essay:** Stillman and Eastwick-Field.

WILLIS, Peter. Contributor. Lecturer in Architecture, University of Newcastle. Editor of *Furor Hortensis: Essays on the History of the English Landscape Garden in Memory of H. F. Clark*, 1975; *The Genius of the Place: The English Landscape Garden 1620–1820*, 1975; and author of *New Architecture in Scotland*, 1977; *Charles Bridgeman and the English Landscape Garden*, 1977. **Essays:** Leslie Martin; Peter Womersley.

WINTER, John. Contributor. Architect in private practice, London. Tutor, University College London and Cambridge University. Author of *Modern Buildings*, 1968; *Industrial Architecture*, 1969; *Power Plant Siting*, 1982. **Essays:** Felix Candela; Amyas Connell; Charles Eames; Craig Ellwood; Norman Foster; Ernö Goldfinger; Myron Goldsmith; Victor Gruen; Philip Johnson; Arthur Korn; Colin Lucas; Robert Maillart; Jean Prouvé; Antonin Raymond; Gerrit Rietveld; Skidmore, Owings and Merrill; Raphael Soriano.

WINTER, Robert. Contributor. Professor of History, Occidental College, Los Angeles. Chairman, Pasadena, California Cultural Heritage Commission; Vice-President, Los Angeles Cultural Heritage Board. Author (with David Gebhard) of *A Guide to Architecture in San Francisco and Northern California*, 1974, and *A Guide to Architecture in Los Angeles and Southern California*, 1977. **Essay:** Whitney R. Smith.